P9-AFP-914

THE OXFORD ENGLISH DICTIONARY

SECOND EDITION

THE OXFORD ENGLISH DICTIONARY

First Edited by

JAMES A. H. MURRAY, HENRY BRADLEY, W. A. CRAIGIE
and C. T. ONIONS

COMBINED WITH

A SUPPLEMENT TO THE OXFORD ENGLISH DICTIONARY

Edited by

R. W. BURCHFIELD

AND RESET WITH CORRECTIONS, REVISIONS
AND ADDITIONAL VOCABULARY

THE OXFORD ENGLISH DICTIONARY

SECOND EDITION

Prepared by

J. A. SIMPSON *and* E. S. C. WEINER

VOLUME IV

creel–duzepere

CLARENDON PRESS · OXFORD

1989

Oxford University Press, Walton Street, Oxford OX2 6DP
Oxford New York Toronto
Delhi Bombay Calcutta Madras Karachi
Petaling Jaya Singapore Hong Kong Tokyo
Nairobi Dar es Salaam Cape Town
Melbourne Auckland
and associated companies in
Berlin Ibadan

Oxford is a trade mark of Oxford University Press

British Library Cataloguing in Publication Data
Oxford English dictionary.—2nd ed.
1. English language-Dictionaries
I. Simpson, J. A. (John Andrew), 1953-
II. Weiner, Edmund S. C., 1950-
423
ISBN 0-19-861216-8 (vol. IV)
ISBN 0-19-861186-2 (set)

Library of Congress Cataloging-in-Publication Data
The Oxford English dictionary.—2nd ed.
prepared by J. A. Simpson and E. S. C. Weiner
Bibliography: p.
ISBN 0-19-861216-8 (vol. IV)
ISBN 0-19-861186-2 (set)
1. English language—Dictionaries. I. Simpson, J. A.
II. Weiner, E. S. C. III. Oxford University Press.
PE1625.087 1989
423—dc19 88-5330

Data capture by ICC, Fort Washington, Pa.
Text-processing by Oxford University Press
Typesetting by Filmtype Services Ltd., Scarborough, N. Yorks.
Manufactured in the United States of America by
Rand McNally & Company, Taunton, Mass.

KEY TO THE PRONUNCIATION

THE pronunciations given are those in use in the educated speech of southern England (the so-called 'Received Standard'), and the keywords given are to be understood as pronounced in such speech.

I. *Consonants*

b, d, f, k, l, m, n, p, t, v, z *have their usual English values*

g as in *go* (gəʊ)
h ... *ho!* (həʊ)
r ... *run* (rʌn), *terrier* ('tɛrɪə(r))
(r) ... he*r* (hɜː(r))
s ... *see* (siː), *success* (sək'sɛs)
w ... *wear* (wɛə(r))
hw... *wh*en (hwɛn)
j ... *yes* (jɛs)

θ as in *th*in (θɪn), ba*th* (bɑːθ)
ð ... *th*en (ðɛn), ba*th*e (beɪð)
ʃ ... *sh*op (ʃɒp), di*sh* (dɪʃ)
tʃ ... *ch*op (tʃɒp), di*tch* (dɪtʃ)
ʒ ... vi*s*ion ('vɪʒən), dé*j*euner (deʒøne)
dʒ ... *judge* (dʒʌdʒ)
ŋ ... si*ng*i*ng* ('sɪŋɪŋ), thi*n*k (θiŋk)
ŋg ... fi*ng*er ('fɪŋgə(r))

(FOREIGN AND NON-SOUTHERN)

ʎ as in It. serra*gli*o (ser'raʎo)
ɲ ... Fr. co*gn*ac (kɔɲak)
x ... Ger. a*ch* (ax), Sc. lo*ch* (lɒx), Sp. fri*j*oles (fri'xoles)
ç ... Ger. i*ch* (ɪç), Sc. ni*ch*t (nɪçt)
ɣ ... North Ger. sa*g*en ('zaːɣən)
c ... Afrikaans baardmanne*tj*ie ('baːrtmanəci)
ɥ ... Fr. c*u*isine (kɥizin)

Symbols in parentheses are used to denote elements that may be omitted either by individual speakers or in particular phonetic contexts: e.g. *bottle* ('bɒt(ə)l), *Mercian* ('mɜːʃ(ɪ)ən), *suit* (s(j)uːt), *impromptu* (ɪm'prɒm(p)tjuː), *father* ('fɑːðə(r)).

II. *Vowels and Diphthongs*

SHORT

ɪ as in p*i*t (pɪt), -n*e*ss, (-nɪs)
ɛ ... p*e*t (pɛt), Fr. *sept* (sɛt)
æ ... p*a*t (pæt)
ʌ ... p*u*tt (pʌt)
ɒ ... p*o*t (pɒt)
ʊ ... p*u*t (pʊt)
ə ... *a*nother (ə'nʌðə(r))
(ə) ... beat*e*n ('biːt(ə)n)
i ... Fr. s*i* (si)
e ... Fr. b*é*b*é* (bebe)
a ... Fr. m*a*ri (mari)
ɑ ... Fr. b*â*timent (bɑtimɑ̃)
ɔ ... Fr. h*o*mme (ɔm)
o ... Fr. *eau* (o)
ø ... Fr. p*eu* (pø)
œ ... Fr. b*oeu*f (bœf) c*oeu*r (kœr)
u ... Fr. d*ou*ce (dus)
ʏ ... Ger. M*ü*ller ('mʏlər)
y ... Fr. d*u* (dy)

LONG

iː as in b*ea*n (biːn)
ɑː ... b*ar*n (bɑːn)
ɔː ... b*or*n (bɔːn)
uː ... b*oo*n (buːn)
ɜː ... b*ur*n (bɜːn)
eː ... Ger. Schn*ee* (ʃneː)
ɛː ... Ger. F*äh*re ('fɛːrə)
aː ... Ger. T*a*g (taːk)
oː ... Ger. S*oh*n (zoːn)
øː ... Ger. G*oe*the ('gøːtə)
yː ... Ger. gr*ü*n (gryːn)

NASAL

ɛ̃, æ̃ as in Fr. f*in* (fɛ̃, fæ̃)
ɑ̃ ... Fr. fr*an*c (frɑ̃)
ɔ̃ ... Fr. b*on* (bɔ̃)
œ̃ ... Fr. *un* (œ̃)

DIPHTHONGS, etc.

eɪ as in b*ay* (beɪ)
aɪ ... b*uy* (baɪ)
ɔɪ ... b*oy* (bɔɪ)
əʊ ... n*o* (nəʊ)
aʊ ... n*ow* (naʊ)
ɪə ... p*eer* (pɪə(r))
ɛə ... p*air* (pɛə(r))
ʊə ... t*our* (tʊə(r))
ɔə ... b*oar* (bɔə(r))

aɪə as in f*ie*ry ('faɪərɪ)
aʊə ... s*our* (saʊə(r))

The incidence of main stress is shown by a superior stress mark (') preceding the stressed syllable, and a secondary stress by an inferior stress mark (ˌ), e.g. *pronunciation* (prəˌnʌnsɪ'eɪʃ(ə)n).

For further explanation of the transcription used, see *General Explanations*, Volume I.

LIST OF ABBREVIATIONS, SIGNS, ETC.

Some abbreviations listed here in italics are also in certain cases printed in roman type, and vice versa.

a. (in Etym.)	adoption of, adopted from
a (as *a* 1850)	*ante*, 'before', 'not later than'
a.	adjective
abbrev.	abbreviation (of)
abl.	ablative
absol.	absolute, -ly
Abstr.	(in titles) *Abstract, -s*
acc.	accusative
Acct.	(in titles) *Account*
A.D.	*Anno Domini*
ad. (in Etym.)	adaptation of
Add.	Addenda
adj.	adjective
Adv.	(in titles) *Advance, -d, -s*
adv.	adverb
advb.	adverbial, -ly
Advt.	advertisement
Aeronaut.	(as label) in Aeronautics; (in titles) *Aeronautic, -al, -s*
AF., AFr.	Anglo-French
Afr.	Africa, -n
Agric.	(as label) in Agriculture; (in titles) *Agriculture, -al*
Alb.	Albanian
Amer.	American
Amer. Ind.	American Indian
Anat.	(as label) in Anatomy; (in titles) *Anatomy, -ical*
Anc.	(in titles) *Ancient*
Anglo-Ind.	Anglo-Indian
Anglo-Ir.	Anglo-Irish
Ann.	Annals
Anthrop., Anthropol.	(as label) in Anthropology; (in titles) *Anthropology, -ical*
Antiq.	(as label) in Antiquities; (in titles) *Antiquity*
aphet.	aphetic, aphetized
app.	apparently
Appl.	(in titles) *Applied*
Applic.	(in titles) *Application, -s*
appos.	appositive, -ly
Arab.	Arabic
Aram.	Aramaic
Arch.	in Architecture
arch.	archaic
Archæol.	in Archæology
Archit.	(as label) in Architecture; (in titles) *Architecture, -al*
Arm.	Armenian
assoc.	association
Astr.	in Astronomy
Astrol.	in Astrology
Astron.	(in titles) *Astronomy, -ical*
Astronaut.	(in titles) *Astronautic, -s*
attrib.	attributive, -ly
Austral.	Australian
Autobiogr.	(in titles) *Autobiography, -ical*
A.V.	Authorized Version
B.C.	Before Christ
B.C.	(in titles) British Columbia
bef.	before
Bibliogr.	(as label) in Bibliography; (in titles) *Bibliography, -ical*
Biochem.	(as label) in Biochemistry; (in titles) *Biochemistry, -ical*
Biol.	(as label) in Biology; (in titles) *Biology, -ical*
Bk.	*Book*
Bot.	(as label) in Botany; (in titles) *Botany, -ical*
Bp.	Bishop
Brit.	(in titles) *Britain, British*
Bulg.	Bulgarian
Bull.	(in titles) *Bulletin*
c (as *c* 1700)	*circa*, 'about'
c. (as 19th c.)	century
Cal.	(in titles) *Calendar*
Cambr.	(in titles) *Cambridge*
Canad.	Canadian
Cat.	Catalan
catachr.	catachrestically
Catal.	(in titles) *Catalogue*
Celt.	Celtic
Cent.	(in titles) *Century, Central*
Cent. Dict.	*Century Dictionary*
Cf., cf.	*confer*, 'compare'
Ch.	Church
Chem.	(as label) in Chemistry; (in titles) *Chemistry, -ical*
Chr.	(in titles) *Christian*
Chron.	(in titles) *Chronicle*
Chronol.	(in titles) *Chronology, -ical*
Cinemat., Cinematogr.	in Cinematography
Clin.	(in titles) *Clinical*
cl. L.	classical Latin
cogn. w.	cognate with
Col.	(in titles) *Colonel, Colony*
Coll.	(in titles) *Collection*
collect.	collective, -ly
colloq.	colloquial, -ly
comb.	combined, -ing
Comb.	Combinations
Comm.	in Commercial usage
Communic.	in Communications
comp.	compound, composition
Compan.	(in titles) *Companion*
compar.	comparative
compl.	complement
Compl.	(in titles) *Complete*
Conc.	(in titles) *Concise*
Conch.	in Conchology
concr.	concrete, -ly
Conf.	(in titles) *Conference*
Congr.	(in titles) *Congress*
conj.	conjunction
cons.	consonant
const.	construction, construed with
contr.	contrast (with)
Contrib.	(in titles) *Contribution*
Corr.	(in titles) *Correspondence*
corresp.	corresponding (to)
Cotgr.	R. Cotgrave, *Dictionarie of the French and English Tongues*
cpd.	compound
Crit.	(in titles) *Criticism, Critical*
Cryst.	in Crystallography
Cycl.	(in titles) *Cyclopædia, -ic*
Cytol.	(in titles) *Cytology, -ical*
Da.	Danish
D.A.	*Dictionary of Americanisms*
D.A.E.	*Dictionary of American English*
dat.	dative
D.C.	District of Columbia
Deb.	(in titles) *Debate, -s*
def.	definite, -ition
dem.	demonstrative
deriv.	derivative, -ation
derog.	derogatory
Descr.	(in titles) *Description, -tive*
Devel.	(in titles) *Development, -al*
Diagn.	(in titles) *Diagnosis, Diagnostic*
dial.	dialect, -al
Dict.	Dictionary; *spec.*, the *Oxford English Dictionary*
dim.	diminutive
Dis.	(in titles) *Disease*
Diss.	(in titles) *Dissertation*
D.O.S.T.	*Dictionary of the Older Scottish Tongue*
Du.	Dutch
E.	East
Eccl.	(as label) in Ecclesiastical usage; (in titles) *Ecclesiastical*
Ecol.	in Ecology
Econ.	(as label) in Economics; (in titles) *Economy, -ics*
ed.	edition
E.D.D.	*English Dialect Dictionary*
Edin.	(in titles) *Edinburgh*
Educ.	(as label) in Education; (in titles) *Education, -al*
EE.	Early English
e.g.	*exempli gratia*, 'for example'
Electr.	(as label) in Electricity; (in titles) *Electricity, -ical*
Electron.	(in titles) *Electronic, -s*
Elem.	(in titles) *Element, -ary*
ellipt.	elliptical, -ly
Embryol.	in Embryology
e.midl.	east midland (dialect)
Encycl.	(in titles) *Encyclopædia, -ic*
Eng.	England, English
Engin.	in Engineering
Ent.	in Entomology
Entomol.	(in titles) *Entomology, -logical*
erron.	erroneous, -ly
esp.	especially
Ess.	(in titles) *Essay, -s*
et al.	*et alii*, 'and others'
etc.	et cetera
Ethnol.	in Ethnology
etym.	etymology
euphem.	euphemistically
Exam.	(in titles) *Examination*
exc.	except
Exerc.	(in titles) *Exercise, -s*
Exper.	(in titles) *Experiment, -al*
Explor.	(in titles) *Exploration, -s*
f.	feminine
f. (in Etym.)	formed on
f. (in subordinate entries)	form of
F.	French
fem. (*rarely* f.)	feminine
fig.	figurative, -ly
Finn.	Finnish
fl.	*floruit*, 'flourished'
Found.	(in titles) *Foundation, -s*
Fr.	French
freq.	frequent, -ly
Fris.	Frisian
Fund.	(in titles) *Fundamental, -s*
Funk or *Funk's Stand. Dict.*	*Funk and Wagnalls Standard Dictionary*
G.	German
Gael.	Gaelic
Gaz.	(in titles) *Gazette*
gen.	genitive
gen.	general, -ly
Geogr.	(as label) in Geography; (in titles) *Geography, -ical*

LIST OF ABBREVIATIONS, SIGNS, ETC.

Geol.	(as label) in Geology; (in titles) *Geology, -ical*
Geom.	in Geometry
Geomorphol.	in Geomorphology
Ger.	German
Gloss.	Glossary
Gmc.	Germanic
Godef.	F. Godefroy, *Dictionnaire de l'ancienne langue française*
Goth.	Gothic
Govt.	(in titles) *Government*
Gr.	Greek
Gram.	(as label) in Grammar; (in titles) *Grammar, -tical*
Gt.	Great
Heb.	Hebrew
Her.	in Heraldry
Herb.	among herbalists
Hind.	Hindustani
Hist.	(as label) in History; (in titles) *History, -ical*
hist.	historical
Histol.	(in titles) *Histology, -ical*
Hort.	in Horticulture
Househ.	(in titles) *Household*
Housek.	(in titles) *Housekeeping*
Ibid.	*Ibidem*, 'in the same book or passage'
Icel.	Icelandic
Ichthyol.	in Ichthyology
id.	*idem*, 'the same'
i.e.	*id est*, 'that is'
IE.	Indo-European
Illustr.	(in titles) *Illustration, -ted*
imit.	imitative
Immunol.	in Immunology
imp.	imperative
impers.	impersonal
impf.	imperfect
ind.	indicative
indef.	indefinite
Industr.	(in titles) *Industry, -ial*
inf.	infinitive
infl.	influenced
Inorg.	(in titles) *Inorganic*
Ins.	(in titles) *Insurance*
Inst.	(in titles) *Institute, -tion*
int.	interjection
intr.	intransitive
Introd.	(in titles) *Introduction*
Ir.	Irish
irreg.	irregular, -ly
It.	Italian
J., (J.)	(quoted from) Johnson's *Dictionary*
(Jam.)	Jamieson, *Scottish Dict.*
Jap.	Japanese
joc.	jocular, -ly
Jrnl.	(in titles) *Journal*
Jun.	(in titles) *Junior*
Knowl.	(in titles) *Knowledge*
l.	line
L.	Latin
lang.	language
Lect.	(in titles) *Lecture, -s*
Less.	(in titles) *Lesson, -s*
Let., Lett.	letter, letters
LG.	Low German
lit.	literal, -ly
Lit.	Literary
Lith.	Lithuanian
LXX	Septuagint
m.	masculine
Mag.	(in titles) *Magazine*
Magn.	(in titles) *Magnetic, -ism*
Mal.	Malay, Malayan
Man.	(in titles) *Manual*
Managem.	(in titles) *Management*
Manch.	(in titles) *Manchester*
Manuf.	in Manufacture, -ing
Mar.	(in titles) *Marine*

masc. (*rarely* m.)	masculine
Math.	(as label) in Mathematics; (in titles) *Mathematics, -al*
MDu.	Middle Dutch
ME.	Middle English
Mech.	(as label) in Mechanics; (in titles) *Mechanics, -al*
Med.	(as label) in Medicine; (in titles) *Medicine, -ical*
med.L.	medieval Latin
Mem.	(in titles) *Memoir, -s*
Metaph.	in Metaphysics
Meteorol.	(as label) in Meteorology; (in titles) *Meteorology, -ical*
MHG.	Middle High German
midl.	midland (dialect)
Mil.	in military usage
Min.	(as label) in Mineralogy; (in titles) *Ministry*
Mineral.	(in titles) *Mineralogy, -ical*
MLG.	Middle Low German
Misc.	(in titles) *Miscellany, -eous*
mod.	modern
mod.L	modern Latin
(Morris),	(quoted from) E. E. Morris's *Austral English*
Mus.	(as label) in Music; (in titles) *Music, -al; Museum*
Myst.	(in titles) *Mystery*
Mythol.	in Mythology
N.	North
n.	neuter
N. Amer.	North America, -n
N. & Q.	*Notes and Queries*
Narr.	(in titles) *Narrative*
Nat.	(in titles) *Natural*
Nat. Hist.	in Natural History
Naut.	in nautical language
N.E.	North East
N.E.D.	*New English Dictionary*, original title of the *Oxford English Dictionary* (first edition)
Neurol.	in Neurology
neut. (*rarely* n.)	neuter
NF., NFr.	Northern French
No.	Number
nom.	nominative
north.	northern (dialect)
Norw.	Norwegian
n.q.	no quotations
N.T.	New Testament
Nucl.	Nuclear
Numism.	in Numismatics
N.W.	North West
N.Z.	New Zealand
obj.	object
obl.	oblique
Obs., obs.	obsolete
Obstetr.	(in titles) *Obstetrics*
occas.	occasionally
OE.	Old English (= Anglo-Saxon)
OF., OFr.	Old French
OFris.	Old Frisian
OHG.	Old High German
OIr.	Old Irish
ON.	Old Norse
ONF.	Old Northern French
Ophthalm.	in Ophthalmology
opp.	opposed (to), the opposite (of)
Opt.	in Optics
Org.	(in titles) *Organic*
orig.	origin, -al, -ally
Ornith.	(as label) in Ornithology; (in titles) *Ornithology, -ical*
OS.	Old Saxon
OSl.	Old (Church) Slavonic
O.T.	Old Testament
Outl.	(in titles) *Outline*
Oxf.	(in titles) *Oxford*
p.	page
Palæogr.	in Palæography

Palæont.	(as label) in Palæontology; (in titles) *Palæontology, -ical*
pa. pple.	passive participle, past participle
(Partridge),	(quoted from) E. Partridge's *Dictionary of Slang and Unconventional English*
pass.	passive, -ly
pa.t.	past tense
Path.	(as label) in Pathology; (in titles) *Pathology, -ical*
perh.	perhaps
Pers.	Persian
pers.	person, -al
Petrogr.	in Petrography
Petrol.	(as label) in Petrology; (in titles) *Petrology, -ical*
(Pettman),	(quoted from) C. Pettman's *Africanderisms*
pf.	perfect
Pg.	Portuguese
Pharm.	in Pharmacology
Philol.	(as label) in Philology; (in titles) *Philology, -ical*
Philos.	(as label) in Philosophy; (in titles) *Philosophy, -ic*
phonet.	phonetic, -ally
Photogr.	(as label) in Photography; (in titles) *Photography, -ical*
phr.	phrase
Phys.	physical; (*rarely*) in Physiology
Physiol.	(as label) in Physiology; (in titles) *Physiology, -ical*
Pict.	(in titles) *Picture, Pictorial*
pl., plur.	plural
poet.	poetic, -al
Pol.	Polish
Pol.	(as label) in Politics; (in titles) *Politics, -al*
Pol. Econ.	in Political Economy
Polit.	(in titles) *Politics, -al*
pop.	popular, -ly
Porc.	(in titles) *Porcelain*
poss.	possessive
Pott.	(in titles) *Pottery*
ppl. a., pple. adj.	participial adjective
pple.	participle
Pr.	Provençal
pr.	present
Pract.	(in titles) *Practice, -al*
prec.	preceding (word or article)
pred.	predicative
pref.	prefix
pref., Pref.	preface
prep.	preposition
pres.	present
Princ.	(in titles) *Principle, -s*
priv.	privative
prob.	probably
Probl.	(in titles) *Problem*
Proc.	(in titles) *Proceedings*
pron.	pronoun
pronunc.	pronunciation
prop.	properly
Pros.	in Prosody
Prov.	Provençal
pr. pple.	present participle
Psych.	in Psychology
Psychol.	(as label) in Psychology; (in titles) *Psychology, -ical*
Publ.	(in titles) *Publications*
Q.	(in titles) *Quarterly*
quot(s).	quotation(s)
q.v.	*quod vide*, 'which see'
R.	(in titles) *Royal*
Radiol.	in Radiology
R.C.Ch.	Roman Catholic Church
Rec.	(in titles) *Record*
redupl.	reduplicating
Ref.	(in titles) *Reference*
refash.	refashioned, -ing
refl.	reflexive
Reg.	(in titles) *Register*

reg.	regular
rel.	related to
Reminisc.	(in titles) *Reminiscence, -s*
Rep.	(in titles) *Report, -s*
repr.	representative, representing
Res.	(in titles) *Research*
Rev.	(in titles) *Review*
rev.	revised
Rhet.	in Rhetoric
Rom.	Roman, -ce, -ic
Rum.	Rumanian
Russ.	Russian
S.	South
S.Afr.	South Africa, -n
sb.	substantive
sc.	*scilicet*, 'understand' or 'supply'
Sc., *Scot.*	Scottish
Scand.	(in titles) *Scandinavia, -n*
Sch.	(in titles) *School*
Sc. Nat. Dict.	*Scottish National Dictionary*
Scotl.	(in titles) *Scotland*
Sel.	(in titles) *Selection, -s*
Ser.	Series
sing.	singular
Sk.	(in titles) *Sketch*
Skr.	Sanskrit
Slav.	Slavonic
S.N.D.	*Scottish National Dictionary*
Soc.	(in titles) *Society*
Sociol.	(as label) in Sociology; (in titles) *Sociology, -ical*
Sp.	Spanish
Sp.	(in titles) *Speech, -es*
sp.	spelling
spec.	specifically
Spec.	(in titles) *Specimen*
St.	Saint
Stand.	(in titles) *Standard*
Stanf.	(quoted from) *Stanford Dictionary of Anglicised Words & Phrases*

str.	strong
Struct.	(in titles) *Structure, -al*
Stud.	(in titles) *Studies*
subj.	subject
subord. cl.	subordinate clause
subseq.	subsequent, -ly
subst.	substantively
suff.	suffix
superl.	superlative
Suppl.	Supplement
Surg.	(as label) in Surgery; (in titles) *Surgery, Surgical*
s.v.	*sub voce*, 'under the word'
Sw.	Swedish
s.w.	south-western (dialect)
Syd. Soc. Lex.	Sydenham Society, *Lexicon of Medicine & Allied Sciences*
syll.	syllable
Syr.	Syrian
Syst.	(in titles) *System, -atic*
Taxon.	(in titles) *Taxonomy, -ical*
techn.	technical, -ly
Technol.	(in titles) *Technology, -ical*
Telegr.	in Telegraphy
Teleph.	in Telephony
(Th.),	(quoted from) Thornton's *American Glossary*
Theatr.	in the Theatre, theatrical
Theol.	(as label) in Theology; (in titles) *Theology, -ical*
Theoret.	(in titles) *Theoretical*
Tokh.	Tokharian
tr., transl.	translated, translation
Trans.	(in titles) *Transactions*
trans.	transitive
transf.	transferred sense
Trav.	(in titles) *Travel(s)*
Treas.	(in titles) *Treasury*
Treat.	(in titles) *Treatise*
Treatm.	(in titles) *Treatment*
Trig.	in Trigonometry

Trop.	(in titles) *Tropical*
Turk.	Turkish
Typog., *Typogr.*	in Typography
ult.	ultimately
Univ.	(in titles) *University*
unkn.	unknown
U.S.	United States
U.S.S.R.	Union of Soviet Socialist Republics
usu.	usually
v., vb.	verb
var(r)., vars.	variant(s) of
vbl. sb.	verbal substantive
Vertebr.	(in titles) *Vertebrate, -s*
Vet.	(as label) in Veterinary Science; (in titles) *Veterinary*
Vet. Sci.	in Veterinary Science
viz.	*videlicet*, 'namely'
Voy.	(in titles) *Voyage, -s*
v.str.	strong verb
vulg.	vulgar
v.w.	weak verb
W.	Welsh; West
wd.	word
Webster	*Webster's* (*New International*) *Dictionary*
Westm.	(in titles) *Westminster*
WGmc.	West Germanic
Wks.	(in titles) *Works*
w.midl.	west midland (dialect)
WS.	West Saxon
(Y.),	(quoted from) Yule & Burnell's *Hobson-Jobson*
Yrs.	(in titles) *Years*
Zoogeogr.	in Zoogeography
Zool.	(as label) in Zoology; (in titles) *Zoology, -ical*

Signs and Other Conventions

Before a word or sense

† = obsolete
‖ = not naturalized, alien
¶ = catachrestic and erroneous uses

In the listing of Forms

1 = before 1100
2 = 12th c. (1100 to 1200)
3 = 13th c. (1200 to 1300), etc.
5–7 = 15th to 17th century
20 = 20th century

In the etymologies

* indicates a word or form not actually found, but of which the existence is inferred
:— = normal development of

The printing of a word in SMALL CAPITALS indicates that further information will be found under the word so referred to.

.. indicates an omitted part of a quotation.

- (in a quotation) indicates a hyphen doubtfully present in the original; (in other text) indicates a hyphen inserted only for the sake of a line-break.

PROPRIETARY NAMES

THIS Dictionary includes some words which are or are asserted to be proprietary names or trade marks. Their inclusion does not imply that they have acquired for legal purposes a non-proprietary or general significance nor any other judgement concerning their legal status. In cases where the editorial staff have established in the records of the Patent Offices of the United Kingdom and of the United States that a word is registered as a proprietary name or trade mark this is indicated, but no judgement concerning the legal status of such words is made or implied thereby.

creel (kriːl), *sb.*[1] Forms: 5–6 crele, creill(e, 5 crelle, 6 creil, krele, kreil, 7 creele, (8 crail), 8– creel. [Originally northern, and chiefly Scotch; etymology uncertain.

The OIr. *criol* chest, coffer, has been compared: but the vowel of *creel* appears to be not *ī*, but *ē* or *ei*, *ai*. OF. *greille*:—L. *crāticula* fine hurdle-work, may have had a variant **creille*.]

1. A large wicker basket; formerly applied to the large deep baskets, coupled in pairs across the backs of horses, for the transport of goods; now applied to a basket used for the transport of fish and borne upon the back, to a potato-basket, and the like.

c **1425** Wyntoun *Cron.* viii. xxxviii. 51 A payr of Coil Crelis. *c* **1440** *Promp. Parv.* 101 *Crelle*, baskett or lepe, *cartallus*, *sporta*. *c* **1475** *Rauf Coilʒear* 367 He kest twa Creillis on ane Capill, with Coillis anew. **1508** Dunbar *Flyting w. Kennedie* 229 Cager aviris castis bayth coillis and creilis. **1560** Rolland *Crt. Venus* iii. 595 ʒe him hang ouir ʒour wallis in a creill. **1564** *Wills & Inv. N.C.* (Surtees) 224 A basket and iij kreles. **1610** Healey *St. Aug. Citie of God* 251 There was also the Vanne which is otherwise called the Creele. *c* **1730** Burt *Lett. N. Scotl.* (1818) I. 330 The horse laden with creels, or small panniers. **1806** *Gazetteer Scot.* (ed. 2) 194 Fishermen, whose wives carry the fish in wicker-baskets, or creels to Edinburgh. **1811** Willan *W. Riding Gloss.* (E.D.S.), *Creel*, two semi-circular wicker baskets joined by cords which admit of their closing to hold hay. A man having the creel strapped over his shoulders, conveys provender to sheep. **1860** G. H. K. *Vac. Tour* 121 When the father of the last Lord Reay..changed his residence..his son was put into a creel on one side of a pony, and counterbalanced by his younger brother, the admiral, in another. **1869–78** in Dial. Glossaries of *Cumberland*, *Lonsdale*, *Swaledale*, *Whitby*, *Holderness*, *N.W. Linc.* **1884** Q. Victoria *More Leaves* 206 An old fishwife, with her creel on her back.

b. A modern term for an angler's fishing-basket.

1842 *Proc. Berw. Nat. Club* II. 4 Ere the Creel was half stocked. **1874** C. S. Keene *Let.* in *Life* (1892) 159, I hope you had a good time with rod and creel. **1884** W. C. Smith *Kildrostan* i. i. 227 It is not every fish you hook that comes to the creel.

2. A contrivance made of wickerwork used as a trap for catching fish, lobsters, etc.

1457 *Sc. Acts Jas. II* (1597) §87 That na man in smolt time set veschelles, creilles, weires, or ony vther ingine to let the smoltes to goe to the Sea. **1533–4** *Act 25 Hen. VIII*, c. 7 No person shal take in any lepe, hiue, crele..fier, or any other engine..the yonge frie..of any kinde of salmon. **1536** Bellenden *Cron. Scot.* (1821) I. p. xxxiv, The peple makis ane lang mand, narrow halsit, and wyid mouthit..als sone as the see ebbis, the fische ar tane dry in the crelis. **1596** Dalrymple tr. *Leslie's Hist. Scot.* 42 Nocht sa mekle fishe thay with nettis, as with skepis, or long kreilis win with wickeris in the form of a hose. **1758** Binnell *Descr. Thames* 111 With any Nets, Trammel, Keep, Wore, Creel, or other Device. **1775** Adair *Amer. Ind.* 403 Catching fish in long crails, made with canes and hiccory splinters, tapering to a point.

3. ***to coup the creels***: in various *fig.* uses; to fall or tumble over; 'to tumble heels over head, to die' (Jamieson); to meet with a mishap. ***in a creel***: in a state of temporary mental aberration.

1715 Ramsay *Christ's Kirk Gr.* ii. xvii, Whan he was strute twa sturdy chiels..Held up frae cowping o' the creels The liquid logic scholer. **1785** Burns *To William Simpson* iii, My senses wad be in a creel, Should I but dare a hope to speel, Wi' Allan, or wi' Gilbertfield. **1816** Scott *Old Mort.* vi, 'The laddie 's in a creel!' exclaimed his uncle. **1818** —— *Rob Roy* xx, If folk..wad needs be couping the creels ower through-stanes. *a* **1835** Hogg *Tales & Sk.* III. 206 If you should..coup the creels just now..it would be out of the power of man to get you to a Christian burial. **1871** C. Gibbon *Lack of Gold* xvii, 'The lassie's head's in a creel', cried Susan.

4. *attrib.* and *Comb.*, as ***creel-hawking***, ***-pig***; ***creel-like*** adv.; **creel-house**, a house or hut with the walls made of wickerwork covered with clay; **creel-man**, a man who transports goods in creels.

1865 J. G. Bertram *Harvest of Sea* (1873) 310 The system ..followed by the fishwives in the old days of *creel-hawking. **1876** Robinson *Whitby Gloss.*, **Creel-house*, a wicker hut with a sodded roof. **1878** Mackintosh *Hist. Civiliz. Scot.* I. Introd. 134 Till recently crell houses were used in some parts of the Highlands. **1638–9** in Maidment *Sc. Pasquils* (1868) 66 He..*creel lyke lives in the fyre of contentione. **1883** J. Beath *Bishopshire Lilts* 14 Stridelegs on the *creelman's ass. **1880** *Antrim & Down Gloss.*, **Creel-pig*, a young pig, such as is taken to market in a creel or basket.

creel (kriːl), *sb.*[2] [Perh. the same word as preceding; but evidence is wanting.]

1. A framework, varying in form according to its purpose (see quots.). (Cf. CRATCH, 4.)

1788 W. Marshall *Yorksh.* (1796) II. 222 The feet of the sheep being bound, it is laid upon a bier—provincially, a 'creel'. *Ibid.* Gloss., *Creel*, a kind of bier, used for slaughtering and salving sheep upon. **1821** J. Hunter *MS. Gloss.* in Addy *Sheffield Gloss.*, *Creel*, a light frame-work placed overhead in the kitchen or other room of an ordinary farmhouse, on which oatcakes are placed. [So **1883** in *Huddersf. Gloss.*] **1869** *Lonsdale Gloss.*, *Creel*..a barred stool on which sheep are salved and clipped, pigs are killed, etc. **1877** *Holderness Gloss.*, *Creel.*, a plate-rack..a food-rack for sheep; a butcher's hand-barrow. **1877** *N.W. Linc. Gloss.*, *Creel*, a wooden rack in which plates are put to dry. A frame in which glaziers carry glass.

2. *Spinning.* A frame for holding the paying-off bobbins in the process of converting the 'sliver' into 'roving', or the latter into yarn. Hence also ***creel-frame***.

1835 Ure *Philos. Manuf.* 225 The roller-pair..receives the fine rovings from bobbins placed on skewers or upright pins in the creel behind. **1851** *Art Jrnl. Catal. Gt. Exhib.* p. vii**/1 The bobbins..are placed in a wooden frame called a 'creel', so that they will revolve. **1879** *Cassell's Techn. Educ.* IV. 209/1 The rove creels..stand about six or seven feet high.

b. (See quot.) *north. dial.*

1869 *Lonsdale Gloss.*, *Creel*, a frame to wind yarn upon.

creel (kriːl), *v.* [f. CREEL *sb.*[1]]

1. *Sc.* To put into a creel; also *fig.*

1513 Douglas *Æneis* iv. Prol. 32 Men sayis thow bridillit Aristotle as ane hors, And crelit wp the flour of poetry. **1808–79** Jamieson, *Creil*, to put into a basket..'He's no gude to creel eggs wi',' i.e. not easy, or safe, to deal with.

2. *Angling.* To get (a fish) into the basket; to succeed in catching. Cf. 'to *bag* game'.

1844 J. T. Hewlett *Parsons & W.* v, I creeled him, and tried again. **1892** *Field* 18 June 922/3 My friend..creeled nearly twice as many trout.

3. *Sc.* In certain marriage customs: To make (a newly married man) go through some ceremony with a creel; *esp.* to make him carry a creel filled with stones, till his wife releases him. Cf. Brand *Pop. Antiq.* (1870) II. 55.

1792 *Statist. Acc. Scot.* II. 80 The second day after the Marriage a Creeling, as it is called, takes place. **1845** *New Statist. Acc. Scot.*, *Berwicksh.* 59 All the men who have been married within the last 12 months are creeled. *Ibid.* 263 An ancient..local usage called creeling is still kept up here. **1890** *Glasgow Times* 3 Nov. 3/4 A miner..having got married..his fellow-colliers..went through the process of creeling him.

creeler (ˈkriːlə(r)). [f. CREEL *sb.*[2] + -ER[1].] A young person who attends to the creel of a spinning machine.

1864 R. A. Arnold *Cotton Fam.* 32 A minder and a creeler engaged in manufacturing with a self-acting mule. **1882** *Manchester Guardian* 19 May, The relationship between spinners and their creelers and piecers.

ˈcreelful. As much as fills a creel.

1824 Scott *Redgauntlet* ch. vii, A creelfu' of coals. **1873** G. C. Davies *Mountain & Mere* xviii. 157 The creelfuls of trout I have caught.

creem (kriːm), *v. dial.* Also **cream**, **crim**. [Of obscure etymology: possibly two or even three distinct words are here included. The various senses belong to distinct parts of England.

The variant *crim* has suggested identity with OE. *crimman* to squeeze, press (cf. sense 2); but the evidence does not show that *crim* is the earlier form, rather the contrary: and it is not easy to see how *creem* with its long vowel could arise from the ablaut series *krim-*, *kram*, *krum-*.]

1. *trans.* To put, place, or deposit secretly or surreptitiously. (*northern.*)

1674 Ray *N.C. Words* 12 *Creem it into my hand*: Put it in slily or secretly. *Chesh.* *a* **1700** B. E. *Dict. Cant. Crew*, *Creeme*, to slip or slide anything into another's Hand. **1746** Collier (Tim Bobbin) *View Lanc. Dial.* Wks. (1862) 53, I creemt Nip neaw on then o Lunshun. **1887** *S. Cheshire Gloss.*, *Creem*, to hide. 'Creem it up', put it out of sight, hide it in your dress or pocket..It is a rare word, and rapidly becoming obsolete.

2. To squeeze; to hug. (*Devon* and *Cornw.*)

1746 *Exmoor Courtship* (E.D.S.) 326 Tha hast a creem'd ma Yearms and a most bost ma neck. **1864** Capern *Devon Provinc.*, He creemed my hand. **1880** *W. Cornwall Gloss.*, *Creem*, to squeeze, to mash..To hug in wrestling. **1880** *E. Cornwall Gloss.*, *Creem*, to squeeze.

3. *intr.* To shiver. *trans.* To cause to shiver, to chill. Hence **ˈcreemed** *ppl. a.*, chilled and shivering. (*south-western.*)

1847–78 Halliwell, *Crim*, to shiver. *I. Wight.* **1880** *E. Cornwall Gloss.*, *Creem*..is metaphorically used to describe that sensation of rigor or creeping of the flesh, known as goose flesh, *cutis anserina*. 'Creemed wi' the cold'. **1880** Mrs. Parr *Adam & Eve* iv. 44 Do 'ee go near to the fire.. you looks all creemed with the cold, and as wisht as can be. **1888** *W. Somerset Word-bk.*, *Creamy*..to shiver, to shudder.

creem, *sb. dial.* [f. prec.] A shiver proceeding from cold, indisposition, etc.

1847–78 Halliwell, *Cream*..a cold shivering. *Somerset.* **1880** *W. Cornwall Gloss.*, *Creem*, *Crim*, a shiver; a creeping of the flesh. 'I feeled a crim coom o'er me'. **1888** *W. Somerset Word-bk.*, *Cream*, a shiver..a shivering state.

Hence **creemy** *a. dial.*, shivering, shuddering.

creem, obs. f. CREAM *sb.*[2]

creen, obs. form of CAREEN. ***on the creen***: ready to turn either way on receiving an impulse.

1798 T. Jefferson *Writ.* (1859) IV. 234 [To] decide the future turn of things, which are at this moment on the creen. *Ibid.* 236 Stopping the movement in the Eastern States, which were on the creen.

creengle, obs. f. CRINGLE.

creep (kriːp), *v.* Pa. t. and pa. pple. **crept** (krɛpt). Forms: see below. [A common Teutonic strong vb.: OE. *créopan* = OS. *criopan*, OFris. *kriapa* (NFris. *krepen*, Satl. *kriope*), ON. *krjúpa* (Sw. *krypa*, Da. *krybe*):—OTeut. **kreupan*. As with some other verbs of the same class (cf. BOW, BROOK, LOUT), the present has in some of the langs. *ú* for *eu*, as OLG. *krúpan*, MDu. *crúpen*, Du. *kruipen*, MLG., LG. and EFris. *krûpen*, MG. *krûfen*, *kraufen*. In OHG. replaced by *chriohhan*, MHG. and mod.Ger. *kriechen*, repr. a type *kreukan*, the relation of which to *kreupan* is uncertain.

The OTeut. conjugation was, pres. *kreupan*, pa. t. *kraup*, pl. *krupun*, pa. pple. *krupan*; whence OE. pres. *créopan* (3rd sing. *críepþ*), pa. t. *créap*, pl. *crupon*, pa. pple. *cropen*. The OE. pres. *créopan*, ME. *crēpen* (close *ē*), has regularly given the modern *creep*; occasional ME. instances of *crope* are app. errors. The pa. t. sing. *créap* regularly gave ME. *crêp* (open *ê*), spelt also *crepe*, *creep(e*, which was in general use to the 15th c., and survives with short vowel in the dialectal *crep*. The plural *crupon*, *crupe(n*, became in the 13th c. *cropen*, *crope*, after the pa. pple.; and this passed also into the sing. as *crope*, the prevailing type of the tense to the 16th c., after which it gradually dropped out of literary use, though still widely used in English and U.S. dialects. In the northern dial., the form adopted in the 13th c. was *crap* (after the pa. t. of other classes), which is still Scotch. But already before 1400, weak forms *creep-ed* and *crep-t*, began to take the place of all these, the second of which has since 16th c. gradually attained to be the standard form, leaving *crep*, *crope*, *crop*, *crup*, *crap*, as only dialectal. The pa. pple. *cropen* continued till the 17th c. in literary use, and to the 19th c. in the northern dial. where the vowel is still short *croppen*, *cruppen*; in the south it became in 13th c. *crope*, also literary Eng. to the 18th c.; but a weak form *crepid*, *creeped* began to appear in the 14th c., and in the form *crept*, identical with the pa. t., has been the dominant form since the 16th c.]

A. Illustration of Forms.

1. *Pres. tense.* 1 **créopan, críopan, (crýpan)**, 1–3 *3rd sing.* **criep(e)ð**; 2–4 **creope(n, (kreope(n)**; 2–6 **crepe(n**, (3–6 **crope**, 4 **cryepe**); 4–5 **krepe**, 4–7 **creepe**, (6 **creape**), 7– **creep**, (*Sc.* 5– **creip**).

c **1000** Ælfric *Gram.* xxviii. (Z.) 170 *Repo* ic creope. *c* **1175** *Lamb. Hom.* 23 Hwa creopeð þer-in? *c* **1200** *Trin. Coll. Hom.* 199 þe neddre..criepeð..þureh nerewe hole. *a* **1250** *Owl & Night.* 819 þe fox can crepe [*v.r.* crope] bi þe heie. *c* **1305** *Edmund Conf.* 107 in *E.E.P.* (1862) 73 Makede hire redi to kreopen in. **1393** Langl. *P. Pl.* C. xxi. 475 Arys ..and creop on kneos to þe croys. **1483** *Cath. Angl.* 81 To Crepe, *repere*. **1570** Levins *Manip.* 70 To creepe, *repere*. **1583** Hollyband *Campo di Fior* 137 Why creape you on the grounde? **1667** Milton *P.L.* ii. 950 And swims or sinks, or wades, or creeps, or flyes.

2. *Past tense.* α. *sing.* 1–3 **créap**, 3 **(creop)**, 3–5 **crep, crepe**, 4–5 **creep(e**, 9 *dial.* **crep**; *pl.* 1 **crupon**, 2–3 **crupen**.

c **1000** Ælfric *Hom.* II. 394 (Bosw.) Heo creap betwux ðam mannum. *a* **1100** *O.E. Chron.* an. 1083 Sume crupon under. *a* **1225** *Leg. Kath.* 908 [He] com ant creap in ure. *c* **1250** *Gen. & Ex.* 2924 Ðor crep a dragun. **1340–70** *Alisaunder* 1009 þer crep oute an addre. *c* **1386** Chaucer *Reeve's T.* 306 She creepe [*v.rr.* (MSS. **1435–75**) creep, crepe, crep, crepte] in to the clerk. **1881** *Leicester Gloss.*, *Crep*, pt. and p.p., crept.

β. *pl.* 3–4 **cropen**, 3– **crope**; *sing.* 4 **crop, croup**, 5– **crope** (*sing.* & *pl.* 6 **croape**, *dial.* 7–9 **crop**, 9 **crup**).

c **1275** Lay. 18472 Somme hii crope [*c* **1205** crupen] to þan wode. *c* **1290** *S. Eng. Leg.* 170/2217 Heo..cropen al-so ase ametene al aboute. *a* **1300** *Cursor M.* 2303 (Cott.) þaa wigurs croup þe warlau in. *c* **1420** *Avow. Arth.* lxv, The caytef crope in-to a tunne. **1535** Coverdale *1 Sam.* xiii. 6 They crope in to caues and dennes. **1572** R. H. tr. *Lauaterus' Ghostes* (1596) 207 Divers errours croape into the Church. **1606** Birnie *Kirk-Buriall* (1833) 14 Before the Kirk-buriall crop in. **1672** Sir C. Wyvill *Triple Crown* 160 He crope quietly on again. *a* **1734** North *Exam.* i. iii. §144 (1740) 217 Another Witness crope out against the Lord Stafford. **1831** Landor *Fra Rupert* Wks. 1846 II. 577 His dog soon crope betwixt us. **1883** C. F. Smith *Southernisms* in *Trans. Amer. Philol. Soc.* 47 *Crope*, preterit and past participle of *creep*, is common among the negroes and poorer whites.

γ. *north.* 3–9 **crap**, (4–5 **crape**).

c **1205** Lay. 29282 þe sparewe innene crap. *c* **1450** Henryson *Mor. Fab.* 44 To an Caue he crape. **1513** Douglas *Æneis* ii. v. (iv.) 48 And crap in wnder the feit of the goddes. *a* **1605** Montgomerie '*Since that the Hevins*' 41 With my king in credit once I crap. **1795** Macneill *Will & Jean* iii, Gloamin..crap ower distant hill and plain.

δ. 4–5 **creped, -id, crepped, (kreppet)**, 7–9 **creeped**, (4– *Sc.* **creipit**).

c **1300** *K. Alis.* 390 On hire bed twyes he leped, The thridde tyme yn he creped. **14..** *Chaucer MS.* [see B 1]. **1634** Massinger *Very Woman* iv. iii, How the devil Creeped he into my head? **1807** [see B. 1]. *Mod. Sc.* A fox creepit [or crap] through the hole.

ε. 4– **crept(e.**

c **1350** *Cursor M.* 15388 (Fairf.) Crepped in him Sathanas [*Trin. MS.* crepte, *Cott.* crep, *Gött.* croupe]. *c* **1350** *Will. Palerne* 2235 And crepten into a caue. **1548** Hall *Chron.* 169 Whereunto..[this] tended and crept up. **1632** Lithgow *Trav.* iv. (1682) 141 He crept in favour with Christians. **1860** Tyndall *Glac.* i. xi. 69 We crossed crevasses and crept round slippery ridges.

3. *Pa. pple.* α. 1–7 (*north. dial.* –9) **cropen**, 5–6 *Sc.* **croppin, croipin**, (6 **crepen**, 9 *north. dial.* **croppen, cruppen**, *Yorksh.* **creppen**).

c **1205** Lay. 5671 þa ilke þe aniht weoren atcropene. *c* **1386** Chaucer *Frankl. T.* 886 As thou..were cropen out of the ground. **1423** Jas. I. *Kingis Q.* clxxxii, Quho that from hell war croppin onys in hevin. **1481** Caxton *Reynard* (Arb.) 17 He had cropen therein. *a* **1553** Philpot *Wks.* (1842) 336 Corruptions have crepen into the people. **1563** Winȝet *Four Scoir Thre Quest.* Wks. 1888 I. 132 Abuiss..croipin in the Kirk. *a* **1572** Knox *Hist. Ref.* Wks. 1846 I. 401 Frensche men ar croppin in of lait. **1621** Markham *Prev. Hunger* (1655) 32 Cropen away and hidden. **1698** Lister in *Phil. Trans.* XX. 247 [They] would have cropen away. **1790** Mrs. Wheeler *Westmrld. Dial.* (1821) 23 Sic pride croppen intul Storth an Arnside. **1855** Robinson *Whitby Gloss.*, *Croppen* or *Cropen*, crept. 'Where hae ye gitten croppen to?'

β. 3–4 **ycrope, ycrop,** 3–8 **crope,** (4–5 **crepe**).

c **1275** LAY. 5671 Þat weren awei crope. *c* **1325** *Coer de L.* 3473 In the erthe they wolde have crope. *c* **1330** *Arth. & Merl.* 7229 Whider-ward were ye y-crope. *c* **1440** CAPGRAVE *Life St. Kath.* III. 404 If he ware Crope thorow þe ȝate. **1595** MARKHAM *Sir R. Grinvile, To the fayrest* i, A Heauenlie fier is crope into my braine. **1642** ROGERS *Naaman* 71 The Lord speakes of those..despised men, crope out of captivity. *a* **1734** NORTH *Examen* 273 (D.) The Captain was just crope out of Newgate.

γ. 4–5 **crepid,** 7–9 **creeped.**

c **1430** CHAUCER *Reeve's T.* 339 (Camb. MS.) He wende a crepid by hese felawe Ion [5 *MSS.* cropen, *Harl.* crope]. **1761** HUME *Hist. Eng.* I. xvi. 396 Intestine faction had creeped into the Government of France. *Mod. Sc.* It has creepit oot.

δ. 6– **crept.**

1535 COVERDALE *1 Macc.* vi. 11 Some y[t] were crepte in to dennes. **1611** BIBLE *Jude* 4 There are certaine men crept in vnawares. **1634** SIR T. HERBERT *Trav.* 195 Mahomet has a little crept among them. **1855** TENNYSON *Maud* III. vi. i, My life has crept so long on a broken wing.

4. The Perfect Tense was formerly, as in *go, come,* etc., formed with *be* to express result: he *is cropen* or *crept* in.

c **1205–1423** [see 3 *a* above]. **1534** TINDALE *Jude* 4 For ther are certayne craftely crept in. **1545** JOYE *Exp. Dan.* vii. iij b, Oute of poore scoles & cloysters are these beggers cropen vp. **1650** EARL MONM. tr. *Senault's Man bec. Guilty* 338 As soon as they are crope out from their Spring-head. **1706** A. BEDFORD *Temple Mus.* vii. 151 No Errors are crept into the ..Text. **1711** ADDISON *Spect.* No. 57 ¶4 That Party-Rage which..is very much crept into their Conversation. *a* **1734** [see 3 β].

B. Signification.

1. a. *intr.* To move with the body prone and close to the ground, as a short-legged reptile, an insect, a quadruped moving stealthily, a human being on hands and feet, or in a crouching posture.

Formerly said of snakes, worms, and other creatures without limbs, for which *crawl* is now more usual, though in some cases either may be used: see CRAWL *v.*

c **888** K. ÆLFRED *Boeth.* xxxvi. §4 Oþer næfþ his fota ȝeweald þæt he mæȝe gan..and onginþ creopan [*Bodl. MS.* crypan] on ðone ilcan weȝ. *c* **1000** ÆLFRIC *Hom.* II. 488 (Bosw.) Him comon to creopende fela næddran. *c* **1205** LAY. 29313 Þe king him gon crepen an heonden and a futen. *c* **1386** CHAUCER *Reeve's T.* 339 He wende haue cropen [*MS. Camb.* crepid, *Harl.* crope] by his felawe Iohn, And by the Millere in he creepe [*v.rr.* creep, crape, crepede, crept] anon. **1413** LYDG. *Pilgr. Sowle* IV. xxxiii. (1483) 82 The serpent..shold..crepe vpon his breste. **1598** SHAKS. *Merry W.* IV. ii. 59 Creepe into the Kill-hole. **1611** FLORIO, *Carponare,* to creepe on all foure. **1634** SIR T. HERBERT *Trav.* 213 Land Tortoyses so great that they will creepe with two mens burthens. **1705** BERKELEY *Cave of Dunmore* Wks. IV. 509 We were forced to stoop, and soon after creep on our knees. **1735** SOMERVILLE *Chase* III. 146 See there he [the fox] creeps along; his Brush he drags. **1807** ROBINSON *Archæol. Græca* III. vi. 227 A person accused creeped on his hands through the fire. **1864** TENNYSON *Aylmer's F.* 852 [There] the slow-worm creeps.

†b. Proverbially contrasted with *go* (= 'walk').

c **888** K. ÆLFRED *Boeth.* xxxvi. §4 Se biþ mihtiȝra se ðe gæþ þonne se þe criepð [*Bodl. MS.* crypþ]. *c* **1400** *Sowdone Bab.* 267 The Dikes were so develye depe..Ouer cowde thai nothir goo nor crepe. *c* **1460** *Towneley Myst.* 114 Kynde wille crepe Where it may not go. **1562** J. HEYWOOD *Prov. & Epigr.* (1867) 135 Children must learne to créepe ere they can go. **1663** BP. PATRICK *Parab. Pilgr.* 304 The most imperfect souls, who are not as yet able to go, but only to creep in the way to heaven. **1741** RICHARDSON *Pamela* III. 352 And besides, as the vulgar saying is, One must creep before one goes! **1836** *Backwoods of Canada* 57, I used to hear when I was a boy, 'first creep and then go!'

†c. ***to creep to the cross*** (also ***to creep the cross***): spec. used of the Adoration of the Cross, in the Roman Service for Good Friday. *Obs.*

c **1200** *Trin. Coll. Hom.* 95 Crepe to cruche on lange fridai. **1377** LANGL. *P. Pl.* B. XVIII. 428 Ariseth..And crepeth to þe crosse on knees. *c* **1449** PECOCK *Repr.* 269 Not as thouȝ thei crepiden thanne & there to noon other thing saue to the Ymage, but that thei aftir her ymaginacioun crepiden to the persoon of Crist. *a* **1500** *Ratis Raving* II. 129 Nocht our oft creip the corss one kneis. **15..** in Boorde *Introd. Knowl.* (1870) Introd. 92 The Usher to lay a Carpett for the Kinge to Creepe to the Crosse upon. **1554** BALE *Decl. Bonner's Articles* D iv b, To creape to the Crosse on Good Friday featly. **1586–92** WARNER *Alb. Eng.* 115 (N.) We kiss the pix, we creepe the crosse, our beades we over-runne. **1606** SHAKS. *Tr. & Cr.* III. iii. 73 To come as humbly as they vs'd to creepe To holy Altars. **1630** J. TAYLOR *Wks.* (N.), Because they would not creepe unto the crosse, And change Gods sacred Word for humane drosse.

2. a. To move softly, cautiously, timorously, or slowly; to move quietly and stealthily so as to elude observation; to steal (*into, away,* etc.).

c **1175** *Lamb. Hom.* 23 And þer beo analpi holh þat an mon mei crepan in. **1393** GOWER *Conf.* I. 198 This lady tho was crope a side As she, that wolde her selven hide. *c* **1470** HENRY *Wallace* VI. 627 Full law thai crap, quhill thai war out off sicht. **1577** B. GOOGE *Heresbach's Husb.* I. (1586) 6 The Fathers forsaking the Plough..began to creepe into the Toune. **1600** SHAKS. *A.Y.L.* II. vii. 146 The whining Schoole-boy..creeping like snaile Vnwillingly to schoole. **1705** ADDISON *Italy* 9 We here took a little Boat to creep along the Sea-shore as far as Genoa. **1850** TENNYSON *In Mem.* vii. 7 Like a guilty thing I creep At earliest morning to the door. **1873** BLACK *Pr. Thule* XXV. 421 If this wind continues, we can creep up to-morrow to Loch Roag.

b. Of things: To move slowly.

1650 FULLER *Pisgah* II. x. 214 Where the brook Zorek creeps faintly out of the Tribe of Judah. **1752** YOUNG *Brothers* II. i, Go, fool, and teach a cataract to creep! **1867** WHITTIER *Tent on Beach* xxiv, The mists crept upward chill and damp. **1878** HUXLEY *Physiogr.* 178 The sea-bottom over which the cold water creeps.

c. *trans.* To introduce gradually; slowly to increase (an amount of light, volume of music, etc.). Const. *in.* Cf. FADE *v.*[1] 9.

1949 T. RATTIGAN *Harlequinade* in *Playbill* 57 They've crept in numbers two and three [*sc.* spotlights] too early. **1960** N. KNEALE *Quatermass & Pit* III. 97 Creep in music.

3. *fig.* (of persons and things). **a.** To advance or come on slowly, stealthily, or by imperceptible degrees; to insinuate oneself *into*; to come *in* or *up* unobserved; to steal insensibly *upon* or *over.*

c **1340** *Cursor M.* 14147 (Trin.) Þat sekenes crepte to heued & fote. *c* **1380** WYCLIF *Wks.* (1880) 296 Þise newe ordris, þat ben cropen in wiþ-oute grounde. *c* **1430** *Hymns Virg.* (1867) 84 Now age is cropen on me ful stille. *c* **1430** LYDG. *Chron. Troy* I. i, So ferre he was cropen into age. **1533** Q. CATH. PARR tr. *Erasm. Commune Crede* 74 b, By unlawfull plesure crope in the death and destruction of mankynde. **1565** GOLDING *Ovid's Met.* VI. (1593) 172 Sleepe upon my carefull carcasse crope. **1647–8** COTTERELL *Davila's Hist. Fr.* (1678) 19 These opinions..crept up, till they were universally embraced. **1702** DE FOE *Shortest Way w. Dissenters* in Arb. *Garner* VII. 593 How they crope into all Places of Trust and Profit. **1709** STEELE *Tatler* No. 61 ¶1 Among many Phrases which have crept into Conversation. **1837** W. IRVING *Capt. Bonneville* I. 250 Despondency began to creep over their hearts. **1869** TROLLOPE *He Knew* liii. (1878) 293 When these sad weeks had slowly crept over her head. **1875** JOWETT *Plato* (ed. 2) III. 301 The licence of which you speak very easily creeps in.

b. To move timidly or diffidently; to proceed humbly, abjectly, or servilely, to cringe; to move on a low level, without soaring or aspiring. Cf. CREEPING *ppl. a.*

1581 MARBECK *Bk. of Notes* 623 So lowe crope they on the ground, that when they heare the name of the Sabboth, they remember nothing but the seauenth day. **1596** SPENSER *State Irel.* Wks. (Globe) 614/1 When they are weary of warres..then they creepe a litle perhaps, and sue for grace. **16..** DRYDEN (J.), It is evident he [Milton] creeps along sometimes for above an hundred lines together. **1709** POPE *Ess. Crit.* 347 And ten low words oft creep in one dull line. **1735** —— *Prol. Sat.* 333 Wit that can creep, and pride that licks the dust. **1782** COWPER *Conversation* 145 Where men of judgment creep, and feel their way, The positive pronounce without dismay. **1856** EMERSON *Eng. Traits, Manners* Wks. (Bohn) II. 46 Don't creep about diffidently. **1874** BLACKIE *Self-cult.* 89 Where aspiration is wanting, the soul creeps.

4. a. Of plants: To grow with the stem and branches extending along the ground, a wall, or other surface, and throwing out roots or claspers at intervals. **b.** Of roots or subterranean stems: To extend horizontally under ground.

1530 TINDALE *Pract. Prelates* Wks. 1849 II. 270 [Ivy] creepeth along by the ground till it find a great tree. **1580** BARET *Alv.* C 1597 To creepe, to run as rootes do in the ground, *repo.* **1672–3** GREW *Anat. Plants* II. I. i. §9 The Motions of Roots are..sometimes Level, as are those of Hops..and all such as properly Creep. **1697** DRYDEN *Virg. Georg.* IV. 182 Cucumers along the Surface creep. **1717** POPE *Eloisa* 243 Where round some mould'ring tow'r pale ivy creeps. **1837** DICKENS *Pickw.* vi, Oh, a dainty plant is the Ivy green, That creepeth o'er ruins old!

†c. Said of the ramification of blood-vessels, etc. *Obs.* Cf. CRAWL *v.* 4.

1668 CULPEPPER & COLE *Barthol. Anat.* I. xxviii. 67 Those [blood-vessels] which come from above do creep all the womb over. **1774** GOLDSM. *Nat. Hist.* (1776) III. 97 As they [blood-vessels] creep along the side of the branches [of the horns].

d. *fig.* To extend like a creeping plant.

1856 STANLEY *Sinai & Pal.* ii. (1858) 138 Vineyards creep along the ancient terraces. **1859** JEPHSON *Brittany* iii. 24 Up this cliff creeps the town, capped by the fine old church.

e. Of a liquid: to spread over or cover a surface as a thin film; *esp.* (of a salt solution) to rise on the sides of the containing vessel, depositing crystals of the salt; (of the dissolved salt) to be deposited in this way.

1888 J. A. FLEMING *Short Lect. Electr. Artisans* (ed. 2) 208 Difficulty sometimes occurs from the gradual 'creeping' up of the salts around the stopper. **1900** *Nature* 4 Oct. 562/1 Dr. Trouton gave a short account of his experiments on the creeping of liquids, and on the surface tensions of mixtures. He has found that the tendency of certain liquids to creep up the sides of their containing vessels is due to such liquids being mixtures. **1902** W. R. COOPER *Prim. Batteries* 195 When evaporation of a salt takes place in a glass vessel, crystals form on the vessel near the surface of the solution; and..the crystals grow upwards and finally grow over the top of the vessel. This 'creeping', as it is termed, is avoided in Leclanché cells by dipping the tops of the glass pots into ozokerite or paraffin wax. **1909** *Cent. Dict. Suppl.* s.v. *Oil-thrower,* Oil creeping along the shaft from the journal is thrown off. **1957** *Encycl. Brit.* XIV. 186/2 If an open vessel containing helium II is suspended inside the vacuum flask, ..the liquid creeps over the edge, and drops off the bottom of the vessel. **1958** J. J. BIKERMAN *Surface Chem.* (ed. 2) i. 89 The well-known phenomenon of creeping of solutions or crystal climbing probably involves the relation between surface tension and concentration.

5. a. *trans.* = *creep along* or *over. rare.* (Cf. also *creep the cross* in 1 c.)

1667 MILTON *P.L.* VII. 523 And every creeping thing that creeps the ground. **1727** DYER *Grongar Hill* 78 Whose ragged walls the ivy creeps. **1738** WESLEY *Hymns, 'O Thou whose Wisdom'* iii, The meanest Worm that creeps the Earth. **1821** CLARE *Vill. Minstr.* I. 130 Black clouds crept the southern hill.

b. *trans.* and *intr.* To rob (stealthily); to use stealth. *Criminals' slang* (orig. *U.S.*).

1914 in JACKSON & HELLYER *Vocab. Criminal Slang.* **1928** M. C. SHARPE *Chicago May* (1929) xxxi. 259 Panelling, or creeping, only carries eighteen months, because the John went to the room of his own accord. **1955** P. WILDEBLOOD *Against Law* III. 119 You could creep that drum six-handed, with jelly and all, and she'd think it was mice. **1958** [see CREEP *sb.* 1 e].

6. *intr.* Of the skin or flesh, less usually of the person himself: To have a sensation as of things creeping over the skin; to be affected with a nervous shrinking or shiver (as a result of fear, horror, or repugnance).

a **1300** *Cursor M.* 3567 (Cott.) Quen þat [he] sua bicums ald..It crepes crouland in his bak. *c* **1400** *Rom. Rose* 2558 Whanne thou wenest for to slepe, So fulle of peyne shalt thou crepe. **1727** SWIFT *Gulliver* III. vii. 223 Something in their countenances that made my flesh creep with a horror I cannot express. **1840** DICKENS *Barn. Rudge* xvii, You make my hair stand on end, and my flesh creep. **1879** G. MEREDITH *Egoist* xxviii. (1889) 266 He had such an air of saying 'Tom's a-cold', that her skin crept in sympathy. **1882** *Mrs. Raven's Tempt.* I. 310 It makes me quite creep.

7. *Naut.,* etc. To drag with a creeper for anything at the bottom of the water.

1813–14 *Act 54 Geo. III,* c. 159 §10 No person..shall.. creep or sweep for anchors [etc.]..supposed to be lost in any of the ports. **1830** MARRYAT *King's Own* ix, There the cargo is left, until they have an opportunity of going off in boats to creep for it, which is by dragging large hooks at the bottom until they catch the hawser. **1888** T. HARDY *Wessex Tales* II. 143.

8. Of metal rails, etc.: To move gradually forward under the continuous pressure of heavy traffic in the same direction, or as a result of periodical expansion and contraction on a gradient. Also, to increase very gradually in length under excessive stress.

1872 W. S. HUNTINGTON *Road-Master's Assistant* (ed. 2) 29 The rails in creeping have a tendency to move towards the foot of the grade. **1885** *Science* V. 344/2 In some places the rails move longitudinally or 'creep'. On long inclines or grades the track may creep down hill. **1887** *Engineer* LXIV. 9 Now I have the fish bolts loosened I am threatened with a creeping of the line. **1890** *Daily News* 31 Dec. 2/5 The very curious 'creeping' action of lead upon a roof was also shown by means of a model... In the experiment the lead, first heated and then cooled, was made to creep a perceptible space. **1899** J. A. EWING *Strength Mater.* 24 When a load exceeding the elastic limit is applied the strain which occurs at once is followed by a continued 'creeping' or supplementary deformation. **1911** —— in *Encycl. Brit.* XXV. 1014/1 The elastic limit is the point..at which a tendency to creep is first seen. **1924** F. C. LEA in *Proc. Inst. Mech. Engin.* II. 1053 The problem is to find the safe stress at which the material will not change form or creep. *Ibid.* 1072 At 11.40 a.m. on the 11th the specimen had crept 0·2 millimetre, but at 11.40 a.m. on the 14th the creeping had ceased. **1955** *Oxf. Jun. Encycl.* VIII. 286/2 Under this smaller but continuous burden the metal gradually deforms or 'creeps', and eventually breaks.

9. *Coal-mining.* To suffer a 'creep'.

1851 GREENWELL *Coal-trade Terms Northumb. & Durh.* 19 The softer the thill, the greater the liability to creep. **1861** *Trans. N. Eng. Inst. Min. Engineers* IX. 24 [It] had evidently brought on a heavy creep as shown on the section of crept bords.

10. Of soil, talus, etc.: to undergo creep (sense 7 a); to move imperceptibly *en masse.*

1889 *Geol. Mag.* VI. 257 The whole outer layer of the soilcap will..creep slightly downwards. *Ibid.* 260 The creeping of the soilcap through the action of frost. **1918** *Econ. Geol.* XIII. 609 In many places hillside surficial material seems to be creeping up instead of down—perhaps due to swelling by weathering of the surface portions of certain underlying beds. **1965** HATCH & RASTALL *Petrol. Sedim. Rocks* (ed. 4) II. v. 77 If a rock fragment on a slope is moved by its own expansion or that of the pore-water it may be exposed to the pull of gravity. It will then creep slightly downhill.

11. Of a rubber tyre. (Cf. CREEP *sb.* 9.)

1903 *Motoring Ann.* 300 It is claimed for the Collier tyre that it cannot possibly creep. **1908** *Westm. Gaz.* 25 Feb. 4/2, I understand that they have a great tendency to creep.

12. Of a belt or rope: to slip or slide backwards on the pulley. (Cf. CREEP *sb.* 8.)

1922 F. V. HETZEL *Belt Conveyors* 124 A poorly made belt ..will creep more and cause more wear than a good belt.

creep (kriːp), *sb.* [f. the verb.]

1. a. The action of creeping; slow or stealthy motion. (*lit.* and *fig.*)

1818 KEATS *Endym.* I. 679 Until a gentle creep, A careful moving caught my waking ears. **1842** WORDSW. *'Lyre! though such power',* Or watch..The current as it plays In flashing leaps and stealthy creeps Adown a rocky maze. **1862** THORNBURY *Turner* I. 264 There is a fine sense of terror and danger and adventure in Jason's stealthy creep.

†b. *Hawking.* See quot. *Obs.*

1486 *Bk. St. Albans* D j b, Yowre hawke fleeth at or to the Creepe when ye haue yowre hawke on yowre fyst and crepe softely to the Ryuer or to the pit, and stelith softeli to the brynke therof, and then cry huff, and bi that meane Nym a fowle.

c. †(*a*) A creeping fellow; a sneak. *dial. Obs.* (*b*) *slang* (orig. *U.S.*). A despicable, worthless, stupid, or tiresome person. Cf. CREEPER 1 b.

a **1876** E. LEIGH *Gloss. Cheshire* (1877) 52 *A Creep*.., a creeping fellow. **1886** BRIERLEY *Cast upon World* xviii. 218 His whole get-up so suggestive of what in those days was called a 'creep', that I could not help regarding him with additional loathing. **1935** *Jrnl. Abnormal Psychol.* XXX. 362 *Creep,* a worthless person. **1938** *New Republic* 7 Sept. 129/1 The man..is nothing but a creep. **1951** [see CHARGE *sb.* 3 d]. **1954** WODEHOUSE *Jeeves & Feudal Spirit* i. 7 They were.. creeps of the first water and would bore the pants off me.

1958 *Spectator* 9 May 588/3 A pathetic fat city creep comes making eyes at the daughter. **1960** H. PINTER *Room* 117, I get these creeps come in, smelling up my room. **1966** *Punch* 16 Feb. 241 'Maurice Thew School of Body-building'? That'll be that phoney creep upstairs.

d. A stealthy robber; a sneak thief; esp. one who works in a brothel. *Criminals' slang* (orig. *U.S.*). Cf. *creep joint* (6).

1914 in JACKSON & HELLYER *Vocab. Criminal Slang.* **1928** M. C. SHARPE *Chicago May* (1929) xxxi. 255, I have been a badger, pay-off, note-layer, creep, panel, and blackmailer. **1960** *Observer* 25 Dec. 7/6 A creep is a highly expert thief... He is so quiet that he can move about a house for hours without waking anybody.

e. Stealthy robbery; petty thieving; esp. in a brothel. So *at* or *on the creep*: engaged in stealthy robbery. Also *attrib. Criminals' slang* (orig. *U.S.*).

1928 M. C. SHARPE *Chicago May* (1929) xxxi. 257 She may decide to shift to the creep or panel game. **1931** C. RIMINGTON *Bon Voyage Bk.* 89/2 *At the creep*, picking lady's skirt pocket while walking. **1938** F. D. SHARPE *Flying Squad* i. 15 Billy's at 'the Creep' means that Billy earns his living stealing by stealth from tills whilst a shop is momentarily unwatched, or from a warehouse. **1958** F. NORMAN *Bang to Rights* III. 121 A geezer who got captured while he was out on the creep, he used to go out and creep about all over the place trying to find things to knock off. One of his favourite stokes was creep offices [*sic*] in the city.. during the lunch hour.

2. A sensation as of things creeping over one's body; a nervous shrinking or shiver of dread or horror. Usually in *pl.*, *the creeps* or *cold creeps* (colloq.).

1849 DICKENS *Dav. Copp.* iii. 29 She was constantly complaining of the cold, and of its occasioning a visitation in her back which she called 'the creeps'. **1862** LYTTON *Haunted & Haunters* in *Str. Story* (1866) II. 391, I felt a creep of undefinable horror. **1879** A. FORBES in *Daily News* 21 Aug. 5/3 It gives you the creeps all down the small of the back. **1884** *Athenæum* 15 Mar. 340/1.

3. *Coal-mining.* The slow continuous bulging or rising up of the floor of a gallery owing to the superincumbent pressure upon the pillars. 'Also any slow movement of mining ground' (Raymond *Mining Gloss.* 1881).

1813 *Ann. Philos.* II. 285 The pitmen were proceeding.. through the old workings..the proper road being obstructed by a creep. **1867** W. W. SMYTH *Coal & Coal-mining* 132 The creep.. arises when the thill or underclay is soft, and the proportion of pillars to bords such that after a time a downward movement takes place; the pillars then force the clay to rise upwards in the bords. **1867** *Ann. Reg.* 176 He advised that it should be buried in some of the creeps or crevices of some old pit-workings.

4. A low arch under a railway embankment; an opening in a hedge or other enclosure, for an animal to creep or pass through. Cf. CREEP-HOLE. Also, an enclosure in which young animals may feed, with an entrance too small to admit the mother. So *creep-feed*, *-feeding*; *creep-feed* v.

1819 *Sporting Mag.* IV. 209, I have heard that they [*sc.* pheasants] of late have been snared in creeps, like hares. **1875** W. MCILWRAITH *Guide Wigtownsh.* 37 A creep for cattle, on the Wigtown Railway. **1884** R. JEFFERIES *Red Deer* x. 188 Through this hedge [poachers] leave holes, or 'creeps', for the pheasants to run through. **1886** C. SCOTT *Sheep-Farming* 92 To fatten lambs rapidly, the utmost care must be given to their feeding. When folded on green crops they should feed in advance of the ewes, by having 'creeps' provided. **1924** *Chambers's Jrnl.* Jan. 49/2 The rabbits have their chosen creeps through the greenery below. **1950** *N.Z. Jrnl. Agric.* Jan. 63/1 Creep feeding. From the earliest age piglets will take extra feed. *Ibid.* Apr. 371/3 A creep in which the suckers can feed away from the sow is a necessity. **1960** *Farmer & Stockbreeder* 16 Feb. 50 The piglets.. will already be creep-feeding. *Ibid.* 22 Mar. 136/2 A suitable creep-feed mixture would be 2 parts cracked beans, 1 part crushed wheat, 3 parts crushed oats, 2 parts ground barley. **1964** R. JEFFRIES *Embarrassing Death* ii. 18 He could see sheep creep-feeding in one field.

5. = CREEPER 5.

1889 *Chamb. Jrnl.* Jan. 28/2 Boatmen went to work with creeps or drags to search for the body.

6. *attrib.* and *Comb.*, as †*creep-window* (cf. sense 4); (sense 10) *creep-rate*, *-resistance*, *-resistant* adj., *-strain*, *-stress*, *-test*, *-testing*; **creep curve**, a curve showing the rate, circumstances, etc. of creep (sense 10); **creep joint** *U.S. slang*, (*a*) a brothel or unwholesome apartment-house, esp. one where patrons are robbed; (*b*) a gambling-game operating in a different location each night; **creep limit, strength**, the maximum stress to which material, esp. metal, can be subjected without 'creep' (see sense 10). Also CREEP-HOLE, CREEP-MOUSE.

1931 H. J. TAPSELL *Creep of Metals* iii. 31 The form of the creep curve for materials at normal service temperature. **1928** M. C. SHARPE *Chicago May* (1929) ii, New York was full of creep joints at that time [*c* 1896]. **1930** *Amer. Mercury* Dec. 455/1 *Creep-joint*, a gambling house that moves to a different apartment each night. **1946** MEZZROW & WOLFE *Really Blues* i. 3 Earned my Ph.D. in more creep joints and speakeasies and dancehalls than the law allows. **1950** A. LOMAX *Mr. Jelly Roll* (1952) 50 Creep joints where they'd put the feelers on a guy's clothes. **1940** *Chambers's Techn. Dict.* 208/1 Creep limit. **1931** H. J. TAPSELL *Creep of Metals* iii. 31 Ultimate failure of a material would result however small the initial creep rate may be. **1937** *Jrnl. R. Aeronaut. Soc.* XLI. 378 Cast alloys have better creep resistance than forged. **1947** *Mech. Engin.* LXIX. 273 The scarcity of creep-resistant materials for blades and rotors working at high temperature. **1960** *Times* 16 Mar. (Canberra Suppl.) p. vii/1 The use of high-strength alloy creep-resistant steels for the tubes and supports. **1948** *Jrnl. R. Aeronaut. Soc.* LII. 2/2 Strain deviations.. are regarded as 'creep strains'. **1929** TAPSELL & REMFRY (*title*) The 'creep' strength of a 'high nickel-high chromium steel', between 600° and 800° C. **1957** *Times Surv. Brit. Aviation* Sept. 27/4 American writers have claimed an increase in creep strength of 20 per cent. by vacuum-melting. **1934** *Jrnl. R. Aeronaut. Soc.* XXXVIII. 205 When selecting a light alloy material for aero engine design.. it is important to consider the creep stress of the material concerned. *Ibid.* 408 Magnesium alloys under creep test. **1931** H. J. TAPSELL *Creep of Metals* i. 3 The experimental refinements now found necessary in creep-testing. **1664** ATKYNS *Orig. Printing* Ded. Bj, The least Creep-window robs the whole House; the least Errour in War is not to be redeemed.

7. *Geol.* (Cf. 3.) **a.** A slow, imperceptible movement *en masse* of soil, talus, etc., usu. downhill under the influence of gravity but freq. with other processes (such as successive freezing and thawing) contributing to the effect.

1889 *Geol. Mag.* VI. 260 The normal rise of the surface particles was about $\frac{1}{49}$ of the depth of the frozen soil, and their creep about $\frac{1}{185}$ of the same depth. **1897** W. B. SCOTT *Introd. Geol.* iv. 82 Each freezing causes the fragments to rise slightly..and each thawing produces a reverse movement; hence the slow creep down the slope. **1897** [see *soil-creep*, SOIL *sb.*[1] 10]. **1938** C. F. S. SHARPE *Landslides* iii. 21 The general term creep may be defined as the slow down-slope movement of superficial soil or rock debris, usually imperceptible except to observations of long duration. **1942** C. A. COTTON *Geomorphol.* (ed. 3) iii. 29 Evidence of creep may be seen where trees and posts have been tilted from the vertical. **1960** B. W. SPARKS *Geomorphol.* iv. 47 Rock creep is a movement of jointed blocks, partly as the result of soil creep and partly as a result of sliding. **1966** R. COMMON in G. H. Dury *Ess. Geomorphol.* 53 Shearing stresses in the material of a slope cause creep when they exceed the 'fundamental' shearing resistance.

b. A slow displacement of strata or the earth's crust by expansion or contraction or under compressive forces.

1900 [see *crust-creep* s.v. CRUST *sb.* 13b]. **1903** T. M. READE *Evol. Earth Struct.* ix. 134 The horizontal expansion .. will produce, by small increments and minor alterations, a creep, ending in an anticlinal fold. **1906** CHAMBERLIN & SALISBURY *Geol.* III. 312 Continental creep along the steep slope between the continental platforms and the oceanic basins. **1942** E. M. ANDERSON *Dynamics of Faulting* viii. 182 A general 'creep' of the surface towards the mountain axis is supposed by others to be an essential part of the process of orogeny. **1964** L. U. DE SITTER *Struct. Geol.* (ed. 2) xi. 149 Very accurate geodetic surface measurements across the San Andreas fault.. have shown that slow creep at an annual rate of 1 cm does take place along the fault line.

8. The slip of the belt on the pulley drum, or wheel over which it runs.

[**1888** *Lockwood's Dict. Mech. Engin.* 95 *Creeping*, the very slight loss of speed which results when drums are driven by rope gearing, due to the slipping of the rope.] **1909** W. C. UNWIN *Machine Design* I. 448 (*heading*) Creep of belt.

9. A creeping motion between the rim of a wheel and a rubber tyre. Cf. CREEP *v.* 11.

1908 *Westm. Gaz.* 5 Mar. 4/3 The rims of the R.W. wheel allow no creep with a properly inflated tyre.

10. The continuous deformation of a material (esp. a metal) under stress, esp. at high temperatures. Cf. CREEP *v.* 8.

1924 F. C. LEA in *Proc. Inst. Mech. Engin.* II. 1066 At stresses slightly above this the creep was continuous and the bar broke. *Ibid.* 1072 It will thus stand a higher stress without creep. **1931** H. J. TAPSELL *Creep of Metals* iii. 31 Creep may be defined as the deformation of a material occurring with time under and due to an externally applied stress whether the deformation be of the nature of plastic or of viscous flow. **1943** E. G. COUZENS in R. S. Morrell *Synthetic Resins* (ed. 2) xvii. 544 Flow takes place in two stages—creep, which is greatest following elastic deformation, and cold flow. **1952** *Jrnl. Iron & Steel Inst.* CLXXI. 333/2 In these materials creep was found to be primarily a process of slip in the austenite crystals. **1956** *Gloss. Terms Concrete (B.S.I.)* 16 *Creep*, a slow inelastic deformation or movement of concrete under stress. **1957** *Brit. Commonw. Forest Terminol.* II. 51 *Creep*, the increase in strain with time due to elastic after-effect and plastic deformation. **1970** *Fremdsprachen* 44 An uncertainty about the effect of creep and shrinkage.

creepage ('kriːpɪdʒ). [f. CREEP *v.* + -AGE.] Gradual movement; *spec.* leakage of electricity.

1903 *Electr. World & Engin.* 7 Nov. 777 (Cent. D. Suppl. s.v. *Oil-thrower*), Special oil throwers are provided to prevent the creepage of oil along the shaft. **1958** *Which?* I. II. 22/1 We tested the motor for safety... This included brush, creepage and wiring compliance. **1966** *McGraw-Hill Encycl. Sci. & Technol.* VII. 158/2 These [insulators] are made of glazed porcelain, with a series of skirts to lengthen the creepage paths and provide maximum resistance to flash-over.

creeper ('kriːpə(r)). Forms: 1 créopere, 4–6 creper(e, 6 crepar, 6– creeper. [f. CREEP *v.* + -ER.]

1. a. One who creeps. (In quot. 1883, a child too young to walk.)

a **1000** *Glostr. Frag.* 12. 17 (Bosw.) Seo ealde cyrce wæs eall behangen mid criccum and mid creoperа sceamelum. *c* **1440** *Promp. Parv.* 101 Crepere, or he þat crepythe, *reptor*. **1556** J. HEYWOOD *Spider & F.* lx. 35 A creper with spiders, and a flier with flise. **1682** OTWAY *Venice Pres.* v. ii, All us little creepers in 't, called men. **1883** J. PARKER *Apost. Life* II. 256 The door must not be shut..until the last little creeper has been brought in and sat at the Father's table.

b. *fig.* One who moves stealthily, timidly, or abjectly, or proceeds in a mean and servile way.

1589 PUTTENHAM *Eng. Poesie* III. xxiv. (Arb.) 299 Sometimes a creeper, and a curry-fauell with his superiours. **1598** FLORIO, *Insinuatore*, a craftie slie creeper into ones bosome, fauor or minde. *c* **1605** ROWLEY *Birth Merl.* III. vi, A gilded rascal, A low-bred despicable creeper. **1631** BRATHWAIT *Eng. Gentlew.* (1641) 360 They were..no strutters in the streets, but despicable creepers. **1811** LAMB *Trag. Shaks.*, The servilest creeper after nature that ever consulted the palate of an audience.

†**c.** *slang.* A 'penny-a-liner'; see quot.

1824 W. IRVING *T. Trav.* I. 241 A creeper is one who furnishes the newspapers with paragraphs at so much a line. **1825** T. LISTER *Granby* lx. (1836) 425 Persons, called, in the slang of the trade, 'creepers', whose business it is to prowl about, collecting incidents for the newspapers.

d. *pl.* (*a*) The feet; (*b*) shoes with soft soles. Also *attrib.* (in *sing.*). Cf. *brothel-creeper. slang* (orig. *U.S.*).

1889 BARRÈRE & LELAND *Dict. Slang* I. 280/1 *Creepers* ..(American), the feet. **1904** 'No. 1500' *Life in Sing Sing* 247 *Creepers*, soft shoes worn by burglars, sneak-thieves and prison guards. **1924** G. C. HENDERSON *Keys to Crookdom* 402 *Creepers*, rubber-soled shoes. Also called sneaks. **1951** *Sunday Pictorial* 29 Oct., Fancy shoes with thick crepe-rubber wedge soles which are known to connoisseurs as 'creepers'. **1955** E. BLISHEN *Roaring Boys* IV. 210 He pointed to my shoes, which were new and crape-soled. 'They're creepers... Real up-to-the-minute yobo's thick-soled creepers.' **1961** M. DICKENS *Heart of London* I. 67 The two-inch soles of their 'creeper' shoes.

2. a. An animal that creeps, a creeping thing, an insect or reptile; *spec.* (in vulgar speech) a louse.

1577 B. GOOGE *Heresbach's Husb.* III. (1586) 147b, You shall be sure to have neither Mite nor Creeper in your Cheese. **1609** BIBLE (Douay) *Gen.* vii. 21 Al creepers, that creepe upon the earth. **1651** *Miller of Mansf.* 8 Hast any Creepers within thy gay Hose? **1673** S. C. *Rules of Civility* 61 'Tis unbecoming.. to scratch.. as if there were Creepers upon our backs. **1840** HOOD *Up the Rhine* 200 A mounted gendarme would probably disdain to pursue a creeper.

b. *Angling.* The larva of the Stone-fly.

1867 F. FRANCIS *Angling* (1876) 264 The crab or creeper is the larva of the stone fly.

c. *Poultry-rearing.* 'One of a breed of fowls with legs so short that they jump rather than walk'.

1847 W. B. DICKSON *Poultry* 15 The Dwarf Fowl, or Creeper (*Gallus Bankiva*, S. *pumilio*, Temminck, *Le Coq Nain*, Buffon). **1885** in ANNANDALE.

3. A name given to many small birds, of different families, which run or climb up and down the branches of trees and bushes; *esp.* the common Brown Creeper or Tree-creeper, *Certhia familiaris*.

1661 LOVELL *Hist. Anim. & Min.* Introd., Birds..not melodious, as the..witwal, creeper, wren. **1674** RAY *Eng. Birds* 84 The Creeper or Ox-eye Creeper. **1766** PENNANT *Zool.* (1768) I. 193 The creeper.. next to the crested wren is the least of the British birds. **1863** BATES *Nat. Amazon* vii. (1864) 203 Many pretty little blue and green creepers of the Dacnidæ group were daily seen feeding on berries. **1882** *Proc. Berw. Nat. Club* IX. 553 No Gold-crests or Creepers, and rarely any Wrens were seen.

4. a. A plant that creeps along the ground, or (more usually) one that ascends a supporting surface, as ivy and the Virginian Creeper (*Ampelopsis hederacea*); a climber.

1626 BACON *Sylva* §536 They are Winders and Creepers; as Ivy, Briony, Hops, Woodbine. **1712** tr. *Pomet's Hist. Drugs* I. 31 This Plant is a Creeper, and twines or lashes itself round any Tree that is near it. **1721** BRADLEY *Wks. Nature* 37 The Ivy, and Virginia Creeper. **1818** KEATS *Endym.* II. 416 The creeper, mellowing for an autumn blush. **1860** GOSSE *Rom. Nat. Hist.* 60 Primeval labyrinths of giant trees, tangled with ten thousand creepers.

b. (*pl.*) *Arch.* 'Leaves or clusters of foliage used in Gothic edifices to ornament the angles of spires, pinnacles, and other parts; crochets.'

1864 in WEBSTER.

5. A kind of grapnel used for dragging the bottom of the sea or other body of water.

In first quot. app. used of a grappling-iron.

? *a* **1400** *Morte Arth.* 3667 Cogge appone cogge, krayers and oþer, Castys crepers one crosse als to þe crafte langes. **1536** BELLENDEN *Cron. Scot.* (1821) II. 106 He perist in Loch Tay.. His body was found be creparis. **1730** CAPT. W. WRIGLESWORTH *MS. Log-bk. of the 'Lyell'* 24 July, We sweaped with a Creeper for the Hawser, which we got hold of. **1769** FALCONER *Dict. Marine* (1789), *Creeper*, an instrument of iron resembling a grappling, having a shank and four hooks or claws.. It is used to throw into the bottom of any river or harbour.. to hook and draw up any thing.. lost. *a* **1825** FORBY *Voc. E. Anglia*, *Creepers*.. 2. Grapnels to bring up any thing from the bottom of a well or pond. **1875** WILCOCKS *Sea-Fisherman* (ed. 3) 40 The Grapnel or Creeper Sinker is much used off Dartmouth.. on account of the strength of the tidal currents.. These creepers have five claws. **1888** T. HARDY *Wessex Tales* II. 143.

†**6.** A small iron 'dog', of which a pair were placed on a hearth between the andirons. *Obs.*

1556 *Inv. Goods* in *Archæol.* XXXVI. 289 A payre of crepers. **1565** *Richmond. Wills* (Surtees) 178, j. olde brandrethe..j. iron creper. **1629** *Inv.* in *Trans. Essex Archæol. Soc.* III. II. 167, i pr creepers, fire shovell and tonges. **1661** PRYNNE *Exam. Exub. Com. Prayer* 106 The little Creepers, not the great Brass shining Andirons, bear up all the wood, and heat of the fire. **1833** J. HOLLAND *Manuf. Metal* II. 162 The andirons proper.. and what were denominated *creepers*, a smaller sort, with short necks or none at all.

7. *local.* **a.** A kind of patten or clog worn by women. **b.** A piece of iron with points or spikes, worn under the feet to prevent slipping on ice, etc.

1721 BAILEY, *Creepers*, a sort of Galoshes, between Clogs and Pattens, worn by Women. *a* **1825** FORBY *Voc. E. Anglia*, *Creepers*, 1. Low pattens mounted on short iron stumps, instead of rings. **1860** BARTLETT *Dict. Amer.*, *Creepers*, pieces of iron, furnished with sharp points and strapped under the feet, to prevent one falling when walking upon ice. **1887** *Newcastle Wkly. Chron.* 1 Jan. 4 Ice-creepers are now on sale in certain shops of Newcastle.

8. = CREEP *sb.* 4.

1845 *Jrnl. R. Agric. Soc.* VI. I. 189 That..lambs may..have more liberty, and pick out the shortest and sweetest of the keep, I have 'creepers' placed to enable them to do so.

9. **a.** An apparatus for conveying grain in corn-mills, a conveyor. **b.** An endless moving feeding-apron, in a carding-machine.

1847 *Engineer & Mach. Assistant* (*Descr. Plates*) 92 The creeper..constructed by Mr. Fairbairn. **1865** SIR W. FAIRBAIRN *Mills & Mill-work* II. 140 The creeper consists of a long enclosed screw with a wide pitch and projecting thin threads enclosed in a wooden box or trough.

10. A small iron frying-pan with three legs; also called a spider. (*U.S. local.*)

1880 in WEBSTER *Supp.*

11. A pupil in the tea-planting trade, esp. in Ceylon.

1893 *Field* 8 Apr. 510/3 'Creepers', as they are called, are constantly coming out to learn tea. **1894** *Standard* 2 Jan. 5 A 'creeper', it seems, is the technical term for a pupil whose parents pay a high premium to have him taught the art and mystery of tea-planting in Ceylon. **1921** LD. F. HAMILTON *Here, There & Everywhere* ii. 48 [In Ceylon] Planters are divided locally into three categories: the managers,..the assistants,..and the premium-pupils, known as 'creepers'. **1931** E. SUTTON tr. *Fauconnier's Soul of Malaya* I. iii. 30 The conceit of these blasted little creepers!

12. *Cricket.* A ball which keeps low after pitching.

1848 *Punch Almanack* May-June, Till some 'ripper' or 'creeper' gives the great wicket-keeper A chance. **1927** *Daily Tel.* 14 June 6/1 A 'creeper' from Larwood got rid of Twining. **1963** *Times* 17 May 4/5 Ormrod had to deal with three astonishing creepers from the lively Arnold.

13. *Comb.*, as (sense 4) ***creeper-clad, creeper-covered*** adjs.

1884 G. ALLEN *Philistia* I. 292 His pretty latticed creeper-clad window. **1888** *Daily News* 25 June 6/3 The cool woods and creeper-covered rocks.

b. creeper bridge, rope, a bridge or rope of twisted creepers stretched across a tropical river; **creeper chain** *Mining*, an endless chain fitted with grips or hooks for traction of mine-cars, etc.

1892 H. W. HUGHES *Coal-mining* 383 No better appliance has been introduced for minimising the cost of conveying tubs about the heapstead than that known as the 'finger' or 'creeper' chain... It consists of an endless chain travelling under the tubs, provided at intervals with vertical projecting pieces of iron fastened to the links. **1894** *Westm. Gaz.* 16 Jan. 5/3 A creeper rope tied from bank to bank. **1909** *Ibid.* 30 Dec. 5/4 We finally managed to get another creeper bridge between the island and the opposite bank, and hauled the women and children to a place of safety.

Hence **'creepered** *ppl. a.*, having (Virginia) creeper growing on the walls; **'creeperless** *a.*, without such a creeper.

1894 *Pall Mall Gaz.* 20 July 3/3 Down in the hollow is a glimpse of the creepered farmhouse. **1938** L. MACNEICE *Earth Compels* 21 A chart of tropic Swamp and twilight Of creepered curtains. **1904** H. G. WELLS *Food of Gods* I. ii. §1 The little house was creeperless.

creep-hole ('kri:phəʊl). [f. CREEP *v.* or *sb.* + HOLE.] A hole by which one creeps in or out; 'a hole into which any animal may creep to escape danger' (J.). Also *fig.* (cf. *loop-hole*).

1646 *Game of Scotch & Eng.* 20 How willing our brethren are to get a creep-hole, and how they shufle and cut to strugle themselves out of the Bryers. **1681** W. ROBERTSON *Phraseol. Gen.* (1693) 560 A poor shifting excuse, a miserable come-off, a very creep-hole. **1876** T. HARDY *Hand Ethelb.* I. 53 A screen of ivy..across the front of the recess..a small creep-hole being left for entrance and exit.

creepie ('kri:pɪ). *Sc.* and *dial.* Also creepy. [f. CREEP *v.* + -Y or -IE, denominative.]

1. **a.** A low stool. Also ***creepie-stool, creepy stool.***

1661 *Mercurius Caledonius*, To assemble all her Creels, Basquets, Creepies, Furmes. *a* **1756** *Sc. Song, Logie o' Buchan*, I sit on my creepie and spin at my wheel. **1859** DICKENS *Haunted House* VII. 34 He sat between his parents ..and Bessy on the old creepie-stool. **1865** *Reader* 18 Nov. 579/3 Carrying her creepie in one hand and her milking-pail in the other. **1892** JANE BARLOW *Irish Idylls* vii. 178 Pat, set the ould creepy stool for Mrs. Doyne. **1903** W. B. YEATS *Hour-Glass* (1904) 3 A creepy stool near it. **1922** JOYCE *Ulysses* 43 Fiacre and Scotus on their creepystools in heaven.

b. 'It sometimes denotes the stool of repentance' (Jamieson). Also ***creepie-chair.***

1718 RAMSAY *Christ's Kirk Gr.* III. viii, It's a wise wife that kens her weird, What tho' ye mount the creepy? **1794** BURNS *Rantin Dog* iii, When I mount the creepie-chair, Wha will sit beside me there?

2. A small speckled fowl. (*U.S. local.*)

1854 *Trans. Penns. Agric. Soc.* 163 The variety of poultry exhibited..comprising, in the tribe of barn-yard fowls,..the Frizzle; the Creely and the Creepy.

creeping ('kri:pɪŋ), *vbl. sb.* [-ING[1].]

1. **a.** The action of moving on the ground, as a reptile, or a human being on hands and knees.

a **700** *Epinal Gloss.* 696 *Obreptione*, criopungae. *c* **1440** *Promp. Parv.* 101 Crepynge, *repcio, reptura.* **1580** HOLLYBAND *Treas. Fr. Tong, Rampement..sur terre*, a raumping or creeping on the ground. **1813** L. HUNT in *Examiner* 19 Apr. 242/2 Creepings in dust and wadings through mire.

b. ***creeping to the cross***: see CREEP *v.* 1 c.

15.. in Boorde *Introd. Knowl.* (1870) Introd. 92 The Order of the Kinge, on Good Friday, touchinge the..creepinge to the Crosse. **1511** *Will of Osborn* (Somerset Ho.), At the tyme of the creping of the crosse. **1583** BABINGTON *Commandm.* ii. (1637) 23 With crossings and creepings, Paxes and Beads. **1924** C. MACKENZIE *Heavenly Ladder* x. 145 The only thing he regretted about this Good Friday was his cowardice over the ceremony of creeping to the Cross. **1957** *Oxf. Dict. Chr. Ch.* 1411/2 *Veneration of the Cross*, a ceremony of the Latin Rite for Good Friday, sometimes also called Creeping to the Cross.

2. *transf.* and *fig.* The action of moving slowly, stealthily, or in a servile manner.

1565 T. STAPLETON *Fortr. Faith* 153 The creping in of these cancred heresies. **1665** BOYLE *Occas. Refl.* Introd. Pref. (1675) 22 A Writer in some cases may be allowed to..forbear Soaring, as well as avoid Creeping. **1736** NEAL *Hist. Purit.* III. 463 After great creepings and cringings to Archbishop Laud, he became his creature. **1840** THACKERAY *Catherine* xi, The man was well fitted for the creeping and niggling of his dastardly trade.

3. The sensation as of something creeping on the skin; cf. FORMICATION.

1799 MAD. D'ARBLAY *Lett.* 25 July, Your creepings are surely the effect of overlabour of the brain. **1855** ROBINSON *Whitby Gloss.*, *Creepings*, cold shivery sensations. **1879** B. TAYLOR *Stud. Germ. Lit.* 362 We feel a creeping of the nerves.

4. Dragging with creepers or grapnels.

1886 *Pall Mall G.* 7 Sept. 2/1 When they [ironclads] attempted to follow up the clearance effected by creeping and countermining, and to make the passage of the channel.

5. In Canada: Stalking the Moose-deer, etc.

1869 C. HARDY *Forest Life Acadie* vi. 134 At the present day the animal [Cariboo] is shot by stalking or 'creeping' as it is locally termed, that is, advancing stealthily and in the footsteps of the Indian. **1879** LD. DUNRAVEN in *19th Cent.* July 60 Creeping or 'still hunting' as it would be termed in the States is as nearly as possible equivalent to the ordinary deer-stalking.

6. *Comb.* **creeping-hole** = CREEP-HOLE; **creeping-sheet** (see quot.).

1665 J. WEBB *Stone-Heng* (1725) 204 The Works of greatest Magnificence..this Doctor talks of, extended to no more than..a creeping Hole at best. **1849** *Sk. Nat. Hist., Mammalia* IV. 72 Each burrow [of the hamster] has at least two openings, one descends obliquely, the other perpendicularly. The former is termed the 'creeping-hole'. **1874** KNIGHT *Dict. Mech.*, *Creeping-sheet*, the feeding-apron of a carding-machine.

creeping ('kri:pɪŋ), *ppl. a.* [f. as prec. + -ING[2].]

1. That creeps (as a reptile).

c **1000** ÆLFRIC *Gen.* i. 25 And eall creopende cynn on heora cynne. *a* **1300** *Cursor M.* 19849 (Cott.) All maner crepand beist. **1483** *Cath. Angl.* 81 A Crepynge beste, *reptile.* **1611** BIBLE *Gen.* viii. 19 Euery beast, euery creeping thing, and euery fowle. **1667** MILTON *P.L.* VII. 452 Cattel and Creeping things, and Beast of the Earth. **1784** COWPER *Task* VI. 568 The creeping vermin, loathsome to the sight.

2. *transf.* and *fig.* **a.** Moving slowly, stealthily, or by imperceptible degrees. Also applied to a flaw or crack in steel.

c **1340** *Cursor M.* 3567 (Fairf.) Wiþ crepinge croulis in his bake. **1590** SPENSER *F.Q.* I. v. 12 The creeping deadly cold. **1600** SHAKS. *A.Y.L.* II. vii. 112 The creeping houres of time. **1700** DRYDEN *Sigism. & Guisc.* 748 The creeping death Benumbed her senses first, then stopped her breath. **1870** EMERSON *Soc. & Solit.*, *Farming* Wks. (Bohn) III. 59 The invisible and creeping air. **1882** *Syd. Soc. Lex.*, *Creeping sickness*, a form of chronic Ergotism. **1902** *Daily Chron.* 1 May 6/3 From an examination of the broken parts a 'creeping' flaw was found in the cross-section. **1914** H. BREARLY *Case-hardening Steel* 110 Such cracks, generally spoken of as 'creeping cracks', are not often found in brittle material.

b. Moving timidly or abjectly; acting meanly or servilely; cringing. ***creeping Jesus***, a person who slinks about or hides himself from fear of being ill-treated; an abject, sycophantic, or servile person; one who is hypocritically pious. *slang.*

a **1618** RALEIGH *Instruct. Sonne* iii. in *Rem.* (1661) 89 Flatterers..are ever base, creeping, cowardly persons. **1706** JER. COLLIER *Refl. Ridic.* 112 Others of a mean and creeping Soul. **1769** GRAY *Ode for Music* 9 Nor Envy base nor creeping Gain. *c* **1818** BLAKE *Everlasting Gospel* in *Wks.* (1927) 137 If he [*sc.* Christ] had been Antichrist, Creeping Jesus, He'd have done any thing to please us. **1827** —— *Lett.* in *Wks.* (1927) 1138 God keep you and me from the divinity of yes and no too—the yea, nay, creeping Jesus. **1854** H. MILLER *Sch. & Schm.* xv. (1860) 159/1 The mean vices, —such as theft, and the grosser and more creeping forms of untruthfulness and dishonesty. **1871** G. P. R. PULMAN *Rustic Sketches* (ed. 3) 88 Creeping-jesus, applied to a person who seeks to hide himself in pursuit of sport or otherwise. 'Jack crawled ãäder the weeld ducks lik' a creeping-jesus.' **1934** R. CAMPBELL *Broken Record* 56 The Zulus naturally despise the creeping Jesus type who sucks up to them. **1937** 'G. ORWELL' *Road to Wigan Pier* x. 194 The outer-suburban creeping Jesus. **1945** A. HUXLEY *Time must have Stop* xxiv. 226 That fool who believed in Gaseous Vertebrates, that creeping Jesus who tried to convert people to his own idiocies! **1966** 'L. LANE' *ABZ of Scouse* 23 *Creepin' Jesus*, applied to a person who enjoys bad health or constant misfortune; somebody who solicits sympathy by wearing an air of patient martyrdom.

c. ***creeping barrage*** (Mil.): see BARRAGE *sb.* and add examples.

1916 H. W. YOXALL *Let.* 22 Sept. in *Fashion of Life* (1966) iv. 32 The creeping barrage which went in front of our assaulting lines was almost geometrically straight, and lifted each time to the second. **1919** G. K. ROSE *2/4th Oxf. & Bucks Lt. Infty.* 129 Our methods of attack..consisted, broadly speaking, in the advance of lines of Infantry behind a creeping barrage. **1957** *Encycl. Brit.* VI. 663/2 The limitation of the standing barrage was that the curtain of shells did not move with the troops; and while a creeping barrage made short bounds of 50 to 100 yards, a jumping barrage made longer ones.

d. ***creeping paralysis***: locomotor ataxia. Also *fig.*

1913 in DORLAND *Med. Dict.* (ed. 7) s.v. *Paralysis.* **1925** W. DEEPING *Sorrell & Son* i. 10 He remembered that he had won his M.C. by 'doing something' as a protest against the creeping paralysis of intense fear. **1926** H. J. LASKI *Let.* 30 May (1953) II. 843 The miners are still out, and industry, as a result, is afflicted with a kind of creeping paralysis. **1932** *Discovery* Apr. 112/1 A single glance at the film gives information concerning creeping paralysis (disseminated sclerosis). **1964** G. DURRELL *Menagerie Manor* v. 103 The creeping paralysis, a terrible complaint that attacks principally the New World monkeys.

3. Having the sensation of a nervous shiver.

[Cf. **1340** in 2 a.] **1814** BYRON *Corsair* III. x, So thrill'd —so shudder'd every creeping vein. **1815** —— *Hebrew Mel.*, '*A Spirit pass'd*' 5 Along my bones the creeping flesh did quake. **1881** G. M. BEARD *Sea-sickness* 24 Creeping chills up and down the spine.

4. **a.** Of plants: Having a stem or stems which extend themselves horizontally along the surface of the ground, and throw out roots at intervals. It is often popularly applied, instead of 'climbing' or 'clinging', to plants that cling to and ascend trees, walls, or hedges: cf. CREEPER 4.

creeping root, a popular name for a rhizome or subterranean stem that grows horizontally and throws out shoots and roots at the joints, as in Wild Convolvulus.

[**1552** HULOET, Creapyng here and there lyke a vyne, *errans.*] **1697** DRYDEN *Virg. Past.* ix. 57 With..creeping Vines on Arbours weav'd around. **1784** COWPER *Task* IV. 762 The casements lined with creeping herbs. **1807** J. E. SMITH *Phys. Bot.* 111 *I*[*ris*] *florentina* and *I. germanica*..have more properly creeping roots. **1810** SCOTT *Lady of L.* I. xi, Creeping shrubs of thousand dyes. **1882** VINES *Sachs' Bot.* 156 The underground creeping shoots of *Pteris aquilina.*

b. In the names of many plants with aerial creeping stems, as ***creeping ivy*** (the procumbent form of *Hedera Helix*), ***creeping Jack***, a local name of *Sedum acre*, ***creeping Jenny*** (*Lysimachia Nummularia*, and other plants), ***creeping sailor*** (*Saxifraga sarmentosa* and *Sedum acre*), ***creeping wheat*** (*Triticum repens*), etc.; ***creeping willow***, a shrub, *Salix repens*, native to Europe and Asia.

1776 WITHERING *Brit. Plants* (1796) III. 683 Creeping Mouse-ear. Mouse-ear Hawkweed. **1816** KEITH *Phys. Bot.* I. 45 The common Creeping Cinquefoil. **1819** W. C. WENTWORTH *Descr. N.S.W.* 91 The creeping wheat, however, may be sown in the commencement of February. *Ibid.* 92 To the farmer..who keeps large flocks of sheep, the cultivation of the creeping wheat is highly advantageous; since in addition to its yielding as great a crop as any other species of wheat, it supersedes the necessity of growing..food for the support of his stock. **1861** MISS PRATT *Flower. Pl.* VI. 124 Creeping Wheat, or Couch-grass. **1882** *Garden* 12 Aug. 138/2 The common Money-wort, or Creeping Jenny as it is called. **1894** W. ROBINSON *Wild Garden* (ed. 4) xvi. 262 Dwarf willows..such as the Creeping Willow in its various forms, and the Woolly Willow, a dwarf silvery shrub. **1952** A. G. L. HELLYER *Sanders' Encycl. Gardening* (ed. 22) 434 [*Salix*] *repens*, 'Creeping Willow', to 3 ft., Britain, Europe, Asia.

creepingly ('kri:pɪŋlɪ), *adv.* [f. prec. + -LY[2].] In a creeping manner. *lit.* and *fig.*

1548 THOMAS *Ital. Dict.*, *Carpone*, creepyngly, as he that goeth on all fower. **1573** TUSSER *Husb.* (1878) 17 Age comming on so creepinglie. **1675** PHILLIPS *Theatr. Poet.* Pref. (T.), That the poem be not..creepingly low and insipid. **1816** L. HUNT *Rimini* III. 460 Pretending not to see The latter [satyrs] in the brakes come creepingly.

creeple, obs. f. CRIPPLE.

'creep-mouse. [f. stem of CREEP *v.* + MOUSE.]

A. *sb.*

†1. A creeping mouse: a term of endearment.

1540 PALSGRAVE tr. *Fullonius' Acolastus* R ij a, I con the thank my lyttell sparowe, or my pretye crepemous.

2. A nursery play with a child.

1689 J. CARLILE *Fortune-hunters* 25 Not so old but I can play at creep Mouse yet; creep, Mouse, creep, catch her.

B. *adj.* [Cf. *break-neck.*] That creeps like a mouse so as to escape notice; furtive, timid, shy.

1766 *Goody Two-Shoes* (1882) 58 Not seeing such a little creep-mouse Girl as Two-Shoes. **1814** JANE AUSTEN *Mansf. Park* (1816) I. xv. 304 You may be as creepmouse as you like, but we must have you to look at. **1860** EMERSON *Cond. Life*, *Behaviour* Wks. (Bohn) II. 387 Here are creep-mouse manners, and thievish manners.

creepy ('kri:pɪ), *a.* [f. CREEP *v.* or *sb.* + -Y.]

1. Characterized by creeping or moving slowly.

1794 SULLIVAN *View Nat.* II. 95 It is a creepy fluid. **1860** *All Year Round* No. 49. 538 She is rarely still, though I am bound to say she is creepy gentleness itself. **1889** J.

ABERCROMBIE *E. Caucasus* 180 An artistically embroidered coverlet tenanted..by countless swarms of creepy insects.

2. Having a creeping of the flesh, or chill shuddering feeling, caused by horror or repugnance.

1831 *Cat's Tail* 30, I feel somehow quite creepy at the thought of what's coming. **1863** LD. LYTTON *Ring Amasis* II. 38 There comes over him, all at once, a sort of cold, creepy shudder. **1882** *Macm. Mag.* 444 To confess that he has felt 'creepy' on account of certain inexplicable sounds.

b. *transf.* Tending to produce such sensations.

1883 G. LLOYD *Ebb & Flow* II. 236 The whole place seemed lonely, and, as Mildred whispered to Pauline, 'creepy'. **1892** *Spectator* 2 Apr. 470/1 A really effective romance of the creepy order.

creepy-crawly, *a.* That creeps and crawls. Also *transf.* and *fig.*, sneaking, servile; (of feelings, etc.) full of eerie or uncanny suggestion; of or pertaining to creeping or crawling insects. Also as *sb.* (chiefly *pl.*), such an insect, animal, etc.; a creepy-crawly feeling.

1858 C. M. YONGE *Christmas Mummers* iv. 37 The pink scarf came back in his mind, as clear..as if the silver creepey-crawleys and long-barbed flowers had all arranged themselves into the letters *thief*. **1861** J. PYCROFT *Agony Point* ix. (1862) 99 Ride and drive! yes,—creepy crawly! creepy crawly! **1890** F. W. ROBINSON *Very Strange Family* 85 'You and that creepy-crawley lawyer.' **1891** 'L. MALET' *Wages of Sin* VII. iii, I'm ever so hungry, and there's cold creepy-crawlies running up my legs. *a* **1893** *Mod.* A creepy-crawly feeling came over me. **1902** *Daily Chron.* 5 Dec. 4/5 The creepy-crawly atmosphere of 'Wuthering Heights'. **1907** *Ibid.* 1 Apr. 4/4 His way is mostly the creepy-crawly way... There's nothing heroic, or splendid, or even dignified, about his methods. **1909** G. B. SHAW *Let.* 14 Apr. (1956) 152 We..are back again in Algeria, but under creepy-crawly circumstances... We are in a frightful place. **1923** D. H. LAWRENCE *Kangaroo* vi. 133 She had puppies—four darling queer little things—tiny little creepy-crawlies. **1960** *Woman* 5 Mar. 29/2 Mice, spiders, moths and other creepy-crawlies. **1966** AUDEN *About House* 24 The lair, maybe, Of creepy-crawlies or a ghost.

creer, var. of CRAYER.

crees, var. CREST[3] *Obs.*, a kind of linen cloth.

creese, crease, varr. KRIS, Malay dagger.

creese, crease, kris, *v.* Forms: see prec. [f. prec.] *trans.* To stab or kill with a creese. Hence **'creesing** *ppl. a.* and *vbl. sb.*

1602-5 E. SCOT *Disc. Java* in Purchas *Pilgrims* (1625) I. 175 This Boyhoy we tortured not, because of his confession, but crysed him. **1727** A. HAMILTON *New Acc. E. Ind.* II. xlvi. 158 One [Malay] of them runs to the King, and crest him to the Heart. **1857** S. OSBORN *Quedah* vi. 79 They..constantly saw their countrymen creesed before their eyes. **1883** G. M. FENN *Middy & Ensign* xxix. 181 They having been krissed and their bodies thrown into the river.

creeses, obs. and dial. pl. of CRESS.

creesh, creish (kriːʃ), *sb.* *Sc.* 6 creische, cresche, 7-9 creish, 8 creisch, kreish, 9 creesh, cresh. [a. OF. *craisse, cresse* = *graisse, gresse* fat, grease:—L. *crassa*, fem. of *crassus* thick, fat, gross, in late L. also *grassus* (see Du Cange). In Gael. *créis* (kreːʃ), *s* with a 'small' vowel being always (ʃ); several instances of a similar change occur in Lowland Sc.; cf. also *gresche* = GREASE.]

1. Grease, fat.

a **1400** *Burgh Lawis* lxviii, Woll, nowte cresche or swyne sayme. **1500-20** DUNBAR *Dance Sevin Synnis* 99 In creische that did incress. **1513** DOUGLAS *Æneis* VII. xi. 61 Fat cresche or same. **1862** HISLOP *Proverbs Scot.* 41 Butter's king o' a' creesh.

2. A 'lick', a stroke. Cf. ANOINT *v.* 5.

a **1774** FERGUSSON *Poems* (1789) II. 93 (Jam.) Now some for this, wi' satire's leesh, Has gi'en auld Edinbrough a creesh. **1833** MOIR *Mansie Wauch* xxii. (1849) 172 Give the beast a good creish.

creesh (kriːʃ), *v.* *Sc.* Forms: see prec. [f. CREESH *sb.*; cf. F. *graisser.*] *trans.* To grease. *to creesh the loof* (fig.): 'to grease the palm', i.e. with a douceur. Cf. *to grease (a person) in the hand* (see GREASE *v.*).

1721 KELLY *Scot. Prov.* 237 (Jam.) Like the Orkney butter, neither good to eat, nor to creisch wool. *a* **1774** FERGUSSON *Hallowfair* Poems (1845) 13 He'll take the hint and creish her loof Wi' what will buy her fairin. **1816** SCOTT *Antiq.* x, 'Would ye creesh his bonny brown hair wi' your nasty ulyie?' **1843** BETHUNE *Sc. Fireside Stor.* 48 If he was only able to creish the clerk's loof.

creeshy ('kriːʃɪ), *a.* *Sc.* [f. CREESH *sb.* + -Y[1]. In Gael. *créisidh* ('kreːʃi).] Greasy.

1535 LYNDESAY *Satyre* 140, I ken weill, be his creischie mow, He hes bene at ane feast. *a* **1605** POLWART *Flyting w. Montgomerie* 747 Creishie soutter, shoe cloutter, minch moutter. **1786** BURNS *Ordination* i, Wabsters..pour your creeshie nations..Swith to the Laigh Kirk. **1891** *Pall Mall G.* 28 Dec. 2/2 But filthy lucre is the name For Scotland's creeshy pounds.

b. *subst.*

1890 *Scot. N. & Q.* Aug. 53 Creeshie was the name given to boys and girls who worked in the carding and spinning departments [of woollen mills].

creesome, obs. form of CHRISOM.

creest(e, creete, obs. ff. CREST, CREAGHT.

creevish, crefish, -fysshe, obs. ff. CRAYFISH *sb.*

creeze, var. KRIS, Malay dagger.

creft, crefti, -y, obs. ff. CRAFT, CRAFTY.

crei, -en, early var. of CRY.

creil(le, obs. f. CREEL, and var. CRILE *Obs.*

†**creis**, *v.* *Sc. Obs.* To curl. (Jamieson.)

[Only in the following passage, the sense of which is doubtful.]

1513 DOUGLAS *Æneis* XII. ii. 125 Hys crysp and ȝallow hayr, That are mayd creis, and curlis now sa weill.

creitzer, obs. form of KREUTZER.

creke, obs. f. CRATCH, CREAK, CREEK.

creket(t, -kytt, obs. ff. CRICKET.

crele, crelle, obs. ff. CREEL.

crem, obs. form of CREAM *sb.*[1]

‖**crémaillère** (kremɑjɛr). [Fr.; formerly *cramaillère* a crook with a rack or notches for hanging pots over a fire, a toothed rack, any indented piece, deriv. of *cramail*:—late L. *cramāculum* (Capit. Charlemagne *De Villis* 42) in the first of these senses. Perh. f. Du. *kram* hook, or some cognate word. The two following technical applications of the Fr. word appear in Eng.]

1. *Field-fortif.* An indented or zigzag form of the inside line of a parapet, giving opportunity for bringing a greater fire to bear upon the defile. (Stocqueler.)

1828 J. M. SPEARMAN *Brit. Gunner* 264 These hurdles..are very useful in forming the teeth of the cremaillères in the saliant angles of fieldworks. **1859** F. A. GRIFFITHS *Artil. Man.* (ed. 9) 273 Lengthen the lines by cremaillères.

2. *Watch-making.* (See quot.)

1884 F. J. BRITTEN *Watch & Clockm.* 69 Cremaillere..[is] the winding rack of a repeating watch.

cremar(e, obs. f. CRAMER, *Sc.*, pedlar, etc.

cremaster (kriː'mæstə(r)). Pl. **-ers**, also ‖**-eres**. [a. Gr. κρεμαστήρ suspender (or spec. in Anatomy, as in sense 1), f. κρεμα- to hang.]

1. *Anat.* The muscle of the spermatic cord, by which the testicle is suspended.

1678 PHILLIPS, *Cremaster*, the Muscle, that holds up the Stones. *a* **1693** URQUHART *Rabelais* III. xxvi. 218. **1842** E. WILSON *Anat. Vade M.* 187 The Cremaster, considered as a distinct muscle, arises from the middle of Poupart's ligament. **1881** MIVART *Cat* 243 One delicate layer..forming what is known as the cremaster muscle.

2. *Entom.* A name given by Kirby to the hook-like processes on the posterior extremity, by which many lepidopterous chrysalids suspend themselves; extended to the dorsal process or tip of the abdomen of the pupa of any insect that undergoes complete metamorphosis.

1888 ROLLESTON & JACKSON *Anim. Life* 153 Pupa of Privet Hawk Moth..The tenth somite..bears..the cremaster..covered with spines which vary much in different specimens.

†**cre'masteral**, *a.* *Obs. rare*[−1]. [f. prec. + -AL[1].] = next.

1681 tr. *Willis' Rem. Med. Wks.* Vocab., *Cremasteral*, muscles belonging to the testicles.

cremasteric (krɛmæ'stɛrɪk), *a.* [f. as prec. + -IC.] Of or pertaining to the cremaster.

1882 *Syd. Soc. Lex.*, *Cremasteric artery*, a thin branch of the deep epigastric artery.

cremate (kriː'meɪt, krɪ-), *v.* [f. L. *cremāt-* ppl. stem of *cremāre* to burn, consume by fire, cremate.] To consume by fire, to burn; *spec.* to reduce (a corpse) to ashes. Hence **cre'mated** *ppl. a.*; **cre'mating** *vbl. sb.* and *ppl. a.*

1874 F. HALL in *Nation* (N.Y.) XIX. 425/1 *Satî*, or a woman who is cremated with her husband. **1878** *Ann. Reg.* 127 The construction of a cremating apparatus. **1889** *Ibid.* 18 The body of the Marquess of Ely was cremated at Woking. **1889** *Pall Mall G.* 26 Dec. 6/2 Mortuary urns containing cremated Greeks' ashes.

cremation (kriː'meɪʃən, krɪ-). [ad. L. *cremātiōn-em*, n. of action f. *cremāre* (see prec.).]

1. The action of burning or cremating; *spec.* the reduction of a corpse to ashes as a way of disposing of it in lieu of interment; an instance of this practice.

1623 COCKERAM, *Cremation*, Burning. **1658** SIR T. BROWNE *Hydriot.* ii. 4 The Solemnities, Ceremonies, Rites of their Cremation or enterrment, so solemnly delivered by Authors. **1758** JOHNSON *Idler* No. 87 ¶4 The custom of voluntary cremation is not yet lost among the ladies of India. **1851** D. WILSON *Preh. Ann.* II. III. vi. 160 When cremation was abandoned for inhumation. **1882** *Pall Mall G.* 6 June 1/2 The cremation of Garibaldi..is to be carried out in accordance with his last will and testament. **1884** *Pall Mall G.* 7 Mar. 3/2 Mr. Justice Stephen's recent decision that cremation..is a legal proceeding has..stirred the Cremation Society of England to be up and doing.

2. *attrib.* and *Comb.*, as ***cremation-burial, -cemetery, grave***.

1913 E. T. LEEDS *Archaeol. Anglo-Saxon Settlements* iii. 58 The number of cremation burials occurring at Frilford is uncertain. **1934** *Essays & Studies* XIX. 150 The description of the last rites paid to Beowulf shows that his was a cremation-burial. **1955** WOOLLEY *Alalakh* vi. 211 Cremation burial in Sq. M 13. **1907** H. M. CHADWICK *Origin Eng. Nation* iv. 74 The cremation cemeteries at Croydon and Beddington are also perhaps inconclusive. **1960** P. H. REANEY *Orig. Eng. Place-Names* 102 Repton..situated above the right bank of the Trent in a district where cremation-cemeteries have been found. **1950** H. L. LORIMER *Homer & Monum.* vi. 346 Of two Early Geometric cremation graves found..in the Agora one contained a pair of large fibulae.

Hence **cre'mationism**, *nonce-wd.*, the advocacy or 'cause' of cremation. **cre'mationist**, one who advocates cremation as a means of disposing of the bodies of the dead.

1884 *Fargo* (Minnesota) *Argus* Feb., Cremationism is on the increase. **1875** F. S. HADEN *Earth to Earth* 6 The Cremationists, whose position I..think untenable. **1885** *Manch. Exam.* 22 June 5/3 The revelations made..excited the cremationists immensely.

cremator (kriː'meɪtə(r), krɪ-). [a. L. *cremātor* (Tertullian), agent-noun f. *cremāre*; see CREMATE.]

1. One who cremates or practises cremation of corpses.

1881 *London Post Off. Direct.* 1553 (Trades Division) Cremators. **1884** *Pall Mall G.* 1 May 2/1 It is the boast of the skilful cremator that under his supervision the contents of the barrel are never exposed to view. **1885** *Academy* 16 May 342/3 It is..erroneous to describe the aborigines of British Columbia as 'cremators'. Only a few of the Northern tribes burn their dead.

2. A crematory furnace: **a.** for the combustion of rubbish; **b.** for the cremation of dead bodies.

1877 *Chr. World* 12 Oct. 1/2 Models of hospitals, sewer works, and..cremators. **1881** *Scribn. Mag.* XXII. 799 To enable the housekeeper..to dispose of the refuse in a quick and cleanly manner, a small cremator, or destructor, has been introduced. **1883** *Pall Mall G.* 5 Dec. 10/2 The furnace, or 'cremator', built close to the deceased's house, was on the banks of the River Stour.

crema'torial, *a.* [f. next + -AL[1].] Of or pertaining to a crematory or to cremation.

1887 *Chicago Advance* 17 Feb. 112 The Crematorial Association of Philadelphia is about to erect the largest crematory in the world.

crematorium (krɛmə'tɔərɪəm). [mod.L., in form f. *cremāt-us, cremātōr-*, derivs. of *cremāre* to burn.] = CREMATORY *sb.*

1880 *Times* 9 Oct., In the cemetery of Milan, near the Crematorium erected a few years ago, a Cinerarium is to be erected for the preservation of the ashes of the dead. **1884** *St. James's Gaz.* 8 Feb. 4/2 The new building will be the second public crematorium in the United States.

crematory ('krɛmətərɪ), *a.* and *sb.* [f. L. type **cremātōri-us*, f. *cremātor*: see above.]

A. *adj.* Of or pertaining to cremation.

1884 *Manch. Guard.* 26 Sept. 5/4 Belief in the crematory process as a sanitary measure. **1886** MORLEY *Life Geo. Eliot* Crit. Misc. III. 94 Leaving as little work, to the literary executor, except of the purely crematory sort, as did, etc. **1889** *Chambers' Encycl.* III. 556 Crematory furnaces..have been erected.

B. *sb.* A place or establishment for cremation; *spec.* an erection for the incineration of corpses.

1876 L. TOLLEMACHE in *Fortn. Rev.* Jan. 118 The aspect of death might be a little softened, if cemeteries gave place to crematories. **1885** *Times* 27 Mar. 10 Yesterday morning the crematory erected at St. John's, Woking, Surrey, was made use of for the first time.

crème (krɛːm, kreɪm), *sb.* Also **crême**. [Fr., = CREAM *sb.*[2]] **1.** A cream (CREAM *sb.*[2] 2 a) or custard. So ***crème brûlée***, one topped with caramelized sugar; ***crème caramel***, a custard coated with caramel; ***crème Chantilly*** [cf. CHANTILLY 3], whipped cream sweetened and flavoured with vanilla; ***crème renversée***, a custard turned out of a mould.

1845 E. ACTON *Mod. Cookery* xx. 442 Crême à la Comtesse..is a very delicate kind of sweet dish, which..may be rendered more recherché by a flavouring of maraschino. **1846** A. SOYER *Gastronomic Regenerator* 528 *Crême au Caramel*... Have three quarters of a pint of milk in which you have boiled an ounce of isinglass, pour it upon the caramel. **1865** M. B. CHESNUT *Diary* 5 Apr. (1905) xx. 376 We keep a cookery book on the mantelpiece, and when the dinner is deficient we just read off a pudding or a *crême*. **1868** E. ACTON *Mod. Cookery* xxiii. 484 The French make their custards, which they call *crêmes*, also in small china cups. **1886** M. CLARK tr. *Brisse's 366 Menus* 163 Crème brûlée. Burnt cream. [*Ibid.* 324 Crème à la Chantilly. Cream à la Chantilly. **1888** MRS. BEETON *Bk. Househ. Managem.* xxxi. 828 Caramel Pudding. (Fr.—Crême Renversée.)] **1906** *Ibid.* lxv. 1730 Crême Caramel renversée. Caramel Pudding. **1908** C. H. SENN *Menu Book* 273 [*Crème*] *Chantilly*, whipped double cream, with vanilla flavour. **1909** *Cent. Dict.* Suppl., *Crême brulée*, caramel or browned sugar with cream. **1912** H. H. MUNRO *Unbearable Bassington* xv. 271 Jerome and the girls don't want to eat any more *crême renversée*. **1914** C. MACKENZIE *Sinister St.* II. III. v. 592 Our crême caramel is a much showier sweet than anything they've got at the House. **1930** A. BENNETT *Imperial Palace* lx. 478 Evelyn heard the order: vermicelli soup,..cutlets,..crême caramel. **1935** *Punch* 9 Jan. 33/1 Oh, many a *crème* have I consumed. **1949** 'C. HARE' *When Wind Blows* 153

Spooning into his mouth the last of the tasteless crême caramel which the club almost invariably provided by way of a sweet. **1958** R. GODDEN *Greengage Summer* ix. 95 Meringues with crème chantilly. **1959** *Listener* 6 Aug. 227/2 To make the *crême brulée* take 1 pint of double cream, 6 oz. of caster sugar, 4 egg yolks, and vanilla essence. **1970** SIMON & HOWE *Dict. Gastronomy* 143 *Crème pâtissière*, also known as confectioner's custard or baker's custard, this is a thick French custard or cream used to fill tartlets, cream horns or puff creams.

b. A name for various syrupy liqueurs, as ***crème de menthe*** (peppermint), ***crème de vanille, crème de noyau, crème de cacao***. (Cf. CREAM *sb.*[2] 2 e.)

a **1821** KEATS *Cap & Bells*, in *Poet. Wks.* (1907) 472 The least drop of *crème de citron*, crystal clear. *c* **1870** in H. W. ALLEN *3 Saint James's St.* (1950) viii. 186/2 Liqueurs.. Creme de Noyau—10/-. **1877** *Cassell's Dict. Cookery* 382/2 Noyau, or Crême de Noyau, is a sweet cordial flavoured with bitter almonds. **1892** T. F. GARRETT *Encycl. Pract. Cookery* I. 477/1 *Crêmes*, a French term applied to certain cordials and liqueurs, to indicate the cream-like smoothness of these manufactures. **1903** *Daily Mail* 11 Sept. 3/3 Crême de menthe, with its strong peppermint flavour, is the one almost exclusively favoured by ladies. **1930** E. WAUGH *Labels* 26 Shady young men in Charvet shirts sit round the bar repairing with powder-puff and lipstick the ravages of grenadine and *crême de cacao*. **1930**, **1958** [see ALEXANDER *sb.*[2]]. **1961** I. FLEMING *Thunderball* x. 112 A tall glass of his favourite drink—crème de menthe frappé with a maraschino cherry on top.

c. ***crème de riz***, a fine rice-flour; ground rice.

1896 MRS. A. B. MARSHALL *Cookery Bk.* (ed. 2) 15 (Advt.), Marshall's Crème de Riz.. highly prized for Cakes, Puddings, Blancmanges. **1960** E. DAVID *Fr. Prov. Cooking* 97 *Crème de Riz*, Ground Rice.

2. Phr. ***crème de la crème***, the élite, the very pick of society.

1848 F. A. KEMBLE *Let.* 22 Jan. in *Rec. Later Life* (1882) 336 The.. pretensions of an Austrian *crème de la crème* are comprehensible and consistent. **1860** *Once a Week* 28 July 119/2 The elders—the *crême de la crême*, or those initiated into the highest mysteries of the sect. **1867** S. W. BAKER *Nile Tribut.* xvii. 451 The society in this district was not *crême de la crême*. **1898** B. L. FARJEON *Miriam Rozella* xi, Need I say that he and Lady Laverock move in the best society, and are *crême de la crême*? **1920** D. H. LAWRENCE *Lost Girl* i. 8 In his palmy days, James Houghton was *crême de la crême* of Woodhouse society. **1967** R. SHAW *Man in Glass Booth* vi. 70, I love you all for you are the finest of your kind, the crème de la crême Americaine.

†**creme**, *v. Obs.* [f. *creme*, CREAM *sb.*[1]] = CHRISM *v.*

1398 TREVISA *Barth. De P.R.* IX. xxxi. (1495) 367 Crysma .. with the whyche chyldern ben cremyd and enoynted.

creme, obs. form of CRAME, CREAM.

cremesin(e, -yn(e, -ye, obs. ff. CRIMSON, CRAMOISY.

†**'cremetous, cremeuse**, *a. Obs. rare.* [a. OF. *cremeteus* and *cremeus* fearful, timid, f. root of OF. *cremer, cremir*, now *craindre* to fear.] Fearful, timid.

c **1477** CAXTON *Jason* 26 b, As cremetous and doubting the recountres of reffuse. *Ibid.* 14 b, They of Oliferne were so cremeuse.. and durst not come out.

[**cremett, -it(t.** Error for EREMITE, inmate of a hospital.

1624 *Will* in *Ripon Ch. Acts* (Surtees) 363, I give sixteene cremets here, in Well, fower markes. *Note*, This word occurs occasionally in the older registers at Well, applied to the inmates of the hospital, 'eermits' once. **1709** in *Thoresby's Corr.* II. 221 The word Cremits in your old deed relating to the Hospital at Well, is doubtless, or should be, Eremits. **1736** DRAKE *Eboracum* 284 The Eremites, or Hermits, in the north were corruptly called Cremitts; and there is an annual rent.. called Cremitt-money at this day.]

†**cremeur.** *Obs.* [OF. *cremeur* 'feare, dreade' (Cotgr.), f. OF. *cremer*: see CREMETOUS, CREMEUSE, *a.*] Dread.

1485 CAXTON *Chas. Gt.* 46 Kynge of Fraunce and lord of so grete cremeur.

†**'cremify**, *v. Obs.*[−1] [f. F. *crème* or med.L. *crema*, CREAM + -FY.] *trans.* To make creamy, cause to form cream.

1638 NABBES *Tottenham Crt.* IV. 7 Isinglasse and other ingredients to cremifie the soure milke.

†**cremil**, *sb. Obs.* Forms: 4 cremyle, -ell, 4–5 cremyl(l, 5 crymell, -yll. [Connexion with '*crummle* to plait' (Halliwell), and *crimple*, has been suggested. Cf. next word.]

A word used in connexion with certain textile fabrics; often applied *attrib.* to their borders; 'meaning, apparently, open work or lace, or perhaps a fringe' (W. H. Stevenson, in *Nottingham Borough Records* II. Gloss. s.v.).

1393 *Will of Kent* (Somerset Ho.), Flameolum de Cremyle. **1408** in *Nottingham Rec.* II. 52 Pro ij plyces de coton cremyll, ijs. vjd. **1428** *Will of Lyte*, Flameolum vocatum crymell. **1448** *Will of Stapilton*, j crymyll kyrchief. **1483** *Act 1 Rich. III*, c. 8 §18 The making of any Cloths called Florences, with Cremil Lists. **1511–2** *Act 3 Hen. VIII*, c. 6 §3 Wollen clothes called Bastardes made with cremyll Lystes. [**1885** FAIRHOLT *Costume* II. 136 *Cremyll*, cotton open work, or lace.]

†**cremil, crimil**, *v. Obs.* [cf. prec.] *trans.* ? To plait, to crimp.

1377 LANGL. *P. Pl.* B. xv. 223 Ac in riche robes rathest he walketh, Ycalled and ycrimiled [*v.r.* i-crymeled, y-crymyled, ycrymaylid, crymailed] and his crowne shaue.

†**cremitoried**, *ppl. a. Obs.* (Meaning obscure.)

1608 MIDDLETON *Trick to catch* IV. v, Out, you babliaminy, you unfeathered cremitoried quean, you cullisance of scabiosity.

cremmyn, obs. form of CRAM *v.*

Cremnitz ('krɛmnɪts). Also **Kremnitz.** [f. *Kremnitz* (formerly also *Cremnitz*), the German name of Kremnica, a town of eastern Czechoslovakia (formerly Körmöczbánya, Hungary).] Used *attrib.* to designate a white lead pigment used as a paint base.

1874 A. A. FESQUET tr. *Riffault's Manuf. Colors* ii. 56 The Clichy or chemical white lead is less dense and possesses less body than the Kremnitz white. **1880** W. J. MUCKLEY *Char. & Use Colours* 28 *Cremnitz White*, is sometimes known as Vienna White. It is very bright in appearance, even surpassing Flake White, but not so dense in body. It is a preparation of lead. **1934** H. HILER *Technique of Painting* ii. 99 *White lead*, the most important pigment in general use in the fine arts at the present time. It is also called.. *Cremnitz White.*

cremnophobia (krɛmnəʊ'fəʊbɪə). *Path.* [mod.L., f. Gr. κρημνός overhanging cliff: see -PHOBIA.] A morbid dread of precipices or steep places.

1903 in DORLAND *Med. Dict.* (ed. 3). **1908** G. B. SHAW *Sanity of Art* 97 [Nordau] is started off by the termination 'phobia' with a string of Agoraphobia.., Belenophobia, Cremnophobia.

cremocarp ('krɛməʊkɑːp). *Bot.* [irreg. f. Gr. κρεμα- to hang, κρεμαστός suspended, hanging + καρπός fruit.] A species of fructification, occurring in the Umbelliferæ, in which the simple inferior fruit divides into two indehiscent one-seeded mericarps, which remain for some time suspended by their summits from the central axis.

1866 in *Treas. Bot.* 345. **1870** BENTLEY *Bot.* 312 The Cremocarp is an inferior, dry, indehiscent, two-celled, two-seeded fruit. **1885** BENNETT & DYER *Sachs' Bot.* II. v. 537 A Cremocarp, where the fruit breaks up into two one-seeded halves or mericarps by the splitting of the dissepiment or 'carpophore' along its length.

Cremona[1] (kriː'məʊnə). Name of a town in Lombardy, where the art of violin-making reached its highest perfection in the 17th and early 18th century. *attrib.* Pertaining to or made at Cremona, as in ***Cremona fiddle, school, violin***; *absol.* A violin made there. Also (from Fr.) †**'Cremone.** Hence **Cremo'nese** *a.*

1762 STERNE *Tr. Shandy* V. xv. 68 I'll stake my Cremona to a Jew's trump. **1784** SHERIDAN *Life of Swift* (T.), A lady whisking about her long train.. threw down and broke a fine Cremona fiddle. **1798** HARRINGTON *Retort Courteous*, 'Twas thieving Pindar, 'tis well known, Swindled his Godship's old Cremone. **1875** EMERSON *Lett. & Soc. Aims, Quot. & Orig.* Wks. (Bohn) III. 214 The Bible.. is like an old Cremona; it has been played upon by the devotion of thousands of years. **1880** P. DAVID in Grove *Dict. Mus.* I. 416 'A Cremona', or 'a Cremonese violin' is often incorrectly used for an old Italian instrument of any make.

cre'mona[2]. [Corruption of KRUMMHORN, CROMORNE.] An organ reed-stop of 8-foot tone.

1660 *Specif. of Organ, Whitehall* in Grove *Dict. Mus.* II. 591 Choir Organ.. 14. Cremona. **1880** P. DAVID in Grove *Dict. Mus.* I. 416 'Cremona', as applied to an organ stop, is a mere ignorant corruption of 'Krumhorn'. **1880** E. J. HOPKINS *ibid.* II. 74 Krummhorn (i.e. crooked-horn), Cromorne, Cremona.. The Cremonas in the organs built by Father Smith (1660).. were doubtless 'voiced' to imitate the .. now obsolete crooked-horn.

‖**cremor.** In 7 cremour. [a. L. *cremor* thick juice obtained by steeping, pressure, or decoction, broth, pap (? related to *cremāre* to burn), and obs. F. *cremeur* 'a creamie or milkie disposition or humor' (Cotgr.), where the sense is app. influenced by *crème* cream.]

a. A thick juice or decoction; a liquid of this consistency: a broth, pap. **b.** By erroneous association with F. *crème*, CREAM *sb.*[2], a scum gathering on the top of a liquid.

1657 TOMLINSON *Renou's Disp.* 163* Of their cremour may be made a certain sorbicle. **1657** *Phys. Dict.*, *Cremor*, the top or flower of any liquor or cream of milk, yeast, the juyce of steeped barley, &c. **1691** RAY *Creation* (1714) 27 The food is swallowed into the stomach, where, mingled with dissolvent juices, it is reduced into a Chyle or Cremor. **1757** WALKER in *Phil. Trans.* L. 128 When the water was exposed for some days to the air, there was a cremor separated from it of a shining chalybeat colour. **1851–60** MAYNE *Expos. Lex.*, *Cremor*, cream; also, any substance floating on, and skimmed from the surface of a fluid; also, a thick decoction of barley.

c. ***cremor of tartar*** (= *cremor tartari*): cream of tartar; see CREAM *sb.*[2] 4.

1656 RIDGLEY *Pract. Physick* 201, Cremor Tartar dissolved in steeled Wine. **1756** NUGENT *Gr. Tour, France* IV. 16 The chief commodities of this country.. verdigrease, cremor tartari, &c.

cremorne (organ-stop): see CROMORNE.

cremosin, -oysin, cremsin, -ysyn, cremysy, obs. ff. CRIMSON, CRAMOISY.

†**cremp**, *v. Obs. rare.* [Only known in early ME.; prob. a. MDu. or LG. *kremp-en* (:—*kramp-jan*), causal of *krimp-en*; cf. CRAMP.] *trans.* To contract, restrain.

a **1250** *Owl & Night.* 1785 Ȝef the thincth that ich misrempe, Thu stond aȝein and do me crempe. [*Ibid.* 509 A sumere chorles awedeth, And vorcrempeth, and vorbredeth.]

cren, obs. Sc. form of CRANE.

‖**crena** ('kriːnə). *Bot., Zool.*, etc. [mod.L. *crēna* incision, notch, corresp. to It. *crena* notch, nocke (Florio, 1598), F. *crene, crenne* (16th c.); R. Estienne *Petit Dict.* 1543 has 'un cren ou crenne, *crena*'.

The history of this word is very obscure; L. *crēna* incision, notch, was formerly read in Pliny, *H. N.* XI. 37. 68 § 180; but it is now held to be an error, so that the word remains without ancient support. But the word, with its derivative *crēnātus*, has been used freely in mod.L. since the 16th c. From same date F. has also *cren, cran* sb., and *crener* v., *crené* pa. pple. An earlier date for the vb. is implied by the sbs. *crenée* (:—*crēnāta*) = 'crenel', and *creneure* (:—*crēnātūra*) crenature, 12th c. in Godef. For *cren* a still higher antiquity is implied by the diminutives *crenet* and *crenel* (12th c. in Littré): see CRENEL. Herewith Diez associates also Rumansch *crenna*, Lombardian *crena*, Piedm. *cran.* But the origin of *crena* remains uncertain.]

1. An indentation, a notch; *spec.* in *Bot.* one of the notches on a toothed or crenated leaf; *Anat.* the depression or groove between the buttocks; the longitudinal groove on the anterior and posterior surface of the heart (*Syd. Soc. Lex.*).

2. A crenated tooth, a scallop; *spec.* in *Bot.* a round or convex tooth on the margin of a leaf, etc., = CRENATURE, CRENEL; *Entom.* a rounded raised mark resembling a wrinkle on a surface or margin; *Anat.* each of the serrations on the edge of the external table of the cranial bones by which these fit together in the sutures (*Syd. Soc. Lex.*).

crenate ('kriːnət), *sb. Chem.* [f. CREN-IC + -ATE[4].] A salt of crenic acid.

1838 T. THOMSON *Chem. Org. Bodies* 152 Crenate of manganese. **1863–72** WATTS *Dict. Chem.* II. 103 The apocrenates of the alkalis resemble the crenates, excepting that they are black.

So **'crenated** *a.*

1838 T. THOMSON *Chem. Org. Bodies* 152 Crenated peroxide of iron. Obtained when crenic acid is mixed with a neutral sulphated peroxide or chloride of iron.

crenate ('kriːneɪt), *a. Bot., Zool.*, etc. [ad. mod.L. *crēnātus*, f. CRENA. Junius *Nomenclator* 1577 has '*Folium crenatum*, pinnatum, feuille crenée'.] Having the edge notched or toothed with rounded teeth; finely scalloped.

1794 MARTYN *Rousseau's Bot.* xxii. 307 Cat-mint has the middle division of the lower lip [of the corolla] crenate. **1836** TODD *Cycl. Anat.* I. 711/2 When these projections and notches are very fine, the shell is said to be crenate. **1870** BENTLEY *Bot.* 152 When the teeth are rounded the leaf is crenate.

b. In comb. = CRENATO-.

1870 HOOKER *Stud. Flora* 129 Leaves.. crenate-dentate. *Ibid.* 330 Leaves.. shining, crenate-serrate, ciliate.

Hence **'crenately** *adv.*

1864 T. MOORE *Brit. Ferns* 47 Lobes of the pinnæ.. with .. a crenately toothed margin.

'crenate, *v. rare.* [f. CRENATE *a.*: cf. 16th c. F. *créner*.] To produce crenations; to 'mill' the edge of (coin).

1868 SEYD *Bullion* 279 The stamping and crenating are done at one stroke.

crenated ('kriːneɪtɪd), *ppl. a.*

1. *Bot., Zool.*, etc. = CRENATE *a.*

1688 R. HOLME *Armoury* II. 115/1 Crenated Leaves [are] such as are jagged and notched. **1826** KIRBY & SP. *Entomol.* (1828) IV. xxxviii. 39 The margin of the lips is crenated. **1857** BIRCH *Anc. Pottery* (1858) I. 83 Flat plate beads.. which occasionally are crenated.

†**2.** = CRENELLATED. *Obs. rare.*

1822 J. HODGSON in J. Raine *Mem.* (1857) I. 401 Crenated battlements.

crenation (kriː'neɪʃən). *Bot., Zool.*, etc. [f. CRENATE: see -ATION.] A crenated formation; a rounded toothing, *e.g.* on the margin of a leaf or shell; scalloping; a crenature.

1846 DANA *Zooph.* (1848) 490 The polyps.. have twelve short tentacles.. in some species they are mere crenations to the disk. **1875** H. C. WOOD *Therap.* (1879) 317 A well-marked stellar crenation. **1884** BOWER & SCOTT *De Bary's Phaner.* 376 In many teeth and crenations of the leaf.

crenato- (kriː'neɪtəʊ), combining form of mod.L. *crēnātus* CRENATE; crenately, crenate-.

1845 LINDLEY *Sch. Bot.* vii. (1858) 124 Leaves.. doubly and evenly crenato-serrate. **1846** DANA *Zooph.* (1848) 304 It is represented as crenato-denticulate [= crenately-toothed]. **1866** *Treas. Bot.* 346 *Crenato-serrate*, when serratures are convex, and not straight.

crenature ('krɛnətjʊə(r), 'kriːn-). *Bot.* & *Zool.* [f. mod.L. *crēnāt-us* + -URE: cf. OF. *creneure.*] A rounded tooth or denticulation on the margin of a leaf, etc. Also sometimes applied to the notches or indentations between the teeth.

1816 KIRBY & SP. *Entomol.* (1843) I. 389 Mining into the very crenatures between the two surfaces of the leaf. **1845** LINDLEY *Sch. Bot.* iv. (1858) 26 Leaflets 3-lobed, with ovate, rounded crenatures. **1872** OLIVER *Elem. Bot.* II. 177 The leaves..produce young plants from buds originating in the notches (*crenatures*) of the margin.

crenel, crenelle ('krɛnəl, kriː'nɛl), *sb.* Forms: 5 (*pl.* creneuls, creneaux), 8–9 crennel, 9 crenel, -ell(e. [a. OF. (12th c.) *crenel*, pl. *creniaus* (mod.F. *créneau, -eaux*). OF. variants were *kernel, karnel*, whence also Eng. CARNEL, KERNEL q.v. The Fr. word is app. dim. of *cren, cran* notch (of which however Littré has no example before 15th c.); see CRENA and cf. CRANNY.]

1. One of the open spaces or indentations alternating with the merlons or cops of an embattled parapet, used for shooting or launching projectiles upon the enemy; an embrasure: see BATTLEMENT. In *pl.* = Battlements, embattled parapet.

1481 CAXTON *Godfrey* 179 It shold be fasted to the creneaux of the walle, with good and stronge crochettes of yron. *Ibid.* cxx. 181 Thenne cam to the creneuls, and put oute his heede and called his peple. **1774** T. WEST *Antiq. Furness* (1805) 371 The walls..in most castles, were topped by a parapet, and a kind of embrasures called crennels. **1813** SCOTT *Trierm.* III. ix, Crenell and parapet appear. **1819** —— *Leg. Montrose* x, The..palisades should be artificially framed with re-entering angles and loop-holes, or crenelles, for musketry. **1877** DIXON *Diana* II. VII. i. 174 A high curtain of masonry, pierced by many windows, some mere crennels of defence, others embayed and mullioned.

2. *Bot.* = CRENATION, CRENATURE.

1835 LINDLEY *Introd. Bot.* (1848) I. 271 When the..teeth are rounded, they become crenels.

crenel ('krɛnəl), *v. rare.* Also crennel. [a. F. *créneler*, f. OF. *crenel*: see prec. Cf. the parallel forms CARNEL, KERNEL.] *trans.* **a.** To embattle, to crenellate; also *fig.* See also CRENELLED. †**b.** To indent the edge of (a coin), *obs.*

[*c* **1330**, **1377**, see CRENELLED. **1610** HOLLAND *Camden's Brit.* I. 753 Licence to fortifie and kernel his mansion house.] **1697** EVELYN *Numism.* vii. 225 Crenneling of the small and thinner [moneys]. **1840** BROWNING *Sordello* I. 284 The runnel slipped, Elate with rains..He..yet trod..on the stubs of living rock Ages ago it crenneled. **1883** H. E. JERNINGHAM *Norham Castle* 170 A special licence..for the towers to be crennelled.

crenelet ('krɛnɪlɪt). *rare.* [f. CRENEL *sb.* + -ET[1].] A small crenel or embrasure.

1860 READE *Cloister & H.* xliii. II. 278 With far more freedom..than they could shoot..through the sloping crenelets of the higher towers.

crenellate, -elate ('krɛnɛleɪt), *v.* [f. F. *crénel-er* + -ATE. The *l* has been doubled partly after *crenelled*; partly perh. after assumed L. **crēnella*, dim. of *crēna.*] *trans.* To furnish with battlements, to embattle; to furnish with embrasures or loopholes.

1851 TURNER *Dom. Archit.* 157 *note*, Laurence de Ludlow had licence to crenellate his mansion of Stoke-Say. **1877** CLERY *Min. Tact.* xvii. 261 Walls that have been loopholed or crenelated afford material aid.

Hence **'crenellated, crenelated** *ppl. a.*, embattled.

1823 CRABB *Technol. Dict.*, *Crenellated parapet* (*Fort.*). **1848** LYTTON *Harold* IV. vii, Crenellated castles. **1869** tr. *Lenormant's Anc. Hist. East* I. IV. iv. 459 The roofs of Assyrian edifices were flat and terraced, surrounded by a crenelated battlement.

transf. **1881** *Athenæum* 4 June 754 Crenellated mountain tops half clad in snow.

crenellation, -elation (krɛnɛ'leɪʃən).

1. The action of crenellating or providing with battlements; the condition of being crenellated.

1874 STUBBS *Const. Hist.* (1875) III. xxi. 536 The fortification or crenellation of these houses or castles.

2. *concr.* Embattled work; a battlement.

1849 LYTTON *Caxtons* XII. vi. (D.), Octavo ramparts flanked with quarto crenellations. **1864** BURTON *Scot Abr.* I. v. 294 The Scots laird..perched projecting crenelations or bastions on the top corners of his tower.

3. A notch or indentation.

In mod. Dicts.

‖**crenellé, -elee**, *a. Her. Obs.* [a. F. *crénelé* CRENELLED.] Having the edge indented like a battlement; EMBATTLED.

1586 FERNE *Blaz. Gentrie* 179 These bendes..are notched or nicked which thing the French worde Crenelle doth very aptlye signifie. **1610** GUILLIM *Heraldry* II. v. (1632) 65 Hee beareth Gules, a Cheefe Crenelle, Argent.

crenelled, creneled ('krɛnəld), *ppl. a.* [f. CRENEL *v.* + -ED. Cf. F. *crénelé* (12th c. in Littré).]

1. Embattled, crenellated; having embrasures.

[*c* **1330** R. BRUNNE *Chron. Wace* (Rolls) 14646 Castels.. bretaxed and carneled. **1377** LANGL. *P. Pl.* B. VI. 78 See KERNELED.] **1832** *Blackw. Mag.* XXXI. 787 Crenelled battlements. **1863** KINGLAKE *Crimea* (1877) IV. xiii. 355 With a crenelled wall for muskets.

2. Having a notched or indented edge; in *Bot.* = CRENATE *a.*

1727 BRADLEY *Fam. Dict.* s.v. *Elder Tree*, Leaves.. sticking to short Stalks, and crenell'd on the Edges. **1769** *Char.* in *Ann. Reg.* 36/1 An instrument with a crenelled edge. **1836** *Penny Cycl.* V. 242 The calyx is five-lobed..the disk a fleshy crenelled cup.

crengle, obs. form of CRINGLE.

crenic ('kriːnɪk), *a. Chem.* [f. Gr. κρήνη spring, fountain + -IC.] In ***crenic acid***, an organic acid, existing, according to Berzelius, in vegetable mould, and in ochreous deposits of ferruginous waters. (Watts.)

1838 T. THOMSON *Chem. Org. Bodies* 147 Crenic Acid was discovered by Berzelius in the year 1832. **1863–72** WATTS *Dict. Chem.* II. 103 Mulder represents crenic acid by the formula $C_{12}H_{12}O_8$.

crenitic (kriː'nɪtɪk), *a. Geol.* [f. Gr. κρήνη spring of water + -ITE + -IC.] (See quot.)

1884 T. STERRY HUNT in *Trans. R. Soc. Canada* II. III. 35 This newly proposed explanation of the origin of crystalline rocks, through the action of springs bringing up mineral matters from below, might be called the *crenitic* hypothesis, from the Greek κρήνη, a fountain or spring. **1886** *Ibid.* IV. III. 21 As a result of this continued process, the crenitic products themselves will naturally show a diminution in the proportion of silica and potash. *Ibid.* 35 The enormous thickness of crenitic rocks which..make up the pre-Cambrian terranes.

crenkled, obs. form of CRINKLED.

crennel, var. of CRENEL.

crenulate ('krɛnjuːlət), *a.* [ad. mod.L. *crēnulātus*, f. *crēnula*, dim. of *crēna* (see CRENA) + -ATE[1]. In mod.F. *crénulé.*] **1.** *Zool.* and *Bot.* Having the edge divided into minute rounded teeth; finely notched or scalloped: said of a leaf, a shell, etc.

1794 MARTYN *Rousseau's Bot.* xxvii. 414 The second has the lip of the nectary crenulate. **1846** DANA *Zooph.* (1848) 136 Margin of base crenulate. **1872** OLIVER *Elem. Bot.* App. 309 Lower petal..3-lobed..lateral lobes usually.. crenulate.

2. *Geogr.* Of a shoreline: having many small irregular bays formed by the action of waves on softer rock.

1919 D. W. JOHNSON *Shore Processes* vi. 278 Early in the youth of the shoreline the curves will be changed to sharply and irregularly crenulate lines by differential wave erosion. .. We may call a shoreline of this character a crenulate shoreline. **1937** WOOLDRIDGE & MORGAN *Physical Basis Geogr.* xxi. 349 All variations in rock hardness, and divisional planes, are picked out by the waves, and the line of the exposed portions of the shore becomes complex or crenulate. **1967** D. G. FRY tr. *Zenkovich's Processes Coastal Devel.* viii. 492 A crenulate coastline often develops in igneous rocks, where there is alternation of veins and dykes of different compositions, and of zones of jointing.

crenulated ('krɛnjuːleɪtɪd), *ppl. a. Zool.* and *Bot.* [f. as prec. + -ED.] = prec.

1807 ROXBURGH in *Asiatic Res.* IX. 380 A fleshy crenulated cup. **1870** BENTLEY *Bot.* 152 When the leaf is minutely crenated it is said to be crenulated.

crenulation (krɛnjuː'leɪʃən). *Zool.* and *Bot.* [f. as prec. + -ATION.] A crenulated formation; a minute rounded marginal tooth or crenation.

1846 DANA *Zooph.* (1848) 391 The lamellæ are marginal crenulations. **1881** R. B. WATSON in *Jrnl. Linn. Soc.* XV. 452 Forming on the upper whorls infrasutural crenulations.

crenulato-, combining form of mod.L. *crēnulātus* CRENULATE; cf. CRENATO-.

1846 DANA *Zooph.* (1848) 247 Lamellæ crenulato-dentate. **1852** —— *Crust.* I. 300 Carapax transversely crenulato-lineolate.

creodont ('kriːəʊdɒnt). *Palæont.* [f. mod.L. *Creodonta* (E. D. Cope 1875, in *Proc. Acad. Nat. Sci. Philadelphia 1875*, 446), f. Gr. κρέας flesh + ὀδοντ-, ὀδούς tooth.] A member of the Creodonta, a sub-order of extinct carnivorous mammals, which lived during the Palæocene, Eocene, and Oligocene epochs. Also *attrib.* or as *adj.*

1891 FLOWER & LYDEKKER *Mammals* 607 The more typical Creodonts appear..to be..closely related to the true Carnivora. **1903** H. JOHNSTON *Brit. Mammals* 115 No Creodont..has ever been discovered which possessed more than three true molars. *Ibid.* 188 The Creodont Carnivores. **1968** A. S. ROMER *Procession of Life* xv. 245 The Palaeocene and Eocene epochs..saw the rise of a variety of archaic flesh-eaters, often grouped (there were several families of them) as the creodonts.

creoice, -oise, -oix, -oiz: see CROISE *v.*, CROSS.

creoicerie, var. CROISERIE *Obs.*, crusade.

Creole ('kriːəʊl), *sb.*, *a.* Also 7–8 criole. [a. F. *créole*, ad. Sp. *criollo*, native to the locality, 'country'; believed to be a colonial corruption of **criadillo*, dim. of *criado* 'bred, brought up, reared, domestic', pa. pple. of *criar* to breed, etc.:—L. *creāre* to CREATE. According to some 18th c. writers originally applied by S. American negroes to their own children born in America as distinguished from negroes freshly imported from Africa; but D'Acosta, 1590, applies it to Spaniards born in the W. Indies.]

A. *sb.* In the West Indies and other parts of America, Mauritius, etc.: *orig.* A person born and naturalized in the country, but of European (usually Spanish or French) or of African Negro race: the name having no connotation of colour, and in its reference to origin being distinguished on the one hand from born in Europe (or Africa), and on the other hand from aboriginal.

a. But now, usually, = *creole white*, a descendant of European settlers, born and naturalized in those colonies or regions, and more or less modified in type by the climate and surroundings.

The local use varies: in the European colonies of the W. Indies it is usually applied to the descendants of any Europeans there naturalized; in Mauritius to the naturalized French population. It is not now used of the people of Spanish race in the independent South American states, though sometimes of the corresponding natives of Mexico, and in the U.S. it is applied only to the French-speaking descendants of the early French settlers in Louisiana, etc.

1604 E. GRIMSTONE tr. *D'Acosta's Hist. W. Indies* IV. xxv. 278 Some Crollos (for so they call the Spaniards borne at the Indies). **1697** DAMPIER *Voy.* (1698) I. iv. 68 An English Native of St. Christophers, a Cirole, as we call all born of European Parents in the West Indies. **1737** *Common Sense* (1738) I. 280 As to his Birth and Parentage, I cannot say whether he is a Native American or a Creole, nor is it material. **1760–72** tr. *Juan & Ulloa's Voy.* (ed. 3) I. I. iv. 29 The Whites may be divided into two classes, the Europeans, and Creoles, or Whites born in the Country. *Ibid.* II. IX. vii. 375 (*Nova Scotia*) French families, some Europeans, and others Creoles of the place itself and from..Newfoundland. **1832** MARRYAT *N. Forster* xx, [She] was a creole—that is, born in the West Indies, of French parents. **1836** W. IRVING *Astoria* (1849) 199 A French Creole; one of those haphazard wights of Gallic origin, who abound upon our frontier, living among the Indians like one of their own race. **1864** *Sat. Rev.* 21 May, [In Mexico] there are about a million.. Creoles—that is, whites of pure Spanish extraction.

b. Now less usually = *creole negro*: A negro born in the West Indies or America, as distinguished from one freshly imported from Africa.

1748 *Earthquake of Peru* iii. 240 Criollos signifies one born in the Country; a Word made by the Negroes, who give it to their own Children born in those Parts. **1760–72** tr. *Juan & Ulloa's Voy.* (ed. 3) I. I. iv. 31 The class of Negroes is..again subdivided into Creoles and Bozares. **1863** BATES *Nat. Amazon* i. (1864) 19 The term 'Creole' is confined to negroes born in the country.

2. A creolized language.

1879 L. HEARN *Creole Sk.* (1924) 54, I explique myself to her, and she tell me in Creole—[etc.]. **1958** C. F. HOCKETT *Course Mod. Ling.* xlix. 423 There are several examples of creoles in the Caribbean area, spoken largely by the descendants of escaped Negro slaves. **1962** *Listener* 22 Nov. 868/3 A number of people working on Creoles met in Jamaica in 1959, and agreed to adopt Robert Hall's distinction between Creoles and Pidgins: a Pidgin is a first-generation *lingua franca*..spoken by everybody as a *second* language; when in subsequent generations it becomes the *first* language of a community, it is a Creole. **1965** *Tablet* 22 May 587/2 Haiti, it appears, may soon have its vernacular, Creole, in the Mass. They already have a Creole missal... Chants, responses, and readings in Creole are to be found in it.

B. *attrib.* or *adj.*

1. **a.** Of persons: Born and naturalized in the West Indies, etc., but of European (or negro) descent; see A. Now chiefly applied to the native whites in the West Indies, the native French population in Louisiana, Mauritius, etc.

1748 *Earthquake of Peru* iii. 230 A Criole Negro-Woman. **1771** SMOLLETT *Humph. Cl.* (1815) 34 Two negroes, belonging to a Creole gentleman, who..began to practise upon the French-horn. **1827** O. W. ROBERTS *Centr. Amer.* 28 Creole descendants of Spanish adventurers. **1862** J. M. LUDLOW *Hist. U.S.* 316 *note*, There are creole whites, creole negroes, creole horses, &c.; and creole whites are, of all persons, the most anxious to be deemed of pure white blood.

b. Of animals and plants: Bred or grown in the West Indies, etc., but not of indigenous origin.

1760–72 tr. *Juan & Ulloa's Voy.* (ed. 3) [I. IV. vii. 162 The *criollo* or natural bread being unripe plantains..roasted.] *Ibid.* II. VII. i. 17 Fruits..of the Creole kind, being European fruits planted there, but which have undergone considerable alterations from the climate. **1836** MACGILLIVRAY tr. *Humboldt's Trav.* xiv. 168 Three species of sugar-cane, the old Creole, the Otaheitan, and the Batavian. **1885** LADY BRASSEY *The Trades* 263 The active little animals known as 'creole' horses.

2. Belonging to or characteristic of a Creole.

1828 G. W. BRIDGES *Ann. Jamaica* II. x. 9 A trait in the Creole character. **1839–40** W. IRVING *Wolfert's R.* (1855) 27 In an old French creole village. **1884** W. H. BISHOP in *Harper's Mag.* Mar. 516/2 The people speak creole French.

3. *Comb.*, as **creole-crab**, a West Indian species of crab.

1756 P. BROWNE *Jamaica* (1779) 422 The larger hairy Creole-Crab with prickly claws.

Creolian (kriː'əʊlɪən), *sb.* and *a.* ? *Obs.* Also 8 criolian, 9 creolean. [f. CREOLE + -IAN.]

†**A.** *sb.* = CREOLE A. *Obs.*

1702 *Paradoxes of State* 13 The American Creolians. **1748** *Earthquake of Peru* iii. 239 The Spaniards..born in America of white Parents, who are called Crioli or Criolians. **1766**

GOLDSM. *Vic. W.* xx, The moment.. a Creolian arrives from Jamaica.. I strike for a subscription. **1827** SCOTT *Napoleon* ii, This lady was a Creolian.

B. *adj.* = CREOLE B. ? *Obs.*

1726 SHELVOCKE *Voy. round World* 96 A mixed breed of Creolian Spaniards. **1793** GODWIN *Polit. Just.* (1796) II. 94 Born a manorial serf or a Creolian negro. **1842** ORDERSON *Creoleana* Pref., The customs.. of Creolean society.

'creolism. [f. CREOLE + -ISM.] The fact of being a Creole; Creole descent.

1788 J. RAMSAY *Object. Abol. Slave Tr. Answ.* (ed. 2) 49 The farther back the negroe could trace his Creolism, the more he valued himself. **1812** *Ann. Reg.* (1810) 596 They [negroes] feel pride and consequence in being born in a new hemisphere, and conceive that to Creolism is attached a degree of dignity. **1893** *Athenæum* 7 Oct. 484/1 Though he had been born in Misiones (Paraguay), yet, as the son of a lieutenant-governor of a department and removed to Spain at an early age, he did not suffer from the disabilities of creolism.

creolization (ˌkriːəlaɪˈzeɪʃən). [f. next + -ATION.] **a.** The production of a Creole race; racial modification in the case of Creole animals or plants.

1890 *Harper's Mag.* Feb. 416/1 Those extraordinary influences of climate and environment which produce the phenomena of creolization.

b. The fact or process of being creolized.

1934 PRIEBSCH & COLLINSON *German Lang.* I. ii. 35 The complete Creolization of Afrikaans has been prevented by contact with the Dutch of the Bible and literature. **1958** P. GAMMOND et al. *Decca Bk. Jazz* xxi. 262 Lyttelton.. recorded three brilliant Creole-styled versions of Tin Pan Alley songs.. all.. of which, by a process of 'Creolization', became better jazz than many a so-called New Orleans tune recorded.. by revivalists. **1969** *Language* XLV. 659 Its incipient creolization provides scholars with a unique opportunity to observe the dynamics of linguistic change.

'creolize, *v.* [f. CREOLE + -IZE.]

1. *intr.* To 'do' the Creole: see quot.

1818 J. M'LEOD *Voy. of Alceste* 280 The ladies.. generally creolize the whole day in a delectable state of apathy.. Creolizing is an easy and elegant mode of lounging in a warm climate.

2. a. *trans.* To render Creole; to naturalize in the West Indies or adjacent regions.

1834 T. WENTWORTH *West India Sketch Bk.* II. 219 Those.. have become *creolized,* or removed from the physical characteristics of the African.

b. *Philol.* To make into a creolized language.

1958 C. F. HOCKETT *Course Mod. Ling.* xlix. 423 An artificial language.. can be creolized. **1964** *English Studies* XLV. 383 The English dialects were never creolized.

creolized (ˈkriːəʊlaɪzd), *ppl. a.* [-ED[1].] **1.** Naturalized in the West Indies or Louisiana.

1880 G. W. CABLE *Grandissimes* iii. 20 The most throughly Creolized Américain.

2. *creolized language*: a language which has developed from that of a dominant group, first being used as a second language, then becoming the usual language of a subject group, its sounds, grammar, and vocabulary being modified in the process.

1932 W. L. GRAFF *Lang.* p. xxxiv, *Creolized language,* a language of a civilized people, especially European, mixed with that of one or more savage tribes. **1933** BLOOMFIELD *Language* xxvi. 474 In some cases.. a subject group gives up its native language in favour of a jargon... When the jargon has become the only language of the subject group, it is a creolized language. **1949** *Archivum Linguisticum* I. II. 155 It is likewise undeniable in the formation of pidginised languages and of their developments into creolised languages.

creop, obs. form of CREEP.

creophagous (kriːˈɒfəgəs), *a.* Also kreo-. [f. Gr. κρεοφάγ-ος (f. κρεας, κρεο- flesh + -φαγος eating) + -OUS.] Flesh-eating; carnivorous. So **cre'ophagist** (-dʒɪst), one who uses flesh as food; **cre'ophagism** (-dʒɪz(ə)m), **cre'ophagy** (-dʒɪ) [Gr. κρεοφαγία], the eating of flesh.

1881 *Sat. Rev.* LII. 569 The average kreophagist is by no means convinced that kreophagy is the perfect way in diet. *Ibid.* 570 Kreophagism leads to alcoholism. *Ibid.*, The ruling tribes and castes of Europe have invariably been kreophagous. **1885** RAY LANKESTER in *Encycl. Brit.* XIX. 831/2 Exceptional creophagous Protophytes, parallel at a lower level of structure to the insectivorous Phanerogams.

creosol (ˈkriːəsɒl). *Chem.* Also creasol. [f. CREOS(OTE + -OL.] A colourless highly refracting liquid ($C_8H_{10}O_2$) with aromatic odour and burning taste, forming the chief constituent of creosote.

1863–72 WATTS *Dict. Chem.* II. 103 *Creosol,* the principal constituent of wood-creosote. **1873** —— *Fownes' Chem.* 806 Creasol is a diatomic phenol from guaiacum.

Hence **'creosyl** [-YL], the radical of creosol, as in *creosyl chloride* C_8H_9OCl.

1872–9 WATTS *Dict. Chem.* VI. 595 Creosyl chloride.. is a limpid strongly refracting oily liquid.

creosote (ˈkriːəsəʊt), *sb.* Also creasote, kreo-, krea-. [mod. f. Gr. κρεο-, comb. form of κρέας flesh + σώζειν to save: cf. σωτήρ saviour; the formation was intended to mean 'flesh-saving'; but the Gr. for this would have been κρεο(σ)σόος.]

1. A colourless oily liquid, of complex composition, with odour like that of smoked meat, and burning taste, obtained from the distillation of wood-tar, and having powerful antiseptic properties; discovered by Reichenbach in 1832.

1835 ELLIOTSON in *Trans. Med.-Chirurg. Soc.* 235 It is now a year since I began my trials of Creosote. **1860** G. H. K. *Vac. Tourist* 164 The creosote distilled from the peat soon rendered the fish safe from decay.

b. Sometimes commercially applied to CARBOLIC ACID, also distinguished as *coal-tar creosote.*

1863–72 WATTS *Dict. Chem.* IV. 389 Commercial creosote often consists almost entirely of phenol, but the true creosote, obtained by the distillation of wood, is a totally different substance.

2. *attrib.* and *Comb.*, as ***creosote-oil, -tank, creosote-like*** adj.; **creosote-bush, -plant,** a Mexican shrub (*Larrea mexicana,* N.O. *Zygophyllaceæ*) having a strong smell of creosote.

1851 MAYNE REID *Scalp Hunt.* xxvi, We passed.. thickets of creosote bushes. **1866** *Treas. Bot.* 660 *L[arrea] mexicana,* the Creosote plant of the Americans.. its strong creosote-like odour renders it so repulsive that no animal will touch it. **1889** G. FINDLAY *Eng. Railway* 46 Timber, into which creosote oil has been forced under pressure.

'creosote, *v.* [f. prec. sb.] *trans.* To impregnate with creosote, as a preservative.

1846 A. SUCKLING *Hist. Suffolk* 75 The timber being creasoted.. to keep out the worm. **1881** WHITEHEAD *Hops* 37 The practice of creosoting the butt ends preserves them from decay.

Hence **creosoted** *ppl. a.*, **creosoting** *vbl. sb.*; **'creosoter,** one engaged in creosoting timber.

1862 *Rep. Directors E. Ind. Railw. Comp.* 16 Creosoted sleepers. **1863** *Reader* 14 Feb., If the method of creosoting were introduced in India. **1889** *East. Morning News* 12 Apr. 2/9 W. F. W. of Grimsby, late creosoter. **1892** *Daily News* 24 Feb. 6/3 The line.. is laid upon piles of creosoted American pitch-pine.

creosotic, erroneous form of CRESOTIC.

crep, obs. pa. t. of CREEP.

crepan, erron. f. TREPAN *sb.* and *v.*

crepance. *Farriery.* ? *Obs.* Also 7 *pl.* crepanches, 8 (*mispr.*) **crepane.** [In 17th c. *crepanches, crepances,* ad. It. *crepacci* pl., 'the scratches, cratches, or rats-tailes in a horse... little chaps or rifts about the cronet of the horses hoofe' (Florio, 1598), f. *crepare* to crack, chap:—L. *crepāre* to crack, etc.] A sore or wound on a horse's foot; see quots.

1610 MARKHAM *Masterp.* II. lxxxvi. 366 The Scratches, Crepanches, or Rats-tailes.. are long, scabby, dry chaps, or rifts.. on the hinder legges, just from the fetlocke vnto the place of the Curbe. **1727** BRADLEY *Fam. Dict., Crepances,* Ulcers in the Fore-part of a Horse's foot.. caused by a Hurt receiv'd in leaping over a Bar, or the like. **1755** JOHNSON, *Crepane* [a misprint copied in later Dicts.]. **1823** CRABB *Techn. Dict., Crepance* (*Vet.*), a chop, or scratch in a horse's leg.. which often degenerates into an ulcer.

[crepane. Error for CREPANCE.

1755 JOHNSON [citing *Farrier's Dict.*; but *The Farrier's and Horseman's Dictionary* by N.B., **1726**, has *crepance*]. Hence in later Dicts.]

†'crepature. *Obs.* [ad. L. *crepātūra* fissure, crack, f. *crepāre* to crack, creak: see -URE.]

1. *Med.* **a.** A rupture, hernia; **b.** A wound, crack, or chap in the skin.

c **1400** *Lanfranc's Cirurg.* 170 After þe tyme þat þe wounde were souded þere wolde leve a crepature. *Ibid.* 292 Cure cancris & festris & al maner crepaturis. **1582** HESTER *Secr. Phiorav.* II. xxi. 100 To helpe the crepature or chappes make this Unguent.

2. (See quots. App. some error.)

[**1706** PHILLIPS (ed. Kersey), *Crepatura* (Lat.), a Term used by Apothecaries, for the boiling of Barley or any other thing 'till it crack.] **1721** BAILEY, *Crepature* (in Physick) is when any thing is boiled till it cracks.

crepaud(e, -awnde, var. CRAPAUD, *Obs.*

‖crêpe (krɛp). [F. *crêpe,* in 16th c. *crespe*:—L. *crispa* curled.] **1.** The French word for CRAPE (used in that language in the early wider sense, and including *crêpe anglais,* which is called *crape* in English), often borrowed as a term for all crapy fabrics other than ordinary black mourning crape.

crêpe de chine (China crape), a white or other coloured crape made of raw silk. *crêpe lisse,* smooth or glossy crape, which is not *crêpé* or wrinkled. Also *attrib.*

1797 *Wynne Diaries* 13 Jan. (1937) II. 151 After having equipped ourselves, the Bride and me, in a Nuptial garment, (white crepe), we went to Lady Hamilton's. **1825** *Ladies Pocket Mag.* I. 140 Dress of white *crêpe-lisse,* trimmed at the border with an ornament of puckered tulle. **1872** *Young Englishwoman* Oct. 540/1 These tunics are also made of white crêpe de chine. **1881** *Truth* 19 May 686/2 A dress.. of white crêpe, with silk embroidery of jasmine and honeysuckle. **1887** *Daily News* 11 May 5/8 This blossom-dress was lightly veiled with crêpe of wale rose-pink. **1887** *Times* (Weekly Ed.) 23 Sept. 15/4 A costume of pearl satin and crêpe de chine. **1907** *Daily Chron.* 15 July 8/4 The crêpe de soie.. is of the plainer kind, without a printed border. **1909** *Westm. Gaz.* 6 Mar. 15/1 Crêpe eclair is a silken fabric. **1923** *Weekly Dispatch* 11 Feb. 15 This dinner gown of amber crepe Romain. **1923** *Daily Mail* 14 Feb. 6 A very pretty gown of blue crêpe romaine. *Ibid.* 19 Apr. 8 The bride's gown was of white crêpe perle. **1925** *Good Housekeeping* Apr. 142/3 The crêpe twist [of acetate silk]. **1925** E. SITWELL *Poor Young People* 3 Wear crêpe de Siam, barèges Isabelle. **1928** *Sunday Express* 8 July 3 Crepe malika, a lovely material,.. is one of the few innovations which are finding favour with the most important dress artists. **1951** *Good Housek. Home Encycl.* 231/2 Dull-finished fabrics, such as crêpe suède.

2. In full ***crêpe rubber.*** India-rubber rolled into thin sheets with a corrugated surface.

1907 *Brit. Trade Jrnl.* 1 Sept. in W. H. Johnson *Para Rubber* (ed. 2, 1909) 117 After the crêpe rubber has left the vacuum drier. *Ibid.* 118 The first packing of the crêpe in the box. **1909** W. H. JOHNSON *Para Rubber* (ed. 2) 114 The manufacture of crêpe rubber.. consists in passing the freshly coagulated rubber through a washing machine. **1914** H. BROWN *Rubber* 75 The corrugated sheet known as crêpe... The crêpe rubber, after drying, is sometimes converted into blocks by submitting it to pressure in steel moulds. **1926** *Blackw. Mag.* Apr. 575/2 Coarser qualities of rubber are always made into crêpe. **1937** H. BARRON *Mod. Rubber Chem.* v. 55 Since the beginning of this century smoked sheet and pale crêpe have virtually monopolised the field of raw rubber as raw materials for manufacture. **1963** A. S. CRAIG *Rubber Technol.* iii, For crepe rubber production the slabs are given much more severe treatment, being passed.. through a series of mills the rolls of which are grooved and are turning at slightly different speeds.

3. A small, thin pancake. (Cf. CRISP *sb.* 3.) So **crêpe Suzette** (usu. in pl.), a pancake served in a hot sauce, often containing a liqueur.

[**1877** E. S. DALLAS *Kettner's Bk. of Table* 143 *Crêpe.*—The French for pancake. **1907** A. ESCOFFIER *Mod. Cookery* xx. 723 *Suzette Pancakes.* Make these from preparation A [basic recipe], flavoured with curaçoa and tangerine juice. Coat them.. with softened butter, flavoured with curaçao and tangerine juice.] **1922** C. H. SENN *Luncheon & Dinner Sweets* 63 Pancakes à la Suzette. (Crêpes Suzette.) **1924** A. E. M. FOSTER *London Restaurants* 87 Crêpe Suzette is another special dish. **1928** *Vanity Fair* Sept. 31/1 Crêpes Suzettes are pancakes raised by Cunard to a remarkable point of perfection. **1951** *Good Housek. Cookery Bk.* (1957) 304/2 Add the liqueur and brandy to the sauce, and replace the folded crêpes in the pan. **1961** *Guardian* 27 Dec. 2/4 Henri Charpentier, creator of Crêpes Suzette.., died at Redondo Beach, California, on Sunday, aged 81.

4. *Comb.*: **crêpe-hanger** *U.S. slang* = *crape-hanger* (CRAPE *sb.* 3 b); **crêpe paper,** a thin crinkled paper resembling crêpe; **crêpe ring** *Astr.* = *crape ring* (CRAPE *sb.* 3 b); **crêpe sole** [SOLE *sb.*[1] 2], the underside of a shoe covered with crêpe rubber; so **crêpe-soled** *a.*

1930 *N. & Q.* CLIX. 119/1 In an American novel, the writer refers to a man as a mere 'crêpe-hanger'. *Ibid.* 232/1 A crepe-hanger is the ultimate in depressing persons... The expression derives from the lugubrious undertaker's assistants who put up black decorations for a funeral. [**1895** *Montgomery Ward Catal.* 123/3 Crepe tissue paper.] **1897** *Sears, Roebuck Catal.* 333/1 Assorted imported tissue, 2 pieces crepe paper. **1903** K. D. WIGGIN *Rebecca* (1904) xiii. 140 The [lamp] shade.. was of crinkled crêpe paper. **1915** *Chemists' Windows* 27 Crêpe paper or plain stiff materials have enough 'body' to remain in pleat. **1959** I. & P. OPIE *Lore & Lang. Schoolchildren* xii. 258 The Maypoles consisted of a pram wheel decorated with crepe paper and streamers. **1959** *Listener* 17 Sept. 429/1 The innermost ring, C, is more generally known as the Crêpe or Dusky Ring. **1926–7** *Army & Navy Stores Catal.* 654/1 The 'Glastonbury' Slipper Boot in buff sheepskins.. thin crêpe sole. **1936** G. GREENE *Journey without Maps* III. iv. 267 A pair of gym shoes with crêpe soles. **1941** V. WOOLF *Between Acts* 232 Crepe soles?.. They last much longer and protect the feet. **1935** HEMINGWAY *Green Hills Afr.* (1936) I. i. 22 We went quietly. I had on these crêpe-soled boots. **1953** H. CLEVELY *Public Enemy* x. 62 He.. put on.. a pair of crêpe-soled sandals.

Hence **crêpe** *v.* [F. *crêper*], to frizz, to put up in curl-papers. **crêpé** *a.* [F.], frizzed. **crêpy** *a.* (also **crepey, crepey**), of the nature of crêpe; resembling crêpe.

1818 SCOTT *Hrt. Midl.* xl, It was a pity to waste so much paper, which might crepe hair, pin up bonnets, and serve many other useful purposes. **1828** LYTTON *Pelham* I. xvi. 113 Her own grey hair *crêpé*, and surmounted by a high cap of the most dazzling *blonde.* **1862** H. MARRYAT *Year in Sweden* II. 41 Grayish hair, frizzed, in short crêpé curls. **1892** *Pall Mall G.* 23 June 1/3 A full vest of white crêpy stuff. **1941** C. MCCULLERS in *55 Short Stories fr. N. Yorker* (1952) 320 The jockey.. scrutinized the room with pinched, crêpy eyes. **1946** E. TAYLOR *Palladian* vii. 69 The inside of her arm showed grey and crêpy. **1959** P. H. JOHNSON *Humbler Creation* xlii. 281 The skin of her throat seemed to her a little crepey, so she massaged it with cold cream.

crepe, crepel, -ill, obs. ff. CREEP, CRIPPLE.

crêpeline (ˈkreɪpəliːn). Also crêpoline. [Fr., dim. of *crêpe* CRÊPE.] A light thin material of silk, or silk and wool, used for women's dresses.

1873 *Young Englishwoman* Apr. 202/2 Crêpeline, a material only to be found at the Halle des Indes [in Paris]. **1882** CAULFEILD & SAWARD *Dict. Needlework* 93/2 *Crêpeline, Crêpon,* or *Crape Cloth,* a dress material, having a silken surface, much resembling crape, but considerably thicker. **1898** *Daily News* 10 Dec. 6/3 Another novelty is crêpoline cloth,.. as soft as cashmere. **1909** *Westm. Gaz.* 9 Oct. 15/1 Crêpolines, silk combined with wool.

crepidarian (krɛpɪˈdɛərɪən), *a. nonce-wd.* [f. L. *crepidāri-us* shoemaker + -AN.] Of or pertaining to a shoemaker.

1819 L. HUNT *Indicator* No. 8 (1822) I. 64 His crepidarian sculptures indeed are not so well.

†**crepine, crespin(e.** *Obs.* Also 6 crispyne, krippin, creppin, 6–7 crippin. [a. OF. *crespine*, mod.F. *crépine* (Pr. *crespina*), f. *crespe, crêpe*: see CRÊPE, CRAPE.]

1. a. A net or caul (of gold or silver thread, silk lace, etc.) for the hair, formerly worn by ladies. **b.** A part of a hood. **c.** A fringe of lace or network for a dais, baldachin, bed, etc.

c **1532** DEWES *Introd. Fr.* in *Palsgr.* 907 The crispynes, *les crespines.* **1566** ADLINGTON *Apuleius* II. ix. (1596) 25 Diuers (..to shew their grace and feature) wil cast off their partlets, collars, habilimentes, frontes, cornets and krippins. **1578** *Gifts to Queen* in Nichols *Progr.* II. 73 By the Lady Ratclif, five creppins of lawne. **1592** LYLY *Mydas* I. ii, Earerings, borders, crippins, shadowes. **1611** COTGR., *Crespine*, the Crepine of a French hood. **1662** J. DAVIES tr. *Mandelslo's Trav. E. Ind.* 64 On their heads they [Guzuratta women] have onely a thin cap, or cover them with a crepine of Lawn wrought with Gold. **1708** MOTTEUX *Rabelais* IV. lii. (1737) 214 The Crepines of their Hoods, their Ruffles. **1721** C. KING *Brit. Merch.* II. 230 Beds, Matrasses, Hangings, Coverlids, Quilts, Crespins, Fringes, and Molets of Silk. **1860** FAIRHOLT *Costume* Gloss., *Crespine*, the golden net-caul worn by ladies in the fourteenth and fifteenth centuries ..The *crespine* still exists in name and fact in Italy.

2. *Cookery.* See quot. [Cf. F. *crépine* the caul enveloping the viscera of an animal.]

1726 *Dict. Rust.* (ed. 3) *Crepine*, a sort of farce wrapp'd up in a Veal cawl.

crépinette (kreɪpɪˈnɛt). [Fr., dim. of *crépine*: see CREPINE 2.] Minced meat with sauce or farce, wrapped in pieces of pork caul.

1877 E. S. DALLAS *Kettner's Bk. Table* 143 *Crêpinette*, a flat sausage enveloped in pig's caul. **1889** *Mrs. A. B. Marshall's Cookery Book* 123 Crépinettes à la Ferdinand. **1907** A. ESCOFFIER *Mod. Cookery* 462 Shape the *crépinettes* thus formed rectangularly. **1911** FRANCATELLI *Mod. Cook* 331 Crepinettes of Partridge à la d'Estaing. **1951** *Good Housek. Home Encycl.* 426/2 Meat and Ham Crépinettes.

crêping (ˈkreɪpɪŋ), *vbl. sb.*

1. The crimping or frizzing of hair.

1889 *Daily News* 30 Dec. 6/6 The mistake of too tightly crimping—or, to use the new word, crêping—the hair. **1966** J. S. COX *Dict. Hairdressing* 41/2 *Creping* 1. Weaving and boiling hair to transform it into crêpe hair. 2. Crimping.

2. The production of crêpe rubber.

1909 W. H. JOHNSON *Para Rubber* (ed. 2) 123 A large size pair of breaking-up and crêping machines.

crepis (ˈkriːpɪs). **1.** *Bot.* [mod.L. (Linnæus *Genera Plantarum* (1737) 240), ad. Gr. κρηπίς, Theophrastus's name for another plant.] A plant of the large genus of herbs so called, belonging to the family Compositæ and including a few cultivated species.

1822 LOUDON *Encycl. Gardening* Index 1383/2 Crepis,.. of easy culture. **1904** R. J. FARRER *Garden Asia* 246 Twinkling gold of crepis. **1919** —— *Eng. Rock-Garden* I. 243 No Crepis is worthy of admission to the rock-garden.. except the following: *C. incisa*..; *C. rubra*..; and *C. lagoseris.* **1948** A. G. L. HELLYER *Amateur Gardener* viii. 199 Most species of crepis are weeds and all have flowers like small dandelions.

2. *Biol.* [ad. Gr. κρηπίς base.] A sponge-spicule forming the central axis of a desma.

1900 E. A. MINCHIN in Lankester *Treat. Zool.* II. 134 Each desma is formed typically by secondary deposits of silica upon a true spicule termed the *crepis* or foundation. **1940** L. H. HYMAN *Invertebrates* I. vi. 299 The deposited silica at first follows the shape of the crepis. **1963** I. F. & W. D. HENDERSON *Dict. Biol.* (ed. 8) 124/1 *Crepis*, the fundamental spicule by deposition of silica upon which a desma is formed.

‖**crepiˈtaculum.** *Zool.* [L. a rattle.] (With American Zoologists) The rattle of the rattle-snake.

crepitant (ˈkrɛpɪtənt), *a.* [ad. L. *crepitānt-em*, pr. pple. of *crepitāre* to crackle: also in mod.F.]

1. Making a crackling noise: crackling, crepitating.

1855 BROWNING *Master Hugues* xvi, One is incisive, corrosive; Two retorts, nettled, curt, crepitant. **1862** H. W. FULLER *Dis. Lungs* 249 The inflamed lung..is heavier and less crepitant under the finger. **1873** HOLLAND *A. Bonnic.* 192 There came close to my ear a curious crepitant rustle.

2. *Entom.* That crepitates (see CREPITATE 2).

1826 KIRBY & SP. *Entomol.* xlvii. (1828) IV. 401 That [subtribe] to which the crepitant Eutechina belong.

crepitate (ˈkrɛpɪteɪt), *v.* [f. L. *crepitāt-*, ppl. stem of *crepitāre* to crackle, frequentative of *crepāre* to crack, creak: see -ATE.]

†**1.** *intr.* To break wind. *Obs.*

1623 COCKERAM, *Crepitate*, to winde or fart. **1768** *Life & Adv. Sir B. Sapskull* I. 149.

2. *Entom.* Of certain beetles: To eject a pungent fluid suddenly with a sharp report. (Cf. BOMBARDIER 4.)

1826 KIRBY & SP. *Entomol.* xli. (1828) IV. 149 The substance which they emit when they crepitate.

3. To make a crackling sound, to crackle: *spec.* of the tissue of the lungs (also used of the action accompanying or producing this sound; cf. CREPITATION 2).

1853 *Fraser's Mag.* XLVII. 559 That [salt]..bears the heat of the fire without crepitating. **1877** ROBERTS *Handbk. Med.* (ed. 3) I. 378 The part affected is enlarged; crepitates imperfectly. **1888** *Harper's Mag.* Apr. 741 The immense hall rises,—oscillates,—..crepitates,—crumbles into ruin.

4. To rattle: said of the sound made by the *crepitaculum* of the rattle-snake. (Cf. CREPITATION 3.)

Hence ˈ**crepitating** *vbl. sb.* and *ppl. a.*

1852–9 TODD *Cycl. Anat.* IV. 595/1 The crepitating sensation caused by the friction of the head of the humerus against the under surface of the acromion. **1853** KANE *Grinnell Exp.* xxxiv. (1856) 307, I felt a something move. The something had a crepitating, insectine wriggle. **1883** *Knowledge* 13 July 18/2 Starch..on being pressed between the fingers, produces a peculiar sound known as 'crepitating'.

crepitation (krɛpɪˈteɪʃən). [n. of action f. L. *crepitāre*: see prec. and -ATION. So F. *crépitation* (Paré 16th c.).]

1. A crackling noise; crackling.

1656 BLOUNT *Glossogr.*, *Crepitation*,..a creaking, crashing, or ratling noise. **1676** GREW *Luctation* i. §6 in *Anat. Plants* i. (1682) 239 *Crepitation*, when they make a kind of hissing and sometimes a crackling noise. **1711** J. GREENWOOD *Eng. Gram.* 193 *Spatter*..implies a more clear crepitation or crackling. **1864** R. F. BURTON *Dahome* II. 329 Rattling, crackling thunder, with prolonged electric crepitations. **1879** G. PRESCOTT *Sp. Telephone* 127 We hear a dry noise, a crepitation similar to that of the spark.
fig. **1805** SOUTHEY in Robberds *Mem. W. Taylor* II. 7 The Anti-jacobin crepitations never reach me.

2. *Med.* and *Path.* The slight sound and accompanying sensation caused by pressure on any portion of cellular tissue in which air is collected, or by the entrance of air into the lungs in a certain stage of inflammation; also, the noise and sensation observed in the grating together of the ends of fractured bones; the crackling noise sometimes observed in gangrenous parts when examined with the fingers; the cracking of a joint when pulled. (*Syd. Soc. Lex.*)

1834 J. FORBES *Laennec's Dis. Chest* 11 Sometimes in cases of emphysema of the lungs..a species of dry crepitation is felt by the hand. **1836** TODD *Cycl. Anat.* I. 157/1 His right leg presented all the signs of fracture of the fibula..such as ..depression and crepitation above the outer ankle. **1878** T. BRYANT *Pract. Surg.* I. 47 When suppuration or sloughing of the cellular tissue has taken place, fluctuation or crepitation will be detected, or the parts feel boggy.

3. The action of rattling: see CREPITATE 4.

1878 COUES *Bull. U.S. Geol. Surv.* IV. 263 The rattle of the Crotalus cannot be distinguished from the crepitation of the large Western grasshopper.

4. The breaking of wind; *crepitus ventris. rare.*

1822 *Blackw. Mag.* XII. 599 Openly venting their crepitations and eructations at table.

crepitous (ˈkrɛpɪtəs), *a. Med.* and *Path.* [f. L. *crepitus* (see next) + -OUS.] Of the nature of, or such as to produce, crepitus.

1822–34 GOOD *Study Med.* (ed. 4) II. 122 That crepitous dilatation of the pulmonary cells, so strongly marked in infancy. **1836** TODD *Cycl. Anat.* I. 604/1 The structure of the lungs is more flabby and less crepitous than natural.

‖**crepitus** (ˈkrɛpɪtəs). [L., verbal sb. f. *crepāre* to crack, rattle, creak, etc.]

1. *Med.* and *Path.* = CREPITATION 2.

1807–26 S. COOPER *First Lines Surg.* (ed. 5) 275 Great unnecessary pain [has] frequently been occasioned by the custom of feeling for a crepitus, and moving the [fractured] limb about..in order to produce it. **1878** A. HAMILTON *Nerv. Dis.* 115 There is crepitus or rattling in the breathing. **1882** *Syd. Soc. Lex.*, *Crepitus*, the crackling noise occasioned by pressing a part of the body when air is collected in the cellular tissue.

2. The breaking of wind: usually *crepitus ventris.*

1882 *Syd. Soc. Lex.*, *Crepitus*, term for the discharge upwards, or rejection downwards, of gas or flatus from the stomach and bowels.

creple, creppell, -le, obs. ff. CRIPPLE.

‖**crépon** (ˈkreɪpɔ̃, ˈkrɛpən). [F. *crépon*, in 16th c. *crespon*, deriv. of *crespe, crêpe* CRAPE.] A stuff resembling crape, but of firmer substance, made of fine worsted, silk, or a combination of the two.

1887 *Pall Mall G.* 19 Dec. 8/2 The bridesmaids..wore dresses of Liberty silk and crépon. **1890** *Daily News* 13 Sept. 3/1 Such a girl wore lately a pale blue crépon dress.

crept (krɛpt), *ppl. a.* Pa. pple. of CREEP *v.*; *spec.* in *Coal-mining*, that has been subjected to a 'creep'.

1628 J. DOUGHTY *Sermon* 25 A crept in falshood. **1861** *Trans. N. Eng. Inst. Min. Engineers* IX. 24 [This] had evidently brought on a heavy creep as shown in the section of crept bords. **1867** W. W. SMYTH *Coal & Coal-mining* 132 The workings are closely filled with rubbish, and there remain the isolated crept pillars, only accessible by fresh and dangerous workings.

crept, pa. t. and pa. pple. of CREEP *v.*

crepul, obs. form of CRIPPLE.

†**creˈpundian.** *Obs. rare.* Also crepundio [? -on]. [f. L. *crepundia* a rattle, a child's toy.]

1. ? A rattler or empty talker. **2.** A childish toy.

1589 NASHE *Greene's Menaphon* (Arb.) 8 Our quadrant crepundios [**1616** -ous], that spit *ergo* in the mouth of euerie one they meete. **1655** G. EMMOT *North. Blast* 4 Arrayed with Cope and Vestment, and many other feat Crepundians.

crepuscle (krɪˈpʌs(ə)l, ˈkrɛpəs(ə)l). [mod. ad. L. *crepuscul-um* twilight: see below.] Twilight.

1665 *Phil. Trans.* I. 122 The reputed Citizens of the Moon might see our Crepuscle. **1860** MRS. BYRNE *Undercurrent* I. 207 At early dawn or dusty noon, in foggy crepuscle or gloomy midnight.

crepuscular (krɪˈpʌskjuːlə(r)), *a.* [f. L. *crepuscul-um* + -AR. Cf. F. *crépusculaire.*]

1. Of or pertaining to twilight.

1755 B. MARTIN *Mag. Arts & Sc.* I. i. 3 The Difference.. between the crepuscular and the Noon-tide Light. **1791** E. DARWIN *Bot. Gard.* I. Notes 12 The crepuscular atmosphere, or the region where the light of the sun ceases to be refracted to us, is estimated..to be between 40 and 50 miles high. **1876** G. F. CHAMBERS *Astron.* 67 A faint crepuscular light extending beyond the cusps of the planet.

2. *fig.* Resembling or likened to twilight; dim, indistinct.

1668 *Phil. Trans.* III. 730 And perhaps I might have lost the Crepuscular remains of my Sight. **1860** J. P. KENNEDY *W. Wirt* II. ix. 157 [The law is] at best, a crepuscular labyrinth. **1879** H. JAMES *Hawthorne* 132 The crepuscular realm of the writer's own reveries.

b. *esp.* Resembling or likened to the morning twilight as preceding the full light of day; characterized by (as yet) imperfect enlightenment.

1679 PULLER *Moder. Ch. Eng.* (1843) 254 Proportionable to the first crepuscular and duskish light of those times. **1797** W. TAYLOR in *Monthly Rev.* XXIV. 509 The favourable influence even of a partial and crepuscular day on the morals..and the happiness of the people. **1842** MOTLEY *Lett.* (1889) I. 96 The state of crepuscular civilization to which they have reached. **1852** *Fraser's Mag.* XLVI. 679 That crepuscular period, when the historical sense was scarcely brought to a full state of activity.

3. *Zool.* Appearing or active in the twilight.

1826 KIRBY & SP. *Entomol.* xlix. (1828) IV. 525 Crepuscular insects. **1877** COUES & ALLEN *N. Amer. Rodentia* 653 Animals..of crepuscular or nocturnal habits.

crepuscule (krɪˈpʌskjuːl, ˈkrɛpʌskjuːl). Now *rare.* [a. F. *crépuscule*, ad. L. *crepusculum*: see below.] Twilight.

c **1391** CHAUCER *Astrol.* II. §6 The spring of the dawyng and the ende of the euenyng, the which ben called the two crepusculus. *Ibid.* §9 Know the quantite of thi crepusculis. **1789** MRS. PIOZZI *Journ. France* II. 202 The crepuscule [is] less abrupt in its departure. **1819** H. BUSK *Banquet* II. 41 Coeval with the crepuscule of morn. **1866** J. B. ROSE tr. *Ovid's Fasti* v. 183 And when the doubtful crepuscule is gone The Hyades appear.

crepusculine (krɪˈpʌskjuːlaɪn, -lɪn), *a.* and *sb. rare.* [a. F. *crépusculin, -ine*, ad. med.L. *crepusculīn-us*, f. *crepuscul-um*: cf. L. *matutīnus, vespertīnus*: see -INE.]

A. *adj.* Pertaining to twilight; illuminated by twilight, dim, dusky.

1549 *Compl. Scot.* vi. 38 Aurora..hed persit the crepusculyne lyne matutine of the northt northt est orizone. **16..** in Sprat *Hist. R. Soc.* 314 (T.) To take in more or less light..to fit glasses to crepusculine observations. **1876** G. MEREDITH *Beauch. Career* (1889) 309 The line of downs ran luminously edged against the pearly morning sky, with its dark landward face crepusculine yet clear in every combe.

†**B.** *sb.* The (morning) twilight. *Obs.*

1549 *Compl. Scot.* 53 In the mornyng..it is callit lucifer, be cause it auancis the day befor the crepusculine.

crepusculous (krɪˈpʌskjuːləs), *a.* [f. L. *crepuscul-um* + -OUS.] Of the nature of twilight; dim, dusky, indistinct. (*lit.* and *fig.*)

1646 SIR T. BROWNE *Pseud. Ep.* 343 A close apprehension of the one, might perhaps afford a glimmering light and crepusculous glance of the other. **1665** GLANVILL *Sceps. Sci.* xxii. 140 The beginnings of Philosophy were in a crepusculous obscurity; and its yet scarce past the Dawn. **1822** ELIZA NATHAN *Langreath* II. 268.

‖**crepusculum** (krɪˈpʌskjuːləm). [L. = twilight, a diminutive formation, related to *creper* dusky, dark, *creperum* darkness.] Twilight, dusk.

1398 TREVISA *Barth. De P.R.* IX. xxiv. 361 The euentyde highte Crepusculum..whanne it is nat certaynly knowe bytwene lyght and derknesse. **1430** LYDG. *Chron. Troy* III. xxiii, The same time..That clerkes call Crepusculum at eue. **1638** WILKINS *New World* I. (1684) 176 By Observing the height of that Air which causeth the Crepusculum, or Twilight. **1840** DE QUINCEY *Rhet.* Wks. X. 34 Which interval we regard as the common crepusculum between ancient and modern history. **1853** KANE *Grinnell Exp.* xxxv. (1856) 313 The twilight too, that long Arctic crepusculum, seemed..disproportionally increased in its duration.

cres., cresc., *Music*, abbrev. of CRESCENDO *sb.*

cresce, var. of CREASE *v.*[1] and *sb.*[1] *Obs.*, increase.

†**crescence.** *Obs.* [ad. L. *crēscentia*, f. *crēscent-em*: see CRESCENT and -ENCE. Cf. OF. *creissance*, mod.F. *croissance.*] Growth, increase.

1602 FULBECKE *2nd Pt. Parall.* 60 In their cressence in the wombe, there is but one operation of nature. **1660** tr.

Paracelsus' Archidoxis I. IX. 129 There are found to be many superfluous Crescences. **1736** BROOKE *Univ. Beauty* III. 322 And towards the morn's attractive crescence bend.

‖**crescendo** (kreʃˈʃɛndo, krɪˈʃɛndəʊ), *sb. Mus.* [It. *crescendo* increasing, pr. pple. of *crescere* to increase:—L. *crēscĕre* (cf. CRESCENT *sb.*).]

1. A musical direction indicating that the tone is to be gradually increased in force or loudness (abbrev. *cres.*, *cresc.*). As *sb.*: A gradual increase of volume of tone in a passage of a piece of music; a passage of this description.

1776 'J. COLLIER' *Mus. Trav.* 60, I stood still some time to observe the diminuendo and crescendo. **1789** BURNEY *Hist. Mus.* III. 530 Domenico Mazzocchi [1626-40]..first..invented characters of *crescendo*, *diminuendo*, etc. **1812** W. CROTCH *Elem. Mus. Comp.* 112 The peculiar characteristic of the piano forte is its power of varying degrees of loudness and softness, either suddenly or by crescendo, diminuendo, rinforzando, etc. **1826** R. A. R. in Hone *Every-day Bk.* II. 1171 Let these notes be played..with perfect *crescendos* and *diminuendoes*. **1889** *Chambers' Cycl.* III. 557 The swell of a good organ produces a most perfect crescendo.

b. *transf.* A gradual increase in loudness of voice.

1865 *Pall Mall G.* 22 Apr. 11 He has not the force..to represent the climbing crescendo of unjust anger and despairing sarcasm. **1882** MRS. RIDDELL *Pr. Wales' Garden-Party* 45 'Do you mean that Sir Henry is dead?' interposed Susan, in a gradual crescendo.

c. *fig.* A progressive increase in force or effect.

1785 in *Sel. Papers Twining Family* (1887) 123 The crescendo of mountains, as we went up the lake, pleased me as much, I think, as any crescendo of sound can have pleased you. **1884** SYMONDS *Shaks. Predecessors* v. 205 Its chief merit as a play is the crescendo of its interest. **1886** F. HARRISON *Choice Bks.* (1888) 30 The intense crescendo of the catastrophe, the absolute concentration of interest.

d. *attrib.* or as *adj.*

1859 *Sat. Rev.* VII. 430/2 A crescendo series of appeals to the Chairman to call the Commission together. **1870** MISS BRIDGMAN *R. Lynne* II. iii. 70 'Borrow one!' said Dicky in a crescendo tone of amazement.

e. *colloq.* (orig. *U.S.*). The peak of an increase in volume, force, or intensity; a climax. Esp. in phr. ***to reach a crescendo***.

1925 F. SCOTT FITZGERALD *Great Gatsby* iii. 68 The caterwauling horns had reached a crescendo and I turned away and cut across the lawn toward home. **1939** WODEHOUSE *Uncle Fred in Springtime* iv. 54 The babble at the bar had risen to a sudden crescendo. **1946** *R.A.F. Jrnl.* May 170 The crescendo came when more than sixteen hundred bombers battered the coastal defences. **1958** L. URIS *Exodus* (1959) I. xxvii. 169 At the end of the second week the Jews were still holding fast and the clamour in the press was reaching a crescendo. **1961** E. E. GOLAY *Organizing Local Church* v. 57 The total process of evangelism reaches the crescendo when the group of new members stands before the congregation to declare publicly their faith. **1975** *Economist* 16 Aug. 8/1 It was in relation to the annual increment arrangements of the civil service pay system that your attack reached its crescendo of unfairness.

creˈscendo, *v.* [f. the sb.] *intr.* To increase gradually in loudness or intensity.

1900 *Westm. Gaz.* 2 July 2/1 A faint whir crescendoes rapidly into the shrill whoop of a steam-siren. **1901** *Ibid.* 12 Nov. 2/1 The trolly-cars, with their booming note which crescendoes up the scale with increasing speed and diminuendoes with the slackening of it. **1903** R. LANGBRIDGE *Flame & Flood* xvi, A bubbling torrent of vituperation that crescendoed as she leapt in air..and decrescendoed, as..she turned away. **1927** *Daily Express* 24 Oct. 10/3 'The season'..starts in November, crescendoes to its height in January and February, to die away in April. **1969** *Daily Tel.* 3 Feb. 12/3 As well as the nudity story which crescendoed up from Italy to swamp much of the Paris after-dark fashion, there is real news.

crescent (ˈkrɛsənt), *sb.* Forms: α. 4-7 **cressant**, 5 **cressaunt**, 5-7 **cressent**, (8 **cresent**); β. 6-7 **croissant**, 7 **croy-**, **croisant**; γ. 7- **crescent**. [ME. *cressant*, in 16th c. also *croissant*, a. OF. *creissant*, mod.F. *croissant* (:—L. *crēscent-em*), pr. pple. of OF. *creistre*, mod. *croître*:—L. *crēscĕre* to grow. In 17th c. assimilated to the L. spelling, already used in the adj.: see next.

L. *crescens* meant simply 'growing, waxing'; Columella has *luna crescens*, the waxing moon, *luna decrescens*, the waning moon; but these words had no reference to shape; sense 2 was a mediæval development, app. in French.]

1. The waxing moon, during the period between new moon and full. [Cf. OF. *creissant* the waxing of the moon, the first half of the month.] Also *fig.*

1530 PALSGR. 210/2 Cressent, the newe mone as long as it is nat rounde, *cressant*.

1620 FELTHAM *Resolves* xxviii. 88 Thus while he sinnes, he is a Decressant; when he repents, a Cressant. **1640** FULLER *Joseph's Coat* viii. (1867) 192 They are crescents in their waxing, full seas in their flowing. **1649** G. DANIEL *Trinarch., Hen. IV*, ccxxvii, A worke 'bove Nature's power, To make his Crescent Orbed in an Hower.

2. The convexo-concave figure of the waxing or the waning moon, during the first or last quarter, especially when very new or very old.

The crescent of the waxing moon has its horns to the spectator's left, that of the waning moon has them to his right.

1578 LYTE *Dodoens* IV. xxxi. 489 Turned rounde like a croissant or newe moone. **1590** SHAKS. *Mids. N.* v. i. 246 Hee is no crescent, and his hornes are inuisible. **1611** COTGR., *Croissant*, the halfe-moone; in Blazon, a Cressant. **1616** SURFL. & MARKH. *Country Farme* 24 If the higher horne of the said croisant be more obscure and darke than the lower. **1726** AMHERST *Terræ Fil.* xliv. 232 Phœbe's pale cresent. **1824** W. IRVING *T. Trav.* II. 349 The bright crescent of the moon. **1842** TENNYSON *Audley C.*, A moon, that, just In crescent, dimly rain'd about the leaf Twilights of airy silver.

3. A representation or figure of this phase of the moon: **a.** as an ornament or embellishment. (App. the earliest sense in English.)

1399 *Mem. Ripon* (Surtees) III. 132 Super feretrum Sancti Wilfridi de diversis ornamentis per dictum Johannem deauratis viz. j curc et j anulo et j cressant ex dono Willelmi Bedell. **1483** *Cath. Angl.* 81/1 A Cressent a bowte þe nek, *torques*, *lunula*. **1548** HALL *Chron.* 74 b, This cresant was couered with frettes and knottes made of Iue busshes. **1647** R. STAPYLTON *Juvenal* 127 On his black shooe a silver cressent's worn. **1885** BIBLE (R.V.) *Judg.* viii. 21 Gideon..took the crescents that were on their camels' necks.

b. *Her.* as a charge: see quot. 1882.

1486 *Bk. St. Alban's, Her.* Biij b, The ix. baage is Cressauntis that is to say halfe the moone. *c* **1500** *Sc. Poem Heraldry* 44 in *Q. Eliz. Acad., etc.* 95 The fader the hole [arms], the eldast son deffer[e]nt, quhiche a labelle; a cressent the second; third a molet, etc. **1603** DRAYTON *Bar. Wars* II. xxiv, The Noble Percy..With a bright Cressant in his Guide-home came. **1882** CUSSANS *Her.* 102 A Half-Moon, with the horns directed upwards, is a crescent..A Crescent with the horns directed towards the Dexter, is said to be Increscent; and if towards the Sinister, Decrescent.

c. Adopted as a badge or emblem by the Turkish sultans, and used within their dominions as a military and religious symbol; hence *fig.* the Turkish power, and, as this has been to Christendom in recent times the most formidable and aggressive Mohammedan power, used rhetorically to symbolize the Mohammedan religion as a political force, and so opposed to the Cross as the symbol of Christianity.

The attribution of the *crescent* by modern writers to the Saracens of Crusading times and the Moors of Spain is a historical and chronological error.

1589 PUTTENHAM *Eng. Poesie* II. (Arb.) 117 Selim Emperour of Turkie gaue for his deuice a croissant or new moone, promising to himself increase of glory and enlargement of empire. **1614** SELDEN *Titles Hon.* 162 With the Mahumedan Turks, the Croissant..as a Religious symbole, is..commonly set on the top of their Meschits, Seraglias, Turrets and such like. **16..** MARVELL *Britannia & Raleigh*, Her true Crusada shall at last pull down The Turkish crescent and the Persian sun. **1684** *Scanderbeg Rediv.* iv. 90 The Crescent gave way to the Cross, the Turks were broken to pieces. **1789** MRS. PIOZZI *Journ. France* II. 43 Why do you dress up one..with a turban and crescent? **1811** SCOTT *Vis. Don Roderick* I. xxvii, Before the Cross has waned the Crescent's ray. **1823** LOCKHART *Anc. Sp. Ball., Flight fr. Granada* ii, Down from the Alhambra's minarets were all the crescents flung. **1855** H. REED *Lect. Eng. Hist.* iv. 120 To raise the Christian banner, over the crescent of the Saracens. **1886** F. HARRISON *Choice Bks.* (1888) 331 The Crescent was advancing steadily upon Europe.

d. used as the badge of an order of knighthood or as a decorative order.

An order of the Crescent was instituted by Charles I of Naples and Sicily in 1268, and revived or reinstituted by René of Anjou in 1464. A Turkish decoration or order of the Crescent for foreigners was instituted by Sultan Selim after the Battle of Aboukir in 1799, being first conferred on Nelson.

4. A figure or outline of anything of this shape.

[**1572** GASCOIGNE *Flowers* (R.), The Christian crew came on in forme of battayle pight, And like a cressent cast themselues preparing for to fight. **1653** H. COGAN tr. *Pinto's Trav.* xxiv. 88 A very fair Port..extending it self in the form of a Crescent.] **1672** *Descr. Lake of Geneva* in *Phil. Trans.* VII. 5043 This Lake hath the figure of a Croissant..This Croissant where 'tis largest, which is from Morges to Thonon, is about Five good Leagues over. **1797** BEWICK *Brit. Birds* (1847) I. 130 The breast is distinguished by a crescent of pure white. **1837** DISRAELI *Venetia* I. i, The centre of a crescent of woods. **1838** THIRLWALL *Greece* II. 281 As they came near they bent their line into a crescent.

5. A row of houses built in the form of the inner bow of a crescent moon or arc of a circle.

First used in the name of 'the Royal Crescent' at Bath, afterwards used elsewhere, and hence as a generic name.

1766 ANSTEY *Bath Guide* 45 Old Stucco has just sent A plan for a house to be built in the Crescent. **1788** *Birm. Gaz.* 17 Nov., A plan, elevation and section of the intended building to be called the Crescent. **1837** DICKENS *Pickw.* II. xxxv. 163 There were blown into the Crescent a sedan-chair, with Mrs. Dowler inside. **1868** *Lessons Mid. Age* 299 The handsome streets, crescents and terraces which form the west end of Glasgow.

6. A small crescent-shaped roll of bread. (*U.S.*) More fully, ***crescent roll***. (Cf. CROISSANT.)

1886 *Century Mag.* XXXII. 939 At noon I bought two crisp 'crescents', which I ate sometimes at a shop counter. **1899** *Daily News* 23 Sept. 3/1 Crescent rolls and hot milk. **1951** E. PAUL *Springtime in Paris* v. 106 Coffee cups, saucers and crisp crescent rolls in our hands.

7. A Turkish musical instrument consisting of a staff with arms, ornamented with a crescent on the top, and bearing bells or jingles.

In mod. Dicts.

8. A disease in a horse's foot (see quots.).

1725 BRADLEY *Fam. Dict.* s.v., Crescents..are really nothing but the Bones of the little Foot that has left its Place, and fallen downwards, and the Sole at the Toe appears round, and the Hoof above shrinks in. **1823** CRABB *Techn. Dict.*, *Crescent*, a defect in the foot of a horse when the coffin-bone falls down, and presses the sole outwards.

9. *Lace-making.* (See quot.)

1882 CAULFEILD *Dict. Needlework* s.v., These crescents are raised Cordonnets that enclose the flat stitches of needle point laces or join the separate pieces of work together.

10. *Comb.*, as ***crescent-formed***, ***-lit***, ***-pointed***, ***-shaped*** adjs.; ***crescent-like***, ***-wise*** advs.

a **1631** DRAYTON *Wks.* II. 761 (Jod.) As, crescentlike, the land her breadth here inward bends. **1776** WITHERING *Brit. Plants* (1796) I. 316 Keel crescent-shaped, compressed. **1801** SOUTHEY *Thalaba* III. xxxviii, The Sun, Whose crescent-pointed horns Now momently decrease.

crescent (ˈkrɛsənt), *a.* [ad. L. *crēscent-em*, pr. pple. of *crēscĕre* to grow, increase: see -ENT. In II mostly attrib. use of prec.]

I. 1. Growing, increasing, developing. (Often with some allusion to the moon.)

1574 HYLL *Conject. Weather* i, When all cressent things do bud forth. **1606** SHAKS. *Ant. & Cl.* II. i. 10 My powers are Cressent, and my Auguring hope Sayes it will come to th' full. *a* **1624** CRAKANTHORP *Vigil. Dormitans* 188 In the first the Pope was but Antichrist nascent, in the second Antichrist crescent, in the third Antichrist regnant. **1834** WORDSW. *Lines on Portrait* 47 Childhood here, a moon Crescent in simple loveliness serene. **1845** DE QUINCEY *Coleridge & Opium* Wks. 1890 V. 196 The wrath of Andrew, previously in a crescent state, actually dilated to a plenilunar orb. **1859** TENNYSON *Elaine* 447 There is many a youth Now crescent, who will come to all I am And overcome it.

II. 2. Shaped like the new or old moon; convexo-concave, lunulate.

1603 HOLLAND *Plutarche's Rom. Quest.* (1892) 33 The moone..beginneth to show herself croissant in the evening. **1635** PAGITT *Christianogr.* 100 Marked with the Moone Crescent, which is the Turkish Ensigne. **1667** MILTON *P.L.* I. 439 With these in troop Came..Astarte, Queen of Heav'n, with crescent Horns. **1725** TURNER in *Phil. Trans.* XXXIII. 411 An Insect..with..a crescent or forked Tail. **1831** BREWSTER *Newton* (1855) I. xi. 273 Galileo discovered that Venus had the same crescent phases as the waxing and the waning moon. **1860** RUSSELL *Diary India* I. 359 New Orleans is called the 'crescent city' in consequence of its being built on a curve of the river.

ˈcrescent, *v. nonce-wd.* [f. CRESCENT *sb.*]

1. *trans.* To form into a crescent: see CRESCENTED.

2. To border or surround crescent-wise.

a **1809** MISS SEWARD *Lett.* VI. 195 (T.) A dark wood crescents more than half the lawn.

crescentade (krɛsənˈteɪd). [f. CRESCENT *sb.* 3 c. + -ADE, after *crusade*.] *properly*, A religious war waged under the Turkish flag; *rhetorically*, a *jihād* or holy war for Islam.

1868 G. DUFF *Pol. Surv.* 65 The further advance of the White Czar may yet be met by a crescentade, preached from the Caspian far away into the least known regions of China. **1884** *Standard* 14 Nov. 5/4 He would then lead a crescentade to drive the English out of Egypt. **1888** M. MACCOLL in *Contemp. Rev.* Apr. 541 This reactionary crescentade against every attempt at intellectual or moral progress beyond the Koran.

Hence **crescenˈtader**.

1880 *Blackw. Mag.* Mar. 368 Carried on a litter in rear of his crescentaders.

crescented (ˈkrɛsəntɪd), *ppl. a.* [f. CRESCENT *sb.* + -ED.]

1. Formed as a crescent or new moon.

1818 KEATS *Endym.* IV. 432 'Tis Dian's: lo! She rises crescented. **1835** WILLIS *Pencillings* I. iii. 25 The crescented shore of this lovely bay. **1876** G. F. CHAMBERS *Astron.* I. iv. 60 Becoming more and more crescented, it approaches the inferior conjunction.

2. Ornamented, or charged, with crescents.

1818 TODD *Dict.* s.v. *Crescent* v., The old heraldick adjective *crescented*, i.e. having a crescent.

3. Adorned with the crescent moon. *nonce-use.*

c **1825** BEDDOES *Apotheosis* Poems 98 Crescented night, and amethystine stars, And day, thou god and glory of the heavens, Flow on for ever!

crescentic (krəˈsɛntɪk), *a.* [f. L. *crēscent-em*, taken in sense of CRESCENT *sb.* + -IC.] Having the form of a crescent or new moon; crescent-shaped.

1836 TODD *Cycl. Anat.* I. 308/1 A large crescentic membraneous flap, or valve. **1885** H. O. FORBES *Nat. Wand.* IV. App. 364 Feathers..tipped with crescentic spots of white.

crescentically (krəˈsɛntɪkəlɪ), *adv.* [f. prec. + -AL[1] + -LY.] Crescent-wise.

1873 *Trans. Amer. Philos. Soc.* XIII. 113 Fifth segment truncate, sixth crescentically emarginate.

crescentiform (krəˈsɛntɪfɔːm), *a.* [f. L. *crēscent-em* + -(I)FORM.] Shaped like a crescent; crescent-shaped.

In mod. Dicts.

crescentoid (ˈkrɛsəntɔɪd), *a.* [f. CRESCENT + -OID.] = prec.

1887 E. D. COPE *Origin of Fittest* 250 Neither kind of tubercles crescentoid, but united in pairs.

crescentric (krəˈsɛntrɪk), *a. rare.* [f. L. *crescent-em* with second element after CENTRIC *a.*] = CRESCENTIC *a.*

1851 H. MELVILLE *Moby Dick* III. i. 6 And swimming on, in one solid, but still crescentric centre. **1896** *Naturalist* Oct. 338 The beautiful crescentric mounds around York.

crescive ('krɛsɪv), *a.* [f. L. *crēsc-ĕre* to grow + -IVE.] Growing, in the growing stage.

1566 DRANT *Wail. Hierim.* K vij b, The dragons..With propper brestes..do nurse theyr cresyve yonge. **1599** SHAKS. *Hen. V*, I. i. 66 Vnseene, yet cressiue in his facultie. **1824** T. HOGG *Carnation* 203 To..renovate their crescive faculties.

crescograph ('krɛskəgrɑːf, -æ-). [irreg. f. L. *crescĕre* to grow + -O + -GRAPH.]
An instrument invented by Sir Jagadis Chunder Bose (1858–1937), Indian plant physiologist, for recording the rate of growth in plants.

1918 J. C. BOSE *Life Movements in Plants* I. 157 High Magnification Crescograph. *Ibid.* 169 Magnetic Crescograph. **1919** *Ibid.* II. 255 Balanced Crescograph. **1919** —— in *Proc. R. Soc.* B. XC. 365 (*heading*) Researches on growth and movement in plants by means of the high magnification crescograph. **1957** *Encycl. Brit.* III. 926/1 He [*sc.* Bose]..invented many delicate and sensitive instruments, such as his crescograph for recording plant growth, magnifying a small movement as much as 10,000,000 times.

†**crese**, *v. Obs.* ? To crease; or to crush.

*c*1420 *Pallad. on Husb.* v. 77 Thai wol be crispe her seede yf that me crese, Or with a roll or feet hem sprongen brese.

crese, obs. f. CREASE; var. of KRIS.

'**creshawk.** *dial.* [perh. formed after F. *cresserelle* kestrel.] The kestrel.

1802–33 MONTAGU *Ornith. Dict.* 275 Kestrel, Creshawk. **1885** SWAINSON *Prov. Names Birds*, Creshawk (Cornwall).

creshett, obs. f. CRESSET.

cresme, cresment: see CHRISM, CREASEMENT.

cresol ('krɛsɒl). *Chem.* Also **cressol.** [f. *cres-* modification of initial part of *creos-ote* + -OL.] An aromatic alcohol of the Benzene group (C_7H_8O), occurring along with carbolic acid in coal-tar and creosote.

There are three isomeric substances having this composition, distinguished as *ortho-*, *meta-*, and *para-cresol*.

1869 ROSCOE *Elem. Chem.* 413 *Cressol*, a crystallizable solid, homologous with phenol. **1872** WATTS *Dict. Chem.* VI. 508 The red powder known in commerce as *Victoria-yellow* or *Aniline-orange* is a nearly pure salt of dinitro-cresol.

Hence '**cresolene**, $C_6H_5CH_3O$, a product of coal-tar, related to carbolic acid, used to impregnate the air in sick-rooms, etc., with disinfecting fumes. **cre'sotic** *a.* in (***ortho-, para-, meta-***) ***cresotic acid*** ($C_8H_8O_3$), obtained from the corresponding cresols.

1863–72 WATTS *Dict. Chem.* II. 106 Cresotic acid produces a deep violet colour with sesquichlorate of iron.

cresom, obs. f. CHRISOM.

cress (krɛs). Forms: 1 cresse, cerse, cærse, 1–6 kerse, 4 carse, crasse, kers, cres, 4–8 cresse, 6 kars, 6–7 karsse, 6– cress. Pl. 1 -an, 2–5 -en; 5–6 kersis, 5– cresses, 6–7 creeses (still *dial.*). [OE. *cresse*, *cerse* = OLG. **kressa* fem., MDu., MLG. *kerse*, Du. *kers* (also MLG. *karse*, LG. (Bremen) *kasse*), OHG. *chressa* f. (*chresso* m.), MHG. and mod.Ger. *kresse*, app. of native origin:—OTeut. **krasjôn-*, from root of OHG. *chresan* to creep, as if 'creeper'. The Da. *karse*, Sw. *krasse*, Norw. *kars*, Lettish *kresse*, Russ. *kress*, appear to be adopted from Ger. For the metathesis of *r*, in *cresse*, *cerse*, cf. GRASS.

The synonymous Romanic words, It. *crescione*, F. *cresson*, Picard *kerson*, Cat. *crexen*, med.L. *crissonus* (9th c. Littré) are generally held to be from German, though popularly associated with L. *crēscĕre* to grow (as if from a L. type *crēsciōn-em*) with reference to the rapid growth of the plant.]

1. The common name of various cruciferous plants, having mostly edible leaves of a pungent flavour. (Until 19th c. almost always in pl.; sometimes construed with a verb in the singular.)

a. *spec.* garden cress, *Lepidium sativum*, or WATERCRESS, *Nasturtium officinale*.

*a*700 [see b]. *c*1000 *Sax. Leechd.* I. 116 Ðeos wyrt..þe man nasturcium, & oðrum naman cærse nemneð. *Ibid.* II. 68 Do earban to and cersan and smale netelan and beowyrt. **1393** LANGL. *P. Pl.* C. IX. 322 With carses [*v.r.* crasses, cresses] and oþer herbes. *c*1420 *Pallad. on Husb.* II. 218 Now cresses sowe. *c*1450 *Alphita* (Anecd. Oxon.) 39 Cressiones, *gall.* cressouns, *anglice* cressen. **1533** ELYOT *Cast. Helthe* (1541) 9 b, Onyons, Rokat, Karses [**1561** Kersis]. **1548** TURNER *Names of Herbes* 55 Nasturtium is called..in englishe Cresse or Kerse. **1578** LYTE *Dodoens* v. lix. 623 Cresses are commonly sowen in all gardens. **1664** EVELYN *Kal. Hort.* (1729) 195 Sow also Carrots, Cabbages, Cresses, Nasturtium. **1730–6** BAILEY (folio), *Cresses*, an Herb us'd in Sallets; It has no Singular Number. **1770** GOLDSM. *Des. Vill.* 132 To strip the brook with mantling cresses spread. **1830** TENNYSON *Ode to Memory* 59 The brook that loves To purl o'er matted cress and ribbed sand. **1855** —— *Brook* 181, I loiter round my cresses.

b. With defining words, applied to many different cruciferous plants, and occasionally to plants of other Natural Orders resembling cress in flavour or appearance: as

American or ***Belleisle cress***, *Barbarea præcox*; ***Australian c.*** = *golden c.*; ***bank c.***, *Sisymbrium officinale*, also *Barbarea præcox*; ***bastard c.***, *Thlaspi arvense*; ***bitter c.***, the genus *Cardamine*, esp. *C. amara*; ***brown c.*** = WATERCRESS; ***churl's c.***, *Lepidium campestre*; ***cow-c.*** = prec.; also *Helosciadium nodiflorum* and *Veronica Beccabunga* (Brit. & Holl.); ***dock-c.***, *Lapsana communis*; ***French c.***, *Barbarea vulgaris*; ***garden c.***, *Lepidium sativum*; ***golden c.***, a variety of prec.; ***Indian c.***, the genus *Tropæolum*; ***lamb's c.***, *Cardamine hirsuta*; ***land c.***, *Barbarea vulgaris*, *B. præcox*, and *Cardamine hirsuta*; ***meadow c.***, *Cardamine pratensis*; ***mouse-ear c.***, *Arabis Thaliana*; ***penny-c.***, *Thlaspi arvense*; ***pepper-c.***, *Teesdalia nudicaulis* (Miller *Plant-n.*); ***Peter's c.***, *Crithmum maritimum* (Treas. Bot.); ***rock c.***, the genus *Arabis*; also *Crithmum maritimum* (Treas. Bot.); ***Spanish c.***, *Lepidium Cardamines*; ***spring c.***, *Cardamine rhomboidea*; ***swine's c.***, *Senebiera Coronopus*; ***Thale c.***, *Arabis Thaliana*; ***tooth-c.***, the genus *Dentaria*; ***tower c.***, *Arabis Turrita*; ***town c.***, *Lepidium sativum*; ***violet c.***, *Ionopsidium acaule*; ***wall c.***, the genus *Arabis*; ***wart c.*** = *swine's cress*; ***winter c.***, the genus *Barbarea*; ***wild c.***, species of *Thlaspi*; ***yellow c.***, *Nasturtium palustre* and *N. amphibium*.

*a*700 *Epinal Gloss.* 676 *Nasturcium*, tuuncressa. *a*800 *Erfurt Gloss.* 676 *Nasturcium*, leccressae. *c*1000 *Sax. Leechd.* II. 94 Eacersan ȝetrifula oððe ȝeseoð on buteran. *c*1420 *Liber Cocorum* (1862) 42 Town cresses, and cresses that growene in flode. **1548** TURNER *Names of Herbes* 44 Irio is named in greeke Erisimon, in englishe wynter cresse. **1562** —— *Herbal* II. 20 b, It may be called in Englishe way-cresses, wilde cresses, or sciatica cresses, because the herbe is good for the sciatica. **1578** LYTE *Dodoens* I. lxiv. 95 We do now call it *Coronopus Ruellij*..in some places of England they call it Swynescressis. *Ibid.* v. lix. 623 This herbe is called..in English, Cresses, Towne Kars, or Towne Cresses. *Ibid.* v. lxii. 627 There be foure kindes of wilde Cresse, or Thlaspi, the which are not..vnlyke cresse in taste. **1597** GERARD *Herbal* II. xiv. (1623) 253 This beautiful plant is called..in English Indian Cresses. *Ibid.*, Banke Cresses is found in stonie places. **1620** VENNER *Via Recta* vii. 158 Water-Cresse, or Karsse, is.. of like nature..as Towne-Karsse is. **1711** PETIVER in *Phil. Trans.* XXVII. 381 The largest of these Leaves resemble our Wart or Swines Cress. **1851** BALFOUR *Bot.* §822 The unripe fruit of *Tropæolum majus*, common Indian cress, has been pickled and used as capers. **1866** *Treas. Bot.* 347 *Australian Cress*, the Golden Cress, a broad yellowish-leaved variety of *Lepidium sativum*.

†**2.** As the type of something of little worth or significance; in such phrases as ***not worth a cress*** (***kerse***), ***not to count*** (***a thing***) ***at a cress.*** *Obs.* (Cf. *rush*, *straw*.)

*c*1325 *E.E. Allit. P.* A. 343 For anger gaynez þe not a cresse. **1377** LANGL. *P. Pl.* B. x. 17 Wisdome and witte now is nouȝt worth a carse [*v.r.* kerse]. *c*1380 *Sir Ferumb.* 5443 þe Amerel ne dredeþ hym noȝt..þe value of a kerse. *c*1386 CHAUCER *Miller's T.* 570 Of paramours ne sette he nat a kers. *a*1440 *Sir Degrev.* 191 Y counte hyme nat at a cres.

3. *attrib.* and *Comb.*, as ***cress-flower, -green, -taste***; **cress-rocket**, a name for the cruciferous genus *Vella* (*Treas. Bot.* 1866).

1707 FLOYER *Physic. Pulse-watch* 332 The Cresse Tastes, Mustard-Seed, Spirit of Scurvy-Grass. **1813** HOGG *Queen's Wake* ii. Wks. (1876) 32 And pu' the cress-flower round the spring. **1883** *Cassell's Fam. Mag.* Oct. 698/2 The velvet is the new cress-green..known by the name of 'cresson'.

cress, var. of CREASE, CREST³; obs. f. KRIS.

cressant, -ent, obs. ff. CRESCENT.

cressed ('krɛsɪd, krɛst), *a.* [f. CRESS + -ED².] Furnished or adorned with cresses.

1860 RUSKIN *Mod. Paint.* V. VII. iv. 139 Cressed brook and ever-eddying river.

†'**cresser.** *Obs. rare.* A small ladle or scoop.

1656 W. D. tr. *Comenius' Gate Lat. Unl.* ¶ 366 If any thing groweth hot and boileth, hee keeleth it with a cresser [*trulla futat*], lest it boyle over.

cresset ('krɛsɪt). Also 4 crassete, 5 crescette, cresette, cresset, -yt, 5–6 cressette, 5–7 -ett, 6 cres(s)hett(e, 7 cressit. [a. OF. *craicet*, *craisset*, *cresset* in same sense.]

1. A vessel of iron or the like, made to hold grease or oil, or an iron basket to hold pitched rope, wood, or coal, to be burnt for light; usually mounted on the top of a pole or building, or suspended from a roof. Frequent as a historical word; in actual use applied to a fire-basket for giving light on a wharf, etc.

1370 *Mem. Ripon* (Surtees) II. 130, j long cresset. **1393** GOWER *Conf.* III. 217 A pot of erthe, in which he tath A light brenning in a cresset. *c*1477 CAXTON *Jason* 85 The cite as light as it had ben daye by the clarte..of torches, cresettes and other fires. **1523** LD. BERNERS *Froiss.* I. cccc. 694 The erle..was comyng..with a great nomber of cressettes and lyghtes with hym. **1535** COVERDALE *Ecclus.* xlviii. 1 Then stode vp Elias the prophet as a fyre, and his worde brent like a creshett. **1574** tr. *Marlorat's Apocalips* 29 As a cresset set vp in a hauen, to shew the hauen a far of. **1656** BLOUNT *Glossogr.*, *Cresset*, an old word used for a Lanthorn or burning beacon. **1667** MILTON *P.L.* I. 728 Blazing Cressets fed With Naphtha and Asphaltus. **1782** FALCONER *Shipwr.* III. 202 Where beauteous Hero from the turret's height Display'd her cresset. **1814** SCOTT *Ld. of Isles* I. xxiv, Soon the warder's cresset shone. **1853** DICKENS *Reprinted Pieces* (1866) 221 Here and there, a coal fire in an iron cresset blazed upon a wharf.

†**b.** A cavity in a cresset-stone. *Obs.*

1593 *Rites & Mon. Ch. Durh.* (Surtees) 72 A four square stone, wherein was a dozen cressets wrought..being ever filled and supplied with the cooke as they needed, to give light to the Monks.

2. *transf.* and *fig.*; cf. *torch.*

1578 *Chr. Prayers in Priv. Prayers* (1851) 445 Unto the spiritual world the cresset is thy wisdom. **1581** MARBECK *Bk. of Notes* 154 So doth our Sauiour saie of Iohn Baptist, that he was a burning and blasing cresset. **1604** DRAYTON *Owle* 1140 The bright Cressit of the Glorious Skie. **1826** SCOTT *Woodst.* xxxiii, The moon..hung her dim dull cresset in the heavens. **1877** BRYANT *Constellations* 13 The resplendent cressets which the Twins Uplifted.

3. *Coopering.* A fire-basket used to char the inside of a cask.

1874 in KNIGHT *Dict. Mech.*

4. *local.* 'A kitchen utensil for setting a pot over the fire' (Bailey (folio), 1730–6).

5. *attrib.* and *Comb.*, as ***cresset-lamp***; **cresset-stone**, a flat stone with cup-shaped hollows for holding grease to be burnt for light. See also CRESSET-LIGHT.

1875 FARRAR *Silence & V.* v. 90 The stars its cresset lamps.

[**cresset.** In *water cressets*, error for *water cresses* (WATERCRESS).

1586 T. B. *La Primaud. Fr. Acad.* (1589) 669 A poore woman that sold Water cressets [so in ed. 1618]. **1730–6** BAILEY (folio), *Creset*, an Herb.]

cresset, obs. var. of KRIS, Malay dagger.

†'**cresset-light.** *Obs.* or *arch.* A blazing cresset; the light of a cresset; a beacon-light.

1525 in *Vicary's Anat.* (1888) App. iii. 170 To be furnyssed with his Watche..with Cressett light borne before them. **1587** FLEMING *Contn. Holinshed* III. 1271/2 John Cassimere..conueied by cresset light and torch light to sir Thomas Greshams house. **1610** *Histrio-m.* II. 269 Come Cressida, my Cresset light, Thy face, doth shine both day and night. **1729** SHELVOCKE *Artillery* v. 356 Those who ..ran about like mad People with Cresset-Lights of Sulphur and Dirt. *a*1835 MOTHERWELL *Merry Gallant*, In the Midnight Watch..When cresset lights all feebly burn.

cressol, var. of CRESOL.

‖**cresson** (krɛsɔ̃). [Fr.; = CRESS.]

†**1.** = CRESS. *Obs. rare.*

1657 TOMLINSON *Renou's Disp.* 13 As much abhorred Cabbages, as himself did the Cressons.

2. A shade of green used for ladies' dresses.

1883 *Cassell's Fam. Mag.* Oct. 698/2 The velvet is the new cress-green..known by the name of 'cresson' or water-cress. **1884** *Girl's Own Paper* 29 Nov. 136/1 The newest greens are called cresson and 'fir-green'.

cresswort ('krɛswɜːt). *Bot.* [CRESS.] A book-name for any plant of the N.O. *Cruciferæ*.

1854 LINDLEY *Sch. Bot.* (ed. 14) 32 Order V. Cruciferæ, or Brassicaceæ—Cressworts. **1882** *Garden* 24 June 439/3 *Hutchinsia petræa* is an early spring Cresswort.

cressy ('krɛsɪ), *a.* [f. CRESS + -Y.] Abounding in cresses.

1859 RUSKIN *Two Paths* 214 Rustic bridges over cressy brooks. **1859** TENNYSON *Geraint & Enid* 1324 Cressy islets white in flower.

cressyl, -ic, var. of CRESYL, -IC.

crest (krɛst), *sb.*¹ Forms: 4–7 creste, 4– crest; also 4–6 creest(e, 4–7 crist(e, 5 krest(e, creyste, 5–7 creast, 6 *Sc.* creist. [ME. a. OF. *creste* (13th c. in Littré, also *creiste*), mod.F. *crête*, = Pr., Sp., It. *cresta*:—L. *crista* tuft, plume.]

1. a. A 'comb', a tuft of feathers, or similar excrescence, upon an animal's head.

1387 TREVISA *Higden* (Rolls) II. 197 (Mätz.) He..had anon igrowe a spore on þe leg, and a crest on þe heed, as it were a cok. **1398** —— *Barth. De P.R.* XVIII. xxxiii. (1495) 795 A certen fysshe hauynge a creste lyke to a sawe. **1393** GOWER *Conf.* II. 329 A lappewinke made he was..And on his heed there stont upright A crest in token of a knight. *c*1440 *Promp. Parv.* 102 Creste, of a byrdys hede, *cirrus.* **1513** DOUGLAS *Æneis* XII. Prol. 155 Phebus red fowle hys corall creist can steir. **1667** MILTON *P.L.* IX. 525 Oft he [the serpent] bowd His turret Crest. **1781** COWPER *Truth* 476 The subtlest serpent with the loftiest crest. **1842** TENNYSON *Locksley Hall* 18 In the Spring the wanton lapwing Gets himself another crest.

b. *fig.* In phrases, such as to ***erect, elevate, let fall one's crest***, used as a symbol of pride, self-confidence, or high spirits. Cf. CRESTFALLEN.

1531 TINDALE *Exp. 1 John* 27 When the byshoppes sawe that..they beganne to set up theyr crestes. **1606** SHAKS. *Tr. & Cr.* I. iii. 380 And make him fall His crest. **1614** RALEIGH *Hist. World* III. 80 Then began the Argives to let fall their crests and sue for peace. **1796** BURKE *Regic. Peace* iii. Wks. VIII. 318 That this faction does..erect its crest upon the engagement. **1851** GALLENGA *Italy* 481 After a short explanation..their crests fell, and..all went away satisfied.

c. Any feathery-like tuft or excrescence: applied *e.g.* to the tail of a comet.

1387 TREVISA *Higden* (Rolls) VII. 33 Stella comata, þat is, a sterre wiþ a briȝt shynynge crest. **1494** FABYAN *Chron.* VI. cxlix. 135, .Ii. blasynge starrys, or .ii. starrys with crestis.

2. An erect plume or tuft of feathers, horse-hair, or the like, fixed on the top of a helmet or head-dress; any ornament or device worn there as a badge or cognizance.

*c*1380 *Sir Ferumb.* 622 Al anoneward þe helm an heȝ ys crest a bar adoun & þe cercle of gold þat sat þer-bey. *c*1435 *Torr. Portugal* 1128 The creste, that on his hede shold stond, Hit was all gold shynand. **1605** CAMDEN *Rem.*, *Armories* (R.), Creasts being the ornaments set on the eminent toppe of the healme..were vsed auntiently to terrifie the enemy, and therefore were strange deuises or figures of terrible shapes. **1824** MACAULAY *Ivry*, A thousand knights are pressing close behind the snow-white crest. **1874** WHITTIER *Eagle's Quill from Lake Superior* ix, War-chiefs with their painted brows, And crests of eagle wings.

3. a. *Her.* A figure or device (originally borne by a knight on his helmet) placed on a wreath, coronet, or chapeau, and borne above the shield and helmet in a coat of arms; also used separately, as a cognizance, upon articles of personal property, as a seal, plate, note-paper, etc.

As it represents the ornament worn on the knight's helmet, it cannot properly be borne by a woman, or by a corporate body, as a college or city. (It is a vulgar error to speak of the arms or shields of such bodies as *crests*.)

a **1400–50** *Alexander* 1837 (Ashmole MS.) To Darius.. enditis he a pistill, A crest clenly inclosid þat consayued þis wordis. **1431** *E.E. Wills* (1882) 88 A faire stone of Marble with my creste, myn armes, my vanturs. **1572** BOSSEWELL (*title*), Workes of Armorie deuided into three Bookes, entituled.. of Cotes and Creastes. **1596** SHAKS. *Tam. Shr.* II. i. 226 What is your Crest, a Coxcombe? **1622** PEACHAM *Compl. Gentl.* i. (1634) 15 Mine old Host at Arnhem.. changed his Coate and Crest thrice in a fortnight. **1837** HOWITT *Rur. Life* II. iv. (1862) 120 A crescent,—the crest of the Northumberland family.

b. *fig.*

c **1425** *Fest. Church* 66 in *Leg. Rood* (1871) 212 Whan kyngis sone bare fleisshly creste. **1592** LYLY *Midas* v. ii, Melancholy is the creast of courtiers' armes. **1650** BULWER *Anthropomet.* 173 Who have nothing but long Nails as the Crests of idle Gentility.

c. *Archery.* A series of narrow coloured bands painted around the shaft of an arrow below the fletching, used as an identifying mark.

1929 A. W. LAMBERT *Mod. Archery* xii. 108 This protective painting is elaborated to serve as a decoration of heraldic nature, termed the crest. **1939** P. H. GORDON *New Archery* xviii. 271 The crest is an arrangement of bright paint bands about the chest of the shaft.

4. The apex or 'cone' of a helmet; hence, a helmet or head-piece.

c **1325** *Coer de L.* 275 Upon hys crest a raven stode. *c* **1386** CHAUCER *Sir Thopas* 195 Vpon his crest he bar a tour. **14..** *Voc.* in Wr.-Wülcker 782 *Hic conus*, a crest. **1590** SPENSER *F.Q.* I. ii. 11 On his craven crest A bounch of heares discolourd diversly. **1595** SHAKS. *John* II. i. 317 There stucke no plume in any English Crest, That is remoued by a staffe of France. **1667** MILTON *P.L.* IV. 988 On his crest Sat horror plum'd. **1740** SOMERVILLE *Hobbinol* II. 416 On his unguarded Crest The Stroke delusive fell. *a* **1839** PRAED *Poems* (1864) I. 22 The feathers that danced on his crest.

5. a. The head, summit, or top of anything.

1382 WYCLIF *Ex.* xxviii. 23 Two goldun ryngis, the whiche thow shalt putte in either creeste of the broche. **1513** DOUGLAS *Æneis* XII. Prol. 128 Hevynly ylleis.. Oppynnyt and schew thar creistis redymyte. **1632** LITHGOW *Trav.* (1682) 71 The Northern wind.. doth first murmur at this aspiring Oke, and then striketh his Crest with some greater strength. **1635** QUARLES *Emblems* v. xi, The drooping crests of fading flow'rs. **1859** TENNYSON *Enid* 827 The giant tower, from whose high crest, they say, Men saw the goodly hills of Somerset. **1871** ROSSETTI *Troy Town* xii, His arrow's burning crest.

b. *esp.* The summit of a hill or mountain.

c **1340** *Gaw. & Gr. Knt.* 731 Þer as claterande fro þe crest þe colde borne rennez. ? *a* **1400** *Morte Arth.* 882 Appone the creste of the cragge. **1470–85** MALORY *Arthur* v. v, And wente forth by the creast of that hylle. **1601** HOLLAND *Pliny* I. 83 The very pitch and crest of the hill, the Scyto-tauri do hold. **1681** COTTON *Wond. Peake* 5 At a high Mountains foot, whose lofty crest O're looks the Marshy Prospect. **1799** WELLINGTON in Gurw. *Desp.* I. 22 Strongly posted on the elevated crest of a rocky ridge. **1818** SHELLEY *Rev. Islam* IV. xxxii, O'er many a mountain chain which rears Its hundred crests aloft.

c. *fig.* The most excellent, the crown. *rare.*

c **1325** *E.E. Allit. P.* A. 855 Of spotlez perlez þa[y] beren þe creste. **1838** DE QUINCEY *The Avenger* Wks. 1890 XII. 239 And yet to many it was the consummation and crest of the whole. **1873** LOWELL *All Saints* 1 One feast, of holy days the crest.. All-Saints.

6. *Arch.* **a.** The finishing of stone, metal, etc., which surmounts a roof-ridge, wall, screen, or the like; a cresting; sometimes applied to the finial of a gable or pinnacle. **b.** Short for *crest-tile* (see 11).

1430 LYDG. *Chron. Troy* II. xi, To reyse a wall With batayling and crestes marciall. **1513** *Will of J. Hutton* (Somerset Ho.), Crest of the Highe Aulter. *c* **1530** LD. BERNERS *Arth. Lyt. Bryt.* (1814) 188 Than Arthur.. slypped downe thereby tyll he came to the crest of the wall. **1596–7** S. FINCHE in Ducarel *Hist. Croydon* App. (1783) 155 The crests as heigh for the safegarde of the windoes. **1601** HOLLAND *Pliny* II. 526 Supposing verily there had been tiles and crests indeed. **1610** W. FOLKINGHAM *Art of Survey* I. vii. 14. **1626** BACON *Sylva* §537 Moss groweth chiefly upon Ridges of Houses.. and upon the Crests of Walls. **1866** ROGERS *Agric. & Prices* I. xx. 491 As a rule, crests cost as much by the hundred as plain tiles do by the thousand.

7. An elevated ridge. **a.** The lofty ridge of a mountain which forms its sky line, and from which the surface slopes on each side; the summit line of a *col* or pass; the ridge of a hedge-bank or the like. **b.** *Fortif.* The top line of a parapet or slope. **c.** A balk or ridge in a field between two furrows. **d.** The curling foamy top or ridge of a wave; the highest part of any undulation.

c **1440** *Promp. Parv.* 102 Creyste, of londe eryyde, *porca.* **1830** E. S. N. CAMPBELL *Dict. Mil. Sc.* 21 Four feet and a half below the crest of the Parapet. **1850** LAYARD *Nineveh* vii. 151 Two vast rocks formed a kind of gateway on the crest of the pass. **1854** *Jrnl. R. Agric. Soc.* XV. I. 19 Crests, cradges, and ward-dykes [were] constructed to hold off fen-waters. **1864** EARL DERBY *Iliad* IV. 485 First curls the ruffl'd sea With whit'ning crests. **1865** GEIKIE *Scen. & Geol. Scot.* vi. 118 From a rounded and flattened ridge it narrows into a mere knife-edged crest, shelving steeply into the glens on either side. **1878** HUXLEY *Physiogr.* 214.

e. Chiefly *Electr. Engin.* A point in a wave-form at which the varying quantity is a maximum. Hence **crest factor**, the ratio of the maximum value (***crest value***) of an alternating current or voltage to its root-mean-square value; **crest voltmeter**, any instrument for measuring the maximum value of an alternating voltage. (Cf. PEAK *sb.*[2])

1875 *Encycl. Brit.* I. 111/1 [*Acoustics.*] The wave represented by the dotted line, which.. has its crests. **1914** H. PENDER *Amer. Handbk. Electr. Engineers* 1297 Crest-factor or peak-factor is the ratio of the crest or maximum value to the r.m.s. value. *Ibid.*, The crest value of a sine-wave is $\sqrt{2}$. **1916** *Trans. Amer. Inst. Electr. Engin.* XXXV. I. 115 The crest voltmeter is a direct-reading instrument, reading either the r.m.s. value of a sine wave having the same crest as a high voltage wave to which it is connected, or the true crest value, depending upon its calibration. **1961** *Listener* 9 Nov. 767/2 With an alternating current system, the insulation has to withstand the maximum value of the crest of the voltage wave; and that crest value is higher than the *useful* value, and so some of the expensive insulating capacity is wasted. In a direct current system the crest value of the voltage *is* the useful value, so there is no waste of insulation.

8. a. The ridge or surface line of the neck of a horse, dog, or other animal; sometimes applied to the mane which this part bears.

1592 SHAKS. *Ven. & Ad.* 272 His braided hanging mane Upon his compass'd crest now stand on end. **1614** MARKHAM *Cheap Husb.* I. i. (1668) 2 Chuse a horse with a deep neck, large crest. **1724** *Lond. Gaz.* No. 6286/3 Stolen .. a.. Gelding.. with Saddle Spots upon his Crest. *a* **1849** SIR R. WILSON *Autobiog.* (1862) I. ii. 89 My little mare received.. a musket-ball through the crest of her neck. **1872** RUSKIN *Eagle's N.* §227 The crest, which is properly the mane of lion or horse.

†b. The dewlap of an ox. *Obs.*

1607 TOPSELL *Four-f. Beasts* (1673) 58 A long, thick, and soft neck; his crest descending down to the knee.

9. a. A raised ridge on the surface of any object.

1611 COTGR. s.v. *Areste*, The Crest, of a sword, &c.; a sharpe rising in the middle thereof.

b. *Anat.* A ridge running along the surface of a bone, as the *frontal*, *occipital*, *parietal* (or *sagittal*) *crests* of the skull, the *lacrymal*, *nasal*, and *turbinated crests* in the face, the *iliac*, *pubic*, and *tibial crests*, etc.

1828 STARK *Elem. Nat. Hist.* I. 152 Horns.. slightly bent outwards and forwards, the frontal crest passing behind them. **1831** R. KNOX *Cloquet's Anat.* 149 These surfaces are separated by three edges. The anterior.. is called the Crest (*crista tibiæ*). **1872** MIVART *Elem. Anat.* 178 The ilium has a wide outer surface, the upper border of which is termed the 'crest'.

c. ***dental crest***: 'the ridge of epithelium which, at the earliest stage of the development of the teeth, covers in the dental groove, and from the lower layers of which the enamel organ is developed' (*Syd. Soc. Lex.* 1882).

d. *Bot.* and *Zool.* A formation resembling a crest or ridge, on the surface of an organ.

1597 GERARD *Herbal* I. i. (1633) 2 Leafe, Sheath, eare, or crest. **1830** LINDLEY *Nat. Syst. Bot.* 145 The keel [of *Polygala*] has an appendage.. called technically a crest, and often consisting of one or even two rows of fringes or divisions. **1870** HOOKER *Stud. Flora* 392 *Luzula pilosa*.. crest of seeds long curved terminal. **1875** BENNETT & DYER *Sachs' Bot.* 540 When outgrowths occur on the seed, either along the raphe.. or as a cushion covering the micropyle.. they are variously called *Crest*, *Strophiole*, or *Caruncle*.

e. (See quot. 1954.)

1916 C. E. ALLEN *Machinery's Screw Thread Bk.* 3 The crest is the prominent part of the thread, of either the male screw or of the female screw. **1954** *Defs. for use in Mech. Engin.* (*B.S.I.*) 16 *Crest*, that part of the surface of a thread which connects adjacent flanks at the top of the ridge.

†10. The middle line of fold in broad-cloth.

1483 *Act 1 Rich. III*, c. 8 §4 Every hole wolen Cloth called brode Cloth shall hold and conteyn in leenght xxiiij yerdes .. to be measured by the Crest of the same Cloth.

11. *Comb.*, as ***crest-bearer***, ***-feather***, †***-front***; ***crest-like***, ***-lopped***, ***-wounding*** adjs.; **crest-board**, a board which forms the crest or finishing of any projecting part of a building; **crest-line**, (*a*) a series of ridges; (*b*) the sky-line of a ridge (cf. 7 a); †**crest-risen**, †**crest-sunk** *a.* (cf. 1 b and CREST-FALLEN); **crest-tile**, a bent tile used to cover the crest or ridge of a roof; **crest-wreath** (in *Her.*), the wreath or fillet of twisted silk which bears the crest.

1883 *Pall Mall G.* 27 Dec. 3/2 The united crest of France and Navarre.. supported by two angels as *crest-bearers. **1881** *Mechanic* §985 If a gutter be made.. the front may be finished with a *crest-board. **1836** TODD *Cycl. Anat.* I. 291/2 To elevate the *crest-feathers. **1890** LD. LUGARD *Diaries* (1959) I. ii. 96 The house.. does not run parallel with the *crest line, so.. I am bound to make the Stockade skew-wise a bit. **1901** 'LINESMAN' *Words by Eyewitness* (1902) 49 From the encircling rim are darting innumerable spurts of flame.. from the rifles of the men clinging like flies to the crest-line. **1915** *Blackw. Mag.* Jan. 9/2 Hardly had we rejoined the battalion, which was formed up behind a second crest-line.., when a tremendous shell fire began to fall. **1611** COTGR., *Accresté*.. also, cockit, proud, lustie, *creast-risen. **1618** BRATHWAIT *Descr. Death* 271 Chapfalne, *crest-sunke, drie-bon'd anatomie. **1477** *Act 17 Edw. IV*, c. 3 Thaktile, roftile, ou *crestile. **1611** COTGR., *Enfaistau*, a Ridge-tyle, Creast-tyle, Roofe-tyle. **1876** GWILT *Archit.* Gloss. s.v., In Gothic architecture, crest tiles are those which, decorated with leaves, run up the sides of a gable or ornamented canopy. **1593** SHAKS. *Lucr.* 828 O vnfelt sore, *crest-wounding priuat scarre! **1864** BOUTELL *Heraldry Hist. & Pop.* xvii. 265 This *Crest-Wreath first appears a little before the middle of the 14th century.

†**crest**, *sb.*[2] *Obs.* [ad. It. *cresta* (and pl. *creste*) 'a disease.. called the piles or hemorrhoides' (Florio); a specific use of *cresta* tuft: see prec.] The disease called piles; also, corns.

1569 R. ANDROSE tr. *Alexis' Secr.* IV. III. 46 Against the crestes of the piles in the fundiment. **1651** *Surgions Direct.* IX. 244 This kind of Tumor is called.. Cornes in English; and I thought it good to call them Crest, because they are alwayes growing.

†**crest**, *sb.*[3], **cress.** *Obs.* Forms: 5 crees, 5–6 crest(e, cres, cress(e. In ***crest-cloth***: some kind of linen cloth.

c **1430** *Two Cookery-bks.* 38 Take Rys.. bray hem smal y-now; & þerow a crees bunte syfte hem. **1436** *Pol. Poems* (Rolls) (1859) II. 164 Creste clothe, and canvasse. **1488** *Will of Elis Brown* (Somerset Ho.), A pece of new creste clothe conteygnyng xxiij ellys. **1507** in Kerry *St. Lawr., Reading* (1883) 234 Paied for ij ells di. of crescloth for to make Eve a cote—xd. **1611** in Heath *Grocers' Comp.* (1869) 92 In any kerchief, koyfe, crest cloth or shaddow.

b. A piece or fixed quantity of this cloth.

1459 *Will of Lyghtfote* (Somerset Ho.), Crestes panni linei vocat[i] crestcloth. **1488** *Will of Jonys*, j cresse de cressecloth. [**1866** ROGERS *Agric. & Prices* IV. 555 In the earlier years the 'crest' appears to be a recognised quantity [of linen cloth].]

crest (krɛst), *v.* [f. CREST *sb.*[1] Cf. CRESTED.]

1. *trans.* To furnish with a crest; to put a crest, cresting, or ridge on (a building).

c **1440** *Promp. Parv.* 102 Crestyn, or a-rayyn wythe a creste (PYNSON, or sette on a creest), *cristo.* **1814** SOUTHEY *Roderick* v, The Christian hand.. had with a cross Of well-hewn stone crested the pious work. **1851** TURNER *Dom. Archit.* II. v. 215 The Sheriff.. is ordered to crest with lead all the passages at Clarendon.

2. To serve as a crest to; to surmount as a crest; to top, to crown.

1606 SHAKS. *Ant. & Cl.* v. ii. 83 His legges bestrid the Ocean, his rear'd arme Crested the world. **1795** SOUTHEY *Joan of Arc* VII. 11 Broad battlements Crested the bulwark. **1856** RUSKIN *Mod. Paint.* II. IV. iii. §16 The clinging wood climbing along their ledges and cresting their summits.

b. 'To mark with long streaks, in allusion to the streaming hair of the crest' (Todd).

1596 SPENSER *F.Q.* IV. i. 13 Like as the shining skie in summers night.. Is creasted all with lines of firie light.

3. To reach the crest or summit of (a hill, rising ground, wave, etc.).

1851 J. H. NEWMAN *Cath. in Eng.*, In this inquisitive age, when the Alps are crested, and seas fathomed. **1877** KINGLAKE *Crimea* VI. vi. 75 The.. Ravine [was] forbiddingly hard to crest. **1860** MAYNE REID in *Chamb. Jrnl.* XIV. 172 As we crested each swell, we were freshly exposed to observation.

4. *intr.* To erect one's crest, raise oneself proudly. Now *dial.*

1713 *Guardian* No. 56 ¶6 The bully seemed a dunghil cock, he crested well, and bore his comb aloft. **1791** BOSWELL *Johnson* 5 Oct. an. 1773, The old minister was standing with his back to the fire, cresting up erect.

5. *intr.* Of waves: To form or rise into a crest; to curl into a crest of foam.

1850 BLACKIE *Æschylus* II. 235 Where wave on wave cresting on Bristles with angry breath. **1882** GEIKIE *Text-bk. Geol.* III. II. ii. §6 The superficial part of the swell.. begins to curl and crest as a huge billow.

crest, obs. var. of KRIS, Malay dagger.

crested ('krɛstɪd), *ppl. a.* Also 6 creasted, 6–8 cristed. [f. CREST *sb.* and *v.* + -ED. Cf. OF. *cresté*, L. *cristātus*.]

1. Furnished, topped, or adorned with a crest; wearing or having a crest.

c **1380** *Sir Ferumb.* 4541 With an hard crested serpentis fel. **1481** CAXTON *Myrr.* II. xvi. 102 The huppe or lapwynche is a byrde crested. *c* **1620** Z. BOYD *Zion's Flowers* (1855) 135 With cristed plumes they fiercely other smite. **1667** MILTON *P.L.* VII. 443 The crested Cock. **1810** SCOTT *Lady of L.* I. Introd. ii, Fair dames and crested chiefs. **1851** C. L. SMITH tr. *Tasso* II. lxxxiv, This makes the billow smooth its crested head.

b. *spec.* Applied to many species of animals and plants distinguished by a crest; = L. *cristatus*, *-a.*

1796 STEDMAN *Surinam* II. xxvii. 300 The crested eagle. **1802** BINGLEY *Anim. Biog.* (1813) II. 347 The Crested Penguins are inhabitants of several of the South Sea islands. **1861** MISS PRATT *Flower. Pl.* VI. 98 Crested Dog's-tail. **1882** *Garden* 16 Sept. 258/3 The Crested Male Fern.

c. *fig.* (Cf. CREST *sb.*[1] 1 b.)

1618 BOLTON *Florus* IV. ix. 307 The miserable overthrow of Crassus made the Parthians higher crested. **1757** GRAY *Bard* I. i, The crested pride Of the first Edward.

2. *Her.* Having a crest of a different tincture from that of the body.

1572 BOSSEWELL *Armorie* II. 60b, A Basiliske displayed, Emeraude, cristed, Saphire. **1766–87** PORNY *Her.* Gloss.

†3. Having raised lines or *striæ*, ribbed. *Obs.*

1578 LYTE *Dodoens* I. xxx. 42 The stalkes [of Rhubarb] are straked and crested. **1834** PLANCHÉ *Brit. Costume* 268 Mandillians.. some plaited and crested [striped] behind.

4. Having a raised ridge. (See CREST *sb.* 9.)

1857 HENFREY *Bot.* Index, Crested petals. **1856** A. R. WALLACE in Huxley *Man's Place Nat.* I. (1863) 40–1 Single-crested and double-crested skulls.

† **'crestel.** *Obs. rare*⁻¹. [app. dim. of CREST *sb.*: see -EL. Cf. OF. *crestel*, *cretel* a battlement.] ? = CREST.

c **1320** *Sir Beues* 4175 To Beues he smot a dent ful sore, þat sercle of gold & is crestel Fer in to þe mede fel.

Cresten, var. of CHRISTEN *a. Obs.*, Christian.

† **'crest-fall,** *sb. Obs. rare.* [A back-formation from CREST-FALLEN.] The distemper of a horse that is crest-fallen.

1609 ROWLANDS *Knave of Clubbes* (1843) 44 For any Iade he phisicke had.. The Iampasse, crest-fall, withers greife.

† **crest-fall,** *v. Obs. rare.* [f. as prec.] *trans.* To make crest-fallen.

1611 COTGR. s.v. *Rosse*, It would anger a Saint, or crest-fall the best man liuing, to be so vsed.

crest-fallen ('krɛstˌfɔːlən), *ppl. a.*
1. With drooping crest; *hence*, cast down in confidence, spirits, or courage; humbled, abashed, disheartened, dispirited, dejected.

1589 *Pappe w. Hatchet* D iv b, O how meager and leane hee lookt, so creast falne, that his combe hung downe to his bill. **1593** SHAKS. *2 Hen. VI*, IV. i. 59 Let it make thee Crest-falne, I, and alay this thy abortiue Pride. **1668** MARVELL *Corr.* cv. Wks. 1872–5 II. 264 He is here a kind of decrepit young gentleman and terribly crest-falln. **1860** THACKERAY *Four Georges* iii. (1876) 69 Slinking back into the club somewhat crestfallen after his beating.

2. Of a horse: see quot. 1725.

1696 *Lond. Gaz.* No. 3217/4 A grey Gelding.. black mane and tail, and a little Crest-fallen. **1725** BRADLEY *Fam. Dict.*, *Crestfallen*, a Distemper in Horses, when the Part on which the Main grows, which is the upper Part thereof, and call'd the Crest, hangs either to one Side or the other, and does not stand upright as it ought to do.

Hence **'crestˌfallenly** *adv.*, **'crestˌfallenness.**

1854 LYTTON *What will he* IV. i, That ineffable aspect of crestfallenness! **1880** MISS BROUGHTON *Sec. Th.* I. I. ii. 28 The Squire is crestfallenly eying the shipwreck of his hopes. **1890** —— *Alas!* II. xxiv. 125 A look of mortification and crestfallenness.

Crestin, -yn, var. of CHRISTEN *a. Obs.*, Christian.

cresting ('krɛstɪŋ), *vbl. sb.* [f. CREST *sb.* (sense 6) + -ING¹.] **1.** *Arch.* An ornamental ridging to a wall or roof.

1869 *Builder* 18 Dec. 998/2 The lines of a building are best followed by.. placing crestings where objects would be artistically enriched by them. **1870** F. R. WILSON *Ch. Lindisf.* 48 Roofs.. finished with ornamental tiled cresting.

2. Ornamental edging on a chair, settee, etc. Also *attrib.*, as ***cresting rail.***

1908 P. MACQUOID *Hist. Eng. Furnit.* IV. viii. 241 Sometimes the whole of the splat was formed of crossed diagonal lines.. and the panel of the cresting lightly carved in place of painting. **1941** *Burlington Mag.* June 187/1 The back [of the *Director* chair] was of a light and elegant design with graceful curves to the splat and cresting rail. **1963** *Times* 2 Mar. 11/7 Compared with *Director* designs, the Portuguese cresting rail is deeper, generally less pierced, and treated much more as a pediment.

crestless ('krɛstlɪs), *a.* [See -LESS.] **1.** Without a crest; not bearing a crest.

1591 SHAKS. *1 Hen. VI*, II. iv. 85 Spring Crestlesse Yeomen from so deepe a Root? **1828** SCOTT *F.M. Perth* xiii, Like the crestless churls of England. **1891** *Standard* 14 May 5/2 Armless, and crestless, and mottoless.

2. *gen.* Without a tuft, top, ridge, or the like.

1889 in *Cent. Dict.* **1908** A. S. M. HUTCHINSON *Once Aboard the Lugger* I. ii. 33 It welled, rose-deeply;.. crestless, flinging no intoxicating spume. **1908** *Daily Chron.* 31 Aug. 7/2 Great shiny blue crestless jays flitted over the scrub.

crestlet ('krɛstlɪt). *nonce-wd.* A little crest.

1889 *Repent. P. Wentworth* III. xvi. 274 The sparkling expanse broken.. by jets and crestlets of foam.

† **Crestmarine.** *Herb. Obs.* [a. F. *creste-marine*, *crête-marine*, in 16th c. also *criste-marine*, in the Herbals *Creta marina*, the first element being a perversion of *crithmum*, Gr. κρίθμον, κρῆθμον, in mod. Bot. *Crithmum maritimum*.] An old name of Samphire.

1565–73 COOPER *Thesaurus*, *Batis*, an herbe called.. of the Frenchmen Crestmarine, in English Sampiere. **1578** LYTE *Dodoens* V. xxi. 578 They keepe.. branches of Crestmarin or Sampier in brine or pickle, to be eaten lyke cappers. **1611** COTGR., *Creste marine*, Sampier, sea Fennell, Crestmarine.

† **'cresty,** *a. Obs.* [f. CREST *sb.*² + -Y.] Of the nature of or affected with piles.

1569 R. ANDROSE tr. *Alexis' Secr.* IV. II. 13 Against the Hemerodes and crestie swellings of the fundiment. **1598** FLORIO, *Crestoso*, crestie, full of the piles or hemorrhoides.

† **crestyn.** *Obs. rare*⁻¹. [a. OF. *crestin*, *cretin* in same sense.] A sort of pannier.

a **1400–50** *Alexander* 4687 As gud ware crestyns of clathe þe caryon to serue.

† **'creswell.** *Obs.* [? Cf. WELT.]

1721 BAILEY, *Creswell*, the broad Edge or Verge of the Shoe-Sole, round about.

Creswellian (krɛz'wɛlɪən), *a. Archæol.* [f. the name of *Creswell* Crags in Derbyshire (see quot. 1926) + -IAN.] Pertaining or belonging to a cultural period of the Mesolithic or late Palæolithic, represented only in Britain and roughly contemporary with the Magdalenian period. Also *ellipt.* as *sb.*

1926 D. A. E. GARROD *Upper Palaeolithic Age* III. 194, I would suggest that this industry is sufficiently well characterized to deserve a name.. to differentiate it.. from the classical Magdalenian of France.. [and] the true Upper Aurignacian. I propose tentatively 'Creswellian', since Creswell Crags is the station in which it is found in greatest abundance and variety. **1948** KROEBER *Anthropol.* (ed. 2) xvi. 661 Some authors.. prefer to give local designations to these marginal local phases contemporary with the Magdalenian period of France. Such are Creswellian, Grimaldian and (late) East Gravettian for England, Italy and the Danube respectively. **1969** K. P. OAKLEY *Frameworks for dating Fossil Man* (ed. 3) II. ii. 167 Other Epi-Gravettian cultures developed contemporaneously in various parts of Europe, notably the Creswellian in Britain.

cresyl ('krɛsɪl). *Chem.* Also **cressyl.** [f. CRES-OL + -YL.] The radical C_7H_7 of cresol. **'cresylate,** a salt of cresylic acid. **cre'sylic** *a.*, of cresyl, in ***cresylic acid*** = CRESOL.

1863–72 WATTS *Dict. Chem.* II. 107 With pentachloride of phosphorus, cresylic alcohol yields chloride of cresyl, C_7H_7Cl. *Ibid.*, A mass of slender needles of cresylate of potassium or sodium. **1869** E. A. PARKES *Pract. Hygiene* (ed. 3) 360 The fumes contain carbolic and cresylic acids.

cret, crete, var. of CREAGHT, *Obs.*

cretaceo- (kriː'teɪʃ(ɪ)əʊ), combining form of CRETACEOUS, = 'cretaceous and ——', as in ***cretaceo-oolitic, cretaceo-tertiary*** adjs.

1880 RAMSAY in *Times* 26 Aug. 5/4 In.. Cretaceo-Oolitic .. times. **1881** *Rep. Geol. Explor. N. Zealand* 117 The Cretaceo-Tertiary rocks.

cretaceous (kriː'teɪʃəs), *a.* and *sb.* Also with cap. initial in *Geol.* senses. [f. L. *crētāce-us* chalk-like, chalky, f. *crēta* chalk: see -ACEOUS.]

A. *adj.* **1.** Of the nature of chalk; chalky.

c **1675** GREW (J.), The cretaceous salt. **1708** J. PHILIPS *Cyder* I. 54 Nor from the sable Ground expect Success Nor from cretaceous, stubborn and jejune. **1710** T. FULLER *Pharm. Extemp.* 119 A cretaceous Electuary. **1841–71** T. R. JONES *Anim. Kingd.* (ed. 4) 787 The lining membrane.. secretes cretaceous matter.

b. Chalk-like. *humorous.*

1808 SYD. SMITH *Plymley's Lett.* vi, I love not the cretaceous and incredible countenance of his colleague.

2. *Geol.* Belonging to or found in the Chalk formation. So ***cretaceous group, series, system. cretaceous period***: the period during which these strata were deposited.

1832 DE LA BECHE *Geol. Man.* (ed. 2) 307 The cretaceous rocks of south-eastern England. **1854** F. C. BAKEWELL *Geol.* 56 The chalk and its associated sands have been termed the 'cretaceous system'. **1863** LYELL *Antiq. Man* 335 During the oolitic and cretaceous periods.

B. *sb.* (usu. with *the*). *Geol.* The Cretaceous system or period.

1851 LYELL *Man. Elem. Geol.* (ed. 3) xvii. 209 (*heading*) Upper Cretaceous. I. Maestricht beds and Faxoe limestone. **1906** CHAMBERLIN & SALISBURY *Geol.* III. 160 In the Black Hills, the Cretaceous has in some places a thickness of no more than 1000 feet. *Ibid.* 162 The Appalachian mountains,.. which had been reduced to a peneplain by the close of the Cretaceous. **1910** *Encycl. Brit.* VII. 415/1 There is a very general unconformity and break between the Lower and Upper Cretaceous. *Ibid.*, With the opening of the Cretaceous in Europe there commenced a period of marine transgression. **1960** L. D. STAMP *Britain's Struct.* (ed. 5) xii. 139 These strata form.. transition beds between the Cretaceous and the Tertiary.

cre'taceously *adv.*, in the manner of chalk.

1864 in WEBSTER. **1882** *Syd. Soc. Lex.*, *Cretaceously-pruinose*, having a white shining incrustation.

cretals, obs. aphetic f. DECRETALS.

c **1380** *Antecrist* in Todd 3 *Treat. Wyclif* 129 þe cretals and þe clementynes.

Cretan ('kriːtən), *a.* and *sb.* [ad. L. *Crētānus.* The forms used in the various translations of the Bible are, in Acts ii. 11 *Cretes* (Middle English (*a* 1400, ed. A. C. Paues), Geneva and A.V.), in Titus i. 12 *Cretayns* (Tindale and Coverdale), *Cretyans* (Cranmer), *Cretians* (Geneva and A.V.); Reims and Douay have *Cretensians*, and R.V. *Cretans* in both places.] **A.** *adj.* Of or belonging to the island of Crete in the Mediterranean. **B.** *sb.* A native of Crete.

Cretan bull, the bull beloved by Pasiphæ. ***Cretan carrot***, the plant *Athamanta cretensis*, used in medicine. ***Cretan hemp***, bastard hemp.

[*c* **893** K. ALFRED *Oros.* I Hu Cretense & Atheniense, Creca leode, him betweonum wunnon.] **1579** NORTH *Plutarch's Lives* 276 This was but a fraude and a Cretan lye, to deceaue the Cretans with. **1596** SHAKS. *Tam. Shrew* I. i. 175 When with his knees he kist the Cretan strond. **1654** OGILBY *Virgil*, *Bucolicks* v. 24 *note*, That excellent Cretan Archer. **1797** *Encycl. Brit.* V. 532/2 In order to distinguish the true Cretans from strangers, they were named *Eteocretes*. **1819** SHELLEY *Peter Bell 3rd* III. xiii, Lunches and snacks so aldermanic.. Where reigns a Cretan-tongued panic. **1820** —— *Œd. Tyr.* II. ii. 3 What though Cretans old called thee City-crested Cybele? **1821** T. CAMPBELL in *New Monthly Mag.* II. 438 (*title*) Song of Hybrias the Cretan. [**1829** LOUDON *Encycl. Plants* 506 *Oríganum Dictámnus*, Dittany of Crete.] **1868** S. HEREMAN *Paxton's Bot. Dict.* 164/2 Cretan carrot. **1874** HARDY *Far fr. Mad. Crowd* xxv, He was perfectly truthful toward men, but to women lied like a Cretan. **1880** E. GLAISTER *Needlework* viii. 94 Another good style of pattern for tidies is to be found in the Cretan work.. which.. was brought to London three or four years ago. **1881** C. C. HARRISON *Woman's Handiwork* III. 157 Cutting Cretan embroidery into strips. **1902** *Encycl. Brit.* XXVII. 273/1 In the palace at Knossós.. have been found a large number of clay tablets.. inscribed with the indigenous Cretan character. **1915** *Edin. Rev.* Jan. 127 Compare the Cretan and Dionysiac Oreibasiai or Mountain-Rites. **1952** A. G. L. HELLYER *Sanders' Encycl. Gardening* (ed. 22) 97 *Celsia.. cretica*, 'Cretan Mullein', yellow, 3 to 5 ft., Medit. Region. *Ibid.* 344 *Origanum.. Dictamnus*, 'Cretan Dittany', pink, summer, 1 ft., Crete. *Ibid.* 502 *Valeriana.. Phu*, 'Cretan Spikenard', white, Aug., 2 ft., Caucasus. **1955** *Times* 6 Aug. 3/5 An important inscribed baked clay tablet .. carries three lines of Cypro-Minoan script to which the date 1300 B.C. is attributed. It shows an affinity with the Cretan linear script found by Sir Arthur Evans at Knossos.

† **cretated,** *pa. pple. Obs.*⁻⁰ [f. L. *crētātus.*]

1730–6 BAILEY (folio), *Cretated*, chalked.

cretche, obs. form of CRATCH.

crete¹ (kriːt). [Cf. OF. *cretin* basket; also Teutonic words mentioned under CRADLE *sb.*]

† **1.** = CRADLE *sb.* I. *Obs.*

1340 *Ayenb.* 137 þe litel childe.. þet wepþ ine his crete.

2. = CRADLE *sb.* 7. *dial.*

1887 *Kentish Dial.*, *Creet*, a cradle, or frame-work of wood, placed on a scythe when used to cut corn. **1892** *Auctioneer's Catal. Farm Sale near Minster, Kent*, Scythe and crete.

† **crete**². *Obs. rare.* The septum or division between the nostrils.

1541 COPLAND *Guydon's Quest. Chirurg.*, There are.. other small bones lesse pryncypalles.. as is the bone of the crete that deuyde the nosethyrlles.

crethe, = CRETE¹, or error for *creche*, CRATCH.

cretic ('kriːtɪk), *a.*¹ and *sb.* [ad. L. *Crētic-us* of Crete, Cretan, f. *Crēta* Crete.]

A. *adj.* Belonging to Crete, Cretan; applied in Gr. and Lat. prosody to a particular metrical foot, or to verse characterized by these. **B.** *sb.* (without capital) A metrical foot consisting of one short syllable between two long; = AMPHIMACER.

[**1586** W. WEBBE *Eng. Poetrie* (Arb.) 69 Creticus of a long, a short, and a long, [as] *daungerous*.] **1603** HOLLAND *Plutarch's Mor.* lxviii. 1257 The Prosodiaque & also the Creticke. **1697** BENTLEY *Phal.* (T.), The first verse here ends with a trochee, and the third with a cretick. **1867** JEBB *Sophocles' Electra* (1870) 39/1 Although τῶνδέ μοι form a cretic foot, a spondee is still admissible in the 5th place, because the word γάρ preceding the cretic is a monosyllable. **1885** GILDERSLEEVE *Pindar* Introd. 73 The passionate cretics that abound in that.. play [the *Acharnians*].

† **cretic** ('kriːtɪk), *a.*² *Obs. rare.* [f. L. *crēta* chalk + -IC.] Chalk-like; of the hardness of chalk.

1811 PINKERTON *Petral.* 302 Hardness, cretic. Fracture, slaty.

† **'Creticism.** *Obs.* Cretan behaviour, *i.e.* lying.

1614 RALEIGH *Hist. World* V. v. §2. 650 *marg.*, So diligent .. [an] Architect of Lies: in regard whereof I may not denie him the commendation of Creticisme. **1656** [see CRETISM].

cretifaction (kriːtɪ'fækʃən). (*erron.* crete-.) [f. L. *crēta* chalk + -FACTION.] = next.

1866 A. FLINT *Princ. Med.* (1880) 58 Calcareous degeneration, calcification, or cretefaction.

cretification (ˌkriːtɪfɪ'keɪʃən). [n. of action f. CRETIFY.] Deposition of salts of lime in a tissue of the animal body; calcareous degeneration.

1852–9 TODD *Cycl. Anat.* IV. 537/2 Its appearances sometimes approximate to those of the cretification. **1874** JONES & SIEV. *Pathol. Anat.* 64 Saline earthy matter may be deposited.. inducing a state.. named cretification.

cretify ('kriːtɪfaɪ), *v.* [f. L. *crēta* chalk + -FY, repr. a L. type *crētificāre.*] *trans.* To impregnate with salts of lime.

1859 TODD *Cycl. Anat.* V. 419/2 The cretified contents of old abscesses.

cretin ('krɛtɪn, formerly 'kriːtɪn). [a. F. *crétin* (in *Encycl.* 1754), ad. Swiss patois *crestin*, *creitin*:—L. *Christiānum* CHRISTIAN, which in the mod. Romanic langs. (as sometimes *dial.* in Eng.) means 'human creature' as distinguished from the brutes; the sense being here that these beings are really human, though so deformed physically and mentally. (Cf. *natural.*) So, according to Hatzfeld and Darmesteter, the Cagots are called in Béarn *crestiaas.*] One of a class of dwarfed and specially deformed idiots found in certain valleys of the Alps and elsewhere. Also in weakened sense (esp. in form *crétin*): a fool, one who behaves stupidly. Also *attrib.* and *transf.*

1779 W. COXE in *Ann. Reg.* II. 92 *note*, The species of idiots I have mentioned.. who are described by many authors as peculiar to the Vallais, are called Cretins. **1834** MEDWIN *Angler in Wales* I. 239 The Cretin is hardly a human being..They have all immense heads and more immense goitres. **1879** KHORZ *Princ. Med.* 4 The offspring of persons with goître are cretins without goître. **1884** W. JAMES *Coll. Ess. & Rev.* (1920) 270 Bodily commotions.. may be experienced in their fulness by *Crétins* and Philistines in whom the critical judgment is at its lowest ebb. *a* **1930** D. H. LAWRENCE *Pornography* (1936) 75 The blood in the body stands still, before such *crétin* ugliness. **1933** J. JOYCE *Let.* 13 Aug. (1966) III. 282 The crétin of a concierge ..has misdirected half my mail. **1961** I. JEFFERIES *It wasn't Me* ix. 123, I know I'm a moron and a cretin like you're always calling people.

Hence ˈ**cretinage**.

1820 H. MATTHEWS *Diary of Invalid* 314 Cretinage seems also to be peculiar to mountainous regions.

cretinism (ˈkriːtɪnɪz(ə)m). [f. prec. + -ISM: in mod.F. *crétinisme*.] The condition of a cretin; a species of imperfect mental and physical development, or combination of deformity and idiocy, endemic in some valleys of the Alps and elsewhere.

1801 *Med. Jrnl.* V. 176 Physical and moral remedies that may be employed in preventing the Wen and Cretinism. **1891** *Lancet* 3 Oct., Cretinism is becoming more common in the Pyrenean and Alpine valleys.

So ˈ**cretinist**.

1858 G. SMITH in *Oxford Ess.* 266 Some of his [Newman's] party displayed in University matters something of that 'cretinist' tendency which they have since developed in its natural sphere.

cretinize (ˈkriːtɪnaɪz), *v.* [f. as prec. + -IZE: mod.F. *crétiniser*.] *trans.* To reduce to the condition of a cretin. Hence **cretinized** *ppl. a.*

1846 R. FORD *Gath. Spain* xxiv. 338 The Spanish Bourbons, when not 'cretinised' into idiots, are creatures composed to cunning and cowardice. **1858** *Sat. Review* V. 16/2 No Jesuit, seeking to cretinize humanity for pious purposes. **1869** *Daily News* 30 June, Society as usually understood..would cretinize an archangel.

1876 FREEMAN *Hist. & Archit. Sk.* 315 The wretched look of the dwarfed, diseased, and cretinized inhabitants.

cretinoid (ˈkrɛtɪnɔɪd), *a.* [See -OID.] Resembling a cretin or cretinism.

1874 W. GULL in *Trans. Clin. Soc.* VII. 180 (*title*) On a Cretinoid State supervening in Adult Life in Women. **1886** *Buck's Handbk. Med. Sci.* II. 20 Myxœdema..Cretinoid disease. **1966** *Jrnl. Clin. Endocrinol. & Metabolism* XXVI. 111/2 The appearance of the face was typical for a cretinoid child, with a large, protruding tongue and heavy features.

cretinous (ˈkriːtɪnəs), *a.* [f. as CRETIN + -OUS.] Of or pertaining to a cretin; of the nature of cretinism.

1839 TODD *Cycl. Anat.* II. 471/2 The..cretinous affections..are striking examples of the effect of hereditary influence combined with that of..situation. **1863** RUSKIN *Munera P.* (1880) 146 The whole nature of slavery being one cramp and cretinous contraction.

cretion (ˈkriːʃən). *Roman Law.* [ad. L. *crētiōn-em*, n. of action from *cernĕre* to decide, resolve: see CERN.] Declaration of acceptance of an inheritance (see CERN *v.*); *transf.* the period or term allowed for this.

1880 MUIRHEAD *Gaius* II. §166 If the individual so instituted desire to be heir, he must cern within the time for cretion. **1880** —— *Ulpian* xxii. §27 Cretion is a certain.. time allowed to the instituted heir for deliberating whether or not it will be for his advantage to enter to the inheritance.

Hence ˈ**cretionary** *a.*, of or belonging to cretion.

1880 MUIRHEAD *Ulpian* xxii. §30 Failing to cern within the cretionary period.

†ˈ**Cretism.** *Obs.*$^{-0}$ [ad. Gr. Κρητισμός Cretan behaviour, lying, f. κρητίζειν: see next, and cf. Fr. *cretisme* (Cotgr.).] (See quot. and CRETICISM.)

1656 BLOUNT *Glossogr.*, *Creticism* or *Cretism*, the Art of coyning or inventing lyes. Hence in later and mod. Dicts.

†**Cretize** (kriːtaɪz), *v. Obs.* or *arch.* [ad. Gr. κρητίζειν to play the Cretan, to lie, cheat, f. Κρήτη Crete. (Cf. *Titus* i. 12.)]

1. *intr.* To play the Cretan, *i.e.* to lie, tell lies.

a **1653** GOUGE *Comm. Hebr.* vi. 17 To lye, was in a proverbiall speech, said, to cretize, or play the Cretian. **1842** *Blackw. Mag.* LI. 17 He 'bounced' a little, he 'Cretized'.

†**2.** *trans.* To overreach or outdo by lying. *Obs.*

a **1673** J. CARYL in Spurgeon *Treas. Dav.* Ps. xviii. 26 He will Cretize the Cretians, supplant the supplanters.

†**cretone, cretoyne.** *Obs.* Also 5 critone. [a. OF. *cretonné*: see Godefroy.] A kind of seasoned soup or pottage in which rabbits, fowls, etc. were boiled.

?*a* **1400** *Morte Arth.* 197 Connygez in cretoyne. *c* **1420** *Liber Cocorum* (1862) 8 Chekyns in cretone [*printed* -ene]. *c* **1440** *Anc. Cookery* in *Househ. Ord.* (1790) 431 Critone to Potage.

‖**cretonne** (krətɔn, ˈkrɛtɒn). [a. F. *cretonne* (in Savary *Dict. du Comm.* 1723), according to Hatzfeld and Darmesteter from *Creton*, a village of Normandy, famous for its linen manufactures.]

The French name of a strong fabric of hempen warp and linen woof; applied in England to a stout unglazed cotton cloth printed on one or both sides with a pattern in colours, and used for chair covers, curtains, and the like.

1870 DASENT *Annals Eventf. Life* II. viii. 134 Chair-covers and sofa-covers, chintz or tammy,—*crétonnes* were not then invented. **1886** *Funny Folks Ann.* 47 In chintz, silk, velvet, rep, cretonne, and satin brocatelle.

attrib. **1887** R. N. CAREY *Uncle Max* xix. 149 Pretty cretonne curtains.

†**creˈtose,** *a. rare*$^{-0}$. [Cf. next.] Chalky.

1775 ASH, *Cretose*, chalky, full of chalk.

cretous (ˈkriːtəs), *a. rare.* [ad. L. *crētōs-us*: see prec. and -OUS.] = prec.

1805 LUCCOCK *Nat. Wool* 280 Hills of a cretous texture.. divide Hertfordshire from..Bedford and Cambridge.

creu, obs. pa. t. of CROW *v.*[1]

creu-: see CREV- in CREVICE, etc.

†**creue,** *v. Obs. rare.* [f. OF. *creü, creüe*, pa. pple. of *croistre* to grow.] *intr.* To grow.

c **1450** *St. Cuthbert* (Surtees) 6914, þe erle..gart sone downe be hewed All þe wod þat þare creued.

creuell, creuett, obs. ff. CRUEL, CRUET.

creul, creuse, obs. ff. CRAWL *v.*, CRUSE.

creutzer, obs. form of KREUTZER.

crevace, crevasse, obs. ff. CREVICE.

crevasse (krɪˈvæs), *sb.* [a. mod.F. *crevasse* = OF. *crevace* CREVICE. This F. form has been adopted by Alpine climbers in Switzerland in sense 1, and in U.S. from the French of Louisiana, etc., in sense 2; these being too large for the notion associated with the corresponding Eng. form *crevice*.]

1. a. A fissure or chasm in the ice of a glacier, usually of great depth, and sometimes of great width.

1823 F. CLISSOLD *Ascent Mt. Blanc* 12 The crevasses are supposed to be, in some places, several hundred feet deep. **1872** C. KING *Mountains Sierra Nev.* xi. 231 A glacier, riven with deep crevasses, yawning fifty or sixty feet wide.

b. *transf.* Any similar deep crack or chasm.

1859 R. F. BURTON *Centr. Afr.* in *Jrnl. Geog. Soc.* XXIX. 213 The broad open prospect of this vast crevasse. **1863** DICEY *Federal St.* I. 20 The struggles of the floundering horses to drag the carriages out of the ruts and crevasses.

2. *U.S.* A breach in the bank of a river, canal, etc.; used *esp.* of a breach in the *levée* or artificial bank of the lower Mississippi. Also *fig.*

1814 H. M. BRACKENRIDGE *Views Louisiana* 179 The terrors excited by a *crevasse* or breaking of the levee. **1819** *Edin. Rev.* XXXII. 240 A breach in the *levée*, or a *crevasse*, as it is termed, is the greatest calamity which can befal the landholder. **1850** B. TAYLOR *Eldorado* i. (1862) 7 The crevasse, by which half the city had lately been submerged, was closed. **1850** *Congressional Globe* App. 149/2 A moral crevasse has occurred: fanaticism and ignorance..have accumulated into a mighty flood. **1897** G. W. CABLE *Old Creole Days* 104 The Anglo-American flood that was presently to burst in a crevasse of immigration upon the delta.

crevasse (krɪˈvæs), *v.* [a. F. *crevasse-r* to form into crevasses, f. *crevasse* sb.] To fissure with crevasses. Chiefly in **creˈvassed** *ppl. a.*, having crevasses; fissured, as a glacier.

1855 J. D. FORBES *Tour Mt. Blanc* viii. 100 It is not much crevassed. **1856** KANE *Arct. Expl.* II. xxvii. 271 A steep crevassed hill. **1892** *Pall Mall G.* 5 Aug. 6/1 The glaciers.. are crevassed to the very foot.

crevassing (krɪˈvæsɪŋ), *vbl. sb.* [f. CREVASSE *v.* + -ING[1].] Formation of crevasses.

1856 KANE *Arct. Expl.* I. 459 *note*, Abrupt fractures and excessive crevassing. **1860** TYNDALL *Glac.* II. x. 281 This cannot be the true cause of the crevassing.

crevat, obs. form of CRAVAT.

creve, *v. Obs.* (or *dial.*). [a. F. *creve-r* to burst, split:—L. *crepāre* to crackle, crack.]

†**1.** *intr.* To burst, to split. *Obs.*

c **1450** *Mirour Saluacioun* 2941 The roches..creved both vppe and doune.

2. (Also *creave, creeve*) Earlier and now dial. form of CREE *v.*

Crèvecœur (ˈkrɛvkœr). [Fr., = heart-break (see quot. 1909).] A variety (usually black) of the domestic fowl of French origin, resembling the houdan in body, but characterized by a comb consisting of two large coral-red horns. Also abbrev. **Crève** (**Crêve**).

1855 *Poultry Chron.* III. 285 The Crèvecœur fowls. *Ibid.* 286 The Crèvecœurs exhibited at Baker Street. **1873** L. WRIGHT *Bk. Poultry* xxvi. 415 The Crêve is the bulkiest in appearance of all the French races. **1883** *Daily News* 3 Oct. 2/2 The pretty Houdans and Crèvecœurs. **1904** S. W. THOMAS in *L. Wright's Bk. Poultry* xxxi. 452/1 The spiral crest is gone, and so is the Crêve comb. *Ibid.* 456/1 The very finest Crêves even now attain greater size than the largest Houdans. **1909** T. W. STURGES *Poultry Man.* xvii. 527 The Crève-Cœur..is one of the oldest of the French breeds... They derive their name from the peculiar shape of the comb (Crève-cœur..split hearts), the comb being like a V with a broad base and filled up half its height with a protuberant growth of flesh.

creves, obs. f. CRAYFISH *sb.*, CREVICE.

[**crevet.** App. an error for CRUSET, crucible.

1658 PHILLIPS, *Crevet*, or *Cruset*, from the French word *Creux*, hollow, a Goldsmiths melting pot. [So all edd. to 1706.] **1721** BAILEY, *Crevet, Cruset*, a Melting Pot used by Goldsmiths. **1823** CRABB *Technol. Dict.*, *Crevet*, a melting pot used by goldsmiths. [Hence in WORCESTER and some later Dicts.] **1881** RAYMOND *Mining Gloss.*, *Crevet*, a crucible.]

crevette (krəˈvɛt). [Fr., = shrimp.] A deep shade of pink, shrimp-pink.

1884 *Cassell's Fam. Mag.* May 371/1 Blues, greens.. salmon-pink, and the deeper crevette, or shrimp-pink. **1890** *Daily News* 5 July 3/4 Costumes of the colours known as crevette and eau-de-Nil.

crevice (ˈkrɛvɪs), *sb.* Forms: 4 crevace, -yce, 4-5 creveys, (creu-), cravas(e, (crau-), 4-6 creves, (creu-), 4-7 crevesse, (creu-), 5 creveis, creuys, crayues, (cref(f)eys, crefes), 5-6 craues, 6 crevisse, craivesse, 5-7 creuice, 6-7 creuis, (crev-), 7 creuas, crevasse, creuise, 7-8 crevise, 8 crivess, 5- crevice. [ME. *crevace*, a. OF. *crevace*, mod.F. *crevasse*:—late L. *crepātia*, f. L. *crepāre* to creak, rattle, crack: cf. CREVE. Already in the 14th c. the stress began to be shifted to the first syllable, and the unaccented second syllable to be weakened to *-esse, -isse, -ice*. The mod.F. form has been re-adopted in CREVASSE *sb.*]

1. A crack producing an opening in the surface or through the thickness of anything solid; a cleft, rift, chink, fissure.

c **1340** *Gaw. & Gr. Knt.* 2183 A creuisse of an olde cragge. **1382** WYCLIF *Nehem.* iv. 7 The chinys or cravasis begunnen to be closid. *c* **1384** CHAUCER *H. Fame* 2086 Hyt gan out crepe at somme crevace. *c* **1400** *Lanfranc's Cirurg.* 134 If þe creveis [*MS. B.* creffeys] perse not þe brayn scolle. **1552** HULOET, Craues or creues. *Vide* in chyncke. **1562** TURNER *Herbal* II. (1568) 167 b, With a barcke gapynge and havinge crevisses. **1592** W. PERKINS *Case Consc.* (1619) 202 Hee sees but one little beame of the Sunne, by a small creuise. *a* **1628** PRESTON *New Covt.* (1634) 77 There was but a little crevis opened. **1678** tr. *Gaya's Arms War* 73 Care must be had that there be no Cracks, Flaws, Crevasses, nor Honey Combs in her Cylender. **1712** STEELE *Spect.* No. 266 ¶4 To peep at a Crevise, and look in at People. **1774** GOLDSM. *Nat. Hist.* (1776) VII. 286 In winter it lies hid in the crevices of walls. **1860** TYNDALL *Glac.* II. xx. 335 Water..percolating freely through the crevices..to all depths of the glacier.

b. *spec.* in *Mining.* A fissure in which a deposit of ore or metal is found. Also *attrib.*

1872 RAYMOND *Statist. Mines* 262 The crevice is filled with a mixture of carbonate of lead and bunches of undecomposed galena. **1870** ATCHERLEY *Boërland* 175 Gold ..known as 'crevice gold', from..being picked out of crevices in the bed-rock.

c. Rarely = CREVASSE *sb.*, in a glacier.

1852 ALB. SMITH in *Blackw. Mag.* LXXI. 53 Tairraz, who preceded me, had jumped over a crevice.

†**2.** A deep furrow or channel. *Obs.* Cf. CREVICED.

(Quot. 1609 is doubtful).

1580 BARET *Alv.* C 1610 Leaues, wherein Creuises, or smal lines are seene..*folia striata.* **1609** W. M. *Man in Moone* (1849) 18 Pish, your band hangeth right enought, what, yet more crevises in your stockings?

†ˈ**crevice,** *v.* [f. prec., or ad. F. *crevasser*: see CREVASSE *v.*] *trans.* To make crevices in; to fissure, crack, split. *Obs.* exc. in pa. pple. CREVICED.

1624 WOTTON *Elem. Archit.* in *Reliq. Wotton.* (1672) 20 They [the stones] are more apt..to pierce with their points ..and so to crevice the Wall.

crevice, obs. form of CRAYFISH *sb.*

creviced (ˈkrɛvɪst), *ppl. a.* Also 6 creuised, -ished, 6-8 crevissed, 7 -assed. [f. CREVICE *sb.* or *v.* + -ED.] Having crevices, chinks, or cracks; fissured. †**b.** Deeply furrowed or channelled. †**c.** Indented (of leaves, etc.).

1558-68 WARDE tr. *Alexis' Secr.* (1568) 10 b, A kynde of poulse corne..havynge..the codde crevised about. **1578** LYTE *Dodoens* v. xii. 561 Long narrow leaues, sometimes creuished or slightly toothed about the edges. **1583** J. HIGGINS tr. *Junius' Nomenclator* (N.), *Columna striata*..a carved or crevissed pillar, with long strakes or lines made therin. **1678** tr. *Gaya's Arms War* 22 It is screwed and rifled; that is to say, wrought and crevassed in the inside from the Muzzel to the Breech, in form of a Screw. **1725** BRADLEY *Fam. Dict.* s.v. *Jujube-tree*, A rough, rugged and crevissed Bark. **1806** J. GRAHAME *Birds of Scotl.* 71 Some green branch That midway down shoots from the creviced crag. **1861** MRS. NORTON *Lady La G.* I. 44 The prisoned streamlet..undermining all the creviced bank.

crevicing (ˈkrɛvɪsɪŋ), *vbl. sb.* (See quots. and CREVICE *sb.* 1 b.) Also *attrib.*

1851 *Alta California* (San Francisco) 17 July 2/2 The early adventurers in the gold-diggings required simply..a strong sheath-knife for 'crevicing'. **1876** J. MILLER *First Fam'lies* ix. 68 A lot of picks and pans, and tom irons, and crevicing spoons, that lay up against the wall. **1886** J. W. ANDERSON *Prospector's Handbook* 117 Crevicing—Collecting gold in the crevices of rock. **1888** C. D. FERGUSON *Exp. Forty-niner* ix. 129 It was all crevicing, that is, working the crevices in the rocks. **1948** P. JOHNSTON *Cities Calif. Gold Rush* 41/2 As crevicing was better up the fork, they broke camp, and moved to Zumwalt Flat.

crevis(e, ish(e, -isse, -ys(e, obs. ff. CRAYFISH *sb.*, CREVICE.

crew (kruː), *sb.*[1] Forms: 5-7 crue, 5-6 crewe, 6- crew. [a. OF. *creue* increase, augmentation, reinforcement, sb. fem. f. pa. pple. of *croistre* to grow, increase, etc.; perh. in part aphetic form of *acrewe*, ACCRUE, which easily became *a crue*.

Documentary evidence for *acrewe* (in Eng.) is not known of so early a date as that for *crewe*. In the general sense, both words go back to an early date in OF.; but in the special sense 'military reinforcement' Godefroy's examples of *creue*, *acreue* are only of 1554-8.]

I. †**1.** An augmentation or reinforcement of a military force; hence, a body of soldiers organized for a particular purpose, as to garrison a fortress, for an expedition, campaign, etc.; a band or company of soldiers. *Obs.*

1455 *Rolls of Parl.* 34 Hen. VI, c. 46 The wages of ccc men ordeigned to be with him for a Crue over the ordinary charge abovesaid. **1494** FABYAN *Chron.* VII. 444 The Frensh kynge sent soone after into Scotlande a crewe of Frenshe-men, to ayde suche enemyes as Kyng Edwarde there had. **1548** HALL *Chron.* 175 b, Sir Simon Mondford with a great crew, was appoynted to keep the dounes and the five Portes. **1550** *Acts Privy Council E.* (1891) III. 5 It was thought necessarie to encrease the crewe of Berwicke with a more nombre of men. **1577-87** HOLINSHED *Chron.* III. 808/2 To be generall of the crue..sent into Spaine.

2. By extension: Any organized or associated force, band, or body of armed men.

1570 LEVINS *Manip.* 94 A crewe, *caterua*. **1575** CHURCHYARD *Chippes* (1817) 134 To foster and nourishe this crue of men in the marshall arte and rules of warre. **1608** SHAKS. *Per.* v. i. 176 A crew of pirates came and rescued me. **1667** MILTON *P.L.* XII. 38 A crew, whom like Ambition joyns With him or under him to tyrannize. **1786** GILPIN *Mts. & Lakes Cumbld.* (1788) II. 128 Those crews of outlawed banditti, who under the denomination of Moss-troopers, plundered the country. **1866** KINGSLEY *Herew.* i. (1875) 25 He had fallen in with Hereward and his crew of house-carls.

3. a. A number of persons gathered together in association; a company.

1579 LYLY *Euphues* (Arb.) 51 Don Ferardo one of the chiefe gouernours of the citie..had a courtly crew of gentlewomen soiourning in his pallaice. **1590** SPENSER *F.Q.* I. iv. 7 There a noble crew Of lords and ladies stood on every side. **1632** MILTON *L'Allegro* 38 Mirth, admit me of thy crew. **1641** BROME (*title*), A Joviall Crew, or the Merry Beggars. **1732** LEDIARD *Sethos* II. VII. 104 About break of day..this monstrous tatter'd crew entered the city. **1832** W. IRVING *Alhambra* I. 188 As gaunt and ragged as a crew of gypsies.

b. *transf.* An assemblage of animals or things.

1607 ROWLANDS *Dr. Merrie-man* (1609) 15 A Crew of Foxes, all on theeuing set, Togeather at a Countrie Hen-roost met. **1674** N. FAIRFAX *Bulk & Selv.* To Rdr., The same bodies crew of atoms. **1704** SWIFT *Batt. Bks.* (1711) 246 Excrescencies in form of Teats, at which a Crew of ugly Monsters were greedily sucking. **1877** *N.W. Linc. Gloss.*, *Crew*, a confused crowd. It may be applied to lifeless things as well as living. 'You nivver seed such a crew o' plough-jags as we hed to-year'.

4. A number of persons classed together (by the speaker) from actual connexion or common characteristics; often with derogatory qualification or connotation; lot, set, gang, mob, herd.

1570 B. GOOGE *Pop. Kingd.* III. 281 The supper serueth for desertes, with papistes euery where..And is not this a goodly crewe? **1581** MULCASTER *Positions* v. (1887) 35 A crew of excellent painters. **1593** SHAKS. *2 Hen. VI*, II. ii. 72 Winke at the Duke of Suffolkes insolence, At Beaufords Pride, at Somersets Ambition, At Buckingham, and all the Crew of them. **1628** PRYNNE *Loue-lockes* 27 They would be singular and different from the vulger Crue. **1778** FOOTE *Trip Calais* II. Wks. 1799 II. 358 *Lady Kitty*..You want some tale to run tattling with to the rest of the crew. *Hetty.* Crew? I don't understand what your Ladyship means by the crew; tho' we are servants, we may be as good Christians as other people, I hope. **1884** W. C. SMITH *Kildrostan* 80 All the ravenous crew Of jobbers and promoters.

II. Specific or technical uses, from 2.

5. a. A body or squad of workmen engaged upon a particular piece of work, or under one foreman or overseer; a gang.

In U.S. and Canada *esp.* one of the companies or gangs of men engaged together in lumber-cutting, in working a railway train, etc.

1699 DAMPIER *Voy.* II. II. 88, I was yet a Stranger to this work, therefore remained with 3 of the old Crew to cut more Logwood. **1701** *Aberdeen Burgh Rec.* 21 Apr., Divisions into crews for carying sting burdens. **1808** FORSYTH *Beauties Scotl.* V. 434 Every four men, which is called a crew, are said to quarry one hundred and four thousand slates in a year. **1860** *Harper's Mag.* XX. 444 A crew consists of from twenty to thirty men in charge of the 'Boss', of whom two are experienced choppers, two barkers and sled-tenders, etc. **1878** *Lumberman's Gaz.* 9 Feb., Logging crews are coming out of the woods there.

b. A team of people concerned with the technical aspects of film-making, recording, etc., for a particular production; freq. with narrower description of function, as *camera crew* (CAMERA 3 d), *sound crew* (SOUND *sb.*[3] 8 b), etc.

1954 [see *cue card* s.v. CUE *sb.*[2] 5]. **1962** *Movie* Nov. 28/1 With a good crew, I can work much faster outside than I ever could in the studio. **1976** *National Observer* (U.S.) 8 May 22/4 I had never worked with a crew before—just friends. And here were 40 or 50 people, actors and crew, suddenly looking to me to tell them what to do. **1982** A. ROAD *Dr. Who* 22/1 In the foyer members of the crew are gathering.

6. a. *Naut.* A gang of men on a ship of war, placed under the direction of a petty officer, or told off for some particular duty, as manning a boat, etc.

1692 *Order* in J. Love *Mariner's Jewel* (1724) 120 Quarter-Gunner, Carpenter's Crew, Steward, Cook. *a* **1700** B. E. *Dict. Cant. Crew*, *Crew*, the Coxon and Rowers in the Barge or Pinnace, are called the *Boats-crew*, in distinction from the Complement of Men on Board the Ship, who are term'd the *Ships-Company*, not *Crew*. **1712** W. ROGERS *Voy.* 7 Henry Oliphant, Gunner, with eight Men call'd the Gunners Crew. **1726** SHELVOCKE *Voy. round World* (1757) 18 To order the cooper and his crew to trim the casks. **1836** MARRYAT *Midsh. Easy* xxv, Among the boat's crew taken with him by Captain Wilson. **1868** SMYTH *Sailor's Word-bk.* 222 There are in ships of war several particular crews or gangs, as the gunner's, carpenter's, sailmaker's, blacksmith's, armourer's, and cooper's crews.

b. *Naut.* The whole of the men belonging to and manning a ship, boat, or other vessel afloat. (Now the leading sense.)

In a general sense the ship's crew includes all under the captain, but in a more restricted sense it is applied to the men only, to the exclusion of the officers.

1694 SMITH & WALFORD *Acc. Sev. Late Voy.* II. (1711) 170 Whoever of a Ships Crew sees a dead Whale, cries out Fish mine. **1699** DAMPIER *Voy.* II. II. 86 Supposing the Captain and Crew would soon be with him. **1726** *Adv. Capt. R. Boyle* 176, I did not know how to dispose of the Ship and the rest of the Crew. **1796** H. HUNTER tr. *St. Pierre's Stud. Nat.* (1799) I. p. liv, The corrupted air..carries off the seamen of our trading vessels by whole crews at once. **1817** W. SELWYN *Law Nisi Prius* (ed. 4) II. 904 Whether the ship was thus destroyed..by the captain and crew. **1847** GROTE *Greece* I. xl. (1862) III. 447 The Egyptians..had captured five Grecian ships with their entire crews. **1893** *Whitaker's Almanac* 617 The stroke oar in the Oxford crew..Both crews came to Putney on the same day.

c. *Aeronaut.* In full *air crew* (see AIR *sb.*[1] III. 4). The persons manning an aircraft or spacecraft.

1917 'CONTACT' *Airman's Outings* 79 But the airman has experience of what the aeroplane crews must be going through, and his thought is all for them. **1960** *Aeroplane* XCVIII. 422/1 The crew chief, in fact, is the sixth member of the V-bomber flight crew, and is taken on all sorties which entail landing away from base. **1969** *Listener* 1 May 605/2 Eugene Cernan, one of the three-man crew of Apollo 10, due to be launched on 18 May.

7. crew (hair-)cut orig. *U.S.*, a closely cropped style of hair-cut for men (app. first adopted by boat crews at Harvard and Yale Universities); also *transf.* and *fig.*; also ***crew-cropped*** adj.; **crew neck, neckline** orig. *U.S.*, a round neckline of a garment, esp. a sweater, fitting closely to the throat as on vests worn by oarsmen; so ***crew-necked, -shaped*** adjs.

1938 HEMINGWAY *Fifth Column* (1939) 111 Wilson noted his crew-cropped hair. **1942** R. KING *Design in Evil* iv. 41 A steward..with a sparkling crew cut of chestnut hair. **1944** D. W. BROGAN *Amer. Problem* iv. 69 Crew-cut hair and brogues. *a* **1953** DYLAN THOMAS *Quite Early One Morning* (1954) 68 He is vigorously welcomed at the station by an earnest crew-cut platoon of giant collegiates. **1958** *Times* 20 Jan. 11/3 The mature version of the intellectual crew-cut is, with sad inevitability, the egg-head. **1962** *Listener* 18 Jan. 138/2 These new works sometimes convey nautical accents through the use of ship-shape and Bristol-fashioned wood, planed and crew-cut wood surfaces. **1940** *Time* 11 Nov. 76/2 Doe-eyed Lucille Ball..gets the affections of Richard Carlson, whose crew haircut makes him the first genuine-looking Princeton undergraduate in cinema history. **1946** 'P. QUENTIN' *Puzzle for Fiends* x. 98 A young man with a blond crew haircut. **1940** *Illustr. London News* CXCVII. 385 (Advt.), The windcheater..famous wind-resisting-pullover of close-textured cotton with fleecy inner surface. Crew neck. **1944** U. SINCLAIR *Presidential Agent* (1945) ii. 36 The President was lying in bed, wearing pyjamas..covered by a knitted blue sweater, crew-neck style. **1957** J. BRAINE *Room at Top* vi. 51 A yellow crew-neck sweater and a golf jacket. **1950** *Here & Now* (N.Z.) Dec. 25/1 The war was fought for the right of every man to wear crew-necked jerseys and every woman to wear black-lace panties. **1939** M. B. PICKEN *Lang. Fashion* 39/2 *Crew neckline*, round, high neckline, as in a sweater. **1935** *Amer. Speech* X. 193/1 Young girls *went nautical* last fall in dresses that were 'deeply pleated fore and aft'. The necks were *crew shaped* and the pockets were *anchored*.

crew (kruː), *sb.*[2] *dial.* Also creuh, crow, crough, crue. [app. of British origin: cf. earlier Welsh *creu*, *crau*, whence the singulative mod.W. *crewyn*, *crowyn* pen, sty, hovel, Cornish *crow* sty, hovel, hut, *crow moh* pig-sty, now in Cornwall a 'pig's crow', Breton *kraou* stable, stall, sheep-cote; Irish *cró* pen, hut, hovel; cf. CROO.]

1. A pen, cote, or fold for animals, as pigs, sheep, fowls.

1669-81 WORLIDGE *Dict. Rust.*, *Swyn-hull*, or *Swine-crue*, a hog sty. **1863** MORTON *Cycl. Agric.* Gloss., *Pig's-crough* (Cornw.), pig-stye. **1878** *Cumbrld. Gloss.*, *Swine creuh*, a pig-sty; a dirty hull or house. 'Her house is na better ner a swine creuh'. **1879** *Shropshire Word-bk.*, *Crew*, a pen for ducks and geese. [So in *Cheshire* and *Sheffield Gloss.*]

b. Hence *crew-yard*, a close or yard with sheds for cattle.

1778 T. BATEMAN *Agistm. Tithe* (ed. 2) 61 Confined to the House, or in a crew-yard. **1867** *Stamford Mercury* 20 Sept. (in *N.W. Linc. Gloss.*), With hay and straw, and use of crews and sheds..with the use of the crew-yards until the 5th of April next. **1881** *Gainsburgh Times* 21 Jan., The crew-yard will soon be required.

2. (In Cornwall *crow*.) A hut, a cabin.

1880 *W. Cornwall Gloss.*, *Crow*, (as in *crowd*), a hut; a small house.

crew (kruː), *v.* [f. CREW *sb.*[1]] *trans.* and *intr.* To act as (a member of a) crew of a ship, aircraft, etc.; to assign to a crew. Hence **crewing** *vbl. sb.*, the work of such a crew, or of one of its members.

1935 'A. ANDREWS' *Blue Tunnyman* vi. 93 Of the many racing men for whom I crewed, no one taught me more than Mr. J. Paine..in a converted Bristol pilot cutter. **1944** 'N. SHUTE' *Pastoral* v. 107 Bad luck on the chaps that had to crew for him. **1947** *Daily Tel.* 7 May 5/1 He criticises the crewing of the aircraft... Air Cmdre. Brown attributes the accident to..bad crewing, the navigator being the only one of the four operational members who knew the route. **1955** *Times* 13 June 12/2 The Swallow class boat Blue Phantom, crewed by the Glanville twin brothers. *Ibid.* 16 June 8/2 Arrangements had been made for the crewing of the ship to ensure this. **1957** RAWNSLEY & WRIGHT *Night Fighter* i. 19 When it came to my turn to be crewed up it was..no surprise to me to learn that I had been allocated to the youngest pilot in the squadron. **1967** *Jane's Surface Skimmer Systems 1967-68* 30/1 It..can be crewed by personnel experienced in the operation of these craft.

crew, pa. t. of CROW *v.*[1]

†**crewe.** *Obs. rare*[−1]. [a. OF. *crue.*] A pot.

1579 SPENSER *Sheph. Cal.* Feb. 209 Often crost with the priestes crewe [*gloss.* holy water pott] And often halowed with holy-water dewe.

crewel ('kruːəl), *sb.*[1] Forms: 5-6 crule, 6 crewle, crulle, cruele, croole, croylle, (crue, crewe), 6-7 crewell, 6-8 cruel(l, 7- crewel. [Of obscure origin: app. the earliest forms were monosyllabic, *crule*, *crewle*, *croole*, some of which are still dialectal.

Connexion with *crull*, s.w. dial. form of CURL, or its Du. cognate *krul* a curl, *krullen* to curl, has been suggested; but the vowel sounds do not agree.]

1. A thin worsted yarn, (according to Bailey) of two threads, used for tapestry and embroidery; also formerly for making fringes, laces, vestments, hosiery, etc.

These yarns, being produced in different colours and used in combination in the making of one article, are often spoken of in the plural. The name is also applied to the balls or bobbins on which the yarn is wound up for use. The name appears to have become obsolete about 1800, except in dialects, and to have been reintroduced to general use about 1860 in connexion with CREWEL-WORK, q.v.

1494 in Rogers *Agric. & Prices* 560/2, 11 oz. Crule. **1496** *Ibid.* /4, 3 lbs. Crule of different colours. **1502** *Privy Purse Exp. Eliz. York* (1830) 83 Itm for blake crewle to purfulle the rosys vj d. **1553** *Inv. Ch. Goods* in *Ann. Litchfield* IV. 38, ij coopes, on of redd silke, thother of cheked crulle. *c* **1555** *Inv.* in H. Hall *Eliz. Soc.* (1887) 150 A lytle stoole covered withe Nedle worcke checkerid wth white, blewe, & tawnye cruell. **1567** *Wills & Inv. N.C.* (Surtees) 250, ij longe guishings of croole wrowght wth the nedle, & a carpett clothe that is in workinge with crooles for the same. **1571** *Ibid.* 364, viij lbs. of sewing crewle. **1625** FLETCHER *Noble Gent.* v. i, An old hat..and on it for a band A skeine of crimson cruell. **1653** WALTON *Angler* 115 A May-flie, you may make his body with greenish coloured crewel. **1755** JOHNSON, *Crewel*, yarn twisted and wound on a knot or ball. *c* **1750** in H. Walpole *Vertue's Anecd. Paint.* (1789) IV. 144 While crewel o'er the canvass drawn Became a river or a lawn. **1787** MRS. TRIMMER *Œcon. Charity* 79 Binders herring-boned with coloured Cruel. **1855** ROBINSON *Whitby Gloss.*, *Crules* worsted of all-colours for fancy needle-work. **1858** SIMMONDS *Dict. Trade*, *Crewel*, worsted twisted in knots, and sold for tapestry, and embroidery work; now called Berlin wool. **1865** *Cornh. Mag.* Feb. 216 In rising to receive him, she threw down her basket of crewels.

β. The forms *crewe*, *crue* occur: perh. as scribal errors.

1552-3 *Inv. Ch. Goods* in *Ann. Litchfield* IV. 10 In this chapell a vestement of grenne crewe, a vestement of redd crue, a cope of grenne crue. *Ibid.* 41 Vestements of crewe.

2. Short for CREWEL-WORK.

Mod. You might do it in crewel.

3. *attrib.* †**a.** Made of crewel. *Obs.* or *dial.*

1550-1600 [see CADDIS[1] 2 b]. **1596** NASHE *Saffron Walden* 10 To buy him cruel strings to his bookes. **1599** PORTER *Angry Wom. Abingd.* in Hazl. *Dodsley* VII. 286 He will have His cruel garters cross about the knee. **1605** SHAKS. *Lear* II. iv. 7. **1633** SHIRLEY *Bird in Cage* IV. ii, I speak the prologue to our mixed audience of silk and crewel gentlemen in the hangings [*i.e.* the tapestry figures]. **1867** F. FRANCIS *Angling* i. (1880) 42 A yellow crewel body with red hackle and dun turkey wing.

b. Pertaining to or embroidered with CREWEL-WORK: ***crewel yarn*** = sense 1.

1598 FLORIO *Worlde of Wordes* 260/3 *Passamano d'accia*, statute lace, crewell lace. **1880** L. HIGGIN *Handbk. Embroidery* iii. 19 'Stem stitch' (wrongly called also, 'crewel stitch', as it has no claim to being used exclusively in crewel embroidery). **1882** MISS BRADDON *Mt. Royal* II. iv. 58 Throwing back his dark head upon a crewel anti-macassar. **1887** *Daily News* 21 Nov. 2/7 There is a moderate business doing..in knitting and crewel yarns.

Hence **'crewel** *v. trans.* (*dial.*) to ornament with crewel-work embroidery: see also quot. 1869. **'crewelist**, one who works crewel-work. **'crewellery**, crewel-work collectively. (All recent.)

1869 *Lonsdale Gloss.*, *Crewel*, to cover a ball or other object with particoloured worsted worked in a peculiar manner. **1876** *Mid. Yorksh. Gloss.*, *Creal*, to wind twine, or anything of the kind, is to creal it..The process of doing samplers, or other worsted needle-work, is spoken of as crealing. **1881** *Standard* 16 July 5/2 She was unable to dispose of her crewellery, her fans. **1880** *Daily Tel.*, Wanted a good crewelist.

crewel[2], **cruel.** A local name of the Cowslip in Devon and Somerset.
1847–78 in HALLIWELL.

crewel, obs. form of CRUEL.

crewels ('kru:əlz), *sb. pl. Sc.* Also **cruels.** [f. F. *écrouelles* scrofula.] The king's evil, scrofula.
1660 J. LAMONT *Diary* (1815) 154 (Jam.) The Lady Balcleuch.. had the cruells in hir arme. **1721** WODROW *Hist.* II. 445 (Jam.) His right hand and right knee broke out in a running sore, called the cruels. **1818** SCOTT *Hrt. Midl.* xlvii, Having a beloved child sick to death of the Crewels. **1824** —— *St. Ronan* ii, 'A puir body's bairn that had gotten the cruells.' **1880** *Antrim and Down Gloss.*, *Cruels*, the king's evil.

'crewel-work. *lit.* Work done with crewels or worsted yarns; applied to a species of embroidery which became fashionable about 1860, in which a design is worked in worsted on a background of linen or cloth.
1863 E. J. MAY *Stronges of N.* 13 In one of the windows by a small table, occupied in some crewel work, sat the venerable lady. **1885** E. GARRETT *At Any Cost* xiv. 255 Bending over her crewel work.

crewet, -ette, obs. forms of CRUET.

crewless ('kru:lɪs), *a.* [f. CREW *sb.*[1] + -LESS.] Without a crew.
1889 *Standard* 26 Mar., The schooner floated helmless and crewless.

crewman ('kru:mən). [CREW *sb.*[1] + MAN *sb.*[1]] A member of a crew (senses 5 and 6).
1937 *Sun* (Baltimore) 2 July 1/6 Captain Gray.. will share the 22½-ton Sikorsky flying boat with six other crew-men. **1950** J. DEMPSEY *Championship Fighting* 179, I never rowed in a crew. But I do know that crewmen have a rhythm or 'beat' to which they time their strokes. **1961** *Flight* LXXX. 284/1 A Mercury spacecraft carrying special instrumentation and a 'crewman simulator'. **1964** *English Studies* XLV. 4 The crewmen of the Tuscan vessel which carried him to Corsica.

crewse, crewyse, obs. ff. CRUSE.

creyance, creyme, obs. ff. CREANCE, CREAM.

creyer, creyfish: see CRAYER, etc.

creyse, -ery, var. of CROISE, CROISERIE.

creyste, obs. form of CREST.

criance, obs. form of CREANCE.

‖**criant** (krijɑ̃), *a.* [a. F. *criant* crying, loud, pr. pple. of *crier* to CRY.] 'Loud', garish.
1876 'OUIDA' *Winter City* i. 9 A *criant* bit of furniture hurt her as the grating of a false quantity hurts a scholar. **1884** *Tablet* 24 May 805/1 There is nothing garish or *criant* in either of these glorious canvases.

‖**criard** (krijar), *a.* Also in fem. form **criarde.** [Fr.] Shrill; 'loud'; garish (cf. prec.).
1840 THACKERAY in *Fraser's Mag.* July 120/1 His pictures are chiefly effects of sunset and moonlight; of too *criarde* a colour as regards sun and moon. **1889** G. B. SHAW *London Music in 1888–89* (1937) 260 His voice is high pitched and a little *criarde*. **1924** *Blackw. Mag.* June 774/1 Man and label were equally *criard*. *Ibid.* Aug. 237/1 The palace furniture was equally *criard*.

criature, obs. f. CREATURE, CREATOR.

crib (krɪb), *sb.* Forms: 1, 4– crib; also 1, 5–6 cryb, 3–7 cribbe, 4 kribbe, 4–5 crybe, 4–6 crybbe, 5 crebe, 7 cribb, krib(b, (crub). [A common WGer. sb.: OE. *crib(b)* fem. = OFris. *cribbe*, OS. *kribbja* (MDu. *cribbe*, Du. *krib*, *kribbe*), OHG. *chrippa* (MHG. and mod.G. *krippe*). Supposed to be etymologically related to MHG. *krebe* masc. basket, which may again stand in ablaut relation to *korb*, CORF: see Kluge, Franck.]

I. 1. a. A barred receptacle for fodder used in cowsheds and fold-yards; also in fields, for beasts lying out during the winter; a CRATCH. (In nearly all early quots. applied to the manger in which the infant Christ was laid; cf. CRATCH *sb.*)
a **1000** *Crist* 1426 (Gr.) Ic læᵹ cildᵹeonᵹ on crybbe. *c* **1200** ORMIN 3711 Te Laferrd Jesu Crist Wass leȝȝd inn asse cribbe. *a* **1300** *Cursor M.* 11253 (Cott.) In a crib he sal be funden. **1340** HAMPOLE *Pr. Consc.* 5200 Born.. and layd.. In a cribbe, bytwen an ox and an asse. *c* **1400** *Apol. Loll.* 97 þe oxe knowiþ his weldar, and þe as þe crib of his lord. **1535** COVERDALE *Job* xxxix. 9 Wyll the vnicorne be so tame as.. to abyde still by thy cribbe? **1577** B. GOOGE *Heresbach's Husb.* III. (1586) 142 b, Serpents, that many tymes lie hid under their [sheep's] Cribbes. **1602** SHAKS. *Ham.* v. ii. 87 Let a Beast be Lord of Beasts, and his Crib shall stand at the Kings Messe. **1712** POPE *Messiah* 79 The steer and lion at one crib shall meet. **1847** MARRYAT *Childr. N. Forest* v, The animal could move about a little and eat out of her crib. **1884** *West Sussex Gaz.* 25 Sept. Advt., Circular iron and oak bullock cribs.

b. (Orig. in *R.C. Ch.*) A representation of the manger in which the infant Christ was laid, erected in churches.
1885 *Catholic Dict.* s.v., The present custom of erecting a crib in the churches at Christmas time.. began during the thirteenth century.

c. *Astron.* The star-cluster *Præsepe* in Cancer.
1551 RECORDE *Cast. Knowl.* (1556) 266 Cancer containing 8 stars, beside a cloudy tract which is named yᵉ Manger or Crybbe. *a* **1718** R. CUMBERLAND *Orig. Gentium Antiq.* (1724) 93 The constellation Cancer, in which the Aselli and their crib is plac'd.

2. 'The stall or cabin of an ox' (J.).
a **1340** HAMPOLE *Psalter* 512 Nete sall noght be in kribbis. **1611** BIBLE *Prov.* xiv. 4 Where no Oxen are, the crib is cleane. **1841** LANE *Arab. Nts.* I. 13 The Merchant.. went to the bull's crib, and sat down there, and the driver came and took out the bull. **1879** *Cassell's Techn. Educ.* IV. 416/2 The calf-house.. should be.. divided into separate sparred cribs or hutches. **1884** *Cheshire Gloss.*, *Crib*, a small cote to put young calves in.

3. a. A small habitation, cabin, hovel; a narrow room; *fig.* a confined space. In N.Z. now esp. a small house at the seaside or at a holiday resort.
1597 SHAKS. *2 Hen. IV*, III. i. 9 Why rather (Sleepe) lyest thou in smoakie Cribs.. Then in the perfum'd Chambers of the Great? **1840** CLOUGH *Amours de Voy.* I. 6 The world.. Whithersoever we turn, still is the same narrow crib. **1862** C. R. THATCHER *Dunedin Songster* No. 1. 5 The weather and time had so peppered that tumbledown crib, I declare. **1886** BESANT *Childr. Gibeon* II. vi, There were no confessional cribs and no candles. **1887** HALL CAINE *Deemster* xxviii. 185 Shutting himself in this dusty crib, the Bishop drew from under the bed a glass-covered case. **1929** W. SMYTH *Bonzer Jones* xvii. 213 'Here's my crib,' he announced. **1947** 'A. P. GASKELL' *Big Game* 88 If it's fine George will be taking them up to his crib. **1962** *Guardian* 21 July 6/4 An index to social status in New Zealand.. is possession of the seaside bach (in Southland, the crib). **1963** *Truth* (N.Z.) 24 Sept., 'You know my sea-side summer bach?' 'Bach? What the South Islanders call a crib?' **1970** D. M. DAVIN *Not Here, Not Now* II. ix. 115 Then back to the crib again, set off the road in the bush.

b. *Thieves' slang.* A dwelling-house, shop, public-house, etc. ***to crack a crib***: see CRACK *v.* 11.
1812 J. H. VAUX *Flash Dict.*, *Crib*, a house, sometimes applied to shops. **1838** DICKENS *O. Twist* xix, Now, my dear, about that crib at Chertsey. **1844** J. T. HEWLETT *Parsons & W.* xxii, The grocer's crib, as he called it.

c. A lock-up; a bridewell. *local.*
1847–78 in HALLIWELL. **1879** in *Shropshire Word-bk.*

d. *slang* (chiefly *U.S.*). A saloon, 'low dive', or brothel. Also ***crib-house, -joint.***
c **1857** B. A. BAKER *Glance at N.Y.* 23 Let's take a drink; there's a crib open. **1882** *Sydney Slang Dict.* 3/2 *Drum*, or *crib*, house of ill repute. **1901** 'J. FLYNT' *World of Graft* 219 *Crib*, gambling dive. **1926** J. BLACK *You can't Win* (1927) xiv. 199 I'll make the cribs myself. I'm dynamite with them old brums in the cribs. **1930** J. DOS PASSOS *42nd Parallel* 320 The little lighted cribhouses. **1932** B. DE VOTO *Mark Twain's Amer.* vi. 124 The palaces blended with scores of dance halls.. parlor houses, cribs. **1958** P. GAMMOND et al. *Decca Bk. Jazz* iii. 42 Forced into the dives and crib-joints of the red-light district of New Orleans.

4. *fig.* A 'berth', 'place', situation. *slang.*
1865 HATTON *Bitter Sweets* vii, It's a snug crib this.

5. a. A small rectangular bed for a child, with barred or latticed sides. (Sometimes *loosely* = cradle.)
1649 *Bury Wills* (1850) 220 One trundle bedstead and an halfe trundle bedstead, a cribb. **1828** WEBSTER, *Crib*.. 6. A small frame for a child to sleep in. **1832** HT. MARTINEAU *Weal or Woe* vii. 86 Fergus was kneeling at the foot of the child's crib. **1857** W. COLLINS *Dead Secret* (1861) 77 Having a nurse to engage and a crib to buy.

†**b.** *transf.* Child, baby. *Obs.* Cf. CRIBBER 1.
1702 LADY MARY COKE in *Cowper MSS.* II. 447 (*Hist. MSS. Comm.*) Your Crib is well, and all are yours. *Ibid.* 453 Inquire me out a nursery maid, because your crib is weaning.

6. *fig.* †**a.** A close-fisted person, one who keeps a tight hold of what he has. *Obs.*
1622 MABBE tr. *Aleman's Guzman d' Alf.* I. 251 That his wife be close-fisted, a very Crib.

b. *dial.*, *Austral.*, and *N.Z.* Food, provisions; a light meal or snack; a piece of bread, cake, etc. Freq. *attrib.*
1641 BROME *Jov. Crew* II. Wks. 1873 III. 388 Here's Pannum and Lap, and good Poplars of Yarrum To fill up the Crib, and to comfort the Quarron. **1825** JAMIESON Suppl. *s.v.*, Haste ye, and gi'e me ma.. *crib*, Guidwife. **1872** *N. & Q.* 4th Ser. IX. 47/1 The gift.. was generally a small cake.. and was called the 'christening crib'—a *crib* of bread or cake being a provincialism for a *bit* of bread, &c. **1880** M. A. COURTNEY *Gloss. Cornwall* 15/2 *Crib*, a crust of bread; fragments of meat. 'Eat up your cribs.' **1881** RAYMOND *Mining Gloss.*, *Crib*.. 3. A miner's luncheon. **1889** *Daily News* 4 Apr. 4/8 In the pocket of each of the garments was a pasty and a 'crib' (apparently a small loaf). **1904** 'G. B. LANCASTER' *Sons o' Men* 159 Sereld.. growled because someone had spilt tobacco-ash into his crib—which is bushman for dinner. **1908** *Westm. Gaz.* 13 May 6/1 Half an hour's 'crib' time [at Blackball, N.Z.] is also granted. **1926** K. S. PRICHARD *Working Bullocks* xi. 108 Red picked up his crib-bag. **1928** J. DEVANNY *Dawn Beloved* xxx. 273 He stopped.. to hang up his towel and crib tin. **1942** A. L. ROWSE *Cornish Childhood* ii. 30 He used to take it to work with him and at crib-time (i.e. lunch-time) would entertain his fellows with it. **1947** A. VOGT in D. Davin *N.Z. Short Stories* (1953) 364 Ben went to work [in the bush] each day like the rest of the men, with his crib and oil-skin. **1954** *Coast to Coast 1953* 37 Jacques was holding out his crib. 'Time to eat.'.. Crib over, the men rolled cigarettes. **1971** J. TURNER *Stone Dormitory* iii. 30 'Just come in for me crib. It's time.'.. 'It's ready for you, Tom,' she said, putting the bread and cheese and tea before him.

II. †**7. a.** A wickerwork basket, pannier, or the like. In quot. 1648 a bag. *Obs.*
1387 TREVISA *Higden* (Rolls) IV. 353 þey putte hym in a litel cribbe i-schape as a litel bote. **1398** —— *Barth. De P.R.* XIX. cxxviii. (1495) 934 Fiscella is a lytyll euenlonge crybbe or a panyer woue wyth smale roddes of wylow. **1648** DAVENANT *Long Vac. London*, With canvas crib To girdle tied.. Where worms are put, which must small fish Betray at night to earthen dish. **1676** WORLIDGE *Cyder* (1691) 112 You may have a Basket or Crib.. and put Straw round it in the inside.

b. The BIN used in hop-picking.
c **1830** MRS. SHERWOOD in *Houlston Tracts* III. lxxii. 10 Come along this way to the crib (that is, the sheet or cloth into which the hop blossoms are cut).

†**8.** A crate or measure of glass. *Obs.* Cf. CRATE 2 b, CRADLE *sb.* 6 c.)
1688 R. HOLME *Armoury* III. 385/1 A Load of Glass is two Kribbs; a Krib is 100 or 150 Foot of cut Glass.

9. *Salt-making.* An apparatus like a hay-rack in which the salt is placed to drain after boiling. ? *Obs.*
c **1682** J. COLLINS *Making of Salt* 54 The Liquor that Dreynes from the Salt in the Cribs is a sort of Bittern. **1753** CHAMBERS *Cycl. Supp.* s.v., *Crib* in the English Salt Works.. These cribs are like hay-racks, wide at the top, and tapering to a narrow bottom, with wooden ribs.. placed so close, that the salt cannot easily fall through them.

10. a. A wickerwork contrivance for catching salmon; a CRUIVE.
1873 *Act 36–7 Vict.* c. 71 Sched. III, License Duties.. For each.. weir.. box, crib, or cruive. *Ibid.* § 17 Any legal fishing mill dam not having a crib, box, or cruive.

b. The enclosure for trapped fish in a pound-net. *U.S.*
1873 *Rep. U.S. Fish Commission* I. 264 The pound-nets.. have several parts, termed the 'leader', the 'heart', the 'pot', 'bowl', or 'crib', and the 'tunnel'. *a* **1884** KNIGHT *Dict. Mech.* Suppl. 231/1 *Crib* (Fishing), the bowl or pound of a Pound Net.

11. A framework of bars or spars for strengthening, support, etc.; see quots. Cf. CRADLE *sb.* 6.
1693 *Phil. Trans.* XVII. 895 Preserving the Banks of Rivers, by building Wings or Cribs to break the force of the Water. **1708** S. MOLYNEUX *Ibid.* XXVI. 38 A large Tub.. of Wood inclosed with a Crib made of Brick and Lime. **1883** F. M. CRAWFORD *Mr. Isaacs* iii. 49 As the crib holds the ship in her place while she is building.

12. *Mining.* A framework of timber, etc., lining a shaft, to prevent the earth from caving in, or water from trickling through.
1839 *Ann. Reg.* 41 It was necessary to construct what is termed a crib; that is a cylinder corresponding to the dimensions of the shaft. **1851** GREENWELL *Coal-trade Terms Northumb. & Durh.* 19 Common cribs are circles of wood, usually oak, from 4 to 6 inches square, and are used to support the sides of a pit when the stone is bad. **1881** *Pop. Sc. Monthly* XIX. 28 A shaft or crib is sunk.. to prevent the sides from caving in.

13. A rectangular frame of logs or beams strongly fastened together and secured under water to form a pier, dam, etc.; sometimes including the superstructure raised upon it. (*Canada & U.S.*)
1816 [see *crib-dam*]. **1867** *Harper's Weekly* 20 Apr. 252/4 The flood-gates of the 'crib' were opened. **1874** KNIGHT *Dict. Mech.*, *Crib*.. 6. A structure of logs to be anchored with stones. Cribs are used for bridge-piers, ice-breakers, dams, etc. **1881** *Proc. Inst. Civ. Engineers* LXIII. 268 (*Cribwork in Canada*) Cribs are merely open or close boxes, made of timbers strongly framed together. **1884** *Pall Mall G.* 10 Oct. 7/2 Fourteen men were employed at a crib in the lake at the outer end of the tunnel.

14. A small raft of boards or staves to be floated down a small stream, a number of which are made up into a large raft. (*Canada & U.S.*)
1813 W. JOHNSON *Reports* X, Light cribs of boards would float over the dam in safety. **1880** *Lumberman's Gaz.* 28 Jan., When the streams get wide enough the 'sticks' are made into 'cribs', and these, again, are made up into 'rafts'.. Cribs are formed of about 20 sticks of timber fastened between two logs called 'floats'.

15. A bin or place with sparred or slatted sides for storing Indian corn (= CORN-CRIB b); also for salt and other commodities. *U.S.*
1823 J. D. HUNTER *Captiv. N. Amer.* 258 The corn [is preserved] in cribs, constructed of small poles and bark of trees. **1828** WEBSTER, *Crib*.. 5. A small building, raised on posts, for storing Indian corn. **1864** *Ibid.*.. 4. A box or bin for storing grain, salt, etc.

III. 16. *Cards.* **a.** The set of cards made up of two (or one) thrown out from each player's hand, and given to the dealer, in the game of cribbage. **b.** Also, short for CRIBBAGE. (*colloq.*)
1680 COTTON *Compl. Gamester* viii, Sometimes it so happens that he is both bilkt in hand and crib. **1870** HARDY & WARE *Mod. Hoyle* 79 (*Cribbage*) The players.. each throw out two [cards] for the crib, face downwards.. The four cards constituting 'crib' belong to the dealer. *Ibid.* 80 Having counted his hand, the dealer proceeds in like manner to count his crib. **1885** *Standard* 3 Apr. 2/6 He had played.. at 'whist' and 'crib'.

IV. Senses from CRIB *v.*

17. The act of 'cribbing'; a petty theft. (See CRIB *v.* 7.) *rare.*
1855 BROWNING *Fra Lippo Lippi* 148 To confess Their cribs of barrel-droppings, candle-ends.

18. Something 'cribbed' or taken without acknowledgement, as a passage from an author; a plagiarism. (*colloq.*)
1834 MEDWIN *Angler in Wales* I. 207 That's a crib from Waller, I declare. **1876** A. M. FAIRBAIRN in *Contemp. Rev.* June 130 It was a crib from himself.

19. A translation of a classic or other work in a foreign language, for the illegitimate use of students. (*colloq.*)

1827 LYTTON *Pelham* I. ii. 11, I could read Greek fluently, and even translate it through the medium of the Latin version technically called a crib. **1861** HUGHES *Tom Brown at Oxf.* xxxix. (1889) 375 Schoolboys caught by their master using a crib.

20. A complaint, grumble. *colloq.*

1943 HUNT & PRINGLE *Service Slang* 26 People have their own pet cribs.

V. 21. *attrib.* and *Comb.*, as ***crib timber-work*** (see sense 13); **crib-bite** *v. intr.*, to have the practice or habit of crib-biting; **crib-biter**, a horse addicted to crib-biting; also *fig.*; also, a grumbler; **crib-biting**, the vice or morbid habit of seizing the manger (or other object) with the teeth and at the same time noisily drawing in the breath (*wind-sucking*); **crib-breakwater** *U.S.*, a breakwater made of cribwork; **crib-bridge**, a bridge whose piers are formed of cribs (see CRIB *sb.* 13); **crib-cracker** *slang*, a burglar (see CRIB *sb.* 3 b); so ***crib-cracking***; **crib-dam** *U.S.*, a dam formed of cribs; **crib-muzzle**, a muzzle worn by a horse to prevent crib-biting; **crib-rail**, a transverse member of the frame of a railway coach; **crib-strap** (see quot.); **cribwork**, work consisting or formed of cribs (sense 13); also *attrib.*

1844 *Crib-bite [see WIND-SUCK *v.*]. **1809** *Sporting Mag.* XXXIV. 190 A bay horse..found to be a *crib-biter. **1832** MARRYAT *N. Forster* xl, I have lately used iron pens, for I'm a devil of a crib-biter. **1860** HOTTEN *Dict. Slang* (ed. 2) 124 *Crib biter*, an inveterate grumbler; properly said of a horse which has this habit, a sign of its bad digestion. **1831** *Ann. Reg.* 25 Horses had the habit of *crib-biting in very different degrees. **1879** *Rep. Chief of Engineers, U.S. Army* II. 1588 (Knight), *Crib breakwater. **1899** *Westm. Gaz.* 8 Dec. 2/1 What military engineers call a '*crib' bridge. **1879** *Punch* 3 May 201/1 A bludgeon as big As a *crib-cracker's nobby persuader. **1883** G. R. SIMS *How the Poor Live* ii. 10 His talents as a 'cribcracker', and his adventures as a pickpocket. **1906** *Daily Chron.* 5 Dec. 6/6 The house is adequately protected against burglars and is proof against the amateur crib-cracker. **1852** *Punch* 9 Oct. 161/1 He..From cly-faking to *crib-cracking turned. **1816** *Niles' Reg.* IX. Suppl. 164/2 These dams are built with timber, in the manner of *crib dams, secured to the rocks below with iron bolts. *a* **1884** KNIGHT *Dict. Mech.* Suppl. 231/1 **Crib muzzle* (Manège), a muzzle used to correct the equine habit of cribbing. **1958** *Engineering* 14 Mar. 344/1 The body pillars, cantrail and *cribrails are in 12 s.w.g. **1874** KNIGHT *Dict. Mech.*, **Crib-strap* (*Menage*), a neck-throttler for crib-biting and wind sucking horses. **1884** *Harper's Mag.* Sept. 621/2 Sluices.. are constructed through a mass of *crib timber-work. **1873** ROBERTSON *Engin. Notes* 56 *Cribwork..consists of logs notched on to each other in layers at right angles. **1881** *Proc. Inst. Civ. Engineers* LXIII. 271 A cribwork pier is easily ripped up and removed by an ordinary spoon dredge.

crib (krɪb), *v.* [f. CRIB *sb.*]

†**1.** *intr.* ? To feed at a crib. (In quot. humorously of persons.) *Obs. rare.*

c **1460** *Towneley Myst.* 89, I fare fulle ylle, At youre mangere..Syrs, let us cryb furst for oone thyng or oder.

2. a. *trans.* To shut up as in a crib or small compartment; to confine within a small space or narrow limits; to hamper. (In modern use generally as an echo of Shaks.; cf. CABIN *v.* 3.)

1605 SHAKS. *Macb.* III. iv. 24 Now I am cabin'd, crib'd, confin'd, bound in. **1743** E. POSTON *Pratler* (1747) I. 151 How must that which is boundless..be confin'd and cribb'd up within the narrow Limits of my..finite Capacity! **1826** DE QUINCEY *Lessing* Wks. XIII. 236 The mind of Lessing was not cribbed and cabined within the narrow sphere of others. **1876** BLACKIE *Songs Relig. & Life* 34 Vainly the narrow wit of narrow men Within the walls which priestly lips have blest..Would crib thy presence.

b. To lock up, imprison. *local.* (CRIB *sb.* 3 c.)

1849 C. BRONTË *Shirley* xxxii, They should be arrested, cribbed, tried, and brought in for Botany Bay.

c. To place (Indian corn, etc.) in a crib. *U.S.*

1719 J. HEMPSTEAD *Diary* (1901) 93, I went to Stonington and Stephen to Cribb the Corn. **1831** J. M. PECK *Guide for Emigrants* II. 151 The value of the crop, then, before it is cribbed, is one hundred and twenty-five dollars. **1874** E. EGGLESTON *Circuit Rider* i. 17 Now, boys, crib your corn. **1939** *These are our Lives* 256 The buyers would crib eight and ten thousand bushel of wheat and corn.

3. *intr.* To lie as in a crib. (CRIB *sb.* 5.) *Obs.*

1661 GAUDEN *Anti-Baal-Berith* 35 (L.) Who sought to make the..bishops to crib in a Presbyterian trundle-bed.

4. *trans.* To furnish with cribs. (CRIB *sb.* 1.)

1669 WORLIDGE *Syst. Agric.* v. §2 (1681) 67 A large Sheep-house for the housing of Sheep in winter, which may be Sheep-cribbed round about and in the middle too, to fother them therein.

5. To furnish with a crib or framework of timber. (CRIB *sb.* 11–13.)

1861 *Times* 29 Aug., The [oil-] wells are sunk and cribbed to a depth of from 40 to 60 feet. **1862** *Ibid.* 21 Jan., The shaft of the [coal-] pit was cribbed round with oak timber.

6. To make up (timber) into cribs or small rafts. *U.S.* (CRIB *sb.* 14.)

1876 in *Minnesota Rep.* (1880) XXV. 524 Any person who may do..any manual labour in cutting, cribbing or towing any logs or timber in this state.

7. *colloq.* To pilfer, purloin, steal; to appropriate furtively (a small part of anything). [Prob. orig. *thieves' slang*, connected with sense 7 of the sb.]

1748 DYCHE *Dict.*, *Crib*, to withhold, keep back, pinch, or thieve a part out of money given to lay out for necessaries. **1772** FOOTE *Nabob* I. Wks. 1799 II. 298 A brace of birds and a hare, that I cribbed this morning out of a basket of game. **1795** *Hull Advertiser* 31 Oct. 4/2 We would never have cribb'd your papers. **1825** COBBETT *Rur. Rides* 28 Bits of ground cribbed..at different times from the forest. **1862** MRS. H. WOOD *Mrs. Hallib.* II. xii. 204 We crib the time from play-hours. **1884** *Times* (Weekly Ed.) 17 Oct. 2/3 How many Tory seats he can crib there.

absol. **1760** C. JOHNSTON *Chrysal* (1822) I. 174 Cribbing from the till. *a* **1839** PRAED *Poems* (1864) II. 8 Both of old were known to crib, And both were very apt to fib!

8. *colloq.* To take or copy (a passage, a piece of translation, etc.) without acknowledgement, and use as one's own; to plagiarize.

1778 J. HOME *Alfred* Prol., And crib the prologue from the bill of fare. **1844** J. T. HEWLETT *Parsons & W.* xlvii, Flogged for cribbing another boy's verses. **1862** SALA *Accepted Addr.* 168 Antiquarian anecdotes (cribbed from Hone, etc.).

absol. **1862** SHIRLEY *Nugæ Crit.* vi. 266, I rather suspect that Homer..cribbed without..compunction from every old ballad that came in his way. **1892** *Pall Mall G.* 19 Oct. 3/1 At school..it was dishonourable to 'crib' because it would be to unfairly injure..others.

9. a. *intr.* Of horses: To practise crib-biting.

1864 in WEBSTER. **1892** *Field* 26 Nov. 820/2 No horse would crib after using this strap.

b. To complain, to grumble. *colloq.* Cf. *crib-biter.*

1925 in FRASER & GIBBONS *Soldier & Sailor Words.* **1957** L. P. HARTLEY *Hireling* xi. 90 She calls on the neighbours, she's out half the time and doesn't answer the telephone, and when I start cribbing she just laughs.

cribbage ('krɪbɪdʒ). Also 7–9 **cribbidge.** [f. CRIB *sb.* and *v.* + -AGE.

In sense 1, *cribbage* is known earlier than any recorded instance of CRIB *sb.* 16; but this is perh. only accidental.]

1. A game at cards, played by two, three, or four persons, with a complete pack of 52 cards, five (or six) of which are dealt to each player, and a board with sixty-one holes on which the points are scored by means of pegs; a characteristic feature being the 'crib', consisting of cards thrown out from each player's hand, and belonging to the dealer.

1630 BRATHWAIT *Eng. Gentlem.* (1641) 126 In games at Cards..the Cribbage [requires] a recollected fancy. **1674** S. VINCENT *Gallants Acad.* 68 Such Ladies with whom you have plaid at Cribbidge. **1711** PUCKLE *Club* ⁋123 Guess then the numbers of frauds there are at Picquet, Gleck.. Basset, Cribbidge, and all the rest of the games upon the cards. **1768** GOLDSM. *Good-n. Man* III. i, Men that would go forty guineas on a game of cribbage. **1820** *Hoyle's Games Impr.* 149 Mode of playing five-card cribbage..Eight-card cribbage is sometimes played; but very seldom. **1840** DICKENS *Old C. Shop* xxiii, He proposed a game of four-handed cribbage.

2. The action of 'cribbing', or that which is 'cribbed'; plagiarism. (*colloq. rare.*)

In first quot. with play on sense 1.

1830 *Blackw. Mag.* XXVII. 146 You think you are writing poetry, while you are only playing at cribbage. **1852** *Ibid.* LXXII. 681 The only tolerable parts of the book were palpable cribbages from poor Ruxton.

b. Something 'cribbed' or stolen.

1862 H. MARRYAT *Year in Sweden* II. 54 Gustaf Adolf.. signed his abdication on an inlaid table—a Thirty Years War cribbage,—which stands under this very picture.

3. *attrib.* and *Comb.*, as ***cribbage-card, -peg, -player, -table***; **cribbage-board**, the board used for marking at cribbage; **cribbage-faced** *a.* (see quot.).

1755 MRS. DELANY *Let. Mrs. Dewes* 17 Nov., My brother is in great request at the cribbage-table. **1769** MRS. RAFFALD *Eng. Housekpr.* (1778) 205 To make Cribbage Cards in Flummery. **1785** GROSE *Dict. Vulg. T.*, *Cribbage-faced*, marked with the small-pox, the pits bearing a kind of resemblance to the holes in a cribbage-board. **1810** *Reformist* II. 104 That skinny cribbage-faced little devil in pink. **1821** LAMB *Elia, Old Benchers*, [He] turned cribbage-boards, and such small cabinet toys, to perfection. **1824** MISS MITFORD *Village* 1st Ser. (1863) 217 We cribbage-players are as well amused as they. **1839** *36 Years Seafaring Life* 46 Written in legible characters on his old cribbage face.

cribbed (krɪbd, 'krɪbɪd), *ppl. a.* [f. CRIB *v.* + -ED[1].] Confined in a crib, etc. (see CRIB *v.*); *fig.* confined within narrow space or limits.

1863 W. PHILLIPS *Speeches* xii. 266 This limited, cribbed, cabined, isolated American civilization. **1871** MORLEY *Voltaire* (1886) 44 The narrowness of the cribbed deck that we are doomed to tread.

cribber ('krɪbə(r)). *rare.* [f. CRIB *sb.* and *v.*]

†**1.** The occupant of a child's crib; a young child. *Obs. nonce-use.* (Cf. CRIB *sb.* 5 b.)

1701 LADY M. COKE in *Cowper MSS.* II. 415 (*Hist. MSS. Comm.*) If my little cribber could speak.

2. One who 'cribs' or appropriates clandestinely; one who uses a crib (sense 19). *colloq.*

1892 *Pall Mall G.* 19 Oct. 3/1 He can study the records of historic cribbers.

cribbing ('krɪbɪŋ), *vbl. sb.* [f. CRIB *v.* (and *sb.*) + -ING[1].]

1. The action of the verb CRIB.

1791 BENTHAM *Panopt.* 122 Cribbing, a vice thought hitherto congenial to schools. **1892** *Pall Mall G.* 25 June 7/2 The cribbing and warehousing of grain.

2. = Crib-biting: see CRIB *v.* 9.

1864 in WEBSTER.

3. That which is 'cribbed' or pilfered.

1837 MAJOR RICHARDSON *Brit. Legion* ix. (ed. 2) 225 A horse he had contrived to purchase out of his cribbings from me.

4. *Mining.* Timbering forming the lining of a shaft, etc.; cribwork.

1841 J. HOLLAND *Collieries* (ed. 2) 181 The sinking is then resumed, and..another circuit of cribbing is laid.

†**5.** *Thieves' cant.* Provender, provisions. *Obs.*

1641 BROME *Jov. Crew* II. Wks. 1873 III. 388 For all this bene Cribbing and Peck let us then, Bowse a health to the Gentry Cofe of the Ken.

cribble ('krɪb(ə)l), *sb.* ? *Obs.* Also 6 **cryble**, cribel, 6–9 **crible.** [a. F. *crible* (for **cribre*) 13th c., ad. L. *crībrum* (dim. *crībellum*) sieve.]

1. A sieve.

1565–73 COOPER *Thesaurus*, *Capisterium*, a crible or sive to clense corne. **1706** PHILLIPS, *Cribble*, a kind of Sieve to purge Corn. **1881** in RAYMOND *Mining Gloss.*

†**2.** That which remains in the sieve after the fine flour is sifted out; bran or coarse meal; *spec.* applied to a particular quality of coarse meal. *Obs.*

1552–71 [see b.]. **1599** MINSHEU, *Farro*, bran, the cribble of meale that is boulted or sifted out. **1629** CHAPMAN *Juvenal* v. 139 With your familiar crible to be fed. **1674–91** RAY *S. & E.C. Words* 94 *Crible*; course Meal, a degree better than Bran.

b. *attrib.*, as in †***cribble bread***, bread made of this coarse meal.

1552 HULOET, Bread called chete breade, raunged bread, or cribel bread. **1571** GOLDING *Calvin on Ps.* xxiii. 5 A shiver of cryble bred. **1577** tr. *Bullinger's Decades* (1592) 243 Because wee will not eate common cribble breade. **1701** S. JEAKE *Arithmetick* 74 Bread made of whole Wheat is sometimes called Cribble or Fine Ravel Bread.

cribble, *v.* ? *Obs.* [f. prec.: cf. F. *cribler.*] *trans.* To pass through a sieve, to sift.

1558–68 WARDE tr. *Alexis' Secr.* (1580) I. v. 87 b, Take plaster called Gypsum, cribled or sifted. **1601** HOLLAND *Pliny* II. 520 The same must bee cribled or serced afterwards, and beaten to pouder.

'cribbled, *ppl. a.* [f. F. *criblé*, f. *crible* sieve.] Composed of or decorated with minute punctures, as a surface of metal or wood, the ground of an engraving, or the like.

1891 *N.Y. Nation* 12 Nov. 376 The French style leaned to strong contrasts of black and white, or to closer engraving on cribbled backgrounds.

†**cribe.** *Obs.* = CRIBBLE *sb.* and *v.*

1570 LEVINS *Manip.* 113 A cribe, *cribrum*. *Ibid.*, To cribe, *cribrare*. **1677** GALE *Crt. Gentiles* II. IV. 509 Σινίον is a cribe or sieve.

cribellum (krɪ'bɛləm). *Zool.* [L. *cribellum*, dim. of *cribrum* sieve.] An additional spinning organ, having numerous fine pores, situated in front of the spinnerets in certain spiders. Also **'cribellate(d)** *adjs.*, having a cribellum.

1888 ROLLESTON & JACKSON *Forms Anim. Life* 524 In a few Spiders a chitinoid plate, the cribellum, lies in front of the spinnerets. **1926** T. H. SAVORY *Brit. Spiders* 97 The British cribellated spiders. **1951** LOCKET & MILLIDGE *Brit. Spiders* I. iii. 28 The presence of the cribellum is of importance in classification and the whole group is usefully divided into cribellate and ecribellate spiders. **1958** [see CALAMISTRUM].

‖**criblé** (krible), *sb.* (and *a.*). [Fr.: see CRIBBLED *ppl. a.*] A type of engraving on wood or metal (see quots.). Also as *adj.*, engraved in this way, = CRIBBLED *ppl. a.*

1879 *Encycl. Brit.* VIII. 437/1 A kind of wood engraving ..called the *criblé*... It means, *riddled with small holes*... The effect of light and dark is produced in this kind of engraving by sinking a great number of round holes of different diameters in the substance of the wood, which, of course, all come white in the printing. **1960** G. A. GLAISTER *Gloss. Bk.* 91/2 *Criblé*, minute punctures or depressions made in surfaces of wood or metal... Criblé backgrounds can be used to lighten borders which would appear too dark.

cribo ('kraɪbəʊ, 'krɪbəʊ). [Origin unknown.] A large harmless snake, *Drymarchon corais*, found in tropical North, South, and Central America and the West Indies; also called *gopher snake* (*s.v.* GOPHER *sb.*[1] 4) and *indigo snake* (*s.v.* INDIGO C 2.).

1871 KINGSLEY *At Last* I. ii. 78 This snake..has no power against another West Indian snake, almost equally common, namely, the Cribo. **1918** W. H. HUDSON *Far Away* xii. 176 The Cribo of Martinique..kills and swallows the deadly fer-de-lance. **1957** A. H. & A. A. WRIGHT *Handbk. Snakes U.S. & Canada* I. 204 Mexican indigo snake... Other common names: Black gopher snake, blue bull snake, blue gopher snake, corais, cribo.

cribrate ('kraɪbreɪt), *a. Nat. Hist.* [f. L. *crībrum* sieve, after *caudate*, etc.: see -ATE[2].] Perforated like a sieve with small holes.

1846 DANA *Zooph.* (1848) 430 Thin cribrate parietes.

†**'cribrate,** *v. Obs.* [f. ppl. stem of L. *crībrāre* to sift, f. *crībrum* sieve.] *trans.* To sift; also *fig.*

a **1631** DONNE *Lett.* (1651) 308, I have cribrated, and re-cribrated, and post-cribrated the Sermon. **1657** TOMLINSON *Renou's Disp.* 633 Cribrated flower of white Orobs. **1669**

WORLIDGE *Syst. Agric.* xiv. §1 (1681) 307 It distils in minute drops, as it were cribrated through the thick Air.

† **cri'bration.** *Obs.* [n. of action f. prec.: see -ATION.] Sifting; also *fig.*

1612 WOODALL *Surg. Mate* Wks. (1653) 270 Cribration is the preparation of medicaments by a sive or searce. *a* **1631** DONNE in *Select.* (1840) 224 In the cribration and sifting of our consciences. **1676** *Phil. Trans.* XI. 772 The Chyle, which by various cribrations and circulations, at last comes to constitute the whole mass of bloud.

cribriform ('kraɪbrɪfɔːm, 'krɪb-), *a.* [a. mod.L. *crībriform-is* sieve-shaped; see prec. and -FORM.] Having the form or appearance of a sieve; perforated with numerous small holes; esp. in ***cribriform plate***, the bony plate forming the front part of the ethmoid bone, through which the olfactory nerves pass to the nasal cavity.

1741 MONRO *Anat. Bones* (ed. 3) 80 The cribriform part of the *Os Ethmoides.* **1847** YOUATT *Horse* vi. 118 The cribriform or sieve-shaped plate..perforated by a multitude of little holes, through which the nerve connected with smelling passes and spreads over the nose. **1880** GRAY *Struct. Bot.* iii. §3. 77 Cribriform or Sieve-cells, a sort of ducts the walls of which have open slits, through which they communicate with each other.

cribrose (kraɪ'brəʊs), *a.* [f. L. type **cribrōs-us*, f. *crībrum* sieve: see -OSE.] Sieve-like, perforated.

1857 BERKELEY *Cryptog. Bot.* §181. 203 Algæ..which present..a clathroid, cancellated, or cribrose frond. **1866** *Treas. Bot.*, *Cribrose*, pierced (like a sieve) with numerous close small apertures.

† **'cribrous,** *a. Obs.* [ad. L. type **cribrōs-us*: see prec. and -OUS.] = prec.

1674 *Phil. Trans.* IX. 195 New passages through the crevices and cribrous parts. **1681** tr. *Willis' Rem. Med. Wks.*, Vocab.

cric, crice, obs. ff. KRIS, Malay dagger.

crice, var. of CRIKE. *Obs.*

Crichton ('kraɪt(ə)n). The surname of James *Crichton* of Clunie (1560-85?), a Scottish prodigy of intellectual and knightly accomplishments; freq. qualified by *admirable*, it is used allusively for any person who excels in all kinds of studies and pursuits. Hence ***Admirable Crichtonism***; also ***Crich'tonian*** adj.

The epithet which became traditional was first applied in Johnstone's *Heroes Scoti* (1603) 41 Iacobus Critonius Clunius, Musarum pariter ac Martis alumnus, omnibus in studiis, ipsis etiam Italis admirabilis. In English it appeared first in Urquhart's *Jewel* (1652) 112 The admirable Crichtoun..did..present himself to epilogate this his almost extemporanean Comedie.

1812 T. AMYOT *Life of Windham* I. 139 [Windham] was the admirable Crichton of his age and country. *a* **1845** BARHAM *Ingol. Leg.* 3rd Ser. (1847) 264 Like a small boy at Eton, Who's not quite a Crichton. **1889** *Blackw. Mag.* CXLVI. 707/1 The..endless resource and Admirable Crichtonism of Robert Hazel. **1890** *Punch* 11 Jan. 15/2 *Algy.* .. You lucky dog, you possess all the accomplishments I lack! *Jim.*.. Oh, nonsense! Why, you're making me out a regular *Crichton*! **1900** *Academy* 3 Feb. 99/2 Matthew, the self-taught, listening intelligently to a German song while he is swimming, is a little too Crichtonian. **1914** 'IAN HAY' *Lighter Side School Life* ii. 47 In addition to all this, he must be an Admirable Crichton. **1914** J. M. BARRIE (*title*) The admirable Crichton. **1953** A. CHRISTIE *Pocket Full of Rye* iv. 30 Inspector Neele raised his eyebrows. 'The admirable Miss Crichton.' 'I find one must *know* how to do everything oneself.' **1959** *Listener* 5 Feb. 244/1 Other people, in some sort of Admirable Crichton situation, in fact exercise authority even though they are not in authority.

crichtonite ('kraɪtənaɪt). *Min.* [Named after Dr. Crichton.] A variety of menaccanite.

1822 CLEVELAND *Min.* 705. **1868** DANA *Min.* 143.

crick (krɪk), *sb.*[1] Forms: 5 crykke, cryk, 6-7 cricke, (8 creek, 9 creak), 6- crick. [Of uncertain origin; prob. onomatopœic, expressing the sudden check which the spasm causes; cf. next, and STITCH. It may owe its form partly to association with CROOK, which has this sense in Craven dialect: cf. the Sc. *cleik* similarly used, 'cleik in the back' (Jam.).]

A painful spasmodic affection of the muscles of the neck, back, or other part, appearing as a sudden stiffness which makes it more or less impossible to move the part.

c **1440** *Promp. Parv.* 103/1 Crykke, sekenesse (or crampe), *spasmus,..tetanus.* *c* **1460** *Rel. Ant.* II. 29 Thou might stomble, and take the cryk. **1598** FLORIO, *Adolomato*, troubled with a cricke or wrinch in the necke or backe. **1639** FULLER *Holy War* Ep. Ded. (1840) 6 To have such a crick in his neck that he cannot look backward. **1668** R. L'ESTRANGE *Vis. Quev.* (1708) 173 'Tis nothing..but a Crick she has got in her Back. **1749** MRS. DELANY *Life & Corr.* II. 520 A violent creek has seized Mr. Monck's neck, and he can't stir. **1856** WHYTE MELVILLE *Kate Cov.* xiv, You..study the thermometer till you get a crick in your neck.

b. Applied to a disease of horses.

1607 TOPSELL *Four-f. Beasts* (1673) 284 The crick in the neck..is when the horse cannot turn his neck any manner of way, but hold it still right forth. **1727** BRADLEY *Fam. Dict.*, *Flanks*, a Distemper in Horses, the same being a Wrench, Crick, Stroke, or other Hurt got in his Back.

c. *attrib.*

1774 MRS. HARRIS in *Priv. Lett. Ld. Malmesbury* I. 276 She has had what was formerly named a *crick* neck, but the modern phrase now for those vulgar things is rheumatism.

† **crick,** *sb.*[2] *Obs.* [app. the same as F. *cric*, an instrument composed of a toothed wheel, which gives motion to a notched bar: see Hatzfeld s.v. *Cric.*] The instrument or appliance for bending a cross-bow; the gaffle.

1530 PALSGR. 210/2 Cricke to bende a crosbowe with, *cranequin.* [**1874** KNIGHT *Dict. Mech.*, *Crick*, a small jack-screw.]

crick, *sb.*[3] A variant of CREEK *sb.*[1]

crick, *sb.*[4] Short for CRICKET: cf. also GRIG.

1616 SHELDON *Mir. of Antichrist* 323 (T.) A merry cricke and boon companion. **1818** TODD, *Crick*..3. A corruption of cricket..*Crick* is used for *cricket* in the old song of *Take thy old Cloak about thee.*

crick (krɪk), *v.*[1] [f. CRICK *sb.*[1]] *trans.* To give a crick or wrench to (the neck, etc.).

1861 MAYHEW *Lond. Lab.* III. 90/2 He used to take my legs and stretch them, and work them round in their sockets ..That is what they called being 'cricked'. **1884** J. COLBORNE *Hicks Pasha* 48, I can't say I saw it, as I did not want to crick my neck.

crick, *v.*[2] [Echoic, or perh. a. F. *criquer.* It implies a less shrill and prolonged sound than *creak.*] To make a sharp abrupt sound, as a grasshopper. Hence **'cricking** *vbl. sb.*

1601 HOLLAND *Pliny* I. 353 Others make a cricking with a certain long traine, as the Grashoppers. *a* **1693** URQUHART *Rabelais* III. xiii. 107 The..mumbling of Rabets, cricking of Ferrets.

crick-crack, *sb., v., adv.* [Onomatopœic reduplication of CRACK. Cf. F. *cric crac*, and Du. *krikkrakken* to crackle.] A representation of a repeated sharp sound. (In quot. 1600 perh. = CRACKER 6.)

1565-73 COOPER *Thesaurus* s.v. *Crispans, Crepitus crispans*, a sowne or noyse goying by stoppes: as, cricke, cracke, crocke: ticke, tacke, etc. **1600** *Maides Metam.* II. in Bullen *O. Pl.* I. 126 They come of crick-cracks, and shake their tayles like a squib. **1856** DOBELL *Eng. in Time of War*, '*Lady Constance*', Hear his pistol cric-crac! Hear his rifle ping-pang! **1870** MISS BRIDGMAN *Ro. Lynne* II. viii. 166 Her dress caught in a twig, and crick-crack went 'the abominable thing'.

So † **crick-crackle** *v.*, to emit a series of sharp crackling sounds.

a **1618** SYLVESTER *Du Bartas* II. IV. IV. *Decay* 635 A fire in stubble, Which, sodain spreading..Crick-crackling quickly all the Country wastes.

cricke: see KRIS.

cricket ('krɪkɪt), *sb.*[1] Forms: 4-5 cri-, cryket(te, -at, crekytt, 5-6 creket(te, 7 kricket, crecket, 6- cricket. [a. OF. *criquet*, *crequet* (Marie de France, 12th c.) cicada, cricket, related to *criquer* 'to creake, rattle, crackle' (Cotgr.), and to MDu. *crekel*, Du. and LG. *krekel* cricket; all derivatives of an echoic *krik-*, imitating a sharp, abrupt, dry sound, such as is made by this insect.]

1. Any saltatorial orthopterous insect of the genus *Acheta* or of the same tribe; the best-known species are the common house-cricket, *Acheta domestica*, 'an insect that squeaks or chirps about ovens and fireplaces' (J.), the field-cricket, *A. campestris*, and mole-cricket, *Gryllotalpa vulgaris.*

In ME. identified with the fabulous *Salamander.*

c **1325** *Gloss. W. de Biblesw.* in Wright *Voc.* 164 *La salemaundre*, a criket. **1377** LANGL. *P. Pl.* B. XIV. 42 Fissch to lyue in þe flode and in þe fyre þe crykat. **1398** TREVISA *Barth. De P.R.* XVIII. ix. (1495) 760 The Crekette hyght Salamandra: for thys beest quenchyth fyre and lyueth in brennynge fyre. **1530** PALSGR. 210/2 Cricket a worme, *cricquet, gresillon.* **1605** SHAKS. *Macb.* II. ii. 16, I heard the Owle schreame, and the Crickets cry. **1632** MILTON *Penseroso* 82 Far from all resort of mirth, Save the cricket on the hearth. **1727** BRADLEY *Fam. Dict.* s.v. *Dropsy*, Five grains of the Ashes of Crickets, little Animals found in Baker's Ovens. **1795** SOUTHEY *Hymn to Penates*, Where by the evening hearth Contentment sits And hears the cricket chirp. **1846** DICKENS (*title*), The Cricket on the Hearth. **1859** TENNYSON *Elaine* 106 The myriad cricket of the mead.

b. Used for CICADA. (Cf. BALM-CRICKET.)

1864 EARL DERBY *Iliad* III. 181 In discourse Abundant, as the cricket, that on high From topmost boughs of forest tree sends forth His delicate music.

c. *transf.* of a person.

1612 BEAUM. & FL. *Coxcomb* IV. iii, Shee'le talke some times; 'tis the maddest cricket!

d. Prov. phrase. ***as merry*** (etc.) ***as a cricket.***

1592 G. HARVEY *Pierce's Super.* 158 As pleasant as a cricket. **1596** SHAKS. *1 Hen. IV*, II. iv. 100 *Prin.* Shall we be merry? *Poin.* As merrie as Crickets, my Lad. **1720** AMHERST *Ep. Sir J. Blount* 11 Make me merry as a Cricket. **1873** HOLLAND *A. Bonnic.* xvi. 253 Mullens had become as cheerful and lively as a cricket.

2. U.S. ***savannah cricket*** (cf. *cricket-frog* in 3).

1796 MORSE *Amer. Geog.* I. 217 There is yet an extremely diminutive species of frogs, called by some, Savannah crickets, whose notes are not unlike the chattering of young birds or crickets.

3. *Comb.*, as ***cricket-hole***; **cricket-bird,** a local name for the grasshopper warbler (*Locustella nævia*); **cricket-frog,** a name for small tree-frogs of the genus *Hylodes*, which chirp like crickets; **cricket-teal,** a local name for the garganey (*Querquedula circia*).

1483 *Cath. Angl.* 80 Crekethole, *grillarium.*

cricket ('krɪkɪt), *sb.*[2] Also 6 crecket, 7 krickett. [Etymology uncertain.

The word occurs in a document of 1598 (see below), and the evidence then given takes the game back to the end of the reign of Henry VIII. The word appears to be the same as F. *criquet* given by Littré as 'jeu d'adresse', by Godefroy as 'bâton servant de but au jeu de boules', with a quot. of 1478, 'Le suppliant arriva en ung lieu ou on jouoit a la boulle, pres d'une atache [vine-stake] ou criquet'. It has been surmised that it is the same as CRICKET *sb.*[3], and the game a development of that known as STOOL-BALL, to which there are many references from 1567 to 1725, as a game at which girls and women especially played; but this is very doubtful: *cricket*, a stool, is itself not in evidence till a later date. *Cricket* cannot be a deriv. of OE. *crycc* 'knobbed staff', for here the *cc* was palatal and gave ME. *crytch*, crutch; but F. *criquet* might be a deriv. of the cognate M.Flem. *krick*, *kricke*, 'baston à s'appuyer, quinette, potence'. Many changes have been made in the character of the game since the 17th c. when the *bats* were hockey-sticks, the wicket of two stumps with one long bail, and the ball trundled or 'bowled' along the ground. Cf. BAIL *sb.*[4], BAT *sb.*[2], BOWL *v.*, WICKET.]

1. a. An open-air game played with ball, bats, and wickets, by two sides of eleven players each; the batsman defends his wicket against the ball, which is bowled by a player of the opposing side, the other players of this side being stationed about the 'field' in order to catch or stop the ball.

1598 *Guild Merchant Bk.* (MS. in Guildford Borough Records), John Denwick of Guldeford..one of the Queenes Majesties Coroners of the County of Surrey being of the age of fyfty and nyne yeares or there aboute..saith upon his oath that hee hath knowen the parcell of land..for the space of Fyfty years and more, and..saith that hee being a schollar in the Free schoole of Guldeford, hee and several of his fellowes did runne and play there at Creckett and other plaies. [Cf. *History of Guildford* (1801) 203.] **1611** COTGR., *Crosse*..also, a Cricket-staffe; or, the crooked staffe wherewith boyes play at Cricket. *Crosser*, to play at Cricket. **1653** URQUHART *Rabelais* I. xxii, At cricket. **1662** J. DAVIES *Voy. Ambass.* 297 A certain Game, which the Persians call Kuitskaukan, which is a kind of Mall, or Cricket. **1676** H. TEONGE *Diary* (1825) 159 Wee had severall pastimes and sports, as duck-hunting..handball, krickett, scrofilo. **1712** ARBUTHNOT *John Bull* IV. iv, When he happened to meet with a foot-ball, or a match at cricket. **1781** COWPER *Lett.* 28 May, When I was a boy I excelled at cricket and foot-ball. **1881** *Daily News* 9 July 2 The cricket was very slow for a time. **1888** PARDON *Wisden's Almanac* 111 Mr. W. G. Grace played excellent cricket.

b. The playing of the game of cricket.

1851 J. PYCROFT *Cricket Field* x. 200 Have me to bowl.. Box to keep wicket, and Pilch to hit, and then you'll see Cricket. **1857** HUGHES *Tom Brown* II. viii, Such a catch hadn't been made in the close for years... 'Pretty cricket,' says the Captain. **1898** RANJITSINHJI *With Stoddart's Team* (ed. 3) x. 209 The dropped chances were the result of poor cricket on the part of the fieldsmen. **1904** P. F. WARNER *Recov. Ashes* viii. 150 The rain came down in torrents, and no cricket took place until 2.15.

c. Cricket as it should properly be played; hence *fig.*, fair play; honourable dealings with opponents or rivals; esp. in phr. ***not cricket***; so ***to play cricket***, to act fairly; to 'play the game'.

1851 J. PYCROFT *Cricket Field* xi. 210 We will not say that any thing that hardest of hitters..does is not cricket, but certainly it's anything but *play.* **1867** J. LILLYWHITE *Cricketers' Compan.* 13 Do not ask the umpire unless you think the batsman is out; it is not cricket to keep asking the umpire questions. **1900** *Westm. Gaz.* 5 June 2/2 We should be very much surprised if the Duke really thought that to dissolve would be 'cricket'. *Ibid.* 31 July 1/3 We believe that the feeling is very widespread that it would not be 'cricket' to get back to power again as the result of an appeal to the country. **1911** W. DE MORGAN *Likely Story* 313 It is scarcely fair play to make a merit of patience—isn't cricket, as folk say nowadays. **1922** *Daily Mail* 14 Nov. 10, I appeal to the Conservatives to do what is patriotic and honourable and to play 'cricket'. **1930** 'VAN DINE' *Scarab Murder* 20 It didn't seem cricket to leave the poor devil there. **1955** *Times* 21 July 5/7 When one was called to the Bar one was a public menace but one learnt what was and was not cricket during the period of pupilage.

2. *attrib.* and *Comb.*, as ***cricket-ball***, ***-cap***, ***-club***, ***-field***, ***-ground***, ***-jacket***, ***-match***, ***-pitch***, ***-player***, ***-playing***, † ***-staff***, ***-week***; **cricket-bag,** a long bag in which a cricketer's equipment is carried; **cricket-shoes,** shoes specially designed for wear on the cricket-field, usually having spiked soles.

1868 *Saint Pauls* II. 549 At Florence, Rome, or Naples, the unwonted spectacle of *cricket-bags may startle the natives. **1904** P. F. WARNER *Recov. Ashes* xiii. 244 The rubber was won: the 'ashes' were in my cricket-bag. **1658** E. PHILLIPS *Myst. Love & Eloq.*, Would my eyes had been beat out of my head with a *cricket ball. **1750** JOHNSON *Rambler* No. 30 ¶6 Sometimes an unlucky boy will drive his cricket-ball full in my face. **1909** *Daily Chron.* 10 Feb. 5/3 A neighbouring cricket-ball factory. **1873** L. TROUBRIDGE *Jrnl.* in J. Hope-Nicholson *Life amongst Troubridges* (1966) ii. 9 A blue and white *cricket cap on the back of his head. **1916** E. F. BENSON *David Blaize* iii. 35 The school eleven cricket-cap which he had won last week. **1731** *Daily Advertiser* 29 June, Eleven Gentlemen of Kent, belonging to Esquire Steed's *Cricket-Club. **1755** (*title*), The Game at

Cricket, as settled by the Several Cricket Clubs. **1887** F. GALE *Game of Cricket* 153 Cricket clubs are very much larger affairs than they used to be. **1787** in H. T. Waghorn *Cricket Scores* (1899) Frontispiece, Representation of the Noble Game of Cricket, as played in the celebrated *Cricket Field near White Conduit House. **1884** HON. I. BLIGH in *Lillywhite's Cricket Ann.* 3 An eleven on an Australian cricket-field. **1825** in Hone *Everyday Bk.* I. 636, I was stunned with shouts..from the *cricket ground. **1827** E. NEALE *Living & Dead* 163 A dozen different *cricket jackets. **1903** *Cricket* 30 Apr. (Advt.), Cricket Jackets. Navy, Melton, Trimmed Ribbon, or Cord. **1677** in T. Barrett-Lennard *Fam. Lennard & Barrett* (1908) 317 The *crekitt match at ye Dick^er^. **1747** *Scheme Equip. Men of War* 37 In as great Esteem in London, as Cricket Matches are at this Day. **1955** *Times* 9 May 15/1 One travels not only to see a cricket match as such. **1890** *Cricket pitch [see PITCH *sb.*² 13]. **1654** in *N. & Q.* (1924) CXLVII. 325/1 *Cricket players on ye Lord's Day. *a* **1787** JENYNS *Imit. Hor. Epist.* II. i. (R.) Hence all her [England's] well-bred heirs Gamesters and jockies turn'd, and cricket players. **1851** J. PYCROFT *Cricket Field* xi. 214 Pugilists have rarely been cricket players. **1700** *Post Boy* 30 Mar. in *N. & Q.* 10th Ser. (1904) II. 394/2 Gentlemen, or others, who delight in *Cricket-playing. **1894** W. B. YEATS *Let.* 6 Aug. (1954) 234 Those vigorous fair-haired, boating, or cricket-playing young men. **1906** A. E. KNIGHT *Complete Cricketer* ix. 323 The Need of Cricket Playing. **1849** 'BAT' *Cricketer's Manual* (Advt.), Spiked soles for *cricket shoes. **1908** W. E. W. COLLINS *Country Cricketer's Diary* ii. 27, I should doubt whether he ever owned a pair of cricket-shoes in his life. **1611** *Cricket-staffe [see above]. **1873** LD. W. P. LENNOX *Recoll. 1806–73* II. v. 106 Few gatherings are more delightful than the one that takes place annually at Canterbury during the *cricket week. **1916** E. F. BENSON *David Blaize* xiii. 256 There's a cricket week at Baxminster, and they've asked me to play in two matches. **1968** R. V. BESTE *Repeat Instructions* xi. 121 A local festivity such as a cricket week.

cricket ('krɪkɪt), *sb.*³ Also 7 -it, krickett. [This and the parallel form CRACKET appear in the 17th c. Cf. also CROCK *sb.*⁵; the ulterior history is unknown.

Connexion has been suggested with LG. *kruk-stool*, pl. *-stöle*, according to the *Bremische Wörterbuch* 1767, 'the movable seats in churches for women of the lower ranks.']

A low wooden stool; a foot stool. Now *local.*

a **1643** W. CARTWRIGHT *Lady Errant* v. i. (1651) 69 I'l stand upon a Crickit, and there make Fluent Orations to 'em. **1688** R. HOLME *Armoury* III. 291/2 A kind of low footed stool, or Cricket as some call it. **1691** SHADWELL *Scowrers* 11, I went thither [to Westminster Hall], expecting to find you upon a Cricket, civilly taking Reports. **1713** *Guardian* No. 91 That he..hath privily conveyed any large book, cricket, or other device under him, to exalt him on his seat. **1740** GRAY *Wks.* (1827) 78 Nine chairs..five stools, and a cricket. **1848** MRS. GASKELL *M. Barton* xxiv, Mary drew her little cricket out from under the dresser, and sat down at Mrs. Wilson's knees. **1880** MISS YONGE *Bye Words* 220 He gave us each a little cricket to sit upon.

b. Also *cricket-stool.* (Cf. Sc. *crackie-stool.*)

1694 S. JOHNSON *Notes on Lett. Bp. Burnet* 1. 104 [She] threw her Cricket-stool at his Head. **1708** MOTTEUX *Rabelais* IV. xxx. (1737) 126 His Reason, like a Cricket Stool.

cricket ('krɪkɪt), *v.* [f. CRICKET *sb.*²] *intr.* To play cricket.

c **1809** BYRON in *Lett. & Jrnls.* (1830) I. 63 [At Harrow] I was always cricketing—rebelling—fighting—rowing. **1847** TENNYSON *Princ.* Prol. 159 They boated and they cricketed. **1861** G. MEREDITH *Evan Harrington* I. xv. 294 You can cricket, and you can walk.

cricketana (krɪkɪ'tɑːnə). [f. CRICKET *sb.*² + ANA *suff.*] **a.** Literature, sayings, or items of gossip about cricket. **b.** Collectable objects associated with cricket; cricket memorabilia.

1862 *London Society* Aug. 114 (*heading*) Cricketana. No. I.—The Two 'All England' Elevens. **1944** BLUNDEN *Cricket Country* 48 After this I seldom heard any cricketana. **1950** W. HAMMOND *Cricketers' School* ix. 89 Collection of cricket books, prints, autographs, photographs and general cricketana. **1979** *Sunday Mail* (Brisbane) 1 Apr. 34/2 Phillips is holding a second sale of cricketana. This time, they are offering tennis and golf 'antiques' too. **1980** *Country Life* 3 Apr. (Phillips Sales Preview) p. xv. (*caption*) *Cricketana*... A Bilston enamel patchbox, the cover decorated with a view of a cricket match. **1987** *Times* 13 June 24/1 The newly formed Cricket Memorabilia Society..is an organization founded this year for those strange people.. who express their devotion to the game by collecting caps, bats, books,..tour brochures, videos or any other items of what they call 'cricketana'.

† **cricket-a-wicket.** *Obs.* (See quots.)

1598 FLORIO, *Sgrillare*, to make a noise as a cricket, to play cricket-a-wicket, and be merry. *Ibid.*, *Tarabara*, higledi-pigledie, helter skelter, cricket a wicket. **1611** —— *Frittfritt*, as we say cricket a wicket, or gigaioggie.

cricket-bat. 1. = BAT *sb.*² 3 a.

1743 BULKELEY & CUMMINS *Voy. S. Seas* 130 The Indians had nothing in their Hands but a Club, like to our Cricket-Batts. **1860** *All Year Round* No. 53. 58, I observe a sheaf of cricket-bats in the corner. **1900** *Daily News* 9 June 6/5 Each has been engaged on his particular branch of the work of cricket bat making. **1964** W. L. GOODMAN *Hist. Woodworking Tools* 37 The cricket-bat maker's side-axe.

2. *cricket-bat willow* = *bat-willow* (see BAT *sb.*² V).

1926 G. C. DRUCE *Flora of Bucks.* 314 Salix alba, var. caerulea. Cricket-bat Willow. This occurs as a female planted tree, sometimes 100 ft. high. **1933** *Discovery* Feb. 66/1 There is more than one botanical variety being grown under the name of 'cricket-bat willow'. **1955** G. GRIGSON *Englishman's Flora* 257 Cricket bats, from the Cricket Bat willow, which is *Salix alba* var. *coerulea.*

cricketer ('krɪkɪtə(r)). [f. CRICKET *sb.*² or *v.* + -ER¹.] One who plays cricket.

c **1742** J. LOVE *Cricket* 4 The robust Cricketer, plays in his Shirt. **1773** *Gentl. Mag.* XLIII. 451 To see the Surrey cricketers Out-bat them and out-bowl. **1861** HUGHES *Tom Brown at Oxf.* xxv. (1889) 237 A coach covered with cricketers returning from a match drove past the window.

cricketess: see CRICKETRESS.

cricketing (krɪkɪtɪŋ), *vbl. sb.* [f. as CRICKETER + -ING¹.] Playing cricket.

1771 in H. T. Waghorn *Cricket Scores* (1899) 74 After the cricketing there was a match at running. **1772** *Ibid.* 78 A cricket-match was played in Mr. Louch's cricketing-field. **1808** HUGHSON *London* V. 257 A handsome plain.. appropriated to cricketings and similar diversions. **1884** W. C. SMITH *Kildrostan* 68 Some of them prefer Boating or boxing, cricketing or hunting. **1955** *Times* 16 July 2/5 One of the great events of the cricketing year.

attrib. **1824** MISS MITFORD *Village* Ser. I. (1863) 205 Joel ..arrayed in a new jacket, and thin cricketing-pumps.

'cricketing, *ppl. a.* [f. as prec. + -ING².] That plays cricket.

1823 M. R. MITFORD in *Lady's Mag.* July 386/1 One club of cricketing dandies encounters another such club. **1850** 'BAT' *Cricketer's Man.* 31 Kent, Surrey, and Hampshire.. had the credit of being the only cricketing counties. **1880** *Birm. Weekly Post* 2 Oct. 1/6 The late Mr. G. F. Grace, one of the three celebrated cricketing brothers.

cricketress ('krɪkɪtrɪs). Also *erron.* cricketess. [f. CRICKETER + -ESS.] A female cricketer.

1886 *Halstead Gaz.* 16 Sept. 4/5 One of the fair 'Cricketesses'. **1890** *Pall Mall G.* 2 June 2/2 Miss Austen played cricket..All Alfred Mynn's sisters were famous cricketresses. **1963** *Times* 20 Apr. 3/7 (Advt.), Since '63 you've saved the guesses Of cricketers and cricketesses.

crickety ('krɪkɪtɪ), *a.* [f. CRICKET *sb.*¹ + -Y.] Cricket-like.

1835 *Fraser's Mag.* XII. 497 The small cricketty sound of the beetle. **1846** HAWTHORNE *Mosses* II. vii. 119 He has that cricketty sort of liveliness.

crickey, var. CRIKEY *int.*

'cricking, *vbl. sb.* See CRICK *v.*²

crickle ('krɪk(ə)l), *v.* [Echoic.] *intr.* To make a sharp, thin sound; to make a succession of sharp sounds. Hence **'crickle** *sb.*

1883 STALLYBRASS tr. *Grimm's Teut. Myth.* III. 929 You hear him [*sc.* the wild hunter] bluster in the air, so that it 'crickles and crackles'. **1926** *U.F. Ch. Mission Rec.* Aug. 361/1 There ran a crickle of wind in the thatch.

crickle-crackle. [Redupl. of CRACKLE: cf. CRICK-CRACK.] Repetition of crackling.

1637 N. WHITING *Hist. Albino & Bellama* 130 (N.) We this night With crickle-crackle will the gobblins fright. **1914** W. J. LOCKE *Fortunate Youth* xiii, I like to feel that He's in the wind or in the crickle-crackle of the earth.

† **'crickling,** *vbl. sb. nonce-wd.* Onomatopœic modification of *crackling*, expressing a lighter or more slender sound. With quot. 1644 cf. CRICK *sb.*¹

1577 DEE *Relat. Spir.* I. (1659) 93 The frame of the stone gave a crickling, no hand touching it. *a* **1644** QUARLES *Virgin Widow* IV. i. Wks. (Grosart) III. 305/1 Has any Courtier lost his haire? Or finds a crickling in his hammes?

crico- ('kraɪkəʊ), comb. form of Gr. κρίκος = κίρκος ring, used in *Anat.* in sense 'pertaining to or connected with the cricoid cartilage', as **crico-ary'tenoid** *a.*, pertaining to the cricoid and arytenoid cartilages; also *sb.* (*sc.* muscle); **crico-'thyroid** *a.*, pertaining to the cricoid and thyroid cartilages; also *sb.* (*sc.* muscle); hence **crico-'thyroidean** *a.*; so ***crico-pharyngeal, -tracheal.*** **cri'cotomy,** the operation of dividing the cricoid cartilage.

1842 E. WILSON *Anat. Vade M.* 272 The crico-thyroidean membrane. **1847** TODD *Cycl. Anat.* III. 101/1 The crico-thyroid muscles. **1878** T. BYRANT *Pract. Surg.* (1879) II. 31 The crico-thyroid arteries.

cricoid ('kraɪkɔɪd), *a.* and *sb. Anat.* [ad. mod.L. *cricoīdēs*, a. Gr. κρικοειδής ring-shaped, f. κρίκο-ς = κίρκος ring + -ειδής -form. Formerly used in L. form.]

A. *adj.* Ring-shaped; applied *spec.* to the ring-shaped cartilage which forms the lower and back part of the larynx.

[**1727–51** CHAMBERS s.v., The cartilage cricoides.] **1746** R. JAMES *Introd. Moufet's Health's Improv.* 5 The broad posterior Surface of the Cricoide Cartilage. **1861** F. H. RAMADGE *Curab. Consumpt.* 36 Between the first ring of the trachea and the cricoid cartilage.

B. *sb.* The cricoid cartilage.

[**1706** PHILLIPS (ed. Kersey), *Cricoides*, the Gristle of the Larynx, or top of the Wind-pipe, shaped like a Ring. **1727–51** CHAMBERS s.v. *Crico-arytænoidæus*, In the posterior and lower part of the cricoides.] **1842** E. WILSON *Anat. Vade M.* 492 The Cricoid is a ring of cartilage, narrow in front and broad behind. **1872** HUXLEY *Phys.* vii. 179 A great ring of Cartilage, the Cricoid, which forms, as it were, the top of the windpipe.

cri'coidean, *a.* = CRICOID. (*Syd. Soc. Lex.*)

‖ **cri de cœur** (kridəkœr). Also cri du cœur. [Fr., lit. 'cry of' or 'from (the) heart'.] An utterance of distress or anguish; also *fig.*

1905 G. K. CHESTERTON in *Daily News* 1 July 6/4 After this innocent cri de cœur of mine, I thought at first there would be a fight. **1909** BEERBOHM *Yet Again* 125, I could no more 'dash off' this my *cri de cœur* than I could an elegy on a broomstick I had never seen. **1928** D. H. LAWRENCE *Lady Chatterley* vii. 88 She needed help, and she knew it; so she wrote a little 'cri du cœur' to her sister. **1950** A. L. ROWSE *Eng. of Eliz.* x. 414 The Bishop's pathetic *cri de cœur.*

crie, obs. form of CRY.

cried (kraɪd), *ppl. a.* [f. CRY *v.* + -ED.] Proclaimed by crying or loud calling, announced.

Chiefly in *cried fair* (Sc.), a fair proclaimed by public announcement; ***cried up***, extolled: the opposite of ***cried down*** or *decried.*

1642 FULLER *Holy & Prof. St.* III. xxii. 213 A cried-up Beauty makes more for her own praise then her husbands profit. *a* **1679** EARL ORRERY *Tryphon*, Epilogue, A cry'd-down play. **1813** G. ROBERTSON *Agric. Surv. Kincard.* xvi. 407 Drumlithie Michael fair for cattle..followed..by what is called a Cried fair, so distinguished, by being audibly proclaimed at this. **1837** LOCKHART *Scott* (1839) VII. 85 Sir Walter's house was in his own phrase 'like a cried fair' during several weeks after the King's departure. **1886** MRS. CADDY *Footsteps Jeanne D'Arc* 228 Another of these much-cried-up spires.

cried, created: see CREE *v.*¹

criell: see CRYAL.

crier ('kraɪə(r)). Forms: 4–5 criere, -are, -our, cryour, 5–6 cryar, 6 criar, 5–9 cryer, 4– crier. [ME. *criere*, a. OF. *criere*, nom. of *crieur*, agent-n. f. *crier* to CRY: see -ER.]

1. *gen.* One who cries.

c **1380** WYCLIF *Serm.* Sel. Wks. II. 11 Joon was a vois of a Criere in desert. **1593** NASHE *Christ's T.* (1613) 105 You are none of these cryers vnto God. **1748** RICHARDSON in *Four C. Eng. Lett.* 196 Simplicity is all their cry; yet hardly do these criers know what they mean by the noble word. **1767** S. PATERSON *Another Trav.* II. 5 Some will join the cryers-up, and others the cryers-down. **1892** *Harper's Mag.* 269/1 You were always a pretty crier, mother.

2. *spec.* **a.** An officer in a court of justice who makes the public announcements, acts as preserver of order, etc.

[**1292** BRITTON I. xxii. §18 Et des criours, si nul prenge plus qe le establisement de noster estatut.] *c* **1400** *Apol. Loll.* 8 If a bedel, or criare, schewe þe fre graunt of his lord. **1541** *Act 33 Hen. VIII*, c. 12 §19 The saide clerkes..shal.. appoint a criar to make proclamacions, and to call the iuries, and to do other thinges as becometh a criar of a court to do. *a* **1633** AUSTIN *Medit.* (1635) 195 The Crier goes before the Judge. **1768–74** TUCKER *Lt. Nat.* (1852) II. 445 Their crier calls out, 'Make way for the grand jury!' **1882** SERJT. BALLANTINE *Exper.* xvi. 158 A remark made by the crier of the court to a friend.

b. One appointed in a town or community to make public announcements; a COMMON, or TOWN *crier.*

1387 TREVISA *Higden* (Rolls) I. 247 (Mätzn.) A cryour schulde stonde vppon a toure, and..he schulde crie: *Calo.* *a* **1400** *Barlaam & Josaphat* 348 A Crior to stonde þer ate Wiþ a Trompe for to blowe þat alle men mihte hit wel i knowe. *c* **1440** *Promp. Parv.* 103/1 Cryar, he þat cryethe yn a merket, or in a feyre, *declamator, preco.* *a* **1533** LD. BERNERS *Huon* xxvii. 84 Get a cryer and make to be cryed in euery merket place and strete. **1680** *Lond. Gaz.* No. 1529/4 Whoever can give notice of him to..the City Cryer, they shall be well rewarded. **1726** LEONI *Alberti's Archit.* II. 6 b, All common Cryers were excluded from the Temple. **1837** W. IRVING *Capt. Bonneville* II. 265 Repeated by a crier for the benefit of the whole village.

c. One who cries goods for sale: †(*a*) as auctioneer or agent for others (*obs.*); (*b*) as hawker on his own account.

1553 GRIMALDE *Cicero's Offices* (1556) 107 To put the goodes of the citizens in ye cryers mouthe. **1598** FLORIO, *Incantare*..to sell goods by a crier, at who giues most. **1653** H. COGAN *Pinto's Trav.* iv. 8, I was the first that was put to sale: whereupon, just as the Cryer was offering to deliver me unto whomsoever would buy me. **1727** POPE *Art of Sinking* 115 Common cryers and hawkers, who by redoubling the same words persuade people to buy their oysters, green hastings, or new ballads. **1843** LYTTON *Last Bar.* II. i, The whole ancient family of the London criers. *c* **1850** *Arab. Nts.* (Rtldg.) 683 He saw a crier going about with a carpet.. which he offered to put up for sale.

†**3.** ? A kind of small bell used as a call. *Obs.*

1467 *Will of Langewith* (Somerset Ho.), A small belle called a cryer.

crik (*to cry crik*): see CREAK *v.* 5.

† **crike.** *Obs.* Also 4 crice. [a. ON. *kriki* 'crack, corner, recess', used also of parts of the body, as in *handarkriki* arm-pit, *lærkriki*, Du. *laarkrig* the groin. Cf. CREEK *sb.*¹ 4.]

1. The anal cleft, *rima podicis.*

c **1300** HAVELOK 2450 On a scabbed mere, His nese went [=turned] un-to the crice, So ledden he þat fule swike.

2. A variant of CREEK *sb.*¹ in various senses.

† **criket.** *Obs.* [f. *crike*, CREEK + -ET¹, corresponding to a possible F. *criquette*, dim. of *crique.*] A small creek.

1538 LELAND *Itin.* III. 38 There is a Criket betwixt Poulpirrhe and Low.

crikey ('kraɪkɪ), *int. colloq.* or *slang*. Also crickey, cricky; see also CRACKEY *int.*. [As this alliterates with *Christ*, or L. *Christe!* it was perh. originally one of the alliterative or assonant substitutes for sacred names, used to avoid the appearance of profanity: cf. CRIMINE.] An exclamation of astonishment.

1838 *Actors by Daylight* I. 24 Crikey, oh crikey! How very flat, stale and abominable Seem to me all the acting of this world. **1842** BARHAM *Ingol. Leg., Auto-da-fé*, It would make you exclaim..if an Englishman, Crikey! **1884** *Harper's Mag.* Oct. 693/1 Cricky! didn't she go it, though! **1922** JOYCE *Ulysses* 223 Crickey, is there nothing for us to eat? **1924** D. H. LAWRENCE & SKINNER *Boy in Bush* 85 Crickey! Stop up another night! It'ud make ye sawney. **1960** J. RAE *Custard Boys* I. i. 16 Crikey, I thought, he's tough.

crile. *north. dial.* Also 7 creil, 7–8 croyll, croil. [Cf. Du. *kriel* dwarf; the forms present phonetic difficulties.] A dwarfed or stunted person.

a **1605** MONTGOMERIE *Flyting* 295 That cruiked, camschoche croyll, vncristned, they curse. **1691** TOMLINSON in Ray *N.C. Words, Creil*, a short, stubbed, dwarfish man. *Northumb.* **1728** RAMSAY *Fables & Tales, Ep. Duncan Forbes* viii, Thy wit's a croil, thy judgment's blind. **1818** HOGG *Brownie of B.* I. 13 (Jam.) A wee bit hurklin crile.

†**crim**, *v. Obs.* or *dial.* In 5 **kreme, kryme,** 6 **crym(me,** 8 **cream.** [The form would be satisfied by an OE. **crymman*:—**krumjan*, f. *cruma*, CRUMB, *sb.*, q.v.] *trans.* To crumble (bread, etc.); to scatter crumbs upon or into (a dish). **b.** *intr.* To crumble, fall to pieces.

c **1430** *Two Cookery-bks.* 35 Take hard ȝolkys of Eyroun, & kryme a gode quantyte þer-to. **1530** PALSGR. 501/2, I crym breed into a dysshe..Thou haste eaten thy potage or I can crymme my dyssche. **1736** PEGGE *Kenticisms, Cream*, to crumble. Hops, when they are too much dried, are said to cream, i.e. to crumble to pieces. 'To cream one's dish', to put the bread into it, in order to pour the milk upon it. **1880** in PARISH & SHAW *Kentish Gloss.* (? from Pegge).

crim, *sb. U.S.* and *Austral. slang* abbrev. of CRIMINAL *sb.* 2.

1909 in WEBSTER. **1953** K. TENNANT *Joyful Condemned* xxii. 212 Some of the fellow crims remarked on it in filthy language. **1970** *Tel.* (Brisbane) 29 June 4/1 (*headline*) Crims 'in turmoil'.

crimble, earlier form of CRUMBLE *v.* now *dial.*

crimble, *v. dial.* [Related to the root vb. **crimb-an*, OE. *crimman* to press, compress, and to *crumb* adj. contracted, bent, crooked, in the same way as *crimple* is to *crimp* vb. and *crump* adj.[1]: see CRIMPLE *v.* 2.] *intr.* To shrink, cringe, go shrinking from observation.

a **1825** FORBY *Voc. E. Anglia, Crimble*, to creep about privily, to sneak, to wind along unperceived. **1884** *Cheshire Gloss., Crimble*, to sneak out of an engagement. **1887** *S. Cheshire Gloss., Crimble, intr.* to cringe, to lift and draw together the shoulders..to avoid certain places, pick one's way.

crim. con. Abbreviation of *criminal conversation*, i.e. adultery. (See CRIMINAL *a.* 1.)

1770 FOOTE *Lame Lover* I. Wks. 1799 II. 56 You would not insinuate that she has been guilty of crim. con.? **1803** SOUTHEY *Eclogues* ix, His dead father; did no murder; Never sustain'd an action for crim. con. **1858** LD. ST. LEONARDS *Handy Bk. Prop. Law* xii. 77 The action of crim. con., that disgrace to the nation, has been abolished.

crime (kraɪm), *sb.* Also 4–6 **cryme.** [a. F. *crime*, in 12th c. *crimne*, ad. L. *crīmen* judgement, accusation, offence, f. root of *cer-n-ĕre*, *crē-tum* to decide, give judgement, etc.]

1. a. An act punishable by law, as being forbidden by statute or injurious to the public welfare. (Properly including all offences punishable by law, but commonly used only of grave offences.)

1382 WYCLIF *Acts* xxxiii. 29 Hauynge no cryme worthi the deeth, or bondis. *c* **1400** MAUNDEV. (1839) xxviii. 287 Ȝif the kyng him self do ony homycydie, or ony cryme. **1526** TINDALE *Acts* xxv. 16 The Cryme wher of he is accused. **1607** SHAKS. *Timon* III. v. 83 If by this Crime, he owes the Law his life. **1769** BLACKSTONE *Comm.* IV. 5 A crime, or misdemesnor, is an act committed, or omitted, in violation of a public law, either forbidding or commanding it. **1832** AUSTIN *Jurispr.* (1879) I. xix. 417 An offence which is pursued at the discretion of the injured party or his representative is a civil injury. An offence which is pursued by the Sovereign or by the subordinates of the Sovereign is a Crime. **1867** *Manch. Examiner* 10 Oct., With the moralist bribery is a sin; with the legislator a crime.

¶ ***a blunder worse than a crime***: see BLUNDER *sb.* 2.

b. *collective sing.* Action of such kind viewed collectively or abstractly; violation of law.

1485 CAXTON *St. Wenefr.* 3 Hast slayn by cryme as an homycyde this noble vyrgyn. **1760** GOLDSM. *Cit. W.* lxxiii, I was imprisoned, though a stranger to crime. **1879** FROUDE *Cæsar* viii. 72 Men steeped in crime. **1891** GLADSTONE in *Daily News* 3 Oct. 6/3 When they talk of crime in Ireland you must understand that the word bears a totally different meaning to what the word means in England.

2. a. More generally: An evil or injurious act; an offence, a sin; *esp.* of a grave character.

1514 BARCLAY *Cyt. & Uplondyshm.* (Percy Soc.) 11 Longe after this began this cursed cryme. **1526** *Pilgr. Perf.* (W. de W. 1531) 238 b, All yͤ crymes of yͤ tonge, as sclaunders.. and prevy backbytynges. **1604** SHAKS. *Oth.* v. ii. 26 If you bethinke your selfe of any Crime Vnreconcil'd as yet to Heauen, and Grace. **1667** MILTON *P.L.* I. 214 That with reiterated crimes he might Heap on himself damnation. **1706** ADDISON *Poems, Rosamond* I. i, 'Tis her crime to be loved, 'Tis her crime to have charms. **1842** MIALL *Nonconf.* II. 1 If in future we should go astray, we can plead no excuse in extenuation of the crime.

b. *collective sing.* Wrong-doing, sin.

c **1440** *Gesta Rom.* xxii. 74 (Harl. MS.) For no man may lyve withoute cryme. **1590** SPENSER *F.Q.* II. xii. 75 Whilest louing thou mayst loued be with equall crime. **1667** MILTON *P.L.* I. 79 One next himself in power, and next in crime. **1865** WHITTIER *Laus Deo* ii, Ring, O bells! Every stroke exulting tells Of the burial hour of crime.

†**3.** Charge or accusation; matter of accusation.

c **1386** CHAUCER *Sec. Nun's T.* 455 For we bere a cristen name Ye putte on vs a cryme and eek a blame. **1526** *Pilgr. Perf.* (1531) 66 b, To whome, they beynge most innocent, hath ben put the cryme of fornicacyon. **1568** GRAFTON *Chron.* II. 92 The common people raysed a great cryme upon the Archbishop. **1667** MILTON *P.L.* IX. 1181, I rue That errour now, which is become my crime, And thou th' accuser.

4. *Comb.* ***crime-drama, fiction, film, magazine, -mystery, novel, play, -preventers, -prevention, -proneness, -romance, -story***; ***crime-promoting, -prone, -stained*** adjs.; **crime-buster** *slang*, one who represses organized crime; **crime reporter**, a reporter (sense 2 b) who describes crimes and the trials of criminals; **crime sheet**, in the army, a list in which the names of offenders and their offences are entered; **crime wave**, a sharp rise in the incidence of crime; **crime-writer**, an author who writes about fictional crimes; hence ***crime-writing***.

1952 *Manch. Guardian Weekly* 31 July 7/1 The tall prim *crime-buster came forward. **1962** K. ORVIS *Damned & Destroyed* i. 9 A man who takes pleasure in being called crime-buster promotes without delay to put vice on ice in Montreal. **1933** P. GODFREY *Back-Stage* ix. 119 An English school of *crime-drama arose and flourished. **1924** C. S. MONTANYE in *Saucy Stories* Jan. 41/2, I write *crime fiction for the magazines. **1936** *Daily Tel.* 16 Oct. 7/2 'Middle Class Murder' is first-class crime fiction. **1935** *Ann. Reg. 1934* II. 307 A cinema in Chicago where he was enjoying a '*crime film'. **1940** J. CARY *Charley is My Darling* xi. 63 Charley is telling stories out of some *crime magazine. **1906** *Daily Chron.* 26 May 7/5 The many strange features of the case certainly make it one of the most remarkable *crime-mysteries which have occupied the attention of the London police for some years. **1889** *Sat. Rev.* 16 Mar. 329/1[These] are both *crime-novels. **1952** GRANVILLE *Dict. Theatr. Terms* 53 **Crime play*, a thriller featuring murder, theft, or crime generally. **1888** *Pall Mall G.* 10 Oct., The thief-takers and *crime-preventers of London. **1928** HECHT & MACARTHUR *Front Page* II. 71 The time to catch 'em is while they're little kids. That's the whole basis of my *crime prevention theory. **1944** 'G. ORWELL' in *Horizon* Oct. 240 The distinction between crime and crime-prevention practically disappears. **1823** MILL *Autobiogr.* (1924) 273 The Catholic priesthood added..the *crime-promoting doctrine of indulgences. **1960** L. T. WILKINS *Delinquent Generations* 1 Children born during the war might be more *crime-prone than others. *Ibid.* 8 The greatest '*crime-proneness' is thus found to be associated with that birth group. **1936** 'J. TEY' *Shilling for Candles* xix. 200 He.. might be only a *crime reporter, but he knew just as much about crime..as any police force. **1951** WODEHOUSE *Old Reliable* iv. 48 Bill in her time had been..crime reporter, sob sister, [etc.]. **1906** *Daily Chron.* 15 May 3/5 All the stock characters of..*crime-romance are here. **1915** D. O. BARNETT *Lett.* 41 Spent the morning filling up '*crime sheets' with all their offences. **1917** EMPEY *From Fire Step* 150 The Sergeant-Major keeps what is known as the Crime Sheet. When a man commits an offence, he is 'Crimed'—that is, his name, number, and offence is entered on the Crime Sheet. [**1886** AINSLIE *Reynard the Fox*, The rascal Reynard, crime-bestained.] **1898** *Westm. Gaz.* 14 July 2/1 She wondered..what manner of hideous *crime-stained countenance that paper hid. **1934** J. CARTER *New Paths in Book Coll.* 35 Mystery stories, *crime stories, spy stories. **1936** 'G. ORWELL' *Keep Aspidistra Flying* xi. 295 Fools demanding crime-stories and sex-stories and romances. **1920** *Times* 21 Jan. 12/1 (*headline*) *Crime Wave. Murder, robbery and theft. **1945** *Daily Mirror* 8 Dec. 1/4 Scotland Yard..made a new move in its war against the mounting crime wave. **1946** 'M. INNES' *What happened at Hazelwood* III. i. 169 Amateur *crime-writers are just as painfully incompetent as amateur actors. **1959** *Times Lit. Suppl.* 24 Apr. 238/5 A category-debate about whether *crime-writing ought to grow closer to the straight novel and away from the master-mind detective story.

crime, *v.* [cf. OF. *crimer*, f. *crime*.] *trans.* To charge with a crime or offence; to accuse. Now esp. in army use.

1570 LEVINS *Manip.* 132/30 To cryme, *criminari*. **1621** W. SCLATER *Tythes* (1623) 140 [They] would..not crime him of couetousness in that demand. **1890** W. G. BROWNE in *19th Cent.* Nov. 846 He was crimed (i.e. charged before the colonel) with 'filthy dirtiness and disorderliness on parade'. **1917** [see *crime sheet*]. **1929** C. E. MONTAGUE in *Mercury Story Bk.* 178 You know, Sergeant, the sort of a squadroon it is where a man's never crimed. **1957** N. SQUIRE *Theory of Bidding* 213 East here has used his judgment... He has been slightly optimistic but cannot be crimed. **1957** E. HYAMS *Into the Dream* 91 He'd crime a man as soon as look at him.

Crimean (kraɪ'miːən), *a.* [f. *Crimea*, name of a peninsula lying between the Sea of Azov and the Black Sea, the chief seat of a war (1854–6) between Russia and Turkey (with its allies).] Of, pertaining to, or characteristic of the Crimea; ***Crimean Gothic***, name given to an East Germanic language, supposedly a dialect or descendant of Gothic, which continued to be used in the Crimea down to the sixteenth century; ***Crimean shirt***, a shirt worn by workers in the Australian and New Zealand bush (also *Crimea shirt*).

[**1591** G. FLETCHER *Russe Commonw.* XIX. 72ᵛ Some thinke that the Turkes tooke their beginning from the nation of the Chrim Tartars.] **1855** F. NIGHTINGALE *Let.* in C. Woodham-Smith *F. Nightingale* (1951) x. 231, I have now had all that this climate can give. Crimean fever. Dysentery. Rheumatism. **1855** (*title*) The illustrated Crimean war song-book of the allies. **1862** R. HENNING *Let.* 29 Aug. (1966) 96 He..had seen fit to array himself in a Crimean shirt which he put on *over* his other clothes. **1893** K. MACKAY *Out Back* (ed. 2) I. ix. 108 Crimean shirts, tight-cut moles, and light square-toed bluchers completed their costume. **1895** 'R. BOLDREWOOD' *Crooked Stick* iii. 80 A young man, whose Crimean shirt and absence of necktie denoted..the presumed abandon of bush life. **1899** M. BEERBOHM in *Sat. Rev.* 14 Jan. 45/1 An actor made up as a young 'swell', with glengarry, cheroot, and 'Crimean beard'! **1902** W. SATCHELL *Land of Lost* ii. 14 He wore a blue Crimea shirt open at the throat. **1913** J. D. JONES tr. *Loewe's Germanic Philol.* I. v. 16 Crimean Gothic can have been no real Gothic dialect, as it did not undergo the different changes common to East and West Gothic. **1927** M. M. BENNETT *Christison* x. 110 Christison gave Mickey a Crimean shirt. **1943** C. L. WRENN *Word & Symbol* (1967) 137 The famous 'Crimean Gothic'..rests on no other foundation than that of a hastily-written list of some seventy words and phrases which Busbecq thought he heard from two men who had been in the Crimea. **1958** A. S. C. ROSS *Etymology* II. 74 Germanic ..falls into three groups, the first containing only Gothic (texts of IV and VI C. A.D., also fragments of Crimean Gothic recorded 1560 A.D.), the other two being North and West Germanic. **1971** *Times* 1 Jan. 11/3 If some Baptists or Crimean Tatars or dissident writers tried to hijack an aircraft they would almost certainly be more severely dealt with than ordinary citizens.

crimeful ('kraɪmfʊl), *a.* [f. CRIME *sb.* + -FUL.] Full of or laden with crime; criminal.

1593 SHAKS. *Lucr.* 970 This cursed, crimefull night. **1602** —— *Ham.* IV. vii. 7 These feates, So crimefull, and so Capitall in Nature. **1877** TENNYSON *Harold* v. i, Bolts that fall on crimeful heads.

crimeless ('kraɪmlɪs), *a.* [f. as prec. + -LESS.] Free from crime; faultless, innocent.

1593 SHAKS. *2 Hen. VI*, II. iv. 63 So long as I am loyall, true and crimelesse. **1621** W. SCLATER *Tythes* (1623) 121 To pleade himselfe crimelesse of all irreuerence. **1834** *Tait's Mag.* I. 372 A nobler aim,—To be—the crimeless Washington of France! **1887** *Daily News* 25 July 4/7 Examples of crimeless districts.

Hence **'crimelessness.**

1887 *United Ireland* 2 Apr. 5/2 Evidence of the absolute crimelessness of the country.

‖**crime passionnel** (krim pasjɔnɛl). Also **crime passionel.** [Fr.] A crime due to passion; *spec.* a murder resulting from jealousy.

1910 *Encycl. Brit.* X. 86/1 In cases of what is termed 'crime passionel', French juries..almost invariably find extenuation. **1912** J. MASEFIELD *Widow in Bye Street* VI. 84 Two lawyers talked statistics, '"Crime passionel" in Agricultural Districts'. **1930** *Punch* 7 May 529/3 We too find the literature of the *crime passionnel* a trifle soporific. **1943** M. F. RODELL *Mystery Fiction* v. 35 The *crime passionel*, the crime of jealousy committed on the spur of the moment, makes poor material. **1955** *Times* 13 July 6/5 The case of Mrs. Ellis has..demonstrated in an extreme degree the fundamental difference between French and English law in relation to the *crime passionel*. **1969** *Times* 17 Nov. 6/6 A woman has been murdered in a *crime passionnel*.

crimes (kraɪmz), *int.* Later modification of CRIMINE *int.*

1874 in HOTTEN *Slang Dict.* s.v. *Crikey*. **1891** FARMER *Slang*, Crimini, Criminey, or Crimes. **1929** E. RAYMOND *Family that Was* II. ii, Crimes! I'm moving in the Upper Ten, I think.

crimesin, -yn(e, obs. ff. CRIMSON.

†**'criminable**, *a. Obs.* [f. L. type **crīminābilis*, f. *crīmināre* to criminate: see -BLE.] Indictable. Hence **'criminably** *adv.*, as a criminal.

1560 ROLLAND *Crt. Venus* IV. 495 Crimes criminabill. **1533** BELLENDEN *Livy* III. (1822) 223 To be accusit criminably.

criminal ('krɪmɪnəl), *a.* and *sb.* Also 5 **crymynalle, -el(l, cryminall, -el,** 6–7 **criminall.** [a. F. *criminel* (in Ch. de Roland, 11th c.), ad. L. *crīmināl-is* of or pertaining to crime; f. *crīmen* CRIME. See -AL[1].]

A. *adj.*

1. Of the nature of or involving a crime; more generally, of the nature of a grave offence, wicked.

criminal conversation (CONVERSATION 3): adultery, in the legal aspect of a *trespass* against the husband at common law. (*Obs.* in England since 1857.)

1430 LYDG. *Chron. Troy* II. xiii, She..a syn committed that was cryminall. **1590** SPENSER *F.Q.* I. iii. 16 Pillage.. which he had got abroad by purchas criminall. **1611** SHAKS. *Wint. T.* III. ii. 90 No Father owning it (which is indeed More criminall in thee, then it). **1759** JOHNSON *Rasselas* xxix, Ignorance, when it is voluntary, is criminal. **1768** BLACKSTONE *Comm.* III. 139 Adultery, or criminal conversation with a man's wife. **1817** W. SELWYN *Law Nisi Prius* (ed. 4) II. 710 A criminal neglect of duty. **1892** F.

Pollock *On Torts* (ed. 3) 210 Against an adulterer the husband had an action at common law, commonly known as an action of criminal conversation. In form it was generally trespass *vi et armis*, on the theory that 'a wife is not, as regards her husband, a free agent or separate person'.. Actions for criminal conversation were abolished in England on the establishment of the Divorce Court in 1857.

2. a. Relating to crime or its punishment.

1474 Caxton *Chesse* 25 Some causes ben crymynel and somme ben cyuyle. **1590** Sir J. Smyth *Disc. Weapons* **ij, Good lawes, civil and criminall. **1686** J. Sergeant *Hist. Monast. Conventions* 146 Having under him two Civil-Lieutenants..and one Lieutenant Criminal, with many Judges. **1745** *Fortunate Orphan* 200 She..sent immediately for the Judge Criminal. **1776** Gibbon *Decl. & F.* I. xvi. 390 They no longer possessed the administration of criminal justice. **1846** McCulloch *Acc. Brit. Empire* (1854) II. 173 The highest court of criminal judicature known to the laws of England is the House of Lords. **1887** Lowell *Democr.* 29 An experienced criminal lawyer.

b. ***criminal court***, a court (first in Scotland) having jurisdiction over criminal prosecutions.

[**1597** *Lawes & Actes* Table, s.v. *Courtes*, All Courtes, Civill and Criminall, suld be fensed at elleven houres before noone.] **1678** Mackenzie *Laws & Customes* 5 The decisions of our Criminal Court..do bind the same or succeeding Judges. **1788** *Desp. Paris* II. 53, I herewith send your Lordship the Resolutions of the Châtelet (one of the Criminal Courts). **1834** *Act* 4–5 *Will. IV* c. 36 §1, That the Lord Mayor.., the Lord Chancellor.., and all the Judges.. shall be and be taken to be the Judges of a Court to be called the 'Central Criminal Court'. **1910** *Encycl. Brit.* VII. 322/2 *Criminal Courts.*—(1) The lowest is that of the justice of the peace, sitting..to determine in a summary way certain specified minor offences.

c. ***criminal code***, a system of jurisprudence to be applied in criminal cases.

1788 *Desp. Paris* II. 91 Great offers have been made to the Grand Conseil to induce that Tribunal to recognize the new Criminal Code. **1829** *Observer* 19 Apr. 1/4 It is in vain that we pass measures for modifying the severity of our Criminal Code. **1878** *Times* 18 July 10/3 The Criminal Code.—The course..taken with reference to the Criminal Code Bill, of referring it to a Commission..will give..the assurance of a most acute and careful investigation.

3. a. Guilty of crime or grave offence.

c **1489** Caxton *Blanchardyn* xxix. 110 The vntrewe and crymynel tyraunt Alymodes. **16..** Rogers (J.), The neglect ..renders us criminal in the sight of God. **1644** Prynne *Moder. Apol.* 1 Being..taxed by Master Iames Howell..as criminall of offering him very hard measure. **1726** *Adv. Capt. R. Boyle* 362 If criminal Persons were sent over there, they would find Employment. **1741** Watts *Improv. Mind* I. iv. §14 Let us search our hearts..and enquire how far we are criminal. **1851** Hussey *Papal Power* iii. 144 Criminal clerks had not yet..exemption allowed them from all civil tribunals.

†**b.** Of beasts: Savage, fierce, malignant. *Obs.*

c **1477** Caxton *Jason* 86 The most terrible and most crymynel dragon. **1481** —— *Myrr.* II. vi. Kij, Bestes..so righte stronge & crymynell that no men dare approche them.

B. *sb.* †**1.** A person accused of a crime. *Obs.*

1634 W. Tirwhyt tr. *Balzac's Lett.* 18 The number of Judges is not much inferiour to that of Criminals. **1681** Dryden *Sp. Fryar* (J.), Was ever criminal forbid to plead?

2. A person guilty or convicted of a crime.

a **1626** Bacon (J.), Ruined..by justice and sentence, as delinquents and criminals. **1651** Hobbes *Leviath.* II. xxvii. 157 In the violation of the Law, both the Author, and Actor are Criminalls. **1772** Priestley *Inst. Relig.* (1782) I. 53 Take notice of crimes, and punish the criminals. **1883** G. Lloyd *Ebb & Flow* II. 210 Going with the criminal to execution.

criminaldom ('krɪmɪnəldəm). *nonce-wd.* The realm of criminals; criminals collectively.

1887 *Spectator* 5 Nov. 1515 The very dregs of French criminaldom.

criminalism ('krɪmɪnəlɪz(ə)m). The condition or practice of a criminal.

1877 Besant & Rice *Son of Vulc.* I. VIII. 84 Sunk into the slough of habitual criminalism. **1891** *Daily News* 13 May 7/1 A Past Master in the Art of Convicted Criminalism.

criminalist ('krɪmɪnəlɪst). [mod. f. L. *crīmināl-is* CRIMINAL + -IST. Cf. F. *criminaliste* (1715 in Hatzfeld).] One versed in criminal law; a writer on criminal law.

a **1631** Donne *Ess.* (1651) 97, I haue read in some of the Criminalists. **1831** *Edin. Rev.* LIV. 188 Consulting the.. criminalists of different nations. **1892** *N.Y. Nation* 15 Sept. 203/3 The theories advanced by the anthropological school of criminalists.

criminalistic (ˌkrɪmɪnə'lɪstɪk), *a.* [f. CRIMINAL *a.* and *sb.* or CRIMINAL(ISM + -ISTIC; cf. next.] Of or pertaining to criminalism; with a tendency towards criminality.

1924 F. H. Allport *Social Psychol.* vi. 136 The converse, that all who have such attitudes are criminalistic, is far from true. **1936** S. & E. Glueck *Preventing Crime* i. 3 The more 'inflammables' (such as poverty, broken and distorted home life..and the like) that can be removed from the environment of childhood and youth, the less possibility is there of criminalistic conflagration. **1945** —— *After-conduct of Discharged Offenders* vii. 84 The acquisition of a certain degree of maturation..is significantly related to changes in criminalistic behaviour. **1967** A. Boucher *Best Amer. Detective Stories* 221 Locard was ..one of the great initiators of modern criminalistic science.

criminalistics (ˌkrɪmɪnə'lɪstɪks), *sb. pl.* [ad. G. *kriminalistik* (Gross 1897), f. CRIMINAL *a.* and *sb.* + -ISTIC.] (See quot. 1949.)

1949 O'Hara & Osterburg *Criminalistics. The Application of the Physical Sciences to the Detection of Crime* p. x, The authors have decided, for the purposes of the present text, to use the name *criminalistics* in referring to the work of the police laboratory. This is not entirely a neologism. The words *Kriminalistik*, *criminalistique*, and *criminalistica* are in common use in continental Europe... We shall define *criminalistics* as that science which applies the physical sciences in the investigation of crimes. **1961** L. Radzinowicz *In Search of Criminology* ii. 34 Too large a place was assigned to the technical aspects of criminalistics.

criminality (krɪmɪ'nælɪtɪ). [ad. F. *criminalité* or med.L. *crīminālitās* (see Du Cange), f. *crīminālis* CRIMINAL: see -ITY.] The quality or fact of being criminal.

1611 Cotgr., *Criminalité*, Criminalitie; a criminal action, case, or cause. **1774** Pennant *Tour Scot. in 1772*, 345 From habit it lost all the appearance of criminality. **1869** Lecky *Europ. Mor.* I. iii. 474 That doctrine of the criminality of error. **1869** J. Greenwood *7 Curses Lond.* 133 The growth of juvenile criminality.

b. (with *pl.*) A criminal act or practice.

1849 Stovel *Canne's Necess.* Introd. 30 Alleged as a chief point in the criminalities imputed to the Welsh.

criminally ('krɪmɪnəlɪ), *adv.* [f. CRIMINAL *a.* + -LY[2].]

1. According to criminal law.

1560 *1st Bk. Discip. Ch. Scot.* vii. (1836) 49 If any of the university be criminally persued. **1651** W. G. tr. *Cowel's Inst.* 210 It is in his choise..whether he will prosecute the party civilly or criminally. **1699** Ludlow *Mem.* III. 110 (R.) They thought not convenient to proceed against him criminally. **1885** *Law Reports 14 Q. Bench Div.* 202 The Attorney General..was entrusted by the constitution to sue for the King, either civilly or criminally.

2. In a criminal manner; so as to constitute crime.

16.. Rogers (J.), As our thoughts extend to all subjects, they may be criminally employed on all. **1758** S. Hayward *Serm.* xvii. 505 David..when he fell so criminally and so publickly. **1848** Macaulay *Hist. Eng.* I. 537 The earl's conduct..had been, as he afterwards thought, criminally moderate. **1886** *Law Times* LXXXI. 178/1 The co-respondent..proved that he had not been criminally intimate with the respondent.

†'**criminalness.** *Obs.* [f. as prec. + -NESS.] Quality or state of being criminal; = CRIMINALITY.

a **1660** Hammond *Wks.* II. 131 (R.) To..excuse our schism, or avert the criminalness of it. **1698** R. Fergusson *View Eccles.* 50 A proof of his Criminalness. **1755** in Johnson. **1775** Ash [see CRIMINALTY].

criminaloid ('krɪmɪnəlɔɪd). [f. CRIMINAL *sb.* + -OID.] A man with a tendency towards crime; a first offender as opposed to a habitual criminal.

1895 tr. *Lombroso & Ferrero's Female Offender* 308 A middle type between criminaloids and born criminals. **1909** *Westm. Gaz.* 5 Jan. 2/1 The common incarceration of offenders manufactures the criminal out of the juvenile, the criminaloid and the single offender.

†'**criminalty.** *Obs.* = CRIMINALITY.

1775 Ash, *Criminalty* (*not much used*), Criminalness. **1797** *Hist.* in *Ann. Reg.* 15/1 These were acts of criminalty for which..they would find no mercy.

criminate ('krɪmɪneɪt), *v.* [f. L. *crīmināt-*, ppl. stem of *crīminārī*, or *crīmināre* to accuse, charge with crime, f. *crīmen* CRIME.]

1. *trans.* To charge with crime; to represent as criminal.

1645 Pagitt *Heresiogr.* (1646) 62 They criminate the Dutch and French Churches. **1793** Gouv. Morris in Sparks *Life & Writ.* (1832) II. 386, I suppose the public servants will be criminated. **1816** Keatinge *Trav.* (1817) I. 134 We must begin in self-justification..by criminating those whom we mean to destroy. **1855** Macaulay *Hist. Eng.* III. 699 The noble penitent then proceeded to make atonement for his own crime by criminating other people.. guilty and innocent.

2. To prove (any one) guilty of crime; to incriminate.

1665 Glanvill *Sceps. Sci.* xii, Whom, I would not justifie myself, to criminate. **1791** *State Papers* in *Ann. Reg.* 160* They cannot be examined, criminated, or judged..with respect to what they have said, written, or performed. **1841** J. T. Hewlett *Parish Clerk* I. 129 Determined not to criminate himself by any allusion to the circumstance.

3. To represent or censure (a thing or action) as criminal; to blame severely, condemn.

a **1677** Ld. North *Light in Way to Paradise* (1682) 29 (T.) As for our church liturgy it is now criminated by many as idolatrous. **1792** W. Roberts *Looker-on* No. 43 (1794) II. 138 To criminate the motives and actions of mankind. **1828** D'Israeli *Chas. I*, I. xii. 327 Eliot descends to criminate the Duke's magnificent tastes.

Hence '**criminating** *ppl. a.*

a **1656** Ussher *Ann.* vi. (1658) 427 Spoken with a sterne countenance and criminating voice. **1786** Burke *W. Hastings* Wks. 1842 II. 210 Applying no stronger or more criminating epithets than those of 'improper, unwarrantable, and highly impolitick'. **1801** Mar. Edgeworth *Belinda* iii, A long criminating and recriminating chapter.

crimination (krɪmɪ'neɪʃən). [ad. L. *crīminātiōn-em*, n. of action from *crīmināre*: see prec.] The action of charging with a crime or grave offence; severe accusation or censure.

1583 Fulke *Defence* xvii. 512 You have placed your crimination in the first chapter. **1654** Trapp *Comm. Ps.* lxix. 4 Loaden with many calumnies and false criminations. **1786** Burke *W. Hastings* Wks. 1842 II. 231 The said Hastings hath established divers matters of weighty and serious crimination against himself. **1848** Macaulay *Hist. Eng.* II. 250 The criminations and recriminations of the adverse parties.

criminative ('krɪmɪnətɪv), *a.* [f. L. ppl. stem *crīmināt-* + -IVE.] Tending to or involving crimination; that charges with crime or grave offence; accusatory.

a **1734** North *Lives* I. 214 In such cases the courtiers are ..criminative against the judges..as being morose, ill-bred, and disrespectful. **1818** Jas. Mill *Brit. India* II. v. viii. 680 Their criminative representations against Macartney. **1849** Grote *Greece* II. lix. (1862) V. 248 The criminative orators were omnipotent.

criminator ('krɪmɪneɪtə(r)). [a. L. *crīminātor*, agent-n. from *crīmināre*: see CRIMINATE.] One who criminates, or charges with crime.

1609 Bible (Douay) *Lev.* xix. 16 Thou shalt not be a criminatour, nor a whisperer among the people. **1653** R. Baillie *Disswasive Vindic.* (1655) 76 A false Criminator. **1812** Shelley *Let. to E. Hitchiner*, The opinion of the world is not the likeliest criminator to impeach their credulity.

criminatory ('krɪmɪnətərɪ), *a.* [f. L. type *crīminātōrius*, f. *crīminātor*: see prec. and -ORY.] Involving or relating to crimination.

1576 Fleming *Panopl. Epist.* Bivb, An epistle.. Criminatorie. **1811** *Ann. Reg.* 1809, 159 A criminatory charge against an individual. **1868** E. Edwards *Raleigh* I. xviii. 370 No evidence criminatory of his master had been obtained from him.

crimine, -iny ('krɪmɪnɪ), *int.* Also **crimeny, -ini.** [perh. It. *crimine* crime, etc., as an ejaculation; but cf. CRIKEY, and the kindred ejaculation *jiminy*, GEMINI.] A vulgar exclamation of astonishment: now somewhat archaic.

1681 Otway *Soldier's Fort.* I. i, O crimine! Who's yonder? **1693** Southerne *Maid's last Prayer* III. i, O crimine! I see I must be plain with thee. *c* **1816** Byron (L.), Crimini, jimini! Did you ever hear such a nimminy pimminy Story as Leigh Hunt's *Rimini*? **1865** E. C. Clayton *Cruel Fortune* II. 184 Criminy!—Raymond tight. I am astonished.

†'**criminist.** *Obs.* ? = CRIMINALIST.

a **1631** Donne *Ess.* (1651) 53 Criminists have commanded Heresie, which is but Election..to..undertake a capitall and Infamous signification.

criminology (krɪmɪ'nɒlədʒɪ). [f. L. *crīmin-* CRIME + -(O)LOGY.] The science of crime; that part of anthropology which treats of crime and criminals.

1890 *Athenæum* 6 Sept. 325/2 We share Dr. Topinard's dislike of the term 'criminal anthropology', and may adopt the term 'criminology' till a better can be found. **1891** *Sat. Rev.* 28 Mar. 398/1 An examination and refutation of the new Italian 'criminology'.

So **crimino'logical** *a.*, **crimi'nologist**.

1857 *Sat. Rev.* III. 271/2 In the author of *Dark Deeds* we have a criminologist of a third sort. **1890** *Athenæum* 6 Sept. 325/3 The object of the criminologist is, first, to establish the existence and define the characteristics of a physical criminal type or types; second, to investigate the psychical phenomena associated with criminality. **1892** *Monist* II. 314 M. G. Tarde, the great criminologist..reviews the penological and criminological literature of recent times.

†**criminose**, *a.* *Obs.*$^{-0}$ [Cf. next]. Hence **criminosity**.

1727 Bailey vol. II., *Criminose*, ready to blame or accuse. *Criminosity*, Reproach, ill Report. **1775** in Ash.

criminous ('krɪmɪnəs), *a.* Also 5 **crymynous**, 6 **crimynous, cryminous**, *Sc.* **criminois.** [a. AFr. *criminous* = OF. *crimineux* (15th c. in Godef.), ad. L. *crīminōsus*, f. *crīmen* CRIME.]

†**1.** Of the nature of a crime; full of or marked by crime or grave offence; criminal. ? *Obs.*

1483 Caxton *Æsop* (1889) 63 The sayd shepherd commysed a crymynous dede. **1562** *Act 5 Eliz.* c. 23 §1 To continue their sinful and criminous Life. **1593** Norden *Spec. Brit. M'sex* I. 8 Carping at euerie fault, holding the smallest errour..verie criminous. **1674** P. du Moulin *Papal Tyranny* 47 A deeply criminous forgery. **1858** *Sat. Rev.* VI. 204/1 My criminous iambics.

2. Of persons: Guilty of crime. Now chiefly in the technical ***criminous clerk*** (see CLERK *sb.* 1).

1535 Stewart *Cron. Scot.* III. 535 Of his men War criminois vther nyne or ten. **1583** Stubbes *Anat. Abus.* II. (1882) 107 To giue sentence..vpon any criminous person. **1611** Speed *Hist. Gt. Brit.* IX. vi. (1632) 504 That Clerks criminous should be tried before secular Judges. **1659** Hammond *On Ps.* li. 4 Paraphr. 262 The most criminous rebell. **1722** Bp. Wilson in Keble *Life* xvi. (1863) 497 Tending to the encouragement of the criminous and refractory. **1847** Maskell *Mon. Rit.* III. p. cxxix, Of punishing criminous clerks. **1892** *Times* 29 Apr. 9/2 Bishops at present have to get rid of criminous clerks at a cost which is almost prohibitory.

†**3.** Of or relating to crime; accusing of crime; involving crimination. *Obs.*

1533 More *Debell. Salem* Wks. 995/2 Concerning great crimynous wytnesses to be taken in great criminal causes. **1600** Holland *Livy* II. vii. 48 Exposed unto criminous slanders. **1650** Bulwer *Anthropomet.* 124 Some..dare to make this criminous proposition against very Nature.

'**criminously**, *adv.* [f. prec. + -LY[2].]

1. In a criminous manner; criminally.

1640 Bp. Hall *Episc.* III. iv. 239 It ought to seeme incredible..that this man, who is Gods Priest, should live criminously. **1654** Hammond *Answ. Animadv. Ignat.* i. 10 So criminously guilty of it.

†**2.** With reference to crime; by way of crimination. *Obs.*

1603 KNOLLES *Hist. Turks* (1621) 1325 These wordes tooke crimonously in that place. **1625** tr. *Camden's Hist. Eliz.* I. (1688) 112 By accusing her criminously.

'criminousness. [f. as prec. + -NESS.] The state or quality of being criminous; criminality.

1648 *Eikon Bas.* 4, I could never be convinced of any such Criminousness in him. *a* **1715** BURNET *Own Time* II. 312 His words had no sort of criminousness, much less of treason in them. **1874** BP. MAGEE in *Rep. Comm. Ch. Patronage, Evid.* Quest. 31. 5 Within what limit of time would the bishop be allowed to allege criminousness on the part of a clerk?

crimison, crimosin(e, etc., obs. ff. CRIMSON.

crimmer, var. KRIMMER.

crimp (krɪmp), *sb.*[1] [Of uncertain origin.

(It might be connected with CRIMP *v.*[1], if the primary sense were 'to press or impress' (seamen, etc.); but this is very doubtful, for the general notion running through the senses appears to be that of 'agent, intermediary, broker, procurer'.)]

†**1.** Of doubtful meaning: used in reproach or derision. *Obs.*

1638 FORD *Fancies* I. ii, *Int.* What? thou fatten'st apace on capon still? *Spa.* Yes, crimp; 'tis a gallant life to be an old lord's pimp-whiskin.

2. An agent making it his business to procure seamen, soldiers, etc., esp. by seducing, decoying, entrapping, or impressing them.

Since the passing of the Merchant Shipping Act of 1854, applied to one who infringes sub-section 1 of this Act, *i.e.* to a person other than the owner, master, etc., who engages seamen without a license from the Board of Trade.

1758 J. BLAKE *Plan Mar. Syst.* 44 When a master of a ship ..hath lost any of his hands, he applies to a crimp..who makes it his business to seduce the men belonging to some other ship. **1796** STEDMAN *Exped. Surinam* II. 28 Trepanned into the West India Company's service by the crimps or silver-coopers as a common soldier. **1836** MARRYAT *Midsh. Easy* xxxviii. 144 Offering three guineas ahead to the crimps for every good able seaman. **1842** —— *P. Keene* xx. (1863) 173, I hear there are plenty of good men stowed away by the crimps at different places. **1839-40** W. IRVING *Wolfert's R.* (1855) 235 Sallying forth at night..he came near being carried off by a gang of crimps. **1887** *Spectator* 21 May 691/2 In the high and palmy days of the crimp, the pirate, the press-gang.

b. *transf.* and *fig.*

1789 WOLCOTT (P. Pindar) *Ep. Falling Minis.* Wks. 1812 II. 115 That sends to counties, borough-towns, his Crimps Alias his vote-seducing Pimps. **1794** —— *Rowl. for Oliver*, ibid. 198 Cupid's trusty crimp, By mouths of vulgar people christen'd pimp. *c* **1860** WRAXALL tr. *R. Houdin* xv. 207 Nothing..can shake off the grip of these skilful crimps [theatrical agents].

†**3.** An agent or contractor for unloading coal-ships; a broker. *Obs.*

a **1700** B. E. *Dict. Cant. Crew, Crimp*, one that undertakes for or agrees to unlade a whole ship of coals. **1754** STRYPE *Stow's Surv.* II. v. xiv. 319/1 Any Coal owner may employ ..crimps or Factors, not being lightermen or buyers of Coals for sale. **1769** *De Foe's Tour Gt. Brit.* II. 151 The Brokers of these Coals are called Crimps: The Vessels they load their Ships with at Newcastle, Keels. **1791** HUDDESFORD *Salmag.* (1793) 109 Crimps, and coal-heavers.

†**4.** *to play crimp*: see quots. *Obs.*

a **1700** B. E. *Dict. Cant. Crew, To play Crimp*, to lay or bet on one side, and (by foul play) to let t'other win, having a share of it. *Run a Crimp*, to run a Race or Horse-match.. knavishly. **1719** D'URFEY *Pills* II. 53 Let Jades that are founder'd be bought, Let Jockeys play Crimp to make sport. *Ibid.* 54 Another makes Racing a Trade..And many a Crimp Match has made, By bubbing another Man's Groom.

5. *Comb.*, as *crimp-like*, *-match* (see 4, quot. 1719).

1794 WOLCOTT (P. Pindar) *Rowl. for Oliver* Wks. II. 307 Crimp-like, for other regions, troops engaging.

crimp, *sb.*[2] [prob. f. CRIMP *v.*[1]] An obsolete game at cards.

1632 B. JONSON *Magn. Lady* II. i, Let her..Laugh and keep company at gleek or crimp. **1689** SHADWELL *Bury F.* I. i, Gallantry, mix'd now and then with Ombre, Crimp, Comet, or Incertain. **1703** *Eng. Lady's Catech.* in J. Ashton *Soc. Life Q. Anne* 70 Lost five Guineas at Crimp. **1710** ADDISON *Tatler* No. 250 ¶9 To find them about Midnight at Crimp and Basset. **1867** OUIDA *C. Castlemaine* (1879) 3 Regretted the loss of ten guineas at crimp.

attrib. **1712** ADDISON *Spect.* No. 457 ¶3 The private Transactions of the Crimp Table.

crimp (krɪmp), *sb.*[3] [f. CRIMP *v.*[1]]

1. a. *pl.* Crimped tresses: cf. 'curls'. *U.S.* Also *sing.*, a curl or (artificial) wave of the hair.

1867 A. D. WHITNEY *L. Goldthwaite* v. 97 I've brushed out half my crimps. **1870** L. M. ALCOTT *Old-Fashioned Girl* i. 1. It's too wet. Shouldn't have a crimp left if I went out such a day as this. **1883** *Century Mag.* XXV. 525/1 The Shaker sisters don't wear crimps. **1888** *Chicago Advance* 13 Dec., Crimps that had ceased to be crimpy.

b. (See quot. 1863.) orig. *U.S.*

1863 H. S. RANDALL *Pract. Shepherd* (ed. 7) vii. 75 Regularity and distinctness of 'crimp'—that curved and graceful form and arrangement of the locks and fibers in the sheared fleece which indicate extreme pliancy. **1874** *Rep. Vermont Board Agric.* II. 410 Fineness of fiber can be judged by its appearance to the eye, by its feeling when touched and by its fineness of crimp. *Ibid.* 411 Style of wool is judged by its crimp; the number of crimps to an inch of very fine wool is from twenty-seven to twenty-nine. **1956** G. BOWEN *Wool Away!* (ed. 2) xii. 143 The wool..is remarkably heavy, with..a very pronounced crimp.

c. *to put a crimp in* or *into*: to thwart or block; to impair or interfere with. *U.S. slang.*

1896 ADE *Artie* xii. 106 They'll put a crimp in him if things come their way. **1911** H. S. HARRISON *Queed* xxv. 321 They never forgive a man who puts a crimp into the party. **1918** *Nation* (N.Y.) 7 Feb. 166/1 All plans passed through their hands, and they took particular pleasure in putting a crimp into the Fire God. **1939** WODEHOUSE *Uncle Fred in Springtime* vi. 80 My prestige in the home is already low, and a substantiated charge of being A.W.O.L. would put a further crimp in it. **1969** *New Yorker* 27 Dec. 26/3 Finally, a giant black panther leaps upon me and devours my mind and heart. This puts a terrific crimp in my evening.

†**2.** Phrase. *to be in the crimps*: see quot. *Obs.*

1688 MIEGE *French Dict.* s.v., *To be in the Crimps*, or to be well set out in Clothes, *être bien paré*.

crimp (krɪmp), *a.* [app. radically allied to CRIMP *v.*[1]; perh. originally with the notion 'yielding to pressure, easily compressed'; cf. however MHG. *krimpf* crooked, curved (Kluge), and CRISP *a.* for the transition from 'curled, curly, crimped' to 'brittle, friable'. Cf. also CRUMP *a.*]

1. 'Friable, brittle, easily crumbled, easily reduced to powder' (J.); crisp.

1587 CHURCHYARD *Worth. Wales* (1876) 28 So fresh, so sweete, so red, so crimp withall As man may say, loe, Sammon here at call. **1699** EVELYN *Acetaria* (1729) 176 They will keep longer, and..eat crimp, and well tasted. **1708** J. PHILIPS *Cyder* II. (1727) 50 Now the Fowler..with swift early steps Treads the crimp Earth. **1725** BRADLEY *Fam. Dict.* s.v. *Sallet*, Slices of the whitened stems which being crimp and short are eaten with oil, vinegar, salt, and pepper. **18..** MRS. CAMERON *Careless Boy* 12 The grass was crimp and white with the hoar frost.

b. Hence *crimp-meat.*

1656 W. D. tr. *Comenius' Gate Lat. Unl.* ¶365 Som things also hee broileth on a gridiron, or frieth on a frying-pan, but if overmuch, they becom crimp-meat.

†**2.** *fig.* 'Not consistent, not forcible: a low cant word' (J.) *Obs.*

[But this alleged sense is founded only on the following passage, in which some edd. have *scrimp* = 'scant, limited, very sparing', which seems a better reading.]

1712 ARBUTHNOT *John Bull* II. iv, The evidence is crimp; the witnesses swear backwards and forwards, and contradict themselves.

3. Said of hair, feathers, etc.: Crimped.

1764 ANNA SEWARD in *Poet. Wks.* (1810) I. p. cxv, A bag wig, in crimp buckle, powdered white as the new shorn fleece. **1784** *New Spectator* iii. 4/2 The head is adorned.. with crimp feathers.

4. *Comb.*, as *crimp-frilled.*

1821 CLARE *Vill. Minstr.* II. 131 Crimp-frill'd daisy.

crimp (krɪmp), *v.*[1] [Corresponds to MDu. *crimpen* intr., to contract or draw oneself together, to shrink, become wrinkled or shrivelled (with cold, etc.), with weak causal *krempen, krimpen* to draw together, shrivel up, wrinkle, Du. *krimpen* to shrink, shrivel, diminish, E.Fris. *krimpen* trans. and intr., to crook, wind, draw in or together, shrink, become tight, compressed, shorter, or less, Da. *krympe* trans., to wrinkle, shrink (cloth), Sw. *krympa* to shrink, to sponge; OHG. *chrimphan*, MHG. *krimpfen* to draw oneself together convulsively. For ulterior etymology, see the note to CRAMP *sb.*[1] Not known in OE.; the only ME. example found is that in the intr. sense 1; otherwise the verb belongs to the 17–19th c., and may be the causal derivative.]

1. *intr.* To be compressed, pinched or indented (as e.g. the body of insects). (In ppl. a. *crimping.*)

1398 TREVISA *Barth. De P.R.* XVIII. i. (1495) 741 Beestys with crympynge body haue sharpe wytte and felynge..as bein and amptes that here and smel aferre.

†**2.** *trans.* To curl. (In pa. pple. *crimped.*) *Obs.*

1698 TYSON in *Phil. Trans.* XX. 112 The Verge or Rime of the outward Ear seem'd to be crimp'd. **1730-36** BAILEY (folio), *Crimpt*, curled.

3. To compress or pinch into minute parallel plaits or folds; to frill.

1712 ARBUTHNOT *John Bull* III. i, Crimpt ribbons in her head-dress. **1838** DICKENS *O. Twist* xiv, To crimp the little frill that bordered his shirt-collar. **1848** THACKERAY *Bk. Snobs* xxvii, The maid is crimping their..ringlets with hot tongs. **1859** LEWES *Sea-side Stud.* 157 By crimping or dividing the edge of the cup, prehensile organs of less or greater length and power arising thereby. **1861** SALA *Dutch Pict.* xix. 295 [She] thought far too much of crimping her tresses.

b. To wrinkle or crumple minutely, to crisp the surface of.

1772 W. BAILEY *Descr. Useful Machines* I. 229 The Italian method of crimping crapes. *Ibid.* I. 230 A large specimen of crape crimped and manufactured exactly like the Italian. **1821** CLARE *Vill. Minstr.* I. 209 The breeze, with feather-feet, Crimping o'er the waters sweet. **1883** E. PENNELL-ELMHIRST *Cream Leicestersh.* 398 The crimping, woolly effect of half a gale from the south-west.

c. *Techn.* To make flutings in (a brass cartridge case), so as to turn the end inward and back upon the wad, in order to confine the charge; to corrugate.

4. To cause (the flesh of fish) to contract and become firm by gashing or cutting it before *rigor mortis* sets in.

1698 LEEUWENHOEK in *Phil. Trans.* XX. 174 The Muscles of a Fish that has been dead for a good while, do not contract themselves when they are cut in Pieces, which we call Krimping. **1743** *Lond. & Country Brew.* III. (ed. 2) 170 The Cook cuts [a fresh Cod] into several small Pieces, in order, as they call it, to crimp it, by letting them lie in hard cold Spring-Water about an Hour. **1789** G. KEATE *Pelew Isl.* 302 The grey mullet, which they crimped, and frequently eat raw. **1804** A. CARLISLE in *Phil. Trans.* XCV. 23 The remarkable effects of crimping fish by immersion in water, after the usual signs of life have disappeared. **1867** F. FRANCIS *Angling* i. (1880) 39 Small chub..if crimped and fried dry, are by no means so bad.

b. *transf.* To slash, to gash.

1855 MOTLEY *Dutch Rep.* (1861) II. 359 Those who attempted resistance were crimped alive like fishes and left to gasp themselves to death in lingering torture. **1865** LUBBOCK *Preh. Times* xiii. (1869) 435 Among the females.. the only ceremony of importance was scarring the back. Eyre indeed calls it tattooing, but 'crimping' would be, I think, a more correct expression.

5. *spec.* To bend or mould into shape (leather for the uppers of boots, or for a saddle).

1874 KNIGHT *Dict. Mech.* 648/1 The curved bar which supports the form upon which the leather is crimped.

6. 'To pinch and hold; to seize' (Webster).

(No quotation given or source named.)

crimp (krɪmp), *v.*[2] [f. CRIMP *sb.*[1]] To impress (seamen or soldiers); to entrap, to decoy.

1812 WELLINGTON in Gurw. *Desp.* IX. 233 Plundering corn and crimping recruits. **1831** CARLYLE *Misc.* (1857) II. 326 Clutching at him, to crimp him or impress him. **1867** GOLDW. SMITH *Three Eng. Statesmen* (1882) 187 The cruel folly which crimps a number of ignorant and innocent peasants, dresses them up in uniform..and sends them off to kill and be killed. **1884** *Pall Mall G.* 26 Jan. 2/1 The Egyptian Government crimped negroes in the streets of Cairo.

fig. **1839** *Standard* Feb. 11 Why not create customers in the Queen's dominions..instead of trying..to crimp them in other countries?

crimp (krɪmp), *v.*[3] *nonce-wd.* [Partly echoic, but having associations with the primary sense of CRIMP *v.*[1]] To make a crisp sound, as in the compression of slightly frozen snow under the feet.

1834 GLEIG *Country Curate* II. xv. 267 A sound came upon me as of footsteps crimping through the snow.

†**crimp,** *v.*[4] *Obs. slang.* = To 'play crimp': see CRIMP *sb.*[1] 4.

a **1700** B. E. *Dict. Cant. Crew, He crimps it*, he plays booty. *A Crimping Fellow*, a sneaking Cur. So **1725** in *New Cant. Dict.*

crimpage ('krɪmpɪdʒ). [f. CRIMP *sb.*[1] + -AGE.] A payment made to a crimp for his services.

1754 STRYPE *Stow's Surv.* II. v. xiv. 319/1 Any coal owner may employ..crimps or factors..to dispose of their loadings and pay their crimpage or factorage. **1800** COLQUHOUN *Comm. Thames* xvi. 528 The Captain pays them two guineas crimpage. **1815** MAULE & SELWYN *Reports* III. 484 Disbursements..for crimpage to replace deserters during the repairs.

crimped (krɪmpt), *ppl. a.* Also crimpt.

†**1.** Curled: see CRIMP *v.*[1] 2. *Obs.*

2. Compressed or folded into minute parallel ridges or plaits, frilled.

1712 [see CRIMP *v.*[1] 3]. **1792** *Minstrel* (1793) II. 172 Her crimpt lips relaxed to something like a smile. **1809** PINKNEY *Trav. France* 38 Madame in a high crimped cap. **1860** TYNDALL *Glac.* I. xxi. 147 Many cells had also crimped borders. **1871** —— *Fragm. Sc.* (1879) I. vii. 238 The edge of the cataract is crimped by indentations. **1886** SHELDON tr. *Flaubert's Salammbô* 44 Gold spangles glittered in the crimped hair.

3. Of fish; see CRIMP *v.*[1] 4.

1791 HUDDESFORD *Salmag.* (1793) 145 Crimpt cod, and mutilated mackarel. **1798** CANNING, etc. *Progress of Man* 28 in *Anti-Jacobin* 19 Feb., Cools the crimpt cod. **1804** A. CARLISLE in *Phil. Trans.* XCV. 23 The specific gravity of the crimped fish was greater than that of the dead fish.

crimper[1] ('krɪmpə(r)). [f. CRIMP *v.*[1] + -ER[1].]

1. a. One who crimps.

1819 *Blackw. Mag.* VI. 244 Crimpers of salmon.

b. A hairdresser. *slang.*

1968 D. GRAY *Died in Red* ix. 52 She was then put under a drier. Twenty minutes or so later she was again taken to the stylist (or crimper as they called themselves). **1968** 'E. TREVOR' *Place for Wicked* i. 6 He'd opened up as a crimper ..decorating the salon and supervising the work himself.

2. The name of several machines and instruments used in crimping.

a. An apparatus consisting of a pair of fluted rollers, for crimping cloth or the like. **b.** A machine for bending wire in a sinuous form in preparation for the weaving of wire-cloth. **c.** A toilet instrument for crimping the hair. **d.** A machine for crimping leather on a curved board for the uppers of boots and shoes. **e.** An apparatus for bending or moulding leather into various shapes for saddles and harness. **f.** A small machine or apparatus used by cartridge-makers for 'crimping' brass cartridge-cases.

1877 E. S. PHELPS *Story of Avis* ii. 31, I think I could have patented a crimper that would make a simpler system of punctuation in your finger than this. **1881** GREENER *Gun* 425 This may be prevented by using an indented case, or closing in with a patent crimper specially made for these brass cases.

crimper[2]. [f. CRIMP *v.*[2] + -ER[1].] One who crimps (seamen); = CRIMP *sb.*[1] 2.

1868 *Morn. Star* 7 Jan., The river police..engaged in defending 'poor Jack' from the machinations of the crimpers.

crimping ('krɪmpɪŋ), *vbl. sb.*[1] [f. CRIMP *v.*[1]]

1. The action of CRIMP *v.*[1]; the product of this action; a succession of small folds, frills or flutings.

1755 *Songs Costume* (Percy Soc.) 237 Ornament it well with gimping, Flounces, furbelows, and crimping. **1853** KANE *Grinnell Exp.* xlii. (1856) 386 Presently..you see a slight crimping, followed by a dotted..appearance on the ice. **1865** LUBBOCK *Preh. Times* iv. (1878) 104 The 'crimping' along the edges. **1870** *Spectator* 13 Aug. 976 The beautiful conchoidal waves, crimpings, and ripple-work displayed on the surface of tools and weapons in Scandinavia.

2. The causing of muscular contraction in fishes by dividing or gashing their flesh.

1698 [see CRIMP *v.*[1] 4]. **1776** HUNTER in *Phil. Trans.* LXVI. 415 *note*, Cutting fish into pieces while yet alive, in order to make them hard, usually known by the name of crimping. **1805** A. CARLISLE *Ibid.* XCV. 23 Many transverse sections of the muscles being made, and the fish immersed in cold water, the contractions called crimping take place. **1873** E. SMITH *Foods* 111 Crimping should be performed immediately after the fish has been caught, and before the rigor mortis has set in.

3. *Comb.*, as ***crimping board, -iron, -machine, -pin***, instruments for crimping frills, cap-borders, hair, etc.

1837 W. JENKINS *Ohio Gaz.* 158 A last factory, producing 14,000 lasts, 200 boot trees, and 200 crimping boards per annum. **1858** SIMMONDS *Dict. Trade*, *Crimping-iron, crimping-pin.* **1877** PEACOCK *N.W. Linc. Gloss.*, *Crimping-machine*, an instrument with two indented rollers, in which heaters can be placed..It is used for 'crimping' women's frills and cap-borders. **1969** E. H. PINTO *Treen* 150 Crimping boards and their correspondingly grooved or serated rollers..were used for forming the minute crimpings, gatherings or ruckings, on 17th- and early 18th-century fabrics.

'crimping, *vbl. sb.*[2] [f. CRIMP *v.*[2] + -ING[1].]

1. The decoying and confining of men, in order to force them into the army, navy, or merchant service: see CRIMP *sb.*[1] 2.

1795 *Hull Advertiser* 26 Sept. 4/2 We are sorry to find that the infamous practice of Crimping is not yet put a stop to. **1806** *Weekly Polit. Rev.* 27 Dec. 946 Men..who do not possess the necessary rascality for crimping. **1848** MACAULAY *Hist. Eng.* I. 336 This demand was partly supplied by a system of crimping and kidnapping at the principal English seaports.

2. *attrib.* and *Comb.*, as in ***crimping system***; **crimping-house**, a house constructed or used for crimping seamen or soldiers.

1795 *Hull Advertiser* 18 July 2/3 A false impression..of persons being kidnapped in a Crimping-house. **1828** *New Sailor's Mag.* 150 All the ramifications of the crimping system in London were then developed. **1858** POLSON *Law & L.* 148 A mob assembled in Holborn, threatening to pull down a Crimping-house.

'crimping, *ppl. a.*[1] [f. CRIMP *v.*[1] + -ING[2].]

1. Pinched: see CRIMP *v.*[1] 1.

2. That crimps or curls in minute creases.

'crimping, *ppl. a.*[2] [f. CRIMP *v.*[2] + -ING[2].] That impresses or entraps seamen, etc.

1820 SOUTHEY *Life of Wesley* II. 470 They were persuaded..by the crimping skipper to join the party. **1836** DISRAELI *Lett. Runnymede* 105 Your fellow-countrymen whom your crimping Lordship inveigled into a participation in the civil wars of Spain.

Hence **'crimpingly** *adv.*

1838 *Tait's Mag.* V. 206, I hold it to have been wickedly, deceitfully, fraudulently, crimpingly, kidnappingly done.

crimple, *sb.* [Cf. next, and CRUMPLE *sb.*] A crease, wrinkle, or fold; a crinkle. Now *dial.* and *U.S.*

c **1440** *Promp. Parv.* 103 Crympylle or rympylle, *ruga.* **1844** *Lowell* (Mass.) *Offering* IV. 148 My paper is full, and I can only say ribbons, bows,..wimples, and crimples. **1862** C. C. ROBINSON *Dial. Leeds* 278 Where the breadth of muslin was narrow the 'crimple' was made by means of a penknife and the thumb. **1881** S. P. MCLEAN *Cape Cod Folks* vi. 131 Teacher,..how shiny those crimples in your hair look, with that streak of sun lighting on 'em!

crimple, *v.* Also 5-6 **crymple**. [The early form *crymple* (if *y* is original) corresponds to Ger. dial. *krümpeln* to crumple; but *crimple* (with *i*) may be in its origin a dim. and iterative of CRIMP *v.*[1]; in later use *crimple* appears to be treated as a secondary form of *crumple*, expressing something finer and more attenuated; cf. *sip, sup, drip, drop*, etc.; also *crinkle, crunkle*. (See note to CRAMP *sb.*[1])]

†**1.** *intr.* To be or become incurved, or drawn together; hence to stand or walk lame from this or similar cause. Cf. CRIPPLE. *Obs.*

1398 TREVISA *Barth. De P.R.* XVIII. xxxix. (1495) 801 The token therof is that the hynder membres crymplyth togyders and ben constreyed. **1694** *Lond. Gaz.* No. 3007/4 Lost..a thick black Nag..stands crimpling on his near Leg behind. **1730-6** BAILEY (folio), *Crimpling*, as to go crimpling, i.e. as if the feet were tender.

2. *intr.* and *trans.* To wrinkle, crinkle, curl. Now *dial.*

c **1440** *Promp. Parv.* 103 Crymplyn or rymplyn, *rugo.* **1600** F. WALKER *Sp. Mandeville* 10a, The hair was so curled, that it crimpled round like Ringes. **1676** WISEMAN *Surgery* (J.), He passed the cautery through them, and accordingly crimpled them up. **1821** CLARE *Vill. Minstr.* I. 138 While the flood's triumphing care Crimpled round its guarded home. **1881** *Leicester Gloss.*, *Crimple*, to crumple, to wrinkle.

crimpled ('krɪmp(ə)ld), *ppl. a.* [f. CRIMPLE *v.* + -ED[1].] Wrinkled, crinkled, curled; finely crumpled; minutely wrinkled or creased.

c **1440** *Promp. Parv.* 103 Crympled, or rympled, *rugatus.* **1562** TURNER *Herbal* II. 36a, Lyke vnto a lefe of the crympled lettuce. **1578** LYTE *Dodoens* III. lxx. 411 Liuerwort..hauing wrinckled or crimpled leaues layde one vpon another. **1846** DANA *Zooph.* (1848) 170 The under surface of the corallum is crimpled and striate. **1882** *Garden* 29 July 85/3 Blossoms..exquisitely fringed and crimpled at the margins.

Crimplene ('krɪmpliːn). Also **crimplene**. A proprietary name for a type of synthetic yarn and fabric, noted for its crease-resistant properties, used esp. for knitted and jersey clothing.

1959 *Trade Marks Jrnl.* 11 Nov. 1174/1 *Crimplene*, all goods in Class 24. Imperial Chemical Industries Limited. **1961** *Times* 30 May (I.C.I. Suppl.) p. vi/5 'Crimplene' is 'Terylene' expressly made to be knitted. **1965** *Guardian* 31 Mar. 17/2 The polyester fibre, in its 'Crimplene' guise..has had advantages over the other fibres in the double jersey market owing to the fashionable fancy surface effects for which it is suitable. **1971** 'D. DEVINE' *Dead Trouble* vii. 65 Alma came out to greet Neville, wearing dark blue crimplene flare trousers and a white sweater. **1978** *Dumfries Courier* 20 Oct. 27/4 (Advt.), Large selection of plain fabrics, crimplene fabrics and vinyl plains and prints. **1984** *Mail on Sunday* (Colour Suppl.) 2 Dec. 19/3 A highly improbable headmistress—off-white crimplene suit, shoulder-length auburn perm, tarty high-heeled shoes and glossy pink lips—gave a highly improbable welcome speech.

'crimpness. [f. CRIMP *a.* + -NESS.] The quality of being crimp; friability.

1699 EVELYN *Acetaria* (1729) 178 Some eat them [potatoes] with sugar together in the skin, which has a pleasant crimpness.

crimpy ('krɪmpɪ), *a.* [f. CRIMP *sb.*[3] or *v.*[1] + -Y[1].] Having a crimped appearance; frizzy.

1888 [see CRIMP *sb.*[3] 1]. **1894** *Daily News* 24 July 5/7 The special petroleum wash dried more quickly..and left the hair more crimpy. **1923** E. BOWEN *Encounters* 91 A woman, with bright crimpy hair.

crimson ('krɪmz(ə)n), *a.* and *sb.* Forms: 5-6 **cremesin(e, -yn(e, -ysyn, crimesin, -yne, crymysyn, -esyn, -asyn(e, cramoysin, -en, -mysin, cremoysin, (crenseyn), 6 cremosin, crimison, -ozen, (chrymesyn), cremsin, crymsen, -on(e, 6-7 crimosin(e, -yn(e, crymosen, -in(e, crimsin, (7 crimzon, -sone), 6- crimson.** [The 15th c. *cremesin(e* corresponds exactly to early Sp. *cremesin* (cited 1403-12), early It. *cremesino* and med.L. *cremesīnus*, variants (by metathesis of *r*) of med.L. *kermesīnus, carmesīnus*, It. *chermesino, carmesino*, Sp. *carmesin* (16th c.), f. It. *chermisí, cremesí*, Sp. *carmesí* (cited 1422), (a. Arab. *qermazī, qirmazī*: see CRAMOISY) + suffix *-ino*, L. *-īnus*: see -INE. Thence our 16th c. variants. The corresponding 15-16th c. F. form was *cramoisin* (Littré), whence occasional Eng. *cramoysine*; the disturbing influence of this probably appears also in *cremosin, crimosin, crimison, crimson.*]

A. *adj.* **1.** The name of a colour: of a deep red somewhat inclining towards purple; of the colour of an alkaline infusion of cochineal.

Historically, the colour obtained from the Kermes or Scarlet Grain insect, at first chiefly used in dyeing fine cloth and velvet (F. *velours cramoisi*), in connexion with which this shade of red was first distinguished in English.

c **1440** *Partonope* 5976 A mantel..Of rede saten full good cremesyn. **1462** *Mann. & Househ. Exp.* 149 A jaket off crymysyn clothe. **1517** *Test. Ebor.* (Surtees) V. 86 My gowne of crymsen velwett. **1548** HALL *Chron.* 116b, All appareled in Crimosyne clothe. **1549** CHALONER *Erasmus on Folly* O iv b, This cramoysen gowne. **1568** TURNER *Herbal* III. 16 It hath a cremesin color. **1577** B. GOOGE *Heresbach's Husb.* II. (1586) 67 Some of them glitter with a perfect crimson dye. **1579** SPENSER *Sheph. Cal.* II. 130 Dyed in Lilly white and Cremsin redde. **1626** BACON *Sylva* §224 Two Lanthorns..the one a Crimsin, and the other an Azure. **1670-98** LASSELS *Voy. Italy* I. 68 Velvet coats of crimosin colour. **1860** RUSKIN *Mod. Paint.* V. VII. i. §8. 110 Why..are the most distant clouds crimsonest? **1866** KINGSLEY *Herew.* x. 186 She turned deadly pale and then crimson.

2. *fig.* Often used with reference to blood; sanguinary.

a **1681** SIR G. WHARTON *Wks.* (1683) 340 Why may not I some Crimson Lines leave out, To save my Ankles from the Prison-gout? **1777** SIR W. JONES *Pal. Fortune* 19 Crimson conquest glow'd where'er he trod. **1872** BLACKIE *Lays Highl.* 81 The crimson crime, The basest in the book of Time.

B. *sb.* (The *adj.* used absolutely.)

1. The colour or pigment.

a **1400** *Cov. Myst.* (Shaks. Soc.) 241 The most costyous cloth of crenseyn. **1494** FABYAN *Chron.* VII. 523 Cladde in one lyuerey of browne..and..in blewe and cremesyne. **1509-10** *Act 1 Hen. VIII*, c. 14 Of the Colour of Crymesyn or blewe. **1599** SHAKS. *Hen. V*, V. ii. 323 Ros'd ouer with the Virgin Crimson of Modestie. *a* **1691** BOYLE *On Colours* (J.), Crimson seems to be little else than a very deep red with an eye of blue. **1791** HAMILTON *Berthollet's Dyeing* II. II. III. v. 195 These salts..have the property of changing the colour of scarlet to crimson. **1816** J. SMITH *Panorama Sc. & Art* II. 537 For pale crimsons the quantity of cochineal is reduced. **1860** TYNDALL *Glac.* I. xxiv. 175 The western heaven glowed with crimson.

†**2.** Crimson cloth. *Obs.*

14.. *Epiph.* in *Tundale's Vis.* 114 Was ther any veluet or crymysyn. **1490** CAXTON *Eneydos* xvi. 63 A sleue..of fyne cremoysin alle drawen ouer wyth golde wyer. **1561** DAUS tr. *Bullinger on Apoc.* (1573) 144b, Not..clothed in..veluet, sattin, or damaske, or crimosine ingrayned, but in sacke-cloth. **1595** SPENSER *Epithal.* 228 Like crimsin dyde in grayne. **1611** COTGR., *Alchermes*, a graine wherewith Crimzons are dyed.

C. *Comb.*, as ***crimson-barred, -coloured, -dyed, -scarfed, -tipped, -warm*** adjs.; also with colours, expressing blended shades, as ***crimson-carmine, -lake, -purple, -violet***, etc.

1598 SYLVESTER *Du Bartas* II. I. I. (1641) 86/1 A crimsin-coloured juice. **1683** tr. *Erasmus' Moriæ Enc.* 56 Those crimson-died crimes. **1786** BURNS *Mountain Daisy*, Wee, modest, crimson-tipped flow'r. **1812** BYRON *Ch. Har.* II. lviii, The crimson-scarfed men of Macedon. **1877** BLACK *Green Past.* xii. (1878) 98 The..crimson-tipped bird's-foot trefoil. **1882** *Garden* 24 June 435/3 Flaked with crimson-purple.

crimson ('krɪmz(ə)n), *v.* [f. CRIMSON *a.*]

1. *trans.* To make crimson, impart a crimson colour to.

1601 SHAKS. *Jul. C.* III. i. 206 Heere thy Hunters stand.. Crimson'd in thy Lethee. **1743-6** SHENSTONE *Elegy* xx. 55 Stain'd with blood, and crimson'd o'er with crimes. **1768** MAD. D'ARBLAY *Early Diary* 20 May, My cheeks are crimsoned with the blush of indignation. **1877** A. B. EDWARDS *Up Nile* iv. 102 A gorgeous sunset was crimsoning the palms and pigeon-towers of Bedreshayn.

2. *intr.* To become crimson; *esp.* in blushing.

1805 SOUTHEY *Madoc in Art.* xvii, See his cheek! How it hath crimson'd at the unworthy thought! **1822-56** DE QUINCEY *Confess.* Wks. V. 89 The ancient collegiate church ..beginning to crimson with the deep lustre of a cloudless July morning. **1862** MRS. H. WOOD *Mrs. Hallib.* I. xv. 79 Jane's pale face crimsoned at the idea of parting with it.

Hence **'crimsoned, 'crimsoning** *ppl. adjs.*

1730-46 THOMSON *Autumn* 1090 The moon..Shows her broad visage in the crimsoned east. *a* **1853** ROBERTSON *Lect.* ii. (1858) 57 A crimsoned cheek. **1861** MRS. NORTON *Lady La G.* IV. 378 As the fresh bud a crimsoning beauty shows. **1879** R. H. HORNE *Orizaba* in *Poems of Places* 147 They mark the crimsoning sunrise tinge The clouds.

'crimsoning, *vbl. sb.* [f. CRIMSON *v.* + -ING[1].] Crimson colour or colouring.

1873 G. M. HOPKINS *Jrnl.* 3 Nov. (1959) 240 Balks of grey cloud searched with long crimsonings. **1898** —— *Poems* (1930) 147 When the Rose ran in crimsonings down the Cross-wood.

'crimsonish, *a. nonce-wd.* Somewhat crimson.

1760 MRS. DELANY *Life & Corr.* (1868) III. 592 A rich crimsonish and purpleish curtain.

crimsony ('krɪmzənɪ), *a.* [f. CRIMSON *a.* + -Y[1].] Somewhat crimson; resembling crimson.

1844 *Florist's Jrnl.* V. 17 The flowers differ in having the violaceous tint not *upon* the crimsony scarlet..but really *mixed* with the crimson in the texture of the flower. **1905** HOLMAN HUNT *Pre-Raph.* II. 70 With a crimsony lustre. **1909** M. B. SAUNDERS *Litany Lane* I. vi, The dim crimsony browns, the curious blue-greens.

crin (krɪn, ‖krɛ̃). [Fr., = horsehair.] A fabric made from horsehair alone or combined with some other fibre; = CRINOLINE *sb.* 1 a; so ***crin végétal***, vegetable horsehair (see VEGETABLE *a.* 7 a).

[**1858** SIMMONS *Dict. Trade*, *Crin*, the French name for horsehair.] **1875** *Encycl. Brit.* I. 565/1 The most important fibre is the *crin vegetal*, or vegetable horse hair, produced from the dwarf palm (*Chamærops humilis*), with which a vast portion of the uncultivated parts of the country [*sc.* Algeria] is covered. **1900** *Daily News* 9 June 6/6 The crin or horsehair (sometimes called crinoline) hat is poetic enough. **1900** *Traveller* 4 Aug. 112/2 A big floppy *crin* hat, trimmed with..black lace. **1909** *Westm. Gaz.* 3 June 8/3 There is a large hat of black crin. **1923** *Daily Mail* 9 Feb. 11 A similar shape of blue crin straw and satin ribbon. **1963** *Times* 3 June 11/5 A beret of crin sprinkled with chenille bobbles.

crinal ('kraɪnəl), *a. rare.* [ad. L. *crīnāl-is*, f. *crīn-is* hair.] Of or pertaining to the hair.

1656 in BLOUNT *Glossogr.* **1859** R. F. BURTON *Centr. Afr.* in *Jrnl. Geog. Soc.* XXIX. 317 The crinal line is low, and often encroaches upon the temples. **1876** —— *Gorilla L.* I. 204 A fashion of crinal decoration quite new to me.

cri'nanthropy. *nonce-wd.* [f. Gr. κρίν-ειν to judge + ἄνθρωπος man: after *misanthropy*.] Judgement or criticism of men. Hence **cri'nanthropist**, one who judges mankind.

1891 E. A. ABBOTT *Philomythus* 60 That critical attitude which I have called crinanthropy. *Ibid.*, Judging men and hating men, crinanthropy and misanthropy. *Ibid.* 61 For one misanthropist there are a thousand or ten thousand crinanthropists.

'crinate, by-form of CRINITE, haired, hairy.

'crinated, *a.* = prec.
1730–6 BAILEY (folio), *Crinated*, having long Locks. *Crinated Roots* (in Botany) such as shoot into the ground in many small fibres or hairs. **1775** in ASH; and in mod. Dicts.

crinatory, var. of CRINITORY.

crinc-: see CRINK-.

crinch by-form of CRINGE *v.*

crinch *v.*, dial. var. of CRUNCH.

crine (kraɪn), *sb. rare.* [a. It. *crine* or ad. L. *crīn-is* hair: cf. F. *crin* hair, horse-hair.]
1. Hair, head of hair. Also *attrib.*
1614 SYLVESTER *Du Bartas, Bethulia's Rescue* I. 160 Priests, whose sacred Crine Felt never Razor. **1768** *Bristol Jrnl.* Oct., Hose of Goatskyn, Crinepart outwards. **1865** *Athen.* No. 1969. 119/3 Both crines look like ill-made wigs.
2. *Hawking.* = CRINET 2.
1883 SALVIN & BRODRICK *Falconry Brit. Isles* Gloss. 150.

crine (kraɪn), *v. Sc.* [app. a. Gael. *crìon* to wither, f. *crìon* dry, withered.]
1. *intr.* To shrink, shrivel, contract from dryness.
1501 DOUGLAS *Pal. Hon.* III. 845 All wycht but sycht of thy gret mycht ay crinis. **1724** RAMSAY *Evergreen, Interl. Droichs* xiii, I am crynit in for eild. **1818** SCOTT *Hrt. Midl.* xxxix, 'And mine bairns hae been crining too, mon.' **1849** MRS. CARLYLE *Lett.* II. 62 He had grown old like a golden pippin, merely crined, with the bloom upon him. *Mod. Sc.* The meat (in stewing) has crined into very little.
b. *trans.*
1847 *Whistlebinkie* (Sc. Songs) (1840) II. 165 The drouth it had krined up and slackened the screw. **1878** DICKINSON *Cumbrld. Gloss.*, *Crine*, to overdo in frying or roasting.
†2. To sweat or clip (coin). *Obs. rare*⁻¹.
1513 DOUGLAS *Æneis* VIII. Prol. 97 Sum trachour crynis the cunȝe, and kepis corn stakis.
Hence **crined** *ppl. a.*, shrunken, shrivelled.
1861 RAMSAY *Remin.* 2nd Ser. 121 A very little 'crined' old man.

crined (kraɪnd), *a. Her.* [f. CRINE *sb.* + -ED².] Of a charge: Wearing hair; having the hair of head or mane tinctured differently from the body.
1572 BOSSEWELL *Armorie* II. 46b, S. beareth Sable, a Sphinx d'argent, crined, and penned d'Or. **1864** BOUTELL *Heraldry Hist. & Pop.* xix. §3 (ed. 3) 363 An unicorn arg., armed, unguled and crined or.

[**crinel.** Error for CRINET 2, small hair-like feathers which grow about the cere of a hawk.
1730–6 BAILEY (folio), Crinels, Crinets [with definition of *Crinet* from 1721 Bailey]. Hence in **1775** ASH, **1823** CRABB *Technol. Dict.*, **1846** WORCESTER, **1864** WEBSTER, OGILVIE (Annandale), and *Century Dict.*]

†**crinet.** *Obs.* [dim. of F. *crin* hair: see -ET¹.]
1. A hair.
1572 GASCOIGNE *Flowers* Wks. (1587) 67 The heeres were not of gold But of some other metall farre more fine Wher of ech crinet seemed to behold Like glistering wyars.
2. *Hawking.* (*pl.*) The small hair-like feathers which grow about the cere of a hawk. (Also written *crinites*; now called *crines.*)
1486 *Bk. St. Albans* Bj b, Ther be oon an hawke long smale blake federis like heris abowte the sere & thossame be calde Crinettis of yᵉ hawke. **1610** GUILLIM *Heraldry* III. xx. (1660) 223. **1792** OSBALDISTON *Brit. Sportsman* 130/1 *Crinets* or *Crinites*, with falconers, small black feathers in hawks.
3. = CRINIÈRE. (Cf. CRANET¹.)
1586 FERNE *Blaz. Gentrie* 336 Vpon any sadle, crinet, bard, chapperon, cooperison or other indument.

cringe (krɪndʒ), *v.* Also 3–5 **crenge, crenche,** 6 **crintch,** 7 **crindge, cring, chringe,** (9 *dial.* **crinch**). [*Cringe* (*crintch*), first found in 16th c., appears to be a phonetic modification (with ordinary Eng. change of *eng, enge*, to *ing, inge*, as in *hinge, singe, wing*: see CLINK *v.*²) of an earlier *crenge*, found with variant *crenche* early in 13th c. *Crenge, crenche*, represent OE. **cręngcean*, **cręncean* (:—**krangjan*, **krankjan*), causal deriv. of the strong verb found in OE. with the double form *cringan, crincan* to draw oneself together spasmodically, to contract or shrink together into a bent or crooked position: see CRANK *sb.*¹ Primarily then *crengen, crenchen* was transitive, but already in 13th c. we find 'cringe with the neck'.]
†1. *trans.* To compress, draw together, or draw in (any part of the body) as in shrinking from pain or danger; to contract, distort (the neck, face, etc.). *Obs.*
1598 BP. HALL *Sat.* IV. ii, He can..make a Spanish face with fauning cheere..shake his head, and cringe his necke and side. **1606** SHAKS. *Ant. & Cl.* III. xiii. 100 Whip him, Fellowes, Till like a Boy you see him crindge his face, And whine aloud for mercy. *c* **1630** J. TAYLOR (Water P.) *Red Herring*, They cringing in their necks, like rats, smothered in the hold, poorly replied.
2. *intr.* **a.** To draw in or contract the muscles of the body involuntarily; to shrink. **b.** To shrink in or away (as with fear); to cower.
a **1225** *St. Marher.* 9 (MS. B.) [The dragon] bigon to crahien ant to crenge wið swire [*MS. R.* crenchen mit swire]. *a* **1455** HOLLAND *Houlate* 956 He crepillit, he crengit, he carfully cryd. **1597** R. LICHFIELD *Trimming of T. Nashe* (N.), What makes you sit downe so tenderly? You crintch in your buttocks like old father *Pater patriæ*. **1684** BUNYAN *Pilgr.* II. 69 The Boys that went before were glad to cringe behind, for they were afraid of the Lions. **1719** D'URFEY *Pills* IV. 125 We have no twinge to make us cringe Or crinkle in the Hams. *c* **1750** J. NELSON *Jrnl.* (1836) 4 The words made me cringe, and my flesh seemed to creep on my bones. **1847** TODD *Cycl. Anat.* III. 68/1 He was sensible..of something 'cringing' in the lower part of the thigh. **1861** G. F. BERKELEY *Sportsm. W. Prairies* vii. 101 The last two cows had to 'cringe' or tuck in their tails and haunches to avoid the 'catcher'.
3. *intr.* To bend the body timorously or servilely; to cower. Often applied derisively or depreciatively to bowing, with the implication of attendant servility or cowardice. Const. *to* (a person).
1575–97 [see CRINGING *ppl. a.*]. **1621–51** BURTON *Anat. Mel.* I. ii. III. xv. 129 They cannot..carve at Table, chringe and make congies. **1647** H. MORE *Song of Soul* I. I. lxiii, Thus cring'd he toward th' East. *c* **1680** BEVERIDGE *Serm.* (1729) I. 48 An opinion that to bow or cringe (as they profanely call it) before Almighty God is superstition. **1853** LYNCH *Self-Improv.* v. 123 You should bow to most people, but cringe to nobody.
4. *fig.* To behave obsequiously or with mean submissiveness; to show base or servile deference.
c **1620** H. ANDERSON *Law of Christ*, Cringing to those that from all virtue run. **1660–72** WOOD *Life* (Oxf. Hist. Soc.) I. 359 The most ready men to cring to and serve these times. **1855** MACAULAY *Hist. Eng.* III. 105 Their chief business.. had been to teach the people to cringe and the prince to domineer.
5. *trans.* †**a.** To bow deferentially to (a person). **b.** To bow a person in or out with cringes.
1609 W. M. *Man in Moone* (1849) 17 Your tradesmen, which now cappe and cringe you. **1660** H. MORE *Myst. Godliness* v. xiv. 169 Cringing and courting..not only Christ, but the blessed Virgin. **1822** BYRON *Werner* I. i. 441 Hence, and bow and cringe him here!

cringe (krɪndʒ), *sb.* [f. CRINGE *v.*]
1. A deferential, servile, or fawning obeisance. Often a hostile or derisive name for a bow.
1597 *1st Pt. Return fr. Parnass.* v. iii, That better doe rewarde each scriveners pen, Each tapsters cringe, each rubbinge ostler. **1603** B. JONSON *Sejanus* I. i, He is the now court God, and well applyed With sacrefice of Knees, of Crookes, and Cringe. **1624** GATAKER *Transubst.* 113 Where are all those crossings and bendings, and cringes and turnings? **1700** R. PEARSON *Naaman Vind.* 10 Nor could he hope, by a few external Cringes..to expiate for his notorious neglect. **1751** JOHNSON *Rambler* No. 180 ¶1 The professors ..flocked round him with all the cringes of awkward complaisance. **1852** THACKERAY *Esmond* I. (1876) 2 Performing cringes and congees like a court-chamberlain.
2. *fig.* A cringing or obsequious act.
1610 HEALEY *St. Aug. Citie of God* v. xxiv, Puffed up with ..the cringes of their subjects. **1751** JOHNSON *Rambler* No. 180 ¶12 To purchase favour by cringes and compliance.

cringeling ('krɪndʒlɪŋ). *rare.* [f. CRINGE *v.* + -LING.] A cringing creature. Also *attrib.*
a **1693** URQUHART *Rabelais* III. xxvi. 216 Cringeling cock. **1798** W. TAYLOR in Robberds *Mem.* I. 219 Their monument [must] no tyrant's cringeling rear. **1807** —— *Ann. Rev.* V. 569 Among those cringelings who have assisted sovereigns to extend their power.

cringer (krɪndʒə(r)). [f. as prec. + -ER¹.] One who cringes; an obsequious or servile creature.
1597 *1st Pt. Return fr. Parnass.* IV. i. 1236 This ladye-munger, this meere rapier and dagger, this cringer. *a* **1649** DRUMM. OF HAWTH. *Skiamachia* Wks. (1711) 199 Cringers to crucifixes, approvers of purgatory. **1799** W. TAYLOR in *Monthly Rev.* XXIX. 102 Cringers to fortune, birth and power. **1859** SALA *Tw. round Clock* (1861) 336 The decorations that are shared by footmen and backstairs cringers.

cringing ('krɪndʒɪŋ), *vbl. sb.* [-ING¹.]
1. The action of shrinking timorously, or of bowing or bending the body servilely; servile or obsequious behaviour. Often applied contemptuously to bowing.
1634 W. TIRWHYT tr. *Balzac's Lett.* 248 A Country.. where all men grow crooked with extreame cringeing. **1660** MILTON *Free Commw.* 429 Among the perpetual bowings and cringings of an abject People. **1727** A. HAMILTON *New Acc. E. Ind.* I. xiii. 156 Making some decent Cringings towards the Tomb. **1767** T. HUTCHINSON *Hist. Mass. Bay* II. 214 His cringing to Randolph..was a spot in his character. **1847** L. HUNT *Jar Honey* (1848) 199 The studied cringing so common in Naples is rare here.
2. Muscular contraction, shrinking.
1727–51 CHAMBERS *Cycl.* s.v. *Amble*, Though the amble be gained, it must be slow and unsightly; because attended with a cringing in the hind-parts.

'cringing, *ppl. a.* [f. as prec. + -ING².] That cringes, that shrinks or bends the body timorously or servilely; that behaves with servile deference.
1575 G. HARVEY *Letter-bk.* (Camden) 98 His cringeinge side necke, eies glauncinge, fisnamy smirkinge. **1597** *1st Pt. Return fr. Parnass.* Prol., Youe cringinge parasite. **1680** OTWAY *Orphan* I. i, A huffing shining flatt'ring cringing Coward. **1746–7** HERVEY *Medit.* (1818) 209 In a state of abject and cringing dependence. **1869** FREEMAN *Norm. Conq.* (1876) III. xiii. 297 He began in a tone of almost cringing loyalty.

cringingly ('krɪndʒɪŋlɪ), *adv.* [f. prec. + -LY².] In a cringing manner.
1853 *Fraser's Mag.* XLVIII. 329 'My wife never was a good walker,' said Roberts, cringingly. **1861** TROLLOPE *Barchester T.* 104 Nevertheless he was..cringingly civil.

'cringingness. [f. as prec. + -NESS.] Cringing quality, timid servility.
1695 *Whether Preserv. Protest. Relig. Motive of Revol.* 22 With a flattering as well as a mean Cringingness. **1821** *Blackw. Mag.* IX. 508 There is..less of plebeian cringingness and adulation in his works.

cringle ('krɪŋg(ə)l). Also 7 **creengle,** 8 **crengle, crencle.** [app. of LG. origin: cf. Ger. (mostly LG. and MG.) *kringel*, MLG. and mod.LG. also *krengel*, dim. of *kring* circle, ring. Cf. Icel. *kringla* disc, circle, orb. From the verbal stem *kring-*: see CRANK *sb.*¹, and cf. CRINKLE.]
1. *Naut.* A ring or eye of rope, containing a thimble, worked into the bolt-rope of a sail, for the attachment of a rope.
1627 CAPT. SMITH *Seaman's Gram.* v. 22 Creengles are little ropes spliced into the Bolt-ropes of all sailes belonging to the maine and fore mast, to which the bolings bridles are made fast. **1762** FALCONER *Shipwr.* II. 330 Each earing to its cringle first they bend. **1804** A. DUNCAN *Mariner's Chron.* Pref. 15 *Bunt-Lines*, ropes fastened to cringles on the bottom of square sails, to draw them up to the yards. **1867** SMYTH *Sailor's Word-bk.* s.v., Cringles should be made of the strands of new bolt-rope.
b. Also in rural use: see quot.
1787–95 W. MARSHALL *Norfolk* Gloss., *Cringle*, a with or rope for fastening a gate. Hence **1847–78** in HALLIWELL.
2. = CRINKLE. *dial.*
1807 VANCOUVER *Agric. Devon.* (1813) 298 This plain..is generally without creeks or cringles, and forms one compact and even surface. **1877** *N.W. Linc. Gloss.* s.v. *Crinkle*, A brook in Roxby parish, the course of which is very circuitous, is called *Cringlebeck* [in 12–13th c. *Cringelbec*].
Hence **'cringle** *v. dial.*
1787–95 W. MARSHALL *Norfolk* Gloss., *Cringle up*, to fasten with a *cringle*. See above.

†**cringle-crangle,** *a., adv.* and *sb. Obs.* exc. *dial.* [Frequentative reduplication of CRANGLE; cf. CRINKLE-CRANKLE.]
A. *adj.* Winding in and out, twisted, having twists and turns. Also *advb.*
1606 CHAPMAN *Gentl. Usher* Plays 1873 I. 261 The busky groues..With cringle-crangle hornes do ring alowd. **1781** J. HUTTON *Tour to Caves* Gloss., *Cringle-crangle* adv., zig-zag. **1869** *Lonsdale Gloss.*, *Cring'l-crang'l*, zig-zag.
B. *sb.* A zigzag; a mass of twists and turns.
16.. *English Rogue* 111 (N.), I had prepared a deal of scribble or cringle crangle, and so from thence began to take the height of her fortune. **1739** *Poor Robin* (N.), When Don Phœbus enters that cringle-crangle which the rablers would have to be a pair of heavenly scales.

cringy ('krɪndʒɪ), *a. rare.* [f. CRINGE + -Y.] Having the attribute of cringing.
1880 *Blackw. Mag.* Mar. 321 An oily cringy voice in which there is a strong dash of insolence.

crini-, stem of L. *crīnis* hair: used as comb. form in a number of formations (chiefly nonce-wds.): **crini'cultural** *a.*, of or pertaining to the growth or culture of hair. **cri'niferous** *a.*, bearing hair. **'criniger** (*Ornith.*), a genus of African and Asiatic birds allied to the Thrush, so called from the stiff bristly hairs or setæ on their bills. **cri'nigerous** *a.*, bearing or wearing hair, hairy. **cri'niparous** *a.*, hair-producing. **cri'nivorous** *a.*, hair-devouring.
1837 *New Monthly Mag.* XLIX. 550 Those criniferous appendages to the head worn by the bucks of that period. **1656** BLOUNT *Glossogr.*, *Crinigerous*, that hath or weareth hair. **1755** in JOHNSON. **1819** H. BUSK *Vestriad* III. 720 Her front crinigerous, each hair a snake. **1798** *Anti-Jacobin, Progr. Man* 38 *note*, Bears' grease or fat..supposed to have a criniparous or hair-producing quality. **1837** WHEELWRIGHT tr. *Aristophanes* II. 151 But worms crinivorous have eat my crests.

Crinid ('krɪnɪd, kraɪ-). *Zool.* [f. Gr. κρίνον lily + -ID.] *pl.* A family of the *Crinoidea* containing the typical crinoids with branching arms.
1862 DANA *Man. Geol.* II. 161 The Crinids closely resemble a Comatula..a modern Crinid..ancient Crinids or Encrinites. **1877** LE CONTE *Elem. Geol.* II. (1879) 299 Stemmed Echinoderms or Crinoids may be divided into three families, viz. 1. Crinids; 2. Cystids; 3. Blastids.

‖**crinière** (krinjɛr). [F., f. *crin* (horse) hair; corresp. to a L. type **crināria*. In 16th and 17th c. anglicized as *crinier*.] The part of the 'bards' or protective covering of a war-horse which covered the ridge or back of the neck and the mane.
1598 BARRET *Theor. Warres* v. ii. 141 His horse barded with a sufficient Pectron, crinier. **1622** F. MARKHAM *Bk. War* v. ii. §4 The Horses head, breast and buttocke barbed with Pectron, Trappings, Crinier, and Chieffront. **1847–78** HALLIWELL, *Cranet*, small crinière.

†**cri'nital,** *a. Obs. rare*⁻¹. = CRINITE *a.*, having hair: applied to a comet.
1583 STANYHURST *Aeneis* II. (Arb.) 66 He the star crinital adoreth.

crinite ('kraɪnaɪt), *a.* [ad. L. *crīnīt-us* hairy, f. *crīnis* hair.] Hairy; having a hairy or hairlike appendage; *spec.* in *Bot.* and *Zool.* having tufts of hairy growth on the surface.

1600 FAIRFAX *Tasso* XIV. xliv, How comate, crinite, caudate starres are fram'd I knew. **1654** GAYTON *Pleas. Notes* IV. 248 The Cane, like to a blazing Starre Crinite, Greater appear'd. **1852** DANA *Crust.* I. 436 Flagellum of outer antennæ more or less crinite, often long ciliate.

crinite ('krɪnaɪt, kraɪ-), *sb. Geol.* [f. Gr. κρίνον lily + -ITE.] A fossil crinoid; an encrinite.

'crinitory, *a. rare.* [f. L. *crīnītus* hairy + -ORY.] Of the nature of hair, hairy.

1836 T. HOOK *G. Gurney* II. 153 Away came every vestige of its crinitory covering.

crink, *sb.* Also 6–7 krink(e. [f. CRINK *v.*, or directly from vb. stem *crinc-an*: see CRANK *sb.*[1]]

1. A twist, bend, or winding; a winding crevice, furrow, or channel. Cf. CRANK *sb.*[2] I. Now *dial.*

1565 GOLDING *Ovid's Met.* VIII. (1593) 186 A house with many nooks and krinkes. **1688** R. HOLME *Armoury* II. 188/1 Gutters are the Slifters, or Krinks, in the beam of a Stags horn. **1888** *Sheffield Gloss., Crink,* a twist or bend.

†**2.** *fig.* An intricate turn or twist of thought or speech; a tortuous shift or sleight. *Obs.*

1565 GOLDING *Ovid's Met.* VII. (1593) 176 The krinks of certaine prophesies surmounting farre above The reach of ancient wits to read. **1583** —— *Calvin on Deut.* xv. 89 Such a crink was practised against mee. **1587** —— *De Mornay* xx. 313 To take away the doubts, and to auoyde the krinks inuented anew by certaine Libertines.

3. *dial.* (See quots.)

1888 *Berksh. Gloss.* s.v. *Cranks,* A person is said to be full of 'crinks and cranks' when generally complaining of ill health. [**1883** *Hampsh. Gloss., Crink-crank* words are long words . . not properly understood.]

crink (krɪŋk), *v.*[1] Also 6 **krink**. [possibly a survival of OE. *crincan* to contract or draw oneself together in a bent form (see CRANK *sb.*[1]), but more prob. repr. an earlier **crenk* :—*krankjan*, causal deriv. of *crincan*. In mod. use, however, perh. formed anew from *crinkle.*] Hence **'crinking** *vbl. sb.* and *ppl. a.*

1. *trans.* To bend or twist; to form into furrows or wrinkles; to crinkle. *dial.*

1821 CLARE *Vill. Minstr.* II. 93 As the wakening wind . . o'er the water crink'd the curdled wave. **1888** *Sheffield Gloss., Crink,* to twist, or wrench painfully. 'I've crinked my neck.' . . When a man bends a piece of iron by hammering it he is said to crink it.

†**2.** *intr.* (*fig.*) To use tortuous shifts or sleights.

1583 GOLDING *Calvin on Deut.* xxxix. 231 If wee vse any craftinesse or krinking. *Ibid.* 234 He which thinketh to further himselfe by his crinking, pilling and deceyuing.

crink, *v.*[2] [Echoic: cf. *creak, crick, crinkle,* etc.] *intr.* To make a sound in which cricking and chinking blend. Hence **'crinking** *ppl. a.*

1860 GOSSE *Rom. Nat. Hist.* 174 The noisy cicadæ that . . make the woods ring with their pertinacious crinking. *Ibid.* (ed. 7) 105 Those crinking merry-voiced denizens of our summer-fields.

crinkle ('krɪŋk(ə)l), *sb.* [prob. f. CRINKLE *v.*, but the sb. may be the earlier: cf. Du. and LG. *krinkel* curve, flexure, crookedness, curvature, dim. of *kring, krink* circle, etc.]

1. A twist, winding, or sinuosity; a wrinkle or corrugation, as in a rumpled or rippling surface.

1596 NASHE *Saffron Walden* 50 The vnflattered picture of Pedantisme, that hath no one smile or crinkle more than it should. **1598** FLORIO, *Tortuoso,* crooked, winding, full of crinkles and crankles. **1621–51** BURTON *Anat. Mel.* I. i. II. iv. 17 Ilion the third [gut], which consists of many crinckles. **1768–74** TUCKER *Lt. Nat.* (1852) I. 563 The crinkles in this glass making objects appear double. **1871** MISS BRADDON *Lovels* xvi. 128 To blow the crinkles out of their luxuriant hair. **1885** RUNCIMAN *Skippers* 2 His oilskins . . poured multitudinous streams from all their crinkles.

†**2.** A ring or circle. *Obs. rare*[−1]. (Cf. CRINGLE.)

1703 *Art's Improv.* I. 19 Of the Crincles or Rings which are seen at the end of Trees when Saw'd off.

3. crinkle-cut *a.*: of potato chips, etc., cut with corrugated or crinkly, as opp. to straight, sides (cf. CHIP *sb.*[1] 2 b).

1968 *Times* 29 Nov. p. xi/1, If muzak be the food of love, no wonder it is commonly to be found—whether in supermarkets or eateries—among the frozen mint-flavoured peas and the crinkle-cut chips. **1969** [see *hash browns* s.v. HASH *sb.*[1] 6]. **1984** S. TOWNSEND *Growing Pains A. Mole* 59 He went to the pub and had a microwave mince and onion pie and crinkle-cut chips.

crinkle ('krɪŋk(ə)l), *v.* Also 4 cr-, **krenkle, cr-, krynkle,** 6 **crencle.** [Frequentative derivative from stem of OE. *crincan*; see CRANK *sb.*[1], and cf. CRANKLE. As the ME. form is sometimes *crenkle* (see CRINKLED), the type seems to be **crankil-*, whence **crenclian.*]

I. 1. *intr.* To form numerous short twists or turns; to wind or twist in its course; to contract surface wrinkles or ripples; to wrinkle or shrink *up*.

c **1385**, *a* **1529** [see CRINKLED]. **1577**, **1621** [see CRINKLING *vbl. sb., ppl. a.*]. *a* **1600** *Boy & Mantle* xxviii. in Child *Eng. & Sc. Pop. Ball.* (1884) II. 273/1 Vpp att her great toe, itt [the mantle] began to crinkle and crowt. **1864** MRS. GATTY *Parables fr. Nat.* 4th Ser. 12 The last leaves . . had crinkled up and turned brown. **1873** LOWELL *Among my Bks.* Ser. II. 132 It [a stream] seemed to ripple and crinkle. **1876** *Mid-Yorksh. Gloss., Crinkle,* to bend tortuously. Of a twisting pathway, it will be said: 'It crinkles round, but goes straight at after'. [In Dial. Glossaries of *Cheshire, Lincolnsh., Leicestersh.,* etc. = 'to wrinkle, crumple, shrink, shrivel up'.]

2. To bend shrinkingly or obsequiously with the legs or body; to cringe. *Obs.* exc. *dial.*

1633 SHIRLEY *Bird in Cage* II. i, The other signor crinkles in the hams, as he were studying new postures against his turn comes to salute me. **1633** FORD *'Tis Pity* I. ii, I like him the worse, he crinkles so much in the hams. **1719** [see CRINGE *v.* 2]. **1825** BROCKETT *Gloss. N. Country Words, Crinkle,* to wrinkle, to bend under a load. **1875** *Lanc. Gloss., Crinkle,* to bend under a weight.

b. *fig.* To turn aside, to shrink or recede from one's purpose. *Obs.* exc. *dial.*

1610 B. JONSON *Alch.* III. v, He that hath pleas'd her Grace Thus farre, shall not now crinckle for a little. **1703** THORESBY *Let. to Ray, Crinkle,* to crouch; to yield sneakingly. **1781** J. HUTTON *Tour to Caves* Gloss., *Crinckle,* to recede, or fall off from a promise or purpose. **1873** *Swaledale Gloss., Crinkle,* to recede from an avowed resolution or the performance of a promise.

3. *trans.* To twist or bend (anything) to and fro, or in and out; to wrinkle, crumple; to crimp (the hair). (See also CRINKLED *ppl. a.*)

a **1825** FORBY *Voc. E. Anglia, Crinkle, Crunkle,* to wrinkle, twist, plait, or rumple irregularly. **1856** MRS. BROWNING *Aur. Leigh* VIII. (1857) 358 The flames through all the casements pushing forth, Like red-hot devils crinkled into snakes. **1871** MISS BRADDON *Lovels* xvi. 128 Miss Granger was too perfect a being to crinkle her hair. **1888** *Berksh. Gloss., Crinkle,* to crease; to rumple.

II. 4. *intr.* To emit sharp thin ringing sounds; to move with these sounds. [Cf. CRINK *v.*[2]]

1856, etc. [see CRINKLING *ppl. a.* II]. **1878** R. W. GILDER *Poet & M.* 19 Small brooks crinkle o'er stock and stone.

'crinkle-'crankle, *sb., a.* and *adv.* Chiefly *dial.* [Frequentative reduplication of CRANKLE: cf. CRINGLE-CRANGLE.]

A. *sb.* A winding in and out, a zigzag, sinuosity.

1598 FLORIO, *Sinuoso* . . that is full of creekes, bosomes, or crinkle-crankles. **1620** THOMAS *Lat. Dict., Sinuosus* . . that hath many turnings . . full of crinckle cranckles.

B. *adj.* and *adv.* (Twisting) in and out, zigzag.

1840 SPURDENS *Suppl. Voc. E. Anglia, Crincle-crancle* adv., like a corkscrew. **1869** *Lonsdale Gloss., Crinkle-crankle, Crinklety-cranklety,* adv., zig-zag. **1881** *Leicestersh. Gloss., Crinkle-crankle* adj. and adv., zig-zag; sinuous.

Hence **crinkle-crankled** *ppl. a.* †**cricnledum and crancledum,** tortuously.

1858 MOTLEY *Corr.* 4 July, With a wonderful profusion of gilt flaxen crinkle-crankled hair. **1660** H. PETERS in Bp. Kennett *Register* 35 This was still the Lord's right way who led His people cricnledum and crancledum.

crinkled ('krɪŋk(ə)ld), *ppl. a.* [f. CRINKLE *v.*]

a. That has been crinkled; see CRINKLE *v.* I.

c **1385** CHAUCER *L.G.W.* 2012 *Ariadne,* And for the hous is krynkeled [*v.rr.* crenkled, ycrynklid, ykrenkled] two and fro And hath so queynte weyis for to go. *a* **1529** SKELTON *El. Rumminge* 17 Her face all bowsy Comely crynklyd Woundersly wrynkled. **1611** BARRY *Ram-Alley* IV. i. in Hazl. *Dodsley* X. 339 An old crazed man . . With little legs and crinkled thighs. **1850** L. HUNT *Autobiog.* II. x. 30 His hat . . looking sadly crinkled and old. **1862** *Macm. Mag.* Apr. 30 The arum['s] . . rigid spike and crinkled leaves.

b. crinkled (tissue) paper, paper that is crinkled, made in various colours, and used for making paper flowers and for decorative purposes; = *crêpe paper.*

1895 *Army & Navy Co-op. Soc. Price List* 526 Crinkled tissue paper. For making Fancy Lamp Shades. **1921** *Dict. Occup. Terms* (1927) §559 Crinkled paper machine operator. **1929** E. BOWEN *Last September* viii. 91 She used to plait hats out of crinkled paper.

†**crinklepouch.** *Obs. slang.* A sixpence.

1593 *Bacchus Bountie* in *Harl. Misc.* (Malh.) II. 270 With the expence of an odde Crinclepouch, wash yourselues within and without.

'crinkle-root. *U.S.* = PEPPERWORT 1 b.

1847 *Knickerbocker* XXIX. 377 Sassafras is 'coming good' now too in the woods; and so is 'crinkle-root'. **1899** H. VAN DYKE *Fisherman's Luck* iv. 74 Crinkle-root is spicy, but you must partake of it delicately, or it will bite your tongue.

crinkliness ('krɪŋklɪnɪs). [f. CRINKLY *a.* + -NESS.] Crinkly condition.

1927 R. A. FREEMAN *Certain Dr. Thorndyke* xv. 228 Mr. Wamploe's advice produced on Polton's countenance a smile of most extraordinary crinkliness.

crinkling ('krɪŋklɪŋ), *vbl. sb.* [-ING[1].]

I. The action of the verb CRINKLE; twisting to and fro; wrinkling, crumpling, etc. Also *concr.*

1577 HARRISON *Desc. Britaine* I. xiv. in *Holinshed,* The Wyuer . . no riuer in England . . fetcheth more or halfe so many windlesses and crinklings. **1602** *2nd Pt. Return fr. Parnass.* III. iv. (Arb.) 46 The curious crinkling of a silke stocking. **1709** W. KING *Art of Cookery* 138 Who'cares for all the crinkling of the pye? **1891** *Daily News* 20 May 3/1 Much of the crêpon is crinkled like the surface of cream . . Sometimes this crinkling runs in stripes.

II. The emitting of sharp thin sounds.

1880 *7th Rep. Topog. Surv. Adirondack Region* 157 The sharp 'crinkling' of the runners of the large hand-sleds.

'crinkling, *ppl. a.* [f. as prec. + -ING[2].]

I. That crinkles; see CRINKLE *v.* I.

1577 HARRISON *Desc. Brit.* I. xv, Manifold Water, so called bicause of the sundrie crinckling rills that it receiueth. **1621** MOLLE *Camerar. Liv. Libr.* IV. ii. 227 Running with a crinkeling course as far as Lions. **1648** JOS. BEAUMONT *Psyche* IX. xxx. (R.), Her legs are two faint crinkling props.

II. Emitting sharp thin sounds.

1856 MRS. BROWNING *Aur. Leigh* v. Poems VI. 191 All the rooms Were full of crinkling silks. **1865** MISS MULOCK *Christian's Mistake* 69 As she stepped with her light, firm tread across the crinkling snow. **1880** WEBB *Goethe's Faust* III. viii. 168 With the crinkling sand the floor to strow.

'crinkling, crinchling, *sb. dial.* [f. CRINCH *v.*, or CRINK *v.* + -LING.]

a **1825** FORBY *Voc. E. Anglia, Crinchling,* a small apple. **1881** *Suppl. Oxfordsh. Gloss., Crinklin',* a small wrinkled apple.

crinkly ('krɪŋklɪ), *a.* [f. CRINKLE *sb.* + -Y.]

a. Full of crinkles.

1866 LOWELL *Biglow P.* Poems 1890 II. 212 His veins 'ould run All crinkly like curled maple. **1882** MISS BRADDON *Mnt. Royal* II. viii. 159 Unfolding crinkly green leaves.

b. Characterized by a succession of crinkling sounds.

1827 J. WILSON *Noctes Ambr.* in *Wks.* (1855) I. 330 Does my voice come from my heart in a crinkly cough, as if the lungs were rotten? **1911** HUGH WALPOLE *Mr. Perrin* iii, The white, crinkly sound of the silk of her dress against the table.

So **crinkly-crankly.**

1891 ATKINSON *Last of Giant-Killers* 8 In the rough, crumpled, crinkly-crankly part.

†**crinkum, crincum.** *Obs. slang.* Also 7 crinkom, 8 crinckam. Also GRINCOME, q.v. In *pl.* A name for the venereal disease.

1618 HORNBY *Sco. Dronk.* (1859) 13 Some will haue his nose most rich bespread With pearles and crinkoms mixt with crimson red. *a* **1700** B. E. *Dict. Cant. Crew, Crinkums,* the French Pox. **1708** MOTTEUX *Rabelais* v. xxi. (1737) 96. **1719** D'URFEY *Pills* I. 147 The Old Queen has got the Crincums.

'crinkum-'crankum, *sb.* (*a.*) Also crincum-crancum. A word applied playfully to anything full of twists and turns, or intricately or fancifully elaborated. Cf. *gim-crack, knick-knack.*

In first quot. app. a meaningless euphemism (cf. prec.). In quot. 1761 = CRINKLE-CRANKLE.

[**16..** *Old Rime* in Blount *Law Dict.* 1670 s.v. *Free-bench,* Here I am . . Like a Whore as I am. And for my *Crincum Crancum* Have lost my *Binkum Bankum.*] **1761** COLMAN & GARRICK *Cland. Marriage* II. ii. (L.) Here's none of your straight lines here—but all taste—zigzag—crinkum-crankum—in and out. **1778** MISS BURNEY *Evelina* (1794) I. 105 We shall see some crinkum-crankum or other for our money. **1793** BURNS *Let. to Thomson* Aug., That crinkum-crankum tune, 'Robin Adair'. **1840** HOOD *Up the Rhine* 103 All sorts of engine-turning, and filagree-work, and crinkum-crankum. **1864** *Sat. Rev.* 10 Dec. 731/2 Those scientific crinkum-crankum hives, from which bees with difficulty get out, and with more difficulty get in.

crinoid ('krɪnɔɪd, kraɪ-), *a.* (*sb.*) *Zool.* [ad. Gr. κρινοειδής lily-like. As a sb. the latinized plural forms *crinoidea, crinoida* are used in Zool.]

A. *adj.* Lily-shaped; applied to an order (chiefly fossil) of echinoderms, having a calyx-like body, stalked and rooted. **B.** *sb.* A member of this order.

1836 TODD *Cycl. Anat.* I. 109/2 Some are fixed, as the crinoid echinoderma. **1847** ANSTED *Anc. World* iii. 26 Animals . . called Crinoids. **1871** HARTWIG *Subterr. W.* ii. 17 The Crinoids, or Sea-lilies, now almost entirely extinct.

Hence **cri'noidal** *a.*, of or pertaining to the *Crinoida* or *Crinoidea,* an order of Echinodermata. **cri'noidean,** a member of the Crinoidea.

1849 DANA *Geol.* ix. (1850) 494 The rarity of Crinoidal remains. **1882** GEIKIE *Text Bk. Geol.* II. II. vi. 168 *Crinoidal (Encrinite) Limestone,* a rock composed in great part of crystalline joints of encrinites. **1835** KIRBY *Hab. & Inst. Anim.* II. xiii. 11 Lamarck has placed the Crinoïdeans . . in the same order with his Floating Polypes. **1851** RICHARDSON *Geol.* 227 The most perfect type of crinoidean.

crinolette (krɪnəʊ'lɛt). [dim. f. CRINOLINE.] A sort of bustle or contrivance for distending the back of a woman's skirt.

1881 *World,* 27 July 15/1 The crinoline projected hideously at the side, whereas the crinolette will only stick out at the back. **1883** *Times* 1 Jan. 4/2 Why has the crinolette, making such grotesque protuberances, been allowed to thrust itself into the fashions of 1883?

Hence **crino'letted** *a.*

1885 *Pall Mall G.* 15 June 4 They will not give up corsets and crinoletted skirts.

crinoline ('krɪnəʊliːn, -əlɪn). [a. mod.F. *crinoline,* f. L. *crīnis* hair, in sense of F. *crin* horse-hair + *līnum* thread, a manufacturer's name intended to express its composition with warp of thread and woof of horse-hair.]

1. A stiff fabric made of horse-hair and cotton or linen thread, formerly used for skirts (see 2), and still for lining, etc. (For the latter purpose the name is also applied to imitations made of stiffened muslin, etc.)

1830 *World of Fashion* Aug. 180 The new stuff called *crinoline*; it was at first announced as a material for shoes and *bottines* only, then for bonnets; now it is offered for dresses. **1848** THACKERAY *Bk. Snobs* xxv, Crinoline or its substitutes is not an expensive luxury.

b. This material or its substitutes (*e.g.* whalebone or iron hoops) as used to expand a petticoat: see next.

1848 THACKERAY *Bk. Snobs* xxxii, I saw them to-day, without any crinoline, pulling the garden-roller. **1859** *All Year Round* No. 33. 161 We hear..of a woman in crinoline being blown off a narrow ledge into the water. **1885** KATH. O'MEARA *Madame Mohl* ii. 117 A short skirt, guiltless of the faintest suspicion of crinoline.

2. A stiff petticoat made of this stuff, worn under the skirt of a woman's dress in order to support or distend it; *hence*, a petticoat lined with, or consisting of, a framework of whalebone, steel hoops, etc., worn for the same purpose; a hoop-petticoat.

1851 *Punch's Almanac* 9 Mrs. H. came out this morning in her crinoline, as if she was not big enough already! **1869** TROLLOPE *He Knew* vii. (1878) 38 In the days of crinolines she had protested that she had never worn one.

3. *transf.* **a.** A contrivance worn by divers.

1870 *Instr. Mil. Engineering* I. 351 The crinoline should be used in deep water..it is placed round the body and tied in front of the stomach..it..enables him to breathe more freely.

b. A netting fitted round war-ships as a defence against torpedoes. Chiefly *attrib.*

1874 *Times* 23 Feb. in *Ure's Dict. Arts* (1875) II. 207 A strong crinoline framework of booms and spars built up round her. **1885** *Times* 30 Apr. 10/6 Her crinoline defences against torpedoes. **1887** *Pall Mall G.* 5 July 5/1 When the Légé torpedo is drawn up against the crinoline of an ironclad it impinges upon it and is then drawn under the crinoline by the wire.

4. *attrib.*, as ***crinoline cloth, hat*** (made of cotton braid, and then stiffened like straw), ***steel, wire.***

1848 THACKERAY *Van. F.* III. iii. 38 Crinoline-petticoats. **1850** *Harper's Mag.* I. 144 Crinoline hats of open pattern.. are worn to the opera. **1868** ROGERS *Pol. Econ.* viii. (ed. 3) 78 Fifty tons of crinoline wire were turned out weekly from factories. **1882** *Worcester Exhib. Catal.* iii. 54 Horse-hair crinoline cloth. **1891** *Leeds Mercury* 27 Apr. 4/7 A wide-brimmed pale-grey crinoline straw hat.

Hence **'crinoline** *v.*, to stiffen or provide with crinoline. **'crinolined** *ppl. a.*, wearing crinoline or a distended petticoat (also *fig.*).

1855 DE QUINCEY in H. A. Page *Life* (1877) II. xviii. 111 But afterwards..he buckramed or crinolined his graceful sketch with an elaborate machinery of gnomes and sylphs. **1862** T. A. TROLLOPE *Marietta* I. xi. 210 Crinolined lady. **1927** E. SITWELL *Rustic Elegies* 78 Like the crinolined waterfalls. **1930** —— *Coll. Poems* 222, I sat at my dressing-table—that chilly Palely crinolined water-lily. **1934** LD. BERNERS *First Childhood* 200 A crinolined damsel seated at the piano.

crinosity (kraɪˈnɒsɪtɪ). *rare.* [f. L. type **crīnōsitās*, f. **crīnōsus* hairy, f. *crīnis* hair.] Hairiness.

1656 BLOUNT *Glossogr.*, *Crinosity*, hairiness. **1730–6** in BAILEY (folio). **1755** in JOHNSON. **1825** *New Monthly Mag.* XIII. 424 None of the ancients, as I see, Laid claim to our crinosity. **1832** L. HUNT *Sir R. Esher* (1850) 95 The royal crinosity was naturally a deep black.

So **cri'nose** *a.*, having much or long hair.

1730–6 in BAILEY (folio); whence in JOHNSON and mod. Dicts.

crio- = Gr. κριο-, comb. form of κριός ram: in some technical terms, as **crio'cephalous** *a.* [Gr. κεφαλή head], having a ram's head (said *e.g.* of a sphinx). **cri'ocerate** *a.* [Gr. κέρας horn], akin to the genus *Crioceras* of fossil cephalopods, having the whorls discrete, so as to resemble a ram's horn. **crio'ceratite**, a fossil of the genus *Crioceras*, a ram's-horn ammonite. **crio-cera'titic** *a.*, pertaining to, or of the nature of, a crioceratite. **'criophore**, a statue or other representation of a figure carrying a ram (1909 in WEBSTER); so **cri'ophoric, cri'ophorous** *adjs.* **'criosphinx**, a sphinx having a ram's head, one of the three types of the Egyptian sphinx.

1832 G. LONG *Egypt. Antiq.* I. x. 213 A row of crio-sphinxes..with a ram's head and lion's body. **1847** ANSTED *Anc. World* x. 244 The shell called Crioceratite.. corresponds with the Ammonite, much as the Spirula corresponds with the Nautilus. **1921** G. A. F. KNIGHT *Nile & Jordan* xiii. 160 Criophorous sphinxes lined the avenues of Thebes and other cities. **1952** *Jrnl. Theol. Stud.* III. 90 The criophoric figures, such as those of Hermes, which anticipate later Christian representations of the Good Shepherd.

criollo (krɪˈɒləʊ). [a. Sp. *criollo* native to the locality: see CREOLE.] A variety of cocoa tree, *Theobroma cacao*, native to Central America; also, a name for high-quality cocoa or cocoa beans. Also *attrib.*

1908 H. H. SMITH *Cacao Planting* 39 Strong growing forastero or calabicillo, bearing the finest criollo beans. *Ibid.*, Good buds from pure criollo stocks. **1929** *Encycl. Brit.* V. 947/1 The finest type of bean the criollo, is grown in Venezuela, Ceylon, Java, Samoa, Madagascar and Nicaragua; but in Ceylon, and other places, criollo is being replaced by forastero. *Ibid.* XXIII. 52/1 There are two grades of Venezuelan cacao—the *criollo* or native, and the *trinitario* or Trinidad. **1955** D. H. URQUHART *Cocoa* ii. 15 Cross-fertilization took place with the Criollo trees and when seedlings were raised from them they were no longer pure Criollo. *Ibid.* xiii. 156 Criollos and allied types were the cocoas with distinctive flavour.

crion, criour, obs. ff. CRAYON, CRIER.

‖**'crious,** *a. Obs.* [ME. and AF. *crious* = OF. *crieus*, f. *crier* to CRY: see -OUS.] Clamorous.

1382 WYCLIF *Prov.* ix. 13 A fool womman and crious [**1388** full of cry; L. *clamosa*].

crip. *U.S.* colloq. abbrev. of CRIPPLE *sb.*

1918 'A—No. 1' *Mother Delcassee of Hoboes* 43 *Straight crip*, actually crippled or otherwise afflicted. *Phoney crip*, self-mutilated or simulating a deformity. *Ibid.* 84 Going to play the 'phoney crip' act for a spell, Dallas Bob? **1942** BERREY & VAN DEN BARK *Amer. Thes. Slang* §120/2 *Crip*, a crippled animal. **1950** HEMINGWAY *Across River* viii. 62 He only loved people, he thought, who had fought or been mutilated... So I'm a sucker for crips, he thought.

crip, obs. var. of SCRIP.

cripes (kraɪps), *int.* Vulgar perversion of CHRIST in the exclamation (*by*) *cripes!* (Cf. CRIMES *int.*)

1910 A. H. DAVIS *From Selection to City* xii. 107 'By cripes!' he gasped,..'I've lost th'..th' *cheques*!' **1911** L. STONE *Jonah* I. ix. 100 Stinky spat on his hands, and seized the wooden mallet. Cripes! he would show Pinkey which was the better man of the two. **1919** E. H. JONES *Road to En-Dor* i. 2 'What's the suggestion?' Alec asked. 'Spooking,' said I. 'Cripes!' said Alec. **1929** *Sunday Dispatch* 13 Jan. 2/4 You've sold me a pup! But, by cripes, I'll..let you have it back. **1930** J. B. PRIESTLEY *Angel Pavement* iv. 177 That's what it was—oh, cripes!—awful hole! **1937** N. MARSH *Vintage Murder* vi. 59 By cripes,..I'm sorry. **1952** A. F. GRIMBLE *Pattern of Islands* 68 The captain goggled at me for a second, 'Cripes!' he said.

†**crippid,** *ppl. a. Obs.* Perh. var. of CRIMPED = pinched, squeezed.

1382 WYCLIF *Lev.* xxii. 24 Al beeste..with al to-broken or crippid or kitt..ballokes [L. *contritis vel tusis vel sectis.. testiculis*].

crippin, var. of CRESPINE.

cripple (ˈkrɪp(ə)l), *sb.* and *a.* Forms: 1 crypel, 3–4 crupel (-y-), 4 cruppel, crepil, -ul, 4–5 cripel, -il, 4–7 crepel, 5 crypylle, crebull, 5–6 crepell, -ill, -yl(le, 6 crippil, crypple, crepple, -ell, 6–7 creeple, creple, criple, 7 creaple, 7– cripple. [OE. *crypel* (known only in Lindisf. Gosp.) = OFris. *kreppel*, MDu. *crōpel, crēpel*, Du. *kreupel*; MLG. *krōpel, krēpel*, LG. *kröpel*; MHG. *krüppel, krüpel*, MG. 11th c. *crupel* (from LG.), Ger. *kruppel*, dial. *krippel*; ON. *kryppill*, Norw. *krypel*; all:—OTeut. **krupilo-*, f. *krup-* ablaut stem of *kriupan* to CREEP; either in the sense of one who can only creep, or perhaps rather in that of one who is, in Scottish phrase, 'cruppen together', *i.e.* contracted in body and limbs.]

A. *sb.* **1. a.** One who is disabled (either from birth, or by accident or injury) from the use of his limbs; a lame person.

*c***950** *Lindisf. Gosp.* Luke v. 24 Cuoeð ðæm cryple..aris. *c***1290** *S. Eng. Leg.* I. 51/157 Tweie crupeles þat in heore limes al fur-crokede were. *c***1374** CHAUCER *Troylus* IV. 1458 It is ful hard to halten unespied Bifor a crepul, for he kan the craft. **1480** CAXTON *Chron. Eng.* cci. 182 God hath yeuen therto to crepels hir goyng and to croked hir hondes. **1586** A. DAY *Eng. Secretary* II. (1625) 22 Of ancient time it hath often been said, that it is ill halting before a Creple. **1611** BIBLE *Acts* xiv. 8 A creeple from his mothers wombe. **1684** BUNYAN *Pilgr.* II. Introd. 229 These strings..will such Musick make, They'l make a Cripple dance. **1747** WESLEY *Prim. Physic* (1762) 93 One who was quite a Cripple, having no strength left either in his Leg, Thigh, or Loins. **1865** TROLLOPE *Belton Est.* xiii. 142 A poor cripple, unable to walk beyond the limits of her own garden.

b. A cattle disease. Also in *pl. dial.* and *Austral.*

1897 *Penrith Obs.* 7 Dec. (E.D.D.), Ass t'coo doctor what ails a coo when it'll eat a body's kytle, er owt else but gerse —that's cripple. **1929** *Times* 1 July 15/6 Lack of minerals in pastures causes innumerable diseases, such as..'cripples'.. in Australia.

2. *techn.* **a.** = *cripple-gap* (see 5), where app. *cripple* = 'creeping'. **b.** A temporary staging used in cleaning or painting windows: cf. CRADLE *sb.*

1648 A. EYRE *Diary* (Surtees) 106 He opened a cripple and putt his sheepe on to the New field. **1887** *Even. News* 11 May 3/6 The jury..recommended the use of ladders, or of the recognised machine known as a 'cripple'.

3. *U.S.* (*local.*) **a.** A dense thicket in swampy or low-lying ground. **b.** A lumberman's term for a rocky shallow in a stream.

1675 *New Jersey Archives* (1880) I. 115 The great Swamp or Cripple which backs the said two Necks of land. **1705** in *Corr. Penn. & Logan* I. 234 About 300 acres, 100 upland, the rest swamp and cripple that high tides flow over. **1832** J. F. WATSON *Tales Olden Time* 57 Through that cripple browsed the deer. **1942** *Sat. Even. Post* 5 Sept. 11/1 When they came to the cripple he sloshed straight through.

4. *slang.* A sixpence. Cf. BENDER 6.

1785 GROSE *Dict. Vulgar Tongue*, *Cripple*, six pence, that piece being commonly much bent and distorted. **1885** *Househ. Words* 20 June 155 (Farmer) The sixpence..is called a bandy, a 'bender', a cripple.

5. *Comb.*, as ***cripple-lame*** adj.; **cripple-gap, -hole** (*dial.*), see quot. and cf. 2a; **cripple-stopper** (*colloq.*), a small gun for killing wounded birds in wild-fowl shooting.

1595 MARKHAM *Sir R. Grinvile* lix, Dismembred bodies perish cripple-lame. **1847–78** HALLIWELL, *Cripple-gap*, a hole left in walls for sheep to pass through. *North.* Also called a *cripple-hole*. **1881** GREENER *Gun* 553 Armed with a big shoulder-gun and a 'cripple-stopper'. **1886** *Pall Mall G.* 24 Aug. 4/2 The Crane gun..being used with ball and slugs for..cripple-stopping.

B. *adj.* Disabled from the use of one's limbs; lame. *Obs.* or *dial.*, exc. in *attrib.* use of prec.

*c***1230** *Hali Meid.* 33 Beo he cangun oðer crupel. *a***1300** *Cursor M.* 22829 (Gött.) Ani man..crepil or croked. **1535** COVERDALE *Matt.* xviii. 8 It is better for yᵉ to entre in vnto life lame or crepell. **1599** SHAKS. *Hen. V*, IV. Prol. 20 And chide the creeple tardy-gated Night, Who..doth limpe So tediously away. *a***1649** DRUMM. OF HAWTH. *Poems* Wks. (1711) 56 That criple folk walk not upright. *c***1860** WHITTIER *Hill-top* viii, My poor sick wife, and cripple boy.

cripple (ˈkrɪp(ə)l), *v.* [f. CRIPPLE *sb.* Cf. Ger. *krüppeln*, trans. and intr. in senses 1 and 3.]

1. *trans.* To deprive (wholly or partly) of the use of one's limbs; to lame, disable, make a cripple of.

*a***1300** [see CRIPPLED]. **1607** SHAKS. *Timon* IV. i. 24 Thou cold Sciatica, Cripple our Senators, that their limbes may halt As lamely as their Manners! **1791** HUDDESFORD *Salmag.* (1793) 119 Falling in his drunken fits, Crippled his Nose. **1859** KINGSLEY *Misc.* (1860) II. 326 Sailors..crippled by scurvy or Tropic fevers.

2. *transf.* and *fig.* To disable, impair: **a.** the action or effectiveness of material objects, mechanical contrivances, etc.

1694 SMITH & WALFORD *Acc. Sev. Late Voy.* I. (1711) 75 The Grass and Trees are much weather-beaten, worn away, and crippled. **1725** W. HALFPENNY *Sound Building* 22 So, that the Mason..shall twin their Arches thereon without crippling them. **1805** NELSON in Nicolas *Disp.* VII. 153 *note*, The lower masts, yards and bowsprit all crippled. **1871** MACDUFF *Mem. of Patmos* xviii. 247 No sickness..crippling the warrior on the very eve of conquest.

b. a person in his resources, means, efforts, etc., or immaterial things, as trade, schemes, strength, operations, etc.

1702 C. MATHER *Magn. Chr.* III. III. Introd. (1852) 531 To creeple all the learned, godly, painful ministers of the nation. **1751** JOHNSON *Rambler* No. 173 ¶1 The mind..is crippled..by perpetual application to the same set of ideas. *a***1809** J. PALMER *Like Master Like Man* (1811) II. 56 He was ..crippled of present means. **1856** FROUDE *Hist. Eng.* (1858) I. iv. 289 The nobility, crippled by the wars of the Roses. **1880** L. OLIPHANT *Land of Gilead* x. 304 The trade..is crippled by the difficulty of transport.

3. *intr.* To move or walk lamely; to hobble. (Now chiefly *Sc.*)

*c***1220** *Bestiary* 130 He crepeð cripelande forth. *a***1455** HOLLAND *Houlate* 956 He crepillit, he crengit, he carfully cryd. **1649** G. DANIEL *Trinarch., Rich. II*, cclxxix, The King (who creepled till he came before This Shrine) walkes vpright now. **1828** SCOTT *F.M. Perth* viii, Her discomfited master..was crippling towards him, his clothes much soiled with his fall. **1878** W. C. SMITH *Hilda* (1879) 239 The wounded..cripple through the street.

crippled (ˈkrɪp(ə)ld), *ppl. a.* [f. prec. + -ED.] Deprived of the use of one's limbs; lame, disabled; also *transf.* and *fig.*: see the verb.

*a***1300** *Cursor M.* 19048 (Cott.) Þar sagh þai lij, A man was criplid in þe parlesi. **1591** PERCIVALL *Sp. Dict.*, *Contrecho*, weake, cripled. **1674** N. FAIRFAX *Bulk & Selv.* 173 It has no crutches to lean its crippled burden on. **1779–81** JOHNSON *L.P.*, *Somervile*, If blank verse be not tumid and gorgeous, it is crippled prose. **1810** ROWLEY in *Naval Chron.* XXV. 162 One of them..had a crippled frigate in tow. **1864** EARL DERBY *Iliad* I. 712 The crippled Vulcan, matchless architect.

'crippledom. [See -DOM.] The condition of being a cripple. So **cripplehood, crippleness.**

1860 READE *Cloister & H.* (1861) III. 72 What with my crippledom and thy piety..we'll bleed the bumpkins. **1883** W. H. RUSSELL in *19th Cent.* Sept. 495 Emerging rapidly from a state of crippledom to one of comparative activity. **1864** DASENT *Jest & Earnest* (1873) I. 168 One cripple of such commanding cripplehood. **1755** JOHNSON, *Crippleness*, lameness; privation of the limbs. *Dict.*

crippler (ˈkrɪplə(r)). [f. CRIPPLE *v.* + -ER¹.]

1. One who or that which cripples.

1648 EARL WESTMRLD. *Otia Sacra* (1879) 166 His sounder feet with swathes he ties, And seems to goe in pain as far, As art can prove a Crippeler. **1890** *The Voice* (N.Y.) 21 Aug., A great crippler to the saloon power in..politics.

2. (See quot.)

1874 KNIGHT *Dict. Mech.*, *Crippler*, a board with a corrugated under-surface..used in boarding or graining leather.

crippling (ˈkrɪplɪŋ), *vbl. sb.* The action of the verb CRIPPLE.

1598 FLORIO, *Zoppicamento*, a halting, a cripling, a limping. **1836** W. IRVING *Astoria* II. 285 The crippling of the feet of females in China.

'crippling, *ppl. a.* That cripples: see CRIPPLE *v.*

1598 FLORIO, *Zótto*..a limping or cripling fellow. **1814** WORDSW. *Excursion* I. Wks. (1888) 422/2 To meet The hour of accident or crippling age. **1859** DICKENS *T. Two Cities* I. v, The crippling stones of the pavement.

cripplingly ('krɪplɪŋlɪ), *adv.* [f. prec. + -LY².] So as to cripple or disable.

1899 *Daily News* 18 Feb. 6/3 The new skirts are very long, cripplingly so. **1927** *Daily Express* 4 Nov. 3/4 The damage, the cost, the contamination are cripplingly unbearable. **1955** *Times* 1 July 16/3 The standard rate of income tax.. remains at a cripplingly high level.

'**cripply,** *a. Obs.* exc. *dial.* [f. CRIPPLE + -Y.] Somewhat crippled.

1775 *Mad. D'Arblay's Early Diary* 18 Apr., Tho' fingers are crippley and left arm lame. **1839** MRS. F. TROLLOPE *M. Armstrong* iii. (D.) 'He's so cripply, he beant to work no more.' **1876** *Whitby Gloss.*, *Cripply*, tending to lameness.

crips, obs. and dial. form of CRISP.

cript(e, criptic, obs. var. CRYPT, CRYPTIC.

cris, obs. f. KRIS, Malay dagger.

crise (kriːz). Also 6 cryse. [a. F. *crise* crisis (Paré 16th c.).] = CRISIS. Also in various French phrases, esp. ***crise de*** (or ***des***) ***nerfs***, an attack of nerves, a fit of hysterics.

1541 R. COPLAND *Galyen's Terap.* 2 D iij, They haue wel and parfytly knowen the contemplacyon of the Cryse. **1643** R. BAILLIE *Lett. & Jrnls.* (1841) II. 90 This seems to be a new period and crise of the most great affaire. *c* **1750** SHENSTONE *Progr. of Taste* IV, Behold him, at some crise, prescribe, And raise with drugs the sick'ning tribe! **1768** Ross *Helenore* 52 (Jam.) [She] thinks her wiss is now come to the creeze. **1921** W. J. LOCKE *Mountebank* xxi. 272 Reason enough for a *crise de nerfs*. Even I, who had nothing to do with it, found my equilibrium disturbed. **1922** M. ARLEN *Piracy* II. i. 72 'Virginia has got a *crise*,' Lois Lamprey commented. **1923** W. J. LOCKE *Moordius & Co.* vii. 96 Sometimes these *crises de nerfs* are dangerous. **1933** 'G. ORWELL' *Down & Out* xx. 148 The cook usually had a *crise de nerfs* and a flood of tears. **1946** E. TAYLOR *Palladian* v. 49 When the time came for her to go to the party.. there would be a painful *crise de nerfs*. **1962** GREGOR & NICHOLAS *Moral & Story* v. 133 The *crise de conscience* that faces the serious contemporary novelist. **1962** N. MARSH *Hand in Glove* ii. 44 I'm afraid your Pixie has created a parochial *crise*. **1962** *Punch* 23 May 808/1 When there is a *crise d'amour* it is very peaceful for me. **1963** A. HARTLEY *State of England* iii. 79 The Algerian *crise de conscience* that dissolved the authority of the French state. **1970** P. BAIR *Tribunal* III. v. 201 What then caused this *crise de conscience*? **1970** *New Yorker* 10 Oct. 178/2 She has been a splendid advertisement for the benefits of a happy marriage—conspicuously more relaxed, far less subject to those old *crises des nerfs*.

crisis ('kraɪsɪs). Pl. crises, *rarely* crisises. [a. L. *crisis*, a. Gr. κρίσις discrimination, decision, crisis, f. κρίν-ειν to decide.]

1. *Pathol.* The point in the progress of a disease when an important development or change takes place which is decisive of recovery or death; the turning-point of a disease for better or worse; also applied to any marked or sudden variation occurring in the progress of a disease and to the phenomena accompanying it.

1543 TRAHERON *Vigo's Chirurg.* VI. i. Dict. Terms, *Crisis* sygnifyeth iudgemente, and in thys case, it is vsed for a sodayne chaunge in a disease. **1548** HALL *Chron.* 80 When the crisis of his sicknes was past and that he perceived that helth was overcome. **1625** HART *Anat. Ur.* I. ii. 21 Then shall the sicke.. by the vertue and power of a happy Crisis, saile forth into the hauen of health. **1685** BOYLE *Enq. Notion Nat.* 222, I observe that Crises's, properly so call'd, do very seldom happen in other than Feavers. **1748** SMOLLETT *Rod. Rand.* xxxiv, When he found I had enjoyed a favourable crisis, he congratulated me. **1856** KANE *Arct. Expl.* II. viii. 87 Brooks.. and Thomas have seen the crisis of their malady.

†**2.** *Astrol.* Said of a conjunction of the planets which determines the issue of a disease or critical point in the course of events. (Cf. CRITICAL 4.)

1603 SIR C. HEYDON *Def. Jud. Astrol.* 474 When the Moone comes to the 22 of Gemini, shee shall there begin to worke a dangerous Crisis, or alteration.. so preuenting her ordinarie working. **1663** BUTLER *Hud.* I. i. 611 They'll feel the Pulses of the Stars, To find out Agues, Coughs, Catarrhs; And tell what Crisis does Divine The Rot in Sheep, or Mange in Swine.

3. *transf.* and *fig.* A vitally important or decisive stage in the progress of anything; a turning-point; also, a state of affairs in which a decisive change for better or worse is imminent; now applied *esp.* to times of difficulty, insecurity, and suspense in politics or commerce.

1627 SIR B. RUDYARD in Rushw. *Hist. Coll.* I. (1659) 301 This is the Chrysis of Parliaments; we shall know by this if Parliaments live or die. *a* **1661** FULLER *Worthies* I. 204 The time betwixt Wicklife and Trevisa was the Chrisis of the English tongue. **1715** M. DAVIES *Ath. Brit.* I. 346 Great Crisises in Church and State. **1769** *Junius Lett.* i. 10 To escape a crisis so full of terror and despair. **1848** MILL *Pol. Econ.* III. xii, There is said to be a commercial crisis when a great number of merchants and traders, at once, either have, or apprehend that they shall have, a difficulty in meeting their engagements. **1860** TYNDALL *Glac.* I. xxvii. 202 The layer of snow had been in a state of strain, which our crossing brought to a crisis. **1875** JOWETT *Plato* (ed. 2) III. 174 The ordinary statesman is also apt to fail in extraordinary crises. **1886** STUBBS *Lect. Med. & Mod. Hist.* xvi. 365 Foreign transactions.. most tedious because they go on without crisises and without issues.

†**4.** Judgement, decision. *Obs.*

1621 W. SCLATER *Quæst. Tythes* (1623) 198 His Crisis so exact will with greatest scorne reiect [etc.]. **1643** HERLE *Answ. Ferne* 2 Consciences *Synteresis*, and *Syneidesis*.. can warrant her to passe her Crisis or conclusive judgement. **1683** CAVE *Ecclesiastici* Pref. 3 We have not made.. a Crisis and Censure of every single Tract. **1715** M. DAVIES *Ath. Brit.* I. 11.

†**5.** A point by which to judge; a criterion, token, sign. *Obs.*

1606 SIR G. GOOSECAPPE II. i. in Bullen *O. Pl.* III. 33 The Crises here are excellent good; the proportion of the chin good.. the wart above it most exceeding good. **1641** H. P. *Quest. Div. Right Episc.* Ep. Ded. 2 Let your gracious acceptance of the same be as strong a crisis that your Grace is not a prejudging factious enemie. **1657** S. PURCHAS *Pol. Flying-Ins.* I. v. 12 Whereas the others beauty and lustiness is a Crysis of their youth, not their idleness.

6. *attrib.* and *Comb.*

1841 *Times* 11 May 5/1 It may disappoint the crisis-mongers to hear us say so. **1896** *Westm. Gaz.* 23 June 3/1 All the aspects of a crisis night. **1898** *Ibid.* 4 Jan. 2/2 A Tory Government was 'crisis proof'. **1898** *Ibid.* 26 Mar. 5/1 The 'crisis'-less years of the late Liberal Government. **1898** *Ibid.* 24 June 2/3 The Near and not the Far East.. was the crisis-centre. **1900** *Ibid.* 11 May 2/2 A crisis-avoiding peace-compelling Government. **1903** *Ibid.* 3 Jan. 2/3 A Crisis Fund, amounting to nearly two millions. **1938** E. WAUGH in *Tablet* 23 July 112/1 The crisis-minded always maintain that the problems of their particular decade are unique and insuperable. **1938** *Punch* 10 Aug. 163/1 How many of these people are crisis-conscious? **1939** WYNDHAM LEWIS *Let.* 5 Oct. (1963) 266 In the crisis-days prior to the war. **1940** W. EMPSON *Gathering Storm* 65 The point is to join up the crisis-feeling to what can be felt all the time in normal life. **1960** *Times* 24 Oct. (Financial Rev.) p. viii/6 Switzerland.. has been a normal haven for 'crisis' money. **1965** H. KAHN *On Escalation* xiii. 245 Crisis-management problems.

crisle, obs. f. CRIZZLE *v.*, to scale.

crismatory, crisme, crisome: see CHRISM-.

criso-, obs. form of CHRYSO-.

†**crisol.** *Obs.* Also **chrysoll, -sole.** [a. Sp. *crisol*: see DIEZ, s.v. *Crisuelo*.] A crucible.

1622 MABBE tr. *Aleman's Guzman d'Alf.* II. 86 Death, which is the Chrysoll wherein wee must at last be all melted. *Ibid.* II. 238, I did put all the gold into a great Crisoll.

crisp (krɪsp), *a.* Forms: 1– crisp; also 1 cyrps, 3–5 crips, 4–7 crispe, 5 cryps(e, cryspe, kyrspe. [OE. *crisp*, *cyrps*, ad. L. *crispus* curled. Cf. OF. *crespe* curled, mod.F. *crêpe*; but this does not appear to have influenced the Eng. word in form. The sense development of branch II is not clear: cf. however CRIMP *a.*, and the quot. from Cotgr. Some onomatopœic influence associated with the action of pronouncing *crisp* is to be suspected.]

I. In senses of L. *crispus*.

1. Of the hair: Curly; now applied *esp.* to stiff, closely curling, or frizzy hair; †also, having or wearing such hair.

c **900** *Bæda's Hist.* v. ii, Se ȝunga wæs ȝeworden hale lichoman.. and hæfde crispe loccas fægre. *c* **1000** in Thorpe's *Hom.* I. 456 (Bosw.) He is blæcfexede and cyrps. *c* **1290** *S. Eng. Leg.* I. 319/687 Blac with cripse here. *c* **1386** CHAUCER *Knt.'s T.* 1307 His crispe heer lyk rynges was yronne. **1398** TREVISA *Barth. de P.R.* IV. ii. (1495) 80 Lytyll heere and cryps as in blomens countree. *c* **1400** *Lanfranc's Cirurg.* 179 Wynde alle þese þingis & frote þe heeris and þei wolen bicome crisp. **1583** STANYHURST *Aeneis* II. (Arb.) 65 A certeyn lightning on his headtop glistered harmelesse, His crisp locks frizeling. **1626** BACON *Sylva* §852 Buls are more Crispe upon the Fore-Head than Cowes. **1777** COOK *Voy. S. Pole* III. vi, Their hair.. black and brown, growing to a tolerable length, and very crisp and curly. **1859** R. F. BURTON *Centr. Afr.* in *Jrnl. Geogr. Soc.* XXIX. 317 The hair of these races has invariably a crisp, short, and stiff curl.

2. a. Having a surface curled or fretted into minute waves, ripples, folds or wrinkles.

1398 TREVISA *Barth. de P.R.* (Tollem. MS.) XIII. xv, The ponde.. with crispe water and calm, and nouȝt with stronge wyndes. *c* **1400** MAUNDEV. (1839) xv. 168 The peper.. þei putten it vpon an owven and þere it waxeth blak and crisp [*Roxb.* ed. blakk and runklid]. *c* **1430** LYDG. *Min. Poems* (Percy Soc.) 199 The kyrspe skyn of hyr forheed, Is drawyn up and on trustily bownde. **1596** SHAKS. *1 Hen. IV*, I. iii. 106 Swift Seuernes flood.. hid his crispe-head in the hollow banke. **1610** —— *Temp.* IV. i. 130 You Nimphs cald Nayades of yᵉ windring brooks.. Leaue your crispe channels. **1823** BYRON *Juan* IX. lxxviii, The elder ladies' wrinkles curl'd much crisper. **1877** BLACK *Green Past.* xxix. (1878) 235 The crisp white crest of the running waves.

b. *Bot.* = CRISPATE, CRISPED 2 b.

1753 CHAMBERS *Cycl. Supp.* s.v. *Leaf*, *Crisp leaf*.. that which is undulated or folded over and over at the edge. **1776** WITHERING *Brit. Plants* (1796) III. 847 *Hypnum crispum*.. leaves crisp, transversely waved.

†**3.** Applied to some fabrics: perh. of crape-like texture. Cf. CRISP *sb. Obs.*

a **1300** *Cursor M.* 28018 (Cott.) Yee leuedis.. wit curchefs crisp and bendes bright. **1387** TREVISA *Higden* (Rolls) I. 401 A crisp breche wel fayn [*crispa femoralia*]. **1393** *Will* in A. Gibbons *Early Linc. Wills* (1888) 85 Omnes meos crispcouerchifes.

†**4.** Apparently = Smooth, shining, clear. *Obs.*

[Cf. Cotgr. '*Crespu*, curled, frizled, ruffled, crisped; sleeked, shining'; '*Cresper*.. also, to sleeke, make to shine or glitter'.]

1565 GOLDING *Ovid's Met.* IX. (1593) 211 My cleere crispe legs [L. *crura micantia*] he striveth for to catch. **1607** SHAKS. *Timon* IV. iii. 183 All th' abhorred births below crispe Heauen. **1623** FLETCHER *Bloody Bro.* IV. ii, You must leave your neat crisp Claret, and fall to your Cyder a while.

II. 5. a. Brittle or 'short' while somewhat hard or firm in structure (usually as a good quality); said *esp.* of hard things which have little cohesion and are easily crushed by the teeth, etc.

1530 PALSGR. 501/1, I crasshe, as a thynge dothe that is cryspe or britell bytwene ones tethe. **1611** COTGR., *Cresper*, to crackle or creake, as new shooes; or drie stickes that are laid in the fire; also, to crash between the teeth (a thing thats crispe or brittle). **1626** BACON *Sylva* §231 In Frostie weather.. the Wood or String of the Instrument.. is made more Crispe, and so more porous and hollow. **1749** F. SMITH *Voy. Disc. N.-W. Pass.* II. 15 The Snow was of a greyish Colour, crisp on the Top. **1766** GOLDSM. *Vic. W.* xvi, If the cakes at tea eat short and crisp, they were made by Olivia. **1822** LAMB *Elia*, *Roast Pig*, The crisp.. not over-roasted crackling. **1866** *Treas. Bot.* 79/1 Celery.. the sweet, crisp, wholesome, and most agreeable of our cultivated vegetables.

b. From *crisp snow* or *frost*, transferred by association to a brisk frosty day, to frosty air, and thence to bracing air generally.

1869 LADY BARKER *Station Life N. Zeal.* xv. (1874) 109 The peculiar fresh crisp feeling which the atmosphere always has here the moment the sun sets. **1873** MRS. ALEXANDER *Wooing o't* xxv, All that Christmas Day ought to be, clear, crisp, bright. **1883** ANNA K. GREEN *Hand & Ring* xxxiv, The crisp frosty air had put everybody in a good humour.

6. *transf.* and *fig.* Applied vaguely to anything possessing qualities more or less characteristic of crisp substances: **a.** stiff, firm, as opposed to limp.

1851 MAYNE REID *Scalp Hunters* iv. 29 The 'crop, crop' of our horses shortening the crisp grass. *a* **1859** L. HUNT (Webster), It [laurel] has been plucked nine months, and yet looks as hale and crisp as if it would last ninety years. **1868** DILKE *Greater Brit.* I. 133 The 'blue grass' has high vitality.. this crisp turf at once springs up, and holds the ground for ever.

b. *fig.* Short, sharp, brisk, decided in manner. (Cf. an analogous use of 'flabby' as the opposite.) Also, clean, neat; clearly defined.

1814 MACKINTOSH in *Life* (1836) II. 300 Ward said Constant was very 'crisp'. **1857** W. COLLINS *Dead Secret* II. i. (1861) 31 Such a crisp touch on the piano. **1873** HALE *In His Name* iii. 10 What he said was crisp and decided. **1884** *Athenæum* 6 Dec. 739/2 The crisp draughtsmanship of Mr. H. P. Riviere's Arch of Constantine, Rome. **1884** H. D. TRAILL in *Macm. Mag.* Oct. 441/2 His crisp antithetic manner is the perfection of style. **1937** D. M. JONES *In Parenthesis* IV. 97 The sky overhead looked crisp as eggshell. **1961** *Listener* 21 Dec. 1069/1 The superbly detailed capitals, as crisp now as they were 150 years ago. **1963** *Ibid.* 24 Jan. 160/1 A rational, crisp, glass-and-rectangular-framework architecture.

7. *Comb.*, as ***crisp-haired, -withered.***

c **1400** *Destr. Troy* 3757 Crispe herit was the kyng, colouret as gold. **1677** HALE *Prim. Orig. Man.* II. vii. 200 The Ethiopian black, flat-nosed and crisp-haired. **1868** LD. HOUGHTON in *Select. fr. Wks.* 201 Crisp-wither'd hung the honourable leaves.

crisp (krɪsp), *sb.* Also 5–6 **crysp, kirsp, kyrsp,** 6–7 **crispe.** [app. f. the adj.; cf. 16th c. F. *crespe* crape or material for veils, mod.F. *crêpe* crape. In the entries in the *Testamenta Eboracensia* 'cryspe' appears to interchange with 'cypres' = Cyprus lawn: see CYPRUS.]

†**1.** Some thin or delicate textile fabric, used *esp.* by women for veils or head-coverings; ? a crape-like material. Cf. CRISP *a.* 3. *Obs.*

1397 *Test. Ebor.* I. 220 Flameolam me' de crispo. **1402** *Ibid.* I. 289, ij flameola de cipres. **1415** *Ibid.* I. 382 Flameolum de krespe. *c* **1460** *Towneley Myst.* 313 And Nelle with hir nyfyls of crisp and of sylke. **1498** *Ld. Treas. Acc. Scot.* I. 392 Item, for xxiiij elne of kyrsp to hir for ilk elne iijs iiijd. **1500-20** DUNBAR *Tua Mariit Wemen* 23 Curches.. of kirsp cleir and thin. *c* **1600** BUREL in Watson *Coll. Sc. Poems* II. 13 (Jam.) A robe Of clenely crispe, side to his kneis. **1619** PURCHAS *Microcosmus* xxvii. 268 The new deuised names of Stuffes and Colours, Crispe, Tamet, Plush.. Callimanco, Sattinisco.

†**2.** A head-covering or veil made of this material. *Obs.*

1584 HUDSON tr. *Du Bartas' Judith* IV. (1608) 57 Upon her head a silver crispe she pind Loose waving on her shoulders with the wind. **1593** GREENE *Mamillia* II. Poems (Rtldg.) 316 Needless noughts, as crisps and scarfs, worn a la morisco. **1597** MONTGOMERIE *Cherrie & Slae* 113 Ane cleinlie crispe hang ouir his eyes [Latinized by Dempster *Involvens nivea de sindone lumina velo*].

†**3.** A crisp kind of pastry made by dropping batter into boiling fat. [So OF. *crispes* in W. de Biblesworth.] *Obs.*

? *c* **1390** *Form of Cury* 73 Cryspes. *a* **1422** *Dinner Hen. V* in *Q. Eliz. Acad.*, etc. 91 Cryspes fryez. *c* **1430** *Two Cookery-bks.* 44 Cryspes. **1450** *Ibid.* 93 Cryspes.

†**4.** A curl (of hair); *esp.* a short or close curl. *Obs.*

1634 SIR T. HERBERT *Trav.* (1638) 325 They.. weare their hayre pretty long, and about their crispes wreath a valuable Sash or Tulipant. *c* **1680** *Roxb. Ball.* VI. 278 Those bright locks of hair Spreading o're each ear, Every crisp and curle.

5. The 'crackling' of roast pork. *Obs.* exc. *dial.*

1675 T. DUFFETT *Mock Tempest* II. ii, Methinks I hear a great she Devil, call for [a] Groats worth of the Crispe of my Countenance. **1847-78** HALLIWELL, *Crisp*, pork crackling. *South.*

6. An overdone piece of anything cooked, fried, or roasted; usually in phr. ***to a crisp.*** Also *transf.* orig. *U.S.*

a **1852** F. M. WHITCHER *Widow Bedott Papers* (1856) xxix, One time, they'll burn their bread to a crisp. **1852** H. MELVILLE *Pierre* XII. ii. 263 Burn it till it shriveled to a crisp!

1899 W. C. MORROW *Bohem. Paris* 44 It was some-time before Haidon could realize that he was not burned to a crisp. **1911** H. S. HARRISON *Queed* xxi. 258, I became absorbed in a book I was reading, and Jim came back to find the bacon a crisp. **1959** A. HUXLEY *Let.* 29 Nov. (1969) 881 Temperatures are in the eighties—..the vegetation..is burnt to a crisp. **1968** K. WEATHERLY *Roo Shooter* 35 The hot weather continued and the feed had dried to a crisp.

7. In full *potato crisp*. A thin sliver of potato fried until crisp and eaten cold. Usu. in *pl.* of such food produced commercially.

1929 *Star* 21 Aug. 13/3 Potato Crisp Factory. **1935** H. NICOLSON *Let.* 3 Sept. (1966) I. 213 We went to Harry's Bar ..and there was a Pekinese being fed with crisps. **1950** T. S. ELIOT *Cocktail Party* I. 12 Potato crisps? No I can't endure them. **1953** 'N. BLAKE' *Dreadful Hollow* 43 It [*sc.* a public bar] held only one occupant, who was eating out of a packet of crisps. **1961** 'T. HINDE' *For Good of Company* iv. 41 She ..sloped her little red mouth and let a fingerful of crisps into it.

crisp (krɪsp), *v.* [f. CRISP *a.*: cf. L. *crispāre* to curl, crisp, crimp, f. *crispus.*]

1. a. *trans.* To curl into short, stiff, wavy folds, or crinkles; to crimp.

1340 [see CRISPED 1]. **1565–73** COOPER *Thesaurus, Calamistrum*..a pinne of wodde or yvory, to trime or crispe heare. **1617** B. JONSON *Vis. Delight*, As Zephyr blows.. The rivers run as smoothed by his hand: Only their heads are crisped by his stroke. **1632** J. HAYWARD tr. *Biondi's Eromena* 52 A blacke gowne..lined quite through with white silke cipres, pleated and crisped about the necke, with a deepe fringe. **1644** BULWER *Chirol.* To Rdr. A v b, We..wrinkle our forehead in dislike, crispe our nose in anger. **1747** HERVEY *Winterpiece* (1813) 365 It has..crisped the travellers locks. **1821** BYRON *Sardan.* I. ii. 6 There is A cooling breeze which crisps the broad clear river. **1837** T. HOOK *Jack Brag* vi, Every curl was crisped into its own peculiar place. **1849** RUSKIN *Sev. Lamps* iii. §22. 90 The leaf being..rendered liny by bold marking of its ribs and veins, and by turning up and crisping its edges.

b. To fold (cloth) which has just been woven.

1892 in *Eng. Dial. Dict.* **1927** *Daily Tel.* 21 June 8 The cloth may be crisped (folded lengthwise), rolled or lapped.

2. *intr.* To curl in short stiff curls.

1583 T. WATSON *Centurie of Loue* xx, Although his beard were crisping hard. **1597** GERARDE *Herbal* II. xxxvi. §12. 247 The leaues..do somewhat curle or crispe. **1777** tr. FORSTER *Voy. round World* I. 17 Their black hair naturally falls in ringlets, and begins to crisp in some individuals. **1815** SCOTT *Guy M.* iii, The quiet bay, whose little waves, crisping and sparkling to the moonbeams, rolled, etc. **1852–9** TODD *Cycl. Anat.* IV. 10/1 The shell..exposed to heat..crisping up..like horn.

3. a. *trans.* To make crisp, 'short' or brittle.

[**1658** WILLSFORD *Nature's Secrets* 52 The ground..will be hoary..the grass crisped with the Frost.] **1815** SCOTT *Guy M.* xxviii, The snow..crisped by..a severe frost. *c* **1854** THACKERAY *Wolves & Lamb* I, She crisped my buttered toast.

b. *transf.* and *fig.* Cf. CRISP *a.* 5 b, 6.

1833 ARNOLD *Lett.* in Stanley *Life* I. vii. 286 When we live in uncongenial society, we are apt to crisp and harden our outward manner, to save our real feelings from exposure. **1877** MRS. OLIPHANT *Makers Flor.* i. 3 The fresh island air crisped by the sea.

4. *intr.* To become crisp.

1805 A. SCOTT *Poems* 63 (Jam.) The nights were lang, Wi' frost the yird was crispin'. **1849** C. BRONTË *Shirley* ix, The air chilled at sunset, the ground crisped.

5. *trans.* To crush a firm but brittle substance. *rare.*

1824 MISS FERRIER *Inher.* lxviii, Hearing the sound of wheels crisping the gravel as they rolled slowly round.

†**crispage.** *Obs.*—[0] [a. F. *crespage*, now *crépage*, f. *crêper.*] 'The frizzle or curledness of crape' (Bailey, folio—Suppl. at end of Pref.).

crispate (ˈkrɪspeɪt), *a.* [ad. L. *crispātŭs*, pa. pple. of *crispāre* to curl.] Crisped; *spec.* in *Bot.* and *Zool.*, having the margin curled or undulated.

1846 DANA *Zooph.* (1848) 183 Corallum..crispate, sublobate.

crispation (krɪˈspeɪʃən). [n. of action, f. L. *crispāre* to curl: see -ATION.] Curling, curled condition; formation of slight waves, folds, or crinkles; undulation.

1626 BACON *Sylva* §852 Some differ in the Haire..both in the Quantity, Crispation, and Colours of them. *Ibid.*, Heat causeth Pilosity and Crispation. **1668** CULPEPPER & COLE *Barthol. Anat.* I. xxvii. 64 Dismissing its wrinkled Crispations, and becoming very broad. **1714** DERHAM *Astro-Theol.* v. ii. *note*, The motion of the air and vapours, makes a pretty crispation, and rouling. **1842** PRICHARD *Nat. Hist. Man* (1855) I. 96 A difference in the degree of crispation, some European hair being also very crisp.

b. 'A slight contraction of any part, morbid or natural, as that of the minute arteries in a wound when they retract, or of the skin in the state called goose-skin' (Mayne, *Expos. Lex.*).

1710 T. FULLER *Pharm. Extemp.* 150 Painful Crispations of the Fibres. **1871** M. COLLINS *Mrq. & Merch.* II v. 134 She could not think of marrying him without a shudder, a crispation from head to foot. **1887** O. W. HOLMES in *Atlantic Monthly* July 118/1 Few can look down from a great height without creepings and crispations.

c. Applied to the minute undulations on the surface of a liquid, produced by vibrations of the containing vessel, or by sound-waves.

1831 FARADAY *Exp. Res.* xlvi. 329 The well-known and peculiar crispations which form on water at the centres of vibration. **1891** *Century Mag.* May 37 Upon singing.. through the tube..beautiful crispations appear upon the surface of the liquid, which vary with every change of tone.

ˈ**crispature.** *rare.* [f. L. *crispāt-*, ppl. stem of *crispāre* + -URE.] Crisped condition; crispation.

1745 P. THOMAS *Jrnl. Anson's Voy.* 167 The Spaniards.. slice it [bread-fruit] and expose it to the Sun, and when baked thereby to a Crispature, reserve it as Biscuit. **1756** C. LUCAS *Ess. Waters* I. 157 A tension, or crispature, or a relaxation of the fibres [will] be produced. **1866** *Treas. Bot.*, *Crispature*, when the edge is excessively and irregularly divided and puckered; also when the surface is much puckered and crumpled. Good examples are afforded by 'curled' endive, 'curled' kale, and the like.

crispbread (ˈkrɪs(p)brɛd). [f. CRISP *a.* 5 a + BREAD *sb.*] A food made from crushed whole grains such as rye and wheat, prepared in the form of thin crisp biscuits.

1926–7 *Army & Navy Stores Catal.* 61/1 Ryvita (Crisp-bread)—pkt. 1/6. **1927** *Lancet* 11 June 1244/2 *Vita-wheat Crisp Bread*... The crisp bread has a pleasant texture and flavour. **1928** *Daily Mail* 25 July 8/5 (Advt.), This crisp-bread [Vita-Wheat] keeps you slim. **1951** *Good Housek. Home Encycl.* 427/1 Crispbread may be substituted for bread or toast at most meals, and is enjoyed with cheese.

crisped (krɪspt, -pɪd), *ppl. a.* [f. CRISP *v.*]

1. Of hair: Closely and stiffly curled.

c **1340** *Gaw. & Gr. Knt.* 188 þe mane of þat mayn hors.. Wel cresped & cemmed. **1432–50** tr. *Higden* (Rolls) I. 53 More blacke of skynne, more crispedde in heire. **1596** SHAKS. *Merch. V.* III. ii. 92 Those crisped snakie golden locks. **1637** R. HUMFREY tr. *St. Ambrose* I. 137 Cupids yonkers with their crisped, powdred, and perfumed lockes. **1842** PRICHARD *Nat. Hist. Man* 99 [Hair] sometimes straight and flowing, at others considerably curled and crisped.

2. Having a surface curled into minute waves, folds or puckers.

1603 DEKKER *Grissil* (Shaks. Soc.) 9 Canst drink the waters of the crisped spring? **1609** BIBLE (Douay) *1 Kings* vii. 26 The leafe of a crisped lilie. **1665** *Phil. Trans.* I. 87 Having three Auricles or crisped Angles. **1818** KEATS *Endym.* IV. 95 The wind that now did stir About the crisped oaks full drearily. **1849** THOREAU *Week on Concord* Monday 123 A million crisped waves come forth.

b. Said of a crinkled margin.

1802 BEDDOES *Hygëia* VIII. 119 [The liver] has its edges crisped till they bend forwards. **1870** HOOKER *Stud. Flora* 276 *Orobanche rubra*..lobes of lip toothed and crisped. **1870** BENTLEY *Bot.* 153 When the margin is very irregular, being twisted and curled, it is said to be crisped or curled.

3. Made crisp or brittle; 'short' in texture; also in manner, style, etc.

1628 FELTHAM *Resolves* II. xx, Hee that reades the Fathers shall finde them as if written with a crisped pen. **1769** MRS. RAFFALD *Eng. Housekpr.* (1778) 102 Garnish with crisped parsley and fried oysters. **1832** HT. MARTINEAU *Each & All* ii. 26 Young ash plantations, miles long, with their shoots crisped and black.

¶**4.** Applied to trees: sense uncertain.

1634 MILTON *Comus* 984 Along the crisped shades and bowers. **1648** HERRICK *Hesper.*, *Cerem. Candlemas-Eve*, The crisped yew.

crispen (ˈkrɪspən), *v.* [f. CRISP *a.* + -EN[5].] **a.** *trans.* To make (more) crisp or brittle. **b.** *intr.* To become crisp(er).

1961 in WEBSTER. **1977** *Washington Post* 6 May D13 Hatched lines remain distinct rather than coalescing into dark forms. The fact that they are held distinct by the paper allows Rembrandt to crispen and clarify the lines of the image. **1984** *Financial Times* 15 Sept. 11/6 Wash the lettuce leaves and place them in the refrigerator to crispen until needed. **1985** *Christian Science Monitor* 19 Sept. 17/1 Fall is a favorite time of hikers: Woods and mountains undulate with long files of people as autumn's tang crispens the air.

crisper (ˈkrɪspə(r)). [f. CRISP *v.* + -ER[1].] **a.** One who or that which crisps or curls; *spec.* an instrument for friezing or crisping cloth.

1835 BOOTH (cited by WORCESTER). **1874** KNIGHT *Dict. Mech.*, *Crisper*, an instrument for crisping the nap of cloth; i.e. covering the surface with little curls, such as with petersham or chinchilla. A crisping iron.

b. A container in a refrigerator in which vegetables and fruit can be kept crisp and fresh.

1960 *Housewife* May 92/2 A..moisture-seal crisper, in which to store your fruit and vegetables. **1960** *Sunday Express* 15 May 17/6 Full-width crisper for fruit and vegetables.

†**crisphede.** *Obs.*—[0] Crispness.

c **1440** *Promp. Parv.* 103 Cryspheed, or cryspeness, *crispitudo.*

ˈ**crispin.** A name given to a shoemaker, in allusion to Crispinus or St. Crispin, the patron saint of shoemakers; also sometimes adopted by the members of trades-unions or benefit societies of shoemakers. *St. Crispin's lance*: a shoemaker's awl.

[**1611** COTGR. s.v. *Crespin*, *Lance de S. Crespin*, an Awle.] *c* **1645** HOWELL *Lett.* (1650) I. 417 A good shoemaker that can manage St. Crispin's lance handsomely. **1726** AMHERST *Terræ Fil.* x. 47 What a pretty set of tradesmen..should we have..if gentle crispin was appointed to teach the art and mystery of basket-making. **1756** W. TOLDERVY *Hist. Two Orphans* IV. 7 In company with an honest crispin who dealt very considerably in politicks. *a* **1845** HOOD *My Son & Heir* xix, A Crispin he shall not be made.

ˈ**crispiness.** [f. CRISPY *a.* + -NESS.] The quality of being crispy; crispness.

a **1648** DIGBY *Closet Open.* (1677) 147 Give the top [of the pudding] a yellow crispiness. **1890** *Harper's Mag.* Oct. 670/2 The frilled and ruffled crispiness of its fittings.

crisping (ˈkrɪspɪŋ), *vbl. sb.* [f. CRISP *v.* + -ING[1].] The action of the verb to CRISP; curling.

1400–1568 [see b.]. **1669** E. MONTAGUE *Art of Mettals* II. xix. (1674) 67 That some little hairyness, or crisping encompasseth the Pellets of Quicksilver. **1683** (*title*), England's Vanity..wherein Naked Breasts and Shoulders ..Long Perriwigs..Curlings, and Crispings, are condemned.

b. *Comb.*, as in *crisping-crook*, *-iron*, *-pin*, *-tongs*, instruments for crisping or curling the hair, etc.

? *a* **1400** *Morte Arthur* 3353 The krispane kroke to my crowne raughte. **1483** *Cath. Angl.* 83 A Cryspyngeyren, *acus.* **1568** BIBLE (Bishops') *Isa.* iii. 20 The wimples, and the crisping pinnes. *c* **1618** FLETCHER *Q. Corinth* IV. i, Never powder, nor the crisping-iron, Shall touch these dangling locks. **1637** POCKLINGTON *Altare Chr.* 42 Fetch me my Crisping pinnes to curle my lockes. **1772** *Ann. Reg.* 220 Cease, with crisping tongs, to tare And torture thus thy flowing hair. **1874** [see CRISPER].

ˈ**crisping,** *ppl. a.* [f. as prec. + -ING[2].] That crisps. *trans.* and *intr.*

1581 J. BELL *Haddon's Answ. Osor.* 471 This curious cripsing and blazing bravery of hawtye speech. **1778** *Phil. Surv. S. Irel.* 374 The crisping and drying quality of E., N., and N.E. winds. **1851** RUSKIN *Stones Ven.* (1874) I. App. 389 The small crisping waves which break upon the shore.

crispish (ˈkrɪspɪʃ), *a.* [f. CRISP *a.* + -ISH[1].] Somewhat crisp.

1930 WODEHOUSE *Very Good, Jeeves!* vi. 142 When not pleased Aunt Dahlia, having spent most of her youth in the hunting-field, has a crispish way of expressing herself. *a* **1948** E. ANDERSON in B. James *Austral. Short Stories* (1963) 333 Pork..with its crispish, tannish, delectable-looking strips of crackling.

†**crispiˈsulcant,** *a.* *rare*—[0]. [ad. L. *crispisulcāntem.*] Undulating or serpentine.

1727 BAILEY vol. II., *Crispisulcant*, coming down wrinkled; spoken of Lightening. Hence in JOHNSON etc.

ˈ**crispite** (ˈkrɪspaɪt). *Min.* [Named 1797, from *Crispalt*, St. Gothard, Switzerland + -ITE.] A kind of Rutile; = SAGENITE.

1814 in T. ALLAN *Min. Nomen.* **1868** in DANA *Min.* 159.

†ˈ**crispitude.** *Obs.*—[0] [ad. L. *crispitūdo*, f. *crispus* curled.] 'Curledness' (Blount 1656).

†**crisple,** *v.* *Obs. rare.* [dim. of CRISP *v.*: see -LE.] To crisp, curl, or undulate minutely; to ripple. So **crisple** *sb.*, a minute curl or undulation. ˈ**crispling** *vbl. sb.* and *ppl. a.*

1594 CAREW *Tasso* (1881) 80 The winde new crisples makes in her loose haire, Which nature selfe to waues recrispelled. **1604** T. WRIGHT *Passions* II. ii. 59 A calme Sea, with sweete, pleasant, and crispling streames. *Ibid.* v. §2. 168 The shaking or artificiall crispling of the aire (which is in effect the substance of musicke).

crisply (ˈkrɪsplɪ), *adv.* [f. CRISP *a.* + -LY[2].] In a crisp manner; with crispness.

1824 MISS MITFORD *Village* Ser. I. (1863) 18 The roads, in spite of the slight glittering showers, crisply dry. **1859** R. F. BURTON *Centr. Afr.* in *Jrnl. Geog. Soc.* XXIX. 196 The hair curls crisply. **1881** *Athenæum* 13 Aug. 197/2 What [they] have to say is..clearly and crisply phrased.

crispness (ˈkrɪspnɪs). [f. CRISP *a.* + -NESS.] The state or quality of being crisp.

c **1440** [see CRISPHEDE]. **1635–67** COWLEY *Davideis* III. *Note* 25 The..crispness of the wood. **1799** SOUTHEY *Lett.* (1856) I. 83 The colour of the hair, its quality and its crispness. **1865** DICKENS *Mut. Fr.* I. v, An unwholesomely-forced lettuce that had lost in colour and crispness what it had gained in size. **1885** *Bookseller* July 662/2 The tale is told with the crispness and sparkle of this author's popular style.

crispy (ˈkrɪspɪ), *a.* [f. CRISP *a.* + -Y.]

1. Curly, wavy; undulated; = CRISP *a.* 1 and 2.

1398 TREVISA *Barth. de P.R.* v. xv. (1495) 121 By grete heete the heer of the berd and of the heed ben cryspy and curlyd. **1594** KYD *Cornelio* IV. in Hazl. *Dodsley* V. 229 Turn not thy crispy tides like silver curl, Back to thy grass-green banks to welcome us. **1678** JORDAN *Triumphs Lond.*, A fair bright crispy curl'd flaxen hair. **1819** H. BUSK *Banquet* III. 502 The Arctic frost That chains the crispy wave on Zemla's coast. **1870** MORRIS *Earthly Par.* I. I. 381 Ye shall behold I doubt not soon, his crispy hair of gold.

2. a. Brittle or 'short'; = CRISP *a.* 5.

1611 COTGR., *Bressaudes*, the crispie mammocks that remaine of tried hogs grese. *c* **1720** W. GIBSON *Farriers Dispens.* xv. (1734) 280 Boil..till..the Worms are grown crispy. **1871** NICHOLS *Fireside Science* 92 A black, crispy mass of charcoal.

b. *crispy noodles*, crisp fried noodles served with Chinese food.

1940 A. SIMON *Concise Encycl. Gastronomy* II. 55/2 'Crispy Noodles'... Roll this dough out very thinly and cut into strips as thin as spaghetti... Throw into boiling oil or frying fat, frying a delicate brown. **1961** B. ALDISS *Primal Urge* ii. 41 They ate their chow mein, sweet and sour pork and crispy noodles. **1969** *Guardian* 27 Dec. 13/3 He took ..[a] job..as a waiter in a Chinese restaurant..fetching and carrying No. 31 with crispy noodles and No. 13 with soft.

3. Pleasantly sharp, brisk; = CRISP *a.* 5 b.

1841 *Fraser's Mag.* XXIII. 314 The crispy coolness of fair Eve.

criss (krɪs). [Variant form of w. midl. dial. *cress* = CREASE *sb.*[2] (sense 3).] The curved top of the stand on which tiles are made.

1881 *Instr. Census Clerks* (1885) 87 Brick, Tile-Maker, Burner, Dealer, Criss Maker. **1921** *Dict. Occup. Terms* (1927) §474 *Criss maker* (tile making); a carpenter who makes criss.

Crissake(s), var. CHRIS(S)AKE. Also c-. orig. *U.S.*

1923 J. DOS PASSOS *Streets of Night* i. 13 Go ahead, Fanshaw, for crissake, we can't wait here all day. **1930** —— *42nd Parallel* 72 Say wake up Ike for crissake. **1939** C. R. COOPER *Designs in Scarlet* v. 74 Get screwball for Crissakes, get wacky! **1959** H. HOBSON *Mission House Murder* xii. 81 For Crissake, Ma.

'crissal, *a. Ornith.* [ad. mod.L. *crissālis* (used by Vigors, *Ornithol. of Capt. Beechy's Voy.* 19, in specific name of a Finch), f. *crissum*: see below. Used chiefly in U.S.]

1. Pertaining to the crissum, as the ***crissal region***.

2. Characterized by the colouring of the under tail-coverts, as ***crissal thrush*** or ***thrasher***, the Red-vented Thrush or Thrasher.

1872 COUES *Key to N. Amer. Birds* 75 Crissal Thrasher.

criss-cross ('krɪskrɒs, -ɔː-), *sb.* [A phonetic reduction of CHRIST(S)-CROSS: but in some late senses used with unconsciousness of the origin, and treated merely as a reduplication of *cross*; cf. *mish-mash*, *tip-top*, *zig-zag*, etc.]

1. = CHRIST-CROSS, in various senses, q.v.

2. a. [f. CRISS-CROSS *v.*] A transverse crossing.

1876 R. F. BURTON *Gorilla L.* I. 2 When the current, setting to the north-west, meets a strong sea-breeze from the west, there is a criss-cross, a tide-rip.

b. A network of intersecting lines.

1881 C. DE KAY *Vision of Nimrod* x. 179 The country gleaming With silvery crisscross of canals. **1901** *Daily Express* 28 Aug. 4/6 A great boulevard..hemmed in all round by the criss-cross of narrower streets. **1928** A. BENNETT *Strange Vanguard* xxxii. 214 A criss-cross of streets dotted with a thousand towers. **1944** S. PUTNAM tr. *E. da Cunha's Rebellion in Backlands* i. 8 An irregular line of low hills..forms a confused crisscross over the entire breadth of the Campos.

c. *fig.* The state of being at cross-purposes.

1907 *Daily Chron.* 23 Feb. 3/1 The practice of one manufacturing country assisting another with the sinews of war was described by Mr. Zangwill as 'a topsy turvy criss-cross, and Gilbertian'. **1909** *Westm. Gaz.* 20 Sept. 2/3 The absurd criss-cross of the authorities who look after us at playtime.

3. *U.S.* (See quot.)

1860 BARTLETT *Dict. Amer.*, *Criss-cross*, a game played on slates by children at school; also called Fox and Geese.

Hence **criss-cross-row**: see CHRIST-CROSS-ROW.

criss-cross ('krɪskrɒs, -ɔː-), *a.* and *adv.* [See prec.; now treated as a mere reduplication of *cross*; cf. *zig-zag*.]

A. *adj.* Arranged or placed in crossing lines, crossing, crossed; marked by crossings or intersections. **B.** *adv.* In the manner of crossing lines, crosswise; *fig.* in a contrary way, awry, askew.

1846 HAWTHORNE *Mosses* I. vii. 132 His puckered forehead unravels its entanglement of criss-cross wrinkles. **1864** THOREAU *Maine W.* iii. 244 Others prostrate and criss-across. **1879** F. CONDER *Tentwork Pal.* 352 A regular criss-cross pattern, never seen in the later masonry.

criss-cross ('krɪskrɒs, -ɔː-), *v.* [See prec.]

1. *trans.* To mark with crossing lines, to cross repeatedly; to trace in crossing lines.

1818 KEATS in *Life & Lett.* I. 112 To criss-cross the letter. **1871** LE FANU *Ten. Malory* lxvii. 391 A pretty portrait.. criss-crossed over with little cracks. **1883** *Harper's Mag.* 826/2 The passing vessels criss-cross the white lines of their wakes upon it like pencil-marks on the slate.

2. *intr.* To intersect or cross repeatedly; also *fig.*

1953 G. E. M. ANSCOMBE tr. *Wittgenstein's Philosophical Investigations* I. §66, We see a complicated network of similarities overlapping and criss-crossing. *Ibid.*, The various resemblances between members of a family.. overlap and criss-cross in the same way.

crisse, obs. f. KRIS, Malay dagger.

crissel, cristle, obs. ff. GRISTLE, CRIZZLE.

‖**crissum** ('krɪsəm). *Ornith.* [mod.L. (1811 Illiger, *Prodromus* 166), f. *crissāre* 'clunem movere'.] The anal region of a bird under the tail; the vent-feathers or lower tail-coverts.

1874 COUES *Birds N.W.* 314 There is more dark color on the crissum.

Crist, Cristante, Cristen, etc., obs. ff. CHRIST, CHRISTIANITY, CHRISTEN, etc.

crist(e, cristed, obs. ff. CREST, -ED.

crista ('krɪstə). Pl. cristæ. [L., = crest.] A ridge or crest; *spec.* in various anatomical and zoological senses.

1849–50 J. WEALE *Dict. Terms Archit.*, *Crista*, a crest; the apex or highest part of a shrine. **1889** *Jrnl. Morphology* III. 300 The crista, a cord-like ridge running the full length of the dorsal surface of the capsule. **1940** *Proc. R. Soc.* B. CXXIX. 257 The possibility of a two-way response of the cristae. **1964** J. Z. YOUNG *Model of Brain* vi. 97 Each [statocyst] contains three main types of receptor: (1) a macula, vertically placed and carrying a statolith; (2) a ridge of cells with long hairs, the crista; [etc.].

cristal(l, cristalline, etc., obs. ff. CRYSTAL, -INE, etc.

cristate ('krɪsteɪt), *a. Nat. Hist.*, etc. [ad. L. *cristāt-us*, f. *crista* CREST: see -ATE.] Having a crest, crested; in the form of a crest.

1661 LOVELL *Hist. Anim. & Min.* Introd., The..larke, cristate, and not cristate. **1859** TODD *Cycl. Anat.* V. 768 *Index*, Cristate process of the ethmoid bone.

cristated ('krɪsteɪtɪd), *a.* = prec.

1727 BAILEY vol. II., *Cristated*, having a crest or comb. **1757** tr. *Henckel's Pyritol.* 23 Pyrites..oval, clustered, cristated. **1794** KIRWAN *Min.* I. 244 Sometimes also in the form of a cockscomb and hence called cristated.

cristobalite (krɪ'stəʊbəlaɪt). *Min.* Also erron. christobalite, crystobalite. [ad. G. *cristobalit* (G. vom Rath 1887, in *Neues Jahrbuch für Min.* I. 198), f. the name of Cerro San *Cristóbal*, near Pachuca, Mexico, where it was first found: see -ITE[1].] One of the three main forms of silica (the others being quartz and tridymite), formed at high temperatures as ***high-cristobalite*** and changing at lower temperatures to a structurally related metastable polymorph, ***low-cristobalite***, which occurs both massive (e.g. in opal) and as small, usu. octahedral, crystals.

1888 *Min. Mag.* VIII. 36 A New Mineral. Cristobalite... An analysis..gave 91 per cent. of silica and 6 per cent. of oxide of iron and alumina. **1920** *Brit. Museum Return* 144 Artificial minerals (cristobalite, fayalite, rhodonite, apatite, spinel..) from furnace slags. **1935** *Discovery* July 206/1 When ware is fired above a certain temperature a very large number of extremely fine crystals of a mineral (crystobalite) are formed. **1959** *Chambers's Encycl.* IX. 423/1 Both cristobalite (stable 1,470°–1,710° C) and tridymite (stable 870°–1,470° C) are known to occur in certain natural lavas. **1962** C. FRONDEL *Dana's Syst. Min.* (ed. 7) III. 287 In recent years..study has shown that opal..is a submicrocrystalline aggregate of crystallites of cristobalite.

†**cristy gray, cristigrey.** *Obs.* A term applied to some kind of fur: cf. GRAY, GREY.

1404 *Will of Wynyngton* (Somerset Ho.), Togam meam.. furratam de cristigrey. **1422** *E.E. Wills* (1882) 50 A gown furred with Cristy gray. **1474** in *Ld. Treas. Acc. Scot.* I. 36, v tymire of cristy gray..to lyne a gowne of blac dammask to the Qwene.

crisum, crisyme, obs. ff. CHRISOM.

crit. †**1.** Short for CRITIC. *Obs.*

1743 FIELDING *Wedding-day* Prol., Smoke the author, you laughing crits.

2. Short for CRITICISM 2, 3, CRITIQUE 1. *colloq.*

1908 D. H. LAWRENCE *Let.* 13 May (1962) I. 11, I could write crits.—but..who would have 'em? **1952** W. GRANVILLE *Dict. Theatr. Terms* 53 *Crit*, short for *critique* or the notice of a first-night performance. **1966** R. TRICKETT *Elders* vi. 78 Someone had written a practical crit. of Collier's poem with an interpretation of that rather obscure stanza. **1970** K. GILES *Death in Church* iii. 69 The inquest stuff won't be so bad, more like a send-up than a crit.

3. Short for *critical mass* or *size* (see CRITICAL *a.* 7b). *colloq.* (orig. *U.S.*).

1957 in *Gloss. Terms Nuclear Sci.* (Nat. Res. Council, U.S.) 39/1. **1958** [see CRITICAL *a.* 7b].

critch, variant of CRATCH, rack.

criterial (kraɪ'tɪərɪəl), *a.* [f. CRITERI(ON, or pl. *criteri(a*, + -AL[1].] Of, according to, or pertaining to criteria; constituting a criterion or criteria.

[**1893** in *N.E.D.* s.v. *Criterional a.*, etym.] **1957** *Psychol. Rev.* LXIV. 123/2 On the basis of certain defining or criterial attributes in the input..there is a selective placing of the input in one category of identity rather than another. **1962** U. WEINREICH in Householder & Saporta *Probl. Lexicogr.* 33 The word 'especially' preceding the statement of a condition indicates that what follows is less criterial than the rest. **1967** *Philos. Rev.* LXXVI. 49 This criterial account of perception statements embodies an observation of several contemporary philosophers. **1975** T. PARSONS in Glazer & Moynihan *Ethnicity* 56 In spite of the difficulty of being specific about criterial features and components, what social scientists have called ethnic groups do not belong to a relatively distinct sociological type. **1983** BROWN & YULE *Discourse Analysis* vi. 196 It seems to be the case then that 'texture', in the sense of explicit realisation of semantic relations, is not criterial to the identification and co-interpretation of texts.

†**cri'terie.** *Obs. rare.* An adapted form of CRITERION.

1655–60 STANLEY *Hist. Philos.* III. III. 38 Man is the criterie of all things. *Ibid.* (1701) 477 We say the Criterie of Scepticism is the Phænomen.

criteriological (kraɪˌtɪərɪə'lɒdʒɪkəl), *a.* [f. next + -ICAL.] Pertaining to criteriology; dealing with criteria. Hence **criˌterio'logically** *adv.*

1936 *Downside Rev.* LIV. 110 A criteriological problem —the difference between sense perception and rational knowledge. **1938** R. G. COLLINGWOOD *Princ. Art* viii. 171 A science of thought must be 'normative', or (as I prefer to call it) 'criteriological', i.e. concerned not only with the 'facts' of thought but also with the 'criteria' or standards which thought imposes on itself. *Ibid.*, Forms of thought can be dealt with only 'criteriologically'.

criteri'ology. [f. next: see -LOGY.] **a.** The doctrine of a criterion (of knowledge, etc.).

1884 *Athenæum* 14 June 753/1 An outline of what may be termed criteriology, the relation of thought to reality as regards its validity.

b. The study of criteria, esp. as a branch of logic.

1934 *Theology* XXIX. 48 St. Thomas..places his theodicy before his criteriology. **1940** R. G. COLLINGWOOD *Ess. Metaph.* xi. 119 The methods it [*sc.* psychology] has developed in its history as a science of feeling preclude it from dealing with the problems of criteriology. It has nothing to say about truth and falsehood. **1955** *Jrnl. Philos.* LII. 564, I propose here merely the outlines of a criteriology.

criterion (kraɪ'tɪərɪən). Pl. criteria; less commonly -ons. [a. Gr. κριτήριον a means for judging, test, standard, f. κριτής judge. In 17th c. often written in Gr. letters.]

†**a.** An organ, faculty or instrument of judging.

1647 H. MORE *Poems* Pref., Wits that have..so crusted and made hard their inward κριτήριον by over-much and trivial wearing it. **1678** CUDWORTH *Intell. Syst.* 23 According to Empedocles, the Criterion of Truth is not Sense but Right Reason.

b. A test, principle, rule, canon, or standard, by which anything is judged or estimated.

1622 BP. HALL *Serm.* 15 Sept. Wks. (1627) 490 All the false κριτηρια that vse to beguile the iudgment of man. **1661** FULLER *Worthies* I. 129 The moving hereof [a statue] was made the Criterion of womens chastity. **1768** BLACKSTONE *Comm.* III. 330 Some mode of probation or trial, which the law of the country has ordained for a criterion of truth and falshood. **1788** MRS. HUGHES *Henry & Isab.* I. 17 Regular uniformity and the straight line were the criterions of taste and beauty. **1795** *Fate of Sedley* I. 168 Lord Stokerland [is] the criterion of gallantry and politeness. **1856** FROUDE *Hist. Eng.* (1858) I. i. 18 We have no criterion by which, in these matters, degrees of good and evil admit of being measured.

†**c.** A distinguishing mark or characteristic attaching to a thing, by which it can be judged or estimated. *Obs.*

1613 JACKSON *Creed* I. v. Wks. I. 37 This sincerity in teaching..is the true κριτήριον or touchstone, the livery or cognizance of a man speaking by the Spirit of God. **1678** GALE *Crt. Gentiles* III. 138 Take these Criteria or distinctive notes of Durandisme.

cri'terional, *a. nonce-wd.* [f. prec. + -AL[1]; irreg. for CRITERIAL, which is not evidenced until 20th c.] Of or relating to a criterion.

1830 COLERIDGE *Table-t.* 23 Sept., There are two kinds of logic: 1. Syllogistic, 2. Criterional..The criterional logic, or logic of premisses, is, of course, much the most important; and it has never yet been treated.

‖**criterium** (kraɪ'tɪərɪəm). Latinized form of Gr. κριτήριον CRITERION, occas. used in English.

a **1631** DONNE *Serm.* lxi. 612 This is our Criterium and onely this; hereby we know it. *a* **1734** NORTH *Exam.* I. iii. §62 (1740) 170 It ever was and will be a certain Criterium of Truth, to be easy..clear and intelligible. **1867** LEWES *Hist. Philos.* I. 181 There is no criterium of truth.

crith (krɪθ). *Physics.* [f. Gr. κριθή barley-corn, the smallest weight.] The weight of 1 litre of hydrogen at standard pressure and temperature; proposed by Hofmann as the unit of weight for gaseous substances.

1865 A. W. HOFMANN *Introd. Mod. Chem.* 131 For this purpose I venture to suggest the term *crith* derived from the word κριθή signifying a barley-corn. **1870** *Eng. Mech.* 21 Jan. 464/1 The 'Crith'..is the weight of one litre of Hydrogen at 0· cent., and 0·76 m. pressure = 0·0896 gramme.

†**cri'thology.** *Obs.*[—0] [ad. Gr. κριθολογία the gathering of barley, f. κριθή barley-corn.] (See quot.)

1656 BLOUNT *Glossogr.*, *Crithology*..the office of gathering the first fruits of Corn.

crithomancy ('krɪθəʊmænsɪ). [f. Gr. κριθή barley-corn + μαντεία divination (see -MANCY); cf. κριθόμαντις one who divined by barley.] Divination by meal strewed over animals sacrificed.

1652 GAULE *Magastrom.* 165 *Crithomancy*, [divining] by grain or corn. **1884** J. C. BOURKE *Snake Dance of Moquis* xv. 165 The use of this sacred meal closely resembles the crithomancy of the ancient Greeks.

†**critic**, *a. Obs.* Also 6 creticke, 6–7 criticke, 7–8 -ick, -ique. [ad. L. *critic-us* (orig. as a medical term), a. Gr. κριτικός critical, f. κριτός decerned, κριτής a judge; f. κρί-ν-ειν to decide, judge. Partly

after F. *cretique* (1372, Corbichon), *critique* (*a* 1590 Paré) both in medical use.]

†1. *Med.*, etc. Relating to or involving the crisis of a disease, etc.; = CRITICAL 4, 5. *Obs.*

1544 PHAER *Regim. Lyfe* (1553) Gjb, If it ['jaundis'] appeare in the vj day, beyng a day iudiciall or creticke of the ague. **1601** WEEVER *Mirr. Mart.* C viij b, If euer sheild-shapt Comet was portent Of Criticke day, foule and pernitious. **1605** DANIEL *Queen's Arcadia* III. i, Of Symptoms, Crycis, and the Critick Days.

2. Judging captiously or severely, censorious, carping, fault-finding.

1598 FLORIO, *Critico*, criticke, judging mens acts and works written. **1621** R. JOHNSON *Way to Glory* 25 That..is now, in this criticke age, called in question, etc. *a* **1667** COWLEY *Elegy on J. Littleton*, In 's Body too, no Critique Eye could find The smallest Blemish.

3. Skilful in judging, *esp.* about literary or artistic work; belonging to criticism; = CRITICAL 3.

1626 W. SCLATER *Expos. 2 Thess.* (1629) 144 A criticke Scholiast vpon the Reuelation. **1635** N. CARPENTER *Geog. Del.* II. v. 67 Learned diuines and criticke expositours. **1677** GALE *Crt. Gentiles* II. iii. 87 A critic judgement is made by experience and prudence and Reason or discourse. **1709** POPE *Ess. Crit.* 111. 153 Critic Learning flourish'd most in France. **1834** *Fraser's Mag.* X. 19 Matters historic, critic, analytic, and philologic. **1850** TENNYSON *In Mem.* cviii, The critic clearness of an eye, That saw thro' all the Muses' walk.

critic ('krɪtɪk), *sb.*[1] Also 7 crittick, criticke, -ique, 7–8 critick. [ad. L. *critic-us* sb., a. Gr. κριτικός a critical person, a critic, subst. use of the adj.; perh. immediately after F. *critique*: see prec. In early times used in the L. form:

1583 FULKE *Defence Eng. Bible* (Parker Soc.) 381 The prince of the *Critici*. **1609** HOLLAND *Amm. Marcell.* XXII. xi. 206, I am here forced even against my will to be after a sort *Criticus*..but to find out a truth.]

1. One who pronounces judgement on any thing or person; *esp.* one who passes severe or unfavourable judgement; a censurer, fault-finder, caviller.

1588 SHAKS. *L.L.L.* III. i. 177, I that haue beene loues whip..A Criticke, Nay, a night-watch Constable. **1598** FLORIO *Ital. Dict.* To Rdr., Those notable Pirates in this our paper-sea, those sea-dogs, or lande-Critikes, monsters of men. **1606** DEKKER *Newes from Hell*, Take heed of criticks: they bite, like fish, at anything, especially at bookes. **1692** E. WALKER *Epictetus' Mor.* xlix, Nor play the Critick, nor be apt to jeer. **1702** *Eng. Theophrast.* 5 How strangely some words lose their primitive sense! By a Critick, was originally understood a good judge; with us nowadays it signifies no more than a Fault finder. **1766** FORDYCE *Serm. Yng. Wom.* (1777) I. iv. 192 We are never safe in the company of a critic.

2. One skilful in judging of the qualities and merits of literary or artistic works; one who writes upon the qualities of such works; a professional reviewer of books, pictures, plays, and the like; also one skilled in textual or biblical criticism.

1605 BACON *Adv. Learn.* I. vii. §21 Certaine Critiques are used to say..That if all sciences were lost, they might bee found in Virgill. **1697** BENTLEY *Phal.* Introd., To pass a censure on all kinds of writings, to shew their excellencies and defects, and especially to assign each..to their proper authors, was the chief Province of the ancient Critics. **1780** JOHNSON *Lett. Mrs. Thrale* 27 July, Mrs. Cholmondely..told me I was the best critick in the world; and I told her, that nobody in the world could judge like her of the merit of a critick. **1825** MACAULAY *Ess. Milton* Ess. (1854) I. 3/1 The poet, we believe, understood the nature of his art better than the critic [Johnson]. **1870** DISRAELI *Lothair* xxxv, You know who the Critics are? The men who have failed in Literature and Art.

3. *Comb.* (freq. in appositive use).

1680 LD. ROCHESTER *Poems* 16 A great Inhabiter of the Pit; Where Critick-like, he sits and squints. **1754** W. COWPER in W. Hayley *Life W.C.* (1803) I. 16 This simile were apt enough, But I've another, critic-proof! **1906** *Westm. Gaz.* 29 Sept. 14/2 There have been murmurs..against the critic-dramatist. **1938** H. READ *Coll. Ess. Lit. Crit.* I. i. 17 When such a critic-poet attempts to probe down into such a fundamental question as the form and structure of poetry. **1965** *Canadian Jrnl. Linguistics* Fall 40 Critic-centred comments on the text.

†'**critic**, *sb.*[2] *Obs.* Also in 7 -icke, 7–8 -ick, 8–9 CRITIQUE q.v. [app. ad. F. *critique* fem. (used in this sense by Molière and Boileau), ultimately ad. Gr. ἡ κριτική the critical art, criticism (cf. It. *critica* 'arte of cutting of stones', Florio 1598). Early in the 18th c. this began to be spelt as in Fr. *critique*, a spelling which in spite of Johnson and the Dictionaries, has become universal; in the 19th c. it has received a quasi-French pronunciation also: see CRITIQUE, chiefly used in sense 2, while sense 1 is now expressed by CRITICISM.]

1. The art or action of criticizing; criticism; an instance of this. Also in *pl.* (cf. *metaphysics*.)

1656 *Artif. Handsomeness* (1662) 216 A Satyrical Critick upon the very Scriptures. **1657** HOBBES *Stigmas* Wks. 1845 VII. 389 Grammar and Criticks. **1676** ETHEREDGE *Man of Mode* III. iii, Wee'l make a Critick on the whole Mail Madam. **1690** J. LOCKE *Hum. Und.* IV. xx, They would afford us another sort of Logick and Critick. **1697** BENTLEY *Phal.* 69, I do not expect from our Editors much sagacity in way of Critic. **1710** STEELE *Tatler* No. 45 ¶4 That Sort of Drama is not..thought unworthy the Critick of learned Heads. **1755–73** JOHNSON, *Cri'tick*, Science of Criticism [Todd 1818 alters to *Critique*].

2. An essay in criticism of a literary work, etc.; a critical notice or review; now CRITIQUE.

1709 POPE *Ess. Crit.* 571 Own your errors past, And make each day a critick on the last. **1710** STEELE *Tatler* No. 115 ¶1, I shall not fail to write a Critick upon his Performance. **1755–73** JOHNSON, *Cri'tick*, a critical examination; critical remarks [Todd 1818 alters to *Critique*]. **1766** ELIZ. GRIFFITH *Lett. Henry & Frances* III. 4, I shewed your Critic upon the Series to the Bishop of ——.

†**critic**, *v. Obs.* In 7 -icke, 8 -ick, -ique.

1. *intr.* To play the critic, pass judgement (*on* something).

1607 A. BREWER *Lingua* IV. ix. (R.) Nay, if you begin to critic once, we shall never have done. **1629** LIGHTFOOT *Erubhin* ii, On which words I can criticke onely with deepe silence. *a* **1698** TEMPLE (J.), They do but..comment, critick, and flourish upon them.

2. *trans.* To pass judgement upon, criticize; *esp.* (in earlier use) to criticize unfavourably, censure.

1697 DRYDEN *Virg.* Life (1721) I. 71 Those who can Critick his Poetry, can never find a Blemish in his Manners. **1706** COLLIER *Refl. Ridic.* 307 'Tis playing the Pedant unseasonably to critick things. **1735** POPE *Ep. Lady* 81 As Helluo..Critick'd your wine and analysed your meat. **1751** [see CRITIQUE *v.*].

'**criticable**, *a. rare.* [f. CRITIC *v.* or F. *critiquer* + -ABLE.] Criticizable.

1889 J. M. ROBERTSON *Ess. Crit. Method* 71 Criticism is thus seen to be in itself criticable literature.

critical ('krɪtɪkəl), *a.* [f. L. *critic-us* (see CRITIC *a.*) + -AL[1].]

1. Given to judging; *esp.* given to adverse or unfavourable criticism; fault-finding, censorious.

1590 SHAKS. *Mids. N.* v. i. 54 That is some Satire keene and criticall. **1604** —— *Oth.* II. i. 120, I am nothing, if not Criticall. **1665–9** BOYLE *Occas. Refl.* III. vi. (1675) 157 The more Witty and Critical sort of Auditors. **1683** D. A. *Art Converse* 49 Those that are of a too critical humour approve of nothing. **1828** SOUTHEY *Ballads, Brough Bells*, 'What! art thou critical?' quoth he; 'Eschew that heart's disease'. **1881** RUSSELL *Haigs* Introd. 3 It was not in his nature to be either critical or indifferent.

†2. Involving or exercising careful judgement or observation; nice, exact, accurate, precise, punctual. Now *Obs.* (or merged in other senses).

1650 SIR T. BROWNE *Pseud. Ep.* II. v, Exact and critical trial should be made..whereby determination might be settled. **1654** WHITLOCK *Zootomia* 186 He is not criticall and exact in Garbes and Fashions. **1692** RAY *Disc.* II. v. (1732) 272, I can hear of nobody that was so critical in noticing the Time. **1716** CIBBER *Love makes Man* v. iii, Well, Madam, you see I'm punctual..I'm always critical—to a Minute. [**1806** HERSCHEL in *Phil. Trans.* XCVI. 463 The air is beautifully clear, and proper for critical observations. **1832** *Regul. Instr. Cavalry* II. 37 A critical dressing need not be required.]

3. **a.** Occupied with or skilful in criticism.

1641 J. JACKSON *True Evang. T.* I. 69 The Millenaries, a sect of learned, and criticall Christians. **1766** ENTICK *London* IV. 165 Of which a critical writer remarks [etc.]. **1871** MORLEY *Voltaire* (1886) 26 Molière is only critical by accident.

b. Belonging or relating to criticism.

1741 MIDDLETON *Cicero* II. VIII. 237 Cæsar was conversant also with the most abstruse and critical parts of learning. **1768** W. GILPIN *Ess. Prints* 169 How far the works of Hogarth will bear a critical examination. **1843** MACAULAY (*title*), Critical and Historical Essays. **1867** FREEMAN *Norm. Conq.* (1876) I. App. 585 He shows a good deal of critical acumen.

c. ***critical theory*** [tr. G. *kritische Theorie*, M. Horkheimer (1937) in *Zeitschr. f. Sozialforschung* 245], a dialectical critique of society (esp. of the theoretical bases of its organization) associated with the leaders of the Institute for Social Research at Frankfurt (the Frankfurt School).

1968 J. J. SHAPIRO tr. *H. Marcuse's Negations* iv. 155 The rigorously scientific character that critical theory has always made a criterion of its concepts. **1972** M. J. O'CONNELL tr. *Horkheimer's Crit. Theory* 207 The separation between individual and society in virtue of which the individual accepts as natural the limits prescribed for his activity is relativized in critical theory. **1973** M. JAY *Dialectical Imagination* ii. 41 At the very heart of Critical Theory was an aversion to closed philosophical systems... Critical Theory ..was expressed through a series of critiques of other thinkers and philosophical traditions. **1977** A. GIDDENS *Stud. in Social & Polit. Theory* i. 65 If there is a single dominating element in critical theory, it is the defence of Reason (*Vernunft*) understood in the sense of Hegel and classical German philosophy. **1985** R. J. SIEBERT *Crit. Theory Relig.* p. xi, J. Habermas's theory of communicative praxis..the most advanced stage in the development of the critical theory of subject, society, history and religion, initiated..by M. Horkheimer..and others in..the so-called Frankfurt School.

4. *Med.* (and *Astrol.*) Relating to the crisis or turning-point of a disease; determining the issue of a disease, etc.

1601 HOLLAND *Pliny* XVII. ii. I. 500 The foure decretorie or criticall daies, that give the dome of olive trees, either to good or bad. **1602** W. VAUGHAN *Nat. Direct.* 47 The Moone ..passeth almost euery seuenth day into the contrary signe of the same quality..and..bringeth the criticall daies. **1684** tr. *Bonet's Merc. Compit.* III. 72 You may reckon it [the Head-ach] critical, if in a Fever it fall upon a critical day. **1733** CHEYNE *Eng. Malady* II. viii. §7 And so the Fever terminates in a critical Abscess. **1843** T. WATSON *Lect. Physic.* iv. (1857) 53 The moment of exhalation is very transient..It is evidently critical, for the congestion is relieved.

5. Of the nature of, or constituting, a crisis: **a.** Of decisive importance in relation to the issue. *spec.* ***critical path***: the most important sequence of stages in an operation, determining the time needed for the whole operation; freq. *attrib.*

1649 BP. REYNOLDS *Hosea* iv. 65 Mercies are never..so seasonable as in the very turning and criticall point. **1673** S. C. *Art of Complaisance* 25 There is in the Court, as there is said to be in Love, one critical minute. **1786** T. JEFFERSON *Writings* (1859) II. v. 5 That month, by producing new prospects, has been critical. **1833** ALISON *Hist. Europe* II. vii. §100 Three hundred horse, at that critical moment, might have saved the monarchy. **1871** BLACKIE *Four Phases* i. 145 *note*, Socrates taught that on great and critical occasions he was often directed by a mysterious voice. **1959** in *Jrnl. Industr. Engin.* (1962) XIII. 508/2 (*title*) Critical Path planning and scheduling. An Introduction. **1960** SAYER et al. in *Factory* July 75/1 The critical path technique forces management to recognize planning and scheduling as two distinct functions. For example, the planning of sequence of roof construction on a building job would be done as a separate critical path analysis operation. **1964** C. DENT *Quantity Surveying by Computer* vii. 114 The critical path schedule indicates to what extent an operation may be delayed before the job becomes 'critical', i.e. before the completion date must be put forward. **1964** K. G. LOCKYER *Introd. Critical Path Analysis* i. 2 In 1958, the E.I. du Pont de Nemours Company used a technique called the Critical Path Method (CPM) to schedule and control a very large project. *Ibid.* 6 This determining sequence is critical to the performance of the project, and is hence known as the *Critical Path.* **1970** *Daily Tel.* 13 Oct. 21/4 The critical path through a diagram..is the one which takes the longest, because it is on that route the time for completing the whole operation depends.

b. Involving suspense or grave fear as to the issue; attended with uncertainty or risk.

1664 EVELYN *Kal. Hort.* (1729) 198 Acquaint them [tender-plants] gradually with the Air..for this change is the most critical of the whole year. **1767** *Junius Lett.* iv. 25 Considering the critical situation of this country. **1836** W. IRVING *Astoria* I. 149 The relations between [them]..were at that time in a critical state; in fact, the two countries were on the eve of a war. **1883** *Manch. Guardian* 17 Oct. 5/2 Mrs. H——'s throat was badly cut, and her condition is deemed critical.

6. Tending to determine or decide; decisive, crucial.

1841 MYERS *Cath. Th.* IV. vii. 201 The alterations..in our conceptions of the material Universe..are critical instances of the influence [of]..Natural Philosophy..over Scholastic Theology. **1860** TYNDALL *Glac.* II. i. 230 Here..we have a critical analogy between sound and light.

7. *Math.* and *Physics.* **a.** Constituting or relating to a point at which some action, property or condition passes over into another; constituting an extreme or limiting case; as ***critical angle***, in *Optics*, that angle of incidence beyond which rays of light passing through a denser medium to the surface of a rarer are no longer refracted but totally reflected; ***critical damping***, damping which is just sufficient to prevent oscillations; ***critical point*** or ***temperature*** for any particular substance, that temperature above which it remains in the gaseous state and cannot be liquefied by any amount of pressure; ***critical potential*** = *ionization potential*; ***critical pressure***, the pressure required to liquefy a gas at its critical temperature; ***critical state***, the state of a substance when it is at its critical temperature and critical pressure; ***critical volume***, the volume of unit mass of a substance at its critical temperature and pressure.

1841 J. R. YOUNG *Math. Dissert.* Pref. 7 Even in the extreme and critical case of the problem. **1869** T. ANDREWS in *Phil. Trans.* CLIX. 583 Below the critical temperature this distinction is easily seen to have taken place. **1873** W. LEES *Acoustics* II. iii. 53 This angle is called the limiting or critical angle of refraction. **1876** TAIT *Rec. Adv. Phys. Sc.* xiii. 336 The temperature rises to the critical point, *i.e.* the temperature at and above which the presence of liquid and vapour together becomes impossible. **1879** *Encycl. Brit.* VIII. 732/1 Clerk Maxwell has calculated that the critical temperature for water should be about 434° C., the critical pressure about 378 atmospheres, and the critical volume about 2·52 cubic [*printed* cubit] centimetres per gramme. **1881** T. MATTHIEU WILLIAMS in *Knowledge* No. 8. 157 That Jupiter is neither a solid, a liquid, nor a gaseous planet, but a critical planet. **1884** *Phil. Mag.* XVIII. 212 These cooling agents may be said to lower the temperature sufficiently to produce liquid oxygen, provided a pressure of the gas above the critical pressure, which is 50 atmospheres, is at command. **1899** T. O'C. SLOANE *Liquid Air* i. 20 When a gas is at the critical temperature and at the critical pressure also, the least increase of pressure or decrease of temperature will convert it into a liquid. When in this condition, ready to be a gas or a liquid, it is said to be in the critical state. **1908** K. EDGCUMBE *Industr. Electr. Meas. Instrum.* 35 It is easy to determine how nearly a given instrument approaches the point of critical damping, by noting how much the pointer overshoots a reading as it flies up to it. **1916** *Physical Rev.* VII. 687 To determine this critical potential more accurately, and..to demonstrate whether or not ionization took place there, current-potential curves were made. **1922** GLAZEBROOK *Dict. Appl. Physics* II. 373/2 In galvanometers of the Thomson type the damping due to induced currents is small, and if critical damping is desired the retardation by air friction must be capable of adjustment. **1931** *Rev. Mod. Physics* III. 347 Bohr's theory was so quickly supported by the experiments on critical potentials. **1933** in J. K. Henney *Radio Engineering Handbk.* §7. 146 The smallest amount of damping which will cause the coil to come to rest with no oscillation whatever is called the critical damping, and the coil is said to be critically damped. **1947** *Sci. News* V. 164 No amount of compressing will liquefy it [*sc.* a gas] as long as it is hotter than this critical temperature.

b. ***critical mass*** or ***size***: in Nuclear Physics, the minimum mass or size of fissile material required in a nuclear reactor, bomb, etc., to sustain a chain reaction.

1940 in M. Gowing *Britain & Atomic Energy 1939–1945* (1964) 391 For a sphere well above the critical size the loss through neutron escape would be small. **1941** *Ibid.* 402 For a low critical mass, the material must be as dense as possible. **1945** *Statements relating to the Atomic Bomb* (*H.M.S.O.*) 16 This estimate was very rough and the critical size was known only to a factor of three. **1946** E. S. C. SMITH et al. *Appl. Atomic Power* 202 No explosion occurs at all unless the mass of the fissionable material exceeds the critical mass. **1958** J. CLEUGH tr. *Jungk's Brighter than Thousand Suns* xii. 191 The determination of this 'critical size'—referred to simply as 'crit' in the Los Alamos jargon—had been one of the chief problems studied by the theoretical department.

c. *Nuclear Physics.* Of a nuclear reactor: maintaining a self-sustaining chain reaction; esp. in phr. ***to go critical***, to reach the stage of maintaining such a reaction. Also *transf.*

1949 H. SOODAK in C. Goodman *Sci. & Engin. Nuclear Power* II. viii. 91 For a critical pile, the fundamental mode, j = 1, is constant in time whereas the higher modes decay. **1955** *Ann. Reg. 1954* 393 At Harwell the more important news of reactors was that 'Zephyr' became critical in February. **1955** *Sci. News Let.* 6 Aug. 83/1 The possibility of really putting atoms to work for the good of the world will go 'critical', to use a term applicable to the atomic reactor. **1957** *New Scientist* 26 Dec. 6/2 The prototype reactor went critical at the end of 1954. **1970** *Nature* 21 Nov. 704/1 Sizewell B will be the largest nuclear power station in Britain when the last of its four reactors goes critical in 1977.

8. *Zool.* and *Bot.* Of species: Distinguished by slight or questionable differences; uncertain or difficult to determine.

1854 WOODWARD *Mollusca* III. (1856) 360 Most of these are minute or 'critical' species. **1858** *Jrnl. R. Agric. Soc.* XIX. I. 104 Crossing often renders certain species of plants very 'critical'. **1884** *Jrnl. Bot.* XXII. 128 When he..ran down some less familiar or critical species.

9. *Comb.*, as ***critical-minded*** adj.

1899 W. JAMES *Talks Teachers Psychol.* i. 6 Where the disciples are not independent and critical-minded enough. **1956** A. TOYNBEE *Historian's Approach to Religion* x. 128 Philosophies have been apt to arise in..critical-minded, disillusioned social milieux.

criticality (krɪtɪˈkælɪtɪ).

1. a. The quality of being critical. **b.** A critical remark, criticism. **c.** A critical moment, crisis.

1756 GRAY *Lett.* Wks. 1884 II. 299 [I] hope to despatch you a packet with my criticalities entire. **1843** CARLETON *Traits* I. 143 At this criticality every eye was turned from the corpse to the murderer.

2. *Nuclear Physics.* The state or quality of being critical (see CRITICAL *a.* 7 c). Also *attrib.*

1950 *U.S. Atomic Energy Commission, AECD 3024* (*title*) Conditions for criticality in certain types of nuclear reactors, by D. S. Selengut. **1952** *Sci. News Let.* 20 Dec. 391/3 A pilot reactor..started operation and reached criticality. **1955** *Ibid.* 16 Apr. 248/1 During these experiments, known as criticality tests, the familiar blue glow of the irradiated fuel elements will be visible under the water. **1956** *Sunday Times* 14 Oct. 10/2 This miscalculation in the quantity of fuel needed to achieve 'criticality' has brought other problems.

critically (ˈkrɪtɪkəlɪ), *adv.* [f. CRITICAL + -LY[2].] In a critical manner.

1. With critical judgement or observation; nicely, accurately, precisely.

1654 WHITLOCK *Zootomia* 504 Though not Critically translated. *a* **1660** HAMMOND *Wks.* IV. 498 (R.) Would we but look critically into ourselves. **1719** DE FOE *Crusoe* (1840) I. xv. 265, I inquired of him more critically, what was become of them? **1870** MISS BRIDGMAN *R. Lynne* I. xvii. 285 Miss Gladwin eyed her critically. **1883** A. ROBERTS *O.T. Revision* viii. 168 A critically revised text of the Septuagint translation.

†**2. a.** With exactness in regard to time, place, etc.; exactly, precisely, punctually. *Obs.*

1655 FULLER *Ch. Hist.* I. i. §15 Others more warily affirm, that it doth not punctually and critically bud on Christmas day. **1722** DE FOE *Col. Jack* (1840) 272 An account, which ..was critically just. **1802** PALEY *Nat. Theol.* iii. §2 The point of concourse..must fall critically upon the retina, or the vision is confused. **1853** KANE *Grinnell Exp.* xl. (1856) 363 This hole was critically circular.

b. So as to determine or decide; decisively. *rare.*

1857 KEBLE *Euchar. Adorat.* 36 This..is no exception, but critically confirms our allegation.

†**3.** At or in relation to the crisis of a disease.

1655 CULPEPPER *Riverius* I. xiv. 50 If the humors be cast down thither critically by Nature. *c* **1670** SIR T. BROWNE *Let. to Friend* xi, That..distemper of little children.. wherein they critically break out with harsh Hairs on their backs, which takes off the unquiet symptoms.

†**4.** At a critical moment; in the nick of time.

1693 CONGREVE *Double Dealer* I. i, Here's the coxcomb most critically come to interrupt you. **1755** *Mem. Capt. P. Drake* I. iv. 33 The Hatches were opened, and indeed very critically, for a Minute's Confinement longer would have terminated in our Destruction. **1799** T. JEFFERSON *Writ.* (1859) IV. 263 Could these debates be ready to appear critically, their effect would be decisive.

5. In a critical situation or condition; perilously, dangerously.

1815 W. H. IRELAND *Scribbleomania* 192 *note*, Thus critically circumstanced. **1856** KANE *Arct. Expl.* I. xxv. 329 The toppling ice..critically suspended, met above our heads. **1889** *Pall Mall G.* 30 Apr. 6/3 The Swazi King is critically ill.

6. *Physics.* In a critical state: see CRITICAL 7.

1881 T. M. WILLIAMS in *Knowledge* No. 8. 157 Elementary substances may exist as solids, liquids, or gases, or critically, according to the conditions of temperature and pressure.

7. *Comb.*, as ***critically-minded*** adj.; also *absol.*

1906 *Daily Chron.* 1 May 3/3 The critically-minded might find fault with some of the drawing. **1938** *Mind* XLVII. 196 Has there ever been a philosopher against whom critically-minded successors have not been able to bring the charge of unconscious self-contradiction?

criticalness (ˈkrɪtɪkəlnɪs). [f. as prec. + -NESS.] The quality or condition of being critical.

1649 FULLER *Just Man's Fun.* 9 The harlot..tunes her self to the criticalness of all complacencie. **1693** BURNET *Let. Bp. Lloyd* in *Brit. Mag.* XXXV. 371 That Criticalness..in marking all dates so punctually. **1794** GODWIN *Cal. Williams* 10 Struck with the criticalness of the situation. **1822** LAMB *Elia, Roast Pig*, Satisfactory to the criticalness of the censorious palate.

criticaster (krɪtɪˈkæstə(r)). [See -ASTER.] A petty or inferior critic. (Used in contempt.)

1684 N. S. *Crit. Enq. Edit. Bible* viii. 51, I perceived that note to be added by some Jewish Criticaster. **1810** SOUTHEY in *Q. Rev.* III. 457 While the criticasters..were pronouncing sentence of condemnation upon it. **1872** SWINBURNE *Under Microscope* 36 The rancorous and reptile crew of poeticules who decompose into criticasters.

Hence **critiˈcasterism**, **critiˈcastry**, *nonce-wds.*

1805 SOUTHEY in Robberds *Mem. W. Taylor* II. 87 Whose criticasterisms have long annoyed me. **1887** F. HALL in *N.Y. Nation* XLIV. 516/1 His criticastry takes no stigmatic note of 'was being done away'.

criticiasis. *Jocular nonce-wd.* [f. CRITICI(SM + -ASIS.] Criticism regarded as a disease.

1874 SWINBURNE *Let.* 5 Mar. (1959) II. 287 The awful dropsy of criticiasis of verbal emendation is dangerous when it becomes incurable.

criticism (ˈkrɪtɪsɪz(ə)m). [f. CRITIC or L. *critic-us* + -ISM: prob. formed in conjunction with *criticize*, of which it is the n. of action. Adopted in French in 19th c. as *criticisme* (in sense 2 c below).]

1. The action of criticizing, or passing judgement upon the qualities or merits of anything; *esp.* the passing of unfavourable judgement; fault-finding, censure.

1607 DEKKER *Knt.'s Conjur.* To Rdr., Therfore (reader) doe I..stand at the marke of criticisme (and of thy bolt) to bee shot at. **1637** HEYWOOD *Royal Ship* 42 They would not allow it..But..it was rather their Criticisme than my ignorance. **1683** D. A. *Art Converse* 45 Criticism or a censorious humour, condemning indifferently every thing. **1736** BUTLER *Anal.* II. vii. 361 This..gives the largest scope for criticism. **1863** GEO. ELIOT *Romola* III. x, These acts.. were not allowed to pass without criticism. **1875** JOWETT *Plato* (ed. 2) IV. 44 No philosophy has ever stood this criticism of the next generation.

2. The art of estimating the qualities and character of literary or artistic work; the function or work of a critic.

1674 DRYDEN *Pref. State of Innocence* Wks. 1821 V. 106 Criticism, as it was first instituted by Aristotle, was meant a standard of judging well; the chiefest part of which is, to observe those excellencies which should delight a reasonable reader. **1709** POPE *Ess. on Crit.* 101 Then criticism the muse's handmaid proved. **1719** J. RICHARDSON (*title*), The Connoisseur: an Essay on the whole Art of Criticism as it relates to Painting. **1865** M. ARNOLD *Ess. Crit.* i. 38, I am bound by my own definition of criticism: a disinterested endeavour to learn and propagate the best that is known and thought in the world. **1878** DOWDEN *Stud. Lit.* 413 The effort of criticism in our time has been..to see things as they are, without partiality, without obtrusion of personal liking or disliking.

b. *spec.* The critical science which deals with the text, character, composition, and origin of literary documents, *esp.* those of the Old and New Testaments.

textual criticism: that whose object is to ascertain the genuine text and meaning of an author. ***higher criticism***: see quot. 1881.

1669 GALE *Crt. Gentiles* I. I. x. 51 The Knowledge of Languages, anciently stiled Grammar, and lately Criticisme. **1748** HARTLEY *Observ. Man* I. iii. 356 Criticism ..may be defined the Art of restoring the corrupted Passages of Authors, and ascertaining their genuine Sense. **1836** R. KEITH tr. *Hengstenberg's Christol.* I. 414 A fundamental principle of the higher criticism. **1864** FROUDE *Short Stud.* (1891) I. 241 (*title*), Criticism and the gospel history. **1875** SCRIVENER *Lect. Grk. Test.* 7 The problem which Textual criticism sets itself to solve. **1881** ROBERTSON SMITH *Old Test. in Jewish Ch.* (1892) 90 A series of questions affecting the composition, the editing, and the collection of the sacred books. This class of questions forms the special subject of the branch of critical science which is usually distinguished from the verbal criticism of the text by the name of Higher or Historical Criticism.

c. *Philos.* The critical philosophy of Kant.

So called from its being based on a critical examination of the faculty of knowledge.

1867 J. H. STIRLING tr. *Schwegler's Hist. Philos.* (ed. 8) 216 Kant..possessed the clearest consciousness of the relation of criticism to all preceding philosophy. **1889** CAIRD *Kant* I. 2 [Kant] opposes Criticism to two other forms of philosophy, Dogmatism and Scepticism.

3. (with *pl.*) An act of criticizing; a critical remark, comment; a critical essay, critique.

1608 CHAPMAN *Byron's Conspir.* I. i, There are a number more Of these State Criticismes: That our personall view May profitably make. **1683** DRYDEN *Life Plutarch* 14 Philosophical questions and criticisms of humanity were their usual recreations. **1756** C. LUCAS *Ess. Waters* I. Pref., Some..have..got their criticisms ready for the press. **1872** E. PEACOCK *Mabel Heron* I. v. 75 Very much disposed to make free criticisms. **1875** JOWETT *Plato* (ed. 2) V. 22 A criticism may be worth making which rests only on probabilities or impressions.

†**4.** A nice point or distinction, a minute particular, a nicety; a subtlety; in bad sense, a quibble.

a **1616** BEAUM. & FL. *Lit. Fr. Lawyer* I. i, This godly calling [of Duellist] Thou hast follow'd five-and-twenty yeares, and studied The criticismes of contentions [*i.e.* duelling]. **1658** SIR T. BROWNE *Gard. Cyrus* iii. 50 To set Seeds in that posture, wherein the Leaf and Roots may shoot right..were a Criticisme in Agriculture. **1663** J. SPENCER *Prodigies* (1665) 82 For the omission of some petty criticisms in their Rites. **1683** CAVE *Ecclesiastici, Athanasius* vi. §12. 108 Not sufficiently understanding the Criticisms of the Greek Language.

criticist (ˈkrɪtɪsɪst). [f. CRITIC(ISM + -IST.] An adherent of the critical philosophy of Kant (cf. CRITICISM 2 c). Also *attrib.*

1889 in *Cent. Dict.* **1892** *Monist* II. 295 The conceptions of philosophy held by the criticist, the positivist, and the evolutionist. **1898** W. JAMES *Let.* 15 June (1920) II. 74 It confirms the 'criticist' views of the philosophy of history. *c* **1905** C. S. PEIRCE *Sel. Writings* (1940) 299 It is difficult to find a Criticist who does not hold to more fundamental beliefs than any Critical Common-sensist does.

ˈcritiˈcizable, *a.* [f. CRITICIZE *v.* + -ABLE.] That may be criticized; open to criticism.

1863 HAWTHORNE *Our Old Home, Glimpses Eng. Poverty* (1879) 327 A few criticisable peculiarities in her talk and manner. **1888** BRYCE *Amer. Commw.* II. II. lii. 299 American cities are justly criticizable for many defects.

criticize (ˈkrɪtɪsaɪz), *v.* Also **-ise.** [f. CRITIC or L. *critic-us* + -IZE.]

1. *intr.* To play the critic; to pass judgement upon something with respect to its merits or faults. (Often connoting unfavourable judgement.)

1649 MILTON *Eikon.* xxiv. 491 To let goe his Criticizing about the sound of Prayers. **1681** DRYDEN *Abs. & Achit.* Introd. (1708) 2 They, who can criticize so weakly, as to imagine I have done my worst. **1753** MRS. DELANY *Let. Mrs. Dewes* 7 Apr., Her character is pretty; though had I time I could criticise. *a* **1862** BUCKLE *Civilis.* III. v. 316 They who criticize are unable to discern the great principle which pervades the whole.

†**b.** with *on* or *upon*; = sense 2. *Obs.*

1657 J. SERGEANT *Schism Dispach't* 15 Who can most dexterously and artificially criticize upon words. **1748** HARTLEY *Observ. Man* I. ii. ¶61. 213 We criticize much upon the Beauty of Faces. **1790** BURKE *Fr. Rev.* 244 To criticise on the use that is made of it. **1810** SOUTHEY in *Life* (1850) III. 277 It requires a knowledge of that art to criticise upon the structure of verse.

2. *trans.* To discuss critically; to offer judgement upon with respect to merits or faults; to animadvert upon.

1665 SIR T. HERBERT *Trav.* (1677) 354 Concerning the word *Tharsish*, so much criticiz'd, it is *Verbum ambiguum* and admits a various sence. **1724** BOLINGBROKE in *Swift's Lett.* (1766) II. 39 The verses I sent you are very bad..you would do them too much honour, if you criticized them. **1855** PRESCOTT *Philip II*, I. II. v. 193 Men began boldly to criticize the rights of kings and the duties of subjects. **1880** MACCORMAC *Antisept. Surg.* 49, I will now pass on to criticise a paper recently published.

b. To censure, find fault with.

1704 SWIFT *T. Tub* Concl., To criticise his gait, and ridicule his dress. **1779** JOHNSON *Lett. Mrs. Thrale* 11 Oct., The gout that was in my ankles when Queeney criticised my gait. **1884** tr. *Lotze's Logic* 131, I am not afraid that anyone will criticise this..on the ground that it has nothing to do with logic.

Hence **ˈcriticizing** *vbl. sb.* and *ppl. a.*; **ˈcritiˌcizingly** *adv.*

1649 [see CRITICIZE 1]. **1772** MAD. D'ARBLAY *Early Diary* (1889) I. 161 So criticising an eye. **1859** SALA *Tw. round Clock* (1861) 115 They..eye her approvingly, and the bridesmaids criticisingly.

criticizer (ˈkrɪtɪsaɪzə(r)). One who criticizes; a critic.

a **1680** CHARNOCK *Disc. God's Knowledge* Wks. 1684 I. 285 He is therefore called a 'discerner' or criticiser of the heart. **1731** BLACKWALL *Sacred Class.* II. 265 (T.) Pert criticisers and saucy correctors of the original. **1794** *Hist.* in *Ann. Reg.* 35 Severe criticisers of the conduct of the allies.

ˈcritickin. *nonce-wd.* A small or petty critic.

a **1843** SOUTHEY *Doctor* lxxii, Mr. Critickin,—for as there is a diminutive for cat, so should there be for critic,—I defy you. *Ibid.* Interch. xix, Critics, critickins, and criticasters.

criticling (ˈkrɪtɪklɪŋ). [See -LING.] = prec.

1755–6 *Old Maid* No. 18 (1764) 156, I shall therefore say ..to the Criticlings [etc.]. **1816** J. GILCHRIST *Philos. Etym.* 185 Criticlings may drawl and drivel..about the earliest authors being most original. **1883** *Lit. World* (U.S.) 16 June 194/1 Thus criticlings at Tennyson may yelp.

'critico-, combining form (after Gr. κριτικο-), = critically, critical and...: as in **critico-historical, -poetical, -theological**, etc., adjs.

1817 T. L. PEACOCK *Melincourt* xxxix, The members of this critico-poetical council. **1823** PARR *Wks.* 1828 VII. 282 Some critico-theological matter on Deuteronomy. **1878** *N. Amer. Rev.* CXXVII. 162 Stronger than his critico-historical [conscience].

b. Also used as a base for nonce-words, as **criti'cometer**, a measurer of critics or criticism. **,critico'phobia**, fear or horror of critics.

1883 *Athenæum* 20 Oct. 493/1 We thus obtain a scientific measurement of the thought..and the criticometer is before us. **1836** *Fraser's Mag.* XIII. 338 A peculiar sensitiveness (technically called criticophobia) has possessed the mind of every great author.

'criticule. *nonce-wd.* [See -ULE.] A small or petty critic.

1889 F. HALL in *N.Y. Nation* XLVIII. 97/1, The criticule whose callowness I have scrutinized.

critique (krɪ'tiːk). [A gradual alteration of the 17–18th c. *critick*, CRITIC *sb.*[2], after French.

Critique occurs in Addison's *Dial. Medals* (publ. in Wks. 1721), and Pope so altered his spelling in 1729. It became general in the 18th c., though Johnson and most of the dictionaries to the end of the century adhered to *critick*. Todd substituted *critique* in his ed. of J. in 1818; the modern pronunciation and stress after F. (or Ger.) appears in 1815.]

1. An essay or article in criticism of a literary (or more rarely, an artistic) work; a review.

1702–21 ADDISON *Dial. Medals* Wks. 1721 I. iii. 532, I should as soon expect to see a Critique on the Posie of a Ring, as on the Inscription of a Medal. **1729** POPE *Dunc.* I. 173 Not that my quill to Critiques was confin'd [in ed. **1728** Not that my pen to Criticks was confin'd]. **1793** COWPER *Lett.* 17 Feb., I have read the critique of my work in the *Analytical Review*. **1820** BYRON *Blues* I. 22, I just had been skimming a charming critique. **1882** PEBODY *Eng. Journalism* xix. (1882) 143 Turning out articles and critiques upon the topics of social life, of art, or literature.

2. The action or art of criticizing; criticism.

1815 W. H. IRELAND *Scribbleomania* 46, I deem such the basis of candid critique. **1856** MEIKLEJOHN tr. *Kant's Crit. P.R.* 15 Idea and division of a particular science, under the name of a Critique of Pure Reason. **1866** J. MARTINEAU *Ess.* I. 51 The critique of nature in detail is quite beyond us.

critique (krɪ'tiːk), *v. trans.* **a.** To write a critique upon; to review, criticize. (In quot. 1751 prob. stressed *'critique*: cf. CRITIC *v.*)

1751 *Hist. Pompey the Little* p. vii, The worst ribaldry of Aristophanes shall be critiqued and commented on. **1815** W. H. IRELAND *Scribbleomania* 2 Some writers there are who ..all subjects critique. **1831** *Fraser's Mag.* IV. 3 Hogg's tales are critiqued by himself in Blackwood.

b. More generally, to judge critically, to make a critical assessment of or comment on (an action, person, etc.), not necessarily in writing. Chiefly *U.S.*

1969 *New Yorker* 19 Apr. 81/1 A football coach critiquing a fumble on a film of a game. **1972** *Jrnl. Social Psychol.* LXXXVII. 160 If we, as scientists, critique society, does our ethical commitment stop there? **1973** *N.Y. Times* 21 Jan. IV. 4/1, I would not try to critique what Governor Rockefeller said to his legislature. **1975** *New Yorker* 24 Mar. 32/3 You can watch..a videotape of your own tennis game ..to critique your serve. **1978** *Detroit Free Press* 2 Apr. E6/1 Clark is not about to critique the Lions publicly. **1986** *Washington Post* 20 Mar. D5/4 The home economics supervisor who is overseeing and critiquing the progress of 'Dynamics' for District Public Schools, has commented [etc.].

Hence **cri'tiquing** *vbl. sb.*

1975 P. STONE in *Hard Cheese* Nov. 43 The substantive matter was divided into two sections—the first dealing with the sociology of education in terms of critiquing, and, by so doing, illustrating how critique is possible. **1982** *Washington Post* 13 June F1/1 Critiquing for the books is another matter.

†**'critism.** *Obs. rare*[−1]. [f. Gr. κριτής judge + -ISM.] = CRITICISM. So †**'critist**, †**'critize** *v.* [= Gr. *κριτίζειν].

1651 *Reliq. Wotton.* 40 There being then no such Critismes as interpreted [this]..a conspiracy against the State. **1602** DEKKER *Satirom.* Wks. 1873 I. 211 You are growne a piece of a Critist. **1631** DONNE *Polydoron* Pref., They may find their humours here critiz'd. *a* **1677** BARROW *Wks.* 1687 I. 511 We need not critize on the words, the sense being plain.

'critling. *dial.* [See -LING, and cf. CRITON, CRATLING.]

†**1.** (See quot. 1611.) *Obs.* **2.** The refuse of lard or grease; = next: cf. CRACKLING *sb.* 3.

1611 COTGR., *Bourgeons*, writlings, or critlings; the smaller and most vntimely apples or peares. **1851** MAYHEW *Lond. Labour* I. 196 Spice to give the critlings a flavour, critlings being the refuse left after boiling down the lard.

'criton. *Obs.* exc. *dial.* Also 4 critoun, 9 *dial.* critten. [a. F. *cretons* 'the crispie peeces or mammockes remaining of lard, that hath beene first shred..then strained, etc.' (Cotgr.)] The refuse of lard or grease; = CRACKLING *sb.* 3.

1388 WYCLIF *Ps.* ci[i]. 4 My boonus han dried vp as Critouns [**1382** croote; Vulg. *cremium*; *marg.* critons], that is, that that dwellith in the panne of the friyng. **1888** *Berkshire Gloss.*, *Crittens*, small pieces of lean meat strained from lard when it is melted.

critter ('krɪtə(r)). Also 9 crittur. Widespread dial. and jocular var. CREATURE; *spec.* an ox or cow; a horse; a chicken; a person (usu. disparaging).

1815 D. HUMPHREYS *Yankey in Eng.* 41 Cooking for the crew, and taking care of the dum critturs. **1827** A. SHERWOOD *Gaz. Georgia* 139 *Beast*, or *crittur*, for horse. **1834** S. SMITH *Sel. Lett. Downing* 86 Bears and wolves and sich kind of critters. **1834** C. A. DAVIS *Lett. J. Downing* 19 There he [*sc.* Capt. Finny] was, sure enough: the crittur had just come out of his bush-pasture. *Ibid.* 31 There was that crittur Mr. Van Buren. **1853** R. S. SURTEES *Sponge's Sp. Tour* xiv. 73 One of your poor pryin', inquisitive critturs, what's always fancyin' themselves cheated. *Ibid.* xxvii. 166, I saw the critter's great pecker steadily down in his plate. **1853** FELTON *Fam. Lett.* xxvii. (1865) 249 The upper story ..occupied by..the family, and the rooms below by the animals, or as a Yankee would call them, the *critters*. **1855** D. G. ROSSETTI *Let.* 11 May (1897) 126 That magnanimous crittur seems to have restored him his confidence. **1856** GEO. ELIOT *Let.* 6 June (1954) II. 253 A charming little zoological curate here, who..is most good-natured in lending and giving apparatus and 'critturs' of all sorts. **1862** G. DU MAURIER *Let.* Apr. (1951) 127 My talk is rather an institution among critters who are like to each other. **1923** 'B. M. BOWER' *Parowan Bonanza* vi. 65 She..can sling a pack or rope a critter better than lots of men that draw wages for doing it. **1926** E. M. ROBERTS *Time of Man* (1963) 321 'You came a-horseback?' Jasper said. He was moved almost beyond speech by this expression of loyalty. 'A-horseback I reckon.' 'Yes, we rode our critters.' **1942** M. CAMPBELL *Cloud-Walking* 32 He dozed off till Sary's chickens crowed for morning... Then he stirred to light a fire in the cook room and go out to the lot to feed the critters about the place. **1956** 'N. SHUTE' *Beyond Black Stump* 143 I'd have said it wasn't possible. I mean, to tame a critter like that.

crivens ('krɪvənz), *int. dial.* or *slang.* Also crivvens. [Vulgar corruption of CHRIST; perh. infl. by *heavens* (HEAVEN *sb.* 6 d).] An exclamation of astonishment or horror.

1917 A. S. NEILL *Dominie Dismissed* viii. 101 Crivens! What a fine essay that wud mak! **1927** *Scots Observer* 2 July 11/2 'Crivens!' ejaculated Oddfish, 'Are they awa' again?' **1935** G. BLAKE *Shipbuilders* iv. 88 Holy crivvens, I nearly broke my flakin' back. *Ibid.* 89 Crivvens, boy, it's great to see one of the old crush!

crize, obs. f. KRIS, Malay dagger.

crizzle ('krɪz(ə)l), *v.* Also 7 crisle, crizle, crizel, 8–9 crizel, 9 crissel. [Origin obscure: perh. dim. of CRAZE *v.* Cf. F. *crisser* to crackle.]

1. *intr.* To become rough on the surface, as some kinds of stone or glass by scaling, or as water when it begins to freeze, etc.

1673 RAY *Journ. Low C.* (1738) II. 462 Those stones will last well enough, till they shall be removed into a rougher [air]: But then they'll crizle and scale. **1676** *Lond. Gaz.* No. 1136/4 Some of the..Flint Glasses..have been observed to crizel and decay. **1753** CHAMBERS *Cycl. Supp.* s.v. *Crizzelling*, The glass thus made..is subject to crizzel. **1821** CLARE *Addr. to Plenty* (1821) 55 View the hole the boys have broke, Crizzling, still inclin'd to freeze. **1881** *Leicestersh. Gloss.*, *Crizzle*, to crisp; to grow hard and rough with heat or cold.

2. *trans.* To cause to 'crizzle'; to roughen or crumple the surface of.

1821 CLARE *Vill. Minstr.* II. 26 White frost 'gins crizzle pond and brook. **1876** *Whitby Gloss.*, *Crizzle*, to broil. *Crizzled*, hardened or crisped as the land is in a droughty season. **1877** *N.W. Linc. Gloss.*, *Crisseled up*, twisted up as leaves are by cold.

Hence **'crizzle** *sb.* (see quot.); **'crizzled** *ppl. a.*; **'crizz(e)l(l)ing** *vbl. sb.*

1624 FORD & DEKKER *Sun's Darling* v. i, To feel the ice fall from my crisled skin. **1677** R. PLOT *Oxfordshire* ix. 253 The glasses made of these being subject to that..fault called Crizelling. **1876** *Whitby Gloss.*, *Crizzles*, the rough sunburnt places on the face and hands in scorching weather. **1937** *Burlington Mag.* Nov. 217/1 The interior decay has taken the form of what in seventeenth-century England was called 'crizzelling'. *Ibid.* 218/2 The bowl was..extensively crizzled.

‖**cro** (kroː). *Celtic Antiq.* Also 5 croy. [Irish *cró* death, blood, blood-wyte.] 'The compensation or satisfaction made for the slaughter of any man, according to his rank' (Jam.).

13.. *Reg. Maj.* IV. xxx. Sc. Stat. I. 640 Quid sit le cro quod anglice dicitur Grant befor the Kyng. **1426** *Sc. Acts Jas. I* (1566) § 104 (Jam.) To pay..the croy to the narrest of the kin of the slaine man. **1609** SKENE *Reg. Maj.* 74 It is statute be the King, that Cro of ane Erle of Scotland is seven tymes twentie kye. **1614** SELDEN *Titles Hon.* 286 Where Earles, Earles sonnes, Thanes, Ochierns and the like are distinguisht by their Croes. **1872** E. W. ROBERTSON *Hist. Ess.* 135 The Cro, or Wergild, of the Thane.

croak (krəʊk), *sb.* Also 8 croke. [See CROAK *v.*]

1. The deep hoarse sound made by a frog or raven. Also *transf.* and *fig.*

1561 DAUS tr. *Bullinger on Apoc.* (1573) 225 b, They play the waterfrogs, singyng croake croake. **1632** ROWLEY *Woman never vext* III. in Hazl. *Dodsley* XII. 160 O thou fatal raven! let me pull thine eyes out For this sad croak. **1766** PENNANT *Zool.* (1812) II. 157 (*Puffin Auk*) The hoarse, deep, periodical croak of the corvorants. **1861** TROLLOPE *Barchester T.* xliv, 'I told you so, I told you so!' is the croak of a true Job's comforter.

2. *Hawking.* (See quot. 1891.) Also *pl.* (Cf. CROCK *sb.*[4])

1707 FLOYER *Physic. Pulse-Watch* (1710) 400 The Croke is evidently an Asthmatic Disposition produced by hard flying. *Ibid.* 401 The Noise called the Croke was made by Expiration and not by Inspiration. **1891** HARTING *Gloss. Falconry*, *Croaks*, or *Kecks*, Fr. *crac*, a disease of the air-passages, analogous to a cough, and so called from the sound the bird makes during any exertion, such as bating, or flying.

croak (krəʊk), *v.* Forms: (5 crok) 6–8 croke, 6–7 croake, 7– croak. [*Croak* sb. and vb. appears only about 1550; the 15th c. *crok* is not its exact equivalent phonetically; in the same sense ME. had also *crouke*, *crowke*: see CROOK *v.*[2] It is possible that *croak*, with the northern parallel form *crake*, *craik*, goes back to an OE. **crácian*, of which the recorded *cræcetian* to croak (said of ravens) may be a diminutive; but it is on the whole more probable that *crouke*, *crok*, *croak*, with *crake*, *creak*, *crick*, are later formations imitating or suggesting varieties of animal and other sounds.]

1. a. *intr.* To utter a deep, hoarse, dismal cry, as a frog or a raven.

c **1460** *Towneley Myst.* 99 Sely Capyll, oure hen..She kakyls, Bot begyn she to crok, To groyne or to clok. **1557** *Tottell's Misc.* (Arb.) 200 Thou dunghyll crowe that crokest agaynst the rayne. **1595** SPENSER *Epithal.* 349 Th' vnpleasant quyre of frogs still croking. **1602** MARSTON *Antonio's Rev.* III. iii. Wks. 1856 I. 111 Now croakes the toad. **1697** DRYDEN *Virg. Ecl.* I. 26 The hoarse Raven..By croaking from the left presag'd the coming Blow. **1835** W. IRVING *Tour Prairies* 277 Ravens..flapping about and croaking dismally in the air. **1877** A. B. EDWARDS *Up Nile* xxii. 699 Meanwhile the frogs croaked furiously.

b. Of a hawk: see CROAK *sb.* 2.

1575 TURBERV. *Faulconrie* 250 You may perceyve these woormes to plague and trouble your hawke when she croakes in the night. **1618** LATHAM *2nd Bk. Falconry* (1633) 23 It breedeth much winde in them, the which..will appeare often with a rising in the gorge, and a noyse withall of croking.

2. *transf.* Of persons: †To groan or cry (*obs.*); to speak with a hoarse, hollow utterance; *fig.* to speak in dismal accents, talk despondingly, forebode evil (like the raven).

c **1460** *Towneley Myst.* 108, I thoght Gylle began to crok, and travelle full sad. **1606** SHAKS. *Tr. & Cr.* v. ii. 191 Would I could meete that roague Diomed, I would croke like a Rauen: I would bode, I would bode. **1797** BURKE *Regic. Peace* iii. Wks. VIII. 389 They, who croak themselves hoarse about the decay of our trade. **1806** METCALFE in Owen *Wellesley's Desp.* 807 Without croaking, it may be observed that our government is upon a dangerous experiment. **1852** MRS. STOWE *Uncle Tom's C.* xxii. 222 'Don't be croaking, cousin—I hate it!' he would say.

†**3.** Of the stomach or bowels: To make a rumbling noise. *Obs.*

1547 [see CROAKING *vbl. sb.* 1]. **1611** COTGR., *Gribouiller*, to rumble or croake (as the guts doe through windinesse). **1682** N. O. *Boileau's Lutrin* IV. 330 My eager stomach crokes, and calls for Dinner! *a* **1704** T. BROWN *Sat. Fr. King* Wks. 1730 I. 60 When my starv'd entrails croke.

4. *trans.* To utter or proclaim by croaking.

1605 SHAKS. *Macb.* I. v. 40 The raven himselfe is hoarse That croakes the fatall entrance of Duncan. **1791** *Ep. to J. Priestley* in *Poet. Reg.* (1808) 401 Now half the bench of Bishops we may meet, Croaking 'old clothes' about St. James's Street. **1847** TENNYSON *Princ.* IV. 106 Marsh-divers, rather, maid, Shall croak thee sister. **1879** FROUDE *Cæsar* xiii. 178 Bibulus, as each measure was passed, croaked that it was null and void.

5. *intr.* **a.** *slang.* To die.

1812 in J. H. VAUX *Flash Dict.* **1851** MAYHEW *London Lab.* I. 424/1 They go mouching along as if they were croaking. **1873** *Slang Dict.*, *Croak*, to die—from the gurgling sound a person makes when the breath of life is departing. **1896** A. MORRISON *Child of Jago* xxviii. 272 Run, for Gawd's sake, or the woman'll croak! **1961** 'J. WELCOME' *Beware of Midnight* ii. 33 Your old man has croaked and left you the lot.

b. *trans.* To kill; to murder; to hang. *dial.* or *slang.*

1823 P. EGAN *Grose's Dict. Vulgar Tongue*, *Croaked*, hanged. A flash term among keepers of prisons, who, speaking of a thief that was executed, observe, 'He was *croaked*.' **1848** *Ladies' Repository* VIII. 316/1 *Croak*, to murder. **1877** F. Ross et al. *Gloss. Holderness*, *Crooak*,..N. and E., to kill. **1910** E. A. WALCOTT *Open Door* vii. 83 'I never done it!' he gasped. 'I never hurt nobody. Who's been croaked?' **1930** *Punch* 26 Feb. 236 It was fairly clear that he had been croaked. **1945** L. A. G. STRONG *Othello's Occupation* 123 Who croaked Enameline?

croaker ('krəʊkə(r)). Also 7–8 croker. [f. CROAK *v.* + -ER.]

1. An animal that croaks; applied *spec.* to several North American fishes, also to the Mole Cricket.

1651 OGILBY *Æsop* (1665) 11 While the long Vale with big-voiced Croakers [*i.e.* frogs] rings. **1676** T. GLOVER *Virginia* in *Phil. Trans.* XI. 625 In the Creeks are great store of small fish, as Perches, Crokers, Taylors, Eels. **1784** MORTIMER *Carolina* ibid. XXXVIII. 315 *Perca marina*..the Croker. **1868** WOOD *Homes without H.* viii. 158 The Mole Cricket, called in some places the Croaker or Churr-worm on account of the peculiar sound which it produces. **1883** *Fisheries Exhib. Catal.* (ed. 4) 170 Salt-water fishes.. Grunts, Croakers, and Drummers..the three last deriving their names from the sounds they utter when caught.

2. *transf.* One who talks dismally or despondingly, one who forebodes or prophesies evil.

1637 BASTWICK *Litany* I. 20 A malignant and corrupt.. brood of Crokers. **1771** FRANKLIN *Autobiog.* Wks. 1840 I. 79 There are croakers in every country, always boding its ruin. **1850** T. A. TROLLOPE *Impress. Wand.* v. 57 A few timid croakers shake their heads.

3. *slang.* (See quot.)

1873 *Slang Dict.*, *Croaker*, a dying person beyond hope; a corpse. **1892** *Star* 28 May 2/7 The cow was a 'croker', a beast killed to save it from dying.

4. *slang.* A doctor, physician; esp. a prison doctor. Now chiefly *U.S.* Cf. CROCUS 4.

1859 in HOTTEN *Dict. Slang* 26. **1889** BARRÈRE & LELAND *Dict. Slang* I. 281/1 One man who had put his name for the 'butcher' or *croaker*, would suddenly find that he had three ounces of bread less to receive. **1931** 'DEAN STIFF' *Milk & Honey Route* vii. 71 Every doctor, known among the hobos as the 'croaker' or 'pill peddler'. *a* **1935** D. RUNYON *More than Somewhat* (1937) 12 She..goes..to get a croaker to see if my wounds are fatal. **1946** MEZZROW & WOLFE *Really Blues* vii. 95 The most he needed was some bicarbonate of soda and a physic, not a croaker.

croakery ('krəʊkərɪ). *nonce-wd.* [f. CROAK *v.* or CROAKER: see -ERY.] Croakings collectively.

1865 CARLYLE *Fredk. Gt.* (1873) VI. XVI. vi. 193 Freidrich, in answer to new cunning croakeries and contrivances..has answered him like a king. **1867** —— *Remin.* (1881) II. 186 A croakery of crawling things, instead of a speaking by men.

croakily ('krəʊkɪlɪ), *adv.* [f. CROAKY *a.* + -LY[2].] In a croaky manner.

1858 CARLYLE *Fredk. Gt.* (1865) II. v. vii. 125 Immortal Wolf, croakily satirical withal, had defended himself.

croaking ('krəʊkɪŋ), *vbl. sb.* [f. CROAK *v.*]

1. The action of making a deep hoarse sound.

1547 BOORDE *Brev. Health* cccix. 100 b, In Englyshe it is named crokyng or clockyng in ones bely. *a* **1610** HEALEY *Epictetus' Man.* xxiv. (1636) 29 The croaking of the Raven. **1840** R. DANA *Bef. Mast* ix. 22 The frogs set up their croaking in the marshes.

2. *fig.* Talking dismally or foreboding evil.

1787 J. WEDGWOOD *Let.* 16 June (1965) 305, I rejoice to find that all croaking against the treaty is at an end everywhere. **1810** WELLINGTON in Gurw. *Desp.* VI. 417 The croaking which already prevails in the army. **1836** MARRYAT *Midsh. Easy* xxvii. 106 All this comes from your croaking —you're a Mother Cary's chicken.

'croaking, *ppl. a.* [f. as prec. + -ING[2].] That croaks. (*lit.* and *fig.*)

1607 TOPSELL *Serpents* (1653) 719 The croaking Frogs made such a noise, as he could take no rest. **1662** STILLINGFL. *Orig. Sacr.* II. i. §2 An innumerable company of croaking Enthusiasts. **1780** MAD. D'ARBLAY *Lett.* 24 Aug., A croaking prophet, foretells nothing but utter destruction. **1885** *Manch. Exam.* 27 Feb. 5/4 [His] voice itself was pitched in a low and croaking key.

croaky ('krəʊkɪ), *a.* [f. CROAK *sb.* or *v.* + -Y.]

1. Characterized by croaking; given to croaking.

1851 CARLYLE *Sterling* II. iv, His voice was croaky and shrill. **1854** DICKENS *Lett.* (ed. 2) I. 363 A croaky voice.

2. *Naut.* (See quot.)

c **1850** *Rudim. Navig.* (Weale) 112 *Croaky*, a term applied to plank when it curves or compasses much in short lengths. **1867** in SMYTH *Sailor's Word-bk.*

† croan, croane, *a. Obs.* perh. an attrib. use of CRONE *sb.*

1577 tr. *Bullinger's Decades* (1592) 498 He..liued in..the studie of the sacred Scriptures, euen to his croane and crooked age. **1746** *Brit. Mag.* 53 Coaches..filled with several Croan Matrons, Town Ladies, etc.

croane, obs. f. CRONE.

† croape, *v. Obs.* Also crope. [Cf. CROUP.] *intr.* To croak.

c **1500** KENNEDY *Flyting w. Dunbar* 393 Cursit croapand craw. **1549** *Compl. Scot.* vi. 39 The ropeen of the rauynis gart the crans crope. **1593** B. BARNES *Parthenophil* in Arb. *Garner* V. 481 Bulls bellow through the wood! Ravens croape! **1600** ABP. ABBOT *Exp. Jonah* 471 He feedeth the young ravens who do cry or croape.

croape, obs. pa. t. of CREEP.

croaper, obs. form of CRUPPER.

Croat ('krəʊæt). [ad. mod.L. (pl.) *Croatæ* (F. *Croate*, G. *Kroat*), ad. Serbo-Croatian *Hrvat*, formerly pronounced (xr̩'wat). Cf. CRAVAT *sb.* (from a later variety of pronunciation).] **a.** A native or inhabitant of the former Austrian province of Croatia, now forming part of Yugoslavia; one of a race descended from the people which occupied that country in the seventh century. **b.** A soldier of a former French cavalry regiment, composed mainly of Croats. **c.** The language of the Croats. Also *attrib.* or as *adj.*

1702 *Milit. Dict.*, *Croat*, properly the People of Croatia; but in *France* there is a Regiment of Horse so call'd... These *Croats* are commanded upon all desperate Service. **1749** FIELDING *Tom Jones* VI. ii, Brother, you are absolutely a perfect Croat; but as those have their Use in the Army of the Empress Queen, so you likewise have some Good in you. *c* **1790** *Encycl. Brit.* V. 555/2 The Croats derive their origin from the Sclavi. **1815** *Wynne Diaries* 28 Sept. (1940) III. 386 We passed a Croat Regiment, the women that follow'd it were perfect Gypsies. **1862** *Chambers's Encycl.* III. 324/2 The Croatians are warlike, but the name Croats is employed to designate light-cavalry regiments in the imperial army, in which Magyars and others are mingled with true Croatians. **1920** H. A. L. FISHER *Studies Hist. & Pol.* 207 Croat and Slovene newspapers. **1942** L. B. NAMIER *Conflicts* 48 In Yugoslavia the conflict between Croats and Serbs..offered the Nazis rich opportunities for political intrigue. **1959** J. REMAK *Sarajevo* iii. 42 Franz Ferdinand replied..ending with a sentence spoken in Croat.

Croatian (krəʊ'eɪʃ(ɪ)ən), *sb.* and *a.* [f. mod.L. *Croatia*, f. *Croatæ*: see prec. and -IAN.] **A.** *sb.* **a.** A Croat. **b.** The language of the Croats, belonging to the Balto-Slavic group. **B.** *adj.* Of or pertaining to Croatia or the Croats.

1555 EDEN *Decades* (Arb.) 290 The Bohemians, Croatians, and Sclauons. **1607** TOPSELL *Four-f. Beasts* 160 The Croatian Dog, resembling a Wolfe in haire and bignesse. **1748** JOHNSON *Van. Hum. Wishes* 20 The fierce Croatian, and the wild Hussar. **1822** [see WEND *sb.* 2]. **1837** *Penny Cycl.* VIII. 161/2 The Damascene plum furnishes the favourite drink of the Croatians. *Ibid.*, The Croatian language is a dialect of the Sclavonian. **1876** [see SLAV *sb.*]. **1855** *Encycl. Brit.* XVIII. 785/1 There are two main branches of Slavonic. The so-called Southern or South-Eastern branch embraces Russian, Ruthenian (in Galicia), Bulgarian, Servian, Croatian, and Slovenian. **1921** *Glasgow Herald* 8 Jan. 6 Their intrigues with the Croatian separatists. **1936** A. W. CLAPHAM *Romanesque Archit.* iii. 70 The native product of Croatian culture.

† crob, *sb. Obs.* In 6 crobbe. *pl.* 'The knops of leafy buds, used as pendants from the roof' (Halliwell).

1548 HALL *Chron.* (1809) 639 The Vautes in orbes with Crobbes dependyng.

† crob, *v. Obs.* Also 6 crobb. = CROAK *v.*

c **1350** *N. Eng. Leg.* in Horstmann *Alteng. Leg.* II. 149/252 I leue to crakes þat crobbes & cryes. *c* **1450** *St. Cuthbert* (Surtees) 2380 þe crawe..Reufully sho crobbed and cryed. *c* **1475** *Cath. Angl.* 83 (MS. A), To Crobe, *crocitare vel crocare, coruorum est.* A Crobbynge of rauens. **1566** DRANT *Horace's Sat.* A iij, Still, still thy stomake crobbs.

‖ croc[1], † crock (krɒk). [OF. *croc* hook = Pr. *croc*, It. *crocco*, med.L. *croccus*, of uncertain origin.] A hook: in ***harquebus à*** (of) ***croc***, a harquebus with a hook or crook by which it was fixed to its rest or support when fired: see HARQUEBUS.

croc[2] (krɒk). Colloq. abbrev. of *crocodile*.

1. = CROCODILE *sb.* 1 a.

1884 C. B. LEWIS *Sawed-off Sketches* 133 'You'll be sure to agree with me,' muttered the old Croc. as he chewed him down. **1921** *Blackw. Mag.* Jan. 102/1 The 'croc' is the one African animal regarding which nobody has any idea of sportsmanship. **1925** *Ibid.* Sept. 419/1 With loud yells to scare away any crocs that might be lurking round. **1936** P. M. CLARK *Autobiogr. Old Drifter* x. 135 Leaving the corpses of many crocs lying about behind us. **1964** C. WILLOCK *Enormous Zoo* iv. 60 The head of a croc spear is detachable, like that of an old-fashioned whaler's harpoon.

b. = CROCODILE *sb.* 1 c; esp. in phr. ***mock croc***, imitation crocodile-skin.

1963 *Honey* Oct. 59 Boots—in mock-croc. *Ibid.* 69/4 Mock-croc bag. **1967** *Woman* 9 Dec. 11/2 Chic burgundy mock croc shoes.

2. = CROCODILE *sb.* 4.

1948 'J. TEY' *Franchise Affair* ii. 27 An ordinary sort of girl, after all. Not the sort you would notice in a croc. **1958** *Listener* 6 Nov. 722/2 Walking in a school croc.

crocalite ('krɒkəlaɪt). *Min.* [Named 1797, app. from κρόκος saffron + -LITE.] A red variety of NATROLITE, occurring in small amygdules.

1808 T. ALLAN *Names of Min.* 24 Crocalite. **1844** ALGER *Phillips' Min.* 202 Crockalite.

crocard, var. of CROCKARD *Obs.*

† cro'cation. *Obs.*[−0] [L. *crocātio* croaking, cawing.] See CROCITATION.

croce, original form of CROSE, crosier.

croce, obs. var. of CROSS.

† 'croceal, *a. Obs.* [f. L. *croce-us* saffron-coloured + -AL[1].] = CROCEOUS.

1647 LILLY *Chr. Astrol.* vii. 52 The Red and Yellow, or Croceall, or Sorrell colour.

'crocean, *a.*[1] [cf. prec.] = CROCEOUS.

1621 QUARLES *Argalus & P.* III. Wks. (Grosart) III. 269/1 And from the pillow of his Crocian bed Don Phœbus rouzes his refulgent head. **1638** —— *Hieroglyph.* xv. III. 196/2 Rising in glory from his Crocean bed. **1900** F. THOMPSON *Sel. Poems* 21 The crocean and amethystine In their pristine Lustre linger on its coat.

Crocean ('krəʊtʃɪən, 'krəʊsɪən), *a.*[2] (and *sb.*). Also Crocian. [f. *Croce* (see below) + -AN.] Of, pertaining to, or characteristic of the Italian philosopher and statesman Benedetto Croce (1866–1952) or his idealistic 'philosophy of the spirit'. Also *sb.*, a follower of Croce or of his philosophy.

1921 HANNAY & COLLINGWOOD tr. *Ruggiero's Mod. Philos.* 357 This is the new conception of reality that emerges from the very heart of the Crocian philosophy. **1925** *Glasgow Herald* 16 Apr. 4 The French 'Symboliste' poets also are open to attack along Crocean lines. M. Paul Valéry..is not a Crocean. **1926** *Ibid.* 2 Apr. 5 The Crocean doctrine that art is expression and that all expression is art. **1958** *Listener* 10 July 61/1 A historian of the Crocean persuasion.

croceate ('krəʊsɪeɪt, -ʃɪeɪt), *a.* [f. L. *croce-us* + -ATE: cf. *roseate.*] **a.** Pertaining to saffron. **b.** Saffron-coloured, CROCEOUS.

1866 J. B. ROSE *Virg. Georg.* I. 56 Tmolus doth supply Its croceate odours. **1867** —— *Æneid* 262 From Tithon's croceate bed Aurora springs. *Ibid.* 268 The croceate garb.

† croceous ('krəʊsɪəs, -ʃɪəs), *a. Obs.* [f. L. *croce-us* saffron-coloured, f. *crocus* saffron + -OUS.] Saffron-coloured; deep reddish yellow.

1657 TOMLINSON *Renou's Disp.* 688 The first water will be white..the third croceous. **1688** R. HOLME *Armoury* II. 311/2 Croceous is a saffron yellow.

crocer(e, obs. form of CROSIER.

crocetin: see CROCIN.

† croche, *sb.*[1] *Obs.* Also 5–6 crotche, crowche, 6 cruche. [Etymologically the same as *croce*, CROSE; *croche* being the Old Northern French equivalent of Central OF. *croce*. The form *crowche* is perh. a phonetic development (cf. *poche*, *pouch*); in *cruche* there may be a blending with CRUTCH.]

1. A pastoral staff, crook, crosier.

14.. *Nominale* in Wr.-Wülcker 721/38 (*Nom. Rer. Ecclesiast.*), *Hoc pedum*, a crowche. *c* **1450** *St. Cuthbert* 6249 A biscop..with his croche. **1483** CAXTON *Gold. Leg.* 123/1 Thenne saynt basille..cam to the chyrche and knocked a stroke wyth hys croche. **1490–9** *Promp. Parv.* 104 (H., P.) Croke or schoke [H. *c* **1490**, P. **1499** crotche, **1516** croche], *pedum, cambuca.* **1536** *Inv. Whalley Abbey* (*Trans. Hist. Soc. Lanc.* N.S. VII. 107), j crowche of silver and gilt with a staff of silver. **1539** *Inv.* in Burton *Mon. Ebor.* 144 One cruche-head gilt..the staff of the Cruche, gilt. **1563** BP. PILKINGTON *Burn. Pauls* (Parker Soc.) 584 They have not the cruche and mitre as the old bishops had.

2. A stick having a head to lean on; a lame man's staff, a crutch. Cf. CROSE 2.

In this sense not easily separated from CRUTCH, q.v.

14.. *Voc.* in Wr.-Wülcker 810/25 *Hoc sustentaculum, hoc podium*, a croche. *c* **1500** *Merchant & Son* in Halliwell *Nugæ Poet.* 32 An olde man, wyth crochys twayne.

¶ See also CROTCH.

croche, *sb.*[2] [a. F. *croche* spur on a fruit tree, etc.:—Rom. **crocca*: cf. med.L. *crocha* hook (Du Cange); from same radical as CROC[1].] One of the 'buds' or knobs at the top of a stag's horn.

1575 TURBERV. *Venerie* 54 These litle buddes or broches which are about the toppe are called Croches. **1583** STANYHURST *Aeneis* I. (Arb.) 23 Chiefe stags vpbearing croches high from the antlier hauted. **1630** J. TAYLOR (Water P.) *Wks.* I. 93/1 The hornes haue many dogmaticall Epithites, as..the Burs, the Pearles, the Antliers..and the Croches. **1774** GOLDSM. *Nat. Hist.* (1862) I. II. v. 325. **1884** JEFFERIES *Red Deer* iv. 71.

† croche, *v. Obs.* [a. F. *crocher* to hook, catch with hooks or claws (f. *croche*); and aphetic form of *acroche*, ACCROACH.]

1. *trans.* To hook, catch with hooks.

a **1225** *Juliana* 35 Make me war and wite me wið his crefti crokes, þat ha me ne crochen [*printed* crechen].

2. = ACCROACH, ENCROACH.

c **1380** WYCLIF *Serm.* Sel. Wks. I. 139 Pharisees..haue crochid to þem þe chesynge of many heerdis in þe chirche. **1592** *Manch. Court Leet Rec.* (1885) II. 60 Roberte Janye hathe Croched..vppon the hye..streete.

croche, obs. form of CROTCH, CROUCH *v.*

crochebake: see CROUCHBACK.

† croched, *ppl. a. Obs.* [f. CROCHE *v.* and *sb.* + -ED. Cf. F. *crochu.*]

1. Crooked, twisted.

c **1300** *K. Alis.* 7099 Wilde swyn And croched dragons.

2. Having 'croches': see CROCHE *sb.*[2]

1598 MANWOOD *Lawes Forest* iv. §6 (1615) 46 a, A Hart.. whether he be croched, palmed, or crowned.

crocherd(e, obs. form of KREUTZER.

crochet ('krəʊʃeɪ, 'krəʊʃɪ), *sb.* [F. *crochet*, dim. of *croche*, *croc* hook.]

1. A kind of knitting done with a hooked needle; material so made.

1848 CLOUGH *Bothie* I. 42 A shirt as of crochet of women. **1879** E. GARRETT *House by Works* II. 39 Sundry trifles of simple cambric or crochet with which to brighten her worn, plain gowns.

2. *attrib.* and *Comb.*, as ***crochet-cotton***, ***edging***, ***-hook***, ***-lace***, ***-needle***, ***-pin***, ***-sampler***, ***-type*** (see quot.), ***-work***.

1846 C. MEE *Crochet Expl. & Illustr.* 2nd Ser. 151 Three reels of No. 12 *crochet cotton will be sufficient. **1873** *Young Englishwoman* Feb. 91/1 Work with crochet cotton No. 30 in a chain the required length. **1849** *Family Friend* I. 78/2 The Penelope *Crochet Hook is invented by Mrs. Warren. **1860** *Ladies' Companion* 37 A coarse Crochet Hook. **1881** *Instr. Census Clerks* (1885) 44 Crochet Hook Maker. **1849** CLARIDGE *Cold Water Cure* 130 A *crochet-needle was, by accident, driven into the side of a young lady. **1909** *Daily Chron.* 8 Dec. 9/2 By putting the *crochet-pin into the upper half of the stitch. **1848** MISS LAMBERT (*title*), My *Crochet Sampler. **1874** KNIGHT *Dict. Mech.*, *Crochet-type, type with fancy faces, to set up in imitation of lace, crochet, or worsted work. **1856** MRS. BROWNING *Aur. Leigh* 38 And should I sit down to the *crochet work?

crochet (ˈkrəʊʃeɪ, ˈkrəʊʃɪ), *v.* [f. prec. sb.] **a.** *intr.* To work with a crochet-needle. **b.** *trans.* To make or knit in crochet. Hence **crocheting** (ˈkrəʊʃɪɪŋ, ˈkrəʊʃeɪɪŋ) *vbl. sb.*, crochet-work.

1858 MRS. CARLYLE *Lett.* II. 384 She had crocheted..a large cover for the drawing-room sofa. **1883** *Mem. Mrs. Sutherland* 60 The sewing and crocheting department. **1891** *Daily News* 31 Dec. 5/5 The Queen has contributed a..shawl of her own crocheting. **1901** *Daily Chron.* 17 Sept. 7/1 She..at once took up her crocheting. **1921** *Dict. Occup. Terms* (1927) §375 A crocheting machine to make lace.

crochet, obs. var. of CROTCHET.

‖**crocheteur.** *Obs.* Also 6 -tor. [F.; f. *crochet* hook.] 'A porter or common burthen-bearer' (Cotgr.).

1579 J. STUBBES *Gaping Gulf* B v, The sayntes of God ledde to the shambles..by vile crochetors or porters. **1613** BEAUM. & FL. *Honest Man's Fort.* III. ii, I would have hired a chrocheteur for two cardecues.

crociary (ˈkrəʊʃɪərɪ). *Eccl.* [ad. med.L. *crociarius*, f. *crocia* crosier.] 'The person who carried the crosier before the abbot or bishop' (Ash 1775).

†**crociate.** *Obs.* [ad. It. *crociata*, f. *croce* cross.] Taking the cross; = CRUSADE.

1607 DONNE *Lett.* (1651) 140 In the Crociate for the warres in the Holy Land.

crociate, *v.*: see CROCITATE.

crocidolite (krəʊˈsɪdəlaɪt). *Min.* [Named 1831 f. Gr. κροκίς, κροκιδ-, var. of κροκύς the nap of woollen cloth + λίθος stone (-LITE).] A fibrous silicate of iron and sodium, called also *blue asbestos*; sometimes massive or earthy. Also applied to a yellow fibrous mineral produced by natural alteration from the blue crocidolite, and much used for ornament.

1835 SHEPARD *Min.* 297 Krocidolite. **1887** *Daily Tel.* 7 June 7 The new crocidolite, which is only a compressed asbestos, displays sheens and radiances of gold and bronze and green like satin changed to stone. **1888** *Catholic Press* 7 Apr. 419 A cross made of South African gold, mounted in crocidolite and ivory.

crocin (ˈkrəʊsɪn). *Chem.* [f. L. *croc-us* saffron + -IN.] A red powder, the colouring matter of Chinese Yellow pods, the fruit of *Gardenia grandiflora*, with which the robes of Chinese mandarins are dyed. A supposed product of the action of hydrochloric acid on crocin is ˈ**crocetin**.

1863–72 WATTS *Dict. Chem.* II. 108.

crocine (ˈkrəʊsɪn, -aɪn), *a.* [ad. L. *crocin-us*, f. *crocus*.] Of, or consisting of, crocuses.

1812 HAWORTH in *Trans. Hort. Soc.* I. 130, I have seldom observed these crocine hedgehogs produce many flowers.

†ˈ**crocitate,** *v. Obs.*⁻⁰ [f. L. *crocitāre*, freq. of *crōcīre* to croak loudly: see -ATE.] *intr.* To croak or caw. Hence †**crociˈtation.**

1623 COCKERAM, *Crociate*, to cry like a rauen. **1656** BLOUNT *Glossogr.*, *Crocation*, the kawing of Crows, Rooks, or Ravens. *Crocitation*, *Idem*.

crock (krɒk), *sb.*[1] Forms: 1 crocca, 3 krocke, 3–7 crocke, 4 crokk(e, 5–6 crok, 6– crock. [OE. *croc(c* and *crocca* masc., earthenware pot or pitcher, related to Icel. *krukka* f. (Da. *krukke*, Sw. *kruka*) in same sense; and perh. more remotely to CROH, and CROUKE. Whether the Celtic words, MIr. *crocan*, Gael. *crogan* (see CROGGAN), Welsh *crochan* 'pot', are related, is not determined.]

1. An earthen pot, jar, or other vessel.

c **1000** *Sax. Leechd.* I. 238 Do [the herbs] on anne niwne croccan. *a* **1225** *Ancr. R.* 346 Kulle al ut þet is iðe krocke. **1399** LANGL. *Rich. Redeles* II. 52 Cast adoun the crokk the colys amyd. **1542** *MS. Acc. St. John's Hosp., Canterb.*, For a crock to put mylk in jᵈ. **1596** SPENSER *F.Q.* v. ii. 33 The vulgar did about him flocke..Like foolish flies about an hony-crocke. **1674** RAY *S. & E.C. Words* 63 *Crock*, an Earthen pot to put butter or the like in. **1709** STEELE *Tatler* No. 37 ¶3 His Whip throws down a Cabinet of China: He cries, What! Are your Crocks rotten? **1848** KINGSLEY *Saint's Trag.* IV. ii. 121 Her only furniture An earthen crock or two.

2. A pot of iron or other metal. (*S.W. of Eng.*)

c **1475** *Exeter Tailors' Gild* in *Eng. Gilds* 320 A brasen krocke of ij galons and more, a pache clowted in the brem with laten. **1605** in Wadley *Bristol Wills* (1886) 269 The lesser brasse Crocke. **1746** *Exmoor Courtship* (E.D.S.) 88 Thare be more..than can boil tha crock. **1885** E. C. SHARLAND *Ways & Means Devonsh. Vill.* 60 A pie made in a crock—the big kettle you see hanging over the fire in farm-houses. **1888** *W. Somerset Word-bk.*, *Crock*..a cast-iron cooking-pot only..It has a loose bow-handle..and three little legs.

3. A broken piece of earthenware, a potsherd, such as is used to cover the hole in a flower-pot.

1850 *Florist* 84 Turn it out of the pot, remove the crocks. **1851** GLENNY *Handbk. Fl. Gard.* 10 Put a layer of crocks to reach one-third of the height of the pot.

4. *Comb.*, as *crock-butter*; **crockman,** a seller of crockery; **crock-saw,** an iron bar with teeth like a saw, suspended over a fire-place to carry 'crocks' or pots; **crock-stick,** a stick used to stir a pot, support the lid, etc.; a 'thivel'.

14.. *Metr. Voc.* in Wr.-Wülcker 626/8 *Contus*, crokstyke. **1792** J. WOLCOTT (P. Pindar) *Ode to Acad. Chair* Wks. 1812 III. 49 Get thyself to Skewers and Crock-sticks turn'd. **1851** MAYHEW *Lond. Labour* II. 44 His avocation as a crockman. **1869** BLACKMORE *Lorna D.* xiv. (ed. 12) 84 Master Huckaback stood up, without much aid from the crock-saw. **1879** *Shropshire Gloss.*, *Crock-butter*, butter salted and put down in a crock for winter use.

crock (krɒk), *sb.*[2] *Obs.* exc. *dial.* [Derivation doubtful; by Ray app. identified with prec.] Smut, soot, dirt.

1657 H. CROWCH *Welsh Trav.* 496 Was all bedawb'd hurself with crock. **1674** RAY *S. & E.C. Words* 63 *Crock*, to black one with soot or black of a pot or kettle or chimney-stock, this black or soot is also substantively called *Crock*. **1861** DICKENS *Gt. Expect.* vii, The boy grimed with crock and dirt. **1875** *Sussex Gloss.*, *Crock*, a smut or smudge. **1883** *Harper's Mag.* Apr. 665/1 New England expressions here are..'You have a crock on your nose', for a smut.

crock (krɒk), *sb.*[3] Chiefly *Sc.* Also 6 crocke, 6–8 crok. [Cf. Norw. *krake*, *krakje* a sickly, weakly, or emaciated beast (Aasen), Sw. *krake*, Da. *krak*, *krakke*; LG. *krake*, *krakke*, NFris. *krack* a sorry, broken-down horse; MDu. *kraecke*, MFlem. *krake* a broken-down horse or house; EFris. *krakke* a broken-down horse, house, or old man: all app. related to CRACK *v.*]

1. An old ewe, or one that has ceased bearing. Also *crock ewe*.

1528 LYNDESAY *Dreme* 893 Quho wyll go sers amang sic heirdis scheip, May habyll fynd mony pure scabbit crok. **1570** LEVINS *Manip.* 158 A crocke, shepe, *adasia*. **1724** RAMSAY *Tea-t. Misc.* (1733) II. 182 Twa croks that moup amang the heather. **1785** BURN *Twa Herds* i, Wha will tent the waifs and crocks? **1842** BISCHOFF *Woollen Manuf.* II. 139 The crock ewes.

2. An old broken-down horse.

1879 *Daily News* 7 Mar. 6/1, I was riding a broken-kneed old crock. **1892** R. BOLDREWOOD *Nevermore* III. xxii. 131 That horse of hers..I'd like to have..instead of my old crock.

3. *slang.* Used contemptuously of persons. Now usu. a broken-down or physically debilitated person; an invalid; a hypochondriac. *colloq.* or *dial.*

1876 O. MADOX-BROWN *Dwale Bluth* II. v. 158 Hare sher cumes at learst... Th'little doiling crock! **1880** W. H. PATTERSON *Gloss. Antrim & Down* 25 *Crock*, *sb.* a derisive term for a person who fancies himself ailing or delicate. **1889** *Illustr. Bits* 13 July 4/2 You are getting a bit of a crock—failing fast, I should say. **1891** FARMER *Slang Dict.*, Applied to men and things, *crock* is synonymous with worthlessness and folly. **1920** R. MACAULAY *Potterism* IV. iii. 149 Shall we be a race of clever crocks, or..be robust imbeciles? **1922** C. E. MONTAGUE *Disenchantment* iv. 58 Chance ..gave me the job of marching parties of crocks, total and partial, real, half-real, and sham, across..to the place where the faculty did its endeavour to sort them. **1969** *Sci. Amer.* Feb. 69/2 Physicians..blame the patient by labeling him a 'crock'—medical slang for a neurotic complainer.

4. *slang.* An old, worn-out vehicle, ship, bicycle, etc.; esp. as *old crock*.

1903 KIPLING *Traffics & Discoveries* (1904) 123 But if those cruisers are crocks, why does the Admiral let 'em out of Weymouth at all? **1905** G. B. SHAW in *Grand Mag.* Feb. 116 An old crock of a 1904 six-cylinder car. **1914** A. BENNETT *Price of Love* xii. 242 I'm going to buy you a bike. I've had enough of that old crock I borrowed for you. **1935** H. G. WELLS *Things to Come* ix. 71, I understand you want all of these out-of-date crocks of yours..to fly again. **1959** I. & P. OPIE *Lore & Lang. Schoolch.* iii. 55 When boys see an antiquated machine [*sc.* bicycle] they shout:..'Sell that crock and buy a bike.'

†**crock,** *sb.*[4] *Obs. Hawking.* = CROAK *sb.* 2.

1615 LATHAM *Falconry* (1633) 80 Whereof commeth the Crocke and diuers other diseases. *a* **1667** SKINNER *Etym.*, *Crock*, morbus accipitrum.

So **crock** *v.*[3]

1615 LATHAM *Falconry* xxviii, A Hawke..before shee cold be conueniently taken to the fist, hath euen crockt again and again.

crock (krɒk), *sb.*[5] *Obs.* or *dial.* Also crook, cruk. [app. related to CROOK *sb.*, but the phonology is obscure.] (See quots.)

1570 LEVINS *Manip.* 158/15 Yᵉ Croks of a house, *bijuges*. **1828** *Craven Dial.* I. 93 *Crockes*, two crooked timbers, of a natural bend, forming a Gothic arch. They generally rest in large blocks of stone. Many roofs of this construction are still remaining in ancient farm-houses and barns. **1886** *Cheshire Gloss.*, *Crooks*, the main timbers of an old black and white house. **1890** S. O. ADDY (Sheffield) *Note*, *Cruks pl.*, the arched oaken timbers which support the roofs of some old houses. These timbers rise from the ground and reach to the ridge of the roof.

†**crock,** *sb.*[6] *Obs.* or ? *dial.* [Origin unknown: prob. related to CRICKET[3].] ? A low stool.

1709 ADDISON *Tatler* No. 116 ¶1, I..seated her upon a little Crock at my Left Hand. [Cf. **1873** *Swaledale Gloss.*, *Crocket*, a small wooden stool.]

crock, *v.*[1] *Obs.* exc. *dial.* [f. CROCK *sb.*[1]] *trans.* To put up in a crock or pot; see also quot. 1887.

1594 LYLY *Moth. Bombie* III, Wit would worke like waxe & crocke up gold like honey. **1859** *Jrnl. R. Agric. Soc.* XX. I. 51 Butter is crocked for winter supply. **1887** *Kentish Gloss.*, *Crock*, to put away; lay by; save up; hide..'Crocking it [butter] up till it's no use to nobody.'

crock, *v.*[2] *Obs.* exc. *dial.* [f. CROCK *sb.*[2]] **a.** *trans.* To smut with soot or grime; to soil, defile. Hence **crocked** *ppl. a.*

1642 ROGERS *Naaman* 355 He shall take thee from among the crokt pots. *Ibid.* 860 Suffers them to be crockt among the pots. **1655** GURNALL *Chr. in Arm.* (1669) 100/2 The Collier and Fuller..what one cleanseth, the other will crock and smutch. **1674** in RAY *S. & E.C. Words* 63 [see CROCK *sb.*[2]]. **1838** DICKENS *Nich. Nick.* (1839) 413 Without blacking and crocking myself. **1860** O. W. HOLMES *E. Venner* xxii, They'll 'crock' your fingers.

fig. *c* **1680** HICKERINGILL *Hist. Whiggism* Wks. 1716 I. 20 He crocks every Man in the mouth (with his Pen) that stands in the way of Popish Designs.

b. *intr.* To give off 'crock' or smut.

In mod. Dicts.

c. To impart colour or dye to other articles, to stain: said also of the colour.

1855 *Knickerbocker* XLV. 566 A pair of green gloves..had 'crocked off' very generously to whatever was in contact with them. **1885** A. WATT *Leather Manuf.* 322 The clear colours do not 'crock' so easily, and the little that does come off is hardly noticeable. **1895** *Montgomery Ward Catal.* 3/1 This black is perfectly fast color and will not crock.

crock, *v.*[3]: see after CROCK *sb.*[4]

crock, *v.*[4] *colloq.* [f. CROCK *sb.*[3]] *intr.* To become feeble, collapse, give way, break down. Also *trans.*, to cause to collapse; to injure or disable. Often with *up*. Hence **crocked** *ppl. a.*[1], hurt, damaged, disabled; **crocking** *vbl. sb.*, collapsing, breaking down.

1846 J. T. & W. E. BROCKETT *Gloss. N. Country Words* I. 114 *Crock*, to grow little in bulk, to suffer decay from age. **1893** *Idler* Mar. 221 An oarsman who is likely to 'crock up'. **1896** *Westm. Gaz.* 12 Dec. 2/1 Smith has crocked his knee. **1900** *Ibid.* 17 Dec. 8/2 The northern player, who is less likely to get 'crocked' than the Richmond man. **1906** *Daily Tel.* 23 Aug. 9/7 He limped out to bat, after remaining in obscurity as a crocked player for half a day. **1926** *Spectator* 12 June 983/1 Dressing is accomplished quickly considering my crocked-up hand. **1928** *Observer* 19 Feb. 28/6 Slogging home against the present stream would safeguard a crew against crocking later on. **1960** *Times* 22 Oct. 8/6, I had 'crocked' my knee at hockey.

crock: see CROC[1].

crockadell, obs. form of CROCODILE *sb.*

crockadore, obs. form of COCKATOO.

1697 DAMPIER *Voy.* (1698) I. xvi. 442, 458.

†**crockard.** *Obs.* Also 4–5 crocard(e. [Anglo-F. *crokard*: of uncertain origin.] A kind of foreign money, decried as base under Edward I.

1300 *Act 27 Edward I*, Mauveises monees que sunt appellez Pollardz et crokardz. **1387** TREVISA *Higden* (Rolls) VIII. 289 Kyng Edward dampned sodeynliche fals money þat was styliche i-brouȝt up: men cleped þe money pollardes, crocardes and rosaries. **1494** FABYAN *Chron.* VII. 401. **1605** CAMDEN *Rem.* (1657) 186 Afterward crocards and pollards were decried down to an halfe penny. **1769** BLACKSTONE *Comm.* IV. 98 Pollards and crockards, which were foreign coins of base metal.

†**crocked** (krɒkt), *a. Obs.* Affected with crock (see CROCK *sb.*[4]).

1707 FLOYER *Physic. Pulse-Watch* (1710) 405 The crocked Hawks, and broken-winded Horses.

crocked (krɒkt), *ppl. a.*[2] *slang* (orig. *U.S.*). [Perh. f. CROCK *v.*[4]] Drunk; intoxicated.

1927 in *New Republic* 9 Mar. 71/2. **1957** KEROUAC *On Road* (1958) 76, I had traveling money and got crocked in the bar. **1970** *Guardian* 9 Apr. 1/2 The curtain fell and the audience retired to get crocked.

†**crocker**[1]. *Obs.* Also 6 croker. [f. CROCK *sb.*[1] + -ER[1].] A potter.

c **1315** SHOREHAM 106 Wat helpth hyt the crokke..Aye the crokkere to brokke, Wy madest thou me so? **1382** WYCLIF *Jer.* xviii. 3 Y cam doun to the hous of the crockere [**1388** pottere]. **1562** J. HEYWOOD *Prov. & Epigr.* (1867) 43 As koy as a crokers mare. **1703** T. N. *City & C. Purchaser* 46 Something like to common Crockers Earth.

crocker[2]. A local name of the Black-headed Gull.

(The 16th c. *crocard* may be the same word.)

a **1547** in *Househ. Ord.* (1790) 223 Crocards and Oliffs, 3s. 4d. [See *Archæol.* III. 157.] **1885** SWAINSON *Prov. Names Birds* 209 Black-headed Gull (*Larus ridibundus*)—Crocker.

crockery (ˈkrɒkərɪ). [f. CROCKER[1]: see -ERY.]

1. Crocks or earthen vessels collectively; earthenware; *esp.* domestic utensils of earthenware.

1755 JOHNSON, *Crockery*, earthen ware. **1835** MARRYAT *Jac. Faithf.* x, Now, Tom, my hearty, bring out the crockery. **1883** G. LLOYD *Ebb & Flow* II, I shall sell all my crockery and bric-à-brac.

2. *Comb.*, as **crockery-ware** = CROCKERY.

1719 DE FOE *Crusoe* (1840) II. xiv. 286 They [the Chinese] told me such incredible things of their performance in crockery-ware. **1782** MISS BURNEY *Cecilia* v. ix, Where would be all this smart crockery work for your breakfast? **1840** R. DANA *Bef. Mast* xiii. 28 We had..hard-ware, crockery-ware, tin-ware, cutlery.

crocket[1] (ˈkrɒkɪt). Also 4 croket. [a. AF. *croket*, *croquet*, northern Fr. form of F. *crochet* (used in senses 1 and 2), dim. of OF. *croche*, ONF. *croque*: see CROCHET, CROQUET.]

†**1.** A curl or roll of hair formerly worn. *Obs.*

1303 R. BRUNNE *Handl. Synne* 3208 Be nat proude of þy croket [*trop geluz de sun croket*]. *c* **1325** *Poem Times Edw. II* in *Pol. Songs* (Camden) 329 He set upon a koife, and kembeth the croket. **1393** GOWER *Conf.* II. 370 His croket kempt and theron set An ouche, with a chapelet.

2. *Arch.* 'One of the small ornaments placed on the inclined sides of pinnacles, pediments, canopies, etc. in Gothic architecture' (Gwilt); usually in the form of buds or curled leaves, sometimes of animals. (Also *crochet*, CROTCHET 4.)

[**1394** *P. Pl. Crede* 174: see CROTCHET.] **1673** E. BROWN *Trav. Germ.* (1677) 80 This Spire hath the largest Crockets I have observed in any. *a* **1682** SIR T. BROWNE *Posth. Wks.* (1712) 34 Eight leaves of stone spreading outward, under which begin the eight rows of crockets. **1811** MILNER *Eccl. Archit. Eng.* 104 Adorned with the representation of foliage along the jambs called crockets. **1849** FREEMAN *Archit.* 296 Rows of canopied niches, with crocket and finial. **1874** PARKER *Goth. Archit.* 321 Gloss., *Crocket*..supposed to be derived from the resemblance to a shepherd's crook.

3. One of the terminal 'buds' or knobs on a stag's horn; = CROCHE *sb.*[2]

1870 BLAINE *Encycl. Rural Sports* §1796 His [the stag's] crockets are the upright points of his horns. **1873** BLACK *Pr. Thule* xxv. 414 You will discourse..of the span and the pearls, of the antlers and the crockets.

4. *attrib.* and *Comb.* (in sense 2): = 'decorated with, or characterized by, crockets'.

1703 T. N. *City & C. Purchaser* 155 Arches are made use of in crocket Windows. *Ibid.* 194 Crocket-work, (or Fret-work, as some Glaziers call it). **1879** SIR G. SCOTT *Lect. Archit.* I. 153 During the first half of the thirteenth century these crocket capitals were brought to very high perfection.

†**crocket**[2]. *Obs.*—[1] Diminutive of CROCK *sb.*[1]

1658 W. BURTON *Itin. Anton.* 160 Besides other Crockets and earthen Vessels.

crocketed ('krɒkɪtɪd), *a.* [f. CROCKET[1].]

1. *Arch.* Having, or decorated with, crockets.

1816 RICKMAN in J. Smith *Panorama Sc. & Art* I. 146 The second canopy is the ogee..This..is sometimes crocketed, and sometimes not. **1878** F. S. WILLIAMS *Midl. Railw.* 448 The..crocketed pinnacles of the church.

2. Of a stag's horn: Having crockets.

1875 'STONEHENGE' *Brit. Sports* I. x. §1 With one horn crocketed and the other single.

'**crocketing.** [f. as prec. + -ING[1].] Decoration with crockets; crocket-work.

1851 RUSKIN *Stones Ven.* I. Pref. 8 Then come..the crocketings of the upper arches.

Crockford ('krɒkfəd). **1.** (Usu. *Crockford's.*) The name of an exclusive gambling club opened in St. James's Street, London, in 1827 by William Crockford (1775–1844). Also *transf.*

1827 W. MAGINN *Whitehall* II. iii. 117 The Opera was crowded... Tattersall's was crammed—Crockford's crowded. **1838** H. C. ROBINSON *Diary* 27 Apr. (1967) 188 D'Orsay looked haggard as if he had been unlucky at Crockford's. **1867** 'OUIDA' *Under Two Flags* I. vii. 136 They had brought..dice for hazard..and were turning the unconscious Star and Garter into an impromptu Crockford's. **1966** J. CLEARY *High Commissioner* vi. 131 It's *the* gambling club. A sort of millionaire's Crockford's.

2. A colloquial designation of 'Crockford's Clerical Directory', a reference book for the clergy and the Church of England, first issued in 1860 by John Crockford (1823–65). (Occas. *Crockford's.*) Also *fig.*

1891 S. WEYMAN *New Rector* I. i. 9 In more distant vicarages..there were..anxious searchings of the 'Guardian' and Crockford. **1909** H. G. WELLS *Tono-Bungay* I. i. 16 There was an old peerage and a Crockford together with the books of recipes. **1947** [see ALL C. 2c]. **1970** K. GILES *Death in Church* i. 22 'I'll look it up in *Crockford's*.'..Harry wondered whether the compiler of the clerical Who's Who had..been related to the gambler.

†**crockling,** *vbl. sb. Obs.*—[1] [Cf. CROAK.] Used to express the noise made by cranes.

1573 TWYNE *Æneid* x. Eejb, Herds of cranes With crockling casting signes.

crocky ('krɒkɪ), *a.*[1] *dial.* [f. CROCK *sb.*[2] + -Y.] Smutty, sooty.

a **1825** in FORBY *Voc. E. Anglia.* Hence in WORCESTER and mod. Dicts.

crocky ('krɒkɪ), *a.*[2] [f. CROCK *sb.*[3] + -Y[1].] That is a crock; broken-down, physically enfeebled.

1880 W. H. PATTERSON *Gloss. Antrim & Down* 25 *Crocky, adj.* fanciful about his health; hippish. **1906** *Westm. Gaz.* 18 Sept. 10/1 Among the parts of a crocky engine. **1907** A. CONAN DOYLE *Through Magic Door* 109 The crockiest of spectators had a better chance of life than the magnificent young athlete. **1920** R. MACAULAY *Potterism* IV. iii. 149 Crocky imbeciles.

crocodile ('krɒkədaɪl), *sb.* Forms: α. 4–5 cokadrille, -yll(e, cokedril, -ill(e, 4–6 cocodrill(e, -yll(e, 5 cocodrile, coko-, coquodrille, cockadrylle, 5–6 cocadryll(e; β. 6– crocodile, (6 crocodrille, 6–7 -dil(l, 7 crockadell, crocadile, crokidile, -odile, 8 crocodyle). [ME. *cocodrille, cokadrill*, etc. a. OF. *cocodrille* (13–17th c.) = Pr. *cocodrilh*, Sp. *cocodrilo*, It. *coccodrillo*, med.L. *cocodrillus*, corruption of L. *crocodīlus* (also *corcodilus*), a. Gr. κροκόδειλος, found from Herodotus downward. The original form after Gr. and L. was restored in most of the mod. langs. in the 16–17th c.: F. *crocodile* (in Paré), It. *crocodillo* (in Florio), Sp. *crocodilo* (in Percival).]

1. a. A large amphibious saurian reptile of the genus *Crocodilus* or other allied genera. The name belongs originally and properly to the crocodile of the Nile (*C. niloticus* or *vulgaris*); but is extended to other species of the same or allied genera, and sometimes to the whole of the *Crocodilia*, including the Alligators of America and the Gavial or 'crocodile' of the Ganges.

c **1300** *K. Alis.* 6597 What best is the cokadrille. **1382** WYCLIF *Lev.* xi. 29 A cokedril..that is a beest of foure feete, hauynge the nether cheke lap vnmeuable, and meuynge the ouere. **1483** CAXTON *Cato* E viii b, The cockadrylle is so stronge and so grete a serpent. *a* **1533** LD. BERNERS *Huon* xxxvi. 112 The grete multytude of serpentes and cocodrylles. **1578** T. N. tr. *Conq. W. India* 184 Crocodrilles which they call Caymanes or Lizards of twenty foote long, with such Scales..as a Dragon hathe. **1684** EVELYN *Diary* 22 Oct., A crocodile, brought from some of the West India Islands, resembling the Egyptian Crocodile. *a* **1711** KEN *Hymnotheo* Poet. Wks. 1721 III. 271 As a young Brood of Crocodiles, who swim In Ganges stream. **1842** H. MILLER *O.R. Sandst.* iii. (ed. 2) 63 Some huge salamander or crocodile of the Lias. **1847** CARPENTER *Zool.* §491 This family..is divided into three genera, the Crocodiles, Alligators and Gavials..The true crocodiles are inhabitants of Africa, India, and the hotter parts of America.

†**b.** Formerly applied with qualifications to various small saurians or lizards. *Obs.*

1607 TOPSELL *Four-f. Beasts* (1673) 693 A Scink or a Crocodile of the earth. *Ibid.*, Of the Land Crocodile of Bresilia.

c. = *crocodile-skin* (see also quot. 1968).

1907 *Yesterday's Shopping* (1969) 389/2 The 'Gadabout' writing case... Crocodile, lined sheep..67/6. **1908** *Daily Chron.* 15 Aug. 3/2 A large crocodile letter-case. **1908** *Westm. Gaz.* 19 Nov. 4/2 All the upholstering is in crocodile. **1968** J. IRONSIDE *Fashion Alphabet* 237 Many so-called 'crocodile' accessories are in fact made from alligator skins, crocodile being particularly difficult to tan and preserve.

2. a. The crocodile was fabulously said to weep, either to allure a man for the purpose of devouring him, or while (or after) devouring him; hence many allusions in literature. (See also 5.)

c **1400** MAUNDEV. (1839) xxviii. 288 In that contre..ben gret plentee of Cokadrilles..Theise Serpentes slen men, and thei eten hem wepynge. **1565** *Sir J. Hawkins' Voy.* in Hakluyt (1600) III. 512 In this riuer we saw many Crocodils ..His nature is euer when hee would haue his prey, to cry and sobbe like a Christian body, to prouoke them to come to him, and then hee snatcheth at them. **1590** SPENSER *F.Q.* I. v. 18. **1604** SHAKS. *Oth.* IV. i. 257 If that the Earth could teeme with womans teares, Each drop she falls, would proue a Crocodile. **1607** TOPSELL *Serpents* (1608) 688. **1623** COCKERAM III. s.v. **1676** D'URFEY *Mad. Fickle* III. iii, More false than Crocodils, That mourn the Slain, and yet delight to kill 'em. **1700** BLACKMORE *Paraphr. Job* v. 23 His plighted faith the crocodile shall keep, And seeing thee, for joy sincerely weep.

b. Hence *fig.* A person who weeps or makes a show of sorrow hypocritically or with a malicious purpose.

1595 BARNFIELD *Cassandra* lxii, He..Sweetely salutes this weeping Crocodile. **1609** B. JONSON *Sil. Woman* v. iv, O, my nephew knowes you belike: away crocodile. **1665** SIR T. HERBERT *Trav.* (1677) 199 Down he goes without hostages, where he finds the Crocodile ready to embrace him with tears of joy. **1863** READE *Hard Cash* xliii, The amorous crocodile shed a tear, and persisted in her double-faced course.

3. *Logic.* Name of an ancient sophism or dilemma; see CROCODILITE.

1727–51 CHAMBERS *Cycl.*, *Crocodile*, in rhetoric, a captious sophistical kind of argumentation. **1798** EDGEWORTH *Pract. Educ.* II. xxiii. 673 Many argue..with great..precision, who might..be caught on the horns of a dilemma, or who would..fall victims to the *crocodile*. **1884** tr. *Lotze's Logic* 295 Equally curious is the old dilemma of the crocodile.

4. *colloq.* (orig. *humorous*). **a.** A girls' school walking two and two in a long file. Also of a boys' school, etc.

(In use before 1870.) **1891** H. ATTERIDGE in *Little Folks* Nov. 326/1 He saw what boys sometimes call 'a crocodile'—a girls' school out for a walk. **1898** J. K. JEROME *Second Thoughts* 311 We came upon a girls' school walking two and two,—a 'crocodile', they call it. **1922** *Blackw. Mag.* Oct. 487/2 The crocodile of small boys in the streets. **1926** I. M. PEACOCKE *His Kid Brother* ii. 37 To walk in a 'crocodile' of orphans. **1950** F. A. SWINNERTON *Flower for Catherine* 107 One saw her leading the long lines of schoolgirls which are called 'Crocodiles'. **1968** M. BRAGG *Without City Wall* xx. 201 The crocodile rows of little children.

b. A long procession of moving objects close together. Also *fig.*

1912 H. G. WELLS *Marriage* ii. 55 She drove her little crocodile of primly sensible thoughts to their sane appointed conclusion. **1928** *Manch. Guardian Weekly* 17 Aug. 136/2 Those roads which..do not carry an endless and snorting crocodile of cars. **1930** R. PERTWEE *Pursuit* I. xi. 55 Transport would pile up before and behind you in a ceaselessly cursing crocodile.

5. *attrib.* and *Comb.*, often with allusion to the fabled weeping of the crocodile (see 2), *esp.* in *crocodile tears*; *crocodile-like* adj.; **crocodile-bird**, the Egyptian black-headed plover, *Pluvianus ægyptius*, so called from its habit of eating the insect parasites of the crocodile, probably the trochilos of ancient writers; **crocodile shears**, shears used in cutting into lengths and removing the faulty ends of steel or iron bars; **crocodile squeezer**, a machine with a pivoted upper jaw, used in the process of removing impurities from metals by the application of pressure.

1806 G. S. FABER *Dissert.* II. 343 With a *crocodile affectation of clemency. **1868** A. C. SMITH *Attractions Nile* II. 255 *Charadrius spinosus*..in all probability the true '*crocodile bird' or *trochilus* of Herodotus. **1966** C. SWEENEY *Scurrying Bush* x. 142 The Egyptian 'Plover' (*Pluvianus aegyptius*) or crocodile bird has been the centre of controversy. **1678** *Yng. Man's Call.* 156 Believe him not: his *crocodile flatteries have undone thousands. **1716** M. DAVIES *Athen. Brit.* III. *Crit. Hist.* 5 To a greater advantage of the *Crocodyle-Jesuits. **1621** in W. Foster *Eng. Factories India 1618–21* (1906) 347 These viprous, dessemblinge, and *crockadillike currs. **1897** A. PAGE *Afternoon Ride* x. 61 A large iguana, almost crocodile-like in its proportion. **1884** W. H. GREENWOOD *Steel & Iron* 347 Puddled bars are..sheared hot either by *crocodile or guillotine shears. **1887** *Pall Mall G.* 2 Mar. 6/1 The *crocodile-skin bag may perhaps be called fashionable. **1884** W. H. GREENWOOD *Steel & Iron* 301 The single alligator or *crocodile squeezer has two broad flat jaws. *Ibid.* 302 The crocodile squeezer makes about 60 strokes per minute. **1563** GRINDAL in Strype *Life* (1710) I. vii. 78, I begin to fear, lest his humility..be a counterfeit humility, and his tears *crocodile tears. **1623** COCKERAM III. s.v., Thence came the Prouerb, he shed Crocodile teares, *viz.* fayned teares. **1863** SALA *Capt. Dangerous* xvii, Saying with crocodile tears, that he was not the first who had an undutiful son. **1892** *Temple Bar* July 348 Narrow gauge stock had also been conveyed westward in 'crocodile' trucks—ones with very low bodies.

Hence '**crocodile** *v.* (from sense 4).

1889 [Implied in CROCODILING *vbl. sb.* 1]. **1936** M. FRANKLIN *All that Swagger* xii. 116 The school crocodiled abroad with its instructresses. **1960** *News Chron.* 15 Mar. 4/5 The girls crocodile in, a mistress at head and tail. **1969** *Guardian* 25 July 9/5 The diminutive school-girls crocodiling through the Commonwealth Institute.

crocodilian (krɒkə'dɪlɪən), *a.* and *sb.* Also 7–9 -ean. [f. L. *crocodīl-us* + -IAN.]

A. *adj.* †**1.** Like a crocodile; making a hypocritical show of grief; treacherous. *Obs.*

1632 LITHGOW *Trav.* x. (1682) 454 The Soul-betraying Tears of her Crocodilean Sex. **1635** QUARLES *Embl.* I. iv. (1818) 27 O what a crocodilian world is this, Compos'd of treach'ries, and insnaring wiles.

2. Of, pertaining to, or of the nature of, a crocodile; belonging to the crocodile family of reptiles.

1836 TODD *Cycl. Anat.* I. 601/1 The crocodilian family. **1890** *Q. Jrnl. Geol. Soc.* May 284 An undoubtedly crocodilian jaw.

B. *sb.* An animal of the crocodile family.

1837 W. BUCKLAND *Geol.* I. 251 *note*, The modern broad-nosed Crocodileans. **1870** A. L. ADAMS *Nile Valley & Malta* 129 [Fossil] jaws of undetermined crocodilians.

†'**crocodiline,** *a. Obs. rare.*—[0] [ad. L. *crocodīlinus.*] = CROCODILIAN *a.*

1730–6 BAILEY (folio), *Crocodiline*, like a crocodile; also sophistical. Hence **1755** in JOHNSON.

crocodiling ('krɒkədaɪlɪŋ), *vbl. sb.* [f. CROCODILE *sb.* or *v.* + -ING[1].]

1. Walking in a crocodile (CROCODILE *sb.* 4).

1889 *Pall Mall G.* 25 Apr. 6/1 He urged..the desirability of substituting lawn tennis..and even cricket, for the everlasting 'crocodiling' about the streets, which is so dear to the hearts of all schoolmistresses.

2. = ALLIGATORING *vbl. sb.*

1932 *Paint Manufacture* II. 245/2 (*caption*) Common Stopper Defects. A. 'Crocodiling' of Hard Stopper Applied over Soft Primer. **1953** [see ALLIGATORING *vbl. sb.*].

†'**crocodilite.** *Logic. Obs.* [ad. L. *crocodīlītēs.*] Name of an ancient sophism: see quot. 1655.

[**1551** T. WILSON *Logike* (1580) 85 b, Crocodilites, is suche a kinde of subtiltie, that when we have graunted a thyng to our adversarie..the same tourneth to our harme afterwarde.] **1624** H. MASON *Art of Lying* ii. 35 This muddy Nylus so fertile of Crocodiles, I mean of this sophistique Crocodilites, whereby vnware men are ouer-reached and caught. **1655–60** STANLEY *Hist. Philos.* (1701) 316/2 The Crocodilite, so named from this Ægyptian Fable: A Woman sitting by the side of Nilus, a Crokodile snatch'd away her Child, promising to restore him, if she would answer truly to what he asked; which was, Whether he meant to restore him or not? She answer'd, Not to restore him, and challenged his promise, as having said the Truth. He reply'd, that if he should let her have him, she had not told true.

Hence **croco'dility**, 'a captious or sophistical mode of arguing' (Webster 1848).

crocoite ('krəʊkəʊaɪt). *Min.* [Named 1838 by Berthier *crocoise*, f. Gr. κροκόεις saffron-coloured; altered by Dana in 1844 to *crocoisite*, and in 1868 to *crocoite*.] Native chromate of lead, a mineral of a red or orange colour.

1844 ALGER *Phillips' Min.* 554 Crocoise. **1861** DANA *Min.* 629.

croconic (krəʊ'kɒnɪk), *a. Chem.* [f. L. *croc-us* saffron + *-on* (meaningless) + -IC.] In *croconic acid* ($C_5H_2O_5$), an inodorous, strongly acid substance, obtained in the form of yellow crystals or powder. Hence **'croconate**, a salt of this acid.

1838 T. THOMSON *Chem. Org. Bodies* 17 Croconic Acid. **1854** *Orr's Circ. Sc.* Chem. 402 The croconate..of potash. **1863–72** WATTS *Dict. Chem.* II. 110 The croconates, $C_5M_2O_5$, are yellow (hence the name of the acid).

crocus ('krəʊkəs). [a. L. *crocus*, a. Gr. *κρόκος* the crocus, and its product saffron: app. of Semitic origin; cf. Heb. *karkōm*, crocus, saffron, Arab. *kurkum*, saffron, turmeric. See Lacaita, *Etymology of Crocus and Saffron*, 1886. Not known as an Eng. name to the 16th c. herbalists, though OE. had *croh* saffron, Ir. and Gael. *croch*, from Latin.]

1. A genus of hardy dwarf bulbous plants, N.O. *Iridaceæ*, natives of southern and central Europe, the Levant, and Western Asia, and commonly cultivated for their brilliant flowers, which are usually deep yellow or purple, and appear before the leaves in early spring, or in some species in autumn. The autumnal species, *C. sativus*, yields SAFFRON.

[**1398** TREVISA *Barth. de P.R.* XVII. xli. (1495) 626 Saffron hyghte *Crocus* and is an herbe. **1578** LYTE *Dodoens* II. lv. 216 Saffron is called..in latine *Crocus*. **1599** GERARDE *Catalogus*, *Crocus vernus flore luteo*, Saffron of the spring with Yellow flowers.] *a* **1639** WOTTON *Poems*, 'On a Bank' (Aldine ed.) 101 The fields and gardens were beset With tulips, crocus, violet. **1682** WHELER *Journ. Greece* IV. 318 White and Yellow Crocus grows wild here. **1728–46** THOMSON *Spring* 529 Fair-handed Spring..Throws out the snowdrop and the crocus first. **1832** TENNYSON *Œnone* 94 At their feet the crocus brake like fire. **1885** BIBLE (R.V.) *Isa.* xxxv. 1 The desert shall..blossom as the rose [*marg.* Or, autumn crocus].

†**2.** Saffron; the stigma of *Crocus sativus*. *Obs.* (In OE. *croh*.)

c **1000** *Saxon Leechd.* II. 244 Meng wiþ croh. **1659** GAYTON *Longevity* 54 Half a Crown in Crocus and Squills Wine. **1710** *Lond. Gaz.* No. 4658/4 Two Bales of Crocus.

3. a. *Old Chem.* A name given to various yellow or red powders obtained from metals by calcination; as ***crocus of antimony*** (*crocus antimonii* or *c. metallorum*), a more or less impure oxysulphide of antimony; ***crocus of copper*** (*c. veneris*), cuprous oxide; ***crocus of iron*** (*c. martis*; also in 15th c. *crokefer*), sesquioxide or peroxide of iron.

[**1471** RIPLEY *Comp. Alch.* Adm. vi. in Ashm. (1652) 190, I provyd..the Scalys of Yern whych Smethys do of smyte, Æs Ust, and Crokefer which dyd me never good.] **1640** WATTS tr. *Bacon's Adv. Learn.* v. ii. 194 If iron were reduced to a crocus. **1641** FRENCH *Distill.* v. (1651) 135 Quench it in the Oil of *Crocus Martis* made of the best steele. **1728** NICHOLS in *Phil. Trans.* XXXV. 481 Both these..Stones scrape into a deep Crocus. **1753** *Scots Mag.* XV. 40/1 He had put this piece of crocus metallorum into the water. **1799** G. SMITH *Laboratory* I. 92 Take..crocus of copper an ounce and a half. **1842** E. TURNER *Elem. Chem.* (ed. 7) 498 The pharmaceutic preparations known by the terms *glass*, *liver*, and *crocus* of antimony.

b. The name is still applied to the peroxide of iron obtained by calcination of sulphate of iron, and used as a polishing powder.

a **1861** *Hunter MS.* in *Sheffield Gloss.*, *Crocus*, a red oxide used for polishing cutlery. **1874** KNIGHT *Dict. Mech.*, *Crocus*, a polishing powder composed of peroxide of iron. It is prepared from crystals of sulphate of iron, calcined in crucibles. The portion at the bottom, which has been exposed to the greatest heat, is the hardest, is purplish in color, and is called crocus..The upper portion is of a scarlet color, and is called rouge.

4. *slang.* A quack doctor.

[It has been surmised that this originated in the Latinized surname of Dr. Helkiah Crooke, author of a *Description of the Body of Man*, 1615, *Instruments of Chirurgery*, 1631, etc.] **1785** GROSE *Dict. Vulgar Tongue*, *Crocus* or *Crocus Metallorum*, a nickname for the surgeons of the army and navy. **1851** MAYHEW *Lond. Labour* I. 217. **1877** BESANT & RICE *Son of Vulcan* I. ix. 100 Such were the 'crocuses', who lived by the sale of pills and drugs—a pestilent tribe.

5. *attrib.* and *Comb.*, as ***crocus-bag***, ***-bed***, ***-bordered*** adj., ***-flower***, ***-powder*** (= 3 b), ***-scent***.

1699 J. DICKENSON *Jrnl. Travels* 30 [For clothing] I..had a Crocus Ginger-bag. **1873** J. H. WALSH *Dom. Econ.* (1877) 365/2 Crocus-powder is made by calcining sulphate of iron and salt. **1878** O. WILDE in *Irish Monthly* Apr. 211 The crocus-bed is a quivering moon of fire. **1885** STALLYBRASS tr. *Hehn's Wand. Plants & Anim.* 198 Helena takes with her..her..crocus-bordered veil. *Ibid.* 200 When Roman luxury was at its height, crocus-scent and crocus-flowers were used as lavishly as rose-leaves. **1891** 'M. O'RELL' *Frenchm. Amer.* 60 A..crocus-bed effect.

crocused ('krəʊkəst), *a.* [f. prec. + -ED².] Bedecked with crocuses.

1856 RUSKIN *Mod. Paint.* III. IV. xiv. §10 The crocused slopes of the Chartreuse.

crod, obs. pa. pple. of CROWD *v.*

crod(de, crode, obs. ff. CURD, CORRODE.

croe, -foote, crofote, obs. ff. CROW, -FOOT.

Crœsus ('kri:səs). The Latin form of the name of a king of Lydia (Gr. *Κροῖσος*) in the sixth century B.C., who was famous for his riches, used allusively in phrases, as ***Crœsus' wealth***, ***as rich as Crœsus***, and hence typically for 'a very rich person'.

1390 GOWER *Confessio Amantis* v. 4730 in *Compl. Wks.* (1901) III. 75 If the tresor of Cresus And al the gold Octovien, Forth with the richesse Yndien Of Perles and of riche stones, Were al togedre myn at ones. **1577** T. KENDALL *Flowers of Epigrams* fol. 21ʳ, As riche as Cresus Affric is. **1578** G. WHETSTONE *Remembraunce of G. Gaskoigne* sig. B1, What auailes..King Cressus welth. **1650** TRAPP *Comm. Prov.* xxx. 8, I shall not envie the richest Crœsus or Crassus upon earth. **1707** [see RICH *a.* 2a]. **1754** H. WALPOLE *Lett.* (1857) II. 389 A contest between two young Crœsus's, Lord Thanet and Sir James Lowther. **1883** M. E. BRADDON *Golden Calf* xii, Ida, left alone amidst all the fascinations of the chief shop in a smart county town, and feeling herself a Crœsus. **1924** C. MACKENZIE *Old Men of Sea* (1963) xix. 245 We could have sailed in the poor old *Able and Willing*, and been rich as Creases all our lives. **1931** J. T. ADAMS *Epic of America* vii. 185 There he was, rich as Crœsus, and dictating to the government.

croft (krɒft), *sb.*¹ Also 5 ? crofe, croofte, 5–6 crofft(e, 5–7 crofte, 6–9 *Sc.* craft. [OE. *croft* enclosed field, app. corresp. to Du. *kroft*, *krocht* prominent rocky height, high and dry land, field on the downs. Ulterior etymology unknown.]

1. A piece of enclosed ground, used for tillage or pasture: in most localities a small piece of arable land adjacent to a house.

Ray, *N.C. Words* 133, notices that in the north it implied adjacency to a dwelling-house, but that this attribute did not attach to its general English use. Cf. the Cornish use in quot. 1880, and the quot. from Milton 1634, which suggests the Dutch sense.

969 *Cod. Dipl.* III. 37 (Bosw.) Æt ðæs croftes heafod. *c* **1290** *S. Eng. Leg.* I. 478/558 Ase he stod in is crofte. **1362** LANGL. *P. Pl.* A. VII. 35 For þei [birds] comen into my croft and croppen my whete. **1483** *Cath. Angl.* 83 Crofte, *confinium*. **1486** *Bk. St. Albans* F v b, Who that..closith his croofte wyth cheritrees. **1523** FITZHERBERT *Surv.* 1b, A curtylage is a lytell croft or court..to put in catell for a tyme. **1604** in *Eng. Gilds* (1870) 437 All ould tenants shall haue a croft and a medow. **1634** MILTON *Comus* 531 Tending my flocks hard by i' th' hilly Crofts That brow this bottom glade. **1718** BP. HUTCHINSON *Witchcraft* xv. (1720) 268 In a croft or close adjoining to his Father's House. **1794** WORDSW. *Guilt & Sorrow* xxiv, A little croft we owned—a plot of corn. **1818** SCOTT *Hrt. Midl.* viii, To occupy her husband's cottage, and cultivate..a croft of land adjacent. **1842** TENNYSON *Two Voices*, Thro' crofts and pastures wet with dew. **1864** *Glasgow Herald* 16 May, The croft is now generally the best land of the farm, and every farm almost has its croft. **1880** *W. Cornwall Gloss.*, *Croft*, an enclosed common not yet cultivated.

b. *fig.*

c **1460** *Towneley Myst.* 314 Com to my crofte Alle ye..Welcom to my see. **1588** A. KING tr. *Canisius' Catech.* 184b, Quhilk proues..vs to be as fruictful tries in the croft or feild of the kirk. **1636** JAMES *Iter Lanc.* (1845) 360 Happie they whose dwelling's in Christs crofte.

c. ***toft and croft***: a messuage with land attached: see TOFT¹.

2. A small agricultural holding worked by a peasant tenant; *esp.* that of a CROFTER in the Highlands and Islands of Scotland (see quot. 1851).

1842 ALISON *Hist. Europe* XIV. xcv. §53 It has covered the country, not with Tuscan freeholds, but with Irish crofts. **1851** *2nd Rep. Relief of Destit. Highlands* 1850, 42 The crofting system was first introduced, by the arable part of the small farms previously held in common being divided among the joint tenants in separate crofts, the pasture remaining in common. **1883** A. R. WALLACE *Land National.* in *Macm. Mag.*, The Highland crofters are confined to miserably small holdings—the largest croft in Skye..being seven acres. **1884** *Spectator* 17 May 642 In some parts of North Uist there are no crofts in individual ownership.

3. *attrib.* and *Comb.*, as **croft-bleaching**, bleaching by exposure on the grass; **croft-land**, 'the land of superior quality, which, according to the old mode of farming, was still cropped' (Jam.).

1791 *Statist. Acc. Dumfr.* I. 181 (Jam.) Lime and manure were unknown, except on a few acres of what is called croft-land, which was never out of crop. **1796** *Trans. Soc. Enc. Arts* XIV. 154 Waste land, consisting of marsh, croft, and sandy soils. **1875** URE *Dict. Arts* I. 366 After being altered by the action of chlorine, or by insolation or croft-bleaching. **1878** *Cumbrld. Gloss.*, *Croft land*, a range of fields near the house, of equally good quality with the croft.

croft, *sb.*² *rare.* [Cf. Du. *krocht*, MDu. *crochte*, *crofte*, MLG. *kruft*, OHG. *chruft*, ad. L. *crupta*, *crypta*.] A crypt, vault, cavern.

1470–85 MALORY *Arthur* XVII. xviii, Thenne he loked in to a Crofte vnder the mynster and there he sawe a Tombe. **1861** TEMPLE & TREVOR *Tannhäuser* 88 From low-brow'd caves, and hollow crofts Under the hanging woods, there came..A voice of wail. **1887** *Kentish Gloss.*, *Croft*, a vault.

croft, corruption of CARAFE.

1852 M. W. SAVAGE *R. Medlicott* III. xiii. (D.), The Bishop..pushed the croft to the Vicar.

croft (krɒft), *v.* [f. CROFT *sb.*¹] To expose (linen, etc.) on the grass to sun and air, as part of the process of bleaching. Hence **'crofting** *vbl. sb.*

1772 [cf. CROFTER²]. **1875** URE *Dict. Arts* I. 367 One exposure may not be found enough; another washing and another crofting are then needed. *Ibid.* 391 Washed and spread out on the green, or crofted.

crofter¹ ('krɒftə(r)). Also *Sc.* crafter. [f. CROFT *sb.*¹ + -ER¹. In Gael. *croitear*, from Eng.] One who rents and cultivates a croft or small holding; *esp.* in the Highlands and Islands of Scotland, one of the joint tenants of a divided farm (who often combines the tillage of a small croft with fishing or other vocation).

1799 MARSHALL in J. Robertson *Agric. Perth* 353 Every man, whether farmer, crafter, cotter or villager. **1811** G. S. KEITH *Agric. Surv. Aberd.* Prel. Obs. 14 There cannot be..too few large crofters, who hold their grounds of the farmers. **1862** SHIRLEY *Nugæ Crit.* i. 34 Flat, dreary, up-lying moors, with the thatched cottage of the crofter, and his scanty patch of cultivation. **1880** *Macm. Mag.* No. 245. 410 The crofter with his few acres well cultivated, produces a larger yield per acre than the large farmer.

attrib. **1848** *3rd Rep. Relief of Destit. Highlands* 68 The state and condition of the Crofter population of Sutherland Proper.

Hence **'crofterdom** *nonce-wd.*

1873 *Blackw. Mag.* July 100/2 One dead level of crofterdom.

'crofter². [f. CROFT *v.*] One who crofts or bleaches linen on the grass.

1772 *Manchester Directory* 53 Alphabetical list of the Crofters or Whitsters.

crofterize ('krɒftəraɪz), *v.* [f. CROFTER¹ + -IZE.] *trans.* To convert into a croft-tenancy. So **,crofteri'zation**, **'crofterizing** *vbl. sb.*

1907 *Times* 7 Oct. 9/4 Nor do the Scottish Lowlands..desire the crofterization of the Lowland counties. **1908** *Ibid.* 11 Mar. 11/5 Amendments which shall not interfere with the crofterizing of the Scottish Lowlands.

crofting ('krɒftɪŋ), *vbl. sb.* [f. CROFT *sb.*¹]

1. 'The state of being successively cropped; the land itself which is cropped in this way.' (Jam.)

1743 MAXWELL *Sel. Trans.* 12 (Jam.) By turning this croft-land into grass, the labour and manure..may be employed in improving..the other third part, and bringing it into crofting. *Ibid.* 213 (Jam.) The lands are generally divided into Crofting and Outfield-land. *Ibid.* 216 (Jam.) They shall dung no part of their former Crofting.

2. The practice or system of croft-tenancy; *concr.* the holding of a crofter.

1851 [see CROFT *sb.*¹ 2]. **1860** G. H. K. *Vac. Tourists* 158 Land under cultivation [in Sutherland]..not only in the form of large farms, but of cotters' croftings. **1886** *Times* 5 Feb. 4/6 *heading*, Crofters and Crofting.

attrib. **1884** *Pall Mall G.* 10 May 1/2 The Royal Commissioners on the crofting system of the Highlands.

So **'crofting** *ppl. a.*

1884 MRQ. OF LORNE in *Pall Mall G.* 10 May 2/2 The condition of the crofting class. **1888** *Pall Mall G.* 18 Jan. 7/2 A large farm..cleared of its crofting tenants.

crognet, var. of CRONET 2.

†**croh.** *Obs.* In 3 croo. [OE. *crōᵹ*, *crōh* small vessel, cognate with OHG. *chruog*, MHG. *kruoc(g)*, Ger. *krug* pitcher, jug, mug:—OTeut. **krôgo-z*. Cf. CROCK *sb.*¹] A pitcher, a water-pot.

a **700** *Epinal Gloss.* 584 *Lagoena* crooᵹ [so in *Erfurt*, *Leyden*; *Corpus* 1171 croᵹ]. *c* **1050** *Voc.* in Wr.-Wülcker 298/17 *Lagena* croᵹ. —— *Glosses* ibid. 431/36 *Lagena* croh. *c* **1230** *Hali Meid.* 39 þe croh eorneð iþe fur & te cheorl chideð. *c* **1250** *Old Kentish Serm.* in *O.E. Misc.* 29 Fol vellet..þos Ydres, þet is to sigge þos Croos, oþer þos faten of watere.

croh, OE. form of CROCUS (sense 2), saffron.

Crohn's disease ('krəʊnz dɪ'zi:z). *Path.* [f. the name of B. B. *Crohn* (1884–1983), U.S. pathologist, who with others described it in 1932 (*Jrnl. Amer. Med. Assoc.* 15 Oct. 1323).] A chronic, sometimes fatal, inflammatory disease of the gastro-intestinal tract, esp. the ileum and colon, characterized by ulcers, fissuring, and fistulæ.

1935 *Trans. Med. Soc. London* LVIII. 94 (*heading*) Two cases of Crohn's disease. **1936** *Lancet* 24 Oct. 980/2 A case of regional ileitis has been described which conforms clinically and pathologically to Crohn's disease. **1966** WRIGHT & SYMMERS *Systemic Path.* I. xvi. 530/1 Whatever the fundamental cause of Crohn's disease may be, there is pathological evidence that the condition is a disease of lymphoid tissue. **1977** *Cleethorpes News* 27 May 1/5 John suffers from the often fatal Crohn's disease. **1985** *Brit. Med. Jrnl.* 1 June 1628/2 A small bowel resection was performed...Histology confirmed Crohn's disease.

croice, var. of CROISE, CROSS.

croil, var. of CRILE (*north.*), dwarf.

croin, Sc. form of CROON.

crois, an early synonym of CROSS, q.v.

croisad(e, -ada, -ado, earlier forms of CRUSADE.

†**croisard.** *Obs.* [f. stem of F. *croisade* (see the following words) + -ARD. Cf. CRUSARD.] A crusader.

1766 SMOLLETT *Trav.* 92 Fanatic croisards. **1838** G. S. FABER *Inq. Anc. Vallenses* 270 The unchristian zeal of the misnamed holy croisards.

†**croise**, *v.* *Obs.* Forms: 3 creoise, -oyse, -oice, -oyce, creyse, croice, 4 croyss, croyce, 4–7 croise,

5 croyse, (6 croisy). [a. OF. *cruisier, croisier*:—L. *cruciāre*, f. *cruc-em* cross.]

1. *trans.* To mark with the sign of the cross; to make the sign of the cross upon or over.

a **1225** *Ancr. R.* 64 Creoiseð..our muð, earen & eien, & te breoste eke. *c* **1290** *S. Eng. Leg.* I. 433/72 Creoyce þare-with þi fore-heued. *Ibid.* 433/78 To creoici þri3es is fore-heued: and is breoste. *c* **1380** *Sir Ferumb.* 4913 þan þankeþ he god eft of ys sond, & croycede ys fysage with ys hond. *c* **1470** HENRY *Wallace* VIII. 1195 Than Wallace thocht it was no tyme to ly; He croyssit him, syne sodeynli wp rais.

2. To mark with a cross by way of giving sanctity to a vow; *refl.* and *pass.* to take or receive the mark of the cross in solemnization of a vow; *esp.* to take the cross to fight against the Saracens, or other foes of Christianity, real or reputed.

1297 R. GLOUC. (Rolls) 8068 Pope..Urban..prechede of þe croyserie, and croysede moni mon. *Ibid.* 9882 & naþeles hii croicede hom þuder vor to wende. *Ibid.* 10586 Manie in hor bare fless hom late croici vaste, To libbe uor him and deie, Lowis out to caste. *c* **1325** *Coer de L.* 1693 Kyng Rychard is a pylgryme, Croyssyd to the Holy Lande. *c* **1330** R. BRUNNE *Chron.* (1810) 226 Lowys..Himself þe first was croised on his flessh. **1480** CAXTON *Chron. Eng.* clxxiii. 156 He had thought for to haue gone in to holy land..for encheson that he was croysed long tyme before. **1563-87** FOXE *A. & M.* (1684) I. 508/2 Unto this Bishop of Norwich the Pope had sent his Bulls..to Croisy whomsoever would go with him into France, to destroy the Antipope. **1586** J. HOOKER *Girald. Irel.* in *Holinshed* II. 50/2 Manie..were croised to the seruice of Christ. **1639** FULLER *Holy War* IV. xi. (1840) 196 And thereupon was croised, and..bound himself..to sail to the Holy Land.

3. To crucify.

a **1300** *Cursor M.* 19445 (Cott.) He sagh him [Christ] croised. *a* **1400** *Leg. Rood* (1871) 133 Feet and fayre hondes þat nou ben croised. *c* **1450** *Mirour Saluacioun* 4339 Barthelmewe slayne alle qwhikke and petere postle croisid.

Hence †**croised** *ppl. a.*, furnished or marked with a cross; having taken the cross.

1586 FERNE *Blaz. Gentrie* 215 A croysed staffe and allowed to them as a crosse. **1639** FULLER *Holy War* III. xxii. (1840) 158 Three hundred thousand of these croised pilgrims lost their lives in this expedition.

croise, *sb.*: see CROISES.

†**croisee, -ie, -y.** *Obs.* Also 5 croysee, -ye, 6 -ie, croisey, crosey. [a. OF. *croisée, -iée, -ie*, the native French form = med.L. *cruciāta*, It. *crociata*, Sp. *cruzada*, Pr. *crozada*, which was in the 16th c. displaced by *croisade*, with the adapted ending -ADE from the southern langs.] A crusade.

1482 CAXTON *Polycron.* VIII. v, Syre Henry spencer bisshop of norwiche wente..with a Croysye in to Flaundres. *Ibid.* VIII. xi, The pope gaf oute a croysye ageynst them [Hussites]. **1523** LD. BERNERS *Froiss.* I. xxvii. (*heading*), Other kynges toke on them the Croisey to the holy lande. **1549** THOMAS *Hist. Italie* 124 Manfredo lette crie a Croysie. **1608** GOLDING *Epit. Frossard* I. 37 The Pope.. commaunded a croysie to be preached against them. **1615** W. HULL *Mirr. Maiestie* 69 At the sute of them that were marked for the Croyssie.

croiser, -ier, obs. ff. CROSIER.

†**croiserie, -ry.** *Obs.* Forms: 3 creoicerie, -oy-, 3-5 croiserie, croy-, -rye, 4 croserie. [a. OF. *croiserie*, f. *crois* CROSS.] Crusading; a crusade.

c **1290** *S. Eng. Leg.* I. 440/331 To prechi of þe creoicerie a-boute in þe londe. **1297** R. GLOUC. (Rolls) 7091 þe pope sende croiserie in to þe holi lond. *c* **1380** WYCLIF *Serm.* Sel. Wks. I. 116 Croiserye ne assoilinge..shal not as þe day of dome reverse Cristis sentens. **1475** *Bk. Noblesse* 10 King Richarde the first..whiche in a croiserie went in to the holy londe.

†'**croises, 'croisees**, *sb. pl. Obs.* [a. F. *croisés*, in OF. *croisiés*:—L. *cruciātōs*, f. *croisier*: see CROISE *v.* 2.] Those who have been 'croised', crusaders. (App. sometimes used by modern writers as an archaism for *Crusades*, and supplied with erroneous singular *croise*.)

1656 BLOUNT *Glossogr.*, *Croises* (*cruce signati*), pilgrims. See *Croysado*. *c* **1750** SHENSTONE *Ruined Abbey* 248 How oft he blew The croise's trumpet. **1751** JORTIN *Eccl. Hist.* (R.), To instruct the croisez, to comfort them. **1779** *Archæol.* V. 19 (D.) When the English croisees went into the East in the first Crusade. **1846** *P. Parley's Ann.* VII. 18 The wars of the croises.

‖**croisette.** [F. *croisette*, dim. of *croix* CROSS.] A small cross.

1688 *Lond. Gaz.* No. 2311/4 A Croisett of Diamonds. **1906** *Daily Chron.* 11 Oct. 3/2 To pay to the Administration, in the form of a tax, a certain number of croisettes—brass rods in the form of a St. Andrew's cross. **1920** A. STRATTON *Engl. Interior* 72 French doorways of the Louis XIV. period, with surrounding architraves broken at the top with *croisettes* and surmounted by a frieze.

croissant (krwasɑ̃). [Fr. (see CRESCENT *sb.*).] = CRESCENT *sb.* 6.

1899 W. C. MORROW *Bohem. Paris* 139 The odor of hot rolls and croissants. **1928** R. MACAULAY *Keeping up Appearances* i. §2 Foaming coffee and milk, the crusty roll, the little tender croissant. **1958** X. FIELDING *Corsair Country* 96 We're having coffee and croissants in the sort of square you would come across in any of the larger French Mediterranean seaports. **1970** *New Yorker* 6 June 64/2 Resident jockeys..were being offered..the French racing papers, with their coffee and croissants.

croissant, earlier form of CRESCENT.

croissard, obs. incorrect form of CRUSADE.

‖**Croix de Guerre** (krwadəgɛːr). Also **croix de guerre**. [Fr., lit. 'cross of war'.] A French medal first awarded during the war of 1914–18 (see quot. 1922).

1915 *Daily Chron.* 4 Aug. 7/7 M. Poincaré conferred upon King Albert himself the French Croix de Guerre. **1917** T. E. LAWRENCE *Home Lett.* (1954) 345 The French Government has stuck another medal on to me: a croix de guerre this time. **1922** *Encycl. Brit.* XXXI. 892/2 The *Croix de Guerre.*—Established in 1915 to commemorate individual mentions in despatches during the war 1914–18. The cross was awarded to soldiers or sailors of all ranks..who were mentioned in orders of the day for an individual feat of arms. .. The ribbon..is green with narrow red stripes. **1944** H. G. WELLS *'42 to '44* 78 A girl in M.T.C. uniform with the gold leaf of the Croix de Guerre over her pocket. **1960** G. MARTELLI *Agent Extraordinary* ii. 34 Dressed usually in a neat dark blue suit only distinguished by the ribbon of the Croix de Guerre.

cro'jack, abbreviation of CROSS-JACK.

crok, obs. f. CROAK *v.*, CROCK.

croke, obs. f. CROAK, CROOK.

croke. *Obs.* exc. *dial.* [Etymology uncertain. Cf. CORK *sb.*[3]] Core of a fruit; refuse, dross.

c **1450** *Nominale* in *Wr.-Wülcker* 719/6 *Partes fructuum*.. *Hec arula* the crok. **1847-78** HALLIWELL, *Croke*, refuse; the bad or useless part of anything. *Linc.* **1886** *S.W. Linc. Gloss.*, *Croke*, refuse: as 'It's only an old croke'.

crokefer, crocus of iron: see CROCUS 3.

†'**croker.** *Obs. rare.* [app. f. CROC-US + -ER[1].] A cultivator or seller of saffron.

1577 HARRISON *England* III. viii. (1877) II. 57 The crokers or saffron men.

Crokerism ('krəʊkərɪz(ə)m). [f. the surname *Croker* + -ISM.] **1.** The political principles of John Wilson Croker (1780–1857).

1851 CARLYLE *New Lett.* (1904) II. 114, I was reading in the *Quarterly Review*:—very beggarly Crokerism, all of copperas and gall and human baseness. **1927** *Observer* 9 Oct. 16/4 When Randolph Churchill set out to revive his party, what did he do? He swept away Crokerism.

2. In U.S. politics, the political following and influence of Richard Croker (1841–1922), who made himself master (*c* 1888) of the Tammany organization and subsequently attained to great power in the government of the state of New York. Hence '**Crokerist**, an adherent of Crokerism; also *attrib.*

1897 *Daily News* 4 Nov. 3/4 Evidence..that Crokerism had brought New York to almost the lowest possible point. **1900** *Westm. Gaz.* 27 Oct. 6/2 Mr. Roosevelt..urged..the killing of Crokerism in the State. **1901** *Daily Chron.* 3 Oct. 5/7 The supporters of Crokerism and corruption..are opposed by the advocates of good government with freedom from bosses. *Ibid.* 1 Nov. 6/3 He will..vote the whole Fusionist 'ticket' or the whole Crokerist 'ticket' as it is offered to him.

croket, crokt: see CROCKET, CROCK *v.*[2]

crol(le, var. of CRULL *Obs.*, curly.

crom, crome, obs. ff. CRAM, CRUMB.

Cro-Magnon (krəʊ'mænjɔ̃, krəʊ'mægnən). Also **Cromagnon**. [The name of a hill of Cretaceous limestone in the Dordogne department of France in a cave at the base of which skeletons of *Homo sapiens* were found in 1868 among deposits of Upper Palæolithic age; it had previously been supposed that modern man did not exist in Palæolithic times.] Used, chiefly *attrib.*, to designate a group of mankind characterized by a long low skull, a wide face, and wide orbits having upper and lower borders close to one another and almost parallel; the stature is moderate or tall.

The group persisted in Mesolithic and Neolithic times, and some authorities consider that it survived in the Guanches of the Canary Islands. Similar skeletal features can be detected in certain modern European and north African peoples.

1869 P. BROCA in Lartet & Christy *Reliq. Aquit.* (1875) ix. 99 The general characters of the Cro-Magnon race. **1869** A. DE QUATREFAGES *Ibid.* 124 The Cro-Magnon skulls introduce new elements into the question of European origins. **1874** *Leisure Hour* 31 Oct. 697 Outline of Cro-Magnon skull as seen in front. **1882** *Amer. Antiquarian* Apr.-July 242 Cromagnon skulls in Bavaria. **1912** R. MUNRO *Palæolithic Man* 200 All the skeletons of the Cro-Magnon type found in the Grimaldi caves. **1927** HALDANE & HUXLEY *Anim. Biol.* xiii. 331 Cromagnon man. **1934** *Discovery* Mar. 79/2 All comparisons between individual moderns and individual Greeks or Cro-Magnons, are beside the mark in a discussion of the meaning of human progress as a whole. **1939** R. CAMPBELL *Flowering Rifle* II. 53 To sink these new Cromagnons out of sight.

cromatick, obs. form of CHROMATIC.

crombec ('krɒmbɛk). [Used in this form by Le Vaillant *Histoire naturelle des oiseaux d'Espagne* 1802; f. Du. *krom* crooked + *bek* BEAK *sb.*] A popular name for African warblers of the genus *Sylvietta*.

[**1875-84** LAYARD *Birds S. Afr.* 303 Sylvietta rufescens... The 'Stomp-stertje' of the Dutch colonists, and the 'Crombec' of Le Vaillant.] **1901** STARK & SCLATER *Birds S. Afr.* II. 117 Sylviella [*sic*] pallida. The Zambesi Crombec. **1908** HAAGNER & IVY *Sk. S. Afr. Bird Life* 80 The Crombec (*Sylviella rufescens*), known to the farmers as the Stomp-stertje (Stump-tail), is ash-grey above and tawny-buff below. **1955** MACKWORTH-PRAED & GRANT *Birds E. & N.E. Afr.* II. 423 Crombecs or Stump-tails... Called Crombecs by the early Dutch settlers in South Africa because of their curved bills.

Crombie ('krɒmbɪ). Also **crombie**. The name of J. & J. *Crombie* Ltd., a Scottish firm of cloth-makers, used to designate a type of overcoat, jacket, etc., made by them. Hence ***Crombie-coated*** adj.

1951 *Trade Marks Jrnl.* 17 Jan. 67/1 Crombie Product... Men's and boys' coats, suits, jackets..all made from piece goods wholly or substantially of wool, worsted or hair. J. & J. Crombie Limited, Grandholm Works, Woodside, Aberdeen, Scotland; Manufacturers and Merchants;—7th September, 1949. **1957** J. BRAINE *Room at Top* x. 95 A young man in a Crombie overcoat came through the door. **1957** *Times* 11 Sept. 3/1 Visiting Americans lured by the theatre's magic name come crombie-coated to tread heavily on Yeats's dreams. **1963** *Guardian* 16 Jan. 9/7 A man in a heavy black Crombie glared at the loud-speaker.

cromble, obs. form of CRUMBLE.

crome, cromb (krəʊm, kruːm), *sb.* Now *local.* Also 5 croumbe, cromp, 9 *dial.* croom, craam. [repr. an OE. **cramb*, **crǫmb* f. (cf. *wamb, womb*):—WG. *kramba*, whence also MDu. and LG. *kramme*, Du. *kram* hook, crook ('*kramme*, harpago' Kilian); f. *kramb-* grade of **krimb-an*: see note to CRAMP *sb.*[1]] A hook, a crook; *esp.* 'a stick with a hook at the end of it, to pull down the boughs of a tree, to draw weeds out of ditches,' etc. (Forby). †In early use, also = Claw, talon.

a **1400** in *Leg. Rood* 139 Lord send us þi lomb Out of þe wildernesses ston, To fende vs from þe lyon cromp. *c* **1440** *Promp. Parv.* 104 Crombe, or crome [P. crowmbe], *bucus* [v. r. *uncus, arpax*]. **1533** *Richmond Wills* (Surtees) 11 A ladyll and a flech crome. **1561** BECON *Sick Man's Salve* 257 Some rent apeaces w^t^ whot burning yron cromes. **1573** TUSSER *Husb.* (1878) 38 A sickle to cut with, a didall and crome For draining of ditches, that noies thee at home. **1770-4** A. HUNTER *Georg. Ess.* (1804) II. 351 They are drawn out by crombes, forks, &c. **1846** SPURDENS *Suppl. to Forby* s.v. *Croom*. Forby has *crome* a crook. We have *muck-crooms, fire-crooms, mud-crooms*, as well as *croom-sticks*. **1862** BORROW *Wild Wales* I. 231 A thin polished black stick with the crome cut in the shape of an eagle's head. **1869** *Lonsdale Gloss.*, *Craam*, an instrument with three curved prongs, used by cocklers to take cockle with.

crome, cromb, *v.* Now *local.* [f. prec. sb.] *trans.* To seize or draw with a crook; to hook.

1558 PHAER *Æneid* VI. Rij, With crokid beake, and croming pawes. *a* **1825** FORBY *Voc. E. Anglia*, *Crome*, to draw with a crome. **1868** J. TIMBS *Eccentr. Anim. Creation* 48 In 1863..Children described them [Mermaids] as 'nasty things that crome you into the water'. **1891** *Blackw. Mag.* Mar. 311 We were warned never to go near its edge, lest the mermaid should come and crome us in.

Cromer ('krəʊmə(r)). [The name of a town on the Norfolk coast.] ***Cromer Forest Bed***: the name of a series of deposits which outcrops on the coast at Cromer, comprising two freshwater beds which enclose the Forest Bed proper, an estuarine bed of clay containing the transported remains of trees and rich in plant and animal fossils.

From its position (see quot. 1964) the series was formerly thought to be pre-glacial, of Pliocene age, but it is now generally thought to have been deposited during the first (antepenultimate) interglacial, in the early Pleistocene, and its flora and fauna are taken as typical of this interglacial in Britain.

[**1840** C. LYELL in *Phil. Mag.* 3rd Ser. XVI. 377 A general subsidence..must have taken place..in order to explain the submergence and burial of the trees of which the stools are found *in situ*; and this forest bed could not have been brought up again..to the level of low water, without a subsequent upheaval.] **1863** —— *Antiquity of Man* 511/1 Cromer forest bed. **1882** C. REID *Geol. Country around Cromer* iii. 8 The so-called 'Cromer Forest-bed', celebrated for the number and variety of the fossil mammals which it has yielded. **1902** *Encycl. Brit.* XXXI. 439/2 The latest Pliocene, or pre-Glacial, flora of northern Europe is best known from the Cromer Forest-bed of Norfolk and Suffolk, a fluvio-marine deposit which lies beneath the whole of the Glacial deposits of these counties. **1946** L. D. STAMP *Britain's Struct.* xiv. 156 The Cromer Forest Bed series which we mentioned as the youngest Pliocene beds in Britain are claimed by some as early Pleistocene. **1964** K. P. OAKLEY *Frameworks for dating Fossil Man* I. 102 The Cromer Forest Bed was for long regarded by British geologists as 'pre-glacial', for it is overlain by the oldest known glacial deposits in East Anglia... In 1950 Woldstedt published Thomson's pollen-diagram of the Cromer Forest Bed which showed that it was undoubtedly interglacial in character.

Cromerian (krəʊ'mɪərɪən), *a.* and *sb.* [f. prec. + -IAN.] **A.** *adj.* **1.** *Geol.* and *Palæont.* **a.** Epithet of the Cromer Forest Bed series (see prec.);

hence, of, pertaining to, or characteristic of this series.

1900 F. W. HARMER in *Q. Jrnl. Geol. Soc.* LVI. 725 The so-called Forest-bed Series of the Cromer and Kessingland coasts..may be known as Cromerian. **1925** A. KEITH *Antiquity of Man* (ed. 2) I. xv. 304 The Cromerian beds tell us of the mild climate of the last phase of the Pliocene period. **1931** *Discovery* Mar. 85/1 The Cromerian flora is practically the same as that in East Anglia to-day. **1964** [see 1 b].

b. Epithet of a stage (and the corresponding age) in the Lower Pleistocene, and also of the first (antepenultimate) interglacial in Britain (generally identified with the Günz-Mindel Interglacial of Europe); hence, of or contemporaneous with this stage or interglacial.

1922 OSBORN & REEDS in *Bull. Geol. Soc. Amer.* XXXIII. 431 Certain surviving marine deposits of the north of Europe may be correlated with those of the Mediterranean, as follows: 1. Sicilian Stage of the Mediterranean = Cromerian Stage of the North Sea basin and Baltic. *Ibid.*, Along the German-Baltic coast Depéret recognizes marine faunal beds of Sicilian-Cromerian age. **1956** R. G. WEST et al. in *Phil. Trans. R. Soc.* B. CCXXXIX. 344 The Cromer Forest Bed or Cromerian Interglacial is considered to be equivalent to the..Günz/Mindel Interglacial of Europe. **1964** K. P. OAKLEY *Frameworks for dating Fossil Man* I. 109 In China the industry of Peking Man is associated with a fauna which was for long identified as Cromerian, whereas new evidence indicated that it is of Mindel II age... It is therefore most important to distinguish between a horizon of Cromerian *age* (*i.e.* dating from the Günz-Mindel Interglacial) and one containing elements of Cromerian *fauna*. **1967** D. H. RAYNER *Stratigr. Brit. Isles* xii. 378 The Cromerian stage refers to the Cromer Forest Bed and associated sediments of north Norfolk. **1968** R. G. WEST *Pleistocene Geol. & Biol.* xiii. 305 Compared with the succeeding interglacials the Cromerian vegetational history is distinct in the absence or scarcity of *Hippophaë* in the late-glacial zone. **1969** *Proc. Geol. Soc. Lond.* Aug. 152 It is recommended that for the Pleistocene and Holocene of the British Isles the following ages/stages be adopted as a regional scale... Pleistocene:..Anglian, Cromerian, Beestonian [etc.].

2. *Archæol.* Of, pertaining to, or characteristic of an ancient culture or people formerly supposed to be represented by remains (now not generally held to be artefacts) found in some Pliocene deposits near Cromer.

1922 OSBORN & REEDS in *Bull. Geol. Soc. Amer.* XXXIII. 424 Beneath the Forest Bed there has been discovered recently by J. Reid Moir a bed of giant flints of human manufacture, an industry which may be termed Cromerian. **1934** L. S. B. LEAKEY *Adam's Ancestors* v. 98 (*caption*) Two sides of a Cromerian flake tool. **1946** F. E. ZEUNER *Dating Past* vi. 185 The Cromerian industry..is particularly well-known from the so-called 'foreshore site', a flint spread exposed at low-water. **1964** K. P. OAKLEY *Frameworks for dating Fossil Man* II. vi. 219 All these flakes are in a highly battered condition. They have been compared with the very dubious 'Cromerian industry' in Britain.

B. *sb.* **1.** *Archæol.* One of the 'Cromerian' people.

1921 J. R. MOIR in *Jrnl. R. Anthrop. Inst.* LI. 387 These large flint masses represent the cores from which the ancient Cromerians obtained the raw material in the manufacture of their artefacts. **1925** A. KEITH *Antiquity of Man* (ed. 2) I. xv. 305 In 1920, Mr Moir discovered a 'working floor', a site used for the knapping of flint implements by early Cromerians.

2. *Geol.* The Cromerian stage or age or the Cromerian interglacial.

1957 J. K. CHARLESWORTH *Quaternary Era* II. xxix. 598 In East Anglia, by referring the Cromerian to the Pliocene and at the same time to an interglacial epoch, as is commonly done.., the glacial beginnings are thrust into the earlier horizons. *Ibid.* xxxii. 692 The Cromerian saw the European facies fully established. **1968** R. G. WEST *Pleistocene Geol. & Biol.* xiii. 305 The flora is very similar to that of the Cromerian in its paucity of exotic genera.

cromfordite ('krɒmfədaɪt). *Min.* [Named 1858 from Cromford, Derbyshire, where first found.] A synonym of phosgenite or chlorocarbonate of lead.

1861 BRISTOW *Gloss. Min.* 99. **1868** DANA *Min.* 703.

cromie, obs. form of CRUMMIE.

cromlech ('krɒmlɛk). Also 7 **kromlech**, 8–9 **cromleh**, 9 **cromleac**. [a. Welsh *cromlech* (in Irish and Gael. *cromleac*, *-leachd*), f. *crom*, fem. of *crwm* 'crooked, bowed, bent, curved, concave, convex' + *llech* (flat) stone.]

A structure of prehistoric age consisting of a large flat or flattish unhewn stone resting horizontally on three or more stones set upright; found in various parts of the British Isles, *esp.* in Wales, Devonshire, Cornwall, and Ireland. Also applied to similar structures in other parts of the world.

This is the application of the word in Welsh. In Brittany such structures are called *dolmen* (= table-stones), while *cromlech* is the name of a circle of standing stones. As a common noun *cromlech* is known in Welsh only from *c* 1700, but as a proper name, or part of one, it occurs in Owen's *Pembrokeshire*, and in several place-names believed to be ancient. In Cornish it is known earlier; a grant in Bp. Grandison's Register at Exeter (1328–1370), purporting to be from Æthelstan to Buryan, 943 (Birch, *Cartul. Sax.* II. 527), mentions in the boundaries 'fossa quæ tendit circa Rescel cromlegh'. See Silvan Evans *Welsh Dict.*

1603 OWEN *Pembrokesh.* I. xxvi. (1892) 251 An other thinge worth the noteinge is the stone called *Maen y gromlegh* vpon *Pentre Jevan* lande; yt is a huge and massie stone mounted on highe and sett on the toppes of iij other highe stones, pitched standinge vpright in the grounde. **1695** J. DAVIES in *Camden's Brit.* (ed. Gibson) 676 In Bod-Owyr..we find a remarkable *Kromlech*..These..are thought to have received the name of *Cromlecheu*, for that the Table or covering-Stone is, on the upper side, somewhat gibbous or convex. **1740** STUKELEY *Stonehenge* vii. 33 It was one of those stones which the Welsh call *Crwm-Lecheu* or bowing stones. **1766** *Ann. Reg.* 297 The huge, broad, flat stones, raised upon other stones set up on end for that purpose, now called Cromlechs. **1851** D. WILSON *Preh. Ann.* (1863) I. iii. 92 The cromlech, which is now universally recognised as a sepulchral monument. **1859** JEPHSON *Brittany* xi. 181 Scattered over its wide and arid plains, are cromlechs, dolmens, menhirs.

cromme, obs. form of CRUMB.

crommel, erroneous form of CROMLECH.

1848 LYTTON *Harold* I. i, An ancient Druidical crommel. **1849** —— *King Arthur* XII. xli, Grey crommell stones.

cromorne (krəʊ'mɔːn). [a. F. *cromorne*, corruption of Ger. *krummhorn* crooked horn.] A reed-stop on an organ; = KRUMMHORN, CREMONA[2].

1710 *Specif. Organ Salisbury Cath.* in Grove *Dict. Mus.* II. 595, 32. Vox Humana. 33. Cromhorn. **1880** E. J. HOPKINS ibid. II. 74 Krummhorn, Cromorne, Cremona, Clarionet, Corno-di-Bassetto..An Organ Reed Stop of 8 feet size of tone.

cromp, obs. var. or by-form of CROME.

crompe, for *corompe*, CORRUMP *v.*

a **1450** *Knt. de la Tour* (1868) 71 Lecherye..stinkithe and crompithe vnto heuene.

crompid (cake): see CRUMPET.

crompie, crompeled, obs ff. CRUMPLE, -ED.

crompster, var. CRUMSTER *Obs.*, small ship.

Cromwell ('krɒmwɛl). [See CROMWELLIAN *a.* and *sb.*] **1.** In full ***Cromwell shoe***. A shoe of the type supposedly worn by Oliver Cromwell, usu. having a large buckle or bow.

1879 M. E. BRADDON *Vixen* I. iv. 86 The girl..made rather a pretty picture... The tawny hair, black velvet frock ..and broad-toed Cromwell shoes. **1952** C. W. CUNNINGTON *Eng. Women's Clothing Pres. Cent.* ii. 36 *Shoes*: ..the Cromwell with two straps. **1963** A. GERNSHEIM *Fashion & Reality* II. 93 Buckled Cromwell shoes..were also popular [about 1911].

2. In full ***Cromwell chair***. = *Cromwellian chair* (see next).

1868 C. L. EASTLAKE *Hints Household Taste* iii. 80 Perhaps the most satisfactory type [of dining-room chair] is that which is commonly known in the trade as the 'Cromwell' chair. Its form is evidently copied from examples of the seventeenth century. **1881** C. C. HARRISON *Woman's Handiwork* III. 191 A square Puritan 'Cromwell' in oak, severely plain save for its dark cushion in maroon plush. *Ibid.* 192 The large, square-seated 'Cromwell' chair. **1969** J. GLOAG *Short Dict. Furnit.* (ed. 3) 275 *Cromwell chair*, mid-19th century trade term for a dining-room chair, copied or adapted from a mid-17th century prototype.

Cromwellian (krɒm'wɛlɪən), *a.* and *sb.*

A. *adj.* Of or pertaining to Oliver Cromwell, who became Protector of the Commonwealth of England in 1653. *spec.* Designating a type of chair (see quots.).

1905 A. HAYDEN *Chats on Old Furnit.* iii. 96 There is a style of chair, probably imported from Holland, with leather back and leather seat which is termed 'Cromwellian'. **1948** H. GORDON *Old Eng. Furnit.* iv. 33 In the ten years or so of the Commonwealth régime..furniture was extremely plain, and the chair that is generally labelled 'Cromwellian' may well have been a Puritan model. **1970** G. SAVAGE *Dict. Antiques* 108/2 *Cromwellian chair*, a modern term to describe a plain chair of Spanish design slightly decorated with turning, with slung leather seat and back, the leather held in place with large-headed studs.

B. *sb.* An adherent or partisan of Cromwell; one of the settlers in Ireland at the 'Cromwellian Settlement' of 1652, or of their descendants.

1725 SWIFT *Riddle*, A damn'd cromwellian knock'd me down. **1855** MACAULAY *Hist. Eng.* IV. 112 The stern Cromwellian, now..left the undisputed lord of the blood-stained and devastated island.

So also **'Cromwellate** (cf. *Protectorate*), **Crom'welliad**, **'Cromwellism**, **'Cromwellist**, **'Cromwellite**, **'Cromwellized**.

1835 *Fraser's Mag.* XII. 128 Of the time of Charles I and the Cromwellate. **1850** CARLYLE *Latter-day Pamph.* viii. 20 Puritan Cromwelliads on the great scale. **1685** SOUTH *Serm.* '*Will for Deed*' I. 275 When Rage and Persecution, Cruelty and Cromwellism were at that diabolical Pitch. **1881** PARNELL in *Daily News* 3 Oct. 6/3 The Gospel of Puritanism which might be called Cromwellism. **1649** C. WALKER *Hist. Independ.* II. 195 They joyned but to prevent the Cromwellists. **1648** 'MERCURIUS PRAGMATICUS' *Plea for King* 12 Even the very Cromwelites. **1648** C. WALKER *Hist. Independ.* I. 34 How faithfull then! How perfideous and Cromwellized are they now!

cron, obs. f. CRANE, CROWN *sb.* and *v.*

cronach, var. of CORONACH.

cronacle, -akle, obs. ff. CHRONICLE.

cronall, -el, -ation, obs. ff. CORONAL, -ATION.

croncled, obs. form of CRUNKLED.

crone (krəʊn), *sb.* Also 4 **krone**, 6 **croen**, 6–7 **croane**, 7 **chrone**. [In the sense 'old ewe' the word appears to be related to early mod.Du. *kronje*, *karonje*, 'adasia, ouis vetula, rejecula' (Kilian), believed to be the same word as *karonje*, *kronje*, MDu. *caroonje*, *croonje* carcass, a. NFr. *carogne* carcass: see CARRION. As applied to a woman, it may be an Eng. transferred application of 'old ewe' (though the evidence for the latter does not yet carry it back so early); but it was more probably taken directly from ONF. *carogne* (Picard *carone*, Walloon *coronie*) 'a cantankerous or mischievous woman', cited by Littré from 14th c. App. rare in the 18th c., till revived by Southey, Scott, and their contemporaries.]

1. A withered old woman.

c **1386** CHAUCER *Man of Law's T.* 334 This olde Sowdones, þis cursed crone [*v.r.* krone]. **1572** GASCOIGNE *Flowers, Divorce Lover*, That croked croane. **1586** WARNER *Alb. Eng.* II. x, Not long the croen can liue. **1621–51** BURTON *Anat. Mel.* III. ii. VI. v. (1676) 372 She that was erst a maid as fresh as May, Is now an old Crone. **1640** BRATHWAIT *Boulster Lect.* 151 This decrepit chrone. **1733** POPE *Ep. Cobham* 242 The frugal Crone, whom praying priests attend. **1795** SOUTHEY *Vis. Maid of Orleans* III. 28 There stood an aged crone. **1848** MACAULAY *Hist. Eng.* II. 258 An ancient crone at war with her whole kind. **1873** W. BLACK *Pr. Thule* iv. 57 Some old crone hobbling along the pavement.

b. Rarely applied to a worn-out old man.

In quot. 1844 = 'old woman', applied contemptuously.

1630 BRATHWAIT *Eng. Gentlem.* 457 A miserable crone, who spares when reputation bids him spend. **1822** W. IRVING *Braceb. Hall* (1849) 391 The old crone lived in a hovel..which his master had given him on setting him free. **1844** DISRAELI *Coningsby* II. i, The Tory party..was held to be literally defunct, except by a few old battered crones of office.

2. An old ewe; a sheep whose teeth are broken off. Also ***crone sheep***.

1552 HULOET, Crone or kebber sheape, not able to be holden or kepte forth, *adaria, adasia*. *a* **1577** GASCOIGNE *Dulce bellum* Wks. (1587) 127 The sheepmaster his olde cast croanes can cull. **1674** RAY *S. & E.C. Words* 63 *Crones*, old Ewes. **1767** A. YOUNG *Farmer's Lett. People* 217 Fifteen old crones sold fat, with their lambs. **1805** R. W. DICKSON *Pract. Agric.* (1807) II. 678 The crones are..constantly sold at four or five years old. **1854** *Jrnl. R. Agric. Soc.* XV. II. 344 In many districts, as on the heath lands of Norfolk, it often happens that..the centrally-placed teeth are broken across their bodies, by the rough plants on which the sheep graze. Such animals are called 'crones'.

†**crone**, *v. Obs.* [f. the sb.] *trans.* To pick out and reject (the old sheep) from a flock. Also *transf.*

1461 MARG. PASTON in *Paston Lett.* No. 429. II. 74 It is time to crone your old officers. **1552** HULOET, Crone out olde sheape, *adarias pascere, uel reijcere, reieculas carpere*. **1573** TUSSER *Husb.* (1878) 127 Now crone your sheepe, fat those ye keepe.

crone, crone-berry, dial. var. of CRANBERRY. [In Gerarde perh. from LG.]

1597 GERARDE *Herbal* App. to Table, Croneberries, *Vaccinia palustria*. **1744** WILSON *Syn.*, Croan-berries. **1878** *Cumbrld. Gloss.* (Central), *Crones*, cranberries.

crone, obs. f. CRANE, CROON, CROWN *sb.* and *v.*

cronecle, obs. form of CHRONICLE.

cronel, croner, obs. ff. CORONAL, -ER.

†**cronet, cronett**. *Obs.* A syncopated form of CORONET: cf. CROWNET.

1. = CORONET 1, 2.

1533 WRIOTHESLEY *Chron.* (1875) I. 20 A rich cronett..on her hedde. **1602** WARNER *Alb. Eng.* IX. xlviii, That Castill from a Cronet leapt, thinks manie Crownes not much.

2. The head of a tilting spear; usually with three or four spreading points; = CORONAL *sb.* 3.

1519 HORMAN *Vulg.* 283 b, They haue nat sharpe sperre heeydis, but blunt cronettis. **1730–6** BAILEY (folio), *Cronet, Crognet*, is the iron at the end of a tilting spear. (Hence in mod. Dicts.)

3. Some part of the armour of a horse.

1633 SHIRLEY *Tri. Peace* Introd., Four horses..their.. chamfron, cronet, petronel, and barb, of rich cloth of silver.

4. *Farriery.* The lowest part of the pastern of a horse; also the tuft of hair growing on this part, and the coronary bone; = CORONET 5.

1610 MARKHAM *Masterp.* II. ii. 214 He hath foure veines about the cronets of his hoofes..called the cronet veines. **1688** R. HOLME *Armoury* II. 154/1 The Cronet, is the Hair as groweth over the top of the hoof. [Hence in BAILEY.] **1725** BRADLEY *Fam. Dict.* s.v. *Ris*, A hard swelling round the Cronet of the Hoof.

5. *Arch.* A name for the architrave.

1665 J. WEBB *Stone-Heng* (1725) 7 So hath he the Architraves by two several Terms, *viz.* overthwart Pieces, and Cronets.

†**cronge.** *Obs. rare*⁻¹. 'A hilt or handle' (Halliwell).

1577 HARRISON *England* II. xxii. (1877) I. 345 The people go..into their fens and marises with long spits, which they dash here and there vp to the verie cronge into the ground.

Cronian ('krəʊnɪən), *a.* [f. Gr. Κρόνι-ος belonging to Cronos (Saturn) + -AN.] ***Cronian Sea***: the northern frozen sea.

1667 MILTON *P.L.* x. 290 Two Polar Winds blowing adverse Upon the Cronian Sea.

†**cronicall, -ychall,** short for ACRONYCHAL.

1647 H. MORE *Song of Soul* II. iii. III. lxxii, Saturn, Jove, and Mars.. When they go down with setting Cronicall. —— *Interp. Gen.* 425 *Cronychall*, or *Acronychall*, that is ἀκρόνυχος, vespertine.

†**cronicle.** *Obs. rare*⁻¹. [Cf. CROWNACLE, CORONACLE.] A coronet.

1568 GRAFTON *Chron.* II. 801 The Duchesse..in her robes of estate, and on her head a Cronicle of Golde.

cronicle, -ikle, etc., obs. ff. CHRONICLE.

†**cronie, crony.** *Obs.*⁻¹ App. a variant of (or ? error for) CRONE.

1621 BURTON *Anat. Mel.* II. iii. VII. 428 Marry not an old Cronie [*ed.* **1660** Crony] or a foole for money.

cronike, -ique, var. CHRONIQUE *Obs.*

cronk (krɒŋk), *sb. dial.* [Echoic: cf. Icel. *krúnk* the raven's cry.] The croak of a raven; = CRUNK; in U.S. applied to the cry of the wild-goose.

1878 Cumbrld. Gloss., *Cronk*, the hollow note uttered by the raven when on the wing.

cronk (krɒŋk), *a. Austral. colloq.* [Cf. CRANK *a.*³ 3 and 4.] Of a horse: unfit to run in a race, or dishonestly run as though unfit; said also of the race. Hence *gen.*, unsound, liable to collapse; also, obtained by fraud.

1891 N. GOULD *Double Event* xvii, He'd never ride another 'cronk' race, he vowed. **1892** *Bulletin* (Sydney) 12 Nov. (Funk), 'Cronk' financial institutions. **1893** *Herald* (Melbourne) 4 July 2/7 (Morris), The word 'cronk', Mr. Finlayson explained, meant 'not honestly come by'. **1900** H. LAWSON *On Track* 39 'It's always the way!'..'I knew the beggar would turn up!..And the only cronk log we've had, too!' *Ibid.* 157 Generosity isn't understood nowadays, and what the people don't understand is either 'mad' or 'cronk'. **1930** *Bulletin* (Sydney) 8 Oct. 20/4 Snip Sinker..was mostly too lazy or 'ad a cronk wrist or a kink in his back when there were big guns on the board.

cronkeled, obs. var. of CRUNKLED.

cronography, cronology, etc.: see CHRON-.

cronstedtite ('krɒnstɪtaɪt). *Min.* [Named after Cronstedt, a Swedish mineralogist: see -ITE.] A hydrous silicate of iron and manganese.

1823 W. PHILLIPS *Min.* 227 Cronstedite..is described..as occurring both massive and crystallized.

crony ('krəʊnɪ), *sb.* Also 7-8 chrony, 7 cronee, 7-9 croney, cronie. [Found first after 1660. According to Skinner 1671 'vox academica', *i.e.* a term of university or college slang. No connexion with *crone* has been traced.]

An intimate friend or associate; a 'chum'.

1665 PEPYS *Diary* 30 May, Jack Cole, my old schoolfellow..who was a great chrony of mine. **1678** BUTLER *Hud.* III. ii. 1269 The Scots, your constant Cronies, Th' Espousers of your Cause, and Monies. **1710** STEELE *Tatler* No. 266 ¶2 This is from Mrs. Furbish..an old School-Fellow and great Crony of her Ladyship's. **1818** SCOTT *Old Mort.* xi, The poor lad—my old cronie's son! **1857** W. COLLINS *Dead Secret* III. ii. (1861) 78 Her father and the doctor had been old cronies. **1864** THACKERAY *D. Duval* VI. (1869) 85 My schoolfellow..became a great crony of mine.

b. *attrib.*

1663 BUTLER *Hud.* I. iii. 188 He beat his Breast, and tore his Hair, For loss of his dear Crony Bear. **1713** SWIFT *Poems, Elegy on Partridge*, Not one of all his crony stars To pay their duty at his herse! *a* **1845** HOOD *Ode Clapham Acad.* x, Some run..some twine Their crony arms.

crony ('krəʊnɪ), *v.* [f. the sb.] *intr.* To associate (*with*) as a crony.

1826 DISRAELI *Viv. Grey* I. v, I wonder whom Grey will crony with this half. **1830** LYTTON *P. Clifford* xii, Melancholy ever cronies with sublimity. **1873** *St. Paul's Mag.* II. 712 The Earl of Delamere and Rollo cronied so completely, to use a schoolboy's word, that Elinor saw very little of her father.

cronyism ('krəʊnɪɪz(ə)m). Also **croneyism.** [f. CRONY *sb.* + -ISM.] **a.** Friendship; the ability or desire to make friends. **b.** (Chiefly *U.S.*) The appointment of friends to government posts without proper regard to their qualifications.

1840 A. CONOLLY *Let.* July in F. MacLean *Person from England* (1958) 43 It *must* end in my going to Khokund, probably *via* Khiva with the Envoy thence, Yakoob Bai, with whom I have established great croneyism. **1922** W. DE LA MARE in *Boswell's Life of Johnson* p. xix, Johnson's oddities, his queer habits, his cronyism, his truculence, his wit, his frailties. **1950** *Collier's Mag.* 24 June 78/1 [He] sets a heap of store by the solemn vows of cronyism. **1952** *N.Y. Times* 17 Aug. 8E/1 The amount of politically entrenched bureaucracy that has earned for Mr. Truman's regime its sorry reputation for corruption, cronyism, extravagance, waste and confusion. **1968** *Guardian* 13 July 9/5 The Congress would be more amenable to the argument that 'cronyism' should give way to the next President's right to choose his own Chief Justice.

†**croo** (kruː), *v. Obs.* [Echoic: cf. COO, CROOD.] = CROOD.

1611 COTGR., *Roucoler*, to croo like a Doue or Queest. *Roucoulement*, the crooing of Doues. **1706** PHILLIPS, To *Croo* or *Crookel*, to make a Noise like a Dove, or Pigeon.

croo, *sb. Sc.* (and *Irish*). Also 7 crue. [a. Gael. *cró* sheepcot, wattled fold, hut, hovel, cottage, OIrish *cró* sty, pen, cote, hovel: cf. CREW *sb.*², also Icel. *kró* small pen, fold for lambs, which may be from Celtic, and is the source of the Shetland form.]

1. A hovel, hut, or cabin.

1570 *Tressoun of Dumbartane* in *Satir. Poems Reform.* (1890) 172 The Inglis men raid neir For all your craking, caigit within ane Cro [*rime* to]. **1880** *Antrim & Down Gloss.*, *Croo*, a poor, filthy cabin.

attrib. **17..** *Jacobite Songs*, '*When the King comes*', I may sit in my wee croo house.

2. A sty.

1825 in JAMIESON. **1880** *Antrim & Down Gloss.*, *Pig-croo*, a pig-sty.

3. A fold, a pen for sheep. *Shetland.*

1795 SIR J. SINCLAIR *View Agric. North C. Scotl.* App. 29 The proprietors..gather their sheep in folds or what are termed here punds and crues. **1856** ELIZA EDMONDSTON *Sk. & Tales Shetland* xiv. 173 Driven to small ponds (or croos) for the purpose of being counted, marked [etc.]. **1866** T. EDMONDSTON *Shetland Gloss.* (Philol. Soc.), *Crû*, a small enclosure.

crooch(e, obs. form of CROUCH *v.*

crood, croud, *v. Sc.* Also 6 crowd. [Echoic.] *intr.* To make the murmuring sound of a dove. (Also, to croak: see quot. 1710.)

1513 DOUGLAS *Æneis* XII. Prol. 237 The cowschet crowdis and pirkis on the rys. **1619** Z. BOYD *Last Battell* (1629) 299 (Jam.) Turtles crouding with sighes and grones. **1710** RUDDIMAN *Gloss. to Douglas' Æneis*, *Crowde*, to curr like a dove. We now use it *Scot.* for the noise of frogs. **1785** BURNS *To W. Simpson* xii, While thro' the braes the cushat croods With wailfu' cry!

croodle ('kruːd(ə)l), *v.*¹ *Sc.* [f. prec.] *intr.* To make a continued soft low murmuring sound; *esp.* to coo as a dove. Hence **'croodling** *ppl. a.*

17.. *The Croodlin Doo* in Child *Eng. & Sc. Ballads* II. 363 My little wee croodlin doo. *a* **1810** TANNAHILL *Bonnie Wood* Poems (1846) 132 The cushat croodles amourously. **1890** *Univ. Rev.* 15 Oct. 195 She made a queer little croodling sound of comfort.

croodle ('kruːd(ə)l), *v.*² *dial.* Also crowdle, cru(d)dle. [Of uncertain origin. It has been viewed as a dim. of *crowd*; but its dialectal phonology, e.g. W. Yorkshire *crooidle*, takes it back to a ME. *crōdle* with long *o*. In modern use, app. influenced by association with various other words, e.g. *crouch*, *cludder*, *cuddle*.]

intr. To cower or crouch down; to draw oneself together, as for warmth; to cling close together, or nestle close to a person.

1788 W. MARSHALL *Yorksh.* Gloss., *Crowdle*, to creep close together, as children round the fire, or chickens under the hen. **1821** CLARE *Vill. Minstr.* II. 183 On the pale traveller's way, Who, croodling, hastens from the storm. **1857** KINGSLEY *Two Y. Ago* x, 'There', said Lucia, as she clung croodling to him. **1858** —— *Winter Gard.* Misc. I. 136 As a dove, to fly home to its rest, and croodle there. **1884** *Chesh. Gloss.*, *Croodle*, (1) to snuggle, as a young animal snuggles against its mother; (2) to crouch down.

crooe, obs. form of CROW.

crook (krʊk), *sb.* and *a.* Forms: 3-4 croc, 3-6 croke, 4-5 *Sc.* and *north.* cruk, 4-6 crok, kroke, 5-6 cruke, 5-8 crooke, 6-9 *Sc.* cruik, 4- crook. [ME. *crōk*, *crōc*, app. a. ON. *krókr* (Sw. *krok*, Da. *krog*) crook, hook, barb, trident; unknown elsewhere in Teutonic, but app. belonging to the same ablaut series (*krak-*, *krôk*), as OHG. *chracho*, *chracco* hook; cf. ON. *kraki* boat-hook.

The parallelism of form and meaning with CROCHE, CROSE, is notable in sense 4. Relationship between the ablaut series *krak-*, *krôk*, and that to which *crutch* belongs, cannot at present be asserted.]

A. *sb.* **1.** An instrument, weapon, or tool of hooked form; a hook. *spec.* †**a.** A reaping-hook, sickle; **b.** A hook for grappling or catching; **c.** A hook or bent iron on which anything is hung; *e.g.* one of the iron hooks on which a gate hangs: *esp.* in 'crooks and bands' (see BAND *sb.*¹ 3); a hook in a chimney for hanging a pot or kettle on, a pot-hook; hence phr. ***as black as the crook*** (Sc.).

c **1290** *S. Eng. Leg.* I. 99/241 And hire bresten fram hire bodi with Irene crokes rende. *a* **1300** *Cursor M.* 18104 (Cott.) He..brast þe brasen yates sa strang, And stelen croc þat þai wit hang. *c* **1325** *E.E. Allit. P.* A. 40 Quen corne is coruen with crokez kene. *c* **1385** CHAUCER *L.G.W.* 640 *Cleopatras*, In gooth the grapenel so ful of crokis. *c* **1420** *Pallad. on Husb.* I. 1161 Rakes, crookes, adses, and bycornes. **1453** *Mem. Ripon* (Surtees) III. 160 Pro nayles et crokes emptis pro magnis portis. **1522** *Test. Ebor.* (Surtees) V. 153, j blake worsted kirtle, and the gretter golde crokes. **1587** *Vestry Bks.* (Surtees) 26 For fowre bands & crookes, vj d. **1588** A. KING tr. *Canisius' Catech.* 177 As ane dur is tourned on the cruuks (quhilk in latin ar called *cardines*). **1600** SURFLET *Countrie Farme* I. xxiv. 152 Hang them [pigs when killed] to the crookes set vp in some vaulted roofe. *a* **1774** FERGUSSON *Election* Poems (1845) 40 Till, in a birn, beneath the crook, They're singit wi a scowder. **1826** SCOTT *Diary* 17 Jan., With a visage as black as the crook. **1848** *Jrnl. R. Agric. Soc.* IX. II. 420 The ends of each rafter are turned in the form of a gate-crook. **1858** R. S. SURTEES *Ask Mamma* lvi. 256 From whose lofty ceiling hung the crooks, from whence used to dangle the..legs of..mutton.

†**2.** A crooked claw, as of a beast or fiend; passing into sense 'clutch'. (Cf. CLUTCH *sb.*¹ 1-3.)

In reference to fiends the sense is often doubtful; some hooked or barbed instrument may have been meant.

a **1225** *Ancr. R.* 102 (Cleop. MS.) þe cat of helle..drouh al ut..wið crokede crokes. *Ibid.* 174 Uorte worpen upon ou his crokes [*MS. T.* hore clokes, *MS. C.* hise cleches]. *a* **1300** *Cursor M.* 23252 (Cott.) Strang paine es it on þam to loke, and namli laght vntil þair crok. *Ibid.* 25060 þas oþer þat his lagh forsok, he kest þam in þat feindes croke. *a* **1400** *Cov. Myst.* 209 Out of thi [Satan's]..cruel crook By Godys grace man xal be redempt. **14..** in *Pol. Rel. & L. Poems* (1866) 98 The deville caught him in his croke.

†**3.** A barbed spear. (So in ONorse.) *Obs.*

c **1435** *Torr. Portugal* 1590 He bare on his nek a croke..It was twelfe ffeete and more. *Ibid.* 1604 Sith he pullith at his croke, So fast in to the flesh it toke That oute myȝt he gete it nought.

4. a. A shepherd's staff, having one end curved or hooked, for catching the hinder leg of a sheep.

c **1430** LYDG. *Chorle & Byrde* xlviii. in Ashm. 223 A Chepys Croke to the ys better than a Launce. *c* **1440** *Promp. Parv.* 104 Croke, or scheype hoke, *pedum.* **1635** COWLEY *Davideis* I. 2, I Sing the Man who Judah's Scepter bore In that right hand which held the Crook before. **1720** GAY *Dione* III. ii, Leaning on her crook Stood the sad nymph. **1883** E. PENNELL-ELMHIRST *Cream Leicestersh.* 240 Where the sickle holds the place of the shepherd's crook.

b. The pastoral staff of a bishop, abbot or abbess, shaped like a shepherd's staff; a crosier.

c **1386** CHAUCER *Friar's T.* 19 (Tyrwh.) Er the bishop hent hem with his crook [*Harl. & 6-text* hook]. *c* **1430** *Pilgr. Lyf Manhode* III. xxiv. (1869) 149 This crook and this S shewen wel that j am an abbesse. **1851** LONGF. *Gold. Leg.* I. ii. 23 The Priests came flocking in..With all their crosiers and their crooks.

5. a. Any hooked or incurved appendage, *e.g.* a tendril of a plant, one of the hooks on the fruit of the burdock, etc.; the curved or hooked part of anything, *e.g.* of a walking-stick; the 'crosier' of a fern.

1398 TREVISA *Barth. de P.R.* XVII. clxxvii. (1495) 717 Those bondes or crokes of the vyne by the whyche it takyth and byclypppyth trees and stalkes. **1578** LYTE *Dodoens* I. viii. 15 Upon the braunches there groweth small bullets..garnisshed full of little crookes or hookes. **1665** HOOKE *Microgr.* 2 The..thorns, or crooks, or hairs of leaves. **1850** *Florist* Mar. 87 The young fronds of the..Ferns uncurling their crooks.

†**b.** A curl or roll of hair formerly worn. *Obs.* (Cf. CROCKET¹ 1.)

c **1308** *Sat. People Kildare* x. in *E.E.P.* (1862) 154 þo3 ȝur crune be ischave, fair beþ ȝur crokes [*rime* bokes]. *c* **1325** *Poem Times Edw. II* in *Pol. Songs* (Camden) 327 A myrour and a koeverchef to binde wid his crok [*rime* bitok]. ? *a* **1400** *Morte Arth.* 3352 Cho kembede myne heuede That the krispane kroke to my crownne raughte. [**1721** BAILEY, *Crok*, the turning up of the hair into curls.]

c. A crooked or incurved piece of timber.

1802 *Naval Chron.* VIII. 373 The..futtocks are all got from natural grown crooks. **1806** *Hull Advertiser* 11 Jan. 2/2 Oak Timber, consisting of Knees and Crooks, peculiarly well adapted for Ship Building.

d. *Bell-founding.* (See quots.)

1857 LUKIS *Acc. Ch. Bells* 21 The crook is a kind of compass formed of wood, and is used for making the moulds. **1872** ELLACOMBE *Ch. Bells Devon* I. 7 The core is first..moulded as described by the action of the crook.

6. A small space, or piece of ground, of a crooked shape; an odd corner, nook.

1417 *Searchers Verdicts* in *Surtees Misc.* (1890) 11 A cruke of Robert Feriby grund. *c* **1430** *Pilgr. Lyf Manhode* I. lvi. (1869) 34 In sum anglet or in sum..crook or cornere. **1717** *N. Riding Rec.* VIII. 23 Other small parts [of a farm] called crookes and crinkles. **1839-40** W. IRVING *Wolfert's R.* (1855) 33 It was full of nooks and crooks, and chambers of all sorts and sizes.

†**7.** *pl.* Brackets (in printing), parentheses. *Obs.* (Cf. CROTCHET 8.)

1641 MILTON *Ch. Govt.* I. (1851) 116 Though it be cunningly interpolisht..with crooks and emendations. **1762** STERNE *Tr. Shandy* VI. xxxi, Among my father's papers, with here and there an insertion of his own, betwixt two crooks, thus [ ].

8. *Musical Instr.* **a.** An accessory piece of curved tubing to be added to a metal wind instrument, as a horn or cornet, to lower the pitch, so as to adapt it to the key of the piece of music in which it is to be used. **b.** The crooked metal tube connecting the body with the reed of a bassoon.

1842 S. LOVER *Handy Andy* xviii, The trumpeter..pulling out one crook from another. **1880** GROVE *Dict. Mus.* I. 150 [The bassoon] consists of five pieces..the crook, wing, butt, long joints, and bell. *Ibid.* I. 750 The difference of pitch [in the Horn] being provided by the various crooks.

9. A support or frame of wood, bent in a particular way, formerly slung in pairs panier-wise across the saddle of a pack-horse for carrying loads. (*Somerset* and *Devon*.)

1657 LIGON *Barbadoes* (1673) 89 Small pack-saddles, and crooks..laying upon each Crook a faggot. *c* **1710** CELIA

Fiennes *Diary* (1888) 225 Carryages on horses backes.. with sort of crookes of wood like yokes either side.. in which they stow y[e] corne and so tie it with cords. **1791** J. Collinson *Hist. Somerset* II. 34 The crops are.. carried in with crooks on horses. **1850** *Jrnl. R. Agric. Soc.* XI. II. 739 The corn is often harvested in crooks on horses' backs. **1888** Elworthy *W. Somerset Word-bk.* s.v., It used to be as common to say 'I'll send a horse and crooks' as it is now to say 'horse and cart'. [They] are now very rarely seen.

10. a. The act of crooking; *esp.* a bending of the knee or of the body in sign of reverence (*obs.*).

c **1330** R. Brunne *Chron. Wace* (Rolls) 1816 Ffor-setten byfore, and eke byhynde, Wyþ crokes ilkon oþer gan bynde. **1603** B. Jonson *Sejanus* I. i, He is now the court god; and well applied With sacrifice of knees, of crooks, and cringes. **1857** Hughes *Tom Brown* I. iii, A well-aimed crook of the heel or thrust of the loin.

b. In polo, an act of crooking an opponent's stick (see crook *v.*[1] 6).

1935 *Times* 18 June 5/5 Captain Ansell.. scored with a 60 yards penalty given for a foul crook.

11. A bending or curve, a convolution, *e.g.* of a river, path, the intestines, etc.

1486 *Bk. St. Alban's* E vij b, Of the nomblis.. theys oder crokes and Roundulis bene. **1558** Phaer *Æneid* II. (R.), Through lanes and crokes and darknes most we past. **1585** James I *Ess. Poesie* (Arb.) 16 Sea eylis rare, that be Myle longs, in crawling cruikis of sixtie pace. **1609** C. Butler *Fem. Mon.* v. (1623) M ij, Let it downe by a cord tied to some crooke of the bough. **1686** Burnet *Trav.* v. (1750) 253 The Rhine maketh a Crook before it. **1885** *Harper's Mag.* Mar. 594/1 Old homely ways, whose crooks.. she knew by heart. **1887** Stevenson *Underwoods* I. xiv. 29 The crooks of Tweed.

†**12.** *fig.* A crooked piece of conduct; a trick, artifice, wile; deceit, guile, trickery. *Obs.*

c **1200** Ormin 11635 þa wære he þurrh þe deofless croc I gluternesse fallenn. *a* **1225** *Leg. Kath.* 125 Wið alle hise crefti crokes. *a* **1300** *Cursor M.* 740 (Cott.) þe nedder.. þat mast kan bath on crok and craft. **1393** Gower *Conf.* III. 161 He soughte nought the worldes croke [*rime* boke] For veine honour ne for richesse. *c* **1460** *Towneley Myst.* 145 Withe sich wylys and crokes. *a* **1556** Cranmer *To Gardiner* (T.), For all your bragges, hookes, and crookes, you have such a fall. **1594** Willobie *Avisa* 35 The wise will shunne such craftie crookes.

13. One whose conduct is crooked; a dishonest person, swindler, sharper. orig. *U.S. colloq.* Now esp. a professional criminal or an associate of criminals.

1879 *Chicago Tribune* 6 Feb. 5/2 The *Times* still continues its attacks upon the Government officials in the interest of the Pekin and Peoria crooks. **1882** *Sydney Slang Dict.* 3/1 *Crook*, a thief and burglar. One who gets his living on the best. **1886** *American Local Newspr.*, The photographs of several English cracksmen along with one of a New York crook. **1891** H. Campbell *Darkness & Daylight* 470 Gamblers, pickpockets and other 'crooks' abound. **1891** *The Sun* (N.Y.) 19 June 6/4 (Funk), The slang word 'crook' now bids fair to be recognized in the statutes and consequently to be adopted as good English in the courts of law. A bill regulating admissions to the prison at Marquette excludes, among other classes of individuals specified, those known to be 'crooks' in police parlance. **1896** *Westm. Gaz.* 17 July 2/1 A crook what kep a little crib Dad went to when things was too lively. **1903** *Daily Chron.* 3 Nov. 5/4 All the saloon-keepers, and gamblers, and crooks, and confidence men, in fact all the predatory elements of society are.. working for a Tammany victory. **1909** *Ibid.* 19 June 3/2 The people here .. are clever and rather interesting scamps. Were they on a slightly lower social level they would be called 'crooks'. **1949** [see crookery]. **1953** 'M. Innes' *Christmas at Candleshoe* xiii. 150 'The fact is that a gang of crooks——' 'I beg your pardon?' Miss Candleshoe is wholly at sea. 'The fact is that a band of robbers is prowling about outside this house now.'

14. *dial.* **a.** 'The crick in the neck; a painful stiffness, the effect of cold'. *Craven Gloss.* 1828. **b.** 'A disease of sheep, whereby their heads are drawn on one side.' *Ibid.*

15. *Phrases.* **a.** †*on crook, a-crook*: crookedly, in a crooked course. *Obs.* ***on the crook***: dishonestly. *slang.*

1387 Trevisa *Higden* (Rolls) II. 53 Humber.. renneþ first a crook out of þe south side of York. *c* **1425** *Hampole's Psalter* Metr. Pref. 38 Many out of bales brow3t, þ[t] in lywyng went on croke. **1500–1881** [see acrook]. **1879** *Macm. Mag.* 503 (Farmer) Which he had bought on the crook.

b. ***crook in one's lot***: something untoward or distressing in one's experience: an affliction, trial. *Sc.*

a **1732** T. Boston (*title*), The Crook in the Lot; or the Wisdom and Sovereignty of God displayed in the afflictions of men. *Ibid.* (1767) 14 The crook in the lot is the special trial appointed for every one. **1818** Scott *Hrt. Midl.* xii, I trust to bear even this crook in my lot with submission. **1835** Mrs. Carlyle *Lett.* I. 32 It is positively a great crook in my present lot.

16. ***by hook or by crook***: see hook.

B. *adj.* **1. a.** [Arising probably from dissolution of the combinations *crook-back*, etc., in which *crook-* was perhaps originally the sb., or the vb. stem; though it may have been shortened from *crookt*, *crooked*: cf. C b.] = crooked.

1508 Dunbar *Tua Mariit Wemen* 275 Weil couth I claw his cruke bak. **1647** H. More *Insomn. Philos.* xxiv, Interpreting right whatever seemed crook.

b. 'Bent', stolen. *Criminals' slang.*

1900 *Sessions' Paper Central Criminal Court* CXXXII. 462, I brought it from you b—— straight; I did not know it was *crook*.

2. *Austral.* and *N.Z.*

a. Of things: bad, inferior; out of order, unsatisfactory; unpleasant, dreadful.

1898 *Bulletin* (Sydney) 17 Dec. Red Page/2, *Krook* or *kronk* is bad. **1915** E. G. Pilling *Anzac Memory* (1933) iv. 62 Had a very crook night, sickness, cramp, dysentery. **1917** E. Miller *Camps, Tramps & Trenches* (1939) ix. 52 The rifle issued to me was a crook one that fired high and left. **1918** *N.Z.E.F. Chrons.* 5 July 250/2 It's crook to stay for years. **1929** W. Smyth *Girl from Mason Creek* xv. 163 'Cow of a job,' he muttered... 'It's a bit crook for yer.' **1931** V. Palmer *Separate Lives* 271 It can't be helped now. When things go crook in the beginning [etc.]. **1934** A. Russell *Tramp-Royal in Wild Australia* xvii. 106, I wasn't feeling too well at the time—too much crook water an' not enough decent tucker, I suppose. **1945** J. Henderson *Gunner Inglorious* iii. 18 A cigarette first thing in the morning before a cup of tea, tastes crook. **1947** 'A. P. Gaskell' *Big Game* 32 Isn't it crook about Keith and Gordon [being killed]? **1958** 'N. Shute' *Rainbow & Rose* 64, I never knew it [*sc.* the weather] to be so crook. **1968** K. Weatherly *Roo Shooter* 111 You know how the old wagon is crook in water.

b. Dishonest, unscrupulous, 'crooked'.

1911 L. Stone *Jonah* I. xi. 132 Yous don't think any worse o' me 'cause Lil's crook, do yer? **1916** 'Anzac' *On Anzac Trail* 44 Protesting.. in lurid language against what they styled 'a crook trick'. **1929** C. C. Martindale *Risen Sun* 173 When sport goes crook, what can remain wholesome? **1933** *Bulletin* (Sydney) 6 Sept. 8/2 They think.. that the system is 'crook'. **1936** F. Sargeson *Conversation with Uncle* 18 They said it [*sc.* pulling a race-horse] was a crook business right through. **1953** J. W. Brimblecombe in J. C. Reid *Kiwi Laughs* (1961) 178 His mentor had a crook deal put over him.

c. Irritable, bad-tempered, angry; esp. in phr. ***to go crook*** (*at* or *on*), to become angry (at); to lose one's temper (with); to upbraid, rebuke.

1911 L. Stone *Jonah* II. iv. 190 Yer niver 'ad no cause ter go crook on me, but I ain't complainin'. **1916** C. J. Dennis *Songs of Sentimental Bloke* 78 An' there I'm standin' like a gawky lout.. An' wonders wot 'e's goin' crook about. **1933** P. Cadey *Broken Pattern* xviii. 197 If Phœbe's gone crook at you.. she's had some good reason for it. **1937** N. Marsh *Vintage Murder* vii. 70 See him when he goes crook!.. His eyes fairly flashed. **1946** P. Freedman in *Coast to Coast 1945* 136 Her ma's always going crook because I break the plaster. **1959** *Listener* 15 Jan. 115/2, I cut off his boot to stop the foot swelling. I remember he went crook on me: he said they were new, and I'd darn well have to buy him a new pair. **1964** P. White *Burnt Ones* 295 When his mum went crook, and swore, he was too aware of teeth, the rotting brown of nastiness.

d. Ailing, out of sorts; injured, disabled.

1916 C. J. Dennis *Songs of Sentimental Bloke* 88, I sneaks to bed, an' feels dead crook. **1916** *Oil Sheet* Dec. 7 Now I've just been vaccinated, and am feeling pretty 'crook'. **1934** A. Russell *Tramp-Royal in Wild Australia* xxvii. 178 An' when Dick says he's crook, he's crook. He's out there alone, you know. **1937** N. Marsh *Vintage Murder* viii. 94 Letting him out just because he kidded he felt crook. *Ibid.* x. 116 'He was looking horribly crook.' 'Ill?' asked Alleyn cautiously. 'Too right, sir.' **1938** 'R. Hyde' *Nor Years Condemn* 208 A crook knee and arm. **1952** N. Donnan in *Coast to Coast 1951–52* 141, I got a crook hip, I can't do heavy work now. **1956** P. White *Tree of Man* 55 'She's crook. It looks like the milk fever,' he said. **1960** B. Crump *Good Keen Man* 45 It saves you from getting the crook guts, boy. *Ibid.* 49 He said he wasn't crook or anything. **1968** K. Weatherly *Roo Shooter* 28 If I don't go out at least five nights a week the cook thinks I'm crook and gets all worried.

C. *Comb.*, as ***crook-like*** adj.; **crook-saddle**, a saddle with crooks for carrying loads (cf. 9).

1700 *Acc. St. Sebastian's* in *Harl. Misc.* I. 413 Their iron bars are brought to the town on horses or mules, on crook-saddles. **1797** *Statist. Acc. Scot.* XIX. 248 (Stornoway) Horse-loads are.. carried in small creels, one on each side of the horse, and fixed by a rope to the crook-saddle. **1888** F. G. Lee in *Archæol.* LI. 356 A bishop or abbot holding a crook-like pastoral staff.

b. Parasynthetic combs., as ***crook-billed***, ***-fingered***, ***-kneed***, ***-legged***, ***-lipped***, ***-nosed***, ***-shouldered***, ***-sided***, ***-sterned***, ***-toothed*** adjs. See also crook-back, -backed, crook-neck, -necked.

Crooked- was used in the same way from Wyclif onwards.

1580 Hollyband *Treas. Fr. Tong*, *Bossu*, downe backed, crooke shouldered. **1590** Shaks. *Mids. N.* IV. i. 127 My hounds are.. Crooke kneed, and dew-lapt, like Thessalian Buls. **1591** Percivall *Sp. Dict.*, *Cancajoso*, crooklegged. **1591** Sylvester *Du Bartas* I. v. 515 Crook-tooth'd Lampreys. **1598** Chapman *Iliad* II. 684 The crooke-stern'd [ed. *c* **1611** crookt-stern'd] shippes. **1684** tr. *Bonet's Merc. Compit.* IX. 334 Oftentimes Children about two years old, when they begin to go, are crook-legged. **1775** S. Crisp in *Mad. D'Arblay's Early Diary* II. 36 Reduc'd to a level with crook-finger'd Jack!

crook, var. of crock *sb.*[5]

crook (krʊk), *v.*[1] Forms: 3–6 **croke**, 4– **crook(e**, (6 **croock**). [f. crook *sb.*]

1. a. *trans.* To bend into an angular or curved form; to distort from a straight line; to curve.

c **1175** *Lamb. Hom.* 61 Gif he binimeð us ure sihte.. oðer us crokeð on fote oðer on honde. **1382** Wyclif *Ps.* lxviii. 24 The rig of hem euermor crooke thou in. **1398** Trevisa *Barth. de P.R.* XVIII. xix. (1495) 778 Whan camelles take charge vpon them thenne they bende and croke the knees. **1602** Shaks. *Ham.* III. ii. 66 And crooke the pregnant hindges of the knee. **1651** *Raleigh's Ghost* 21 The star of Venus.. crooking it self into hornes, as the moon doth. **1862** T. Morrall *Needle-making* 23 Hardening needles in oil instead of water, as the oil did not crook them so much. **1875** Blackmore *A. Lorraine* III. v. 69 The air was so full of rheumatism that no man could crook his arm to write a sermon.

†**b.** To curl (hair). *Obs. rare.*

1340 *Ayenb.* 177 þe men þet doþ zuo grat payne ham to kembe.. and ine hare here wel to croki.

c. ***to crook one's mou'*** (Sc.): to distort the mouth in expression of displeasure or ill temper.

1724 Ramsay *Tea-t. Misc.* (1733) I. 86 O kend my minny I were wi' you Illfardly wad she crook her mou. **1803** Mayne *Glasgow* 31 (Jam.) They, scornfu', toss their head ajee, And crook their mou'.

d. ***to crook one's elbow*** or ***little finger***: to drink alcoholic liquor (esp. with implication of excess). *slang.*

1825 Jamieson Suppl. I. 271/2 *To crook the elbow*; as, She *crooks* her *elbow*, a phrase used of a woman who uses too much freedom with the bottle, q. bending her elbow in reaching the drink to her mouth. **1836** *Public Ledger* (Philadelphia) 2 Aug. (Th.), William Martin was fined for, as he quaintly expressed it, crooking his little finger too often. **1859** Bartlett *Dict. Amer.* (ed. 2) s.v., To crook one's elbow or one's little finger, is to tipple. **1875** Besant & Rice *With Harp & Crown* xix, The secretary.. might have done great things in literature but for his unfortunate crook of the elbow. As he only crooks it at night, it does not matter to the hospital. **1924** J. Masefield *Sard Harker* III. 251 Sir James has sacked his old man for crooking his little finger: going on the jag, in other words.

†**2.** *fig.* To bend or turn out of the straight course, or from the direct meaning or intention; to pervert, 'twist'. *Obs.*

a **1340** Hampole *Psalter* lvi. 8 þai crokid my saule: that is, thai thoght to draghe it fra the luf of god in til the erth. **1382** Wyclif *Ps.* lvi. 7 Thei myche crookeden [*incurvaverunt*] my soule. **1393** Gower *Conf.* II. 144 That she may.. Ne speke o word, ne ones loke, But he ne wil it wende and croke, And torne after his own entent. **1545** Ascham *Toxoph.* I. (Arb.) 58 There is no one thinge yat crokes youth more than suche unlefull games. **1607–12** Bacon *Ess.*, *Wisdom* (Arb.) 184 Hee crooketh them to his owne endes. **1646** J. Gregory *Notes & Obs.* (1650) 83 The more part.. crooke the Prophesie to the Patriarch Abraham.

3. *intr.* To have or take a crooked form or direction; to be or become crooked; to bend, curve.

a **1300** *Song of Yesterday* 98 in *E.E.P.* (1862) 135 Me meruayles.. þat god let mony mon croke and elde. **1398** Trevisa *Barth. de P.R.* VI. i. (1495) 187 In olde aege the body bendyth and crokyth. *c* **1510** Barclay *Mirr. Gd. Manners* (1570) B vj, Soone crooketh the same tree that good camoke wilbe. **1579** Fenton *Guicciard.* VIII. (1599) 350 A riuer both large and deepe.. goeth crooking on the left hand. **1661** Lovell *Hist. Anim. & Min.* 106 Their hornes crook backwards to their shoulders. **1876** C. D. Warner *Wint. Nile* 240 Fingers that crook easily.

†**4.** *intr.* To bend the body in sign of reverence or humility; to bow. *Obs.* or *arch.*

c **1320** R. Brunne *Medit.* 149 He stode krokyng [*v.r.* croked] on knees knelyng Afore hys cretures fete syttyng. **1645** Rutherford *Tryal & Tri. Faith* (1845) 312 That the Sinner may halt and crook. **1841–4** Emerson *Ess.*, *Prudence* Wks. (Bohn) I. 100 They will shuffle and crow, crook and hide.

†**5.** *intr.* To turn or bend aside out of the straight course (*lit.* and *fig.*). *Obs.*

c **1380** Wyclif *Wks.* (1880) 230 He schal not croke in-to þe ri3tte side ne in-to þe left side. **1483** Caxton *Gold. Leg.* 87/4 Goyng right without crokyng. **1545** Ascham *Toxoph.* II. (Arb.) 157 It [the snow] flewe not streight, but sometyme it crooked thys waye sometyme that waye. **1607** Topsell *Serpents* (1653) 743 He must not run directly forward, but winde to and fro, crooking like an Indenture.

6. *trans.* In polo, to catch hold of (an opponent's stick) with one's own stick, so as to interfere with his play.

1890 G. J. Younghusband *Polo in India* ii. 21 No player shall crook his adversary's stick unless he is on the same side of the pony as the ball, or immediately behind. **1898** T. B. Drybrough *Polo* xi. 268 'Crooking' means 'interposing' a stick between the ball and an adversary's stick.. so as to 'hook' and arrest it. **1902** *Encycl. Brit.* XXXI. 820/2 They have no off side [in American polo], and it is not permitted to crook the stick of an adversary.

†**crook,** *v.*[2] *Obs.* Forms: 4–7 **crouk(e**, 5 (9 *dial.*) **crowk**, 6–7 **crooke**. [Echoic: cf. croak.

The phonetic relations between *crouke*, *crowke*, 17th c. *crook*, and mod. north dial. *crowk* are not clear.]

1. *intr.* To croak. Rarely *trans.*

a **1325** *E.E. Allit. P.* A. 459 He [the raven] croukez for comfort when carayne he fyndez. *c* **1440** *Promp. Parv.* 105 Crowken, as cranes, *gruo*. Crowken, as todes, or frosshes, *coaxo*. **14..** *Metr. Voc.* in Wr.-Wülcker 623 A lytulle frogge crowkyt. **1607** Walkington *Opt. Glass* 150 They crouke harshly. **1617** Wither *Fidelia*, Fatall Ravens that.. Crooke their black Auguries. **1878** *Cumbrld. Gloss.*, *Crowk*, to croak. 'The guts crowk' when the bowels make a rumbling noise.

2. To coo or crood, as a dove. Cf. crookle.

1586 W. Webbe *Eng. Poetrie* (Arb.) 75 Neither.. thy beloude Doues.. Nor prettie Turtles trim, vvill cease to crooke. **1611** Cotgr., *Geindre*.. to crooe, crooke, or mourne as a doue.

crook-back (ˈkrʊkbæk). [See crook *a.*]

†**1.** A crooked back. *Obs.*

1508 [see crook *a.*]. **1709** Swift *Merlin's Proph.*, *Bosse*, is an old english word for hump-shoulder, or crook-back. **1710** Palmer *Proverbs* 98 The deformity of a squint eye, red hair, or a crook-back.

2. One who has a crooked back; a hunchback.

1494 Fabyan *Chron.* VII. 330 Edmunde, that is of wryters surnamed Crowke backe.. was put by.. for his deformytye. **1577** *St. Aug. Manual* 51 Any lame man, any crooke backe. **1593** Shaks. *3 Hen. VI*, II. ii. 96, I Crooke-back, here I stand to answer thee. **1648** Gage *West. Ind.* xii. (1655) 45 Dwarfes, crook-backs or any monstrous persons.

crook-backed (ˈkrʊkbækt), *a.* [f. prec. + -ed.] Having a crooked back: hunchbacked.

1477 Earl Rivers (Caxton) *Dictes* C ij a, The said ypocras was of littel stature, grete heded, croke backed. **1513** More in Grafton *Chron.* II. 758 Richard the thirde sonne..was..crooke backed, his left shoulder much higher then his right. **1611** BIBLE *Lev.* xxi. 20 Or crooke-backt or a dwarfe. **1826** MILMAN *A. Boleyn, Landing at Tower*, Those poor babes, their crook-back'd uncle murder'd.

'crookdom. [f. CROOK *sb.* 13 + -DOM.] The realm of crooks.

1921 *Glasgow Herald* 23 Apr. 4 The brilliant amateur investigator, whose uncanny intuition and superman brain have paralysed the ranks of 'crookdom'. **1929** *Daily Express* 7 Jan. 9 Story of a careless young athlete's adventures in crookdom.

crooked ('krʊkɪd), *a.* Forms: 3–6 **croked**, 4–6 **-id, -yd,** (4 **kr-**), 5 **cruked,** (**crowkyt**), 6 *Sc.* **crukit,** 7 (*Shaks.*) **crook'd,** 4– **crooked.** [Partly pa. pple. of CROOK *v.*, partly f. CROOK *sb.* + -ED, as in *hunched*, etc.: the formation from the sb. may even have been the earlier.]

1. a. Bent from the straight form; having (one or more) bends or angles; curved, bent, twisted, tortuous, wry. Applied to everything which is not 'straight' (of which *crooked* is now the ordinary opposite).

a **1225** *Ancr. R.* (MS. Cleop.) þe cat of helle..wið crokede crokes. **1382** WYCLIF *Isa.* xxvii. 1 Leuyathan a crokid wounde serpent. **1393** LANGL. *P. Pl.* C. III. 29 Shal neuere ..on croked kene þorne kynde fygys wexe. *a* **1450** *Knt. de la Tour* 23 Al her lyff after she hadd her nose al croked. *c* **1460** *Medulla Gram.* (in *Promp. Parv.* 80), *Cambuca*, a buschoppys cros or a crokid staf. **1534** TINDALE *Luke* iii. 5 Crocked thinges shalbe made streight. **1551** RECORDE *Pathw. Knowl.* I, All other lines, that go not right forth..but boweth any waye..are called Croked lynes. **1591** LYLY *Sappho* II. i, Juniper, the longer it grew, the crookeder it wexed. **1607** SHAKS. *Cor.* II. i. 62 If the drinke..touch my Palat aduersly, I make a crooked face at it. **1642** FULLER *Holy & Prof. St.* II. xvi. 111 Shipwrights and boat makers will choose those crooked pieces of timber. **1717** BERKELEY *Tour in Italy* §27 Streets open..but crooked. **1810** SCOTT *Lady of L.* I. xxiii, That falchion's crooked blade.

b. *crooked stick*: see STICK *sb.*[1] 12.

2. a. Of persons: Having the body or limbs bent out of shape; deformed; bent or bowed with age. Hence *transf.* as an epithet of *age*.

c **1290** *S. Eng. Leg.* I. 34/18 He..maude hole..Meseles and þe crokede. **1377** LANGL. *P. Pl.* B. XI. 186 Ac calleth þe careful þer-to þe croked and þe pore. **1430** LYDG. *Chron. Troy* IV. xxx, In my croked age. *a* **1533** LD. BERNERS *Huon* xxiii. 68 The crokyd dwarfe. **1628** MILTON *Vacation Exerc.* 69 A Sybil old, bow-bent with crooked age. **1718** *Freethinker* No. 92. 258 You would have thought she had been crooked from her Infancy. **1865** DICKENS *Mut. Fr.* II. xv, A pert crooked little chit.

†**b.** of an old decrepit horse. *Obs.*

1470–85 MALORY *Arthur* x. lxxxiv, Whan that knyghte sawe sire palomydes bounden vpon a croked courser. *a* **1533** LD. BERNERS *Gold. Bk. M. Aurel.* (1546) Q, There is not so croked a hors.

3. *fig.* **a.** The reverse of 'straight' in figurative senses (*esp.* with reference to moral character and conduct); deviating from rectitude or uprightness; not straightforward; dishonest, wrong, perverse; perverted, out of order, awry.

a **1225** *Ancr. R.* 102 þe cat of helle..mid clokes of crokede & of kene uondunges. *a* **1340** HAMPOLE *Psalter* xxxi. 14 Krokid of hert ere þa. **1508** FISHER *Wks.* (1876) I. 240 The wyll of some is so croked. **1591** SHAKS. *Two Gent.* IV. i. 22 If crooked fortune had not thwarted me. **1611** BIBLE *Deut.* xxxii. 5 They are a peruerse and crooked generation. **1660** H. MORE *Myst. Godliness* V. xvii. 204 A very crooked Objection both from the Jew and Atheist. **1711** POPE *Temp. Fame* 411 Of crooked counsels and dark politicks. **1749** FIELDING *Tom Jones* VII. xv, This young gentleman, though somewhat crooked in his morals, was perfectly straight in his person. **1875** JOWETT *Plato* (ed. 2) IV. 245 Perfect in the practice of crooked ways.

b. *colloq.* Dishonestly come by; made, obtained, or sold in a way that is not straightforward.

1864 HOTTEN *Slang. Dict.* (ed. 3) 112 *Crooked*, a term used among dog-stealers, and the 'fancy' generally, to denote anything stolen. **1876** *N. Amer. Rev.* CXXIII. 301 Another house testified..that half its entire annual product was 'crooked'. **1891** FARMER *Dict. Amer.*, *Crooked whiskey*, illicitly distilled whiskey upon which no excise has been paid. **1892** R. BOLDREWOOD *Nevermore* I. x. 180 He was riding a crooked horse when he was took. **1898** *Daily News* 27 Aug. 6/6 Telling him that he rather thought he had bought 'a crooked lot'. **1902** *Daily Chron.* 26 Aug. 6/6 In the event of his being found..to be dealing in 'crooked' things, or refusing to give information as to where he got his stuff.

c. *Austral.* and *N.Z. slang.* = CROOK *a.* 2 c; esp. in phr. ***crooked on***, angry at. Usu. pronounced (krʊkt).

1944 L. GLASSOP *We were Rats* I. viii. 48 Ya oughtn' ter feel crooked on things. I s'pose it's because Bertha's outa town? **1957** 'N. CULOTTA' *They're a Weird Mob* (1958) vi. 86 'Are you not ashamed of yourself?' 'Yeah, I'm real crooked on me.'

4. quasi-*adv.* In a crooked course or position; not straight.

1545 ASCHAM *Toxoph.* (R.), If the younge tree growe crooked. **1549** *Compl. Scot.* xix. 159 Sche ȝeid crukit, bakuart, and on syd. **1864** MRS. CARLYLE *Lett.* III. 220 Pictures..which were hung up all crooked.

5. *Comb.*, as **crooked-bill**, a name for the AVOCET; †**crooked-rig** (*rig* = back), crook-back; **b.** parasynthetic, as ***crooked-backed, -clawed, -eyed, -houghed, -legged, -lined, -lipped, crooked-neck(ed)*** (*spec.* applied to a variety of squash: cf. CROOK-NECK; *U.S.*), ***-pated, -shouldered***, etc. adjs.

1382 WYCLIF *Lev.* xxi. 20 If crokid rigge or bleer eyed. *a* **1533** LD. BERNERS *Huon* xxi. 63 He is..crokyd shulderyd. **1600** SHAKS. *A.Y.L.* III. ii. 86 A crooked-pated olde..Ramme. **1691** *Lond. Gaz.* No. 2691/4 A dark brown-bay Mare..crooked Legg'd behind. **1705** BOSMAN *Guinea* 264 Crooked-bills and several sorts of Snipes. **1784** *Massachusetts Spy* 22 Apr. 1/1 Crooked neck squash. **1796–1801** FESSENDEN *Orig. Poems* (1806) 134 Like a nice crook'd neck'd squash on the ground. **1853** HICKIE tr. *Aristoph.* (1887) I. 321 These here crooked-clawed birds. **1865** TROLLOPE *Belton Est.* xiii. 142 Small and crooked-backed. **1871** C. D. WARNER *Summer in Garden* viii. 104 The summer squash..was nearly all leaf and blow, with only a sickly crooked-necked fruit after a mighty fuss.

crookedly ('krʊkɪdlɪ), *adv.* [f. CROOKED + -LY[2].] In a crooked manner (see the adj.).

c **1374** CHAUCER *Anel. & Arc.* 171 She..al crampisshed hir limmes crokedly. **1398** TREVISA *Barth. de P.R.* XVIII. ix. (1495) 760 Some serpentes crepyth and glydyth..crokydly. *c* **1400** *Lanfranc's Cirurg.* 140 þe ȝ ȝen to loke asquynt eiþer crokidliche. **1578** *Chr. Prayers* in *Priv. Prayers* (1851) 437 That we talk not smoothly, and walk crookedly. **1655** DIGGES *Compl. Ambass.* 161 The..Ambassador..used himself very crookedly, perniciously, and maliciously against the State. **1785** *Phil. Trans.* LXXV. 219 A crookedly branching nebula. **1866** MRS. GASKELL *Wives & Dau.* xi, A shawl crookedly put on. **1874** MAHAFFY *Soc. Life Greece* iii. 60 *footn.*, The men who..decide crookedly in the agora and banish justice.

crookedness ('krʊkɪdnɪs). [f. as prec. + -NESS.] The quality or state of being crooked.

1. *lit.* **a.** *generally.*

1398 TREVISA *Barth. de P.R.* XVII. iv. (1495) 605 The fer stretchyth vpryght wythoute ony crokydnesse. **1447** BOKENHAM *Seyntys* (Roxb.) 257 Lyht..rhyt furth procedyth wyth owte crokydnesse. **1677** HALE *Prim. Orig. Man.* I. ii. 55 The apparent crookedness of the Staff in a double medium of Air and Water. **1858** HAWTHORNE *Fr. & It. Jrnls.* (1872) I. 16 This legend may account for any crookedness of the street.

b. Bodily deformity.

1398 TREVISA *Barth. de P.R.* v. xxviii. (1495) 138 The cause of shrynkynge and crokidnes of the honde. **1547** BOORDE *Brev. Health* clxiv. 59 Crokednes or curvytie in the backe or shoulders. **1692** LOCKE *Educ.* Wks. 1812. IX. 14 Narrow breasts..ill lungs, and crookedness, are the..effects of hard boddice and clothes that pinch.

†**c.** *Math.* Curvature. *Obs. rare.*

1651 HOBBES *Leviath.* II. xxvii. 156 All deviation from a strait line is equally crookednesse. **1656** tr. *Hobbes' Elem. Philos.* (1839) 294 The crookedness of the arch of a circle is everywhere uniform.

2. *fig.* Deviation from rectitude; moral obliquity; perversity, etc.: see CROOKED 3.

c **1380** WYCLIF *Serm.* Sel. Wks. I. 273 Sich crokidnesse bringiþ aȝen derknesse of mannis liif. **1576** FLEMING *Panopl. Epist.* 393 The crookednesse of my lucke. **1673** *Lady's Call.* II. i. 59 Youth..easily warps into a crookedness. **1803** WELLINGTON in Gurw. *Desp.* II. 351 There is a crookedness in his policy. **1875** MANNING *Mission H. Ghost* xi. 305 Moral obliquities bring on a crookedness which hinders the faculty of discerning the rectitude of God's truth.

3. (with *pl.*) An instance of crookedness; a crooked or bent part. Also *fig.* A 'crooked' piece of conduct.

1654 WHITLOCK *Zootomia* 496 As Carpenters bring the square to great unweildy crookednesses, that cannot be moved to it. **1766** PENNANT *Zool.* (R.) x, A variety of trout, which is naturally deformed, having a strange crookedness near the tail. **1869** TROLLOPE *He Knew* xxviii. (1878) 159 He lived by the crookednesses of people.

crookedy ('krʊkɪdɪ), *a. rare.* [f. CROOKED *a.* + -Y[1].] Crooked.

1907 F. CAMPBELL *Shepherd of Stars* xv. 170, I call it a very crookedy sort of tune. **1938** M. K. RAWLINGS *Yearling* xvii. 203 I've lost my boy. My pore crookedy boy.

†**'crooken,** *v. Obs.* Also 6 **croken.** [A secondary form of CROOK *v.*: cf. *straighten.*]

1. *trans.* To make crooked; *fig.* to pervert.

1552 HULOET, Croken, or make croked. **1563** *Homilies* II. *Idolatry* II, Saint Augustine..sayth..images be of more force to croken an unhappye soule then to teache and instruct it. **1621** SANDERSON *Serm.* (1681) 25 [They] rather choose to crooken the Rule to their own bent. **1680** BAXTER *Cath. Commun.* (1684) 9 By crookening it to any carnal interest. **1825** C. CROKER *Fairy Leg.* 303 When I got up, my back was crookened. **1828** in *Craven Gloss.*

2. *intr.* To be or become crooked; to bend.

1603 HOLLAND *Plutarch's Mor.* 1201 It bendeth not, it crookeneth not. **1681** CHETHAM *Angler's Vade-m.* i. §1 (1689) To keep them from warping or crookning.

†**'crooken,** *ppl. a. Obs. rare.* [f. prec., after analogy of strong vbs., e.g. *broken.*] Crooked.

1589 *Gold. Mirr.* (1851) 52 Cho ho hath croken bill her maister left astray?

crookery ('krʊkərɪ). [f. CROOK *sb.* 13 + -ERY 2.] The state or condition of being a crook; the dealings or behaviour of crooks; the world of crooks (see CROOK *sb.* 13).

1927 *Observer* 15 May 15/2, I do not call it good 'crookery' when the situation can only be made by turning out the light. **1928** *Daily Express* 22 June 10/3 If a boy came to me and said: 'I have received a call to crookery.' **1949** 'J. TEY' *Brat Farrar* x. 81 A very..intelligent crook. On the highest level of crookery. **1962** 'E. FERRARS' *Busy Body* vi. 67 They probably want to use you as an alibi for Tom while Tom's up to crookery of some sort. **1967** M. STAND *Diana is Dead* vii. 104 'You seem to know a lot about crookery,' the sergeant said.

Crookes (krʊks). The name of Sir William *Crookes* (1832–1919), English scientist, used attrib. or in the possessive to designate phenomena observed and apparatus invented by him. **Crookes** or **Crookes's (dark) space**, the dark space between the negative glow and the cathode of a vacuum tube, observed when the pressure is very low; also called *cathode dark space, cathodic dark space.* **Crookes** or **Crookes's glass**, a type of glass which protects the eyes from intense radiation, bright sunlight, etc. **Crookes** or **Crookes's layer**, (*a*) the layer of vapour underlying any mass or liquid in the spheroidal state, insulating it from the surface on which it rests; (*b*) = *Crookes* (*dark*) *space.* **Crookes** or **Crookes's radiometer**: see RADIOMETER 2. **Crookes rays**, = *cathode rays.* **Crookes's tube**, a highly evacuated tube in which stratified electric discharges can be observed.

1884 A. DANIELL *Princ. Physics* 325 Let us now suppose that the particles recoiling from the heated surface do not meet other molecules, but impinge on the walls of the vessel. A layer of particles in such a condition is called a Crookes' layer. **1885** *Encycl. Brit.* XIX. 249/1 In Crookes's radiometer the free path is very long. **1889** *Cent. Dict.*, *Crookes's tubes.* **1892** G. F. BARKER *Physics* 329 The layer of vapor which has to support the drop is called a Crookes layer. **1893** J. J. THOMSON *Recent Res. Electr. & Magn.* 108 Next to this [*sc.* the negative electrode] there is a comparatively dark region..called sometimes 'Crookes' space' and sometimes the 'first dark space'. **1896** *Daily News* 29 May 5/2 The rays which produce the fluorescence are certainly the Crookes rays. **1902** *Encycl. Brit.* XXVIII. 47/2 The Crookes dark space. **1906** *Amer. Jrnl. Sci.* 4th Ser. XXII. 312 The extremely tenuous condition of the residual elementary gas or gases in a Crookes tube. **1910** *Hawkins's Electr. Dict.*, *Crookes' Effect*, the radiant effect produced in a vacuum glass tube in which the exhaustion has been carried to a high degree, when electricity is discharged through it between suitable electrodes. **1918** J. H. PARSONS *Dis. Eye* (ed. 3) x. 184 Smoked or orange tinted (not blue) glasses..are most efficacious when made with Crookes's glass. **1927** L. B. LOEB *Kinetic Theory of Gases* vii. 241 The Crookes radiometer, so often seen in opticians' windows, consisting of a set of mica vanes blackened on one face and mounted on an axis so that they are free to rotate inside a partially evacuated glass vessel and which rotate when radiation falls on them. **1931** *Glass* Dec. 509/1 Several Crookes glasses were shown. **1958** C. G. WILSON *Electr. & Magn.* xii. 365 At a pressure of 10^{-2} mm. Hg. or less, the Faraday Dark Space and Negative Glow disappear and the Crooke's [*sic*] Dark Space almost fills the tube.

Hence **Crookesian** ('krʊksɪən) *a.*, pertaining to Crookes or to instruments invented by him (*rare*).

1899 *Science Siftings* XVI. 117/2 The Crookesian scale-pan. *Ibid.*, Crookesian radiometer.

crookesite ('krʊksaɪt). *Min.* [ad. Sw. *crookesit* (A. E. Nordenskiöld 1867, in *Öfv. K. Vet.-Akad. Förh. 1866* XXIII. 366), f. CROOKES (the discoverer of thallium): see -ITE[1].] A brittle, lead-grey selenide of copper, thallium, and silver.

1868 J. D. DANA *Syst. Min.* (ed. 5) II. ii. 40 Crookesite... Massive, compact; no trace of crystallization. **1946** J. R. PARTINGTON *Gen. & Inorg. Chem.* xvi. 431 The only minerals rich in thallium are crookesite (17 p.c. Tl, with Se, Cu, Ag) and lorandite.

crooking ('krʊkɪŋ), *vbl. sb.* [f. CROOK *v.*[1] + -ING[1].] The action of the verb CROOK; bending from the straight line; a bend, curve, curvature.

c **1380** WYCLIF *Serm.* Sel. Wks. II. 287 þis crokyng bi litil and litil is now cropen ferre fro Cristis lawe. **1483** *Cath. Angl.* 85 A Crukynge of þe water, *meandir.* **1551** RECORDE *Pathw. Knowl.* II. Introd., In true streightenes without crokinge. **1562** PHAER *Æneid.* ix, The horsmen kest them selfs in crokings knowen of quainted ground. **1607** TOPSELL *Four-f. Beasts* (1673) 48 Rivers..[that] by their crooking and winding..imitate the fashion of a horn.

'crooking, *ppl. a.* That crooks or bends.

1382 WYCLIF *Job* xxvi. 13 The eche side krokende edder. **1607** TOPSELL *Four-f. Beasts* (1673) 327 A deep, hollow, crooking ulcer.

crookish ('krʊkɪʃ), *a.* [f. CROOK *sb.* 13 + -ISH[1] 2.] Pertaining to or characteristic of a crook (CROOK *sb.* 13) or crooked behaviour, dealings, etc.

1927 *Spectator* 17 Dec. 1083 At the Royalty, *The Crooked Billet*—terrifyingly, confusingly crookish, with a throat-cutting scene against which I warn nervous parents. **1934** E. BOWEN *Cat Jumps* 89 Marianne's coupé had been run up on to the rough grass..with its lights out. Its air was lurking and crookish. **1937** —— *Coll. Impressions* (1950) 117 *The Alchemist*, with its crookish hilarity.

†**'crookle,** *v.*[1] *Obs. rare.* [dim. of CROOK *v.*[1]: cf. *crinkle.*] *intr.* To crook or bend in a curve.

1577 B. GOOGE *Heresbach's Husb.* III. (1586) 138 The hornes must rather crookle inward, then growe straight up.

†**'crookle,** *v.*[2] *Obs. rare.* [dim. of CROOK *v.*[2]] *intr.* To coo as a pigeon.

1580 BARET *Alv.* C 1673 To Crookle like a doue, or pigeon. **1617** MINSHEU *Ductor*, To *Crookle* like a pigeon, [Fr.] *gemir.* **1706** PHILLIPS (ed. Kersey), *Croo* or *Crookel*, to make a Noise like a Dove, or Pigeon.

crookless ('krʊklɪs), *a.* Without a crook.
1849 ROCK *Ch. of Fathers* II. vi. 199 This bordon or crookless staff.

'crook-neck. *U.S.* [CROOK *sb.* C.] A name given to varieties of squash (*Cucurbita maxima*) having the neck or narrow basal part recurved.
1848 LOWELL *Biglow P.* Poems 1890 II. 10 Agin' the chimbly crooknecks hung. **1860** EMERSON *Cond. Life, Wealth* (1861) 66 The cantelopes, crook-necks, and cucumbers.

crook-necked, *a.* Having a crooked neck; spec. *U.S.*, applied to a variety of squash (cf. CROOK-NECK and CROOKED *a.* 5 b).
a **1529** SKELTON *El. Rummyng* 427 Croke necked like an owl. **1818** *Massachusetts Spy* 11 Nov. (Th.), Upwards of ten tons of the best crook-necked winter Squashes. **1945** *New Eng. Homestead* 27 Oct. 3/2 They are..the size of a summer crooknecked squash.

crool (kru:l), *v. rare.* [app. an onomatopœic formation, associated initially with the imitative group, *croo, crood, croodle, crook, crookle, croak*, and perhaps with *croon*, with echoic fashioning of the latter part.] *intr.* To make an inarticulate sound more liquid and prolonged than a croak.
1580 BARET *Alv.* C 1672 To Croole, mutter, or speake softe to ones selfe: to rumble. **1617** MINSHEU *Ductor*, To *Croole*, mutter, or speake softly to himselfe. **1851** S. JUDD *Margaret* xiv. (1871) 102 Frogs..crooled, chubbed, and croaked. **1892** *Sunday Mag.* June 425/1 Baby is lying in mother's lap, crooling and gurgling.

crool (kru:l), *sb. rare.* [f. the vb.] The sound described under CROOL *v.*; = COOING *vbl. sb.* 1.
1938 W. DE LA MARE *Memory* 71 The monotonous crool of a dove.

croompled, obs. form of CRUMPLED.

croon (kru:n), *v.* Chiefly *Sc.* Forms: 5-9 *Sc.* croyn, (5-7 croyne, 9 croin), 6 *Sc.* cruin, 6-9 crune, 8- croon. [Originally only northern, chiefly Sc. (krøn, krʏn), whence in 19th c. Eng. mainly since Burns. It corresponds to Du. *kreunen* to groan, whimper, MDu. *krônen* to lament, mourn loudly, groan, MLG. *kronen* to growl, grumble, scold, EFris. *krōnen* to cause to weep; cf. also OHG. *chrônnan*(:—*njan*), *chrônan*, MLG. *kroenen* to chatter, prattle, babble, and *chrôn, crôn* adj. talkative, chattering, noisy. There is no trace of the word in OE., and it appears to be one of the LG. words that came into Sc. early in the ME. period: its form is that of a word in ME *ō̄*. (In *Towneley Myst.*, as in MSc., *oy* = *ō̄*.)]

1. *intr.* To utter a continued, loud, deep sound; to bellow as a bull, to roar, low; to boom as a bell. *Sc.* or *north. dial.*
1513 DOUGLAS *Æneis* VI. iv. 40 The ground begouth to rummys, croyn, and ring, Vndir thair feit [*sub pedibus mugire solum*]. **1588** [see CROONING *ppl. a.*]. **1611** COTGR. s.v. *Reer*, In tearmes of hunting we say, that the red Deere bells, and the fallow troytes or croynes. **1674-91** RAY *N.C. Words* 140 To Crune, *mugire*. **1787** BURNS *Holy Fair* xxvi, Now Clinkumbell, wi' rattlin tow, Begins to jow an' croon. **1813** HOGG *Queen's Wake* ii. Wks. (1876) 35 Even the dull cattle crooned and gazed. **1828** SOUTHEY *Brough Bells* Poems VI. 227 That lordly Bull of mine..How loudly to the hills he crunes, That crune to him again.

2. a. To utter a low murmuring sound; to sing (or speak) in a low murmuring tone; to hum softly. *spec.* to sing popular sentimental songs in a low, smooth voice, esp. into a closely-held microphone (see quot. 1959 s.v. *crooning* below).
(The earlier quots. may have been ironical or humorous uses of sense 1.)
c **1460** *Towneley Myst.* 116 *Primus P.* For to syng..I can. *Sec. P.* Let se how ye croyne. Can ye bark at the mone? **1578** *Gude & Godlie Ballates* (1868) 179 The Sisters gray befoir this day, Did crune within thair cloister. *a* **1818** MACNEIL *Poems* (1844) 56 Whan, crooning quietly by himsel', He framed the lay. **1832** MOTHERWELL *Jeanie Morrison* vii, To wander by this green burnside, And hear its waters croon. **1877** A. B. EDWARDS *Up Nile* xix. 571, I hear a mother crooning to her baby. **1920** *Catal. Victor Records*, Standard Songs. 'Croon, Croon, Underneat' de Moon' (Clutsam). **1931** H. ARLEN (title of song in the musical production *You Said It*) Learn to croon. **1933** *Punch* 2 Aug. 122/1 Bing Crosby the crooner..croons to his feminine class and is crooned to in reply. **1940** *War Illustr.* 5 Jan. p. ii/2, I used to sup while Roy Fox's 'boys' played joyously with Les Allen 'crooning'.

b. To make murmuring lament or moan. *Sc.* or *north. dial.*
1823 GALT *Entail* I. ii. 11 Frae the time o' the sore news, she croynt awa, and her life gied out like the snuff o' a can'le. **1830** —— *Lawrie T.* I. ii. 6 Croining and dwining, peaking and pining, at the fire-side. **1880** *Antrim & Down Gloss.*, *Croon*, to lament, wail.

3. *trans.* To sing (a song, tune, etc.) in a low murmuring undertone; to hum. *spec.* to sing (a song, etc.) in a low, smooth voice (cf. CROOL *sb.*).
1790 BURNS *Tam O' Shanter* 84 Whiles crooning o'er some auld Scots sonnet. **1848** DICKENS *Dombey* (C.D. ed.) 60 Paul sometimes crooning out a feeble accompaniment. **1872** HOLLAND *Marb. Proph.* 60 Over the cradle the mother hung Softly crooning a slumber song. **1915** C. LEAN (title of song in the musical production *The Blue Paradise*) The tune they croon in the U.S.A. **1925** H. D. KERR (*title of song*) Croon a little lullaby. **1931** DURANTE & KEFOED *Night Clubs* 227 His band stressed the soft notes, and Rudy [Vallée] crooned his way right into the heart of the nation. **1932** *Amer. Speech* VII. 250 Bing Crosby plaintively croons that he has 'Found a Million Dollar Baby in the Five and Ten Cent Store'. **1933** *Fortune* Aug. 47/2 Their use of 'jazz' includes both Duke Ellington's Afric brass and Rudy Vallée crooning *I'm a Dreamer, Aren't We All?*

Hence **'crooning** *vbl. sb.* and *ppl. a.*
1588 A. HUME *Hymns, Triumph of the Lord* 234 (Bannatyne Club) 41 Be cruining Bulls of heigh and haughtie minde. **1828** SOUTHEY *Brough Bells*, That cruning of the kine. **1859** GEO. ELIOT *A. Bede* xviii, The cocks and hens..made only crooning subdued noises. **1872** BLACK *Adv. Phaeton* xix. 270 As soft and musical as the crooning of a wood-pigeon. **1923** B. JAMES (*title of song*) Carolina Mammy. A real Southern mammy song—the crooning kind. **1927** *Melody Maker* Aug. 784/3 'Muddy Water' has a feature in a sweet crooning vocal introduction. **1929** *Ibid.* Dec. 1139/3 His crooning style of singing. **1931** *Musical Courier* (N.Y.) in *Oxf. Compan. Mus.* (1938) 1018/2 No jazz or cheap crooning stuff had a place in her repertoire. **1932** *Literary Digest* 30 Jan. 23/2 'You can't help thinking badly of any man who would degrade himself whining in that way ..' he said of crooning. **1935** WODEHOUSE *Blandings Castle* v. 116 Everybody knows what Crooning Tenors are... They sit at the piano and gaze into a girl's eyes and sing in a voice that sounds like gas escaping from a pipe about Love and the Moonlight and You. **1959** *Chambers's Encycl.* XII. 570/2 In that type of vocal performance known as 'crooning' the lower range of the voice is chiefly used, and that more in the manner of conversation than of singing, though falsetto notes are often introduced. There is a noticeable gliding or sliding from one pitch to another and the intonation is often deliberately indefinite... Characteristic also is a certain oscillation or catch in the voice as it comes to rest momentarily upon a sustained sound.

croon (kru:n), *sb.* Chiefly *Sc.* Also 6 crone, 8-9 crune. [f. CROON *v.*]

1. A loud, deep sound, such as the bellow of a bull or the boom of a large bell. *Sc.* or *north. dial.*
1513 DOUGLAS *Æneis* XII. xii. 56 Lyke as twa bustuus bullis..Ruschand togiddir with cronys and feirfull granis. **1785** BURNS *Halloween* xxvi, The Deil, or else an outler Quey, Gat up an' gae a croon. **1813** HOGG *Queen's Wake* 204 The bittern mounts the morning air, And rings the sky with quavering croon. **1858** M. PORTEOUS *Souter Johnny* 14 The bell's last croon.

2. A low murmuring or humming sound, as of a tune hummed in an undertone.
1725 RAMSAY *Gentle Sheph.* II. ii, She [a witch] can o'ercast the night, and cloud the moon, And mak the deils obedient to her crune. **1837** R. NICOLL *Poems* (1843) 82 The cushat's croon. **1865** KINGSLEY *Herew.* xii, She thought over the old hag's croon.

crooner ('kru:nə(r)). [f. CROON *v.* + -ER.]
a. One who croons. In *Sc.* a name for a fish, the Grey Gurnard (*Trigla gurnardus*), from the noise it makes when landed.
1808 in JAMIESON. **1838** *Proc. Berw. Nat. Club* I. 170 *Trigla gurnardus*..the Gurnett or Crooner. **1884** G. H. BOUGHTON in *Harper's Mag.* Dec. 73/1 We..discovered each other—the crooner and I.

b. *spec.* A singer who croons (see CROON *v.* 2 a).
1930 *Vanity Fair* July 57 Just call them Crooners. **1932** THORNE SMITH *Bishop's Jaegers* (1934) 314 That sound..is made nightly by one of the nation's most popular crooners. **1933** [see CROON *v.* 2 a]. **1948** *Penguin Music Mag.* Feb. 25 The B.B.C. could start the campaign by refusing to make 'stars' of its crooners. **1954** *Granta* 6 Nov. 23/1 Dickie Valentine turns out, from his old cuttings, to be a crooner, as I had suspected.

crooningly ('kru:nɪŋlɪ), *adv.* [f. CROONING *ppl. a.* + -LY[2].] In a crooning manner.
1902 *Munsey's Mag.* Apr. 42 'Ah, no, ah, no,' she said crooningly, as if she comforted the child. **1928** D. L. SAYERS *Unpleasantness at Bellona Club* iii. 31 A melody of Parry's formed itself crooningly under his fingers.

croop(e, var. of CROUP.

crooper, obs. form of CRUPPER.

croos, var. of CROSE *Obs.*, crosier.

†croose, *v. Obs.* Also 6 crowse. [? a. OF. *croussir, crusir*: see CRUSH.] To crush.
1567 DRANT *Horace Epist.* II. i. F viij, He that did crowse and culpon once Hydra of hellish spyte [Lat. *diram qui contudit hydram*]. **1611** COTGR., *Esmarmeler*, to crush, croose, or burst in peeces. **1674** N. FAIRFAX *Bulk & Selv.* 130 They can't strike sail, or notch the wheels, and croose the springs, at work within them, in a trice.

croose, -ly, var. of CROUSE, -LY.

croosie, var. of CRUISIE *Sc.*

†croot[1]. *Obs. rare.* [In first quot. perhaps the same word as Sc. *croot, cruit* (krʏt) the smallest pig in a litter, a diminutive child or person, and north. dial. *crut* dwarf. Cf. also Welsh *crwt* boy, lad, chap, little fellow.] (See quots.)
1614 T. FREEMAN *Rubbe & Great Cast* xliv. C iv, Caspia, the decrepit old rich Croot [*rime* boot]. **1808-25** JAMIESON, *Croot*, a puny feeble child; the smallest pig in a litter, etc. **1825** BROCKETT *Gloss. N.C. Wds.*, *Crut*, a dwarf, or anything curbed in its growth. **1883** *Huddersfield Gloss.*, *Crut*..in some parts means a dwarf.

†croot[2]. *Mining. Obs.* [? F. *croûte* crust.] 'A substance found about the ore in the lead mines at Mendip, being a mealy, white, soft stone, matted with ore' (Chambers *Cycl.* Suppl.).
1668 *Phil. Trans.* III. 770 There is Sparr and Caulk about the Ore; and another substance, which they call the Crootes which is a mealy white stone, marted with Ore and soft. *Ibid.* It terminates in a dead Earth Clayie, without Croot or Sparr. **1759** B. MARTIN *Nat. Hist. Eng.* I. 67.

croot, var. of CROUT *v.*

crootche, obs. form of CROUCH.

†croote. *Obs.* = CRITON.
1382 WYCLIF *Ps.* ci. 4 My bones as croote han dried.

crop (krɒp), *sb.* Forms: 1- crop; also 1-6 cropp, 3-7 croppe, 4-7 crope, (5 crowpe, croupe, in sense 1), 7-9 *Sc.* and *dial.* crap. [OE. *crop(p* = OLG. **crop(p*, MDu. *crop(p*, MLG., LG. and Du. *krop*, OHG. *chropf*, MHG., Ger. *kropf*, 'swelling in the neck, wen, craw of a bird', in ON. *kroppr* hump or bunch on the body, Sw. *kropp* the body, Da *krop* swelling under the throat. These various applications indicate a primitive sense of 'swollen protuberance or excrescence, bunch'. The word has passed from German into Romanic as F. *croupe*, and It. *groppo*, F. *groupe*: see CROUP, GROUP. OE. had only sense 1, 'craw of a bird', and 3, 'rounded head or top of a herb'; the latter is found also in High German dialects (Grimm, *Kropf* 4 *c*); the further developments of 'head or top' generally, and of 'produce of the field, etc.', appear to be exclusively English. The senses under IV are new formations from the verb, and might be treated as a distinct word.]

I. A round protuberance or swelling, the craw.

1. a. A pouch-like enlargement of the œsophagus or gullet in many birds, in which the food undergoes a partial preparation for digestion before passing on to the true stomach; the craw.
c **1000** ÆLFRIC *Lev.* i. 16 Wurp þone cropp & þa federa wiðæftan þæt weofod. **1398** TREVISA *Barth de P.R.* v. xliv. (1495) 161 The mete of fowles is kepte in the croppe as it were in a propre spence. **14..** WYCLIF (MS.S.) *Lev.* i. 16 The litil bladdir of the throte or the cropp. *c* **1440** *Promp. Parv.* 101/1 Crawe, or crowpe of a byrde. **1486** *Bk. St. Albans* C vij b, Hawkys that haue payne in theyr croupes. **1555** EDEN *Decades* 16 He commaunded the croppe to bee opened of suche as were newely kylled. **1607** TOPSELL *Serpents* (1653) 740 They have a crap on the belly from the chin to the breast, like the crap of a Bird. **1780** COWPER *Nightingale & Glowworm* 12 Stooping down..He thought to put him in his crop. **1870** ROLLESTON *Anim. Life* Introd. 52 The oesophagus..often expands into a crop.

b. An analogous organ in other animals.
1836 TODD *Cycl. Anat.* I. 535/1 In the *Nautilus* it [the gullet] is dilated into a pyriform crop. **1881** DARWIN *Earthworms* i. 17 In most of the species, the œsophagus is enlarged into a crop in front of the gizzard.

†c. The dewlap of an ox; a wen in the neck.
1591 HORSEY *Trav.* (Hakluyt Soc.) 220 A goodly fare white bull..his crop or gorg hanging down to his knees before him. **1599** A. M. tr. *Gabelhouer's Bk. Physicke* 89/2 When anye man hath a croppe growinge on him..applye it on the Croppe, and it helpeth.

2. *transf.* and *fig.* The stomach or maw; also the throat. Now *Sc.* and *dial.* Cf. GIZZARD.
c **1325** *Pol. Songs* (Camden) 238 The knave crommeth is crop Er the cok crawe. *a* **1400** *Cov. Myst.* xxiii. (Shaks. Soc.) 217 I xal this daggare putt in his croppe. *a* **1575** *Wife lapped* 88 in Hazl. *E.P.P.* IV. 184 Which sore would sticke then in thy crop. **1737** RAMSAY *Sc. Prov.* (1776) 31 (Jam.) He has a crap for a' corn. **1808-25** JAMIESON s.v., *That'll craw in your crap*, that will be recollected to your discredit, it will be matter of reproach to you. **1876** *Mid-Yorksh. Gloss.*, *Crop*, applied to the throat, or locality of the windpipe. One who manifests hoarseness is alluded to as having a 'reasty crop'.

II. The (rounded) head; the top part.

†3. a. The 'head' of a herb, flower, etc., *esp.* as gathered for culinary or medicinal purposes; a cyme; an ear of corn, a young sprout, etc. *Obs.*
a **700** *Epinal Gloss.* 60 *Acitelum*, hramsa crop. *c* **950** *Lindisf. Gosp.* Luke vi. 1 Ðegnas his ða croppas eton. *c* **1000** ÆLFRIC *Gloss.* in Wr.-Wülcker 135, *Tursus, cimia*, crop. *Ibid.* 149 *Cima*, crop. *c* **1350** in *Archæol.* XXX. 356 Take sanycle and yᵉ crop of brembelys..Yᵉ crop of yᵉ reednettyle. **1536** BELLENDEN *Cron. Scot.* (1821) I. p. xlii, Mure cokis and hennis, quhilk etis nocht bot seid, or croppis of hadder. **1601** HOLLAND *Pliny* II. 97 When the Nettle is young..they vse to eat the crops therof for a pleasant kind of meat. **1686** W. HARRIS tr. *Lemery's Chym.* (ed. 3) 572 Take two pounds of Rosemary Flowers, the Leaves of Rosemary, the crops of Thyme, Savory, Lavender, etc. **1785** BURNS *Earnest Cry* xxxi, Whare ye sit, on craps o' heather.

b. *Arch.* A bunch of foliage terminating a pinnacle, etc.; a finial.
1478 BOTONER *Itin.* (Nasmith 1778) 282 A le gargayle usque le crope qui finit le stone-work. **1846** *Ecclesiologist* V. 214 The 'crop' is a bunch of foliage surmounting a crocketed canopy, and resulting from the concurrence of the two topmost crockets. **1848** B. WEBB *Cont. Eccles.* 60 With crockets and a crop above a two-light window.

†4. The 'head' or top of a tree. Sometimes (with *pl.*), A topmost branch. *Obs.*
a **1300** *Signs bef. Judgem.* in *E.E.P.* (1862) 10 þe sefþe dai hit [the tree] sal grow aȝe har crop adun har rote an hei. **1387** TREVISA *Higden* (Rolls) I. 81 In Inde a crop of a figge tree is so huge..þat meny companyes of men may sitte at þe mete

wel i-now þere vnder. **1399** *Pol. Poems* (Rolls) I. 365 Hewe hit downe crop and rote. *c* **1440** *Gesta Rom.* lxv. 186 (Add. MS.) He sawe the Ape..in the croppe of a tree. **1549** *Compl. Scot.* xiv. 121 Tha band his tua armis vitht cordis to the crops of ane of the treis. **1558** PHAER *Æneid.* VI. P iv b, So from the tree the golden braunche did shewe..Æneas..caught a crop with much ado.

5. *fig.*, esp. in phr. ***crop and root***, implying the completeness or thoroughness of anything: cf. 'root and branch'. Now *Sc.*

a **1310** in Wright *Lyric P.* xxxvi. 100 Fals y wes in crop ant rote. *c* **1374** CHAUCER *Troylus* v. 25 She that was sothfaste crop and moore Of al his lust or ioyes here-to-fore. **1393** LANGL. *P. Pl.* C. XXIII. 53 Antecrist cam þenne and al þe crop of treuthe Turned tyte vp-so-doun. *c* **1460** *Towneley Myst.* 96 Haylle, David sede! Of oure crede thou art crop. **1513** DOUGLAS *Æneis* XII. x. 116 Baith crop, and ruyte, and heyd of sik myscheif. *a* **1670** SPALDING *Troub. Chas. I* (1792) I. 100 (Jam.) To..sweep off the bishops of both kingdoms crop and root. **1768** ROSS *Helenore* 30 (Jam.), I tauld you crap and root, Fan I came here.

6. *gen.* The top of anything material. *Sc.*

1513 DOUGLAS *Æneis* I. iii. 91 Our slidand lychtlie the croppis of the wallis [= waves]. **1808–25** JAMIESON s.v. *Crap*, *The crap of the earth*, the surface of the ground..*The crap of the wa'*, the highest part of it in the inner side of a house. The cones of firs are called *fir-craps*. **1834** H. MILLER *Scenes & Leg.* xviii. 270 A grip that would spin the bluid out ot the craps o' a child's fingers. **1868** G. MACDONALD *R. Falconer* I. 271 She proceeded..to search for them in the crap o' the wa', that is, on the top of the wall where the rafters rest.

7. *spec.* **a.** 'The top or uppermost section of a fishing-rod' (Jamieson). Now *Sc.*

a **1450** *Fysshynge wyth an Angle* (1883) 8 Set your crop an honful withyn þe ovir ende of ȝowr stafe. Than arme ȝowr crop at þe ovir ende..with a lyn of vi herys. **1496** *Bk. St. Albans* H v, But kepe hym ever under the rodde..soo that your lyne may susteyne and beere his lepys and his plungys with the helpe of your cropp and of your honde. **1808–25** JAMIESON s.v., The crap of a fishing-wand.

b. The upper part of a whip; hence the whole stock or handle of a whip.

1562 BULLEYN *Def. agst. Sickness, Sicke Men* (1579) 8 b, A long whipstocke with croppe and laniarde. **1706** PHILLIPS (ed. Kersey), *Crop*..the Handle of a Coach-man's Whip. **1781** P. BECKFORD *Hunting* (1802) 42 The whips I use are coach-whips, three feet long, the thong half the length of the crop. **1846** EGERTON-WARBURTON *Hunting Songs*, '*Tantivy Trot*', Here's to the music in three feet of tin, Here's to the tapering crop, Sir. **1856** LEVER *Martins of Cro' M.* 33 He admonished the wheeler with the 'crop' of his whip.

c. *esp.* A short straight whipstock with a handle and a short leather loop in place of the lash, used in the hunting field; more fully *hunting-crop*.

1857 CAPT. LAWRENCE *Guy Livingstone* iv. 30 Hunting-crops and heavy cutting-whips. **1887** SIR R. H. ROBERTS *In the Shires* i. 13 His crop had fallen out of his hands.

III. The produce of the field, etc. [from 3].

8. a. The annual produce of plants cultivated or preserved for food, *esp.* that of the cereals; the produce of the land, either while growing or when gathered; harvest.

[*c* **1213** in Madox *Form. Anglic.* ccxxii, Donec inde duos croppos perceperint.] *a* **1300** *Cursor M.* 3103 (Cott.) O corn, o crop, aght and catell [*Trin.* Of crop of corn & oþere catel] To godd his tend þar gafe he lele. *c* **1450** *St. Cuthbert* (Surtees) 8280 þare he gaue all stayndrope With purtenance, wode and croppe. **1546** *Supplic. of Poore Commons* 71 No man myght..gleane his grounde after he had gathered of his croppe. **1596** BP. W. BARLOW *Three Serm.* i. 28 Bewitch not by any Charme any other man's Crop. *a* **1656** BP. HALL *Rem. Wks.* (1660) 121 The Husbandman looks not for a crop in the wild desart. **1818** CRUISE *Digest* (ed. 2) II. 109 He was not even entitled to reap the crop, as other tenants at will were.

b. ***in, under, out of crop***: i.e. the condition of bearing crops; tillage, cultivation.

1791 *Statist. Acc. Dumfr.* I. 181 (Jam. s.v. *Croft-land*) A few acres of what is called croft-land, which was never out of crop. **1806** *Gazetteer Scot.* (ed. 2) 58 The surface is in general level, and about three-fourths are under crop. **1892** *Times* (Weekly Ed.) 16 Dec. 8/1 Including 75,833 acres in crop and grass.

9. a. With qualification or contextual specification: The yield or produce of some particular cereal or other plant in a single season or in a particular locality. ***the crops***: the whole of the plants which engage the agricultural industry of a particular district or season.

black crop: a crop of beans or peas, as opposed to one of corn. ***green crop***: a crop cut in its green state for fodder; also, a crop which does not turn white in ripening, as roots, potatoes, etc. ***white crop***: a crop which whitens in ripening; a corn or grain crop.

[**1322** *Literæ Cantuar.* (Rolls) I. 82 Cum cropa frumenti..cropa vescarum..et cropa avenarum.] *c* **1440** *Promp. Parv.* 104 Croppe of corne yn a yere (ȝere K.), *annona.* **1530** PALSGR. 211/1 Croppe of corne, *leuee de terre.* **1611** CORYAT *Crudities* 124 They turned in their stubble to sow another croppe of wheate in the same place. **1789** MRS. PIOZZI *Journ. France* I. 8 No crops are yet got in. **1807** VANCOUVER *Agric. Devon* (1813) 156 The common course of crops through this district may be stated—as, wheat, barley, oats, clover with hievre, first year mown. **1816** KEATINGE *Trav.* (1817) II. 182 The ground..is only sown with a white crop one year, and the next with a green one to cut for fresh fodder, as lucerne, sanfoin, trefoil or clover. **1849** HELPS *Friends in C.* II. 91 Many a long talk about the crops and the weather. **1852** MRS. STOWE *Uncle Tom* xxxvi, You'll lose your bet on the cotton-crop.

b. The annual or season's yield of any natural product.

a **1825** FORBY *Voc. E. Anglia*, *Crop*, annual produce, as well animal as vegetable. We talk of crops of lambs, turkeys, geese, etc. **1879** *Lumberman's Gaz.* 15 Oct., Cutting their next season's crop of logs. **1884** *Cassell's Fam. Mag.* Feb. 188/1 The total annual ice-crop of the States is twenty million tons.

10. The entire skin or hide of an animal tanned. Also short for *crop-hide*, *crop-leather*: see 22. (Cf. *englische kröpfe* and *kropfen* in Grimm 2395, 2400.)

1457 *Bury Wills* (Camden) 13 Togam meam penulatam cum croppes de grey [? badger skins]. **1486** *Will of Marsh* (Somerset Ho.), Togam..furratam cum croppys. **1856** R. GARDINER *Handbk. Foot* 50 The soles should be of the best English crop or dintle. **1858** SIMMONDS *Dict. Trade*, *Crop*..in the leather trade, the commercial name for an entire hide.

11. *transf.* and *fig.* That which grows out of or is produced by any action; the 'fruit'; a supply produced or appearing.

c **1575** FULKE *Confut. Doct. Purg.* (1577) 424 The latter end of this chapter hath one croppe of his olde custome. **1587** *Mirr. Mag.*, *Malin* v, Insteade of rule hee reapes the crop of thrall. **1590** SPENSER *F.Q.* I. iv. 47 When..I..hop'd to reape the crop of all my care. **1680** OTWAY *Hist. Caius Marius* Prol., From the Crop of his luxuriant Pen. **1799** *Med. Jrnl.* II. 135 This morning there is a plentiful crop [of pustules] on every part of her body. **1830** CUNNINGHAM *Brit. Paint.* I. 322 The annual academical crop of beardless youths. **1862** GOULBURN *Pers. Relig.* IV. x. (1873) 335 [This] has given rise to a crop of petty discussions.

12. *Tin-mining.* The best quality of tin-ore obtained after dressing; more fully ***crop-ore***, ***-tin***.

1778 W. PRICE *Min. Cornub.* 218 The crop and leavings of Tin. The first is the prime Tin. *Ibid.* 319 The finest black Tin is called the Crop. **1884** ERICHSEN *Surgery* (1888) 348 Two pits are formed; in the one nearest the mill the purer and heavier part of the ore, or crop, is deposited.

IV. [f. CROP *v.*] The act of cropping or its result.

13. The cropping or cutting of the hair short; a style of wearing the hair cut conspicuously short; a closely cropped head of hair.

1795 WOLCOTT (P. Pindar) *Hair Powder* Wks. 1812 III. 289 His Curling-irons breaks and snaps his Combs..For dead is Custom 'mid the world of crops. **1844** DICKENS *Mart. Chuz.* ii, She wore it [her hair] in a crop, a loosely flowing crop. **1853** County crop [see COUNTY[1] 8 b]. **1856** J. W. COLE *Mem. Brit. Gen. Penins. War* I. i. 38 Giving up the time-honoured powder and queue, and wearing a crop. **1878** *Punch* I. 21 Newgate crop.

14. A mark made by cropping the ears of animals; an ear-mark.

1675 *Lond. Gaz.* No. 1007/4, 39 fat sheep..cropped in both ears; but the farther ear is a hollow crop. **1887** *Scribn. Mag.* II. 508/2 *Crop*, an ear-mark.

†**15.** A crop-eared animal; a person who wears his hair cropped. (In quot. 1811 = CROPPY[2]).

1689 *Lond. Gaz.* No. 2422/4 And also a sorrel Crop. *a* **1700** B. E. *Dict. Cant. Crew*, *Crop*, one with very short Hair; also a Horse whose Ears are cut. *Ibid.*, *Prickear'd Fellow*, a Crop, whose Ears are longer than his Hair. **1811** E. LYSAGHT *Poems* 97 'That's true' says the Sheriff, 'for plenty of crops Already I've seen on the pavement.'

16. a. A piece cropped or cut off from the end.

1874 J. A. PHILLIPS *Elem. Metal.* (1887) 367 The rails are sawn to the proper length, giving a short piece or crop from either end. **1890** *Nature* 2 Oct. 555 Steel rails occasionally fail at the ends owing to insufficient 'crop' being cut off the rolled rail.

b. Applied to certain cuts of meat.

a **1825** FORBY *Voc. E. Anglia*, *Crop*..a joint of pork, commonly called the spare-rib. **1868** C. J. ATKINSON *Cleveland Gloss.*, *Crop*, a joint cut from the ribs of an Ox, and with the bones shortened. **1880** WEBSTER *Supp.*, *Crop*, the region above the shoulder in the ox.

17. The noise made by an animal in cropping grass, etc. (Cf. CRUMP.)

1851 MAYNE REID *Scalp Hunt.* iv. 29 The 'crop, crop' of our horses shortening the crisp grass.

18. *Min.* and *Geol.* † **a.** The cropping up or out of a stratum, vein, etc. *Obs.* **b.** An outcrop.

1679 [see CROP *v.* 10]. **1719** STRACHEY in *Phil. Trans.* XXX. 968 For Discovery of Coal, they first search for the Crop, which..sometimes appears to the Day, as they term it. **1789** J. WILLIAMS *Nat. Hist. Min. Kingd.* (1810) I. 116, I have traced the crops or outward extremities of these coals. **1879** DIXON *Windsor* I. ii. 11 A crop of rock, starting from a crest of rock.

19. (See quot.)

1858 SIMMONDS *Dict. Trade*, *Crop*..a fixed weight in different localities for sugar, tobacco, and other staples..the usual recognized weight of a crop-hogshead of tobacco is from 1000 to 1300 lbs. nett.

20. ***neck and crop***: see NECK.

V. *attrib.* and *Comb.*

†**21.** *attrib.* Having the ears, hair, etc. cropped.

1663 PEPYS *Diary* 1 May, Galloping upon a little crop black nag. **1785** SARAH FIELDING *Ophelia* II. i, I had rather have..my crop horse. **1825** LOCKHART *Let.* 24 Aug. in *Life Scott*, They have crop heads, shaggy, rough, bushy.

22. *Comb.*, as (sense 1) ***crop-like***, ***-shaped*** adjs.; (senses 8–9) ***crop-farming***, ***-land***; ***crop-producing*** adj.: parasynthetic, as ***crop-headed***, ***-haired***, ***-nosed***, ***-tailed***; **crop-bound** *a.*, (of birds) unable to pass food through the crop; †**crop-doublet**, a short doublet; **crop-duster**, an aircraft used for sprinkling insecticide, fertilizer, etc., on crops; a person who flies such a aircraft; **crop-dusting** (see DUSTING *vbl. sb.* 1 b); **crop-end**, a piece of metal cut off a bar of rolled iron or steel to remove imperfections and to reduce the bar to standard length; **crop-head**, a crop-end cut from that end of a bar of iron or steel which is at the top during the process of cooling and where most of the imperfections occur; **crop-hide**, a hide, *esp.* a cow- or ox-hide, tanned whole and untrimmed; **crop-leather** (see quot.); **crop-mark** *Archæol.* (see quot. 1956); also *attrib.*; so ***crop-marking***; **crop movement** (see MOVEMENT *sb.* 8); **crop-ore** (see 12); **crop-over**, in the West Indies, the end of the sugar-cane harvest on a plantation, and the accompanying celebrations; **crop-plant**, a plant cultivated for food; †**crop-side**, the outcrop of a stratum on a slope; **crop-sole**, sole leather obtained from crop-hides; **crop-spraying**, the spraying of crops with insecticide or the like; also *attrib.* or *ppl. a.*; **crop-tin** (see 12); **crop-wall** (*Sc.*), the crop of the wall (cf. 6); †**crop-weed**, the knapweed, *Centaurea nigra*; **crop-wood** (*dial.*), the branches lopped off a felled tree. Also CROP-EAR, -EARED, -SICK.

1854 *Poultry Chron.* I. 136 '*Crop-bound' fowls. **1897** *Daily News* 29 Dec. 7/2 The bird..had become crop-bound, and in order to remove the obstruction an incision five inches long was made in the crop. **1640** SHIRLEY *Const. Maid* I. i. (D.), Hospitality went out of fashion with *crop-doublets and cod-pieces. **1939** *Collier's* 24 June 17/1 These are the *crop dusters. **1966** *Punch* 8 June 832/3 The first cropduster to be produced in partnership, this nippy little machine can carry..liquid DDT. **1880** *Encycl. Brit.* XIII. 332/1 Cuttings, '*crop ends', and 'scrap' of various kinds, often not very largely inferior in value to the bar iron. **1884** W. H. GREENWOOD *Steel & Iron* xvi. 347 Cutting off the rough or crop-ends of puddled, finished, or other bars. **1887** *Contemp. Rev.* May 701 Southern Minnesota has outlived the wheat growing and *crop-farming period. **1879** F. W. ROBINSON *Coward Consc.* II. xxi, He glanced..at a *crop-haired individual. **1903** *Sci. Amer.* Suppl. 21 Feb. 22687 The rough ends—'*crop heads'—are cut off and are placed by an electric crane in a car for shipment to any part of the works. **1842** BROWNING *Cavalier Tunes* ii, Bidding the *crop-headed Parliament swing. **1794** *Hull Advertiser* 20 Sept. 4/1 Leather..*Crop Hides for Cutting. **1802** *Hull Packet* 28 Sept. 2/2 A good assortment of horse, calf, and crop hides. **1846** MCCULLOCH *Acc. Brit. Empire* (1854) I. 211 Thousands of acres of *crop-land are sometimes laid under water. **1858** SIMMONDS *Dict. Trade*, **Crop-leather*, *Crops*, leather made from thin cow hides, used chiefly for pumps and light walking-shoes. **1935** *Proc. Prehist. Soc.* I. 157 The two fields showing *crop marks. **1947** J. & C. HAWKES *Prehist. Britain* vii. 161 Two of the most spectacular discoveries made by this crop mark method are the Bronze Age temple of Arminghall and the Roman town of Caistor-by-Norwich where every building was clearly planned in pale lines in the corn. **1956** J. K. S. ST. JOSEPH in R. L. S. Bruce-Mitford *Recent Archaeol. Excavations in Brit.* 275 In spring and early summer, differences in colour, density or luxuriance of growth commonly develop in response to hidden differences in the soil. These 'crop-marks', as they are termed, reveal to an observer, often in the finest detail, buried remains of which no trace can be seen on the surface. **1937** *Oxoniensia* II. 13 Under corn or grass however it becomes covered with very distinct *crop-markings, as can be seen from the air-photographs. **1909** *Westm. Gaz.* 14 June 12/1 The *crop movement began very early last year, and the farmers were paid for their wheat and other products promptly. **1894** G. ROBSON *Missions United Presb. Ch.* 35 The grinding routine of slavery was relieved at '*crop-over' and Christmas-time by boisterous revels. **1906** *Westm. Gaz.* 2 June 11/2 Burrowing into the roots of grasses, *crop-plants, and trees. **1958** *Listener* 28 Aug. 301/2 The herd-animals and crop-plants which were destined to form the main basis of modern food-production. **1839** TODD *Cycl.* II. 970/2 The œsophagus..expanded into a large *crop-shaped bag. **1717** E. BARLOW *Surv. Tide* (1722) 11 The Water..descending from the *Crop-side is lodg'd therein. **1824** *Mechanic's Mag.* No. 43. 238 The best method of finishing or striking *cropsole leather. **1881** *Chicago Times* 11 June, The largest advance in leather has been in crop sole. **1956** *Farm Implement & Machinery Rev.* 1 Apr. 2146/1 *Crop spraying is carried out to remove the injurious influences which adversely affect yields. **1959** *Daily Tel.* 15 Oct. 20/5 Three crop-spraying helicopters. **1970** *East African Standard* 23 Jan. 12/6 'What's crop-spraying?' asked his mother. 'Well, you fly low over cultivated fields and spray the crops with weed-killer solution from the aircraft,' explained Bill. **1689** *Lond. Gaz.* No. 2427/4 One black brinded Bull-Bitch, crop Ear'd, *crop Tailed, black Mouth'd. **1884** *Times* (Weekly ed.) 29 Aug. 14/2 The..crop-tailed little Kerry nag. **1892** *Blackw. Mag.* Oct. 481 The timbers..went down open to the *Crap-wa' or angle at the eaves. **1597** GERARDE *Herbal* App. to Table, *Crop weed is *Iacea nigra.* **1884** HOLLAND *Cheshire Gloss.*, *Crop*, or **Crop-wood*, the branches of a felled tree.

crop (krɒp), *v.* Forms: 3–6 croppe, (6 cropp), 6–9 *dial.* crap, 7 crope, 4– crop. [f. CROP *sb.*]

1. *trans.* To cut off or remove the 'crop' or head of (a plant, tree, etc.); to poll, to lop off the branches of (a tree).

a **1225** *Ancr. R.* 86 Ase þe wiði þet spruteð ut þe betere þet me hine ofte croppeð. **1399** *Pol. Poems* (Rolls) I. 363 Crop hit welle, and hold hit lowe, or elles hit wolle be wilde. *c* **1420** *Pallad. on Husb.* v. 92 So cropped for to sprynge he wol not ceese. **1523** FITZHERB. *Husb.* §132 Yf a tree be heded and vsed to be lopped and cropped at euery .xii. or .xvi. yeres ende. **1688** R. HOLME *Armoury* II. 85/2 A Tree is..cropped, when all its Boughs are cut off. **1881** *Oxfordshire Gloss. Supp.*, *Crap*, to crop or trim hedges. **1884** *Cheshire Gloss.*, *Crop*, to cut the branches from a felled tree.

2. a. To pluck off, remove, or detach (any terminal parts of a plant); to snip off (twigs, leaves, etc.).

c **1420** *Pallad. on Husb.* III. 415, I must..ther it growed, croppe a plante of peche. **1579** SPENSER *Sheph. Cal.* Feb. 58 My budding braunch thou wouldest cropp. **1611** BIBLE *Ezek.* xvii. 4 Hee cropt off the top of his yong twigs. **1693** EVELYN *De la Quint. Compl. Gard.* Dict., *To crop*, is to break or pinch of useless Branches without cutting. **1726** LEONI *Alberti's Archit.* I. 24 a, Leaves of Trees cropt in the wane of the Moon.

b. To gather, pluck, pick, or cull (a fruit, flower, or other produce of a plant). *arch.* or *dial.*

c **1450** MYRC 1502 Hast þow I-come in any sty And cropped ȝerus of corne þe by. **1593** SHAKS. *Rich. II*, II. i. 134 To crop at once a too-long wither'd flowre. **1667** MILTON *P.L.* v. 68 O Fruit Divine, Sweet of thy self, but much more sweet thus cropt. **1680** OTWAY *Orphan* IV. vii, A cruel Spoiler came, Cropt this fair Rose. **1809** CAMPBELL *Gertr. Wyom.* III. xxxvii, The hand is gone that cropt its flowers.

c. Said of animals biting off the tops of plants or herbage in feeding; also *absol.*

1362 LANGL. *P. Pl.* A. VII. 35 Þei comen in-to my croft, And croppen my Whete. *a* **1500** *Mourning of Hare* (Hartshorn *Metr. Tales* 1829), I dar not sit to croppe on hawe. **1583** STANYHURST *Aeneis* III. (Arb.) 77 Neere, we viewd..goats..cropping carelesse, not garded of heerdman. **1644** QUARLES *Barnabas & B.* 70 Sheep..that crop the springing grass. **1697** DRYDEN *Virg. Past.* x. 9 Sing, while my Cattel crop the tender Browze. **1717** POPE *Iliad* XI. 686 As the slow Beast..Crops the tall Harvest. **1850** LYNCH *Theo. Trin.* v. 80, [I] listened to the browse of the sheep as they cropped the grass.

†**d.** To feed on, eat. *Obs.* Cf. L. *carpere.*

1377 LANGL. *P. Pl.* B. xv. 394 Makometh..Daunted a dowue and day and nyȝte hir fedde; þe corne þat she cropped he caste it in his ere.

3. To gather as a crop; to reap.

1601 B. JONSON *Poetaster* I. i, Or crooked sickles crop the ripen'd eare. **1608** MIDDLETON *Peacemaker* Wks. 1886 VIII. 329 The frolic countryman opens the fruitful earth, and crops his plenty from her fertile bosom. **1870** LOWELL *Among my Bks.* Ser. I. (1873) 310 He not only sowed in it the seed of thought..but cropped it for his daily bread.

4. *fig.* (from 1 to 3). To cut off, lop off; to reap.

1549 CHALONER *Erasmus on Folly* Pij a, Those who through the divells instinction dooe go about to croppe Peters patrimonie. **1594** SHAKS. *Rich. III*, I. ii. 248 On me That cropt the Golden prime of this sweet Prince. **1659** *Vulg. Errors Cens.* 49 Too tender a bud to be cropp'd by Death. **1660** R. COKE *Justice Vind.* 4 Sophisters cropping of the inventions of other Men. **1837** CARLYLE *Fr. Rev* III. v. iii, By the hundred and the thousand, men's lives are cropt.

5. *intr.* To bear or yield a crop or crops; also with *compl.*

1606 SHAKS. *Ant. & Cl.* II. ii. 233 She made great Cæsar lay his sword to bed, He ploughed her, and she cropt. **1839** STONEHOUSE *Axholme* 397 No land would crop better than this mixture of warp and peat earth. **1877** BLACKMORE *Cripps* iii. 18 Oakleaf potatoes..warranted to beat the ashleaf by a fortnight, and to crop tenfold as much.

6. a. *trans.* To cause to bear a crop; to sow or plant with a crop; to raise crops on. Also *intr.*, to cultivate land; to work as a farmer. Chiefly *U.S.*

[**1573** TUSSER *Husb.* (1878) 44 Few after crop much, but noddies and such.] **1607** *Relat. Disc.* in Arb. *Capt. Smith's Wks.* p. xlix, A plaine lowe grownd prepared for seede, part whereof had ben lately cropt. **1792** A. YOUNG *Trav. France* (1794) II. x. 28 A field, entirely cropped with mulberries. **1844** *Jrnl. R. Agric. Soc.* V. I. 162 It is usually cropped on the four-field or Norfolk course. *a* **1847** in H. Howe *Hist. Coll. Ohio* (1847) 357 He came down the Ohio to Cincinnati, and cropped the first season on Zeigler's stone house farm. **1868** ROGERS *Pol. Econ.* xxii. (1876) 293 More land would be cropped with barley. **1903** *Dialect Notes* II. 310, I am cropping with Mr. Brown this year.

b. *trans.* To grow or rear as a crop.

1921 *Discovery* Feb. 48/1 The pest..remains in existence until potatoes are again cropped in the field.

7. To cut off the top or extremity of (the ears, tail, etc.), to cut off short; *esp.* to cut the ears of animals as a means of identification, and of persons as a punishment.

1607 TOPSELL *Four-f. Beasts* (1673) 172 Stayeth his crying by cropping off the head. **1611** SHAKS. *Cymb.* II. i. 14 Nor crop the eares of them. **1724** SWIFT *Riddle*, My skin he flay'd, my hair he cropt. **1796** BP. WATSON *Apol. Bible* 257 Having their ears cropt for perjury. **1836** W. IRVING *Astoria* II. 36 As soon as a horse was purchased, his tail was cropped. **1864** H. AINSWORTH *John Law* IV. vii. (1881) 212 That..puppy ought to have had his ears cropped for his impertinence.

8. *spec.* **a.** To cut or clip short the ears, etc. of (an animal, person, etc.).

1578 in W. H. Turner *Select Rec. Oxford* 396 One grey..mare, crapped on the further yeare. **1675** *Lond. Gaz.* No. 1007/4, 39 fat sheep..cropped in both Ears. **1764** FOOTE *Patron* I. i, And so get cropped for a libel. **1787** 'G. GAMBADO' *Acad. Horsemen* (1809) 24 A horse's ears cannot well be too long..Were he cropt, and that as close as we sometimes see them now a days, [etc.].

b. To cut the hair of (a person) close.

1796 *Hull Advertiser* 21 May 4/4 To crop, or not to crop, that is the question..and by a crop to say we end The head-ach. **1858** CARLYLE *Fredk. Gt.* (1865) II. IV. xi. 42 Crop him, my jolly Barber; close down to the accurate standard.

c. To clip the nap of (cloth); to shear.

1711 [implied in CROPPER[2] 2]. **1839** CARLYLE *Chartism* viii. 168 The Saxon kindred burst forth into cotton-spinning, cloth-cropping. **1879** *Cassell's Techn. Educ.* IV. 343/1 Cloth is usually 'raised' twice and 'cropped' several times.

d. To cut down the margin of (a book) closely.

1824 DIBDIN *Libr. Comp.* 378 Copies are usually cropt. I never saw it uncut. **1885** C. PLUMMER *Fortescue's Abs. & Lim. Mon.* Introd. 88 The manuscript..has been a good deal cropped by the binder.

e. (See quot.)

1851 GREENWELL *Coal-trade Terms Northumb. & Durh.* 20 *Crop*..to leave a portion of coal at the bottom of a seam in working.

9. In mining districts (Durham, S. Wales, etc.): To dock, to fine.

1891 *Labour Commission*, Glossary of Terms.

10. a. *intr. Min.* and *Geol.* Of a stratum, vein, etc.: To come *up* to the surface; to come *out* and appear on the side of a slope, etc.

1665 D. DUDLEY *Metal. Martis* (1854) 27 The Coles Ascending, Basseting, or as the Colliers term it, Cropping up even unto the superfices of the earth. **1679** PLOT *Staffordsh.* (1686) 130 The coal which has cropt to the same point of its first diping..before it has reach't the surface and cropt out, has taken another dip agreeable to the first, and then again another crop agreeable to the former. **1698** ST. CLAIR in *Phil. Trans.* XX. 379 A Vein of Bitumen or Naphtha that cropes (as the Miners call it) only here. **1792** *Trans. Soc. Enc. Arts* X. 136 Where the different strata or measures crop out. **1855** LYELL *Elem. Geol.* v. (ed. 5) 55 The ridges of the beds in the formations a, b, c, come out to the day, or, as the miners say, *crop out* on the sides of a valley. **1880** *Academy* 26 June 468 The mainland has a foundation of older rock which crops up in many places.

b. *fig.* ***to crop up***: to come up or turn up unexpectedly or incidentally, in the field of action, conversation, or thought.

1844 DISRAELI *Coningsby* II. vi, We shall have new men cropping up every session. **1888** BURGON *Lives 12 Gd. Men* I. ii. 143 The subject..having once cropped up in Exeter College common-room.

c. *fig.* ***to crop out*** (rarely *forth*): to come out, appear, or disclose itself incidentally.

1849 S. R. MAITLAND *Ess.* 288 The charge against the prisoner..crops out in the sequel. **1853** KANE *Grinnell Exp.* I. (1856) 486 Some of their superstitions, which crop out now and then through their adopted faith. **1868** BROWNING *Ring & Bk.* II. 174 All such outrage crop forth I' the course of nature.

11. To remove the crop of (a bird).

1741 *Compl. Fam. Piece* I. ii. 139 Pull, crop, and draw your Pidgeons.

12. ***to crop the causey*** (Sc.): to take or keep the 'crown of the causey', to walk boldly in the centre or most conspicuous part of the street.

a **1670** SPALDING *Troub. Chas. I* (1792) I. 176 All the Covenanters now proudly crop the cawsy. **1887** BALLOCH *Pynours* iv. 34 The merchant burgesses as a class proudly cropt the causey.

crop, var. of CRAP *sb.*[2]

crop, crope, obs. pa. t. and pa. pple. of CREEP.

cropar, obs. form of CRUPPER.

crope, *v.*: see CROAPE, CROUP.

†**ˈcrop-ear.** *Obs.* [Cf. CROP *sb.* 21, *v.* 7.] An ear that has been cropped; hence, a crop-eared animal or person.

1596 SHAKS. *1 Hen. IV*, II. iii. 72 What Horse? a Roane, a crop eare, is it not. **1618** ROWLANDS *Sacred Mem.* 49 He made a crop-eare of the High-Priests man. **1694** *Lond. Gaz.* No. 3014/4 A little..Grayhound bitch, with crop Ears. **1702** VANBRUGH *False Friend* III. ii, See that crop-ear there, that vermin, that wants to eat at a table would set his master's mouth a-watering!

crop-eared (ˈkrɒpˌɪəd), *a.* [f. prec. + -ED.]

1. Having the ears cropped; *esp.* in dogs, horses, etc., as a means of identification, and in persons as a punishment.

1530 *Wells Wills* (1890) 194, ij cropyired heyfers. **1626** B. JONSON *Masque of Owls*, A crop-ear'd scrivener, this..He had his ears in his purse. **1629** DAVENANT *Albovine* Wks. (1673) 430 Crop-ear'd too, like Irish Nags. **1706** *Lond. Gaz.* No. 4234/4 A Black Dutch Dog, crop Ear'd. **1841** LYTTON *Nt. & Morn.* I. i, He purchased a crop-eared Welsh cob.

2. Having the hair cut short, so that the ears are conspicuous.

This and related terms (cf. quot. 1641–2 in CROPPED 4), applied to the Puritans or 'Round-heads', were probably intended by their opponents to associate them with those whose ears had been cut off as a punishment.

1680 WOOD *Life* (Oxf. Hist. Soc.) II. 477 Others say he was a crop-ear'd rogue. *a* **1700** B. E. *Dict. Cant. Crew*, *Crop-ear'd-Fellow*, whose Hair is so short it won't hide his Ears. **1760** FOOTE *Minor* I, The sleek, crop-eared prentice. **1816** SCOTT *Old Mort.* viii, If I were to give the law, never a crop-ear'd cur of the whole pack should bark in a Scotch pulpit. *a* **1839** PRAED *Poems* (1864) I. 354 Out on the crop-eared boor, That sent me with my standard on foot from Marston Moor.

cropen, obs. pa. pple. of CREEP.

croper(e, -ier, -ore, -our, obs. ff. of CRUPPER.

ˈcrop-ˌfull, *a.* [f. CROP *sb.* 1–2 + FULL.] Having the crop or stomach filled; filled to repletion.

1632 MILTON *L'Allegro* 113 And crop-full out of doors he flings Ere the first cock his Matin rings. **1801** *Sporting Mag.* XVII. 121 Not having received that crop-full surfeit that you have. **1846** LANDOR *Imag. Conv.* Wks. I. 68 Let poets be crop-full of jealousy.

cropless (ˈkrɒplɪs), *a.* [f. CROP *sb.* + -LESS.] Without a crop; having no crop.

a **1845** HOOD *Answ. Pauper* iv, What's weather to the cropless? You Don't farm. **1855** MACGILLIVRAY *Nat. Hist. Dee Side* 286 The brown peat forms the soil, crumbled and cropless.

†**cropling.** *Obs.* An inferior kind of stock-fish.

1274 *Stat. de Poltria et Pisce.* Lib. Horn fol. 312, 313 [in *Stow's Surv.* (ed. Strype 1720) II. v. xxvii. 366/2, Anno 1274, Saving a Cropling of which three of the better sort for 1[d]]. **1662** *Stat. Ireland* (1765) II. 449 Croplings, the hundred, containing six score 13[s]. 4[d].

cropon, -oun, etc.: see CROUPON, rump.

cropped (krɒpt), *ppl. a.* Also **cropt.** [f. CROP *v.* and *sb.* + -ED.]

1. Cut off; cut short; plucked, lopped, pruned.

1558 PHAER *Æneid.* VI. (R.), Lothly croppid nose. **1623** DRUMM. OF HAWTH. *Flowers of Sion* (R.), Like a crop'd rose that languishing doth fade. **1687** *Lond. Gaz.* No. 2289/7 A plain brown cropt Nag. **1856** R. W. PROCTER *Barber's Shop* xxi. (1883) 209 [They] shook their cropped heads in the faces of the dainty Cavaliers.

2. Sowed or planted with crops.

1840 T. A. TROLLOPE *Summ. Brittany* I. 189 The flat and richly cropped district of the marshes.

3. Having a crop. Chiefly in *comb.*, as ***full-cropped***.

1486 *Bk. St. Albans* A vj b, Ye shall say yowre hawke is full goorged and not cropped.

4. *Comb.* †***cropped-eared*** = CROP-EARED 2.

1641–2 D. LEWIS in Rushw. *Hist. Coll.* (1721) IV. III. I. 482 A company of prick-eared and cropt-eared Rascals.

croppen, -in, north. dial. pa. pple. of CREEP.

cropper[1] (ˈkrɒpə(r)). [f. CROP *sb.*[1] + -ER[1].] A breed of pigeons having the power of greatly distending or puffing up their crops; a pouter.

1655 WALTON *Angler* 101 There be Cropers, Carryers, Runts. **1678** RAY *Willughby's Ornith.* II. xv. §2 Pigeons..croppers, so called because they can and usually do by attracting the air blow up their crops to that strange bigness that they exceed the bulk of the whole body beside. **1774** GOLDSM. *Nat. Hist.* (1862) II. IV. viii. 126. **1850** E. S. DIXON in Tegetmeier *Pigeons* v. (1867) 54 Pouters..Provincially they are called Croppers. **1891** *Daily News* 7 Jan. 3/4 Those Norwich croppers are not half so puffed up as they seem.

ˈcropper[2]. [f. CROP *sb.* or *v.* + -ER.]

1. One who or that which crops. *spec.* a shearing machine in iron and steel work; also, the workman who operates it.

1483 *Cath. Angl.* 84 A Cropper, *decimator.* **1881** *Sat. Rev.* No. 1319. 182 One can imagine Cicero..imploring the binder to leave the rough edges, and imploring in vain..But..binders were often slaves, and an angry amateur would throw the cropper to feed the lampreys. *a* **1884** KNIGHT *Dict. Mech.* Suppl., *Cropper*, a powerful hand machine for shearing off bolts or rod iron. **1921** *Dict. Occup. Terms* (1927) §279 *Cropper* (iron and steel rolling); forge cropper, mill cropper and shearer; a shearer or a hot sawyer who cuts off badly shaped ends of finished bars of iron or steel after rolling. **1937** *Times* 13 Apr. p. xxxviii/1 Portable hand-lamps, bolt croppers, insulated pliers.

2. A workman who shears the nap of cloth; a cloth-shearer; also, a machine for doing this.

1711 THORESBY *Diary* (1830) II. 89 A fund for the aged and poor croppers at 2d or 4d per cloth. **1888** F. PEEL *Luddites* 42 The discontented croppers of Liversedge.

3. One who raises a crop, or successive crops.

Locally in U.S. and elsewhere used more or less specifically: see quots.

1573 TUSSER *Husb.* (1878) 44 What croppers bee here learne to see. *Ibid.* 50 Though breadcorne and drinkcorn such croppers do stand: count peason or brank, as a comfort to land. **1850** *Jrnl. R. Agric. Soc.* XI. II. 727 The land is occupied by tenants called Croppers, who pay rents amounting to 5*l.* or 6*l.* per acre, which they are enabled to pay by never letting the land lie idle, and growing crops of vegetables in rapid succession, which they carry to the Bristol market. **1886** *Q. Rev.* Oct. 109 A cropper hires for two years, at a low rent from a squatter, a bit of waste land, undertaking to clear it and grow wheat upon it. After this it is ready for English grass. To succeed, a cropper must work hard with his own hands. **1889** FARMER *Dict. Amer.*, *Cropper*, a farmer on commission, the consideration being..calculated by the proprietor on the basis of the crop produced.

4. A plant which yields a crop. (Usually with qualification.)

1845 *Jrnl. R. Agric. Soc.* VI. II. 352 The best croppers for feeding cattle. **1882** *Garden* 14 Jan. 19/3 Apples and Pears..having the stamp of excellent croppers.

5. *Comb.* **cropper-worker**: One who works a cropping-machine (for cloth).

1891 *Labour Commission*, Glossary of Terms.

ˈcropper[3]. *colloq.* [perh. from phrase *neck and crop.*] A heavy fall; usually in phr. *come (fall, get) a cropper*: often *fig.*

1858 R. S. SURTEES *Ask Mamma* liii. 244 [He] rode at an impracticable fence, and got a cropper for his pains. **1874** HOTTEN *Slang Dict.* 133 *Cropper*, 'to go a cropper', or 'to come a cropper', *i.e.*, to fail badly. **1874** TROLLOPE *Way We live Now* (1875) I. xxxviii. 241 He would 'be coming a cropper rather', were he to marry Melmotte's daughter for her money, and then find that she had got none. **1877** H. A. LEVESON *Sport Many Lands* 464 My horse put his foot in a hole and came down a cropper. **1951** T. RATTIGAN *Who is Sylvia?* I. 230 We bachelors welcome competition from married men. We so much enjoy watching them come the inevitable cropper. **1963** *Times* 30 Jan. 1/7, I came a proper cropper, dearie, all black and blue I was.

cropper[4]. *Printing.* The name given to a small printing-machine, the Minerva platen, after H.

S. Cropper, the inventor (1866). Also attrib., as *cropper boy, -hand, -machine, work.*

1881 *Instr. Census Clerks* (1885) 40 Letter-Press Printing: ..Cropper Hand. **1888** JACOBI *Printers' Vocab.* 28 *Cropper,* a short term for the 'cropper' small printing platen machine. **1892** *Daily News* 23 Sept. 8/6, Printers' Advt., Cropper hand wants work. **1896** *Daily News* 30 Oct. 10/6 Compositor (young). Jobbing and cropper. **1901** *Daily Chron.* 3 Dec. 9/7 Printers.—Young man seeks Situation in machine room; good reference for Cropper work. **1903** *Ibid.* 4 Mar. 9/7 Printers.—Cropper boy wanted. **1921** *Dict. Occup. Terms* (1927) §529 *Machine minder,* platen; cropper hand; has charge of platen machine.

cropper(e, obs. form of CRUPPER.

ˈcroppie. *U.S.* Also croppy. [App. f. F. dial. *crape* or LG. *krape.*] Any of several North American freshwater fishes (see quot. 1889). Cf. CRAPPIE.

1856 *Spirit of Times* 20 Sept. 43/1 Rock and black bass, croppy, and the common sunfish. **1889** FARMER *Americanisms, Croppie,* a local name for a species of green bass found in Lake Minnetonka. **1892** *Gentlewoman's Bk. Sports* I. 73 We caught bass, croppie, sun perch and pickerel. **1920** S. LEWIS *Main St.* 18 A fisherman..holding up a string of croppies.

croppin, -ing, *sb. Sc.* Also crap-. The crop or craw of a fowl; also, *transf.* the stomach.

1737 RAMSAY *Sc. Prov.* (1776) 40 (Jam.), I never loo'd meat that craw'd in my crapine. **1822** HOGG *Perils of Man* II. 190 (Jam.) Jocks crappin began to craw.

cropping (ˈkrɒpɪŋ), *vbl. sb.* [f. CROP *v.* + -ING[1].] The action of the vb. CROP.

1. a. The action of polling or pruning; the gathering of the crop, etc.

1616 SURFL. & MARKH. *Country Farme* 550 The cropping or gathering of this Maslin. **1705** HICKERINGILL *Priestcraft* Wks. 1716 III. 193 Answer it all with a cropping of Ears, Pillory [etc.]. **1855** MOTLEY *Dutch Rep.* (1861) I. 229 The cropping of the ears or the slitting of nostrils..practised upon the Puritan fathers of New England. **1870** H. MACMILLAN *Bible Teach.* iii. 56 Blossoms are often prevented from forming by the cropping of animals.

b. The shearing of cloth; also *attrib.*

1835 URE *Philos. Manuf.* 131 The cropping or shearing-machine. *Ibid.* 197 Shearing, or Cropping, is the next operation. **1888** F. PEEL *Risings of Luddites* 10 The old method of finishing by hand, or cropping as it was called.

c. *concr.* That which is cropped; the wood lopped from trees, etc.

1768 *Case of Jeffry Ruffle* (Erskine *v.* Ruffle & Brewster) 7 The Defendant..had ten loads of croppings in the same year. **1795** *Hull Advertiser* 10 Oct. 4/1 Green lanes where my poor ass may light of good croppings.

d. *Metal-working.* The operation of cutting off the ends of an ingot, bar, etc., to remove the pipe and other defects (see also quot. 1904).

1904 GOODCHILD & TWENEY *Technol. & Sci. Dict.* 139/2 *Cropping,* cutting the ends of bars, rails, etc.; especially cutting iron bars into lengths suitable for making into a fagot. **1930** *Engineering* 21 Mar. 385/2 Piping was avoided, so that no serious amount of cropping was needed. **1968** *Gloss. Terms Mechanized & Hand Sheet Metal Work* (*B.S.I.*) 7 *Cropping,* separation of a semi-complete or complete workpiece. *Ibid.,* Cropping tool.

2. The raising of crops from land; also crops collectively.

1806 *Gazetteer Scot.* (ed. 2) 317 The farmers..by incessant cropping, have reduced the land to a sort of *caput mortuum.* **1861** *Times* 27 Sept., A climate more favourable to the growth of grass and green cropping.

3. *Min.* and *Geol.* The rising of strata to the surface; the portion of a stratum which appears on the surface, an out-crop; *fig.* the act of rising into view or into prominence. Also with *up, out.*

1679 PLOT *Staffordsh.* (1686) 129 Their rise, croping or basseting. **1831** J. HODGSON in J. Raine *Mem.* (1858) II. 210 On a slope of the croppings of the lowest beds of the mountain limestone. **1847** EMERSON *Repr. Men, Shaks.* Wks. (Bohn) I. 355 The cropping out of the original rock.

4. *Comb.,* as **cropping shears** = *crocodile shears.*

1873 *Spon's Dict. Engin.* VI. 2122 Two pairs of cropping shears at 55 revolutions a minute. **1884** W. H. GREENWOOD *Steel & Iron* xvi. 348 The crocodile, cropping, or alligator shears.

ˈcropping, *ppl. a.* [-ING[2].] That crops (in various senses of the verb).

1851 *Beck's Florist* Sept. 197 Natural cropping clefts, and romantic rocky spots. **1888** *Daily News* 17 Oct. 4/5 The best cropping apple in existence is Keswick.

†**ˈcroppy**[1]. *Obs. rare.* [dim. of CROP *sb.* 1–2.] Throat, stomach, maw.

a **1529** SKELTON *El. Rummyng* 561 This ale, sayde she, is noppy..It coleth well my croppy.

croppy[2] (ˈkrɒpɪ). [f. CROP *sb.* 13 or *v.* 8 b.] **a.** One who has his hair cropped short; applied *esp.* to the Irish rebels of 1798, who wore their hair cut very short as a sign of sympathy with the French Revolution. Also *croppy-boy.*

1798 *Ballad* in Madden *Lit. Rem. United Irishmen* (1887) 122 Down Croppy, down Orange, down great, and down small. *c* **1801** *Remin. fugitive Loyalist* in *Eng. Hist. Rev.* July (1886) 539 Several of them..swore they would die with me or make the 'Croppies lie down', alluding to a loyal song in which the rebel party was so styled. *c* **1830** (*title*) The Croppy Boy. **1861** MAY *Const. Hist.* (1863) II. xvi. 536 The wretched 'croppies' were scourged, pitch-capped, picketed ..and shot. **1898** *Westm. Gaz.* 14 Jan. 2/2 What form of higher education you deem at once most suitable for Croppy Boys and least objectionable..to their Protestant overseers. **1949** D. M. DAVIN *Roads from Home* 59 A line of papists and croppy-boys and Galway rebels.

b. *Austral.* A convict.

1800 J. ELDER *Jrnl.* 25 Dec. in *Austral. Lit. Stud.* (1966) II. 215 An attack from the Irish Croppies. **1830** R. DAWSON *Present State of Australia* viii. 299 He had a constable's staff, and considered himself..as a look-out constable for *croppy,* (as they always call the runaway convicts). **1848** H. W. HAYGARTH *Bush Life in Australia* i. 9 Mr. Longbow..was.. robbed..by the well-known 'croppies'—'Black Joe' or 'Irish Jem'.

¶ The following appear in Dictionaries.

1847–78 HALLIWELL, *Croppy,* a Roundhead. **1873** *Slang Dict., Croppie,* a person who has had his hair cut, or *cropped,* in prison. Formerly those who had been cropped (i.e. had their ears cut off and their noses slit) by the public executioner were called *croppies;* then the Puritans received the reversion of the title.

†**ˈcropshin.** *Obs.* Another form of *copshen,* CORPION, a herring of inferior quality.

1599 NASHE *Lenten Stuffe* 63 It was but a cropshin, (one of the refuse sort of Herrings,) and this Herring or this Cropshin was sensed..in the smoake. **1601** B. JONSON *Poetaster* I. ii, Th' art in the right, my venerable Cropshin.

ˈcrop-sick, *a. Obs.* exc. *dial.* [f. CROP *sb.* 1–2 + SICK *a.*] Disordered in stomach, *esp.* as a result of excess in eating and drinking. Often *fig.*

1624 MIDDLETON *Game at Chess* III. ii, My merit doth begin to be crop-sick For want of other titles. *a* **1625** BOYS *Wks.* (1629) 400, People, who being Crop-sicke, doe not hunger after the righteousnesse of Gods kingdome. **1703** OLIVER in *Phil. Trans.* XXIII. 1408 A Prussian Boor; who being Crop-sick..thrust the Haft of his Knife down his Throat. **1748** RICHARDSON *Clarissa* (1811) VI. 350 A man in ill health, and crop-sick. **1845** *Blackw. Mag.* LVIII. 369 In his appeal from Philip drunk to Philip sober, Philip cannot, crop-sick, but nauseate the thought. **1878** *Cumbrld. Gloss., Crop-sick,* disordered in the stomach.

Hence **ˈcrop-sickness.**

1654 WHITLOCK *Zootomia* 126 One that scarce knew any but Crop-sicknesse. **1788** V. KNOX *Winter Even.* I. III. ii. 241 As soon as they were recovered of their own crop-sickness.

cropure, obs. form of CRUPPER.

†**crop-ward.** *Obs. rare*$^{-1}$. [f. CROP *sb.* 4 + -WARD.] In phr. *to the crop-ward* = towards the 'crop' or top (of a tree).

c **1425** LANGL. *P. Pl.* C. XIX. 108 (MS. T.) Elde clomb to the cropward.

cropyn, obs. var. of CROUPON.

croquet (ˈkrəʊkeɪ, -kɪ), *sb.* [Supposed to be a. NorthFr. *croquet,* dial. form of *crochet,* dim. of *croc, croche* crook, found in ONF. in sense of 'shepherd's crook' (Du Cange s.v. *crochetum,* Littré and Hatzfeld s.v. *Crochet*); and used in some modern F. dialects in sense of 'hockey-stick'.

Authorities for this use of *croquet* in Brittany are given by Dr. Prior *Notes on Croquet* (1872) 51/2. In *The Reader* of 29 Oct. 1864, F. J. Foot, of the Geological Survey, stated that the game had been played under this name (though this is perhaps doubtful) near Dublin in 1834–5: see also quot. 1877. From Ireland the game and name were introduced into England in 1852, where between 1858 and 1872 Croquet attained great popularity.]

1. A game played upon a lawn, in which wooden balls are driven by means of wooden mallets through iron arches or 'hoops' fixed in the ground in a particular order.

It resembles more or less the ancient game of CLOSH, and the more recent one of PALL-MALL, in both of which a ball had to be driven through an arch or hoop, in the former by a spade-shaped *beytel,* in the latter by a mallet.

1858 *Field* 10 July 33/3 There is no game which has made such rapid strides in this county [Co. Meath] within a few years as croquet. *Ibid.* 27 Nov. 437/2 The game [croquet].. was introduced into the North of Ireland some twelve years ago from a French convent. **1862** TROLLOPE *Small Ho. Allington* ii, 'I haven't had a game of croquet yet', said Mr. Crosbie. **1864** *Daily Tel.* 4 June, Croquet, a fashionable game everywhere, is adopted permanently at Cambridge. **1877** *Encycl. Brit.* VI. 608 Mr. Dickson, an ivory turner of Gracechurch Street, London, remembers having made a set of croquet implements for Ireland over 40 years ago.

2. The action of croqueting a ball in the game of croquet (see CROQUET *v.*).

1874 J. D. HEATH *Croquet Player* 8 This hitting of one ball by another..[and] the consequent 'croquet', in which the two balls are placed together, and struck so as to move them both. *Ibid.* 14 To croquet, or take croquet.

3. *attrib.* and *Comb.,* as *croquet-ground, -hoop, -mallet, -match, -player,* etc.

1868 DILKE *Greater Brit.* II. 246 Few with flat ground enough for more than..a quarter of a croquet-ground. **1879** E. GARRETT *House by Works* I. 128 To put in an appearance at the Pride's next croquet match.

croquet (ˈkrəʊkeɪ, -kɪ), *v.* Pa. t. and pple. croqueted (krəʊkeɪd); also croqueed, -éd, -ed. [f. prec. sb.] In the game of croquet: To drive away a ball, after hitting it with one's own, by placing the two in contact and striking one's own ball with the mallet. (*trans.* and *absol.*)

1858 *Field* 21 Aug. 148/3 He may croquet any number of balls. **1864** MISS YONGE *Trial* II. 123 Ethel would just have to be croqued all through by her partner. **1874** J. D. HEATH *Croquet Player* 35 In this, the striker's or rear ball passes, and goes a longer distance than the other or croqueted ball.

‖**croquette** (krəʊˈkɛt). Also 8 croquet. [F., f. *croquer* to crackle under the teeth, to crunch.] A ball or mass of rice, potato, or finely minced meat or fish, seasoned and fried crisp.

1706 PHILLIPS (ed. Kersey), In Cookery, Croquets are a certain Compound made of delicious Stuff'd Meat, some of the bigness of an Egg, and others of a Walnut. **1869** J. GRANT *Secret Disp.* 161 A dinner of shee (which is identically Scotch broth), croquettes, with purée of beet-root. **1883** *Harper's Mag.* Apr. 654/1 Croquettes of canned salmon.

‖**croquis** (krɔki). [Fr.] A rough draft; a sketch, study.

1805 C. JAMES *Mil. Dict.* (ed. 2), *Croquis,* Fr. a rough sketch taken of any thing. **1888** *Athenæum* 7 Jan. 23/2 The volume will be illustrated with etchings and *croquis.* *a* **1895** F. LOCKER-LAMPSON in T. H. Ward *Eng. Poets* (1918) V. 525 He sent her this copy containing His comical little *croquis.* **1912** C. MACKENZIE *Carnival* xxi. 248 So Ronnie sat there, making little *croquis* of Jenny with soft outlines elusive as herself.

‖**crore** (krɔə(r)). *Anglo-Indian.* Also 7 carror, kraur, courou, kourou, crou, crow. [ad. Hindī *kǎrōṛ, krōṛ:*—Prakrit *kroḍi,* Skr. *koṭi.*] Ten millions, or one hundred lakhs (usually of rupees).

1609 HAWKINS in Purchas *Pilgrims* I. 216 (Y.) The King's yeerely Income of his Crowne Land is fiftie Crou of Rupias, every Crou is an hundred Leckes. **1678** J. PHILLIPS *Tavernier's Trav.* II. I. ii. 22, 100000 Roupies make a Lekke. 100000 Lekks make a Kraur. **1696** OVINGTON *Voy. Suratt* 189 (Y.) A kourou is an hundred thousand lacks. **1753** HANWAY *Trav.* (1762) II. XIV. v. 362 *note,* A crore is an hundred lacks, or one million two hundred and fifty thousand pounds. **1859** LANG *Wand. India* 109, I would give a crore of rupees (one million sterling) to see her only for one moment. **1876** A. ARNOLD in *Contemp. Rev.* June 42 His father had five Persian crores of soldiers (2,500,000 men).

crosbite, var. CROSSBITE *Obs.,* to cheat.

Croscrist, the Cross of Christ, cross-row, or alphabet: see CROSS *sb.* 4 b.

†**crose, croce.** *Obs.* Also 5 croos, (cros), 5–6 crosse. [a. OF. *croce* (pronounced krɔtsə), in *Roland* 11th c.; from 14th c. onward *crosse;* corresponding to Pr. *crossa,* OSp. *croza,* It. *croccia:*—late L. type **croccia, croccea,* a derivative of late L. **croccus,* It. *crocco,* in F. *croc* crook, hook. (See CROC[1].) Cf. the various med.L. forms for 'pastoral crook' or 'episcopal staff' in Du Cange, *croca, croqua, crocea, crocia, croccia, crochia, crossa, crossea.* In English there was a doublet form CROCHE from Norman French. These words are quite distinct from L. *crux* CROSS, and its derivatives, with which they have never been confused in any Romanic language: thus OF. *croce* and *crois* (*cruiz*), mod.F. *crosse* and *croix,* Pr. *crossa* and *crotz,* OSp. *croza* and *cruz,* It. *cròccia* and *cróce,* med.L. *croccia* and *crux.* In ME. also, *croce* was quite distinct from *crois, croys, croyce;* but after the Norse form of the latter word, *cros,* CROSS, prevailed, there was a tendency for *croce* and *cross* to run together as *crosse,* which resulted in the obsolescence of *croce.* (See copious examples by Rev. J. T. Fowler in *Archæologia* LII.)]

1. The pastoral staff or crook of a bishop or abbot; a crosier.

c **1330** R. BRUNNE *Chron. Wace* (Rolls) 8921 He gaf.. Croces [*v.r.* kroces] riche to clerkes of pris..York he gaf to seint Saunson. **1377** LANGL. *P. Pl.* B. VIII. 94 A bisschopes crosse [C. XI. 92 croce], Is hoked in þat one ende to halie men fro helle. A pyke is on þat potente to pulte adown þe wikked. **1387** TREVISA *Higden* (Rolls) VII. 473 Croces. *c* **1430** *Pilgr. Lyf Manhode* III. vi. (1869) 139 Of a bishoppes croos [*v.r.* croce] he made his howwe and his pikoyse. Pikoise was the sharpe ende, and howwe was the krookede end. *c* **1440** *Promp. Parv.* 103 Croce of a byschope, *pedum, cambuca, crocea.* **1460** CAPGRAVE *Chron.* 134 Cam prelatis, with here crosses and croses. **1528** TINDALE *Obed. Chr. Man* 87 b, Is not that shepherdes hoke, the Bisshopes crose, a false signe. **1617** MINSHEU *Ductor, Croce,* is a Shepheards Crooke in our old English tongue. Hence the staffe of a Bishop..is called the Crocer, Crocier, or Crosier.

β. In 16th c., confounded in form with *cross.*

1528 ROY *Rede me* (Arb.) 31 Which with myters, crosses, and copes, Apere lyke gaye bisshops and popes. *Ibid.* 56 Before hym [Wolsey] rydeth two prestes stronge And they beare two crosses right longe [*i.e.* a crose as bishop and a cross as archbishop]. **1530** PALSGR. 211/1 Crosse, *croix.* Crosse for a bysshoppe, *crosse.* **1552** WRIOTHESLEY *Chron., Allhallows Day,* The prebendaries of Pawles left of their hoodes, and the Bishops their crosses.

2. A staff; = CROCHE 2.

c **1386** CHAUCER *Wife's Prol.* 484 By seint Joce [*v.r.* Iose] I made hym of the same wode a croce [*so 4 MSS.,* 3 crose]. *c* **1400** *Voc.* in Wr.-Wülcker 603/41 *Podium,* a croos.

3. *Comb.* **crose-staff,** = sense 1: cf. *crosier-staff,* CROSIER 2 b.

1549 *Chron. Gr. Friars* (Camden) 60 The byshoppe of Cauntorbery..dyd the offes hym selfe in a cope and no vestment, nor mytter, nor crosse, but a crose staffe. **1553**

Ibid. 84 Many byshoppes with their myteres on their heddes and crose-stavys in their honddes. **1566** in Peacock *Eng. Ch. Furniture* (1866) 71 Banner pooles and crose staves — made awaie the same tyme.

croser, obs. form of CROSIER.

croset, -ette, obs. var. of CRUSET, a crucible.

crosette (*Arch.*), var. of CROSSETTE.

croshabell. *Obs.* exc. *dial.* (See quots.)

a **1598** PEELE *Jests* Wks. (Rtldg. 614) (*title*), How George gulled a Punk, otherwise called a croshabell. *Ibid.* 616 In Italian called a curtezan, in Spain a margerite..now the word refined being latest, and the authority brought from.. the fruitful county of Kent, they call them croshabell, which is a word but lately used.

crosier, crozier ('krəʊʒ(ɪ)ə(r)). Forms: 4-5 crocer, 4-7 croser, 5 crocere, croycer, crosyar, 5-6 croyser, croiser, 6 crosiar, crosyer, crossier, -ear, (7 croisier), 6- crosier, 9 crozier. [Here two words appear to be confounded, the types of which were respectively OF. *crocier, crossier, crosser* 'qui porte la crosse', med.L. *crociārius* bearer of a *crocia*, 'croce', or 'crose', and F. *croisier*, L. type **cruciārius* one who bears or has to do with a cross (*crux, croix*). The Anglo-French and ME. forms of these were *crocer* or *croser*, and *croiser*, respectively; but the distinction was lost in the 15-16th c., when the words *cross* and *crose* began to be confounded as *crosse*: see CROSE. In the 16th c. *crosier's* or *crosier-staff* was a common term for the episcopal crook, borne by the *crociarius*, and at length the crook itself was called the *crosier*. Many 19th c. ecclesiastical antiquaries have erroneously transferred the name to the cross borne before an archbishop.

The history of the application of *crosier(s) staff* and *crosier* to the episcopal crook, is not quite clear. The former appellation seems pretty obviously due to the fact that the crook or staff was borne by the 'crocer' or 'crosier', *crociarius*, and the latter use may have been short for *crosier-staff* (the two words being treated as if in apposition); but there is a possibility that both *crosier-staff* and *crosier* are due to a vulgar perversion of the L. form *crocia*. In any case, we have to remember that the ME. name *croce, crose* was now becoming confounded with *cross* 'crux', and that some new distinctive term was wanted for the *crocia*, which was found in *crosier-staff* and *crosier*. See Rev. J. T. Fowler in *Archæologia* LII, 'On the Use of the Terms *Crosier, Pastoral Staff*, and *Cross*'.]

†**1.** A cross-bearer, one who bears a cross before an archbishop. *Obs.* (prop. croiser.)

[The first quot. may belong to 2; but cf. texts A and B v. 11.]

1393 LANGL. *P. Pl.* C. VI. 113 Reson reuested ryȝt as a pope, And conscience his crocer [*v.rr.* croser, croycer, croyser] by-fore þe kynge stande. *c* **1440** *Promp. Parv.* [see sense 2]. **1483** *Cath. Angl.*, A Croser, *cruciferarius, crucifer.* **1483** CAXTON *Gold. Leg.* 108 a/1 One syre edward gryme that was his croiser put forth his arme wyth the crosse to bere of the stroche. **1515** in Fiddes *Wolsey* II. (1726) 201 The Bishop of Rochester was Crosier to my Lord of Canterbury during the Masse. **1570-6** LAMBARDE *Peramb. Kent* (1826) 78 In broade streetes..their cross-bearers should go togither, but yet in narrow lanes..the crossier of Canterbury should go before..for feare of iustling. **1586** HOLINSHED *Ireland* 32 The canon law, that admitteth the crosier to beare the crosse before his archbishop in an other prouince. **1858** J. PURCHAS *Direct. Anglicanum* 18 The Archiepiscopal Cross is never carried by the Archbishop, but by one of his chaplains chosen to act as Cross-bearer or 'croyser'.

†**2.** The bearer of a bishop's crook or pastoral staff. *Obs.* (prop. crocer, croser.)

(Quot. 1380 is placed here, because the date appears to be too early for sense 3.)

[**1290** in Jacob *Law Dict.* s.v. *Crociarius*, Clericus Episcopi Dunelm. quem vulgo Crociarium ejus vocant.] *c* **1380** WYCLIF *Wks.* (1880) 210 ȝe prelatis..cloþen fatte horsis & gaie sadlis & bridlis & mytris & croceris wiþ gold & siluer & precious stonys. *c* **14..** *Voc.* in Wr.-Wülcker 569/45 *Cambucca*, a busshoppys cros; *Cambuccarius*, a Croser. *Ibid.* 603/40 *Podium*, a croos. *Podiarius*, a Croser. *c* **1440** *Promp Parv.* 104 Crocere, *crociarius, cambucarius, crucifer, pedarius, cruciferarius.* *c* **1450** *Two Cookery-bks.* 68 þe Bisshoppe in pontificalibus; his Croser kneling behinde him, coped. **1558** MACHYN *Diary* 171 My lord of London crossear, Master Mortun, on of the gray ames of Powlles.

†**b.** Hence, apparently, ***crosier's staff, crosier staff***, the episcopal staff or crook. *Obs.*

1488 *Inv.* in *Archæol.* XLV. 119 A miter for a bisshop.. and a croyser staffe hed gilte thereto. *c* **1511** *1st Eng. Bk. Amer.* (Arb.) Introd. 31/1 Theyr bysshops..with the croysers staffe and rynges. **1570** B. GOOGE *Pop. Kingd.* I. (1880) 10 a, His Crosiar staffe in hande he holdes upright. **1611** SPEED *Hist. Gt. Brit.* IX. iv. §53 The Bishops with their Crosier staues. **1630** PAGITT *Christianographie* III. (1636) 31 Investure by a Ring and Croziers staffe. **1733** *Rites & Mon. Ch. Durh.* 19 Crosier staff [*so ed.* **1767** p. 18].

†**c.** Identified with the *lituus* of Roman Augurs.

1585 HIGINS tr. *Junius' Nomenclator* 313 *Lituus*, a crosier's staffe, or a Bishop's staffe. **1600** HOLLAND *Livy* x. vii. 356 With a croiser staffe [*lituo*], and his head vailed..to take Augurie by flight of birds.

3. The pastoral staff or crook of a bishop or abbot. (= med.L. *crocea, crocia.*)

1500 *Inv. Ch. Goods St. Dunstan's Canterb.* in *Archæol. Cant.* (1886) XVI. 315 A vestment for Saint Nicholas tyme with crosyar and myter. **1539** *Inv. St. Osyth's Priory* (in *Trans. Essex Archæol. Soc.* V. 55), Item a Crosyer of sylver gylte. **1570-6** LAMBARDE *Peramb. Kent* (1826) 223 A great dispute..not for the Crosse (for that is the Archbishops warre) but for the Crosier of the Bishop of Rochester. **1610** GUILLIM *Heraldry* (1679) 206 The..Shepherd of whose Crook this Croysier hath a resemblance. **1782** PRIESTLEY *Corrupt. Chr.* II. x. 251 The crosier, or pastoral staff, was the lituus of the Roman augurs. **1827** PRAED *Poems* (1865) I. 243 A pious priest might the Abbot seem, He had swayed his crozier well. **1846** SIR J. STEPHEN *Eccl. Biog.* (1850) I. 53 To place the Sceptre on a level with the Crosier. **1862** J. EADIE *Eccl. Cycl.* (ed. 2) s.v., The crosier bequeathed by William of Wykeham to New College, Oxford.

¶**b.** Applied erroneously to the cross of an archbishop. (Rare before 19th c.: two 18th c. instances.)

1704 COCKER *Eng. Dict.*, *Crosier*, an Arch Bishops staff. **1796** GOUGH *Sepul. Mon.* II. 129 (Referring to monument of Abp. Chichele), The crosier of metal and probably of later date..surmounted by a cross patée. **1819** REES *Cyclop.* s.v., The crosier of an archbishop consists of a lofty processional cross with a single bar to it. **1834** M. H. BLOXHAM *Mon. Archit.* 34 The pastoral staff has often been confounded with the crosier; the latter was, however,..a staff, headed with a cross instead of a crook, and this was carried by the Archbishops. **1848** MRS. JAMESON *Sacr. & Leg. Art* (1850) 105 The staff or crosier, surmounted by a cross. **1876** SCUDAMORE *Notitia Euchar.* 110 We have said nothing of the Crosier borne before an Archbishop. **1880** SMITH & CHEETHAM *Dict. Chr. Antiq.* 1567.

4. *transf.* (from 3). **a.** The curled top of a young fern.

[**1831** J. DAVIES *Manual Mat. Med.* 425 Leaves alternate, rolled up like a crosier before their expansion.] **1874** LYELL *Elem. Geol.* xv. 230 The Croziers of some of the young Ferns are very perfect.

b. The flat convolute shell of the cephalopod *Spirula*.

1840 F. D. BENNETT *Whaling Voy.* ii. 69 A great number of the elegant shells (formerly named Croziers) contained in the body of that curious nondescript animal, the *Spirula Australis*. *Ibid.* 102 Incredible quantites of croziers, or shells of the *Spirula* cephalopod.

†**5.** The constellation of the Southern Cross; *pl.* the four stars of this constellation: cf. CROSS 12. *Obs.* [ad. OSp. *cruciero*, Sp. *crucero*, cross-bearer, Southern Cross.]

1555 EDEN *2nd Voy. to Guinea* in *Decades* 351 In xv. degrees we dyde neere the crossiers [*margin*, The crosiers or cross starres]. **1594** [see CROSS 12]. **1665** G. HAVERS *P. della Valle's Trav. E. India* 337 A Constellation of four starrs, the Mariners call the Crosiers; these stars appear like a Cross. **1670** NARBOROUGH *Jrnl.* in *Acc. Sev. Late Voy.* I. (1711) 25 The Crosers, Stars of the first and second Magnitude, are good for Observation. **1727-51** CHAMBERS *Cycl.*, *Crosier* in Astronomy, four stars in form of a cross; by help whereof those who sail in the southern hemisphere find the antarctic pole.

6. *attrib.* and *Comb.*, as ***crozier bud, head*** (cf. 4 a); ***crozier-like*** adj.

1862 BURTON *Bk. Hunter* (1863) 24 The handle was of a peculiar crosier-like formation. **1885** MRS. LYNN LINTON *Chr. Kirkland* II. 42 The crozier heads of forth-coming, far-spreading fronds. **1891** *Moore's Almanack* 10 The bursting ferns their crozier buds unfold.

crosier [Sp. *crucero*], early f. CRUISER.

'crosiered, *a.* Having or bearing a crosier.

1727-51 CHAMBERS *Cycl.* s.v. *Abbot*, Croziered Abbots, are those who bear the crozier, or pastoral staff. **1798** W. TAYLOR *Monthly Mag.* V. 368 Not the..harmless crosier'd hand.

croslet, erroneous form of CORSLET.

1697 DRYDEN *Æneid* (J.), The croslet some and some the cuishes mould. **1825** HONE *Every-day Bk.* I. 445 Shirts of mail and croslets.

croslet, obs. form of CROSSLET.

cross (krɒs, krɔːs), *sb.* Also crois, croice; corse: see below. [English has had several types of this word, derived by different channels from L. *cruc-em* (nom. *crux*, in late L. *crucis*, It. *croce*, Pr. *crotz*, Sp. *cruz*, OF. *cruiz, croiz*, later *crois*). The native name was OE. *ród*, ROOD; but in late OE. the L. word appears to have been adopted in the form *crúc* (with final *c* palatalized, according to Italian pronunciation), whence ME. *crūche, crouche*. At a date perhaps earlier, the form *cros* appeared in the N. and E. of England, being app. the Norse *kross*, adopted from OIrish *cros* (pl. *crosa*), ad. L. *cruc-em*. In OE., *cros* is known only in local nomenclature, as *Normannes cros*; cf. such northern place-names as *Crosby, Crosthwaite*, etc.; according to Wace (*c* 1175) *Olicrosse!* (= *háliȝ cros*), referring app. to the Holy Rood of Waltham, was the battle-cry of Harold at Hastings. After the Conquest, the OF. *croiz, crois* was introduced as *croiz, crois, croys*, later *croice*, and in early ME. southern writers was the more frequent form; but it became obs. in the 15th c., leaving the northern *cros* (*crosse, cross*) as the surviving type. The later Norse (Danish, Norwegian, Swedish) *kors* appears in Scotland and Northumbria as *corse, cors, corss*, and still lingers in Scotland both in proper names (e.g. Corserig, Corstorphine, etc.) and dialect speech.

Although *cros, croice, corse*, might, in view of their immediate derivation, be treated as distinct words, it is most convenient in tracing the sense-development to deal with them together: CROUCH is treated separately.]

A. Forms. α. 1-6 cros, 4-7 crosse, (4-5 croos, 4-7 croce, 5-6 crose), 5- cross.

963-84 *Recd. of Gifts of Bp. Aðelwold to Medeshamstede* in Birch *Cartul. Saxon.* III. 367 Of þam twam hundredum þe secæð into Normannes cros man aȝeaf, etc. *c* **1175** WACE *Roman de Rou* 13, 119 Olicrosse sovent crioent..Olicrosse est en engleiz Ke Sainte Croix est en franceiz. *c* **1205** LAY. 31386 He lette sone arere a muchel cros and mare. *a* **1300** *Cursor M.* 21637 (Cott.) Meracles o þe cros [*F.* crossis, *G.* crois, *E.* croicis] might. *a* **1340** HAMPOLE *Psalter* xvi. 12 In þe crosse hyngand. *c* **1380** WYCLIF *Sel. Wks.* III. 109 þe peple cryde, Do him on þe croos. **1382** —— *Phil.* ii. 8 The deeth of cross [*many MSS.* the cros]. **1588** A. KING tr. *Canisius' Catech.* 189 The deathe of the croce. **1611** BIBLE *John* xix. 25 Stood by the crosse of Iesus. **1654** J. NICOLL *Diary* (1836) 125 At the Mercat Croce of Edinburgh. **1685** EVELYN *Diary* 16 Sept., The true Crosse.

β. 3-4 croiz, croyz, creoiz, creoice, creoix, 4-5 (6 *Sc.*) crois, croys, croyce, croice.

a **1225** *Ancr. R.* 18 A large creoiz. *Ibid.* 46 And þeonne vour creoices. *Ibid.* 346 Ualleð..a creoix. *c* **1275** *O.E. Misc.* 50 Lyht adun of þe croyz. *a* **1300** *Leg. Rood* 34 And boþe croys [*c* **1350** þe twey croyses] eke þer-wiþ. *a* **1300** *Cursor M.* 21792 (Cott.) Beside þe crois [*v.r.* croice, cros, croz]. *c* **1300** *Beket* 1884 With croiz and with tapres. *c* **1394** *P. Pl. Crede* 805, & on þe crois dyede. **1413** LYDG. *Pylgr. Sowle* IV. xx. (1483) 67 He hanged..vpon the croys. *c* **1450** *Mirour Saluacioun* 2491 How crist bere..the croice.

γ. 5-6 cors, 5-7 corss, (6 corsz, corce), 5- corse.

c **1425** WYNTOUN *Chron.* v. x. 78 (Jam.) Elane that syne fand the Cors. *c* **1470** HENRY *Wallace* II. 22 Wallace..ȝeid to the merkat cors. **1533** GAU *Richt Vay* 29 The wisdome of the corsz. *Ibid.* 44 Apone the cors. **1535** STEWART *Cron. Scot.* II. 363 (*title*) How Sanct Andro apperit, and of his Cors in the air. *Ibid.* Sanct Androis corce. *Ibid.* Quhat that corss suld mene. **1615** [see 13] Corss. **1786** BURNS *To J. Kennedy* i, Mauchline corse. **1813** [see 7 c] Corse.

B. Signification. **I.** The instrument of crucifixion with its representations and *fig.* applications.

1. A kind of gibbet used by the ancients (and in later times by some non-Christian nations); a stake, generally with a transverse bar, on which they put to a cruel and ignominious death certain criminals, who were nailed or otherwise fastened to it by their extremities.

The general sense does not appear in Eng. so early as the specific (2), being mostly of modern occurrence in works on Ancient History: but early mention of the *cross* occurs also in Christian Martyrology and Saints' Lives. In the Vulgate *crux* is applied widely to any gibbet or gallows on which malefactors were hung, and is there also literally rendered *cros, crosse* by Wyclif.

a **1300** *Cursor M.* 21533 (Cott.) He fand tua crosses [*v.r.* croices]. **1382** WYCLIF *Gen.* xl. 19 Pharao shal..honge thee in the crosse. —— *Esther* v. 15 Aman..comaundide to be maad redi an heiȝ cros. **1460** CAPGRAVE *Chron.* (1858) 60 Andrew was..martired on a crosse. **1483** *Cath. Angl.* 84 To do on Crosse, *crucifigere.* **1741** EARL OF HARDWICKE in *Athenian Lett.* (1792) II. 115 Apollonides the physician was condemned to the cross, and executed just before we left Susa. **1827** HEBER *Hymn*, '*The Son of God*', Twelve valiant saints, their hope they knew, And mock'd the cross and flame. **1844** THIRLWALL *Greece* VIII. 205 The body of Cleomenes was flayed and hung on a cross.

2. *spec.* **a.** The particular wooden structure on which Jesus Christ suffered death, believed to have consisted of an upright post, with a horizontal crossbar; the holy rood. (Often written with capital C.)

The identical cross is believed by large bodies of Christians to have been found buried in the ground, by Helena, mother of the Emperor Constantine, in 326; hence, the legend of its finding or *invention*, the adoration of the fragments of it, and stories of miracles wrought by it, play an important part in the religious literature of the Middle Ages. In this connexion the word is often qualified as *holy, real, true, Saint Cross. Stations, way of the Cross*: see STATION, WAY. The antecedent history of this sense in English is found under the earlier name ROOD.

c **1275** *O.E. Misc.* 48 Do a rode! do a rode! *Ibid.* 50 Lyht adun of þe croyz. *c* **1290** *S. Eng. Leg.* I. 3/78 Huy founden roden þreo..þo nusten huy of þe þreo þo holie croyz þat huy souȝten ȝwich it miȝte beo. *a* **1300** *Cursor M.* 8507 (Cott.) þe croce [*F., T.* cros, *G.* crois] O ihesu crist. *a* **1340** HAMPOLE *Psalter* xxi. 1 Crist..when he hyngid on þe crosse. *c* **1386** CHAUCER *Pard. T.* 623 By the croys [*so 2 MSS.*, 3 cros, 2 crosse] which þat seint Eleyne fond. **1470-85** MALORY *Arthur* XXI. vii, Somme men say..that kyng Arthur..shal come ageyn & he shal wynne the holy crosse. **1535** COVERDALE *John* xix. 19 Pilate wrote a superscripcion and set vpon the crosse. **1596** SHAKS. *1 Hen. IV*, I. i. 26 Those blessed feete..nail'd on the bitter Crosse. **1685** EVELYN *Diary* 16 Sept., A little fragment, as was thought, of the true Crosse. **1782** PRIESTLEY *Corrupt. Chr.* I. IV. 387 Images.. according to the form of the venerable cross. **1844** E. B. G. WARBURTON *Crescent & Cross* xxii. (1859) 239 The hole in the rock where the Cross stood. **1867** BP. FORBES *Expl. 39 Art.* xxxi. (1881) 616 On the Cross, the full satisfaction was paid.

†**b.** *by* (*God's*) *cross*, as an oath. *Obs.*

c **1420** *Anturs of Arth.* viii, These knyȝtes are vn-curtas, by cros, and by crede! **1575** J. STILL *Gammer Gurton* v. ii, Else had my hens be stol'n..by Gods cross.

†**c.** A prayer used in the adoration of the cross. *Obs.*

a **1225** *Ancr. R.* 28 Seie sumne oðer of ðe creoiz.

3. a. The sign of the cross made with the right hand, as a religious act.

a **1225** *Leg. Kath.* 728 Heo wið Cristes cros cruchede hire ouer al. *a* **1225** *Ancr. R.* 18 Makieð on ower muþe mit te þume a creoiz. *a* **1300** *Cursor M.* 18338 (Cott.) þe lauerd lift hand.. And on adam a croice he made. *c* **1450** *St. Cuthbert* (Surtees) 781 þe childe a crosse þar on made. **1548–9** (Mar.) *Bk. Com. Prayer, Baptisme,* Then he shall make a crosse upon the childes forehead and breste. **1816** SCOTT *Harold* v. xvii, He sign'd the cross divine. **1861** SIR H. W. BAKER *Hymn, ''Tis done; that new and heavenly birth'* ii, 'Tis done; the Cross upon the brow Is marked for weal or sorrow now.

b. The full expression, ***sign of the cross***, is now usual.

c **1315** SHOREHAM 15 Ich signi the with signe of croys, And with the creme of hele Confermi. **1470–85** MALORY *Arthur* XIV. ix, He made a sygne of the crosse in his forhede. **1548–9** (Mar.) *Bk. Com. Prayer, Baptisme,* Receyue the signe of the holy Crosse. **1645** EVELYN *Diary* May, In the Greek Church they made the signe of the Crosse from the right hand to the left; contrary to the Latines and the Schismatic Greekes. **1857** MRS. GATTY *Parables from Nat.* Ser. II. (1868) 23 If it had not thundered, the peasant had not made the sign of the cross.

†**c.** ***to fall on cross, a cross,*** [= MHG. *an ein crütze vallen*]: to fall cross-wise with outstretched arms, in supplication. *Obs.*

a **1225** *Ancr. R.* 346 Ualleð biuoren ower weoued a creoix to þer eorðe. *c* **1330** *Arth. & Merl.* 7315 Fel on croice.. And seyd sir for Godes gras, Thine help.

4. a. A representation or delineation of a cross on any surface, varying in elaborateness from two lines crossing each other to an ornamental design painted, embroidered, carved, etc.; used as a sacred mark, symbol, badge, or the like.

a **1225** *Ancr. R.* 50 þe cloð in ham [the windows] beo twouold: blac cloð; þe creoiz hwit wiðinnen & wiðuten.. þus bitockneð hwit croiz þe ward of hwit chastite. *a* **1300** *Cursor M.* 21678 (Cott.) O þat blisced lambs blod A cros was mad in signe o rode. **1470–85** MALORY *Arthur* XIII. xi, Therupon that sheld he made a crosse of his owne blood. **1535** STEWART *Cron. Scot.* II. 266 Forbad also in paithment or in streit To mak ane cors quhair men ȝeid on thair feit. **1591** SPENSER *M. Hubberd* 195 In a blew jacket with a crosse of redd. **1645** EVELYN *Diary* 15 Feb., Shut up with broad stones, and now and then a crosse or a palme cut in them. **1700** J. JACKSON 24 Apr. in *Pepys' Diary & Corr.* (1879) VI. 218 His [the Pope's] slipper of crimson velvet, with a gold cross embroidered upon it. **1823** LOCKHART *Anc. Sp. Ball., Dragut* i, The cross upon yon banner.. It is the sign of victory—the cross of the Maltese. **1871** MORLEY *Voltaire* (1886) 344 To write letters to his episcopal foe, signed with a cross and his name: '+ *Voltaire, Capucin indigne*'.

†**b.** ***cross of Christ***, also ***croscrist***: the cross prefixed to the alphabet or CROSSROW; the alphabet itself as the first step in learning. *Obs.*

c **1450** *Bk. Curtasye* 144 in *Babees Bk.* 303 This lessoun schalle þy maistur þe merke Croscrist þe spede in alle þi werke. **1526** *Pilgr. Perf.* (W. de W. 1531) 290 To turne agayne to theyr A. B. C. and lerne the crosse of Chryst agayne.

c. ***to take*** (†***fong*** or ***nim***) ***the cross***: to accept the sign or badge of a cross in ratification of a vow, to engage in a crusade.

For the history of this see CROISE *v.*

c **1290** *Beket* 7 in *S. Eng. Leg.* I. 106 Gilbert Bekat.. him bi-þouȝte þe Croiz for-to fo In-to þe holie land. **1297** R. GLOUC. (1724) 346 Roberd duc of Normandye þe croys nom atten ende, And ȝarked hym wyþ oþere to þe holylonde to wende. *c* **1330** R. BRUNNE *Chron.* (1810) 226 Sir Edward toke the croice, for his fader to go. **1568** GRAFTON *Chron.* II. 80 Baldwyn.. preached, and exhorted men to take the Crosse. **1882** FREEMAN *Reign Will. Rufus* I. iv. §6. 562 Bohemond took the cross, and rent up a goodly cloak into crosses for his followers.

5. A model or figure of a cross as a religious emblem, set up in the open air or within a building, worn round the neck, etc.

c **1205** LAY. 31386 He lette sone arere a muchel cros and snare. **1470–85** MALORY *Arthur* XVII. xv, One helde a candel of waxe brennyng and the other held a crosse. **1501** *Bury Wills* (1850) 88, I bequeth to the parson of Berkhamstede a Seynt Antony crosse. **1568** GRAFTON *Chron.* II. 801 The Byshops delivered to the king.. the Ball with the Crosse in his left hande. **1648** *Ord.* 29 Aug. in Scobell *Acts & Ord.* (1658) I. cxviii. 175 Worshippers of Images, Crosses, Crucifixes, or Reliques. **1878** EDITH THOMPSON *Hist. Eng.* iii. 16 At.. Heavenfield.. Oswald set up a wooden cross—the first Christian sign reared in Bernicia.

6. A staff surmounted by the figure of a cross, borne in religious processions, and *esp.* as an emblem of office before an archbishop.

c **1290** *Beket* 1848 in *S. Eng. Leg.* I. 159 Seint Thomas.. to Caunterburi him drouȝ.. With croyz and with taperes þe contreie a-ȝein him drouȝ. **1460** CAPGRAVE *Chron.* 134 Prelatis, with here crosses and croses. *c* **1465** *Eng. Chron.* (Camden 1856) 94 Thomas Bourchier archebysshop of Caunterbury.. wythe hys crosse before hym, went forthe.. toward Londoun. **1568** GRAFTON *Chron.* II. 75 A great contention arose.. whether the Archebishop of Yorke might beare his Crosse in the Diocesse of Cauntorbury or no. **1645** EVELYN *Diary* 11 Apr., Some of the religious orders and fraternities sung.. the lights and crosses going before. **1814** SCOTT *Ld. of Isles* II. xxii, With many a torch-bearer before, And many a cross behind. **1849** ROCK *Ch. of Fathers* II. 232 An archbishop is seen figured leaning on the staff of his cross.

7. a. A monument in the form of a cross, or having a cross upon it, erected in places of resort, at crossways, etc., for devotional purposes, or as a devout or solemn memorial of some event, as a grave-stone, and the like.

Often also serving to indicate a preaching or meeting place, and qualified as *market-, preaching-, weeping-cross*, for which see these words.

c **1420** *Sir Amadace* xxx, Quen he come sex mile the citè fro, A crosse partut the way a-toe. **1470–85** MALORY *Arthur* IV. v, He.. rode longe in a forest tyll they came to a crosse, and there alyȝt and sayd his prayers deuoutely. **1535** STEWART *Cron. Scot.* II. 677 Into Stanemure ane cors of stane wes set, Quhair the merchis of thir tua kingis met. **1596** SHAKS. *Merch. V.* v. i. 31 She doth stray about By holy crosses where she kneeles and prayes For happy wedlocke houres. **1643** EVELYN *Diary* Nov., In the way were faire crosses of stone carv'd with fleurs de lys at every furlong's end. **1851** D. WILSON *Preh. Ann.* II. IV. iv. 283 Memorial crosses, graven with inscriptions in the Northern Runes.

b. *spec.* The monument of this kind occupying a central position in a town or village, formerly used as a centre for markets, meetings, proclamations, etc.; a market-cross.

c **1465** *Eng. Chron.* (Camden 1856) 75 [Bp. Pocock] vtterly abiured, reuoked, and renounced the sayde articles opynly at Powles Crosse. **1553** *Chron. Gr. Friars* (Camden) 80 The xix. day of [July].. was proclamyd lady Ma[ry to] be qwene of Ynglond at the crose in Cheppe. **1554** *Chron. Q. Mary* (Camden 1850) 78 Ther preched at Poles crosse one doctour Watson. **1596** SHAKS. *Tam. Shr.* I. i. 137 To be whipt at the hie crosse euerie morning. **1611** COTGR. s.v. *Sing*, Thou hast not cried it at the crosse. **1702** *Lond. Gaz.* 3869/3 The Mayor and all the Company went.. to the two Crosses, where Bonfires were prepared. **1786** BURNS *To J. Kennedy* i, If foot or horse E'er bring you in by Mauchline Corse. **1829** SCOTT *Rob Roy* Introd., Birrell.. reports that he was hanged at the Cross. **1848** MACAULAY *Hist. Eng.* I. 480 The newly elected members went in state to the City Cross.

c. A market-place, market. Now only *local.*

1577 HARRISON *England* II. xviii. (1877) I. 298 They begin to sell.. by the bushell or two.. therby to be seene to keepe the crosse. **1587** *Ibid.* 300 The crosses sufficientlie furnished of all things. **1724** RAMSAY *Tea-t. Misc.* (1733) I. 61 When ye gae to the cross then.. Buy me a pacing horse then. **1813** PICKEN *Poems* I. 906 (Jam.) The cadies rang'd about the Corse For messages ay ready.

8. *fig.* Used as the ensign and symbol of Christianity; the Christian religion, *esp.* when opposed to other religions. (In later use it becomes more *fig.*, as in *messenger, preacher, servant of the cross*: cf. next.)

soldier, warrior of the Cross: a crusader; hence *fig.* one actively zealous for the advancement of Christianity.

c **1325** *Poem Times Edw. II*, 249 in *Pol. Songs* (Camden) 334 Hii sholde gon to the Holi Lond.. And fihte there for the croiz. **1593** SHAKS. *Rich. II*, IV. i. 94 Streaming the Ensigne of the Christian Crosse, Against black Pagans, Turkes, and Saracens. **1659** B. HARRIS *Parival's Iron Age* 81 Let us now take leave of the Countries, of the Half Moon.. and return.. into those of the Crosse. **1756–7** tr. *Keysler's Trav.* (1760) II. 199 Constantine, in acknowledgment of his signal victory obtained by the cross, was baptized on this spot. **1812** BYRON *Ch. Har.* I. xxxv, Red gleam'd the cross, and waned the crescent pale. **1830** J. B. WATERBURY *Hymn*, Soldiers of the Cross, arise. **1892** *Q. Rev.* Jan. 61 A Sufi.. is, by profession, tolerant or even sympathetic in the presence of the Cross.

9. *fig.* The crucifixion and death of Christ as the culmination of His redemptive mission, and the central fact of the Christian religion; the atonement wrought on the cross.

c **1380** WYCLIF *Wks.* (1880) 45 By þyn holy crois þu hast aȝen bouȝt þe world. **1382** —— *1 Cor.* i. 18 For the word of the cros is folye sothli to men perischinge. **1549** *Bk. Com. Prayer, Litany*, By thy crosse and passion.. Good lorde deliuer us. **1603** *Const. & Canons Eccles.* No. 30. **1611** BIBLE *1 Cor.* i. 18 The preaching of the Crosse. **1782** COWPER *Progr. Err.* 622 The Cross once seen is death to every vice. **1845** G. A. POOLE *Churches* iv. 27 The doctrine of the cross, as the one great rule and hope of the world. **1891** T. MOZLEY *The Son* xxxvii. 232 Rome, which insists more on the cross than on the divine character, the divine life, and the divine teaching.

10. a. A trial or affliction viewed in its Christian aspect, to be borne for Christ's sake with Christian patience; often in phr. ***to bear, take one's cross***, with reference to Matt. x. 38, xvi. 24, etc.

1382 WYCLIF *Matt.* x. 38 He that takith nat his crosse, and sueth me, is not worthi of me. **1528** TINDALE *Obed. Chr. Man* Doctr. Treat. (Parker Soc.) 310 Mark what a cross God suffered to fall on the neck of his elect Jacob. **1550** CROWLEY *Last Trump* 62 Though thou shouldest perishe for fode, yet beare thou thy crosse patientlie. **1644–5** *Direct. Publ. Prayer* in Scobell *Acts & Ord.* (1658) I. li. 79 To pray for.. the sanctified use of blessings and crosses. **1669** PENN (*title*), No Cross no Crown; a Discourse shewing.. that the.. daily bearing of Christ's Cross, is the alone way to the rest and kingdom of God. **1779** COWPER *Olney Hymns* xxviii, We learn our lighter cross to bear. **1920** A. HUXLEY *Limbo* 184 You must try and be strong and bear it bravely. We all have our cross to bear. **1963** A. HERON *Towards Quaker View of Sex* iv. 40 They must practise self-denial and 'bear their cross'.

b. In a general sense: A trouble, vexation, annoyance; misfortune, adversity; sometimes (under the influence of the verb) anything that thwarts or crosses. Cf. sense 27.

1573 TUSSER *Husb.* (1878) 17 To banish house of blasphemie, least crosses crosse vnluckelie. **1580** SIDNEY (J.), Wishing unto me many crosses and mischances in my love, whensoever I should love. **1614** BP. HALL *Recoll. Treat.* 120 Crosses, after the nature of the Cockatrice, die if they be forseene. **1649** —— *Cases Consc.* (1650) 224 Camillus.. wished some great crosse might befall Rome for the tempering of so high a felicity. **1693** *Mem. Cnt. Teckely* IV. 10 If it has met with some Crosses of Fortune, it is not in a danger for all that to be overthrown. **1712** ARBUTHNOT *John Bull* III. x, After all his losses and crosses. **1853** C. BRONTË *Villette* xxxvii, Doubtless they knew crosses, disappointments, difficulties. **1866** MRS. H. WOOD *St. Martin's Eve* iii. (1874) 19 Her usual crosses had been but light ones, which she scolded or talked away.

II. Any figure or object of this shape.

11. a. Any object, figure, or mark of the same shape as the instrument of crucifixion, *i.e.* of two bars or lines crossing each other, used as a sign, ornament, etc. †***cross in the hands***: a finger-post.

For the various kinds of crosses, see sense 18.

c **1400** *Lanfranc's Cirurg.* 294 Wiþ an hoot iren make a cros upon þe middil of þe passioun as depe as þe deed fleisch is. **1547** in *Vicary's Anat.* (1888) App. iii. 161 Euerye householder.. whych.. hath bein vysyted with the plage.. shall cause to be fyxed.. a certein Crosse of saynt Anthonye devysed for that purpose, etc. **1563** FULKE *Meteors* (1640) 45 Raynebowes.. crosses, and divers lights.. by divers refractions and reflections of beames. **1626** BACON *Sylva* §494 They make a little Cross of a Quill. **1643** EVELYN *Diary* 24 Dec., The body of the Church formes a Crosse. **1762** FOOTE *Orator* I, A cross in the hands, with letters to direct you on your road. **1771** —— *Maid of B.* I, Pushing forth his fingers like a cross in the hands to point out the different roads on a common. **1776** WITHERING *Brit. Plants* (1796) I. 296, 4 petals, forming a cross. **1828** *Jane Seaton* ix. (ed. 2) 61 Her only ornament, a golden chain with a Cornelian Cross attached to it.

b. A similar mark or sign of small size used to mark a passage in a book, etc.; a mark made, in place of his signature, by one who cannot write.

In the latter case originally belonging to 4.

c **1391** CHAUCER *Astrol.* I. §5 The whiche lyne, from a lityl croys + in the bordure vn-to the centre of the large hole. **1562** J. HEYWOOD *Prov. & Epigr.* (1867) 36 Now will I make a crosse on this gate. **1588** J. MELLIS *Briefe Instr.* F ij b, In the margent.. yee shall set a crosse + which signifieth the error to rectify in the proper place. **1687** W. SHERWIN in *Magd. Coll.* (Oxf. Hist. Soc.) 225 Charnock.. crossed all their names. They.. struck off their crosses. **1853** LYTTON *My Novel* v. ix, He sate.. with his steel-pen in his hand, and making crosses here and notes of interrogation there.

c. A natural cross-shaped marking.

1824 BEWICK *Hist. Quadrupeds* (ed. 8) 239 It has the Mule-cross on the withers like most of the Barbary Caracals. **1855** WOOD *Anim. Life* (ed. 2) 420 There is also a black mark running along the spine, and another crossing the shoulders, the two forming a cross.

12. A constellation within the Antarctic Circle, in which four bright stars are arranged somewhat in the figure of a cross; more fully ***Southern Cross.***

1555 EDEN *Decades* 239 The starres cauled the Crosse, are seene very hyghe. *Ibid.* 253. **1594** BLUNDEVIL *Exerc.* IV. xix. (ed. 7) 473 There are lately found out.. foure other Images towards the South Pole, as the Crosse or Crosier, the South Triangle. **1671** NARBOROUGH *Jrnl.* in *Acc. Sev. Late Voy.* (1711) 48 A small black Cloud, which the foot of the Cross is in. **1700** S. L. tr. *Fryke's Voy. E. Ind.* 353 We saw again the Northern Star to our great Joy; till then we had only the Southern Cross in sight. **1868** LOCKYER *Heavens* (ed. 3) 333 The Southern cross—the pole-star of the South. **1892** R. KIPLING *Barrack-room Ball, Eng. Flag* ix, Where the lone wave fills with fire beneath the Southern Cross.

13. Formerly in Scotland: A signal (app. orig. a cross formed of two sticks charred and dipped in blood) sent through the district to summon the inhabitants: see CROSTARIE, FIRE or FIERY CROSS.

1615 *Act Bailiary* in Barry *Orkney* (1805) App. 458 (Jam.) Ilk house and family shall carefully and diligently direct the corss.. to his next neighbours, with ane sufficient bearer, for admonishing the people.. to conveen. **1848** MACAULAY *Hist. Eng.* (1871) I. v. 269 The mysterious cross of yew, first set on fire, and then quenched in the blood of a goat, was sent forth to summon all the Campbells, from sixteen to sixty.

14. a. A part of an anchor, hinge, or other object, which occupies a position transverse to the main part. †**b.** The cross-piece dividing the blade of a sword, etc. from the hilt, and serving as a guard to the hand; the cross-guard. *Obs.*

1470–85 MALORY *Arthur* IX. xxxix, Kynge Marke.. kneled adoune and made his othe vpon the crosse of the suerd. *c* **1477** CAXTON *Jason* 102 b, His swerde.. into the paunche of the dragon up to the crosse. **1590** SIR J. SMYTH *Disc. Weapons* 4 Short arming Daggers of convenient forme and substance, without hilts, or with little short crosses. **1703** MOXON *Mech. Exerc.* 18 When the Joint.. on the Tail, is pind in the Joint.. in the Cross, the whole Hinge is called a Cross-Garnet. **1709** *Lond. Gaz.* No. 4570/4 Lost.. a piece of Anchor, being the Cross and a peice of the Shank.

†**15.** The transept or cross aisle of a cruciform church. *Obs.*

1658 DUGDALE *St. Paul's* 160 And afterwards bestowed four thousands pounds in repairing of the South Cross. **1702** *Lond. Gaz.* No. 3804/2 The House of Commons were seated.. in the North Cross of the Abbey.

16. A surveyor's instrument; a CROSS-STAFF.

1669 STURMY *Mariner's Mag.* II. xiii. 81 Taking off one of the Crosses, and setting the Staff again. **1807** HUTTON *Course Math.* II. 56 The cross consists of two pair of sights set at right angles to each other, on a staff having a sharp point at the bottom, to fix in the ground.

17. *Horse-breaking.* A 'dumb jockey' shaped like the letter X, buckled across the back of a young horse, and having the reins of the snaffle bridle fastened to it, to make him carry his head properly.

1833 *Reg. Instr. Cavalry* I. 74 In order to bring the horse to.. carry his head properly.. the cross may be used.

III. In Heraldry, Insignia of Knighthood, Numismatics, etc.

18. a. *Her.*, etc. A conventional representation of the Christian symbol, or some modification of it, or of two crossing bars, used as an ordinary or charge, as an ornamental figure in art, etc.

Numerous modifications of the form are recognized, some of them being used as religious symbols; the chief forms are **Celtic cross**: see CELTIC *a.* 2; **Greek cross**, an upright cross with limbs of equal length; **Latin cross**, in which the lower limb is longer than the others; **St. Andrew's cross, or cross saltier**, a cross shaped like the letter *X*; **cross of St. Anthony** or *tau cross*, in which the transverse bar lies on the top of the upright, like the letter *T*. Developments of these are the **cross patée** or **formée**, in which the limbs are very narrow where they are conjoined, and gradually expand, the whole forming nearly a square; **Maltese cross, cross of Malta** or **cross of eight points**, a modification of the preceding, in which the extremity of each limb is indented. Subordinate forms are **cross crossed**, a cross with each arm crossed, reaching the edges of the shield; **cross of chains**, a cross composed of four chains fixed to a central annulet; **cross of four leaves**: see QUATREFOIL; **cross of Jerusalem**, a cross having each arm capped by a cross-bar; **cross of Lorraine**, a cross with two horizontal arms, combining the Greek and Latin crosses; **cross of St. Andrew**: see above; *spec.* the saltier-cross of Scotland, white on a blue ground; **cross of St. George**, the Greek cross, red on a white ground, as used on the English flag; **cross of St. James**, a Latin cross figured as a sword; **cross of St. Julian**, a saltier cross having the arms crossed; **cross of St. Patrick**, the saltier cross of Ireland, red on a white ground; **cross of Toulouse**, a Maltese cross with a point projecting from each indentation; **Buddhist cross**, the gammadion or fylfot, 卍; **capital cross**, a Greek cross having each extremity terminated in an ornament like a Tuscan capital; **Capuchin cross**, a cross having each arm terminated by a ball or disc; ANSATE *c.*, CABLED *c.*, *cross* BEZANTY, FLORY, etc.: see these words.

1486 *Bk. St. Albans, Her.* B iij b, Cros fixyly, Cros paty Cros croslettis and Cros flory. *Ibid.* C j a, The cros is the moost worthi signe emong al signys in armys. **1610** GUILLIM *Heraldry* IV. i. (1660) 270 Called a Crosse-Avellane, from the resemblance it hath of a Philbert Nut. **1615** CROOKE *Body of Man* 350 [They] doe mutually intersect themselues in the manner of a Saint Andrewes crosse, or this letter X. **1654** *Ord.* in Scobell *Acts & Ord.* II. ix. (1658) 294 The Arms of Scotland, viz. a Cross, commonly called Saint Andrews Cross. **1702** *Lond. Gaz.* No. 3840/2 A Flag with St. George's Cross was displaied on the Tower. **1797** HOLCROFT *Stolberg's Trav.* (ed. 2) II. xlvi. 114 The long cross..has been called the Latin cross. **1844** F. A. PALEY *Church Restorers* 15 A cross pattée between four lions combatant. **1882** CUSSANS *Her.* iv. 59 No Ordinary is subject to so many modifications of form as the Cross. *Ibid.* 60 Gwillim mentions thirty-nine different Crosses..and Robson no less than two-hundred and twenty-two.

b. *per* or *in cross* (Her.): in the form or figure of a cross.

1562 LEIGH *Armorie* (1579) 78 He beareth party per Crosse wauey Sable, and Argent. **1572** BOSSEWELL *Armorie* II. 37 b, Verte, fiue fermaulx in Crosse. **1610** GUILLIM *Heraldry* V. i. (1611) 238 He beareth parted per Crosse Gules and Argent.

19. A figure of the cross used as the ensign of a religious order of knights, as the Knights of Malta; hence widely adopted as a decoration in many orders of knighthood; also, a wearer of such a cross.

Grand **(†*Great*)** ***Cross***: a decoration of the highest class of such an order, or the person wearing it. ***Victoria Cross***: a British decoration for members of the Army and Navy, instituted Feb. 5th, 1856, as a reward for personal valour.

1651 EVELYN *Diary* 7 Sept., Crosses of the Order of the Holy Ghost. *Ibid.*, The Chevalier Paul..his Malta Cross was esteem'd at 10,000 crounes. **1796** MORSE *Amer. Geog.* II. 444 Out of the 16 great crosses, the great master [of Knights of St. John] is elected. **1855** MACAULAY *Hist. Eng.* IV. 261 This prince had set his heart on some childish distinction, a title or a cross. **1887** *Daily News* 16 July 5/3 He is a Grand Cross of St. Vladimir. **1889** *Whitaker's Alm.* 97 The Most Honourable Order of the Bath..Military Knights Grand Cross. *Ibid.* 98 Civil Knights Grand Cross ..Honorary Knights Grand Cross.

†20. *Numism.* The figure of a cross stamped upon one side of a coin; hence, a coin bearing this representation; a coin generally. *Obs.*

c **1330** R. BRUNNE *Chron.* (1810) 239 Edward did smyte rounde peny, halfpeny, ferthyng..þe kynges side salle be þe hede & his name writen. þe croyce side what cite it was in coyned & smyten. *a* **1420** HOCCLEVE *De Reg. Princ.* 685 The feende, men seyne, may hoppe in a pouche, Whan that no crosse therein may appeare. **1530** PALSGR. 211/1, Crosse of coyne, *la croix d'une piece d'argent.* **1594** NASHE *Unfort. Trav.* Wks. 1883–4 V. 34 His purse was..I thinke verily a puritane, for it kept it selfe from anie pollution of crosses. **1638** HEYWOOD *Wise Woman* I. i. Wks. 1874 V. 281 Ile play the Franck gamester..I will not leave my selfe one Crosse to blesse me. **1667** DRYDEN *Wild Gallant* I. ii, I have not a cross at present. **1766** GOLDSM. *Vic. W.* xxi, She has been here a fortnight, and we have not yet seen the cross of her money. *Ibid.*, To come and take up an honest house, without cross or coin to bless yourself with. **1797** *Sporting Mag.* IX. 312 Neither a bun to put in their belly, nor a cross to put in their pockets.

21. cross and (or) pile [F. *croix et (ou) pile*].

a. The obverse and (or) reverse side of a coin; head or tail; hence sometimes standing for: a coin, money. *arch.*

1393 [see CROUCH *sb.*[1]]. **1584** R. SCOT *Discov. Witchcr.* XIII. xxx. 277 How to know whether one cast crosse or pile by the ringing. **1618** FLETCHER *Chances* v. ii, Compel'd with crosse and pile to run of errands. **1698** SIDNEY *Disc. Govt.* iii. §30 (1704) 362 He had neither cross nor pile. **1718** J. CHAMBERLAYNE *Relig. Philos.* I. xvi. §16 If an equal Number of Pieces of Money were thrown up into the Air, the Chance of their falling Cross or Pile..would be equal. *a* **1856** LONGF. *Friar Lubin* ii, To mingle..The goods of others with his own, And leave you without cross or pile.

†b. *fig.* The two sides of anything; one thing and its opposite. *Obs.*

c **1450** *Pol. Poems* (1859) II. 240 Crosse and pyle standen in balaunce; Trowthe and resoun be no thynge stronge. *a* **1613** OVERBURY *Newes, Countrey Newes* Wks. (1856) 175 That good and ill is the crosse and pile in the ayme of life. **1663** COWLEY *Cut. Colman St.* v, I knew well enough 'twas you; what did you think I knew not Cross from Pile?

†c. 'Head or tail', *i.e.* 'tossing up' to decide a stake, or anything doubtful, by the side of a coin which falls uppermost; 'pitch and toss'; *fig.* a matter of mere chance, a 'toss-up'. (Usually with *cast, throw, toss.*) *Obs.*

[*a* **1327** *Wardrobe Rolls Edw. II* (*Antiq. Repository* II. 58), Item paie illoq a Henri Barber le Roi pour Den[rs] qu il a presta au Roi pur Jewer a cros a Pil de Donn v *s.*] **1597** *1st Pt. Return fr. Parnass.* II. i. 768 Schoolmaister, cross or pile nowe for 4 counters? *c* **1645** *Vox Turturis* 23 They had a Custome, when buyer and seller could not agree, to..cast crosse and pile. **1672** WYCHERLEY *Love in a Wood* III. ii, I'll throw up cross or pile who shall ask her. **1685** *Answ. to Dk. Buckhm. on Liberty of Consc.* 36 Thirdly, whether it be not Cross and Pile, whether a man who may be of any and of all Religions, will be of any, or of none at all? **1709** STEELE *Tatler* No. 39 ¶ 8 There will be no fear of foul Play, if they throw up Cross or Pile who should be shot. **1798** T. JEFFERSON *Writ.* IV. 227 The question of war and peace depends now on a toss of cross and pile.

†d. *fig.* Pitch and toss. *Obs.*

1571 HANMER *Chron. Irel.* (1633) 134 Safer to sit, then upon an Irish Pillion that playeth cross and pile with the rider.

†e. *advb. phr.* By mere chance. *Obs.*

1648 HERRICK *Hesper.*, *Crosse and Pile*, Faire and foule days trip crosse and pile; the faire Far lesse in number then our foule dayes are. *a* **1712** W. KING *Poems, Stumbling Block* 50 The sceptics hypothetic cause..That cross or pile refin'd the chaos.

IV. Senses derived from CROSS *a.*, *v.*, *adv.*

†22. a. A crossing or crossed position: hence the advb. phrase, ***on cross, o cross, a cross*** = crossed, crossing, crosswise: see ACROSS, CROSS *adv. Obs.*

a **1300** *Cursor M.* 21693 (Cott.) He heild his hend on croice [*Edin. MSS.* o croice]. **1551** RECORDE *Pathw. Knowl.* I. xxviii, From those ij. prickes erect two perpendiculars, which muste needes meet in crosse. **1555** EDEN *Decades* 351 They [stars of the S. Cross] are not ryght a croise in the mooneth of Nouember. **1642** *Disput. betw. Devill & Pope* (Brand), A taylor must not sit with legs on crosse. **1659** B. HARRIS *Parival's Iron Age* 54 The King..stood not with his arms a crosse.

b. *on the cross*: diagonally, obliquely across the texture, on the bias. (Cf. BIAS *sb.* I.)

1872 *Young Englishwoman* Nov. 594/1 Bows of dark blue velvet cut on the cross. **1887** [BARING-GOULD] *Golden Feather* iv. 9 The piece of carnation velvet cut on the cross for trimming Jessamy's bonnet. **1955** 'C. BROWN' *Lost Girls* x. 107 The skirt was cut on the cross. **1968** J. IRONSIDE *Fashion Alphabet* 79 Garments cut on the cross or bias have 'give' as the bias is stretchy.

c. *Theatr.* A movement from one part of the stage to another in acting.

1838 *Actors by Daylight* I. 214 He was..well versed in all the crosses and recrosses necessary to impose on the million. **1896** G. B. SHAW *Our Theatres in Nineties* (1932) II. 129 At the end of each of his first vehement speeches, he strode right down the stage and across to the prompt side of the proscenium on the frankest barnstorming principles, repeating this absurd 'cross'—a well-known convention of the booth for catching applause—three times.

d. *Boxing.* A blow that crosses over the opponent's lead. Also *transf.*

1906 E. DYSON *Fact'ry 'Ands* xvii. 233 Ther revolvin' arm ..got home a left lead 'n 'er right cross. **1938** D. RUNYON *Take it Easy* 26 What she lays on his brow is a beautiful straight right cross. **1950** J. DEMPSEY *Championship Fighting* xxii. 144 The right cross, deadliest of all counter-punches, is used when a left-jabber becomes careless.

e. *Association Football.* A cross-pass.

1961 *Times* 29 Sept. 4/3 They quickly turned the screw, with three goals—by Pointer, side-footing in Douglas's cross. **1962** *Times* 12 Mar. 3/2 Greaves failed to stroke home one of his crosses. **1968** *Listener* 23 May 682/1 For a high cross a well-trained full-back..is good enough—though not for the kind of calculated low cross George Best engineered for Billy Foulkes's decisive goal against Real Madrid.

†23. Cross-measurement. *Obs. rare.*

1630 *R. Johnson's Kingd. & Commonw.* 132 The Crosse of London is every way longer, than any you make in Paris.. By this word Crosse, I meane, from Saint Georges in Southwark, to Shoreditch, South and North; and from Westminster to Whitechapell West and East.

24. The point where two lines or paths cross each other; a crossing, cross-way.

1546 BP. GARDINER *Decl. Art. Joye* xv, I..do the offyce of an hande, at a crosse, to saye this is the ryght waye. **1891** G. MEREDITH *One of our Conq.* II. xii. 287 To drive two vessels at the cross of a track into collision.

25. *Electr.* The accidental contact of two lines or circuits so that a portion of the electric current is diverted or crosses from one to the other.

1870 F. L. POPE *Electr. Tel.* v. (1872) 63 The effects of weather crosses usually manifest themselves upon the occurrence of a shower.

26. The writing or marking by which a cheque is crossed.

1876 *Ann. Reg.* [51] The cross on the cheque did not restrain its negotiability.

27. *fig.* A crossing or thwarting: cf. also 10 b.

1599 SHAKS. *Much Ado* II. ii. 4 Any barre, any crosse, any impediment, will be medicinable to me..How canst thou crosse this marriage? **1621–51** BURTON *Anat. Mel.* I. iii. I. ii. 187 If crossed, that cross, etc. **1873** DIXON *Two Queens* IV. XIX. vii. 40 Anne was suffering from a cross in love.

28. a. An intermixture of breeds or races in the production of an animal; an instance of cross-fertilization in plants.

1766 PENNANT *Zool.* (1768) I. 18 Improved by a cross with the foreign kind. **1819** BYRON *Juan* I. lviii, This heathenish cross restored the breed again. **1859** *All Year Round* No. 29. 58 The Bakewell..sheep..is..a creature from a series of judicious crosses of divers long-woolled breeds.

b. An animal or plant, or a breed or race, due to crossing.

1760 *Phil. Trans.* LI. 834 The bird..is an accidental cross, as we sportsmen term it, between a pheasant and turkey. **1834** MEDWIN *Angler in Wales* I. 253 This little feather-legged bantam..is certainly a cross from the grouse. **1868** *Perthshire Jrnl.* 18 June, The large stock of black cattle and crosses. **1871** NAPHEYS *Prev. & Cure Dis.* I. i. 47 The mulatto, a cross between it [the black race] and the white race.

c. *fig.* An instance of the mixture of the characteristics of two different individuals; something intermediate in character between two things.

c **1796** MISS CRANSTOUN in Lockhart *Scott* vii, Walter Scott is going to turn out a poet—something of a cross I think between Burns and Gray. **1852** R. S. SURTEES *Sponge's Sp. Tour* xxii. 112 [He] was a cross between a military dandy and a squire. **1891** FREEMAN *Sk. French Trav.* 125 The west front, a cross between Wells and Holyrood.

29. *slang.* That which is not fair and 'square': dishonest or fraudulent practices.

a cross: a contest or match lost by collusory arrangement between the principals; a swindle. ***on the cross***: in a dishonest, fraudulent manner; ***to be*** or ***go on the cross***: to be a thief, live by stealing. ***to shake the cross***: to give up thieving.

1802 *Sessions' Paper* June 334/2, I got it on..the cross. **1812** J. H. VAUX *Flash Dict.*, *Cross*, illegal or dishonest practises in general are called *the cross*, in opposition to *the square*..Any article which has been irregularly obtained, is said to have been got upon the cross. **1829** *Chron.* in *Ann. Reg.* 21/1 It was decided that it should be a decided 'cross'. —That is, it was decided beforehand that the match was to be lost. **1848** THACKERAY *Van. Fair* lv, A conversation.. about the fight between the Butcher and the Pet, and the probabilities that it was a cross. **1861** H. KINGSLEY *Ravenshoe* lx, The young woman..may be on the cross. **1878** *Tinsley's Mag.* XXIII. 300 Never to act on the square, but invariably on the cross. **1883** 'MARK TWAIN' *Life on Mississippi* lii, If I would shake the cross and live on the square for three months. **1889** BOLDREWOOD *Robbery under Arms* xii. (1890) 85 It's the hardest earned money of all, that's got on the cross. **1915** A. CONAN DOYLE *Valley of Fear* II. iii. 201 It's mum with me so long as I see you living on the straight..But, by gum, if you get off on the cross after this it's another story. **1917** —— *His Last Bow* viii. 293 There's a stool pigeon or a cross somewhere, and it's up to you to find out where it is.

V. Elliptical uses.

†30. Short for CROSS-SAIL, a square-sail. *Obs.*

1513 DOUGLAS *Æneis* IV. viii. 21 Marynaris glaid layis thair schippis onder cros. *Ibid.* v. xiv. 3 Heis heich the cros.

31. *Irish Hist.* = CROSS-LAND.

1612 DAVIES *Why Ireland etc.* (1787) 107 The King's writ did not run in those counties..but only in the church-lands lying within the same, which were called the Cross, wherein the King made a sheriff: and so, in each of these counties palatine there were two sheriffs, one of the Liberty, and another of the Cross. **1879** O'FLANAGAN *Munster Circuit* 3 They could hear and determine all complaints throughout the province of Munster, and the crosses and liberties of Tipperary and Kerry.

VI. *Comb.* See CROSS- I. below.

cross (krɒs, krɔːs), *v.* Pa. t. and pple. crossed, crost (krɒst, -ɔː-). [f. CROSS *sb.*: cf. also CROISE *v.*, and F. *croiser*, Ger. *kreuzen*.]

†1. *trans.* To crucify. *Obs.*

c **1340** *Cursor M.* 24354 (Fairf.) [He] þat crossed was, was al mi care. *c* **1440** *Gesta Rom.* lii. 232 (Harl. MS.) Now Criste is i-bounde, scorgide, ande crosside. *c* **1550** CHEKE *Matt.* xxvi. 2 Y[e] son of man schal be deliverd to be crossed. *Ibid.* xxvii. 30 Yei..caried him awai to be crossed.

2. a. To make the sign of the cross upon or over.

c **1430** *Pilgr. Lyf Manhode* I. xi. (1869) 8 Thilke shal also crosse thee. *c* **1440** CAPGRAVE *Life St. Kath.* IV. 1318 The mayde..crossed hir hed, hir mowth and hir brest. **1547** BOORDE *Brev. Health* 4, I..weke of faith and afeard, crossed my selfe. **1548–9** *Bk. Com. Prayer, Confirmacion*, Then the Bushop shall crosse them in the forehead. **1608** BP. HALL *Char. Vertues & V.* II. 87 This man dares not stirre foorth till his brest be crossed, and his face sprinckled. **1719** DE FOE *Crusoe* (1840) II. vi. 121 They crossed it, and blessed it. **1827** O. W. ROBERTS *Narr. Voy. Centr. Amer.* 228 He crossed himself, and expressed much surprise. **1867** WHITTIER *Tent on Beach, Brother of Mercy* 73 The pale monk crossed His brow.

b. ***to cross a fortune-teller's hand with silver***: to describe crossing lines on her hand with a silver coin given by the consulter: hence to give money to.

1711 ADDISON *Spect.* No. 130 ¶ 1 An honest Dairy-maid who crosses their Hands with a Piece of Silver every Summer. **1766** GOLDSM. *Vic. W.* x. **1821** CLARE *Vill. Minstr.* I. 54 Crossing their hands with coin..How quak'd the young to hear what things they knew. **1838** D. JERROLD *Men of Char.* I. 137 Every domestic..had crossed her [the fortune-teller's] hand and looked on future life.

†3. a. To mark with a cross in sign of a vow; *esp.* of the vow to wrest the Holy Land from the Saracens; = CROISE 2. *Obs.*

1481 CAXTON *Godfrey* xvi, Whan one of the grete barons was croysed so on his sholdre..alle the peple of the contre that were also crossyd cam to hym, and chees hym for theyr captayne. **15..** *Coer de L.* 2131 (from a printed copy) For he is crossed a pilgrim. **1610** BP. CARLETON *Jurisd.* 210 The Souldiers which were crossed for the holy warres.

b. *to cross one's heart*, to make the sign of the cross over one's heart, to attest the truth or sincerity of a statement, promise, etc.; freq. in phr. ***cross my heart*** (***and hope to die***).

1908 S. Ford *Side-stepping with Shorty* xx. 314, I wouldn't touched [*sic*] another thing; cross m' heart, I wouldn't! **1922** 'K. Mansfield' *Garden Party* 24 'Promise not to tell.' They promised. 'Say, cross my heart straight dinkum.' **1926** R. Macaulay *Crewe Train* x. 184 'Let's both swear.' 'Cross my heart and hope to die. Now what about bed?' **1952** A. Wilson *Hemlock & After* iii. 167 Cross her heart, might she die if she sneaked.

4. a. To cancel by marking with a cross or by drawing lines across; to strike out, erase. (*lit.* and *fig.*) Const. *off*, *out*.

[Cf. **1472** *Paston Lett.* No. 696 III. 47.] **1483** *Cath. Angl.* 84 To Crosse, *cancellare*. *c* **1515** *Everyman* in Hazl. *Dodsley* I. 136, I cross out all this. *c* **1600** Day *Begg. Bednall Gr.* I. i, Heres my Bill, I pray see me crost. **1614** Bp. Hall *Recoll. Treat.* 639 The debt is paid, the score is crossed. **1628** W. Pemble *Worthy Rec. Lord's Supper* 43 To have gotten the debt-book crossed. **1813** Southey *Ballads, March to Moscow* 8 And Krosnoff he cross'd them off. **1858** Hawthorne *Fr. & It. Jrnls.* I. 151 Crossed out of the list of sights to be seen.

b. In College usage; see quots.

1576 in W. H. Turner *Select. Rec. Oxford* 380 Every suche person..shalbe dyscharged of the same house, and have hys hedd crossed heare. **1825** C. M. Westmacott *Eng. Spy* I. 156, I move that we have him crossed in the buttery. **1865** *Cornh. Mag.* Feb. 228 There is a very absurd punishment termed 'crossing a man at the buttery', which means that a × is set against his name to prohibit the butler from serving him. **1884** *Weekly Reg.* 18 Oct. 503/2 If you did not go he 'crossed' you, thereby cutting off all your supplies of food.

5. a. To lay (a thing) across or athwart another; to set (things) across each other; to place crosswise. Also, to place (one limb) *over* another.

to cross swords: to engage in fighting with swords; also *fig.* † *to cross legs* or *shins* (i.e. in wrestling; hence *fig.*).

c **1489** Caxton *Sonnes of Aymon* xxii. 471 He..layd hymselfe doun on a bed wyth his legges crossed. **1526** *Pilgr. Perf.* (W. de W. 1531) 259 b, Whan he casteth the stole aboute his necke, and crosseth it before his brest. **1581** Styward *Mart. Discipl.* II. 110 If your battaile be assalted with horse, then couch and crosse your pikes. **1645** Bp. Hall *Remedy Discontents* 148 We must meet with rubs; and perhaps crosse shinnes, and take fals too. **1653** E. Chivenhale *Cath. Hist.* 476 He hath crossed legs with himself, and given himself the fall. **1751** R. Paltock *P. Wilkins* xii, Thus I proceeded, crossing, joining, and fastening all together, till the whole roof was..strong. **1816** Scott *Old Mort.* xvi, Few men ventured to cross swords with him. **1826** Disraeli *Viv. Grey* vi. vi, His arms crossed behind him. **1881** C. E. L. Riddell *Senior Partner* I. ii. 29 She crossed her soft white hands one over the other. **1886** Mrs. Lynn Linton *P. Carew* viii, They rarely met without crossing swords on one matter if not another. **1886** 'Maxwell Gray' *Silence of Dean Maitland* II. i, Staring at the sky, with one leg crossed over the other. **1902** 'H. S. Merriman' *Vultures* xxv. 223 The captain..crossed one leg over the other.

b. *Naut.* To set in position across the mast; hoist (a cross-sail): said formerly of sails, later of yards of a square-rigged vessel. Cf. cross-sail.

1393 Gower *Conf.* I. 81 And forþ þei wenten into schipe And crossen seil and made hem ȝare Anon as þogh þei wolden fare. *c* **1530** Ld. Berners *Arth. Lyt. Bryt.* (1814) 250 A fayre ryuer, wherein were manye shyppes, some vnder sayle, and some redye crossed. **1627** Capt. Smith *Seaman's Gram.* ix. 38 Crosse your yards. **1840** Dana *Before the Mast* v. (1854) 22 The wind having become light, we crossed our royal and skysail yards.

c. *Telephony.* To make a connection between (telephone or telegraph wires of different lines or circuits); freq. used in *pass.* of accidental connections. Also *transf.*, implying a misunderstanding. Also **crossed** *ppl. a.*, **crossing** *vbl. sb.*

1884 *Telegraphic Jrnl.* 31 May 469/1 (*caption*) Crossed wires. **1910** H. Belloc *Pongo & Bull* iii. 56 'Don't mind me, Eddie, the wires were crossed.' And with this meaningless but sufficient phrase, he jammed the receiver down again. **1910** *Hawkins's Electr. Dict.* 100/2 *Crossing wires*, a temporary expedient when a defective section is found to exist in a telegraph circuit, for preserving the continuity of the circuit by crossing the wire over to a neighboring line till the fault is remedied. **1931** Wodehouse *If I were You* i. 12 'There's a lunatic at the other end of the wire who keeps calling me Little Bright Eyes.' 'I fancy the wires must have become crossed, m'lady.' **1932** —— *Hot Water* ii. 57 Can we by any chance have got the wires crossed?..It *was* the idea, wasn't it, that we should pile on to a pot of tea together? **1936** —— *Laughing Gas* vii. 78 An unforeseen crossing of the wires in the fourth dimension. **1958** *Listener* 11 Dec. 976/1 This crossing of the political wires had many repercussions in politics.

6. a. Of things: To lie or pass across; to intersect.

c **1391** Chaucer *Astrol.* I. §5 Over-thwart this..lyne, ther crosseth hym a-nother lyne. **1703** Moxon *Mech. Exerc.* 149 Set another Board..so that..they cross one another. **1774** Goldsm. *Nat. Hist.* (1776) II. 148 The rays..must cross each other in the central point. **1840** Lardner *Geom.* 65 The point X, where they [lines] cross each other.

b. *intr.*

1697 [see crossing *ppl. a.*]. **1869** Ouseley *Counterp.* vi. 30 It is allowable..to let the parts cross, so that the upper part should be below the lower part for a note or two. *Mod.* At the spot where two roads cross.

c. *trans.* To sit across, bestride (a horse, etc.). *colloq.*

1760 R. Heber *Horse Matches* ix. 31 Ill bred riders crossing Queen Mab. **1781** Cowper *Retirement* 467 To cross his ambling pony day by day. **1835** Sir G. Stephen *Search of Horse* i. 7 The 'sweetest little park horse that ever was crossed'. **1876** Trevelyan *Macaulay* (1883) I. 123 He seldom crossed a saddle, and never willingly.

7. a. To draw a line across (another line or surface); to mark with lines or streaks athwart the surface; to write across (a letter). Also *absol.*

1703 Moxon *Mech. Exerc.* 324 Then cross this Line at right Angles with the Line CF. **1797** Bewick *Brit. Birds* (1847) I. 65 With spots of white, crossed with zigzag lines. **1816** Jane Austen *Emma* II. i. 7, I..must.. apologise for her writing so short a letter..in general she fills the whole paper and crosses half. **1819** Keats *Let.* 3 Oct. (1958) II. 221 Brown has a few words to say to you and will cross this. **1849** Thackeray in *Scribn. Mag.* I. 557/1, I have..crossed the t's and dotted the i's. **1850** Mrs. Carlyle *Lett.* II. 115 A letter..two little sheets all crossed! **1924** R. Macaulay *Orphan Island* xiv. §2. 176 Miss Smith had the sloping, flowing hand of the ladies of her period, and often crossed and recrossed.

b. *Farming.* To cross-plough; also *intr.* To admit of being crossed-ploughed.

1796 *Hull Advertiser* 13 Feb. 1/4 The strong lands..are much chilled..and will cross badly..for want of dry winds. **1859** *Jrnl. R. Agric. Soc.* XX. I. 213, I have broken up 201 acres, and have crossed 128 acres. **1864** *Ibid.* XXV. II. 298 In the month of May I cross the work by steam, going down this time to twelve inches.

c. *Banking. to cross a cheque*: to write across the face the name of a banking company, or simply the words '& Co', between two lines, to be filled up with the name of a banking company, through whom alone it may be paid.

The crossing of cheques originated at the Clearing House, the name of the bank presenting the cheque being written across it to facilitate the work of the clearing-house clerks. See *Exchequer Reports* (1853) VII. 402.

1834 Barnewell & Adolphus *Reports* IV. 752 Across the face of the cheque he had written the name of Martin & Co. A cheque so crossed, if presented by any person but the banker whose name is written across, is not paid without further enquiry. **1855** *Ann. Reg.* 192 He..requested that he would cash it [a cheque] for him, as it was crossed. **1866** Crump *Banking* iii. 83 Should the cheque be delivered to the payee, it is a good plan to ask for his banker's name, and cross it.

8. To pass over a line, boundary, river, channel, etc.; to pass from one side to the other of any space. **a.** *trans.*

1583 Foxe *A. & M.* App. 2136/2 Intendyng..to have crossed the seas into Fraunce. **1591** Shaks. *Two Gent.* I. i. 22 How yong Leander crost the Hellespont. **1667** Milton *P.L.* II. 920 No narrow frith He had to cross. **1709** Steele *Tatler* No. 48 ¶4 They crossed Cornhill together. **1860** Tyndall *Glaciers* I. iii. 27 Our aim being to cross the mountains. **1873** Black *Pr. Thule* xiii. 196 White clouds were slowly crossing a fair blue sky. *Mod.* After crossing the Equator, the ship was becalmed.

b. *intr.* Also with *over*. (In early use said of hunted beasts which wheel round and cross their own track.) *spec.* in *Cricket*: (*a*) in fielding, to cross to the other side of the wicket at the end of an over, or when a left-handed batsman replaces a right-handed one at the crease or vice versa; (*b*) of a bowler: to go across at the end of an over in order to bowl from the opposite wicket, thus bowling two overs in succession (*no longer permitted*).

1486 *Bk. St. Albans* E ij b, When ye hunt at the Roo..He crosses and tresones yowre howndys befoore. **1530** Palsgr. 502/1, I crosse over the waye. **1594** Shaks. *Rich. III*, I. iv. 10, I..was embark'd to crosse to Burgundy. **1632** Lithgow *Trav.* IX. (1682) 384 Crossing over in a Boat to the Town of Putzolo. **1711** Addison *Spect.* No. 63 ¶7, I left the Temple, and crossed over the Fields. **1848** Macaulay *Hist. Eng.* I. 559 The only ford by which the travellers could cross. **1867** G. H. Selkirk *Guide to Cricket-Ground* iv. 59 Avoiding the necessity of the field crossing over so frequently. **1877** C. Box *Eng. Game Cricket* 447 To cross over is to change wickets, which a bowler is permitted to do twice in an innings. **1883** *Daily Tel.* 15 May 2/7 Peate [bowler at cricket] now crossed over to the other end. **1908** W. E. W. Collins *County Cricketer's Diary* ix. 162 'He's not quite so good [a bowler] as I thought,' he confided..as we crossed over.

c. *causal.* To carry across.

1804 Monson in Owen *Wellesley's Desp.* 525 Finding the river fordable, I began to cross my baggage. **1882** H. S. Holland *Logic & Life* (1883) 14 It shifts and moves and crosses them from place to place.

d. *intr. Biol. to cross over*: of segments of chromatids of homologous chromosomes: to interchange and recombine during synapsis; to undergo crossing-over (see crossing *vbl. sb.* 11).

1915 T. H. Morgan et al. *Mechanism of Mendelian Heredity* iii. 59 Sex linked factors cross over from each other. **1916** *Jrnl. Genetics* V. 284 If..for every chromosome which crosses over in this definite way, another similar chromosome in another nucleus does not cross over at all, [etc.]. **1920** [see cross-over 4]. **1949** Darlington & Mather *Elem. Genetics* iii. 45 The chromosomes, or rather their constituent chromatids, cross-over and separate in germ cell formation just as the genes segregate and recombine.

e. *euphem.* To die.

1930 'R. Crompton' *William's Happy Days* ix. 224 My dear, dear little four-footed friend..'E crossed over last week. **1935** N. Collins *3 Friends* xvii. 265 Just before she crossed over she mentioned your name.

9. a. Of things: To extend across from side to side.

1577 B. Googe *Heresbach's Husb.* IV. (1586) 171 b, They must have warme Houses, as your Pigions have, crossed through with small Pearches. **1631** Gouge *God's Arrows* IV. xv. 399 The maine Summier which crossed the garret. **1832** *Stat. 2 & 3 Wm. IV*, c. 64 Sched. O. 48 The said railroad.. crosses a small stream.

b. *intr.*

1613–39 I. Jones in Leoni *Palladio's Archit.* (1742) II. 43 A Wall that crosses from the said Wall to the Cornice. **1653** H. Cogan tr. *Pinto's Trav.* xxxiv. 137 Canals..crossing through the length and bredth of the City.

10. a. To meet and pass; to pass (each other) in opposite directions; to meet in passing.

1782 Miss Burney *Cecilia* IV. i, She was crossed upon the stairs by Mr. Harrel, who passed her [etc.]. **1822** Lamb *Elia* Ser. I. *Dream Children*, Now and then a solitary gardening man would cross me. **1854** Lowell *Jrnl. in Italy* Prose Wks. 1890 I. 185 Swallows swam in and out with level wings, or crossed each other.

b. Of two letters or messengers: To pass each other on their way between two persons, who have written to each other at the same time. *trans.* and *intr.*

1793 Twining *Recreat. & Stud.* (1882) 173, I am always angry at this crossing of letters. **1819** Miss Mitford in L'Estrange *Life* II. iii. 71 Our letters always cross, my dear Sir William. **1848** Macaulay *Hist. Eng.* II. 530 This paper on its way to Whitehall crossed the messenger who brought to Portsmouth the order. **1860** Mrs. Carlyle *Lett.* III. 19 A letter from me would have crossed yours..on the road.

11. a. To meet or face in one's way; *esp.* to meet adversely; to encounter. *arch.*

1598 Grenewey *Tacitus' Ann.* III. ix. 77 The legions.. which Visellius, and C. Silius, had set to crosse them, droue them backe. **1602** Shaks. *Ham.* I. i. 127 Ile crosse it, though it blast me. **1628** Earle *Microcosm., A Sharke* (Arb.) 36 Men shun him..and he is never crost in his way, if there be but a lane to escape him. **1631** E. Pelham *God's Power & Prov.* in *Collect. Voy.* (Church.) IV. 821/2 Tho' cross'd sometimes with contrary Winds homeward bound. **1797** Mrs. Radcliffe *Italian* i, He was gone before I could cross him. **1813** Bryon *Giaour* 1084 He knew and crossed me in the fray.

fig. **1581** Mulcaster *Positions* xxxvi. (1887) 134 There be two great doubtes which crosse me.

b. To come across (see come *v.* 38), to meet with, to come upon in one's way. *rare.*

1684 R. H. *Sch. Recreat.* 19 If the Hound chance to cross them, Sport may be had. But no Rule can be prescribed how to find or hunt them. **1857** Ruskin *Pol. Econ. Art* 20 We can hardly read a few sentences on any political subject without running a chance of crossing the phrase 'paternal government'.

12. *to cross the path of* (*any one*): to meet him in his way, to come in the way of; often implying obstruction or thwarting; also, to pass across his path in front of him. ***to cross the bows of*** (***a ship***): to pass across her path immediately in front of her.

1608 Bp. Hall *Char. Vertues & V.* II. 88 This man..if but an hare crosse him the way, he returnes. **1818** W. Irving *Sketch Bk., Leg. Sleepy Hollow* (1865) 426 He would have passed a pleasant life..if his path had not been crossed..by a woman. **1841** De Quincey *Lond. Remin.* vi. Wks. 1890 III. 182 Suppose them insolently to beard you in public haunts, to cross your path continually. **1883** *Law Times Rep.* XLIX. 332 The *Margaret*..attempted to cross the bows of the *Clan Sinclair*. **1892** R. Boldrewood *Nevermore* III. xx. 66 Let him cross my path again at his peril.

13. ***to cross one's mind***, etc. (rarely ***to cross one***): to occur suddenly or momentarily to one, as if flashed across the mind.

1768 Sterne *Sent. Journ., Snuff-box*, The good old monk was within six paces of us, as the idea of him cross'd my mind. **1818** Scott *Hrt. Midl.* xxvii, No notion, therefore, of impropriety crossed her imagination. **1834** Medwin *Angler in Wales* I. 258 Such an idea never crossed one of our minds. **1861** Dickens *Gt. Expect.* li, A misgiving crossed me that Wemmick would be instantly dismissed.

14. *fig.* **a.** To thwart, oppose, go counter to.

c **1555** J. Rogers in Foxe *A. & M.* (1846) VI. 608 He but chasteneth his dearlings and crosseth them for a small while ..as all fathers do with their children. **1588** J. Udall *Demonstr. Discip.* (Arb.) 72 He that loueth Christ, cannot crosse the course of the Gospel. **1631** Gouge *God's Arrows* IV. x. 388 It is..better that our purpose and desire be crossed. **1673** Temple *Ireland* Wks. 1731 I. 113 Without crossing any Interest of Trade in England. **1711** Steele *Spect.* No. 2 ¶1 He was crossed in Love. **1722** De Foe *Relig. Courtsh.* I. i. (1840) 10 He will never cross her in small Matters. **1848** Macaulay *Hist. Eng.* II. 255 He therefore determined to cross those designs. **1876** F. E. Trollope *Charming Fellow* I. xi. 149, I never cross her, or talk to her much when she is not feeling well.

†**b.** To bar, debar, preclude *from*. *Obs. rare.*

1593 Shaks. *3 Hen. VI*, III. ii. 127 To crosse me from the Golden time I looke for. *a* **1650** W. Bradford *Plymouth Plant.* (1856) 329 He in yᵉ end crost this petition from taking any further effecte in this kind.

†**c.** To contradict, contravene, traverse (a sentence, statement, etc.). *Obs.*

1589 Greene *Menaphon* (Arb.) 42 When I alledged faith, she crost me with Æneas. **1614** Bp. Hall *Recoll. Treat.* 848 They..will be crossing every thing that is spoken. **1675** Brooks *Gold. Key* Wks. 1867 V. 55 One divine sentence cannot cross and rescind another. **1687** Dryden *Hind & P.* III. lxviii. 4 A sort of Doves..Who cross the Proverb, and abound with Gall. **1702** Charlett *Let.* in *Pepys' Diary* 26 Sept., Which makes travel so easy, as to cross a sentence of Lord Burghley's [to the contrary].

d. *slang.* To cheat or double-cross; to act dishonestly in or towards; cf. cross *sb.* 29. Also *intr.* (see quot. 1925).

1823 in P. Egan *Grose's Dict. Vulgar T.* *a* **1891** Henley & Stevenson *Deacon Brodie* III. iv, in Farmer *Slang* (1891) II. 218/1 What made you cross the fight, and play booty with your own man? **1925** *Flynn's* 10 Jan. 877/2 *Cross*, to squeal;

to betray... To deceive; to cheat one's pals. **1938** G. GREENE *Brighton Rock* II. ii. 86 It wouldn't have happened if we hadn't been crossed. A journalist thought he could put one over on us. **1960** 'W. HAGGARD' *Closed Circuit* xv. 179 He'd been using us; he'd crossed us; and he knew too much for safety.

†**15. a.** *intr. to cross with*: to go counter to. *Obs.*

a **1586** SIDNEY (J.), Men's actions do not always cross with reason. *a* **1641** BP. MOUNTAGU *Acts & Mon.* (1642) 150 Yet that crosseth not with abbreviation, but confirms it rather. *a* **1662** HEYLYN *Life Laud* (1668) 156 When it seemed.. to cross with the Puritan Interest.

†**b.** *to cross upon* (or *on*): (*a*) to oppose, go counter to; (*b*) to come across, come upon. *Obs.*

a **1678** FELTHAM *Resolves*, etc. (1709) 552 So long as we cross not upon Religion. **1701** COLLIER *M. Aurel.* (1726) 246 He that crosses upon this design, is prophane in his contradiction. **1748** WALPOLE *Lett. to G. Montagu* (1891) II. 121 In this search I have crossed upon another descent. **1750** CHESTERF. *Lett.* II. ccxx. 349 He is in hopes of crossing upon you somewhere or other. **1824** MISS. L. M. HAWKINS *Mem.* I. 25 *note*, One day suddenly crossing on the gentleman.

16. a. *trans.* To cause to interbreed; to modify (a race) by interbreeding; to cross-fertilize (plants).

1754 WARBURTON *Letters* (1809) 174 As that people [the Jews] had no commerce with any other, there was a necessity of crossing the strain as much as possible. **1774** GOLDSM. *Nat. Hist.* (1776) III. 282 This variety seems formed by crossing the breed of such as are imported from various climates. **1802** *Ann. Reg.* 353 The advantage which has resulted from crossing the breed of cattle. **1851** *Beck's Florist* 142 Cross such flowers as appear likely to yield the most desirable colours and shapes. **1883** STEVENSON *Silverado Sq.* (1886) 51 A setter crossed with spaniel. *absol.* **1842** BISCHOFF *Woollen Manuf.* II. 141 They have been generally crossing for bigger sheep, and.. have produced a coarser kind of wool.

b. *intr.* To breed together, being of distinct races or breeds, to interbreed.

18.. COLERIDGE (Webster), If two individuals of distinct races cross, a third is invariably produced differing from either. **1845** *Jrnl. R. Agric. Soc.* VI. II. 453 These [mares] do not cross well with the thorough-bred stallions.

cross (krɒs, krɔːs). *a.* [Originally an attrib. or elliptical use of CROSS *adv.*, some participle (e.g. *lying*, *passing*, *coming*, etc.) being understood.]

No clear line can be drawn between this and various uses of CROSS- in combination, the employment of the hyphen being in many cases unfixed. See CROSS- 4, 5, 9.

1. a. Lying or situated athwart the main direction; transverse; passing from side to side. Also said *fig.* of things to which spatial relations are transferred.

1523 FITZHERB. *Surv.* xx. (1539) 41 Built with two crosse chambers of stone. **1570** *Act 13 Eliz.* c. II §2 Vessels with cross Sails. **1583** STANYHURST *Aeneis* II. (Arb.) 66 Through crosse blynd allye we iumble. **1601** SHAKS. *Jul. C.* I. iii. 50 The crosse blew Lightning. **1719** DE FOE *Crusoe* I. xv. 253 Tying the string to the cross stick. **1761** MRS. F. SHERIDAN *S. Bidulph* III. 255 The road for carriages between the two houses, being a cross one, was very bad. **1867** A. BARRY *Sir. C. Barry* vi. 230 The cross roofs connecting them with the main building.

fig. **1826** DISRAELI *Viv. Grey* III. viii, How many cross interests baffle the parties. **1848** MILL *Pol. Econ.* III. vii. §1 It is easier to ascertain.. the relations of many things to one thing, than their innumerable cross relations with one another. **1868** M. PATTISON *Academ. Org.* v. 146 Our position will not be confused by a cross issue.

b. Passing or lying athwart each other; crossing, intersecting.

1602 MARSTON *Ant. & Mel.* Induct., As crosse as a pair of tailors' legs. *a* **1619** FOTHERBY *Atheom.* II. xi. §2 (1622) 313 They runne in crosse courses; and yet doe not crosse one another, in their courses. **1653** *Cloria & Narcissus* I. 84 To sit with his armes crosse, looking up at the heavens. *a* **1742** BENTLEY (J.), When they.. advance towards one another in direct lines, or meet in the intersection of cross ones. **1799** G. SMITH *Laboratory* II. 34 This is generally performed by little cross etchings, one over another. **1830** E. S. N. CAMPBELL *Dict. Mil. Sc.* 231 The honorable badge of a Regimental Colour supported by two cross Swords.

fig. **1684** R. H. *Sch. Recreat.* 91 The second is called Cross, so are its methods cross and intricate.

c. Of the wind: Blowing across the direct course, contrary. Also *fig.* (See CROSS-WIND.)

Sometimes with a blending of sense 4: adverse.

a **1617** BAYNE *On Eph.* (1658) 49 Every wind, even the crossest shall help us to the haven. **1676** TEONGE *Diary* (1825) 195 The wind crosse and very high all these days. **1763** JOHNSON *Lett. to G. Strahan* 14 July, My friendship is light enough to be blown away by the first cross blast.

d. Of the sea: said when the waves run athwart the direction of the wind, or when two sets of waves cross each other, owing to change of wind. Also *cross-surge*, *-swell*, *-tide*.

1823 SCORESBY *Jrnl.* 375 A mountainous sea, rendered awfully heavy and cross by the sudden changing of the wind. **1864** DICKENS *Mut. Fr.* I. I. xiv. 133 In the cross-swell of two steamers. **1866** *Daily Tel.* 18 Jan. 4/3 The terrific cross-sea constantly broke over her. **1867** SMYTH *Sailor's Word-bk.*, *Cross-sea*, a sea not caused by the wind then blowing. *Ibid.*, *Cross-swell*, this is similar to a cross-sea, except that it undulates without breaking violently. *Ibid.*, *Cross-tide*, the varying directions of the flow amongst shoals that are under water. **1891** KIPLING *Light that Failed* xv. 311 A boisterous little cross-swell swung the steamer disrespectfully by the nose. **1899** —— *Five Nations* (1903) 9 'Twixt wrench of cross-surges or plunge of head-gale. **1903** *Q. Rev.* Apr. 486 Like vortices upon a surface of water swept by violent cross-tides.

e. *Cricket.* Applied to a bat held in a slanting position. Cf. CROSS- A. 8.

1871 F. GALE *Echoes from Old Cricket Fields* 25 If you hit her you could only do it with a cross bat. **1891** W. G. GRACE *Cricket* viii. 224 Playing with a straight bat is more likely to protect your wicket than playing with a cross bat. **1928** *Daily Express* 12 Nov. 3/4 One amazing cross-bat shot, head high.. over cover's head to the boundary.

†**2.** Diagonally opposite in position (as in a quadrilateral). *Obs. rare.* Cf. CROSS-CORNER.

1646 SIR T. BROWNE *Pseud. Ep.* III. v. 115 The progression of quadrupeds being performed *per Diametrum*, that is the crosse legs moving or resting together.

3. Contrary, opposite, opposed (*to* each other, or *to* something specified). (Now rarely predicative.)

1565 CALFHILL *Answ. to Martiall* (Parker Soc.) 72, I am ashamed of your too cross and overthwart proofs. **1602** FULBECKE *1st. Pt. Parall.* Introd. 5 There is nothing in it which to the Law of God is crosse or opposite. **1631** MAY tr. *Barclay's Mirr. Mindes* II. 220 Where they begin a little to differ, they will afterwards be crosse in all things from those men. **1646** E. F[ISHER] *Mod. Divinity* 24 As if he were reduced to.. straits.. by the crosse demands of his severall attributes. **1674** HICKMAN *Quinquart. Hist.* (ed. 2) 171 Is this Election cross to that of the Calvinists? *a* **1787** LOWTH *Serm. & Rem.* 414 Giving me answers so very cross to the purpose. **1865** BUSHNELL *Vicar. Sacr.* III. iv. (1868) 307 It is cross to our humanly selfish habit.

4. Of events, circumstances, or fortune: Adverse, opposing, thwarting; contrary to one's desire or liking; unfavourable, untoward.

1565 CALFHILL *Answ. to Martiall* (Parker Soc.) 113 For when the Cross was most magnified, we had cross luck among. **1586** A. DAY *Eng. Secretary* II. (1625) 69 Frame your selfe to beare all other crosse matters. **1607** DEKKER *Northw. Hoe* II. Wks. 1873 III. 24 Such crosse fortune! **1676** DRYDEN *Aurengz.* III. 1078 With Fate so cross One must be happy by the other's loss. **1690** W. WALKER *Idiomat. Anglo-Lat.* 126 We had such cross weather. **1725** DE FOE *Voy. round World* (1840) 302 We had but a cross voyage.. having contrary winds.. and sometimes bad weather. **1780** MAD. D'ARBLAY *Lett.* 14 Dec., Some.. cross accident for ever frustrates my rhetorical designs.

5. Of persons, their dispositions, actions, etc.: †**a.** Given to opposition; inclined to quarrel or disagree; perverse, froward, contrarious. *Obs.* or *arch.*

1588 SHAKS. *Tit. A.* II. iii. 53 Be crosse with him, and Ile goe fetch thy Sonnes to backe thy quarrel. **1594** —— *Rich. III*, III. i. 126 My Lord of Yorke will still be crosse in talke. **1603** KNOLLES *Hist. Turks* (1638) 304 No man.. vnto his friends more friendly, or vnto his enemies more crosse and contrarie. **1685** BAXTER *Paraphr. N.T. Matt.* xi. 16–17 You are cross to us whatever game we play. **1770** FOOTE *Lame Lover* ii. Wks. 1799 II. 73, I hope you won't go for to tell him.. Indeed, Sir, but I shall.. No, sister, I'm sure you won't be so cross. **1851** C. L. SMITH tr. *Tasso* IV. xxi, How vain are all thy judgements, and how cross.

b. Ill-tempered, peevish, petulant; in an irritable frame of mind, out of humour, vexed. (*colloq.*).

1639 T. B. *Admirable Events* 341 The stepmother beholds me with crosse lookes. **1676** WYCHERLEY *Pl. Dealer* III. i, If she gives me but a cross word, I'll leave her to-night. **1711** SWIFT *Jrnl. to Stella* 17 Nov., I just heard of the stir as my letter was sealed.. and was so cross I would not open it to tell you. **1771** MAD. D'ARBLAY *Early Diary* (1889) I. 120 He is equally ugly and cross. **1796** JANE AUSTEN *Pride & Prej.* II. x, I have never had a cross word from him in my life. **1835** MARRYAT *Jac. Faithf.* viii, I can't bear to be cross to him. **1860** SALA *Lady Chesterf.* 43 The crossest of old maids.

c. Phr. *as cross as two sticks* (with play on sense 1 b).

1842 S. LOVER *Handy Andy* ii. 24 The renowned O'Grady was according to her account as cross as two sticks. **1855** LD. HOUGHTON in *Life* I. xi. 518 [He] has been as cross as two sticks at not having been asked to dinner at Court.

6. a. Involving interchange or reciprocal action.

App. not used predicatively, and often hyphened as a case of combination (which is preferable).

1581 LAMBARDE *Eiren.* II. iv. (1588) 164 In some cases.. there may be a double (or crosse) restitution awarded. **1664** DRYDEN *Rival Ladies* I. ii, For hapning both to Love each other Sisters, They have concluded it in a cross Marriage. **1876** DOUSE *Grimm's Law* xxxix. 81 The.. phenomenon of a cross-transfer of a foreign sound to native words and a native sound to foreign words.

b. *Book-keeping.* Applied to accounts between two parties each of which has claims upon the other; also, to formal entries transferring amounts from one account to another, or made on opposite sides of an account so as to neutralize each other. (Here also *cross-* is more usually hyphened.)

1893 GLADSTONE *Sp. in Parliament* 12 Feb., We hope to escape cross accounts and cross payments on revenue accounts [i.e. between Imperial and Irish revenue].

7. Of animals and plants: Cross-bred; hybrid.

1886 *York Herald* 7 Aug. 1/3 Sale of Cross Lambs. **1889** BOLDREWOOD *Robbery under Arms* (1890) 12 'Clearskins' and 'cross' beasts.

8. *slang.* Dishonest; dishonestly come by. (Opposed to *square* or *straight*.) Cf. CROOKED 3 b, and CROSS *sb.* 29.

1812 J. H. VAUX *Flash Dict.* in *Mem.* (1819) II. 165 Any article which has been irregularly obtained.. is emphatically termed *a cross article*. **1882** *Sydney Slang Dict.* 3/1 *Cross cove*, a thief. *Ibid.* 10/2 Four deaners for lush for the cross coves and their blowers. **1890** 'R. BOLDREWOOD' *Miner's Right* II. xv. 62 He believed all the 'cross boys' of all the colonies were congregated here. **1892** —— *Nevermore* I. ix. 168 'Selling him a cross horse as any man might have knowed was too good for them to own on the square.' *Ibid.* I. x. 179 'He don't know a cross cove from a straight 'un.'

¶ See also CROSS- II.

cross (krɒs, krɔːs), *adv.* Now *rare.* [Aphetic form of ACROSS, orig. a phrase *on cross*, *a-cross*: cf. *adown*, *down*, etc.]

†**1.** From side to side, whether at right angles or obliquely; across, athwart, transversely. *Obs.*

[*a* **1400–50** *Alexander* 4872 And þai croke ouire crosse to cache þaim anothire.] **1577** B. GOOGE *Heresbach's Husb.* IV. (1586) 178 b, Cast bowes of Willowe crosse.. That may preserve the fainting Bee, that in the flud doth fall. **1620–55** I. JONES *Stone-Heng* (1725) 47 The Pict's Wall, extending cross over our Island. **1641** BEST *Farm. Bks.* (Surtees) 126 The boards lyinge thus crosse, one chesse one way and another another. **1699** BENTLEY *Phal.* §2. 39 The Arundel Marble lies cross in our way. **1719** DE FOE *Crusoe* I. 127, I now resolv'd to travel quite cross to the Sea-Shore on that Side. **1793** SMEATON *Edystone L.* §53 Courses of timber alternately cross and cross.

†**2.** In a contrary way, in opposition *to*. *Obs.*

1614 T. ADAMS *Devil's Banquet* 217 Jesus Well: whose bottome.. was in Heauen; whose mouth and spring downewards to the earth: crosse to all earthly fountaines. **1638** CHILLINGW. *Relig. Prot.* I. v. §84. 288 To foist in two others, clean crosse to the Doctor's purpose. **1718** HICKES & NELSON *J. Kettlewell* II. xlix. 153 Every Thing was carried cross to his Intentions. *a* **1732** T. BOSTON *Crook in Lot* (1805) 33 The crook of the lot will.. be found to lie cross to some wrong bias of the heart.

3. In an adverse or unfavourable way; contrary to one's desire or liking; awry, amiss; = ACROSS *adv.* 4. *Obs.* or *colloq.*

1603 KNOLLES *Hist. Turks* (1621) 164 Things falling out crosse with the old Emperour. **1646** P. BULKELEY *Gospel Covt.* I. 156 Though things goe crosse against us. **1691** NORRIS *Pract. Disc.* 248 There is yet another thing.. which lies very cross upon our Minds. **1703** *Lond. Gaz.* No. 3937/3 The Tide fell cross in the night. **1883** G. LLOYD *Ebb & Flow* II. 300, I wonder why things do go so cross in this world.

¶ See also CROSS- III.

cross, *prep.* [CROSS *adv.* with object expressed.] = ACROSS *prep.* Now *dial.* or *poetic*: in the latter case commonly written *'cross*, as a recognized abbreviation.

cross lots, more commonly *across lots* (U.S.): across the lots or fields as a short cut: cf. CROSS-COUNTRY.

1551 RECORDE *Pathw. Knowl.* I. xxii, Draw a corde or stryng line crosse the circle. **1591** SHAKS. *2 Hen. VI*, IV. i. 114, I charge thee waft me safely crosse the Channell. **1684** EVELYN *Diary* 24 Jan., Hardly could one see crosse the streetes. **1703** MOXON *Mech. Exerc.* 135 Cut into the Girder three Inches cross the Grain of the Stuff. **1761** FOOTE *Liar* I, Hallooing to a pretty fellow cross the Mall. *c* **1777** BEATTIE *Hares* 196 The scatter'd clouds fly 'cross the heaven. **1821** CLARE *Vill. Minstr.* I. 201 Whether sauntering we proceed Cross the green, or down the mead.

¶ See also CROSS- IV.

cross- in *comb.* is used in many relations, substantive, adjective, adverbial, and prepositional (rarely verbal), sometimes difficult to separate, and in various senses. In some of these the combination is very loose, the use of the hyphen being almost optional.

This is especially so when *cross* is capable of being viewed as an adjective, in which construction the hyphen would not be used, e.g. *cross road* or *cross-road*, *cross reference* or *cross-reference*. As a rule, the use of the hyphen implies specialization of the combination, either usually, or in the particular instance in which it occurs.

A. General uses in combination.

I. From CROSS *sb.*

1. *objective*: **a.** with *pr. pples.*, forming adjs., as ***cross-adoring***, ***-kissing***; **b.** with vbl. sbs., forming sbs., as ***cross-bearing***; **c.** with agent-n., as ***cross-adorer***, ***-keeper***; CROSS-BEARER.

a **1631** DRAYTON *Wks.* IV. 1311 (Jod.) The cross-adoring fowls. **1637** WHITING *Albino & Bell.* 16 The cross-adorers he, with crossing, catches. **1728** MORGAN *Algiers* II. v. 310 Cross-kissing Christians. **1824** SOUTHEY *Bk. of Ch.* (1841) 243 Latimer was.. Cross-Keeper in the University.

2. *instrumental* and *locative*, with pples., and adjs. forming adjs., as ***cross-crowned***, ***-marked***; CROSS-FIXED.

1839 BAILEY *Festus* xix. (1848) 206 A winged orb, cross-crowned.

3. *attrib.* **a.** Of or pertaining to the Cross or a cross, as ***cross-legend***, ***-shaft***, ***-side***, ***-step***, ***-worship***; CROSS-CLOTH 1, -DAYS, -WEEK, etc.; **b.** Of the shape, appearance, or nature of a cross; having a cross-bar or transverse part; as CROSS-BOW, -FISH, -GARNET, -STITCH, etc.; **c.** Marked or stamped with the figure of a cross, as †***cross-back***; CROSS-BUN, -DOLLAR, -FOX, etc.

c **1330** [see CROSS *sb.* 19], þe croice side. **1611** SPEED *Hist. Gt. Brit.* VII. ii. 199 [They] wore continually vpon their backes a red Crosse, whereby the name Crosse-back.. was to them attributed. **1827** CLARE *Sheph. Cal.* Aug. 75 Placed on the circling Cross-steps. **1889** *Archæol. Æliana* XIII. 265 The Birtley cross-slab.

II. From CROSS *a.*

4. a. *gen.* Having a transverse direction; transverse; going across something; as ***cross-arm***, ***-band***, ***-brace***, ***-bracing***, ***-gate***, ***-pole***, ***-rod***, ***-strap***; CROSS-BAR, -BEAM, -PIECE, -SAIL, etc.; **b.**

spec. Transverse to the direction in which the main or principal thing of the kind lies, and thus often a branch of it, or otherwise subordinate to it, as ***cross-barrel, -drain, -furrow, -lane, -lode, -passage, -timber, -trench, -turnpike, vein, -wall***; CROSS-COURSE, -PATH, -ROAD, -STREET, -WAY, etc.; **c.** Crossing or intersecting each other, as ***cross-hand, -reef***; CROSS-BONES, -KEYS.

1590 SIR J. SMYTH *Disc. Weapons* *** iij, With trenches, cross-trenches, gabions, and diverse other. **1626** BACON *Sylva* §120 As if you should make a Cross-barrel hollow, thorow the Barrel of a Piece. **1725** *Manchester Rec.* (U.S.) I. 165 Southerly by the Towns land cal'd the Pasonage land as the Cross wall now stands. **1757** DA COSTA in *Phil. Trans.* L. 233 These cross-loads are generally filled with fragments of ..minerals. **1760** *Patrington Haven Act* 13 Pass through the said turnpikes or cross gates. **1787** WOLCOTT (P. Pindar) *Ode Upon Ode* Wks. 1794 I. 401 Great in tattoo..and cross-hand roll. **1823** COBBETT *Rur. Rides* (1885) I. 377 We did not take the cross-turnpike till we came to Whitchurch. *a* **1826** FAREY *Steam Eng.* (1827) 678 On the upper end of the piston rod..a horizontal cross-rod..is fixed. **1829** SOUTHEY *Pilgr. to Compostella* 111, Perch'd on a cross-pole hoisted high. **1834** STEPHENS in *Brit. Husb.* I. 474 A drain must be carried along..with outlets to the cross-drains. **1845** *Gloss. Gothic Archit.* I. 317 A variety of cross-braces above the tie-beams. **1849** RUSKIN *Sev. Lamps* ii. §10. 38 Set as stays and cross-bands. **1853** HICKIE tr. *Aristoph.* (1872) II. 409 The cross-straps pinch the little toe of my wife's foot. **1866** THOMAS HOWARD *Hist. Inglewood Reefs* ix. 51 What is known as a cross reef, that is two reefs, the one intersecting the other. **1881** JOWETT *Thucyd.* I. 20 Strengthening the old ships with cross-timbers. **1884** MRS. F. MILLER *Life Ht. Martineau* 148 She set up a cross-pole fence around her estate. **1906** D. V. ALLEN in P. Galvin *N.Z. Mining Handbook* 54 At the intersection of cross-reefs carrying sulphides. **1908** *Westm. Gaz.* 1 Aug. 7/2 He attempted to run back, but the cross-wall was immediately behind him. **1909** *Cent. Dict.* Suppl., Cross-arm. **1909** WEBSTER, Cross bracing. **1925** *Bell Syst. Techn. Jrnl.* IV. 524 Individual wires mounted on separate insulators attached to cross-arms on poles. **1926** F. W. CROFTS *Insp. French & Cheyne Myst.* x. 134 They reached the cross-lane at Earlswood. **1940** *Chambers's Techn. Dict.* 204/1 *Counter-bracing*, the provision of two diagonal tie-rods in the panels of a frame girder or other structure. Also called *cross-bracing*. **1951** *Archit. Rev.* CIX. 140/2 An uncompromising system of concrete cross-walls is used, based on a method of construction developed in Denmark during the war. **1958** C. TOMLINSON *Seeing is Believing* (1960) 19 The wind eludes them Streaking its cross-lanes over the uneasy water. **1964** *Listener* 11 June 950/1 Each pier of each ring is led back to the others by brick cross-bracing, making up as it were the spokes of a set of colossal wheels.

5. Also said of things in motion or involving motion, as ***cross-current*** (also *fig.* and *attrib.*), ***-ice, -traffic, -train***; CROSS-POST.

1598 FLORIO *Worlde of Wordes* 430/3 *Trauérsa*,..a crosse currant of waters. **1823** SCORESBY *Jrnl.* 469 *Cross-ice*, loose ice, affording a dubious and difficult passage to a ship. **1849** MRS. CARLYLE *Lett.* II. 57, I had to wait..for the cross-train to Haddington. **1891** MEREDITH *One of our Conq.* II. x. 254 It was a happy cross-current recollection. **1899** MORLEY in *Westm. Gaz.* 18 Jan. 5/1 There have been cross-currents, and it was impossible either inside the House of Commons or elsewhere that Sir William Harcourt could speak with the authority of a united party. **1899** *Westm. Gaz.* 26 Jan. 2/2 Cross-current politics. **1925** T. DREISER *Amer. Trag.* (1926) I. xix. 140 Several precious moments were lost as the cross-traffic went by. **1948** [see CROSS-TOWN *a.*]. **1952** C. DAY LEWIS tr. *Virgil's Aeneid* XI. 242 In the middle of these cross-currents, when partisan feeling had reached High pressure..the envoys returned.

¶ With *vbl. sbs.* and nouns involving action: see 9.

III. From CROSS *adv.*

6. With *verbs*, forming compound verbs, meaning to do something **a.** across, or cross-wise, or in a direction or way traversing another, as ***cross-bond, -carve, -fetter, -pile, -swim, -tie***; CROSS-CUT, -PLOUGH, etc.; **b.** in a way that crosses recognized or ordinary lines of affinity, as ***cross-pollinate***; CROSS-BREED, -COUPLE, -FERTILIZE; **c.** in a way that crosses or traverses another action, as CROSS-EXAMINE, -QUESTION, etc.; **d.** so that two actions mutually cross each other, the one being the counterpart of the other, or done in return or reciprocation for the other, as ***cross-disguise, -invite, -petition***.

1590 SYLVESTER *Du Bartas Yvry* Wks. (Grosart) II. 249 And fiery-fierce and stout, A hundred wayes cross-carves the Field about. *a* **1618** —— *Mottoes* 329 The world and Death one day them cross-disguised To cosen Man. **1613** T. MILLES *Treas. Anc. & Mod. Times* 75/1 Although the Seas were very..tempestuous, yet he would Crosse-swim them, without any feare. **1645** J. BOND *Occasus Occid.* 35 Hee doth fetter, and..crosse-fetter him. *a* **1734** NORTH *Lives* II. 62 His lordship chose to be so far rude as not to cross invite, rather than bear the like consequences of such another intercourse. **1761** STERNE *Tr. Shandy* III. viii. 25 He tied and cross-tied them all fast together. **1862** SMILES *Engineers* II. 429 These [stones] were to be carefully set by hand, with the broadest ends downwards, all crossbonded or jointed. **1878** *Lumberman's Gaz.* 25 Dec. 446 The amount of lumber now cross-piled on the several mill docks. **1904** *Westm. Gaz.* 7 Dec. 7/2 The husband denied various acts described as cruelty by the wife, and cross-petitioned for judicial separation. **1920** *Chambers's Jrnl.* 13 Mar. 238/1 Budding and cross-pollenating. **1923** *Daily Mail* 28 Feb. 5 Her husband..cross-petitions for the dissolution of his marriage.

7. With *pr. pples.*, or adjs. of this form, forming adjs., as ***cross-flowing, -jingling, -pulling, -running***.

1634 MILTON *Comus* 832 The flood That stayed her flight with his cross-flowing course. **1641** —— *Reform.* I. (1851) 31 The fantastick, and declamatory flashes; the crosse-jingling periods which cannot but disturb, and come thwart a setl'd devotion. **1835** MARRYAT *Pirate* iv, This gale and cross-running sea are rather too much for boats. **1854–6** PATMORE *Angel in Ho.* I. I. x, Cross-pulling vices, tied Like Samson's foxes, by the tails.

8. With *pa. pples.*, or adjs. so formed, forming adjs., as ***cross-batted*** (cf. CROSS *a.* 1 e), ***-fissured, -folded, -gagged, -laced, -latticed, -striped***; CROSS-BRED, -GARTERED, etc.

(Often approaching or passing into 11.)

1577 B. GOOGE *Heresbach's Husb.* I. (1586) 23 b, The Harrowe, is an instrument crosse lettused, to breake the Cloddes. **1599** NASHE *Lenten Stuffe* (1871) 49 They would..stand cross-gagged, with knives in their mouths. **1624** T. SCOTT *Vox Dei* 41 To sitt with our armes crosse-folded. **1649** G. DANIEL *Trinarch., Hen. V*, clxxvi, Clad..in cross-stript Motley. **1865** KINGSLEY *Herew.* iv, Scarlet stockings cross-laced with gold braid up to the knee. **1869** PHILLIPS *Vesuv.* vii. 198 It was originally more cross-fissured than the other. **1955** MILLER & WHITINGTON *Cricket Typhoon* xii. 230 Caught at deep mid-on from a cross-batted swipe. **1955** *Times* 12 July 12/1 An astonishing cross batted slash through the covers. **1968** *Listener* 11 July 61/2 It is a passive, cross-batted reaction to the short ball from a fast bowler.

9. With *vbl. sbs.* and nouns involving action, in the various senses found with the vb. (see 6), as ***cross-alliteration, -peal, -planking, -striation, -stroke, -tabulation, -ventilation; cross-appeal, -association, -belief, -claim, -suit, -summons; cross-blow, -protection, -raiding, -resistance***; CROSS-ENTRY, etc.

Here *cross-* becomes practically equivalent to an adjective, though originating, as in 6, 7, 8, in the adverb.

1684 R. H. *Sch. Recreat.* 91 There are two kinds of Changes, viz. Plain Changes, and Cross-peals..the second is called Cross, so are its methods cross and intricate. **1749** LAVINGTON *Enthusiasm* (1754) I. 151 All the ridiculous Ceremonies of Puff, Cross-Puff, Impuff, and Expuff. **1819** *Edin. Rev.* XXXII. 124 That cross-play of selfishness and vanity. **1869** E. A. PARKER *Pract. Hygiene* (ed. 3) 128 A thorough cross-ventilation by opposite windows. **1884** *Law Reports* 9 App. Cases 571 Appeal and cross-appeal from a judgment of the Supreme Court. **1885** H. T. ATKINSON in *Law Rep.* 14 Q. Bench Div. 923 Cross-claims for damages could only be set up in different actions. **1890** J. CORBETT *Sir F. Drake* ix. 124 It was no mere cross-raiding on which he was bent. **1892** J. C. BLOMFIELD *Hist. Heyford* 4 A couple of trees were laid down, and a cross-planking fixed upon them. **1899** W. JAMES *Talks* x. 98 As cross-associations multiply and habits of familiarity and practice grow, the entire system of our objects of thought consolidates. **1923** *Daily Mail* 28 Feb. 5 In this case there are cross-suits. One, by the wife.., her husband..cross-petitions for the dissolution of his marriage. **1926** J. S. HUXLEY *Ess. Pop. Sci.* xviii. 282 The histological character of the cells had changed, cross-striations arising in them. **1927** *Daily Express* 17 Aug. 7 I hope that I shall live to see the day when motorists will be able to take out cross-summonses against careless pedestrians. **1934** PRIEBSCH & COLLINSON *German Lang.* x. 375 Ingeniously adapting *b*, by a cross-stroke, e.g. *geban*..to designate the voiced labial spirant (*v*). **1938** R. GRAVES *Coll. Poems* p. xv, I found the strictly matching consonantal sequences of Welsh bardic poetry too crabbed for English, but modified them to cross-alliteration. **1949** R. K. MERTON *Social Theory* 15 Paradigms, by their very arrangement, suggest the *systematic* cross-tabulation of presumably significant concepts. **1951** WHITBY & HYNES *Med. Bacteriol.* (ed. 5) xii. 195 Sera prepared against either organism will..afford cross-protection in mice. **1956** *Ibid.* (ed. 6) x. 135 *Tetracycline Derivatives*... Acquired resistance common, with cross-resistance to all members of group. **1961** *Lancet* 2 Sept. 521/1 Cross-resistance between different penicillins is not necessarily absolute.

IV. From CROSS *prep.*

10. With *object sbs.*, forming adjs., with sense **a.** Crossing, across, as ***cross-channel*** (see B), ***-river***; CROSS-TOWN, CROSS-COUNTRY; **b.** Adverse to, as †***cross-bliss***; CROSS COURSE *a.*

1589 WARNER *Alb. Eng.* v. xxvii. 135 This crosse-blisse world of ours. **1888** *Pall Mall G.* 15 Feb. 12/1 The Greenwich Ferry Company..Cross-river communication for vehicular traffic.

V. 11. Parasynthetic derivatives, as **a.** ***cross-handled; cross-shaped***, having the shape of a cross; CROSS-HEADED, -HILTED; **b.** ***cross-armed, fingered***, having the arms, etc. crossed; CROSS-HANDED, -LEGGED, etc.

1601 HOLLAND *Pliny* II. 304 With hand in hand, cross-fingered one between another. **1621** LADY M. WROTH *Urania* 485 Then I..walked cross armed, sighed, cast vp mine eyes. **1670** *Moral State Eng.* 83 Cross-arm'd Lovers. **17..** TOLLET *On Shaks.* (Jod.), The cross-shaped flower on the head of this figure. **1881** *Daily News* 8 Nov. 5/7 In the cross-armed and somewhat downcast attitude which he has assumed throughout the trial. **1896** *Daily News* 15 June 7/1 The familiar cross-handled baskets of the fruit. **1912** T. OKEY *Art of Basket-making* vii. 74 The basket is to be covered as well as cross-handled.

B. Special combinations (with quots. in alphabetical order): **cross-accent** *Mus.* = SYNCOPATION 3; **cross-action** (*Law*), an action brought by the defendant against the plaintiff or a co-defendant in the same action: cf. CROSS-BILL; **cross-and-jostle**, applied to a race in which the riders cross each other's paths and jostle each other, getting to the winning-post as they like, by fair riding or foul; also *fig.*; †**cross-arrow**, an arrow shot from a cross-bow; **cross-axle** (see quot.); **cross-banded** (*Carpentry*), see quot.; **cross-bedding** (*Geol.*), apparent lines of stratification crossing the real ones, false bedding; †**cross-bell**, the bell rung at the Elevation of the Host; **cross-belt**, orig. a belt worn over both shoulders, and crossing in front of the breast; also, in later use, a single belt passing obliquely across the breast; hence **cross-belted** *a.*; **cross-birth**, a birth in which the child is presented in a position transverse to the uterus; **cross-bit** = CROSS-PIECE; †**cross-blow**, a counter-blow; also a blow indirectly dealt; **cross-border** *a.*, that forms a border across a fabric, etc.; so *cross-bordered* adj.; **cross-break**, a break across a lode of ore or strata of rocks; **cross-catalogue** *v.*, to catalogue under a heading or division that crosses another; to cross-index; **cross cause**, (*a*) a hindrance (*Obs. rare*); (*b*) *Law*, a cause in which each of the litigants has a suit against the other; **cross-channel** *a.*, passing or situated across the (English or other) channel; **cross-check** *v. trans.*, (*a*) *Ice Hockey*, to obstruct by holding one's stick across an opponent (Webster, 1934); (*b*) to check (an observation, theory, etc.) by an alternative method of verification; so as *sb.*; **cross-chock** (see quot.); **cross-colouring** *Geol.*, colour-markings in strata caused by the introduction of extraneous matter by the action of water; **cross-correlation**, a correlation between two distinct series of measurements, events, etc., ordered in time or space; **cross-correspondence** *Spiritualism* (see quot. 1909); **cross-court** *a.*, of a stroke in tennis, rackets, etc.: hit diagonally across the court; so as *v. trans.*, to hit diagonally across the court; **cross-cousin**, one of two cousins who are the children of a brother and a sister respectively; also *attrib.* in *cross-cousin marriage*; **cross-cropping** (see quot.); **cross-cultural** *a.*, pertaining to or involving different cultures or comparison between them; †**cross-dagger**, an obsolete coin; **cross-dating**, the establishment of the date of one archæological site or level by correlation with another; also in dendrochronology (see quot. 1946); so **cross-date** *v. trans.* and *intr.*; **cross-dog** (see DOG); **cross-dressing** = TRANSVESTISM; hence [as back-formation] **cross-dress** *v. intr.* , to dress in clothes of the opposite sex, as a transvestite; **cross-dresser**; **cross-fade** *v. trans.* and *intr.* (*Broadcasting* and *Cinemat.*), to 'fade in' one sound or picture while 'fading out' another; so as *sb.*; so **cross-fading** *vbl. sb.*; **cross-fam** *v. slang* (see quot.); **cross-fault** *Geol.*, a fault which crosses the strike of the displaced strata; **cross-ferry** = FERRY *sb.*[1] 2, 3; **cross-file** (see quot.); **cross-fishing**, fishing with a line with many hooks attached extending across a stream; cf. CROSS-LINE 2; **cross-flute**, a transverse flute (see FLUTE *sb.*[1] 1); **cross-frog**, the arrangement where one line of rails crosses another, each of the rails being notched to admit the flanges of wheels on the crossing rail; †**cross-grinded** *a.*, cross-vaulted, having two arches or vaults intersecting each other; **cross-guard**, a sword-guard consisting of a short transverse bar; †**cross-hack** *v.*, to hack or cut with crossing lines; hence †**cross-hacking**; **cross-hair** = SPIDER-LINE; **cross-hap**, adverse fortune or occurrence; **cross-house**, a house at or by a cross; a house standing crosswise to others; also *fig.*; **cross-index** *v.*, to index under another heading as a cross-reference; **cross-influence**, interchange of influences or tendencies; **cross-kick** *v. intr.*, in football, to kick the ball across the field; also as *sb.*; **cross-legs**, (*a*) crossed legs; also quasi-*adv.*; (*b*) (*Obs. slang*) a tailor (cf. quot. 1602 s.v. CROSS *a.* 1 b); †**cross-letter**, a letter crossing the main routes, and carried by the cross-post; **cross-license** *v. trans.*, 'to give a license to another to use (a patent or invention) in return for a similar license' (Webster, 1961); also *intr.* and as *sb.*; hence **cross-licensing** *vbl. sb.*; **cross-lift** *v.* (see quot.); †**cross-like** *a.*, like or resembling a cross; **cross-linguistic** *a.*, pertaining to or involving different languages or comparison between them; **cross-link** *sb.*, **-linkage** *Chem.*, a chemical bond, or an atom or short chain of atoms, which connects two (long) chains in a polymer or other complex molecule; so **cross-link** *v. trans.*, to connect by cross-links, to bring about cross-linking in; *intr.*, to form a cross-link (*with*); **cross-linked** *ppl. a.*; **cross-linking**, *vbl. sb.*, the formation of cross-links; also, a network or system of cross-links; **cross-lock** *a.*, applied to an invention by which a carriage, etc. is enabled to 'lock' or turn on the main-pin in a particular way; **cross-lode** (see 4); **cross-loop**, a loop-hole in a fort in the form of a cross so as to give free range horizontally and vertically to an archer, etc.; **cross-match** *v. trans.* (*Med.*), to test the compatibility of (the blood of a blood-donor and a recipient); also said of the individuals; so as *sb.*; hence **cross-matching** *vbl. sb.*; **cross-member**, a strut fastened across the length of the chassis of a motor-car, etc.; **cross-mint**, the species *Mentha crispa*; **cross-modulation**, electrical intermodulation; *esp.* the introduction into one signal of new frequencies from another, unwanted, modulated signal; **cross-mouth** *a.*, having a transverse mouth; **cross-mouth chisel**, a cylindrical boring chisel with a diametrical blade; also ***cross-mouthed chisel***; †**cross-naming**, metonymy; **cross-oylet** = *cross-loop*; **cross-pass**, a pass across the field in football; **cross-peen** (also **-pane**, **-pein**), a hammer in which the peen runs crosswise to the direction of the handle; †**cross-penny**, a (silver) penny bearing a cross (cf. CROSS *sb.* 19); a kreutzer; **cross-ply** *a.*, designating a tyre in which the layers of fabric are laid with the cords at right angles across one another; also *ellipt.* as *sb.*; †**cross-providence**, an adverse dispensation or dealing of providence; **cross-quarters** (*Arch.*), an ornament of tracery in the form of a cruciform flower; **cross-rail**, a horizontal rail of a door or other framework; **cross-reel** *v. trans.*, to wind (yarn) on a reel with a reciprocating movement; so ***cross-reeling*** vbl. sb.; **cross-rhythm** *Mus.*, the simultaneous use of more than one rhythm; **cross-rib**, (*a*) *Arch.* (see quots.); (*b*) in a side of beef, a sternal rib running crosswise to the body; **cross-saddle**, a saddle on which the rider sits astride; also as *adv.*, on a cross-saddle, astride; **cross-sea** (see CROSS *a.* 1); **cross-seizing** *Naut.*, a seizing in which a number of turns of rope cross an equal number in the opposite direction; **cross-shed** (see quot. *a* 1877); **cross-shoot, -shooting**, a shooting or shot at anything moving across the field of sight; **cross-shot**, (*a*) = prec.; (*b*) *Lawn Tennis*, a shot that sends the ball diagonally across the court; **cross-sleeper**, a sleeper laid transversely across a tramway or railway track as a support for the rails; also as *adj.*; **cross-spider**, the common British garden spider *Epeira diadema*, so called from the cross-like mark on its anterior surface; **cross-talk** (*Telephone*), (*a*) see quot. 1887; in wider use, any unwanted transfer of signals from one circuit, channel, etc., to another; also, in *Radio*, a reproduced signal due to waves that are not of the frequency to which the receiver is tuned; (*b*) altercation, repartee, back-chat; conversation; also *attrib.*; so **cross-talker**; **cross-tig**, a variety of the game 'tig' in which another player running across between pursuer and pursued is pursued in his turn; **cross-tining** (*dial.*), cross-harrowing: see CROSS *v.* 7 b; **cross-tube** (see quot. 1888); **cross-valve**, a valve placed where a pipe has two cross-branches; **cross-vigil** (see quot.); **cross-vine**, a climber of the southern U.S., in which a section of the stem shows a cross-like appearance; **cross-volley** *Lawn Tennis*, a volley that sends the ball diagonally across the court; **cross-voting**, voting not according to party lines, in which some of the votes of each party are given on the other side; **cross-ward**, a cross-shaped ward of a lock; **cross-weaving**, weaving in which the warp-threads are crossed in regular order; **cross-webbing**, webbing drawn over the saddle-tree to strengthen the seat of a saddle; **cross-winding**, (*a*) a twisting of the surface of masonry, or the like; (*b*) the winding of yarn on a reel in such a way that the strands of one layer cross those of the previous layer at an acute angle; **cross-wire**, a wire that crosses; *spec.* = *cross-hair*; **cross-wood**, a West Indian shrub *Jacquinia ruscifolia*; †**cross-work**, transverse work; adverse action; †work with crosses; †**cross-wounded** *ppl. a.*, pierced through with a wound; **cross-yard**, a pole or spar fastened cross-wise.

1934 C. Lambert *Music Ho!* iii. 219 It is often suggested that jazz rhythm..ends by becoming monotonous through its being merely a series of irregular groupings and *cross-accents over a steady and unyielding pulse. **1959** D. Cooke *Lang. Music* v. 265 Driving duple rhythm (with triplets in chaotic cross-accent). **1962** *Listener* 31 May 969/3 Cross-accents and polyrhythms frequently suggest a concerto-like opposition of the various instrumental sounds individually or in groups. **1868** J. H. Blunt *Ref. Ch. Eng.* I. 393 He had begun a *cross action..against the clergyman. **1841** Gen. Thompson *Exerc.* (1842) VI. 52 And because there would be no use in two thousand men agreeing to die upon half the food that can keep soul and body together, they either toss up for it or play a *cross-and-jostle match. **1611** Beaum & Fl. *King & No K.* II. i, I was run twice through the body, and shot i' th' head with a *cross arrow. **1874** Knight *Dict. Mech.*, **Cross-axle*, 1. a shaft, windlass, or roller worked by opposite levers; as the copper-plate printing-press, etc.; 2. (*Railroad Engineering*) a driving-axle with cranks set at an angle of 90° with each other. **1875** Gwilt *Archit.* Gloss. s.v., Handrailing..is said to be *cross-banded when a veneer is laid upon its upper side, with the grain of the wood crossing that of the rail, and the extension of the veneer in the direction of its fibres is less than the breadth of the rail. *c* **1450** Lydg. *Mer. Missæ* 69 Whan he ryngythe the *crosbelle. **1797** Nelson in Nicolas *Disp.* II. 416 It is recommended..that all [the seamen] should have canvas *cross-belts. **1858** W. Ellis *Visits Madagascar* xiii. 372 The men wore the white cloth..round their loins, with cross-belts, and cartouche boxes over their naked shoulders. **1590** Nashe *Pasquil's Apol.* I. D iij, Theyr *crosse-blowe of *Fellowe labourers* will not saue theyr ribbes, if they be no better Fencers. **1607** Hieron *Wks.* I. 449 A counter-buffe, or crosse-blow, to the plots..of carnall and worldly-wise men. **1894** T. W. Fox *Mech. Weaving* 156 If a *cross-border machine is employed, a considerable saving in cards results in the manufacture of handkerchiefs..with a border all round. *Ibid.*, Certain classes of fabrics, such as cross-bordered, swivel, and compound. **1909** *Westm. Gaz.* 30 Mar. 11/4 Low values caused by *cross-breaks. **1890** G. Saintsbury *Ess.* 17 [He] catalogues books as folio, quarto, octavo, and so forth, and then *cross-catalogues them as law, physic, divinity and the rest. **1891** *Athenæum* 18 July 94/2 Librarians should therefore cross-catalogue..the work under these headings. **1696** J. Sergeant *Meth. Sci.* III. viii. 323 Multitudes of *Cross-causes may intervene, hindering that Effect from following. **1768** Blackstone *Comm.* III. xxvii. 451 When there are cross causes, on a cross bill filed by the defendant against the plaintiff in the original cause, they are generally contrived to be brought on together, that the same hearing and the same decree may serve for both of them. **1891** *Scot. Leader* 12 Dec. 4 Heavy weather was experienced by the *cross-channel steamers. **1892** *Daily News* 8 Oct. 7/4 Belfast..White linens for home and cross-Channel markets. **1940** *Economist* 24 Feb. 341/1 Certain *cross checks operated by the authorities suggest that the extent of evasion of the Regulations..has been commendably small. **1951** *N.Y. Times* 24 June E9/7 Experiments designed to cross-check important results. **1953** *Ibid.* 18 Jan. S3/6 An Associated Press cross-check..showed them..in support of the..action. **1960** E. H. Gombrich *Art & Illusion* viii. 274 We now know that touch is only one of a whole battery of cross checks at our disposal. **1962** A. Nisbett *Technique Sound Studio* xiii. 225 This front-line audience can be of immense value to him in cross-checking his calculation or intuition. **1968** *Globe & Mail* (Toronto) 5 Feb. 20/3 Penalties..Watson (P) (cross-checking). **1823** Crabbe *Technological Dict.*, **Cross-chocks* (*Mar.*)..pieces of timber fayed across the dead-wood in midships, to make good the deficiency of the lower heels of the futtock. **1901** *Science* 31 May 869/2, I scarcely dare assert that it might not be secondary *cross-coloring. **1920** H. E. Howard *Territory in Bird Life* iv. 133 Here we have a direct relationship..which at first sight appears to be exclusive of *cross-correlation. **1965** *Math. in Biol. & Med.* (*Med. Res. Council*) I. 37 The computer is being used to apply the mathematical techniques of autocorrelation and cross-correlation to the interpretation of the EEG in the treatment of temporal lobe epilepsy. **1970** *Nature* 26 Dec. 1299/1 A simple check for the effects of such coupling is to look for differences in the cross correlation between records from different aerials. **1904** J. G. Piddington in *Proc. Soc. Psychical Res.* XVIII. 294 (*heading*) *Cross-correspondences between the trance-utterances and script of Mrs. Thompson and those of other mediums. **1909** O. Lodge *Survival of Man* xii. 182 Cross-correspondence—that is, the reception of part of a message through one medium and part through another—is good evidence of one intelligence dominating both automatists. **1938** H. F. Saltmarsh (*title*) Evidence of personal survival from cross correspondences. **1915** M. E. McLoughlin *Tennis as I play It* (1916) xi. 235 The net-man is in line with the angle of almost all *cross-court shots. **1923** *Daily Mail* 30 June 11 He cross-courted both returns with his backhand. **1960** *Times* 10 June 18/6 He..hit his cross-court drive..to within inches of the line. **1889** E. Tylor in *Jrnl. Anthrop. Inst.* XVIII. 263 The child of the brother may marry the child of the sister. It seems obvious that this '*cross-cousin marriage', as it may be called, must be the direct result of the simplest form of exogamy. **1932** *Brit. Jrnl. Psychol.* Jan. 265 All ortho-cousins are forbidden, while cross-cousins are considered suitable mates. **1970** E. Leach *Lévi-Strauss* 121 A cross-cousin is a cousin of the type 'mother's brother's child' or 'father's sister's child'. **1847** *Jrnl. R. Agric. Soc.* VIII. I. 34 The miserable system of *cross-cropping, or taking two or more white straw crops in succession. *a* **1942** B. Malinowski *Sci. Theory Culture* (1944) iii. 18 There is the comparative method, in which the student is primarily interested in gathering extensive *cross-cultural documentations. **1949** M. Mead *Male & Female* ii. 26 All people who have had the good fortune to learn several languages in childhood have a precious degree of..cross-cultural understanding. **1701** S. Jeake *Body Arith.* 142 *Cross Daggers of Scotland, New Value 11s. 8d. **1937** W. S. Glock *Princ. & Methods Tree-Ring Analysis* I. 16 Two ring sequences that *cross-date were synchronous in formation and effectively duplicate each other in whole or in part... Cross-dating as generally practiced is the establishment of the time identity in ring groups in two different trees by means of very high and convincing structural correlation between them. **1939** G. Clark *Archaeol. & Society* v. 142 As a basis he studied living trees, cross-dating many trees of the same age to make sure of eliminating individual or purely topographical variations. **1946** F. E. Zeuner *Dating the Past* i. 11 *Cross-dating.* Having constructed a number of plots of individual trees one proceeds to 'cross-date' them. This is the term used by dendrochronologists for correlating the ring-series of one tree with that of another. **1950** G. E. Daniel *100 Yrs. Archaeol.* iv. 148 The synchronological technique of cross-dating. **1862** Smiles *Engineers* I. 283 The workmen erected another pier, using much timber in *cross-dogs, bars, and braces. **1966** H. Benjamin *Transsexual Phenomenon* ii. 12 Men in whom the desire to *cross-dress is often combined with other deviations. **1979** P. Ackroyd *Dressing Up* i. 27/2 When cross-dressed, the transvestite..'achieves a completely emotional identification which is sexually abnormal but aesthetically correct'. **1984** *Listener* 12 July 7/3 She had never accepted his desire to cross-dress, regarding him as 'perverted' and 'disgusting'. **1976** *National Observer* (U.S.) 16 Oct. 10/3 Not all of these '*cross-dressers', however, are satisfied just to wear feminine finery and assume female mannerisms. **1911** E. Carpenter in *Amer. Jrnl. Relig. Psychol. & Educ.* July 228 *Cross-dressing must be taken as a general indication of, and a cognate phenomenon to, homosexuality. **1928** H. Ellis *Studies Psychol. Sex* VII. 12 But Hirschfeld's conception of the anomaly scarcely appeared to me altogether satisfactory. Transvestism or cross-dressing fails to cover the whole of the ground. **1950** London & Caprio *Sexual Deviations* i. 20 Moll classified various varieties of transvestism as follows: ..(2) homosexual cases, in which cross-dressings constituted part of the contrary state; (3) heterosexual cases, where the sexual impulse is normal and in which cross-dressing constitutes part of a contrary sexual state [etc.]. **1971** *Daily Tel.* (Colour Suppl.) 10 Dec. 21/4 Many transexuals are also transvestites, with cross-dressing an essential part of their all-out desire to assume the opposite role. **1985** *Times* 21 Jan. 8/6 Androgynous clothing is a challenge to fixed concepts of femininity/masculinity, and once that demarcation line was established in Christian society, cross-dressing became subversive. **1937** *Printers' Ink Monthly* Apr. 50/2 **Cross-fade*, where one section of sound (musical or otherwise) is faded in while another is faded out. **1940** *Publishers' Weekly* 5 Oct. 1405 Cross fade on cue. **1953** K. Reisz *Technique Film Editing* ii. 187 The dubbing editor should be able to cross-fade from the dialogue to the music track at any time. **1957** Manvell & Huntley *Film Music* iii. 78 The turning of the page at a crossfade or cut can be helped by music's power. **1931** T. H. Pear *Voice & Personality* vi. 61 The process called by radio-play producers '*cross-fading'. **1812** J. H. Vaux *Flash Dict.*, To **cross-fam* a person, is to pick his pocket by crossing your arms in a particular position. **1900** *Geogr. Jrnl.* XVI. 461 Both longitudinal and *cross-faults..in the Eastern Alps. **1964** L. U. de Sitter *Struct. Geol.* (ed. 2) xiv. 193 The simplest kind of fault is the normal cross-fault, perpendicular to the axis. **1900** *Westm. Gaz.* 2 May 10/1 Nine *cross-ferries, two of which carry vehicular traffic. **1903** *Daily Chron.* 20 Feb. 6/7 Vehicular cross-ferry traffic was suspended. **1874** Knight *Dict. Mech.*, **Cross-file*, a file used in dressing out the arms or crosses of fine wheels. It has two convex faces of different curvatures. **1867** B. Osborne in *Morn. Star* 9 Apr., There is a thing called *cross-fishing, where one line is used with different coloured baits, and where both sides of the stream are swept. **1876** Stainer & Barrett *Dict. Mus. Terms* 172/2 *Cross-flutes were known to the Greeks by the name plagiaulos (πλαγίαυλος), and to the Romans as *tibia obliqua*. **1902** *Westm. Gaz.* 2 July 2/3 How this the flute, and that the cross-flute wrought. **1715** Leoni *Palladio's Archit.* (1742) I. 62 The Portico with a *cross-grinded Arch. **1874** Boutell *Arms & Arm.* ix. 173 The simplest variety of hilt..has..the pommel..the barrel..and the *cross-guard. **1608** Plat *Garden of Eden* (1653) 158 *Crossehack your cherry trees..in the new moon next after Christmas. *Ibid.* 159 All the *cross-hackings here mentioned. *a* **1884** Knight *Dict. Mech.* Suppl. 322/1 A telescope fitted with a *cross hair. **1917** J. H. McConkey *End of Age* 50 The cross-hairs of God's telescope of prophecy are centered upon it. **1881** Duffield *Don Quix.* I. 142 You need not fear any *cross-hap. *a* **1625** Boys *Wks.* (1629) 165 Many are so blinded with the sunshine of prosperity that they see..no such schoole as the *Crosse-house. **1875** W. McIlwraith *Guide Wigtownshire* 58 At either end of the wide part of this street there is a cross-house. **1892** *Law Times* XCII. 196/1 'Mayor's Court' should be *cross-indexed as 'Lord Mayor's Court'. **1931** G. Stern *Meaning & Change of Meaning* i. 13 The 'big' words are especially liable to sense-loans and *cross-influences. **1942** A. Koestler in *Horizon* V. 390 The revolution in physics has certainly affected the artist..and similar cross-influences are easy to discover. **1927** *Daily Tel.* 10 Feb. 16/7 You must swerve..or feint (or even *cross-kick) at an unexpected moment. **1954** J. B. G. Thomas *On Tour* vi. 66 Dobbin..cross-kicked into the middle. **1960** T. McLean *Kings of Rugby* xi. 179 A crosskick by Brown. **1823** in *Spirit of Public Jrnls. 1823* (1825) 59 Although the world has with one assent, agreed to consider the race of **cross-legs* as the most peacable and innocent set of people. **1889** Wilde *House of Pomegranates* (1891) 39 Sitting down cross-legs, in a circle. **1912** W. de la Mare *Listeners* 9 Then from his crosslegs he gets down. **1921** D. H. Lawrence *Let.* in E. & A. Brewster *Reminisc. & Corresp.* (1934) 24 If only you crossed the spoon and fork in front to look like two cross-legs. **1787** *Hist. Eur.* in *Ann. Reg.* 134 The *cross letter postage, which had been for many years let out to Mr. Allen. **1964** M. Gowing *Brit. & Atomic Energy 1939–1945* vii. 208 He did not believe that any agreement between Governments for free *cross-licensing was necessary. **1965** *Economist* 18 Dec. 1330/3 Part of the cross-licensing agreement. **1859** F. A. Griffiths *Artil. Man.* (ed. 9) 110 To *cross lift a gun, or carriage is to move it in a direction nearly at right angles to its axis. **1649** tr. *Behmen's Epist.* (1886) v. §29 It maketh a *cross-like birth. **1685** H. More *Paralip. Prophet.* 290 Otherwise the Perimeter of the House had been Cruciform or Cross-like. **1954** J. H. Greenberg in H. Hoijer *Lang. in Culture* I. 6 A matter which might be tested by *cross-linguistic comparisons. **1964** R. H. Robins *Gen. Linguistics* 208 Cross-linguistic appeals to equivalents or earlier forms in other languages are wholly irrelevant. **1936** Blaikie & Crozier in *Ind. Engin. Chem.* XXVIII. 1159/2 The number of *cross links in different soluble polymers will vary and be less than in the insoluble variety. **1937** Norrish & Brookman in *Proc. R. Soc.* A. CLXIII. 207 The production of these cross-linkages as determined by the formation of insoluble polymers appears to depend upon the electron attracting or repelling properties. *Ibid.* 207 Isoprene was used in an attempt to obtain a cross-linked polymer with styrene, since isoprene must possess this cross-linking property. *Ibid.* 219 Styrene will not form an insoluble co-polymer with the ether, although a small amount of cross-linking must occur. **1941** P. J. Flory in *Jrnl. Amer. Chem. Soc.* LXIII. 3100/2 Gelation occurs when the cross-linking index *y* (equal to the number of structural units which are cross-linked per chain) is equal to unity. **1963** J. Osborne *Dental Mech.* (ed. 5) xi. 240 A cross-linking agent may be added to the monomer. On polymerization such a substance cross-links in at least two directions with methyl methacrylate. **1970** *Nature* 6 June 939/2 This results in cross-linking which binds together the polymer chains within the enlarged crystallites. *Ibid.*, Cross-linking polymers by γ-irradiation is known to decrease crystallinity. **1843** *Jrnl. R. Agric. Soc.* IV. II. 492 Spring-waggon on the equirotal *cross-lock principle. **1930** *Ann. Surg.* XCI. 487 In five cases, in which the donor and the recipient were of the same group, there was agglutination when the bloods were *cross-matched. **1937** KRACKE & GARVER *Dis. Blood* xxxix. 433 It is..advisable to cross match the prospective donor and recipient to eliminate any possibility of an untoward reaction... In performing a cross match either the slide or the test tube method..may be used. *Ibid.*, The latter [is ascertained] by cross matching (donor vs. recipient). **1961** *Lancet* 19 Aug. 381/1 Early assessment allows more time for accurate cross-matching, and makes emergency transfusion safer. **1922** *Autocar* 10 Nov. 982 Another feature is the mounting of the steering box on the front *cross-member of the chassis. **1962** *Which?* (Car Suppl.) Oct. 138/1 We had to replace the front suspension cross-member. **1597** GERARDE *Herbal* II. ccxv. §2. 552 *Mentha cruciata*, *Crosse Mint, or curled Mint. **1933** J. M. STINCHFIELD in K. Henney *Radio Engin. Handbk.* viii. 204 *Cross-modulation and modulation distortion in the r-f stages of a receiver. **1942** *Electronic Engin.* XV. 285 This method..prevents cross-modulation of the two input voltages due to a common cathode impedance. **1958** W. F. LOVERING *Radio Communication* xiii. 319 The cross-modulation component is..most likely to occur when the interfering signal is that from a strong local station. *a* **1877** KNIGHT *Dict. Mech.* I. 650/1 **Cross-mouth chisel*, a boring-chisel of a cylindrical form with a diametrical blade. **1896** *Daily News* 26 Sept. 3/5 Cross-mouthed chisels of hardest tool steel. **1589** PUTTENHAM *Eng. Poesie* III. (Arb.) 189 Single words haue their sence and vnderstanding altered and figured many wayes, to wit, by transport, abuse, *crosse-naming..change of name. **1857** TURNER *Dom. Archit.* III. II. vii. 341 In each side of the central buttress is a slit, and above it a *cross-oylet. **1929** *Daily Express* 7 Nov. 19/2 A *cross-pass from right-winger T. Maskell was retrieved just beyond the far post by his opposite number. **1961** *Times* 25 May 4/2 Hitchens headed into the top corner on the bounce a long cross-pass from Armfield. *a* **1877** KNIGHT *Dict. Mech.* II. 1647/2 (*caption*) *Cross peen for coopers. **1957** R. LISTER *Decor. Wrought Ironwork* ii. 11 If the pane is placed in a position running relatively across this hole instead of running parallel to it, it is called a *cross-pane*. **1958** *Listener* 24 July 143/1 Do not buy a crosspein hammer that is too small. **1847** *Secr. Soc. Mid. Ages* 343 He then threw a *cross-penny..to the court, and went his way. **1965** GOUGH & UDALL *Radial Ply Tyres* 1 (*caption*) A conventional *cross-ply tyre in section. **1968** *Listener* 18 July 95/2 Try not to mix radials with cross-plies. **1970** M. EDWARDS *Car Handyman* viii. 104 A cross-ply tyre is one in which the plies of the tyre, or the beads, cross over. .. Usually, if the marking is in inches, say 5·20 × 10, then the tyre is a cross-ply. **1720** WELTON *Suffer. Son of God* II. xiv. 377 Looking upon Afflictions and *Cross-Providence with Esteem. **1836** DICKENS *Sk. Boz* II. 95 A tent bedstead without hangings or *cross-rails. **1880** *Spon's Encycl. Industr. Arts* II. 739 In the interior of the framework, is fitted a conical grid, having its apex downwards, and resting on a cross-rail at a short distance from the bottom. **1902** *How to make Useful Things* 13/2 The bottom cross-rail is.. 3¼ in. less in length than the width of the end of the fowl-house. **1890** *Nasmith Mod. Cotton Spinning Mach.* xiii. 267 The hanks being reeled, they are, if *cross reeled, dyed or bleached, and, if in leas, bundled. **1926** WHITEMAN & MCBRIDE *Jazz* xi. 231 Six hundred fox-trotters.. automatically were dancing in *cross rhythm. **1927** *Melody Maker* Sept. 845/3 Brahms..employed syncopation and cross-rhythms about a century before modern 'syncopated orchestras' were dreamed of. **1946** A. HUTCHINGS in A. L. Bacharach *Brit. Music of our Time* xvi. 205 They lacked the vigour which comes from cross-rhythm, or counterpoint. **1858** *Dict. Archit.* (*Archit. Publ. Soc.*), **Cross rib* (Fr. *arc doubleau*), a rib from one pier or pillar across to its respond, square with the vault to which the rib belongs... Willis calls it the transverse rib, and it is often called the arch rib. **1902** R. STURGIS *Dict. Archit.* III. 289 The wall ribs (*formerets*) and cross ribs (*arcs doubleaux*) were..pointed. **1897** W. E. NORRIS *Clarissa Furiosa* xxxiii. 293 His daughter..would.. ride to hounds in a *cross-saddle. **1897** *Westm. Gaz.* 22 Dec. 4/2 The cross-saddle position assumed by women on 'bikes'. **1905** *Daily Chron.* 1 Aug. 3/3 One of our Royal Princesses is to be taught to ride cross-saddle. **1930** S. G. GOLDSCHMIDT *Fellowship of Horse* ix. 131 Cross-saddle riding for women is not making the progress it should. *Ibid.* 136 The prejudice against the cross-saddle. **1883** *Man. Seamanship for Boys* 109 A *Cross Seizing is used when the rigging is turned in with the end up. *a* **1877** KNIGHT *Dict. Mech.* I. 650/1 **Cross-shed*, the upper shed of a gauze-loom. **1894** T. W. FOX *Mech. Weaving* 225 *O* shows the lifting for an open shed, and *c* that for a cross shed. **1766** T. PAGE *Art of Shooting* 35 If you take aim a foot before a *cross shoot at forty yards. *Ibid.* 34 A hint concerning cross-shooting. **1789** *Ess. Shooting* (1791) 215 To avoid missing a *cross shot, whether it be flying or running. **1889** H. W. W. WILBERFORCE *Lawn Tennis* xii. 43 It may be a difficult cross-shot. **1902** *Westm. Gaz.* 1 July 4/3 His cross-shots to the left-hand corner swift and sure. **1841** *Penny Cycl.* XIX. 255/1 The use of *cross-sleepers..needs little remark. **1888** *Encycl. Brit.* XXIII. 506/2 The rail was spiked through to a longitudinal timber laid on cross sleepers. **1892** *Pall Mall G.* 14 May 4/3 We have what we call upon certain sections the cross-sleeper road. **1883** J. G. WOOD in *Gd. Words* Dec. 761/1 A Diadem or *Cross Spider comes running over her web. **1887** *Soc. Telegr. Engin. Jrnl.* XVI. 433 The annoyance caused by induction, known commonly by the name of '*cross-talk'. **1891** *Times* 12 Jan., To suppress the sputtering noises, or 'cross-talk', induced in the line by currents passing through some neighbouring telegraph or telephone line. **1909** 'I. HAY' *Man's Man* viii. 132 A carefully rehearsed 'cross-talk' dialogue between two knock-about artistes of the Variety firmament. **1910** *Hawkins's Electr. Dict.*, *Cross talk*, conversation over one telephone circuit overheard in the telephone of another circuit, when their wires run side by side. This fault is due almost entirely to electrostatic induction. **1917** 'I. HAY' *Carrying On* i. 18 Each bus is in charge of the identical pair of cross-talk comedians who controlled its destinies in more peaceful days. **1923** WODEHOUSE *Adventures of Sally* xv. 184 As brisk and snappy as any cross-talk between vaudeville comedians. **1930** *Times Lit. Suppl.* 27 Mar. 276/3 Some of the crosstalk of the American shop-girls is entertaining. **1932** F. E. TERMAN *Radio Engin.* xiii. 470 The first kind of cross-talk is produced by heterodyne detection of two signals having a frequency difference lying within the tuning range of the receiver. *Ibid.* 471 Cross-talk [of the second kind] is caused by the unwanted signal modulating the carrier wave of the desired signal. **1955** *Times* 27 July 8/2 There was a good deal of cross-talk on the origin of recent rumours about sterling. **1957** R. W. G. HUNT *Reproduction of Colour* xii. 163 Hence *cross-talk* (that is, interference between the luminance and chrominance signals) in band-sharing systems..is minimized. **1961** A. WILSON *Old Men at Zoo* vi. 306, I thought that I should scream if I had to live with this cross talk act for long. **1970** *Which?* Apr. 114 The crosstalk rating shows how well the stereo channels were separated, so that signals on one channel did not affect the other. **1907** *Daily Chron.* 1 May 6/4 Those pioneer *cross-talkers, the Christy Minstrels. **1876** GRANT *Burgh Sch. Scotl.* II. v. 180 '*Cross-tig', and 'Scotch and English Jackson'..are played at Arbroath high school. *a* **1884** KNIGHT *Dict. Mech.* Suppl. 232/1 **Cross tube boiler*. In the usual vertical form, this boiler has one or more horizontal cross tubes..placed across the fire-box. **1888** *Lockwood's Dict. Mech. Engin.*, *Cross tubes*, the heating tubes in a steam boiler—usually applied to boilers of the vertical type. **1932** *Times Lit. Suppl.* 28 Jan. 55/3 The *Cross-vigil (cros-figell), that is, praying for lengthened periods with the arms outstretched in the form of a cross. **1905** *Daily Chron.* 20 Mar. 3/3 The American *cross-volleys which may bring the English players a little nearer the net in doubles. **1884** *Manch. Exam.* 9 Apr. 5/2 The *cross voting was so exceptionally slight that only one Liberal voted with the Conservatives. **1703** MOXON *Mech. Exerc.* 29 You may easily file your *Cross, or Hook-wards, wider or deeper. **1843** *Penny Cycl.* XXVII. 179/1 **Cross weaving*.—This term may be conveniently applied to those varieties of woven fabric in which the warp-threads..cross over or twist around one another, thus forming a plexus or interlacing independent of that produced by the weft. *a* **1877** KNIGHT *Dict. Mech.* I. 650/2 *Cross-weaving loom*, a loom for weaving with a crossed warp. **1816** J. SMITH *Panorama Sc. & Art* I. 27 Those twistings of the surface which are technically termed *cross-windings. **1823** P. NICHOLSON *Pract. Build.* 341 A thin board, planed true, to point out cross-windings and other inequalities of surface. **1892** NASMITH *Students' Cotton Spinning* 360 Cross winding is resorted to when the hank is to be dyed. **1866** *Cross wire [see SPIDER-LINE]. **1882** J. SMITH *Economic Plants* 143 It derives its name of *Crosswood from..its branches being produced in whorls of four, thus forming a cross. **1434** *E.E. Wills* (1882) 101 A good bordcloth with *crosse werk. **1627** F. E. *Hist. Edw. II* (1680) 12 There might be some cross-work might blast his project. **1582** T. WATSON *Centurie of Loue* lxi, My Hart *croswounded with desire. **1634** SIR T. HERBERT *Trav.* 193 They erect a Tree, with a *crosse-yard fastned to it.

crossable ('krɒsəb(ə)l, -ɔː-), *a.* [f. CROSS *v.* + -ABLE.] That can be crossed.

1865 CARLYLE *Fredk. Gt.* VII. XVIII. viii. 233 Plank or raft bridge there..will be crossable tomorrow. **1889** *Pall Mall G.* 22 Apr. 7/2 To make it crossable for passengers on foot.

cross-action: see CROSS- B.

crossado, non-naturalized form of CRUSADE.

† **cross-aisle**, *Obs.*, transept: see AISLE 3.

† **crossaundre**. *Obs.* (see quot.)

1519 HORMAN *Vulg.* 240 With great pylys of alder rammed downe, and with a frame of tymbre called a crossaundre [*fistuca*].

cross-axle: see CROSS- B.

cross-banded: see CROSS- B.

cross-bar ('krɒsbɑː(r), 'krɔːs-), *sb.* [CROSS- 4.]

1. a. A transverse bar; a bar placed or fixed across another bar or part of a structure. *spec.* The horizontal bar of a bicycle frame; also, in *Football*, the horizontal bar between the goal-posts.

1562 *Churchw. Acc. Eltham* in Stahlschmidt *Bells of Kent* (1887) 271 A crosbar for the bell. **1611** [see CROSS-BARRED]. **1823** CRABBE *Techn. Dict. Cross-bars* (*Mar.*), round pieces of iron, bent at each end, and used as levers to turn the shanks of the anchor. **1856** KANE *Arct. Expl.* II. xxvi. 267 We had already cut up and burned the runners and cross-bars of two sledges. **1857** T. HUGHES *Tom Brown* v. 120 There it flies, straight between the two posts, some five feet above the cross-bar, an unquestioned goal. **1956** M. GOLESWORTHY *Encycl. Assoc. Football* 36 The crossbar over the goalmouth was first introduced into Football Association rules in 1875. **1966** T. SIMPSON *Cycling is my Life* v. 38 My left leg was still fastened to the pedal by the toe-strap and then bent over the cross-bar with me lying across the front wheel. **1967** S. BECKETT *Film* 32 Two bicycles ridden by men with girl passengers (on crossbar).

† **b.** = *cross-bar shot*: see 5. *Obs.*

1557 W. TOWRSON in Hakluyt *Voy.* (1589) 120 We sent them some of our stuffe, crosse barres and chaine shot and arrowes. **1712** E. COOKE *Voy. S. Sea* 351 We fir'd above 300 great Shot, about 50 Cross Bars.

2. A transverse line or stripe: cf. BAR *sb.*[1] 5.

1599 SANDYS *Europæ Spec.* (1632) 238 In their crossings.. the Greeke..begins his crosse-barre on the right side, and the Latin on the left. **1694** RAY in *Lett. Lit. Men* (Camden) 200 A tail..marked with crosse-bars. **1937** R. H. STETSON in *Mélanges ling. et phil. offerts à J. van Ginneken* 355 In Continental usage the 7 has a cross-bar. **1957** N. R. KER *Catal. MSS. containing Anglo-Saxon* p. xxxi, The form and position of the cross-bar [of ð] often vary.

† **3.** The 'bar sinister', the heraldic mark of illegitimacy. *Obs.*

1655 FULLER *Ch. Hist.* I. v. §13 To shew that no Crosse-barre of Bastardy..can bolt Grace out of that Heart, wherein God will have it to enter. **1732** *Gentleman Instr.* (ed. 10) 11 (D.) Few are in love with Cross-bars, and to be brother to a by-blow is to be a bastard once removed.

† **4.** *fig.* An impediment, hindrance, obstruction; an untoward circumstance, misfortune. *Obs.*

1583 STANYHURST *Aeneis* II. (Arb.) 46 Hence grew my cros-bars. **1616** R. C. *Times' Whistle* iii. 1151 But now this boy, which stands as a crosse-barre Twixt him and home, doth all his fortunes marre.

5. *Comb.*, as ***cross-bar window***; **cross-bar shoe** = *bar-shoe* (see BAR *sb.*[1] 30); **cross-bar shot**, orig. a ball with a bar projecting on each side of it; later, a projectile which expanded on leaving the gun into the form of a cross, with one quarter of the ball at each radial point: cf. BAR-SHOT.

1675 *Lond. Gaz.* No. 1030/4 A light gray Mare..lame in the neer Foot before, and a *Cross-bar shoe under the same Foot. **1591** RALEIGH *Last Fight Rev.* (Arb.) 19 Discharged with *crossebar shot. **1627** CAPT. SMITH *Seaman's Gram.* xiv. 67 Crosbar-shot is also a round shot, but it hath a long spike of Iron cast with it as if it did goe thorow the middest of it. **1768-74** TUCKER *Lt. Nat.* (1852) I. 453 Something like the chain or cross bar shot used in sea engagements, only instead of a bar between, the whole consisted of seven balls. **1867** SMYTH *Sailor's Word-bk.*, *Cross-bar-shot*..when folded it presented a..complete shot.

cross-bar ('krɒs,bɑː(r), ,krɒs'bɑː(r), krɔːs-), *v.* [f. prec.]

1. *trans.* To furnish with cross-bars; to put or set bars across.

1616 SURFL. & MARKH. *Country Farme* 318 These hiues you must crosse-barre within with clouen sticks. *Ibid.* 703.

b. To mark with cross-bars; to draw bars or stripes across.

1805 W. TAYLOR in Robberds *Mem.* II. 97 And suppose you have received it and cross-barred it [a manuscript] where necessary. **1861** THORNBURY *Turner* (1862) I. 336 Some glancing sunshine cross-barring a sail.

† **2.** *fig.* To obstruct, bar the way of. *Obs.*

1680 *Hon. Hodge & Ralph* 22 There's an unlucky Gentleman, that Cross-bars them in their designs.

'cross-barred, *ppl. a.* [f. prec. sb. or vb. + -ED.] Furnished with cross-bars, having bars placed across; marked with cross-bars or stripes.

1611 COTGR., *Croisée*, the crosse-barre of a window; also, a window so crosse-barred. **1624** HEYWOOD *Gunaik.* v. 225 A horse-litter seeled and crosse-bard with gads of steele and plates of yron. **1667** MILTON *P.L.* IV. 190 Substantial dores, Cross-barrd and bolted fast. **1677** *Lond. Gaz.* No. 1245/4 The other [Gown] purple and white single Crossbarr'd Lutestring. **1712** ADDISON *Spect.* No. 311 ¶1 Her Chamber Windows are cross-barred. **1891** *Daily News* 7 Sept. 3/3 [The gown] was grey, crossbarred down the back and front with broad bands of black velvet.

'cross-beak. = CROSS-BILL.

1688 R. HOLME *Armoury* II. 242/1 The Crosbeak is a thick and short Billed Bird. **1789** G. WHITE *Selborne* II. vii. (1853) 176 Considerable flocks of crossbeaks.

cross-beam ('krɒsbiːm, 'krɔːs-). [CROSS- 4.] A beam placed across some part of a structure or mechanism; a transverse beam.

1594 T. B. *La Primaud. Fr. Acad.* II. 96 They want neither the bellowes, nor the crosse-beame, nor the cordes..nor the organ pipes. **1611** COTGR., *Traversin*, A crosse-beame, or peece of timber, in a ship, etc. **1706** PHILLIPS (ed. Kersey), *Cross-piece* or *Cross-beam*, a Beam laid a-cross another: In a Ship, it is a great piece of Timber that goes a-cross two other pieces call'd Bitts, and to which the Cable is fasten'd when the Ship rides at Anchor. **1825** WOOD *Railroads* 146 The piston rods..are attached to the cross-beams [in Stephenson's Killingworth locomotive]. **1844** DICKENS *Mart. Chuz.* xxxi, The old oak roof supported by cross-beams.

cross-bearer ('krɒs,bɛərə(r), 'krɔːs-). [CROSS- 1.]

I. One who bears, wears, or carries a cross.

1. An attendant who carries a cross in a procession or religious ceremony; he who bears an archbishop's cross before him.

1568 GRAFTON *Chron.* II. 58 Thomas Becket..through the instigation of certain about him, but chiefely of his crosse-bearer. **1644** EVELYN *Diary* 23 Nov., The Crosse-bearer on horseback, with two Priests at each hand on foote. **1726** AYLIFFE *Parergon* 94 He has..the Bishop of Rochester (Time was) for his Cross-bearer. **1840** HOOD *Up the Rhine* 186 Besides a cross-bearer and flag-bearer, there were..a score of regular attendants all carrying lighted tapers.

2. One who wears a cross in sign of a vow; *spec.* applied to certain officers of the Inquisition pledged to prosecute heretics.

1731 CHANDLER tr. *Limborch's Hist. Inquis.* I. 191 There is another sort of them, called Cross-Bearers, instituted by Dominick, to whom he gave such Constitutions..as obliges them vigorously to prosecute Hereticks.

3. *fig.* One who 'takes up his cross' and follows Christ.

1540 COVERDALE *Fruitf. Less.* i. Wks. (Parker Soc.) I. 294 Make us true cross-bearers and followers of thee.

II. ***'cross-'bearer***. [from CROSS *a.*, CROSS- 4.]

4. (See quot.)

1874 KNIGHT *Dict. Mech.*, *Cross-bearer*, the transverse bars supporting the grate-bars of a furnace.

'cross-'bearings. *Naut.* [CROSS *a.* or *adv.*] The bearings of two or more points taken from a point of reference so as to give their angular distance from each other, or, when their positions are known, to plot the position of a ship on a chart.

1809 Visc. Valentia *Voy. India, etc.* (1811) II. viii. 342 Its distance was ascertained to be seventy miles, by a set of cross bearings taken from the island. **1857** R. Tomes *Amer. in Japan* xiii. 310 On taking the cross-bearings, it was found ..that the ships had not shifted their places a mile.

cross-bedding, -belt: see cross- B.

'cross-'bench. [cross *a.*, cross- 4.] A bench placed at right angles to other benches. *spec.* In the House of Lords, at Westminster, certain benches so placed, on which independent or neutral members sometimes sit.

1846 J. Baxter *Libr. Pract. Agric.* (ed. 4) I. p. xvii, He seated himself upon the cross benches, an unusual position to take in the House of Lords. **1849** Ht. Martineau *Hist. Eng.* I. 15 The cross-benches of neutrality in the House of Commons. **1884** *Pall Mall G.* 15 Feb. 3/1 Lord Granville's answer to Lord Wemyss's demand for more cross-benches is one of the neatest things on record.

b. *attrib.*, esp. in the phrase ***cross-bench mind.***

1884 Ld. Granville *Sp. in Ho. Lords* (*Pall Mall G.* 15 Feb. 3/1), Individually.. I have no great sympathy with the cross-bench mind.. While.. I prefer a good Liberal I am afraid I also prefer even a good Tory to those who are neither fish, fowl, flesh, nor good herring. **1884** Dk. Argyll *Sp. in Ho. Lords* 7 July, It would be well for this House if a great majority of its members had the cross-bench mind.

Hence **,cross-'bencher**, one who occupies a cross-bench, or asserts his independency of party; **,cross-'benchedness**.

1885 *Contemp. Rev.* Mar. 456 Though posing as a cross-bencher, the author writes in a strong Tory spirit of Nationalism. **1885** *Sat. Rev.* 24 Jan. 101/2 Cross-benchedness has not exactly been justified of all her children.

'cross-'bias, *sb.* [cross *a.*] A bias or inclination running athwart or counter to another.

1678 Marvell *Growth Popery* Wks. 1875 IV. 357 So various were the several interests, and crossbiasses.

So **cross-'bias** *v.*, to give a cross-bias to. **cross-'biased** *ppl. a.*, subject to cross-biases. †**cross-'biasness**, tendency to go athwart or contrary, waywardness.

1633 G. Herbert *Affliction* ix, *Temple* 39 Thus doth thy power crosse-bias me. **1652** Benlowes *Theoph.* xii. lxi. 227 Cross-biasnesse to Grace our ruine spinn'd. **1844** Marg. Fuller *Wom. 19th C.* (1862) 386, I leave Italy.. hoping.. to return, but fearing that may not be permitted in my 'cross-biased' life.

crossbill ('krɒsbɪl, 'krɔːs-). [cross *a.* 1 b.] A bird of the genus *Loxia* (family *Fringillidæ*), having the mandibles of the bill curved so as to cross each other when the bill is closed; found in the north of Europe and America, and in Japan. The Common Crossbill is *L. curvirostra.*

*a*1672 Willughby *Ornith.* 248. **1713** Derham *Phys. Theol.* (1723) 193 The *Loxia*, or Cross-Bill, whose Bill is thick and strong, with the Tips crossing one another. **1766** Pennant *Zool.* (1768) II. 279 The Grosbeak and Crossbill come here but seldom. **1829** E. Jesse *Jrnl. Nat.* 182 That rare bird the Crossbill.. occasionally visits the orchards.

Hence **'cross-billed** *a.*, having the mandibles crossed, like the birds of the genus *Loxia.*

1766 Pennant *Zool.* (*heading*), Cross-billed Grosbeak.

cross-bill, cross bill. *Law.* [cross *a.* 6, cross- 9.] A bill filed in Chancery by a defendant against the plaintiff or other co-defendants in the same suit. **b.** A bill of exchange given in consideration of another bill (Wharton).

1637 in *Select. Harl. Misc.* (1793) 315 That their honours will be pleased to accept of a cross bill against the prelates. **1678** Butler *Hud.* iii. iii. 655 Who, putting in a new cross-bill, May traverse th' action. **1768** Blackstone *Comm.* III. 448 If he [the defendant] has any relief to pray against the plaintiff, he must do it by an original bill of his own, which is called a cross bill. **1883** *Law Rep.* 11 Q. Bench Div. 466 A counter-claim is like a cross-bill under the former practice in equity, which fell with the original bill.

cross-birth: see cross- B.

†**'cross,bite,** *v. Obs.* Also 6–7 crosbite. [cross- 6.]

1. *trans.* To bite the biter; to cheat in return; to cheat by outwitting; to 'take in', gull, deceive.

1532 *Dice-Play* (Percy Soc.) 30 If ye lack contraries, to crosbite him withall, I shall lend you a pair of the same size that his cheats be. **1591** Greene *Disc. Coosnage* To Reader, When a broaking knaue cross-biteth a Gentleman with a bad commoditie. **1672** Wycherley *Love in Wood* v. vi, Fortune our foe.. By none but thee our projects are cross-bit. **1717** Prior *Alma* iii. 365 As Nature slily had thought fit, For some by-ends to cross-bite wit. **1823** Scott *Peveril* xxviii, If your Grace can.. throw out a hint to crossbite Saville, it will be well.

2. To attack or censure bitingly or bitterly.

1571 Golding *Calvin on Ps.* xii. 5 He crossbyteth the courtly clawebackes [sed aulicos caluminiatores perstringit]. **1581** Rich *Farewell* (1846) 154 She.. would crossbite hym with tauntes and spitefull quippes. **1685** F. Spence *House of Medici* 416 The Pope.. unwilling to incense him by fruitlesly cross-biting his election. **1697** Collier *Ess. Mor. Subj.* ii. (1709) 74 Cross biting a Country Evidence, and frighting him out of Truth, and his Senses.

Hence †**'crossbite** *sb.*, a cheat, trick, swindle, deception; †**'crossbiter**, one who 'crossbites', a swindler; †**'crossbiting** *vbl. sb.* and *ppl. a.*

1591 Greene *Disc. Coosnage* To Rdr., When the nip, which the common people call a cutpurse, hath a cros-bite by some bribing officer. **1692** Wagstaffe *Vind. Carol.* xxvi. 120 Unless he could give them the Cross-bite. **1711** Puckle *Club* (1817) 98 Besides the danger of a cross-bite. **1592** Greene *Groat's W. Wit* D iv b, The legerdemaines of nips, foysts, conicatchers, crosbyters. **1656** Earl Monm. *Advt. fr. Parnass.* 185 Dame Nature, who greatly hates cheaters, and crosbiters. **1576** Whetstone *Rocke of Regard* 50 (N.) Crosbiting, a kind of cousoning under the couler of friendship. **1615** Chapman *Odyss.* xv. 551 The cross-biting Phoenicians. **1674** Cotton *Compl. Gamester*, They effect their purpose by cross-biting, or some other dexterity. *a*1734 North *Exam.* i. ii. §l. (1740) 55 Affronts, Tergiversations, Crossbitings, personal Reflections, and such like.

'cross-bond. *Brick-laying.* [cross *a.*] A bond in which a course of 'stretchers' alternates with one of alternate 'stretchers' and 'headers' so as to break joint with it and also with the next row of stretchers.

1876 *Encycl. Brit.* IV. 461/2 The mediæval brick buildings in north-east of Germany are worked in Flemish bond, or as it is there called 'cross-bond'.

'cross-bones, *sb. pl.* [cross- 4 c.] A figure of two thigh-bones laid across each other in the form of the letter X, usually placed under the figure of a skull, as an emblem of death.

1798 Canning, etc. *Anti-Jacobin, Rovers*, A subterranean vault.. with coffins, 'scutcheons, death's heads and cross-bones. **1826** Miss Mitford *Village* Ser. ii. (1863) 898 She was a perpetual *memento mori*; a skull and cross-bones would hardly have been more efficacious. **1885** Runciman *Skippers & Sh.* 86 Half a score of us had been under the crossbones [i.e. pirate's flag].

cross-bow ('krɒsbəʊ, 'krɔːs-). [cross- 3 b.]

1. A mediæval weapon consisting of a bow fixed across a wooden stock, having a groove or barrel for the missile and a mechanism for holding and releasing the string, used for shooting bolts, stones, arrows, etc.; an arbalest.

1432–50 tr. *Higden* I. 297 Crosse bawes or staffe slynges. **1548** Hall *Chron.* 90 Then the arrowes flewe out of the long bowes.. the quarrelles out of the crosse bowes. **1581** J. Bell *Haddon's Answ. Osor.* 147 Stones.. violently whirled out of a Crossebow. **1678** tr. *Gaya's Arms War* 40 The Ancients had two kinds of Cross-bows, the one which shoot Darts or Quarrels, and the other which threw Stones: these were called *Balistae*, and the other *Catapultae.* **1798** Coleridge *Anc. Mar.* i. xx, With my cross-bow I shot the Albatross. *a*1862 Buckle *Misc. Wks.* (1872) I. 343 The cross bow is said to have been used in the battle of Hastings.

2. *transf.* (*pl.*) Men armed with cross-bows; crossbowmen, as a force.

*c*1511 *1st Eng. Bk. Amer.* (Arb.) Introd. 34/2, .x. M. knyghtes on horsbacke .vi. M. Crosse bowes. *a*1533 Ld. Berners *Huon* cxxix. 473 Theyr botys well garnysshyd with men, archars and crosbowes. **1599** Hakluyt *Voy.* I. 20, 50 men of warre.. together with 20 crossbowes.

3. *attrib.* and *Comb.*, as ***cross-bow case, -maker, match, rack, shot.***

1530 Palsgr. 211/1 Crosbowe case, *carquas.* Crosbowe maker, *arcbalestrier.* **1570** Dee *Math Pref.* 35 The force of the Crossebow Racke is.. here, demonstrated. **1632** J. Hayward tr. *Biondi's Eromena* 150 Having one arme little better than lost by a Crosbow-shot. **1676** *Lond. Gaz.* No. 1121/6 Samuel Smith Crosbow-Maker near Temple-bar, London. **1845** S. Austin *Ranke's Hist. Ref.* II. 189 A great cross-bow match at Heidelberg.

†**crossbower** ('krɒsbəʊə(r), 'krɔːs-). *Obs.* [f. prec. + -er.] = next.

1590 Sir J. Smyth *Disc. Weapons* 45 b, Crosse-bowers and Archers on horsebacke. *a*1618 Raleigh *Invent. Shipping* 22 The French had 12000 Crosbowers Genowaies by Sea.

crossbowman ('krɒsbəʊmən, 'krɔːs-). An archer with a crossbow; a soldier armed with a crossbow.

*c*1500 *Melusine* 132 A thousand men of armes, & C crosbowe men. **1632** J. Hayward tr. *Biondi's Eromena* 11 He armed her with twise as many crossebow-men as souldiers. **1777** Robertson *Hist. Amer.* (1778) II. v. 9 Thirty-two were cross-bow-men. **1843** Prescott *Mexico* (1850) I. 372 The artillery, the arquebusiers, and crossbowmen, were to support one another.

'cross-bred, *ppl. a.* [Cf. next and cross- 8.] Bred from parents of different species or varieties; hybrid, mongrel. (Also *absol.* as *sb.*) Also, (designating) wool from cross-bred sheep.

1856 *Farmer's Mag.* Jan. 70 In regard to cross-bred animals. **1880** Grant & Foster *N.Z.* iv. 42 The weight of these [fleeces] in the grease seemed to average about 5½ or 6 lbs., while that of the cross-breds were [*sic*] very little heavier. **1887** *Daily News* 1 Dec. 2/1 Whether the Hereford is to beat the Devon, or the cross-bred the Highlander. **1892** *Ibid.* 1 Feb. 2/7 Wools, both Botany and cross-breds. **1899** *Daily News* 7 Mar. 8/6 Fine crossbreds are also fairly firm, but the stronger descriptions, and English wools generally, are in small demand. **1941** [see *auto-sex* s.v. auto-]. **1955** [see come-back *sb.*[2] 4]. **1962** *Economist* 11 Aug. 548/2 New Zealand's crossbred wools have drifted lower again.

'cross-'breed, *v.* [cross *adv.*] To breed across the lines which separate varieties or races; to breed (animals or plants) from individuals of different species or races. Hence **'cross-,breeding** *vbl. sb.*

1675 Wycherley *Country Wife* ii. i, They are come to think cross breeding for themselves best, as well as for their dogs and horses. **1932** *Discovery* Mar. 73/2 There was a certain amount of selection and cross breeding [of crops] towards the end of the nineteenth century. **1955** *Sci. News Let.* 23 July 50 That individual is separated from the rest, then bred and cross-bred to develop a pure-breeding strain. **1955** *Bull. Atomic Sci.* Sept. 242 FAO technicians are cross-breeding the rice strain Japonica.. with the native Indica species of Southeast Asia and India.

cross-breed ('krɒsbriːd, 'krɔːs-), *sb.* [Cf. prec. and cross *a.*] A breed of animals (or plants) produced by crossing; a mongrel or hybrid breed; *transf.* an animal of such a breed. Also *fig.*

1774 Wilkes *Corr.* (1805) IV. 185 The family of monsieur Louvet.. emigrated to England; and made a cross-breed with those who [etc.]. **1844** Disraeli *Coningsby* iii. v, It seems to me a barren thing, this Conservatism, an unhappy cross-breed; the mule of politics that engenders nothing. **1890** *Spectator* 13 Dec., Both prizes for the cross-breeds were won by crosses of shorthorn with the Scotch breeds.

'cross-'bun. [cross- 3 c.] A bun indented with a cross, commonly eaten on Good Friday.

1733 *Poor Robin's Almanack* in Brand *Pop. Antiq.* (1873) I. 154 Good Friday comes this month, the old woman runs With one or two a penny hot cross buns. **1791** Boswell *Johnson* 9 Apr. an. 1773 Being Good Friday, I breakfasted with him on tea and cross-buns. **1859** Sala *Tw. round Clock* (1861) 80 What becomes of all the cold crossbuns after Good Friday?

'cross-'buttock, *sb.* [app. f. cross *prep.* + buttock; in form an adj. used absolutely.] A peculiar throw over the hip made use of in wrestling and formerly in pugilism: see quot. 1808.

[**1690** D'Urfey *Collin's Walk* ii. 74 (Farmer) When th' hardy Major.. To make quick end of fight prepares, By Strength ore buttock cross to hawl him, And with a trip i' th' Inturn maul him.] **1714** [see buttock *sb.* 6]. **1749** Fielding *Tom Jones* xiii. v, All the various stops, blows, cross-buttocks, &c. incident to combatants. **1808** *Sporting Mag.* XXX. 247 A cross-buttock in pugilism is, when the party, advancing his right leg and thigh, closes with his antagonist, and catching him with his right arm, or giving a round blow, throws him over his right hip, upon his head. **1886** *Times* 24 Apr. 5/5 Clark won easily,.. throwing his man with a cross-buttock.

Hence **'cross-'buttock** *v. trans.*, to throw with a cross-buttock (also *fig.*); **'cross-'buttocker**, one who cross-buttocks; a cross-buttock.

1826 Disraeli *Viv. Grey* vi. i, An unexpected cross-buttocker floored the incautious and unscientific Grafenberg. **1878** Browning *Poets Croisic* 107 Hardly that humbug Could thus cross-buttock thee. **1889** W. Armstrong *Wrestling* (Badm. Libr.) 199 Should the stroke fail there is no help for the unfortunate cross-buttocker. *Ibid.* A much tighter hold is required for the purpose of cross-buttocking your man.

†**'cross-'caper.** *Obs.* [cross- 9.] ? Some kind of caper or movement in dancing; cf. cross-cut, cross-point *sb.* Said usually of a tailor, and often *fig.* in application.

1622 Massinger *Virg. Mart.* iv. i, Had a tailor seen her At this advantage, he, with his cross capers, Had ruffled her by this. **1627** F. E. *Hist. Edw. II* (1680) 31 His ends go not their ways, but with Cross-capers. **1634** Ford *P. Warbeck* ii. iii, *Sketon* [a tailor]. For fashioning of shapes and cutting a cross-caper, turn me off to my trade again. **1783** Ainsworth *Lat. Dict.* (Morell) i. s.v. *Caper*, A cross caper, *Subsultatio.*

Hence †**cross-'caperer**.

1607 Dekker *Knts. Conjur.* (1842) 36 All the crosse-caperers beeing plac'd in strong rankes and an excellent oration cut out.. perswading them to sweat out their braines in deuising new cuts, new French collers [etc.].

cross-catalogue, -channel, -chock: see cross- B.

†**'cross-cloth.** *Obs.* [cross- 3, 4.]

1. *Eccl.* A cloth or hanging before the rood.

1541 *Churchw. Acc. St. Giles, Reading* 61 For emendyng of the Crosse clothe iiij[d]. **1550** in Glasscock *Rec. St. Michael's, Bp. Stortford* (1888) 134 Item 1 cros clothe of sylke and another of Pewke. **1566** in Peacock *Eng. Ch. Furniture* (1866) 32 Item one crose clothe—made awaie.

2. A linen cloth worn across the forehead.

1580 North *Plutarch* (1676) 41 The Nurses also of Sparta use.. to bring up their Children, without swadling.. or having on their heads Cross-clothes. **1589** *Pappe w. Hatchet* D iv b, Ile make him pull his powting crosscloath ouer his beetle browes. **1617** Moryson *Itin.* iii. iv. i. 168 Many weare such crosse-clothes or forehead clothes as our women use when they are sicke. **1699** F. Bugg *Quakerism Exp.* 20 Two Neckcloths, and four double Cross-cloths for a Woman.

†**'cross-clout.** *Obs.* = prec. 2.

17.. *Chrispine & Chrispianus* (N.), Head bands, swaddle bands, cross clouts, bibs.

'cross-co,nnect, *v. Electr.* [cross- 6 a.] *trans.* To interchange the connections of (electric wires); to connect (each of a set of two or more wires or terminals) to a different wire or terminal of another set. Also in *ppl. a.* and *vbl. sb.* Hence **'cross-co,nnection**, the arrangement of wires in this way; **'cross-co,nnector**, a device used to effect this.

a **1877** KNIGHT *Dict. Mech.* III. 2512/2 To cross-connect wires is to interchange them, so that a current from one wire is shifted to another at one station and then back again at a farther station, to work around a faulty station. **1884** F. KROHN tr. *Glaser de Cew's Mag.- & Dyn.-Electr. Mach.* 261 The segments of the collector are internally cross connected. **1893** W. P. MAYCOCK *Electric Lighting* II. vii. 205 The armature is cross connected to avoid the use of 4 brushes, the cross-connectors consisting of copper rings with two lugs. **1893** SLOANE *Electr. Dict.* 157 *Cross-connecting board*, a special switch board used in telephone exchanges and central telegraph offices. Its function is, by plugs and wires, to connect the line wires with any desired section of the main switchboard. **1893** G. KAPP *Dynamos* viii. 176 A four-pole cylinder armature with cross-connections. **1910** *Hawkins's Electr. Dict.*, *Cross connected dynamo*, a dynamo having the coils of its armature connected to corresponding bars of the commutator. **1967** D. H. HAMSHER *Communications Syst. Engin. Handbk.* xxi. 10 Cross connection is a method of.. connecting a terminated cable pair to any one of a group of other cable pairs similarly connected. *Ibid.*, Weather-proof terminals with prewired and soldered conductors of plastic-insulated wires are designed to cross-connect circuits at any one location.

'cross-'corner. [CROSS *a.*] The corner of a quadrilateral diagonally opposite to another. ***at cross-corners with***: *fig.* directly opposite or contrary to. Hence (*nonce-wd.*) **cross-'cornerness.**

1809-12 MAR. EDGEWORTH *Absentee* ix, Set the sea-cale at this corner, and put down the grass cross-corners. **1892** MRS. LYNN LINTON in *New Review* Feb. 225 Private idiosyncrasies which.. place them at cross-corners with the rest of their race. **1884** *Illustr. Lond. News* 10 May 442/2 Pondering.. on the cross-cornerness of things in general.

'cross-,counter. *Boxing.* [f. CROSS- 5 + COUNTER *sb.*[5] 3.] (See COUNTER *sb.*[5] 3.) Hence as *v. trans.* and *intr.* Also *fig.*

1864 'MARK TWAIN' *Sketches of Sixties* (1927) 149 The skirmishers fight shyly up to each other, counter and cross-counter, feint and parry. **1889** E. B. MICHELL *Boxing* 166 The answer to this cross-counter is to deliver the right at the face of the counterer. **1897** *Encycl. Sport* (1901) I. 134/2 That most effective of manœuvres, though difficult of execution, the right hand cross-counter. *Ibid.* 137/1 Should he show a tendency to counter at the body or cross-counter at the head, you may find an opening for an upper-cut. **1907** W. DE MORGAN *Alice-for-Short* xxvi. 276 As this and much more cross-countered continually with the dialogue about Alice's squashy days, Mrs. Heath had good excuse for misunderstanding.

'cross-country, *a.* [CROSS- 10.] **a.** Across the country transversely to the great highways; across the fields, etc., instead of following the roads.

1767 S. PATERSON *Another Traveller!* I. 316 We had a cross-country road back to Alost. **1786** COWPER *Gratitude* 20 These carpets.. Oh spare them, ye knights of the boot, Escaped from a cross country ride! **1885** H. O. FORBES *Nat. Wandr. E. Archip.* 191 The main cross-country road to Bencoolen.

b. Applied to flying across the country. Also *absol.*, a cross-country flight.

1909 *Daily Chron.* 9 Sept. 1/6 The first cross-country flight of note was made by M. Farman on October 30, 1908. **1948** 'N. SHUTE' *No Highway* xi. 287 He.. had hit a hill, like any pupil on his first cross-country.

'cross-'couple, *v.* [CROSS- 6.] *trans.* To couple things that do not naturally go together. Hence **†'cross-'couple** *sb.*, **'cross-'coupling** *vbl. sb.*, Puttenham's term for the rhetorical figure *synœciosis*, 'whereby heterogeneous things were combined or attributed to one person.'

1589 PUTTENHAM *Eng. Poesie* III. xix. (Arb.) 216 Another figure which.. may well be called.. the Crosse-couple [*marg.* Syneciosis, or the Crosse copling]. **1681-6** SCOTT *Chr. Life* II. 363 There will be no more.. such cross-coupling of Prosperity with Vice and Misery with Virtue.

'cross-course, *sb. Mining.* [CROSS- 4.] A vein or lode (usually barren) intersecting the regular vein or lode at an angle; also = CROSS-CUT *sb.* 2.

1802 PLAYFAIR *Illustr. Hutton. Th.* 254 Intersected nearly at right angles by other mineral veins called Cross Courses. **1882** *Rep. Geol. Explor.* 13 A short cross-course was put in intersecting the lode.

†'cross-course, *a. Obs.* [CROSS- 10.] Running athwart the straight course of things.

1632 C. DOWNING *State Eccl. Kingd.* (1634) 51 All was made sure.. by the elective assent of the supreme Nobilitie, without any cross-course conditions (as falls out) when the souldiers or people elect.

'cross-'crosslet. *Her.* [Cf. CROSSLET 2.] A cross having the extremity of each arm in the form of a small cross.

1486 *Bk. St. Albans, Her.* B iij b, Cros croslettis and Cros flory. *c* **1630** RISDON *Surv. Devon.* §128. (1810) 134 Three lions between six cross croslets. **1864** BOUTELL *Heraldry Hist. & Pop.* xxi. §5 (ed. 3) 361 A chevron between three crosses-crosslets sa.

'cross-cut, *sb.* [CROSS- 4 a, b.]

1. (Usually *cross cut*.) A cut or cutting across or from side to side; a direct path between two points, transverse or diagonal to the main way.

1800 *Spirit Pub. Jrnls.* IV. 186 If you have occasion to travel frequently to one place, take all the cross cuts. **1837** R. ELLISON *Kirkstead* 27 Deep cross-cuts lurk the treacherous shrubs below. **1876** BANCROFT *Hist. U.S.* V. xiv. 492 He knew the by-ways.. and the cross-cuts and roads as far as Brunswick.

2. *Mining.* A cutting across the course of a vein, or across the general direction of the workings.

1789 J. WILLIAMS *Min. Kingdom* (1810) I. 312 It is.. proper to push forward cross cuts from your first trench every way. **1851** GREENWELL *Coal-trade Terms Northumb. & Durh.* 20 Crosscut, an excavation driven at an acute angle to the direction of the cleavage or cleat. **1872** RAYMOND *Statist. Mines* 326 A cross-cut is being run from the main shaft.. 95 or 100 feet below the surface.

3. A step in dancing.

1842 DICKENS *Amer. Notes* (1850) 62/2 Single shuffle, double shuffle, cut and cross-cut.

4. Short for *cross-cut file*: see next, 2.

1831 J. HOLLAND *Manuf. Metal* I. 302 For working iron.. the single lines are closely cut over diagonally and the file becomes a cross-cut.

5. Short for *cross-cut saw*.

1848 E. ATKINSON *Otago Jrnl.* III. 46 Pit-saws; whit saws; and crosscuts, and files for ditto. **1853** 'P. PAXTON' *Yankee in Texas* 89 Felling trees, handling cross-cuts, rolling blocks. **1942** L. RICH *We took to Woods* (1948) 55 Excellence on a two-man cross-cut has nothing to do with size and strength.

6. *Cinemat.* (See CROSS-CUT *v.* 2.)

'cross-cut, *a.*

1. Adapted for cross-cutting.

1828 WEBSTER, *Crosscut-saw*, a saw managed by two men, one at each end for sawing large logs or trees across. **1874** KNIGHT *Dict. Mech.*, *Cross-cut Chisel*, a chisel with a narrow edge and considerable depth, used in cutting a groove in iron. **1880** *Blackw. Mag.* Feb. 173 Large trees mostly sawn down by the cross-cut saw.

2. [CROSS- 8.] Cut across or transversely; having transverse cuts; *esp.* of a file, having two sets of teeth crossing each other diagonally.

1833 J. HOLLAND *Manuf. Metal* II. 127 The files used by the whitesmith upon cold work are mostly of the cross-cut description. **1883** E. PENNELL-ELMHIRST *Cream Leicestersh.* 135 A deep cross-cut fallow.

,cross-'cut, *v.* [CROSS- 6.] **1.** *trans.* To cut across or transversely.

1590 SPENSER *F.Q.* III. x. 59 A.. humour rancorous.. That.. Cros-cuts the liver with internall smart. **1655** CULPEPPER *Riverius* II. iii. 67 In a Medium [in Optics] that is Convex and thick, the species are.. broken, and as it were cross-cut. **1793** SMEATON *Edystone L.* §108 The quarry-men proceed to cross-cut the large flats. **1846** J. BAXTER *Libr. Pract. Agric.* (ed. 4) I. 377 The plough.. drawn across the field, and cross-cutting the uncut ribs of grass.

2. *Cinemat.* To subject (a film or films) to cross-cutting (see quot. 1933). Also *intr.* and *transf.* Hence as *adj.* and *sb.*

1933 A. BRUNEL *Filmcraft* 95 You may need part of a rejected take because you are cross-cutting that scene. *Ibid.* 97 After you have eliminated the scene numbers.. you can begin to make the simpler cross-cuts. *Ibid.* 156 *Cross-cut*, to alternate in editing two or more scenes—as when one has two close-ups of characters facing each other. **1957** MANVELL & HUNTLEY *Film Music* ii. 40 The two scenes of the dancing action were hastily lengthened and cross-cut to give a rhythm. **1958** *Times Lit. Suppl.* 5 Dec. 698/1 Haddock's gestures as he tells the story exactly match and are cross-cut with those of the Chevalier de la Hadoque slashing away at the ruffians boarding his ship. **1962** *Listener* 30 Aug. 328/1 A montage sequence.. with shots of Eton, night-club frolics.. cross-cut against back-street slums. **1967** *Spectator* 30 June 772/1 The author has developed an impressive, cinematic technique for telling this story, crosscutting rapidly from episode to episode.

'cross-,cutter. *Forestry.* [f. CROSS-CUT *v.* + -ER[1].] One who uses a cross-cut saw.

1902 *N.Z. Illustr. Mag.* Feb. 374/1 Having severed the head from the trunk, the crosscutter's work is considered accomplished, and they pass on to another tree. **1936** 'A' in A. M. RUST *Whangarei & Dist. Early Rem.* 163 Hundreds of bushmen, loggers, jackers, bullock-drivers, cross-cutters and rafters were employed.

'cross-,cutting, *vbl. sb.* [f. CROSS-CUT *v.* + -ING[1].] **1.** The action of cutting across.

1805 R. W. DICKSON *Pract. Agric.* I. 345 Repeated cross-cuttings with the plough and harrowings. **1896** *Daily News* 16 Dec. 8/4 He had done 326 feet of cross-cutting still in ore.

2. *Cinemat.* The action or process of alternating two or more sequences in editing a film. Also *transf.*

1938 G. H. SEWELL *Amat. Film-making* x. 98 Such a device of alternating shots of two ideas is known as cross cutting. **1954** *Encounter* Aug. 52/2 *Intolerance*.. set a standard of screen narrative by cross-cutting and contrapuntal action never since surpassed. **1958** *Times Lit. Suppl.* 21 Feb. 97/4 The manipulation of a rather complex plot is unsure, the cross-cutting inexpert. **1963** *Movie* Feb. 31/1 These angles, which are constantly cut together, have been selected in deliberate opposition to conventional cross-cutting.

†'cross-days, *sb. pl. Obs.* [CROSS- 3 a.]

1. The Rogation Days, or three days preceding Ascension Day.

1501 *Plumpton Corr.* 152 From Lyncolns Inn, at London, this tuesday in the crose dayes. **1641** BEST *Farm. Bks.* (Surtees) 9 The onely time for putting of fatte weathers is aboute Easter and Crosse days.

2. Days of persecution when the 'cross' has to be borne. (Probably with allusion to sense 1.)

1554 PHILPOT *Exam. & Writ.* (Parker Soc.) 246 Wherefore contend in these cross days, which be the love-days of God towards us.

'cross-di'vision. [CROSS- 9.] The division of any group according to more than one principle of division at the same time, so that the species cut across one another and produce confusion; an instance of such an intersecting division.

1828 WHATELY *Rhet.* in *Encycl. Metrop.* 246/1 Arguments are divided according to several different principles.. And these cross-divisions have proved a source of endless perplexity to the Logical and Rhetorical student. **1887** FOWLER *Deduct. Logic* 60 A division.. of men into Frenchmen, Asiatics, the unproductive classes, and barbarians, would be a cross-division.

†'cross-dollar. *Obs.* [CROSS- 3 c.] A Spanish dollar, having a cross on the reverse (as was the case at the end of the 17th c.).

1689 *Lond. Gaz.* No. 2444/4 About 40*l.* in Spanish Money and Cross Dollars. **1704** *Ibid.* 4029/1 Cross Dollars, Eighteen Peny-weight, Four Shillings and Four Pence Three Farthings.

'cross-dye, *v. trans.* (See quots.) Hence **'cross-dye** *sb.*, a colour used in cross-dying; **'cross-dyeing** *vbl. sb.*

1885 J. J. HUMMEL *Dyeing Textile Fabrics* 466 The cotton warp may be dyed black, brown, dark blue, drab, &c., before weaving, in which case only the woollen or worsted weft is dyed subsequently. The finished goods are then said to be 'cross-dyed'. **1901** F. BEECH *Dyeing Cotton Fabrics* iii. 79 This hawking machine will be found useful.. in dyeing cotton cloths with such dyes as.. Cross-dye blacks. *Ibid.* v. 220 Before the introduction of the direct dyes the method usually followed.. is that known as cross dyeing. **1961** BLACKSHAW & BRIGHTMAN *Dict. Dyeing* 54 *Cross dyeing*, the dyeing of one component of a mixture of the fibres after at least one of the others has been dyed already. *Ibid.*, The criteria are that the dyed yarn shall not change in shade or bleed into other fibres when the latter are cross dyed.

crosse (krɒs). [a. F. *crosse*:—OF. *croce* = It. *croccia*, hockey-stick, etc.: see CROSE.] The implement used in the game of lacrosse for catching and throwing the ball, consisting of a long shank curved round at the end, with a net stretched across from the curve to the shank. Also called *lacrosse-stick*.

1867 *Ball Players' Chron.* 20 June 5/4 It is played with a 'crosse', each player carrying one. **1892** *Photogr. Ann.* II. 51 We remember at a lacrosse match taking a shot at the moment a goal was scored, and the 'crosses' were being shied into the air by the jubilant scorers. **1909** *Westm. Gaz.* 23 Sept. 12/3 French is a fine sturdy player, but he is inclined to use only one hand on his crosse.

crosse, var. of CROSE *Obs.*, crosier.

crossear, -ier, obs. ff. CROSIER.

crossect (krɒsˈsɛkt), *v.* [f. CROSS + L. *secāre, sectum* to cut.] *trans.* To divide transversely.

1860 TROLLOPE *Castle Richmond* III. iv. 69 These had since been bisected and crossected, and intersected. **1927** *Glasgow Herald* 1 Sept. 8 The Exchequer crossects our income.

crossed (krɒst, krɔːst), *a.* Also crost. [f. CROSS *sb.* and *v.* + -ED.]

1. Marked with a cross, or with the sign of the cross; bearing or wearing a cross; having taken the cross. † ***crossed friars***: = CRUTCHED *friars*.

1494, 1530 [see CRUTCHED]. **1529** *Test. Ebor.* (Surtees) V. 276 To be beried.. under a crossed stone. **1625** PURCHAS *Pilgrims* II. 1226 Many crossed Nobles were assembled at Lions, to goe to the Holy Land. **1774** GOLDSM. *Nat. Hist.* (1776) III. 341 The animal is called the crost fox. **1795** tr. *Mercier's Fragments* II. 426 Her crossed and mitred son. **1851** DICKENS *Child's Hist. Eng.* xv. 124 White-crossed.. they rushed into the fight.

2. Placed or lying across each other; marked with lines drawn across; (of a letter) written with lines crossing at right angles. Of a cheque: marked with two parallel lines (see quot. 1957 and CROSS *v.* 7 c).

1834 MEDWIN *Angler in Wales* I. 235 A line.. to which they attach several large crossed hooks. **1834** J. B. BYLES *Law of Bills* (ed. 2) x. 129 Crossed checks. It is common practice in the city of London, to write across the face of a check the name of a banker. **1836** MRS. GASKELL *Let.* 12 May (1966) 8 None of your nimini-pimini notes, but a sensible nonsensical crossed letter. **1865** TROLLOPE *Belton Est.* i. 8 She did not.. correspond with other girls by means of crossed letters. **1876** B. T. BOSANQUET (*title*) Crossed cheques: the object of crossing, with suggestions as to the amendments required in the statutes relating thereto. **1877** *Punch* LXXII. 280/1 'Crossed cheques' are only payable through bankers. **1957** *Encycl. Brit.* V. 413/1 The form [of a cheque] may be printed 'crossed'; two lines being printed across it. A cheque so crossed can only be cashed through a banker. **1966** *Listener* 25 Aug. 291 (Advt.), Order through your bookseller or send crossed cheque.

3. *fig.* Thwarted, opposed, etc.

1621 LADY M. WROTH *Urania* 203 All fortunes pass'd in my cross'd loue. **1691** tr. *Emilianne's Frauds Rom. Monks* 227 How great a change crost Desires are able to produce in the Body of man. **1798** LANDOR *Gebir* Wks. 1846 II. 488 Lest.. crost ambition lose his lofty aim.

†b. Having a 'cross' to bear; afflicted. *Obs.*

a **1732** T. BOSTON *Crook in Lot* (1805) 99 The afflicted crossed party.. is a gainer thereby, if his spirit is brought down to it.

4. ***crossed (out)***: **a.** obliterated or cancelled by crossing lines; **b.** *Watchmaking*: see quot. 1874.

1874 KNIGHT *Dict. Mech.*, *Crossed out*, when the web of a wheel is sawed and filed away so as to leave a cross of four spokes or arms, it is said to be crossed out. **1884** F. J. Britten *Watch & Clockm.* 69 [A] crossed out wheel.

† **'crosser¹**. *Obs. rare*⁻¹. [f. cross *sb.*: cf. crucible, crusie.] A small lamp.

1483 *Cath. Angl.* 84 A Crosser, *crucibulum, lucubrum.*

crosser² ('krɒsə(r), 'krɔːsə(r)). [f. cross *v.* + -er¹.] One who crosses, in various senses; one who makes the sign of the cross; one who thwarts, opposes, or contravenes; one who passes over, etc.

1565 Calfhill *Answ. Treat. Crosse* (1846) 82, I know the most crossers are not the best Christians. **1598** Chapman *Iliad* i. 229 Any crosser of thy lust. **1654** Whitlock *Zootomia* 104 An obstinate crosser of men wiser than himselfe. **1876** Birch *Rede Lect. Egypt* 23 The crossers of the desert.

† **'crosset¹**. *Obs.* [ad. F. *croisette*, dim. of *croix* cross.] A small cross; = crosslet.

1610 Guillim *Heraldry* ii. vii. (1660) 84 He beareth Gules, a Fesse between three Crossets. **1656** Heylin *Surv. France* 137 They..beat down all those little crossets.

† **'crosset²**. *Obs.* [ad. F. *crossette*: see next.] A slip or cutting of a plant, cut under a joint with a small projecting knob left to form an eye.

1616 Surfl. & Markh. *Country Farme* 596 To make good choice therefore of crossets to plant new vines of. *Ibid.* 597 The crossets do put forth rootes of themselues.

‖ **crossette** (krɒ'sɛt). *Arch.* [F. *crossette*, in 16th c. *crocette*, dim. of *croce*, *crosse* crutch, crook, staff, etc.: see crose.] A projection or ear in the architrave or casing around a door- or window-opening, at the junction of the jamb and head; also a shoulder or ledged projection in the voussoir of a built-up architrave or flat arch, which rests in a corresponding recess in the adjoining voussoir and strengthens the construction; see quot. 1819.

1730–6 Bailey (folio), *Crosette*..the returns in the corners of..door cases or window-frames. **1819** P. Nicholson *Archit. Dict.* I. 303 *Crosettes*, in the decorations of apertures, the trusses or consoles on the flanks of the architrave, under the cornice. **1853** in *Archit. Publ. Soc. Dict.* **1876** Gwilt *Archit.* Gloss., *Crossettes*..the small projecting pieces..in arch stones, which hang upon the adjacent stones.

ˌcross-e'xamine, *v.* [cross- 6c.]

1. *trans.* To examine by cross-questioning; to examine by questions adapted to check the results of previous examination; to examine minutely or repeatedly. (In quot. 1664 *humorous*.)

1664 Butler *Hud.* ii. iii. 1137 A Monster..Had cross-examin'd both our Hose, And plunder'd all we had to lose. **1667** *Decay Chr. Piety* (J.), If we may but cross-examine and interrogate their actions against their words, these will soon confess the invalidity of their solemnest confessions. **1848** Macaulay *Hist. Eng.* II. 94 The accused party was furnished with no copy of the charge. He was examined and crossexamined.

2. *spec.* To subject (a witness who has already given evidence on behalf of one side in a legal action) to an examination by the other side, with the purpose of shaking his testimony or eliciting from him evidence which favours the other side.

1697 in *Cumbrld. & Westm. Archæol. Soc. Trans.* VIII. 101 This Exceptant did then by his Councell..Crosse Examine the Witnesses produced..on the Respondents behalfe. **1752** J. Louthian *Form of Process* (ed. 2) 207 The Prosecutor first examines the Witnesses produced against the Prisoner, and then the Prisoner may cross-examine them. **1755** Johnson, *Cross-examine*, to try the faith of evidence by captious questions of the contrary party. *Mod.* The witness was severely cross-examined, but without shaking her evidence on any material point.

Hence **ˌcross-exami'nation**, the action of cross-examining; **ˌcross-e'xaminer**, **ˌcross-e'xamining**.

1827 Bentham *Ration. Evid.* Wks. 1843 VI. 378 Completeness of the mass of evidence..is..an object at which, by cross-examination and a variety of other means, English procedure never ceases to aim. **1838** *Penny Cycl.* X. 103/1 In a court of common law..the cross-examination of a witness follows and is founded upon what the witness has stated in his examination in chief. **1864** Bowen *Logic* xiii. 429 Very few..can be trusted to report their own observations, until they have undergone a severe cross-examination. **1838** Dickens *O. Twist* xxxi, 'Why not?' demanded Rose. 'Because, my pretty cross-examiner' replied the doctor: 'because..there are many ugly points about it.' **1875** Jowett *Plato* (ed. 2) I. 266 On whom Socrates tries his cross-examining powers.

'cross-eye. [cross- 4c.] **a.** *pl.* Squinting eyes. **b.** That sort of squint in which the eyes are turned inwards so that the axes of vision cross each other; internal strabismus.

1826 Miss Mitford *Village* Ser. ii. (1863) 302, I cannot abide these 'cross-eyes', as the country people call them; though I have heard of ladies who..admired those of Mr. Wilkes.

Hence **'cross-eyed** *a.*, squinting.

1791 Cowper *Iliad* ii. 260 Cross-eyed he was. **1816** W. Taylor in *Monthly Mag.* XLII. 139 A cross-eyed effort, which criticism should blush to admire. **1892** R. Kipling *Barrack-room Ball., Yng. Brit. Soldier* x.

'cross-'fertilize, *v. Bot.* [cross- 6.] *trans.* To fertilize by pollen from another flower or plant.

1876 Darwin *Cross-Fertil.* i, The flowers of most kinds of plants are constructed so as to be..cross-fertilised by pollen from another flower.

fig. **1889** Jacobs *Æsop* p. xvii, European literature was being crossfertilized by new germs from the East.

Hence **'cross-ferti'lizable** *a.*; **'cross-fertili'zation** (also *fig.*).

1882 Gray in *Eclectic Mag.* XXXV. 735 Blossoms cross-fertilizable by insects. **1876** Darwin *Cross-Fertil.* i Cross-fertilization is sometimes ensured by the sexes being separated. **1879** Lubbock *Sci. Lect.* ii. 35 To secure cross-fertilisation..winged insects are almost necessary, because they fly readily from one plant to another. **1900** *Westm. Gaz.* 26 Jan 3/3 Nearly all eighteenth-century art in France and England hangs ultimately upon him; and, by their cross-fertilisation, how much of modern art too! **1928** C. H. Dodd *Authority of Bible* ix. 196 Alexander's conquests had brought the old order to an end. There was a mingling of cultures, a cross-fertilization of East and West. **1944** J. S. Huxley *On Living in Rev.* p. vii, The compulsory cross-fertilization of ideas. **1970** *Daily Tel.* 22 Apr. 21/5 The companies are now starting on the cross-fertilisation process, exchanging information, identifying common projects.

cross-file: see cross- B.

'cross-'fire. [cross- 9.] *Mil.* Lines of fire from two or more positions crossing each other. Also *fig.* So **'cross-firing** *vbl. sb.*

1837 Dickens *Let.* 22 June (1965) I. 276 This cross-firing of notes makes me smile. **1860** Gen. P. Thompson *Audi Alt.* III. cxxvii. 83 Exposed to a cross fire of musquetry or matchlocks. **1873** Black *Pr. Thule* xiv. 217 A continual cross-fire of small pleasantries. **1884** J. Hall *A Chr. Home* 160 And so the firing and the cross-firing proceed where all should be peace.

'cross-fish. [cross- 3b.] A starfish of the genus *Uraster*; the common 5-fingered star-fish.

1805 Forsyth *Beauties Scotl.* I. 459 The corse fish prey on oysters, and likewise on muscles. **1862** Ansted *Channel Isl.* ii. ix. (ed. 2) 237 The cross-fish..the *cribella*, the sun-stars ..are all represented.

† **'cross-fixed**, *pa. pple. Obs.* [cross- 2.; after L. *crucifixus*.] Fixed on a cross, crucified.

a **1618** Sylvester *Mysterie of Myst., The Sonne* 29 Tempted, tormented, mockt, condemn'd, Crosse-fixed, dead, buried. **1849** J. A. Carlyle *Dante's Inferno* xxiii. 280 To my eyes came one [Caiaphas] cross-fixed [*crocifisso*] in the ground with three stakes.

'Cross-flower. [cross- 3a.] A name proposed by Gerarde for Milkwort (*Polygala*).

1597 Gerarde *Herbal* ii. clx. §6. 450 Milke woort..doth specially flourish in the Crosse or..Rogation weeke..in English we may cal it Crosse flower. **1822** K. Digby *Broadst. Hon.* (1846) II. 364 Cross-flower, or rogation-flower.

'cross-fox. [cross- 3c.] A variety of the fox, having a dark marking along the back and another across the shoulders, forming a cross.

[**1774** Crost fox: see crossed i.] **1830** *Gardens of Zool. Soc.* I. 221 The Cross Fox of America. **1862** H. Marryat *Year in Sweden* I. 480 An animal..called the cross-fox, from its bearing a distinct black cross on the shoulders.

cross-frog: see cross- B.

† **'crossful**, *a. Obs.* [f. cross *sb.* or *v.* + -ful, after *bashful*, *wakeful*.] Given to crossing or thwarting.

c **1680** *Doubting Virgin* in *Roxb. Ball.* IV. 344, I wonder young-men are so crossful, since Virgins are so full of love?

'cross-'garnet. [cross- 3b.] 'A species of hinge formed thus ⊢, with the vertical part fastened to the style or jamb of the doorcase, and the horizontal part to the door or shutter' (Gwilt).

1659 Willsford *Scales Comm., Archit.* 25 Crosse garnet hinges are usually not so strong. **1663** Gerbier *Counsel* 95 Hung with cross-garnets. **1703** Moxon *Mech. Exerc.* 18 When the Joint..on the Tail, is pind in the Joint..in the Cross, the whole Hinge is called a Cross-Garnet. **1881** *Every Man his own Mechanic* §836 A pair of T hinges, sometimes called cross-garnets, must be screwed to the jamb.

† **'cross-'gartered**, *ppl. a. Obs.* [cross- 8.] Having the garters crossed on the legs. (See Aldis Wright's note to Shaks. *Twel. N.*) So **'cross-'gartering** *vbl. sb.*

[**1585** Higins tr. *Junius' Nomenclator* 168 *Fasciæ crurales*, hose garters going acrosse or ouerthwart, both aboue and beneath the knee. **1599** Porter *Angry Wom. Abingd.* (Percy Soc.) 25, I warrant yee, heele haue His cruell garters crosse about the knee.] **1601** Shaks. *Twel. N.* ii. v. 167 And wish'd to see thee euer crosse garter'd. *Ibid.* iii. iv. 23 This does make some obstruction in the blood, this crosse-gartering. *a* **1613** Overbury *Char., Footeman*, More upright than any cross-gartered gentleman-usher. **1628** Ford *Lover's Mel.* iii. i, As rare an old youth as ever walked cross-gartered.

'cross-grain. [cross- 4b.]

1. A grain running across the regular grain of any substance.

1681 Grew *Musæum Reg. Soc.* 282 Between the Grain and the Vein of a Diamond, there is this difference, that the former furthers; the latter, being so insuperably hard, hinders the splitting of it. Altho..a Vein, sometimes is nothing else, but a Cross-Grain.

2. The grain (of wood, etc.) cut across.

1880 *Libr. Univ. Knowl.* (N.Y.) XI. 404 A wood pavement must expose the cross-grain of the wood.

cross-grained ('krɒsgreɪnd, 'krɔːs-), *a.* [Parasynthetic deriv. of prec.]

1. Of wood: Having the grain or fibre arranged in crossing directions, or irregularly, instead of running straight longitudinally.

1673–4 Grew *Anat. Plants* iii. ii. vii. §5 Elm..is the most Cross-grain'd Timber: that is, cleaveth so unevenly.. according to the cross Position of the said Vessels. **1703** Moxon *Mech. Exerc.* 110 Stuff is Cross-grain'd when a.. Branch shoots out on that part of the Tree; For the..Grain of that branch..runs a-cross the Grain of the Trunk. **1873** J. Richards *Wood-working Factories* 104 Knives for working hard or cross-grained lumber.

2. *fig.* Of opposed nature or temper; given to opposition, contrarious; difficult to deal with, intractable; perverse, refractory, queer-tempered. (Said of persons and things.)

1647 *Case Kingd.* 16 So cross-grain'd to all Novelty. **1652** Wharton *Rothomanne's Chirom.* Ded., The many Discouragements and Cross-grain'd Events I have Laboured under. **1773** Goldsm. *Stoops to Conq.* 111, Was there ever such a cross-grain'd brute, that won't hear me? **1850** Trollope *Impress. of Wand.* xiii. 204 He would think you a pestilent, cross-grained fellow. **1883** Stevenson *Treasure Isl.* v. xxiii. (1886) 184 She [the boat] was the most cross-grained lop-sided craft to manage.

3. *advb.* Across the grain. (*lit.* and *fig.*)

1703 Moxon *Mech. Exerc.* 69 Working still Cross-grain'd. **1825** Lamb *Elia, Convalescent*, Things went cross-grained in the Court yesterday.

Hence **cross-'grainedness**.

1652 Wadsworth tr. *Sandoval's Civ. Wars Spain* 273 By reason of the pervers Cross-grainedness of those of the Junta. **1673** S. Dugard *Marriages Cousin Germ.* 65 The ill nature of the Wife, or the Cross-graindnesse of the Husband. *a* **1734** North *Lives* III. 279 A fanatic, whereof the composition was crossgrainedness, ambition, and malice. **1867** Trollope *Chron. Barset* II. lviii. 154 She.. could only lament..over..the cross-grainedness of men.

cross-guard: see cross- B.

'cross-'hackle, *v.* [cross- 6.] *trans.* To cross-question vexatiously or persistently: cf. hackle. Hence **'cross-'hackling** *vbl. sb.*

1826 J. Banim *O'Hara Tales* Ser. ii. *Peggy Nowlan*, We can cross-hackle her on the head of it. **1886** P. Fitzgerald *Fatal Zero* xxx. (1888) 187 The good-humoured way in which I have borne all this cross-hackling.

'cross-'handed, *a.* [cross- 11.] Having the hands crossed; commonly used *advb.*

1836 W. Irving *Astoria* I. 165 The merchant fishermen.. passed the objects of traffic, as it were, cross-handed. **1882** *Century Mag.* XXIV. 708/1 The gaunt women..[are] rowing 'cross-handed'.

'cross-'handled, *a.* [cross- 11.] Having a handle in the form of a cross.

1801 Scott *Fire-King* xiv, He has thrown by his helmet, and cross-handled sword. **1883** J. Hawthorne *Fort. Fool* i. xxv, Limping cleverly along with the help of his two cross-handled staves.

'cross-ˌhatch, *v.* [cross- 6.] To engrave or hatch a surface with parallel lines in two series crossing each other; *esp.* to shade an engraving or drawing by this method. Hence **'cross-ˌhatched** *ppl. a.*; **'cross-ˌhatching** *vbl. sb.*, the process of marking with crossing sets of parallel lines; the effect so produced.

1822 Bewick *Mem.* 239 Some impressions from wood-cuts done long ago, with cross-hatching. **1860** *Cornh. Mag.* No. 3. 271 A certain kind of cross-hatching went out with A. Durer. **1873** Geikie *Gt. Ice Age* vi. 74 Such cross-hatchings ..seem to be confined to the lowland districts. **1888** W. E. Henley *Bk. of Verses* 46 The long lines of lofty, gray houses! Cross hatched with shadow and light.

So **'cross-ˌhatch** *sb.* = cross-hatching; **'cross-ˌhatcher**, one who executes cross-hatching.

1860 *Cornh. Mag.* No. 3. 271 With the engravers the 'cross-hatch' and the 'double cypher'..were secrets. **1870** *Spectator* 19 Nov., 1384 All the stipplers and cross-hatchers in England.

'cross-ˌhead, *sb.* [cross- 4.]

1. a. The bar at the end of the piston-rod of a steam-engine, which slides between straight guides, and communicates the motion to the connecting-rod, etc.

1827 *Mech. Mag.* VIII. 2 Can the cross-head, side rods, cranks, shaft..be reduced? **1861** T. L. Peacock *Gryll. Gr.* xx. 179 Vibrating..with one invariable regulated motion like the cross-head of a side-lever steam engine.

attrib. **1850** Weale *Dict. Terms*, *Cross-head guides*, in locomotive engines, the parallel bars between which the cross-head moves. *Cross-head blocks*..the parts which slide between the parallel guides.

b. Any beam across the top of a piece of mechanism.

1844 H. Stephens *Bk. Farm* I. 417 The draught shackle ..is held in its place upon the cross-head..by the draught-bolt. *Ibid.* II. 134 The handle..terminates in a crosshead. *a* **1884** Knight *Dict. Mech.* Suppl., *Cross Head*, a cruciform-shaped four-handled bar, at the upper end of a drill-rod or earth-auger. **1884** *Science* III. 314 Two side-screws, carrying the top crosshead. **1888** *Encycl. Brit.* XXIII. 151/1 Thus avoiding torsion of the polar axis at the expense of greatly increased length of the cross-head. **1901** Merwin & Webster *Calumet 'K'* xvi. 322 Another endless series of cups was carrying the wheat aloft. It went over the cross-head and down a spout.

2. A heading to a paragraph printed across the page or column in the body of an article.

1888 *Pall Mall G.* 1 Sept. 11/2 In two cases Mr. Knowles allows frequent 'cross-heads'. **1964** *Friend* 4 Sept. 1067/2 The memorandum continues (and from this point, inserting only crossheads, we quote it in full): We cannot [etc.].

3. *Mining.* A heading running across a vein.

1877 R. W. RAYMOND *Statist. Mines & Mining* 197 At the point of connection the eastern limit of the south vein is defined by a cross-head.., and to the east of this cross-head no trace of the fissure has as yet been found.

4. cross-head brasses *pl.*, the brass bearings of the cross-head of a steam or other engine; **cross-head pin**, the pin by which the connecting-rod is attached to the piston-rod.

1865 *Daily News* 26 July 3/1 No. 80 torpedo boat.. broke down owing to a defect in the crosshead brasses. **1887** D. A. LOW *Machine Drawing* xii. 51 The cross-head pin need not be drawn separately. **1889** HASLUCK *Model Engin. Handybk.* viii. 91 The hole in cross-head must be broached out till the cross-head pin will nearly fit it.

Hence **'cross-head** *v.*, to furnish with a cross-head (sense 2).

1890 *Pall Mall G.* Jan., The *Tablet*.. cross-heads one of its paragraphs 'The Need of the Confessional'. **1908** 'IAN HAY' *Right Stuff* iii. 42, I doubt now if I could write out twenty lines of 'Paradise Lost' without cross-heading them.

'cross-ˌheaded, *a.* [CROSS- 11.] Having the head or top in the form of a cross.

1866 HOWELLS *Venet. Life* xvi. 243 The cross-headed staff.

'cross-ˌheading. [CROSS- 4.] **1.** *Mining.* A transverse heading (see quots.).

1883 H. M. CHANCE *Rep. Mining Methods in Anthrac. Coal Fields* 533 *Cross-heading*, a passage driven for ventilation from the airway to the gangway, or from one breast through the pillar to the adjoining working. **1904** GOODCHILD & TWENEY *Technol. & Sci. Dict.* 140/2 *Cross Heading*, a drift or passage from one level to another for ventilating purposes.

2. = CROSS-HEAD *sb.* 2.

1898 G. B. SHAW *Our Theatres in Nineties* (1932) III. 378 The interview, the illustration and the cross-heading, hitherto looked on as American vulgarities impossible to English literary gentlemen, invaded all our papers. **1967** *Listener* 16 Nov. 634 It's my great opportunity to be listed under the magical cross-heading 'from Professor Ayer and others'.

'cross-ˌhilted, *a.* [CROSS- 11.] Having a hilt which forms a cross with the blade and handle.

1661 EVELYN *Tyranus* in *Mem.* (1871) 751, I.. had rather see a glittering stone to hasp it there, than the long cross hilted knots now worn. **1878** B. TAYLOR *Deukalion* II. iii. 68 Cross-hilted swords.

crossiade, obs. form of CRUSADE.

cross-index: see CROSS- B.

crossing ('krɒsɪŋ, 'krɔːs-), *vbl. sb.* [f. CROSS *v.*] **1.** The marking with or making the sign of the cross.

1530 PALSGR. 211/1 Crossyng, *croisee*. **1548–9** (Mar.) *Bk. Com. Prayer, Offices* 37 As touching kneeling, crossing.. and other gestures. **1884** *Evangelical Mag.* Jan. 9 As many genuflexions.. and as many crossings as ever.

2. The action of drawing lines across; striking out, erasure; writing across other writing. ***crossing off*** or ***out***: striking off (an item), striking out (a word or entry) by drawing a cancelling line across it.

a **1652** J. SMITH *Sel. Disc.* vii. 366 By procuring the crossing of all the debt-books of our sins. **1822** SHELLEY *Let.* 18 June (1964) II. 715, I intend to indulge myself in plenty of paper and no crossings. **1848** CLOUGH *Bothie* IV. 178 Your letter.. was written in scraps with crossings and counter-crossings. **1866** CRUMP *Banking* iv. 90 The alteration or erasure of a crossing [of a cheque] is a forgery.

3. a. The action of passing across; intersecting; traversing; passage across the sea, a river, etc.

1575 TURBERV. *Venerie* 123 The crossings and doublings of the deare. **1768–74** TUCKER *Lt. of Nat.* (1851) I. 76 To follow.. all the twistings, and crossings, and entanglements in those intricate subjects. **1805** SOUTHEY *Madoc in Azt.* xxi, The complex crossings of the mazy dance. **1891** J. E. H. THOMSON *Bks. wh. influenced our Lord* II. i. 271 The crossing of the great and wide sea.

b. The action of crossing the path of another rider so as to obstruct him. Also *fig.* Cf. *cross and jostle* in CROSS- B.

1796 *Hull Advertiser* 23 Apr. 3/3 All the crossings and jostlings which the barrack-master.. experienced. **1891** *Daily News* 5 Nov. 3/3 May Rose, whose jockey.. for boring and crossing, was suspended for the remainder of the meeting.

4. The place where two lines, tracks, bands, or the like, cross; intersection.

1828 SCOTT *Jrnl.* (1890) II. 163 The ceiling.. is garnished, at the crossing and combining of the arches, with the recurring heads of Henry VIII and Anne Boleyn. **1874** BOUTELL *Arms & Arm.* iv. 61 A ring, placed at the crossing of the two strengthening bands.

5. *spec.* **a.** The intersection of two streets, roads, lines of railway, etc. ***level crossing***: the intersection of a road and a railway, or of two railways, on the same level.

1695 DRYDEN *Observ. Painting.* Wks. 1808 XVII. 401 Statues.. in the crossing of streets, or in the squares. **1700** S. L. tr. *Fryke's Voy. E. Ind.* 179, I was always upon my guard at Turnings and Crossings of Streets. **1840** F. WHISHAW *Railways Gt. Brit.* 24 Where gates are fixed at the level road crossings. **1889** G. FINDLAY *Eng. Railway* 51 The intersection of one rail with another at any angle is termed a 'crossing', and these crossings are so constructed with wing rails and check rails as to guide the flange of the wheel, and ensure its taking the required direction.

b. *Eccl. Arch.* That part of a cruciform church where the transepts cross the nave.

1835 WHEWELL *Archit. Notes German Ch.* i. 45 *note*, The portion of the building.. over that space in the ground plan where the transept crosses the nave is called the crossing. **1874** MICKLETHWAITE *Mod. Par. Churches* 13 If the pulpit be in the crossing.

6. The place at which a street, river, etc. is crossed by passengers.

1632 LITHGOW *Trav.* x. (1682) 426 Giving back to Toledo, I crossed the crossing Siera de Morada. **1763** JOHNSON 28 July in *Boswell*, Sweeping crossings in the streets. **1869** TROLLOPE *He Knew, etc.* xxvi. (1878) 145 The fellow that sweeps the crossing.

7. *Venery.* (See quot.)

1611 COTGR., *Salade*.. the young head of a Deere (long, tender, woollie, and but beginning to braunch) tearmed by our Woodmen, the crossing.

8. A thwarting, opposing, or contravening.

1580 LYLY *Euphues* (Arb.) 377 Yᵉ iarres and crossings of friends. **1596** SHAKS. *1 Hen. IV*, III. i. 36 Cousin: of many men I doe not beare these crossings. **1669** WOODHEAD *St. Teresa* I. Pref. (1671) 20 Macerations of the Body, and crossings of the Will. **1692** RAY *Dissol. World* II. ii. (1732) 83 It is a Crossing of Proverbs making Rivers to ascend to their Fountains.

9. The raising of animals or plants from individuals of different races; cross-breeding.

1851 *Beck's Florist* 170 We commenced a series of 'crossings', with the view of remedying the.. earliness of blooming and susceptibility to frost. **1879** tr. *De Quatrefages' Hum. Spec.* 63 This crossing.. is differently named according to whether it takes place between different races or different species.

10. Cheating, dishonest practice: see CROSS *sb.* 29.

1592 GREENE *Def. Conny Catch.* (1859) 18 Is our crossing at cardes more perillous to the commonwelth than this cossenage for land?

11. *Comb.*, as ***crossing-keeper***, ***-place***; **crossing-gate**, a gate at a level crossing which is closed to road traffic when a train is due; **crossing-over** *Biol.*, the formation of a genotype exhibiting characters derived from both parents when the characters are known to be linked; hence also, the interchange of segments between chromatids of homologous pairs of chromosomes which causes this breakdown of linkage; **crossing-sweeper**, a person who sweeps a (street-) crossing.

1929 *Star* 21 Aug. 7/2 The railway crosses the road in several places without *crossing-gates. **1921** D. H. LAWRENCE *Sea & Sardinia* iv. 128 At a level crossing the woman *crossing-keeper darted out vigorously with her red flag. **1912** T. H. MORGAN & E. CATTELL in *Jrnl. Exper. Zoöl.* XIII. 79 In certain combinations, the relation between linkage and breaking of the linkage ('*crossing-over' as we shall call it) is shown at once. *Ibid.* 91 There were seven cases of crossing-over in color, all males, in a total of 872 males. **1937**, **1949** Crossing-over [see ASYNAPSIS]. **1786** *Francis* II. 43 Employed in procuring a clean *crossing-place at the head of the Haymarket. **1876** BANCROFT *Hist. U.S.* V. xiii. 471 His forces.. guarded the crossing-places from the falls at Trenton to below Bristol. **1840** DICKENS *Old C. Shop* xix, Making himself as cheap as *crossing-sweepers.

'crossing, *ppl. a.* [f. as prec. + -ING².] That crosses, in various senses: see the verb.

1587 FLEMING *Contn. Holinshed* III. 1292/1 By meane of some crossing causes in the citie. **1626** W. SCLATER *Exp. 2 Thess.* (1629) 185 Onely consider how crossing to the whole Counsell of God.. that proud dreame is. **1718** POPE *Iliad* xx. 479 The crossing belts unite behind. **1875** BEDFORD *Sailor's Pock. Bk.* iii. (ed. 2) 64 Whenever a green light is opposed to a red light.. the ships carrying the lights are crossing ships.

ˌcross-in'terrogate, *v. Law* [CROSS- 6.] *trans.* To cross-question.

1752 J. LOUTHIAN *Form of Process* (ed. 2) 107 Advocates.. may cross-interrogate the Witnesses.

Hence **ˌcross-inte'rrogatory,** cross-question, cross-examination.

1774 tr. *Helvetius' Child of Nat.* I. 95, I put artlessly some cross interrogatories to him. **1841** CDL. WISEMAN *Remarks Let. fr. W. Palmer* 67 To investigate juridically, on oath, and by cross-interrogatory.

crossish ('krɒsɪʃ, 'krɔːs-), *a. colloq. rare.* [f. CROSS *a.* 5 b + -ISH.] Rather cross or peevish.

1741 RICHARDSON *Pamela* (1824) I. xxxii. 55 Jane.. sometimes used to be a little crossish. **1849** LYTTON *Caxtons* 120, I found my mother indisputably crossish.

cross-jack, cro'jack ('krɒsdʒæk, 'krɔːs-; 'krɒdʒək). *Naut.* A square sail bent to the lower yard of the mizen-mast.

1626 CAPT. SMITH *Accid. Yng. Seamen* 17 A drift sayle, a crosiack, a netting sayle. **1769** FALCONER *Dict. Marine*, *Cross-jack*, pronounced *crojeck*, a sail extended on the lower yard of the mizen-mast.. This sail.. is.. very seldom used. **1820** SCORESBY *Acc. Arctic Reg.* II. 197 In 1816, I fitted a main-sail and cross-jack in the same way. **1858** *Merc. Marine Mag.* V. 19 The sail taken off was the cross-jack and main-sail.

b. *attrib.*, as ***cross-jack brace***; **cross-jack yard** (see quot. 1867); **cross-jack-eyed** *a.* (*Sailors' slang*) = CROSS-EYED.

1627 CAPT. SMITH *Seaman's Gram.* iii. 17 The Crossieacke Yard and Spretsaile Yard to be of a length. **1840** R. DANA *Bef. Mast* xxiii. 69, I was stationed at the weather cross-jack braces. **1867** SMYTH *Sailor's Word-bk.*, *Cross-jack-yard*.. the lower yard on the mizen-mast, to the arms of which the clues of the mizen top-sail are extended.. It is now very common in merchant ships to set a sail called a cross-jack upon this yard. **1892** *Eng. Illustr. Mag.* IX. 849 Haul in your weather cro'jack brace!

cross keys, cross-keys. [CROSS- 4 c.] Keys borne crosswise, as in the Papal arms.

c **1550** BALE *K. Johan* 32 Where is yowr thre crounnys, yowr crosse keys and yowr cope. **1583** *Exec. for Treason* (1675) 32 No nor their Cross-keys, or double edged Sword, will serve their turns. **1646** EVELYN *Diary* (1871) 192 The Citty arms [of Geneva], a demie eagle and a crosse between crosse-keys. *Mod.* An inn with the sign of the Cross Keys.

†**'cross-land.** *Obs.* [Cf. CROSS *sb.* 31.] *Irish Hist.* Land belonging to the Church in the Irish counties palatine.

The second quot. is doubtful in sense.

1568 *Stat. Irel.* (1621) 298 (*Act 11 Eliz.*) That all crosse landes and cleargie of this Realme shall be yearely charged .. with like subsidie. **1597** *1st Pt. Return fr. Parnass.* v. ii, When they shall.. see a hare at a crossland.. they shall want there oulde poet to emparte it to the worlde.

'cross-leaved, *a. Bot.* [CROSS- 11.] Having the leaves arranged in fours cross-wise.

1860 TYAS *Wild Fl.* 5 The cross-leaved and fine-leaved heath. **1861** MISS PRATT *Flower. Pl.* III. 151 Cross-leaved Bedstraw.

cross-legged ('krɒsˌlɛgd, 'krɔːs-), *ppl. a.* [CROSS- 11.] Having the legs crossed (usually of a person in a sitting posture).

c **1530** LD. BERNERS *Arth. Lyt. Bryt.* (1814) 252 Some sytting before their owne dores, croslegged. **1697** DAMPIER *Voy.* (1698) I. xii. 329 They use no Chairs, but sit cross-legg'd like Taylors on the floor. **1867** WHITTIER *Tent on Beach* xiv, In the tent-shade.. [He] Smoked, cross-legged like a Turk, in Oriental calm.

b. Having one leg laid across the other.

1631 WEEVER *Anc. Fun. Mon.* 274 An armed knight crosse legged is to bee seene. **1762–71** H. WALPOLE *Vertue's Anecd. Paint.* (1786) IV. 207 Bishops in cumbent attitudes and cross-legged templars. **1850** COOPER *Hist. Winchelsea* 132 Canopied tombs of cross-legged secular warriors.

In this sense sometimes **'crossed-legged.**

1845 G. A. POOLE *Churches* xii. 118 *note*, All these figures of crossed-legged persons have been popularly referred to Templars. **1864** BOUTELL *Heraldry* ix. 54 The shield of a crossed-legged knight in the Temple Church.

Hence **cross-leggedness,** *nonce-wd.*

1852 G. W. CURTIS *Wand. Syria* 236 He naturally fell into the cross-leggedness of oriental sitting.

crossless ('krɒslɪs, 'krɔːs-), *a.* [f. CROSS *sb.* + -LESS.] Without a cross (in various senses of the word; as *e.g.* †without a coin, penniless).

1490 CAXTON *Eneydos* xvi. 63 A bystorye or wepen crysolite, as it were a lityl swerde crosseles. **1600** ROWLANDS *Let. Humours Blood* xxviii. 34 Three high-way standers, haueing cros-lesse cursse. **1630** J. TAYLOR (Water P.) *Wks.* II. 256/2 Where man doth man within the Law betosse, Till some go croslesse home by Woodcocks Crosse. **1891** *Ch. Times* 4 Sept. 844/2 A Crossless Church, a religion without austerity, has never yet made headway.

†**'crosslet¹.** *Obs.* Forms: 4–6 cros-, 4–7 crosse-, 7 crosslet; also 4 **croslette, crosel(l)et(t, crosselette, croislet; cres(e)let(e, cresselet, crescellette.** [app. dim. of OF. *croiseul* night-lamp, CRUCIBLE. Besides *croiseul*, in Cotgr. *cruzeul*, *crusol*, OF. had also the parellel dim. forms *croisel*, *crosel*, *cruseau*, and later F. *croiset*, now *creuset* (see CRUSET); both endings appear to be present in *croselet*. F. had also a variant *creseul*: cf. our variants in *cres-*. The sense 'lamp' is app. not recorded in Eng.] A crucible.

c **1386** CHAUCER *Can. Yeom. Prol. & T.* 240 And sondry vessels maad of erthe and glas.. Violes, crosletz, and sublymatories [*v.r.* croslets, -is, creseletes, -ys, creslettes, crescellettes]. *Ibid.* 600 The coles for to couchen al aboue The croslet [*v.r.* croslet, crosselette, croislet, cresselet]. **1584** R. SCOT *Discov. Witchcr.* XIV. i. 295 Their.. alembicks, viols, croslets, cucurbits. **1592** LYLY *Galathea* II. iii, Blowing of bellowes.. and scraping of croslets. **1610** B. JONSON *Alch.* I. iii, Your crosse-lets, crucibles, and cucurbites.

crosslet² ('krɒslɪt, 'krɔːs-). Also 6 **crosselette,** 7–8 **crosselet,** 6–9 **croslet.** [a. Anglo-F. *croiselette*, dim. of OF. *crois* cross: cf. OF. *croisette*, and for form OF. *femmette*, later *femmelette*, f. *femme*.]

1. *Her.* A small cross; see also quot. 1661.

[**1300** *Siege of Caerlaverock* 16 Ky les armes ot vermeillettes O blanc lyon et croisselettes.] **1538** LELAND *Itin.* II. 93 Crosselettes of Golde many intermist in one yn a Feld.. Gules. **1590** SPENSER *F.Q.* I. vi. 36 Her champion trew, That in his armour bare a croslet red. **1661** MORGAN *Sph. Gentry* II. i. 11 The Cross Croslet or Crossed, for brevity of blazon, you may term Croslets only. **1727–51** CHAMBERS *Cycl.* s.v., In heraldry.. we frequently see the shield covered with crosselets.. Crosses themselves frequently terminate in crosselets. **1864** BOUTELL *Heraldry Hist. & Pop.* xv. 175 Charging his lion and his crosslets on a field ermine.

2. *gen.* A small cross (used as an ornament, etc.).

1802 W. TAYLOR in Robberds *Mem.* I. 420 Crosslets glitter on the necks of the ladies. **1823** LOCKHART *Anc. Sp. Ball., Young Cid* ii, There is no gold about the boy, but the crosslet of his sword.

†**3.** = CROSS-CLOTH 2. *Obs.*

1607 *Lingua* IV. vi. in Hazl. *Dodsley* IX. 426 Bandlets, fillets, crosslets, pendulets. *a* **1688** VILLIERS (Dk. Buckhm.) *Instalment* Wks. 1705 II. 88 He..tore His pert Wif's Croslet off.

4. *attrib.* Shaped like a crosslet.

1820 J. HODGSON in J. Raine *Mem.* (1857) I. 291 The battlements, and crosslet loopholes of the castle.

Hence **'crossleted** *ppl. a.*, bearing or adorned with a crosslet.

1801 SCOTT *Fire-King* xxxiv, The scallop, the saltier, and crossleted shield. **1846** RUSKIN *Mod. Paint.* II. III. II. v. §20 His hand fallen on his crossleted sword. **1858** *Ecclesiologist* XIX. 209 A crossleted banner.

crosslet, obs. var. CROSLET = CORSLET.

'cross-light. [CROSS- 4] A light which comes athwart the direction of another light and illuminates parts which it leaves in shade; in *pl.* lights whose rays cross each other. Often *fig.*

1851 H. MELVILLE *Whale* iii. 11 Every way defaced in the unequal cross-lights in which you viewed it. **1875** JOWETT *Plato* (ed. 2) III. 25 There is no use in turning upon him the cross lights of modern philosophy. *Mod.* The windows on other sides are to be darkened, so as to avoid cross-lights.

Hence **'cross-,lighted** *ppl. a.*

1884 *Nonconf. & Indep.* 3 July 642/1 Mr. Biggar in his odd, crosslighted way, voting against his own party.

'cross-line. [CROSS- 4, CROSS *a.* 1 b.]

1. A line drawn across another.

c **1391** CHAUCER *Astrol.* I. §12 Next the forseide cercle.. vnder the cros-lyne. **1768** W. GILPIN *Ess. Prints* 60 In engraving and etching we must get over the prejudices of cross lines, which exist on no natural bodies. **1804** SOUTHEY *Lett.* (1856) I. 253 The ceiling has all the crosslines of the trowel.

2. *Fishing.* A line stretched across the river or stream, used in *cross-fishing* (see CROSS- B.).

1891 *Daily News* 9 Feb. 6/3 The Irish fishermen still use the crosslines.

Hence **'cross-line** *v.*, to mark with cross-lines; **'cross-,lining** *vbl. sb.*, (*a*) (see quot. 1816); (*b*) = *cross-fishing*.

1598 BARRET *Theor. Warres* IV. i. 119 It were good for vs to crosselyne him what we may. *Margin*, The proud Spaniardes Mappa Mundi to be crossed. **1816** J. SMITH *Panorama Sc. & Art* II. 779 A white ground and black lines, reticulated work, which is technically called *cross-lining*.. becomes to the wood-engravers of the present day an undertaking of immense labour. **1897** *19th Cent.* Aug. 199 Cross-lining for trout has lately been prohibited. **1900** *Daily News* 16 Aug. 3/2 A large landowner, who has..succeeded in stopping cross-lining on Lough Corrib. **1907** *Westm. Gaz.* 13 Dec. 4/2 A daring spirit suggested the project of cross-lining.

cross-lode, -loop: see CROSS- B.

cross lots, cross-lots, *advb. phr. U.S.* Also cross-lot. [See CROSS *prep.* and LOT *sb.* 6 a.] By a short cut. Also *attrib.*

1825 J. NEAL *Bro. Jonathan* I. 138 They could push on, a pooty, tedious, clever bit furder, cross lots—they could. **1874** 'MARK TWAIN' & C. D. WARNER *Gilded Age* xxi. 154 The cross-lots path she traversed to the Seminary. **1889** 'MARK TWAIN' *Yankee* xx. 241 After three hours of awful crosslot riding he had overhauled his game. **1922** A. BROWN *Old Crow* 469 They might even go over to Mountain Brook by the path ''cross lots'.

crossly ('krɒslɪ, 'krɔːs-), *adv.* [f. CROSS *a.* + -LY[2].]

†**1.** Athwart, crosswise, transversely, so as to cross or intersect. *Obs.*

1598 FLORIO, *Travérso*, a crosse, a thwart, crosly, thwartly. **1614** T. BEDWELL *Nat. Geom. Numbers* iv. 71 The base and height of the extremes crossely multiplied. **1774** BURKE *Amer. Tax.* Wks. II. 420 He put together a piece of joinery, so crossly indented and whimsically dovetailed.

†**2.** In a way that crosses ordinary affinities. *Obs.*

1611 BEAUM. & FL. *Philaster* II. iv, If he have any child, It shall be crossly match'd. **1660** tr. *Amyraldus's Treat. conc. Relig.* II. iii. 184 Crossely coupling prosperity with Vice, and Misery with Virtue.

3. In a way that is cross, contrary, or opposite; adversely, unfavourably.

1593 SHAKS. *Rich. II*, II. iv. 24 And crossely to thy good, all fortune goes. **1596** DRAYTON *Leg.* ii. 407 Since with me it fell so crosly out. *a* **1694** TILLOTSON (J.), He..acts as untowardly, and crossly to the reason of things, as can be imagined. **1856** MISS WINKWORTH *Tauler's Life & Serm.* vi. 220 Whether things go smoothly or crossly with them.

4. Perversely, peevishly, ill-humouredly.

1730–6 BAILEY (folio), *Crossly*, peevishly, untowardly. **1770–90** DOROTHY KILNER *Jemima Placid* in *Storehouse of Stories* (1870) 254 Miss Sally..desired her to..make room for her, which Miss Nelly very crossly refused. **1852** JAMES *Pequinillo* I. 59 'Don't undress me', said Julian rather crossly.

'cross-multipli'cation. *Arith.* [CROSS- 9.] = DUODECIMALS.

1703 T. N. *City & C. Purchaser* 123 Cross-Multiplication is the Multiplying of Feet and Inches by Feet and Inches. **1751** CHAMBERS *Cycl.*, *Cross-multiplication*..so called because the members are multiplied cross-wise. **1836** J. GRAY *Arith.* 95 Duodecimals, or Cross multiplication, is a rule by which artificers cast up the contents of their work.

crossness ('krɒsnɪs, 'krɔːs-). [f. CROSS *a.* + -NESS.]

1. The state or quality of being cross, transverse, or athwart; 'transverseness, intersection' (J.).

1605 BACON *Adv. Learn.* II. xxiii. 107 To keep them [laws] from being..too ful of multiplicitie and crossnesse. **1750** WALPOLE *Lett. G. Montagu* (1891) II. 211 Lord Petersham, with his hose and legs twisted to every point of crossness.

2. The state of being contrary or opposed; opposition, adverseness.

1641 *Disc. Pr. Henry* in *Harl. Misc.* (Malh.) III. 525 Through any crossness of cards or chance. **1674** HICKMAN *Quinquart. Hist.* (ed. 2) 171 Let us see whether there be any such crossness or no. **1736** CARTE *Ormonde* II. 449 There being besides crossness of interests, some private piques between the Prince and him.

b. of the wind: cf. CROSS *a.* 1 c.

1646 LD. DIGBY *Let.* in Carte *Ormonde* (1735) III. 456 The crossness of the winds to the shipping which they expected. *a* **1674** CLARENDON *Hist. Reb.* XII. (1704) III. 251 That the crossness of the Wind only hinder'd the arrival of those Supplies.

3. a. Disposition to oppose or be contrary; perverse tendency, disposition, or temper.

1599 SHAKS. *Much Ado* II. iii. 184 She will die if hee wooe her, rather than shee will bate one breath of her accustomed crossenesse. *a* **1677** BARROW *Serm.* Wks. 1716 I. 7 A peevish crossness and obstinate repugnancy to received laws. **1768–74** TUCKER *Lt. Nat.* (1852) II. 372 The scoffer and caviller move as much by impulse of vanity as crossness.

b. Peevishness, ill-humour.

1741 RICHARDSON *Pamela* I. 61, I am vex'd his Crossness affects me so. **1823** LAMB *Elia* (1860) 160, I missed his kindness, and I missed his crossness, and wished him to be alive again. **1862** MRS. H. WOOD *Mrs. Hallib.* I. v. 28, I beg your pardon for my crossness, but you put me out of temper.

crossopterygian (krɒsɒptə'rɪdʒ(ɪ)ən), *a.* and *sb. Zool.* [f. mod.L. *crossopterygii* or *-ia* (f. Gr. κροσσό-ς tassel, *pl.* fringe, κροσσωτός fringed + πτέρυξ, πτερύγιον fin) + -AN.]

A. *adj.* Belonging to the sub-class *Crossopterygia* or sub-order *Crossopterygidæ* of Ganoid fishes, so called from the arrangement of the paired fins to form a fringe round a central lobe. **B.** *sb.* A fish of this class.

Most of these fishes are extinct, but the genus *Polypterus* is still found in the Nile and other African rivers.

1861 HUXLEY *Ess. Devonian Fishes* 25 (*Mem. Geol. Surv. Gt. Brit.*) Thus both ends of the Crossopterygian series appear..to be cut off from the modern representatives of the suborder. *Ibid.*, Polypterus, however, is clearly related to the rhombiferous Crossopterygians. **1871** —— *Anat. Vert. Anim.* iii. 171 The most ancient Crossopterygian Ganoids.

crossopte'rygious, *a. Zool.* [f. as prec. + -OUS.] = prec. A.

cross-over ('krɒs,əʊvə(r), 'krɔːs-). [from verbal phrase *to cross over*.]

1. a. *Textile Fabrics.* A fabric having the design running across from selvedge to selvedge, instead of along the length.

1795 *Hull Advertiser* 23 May 1/2, 1273 yards of..cotton cross-over. **1860** *All Year Round* No. 53. 63 The barragons ..quiltings, and cross-overs..for which Bolton was famous.

b. *Calico-printing.* A bar or stripe of colour printed across another colour.

1875 URE *Dict. Arts* IV. 326 Printed as a crossover, it darkens the indigo where it falls.

2. A woman's wrap (usually knitted, or of crochet-work) worn round the shoulders and crossed upon the breast.

1868 (The name was then in current use.) **1884** MRS. COOTE *Sure Harvest* vi. 69 Mrs. Timmins will never lose her rheumatism till she has a warm cross-over to wear over that thin old dress. **1886** BESANT *Childr. Gibeon* I. ii, She would wear a grey ulster or a red crossover.

3. A connexion between the up and down lines of a railway by which trains are shunted from one to the other. Also of a tramway.

1884 *Harper's Mag.* July 272/2 The incoming trains approach the city on the western track until they reach the 'cross-over', which throws them to the eastern track. **1895** *Daily News* 15 Oct. 3/2 At the starting point are four crossovers to suit any arrangement of traffic. **1901** *Westm. Gaz.* 29 Nov. 10/2 The castings necessary for the crossovers on electric tramways. **1928** *Daily Express* 22 Nov. 11/1 The cross-overs available were at Beckenham Junction and Penge. **1967** C. J. FREEZER *Model Railway Terminol.* 5/1 A train proceeding in its correct direction along the main line can run directly over the facing crossover, or must reverse to cross over a trailing crossover.

4. *Biol.* (*a*) An instance of the process of crossing-over (see CROSSING *vbl. sb.* 11); (*b*) an individual having characters inherited by crossing-over. Also *attrib.*

1912 T. H. MORGAN & E. CATTELL in *Jrnl. Exper. Zoöl.* XIII. 91 The sum of the 'straight' males is 580, while that of the cross-overs is 292. **1916** *Jrnl. Genetics* V. 285 The cross-overs appear to occur in numbers exactly proportional to the distance apart of the factors concerned. **1916** *Genetics* I. 134 Of these thirteen cases which involved crossing over, twelve were crossovers in only one chromosome and were non-crossovers in the other. *Ibid.* 135 A crossover chromosome. **1919** R. C. PUNNETT *Mendelism* (ed. 5) xii. 144 It is upon the proportion of 'crossover' gametes as compared with 'non-crossover' gametes that the distances between the factors along the chromosomes have been determined. **1920** L. DONCASTER *Introd. Cytology* 224 The American investigators call these exceptional combinations cross-overs, since in the combinations of *Ab* and *aB*, *A* and *a* are regarded as having crossed over from their normal combinations and to have exchanged places. **1964** D. MICHIE in G. H. Haggis *Introd. Molecular Biol.* vii. 203 Ultra-fine genetic analyses using fast-breeding micro-organisms are capable of charting the distribution of cross-over events over exceedingly short chromosomal intervals.

5. a. *attrib.* or as *adj.* That crosses over; characterized by crossing over or having a part that crosses over another.

1893 'M. GRAY' *Last Sentence* III. ii, White pinafore, cross-over shawl, and velvet hat. **1905** *Westm. Gaz.* 8 July 13/2 The cross-over bodice. **1906** *Ibid.* 15 Feb. 4/1 A cross-over ring set with a large brilliant and a cabochon emerald. **1939** F. THOMPSON *Lark Rise* i. 8 They stood at corners in their big white aprons and crossover shawls. **1968** *Economist* 11 May 18/3 Both Governor Branigin and Senator McCarthy were (on different pretexts) soliciting Republican 'crossover' votes.

b. cross-over block, road (see quots.).

1893 SLOANE *Electr. Dict.* 158 *Cross-over block*, a piece of porcelain or other material shaped to receive two wires which are to cross each other. **1888** *Lockwood's Dict. Mech. Engin.*, *Cross-over road*, a short diagonal line of rails on permanent way, provided with a pair of points or switches at each end, and connecting two parallel lines of rails together. **1893** *Athenæum* 8 July 68/1 'Crossings' imply something more than merely the gaps left in the rails for a cross-over road. **1896** *Daily News* 18 Dec. 8/2 He let the goods train on to the up main line, but did not pull over the cross-over road points for the goods train to go across to the down line.

'cross-patch. *colloq.* [f. CROSS *a.* 5 + PATCH.] A cross, ill-tempered person. (Usually applied to a girl or woman; Scott makes it masculine.)

a **1700** B. E. *Dict. Cant. Crew*, *Crosspatch*, a peevish Person. **1775** MAD. D'ARBLAY *Early Diary* 28 Feb., 'You little cross patch', cried I. **1818** SCOTT *Hrt. Midl.* xxix, 'The keeper's a cross-patch, and he maun hae it a' his ain gate.' **1874** LISLE CARR *Jud. Gwynne* I. vii. 206 She's a nasty cross-patch.

'cross-path. [CROSS- 4 b.] A path that crosses between two roads or points. Also *fig.*

1558 PHAER *Æneid.* IV. L ij b, Diana deepe, whose name by night al townes in crospathes crie. **1587** GOLDING *De Mornay* xxiv. 373 To light him in the way of welfare, and to turne him from all crosspathes and bywaies. **1768–74** TUCKER *Lt. Nat.* (1852) II. 415 Taking good caution that in his necessary deviations from the solid road of reason he does not tear up the ground of any cross paths.

cross-pawl: see CROSS-SPALL.

'cross-piece. [CROSS- 4.]

1. A piece of any material placed or lying across anything else.

1607 TOPSELL *Serpents* (1653) 785 With many lines and different crosse pieces. **1715** LEONI *Palladio's Archit.* (1742) I. 89 Over these rows of piles were plac'd Joysts..(those Joysts so placed are vulgarly call'd cross-pieces). **1827** G. HIGGINS *Celtic Druids* 212 The single Lithos, or upright stone or pillar..with a cross-piece on the top. **1853** SIR H. DOUGLAS *Milit. Bridges* (ed. 3) 239 A second row of beams was laid on cross-pieces placed athwart the first.

b. *Ship-building.* (See quots.)

1706 [see CROSS-BEAM]. **1769** FALCONER *Dict. Marine*, *Cross-piece*, a rail of timber extended over the windlass of a merchant-ship from the knight-heads to the belfry..It is stuck full of wooden pins, which are used to fasten the running-rigging. *c* **1850** *Rudim. Navig.* (Weale) 113 *Cross-pieces*, the pieces of timber bolted athwartships to the bitt-pins, for taking turns with the cable, or belaying ropes to. *c* **1860** H. STUART *Seaman's Catech.* 66 'Cross pieces'.. placed across the keel, which is let into them; they assist to form what is called the floor.

c. A small transverse piece forming the cross-guard of a sword or dagger.

1874 BOUTELL *Arms & Arm.* ii. 12 There is no guard for the hand, nor is the hilt separated from the blade by any cross-piece.

d. *Anat.* The corpus callosum, or transverse mass connecting the two hemispheres of the brain.

†**2.** [CROSS *a.* 5.] A perverse or ill-tempered person. *Obs.* Cf. CROSS-PATCH.

1614 WILSON *Inconst. Lady* (N.), The rugged thoughts That crosse-peece of your sex imprinted in mee. **1694** ECHARD *Plautus* 92 Since y' had the good luck t' outlive that Cross Piece [your wife].

'cross-,plough, *v.* [CROSS- 6.] *trans.* To plough (a field) across the furrows of a former ploughing. Hence **'cross-,ploughing** *vbl. sb.*

c **1644** G. PLATTES in *Hartlib's Legacy* (1655) 187 He ploughed [it] up at Michaelmass..and afterward cross ploughed it. **1759** tr. *Duhamel's Husb.* I. vi. (1762) 15 Let the whole field be cross-plowed. **1842** *Jrnl. R. Agric. Soc.* III. I. 163, I immediately ploughed it in; and about Christmas I cross-ploughed it. **1844** *Ibid.* V. I. 40 As soon as the land is sufficiently dry it receives two deep cross-ploughings.

'cross-point, *sb.* [CROSS *a.* 2: see POINT.]

†**1.** Name of a step in dancing. *Obs.*

a **1592** GREENE *James IV*, IV. iii, Nay but, my friends, one hornpipe further, a refluence back, and two doubles forward: what, not one cross-point against Sundays? **1602** *2nd Pt. Return fr. Parnass.* II. vi. (Arb.) 32 Seeing him practise his lusty pointes, as his crospoynt backcaper.

2. One of the points of the compass intermediate between two cardinal points.

1709 *Tatler* No. 42 When the Wind is in a cross Point. **1865** F. HALL in Wilson *Vishńu Puráńa* II. 241 *note*, All the cardinal points, and so the cross-points.

3. *pl.* The points of a railway cross-over.

1896 *Westm. Gaz.* 13 July 2/2 When the train has to pass over cross-points.

ˈcross-polliˈnation. *Bot.* [CROSS- 9.] = CROSS-FERTILIZATION of plants.

1882 VINES *Sachs' Bot.* 913 The contrivances for cross-pollination in Orchids.

†**ˈcross-post.** *Obs.* [CROSS- 5.] The post which carried letters on cross-country routes.

[**1720** *Lond. Gaz.* 16 Apr., General Post-Office, London, April 12, 1720.. His Majesty's Attorney-General, having granted to Ralph Allen.. a Farm of all the Bye-Way or Cross-Road Letters throughout England.] **1750** COVENTRY *Pompey Litt.* II. iii. (1785) 52/1 All the tramantanes that come by the cross-post. **1880** L. STEPHEN *Pope* 146 Allen, who had made a large fortune by farming the cross-posts.

ˈcross-ˈpurpose. [As now used, f. CROSS *a.*, CROSS- 4: but in early use *cross* appears to have been a preposition (cross or contrary to the purpose): cf. *cross-bliss* (CROSS- 10), CROSS-COURSE *a.*]

1. Contrary or conflicting purpose; contradictoriness of intention.

1681 COTTON *Wond. Peak* 59 We altogether in confusion spoke: But all cross purpose, not a word of sence. **1711** SHAFTESB. *Charac.* (1737) I. 305 To allow benefit of clergy, and to restrain the press, seems to me to have something of cross-purpose in it. **1797** BURKE *Regic. Peace* iii. Wks. VIII. 340 Before men can transact any affair, they must have a common language to speak.. otherwise all is cross-purpose and confusion. **1824** SCOTT *St. Ronan* xxxi, He.. makes signs, which she always takes up at cross-purpose.

2. *pl.* The name of a parlour game: cf. CROSS-QUESTION *sb.* c. Often *fig.*

1666 PEPYS *Diary* 26 Dec., Then to cross purposes, mighty merry; and then to bed. **1698** FARQUHAR *Love & Bottle* IV. i, I won't pay you the kisses you won from me last night at cross-purposes. **1712** STEELE *Spect.* No. 504 ¶1 The agreeable Pastime in Country-Halls of Cross-purposes, Questions and Commands, and the like. **1768–74** TUCKER *Lt. Nat.* (1852) II. 545 In the common way of playing at cross purposes, where each party has a quite different sense of the subjects and arguments handled between them. **1860** MRS. CARLYLE *Lett.* III. 55 Was there ever such a game at cross-purposes as this correspondence of ours.

3. *to be at cross-purposes*: (of persons) to have plans intended for the same end, but which cross and interfere with each other; to act counter from a misconception by each of the other's purpose. (Perh. derived from the game.)

1688 MIEGE *Fr. Dict.* s.v. *Cross*, Cross Purposes, *contradictions.* **1769** *Junius Lett.* xvi. 72 No man, whose understanding is not at cross-purposes with itself. **1822** HAZLITT *Table-t.* Ser. II. vi. (1869) 135 Such persons.. are constantly at cross-purposes with themselves and others. **1868** ROGERS *Pol. Econ.* vi. (ed. 3) 59 Like some married people, they have been at cross purposes when they should have been at one.

cross-quarters: see CROSS- B.

ˈcross-ˈquestion, *sb.* [Orig. two words: cf. CROSS *a.* 1, CROSS- 9.] **a.** A question put by way of cross-examination. †**b.** A question on the other side; a question in return.

a **1694** TILLOTSON *Serm.* lxxv. (1748) V. 1191 Now that this question is answered, one might methinks ask him a cross question or two. **1705** FARQUHAR *Twin Rivals* IV. i, Have you witnesses?.. Produce him.. But you shall engage first to ask him no cross questions. **1834** MEDWIN *Angler in Wales* I. 269 Chatting with her on the way, and endeavouring, by cross-questions.. to elicit some information.

c. *cross-questions and crooked answers*: a game of questions and answers in which a ludicrous effect is produced by connecting questions and answers which have nothing to do with one another; as *e.g.* the question of one's neighbour on the right with the answer given to another question by one's neighbour on the left.

1742 J. YARROW *Love at First Sight* 2 As if you had been playing at cross-Questions. **1884** *Illust. Lond. News* Christmas No. 22/1 'I'm afraid, doctor, we are playing at cross-questions and crooked answers.'

ˌcross-ˈquestion, *v.* [CROSS- 6.] *trans.* To interrogate with questions which cross, or tend to check the results of, previous questions, so as to test the consistency and completeness of an account; to question closely or minutely; to cross-examine.

1760 FOOTE *Minor* I. Wks. 1799 I. 234 You will find, by cross-questioning him, whether he is a competent person. **1887** JESSOPP *Arcady* iii. 67 There are moments when the desire to question and cross-question the vanished dead becomes a passionate longing.

Hence **ˌcross-ˈquestioning** *vbl. sb.*; **ˌcross-ˈquestionable** *a.*, capable of being cross-questioned.

a **1839** PRAED *Poems* (1864) II. 8 When on his ranks together spring Cross-buttocks and cross-questioning! **1856** FROUDE *Hist. Eng.* (1858) II. vi. 104 He was submitted to the closest cross-questionings, in the hope that he would commit himself. **1884** J. HAWTHORNE *Pearl-Shell Necklace* I. 48 There was nothing cross-questionable in such an old-wives' tale.

ˈcross-ˌratio. *Math.* [CROSS- 9.] = ANHARMONIC ratio.

1881 TAYLOR *Geom. Conics* 249 An Anharmonic Ratio, or a Cross ratio of the four points. **1882** C. SMITH *Conic Sect.* (1885) 53.

ˈcross-ˈreading. [CROSS- 9.] A reading across the page instead of down the column (of a newspaper, etc.), producing a ludicrous connexion of subjects. Also *fig.*

1768–84 *New Foundling Hospital for Wit* II. *contents*, 'Cross Readings from the Newspapers' [Article at p. 235, signed 'Papyrius Cursor', by Caleb Whitefoord]. **1784** BOSWELL *Johnson* (1887) IV. 322 His [Whitefoord's] ingenious and diverting cross-readings of the newspapers. **1822** HAZLITT *Table-t.* (1852) 247 A large allowance is frequently to be made for cross-readings in the speaker's mind. **1830** MISS MITFORD *Village* Ser. IV. (1863) 139 Stephen spoke of his home, the city; Peggy of hers, the west-end;—and a few mistakes and cross-readings ensued.

cross-reˈfer, *v.* [Back-formation f. CROSS-REFERENCE *sb.*] *intr.* To make a cross-reference or cross-references; to refer or look from one place or publication to another. Also, to contain cross-references.

1879 *Library Jrnl.* IV. 234 Where will you place double subjects? Will you catalogue under both, or cross-refer from one; and from which? **1960** *Twentieth Cent.* Mar. 224 Thus by cross-referring between The Light and the Dark, The New Men and Homecomings, we can work out that in the autumn of 1941 Eliot was falling in love with Margaret Davidson, etc. **1979** G. N. KNIGHT *Indexing* iv. 71 A familiar epithet can be cross-referred from, if prominently alluded to in the text, e.g. Charles the Bold, *see* Charles, Duke of Burgundy. **1979** *Times* 27 Dec. 3/7 Questions are balanced and cross-refer in such a way that it is difficult to cheat. **1985** S. LOWRY *Young Fogey Handbk.* i. 16 Anyone who wants to pursue the.. game further simply has to buy the publications.. and cross-refer.

ˌcross-ˈreference, *sb.* [CROSS- 9.] A reference made from one part of a book, register, dictionary, etc. to another part where the same word or subject is treated of.

1834 H. H. BAKER *Report Catal. Brit. Museum*, It will hence be requisite that a cross-reference from the commentator's name be made to that of the original author. **1839** *Brit. Museum Catal.* Rule 54 Whenever requisite, cross-references to be introduced. **1892** *Bookseller* 17/1 The notes are handy, the cross references plentiful and useful.

ˌcross-ˈreference, *v.* [f. the sb.] *trans.* To provide with a cross-reference or cross-references; to refer *to* by a cross-reference. Hence **ˌcross-ˈreferenced** *ppl. a.*; **ˌcross-ˈreferencing** *vbl. sb.* and *ppl. a.*

1902 H. B. WHEATLEY *How to make Index* iii. 73 If a general heading be divided into sections, and each of these be clearly defined, they should be cross referenced, but not otherwise. *Ibid.* 74 Cross referencing has its curiosities .. 'Cattle *see* Clergy'. **1907** W. JAMES *Let.* 18 May in R. B. Perry *Tht. & Char. W.J.* (1935) II. 506 You.. stop him and cross-reference him and counter on him. **1914** *Cath. Encycl.* XVI. 88 Where several forms of the same name occur, all the references are grouped under one spelling to which the other forms are duly cross-referenced. **1922** *Daily Mail* 7 Dec. 10 It saves the unnecessary labour of cross-referencing. **1955** *Sci. Amer.* Jan. 95/1 Well thought out, clearly printed, skillfully cross-referenced. **1956** *Nature* 3 Mar. 402/2 A series of cross-referencing indexes. **1965** *Math. in Biol. & Med.* (*Med. Res. Council*) II. 47 Although seemingly elaborate, this kind of cross-referencing is really quite natural in view of the facts of human family structure.

cross-remainder (*Law*): see REMAINDER.

ˈcross-road. [CROSS- 4, CROSS *a.* 1, 1 b.]

1. A road crossing another, or running across between two main roads; a by-road.

1719 T. GARDNER (*title*), Pocket Guide to the English Traveller.. of all the Principal Roads and Cross Roads in England and Wales. **1745** *Priv. Lett. Ld. Malmesbury* I. 14 The cross-roads are almost impassible. **1859** W. COLLINS *Q. of Hearts* (1875) 4 One of the loneliest and wildest cross-roads in all South Wales.

2. a. The place where two roads cross each other; the place of intersection of two roads. Also called *the cross roads*, and *dial.* a *four-cross-road.*

(Formerly used as a burial-place for suicides.)

1812 *Examiner* 23 Nov. 739/1 Verdict of the Jury—*Felo de se*.. The body was.. buried in a cross-road, with the customary ceremonies. *a* **1845** HOOD *Faithless Nelly Gray* xvii, And they buried Ben in four cross-roads With a stake in his inside! **1875** W. MCILWRAITH *Guide Wigtownshire* 27 Near the cross-roads are the remains of a cairn.

b. *fig.* (usu. pl.). A point at which two or more courses of action diverge; a critical turning-point.

1795 S. J. PRATT *Gleanings through Wales* I. xv. 238 Join with me.. that they may speedily be conducted from the *cross* roads of life. **1898** *Nat. Rev.* Aug. 908 To place him at the cross roads of starvation and revolt. **1915** *War Illustr.* 6 Mar. 54 Britons at cross-roads of Honour, Glory and Death. **1924** E. Y. MULLINS (*title*) Christianity at the cross roads.

c. Phr. *dirty work at the cross-roads*: see DIRTY *a.* 2 b.

3. *attrib.* **a.** Passing or conveyed by cross-roads. **b.** (Also *cross-roads.*) Situated at the crossing of two roads; *spec.* in *U.S.* with the implication of smallness, cheapness, etc.

1720 [see CROSS-POST] Cross-road Letters. **1725** *Lond. Gaz.* No. 6415/2 The Cross-Road Mail which.. goes between Chester and Exeter. **1785** *Gentl. Mag.* Oct. 838/2 Comptroller of the bye and cross-road letter office. **1845** *Southern Lit. Messenger* XI. 586/1 The country merchant and cross-road store-keeper. **1848** E. BRYANT *Calif.* (1849) 98 The place had something of the air of a cross-roads settlement. **1863** W. PHILLIPS *Speeches* xix. 430 Every cross-road bar-room. **1868** *Putnam's Mag.* June 715/1 Now and then an enterprising specimen of the breed set up a 'cross-roads grocery'. **1869** *Champaign Co.* (Illinois) *Gaz.* 26 May 1/2 Defer the payments we may have promised to Cross-roads politicians. **1905** *Forum* Apr. 485 To place an obstacle in the way of the cross-roads politicians. **1935** *Amer. Speech* X. 5/2 A small crossroads community in Vermont.

†**ˈcross-row.** *Obs.* [CROSS- 3 a: from the figure of the cross (✠) formerly prefixed to it.] The alphabet; = CHRIST-CROSS-ROW.

a **1529** SKELTON *Agst. Venomous Tongues*, In your crosse rowe nor Christ crosse you spede, Your Pater Noster, your Ave, nor your Crede. **1531** TINDALE *Exp. 1 John* 2 A man can by no manes reade, excepte he be taught the letters of the crosserowe. **1594** SHAKS. *Rich. III*, I. i. 55 And from the Crosse-row pluckes the letter G. **1635** SWAN *Spec. M.* i. §3 (1643) 23 By their naturall position in the alphabet or crosse-row. **1681** W. ROBERTSON *Phraseol. Gen.* (1693) 1085 The cross-row, *alphabetum.*

ˈcross-ruff, *sb.* [CROSS- 9.]

†**1.** An obsolete game at cards: see RUFF. *Obs.*

1592 GREENE *Def. Conny Catch.* (1859) 6 As thus I stood looking on them playing at cros-ruffe, one was taken revoking. **1693** *Poor Robin's Alm.* in Brand *Pop. Antiq.* (1870) II. 307 And men at cards spend many idle hours, At loadum, whisk, cross-ruff, put, and all-fours.

2. *Whist.* (See quot. 1862.) Also in *Bridge.*

1862 'CAVENDISH' *Whist* (1870) 28 A Cross-ruff (saw or see-saw) is the alternate trumping by partners of different suits, each leading the suit in which the other renounces. **1885** PROCTOR *Whist* vii. 76 More tricks are usually gained by the cross ruff than the opponents can afterwards make out of their suits. **1905** R. F. FOSTER *Compl. Bridge* 226 Do not let go of the lead until you have made all your trumps separately by the cross ruff on the red suits. **1907** C. S. STREET *Good Bridge* vii. 103 The careless player exhilarated by the success of his devastating cross-ruff continues it once too often. **1926** M. C. WORK *Auction Bridge Complete* II. ii. 330 The Declarer who forces his long trump hand (except to obtain an entry in a cross ruff) is generally playing the game of the adversary.

fig. **1889** *Sat. Rev.* 9 Nov. 515 The trades are to establish a cross-ruff at the expense of the employers.

cross-ruff, *v.* (Stress variable) [f. the sb.] *intr.* To play a cross-ruff. Also *trans.*, to play (a hand) using a cross-ruff. So **cross-ruffing** *vbl. sb.*

1905 R. F. FOSTER *Compl. Bridge* 226 Having no established suit.. he plays to make his trumps separately by cross ruffing. **1918** —— *Foster on Auction* II. 354 Cross-ruffing an entire hand. **1934** L. H. WATSON *Play at Contract Bridge* xvi. 149 If you are going to play a hand by cross-ruffing, you must follow it through. **1958** *Listener* 4 Dec. 965/2 We cannot cross-ruff our way to a high level contract.

†**ˈcross-sail,** *sb. Obs.* [CROSS- 4.]

1. *Naut.* A square-sail, *i.e.* one placed across the breadth of the ship (not *fore-and-aft*); formerly the large mainsail so placed; also a vessel with square-sails.

c **1325** *E.E. Allit. P.* C. 102 Cachen vp þe crossayl, cables þay fasten. *a* **1618** RALEIGH *Invent. Shipping* 30 Any Fleet of crosse sailes, with which they encounter. **1627** CAPT. SMITH *Seaman's Gram.* ix. 40 A crosse saile cannot come neerer the wind than six points.

2. *pl.* Sails (of a windmill) set cross-wise.

1612 STURTEVANT *Metallica* (1854) 75 So a windmillne consisting.. of all his essential parts besides his crosse sales is ineffectuall and not able to grinde corne.

Hence †**ˈcross-sailed** *a.*, ? having the cross-sail set, ready to sail.

1562 J. HEYWOOD *Prov. & Epigr.* (1867) 36 Sens thou art crosse saylde, auale vnhappie booke. **1580** NORTH *Plutarch* (1612) 439 Took ship, finding one crosse-sailed, bound towards Afrike.

†**ˈcross-sail,** *v. Obs.* [CROSS- 6.] *intr.* ? To sail across or over.

1564–78 BULLEYN *Dial. agst. Pest.* (1888) 29 A letter to a Marchaunte Venterer that was crossailed into *Terra Florida.*

cross-sea: see CROSS *a.* 1.

ˈcross-ˈsection, *sb.* Also cross section. **1. a.** The cutting of anything across; a section made by a plane cutting anything transversely. *spec.* = SECTION *sb.* 4 a.

1835 A. GRAY *Lett.* (1893) I. 52 A cross-section shows the same structure as the rattan. **1870** *Spon's Dict. Engin.* II. 389 A front elevation and cross-section of a boiler. **1874** *Ibid.* VIII. 2924 The converting department, shown in ground plan by Fig. 6996, and in cross-section by Fig. 6998. **1878** J. H. BEADLE *Western Wilds* x. 143 Five men were twenty days felling it, the object being to have it sawed into cross-sections to be shipped eastward to Europe. **1884** BOWER & SCOTT *De Bary's Phaner.* 323 The characteristic habit of most Monocotyledonous bundles, which is especially evident in cross-section. **1884** tr. *Lotze's Logic* 265 It is only necessary that the mass be the same at any cross-section of this material line. **1933** *Archit. Rev.* LXXIV. 123 This pictorial cross-section.

b. *fig.* A typical or representative sample, group, etc., or an examination of this.

1903 *Independent* 22 Jan. 210/2 A narrow, timorous artificial treatment of some such limited subject or 'cross-section' of a subject as may be represented 'concretely'. **1904** KIPLING *Traffics & Discoveries* 322 Cross-sections of remote and incomprehensible lives. **1909** H. G. WELLS *Tono-Bungay* I. i. 5 You will ask by what merit I achieved this remarkable social range, this extensive cross-section of the British social organism. **1938** *Ann. Reg. 1937* 275 The New York *Annalist's* index of business activity, covering a wide cross-section of statistically measurable activity. **1952** E. GRIERSON *Reputation for Song* xxvi. 222 The jury, a fair cross-section of the community.

2. *Physics.* Used of the apparent area (measured in barns or millibarns) of a nucleus, atom, elementary particle, etc., as representing the probability of a specified interaction with another particle, etc. Symbol σ.

1921 *Sci. Abstr.* A. XXIV. 393 A method is described whereby the effective cross section of gas molecules is determined by means of slowly-moving electrons having a definite single velocity and definite path. **1938** R. W. LAWSON tr. *Hevesy & Paneth's Man. Radioactivity* (ed. 2) vii. 75 The effective cross-section is equal to the mass absorption coefficient divided by 6×10^{23}, and multiplied by the atomic weight. **1955** R. D. EVANS *Atomic Nucleus* 826 In the wave or field model, the 'cross section' for a particular interaction is the ratio between the rate of energy removal (power) and the incident intensity (power per unit area) per target particle. The cross section can be visualized as an area in the incident wave front... In the corpuscular model, the 'cross section' is the fraction of the incident particles which suffer the specified interaction, divided by the number of target particles per unit area of a thin target. **1960** *Gloss. Atomic Terms* (*H.M.S.O.*) 16 *Cross section*, the apparent size of a nucleus. This varies for many nuclei according to the reaction occurring (capture, fission or scattering) and the speed of the oncoming particle. **1962** *Gloss. Terms Nucl. Sci.* (*B.S.I.*) 30 *Cross section*, of a given nucleus or atom for a given radiation, that area perpendicular to the direction of the radiation which one has to attribute to the nucleus or atom to account geometrically for its interaction with the radiation; or, in other words, the number of those interactions per unit time divided by the radiation flux and the number of nuclei or atoms present. **1967** CONDON & ODISHAW *Handbk. Physics* (ed. 2) IX. viii. 214/2 The intrinsic probability that a reaction will occur is measured by its cross section... All conceivable events that occur when a projectile strikes a nucleus have their separate cross sections. One speaks of the cross section for elastic scattering,..for absorption,..etc. **1971** *Nature* 23 Apr. 523/2 Other processes, such as the $^{16}O(n,\alpha)^{13}C$ reaction, may contribute to the more point-like flashes, but their cross-sections are generally small.

'cross-,section, *v.* [f. the sb.] *trans.* To make a cross-section of; to cut into cross-sections. Hence **,cross-'sectioning** *vbl. sb.*

1876 *Van Nostrand's Eclectic Engin. Mag.* XIV. 394/1 The engineer should have an intimate knowledge of the ground on the line of the work. This is obtained by means of cross-levels taken at right angles to the reference line of the work. .. This work in engineering parlance is cross-sectioning. *Ibid.* 399/2 The finished work can be cross-sectioned and plotted in the same manner as the original ground. **1890** D'OYLE *Notches* 52 They were going down to 'cross-section' the old railway survey which ran through our valley. **1897** *Outing* (U.S.) XXX. 126/2 Much of the ground is.. conveniently bounded and cross-sectioned by roads. **1908** *Westm. Gaz.* 22 Aug. 14/1 The eye would then cross-section its words, reading the lateral parts in indirect vision.

'cross-,sectional, *a.* [f. CROSS-SECTION *sb.* + -AL.] Of or pertaining to a cross-section.

1874 *Spon's Dict. Engin.* VIII. 2931 The difference in cross-sectional area between the two ends of the ram is the area acted upon by the water to lift it. **1896** E. ATKINSON tr. *H. du Bois's Magnetic Circuit* 60, *S* is the cross-sectional area of the bar-magnet. **1916** H. BARBER *Aeroplane Speaks* 94 The cross-sectional dimensions must be correct. **1923** W. E. GIBBS *Clouds & Smokes* 137 The cross-sectional area is many times that of the fume. **1941** *Manch. Guardian Weekly* 14 Mar. 214/3 Material descriptive of conditions at present governing the lives of under-twenties (cross-sectional). **1958** M. ARGYLE *Relig. Behaviour* vi. 38 When age differences in attitudes are found in a cross-sectional survey, it is sometimes possible to account for them by historical factors. **1968** R. A. LYTTLETON *Myst. Solar Syst.* iv. 114 Only about 10^{-5} of its overall cross-sectional area can be producing any reflection.

†'cross-shaped, *a. Obs.* [CROSS- 8.] Of a horse: ? Mis-shapen, ill-shaped.

1703 *Lond. Gaz.* No. 3969/4 A light grey Gelding.. somewhat cross shap'd behind. **1709** *Ibid.* No. 4540/8 A plain strong cross shaped Bay Gelding.

cross-shoot, -shooting, -shot: see CROSS- B.

'cross-,spall, 'cross-,spale. *Ship-building.* [CROSS- 4.] (See quot. 1850.)

c **1850** *Rudim. Navig.* (Weale) 112 *Cross-spales*, deals or fir plank nailed in a temporary manner to the frames of a ship at a certain height, by which the frames are kept to their proper breadths, until the deck-knees are fastened. **1869** SIR E. J. REED *Ship-build.* viii. 154 In many yards the ship is faired by means of ribands and cross-spalls only before the beams are fitted.

cross-spider: see CROSS- B.

cross-'springer. *Arch.* [CROSS- 4.] One of the ribs extending diagonally from one pier to another in groined vaulting.

1816 J. SMITH *Panorama Sc. & Art* I. 163 The cross-springers were ornamented..with carvings of Zigzag and other Norman ornaments. **1843** *P. Parley's Ann.* IV. 293 The cross-springers are perforated into airy forms. **1862** RICKMAN *Goth. Archit.* 144 The great cross-springer rib.

'cross-staff. Also (in sense 1) 6 croystaff.

†1. *Eccl.* An archbishop's cross; also, by confusion, used for CROSE-STAFF, a bishop's crook or crosier. *Obs.* exc. *Hist.*

1460 CAPGRAVE *Chron.* (1858) 156 He [Robt Grostede] appered to the Pope, and smet him on the side with the pike of his crosse staf. **1540** *Inv.* in Greene *Hist. Worcester* II. App. 5 Item, a croystaff of selver and gylt. **1541** BARNES *Wks.* (1573) 246/1 All your holy ornamentes, as your holy myters, your holy crosse-staues, your holy pyllers. **1568** GRAFTON *Chron.* II. 2 He [Becket] taketh from Alexander his Crosyer, the crosse with the Crossestaffe..and caryeth it in himselfe. **1884** TENNYSON *Becket* 188 Shall I not smite him with his own cross-staff?

†2. An instrument formerly used for taking the altitude of the sun or a star. *Obs.*

1594 BLUNDEVIL *Exerc.* III. II. viii. (ed. 7) 386 The Latitude then is to be knowne by the Astrolabe, Quadrant, Crosse-staffe, and by such like Mathematicall instruments. **1669** STURMY *Mariner's Mag.* II. xiii. 80 How to use the Cross-Staff. Set the end of the Cross-Staff to the..Eye.. Then move the Cross..from you or towards you..till that the upper end come upon the..Sun or Star. **1839** MARRYAT *Phant. Ship* ix, The cross-staff at that time was the simple instrument used to discover the latitude.

b. A surveyor's cross, used in taking offsets.

1874 in KNIGHT *Dict. Mech.*

'cross-,stitch, *sb.* [CROSS- 3 b.] **a.** A stitch formed of two stitches crossing each other, thus **X**. **b.** A kind of needlework characterized by stitches crossing each other.

c **1710** C. FIENNES *Diary* (1888) 296 The Chaires, one red damaske, the other Crostitch and tentstitch very Rich. **1737** MRS. PENDARVES *Let.* in *Mrs. Delany's Corr.* 10 Oct. II. 6 Tell me how many pieces of cross-stitch I have left with you. **1856** MRS. BROWNING *Aur. Leigh* I. 16, I learnt cross-stitch, because she did not like To see me wear the night with empty hands.

attrib. **1880** *Birm. Weekly Post* 2 Oct. 1/5 Cross-stitch embroidery is..applied to all sorts of decorative needlework.

Hence **'cross-,stitch** *v.*, to sew or work with cross stitches.

1794 *Rigging & Seamanship* I. 95 All splices are cross-stitched.

'cross-stone. *Min.* [CROSS- 3 b.] A name given to CHIASTOLITE; also to the minerals STAUROLITE and HARMOTOME, from the cruciform arrangement of the crystals.

1770 tr. *Cronstedt's Min.* 83. **1771** HILL *Fossils Arranged* 152. **1796** KIRWAN *Min.* I. 282. **1814** ALLAN *Min. Nomen.* **1851** [see HARMOTOME]. **1868** *Amer. Naturalist* I. 264 A boulder..containing large crystals of staurotide, or cross-stone.

'cross-street. [CROSS- 4, CROSS *a.* 1 b.]

1. A street crossing another, or running across between two main streets; a street at right angles to a main street.

1827 O. W. ROBERTS *Centr. Amer.* 234 The principal streets are terminated by views of the hills..The cross streets are narrower. **1861** DU CHAILLU *Equat. Afr.* ii. 8 There are a few short cross-streets.

†2. The place where two streets cross. *Obs.* (Cf. CROSS-ROAD 2.)

1825 T. JEFFERSON *Autobiog.* Wks. 1859 I. 89 Keeping great fires at all the cross-streets.

'cross-tail. *Mech.* [CROSS- 4.] In a back-action marine steam-engine: A transverse bar which connects the side levers at the end opposite to the cross-head, and to which the connecting-rod is attached.

1839 R. S. ROBINSON *Naut. Steam Eng.* 81 The fork-head or cross-tail..The cross-tail, in shape, resembles the cross-head of the piston, only it is considerably larger and stronger.

'cross-tie. [CROSS- 4.] A transverse connecting piece (of timber, etc.); *spec.* in *U.S.* = TIE *sb.* 7 b.

1813 *Niles' Reg.* III. 323/1 The three large ribs are preserved in their proper relative situations by fifty-four crossties. **1833** in J. R. Commons et al. *Documentary Hist. Amer. Industrial Soc.* (1910) I. 219 Begun laying cross-ties of plantation railroad. **1858** SIMMONDS *Dict. Trade*, *Cross-tie*, a railway sleeper; a connecting band in building. **1886** *Encycl. Brit.* XX. 244/1 The longitudinals are connected and kept to gauge by transoms or cross-ties at intervals. **1890** *Harper's Mag.* May 888/1 Across this ditch two old 'cross-ties' made a bridge to the railway. **1908** *Daily Chron.* 14 Nov. 8/6 A few variations in frame design..taking the form of auxiliary cross-ties and supplementary diagonals. **1948** *Clarke County Democrat* 23 Sept. 1/2 Cross ties and switch ties.

cross-tining: see CROSS- B.

'cross-tongue. [CROSS- 4 a.] A cross-grained tongue of wood used to give extra strength to a joint in woodwork. Hence **'cross-tongue** *v. trans.*, to provide with a cross-tongue.

1876 *Encycl. Brit.* IV. 489/2 Surfaces..formed of inch or inch and quarter boards joined with glue, and a cross or feather tongue ploughed into each joint. **1901** *J. Black's Carp. & Build., Home Handicrafts* 86 In the back and sides the grain of the wood runs vertically, the back being necessarily cross-tongued in two places. **1904** GOODCHILD & TWENEY *Technol. & Sci. Dict.* 141/1 *Cross tongue*, a thin slip of wood with the grain at right angles to its length.

'cross-town, *a.* and *adv.* Also 'cross-town. [CROSS- 10 a.] **A.** *adj.* Lying, leading, or going across a town.

1886 *Fortn. Rev.* 1 Feb. 221 With cross-town tramcars running from side to side. **1894** *Congress. Rec.* 28 May 5413/1, I do not believe that on the L street, or, as it is called, this cross-town road, it is possible for a cable or electric motor to be successfully used. **1900** G. BONNER *Hard-Pan* i. 10 Then he hastened his steps, and a few blocks farther on boarded a cross-town car. **1948** T. SHARP *Oxf. Replanned* iv. 89 Two medieval streets which have also, in the absence of any other single cross-town route, to carry the whole of the cross-traffic of a city of 100,000 inhabitants. **1970** *New Yorker* 9 May 44/1 She gets on the crosstown bus alone.

B. *adv.* Across the town. *U.S.*

1906 'O. HENRY' *Four Million* (1916) xvi. 165 The crowd in the gutter scattered, and the fine hansom dashed away 'cross-town. **1916** H. L. WILSON *Somewhere in Red Gap* 401 A regular old-fashioned horse-car going cross-town.

'cross-tree. [CROSS- 3, 4.]

1. *Naut.* (*pl.*) Two horizontal cross-timbers supported by the cheeks and trestle-trees at the head of the lower and top masts, to sustain the tops on the lower mast, and to spread the top-gallant rigging at the top mast head; affording also a standing-place for seamen.

Formerly sometimes used to include the trestle-trees.

1626 CAPT. SMITH *Accid. Yng. Seamen* 12 The trussell trees or crosse trees. **1627** —— *Seaman's Gram.* iii. 16 The Crosse-trees are also at the head of the Masts, one let into another crosse, and strongly bolted with the Tressell trees. **1753** CHAMBERS *Cycl. Supp.* s.v. *Cross-trees*, They are four in number..but strictly speaking only those which go thwart ships, are called *cross-trees*. **1769** FALCONER *Dict. Marine.* **1836** MARRYAT *Midsh. Easy* xiii. 41. **1871** TYNDALL *Fragm. Science* (ed. 6) I. vi. 214, I climbed the mainmast, and standing on the cross-trees, saw the sun set.

2. a. A gallows; **b.** A cross.

1638 FORD *Fancies* I. ii, Not so terrible as a cross-tree that never grows, to a wag-halter page. **1648** HERRICK *Noble Numbers* Poems (1885) 317 This Cross-tree Here Doth Jesus Bear. *a* **1889** G. M. HOPKINS *Poems* (1948) 265 And where I see the sweet cross-tree I in an instant would be gone. **1934** DYLAN THOMAS *18 Poems* 29 The blood that touched the crosstree and the grail Touched the first cloud and left a sign. **1956** E. MUIR *Coll. Poems* (1960) 228 The archaic peoples in their ancient awe, In ignorant wonder saw The wooden cross-tree on the bare hillside.

†3. A whipple-tree. *Obs.*

1765 DICKSON *Agric.* II. 258 Instead of using a soam, and cross-trees for the second pair, as is commonly done in a four horse plough.

4. *attrib.* **†cross-tree bar** (cf. 3); **†cross-tree yard,** a cross-jack yard.

1692 in *Capt. Smith's Seaman's Gram.* I. xiv. 63 The Cross-tree yard, Cross-tree Braces. **1753** CHAMBERS *Cycl. Supp.*, *Cross-tree-yard*, a yard standing square just under the mizen top. **1787** WINTER *Syst. Husb.* 310 A cross-tree bar must be fixed to the fore standards.

cross-valve: see CROSS- B.

'cross-vault. *Arch.* [CROSS- 3 b.] A compound vault formed by the intersection of two or more simple vaults.

1850 LEITCH *Müller's Anc. Art* §110. 80 The so-called sepulchre of Theron is remarkable on account of..the cross-vault in the interior. **1879** SIR G. G. SCOTT *Lect. Archit.* I. 53 A series of cross gables over the cross vaults.

Hence **'cross-'vaulted** *a.*, **'cross-'vaulting.**

1848 B. WEBB *Cont. Eccles.* 198 The choir is of one bay, cross-vaulted. **1876** GWILT *Archit.* Gloss., *Cross Vaulting*. **1888** FREEMAN in *Archæol. Inst. Jrnl.* XLV. 18 The flat ceiling for the main body and cross-vaulting for the aisles.

cross-vine, -voting: see CROSS- B.

'crosswalk. Also cross walk and with hyphen. [CROSS- 4 a.] **a.** A path or walk that crosses another, esp. in a garden.

1744 F. MOORE *Voyage to Georgia* 30 The Garden is laid out with Cross-walks planted with Orange-trees. **1813** JANE AUSTEN *Pride & Prej.* II. v. 53 Leading the way through every walk and cross walk.

b. *N. Amer.* and *W. Austral.* A pedestrian crossing. Also *fig.*

1853 *Children's Aid Society* (First Public Announcement) Mar., The *girls*...are the cross-walk sweepers, the little apple-peddlers, and candy-sellers of our city. **1904** *N.Y. Even. Post* 16 May 7 The Government service answers very well as a cross-walk in getting over a trying period in a young man's life. **1915** *Amer. City* Sept. 184/2 It was decided to recommend..that the following be adopted for general use. .. Education of the public to use crosswalks at intersections. **1962** *Coast to Coast 1961–62* 173 He went towards the cross walk. He had to wait for the traffic. **1964** M. MCLUHAN *Understanding Media* xxii. 224 Witness the portent of the crosswalk, where the small child has power to stop a cement truck. **1979** P. THEROUX *Old Patagonian Express* (1980) iii. 48 No traffic waited at the red lights, no pedestrians at the crosswalks. **1983** *Austral. Women's Weekly* Aug. 20/3 Pedestrian crossings? Not in Perth. There, a pedestrian crossing is a crosswalk.

'cross-way, *sb.* [CROSS- 4, CROSS *a.* 1 b.]

1. A way or road crossing another, or leading across from one main road to another; a by-way.

a **1490** BOTONER *Itin.* (1778) 176 At the crosse yn Baldwyne strete been IIII crosse wayes metyng. *a* **1533** LD. BERNERS *Huon* lxxxi. 247 We came too a crosse way. **1625–8** tr. *Camden's Hist. Eliz.* II. (1688) 241 The Paths and Cross-ways whereof are scarce known to the Dwellers thereabouts. **1708** MOTTEUX *Rabelais* V. xxvi. (1737) 114 Highways, Crossways, and Byways. **1824** MISS MITFORD *Village* Ser. I.

(1863) 46 The little greens formed by the meeting of these cross-ways.
fig. **1628** GAULE *Pract. Th.* To Rdr. A x, If thou stop, and stumble at the Crosse-wayes of Mysterie. **1720** WELTON *Suffer. Son of God* I. x. 264 Into a many Deviations, and Cross-ways to sin.

†**b.** *allusively.* The way of 'crosses' or afflictions. *Obs.* [CROSS- 3.]
c **1450** tr. *T. à Kempis' Imit.* II. xii. 57 Hov sekist þou a noþer way þan þe kynges hye way, þe crosse wey? All cristys lif was a crosse & a martirdom.

2. The place where roads cross; = CROSS-ROAD 2.
15.. *Knt. of Curtesy* 386 And burie my body in the crosse waie. **1590** SHAKS. *Mids. N.* III. ii. 383 Damned spirits.. That in crosse-waies and floods haue buriall. **1625** K. LONG tr. *Barclay's Argenis* I. i. 4 On the crosse-way issued forth five theeves. **1755** SMOLLETT *Quix.* (1803) I. 37 His imagination suggested those cross-ways that were wont to perplex knights-errant in their choice. **1865** KINGSLEY *Herew.* xix. 235 He went past the crossways.
attrib. **1640** H. MILL *Nights Search* 79 For this cause [suicide] a Crosse-way grave.. Is made for her.

'crossway, *adv.* and *a.* [CROSS- 3, 4.]
A. *adv.* = CROSSWAYS, CROSSWISE.
1611 FLORIO, *Trauerso*.. Also crossely, a thwart, a crosse, crosseway. **1825** SOUTHEY in *Q. Rev.* XXXII. 393 Fabian.. took his own pike cross way, laid it upon those of the enemy.
B. *adj.* Placed or executed crossways.
1829 SOUTHEY *All for Love* iv, With cross-way movement to and fro. **1865** MRS. WHITNEY *Gayworthys* i. (1879) 8 The seven little 'crossway' ruffles that garnish it [the skirt].

crossways ('krɒsweɪz, 'krɔːs-), *adv.* [CROSS- 4 + -WAYS.] = CROSSWISE.
1564 in *Hawkins' Voy.* (1878) 18 Which maketh their townes crosse waies. **1594** T. B. *La Primaud. Fr. Acad.* II. 272 *margin*, Of pleasures which men seeke crosseswayes. **1665** HOOKE *Microgr.* 101 Breaking off a very thin sliver of the Coal cross-ways. **1726** LEONI *Alberti's Archit.* I. 52 a, A defect that runs crossways of the beam. **1871** tr. *Schellen's Spectr. Anal.* ix. 24 A series of dark stripes breaking crossways through the light.

cross-webbing: see CROSS- B.

†**'cross-week.** *Obs.* [CROSS- 3 a.] Rogation week in which the CROSS-DAYS (q.v.) occur.
1530 PALSGR. 211/1 Crosweke, gangeweke, *rovvayson, rogations.* **1577** HOLINSHED *Chron.* II. 141 He sailed over into Normandie in the crosse weeke. **1597** [see CROSS-FLOWER].

'cross-wind. A wind which blows across the direct course; a contrary wind. Also *fig.* (In earlier uses, properly a simple use of CROSS *a.* 1 c and WIND *sb.*[1], but now commonly treated as a single word.)
1725 DE FOE *Voy. round World* (1840) 25 Does the captain think.. because we have met with cross winds, we must never meet with fair ones? **1678** R. L'ESTRANGE *Seneca's Mor.* (1702) 498 Scipio by a Cross Wind, being forc'd into the Power of his Enemies. **1920** L. BAIRSTOW *Appl. Aerodynamics* iv. 141 *Cross-wind force*, the component perpendicular to the lift and to the drag of the total air force on an aircraft or any part thereof. **1935** *Discovery* Feb. 42/2 It now appears doubtful as to whether stabilising fins.. are not a disadvantage, as presenting a greater surface to a cross-wind. **1959** *Manch. Guardian* 14 July 7/2 The pilot.. used a cross-wind to lift the right wing.

cross-winding, -wire: see CROSS- B.

crosswise ('krɒswaɪz, 'krɔːs-), *adv.* [CROSS- + -WISE.]
1. In the form of a cross; so as to intersect.
1398 TREVISA *Barth. De P.R.* IX. xxxi. (1495) 368 On holy Saterdaye newe fyre is fette.. and thus [= incense] is putte therin crossewyse. **1577** B. GOOGE *Heresbach's Husb.* III. (1586) 136 Cut the skinne crossewise. **1686** HORNECK *Crucif. Jesus* x. 178 To put their hands crosswise. **1756** NUGENT *Gr. Tour* II. 333 Four of these streets are built cross-wise. **1774** JOHNSON 23 Aug. in *Boswell*, A church built crosswise. **1839** YEOWELL *Anc. Brit. Ch.* xii. (1847) 136 Four holes arranged crosswise.
†**b.** *on croys-wyse*: by means of a cross, by crucifixion. *Obs. nonce-use.*
1393 LANGL. *P. Pl.* C. XXII. 142 þei.. culled hym on croys-wyse at caluarye.
†**c.** With one crossing another, alternately.
1586 W. WEBBE *Eng. Poetrie* (Arb.) 58 Eche shal containe eyght syllables, and ryme crosse wyse, the first to the thyrd, and the second to the fourth, in this manner.
2. Across, athwart, transversely.
1580 HOLLYBAND *Treas. French Tong*, *Croiser*, to cutte ouerthwarte, or crossewise. **1648** GAGE *West. Ind.* xi. (1655) 38 Great trees newly cut down.. and placed crossewise in the way. **1696** BP. PATRICK *Comm. Ex.* xxviii. (1697) 555 Not cross-wise from shoulder to shoulder; but long-wise. **1881** JOWETT *Thucyd.* I. 144 They cut timber.. and built.. a frame of logs placed cross-wise.
3. *fig.* In a way opposed to the direct or right; perversely, wrongly.
1594 T. B. *La Primaud. Fr. Acad.* II. 272 He may seeke after pleasures crosse-wise, and turne cleane out of the way from reason and iudgement.

'crosswise, *a.* [f. the adv.] Placed or running across; transverse.
1903 *Westm. Gaz.* 10 Sept. 4/2 Its crosswise pelerine. **1927** *Observer* 4 Dec. 16/4 The cross-wise streets.. are growing more and more canyon-like. *Ibid.*, The crosswise thrust of traffic at every block.

cross-wood: see CROSS- B.

'crossword, 'cross-word. [CROSS- 4 c.] In full *crossword puzzle.* A puzzle in which a pattern of chequered squares has to be filled in from numbered clues with words which are written usu. horizontally and vertically, occas. diagonally. Also *attrib.* and *Comb.*
1914 *N.Y. World* 6 Dec. ('Fun') 7/2 Solution to last week's cross-word puzzle. **1924** (*title*) The cross word puzzle book. **1925** *Punch* 1 July 724 The allure of Epstein and Oxford trouserings has been for the few; the Cross-word Puzzle captivated the general. **1925** 'TORQUEMADA' (*title*) Cross-words in rhyme for those of riper years. **1927** *Observer* 3 Apr. 7 Particularly that spot known to crossword solvers as the acnestis. **1935** MRS. H. RICHARDSON *Parody* 5 This parody business is overrated, and he deserts it for a cross-word puzzle. **1970** *Times* 28 Apr. 1/4 A national crossword competition is to be held in Britain this summer .. with The Times crossword puzzles used for heats and finals.
b. *fig.*
1928 GALSWORTHY *Swan Song* II. iv. 141 Religion used to be red-hot politics, then it became caste feeling, and now it's a cross-word puzzle. **1959** R. LONGRIGG *Wrong Number* v. 63, I could see the first few rows of audience: a crossword puzzle of black dinner-jackets, white shirt-fronts, dark dresses, pale shoulders.

crosswort ('krɒswɜːt, 'krɔːs-). [CROSS- 3 + WORT.]
1. A name of various plants having leaves arranged in the form of a cross, or whorl of four; esp. *Galium cruciatum* (also *crosswort bedstraw*); also of the non-British plants *Vaillantia cruciata*, *Eupatorium perfoliatum*, and the genus *Crucianella*. *crosswort gentian*, *Gentiana cruciata.*
1578 LYTE *Dodoens* IV. lxxvii. 541 Croswort is a pale greene herbe, drawing nere to a yellow Popingay colour.. The leaues be.. smal.. alwayes foure growing togither.. in fashion lyke to a Crosse at euery ioynt. **1597** GERARDE *Herbal* II. c. §3. 352 Crossewoort Gentian. **1756** WATSON in *Phil. Trans.* XLIX. 853 Crosswort or Mugweed. **1866** *Treas. Bot.* 352 *Crucianella*, a genus of herbaceous plants, called Crosswort and Petty Madder.
2. *pl.* A book-name for the N.O. *Cruciferæ* (plants with cruciform flowers).
1861 MRS. LANKESTER *Wild Flowers* 29 [A] very extensive and useful family of plants—Cruciferæ or Crossworts. **1884** MILLER *Plant-n.*, *Cross-wort*, any cruciferous plant.

crost, variant spelling of CROSSED.

‖**crostarie** (krɒ'stɑːrɪ). *Sc.* [a. Gaelic *crostàraidh*, *cros-tàra*, called also *crann-tàra*, *-tàraidh* the cross or beam of gathering.] The FIRE-CROSS or FIERY CROSS, used in the Highlands of Scotland to summon the clans to a rendezvous.
1685 *Lond. Gaz.* No. 2037/1 Argile commanded a Crostary to be dispatcht through the whole Country, which is a Sign in a Fiery Stick, commanding and warning every man to rise in Arms with him. **1795** *Statist. Acc. Aberdeen* XIV. 352 (Jam.) A stake of wood, the one end dipped in blood, (the blood of any animal), and the other burnt, as an emblem of fire and sword, was put into the hands of the person nearest to where the alarm was given, who immediately ran with all speed, and gave it to his nearest neighbour.. The stake of wood was named Croishtarich. **1880** BURTON *Reign Q. Anne* I. vii. 328 He sent the Crossterie, popularly called the fiery cross, through the glens.

croste, obs. form of CRUST.

crosyar, -syer, obs. ff. CROSIER.

†**crot, crote.** *Obs.* [Derivation uncertain.
The form has suggested relationship to F. *crotte* (cf. CROTEY), and to mod.Du. *krot*; but difficulties of sense and history attach to both suggestions.]
A particle, bit, atom, individual piece.
a **1300** *Cursor M.* 2378 (Cott.) Abram went.. and wit him loth, his geing, his catel, ilk crot [*Fairf.* crote]. *Ibid.* 9440 If þou haldes mi forbot, þou sal be lauerd ouer ilk crot þat es in erth or paradis. *Ibid.* 27375. *c* **1330** R. BRUNNE *Chron. Wace* (Rolls) 2102 þe host destruyed, ilk a crote. *c* **1425** WYNTOUN *Cron.* VII. viii. 83 þis ilk Pes of Bred.. of it nevyr a Crote.. owre pas my Throt. **1490–9** *Promp. Parv.* 105/1 Crote of a turfe, *glebicula, glebula.*

crotal[1] ('krəʊtəl). [ad. L. *crotalum*, or its F. adaptation *crotale*: see below.]
1. = CROTALUM 1.
1850 LEITCH *Müller's Anc. Art* §388 *note*, A female Bacchante clattering with crotals.
2. *Irish Antiq.* Applied to a small globular or pear-shaped bell or rattle, the nature and use of which are obscure: see quots. Also *attrib.*
[**1156** JOHN OF SALISBURY *Polycrat.* VIII. xii, Crotala quoque dicuntur sonoræ sphærulæ, quæ, quibusdam granis interpositis, pro quantitate sui et specie metalli, varios sonos edunt.] **1790** LEDWICH *Antiq. Ireland* 243 The Chrotal seems not to have been a Bardic Instrument; but the Bell-Cymbal used by the Clergy, and denominated a Crotalum by the Latins. **1845** *Proc. R. Irish Acad.* 135 A communication.. to shew that the article called a crotal.. had properly but one disc, and not two, as represented in Ledwich's Antiquities. **1872** ELLACOMBE *Ch. Bells Devon* 378, I would.. confine the term Crotal to those pear-shaped and globular productions, the exact use of which is evidently very doubtful. *Ibid* 379 Those round crotal bells in figure resemble an apple, and this instrument was evidently intended to make a rattling noise when shaken.

crotal[2] ('krɒtəl), **crottle** ('krɒt(ə)l). Also 8 crottel. [a. Gaelic *crotal*, *crotan* a lichen, *esp.* one used in dyeing.] A name given in Scotland to various species of lichen used in dyeing: cf. CUDBEAR. *attrib.* or *adj.*, of the colour of lichen, golden-brown.
1778 LIGHTFOOT *Flora Scot.* (1789) 818 *Lichen omphalodes.* Dark purple Dyer's Lichen. Cork or Arcell *Anglis*, Crotal *Gaulis.* **1794** *Statist. Acc. Scot.* XII. 113 It [cudbear] was known as a dye-stuff in the Highlands by the name of cookes or crottel some hundred years ago. **1861** H. MACMILLAN *Footnotes fr. Nature* 116 The dyes she herself prepares, by simply boiling in water.. various species of crotal or lichens. **1881** in D. H. Edwards *Mod. Scot. Poets* Ser. III. 999 When ither dykes Wi' crottle are grown gray. **1901** N. MUNRO *Doom Castle* iii. 23 Now the tartan's in the dye-pot, and you'll see about here but *crotal*-colour—the old stuff stained with lichen from the rock. **1907** *Westm. Gaz.* 26 Dec. 2/3 When Autumn wears her crotal gown. **1938** L. MACNEICE *I crossed Minch* II. xii. 165 He showed me some of the stockings and tweeds—one very fine, thick tweed (two blue, two white and the crotal). **1968** *Guardian* 30 Mar. 10/4 The lichen which makes the rich, rust-coloured dye they call crotal.

crotale ('krəʊtəl). [a. F. *crotale* (see CROTAL).] A type of castanet used mainly in Latin-American music; also = CROTALUM. Usu. *pl.*
1938 *Oxf. Compan. Mus.* 702/1 The *Crotales* (Fr.; made of wood or metal) are a variety of castanet. **1949** E. POUND *Pisan Cantos* lxxix. 79 Is there a sound in the forest of pard or of bassarid Or crotale or of leaves moving? **1964** S. BARRETT in Norton & Spacey *Drums & Drumming Today* 30 The gentle tinkle of Crotales.

'crotalid. *Zool.* [f. mod.L. *Crotalidæ.*] A serpent of the *Crotalidæ* or rattlesnake family.

'crotaliform, *a. Zool.* [f. CROTAL-US + -FORM.] Structurally resembling or related to the rattlesnake; as 'the crotaliform serpents'.

'crotalin. *Chem.* [f. CROTAL-US + -IN.] An albuminoid substance found in the venom of the rattlesnake: it is not coagulated at the boiling-point of water. *Syd. Soc. Lex.*

crotaline ('krɒtəlaɪn), *a.* [f. as prec. + -INE.] Of or belonging to the rattlesnake family.
1865 *Athenæum* No. 1950. 344/2 A genus of crotaline serpents. **1882** C. C. HOPLEY *Snakes* xvii. 312 That the sexes [of rattlesnakes] also understand each other through crotaline eloquence is generally believed.

‖**'crotalo.** [It. *crotalo* (in Florio), ad. L. *crotalum*: see below.] = CROTALUM.
a **1682** SIR T. BROWNE *Tracts* (1852) III. 271 All sorts of sistrums, crotaloes, cymbals, tympans, etc., in use among the ancients. **1842** BRANDE *Dict. Sc.*, *Crotalo*, a Turkish musical instrument. Hence in mod. Dicts.

‖**crotalum** ('krɒtələm). *Antiq.* [L.; a. Gr. κρόταλον clapper, castanet, rattle.]
A sort of clapper or castanet used in ancient Greece and elsewhere in religious dances.
1727–51 CHAMBERS *Cycl.* s.v., The crotalum.. consisted of two little brass plates, or rods, which were shaken in the hand. **1822** T. TAYLOR *Apuleius* IX. 194, I was again led forth to the journey.. accompanied by crotala and cymbals. **1864** ENGEL *Mus. Anc. Nat.* 225 Crotala, clappers, or castanets, were made use of by most ancient nations in religious performances.

‖**crotalus** ('krɒtələs). *Zool.* [mod.L., f. Gr. κρόταλον rattle: see prec.] The genus of American serpents containing the typical rattlesnakes.
1834 *Brit. Cycl.* II. I. 180 [Species] of Crotalus, properly so called, which have a rattle or instrument of sound upon the tail. **1864** OWEN *Power of God* 46 The crotalus warns the ear of the American Indian by the rattle of its tail.

crotaphic (krəʊ'tæfɪk), *a. Anat.* [f. Gr. κρόταφος, pl. -οι the temples; cf. F. *crotaphique.*] Of or pertaining to the temples, temporal. **'crotaphite** *a.* [F. *crotaphite* (16th c. Paré), Gr. κροταφίτης], temporal, as in 'crotaphite arteries'; †*sb.* the temporal muscle (*obs.*). **crota'phitic** *a.*, temporal, as in 'crotaphitic nerve', the superior maxillary division of the fifth cerebral nerve.
1653 URQUHART *Rabelais* I. xxv, The crotaphick artery. **1656** BLOUNT *Glossogr.*, *Crotaphites*, the two muscles of the temples. **1713** CHESELDEN *Anat.* III. xv. (1726) 254 Under the crotaphyte muscle. **1841** CRUVEILHIER *Anat.* I. 311 The Temporal muscle or *Crotaphyte*.. occupies the whole of the Temporal fossa. **1839** TODD *Cycl. Anat.* II. 271/2 The 'crotaphitic' and.. the 'buccinator' nerves.

crotaye, var. of CROTEY *Obs.*

crotch (krɒtʃ). Now chiefly *U.S.* or *dial.* Also 6–7 croche. [Etymological history obscure. In form it appears to agree with ME. *croche* shepherd's crook, crosier, ONF. *croche*; but in sense it comes nearer to CRUTCH, of which also, in certain applications, *crotch* appears as a variant. But *crutch* and *crotch* are in current use different words.]
†**1.** A fork: app. the agricultural implement.
1539 TAVERNER *Erasm. Prov.* (1545) 44 Thrust out nature wyth a croche [*Naturam expellas furca*] yet woll she styll runne backe agayne.

†**2.** A fork formerly used for holding a weed down on the ground, while it was cut off or dragged up with the weed-hook. *Obs.*

1573 Tusser *Husb.* (1878) 112 In Maie get a weede hooke, a crotch and a gloue, and weed out such weedes as the corne doth not loue. [**1873** J. Fowler in *Archæol.* XLIV. 179 (*Plate*), A man, in a garden, cutting up thistles from the plants they grow amongst with a weed-hook and crotch. *Ibid.* 207, 220.]

3. A stake or pole having a forked top, used as a support or prop.

1573 Tusser *Husb.* (1878) 64 The strawberies looke to be couered with strawe, Laid ouerly trim vpon crotchis and bows. *Ibid.* 79 For hoppoles and crotches in lopping go saue. **1681** Hickeringill *Vind. Naked Truth* II. 1, A Crazy.. Fabrick that only stands upon Crotches, and Crotchets. **1700** Dryden *Fables, Baucis and Phil.* 160 The crotches of their cot in columes rise [*furcas subiere columnæ*]. **1841** Catlin *N. Amer. Ind.* (1844) I. xxii. 162 Four posts or crotches..supporting four equally delicate rods, resting in the crotches.

†**b.** A forked peg or crook for hanging things on. *Obs.*

1573 Tusser *Husb.* (1878) 36 With crotchis and pinnes, to hang trinkets theron.

c. *Naut.* A forked support for various purposes: see crutch 3.

4. The fork of a tree or bough, where it divides into two limbs or branches.

1573 Tusser *Husb.* (1878) 105 The crotch of the bough. **1641** Best *Farm. Bks.* (Surtees) 120 Some [branches]..that have croches [*printed* creches] will bee for rake-shaftes. **1669** Worlidge *Syst. Agric.* (1681) 323 *Crotch*, the forked part of a Tree useful in many cases of Husbandry. **1758** *Acct. Micmakis*, etc. 83 Branches of trees..stuck in the ground with the crotch uppermost. **1843-4** T. N. Savage in *Boston Jrnl. Nat. Hist.* IV, They [chimpanzees]..build their habitations in trees.. supported by the body of a limb or a crotch. **1854** J. L. Stephens *Centr. Amer.* 374 A platform in the crotch of the tree. **1889** *Century Mag.* Aug. 503/1 *note*, A mass of leaves left..in the crotch of the divergent branches.

5. The 'fork' or bifurcation of the human body where the legs join the trunk. (Not restricted to *U.S.* and *dial.*)

a **1592** Green *Mamillia* ii. Poems (Rtldg.) 316 Some close-breech'd to the crotch for cold. **1615** Crooke *Body of Man* 214 The middle bifurcation at the Crotch. **1817-8** Cobbett *Resid. U.S.* (1822) 156 To be split down the middle, from crown to crotch. **1884** Child *Ballads* II. xxix. 259/1 Three hundred years old, with a beard to the crotch.

6. A bifurcation of road or river.

1767 T. Hutchinson *Hist. Mass. Bay* II. 383 The river to be called by the same name, from the crotch to the mouth. **1857** Holland *Bay Path* xxii, Standing right in the crotch of the roads.

†**7.** *fig.* A dilemma. *Obs.*

1622 Bacon *Hen. VII*, 101 There is a Tradition of a Dilemma that Bishop Morton..vsed, to raise vp the Beneuolence to higher Rates; and some called it his Forke, and some his Crotch [*Ellis & Spedding's ed.* crutch].

8. *Comb.* **crotch-deep** *a.*, up to the 'crotch' or loins; **crotch-stick** (*dial.*), a forked stick; †**crotch-tail**, old name of the Kite.

1844 *Jrnl. R. Agric. Soc.* V. I. 9 Pressing it down closely piece by piece with a small *crotch-stick. **1674-91** Ray *S. & E.C. Words* 94 A *Crotch-tail; a Kite; *Milvus caudâ forcipatâ.* **1865** *Cornh. Mag.* July 41 'Crutch-tail' formerly applied to a Kite. **1885** Swainson *Prov. Names Birds* 137 From its forked tail this bird [the Kite] has received the names of Fork tail, Crotch tail (*Essex*).

crotche, var. of croche *sb.*[1] *Obs.*

crotched (krɒtʃt), *a.* [f. prec. + -ed.] Having a 'crotch' or bifurcation; forked. (Now *U.S.*)

1587 Holinshed *Descr. Brit.* I. xiv. 74/2 A crotched brooke. **1806** A. Young *Agric. Essex* (1813) I. 181 He pins them firmly down with a crotched peg. **1868** Lossing *Hudson* 12 Two crotched sticks. **1882** *Cornh. Mag.* May 580 A shaggy roof of bark upheld by crotched saplings.

crotched-, crotchett-yard, corrupted forms of cross-jack-*yard.*

1867 Smyth *Sailor's Word-bk.*, *Crotched-yard*, the old orthography for *cross-jack-yard*. **1889** *Pall Mall G.* 16 Feb. 4/3 Reeving a 'gin' on tackle affixed to the crotchett yard on board the ship *Sardomene*.

crotchet (ˈkrɒtʃɪt), *sb.*[1] Also 5-6 crochette, 5-9 crochet, 6 corchat, crockchette, chrotchet, 7 crachet, 7 (9 *dial.*) cratchet, 8 crotchett. [ME. a. F. *crochet* hook, dim. of *croche* crook, hook: see crochet.]

I. = crocket.

1. *Arch.* = crocket 2; also *transf.* to buds or branches.

c **1394** *P. Pl. Crede* 174 þe mynstre..Wiþ arches..y-corven Wiþ crochetes on corners wiþ knottes of golde. **1825** Hone *Every-day Bk.* I. 767 The crotchets, or projecting stones on the outside of that..spire. **1892** *Lichfield Mercury* 25 Mar. 8/5 Let us gather one of their [elm trees'] delicate sprays... Every crochet resembles a cluster of spherical beads.

†**2.** = crocket 1. *Obs.* (Cf. F. *crochet.*) In mod. dial. ***cratchet*** = the crown of the head.

1589 *Pappe w. Hatchet* B iv, They will..anatomize..thy bodie from the corne on thy toe, to the crochet on thy head. **1855** Robinson *Whitby Gloss.*, *Cratchet*, the crown of the head. 'Nap his cratchet', crack his crown. **1876** *Mid-Yorksh. Gloss.*, *Cratchet*, the crown of the head.

II. A hook or hooked instrument.

†**3.** A small hook, *esp.* for fastening things; an ornamental hook serving as a brooch or fastening.

c **1430** *Pilgr. Lyf Manhode* III. xxiv. (1869) 149 Of this crochet, S. **1481** Caxton *Godfrey* 179 It shold be fasted to the creneaux of the walle, with good and stronge crochettes of yron. **1483** —— *Gold. Leg.* 134/4 Thenne the tyraunt.. with hokes and crochettis of yron dyde do tere theyr flessh. **1503** *Priv. Purse Exp. Eliz. of York* (1830) 92 For hookes and crochettes..delivered to William Hamerton yeoman of the Warderobe of the beddes. *a* **1618** Sylvester *Du Bartas, Job Triumphant* xli, Canst thou his tongue with steely crotchets thrill. **1690** Evelyn *Mundus Muliebris*, This to her side she does attach With gold crochet, or French pennache. **1703** J. Savage *Lett. Antients* lxxvii. 217 An Imperial Purple Robe on her Shoulders button'd with a Crotchet of Diamonds on her Breast. **1710** Steele *Tatler* No. 245 ¶ 2 A Crochet of 122 Diamonds, set..in Silver.

4. *Surg.* †**a.** A hook-like instrument; **b.** *spec.* an instrument employed in obstetrical surgery.

1750 *Phil. Trans.* XLVII. 83 With a crotchet holding up the integuments [I] keep them from touching. **1754-64** Smellie *Midwif.* II. 448, I sat down with a resolution to deliver either with the forceps or crotchet in order to save the woman's life. **1854** E. Mayhew *Dogs* (1862) 213 Forceps ..are always dangerous..The crochet, a blunt hook..is to be preferred.

5. a. A hook used in reaping: see quot. 1833. ‖**b.** A hook fastened with straps on the back of a porter for carrying parcels. [= Fr. *crochet.*]

1833 J. Holland *Manuf. Metal* II. 58 The crotchet or hook; the workman uses it with the left hand to gather the quantity of corn he intends to cut. **1860** Tyndall *Glac.* I. xxvii. 216 Simond carried my theodolite box, tied upon a crotchet on his back.

6. A natural hook-like organ or process: *spec.* †**a.** 'The tushe, tuske, or fang of a beast' Cotgr. [F. *crochet*]. **b.** One of the minute hooks or claws on the prolegs of many lepidopterous larvæ. **c.** *Anat.* The hook-like extremity of the superior occipito-temporal convolution of the brain.

1678 Phillips s.v., Among Hunters, the chief master Teeth of a Fox, are called Crochets. [Hence **1708** in Kersey and in later Dicts.] **1778** Milne *Dict. Bot.* s.v. *Semen*, Some seeds attach themselves to animals, by means of hooks, crotchets, or hairs. **1802** Paley *Nat. Theol.* xii, In the Ostrich, this apparatus of crotchets and fibres, of hooks and teeth is wanting. **1826** Kirby & Sp. *Entomol.* (1828) III. xxix, The prolegs of almost all Lepidopterous larvæ are furnished with a set of minute slender horny hooks, crotchets, or claws..somewhat resembling fish-hooks. **1876** Quain *Elem. Anat.* (ed. 8) II. 532 Its anterior extremity is rounded into a hook called by Vicq-d'Azyr the 'crotchet', hence its name.

III. Derived and figurative senses.

7. a. *Mus.* A symbol for a note of half the value of a minim, made in the form of a stem with a round (formerly lozenge-shaped) black head; a note of this value. Also *attrib.*

c **1440** *Promp. Parv.* 104 Crochett of songe, *semiminima.* *c* **1460** *Towneley Myst.* 116, *Sec Pastor.* Say what was his song? hard ye not how he crakyd it, Thre brefes to a long. *Tert. Pastor.* Yee mary he hakt it, Was no crochett wrong, nor no thing that lakt it. **1500-20** Dunbar *Poems* (1884) No. 22 iv, The pyet..Fenȝeis to sing the nychtingalis not; Bot scho can nevir the corchat cleif, For harsknes of hir carlich throt. **1597** Morley *Introd. Mus.* 178 He giueth it such a natural grace by breaking a minime into a crotchet rest and a crotchet. **1622** Peacham *Compl. Gent.* xi. (1634) 102 Hee driveth a Crotchet thorow many Minims, causing it to resemble a chaine with the Linkes. **1782** Burney *Hist. Mus.* (ed. 2) II. iv. 303 Notes in a lozenge form:..these, whether the heads were full or open, were at first called minims: but when a still quicker note was thought necessary, the white or open notes only had that title and the black were..by the English [called] Crotchets: a name given by the French with more propriety, from the hook or curvature of the tail, to the ..Quaver. **1850** W. Irving *Goldsmith* 290 He pretended to score down an air as the poet played it, but put down crotchets and semi-breves at random.

b. Often used with playful allusion to sense 9.

1579 Gosson *Apol. Sch. Abuse* (Arb.) 68 They [Musitions] haue euer a crotchet aboue commons, and adde where they liste. **1599** Shaks. *Much Ado* II. iii. 58 Why these are very crotchets that he speaks, Note notes forsooth, and nothing. **1691** Wood *Ath. Oxon.* I. 768 Being possess'd with crotchets, as many Musicians are.

†**8.** A square bracket in typography; = crook 7: formerly also called *hook. Obs.*

1676 Coles, *Crotchet*..also (in printing) the mark of a Parenthesis [ ]. **1748** Richardson *Clarissa* Wks. 1883 VIII. 456 *note*, What is between crotchets, thus [ ], Mr. Belford omitted. **1832** Lindley *Introd. Bot.* 495 A few interpolations, which are distinguished by being included within crotchets [ ].

9. a. A whimsical fancy; a perverse conceit; a peculiar notion on some point (usually considered unimportant) held by an individual in opposition to common opinion.

The original of this sense is obscure: it is nearly synonymous with crank *sb.*[2], senses 3 and 4, and might, like it, have the radical notion of 'mental twist or crook'; but Cotgrave appears to connect it with the musical note, sense 7: '*Crochue*, a Quauer in Musicke; whence *Il a des crochues en teste*, (we say) his head is full of crochets': cf. also 7 b.

1573 G. Harvey *Letter-bk.* (Camden) 46 M. Osburn stud uppon this chrotchet, that he had bene ons there alreddi, and therefore, etc. **1587** Harrison *England* II. xxii. (1877) I. 339 All the od crochets in such a builder's braine. **1603** Shaks. *Meas. for M.* III. ii. 135. **1621-51** Burton *Anat. Mel.* I. iii. I. ii. 187 That castle in the ayr, that crochet, that whimsie. **1628** Wither *Brit. Rememb.* II. 813 How could so fond a crotchet be devised, That God our seriout actions hath despised? **1711** E. Ward *Quix.* I. 37 With fifty Crotchets in his Head. *a* **1772** Wilkie *The Ape, Parrot, etc.* (R.), But airy whims and crotchets lead To certain loss, and ne'er succeed. **1807** Crabbe *Par. Reg.* III. 930 And gloomy crotchets fill'd his wandering head. **1861** M. Arnold *Pop. Educ. France* 165 Opinions which have no ground in reason ..mere crotchets, or mere prejudices.

b. A fanciful device, mechanical, artistic, or literary.

1611 L. Barry *Ram Alley* in Hazl. *Dodsley* X. 366 As for my breath I have crotchets and devices, 'Ladies' rank breaths are often help'd with spices'. **1644** Evelyn *Diary* 8 Nov., He shew'd us his perpetual motions..models, and a thousand other crotchets and devices. **1733** (*title*), Islington; or the Humours of the New Tunbridge Wells..with Serious and Comical Puns, Crotchets, and Conclusions. **1761** Foote *Liar* I. Wks. 1799 I. 290 All the sighing, dying, crying crotchets, that..rhymers have ever produced. **1831** Carlyle *Sart. Res.* II. ix, Nothing but innuendoes, figurative crotchets.

10. *Fortif.* A passage formed by an indentation in the glacis opposite a traverse, connecting the portions of the covered way on both sides of the traverse.

1853 Stocqueler *Milit. Encycl.*

†**11.** *Mil.* 'The arrangement of a body of troops, either forward or rearward, so as to form a line nearly perpendicular to the general line of battle' (Webster 1864). *Obs.*

†**12.** quasi-*adv.* Oddly. *nonce-use.*

1674 N. Fairfax *Bulk & Selv.* 20 Its independency or loosness from God, lies as crotchet every whit, as its being.

13. *Comb.*, as ***crotchet-shaped***; **crotchet-hero** (*humorous*), a musician; **crotchet letter**, one having a hook-shaped hair-line; **crotchet-monger**, one who has crotchets on political and other questions and obtrusively advocates them; hence ***crotchet-mongering***.

1807 W. Irving *Salmag.* (1824) 82 Exhibit loud piano feats Caught from that crotchet-hero, Meetz. **1874** Blackie *Self-Cult.* 60 They are mostly crotchet-mongers and puzzle-brains. **1884** Ray Lankester in *Pall Mall G.* 6 Oct. 1/3 A corkscrew-shaped or a rod-shaped or a crotchet-shaped bacillus. **1887** *Script Letters for Perforating & Sewing*, Crotchet letters b v f r w. **1888** *Charity Organis. Rev.* June 267 The only way for a philanthropist to escape the reproach of crotchet-mongering is to give up trust in legislative crotchets.

†ˈ**crotchet**, *sb.*[2] *Obs.* Also 7 cratchet. [dim. of crotch. (Cf. also crutchet.)]

1. A pole or prop with a forked top; = crotch 3.

1631 Capt. Smith *Advt. Planters* 32 This was our Church, till wee built a homely thing like a barne, set upon Cratchets. **1681** [see crotch 3]. **1756** P. Browne *Jamaica* 25 They live in huts or thatched cabbins sustained by crotchets. **1764** Croker, etc. *Dict. Arts & Sc.* s.v. *Currying*, [Tools used] A crotchet or fork.

2. A forked support or bracket.

1772 W. Bailey *Descr. Useful Machines* I. 255 A Brass Crotchet screwed to the Pedestle and properly fitted to the solid and also to the hollow end of the axis of the machine.

3. *Naut.* = crotch 3 c, crutch 3.

1769 Falconer *Dict. Marine, Crouchants*, the crotchets, or floor-timbers fore and aft in a boat.

ˈ**crotchet**, *v.* [f. crotchet *sb.*[1]] †**a.** To break a longer note up into crotchets (*obs.*). **b.** To affect with crotchets. **c.** To ornament with crotchets or crockets. Hence ˈ**crotcheted**, *ppl. a.*

1587 Harmar tr. *Beza's Serm.* 267 (T.) Not these cantels and morsels of scripture warbled, quavered, and crochetted, to give pleasure unto the ears. *c* **1600** Donne *Elegies* i. *Jealousie*, Drawing his breath, as thick and short, as can The nimblest crocheting Musitian. **1628** Ford *Lover's Mel.* II. ii, You are but whimsied yet, crotcheted, conundrumed. **1892** *Lichfield Mercury* 25 Mar. 8/5 Look up..through the slender branches, crochetted almost to the tips..There is no need to wonder where the architects..got their idea of crochetting the spires and pinnacles of our Cathedral.

crotcheteer (krɒtʃɪˈtɪə(r)). Also crotcheter. [f. crotchet *sb.*[1] + -eer[1].] A person with a crotchet; *esp.* one who pushes or obtrudes his crotchets in politics, etc.

1815 W. H. Ireland *Scribbleomania* 220 As sometimes a brighter orb 'lumines the sphere, So Busby o'er crotcheteers reigns overseer. **1856** *Tait's Mag.* XXIII. 276 Attempts at interference have been hinted at by reckless crotcheters. **1887** Saintsbury *Hist. Elizab. Lit.* vi. 242 A very early example of the reckless violence of private crotcheteers.

ˈ**crotchetiness.** [f. crotchety + -ness.] The quality of being crotchety.

1837 Mill *Let.* May in *Wks.* (1963) XII. 336 His crotchettiness, and his fussiness, and his go-between inclinations. **1860** *Sat. Rev.* 16 June 764/2 The fault to which Examiners are liable is sometimes called crotchetiness, but a better name for it would be vanity. **1877** *Daily News* 9 Oct. 5/2 Amazement at the crotchetiness of his host.

†ˈ**crotchetly**, *a. Obs.* [-ly[1].] = next.

1702 C. Mather *Magn. Chr.* III. iv. v. (1852) 594 Let the reader, here in a crochet, refresh himself with one crochetly passage.

crotchety (ˈkrɒtʃɪtɪ), *a.* [f. crotchet *sb.*[1] + -y.[1]] Given to crotchets; full of crotchets.

1825 Ld. Cockburn *Mem.* 215 He was crotchety, positive and wild. **1867** Bright *Sp. Reform* (1876) 408 All sorts of crotchety people.

b. Of actions, etc.: Of the nature of a crotchet.

1847 Disraeli *Tancred* vi. v, I threw no obstacles in his crotchetty course. **1890** *Spectator* 25 Jan., Crotchety attempts to alter the style and title of the House of Lords.

crote, var. crot *Obs.*, piece, bit.

crotels: see crottels.

crotesco, crotesque: see grotesque.

† **'crotey**, *v. Obs.* [app. a. Anglo-Fr. **croteyer* = OF. **crotoyer*, f. OF. *crote, crotte* dung of hares, etc.] *trans.* and *intr.* Of hares, rabbits, etc.: To evacuate their excrement.

a **1425** *Master of Game* (Bodl. MS. 546 fo. 13 b), The hare ..alwey..croteyeþ yn o manere. *Ibid.* fo. 26 þei [bucks] croteieþ hure fumes yn dyuerse maneres. **1486** *Bk. St. Albans* E iij a, The hare..fymaes and crotis and Roungeth euermoore.

† **crotey**, *sb. Obs.* Also **crotaye, crottoye.** [f. crotey *v.*] In *pl.* = crottels.

a **1425** *Master of Game* (Bodl. MS. 546 fo. 70) ȝif þe croteyes beþ grete and þikke. **1575** Turberv. *Venerie* 65 To iudge an olde harte by the fewmishing, the which they make in brode croteys. **1630** J. Taylor (Water P.) *Wks.* i. 93 1 A Hare or Conneys Crottoyes. **1741** *Compl. Fam. Piece* ii. i. 301 The Croteys or Excrements of a Buck [Hare]. **1807** *Sportsman's Dict.* s.v. *Bear*, [Bears] cast their lesses sometimes in round croteys.

† **'crotising, -izing.** *Obs.* Collective noun in same sense as prec.

1598 [see crottels]. **1677** Plot *Oxfordsh.* 190 The infection of the grass by the urin and crotizing of the Conies. **1686** N. Cox *Gentl. Recr.* 12 Terms for their Ordure..Of a Hare, Crotiles or Crotosing.

Croton ('krəʊtən). [mod.L., a. Gr. κροτών a tick, also the Castor-oil plant *Ricinus communis*, taken in Botany as the name of an allied genus.]

1. *Bot.* A large genus of euphorbiaceous plants, mostly natives of tropical regions, many of the species of which have important medical properties.

1751 Hill *Nat. Hist. Plants* 612 The herbaceous Croton with rhombic leaves and pendulous capsules. **1846** Lindley *Veg. Kingd.* 281 Similar colours are found..in some Crotons. **1847** Youatt *Horse* xiv. 305 The only purgative on which dependence can be placed is the croton.

2. By florists applied to *Codiæum pictum*, a plant closely allied to the Crotons, cultivated in hot-houses for its beautiful foliage.

1881 *Daily News* 29 June 2/7 Crotons, gloxinias, maidenhair, Dracænas, and pitcher plants. **1882** *Garden* 11 Mar. 167/3 Suitable time..for cutting back and striking Crotons.

3. croton oil, a fatty oil existing in the seeds of the East Indian species, *Croton Tiglium*; it is a drastic purgative; **croton chloral** or **c. c. hydrate**, a name of *butyl chloral hydrate*, given in error.

1831 J. Davies *Manual Mat. Med.* 363 Croton Oil. **1875** H. C. Wood *Therap.* (1879) 475 Croton oil is probably the most available of the cathartics. **1876** Harley *Mat. Med.* 346 Croton-chloral Hydrate was first obtained by Kramer and Pinner. **1881** B. W. Richardson in *Med. Temp. Jrnl.* Jan. 79 Croton chloral combined with quinine.

croton-bug. *U.S.* A name given in parts of the U.S. to the Cockroach, *Blatta orientalis*, and other species of the same genus.

The name is said to be derived from the Croton river, Westchester county, N.Y., the suggestion being that these insects became abundant in New York about the time (1842) that the Croton aqueduct brought water to the city.

crotonic (krəʊ'tɒnɪk), *a. Chem.* [f. Croton + -ic.] Of or derived from croton oil; as in ***crotonic acid***, $C_4H_6O_2$, the second member of the acrylic series. So **'crotonate**, a salt of crotonic acid. **'crotonol**, a brown oil obtained from croton oil. **'crotonyl**, the radical C_4H_7 of crotonic acid. **'crotony,lene**, a hydro-carbon, C_4H_6 (liquid below 15° C.), homologous with allylene.

1838 T. Thomson *Chem. Org. Bodies* 433 It owes its purgative qualities to..crotonic acid dissolved in the oil. **1873** Williamson *Chem.* 302 The crotonate which has been extracted from the croton-seed oil. **1880** Cleminshaw *Wurtz' Atom. Th.* 264 The tetratomic radicals, acetylene, allylene, and crotonylene, are known in a free state.

† **crott.** *Obs. rare*$^{-1}$. [a. F. *crotte.*] Dirt.

1657 Howell *Londinop.* 391 And touching streets, the dirt and crott of Paris may be smelt ten miles off.

crottels ('krɒt(ə)lz), *sb. pl.* Also 7 **crotelles, -iles, -els.** [app. dim. f. F. *crote, crotte* (see crot).] The globular dung or excrement of hares, etc.

1598 Manwood *Lawes Forest* iv. §6 (1615) 45/2 Of a Hare [the ordure is called] crottels or cratising. **1660** Howell *Parly of Beasts* 8 (D.) The lesses of a fox, the crotells of a hare. *a* **1700** B. E. *Dict. Cant. Crew, Crotiles*, Hares Excrements. **1711** Puckle *Club* (1817) 90 The spraints of an otter, the crottels of a hare.

crottle, var. crotal².

crottoye, var. crotey *Obs.*

† **crouch**, *sb.*¹ *Obs.* Forms: 1 crúc, 2–3 cruche, 4–5 crouche, crowch(e. [Early ME. *cruche*, app.:—OE. *crúc*, ad. L. *crux, crucis* cross.

OE. *crúc* is known to occur once *c* 1000 in sense 'sign of the cross': its history presents some difficulties. The palatalization of the final *ć* (whence 12th c. *crūche*) suggests that it was a word of early adoption which had undergone the usual phonetic change, as in *circe*, church. But in this case the vowel would have remained short, as in *pic*, pitch, and examples would surely have occurred. The probability is that it is a late learned adaptation of L. *cruci-*, as pronounced by Italians or other Romanic people with *c* as *tch*, and lengthened *ū*: cf. It. *croce*. See Pogatscher §160 (1888). Cf. also OS. *crûci*, OHG. *crûci, crûzi*, mod.G. *kreuz*, and their allied forms, where we have the long *ū*, and *c* repr. by *ts* as in OF. *cruiz*. (Some have thought ME. *cruche* to be of Fr. dial. origin: cf. Bearnese *croutz* cross).]

= cross, in its various early senses: the holy cross, or a representation or figure of it; the sign of the cross; a heraldic cross; the cross on a coin, a coin marked with a cross.

c **1000** *Sax. Leechd.* II. 288 þonne nime he his [petra oleum] dæl, and wyrce cristes mæl on ælcre lime butan cruc on þæm heafde foran se sceal on balzame beon. *c* **1200** *Trin. Coll. Hom.* 95 Crepe to cruche on lange fridai. *a* **1225** *Leg. Kath.* 1171 Ne mahte..his heuenliche cunde..felen..sorhe vpo þe cruche. *c* **1315** Shoreham 15 Ine the foreheved the crouche a-set Felthe of fendes to bermi. **1340** *Ayenb.* 41 The halȝede þinges, þe crouchen [Fr. *les croiz*], þe calices. **1389** in *Eng. Gilds* (1870) 54 In exaltacion of ye holy crouche. **1393** Gower *Conf.* I. 172 Whose tunge nouther pill ne crouche may hire. **1393** *Langl. P. Pl.* C. viii. 167 Meny crouche on hus cloke and keyes of rome. *a* **1400** *Cov. Myst.* (Shaks. Soc.) 355 He deyd on crowche. *a* **1420** Hoccleve *De Reg. Princ.* 680 Loke whethir In this purs there be ony crosse or crouche. **1463**, etc. [see Crouchmas].

crouch (kraʊtʃ), *sb.*² Also 6 crowche. [f. crouch *v.*¹] **a.** An act of crouching; a stooping, bending, or bowing low.

1597 Lyly *Wom. in Moone* ii. i, Thou didst not honor me with kneele and crowche. **1632** Massinger *City Madam* ii. i, The reverence, respect, the crouches, cringes. **1809** Campbell *Gertr. Wyom.* iii. xiv, Nor cougar's crouch I fear'd. **1889** Adm. Maxse in *Pall Mall G.* 29 Jan. 1, Public Opinion, always on the crouch..in order to spring erect.

b. *Athletics.* A method of starting in sprint races in which the runner crouches down on all fours. In full ***crouch start.***

1913 S. A. Mussabini *Compl. Athletic Trainer* 196 The old-fashioned stand-up position enabled the runners to keep 'set' on their marks for a very much longer time than the present-day straining 'crouch' will let them do. *Ibid.* 217 Good level running from the modern 'crouch' start. **1931** F. A. M. Webster *Atheletes in Action* 17 No matter what type of race one is competing in, provided that it calls for a crouch start, the first consideration must be that of generating immediate momentum. *Ibid.* 81 The start is made in the normal 'Crouch' position used by sprinters. **1956** H. Abrahams *Olympic Games Bk.* Pl. facing p. 16 (*caption*) Start of the 100 metres final. T. E. Burke (U.S.A.)..has already adopted the 'crouch' start.

crouch, obs. by-form of crutch.

crouch (kraʊtʃ), *v.*¹ Forms: 4 cruche(n, crouchen, 4–6 crouche, 5–7 croche, 6–7 crowch(e, crooch(e, 6 crootche, croutche, 6– crouch. [First known in end of 14th c.; origin doubtful.

Generally identified with crouk *v.*; but (1) *crouke* and *cruche* come together as distinct words in 2nd quot. 1394; (2) there is no assignable reason for the palatalization of the *k* in *crouk*; cf. the phonetic history of OE. *brúcan, dúcan, lúcan*, etc.; (3) *crouch* is palatalized in all Eng. dialects, Sc. (krutʃ), W. Yorksh. (kraːtʃ) (both meaning ME. *ū*). It is indeed impossible for a word in *-ouch* to be regularly derived from OE., since the same cause that palatalized the *c* in *-úc* would necessarily make umlaut and give *-ýc-*, ME. *-ych, -ich.* There was however an OF. *crochir* to become hooked or crooked, of which Godefroy has a single example, said of the shoulders 'a fet..les espaules crochir.' On the analogy of *pouch, avouch*, etc., this might give Eng. *crouch*, but the lateness of the word is still surprising.]

1. *intr.* To stoop or bend low with general compression of the body, as in stooping for shelter, in fear, or in submission; to cower with the limbs bent. Formerly often applied to the act of bowing low in reverence or deference. Now said also of the depressed and constrained posture assumed by a beast in fear or submission, or in order to make a spring. (To *cower* concerns chiefly the head and shoulders: to *crouch* affects the body as a whole.)

c **1394** *P. Pl. Crede* 302 Lordes loueth hem well, for þei so lowe crouchen. *Ibid.* 751 Kniȝtes croukeþ hem to & crucheþ full lowe. [**14..** *Golagros & Gaw.* 1280 The King crochit with croune, cumly and cleir.] **1548** Gest *Pr. Masse* 121 Without ether crouching or kneling. **1581** J. Bell *Haddon's Answ. Osor.* 322 b, Croochyng and kneelyng to the Crucifixe. **1611** Cotgr., *Tapir*..to crooch, lurke, squat, or ducke vnder. **1653** H. Cogan tr. *Pinto's Trav.* 29 We sat crouching for the space of three whole days upon this rock. **1709** Addison *Tatler* No. 161 ¶5 A Couple of tame Lions lay crouching at her Feet. **1835** Marryat *Jac. Faithf.* xxxi, He crouched behind a lilac-bush. **1840** Dickens *Barn. Rudge* vi, Crouching like a cat in dark corners. **1873** Black *Pr. Thule* vii. 106 Sheila crouched into her father's side for shelter.

2. To bow or bend humbly or servilely; to cringe submissively or fawningly. Chiefly *fig.*

1528 Roy & Barlow *Rede me* (Arb. 59) But they are constrayned to croutche..as it were unto an Emproure. **1577** Hanmer *Anc. Eccl. Hist.* (1619) 327 They crooched vnto the Romanes, and protested loyalty and subiection. **1594** Nashe *Unfort. Trav.* 41 He must faune like a spaniell, crouch like a Jew. **1601** R. Johnson *Kingd. & Commw.* 59 They are croched to, and feared of all men. **1779** J. Moore *View Soc. Fr.* (1789) I. xliv. 375 The free spirit must crouch to the slave in office. **1823** Scott *Quentin D.* xvi, I crouch to no one—obey no one. *a* **1862** Buckle *Civiliz.* (1869) III. iii. 126 They who crouch to those who are above them always trample on those who are below them.

3. *trans.* To bow or bend low (the knee, etc.): often with implication of cringing.

1705 *Lond. Gaz.* No. 4149/4 [She] crouches her hind Fetterlock Joynts when she stands still. **1800** Coleridge *Christabel* 11, She..crouched her head upon her breast. **1815** Moore *Lalla R.* (1824) 207 'Twas not for him to crouch the knee Tamely to Moslem tyranny. **1854** Landor *Lett. American* 26 How long shall a hundred millions of our fellow-creatures crouch their backs before him?

† **crouch**, *v.*² *Obs.* Also 5 crowche, 7 cruch. [f. crouch *sb.*¹: cf. cross *v.*]

1. *trans.* To cross; to sign with a cross.

a **1225** *Leg. Kath.* 728 Heo wið Cristes cros Cruchede hire ouer al. *c* **1386** Chaucer *Miller's T.* 293, I crowche the from elues and from wightes. —— *Merch. T.* 463 And crouched hem, and bad God schuld hem blesse.

2. To cross with lines, etc. *rare.*

c **1620** Z. Boyd *Zion's Flowers* (1855) 125 Bred greefe hath cruch't our cheekes with water furrowes.

crouchant ('kraʊtʃənt), *a.* [f. crouch *v.*¹ + -ant, after *couchant.*] Crouching.

a **1593** H. Smith *Serm.* (1637) 119 To mayntaine his Papists pendant and crouchant which live among Christians. **1850** *Tait's Mag.* XVII. 113/2 Droll fellows.., crouchant under the fancied burdens of waterspouts.

† **'crouchback**, *sb.* and *a. Obs.* (exc. *Hist.*) Also 6 crutch-back, crudge bak, 7 crouched-. [f. stem of crouch *v.*, associated perhaps with F. *croche* crook: cf. crook-back, which is, at least in sense and use, a doublet of this.]

1. A crooked or hunched back. **2.** One who has a crooked back, a hunchback. **b.** *attrib.* or *adj.* Having a crooked back, hunchbacked.

c **1491** in R. Davies *York Records* (1843) 221 That Kyng Richard was an ypocryte, a crochebake, & beried in a dike like a dogge. **1494** Fabyan *Chron.* vii. 366 Sir Edmunde yᵉ kynges other sone, surnamed Crowch Bak. **1519** Douglas *King Hart* ii. liv, A crudge bak that cairfull cative bure. **1592** R. Johnson *Nine Worthies* A iij, Aesope, for all his crutchback, had a quick wit. **1627** Speed *England* xxx. §6 Robert Bossu, the Crouch-backe Earl of that Prouince. **1700** J. Brome *Trav. Eng.* ii. (1707) 66 Crouch-back Robert, Earl [of Leicester]..raised a Rebellion against King Henry II.

(As a cognomen of Edmund, brother of Edward I, it was contended by some 17th c. writers that *Crouchback* meant 'crossed-back', as in *crouched friars*; but this is not compatible with the form crook-back, which goes back to the 15th c., and answers to the 'Edmundus dorsum habuit fractum', attributed to John of Gaunt in the *Continuatio Eulogii* (Rolls, 1863) III. 369. Cf. **1611** Speed *Hist. Gt. Brit.* vii. ii. (1632) 199. **1640** Yorke *Union Hon.* 22. **1677** F. Sandford *Geneal. Hist. Kings Eng.* 103.)

Hence † **'crouch-backed** *a.*

1606 Holland *Sueton.* 211 A man very low of stature and withall crowchbacked. **1630** M. Godwyn tr. *Bp. Hereford's Ann. Eng.* (1675) 148 Crouch-backed Mary [married] to Martin Kayes, groom Porter. *c* **1707** in Maidment *Sc. Pasquils* (1868) 375 The crouch backed Count.

† **crouch-clay.** *Obs.* (Cf. also crouch-ware.)

1726 *Dict. Rust.* (ed. 3) s.v. *Clay, Crouch*, white Clay, Derbyshire, of which the Glass-pots are made at Nottingham.

crouched ('kraʊtʃt, -ɪd), *ppl. a.* [f. crouch *v.*¹ + -ed.] **a.** Bowed, bent together.

1848 J. A. Carlyle tr. *Dante's Inferno* xiv, Sitting all crouched up. **1865** Kingsley *Herew.* xix. (1866) 245 She sat crouched together.

b. *spec.* in *Archæol.* Of a burial: with the body in a crouching posture, usu. on its side.

[**1898** Pitt-Rivers *Excav. Cranborne Chase* IV. 82 On the near side of the collection of interments are seen Nos. 1 and 2 crouched on the right side.] **1915** H. R. Hall *Ægean Archæol.* vi. 160 Primitive *Hockergräber* (crouched burials) have also been found at Tiryns. **1925** A. Keith *Antiquity of Man* (ed. 2) II. iii. 48 This 'crouched' burial had been made by the people who lived on the old land surface and worked the Neolithic flints. **1954** S. Piggott *Neolithic Cultures* ii. 49 A second barrow..contained a crouched skeleton.

crouched, earlier form of crutched (Friars).

'croucher. [f. crouch *v.*¹] One who crouches.

1587 Golding *De Mornay* xviii. (1617) 320 A thousand flatterers, and as many crouchers and cappers. **1884** Tennyson *Becket* 10, I, true son Of Holy Church—no croucher to the Gregories.

'crouchie, -y, *a. Sc.* [f. crouch *v.*¹ or *sb.*² + -y.] = crouch-backed, hunch-backed.

1785 Burns *Halloween* xx, Or crouchie Merran Humphie.

crouching ('kraʊtʃɪŋ), *vbl. sb.* [f. crouch *v.*¹ + -ing¹.] The action of the verb crouch, q.v. Cf. crouch *sb.*² b.

1535 Coverdale *Ecclus.* xii. 11 Though he make moch croutchinge and knelinge. **1581** J. Bell *Haddon's Answ. Osor.* 319 In their croochynges, maskyng Masses, Anthemes. **1814** Byron *Corsair* ii. xiv, The coward crouching of despair. **1904** Graham & Clark *Pract. Track & Field Athletics* ii. 17 To-day practically every one uses the low or crouching start, which experience has proved beyond all question to be the quickest. **1912** E. H. Ryle *Athletics* vi. 89 There are two methods of starting—the old erect posture and the modern crouching or 'all fours' method. **1913** E. W.

HJERTBERG *Athletics in Theory & Practice* II. i. 85 The 'crouching' start has proved its superiority in every respect.

'crouching, *ppl. a.* [f. as prec. + -ING².] That crouches (*lit.* and *fig.*); see the verb.

1600 SHEP. TONIE *Woodmans Walke* in *Eng. Helicon,* Desert went naked in the cold, when crouching craft was fed. **1611** COTGR., *Tapissant,* crooching. **1770** GOLDSM. *Des. Vil.* 355 Where crouching tigers wait their hapless prey. **1867** F. D. MAURICE *Patr. & Lawgivers* x. (ed. 4) 193 They were a set of poor crouching slaves.

Hence **'crouchingly** *adv.*

1831 J. WILSON in *Blackw. Mag.* XXIX. 702 Running crouchingly along the copestones. **1884** E. O'DONOVAN *Story of Merv* iii. 34 They..sat crouchingly around the fires.

†**'Crouchmas.** *Obs.* Also 5 crowche-, 6 crowchmes(se, -mas. [f. CROUCH *sb.*¹ cross + MASS.] The festival of the Invention of the Cross, observed on May 3.

1389 in *Eng. Gilds* (1870) 119 On yᵉ sunday after crouchemesse dai. **1463** *Paston Lett.* No. 472 II. 132 Ye Fryday nexst after Crowchemesse Day. **1530** PALSGR. 804/1 At Crowchmesse, *a la saincte Croyx. Ibid.* 811/2 On Crowchemesse daye, *le jour du saynct Sacrement.* **1573** TUSSER *Husb.* (1878) 110 From bull cow fast till Crowchmas be past. **1706** PHILLIPS (ed. Kersey), *Crouchmas* or *Crouchmas-day,* a Festival kept by Roman-Catholicks in Honour of the Holy Cross. [Hence in BAILEY.] [**1891** *Globe* 28 Dec. 1/5 Martinmas is confined to Scotland; Crouchmas, the feast of the Invention of the Cross, on May 3, is quite obsolete.]

'crouch-ware. *Pottery.* [Of uncertain origin and age: connexion with CROUCH-CLAY, or the converse, is suggested by Solon, *Old English Potter,* but evidence is wanting.] A name applied by collectors to the early salt-glazed pottery of Staffordshire.

1817 W. PITT *Topogr. Hist. Staffordsh.* 415-6 These pieces [of *c* 1700] appear to be composed of the clay found in the coal pits in and near Burslem, then called Can-marl; while others have been found formed of this clay and a mixture of white sand or pounded gritstone procured at Mole Cop, and well covered with a salt glaze. This last is known by the name of Crouch Ware, and proves that at that time the salt glaze had been introduced. **1829** S. SHAW *Hist. Staffordsh. Potteries* 110 We find Crouch ware first made there [Burslem] in 1690..In making Crouch ware, the common brick clay and fine sand from Mole Cop were first used; but afterwards the Can marl and sand; and some persons used the dark grey clay from the coal pits and sand for the body, and salt glaze. **1883** SOLON *Old Eng. Potter* 72.

croud, var. of CROOD *v. Sc.*

croud(e, crouette, obs. ff. CROWD, CRUET.

croudero: see CROWDER.

†**crouk,** *v. Obs. rare.* Also 5 crowke. [Of uncertain origin; but perh. corresponding to Ger. dial. *krauchen* in same sense, which Hildebrand suggests to be:—**krûkan* = *kreukan* (Ger. *kriechen*), like OLG. *krûpan* = *kreupan,* OE. *créopan* to creep. Cf. CROUCH *v.*] *intr.* To bow, to make obeisance.

c **1394** *P. Pl. Crede* 751 Kniȝtes crouken hem to & cruchen full lowe. *c* **1460** *Towneley Myst.* 163 For I [Joseph] can nawthere crowke ne knele [*sc.* to the doctors in the Temple: *Luke* ii. 46].

crouk, var. of CROOK *v.*², to croak.

†**crouke, crowke.** *Obs.* [OE. *crúce* fem. pot, little pitcher, 'urceolus', cognate with OS. *krûka* (MDu. *crûke,* Du. *kruik,* MHG. *krûche,* dial. Ger. *krauche*). The LG. word was prob. the source of F. *cruche,* and the ME. of Welsh *crwc,* which has no Celtic cognates. OTeut. **krûka-* is perh. in ablaut relation to the family of CROCK.] A pitcher, a jug.

a **700** *Epinal Gloss.* 989 *Trulla,* crucae [so *Erf.*; *Corpus* 2051 cruce]. *a* **800** *Corpus Gl.* 2165 *Urciolum,* waetercruce. *a* **1000** *Voc.* in Wr.-Wülcker 281/32 *Urciolum,* cruce. *c* **1386** CHAUCER *Reeve's T.* 238 Whan that dronken was al in the crouke [2 *MSS.* crowke].

croul, obs. f. CRAWL, CURL; var. CROWL *v. Obs.*

croumbe, croum(e, var. CROME, CRUMB.

croun(e, obs. form of CROWN *sb.* and *v.*

crounkil, obs. form of CRUNKLE.

croup, croupe (kruːp), *sb.*¹ Forms: 4- croupe, 7- croup; also 5 crowpe, kroupe, crupe, 5-6 crope, 6 crowp, croope, 7-9 croop, crup. [a. F. *croupe* (in 11-12th c. *crope, crupe*), Pr. *cropa*; of Teutonic origin: cf. CROP *sb.*]

1. The rump or hind-quarters of a beast, *esp.* of a horse or other beast of burden.

c **1300** *K. Alis.* 2447 Tyberye..hutte Salome with his spere, That of the sadel he gan him beore, Over the croupe to the grounde. *c* **1386** CHAUCER *Friar's T.* 261 This carter thakketh his hors upon the croupe. *c* **1450** *Merlin* 118 The kynge loth was so astonyed that he fley ouer his horse crowpe. *a* **1533** LD. BERNERS *Huon* I. 169 Huon lept vp on his crope [ed. **1601** backe]. **1577-87** HOLINSHED *Chron.* III. 896/2 Certeine prelats, whom..they set vpon asses and leane mules, and with their faces reuersed to the crowp of the beasts. **1676** *Lond. Gaz.* No. 1090/4 A Red Roan Gelding..having a small black List over the Withers, and down the Crup. **1774** GOLDSM. *Nat. Hist.* (1862) I. I. i. 250 The Spanish genette..the croup round and large. **1808** SCOTT *Marm.* v. xii, So light to the croupe the fair lady he swung. **1833** *Regul. Instr. Cavalry* I. 74 The crupper.. should admit the breadth of the hand between it and the croup of the horse. **1872** LEVER *Ld. Kilgobbin* xix. (1875) 118 A small bog-boy [was] mounted on the croop behind.

†**b.** ***in croup*** [F. *en croupe*]: upon the croup (of a horse). *Obs.*

1580 HOLLYBAND *Treas. Fr. Tong, Porter en crope,* to haue one behynd him on horse-backe, to beare in croupe. *a* **1676** SIR E. WALKER *Hist. Disc.* (1705) 95 Our Horse taking up the Musquetiers in Croup. [**1820** SCOTT *Monast.* xxix, Preparing to resume her seat *en croupe.*]

c. *humorously.* The rump, posteriors.

c **1475** *Hunt. Hare* 208 Thus sone won hit hym [a man] on the crope. **1664** COTTON *Scarron.* (1692) 37 (D.) Till I had almost gauled my crup. **1678** BUTLER *Hud.* III. i. 1560 But found..his Croop, Unserviceable with Kicks and Blows Receiv'd from hardned-hearted Foes.

2. (*crup*). The hinder end of a saddle. *rare.*

1869 G. BERKELEY *Tales Life & Death* II. 244 Which he tied in a little leather sort of valise, made for the purpose, at the crup of his saddle.

3. *attrib.*

1686 *Lond. Gaz.* No. 2155/4 A croop Saddle and Bridle.

croup (kruːp), *sb.*² [f. CROUP *v.*¹, *lit.* a hoarse croaking.]

1. An inflammatory disease of the larynx and trachea of children, marked by a peculiar sharp ringing cough, and frequently proving fatal in a short time.

Croup was the popular name in the south-east of Scotland, and was introduced into medical use by Prof. Francis Home of Edinburgh in 1765.

1765 F. HOME (*title*), An Inquiry into the nature, cause, and cure of the Croup. **1781** MRS. DELANY *Corr.* 20 June. **1796** *Hull Advertiser* 19 Mar. 2/4 Seven children have lately fallen victims at Highgate to a disorder called the croup. **1866** A. FLINT *Princ. Med.* (1880) 286 The term croup is applied to laryngitis with fibrinous exudation, and it has also been applied to simple laryngitis and to a non-inflammatory affection, namely, spasm of the glottis, occurring in children.

2. The local name of the Northumbrian 'burr' or utterance of *r grasseyé,* with the peculiar modification of pronunciation which it causes.

Mod. (Said by one Northumbrian of another at a Scotch fair) 'That man is from the English side, he has the croup.' (Scotch Shepherd) 'Hoot na! it's only the burr'.

3. *Comb.,* as ***croup-like*** adj.; **croup-kettle** = *bronchitis kettle.*

1799 T. BEDDOES *Contrib. Phys. & Med. Knowl.* 443 Breathing..with such difficulty and croup-like noise, etc. *a* **1884** KNIGHT *Dict. Mech.* Suppl., *Croup kettle,* a small kettle and alcohol lamp for quickly raising a steam for inhalation in cases of croup. **1889** 'MARK TWAIN' *Yankee* xl. 516, I rousted out the croup-kettle myself; for I don't sit down and wait for doctors. **1961** *Brit. Med. Dict.* 790/2 *Bronchitis kettle*..; called also *croup kettle.*

croup, *sb.*³ Short for CROUPIER.

1794 *Sporting Mag.* IV. 43 The croup shuffles another pack in the mean time.

croup (kruːp), *v.*¹ *Obs.* exc. *dial.* Also 6-7 crowp, 7-9 croop(e, 9 *dial.* crowp. [This and the synonymous CROAPE are app. of imitative origin, having associations with *crow, croak,* and with an earlier northern verb *roup, rope,* to call, shout, cry hoarsely, f. ON. *hrópja.*]

1. *intr.* To cry hoarsely; to croak as a raven, frog, crane, etc.

1513 DOUGLAS *Æneis* VII. Prol. 119 Palamedes byrdis crouping in the sky. **1584** T. HUDSON *Judith* in *Sylvester's Du Bartas* (1621) 711 And crowping frogs like fishes there doth swarme. **1616** SURFL. & MARKH. *Country Farme* 25 If the little Frogs croope more than ordinarie. **1654** TRAPP *Comm. Ps.* xiv. 11 As the Raven is said to have crouped from the Capitol when Augustus came to the Empire. **1804** TARRAS *Poems* 44 (Jam.) Ye croopin corbies. **1847-78** HALLIWELL, *Croup,* to croak. *North.* **1855** ROBINSON *Whitby Gloss., To crowp,* to grunt or grumble..'A crowping', that..subdued croaking heard in the bowels from flatulence.

2. 'To speak hoarsely, as one does under the effects of cold' (Jamieson).

3. To make the characteristic hoarse ringing cough of the disease called croup.

1801 *Med. Jrnl.* V. 518 An infant..was heard several times to croup; and its breathing became difficult.

4. To pronounce a rough uvular *r* (*r grasseyé*); to have the Northumberland 'burr'. (The local expression for this; pron. (krup).)

Mod. He croups like a Newcastle man.

†**croup,** *v.*² *Obs.* [from CROUPIER: cf. CROUP *sb.*³] *trans.* To second or back up (a gamester).

1728 VANBR. & CIBBER *Prov. Husb.* II. i, I have a game in my hand, in which, if you'll croup me, that is, help me to play it, you shall go five hundred to nothing.

croup, -e, obs. pa. t. of CREEP.

croupade (kruːˈpeɪd). [a. F. *croupade,* f. *croupe* CROUP *sb.*¹, under the influence of It. *groppata.*] (See quot. 1884.)

1849 W. S. MAYO *Kaloolah* (1850) 171 Forcing him [a horse] to perform a number of lofty croupades. **1884** E. L. ANDERSON *Mod. Horsemanship* II. xvii. 152 The Croupade is a high curvet, in which the hind-legs are brought up under the belly of the horse.

croupal (ˈkruːpəl), *a. Path.* [f. CROUP *sb.*² + -AL¹. Also in mod.F.] Relating to, or of the nature of croup; = CROUPOUS.

1852-9 TODD *Cycl. Anat.* IV. 1258/1 Croupal exudations are sometimes found in the urethra. **1866** A. FLINT *Princ. Med.* (1880) 305 The cough presents..the shrill, ringing, croupal character.

croupe (kruːp). [a. F. *croupe*: see CROUP *sb.*¹]

1. = CROUP *sb.*¹ q.v.

‖**2.** = CROUPADE.

1812 BYRON *Ch. Har.* I. lxxvi, With well-timed croupe the nimble coursers veer. *Note,* The croupe is a particular leap taught in the manège.

‖**3.** The rounded top of a mountain. [So in Fr.]

1808 J. BARLOW *Columb.* I. 268 Hills form on hills and croupe o'er croupe extends.

crouper(e, obs. form of CRUPPER.

croupier (ˈkruːpɪə(r), kruːˈpɪə(r)). Also 8 crouper, croupee, crowpee. [a. Fr. *croupier,* orig. one who rides behind on the croup; hence, one who goes halves with a player at cards or dice and stands behind him to assist him, also he who stands behind the banker to assist at the game of basset, and now at a gaming table as in sense 2.]

†**1.** A second standing behind a gamester to back him up and help him. *Obs.*

1707 WYCHERLEY *Let.* 11 Nov. in *Pope's Letters,* Since I have such a Croupier or Second to stand by me as Mr. Pope.

2. He who rakes in the money at a gaming-table.

1731 *Daily Jrnl.* 9 Jan. (in D'Israeli *Cur. Lit., Gaming*), Two Crowpees, who watch the cards, and gather the money for the bank. **1855** THACKERAY *Newcomes* I. 301 The gambling tables and the cadaverous croupiers and chinking gold. **1884** MAY CROMMELIN *Brown-Eyes* xii. 114 All gone! swept from the green cloth by the coupier's inexorable rake.

3. One who sits as assistant chairman at the lower end of the table at a public dinner.

1785 CRAIG in *Lounger* No. 26 §10 He is no longer *Croupier* at Lord E.'s, his place there being filled up by Tom Toastwell. **1827** T. HAMILTON *C. Thornton* (1845) 76 The honours of the table were performed by my uncle, by whose orders I acted as croupier. *Ibid.* 77 The important office of vice-president or croupier. **1849** THACKERAY *Pendennis* xvi, Hicks officiated as croupier on the occasion.

'croupiness. [f. CROUPY + -NESS.] Croupy condition; tendency to croup.

crouping: see CROUP *v.*¹

†**'croupon.** *Obs.* or *dial.* Forms: 5 cropoun, -on, -owne, -yn, crupoun, cruppon, crovpon, crowpon, -yn, 8 croppin, curpon, -en, -in. [a. OF. *croupon,* augm. or dim. of *croupe,* in OF. *crupe, crope* rump, rear-part: see CROUP I. The mod.Sc. form is *curpon* by metathesis of *r.*] The croup or rump of a horse or other animal; the buttocks or posteriors of the human body; *transf.* the hinder part of a thing; the crupper of the harness.

[*a* **1300** *Gloss. Neckham* in Wright *Voc.* 99 *Clunes,* crupuns.] *c* **1400** *Ywaine & Gaw.* 2468 Fro his [the giant's] hals to his cropoun. *c* **1400** MAUNDEV. (Roxb.) xxxi. 142 A faire beste..his crupoun and his taile er lyke to a hert. *c* **1440** *Promp. Parv.* 105/1 Cropon of a beste, *clunis.* **1483** *Cath. Angl.* 85 A Crovpon [*v.r.* Cruppon], *clunis.* **1722** W. HAMILTON *Wallace* 9 (Jam.) I'd gar their curpons crack. **1725** *New Cant. Dict., Croppin,* the Tail of any Thing; as, The Croppin of the Rotan [= Cart]. **1785** BURNS *Halloween* xviii, The graip he for a harrow taks, And haurls at his curpin.

croupous (ˈkruːpəs), *a. Path.* [f. CROUP *sb.*]

1. Of the nature of, or characteristic of, croup.

1853 PAGET *Lect. Surg. Pathol.* I. 335 Considering croupous exudations to be peculiarly fibrinous. **1888** *Brit. Med. Jrnl.* 10 Mar., Croupous pneumonia.

2. Affected with croup.

1881 T. F. KEANE *Six Months in Meccah* v. 106 [Like] the roars of an enraged croupous lion.

croupy (ˈkruːpɪ), *a.* [f. as prec. + -Y.] = prec.

1834 J. FORBES *Laennec's Dis. Chest* (ed. 4) 113 The croupy or false membrane. **1839-47** TODD *Cycl. Anat.* III. 125/2 On the opening into the windpipe being perfected the croupy breathing disappeared.

crouse (kruːs), *a.* (and *adv.*) *Sc.* and *north. dial.* Forms: 3-4 crus, (3 cruse), 4-6 crous, 4- crouse, (4-5 crows(s, 5 crouss(e, 6-9 crowse, 9 croose). [ME. northern *crūs, crous,* agreeing in form with MHG., MLG., LG. *krûs* crisp, MDu. *kruys* (Kilian) crisp, curly, mod.G. *kraus* crisp, curled, sullen, crabbed, fractious, mod.Du. *kroes* (from LG.) crisp, cross, out of humour, EFris. *krûs* curly, entangled, luxurious, opulent, wanton, jolly. Not found in the earlier stages of any of the langs.; in English only northern, and almost exclusively Sc. (whence the pronunciation with *u*), though borrowed by Drayton and some of his contemporaries, and then rimed with Eng. words in *ou*; also found in Yorkshire dial. with *aa* from *ou.* As only the figurative senses are here found, it appears to be one of the LG. or Frisian words which appeared in the northern dialect early in the ME. period.]

A. *adj.* †**1.** Angry, irate, cross, crabbed. *Obs.*

a **1300** *Cursor M.* 14740 (Cott.) Gains þam he was ful kene and crus, Dos yow, he said, vte of mi hus. *Ibid.* 21882 (Edinb.) To be fuse, ogain þat come þat es sa cruse. *Ibid.* 27740 (Cott.) It [wrath] es a cruel thing and crus.

†**2.** Bold, audacious, daring, hardy, forward, full of defiant confidence, 'cocky'. *Obs.* In later use passing insensibly into 3, as when the crowing cock becomes the type.

a **1300** *Cursor M.* 3044 (Cott.) O him sal gret men cum and crus. *c* **1340** *Ibid.* 23740 (Trin.) Oure flesshe is euer to synne crous. **1535** STEWART *Cron. Scot.* II. 592 None durst be so hardie and so crous To speik of him. **1598** DRAYTON *Heroic. Ep.* 142 Duke Humphry's old allies..Attending their revenge, grow wond'rous crouse [*rime* house]. *c* **1620** A. HUME *Brit. Tongue* (1865) 28 He is the noat of the male; as ..he is a crouse cock; he is a fat wether. **1724** RAMSAY *Tea-t. Misc.* (1733) I. 8 The wooer he step'd up the house And wow but he was wond'rous crouse. **1808** J. MAYNE *Siller Gun* III. 131 Crouse as a cock in his ain cavie. **1862** HISLOP *Prov. Scot.* 16 A man's aye crouse in his ain cause. **1883** *Huddersf. Gloss.*, *Crouse* [pron. *craas*], bold, brave, lively.

3. In somewhat high or lively spirits; vivacious; pert, brisk, lively, jolly.

? *a* **1400** *Chester Pl.* (Shaks. Soc.) I. 51 Heare are beastes in this howse, Heare cattes make yt crousse. **1593** DRAYTON *Eclogues* vii. 73 The little Fly, Who is so Crowse and Gamesome with the flame. **1641** BROME *Jov. Crew* I. Wks. 1873 III. 366 Most crowse, most capringly. **1674** RAY *N.C. Words* 12 *Crowse*, brisk, budge, lively, jolly. **1792** BURNS *Duncan Gray* v, Now they're crouse and cantie baith. **1855** ROBINSON *Whitby Gloss.*, *Crowse*, brisk. 'As crowse as a lop.' **1858** M. PORTEOUS *Souter Johnny* 8 My faith! she was a wife right crouse.

B. as *adv.* Boldly, confidently, briskly, vivaciously: *esp.* in phr. ***to crack*** or ***craw crouse*** (Sc.), to talk boldly or over-confidently.

a **1455** HOLLAND *Howlat* 221 Cryand full crowss. **1681** COLVIL *Whigs Supplic.* (1751) 145 And after thou hast crackt so crouse, Thy mountains do bring forth a mouse. **1786** BURNS *Twa Dogs* 135 The cantie auld folks crackin crouse. *a* **1810** TANNAHILL *Poems* (1846) 11 My trouth but ye craw crouse. **1824** MISS FERRIER *Inher.* lxvi, Some people will maybe not crack quite so crouse by-and-by.

crouse, var. of CROOSE *v.*

'crousely, *adv.* *Sc.* [f. prec. + -LY².] Boldly, confidently, briskly, pertly.

1787 BURNS *Tam Samson's Elegy* vii, Ye cootie moorcocks, crousely craw. **1816** SCOTT *Antiq.* xxxix, Things are ill aff when the like o' them can speak crousely about ony gentleman's affairs.

crousshe, crouste, obs. ff. CRUSH, CRUST.

croustade (krus'tad). [Fr., f. *crouste*, older form of *croûte* CRUST *sb.*] A crisp piece of bread, fried or baked and scooped out to form a mould, to receive a filling of meat or other savoury; also, a hollowed shape of rice or pastry for the same purpose; (see also quot. 1845).

1845 BREGION & MILLER *Pract. Cook* 41 *Croustades*, fried crusts of bread. **1846** SOYER *Gastron. Regen.* 160 Prepare the croustades as above, and make a good purée of fowl. **1865** 'OUIDA' *Strathmore* xi, Congregate at luncheon, and take *croustades* and conversation together! **1892** T. F. GARRETT *Encycl. Pract. Cookery* I. VII. 481/1 The Croustade may be made of bread or paste of any kind. *Ibid.*, Line a dozen small Croustade-moulds with the rolled-out paste. **1960** *Farmer & Stockbreeder* (Suppl.) 16 Feb. 6/2 Croustade of spinach.

crout, *sb.*: see SOUR-CROUT.

crout (kru:t, kraʊt), *v.* *Sc.* Also **croot**. [app. onomatopœic: the initial part being as in *crow*, *croak*, *creak*, and kindred verbs, and the latter part imitative or suggestive of abrupt or grunting sound: cf. also *croud*, CROOD *v.*] *intr.* To make abrupt croaking or murmuring noises; to coo as a dove. Rarely *trans.*

1549 *Compl. Scot.* vi. 60 The dou croutit hyr sad sang. **1613** BP. FORBES *Comm. Rev.* (1614) 158 (Jam.) Men led with the spirit of Satan..sent abroad, as crouting frogges. *a* **1693** URQUHART *Rabelais* III. xiii. 107 The..crouting of Cormorants. **1806** R. JAMIESON *Pop. Ball.* I. 298 (Jam.) And O, as he rattled and roar'd, And graen'd, and mutter'd, and crouted. **1808** JAMIESON s.v., The belly is said to *croot*, when there is a noise in the intestines.

croutch, obs. f. CROUCH, CRUTCH.

‖**croûte** (kru:t). [Fr., = CRUST *sb.*] A crust of bread, toasted or fried, served as a foundation for certain dishes; also = CROÛTON.

[**1841** THACKERAY in *Fraser's Mag.* June 714/1 What do you think was our dinner for six persons?.. Removes. Plompouding; croute de macaroni.] **1906** MRS. BEETON *Bk. Househ. Managem.* lxii. 1657 Croûtes, blocks or shapes of fried bread, used as a basis for dressing salmis, whole birds, etc. **1907** G. A. ESCOFFIER *Mod. Cookery* 782 Set these croûtes in a crown on a round dish, and garnish their midst with a rocky pyramid of plombière ice. **1951** *Good Housek. Home Encycl.* 394/2 It [*sc.* caviare] may also be..served spread on croûtes of fried bread.

crouth(e, var. of CROWD *sb.*¹, fiddle.

‖**croûton** ('kru:tõ). Also **crouton**. [Fr., f. *croûte* CRUST *sb.*] A small piece of toasted or fried bread used in soups and to garnish stewed dishes and minces. Also, any small piece used for garnishing.

1806 J. SIMPSON *Compl. Syst. Cookery* 31 Put a little anchovy essence, squeeze a lemon,..and garnish with croutons. **1846** SOYER *Gastron. Regen.* 60 Put some croûtons in the tureen, with twenty very small *quenelles de volaille*. **1892** T. F. GARRETT *Encycl. Pract. Cookery* I. VII. 481/2 Croûtons of aspic jelly.. are made in almost any shape. *Ibid.*, Croûtons for garnishing or soup. **1907** G. A. ESCOFFIER *Mod. Cookery* 535 Border the dish with neatly-cut *croûtons* of pale jelly. **1921** *Contemp. Rev.* Sept. 374 A purée or cream soup with crackers or croûtons. **1967** C. O. SKINNER *Madame Sarah* xii. 263 She'd taste a morsel or spoonful of every dish, every sauce, every crouton served.

crove, var. of CRUVE, hovel.

crow (krəʊ), *sb.*¹ Forms: 1 crawe, 3-7 crowe, 4- crow, (6 krowe, croo(e, 6-7 croe); *north.* 3-6 crawe, 5- craw. [OE. *cráwe* f., corresp. to OS. *krâia*, MLG. *krâge*, *krâe*, *krâ*, LG. *kraie*, *kreie*, MDu. *kraeye*, Du. *kraai*, OHG. *chrâwa*, *chrâja*, *chrâ*, *crâwa*, *crâ*, MHG. *kræe*, *krâwe*, *krâ*, Ger. *krähe*; a WG. deriv. of the vb. *crâwan*, *crâian* to CROW, q.v.]

1. a. A bird of the genus *Corvus*; in England commonly applied to the Carrion Crow (*Corvus Corone*), 'a large black bird that feeds upon the carcasses of beasts' (Johnson); in the north of England, Scotland, and Ireland to the Rook, *C. frugilegus*; in U.S. to a closely allied gregarious species, *C. americanus*.

a **700** *Epinal Gloss.* 241 *Cornacula*, crauuae. *a* **800** *Erfurt Gl.* 308 *Cornix*, crauua. *a* **800** *Corpus Gl.* 401 *Carula*, crauue. *Ibid.* 538 *Cornix*, crawe. *c* **1000** SPELMAN *Psalms* (Trin. MS.) cxlvi. 10 (Bosw.) Se selþ nytenum mete heora, and briddum crawan cigendum hine. *a* **1250** *Owl & Night.* 1130 Pinnuc goldfinch rok ne crowe Ne dar þar never cumen. *c* **1290** *S. Eng. Leg.* I. 437/196 Blake foule..Ase it crowene and rokes weren. **1382** WYCLIF *Gen.* viii. 7 Noe..sente out a crow. **1486** *Bk. St. Albans* D ij a, A Roke or a Crow or a Reuyn. **1553** EDEN *Treat. Newe Ind.* (Arb.) 17 The Priestes take the meete that is left, and geue it to the crowes to eate. **1575** CHURCHYARD *Chippes* (1817) 108 They wysht at home they had bene keping crooes. **1605** SHAKS. *Macb.* III. ii. 51 Light thickens, and the Crow Makes Wing toth' Rookie Wood. **1766** PENNANT *Zool.* (1812) I. 284 Rooks are sociable birds, living in vast flocks: crows go only in pairs. **1817-18** COBBETT *Resid. U.S.* (1822) 210 They keep in flocks, like rooks (called crows in America). **1842** TENNYSON *Locksley Hall* 68 As the many-winter'd crow that leads the clanging rookery home. **1885** SWAINSON *Prov. Names Birds* 86 *Crow* is common to rook and carrion crow alike.

b. *fig.*

1592 GREENE *Groats-w. Wit* Addr., There is an upstart Crow, beautified with our feathers. *a* **1640** DAY *Peregr. Schol.* Wks. (1881) 57 The devill..sends his black Crowe, Anger, to plucke out his ey. **1649** G. DANIEL *Trinarch., Rich. II*, xxxvi, The Citty Crowes Assemble, and Resolve they would keep out..his ragged rout.

2. With qualifications, as **hooded, Kentish,** or **Royston crow**, *Corvus Cornix*; **red-legged crow**, *C. Graculus*; **fish crow** of America, *C. ossifragus* or *C. caurinus*; CARRION-CROW, etc.; also applied to birds outside the genus or family, as **mire crow, sea crow**, names for *Larus ridibundus*; **scare crow**, the Black Tern (*Hydrochelidon nigra*); **blue crow**, a crow-like jay of N. America, *Gymnocitta cyanocephala*; **piping crows**, the birds of the sub-family *Gymnorhininæ* or *Streperinæ*; and others.

1611 COTGR., *Corneille emmentelée*, the Winter-crow, whose backe and bellie are of a darke ash-colour: we call her a Royston Crow. **1766** PENNANT *Zool.* (1812) I. 286 In England hooded crows are birds of passage. **1844** W. H. MAXWELL *Sports & Adv. Scotl.* (1855) 326 The Laughing Gull..or Black Head..The inhabitants of Orkney call it the 'sea crow'; and in some places it is called the 'mire-crow'. **1875** W. MᶜILWRAITH *Guide Wigtownshire*, These cliffs are frequented by the Cornish chough or red-legged crow.

3. a. In phrases and proverbial sayings, as ***as black as a crow, the crow thinks its own bird fairest*** (or ***white***), etc. ***a white crow***: i.e. a *rara avis*. ***to eat*** (***boiled***) ***crow*** (U.S. colloq.): to be forced to do something extremely disagreeable and humiliating.

1297 R. GLOUC. (1724) 490 So suart so eni crowe amorwe is fot was. *c* **1386** CHAUCER *Knt's. T.* 1834 As blak he lay as any cole or crowe. **1513** DOUGLAS *Æneis* IX. Prol. 78 The blak craw thinkis hir awin byrdis quhite. **1536** LATIMER *2nd Serm. bef. Convoc.* Wks. I. 40 A proverb much used: 'An evil crow, an evil egg.' **1579** GOSSON *Sch. Abuse* (Arb.) 30 For any chaste liuer to haunt them was a black swan, and a white crowe. **1579** FULKE *Confut. Sanders* 675 He triumpheth like a crow in a gutter. **1621-51** BURTON *Anat. Mel.* III. i. II. ii. 421 Every Crow thinks her own bird fairest. **1684** BUNYAN *Pilgr.* II. 98 As fruitful a place, as any the Crow flies over. **1843** 'R. CARLTON' *New Purchase* II. 235 The *rara avis*—the white crow—a good President. [**1851** *San Francisco Picayune* 3 Dec. 1/6, I kin eat a crow, but I'll be darned if I hanker after it.] **1872** *Daily News* 31 July, Both [are]..in the curious slang of American politics, 'boiled crow' to their adherents. **1877** *N. & Q.* 5th Ser. VIII. 186/1 A newspaper editor, who is obliged..to advocate 'principles' different from those which he supported a short time before, is said to 'eat boiled crow'. **1884** 'MARK TWAIN' *Lett.* (1917) II. 443 Warner and Clark are eating their daily crow in the paper. **1885** *Mag. Amer. Hist.* XIII. 199 'To eat crow' means to recant, or to humiliate oneself. **1930** 'E. QUEEN' *French Powder Myst.* xxiv. 196, I should merely be making an ass of myself if I accused someone and then had to eat crow. **1970** *New Yorker* 17 Oct. 39/1, I was going to apologize, eat crow, offer to kiss and make up.

b. ***to have a crow to pluck*** or ***pull*** (rarely ***pick***) ***with any one***: to have something disagreeable or awkward to settle with him; to have a matter of dispute, or something requiring explanation, to clear up; to have some fault to find with him. Formerly also, ***to pluck*** or ***pull a crow with one*** or ***together***.

c **1460** *Towneley Myst.* xviii. 311 Na, na, abide, we haue a craw to pull. **1509** BARCLAY *Shyp of Folys* (1570) 91 A wrathfull woman..He that her weddeth hath a crowe to pull. **1590** SHAKS. *Com. Err.* III. i. 83 If a crow help vs in, sirra, we'll plucke a crow together. **1662** PEPYS *Diary* 18 Nov., He and I very kind, but I every day expect to pull a crow with him about our lodgings. **1668** R. L'ESTRANGE *Vis. Quev.* (1708) 159 We have a Crow to pluck with these Fellows, before we part. **1849** *Tait's Mag.* XVI. 385/1 If there be 'a crow to pluck' between us and any contemporary, we shall make a clean breast of it at once.

c. ***as the crow flies***, etc.: in a direct line, without any of the *détours* caused by following the road.

1800 SOUTHEY *Lett.* (1856) I. 110 About fifteen miles, the crow's road. **1810** *Sporting Mag.* XXXV. 152 The distance ..is upwards of twenty-five miles as the crow flies. **1838** DICKENS *O. Twist* xxv, We cut over the fields..straight as the crow flies. **1873** F. HALL in *Scribner's Monthly* VI. 468/2 It was full eight miles, measured by the crow, to the spot.

d. Colloq. phr. ***stone*** (or ***stiffen***) ***the crows***: an exclamation of surprise or disgust. Esp. *Austral.*

1930 L. W. LOWER *Here's Luck* xxvii. 242 'Stone the crows!' stormed Stanley. **1934** B. PENTON *Landtakers* (1935) II. iii. 120 'Gawd stiffen the crows,' Bill commented bitterly. **1938** J. MOSES *Nine Miles from Gundagai* 82 Stone the crows, what's up, mate? Has Australia got the blues? **1948** C. DAY LEWIS *Otterbury Incident* iv. 46 Cor stone the crows, 'ave a 'eart, young gents. **1953** J. C. TRENCH *Docken Dead* iii. 46 Cor stone the crows, he thought, this could go on till Christmas.

4. *Astron.* To southern constellation *Corvus*, the Raven.

1658 in PHILLIPS. **1868** LOCKYER *Heavens* (ed. 3) 326 Towards the horizon, are distinguished the Balance, the Crow, and the Cup.

5. a. A bar of iron usually with one end slightly bent and sharpened to a beak, used as a lever or prise; a CROW-BAR.

a **1400** *St. Erkenwolde* 71 in Horstm. *Alteng. Leg.* Ser. II. 267 Wyȝt werke-men..Putten prises þer-to..Kaghtene by þe corners wᵗ crowes of yrne. **1458** in Turner *Dom. Archit.* III. 42 Than crafti men for the querry made crowes of yre. **1555** EDEN *Decades* 333 Longe crowes of iren to lyfte great burdens. **1590** SHAKS. *Com. Err.* III. i. 80 Well, Ile breake in: go borrow me a crow. **1676** *Phil. Trans.* XI. 755 The Mine-men do often strike such forcible strokes with a great Iron-crow. **1793** SMEATON *Edystone Lighth.* §206 To detach the stone with an iron Crow. *c* **1850** *Rudim. Navig.* (Weale) 113 Crows are of various sorts; some are opened at the end, with a claw for drawing nails. **1888** RIDER HAGGARD *Col. Quaritch* xl, Driving the sharp point of the heavy crow into the rubble work.

b. Used as an agricultural tool.

1573 TUSSER *Husb.* (1878) 98 Get crowe made of iron, deepe hole for to make. **1574** R. SCOT *Hop Gard.* (1578) 19 Set vp your Poales preparing theyr waye wyth a Crowe of Iron. **1626** A. SPEED *Adam out of E.* xv. (1659) 111 About the body of the Trees make many holes with a crow of Iron. **1731-7** MILLER *Gard. Dict.* s.v. *Vitis*, Having an iron Crow ..a little pointed at the End, they therewith make an Hole directly down.

†**6.** A grappling hook, a grapnel. *Obs.* [Cf. CORVY, F. *corbeau*.]

1553 BRENDE *Q. Curtius* 54 (R.) Certeine instrumentes wherewyth they myght pull downe the workes yᵗ their enemyes made, called Harpagons, and also crowes of iron called Corvi. **1614** SYLVESTER *Bethulia's Rescue* 110 Having in vain summon'd the Town; he..Brings here his Fly-Bridge, there his batt'ring Crow. **1632** J. HAYWARD tr. *Biondi's Eromena* 150 Iron Wolves and Crows to graspe the Ram withall. **1727-51** CHAMBERS *Cycl.*, *Crow*, in the sea-language, a machine with an iron hook, for fastening hold, and grappling with the enemies vessel. **1873** BURTON *Hist. Scot.* V. liii. 34 Their siege-apparatus consisted of ladders with 'craws' or clamps of iron to catch the angles of the trap-rock.

†**7.** An ancient kind of door-knocker. *Obs.* [med.L. *cornix*, Erasmus *Colloq.*, *Puerpera*.]

1579 *Churchw. Acc. Stanford* in *Antiquary* Apr. (1888) 171 For..mending ye perchell and the Crowe. *a* **1632** E. FAIRFAX *Eclogue* iv. (in E. Cooper *Muses Libr.*), Now clad in white I see my porter-crow. **1637** N. WHITING *Albino & Bell.* 22 Who..Knockt at the wicket with the iron crow To whose small neck white phillets here were tyde Which in more ancient dayes did child-bed show. **1846** R. CHAMBERS *Tradit. Edin.* 200 Hardly one specimen of the pin, crow, or ringle now survives in the Old Town.

8. a. *Thieves' slang.* One who keeps watch while another steals.

1851 MAYHEW *Lond. Labour* (1861) iv. 286 (Farmer) If anyone should be near, the 'crow' gives a signal, and they decamp. **1862** *Cornh. Mag.* VI. 648 (Farmer) Occasionally they [women] assist at a burglary—remaining outside and keeping watch; they are then called *crows*.

b. *N.Z., colloq.* A person who pitches sheaves to the stacker.

1888 J. BRADSHAW *N.Z. of To-day* ix. 171 When harvest came..he ought to have taken his place as 'crow' upon the stack. **1913** A. I. CARR *Country Work & Life in N.Z.* v. 11 A 'crow'..whose work consists of passing the fork-fulls thrown up by the carter to the stacker. **1956** J. DARE *Rouseabout Jane* xxiv. 185 When it came to stacking the corn, my job was to be 'crow'.

c. *slang.* A derogatory name for a girl or woman, esp. one who is old or ugly; freq. in phr. ***old crow***.

1925 'H. H. RICHARDSON' *Way Home* (1930) vi. 477 It makes me feel a proper old crow. **1938** RUNYON *Take it Easy* 27 She is by no means a crow. In fact, she is rather nice-looking. **1957** R. C. SHERRIFF *Telescope* II. i. 56 *Mayfield.* There's an old lady named Miss Fortescue... *Ben* (*laughing*). Coo!—I know *that* old crow.

†**9.** *Alch.* A colour of ore, or of substances in a certain state. *Obs.*

1610 B. JONSON *Alch.* II. ii, These bleard-eyes Haue wak'd, to reade your generall colours, Sir, Of the pale citron, the greene lyon, the crow. *Ibid.* II. iii, What colour saies it? *Fac.* The ground black, Sir? *Mam.* That's your crowes-head?

10. *Mining.* Used *attrib.* to denote a poor or impure bed of coal, limestone, etc.; *e.g.* in ***crow bed, chert, coal, lime(stone.*** (Cf. *crow-gold* in 11.) *north.* and *Sc.*

1789 J. WILLIAMS *Min. Kingd.* (1810) I. 62 What is meant by the crawcoal is the crop-coal.. which is always supposed to be a thin one. **1836** J. PHILLIPS *Illustr. Geol. Yorksh.* II. 66 Thus we have Crow chert, Crow limestone, Crow lime. **1852** *Jrnl. R. Agric. Soc.* XIII. I. 208 Small beds of the kind called crow coal (only useful for burning lime).

11. *Comb.*, as ***crow-scaring; crow-like*** adj. and adv.; **crow-bait** *colloq.* (orig. *U.S.*) = *crows'-meat*; *spec.* an old or worn-out horse; †**crow-bird**, a young crow; **crow-blackbird** (*U.S.*), a name for the Purple Grackle (*Quiscalus purpureus*), and allied species; **crow-boy**, a boy employed to scare crows away; **crow-coal** (see 10 above); **crow-corn**, a name for the North American plant *Aletris farinosa*; †**crow-cup** = CROW-STONE; **crow-eater** (*Australian colloq.*), 'a lazy fellow who will live on anything rather than work' (Lentzner); also, a South Australian; **crow-fig**, the berry of the nux vomica tree; **crow-flight, -fly**, a direct course, a straight line (cf. sense 3 c); also quasi-*adv.*; **crow-gold** (see quot.); **crow-herd**, a person employed to guard corn-fields from rooks; **crow-hole**, a hole made with an iron crow; **crow-iron**, a crow-bar; †**crow-keeper** = *crow-herd*; also a scare-crow; **crow-line**, the straight line of a crow's flight; **crows'-meat**, food for crows, carrion; **crow-minder** = *crow-herd*; **crow-needle**, the Umbelliferous plant *Scandix Pecten*; **crow-net**, a net for catching crows and other birds; **crowpeck(s**, †**-pickes** (see quots.); **crow-pheasant**, a large bird of India and China, *Centropus sinensis*; **crow-pick** *v. trans.*, to inspect (coal) and free it from stones and rubbish; hence ***crow-picker***; **crow-purse**, a local name for the empty egg-case of the skate (also Mermaid's-purse); **crow-sheaf** (*Cornwall*), 'the top sheaf on the end of a mow'; **crow-shrike**, a bird of the sub-family *Gymnorhininæ* or Piping Crows; †**crow-spike**, a crow-bar; **crow-starving**, the keeping of rooks from cornfields; **crow-tree**, a tree in a rookery. See also CROW-BAR to CROW-TREAD.

1857 *Spirit of Times* 14 Feb. 382/1 He had a ole ball-face, bob-tail rip, jest' 'bout fit for *crow-bait. **1860** *Marysville* (Calif.) *Appeal* 25 Mar. 2/1 For many moments did the teamster 'cuss' and belabor his crow-baits. **1884** *Harper's Mag.* Oct. 738/2 'Drivin' a black hoss—a reg'lar crowbate.' *a* **1910** 'O. HENRY' *Trimmed Lamp* 73, I think I like your horses best. I haven't seen a crowbait since I've been in town. **1920** J. M. HUNTER *Trail Drivers of Texas* 98 At this I..rounded up my 'crow bait' and pulled out for home. **1957** A. MACNAB *Bulls of Iberia* xiii. 141 He rode out to do the *réjon* act on an ancient crowbait borrowed from the picadors' stable. *a* **1300** *E.E. Psalter* cxlvi. 9 (Mätz.) Mete ..to *crawe briddes [L. *pullis corvorum*] him kalland. **1778** J. CARVER *Travels* 473 The *crow blackbird..is quite black. **1870** LOWELL *Study Wind.* (1886) 13 Twice have the crow-blackbirds attempted a settlement in my vines. **1868** *Lond. Rev.* 28 Nov. 591/2 She warns off comely women from the premises as her *crow-boy does birds from the newly-sown field. **1899** *Daily News* 13 Sept. 7/5 'The land of the *crow-eater' was at no time a convict settlement. **1902** J. H. M. ABBOTT *Tommy Cornstalk* 2 It may have been that, to the early South Australians, means of subsistence came not easily. At any rate they are called 'Crow-eaters'. **1934** Crow-eater [see BANANALAND]. **1967** *Courier-Mail* (Brisbane) 25 July 2 The 'Crow-Eaters' have bustled ahead and watched industrialisation transform their once sleepy-hollow State. **1778** *Crow fig [see NUX VOMICA]. **1830** *Oxford Jrnl.* 30 Oct. 3 He struck her; which exasperated the poor woman so much as to induce her to poison herself with crow-fig. **1895** BLOXAM *Chem.* (ed. 8) 760 Nux-vomica, or crow-fig, contains about 1 per cent of strychnine. **1875** G. M. HOPKINS *Let.* 20 Feb. (1935) 30 A long *crow-flight is between us. **1885** *Science* 7 Aug. 108/2 We clambered over the hills and spurs in the usual crow-flight of the Karens. **1964** *Economist* 17 Oct. 258/1 The road..runs crow-flight straight. **1846** *Wesleyan Methodist Mag.* Jan. 53/1 It lies.. east..at a direct distance, *crow-fly, of about eighty miles. **1929** T. E. LAWRENCE *Home Lett.* (1954) 376 To get to Plymouth (only 300 yards crow-fly) is four and a half miles of bad road! **1878** F. S. WILLIAMS *Midl. Railw.* 370 A bed of chalk, almost like clay, containing many pyrites, locally [at Charlton] termed *crow-gold. **1805** FORSYTH *Beauties Scotl.* II. 86 Many farmers are under the necessity of keeping *crowherds. **1817** *Blackw. Mag.* I. 637/2 One of those blocks is so large..that four men with two *crow-irons could not turn it out. **1562** J. HEYWOOD *Prov. & Epigr.* (1867) 211 Thers no *crowe keeper but thou. **1592** SHAKS. *Rom. & Jul.* I. iv. 6 Skaring the Ladies like a Crow-keeper. *c* **1626** *Dick of Devon* II. iv. in Bullen *Old Pl.* II. 38 Sure these can be no Crowkeepers nor birdscarers from the fruite! **1616-61** HOLYDAY *Persius* (1673) 323 Hoarsly *crow-like caw'st out some idle thing. **1681** OTWAY *Soldier's Fort.* III. i, He shall be *Crows Meats by to-morrow Night. **1837** HT. MARTINEAU *Soc. Amer.* III. 330 A little *crow-minder, hoarse from his late occupation, came in. **1733** W. ELLIS *Chiltern & Vale Farming* xxxvii. 301 *Crow-Needle, bears a white Flower, about half the height of the Corn. **1881** H. & C. R. SMITH *Isle of Wight Words* 46 Crow-needles, *Scandix Pecten.* **1620** J. WILKINSON *Courts Leet* 124 In every parish and tything..a *crow-net provided to kill and destroy crowes, rookes, and choughes. **1870** *Ibis* VI. 234 Among the bamboo-copses and gardens around Kiungchowfoo, and all other towns in Hainan, the *Crow-Pheasant was abundant. **1878** P. ROBINSON *In my Indian Garden* 7 The crow pheasant stalks past with his chestnut wings drooping by his side. **1883** 'EHA' *Tribes on my Frontier* 155 That ungainly object the coucal, crow-pheasant, jungle-crow, or whatever else you like to call the miscellaneous thing. **1964** A. L. THOMSON *New Dict. Birds* 171/2 C[*entropus*] *sinensis*, commonly known in India as the Crow-pheasant, is a large black bird with chestnut wings. **1609** C. BUTLER *Fem. Mon.* vi. (1623) O iij, Barbery, *Crowpickes, Charlocke, Rosemary. **1794** J. DAVIS *Agric. Wilts* (1813) Gloss., Crowpeck, Shepherd's purse. **1886** BRITTEN & HOLL. *Plant-n.*, Crowpecks, *Scandix Pecten.* Hants. **1920** *Glasgow Herald* 13 May 6 To *crow-pick each hutch as it passes the steelyard. **1921** *Dict. Occup. Terms* (1927) §047 **Crow picker*; inspects shale in mine before it is loaded, to see that only clean shale is loaded. **1922** *Glasgow Herald* 12 July 10 Frae crawpickers that craw us O' hauf oor hardwon rakes; ..Deliver us, O Lord! **1693** WALLACE *Orkney* 18 On the shore is to be found..also that which they call the *Crow-Purse: which is a pretty work of Nature. **1897** *Daily News* 15 Jan. 6/1 His first employment was *crow-scaring. **1933** W. DE LA MARE *Lord Fish* 40 He had taken up crow-scaring at seven. **1692** LUTTRELL *Brief Rel.* (1857) II. 456 Great quantities of warlike preparations, as..pickaxes, shovells, *crow spikes, etc. **1848** C. BRONTE *J. Eyre* xv. (D.), I like Thornfield, its antiquity, its retirement, its old *crow-trees and thorn-trees.

crow (krəʊ), *sb.*[2] Also *Sc.* **craw.** [f. CROW *v.*[1]] Crowing (of a cock). Cf. COCK-CROW.

c **1290** *S. Eng. Leg.* I. 137/1090 Bi-fore þe cockes crowe. *c* **1386** CHAUCER *Miller's T.* 489, I shal at cokkes crow Ful pryuely knokken at his wyndowe. **1663** COWLEY *Pindar. Odes, Brutus* iv, One would have thought 't had heard the Morning Crow. **1851** LONGF. *Gold. Leg., Refectory*, The cheery crow Of cocks in the yard below.

b. *transf.* and *fig.*

1859 W. C. BENNET *Baby May*, Crows and laughs and tearful eyes. **1860** GEN. P. THOMPSON *Audi Alt.* III. cxxvii. 85 The folly which got up gasconading crows for war.

crow (krəʊ), *sb.*[3] [Cf. MHG. *kros, krös, kalbskrös, schweinskrös*, etc. mesentery, Du. *kroos, kroost* 'intestina, venter cum intestinis' (Kilian), mod.Du. *kroos* giblets; but also LG. *krage* 'gekröse', mesentery, and its allied forms in Grimm s.v. *kragen* 1962.] The mesentery of an animal.

1662 J. CHANDLER *Van Helmont's Oriat.* 179 The meat and drink ascends into the Chyle or juyce of the stomach, into the juyce of the mesentery or Crow. **1804** FARLEY *Lond. Art of Cookery* (ed. 10), The harslet, which consists of the liver, crow, kidneys, and skirts. *c* **1818** *Yng. Woman's Companion* 2 The liver and crow are much admired fried with bacon.

Crow (krəʊ), *sb.*[4] and *a.* [See quot. 1935.]

A. *sb.* **1.** A North American Indian tribe formerly inhabiting the regions of the Yellowstone and Wind rivers, now occupying a reservation in Montana; a member of this people. **2.** The language of this people, belonging to the Siouan stock.

1801 P. FIDLER in *Amer. Heritage Bk. of Indians* (1961) 324 (*legend on map*) Is.sap.poo. Crow mountain Indians. **1812** J. C. LUTTIG *Jrnl.* 17 Sept. in *Jrnl. Fur-trad. Exped.* (1920) 78 Lecomte..asked them what Nation they were, they answered Crows. **1846** W. G. D. STEWART *Altowan* I. viii. 207 The language used was Crow. **1857** C. KINGSLEY *Two Years Ago* I. iv. 101, I got it in fair fight..by a Crow's tomahawk in the Rocky Mountains. **1877** L. H. MORGAN *Ancient Soc.* III. ii. 440 In Crow my husband's brother's wife is 'my comrade'. **1894** *Outing* (U.S.) May 89/1 Our name 'Crow' for this large and flourishing tribe of Indians.. is a translation of their own totemic name Ab-sár-ra-ké, or Ap-sar-ro-ke. **1900** *Knowledge* 2 July 153/2 Among the other Atlantic stocks are..the Siouans, some of the most famous tribes of the latter being the Sioux or Dakotas, and the Crows. **1907** F. W. HODGE *Amer. Indians* I. 367/2 Crows (trans., through French *gens des corbeaux*, of their own name, *Absároke*, crow, sparrowhawk, or bird people). A Siouan tribe forming part of the Hidatsa group.

B. *adj.* **1.** Of or pertaining to this people or their language.

1804 W. CLARK *Jrnl.* 12 Oct. in Lewis & Clark *Jrnls. Lewis & Clark Exped.* (1904) I. 189 The Chien..or Dog Indians ..[are] at war with the Crow Indians. **1837** W. IRVING *Capt. Bonneville* II. 29 Fitzpatrick..succeeded in prevailing upon the Crow chieftain to return him his horses. **1935** R. H. LOWIE *Crow Indians* 3 The Crow name for themselves is 'Apsâruke', which early interpreters mistranslated as 'gens de corbeaux', 'Crow (or Kite) Indians'. To me the word was explained as the name of a bird no longer to be seen in the country. The squaw-man Leforge defines it as 'a peculiar kind of forked-tail bird resembling the blue jay or magpie' which tradition assigns to the fauna of eastern Nebraska and Kansas at the time the Crow lived there. Apart from this fanciful localization, his and my data thus agree well enough. **1969** W. K. POWERS *Indians of Northern Plains* 246 The Crow hold their annual Sun dance at Lodge Grass, Montana, in June, and the Crow Indian Fair and Rodeo at Crow Agency, Montana, in August.

2. Crow-type or **Crow system**, etc.: a type of kinship terminology, typical of societies with matrilineages, in which sisters and female cousins are classified under three terms, one applied to sister and mother's sister's daughter, another to mother's brother's daughter (and brother's daughter), and the third to father's sister's daughter (and her mother and daughter).

1925 L. SPIER in *Univ. Washington Publ. Anthropol.* I. II. 73 II. Crow Type. In this system the father's sister is an 'aunt' and her female descendants through females are 'aunts'! **1949** F. EGGAN in M. Fortes *Social Structure* 122 They [*sc.* the Hopi] possess a majority of features associated with the classic Crow type. **1964** F. G. LOUNSBURY in W. H. Goodenough *Explor. Cult. Anthropol.* 351 A formal account of the Crow- and Omaha-type kinship terminologies. **1968** *Internat. Encycl. Social Sci.* VIII. 396 Their kinship systems [i.e., those of 'the tribes of the Prairie Plains'] were also 'classificatory', in that lineal and collateral relatives were merged in the terminology, but they utilized the lineage principle to provide a wide extension to the system. There were two subtypes: (*a*) the 'Omaha' system, associated with patrilineal descent, and (*b*) the 'Crow' system, associated with matrilineal descent.

crow (krəʊ), *v.*[1] Pa. t. **crew** (kru:), **crowed.** Pa. pple. **crowed,** [**crown** (krəʊn)]. Forms: 1-2 **crawan, -en,** 3-7 **crowe,** 4- **crow;** *north.* 3-6 **crau,** (**krau**), 4-5 **crawe,** 4- **craw.** *Pa. t.* 1-2 **creow,** 3 **creuȝ,** 3-4 **cru,** 3-6 **creu,** 4 **crwe,** 4-5 **creew,** 4-6 **crewe, krew,** 4- **crew;** also 6- **crowed.** *Pa. pple.* (1 **crawen**), 4-5 **crowe(n,** 7 **crowne,** (9 **crown**); *north.* 6 **crawin,** 8 **crawn;** 6- **crowed.** [OE. *crāwan* strong vb. (*crēow, crāwen*), which in the other WGerm. languages is weak (cf. BLOW): OS. **craian* (MDu. *kraeijen*, Du. *kraaijen*, MLG. *kreien*, LG. *kraien, kreien*), OHG. *chrâian, crâwan, crâen*, (MHG. *crâjen, crâen, kræjen, kræn*, mod.G. *krähen.*) Originally an echoic word, and prob. of WG. origin. The strong pa. t. is still prevalent in sense 1, but in 2, 3 the weak form is used; the strong pa. pple. is only dialectal.]

1. *intr.* To utter the loud cry of a cock.

c **1000** *Ags. Gosp. Matt.* xxvi. 75 Ær þam þe se cocc crawe. *Ibid.* 74 And hrædlice þa creow se cocc. *c* **1290** *S. Eng. Leg.* I. 416/460 At þe furste cocke þat creuȝ. *a* **1300** *Cursor M.* 15945 (Cott.) Þan bigan þe cok to crau. *c* **1386** CHAUCER *Miller's T.* 501 Whan that the firste cok hath crowe anon. **1513** DOUGLAS *Æneis* VII. Prol. 114 Phebus crownit byrd.. thryse had crawin cleir. **15..** *Proph. Welshmen* in Thynne *Animadv.* App. v. (1865) 117 A yong coke that crowed wonderos bould. **1592** SHAKS. *Rom. & Jul.* IV. iv. 3 The second Cocke hath crow'd. **1611** BIBLE *Luke* xxii. 60 While he yet spake, the cocke crew. **1717** BERKELEY *Tour in Italy* Wks. IV. 532 The column..on which the cock stood when he crowed. **1814** SCOTT *Ld. of Isles* v. xiii, The black-cock deem'd it day, and crew. **1834** H. MILLER *Scenes & Leg.* xiv. (1857) 214 The cock had crown. **1842** TENNYSON *Will Waterpr.* xvi, The Cock..Crow'd lustier late and early. **1874** DASENT *Tales fr. Fjeld* 66 He stood on one leg and crew.

†**b.** Rarely of other cries, as that of the raven.

a **1250** *Owl & Night.* 336 Evre croweth thi wrecche crei, That he ne swiketh niȝt ne dai. *c* **1386** CHAUCER *Miller's T.* 191 He syngeth crowyng as a nightyngale. **1483** *Cath. Angl.* 83 To Crowe..*crocitare vel crocare, coruorum est.*

c. quasi-*trans.*

1393 GOWER *Conf.* II. 102 There is no cock to crowe day. **1816** SCOTT *Antiq.* xxi, 'What for the red cock didna craw her up in the morning.'

2. *transf.* Of persons: To utter a loud inarticulate sound of joy or exultation; said *esp.* of the joyful cry of an infant.

1579 SPENSER *Sheph. Cal.* Feb. 40 And crowing in pypes made of greene corne, You thinken to be Lords of the yeare. **1589** GREENE *Menaphon* (Arb.) 28 More he [the baby] crowde, more we cride. **1600** SHAKS. *A.Y.L.* II. vii. 30. **1722** DE FOE *Col. Jack* (1840) 45 He..began to crow and holla like a mad boy. **1782** MAD. D'ARBLAY *Diary* 30 Oct., [The] child..laughed and crowed the whole time. *a* **1863** THACKERAY *D. Duval* iii, [The] baby..would..crow with delight.

3. *fig.* To speak in exultation; to exult loudly, boast, swagger. ***to crow over***: to triumph over.

1522 SKELTON *Why not to Court* 65 Dicken, thou krew doutlesse. **1588** J. UDALL *Demonstr. Discip.* (Arb.) 40 They crow ouer them as if they wer their slaues. **1588** GREENE *Pandosto* (1843) 27 So his wife..beganne to crow against her goodman. **1655** GURNALL *Chr. in Arm.* (1669) 92/1 Hagar.. began to contest with, yea, crow over her Mistress. **1776** JOHNSON *Lett. to Mrs. Thrale* 18 May, He crows and triumphs. **1800** WEEMS *Washington* iii. (1877) 23 The party favoured would begin to crow. **1841** J. H. NEWMAN *Lett.* (1891) II. 337 We must not crow till we are out of the wood. **1844** DICKENS *Mart. Chuz.* xx, I'm not going to be crowed over by you. *Mod.* He crowed over them.

crow (krəʊ), *v.*[2] *S. Afr.* [Transliteration of dialectal Afrikaans *grau, grou*, f. *grawe*, Du. *graven*, with Eng. (k) representing Afrikaans (x)] *trans.* and *intr.* To dig.

1853 F. GALTON *Trop. S. Afr.* iii. 79 This method of digging is called in Dutch patois 'crowing' the ground; thus, 'crow-water', means water that you have to crow for, and not an open well, or spring. **1868** J. G. WOOD *Nat. Hist. Man* I. xxx. 343 The Damaras..will sometimes 'crow' holes eighteen inches..in depth. **1896** H. A. BRYDEN *Tales S. Afr.* 47 With this last implement she can the more easily crow up their dinner.

crowat, obs. form of CRUET.

crow-bar (ˈkrəʊbɑː(r)). [CROW *sb.*[1] 5 + BAR.] **a.** An iron bar with a wedge-shaped end (usually slightly bent and sometimes forked), used as a lever or prise by quarrymen, lumbermen, house-breakers, etc. In earlier use called simply CROW.

1748 in *Documents rel. Colonial Hist. New Jersey* (1883) 1st Ser. VII. 208 Men, armed with clubs, axes & crow bars, came, in a riotous & tumultuous manner. **1825** J. NEAL *Bro. Jonathan* I. 398 [To fetch] a crow-bar. **1862** *Lond. Rev.* 23 Aug. 172 Burglars, using the crowbar, the gimlet, and saw, to burst open doors and shutters.
fig. **1867** *Cornh. Mag.* Apr. 449 Even in progressive England the crowbar of reform spares the village inn.

b. *attrib.*

1885 W. J. FITZPATRICK *Life T.N. Burke* III. 30 *note*, Exterminating landlords, who pulled down the cabins of poor tenants, were called 'the Crowbar Brigade'. **1886** *Pall Mall G.* 26 Apr. 11/2 Evictions..at Knockrush..with sheriff, crowbar brigade, and all.

Hence **ˈcrow-bar** *v.*, to force with a crow-bar.

1853 KANE *Grinnell Exp.* xxix. (1856) 253 We had to send out parties to crow-bar away the ice from our bowsprit.

†**ˈcrow-bells.** *Obs.*

1. *yellow crow-bells*: a name for the daffodil.

1578 LYTE *Dodoens* II. liii. 214 This flower is called.. yellow Crow bels, yellow Narcissus, and bastarde Narcissus.

2. A name for the blue-bell, *Scilla nutans*.

a **1697** AUBREY *Wilts* Royal Soc. MS. p. 126 (Halliwell). These crow-bells have blew flowers, and are common to many shady places in this countrey.

crowberry (ˈkrəʊbərɪ). [prob. a translation of Ger. *krähenbeere*; the northern synonym *crakeberry* (see CRAKE) may be of Norse origin: cf. Da. *kragebær*.]

1. The fruit of a small evergreen heath-like shrub (*Empetrum nigrum*), found on heaths in northern Europe and America; the berry is black and of insipid taste. Also the plant itself.

1597 GERARDE *Herbal* App. to Table, Crow berries, *Erica baccifera*. **1769** J. WALLIS *Nat. Hist. Northumb.* I. viii. 145 Berry-bearing Heath, Crow-berry, or Crake-berry. **1776** WITHERING *Brit. Plants* (1796) II. 177 Black-berried Heath, Black Crow-berries, Crake-berries..in bogs and moorish grounds. **1831** CARLYLE *Sart. Res.* I. i, Apt to run goose-hunting into regions of bilberries and crowberries, and be swallowed up at last in remote peat-bogs. **1837** MACDOUGALL tr. *Graah's E. Coast Greenl.* 32 The walls.. being overgrown with dwarf-willow, crowberry, and whortleberry bushes.

2. a. Extended to plants of the allied genus *Corema* and their fruit. **b.** Erroneously applied in some parts of Britain to the bilberry, *Vaccinium Myrtillus*, and the cowberry, *V. Vitis-Idæa*.

1866 *Treas. Bot.* 351 Broom Crowberry, an American name for *Corema*. **1884** MILLER *Plant-n.*, Broom Crowberry, *Corema (Empetrum) Conradii*. Portugal Crowberry, *Corema lusitanicum*.

ˈcrow-bill. †**1.** A plant. *Obs.*

14.. *Gl. Sloane* 5 in *Sax. Leechd.* III. 320/2 Crowe pil, *acus muscata minor*. **1847–78** HALLIWELL, *Crouwepil*, the herb crane-bill.

2. *Surg.* (Also **crow's bill.**) A forceps for extracting bullets or other foreign bodies from wounds.

1611 COTGR., *Bec de corbin*..a Chirurgions toole, called a Crowes-bill. **1634** T. JOHNSON *Parey's Chirurg.* 440 Plucke it out with your crane or crowes bill. **1688** R. HOLME *Armoury* III. 400/2 Another Instrument of a Chyrurgion, termed a Crow-Bill. **1880** BROWNING *Dram. Idylls, Pietro*, But who wields the crozier down may fling the crow-bill.

crowch(e, var. of CROCHE *sb.*[1], obs. f. CROUCH, CRUTCH.

†**crowd** (kraʊd), *sb.*[1] Now only *Hist.* or *dial.* Forms: α. 4 **croupe**, 4–5 **crouth(e**, 7–9 **crowth**; β. 4–6 **croude**, 4–7 **crowde**, (5 **kroude**, 6 **crouddc**), 6–8 **croud**, 6–9 **crowd**. [a. Welsh *crwth* m. violin, fiddle; also, a swelling or bulging body, a paunch, a kind of round bulging box, akin to *croth* fem. swelling, protuberance, belly, womb. These words correspond as the masc. and fem. of adjs.: cf. *crwm*, *crom* crooked, etc. The fem. form alone is found in the other Celtic langs., but in both senses: cf. Gaelic *cruit* fem. harp, violin, *croit* fem. hump, hunch, Ir. *cruit* fem. violin, and hump, hunch; OIr. *crot* (genit. *croite*, *cruite*, dat. acc. *croit*) harp, cithara, in late L. *crotta* a British musical instrument mentioned by Venantius Fortunatus *c* 600.]

prop. An ancient Celtic musical instrument of the viol class, now obsolete, having in early times three strings, but in its later form six, four of which were played with a bow and two by twitching with the fingers; an early form of the fiddle.

a **1310** *Lyric P.* xvi. 53 Ther nis fiele ne crouth that such murthes maketh. *c* **1330** *King of Tars.* (MS.A.) 503 No minstral wiþ harp no croupe. **1382** WYCLIF *Luke* xv. 25 Whanne he..neiȝede to the hous, he herde a symphonye and a crowde. **1432–50** tr. *Higden* (Rolls) I. 355 And Wales vsethe trumpettes, an harpe, and a crowde. **1509** HAWES *Past. Pleas.* XVI. xi, Harpes, lutes, and crouddes ryght delycyous. **1571** HANMER *Chron. Irel.* (1633) 98 All the instrumentall musicke upon the Harpe and Crowth. **1820** SCOTT *Ivanhoe* xli, Saxon minstrels, and Welsh bards.. extracting mistuned dirges from their harps, crowds, and rotes. **1880** P. DAVID in Grove *Dict. Mus.* I. 422 *Crwth*..or *Crowd*, as far as we know the oldest stringed instrument played with the bow..Bingley heard it played at Carnarvon as late as 1801; but it is now entirely out of use.

b. Hence, a fiddle. Still *dial.*

1622 MIDDLETON, etc. *Old Law* V. i, Enter Fiddlers and others. *Evander*. Stay the crowd awhile. **1664** BUTLER *Hudibras* II. II. 6 That kept their Consciences in Cases, As Fidlers do their Crowds and Bases. *c* **1680** *Roxb. Ball.* VII. 18 When a Fidler wants his Crowd. **1746** *Exmoor Courtship* 84 Es coud a borst tha Croud in Shivers, and tha Crouder too. **1847** in HALLIWELL as *northern*. **1869** in *Lonsdale Gloss.* **1875** in *Lancash. Gloss.* **1880** in *W. Cornwall Gl.* and *E. Cornwall Gl.*

c. *transf.* Applied to the player.

1607 HEYWOOD *Fayre Mayde* Wks. 1874 II. 21 Well, Crowde, what say you to Fiddle now? **1719** D'URFEY *Pills* II. 232 An old Crowd..stood twanging.

†**crowd**, *sb.*[2] *Obs.* Also 4–5 **crudde**, 6 **croude**, **crowde**. [Anglo-Fr. *crudde*, app. corresponding to OF. *crute*, *crote*, later *croute* = Pr. *crota*, It. *grotta*:—late L. *crupta*, *grupta*, for L. *crypta*: see CRYPT. Of the *d* in the AF. and Eng. word no explanation has been found.] An underground vault, a crypt. (Also commonly in *pl.*)

1399 *Mem. Ripon* (Surtees) III. 129 Pro ostio in le Cruddes, 6*d*. **1472** *Ibid.* 225 Lez Cruddes voc. Seint Wilfride nedyll. **1478** BOTONER *Itin.* (Nasmith 1778) 220 Ad introitum ecclesiæ voltæ vocatæ le crowd..Ad descensum voltæ de le croude. **1501** *Will of Barre* (Somerset Ho.), To be buried in the Crowde of Saint John Baptist in Bristow. **1610** HOLLAND *Camden's Brit.* (1637) 700 Within the Church, Saint Wilfrides Needle..A narrow hole this was, in the Crowdes or close vaulted roome under the ground. *Ibid.* I. 703 In a certaine vault or crowdes or a little chappell under the ground. **1658** DUGDALE *St. Pauls* 117 Heretofore called *Ecclesia S. Fidis, in Cryptis* (or [St. Faith] in the Croudes, according to the vulgar expression).

crowd (kraʊd), *sb.*[3] Also 6–7 **croude**, 7 **crowde**, 7–8 **croud**. [f. CROWD *v.*]

1. a. A large number of persons gathered so closely together as to press upon or impede each other; a throng, a dense multitude. (The earlier term from 13th c. was *press*.)

1567 DRANT *Hor. Epist.*, *To Numitius* (R.), Who will, and dare retche forthe his hande, And man the throughe the croude. **1613** SHAKS. *Hen. VIII*, IV. i. 57 Among the crowd i' th' Abbey, where a finger Could not be wedg'd in more. **1632** J. HAYWARD tr. *Biondi's Eromena* 121 Hee perceived through a window..no small crowde of people. **1727** SWIFT *Gulliver* III. ii. 183, I was surrounded by a croud of people. **1847** L. HUNT *Jar Honey* iv, Powers, what a crowd! how shall we get along? **1881** BIBLE *Mark* ii. 4 They could not come nigh unto him for the crowd [**1611** press].

b. *spec.* A mass of spectators; an audience. (Cf. quot. 1613 under sense 1.)

c **1863** E. DICKINSON *Poems* (1968) II. 539 Their [*sc.* balloons'] Ribbons just beyond the eye—They struggle—some—for Breath—And yet the Crowd applaud, below. **1921** *Times* 1 Mar. 16/7 The crowd jeered at Hobbs owing to his slow movements in the field due to his recent injury. **1955** *Manch. Guardian* 30 Apr. 3/6 In recent years the crowd at Wembley Stadium has not seen the game of Rugby League played at its best. **1970** *New Statesman* 9 Oct. 454/3 The crowd was very similar both in behaviour and appearance to the audience that came to the Beaulieu jazz festivals. **1971** *Sunday Times* 31 Jan. 12/1 Tennis players lecture the line judge, appeal to the crowd.

c. A collection of actors playing the part of a crowd; freq. *attrib.*

1899 L. WAGNER *How to get on Stage* 71 Sir Henry Irving when his two sons elected to go on the stage..said..'I could only allow them to stand in the crowd at the Lyceum, to accustom them to the boards, and afterwards procure them an engagement in a touring company.' **1909** J. R. WARE *Passing Eng.* 100/1 What do *I* do? Oh, I go on with the crowd. **1935** J. DELL *Nobody ordered Wolves* v. 69 Her sole ambition had been to do crowd-work. **1936** *Archit. Rev.* LXXX. 192 If you are 'crowd', you go to one of the big communal dressing rooms. **1937** *Ibid.* LXXXII. 286 The interior is designed as a background to this 'crowd-scene'.

2. *transf.* **a.** A large number (*of* persons) contemplated in the mass.

1654 WHITLOCK *Zootomia* 17 The whole crowd of those we converse with, what are they? **1712** STEELE *Spect.* No. 264 ⁋1 Wherein you have Crouds of Rivals. **1848** MACAULAY *Hist. Eng.* I. 331 The principal pulpits..were occupied..by a crowd of distinguished men.

b. The people who throng the streets and populous centres; the masses; the multitude.

1683 TRYON *Way to Health* 630 We ought..not [to] esteem a thing good..because the Multitude do it..for there is scarce a worse guide than the Croude. **1750** GRAY *Elegy* xix, Far from the madding crowd's ignoble strife. **1878** MORLEY *Diderot* I. 225 This passage sounds unpleasantly like an appeal to the crowd in a matter of science.

c. orig. *U.S.* A company; 'set', 'lot'. *colloq.* (Like 'lot', used of an individual, e.g. 'he's a bad crowd'.)

1840 *Congress. Globe* Apr., App. 376/2, I became satisfied that Democracy had but few charms for that crowd. **1857** BORTHWICK *California* 195 (Bartlett) He was one of the most favorable specimens of that crowd. **1883** SWEET & KNOX *Through Texas* 13 He 'always went heeled, toted a derringer, and was a bad crowd generally'. **1889** FARMER *Americanisms* s.v., I don't belong to that crowd, i.e. I don't belong to that set. **1892** BOLDREWOOD *Nevermore* II. xvii. 207 He..got mixed up with a crooked Sydney-side crowd. **1897** KIPLING *Captains Courageous* x. 218 They treat him as one of themselves. Same as they treat me... I'm one of the crowd now. **1933** D. L. SAYERS *Murder must Advertise* ii. 33 The 'varsity crowd don't quarrel like the rest of them. *Ibid.* iii. 41 He used to tag round with that de Momerie crowd. **1939** *Chatelaine* Jan. 19/3 My bridge crowd was over the other night. **1971** *Woman* 23 Jan. 59/1 She was going through a particularly rebellious phase and seemed to be in with a wild crowd.

d. *colloq.* A military unit.

1901 *Westm. Gaz.* 31 Aug. 2/1 My crowd on this day were left flank advance guard. **1929** P. GIBBS *Hidden City* vi. 23 'What was your crowd?'..'East Kents. 8th Battalion.'

e. Colloq. phr. *to pass* (*muster*) *in a crowd*, not to fall so short of the standard as to be noticed; not to be conspicuously below the average (freq. with the implication of mediocrity).

1711 SWIFT *Jrnl. to Stella* 9 Feb. (1948) I. 185 Will she pass in a crowd? Will she make a figure in a country church? **1846** R. FORD *Gatherings from Spain* ix. 94 The rider's.. great object should be to pass in a crowd, either unnoticed, or to be taken for 'one of us'. **1853** DICKENS *Bleak Ho.* xxvi. 259 They were mighty particular. You would pass muster in a crowd, Phil!

3. *transf.* and *fig.* **a.** A great number of things crowded together, either in fact or in contemplation; a large collection, multitude.

1627 SANDERSON *12 Serm.* (1637) 511 In the croude of their vnknowne sinnes. **1728** N. SALMON in *Lett. Lit. Men* (Camden) 361 Amongst such a crowd of Advertisements. **1855** E. FORBES *Lit. Papers* i. 9 A crowd of new thoughts occupies..their minds. **1868** FREEMAN *Norm. Conq.* (1876) II. App. 704 It is signed by a crowd of names.

b. *Naut.* *crowd of sail*: an unusual number of sails hoisted for the sake of speed; a press of sail.

1803 *Phil. Trans.* XCIII. 312 The holes being pressed under water by a crowd of sail on the ship. **1846** RAIKES *Life of Brenton* 124 Several sail of the line appeared off Europa point under a crowd of sail.

4. *Comb.*, as *crowd-control*, *-mind*, *-morality*, *-panic*, *-pleaser*, *-poison*, *-poisoning* (see quot.), *-psychology*, *-suggestion*; *crowd-drawing*, *-pleasing*, *-pulling* adjs. See also sense 1 c and cf. MASS *sb.*[2]

1966 *Truth* (Brisbane) 9 Oct. 41/6 We call them bouncers but the U.S. has another term for those beefy bar room keepers of the peace. They are called *crowd control engineers. **1971** *Times* 4 Jan. 1/3 The debate about crowd control and safety at football stadiums. **1848** J. R. LOWELL *Fable for Critics* 37 He has faith... And this is what makes him the *crowd-drawing preacher. **1923** H. G. WELLS *Men Like Gods* III. ii. 265 Crowds and the *crowd-mind have gone for ever. **1915** A. C. CURTIS (*title*) Politics and *crowd-morality, a study in the philosophy of politics. **1906** *Westm. Gaz.* 22 Jan. 2/2 Fewer processions with banners, fewer *crowd-panics. **1943** *Gen* 16 Jan. 30/1 An up-and-coming fighter is a tearaway chap, a real *crowd-pleaser. **1962** *Times* 26 Feb. (Canada Suppl.) p. xvi/4 One of the biggest *crowd-pleasing sports in Canada is the rough and tumble stock car racing. **1871** NAPHEYS *Prev. & Cure Dis.* I. vii. 197 A peculiar subtle emanation from the human body..which is called *crowd-poison. **1882** *Syd. Soc. Lex.*, **Crowd-poisoning*, the bad condition of health produced by overcrowding of people in a house or houses. **1924** W. B. SELBIE *Psychol. Relig.* 204 The whole subject [*sc.* conversion] is an interesting branch of the study of *crowd psychology. **1955** KEEPNEWS & GRAUER *Pict. Hist. Jazz* ii. 22 Brown..turned the term into a *crowd-pulling asset by billing his group as 'Brown's Dixieland Jass Band'. **1924** W. B. SELBIE *Psychol. Relig.* 157 The whole thing comes from *crowd suggestion.

crowd (kraʊd), *v.*[1] Forms: 1 **crúdan**, 3 **crude**, 4–6 **croude**, 4–7 **crowde**, 7–9 **croud**, 7– **crowd**. [OE. *crúdan*, 3 sing. *crýdeþ*, pa. t. *créad*, pl. **crudon*, pa. pple. **croden*, an original str. vb. (ablaut-series *kreud-*, *kraud-*, *krud-*), not known in the early stages of the other langs., but represented by MDu. *crúden* to press, push, later *kruyden*, *kruyen* (Kilian), Du. *kruien* to push in a wheel-barrow, to drive, WFris. *kroadjen*, EFris. *krôden*, *krüden* (*kröien*, *krüijen*) to push, press, NFris. *krode*, *krojen*, MLG. *krúden*, *kroden*, LG. *krüden*, *krüen*, MHG. *kroten*, *kröten* to oppress, etc.: see *Kroten* in Grimm. As in some other verbs of the same ablaut series, the present had in OE. *ú*, ME. *ū*, *ou*, instead of *éo*. The str. pa. t. *crud* (from pl.), pl. *crodyn* (from pa. pple.) were used in ME.; in the pa. pple., *crod* occurs in 1477, and *crowden* in 17th c.; but the wk. forms in *-ed* prevail from 16th c. The word was comparatively rare down to 1600; it does not occur in the Bible of 1611.]

The primary sense of 'press' (Branch I), has in later Eng. passed into that of the mutual or combined action of multitudes compressed or gathered closely together (II).

I. To press, push, thrust, shove, etc.

†**1.** *intr.* To press, to exert pressure (*on* or *against*).

a **1000** *Riddles* iv. 28 Đonne heah geþring on cleofu crydeþ. *c* **1300** *K. Alis.* 609 And saide to that lady, loude, Withhold! and ageyn croude!

2. a. *intr.* To press, drive, or hasten on: said of a ship (or its crew); in later usage, app. treated as elliptical for *crowd sail* (see 9).

937 *O.E. Chron.* (Parker MS.), Créad cnear on flot. *a* **1300** *K. Horn* 1293 Þat schup bigan to crude, þe wind him bleu lude. *c* **1386** CHAUCER *Man of L.T.* 703 (4 MSS.) In the same schip..Hire and hir yonge sone..He schulde putte, and crowde fro the londe. **1699** DAMPIER *Voy.* II. II. 21 We kept on crouding till Night. **1722** DE FOE *Col. Jack* (1840) 243 Crowding away to the north, [we] got the start of the English fleet. **1890** W. C. RUSSELL *Ocean Trag.* I. i. 16 Is it your intention to crowd on to the Cape and await her arrival there?

b. *trans. to crowd* (a ship) *off.*

1743 BULKELEY & CUMMINS *Voy. S. Seas* 16 [He] desired we would use our utmost Endeavours to crowd the Ship off. **1768** J. BYRON *Narr. Patagonia* (ed. 2) 9 We wore ship..and endeavoured to crowd her off from the land.

c. *trans.* and *intr.* To hurry. *U.S. colloq.*

1838 *Knickerbocker* XII. 506 Well, children, don't *crowd* the old man so; give him time. *a* **1861** T. WINTHROP *John Brent* (1883) v. 43, I might perhaps make it a new story; but I crowd on now to the proper spot where this drama is to be enacted. *Ibid.* xix. 169 He crowded on, more desperately.. as a lover rides for love. **1876** *Rep. Vermont Board Agric.* III. 627 He is for ever crowding and rushing, so as to get some particular piece of work done by such a time.

†**3.** *trans.* To press (anything), to move by pressure, to push, shove; *spec.* to push in a wheel-barrow or hand-cart. (Also *absol.*) Also, to push *back, down* (also *fig.*). *Obs.* exc. *dial.*

c **1330** *Amis & Amil.* 1861 Than Amoraunt crud Sir Amiloun Thurch mani a cuntre, vp and doun. *Ibid.* 1883 He crud his wain into the fen. *c* **1386** CHAUCER *Man of L.T.* 801 (Ellesm.) But in the same ship..Hire and hir yonge sone.. He sholde putte and croude hire fro the lond. **14..** *ABC Poem* 54 in *Pol. Rel. & L. Poems* 245 Cananis hym crodyn to heroudis kyng, þer had he gret scornyng. *c* **1440** *Promp. Parv.* 105 Crowde wythe a barow, *cinevecto.* Crowdyn', or showen, *impello.* **1477** MARG. PASTON in *Paston Lett.* No. 809 III. 215 Sche sent..word..that sche xuld come hedyr ..thoow sche xuld be crod in a barwe. **1674** N. FAIRFAX *Bulk & Selv.* 123 Whence 'tis, that I can crowd a bigger body than I can throw. **1710** J. CLARKE *Rohault's Nat. Phil.* (1729) I. 97 Those little Columns of Water which are longer than the other..will never leave crouding them up, till the surface of the Liquor is come to a Level. **1830** *Massachusetts Spy* 14 July (Th.), He was carting timber, and stepped upon the cart tongue to crowd some sticks back with his feet. **1847** HALLIWELL, *Crowd*, to wheel about. *Norf.* **1874** *Rep. Vermont Board Agric.* II. 732 You are crowding him down to a gold basis. *Ibid.* 764 The excavation was..stopped upon a clean pebbly bottom, into which an iron bar could be crowded down its length. **1880** G. W. CABLE *Grandissimes* xl. 318 He crowded his hat fiercely down over his curls and plunged out.

4. *intr.* To push, or force one's way into a confined space, through a crowd, etc.; to press *forward, up*, etc. Now only *fig.*, as in quot. 1858, and coloured by 5.

a **1415** LYDG. *Temple of Glass* 534 Within þe tempil me þou3te þat I sey Gret pres of folk..To croude and shove —þe tempil was so ful. **1597** SHAKS. *2 Hen. IV*, III. ii. 347 Then he burst his Head, for crowding among the Marshals men. **1602** MARSTON *Antonio's Rev.* II. iii. Wks. 1856 I. 99 Throngs of thoughts crowde for their passage. **1674** N. FAIRFAX *Bulk & Selv.* 138 It cannot stir without asking another bodies leave to crowd by. **1687** A. FARMER in *Magd. Coll.* (Oxf. Hist. Soc.) 72 He crowded into a Dancing Room. **1858** O. W. HOLMES *Aut. Breakf.-t.* xii. 119 The great maternal instinct came crowding up in her soul.

II. Senses in which the notion of physical compression or mutual pressure gradually changes into that of the incommoding effect: cf. THRONG.

5. *intr.* Of persons, etc. in numbers: To press toward a common centre, to gather or congregate closely so as to press upon one another; to come or assemble in large numbers or crowds; to flock, throng. With many advbs. and preps., e.g. *to crowd in; about, after* (a person); *into, to, upon* (a place or thing). Also *fig.*

a **1400** *Pist. Susan* 83 On croppus of canel keneliche þei croude. **1583** STANYHURST *Æneis* iii. (Arb.) 70 Men to vs thick crouded. **1654** WHITLOCK *Zootomia* 408 People not being so hasty to crowde in, or justle them out of these Quarters. *a* **1661** FULLER *Worthies* (1840) III. 409 Multitudes of people crowded to his sermons. **1709** BERKELEY *Th. Vision* §110 There croud into his mind the ideas which [etc.]. **1716** LADY M. W. MONTAGUE *Lett.* 14 Sept., The company crowded away in such confusion, that I was almost squeezed to death. **1840** THIRLWALL *Greece* VII. lvii. 232 The Macedonians crowded about him. **1875** JOWETT *Plato* (ed. 2) III. 197 Suspicions and alarms crowd upon him.

6. *trans.* **a.** To press, thrust, force, cram (things) *in*, or *into* a confined space; †to compress (air, etc.). Also to press (things) in numbers *on* a person. Also *fig.*

1599 SHAKS. *Hen. V*, I. ii. 200 The poore Mechanicke Porters, crowding in Their heauy burthens at his narrow gate. **1606** —— *Tr. & Cr.* I. ii. 23 A man into whom nature hath so crowded humors. **1654** WHITLOCK *Zootomia* 326 We may heare crowd in an Example to be found in the same Book of Justin. **1660** BOYLE *New Exp. Phys. Mech.* xxvii. (1682) 107 A quantity of Air crouded and shut up. **1691** E. TAYLOR *Behmen's Aurora* i. 242 Heat consumeth the Water, cold crowdeth the Air. **1725** DE FOE *Voy. round World* (1840) 122 Nor have I room to crowd many of these things into this account. **1776** G. SEMPLE *Building in Water* 138 Take the utmost Precautions to have..every Thing necessary to crowd in your stuffing. **1848** MACAULAY *Hist. Eng.* II. 504 In revolutions men live fast: the experience of years is crowded into hours. **1856** KANE *Arct. Expl.* II. xxv. 248 Myouk is crowding fresh presents of raw birds on me.

b. To compress; to collect, bring, or pack closely together, as in a crowd.

1612 *Proc. Virginia* vi. in *Capt. Smith's Wks.* (Arb.) 119 The rest..crowded in so small a barge, in so many dangers. **1653** HOLCROFT *Procopius* I. 29 The people being crouded together. **1746** JORTIN *Chr. Relig.* vi. (R.), It would not have entered into their thoughts to have crowded together so many allusions. **1776** WITHERING *Brit. Plants* II. 360 *Aristolochia Clematitis*..flowers crowded, in the bosom of the leaf-stalks. **1881** JOWETT *Thucyd.* I. Introd. 15 A strong individuality..which crowds the use of words, which thinks more than it can express. *Mod.* We were standing crowded together before the picture.

†**c.** To compress (a single thing) *in* a narrow space; to confine. *Obs.*

c **1632** *Poem* in *Athenæum* No. 2883. 121/3 Doe nott thou presume To crowd the Founder in a narrow Tombe. **1672** DRYDEN *Conq. Granada* III. i. 122 Why will you in your Breast your Passion croud. **1707** COLLIER *Refl. Ridic.* 249 They are crowded and wrapt up in themselves.

†**d.** To compress, crush, squeeze *to death* in a crowd. Also *fig. Obs.*

1597 SHAKS. *2 Hen. IV*, IV. ii. 34 The Time (mis-order'd) doth..Crowd vs, and crush vs, to this monstrous Forme. **1598** STOW *Surv.* v. (1603) 25 Many persons were crowded to death. **1647** CLARENDON *Hist. Reb.* I. (1843) 17/1 Great numbers..were crowded to death. **1786** SIR H. CROFT *Abbey of Kilkh.* 99 He was crowded to death with honours.

7. a. To fill or occupy *with* a crowd or dense multitude; to fill to excess or encumbrance; to cram *with.*

1695 WOODWARD *Nat. Hist. Earth* II. (1723) 120, I shall not crowd this Piece with them. **1715** POPE *Pref. to Homer* (Seager), This [subject] he has..crowded with a greater number of councils, speeches, battles, and episodes of all kinds. **1777** W. DALRYMPLE *Trav. Sp. & Port.* cxv, The roads were crouded with little saints and altars. **1848** MACAULAY *Hist. Eng.* I. 597 A port crowded with shipping.

b. To fill as a crowd does, to throng (a place). (The passive of result is *to be crowded with* as in a.; the passive of action *to be crowded by.*)

1646 PAGITT *Heresiogr.* (ed. 3) A iv, They run after these men..crowding the Churches, filling their doors and windows. **1697** DRYDEN *Virg. Georg.* IV. 316 They crowd his Levees, and support his Throne. **1769** ROBERTSON *Chas. V*, III. VIII. 119 A court crowded with armed men. **1883** *Daily News* 30 Oct. 5/3 The trains were crowded by Exhibition visitors. **1884** CHURCH *Bacon* i. 20 The servile and insincere flatterers..who crowded the antechambers of the great Queen.

c. To press upon or beset (a person or place) as a crowd does, to surround, encumber, incommode by pressure of numbers, to crowd upon; also to occupy or encumber *with* a multitude of things.

1614 W. B. *Philosopher's Banquet* (ed. 2) A ij b, Resort shall croud him wheresoere he dwell. **1697** DRYDEN *Virg. Georg.* III. 579 The Men..crowd the chearful Fire. *a* **1735** GRANVILLE (J.), Why will vain courtiers toil, And crowd a vainer monarch for a smile? **1741** JOHNSON *Life Morin*, A man of this temper was not crouded with salutations. **1783** —— *Lett. to Mrs. Thrale* 27 Dec., I am crowded with visits. **1908** E. J. BANFIELD *Confessions of Beachcomber* I. i. 36 Get away from this. Don't crowd a fellow. Go to a rock of your own. **1933** P. GODFREY *Back-Stage* iii. 40 'Crowding' and 'upstaging' are tricks of the selfish actor. To 'crowd' is to stand just close enough to another actor to prevent his making any gesture freely. **1963** 'J. LE CARRÉ' *Spy who came in fr. Cold* vi. 44 They crowded him in the dinner queue. Crowding is a prison ritual akin to the eighteenth-century practice of jostling. It has the virtue of an apparent accident, in which the prisoner's mess tin is upturned, and its contents spilt on his uniform.

†**d.** Said of things: To press upon (one another) in a crowd. *Obs.* exc. *dial.*

1657 AUSTEN *Fruit Trees* I. 65 Frettings and gallings happens to Trees that thrust and croud one another. *a* **1825** FORBY *Voc. E. Anglia, Crowd v.*, to push, shove or press close. To the word, in its common acceptation, number seems necessary. With us, one individual can crowd another. [And so in U.S. (F. Hall).]

e. *U.S. colloq.* 'To urge; to press by solicitation; to dun' (Webster 1828).

f. *to crowd the mourners*: to exercise undue pressure; to push or hurry in an unseemly manner. *U.S. colloq.*

1842 *Spirit of Times* XII. 426 In the second mile, however, Fashion commenced 'crowding the mourners' by brushing down both straight sides. **1904** W. H. SMITH *Promoters* xix. 282, I don't want to crowd the mourners at your end of the line. **1923** *Dialect Notes* V. 205 Keep ca'm now, an' don't crowd the mourners.

g. To approach (a specified age) closely; to verge on. *U.S. colloq.*

1943 *Newsweek* 22 Nov. 52 Reynolds, now crowding 60, would disclose no plans last week. **1960** *Guardian* 5 May 9/6 Groucho is crowding 70, though not very hard. **1961** F. CRANE *Reluctant Sleuth* iv. 33 Bobo's maybe twenty-five. Greene is crowding sixty. **1969** *Guardian* 18 Aug. 9/6 Mae West..confessed to 'crowding sixty'.

8. *crowd out*: to push or force out by pressure of a crowd (*obs.*); to exclude by crowding, or because the crowd is more than the space can hold.

1652 DOROTHY OSBORNE *Lett.* (1888) 30 'Tis very possible the next new experiment may crowd me out again. **1684–90** BURNET *Th. Earth* (J.), According as it [the sea] can make its way into all those subterraneous cavities, and crowd the air out of them. **1841–44** EMERSON *Ess. Over-Soul* Wks. (Bohn) I. 111 [The] cuckoo Crowds every egg out of the nest. **1888** BRYCE *Amer. Commw.* II. lxxiv. 615 They crowd out better men. **1889** *Morning Post* 24 June 2/1 Works sent to the Royal Academy and crowded out.

9. *Naut. to crowd sail*: to hoist an unusual number of sails on a ship; to carry a press of sail for the purpose of speed.

The phrase appears to be derived from sense 2 by confusion or association with the common mod. sense.

1687 *Lond. Gaz.* No. 2251/4 They crowded all the Sail they could possible make after us. **1745** P. THOMAS *Jrnl. Anson's Voy.* 112 In crowding Sail to come up with her. **1844** W. H. MAXWELL *Sport. & Adv. Scotl.* xiii. (1855) 119 Canvass was crowded on the *Clorinde.*

†**crowd**, *v.*[2] *Obs.* Also croud. [f. CROWD *sb.*[1]] *intr.* To play the crowd; to fiddle.

1589 PEELE *Eclogue* 21 Thou art too crank, and crowdest all too high. **1599** MIDDLETON & ROWLEY *Old Law* v. i, Fiddlers, crowd on, crowd on. **1693** SOUTHERNE *Maid's last Prayer* iv. iii, The Knight crowds most splendidly.

†**crowd**, *v.*[3] *Obs.* Also 8 croud. [Cf. CROOD, CROUT.] **1.** *intr.* To crow, as a cock.

1575 J. STILL *Gamm. Gurton* II. ii, Her cock with the yellow legs, that nightly crowded so just. **1752** in *Scots Mag.* Aug. (1753) 401/1 The black cocks were crouding.

2. Variant of *croud*, CROOD *Sc.*, to coo.

†**crowd-**, the stem of CROWD *v.*[1] (see sense 3) in combination, as in **crowd-barrow** (now *dial.*), a wheel-barrow. †**crowd-wain** [= Du. *kruiwagen*, in Kilian *krodewaghen*], a wheel-barrow, a hand cart.

c **1330** *Amis & Amil.* 1858 Thai went..And bought hem a gode croude wain. His lord he gan therin to lain; He no might him bere na mare. *c* **1440** *Promp. Parv.* 105 Crowde, barowyr [? *error for* crowde-barow], *cenivectorium.* **1674** N. FAIRFAX *Bulk & Selv.* 111 By shoving or driving of it forwards, as a slouch does a crowd-barrow. *a* **1825** FORBY *Voc. E. Anglia, Crud-barrow, Crudden-barrow*, a common wheel-barrow, to be shoved forward. **1847–78** HALLIWELL, *Crowd-barrow*, a wheel-barrow. *Norf.*

'crowded, *ppl. a.* [f. CROWD *v.*[1] + -ED.]

1. a. Filled with or thronged by a crowd.

1612 DRAYTON *Poly-olb.* xvii. (R.), His crowded wharfs, and people-pest'red shores. **1637** BASTWICK *Litany* I. 5 They cry out in open Courts and the Crowdest assemblies. **1727–46** THOMSON *Summer* 65 And from the crouded fold, in order, drives His flock. **1855** MACAULAY *Hist. Eng.* IV. 4 Sixteen hundred substantial burghers well armed..kept order in the crowded streets.

b. *fig.* Full of events or experience of life.

1791 T. O. MORDAUNT in *Bee* 12 Oct. 179 One crouded hour of glorious life Is worth an age without a name. **1957** F. KING *Widow* III. iii. 317 The busy and crowded years in India. **1971** *Times* 21 Jan. 10/4 He [*sc.* Compton Mackenzie] records a crowded old age in which flow of writing is as non-stop as social life.

2. Gathered, pressed, or clustered closely together.

1725 POPE *Odyss.* x. 106 Our eager sailors..bound within the port their crouded fleet. **1823** SCORESBY *Jrnl.* 240 We doubled the western point among very crowded ice. **1888** *Pall Mall G.* 2 July 11/1 There was a crowded audience each night.

Hence **'crowdedly** *adv.*, **'crowdedness.**

1846 DANA *Zooph.* (1848) 131 Exterior crowdedly papillose. **1823** *Blackw. Mag.* XIII. 698 The pettiness and crowdedness of its ruins. **1895** W. SCHLICH *Man. Forestry* III. 181 As long as the degree of crowdedness is not too great. **1920** M. WEBB *House in Dormer Forest* I. vi. 65 The phrase pleased him because of its crowdedness. **1923** D. H. LAWRENCE *Birds, Beasts & Flowers* 67, I long to see its [*sc.* the world's] chock-full crowdedness. **1930** O. LODGE in *Aberdeen Press & Jrnl.* 9 Sept. 6/2 The great crowdedness of space.

'crowder[1]. *Hist.* or *dial.* Also 5 crowdere, 6 crouder, -ar, 6–8 crowther. [f. CROWD *sb.*[1] or *v.*[2] + -ER[1].] One who plays a crowd; a fiddler.

c **1450** *Voc.* in Wr.-Wülcker 572/26 *Choricista*, a crowdere. *a* **1533** LD. BERNERS *Gold. Bk. M. Aurel.* (1546) Ii v, Crouders, dauncers, mummers. *a* **1661** FULLER *Worthies* II. 306 Sung but by some blind Crowder. **1731** A. HILL *Adv. Poets* Ep. 4 To tune his Praise..and expect, like his Brother Crowders, to be paid for his Scraping. **1832** J. BREE *St. Herbert's Isle* 19 When mute the harp, nor wandering crowder near.

crowder[2] ('kraʊdə(r)). [f. CROWD *v.*[1] + -ER[1].] One who crowds: see the verb.

1581 J. BELL *Haddon's Answ. Osor.* 462 A certein old crafty Crowder laden throughly with the Popes Bulles raunged the coastes. **1812** H. & J. SMITH *Rej. Addr.* xvii. (1873) 161 Contending crowders shout.

crowdie, crowdy ('kraʊdɪ). *Sc.* and *north. Eng.* Also 7 croudy. [Derivation unknown.

Jamieson conjectured some connexion with GROUT, and Icel. *grautr* porridge; this suits the sense, but leaves phonetic conditions unsatisfied.]

1. Meal and water stirred together so as to form a thick gruel. Frequently used as a designation for food of the brose or porridge kind in general. Jamieson. Now *Obs.* or only traditionally known.

1668 LD. NEWBOTTLE *Cakes o' Croudy* in *Jacobite Songs*, Bannocks of bear meal, cakes of Croudy. **1724** RAMSAY *Tea-t. Misc.* (1733) I. 91 Powsowdy and drummock and crowdy. **1804** ANDERSON *Cumbrld. Ballads* 112 For dinner I'd hev a fat crowdy. **1855** ROBINSON *Whitby Gloss.*, *Crowdy*, oatmeal and water boiled to a paste and eaten with salt, or thinned with milk and sweetened. Spoonmeat in general. **1862** SMILES *Engineers* III. 238 There he [Stephenson] had his breakfast of 'crowdie', which he made with his own hands. It consisted of oatmeal stirred into a basin of hot water.. which was supped with cold sweet milk.

2. In some parts of the north of Scotland, a peculiar preparation of milk.

'In Ross-shire it denotes curds with the whey pressed out, mixed with butter, nearly in an equal proportion' (Jamieson).

1820 *Glenfergus* II. 275 (Jam.) Then came..the remains of a cog of crowdy, that is, of half butter, half cheese. **1938** L. MACNEICE *I crossed Minch* II. xii. 167 For my tea I had.. a large hunk of 'crowdy'. *Ibid.* 168 'Crowdy' is a kind of..

crumbly cream cheese, pure white and with practically no taste. **1946** *Farmhouse Fare* (ed. 2) 274 In Aberdeenshire a delicious crowdie is made from buttermilk.

3. *Comb.*, as *crowdie-time*; **crowdy-mowdy** = CROWDIE 1, 'generally denoting milk and meal boiled together' (Jam.); also humorously as a term of endearment.

1500–20 DUNBAR *Poems, In Secreit Place* 46 My tyrlie myrlie, my crowdie mowdie. **1724** RAMSAY *Tea-t. Misc.* (1733) I. 21 With crowdy mowdy they fed me. **1787** BURNS *Holy Fair* vi, Then I gaed hame at crowdie-time.

crowding ('kraʊdɪŋ), *vbl. sb.* [f. CROWD *v.*[1] + -ING[1].] The action of the verb CROWD q.v., in various senses.

c **1384** CHAUCER *H. Fame* III. 269 Ful moche prees of folke ther nas Ne crowdyng. *c* **1440** *Promp. Parv.* 105 Crowdynge, caryynge wythe a barowe, *cenivectura*. **1665** SIR T. HERBERT *Trav.* (1677) 139 We saw a dozen Persians ride up a breast without crowding. **1814** SCOTT *Wav.* xx, The company numerous even to crowding.

'crowding, *ppl. a.* [f. as prec. + -ING[2].] That crowd, or press closely: see the verb.

1697 DRYDEN *Virg. Past.* IV. 64 In crowding Ranks appear. **1718** ROWE tr. *Lucan* 151 The Crouding Sails from ev'ry Station press. **1853** KANE *Grinnell Exp.* xx. (1856) 160 The crowding tenants of the air, the Brent goose [etc.].

crowdle, cruddle, dial. var. of CROODLE *v.*[2]

crowed (krəʊd), *ppl. a. rare.* = CROW-FOOTED 1.

1851 MAYNE REID *Scalp Hunt.* xx, The eye is grey and slightly crowed at the corner.

crowell, obs. form of CRUEL.

crower ('krəʊə(r)). [f. CROW *v.*[1] + -ER.] A cock that crows; also *transf.* and *fig.* one who crows.

1577 B. GOOGE *Heresbach's Husb.* IV. (1586) 158 Cocks.. good wakers and crowers. **1864** *Daily Tel.* 24 Aug., The Orange party.. the loudest crowers I ever heard.

crowett, obs. form of CRUET.

'crow-flower. A popular name for the buttercup (cf. CROWFOOT). **b.** Applied by Gerarde to the Ragged Robin (*Lychnis Floscuculi*); by Tannahill app. to the wild hyacinth or bluebell (*Scilla nutans*); also in some parts to *Caltha palustris* and *Geranium sylvaticum*.

1597 GERARDE *Herbal* II. clxxxv. 608 Called in English Crow floures, Wilde Williams, Marsh Gilloflours and Cockow Gelloflouers. **1602** SHAKS. *Ham.* IV. vii. 170 With fantasticke Garlands.. Of Crow-flowers, Nettles, Daysies, and long Purples. **1806** E. RUSHTON *Poems* 56 Speckled daisies and crow flowers abounded. *a* **1810** TANNAHILL *Gloomy Winter's now awa'*, Sweet the crawflower's early bell Decks Gleniffer's dewy dell. **1820** CLARE *Poems Rural Life* (1821) 34 From crow-flower's golden cup.

crowfoot ('krəʊfʊt). Pl. -feet, in senses 1 and 2 -foots.

1. A name for various species of *Ranunculus* or Buttercup, properly those with divided leaves; but extended as a book-name to the whole genus.

c **1440** *Promp. Parv.* 105 Crowefote, herbe, *amarusca*. **1562** TURNER *Herbal* II. 114a, Ranunculus is called.. in Englishe Crowfoot or King cup. **1657** W. COLES *Adam in Eden* xlvii. 93 [Wall Pepper] raiseth blisters.. as forcibly as Ranunculus or Crowfoot will do. **1776** WITHERING *Brit. Plants* (1796) I. 7 The leaves of the Ranunculus aquatilis, or Water Crowfoot. **1832** TENNYSON *May Queen* I. 38 And the cowslip and the crowfoot are over all the hill.

2. Applied to other plants of which the leaves or some other part are taken to resemble a crow's foot: **a.** *Geranium pratense*; also called **crowfoot cranesbill, c. geranium.** †**b.** *Plantago Coronopus* and *Senebiera Coronopus*; also **crowfoot plantain. c.** The wild hyacinth, *Scilla nutans* (*north.* and *west.*). **d.** *Orchis mascula* and other species (*Yorks.* etc.). **e.** *Lotus corniculatus* (*Glouc.*). Cf. Britten and Holland *Plant-n.*

1578 LYTE *Dodoens* I. xxxii. 48 The seventh [kind of Geranium] is called in English Croefoote Geranium. *Ibid.* I. lxiv. 93 Of Buckhorne Plantayne.. two kindes of herbes, both comprehended under the name of Crowfoote. The first Crowfoote or Hartshorne, hath long narrow and hearie leaues. *Ibid.* 94 The second Crowfoote hath.. leaues much like to the leaues of the other Crowfoote Plantayne. **1828** *Craven Dial.*, *Crows'-feet Craw-feet*.. 2. Wild hyacinth.

3. = CROW'S-FOOT 1.

1614 J. DAVIES *Eglogue betw. Willy & Wernocke* 133 The crow-feet neere mine Eyne. **1831** *Blackw. Mag.* XXIX. 15 They.. who have served the Muses, till the crow-feet are blackening below their eyes. **1864** LOWELL *Fireside Trav.* 178 Tracing out.. every wrinkle and crowfoot.

4. *Naut.* **a.** A device consisting of a number of small cords rove through a long block or EUPHROE, used to suspend an awning, or to keep the topsail from chafing against the top-rim. **b.** 'A kind of stand, attached to the end of mess-tables, and hooked to a beam above' (Smyth *Sailor's Word-bk.*). **c.** = *beam-arm*: see BEAM *sb.*[1]

1627 CAPT. SMITH *Seaman's Gram.* v. 24 The martnets.. are.. small lines like crowfeet. **1692** —— ed. of *Seaman's Gram.* I. xiv. 65 The Spritsail Topsails Crowfoot. **1730** CAPT. W. WRIGLESWORTH *MS. Log-bk. of the 'Lyell'* 17 Sept., [We] Reeved our Crowfoots. **1769** FALCONER *Dict. Marine.* **1850** WEALE *Dict. Terms*, *Crow-foot*, a number of small lines rove through to suspend an awning. **1867** SMYTH *Sailor's Word-bk.* s.v., *Crowfoot* or *beam-arm* is also a crooked timber, extended from the side of a beam to the ship's side, in the wake of the hatchway, supplying the place of a beam.

5. A kind of embroidery-stitch. Also *attrib.*

The first quot. is doubtful.

[**1649** G. DANIEL *Trinarch., Rich. II*, ccxxvi, Shee's gone to Schoole; her Cross row and Crow feet Hinder the Huswiferye of her Clay-pies.] **1839** H. AINSWORTH *Jack Sheppard* ii, She wore a muslin cap, and pinners with crow-foot edging.

6. *Mil.* A caltrop; = CROW'S-FOOT 3.

1678 tr. *Gaya's Arms War* 102 The Crow-foot, or Casting Caltrop, are Iron Pricks, made in such a manner, that what way soever they be turned they have alwayes the point upwards. **1688** J. S. *Fortification* 125. **1851** D. WILSON *Preh. Ann.* (1863) I. 59 The ploughman turns up the craw-foot, the small Scottish horse-shoe, and the like tokens of [Bannockburn].

7. *Mining.* 'A tool with a side-claw, for grasping and recovering broken rods in deep bore-holes' (Raymond *Mining Gloss.*).

'crow-'footed, *a.*

1. Marked with 'crow's feet' about the eyes.

1834 MEDWIN *Angler in Wales* I. 2 His [eyes] were sunken and crow-footed. **1882** BESANT *Revolt of Man* i. 1 Her face.. was wrinkled and crow-footed in a thousand lines.

2. Having 'crow-steps' or 'corbie-steps'. *Sc.*

1829 *Anniversary*, The house.. presents sundry crow-footed, alias zigzagged, gables.

'crow-'garlic. A wild species of garlic, *Allium vineale*.

a **1387** *Sinon. Barthol.* (Anecd. Oxon.) 10 *Allium agreste*, crawegarlek. **1551** TURNER *Herbal* I. (1568) Biva, The.. crowe garleke or wylde garlyke. **1806** A. YOUNG *Agric. Essex* (1813) I. 8. **1861** MISS PRATT *Flower. Pl.* V. 269 Crow Garlic.. is one of the more common kinds of Garlic.

'crow-hop, *v.* [f. CROW *sb.*[1] + HOP *v.*[1]] *intr.* To hop like a crow; also *fig.* (see quot. 1897). Also as *sb.*, a hopping movement like that of a crow.

1897 *Chicago Tribune* 25 July 15/2 *Crow Hop*, to 'craw-fish'. 'Leedy has crow hopped out of the special session of the Legislature.' **1903** *Wide World Mag.* Apr. 548 The ways they try to throw their riders may be classed under three heads. The first is known as the crow-hop. **1907** S. E. WHITE *Arizona Nights* I. xiv. 207 Sometimes we crow-hopped solemnly around and around the prostrate Schwartz. **1944** R. F. ADAMS *Western Words* 45 *Crow hop*, when a horse jumps about with arched back and stiffened knees at a pretense of bucking.

crowing ('krəʊɪŋ), *vbl. sb.* [f. CROW *v.*[1] + -ING[1].] The action of the verb CROW. **1.** *lit.*

c **1386** CHAUCER *Nun's Pr. T.* 34 Wel sikerer was his crowyng in his logge Than is a clokke. **1483** *Cath. Angl.* 83 A Crowynge of rauens, *cra, vel crocitatus*. **1602** SHAKS. *Ham.* I. i. 157 It faded on the crowing of the Cocke. **1832** W. IRVING *Alhambra* II. 245 The faint crowing of a cock was now heard.

2. *transf.* and *fig.*

1483 CAXTON *Æsop* 133 Ouer moche talkyng letteth and to moche crowyng smarteth. **1573** G. HARVEY *Letter-bk.* (Camden) 34 Two years can hardly slip awai without sum crowing on the on part and more overcrowing on the other. **1860** EMERSON *Cond. Life, Fate* Wks. (Bohn) II. 317 Nothing is more disgusting than the crowing about liberty by slaves, as most men are.

'crowing, *ppl. a.* [f. as prec. + -ING[2].] That crows. In *Path.*, applied to the sound made in inspiration in hooping-cough and croup.

c **1620** Z. BOYD *Zion's Flowers* (1855) 68 Ere crowing Heraulds summon up the daye. **1824** *Blackw. Mag.* XV. 471/1 The joyous, crowing laugh of that little creature. **1828** SCOTT *F.M. Perth* xxii, Her infant.. already black in the face, and uttering the gasping crowing sound, which gives the popular name to the complaint. **1841** TWEEDIE *Libr. Pract. Med.* III. 61 *Laryngismus Stridulus*.. the Crowing Disease.

Comb. **1710** E. WARD *British Hudibras* 123 They'd been so crowing sure Of winning All.

†**'crowish,** *a. rare.* Pertaining to a crow, crow-like.

1552 HULOET, Crowyshe or of a crowe, *coracinus, coruinus*.

crowk(e, var. of CROOK *v.*[2], to croak, CROUKE.

crowkoun, var. of *crawkoun*, CRACON *Obs.*

c **1450** *Nominale* in Wr.-Wülcker 741/10 *De cibis generalibus.. Hoc crimium*, crowkoun.

†**crowl,** *v. Obs.* Also 6 crawle, courl. [app. onomatopœic, having the initial part of *croak* and kindred words, while the latter part expresses prolonged sound: cf. *growl*.] *intr.* To rumble or make a sound in the stomach and bowels. Hence **'crowling** *vbl. sb.*

1519 HORMAN *Vulg.* 36 His bely maketh a great crowlynge. **1530** PALSGR. 502/2 My bely crowleth, I wene there be some padockes in it. *c* **1575** J. STILL *Gamm. Gurton* II. i, My guts they yawle, crawle, and all my belly rumbleth. **1717** *Dict. Rust. Urb. & Bot.*, *Crowling*, a Distemper in Cattel, called by some, The crying and fretting of the Guts, the Signs whereof are the Flux of the Belly and abundance of Phlegm.

†**crow-leek.** *Obs.* A name given, according to Gerarde and later writers, to the wild hyacinth (*Scilla nutans*): by earlier writers sometimes to crow-garlic.

c **1000** ÆLFRIC *Gram.* (Z.) 311 *Hermodactula vel tidolosa* crawan leac. *c* **1000** *Sax. Leechd.* I. 376 Nim.. þa wyrt.. þæt is on ure geþeoda þæt greata crauleac. *a* **1387** *Sinon. Barthol.* (Anecd. Oxon.) 38 *Scordion*, allium agreste, florem habet blauum. Similis est allio ortolano, florem habet indum, angl. Crowelek. *c* **1450** *Alphita* (Anecd. Oxon.) 177 *Scordam*, i. alium agreste.. angl. wildelek uel crauwelek. **1597** GERARDE *Herbal* App. to Table.

crowling ('krəʊlɪŋ). *nonce-wd.* [f. CROW *sb.* + -LING.] A little or young crow.

1609 BP. W. BARLOW *Answ. Nameless Cath.* 327 A more vaine Crowling.. then that Iack-Daw, which Æsop describes. **1887** *Blackw. Mag.* Nov. 705 He is.. ready in a grandmotherly way to think all his crowlings white.

crowling *vbl. sb.*: see CROWL *v.*

crowme, obs. form of CRUMB.

crown (kraʊn), *sb.* Forms: α. (1 corona, acc. -an); 2–4 corune, 4–5 coron(e, coroune, corun, 4–6 coroun, 5 corown(e, 6 coronne; β. 2–4 crune, 4 crun, crone, cron, 4–6 croune, croun, 4–7 crowne, (5 crounne, crowun, 6 crownde), 7– crown. [ME. *croun(e*, earlier *crun(e*, syncopated from *coroune, corune, corone*, a. AF. *corone*, in early ONF. *corune, curune* (central OF. *corone, coronne*, in 13th c. *couronne*) = Pr., Sp., It. *corona*:—L. *corōna* crown, *orig.* wreath, chaplet.

The 11th c. *corona* in the O.E. Chron. was directly from L. The syncopated *crune* was used already in the 12th c.; but the fuller form survived beside it to the 16th c.]

I. 1. a. An ornamental fillet, wreath, or similar encircling ornament for the head, worn for personal adornment, or as a mark of honour or achievement; a coronal or wreath of leaves or flowers.

c **1325** *E.E. Allit. P.* A. 237 A pyȝt coroune ȝet wer þat gyrle, Of mariorys & non oþer ston. **1382** WYCLIF *Ezek.* xxiv. 23 Ȝe shulen haue corowns [Vulg. *coronas*] in ȝoure heedis, and.. ȝe shulen not weile nor wepe. *c* **1386** CHAUCER *Sec. Nun's T.* 221 This aungel had of roses and of lilie Corounes tuo. **1483** *Cath. Angl.* 84 A Crowne, *laurea*. **1592** R. D. *Hypnerotomachia* 65 Nymphes.. about their heades wearing Garlandes and Crownes of Violets. **1610** SHAKS. *Temp.* IV. i. 129 You Nimphs cald Nayades.. With your sedg'd crownes. **1720** OZELL *Vertot's Rom. Rep.* I. IV. 241 He had obtained fourteen Civic Crowns.. three Mural Crowns. **1766** PORNY *Heraldry* (1787) 207 The Romans had ten different Crowns to reward Martial exploits, and extraordinary services done to the Republic as Mural-Crown.. Naval or Rostral-Crown, etc. **1877** J. D. CHAMBERS *Div. Worship* 295 Flowers, sometimes woven into garlands and crowns.

b. *fig.* Chiefly referring to the wreath with which the victor was crowned in the ancient Grecian and Roman games, or to the AUREOLA of a martyr, virgin, or doctor, as victor over the world, the flesh, or the devil; usually the sense is more or less idealized or spiritualized (*e.g.* in ***crown of martyrdom, martyr's crown; no cross, no crown***, etc.), or transferred to any kind of honourable distinction or reward bestowed upon a victor.

c **1175** *Lamb. Hom.* 39 Drihten bihat þon wakiende ane crune þet scal beon seofeside brihtre þene þa sunne. *a* **1225** *Ancr. R.* 160 þeos þreo maner men habbeð ine heouene mid ouer fulle mede—crune upe crune. **1382** WYCLIF *2 Tim.* iv. 8 In the tothir tyme a crowne of riȝtwysnesse is kept to me. —— *Rev.* ii. 10 Be thou feithful vnto the deeth, and I shal ȝiue to thee a coroun of lijf. **1526** *Pilgr. Perf.* (W. de W. 1531) 273 Whiche is onely reserued for the finall crowne and rewarde of all our labours. **1839** YEOWELL *Anc. Brit. Ch.* Pref. (1847) 11 Some.. received the crown of martyrdom during the Diocletian persecution. **1855** H. REED *Lect. Eng. Lit.* v. (1878) 167 His brow, on which four-score years had placed their crown of glory.

[See AUREOLA, quots. 1483, 1626.]

2. *spec.* **a.** The cincture or covering for the head, made of or adorned with precious metals and jewels, worn by a monarch as a mark or symbol of sovereignty; a diadem.

1085 *O.E. Chron.* (Laud MS.), Her se cyng bær his corona and heold his hired on Winceastre. **1111** *Ibid.* On þison geare ne bær se kyng Henri his coronan. *c* **1200** ORMIN 8180 Onn hiss hæfedd wærenn twa Gildene cruness sette. *c* **1250** *Gen. & Ex.* 2638 His corune on his heued he dede. **1297** R. GLOUC. (1724) 376 þre syþe he ber croune a-ȝer. *c* **1385** CHAUCER *L.G.W.* Prol. 216 A quene.. a whit Corone sche ber. *a* **1400–50** *Alexander* 193 With corone & with cony-schantis as it a kynge were. **1535** COVERDALE *Esther* ii. 17 He set the quenes croune vpon hir heade. **1597** SHAKS. *2 Hen. IV*, III. i. 31 Vneasie lyes the Head that weares a Crowne. **1603–4** *Act 1–2 Jas. I*, c. 1 §3 Sithence the Imperial Crown of this Realm descended to you. **1845** S. AUSTIN *Ranke's Hist. Ref.* I. 343 The pope's triple crown. **1870** JEAFFRESON *Bk. abt. Clergy* II. 227 A chief influence in the many forces that put the crown on his son's head.

b. Christ's crown of thorns.

c **950** *Lindisf. Gosp.* John xix. 2 *Coronam de spinis*, of ðornum ða corona *vel* þæt sigbeg of ðornum. *c* **1175** *Lamb. Hom.* 121 Mid þornene crune his heaued wes icruned. **1375** BARBOUR *Bruce* III. 460 The naylis, and the sper, And the croune that Ihesu couth ber. *c* **1400** MAUNDEV. (Roxb.) ii. 7 þat coroun was made of braunches of albespyne. **1611** BIBLE *Matt.* xxvii. 29 When they had platted a crowne of thornes, they put it vpon his head. **1836** MACGILLIVRAY *Humboldt's Trav.* xxii. 315 Beggars carrying a crown of thorns on their heads, asked alms, with crucifixes in their hands.

c. ***crown of thorns*** (***starfish***): a poisonous starfish, *Acanthaster planci* or *A. ellisi*.

1964 *Medical Jrnl. Australia* 18 Apr. 592/2 The 'crown of thorns' starfish is to be found entwined in the branches of living coral, on which it feeds. **1969** *Sci. Jrnl.* Nov. 15/1 The starfish in question, *Acanthaster planci*, is better known as the 'Crown-of-Thorns' starfish since its upper surface is covered with prominent spines. *Ibid.* (*caption*) Starfish, known as the 'Crown-of-thorns', is wreaking havoc amongst coral reefs in the Indian and Pacific Oceans.

3. *fig.* The sovereignty, authority, or dominion of which a crown is the symbol; the rule, position, or empire of a monarch.

Chiefly in phrases in which the sense, originally literal, has ceased to be analysed.

1340–70 *Alex. & Dind.* 978 Emperour alixandre..þe kiddeste y-core þat corone weldus. **1393** Gower *Conf.* III. 167 What emperour was entronized The firste day of his corone. *c* **1460** Fortescue *Abs. & Lim. Mon.* xix, Þat he hath then enriched is crowne with..riches and possescions. **1577** B. Googe *Heresbach's Husb.* I. (1586) 6 Saul from his Asses, and David from his sheepe were called to the crowne. **1590** Shaks. *Com. Err.* I. i. 144 Against my Crowne, my oath, my dignity. **1659** *Vulgar Err. Censured* 27 Osiris King of Egypt thought it not below his crown to have commerce with Physicall rules. **1796** Morse *Amer. Geog.* I. 114 John Cabot..obtained a..commission..to discover unknown lands and annex them to the crown. **1871** Freeman *Norm. Conq.* (1876) IV. xvii. 68 A conqueror whose crown might at any moment be threatened by a Scandinavian rival.

4. *fig.* The wearer of a crown; the monarch in his official character; the supreme governing power of a state under a monarchical constitution.

1579 Tomson *Calvin's Serm. Tim.* 985/2 Hee might haue ben thought to haue beene of the crowne, as the Kings daughters adopted sonne. **1714** Swift *Pres. State of Affairs*, He was treated contemptibly enough by the young princes of France, even during the war; is now wholly neglected by that crown. **1734** tr. *Rollin's Anc. Hist.* (1827) VII. xviii. i. 366 During the interval of this truce a treaty was negotiated between the two crowns. **1780** Burke *Corr.* (1844) II. 338 The resentment of the crown is a serious thing. **1788** Priestley *Lect. Hist.* v. xlvi. 342 The commons..ventured to..give advice to the crown. **1827** Hallam *Const. Hist.* (1876) III. xiv. 90 The assertion of passive obedience to the crown grew obnoxious to the crown itself. **1844** H. H. Wilson *Brit. India* I. 243 The pardon of the Crown was granted.

5. *fig.* That which adorns like a crown; a chief or crowning ornament.

c **1368** Chaucer *Compl. Pite* 75 Ye be also the corowne of beaute. **1382** Wyclif *Prov.* xii. 4 A bisi womman a croune is to hir man. *Ibid.* xvi. 31 The croune of dignete elde, that in the weie of riȝtwisnesse shal be founde. **1611** Shaks. *Wint. T.* iii. ii. 95 The crowne and comfort of my Life (your Fauor) I doe giue lost. **1662** Stillingfl. *Orig. Sacr.* ii. vii. §5 Every place of holy Scripture may have its crown, but some may have their *aureolæ*, a greater excellency. **1829** Southey *All for Love* iii, They were the pride, the joy, The crown of his old age. **1861** Tulloch *Eng. Purit.* iii. 390 It was the very singleness of his spiritual energy, that made his excellence and crown.

II. Something having or bearing the figure or the representation of a crown.

6. a. Any crown-shaped ornament. **b.** A figure of a crown for heraldic or other purposes. **c.** A frequent sign, and hence name, of an inn, alone or in combination, as the *Crown and Sceptre*, *Rose and Crown*, etc.

c **1250** *Gen. & Ex.* 3789 Corunes at ðe alter of bras. **1766** Porny *Heraldry* (1787) 208 The Mural-Crown..Examples of this Crown are frequently met with in Achievements. **1875** W. McIlwraith *Guide Wigtownshire* 55 Bearing two unicorns and a lion rampant and the Crown. **1885** E. B. Evans *Philatelic Handbk.* 118 [1d. stamp] Watermark a Small Crown; imperforate. *Ibid.* 160 Jamaica: Watermark a Pineapple..Wmk. Crown and CC... Wmk. Crown and CA.

d. ***Crown and Anchor***, a gambling game played with three dice each having faces bearing a crown, an anchor, and the four card-suits; the players place their bets on a board or cloth bearing similar figures.

1880 G. A. Sala *America Revisited* (1882) II. vi. 78 The Crown and Anchor booth at Greenwich Fair. **1903** [see banker[2] 4]. **1917** A. G. Empey *From Fire Step* 125 The two most popular games are 'Crown and Anchor' and 'House'. **1935** *Punch's Almanack* CLXXXVIII. p. viii/1 The..new Dukes..played Crown and Anchor in the corridors. **1969** R. C. Bell *Board & Table Games* II. v. 84 The bets are the same as in Crown and Anchor.

7. *Astron.* The name of two constellations, the ***Northern*** and ***Southern Crown***: see corona 8.

[*c* **1385** Chaucer *L.G.W.* 339 *Ariadne*, And in the signe of Taurus men may see The stonys of hire Corone shyne clere.] **1551** Recorde *Cast. Knowl.* (1556) 264 The northe Croune, called also Ariadnes Croune. *Ibid.* 270 There is the Croune of the southe, formed of 13 small starres. **1870** Proctor *Other Worlds* x. 246 Such variable stars as the one which recently blazed out in the Northern Crown.

8. A name of various coins; originally one bearing the imprint of a crown. **a.** *orig.* A translation of the French name *couronne* (*denier à la couronne*), given to a gold coin bearing on the obverse a large crown, issued by Philip of Valois in 1339, or applied to the *écu à la couronne* of Charles VI, issued in and after 1384, in which the shield was surmounted by a crown; and from the 15th to the 18th c. the common English name for the F. *écu*, as well as for other foreign coins of similar value; in more recent times used also for the *krone* of various northern countries. ***Crown of the Sun*** [F. *escu sol*, Cotgr., *écu d'or au soleil*, Littré]: a gold écu much current in England in the 15–16th c., the type of the first English Crown: see b.

1430 Lydg. *Chron. Troy* iv. xxx, The change is not so redy for to make In Lumbarde Strete of crowne nor doket. **1433** Caxton *G. de la Tour* C iij, They dare bye gownes of three or foure score crownes. **1525** Ld. Berners *Froiss.* II. clxvii. [clxiii.] 462 The tresourers made redy the money in Crownes of the Sonne, and put it into foure cofers. **1530** Palsgr. 211/1 Crowne, a pece of golde, *escu.* **1548** Hall *Chron.* (1809) 313 That the French Kyng..should paie..without delaie lxxv M Crounes of the Sunne & yerely l M crounes to be paied at London, whiche, accoumptyng a crowne at iiij s, amounteth to x M l. **1577** Harrison *England* ii. xxv. (1877) i. 364 Of forren coines we haue..the French and Flemish crownes, onlie currant among vs, so long as they hold weight. **1597** Shaks. *2 Hen. IV*, iii. ii. 236 Stand my friend, and heere is foure Harry tenne shillings in French Crownes for you. **1639** Massinger *Unnat. Combat* i. i, Present your bag, crammed with crowns of the sun. **1727–51** Chambers *Cycl.*, *Crown*, in commerce, is a general name for coins both foreign and domestic, of or near the value of five shillings sterling..as the French ecu, which we call the French crown, struck in 1641 for sixty sols, or three livres; also the patagon, dollar, ducatoon, rix-dollar, and piastre, or piece of eight. **1819** Shelley *Cenci* iv. ii, One who thinks A thousand crowns excellent market price For an old murderer's life.

b. A coin (when last minted, silver) of Great Britain of the value of five shillings; hence the sum of five shillings.

The gold 'Crown of the Rose' was coined by Henry VIII in 1526, in imitation of the French Crown of the Sun of Louis XII or Francis I; crowns and half-crowns in silver have been in circulation since the reign of Edw. VI.

1542 Recorde *Gr. Artes* (1575) 197 A Crowne containeth 5s.: & the halfe Crowne 2s. 6d. How bee it there is another Crowne of 4s. 6d., whiche is knowen by the rose side: for the rose hath no Crowne ouer it, as in the other Crowne, but it is enuironed on the 4 quarters with 4 floure deluce. **1577** Harrison *England* ii. xxv. (1877) i. 363 The new gold..Our peeces now currant are..quarters of souereigns (otherwise called crownes) and halfe crownes. **1688** R. Holme *Armoury* iii. 28/2 A Crown, or five Shillings Gold, is the least peece we have in England. **1712** Steele *Spect.* No. 266 ¶2, I..could not forbear giving her a Crown. **1732** Law *Serious C.* vii. (ed. 2) 96 She will toss him half a Crown, or a Crown. **1838** Dickens *O. Twist* xviii, I'll bet a crown!

9. A size of paper, originally watermarked with the figure of a crown.

It measures 15 × 20 inches; in U.S. 15 × 19 inches.

1712 *Act 10 Anne* in *Lond. Gaz.* No. 5018/3 Paper called ..Genoa Crown. **1766** C. Leadbetter *Royal Gauger* ii. xiv. (ed. 6) 372 Large Post, Crown, Printing Foolscap. **1790** Wolcott (P. Pindar) *Benev. Ep. to Sylv. Urban* Wks. 1812 II. 261 His nice discerning Knowledge none deny, On Crown, Imperial, Foolscap, and Demy. **1878** *Print. Trades Jrnl.* xxv. 17 A bulky crown 8vo, selling at threepence.

III. Something having the circular form of a crown or encircling wreath.

†**10. a.** The tonsure of a cleric; cf. corona 5.

c **1205** Lay. 13110 Þe hod hongede adun, alse he hudde his crune. *a* **1300** *Cursor M.* 27251 (Cott.) Or cron þat es o clergi merc. *c* **1325** *Poem Times Edw. II* 115 in *Pol. Songs* (Camden) 329 Some beareth croune of acolyte. *c* **1380** Wyclif *Wks.* (1880) 467 Crounne & cloþ maken no prest. *c* **1449** Pecock *Repr.* iii. xvii. 387 Whanne a persoon is mad first clerk and takith his firste corown for to be therbi oon of the clergie. **1480** Caxton *Chron. Eng.* lxvii. 50 This traytour put vpp on hym an abyte of Relygyon and lete shaue hym a brode crowne. **1533** Elyot *Cast. Helthe* (1541) 80 b, Ashamyd of theyr croune that reverend token of the order of preesthode.

†**b.** ***priest's crown***: a popular name of dandelion seed. *Obs.*

1530 Palsgr. 179 *Barbedieu*, the sede of dandelyon whiche children call preestes crownes. *Ibid.* 258/2 Prestes crowne that flyeth about in somer, *barbedieu*.

11. = corona 1.

1563 Fulke *Meteors* (1640) 41 b, This thick and watry cloud is not..under the Sunne, for then it would make the Circles, called crownes or garlands. **1815** T. Forster *Atmos. Phænom.* 97 Meteorologists have spoken of halos and crowns of light. **1823** Scoresby *Jrnl.* 283 The anthelion..combined with the concentric crowns, has, I believe, been observed by very few.

12. †**a.** A whorl or verticil of flowers. **b.** = corona 7 b. **c.** A circular projection or rim round the top of the fruit of some plants. (See also 25 b.)

1578 Lyte *Dodoens* ii. lxx. 239 The small floures are purple, and grow like Crownes or whorles at the toppe of the stemmes. **1870** Hooker *Stud. Flora* 202 *Chrysanthemum leucanthemum*..Fruits all terete equally ribbed..with a small crown. *Ibid.* 364 *Amaryllideæ*..Perianth superior.. with sometimes a crown at the mouth of the tube. *Ibid.* 365 *Narcissus Pseudo-narcissus*..crown campanulate.

†**13.** A ring. **a.** in *Geom.* **b.** A ring or circle of persons, etc. *Obs.*

c **1611** Chapman *Iliad* xv. 7 With a crown of princes compassed. **1706** Phillips (ed. Kersey) *s.v.*, In Geometry, *Crown* signifies a plain Ring included between two Concentric Perimeters. [Hence in later Dicts.]

14. A circular chandelier; = corona 3.

1845 *Ecclesiologist* Mar. 91 The choir is lighted by two crowns, each carrying six tapers. **1853** Rock *Ch. of Fathers* IV. 28 Beautiful, ornamented metal hoops called 'crowns', which hung from the church's roof. **1877** J. D. Chambers *Div. Worship* 5.

15. *Surg.* The circular serrated edge of a trepan.

1758 J. S. *Le Dran's Observ. Surg.* (1771) 61, I applied the Crown of the Trepan. **1787** C. B. Trye in *Med. Commun.* II. 149, I used a large crown.

16. In med.L. *corona ecclesiæ* was the circular apse of a great church behind the choir; hence, according to some, the name ***Becket's*** or ***St. Thomas's Crown***, given to the eastern apse or circular tower of Canterbury Cathedral. (But the origin of the name is much disputed.)

1703 Somner *Canterbury* 90 Upon the beautifying of St. Thomas's Crown, that is, Becket's Crown, was expended.. 115*l.* 12*s.* **1726** Dart *Canterb.* 30. **1816** Woolnoth *Canterb.* 72 We enter the tower..called Becket's Crown, in which stands the patriarchal chair. **1845** Willis *Canterb. Cath.* 56 *note.*

IV. Something which occupies the position of a crown; the top or highest part of anything, the vertex or vertical surface.

17. a. The top part of the skull; the vertex. (See esp. quot. 1589.)

c **1300** *Havelok* 568 Hise croune he ther crakede Ageyn a gret ston. *a* **1300** *Cursor M.* 5447 (Cott.) He laid his hand a-pon þair cron, And gaue þam serekin beneson. *c* **1380** *Sir Ferumb.* 303 Cristes cors come on hure croun. *c* **1400** *Lanfranc's Cirurg.* 111 Whanne þat þe crounne of þe heed is perfiȝt þe heed is maad in þis maner. *c* **1450** *St. Cuthbert* (Surtees) 923 How cuthbert childe stode on his croune. *c* **1485** *Digby Myst.* (1882) iv. 310 From the Crowne of the hede vnto the too. **1589** Puttenham *Eng. Poesie* iii. (Arb.) 189 In deede crowne is the highest ornament of a Princes head..or els the top of a mans head, where the haire windes about. **1610** Shaks. *Temp.* iv. i. 233 From toe to crowne hee'l fill our skins with pinches. **1816** Keatinge *Trav.* (1817) I. 222 The Arabs..with their bare shaven crowns exposed to its full rays. **1887** Besant *The World went* xiv. 112 He would crack the crown of any man who ventured to make love to his girl.

b. By extension: The head.

1594 Shaks. *Rich. III*, iii. ii. 43 Ile haue this Crown of mine cut from my shoulders, Before Ile see the Crowne so foule mis-plac'd. **1628** Prynne *Love-lockes* 49 Those men who curle their crownes like women. **1692** R. L'Estrange *Josephus, Antiq.* xvii. xiv. (1733) 477 With these Crotchets in his Crown, away he went for Rome. **1728** R. North *Mem. Musick* (1846) 125 A cappriccio came in his crowne to make the like for Paris.

c. The eminence on the head of a whale, in which the blow-holes are situated.

1820 Scoresby *Acc. Arctic Reg.* II. 219 Whales may frequently be seen..elevating and breaking the ice with their crowns. **1822** G. W. Manby *Voy. Greenland* (1823) 45 The pointed part of the head, termed the crown, where the spiracles or blow-holes are situated.

18. The rounded summit of a mountain or other elevation.

1583 Stanyhurst *Æneis* ii. (Arb.) 69 My father to the crowne of mounten I lifted. **1605** Shaks. *Lear* iv. vi. 67 Vpon the crowne o' th' Cliffe. **1725** De Foe *Voy. round World* (1840) 352 The land went ascending up to a round crown or knoll. **1808** Scott *Marm.* iii. xxii, The rampart seek, whose circling crown, etc. **1872** Jenkinson *Guide Eng. Lakes* (1879) 142 A gradual ascent to the crown of the hill.

19. a. The highest or central part of an arch or of any arched surface, as a field ridge, a road, causeway, bridge, etc. ***crown of the causeway***: the central and most prominent part of the pavement or street.

1635 Rutherford *Lett.* (1862) I. 149 Truth will yet keep the crown of the causey in Scotland. **1765** A. Dickson *Treat. Agric.* ii. (ed. 2) 282 When the crown of a ridge is turned into a furrow. **1795** Burke *Regic. Peace* iv. Wks. IX. 122 They will take the crown of the causeway. **1816** Scott *Antiq.* xxi, I keep the crown o' the causey when I gae to the borough. **1856** *Jrnl. R. Agric. Soc.* XVII. i. 328 The crown of the ridge is isolated, raised out of reach of the re-active moisture from below. **1872** O. Shipley *Gloss. Eccl. Terms* 40 Every arch is said to be surmounted if the height of its crown above the level of its impost be greater than half its span. **1877** Mrs. Oliphant *Makers Flor.* v. 127 Marching with honest..steps..holding the crown of the causeway. **1879** Thomson & Tait *Nat. Phil.* I. i. §60 According as the crown of the solar tide precedes or follows the crown of the lunar tide.

b. The arched surface of a bowling-green. (Cf. *crown green*.)

1897 *Encycl. Sport* I. 128/1 In Lancashire each green has a 'crown' varying in rise and slope. **1904** S. Aylwin *Gentle Art of Bowling* iii. 15 Greens with a crown or rise in the centre..are common in many parts of England.

20. The top of a hat or other covering for the head; *esp.* the flat circular top of the modern hat.

1678 Evelyn *Mem.* (1857) II. 126 They had furred caps with coped crowns. **1709** Steele & Swift *Tatler* No. 71 ¶8 From the Crown of his Nightcap to the Heels of his Shoes. **1758** Mitchell in *Phil. Trans.* LI. 225 As broad as a hat crown. **1891** Baring-Gould *In Troub. Land* ii. 28 Tired.. of looking into the crown of her hat.

21. The rounded top of a brewer's copper.

1669 Sturmy *Mariner's Mag.* v. viii. 34 How to Measure a Segment or portion of a Globe or Sphere, which serves for a..Crown in a Brewers Copper. **1712** in *Lond. Gaz.* No. 5006/4 Coppers with..taper Sides..and Crown for the Stilheads.

22. The flattened or rounded roof of a tent or building.

1725 De Foe *Voy. round World* (1840) 268 A large canopy ..spread like the crown of a tent. **1869** Sir E. J. Reed *Shipbuild.* xi. 235 Watertight flats, such as crowns to magazines, platforms, etc. **1887** Stevenson *Underwoods* i. xxxv. 69 Its crown Of glittering glass.

23. The top, with the canons, of a bell.

1756 *Dict. Arts & Sc.* s.v. *Bell*, The pallet or crown which is the cover of the Bell, and supports the staple of the clapper within. **1857** Lukis *Acc. Church Bells* 21 The crown or head of the bell, for the formation of the canons, is then fitted to the top.

24. *Arch.* The uppermost member of a cornice; the corona or larmier; = CORONA 4.

1611 COTGR., *Couronne*..(In Architecture) also, the Corona, crowne, or member of greatest sayle, in a Cornish.

25. In plants: **a.** The leafy head of a tree or shrub; **b.** The cluster of leaves on the top of a pine-apple; **c.** The flattened top of a seed, etc.; **d.** *crown of the root*: the summit of the root whence the stem arises; the subterranean bud of a herbaceous perennial.

1589 PUTTENHAM *Eng. Poesie* III. (Arb.) 189 To call the top of a tree..the crowne of a tree;..because such terme.. is transported from a mans head to a hill or tree, therefore it is called by metaphore, or the figure of transport. **1698** T. FROGER *Relat. Voy.* 59 The Ananas grows like an Artichoak ..It bears a Crown of the same leaves. **1846** J. BAXTER *Libr. Pract. Agric.* (ed. 4) I. 157 Plant some of the largest and best roots early in spring..inserting the crown about two inches below the surface. **1847** *Illust. Lond. News* 17 July 36/3 In preparing to serve a pine-apple, at table, first remove the crown. **1851** GLENNY *Handbk. to Flowergarden* 7 [Primulas] are propagated by dividing the tufts into separate crowns with roots attached. **1857** LIVINGSTONE *Trav.* xviii. 344 It rises thirty or forty feet..and there spreads out a second crown where it can enjoy a fair share of the sun's rays. **1863** *Jrnl. R. Agric. Soc.* XXIV. I. 219 The men cut the plants [carrots] off under the crown, otherwise they will shoot again. **1870** HOOKER *Stud. Flora* 255 *Hyoscyamus*..Capsule ..bursting transversely at the crown.

26. *Farriery.* The CORONET of a horse's hoof.

1611 COTGR., *Couronne*..also, the crowne, top, or beginning of a horses hoofe.

27. The upper part of a deer's horn; the crest, as of a bird.

1774 GOLDSM. *Nat. Hist.* (1862) I. II. v. 325 All the rest which grow afterwards, till you come to the top, which is called the crown, are called royal-antlers.

28. a. *Anat.* That portion of a tooth which appears beyond the gums.

1804 ABERNETHY *Surg. Obs.* 58 The whole crown of the tooth may be destroyed to the level of the gum. **1854** *Jrnl. R. Agric. Soc.* XV. II. 288 The several parts of a tooth are the crown, neck, and fang.

b. *Dentistry.* An artificial structure made to cover or replace the natural crown of a tooth.

1820 L. S. PARMLY *Lect. Nat. Hist. Teeth* iii. 75 The pivot soon wears away the fang. Thus the artificial crown becoming loose, it drops out. **1885** I. E. & R. E. CLIFFORD *Crown, Bar, & Bridge-work* 6 The crown fits over the root like a cap. **1963** J. OSBORNE *Dental Mechanics* (ed. 5) xxiii. 415 Crowns may be of two types, first those that cover the natural crown of the tooth.. Second are those crowns that replace entirely the crown of the natural tooth.

29. In lapidaries' work, the part of a cut gem above the girdle.

1875 URE *Dict. Arts* II. 25 s.v. *Diamond, Crown*, the upper work of the rose, which all centres in the point at the top, and is bounded by the horizontal ribs.

30. The end of the shank of an anchor, or the point from which the arms proceed.

1875 BEDFORD *Sailor's Pock. Bk.* vi. (ed. 2) 216 If anchoring a boat on rocky ground, bend the cable to the crown of the anchor, and stop it to the ring before letting go.

31. a. *Mech.* Any terminal flat member of a structure; the face of an anvil.

b. Short for CROWN-GLASS.

1854 C. TOMLINSON *Cycl. Useful Arts* I. 761/1 Regarding glass as a chemical,..the various kinds have been distributed in the following manner:..2..English crown,.. 3..foreign crown. **1902** *Encycl. Brit.* XXV. 41/2 The experiments of the eminent Jena glass-makers with phosphate crowns and borate flints. *Ibid.*, A triple combination of ordinary crown and flint with a boro-silicate flint. **1966** *McGraw-Hill Encycl. Sci. & Technol.* IX. 351 (*caption*) Heavy flints, flints, light flints, extra-light flints, short crowns, crowns, borosilicate crowns.

c. The boring end of a diamond or similar drill.

1883 *Encycl. Brit.* XVI. 444/1 The working part of the drill consists of the so-called crown, which is a short piece of tube made of cast steel, at one end of which a number of black diamonds are fastened into small cavities.

d. A term used to designate the fineness of wire used in carding operations.

1884 W. S. B. MCLAREN *Spinning* ix. 211 The crown..is the number of wires in 1 inch *along* it.

†**32.** A kind of verse, in which the last line of each stanza is repeated to head the next stanza.

1580 SIDNEY *Arcadia* (1622) 217 Strephon againe began this Dizaine, which was answered vnto him in that kinde of verse which is called the crowne.

33. *fig.* That which crowns anything; the crowning, consummation, completion, or perfection.

c **1611** CHAPMAN *Iliad* II. 104 We fly, not putting on the crown of our so long-held war, Of which there yet appears no end. **1784** COWPER *Task* v. 904 Thou art of all thy gifts thyself the crown. **1806-7** J. BERESFORD *Miseries Hum. Life* (1826) II. x, The crown of the catastrophe. **1884** W. C. SMITH *Kildrostan* 94 The crown of culture is a perfect taste, Which lacking, men are blind and cannot see The higher wisdom.

V. 34. *attrib.* and *Comb.* **a.** Of or pertaining to a regal crown or to the Crown (senses 2-4): as ***crown demesne, due, duty, gleek, government, grant, oath, property, rape, rent, revenue, right, vassal***. **b.** In the translated titles of foreign (chiefly Polish) officials, as ***crown chamberlain, ensign, general, hunter, referendary, standard-bearer, watchmaster***. **c.** Pertaining to the coin, as ***crown cribbage, table, whist***; ***crown-broad*** adj. **d.** Used to designate a quality or brand of an article, as ***crown log, soap, ware***. **e.** Pertaining to the top of the head, corona of a plant, etc., as ***crown bloom, end, lock, set***; ***crown-distempered*** adj. Also ***crown-like*** adj.

1852 *Beck's Florist* 236 Chance *crown-blooms from the general stock. **1830** GALT *Lawrie T.* v. viii. (1849) 226 *Crown-broad buttons. **1704** *Lond. Gaz.* No. 4073/3 The Crown-General Lubomirski and the *Crown-Chamberlain his Brother had made their Submission. **1764** *Priv. Lett. Ld. Malmesbury* I. 105, I played one rubber of *crown cribbage. **1635** QUARLES *Embl.* I. ix. (1718) 37 Like *crown-distemper'd fools, despise True riches. **1875** W. MCILWRAITH *Guide Wigtownshire* 76 McDowall had fallen behind in the payment of certain *crown-dues, and was outlawed. **1684** *Scanderbeg Rediv.* iii. 32 Soon after the *Crown-General Potosky departing this Life. **1687** DRYDEN *Hind & P.* II. 410 You seem crown-gen'ral of the land. **1647** N. BACON *Disc. Govt. Eng.* I. xlvii. (1739) 78 The Popes meaned no less Game than *Crown-glieke with the King and people. **1883** J. FISKE in *Harper's Mag.* Feb. 414/2 The Government of Virginia, after the suppression of the Company in 1624, was a **Crown* government: the governor and council were appointed by the king. **1796** *Hull Advertiser* 3 Sept. 2/3 A parcel of fine wainscot Riga *Crown logs. **1649** MILTON *Eikon.* xxviii. 524 The ancient *Crown-Oath of Alfred. **1874** HELPS *Soc. Press.* iv. 62 Who manages all the *Crown property about here? **1587** *Mirr. Mag., Rudacke* i, *Crownerape accounted but cunning and skill. **1710** *Irish Ho. Com.* 6 June, in *Lond. Gaz.* No. 4706/2 Quit-Rents, *Crown-Rents and Composition Rents. **1614** SELDEN *Titles Hon.* 243 Before him..[was]..the *crown-reuenew accompted. **1592** WARNER *Alb. Eng.* VII. xxxiv. (R.), To whom, from her, the *crowne-right of Lancastrians did accrewe. **1892** *Daily News* 5 Oct. 3/1 The gulf which separates us from those who question the Deity, the atonement, and the crown rights of the Son of God. **1725** BRADLEY *Fam. Dict.* s.v. *Liquorish*, The best sets..are *Crown sets or heads got from the very top of the root. **1684** *Scanderbeg Rediv.* v. 95 Troops under the Command of the *Crown-standard-bearer. **1811** L. M. HAWKINS *C'tess & Gertr.* II. 57 'Ever a *crown-table here, do you know?' **1814** SCOTT *Chivalry* (1874) 26 The nobles and high *crown-vassals. **1881** *Porcelain Works, Worcester* 10 *Crown Ware [superior earthenware], a speciality. **1684** *Scanderbeg Rediv.* iv. 86 The *Crown-Watchmaster was posted next the Neister. **1753** A. MURPHY *Gray's-Inn Jrnl.* No. 34 She plays *Crown Whist.

35. Special combs.: **crown-agent**, agent for the Crown; in Scotland, 'an agent or solicitor who, under the Lord Advocate, takes charge of criminal proceedings' (Bell *Dict. Sc. Law*); **crown-antler**, the topmost antler or ramification of a stag's horn; **crown-bark**, Peruvian bark obtained from *Cinchona officinalis*; **crown-beam**, the cross-joint or cross-beam at the apex of a pair of brace beams; **crown-beard**, a composite plant of the genus *Verbesina*, a native of America; †**crown-benet**, ?a benet who has received the tonsure; **crown-berry**, the Cape cranberry, *Dovyalis rhamnoides*; **crown-bone**, the bone of the 'crown' of a whale, see 17 c; **crown borer**, a drill having a cutter equipped with diamonds or steel teeth for boring purposes; **crown-bud**, the flower-bud of a chrysanthemum shoot that forms after the plant 'breaks' or branches (***first crown bud***) or, if this is removed, the bud that forms on the secondary shoot (***second crown bud***); **crown cap** orig. *U.S.*, a metallic cork-lined stopper designed to be crimped over the top of a bottle; **crown-cases reserved**, criminal cases reserved on points of law for the consideration of the judges; **crown-colony**, a colony in which the legislation and the administration are under the control of the home government; **Crown Court**, (*a*) the court in which the criminal business of an Assize is transacted, as distinguished from the civil court; (*b*) either of two assize courts established in Liverpool and Manchester in 1956; (*c*) the superior English court established in 1971, replacing the criminal assizes and quarter-sessions and incorporating the Crown Courts of Liverpool and Manchester and the Central Criminal Court; **crown-crane**, see CRANE *sb.*[1] 1; †**crown-croacher**, for *crown-encroacher*, one who encroaches on a crown; **crown-daisy**, the old garden Chrysanthemum, *C. coronarium*; †**crown-day**, coronation day; **crown-debt**, a debt due to the Crown, which has preference over all other debts; **Crown Derby**, the Derby (see DERBY 5) porcelain made from about 1784 to 1848, bearing a crown as an additional distinguishing mark; freq. *attrib.*; **crown-eater**, tr. Germ. *kronenfresser*, nickname of the Swiss mercenaries who took service with the French; **crown-fern**, a New Zealand fern, *Blechnum discolor*; **crown fire**, 'a forest fire in which the crowns of the trees are ignited' (Webster, 1909); **crown gall**, a disease of plants caused by the bacterium *Agrobacterium tumefaciens* and characterized by tumours; **crown-gate**, the up-stream or head gate of the lock of a canal, etc.; †**crown-gold**, gold of the quality of which crowns were coined; **crown-graft**, a graft inserted between the inner bark and the alburnum; hence **crown-grafting**; **crown green**, a bowling green which is higher at the middle than at the sides; **crown-head**, in *Draughts*, the marginal row of the board nearest each player, cf. CROWN *v.*[1] 13; **crown-jewels**, the jewels which form part of the regalia; also *fig.*; **crown law**, the part of the common law which relates to the treatment of crimes, the criminal law; **crown lawyer**, a lawyer in the service of the Crown; a lawyer who practises in criminal cases; **crown lens**, a lens made of crown-glass, chiefly used as a component of an achromatic lens; **crown living**, a church living in the gift of the Crown; **crown matrimonial**, a regal crown obtained or claimed through marriage with the sovereign; **crown-mural**, †**-mure**, = MURAL crown; **crown-net** (see quot.); **crown-palm**, *Maximiliana Caribæa*, found on some West Indian islands; **crown-pigeon** = *crowned pigeon*, see CROWNED 6; †**crown-pin**, a pin or stopper to close the top of a hive; **crown-roast** *Cookery*, a roast of pork or lamb consisting of rib-pieces arranged so as to look like a crown; **crown rot**, a disease of rhubarb, caused by the fungus *Erwinia rhapontici*; **crown rust**, a disease of cereals and grasses, caused by the fungus *Puccinia coronata*; **crown-saw**, a kind of circular saw with the teeth on the edge of a hollow cylinder, as in a trepan saw, etc. (cf. sense 15); **crown-sheet**, the upper plate of the fire-box of a locomotive; **crown-shell**, a barnacle or acorn-shell; †**crown-shorn** *a.*, tonsured; **crown-side**, the portion of the Court of Queen's Bench which has to deal with criminal matters, the crown office; **crown solicitor**, a solicitor who prepares criminal prosecutions for the Crown; **crown-sparrow**, a sparrow of the American genus *Zonotrichia*, having a conspicuously coloured crown; **crown-tax**, a tax paid to the Crown; a tribute paid by the Jews to the kings of Syria (see quot.); †**crown-thistle**, a species of Thistle, *Carduus eriophorus* (in some Dicts. erroneously identified with CROWN-IMPERIAL 2); **crown-tile** (see quot.); **crown-tree**, a support for the roof in a coal-mine; **crown-valve**, a dome-shaped valve which works over a box with slotted sides; **crown-witness**, a witness for the Crown in a criminal prosecution instituted by it.

1889 *Whitaker's Alm.* 152 *Crown Agents for the Colonies. *Ibid.* 155 Lord Advocate's Office..Crown Agent in Edinburgh. **1872** J. YEATS *Nat. Hist. Raw Materials of Commerce* II. 234 The pale bark contains most cinchonine, the yellow most quinine; Loxa or *crown bark the largest proportion of quinidine. **1899** J. M. MAISCH *Man. Org. Materia Medica* (ed. 7) 163 Loxa bark or crown bark, chiefly from *C. officinalis*. **1776** G. SEMPLE *Building in Water* 4 The *Crown-Beams..projected from three to five Feet. **1555** SIR J. BALFOUR in C. Innes *Sk. Early Sc. Hist.* (1861) 129 He hes producit ane testimonial of his order of *crowne-bennet. **1907** T. R. SIM *Forests & For. Flora Cape Gd. Hope* 132 '*Crownberry' is in use at East London, and may have originated in the crown-like calyx of *D[ovyalis] rhamnoides*. **1962** WATT & BREYER-BRANDWIJK *Medicinal & Poisonous Plants S. & E. Afr.* (ed. 2) 1386/3 Dovyalis rhamnoides... Cape cranberry, Cranberry, Crownberry. **1792** *Trans. Soc. Encourag. Arts* III. 155 A harpoon..struck the fish in the *crown-bone of the head. **1820** SCORESBY *Acc. Arctic Reg.* I. 454 The upper-jaw, including the 'crown-bone', or skull, is bent. **1902** *Encycl. Brit.* XXXI. 643/1 Attempts are being made to substitute a rotary '*crown' borer for the percussion drill in sinking wells for petroleum. **1900** A. WYNNE in W. D. Drury *Bk. Gardening* v. 140 These growths form buds (termed *crown buds)... If these buds form in July..they are taken out, and another shoot is made, which produces a 'terminal', or second crown, bud. **1962** *Amateur Gardening* 7 Apr. 15/2 Each shoot produces what are known as 'first crown buds'. **1928** *Collier's* 1 Sept. 47/1 Corks, bottle cappers, tubing, *crown caps. **1889** *Whitaker's Alm.* 172 *Crown Cases Reserved Court. Judges.—The Judges of the High Court of Justice. **1845** *Penny Cycl.* Supp. I. 394/1 (Colonial Agents) A person called the agent-general acts for the *crown colonies; but where there is a local legislature the appointment is generally made by it. **1889** *Whitaker's Alm.* 433/1 Hong Kong..the colony is a Crown colony. **1827** F. WITTS *Diary* 19 Apr. (1978) 69, I attended the *Crown Court, and heard a very interesting trial for maliciously shooting with intent to murder. **1955** *Hansard Lords* 23 June 319 Clause 1 establishes the new courts, which are termed 'Crown Courts'. **1967** *Guardian* 17 July 3/1 More crown courts in large urban centres are recommended in the Bar Council's evidence to the Royal Commission on assizes and quarter sessions. **1970** *Hansard Lords* 19 Nov. 1250 Judges of the Crown Court..will consist of the High Court Judges, the existing county court judges, the official referees and all full-time judges with criminal jurisdiction above the level of the stipendiary magistrates. **1977** *Evening Gaz.* (Middlesbrough) 11 Jan. 7/1 Two Middlesbrough youths who attacked another youth in the street were yesterday sent to the Crown Court for sentence. **1587** *Mirr. Mag.* (N.), Sith stories all doe tell in every age, How these *crowne-croachers come to shamefull ends. **1882** *Garden* 14 Jan. 22/3 All the sorts that have chiefly sprung from the *Crown Daisy

..have a preponderance of white and yellow. 1609 Heywood *Brit. Troy* xvi. xcii, He..his neere Neece upon his *Crowne-day rauisht. 1818 Cruise *Digest* (ed. 2) I. 515 An assignment of a term for years will not protect a purchaser from a *crown debt. [1850 J. Marryat *Coll. Hist. Pottery & Porcelain* ix. 181 The Derby porcelain is very transparent... The earliest mark is not known.. subsequently, the mark was a D surmounted by a crown.] 1863 W. Chaffers *Marks & Monograms Pottery* 141 **Crown Derby*. A later mark than the preceding [*sc.* Derby-Chelsea]. 1872 Lady C. Schreiber *Jrnl.* (1911) I. 168 We found some charming Crown Derby custard cups and covers. 1900 E. Glyn *Visits Eliz.* 227 When he saw the best Crown Derby smashed on the floor. 1845 S. Austin *Ranke's Hist. Ref.* III. 65 They demanded the punishment of the 'German-French', the '*crown-eaters'. 1946 W. Martin *Flora N.Z.* iv. 77 At higher altitudes the larger, erect-growing *Crown Fern (*B. discolor*) replaces them. 1960 B. Crump *Good Keen Man* 12 A skinny old sow trotted out of the crown-fern above me. 1938 Weaver & Clements *Plant Ecol.* (ed. 2) ii. 47 **Crown fires* race through the tops of the trees at a high rate of speed. 1900 (*title*) An inquiry into the cause and nature of *crown gall (Arizona Agric. Exper. Station Bull. No. 33). 1950 *N.Z. Jrnl. Agric.* Mar. 229/3 Crown gall (*Bacterium tumefaciens*) in Chinese gooseberries is invariably associated with plants that have been propagated by root grafting or from cuttings. 1961 *Amateur Gardening* 9 Dec. 23 The growths or swellings which have affected your tree of Prunus tibetica are not canker but crown gall. *c* 1530 in Gutch *Coll. Cur.* II. 287 For every ounce channge of the golde betwene *corone golde and fine golde iiijs. iiij*d.* 1712 E. Hatton *Merch. Mag.* 130 Fine Gold to Crown Gold, is in Value, As 1 to .9167. 1727 Bradley *Fam. Dict.* s.v. *Grafting*, A *Crown-graft is very easy to be put in between the Wood and the Rind of the Tree you would graft upon. 1727–51 Chambers *Cycl.* s.v. *Engrafting*, *Crown-grafting is when four or more grafts are put round the stock, between the bark and the rind, somewhat in the manner of a crown. [1902 *Encycl. Brit.* XXVI. 327/2 There are two kinds of green—one the crown, and the other the level.] 1904 S. Aylwin *Gentle Art of Bowling* iii. 15 For a *crown green No. 2 bias..will be sufficient. 1649 Milton *Eikon.* viii, The queen [was gone] into Holland, where she pawned and set to sale the *crown jewels. 1851 H. Melville *Moby Dick* III. xiv. 98 At mid-day, with a blinding sun, all crown-jewels. 1856 Emerson *Eng. Traits, Ability*, Wks. (Bohn) II. 37 The diamond Koh-i-noor, which glitters among their crown jewels. 1895 G. B. Shaw in *Sat. Rev.* 2 Feb., Such crown jewels of dramatic poetry as Twelfth Night and A Midsummer Night's Dream. 1769 Blackstone *Comm.* IV. 3 Our *crown-law is with justice supposed to be more nearly advanced to perfection. 1771 Goldsm. *Hist. Eng.* IV. xxxvii. (Joddr.) The *crown-lawyers received directions to prosecute them for a seditious libel. 1834 P. Barlow in *Phil. Trans.* CXXIV. 202 The *crown lens must be made concave and the flint lens convex. 1845 T. Dick *Pract. Astr.* ii. iv. §6. 244 The predominating refraction of the crown lens disposed the achromatic rays to meet at a distant focus. 1961 R. Auerbach tr. *Boutry's Instrum. Optics* viii. 141 Much more compelling practical considerations will decide our choice, namely which of the four objectives with the crown lens in front..is the simplest to make and to mount. 1872 E. Peacock *Mabel Heron* I. iv. 66 The small *crown living..was given to him. 1864 Burton *Scot Abr.* I. iv. 197 Conferring on the Dauphin the '*crown matrimonial'. 1874 Green *Short Hist.* vii. 378 Mary's scornful refusal of his [Darnley's] claim of the 'crown matrimonial'..drove his jealousy to madness. 1682 Wheler *Journ. Greece* iii. 264 A Figure, with a *Crown-mure, with these Letters about it. 1766 Pennant *Zool.* (1769) III. 272 The fishermen make use of what is called a *crown-net, which is no more than a hemispherical basket, open at top and bottom. 1641 Best *Farm. Bks.* (Surtees) 62 Make the *crowne-pinne very rownde, and fitte for the crowne of the hive. [1912 F. M. Farmer *New Bk. Cookery* 132 Roast crown of pork.] 1934 Webster, *Crown roast. 1962 Crown roast [see best A. 5 a]. 1967 *Vogue* June 132 Crown Roast uses two Best Ends. Your butcher will prepare it for you. 1924 W. A. Millard in *Bull. Agric. Dept., Univ. of Leeds* cxxxiv. 6 Although many minor diseases attack the Rhubarb crop, none is of any importance in Yorkshire excepting that which has thus come to be known simply as 'Rhubarb Disease'. This disease would be better described as Rhubarb *Crown Rot, for it is the crown of the plant which is most generally attacked. 1952 E. Ramsden tr. *Gram & Weber's Plant Dis.* iii. 355/1 No part of a plant with any sign of crown rot should be used for planting. 1899 G. Massee *Text-bk. Plant Dis.* 249 *Crown Rust (*Puccinia coronata*, Corda). A widely distributed rust..met with on wheat, barley, rye, and many wild grasses. 1900 J. Percival *Agric. Bot.* vii. xlviii. 712 Two species of crown 'rusts' are known, namely *Puccinia coronifera*..and *P. coronata*. *Ibid.* 713 The upper cells of the teleutospores in both species are surmounted by a ring or crown of blunt teeth, hence the name crown 'rust'. 1933 *Discovery* Nov. 351/1 Some years crown rust (*Puccinia coronata* Corda) on oats amounted to a really serious menace. 1956 J. G. Dickson *Dis. Field Crops* (ed. 2) xii. 323 Crown rust caused by *Puccinia coronata* Cda. is distributed widely. 1563–87 Foxe *A. & M.* (1684) III. 106 The whole *crownshorn company brought to utter shame. 1768 Blackstone *Comm.* III. 42 The former in what is called the *crown-side or crown-office; the latter in the plea-side of the court. 1845 *Penny Cycl.* Supp. I. 443/1 In Ireland there are officers called *crown solicitors attached to each circuit, whose duty it is to get up every case for the crown in criminal prosecutions. 1535 Coverdale *1 Macc.* xi. 35 The customes of salt and *crowne taxes. 1611 Bible *1 Macc.* x. 29, I release all the Iewes from..crowne taxes. 1706 Phillips (ed. Kersey), A *Crown-thistle or Friers Crown-thistle, a sort of Herb. 1823 P. Nicholson *Pract. Build.* Gloss. s.v. *Tile*, Plane-tiles and *Crown-tiles are of a rectangular form. 1816 J. Hodgson in J. Raine *Mem.* (1857) I. 181 The roof was supported by *crown-trees..of wood. 1851 Greenwell *Coal-trade Terms Northumb. & Durh.* 20 Crowntrees are best made of larch, as being most durable. 1892 *Daily News* 21 Apr. 5/4 The roof of a seven-feet seam of coal required to be supported by what are called 'crown trees'. 1859 Dickens *T. Two Cities* ii. v, You were very sound, Syd, in the matter of those *crown witnesses to-day.

crown (kraʊn), *v.*[1] Forms: α. 3 curune-n, corune-n, 4–5 coroune-n, corone-n, (4 coroun), 5 corowne-n. β. 2–3 crune-n, 3–5 croune-n, (3 crouni, -y), 4–5 cron(e, 4–6 croun(e, (5 kroun), 5–7 crowne, 7– crown. *Pa. pple.* 2–3 icruned, -et, 3 curund, corund, 4 corouned, -de, crund, crond, 4–5 coroned, -de, -d, cround, ycrouned, 5 coronyd, corowned, i-)cronyd, i-, y-)crowned, -yd. [ME. *croune-n*, earlier *crune-n*, syncopated from *corune-n*, *coroune-n*, a. AFr. *coruner*, *corouner*, = OF. *coroner*, from 13th c. *couronner*:—L. *corōnāre*, f. *corōna* crown.]

I. 1. a. *trans.* To place a crown, wreath, or garland upon the head of (a person), in token of victory or honour, or as a decoration, etc.; to adorn with the aureole of martyrdom, virginity, etc. Also, ***to crown the head***, or ***the brows*** (of a person).

c 1175 *Lamb. Hom.* 121 Mid þornene crune his heaued wes i-cruned. *c* 1230 *Hali Meid.* 47 Þu ne schalt been icrunet bute þu beo asailȝet, for godd wole cruni þe. *c* 1300 *Cursor M.* 25368 (Cotton Galba) He þat victori may gete sall be corond [with] wirschippes grete. 1382 Wyclif *2 Tim.* ii. 5 He that stryueth..schal not be crowned, no but he schal fiȝt lawfully. *c* 1385 Chaucer *L.G.W.* Prol. 242 This noble quene, Corouned with white, and clothed al in grene. *c* 1400 Maundev. (Roxb.) ii. 5 He schuld be cround with palme. 1483 *Cath. Angl.* 84 To Crowne, *aureolare*. 1590 Shaks. *Mids. N.* ii. i. 27 But she..Crownes him with flowers, and makes him all her ioy. 1651 Hobbes *Leviath.* iii. xxxv. 219 Hee was crowned in scorn with a crown of thornes. 1711 Steele *Spect.* No. 143 ¶1 Sitting..crowned with Roses in order to make our Entertainment agreeable to us. 1840 Thirlwall *Greece* VII. 255 Many even crowned themselves before the act, as for a joyful solemnity. 1879 J. Todhunter *Alcestis* 114 That I should crown my head, and feast and sing.

b. *transf.* of things.

c 1385 Chaucer L.G.W. Prol. 219 As the dayseye I-corounede is with white levys lite. *Ibid.* 532.

c. To reward or honour (a work of art) with a prize. [After F. *couronner*.]

1885 *Pall Mall G.* 10 Feb. 5/2 M. Wauters's book, which was 'crowned' by the Royal Academy of Belgium.

d. *dial.* or *slang.* To hit (a person) on the head.

1746 P. Lock *Exmoor Scolding* (ed. 3) 6 Chell trim the, chell crown tha, chell vump tha. 1866 R. Hallam *Wadsley Jack* x. 49 Wi' that, sumboddy behint crahn'd me wi' a umbrella. 1919 R. Lardner *Real Dope* iii. 92 If he hadn't been so old I would of crowned him. 1948 A. Baron *From City from Plough* 156 Get off that box..before I crown you with this shovel. 1959 'O. Mills' *Stairway to Murder* xxiii. 234 'Someone crowned me, I take it?' The sergeant nodded. 'With the poker from our own hearth.'

2. *spec.* **a.** To invest with the regal crown, and hence with the character and dignity of a king or ruling prince. Often with complemental object, ***to crown king***, formerly ***to king***.

c 1290 *S. Eng. Leg.* I. 384/256 For-to cloþi him ase an heiȝh kyng, and crouni him with golde. 1297 R. Glouc. (1724) 383 Wyllam..let hym crouny to Kynge. *c* 1325 *E.E. Allit. P.* A. 415 He..Corounde me quene in blysse to brede. 1393 Gower *Conf.* III. 207 He..was coroned king. *c* 1400 *Destr. Troy* 13646 He was corond to kyng. *c* 1470 Harding *Chron.* l. v, To tyme that Kynges to Englande afterward Should coroned bee. 1593 Shaks. *2 Hen. VI*, i. i. 48 And Crowne her Queene of England. 1678 Wanley *Wond. Lit. World* v. i. §75. 466/1 Henry the fifth..went to Rome to be Crowned Emperour by Pope Paschalis the second. 1780 E. Perronet *Hymn, All hail the power of Jesu's name* i, Bring forth the royal diadem, To crown Him Lord of All. 1845 S. Austin *Ranke's Hist. Ref.* I. 83 If the emperor desired to be crowned there.

b. by extension.

1601 Shaks. *Twel. N.* iii. iv. 154 We wil bring the deuice to the bar and crowne thee for a finder of madmen. 1606 —— *Tr. & Cr.* i. iii. 142 Achilles, whom Opinion crownes The sinew, and the fore-hand of our Hoste.

c. To establish as king or sovereign, to enthrone. Usually *fig.*

1596 Shaks. *1 Hen. IV*, iii. i. 217 She will..on your Eye-lids Crowne the God of Sleepe. 1611 Beaum. & Fl. *Philaster* iii. ii, Till He crown a silent sleep upon my eyelid, Making me dream.

3. *fig.* **a.** (the 'crown' being something immaterial.)

c 1175 *Lamb. Hom.* 129 Ure drihten hine crunede mid blisse. *a* 1340 Hampole *Psalter* v. 15 Lord as wiþ a sheld of þi goed wil þou hes corounde vs. 1382 Wyclif *Isa.* xxii. 18 Crounende he shal crowne thee with tribulacioun. 1576 Fleming *Panopl. Epist.* 57 Clawebackes, which crowne him with commendation. 1593 Shaks. *2 Hen. VI*, iii. ii. 71 To be a Queene, and Crown'd with infamie. 1611 Bible *Ps.* viii. 5 Thou..hast crowned him with glory and honour. 1727 De Foe *Syst. Magic* i. i. (1840) 18 Wisdom crowns no man now, except it be with the rage and malice of enemies, with poverty and insult. 1846 Trench *Mirac.* ii. (1862) 124 There a strong faith is crowned and rewarded.

†**b.** *spec.* To reward, remunerate. *Obs.*

c 1461 *Paston Lett.* No. 429 II. 74 It is tyme to crone your old officers.

4. Also predicated of the crown, wreath, aureole, honour, reward, etc.: To cover as a crown does.

1697 Dryden *Virg. Georg.* iii. 50 A double Wreath shall crown our Cæsar's Brows. 1764 Goldsm. *Trav.* 11 Eternal blessings crown my earliest friends.

5. To surmount (something) *with.*

c 1420 *Pallad. on Husb.* i. 379 Thi walles..with brik thou must corone A foote aboute, and sumdel promynent. 1610 Shaks. *Temp.* iv. i. 80 Who..with each end of thy blew bowe do'st crowne My boskie acres. 1798 Ferriar *Illustr. Sterne, Eng. Hist.* 247 We crown the artificial mound with the shivered donjon. 1871 Freeman *Norm. Conq.* (1876) IV. 68 The ancient mound of the East Anglian Kings was now crowned by a castle of the Norman type.

6. a. Of a thing: To occupy the head or summit of (a thing) as a crown does, usually so as to add beauty or dignity; to form a crowning ornament to.

1746–7 Hervey *Medit.* (1818) 184 Ye verdant Woods, that crown our hills, and are crowned yourselves with leafy honours. 1845 M. Pattison *Ess.* (1889) I. 17 The church of St. Genoveva..crowned a height at no great distance. 1858 Hawthorne *Fr. & It. Jrnls.* I. 262 Perugia appeared before us, crowning a mighty hill. 1861 Miss Pratt *Flower. Pl.* III. 183 Corolla with two ears..which remain and crown the fruit. 1874 Micklethwaite *Mod. Par. Churches* 129 The canopy must crown the altar, not conceal it. 1886 Mrs. Flo. Caddy *Footsteps Jeanne D'Arc* 23 Her statue crowns a public fountain.

b. *passive.* To be crowned *with*, rarely *by*.

(In the passive 5 and 6 are scarcely separable.)

1816 J. Smith *Panorama Sc. & Art* I. 152 These [towers]..are generally crowned with fine pinnacles. 1848 Rickman *Archit.* 50 The walls are crowned by a parapet. 1856 Stanley *Sinai & Pal.* ii. (1858) 120 When every hill was crowned with a flourishing town or village. 1858 *Jrnl. R. Agric. Soc.* XIX. ii. 485 The root is crowned by a tuft of leaves.

7. To adorn the surface of (anything) *with* what is beautiful, rich, or splendid. Usually *passive*.

1697 Dryden *Virg. Past.* v. 57 Where..Vales with Violets once were crown'd. 1704 Pope *Pastorals, Spring* 99 The turf with rural dainties shall be crown'd. 1764 Goldsm. *Trav.* 45 Ye glittering towns, with wealth and splendour crown'd.

8. To fill to overflowing, or till the foam rises like a crown above the brim.

1605–31 [see crowned 4].

1697 Dryden *Virg. Past.* v. 108 Two Goblets will I crown with sparkling Wine. *Ibid., Georg.* iv. 208 To..squeese the Combs with Golden Liquor crown'd. 1702 *Roxb. Ball.* VI. 315 Stand about with your glasses full crown'd. 1709 Prior *Poems, Hans Carvel*, The Bowls were crown'd..and Healths went round. 1807 Robinson *Archæol. Græca* iii. iv. 205. 1887 Morris *Odyss.* i. 152 The serving-lads were crowning with drink each bowl and cup.

9. *fig.* To put the copestone to, to add the finishing touch to, to complete worthily. ***to crown all***: as the finishing touch, which confirms and surpasses everything previous.

1606 Shaks. *Tr. & Cr.* iv. v. 224 The end crownes all, And that old common Arbitrator, Time, Will one day end it. 1611 —— *Wint. T.* v. ii. 48 There might you haue beheld one Ioy crowne another. 1613 —— *Hen. VIII*, v. v. 59 No day without a deed to Crowne it. 1659 B. Harris *Parival's Iron Age* 153 The end crowns the work: and it serves for nothing, to have well begun, unless we finish so too. 1665 Sir T. Herbert *Trav.* (1677) 125 To crown all, a Book..was laid upon his Coffin. *c* 1707 in Maidment *Sc. Pasquils* (1868) 374 If the crafty old Peer..Designs to crown all by a finishing trick. 1725 Pope *Odyss.* i. 326 Meditate my doom, to crown their joy. 1741 Shenstone *Judgment of Hercules* 453 Let manhood crown what infancy inspir'd. 1846 Trench *Mirac.* xviii. (1862) 291 This work of grace and power crowned the day of that long debate. 1850 W. Irving *Goldsmith* i. 30 Ordered a bottle of wine to crown the repast. 1871 Blackie *Four Phases* i. 92 To crown all..man alone..can mould the emitted voice into articulate speech.

10. To honour or bless with a successful consummation or issue; to bring (efforts, wishes, etc.) to a successful and happy consummation.

1602 Marston *Antonio's Rev.* v. v. Wks. 1856 I. 138 Fortune crown your brave attempt. 1610 Shaks. *Temp.* iii. i. 69 O heauen..crowne what I professe with kinde euent. 1639 Fuller *Holy War* iii. xxvii. (1840) 167 Inconsiderate projects..if crowned with success, have been above censure. 1697 Dryden *Virg. Past.* iii. 137 Let Pollio's fortune crown his full desires. 1766 Goldsm. *Vic. W.* x, The hours we pass with happy prospects in view are more pleasing than those crowned with fruition. 1870 E. Peacock *Ralf Skirl.* II. 195 Success did not immediately crown his efforts. 1878 Morley *Diderot* I. 31 His wishes should be crowned, if he could procure the consent of his family.

11. To bless, amplify, or endow with honour, dignity, plenty, etc. Now *poetic.*

1535 Coverdale *Ps.* lxiv. 11 Thou crownest the yeare [Wyclif schalt blesse to the croune of the ȝer] with thy good, and thy footsteppes droppe fatnesse. 1577 B. Googe *Heresbach's Husb.* i. (1586) 3 b, Beseeching God..that he wyll crowne the yeere with his plenteousness. 1611 Bible *Ecclus.* xix. 5 He that resisteth pleasures, crowneth his life. 1697 Dryden *Virg. Past.* iv. 78 No God shall crown the Board, nor Goddess bless the Bed. *Ibid.* vii. 57 Come..crown the silent Hours, and stop the rosy Morn. 1863 W. Phillips *Speeches* xi. 252 High purposes which crowned his life.

II. Technical senses.

†**12.** *trans.* To mark (a person) with the tonsure as a sign of admission to the state of a cleric. *Obs.*

c 1290 *Beket* 557 in *S. Eng. Leg.* I. 122 A bonde-man..schal nouȝt with-oute is louerdes leue noȝwere i-crouned beo. 1393 Langl. *P. Pl.* C. vi. 56 Clerkes þat aren crouned.

13. In *Draughts* or *Checkers*, to make (a piece that reaches the opponent's 'crown-head' or marginal line of squares) into a 'king' which can move forward or backward.

This is done by placing on it another piece already off the board, or when the pieces are marked with a crown or other distinguishing mark on one side, by turning this up so as to expose the 'crown'.

1850 *Bohn's Handbk. Games*, He is..made a King by having another piece put on, which is called crowning him. 1863 *Hoyle's Games Modernized, Draughts* 266 When the men of either opponent have made their way to the opposite end of the board..they receive increased power: they are then 'crowned'... Thus crowned the piece may be moved backwards as well as forwards.

14. *Naut.* ***to crown a knot***: to form into a sort of knot by interweaving the strands of the rope so as to prevent untwisting.

1848 G. BIDDLECOMBE *Art of Rigging* 44 Crowning or Finishing a Wall-Knot.

15. *Milit.* To effect a lodgement upon (as upon the covered way in a siege), by sapping upon a glacis near the crest. Webster 1864.

16. *Dentistry.* To put an artificial crown (see CROWN *sb.* 28 b) on (a tooth).

1885 I. E. & R. E. CLIFFORD *Crown, Bar, & Bridge-work* 6 Roots decayed too far for pivoting can be crowned. **1907** *Westm. Gaz.* 23 Oct. 9/1 The teeth were crowned. **1963** C. R. COWELL et al. *Inlays, Crowns, & Bridges* vii. 66 The mobility of any tooth to be crowned must be tested.

III. 17. ***to crown in*** (intr.): to subside and fall in as a crust over an interior hollow.

1880 D. C. MURRAY *Life's Atonement* II. iii. 78 The land had given way and..fallen into the hollow left by some disused coal-mine—had *crowned-in* the country people say.

†**crown**, *v.*[2] *Obs.* exc. *dial.* [Back-formation from CROWNER[2], coroner.] *trans.* To hold a coroner's inquest on.

1602 CAREW *Cornwall* (1769) 112 b, Possesseth sundry large privileges..to wit..crowning of dead persons, laying of arrests, and other Admirall rights. *c* **1630** RISDON *Surv. Devon* §215 (1810) 224 If any man die..in the forest, the coroner of Lidford shall crown him. **1673** *Par. Reg. Hartlepool* in R. E. C. Waters *Parish Registers Eng.* 62 Tho. Smailes was buryed and crowned by a jury of 12 men, and John Harrison supposed to murder him. **1888** in *W. Somerset Word-bk.*

crown, arch. *pa. pple.* of CROW *v.*[1] q.v.

†**'crownacle.** *Obs.* [Cf. CORONACLE.] = CORONAL 3, the head of a spear or lance.

1460 *Lybeaus Disc.* (Percy Fol.) 983 Either smote on others shield the while With crownackles that were of steele [ed. Kaluza 976 With coronals stif and stelde Eiþer smitte oþer in þe scheld.]

crownair, -ar, var. CROWNER, coroner.

'crownal, *sb. Obs.* or *arch.* Also crownel. [A phonetic variant of CORONAL, also *corounal, cronal.*] A coronet; a garland or wreath for the head; = CORONAL *sb.* 1, 2.

c **1500** *Lancelot* 59 Thar was the flour..Wnclosing gane the crownel for the day. **1513** DOUGLAS *Æneis* VII. ii. 111 Hir crownell [*coronam*] picht wyth mony precius stane. **1819** SHELLEY *Ode Assertors of Liberty* v, Bind, bind every brow, With crownals of violet, ivy, and pine. **1865** S. EVANS *Bro. Fabian* 81, I would melt yon crownal into chessmen.

'crownal, *a. rare.* [See prec.] = CORONAL *a.*

1836 *Fraser's Mag.* XIV. 256 Her departure placed the crownal rays Of England's throne upon the house which now..Wears..Its diadem upon an honest brow.

†**crownation.** *Obs.* A by-form of CORONATION, assimilated to CROWN *sb.*

c **1530** LD. BERNERS *Arth. Lyt. Bryt.* (1814) 542 To make purueyaunce for Arthurs crownacion. *c* **1550** *MS. Corp. Chr. Coll. Camb.* No. 105. 235 The crownation of king Edwarde VI..anno 1546. **1604** *Vestry Bks.* (Surtees) 140 For ringing upon the crownation day, iijs. 4d.

crowned (kraʊnd), *ppl. a.* [f. CROWN *v.*[1] and *sb.* + -ED.]

1. Invested with a crown or with royal dignity.

c **1230** *Hali Meid.* 7 To beo cwen icrunet. *c* **1325** *Song Deo Gratias* 41 in *E.E.P.* (1862) 129 Almyhti corteis crouned kyng. **1393** LANGL. *P. Pl.* C. IV. 257 Were ech a kyng ycoroned. *c* **1430** LYDG. *Bochas* II. i. (1554) 41 b, The rudenes of a crowned asse. **1611** SHAKS. *Wint. T.* v. iii. 5 You ..With your Crown'd Brother. **1661** BOYLE *Style of Script.* (1675) 211 Crowned vice. **1695** LUTTRELL *Brief Rel.* (1857) III. 426 As if she were a crowned head. **1756-7** tr. *Keysler's Trav.* (1760) II. 163 Crowned heads, and even popes themselves have stood in awe of it. **18..** CAMPBELL *Men of Engl.* vii, We're the sons of sires who baffled Crowned and mitred tyranny.

2. Surmounted by a crown or the figure of one.

1565 *Act 8 Eliz.* c. 12 §2 The Queen's Highness Seal of Lead, having the Portcullis crowned engraved on the one Side. **1633** T. STAFFORD *Pac. Hib.* iv. (1821) 265 The Harpe Crowned, being the Armes of..Ireland. **1836** J. M. GASKELL in *Ho. Comm.* 30 June, To make the Constitution what Mr. Canning called a crowned republic. **1871** R. ELLIS *Catullus* lxiv. 345 Troy's crown'd city.

†**3.** Consummate, perfect; sovereign. *Obs.*

c **1386** CHAUCER *Sqr's. T.* 518 Al Innocent of his corouned malice. **1621-51** BURTON *Anat. Mel.* II. v. II. iii. 386 'Tis a crowned medicine which must be kept in secret.

4. Brimming, brim-full, abundant, bounteous.

1605 CHAPMAN *All Fools* in Dodsley *O. Pl.* (1780) IV. 186 He shall..carouze one crowned cup To all these ladies health. **1631** SHIRLEY *Traitor* III. ii, And in your crowned tables, And hospitality, will you murder him?

5. Having a crown or top; usually qualified, as ***high-, low-crowned.***

1665 SIR T. HERBERT *Trav.* (1677) 376 An antick sort of hat which is high crown'd. **1778** WESLEY *Let.* in Tyerman *Life* (1871) III. 277 Any woman, who wears either ruffles or a high crowned cap. **1801** W. F. COLLIER *Hist. Eng. Lit.* 177 A..low-crowned hat of Flemish beaver.

6. Having a crown-like excrescence, tuft, etc., on the head or top; crested. Often a specific designation in *Nat. Hist.*, e.g. ***crowned*** or ***crown-pigeon***, *Goura coronata.*

1698 T. FROGER *Relat. Voy.* 65 Another sort of Fruit, which..seems to have the crown'd Head of a clove. **1776** WITHERING *Brit. Plants* (1796) II. 285 *Bupleurum*..fruit egg-shaped, bulging, small, not crowned. **1779** FORREST *Voy. N. Guinea* 95 One of my crowned pigeons escaped. **1802** BINGLEY *Anim. Biog.* (1813) II. 224 The wings of the Crowned Pigeons are armed with an horny excrescence. **1828** STARK *Elem. Nat. Hist.* I. 54 *Cebus cirrifer*..The Crowned Sapajou.

7. Having a crown: in various senses of the sb. ***crowned work*** (Fort.) = CROWNWORK q.v.

1884 JEFFERIES *Red Deer* iv. 70 Crowned heads and forked heads are still spoken of when the antler forks, or when the points draw together in the outline of a crown.

crowner[1] ('kraʊnə(r)). [f. CROWN *v.* + -ER.]

1. One who crowns: in various senses of the vb.

c **1440** *Promp. Parv.* 105 Crownere, or corownere, *coronator.* **1617** FLETCHER *Mad Lover* v. i, Oh, fair sweet goddess, queen of loves..Crowner of all happy nights. **1660** BURNEY *Κέρδ. Δῶρον* (1661) 15 He..is the holy Anointer, the Crowner himself. **1860** PUSEY *Min. Proph.* 564 He who was to be..the sure Foundation and Crowner of the whole building.

2. The crowning act. *U.S.*

1815 *Massachusetts Spy* 31 May (Th. 146), This is the crowner, the cap-sheaf. **1840** R. DANA *Bef. Mast* xxvii. 92 That very night we slipped our cables, as a crowner to our fun ashore. **1860** O. W. HOLMES *Elsie V.* xxv, Wal, if that a'n't the craowner! **1922** ALICE BROWN *Old Crow* xxvii. 320 Isn't that a joke, Rookie? Charlotte would say it's the crowner.

3. A fall on the crown of the head.

1861 W. MELVILLE *Good for Nothing* II. xxvi. 201 A 'crowner' for John, whose horse goes shoulder deep into a hole. **1879** FORBES in *Daily News* 28 June 5/7 The inevitable fate of the rider is an imperial crowner, with, as like as not, his horse on the top of him.

†**crowner**[2]. *Obs.* exc. *dial.* Also 5 *Sc.* -ar(e, -air, 5-6 -ar, 6 -ere. [A popular by-form of CORONER, assimilated to CROWN *sb.*, and corresp. to the med.L. form *corōnātor*: cf. CROWN *v.*[2]]

1. = CORONER. (Now only dialectal, or with allusion to the passage in *Hamlet.*)

c **1425** WYNTOUN *Cron.* VIII. xxiv. 120 Til Elandonan his crownare past, For til arest mysdoaris þare. **1487** *Act 3 Hen. VII*, c. 2 The crowner upon the viewe of the body dede shuld inquire of hym..that had don that deth or murder. **1577** HARRISON *England* II. iv. (1877) I. 102 There are.. crowners, whose dutie is to inquire of such as come to their death by violence. **1602** SHAKS. *Ham.* v. i. 4 The Crowner hath sate on her, and finds it Christian buriall. *Ibid.* 24 *Other.* But is this law? *Clo.* I marry is't, Crowners Quest Law. **1667** PEPYS *Diary* (1877) V. 166 Find the Crowner's jury sitting. **1823** BYRON *Juan* XI. xvii, As soon as 'Crowner's quest' allow'd. **1870** E. PEACOCK *Ralf Skirl.* I. 192 The crowner would be gettin' to hear on it.

2. *Sc.* He who had command of the troops raised in one county. Improperly for *colonel.*

1639 BAILLIE *Letters* (1775) I. 164 Renfrew had chosen Montgomery their crowner. **1654** NICOLL *Diary* (1836) 125 A..feast, prepared by the Toun of Edinburgh for him [Monk] and his speciall crowneris. **1873** BURTON *Hist. Scot.* VI. lxxi. 249 A few trained officers, the most important among whom was Crowner or Colonel Gun.

†**'crownet.** *Obs.* [A by-form of CORONET, CRONET, which in its phonetic history followed the change of *coroune* to CROWN *sb.*] = CORONET.

1. = CORONET 1, 2.

c **1400** *Rom. Rose* 3203 Rounde environ hir crownet Was fulle of riche stonys frett. *c* **1430** LYDG. *Min. Poems* (1840) 6 Withe crounettes of gold. **1538** LELAND *Itin.* I. 17 There lyith on the North side of the High Altare Henry Erle of Lancaster, withowt a Crounet. **1606** SHAKS. *Tr. & Cr.* Prol. 6 The Princes..Sixty and nine that wore Their Crownets Regall. **1613** PURCHAS *Pilgrimage* VIII. vi. 638 With a crownet of Feathers. **1842** L. HUNT *Palfrey* v. 139 King Edward with his crownet on, Sits highest.

fig. **1606** SHAKS. *Ant. & Cl.* IV. xii. 27 Whose Bosome was my Crownet, my chiefe end.

2. Applied to a 'head' of flowers (= CORONET 7 a), or the leafy 'head' of a tree.

1578 LYTE *Dodoens* I. viii. 15 In the middest of those small Burres there groweth forth as it were a little Crownet. **1621** G. SANDYS *Ovid's Met.* xv. (1626) 314 A nest..Vpon the crownet of a trembling Palme.

3. The lowest part of a horse's pastern, or the tuft of hair on this part; = CORONET 5. Cf. CRONET 4.

1616 BULLOKAR, *Crownet*, a little crowne, also a part of a horse hoofe. **1635** MARKHAM *Faithfull Farrier* (1638) 97 With this Salve..annoynt the crownets of the Horses hoofes. **1725** *Lond. Gaz.* No. 6348/3 A bay Mare, with a Crownet upon her near Leg behind.

4. = CORNET *sb.*[1] 4.

1614 MARKHAM *Cheap Husb.* I. lxxv. (1668) 69 Raise up the skin with a crownet, and put in a plate of Lead.

crown-gate, -gold, etc.: see CROWN *sb.* 35.

'crown-,glass. A kind of glass composed of silica, potash, and lime (without lead or iron), made in circular sheets by blowing and whirling.

It is the sort commonly used in Great Britain for windows, and the best quality is used in combination with flint glass to render dioptric instruments achromatic.

1706 PHILLIPS (ed. Kersey), *Crown-glass*, the finest sort of Glass for Windows. **1718** *Freethinker* No. 95. 283 A poor Barber..had above Fifty Shillings Worth of Crown-Glass demolished. **1758** DOLLOND in *Phil. Trans.* L. 740 The crown glass seems to diverge the light rather the least of the two. **1807** T. THOMSON *Chem.* (ed. 3) II. 508 Crown-glass is made without lead. It is therefore much lighter than flint-glass. **1881** *Every Man his own Mechanic* §1678 Crown glass is circular in form with a thick lump called a bull's-eye in the centre.

'crown im'perial.

1. The crown of an emperor, esp. as distinguished from a king's crown.

1542 UDALL *Erasm. Apophth.* I. §164. 136 b, [Diogenes] takyng no lesse pride and glorie of his libertee..then Alexander did of his kyngdome, and croune Emperiall.

2. A handsome species of Fritillary (*Fritillaria Imperialis*), a native of Levantine regions, cultivated in English gardens: it bears a number of pendent flowers collected into a whorl round a terminal leafy tuft.

1611 SHAKS. *Wint. T.* IV. iii. 125 Bold Oxlips, and The Crowne Imperiall. **1625** B. JONSON *Pan's Anniversary* Wks. (ed. Rtldg.) 643/1 Bright crown imperial, kingspear, holyhocks. **1816** KIRKBY & SP. *Entomol.* (1843) II. 147 The conspicuous white nectaries of the Crown Imperial.

3. *Arch.* (See quot.)

1861 BERESF. HOPE *Eng. Cathedr. 19th C.* 244 There is a form of spire peculiar to the northern part of our island..I mean the Crown Imperial, or collection of ribs springing from the four angles, or from the four angles and four central points of a square tower, arching over like the crown from which the name is derived and meeting in a point from which a spire or spirelet springs.

crowning ('kraʊnɪŋ), *vbl. sb.* [f. CROWN *v.*]

1. The action of placing a crown on the head; coronation.

a **1240** *Lofsong* in *Cott. Hom.* 207 Ich bide þe..bi þe þornene crununge. *c* **1300** *Havelok* 2948 The feste of his coruning Laste..Fourti dawes. *c* **1400** *Destr. Troy* 5376 To come to the coronyng of þe kyde lord. **1526** *Pilgr. Perf.* (W. de W. 1531) 253 With the crownynge [of Christ] and other turmentes. *a* **1667** COWLEY *Elegy Anacreon* 52 The Pomp of Kings..At their Crownings. **1868** FREEMAN *Norm. Conq.* (1876) II. x. 513 The walls which beheld their crowning beheld also their burial.

†**b.** As a date: = Reign.

1258 *Eng. Proclam. Hen. III*, In þe twoandfowertiȝþe ȝeare of vre cruninge. **1297** R. GLOUC. (1726) 440.

†**2.** Tonsure. *Obs.*

1393 LANGL. *P. Pl.* C. I. 86 Maisters and doctors, þat han cure vnder cryst and crownynge in tokne.

3. Consummation; completion, fulfilment.

1598 CHAPMAN *Iliad* II. 304 Let two or three, that by themselves advise, Faint in their crowning. **1857** HEAVYSEGE *Saul* (1869) 367 A Power that stands between My purpose and its crowning. **1890** BP. STUBBS *Primary Charge* 55 They are the very crowning of the sin of schism, the forcible rending of the mystical body of the Lord.

4. *Naut.* (See quot.)

1769 FALCONER *Dict. Marine*, *Crowning*, the finishing part of a knot made on the end of a rope. It is performed by interweaving the ends of the..strands..so as they may not become..untwisted.

5. A structure that forms the crown of anything.

1704 *Collect Voy.* (Church.) III. 122/1 The..Row of Seats reaches, with its Crowning or Ornaments, to the.. Roof.

6. The highest part of an arched or convex surface. ***crowning in***: subsidence of an overarching surface. Cf. CROWN *v.* 17.

1888 *Daily News* 4 July 5/2 The 'crowning in' or subsidence of the land is a common enough occurrence in the mining districts.

7. *attrib.*

1829 SOUTHEY *All for Love* IV, On the Crowning-day..A gay procession take..their way. **1871** FREEMAN *Hist. Ess.* Ser. I. viii. 211 He chose Soissons for his crowning-place.

'crowning, *ppl. a.* [f. CROWN *v.* + -ING[2].]

1. That crowns, or bestows a crown.

1611 BIBLE *Isa.* xxiii. 8 Who hath taken this counselle against Tyre the crowning citie [**1885** *R.V. margin*, that giveth crowns].

2. That forms the crown or acme; completing, consummating; highest, most perfect.

1651 CROMWELL *Lett.* 4 Sept. The dimensions of this mercy are above my thought. It is for aught I know a crowning mercy. **1746-7** HERVEY *Medit.* (1818) 62 Heaven's last, best, and crowning gift. **1862** STANLEY *Jew. Ch.* (1877) I. xiv. 270 The crowning event of this period. **1867** A. BARRY *Sir C. Barry* ii. 49 The crowning cornice. **1875** JOWETT *Plato* (ed. 2) I. 386 This last act, or crowning folly.

3. Rising into a crown or rounded summit; arching.

1761 *Lond. Mag.* XXX. 7 No pavement should be laid crowning. **1886** E. S. MORSE *Jap. Homes* i. 28 They are brought to a uniform level, but crowning slightly,—that is, the centre is a little higher than the sides.

crown-land, 'crownland.

1. ('*crown* '*land.*) Land belonging to the Crown, of which the revenue belongs to the reigning sovereign. Mostly in pl. *crown-lands*, the estates of the crown.

a **1625** COPE in Gutch *Coll. Cur.* I. 122 Custody Lands, anciently termed the Crown Lands, answered in the Pipe. **1647** CLARENDON *Hist. Reb.* I. (1843) 2/2 Selling the crown-lands, creating peers for money. **1647** CRASHAW *Steps to Temple* 82 Our crown-lands lie above. **1777** ROBERTSON *Hist. Amer.* VII. (1783) III. 171 By their stated labour the crown-lands were cultivated. **1868** FREEMAN *Norm. Conq.*

(1876) II. App. 563 The estates of the dissolved houses had become crown-land.

2. (*'crownland* = G. *kronland.*) The name of the great administrative provinces of the Austro-Hungarian monarchy.

crown law, living, etc.: see CROWN *sb.* 35.

'crownless, *a.* [f. CROWN *sb.* + -LESS.] Without a crown.

1818 MILMAN *Samor* 322 The Crown'd are crownless, kingdomless the Kings. *a* **1845** HOOD *Retrospective Review* x, The crownless hat, ne'er deem'd an ill.

'crownlet, *sb.* [f. CROWN *sb.* + -LET.] A little or tiny crown.

1805 SCOTT *Last Minstr.* v. ii, The chief, whose antique crownlet long Still sparkled in the feudal song. **1858** CARLYLE *Fredk. Gt.* (1865) II. VI. ii. 141 English crowns, Hanoverian crownlets.

'crownling. *rare.* [f. CROWN *sb.* + -LING.] A scion of the crown, a prince.

1884 TENNYSON *Becket* III. iii, As to the young crownling himself..had I fathered him I had given him more of the rod than the sceptre.

†**'crownment.** *Obs.* Forms: 3-5 corone-, 3 croune-, 4 coron-, 4-6 corown(e)ment. [ME. a. F. *corunement* (now *couronnement*), with phonetic change as in CROWN *sb.*] Coronation.

1297 R. GLOUC. (1724) 433 Of þe kynge's crounement in þe [ix] ȝere. *c* **1330** R. BRUNNE *Chron.* (1810) 35 S. Donstan þe bisshop was at his coronment. *c* **1450** *Mirour Saluacioun* 2391 Ȝe haf herd last tofore of cristis corovnement. *c* **1470** HARDING *Chron.* l. iv, This stone..On whiche yᵉ Scottish Kynges wer brechelesse set At their coronomente. **1592** WYRLEY *Armorie* 120 That th' youthfull Regent, Should haue some news against his corwnment.

Crown office. a. The office in which was transacted, at certain stages, the business of the Crown side of the King's Bench, *i.e.* criminal business and business relating to the prerogative writs of mandamus, *quo warranto*, and prohibition. It is now a department of the Central Office of the High Court of Justice.

1631 WEEVER *Anc. Fun. Mon.* 700 A Clarke or Officer in the Kings Bench, whose function is to frame..Indictments against..offenders..called Clarke of the Crowne office. **1736** C. FORD in *Swift's Lett.* (1768) IV. 161, I indicted him in the crown-office, the terror of the low people. **1842** CHITTY *Practice* III. 30 The Master of the Crown Office transacts a considerable portion of business on the Crown or criminal side of the Court.

b. In Chancery: The office in which the Great Seal is, for most purposes, affixed. It has absorbed other Chancery offices which supervised the sealing of certain documents, *e.g.* the Petty Bag office, from which issued writs for parliamentary elections. The Crown office now transacts all that remains of the common law business of the Chancery.

1863 H. COX *Instit.* I. viii. 111 All elections..take place by virtue of writs issued out of the Crown-office in Chancery. **1892** ANSON *Law & Cust. Const.* II. 149 It is in the Crown Office in Chancery that the Great Seal is, for most purposes, affixed.

crown-paper.

1. A size or make of paper watermarked with the figure of a crown.

1630 J. TAYLOR (Water-P.) *Wks.* (N.), And may not dirty socks from off the feet From thence be turn'd to a crowne-paper sheet? **1807** OPIE *Lect. Art* iv. (1848) 323 Writing.. upon crown, double elephant, or foolscap paper.

†**2.** A paper containing five shillings' worth. *Obs.*

1672 COLLINS in Rigaud *Corr. Sc. Men* (1841) I. 201 To manage the Farthing Office, to deliver out all, that are coined..in crown-papers ready tied up.

crown-piece, 'crownpiece.

1. (*crown-piece.*) = CROWN *sb.* 8 b; in modern use applied to the large silver coin of the value of five shillings.

1648 *Venice Looking-glass* 10 He drew out an halfe crown peece. **1710** STEELE *Tatler* No. 245 ¶2 A Crown-Piece with the Breeches. **1773** WESLEY *Jrnl.* 14 May, Holes larger than a crown-piece. **1844** DICKENS *Mart. Chuz.* iv, Such a trifling loan as a crown piece.

2. (*'crownpiece.*) A piece that forms the crown or top of anything.

1794 W. FELTON *Carriages* (1801) II. 137 The Head Stale or Crownpiece is a Strap..on the top of the horse's head.

'crown-post. The middle post of a trussed roof, which supports the crown of the roof; the king-post.

1703 T. N. *City & C. Purchaser* 122 Crown-post, is that Post, which (in some Buildings) stands upright in the middle..It is also call'd a King-piece. **1703** MOXON *Mech. Exerc.* 159 Crown Post..Also the King-Piece, or Joggle-Piece. **1806** GREGORY *Dict. Arts & Sc.* I. 460. **1823** P. NICHOLSON *Pract. Build.* 221.

Crown prince. [tr. Ger. *kronprinz*, Da. *kronprinds*, Du. *kroonprins*, Sw. *kronprins*, etc.] The prince who is heir-apparent or designate to a sovereign throne, *esp.* in Germany and the Northern European countries. Hence **Crown-'princeship; Crown 'princess,** the wife of a Crown prince.

1791 *Ann. Reg.* 38 The Crown prince was absent by indisposition. **1838** *Penny Cycl.* X. 462/1 The king and the crown prince [of Prussia] were for some time with this corps. **1842** *Ibid.* XXIII. 397/1 The Swedish troops were led by the crown-prince [Bernadotte]. **1863** *Ann. Reg.* 178 The Crown Princess of Prussia (Princess Royal of England) celebrated her birthday by laying the foundation-stone of a new church. **1889** A. LANG *Prince Prigio* xviii. 139 He refused to ..restore Prigio to his crown-princeship! *Mod. Newsp.* Crown Prince of Roumania, of Japan, of Siam.

†**crown-rash.** *Obs.* [f. CROWN *sb.* + RASH; cf. Ger. *kronrasch.*] A particular quality of rash or woollen stuff.

1710 *Lond. Gaz.* No. 4781/1 A free and open Trade for Woollen Stuffs, call'd Crownraches, between..Great Britain, and..Bohemia. [**1891** FLÜGEL *Germ.-Eng. Dict.* 492/1 *Kronrasch*, crown-rashes, English serge.]

crown-saw, -sparrow, etc.: see CROWN *sb.* 35.

'crown-scab. A painful cancerous sore in the coronet of a horse's foot.

1609 ROWLANDS *Knaue of Clubbes* 44 For any Iade he phisicke had..Crowne-scab, and quitter-bone. *c* **1720** W. GIBSON *Farrier's Dispens.* xiv. (1734) 276 Recommended to cure the Crown-Scab, being applied Plaister-wise all round the Coronet. **1792** OSBALDISTON *Brit. Sportsman* 122/2 That there are a great many humours in the coronet, that may occasion the crown-scab, and other sores.

crown-tax, -thistle, etc.: see CROWN *sb.* 35.

'crown-wheel.

a. The balance- or escape-wheel of a vertical watch, the pinion of which is driven by the contrate wheel; but the name is now commonly applied to any wheel with cogs or teeth set at right angles to its plane, *i.e.* a CONTRATE wheel.

1647 J. CARTER *Nail & Wheel* 84 The ballance of the watch..never stirres, but when the crown-wheele, makes it go. **1696** W. DERHAM *Artif. Clockmaker* 5 The Contrate-Wheel is that Wheel in Pocket-Watches which is next to the Crown-Wheel, whose Teeth and Hoop lye contrary to those of other Wheels. **1727-52** CHAMBERS *Cycl.* s.v. *Watch-work*, The crown-wheel, in pocket-pieces, and swing-wheel in pendulums, serving to drive the balance or pendulum. **1807** VANCOUVER *Agric. Devon* (1813) 130 Perpendicular shaft ..[with] crown-wheel of two-inch plank, with six cast iron segments, composing a crown-wheel of 108 cogs. **1829** *Nat. Philos.* I. *Mechanics* II. vii. 30 (U.K.S.) If the teeth be parallel to the axis of the wheel, and therefore perpendicular to its plane, it is called a *crown-wheel*. **1884** F. J. BRITTEN *Watch & Clockm.* 68 The few verge trains with crown wheel of nine have escape pinions of six.

b. *spec.* In the gears of motor vehicles.

1908 *Westm. Gaz.* 29 Dec. 4/1 The transmission [of a motor-car] being by chain,..crown-wheel, and differential gears. **1926** *Amer. Speech* I. 686/2 Automobile nomenclature... American: ring gear... English: crown wheel. **1963** R. F. WEBB *Motorists' Dict.* 70 *Crown-wheel*, the largest bevel gear in the differential..housing.

'crown-work. *Fortif.* Formerly crowned work. See quots.

1677 *Lond. Gaz.* No. 1179/2 The Town..having a large Hornwork with a Halfmoon on each side of it, and a crowned Work before it, all fac'd with Stone and Brick. *Ibid.* No. 1181/4 Retiring into an Half-moon faced with Brick, which was in the middle of the said Crowned work. **1678** tr. *Gaya's Art of War* II. 115 *Couronnement*, or a Crown-work, is a Work made beyond the Horns to gain Ground, and force off the Enemies. **1859** F. A. GRIFFITHS *Artil. Man.* (ed. 9) 262 *A Crown-work* is composed of a bastion between two curtains..terminated by half bastions. It is joined to the body of the place by two long sides.

'crowny, *a. nonce-wd.* [f. CROWN *sb.* + -Y¹.] Of or pertaining to a crown (*e.g.* of the head).

1615 CROOKE *Body of Man* 434 The Coronall suture or crowny seame.

crownycle, -acle, obs. ff. CHRONICLE.

crowp(e, obs. form of CROUP *sb.*¹ and *v.*¹

crowper, obs. form of CRUPPER.

crowpon, -pyn, obs. ff. CROUPON.

'crow-quill. A quill from a crow's wing, used as a pen for fine writing. Also a name for a small fine steel pen used in map-drawing, etc.

1740 GRAY *Let.* Poems (1775) 86 You should take a handsome crow-quill when you write to me, and not leave room for a pin's point in four sides of a sheet royal. **1845** MRS. CARLYLE *Lett.* I. 352 Written on glazed paper with a crow-quill.

fig. **1795** BURKE *Regic. Peace* iv. Wks. IX. 17 Such a poor crow-quill as mine.

attrib. **1878** BROWNING *Poets Croisic* 37 Over the neat crowquill calligraph His pen goes blotting.

crow's-bill: see CROW-BILL.

crowse, var. of CRUSE *sb.*, CROUSE *a.*, CROOSE *v.*

crow's foot, 'crow's-foot.

1. One of the small wrinkles formed by age or anxiety round the outer corner of the eye, 'thought to resemble the impression of the feet of crows' (Todd). Now commonly in *pl.*

c **1374** CHAUCER *Troylus* II. 354 So longe mot ye lyue and alle prowde, Till crowes feet ben growen vnder youre eye. [**1579** SPENSER *Sheph. Cal.* Dec. 136 By myne eie the Crow his clawe dooth wright.] **1579** LYLY *Euphues* (Arb.) 55 When the black Crowes foote shall appeare in their eye. **1611** FLORIO, *Crespatura*..a wrinckling, a withering, as we say a Crowes-foote in a womans face. **1849** E. E. NAPIER *Excurs. S. Africa* II. 79, I begin already to see a few crows feet about the corner of my eyes. **1884** RIDER HAGGARD *Dawn* xvi, The bloodshot eyes and the puckered crow's-feet beneath them.

†**2.** *Naut.* = CROW-FOOT 4. *Obs.*

1627 CAPT. SMITH *Seaman's Gram.* v. 19 Dead mens eyes are blocks..the Crowes-feet reeued thorow them are a many of small lines. **1806** GREGORY *Dict. Arts & Sc.* I. 459 Crow's feet..scarcely of any other use than to make a shew of small rigging.

3. *Mil.* A caltrop; = CROWFOOT 6.

1772 SIMES *Mil. Guide*, *Crows-feet*, an iron of four points ..used against cavalry. **1884** *Daily News* 15 Sept. 5/3 One implement of war of which the British soldier is not proud ..is the 'crow's-foot'.

4. a. A three-pointed figure in embroidery.

1879 *Uniform Reg.* in *Navy List* July (1882) 497/1 Crow's foot of round gold cord on sleeve.

b. A mark or symbol resembling a bird's foot.

1871 *Scribner's Monthly* II. 502 [A chart] adorned at this point by the crowsfeet that call for a chain of mountains.

c. *Textiles.* (See quots.)

1948 J. T. MARSH *Textile Sci.* xiv. 300 Creases should not be allowed to form or they will tend to become fixed in the cloth and form 'crows' feet marks'. **1957** *Textile Terms & Defs.* (ed. 3) 35 *Crowsfeet*, undesirable creases, particularly in crêpe fabrics, that prevent the production of a uniform surface appearance. **1962** J. T. MARSH *Self-smoothing Fabrics* ii. 8 A heat-setting process had a stabilising effect and prevented the subsequent formation of a multiplicity of little wrinkles or crow's-feet marks when the fabric was relaxed.

5. *Mech.* (See quot.)

1874 KNIGHT *Dict. Mech.*, *Crow's-foot.* 1. (*Well-boring.*) A bent hook adapted to engage the shoulder or collar on a drill-rod or well-tube while lowering it into a well or drilled shaft, or to hold the same while a section above it is being attached or detached.

Hence **'crow's-footed, crowsfooted** *ppl. a.*, marked with crow's-feet round the eyes.

1831 T. L. PEACOCK *Crotchet Castle* i, Whose physiognomy..blighted, sallowed, and crow's footed. **1864** SALA in *Daily Tel.* 26 Feb., This dark face, strongly marked, livid and crowsfooted.

crow-silk. [CROW *sb.*¹] A name given to the *Confervæ* and other delicate green-spored Algæ with fine silky filaments, especially to the common freshwater species *Conferva rivularis.*

1721 R. BRADLEY *Works Nat.* 55 About three miles from Colchester there are little Pits..in which they place Baskets of Oysters..to..grow green by feeding upon a sort of Crow-silk, which is in great plenty in those Pits. **1777** LIGHTFOOT *Flora Scot.* II. 976 River Conferva, Crow Silk. **1861** H. MACMILLAN *Footnotes fr. Nature* 166 The various species of confervæ are known in country places by the popular name of crow-silks.

'crow's nest, crow's-nest.

†**1.** *Mil.* ? A fort placed on a height. *Obs.*

1604 E. GRIMSTONE *Hist. Siege Ostend* 163, 2 Frenchmen ..fled vnto the enemies to the crowes neast.

2. *Naut.* A barrel or cylindrical box fixed to the mast-head of an arctic, whaling or other ship, as a shelter for the look-out man.

1818 *Blackw. Mag.* IV. 343 The Crows-Nest is.. generally a cask, fixed near the mast-head, to protect the observer from cold, and enable him to look out for whales, or open pieces of water. **1823** SCORESBY *Jrnl.* 470 *Crow's Nest*..This..was the invention of Captain Scoresby senior, and is now universally used by the northern whalers. **1856** KANE *Arctic Explor.* I. iv. 38, I was able, from the crow's-nest, to pick our way to a larger pool.

3. *N.Z.* (See quot. 1930.)

1930 L. G. D. ACLAND *Early Canterbury Runs* i. 5 To save trouble and disturbing the sheep more than was necessary, 'Crow's nests' were built on some plains stations—platforms on poles or in cabbage trees from which the shepherds could see where the sheep were. **1949** in S. S. Crawford *Sheep & Sheepmen of Canterbury* v. 39.

†**'crowsoap.** *Obs.* [Cf. CROW *sb.* 10.] The plant Soapwort, *Saponaria officinalis*; also applied to some species of *Lychnis.*

a **1387** *Sinon. Barthol.* (Anecd. Oxon.) 37 *Saponaria*, crowsope. **1578** LYTE *Dodoens* II. x. 159 The wilde Campions are called..of some Crowesope.

'crow-step. *Arch.* (In *Sc.* craw-.) = CORBIE-STEP (see CORBIE 3).

1822 SCOTT *Redgauntlet* ch. xx, Reckoning from the crawstep to the groundsill. **1884** A. LANG in *Century Mag.* Jan. 331/1 The houses have the old 'crow-step' on the gable.

attrib. **1839-40** W. IRVING *Wolfert's R.* 12 The crow-step gables were of the primitive architecture of the province.

Hence **'crow-stepped** *ppl. a.*

1853 TURNER *Dom. Archit.* III. II. vii. 300 Several of the gables are crow-stepped.

'crow-stone.

1. The fossil shell *Gryphæa* of the Oolite and Lias.

1677 PLOT *Oxfordsh.* 105 The petrified *Concha oblonga crassa*..found in Worcestershire, and there called Crow-stones, Crow-cups, or Egg-stones.

2. A kind of hard white flinty sandstone in the Yorkshire and Derbyshire coal-fields. Cf. CROW 10.

1778 J. WHITEHURST *Orig. State of Earth* 168 These beds [strata incumbent on coal in Derbyshire] are more white and are commonly called crow-stone. **1811** FAREY *Derbyshire* I.

179-80 The immediate floor of every coal seam within all this large district is..a peculiar kind of hard stone, called Crowstone or Ganister. **1864** J. C. ATKINSON in *Gentlem. Mag., Celtic Refuse-heap at Normanby in Cleveland,* The querns were formed, one..of the so-called white flint, or 'crow-stone' of the neighbourhood [Cleveland].

3. 'The top stone of the gable end of a house' (Halliwell).

crowth, obs. f. CROWD, fiddle.

crow-toe. Also crow-toes; *Sc.* and *north. dial.* craw-tae(s, -tees. A popular name of various plants: an early name of the wild hyacinth (*Scilla nutans*); also applied to *Orchis mascula, Lotus corniculatus,* and the various species of Buttercup. (Cf. CROWFOOT.)

1562 TURNER *Herbal* II. 18 a, Hiacinthus is..common in Englande..and it is called Crowtowes, crowfote, and crow-tese. **1637** MILTON *Lycidas* 143 The tufted crow-toe, and pale jessamine. **1657** W. COLES *Adam in Eden* cclxxviii. 45. **1783** AINSWORTH *Lat. Dict.* (Morrell) I, Crow toes, *Hyacinthi flores.* **1812** J. WILSON *Agric. Renfrewshire* 156 (Jam.) Some of the prevailing weeds in meadows..are, crow-foot, or crow-toe, ranunculus acris, etc. **1864** CAPERN *Devon Provincialism,* Crow-toe, Crowfoot..the..Buttercup. **1873** *Proc. Berw. Nat. Club* VII. 37 A coarse dry herbage, composed of Carices, Crow-toes, &c.

2. = CROWFOOT 6.

1816 SCOTT *Antiq.* iii, Three ancient calthrops, or crawtaes, which had been lately dug up..near Bannockburn.

†**'crow-tread,** *v. Obs. trans.* To tread (a fowl) as crows or rooks were supposed to do; hence *fig.* to subject to ignominious treatment, abuse. Hence **'crow-trod, -trodden** *ppl. adjs.*

1592 G. HARVEY *Pierce's Super.* 6 Who is so forward to accuse, debase, revile, crow-treade another. **1600** N. BRETON *Pasquil's Precession* Wks. (1879) 9 A crauen henne that is crow trodden. **1602** *Content. Liberality & Prodigality* IV. iv. in Hazl. *Dodsley* VIII. 366 O thou vile, ill-favoured, crow-trodden, pye-picked ront! **1614** MARKHAM *Cheap Husb.* (1668) 118. **1649** C. WALKER *Hist. Independ.* II. 8 Cockatrice Eggs laid by their Grandees when they had been Crow-trodden by Armies from abroad. *a* **1652** BROME *Queenes Exchange* v. Wks. 1873 III. 537 What are thou that canst look thus Piepickt, Crowtrod, or Sparrow-blasted?

croy (krɔɪ). *Sc.* [Formed from early Sc. *croys,* pl. of *cro* wattled enclosure for catching fish: cf. CREW², CROO, CRUIVE.] A structure in a river designed to hold back the water and restrict it to a certain channel; also = CRUIVE 4.

[**1493** in *Acts of Lords Auditors of Causes & Complaints 1466–1494* (1839) 179/2 Johne Erskin..dois na wrang In the occupationn of the Croys of montross and fisching of the sammyn.] **1825** in JAMIESON Suppl. *a* **1877** KNIGHT *Dict. Mech.* I. 652/1 *Croy,* a mound or structure projecting into a stream, to break the force of the water on a particular part and prevent encroachments. **1880** *Scottish Naturalist* V. 258 It [*sc.* a cormorant] frequented a croy at Benchill fishing-station. **1908** *Baily's Mag.* May 380 Croys may be convenient for casting from. **1909** W. L. CALDERWOOD *Salmon Rivers Scot.* 70 At Edradynate the system of croy-building has been carefully developed by Mr. H. W. Johnston, so that in one large pool alone..there are eleven croys.

croy, var. of CRO *Obs.*

croyce, croys(e, etc., var. *crois,* CROSS *sb.,* CROISE *v. Obs.*

croycer, -ser, obs. ff. CROSIER, cross-bearer.

croydon ('krɔɪdən). [Named from Croydon in Surrey.] A kind of two-wheeled carriage of the gig class, introduced about 1850, originally of wicker-work, but afterwards made of wood.

1880 *Daily News* 2 Dec. 6/6 A croydon driven by a farmer. **1890** MRS. B. M. CROKER *Two Masters* xxii. 139 As I clambered into the croydon beside her.

†**croydon-sanguine.** *Obs.* 'Supposed to be a kind of sallow colour' (Nares).

(In the first quot. it is associated with Croydon in Surrey, but app. only as a humorous play upon the name.)

1567 R. EDWARDS *Damon & P.* in Hazl. *Dodsley* IV. 80 [To Grim, the collier of Croydon] By'r Lady, you are of a good complexion, A right Croyden sanguine. **1596** HARINGTON *Metam. Ajax* L vij (N.), A complexion inclining to the Oriental colour of a croydon-sanguine. **1630** BRETON *Post w. Packet,* Your Croidon sanguine is a most fine complexion.

croyl. *Obs.* or *dial.* (See quot.)

1836 J. PHILLIPS *Illustr. Geol. Yorksh.* II. 28 Croyl, or indurated clay with shells.

Hence, perhaps, †**croylstone,** a name for native sulphate of barium; cawk.

1728 WOODWARD *Fossils* 18 Croyl-Stone, Craulgum, Crystalliz'd Cauk; likewise from the Peak Lead Mines. In this the Crystalls are very small.

croyll(e, var. of CRILE *Obs.,* obs. f. CREWEL.

croyn(e, Sc. form of CROON.

croysada, -sade, -sado, etc.: see CRUSADE.

croysant, obs. form of CRESCENT.

croysee, var. CROISEE *Obs.,* crusade.

croze (krəʊz), *sb. Coopering.* In 7 croes, crowes. [perh. derived from F. *creux,* OF. *croz,* hollow, cavity, groove, excavation, *creuser,* OF. *croser,* to hollow out, excavate.

Quot. 1706 (repeated in a number of 18th c. Dicts.) appears to be due to a combination of blunders; *crome* is prob. a misprint for *crowe*; and *croe, crowe,* fictitious singulars due to mistaking Cotgrave's *croes, crowes,* for plurals.]

1. The groove at the ends of the staves of a cask, barrel, etc., to receive the edge of the head.

1611 COTGR., *Enjabler,* to rigoll a peece of caske; or, to make the Crowes; also, to make the head fit for the Crowes. *Ibid., Jables,* the croes of a peece of caske; the furrow, or hollow (at either end of the pipe-staues) whereinto the head-peeces be enchased. [**1706** PHILLIPS (ed. Kersey), *Croe* or *Crome*..an Iron-bar or Leaver..also a notch in the Side-boards of a Cask or Tub, where the Head-pieces come in.] **1852** *Board of Fisheries Notice* (May 15), The present cran..The Staves not to be under two Inches, nor to exceed four Inches in breadth, and no croze to be allowed. **1880** *Libr. Univ. Knowl., Barrel-making machinery,* A croze, or groove, to receive the head.

2. A cooper's tool for making the groove in cask staves, etc.

a **1846** WORCESTER cites NEWTON. **1846-50** tr. *Holzapffel's Turning* II. 488 The cooper's croze is used for making the grooves for the heading of casks. **1888** ADDY *Sheffield Gloss., Croze-stock,* the wooden handle into which a croze is fitted.

croze, *v.*¹ *Coopering.* [f. prec. or its F. source.] *trans.* To make the croze in (cask staves, etc.).

1849 *Rep. U.S. Comm. Patents* (1850) 386, I also claim the apparatus for chamfering and howelling and crozing.

Hence **'crozing** *vbl. sb.*; also *attrib.*

1880 *Times* 9 Oct. 10/3 The chining, crozing, and howelling machine. **1883** *Fisheries Exhib. Catal.* 83 Machine for chiming, crozing and howelling casks.

croze, *v.*² *Hat-making.* In felting hats, to refold (a hat-body) so as to present a different surface to the action of the felting-machine.

crozier, -ed: see CROSIER, -ED.

crozle, *v. local. intr.* Of coal: To run together or cake with heat. ***crozling coal***: a caking or bituminous coal.

1811 FAREY *Derbyshire* I. 177 On the banks of the Erewash..crozling or melting coals are very rare. **1834** E. MAMMATT *Ashby Coal-Field* Gloss. 100 *Crozling.*—This takes place when small coal aggregates in burning. **1855** J. PHILLIPS *Man. Geol.,* Derbyshire and Nottinghamshire..Some of the coal is of a 'crozling' or caking nature.

crozzle ('krɒz(ə)l), *sb. dial.* [Relation to prec. obscure.] A cinder.

1819 HUNTER *Hallamsh., Crozzil,* half-burnt coals. **1883** *Almondb. & Huddersf. Gloss., Crozzle,* a hard cinder found in furnaces. **1887** S. O. ADDY in *N. & Q.* 7th Ser. III. 422/2 The [bronze] spear-head bears marks of having been subjected to a hot fire, the point especially having been burnt to a 'crozzil'.

crozzle, *v. dial.* (See quot.)

1876 ROBINSON *Whitby Gloss., Crozzled,* curled. 'Crozzl'd up like a squirrel', huddled together.

‖**cru** (kry). Also crû. [Fr., f. *crû,* pa. pple. of *croître* to grow.] A French vineyard or wine-producing region; the grade of wine produced there. Also *attrib., Comb.,* and *fig.*

1824 tr. *Jullien's Topography of Vineyards & their Products* p. xiii, A wine is called of such a *cru,* meaning a circumscribed spot in a vineyard; it is also used in a more extensive sense, as the *cru* of such a district, &c. **1833** C. REDDING *Mod. Wines* iv. 67 *Cru.* This word is applied in several ways. It means a vineyard, a particular spot in a vineyard, any vine land generally. **1862** C. TOVEY *Wine & Wine Countries* iv. 131 There are in Bordeaux Wines four estates, or growths, classed as first *crûs* or growths. **1867** 'OUIDA' *Under Two Flags* I. vii. 139 He drank the right *cru* and lived in the right set. **1939** F. M. FORD *Let.* 24 Jan. (1965) 309 Chateau Pavie is usually esteemed one of the big cru wines. **1951** R. POSTGATE *Plain Man's Guide to Wine* v. 92 The finest château bottled Premier Cru Classé of Médoc is connected by an insensible progression with the Bordeaux ordinaires. **1962** *Economist* 27 Jan. 334/1 Although most provincial papers are conservative, their conservatism is..not of the same *cru* as..the journalistic norm in Paris. **1963** *Times* 22 Jan. 12/3 Many of the vineyards which are classified as *crus bourgeois supérieurs* or *crus bourgeois*—that is, which did not appear among the first five growths in 1855—have profited by the great advances in viticulture since then. **1966** P. V. PRICE *France, Food & Wine Guide* 172 Just below the classed growths come the *crus bourgeois*..then the *crus artisans.*

cru, obs. f. *crew,* pa. t. of CROW *v.*¹

crualte, -aulte, obs. ff. CRUELTY.

crub. Also 6 crubbe, 7 crubb. [By metathesis for *curb.*] A variant of CURB *sb.,* still in dialect use. See *esp.* quot. 1890.

1565 *Richmond. Wills* (Surtees) 178, 1 brode pan and a crubbe to the same. **1636** *MS. Accts. Hull Charterhouse,* A great brewing copper..set in a wooden crubb. **1890** BARING-GOULD *Old Country Life* 205 The packhorse had crooks on its back and the goods were hung to these crooks..The short crooks called crubs were slung in a similar manner. These were of stouter fabric and formed an angle; these were used for carrying heavy materials.

crubeen (kruː'biːn, 'kruːbiːn). *Anglo-Irish* [ad. Irish *crúibín,* dim. of *crúb* claw, hoof, paw.] The foot of an animal; esp. a (cooked) pig's foot.

1847 W. H. GREGORY *Paddiana* II. 95 Did ye ever see a pair of *crubeens* like them? **1907** G. B. SHAW *John Bull's Other Island* IV. 81 It [*sc.* the pig] put in the fourth speed wid its right crubeen as if it was enthered for the Gordn Bennett [car race]. **1922** JOYCE *Ulysses* 144 Florence MacCabe takes a crubeen and a bottle of double X for supper every Saturday. **1970** M. KENYON *100,000 Welcomes* xii. 96 'No crubeens', said Rafferty, fingering the groceries... 'All I wanted was crubeens.'

cruceato, var. of CRUCIADE, crusade.

†**crucet-hus.** *Obs.* [OE.; *crucet* is app. an adaptation of L. *cruciātus* or its OF. form *cruciet.*] House of torment; see quot.

1137 *O.E. Chron.* Sume hi diden in crucethus ðis in an cæste þat was scort & nareu & un dep & dide scærpe stanes þer inne. [**1839** KEIGHTLEY *Hist. Eng.* I. 122 Some, they put in the crucet-house, that is in a chest that was short, narrow, and not deep, and put sharp stones in it and forced the man in, and so broke all his limbs.]

cruche, obs. f. of CROCHE¹, CROUCH, CRUTCH.

†**cruche¹.** *Obs.* [Cf. F. *crochet* a flat curl gummed to the forehead or temples.] A small curl lying flat on the forehead.

1690 EVELYN *Mundus Muliebris,* Nor cruches she, nor confidents, Nor passagers, nor bergers wants.

cruche² (kruːʃ). [Fr., = pitcher.] = CRUSE.

1856 J. C. ROBINSON *Invent. Objects Mus. Ornamental Art* 26 Cylindrical Mug or Cruche. *Ibid.* 27 Globular brown glazed Flemish or Old English Cruche ('Gray-beard'). **1874** LADY C. SCHREIBER *Jrnl.* (1952) I. 446 Bought our cruche.

cruchet, obs. Sc. form of CROTCHET.

1489 *Barbour's Bruce* x. 401 (MS. E.) That maid a clap, quhen the cleket [*MS. E.* cruchet] Wes festnyt fast in the kyrnell.

†**'cruciable,** *a. Obs. rare.* [ad. L. *cruciābil-is* tormenting, racking, f. *cruciāre* to torture, rack: see CRUCIATE.] Excruciating, racking.

1578 BANISTER *Hist. Man* I. 7 His continuall cruciable payne, and capitall dolour. *Ibid.* 14 Such cruciable tormentes of Rheumaticke incursions.

cruciade, -ada, -at, cruceato. [Obs. forms of CRUSADE, founded on med.L. *cruciata,* It. *crociata,* and allied Romanic forms; Littré has *cruciade* in sense b.] **a.** A crusade. **b.** A papal bull authorizing a crusade or giving privileges to those who engaged therein.

1429 *Petition* in Rymer *Foedera* (1710) X. 419 That I may Publishe..the Cruciat [against Bohemia], whiche is committed unto me of our Holy Fadre..Considered that Cruciats have been late seen in this Land. **1501** HEN. VII in J. Gairdner *Papers Reigns Rich. III & Hen. VII* (Rolls) I. 154 That our said souuerain lord will suffre the cruciade to [proceed] and take effect. **1611** SPEED *Hist. Gt. Brit.* IX. xiii. 59 Few were found open-handed towards this Cruceato [*huic cruce signationi*]. *a* **1670** HACKET *Abp. Williams* II. 196 (D.) The Pope's Cruciada drew thousands of soldiers to adventure into the Holy War.

crucial ('kruːʃɪəl, -ʃ(ɪ)əl), *a.* [a. F. *crucial* (Paré 16th c.), f. L. *cruc-em* cross + -AL¹.]

1. (Chiefly *Anat.*) Of the form of a cross, cross-shaped, as ***crucial incision***; *spec.* the name of two ligaments in the knee-joint, which cross each other in the form of the letter **X**, and connect the femur and tibia; also applied to 'the transverse ligament of the atlas and its upper and lower offshoots combined' (*Syd. Soc. Lex.*).

1706 PHILLIPS (ed. Kersey) s.v. *Incision, Crucial Incision,* the cutting or lancing of an Impostume or Swelling cross-wise. **1767** GOOCH *Treat. Wounds* I. 451 Making an incision quite cross to the bone, from ear to ear; which section is preferable to the crucial, commonly made. **1804** ABERNETHY *Surg. Obs.* 256 Between the condyles of the os femoris and the crucial ligaments. **1859** J. TOMES *Dental. Surg.* 338 In the molar teeth of the lower jaw, the decay sometimes takes a crucial shape. **1861** S. THOMSON *Wild Fl.* III. (ed. 4) 302 The crucial flowers.

2. That finally decides between two rival hypotheses, proving the one and disproving the other; more loosely, relating to, or adapted to lead to such decision; decisive, critical. Freq. in trivial use = 'very important'.

This sense is taken from Bacon's phrase *instantia crucis,* explained by him as a metaphor from a *crux* or finger-post at a *bivium* or bifurcation of a road. Boyle and Newton used the phrase *experimentum crucis.* These give 'crucial instance', 'crucial experiment', whence the usage has been extended. Occasionally the sense intended seems to be 'of the nature of a crux or special difficulty'; see CRUX.

[**1620** BACON *Nov. Org.* II. xxxvi, *Instantias Crucis:* translato Vocabulo a Crucibus, quæ erectæ in Biuijs, indicant & signant viarum separationes. Has etiam Instantias Decisorias & Iudiciales, & in Casibus nonnullis Instantias Oraculi, & Mandati appellare consueuimus. **1672** NEWTON *Light & Colours* i, The gradual removal of these suspicions at length led me to the *Experimentum Crucis.*] [Not in JOHNSON, TODD, or WEBSTER 1828.] **1830** HERSCHEL *Stud. Nat. Phil.* II. vi. 150 What Bacon terms 'crucial instances', which are phenomena brought forward to decide between two causes, each having the same analogies in its favour. **1869** J. MARTINEAU *Ess.* II. 134 Crucial experiments for the verification..of his theory. **1874** HELPS *Soc. Press.* xvi. 226 Showing where, at some crucial point of the story, fraud or delusion might enter. **1957** F. KING *Widow* II. x.

245 That's the crucial time for me, like the first month of a baby. **1963** *New Statesman* 8 Feb. 195/1 What is crucial, of course, is that these books aren't very good. **1968** *Ibid.* 23 Feb. 241/2 Twice at crucial moments in this volcanic tragic comedy he asked us to advise him what to do. **1971** *Times* 19 Jan. 1 (*headline*) Leaders arrange to meet in private before today's crucial debate.

¶ 3. Apparently associated with the trying action of a 'crucible'.

1856 MRS. BROWNING *Aur. Leigh* v. 310 And from the imagination's crucial heat Catch up their men and women all a-flame For action. **1860** *Lit. Churchman* VI. 222/1 This crucial time..which will purge out the dross and tin of popery and dissent.

Hence **'crucially** *adv.*, in a crucial manner.

1879 H. GRUBB in *Trans. R. Dubl. Soc.* 188 Any one can try this crucially for himself.

crucian, crusian ('kru:ʃən). Also 8 **crusion.** [Formed with suffix -AN, and accommodated spelling, from earlier or dial. LG. *karusse, karuse, karutze* (mod.G. *karausche*), cf. Du. *karuts* (Kilian), Da. *karudse*, South Sw. *karussa* (Grimm). An older MG. form was *karas, karaz*, corresp. to Russ., Pol., Boh. *karas*, whence zoological specific name *carassius*. The ultimate source is supposed to be L. *coracīnus*, a. Gr. *κορακῖνος* a black fish like a perch, found in the Nile; but the actual history of the word in the modern langs. is obscure.]

A species of fish, a native of Central Europe, now naturalized in England, of a deep yellow colour, also called ***crucian carp***, and (when lean) ***German*** or ***Prussian carp***; it is closely allied to the Carp, but with the Goldfish is now generally placed in a distinct genus *Carassius*, being *C. carassius*.

1763 C. SMART *Song to David* lvii, And by the coasting reader spy'd, the silverlings and crusions glide, For Adoration gilt. **1771** *Phil. Trans.* LXI. 318 Sometimes crusians and carp, or tench and carp, [are] put together in a pond. **1836** YARRELL *Brit. Fishes* I. 311 The Crucian Carp is found in some of the ponds about London. In Warwickshire it is called Crouger. **1880** GUNTHER *Fishes* 591 The Crucian Carp (*Carassius carassius*) is much subject to variation of form; very lean examples are commonly called 'Prussian Carps'.

†**'cruciar.** *Obs. rare*$^{-1}$. [f. L. *cruciāre* to torture, crucify.] = CRUCIFIER.

c **1400** *Apol. Loll.* 21 He..prayed for his cruciars.

cruciate ('kru:ʃɪət), *a.* Now only in *Zool.* and *Bot.* [ad. med. or mod.L. *cruciāt-us*, f. *crux, crucem* cross: see -ATE.] Formed like a cross, cross-shaped; arranged in the form of a cross.

1826 KIRBY & SP. *Entomol.* (1828) III. xxxv. 539 In numbers of Locusta the prothorax is what Linné terms cruciate. **1835** LINDLEY *Introd. Bot.* (1848) I. 335 The cruciate flower has four valvaceous sepals, four petals, and six stamens. **1870** HOOKER *Stud. Flora* 132 Chrysosplenium ..Capsule..opening at the top by a cruciate mouth.

†**b.** as *sb.* = CRUCIAL incision. *Obs.*

1684 tr. *Bonet's Merc. Compit.* III. 81 He made a Cruciate ..three inches every way.

c. in *Comb.* = CRUCIATO-, as ***cruciate-complicate***.

†**'cruciate,** *pa. pple. Obs.* [ad. L. *cruciāt-us*, pa. pple. of *cruciāre* to torture, rack, torment, f. *crux, crucem*, CROSS.] Tortured.

1504 ATKINSON tr. *T. à Kempis* III. liii. (1893) 241 He is crucyate and turmentyd with penury and nede. **1554** KNOX *Godly Let.* A iij b, I am crucyet for remembraunce of your troubles. **1563-87** FOXE *A. & M.* (1596) 82/1 Pinched and cruciat with sundrie punishments.

cruciate ('kru:ʃɪeɪt), *v.* Also 6 crutiate. [f. *cruciāt-*, ppl. stem of L. *cruciāre*: see prec. Used as a pa. pple. before it became the verb-stem, after which it continued to be used for some time as pa. pple., and in Sc. writers also as pa. t.]

1. *trans.* To afflict with grievous pain or distress; to torture, torment, to EXCRUCIATE. *arch.*

1532 HEN. VIII *Let.* in Burnet *Hist. Ref.* II. 168 Ye do still cruciate the Patient and Afflicte. **1550** BALE *Image Both Ch.* D v b, Thou art..inwardlye crucyated in conscience. **1560** ROLLAND *Crt. Venus* II. 205, xviij. Kings he cruciat. **1609** W. M. *Man in Moone* (1849) 43 Hee cruciateth himself with the thought of her. **1702** C. MATHER *Magn. Chr.* II. App. (1852) 208 She directed her familiar spirits how and where to cruciate the objects of her malice. **1834** H. MILLER *Scenes & Leg.* iv. (1857) 53 To cruciate himself by fancying his cradle his sepulchre.

†**2.** To crucify. *Obs. rare.*

1560 ROLLAND *Crt. Venus* II. 366 Sum said he seruit for to be cruciat. **1658** R. FRANCK *North. Mem.* (1821) 21 He that cruciates his lusts.

3. To mark with crosses, to cross. *nonce-use.*

1877 BLACKMORE *Erema* II. xxxiv. 182 The simple roof is not cruciated with tiles of misguided fancy.

Hence **'cruciated, 'cruciating** *ppl. adjs.*

1643 PRYNNE *Sov. Power Parl.* App. 212 Contrite, cruciated, afflicted Joseph. **1670** MAYNWARING *Vita Sana* i. 5 Cruciating maladies. **1762** KAMES *Elem. Crit.* ii. §6 The pain of an affront [is]..cruciating and tormenting.

'cruciately, *adv.* In a cruciate manner; so as to resemble a cross; crosswise.

cruciation. Now *rare* or *Obs.* [ad. L. *cruciātiōn-em*, n. of action f. *cruciare* to CRUCIATE.] Torture, torment.

15.. *Skelton's Wks., Epit. Dk. Bedford* 85 By cruel crucyation He hath combryd hym sore. **1659** PEARSON *Creed* 297 Which cannot be annihilation, but cruciation only. **1862** MRS. SPEID *Last Years Ind.* 17 The protection of my bonnet saved me from further outrage and cruciation.

cruciato-, combining form of L. *cruciātus*, CRUCIATE *a.*, as in **cruciato-complicate,** 'applied by Kirby to the wings of insects which are at the same time crossed and folded, as those of the *Pentatoma*'; **cruciato-incumbent,** 'applied to the wings of insects when they are crossed but not folded, and when they cover the abdomen, as in the *Apis*' (*Syd. Soc. Lex.*).

†**'cruciatory,** *a. Obs. rare*$^{-1}$. [ad. L. *cruciātōri-us*, f. *cruciātor*, agent-n. f. *cruciāre*: see -ORY.] Torturing, tormenting.

1660 HOWELL *Parly of Beasts* 7 (D.) These cruciatory passions.

crucible ('kru:sɪb(ə)l), *sb.* Forms: 5 **corusible, (kressibulle),** 7- **crucible,** (7 **crus-, chrus-,** 8 **cruzible**). [ad. med.L. *crucibulum, -bolum*, orig. a night-lamp, later a melting pot for metals—the only English sense.

App. a deriv. of L. *crux, crucis* Cross: cf. the kindred words It. *crociuolo*, OF. *croiseul*, later F. *croiset, creuset*, f. It. *croce*, F. *croix*, and see Du Cange, Littré, Hatzfeld, who suggest for the original sense 'lamp with crossed wicks giving 4 flames', but this is doubtful: cf. CRUSELL. A 15th c. Vocabulary in Wright-Wülcker 576/9 has '*Crassipulum, Crassipularium, Crucibolum*, a Cresset', where the two synonyms appear to be derivatives of *crassus* fat, *crassa* grease; but their association with *crucibolum* appears to be due to popular etymology.]

1. A vessel, usually of earthenware, made to endure great heat, used for fusing metals, etc.; a melting-pot.

1460-70 *Bk. Quintessence* 9 In þe corusible ȝe schal fynde þe gold calcyned and reducid into erþe. **1495** *Nottingham Rec.* III. 284 Item kressibulles iiijd. **1605** TIMME *Quersit.* II. iii. 113 Salt-peter remaineth liquid and fusible in a red hote crucible. **1611** COTGR., *Creuset*, a cruzible, cruzet, or cruet; a little earthen pot wherein Goldsmithes melt their siluer, etc. **1776** ADAM SMITH *W.N.* I. i. iv. 26 A part of the metal is melted in the crucible. **1800** HENRY *Epit. Chem.* (1808) 5 Crucibles..are most commonly made of a mixture of fire-clay and sand, occasionally with the addition of plumbago. **1872** J. YEATS *Techn. Hist. Comm.* 51 The gold was fused in clay crucibles.

b. A hollow or basin at the bottom of a furnace to collect the molten metal.

1864 in WEBSTER. **1881** in RAYMOND *Mining Gloss.*

2. *fig.* Used of any severe test or trial.

c **1645** HOWELL *Lett.* (1688) II. 334 In this Limbec and Crusible of Affliction. **1796** H. HUNTER tr. *St.-Pierre's Stud. Nat.* (1799) III. 332 A ship is the crucible in which morals are put to the test. **1884** ANNIE S. SWAN *Dorothea Kirke* xiv. 128 So in the crucible of pain we are purified. **1887** *Spectator* 21 May 683/2 He had lived through the Mutiny, he remembered when all India was in the crucible.

3. *attrib.* and *Comb.*, as ***crucible-earth; crucible-steel***, cast steel.

1664 EVELYN *Kal. Hort.* (1729) 232 Pipes..made of the best Crucible-earth. **1799** G. SMITH *Laboratory* I. 229 Take two pounds of crucible powder, of such as is commonly used for refining of silver. **1879** *Cassell's Techn. Educ.* IV. 371/2 Crucible or cast-steel. **1886** *Pall Mall G.* 29 Sept. 6/2 The cable..will consist of six strands of crucible steel twisted round a Manilla centre.

Hence (*nonce-wds.*) **crucible** *v.*, to put into or melt in a crucible; **crucibled** *ppl. a.* (*fig.* in quot.)

1796 *Mod. Gulliver's Trav.* 164 Crucibled perversion's threefold mask. **1841** J. T. HEWLETT *Parish Clerk* III. 251 Had it been silver, it would doubtless have been crucibled long since.

crucifer ('kru:sɪfə(r)). [a. late L. *crucifer* cross-bearer (applied by Prudentius to Christ).]

1. *Eccl.* An attendant who carries a cross in a procession; a cross-bearer.

1574 *Life 70th Abp. Canterb.* Pref. D iij b, What fees weare bestowed on his crucifer Marshall, and other seruantes. **1865** *Reader* 24 June 706 The procession, headed by a crucifer, left the school-room. **1888** F. G. LEE in *Archæol.* LI. 365 *note*, The bishop of Rochester..is official crucifer to the archbishops of Canterbury.

2. *Bot.* A cruciferous plant: see next.

1846 LINDLEY *Veg. Kingd.* 352 Almost all Crucifers are destitute of bracts. **1872** OLIVER *Elem. Bot.* II. 139 All Crucifers are wholesome, and many are anti-scorbutic.

cruciferous (kru:'sɪfərəs), *a.* [a. late L. *crucifer* cross-bearing + -OUS.]

1. Bearing, wearing, or adorned with, a cross.

1656 BLOUNT *Glossogr.*, *Cruciferous*, he that bears the Cross. **1670** G. H. *Hist. Cardinals* III. III. 317 The Convent of the Cruciferous Fryers. **1875** MASKELL *Ivories* 30 The head of Christ with a cruciferous nimbus.

2. *Bot.* Belonging to the order *Cruciferæ*; bearing flowers with four equal petals arranged crosswise. Also said of the flowers or petals; = CRUCIATE, CRUCIFORM.

1851 GLENNY *Handbk. Fl. Gard.* 25 The flowers being small, white, of the cruciferous form. **1868** DUNCAN *Insect World* iii. 91 The cabbage and most of the cruciferous plants.

crucificial (-'fɪʃəl), *a. rare.* [f. L. *crucem* cross + *-fici-um* making + -AL[1]: cf. *artificial.*] Of or pertaining to making a cross.

1849 THACKERAY *Lett.* Feb., [He] blessed the people, making crucificial signs.

crucified ('kru:sɪfaɪd), *ppl. a.* [f. CRUCIFY + -ED.] Nailed to a cross; see CRUCIFY.

c **1340** HAMPOLE *Prose Tr.* (1866) 10 Haly crosses..are in syngne of Cryste crucyfiede. **1534** TINDALE *1 Cor.* i. 23 But we preache Christ crucified. **1705** PENN in *Pa. Hist. Soc. Mem.* X. 71, I am a crucified man between Injustice and Ingratitude there, and Extortion and Oppression here. **1888** PLUMPTRE *Life of Ken* I. ii. 20 A figure of the Crucified One, not on the cross, but on an anchor, as the emblem of hope.

b. *absol.* A crucified person; *spec.* = Christ.

1548 UDALL, etc. *Erasm. Par. Acts* 37 b, A professoure of the crucified. **1614** BP. HALL *Recoll. Treat.* 643 The crosse was a slow death..whence a second violence must dispatch the crucified. **1827** KEBLE *Chr. Y., Monday bef. Easter* i, So evermore..We own the Crucified in weal or woe.

crucifier ('kru:sɪfaɪə(r)). Also 5 **-our.** [f. as prec. + -ER[1].] One who crucifies.

c **1320** R. BRUNNE *Medit.* 710 For hys crucyfyers mekely he preyd. *c* **1450** *Mirour Saluacioun* 148 Crist..prayed for his crucyfiours. **1686** AGLIONBY *Painting Illust.* 243 The Rage of his Crucifiers. **1838** LYTTON *Leila* II. i, Shall there be no difference between..His disciples and His crucifiers?

b. One who torments or worries.

1870 W. DASENT *Annals Eventful Life* (ed. 4) II. 281 She was never much of a catechiser or crucifier.

‖**cruci'fige.** *Obs.* L. *crucifīge*, crucify (him)! the cry of the Jews to Pilate; formerly sometimes used subst., and transferred to: Popular clamour for the death of a victim.

1393 LANGL. *P. Pl.* C. XXI. 38 And alle þe court cryede crucifige lowde. **1593** PEELE *Edw. I*, 139 If this crucifige do not suffice Send me to heaven in a hempen sacrifice. *a* **1635** NAUNTON *Fragm. Reg.* (Arb.) 27 His Father dying in ignominie, and at the Gallows, his Estate confiscate..by the clamour, and crucifige of the people. **1652** SPARKE *Prim. Devot.* (1663) 215 Their palms are turned into thorns, and their hosannahs into crucifiges.

crucifix ('kru:sɪfɪks), *sb.* [a. OF. *crucefix*, now *crucifix*, = Pr. *crucific*, Sp. *crucifixo*, It. *crocifisso*, ad. L. *cruci fixus*, later *crucifixus*, (one) fixed to a cross, crucified.]

†**1.** The Crucified One; Christ on the cross.

14.. *Prose Legends* in *Anglia* VIII. 155 Þe deþe of þe crucifix [L. *mortem crucifixi*]. **1485** CAXTON *Gold. Leg.* 168/4 To fore the ymage of the crucyfyxe. **1526** *Pilgr. Perf.* (W. de W. 1531) 81 b, Suche may..with mekenes approche to the crucifixe and stande by hym. *a* **1633** AUSTIN *Medit.* (1635) 114 To take up our Crosse, and become, like him, a Crucifix. **1649** JER. TAYLOR *Gt. Exemp.* II. ix. 118 He that sweares by the Crosse, sweares by the Holy Crucifix, that is, Jesus crucified thereon. **1660** —— *Duct. Dubit.* II. iii. Rule ix. §31 The brazen serpent..was but a type and a shadow of the holy crucifix.

2. An image or figure (formerly also a pictorial representation) of Christ upon the cross.

a **1225** *Ancr. R.* 16 Ualleð a cneon to ower crucifix. **1387** TREVISA *Higden* (Rolls) V. 399 Wiþ a crucifix i-peynt in a table. *c* **1430** LYDG. *Bochas* VIII. xiii. (1554) 185 a, Where that euer he hath perceiued Crosse or crucifix, he brake them vengeably. **1553** *Act 1 Mary* Sess. II. c. 3 §4 If anye person..shall..deface..or..breake any aulter..or any crucifixe or Crosse. **1666** PEPYS *Diary* 20 July, To Lovett's, there to see how my picture goes on to be varnished; a fine Crucifix. **1867** GEO. ELIOT *Felix Holt* 3 There was no.. crucifix or image to indicate a misguided reverence. **1885** *Catholic Dict.* (ed. 3) s.v., No crucifix has been found in the Catacombs; no certain allusion to a crucifix is made by any Christian writer of the first four centuries.

¶ Todd, misunderstanding Jeremy Taylor's use of 'holy Crucifix' (in sense 1), inserted a conjectured sense 'The cross of Christ; figuratively, the religion of Christ', an error which has been repeated in the Dictionaries.

The misuse of *crucifix* for 'cross, figure of the cross', is frequent in writers of the 18-19th c.

1806 J. GRAHAME *Birds Scot.* 21 The red brick-wall, with ..many a leafy crucifix adorned. **1827** G. HIGGINS *Celtic Druids* 126, I make a great distinction between a cross, and a human figure nailed to a cross, two things which, under the name of crucifix, are so often confounded. **1848** LYTTON *Harold* XII. vi, The simple imageless crucifix that stood on its pedestal at the farther end of the tent.

†**'crucifix,** *v. Obs. rare.* [f. L. *cruci-fix-*, ppl. stem of *cruci-figĕre*: see CRUCIFY and FIX.] *trans.* To crucify.

1483 CAXTON *G. de la Tour* I vj b, He bare the Crosse for to be theron crucifixed. **1598** SYLVESTER *Du Bartas* II. i. IV. (1641) 108/2 Messias..mockt, beat..crucifixt. **1635** SWAN *Spec. M.* i. §3 (1643) 17 Crucifixt For our foul sinnes.

Hence †**'crucifixer,** crucifier.

c **1450** *Mirour Saluacioun* 1708 Crist praying for his Crucifixours.

crucifixion (kru:sɪ'fɪkʃən). [17th c. ad. mod. (16th c.) L. *crucifixiōn-em*, n. of action f. *crucifi-gere* to CRUCIFY: in F. occasional from *c* 1600, but never yet admitted by the Academy.]

1. a. The action of crucifying, or of putting to death on a cross. **b.** *spec. **the Crucifixion***: that of Jesus Christ on Calvary.

1649 JER. TAYLOR *Gt. Exemp.* III. Ad §15. 132 The accidents happening from the apprehension till the crucifixion of Jesus. *a* **1729** R. MOSS *Serm.* (1738) VIII. 364 The Jews, who had no such legal Punishment as Crucifixion. **1855** MILMAN *Lat. Chr.* III. v. I. 375 The abolition of Crucifixion as a punishment by Constantine was an act..of religious reverence. **1858** J. MARTINEAU *Stud. Chr.* 129 So studiously is every allusion to the crucifixion avoided.

2. *fig.* †**a.** Torture, severe pain or anguish (quot. 1648). **b.** The action of 'crucifying' or mortifying (passions, sins, etc.).

1648 HERRICK *Hesper., To Sycamores*, Do ye prove What crucifixions are in love? *a* **1711** KEN *Hymnarium* Poet. Wks. 1721 II. 111 They'll be my constant Crucifixions here. **1838** PUSEY *Par. Serm.* (1873) III. iii, A crucifixion of our passions, appetites, desires.

c. (See quot.)

1917 A. G. EMPEY *From Fire Step* 149 The famous Field Punishment No. 1. Tommy has nicknamed it 'crucifixion'. It means that a man is spread-eagled on a limber wheel two hours a day for twenty-one days. During this time he only gets water, bully beef, and biscuits for his chow. You get 'crucified' for repeated minor offences.

3. A picture or representation of the Crucifixion of Christ.

1841 W. SPALDING *Italy & It. Isl.* II. 353 The masterpiece..is the celebrated Crucifixion. **1859** JEPHSON *Brittany* viii. 113 An incongruous collection of Crucifixions and Venuses.

cruciform ('kruːsɪfɔːm), *a.* [ad. mod.L. *cruciform-is*, f. *cruc-em* cross: see -FORM.] Of the form of a (right-angled) cross; cross-shaped: *spec.* in *Bot.* of the flowers of cruciferous plants; in *Arch.* of a church built in the form of a cross; in *Anat.* = CRUCIAL 1.

1661 LOVELL *Hist. Anim. & Min.* 215 The cruciforme bone of the head [of a pike]. **1794** MARTYN *Rousseau's Bot.* ii. 29 These corollas are called cruciform or cross shaped. **1807** J. E. SMITH *Phys. Bot.* 268 The natural order of Cruciform plants, composing the Linnæan class *Tetradynamia*. **1827** *Gentl. Mag.* XCVII. II. 499 At Horton Kirby..the Antiquary will find a cruciform church.

Hence ˌ**cruci'formity**, the quality or fact of being cruciform; '**cruciˌformly** *adv.*, in form of a cross.

1846 *Ecclesiologist* V. 219 Forms of symbolism..the cruciformity of churches, for instance. **1834** H. O'BRIEN *Round Towers Ireland* 352 The Pagodas of Benares and Mathura..are cruciformly built.

crucify ('kruːsɪfaɪ), *v.* [a. OF. *crucifier* (12th c.) = Pr. and Sp. *crucificar*, repr. a late pop. L. type **crucificāre* instead of L. *cruci figĕre* to fasten to the cross, subseq. as one word *crucifīgere*.]

1. a. *trans.* To put to death by nailing or otherwise fastening to a cross; an ancient mode of capital punishment among Orientals, Greeks, Romans, and other peoples; by the Greeks and Romans considered specially ignominious.

a **1300** *Cursor M.* 18273 (Cott.) þis ilk iesu to crucifi [*v.r.* crucefie]. **1382** WYCLIF *2 Sam.* xxi. 6 Be there ȝouun to us seuen men of the sonys of hem, that we crucifien hem to the Lord in Gabaa of Saul. —— *John* xviii. 15 Thei cryeden, seyinge, do awey, do awey, crucifie hym. **1494** FABYAN *Chron.* VII. ccxxxiii. 267 About this tyme..ye Iues, vpon Ester Euyn, crucifyed a chyld, named Wyllyam, in ye Cytie of Norwych. **1659** SPENSER *Hymne Heavenly Love* 244 Twixt robbers crucifyde. **1649** JER. TAYLOR *Gt. Exemp.* III. xv, Malefactors and persons to be crucified. **1838** THIRLWALL *Greece* II. 223 He was led to Artaphernes, who immediately ordered him to be crucified.

b. *transf.* †(*a*) To fasten or nail to the pillory (*obs.*); (*b*) see quot. 1890.

1664 BUTLER *Hud.* II. *Let. to Sidrophel* 14 William Pryn's [ears] before they were Retrench'd and crucify'd. **1890** *Pall Mall G.* 12 July 2/1 A man and a woman were sentenced..to..penal servitude..for the crime of 'crucifying' a child. By 'crucifying' was meant tying down the child..and beating the helpless little body with a belt.

2. *fig.* **a.** In religious use: To mortify, with reference to the Crucifixion of Christ; esp. to destroy the power of (passions, sins, the flesh, etc.).

c **1320** R. BRUNNE *Medit.* 608 Beholde þe peynes of þy sauyour, And crucyfye þyn herte with grete dolour. **1340** *Ayenb.* 241 þet word þet..sainte paul zayde..'þe wordle..is y-crucefyed to me and ich to þe wordle'. **1382** WYCLIF *Gal.* v. 24 Thei that ben of Crist, han crucified her fleisch with vices and concupiscencis. **1534** TINDALE *Rom.* vi. 6 Oure olde man is crucified with him also, that the body of synne myght vtterly be destroyed. *a* **1652** J. SMITH *Sel. Disc.* i. 17 The faint strugglings of a higher life within them, which they crucify again by their wicked sensuality. **1814** SOUTHEY *Roderick* XVII, Help me, O my God, That I may crucify this inward foe!

†**b.** To afflict with severe pain or distress; to excruciate. **c.** To torment, to prove a 'crux' to.

1621 BURTON *Anat. Mel.* Democr. to Rdr. 15 As great trouble as to perfect the motion of Mars and Mercury, which so crucifies our astronomers. **1702** J. YOUNG in *Phil. Trans.* XXIII. 1280 After she had been thus crucified four days her Urine also stopt. **1728** POPE *Dunc.* I. 164 Old puns restore, lost blunders nicely seek, And crucify poor Shakespear once a week. **1791–1823** D'ISRAELI *Cur. Lit., Quadrio's Acc. Eng. Poetry*, It might..crucify the critical intuition of the ablest of commentators. **1921** D. H. LAWRENCE *Tortoises* 45 Why were we crucified into sex? **1940** H. L. ICKES *Secret Diary* 10 Aug. (1954) III. 297 He knew he would be crucified when he reached his own country. **1947** A. MILLER *All my Sons* (1958) I. 81 *Ann.* Don't you hold anything against him? *Keller.* Annie, I never believed in crucifying people. **1960** *News Chron.* 15 July 3/3 If I was an hour or two late for filming, I was just about crucified. **1971** *Sunday Times* 24 Jan. 29/5, I do wish David Coleman wouldn't say 'Is the TV action replay *crucifying* referees?' I don't much mind what TV does to referees, but I do mind what it does to the language.

d. To subject to 'crucifixion' (see CRUCIFIXION 2c).

¶**3.** ? To put to the crucible. *Obs.*$^{-1}$

1471 RIPLEY *Comp. Alch.* x. in Ashm. (1652) 178 Whych must be Crusyfyed and examynat.

¶**4.** To cross, place cross-wise. *Obs.*$^{-1}$

1633 SHIRLEY *Bird in a Cage* II. i, I do not despair..You see I do not wear my hat in my eyes, crucify my arms.

crucifying ('kruːsɪfaɪɪŋ), *vbl. sb.* [f. CRUCIFY + -ING[1].] The action of the verb CRUCIFY; crucifixion (for which it was the earlier equivalent).

c **1320** R. BRUNNE *Medit.* 693 My crucyfyyng suffyseþ for alle mankynne. *c* **1450** LONELICH *Grail* xlv. 104 Forto hym it sufficeth no thing Of my ferste Crwcyfyeng. **1607** HIERON *Wks.* I. 273 The crucifying of our affections, which the scripture speaketh of. **1653** HAMMOND *On N.T.* John xix. 17 Christs carrying his crosse was a part of the Roman custome of crucifying.

'**crucifying**, *ppl. a.* [f. as prec. + -ING[2].] That crucifies, tortures, excruciates: see the vb.

1648 W. CARTER *Light in Darkness*, Which is a crucifying thing to sinful flesh. **1694** WESTMACOTT *Script. Herb.* (1695) 17 This crucifying Malady. *a* **1711** KEN *Serm.* Wks. (1838) 131 With a crucifying..remembrance of her crucified Saviour. **1792** R. CUMBERLAND *Calvary* (1803) II. 50 Their crucifying clamor. **1934** S. SPENDER *Vienna* ii. 19 And made invisible by crucifying suns Day after day. **1962** *Listener* 22 Nov. 885/3 We talked of a trend in twentieth-century music that is not fortifying but crucifying. **1964** *Times* 10 Dec. 18/3 The crucifying bottlenecks at the docks.

Hence †'**crucifyingly** *adv.*, excruciatingly.

1826 *Blackw. Mag.* XX. 20 Of all visitations..the most crucifyingly horrible.

†**cru'cigeran**, *a. Obs. rare*$^{-1}$. [f. L. type **cruciger* cross-bearing + -AN.] = next. *crucigeran fox* = CROSS-FOX.

1607 TOPSELL *Four-f. Beasts* 174 The Crucigeran Fox.

†**cru'cigerous**, *a. Obs. rare*$^{-1}$. [f. as prec. + -OUS.] Bearing or marked with a cross.

1658 SIR T. BROWNE *Gard. Cyrus* i. 37 The crucigerous Ensigne carried this figure..after the form of an Andrean or Burgundian cross.

crucilly, crucily: see CRUSILY.

†**cruck**[1]. *Obs.* [Cf. ON. *krukka* pot: see CROCK.] A pail or can.

1688 R. HOLME *Armoury* II. 181/2 For keeping of Swine..Crucks, or Cans, to carry their Meat and Draff in. *Ibid.* III. 335/1 Of some Milk-Maids..I have heard..a Milk Pail called..a Cruck.

cruck[2] (krʌk). [Var. CROCK *sb.*[5], CROOK *sb.* 5c.] One of a pair of curved timbers, forming with other pairs the framework of a house; = CROCK *sb.*[5] Freq. *attrib.*

1898 S. O. ADDY *Evol. Eng. House* ii. 17 A building erected in this way is now said to be 'built on crucks'. **1934** *Archit. Rev.* LXXV. 214/2 The foreign prototypes of the English 'cruck' house. **1948** J. WALTON in *Antiquity* XXII. 179 The development of the cruck framework. *Ibid.*, The cruck buildings of Northern England. **1949** K. S. WOODS *Rural Crafts* IV. xi. 170 Two arched or slanting timbers, called crucks, or crutches,..form each of the gable-ends, and support the roof-tree. **1970** H. BRAUN *Parish Churches* viii. 101 The great halls of the Anglo-Saxons were formed of lines of wide timber arches called 'crucks'.

†'**cruckle**, *v.* Variant of CROOKLE *v.*

1691 J. WILSON *Belphegor* II. iii, Did you never see two Cocks cruckling about one Hen.

crud (krʌd). [*Obs.* and *dial.* var. of CURD *sb.*]

1. See CURD *sb.* 1.

2. A despicable or undesirable person or thing; nonsense, rubbish. Cf. CRUT[3]. *slang* (orig. *U.S.*).

1940 *Amer. Speech* XV. 212 A 'crud' is a fellow who is slovenly in his personal appearance and with his possessions. **1942** BERREY & VAN DEN BARK *Amer. Thes. Slang* §825/23 *Unattractive girl*,..crud, crumb, [etc.]. **1943** *Amer. Speech* XVIII. 153/2 *Crud*, food, usually unpalatable. **1955** 'T. STURGEON' in 'E. Crispin' *Best SF 2* (1956) 147 Would you say that..the writer of all this crud, believes..in what he writes? **1966** 'L. LANE' *ABZ of Scouse* 23 *Crud*, rubbish. **1966** 'K. A. SADDLER' *Gilt Edge* i. 9 Can't stand the man. A real crud.

b. A real or imaginary disease. *slang* (orig. *U.S. Army*).

1945 *Reader's Digest* Apr. 109 We also have what the men call 'crud', a skin outbreak like ringworm. **1945** *Time* 13 Aug. 76 Jungle rot; New Guinea crud; the creeping crud: GI names for any and every kind of skin disease. **1947** *Amer. Speech* XXII. 304/2 *Crud (the)*, this word..is used more commonly than any other single Army or Navy term for imaginary disease. **1948** *Ibid.* XXIII. 295/1 In the Pacific theater, *crud* was colloquial for all kinds of diseases, though it was most often used for the various forms of fungus infection. **1966** F. SHAW et al. *Lern yerself Scouse* 56, *I got Bombay crud*, I am suffering from looseness of the bowels.

c. An undesirable impurity, foreign matter, etc. (see quots.). *slang.*

1950 *Gloss. Terms Nuclear Sci.* (Nat. Res. Council, U.S.) 41/1 *Crud*, a slang term referring to an undesirable impurity or foreign material arising in a process. **1959** *New Scientist* 26 Mar. 696/1 'Crud' (Chalk River Unidentified Deposit), an impolite word applied to rust deposited on the fuel elements in the high radiation zones which exist in the heart of a reactor. **1962** in D. E. Barnes et al. *Newnes Conc. Encycl. Nuclear Energy* 160/2 In corrosion problems crud may be defined as particulate corrosion products..deposited on the surfaces of circulating water systems... The term is also applied to..many other undesirable residues..appearing in plant processes.

crud(de, cruddle, cruddy, obs. or dial. ff. CURD, CURDLE, CURDY.

crudde, var. CROWD *sb.*[2] *Obs.*, crypt.

cruddy ('krʌdɪ), *a.* [*Obs.* and *dial.* var. of CURDY *a.*]

1. See CURDY *a.*

2. Dirty, unpleasant, unsavoury (see also quot. 1952). *slang* (orig. *U.S.*).

1949 D. LEVIN *Mask of Glory* 150 Get the cruddy end of the stick. **1952** BERREY & VAN DEN BARK *Amer. Thes. Slang* (ed. 2) §284/6 *Ill-tempered*,..cruddy. **1960** J. KIRKWOOD *There must be a Pony!* (1961) iv. 32 He had the largest collection of cruddy-looking suède shoes in the world. **1960** W. SHEED *Middle Class Education* (1961) 157 A cruddy wall of fastidiousness. **1962** K. ORVIS *Damned & Destroyed* 144 Is that what's running around in your cruddy mind? **1966** *20th Cent.* Spring 20/2 The company gets cruddier every time I come here. **1970** C. WOOD *Terrible Hard* xiv. 205 We're slavin' our guts out 'ere and the cruddy Brylcreem boys are poncing about playing basketball.

crude (kruːd), *a.* [ad. L. *crūd-us* raw, undigested, unripe, rough, cruel.]

1. a. In the natural or raw state; 'not changed by any process or preparation' (J.); not manufactured, refined, tempered, etc.; of bricks, unbaked.

c **1386** CHAUCER *Can. Yeom. Prol. & T.* 219 In amalgamynge, and calcenynge Of quyksilver, y-clept mercury crude. **1555** EDEN *Decades* 179 [Gold] is so muche the baser, fouler, and more crude. **1666** BOYLE *Formes & Qual.* 134 All these Vitriols, especially that of crude Lead. **1747** WESLEY *Prim. Physick* (1762) 108 Dissolve a Dram of crude Sal Ammoniac. **1822** IMISON *Sc. & Art* II. 115 An ore called crude Antimony, which is a Sulphuret of antimony. **1862** RAWLINSON *Anc. Mon.* I. v. 92 Sometimes the crude and the burnt brick were used in alternate layers. **1883** *Eng. Illust. Mag.* Nov. 89/1 Spelter in the crude form of calamine stone.

b. ***crude oil***, natural mineral oil. So ***crude petroleum.***

1865 *Atlantic Monthly* XV. 389 Wagons laden with crude oil for the refinery. **1896** B. REDWOOD *Petroleum* I. 215 The crude oil of Upper Burma. *Ibid.*, The solid hydrocarbons present in crude petroleum. **1931** *Discovery* Nov. 350/1 Crude-oil rail traction is the successor to steam rail traction. **1970** *Times* 16 Apr. 14/5 The tar lumps are residues of crude oil.

c. ***crude fibre***, the insoluble residue left when vegetable matter is boiled alternately in dilute acids and alkalis, corresponding roughly to its indigestible part.

1895 C. F. CROSS et al. *Cellulose* 165 'Crude Fibre'.—'Rohfaser'. **1910** *Encycl. Brit.* V. 606/2 In the analysis of fodder plants..the residue obtained after successive acid and alkaline hydrolysis is the 'crude fibre' of the agricultural chemist. **1927** R. G. LINTON *Anim. Nutrition & Vet. Dietetics* i. 9 As obtained by ordinary analysis, crude fibre is a mixture of cellulose, lignin, cutin, pentosans, etc. **1965** *Brit. Poultry Sci.* VI. 23/2 There is little detailed information concerning crude fibre digestion by poultry.

†**2.** Of food: Raw, uncooked. *Obs.*

1542 BOORDE *Dyetary* ix. (1870) 250 Of eatynge of crude meate. **1586** COGAN *Haven Health* ccxiii. (1636) 225 He never eat any crude or raw thing, as fruits, herbs. **1658** SIR T. BROWNE *Tracts* i. *Scripture Plants*, Meal of crude and unparched corn. **1796** *Hull Advertiser* 23 Apr. 1/4 The inside [of the potato] will be nearly in a crude state.

3. a. Of food in the stomach, secretions, 'humours': Not, or not fully, digested or 'concocted'.

1533 ELYOT *Cast. Helthe* II. ix, Rape rootes..if they be not perfectly concoct in the stomake, they do make crude or raw iuice in the veynes. **1668** CULPEPPER & COLE *Barthol. Anat.* I. ix. 18 The Venter and the Reticulum..are ordained to hold the crude meat. **1789** W. BUCHAN *Dom. Med.* (1790) 635 Which induces a languid circulation, a crude indigested mass of humours. **1851** CARPENTER *Man. Phys.* 322 In the higher Plants, the ascending or crude sap is to be distinguished from the elaborated or descending sap.

†**b.** *transf.* Characterized by or affected with indigestion; lacking power to digest. *Obs.*

1605 B. JONSON *Volpone* II. i, To fortifie the most indigest and crude stomack. **1634** MILTON *Comus* 476 A perpetual feast of nectar'd sweets, Where no crude surfeit reigns. **1671** —— *P.R.* IV. 328 Deep versed in books and shallow in himself, Crude or intoxicate, collecting toys, And trifles.

4. Of fruit: Unripe; sour or harsh to the taste.

1555 EDEN *Decades* 263 Crude thynges are in shorte tyme made rype. **1637** MILTON *Lycidas* 3, I come to pluck your berries harsh and crude. **1737** WEST *Let.* in *Gray's Poems* (1775) 20 Or, ere the grapes their purple hue betray, Tear the crude cluster from the mourning spray. **1853** C. BRONTE *Let.* in Mrs. Gaskell *Life* xxvi. 418 As the..wasp attacks the sweetest and mellowest fruit, eschewing what is sour and crude.

5. Of a disease, morbid growth, etc.: In an early or undeveloped stage; not matured.

1651 R. WITTIE *Primrose's Pop. Errours* IV. 225 In diseases that are crude, and hard to bee concocted. **1727–51** CHAMBERS *Cycl.* s.v. *Crudity*, That state of the disease, wherein the crude matter is changed, and rendered less peccant..is called *digestion, concoction*, or *maturation*. **1847** TODD *Cycl. Anat.* IV. 107 Tubercle having subsisted for a..time in the firm (or, as it is called, crude) state.

6. Of products of the mind: Not matured, not completely thought out or worked up; ill-digested.

1611 B. JONSON *Catiline* Ded., Against all noise of opinion; from whose crude and airy reports, I appeal to the ..singular faculty of judgement in your lordship. **1646** PAGITT *Heresiogr.* (ed. 3) 71 Being tyed to the *ex tempore* and crude Prayers of the Ministers. **1749** BERKELEY *Let.* Wks. IV. 323, I have thrown together these few crude thoughts for you to ruminate upon. **1826** DISRAELI *Viv. Grey* v. vii, The crude opinions of an unpractised man. **1848** MACAULAY *Hist. Eng.* II. 654 Hasty and crude legislation on subjects so grave could not but produce new grievances.

7. a. Of literary or artistic work: Lacking finish, or maturity of treatment; rough, unpolished.

1763 MALLET in *Crit. Review* (in Boswell *Johnson*) The crude efforts of envy, petulance, and self conceit. **1786** SIR J. REYNOLDS *Disc.* xiii, No Architect took greater care than he [Vanbrugh] that his work should not appear crude and hard. **1831** LAMB *Elia, Ellistoniana*, In elegies, that shall silence this crude prose. **1875** FORTNUM *Majolica* iii. 30 The design, crude and wanting in relief.

b. Of natural objects: Coarse, clumsy.

a **1828** CAMPBELL *Poems, Power of Russia* vi, But Russia's limbs..Are crude, and too colossal to cohere. **1853** KANE *Grinnell Exp.* iii. (1856) 28 A school of fin-backed whales, great, crude, wallowing sea-hogs.

8. Of action or statement: Rough, rude, blunt, not qualified by amenity.

1650 JER. TAYLOR *Serm., Return of Prayers* iii, John Huss ..for the crude delivery of this truth was sentenced by the council of Constance. **1670** COTTON *Espernon* III. x. 510 Surpriz'd at so slight, and so crude an answer.

9. a. Of persons: Characterized by crudeness of thought, feeling, action, or character.

1722-4 SWIFT *Maxims contr. Ireland*, Errors committed by crude and short thinkers. **1837** LYTTON *E. Maltrav.* I. xvi, A crude or sarcastic unbeliever. **1876** GEO. ELIOT *Dan. Der.* IV. xxviii, A cruder lover would have lost the view of her pretty ways and attitudes.

b. Of manners or behaviour: Unpolished, 'rude'.

1876 T. HARDY *Hand of Ethelb.* xiii, To correct a small sister of somewhat crude manners as regards filling the mouth.

10. *Gram.* Applied to a word in its uninflected state, or to that part which is independent of inflexion; *esp.* in ***crude form***, the uninflected form or stem of a word.

1805 COLEBROOKE *Gram. Skr. Lang.* I. 129 The root, or theme, denominated *dhātu*, consists of the radical letters, disjoined from the affixes and augments. It may be called a crude verb. **1808** SIR C. WILKINS *Gram. Skr. Lang.* 36. **1830** G. LONG *Observ. Study Gr. & Lat. Lang.* 37 Λιθο, λογο, must be considered as the roots, or rather the crude forms, both in the formation of the cases, and in that of the compounds. **1844** B. H. KENNEDY *Lat. Gram. Curric.* 129 Besides this root, common to all words of one kindred, every word has a Crude-form or Stem, which represents it independently of any relation to other words. **1875** WHITNEY *Life Lang.* iii. 41 The base or crude-form of an adjective as adverb.

11. *Statistics.* Unadjusted; not corrected by reference to modifying circumstances; spec. ***crude birth-, death-rate***, the total figures before adjustment.

1889 *Jrnl. R. Statistical Soc.* LII. 442 The merest tyro in statistics knows that crude gross numbers are of little value. **1896** *Lancet* 15 Aug. 479/1 The mean crude or uncorrected death-rate. *Ibid.* 479/2 The range of corrected death-rates is far wider than that of crude death-rates. **1945** *New Biol.* I. 30 A crude birth-rate is the annual number of births per thousand living persons. *Ibid.* 36 Determination of the standard mortality rate, as opposed to the crude death-rate, is a simple matter if we know the age composition of the population and specific mortality rates for each year of life. **1965** *Times* 13 Feb. 8/3 These are crude figures, with exports valued f.o.b. and imports c.i.f.

crude (kruːd), *sb.* [f. the adj.] Crude oil (see prec., 1 b).

1904 *Encycl. Americana* XII, s.v. *Petroleum Industry*, The crude..might be found in paying quantities if artesian wells were sunk. **1921** J. E. POGUE *Econ. Petroleum* 79 The details of a complete refinery differ according to the type of crude employed. *Ibid.* 82 Asphaltic crudes such as those of the Gold Coast. **1960** *Times* 11 Apr. 15/5 In 1959 French bottoms carried almost 90 per cent. of the crude reaching France from all sources. **1970** R. JOHNSTON *Black Camels* v. 86 We might be thankful for that crude to feed the refinery.

†**'cruded**, *ppl. a. Obs.* ? Made crude, raw, bloody.

1613 HEYWOOD *Silver Age* III. Wks. 1874 III. 157 These phangs shall gnaw vpon your cruded bones.

†**crude'faction.** *Obs. rare.* [f. L. *crūd-us* crude + -FACTION.] Rendering or becoming crude or unripe.

1655-60 STANLEY *Hist. Philos.* (1701) 565/1 The softning, hardning, crudefaction, ripening of things.

†**cru'delity.** *Obs.* [a. F. *crudélité* (Oresme, 14th c.), ad. L. *crūdēlitās* cruelty, f. *crūdēlis* CRUEL.] = CRUELTY.

1483 CAXTON *Cato* B iij b, The thyrd synne is unmyserycorde and crudelyte. **1527** *St. Papers Hen. VIII*, VI. 585 The shameful crudelities committed by the Emperours armye. **1635** HEYWOOD *Hierarch.* v. 316, 3. The Atrocitie of the punishment. 4. The Crudelitie of the afflicters. **1707** COLLIER *Refl. Ridic.* 287 The Excess of Crudelity.

crudely ('kruːdlɪ), *adv.* [f. CRUDE + -LY².] In a crude manner; see the adj.

1638 CHILLINGW. *Relig. Prot.* I. iii. §12. 132 This proposition so crudely set down..no Protestant will justify. **1669** W. SIMPSON *Hydrol. Chym.* 163 Blood and urine distilled crudely. **1881** H. JAMES *Portrait of Lady* xxxvii, He ..said to her crudely—'Your husband is awfully cold-blooded'.

crudeness ('kruːdnɪs). [f. as prec. + -NESS.] The state or quality of being crude; crudity.

1533 ELYOT *Cast. Helthe* II. xxvii. (1541) 42 b, Abundance of drinke at meale[s]..ingendreth..crudenes in the vaynes. **1635** COWLEY *Davideis* I. 870. **1706** DODWELL in Hearne *Collect.* 22 May, Ye Crudeness of my thoughts. **1837** HALLAM *Hist. Lit.* (1847) I. 375 Long afterwards..when its original crudeness had been mellowed. **1881** *Daily News* 3 Jan. 6/6 Occasional crudenesses of thought and style.

crudge-bak: see CROUCHBACK.

crudification (ˌkruːdɪfɪ'keɪʃən). [f. CRUDE *a.* + -IFICATION; cf. next.] The process or result of making something crude; an example of this.

1910 H. G. WELLS *New Machiavelli* (1911) II. iv. 263 A series of hits and anecdotes and—what shall I call them?—'crudifications' of the issue. **1965** I. A. RICHARDS in *Times Lit. Suppl.* 27 May 438/3 Reading..can also be an occasion for mind-breaking failure, for stultifying confusion, for crudification.

crudify ('kruːdɪfaɪ), *v. rare.* [f. CRUDE *a.* + -IFY.] *trans.* To make crude.

1899 H. JAMES *Notebooks* 15 Feb. (1947) 276 It will be pretty, though, in making that plain, not to crudify the statement of it.

‖**crudités** (krydite), *sb. pl.* [Fr.; cf. CRUDITY 1 b.] A traditional French hors-d'œuvre of mixed raw vegetables.

1960 E. DAVID *French Provincial Cooking* 133 (*heading*) Les crudités. Raw vegetables. *Ibid.*, With a *plat de crudités* is usually served..a slice or two of *pâté de campagne*. **1965** E. O'BRIEN *August is Wicked Month* xv. 179 They had *crudités du pays* to start with..so many kinds of vegetable. **1970** *Sat. Rev.* (U.S.) 18 July 37/3 The hostesses were able to deposit on one tray a *tranche* of excellent pâté, a bowl of *crudités*, a hot steak. **1981** *N.Y. Times Mag.* 21 June 10/3 You like *raw vegetables*? I'll take *crudités*.

crudity ('kruːdɪtɪ). [ad. L. *crūditās*, f. *crūdus* CRUDE, or perh. immediately a. F. *crudité* (14th c.).]

1. The state or quality of being raw, unrefined, untempered, unripe, etc.

1638 RAWLEY tr. *Bacon's Life & Death* (1650) 41 To keep it to the age of a yeare..whereby the water may lose the Crudity. **1655** CULPEPPER *Riverius* x. vi. 296 Waters.. wherein there is Crudity or a Mineral. **1707** FLOYER *Phys. Pulse-Watch* 67 These several degrees of Crudity appear in Grapes. **1729** SHELVOCKE *Artillery* IV. 292 Lead, divested of its Crudity and Grossness by being purified.

b. An instance of this; also *concr.* (in *pl.*) raw products; unripe or uncooked substances.

1626 BACON *Sylva* §326 To say..that if the Crudities, Impurities, and Leprosies of Metals were cured, they would become Gold. **1676** ETHEREDGE *Man of Mode* I. i, In Fee with the Doctors to sell green Fruit to the Gentry, that the Crudities may breed Diseases. **1870** H. MACMILLAN *Bible Teach.*, How to convert these crudities of nature into nutritious vegetables.

2. *Phys.* Of food: The state of being imperfectly digested, or the quality of being indigestible; indigestion; also, in old physiology, imperfect 'concoction' of the humours; undigested (or indigestible) matter in the stomach; *pl.* imperfectly 'concocted' humours. ? *Obs.*

1533 ELYOT *Cast. Helthe* IV. i. (1541) 74 b, Cruditie is a vycious concoction of thynges receyued, they not beinge holly or perfitely altered. **1601** HOLLAND *Pliny* II. 259 The crudities or raw humors lying in the stomack, which cause loathing and abhorring of meat. **1670** COTTON *Espernon* III. XI. 536, I do not think any stomach in the world, but his, could have digested so much crudity. **1684** tr. *Bonet's Merc. Compit.* III. 87 Crudities are the cause of all Catarrhs. **1785** REID *Int. Powers* IV. iv. 387 Crudities and indigestion are said to give uneasy dreams. **1860** EMERSON *Cond. Life, Fate* Wks. (Bohn) II. 327 A crudity in the blood will appear in the argument.

fig. **1611** (*title*), Coryats Crudities, hastily gobled vp in fiue Moneths travells in France, Italy [etc.].

b. The firmness or hardness of morbid matter before it is 'ripe'; the early or immature stage of a disease.

1727-51 CHAMBERS, *Crudity* sometimes denotes that state of a disease, wherein the morbific matter is of such bulk, figure, cohesion, mobility, or inactivity, as creates or increases the disease. **1847** TODD *Cycl. Anat.* IV. 107/2 When tuberculous matter has existed..in the state of firmness or 'crudity'.

3. Of mental products, etc. (also *transf.* of persons): The condition of being immature, undeveloped, ill-digested.

1869 FARRAR *Fam. Speech* i. (1873) 7 Languages in every stage of crudity or development. **1879** GLADSTONE *Glean.* I. 49 He gave no signs of crudity, never affected knowledge he did not possess.

b. (with *a* and *pl.*) An instance of crudity; a crude idea, statement, piece of literary work, etc.

1652 BP. HALL *Rem. Wks.* (1660) 152 They have nothing in them, but cold crudities. **1710** ADDISON *Tatler* No. 239 ¶2 This Author, in the last of his Crudities, has amassed together a Heap of Quotations. **1859** MILL *Liberty* v. (1865) 67/1 Rushing into some half-examined crudity which has struck the fancy. **1879** MORLEY *Burke* 26 The book is full of crudities.

4. Unpolished plainness or 'brutality' of statement or expression: cf. CRUDE 8.

1885 *Spectator* 30 May 704/2 Nor did he recoil from Rabelaisian crudity of expression.

crudle, obs. f. CURDLE, CROODLE.

†**crudwort.** *Obs.* [f. *crud*, dial. form of CURD + WORT.] A name for Yellow Bedstraw or CHEESE-RENNET (*Galium verum*).

15.. in *Lyte's MS.* (Britten & Holl.). **1627** MINSHEU *Ductor* (ed. 2), *Galerion* or Crudwort, an herbe. **1692** COLES, *Galerion*, the herb crudwort.

crudy, obs. form of CURDY.

crue, var. of CREW *sb.*², pen, sty.

cruel ('kruːɪl, -əl), *a.* Forms: 3-7 cruell, 4 cruelle, krewelle, 4-5 crewel(l, cruwel(l, 5 cruail, crowell, 6 creuell, 3- cruel. [a. F. *cruel* (in 10th c. *crudel* = Pr. *cruzel*, *cruel*, Sp. *cruel*, It. *crudele*):— L. *crūdēl-em*, morally rough, cruel, from same root as *crūdus* CRUDE: cf. *fidēlis*.]

1. Of persons (also *transf.* and *fig.* of things): Disposed to inflict suffering; indifferent to or taking pleasure in another's pain or distress; destitute of kindness or compassion; merciless, pitiless, hard-hearted.

1297 R. GLOUC. (Rolls) 2650 Vor so cruel, ne so tirant Ich wene no man ne say. *c* **1385** CHAUCER *L.G.W.* Prol. 377 Ffor he that kyng or lord is naturel Hym oughte nat be tyraunt & crewel. *c* **1450** *Merlin* 27 He be-come so crewell to his peple that thei..a-roos a-geyn hym. **1568** GRAFTON *Chron.* II. 390 Sir John Bushe, which was called a cruell ambicious, and covetous man. **1605** SHAKS. *Lear* III. vii. 56 Because I would not see thy cruell nailes Plucke out his poore old eyes. **1634** MILTON *Comus* 679 Why should you be so cruel to yourself? **1751** JOHNSON *Rambler* No. 175 ¶13 The meanest and cruelest of human beings. **1842** TENNYSON *Walk to Mail* 99 As cruel as a schoolboy ere he grows To Pity. **1871** MORLEY *Misc.* Ser. I. *Carlyle* (1878) 175 The puniness of man in the centre of a cruel and frowning universe.

b. *absol.* = Cruel one.

c **1420** *Anturs of Arth.* 612 Clenly þat crewelle couerde hym on highte. **1575** GASCOIGNE *Pr. Pleas. Kenilw.* (1821) 66 This courteous cruel, and yet the cruelest courteous that ever was. **1632** MASSINGER *Maid of Hon.* I. ii, Farewell then, fairest cruel! **1725** POPE *Odyss.* XXIII. 169 Canst thou, oh cruel, unconcerned survey Thy lost Ulysses on this signal day?

c. Of actions, etc.: Proceeding from or showing indifference to or pleasure in another's distress.

a **1300** *Cursor M.* 16762 + 135 (Cott.) Hou miȝt euer ani man More cruel ded see. **1568** GRAFTON *Chron.* II. 198 The Scottes..slue the people and robbed them in most cruell wise. **1656** J. HAMMOND *Leah & R.* 6 The odiums and cruell slanders cast on those two famous Countries. **1733** in *Swift's Lett.* (1766) II. 191 The cruelest revenge that one can possibly inflict. **1848** MACAULAY *Hist. Eng.* I. 160 The Puritans had..given cruel provocation.

†**2.** Of men, wild beasts, etc.: Fierce, savage.

a **1300** *Cursor M.* 2631 (Cott.) He sal be cruell, fers, and wrath. *c* **1330** R. BRUNNE *Chron.* (1810) 44 An armed knyght ..þat was S. Edmunde, cruelle als a leon. *c* **1400** MAUNDEV. (Roxb.) viii. 30 For drede of crowell wilde bestes. **1535** COVERDALE *Ps.* lvi. 4, I lye with my soule amonge the cruell lyons. **1600** J. PORY *Leo's Africa* 261 The passage unto this mountaine is very difficult, in regard of certaine cruell Arabians.

†**b.** Of actions, etc. (*esp.* of contests): Fierce.

? *a* **1400** *Morte Arth.* 4034 With krewelle contenance thane the kyng karpis theis wordes. *c* **1489** CAXTON *Sonnes of Aymon* iii. 108 Soo beganne the bataylle yet agen more cruell than it hadde be afore. **1548** HALL *Chron.* 160 b, A ferce and cruell encounter. *c* **1630** RISDON *Surv. Devon* §95 (1810) 92 The fight was cruel, and the slaughter great. **1674** *Essex Papers* (Camden) I. 197 Arlington had a Cruel dispute wth Anglesey yesterday, & told him yt he was a Knave.

†**3.** Severe, strict, rigorous. *Obs.*

a **1225** *Ancr. R.* 100 Þis is a cruel word, & a grim word mid alle, þet vre Louerd seið. **1387** TREVISA *Higden* (Rolls) IV. 327 Þey were to cruel [*nimis severi*] and nouȝt compynable among hem self. **1562** WINȜET *Cert. Tractates* Wks. 1888 I. 14, I haue pourit oute my creuell displesour vpon thaim. *a* **1659** OSBORN *Queries* Ep. (1673) Ss v, The crueller Culture of the School. **1670** *N. Riding Rec.* VI. 144 An apprentice.. to be received again.. and the Master to be not too cruel with him.

4. Of conditions, circumstances, etc.: Causing or characterized by great suffering; extremely painful or distressing; *colloq.* = severe, hard.

a **1300** *Cursor M.* 22428 (Cott.) þaa cruel dais and þaa kene. *c* **1384** CHAUCER *H. Fame* I. 36 That cruelle lyfe un-softe Whiche these ilke lovers leden. **1526** *Pilgr. Perf.* (W. de W. 1531) 13 Suffrynge..intollerable turmentes..and moost cruell & bytter deth. **1611** BIBLE *Ex.* vi. 9 They hearkened not vnto Moses, for anguish of spirit, and for cruell bondage. **1662** J. DAVIES *Mandelslo's Trav. E. Ind.* 4 We..had that day very cruel weather. **1710** SWIFT *Jrnl. to Stella* 26 Nov., I have got a cruel cold, and staid within all this day. **1800** WORDSW. *Hart-Leap Well* II. xii, O Master! it has been a cruel leap. **1855** MACAULAY *Hist. Eng.* IV. 545 A fate far more cruel than death befell his old rival. **1862** CARLYLE *Fredk. Gt.* (1865) III. IX. x. 161 But what is crueler upon me than all, is that you are ill.

5. as *adv.* Cruelly, distressingly; hence as a mere intensive = exceedingly, very. *Obs.* exc. *dial.*

1573 G. HARVEY *Letter-bk.* (Camden) 12 Uppon the cruellist could nihts. **1595** SPENSER *Col. Clout* 911 Being to that swaine too cruell hard. **1621** LADY M. WROTH *Urania* 390 Vse mee crueller if that may be. **1632** LITHGOW *Trav.* VII. (1682) 290 The season being cruel hot. **1860** BARTLETT

Dict. Amer., *Cruel*, one of the numerous substitutes for very, exceedingly. **1888** *W. Somerset Word-bk.*, *Cruel*, very; 'cruel good to poor volks'.

6. *Comb.*, as ***cruel-hearted***, ***-looking*** adjs.

1591 Shaks. *Two Gent.* ii. iii. 10 This cruell-hearted Curre. **1836** J. H. Newman in *Lyra Apost.* (1849) 234 Thou cruel-natured Rome! **1863** Miss Braddon *Eleanor's Vict.* (1878) ii. 17 Rather a cruel-looking hand.

†**cruel**, *sb. Obs. rare.* [f. prec.] Cruelty.

c **1440** *Partonope* 7188 God forbid that crewell or vengence In ony woman founde shulde be.

cruel (ˈkruːəl), *v. Austral. slang.* [f. the adj.] *trans.* To spoil; to destroy all chance of success with.

1934 *Bulletin* (Sydney) 1 Aug. 46/3 The game's right enough so long as mugs don't try and play a hand. When they come in that cruels the whole show. **1967** *Courier-Mail* (Brisbane) 17 May 1 He asked yesterday if the purpose of the debate was to 'cruel' his object. **1967** I. Hamilton *Man with Brown Paper Face* iii. 41 I've got a good job and I don't want to cruel it while everything's going for me.

cruel(s, var. of crewel, -els.

cruellie, cruelly (ˈkruːəlɪ), *sb. colloq.* [f. cruel *a.* + -ie, -y⁶.] A cruel joke, remark, comment, etc. Also *attrib.*

1959 *News Chron.* 6 July 3/4 The famous American 'cruellie' joke—example: 'But what did you think of the play, Mrs. Lincoln?'—is on the way out. **1959** *Guardian* 3 Nov. 7/3 'Some of [the greeting cards] are cruellies... They might say on the outside "*Stay the way you are*", and..on the inside.."*Mean, Cruel, Thoughtless*"... ' How about a real cruelly, then, with the gum flavoured with cyanide? **1961** 'J. Ross' *Last August* xiv. 168 Con fancies himself as a psychiatrist... He has the best collection of sick jokes and cruellies.

cruelly (ˈkruːəlɪ), *adv.* [f. cruel *a.* + -ly².] In a cruel manner, with cruelty.

1. With indifference to or delight in another's suffering.

a **1340** Hampole *Psalter* ix. 31 Cruelly he lokes in þaim. *c* **1380** Wyclif *Wks.* (1880) 98 þei pursuen more and cruelliere. *c* **1450** *Mirour Saluacioun* 3957 Absolon toke on boldnesse to slee his brothere cruwelly. **1568** Grafton *Chron.* II. 197 Robbed and brent the Countrie most cruelly. **1653** H. Cogan tr. *Pinto's Trav.* xxii. 77 They were cruelly detained in prison. **1790** Burke *Fr. Rev.* 106 These two gentlemen..were cruelly and publickly dragged to the block, and beheaded. **1845** M. Pattison *Ess.* (1889) I. 28 He ..was cruelly beaten by the soldiers.

†2. Fiercely, savagely. *Obs.*

1375 Barbour *Bruce* xvii. 144 The yngliss men faucht cruelly. *c* **1470** Henry *Wallace* iv. 449 Wallace and his went cruelly thaim agayne. *a* **1533** Ld. Berners *Huon* lxvii. 230 They all fought cruelly. **1598** W. Phillips tr. *Linschoten* in Arb. *Garner* III. 16 These two fleets meeting together, fought most cruelly.

†3. Severely, rigorously, sharply. *Obs.*

c **1430** *Pilgr. Lyf Manhode* iv. xix. (1869) 185 We sende þee..þat..þou hurtle alle þilke so cruelliche [*tres-durement*] þat hauen here hoodes wrong turned. **1535** Coverdale *Ezek.* xxiv. 17 A greate vengeaunce will I take vpon them, and punysh them cruelly. **1577** B. Googe *Heresbach's Husb.* i. (1586) 15 The Bayliffe must beware that he deale not to cruelly, nor to gently with them.

4. Painfully, sorely; excessively.

c **1385** Chaucer *L.G.W.* Prol. 340 Thou shalt repenten this So cruelly, that it shal wele be sene. **1599** Shaks. *Hen. V*, v. ii. 216 But good Kate, mocke me mercifully, the rather ..because I loue thee cruelly. **1653** H. Cogan tr. *Pinto's Trav.* ii. 4 Their ship being shot through and through..and cruelly battered all over. **1780** Mad. D'Arblay *Diary* May, Mrs. Montagu we miss cruelly. **1782** —— *Lett.* Feb., We had waited cruelly for the coach. **1885** *Manch. Exam.* 6 Apr. 5/2 The weather this Eastertide is bright, but cruelly dry and cold.

†**cruelness.** *Obs.* [f. as prec. + -ness.]

1. The quality of being cruel; cruelty.

a **1300** *Cursor M.* 28739 (Cott.) Resun to yield well better is o merci þan of cruelnes [*v.r.* crowelnes]. **1426** Audelay *Poems* 60 Scorgid with creuelnes. **1541** Paynel *Catiline* vi. 10 Consideryng the great cruelnesse of the dede. **1596** Spenser *F.Q.* vi. i. 41 The reproch of pride and cruelnesse.

2. Fierceness, savageness.

1432–50 tr. *Higden* (Rolls) I. 153 Amazones..the cruellenes of whom Hercules did mitigate firste. **1575** Recorde *Ground of Arts* Pref. to Edw. VI, To conuerte wylde people to a myldenesse, and chaunge their furious cruelnesse into gentle curtesye. **1631** *Celestina* iv. 53 Your dogge, for all his fiercenesse, and cruelnesse of nature [etc.].

3. Severity, rigour.

1537 *Inst. Chr. Man* L v b, A good iudge..although he shewe outwardely cruelnesse and rygour, yet inwardly he ought to loue the personne. *a* **1625** Boys *Wks.* (1630) 415 Wise men inuented the game of Chesse to mitigate the cruelnesse of governours.

cruelty (ˈkruːəltɪ). Forms: 3–6 cruelte, (4 cruelete, creweltie), 4–6 crualte, (5 crueltee, 6 cruaulte), 5–7 crueltie, 6– cruelty. [a. OF. *crualté* (later *cruauté*), according to Hatzfeld:—pop. L. type **crūdālitāt-em*, for *crūdēlitāt-em* (see crudelity), whence the other Romanic forms Pr. *cruzeltat*, Sp. *crueldad*, It. *crudeltà*, *-ità*.]

1. a. The quality of being cruel; disposition to inflict suffering; delight in or indifference to the pain or misery of others; mercilessness, hard-heartedness: *esp.* as exhibited in action. Also, with *pl.*, an instance of this, a cruel deed.

a **1225** *Ancr. R.* 268 þus he liteð cruelte mid heowe of rihtwisnesse. *c* **1330** R. Brunne *Chron.* (1810) 78 Of his crueltes he gynnes for to assuage. *c* **1449** Pecock *Repr.* iii. viii. 324 Deedis of cruelte and of vnpitee. **1531** Elyot *Gov.* ii. vii, The vice called crueltie, whiche is contrary to mercye. **1613** Shaks. *Hen. VIII*, v. iii. 76 'Tis a cruelty, To load a falling man. **1655–60** Stanley *Hist. Philos.* (1701) 40/1 All, whom the Cruelty of War suffer'd to escape. **1773** *Observ. State Poor* 43 The cruelty of a Nero, or a Domitian. **1865** Kingsley *Herew.* iii. (1866) 77 Boasting of his fights and cruelties. **1871** R. W. Dale *Commandm.* iii. 83 It would be brutal cruelty to make a jest of the weakness and sufferings of the patients in an hospital.

b. *attrib.*, as ***cruelty-lust***; **cruelty man** (also with capital initials) *colloq.*, an N.S.P.C.C. or R.S.P.C.A. officer.

1925 D. H. Lawrence *Refl. Death Porcup.* 59 His cruelty-lust is directed almost as much against himself as against his victim. **1954** D. V. Donnison *Neglected Child* iv. 82 Workers..had been shut out of houses by people who suspected they had 'put the cruelty man on to them'. **1958** *Sunday Express* 27 Apr. 6/6 The Cruelty Man has been asking questions about Janie. **1970** P. Dickinson *Seals* iii. 68 Mr. Fasting..had larruped Jamie... Mother had wanted to send for the Cruelty Man.

†2. Severity of pain; excessive suffering. *Obs.*

14.. *Circunsision* in *Tundale's Vis.* (1843) 87 With full grete cruelte For us he suffurd circunsysyon Upon the cros. **1634** Sir T. Herbert *Trav.* 168 A tedious sicknesse.. continued with such cruelty, that never any man was brought lower.

†3. Severity, strictness, rigour. *Obs.*

1556 *Aurelio & Isab.* (1608) K v, It sholde be beter to faille a litell in the justice, than to be superflue in crualte. **1636** Blount *Voy. Levant* (1637) 13 The want of crueltie upon delinquents causes much more oppression of the Innocent.

†4. Strength or harshness (of smell); ill savour.

c **1420** *Pallad. on Husb.* xii. 81 Of crueltee noo thing wol in hem [Garlic, etc] smelle.

†**'cruent**, *a. Obs. rare.* [ad. L. *cruent-us* bloody, f. *cru-* root of *cruor* blood (from a wound).] Bloody; *fig.* cruel.

1524 *St. Papers Hen. VIII*, VI. 350 With a cruent and blody hand. **1541** R. Copland *Galyen's Terapeut.* 2 C iv b, [An] vlcere..that is cruent and full of blode. **1657** *Phys. Dict.*, *Cruent*, bloody.

Hence †**'cruently** *adv.*, cruelly.

c **1380** *Antecrist* in Todd 3 *Treat. Wyclif* 120 What is it þenne þat shal encreese cruentlier in þise tourmentis?

†**cruentate**, *a. Obs. rare.* [ad. L. *cruentāt-us*, pa. pple. of *cruentāre* to stain with blood, f. *cruent-us*: see prec.] Blood-stained.

1665 Glanvill *Sceps. Sci.* xxiv. §3 Passing from the cruentate cloth or weapon to the wound.

So †**cruentated** = prec.

1730–6 Bailey (folio), *Cruentated*, embrued, or besprinkled, or bedawbed with blood.

cruentation (kruːɛnˈteɪʃən). [ad. L. *cruentātiōn-em*, n. of action f. *cruentāre* (see prec.); in Tertullian with the sense 'staining with blood'.] 'A term applied to the oozing of blood which occurs sometimes when an incision is made into the dead body'; also formerly to the supposed 'bleeding from the wounds of a dead person in the presence of the murderer' (*Syd. Soc. Lex.*).

†**cru'entous**, *a. Obs. rare.* [f. L. *cruent-us* (see cruent) + -ous.] Bloody. (*lit* and *fig.*)

1648 *Venice Looking-glass* 9 Thus a cruell and most cruentous civill war began. **1651** Howell *Venice* 125 A most cruentous fight pass'd on both sides. **1675** Burthogge *Causa Dei* 301 The insufficiency of cruentous Sacrifices. **1882** *Syd. Soc. Lex.*, *Cruentous*, red like blood; bloody. Formerly applied to the humours or excretions, sputa, sweat, and such like, when mixed with blood.

cruet (ˈkruːɪt). Forms: 3–6 cruett(e, 4–6 cruete, crowet, -ett(e, 5 crewyt, krewette, 5–6 crwet(t, 5–7 crewett(e, 6 cruat, -ytte, crewat, crowat, crouette, 6–8 cruit, 7 creuett, 6–9 crewet, 3– cruet. [ME. *cruete*, *cruette*, appears to repr. an OF. **cruete*, dim. of OF. *cruie*, *crue*, pot, = Gascon *cruga* (cf. Pr. *crugó*), app. f. OLG. *crûca*, MLG. *kruke* f., cognate with OHG. *kruog*, Ger. *krug* m., pot, which appears to have entered the Romanic of Gaul in the two forms **crūca*, **crūga*, whence F. *cruche*, *cruie* respectively. An AF. *cruet* m. of date 1376 is cited in Godef.]

1. A small bottle or vial for liquids, etc.; now only applied to a small glass bottle with a stopper, to contain vinegar, oil, etc. for the table.

1382 Wyclif *Mark* vii. 4 Waischingis of cuppis and cruetis. **1432–50** tr. *Higden* (Rolls) V. 131 A cruette of gold with bawme brennenge faste in hit. **1512** *Act 4 Hen. VIII*, c. 7 §7 Salsellers, goblettes, spones, cruettes or candelstikkes. **1611** Cotgr., *Goutteron*, a Violl, or Cruet wherein Oyle, or Vinegar is serued to the table. **1630** Brathwait *Eng. Gentlem.* (1641) 194 To set an houre-glasse beside us, and observe those precious graines..how swiftly they run thorow the cruet. **1713** *Lond. Gaz.* No. 5086/3 A Sett of Casters with Vinegar Crewets. **1865** Miss Braddon *Only a Clod* v. 27 The landlord..came bustling in..with.. knives and forks, and glasses, and cruets.

2. *Eccl.* A small vessel to hold wine or water for use in the celebration of the Eucharist, or to hold holy water for other uses.

After 16th c. rare until the 19th c., in which the spelling *crewet* is sometimes used.

c **1290** *S. Eng. Leg.* I. 228/318 Weued and chaliz and Cruettes þouruȝ-out cler cristal. **1395** *E.E. Wills* (1882) 5 Twey cruetis..twey siluer basyns for the auter. **1460–5** *Churchw. Acc. St. Andrew's, East Cheap* in *Brit. Mag.* XXXI. 394 For..a kay to the chyrch yard durr and for ij Crewettys. **1550** Bale *Image both Ch.* (1560) B ij, Miters, copes, crosses, cruettes, ceremonies. **1691** Wood *Ath. Oxon.* I. 579 He bequeathed all his books, his two Chalices, his Crewetts, holy water stock [etc.]..to his private chappell in London. **1877** J. D. Chambers *Div. Worship* 259 Two Crewets, one containing the wine and the other water. **1885** Dixon *Hist. Ch. Eng.* III. 450 Cruets and chrismatories.

3. *Comb.* **cruet-stand**, a stand or frame, commonly of silver, for holding cruets and castors at table; also formerly ***cruet-frame***.

1716 *Lond. Gaz.* No. 5437/4 A Cruit Frame, 4 Salts. **1793** W. Roberts *Looker-on* No. 65 Aided by the delicious provocatives of the cruet-stand! **1840** Dickens *Old C. Shop* xxxix, White table-cloth, and cruet-stand complete.

crufe, cruif(e, obs. var. cruive.

Cruft (krʌft). The name of Charles *Cruft* (1852–1938), used in the possessive to designate the dog show founded by him (now administered by the Kennel Club) and held annually in London since 1886. Also as **Cruft's**, **Crufts(')**.

[**1891** *Kennel Chron.* 26 Jan. 2/2 The following shows between 1st Jan. and 31st Dec. in each year only to count: Liverpool, Cruft's Terrier Show [etc.].] **1910** *Encycl. Brit.* VIII. 376/2 The [Kennel] club has control over all the shows held in the United Kingdom,..the actual number of dogs which were entered at the leading fixtures being: Kennel Club show 1789, Cruft's 1768, [etc.]. **1936** 'R. West' *Thinking Reed* xii. 433 The dogs were sitting on each side of him..they looked too like him. She felt as if she were contemplating marrying into Crufts'. **1962** 'J. le Carré' *Murder of Quality* v. 68 My sister is devoted to dogs...She ..was commended at Cruft's. **1970** *Guardian* 6 Apr. 9/1 A girl..is constantly under pressure to groom herself like a Cruft's exhibit. **1984** S. Townsend *Growing Pains A. Mole* 18 He said that Mitzi was being prepared for Crufts and mustn't suffer any stress.

crug (krʌg). *slang.* Food; *spec.* the commons of bread at Christ's Hospital.

The original meaning may be 'crust', in which sense it is used at Christ's Hospital School, Hertford.

1820 Lamb *Elia* Ser. i. *Christ's Hospital*, We were battening upon our quarter of a penny loaf—our crug—moistened with attenuated small beer. **1873** *Slang Dict.*, *Crug*, food. Christ's Hospital boys apply it only to bread.

cruin, Sc. form of croon.

cruise (kruːz), *v.* Also 7 cruse, 7–9 cruize. [First in 17th c.; corresponding alike to Du. *kruisen* to cross, also since 17th c. to cruise, to sail crossing to and fro, '*kruyssen op de Zee*, to traverse and cross the seas' (Hexham, 1678), f. *kruis* cross, and to Sp. and Pg. *cruzar* to cross, to cruise, F. *croiser* to cross, '*croiser la mer* to cruise up and down the Sea' (Miège 1688). The word is thus ultimately identical with croise *v.* and cross *v.*; the current spelling with *ui* seems to be after Dutch; but the vowel sound is as in Sp. and Pg.]

1. a. *intr.* To sail to and fro over some part of the sea without making for a particular port or landing-place, on the look out for ships, for the protection of commerce in time of war, for plunder, or (in modern times) for pleasure.

1651 G. Carteret in *Nicholas Papers* (Camden) I. 236 Van Trump is with his fleete crusinge about Silly. **1668** Etheredge *She Would* ii. i, Two men-of-war that are cruising here to watch for prizes. **1726** Shelvocke *Voy. round World* (1757) 8 Our first place of rendezvous..was the Canary Islands, where we were to cruize ten days for one another. **1748** *Anson's Voy.* i. vii. 70 They were to cruize off that Island only ten days. **1823** Scoresby *Jrnl.* 120 A breeze of wind..under which we cruised the whole day, among floes and drift-ice, in search of whales. **1848** Macaulay *Hist. Eng.* I. 573 Several English men of war were cruising in the Channel.

b. *transf.* and *fig.* Esp. of an aircraft or automobile: to travel at cruising speed; of a taxicab: to travel about at random seeking business.

1698 Farquhar *Love & Bottle* i, Madam, how would you like to cruise about a little? **1742** Young *Nt. Th.* viii. 993 Fancy still cruises, when poor sense is tir'd. **1879** Jefferies *Wild Life in S.C.* 5 Blackbirds will cruise along the whole length of a hedge before finding a bush to their liking. **1915** *Sphere* 5 June 229/2 A craft [*sc.* Zeppelin] which can slip through the air with the speed of an express train and cruise about for thirty-six hours. **1930** 'A. Armstrong' *Taxi!* v. 49 A 'crawling' or 'cruising' taxi being one that meanders along the road..looking for fares. **1934** *Discovery* Dec. 350/2 Aeroplanes like the Handley Page 42 which cruises at a speed of 110 m.p.h. **1959** 'E. Peters' *Death Mask* i. 7 He didn't cross to one of the parked cars..nor halt to look round for a cruising taxi.

c. *trans.* To sail to and fro over.

1687 A. Lovell tr. *Bergerac's Comic. Hist.* ii. 17 Our Predecessors..a Thousand times had cruised the Ocean. **1890** S. Lane Poole *Barbary Corsairs* i. xii. 124 We cruised the waters of the Levant. **1971** *Sunday Times* 3 Jan. 54/8 (Advt.), Board a luxury liner to cruise the most colourful waters in the world. **1971** *Observer* 10 Jan. 37/3 (Advt.), Cruise the lovely Erne waterway.

d. *intr.* and *trans.* To walk or drive about (the streets) in search of a casual sexual (*esp.* homosexual) partner; to solicit (a person), entice. *slang* (orig. *U.S.*).

1904 [implied at CRUISER 1 d]. **1927** [implied at the vbl. sb.]. **1941** in J. N. Katz *Gay/Lesbian Almanac* (1983) 575 *Cruise*, to walk or drive in an automobile.. aimlessly but in certain specific and likely areas, looking.. for a companion for homosexual intercourse. **1946** MEZZROW & WOLFE *Really Blues* (1957) xi. 203 We cruised these two chicks up to Harlem for some ribs. **1968** *Globe Mag.* (Toronto) 13 Jan. 6/3 A homosexual who is cruising.. might make an effeminate gesture as a signal that he is a homosexual. **1970** 'E. QUEEN' *Last Woman* III. 163, I never cruised anyone connected with the college... All my pickups were made far off campus. **1977** C. MCFADDEN *Serial* (1978) vii. 20/1 Whiling away the best years of her life cruising Fourth Street. **1984** *Times Lit. Suppl.* 14 Dec. 1455/4 Male metropolitan homosexuals.. who cruise compulsively.

2. *trans.* and *intr. Forestry.* (See quots.) Chiefly *U.S.*

1879 A. P. VIVIAN *Wanderings in Western Land* 53 Experienced men are sent out into the forests exploring, or to use their own term 'cruising'; their object being.. to find suitable lumber for chopping. **1895** *Outing* (U.S.) XXVII. 218/2, I found he was off 'cruising' (i.e. hunting up good timber tracts). **1919** T. K. HOLMES *Man from Tall Timber* 40 Si and me cruised a part of this timber before ever you fellers come down from Blainesburg. **1953** *Brit. Commonw. Forest Terminol.* I. 35 *To cruise*, surveying of forest land to locate merchantable timber and estimate its quantity..; the estimate obtained in such a survey.

cruise (kruːz), *sb.* Also 8–9 cruize. [f. prec.]

1. a. The action of cruising; a voyage in which the ship sails to and fro over a particular region. *spec.* a voyage taken by tourists. Also *attrib.*

1706 PHILLIPS (ed. Kersey), *Cruise* or *Cruising*, the Course of a Ship. **1728** MORGAN *Algiers* I. ii. 221 A Turkish Half-Galley, armed for the Cruise, touched at a small Port. **1758** J. BLAKE *Mar. Syst.* 64 If they are sent to sea on a foreign voyage, or cruize. *a* **1893** *Mod.* A cruise round the coast. **1906** 'O. HENRY' *Four Million* (1916) 91 The hibernatorial ambitions of Soapy were not of the highest. In them were no considerations of Mediterranean cruises. **1933** N. COWARD *Design for Living* II. iii, That world cruise was a fatal mistake. **1937** R. MACAULAY *I would be Private* 43 Dressed in all those cruise clothes. **1962** *Listener* 11 Jan. 90/2 Cruise-ships and charabancs and monstrous hordes of hikers are blots upon the landscape [in Greece]. **1971** *Sunday Times* 3 Jan. 72/1 Standards on board British cruise liners are generally high.

b. *transf.* and *fig.*

1751 SMOLLETT *Per. Pic.* xiv, 'What, you are on a cruise for a post, brother Trickle, arn't ye?' **1837** W. IRVING *Capt. Bonneville* I. 118 To prosecute their cruise in the wilderness. **1879** LD. DUNRAVEN in *19th Cent.* July 58 We started off to take a little cruise round the edge of the barren.. Cruising is performed on land as well as at sea.

2. A survey or estimate of the amount of timber in a particular area. Cf. prec., sense 2. Chiefly *U.S.*

1911 J. F. WILSON *Land Claimers* viii. 112, I finished the cruise today. **1953** [see CRUISE *v.* 2].

3. Short for *cruise missile* below.

1976 *Listener* 16 Sept. 322/2 A short film about the cruise. **1986** *Church Times* 14 Feb. 14/1 The General Synod debate and resolutions supported neither the unilateralists nor the supporters of Cruise and Trident.

4. Special Comb. **cruise control** orig. *U.S.*, (*a*) *Aeronaut.*, the regulation of the flying speed, etc., of an aircraft in order to achieve maximum fuel efficiency; (*b*) chiefly *N. Amer.*, a device fitted to some motor vehicles which allows the driver to maintain a constant cruising speed on motorways, etc., without depressing the accelerator pedal; the facility for regulating the speed of a motor vehicle in this way; **cruise missile** orig. *U.S.*, a weapon in the form of a guided pilotless jet aircraft carrying a warhead and able to fly at low altitudes.

1949 *Sun* (Baltimore) 17 Oct. 1/5 Some proponents of the B-36 now predict that with '*cruise control' (the technique of getting more mileage out of a gallon of fuel by careful attention to adjustments, airplane flying position, wind and other factors) a range of 12,000 miles or more is in prospect. **1960** *Pop. Sci.* Apr. 95/1 With a lever you can set either for speed warning or automatic cruise control. **1968** *Autocar* 14 Mar. 16/1 Speedostat cruise control now imported from the USA... Fully automatic operation the main feature, with a 'speed-limit' reminder as a useful half-way provision. **1972** *Gloss. Aeronaut. & Astronaut. Terms* (*B.S.I.*) XIII. 2 *Cruise control*, the method of operating an aircraft to produce optimum fuel economy with regard to time or distance, or both. **1977** *National Observer* (U.S.) 1 Jan. 8/5 Two Cadillacs equipped with cruise control, a device that holds a car at a constant speed, have been in accidents allegedly because of a defect in the cruise-control system. **1985** *New Yorker* 22 Apr. 51/3 Plenty of smooth-riding Ford and General Motors sedans loaded with options like cruise control, tilt steering wheels, FM with the AM, a few tape decks and C.B.s, but nothing truly ostentatious. **1959** *Aviation Week* May 85/1 Severest test to date for Bomarc A was a simulated operational launch against North American X-10 test vehicle from the Navaho *cruise missile program. **1976** *National Observer* (U.S.) 7 Feb. 5/2 The cruise missile, essentially, is a sophisticated, unmanned airplane. **1977** *Sci. Amer.* Feb. 20/3 A cruise missile requires continuous guidance, since both the velocity and the direction of its flight can be unpredictably altered by local weather conditions. **1983** *Daily Tel.* 31 Jan. 7/2 The threat to peace was not from the Cruise missile. **1984** *Guardian* 5 Nov. 2/2 The plans could include the use of cruise missiles with conventional warheads to knock out single targets such as bridges or airfields deep behind the enemy front lines.

cruiser (ˈkruːzə(r)). Also (7 crosier), 8 cruzer, 7–9 cruizer. [f. CRUISE *v.* + -ER[1], or immed. a. Du. *kruiser*: cf. also F. *croiseur* (ship and captain), *croisière* a cruise (1696 in Jal), cruising ground, cruising fleet.] **1. a.** A person or a ship that cruises; *spec.* a war-ship commissioned to cruise for protection of commerce, pursuit of an enemy's ships, capture of slavers, etc. In 18th c. commonly applied to privateers. Now, in the British Navy, a class of war-ships specially constructed for cruising.

1679 G. R. tr. *Boyatuau's Theat. World* II. 302 Forty Ships which he took from the Crosiers [? croisers] or Pyrates. **1695** *Lond. Gaz.* No. 3061/1 They have at present 6 Frigats abroad, with some other Cruisers. **1723** DE FOE *Col. Jack* (1840) 191 A French cruiser or privateer of twenty-six guns. **1757** J. LIND *Lett. Navy* Pref. 8 A few cruizers.. would have made us masters of the Mediterranean. **1851** DIXON *W. Penn* ii. (1872) 9 The boldest cruiser in that section of the.. fleet. **1868** G. DUFF *Pol. Surv.* 110 The efforts.. made by our cruisers in these Seas to put down the Slave trade.

fig. **1698** FARQUHAR *Love & Bottle* IV. iii, Ha! There's a stately cruiser [a woman]; I must give her one chase.

b. A yacht constructed or adapted for cruising, as distinguished from a 'racer'; also, a motor-vessel designed for pleasure cruises on the sea, or on rivers, canals, etc. See also *cabin cruiser*.

1879 in É. Bonnaffé *Dict. Anglicismes* (1920). **1888** *Encycl. Brit.* XXIV. 724/2 As to the number of yachts now afloat, cruisers as well as racers, the British yacht fleet.. now numbers.. 3000 yachts. **1971** *Observer* 10 Jan. 37/1 (Advt.), Explore beautiful uncrowded waterways in 2- to 6-berth luxury cruisers. *Ibid.* 37/2 Explore the fascinating inland waterways on a real canal cruiser.

c. One who goes on a pleasure cruise.

1940 *Times* 9 Jan. 6/4 Shovel-board, with which cruisers are familiar on board our liners. **1961** *Guardian* 11 Jan. 5/4 Most 'cruisers' find the time all too short for what they want to do.

d. One who cruises (sense 1 d) in search of a casual sexual partner. Chiefly *U.S.*

1903 H. HAPGOOD *Autobiogr. Thief* (1904) ii. 34 Even the Bowery 'cruisers' (street-walkers) carried them. **1910** —— *Types from City Streets* I. viii. 140 The Bowery girl, the 'cruiser',.. is taught early that 'the world is graft'. **1942** BERREY & VAN DEN BARK *Amer. Thes. Slang* §508/3 *Cruiser*, .. a homosexual who looks for patrons. **1980** *Amer. Speech* LV. 191 With the recent diffusion of the [homosexual] subculture, such [until recently secret or semi-secret] terms are gradually becoming known, for example, queer, queer bitch, aunt, and cruiser.

2. a. In science fiction, an aircraft or spaceship.

1923 E. R. BURROUGHS *Chessmen of Mars* vii. 70 The cruiser 'Vanator' careened through the tempest. **1958** T. GODWIN in 'E. Crispin' *Best SF 3* 94 The cruisers carried the colonists to their new worlds.

b. A police-car that patrols the streets. *N. Amer.*

1929 *Sat. Even. Post* 7 Dec. 68/2 The cruisers are high-powered seven-passenger touring cars manned by a crew of four. **1958** *Ottawa Citizen* 28 May 7/5 To lift all speed regulations from police cruisers chasing law-breaking suspects. **1967** *Boston Sunday Globe* 23 Apr. 25/1 In Weymouth Patrolmen Richard McDonald and Ralph Campbell were injured when a car hit their cruiser.

3. a. (See quot. 1900.) Cf. CRUISE *v.* 2. Chiefly *U.S.*

1893 *Scribner's Mag.* June 695/1 My first day's experience as a 'Cruiser' or 'Landlooker'. **1900** E. BRUCKEN *N. Amer. Forests* 81 A peculiar class of people variously known as woodsmen, cruisers, landlookers, whose business it is to give information as to the existence of pine timber, its location, amount, value. **1921** *Daily Colonist* (Victoria, B.C.) 11 Oct. 9/3 Dave Vanstone.. was on a timber cruising expedition with his two head cruisers. **1946** R. PEATTIE *Pacific Coast Ranges* 232 With his cruiser's eye, he could measure the quantity and the quality of the timber from the water's edge.

b. A long-legged boot such as timber-cruisers often wear. *U.S.*

1902 S. E. WHITE *Blazed Trail* xvii. 125 Dressed in broad hats, flannel shirts, coarse trousers tucked in high-laced 'cruisers'. **1946** *Sat. Even. Post* 11 May 41/1 He was wearing Tillamook light cruisers.

4. *Boxing.* Short for *cruiser-weight* (see 5).

1928 *Daily Tel.* 28 Feb. 16 Poor heavy-weights. Gallant 'cruisers'. **1928** *Daily Chron.* 9 Aug. 11/2 Cuthbert Taylor (flyweight), John Garland (bantam), and Alfred Jackson (cruiser) all survived their preliminary tests.

5. *attrib.* and *Comb.*, as ***cruiser-pinnace***, ***-squadron***; ***cruiser-built*** adj.; **cruiser stern** *Naut.*, a type of ship's stern without an overhang, the projecting part being under the water; **cruiser tank**, a tank (TANK *sb.*[7]) of intermediate weight designed for rapid movement; **cruiser-weight** *Boxing*, for professionals: a weight of more than 11 stone 6 lb. but not exceeding 12 stone 7 lb.; for amateurs: a weight of more than 11 stone 11 lb. but not exceeding 12 stone 10 lb.; light heavy-weight; a boxer of this weight; also *attrib.*

1902 *Westm. Gaz.* 7 May 5/1 Cruiser-built merchantmen. **1934** T. E. LAWRENCE *Let.* 8 June (1938) 806 The new cruiser-pinnaces. **1901** *Westm. Gaz.* 30 July 6/2 Cruiser squadrons. **1915** G. S. BAKER *Ship Form* I. viii. 74 If the water line at the stern is kept too full it results in.. eddymaking, and partly to avoid this a 'cruiser stern' has been adopted in many recent ships. **1950** P. F. ANSON *Scots Fisherfolk* viii. 111 In most modern fishing vessels of the larger type.. a 'cruiser-stern' is now almost universal. **1940** *Illustr. London News* CXCVII. 133 Armoured turrets of 'cruiser' tanks.. can be automatically swung in any direction. **1964** C. WILLOCK *Enormous Zoo* v. 98 The rhino-catchers were used to taking their transport across country at which a cruiser tank might have balked. **1920** *Boxing* 25 Feb. 96/2 Two cruiser-weights.. engaged in a 15 rd. side stake match. *Ibid.* 13 Oct. 163/3 Carpentier.. wants the world's cruiser-weight title. **1922** *Daily Mail* 11 Nov. 11 Jack Bloomfield, the cruiser-weight champion. **1923** *Ibid.* 10 Jan. 9 He will go for the cruiser-weight trophy.

cruiseway (ˈkruːzweɪ). [f. CRUISE *sb.* + WAY *sb.*[1]] An inland waterway intended chiefly for pleasure cruising.

1967 *British Waterways* (Cmnd. 3401) 3 The Government propose that forthcoming legislation should make special provision for two distinct groups of waterways. The first will be those which are to form part of the [British Waterways] Board's commercial division... The second.. will be maintained primarily for powered pleasure craft. They can no longer usefully form part of a commercial transport system and they will be known as cruising waterways—or 'cruiseways'. **1968** *Guardian* 26 July 4/6 The Leeds-Liverpool canal is classified as a cruiseway for all but eight miles of its length. **1971** *Observer* 17 Jan. (Colour Suppl.) 10/4 Barbara Castle's 1968 Transport Bill, which designated a few miles of the [canal] system as cruiseways.

cruisie, cruisken, var. of CRUSIE, CRUSKYN.

cruising, *vbl. sb.* [f. CRUISE *v.*] **a.** The action of sailing to and fro; also *transf.*

1690 *Lond. Gaz.* No. 2532/2 The *Plimouth* is come in from Cruising. **1839–40** W. IRVING *Wolfert's R.* (1855) 219 The chimerical cruisings of Old Ponce de Leon in search of the Fountain of Youth.

b. *spec.* The action of walking or driving about the streets in search of a casual sexual partner (cf. CRUISE *v.* 1 d.) *slang.*

1927 A. J. ROSANOFF *Man. Psychiatry* (ed. 6) 203 In the most respectable class [of homosexuals] are those who do no 'cruising'. **1942** Z. N. HURSTON in A. Dundes *Mother Wit* (1973) 223/2 He had plenty to get across and maybe do a little more cruising besides. **1981** H. CARPENTER *W. H. Auden* I. v. 97 The length of the list might suggest that Auden was in the habit of 'cruising'—picking up boys for casual sex.

c. *attrib.*, as (CRUISE *v.* sense 1 a) ***cruising-ground***, ***-shirt***, ***-trade***, ***-vessel***; (CRUISE *v.* sense 1 b) ***cruising-altitude***, ***-height***; **cruising radius, range**, the maximum distance that the fuel capacity of a ship or aircraft will allow her to travel and return at cruising speed; **cruising speed**, the best economic travelling speed for a ship or vehicle, esp. an aircraft.

1951 *Gloss. Aeronaut. Terms* (*B.S.I.*) III. 19 *Cruising height* (*cruising altitude*), a constant altimeter indication, in relation to a fixed and defined datum, maintained during a flight or portion thereof. **1958** *Listener* 16 Oct. 593/1 The pressurised cabin was subject to cyclic reversals of load as the aircraft climbed to cruising altitude. **1780** CAPT. HOPE in *Lett. S. Hood* (1895) 11 But could not learn what latitude their cruizing ground was in. **1851** MELVILLE *Moby Dick* II. ix. 61 The.. *Pequod* had slowly swept across four several cruising-grounds. **1968** *Globe Mag.* (Toronto) 13 Jan. 7/3 Certain parks.. become known as favorite cruising grounds. **1951** Cruising height [see *cruising altitude* above]. **1956** 'N. SHUTE' *Beyond Black Stump* 237 They were off the ground and climbing up to cruising height. **1927** G. BRADFORD *Gloss. Sea Terms* 45/2 Cruising radius is calculated with two points of view—one, the vessel's capacity in miles without refueling; the other, her capacity to remain at sea expressed in days running at normal speed. **1922** M. LUCKIESH *Bk. of Sky* xxi. 230 These huge flying-machines with a cruising range of a thousand miles. **1959** J. BRAINE *Vodi* vi. 94 One of those woollen shirts with a fastener at the throat—cruising shirts they called them. **1919** *Sphere* 26 Apr. 67/2 The single-engine machine is the faster at full and cruising speeds. **1928** *Daily Chron.* 9 Aug. 3/6 It will have a 'cruising speed' of 15 miles an hour. **1935** P. W. F. MILLS *Elem. Practical Flying* iii, It is usual to describe performances in terms of both maximum and cruising speeds—the latter being the speed at which the aeroplane flies level with the engine running at the cruising revolutions recommended by the makers. **1958** *Listener* 30 Oct. 683/1 You want a car that has.. a high cruising speed. **1720** DE FOE *Capt. Singleton* xiii. (1840) 226 We pretended to carry on our cruising trade. **1878** *N. Amer. Rev.* CXXVII. 382 A cruising-vessel.

cruive (kruːv). Forms: 5 crufe, 5–6 cruif(e, 5–8 cruve, 8 crove, 4– cruive. [Originally Scotch (pronounced krøːv, kryːv), and retaining its Sc. spelling in sense 4, in which it has passed into legal and general use. The various forms point to an original **crōf-*, of which nothing seems to be known. In senses 1 and 2, CROO and *cruive* are synonymous: cf. also CREW *sb.*[2] Sense 4 suggests connexion with *corve*, CORF and its family.]

1. A hovel, cabin. *Sc.*

c **1450** HENRYSON *Fables, Wolf & Lamb* (*Bannatyne Poems*), The pure husband hes nocht But cote and crufe, upone a clout of land. **1725** RAMSAY *Gent. Sheph.* v. iii, I that very day Frae Roger's father took my little crove [*rime* love].

2. A pen for live stock, *esp.* a pig-sty. *Sc.*

c **1575** BALFOUR *Pract.* 588 Gif thair be ony swine cruivis biggit on the fore-gait. **1597** SKENE *De Verb. Sign.* s.v. *Creffera, Hara porcorum*, ane cruife, or ane swines cruif.. quhilk in sum auld buikes is called ane Stye. **1883** *Longman's Mag.* Apr. 648 The neighbours lean over the sow's 'cruive' or sty.

3. A kitchen-garden enclosure. (*Orkney.*)

1876 D. GORRIE *Summ. & Wint. in Orkneys* v. 160 Plantie cruives—deserted cottage kitchen-gardens.

4. A coop or enclosure of wickerwork or spars placed in tide-ways and openings in weirs, as a trap for salmon and other fish.

14.. *Sc. Stat.* I. 469 Al þai þat hes cruffis [*croas*] or fyschingis.. or mylnys in watteris quhar the se cumis and gangis. **1599** A. HUME *Hymnes, Day Estival*, The salmon out of cruives and creels Uphailed into scouts. **1609** SKENE *Reg. Maj.* Treat. 139 To execut the Acts of Parliament made anent Salmond fishing, and cruves. **1769** PENNANT *Tour Scot.* (1771) 117 Beneath are some cruives, or wears, to take Salmon in. **1834** MEDWIN *Angler in Wales* I. 330 The pool .. is too shallow for salmon, who run into the cruives. **1862** *Act* 25-6 *Vict.* c. 97 §6 (6) General regulations with respect to.. The construction and use of cruives.

cruize, cruizie, var. CRUISE, CRUSIE.

cruk(e, obs. form of CROOK.

crule *v. Obs.*: see CRAWL.

†**crull**, *a. Obs.* Also crul, crol(le. [ME., corresp. to Fries. *kroll, krull*, MDu. *crul*, MG. (15th c.) *krul* curly: see Grimm *kroll*. Not recorded in OE.: cf. CURL.] Curly.

c **1300** *K. Alis.* 1999 His hed was crolle, and yolow the here. *c* **1386** CHAUCER *Prol.* 81 A yong Squier.. With lokkes crulle as they were leyd in presse. —— *Miller's T.* 128 Crul [*v.r.* crol, crull, crulle] was his heer.

cruller ('krʌlə(r)). *U.S.* [app. a. Du. *cruller*, f. *crullen* to curl: cf. EFris. *kruller* curl, paper-curl, LG. *kroll-koken* wafer-cakes.] A cake cut from dough containing eggs, butter, sugar, etc., twisted or curled into various shapes, and fried to crispness in lard or oil.

1818 W. IRVING *Sketch-Bk., Leg. Sleepy Hollow*, The doughty dough-nut.. the crisp and crumbling cruller. **1866** HOWELLS *Venet. Life* vi, A species of cruller, fried in oil, which has all seasons for its own. **1890** G. RUDMANI *Royal Baker* (N.Y.) 8 [Recipe].

crum, var. of CRUMB *a.* and *v.*[2] *Obs.*

crumb, (krʌm), *sb.* Forms: 1 cruma, 3-6 cromme, 3-7 crumme, 4-6 crome, 5 crom, crume, crwme, 5-6 crowm(e, 6 crumbe, 7 crumm, 5- crum, 7- crumb. [OE. *cruma* masc., related to MDu. *crūme* f., Du. *kruim*, MLG. *krōme*, LG. *krōme*, mod.Ger. *krume*, these having the vowel long. The ulterior derivation is obscure. The merely graphic *b* began to be added in the 16th c.; but *crum* continued to be the prevalent form to the end of the 18th c., and is recognized in 19th c. Dictionaries. Johnson has *crum, crumb*.

The *b* probably appeared first in the derivative *crumble* (where it has also invaded the pronunciation), after words of F. origin like *humble*; there was also the apparent analogy of OE. words like *dumb*, where *b* was retained in the spelling, though no longer pronounced: cf. *thumb*.]

1. a. A small particle of bread (or other friable food), such as breaks or falls off by rubbing, etc.

c **975** *Rushw. Gosp.* Matt. xv. 27 Welpas ek etaþ of cromum þe þe falleþ of beode. *c* **1000** *Ags. Gosp.* ibid. þa hwelpas etað of þam crumum. *a* **1110** *Voc.* in Wr.-Wülcker 330/13 *Mica* cruma. *c* **1200** ORMIN 1474 Laf þatt iss wiþþutenn crummess. **1303** R. BRUNNE *Handl. Synne* 6645 To ete hys fylle of þe crummes. *c* **1400** *Lanfranc's Cirurg.* 59 A crumme of breed. *c* **1450** *St. Cuthbert* (Surtees) 6758 All Northumbirlande prouynce He thoght as croms of bred to mynce. **1547** *Ordre of Communion*, We be not woorthie.. to gather up the cromes under thy table. **1568** BIBLE (Bishops') *Mark* vii. 28 The childrens crumbes. **1632** SANDERSON *12 Serm.* 472 Every crumme we put in our mouthes. **1797** BEWICK *Brit. Birds* (1847) I. 157 He hops round the house, picks up the crumbs. **1829** G. R. GLEIG *Chelsea Pensioners* (1840) 207 A few crums which remained in our havresacks. **1849** JAMES *Woodman* xi, We feed it with the crumbs from our table.

b. A small particle of anything; a grain, as of dust. *Obs.* exc. *dial.*

1387 TREVISA *Higden* (Rolls) IV. 399 Was neuere founde gobet noþer cromme. *c* **1470** HARDING *Chron.* CXXIV. xii, [He].. for his workes and buyldynges held eche crome. **1560** P. WHITEHORNE tr. *Macchiavelli's Arte of Warre* (1573) Litle peeces or crummes of pitche. **1642** FULLER *Holy & Prof. St.* v. iv. 369 To leave no crumme of dust behind. **1655** H. VAUGHAN *Silex Scint.* I. 92 (Burial of Infant) Softly rest all thy Virgin-Crums! **1883** STEVENSON *Treas. Isl.* III. xiv. (1886) 114 His eye.. gleaming like a crumb of glass.

c. One of the irregularly-shaped and highly porous aggregates of particles found in soil having a crumb structure. (Cf. sense 3 b.)

1906 [see *crumb structure*]. **1914** T. L. LYON et al. *Soils* (1920) vii. 109 The soil particles are not homogeneous as to size, and neither do all the particles function as simple grains, being gathered together in groups called granules, or crumbs. **1961** J. MACBEAN *Soil* iii. 34 Clay soils which are treated with lime to allow of the flocculation or grouping together of the single particles into crumbs.. are warmer and more easily worked.

d. In rayon manufacture (see quots.).

1927 M. H. AVRAM *Rayon Industry* 259 Following the steeping operation the blocks of alkali-cellulose are shredded. In this operation, which is usually carried out in a machine called a shredder or disintegrator, the cellulose is reduced to very finely divided particles called crumbs. **1927** T. WOODHOUSE *Artif. Silk* vi. 54 The action of the internal parts of the kneader breaks up the [alkali-cellulose] sheets effectively into small particles similar to small breadcrumbs, and hence these particles are called 'crumbs'. **1959** *Chambers's Encycl.* V. 643/2 Viscose process... The crumbs are placed in churns where the action of carbon disulphide causes the alkali-cellulose to change to cellulose xanthate.

2. *fig.* **a.** A very small particle or portion (of something immaterial), a 'scrap'.

a **1535** FISHER *Wks.* (1876) 408 [Not] one crum of merit. **1541** BARNES *Wks.* (1573) 225 Some cromme of charitie within them. **1662** FULLER *Worthies, Berks., R. of Wallingford*, This their clock gathering up the least crume of time. **1719** D'URFEY *Pills* V. 76 To beg Some Crumbs of Comfort. **1801** SCOTT *Let. to G. Ellis* 11 May, I think I could give you some more crumbs of information were I at home. **1890** *Dict. Nat. Biog.* XXII. 339 Claverhouse's only crumb of comfort was that he saved the standards.

b. A body-louse. *U.S. slang.*

1863 O. W. NORTON *Army Lett.* (1903) 175 Fortunately, I am not troubled with the 'crumbs' now. **1898** *Scribner's Mag.* XXIII. 440/1 Just then I felt something crawling on my neck. It was a crumb. **1925** J. H. MULLIN *Adv. Scholar Tramp* iii. 46 If there is crumbs hoppin' around on me, I don't want to encourage 'em too much.

c. A lousy or filthy person; an objectionable, worthless, or insignificant person. *slang* (orig. *U.S.*).

1918 H. M. RIDEOUT *Key of Fields* 236 A couple of crumbs want to kill you. **1930** WODEHOUSE *Very Good, Jeeves!* iii. 83 This old crumb would be the occupant of the bed which I was proposing to prod with darning-needles. **1959** H. D. BARTON *Loving Cup* 236 He's an absolute crumb called Stuart Rowlandson. **1970** *Women Speaking* Apr. 5/1 If a man doesn't like a girl's looks or personality, she's a.. crumb.

3. a. The inner part of a loaf, not hardened in baking, and capable of being easily crumbled; the soft part of bread. Opposed to *crust*.

c **1430** *Pilgr. Lyf Manhode* I. xli. (1869) 25, I entermeted me neuere to make cruste ne cromme. *c* **1440** *Anc. Cookery* in *Househ. Ord.* (1790) 441 Pare away the cruste, and stepe the crome in vynegur. **1605** SHAKS. *Lear* I. iv. 217 He that keepes nor crust nor crum. **1726** LEONI *Alberti's Archit.* I. 32 a, Make them thin, that they may have the more Crust and the less Crum. **1869** E. A. PARKES *Pract. Hygiene* (ed. 3) 174 Taking the bread ½ crust and ⅔ crumb.

b. *transf.* Loosened and crumbled earth.

1805 R. W. DICKSON *Pract. Agric.* (1807) I. 16 It will give as much mould, or crumb, in the harrow, as any other furrow. **1881** WHITEHEAD *Hops* 45 There should be a good tilth, or crumb, at least a foot deep.

c. *slang.* Plumpness. Cf. CRUMMY 3.

1844 DICKENS *Mart. Chuz.* xxix, 'Too much crumb, you know', said Mr. Bailey; 'too fat, Poll.'

†**4.** Phr. ***to gather*** (or ***pick***) ***up one's crumbs***: to 'pick up' or recover strength or health; to improve in condition. *Obs.* exc. *dial.*

1588 A. INGRAM in Hakluyt *Voy.* II. II. 130 Our men beganne to gather vp their crums and to recouer some better strength. *c* **1645** HOWELL *Lett.* 2 Feb. an. 1621 Thank God, I.. am recovering and picking up my crums apace. **1840** R. H. DANA *Before Mast* xxvii, [He] had 'picked up his crumbs'.. and [was] getting strength and confidence daily. **1888** *W. Somerset Word-bk.* s.v., A person or animal improving in appearance is said to be picking up his crumbs.

5. *Comb.*, as ***crumb rubber***; ***crumb-catching*** ppl. adj.; **crumb-brush**, a brush for sweeping crumbs from a table; **crumb-cloth**, a cloth laid under a table to catch the crumbs and keep the carpet clean; sometimes laid over the greater part of a carpet; **crumb structure** [tr. G. *krümelstruktur* (E. Wollny 1882, in *Forsch. auf d. Geb. d. Agrik.-Physik* V. 146)], the condition of soil when its particles are aggregated into crumbs (sense 1 c).

1884 HUGH CONWAY in *Eng. Illustr. Mag.* Dec. 176/1 Whittaker came in with the crumb brush. **1607** WALKINGTON *Opt. Glass* Ep. Ded. ¶3 b, Sycophants and crum-catching parasites. **1843** MRS. CARLYLE *Lett.* I. 196 The crumb cloth of the library. **1864** ELIZ. A. MURRAY *E. Norman* I. 6 A rich carpet, covered by a linen crumb-cloth. **1956** *Gloss. Terms Rubber & Rubber-like Materials* (ASTM Spec. Techn. Publ. No. 184) 28 *Crumb rubber.* When vulcanized rubber is milled, it does not become soft and plastic but forms a type of material known as crumb or spring rubber. **1957** *Times* 20 Dec. 17/6 Output of reclaim and crumb rubber for the 12 months was approximately 7 per cent. higher. **1906** E. W. HILGARD *Soils* vii. 109 The word 'Krümelstructur' (crumb-structure), adopted by Wollny for this phenomenon, has both fitness and priority in its favor. *Ibid.* 110 Clay is most frequently the substance which imparts at least temporary stability to the crumbs and crumb-structure. **1926** TANSLEY & CHIPP *Study of Veg.* vii. 116 The 'primary' inorganic particles of soil show a tendency to aggregate into 'compound particles'... This 'crumb structure'.. is found in all good agricultural and good forest soils. **1960** L. D. STAMP *Britain's Struct.* (ed. 5) xi. 96 It is mainly the maintenance of this soil-structure, especially this crumb structure, which the farmer means when he talks about.. 'maintaining a fine tilth'.

†**crumb, crum**, *a. Obs.* exc. *dial.* Also 4 croume, 9 *dial.* crum, crom. [A common WG. adj.: OE. *crumb* = OFris. *krumb* (EFris. *krum, -mme*), OS. *crumb* (MLG. *krum, -mme*, LG. *krumm*); MDu. *cromp, -be, crom(m* (Da. *krom*), OHG. *chrump, -be* (MHG. *krump, -be*, G. 16-17th c. *krumb*, mod.G. *krumm*, Upper G. dial *krump*) crooked:—OTeut. type **krumbo-*, f. *krimb-, kramb, krumb-* to press, squeeze, compress: see CRAMP *sb.*[1] Cf. also Irish *crón*, Welsh *crom*, crooked, bent. This adj., so important in G. and Du., has had very little development in Eng., its place being taken by the kindred CRUMP; it survives to a slight extent dialectally as *crum, crom* crooked, and in the derivatives *crum, crom* vb. (see CRUMB *v.*[2]), *cromster, crummie* q.v.] Crooked.

a **1100** *Misc. Glosses* in Wr.-Wülcker 514/14 *Obunca* þa crumban. *c* **1200** ORMIN 9207 7 all þatt ohht iss wrang 7 crumb shall effnedd beon 7 rihhtedd. *c* **1425** *Seuyn Sag.* (Wr.) 2477 With a lytil croume knyfe. **1866** GREGOR *Banffshire Gloss.* (Philol. Soc.), *Crom*, crooked: as 'the man [has] a crom finger'. Very frequently prefixed, as *crom-taet* (-toed), *crom-fingert, crom-leggit*. **1878** *Cumberld. Gloss.*, *Crum-horn't*.

crumb, crum (krʌm), *v.*[1] Forms: 5 croume, 5-6 crumm(e, crume, crome, 6 cromme, 6-7 crum, 7- crumb. [f. CRUMB *sb.* There was an earlier umlaut form CRIM (:—*crymman*), *cream*, still in dialect use.]

1. *trans.* To break down into crumbs or small fragments, reduce to crumbs. Now *rare.*

c **1430** *Pilgr. Lyf Manhode* IV. xxxiii. (1869) 194 As me þouhte, she bar mete croumed vp on parchemyn. **1565** JEWEL *Repl. Harding* (1611) 457 Into how small mites the Bread may be crummed. **1583** HOLLYBAND *Campo di Fior* 201 Heate them.. before you crume in the bread. *a* **1625** FLETCHER *Mons. Thomas* IV. iv, Crumb not your bread before you taste your porridge. **1882** *Worc. Exhib. Catal.* iii. 38 Machine for crumbing bread.

†**2.** *intr.* To fall into crumbs; to crumble. *Obs.*

1562 J. HEYWOOD *Prov. & Epigr.* (1867) 64 A mud wall.. Cracketh and crummeth in peeces. **1580** NORTH *Plutarch* (1676) 493 Ground.. that.. being troden on, crummeth like white lime. **18..** SOUTHEY (F. Hall).

3. *trans.* To put crumbs into or over; to thicken or cover with crumbs.

[See CRIM *v.*] **1579** FULKE *Heskins' Parl.* 377 As for his bare bread, let him keepe to crome his pottage. **1669** DRYDEN *Wild Gallant* I. ii, Last night good Mrs. Bibber.. crumm'd me a mess of gruel. **1684** BUNYAN *Pilgr.* II. 133 A Dish of Milk well crumbed. **1864** MRS. H. WOOD *Trev. Hold* III. ix. 131 To see a sweetbread egged and crumbed.

Hence **crumbed** *ppl. a.*

c **1430** *Two Cookery-bks.* 55 Melle yt with cromyd Marow, & lay on Sugre y-now.

†**crumb, crum**, *v.*[2] *Obs.* exc. *dial.* Also 5 cromin, 9 *dial.* crom. [f. CRUMB *a.* Not recorded in OE., but cf. OS. *crumban*, MLG. *krummen*, Du. *krommen*, OHG. *chrumbian*, MHG. *krumben*, G. *krümmen* to make crooked, to crook; also MHG. *krumben*, G. dial. *krummen*, to become crooked, f. the corresponding adj. *crumb*, see above.] *trans.* To make crooked or curved; to crook, bend.

c **1490** *Promp. Parv.* 104 (MSS. K., H.) Cromyn [*v.r.* crokyn], *unco.* **1866** GREGOR *Banffshire Gloss.*, *Crom*, to double, to crook.. as 'the tinker crommt up 's leg'.

Hence **crummet, crum't, crommt** *ppl. a. Sc.* [G. *gekrümmt*], crooked, crooked-horned.

1789 D. DAVIDSON *Seasons* 51 (Jam.) Spying an unco crummet beast. **1866** GREGOR *Banffshire Gloss.*, *Crommt*, crooked; [also] same as *crummie*.

†'**crumblable**, *a. Obs. rare.* [f. CRUMBLE *v.* + -ABLE.] = CRUMMABLE, q.v.

crumble ('krʌmb(ə)l), *sb.* Also 6 cromble. [In sense 1, app. dim. of *crumb*: cf. Du. *kruimel*, LG. *krömel*, MG. *krümel* (:—**krumila*), small crumb. In sense 2 treated as vbl. sb. from CRUMBLE *v.*]

1. A small or tiny crumb of anything friable; a particle of dust, etc. *Obs.* or *dial. rare.*

1577 B. GOOGE *Heresbach's Husb.* III. (1586) 146 b, They so shake the milke, as they sever the thinnest parte of it from the thicke, which at the first gather together in little crombles. **1646** J. MAINE *Sermon* (1647) 19 This diversity of Tongues at first broke the world into the severall crumbles and portions of men. **1704** in *Phil. Trans.* XXV. 1552 The Powder or Crumbles of 'em is what we call Bikstone. **1820** CLARE *Poems, Rural Life* (1821) 43 Thou shalt eat of the crumbles of bread to thy fill.

2. a. Crumbling substance; anything of crumbling consistency; fine débris. *rare.*

1860 HAWTHORNE *Marb. Faun* (1879) II. xx. 203 She had trodden lightly over the crumble of old crimes. **1883** JEFFERIES *Story of my Heart* i. 5 The crumble of dry chalky earth I took up and let fall through my fingers.

b. *Cookery.* Food, such as bread or a mixture of flour and fat, in the form of crumbs; a dish made from such crumbs together with fruit, esp. ***apple crumble***. Also *attrib.*

1947 M. GIVEN *Mod. Encycl. Cooking* I. 727 Apple crumble. **1951** *Good Housek. Home Encycl.* 589/1 Canadian or 'crumble' topping for pies. **1958** J. HAWTHORNE *Myst. Blue Tomatoes* xiv. 92 For 'afters' to-day she made them all an apple crumble. *Ibid.*, Her crumbles were delicious. **1958** *Listener* 12 June 995/1 Rhubarb crumble pudding... Rhubarb crumble.

crumble ('krʌmb(ə)l), *v.* Forms: *α.* 5 kremele, 6 crymble, 6-8 crimble; *β.* 6 cromble, croomble, 6- crumble. [The current form *crumble* is known only from late in the 16th c.; being evidently an assimilation to *crumb, crumbly*, etc. of the earlier *crymble, crimble*, the type being an OE. **crymelen* (:—**krumilôn*), f. *cruma* crumb: cf. prec. So Du. *kruimelen*, G. *krümeln*, LG. *krömeln* to crumble.]

1. *trans.* To break down into small crumbs; to reduce to crumbs or small fragments.

c **1420** *Liber Cocorum* (1862) 36 Kremelyd sewet of schepe. **1570** LEVINS *Manip.* 132/2 To crimble, *comminuere.* **1577** HANMER *Anc. Eccl. Hist.* (1619) 118 Commanded him to crimble or soke it. **1641** J. JACKSON *True Evang. T.* I. 7 Bread must be distributed, not crumbled. **1796** MRS. GLASSE *Cookery* xiv. 214 You may crumble white bread instead of biscuit. **1853** PHILLIPS *Rivers Yorksh.* i. 8 Moisture softens and crumbles the shale.

b. To strew or scatter as crumbs.

1547 BOORDE *Brev. Health* cvi. 40 b, Crymble them into a pynt of read wyne. **1803** *Jrnl. Excurs. Swiss Landscapes*, While cabins, single or in clusters, have been crumbled over it.

c. *fig.*

1632 G. HERBERT *Church Porch* xii, O crumble not away thy souls fair heap. **1667** POOLE *Dial. betw. Protest. & Papist* (1735) 81 You are crumbled into a thousand Sects. **1780** BURKE *Sp. Econ. Reform* Wks. 1842 I. 240 To avoid frittering and crumbling down the attention. **1870** FARRAR *Witn. Hist.* ii. (1871) 75 Sufficient.. to crumble the mythical theory of miracles into the dust.

2. *intr.* To fall asunder in small crumbs or particles; to become pulverized.

1577–87 HOLINSHED *Chron.* III. 1137/2 Bulworks, whereof the filling.. did crimble awaie. **1577** B. GOOGE *Heresbach's Husb.* I. (1586) 32 The bread is very drye, and croombleth lyke Sand or Ashes. *a* **1624** BP. M. SMITH *Serm.* (1632) 14 Shall it not breake and crimble betweene your fingers? **1697** EVELYN *Numism.* Introd. 2 Marbles with their deepest inscriptions crumble away. **1703** T. N. *City & C. Purchaser* 256 Their [stones'] edges crimble off. **1816** KEATINGE *Trav.* (1817) I. 224 The earth crumbled under our horses' feet. **1875** BRYCE *Holy Rom. Emp.* xix. (ed. 5) 358 Ready to crumble at a touch.

fig. **1642** FULLER *Holy & Prof. St.* v. xi. 404 They [the Donatists] crumbled into severall divisions amongst themselves. **1868** FREEMAN *Norm. Conq.* (1876) II. vii. 120 His influence was crumbling away.

crumbled ('krʌmb(ə)ld), *ppl. a.* [f. prec. + -ED[1].] Reduced to minute crumbs or fragments; pulverized, disintegrated.

c **1420** [see CRUMBLE *v.* 1]. **1667** MILTON *P.L.* VII. 468 The crumbled earth. **1853** KANE *Grinnell Exp.* xx. (1856) 156 Four circular mounds.. of the crumbled lime-stones.

crumblement ('krʌmb(ə)lmənt). *rare.* [f. as prec. + -MENT.] Crumbling, crumbled condition.

1868 BROWNING *Ring & Bk.* I. 676, I.. turned it over, and recognised, For all the crumblement, this abacus.

crumblet, crumlet ('krʌmlɪt). *rare.* [f. CRUMB *sb.* + -LET.] A little crumb.

1609 C. BUTLER *Fem. Mon.* (1634) 49 Small crumlets of wax.. fallen from the broken Combs. **1830** JENNER *To a Robin*, My board shall plenteously be spread With crumblets of the nicest bread.

'crumbliness. [f. CRUMBLY + -NESS.] The quality of being crumbly.

1807 SOUTHEY *Espriella's Lett.* II. 70 The dust, and the crumbliness of age.

crumbling ('krʌmblɪŋ), *vbl. sb.* [-ING[1].]

1. The action of the verb CRUMBLE.

a **1655** VINES *Lord's Supp.* (1677) 292, I naturally abhor the crumbling of Scripture into crumbs. **1810** SOUTHEY *Kehama* II. xv, He heard the crumbling of the pile.

2. *concr.* (*pl.*) Crumbled particles, débris.

1660 BURNEY *Κέρδ. Δῶρον* (1661) 96 That Royal David.. gathers up the crumblings of it. **1865** SWINBURNE *Atalanta* 2231 As light dust and crumblings from mine urn.

'crumbling, *ppl. a.* [-ING[2].] That crumbles; breaking into small particles.

1577 B. GOOGE *Heresbach's Husb.* II. (1586) 86 b, [That the ground] may be mellowed and made crumbling. **1697** DRYDEN *Virg. Georg.* I. 139 The crumbling Clods. **1769** GRAY *Jrnl. of Tour* 5 Oct., A mass of crumbling slate. **1861** HUGHES *Tom Brown at Oxf.* i. (1889) 6 A venerable old front of crumbling stone fronting the street.

crumbly ('krʌmblɪ), *a.* and *sb.* Forms: 6 cromely, 7 crumly, 8 crumbley, 7– crumbly. [The 16–17th c. forms *crome-ly*, *crum-ly*, imply formation from CRUMB *sb.* + -LY[1]; later pronunciation associates it with CRUMBLE *v.* and -Y.] **A.** *adj.* †**a.** Crumb-like; in crumbs. **b.** That crumbles easily; having a tendency to crumble; friable.

1523 FITZHERB. *Husb.* §100 It wyll.. waxe whyte, and cromely lyke a pomis. **1616** SURFL. & MARKH. *Country Farme* 399 If they find not the earth of their new lodging so light and crumly. **1764** HADLEY in *Phil. Trans.* LIV. 7 The pitch.. was crumbly and soft. **1860** HAWTHORNE *Marb. Faun* iii, Hewn.. out of a dark-red, crumbly stone.

B. *sb.* Also **crumblie**. An elderly person, older than a WRINKLY; *loosely*, any person considered to be old or senile. *slang.*

1976 *Times* 31 Aug. 10/8 The girl's great-grandmother, who died recently at 102, was called 'the crumblie'. **1980** *Daily Tel.* 27 Aug. 11/2 Synonyms and abbreviations require translation if one is not to be left on the conversational sidelines like bewildered pre-senile 'crumblies'. **1984** S. TOWNSEND *Growing Pains A. Mole* 130 At the end of the party Rick Lemon put 'White Christmas' by some old crumblie on the record deck and all the couples danced romantically together.

crumbs (krʌmz), *int.* Also by crum(s), by crumbs. [In phr. *by crum(s)*, a disguised oath.] An exclamation of consternation, dismay, etc.

1892 'Q' *Three Ships* i. 24 She'll not weather Gaffer's Rock. By crum! if she does, they may drive her in 'pon the beach, yet! *a* **1918** W. OWEN *Poems* (1963) 60 *Vrach!* By crumbs, but that was near. **1922** 'R. CROMPTON' *Just—William* viii. 166 'Crumbs!' said William, 'Talk about bad luck!' **1922** F. HAMILTON *P.J.: Secret Service Boy* vii. 277 O crumbs! Did he really say that I didn't mind wearing that rig-out? **1943** H. PEARSON *Conan Doyle* iii. 52 Devil of a temper you've got, Doyle! By Crums, it's hardly safe to go out with you. **1956** S. GIBBONS *Here be Dragons* iv. 74 Nothing like that. Crumbs! I should say not.

crumby ('krʌmɪ), *a.* [f. CRUMB *sb.* + -Y. The earlier spelling was CRUMMY, which is retained in some senses.]

1. Of the nature of crumb: see CRUMMY 2.

1767 *Byron's Voy.* 134 [Bread fruit] when gathered green, and roasted.. has its inside soft, tender, white, and crumby, like bread.

2. Full of crumbs; strewed with crumbs.

1731 BAILEY, vol. II, *Crummy.* **1739** WALPOLE *Let. to R. West* 20 July, Round a littered table, in a crumby room. **1873** MRS. WHITNEY *Other Girls* (1876) 153 Table cloths left.. dragging and crumby.

3. *slang.* (Freq. **crummy.**) Lousy; filthy, dirty, untidy; inferior, shoddy, distasteful. Hence **'crumbiness, 'crumminess.**

1859 HOTTEN *Dict. Slang* 27 *Crummy-doss*, a lousy or filthy bed. **1889** BARRÈRE & LELAND *Dict. Slang* I. 283/2 *Crummy* (army), dirty; applied amongst soldiers to a man's appearance. **1899** KIPLING *Stalky & Co.* 73 'It's a crummy place...' They crawled out, brushed one another clean. **1931** G. IRWIN *Amer. Tramp & Underworld Slang* 58 *Crummy*, verminous; undesirable; inferior or cheap. **1932** J. DOS PASSOS *Nineteen Nineteen* 3 Feeling crummy in the baggy civies, he walked slowly. **1949** H. E. BATES *Jacaranda Tree* vii. 66 The whole thing's a bit crummy. **1949** *Here & Now* (N.Z.) Nov. 27/2 The authentic crumminess of the downtown settings. **1956** R. FULLER *Image of Society* vi. 156 The place soon got to look crumby. **1958** *Spectator* 30 May 705/2 A A crumby seducer. *Ibid.*, Crumby phoneyness. *Ibid.*, There is nowhere free from crumbiness and sex. **1969** I. & P. OPIE *Children's Games* viii. 237 The game has been taken up by the physical training instructors under such crummy names as 'Poison Circle Tag'.

crume, obs. form of CRUMB.

crumen ('kru:mɛn). *Zool.* [ad. L. *crumēna* purse.] The suborbital gland in deer and antelopes, secreting a waxy substance.

1875 W. H. FLOWER in *Proc. Zool. Soc.* 160 There was no suborbital gland or crumen [in a musk-deer]. **1883** [see SUBORBITAL *a.*]. **1902** F. A. BEDDARD in *Cambr. Nat. Hist.* X. xi. 299 There is no crumen or suborbital gland [in the musk-deer].

†**'crumenal.** *Obs. rare.* [f. L. *crumēna* purse.] Used by Spenser and by Henry More, app. in sense 'purse' or 'pouch'.

1579 SPENSER *Sheph. Cal.* Sept. 119 The fat oxe, that wont ligge in the stall, Is now fast stalled in her [= their] crumenall. **1647** H. MORE *Song of Soul* I. III. xix, Thus cram they their wide-gaping Crumenall.

cru'menically, *adv. humorous nonce-wd.* [f. L. *crumēna* purse.] In relation to the purse.

1825 COLERIDGE *Lett., Convers. etc.* II. xl. 178 A Work.. in which I am greatly interested, morally and crumenically.

crumhorn, var. CROMORNE, KRUMMHORN.

1694–6 *Specif. Organ St. Paul's Cath.* in Grove *Dict. Mus.* II. 594, 20. Voice Humane. 21. Crumhorne. **1954** *Grove's Dict. Mus.* (ed. 5) II. 547/1 The body of a crumhorn is a slender tube, almost invariably of boxwood, with the lower end bent up in a hook-like curve. **1966** *New Statesman* 1 July 25/3 A few drones on shawms and crumhorns would have encouraged vocal techniques.

crumlet: see CRUMBLET.

crummable ('krʌməb(ə)l), *a. rare.* [f. *crum*, CRUMB *v.*[1] + -ABLE.] That can be crumbled; friable.

1611 COTGR., *Esmiable*, crummable, crumblable. [Hence in Todd 1818, and in mod. Dicts.]

crummet, *ppl. a. Sc.*: see CRUMB *v.*[2]

crummie, crummy ('krʌmɪ), *sb.* (*a.*) *Sc.* and *north.* Also 8 cromie. [f. *crum*, CRUMB *a.* crooked + *-ie* = -Y[4] dim. and denominative, as in *blacky, brownie, cockie, doddie*, etc.]

A. *sb.* **1.** A cow with 'crumpled' or crooked horns; often a kind of proper name for any cow.

1724 RAMSAY *Tea-t. Misc.* (1733) I. 111 My Cromie is a useful cow. *a* **1774** FERGUSSON *Drink Eclogue* Poems (1845) 52 Crummie nae mair for Jenny's hand will crune. **1824** SCOTT *Redgauntlet* Let. ii, The crummie drank without sitting down. **1876** D. GORRIE *Summ. in Orkneys* I. 39 Old men leading highboned crummies equally grave.

2. A staff with a crooked head.

1808–25 JAMIESON, *Crummie-staff*, *crummie-stick.* **1832–53** *Whistle-Binkie* (Sc. Songs) Ser. II. 111 The carlins coost their crummies til't, Sae vauntingly they vapour'd.

B. *adj.* Having crooked or crumpled horns.

1878 *Cumbrld. Gloss.*, *Crummy*, *crum-horn't*, [having] horns turned towards the eyes.

'crummock. *Sc.* [f. as prec., with dim. suffix -OCK; perh. after Gael. *crómag* any little crooked thing, dim. of *cróm* crooked, bent.] = prec. (in both senses).

1725 RAMSAY *Gent. Shep.* II. i. 4 And sauld your crummock and her bassand quey. **1790** BURNS *Tam o' Shanter* 161 Wither'd beldams.. Lowping an' flinging on a crummock.

crummy ('krʌmɪ), *a.* [f. *crum*, CRUMB *sb.* + -Y. Cf. also CRUMBY.]

†**1.** Crumbly, friable. *Obs.*

1567 MAPLET *Gr. Forest* 69 [The Adder] loueth.. to eate crummie and dry earth. **1611** COTGR., *Court en paste*, short, crummie.. ill cleauing together. **1725** BRADLEY *Fam. Dict.* s.v. *Waters*, A quantity of crummy Earth.

2. Like or of the nature of the crumb of bread, as distinguished from the crust.

1579 J. JONES *Preserv. Bodie & Soule* I. xiv. 26 Breade.. neyther to crustie nor to crummie. **1707** *Curios. in Husb. & Gard.* 255 The crummy part of a hot Loaf. **1844** DICKENS *Mart. Chuz.* viii, A slack-baked, crummy quartern [loaf].

3. *slang.* **a.** Plump, full-figured: usually said of women. Also **b.** Comely, pretty. **c.** Having well-filled pockets, rich.

1718 MOTTEUX *Quix.* I. III. vi, A well-truss'd, round, crummy, strapping Wench. **1748** DYCHE *Dict.*, *Crummy*, full of crumb; also fat, rich, plump, or fleshy. **1768** BUYS *Terms of Art*, *Crummy* (Figuratively), plump or fleshy. 'A Crummy Lass'. **1827** A. FONBLANQUE *Eng. under 7 Administ.* (1837) I. 40 We would.. much rather find the whole House [of Lords] in rich, crummy widows, than let them meddle with our bread. **1861** H. KINGSLEY *Hillyars & Burtons* (Farmer), 'You're crummy.. But you ain't what I'd call fat.' **1877** *N.W. Linc. Gloss.*, *Crummy*, fat, in good condition.

†**4.** Obs. spelling of CRUMBY *a.* 2.

5. Freq. var. of CRUMBY *a.* 3.

†**crump,** *a.*[1] and *sb.*[1] *Obs.* Also 7 cromp. [OE. *crump* = OHG. *chrumph*, MHG. *krumpf*, a by-form, prob. intensive, of OE. *crumb*, OHG. *chrumb* (see CRUMB *a.*), which has largely supplanted the simpler form. There is however a long gap in the history during the ME. period, and it is possible that the 16th c. *crump* resulted from analysis of *crump-back*, *crump-footed*, etc., where *crumped*, *crumpt*, was in earlier use. For the etymological affinities of the group see Note to CRAMP *sb.*[1]]

A. *adj.* **1.** Crooked: said chiefly of the body or limbs from deformity, old age, or disease.

a **800** *Corpus Gloss.* 1411 *Obunca* crump. *c* **1050** *O.E. Gloss.* in Wr.-Wülcker 459 *Obunca* crump. **1591** SYLVESTER *Du Bartas* I. iii. (1641) 21/2 All those steep mountains.. Under first Waters their crump shoulders hid. **1652** GAULE *Magastrom.* 186 Cromp shoulders. **1656** W. D. tr. *Comenius' Gate Lat. Unl.* ¶ 287 A crump-back, swoln throat, and any bunch whatsoever, caus deformitie. **1719** D'URFEY *Pills* I. 34 Bowing low with her back-bone crump.

2. *Comb.*, as **crump-back**, a hunch-back, a crook-back; also ***crump-backed***, ***-footed***, ***-shouldered***, etc.

[Cf. Ger. combinations in *krumm-*, as *krummfusz*, *krumfüszig*, Du. *krom-*, as *krom-voet*, *krom-voetigh* (Kilian).] **1542** UDALL *Erasm. Apoph.* 223 a, Croumpe shouldreed, shorte necked. **1599** WITHALS *Dict.* 96/1 Crumpe-footed, *loripes.* *a* **1661** HOLYDAY *Juvenal* x. 191 Ne're contract With one throat-swoln, gor-bellied, or crump-back'd. **1661** LOVELL *Hist. Anim. & Min.* 153 It helps crump-backs. **1715** tr. *C'tess D'Aunoy's Wks.* 370 She was Hunch-back'd and Crump-shoulder'd both before and behind. **1783** AINSWORTH *Lat. Dict.* s.v. *Back*, Crump backed, *gibbosus, humeris incurvus.*

B. *sb.* **1.** A hunch or hump on the back. *rare.*

1659 TORRIANO, *Scrígno*, a bunch, a crump, a knob upon ones back.

2. A crooked person, a hunch-back.

1698 VANBRUGH *Æsop* II. i, Esop.. that piece of deformity! that monster! that crump! *Ibid.* III. i, If I stand to hear this crump preach a little longer, I shall be fool enough perhaps to be bubbled out of my livelihood. **1719** D'URFEY *Pills* I. 78 Tho' the Crump too that Season, Got Bruges and Ghent by Treason. *c* **1765** FLLOYD *Tartarian T.* (1785) 43/2 Nohoud.. put only one of the crumps into his sack.

crump (krʌmp), *a.*[2] *Sc.* and *north.* [A parallel form of CRIMP *a.* 1; having app. associations with CRUMP *v.*[2], and with CRUMPLE. Cf. CRAMP *sb.*[1]] Brittle or friable under the teeth, easily 'crumped'.

1787 BURNS *Holy Fair* vii, And farls bak'd wi' butter, Fu' crump that day. **1811** WILLAN *W. Riding Gloss.* (E.D.S.), *Crump, crimp*, hard, brittle, crumbling. *a* **1825** FORBY *Voc. E. Anglia*, *Crump, crumpy*.. easily breaking under the teeth. **1878** *Cumbrld. Gloss.*, *Crump*, brittle; crumbling.

†**crump,** *sb.*[2] *Obs.* A variant of CRAMP *sb.*[1]

c **1460** *Towneley Myst.* 308 There I stode on my stumpe I stakerd that stownde: There chachid I the crumpe, yet helde I my grounde Halfe nome.

†**crump,** *sb.*[3] *Obs.* [Cf. CRIMP *sb.*[1]]

a **1700** B. E. *Dict. Cant. Crew*, *Crump*, one that helps Sollicitors to Affidavit men, and Swearers, and Bail, who for a small Sum will be Bound or Swear for any Body. **1725** in *New Cant. Dict.*

crump, *sb.*[4] *dial.* or *colloq.* [f. CRUMP *v.*[2] 3.]

1. A hard hit, given with brisk or abrupt effect.

1850–60 [In use at Cricket]. **1879** *Jamieson's Dict.*, *Crump*, a smart blow, *Clydesdale.* **1891** FARMER *Slang Dict.*, *Crump* (Winchester College), a hard hit; a fall.

2. The explosion of a heavy shell or bomb, or the sound of this; hence, the shell itself; ***crump-hole***, a hole or crater made by a shell. *Soldiers' slang.*

1914 *Times* 10 Dec. 6/1 The heavy shell.. ending in a loud 'crump' as it bursts on the ground. **1915** D. O. BARNETT *Lett.* 180 Suddenly a yellow cloud leaped up three times as high as the tower itself.. and after a bit there was the deuce of a crump. *Ibid.* 220, I got buried by a six-inch crump. **1915** 'BOYD CABLE' *Between Lines* 254 There was some fancy driving past them crump holes in the road. **1917** P. GIBBS *Battles of Somme* 171 The enemy was 'lathering' the field of observation with every kind of 'crump' and shell. **1930** BLUNDEN *Poems* 186 A crump at any moment May blow us to bits. **1961** *Guardian* 3 Apr. 5/4 The steady crump of falling bombs.

3. *Mining.* A violent burst in the floor, walls, or ceiling of a mine.

1925 *Pendleton Reporter* 7 Nov. 8/2 The accident was due to a 'crump'. 'Crumps' are caused through the floor of the mine rising owing to an accumulation of gases below it. **1927** *Command Paper 2946* (Reports XI) 244 Crumps are.. caused by.. great cumulative stress set up by the folding and thrusting of the strata.. which.. causes violent roof-falls and up-thrusting of the floor of the mine. **1967** *Gloss. Mining Terms* (*B.S.I.*) VIII. 8 *Bump* (*crump*), a sudden and heavy release of strain energy in the major body of rock surrounding a mine working, resulting in displacement of the strata.

†**crump,** *v.*[1] *Obs.* [f. CRUMP *a.* or its source: see CRIMP *v.*[1] and CRAMP *sb.*[1] Cf. also G. dial. *krummen, krumpen,* Du. *krommen,* to become crooked, to crook, *krumpfen* to shrivel, shrink up, which are similarly related to G. *krumm, krumpf* adj. Also the transitive *krümmen, krümpen, krumpfen*: see Grimm.]

1. *intr.* To draw itself into a curve, curl, curl up.

c **1325** *Poem Times Edw. II.* 115 in *Pol. Songs* (Camden) 329 Summe bereth croune of acolite for the crumponde crok. **1605** B. JONSON *Volpone* v. ii, But your Clarissimo, old round-backe, he Will crumpe you [= *to* or *for you*], like a hog-louse, with the touch.

2. *trans.* (and *refl.*) To bend (a thing) into a curve, crook, curl up.

1480 [see CRUMPED]. **1743** PARSONS in *Phil. Trans.* XLII. 535 He turns his Tail to the Wall, and, extending his hind Legs asunder, crumps himself up. **1818** KEATS *Extracts from Opera*, A careless nurse.. May have crumpt up a pair of Dian's legs, And warpt the ivory of a Juno's neck.

3. *fig.* ? To ruffle, disturb.

1656 HEYLIN *Surv. France* 158 Who being so often troubled and crumped by them have little cause to afford them a liking.

crump (krʌmp), *v.*[2] [A word imitating the sound made in eating moderately firm and 'short' substances, or in walking over slightly compressed snow, greater firmness and less brittleness being implied than in the use of *crunch* or *crush*. There is possibly some association with CRUMP *a.*[2]; cf. also CRUMPLE *v.* 6.] *trans.* and *intr.*

1. To eat with an abrupt but somewhat dulled sound; applied esp. to horses or pigs when feeding.

1646 H. MORE *Pref. Verses* in *J. Hall's Poems*, A Pig, that roots In Jury-land or crumps Arabick roots. **1760** MISS TALBOT in *Lett. w. Miss Carter* (1808) 484 Two years ago I could as easily have eat an Elephant as a sea biscuit, which I now crump again very comfortably. *a* **1825** FORBY, *Crump*, to eat anything brittle or crimp. **1827** CLARE *Sheph. Cal.* Aug. 74 The restless hogs will.. crump adown the mellow and the green. [**1878** *Cumbrld. Gloss.*, *Crump*, the sound of horses' teeth when eating.]

2. Applied to the sound made by the feet in crushing slightly frozen snow; and to the action which produces it. Cf. CRUMPLE *v.* 6.

1789 D. DAVIDSON *Seasons* 133 (Jam.) To the pliant foot .. the grassy path crumps sonorous. *Ibid.* 151 Close upon her snow-cap'd haunt.. watchful lest his crumping tread Should her untimely rouse. **1820** CLARE *Poems Rural Life, Addr. to Plenty*, And upon the crumping snows Stamps, in vain, to warm his toes.

3. To strike with a brisk or abrupt effect.

[There is a certain analogy of manner between this and the prec. senses.]

1850–60 [In use at Cricket]. **1879** *Jamieson's Dict.*, *Crump*, to smack, to thwack, as 'he's crumpit my croun wi' his stick'. **1889** *Boy's Own Paper* 4 May 496/1 Let me see The way well pitched up balls to crump. **1892** *Sat. Rev.* 2 Jan. 12/2 We could slog to square-leg, or crump to the off.

4. *Soldiers' slang.* **a.** *trans.* To bombard with heavy shells. **b.** *intr.* To fire heavy shells; also, to explode with a 'crump' (see prec., 2). Hence **'crumping** *vbl. sb.*

1915 'BOYD CABLE' *Between Lines* 254 We could hear the blighters crumpin' away back down the road behind us. **1916** *Blackw. Mag.* Jan. 125/1 You may imagine with what methodical solemnity the Bosche 'crumps' the interior of that constricted area. **1919** W. DEEPING *Second Youth* xxiii. 196 Five-point nines were still crumping on the road ahead of them. *Ibid.*, The crumping ceased, and they moved on. **1923** KIPLING *Irish Guards in Great War* I. 170 No. 1 Company of the Irish saw a platoon of Coldstream in front of them crumped out of existence. **1952** E. F. DAVIES *Illyrian Venture* vii. 119 Mortars of about two-inch and three-inch size were crumping irregularly. **1968** J. R. ACKERLEY *My Father & Myself* vii. 66 Shells began to whizz over and crump in the ravine behind.

crump-back: see CRUMP *a.*[1]

†**crumped, crumpt,** *ppl. a. Obs.* [app. f. CRUMP *v.*[1]] **1.** Curved, crooked.

1480 CAXTON *Ovid's Met.* XI. xviii, A fowle.. that hath a crumped bill. **1600** HEYWOOD *Edw. IV*, II. v. iii, Richard, I'll sit upon thy crumped shoulder. **1659** TORRIANO *Ital. Dict.*, *Scrignúto*, crumpt, or hunch-backt as a Camel.

2. *Comb.* **crumpt-shouldered** *a.*, round-shouldered.

1603 HOLLAND *Plutarch's Mor.* 667 A sonne, who was crumpt-shouldred and bunch-backed.

crumper, *sb. dial.* or *colloq.* [f. CRUMP *v.*[2] 3.] A 'whopper', 'whacker', 'thumper'; also a 'thumping' lie, a 'cracker'.

1855 E. WAUGH *Birtle Carter's T.*, *Lanc. Life* (1857) 24 There's some crumpers amoon th' lot. **1881** MISS BRADDON *Asph.* ix. 101 You told me your father was a grocer in Oxford Street. Was not that what school-boys call a crumper?

crumpet ('krʌmpɪt). Also 7 -it. [Not known till late in 17th c.; Wyclif has however *crompid cake* as a rendering of *laganum*, which may be the antecedent of the name:

1382 WYCLIF *Ex.* xxix. 23 A cake of a loof, a crusted cake spreynde with oyle, a crompid cake, of the leepe of therf looues [**1388** a tender cake of o loof, spreynde with oile, paast sodun in watir and after fried in oile, of the panyer of therf looues; Vulgate *tortamque panis unius, crustulam conspersam oleo; laganum de canistro azymorum*].

Crumpid here app. means 'curled up, bent into a curve' (see CRUMP *v.*[1], CRUMPED) as is usual with thin cakes baked on a griddle or iron plate; cf. CRULLER. The crumpet is not necessarily the same now as when it was first so called.]

†**1.** A thin griddle cake: in quots. made of buckwheat meal. *Obs.*

1694 WESTMACOTT *Script. Herb.* (1695) 220 They make Cakes of it [Buck Wheat].. as they do Oat-cakes, and call it Crumpit. **1830** *Withering's Brit. Plants* (ed. 7) II. 449 *footn.*, It [buck-wheat meal].. is made into thin cakes in Shropshire and other parts of England, called crumpits.

[Not in Miss Jackson's *Shropshire Word-bk.* 1879.]

2. A soft cake made of flour, beaten egg, milk, and barm or baking-powder, mixed into batter, and baked on an iron plate. (*Royal Baker*, 1890.) Now usually a soft, round, doughy cake made with flour and yeast, cooked on a griddle or the like and usu. eaten toasted with butter. Cf. PIKELET[1].

1769 MRS RAFFALD *Eng. Housekpr.* (1778) 279 To make Tea Crumpets. Beat two eggs very well, put to them a quart of warm milk and water, and a large spoonful of barm; beat in as much fine flour as will make them rather thicker than a common batter. **1827** HONE *Every-day Bk.* II. 1353 The basket and bell pass.. with muffins and crumpets. **1855** TROLLOPE *Warden* viii, There was dry toast and buttered toast, muffins and crumpets. **1899** WILDE *Importance of being Earnest* I. 22, I had some crumpets with Lady Harbury. **1912** E. H. RYLE *Athletics* iii. 53 The usual indigestible concomitants of a heavy tea—buttered buns and crumpets—ought to be eschewed. **1930** D. L. SAYERS *Strong Poison* ix. 111 Nothing goes so well with a hot fire and buttered crumpets as a wet day without and a good dose of comfortable horrors within. **1969** R. & D. DE SOLA *Dict. Cooking* 78/2 Crumpets are similar to.. muffins but of porous consistency with surface holes.

attrib. **1825** HOOD *Ode to Gt. Unknown*, This is dimpled, Like a pale crumpet face, or that is pimpled.

3. *dial.* = CRUMPLING *sb.* 2, CRUMPY *sb.*

4. *slang.* **a.** The head; esp. in phr. ***balmy*** or ***barmy on*** (or ***in***) ***the crumpet***: wrong in the head, mad: see BALMY *a.* 7, BARMY *a.* 2 b.

1891 [see BALMY *a.* 7]. **1897** W. S. MAUGHAM *Liza of Lambeth* ix. 153 You're all barmy on the crumpet. **1909** H. G. WELLS *Tono-Bungay* III. iii. 356, I heard my aunt admit that one of the Stuart Durgan ladies did look a bit 'balmy on the crumpet'.

b. A trivial term of endearment; also ***old crumpet.***

1900 G. SWIFT *Somerley* 40 You're Ophelia, Scrubby; but don't you go winking at the johnnies in the stalls, you giddy little crumpet! **1920** *Punch* 21 Jan. 45/1 Don't, Percival, old crumpet. **1923** WODEHOUSE *Inimit. Jeeves* ii. 23, I say, old crumpet, did my uncle seem pleased to see you?

c. Women regarded collectively as a means of sexual gratification; *occas.* a woman; sexual intercourse. So ***a bit*** (or ***piece***) ***of crumpet***: a (desirable) woman; a 'bit of fluff'.

1936 J. CURTIS *Gilt Kid* 75 Fancy staying up as late as this and not having no crumpet. **1958** M. PUGH *Wilderness of Monkeys* 37 'Not much crumpet here, tonight,' Maguire said, smiling lecherously at the military man's companion. **1959** S. DELANEY *Taste of Honey* (rev. ed.) II. ii. 81 He's gone off with his bit of crumpet. **1961** D. MOORE *Highway of Fear* i. 11 There's a delightful piece of crumpet.. I'm anxious to set me eyes on again. **1961** *Spectator* 25 Aug. 269 Thigh-slapping accounts of luscious foreign crumpet. **1969** D. LAMBERT *Angel in Snow* iv. 63 Ansell.. watched the couples wistfully. 'Plenty of crumpet here, you know. Why don't you chance your arm?'

'crumpiness. *dial.* [f. CRUMPY *a.* + -NESS.] The quality of being crumpy.

1832 J. WILSON *Noctes* lx. in *Blackw. Mag.* Feb. 259 On her girdle the gudewife heats into crumpiness a fair farl.

crumple, *sb.* In 7 cromple. [Cf. G. *krumpel, krümpel* in same sense, f. *krumm, krumb, krump* crooked; also CRUMPLE *v.*] A crushed fold or wrinkle produced by compression.

1607 DEKKER *Westw. Hoe* Wks. 1873 II. 293 My forehead has more cromples then the back part of a counsellors gowne. **1773** *Gentl. Mag.* XLIII. 584 The best method of taking out the creases and crumples.. without damaging the drawing or colours. **1860** TYNDALL *Glac.* I. xxi. 149 An ice-fall, on one side of which I found large crumples produced by the pressure.

†**crumple,** *a. Obs.* [f. CRUMPLE *v.*] = CRUMPLED: chiefly in comb., as ***crumple-horned*** adj.; **crumple-back** *sb.*, crook-back.

1523 *Act. 14–5 Hen. VIII*, c. 1 White brode wollen clothes with crumpil listes. **1685** STILLINGFL. *Orig. Brit.* v. 275 White Crumple-horned Cows. **1842** S. C. HALL *Ireland* II. 395 The long-horned, or crumple-horned. **1851** S. JUDD *Margaret* II. i. (1871) 178 She had partiality to the crumpleback, Job.

crumple ('krʌmp(ə)l), *v.* Also 4–6 cromple, -pyl, -pull. [In form, a dim. and iterative of CRUMP *v.*[1], for the affinities of which see Note to CRAMP *sb.*[1] As OE. *y* frequently gave later *u*, *crumple* might arise merely as a later form of *crymple, crimple*; but the historical evidence does not favour this.

Found first in pa. pple, which might belong either to an intr. or trans. vb. (cf. *withered, faded*); see CRUMPLED.]

1. *intr.* To become incurved or crushed together; to contract and shrivel up; to become creased or wrinkled by being crushed together.

1528 PAYNEL *Salerne's Regim.* C iij, To crompull to gether like parchement cast in the fire. **1577** STANYHURST *Descr. Irel.* ii. in *Holinshed* I. II. 13 It [aqua vitæ] keepeth and preserueth the veines from crumpling. **1633** T. JAMES *Voy.* 63 The snow.. crumples and so runnes vpon it selfe, that in a few houres it will be fiue or sixe foote thicke. **1681** H. MORE *Exp. Dan.* vi. 193 Hence it is that men crumple so in persecution. **1855** TROLLOPE *Warden* vi, How.. the muslin fluttered and crumpled before Eleanor and another nymph were duly seated at the piano.

2. *trans.* To crook, bend together, contort; in mod. use, *esp.* by crushing.

1613 BEAUM. & FL. *Honest Man's Fort.* II. iii, He would have crumpled, curled, and shrunk [*v.r.* struck] himselfe out of the shape of man. **1615** CROOKE *Body of Man* 268 He sitteth in the wombe crumpled, contracted or bent round. **1630** J. TAYLOR (Water P.) *Trav.* Wks. III. 82/1 The fellow was hanged, who being not choaked.. did stirre his legges, and writhe and crumple his body. **1880** A. R. WALLACE *Isl. Life* vi. 86 The effect.. is to crumple the strata and force up certain areas in great contorted masses.

3. To crush into irregular creases; to ruffle.

1632 MASSINGER & FIELD *Fatal Dowry* IV. i, Plague on him! how he has crumpled our bands! **1711** ADDISON *Spect.* No. 130 ¶2 Sir Roger.. exposing his palm.. they crumpled it into all shapes and diligently scanned every wrinkle. **1825** tr. *De Genlis' Mem.* I. 175 He.. crumpled my gowns, and even tore them. **1838** LYTTON *Alice* I. xii, 'Don't crumple that scarf, Jane'.

4. To wrinkle the smooth surface of; to corrugate, to crinkle.

1858 O. W. HOLMES *Aut. Breakf.-t.* ix. (1883) 179, I could see her.. crumpling the water before her, weather-beaten, barnacled. **1860** MAURY *Phys. Geog. Sea* ix. §445 The Sunbeam has power to wrinkle and crumple the surface of the sea by alternate expansion and contraction of its waters.

5. a. To crush (together) in an irregularly folded state.

1678 CUDWORTH *Intell. Syst.* 479 Huddled up, and as it were crouded and crumpled together. **1862** SALA *Seven Sons* I. xii. 307 She crumpled the cheque in her hand, and walked to the door.

b. ***to crumple up***: to shrivel up by compression; to crush together in a contracted or compressed state. Also *fig.* (usu. *pass.*).

1577 GOOGE *Heresbach's Husb.* IV. (1586) 185 The little Worme, or Grubbe.. lieth crumpled up in the Coame. **1602** MARSTON *Antonio's Rev.* I. v, Are thy moyst entrals crumpled up with griefe Of parching mischiefs? *a* **1682** SIR T. BROWNE *Plants Script.* Tracts 34 Our Rose of Jericho.. though crumpled and furdled up, yet, if infused in water, will swell and display its parts. **1861** HUGHES *Tom Brown at Oxf.* x. (1889) 91 He saw Drysdale crumple up the notes in his hand. **1865** G. MEREDITH *Let.* 11 Aug. (1970) I. 315, I fear that you are crumpled up with this accursed dyspepsia. **1916** A. HUXLEY *Let.* May (1969) 100 The only time they tried to do anything *strong*.. they were absolutely crumpled up.

c. *intr.* (for *refl.*). Also, to give way, collapse.

1858 *Sat. Rev.* VI. 90/2 Years crumple up into nothing, or extend to vast duration. **1898** *Westm. Gaz.* 17 May 2/2 It may be well that the Spanish defeat should not be too immediately overwhelming. It may help to keep Spain stable internally if she does not 'crumple up' at once.

6. Applied to the action and accompanying sound of crushing under foot things moderately brittle; said also *intr.* of the things so crushed. Cf. CRUMP *v.*[2]

1861 WOODS *Pr. of Wales in Canada* 63 The dry, sultry ashes of the forest crumple under your feet. **1868** HAWTHORNE *Amer. Note-Bks.* (1879) I. 92 Fallen leaves and acorns lying beneath; the footsteps crumple them in walking.

7. *fig.* To deprive of strength and energy.

1892 KIPLING *Barrack-room Ballads* 47 For the sickness gets in as the liquor dies out, An' it crumples the young British soldier.

crumpled ('krʌmp(ə)ld), *ppl. a.* [In form, f. CRUMPLE *v.* + -ED; but found much earlier than any finite part of the verb.]

1. Bent together by compression, incurved, crooked (*esp.* of parts of the body bent by malformation or disease).

a **1300** *Cursor M.* 8087 (Cott.) Crumpled knes [T. crompled knees] and boce on bak. *c* **1440** *Bone Flor.* 1979 In the palsye can he schake, And was crompylde and crokyd therto. **1647** H. MORE *Song of Soul* I. III. l, For that old crumpled wight gan go upstraight.

2. Bent spirally, curled. Hence ***crumpled-horn** a.*

14.. *Prose Legends* in *Anglia* VIII. 135 Also seint Paul seiþ not in crumpled [WYCLIF *1 Tim.* ii. 9 writhen] lokkys or golde. **1583** STANYHURST *Æneis* II. (Arb.) 50 Their tayls with croompled knot twisting. ? *a* **1750** *Nursery rime 'House that Jack Built'*, This is the Cow with the crumpled Horn, that tossed the Dog. **1846** J. BAXTER *Libr. Pract. Agric.* (ed. 4) II. 89 Horns short and generally curled, or what some call crumpled horn. **1886** W. G. WOOD-MARTIN, *Lake Dwellings Irel.* I. iv. 77 Specimens of the crania of four distinct breeds ..the straight-horn..the crumpled-horn..the short-horn ..the hornless.

3. Crushed into creases and folds; crushed out of shape, out of smoothness or tidiness.

a. Applied to a wrinkled, creased, or 'tumbled' condition of things flexible, as cloth, paper.

1535 COVERDALE *Job* vii. 5 My skynne is wythered and crompled together. **1664** EVELYN *Kal. Hort.* (1729) 203 Break, and pull off all crumpl'd dry'd Leaves. **166.** PEPYS *Diary* (1879), IV. 179 Finding the cloth laid, and much crumpled..I grew angry. **1877** W. THOMSON *Voy. Challenger* I. iii. 192 The strong brass cylinder..was found collapsed and crumpled like a piece of paper. **1888** ANNA K. GREEN *Behind Closed Doors* ii, Mrs. A. took a small and crumpled note out of her pocket.

b. Applied to strata crushed into folds by lateral pressure; contorted.

1854 HOOKER *Himal. Jrnls.* I. xi. 251 Granite appeared in large veins in the crumpled gneiss. **1862** DANA *Man. Geol.* 650 Crumpled or folded beds of clay.

4. Wrinkled, marked with lines and furrows, such as are caused by compression.

1577 GOOGE *Heresbach's Husb.* II. (1586) 56 The second sort with the croompled leafe. **1578** LYTE *Dodoens* I. xxix. 41 Medesweete..hath leaues..crompled, and wrinckled. **1688** R. HOLME *Armoury* II. 64/2 The Crumpled Plantan is a round crumpled Leaf. **1870** MORRIS *Earthly Par.* I. I. 400 The trembling poppies shed..their crumpled leaves.

b. Of hair. (Cf. CRUMPLING *vbl. sb.*)

1872 MISS THACKERAY *Old Kensington* ii. (ed. 2) 7 Dolly's ..crumpled bronze hair.

'crumpledness. [f. prec. + -NESS.] The quality of being crumpled, crumpled condition.

1805 LUCCOCK *Nat. Wool* 150 If..this compressure of the fleece produces that kind of crumpledness, which is considered as an excellent quality in English wool.

'crumpler. [f. CRUMPLE *v.* + -ER[1].]

1. One who crumples.

1849 *Blackw. Mag.* LXVI. 595 This crumpler-up and defier of empires.

2. A cravat. *dial.*

1869 BLACKMORE *Lorna D.* iii. (ed. 12) 12 If I see a boy make todo about the fit of his crumpler.

3. A fall by which man and horse are doubled up.

1883 E. PENNELL-ELMHIRST *Cream Leicestersh.* 3 A loaded shoulder [in a horse] means a crumpler over timber. **1887** H. SMART *Cleverly won* iii. 20 The mare..would be more frightened by a crumpler than you would. **1891** *Temple Bar Mag.* Jan. 30 The brute broke away with me and came no end of a crumpler over a wire fence.

†**'crumpling,** *sb.* and *a. Obs.* [Cf. G. *krümmling*, dial. *krumling*, *krümpling*, crooked stick, crooked man, etc.: see CRUMB *a.*, CRUMP *a.* But in the sb. sense 2, the word appears to be immediately associated with *crumple* vb. or sb.]

A. *sb.* **1.** A crooked, or deformed person.

a **1825** FORBY *Voc. E. Anglia*, *Crumplin*, a diminutive and deformed person.

2. A small dwarfed and shrivelled apple, cucumber, etc.: see quots.

1658 EVELYN *Fr. Gard.* (1675) 268 Putting each sort in a basket apart: I speak not here of the smallest, and the crumplings. **1693** —— *De la Quint. Compl. Gard.* Dict., *Crumpling*, or Guerkins are small Cucumbers to pickle, called in French *Cornichons*. *a* **1700** B. E. *Dict. Cant. Crew*, *Crumplings*, wrinkled Codlings, usually the least, but sweetest. **1710** *Brit. Apollo* III. 3/1 Ginger-Bread Babies and Crumplins. *a* **1825** FORBY *Voc. E. Anglia*, *Crumplin*, a diminutive and mis-shapen apple. **1888** *W. Somerset Word-bk.*, *Crumpling*, an apple which does not mature, but which shrivels on the tree.

B. *adj.* ? Crooked, shrivelled, deformed.

1666 J. SMITH *Old Age* (1752) 154 The locust and grasshopper are both of them hard cragged crumpling creatures. **1755** CARTE *Hist. Eng.* IV. 595 A little old crumpling fellow who made his fires was the best companion he had.

crumpling ('krʌmplɪŋ), *vbl. sb.* [-ING[1].] The action of the verb CRUMPLE; a crumpled condition. Also *attrib.*, as ***crumpling-irons.***

1855 THACKERAY *Newcomes* I. 233 In Miss Ethel's black hair there was a slight natural ripple..[which others] endeavoured to imitate by art, paper, and I believe crumpling irons. **1862** DANA *Man. Geol.* 650 The folding or crumpling of the clayey layer subjected to the pressure. **1866** A. FLINT *Princ. Med.* (1880) 209 Crumpling and crackling sounds.

crumply ('krʌmplɪ), *a.* [f. CRUMPLE *v.* + -Y[1]: cf. dial. G. *krumplig*, *krumpelicht.*] Full of crumples or wrinkles.

1847-78 HALLIWELL, *Crumply*, wrinkled. *Devon.* **1869** *Lonsdale Gloss.*, *Crumply*, wrinkled.

crumponde: see CRUMP *v.*[1]

crumpy, *sb. dial.* [f. CRUMP *a.*[1] or *sb.*[1] + -Y[4] dim. and denominative.] = CRUMPLING *sb.* 2.

1877 *Holderness Gloss.*, *Crumpy*, a small irregularly shaped apple.

'crumpy, *a. dial.* [f. CRUMP *a.*[2] + -Y[1].] = CRUMP *a.*[2]: see quots.

1808-25 JAMIESON, *Crump*, *crumpie*. *a* **1825** FORBY *Voc. E. Anglia*, *Crump*, *Crumpy*, brittle, dry-baked, easily breaking under the teeth. **1877** *Holderness Gloss.*, *Crumpy*, crisp; [as sb.] the crisp crust of a loaf. **1877** *N.W. Linc. Gloss.*, *Crumpy*, crisp; said of bread or pastry.

†**'crumster, cromster.** *Obs.* Also **crompster.** [f. Du. *krom* crooked: cf. Du. *kromsteve* 'genus navis' (Kilian), f. *krom* + *steve* prow.] A kind of galley or hoy.

1596 RALEIGH *Discov. Gviana* 98 Two or three crumsters or galleys buylt, and furnished vpon the riuer. —— *Invent. Shipping* 28, 200 saile of Crumsters, or hoyes of Newcastle, which each of them will beare six Demiculverins, and foure Sakers. **1600** *Carew MSS.* (1869) 375 Certain ships called 'crompsters'..with other barks and barges.

crunch (krʌnʃ), *v.* [A recent variation of *cranch*, CRAUNCH, perhaps intended to express a more subdued and less obtrusive sound, perh. influenced by association with *crush*, *munch*.]

1. *trans.* To crush with the teeth (a thing somewhat firm and brittle); to chew or bite with a crushing noise.

1814 *Suppl. Grose's Provinc. Gloss.*, *Crunch*, *Cronch*, and *Cranch*, to crush an apple, etc. in the mouth. *North.* **1832** W. IRVING *Alhambra* II. 201 'While I was quietly crunching my crust.' **1859** KINGSLEY *Misc.* (1860) I. 202 A herd of swine crunching acorns.

b. *intr.* or *absol.*

1816 BYRON *Siege Cor.* xvi, Their white tusks crunch'd o'er the whiter skull. **1856** KANE *Arct. Expl.* II. x. 101 Our appetites were good; and..we crunched away right merrily.

2. *trans.* To crush or grind under foot, wheels, etc., with the accompanying noise.

1849 C. BRONTE *Shirley* ii. 24 A sound of heavy wheels crunching a stony road. **1873** *Spectator* 23 Aug. 1069/1 You crunch little heaps of salt at every step.

b. *intr.* or *absol.* **c.** *intr.* for *refl.*

1801 SOUTHEY *Thalaba* VIII. xxii, No sound but the wild, wild wind, And the snow crunching under his feet! **1880** *Blackw. Mag.* Apr. 452 The animal's hoofs crunch on the stones and gravel.

3. *intr.* To advance, or make *one's way*, with crunching.

1853 KANE *Grinnell Exp.* xxiii. (1856) 189 The sound of our vessel crunching her way through the ice. **1856** —— *Arct. Expl.* I. iv. 38 Our brig went crunching through all this jewelry. **1864** LOWELL *Fireside Trav.* 109 As we crunched and crawled up the long gravelly hills.

Hence **crunched** *ppl. a.*, **'crunching** *vbl. sb.* and *ppl. a.*

1840 LYTTON *Pilgr. of Rhine* xix, The crunched boughs.. that strewed the soil. **1848** C. BRONTE *J. Eyre* xviii. (D.), A crunching of wheels..became audible on the wet gravel. **1890** *Century Mag.* Apr. 916/2 Passing a rim of crunching cinder.

crunch, *sb.* (and *a.*) [f. prec.]

A. *sb.* **1. a.** An act, or the action, of crunching.

1836 MARRYAT *Midsh. Easy* xvii. 56 If you will not take us, the sharks shall—it is but a crunch, and all is over. **1856** KANE *Arct. Expl.* I. xxvii. 361 Listening to the half-yielding crunch of the ice beneath. **1867** BAKER *Nile Tribut.* ii, The hippo..caught him in its mouth and killed him by one crunch.

b. A crisis; a decisive point, event, confrontation, etc.; a show-down; esp. in phr. ***to come to the crunch***: to come to the point; to reach a show-down.

1939 W. S. CHURCHILL in *Daily Tel.* 23 Feb. 14/6 Whether Spain will be allowed to find its way back to sanity and health..depends..upon the general adjustment or outcome of the European crunch. **1948** —— *2nd World War* I. xvii. 243 When the imminence of an attack on Czechoslovakia became clear, Beck demanded an assurance against further military adventures. Here was a crunch. **1957** *Economist* 28 Sept. 1002/1 What Sir Winston Churchill would have called the 'crunch' of the economic battle has arrived. *Ibid.* 19 Oct. 200/1 No one is anxious to be the spearhead of the next wages struggle; and..the crunch may not be reached until some time after the turn of the new year. **1960** *Times* 21 July 15/5 Even the holders of Government bonds turn out to be chiefly philanthropic institutions and trade unions when it comes to the crunch. **1963** 'W. HAGGARD' *High Wire* v. 52 When it came to the crunch de Fleury wasn't to be relied on. **1969** 'J. FRASER' *Cock-pit of Roses* xv. 111 Now the crunch. 'How do you know, Andrew? ..' No reply.

c. The principal problem; a sticking-point, an issue which gives rise to conflict or crisis. *colloq.*

1970 *Telegraph* (Brisbane) 20 Feb. 11/5 The chihuahua has vanished... The crunch is that the chihuahua belongs to the boss's wife. **1970** *New Scientist* 23 July 171/1 The real crunch is that there may never be any profits from the RB211-2Z. **1977** *Time Out* 28 Jan. 5/1 First crunch for the case against Mark was that he didn't write the story. **1985** C. MCCULLOUGH *Creed for Third Millennium* v. 135 The real crunch had become the length of time the ground remained unfrozen, but in future years it was likely to become the amount of rain.

2. *pl.* Small pieces resulting from crunching. *rare.*

1833 MOIR *Mansie Wauch* xxiii. (1849) 181 [He] had his pipe smashed to crunches.

B. *attrib.* or as *adj.* Critical, decisive, crucial; involving or arising from a crisis. *colloq.*

1974 *Courier-Mail* (Brisbane) 15 Aug. 4/3 Townley continues to vote Liberal on most crunch issues. **1977** *Sunday Mail* (Brisbane) 17 July 1/10 The president of Houston Oil and Mineral..will arrive..today for crunch talks on the controversial Oaky Creek coal project. **1981** G. BOYCOTT *In Fast Lane* ix. 74 If we were to save the match it would have to be through our own efforts, and the crunch period was approaching fast. **1985** *Times* 19 Jan. 1/2, I believe we are in crunch times.

crunchable ('krʌnʃəb(ə)l), *a.* [f. CRUNCH *v.* + -ABLE.] Capable of being crunched or crushed.

1906 H. G. WELLS *In Days of Comet* I. iv. §3 The coal-cellar..opened, and diffused small crunchable particles about the uneven brick floor.

crunchingly ('krʌnʃɪŋlɪ), *adv.* [f. CRUNCHING *ppl. a.* + -LY[2].] In a crunching manner; with a crunching action or sound.

1849 A. J. SYMINGTON *Harebell Chimes* 24 While there crisp'd 'neath her feet The snow crunchingly. **1927** *Chambers's Jrnl.* 79/1 Carwardine stepped out on to the shingle, with no particular caution as to noise—quite crunchingly, in fact.

crunchy ('krʌnʃɪ), *a.* [f. CRUNCH *v.* or *sb.* + -Y[1].] Fit for crunching or for being crunched; crisp. So **'crunchiness**, the quality of being crunchy.

1892 W. BESANT in *Pictorial World* 6 Feb. 434/2 Showing molars of a whiteness and crunchiness both beautiful and awful. **1928** *Daily Express* 14 June 4 The ripe-corn flavour and delightful 'crunchiness'..make it unusually tempting. **1929** *Ibid.* 3 Jan. 5 The crispest and crunchiest of nuts from Brazil. **1960** *News Chron.* 12 Oct. 8/2 The crisp crunchiness of a breakfast cereal. **1971** *Woman's Own* 6 Feb. 3 (Advt.), Crisp and crunchy biscuits.

crune, var. of CROON; obs. f. CROWN *sb.*

†**crunk,** *v. Obs.* or *dial.* Also 6-7 **crunck(e.** [Cf. Icel. *krúnka* to croak (as a raven).] *intr.* Of some birds: To utter a hoarse harsh cry.

1565-73 COOPER *Thesaurus*, *Gruo*..to crunke like a crane. **1583** STANYHURST *Æneis* IV. (Arb.) 111 The skrich howle.. Her burial roundel dooth ruck, and cruncketh in howling. **1617** MINSHEU *Ductor*, To Cruncke or Crunckle like a Crane.

crunk, *sb. dial.* [f. prec.: cf. Icel. *krúnk* the raven's cry.] A hoarse harsh cry; a croak.

1868 ATKINSON *Cleveland Gloss.*, *Crunk*, the hoarse cry or croak of the raven or carrion crow.

crunkle ('krʌŋk(ə)l), *v.*[1] Chiefly *north. dial.* In 4 **crounkil**, 6 **croncle, -kel.** [A parallel form to CRINKLE, perh. going back to the ablaut-stem *crunc-* of *crinc-an* (see CRANK *sb.*[1]), perh. a later analogical formation: cf. *crimple*, *crumple*.] To wrinkle, rumple, crinkle. **a.** *trans.* Hence **'crunkled** *ppl. a.*

c **1400** *Rowland & O.* 1252 Thi vesage es crounkilde & waxen olde. **1546** PHAER *Bk. Childr.* (1553) Tib, The musherom..called..Jewes eares for it is..croncled and flat, much like an eare). **1578** LYTE *Dodoens* IV. lviii. 519 Leaves a little crompled or cronkeled about the edges. **1788** W. MARSHALL *Yorksh.* Gloss., *Crunkle*, to tumble or rumple, as linen or other cloaths. **1804** TARRAS *Poems* 46 (Jam.) Wi' crunkl't brow, he aft wad think Upo' his barkin faes. **1876** *Whitby Gloss.*, *Crunkle* or *Crinkle*, to rumple or crimp.

b. *intr.*

1826 J. WILSON *Noct. Ambr.* Wks. I. 2 A piece of paper torn out of..a volume crunkling on my knee.

†**crunkle,** *v.*[2] *Obs.* [A diminutive of CRUNK *v.*] To cry like a crane.

1611 COTGR., *Gruïr*, to crunkle, or creake, like a Crane. **1617** [see CRUNK].

crunkle ('krʌŋk(ə)l), *v.*[3] [Echoic.] *intr.* To make a harsh dry sound, as by grinding the jaws. So **'crunkling** *vbl. sb.*

1882 E. A. FLOYER *Unexpl. Balūchistan* 362 The 'crunkling' noise of so many feeding together. **1900** *Westm. Gaz.* 5 Sept. 2/3 The crabs..crunkled loud and long.

crunode ('kru:nəʊd). *Geom.* [Irreg. f. L. *crux* cross + NODE.] A point on a curve where it crosses itself; a node with two real tangents.

1873 SALMON *Higher Plane Curves* 22 In the first case the tangents are both real..such a point is termed a *crunode*.

Hence **cru'nodal** *a.*, having a crunode.

1873 SALMON *Higher Plane Curves* 126 Nodal cubics may obviously be subdivided into crunodal and acnodal.

crunt (krʌnt). *Sc. dial.* [Cf. CRUMP.] 'A blow on the head with a cudgel' (Jam.).

1785 BURNS *To W. Simpson* xxv, An' monie a fallow gat his licks, Wi' hearty crunt. **1819** *St. Patrick* I. 166 (Jam.) Though I got a fell crunt ahint the haffit.

‖**cruor** ('kru:ɔ:(r)). *Phys.* and *Med.* [L. *cruor* blood (when out of the body), gore.] Coagulated blood, or that portion of the blood which forms the clot; gore.

1656 BLOUNT *Glossogr.*, *Cruor*, blood dropping out of a wound. **1705** GREENHILL *Art of Embalming* 3 (T.) Any offensive odour or contaminating cruor. **1843** J. WILKINSON *Swedenborg's Anim. Kingd.* I. ix. 266 The chyle clogged with cruor.

cruorin ('kruːərɪn). *Chem.* [f. prec. + -IN.] The red colouring matter of blood-corpuscles; now called *hæmoglobin.*

1840 BALY tr. *Müller's Physiol.* (ed. 2) I. 133 The solution of cruorin is reddened less strongly by exposure to air. **1871** tr. *Schellen's Spectr. Anal.* 140 By the action of an acid on blood the cruorin is converted into haematin.

crup, *a. dial.* [? var. of CRUMP: cf. CRUP-SHOULDER.] 'Short, brittle, as a *crup* cake; and *fig.*, short or snappish, as a *crup* answer. Still used in Kent' (Todd).

1736 PEGGE *Kenticisms, Crup*, pettish, peevish. **1847-78** HALLIWELL, *Crup*, crisp, short; surly. *South.* **1887** PARISH & SHAW *Kentish Gloss., Crup*, crisp. 'You'll have a nice walk, as the snow is very crup.'

crup(e, var. of CROUP *sb.*[1], hind-quarters.

crup (krʌp), *v.* [f. CRUPPER.] *trans.* To put the crupper on (a horse).

1881 A. C. GRANT *Bush Life Queensland* I. viii. 97 A vicious kick or two when being crupped.

crupel, cruppel, obs. ff. CRIPPLE.

crupen, obs. pa. t. pl. of CREEP.

crupon, -oun, obs. var. of CROUPON.

crupper ('krʌpə(r)), *sb.* Forms: 4 cropere, -ore, -our, -ier, 4-5 -ure, 4-6 croper, 5 croppere, croupere, cruppure, cruper, 5-8 crouper, crowper, 6 cropar, 6-7 cropper, crooper, 7 croaper, (crupyard), 6- crupper. [a. OF. *cropiere* (Anglo-Fr. *cropere*), mod.F. *croupière* = Pr. *cropiera*, Sp. *gropera*, It. *groppiera* (Rom. type **groppāria, -eria*), f. med.L. and It. *groppa*, Pr. *cropa*, OF. *crope, crupe*, mod. *croupe*: see CROUP.]

1. A leathern strap buckled to the back of the saddle and passing under the horse's tail, to prevent the saddle from slipping forwards.

c **1300** *K. Alis.* 3421 Mony trappe, mony croper, Mony queyntise on armes clere. **1470-85** MALORY *Arthur* VII. xvi, The paytrellys sursenglys and crowpers braste. **1523** FITZHERB. *Husb.* § 105 Hurte with a saddle, or with a buckle of a croper. **1672** MARVELL *Reh. Transp.* I. 14 The Preface might have past as well for a Postscript, or the Headstall for a Crooper. **1779** SHERIDAN *Critic* II. ii, His accoutrements, from the bit to the crupper. **1876** *World* V. 14 Tight reins, tight cruppers, tight curbs..are the refuges of incompetence.

2. *transf.* The hind-quarters or rump of a horse; the croup.

[*c* **1386** CHAUCER *Can. Yeom. Prol. & T* 13 A Male twey-foold vpon his croper.] **1591** HARRINGTON *Orl. Fur.* XLVI. c. (R.), And both gaue strokes so sound, As made both horses cruppers kisse the ground. **1598** FLORIO, *Langio*, a disease in a horse about the crupper [**1611** in a horses cropper]. **1632** J. HAYWARD tr. *Biondi's Eromena* 29 They must have taken them up behind them on their horse croppers. **1797** *Sporting Mag.* X. 295 The Crupper, which is round, and reaches from the kidneys to the tail. **1852** TH. ROSS *Humboldt's Trav.* I. viii. 283 The mules lowered their cruppers and slid down the steepest slopes.

†**b.** The rear (of a horse). ***on the crupper***: in the rear, close behind (one's horse). *Obs.*

1627 *Lisander & Cal.* VI. 98 Cloridon..desirous to get the crupper of his enemie's horse, turned his own speedily. **1721** DE FOE *Mem. Cavalier* (1840) 65 The king follows them on the crupper with thirteen troops of horse.

3. The buttocks (of a man). Usually *humorous.*

1594 NASHE *Unfort. Trav.* 71 A close-bellied dublet comming downe..as farre as the crupper. **1630** B. JONSON *New Inn* III. i, He cuts me a back caper with his heels, and takes me just o' the crupper. **1664** COTTON *Scarron.* 104 There as she sate upon her crupper. **1842** BARHAM *Ingol. Leg., Ingol. Penance*, The Knight on his crupper Received the first taste of the Father's *flagellum*.

†**b.** A hind-quarter, haunch (as a joint of meat). *Obs.*

1725 BRADLEY *Fam. Dict.* s.v. *Mutton*, Take a Crupper of ..Mutton. *Ibid.* s.v. *Veal*, A Quarter or Crupper of Veal.

4. *Naut.* **a.** = *crupper-chain*: see 5. **b.** (See quot. 1867.)

c **1860** H. STUART *Seaman's Catech.* 74 The heel of the jib-boom has..a notch for the crupper. **1867** SMYTH *Sailor's Word-bk., Crupper*, the train tackle ring-bolt in a gun-carriage.

5. *Comb.*, as †***crupper-bone, -compliment, -evil***; ***crupper-cramped, -galled*** adjs.; **crupper-chain**, *Naut.* (see quot. 1882); †**crupper-clout**, a clout or cloth to cover the posteriors; **crupper-dock, -loop**, that part of the crupper which passes under the horse's tail.

a **1652** BROME *Queen & Conc.* III. iv, My Back and *Crupper-bone is out of joynt. **1882** *Syd. Soc. Lex., Crupper bone*, the coccyx. **1882** NARES *Seamanship* (ed. 6) 13 **Crupper chain*, a chain passed round the bowsprit and the heel of jib-boom to secure the latter down in its saddle. **1647** STAPYLTON *Juvenal* xiv. 665 [He] puts about His naked middle a cold *crupper-clout. **1630** B. JONSON *New Inn* III. i, I love no *crupper-compliments. [He had just received a kick on the posteriors.] **1641** BROME *Jov. Crew* III. Wks. 1873 III. 395, I am..so *crupper-crampt with our hard lodging. **1794** W. FELTON *Carriages* (1801) II. 133 The *Crupper-dock is mostly stuffed with a tallow candle to make it easy for the horse's tail. **1611** COTGR., *Le mal de cropion*, the Rumpe-euill or *Crupper-euill. **1689** *Lond. Gaz.* No. 2486/4 A dark-brown Horse..*Crupper-galled. **1874** KNIGHT *Dict. Mech.* s.v. *Crupper*, The rounded portion EB is the *crupper-loop.

'**crupper**, *v.* [f. prec. sb.] *trans.* To furnish with a crupper, put a crupper upon.

1787 'G. GAMBADO' *Acad. Horsemen* (1809) 33 Sent on a Sunday into Hyde Park, crupper'd up as tight as need be. **1803** *Sporting Mag.* XXI. 219 So caparisoned, bitted..and cruppered.

†**crup-shoulder, -shouldered.** *Obs.* = CRUMP-*shoulder*, etc.

1589 R. HARVEY *Pl. Perc.* 12 Thinking belike to ride vpon my Crupshoulders. **1599** BRETON *Mis. Mavillia* iv, Hee goes Crup shouldred and sits down by leisure.

crural ('krʊərəl), *a.* (and *sb.*) [ad. L. *crūrāl-is* adj., f. *crūs, crūr-* leg.]

1. Of or belonging to the leg; *spec.* in *Anat.*, as in ***crural artery, nerve, vein, vessels.***

crural arch, the arch formed by Poupart's ligament, beneath which the crural vessels emerge; ***crural canal***, a canal about half an inch long forming the innermost compartment of the crural sheath, through which a femoral hernia passes; ***crural hernia***, a hernia descending beside the crural vessels; ***crural ring***, the upper end of the crural canal; ***crural septum***, the septum of connective tissue normally closing the crural canal at the top; ***crural sheath***, the sheath which encloses the crural vessels as they leave the abdomen.

1599 A. M. tr. *Gabelhouer's Bk. Physicke* 393/2 An excellent Cruralle Playster. **1634** T. JOHNSON *Parey's Chirurg.* 225 The crurall artery arising from the same place whence the crurall veine proceeded. **1676** SHADWELL *Virtuoso* III, If the capricious fly happens not to remove itself by crural motion, or the vibration of its wings. **1708** KEILL *Anim. Secretion* 91 The Blood must stagnate in the Crural Vessels. **1836** TODD *Cycl. Anat.* I. 396/1 Hernia of the bladder at the crural ring is very rare. **1870** R. M. FERGUSON *Electr.* 157 The legs..are skinned, and the crural nerve laid bare.

b. as *sb.* Short for *crural artery, nerve*, etc.

1667 *Phil. Trans.* II. 514 The Umbilical Arteries..said to be derived from the Crurals. **1741** MONRO *Anat. Nerves* (ed. 3) 70 The two Crurals, with the Sciatic..are distributed to the inferior Extremities.

2. Of the nature or form of a leg.

1842 BRANDE *Dict. Sci., Crural*..shaped like a leg or root. Hence in WEBSTER and mod. Dicts.

†**crure.** *Obs. rare.* [ad. L. *crūs, crūr-* leg.] A 'leg' or side of a triangle; = CRUS 1.

1610 W. FOLKINGHAM *Art of Survey* II. v. 55 Proiect a Triangle by producing 2 Crures from the Chords extreames.

crured (krʊəd), *a. Her.* [f. L. *crūs, crūr-* + -ED.] Of a bird borne as a charge: Having the legs of a (specified) tincture different from that of the body; legged.

1804 MANNING & BRAY *Hist. & Antiq. Surrey* I. 631 A Falcon, Or. beaked and crured, Gules.

‖**crus** (krʌs). Pl. **crura** ('krʊərə). [L. *crūs*, pl. *crūra*, leg.]

†**1.** *Geom.* A straight line forming one side of a triangle. *Obs. rare.*

a **1687** H. MORE *Antid. Ath.* I. iv. Schol. (1712) 144 All the Crura's EG, EH, EI, EC, are easily demonstrated to be equal to the Crus E.

2. *Anat.* **a.** The leg or hind limb; *spec.* the part between the knee and the ankle, the shank. **b.** Applied to various parts occurring in pairs or sets and resembling or likened to legs.

crura of the cerebellum, cerebrum, fornix, and ***medulla oblongata***, strands of nerve-fibres in the brain; ***crura of the diaphragm***, two tendinous and muscular bundles, one on each side, connecting the diaphragm with the lumbar vertebræ; ***crura of the penis, of the clitoris***, bodies forming the attachments of those organs, one on each side of the pubic arch. Also applied to the two processes of the *incus* and those of the *stapes* (bones of the ear).

1727-51 CHAMBERS *Cycl., Crus*, among anatomists, denotes all that part of the body which reaches from the buttocks to the toes. *Ibid., Crura of the medulla oblongata*, are two of the four roots whence the medulla oblongata springs, in the brain. **1783** H. WATSON in *Med. Commun.* I. 186 The crura of the diaphragm..were removed. **1845** TODD & BOWMAN *Phys. Anat.* I. 271 The central stem, or crus, around which each hemisphere of the cerebellum is developed.

crus, obs. form of CROUSE.

crusada, obs. f. CRUSADE, CRUSADO.

crusade (kruː'seɪd). Forms: α. 6 croisad, croysade, (croissard), 6-8 croisade, (7 crossiade); β. 7 croisada, (croy-), cruysado, (crossado), 7-8 croisado, croy-; γ. 7-8 crusada, cruz-, 6-8 crusado, cruz-; δ. 8- crusade. [= mod.F. *croisade* (= OF. *croisee*), Pr. *crozada*, Sp. *cruzada*, It. *crociata*, med.L. *cruciata* (*cruzata*), being in the various langs. the fem. noun of action formed on pa. pple. of *cruciāre, crociare, cruzar, croiser* to CROSS, *lit.* a being crossed, a crossing or marking with the cross, a taking the cross: cf. the early F. *croisement*. The earliest and only ME. equivalents were CROISERIE (13th-15th c.), and CROISEE (15-17th c.), from the corresponding OF. words. In 16th c. French, *croisée* was displaced by *croisade*, with the new ending *-ade*, adapted from the -ADA of Provençal and Spanish. This *croisade* appeared in Eng. c. 1575, and continued to be the leading form till c. 1760 (see Johnson's Dict.). About 1600, the Sp. *cruzada* made its appearance under the forms *crusada* and *crusado* (see -ADO); a blending of this with *croisade* produced two hybrid forms, viz. *croisado* (*-ada*), with French stem and Spanish ending, frequent from c. 1611 to 1725, and *crusade*, with Spanish stem and French ending, mentioned by Johnson, 1755, only as a by-form of *croisade*, but used by Goldsmith and Gibbon, and now universal. From 15th to 17th c. occasional attempts to adopt the med.L. and other Romanic forms, as *cruciat, -ada, -ade, cruceat*, were made: see CRUCIADE.]

1. *Hist.* A military expedition undertaken by the Christians of Europe in the 11th, 12th, and 13th centuries to recover the Holy Land from the Mohammedans.

α. **1577** HARRISON *England* III. iv. (1878) II. 29 At such time as Baldwine archbishop of Canturburie preached the Croisad there. **1616** JAS. I. *Remonstr. Right of Kings* Wks. 445 All such..as undertooke the Croisade became the Pope's meere vassals. **1753** CHESTERF. *Lett.* (1774) IV. 6 His history of the Croisades. **1769** BLACKSTONE *Comm.* IV. 416 The knight errantry of a croisade against the Saracens.

β. **1611** SPEED *Hist. Gt. Brit.* IX. xx. (1632) 965 A Croisado against the Turkes. *c* **1645** HOWELL *Lett.* IV. xix. (1892) 592 A Croisada to the Holy Land. **1758** CHESTERF. *Lett.* cxxxi, This gave rise to the Croisadoes, and carried such swarms of people from Europe to the..Holy Land.

γ. **1631** WEEVER *Anc. Fun. Mon.* 793 To preach the Crusado. *a* **1678** MARVELL *Poems, Britannia & Raleigh*, Her true Crusada shall at last pull down The Turkish crescent and the Persian sun. **1765** H. WALPOLE *Otranto* v. (1834) 249 Until his return from the crusado.

δ. **1706** PHILLIPS, *Croisado or Crusade.* *c* **1750** SHENSTONE *Ruined Abbey* 118 Here the cowl'd zealots..Urg'd the crusade. **1755-73** JOHNSON, *Crusade, Crusado*: see *Croisade.* **1781** GIBBON *Decl. & F.* III. lxi. 546 The principle of the crusades was a savage fanaticism. **1841** W. SPALDING *Italy & It. Isl.* II. 318 A single campaign of the first crusade, that of 1099. **1856** EMERSON *Eng. Traits, Relig.* Wks. (Bohn) II. 96 The power of the religious sentiment..inspired the crusades.

b. *transf.* Any war instigated and blessed by the Church for alleged religious ends, a 'holy war'; applied *esp.* to expeditions undertaken under papal sanction against infidels or heretics.

1603 FLORIO *Montaigne* II. xxvii. (1632) 393 George Sechell..who under the title of a Croysada, wrought so many mischiefes. **1624** BP. MOUNTAGU *Gagg* 95 Urban the eight, that now Popeth it, may proclaime a Croisado if hee will. **1681** BURNET *Hist. Ref.* II. 122 Afterwards croisades came in use; against such princes as were deposed by popes. **1875** STUBBS *Const. Hist.* III. xviii. 106 Commander of a crusade against the Hussites.

2. *fig.* An aggressive movement or enterprise against some public evil, or some institution or class of persons considered as evil.

1786 T. JEFFERSON *Writ.* (1859) II. 8 Preach, my dear Sir, a crusade against ignorance. **1839** DE QUINCEY *Recoll. Lakes* Wks. 1862 II. 184 This new crusade against the evils of the world. **1855** MILMAN *Lat. Chr.* (1864) IV. VII. i. 25 Dunstan's life was a crusade..against the married clergy. *Mod.* The Temperance crusade.

†**3.** A papal bull or commission authorizing a crusade, or expedition against infidels or heretics.

1588 (*title*), The Holy Bull and Crusado of Rome, first published by the Holy Father, Gregory the XIII. **1643** PRYNNE *Sov. Power Parl.* App 64 They concluded to crave ayd from all Christian Princes, and a Crossado from the Pope against the Moores. *a* **1677** BARROW *Popes Suprem.* Wks. 1859 VIII. 50 To summon or commissionate soldiers by croisade, &c. to fight against infidels. **1724** T. RICHERS *Hist. R. Geneal. Spain* 247 The Pope, willing to help the King to sustain this War, sent him the Croisade, by which Means he raised 300,000 Ducats. **1771** GOLDSM. *Hist. Eng.* I. 317 The pope published a crusade against the deposed monarch.

†**4.** *Span. Hist.* A levy of money, or a sum raised by the sale of indulgences, under a document called *Bula de la cruzada*, originally for aggression or defence against the Moors, but afterwards diverted to other purposes. *Obs.*

The sale of the indulgences granted under the *Bula* became a permanent source of revenue, held by the kings of Spain in consideration of expenses incurred by them as champions of Catholicism and in the conversion of the American Indians. A board for the collection and administration of these revenues was created in the 16th c. called *Consejo de la Cruzada*, the court or tribunal of the Crusade.

1579 FENTON *Gruicciard.* I. (1599) 30 The moneys gathered in Spaine..vnder colour of the Croysade. *Ibid.* XII. 566 The Pope had transferred to the king of Aragon for two yeares the moneys and collections called the Croissards of the realme of Spaine. **1630** *R. Johnson's Kingd. & Commw.* 531 His Subsidies which he levieth extraordinarily (of late times for the most part turned into ordinary, as his Croisados). **1655** DIGGES *Compl. Ambass.* 288 To suffer a levy of money to be made within his Dominions, termed by the name Crusado, for the maintenance of the Turkish Wars. **1716** in *Lond. Gaz.* No. 5480/3 The President of the Cruzada is ordered to draw up a perfect Account of the intire Produce of the Cruzada, as well in Spain as in the Indies. **1760-72** tr. *Juan & Ulloa's Voy.* (ed. 3) II. VII. xii. 132 Here [Peru] is also a court of inquisition, and of the croisade.

†**5.** A marking with the cross; the symbol of the cross, the badge borne by crusaders. *Obs.*

1613 ZOUCH *Dove* 43 Like the rich Croisade on th' Imperiall Ball. **1641** PRYNNE *Antip.* 299 He tooke up the Crossado and went..with King Richard..to the warres in the holy Land. **1700** TYRRELL *Hist. Eng.* II. 772 He took upon him the Crusado, i.e. Vowed an Expedition to the Holy-Land.

†**b.** *fig.* (with allusion to 'cross' in the sense of trial or affliction). *Obs.*

1654 WHITLOCK *Zootomia* 531 The Noble Order of the Cruysado Heaven bestoweth not on Milk-sops. *Ibid.* 533 The Cruysado, or Crosse of Christ, above all Orders taken up by the Potentates of the World.

6. *attrib.*

1750 CARTE *Hist. Eng.* II. 706 The crusado troops of Cardinal Beaufort. **1764** HARMER *Observ.* XVIII. i. 43 The Croisade army arrived there in the end of May.

crusade, obs. f. CRUSADO, Portuguese coin.

crusade (kruːˈseɪd), *v.* Also croizade. [f. prec. sb.] *intr.* To engage in a crusade, go on a crusade. Also *to crusade it.*

1732 M. GREEN *Grotto* 215 Cease crusading against sense. **1737** OZELL *Rabelais* III. 40 He's going to croizade it. **1765** STERNE *Tr. Shandy* VII. xviii, When.. you have crusaded it thro' all their parish-churches. **1834** GEN. P. THOMPSON *Exerc.* III. 111 Burning heretics at home, except when he was busy crusading abroad. **1873** BROWNING *Red Cott. Nt.-cap* 955 'Duke, once your sires crusaded it, we know.'

crusader (kruːˈseɪdə(r)). Also 8–9 **croisader.** [f. CRUSADE *v.* (or *sb.*) + -ER. Cf. obs. F. *croisadeur* (Cotgr.).] **a.** One who engages in a crusade.

1743 W. WHITEHEAD *Ess. Ridicule*, If, crusaders like, their zeal be rage. **1769** *De Foe's Tour Gt. Brit.* III. 169 Standing cross-legged, like our Effigies of Croisaders in Churches. **1825** FOSBROKE *Encycl. Antiq.* (1843) I. 133 Badge of croisaders. **1866** *Treas. Bot.* 292 The crusaders found Citrons, Oranges, and Lemons very abundant in Palestine.

b. *attrib.* and *Comb.*

1845 E. B. G. WARBURTON *Crescent & Cross* II. xlvi. 238 Such a scene unchanged might that old Crusader-castle have witnessed, six hundred years ago. **1864** J. A. GRANT *Walk across Africa* 143 The drums.. are on the ground, in a line, each having a large white cross on its head—a strange Crusader-like custom. **1906** *Daily Chron.* 6 Apr. 3/5 The finest Crusader ruin extant. **1907** G. L. BELL *Desert & Sown* ix. 198 The great crusader fortress towards which we were going. *Ibid.* 205 The castle is the 'Kerak of the Knights' of Crusader chronicles. **1936** T. E. LAWRENCE (*title*) Crusader castles. **1968** C. FORSYTE *Murder with Minarets* xviii. 119 On one arm of a bay stood what they took to be a Crusader castle.

cruˈsading, *vbl. sb.* [-ING¹.] The action of the verb CRUSADE. Also *attrib.*, passing into *adj.*

1732 [see CRUSADE *v.*]. **1837** CARLYLE *Fr. Rev.* (1872) III. I. i. 10 Not since our Albigenses and Crusadings were over. **1855** MILMAN *Lat. Chr.* (1864) IX. XIV. v. 197 Provençal poetry.. contains some noble bursts of the Crusading religious sentiment. **1879** W. H. DIXON *Royal Windsor* II. v. 50 One of those unfortunate captives of crusading wars.

cruˈsading, *ppl. a.* [-ING².] Engaging in a crusade; belonging to the crusades.

1759 STERNE *Tr. Shandy* II. xvii, The crusading sword of this misguided saint-errant. **1864** BURTON *Scot Abr.* I. iv. 187 The ancient crusading chivalry. **1873** TRISTRAM *Moab* iv. 66 The character of the architecture is Crusading.

‖**crusado**¹ (kruːˈseɪdəʊ). Also 6 cru(e)sadowe, 7–9 cruzado, 8 crusada, (crusad, cruzate, 8–9 crusade). [ad. Pg. *cruzado* lit. 'crossed, marked with the cross'.] A Portuguese coin bearing the figure of a cross, originally of gold, later also of silver; the new crusado is of 480 reis (16¼ grains of gold or 219 grains of silver) = about 2*s.* 4*d.* sterling (1893).

1544 *Will of R. Osborne* (Somerset Ho.), One syde Crusadowes & the other side haulfe Aungelle. **1577** HARRISON *England* II. xxv. (1877) I. 364 Of forren coines we haue.. ducats.. crusadoes [etc.]. **1604** SHAKS. *Oth.* III. iv. 26. **1683** *Brit. Spec.* 267 Eight hundred Millions of Reas, or two Millions of Crusadoes, amounting to about three hundred thousand pounds sterling. **1695** *Lond. Gaz.* No. 3086/2 The Crusado of Portugal.. to pass at 3*sh.* 6*d.* **1727–51** CHAMBERS *Cycl.*, *Cruzado*.. is a Portuguese coin, struck under Alphonsus V about the year 1457, at the time when pope Calixtus sent thither the bull for a croisade, against the infidels. **1853** TH. ROSS *Humboldt's Trav.* III. xxxii. 406 *note*, The value of an arroba of gold is 15,000 Brazilian crusados (each cruzado being 50 sous).

‖**cruˈsado**². *Obs.* [a. Sp. and Pg. *cruzado*, OPg. *crusado*, corresp. to F. *croisé* a crusader, *lit.* a crossed man, one that has received or assumed the sign of the cross: cf. CROISES.] A crusader.

1575 G. HARVEY *Letter-bk.* (Camden) 92 In such gallant bravadoe termes runnith your mill crusadoe rhetorick. **1619** BRENT tr. *Sarpi's Counc. Trent* VIII. (1676) 746 Provision was not made for the Crusadoes. **1625** PURCHAS *Pilgrims* II. VIII. vi. §4. 1267 An Armie of Crusado's.

Hence †**crusado, cruzado** *v.*, to cross, engage as a crusader; = CROISE *v.* 2.

1671 F. PHILIPPS *Reg. Necess.* 327 Which were Cruzadoed or voluntarily went unto the Holy Land.. for recovery of it.

crusado³, var. of *crusada* = CRUSADE.

‖**cruˈsal.** *Obs.* [A term of the *lingua franca* of the Levant = It. *corsale* privateer.] = CORSAIR.

1699 ROBERTS *Voy. Levant* 2, I had heard how miserably men lived in a Crusal. *Ibid.* 3 *Crusal* is a word, mistakingly used for Corsair which in English signifies a Privateer.

†**crusard.** *Obs. rare.* [f. stem of CRUSADE + -ARD: cf. CROISARD.] A crusader.

1753 tr. *Voltaire's Micromegas, etc.* 59 The most politic of all the Crusards [*tous ces croisés*].. was Bohemond. *Ibid.* 90 Saladin.. gave battle to those Crusards near Cæsarea.

cruse (kruːs, kruːz). *arch.* Forms: 5- cruse; also 5 crowse, crowce, crewse, crwce, 5–7 cruce, 6 crouse, cruys(e, crewyse, 7 cruze, criuze, 8 creuse, 8–9 cruise. [A word of which similar forms are found in most of the Teutonic langs.; cf. Icel. *krús* (*a* 1300) pot, tankard, Da. *kruus* mug, jug, cruet, Sw. *krus* mug; also OHG. **krûse* represented by dim. *krûselîn*, MHG. *krûse*, Ger. *krause* pot with a lid, MLG. *hrûs*, *krôs*, LG. *kroos*, *krûs*, *kraus*; MDu. *cruyse*, Du. *kroes*; WFris. *kroes*, EFris. *krôs*, NFris. *kruas*, *kröss*, Wang. *krûs*.

The etymological history is uncertain, as is also the original type, since the LG., Du. and Fris. present forms both in *û* and *ô*; in Eng. also, it is noteworthy that we have beside ME. *u*, modern *u*, where we should expect *ou*. The variant spelling in *ui*, (*uy*) from 16th c. appears to be from Dutch. The historical pronunciation is with *s* (cf. the early *cruce*), which also now predominates; but the spelling with *z* has been occasional since 1600, and a corresponding pronunciation is given by Smart and Cassell, and often heard.]

A small earthen vessel for liquids; a pot, jar, or bottle; also a drinking vessel.

c **1420** *Pallad. on Husb.* I. 584 Twey cruses in oon day. *Ibid.* XI. 349 A cruce into a stene of wyne devise. *c* **1440** *Promp. Parv.* 105 Crowse, or cruse, potte [*P.* crowce or crwce]. **1481–90** *Howard Househ. Bks.* (Roxb.) 404 For drynkyng crewses for howsold viij.d. **1526** SKELTON *Magnyf.* 2192 Then he may drink out of a stone cruyse. **1535** COVERDALE *1 Kings* xvii. 16 The oyle in the cruse fayled not. **1603** B. JONSON *King's Entertainment*, A crystal Cruze fill'd with Wine. **1634** PEACHAM *Gentleman's Exerc.* I. xxvii. 94 In a crucible or melting cruse. **1742** COLLINS *Eclogues* ii. 3 One cruise of water on his back he bore. **1755** JOHNSON, *Cruise*, a small cup. **1817** COLERIDGE *Zapolya* 11, What if I leave these cakes, this cruse of wine Here by this cave. **1892** RAINE *Handbk. York Museum* 167 Cruses and Pottle-pots of black and brown ware.

b. *fig.* (with allusion to 1 Kings xvii. 12–16).

c **1620** Z. BOYD *Zion's Flowers* (1885) 40 Thy cruse of joye is it already spent? **1849** THACKERAY *Pendennis* xx, He had dipped ungenerously into a generous mother's purse, basely and recklessly spilt her little cruse.

cruse, obs. form of CROUSE.

†ˈ**cruseful.** *Obs.* [f. CRUSE + -FUL.] As much as a cruse contains.

1561 HOLLYBUSH *Hom. Apoth.* 15 b, Geve him half a good cruys ful to drinke. *a* **1645** HEYWOOD *Fortune by Land* II. Wks. 1874 VI. 384 Of his smallest beer Not a bare crusful.

†ˈ**crusell.** *Obs. rare*⁻¹. [= med.L. *crusellus*; also MLG. *krusel*, *crusele*, LG. *krüsel*, *krôsel*, *kreusel*, EFris. *krûsel*, an oil-lamp used by country-people, etc., MDu. *kruysel*, *krosel* hanging-lamp; cf. also OF. *croisel*, *croissol*, and other Romanic forms, usually connected with *crux* and associated with *crucibolum*, while the Ger. forms are treated by Hildebrand and others as dim. of *krûse*, CRUSE.] A night-lamp of oil or tallow.

1401–2 *Mem. Ripon* (Surtees) III. 210 Pro lumine habendo in crusell.

†ˈ**cruset.** *Obs.* Also 6 croset, -ette, 7 cruzet. [a. F. *creuset* (Paré 16th c.) crucible.

The ulterior etymology is complicated and uncertain; cf. CRUSELL, and see Hatzfeld, Littré, Diez, Grimm s.v. *Krausel*, Doornkaat-Koolman s.v. *Krusel*. The OF. *croisel*, *croiseul* meant both night-lamp and crucible: cf. CRUSIE.]

A crucible.

See also CRUSIE.

1558–80 WARDE tr. *Alexis' Secr.* I. VI. 115 b, Poure the Siluer out of the croset. *Ibid.* (ed. 1) 118 Set it in the fire in a Goldsmithes croset. **1604** E. G[RIMSTONE] *D'Acosta's Hist. Indies* IV. xiii. 247 They cary the bars of silver unto the Assay maister.. he cuttes a small peece of every one.. and puttes them into a cruset. **1611** COTGR., *Creuset*, a crucible, cruzet, or cruet: a little earthen pot, wherein Goldsmithes melt their siluer. **1755** JOHNSON, *Cruset*, a goldsmith's melting pot. *Phillips.*

crush (krʌʃ), *v.* Forms: 5 crusch-en, -yn, crussh-yn, (crusse), 5–6 crusshe, 6 crousshe, 7 chrush, 6- crush. Cf. CROOSE *v.* [app. a. OF. *croissir*, *croisir*, sometimes *cruis(s)ir*, rarely *crusir*, *croussir*, to gnash (the teeth), to make a crashing or cracking noise, to crash, crack, smash, break; in Cotgr., 1611, 'to cracke, or crash, or crackle, as wood thats readie to breake'; = Cat. *croxir*, Sp. *cruxir*, *crujir* to crackle, to rustle, It. †*croscere*, *crosciare* to crackle, crash, clatter; 'also to squease, to crush, or squash' (Florio); med.L. *cruscire* to crackle (Du Cange). The Romanic word is app. of Ger. origin: see Diez and Mackel, and cf. MHG. *krosen*, *krösen* to gnash with the teeth, make a crackling noise, bruise or crush with a crackling sound, crash, craunch, for which Hildebrand infers an OHG. *chrosôn*, *chrosian*.

The notion of noise present in the foreign words appears also in early uses of *cruss*, *crussh*, but is practically absent from later use, being now expressed by CRASH.]

†**1.** To dash together with the sound of violent percussion, to clash, crash; to make the harsh grating noise of things forcibly smashed or pounded to fragments. *Obs.*

1398 TREVISA *Barth. De P.R.* x. vii. (1495) 379 Cole quenchyd though it greue not wyth brennynge hym that trede theron it makyth crusshynge and grete noyse. *c* **1400** *Destr. Troy* 4752 At yche cornell of þe castell was crusshyng of weppon. *Ibid.* 5852 Crakkyng of cristis, crusshyng of speires. *Ibid.* 7298 There was crie of ken men, crussing of wepyn.

2. *trans.* To compress with violence, so as to break, bruise, destroy, squeeze out of natural shape or condition: said of the effect of pressure whether acting with momentum or otherwise.

? *a* **1400** *Morte Arth.* 1134 He [the geaunt] caughte hyme in armez, And enclosez hyme clenly, to cruschene hys rybbez. *c* **1440** *Promp. Parv.* 106 Crusshyn' bonys, *ocillo.* **1526** *Pilgr. Perf.* (W. de W. 1531) 234 b, The worme yᵗ is crusshed or poysoned. **1611** BIBLE *Job* xxxix. 15 The Ostrich.. leaueth her egges in the earth.. And forgetteth that the foot may crush them. **1665** HOOKE *Microgr.* 33 Some of these I broke.. by crushing it [the stem] with a small pair of Plyers. **1715–20** POPE *Iliad* XII. 83 In one promiscuous carnage crush'd and bruis'd. **1840** F. D. BENNETT *Whaling Voy.* II. 357 The leaves, when crushed, emit a powerful smell of camphor. **1860** TYNDALL *Glac.* I. ii. 9 The shock which would crush a railway carriage.

absol. **1885** MRS. H. WARD tr. *Amiel's Jrnl.* (1891) 18 The wish to crush, roused irresistibly by all that creeps.

b. With advb. extension, defining the result.

1530 PALSGR. 502/2 He hath crousshed his legge with the fall all to peces. **1594** SHAKS. *Rich. III*, V. iii. 111 That they may crush downe with a heauy fall, Th' vsurping Helmets of our Aduersaries. **1628** EARLE *Microcosm.*, *Selfe-conceited Man* (Arb.) 33 He is a bladder blown vp with wind, which the least flaw crushes to nothing. **1665** SIR T. HERBERT *Trav.* (1677) 50 Some.. cast themselves in the way and are crusht to death. **1768** J. BYRON *Narr. Patagonia* 222 We expected.. the roof and walls of our prison to fall in upon us, and crush us to pieces. **1853** KINGSLEY *Hypatia* xxiv. 299 Philammon crushed the letter together in his hand. *Mod.* Crushed flat under the feet of the crowd.

c. To crumple or put out of shape (cloth, a dress, etc.) by pressure or rough handling.

Mod. Her bonnet and dress were all crushed.

d. *intr.* To advance with crushing.

1876 WHITTIER *Lost Occasion* 24 Crushing as if with Talus' flail Through Error's logic-woven mail.

e. *intr.* (for *refl.*) To become violently compressed, squeezed out of shape, or otherwise injured, by outside pressure.

1755 JOHNSON, *Crush*, to be condensed. **1776** WITHERING *Brit. Plants* (1796) IV. 282 Its texture tender, soon crushing and becoming watery when gathered. **1786** T. JEFFERSON *Writ.* (1859) I. 553 Their rotten machine must crush under the trial. **1866** G. MACDONALD *Ann. Q. Neighb.* xxxix. (1878) 506, I heard the hailstones crush between my feet and the soft grass of the lawn.

†**f.** In imprecations. *Obs.*

1770 FOOTE *Lame Lover* I. Wks. 1799. II 60 Crush me if ever I saw any thing half so handsome before!

3. To press or squeeze forcibly or violently. (The force, not the effect, being the prominent notion.) Also with advb. extension, ***to crush against, into, out of, through***, etc.

1592 SHAKS. *Ven. & Ad.* 611 'Fie, fie', he says, 'you crush me, let me go'. **1596** —— *1 Hen. IV.* v. i. 13 To crush our old limbes in vngentle Steele. **1611** BIBLE *Num.* xxii. 25 The asse.. crusht [COVERD. thrust, *Geneva* dasht] Balaams foote against the wall. **1884** SIR N. LINDLEY in *Law Rep.* 9 Probate Div. 205 The salving vessel.. was crushed against the landing-stage.. and was damaged. *Mod.* Too many people were crushed into the carriage. The article was in type but has been crushed out by the pressure of political news.

b. *intr.* (for *refl.*) To advance or make one's way by crushing or pressure.

1755 JOHNSON, *Crush*.. to come in a close body. **1860** *Sat. Rev.* X. 444/1 The multitude which crushes round the Prince.

4. *fig.* **a.** To break down the strength or power of; to conquer beyond resistance, subdue or overcome completely.

1596 SPENSER *State Irel.* Wks. (Globe) 672/2 They use them.. to oppress and crush some of their owne to stubburne free-holders. **1611** BIBLE *Lam.* i. 15 He hath called an assembly against mee, to crush my yong men. **1781** GIBBON *Decl. & F.* III. xlix. 86 His enemies were crushed by his valour. **1838** THIRLWALL *Greece* V. 95 Such an opportunity of crushing or humbling Sparta. **1848** GASKELL *Mary Barton* (1882) 82/1 He sank upon a seat, almost crushed with the knowledge of the consequences of his.. action.

b. Of actions, feelings, etc.: To put down, subdue utterly, extinguish, stamp *out.*

1610 R. NICCOLS *Mirr. Mag.* 573 And at my state with her proud hornes did push In hope my fame.. to crush. **1697** DAMPIER *Voy.* (1698) I. xiii. 371 These disorders might have been crusht. **1720** GAY *Poems* (1745) I. 172 Crush'd is thy pride. **1853** C. KINGSLEY *Hypatia* xxiv. 299 She was to crush the voice of conscience and reason. **1867** SMILES *Huguenots Eng.* i. (1880) 1 Wherever free inquiry showed itself.. the Church endeavoured to crush it. **1875** JOWETT *Plato* (ed. 2) III. 160 The higher feelings of humanity are far too strong to be crushed out.

c. To oppress with harshness or rigour.

1611 BIBLE *Amos* iv. 1 Yea kine of Bashan.. which oppresse the poore, which crush the needy. **1665** SIR T. HERBERT *Trav.* (1677) 293 There the poor are crusht without a cause. **1846** WHITTIER *The Branded Hand* x, Woe to him who crushes the soul with chain and rod.

5. To bruise, bray, break down into small pieces; *esp.* applied to the comminution of ore, quartz, coke, sugar-cane, oil-seeds, etc. in various industrial processes.

1588 GREENE *Pandosto* Ded. (1607) 2 Unicornes being glutted with brousing on rootes of Lycoras, sharpen their stomacks, with crushing bitter grasse. **1667** MILTON *P.L.* v. 345 For drink the grape She crushes. **1830** M. DONOVAN *Dom. Econ.* I. 309 The apples had..been well crushed and pressed. **1839** *Penny Cycl.* XV. 245/1 The lumps of..ore..falling through between the rollers..are completely crushed into small fragments. **1873** C. ROBINSON *N. S. Wales* 18 Cane crushed at the large mills on the Clarence.

6. To force out by squeezing or pressing; to press or squeeze *out*. Also *fig.*

1602 MARSTON *Antonio's Rev.* v. i. Wks. 1856 I. 132 And crush lives sap from out Pieros vaines. *a* **1626** BACON (J.), He crushed treasure out of his subjects purses by forfeitures. **1634** MILTON *Comus* 47 Bacchus, that first from out the purple grape Crushed the sweet poison of misused wine. **1690** DRYDEN *Don Sebastian* (J.), I wanted weight of feeble Moors upon me To crush my soul out.

7. ***to crush a cup of wine, pot of ale***, etc.: to drink, quaff, 'discuss' it: cf. CRACK *v.* 10.

1592 GREENE *Def. Conny Catch.* Wks. (Grosart) XI. 43 If euer I brought my Conny but to crush a potte of ale with mee. **1592** SHAKS. *Rom. & Jul.* I. ii. 86, I pray come and crush a cup of wine. **1822** SCOTT *Nigel* v, You shall crush a cup of wine to the health of the Fathers of the city. **1845** *Whitehall* xxx. 206 They had crushed several pottles of wine.

crush (krʌʃ), *sb.* [f. prec. vb.]

†**1.** The noise of violent percussion; clashing; a crash. *Obs.*

c **1330** R. BRUNNE *Chron. Wace* 2946 When boþe fflutes come at a frosche, þe fyrste hortlyng gaf a gret crusche.

2. a. The act of crushing; violent compression or pressure that bruises, breaks down, injures, or destroys; also *fig.*

1599 T. M[OUFET] *Silkwormes* 63 The hart-breake crush of melancholies wheele. **1601** HOLLAND *Pliny* XXIX. vi (R.) To heale the eares that have caught some hurt either by bruise, crush or stripe. **1611** COTGR., *Escachure*..also, a squash, crush, knocke, or squeeze (whereby a thing is flatted, or beaten close together). **1775** JOHNSON *Western Isl.* Wks. X. 429 A heavy crush of disaster. **1820** SCORESBY *Acc. Arctic Reg.* I. 214 The ice pressed dreadfully around them..but the ship always escaped the heaviest crushes. **1882** SPURGEON *Treas. Dav.* cxxi. 7 Our soul is kept from the dominion of sin..the crush of despondency.

b. In the following perhaps = *crash*, as now often quoted, and as apparently alluded to by Pope: see CRASH *sb.*[1] 2; but it may mean simply 'destruction by crushing'.

1713 ADDISON *Cato* v. i, Unhurt amidst the war of elements, The wrecks of matter, and the crush of worlds. **1848** LOWELL *Biglow Papers* Poems (1890) II. 6 Holding up the star-spangled banner amid the wreck of matter and the crush of worlds.

c. *Coal-mining.* (See quots.)

1851 GREENWELL *Coal-tr. Terms Northumb. & Durh.* 20 *Crush.*—This occurs when both the roof and thill of a seam of coal are hard, and when the pillars, insufficient for the support of the superincumbent strata, are crushed by their pressure. **1881** RAYMOND *Mining Gloss., Crush.* 1. A squeeze, accompanied, perhaps, with more violent motion and effects. 2. A variety of fault in coal.

d. A person with whom one is enamoured or infatuated; an infatuation; so ***to have*** or ***get a crush on***, to be enamoured of, take a strong fancy to. *slang* (orig. *U.S.*).

1884 I. M. RITTENHOUSE *Maud* (1939) 338 Wintie is weeping because her crush is gone. **1895** J. S. WOOD *Yale Yarns* 153 Miss Palfrey..consented to wear his bunch of blue violets. It was a 'crush', you see, on both sides. **1913** *Dialect Notes* IV. 10 (Have a) *crush* (on), to be conspicuously attached to some one. **1914** G. ATHERTON *Perch of Devil* I. 31 Some of the younger married women..get a crush on some other woman's husband. *Ibid.* 186 To be jealous you've got to have a fearful crush. **1928** *Punch* 2 May 484/1 Gervase and Pontefract had had a quiet sort of masculine crush on Joyce for some time. **1929** JELLIFFE & WHITE *Dis. Nervous Syst.* (ed. 5) iii. 335 They tend to be aggressive, domineering and often play the man role with their school-mates, or 'crushes'. **1952** V. GOLLANCZ *My dear Timothy* 212 It is common to make fun of schoolboy and schoolgirl 'pashes' and 'crushes'.

†**3.** A bruise or injury caused by crushing. *Obs.*

1601 HOLLAND *Pliny* II. 350 Contusions, bruses looking black and blew, strokes, crushes, rushes, rubs, and gals. **1617** MARKHAM *Caval.* VII. 67 It is called Nauell-gall, because the crush is vpon the signe iust opposite against the Horses Nauell. **1702** *Lond. Gaz.* No. 3837/4 Lost..a flea-bitten grey Mare, with a Crush on her right Foot in the Hoof behind.

4. a. The crowding together of a number of things, or *esp.* persons, so that they press forcibly upon each other; the mass so crowded together.

1806 SURR *Winter in Lond.* (ed. 3) III. 136 No rank, no sex, could possibly receive exemption from the general crush. **1830** CUNNINGHAM *Brit. Paint.* II. 54 The crush to see it was very great. **1840** DICKENS *Barn. Rudge* xxxvii, A crush of carts and chairs and coaches.

b. A crowded social gathering. *colloq.*

1832 MACAULAY *Lett.* 18 July, I fell in with her at Lady Grey's great crush. **1888** MRS. H. WARD *R. Elsmere* (1890) 439 [The party] isn't a crush. I have only asked about thirty or forty people.

c. A funnel-shaped fenced passage along which cattle, sheep, or horses are driven for branding, dipping, etc. In full ***crush-pen***.

1856 W. ROBERTS *Diary* 18 Dec. in J. H. Beattie *Early Runholding in Otago* (1947) vi. 43 There was no crush pen or drafting race. **1872** C. H. EDEN *My Wife & I in Queensland* iii. 69 A crush, which is an elongated funnel, becoming so narrow at the end that a beast is wedged in and unable to move. **1890** MRS. C. PRAED *Romance of Station* ii, The 'crush', or branding lane. **1892** W. E. SWANTON *Notes on N.Z.* ii. 124 The [unbroken] horses are put in a stockyard, and there roped or driven into a crush. **1895** *Chambers's Jrnl.* 702/2 A crush—that is, long lines of parallel fences just wide enough for one horse to pass at a time—was erected; they were driven into this long lane. **1931** T. A. HARPER *Windy Island* (1934) III. iv. 225 The lean-to in its turn was divided into crush-pens and a large receiving pen. **1936** M. FRANKLIN *All that Swagger* x. 91 Delacy erected trap yards and drafting crushes. **1942** *E. Afr. Ann.* *1941–2* 105/1 Several hundred protesting cattle must be put through the 'crush' and jabbed with the big hypodermic needle.

d. A group or gang of persons; = CROWD *sb.*[3] 2 c; *spec.* a body of troops; a unit of a regiment. *slang* (orig. *U.S.*).

1904 'No. 1500' *Life in Sing Sing* 247 *Crush*, a crowd. **1916** 'BOYD CABLE' *Action Front* 151 You want to ask something about someone in the old crush [*sc.* regiment]. **1924** A. J. SMALL *Frozen Gold* i. 40 Any one of that crush would do murder for no more than that 500 dollars reward. **1927** *Observer* 12 June 10/3 The best recruiter is the man who is pleased with his 'crush'. **1931** R. DARK (*title*) Shakespeare—and that crush.

e. A drink made from the juice of crushed fruit; = SQUASH *sb.*[1] 7.

1919 H. W. MOORE *On Uncle Sam's Water Wagon* 91 Strawberry crush. Wash and mash one pint of fresh strawberries..put three tablespoonfuls into a glass... Fill up the glass with any charged water. **1935** *Economist* 30 Mar. 734/2 The fruit-eating habit..has inclined the public favourably towards fruit juice beverages ('crushes', 'squashes', etc.). **1952** A. BARON *With Hope* 25 Have you seen that place along the front where they sell orange crush? **1959** P. ROTH *Goodbye, Columbus* iii. 37 Smelling still of all the orange crush they'd drunk that weekend.

5. Cartilage, gristle. *dial.*

[= OHG. *cros* in *nasecros*, *ôrcros*, MLG. *krose*, also MHG. *kroszbein*, *kruszbein*, *krusbein*, f. *krosen* to crackle, crunch: cf. CRUSHEL.]

a **1825** FORBY *Voc. E. Anglia*, *Crish*, *Crush*, cartilage, or soft bones of young animals, easily crushed by the teeth. *Ibid.*, *Crush*, *crustle*, gristle.

6. a. *Comb.* (perh. formed on verb-stem), as ***crush-bone***, ***-nosed***. **crush bar**, a bar in a theatre, where the audience may buy drinks during the intervals of the entertainment; **crush barrier**, a barrier erected to restrain a crowd; **crush-pen** (see sense 4 c above); **crush-yard** *Austral.* and *N.Z.*, a yard leading to the crush (sense 4 c); also *fig.* Also CRUSH HAT, -ROOM.

1954 *Granta* 24 Apr. 22/2 Shall I follow the deception of the crush bar into the first world of critical abuse? **1968** V. C. CLINTON-BADDELEY *My Foe Outstretch'd* ii. 50 In the second interval he made his way..round the back of the Grand Circle to the crush bar. **1909** *Westm. Gaz.* 17 Sept. 9/1 To prevent mishap several other crush barriers are erected. **1970** *Guardian* 24 Mar. 11/6 The stations are not equipped with proper crush barriers. **1696** *Lond. Gaz.* No. 3193/4 Lost..a bay Gelding..with a Crush bone on the side of the Nose. **1876** BROWNING *Shop* 9 Some crush-nosed human-hearted dog. **1888** 'R. BOLDREWOOD' *Robbery under Arms* III. xvi. 247 This was the crush-yard and no gateway. I was safe to be hanged in six weeks. **1921** H. GUTHRIE-SMITH *Tutira* xvi. 127 More would have been done but for the number of previously shorn sheep being mixed up with the woolly, making it necessary to fill the crush-yard more often. **1950** *N.Z. Jrnl. Agric.* Apr. 377/2 For handling large herds a crush yard is recommended.

b. *spec.* in *Geol.* with reference to compression, thrust, or shattering of rock, as ***crush-belt***, ***-breccia***, ***-conglomerate***, ***-line***, ***-material***, ***-movement***, ***-plane***, ***-rock***, ***-structure***, ***-zone***.

1893 GEIKIE *Text-bk. Geol.* (ed. 3) VI. I. ii. 703 Dykes of 50 or 60 yards in breadth are reduced, where one of these crush-lines crosses them obliquely, to a thickness of no more than four feet. **1895** G. W. LAMPLUGH in *Q. Jrnl. Geol. Soc.* LI. 564 Essentially, these crush-conglomerates are rocks made up of scattered fragments set in a slaty matrix. *Ibid.* 571 The rocks bordering on the crush-zones. *Ibid.* 574 The crush material is again revealed. *Ibid.* 578 Three..separate zones of the crush-structure. **1903** GEIKIE *Text-bk. Geol.* (ed. 4) I. II. II. vii. 164 Angular fragmentary rubbish..has subsequently been consolidated by some infiltrating cement (Fault-rock, Crush-breccia, Crush-conglomerate). **1903** *Trans. Edin. Geol. Soc.* VIII. 30 The previous investigators of Fassa Valley failed to recognise the presence of the innumerable crush-planes with extremely low hade. **1903** *Nature* 12 Feb. 359/1 This passage-zone had been the great crush-zone of the district. **1904** *Ibid.* 16 June 166/1 The post-Bala crush-movements. **1930** PEACH & HORNE *Geol. Scotl.* 62 The belt of sheared rocks and flinty crush-material. *Ibid.*, The flinty crush-rock weathers with a black or brown surface. **1937** *Discovery* Oct. 324/1 The flint crush belt that runs throughout the length of the Long Island.

crushable ('krʌʃəb(ə)l), *a.* [f. CRUSH *v.* + -ABLE.] Capable of being crushed.

1863 TROLLOPE *Rachel Ray* I. vii. 130 Make yourself comfortable..; you can't crush me. Or rather I always make myself crushable on such occasions. **1887** *Daily News* 6 Jan. 3/1 A less crushable material. **1927** *Daily Express* 12 Dec. 5 Pack as you buy is a useful rule for all but very crushable goods.

†**crush-crash.** *rare*⁻¹. *Obs.* A combination of *crush* and *crash*, having the effect of a reduplication of the latter.

1583 STANYHURST *Æneis* IV. (Arb.) 110 Thee winds scold strugling, the threshing thick crush crash is owtborne.

crushed (krʌʃt), *ppl. a.* [f. CRUSH *v.* + -ED.]

1. a. Bruised or broken by pressure; pressed or squeezed out of shape; *fig.* overwhelmed, subdued utterly.

1599 SHAKS. *Hen. V*, I. ii. 175 That is but a crush'd necessity. **1795** SOUTHEY *Joan of Arc* VIII. 166 The crush'd and mangled corpse. **1851–5** BRIMLEY *Ess.* 248 To awaken his crushed intelligence.

b. Of fabrics: pressed between rollers or otherwise processed to produce an irregular surface.

1895 *Montgomery Ward Catal.* Spring & Summer 598/2 Fine mohair, crushed plush, silk faced tapestry. **1939** M. B. PICKEN *Lang. Fashion* 40/1 *Crushed leather*, novelty treatment giving to leather a round, slightly bumpy grain similar to blistered fabric. **1957** —— *Fashion Doct.* 91/1 *Crushed velvet*, velvet processed to have an irregular surface. **1970** *Observer Mag.* 13 Dec. 35/1 Crushed velvet has a fashionable antiqued look. **1983** *Truckin' Life* Nov. 65/1 The cab is..padded and lined throughout in russet crushed velour. **1984** *Sears Catal.* *1985* Spring/Summer 39 Oversized crushed nylon bag with adjustable shoulder strap.

2. Bruised or broken down into small pieces or powder.

1855 JOHNSTON *Chem. Com. Life* iv. (1879) 58 Crushed bones are strewed over a meadow. **1875** URE *Dict. Arts* III. 943 There are three classes of sugar-refineries in this country, the chief productions of which are, respectively: 1st, Loaf-sugar; 2nd, Crystals..3rd, Crushed sugar.

3. ***crushed morocco*** (*Bookbinding*): morocco leather, grained, shaved thin, pressed between iron plates, and polished. ***crushed strawberry***: the colour of strawberries when crushed or bruised. Similarly ***crushed raspberry***.

1881 C. C. HARRISON *Woman's Handiwork* III. 165 Wine color, pomegranate, Indian-red, crushed strawberry. **1897** [see STRAWBERRY 7]. **1906** S. W. BUSHELL *Chinese Art* II. 40 The brilliant *sang de bœuf*..is now succeeded by its derivative of softer hue,..*peau de pêche* (peach-bloom) or crushed strawberry (*fraise écrasée*). **1931** R. LEHMANN *Let. to Sister* 9 A patch of those crushed-raspberry, button chrysanthemums.

†**crushel, crussel.** *Obs.* [Corresponds to OHG. *crosela*, *kroschela*, MHG. *krosel*, *kroszel*, *kroschel*, MLG. *crosle*, LG. *kroselle* cartilage, gristle, referred by Hildebrand to MHG. and dial. G. *krosen*, *krösen* to gnash the teeth, crackle, craunch, crush with noise. Cf. dial. *crustle*, CRUSH *sb.* 5.] Cartilage, gristle.

c **1440** *Promp. Parv.* 106 Cruschylbone, or grystylbone [P. crusshell]. **1617** MINSHEU *Ductor*, A crussell or gristle.

crusher ('krʌʃə(r)). [f. CRUSH *v.* + -ER[1].]

1. a. One who or that which crushes.

1598 FLORIO, *Premitore*, a crusher. **1611** COTGR., *Escacheur*, a squasher; a beater, or crusher of things flat. **1662** J. SPARROW tr. *Behme's Rem. Wks.*, *Apol. conc. Perfection* 8 The Crusher or bruiser of the Serpent. **1859** SALA *Tw. round Clock* (1861) 62 Crushers of walnuts with silver nut-crackers. **1885** C. F. HOLDER *Marvels Anim. Life* 191 The Port Jackson shark..has crushers instead of teeth.

b. *spec.* One whose trade is to crush some article for economic purposes.

1794 *Hull Advertiser* 9 Aug. 3/4 The Crushers of Rape-seed continue to buy this article very freely. **1841** *Penny Cycl.* XIX. 300/2 Rape..The seed..is then sold to the crushers, who express the oil. **1884** *Law Rep.* 13 Q. Bench Div. 469 Seed crushers and oil refiners.

c. A machine for crushing seed, ore, quartz, etc.

1825 J. NICHOLSON *Operat. Mechanic* 160 For breaking malt, beans, &c. one crusher only is wanted. **1879** ATCHERLEY *Boërland* 172 Mr. Armfield's crusher was in full work.

2. *colloq.* Something which overwhelms or overpowers. Cf. *stunner*.

1840 DICKENS *Old C. Shop* l, It's Destiny, and mine's a crusher! **1849** THACKERAY *Pendennis* iv, 'She *is* a crusher, ain't she now?' **1884** *Chr. Commonwealth* 6 Nov. 53/5 The decision was a crusher on Dr. Phin.

3. An apparatus for recording the pressure exerted on a gun by a charge of powder; also *attrib.* as in ***crusher-gauge***, ***-plug***.

1871 *Standard* 19 Jan., A 'crusher', or small apparatus exposing a copper disc to the pressure over a given surface of the pent-up gases, was inserted in the rear of the 700-pounder bolts. **1871** NOBLE & ABEL in *Phil. Trans.* CLXV. 140 A slight escape of gas past the crusher-gauge.

4. *slang.* **a.** A policeman.

1835 *Sessions' Paper* Aug. 643 'Here are two *crushers*.'.. I looked out of the window, and saw both the policemen. **1841** *Punch* II. 137 There is not one crusher who is proof against the waistcoat pocket. **1851** MAYHEW *Lond. Labour* I. 25 'The blessed crushers is everywhere', shouted one.

b. A ship's corporal or policeman; a regulating petty officer. *Naval.*

1908 'L. YEXLEY' *Inner Life of Navy* ii. 10 Whenever the 'Assembly' sounded, the Police (usually called Corporals or 'Crushers') would run round the decks cutting..at the boys as they rushed up the ladders. **1909** J. R. WARE *Passing Eng.* 100/2 *Crushers*, ships' corporals, who are the rank and file of the master-at-arms. **1912** 'AURORA' *Jock Scott, Midshipman* xiv. 165 One of the 'crushers' has a 'down' on you. **1943** C. S. FORESTER *Ship* 85 A crusher is a member of the ship's police.

crush hat. A soft hat which can be crushed flat; *spec.* a hat constructed with a spring so as to collapse and assume a flat shape; an opera-hat.

1838 DICKENS *Nich. Nick.* xix, Folding his crush hat to lay his elbow on. **1848** THACKERAY *Bk. Snobs* i. **1891** *Punch* 25 Apr. 201/2 Smart new boy in cloak-room has noted gentlemen shutting up their crush hats, and promptly flattens de Jones's best silk topper.

crushing ('krʌʃɪŋ), *vbl. sb.* [f. CRUSH *v.* + -ING[1].] The action of the vb. CRUSH.

†**1.** Crashing, smashing: see CRUSH *v.* 1. *Obs.*

2. Compressing violently so as to bruise or destroy; violent pressure or squeezing. Also *fig.*

1580 HOLLYBAND *Treas. Fr. Tong, Froissement*, a crushing in pieces. **1645** MILTON *Tetrach.* (1851) 195 The crushing.. and the overwhelming of his afflicted Servants. **1694** *Acc. Sev. Late Voy.* II. (1711) 6 Cornelius Seaman lost his Ship by the squeezing and crushing together of the Ice. **1860** TYNDALL *Glac.* I. xviii. 123 The sound produced by the crushing of the fragments. **1890** *Spectator* 31 May, All delays, discomforts and crushings were met with good-humour.

3. *spec.* Bruising or comminution of ore, quartz, oil-seeds, etc. for economic purposes; also *attrib.* and *comb.*, as ***crushing-machine***, ***-mill***, ***-seed***, etc.

1759 SMEATON in *Phil. Trans.* LI. 168 The crushing of rape seed. **1796** *Hull Advertiser* 10 Sept. 2/2 Fifty lasts of fine Koningsburg Crushing Linseed. **1832** BABBAGE *Econ. Manuf.* xxxii. (ed. 3) 337 The Crushing Mill, used in Cornwall and other mining countries. **1872** RAYMOND *Statist. Mines* 43 The crushing for the year is 9,782 tons of quartz.

'crushing, *ppl. a.* [f. as prec. + -ING[2].] That crushes; bruising, overwhelming, etc.

1577 WHETSTONE in *Gascoigne's Steel Glas* (Arb.) 22 Crusshing care. **1593** SHAKS. *Rich. II*, v. v. 34 Crushing penurie. **1855** MACAULAY *Hist. Eng.* IV. 206 The blow must be quick, and crushing. **1876** TREVELYAN *Macaulay* II. ix. 137 A.. crushing censure upon Lord Ellenborough.

'crushingly, *adv.* [f. prec. + -LY[2].] In a crushing manner; so as to crush.

1816 L. HUNT *Rimini* IV. 173 The word smote crushingly. **1881** *Daily Tel.* 20 Oct., Falling slowly but crushingly.

'crush-room. A room or hall in a theatre, opera-house, etc., in which the audience may promenade during the intervals of the entertainment.

1806 SURR *Winter in Lond.* (ed. 3) III. 135 The drawing-room.. actually differed in nothing from the crush-room at the opera on a very crowded night. **1833** MACAULAY *Lett.* 2 Aug., The crush-room of the opera at night. **1855** THACKERAY *Newcomes* I. 278.

crusian, var. of CRUCIAN, species of carp.

crusie, crusy ('kryzɪ, 'krøzɪ). *Sc.* Also cruisie, -zie, -y, -ey, cruzie, croosie. [app. a phonetic repr. of F. *creuset*, CRUSET, or perh. of earlier origin from OF. *croiseul*, *creuseul* (pl. *-eus*), or *croisel*, *cruseau*, with which it agrees in its two senses, while F. *creuset* and Eng. CRUSET have only that of 'crucible'.]

1. A small iron lamp with a handle, burning oil or tallow; also, a sort of triangular iron candlestick with one or more sockets for candles, having the edges turned up on the three sides. (Jamieson.)

a **1774** FERGUSSON *Farmer's Ingle*, The cruizy, too, can only blink and bleer. **1776** C. KEITH *Farmer's Ha'* ix. (Jam.), Meg lights the crusy wi' a match. **1824** SCOTT *Red-gauntlet* Let. iv, A silver lamp, or cruisie, as the Scottish term it. **1892** *Blackw. Mag.* Oct. 487 The croosie, a triangular metal saucer with an upright hook at the base to be hung by.

2. A crucible, or hollow piece of iron with a long handle, used for melting metals. (Jamieson.)

The common sense in South of Scotland; *crusies* were commonly used by stocking-weavers in middle of the 19th c. to melt lead or pewter for setting the needles in their frames.

crusily, -illy ('kruːsɪlɪ), *a. Her.* Also 6 crusule, 7–8 crusuly, 7 crossule, 9 crusillé(e, (crucilly, cily). [a. OF. *crusillié*, var. of *croisillé* (Godef.) 'strewn with crosses or croisettes', f. *croisille*, dim. of *croix* cross.]

Of a field or charge: Covered or strewn with small crosses, usually crosses crosslet.

1572 BOSSEWELL *Armorie* II. 115 b, He beareth Argent, a Cheuron de Ermines, betweene three Inkes molyn, crusule botonie fitchie Sable. **1766** PORNY *Heraldry* Gloss., *Crusily* or *Crusuly*. **1864** BOUTELL *Heraldry Hist. & Pop.* vi. 29 When the Field is covered with small Crosses Crosslets, it is said to be Crusilly. **1882** CUSSANS *Heraldry* viii. 128 Crusillé.

†**cruskyn, cruisken.** *Obs.* or *Sc. dial.* In 4–5 cruskyn, (cruske), 5 curskyn. [= OF. *creusequin*, *crousequin*, mod. Walloon *cruskin*, *creuskin*, prob. a. MFlem. *kruyseken*, *kroesken*, dim. of *kruyse*, *kroes*, CRUSE. The forms in Promp. Parv. may be directly from Flemish. The Gael. *crùisgein* small cruse, oil-lamp, Irish *cruisgin* small pot or pitcher, are adopted words.] A small vessel for holding liquids; hence a liquid measure.

1378 *Inventory* in *Promp. Parv.* 106 Un cruskyn de terre garnis d'argent.. Un pot d'argent blanc au guyse d'un cruskyn. **1408** *Will of Molynton* (Somerset Ho.), Vnum Cruskyn de argento & deauratum. **14..** *Voc.* in Wr.-Wülcker 602/40 [*Picarius, quidam ciphus*, a curskyn]. *c* **1440** *Promp. Parv.* 106 Cruskyn' or cruske, coop of erþe, *cartesia*. **1808** JAMIESON, *Cruisken of whisky*, a certain measure of this liquor, *Angus*.

crusoe[1]. = CRUCIAN, species of carp.

1799 G. SMITH *Laboratory* ii. 264 Method of catching Crusoes, or Crucians.

Crusoe[2] ('kruːsəʊ). One who is shipwrecked on a desert island, like the hero of Defoe's book. Also *attrib.* and *Comb.*, as ***Crusoe life***, ***-like*** adj. and adv. Hence **'Crusoeing**, living like Crusoe.

1888 R. L. STEVENSON in *Scribner's Mag.* Feb. 252/1 And then you might go Crusoeing, a word that covers all extempore eating in the open air. **1907** *Daily Chron.* 3 July 5/5 There he had built himself a habitation, Crusoe-like, out of brushwood. **1908** *Ibid.* 16 July 1/5 Blades of penknives were fashioned into needles, hair-combs were made from bush thorns, and altogether the men led a regular Crusoe life. **1926** *Chambers's Jrnl.* 104/1 No other island.. has accommodated more Crusoes during the last three centuries than Chatham Island. *Ibid.*, There is another and fell aspect of Crusoeing, however—an aspect which most fiction-writers carefully ignore.

†**crusoile.** *Obs. rare*[−1]. [a. OF. *cruseul*, *crusol* crucible: see CRUSELL, CRUSET.] A crucible.

1613 MARSTON *Insat. C'tesse* I. Wks. 1856 III. 111 Thou scum of his melting-pots, thou wert christned in a crusoile with Mercuries water.

crusopasse, -praso, obs. ff. CHRYSOPRASE.

crust (krʌst), *sb.* Forms: 4 crouste, 5 croste, 5–6 cruste, 4– crust. [In some senses ad. L. *crusta*, in others immed. a. OF. *crouste* (mod. *croûte*), Pr. and It. *crosta*:—L. *crusta* hard surface, rind, shell, incrustation. In F. the earliest recorded popular sense is the crust of bread, but medical writers used it in sense 3 after L. at an early date.]

1. a. The outer part of bread rendered hard and dry in baking. Opposed to *crumb*.

a **1330** *Otuel* 954 Anawe of Nubie he smot, That neuere eft crouste he ne bot. **1398** [see CRUSTING *vbl. sb.* 1]. *c* **1430** *Two Cookery-bks.* 53 Saue þe sydys and al þe cruste hole with-owte. **1583** HOLLYBAND *Campo di Fior* 191 Make cleane his bread, If there be either ashes or coles in the cruste. **1620** VENNER *Via Recta* i. 22 The like may be said of the crust of bread. **1825** SCOTT 2 Jan. in *Lockhart*, When we do get bread to eat, we complain that the crust is hard. **1871** *When I was a little Girl* (ed. 2) 25 You know there can't be crust without crumb.

b. (with *a* and *pl.*) The hard outer part of a loaf or roll of bread; a portion of this external part such as belongs to a single slice of bread.

c **1325** in *Pol. Songs* (Camden) 204 A rowȝ bare trenchur, other a crust: The begger that the crust ssal hab. *c* **1420** *Liber Cocorum* (1862) 16 A crust of bread thou bray withalle. *c* **1450** *Two Cookery-bks.* 113 Nym crostes of whyt bred. **1594** SHAKS. *Rich. III*, II. iv. 28 My Vnkle grew so fast, That he could gnaw a crust at two houres old. *a* **1704** R. L'ESTRANGE (J.) Men will do tricks, like dogs, for crusts. **1871** *When I was a little Girl* (ed. 2) 24, I had a piece of bread and butter for my luncheon every morning, and the crust of it was often a serious incumbrance to me.. Bread-crusts are not nice things.

c. By extension: A scrap of bread which is mainly crust or is hard and dry: often applied slightingly to what is much more than crust.

1561 T. NORTON tr. *Calvin's Inst.* Pref., Some.. doe plenteously glut themselves, and other some live with gnawing of poore crusts. **1592** WARNER *Alb. Eng.* VII. xxxvii. (1612) 182 My hap was harder than to owne in that distresse a Crust. **1697** DAMPIER *Voy.* (1698) I. xi. 313 Sauce.. which makes it eat very savory: much better than a crust of Bread alone. **1821** CLARE *Vill. Minstr.* I. 66 Parents.. Who in distress broke their last crust in twain.. that I might be fed. **1837** LYTTON *E. Maltravers* I. i, Bring me a cup of beer, and crust of bread. **1886** H. F. LESTER *Under two Fig Trees* 42 To have a 'crust' as she calls it, or in reality a good deal of cheese and bread and beer.

d. *fig.*

1593 *Tell-Troth's N.Y. Gift* 12 Such crustes of small comfort. **1749** FIELDING *Tom Jones* XI. i. *heading*, A Crust for the Critics.

e. A livelihood, a living. *Austral.* and *N.Z. slang*.

1916 C. J. DENNIS *Songs Sentimental Bloke* 120 *Crust*, sustenance; a livelihood. **1944** G. MCCARTHY in *Coast to Coast* 149 He's still there.. Makin' a crust too. **1949** E. DE MAUNY *Huntsman in Career* ii. 128 'What do you do for a crust?' 'I work on a newspaper.' **1969** *Coast to Coast 1967–8* 100 You'd have to work pretty hard for that, I'd reckon, and your old man too. What does he do for a crust?

2. The paste forming the covering of a pie.

1598 *Epulario* B iv b, Make a crust of thicke past like a Pie crust. **1712** ADDISON *Spec.* No. 482 ¶4 Learning how to season it [a buck], or put it in crust. **1771** GOLDSM. *Haunch of Venison* 54 A pasty; it shall, and it must, And my wife, little Kitty, is famous for crust.

3. A hard dry formation on the surface of the body, caused by a burn, an ulcer, or disease of the skin; a scab or eschar.

1398 TREVISA *Barth. De P.R.* VII. xvii. (1495) 235 A crouste of blood. *c* **1400** *Lanfranc's Cirurg.* 70 We moten brenne þe heed of þe veyne.. wiþ hoot iren & þilke hoot iren myȝte make an hard cruste. **1543** TRAHERON *Vigo's Chirurg.* 275 b, *Eschara* is the herdnes, or cruste y[t] remayneth after the burnynge of a wounde, or ulcer. **1602** SHAKS. *Ham.* I. v. 72 A most instant Tetter barked.. with vile and loathsome crust All my smooth Body. **1876** DUHRING *Dis. Skin* 47 Crusts are effete masses of dried materials composed of the products of disease of the skin.

4. †**a.** The upper or surface layer of the ground. *Obs.*, having passed into **b.** *Geol.* The outer portion of the earth; that part of the body of the earth accessible to investigation.

Used first in accordance with the notion that the interior of the earth was an 'abyss' of waters, subsequently in reference to the theory of an interior in a state of fusion.

1555 EDEN *Decades* 234 An other kynde of Rubies.. found in the mountaynes in the vpper crust or floure of the earth. **1611** SPEED *Theat. Gt. Brit.* xxxiv. (1614) 67/1 In the very crust of the ground, without any deepe digging. **1666** BOYLE in *Phil. Trans.* 2 Apr. 185 The elevation of steams from the Crust or Superficial parts of the Earth. **1747** *Gentl. Mag.* XVII. 433 The whole earth, in the opinion of some philosophers, is but a kind of bridge, or crust to the great body of waters included in it. **1851** HERSCHEL *Stud. Nat. Phil.* III. iv. 294 The rocks and stones which compose the external crust of the globe.

5. a. A more or less hard coating, concretion, or deposit on the surface of anything; an incrustation.

1540 HYRDE tr. *Vives' Instr. Chr. Wom.* I. ix. (R.) Except thou wilt neuer wash out the crust, but goe so with a crust of paynting to bedde. **1618** BOLTON *Florus* III. iv. 176 While they ride upon the false crusts of yce breaking under. **1684** BUNYAN *Pilgr.* II. 138 Precious Stones are covered over with a homely Crust. **1726** LEONI *Alberti's Archit.* I. 58 a, Lay.. over all a Crust made of Sand, Mortar, and Ashes. **1756** C. LUCAS *Ess. Waters* I. 146 It looked more like a saline crust. **1838** THIRLWALL *Greece* III. xxi. 179 The water.. [was] covered with a thin crust of ice. **1869** PHILLIPS *Vesuv.* iv. 121 The crust formed over the lava.

b. ***crust of wine***: see quot.

1863 T. G. SHAW *Wine, etc.* iv. 145 In every wine.. a portion of the vegetable and other matters which constitute its 'distinctiveness' must inevitably be precipitated to the bottom of the vessel; this is called lees in the cask, and crust or deposit in the bottle.

c. orig. *U.S.* The hardened surface of snow suitable for crust-hunting.

1809 A. HENRY *Travels* 146 The crust upon the snow cutting his legs.. to the very bone. **1860** [cf. CRUSTING *vbl. sb.* 2]. **1876** *Forest & Stream* VI. 18/1 We had waited for a 'crust' through days of rain, thaw, and fog. **1890** N. HIBBS in *Big Game N. Amer.* 27 The Moose would come when the crust formed on the snow in the mountains. **1966** T. ARMSTRONG et al. *Gloss. Snow & Ice* 13 *Crust*, a hard snow surface upon a softer layer.

6. The hard external covering of an animal or plant; a shell, test, husk, etc.; *spec.* the hard chitinous integument or 'shell' of Crustaceans.

1615 CROOKE *Body of Man* 121 This Crust is spongie, hauing smal holes.. that by these hollowe passages.. the thinner part of the Chylus might pierce. **1653** WALTON *Angler* 101 This Caterpiller gives over to eat, and.. comes to be coverd over with a strange shell or crust. **1776** WITHERING *Brit. Plants* (1796) I. 322 There is a sort of leathery crust over the seed. **1834** GOOD *Study Med.* (ed. 4) IV. 464 [The skin] was shed annually like the crust of a lobster.

7. *fig.* **a.** Something figured as an outer covering or shell diffcult to penetrate, or merely superficial.

1651–3 JER. TAYLOR *Serm. for Year* (1678) 369 A universal crust of Hypocrisie that covers the face of the greatest part of Mankind. *a* **1655** VINES *Lord's Supp.* (1677) 320 He may be overgrown with a crust, a coldness. *a* **1853** ROBERTSON *Lect.* i. (1858) 105 Break through the crust of his selfishness.

b. Impudence, effrontery. *slang.*

1900 *Dialect Notes* II. 31 *Crust*, forwardness. **1923** WODEHOUSE *Inimitable Jeeves* xiv, The blighter had the cold, cynical crust to look me in the eyeball without a blink. **1954** —— *Jeeves & Feudal Spirit* xi. 97 Actually having the crust to come barging in here!

†**8.** A plank cut from the outside of a tree-trunk.

1486 *Nottingham Rec.* III. 255, iij. crustes.. to ley on þe same Brigge vnder þe gravell. **1563** *Louth Churchw. Acc.* III. 28 (in Peacock *N.W. Linc. Gloss.*) For a crust of a plank to a brigge. **1569** *Nottingham Rec.* IV. 136 For a kruste and a planke.

9. *Angling.* The surface film of water. ? *Obs.*

1653 W. LAUSON *Secr. Angling* in Arb. *Garner* I. 194 If the wind be rough, and trouble the crust of the water. *Ibid.*, This fly.. moved in the crust of the water is deadly in an evening.

10. *Leather Manuf.* The state of sheep or goat skins when merely tanned and left rough preparatory to being dyed or coloured.

1686 *Lond. Gaz.* No 2125/4 About 350 of the best Kids, some ready pared, and some in the Crust not staked. **1882** *Worcester Exhib. Catal.* iii. 50 Crust and coloured skivers.

11. The outer part or 'wall' of a horse's hoof.

1847 YOUATT *Horse* xviii. 372 The crust or wall, is that portion which is seen when the foot is placed on the ground.

†**12.** *fig.* A crusty person. *Obs.*

1594 *Merry Knack* in Hazl. *Dodsley* VI. 539 What an old crust it is!.. I think the villain hath a face hardened with steel. *a* **1640** DAY *Peregr. Schol.* (1881) 44 An old crust, with a back bent like a bowe with carieing tables.

13. a. *Comb.*, as ***crust-hardened***, ***-like*** adjs.; †**crust-clung** *a.* (see quot.); **crust-lizard**, book-name of *Heloderma horridum*; †**crust-roll**, a kind of thin crusted pancake.

c **1430** *Two Cookery-bks.* 46 Cruste Rolle.—Take.. Flowre of whete; nym Eyroun and breke þer-to.. rolle it on a borde also þinne as parchement.. frye hem, and serue forth. **1610** W. FOLKINGHAM *Art of Survey* I. x. 24 Crust-clung and Soale-bound soyles. **1688** HOLME *Armoury* III. 333/2 Crust Clung, or Soil Bound, is an hard sticking together of the Earth, that nothing will grow on it. **1884** *Sat. Rev.* 7 June 741/1 Old crust-hardened politicians.

b. *spec.* in *Geol.* (see 4 b), as ***crust-block***, ***-creep***, ***-fold***, ***-fracture***, ***-lag***, ***-movement***, ***-strain***, ***-stress***, ***-torsion***.

1897 *Geogr. Jrnl.* June 669 There are two primary and permanent kinds of crust-movements. **1900** *Ibid.* Jan. 48 The great Rocky Mountain-Andes fold,..the longest and most continuous crust-fold of the present day. *Ibid.* Oct. 457 That phenomena of crust-torsion were induced by any combination of crust-pressures. *Ibid.*, The original cause of crust-strains. *Ibid.* 460 Old crust-forms and crust-fractures, especially such as allow occasional intrusion and outlet of volcanic material, are determining factors in the distribution of the subsequent deposits. *Ibid.* 461 Gigantic crust-creep of overthrust masses. **1903** *Trans. Edin. Geol. Soc.* VIII. 177 The form of the sill-complex was capable of being re-moulded periodically in harmony with the localised crust-stresses. **1907** *19th Cent.* Aug. 220 The remarkable crust-movements exhibited over a wide area. **1926** *Chambers's Jrnl.* 598/2, I would..hazard also the suggestion that crust-lag may be a potent factor, in conjunction with shrinkage of the earth's crust, in the causation of earth-tremors and earthquakes. **1929** *Encycl. Brit.* II. 980/2 According to current views of the mechanics of mountain-folding, a crust-block of old and hard rocks is always present, which receives the pressure of the thrust causing the folding. **1934** *Nature* 15 Dec. 940/2 In one crust-block (west of the volcano), the tilting occurred in the same direction as before.

crust (krʌst), *v.* [f. prec. sb., after F. *crouster, croûter*, L. *crustāre.*]

1. *trans.* To cover as with a crust, to encrust. **1545** Ascham *Toxoph.* (Arb.) 157 Snowe..whyche was harde and crusted by reason of the frost. **1570** Levins *Manip.* 194/22 To cruste, *crustare.* **1607** Shaks. *Timon* iv. vi. 109 Of Man and Beast, the infinite Maladie Crust you quite o're. **1614** W.B. *Philosopher's Banquet* (ed. 2) 162 The meates become crusted and baked. **1836** Macgillivray tr. *Humboldt's Trav.* ii. 34 Rocks..scantily crusted with lichens. **1892** *Illustr. Mag.* Sept. 879 North winds begin to crust over the pools and streams with ice.

b. *fig.*

c **1616** Chapman *Homer, Battaile of Frogs*, &c. Ep. Ded. (R.), Being crusted with their couetous leprosies. **1767** Johnson *Lett.* 19 Aug., Ill health..has crusted me into inactivity. **1883** Froude *Short Stud.* IV. ii. vi. 250 The truth had been crusted over with fictions.

2. *intr.* To form or contract a crust; to become covered with a crust or hardened surface. Also *fig.*

c **1430** *Two Cookery-bks.* 32 Stere it faste þat it crouste noȝt. **1649** G. Daniel *Trinarch., Hen. IV.* ccclxxxvii, Aged Tyrrannie whose Oyle Crusts in the Lampe. *a* **1698** Temple (J.), The place that was burnt..crusted and healed in very few days. **1765** A. Dickson *Treat. Agric.* 471 The soil..will only crust a little above. **1820** Hazlitt *Lect. Dram. Lit.* 26 The tide of fancy and enthusiasm..settles and crusts into the standing pool of dulness, criticism, and *vertù*.

3. *trans.* To form into a crust; to make hard like a crust.

1671 Narborough *Jrnl.* in *Acct. Sev. Late Voy.* i. (1711) 182 The main Body of Ice that lyeth crusted about the Shore. **1857** W. Collins *Dead Secret* v. v. (1861) 227 The dirt of half a century, crusted on the glass.

4. *U.S.* and *Canada.* To hunt (deer, etc.) on the crust of snow; to crust-hunt.

1860 [see crusting *vbl. sb.* 2]. **1888** *Forest & Stream* XXX. 46/3 The guides and hunters..going over the border ..on the deep snows, and crusting deer and moose. *Ibid.* 165/1 A good deal of crusting deer is being done..this winter.

crusta (ˈkrʌstə). Pl. **crustæ**. The L. original of crust *sb.*, used in some scientific senses and combinations. **a.** *Anat.* The ventral part of the cerebral peduncle. **b.** *Path.* = crust *sb.* 3. **c.** ***crusta fibrosa, c. petrosa***, the cement of a tooth (cement *sb.* 4). **d.** ***crusta lactea***, an eruptive disease of infants at the breast; milk-scab, milk-blotch. **e.** ***crusta phlogistica*** (see quot. 1890).

1806 *Med. Jrnl.* XV. 33 Crusta Lactea..sometimes proves a very severe..disease; in some families attacking every child at the age of a few weeks. **1820** R. Hooper *Med. Dict.* (ed. 4) 266/1 *Crusta*,..a scab. **1848** Dunglison *Med. Dict.* (ed. 7) 238/2 Crusta phlogistica. *Ibid.* 851/1 At the part where the enamel terminates at the cervix of the tooth, the *crusta pertroˈsa, cemenˈtum*, or cortical substance, commences in an extremely thin stratum. **1856** *Crusta lactea* [see *milk-scab* s.v. milk *sb.* 10 a]. **1876** T. Bryant *Pract. Surg.* (ed. 2) I. xiii. 537 The *crusta petrosa* is formed on the gradually elongating root through the agency of the dental sac or capsule which surrounds the forming tooth crown. **1876** *Quain's Elem. Anat.* (ed. 8) II. 555 The lower or superficial part [of the peduncular fibres]..consists almost entirely of white fibres, collected into coarse fasciculi and is named the crusta [earlier edd., crust] or basis, or the fasciculated portion of the peduncle. **1890** Billings *Med. Dict.* I. 353/2 *Crusta fibrosa*, crusta petrosa... *Crusta phlogistica*, inflammatory or buffy coat of blood. **1910** *Encycl. Brit.* IV. 395/2 The ventral part of each crus forms the crusta, which is..the great motor path from the brain to the cord. **1911** *Ibid.* XXVI. 501/1 Surrounding the dentine where it is not covered by enamel is the 'cement' or 'crusta petrosa', a thin layer of bone. **1949** F. W. Jones et al. *Buchanan's Man. Anat.* (ed. 8) v. 266 Cement, or crusta petrosa. This covers the dentine that forms the root of the tooth. *Ibid.* xiii. 1400 The basis pedunculi (crusta)..has a crescentic outline, the concavity of the crescent being dorsal and occupied by the convexity of the substantia nigra.

f. *Antiq.* A thin plate of embossed metal, etc., inlaid on a vessel, wall, or other object.

1842 Brande *Dict. Sci.*, etc., *Crusta*, in gem sculpture, a gem engraved for inlaying on a vase or other object. **1910** *Encycl. Brit.* XIV. 627/2 The *proscenium* of the Odeum was lined with *crustae*, or 'marble-veneering', under one inch thick. **1911** *Ibid.* XXIII. 484/1 The *crustae*, or plaques decorated in repoussé, which were mounted on smooth silver cups. *Ibid.*, Cups adorned with golden *crustae*.

‖**Crustacea** (krʌˈsteɪʃ(ɪ)ə), *sb. pl. Zool.* [mod.L. neuter pl. of *crustāceus* adj. (sc. *animālia*): see below. Introduced by Lamarck, 1801, as a name of the class of animals called by Cuvier, 1798, *les insectes crustacées*: cf. crustaceous 3.] A large class of Arthropodous animals, mostly aquatic, characterized by a hard, close-fitting, usually chitinous shell or 'crust' which is shed periodically; comprising Crabs, Lobsters, Crayfish, Prawns, Shrimps, and many others.

1814 W. E. Leach *Trans. Linn. Soc.* XI. 306 (*title*), Arrangement of the Crustacea, etc. **1828** Stark *Elem. Nat. Hist.* II. 144 The Crustacea..respire by branchiæ..They have a distinct heart provided with circulating vessels. **1848** Carpenter *Anim. Phys.* ii. (1872) 108 Most of the Crustacea, like insects, come forth from the eggs in a state very different from their adult form.

crustaceal (krʌˈsteɪʃ(ɪ)əl), *a. rare.* [f. prec. + -al^{1}.] = crustacean *a.*

1853 Kane *Grinnell Exp.* xvii. (1856) 130 Like all birds feeding on crustaceal life.

crustacean (krʌˈsteɪʃ(ɪ)ən), *a.* and *sb.* [f. as prec. + -an.]

A. *adj.* Belonging to the class Crustacea.

1858 Geikie *Hist. Boulder* v. 81 The most abundant order of Crustacean life.

B. *sb.* An animal of this class.

1835 Kirby *Hab. & Inst. Anim.* II. xiv. 26 Whether the higher Orders of Crustaceans undergo a real metamorphosis. **1873** Dawson *Earth & Man* iii. 54 The Crustaceans, the highest marine animals of the annulose type.

crustaceoid (krʌsteɪʃɪɔɪd), *a. rare.* [f. as prec. + -oid.] Having a resemblance to a crustacean.

1846 Dana *Zooph.* vii. 106 These crustaceoid species.

crustaceˈology. [See -(o)logy.] The scientific study of Crustacea. Hence **crustaceoˈlogical** *a.*, pertaining to crustaceology; **crustaceˈologist**, one versed in crustaceology.

1828 Webster, *Crustalogy*, that part of zoology which treats of crustaceous animals..*Crustaceology*, the word sometimes used, is ill-formed..Who can endure such words as *crustaceological*? **1849** tr. *Cuvier's Anim. Kingd.* 409 *note*, Milne Edwards has not mentioned them in his Review of Crustaceology. *Ibid.* 408 *note*, Anomalous animals..which have long perplexed Crustaceologists. **1876** Page *Advd. Text-bk. Geol.* xiii. 237 A fresh and inviting field to the crustaceologist.

cruˌstaceoˈrubrin. *Chem.* [f. L. *Crustace-a* + *ruber* red + -in.] A red colouring matter found in the bodies of some Crustacea.

1882 in *Syd. Soc. Lex.*

crustaceous (krʌˈsteɪʃəs), *a.* [f. mod.L. *crustāceus*, f. *crusta* crust, hard shell: see -aceous.]

1. a. Pertaining to, or of the nature of, a crust or hard integument. ***crustaceous lichens*** (in *Bot.*): see quot. 1882.

1656 Blount *Glossogr.*, *Crustaceous*..pertaining to the crust, hard shell or pill of any thing. **1664** Power *Exp. Philos.* i. 3 Their crustaceous Tunica Cornea. **1762** B. Stillingfleet *Econ. Nat.* 78 The crustaceous liverworts are the first foundation of vegetation. **1830** Lindley *Nat. Syst. Bot.* 145 The outer integument [of the seed] crustaceous, the inner membranous. **1856** W. L. Lindsay *Pop. Hist. Brit. Lichens* iii. 80 Without a soil prepared..by crustaceous Lichens, there could have arisen no higher vegetation. **1882** Vines *Sachs' Bot.* 319 The Thallus of Lichens is commonly developed in the form of incrustations which cover stones and the bark of trees..These Crustaceous Lichens, as they are termed [etc.]. **1921** A. L. Smith *Lichens* iii. 72 Some crustaceous lichens have a persistently scanty furfuraceous crust.

†**b.** *Path.* Characterized by crusts or scabs.

1801 *Med. Jrnl.* V. 23 The discovery of the crustaceous Cow-pox..The ulcers on the hands and arms assumed the crustaceous form.

2. Of animals: Having a hard integument.

1659 H. More *Immort. Soul* ii. xi. (1662) 108 Wasps and Hornets..the Animal Spirits not easily evaporating through their crustaceous Bodies. **1664** Power *Exp. Philos.* i. 16 Mites in Cheese..It seems they are sheath'd and crustaceous Animals (as Scarabees and such like Insects are). **1826** Kirby & Sp. *Entomol.* (1828) III. xxix. 168 Crustaceous forms in Coleoptera.

3. a. *spec.* in *Zool.* Belonging to the class Crustacea, crustacean.

1646 Sir T. Browne *Pseud. Ep.* iii. xvii. 151 Crustaceous animals, Lobsters, Shrimps, and Crevises. **1677** Plot *Oxfordsh.* 106 The shell-fish of the softer crustaceous kind. **1707** *Curios. in Husb. & Gard.* 320 Testaceous and Crustaceous Fish. **1873** J. G. Bartram *Harvest of Sea* (ed. 3) 300 Old men..setting lobster-pots, doing business in the crustaceous delicacies of the season.

b. Crab-like; like a crustacean.

1842 *Blackw. Mag.* LI. 377 Retiring in a crustaceous or crab-like manner from the Court. **1864** Lowell *Fireside Trav.* 205 Thy poor crustaceous efforts at self-isolation.

Hence **cruˈstaceousness.**

1727 Bailey vol. II, *Crustaceousness*, hardness, like, or being covered with a Shell, as Shell-fish. **1755** in Johnson.

†**cruˈstade.** *Obs.* Also crustate, -arde: see also custard. [Evidently a. F. *croustade*, although this is not given by Godefroy, and is known to Hatzfeld only as a modern word after It. *crostata* 'a kinde of daintie pye, chewet, or such paste meate' (Florio), f. *crostare* to encrust: see -ade.]

A sort of rich pie, made of flesh, eggs, herbs, spices, etc. enclosed in a crust.

? *c* **1390** *Form of Cury* No. 154 Crustardes of Flessh. *ibid.* No. 156 Crustardes of Fysshe. *c* **1420** *Liber Cocorum* 40 Crustate of flesshe. *c* **1440** *Anc. Cookery* in *Househ. Ord.* (1790) 452 Let bake hom as thow woldes bake flaunes, or crustades.

crustal (ˈkrʌstəl), *a.* [f. L. *crusta* + -al^{1}.] Of or pertaining to a crust; consisting of crust; esp. of the crust of the earth or moon.

1860 Worcester cites *N. Brit. Rev.* **1883** A. Winchell *World-Life* (1889) ii. iii. 402 The addition of crustal layers upon the exterior [of the moon]. **1892** C. Lapworth in *Proc. Geogr. Soc.* 697 The many twisting crustal septa of the earth. **1912** [see batholith]. **1924** J. G. A. Skerl tr. *Wegener's Orig. Cont. & Oceans* 14 An explanation of mountain building must take into account immense tangential crustal movements. **1958** *New Scientist* 23 Oct. 1099/2 This boundary or discontinuity between the surface crustal rocks and the mantle. **1970** *Nature* 28 Feb. 845/2 Crustal earthquakes may be caused by what is effectively a gravitational loading of the crust.

crustaˈlogical, cruˈstalogist, crustalogy, synonyms of crustaceological, etc.

Proposed by Webster (1828), and in later Dicts.

crustate (ˈkrʌsteɪt), *a.* [ad. L. *crustāt-us* crusted, incrusted; applied by Pliny to crustacea.] Crusted; crustaceous.

1661 Lovell *Hist. Anim. & Min.* Introd., Exanguine aquaticks, which are either soft, as the Polypus..or Crustate ..as the Lobster. **1882** *Syd. Soc. Lex.*, *Crustate*, having an outer hard rind or shell.

crustated (ˈkrʌsteɪtɪd), *ppl. a.* [f. as prec. + -ed.] Covered with a crust; encrusted.

1780 Von Troil *Iceland* 342 Icelandic springs..the crustated stones formed in them.

crustation (krʌˈsteɪʃən). [n. of action f. L. *crustāre* to crust: see -ation.] The formation of a crust; an incrustation.

1620-55 I. Jones *Stone-Heng* (1725) 25 These, having through long Time, got the very same Crustation upon them. **1698** Keill *Exam. Th. Earth* (1734) 235 The Abyss was enclos'd by a thick Crustation, in which were all the Materials of Earth, Sand, Clay, Gravel [etc.]. **1870** *Eng. Mechanic* 21 Jan. 463/1 To attempt to remove crustations.

crusted (ˈkrʌstɪd), *ppl. a.* [f. crust *sb.* and *v.* + -ed.] Having or covered with a crust, encrusted; †crustaceous (*obs.*); that has deposited a crust, as old port or other wine.

1382 Wyclif *Ex.* xxix. 23 A crustid cake spreynde with oyle. **1579-80** North *Plutarch* (1676) 24 Entring upon the crusted mud, and sinking withall. **1610** Guillim *Heraldry* iii. xxiii. (1611) 170 The Crusted sort of Fishes..viz. Crabs, Lobsters, Creuises, Cuttles, Razers, Shrimpes, &c. **1665** Hooke *Microgr.* 196 The pretty Insect was covered all over with a crusted shell. *a* **1745** Swift *Direct. Servants, Butler*, Musty, or very foul and crusted bottles. **1873** *Forest & Stream* I. 90/2 The crusted snow-drifts. *Mod.* Fine old crusted port.

b. *fig.* (from crusted wine): Antiquated, 'venerable'; often with admixture of the notion 'covered with a crust of prejudice, etc.' *humorous.* Hence **ˈcrustedly** *adv.*

1831 Lytton *Godolphin* vii, His own crusted urbanity and scheming perseverance. **1884** *19th Cent.* Feb. 230 England ..cherishes a fine old crusted abuse as much as it does its port. **1888** *Pall Mall G.* 28 Nov. 4/1 The lengths to which good old crusted bigotry can go.

ˈcruster. *U.S.* and *Canada.* = crust-hunter: see crust *v.* 4, and cf. crusting *vbl. sb.* 2.

188. *Forest & Stream* (quoted in *Cent. Dict.*).

ˈcrust-hunt, *v. U.S.* and *Canada.* [f. crust + hunt *v.*, after *crust-hunter, crust-hunting*, in which *crust-* is in locative relation to the sbs., as in *plain-dweller, sea-faring*, etc.] *intr.* To hunt deer or other large game on the snow, when covered with a frozen crust strong enough to bear the hunter, but not to support the game, which sink in and are easily run down. So **ˈcrust-hunter, ˈcrust-hunting.**

1885 *Forest & Stream* XXIV. 425 Advocates of January crust-hunting. **1888** *Ibid.* XXX. 47/1 Thus eluding..the.. crust-hunters as well as the hound. **1889** *Cent. Dict.*, *Cruster*, one who crust-hunts for game.

crustific (krʌˈstɪfɪk), *a. rare*$^{-0}$.

1727 Bailey vol. II, *Crustifick*, that bringeth a Crust or Skin. Hence in mod. Dicts.

crustily (ˈkrʌstɪlɪ), *adv.* Also 6 crustely. [f. crusty + -ly^{2}.] †**a.** After the manner of, or as a crust (*obs.*). **b.** In a 'crusty' manner; crabbedly, snappishly (*colloq.*).

1578 Banister *Hist. Man.* i. 20 A Cartilage, crustely coueryng either side. **1730-6** Bailey (folio), *Crustily*, peevishly. **1749** Mrs. R. Goadby *Carew* (ed. 2) 229 The Parson..very crustily told him, He had lost his Dog. **1840** Hood *Up the Rhine* 5 [He] asked..rather crustily if he could name a single instance [etc.].

crustiness (ˈkrʌstɪnɪs). [f. as prec. + -ness.]

1. The quality or condition of being crusty. *concr.* a crusty formation, incrustation.

1607 *Topsell Serpents* (1653) 661 Their..quality is to burn the body..and to bring a hard scale or crustinesse upon any part. **1665** MANLEY *Grotius' Low-C. Warres* 269 The upper Crustiness of the Turf was so hardned..that it would endure a few to go over it. *c* **1720** W. GIBSON *Farriers Dispens.* xiv. (1734) 275 They leave such a hardness and crustiness that the part is very apt to..break out into fresh sores.

2. *fig.* Crabbed curtness of manner or temper.
1727 BAILEY vol. II, *Crustiness*..pettishness of Temper. **1822** W. IRVING *Braceb. Hall* (1845) 95 Old Christy forgot his usual crustiness. **1839–40** —— *Wolfert's R.* (1855) 147 An old English gentleman, of great probity, some understanding, and very considerable crustiness.

crusting (ˈkrʌstɪŋ), *vbl. sb.* [f. CRUST *v.* (and *sb.*) + -ING[1].]
1. The action of the verb CRUST; formation of a crust; *concr.* a crust formed, an incrustation.
1398 TREVISA *Barth De P.R.* VII. lix. (1495) 273 Paaste in an ouen..receyueth a maner croustyng in the vtter syde vnder the whiche crouste the paaste is nesshe. **1820** *Blackw. Mag.* VI. 548 The..department in this factitious wine trade, called crusting, consists in lining the interior surface of empty wine-bottles..with a red crust of super-tartarate of potash. **1853** KANE *Grinnell Exp.* xxx. (1856) 261 Put out your tongue, and it instantly freezes to this icy crusting.
2. *U.S.* = CRUST-HUNTING: see CRUST *v.* 4.
1860 GOSSE *Rom. Nat. Hist.* 207 Deer are taken extensively by a process called 'crusting'; that is, pursuing them, after a night's rain followed by frost has formed a crusty ice upon the surface of the deep snow. **1888** *Forest & Stream* XXX. 165/1 A crust sufficiently strong for moose and deer crusting.

ˈcrusting. *ppl. a.* [f. CRUST *v.* + -ING[2].] That crusts or forms a crust; encrusting.
1867 JEAN INGELOW *Story Doom* III. 72 A coverlet made stiff with crusting gems.

†**ˈcrustive,** *a. Obs.* [f. CRUST *v.* + -IVE.] Producing a 'crust' or eschar, escharotic.
1607 TOPSELL *Four-f. Beasts* 429 Medicines..called 'Escharotica', that is to say crustive: which be hot in the fourth degree, and do breed a crust and scarre. **1610** MARKHAM *Masterp.* II. clvi. 461 Medicines to be crustiue.

crustless (ˈkrʌstlɪs), *a.* [See -LESS.] Made without a crust; with the crust removed.
1927 *Daily Tel.* 11 May 18/3 (Advt.), Cheese factory (outside trust), of reputed 'Matterhorne' Gruyere (crustless), also in loaves, desires connection. **1971** *Ibid.* 21 Oct. 17/4 Pass the crustless bread pieces through one small egg beaten up with 4 fl. oz. milk.

cruˈstose, *a.* [ad. L. *crustōs-us*: see next.] Of the nature of a crust; crustaceous; esp. designating a lichen having a thin, closely adhering thallus (now more common than *crustaceous* in this sense).
1879 W. A. LEIGHTON *Lichen-flora of Gt. Brit.* (ed. 3) 509 Crustose, forming a crust. **1882** *Syd. Soc. Lex.*, *Crustose*, thick-skinned. Applied to certain mushrooms which form laminæ like crusts. **1938** G. M. SMITH *Cryptogamic Bot.* I. xv. 515 These lichens are always crustose and with the thallus forming an incrustation that adheres closely to the substratum. **1959** *New Scientist* 5 Feb. 294/1 In a crustose lichen there is an upper cortex and a rather poorly defined gonidial layer of algal cells. **1967** M. E. HALE *Biol. Lichens* i. 10 Lichens are traditionally classified into three growth forms: crustose, foliose and fruticose.

†**ˈcrustous,** *a. Obs.* [a. OF. *crousteus*, mod. F. *croûteux*, ad. L. *crustōs-us* (Pliny), f. *crusta* CRUST.] Of the nature of a crust or scab; crusty.
c **1400** *Lanfranc's Cirurg.* 350 Rotid fleisch & crustous. **1651** BIGGS *New Disp.* ¶238 Before the crustous eschar be taken away.

crusty (ˈkrʌstɪ), *a.* [f. CRUST *sb.* + -Y.]
1. Of the nature of a crust; hard like a crust; characterized by having a crust. *spec.* **a.** Scabby; †**b.** Crustaceous (*obs.*); **c.** Crusted (of wine).
c **1400** *Lanfranc's Cirurg.* 186 If þe mater be fleumatik..& if þe skyn be crusty. **1577** tr. *Bullinger's Decades* (1592) 369 An handfull of corne..or else of crustie breade sodden in a caldron. **1600** HAKLUYT *Voy.* III. 274 (R.) A kinde of crusty shel-fish..hauing a crusty taile. **1666** J. SMITH *Old Age* 173 (T.) The dry, solid, tensile, hard, and crusty parts of the body. **1713** DERHAM *Phys. Theol.* (J.), The egg..its parts within, and its crusty coat without. **1830** MISS MITFORD *Village* Ser. IV. (1863) 136 His loaves, which are crusty, and his temper, which is not. **1853** KANE *Grinnell Exp.* xxviii. (1856) 229 Snow, recent and sufficiently crusty to bear you five paces and let you through the sixth. **1866** *Possibilities of Creation* 77 Good old crusty port.
2. *fig.* Of persons (or their dispositions, etc.): Short of temper; harshly curt in manner or speech: the opposite of suave or affable.
c **1570** PRESTON *Cambyses* in Hazl. *Dodsley* IV. 184 Master Ruff, are ye so crusty? **1598** LYLY *Moth. Bomb.* II. iv, You need not bee crustie, you are not so hard backt. **1606** SHAKS. *Tr. & Cr.* V. i. 5 *Enter Thersites. Achil.* Thou crusty batch of Nature, what's the newes? **1764** FOOTE *Mayor of G.* I. Wks. 1799 I. 174 Come, come, man; don't be so crusty. **1857** MRS. GASKELL *C. Brontë* (1860) 12 A stranger can hardly ask a question without receiving some crusty reply.
†**b.** *fig.* Hardened, stubborn. *Obs.*
1651–3 JER. TAYLOR *Serm. for Year* I. xii. 153 Hardned not by cold, but made crusty and stubborn, by the warmth of the divine fire.

crusulé, -uly, obs. ff. CRUSILY.

†**crusy,** *a. Obs. rare.* [ad. F. *creusé* hollowed.] Concave.
1625 LISLE *Du Bartas* 151 It is concave and convex,..inbent and out-bent, or crusye and bulked.

crut[1]. *Coal-mining.* A roadway driven from the shaft across strata of rock, shale, or other 'waste', to reach a seam of coal. Chiefly used in the Staffordshire coal-field.
1665 D. DUDLEY *Metallum Martis* (1854) 27 The Colliers getting the nethermost part of the Coles first..when they have wrought the Crutes or Staules, (as some Colliers call them) as broad and as far in under the ground, as they think fit [etc.]. **1884** *Pall Mall G.* 26 Aug. 10/1 The defendant was engaged..in the driving of what is technically known as the crut, and was seen to take off the top of his safety lamp and light his pipe.

crut[2]. [? ad. F. *croûte* crust.] The rough part of oak bark.
1847 in CRAIG and mod. Dicts.

crut[3] (krʌt). *U.S. slang.* = CRUD 2 a (in quot. 1940 = excrement). So **ˈcrutting** *a.*, = CRUDDY *a.* 2.
1925 HEMINGWAY *In our Time* (ed. 2) 66 That son of a crutting brakeman. **1937** —— *To have & have Not* III. vii. 130 You miserable little crut. **1940** —— *For whom Bell Tolls* xi. 150 We can eat goat crut in Gredos. **1955** J. P. DONLEAVY *Ginger Man* (1957) viii. 63 Two years in Ireland, shrunken teat on the chest of the cold Atlantic. Land of crut.

crut, var. of CROOT, a dwarf.

crutch (krʌtʃ), *sb.* Forms: 1 crycc(e, 3–5 crucche (ü), 5–6 **cruche, crutche,** 7– **crutch**; *β.* 6 crooch(e, 6– crotch; *γ.* 5–6 crouche, crowch(e, 6 croutch, 6–7 crouch. [OE. *crycc*, (acc. *crycce*) fem., a common Teutonic word = *OLG. *krukkja* (whence MDu. *crucke*, Du. *kruk*, MLG. *krucke, krocke*, LG. *krukke, krück*), OHG. *chruckja, chrucha* (MHG. *kruche, krucke*, Ger. *krücke*), ON. *krykkja* (Norw. *krykkja*, OSw. *krykkia*, Da. *krykke*):—OTeut. *krukjâ-, krukjôn-* f. ablaut stem *kruk-* of *kreuk-* to bend. The ME. change of *y* (y) to *ŭ*, is found also in *clutch, much, trust.* The phonology of the variants is obscure.
For the *crotch* form, cf. CROTCH, as a separate word. *Cruche* may be merely a variant spelling, but it also occurs as a variant of CROCHE *sb.* q.v. *Crooch(e* may belong to *crotch* or to *crouch*: the latter was perh. influenced in form by CROUCH *v.*, but it may represent an early lengthening of the *u* in *cruche, crucche,* with later diphthongization.]
1. a. A staff for a lame or infirm person to lean upon in walking; now a staff with a cross-piece at the top to fit under the armpit (usually ***a pair of crutches***).
c **900** *Bæda's Hist.* IV. xxx[i]. (1891) 380 Mid his crycce hine wreðiȝende. *c* **1205** LAY. 19482 Vder þe lome mon..he wænde mid his crucche us adun þrucche. *c* **1430** *Hymns Virg.* (1867) 81 þan wole no þing us availe but oure bedis and our crucche [*rime* myche]. *c* **1440** *Sir Gowther* 673 We make ..Crokyd here cruches for-sake. **1570** LEVINS *Manip.* 182 A crutche, *grallus.* **1599** SHAKS. *Much Ado* II. i. 373 Time goes on crutches, till Loue haue all his rites. **1684** BUNYAN *Pilgr.* II. 161 He could not Dance without one Crutch in his Hand. **1709** ADDISON *Tatler* No. 103 ¶11, I..gave him a new Pair of Crutches. **1805** *Med. Jrnl.* XIV. 30 He could walk with great ease, and without crutches. **1866** R. M. BALLANTYNE *Shift. Winds* xvi. (1181) 165 He walked with a crutch.
β. **1530** PALSGR. 211/1 Crotche for a lame man, *potence.* **1573** TUSSER *Husb.* lx. (1878) 138 Mans age deuided here ye haue..The next [seven yeers: 71–77], get chaire and crotches to stay.
γ. *c* **1440** *York Myst.* xxv. 376 My man, ryse and caste þe cruchys gode space. —— 380 Lorde! lo, my crouchis whare þei flee. **1582** MUNDAY *Eng. Rom. Life* in *Harl. Misc.* (Malh.) II. 196 Some of them [had] bound up their legs and went on croutches. **1592** SHAKS. *Rom. & Jul.* I. i. 83 (Qo. 1599) A crowch [*Fo.* crutch], a crowch, why call you for a sword? **1611** FLORIO, *Grúccia*..a lame mans crouch or crutchet.
b. *transf.* as the symbol of old age.
1588 SHAKS. *L.L.L.* IV. iii. 245 And giues the Crutch the Cradles infancie. *a* **1592** GREENE & LODGE *Looking Glasse* (1861) 119 From cradle to the crutch.
c. *fig.* A prop, a support.
1602 MARSTON *Antonio's Rev.* Prol. Wks. 1856 I. 72 Your favour will give crutches to our faults. **1606** SHAKS. *Tr. & Cr.* V. iii. 60 Hold him fast: He is thy crutch. **1728** YOUNG *Love Fame* IV. (1757) 115 Who'd be a crutch to prop a rotten peer. **1865** TYLOR *Early Hist. Man.* v. 99 The Egyptians were later..in throwing off the crutches of picture signs.
β. **1581** J. BELL *Haddon's Answ. Osor.* 130 Of what force therfore can this your wyndeshaken crooche be.. whereupon your lame cripled workes do rest? *Ibid.* 230 Osorius underproppeth his Freewill here, with this crooch.
γ. **1635** N. CARPENTER *Geog. Del.* I. iii. 54 This opinion is very feeble, and cannot goe without crouches. **1661** MORGAN *Sph. Gentry* II. vii. 73 He is Potent Counterpotent by the Crouches of providence.
2. A support or prop, with a forked or concave top, for various uses: cf. CROTCH 3.
1645 *Enchirid. Fortif.* 52 The crutches, or forks, against which the arms of each company are set. **1670** EACHARD *Cont. Clergy* 91 Though his house stands not upon crutches. **1703** MAUNDRELL *Journ. Jerus.* (1732) 28 On each hand of every seat were placed Crutches..for the Priest to lean upon. **1772–84** COOK *Voy.* (1790) VI. 2169 The hunters fix their crutches in the ground, on which they rest their firelocks. **1892** GARDINER *Student's Hist. Eng.* 527 Soldier with musket and crutch: from a broadside printed about 1630.

3. Of a saddle: †**a.** Formerly, the raised part in front and at the back of the saddle. *Obs.*
1617 MARKHAM *Caval.* IV. 48 The Garthweb which holdes vp his Tramels behinde the hinder croutch of his Saddle. **1663** BLAIR *Autobiog.* vii. (1848) 93, I was forced to stoop and lie on the very curche of the saddle. **1689** *Depos. Cast. York* (Surtees) 290 And..he could not hold up his head, but it hung below the sadle crutch on the farr side.
b. In modern use: The front of the tree which is made to fork down on each side of the shoulder, and which supports the pommel. Also a forked rest for the leg in a side-saddle.
1874 in KNIGHT *Dict. Mech.*
4. *Naut.* **a.** Applied to various contrivances of a forked shape in a ship or boat, *e.g.* a forked support (of wood or iron) for a boom, mast, spar, etc., when not in use (also called *crotch*); a forked rowlock.
1769 FALCONER *Dict. Marine, Chandeliers de chaloupe*, the crutches of a boat, which sustain the main-boom, or the mast and sail, when they are lowered. **1791** COWPER *Iliad* I. 537 Lowering swift the mast Into its crutch. **1825** H. B. GASCOIGNE *Nav. Fame* 58 The Spanker-Boom then to the Crutch they bear. **1869** F. W. BENNETT *Leaves from Log* 127 One of the men in beaching her lost his brass crutch (rowlock) overboard.
β. **1769** FALCONER *Dict. Marine, Crotches*..are fixed in different places of the ship..to support the spare-masts, yards, &c. **1799** *Naval Chron.* II. 238 A bolt must be fixed in each crotch. **1867** SMYTH *Sailor's Word-bk.*, *Crutch* or *crotch*..stanchions of wood or iron, whose upper parts are forked to receive masts, yards, and other spars, and which are fixed along the sides of gang ways. Crutches are used instead of rowlocks.
b. Crooked timbers (or iron bands replacing them) fitted horizontally inside a vessel at the after end, and bolted to the stern post and the vessel's sides, to give additional strength to the connexion of these parts. They correspond to the *breast-hooks* at the fore-end.
1769 FALCONER *Dict. Marine, Crotches*, a name given to those crooked timbers that are placed upon the keel in the fore and hind parts of a ship, upon which the frame of her hull grows narrower below, as it approaches the stem afore, and the stern post abaft. *c* **1860** H. STUART *Seaman's Catech.* 68 What are the crutches?.. Iron bands which unite the sides of the ship at the stern.
5. In a clock: The fork at the end of the arm which depends from the axis of the anchor-escapement, and receives the pendulum rod between its arms.
1752 ELLICOTT in *Phil. Trans.* XLVII. 490 The pendulum is moved by a piece of steel (call'd the crutch) rivited to one end of the arbor. **1874** KNIGHT *Dict. Mech.* s.v., The pendulum-rod is contained within the limbs of the crutch.
6. a. A handle consisting of a cross-bar like the head of a crutch.
1831 J. HOLLAND *Manuf. Metal* I. 141 The shafts [of the spade, with]..the crutch or open handle, according to preference. **1874** KNIGHT *Dict. Mech.*, *Crutch*..5. (*Founding.*) The cross-handle on the end of a shank (a founder's metal-ladle), by which it is tipped.
b. Chiefly *Austral.* and *N.Z.* (See quot. 1965.)
1916 *N.Z. Jrnl. Agric.* 20 Sept. 228 It is necessary to hold each lot of sheep in the bath for the time necessary to secure thorough immersion. This may be done..by the use of the crutch. **1953** B. STRONACH *Musterer on Molesworth* viii. 55 We had two men on the 'crutch' pushing the sheep's heads under, and seven men at the race. **1965** J. S. GUNN *Terminol. Shearing Industry* I. 18 *Crutch*, a mallet-shaped instrument (like a crutch) used to push sheep under in a swimming dip. Improved dips, especially spray dips, have caused this tool to become obsolete.
7. *Soap-boiling.* A staff with a perforated piece of wood or iron at the end, used to stir the ingredients.
1837 WHITTOCK *Bk. Trades* (1842) 409 A rotatory motion is given the crutch.
8. a. The 'fork' of the human body: see CROTCH 5; **b.** the angle between the two flukes of a whale's flapper or tail-fin.
1748 F. SMITH *Voy. Disc. N.W. Pass.* 163 The Stockings reach up to the Crutch. **1771** FRANKLIN *Autobiog.* (1881) I. 140, I clapped my hand under his crutch, and..pitched him head-foremost into the river. **1842** F. D. BENNETT *Whaling Voy.* II. 156 The tail-fin, or 'flukes'..each half overlaps the other at the central notch, or 'crutch'. **1844** *Regul. & Ord. Army* 154 The Fly to extend from top to within $3\frac{1}{2}$ inches above point of Crutch.
9. *Comb.*, as ***crutch-like*** adj.; **crutch-boots,** tall sea boots; **crutch-cane,** see *crutch-stick*; **crutch-handled** *a.*, having a transverse handle like the head of a crutch; so **crutch-headed** *a.*; **crutch-hole,** a hole to receive a crutch or movable rowlock; **crutch-pin,** the pin of a pendulum crutch; **crutch-stick,** a crutch-handled stick; **crutch-tail**: see CROTCH 8.
1889 P. H. EMERSON *Eng. Idylls* 118, I went down in the cabin, and pulled off my *crutch-boots. **1847** LYTTON *Lucretia* I. i, With a gold-headed *crutch-cane. **1864** H. AINSWORTH *John Law* Prol. iii. (1881) 19 He carried a *crutch-handled cane. **1767** *Babler* I. 113, I..threw by my *crutch headed stick. **1875** BEDFORD *Sailor's Pock. Bk.* vi. (ed. 2) 229 Boats..fitted with a *crutch hole on each quarter where an oar could be worked to assist the rudder. **1772** WOLLASTON in *Phil. Trans.* LXIII. 77 The bottom of the stem, instead of receiving the *crutch-pin, is turned sideways. **1780** in Hone *Every-day Bk.* II. 1478 Walks with a short *crutch stick with an ivory head.

crutch (krʌtʃ), *v.*[1] [f. prec.]

1. a. *trans.* To support as with a crutch or crutches, to prop.

1681 Dryden *Abs. & Achit.* II. 409 Two fools that crutch their feeble sense on verse. **1833** D'Israeli in *New Monthly Mag.* XXXVII. 432 The genius of Moliere..in its first attempts..did not move alone; it was crutched by imitation. **1890** Caine in *Pall Mall G.* 28 June 5/2 This sickly Government, crutched by Lord Hartington and Mr. Chamberlain.

b. with *up*: To prop up, sustain.

1642 R. Carpenter *Experience* II. viii. 193 Howsoever they crutch it up handsomly. **1816** Scott *Old Mort.* Concl., A history, growing already vapid, is but dully crutched up by a detail of circumstances which every reader must have anticipated. **1861** Thornbury *Turner* I. 106 Old crippled buildings..crutched up with posts and logs.

2. *intr.* To go on crutches, to limp. (Also, *to crutch it.*)

1828 J. Wilson in *Blackw. Mag.* XXIII. 810 Up and down..the various steps..do we delight to crutch it. **1847** *Tait's Mag.* XIV. 291 The most apparent 'dodge' on which a statesman ever 'crutched' round a corner.

3. *trans. Soap-boiling.* To stir with a crutch.

1837 Whittock *Bk. Trades* (1842) 410 What the new crutching wheels..will cost..we have no present means of stating.

4. To push (a sheep) into a dip with a crutch (see crutch *sb.* 6 b). Chiefly *Austral.* and *N.Z.*

1886 C. Scott *Sheep-Farming* 135 The hot water tank into which the sheep are put next morning has three divisions, in each of which they are well crutched. **1940** E. C. Studholme *Te Waimate* (1954) xiii. 117 One day whilst trying to 'crutch' (push under) some slippery-backed old ewe..Geoffrey fell in.

5. To cut off the wool or hair from the hind-quarters of (a sheep, dog, etc.). Chiefly *Austral.* and *N.Z.*

1915 J. R. Macdonald *N.Z. Sheepfarming* xxv. 68 If crutching is followed, any wool that might hinder the lambs from sucking may be clipped. **1920** *N.Z. Jrnl. Agric.* 20 July 8 The keeping-lambs are crutched, branded, dipped, and placed out. **1942** R. B. Kelley *Animal Breeding* vii. 76 We find it advantageous also to 'crutch' long-coated bitches. **1946** F. Davison *Dusty* vi. 65 Blowfly season was drawing near. Morrison and Tom were crutching the sheep, cutting away the soiled wool from under their tails, where they would be most likely to be blown.

Hence **ˈcrutching** *vbl. sb.* (also *attrib.*).

1837 [see sense 3]. **1915** [see sense 5]. **1933** L. G. D. Acland in *Press* (Christchurch) 7 Oct. 15/7 When sheep are dipped, they are shoved under with a thing like an inverted crutch. This is called crutching. **1941** *Nature* 5 Apr. 421/2 'Crutching'..consists of shearing the wool away from the area around the tail so that this part keeps clean. **1953** O. E. Middleton in C. K. Stead *N.Z. Short Stories* (1966) 189 But aside from shearing and crutching times, life was good at the station.

†**crutch,** *v.*[2] *Obs.* Misprint or error for cratch, to scratch.

1481 Caxton *Reynard* viii. (Arb.) 15 Bruyn..crutched [Flem. *crassede*] with the hynder feet.

crutch-back: see crouchback.

crutched (ˈkrʌtʃɪd), *ppl. a.*[1] Formerly **crouched.** [f. ME. crouch *sb.*[1] cross, *crouchen*, crouch *v.*[2] to sign with the cross, to cross. The original long *ū* has been shortened before the consonant group: cf. *Dutch*, formerly *Douch.*]

Having or bearing a cross. ***Crutched*** or ***Crouched*** (also *Crossed*) ***Friars*** (*Fratres cruciferi* or *Sanctæ Crucis*): a minor order of friars so called from their bearing or wearing a cross.

According to Hospinianus (*de Orig. Monach.* v. xv. (1609) 163) they were bound to a rule in 1169; but they first appeared in England in 1244, their rule having been 'confirmed' by Pope Innocent IV in 1243. They then bore a cross upon the top of their staves, but subsequently wore a cross of scarlet cloth on the breast of their habit, which Pope Pius II in 1460 appointed to be blue. They were suppressed in 1656. See Newcourt *Repertorium* (1708) I. 328.

[*a* **1259** Matt. Paris *Chron.* anno 1244 Fratres dicti cruciferi, dicti sic, quia cruces in baculis efferebant. **1494** Fabyan *Chron.* VII. 297 In the Towre warde. An howse of crossed freres. **1530** Palsgr. 211/1 Crossed frere, *frere de Saincte-Croix.*] **1570-6** Lambarde *Peramb. Kent* (1862) 299 This suppressed house of crouched Friars at Motindene. **1628** L. Owen *Unmask. Monks* 23 Of the Cruciferi, or Crucigeri, or the Cruched Friers. **1688** R. Holme *Armoury* III. 191/1 Cruciferians..of the vulgar called Cruched Friers ..came into England in the year 1244. **1807** Sir R. Colt Hoare *Tour in Ireland* 270 A Priory..erected in the thirteenth century for Crossbearers, or Crouched Friars.

b. The quarters of this order; hence, the part of a town where their convent formerly existed.

1556 *Chron. Gr. Friars* (Camden) 39 Hys boddy buryd at the Crost Freeres in the qwere. **1666** Pepys *Diary* 6 June, Going through Crouched Friars. **1875** Ure *Dict. Arts.* II. 645 The window-glass manufacture was first begun in England in 1557, in Crutched Friars, London.

crutched (krʌtʃt, -ɪd), *ppl. a.*[2] [f. crutch *sb.* or *v.* + -ed.]

1. Furnished with a crutch, or a handle like the head of a crutch.

1707 E. Ward *Hud. Rediv.* I. xv, A leaning on a Crutched Staff. **1862** Sala *Seven Sons* III. ii. 29 An umbrella with a crutched handle.

2. Supported on a crutch or crutches: see the vb.

crutcher (ˈkrʌtʃə(r)). *Soap-boiling.* [f. crutch *v.* 3 + -er[1].] An apparatus in which the ingredients are stirred with a crutch.

1885 *Sci. American* 11 July 18 The soap is then pumped ..into a crutcher, nearly like a milk churn, where it is mixed thoroughly.

†**ˈcrutchet.** *Obs.* [dim. of crutch: cf. also crotchet[2].] = crutch 1.

1611 Florio, *Gruccia*..a lame mans crouch or crutchet.

crutlins: see cratling.

cruve, cruwel(l, obs. ff. cruive, cruel.

crux (krʌks). [L.: see cross.]

‖**1.** = cross, in heraldic and other expressions. *crux ansata* = tau 2 b (see quot. 1930).

1841 J. G. Wilkinson *Manners & Customs Anc. Egyptians* 2nd Ser. I. xiii. 341 The sign of life (or *crux ansata*) was compelled to submit to the unintelligible name of 'Key of the Nile'. **1896** [see ankh]. **1930** E. A. W. Budge *Amulets & Superstitions* xviii. 340 It is wrong, too, to call the sign ☥, *crux ansata*, the 'handled cross', for whatever object the hieroglyph may represent, it was certainly not a cross or anything like it.

‖**2.** *Astron.* The constellation of the Southern Cross.

1837 *Penny Cycl.* VIII. 198 *Crux*, a southern constellation formed out of Halley's observations by Augustine Royer in his maps published in 1679. **1870** Proctor *Other Worlds* xi. 253 There is in the constellation *Crux*, a pear-shaped vacuity of considerable size.

3. *fig.* **a.** A difficulty which it torments or troubles one greatly to interpret or explain, a thing that puzzles the ingenuity; as 'a textual crux'. Cf. crucify *v.* 2 c. (Used by Sheridan and Swift with the sense 'conundrum, riddle'.)

[Cf. G. *kreuz*, Grimm, 2178 g, (quoted from Herder 1778, and Niebuhr); according to Hildebrand taken from the scholastic Latin *crux interpretum*, etc.]

1718 Sheridan *To Swift* Wks. 1814 XV. 56 Dear dean, since in cruxes and puns you and I deal, Pray, Why is a woman a sieve and a riddle? —— Swift *To Sheridan* Ibid. 61 As for your new rebus, or riddle, or crux, I will either explain, or repay it in trucks. **1830** Sir W. Hamilton *Philos. Perception* Disc. (1852) 69 *note*, Ideas have been the *crux philosophorum*, since Aristotle sent them packing to the present day. **1859** Maurice *What is Revelation* 70 To look upon them as mere cruxes and trivialities which may be left to critics. **1875** Jowett *Plato* (ed. 2) IV. 401 The unity of opposites was the crux of ancient thinkers in the age of Plato. **1888** Dowden in *19th Cent.* XLIII. 336 The consideration of a textual crux in itself sharpens the wits.

b. The chief problem; the central or decisive point of interest.

1888 *Law Times* LXXXIV. 293/2 There remained the point, which was the *crux* of the case, whether the defendant was under any duty towards the plaintiff. **1934** R. Benedict *Patterns of Culture* vii. 232 The crux of the matter is that the behaviour under consideration must pass through the needle's eye of social acceptance. **1944** J. S. Huxley *On Living in Rev.* 179 Culture, not 'race', is, again, the crux of the American problem. **1971** *Sunday Times* 31 Jan. 12/1 The crux, however, is accommodation. This is now widely agreed to be the main determinant of university and polytechnic expansion.

4. *Comb.* †**crux-herrings,** herrings caught after the festival of the Exaltation of the Cross (Sept. 14).

1641 S. Smith *Herringbusse Trade* 7 There are also a sort of Herrings called Crux-Herrings, beginning the 14 of Septemb. being the day noted *exal. Crucis*; these Herrings are made with salt upon salt, and are carefully sorted out. **1727-51** in Chambers *Cycl.*

cruyde, obs. f. curd.

cruysado, cruzada, -ado, obs. ff. crusade, crusado.

[**cruyshage,** *sb.*[1] Error for Du. *cruyshaye*, a species of shark (Marcgraf *Hist. Rer. Nat. Brasil.*, 1648, 181) = *kruis* cross + *haai* shark.

1753 Chambers *Cycl. Supp.*, *Cruyshage*,..the name of a fish of the shark kind, somewhat approaching to that strange fish the zygæna: but much less monstrous, its head being only triangular, or something like the figure of an heart... *Marggrave* p. 132. **1828-32** Webster *Cruyshage*, a fish of the shark kind, having a triangular head and mouth. *Dict. Nat. Hist.* [Hence in 1864 Webster, and some later Dicts.]]

cruzeiro (krʊˈzɛərəʊ). [Pg., lit. 'a small cross'.] The principal monetary unit of Brazil, which superseded the milreis in 1942, = 100 centavos; also, a coin representing this.

[**1927** *Glasgow Herald* 30 Aug. 12 A decree of financial reform was promulgated providing for the stabilisation of exchange on the basis of a new monetary unit to be called the 'cruzeir'.] **1942** *Times* 8 Oct. 9/1 No date has yet been announced for the calling in of the note issue and the substitution of the new currency unit, the cruzeiro for the milreis. **1964** W. McCord in I. L. Horowitz *New Sociology* 427 She..earned a few cruzeiros a day. **1970** *Sci. Jrnl.* May 73/1 The cruzeiro is still far from being stabilized.

crwd, crwth: see crowd *sb.*[1]

crwet(t, crwme, obs. ff. cruet, crumb.

crwth (kru:θ). Also **cruth.** The Welsh form of crowd *sb.*[1]

1837 *Penny Cycl.* VIII. 198/1 *Cruth*, or *Crwth*, a musical instrument of the violin kind, formerly much used in Wales. **1880** [see crowd *sb.*[1]]. **1938** *Oxf. Compan. Mus.* 243/2 It is said that in remote parts of Wales a violin is still called a crwth. **1942** E. Blom *Mus. in Eng.* ii. 20 A crwth or rebec or bass viol player may have indulged boldly in a double stop. *a* **1953** Dylan Thomas *Under Milk Wood* (1954) 20 He intricately rhymes, to the music of crwth and pibgorn.

cry (kraɪ), *sb.* Pl. **cries.** Forms: 3-5 **cri**, 3- **cry.** Also 4-7 **crie, crye,** (4-5 **krie, krye**); *pl.* 4-7 **cryes.** [a. F. *cri* = Pr. Cat. *crit*, Sp. *grito*, It. *grido*, f. stem of *crier* (*cridar, gridare*) to cry.]

I. 1. a. The loud and chiefly inarticulate utterance of emotion; *esp.* of grief, pain, or terror.

c **1275** Lay. 11991 Nas neuere no man..þat i-horde þane cri [*c* **1205** þesne weop] hou hii gradde to þan halwes, þat his heorte ne mihte beo sori for þane deolfulle cri. **1297** R. Glouc. (1724) 139 The cry of þe folk þat me slow, þe oþere broȝte in drede. **1340** Hampole *Pr. Consc.* 478 By þat cry men knaw þan Whether it [the infant] be man or weman. **1393** Gower *Conf.* I. 115 With such weping and with such cry Forth..he goth. *c* **1440** *Ipomydon* 1951 The lady herde hym make suche crye. **1590** Spenser *F.Q.* I. iii. 23 With hollow houling, and lamenting cry. **1604** Shaks. *Oth.* v. i. 38 (Qo.) 'Tis some mischance; the cry is very direful. **1813** Scott *Rokeby* III. xxx, Their wail and their cry.

b. (with *a* and *pl.*). A shout or exclamation of pain, grief, terror, etc.; a scream, shriek, wail.

a **1300** *Cursor M.* 4393 (Cott.) Sco [Potiphar's wife] gaue a cri þat all moght here. *c* **1400** Maundev. (Roxb.) IV. 13 Scho turned agayne with a hidous crie. *a* **1533** Ld. Berners *Huon* lxvii. 231 He herde the cryes & wepynges that she made. **1605** Shaks. *Lear* II. iv. 43 He rais'd the house with loud and coward cries. **1771** Mrs. Griffith tr. *Viaud's Shipwreck* 25 A Dutchman..who had been..the loudest in his plaints and cries. **1840** Dickens *Old. C. Shop* lxxi, He dropped into his chair again, and..uttered a cry never to be forgotten. *c* **1850** *Arab. Nts.* 636 Those mournful cries, which women usually utter on the death of their husbands.

c. An exclamation expressive of any emotion.

1813 Shelley *Q. Mab* vii. 11 The insensate mob Uttered a cry of triumph. **1891** Barrett *Sin of Olga Z.* III. xlvii. 193 He drew her to him with a cry of joy.

d. in *Pathol.* (See quot. 1882.)

1843 Sir T. Watson *Lect. Physic* I. 630 The cry [in epilepsy]..is sometimes a husky groan, but generally a piercing and terrifying scream. **1882** *Syd. Soc. Lex.*, *Epileptic cry*, a peculiar discordant cry or yell occasionally uttered just before the respiration is arrested in an epileptic fit. *Hydrocephalic cry*, a sharp, plaintive cry uttered by a child suffering from hydrocephalus.

†**2. a.** Shouting, calling in a voice loud and uttered with effort. *Obs.*

a **1300** *Cursor M.* 16304 (Cott.) Foluand him wit cri. *c* **1380** *Sir Ferumb.* 5382 Þe Sarazynz after him prikede.. With noyse & eke with crye. *c* **1440** *Promp. Parv.* 102 Crye, *clamor, vociferacio.*

b. A shout, a loud and excited utterance.

c **1380** Wyclif *Sel. Wks.* I. 294 Þis crie is warnynge of aungels. **1568** Grafton *Chron.* II. 63 Altogether with one crie called him on every side Traytor. **1653** H. Cogan tr. *Pinto's Trav.* lviii. 228 Yet could they..neither with their cries, nor menaces, stop them all. **1839** T. Beale *Sperm Whale* 314 Canoes filled with natives..uttering loud cries, and appearing much excited. **1855** Macaulay *Hist. Eng.* IV. 771 The Ayes raised so loud a cry that it was believed that they were the majority.

c. The loud and excited utterance of words; the words as shouted.

1382 Wyclif. *Matt.* xxv. 6 Sothely at myd niȝt a cry was maad, Loo! the spouse cummeth. **1548** Hall *Chron.* 118 b, The people..cried: live king Henry, live king Henry. After whiche crie passed, the noble men..did to hym homage. **1605** Shaks. *Macb.* v. v. 2 The cry is still they come. **1783** *Gentl. Mag.* LIII. II. 822 A cry of Hear him! Hear him! **1837** Carlyle *Fr. Rev.* I. v. vi, There has been a cry every where; To the Bastille! **1839** T. Beale *Sperm Whale* 169 Hearing the loud cry of 'a man overboard'.

d. The united shouting with which seamen, etc. accompany their combined exertions.

c **1440** *Promp. Parv.* 102 Crye of schypmen, that ys clepyd haue howe (P. halowe). **1769** Falconer *Dict. Marine, Hola-ho*, a cry which answers to yoe-hoe. **1850** W. B. Clarke *Wreck of Favorite* 21 By the signal and well known cry—without which, apparently, no British tar..can haul a rope ..they united their strength.

3. An importunate call, a prayer, entreaty; an appeal for mercy, justice, etc.

a **1300** *Cursor M.* 4715 (Cott.) Bi for þe king þai com wit cri, And said, lauerd, þou ha merci. *a* **1300** *E.E. Psalter* ci. 2 Laverd, here þe bede of me, And mi krie mote come to þe. **1382** Wyclif *Prov.* xxi. 13 Who stoppeth his ere at the cri of the pore. **1597** Hooker *Eccl. Pol.* v. lxi. §4 The unresistible cries of suppliants calling upon you for mercy. **1649** Blithe *Eng. Improv. Impr.* (1652) 181 It is my constant cry to my own Husbandmen to take heed of Plough balking. **1704** Pope *Windsor For.* 85 Succeeding Monarchs heard the subjects cries. **1848** Macaulay *Hist. Eng.* I. 147 The cry of the whole people was for a free Parliament.

†**4.** A formal authoritative summons; a 'call'.

a **1300** *Havelok* 270 And forto hauen alle at his cri, At his wille, at his merci. *c* **1330** R. Brunne *Chron.* (1810) 279 Knyghtes, lordes of tounes, and alle com to his crie. *c* **1330** *Amis & Amil.* 207 Than hadde the douke..A douhti knight, at crie. **1483** Caxton *Gold. Leg.* 179/4 Thenne assemblyd alle the cyte of Luques at the crye of the fader.

†**5. a.** An announcement made in public in a loud voice; a proclamation. *Obs.* in general sense.

[**1292** Britton I. xxiii. §13 Qi qe face encountre la crye, qe il eyt la prisoun par un an et un jour.] **1303** R. Brunne *Handl. Synne* 906 Þan commaundede þey, and made a cry.. On satyrday shulde men noun ryngge. *c* **1350** *Will. Palerne* 2249 Wich a cri has he cried..þurch hest of þemperour. *a* **1400-50** *Alexander* 981 He makes a crie þat alle þe curte.. Suld put þaim in to presens. *a* **1502** in Arnolde *Chron.* (1811) 90 Ony man that hangith not out a lanterne..

acordyng to the Mayrs crye. *a* **1533** LD. BERNERS *Huon* liii. 181 Kyng yuoryn made a crye thorow all the cyte that euery man sholde be armed. **1837** SIR F. PALGRAVE *Merch. & Friar* iv. (1844) 139 A grave..personage read..the 'crye', which..announced the appointed meeting of the great Council of the realm.

†**b.** *pl.* The proclamation of banns of marriage; the 'askings'. *Obs.*

c **1315** SHOREHAM 71 Me schal maky the cryes At cherche oppe holy dayȝes thre.

c. The proclamation of wares to be sold in the streets; the words in which wares are cried, as ***London cries.***

1642 HOWELL *For. Trav.* (Arb.) 25 Let his Chamber be street ward to take in the common cry and Language, and [to] see how the Town is serv'd. **1762–71** H. WALPOLE *Vertue's Anecd. Paint.* (1786) III. 239 A book of fencing, the cries of London, and the procession at the coronation of William and Mary were designed by him. **1834** HT. MARTINEAU *Farrers* i. 3 The six o'clock cries are not all over. **1857** E. FITZGERALD *Lett.* (1889) I. 252 Some old Street cry, no doubt.

d. ***hue and cry***: see HUE.

†**6.** The mingled noise of people shouting; clamour, tumultuous noise, outcry. *Obs.*

c **1275** LAY. 27034 þane cry hii of horde of þan Romleode. *c* **1330** R. BRUNNE *Chron.* (1810) 244 þer was contek & crie. *Ibid.* 245 Men said þe wrath & cri com þorgh þe lord Tiptofte. *c* **1400** *Destr. Troy* 5915 Myche clamour & crye was kyde in þe ost. *c* **1440** *Promp. Parv.* 103 Crye, or grete noyse a-mong the peple, *tumultus.*

7. a. Rumour, public report.

1568 GRAFTON *Chron.* II. 340 A crye and noyes went through the Citie, how the king and the Maior were lyke to be slayne. **1604** SHAKS. *Oth.* IV. i. 127 Why, the cry goes, that you marry her. **1608** *Yorksh. Trag.* I. ix, *Knight*..Murder'd his children? *1st Gent.* So the cry goes. **1668** TEMPLE *Let. to Sir J. Temple* Wks. 1731 II. 122 For ought I can judge by the Cry of the Court, he wants it [money] more than I do. **1864** E. CAPERN *Devon Provinc., All the Cry*, the report, something generally talked of.

b. The public voice loudly uttered in approval, denunciation, etc.; the *vox populi.*

1628 EARLE *Microcosm., Vulgar-spirited Man* (Arb.) 70 One that followes meerely the common crye, and makes it louder by one. **1691–8** NORRIS *Pract. Disc.* 85 Vice will always have the Cry of her side. **1692** LOCKE *Toleration* III. ix, He that troubles not his Head at all about Religion, what other can so well suit him as the National: with which the Cry and Preferments go. **1768** W. GILPIN *Ess. Prints* 116 The cry, in his day, ran wholly in favour of antiquity. *a* **1842** ARNOLD *Later Rom. Commw.* (1846) I. iv. 120 The popular cry was loud against him.

8. A form of words in which popular opinion on any matter finds general utterance; an opinion very generally expressed.

1688 S. PENTON *Guardians Instr.* 68 The common Cry is, that it is time enough to learn their Books when they come to be seven or eight years old. **1713** STEELE *Englishman* No. 50. 323 Then the Cry would be, Images were put up for the common and ignorant People to worship. **1786** T. JEFFERSON *Writ.* (1859) II. 9 The general cry that our commerce was in distress. **1848** MACAULAY *Hist. Eng.* I. 387 A cry was..raised that the penny post was a Popish contrivance.

9. a. Something shouted to encourage and rally a party; a watchword; a war-cry, a battle-cry; a rallying cry. *lit.* and *fig.*

1548 HALL *Chron.* 138 b, The lord Talbot made a crye, as though he would assaile the gate. **1591** SHAKS. *1 Hen. VI*, II. i. 79 The Cry of *Talbot* serues me for a Sword. **1744** BERKELEY *Siris* §368 Truth is the cry of all, but the game of a few. **1850** *Tait's Mag.* XVII. 398/2 Their names are no longer 'a cry' and a test. **1883** *Manch. Exam.* 23 Nov. 5/1 A revived Islamism was one of the cries by which Arabi sought to inspire his countrymen.

b. *esp.* A political or electioneering watchword; a legislative proposal or scheme designed as a rallying cry for the members of a party in a contest.

1799 BURKE *Corr.* (1844) II. 264 It would be well if gentlemen, before they joined in a cry against any establishment, had well considered for what purpose that cry is raised. **1831** BREWSTER *Newton* (1855) II. xix. 218 The Tory election cry..was 'the Church in danger'. **1844** DISRAELI *Coningsby* II. i, 'It is a very good cry though, if there be no other' said Tadpole. **1884** GLADSTONE in *Standard* 29 Feb. 2/7 Redistribution is their favourite cry.

10. A fit of weeping: ***a good cry***, an energetic fit of weeping that relieves the feelings (*colloq.*).

1852 J. B. OWEN in Visc. Ingestre *Meliora* I. 138 She was not sure but a good cry would do herself good, too. **1890** *Eng. Illust. Mag.* Christmas No. 162 Mrs. Macdonald had her cry out.

11. The vocal utterance of animals; *esp.* the particular call of any animal.

c **1300** *K. Alis.* 5410 Sory foules..Cry hy hadden als a pecok. **1634** SIR T. HERBERT *Trav.* 213 The Bats..sqweake and call one the other, in most offensive cryes. **1694** *Acc. Sev. Late Voy.* II. (1711) 90 His Cry is like the Cry of some Ravens that I have..heard. **1771** MRS. GRIFFITH tr. *Viaud's Shipwreck* 151 The different species of animals were to be distinguished by their cries. **1841** JAMES *Brigand* iii, The distant cry of a wolf. **1877** C. C. ABBOTT *Waste-Land Wand.* vi. 170 The sora has a cry that is peculiar in its marked resemblance to the rattle of our green frog.

12. a. The yelping of hounds in the chase.

1535 R. LAYTON in *Lett. Supp. Monast.* (Camden Soc. 1843) 71 To kepe the dere within the woode, therby to have the better cry with his howndes. **1749** FIELDING *Tom Jones* XVIII. xiii, Sweeter music than the finest cry of dogs in England. **18..** WHITTIER *King Volmer & Elsie* iv, With cry of hounds and blare of hunter's horn.

b. Hence various phrases: e.g. ***to give cry***, ***to open upon the cry***; ***full cry***, full pursuit; also *fig.*

1589 R. HARVEY *Pl. Perc.* 6 Will you..run vpon a Christen body, with full cry and open mouth? **1649** FULLER *Just Man's Fun.* 13 Hear the whole kennel of Atheists come in with a full crie. **1684** R. H. *Sch. Recreat.* 16 Being in full Cry and main Chase, comfort and cheer them with Horn and Voice. **1710** PALMER *Proverbs* 53 He gives out this cue to his admirers, who are sure to open upon the cry 'till they are hoarse again. **1858** HAWTHORNE *Fr. & It. Jrnls.* II. 32 All offering their merchandise at full cry. **1891** *Rev. of Reviews* July 25 The journalists gave cry after the Prince, like a pack of hounds when they strike the trail of a fox.

13. *transf.* **a.** A pack of hounds.

1590 SHAKS. *Mids. N.* IV. i. 131 My hounds are bred out of the Spartan kinde..A cry more tuneable Was neuer..cheer'd with horne. **1601** YARINGTON *Two Lament. Traj.* III. ii. in Bullen *O. Pl.* IV, The little flocked hound..surer of his sent, Then any one in all the crie beside. **1611** COTGR., *Meute*, a kennell, or crie, of hounds. **1697** G. DAMPIER in *Phil. Trans.* XX. 51 A Gentleman's Cry of Dogs. **1890** *Daily News* 3 Nov. 5/3 With four packs of staghounds, sixteen of foxhounds..besides not a few of those small 'cries' of beagles, which afford such excellent sport in their way.

†**b.** *contemptuously.* A 'pack' (of people).

1602 SHAKS. *Ham.* III. ii. 289 Get me a Fellowship in a crie of Players. *a* **1658** CLEVELAND *London Lady* 35 A small Cry of Tenants.

14. The creaking, crackling noise emitted by some metals, *esp.* tin, when bent.

1882 *Nature* XXV. 374 The cry of tin is due to crystalline structure.

15. Combined with an *adv.*, as ***cry-out***, the act of crying out, exclamation, outcry.

1814 JANE AUSTEN *Mansf. Park* (1886). **1816** —— *Emma* I. viii, A general cry-out upon her extreme good luck. **1852** J. NUTT in Visc. Ingestre *Meliora* I. 199 The constant cry-out was that the filth came from their neighbours.

II. Phrases.

16. ***great*** (or ***much***) ***cry and little wool***: the proverbial outcome of shearing hogs; hence, much noise or fuss with small results, much ado about nothing. Also ***more cry than wool.***

c **1460–1809** [see WOOL *sb.* 1 g]. **1579** GOSSON *Sch. Abuse* (Arb.) 28 As one said at the shearing of hogs, great cry and litle wool, much adoe and smal help. **1625** HART *Anat. Ur.* II. x. 119 *Parturient montes, etc.*..Great cry and little wooll. **1684** T. GODDARD *Plato's Demon* 301 When there is a great cry, there is not always the more wooll. *a* **1893** *Mod. Sc.* Muckle cry an' little woo', As the deil said whan he shore the soo. **1952** V. W. BROOKS *Confident Years* xviii. 197 Her diary was much more cry than wool and Mary MacLane was a startling figure only because the times were so colourless and mild.

†**17.** ***out of*** (or ***without***) ***all cry***: **a.** beyond all cavil or dispute; to a certainty; certain; **b.** (also, ***out of cry***) beyond measure; to excess; desperately.

(Cf. *out of all ho, out of all whooping*, and see HO *sb.*)

1563 GOLDING *Cæsar* (1565) 77 As if the vyctory had bene theyr own out of al cry. **1569** TURBERV. *Poems*, In their countrey downe is rife, and feathers out of cry. **1583** GOLDING *Calvin on Deut.* xxvii. 163 The proofes were so notable as the matter ought to be out of all crie. **1589** NASHE *Martins Months minde* 36 The griefe whereof vext him out of all crie. **1594** *Taming of Shrew* C iv b, For Ile so cram me downe the tarts..out of all crie. **1598** R. BERNARD tr. *Terence* (1607) 54 *Misere hanc amat*, he loues her out a crie. **1598** CHAPMAN *Blind Beggar* Plays (1889) 4/2 Oh! Master, tis..without all cry. **1690** W. WALKER *Idiom. Anglo-Lat.* 125 You commend them out of all cry. **1875** LOWELL *Spenser* Wks. (1890) IV. 347 He sometimes 'hunted the letter', as it was called, out of all cry.

18. ***within cry of***: within calling distance. ***a far cry***: a long way, a very long distance.

1632 LITHGOW *Trav.* IX. (1682) 396 Villages and Houses..each one was within cry of another. **1819** SCOTT *Leg. Montrose* xii, One of the Campbells replied, 'It is a far cry to Lochow'; a proverbial expression of the tribe, meaning that their ancient hereditary domains lay beyond the reach of an invading enemy. **1850** *Tait's Mag.* XVII. 75/1 In those days it was a 'far cry' from Orkney to Holyrood; nevertheless the cry' at length penetrated the royal ear. **1885** *Athenæum* 18 Apr. 498/3 It is a far cry from the ascidian to bookbinding and blue china, yet it is a cry that can be achieved by Mr. Lang.

cry (kraɪ), *v.* Pa. t. and pple. cried (kraɪd). Forms: 3–5 crie-n, (3 creie-n), 4–7 crie, crye, 4– cry, (4 crei, crij, cri, criȝe, criy). *Pa. t.* 3–5 cryde, 4–5 criede, cryede, 4–7 cride, cryed, 4– cried, (4 crijd, crid, creid, 7 cri'd, 7–8 cry'd). [a. F. *crie-r* = Pr. and OSp. *cridar*, It. *gridare*, Sp. *gritar*:—L. *quirītāre* to raise a plaintive cry, to wail, scream, shriek out, cry aloud, bewail, lament, *orig.* (according to Varro) to implore the aid of the *Quirītes* or Roman citizens: 'quiritare dicitur is qui Quiritum fidem clamans implorat'.]

I. 1. *trans.* To entreat, beg, beseech, implore, in a loud and emoved or excited voice. †**a.** with the thing begged as direct object. *Obs.* (Now *cry for.*) Hence *to cry* QUARTER, TRUCE: see these words.

a **1300** *Cursor M.* 20746 (Cott.) þan crijd [*G.* creid] he merci atte last. *Ibid.* 1131 (Gött.) His blod..fines noght wrake to crij [*v.r.* cri, crye, cry]. **1393** LANGL. *P. Pl.* C. VII. 338 Alle..þat with good will Confessen hem and crien mercy. *Ibid.* C. VIII. 109 A bedreden womman To crye a largesse by-fore oure lorde. **1597** SHAKS. *Lover's Compl.* 42 Or monarch's hands that let not bounty fall Where want cries some, but where excess begs all. **1668** PEPYS *Diary* 18 Dec., He became as calm as a lamb, and owned..and cried excuse.

†**b.** with the person addressed as indirect (dative) object, and the thing begged as direct object; *esp.* in ***to cry him mercy***, and analogous phrases. *Obs.* (The earliest known English use.)

a **1225** *Ancr. R.* 44 Crieð him eorne merci & forgiuenesse. *a* **1240** *Lofsong* in *Cott. Hom.* 205 Ich..creie þe leafdi merci. **1297** R. GLOUC. (1724) 381 He..cryde hym mylce & ore. **1393** LANGL. *P. Pl.* C. XXI. 90 þe knyght..cryed iesu mercy. **1483** CAXTON *Gold. Leg.* 81/1 Whan they repente..and crye their god mercy. *a* **1533** LD. BERNERS *Huon* lxxxi. 249 Syr, I crye you mercy for goddes sake doo not to me so grete an outrage. **1672** VILLIERS (Dk. Buckhm.) *Rehearsal* I. i. (Arb.) 29 No, cry you mercy; this is my book.

†**c.** with *on, to him*, in place of the dative. *Obs.*

a **1300** *Cursor M.* 2789 (Gött.) ȝerne on þaim he crid merci. *Ibid.* App. ii. 739 (Brit. Mus. Add. MS.) The folke hem bad mercy to crie to iesu cryst. **1393** LANGL. *P. Pl.* C. XIV. 13 þe kynge cride to abraam mercy. **1795** SOUTHEY *Joan of Arc* VII. 521 This Alençon..Cried mercy to his conqueror.

†**d.** with const. *him* (*to him*) *of* (*grace*). *Obs.*

1362 LANGL. *P. Pl.* A. I. 77 þenne knelede I on my kneos and criȝed hire of grace. [**1393** *Ibid.* C. III. 1 And cryede to hure of grace.]

2. To call in supplication or reverential invocation (*on, upon, unto, to* a person). **a.** *intr. Obs.* or *arch.*

c **1290** *S. Eng. Leg.* I. 15/479 On god huy criden and wepen sore. *a* **1300** *Cursor M.* 6789 Crie to me þei shal And I forsoþe wol here her cal. *c* **1380** WYCLIF *Serm.* Sel. Wks. I. 94 þei maken us dreden and crie on Crist. *c* **1440** *York Myst.* xxxiii. 62 Why crye ȝe so on me? **1550** CROWLEY *Way to Wealth* 213 Crienge and callinge vpon them in thy nede. **1611** SHAKS. *Wint. T.* III. iii. 97 How he cride to mee for helpe. *a* **1850** ROSSETTI *Dante & Circ.* I. (1874) 176 She is cried upon In all the prayers my heart puts up alone.

b. with object sentence containing the utterance, or clause expressing its purport. (Now merged in 3.)

1297 R. GLOUC. (1724) 495 Criinde pitosliche, that he ssolde..abbe reuthe of Cristendom. *a* **1300** *Cursor M.* 4737 (Cott.) Criand..'Ha reuth on vs, þou blisced man'. *c* **1386** CHAUCER *Kni.'s T.* 898 Alle crieden..Haue mercy Lord vp on vs. **1548** HALL *Chron.* 190 b, Criyng on his men to do valiauntly. **1590** SPENSER *F.Q.* I. ii. 21 Shee..with ruefull countenaunce, Cride, Mercy, mercy, Sir, vouchsafe to show. **1659** B. HARRIS *Parival's Iron Age* 149 The Foot..was deserted by the Horse..and cryed to them to stand, and make good their ground. **1697** DRYDEN *Virg. Georg.* IV. 455 He..Thus mourning, to his Mother Goddess cry'd, Mother Cyrene [etc.]. **1886** R. C. LESLIE *Sea-painter's Log* 27 Turning a..deaf ear to the solicitations of admiring companions when they cry, 'Do let I come wi'ye, Bill'.

c. *fig.* (*intr.*) Of things. Cf. 7 and *cry out.*

a **1300** *Cursor M.* 1130 (Cott.) His blod on erth sced lijs Efter wrak to me it crijs. **1552** ASCHAM in *Lett. Lit. Men* (Camden) 12 Mischief..so moche as did crye to God for a generall plage. **1591** SHAKS. *1 Hen. VI*, V. iv. 53 Maiden blood, thus rigorously effus'd, Will cry for Vengeance at the gates of heaven. **1607** —— *Timon* II. i. 20 But tell him, My Vses cry to me. **1711** STEELE *Spect.* No. 258 ¶3 Sir, these Things cry loud for Reformation. **1835** THIRLWALL *Greece* I. ix. 344 Injuries and insults..which cried aloud for vengeance.

3. *intr.* To utter the voice loudly and with exclamatory effort, whether under the influence of emotion, as indignation, fear, pain, surprise, or merely in order to be heard afar, or above any noise that would prevent the ordinary speaking voice from being heard or distinguished; to call aloud (*to* a person), shout, vociferate.

It differs from *bawl, scream, screech, shriek*, in that these describe particular tones used in crying.

a **1300** *Cursor M.* 4401 (Gött.) And quan i crid ful sone i-fledd [*v.r.* he fledde]. *Ibid.* 22607 (Cott.) He sal..Bath cri and brai for dute and drede. **1382** WYCLIF *Acts* xix. 28 Thei..cryeden, seiynge Greet [**1388** is the] Dian of Ephesians. *c* **1386** CHAUCER *Knt.'s T.* 225 Why cridestow? who hath the doon offence? *c* **1400** MAUNDEV. (Roxb.) xxxiii. 151 Grete noyse of waters þat a man may noȝt here anoþer, crie he neuer so hie. *a* **1450** *Knt. de la Tour-Landry* (1868) 9 Men synging and crienge, iaping, and plaieng. **1590** SPENSER *F.Q.* I. v. 33 The damned ghosts in torments fry, And with sharp shrilling shrieks doe bootlesse cry. **1611** BIBLE *Isa.* xxxiv. 14 The satyr shall cry to his fellow. *c* **1684** *Frost of 1683–4* (Percy Soc.) 19 The watermen do loudly cry and bawl. **1824** SCOTT *Redgauntlet* Let. xii, If onybody stops ye, cry on me. **1830** TENNYSON *Mermaid* 26 Call to each other and whoop and cry All night, merrily.

†**b.** in connexion with sale by candle (CANDLE 5 d). *Obs.*

1660 PEPYS *Diary* 6 Nov., We met all, for the sale of two ships by an inch of candle..I observed how..they all do cry, and we have much to do to tell who did cry last.

c. quasi-*trans.* with complemental accusative.

1674 LEIGHTON in *Lauderdale Papers* (1885) III. xxxiii. 55 The germans cri'd their throats dry with calling for a generall Councill.

4. *trans.* To utter or pronounce in a loud exclamatory voice, to call out. The object may be **a.** a description or term for the utterance; **b.** the word or words uttered; **c.** a clause stating their effect.

a. *a* **1300** *Cursor M.* 16388 (Cott.) þis word ai mar and mar to cri all þai be-gan. **1382** WYCLIF *Acts* xix. 32 Othere men cryeden othir thing sothli the chirche was confused. *a* **1533** LD. BERNERS *Huon* lxvii. 230 When he sawe his tyme, he cryed his worde and token. *a* **1635** CORBET *Poems* (1807) 16 What cryes the University?

b. **1382** WYCLIF *Acts* xix. 34 O vois of alle men was maad, criynge..Greet Dian of Ephisians. **1598** SHAKS. *Merry W.* V. v. 209, I went to her in greene, and cried Mum, and she cride budget. **1610** —— *Temp.* II. ii. 53 For she had a tongue ..Would cry to a Sailor goe hang. **1697** DRYDEN *Virg. Georg.* IV. 763 With his last Voice, *Eurydice*, he cry'd. **1709** PRIOR *Despairing Sheph.*, And yet I pardon you, she cry'd. **1749** FIELDING *Tom Jones* v. xii, Lest grave men and politicians..may cry pish at it. **1831** *Blackw. Mag.* XXIX. 564 Ten thousand voices cried, 'The King! The King!'

c. **1668** CULPEPPER & COLE *Barthol. Anat.* I. xviii. 49 He cries that [this Cavity] is so small, that it will hardly admit a little Pea. **1680** OTWAY *Orphan* I. i, He..cries He's old, and willingly would be at rest. **1726** SHELVOCKE *Voy. round World* (1757) 249 This, they cried, was a poor dependance. **1847** TENNYSON *Princess* IV. 463 Some crying there was an army in the land.

d. *spec.* To shout (a war-cry, watchword, or the like).

1375 BARBOUR *Bruce* XV. 497 Than his ensenȝe he can hye cry. **1535** STEWART *Cron. Scot.* II. 78 Loud on hicht he cryit hes his seinȝe. **1548** HALL *Chron.* 103 b, Thei issued out of the castle criyng saienct George, Talbot. **1634** SIR T. HERBERT *Trav.* 188 They presently shake and vibrate their Swords upon their Shields, crying aloud Nayroe.

5. To announce publicly so as to be heard by all concerned; to give oral public notice of, to proclaim; to appoint or ordain by proclamation.

c **1300** *Beket* 2477 Forte the dai were icome, That was icrid into al that lond that he scholde beo up ynome. *c* **1340** *Cursor M.* 5497 (Fairf.) He lete cry a parlement. *c* **1400** MAUNDEV. (Roxb.) Pref. 2 He will ger crie it openly in þe middell of a toune. *c* **1465** *Eng. Chron.* (Camden) 6 He leet crie and ordeyne general justis at Londoun, in Smythfeld. *a* **1533** LD. BERNERS *Huon* liii. 179 The kynge caused to be cryed.. that none sholde by so hardy to speke. **1646** BUCK *Rich. III*, I. 14 Those who cry him so deepe an homicide. **1667** MILTON *P.L.* II. 514 They bid cry With Trumpets regal sound the great result. **1883** *Century Mag.* XXVI. 446/1, I was induced to outbid..bids that were cried by the auctioneer, but that had never been made at all.

absol. **1605** SHAKS. *Lear* v. i. 48 Let but the Herald cry, And Ile appeare againe.

b. To announce (a sale, things for sale); to sell by outcry; to offer for sale by auction or by hawking in the streets.

1393 LANGL. *P. Pl.* C. I. 226 Kokes and here knaues crieden hote pyes, hote! **1483** *Cath. Angl.* 82 To Cry in þe merketh, *preconizare*. **1586** T. B. *La Primaud. Fr. Acad.* 318 Diogenes when he was to be sold for a slave..mocked the Serjeant that cried him to sale. **1632** MASSINGER *Maid of Hon.* III. i, I will cry broom, or cat's-meat, in Palermo. **1677** *Act 29 Chas. II* c. 7 Noe person..shall publickly cry, shew forth, or expose to sale, any wares, merchandizes, fruit, herbs, goods, or chattells. **1701** W. WOTTON *Hist. Rome* 265 He went to the Camp, when he heard the Sale was cry'd, to bid for the Empire. **1875** HOWELLS *Foregone Concl.* I A peasant crying pots of pinks and roses.

Proverb. to cry stinking fish.

1660 JER. TAYLOR *Duct. Dubit.* (1671) 805 Does ever any man cry stinking fish to be sold? **1825** MRS. CAMERON *Crooked Paths* (*Houlston Tracts*, I. xxv. 5) 'Sir,' answered the woman, looking wise, 'nobody cries stinking fish.' **1861** THACKERAY *B. Lyndon* (1878) IV. iii. 444 This was not true; but what is the use of crying bad fish?

c. To give public oral notice of (things lost or found).

1596 NASHE *Saffron Walden* 114 His Master..is readie to ..get his Nouice cride in euerie market Towne in Essex. *a* **1626** BACON *Max. & Uses Com. Law* (1636) 65 [The strayes] to be seized..and to be cryed in three markets adjoyning. **1799** S. FREEMAN *Town Off.* 58 Persons who take up any stray beast, shall cause him to be posted and cried. *a* **1845** BARHAM *Ingol. Leg.*, *Knight & Lady* xiii, We've sent round the Crier, and had him well cried. **1885** SIR J. F. STEPHEN in *Law Times' Rep.* LIII. 782/2 The prisoner found a purse and money, and..heard soon afterwards that it was cried in the street.

d. To proclaim the marriage banns of; to 'ask' in church. (Still in Scotland and New England.)

1775 SHERIDAN *Rivals* v. i, Or perhaps be cried three times in a country church. **1867** LOWELL *Biglow Papers* Ser. II. Introd. *The Courtin'*, An all I know is they wuz cried In meetin', come nex Sunday. **1875** W. MCILWRAITH *Guide Wigtownshire* 123 Loving couples landing on the Saturday got 'cried' on the Sunday, and were married, firm and fast, on the Monday.

e. To read or recite aloud in the streets.

1710 LUTTRELL *Brief Rel.* (1857) VI. 572 The justices have ordered the constables to take up all those that cry such libells. **1855** MACAULAY *Hist. Eng.* III. 503 Broadsides of prose and verse written in his praise were cried in every street.

†**6.** To summon in a loud voice; to call (to come). *Obs.*

c **1420** *Pallad. on Husb.* II. 10 The medes clensed tyme is now to make, And beestes..from hem to crie. **1470–85** MALORY *Arthur* x. li, There he..cryed vnto harneis alle that myghte bere armes.

†**7.** To call for, demand loudly. Also *fig.* of things. *Obs.*

1604 SHAKS. *Oth.* I. iii. 277 Th' Affaire cries hast: And speed must answer it. **1621** FLETCHER *Pilgrim* I. ii, This cries money for reward, good store too. **1798** SOUTHEY *Inscriptions* xv, The innocent blood cried vengeance.

†**8.** To extol; = *cry up*. *Obs.*

1613 SHAKS. *Hen. VIII*, I. i. 27 Now this Maske Was cry'de incompareable. *a* **1625** FLETCHER *Hum. Lieutenant* I. i, When all men cry him. **1628** EARLE *Microcosm.*, *Vulgar-spirited Man* (Arb.) 70 That cries Chaucer for his Money aboue all our English Poets.

9. *intr.* To utter inarticulate exclamations, *esp.* of grief, lamentation, or suffering, such as are usually accompanied with tears; to weep and wail.

1297 R. GLOUC. (1724) 13 Heo cryede and wep with sorwe ynow. *c* **1300** *Seyn Julian* 179 þe Justice bigan to wepe and crie. **1340** HAMPOLE *Pr. Consc.* 475 Bot ligge and sprawel and cry and wepe. *c* **1400** MAUNDEV. (Roxb.) iv. 13 Scho began to crie, as a thing þat had mykill sorowe. *c* **1450** *Merlin* 261 He be-gan to make grete sorow, and cried high and cleer that thei with-ynne vpon the walles myght wele it here. **1590** SPENSER *F.Q.* I. iii. 25 She gan..to..cry, and curse, and raile, and rend her heare. **1599** SHAKS. *Much Ado* III. iii. 69 If you heare a child crie in the night you must call to the nurse, and bid her still it. **1611** BIBLE *Ezek.* xxvi. 15 When the wounded crie, when the slaughter is made in the midst of thee. **1850** TENNYSON *In Mem.* liv. 18 An infant crying in the night: An infant crying for the light: And with no language but a cry. **1884** J. PARKER *Apost. Life* III. 124 You will never persuade the world that Jeremiah did anything but cry.

b. *trans.* with *into*, *out of*, etc.

1746 W. HORSLEY *Fool* (1748) I. 196 We must..not let ..[them] whine and cry us into a tame submission.

10. This passes in later use into: To weep, shed tears; used even where no sound is uttered.

c **1532** DEWES *Introd. Fr.* in *Palsgr.* 939 To crye or wepe, *braire*. **1598** SHAKS. *Merry W.* III. i. 21 'Mercie on mee, I haue great dispositions to cry. *a* **1631** DONNE (J.), Her who still weeps with spungy eyes, And her who is dry cork, and never cries. **1662** PEPYS *Diary* 14 Oct., And she so cruel a hypocrite that she can cry when she pleases. **1742** CHESTERFIELD *Lett.* I. xci. 252 Julius Caesar..even cried when he saw the statue of Alexander the Great. **1840** *P. Parley's Annual* I. 116 What! have you not left off crying yet? I shall give you something to cry for before you go home. **1883** G. LLOYD *Ebb & Flow* II. 108 Poor Pauline, who cried copiously.

b. quasi-*trans. to cry tears, cry one's eyes* or *heart out, cry oneself blind, sick, to sleep*, etc.

1611 SHAKS. *Cymb.* III. iv. 46 And cry my selfe awake? **1704** CIBBER *Careless Husb.* I. i, I could cry my Eyes out. *Ibid.*, I should cry my self sick in some dark Closet. **1831** *Blackw. Mag.* XXIX. 524/1 A sickly infant, which a stern stepmother bids cry itself to sleep. **1862** KINGSLEY *Water Bab.* iv. (1886) 157 He..sat down..and cried salt tears from sheer disappointment. **1864** TENNYSON *Grandmother* x, I cried myself well-nigh blind. **1888** MRS. OLIPHANT *Joyce* I. 169 When she had cried her heart out.

11. *intr.* Of an animal: To give forth a loud call or vocal sound; to utter its characteristic call.

1398 TREVISA *Barth. De P.R.* v. xxiii. (1495) 131 Amonge byrdes and foules..the male cryeth and not the female. *c* **1450** *Voc.* in Wr.-Wülcker 576/44 *Cuculo*, to crye as a Cokow. *Ibid.* 607/3 *Recano*, to crye as a tygre. **1563** FULKE *Meteors* (1640) 51 Frogs crying..forewarne us of a tempest. **1610** SHAKS. *Temp.* v. i. 90 There I cowch when Owles doe crie. **1821** BYRON *Heav. & Earth* iii. 732 Hark, hark! the sea-birds cry! **1839** THACKERAY *Major Gahagan* iv, The camels began to cry.

b. Said of the yelping of hounds in the chase.

1486 *Bk. St. Albans* E viij a, Whi theys houndes all Bayen and cryen. **1601** SHAKS. *Twel. N.* II. v. 135 Sowter will cry vpon't for all this, though it bee as ranke as a Fox. **1602** —— *Ham.* IV. v. 109 How cheerefully on the false Traile they cry, Oh this is Counter you false Danish Dogges.

c. quasi-*trans.*

1796 BURKE *Regic. Peace* i. Wks. VIII. 143 Like importunate Guinea-fowls crying one note day and night.

†**12.** *transf.* Of things inanimate: To emit a wheezing or creaking sound. *Obs.*

1523 FITZHERB. *Husb.* § 10 If it synge or crye, or make any noyse vnder thy fete, than it is to wete to sowe. **1781** [see *Cry out*].

II. Phrases and combinations.

* *Phrases.*

13. In many phraseological expressions, as *to cry* AIM, COCK, CRAVEN, CREAK, CUPBOARD, FIE, HALVES, HARROW, HAVOC, MEW, QUARTER, QUIT, QUITS, QUITTANCE, SHAME, TRUCE, VENGEANCE, etc., for which see these words. *to cry encouragement*: to shout encouraging words. *cry fish*: see 5 b. *cry mercy*: see 1 a, b. *to cry smack*: to give out the sound of a smack. Cf. also sense 17.

1627 W. SCLATER *Exp. 2 Thess.* (1632) 124 He heares not the sweet Busse cry smacke. **1872** RAYMOND *Statist. Mines* 324 Where so many voices cry encouragement, it is well that one should speak warning.

** *With prepositions.*

(For the constructions in which both words have their ordinary senses, see above.)

14. cry against ——. To raise one's voice against; to utter protests or reproofs against; also *fig.* of things.

1382 WYCLIF *Deut.* xv. 9 Lest he crye aȝens thee to the Lord. **1611** BIBLE *Jonah* i. 2 Goe to Nineueh..and cry against it. **1635** SWAN *Spec. M.* vi. § 2 (1643) 185 Reason it self doth crie against it. **1850** TENNYSON *In Mem.* xc. 24, I find not yet one lonely thought That cries against my wish for thee.

15. cry for ——. To beg or call for loudly and imploringly, or with tears; *fig.* to be in pressing need of, to demand in the name of justice (see above 2 c).

a **1300** *Cursor M.* 9610 (Cott.) All þat sco wald for cri or call. **1581** MULCASTER *Positions* xxxviii. (1887) 159 If ye shew a child an apple, he will crye for it. **1599** SHAKS. *Hen. V*, IV. i. 145 Some swearing, some crying for a Surgean. **1860** T. MARTIN *Horace* 96 The toilworn wretch who cries for ease.

†**16. cry of** ——. To hail from, belong to. *Obs.*

c **1314** *Guy Warw.* (A.) 7001 Redi to fiȝtes Wiþ alle þat crie of þat cuntre.

17. cry on, upon ——: see senses 2, 3. Also (obs.), to call upon in the way of appeal, to appeal to; to exclaim against; to choose by acclamation; to invoke or bring by outcry (*fame, honour, hate*, etc.) on or upon. Cf. *cry* SHAME *upon*.

a **1300** *Cursor M.* 6139 (Gött.) þan gan þe folk apon him cri, And said 'do ȝou forth in hey'. *c* **1400** *Destr. Troy* 6504 Then criet he full cantly þe knightes vpon. **1532** MORE *Confut. Tindale* Wks. 396/1 He cryed vpon them to done penaunce. **1547–64** BAULDWIN *Mor. Philos.* (Palfr.) 73 b, All their religiones were wicked and abhominable And therefore some of them cried upon them. **1568** GRAFTON *Chron.* II. 154 This yere fell a great controversie..about the chosyng of the Maior..the Commons..cryed upon Thomas fitz Thomas. **1601** SHAKS. *Twel. N.* v. i. 62 That very enuy..Cride fame and honor on him. **1606** —— *Tr. & Cr.* v. v. 35 His mangled Myrmidons..come to him, Crying on Hector.

*** *With adverbs.*

18. cry back. a. *trans.* To call back. *Sc.*

1864 W. CHAMBERS in *Athenæum* No. 1923. 301/2 Rin and cry back the laird.

b. *intr. Hunting.* To return as on a trail; to hark back; *fig.* to revert to an ancestral type.

19. cry down. a. *trans.* To proclaim (a thing) as unlawful, to forbid, suppress, or condemn by public proclamation; to decry; publicly to disclaim responsibility for.

1457 *Sc. Acts Jas. II* (1597) § 65 That the fute-bal and golfe be vtterly cryed downe, and not to be vsed. **1684** BUNYAN *Pilgr.* II. (1879) 211 Her Husband first cried her down at the Cross, and then turned her out of his Doors. **1692** LUTTRELL *Brief Rel.* (1857) II. 563 The lord mayor sent his officers to cry downe the faire. **1765** BLACKSTONE *Comm.* (1774) I. 278 The king may..decry, or cry down, any coin of the kingdom, and make it no longer current. **1827** HALLAM *Const. Hist.* (1876) I. i. 38 Bad money was cried down, with penalties.

b. To condemn, depreciate, or disparage loudly, vehemently, or publicly.

1598 B. JONSON *Ev. Man in Hum.* I. v, He condemned, and cry'd it downe for the most pyed and ridiculous that ever he saw. **1642** FULLER *Holy & Prof. St.* II. xxi. 135 These cry up Drakes fortune herein to cry down his valour. **1742** FIELDING *J. Andrews* I. xvii, A book which the clergy would be certain to cry down. **1888** RIDER HAGGARD *Meeson's Will* i, Did Meeson's subsidize a newspaper to puff their undertakings, the opposition subsidized two to cry them down.

c. To put down, overcome, silence, by louder or more vehement crying.

1613 SHAKS. *Hen. VIII*, I. i. 137 Ile to the King, And from a mouth of Honor quite cry downe This Ipswich fellowes insolence. *a* **1628** PRESTON *Saints Daily Exerc.* (1629) 103 Our sinnes cry lowder then our prayers, they cry downe our prayers.

20. cry off. *intr.* To exclaim that a negotiation is broken off, on the part of the exclaimer; to announce one's withdrawal *from* a negotiation, treaty, engagement, etc.

1775 SHERIDAN *Rivals* III. i, I should never be the man to bid you cry off. **1857** TROLLOPE *Three Clerks* xxxviii, Would she be the first to cry off from such a bargain? **1890** G. M. FENN *Double Knot* I. Prol. iv. 62 He soon cried off on finding that his challenge was taken up.

21. cry out. To utter loud and (usually) impassioned exclamation; to exclaim. *intr.* and *trans.* Of things: To emit a creaking sound.

1382 WYCLIF *Ecclus.* I. 18 Thanne crieden out the sonus of Aron. **1483** *Cath. Angl.* 82 To Cry owte, *exclamare*. **1535** COVERDALE *Isa.* xii. 6 Crie out, and be glad, thou that dwellest in Sion. **1592** SHAKS. *Rom. & Jul.* III. iii. 109 Art thou a man? thy forme cries out thou art. **1653** H. COGAN tr. *Pinto's Trav.* xix. 67 Threatening, if they cryed out never so little, to kill them all. **1781** ARCHER in *Naval Chron.* XI. 291 Our poor ship grinding, and crying out at every stroke. **1818** BYRON *Juan* I. ccvii, They will not cry out before they're hurt. **1890** A. GISSING *Village Hampden* III. iii. 72 He just cried out a good-night..and set off.

b. Const. *against, at, on, upon* (persons or things objected to); *for* (something wanted); †*to cry out of*, to complain loudly or vehemently of (a matter).

c **1385** WYCLIF *Wks.* (1880) 157 All cristene men schal crie out on þes deuelis blasphemyes. **1548** HALL *Chron.* 14 b, All pore people will rayle and crie out upon us. *Ibid.* 209 b, Which commaundement so vexed..that they cryed out of God. **1568** GRAFTON *Chron.* II. 249 Criyng out of the dammages and great hurtes that they had susteyned. **1579** GOSSON *Sch. Abuse* (Arb.) 41 His crueltie was so loudely cryed out on. **1599** SHAKS. *Hen. V*, II. iii. 29 They say he cried out of Sack. **1630** BP. BEDELL in *Abp. Ussher's Lett.* (1686) 421 He is the..most cried out upon. **1634** SIR T. HERBERT *Trav.* 160 A severe Scholler..cries out against their filthinesse. **1653** H. COGAN tr. *Pinto's Trav.* xv. 48 Crying out for help. *a* **1680** T. BROOKS *Wks.* (1867) VI. 217 Sometimes they cry out of the malice, plots, envy, and rage of men. **1711** tr. *Werenfelsius' Meteors of Stile* 194 You cry out Thief upon a Man. **1722** DE FOE *Plague* (1884 Rtldg.) 218 They wou'd cry out of the Cruelty of being confin'd. **1759** GOLDSM. *The Bee* Wks. (Globe) 366/2 The world.. may cry out at a bankrupt who appears at a ball. **1871** R. H. HUTTON *Ess.* (1877) I. 92 Every living movement of human thought..cries out against it. **1879** MISS YONGE *Cameos* Ser. IV. i. 15 The state of the church cried out for a general council.

†**c.** To be in child-birth. Cf. SHOUT. *Obs.*

1613 SHAKS. *Hen. VIII*, v. i. 67 What, is she crying out? **1668** PEPYS *Diary* 12 July. **1692–1754** [see CRYING 2].

†**d.** To sell out by auction. *Obs.*

1701 *Lond. Gaz.* No. 3748/4 Mr. John Boulte..Pawnbroker..gave his Employment, and cried out his Goods.

e. Colloq. phr. *for crying out loud*, an exclamation expressing astonishment or impatience. orig. *U.S.*

1924 H. C. WITWER *Love & Learn* vi. 148 'For crying out loud' butts in Hazel impatiently. **1933** M. ALLINGHAM

Sweet Danger v. 69 Well for crying out loud!.. That's a nasty scrape. **1941** 'R. WEST' *Black Lamb* (1942) II. 156 For crying out loud, why did you do it?

22. cry up. *trans.* To proclaim (a thing) to be excellent; to endeavour to exalt in public estimation by proclamation or by loud praise; to extol.

1593 DRAYTON *Misery Q. Mary* Wks. 1753 II. 388 When she up is cry'd, Of all angelic excellence the prime. **1631** T. POWELL *Tom All Trades* 144 When your credit is cryed up to the highest. **1648** JENKYN *Blind Guide* iv. 88 You cry up Miracles as you cry down the Word. *a* **1698** TEMPLE (J.), Crying up the pieces of eight. **1711** ADDISON *Spect.* No. 125 ¶5 We often hear a poor insipid Paper or Pamphlet cried up. **1792** BURKE *Corr.* (1844) III. 390 They who cry up the French revolution, cry down the party which you and I.. belong to. **1874** HELPS *Soc. Pressure* v. 73 Isn't it good to hear Milverton cry up the virtue of athletic sports?

†**b.** *intr.* To raise one's voice, shout. *Obs.*

1684 GODDARD *Plato's Demon* 259 Worthy Patriots, who cry up so much for Liberty and Property.

cry-, in many words, obs. f. CRI-.

cryable ('kraɪəb(ə)l), *a.* [f. CRY *v.* + -ABLE, after LAUGHABLE *a.*] That may be cried or wept over.

1897 *Daily News* 22 Mar. 9/4 Tragedy means a cryable play. **1908** S. E. WHITE *Riverman* xxi. 188 What laughable and cryable mistakes she made only those who have encountered a like situation could realize.

†**cryal.** *Obs.* Also cry-, criell. In ***criell heron***, an old name of the Egret or Lesser White Heron.

1565–73 COOPER *Thesaurus*, *Albardeola*..a cryell herne. **1611** COTGR., *Aigrette*..a criell Heron. [**1755** JOHNSON, *Cryal*, the heron [citing Ainsworth]. Hence in mod. Dicts.]

cryance, -aunce, cryature: see CRE-.

cryb, etc.: see CRIB.

'**cry-baby**, *sb.* Also **cry-babby.** [f. CRY *sb.* or *vb.* stem.] A derisive appellation for one who cries childishly.

1852 A. CARY *Clovernook* 274 You had better be still, cry-baby. **1854** M. J. HOLMES *Tempest & Sunshine* xiii. 180, I wouldn't be such a cry-baby, anyway. **1858** A. MAYHEW *Paved with Gold* I. iii. 51 Don't take on like that, for if the chaps see you they are sure to call you 'cry-baby'. **1882** *Advance* 18 May 317 Tom called him a cry-baby, because his eyes were always full of tears. **1891** *Sat. Rev.* 21 Feb. 230/1, 'I declare..that they're cry-baby chaps.' **1922** JOYCE *Ulysses* 532 Crybabby! Crocodile tears! **1969** I. & P. OPIE *Children's Games* ii. 76 There was a girl..with the reputation of a cry-baby.

Hence **cry-baby** *v. intr. U.S. colloq.*

1902 O. WISTER *Virginian* vii. 85, I am not crybabying to the judge. **1966** H. KEMELMAN *Saturday the Rabbi went Hungry* (1967) xxvii. 181 I'd be the last one to crybaby on it.

'**crying**, *vbl. sb.* [-ING[1].]

1. The action of the verb CRY in its various senses; shouting, lamentation, weeping, etc.

a **1340** HAMPOLE *Psalter* iii. 4 His prayere he calles criynge. **1398** TREVISA *Barth. De P.R.* XII. vi. (1495) 416 Cryenge of the owle by nyght. *c* **1400** *Destr. Troy* 10180 The clamor was kene, crying of pepull. **1509** BARCLAY *Shyp of Folys* (1570) 168 Thy crying, foole, shall not wake him out of that sleepe. **1611** BIBLE *1 Sam.* iv. 14 Eli heard the noise of the crying. **1722** DE FOE *Col. Jack* (1840) 24 My crying was over. **1891** F. BARRETT *Sin of Olga Z.* I. viii. 115 There's a good deal of crying! And we mope and look miserable.

2. With adverbs, as ***crying out***, exclamation, calling out, outcry; †*spec.* accouchement (*obs.*); ***crying up***, extolling, laudation, etc.

1483 *Cath. Angl.* 82 A Criynge owte, *exclamacio*. **1676** ALLEN *Address Nonconf.* 158 A zealous crying up one, and crying down another. **1692** LUTTRELL *Brief Rel.* (1857) II. 417 He has ordered all the English nobility and gentry to be present at her crying out. **1715** tr. *C'tess D' Anois' Wks.* 479 Couriers were dispatch'd..to desire them to come to Her Majesty's Crying-out. **1754** RICHARDSON *Grandison* (1812) VI. 323 (D.) Aunt Nell..was at the crying out.

3. *attrib.*, as **crying cold**, a cold that makes the eyes run.

1761 FOOTE *Liar* I. Wks. 1799 I. 290 All the sighing, dying, crying crotchets, that the whole race of rhymers have ever produced. **1843** SIR T. WATSON *Lect. Physic* (1871) II. 55, I found her suffering under what is popularly called a 'crying cold'.

'**crying**, *ppl. a.* [-ING[2].] That cries.

1. Exclaiming, shouting, clamorous; roaring.

1398 TREVISA *Barth. De P.R.* XIII. xxiii. (1495) 455 A cryenge see and an vnpeasyble is peryllous. **1483** *Cath. Angl.* 82 Criynge, *clamans*. **1604** SHAKS. *Oth.* II. iii. 230 My selfe the crying Fellow did pursue. **1697** DRYDEN *Virg. Georg.* I. 495 When crying Cormorants forsake the Sea.

2. Wailing, weeping.

1593 SHAKS. *Lucr.* 814 And fright her crying babe with Tarquin's name. **1848** MACAULAY *Hist. Eng.* I. 380 Annoyed by invalids and crying children.

3. Of evils: That forces itself upon notice, and calls loudly for redress; clamant, notorious.

1607 TOPSELL *Serpents* (1608) 736 Odious crying sins. **1640** *Petit.* in Rushw. *Hist. Coll.* (1692) III. I. 21 Representing Ship-Money as a Great and Crying Grievance. **1660** GAUDEN *God's Great Demonstr.* 52 The cryingest injustice and cruelty in the world. **1711** ADDISON *Spect.* No. 61 ¶5 There is a most crying Dulness on both Sides. **1838** PRESCOTT *Ferd. & Is.* (1846) I. iii. 155 The most crying evil of this period. **1890** F. W. ROBINSON *Very Strange Family* xi. 95 It would be a crying shame, if you could.

advb. **1836–9** DICKENS *Sk. Boz* (1877) 126 These two old men..have made themselves crying drunk.

'**cryingly**, *adv.* [f. prec. + -LY[2].] In the manner of a crying evil; clamantly, markedly.

1818 SOUTHEY *Ess.* (1832) II. 130 The condition of the inferior clergy..still cryingly requires improvement. **1878** SEELEY *Stein* II. 183 There was nothing that was so cryingly unjust or wrong.

crykat, -et(te, obs. ff. CRICKET *sb.*[1]

cryke, obs. form of CREEK *sb.*[1]

crym-: see CRIM-.

crymble: see CRUMBLE.

crymell, -yll, var. of CREMIL *Obs.*

cryne, obs. f. CRINE *v. Sc.*

crynok, obs. f. CRANNOCK, CURNOCK.

cryo- (kraɪəʊ), combining form of Gr. *κρύος* frost, icy cold (cf. KRYO-); as in **cryobi'ology**, the biology of materials cooled to temperatures lower than those at which they normally function; low-temperature biology; hence **cryobi'ologist**, one who studies or is skilled in cryobiology; **cryobio'logical** *a.*, of or pertaining to cryobiology; **cryo'globulin** *Biochem.* (see quots.); **cry'ology** (see quots.); **cryope'dology** (see quot.); **cryo'philic** *a.*, applied to bacteria which flourish at low temperatures; '**cryophyte** (see quots.); **cryopla'nation** (see quot.); **cryo'plankton**, plankton inhabiting snow and ice; **cryo'pump**, a vacuum-pump which produces a very high vacuum by the use of liquefied gases; hence **cryo'pumping** *vbl. sb.*, the use of the cryopump; '**cryosar**, a switching device in computers (see quot. 1959); **cryo'surgery**, surgery using instruments that produce intense cold locally; cryogenic surgery; hence **cryo'surgical** *a.*; **cryotur'bation** [cf. G. *kryoturbat* adj. (C. H. Edelman et al. 1936, in *Verh. van het Geol.-Mijnbouwkundig Genootsch.*, *Nederland*, Geol. Ser. XI. 332)], any physical disturbance to the soil produced by the action of frost on water in the soil.

1960 H. T. MERYMAN in *Ann. N.Y. Acad. Sci.* LXXXV. II. 509 The future of cryobiology is exciting, permitting as it does the attainment of indefinitely suspended animation. **1961** *Lancet* 16 Sept. 657/2 At the cryobiology laboratories ..A. Rowe..demonstrated new apparatus for the..low-temperature storage of bone-marrow. **1962** *Business Week* 16 June 72/1 Cryobiology is the marriage of two separate sciences: cryogenics, or extreme low-temperature physics, and biology. *Ibid.*, Cryobiologists have come up with two ways to preserve cells by freezing. **1964** *Internat. Science & Technol.* June 58/2 The realm of cryobiology encompasses everything below the optimum temperatures at which life functions... The problems of cryobiology stretch all the way from trying to understand what happens to an animal, an insect, or a single cell when it is cooled (or later warmed) to techniques for preserving useful cells like blood or destroying undesirable cells such as those in the brain of a patient suffering from Parkinson's disease. *Ibid.* 66/2 The trouble is that these high rates of heat transfer occur too late —at temperature differences between specimen and fluid that are too low for cryobiological use. **1947** LERNER & WATSON in *Amer. Jrnl. Med. Sci.* CCXIV. 413/1 The term cryoglobulin is..suggested to represent a group of proteins with the common property of precipitating (or gelifying) from cooled serum. **1965** *Oxford Mag.* 25 Feb. 235/2 He [*sc.* Bagratuni] perfected a technique for the assay of cryoglobulins, proteins separating from blood at temperatures below that of the body. **1947** *Jrnl. Glaciology* I. 35 '*Cryology*'. Shortly before the war this new word for the study of glaciology was coined in Central Europe... In America the word 'cryology' is coming into fashion to describe the study of refrigeration. **1961** L. D. STAMP *Gloss. Geogr. Terms* 140/1 At the International Association of Scientific Hydrology in Zurich, Meinzen referred to four divisions of hydrology—potamology, limnology, hydrology ..and cryology (the scientific study of ice and snow). **1946** K. BRYAN in *Amer. Jrnl. Sci.* CCXLIV. 639 *Cryopedology*, the science of intensive frost action and permanently frozen ground including studies of the processes and their occurrence and also the engineering devices which may be invented to avoid or overcome difficulties induced by them. **1942** C. S. MORRIS in *Dairy Industries* VII. 63 (*title*) Cryophilic bacteria as a cause of milk samples failing the methylene blue test. **1962** *Lancet* 5 May 955/2 Where stored blood is used, the greatest danger is its accidental infection with cryophilic bacteria, though this happens only once or twice for each million bottles issued. **1909** GROOM & BALFOUR tr. *Warming's Oecology of Plants* xxxvii. 154 Closely allied to plankton, but of a subsidiary..nature, is the glacial community forming the cryophyte-formation, which is composed of microphytes that are periodically exposed to ice-cold water. **1960** N. POLUNIN *Introd. Plant Geogr.* xv. 490 It is perhaps best to refer to the plants growing on snow or ice as 'cryophytes'. **1946** K. BRYAN in *Amer. Jrnl. Sci.* CCXLIV. 640 *Cryoplanation*, land reduction by the processes of intensive frost-action... Includes the work of rivers and streams in transporting materials delivered by the above process. **1932** FULLER & CONARD tr. *Braun-Blanquet's Plant Sociology* xii. 289 *Cryoplankton*, protista inhabiting snow and ice. **1961** *New Scientist* 25 May 434/2 Cryopumps which involve the liquefaction of hydrogen or helium to produce high vacua over large volumes. **1963** *Ibid.* 11 Apr. 99/1 'Cryopumping'—freezing the air in a chamber. **1959** McWHORTER & REDIKER in *Proc. Inst. Radio Engin.* XLVIII. 1207/1 The cryosar is a new semiconductor device, intended primarily for high-speed computer switching and memory applications, which utilizes the low-temperature avalanche breakdown produced by impact ionization of impurities. The name of the device was derived from 'low-temperature (*cryo*-) switching by *a*valanche and *r*ecombination'. **1962** *Engineering* 5 Jan. 21/3 Cryogenic devices such as..the cryotron and the cryosar. **1962** *New Scientist* 26 July 213 (*heading*) Cryosurgery cures Parkinsonism. **1965** *Observer* 2 May (Colour Suppl.) 14 (Advt.), Union Carbide also manufacture..cryosurgical equipment. **1946** K. BRYAN in *Amer. Jrnl. Sci.* CCXLIV. 633 A recent coinage by Edelman, Florshutz and Jeswiet (1936) is 'cryoturbation'. **1954** *Proc. Prehist. Soc.* XX. 134 At a similar time cryoturbation took place where a clay and sand interface occurred near enough to the surface.

cryoconite (kraɪəʊ'kəʊnaɪt). Also **kryokonite.** [f. CRYO- + Gr. *κόν-ις* dust + -ITE[1].] A grey powder found in layers at the bottom of holes in glaciers, at one time thought to be meteoric in origin but now thought to consist of dust blown by wind from areas beyond the ice margin. Also *attrib.* in ***cryokonite hole***.

1872 A. E. NORDENSKIÖLD in *Geol. Mag.* IX. 356 In the bottom of them [*sc.* holes in the ice filled with water] we found everywhere..a layer..of grey powder, often conglomerated... The substance is not a clay, but a sandy trachytic mineral... I propose for this substance the name Kryokonite. **1889** G. J. WRIGHT *Ice Age N. Amer.* 9 Nordenskiöld attributed the initial melting of ice-surface to accumulations of meteoric dust which he named kryokonite. **1891** *Standard* 9 Feb., The mysterious 'kryokonite' of the vast icefields of Greenland is now believed to be..simply dust blown from America or Europe. **1925** N. E. ODELL in E. F. Norton *Fight for Everest, 1924* 311 On the East Rongbuk Glacier were some rather beautiful examples of the so-called 'cryoconite holes' or 'dust holes', in which small particles of morainic material had melted their way down into the surface of the ice, as is so often to be seen on arctic glaciers especially. **1957** *Gloss. Geol.* (Amer. Geol. Inst.) 69/2 Absorption of radiation by the cryoconite causes ablation and formation of cryoconite holes or Dust wells. **1963** J. L. DYSON *World of Ice* xii. 138 In the bottom of every pit is a fine-grained gelatinous material called cryoconite, consisting partly of dust blown by the wind from areas beyond the ice margin. But cryoconite contains a considerable amount of organic material in the form of several kinds of blue-green algae and fungi. **1967** HAMELIN & COOK *Illustr. Gloss. Periglacial Phenom.* iii. 87 (*caption*) Cryoconite holes.

cryogen ('kraɪədʒɛn). *Chem.* [mod. f. Gr. *κρύο-ς* frost, icy cold + -GEN taken as = producer.] A freezing-mixture, or a substance which when mixed with ice produces a freezing mixture.

1875 F. GUTHRIE in *Proc. Physical Soc.* I. 76 By Cryogen I mean an appliance for obtaining a temperature below 0° C. In this paper it always signifies a freezing-mixture. **1881** WATTS *Dict. Chem.* VIII. 1005 The temperature of the mixture when used as a cryogen.

cryogenic (kraɪəʊ'dʒɛnɪk), *a.* [f. CRYOGEN + -IC.] Of or pertaining to the production or use of very low temperatures.

1902 *Encycl. Brit.* XXX. 287 Within recent years several special cryogenic laboratories have been established. **1933** *Discovery* Mar. 70/1 The ultimate liquid of all low-temperature or 'cryogenic' work—liquid helium. **1960** *Aeroplane* XCVIII. 643/1 A frictionless spinning element as in the cryogenic gyro. **1960** *Guardian* 15 June 6/2 My husband earns his living as a cryogenic physicist. **1962** I. S. COOPER in *Jrnl. Amer. Med. Assoc.* CLXXXI. 600/1 The technique of cryogenic surgery consists of first applying moderate cold to identify the locus of abnormal neural activity and then intense cold to make a circumscribed lesion there. **1967** *Technology Week* 20 Feb. 27 (Advt.), Flight simulation, high energy fuels, system design,..and fabrication of cryogenic support equipment are only a few of the advanced aerospace research..activities currently in progress.

Hence **cryo'genics**, that branch of physics which deals with the production of very low temperatures and their effects on matter.

1958 *Oxf. Univ. Gaz.* 2 Oct. 81/2 Research into He[3] Cryogenics being carried out in the Clarendon Laboratory. **1962** [see *cryobiology* s.v. CRYO-].

cryohydrate (kraɪəʊ'haɪdrət). *Chem.* [f. as CRYOGEN + HYDRATE.] A solid hydrate formed by the combination of a salt or other crystalloid with water (ice) at a temperature below freezing-point.

1874 F. GUTHRIE in *Proc. Physical Soc.* I. 74 At O° C. the ice and the water solidify together, producing the compound body or cryohydrate called ice, which is thus a cryohydrate of water. **1875** *Ibid.* I. 76 By Cryohydrate I mean the body resulting from the union of water with another body, and which hydrate can only exist in the solid form below O° C.

cryohydric (kraɪəʊ'haɪdrɪk), *a.* [f. CRYOHYDRATE + -IC.] Of or pertaining to a 'cryohydrate'; ***cryohydric point*** or ***temperature***, the eutectic point or temperature of a solution of a salt in water.

1890 *Jrnl. Chem. Soc.* LVII. 361 A solution at the cryohydric point is the coldest of the same solvent and dissolved substance obtainable. **1902** G. S. NEWTH *Text-bk. Inorg. Chem.* (ed. 9) I. xiv. 155 Such a solution is known as a constant-freezing solution, or sometimes a cryohydric solution. **1902** *Encycl. Brit.* XXVIII. 569/1 The solution must..become saturated with respect to both ice and salt, and this can only occur at the cryohydric temperature. **1940** GLASSTONE *Physical Chem.* x. 762 The terms cryohydrate and cryohydric point are obsolescent and will not be employed further. **1964** G. W. CASTELLAN *Physical Chem.* xv. 299 The eutectic mixture was originally thought to be a compound. In aqueous systems, this 'compound' was called a cryohydrate; the eutectic point was called the cryohydric point.

cryolite ('kraɪəʊlaɪt). *Min.* [Named 1799 f. Gr. κρυο-ς frost + -LITE.] A native fluoride of aluminium and sodium, found in white or brownish semi-transparent masses or crystals.
It occurs in an extensive bed in Greenland, and is an important source of the metal aluminium.
1801 W. NICHOLSON *Jrnl. Nat. Philos.* Ser. I. V. 212 Before the blowpipe chryolite fuses even before ignition. **1888** *Times* 19 Nov. 10/3 The cryolite mines at Ivigtut.

cryon, obs. form of CRAYON.

‖**cryophorus** (kraɪ'ɒfərəs). [mod.L. in form, f. Gr. κρύο-ς frost + -φορος -bearing, -bearer.] An instrument for illustrating the freezing of water by evaporation; that invented by Wollaston consists of a glass tube with a bulb at each end.
1826 HENRY *Epit. Chem.* I. 134 The instrument invented by Dr. Wollaston, and termed by him the Cryophorus or Frost-bearer. **1863** TYNDALL *Heat* v. §187 (1870) 151.
Hence **cryo'phoric** *a.*, having the nature or function of a cryophorus.
1881 HERSCHEL in *Nature* XXIII. 384 The cryophoric apparatus needed.

cryophyllite (kraɪəʊ'fɪlaɪt). *Min.* [f. Gr. κρύο-ς frost + φύλλον leaf + -ITE.] A species of mica found in granite at Cape Ann, Mass.
1867 *Amer. Jrnl. Sc.* Ser. II. XLIII. 217 On Cryophyllite a new mineral species.

cryoscopy (kraɪ'ɒskəpɪ). Formerly also **kryoscopy**. [f. CRYO- + -SCOPY.] (See quot. 1901[1].) So **cryo'scopic** *a.*, **cryo'scopically** *adv.*
1900 *Rep. Brit. Assoc.* 167 The cryoscopic behaviour of substances possessing constitutions similar to that of the solvent. **1901** *Brit. Med. Jrnl.* 5 Jan., The clinical value of kryoscopy, that is estimation of the osmotic tendency of fluids by means of freezing. *Ibid.*, In renal disease there is a lowering of the kryoscopic index of the urine. **1903** *Nature* 15 Jan. 263/1 The methods of exact cryoscopy. **1908** *Practitioner* Sept. 435 In differential diagnosis, he regards cryoscopic examination as of great importance. **1909** *Ibid.* Nov. 664 Kümmel is satisfied in such cases with the cryoscopy of the blood. **1949** E. P. ABRAHAM in H. W. Florey et al. *Antibiotics* II. xxiii. 872 Its molecular weight, determined cryoscopically. **1964** N. G. CLARK *Mod. Org. Chem.* xxiv. 505 The depression is a constant, characteristic of the particular solvent; it is called the molecular depression constant or cryoscopic constant.

cryostat ('kraɪəʊstæt). [f. CRYO- + -STAT.] An apparatus for maintaining a very low temperature.
1913 *Chem. Abstr.* VII. 2327 A Helium Cryostat. *Ibid.*, Making use of the He cryostat O. [*i.e.* K. Onnes] has detd. the vapor pressure of liquid He. **1917** *Ibid.* 2976 Cryostat for temperatures between 27°K and 55°K. **1946** *Nature* 24 Aug. 272/1 The experiments can be made in an ordinary cryostat. **1969** BROWN & BERTKE *Textbk. Cytology* iii. 19/1 Recently a refrigerated unit to cut frozen sections (cryostat) has become available.
Hence **cryo'static** *a.*; *spec.* ***cryostatic hypothesis*** (see quot.).
1950 A. L. WASHBURN in *Rev. Canadienne Géogr.* IV. 111. 34 Progressive freezing from the surface downward to the permafrost table sets up a large hydrostatic pressure in the unfrozen material that is confined between these surfaces... Because of analogy with a hydrostatic press and because freezing is the initiating factor, the writer suggests that this concept be termed the cryostatic hypothesis.

cryotron ('kraɪəʊtrɒn). *Electronics.* [f. CRYO- + -TRON.] (See quot. 1956.)
1956 D. A. BUCK in *Proc. Inst. Radio Engin.* XLIV. 482 (*heading*) The cryotron—a superconductive computer component. *Ibid.*, The cryotron, in its simplest form, consists of a straight piece of wire about one inch long with a single-layer control winding wound over it. Current in the control winding creates a magnetic field which causes the central wire to change from its superconducting state to its normal state. The device has current gain, that is, a small current can control a larger current; it has power gain so that cryotrons can be interconnected in logical networks as active elements. *Ibid.* 486/2 Cryotron circuitry. **1960** E. DELAVENAY *Introd. Machine Translation* ii. 21 Cryotrons also provide immense storage facilities on a very limited volume of matter. **1965** *New Scientist* 4 Nov. 331/3 Networks of cryotrons for storage..can be built up on one plane in one sequence of operations.

crypse, obs. form of CRISP *a.*

crypt (krɪpt), *sb.* Also 5 cripte, 7 cript. [ad. L. *crypta*: see below. Cf. F. *crypte* (1721, in Hatzfeld), and see GROT, GROTTO. The L. form was commonly used up to the end of the 18th c.; the example of 1432 appears to be isolated.]
†**1.** A grotto or cavern. *Obs.*
1432-50 tr. *Higden* (Rolls) V. 307 The cripte [TREVISA den] of Seynte Michael in the mownte Gargan.
2. An underground cell, chamber, or vault; *esp.* one beneath the main floor of a church, used as a burial-place, and sometimes as a chapel or oratory.
1789 BRAND *Hist. & Antiq. New-Castle-upon-Tyne* I. 368 The chancel of this church stood upon a large vault or crypt. **1841** W. SPALDING *Italy & It. Isl.* II. 36 The devout, as St. Jerome relates, were in the habit of visiting..the tombs of the martyrs in these crypts [the Catacombs]. **1883** S. C. HALL *Retrospect* II. 207 He [Turner] was buried in the crypt of St. Paul's Cathedral.
†**b.** An underground passage or tunnel. *Obs.*
1667 EVELYN *Mem.* (1857) II. 32, I design'd..the plot of his canall and garden, with a crypt thro' the hill.
3. *transf.* and *fig.* Recess, secret hiding-place.
1833 A. FONBLANQUE *Eng. under 7 Administ.* (1837) II. 316 [The Ballot] is..the crypt of political honesty. **1842** TENNYSON *Will Waterproof* xxiii, Fall'n into the dusty crypt Of darken'd forms and faces.
4. *Anat.* A small simple tubular or saccular gland; a secretory pit or cavity, as in a mucous membrane; a follicle. Also applied to the cavities in the jaw-bones in which the teeth are developed.
1840 BALY tr. *Müller's Elem. Physiol.* I. 485 Very shallow depressions, such as the simple crypts of the mucous membranes. **1859** J. TOMES *Dental Surg.* 5 The crypts of the canine teeth.
5. *Comb.*, as ***crypt-house***.
1873 TRISTRAM *Moab* vi. 182 There are many caves which have been used as dwellings, and several crypt houses.

‖**crypta** ('krɪptə). [L., a. Gr. κρύπτη vault, f. κρυπτός hidden, concealed.]
†**1.** = CRYPT *sb.* 1, 2. *Obs.*
1563 *Homilies* II. *Idolatry* III. (1859) 256 Christians had.. caves under the ground called Cryptae, where they for fear of persecution assembled secretly together. **1611** CORYAT *Crudities* 145 In a low crypta or vaulted chappell which is directly under the quire. **1639** in Hearne *Collect.* (Oxf. Hist. Soc.) III. 128 In this of St. Calixtus there are 3 Cryptas one above another. **1703** BATTELY *Antiq. Canterb.* II. 28 They were commonly called Cripta, or rather Crypta.
2. *Anat.* = CRYPT *sb.* 4.
1860 in MAYNE *Exp. Lex.*
b. *Bot.* (See quots.)
1866 *Treas. Bot.*, *Crypta*, the sunken glands or cysts which occur in dotted leaves. **1882** *Syd. Soc. Lex.*, *Cryptæ* ..in Botany, the oil receptacles of a leaf.

cryptæsthesia (ˌkrɪptɪs'θiːzɪə). Also **cryptesthesia**. [f. Gr. κρυπτ-ός CRYPTO- + αἴσθησις perception + -IA[1].] A supernormal faculty of perception, whether clairvoyant or telepathic.
1923 S. DE BRATH tr. *Richet's 30 Yrs. Psychical Res.* II. ii. 64 A single phenomenon which the magnetizers of a past age called 'lucidity' or ' clairvoyance' (*hellsehen*); which is now called telepathy... I propose to name it cryptesthesia. **1926** *Spectator* 9 Oct. 601/2 The dowser..is a person endowed with a subconscious supernormal cryptesthesia.

cryptal ('krɪptəl), *a.* [f. L. *crypta* (see CRYPTA) + -AL[1].] Of, pertaining to, or of the nature of a crypt.
1842 DUNGLISON *Med. Lex.* s.v. *Crypta*, The use of the cryptal or follicular secretion, is to keep the parts..supple and moist. **1860** *All Year Round* No. 56. 139 He led me down to the second cryptal chamber.

cryptanalysis (ˌkrɪptə'nælɪsɪs). orig. *U.S.* [f. CRYPTO- + ANALYSIS.] The art of deciphering a cryptogram or cryptograms by analysis. Hence **cryp'tanalyst**, one who deciphers cryptograms; **ˌcryptana'lytic**, **-ical** *adjs.*, of or pertaining to cryptanalysis.
1921 *Let.* 12 Feb. (Manly Papers, Univ. of Chicago), William F. Friedman. Cryptanalyst. **1923** W. F. FRIEDMAN (*title*) Elements of cryptanalysis. **1934** WEBSTER, Cryptanalyst. **1937** *Reader's Digest* Sept. 52/2 She was responsible for awakening Col. Friedman's interest in cryptanalytical science. **1938** W. F. FRIEDMAN *Military Cryptanalysis* I. 5 Valid, or authentic cryptanalytic solutions cannot and do not represent 'opinions' of the cryptanalyst. **1957** W. S. ALLEN *Ling. Study Lang.* 11 The interest of such material for cryptanalysis and prehistory. **1958** *Antiquity* XXXII. 216 Cryptanalytic, epigraphic and linguistic aspects. **1966** D. KAHN *Codebreakers* i. 7 The only man in the Navy with expertise in three closely related and urgently needed fields: cryptanalysis, radio, and the Japanese language. *Ibid.* xiv. 435 The cryptanalysts of the German Foreign Office, who had long ago cracked the Polish diplomatic code. *Ibid.* 436 The cryptanalytic service of the German Foreign Office.

cryptarch ('krɪptɑːk). *rare.* [f. Gr. κρυπτός hidden, secret + ἀρχός ruler.] A secret ruler. So **'cryptarchy**, secret government.
1800 W. TAYLOR in *Monthly Mag.* VIII. 599 These foreign assistants are, in fact, the cryptarchs of such synods. **1798** —— in *Monthly Rev.* XXV. 511 Yet..this cosmopolitan cryptarchy is coextensive with the habitable world.

crypted ('krɪptɪd), *a. rare.* [f. CRYPT + -ED.] Formed like a crypt, vaulted.
1885 A. J. C. HARE *Russia* iii. 136 A crypted hall and stair lead to the chapter-house.

cryptic ('krɪptɪk), *a.* (*sb.*) Also 7 -ique, 7–8 -ick, 7–8 criptic(k. [ad. L. *cryptic-us*, a. Gr. κρυπτικός fit for concealing, f. κρυπτός hidden; in sense 2, f. CRYPT + -IC.]
A. *adj.* **1. a.** Hidden, secret, occult, mystical.
cryptic syllogism, a syllogism of which the premises are not fully or explicitly stated.
a **1638** MEDE *Wks.* I. (1672) 187 Not in cryptick or mystical terms, or in..a language which they understand not. **1663** J. SPENCER *Prodigies* (1665) 130 Her [Nature's] silent processes and more cryptick methods. *a* **1734** NORTH *Examen* I. iii. ¶ 103. 193 This cryptic Plot. **1882** A. B. BRUCE *Parab. Teaching Christ* I. iv. (1891) 109 His doctrine was open and not cryptic.
b. Mysterious, enigmatic.
1920 A. CHRISTIE *Mysterious Affair at Styles* (1921) iv. 60 'That difficulty will not exist long,' pronounced Poirot quietly. John looked puzzled, not quite understanding the portent of this cryptic saying. **1936** C. S. LEWIS *Allegory of Love* i. 25 How irresistible is that cryptic knight who comes and goes we know not whence or whither, and lures the reader to follow as certainly as he lured the Queen and Kay. **1936** A. CHRISTIE *Cards on Table* xix. 188 He might have amused himself by making some cryptic remark to the doctor and noted the startled awareness in his eye. **1940** N. MARSH *Surfeit of Lampreys* (1941) xv. 225 'What did his lordship say?' 'His lordship is cryptic. He doesn't say much.' **1965** GOWERS *Fowler's Mod. Eng. Usage* 115/1 *Cryptic* might usefully be reserved for what is purposely equivocal.., and not treated as a stylish synonym for *mysterious, obscure, hidden*, and other such words.
2. Of the nature of a crypt or vault. *rare.*
1878 *Masque Poets* 26 The uncrumbled cryptic place Of still sarcophagi. **1882** *Society* 4 Nov. 21/2 One of those coved cryptic rooms found so generally in South Germany.
3. *Zool.* Of markings, coloration, etc.: serving for concealment; protective.
1890 [see ANTICRYPTIC *a.*]. **1933** *Discovery* Sept. 276/2 Bright animal colour..is frequently cryptic. *Ibid.* 277/1 The pattern of tigers, in fact of all cats, and also of zebras, is really cryptic. **1964** V. B. WIGGLESWORTH *Life of Insects* x. 149 By far the most frequent method of concealment among insects living or resting in exposed situations is camouflage, or 'cryptic coloration'.
†**B.** *sb.* A secret or occult method (of communicating knowledge). *Obs.*
1605 BACON *Adv. Learn.* II. xvii. 64 There be also other Diuersities of Methodes..as that..of Concealement, or Cryptique, etc., which I do allowe well of.

cryptical ('krɪptɪkəl), *a.* [f. as prec. + -AL[1].] = prec.
1613 R. C. *Table Alph.* (ed. 3), *Crupticall*, hidden or secret. **1648** BOYLE *Seraph. Love* xxiv. (1700) 145 That.. cryptical Method and Stile of Scripture. **1844** DE QUINCEY *Greece under Romans* Wks. VIII. 318 These cryptical or subterraneous currents of communication.

'cryptically, *adv.* [f. CRYPTICAL *a.* + -LY[2].]
a. In a cryptical manner.
1680 BOYLE *Produc. Chem. Princ.* II. 68 If we take the word Acid..in a familiar sense, without Cryptically distinguishing it from those vapors that are akin to it.
b. *Zool.* Of coloration (cf. CRYPTIC *a.* 3).
1922 *Encycl. Brit.* XXX. 725/2 This revealing coloration ..is as a rule hidden by a cryptically coloured fore wing. **1953** N. TINBERGEN *Herring Gull's World* x. 95 Finding a nest with its cryptically coloured eggs takes some time.

cryptish ('krɪptɪʃ), *a. rare.* [f. CRYPT + -ISH.] Belonging to a crypt or secret place.
1866 J. B. ROSE *Virg. Ecl. & Georg.* 143 The cryptish fire of the Gortygian cavern. **1867** —— *Virg. Æneid* Notes 402 Latinus is the eponym of the secret and cryptish worship.

crypto ('krɪptəʊ). *colloq.* [The combining form CRYPTO- used as a separate word.] A person who conceals his adherence to a certain political group; *spec.* a crypto-communist. Also *transf.*
1946 T. DRIBERG in *Reynolds News* 10 Mar. 2/2 Labour MPs of various shades of opinion—not by any means only the Communist 'fellow-travellers' or so-called 'cryptos'. **1947** W. S. CHURCHILL in *Hansard Commons* 5th Ser. CDXXXVII. 456 Pacifists or 'cryptos', or that breed of degenerate intellectuals. **1949** 'C. HARE' *When Wind Blows* 147 Is there any chance of our being able to find a crypto?.. I mean, another man like Ventry, who can really play the thing but doesn't let on that he can.

crypto- ('krɪptəʊ), before a vowel **crypt-**, combining form from Gr. κρυπτός hidden, concealed, secret. (Not so used in ancient Greek, where the sense was expressed by κρυφο-, κρυφι-.)
1. Forming the first element in many scientific words of modern formation. The more important of these occur in their alphabetical order: others are **'cryptobranch** (-bræŋk), an animal with concealed or covered branchiæ or gills; **crypto'branchiate** *a.*, having the gills concealed; *spec.* applied to certain divisions of crustacea, gastropods, etc. **'cryptocarp**, the sexual fruit of certain sea-weeds, also called CYSTOCARP; hence **crypto'carpic**, **crypto'carpous** *a.*, having the fruit or fruiting organs concealed. **crypto'cephalous** *a.*, having the head concealed. **cryp'tocerous** *a. Entom.*, having concealed 'horns' or antennæ. **crypto'clastic** *a. Min.* (see quot.). **'cryptoclite** *Gramm.* (see quot.). **crypto'crystalline** *a. Min.*, indistinctly or imperfectly crystalline, having the crystalline structure concealed; so **cryptocrystalli'zation**. **crypto'dirous** *a.*, having a concealed or concealable neck; applied to some tortoises with retractile necks. **'cryptodont** *a.* or *sb.*, having the teeth concealed or suppressed; applied to certain palæozoic bivalve molluscs. **crypto'lalic** *a. nonce-wd.*, of the nature of secret speech. **'cryptolin** [L. *oleum* oil] (see quot.). **'cryptolite** *Min.*, native phosphate of cerium found enclosed in crystals of apatite. **cryptom'nesia** [after AMNESIA] (see quot. *a* 1901); hence **cryptom'nesic** *a.* **crypto'monad**, one of a family of infusoria. **crypto'morphite** *Min.*, a native borate of calcium and soda, of cryptocrystalline structure.

crypto'neurous *a.*, having no discernible nervous system. **cryptopen'tamerous** *Entom.*, having one of the five joints of the tarsi minute or concealed. **'cryptophyte** *Bot.*, (*a*) a synonym of cryptogam, or a name for the lowest cryptogams (*rare*); (*b*) (see quots.); hence **crypto'phytic** *a.* **cryp'topia, 'cryptopine** *Chem.*, an alkaloid found in opium. **cryp'torchid, -'orchidism, -'orchism** *Path.* (see quots.). **cryp'tostoma,** *pl.* **-'stomata** *Bot.*, little circular pits found on the surface of some sea-weeds (*Treas. Bot.* 1866). **cryp'tozygous** *a.*, in Craniology, having the zygomatic arches not seen when the skull is viewed from above; hence **cryptozy'gosity.**

1872 G. M. HUMPHRY (*title*) Observations in myology, including the myology of Cryptobranch, Lepidosiren, [etc.]. *Ibid.* 1 The muscles and nerves of the Cryptobranch. **1882** GEIKIE *Text Bk. Geol.* II. II. §III. 88 *Cryptoclastic* or *compact*, where the grains are too minute to reveal to the naked eye the truly fragmental character of the rock. **1875** MARCH *Anglo-Saxon Gram.* 52 Irregular nouns.. disquised by phonetic changes (Cryptoclites). **1862** DANA *Man. Geol.* 72 Crypto-crystalline. **1880** *Encycl. Brit.* XI. 634/1 A cryptocrystalline variety of quartz. **1889** *Sat. Rev.* 26 Oct. 445/1 On some cryptographic or cryptolalic system. **1863–72** WATTS *Dict. Chem.* II. 114 *Cryptolin*, an organic liquid, found.. in cavities of topaz, chrysoberyl, quartz-crystals.. and amethyst.. Cryptolin, when exposed to the air, speedily hardens into a yellowish, transparent, resinous body. **1850** DANA *Geol.* 236 The crystals of.. cryptolite are microscopic. *aa***1901** MYERS *Hum. Pers.* (1903) I. p. xvi, *Cryptomnesia*, submerged or subliminal memory of events forgotten by the supraliminal self. *Ibid.* II. 136 'Cryptomnesia' (as Professor Flournoy calls submerged memory). *Ibid.* 140 This cryptomnesic automatism. **1916** C. E. LONG tr. *Jung's Coll. Papers Analyt. Psychol.* 91 The rudimentary glossolalia of our case has not any title to be a classical instance of cryptomnesia. *Ibid.*, The cryptomnesic image arrives at consciousness through the senses. **1961** W. H. SALTER *Zoar* x. 138 Latent memory (cryptomnesia) is therefore left as an alternative explanation to sheer chance-coincidence. **1847–9** TODD *Cycl. Anat.* IV. 7/2 In the Cryptomonads.. the proboscis is of a similar character. **1861** *Amer. Jrnl. Sc.* Ser. II. XXXII. 9 Cryptomorphite. **1882** *Syd. Soc. Lex.*, *Cryptoneurous*, applied by Rudolphi to a series of animals the nervous system of which is mingled and confounded with the mass which constitutes them, as the zoophytes. **1869** *Biennial Retrospect Med. & Surg.* 475 Messrs. C. and H. Smith have extracted from opium a new alkaloid to which they assign the name *cryptopia*. **1879** WATTS *Dict. Chem.* VI. 514 Cryptopine.. crystallises.. in microscopic six-sided prisms or tables. **1874** *Van Buren's Dis. Genit. Org.* 390 A cryptorchid is an individual whose scrotum contains no testicles. **1882** *Syd. Soc. Lex.*, *Cryptorchidism*, the condition of a *Cryptorchis*. *Cryptorchis*, term for one whose testicles have not descended into the scrotum, but remain in the abdomen. [**1904** *Botanisk Tidsskrift* XXVI. p. xiv, C. Raunkiær gav en Meddelelse om biologiske Typer.. karakteriserede ved Graden og Arten.. iv. Jordplanter, *Kryptofyter*. De overlevende Knopper.. befinder sig nede i Jorden.] **1913** *Jrnl. Ecol.* I. 17 Cryptophytes include plants with their dormant parts subterranean. **1937** *Nature* 18 Dec. 1035/2 Cryptophytes, whose surviving buds, etc., are either beneath the soil or at the bottom of water. **1964** GLEASON & CRONQUIST *Nat. Geogr. Plants* xviii. 229 Cryptophytes (hidden plants) are perennial herbs with their buds well below the surface. **1925** *Glasgow Herald* 23 May 4 The dense cryptophytic life [in the jungle] underneath the thick carpet. **1878** BARTLEY *Topinard's Anthrop.* II. iii. 288 When [[the facial angle] is negative, the [zygomatic] arches are cryptozygous or concealed.

2. From these *crypto-* passes into the status of a separable element, which may be prefixed, **a.** to sbs. of any origin, with the sense 'concealed, unavowed', as in **Crypto-'Calvinist,** a name given in the 16th c. in Germany to those Lutherans who secretly held or sympathized with Calvinistic tenets (= *Philippist*, or *Melanchthonian*), and in France to professing Roman Catholics accused of being secretly Calvinists; hence, **Crypto-'Calvinism,** †**-Cal'vinianism, -Calvi'nistic** *a.* So ***Crypto-Catholic, -Catholicism, -Christian, -communist, -deist, -fascist, -Fenian, -heresy, -heretic, -Jesuit, -Jew, -lunatic, -proselyte, -Royalist, -semite, -Socinian,*** etc.; also ***crypto-insolence***, veiled insolence; **b.** to adjs. with the sense 'secretly, unavowedly', as in ***crypto-splenetic.***

1760 KEYSLER *Trav.* IV. 289 The sword with which secretary Krell was beheaded for his *Crypto-calvinianism. **1856** HARDWICK *Ch. Hist. Reform.* 176 *note*, 'Philippism', or *Crypto-Calvinism, was principally found in the Palatinate. **1764** MACLAINE tr. *Mosheim's Eccl. Hist.* (1884) II. 94 The schemes of the *Crypto-Calvinist, or secret abettors of Calvinism, being thus disconcerted. **1883** BEARD *Reformation* v. 182 Whoever would not subscribe every article of ultra-Lutheran orthodoxy was a Crypto-Calvinist. **1798** W. TAYLOR in *Monthly Rev.* XXVII. 515 The charge of *Crypto-Catholicism. **1800** —— in *Monthly Mag.* VIII. 598 This fraternity of darkness, of crypto-proselytism, crypto-catholicism, and crypto-jesuitism. **1888** *Contemp. Rev.* Apr. 544 The large number of Christians who professed Islam, but remained *crypto-Christians. **1946** *Newsweek* 10 June 44/3 To.. Ernest Bevin these extreme left-wingers with their demands for 'working class unity' appear as fellow travelers. He has denounced them as 'crypto-communists'. **1947** *News Chron.* 8 Apr., He is an extreme Left-Wing Socialist... In the Commons he is, of course, dubbed a 'fellow-traveller' and a 'crypto-communist'. **1961** *Times* 1 Dec. 15/1 A crypto-communist reporter. **1965** *Ibid.* 23 Feb. 10/5 The right wing.. attacked M. Beuve-Méry as a crypto-communist. **1885** H. N. OXENHAM *Short Studies* xxvi. 244 He [Thomas Paine] was already a *crypto-deist. **1937** C. CONNOLLY in L. Russell *Press Gang!* 91 Ah, summer! There's a *crypto-fascist for you! **1942** E. WAUGH *Work Suspended* ii. 86 They're the new hush-hush crypto-fascist department. **1956** D. J. ENRIGHT *Bread rather than Blossoms* 26 A crypto-fascist looks for open war. **1887** PLUMPTRE *Dante's Commedia* II. 382 The symbolic cypher of a *crypto-heresy. **1881** *Spectator* 15 Jan. 77 The *crypto-insolence which so often underlies journalistic argument about Irishmen. **1892** ZANGWILL *Childr. Ghetto* I. 3 The Spanish *crypto-Jews who had reached England via Holland. **1957** *Encycl. Brit.* XXI. 231/2 Portuguese crypto-Jews, that is, descendants of Jews whom the Inquisition had compelled to embrace Christianity but who remained Jews at heart. **1889** *Spectator* 16 Nov., M. Thiers.. allowed many thousand persons, half of them *crypto-lunatics, to be executed. **1837** CARLYLE *Fr. Rev.* III. III. ii, A traitorous *Crypto-Royalist class. **1920** *Punch* 26 May 415/1 Giving dancing lessons to the daughters of profiteers, *Crypto-Semites and other unpropitious persons. **1937** WYNDHAM LEWIS *Blasting & Bombardiering* v. v. 280 This 'young American poet' was undoubtedly a crypto-semite. **1858** CARLYLE *Fredk. Gt.* (1865) II. VI. iv. 170 A weak croaky official gentleman, of a *crypto-splenetic turn.

cryptobiosis (ˌkrɪptəʊbaɪˈəʊsɪs). *Biol.* [f. CRYPTO- + *-biosis* as in ANABIOSIS.] (See quot. 1959.)

1959 D. KEILIN in *Proc. R. Soc.* B. CL. 166, I should like to propose the term cryptobiosis, that is, latent life, for the state of an organism when it shows no visible signs of life and when its metabolic activity becomes hardly measurable, or comes reversibly to a standstill. **1965** *New Scientist* 28 Oct. 270/2 When an organism is in a state of cryptobiosis mechanical injuries are tolerated that would be immediately fatal in the normal state.

cryptobiotic (ˌkrɪptəʊbaɪˈɒtɪk), *a.* [ad. G. *kryptobiotisch* (O. Kuntze *Phytogeogenesis* (1884) iii. 40), f. CRYPTO- + Gr. βιωτικ-ός pertaining to life.]

a. (See quot. 1916.) **b.** = CRYPTOZOIC *a.* 1. **c.** Of or pertaining to cryptobiosis.

1916 B. D. JACKSON *Gloss. Bot. Terms* (ed. 3) 97/2 *Cryptobiotic*, Kuntze's suggested expression for those lowly organisms which appeared in geologic times, but have left no trace of their existence. **1934** S. F. LIGHT in C. A. Kofoid *Termites* iii. 23 Associated with the wood-eating habit of the termites is their cryptobiotic mode of life. They live shut off from the light in enclosed passageways. **1948** T. E. SNYDER *Our Enemy the Termite* (ed. 2) 240 *Cryptobiotic*, living a 'hidden life', a term applied to insects, such as termites, living a life where they are concealed in wood, underground, etc. **1965** *New Scientist* 28 Oct. 270/2 Some further properties of the cryptobiotic state.

cryptococcosis (ˌkrɪptəʊkəˈkəʊsɪs). *Path.* [f. mod.L. *Cryptococcus* + -OSIS.] A disease of man and animals caused by the yeast-like fungus *Cryptococcus neoformans*; torulosis.

1938 *Texas Jrnl. Med.* XXXIII. 310 Systemic cryptococcosis. **1962** *New Scientist* 12 Apr. 46/3 A fungus disease called cryptococcosis, which usually attacks the [koala] bears' central nervous system. **1970** JUBB & KENNEDY *Path. Domestic Anim.* (ed. 2) I. iii. 253/1 Cryptococcosis (European blastomycosis) is a subacute or chronic mycosis, caused by *Cryptococcus neoformans* (*Torula histolytica*), .. which shows, in man, dogs, and possibly other species as well, a marked predilection for the central nervous system.

crypto-communist, -fascist: see CRYPTO- 2 a.

cryptodynamic (ˌkrɪptəʊdɪˈnæmɪk), *a.* [CRYPTO- + Gr. δύναμις power, δυναμικός powerful.]

1. Relating to hidden force.

1816 BENTHAM *Chrestom.* Wks. VIII. 87 Idioscopic or Cryptodynamic Anthropurgics has for its single-worded synonym the unexpressive appellation, Chemistry.

2. Applied to a kind of cycling gear; usually abbreviated ***crypto***; also as *sb.*

1885 *Cyclists' Tour. Club Gaz.* Sept. 12 *Advt.*, The Crypto-Dynamic gear. **1886** *Ibid.* IV. 139 The 'slight friction' incident to the use of the 'Crypto' at speed. **1888** *Encycl. Brit.* XXIII. 560 Two-speed gears are becoming general, among which may be.. mentioned the Crypto-dynamic.

cryptogam (ˈkrɪptəʊgæm). *Bot.* [a. Fr. *cryptogame* adj. and sb., in pl. *-games*, ad. mod.L. *cryptogamæ* (sc. *plantæ*), fem. pl. of *cryptogamus*, f. Gr. κρυπτός hidden + γάμος wedlock; after the Linnæan class-name CRYPTOGAMIA.

Brongniart in 1843 first divided the Vegetable Kingdom into *Cryptogamæ*, and *Phanerogamæ*, whence F. *cryptogames*, Eng. *cryptogams*, etc.]

A plant of the class Cryptogamia.

1847 LINDLEY *Veg. Kingd.* Pref. 17 The substitution of the words Endogens, Cryptogams, Phænogams, etc., for Endogenæ, Cryptogamæ, Phænogamæ, etc. **1883** H. DRUMMOND *Nat. Law in Spir. W.* (1884) 412 From the unicellular cryptogam to the highest phanerogam.

†**'cryptogame,** *a. Obs. rare.* [a. F. *cryptogame*: see prec.] Breeding in secret; see quot.

1774 WHITE *Sand-martin* in *Phil. Trans.* LXV. 275 This species is *cryptogame*, carrying on the business of nidification, incubation, and the support of its young, in the dark.

‖**cryptogamia** (krɪptəʊˈgæmɪə). *Bot.* [mod.L. *Cryptogamia* (Linn. 1735), sb. fem., f. Gr. κρυπτός hidden, concealed + γάμος wedding, wedlock + -ία suffix of state: cf. Gr. ἀγαμία unmarried condition, celibacy; in F. *cryptogamie.*

Like the names of other Linnæan classes and orders, it is a singular noun, and was always so treated in the 18th c.; but in the 19th c., prob. by unthinking confusion with classes and orders of the animal kingdom (e.g. *Vertebrata, Mammalia, Carnivora*) which are adjs. neuter plural, it has been (first apparently by persons not botanists, and afterwards by some botanists also) misused as a noun plural = cryptogams.]

A large division of the vegetable kingdom, being the last class in the Linnæan Sexual system, and comprising those plants which have no stamens or pistils, and therefore no proper flowers; including Ferns, Mosses, Algæ, Lichens, and Fungi.

[**1735** LINNÆUS *Syst. Nat.* (1740) 74 Cryptogamia vegetabilia sæpe suspecta includit. **1737** —— *Gen. Plant.* (1742) 500 Classes xxiv Cryptogamia. Cryptogamia continet Vegetabilia, quorum Fructificationes visui nostro sese subtrahunt. Ordines hujus classis sex constituo.] **1753** CHAMBERS *Cycl. Supp.*, *Cryptogamia*, in botany, a class of plants whose flowers are either wholly invisible, or scarce discernable by the eye. **1794** MARTYN *Rousseau's Bot.* ix. 96 That class is called cryptogamia, from the circumstance of the fructification being concealed, or not obvious. **1861** H. MACMILLAN *Footnotes fr. Nat.* 3 The second great division of the vegetable kingdom, to which the name of cryptogamia has been given.

¶ Erroneously treated as a plural = Cryptogams.

1813 SIR H. DAVY *Agric. Chem.* (1814) 72 Even in the cryptogamia.. as in the more perfect plants. **1856** MISS MULOCK *J. Halifax* (ed. 17) 337 In order to study the cryptogamia. **1885** ANNANDALE *Imperial Dict.*, The Cryptogamia are divided into cellular and vascular cryptogams.

Hence **crypto'gamian** *a.* (1828 in Webster), **crypto'gamic** *a.* (also as *sb.*), **crypto'gamical** *a.*, of or pertaining to the class Cryptogamia or to cryptogams; **cryp'togamist,** a botanist who specially studies cryptogams; **cryp'togamous** *a.*, of the nature of a cryptogam; **cryp'togamy,** cryptogamic condition or relations.

1805 *Edin. Rev.* VI. 134 Among these last [plants] we notice several cryptogamics. **1830** LINDLEY *Nat. Syst. Bot.* 307 The subject of Cryptogamic botany. **1801** *Med. Jrnl.* V. 370 A country rich in cryptogamical plants. **1830** LINDLEY *Nat. Syst. Bot.* 307 Those great cryptogamists whose lives have been devoted to the study of the subject. **1829** JESSE *Jrnl. Nat.* 374 A cryptogamous plant, which I believe to be lichen fascicularis. **1870** BENTLEY *Bot.* 10 Flowerless or Cryptogamous plants. **1796** PENNANT *Hist. Whiteford & Holywell* (T.), The picturesque dingle Nant-y-bi abounds with what the botanists name the cryptogamous plants. The idea of cryptogamy inspired Timæus with ideas of loves of other kind.

cryptogenetic (ˌkrɪptəʊdʒɪˈnɛtɪk), *a. Path.* [f. CRYPTO- + -GENETIC.] Of a disease: of obscure or unknown origin. Also **crypto'genic** *a.*

1908 R. PARK *Mod. Surg.* I. 87 Cryptogenetic or spontaneous septicemia is a term applied to those cases in which the port of entry of the germs is no longer visible—e.g., a hypodermic puncture—or cannot be positively determined. **1908** *Practitioner* Feb. 249–50 Cryptogenic pernicious anaemia... So-called 'cryptogenic' sepsis, or pyaemia. **1962** *Lancet* 27 Jan. 190/1 All cases of liver cirrhosis which cannot be ascribed to abuse of alcohol, occlusive processes of the bile ducts, or hæmochromatosis will be referred to as 'cryptogenetic cirrhosis of the liver'.

cryptogram (ˈkrɪptəgræm). [mod. f. Gr. κρυπτός hidden + γράμμα writing, a letter, but not on Greek analogies: see -GRAM. So mod. F. *cryptogramme.*] A piece of cryptographic writing; anything written in cipher, or in such a form or order that a key is required in order to know how to understand and put together the letters.

1880 *Times* 28 Dec. 10/1 In every case of deciphering—whether it be of a Cypriote inscription of a cryptogram in the agony column. **1888** I. DONNELLY (*title*), The Great Cryptogram: Bacon's Cipher in Shakespeare's Plays.

Hence **crypto'gramic** *a.*, pertaining to or of the nature of a cryptogram. So also **cryptogra'mmatic, -ical** *adjs.*; **crypto'grammic** *a.* = CRYPTOGRAMIC *a.*; **crypto'grammatist; crypto'grammist** = CRYPTOGRAMMATIST.

1884 *Bazaar* 22 Dec. 666/2 Every vowel and consonant in the words of the cryptogramic sentence was represented. **1888** *Scott. Leader* 4 July 4 Mr. Ignatius Donnelly.. with his cryptogramic theory of Shakspere. **1895** *Daily News* 17 Jan. 6/4 To offer insoluble conundrums in cryptogrammatic ellipsis. **1962** C. L. WRENN in Davis & Wrenn *Eng. & Medieval Studies* 314 The cryptogrammatic runes and oghams of the Hackness Cross. **1892** *Athenæum* 13 Feb. 211/2 Mr. Donnelly keeps his cryptogrammatical tendencies in check. **1890** *Ibid.* 8 Mar. 316/3 America will some day produce.. a cryptogrammatist ready to prove that "The Ring and the Book' was written by Lord Tennyson. **1901** *Westm. Gaz.* 3 Jan. 2/3 By a bewildering.. system of.. word-counting he constructed a cryptogrammic theory. **1906** *Daily Chron.* 18 June 3/3 Prophets, cranks, cryptogrammists. **1929** W. J. LOCKE *Ancestor Jorico* vii. 90 In peace times the Admiralty had no use for an expert cryptogrammist.

cryptograph ('krɪptəʊgrɑːf, -græf). [mod. f. as prec. + Gr. -γραφος writing, written; see -GRAPH.]

1. = CRYPTOGRAM.

a **1849** POE *Tales, Gold Beetle*, I could not suppose him [Kidd] capable of constructing any of the more abstruse cryptographs. **1879** FARRAR *St. Paul* I. 641 *note*, Much of the Talmud consists of cryptographs which designedly concealed meanings from persecutors and heretics.

2. a. A kind of type-writer for writing in cipher.

1889 *Daily News* 21 Oct. 3/6 The Wier Cryptograph.. by means of which a small.. type-writer is made to write cryptograms, to be translated mechanically on a similar machine.

b. An enciphering or deciphering device.

1879 C. WHEATSTONE *Sci. Papers* 342 (*heading*) Instructions for the employment of Wheatstone's cryptograph. **1928** *Daily Express* 22 May 2/4 A new invention known as the cryptograph, which could automatically code messages and decode them.

Hence †**cryp'tographal** *a.*, **crypto'graphic** *a.*, of, or of the nature of, cryptography; †**crypto'graphical**, dealing or concerned with cryptography; also **cryp'tographer**, **cryp'tographist**, one who writes in or is skilled in cipher. [All founded on a possible Gr. κρυπτόγραφος: see above.]

a **1691** BOYLE *Wks.* VI. 339 (R.) Neither have I any zeal for the character, as cryptographal or universal. **1641** WILKINS *Mercury* Pref. (1707) 3 Now.. both are grown Such Cryptographers. **1824** J. JOHNSON *Typogr.* II. xii. 478 A cryptographic, secret, or cypher writing. **1870** *Pall Mall G.* 5 Nov. 4 The cryptographic advertisements in the second column of the *Times.* **1694** *Lond. Gaz.* No. 2973/4 Recreations of divers Kinds, viz. Numerical, Geometrical.. Horometrical, Cryptographical. **1753** CHESTERF. *World* No. 24 ¶12 In possession.. of a more brachygraphical, cryptographical, and steganographical secret. *a* **1849** POE *Tales, Gold Beetle*, To divide the sentence into the natural division intended by the cryptographist. **1896** *Daily News* 3 Feb. 3/4 He has.. been very successful as a cryptographer, and published.. what is perhaps the only attempt at a scientific method of analysis of ciphers. **1959** *Chambers's Encycl.* IV. 280/1 The countries at war [in 1914–18] established numerous intercepting stations.. and also a staff of cryptographers.

cryptography (krɪp'tɒgrəfɪ). [a. mod.L. *cryptographia*, f. Gr. κρυπτός hidden + -γραφία writing: see -GRAPHY.] A secret manner of writing, either by arbitrary characters, by using letters or characters in other than their ordinary sense, or by other methods intelligible only to those possessing the key; also anything written in this way. Generally, the art of writing or solving ciphers.

[**1641** WILKINS *Mercury* ii. (1707) 8 There are also different Ways of Secresy. 1. Cryptologia. 2. Cryptographia. 3. Semæologia.] **1658** SIR T. BROWNE *Gard. Cyrus* iii, The strange Cryptography of Gaffarell in his Starry Book of Heaven. **1780** VON TROIL *Iceland* 300 Our gravers of runes even made use of this cryptography in monuments. **1855** *Chamb. Jrnl.* IV. 134 These decipherers gave the high-sounding names of Cryptography, Cryptology.. to their art. **1950** J. KOBLER in *Collier's* 28 Oct., Perhaps the most brilliant feat in all the long history of cryptography was accomplished by our own cryptanalysts. **1957** *Encycl. Brit.* V. 930/1 The.. quite important roles which poor cryptography or good cryptanalysis have played in international relations. **1966** [see next].

cryptology (krɪp'tɒlədʒɪ). [ad. mod.L. *cryptologia*, f. Gr. κρυπτός hidden + -λογια speaking, etc.: see -LOGY.] **a.** 'Secret speech or communication' (Blount 1656); mystical or enigmatical language.

[**1641** WILKINS *Mercury* ii. (1707) 8 Cryptologia, or the Secresy of Speaking, may consist either 1. In the Matter. 2. In the words.] *c* **1645** HOWELL *Lett.* I. III. xxxvii, Cryptology, or Epistolizing in a Clandestin way, is very ancient. **1840** *New Monthly Mag.* LX. 226 Certain advertising individuals.. are most mischievously addicted to another species of cryptology.

b. (See quot. 1966.)

1945 J. S. GALLAND (*title*) An historical and analytical bibliography of the literature of cryptology. **1957** *Encycl. Brit.* V. 923/1 Because of.. the remarkable progress made in communications-electronics technology, cryptology has come to play a very important role in governmental communications. **1966** D. KAHN *Codebreakers* p. xvi, Cryptology is the science that embraces cryptography and cryptanalysis, but the term 'cryptology' sometimes loosely designates the entire dual field of both rendering signals secure and extracting information from them.

cryptomere ('krɪptəʊmɪə(r)). *Biol.* [ad. G. *kryptomer* (E. Tschermak 1904, in *Beih. z. Bot. Centralbl.* XVI. 11), f. CRYPTO- + Gr. μέρος part.] A latent genetic factor or characteristic. So **cryp'tomerism**, the possession of this factor or characteristic.

1906 R. H. LOCK *Rec. Progress Study Variation* viii. 189 The best general name for the class of phenomena we are about to describe is perhaps latency of characters, or cryptomerism. **1909** W. BATESON *Mendel's Princ. Hered.* (ed. 2) v. 93 Factors which may thus exist without making their presence visible have been named by Tschermak 'Cryptomeres'.

cryptomeria (krɪptəʊ'mɪərɪə). [mod.L., f. CRYPTO- + Gr. μέρος part. So named because the seeds are hidden or enclosed by scales.] An evergreen coniferous tree (*C. japonica*) allied to the cypresses, a native of North China and Japan, and now extensively cultivated in England; the Japanese cedar; also, the wood of this tree.

1841 D. DON in *Trans. Linnean Soc.* XVIII. 166 (*heading*) *Cryptomeria*. Ord. Nat. Coniferæ. *Ibid.* 170 The wood in *Cryptomeria* is compact, and the fibrous tissue is composed of very slender vessels. **1852** R. FORTUNE *Journey Tea Countries China* xviii. 304 The beautiful *Cryptomeria*, or Japan cedar. **1863** R. ALCOCK *Capital of Tycoon* I. iv. 103 A long avenue of cryptomerias and pines. **1904** D. SLADEN *Playing the Game* I. xii. 124 An avenue of tall cryptomerias. **1957** C. BROOKE-ROSE *Languages of Love* 45 A false ceiling of wide boards, not, alas, of cryptomeria but of ordinary stained timber. **1966** BOOM & KLEIJN *Glory of Tree* 24/1 The *Cryptomeria* is a very beautiful tree.

cryptonym ('krɪptəʊnɪm). *rare.* [f. Gr. κρυπτός hidden + ὄνομα name: cf. ANONYM.] A private or secret name.

1876 LOWELL *Among my Bks.* Ser. II. *Dante* p. 16 *note*, Only a cryptonym by which heretics knew each other.

So **cryp'tonymous** *a.*, whose name is concealed, anonymous.

1880 SWINBURNE in *Fortn. Rev.* Dec. 719 The cryptonymous railer for his bread.

‖**cryptoporticus** (krɪptəʊ'pɔːtɪkəs). [L., f. Gr. κρυπτός hidden + L. *porticus* gallery.] In ancient architecture, a concealed or enclosed portico; an enclosed gallery having, at the side, walls with openings instead of columns; also a covered or subterranean passage.

1681 COTTON *Wond. Peake* 5 An entry.. such as one as we might well Think it the Crypto-porticus of Hell. **1832** GELL *Pompeiana* II. 61 In one of the most obscure parts of the cryptoporticus. **1877** LL. JEWITT *Half-hrs. Eng. Antiq.* 67 Two courts.. surrounded by a gallery, or cryptoporticus.

cryptous ('krɪptəs), *a. rare.* [f. L. *crypta* + -OUS.] Of the nature of or pertaining to a crypt; cryptal. Cf. CRYPT 4.

1857 BULLOCK *Cazeaux' Midwif.* 42 The internal lips are furnished with a cryptous apparatus.

cryptovolcanic (ˌkrɪptəʊvɒl'kænɪk), *a. Geol.* [ad. G. *kryptovulkanisch* (W. Branco and E. Fraas 1905, in *Abh. K. Preuss. Akad. Wiss.* 57), f. CRYPTO- + VOLCANIC *a.*] ***cryptovolcanic structure***: a nearly circular area not associated with igneous rock but having features suggesting volcanic activity.

1921 W. H. BUCHER in *Bull. Geol. Soc. Amer.* XXXII. 75 The Steinheim Basin.. has thus far been the only known representative of this type of structure, for which Branco and Fraas proposed the term 'cryptovolcanic'. **1954** W. D. THORNBURY *Princ. Geomorphol.* (1962) ix. 211 A rare but interesting type of dome is the cryptovolcanic structure. It is thought to be produced by the sudden release of volcanic gases at depth. *Ibid.* xx. 521 Some alleged cryptovolcanic structures may prove to be meteorite craters. **1969** C. OLLIER *Volcanoes* iii. 33 Gosses Bluff in central Australia may be a cryptovolcanic structure.

cryptoxanthin (krɪptəʊ'zænθɪn). *Chem.* [ad. G. *krypto-xanthin* (R. Kuhn and C. Grundmann 1933, in *Ber. d. Deut. Chem. Ges.* LXVI. 1746), f. CRYPTO- + XANTHIN.] A yellow carotenoid pigment, $C_{40}H_{56}O$, widely found in nature and important as a precursor of vitamin A.

1934 *Chem. Abstr.* XXVIII. 1043 Cryptoxanthin... This new xanthophyll.. constitutes almost ⅓ of the total pigment of the calyxes and berries of *Physalis franchetti*. **1946** *Nature* 24 Aug. 269/2 Carotenoids, such as cryptoxanthin and β-carotene. **1960** FOX & VEVERS *Nature of Animal Colours* v. 76 Other vitamin A precursors are α-carotene, cryptoxanthin (3-oxy-β-carotene), found in many plants as well as in egg-yolk, and echinenone.

cryptozoa (krɪptəʊ'zəʊə), *sb. pl. Zool.* [Back-formation from CRYPTOZOIC *a.*] The group of cryptozoic animals.

1911 A. WILLEY *Convergence in Evolution* iii. 25 Phanerozoa and cryptozoa are two well-marked physiological groups. **1968** *Sci. Amer.* July 108/1 They are examples of the many small animals that lead hidden lives; they are some of the cryptozoa, the animals in hiding.

cryptozoic (krɪptəʊ'zəʊɪk), *a.* [f. CRYPTO- + Gr. ζωή life + -IC.]

1. *Biol.* Defining a class of fauna composed of animals living a concealed or hidden life (see quots.); also, belonging to this class.

1895 A. DENDY in *Rep. 6th Meeting Austral. Assoc. Adv. Sci.* 99 The Cryptozoic Fauna of Australasia... I use the word 'Cryptozoic' for want of a better. **1897** PARKER & HASWELL *Zool.* II. xiv. 601 Cryptozoic forms, which live under stones, logs of wood, etc., such as Land-Planarians, Peripatus, Centipedes, and Woodlice. **1953** R. F. LAWRENCE *Biol. Cryptic Fauna of Forests* ii. 32 Certain examples of cryptozoic forms may take advantage of the shelter provided by human habitations.

2. *Geol.* (Usu. with capital initial.) A name given to the Pre-Cambrian era, now esp. when this is contrasted with the whole of the later part of geological history, from the beginning of the Cambrian to the present day; of or pertaining to the Pre-Cambrian era. Cf. PHANEROZOIC *a.*

1911 *Encycl. Brit.* XXII. 266/2 The name pre-Cambrian is the equivalent of the 'Algonkian'..; the terms.. cryptozoic, eparchaic and others have also been applied to the same period. **1930** G. H. CHADWICK in *Bull. Geol. Soc. Amer.* XLI. 48 Cryptozoic or Cryptobiotic (Precambrian). **1958** R. C. MOORE *Introd. Hist. Geol.* (ed. 2) iv. 59 The first major division of earth history determinable from rocks exposed at the surface is the Cryptozoic Eon. *Ibid.*, It is convenient also to designate the Cryptozoic rocks as Precambrian. **1968** *Courier-Mail* (Brisbane) 19 Nov. 26/8 The Cryptozoic ('hidden life') extends a further 3,000 million years—and yet its rocks show almost no traces of life! **1969** DUNBAR & WAAGE *Hist. Geol.* (ed. 3) vii. 164/1 In rocks so generally devoid of fossils what little indication we have of Cryptozoic environments and climates is derived from the sediments.

cryptozoon (krɪptəʊ'zəʊɒn). *Geol.* [f. CRYPTO- + Gr. ζῷον animal.] A Cambrian reef-forming fossil, believed to be the remains of colonies of calcareous algæ; cf. STROMATOLITE. Also *attrib.*

1883 J. HALL in *36th Ann. Rep. N.Y. State Mus. Nat. Hist.* Plate 6, There occurs a bed of limestone.. the surface being nearly covered by closely-arranged circular or subcircular discs which are made of concentric laminæ... I, therefore, propose the term cryptozoön as a designation for this peculiar form and mode of growth. **1914** *Smithsonian Misc. Coll.* LXIV. 98, I do not know a true Cryptozoön older than the Cambrian fauna. **1936** *Geogr. Jrnl.* LXXXVII. 429 Near Etah a Cryptozoon reef occurs. **1965** M. E. WILSON in K. Rankama *Precambrian* II. 312 Concentric *Cryptozoon*-like structures believed to be of algal origin. **1969** DUNBAR & WAAGE *Hist. Geol.* (ed. 3) viii. 182/2 The name *Cryptozoon*, once given to all Lower Paleozoic stromatolites, is no longer used.

crys, obs. f. KRIS, Malay dagger.

crys-: see also CHRIS-, CHRYS-, CRIS-.

'crysiple, irreg. form of CRUCIBLE.

1651 MORE *2nd Lash* in *Enthus. Triumph.* (1656) 208 Put thy soul into a crysiple, O pragmaticall Chymist.

Cryst(e, etc.: see CHRIST, etc.

crystal ('krɪstəl), *sb.* and *a.* Forms: α. [1 cristalla], 3–7 cristal(l, (4 **crestal**, **-el**, **kristall**, **cristale**, **-talle**); β. 5 **crystalle**, 5–7 **crystall**, 7– **crystal**; γ. 6–7 **christal(l**, 7 **chrystall**, 7–9 **chrystal**. [a. OF. *cristal* (11th c. in Littré) = Pr. and Sp. *cristal*, It. *cristallo*, ad. L. *crystallum*, ad. Gr. κρύσταλλος clear ice, (rock-)crystal, deriv. of κρυσταίν-ειν to freeze, congeal with frost, κρύος frost. Between the 15th and the 17th c. the Eng. spelling was gradually changed after L. to *crystal* (against the practice of the Romanic langs.), and in the 16th c. an erroneous spelling with *chr-* (app. after *chrysolite*, etc.) became frequent.]

A. *sb.*

†**1.** Ice, clear ice. *Obs.* (chiefly a literalism of translation from the Vulgate).

c **1000** *Ags. Ps.* cxlvii. 6 He his cristallum cynnum sendeð. *a* **1340** HAMPOLE *Psalter* cxlvii. 6 He sendis his kristall as morcels. **1382** WYCLIF *Ecclus.* xliii. 22 The cristal freesede fro the watyr. *c* **1400** MAUNDEV. (Roxb.) xvii. 79 Þe water congelez in to cristall. **1535** COVERDALE *Ecclus.* xliii. 20 Whan the colde northwynde bloweth, harde Christall commeth of the water.

2. a. A mineral, clear and transparent like ice; *esp.* a form of pure quartz having these qualities. Now more particularly distinguished from other senses as ***rock-crystal***, formerly also ***crystal of the mountains***. ***Iceland crystal***: old name of Iceland spar.

(By the ancients and in the Middle Ages (rock-)crystal was supposed to be congealed water or ice 'petrified' by some long-continued natural process. There was thus no transfer of sense in applying to it the same name as to clear ice, of which it was viewed as merely another state.)

c **1000** ÆLFRIC *Num.* xi. 7 Swilce coryandran sæd, hwites bleos swa cristalla [Vulg. *coloris bdellii*]. *c* **1290** *S. Eng. Leg.* 228/318 Weued and chaliz and Cruettes þoruȝ-out cler cristal. **1398** TREVISA *Barth. De P.R.* XVI. xxx. (1495) 562 Crystall is a bryght stone and clere wyth watry colour. Men trowe that snowe or yse is made hard in space of many yeres; therfore the Grekys yaue this name therto. *c* **1440** *Promp. Parv.* 103 Crystalle, stone, *cristallus*. **1567** MAPLET *Gr. Forest* 5 b, The Cristall is one of those stones that shyneth in euerie part, and is in colour watrie. Isidore saith, that it is nothing else then a congeled Ise by continuance frosen whole yeares. **1611** BIBLE *Rev.* iv. 6 A sea of glasse like vnto Chrystall. **1647** COWLEY *Mistress, Coldness* iii, Though Heat dissolve the Ice again, The Chrystal solid does remain. **1750** tr. *Leonardus' Mirr. Stones* 84 Crystal, is a Stone like Ice, both in Colour and Transparency, with a pretty good Hardness. **1861** C. W. KING *Ant. Gems* (1866) 93 Crystal is found in very large masses; the largest known to the Romans weighed 50 pounds. **1874** BOUTELL *Arms & Arm.* vi. 85 Of iron, or of bone, stone, crystal, or some other hard substance.

b. The standard type of clearness or transparency, in the phrase 'as clear as crystal' (CLEAR *a.* 3).

a **1300** *Cursor M.* 376 (Fairf.) Water clere als cristale. *c* **1440** *York Myst.* xxxii. 24 My coloure as cristall is clere. **1647** COWLEY *Mistress, My Heart Discov.*, Clear as fair Crystal to the View.

3. Poetically applied to pure limpid water, or other clear transparent substance.

1594 BARNFIELD *Aff. Sheph.* I. xxii, Within the Christall of a Pearle-bright brooke. **1643** DENHAM *Cooper's H.* 322 Proud of his wound to it resigns his blood And stains the crystal with a purple flood. **1767** Sir W. Jones *Seven Fount.* Poems (1777) 43 Birds that..from the brink the liquid crystal sip. **1885** Mrs. H. Ward tr. *Amiel's Jrnl.* 255 The glacier throws off the stones and fragments fallen into its crevasses that it may remain pure crystal.

4. a. (with *a* and *pl.*) A piece of rock-crystal or similar mineral; *esp.* one used in magic art.

1393 Gower *Conf.* III. 112 A cristall is that one, Which that corone is set upon. *c* **1475** *Rauf Coilȝear* 474 Blandit with Beriallis and Cristallis cleir. **1597** Jas. I. *Demonol.* (in Brand *Pop. Ant.* III. 108) The Seer looks into a Chrystal or Berryl, wherein he will see the answer, represented either by Types or Figures. **1669** *Phil. Trans.* IV. 983 At the foot of these mountains are with great labour digg'd out Chrystals. **1769** Sir W. Jones *Pal. Fortune* Poems (1777) 16 She..in th' enchanted crystal sees A bower o'er-canopied with tufted trees. **1816** Scott *Antiq.* xxiii, You have used neither ..crystal, pentacle, magic-mirror, nor geomantic figure. **1882** Stevenson *New Arab. Nts.* (1884) 110 The gardener.. hastily drew together the..jewels..The touch of these costly crystals sent a shiver..through the man's frame.

b. *fig.* Applied to the eyes.

1592 Shaks. *Ven. & Ad.* 963 Her eye seene in the teares, teares in her eye, Both christals, where they viewd ech others sorrow. **1599** —— *Hen. V*, II. iii. 56 Goe cleare thy Chrystalls. *a* **1616** Beaum & Fl. *Cust. County* I. ii, Bid the coy wench..out-blush damask roses, And dim the breaking East with her bright crystals.

c. *fig.* Esp. a prophecy derived from crystal-gazing. Now *rare.*

1902 *Westm. Gaz.* 6 Nov. 2/3 The Cleveland by-election will always be memorable if only for the fact that the crystal has had a new form given to it. **1914** *Concise Oxf. Dict.* Add., *Crystal* colloq., view of the future thus obtained [*i.e.* by crystal-gazing], prophetic utterance. **1931** H. G. Wells *Work, Wealth & Happiness of Mankind* (1932) xii. 596 Favours, buttons, crystal and claptrap: these are the forces that bring the politicians of the great powers of the world to office.

5. Short for ***crystal-glass***: a quality of glass having a high degree of transparency, usually due to its containing a large proportion of oxide of lead; also often a synonym for fine cut glass; hence, glass vessels, decanters, wine glasses, etc. of this quality collectively. [Ger. *krystallglas.*]

1594 T. B. *La Primaud. Fr. Acad.* II. Ep. to Rdr., Humors in the eyes, as it were the christall glasse set in the windowes. *c* **1645** Howell *Lett.* I. xxvii. 53, I was..in Murano, a little Island, wher Crystall-Glasse is made. **1875** Ure *Dict. Arts* II. 659 English manufacturers..in improving the brilliancy of crystal-glass..have injured its fitness for constructing optical lenses.

1668 Lady Chaworth in *12th Rep. Hist. MSS. Comm.* App. v. 10 The King..hath lately made a closet which they call a cabinet of cristall and philigrin. **1735** *Dict. Polygraph, Crystal* is also a name given to a factitious body cast in the glass-houses, also call'd crystal-glass..Of this fritt, you may make common glass, and also Crystal. **1831** Brewster *Optics* viii. 75 Let us take another [prism] of flint glass or white crystal. **1855** Thackeray *Newcomes* II. 294 Eyeing the plate and crystal.

6. (with *a* and *pl.*) A vessel or other article made of this glass; *orig.* called ***a crystal glass***; *esp.* the glass of a watch-case. Also *fig.* applied to the eyes.

1613 Heywood *Braz. Age* II. ii. Wks. 1874 III. 184 Looke on me Adon with a stedfast eye, That in these Christall glasses I may see My beauty. **1656** Sanderson *Serm.* (1689) 370 The breaking of a Christal glass or China dish.

1651 Devenant *Gondibert* VI. xiii, And thence..In a small Christall he a Cordiall drew. **1678** *Lond. Gaz.* No. 1292/4 A Picture of a Lady in Little, in a black Shagrine Case..with a Christal over the Picture. **1873** Morley *Rousseau* II. 43 Tall crystals laden with flowers.

†**7.** The crystalline lens of the eye. *Obs. rare.*

1694 *Acc Sev. late Voy.* II. 135 The Crystal of the Eye is not much bigger than a Pea.

†**8.** *pl.* Transparent vesicular eruptions or pustules appearing in certain diseases. *Obs.*

1661 Lovell *Hist. Anim. & Min.* 327 Hereto belong the crystals, tubercles, rubeols, and rossals. [**1882** *Syd. Soc. Lex.*, *Crystalli*, old name applied to the transparent vesicular eruption of pemphigus; also, to that of varicella.]

9. a. *Chem.* and *Min.* A form in which the molecules of many simple elements and their natural compounds regularly aggregate by the operation of molecular affinity: it has a definite internal structure, with the external form of a solid enclosed by a number of symmetrically arranged plane faces, and varying in simplicity from a cube to much more complex geometrical bodies.

So called because of the resemblance in colour, transparency, and regularity of shape, between native specimens of (rock-) crystal and the forms assumed by salts, etc., in the process of crystallization from a solution, aided by the ancient notion that rock-crystal was itself a substance like ice produced by some process from water.

a **1626** Bacon (J.), If the menstruum be overcharged, within a short time the metals will shoot into certain crystals. **1672** P. F. Lana in *Phil. Trans.* Abr. I. 720 *(title)*, Reflections on an Observation of Signior M. Antonio Castagna concerning the Formation of Crystals. **1704** J. Harris *Lex. Techn.*, *Chrystallization*..by which the Salts dissolved in any Liquor are made to shoot into little prettily figured Lumps or Fragments which they call Chrystals, from their being pellucid or clear like Chrystal. **1876** Page *Adv. Text Bk. Geol.* vii. 126 Granite is composed of crystals of felspar, quartz, and mica. **1878** Huxley *Physiogr.* 59 The term 'crystal' is now applied to all symmetrical solid shapes assumed spontaneously by lifeless matter.

†**b.** Used in the old names of various chemical salts of crystalline form, as ***crystals of alum, copper, Mars*** (= iron), ***silver, tartar, Venus*** (= copper), etc. Now mostly *Obs.*

1662 R. Mathew *Unl. Alch.* § 101. 172 Chrystal of Tartar ..to be had at any Druggist. **1706** Phillips, *Crystals of Silver*..Silver reduc'd into the Form of a Salt by the sharp Points of Spirit of Nitre: These Crystals are us'd by Surgeons to make an Eschar. **1727–51** Chambers *Cycl.*, *Crystals of Mars*..iron reduced into a salt by an acid liquor; used in diseases arising from obstructions. **1730–6** Bailey (folio), *Crystals of Copper*, is a solution of copper in spirit of nitre, evaporated and crystallized to gain the salt; those crystals are used as caustics. **1811** A. T. Thomson *Lond. Disp.* (1818) 501 Take of..crystals of tartar, rubbed to a very fine powder, two ounces. **1882** *Syd. Soc. Lex.*, *Crystals of Venus*, crystallised neutral acetate of copper.

c. ***crystals***: a particular quality of refined crystallized sugar.

1875 Ure *Dict. Arts* III. 943 There are three classes of sugar-refineries in this country, the chief productions of which are, respectively:—1st Loaf-sugar. 2nd Crystals (i.e. large, well-formed, dry white crystals of sugar). 3rd Crushed sugar. **1886** *Daily News* 15 Sept. 2/4 Sugar.. Russian crystals continue active.

d. *spec.* in *Electronics*, a crystalline piece of a semiconductor (such as germanium, silicon, or galena) used in a device on account of its properties of electrical conduction; ***crystal detector***, a detector (sense 3 f) in which a crystal diode is employed to rectify a high-frequency current; a crystal diode used as a detector; ***crystal diode***, a semiconductor diode, esp. one comprising a semiconductor crystal with which a thin metal wire is in point contact; also called ***crystal rectifier***; ***crystal receiver, set***, a receiving set employing a crystal detector.

1907 G. W. Pierce in *Physical Rev.* XXV. 31 *(title)* On crystal rectifiers for..electric oscillations. *Ibid.* 50 Crystal rectifiers employed in the construction of alternating current measuring instruments. **1908** J. A. Fleming *Elem. Man. Radiotelegr.* 332 Crystal detectors. **1913** *Year-Bk. Wireless Telegr.* 419 Crystal Detector, a form of oscillation detector depending on the fact that certain crystals (*e.g.*, carborundum) allow current to pass through them more readily in one direction than in the other. **1917** *Wireless World* June 168 The balanced crystal receiver, by keeping signals at a reasonable strength, enables the operator to receive in conditions which would otherwise make work impossible. **1923** J. A. Fleming *Wireless Telegr. & Teleph.* 20 The most generally used crystal is now galena (sulphide of lead). **1923** Hawkhead & Dowsett *Techn. Instr. Wireless Telegr.* (ed. 3) 129 A good commercial crystal detector.. should rectify with very small changes in potential. *Ibid.* 223 Crystal Receiver. **1924** E. T. Larner *(title)* Crystal sets. **1926** J. A. Fleming *Electr. Educator* I. 379/2 This detector consists of two crystals, zincite and chalcopyrites, in contact. **1943** C. L. Boltz *Basic Radio* xiii. 209 Some years ago thousands of people regularly used crystal sets for listening to broadcast programmes. **1948** *Gloss. Computer Terms* (M.I.T. Servomechanisms Lab. Rep. R-138) 5 Crystal diode. *Ibid.*, *Crystal rectifier*, a circuit component having almost unidirectional current-flow characteristics, usually consisting of a small piece of germanium in contact with a thin wire. **1955** *Sci. News Let.* 11 June 378/3 A crystal diode is a device similar to the transistor. **1959** *Chambers's Encycl.* XI. 475/1 The crystal detector..has found a new application in the field of radar where it is used at frequencies up to about 30,000 Mc/s. **1966** *McGraw-Hill Encycl. Sci. & Technol.* I. 359/2 Modern crystal rectifiers.. represent the simplest and most sensitive of all rectifying devices.

10. 'A very fine wide Durant [a glazed woollen stuff], once an article of export for use in making nuns' veils. Invariably made white' (Beck *Drapers' Dict.*). [Cf. Sp. *cristal* fine shining woollen stuff.]

11. *Her.* = Argent or pearl.

1830 Robson *Brit. Heraldry* III. Gloss., *Crystal*, used by some heralds instead of pearl, to express *argent.*

B. *attrib.* and *adj.*

1. Composed of crystal: **a.** of rock-crystal; **b.** of crystal glass.

c **1325** *E.E. Allit. P.* A. 159 A crystal clyffe ful relusaunt. **1569** tr. *Bellay's Visions* iv. in *Theat. Worldlings*, The chapters Alabaster, Christall frises. *a* **1631** Donne *Poems* (1650) 23 Hither with Crystall vials, lovers come, And take my teares. **1648** Boyle *Seraph. Love* xi. (1700) 59 Your Mistresses Picture, and its Chrystal Cover. **1858** Mrs. Carlyle *Lett.* II. 371 Four bright crystal tumblers. **1860** Emerson *Cond. Life, Behaviour* Wks. (Bohn) II. 383 Geneva watches with crystal faces.

2. a. Clear and transparent like crystal.

1430 Lydg. *Chron. Troy* I. xii. 195 Besyde the riuer of a cristall welle. **1509** Hawes *Past. Pleas.* IV. xviii, Her crystall eyes full of lowlenes. *c* **1576** Thynne *Ld. Burghley's Crest* i. in *Animadv.* App. iv. (1865) 103 With cristalle starres twinklinge in azurd skye. *a* **1652** Brome *Queen* IV. iii, How black and fowl your Sin Is rendred by my Chrystal innocence. **1727–46** Thomson *Summer* 1245 The well-known pool, whose crystal depth A sandy bottom shows. **1853** Kane *Grinnell Exp.* xxx. (1856) 260 The crystal transparency of an icicle.

†**b.** Sometimes with a reference to the crystalline heavens of old Astronomy. *Obs.*

c **1485** *Digby Myst.* (1882) I. 57 A-boue all kynges..vnder the Clowdys Cristall. **1718** Pope *Iliad* XI. 445 Shouts, as he past, the crystal regions rend. **1738** Wesley *Psalms* cxlvii. 2 Shine to his Praise, ye chrystal Skies, The Floor of his Abode.

c. *Comb.*, as ***crystal-clear, -dropping, -flowing, -leaved, -like, -producing, -smooth, -streaming, -winged***, etc. adjs.; ***crystal-wise*** adv.; **crystal ball**, a crystal (sense 4 a) in the shape of a globe, also *fig.*; **crystal clock**, a quartz-crystal clock (see QUARTZ); **crystal-gazing**, concentration of one's gaze on a ball of rock-crystal or the like in order to obtain a telepathic or hallucinatory picture; also *fig.*; similarly **crystal-gaze** *v. intr.*, **crystal-gazer** (cf. *crystal-seer, -seeing*); **crystal-glass**, see CRYSTAL 5, 6; **crystal lattice** (see LATTICE *sb.*); **crystal microphone**, a microphone which depends for its action on the piezo-electric activity of a crystalline substance; **crystal palace**: see PALACE; **crystal-pulling** [cf. G. *kristallisations-geschwindigkeit* used of a similar process by J. Czochralski 1918, in *Zeit. f. physikal. Chem.* XCII. 219], a method of obtaining pure single crystals for use in a junction diode or a transistor by inserting a seed crystal in a melt of germanium or silicon and gradually withdrawing it; also *attrib.*; **crystal-seer**, one who professes to see secrets, etc., in pieces of crystal, so **crystal-seeing** [cf. Germ. *krystallsehen, -seher*]; †**crystal-stone** = A. 2 above; **crystal violet**, a name of one of the aniline dyes; **crystal-vision**, crystal-gazing, or the picture seen by this means.

1855 Browning *Men & Women* II. 31 The sights in a magic *crystal ball. **1964** J. Drummond *Welcome, Proud Lady* xii. 51 Did you see that in your crystal ball..or did Mrs. Dannhauser put you up to it? **1968** G. Butler *Coffin Following* i. 7 In the crystal ball the old woman could see it. *c* **1520** *Everyman* (1890) 898 Now the soule is taken the body fro Thy rekenynge is *crystall clere. **1840** Lowell *Irene* in *Poet. Wks.* (1873) 3 Hers is a spirit deep, and crystal-clear. **1845** Browning *Dram. Rom. & Lyrics* 15 Glasses they'll blow you, crystal-clear. **1859** J. W. Carlyle *Let.* 20 Feb. in *Geo. Eliot's Lett.* (1954) III. 17 A crystal-clear, musical, Scotch stream. **1952** C. Day Lewis tr. *Virgil's Aeneid* XI. 245 The issue you ask our advice on Is crystal-clear and does not require our comments. **1937** *Discovery* Jan. 18/2 A *crystal clock..will increase the accuracy of the gravity observations. *a* **1650** May *Old Couple* II. in Hazl. *Dodsley* XII. 30 Her *crystal-dropping eyes. **1950** W. de la Mare *Inward Companion* 78 And do you rap? Or *crystal-gaze? **1898** A. Lang *Making of Religion* v. 95 The *crystal-gazer. **1920** R. Macaulay *Potterism* III. i. 108 Thought-readers, crystal-gazers, mediums and planchette-writers. **1889** *Proc. Soc. Psychical Res.* V. 507 *Crystal-gazing. **1945** H. Read *Coat Many Colours* xxxi. 151 To ask people to begin looking for profound human emotions..in painted canvas or carved stone seems to me like asking them to indulge in a new kind of crystal-gazing. **1960** *Farmer & Stockbreeder* 12 Jan. 63/1 A suitably cynical note on which to end a session of crystal-gazing. **1926** R. W. Lawson tr. *Hevesy & Paneth's Man. Radioactivity* xxvi. 218 The *crystal lattice has been traversed by about as many α-particles as there are uranium atoms contained in the lattice. **1933** *Chem. Abstr.* XXVII. 1578 A practical application of the observed phenomena is a new *crystal microphone. **1962** A. Nisbett *Technique Sound Studio* 247 *Crystal microphone or gramophone pick-up.* This generates a signal by means of a crystal bimorph. **1952** *Proc. Inst. Radio Engin.* XL. 1339/2 *(caption)* High vacuum melting furnace showing *crystal pulling mechanism. **1960** *Engineers' Digest* XXI. XI. 125/1 Dislocation free single crystals of germanium can be produced by a special method of crystal-pulling. **1962** Simpson & Richards *Junction Transistors* iii. 39 *Crystal pulling*... During this process material from the melt freezes on the seed, building up new rows of atoms whose crystal axes are the same as those of the seed. **1567** Maplet *Gr. Forest* 5 b, The Diamond is..in colour almost *Christallike, but somewhat more resplendishing. **1855** Smedley *Occult Sci.* 323 *Crystal-seeing has now become very common. *Ibid.*, Some *crystal-seers can discover nothing unless certain magical words are pronounced by the operator. **1818** Keats *Endymion* III. 382 How *crystal-smooth it felt. *c* **1386** Chaucer *Pard. Prol.* 19 Thanne shewe I forth my longe *cristal stones. *a* **1490** Botoner *Itin.* (Nasmith 1778) 224 Lapides vocati cristalle-stonys. **1584** R. Scot *Discov. Witchcr.* XV. xii. 344 To have a spirit inclosed into a christall stone or berill glasse. **1889** *Proc. Soc. Psychical Res.* V. 486 Recent experiments in crystal-vision. **1898** A. Lang *Making of Religion* v. 90 Crystal visions, savage and civilised. **1573** G. Harvey *Letter-bk.* (Camden) 103 Her fayer graye eies Shininge *christall wise.

'crystal, *v.* [f. prec.] To make into crystal; to crystallize. ***to crystal over***: to overlay with crystal. Hence **'crystalled** *ppl. a.*

1674 Flatman *Poems, Against Thoughts* 6/3 The Chrystal'd streams. **1715** M. Davies *Athen. Brit.* I. 186 Its top is Crystal'd over with..a transparent and diaphonous Azure. **1848** Lowell *Poems, Sir Launfal* II. Prelude, Diamond drops, That crystalled the beams of moon and sun, And made a star of every one. *c* **1860** —— *Fam. Ep. to Friend* Poems 417/1 Old sorrows crystalled into pearls.

crystallic (krɪ'stælɪk), *a.* [f. Gr. κρύσταλλ-ος + -IC.] Pertaining to crystals or their formation.

18.. Ashburner is cited by *Century Dict.*

crystalliferous (-'ɪfərəs), *a.* [f. L. *crystallum*: see -FEROUS. In mod.F. *cristallifère.*] Containing or yielding crystals.

1882 in *Syd. Soc. Lex.*

crystalliform (krɪ'stælɪfɔːm), *a.* [f. as prec.: see -FORM.] Having a crystalline form.

1796 Kirwan *Min.* I. 447 These crystalliform masses. **1830** Lindley *Nat. Syst. Bot.* 341 Vegetable crystals bounded by right lines, collected into a crystalliform body.

crystalligerous (-ˈɪdʒərəs), *a.* [f. as prec. + -GEROUS.] Bearing a crystal or crystals.

1885 E. R. LANKESTER in *Encycl. Brit.* XIX. 852 In those individuals which produce crystalligerous swarm-spores, each spore encloses a small crystal.

crystallin (ˈkrɪstəlɪn). *Chem.* [f. as prec. + -IN.] An albuminoid substance contained in the crystalline lens of the eye.

1847-9 TODD *Cycl. Anat.* IV. 169/1 There is another modification of protein..called both *globulin* and *crystallin*. **1863-72** WATTS *Dict. Chem. Crystallin* or *globulin*.

crystalline (ˈkrɪstəlɪn, -laɪn), *a.* and *sb.* [a. F. *cristallin*, in 15th c. *cristalin*, and its prototype L. *crystallīn-us*, a. Gr. κρυστάλλιν-ος of crystal, f. κρύσταλλος crystal. The pronunciation (krɪsˈtælɪn), after Latin, is used by Milton, Gray, Shelley, and Palgrave.]

A. *adj.*

1. Consisting of or made of crystal; of the nature of crystal; = CRYSTAL *a.* 1.

1509 HAWES *Past. Pleas.* XXXVIII. x, The cristallyne wyndowes of great bryghtnes. **1553** EDEN *Treat. Newe Ind.* (Arb.) 37 Cristallyne cuppes, and suche other iewelles. **1621-51** BURTON *Anat. Mel.* I. ii. I. ii, Besides those other heavens, whether they bee christalline or watery. **1660** BOYLE *New Exp. Phys.-Mech.* ix. 70 Small Receivers blown of Crystalline Glass. **1779** J. MOORE *View Soc. Fr.* II. lv. 57 Broad crystalline mirrors.

2. a. Clear and transparent like crystal.

c **1440** LYDG. *Secrees* 425 Wellys of philosophye, With Crystallyn sprynges. *a* **1529** SKELTON *Poems, Agst. Garnesche* 99, I yave hym drynk..Of Eliconys waters crystallyne. **1607** WALKINGTON *Opt. Glass* 1 The Sepias inkie humor does make turbulent the cristallinest fountaine. **1671** MILTON *Samson* 541 Nor did the dancing ruby Sparkling, out-poured..Allure thee from the cool crystalline stream. **1742** YOUNG *Nt. Th.* vii. 555 A crystalline transparency prevails. **1821** SHELLEY *Hellas* 698 Built below the tide of war, Based on the crystalline sea. **1871** PALGRAVE *Lyr. Poems* 13 Queen of the crystalline lake.

b. *fig.*

1605 BACON *Adv. Learn.* II. xvii. 65 Rules..howe Chrystallyne they may bee made at the first. **1670** EACHARD *Cont. Clergy* Pref. 4 An incorruptible and pure crystalline church. **1857-8** SEARS *Athan.* xi. 91 A sermon..in which his crystalline style is even more than usually radiant with momentous truths.

3. a. Of the nature of a crystal; having a structure which is the result of crystallization.

1612 WOODALL *Surg. Mate* Wks. (1653) 217 Sal Nitri is the Chrystalline salt purified from grosse Salt-peeter. **1665** HOOKE *Microgr.* 82 A multitude of little Crystalline or Adamantine bodies. **1799** KIRWAN *Geol. Ess.* 136 The crystalline grains are scarcely discernible. **1869** ROSCOE *Elem. Chem.* 191 Many naturally occuring minerals exhibit very perfect crystalline forms.

b. Of rocks: Composed of crystals or crystalline particles: opposed to *amorphous*.

1833 LYELL *Princ. Geol.* III. 334 A more compact and crystalline texture, which will be considered when we speak of the strata termed 'primary'. **1851** RUSKIN *Stones Ven.* (1874) I. viii. 81 The natural crystalline rocks.

4. Of or pertaining to crystals and their formation.

a **1866** WHEWELL (O.), Snow being apparently frozen.. vapour, aggregated by a confused action of crystalline laws. **1871** TYNDALL *Fragm. Sc.* (1879) II. iv. 51 The marvels of crystalline force.

5. *crystalline heaven* (*sphere, circle*): in the Ptolemaic astronomical system, a sphere (later two spheres) supposed to exist between the primum mobile and the firmament, by means of which the precession of the equinox and the motion of libration were accounted for.

1340 HAMPOLE *Pr. Consc.* 7574 Ane other [heven] es, þat clerkes calles cristallyne, þat next oboven þe sterned heven es. **1481** CAXTON *Myrr.* III. xxii. 184 Aboue this..ther is another heuene..lyke as it were of the colour of whyte crystall..And is called the heuen crystalyn. **1549** *Compl. Scot.* vi. 48 The nynte spere, callit the hauyn cristellyne. **1600** FAIRFAX *Tasso* IX. lx. 171 The mouer first and circle Christalline, The firmament, where fixed stars all shine. **1667** MILTON *P.L.* III. 482 They..pass the fixt, And that Crystalline Sphear whose ballance weighs The Trepidation talkt, and that first mov'd. **1796** MORSE *Amer. Geog.* I. 27 Above the starry sphere were imagined to be the two crystalline spheres. **1847** LD. LINDSAY *Chr. Art* I. p. xxxii, The crystalline, or ninth heaven, of pure ether.

6. *crystalline lens* (formerly *humour*): a transparent body enclosed in a membranous capsule, situated immediately behind the iris of the eye; it is the principal agent by which rays of light are brought to a focus on the retina, and it plays an important part in the action of accommodation. *crystalline cones*: the end organs of the apparatus of vision in the *Arthropoda*.

1398 TREVISA *Barth. De P.R.* v. v. (1495) 109 The humour albugines in the eye is more moyst thenne the humour cristallin. **1541** R. COPLAND *Guydon's Quest. Chirurg.*, In the myddes of the eye is..humour crystallyn, by cause it is of colour of Crystall. **1615** CROOKE *Body of Man* 33 The cristalline and glassy humors of the eye. **1794** G. ADAMS *Nat. & Exp. Philos.* II. xvii. 265 The seat of this disorder [cataract] is in the crystalline lens. **1836-39** TODD *Cycl. Anat.* II. 172/1 Within this hollow sphere..is fixed a double convex lens, called the crystalline lens or crystalline humour.

7. *crystalline style* or *stylet*: a transparent rod-like body contained in a sac embedded in the liver of some lamellibranchiate molluscs.

1864 W. HOUGHTON in *Intell. Observ.* No. 32. 70 This body, called the crystalline style. **1866** TATE *Brit. Mollusks* ii. 14 The stomach contains a jelly-like body termed the crystalline style.

B. *sb.* [elliptical uses of the adj.]

1. The crystalline heaven: see A. 5. *arch.*

1413 LYDG. *Pilgr. Sowle* v. i. (1859) 71 The entre, that is the Crystallyn, that yett is not ouerpassed. **1634** HABINGTON *Castara* (Arb.) 19 In a bright orbe beyond the Christalline. **1663** COWLEY *Pindar. Odes, Ecstasie* ix, The Transparent Rocks o' th' Heav'nly Chrystalline. **1840** MRS. BROWNING *Drama of Exile* (1850) I. 6 What if I stand up And strike my brow against the crystalline Roofing the creatures.

2. The crystalline lens or humour: see A. 6.

[**1597** LOWE *Chirurg.* (1634) 142 The second and chiefe principall instrument of the sight is called cristalline.] **1657** W. RAND tr. *Gassendi's Life of Peiresc* II. 97 The Image which was inverted in the Retina was..received by the Crystalline in its right posture. **1682** SIR T. BROWNE *Chr. Mor.* 100 Behold thy self by inward opticks and the crystalline of thy soul. **1793** YOUNG in *Phil. Trans.* LXXXIII. 174 In the ox's eye, the diameter of the crystalline is 700 thousandths of an inch. **1868** J. DUNCAN *Insect World* Introd. 3 These cones..play the part of the crystalline, or lens, in the eyes of animals.

†**3.** A venereal disease characterized by an outbreak of clear pustules; cf. CRYSTAL *sb.* 8. *Obs.*

1674 BUTLER *Hud. to Sidrophel* 51 Recovering Shankers, Chrystallines, And Nodes and Botches in their Rindes.

4. A crystal; a crystalline rock.

1856 MRS. BROWNING *Sonn., Work*, All thy tears..Like pure crystallines. —— *Sonn. from Portuguese* xv, On me thou lookest with no doubting care, As on a bee shut in a crystalline.

†**5.** *Chem.* An obsolete name for ANILINE, called by its discoverer Unverdorben in 1826, *crystallina*.

1838 T. THOMSON *Chem. Org. Bodies* 294 Of crystallina.

6. A light soft dress-material.

1903 *Daily Chron.* 25 July 8/4 Crystalline differs very little from mousseline de soie, for it is a thin fabric with a silky sheen upon it, and a very charming one for afternoon summer frocks. **1923** *Daily Mail* 8 May 14 Soft crepe finish crystalline.

crystallinity (krɪstəˈlɪnɪtɪ). [f. prec. + -ITY.] Crystalline quality or character; amount or degree of crystallization.

1881 C. R. A. WRIGHT in *Encycl. Brit.* XIII. 355 The tendency to crystallinity observable in large masses of cast metal. **1937** *Discovery* Oct. 302/2 Regularity of molecular arrangement (*i.e.*, crystallinity). **1947** *Nature* 4 Jan. 30/1 A displacement of the electric strength temperature curve with decreasing crystallinity. **1958** *Times Rev. Industry* May 52/3 The long hydrocarbon chains..show a high degree of crystallinity.

crystallite (ˈkrɪstəlaɪt). [f. Gr. κρύσταλλ-ος CRYSTAL + -ITE.]

†**1.** *Min.* A name applied to the somewhat crystalline form and structure taken by igneous rocks, lavas, etc. upon fusion and slow cooling.

1805 SIR J. HALL in *Trans. Soc. Edin.* V. 43 (Whinstone and Lava). **1807** T. THOMSON *Chem.* (ed. 3) II. 486 Sir James Hall..has given the whin in this last state the name of *crystallite*, a term suggested by Dr. Hope..The rock on which Edinburgh Castle is built fuses at the temperature of 45° Wedgewood. By rapid cooling it is converted into a glass which melts at 22°; by slow cooling into a crystallite which melts at 35°. *Ibid.* 488 In the crystallite, the component parts having had time to combine according to their affinities. **1852** TH. ROSS tr. *Humboldt's Trav.* I. 101 The fibrous plates of the crystalites of our glass-houses.

2. a. A term proposed by Vogelsang for aggregations, in various forms, of the globulites seen in thin sections of rock under the microscope; Formerly by some identified with, but now distinguished in sense from, MICROLITH, -LITE: a crystallite is of smaller size, does not polarize light, and cannot be referred to any definite species of mineral.

Occas. used (following Vogelsang) for 'embryonic crystals' in other substances (in quot. 1914 the word denotes a branched crystal or dendrite such as forms in freezing metal).

1878 LAWRENCE tr. *Cotta's Rocks Class.* 67 Many rocks.. more or less filled with very minute crystals, or so-called crystallites. **1881** J. W. JUDD *Volcanoes* iii. 53 Those minute particles of definite form, which the microscope has revealed in the midst of the glassy portions of lava, have received the name of microliths, or crystallites. **1910** *Encycl. Brit.* VII. 568/2 Crystallites may also be produced by allowing a solution of sulphur in carbon disulphide mixed with Canada balsam to evaporate slowly. **1914** *Jrnl. Inst. Metals* XI. 65 Most metals only exceptionally form simple polyhedral crystals, but by preference assume the form of branched crystallites. A theory of crystallites was proposed by Vogelsang, who made a special study of these structures in vitreous rocks,..in blast-furnace slags, and in artificial preparations. He observed that by cooling solutions of sulphur in viscous solvents, minute..globules were obtained, which..gradually developed crystalline outlines, so that the typical branched crystallites were thus produced. He therefore..regarded crystallites as 'embryonic crystals'. **1926** G. W. TYRRELL *Princ. Petrol.* v. 81 Crystallites are embryo crystals, not yet organized to full crystalline status. .. Microlites are somewhat larger bodies which can be definitely recognised as minute crystals. **1953** L. E. SPOCK *Guide Study of Rocks* iv. 59 Typical fresh obsidian is glossy and black, owing its darkness to closely spaced crystallites. **1958** A. D. MERRIMAN *Dict. Metallurgy* 49 *Crystallite*... The term is often used in reference to the tiny incipient crystals forming on the solidifying of metals and alloys. **1966** *McGraw-Hill Encycl. Sci. & Technol.* VII. 10/2 Crystallites ..are the most rudimentary forms [of rock grains] and abound in glassy rocks in which rapid consolidation has arrested further growth.

b. An individual crystal or grain in a metal or other polycrystalline substance; also, a part of a quasi-single crystal in which the orientation is uniform and the structure homogeneous. (Orig. an application of the word in the prec. sense, as in quot. 1914.)

1914 *Jrnl. Inst. Metals* XI. 64 The 'crystal grains' of ordinary cast metals arise in this way, their boundaries being produced by the mutual interference of neighbouring crystallites. **1920** *Chem. Abstr.* XIV. 3006 The dissoln. of the eutectic..occurs at the boundaries of the crystallites even of 'pure' metals. **1938** J. NEWTON *Introd. Metallurgy* ii. 27 These small units are individual crystals of the metal or alloy and are called crystallites, crystal grains, or simply grains. **1962** SIMPSON & RICHARDS *Junction Transistors* iii. 39 To minimize the formation of improperly oriented crystallites on the surface of the main crystal..the seed is slowly rotated as it is withdrawn. **1963** W. G. BURGERS in J. J. Gilman *Art & Science of growing Crystals* xxii. 417/1 A normal piece of metal..is usually fine-grained and built up of crystallites (grains) often a few hundredths of a millimeter in diameter.

3. *poetically.* = CRYSTAL *sb.* 2.

1838 S. BELLAMY *Betrayal* 150 Write Upon her walls of crystallite Salvation!

4. A minute part of cellulose or other polymers having the highly ordered structure characteristic of a crystal. Cf. MICELLE.

1926 *Jrnl. Physical Chem.* XXX. 457 Cellulose, in its natural condition, consists of aggregates of crystallites as found in the bast fibres, seed hairs, and other plant tissue as well as in the animal body. **1931** *New Phytologist* XXX. 4 In such fibres as ramie the crystallites are arranged parallel to each other. **1932** *Proc. R. Soc.* B. CIX. 449 The cell-wall of *Valonia ventricosa* is found by X-ray methods to be built up of two main sets of cellulose chains which form crystallites crossing at an angle. **1946** E. I. VALKO in J. Alexander *Colloid Chem.* VI. xxix. 595 A single macro-molecule can.. traverse disorganized regions, so that it belongs to different crystalline regions. As a consequence, the size of the organized regions, i.e., the 'crystallites', is not determined by the length of the macromolecule. **1948** SCHMIDT & MARLIES *Princ. High-Polymer Theory & Pract.* ii. 54 In high polymers these crystallites are not all of the same size and do not possess well-defined faces or edges. **1965** BELL & COOMBE tr. *Strasburger's Textbk. Bot.* (new ed.) I. i. 53 (*caption*) Diagram illustrating the micellar structure of cell walls... Linear macromolecules are grouped to form micellae or crystallites. **1966** M. L. MILLER *Struct. Polymers* x. 493 Each of these crystallites was supposed to consist of a bundle of parallel chains,..with each crystallite so small that a single molecule passed through several crystals... A modern view regards highly crystalline polymers..as a single crystalline phase with defects.

crystallitic (krɪstəˈlɪtɪk), *a.* [f. CRYSTALLITE + -IC.] Of the nature of a crystallite.

1859 A. HARKER *Petrol.* vii. 97 The general mass of the glass is full of very minute crystallitic bodies. *Ibid.*, These are rocks..having the glassy base rich in crystallitic growths.

crystallizable (ˈkrɪstəˌlaɪzəb(ə)l), *a.* [f. CRYSTALLIZE + -ABLE; cf. F. *cristallisable*.] Capable of being formed into or of forming crystals.

1781 J. T. DILLON *Trav. Spain* 235 Alum is a crystallizable salt. **1839** TODD *Cycl. Anat.* II. 405/2 A peculiarly crystallisable compound. **1869** ROSCOE *Elem. Chem.* 149 All crystallizable substances (called crystalloids) can pass in solution through the parchment paper.

Hence **crystalliza'bility**.

1854 J. PEREIRA *Lect. Polar Light* (ed. 2) 276 When.. subjected to heat..it loses its crystallizability. **1875** URE *Dict. Arts* I. 125 The ready crystallisability of alum.

crystallization (ˌkrɪstəlaɪˈzeɪʃən). [n. of action f. CRYSTALLIZE *v.* So F. *cristallisation*.]

1. a. The action of forming crystals, or of assuming a crystalline structure, a process which takes place in many substances while cooling from a state of fusion or solution.

water of crystallization: the water held by certain salts as an essential part of their crystalline structure, which structure is destroyed when the water is lost by evaporation or driven off by heat.

1665 HOOKE *Microgr.* 87 In the Solution and Crystallization of Salts. **1707** *Curios. in Husb. & Gard.* 136 Salts..dissolv'd in Water..separate themselves by Cristalization. **1791** HAMILTON tr. *Berthollet's Dyeing* I. I. III. i. 214 It effloresces, that is, it parts with its water of crystallization in the air, and assumes the appearance of flour. **1878** HUXLEY *Physiogr.* 222 The tree-like form which some bodies assume in the act of crystallisation.

b. *fig.*

1842 MILL *Let.* 8 Feb. (1963) XIII. 498 This will necessarily require..a gradual crystallization of many thoughts at present held in a state of suspension. **1862** HELPS *Organiz. Daily Life* 32 All systems tend to a certain kind of crystallization. **1875** HAMERTON *Intell. Life* VII. ii. (1876) 234 The final fixing, and crystallization of her intellect.

2. *concr.* A crystallized formation or body.

1695 WOODWARD *Nat. Hist. Earth* IV. (1723) 213 All other natural metallick and mineral Crystallizations. **1776** J. KEIR in *Phil. Trans.* XIV. 102 (*title*) On the Crystallizations

observed in Glass. **1836** W. IRVING *Astoria* III. 93 Salt springs..forming beautiful crystallizations.
fig. **1884** *Harper's Mag.* June 56/1 The laws of a nation are the crystallizations of its historical experiences.

crystallize ('krɪstəlaɪz), *v.* [f. CRYSTAL + -IZE: cf. mod.F. *cristalliser* (1680 in Hatzfeld).]

†**1.** *trans.* To convert into crystal or ice; to make crystal. *Obs.*

1598 SYLVESTER *Du Bartas* II. I. *Handy Crafts* 185 When the Winter's keener breath began To crystallize the Baltike Ocean, To glaze the Lakes. **1643** SIR T. BROWNE *Relig. Med.* I. §50 Some of our Chymicks facetiously affirm, that at the last fire all shall be crystallized and reverberated into glasse. **1798** S. ROGERS *Ep. to Friend* Note, Wild Winter ministers his dread controul To cool and crystallize the nectared bowl.

2. To cause to assume a crystalline form or structure, to form into crystals.

1664 *Phil. Trans.* I. 29 By dissolving them..and Crystallizing them. **1665** HOOKE *Microgr.* 82 As Alum, Peter, &c. are crystallized out of a cooling liquor, in which, by boyling they have been dissolv'd. **1756** C. LUCAS *Ess. Waters* I. 69 All salts that are capable of being crystallised are distinguishable by the figures of their crystals. **1876** PAGE *Adv. Text Bk. Geol.* ii. 47 Limestone crystallised by the heat of superincumbent lava.

3. *fig.* To give a definite or concrete and permanent form or shape to (something of an undefined, vague, or floating character).

1663 COWLEY *Pindar. Odes, Muse* iv, This shining Piece of Ice Which melts so soon away..Thy Verse does solidate and Crystallize. **1841** MYERS *Cath. Th.* III. §41. 157 Crystalising into permanent shapes the floating clouds of metaphor. **1875** POSTE *Gaius* IV. Comm. (ed. 2) 485 The forms of Action..as crystallized in the law or in the edict.

4. *intr.* To form (itself) into crystals, become crystalline in structure. ***crystallize out***: to separate in the form of crystals from a solution.

1641 FRENCH *Distill.* iii. (1651) 73 Let it stand two or three dayes..to crystallize. **1646** SIR T. BROWNE *Pseud. Ep.* II. i. 50 Aqua fortis..exhaled and placed in cold conservatories, will crystallise and shoot into white and glacious bodyes. **1718** QUINCY *Compl. Disp.* 4 Salts will not chrystallize, till the Water in which they are dissolv'd is near or quite cold. **1854** J. SCOFFERN in *Orr's Circ. Sc.* Chem. 379 As the solution cools the acid crystallizes out. **1878** GURNEY *Crystallogr.* 7 Each substance will crystallise in its characteristic form.

5. *fig.* To assume a definite or concrete form.

1816 COLERIDGE *Lay Serm.* 318 To make them crystallize into a semblance of growth. **1880** MCCARTHY *Own Times* III. xxxvi. 125 This vague impression crystallised into a conviction.

crystallized ('krɪstəlaɪzd), *ppl. a.* [f. prec.]

†**1.** Made into crystal, made transparent like crystal. *Obs.*

1600 TOURNEUR *Transf. Metam.* lxxxiv, The cristallized fount, That streames along the valley of Artes' mount.

2. Formed into crystals, existing in a definite crystalline form. Also *fig.*

1667 *Phil. Trans.* II. 468 That kind of Vitriol..is affirmed to be found chrystallized in Transylvania. **1800** tr. *Lagrange's Chem.* II. 339 Crystallized verdigrise or acetite of copper. **1871** C. DAVIES *Metr. Syst.* II. 47 Before the mind can grasp, as a crystallized idea, the fractional unit one-tenth.

3. Of fruit, ginger, etc.: preserved by impregnation with sugar, and usually coated with sugar crystals.

1875 L. TROUBRIDGE *Jrnl.* 25 Dec. in J. Hope-Nicholson *Life amongst Troubridges* (1966) 133 Funny little presents they were—mostly boxes of choc. and crystallised fruits. **1882** [see GLACÉ *a.* 2]. **1900** *Lancet* 6 Jan. 49/2 The greengages of crystallised fruit..and candied citron peel, all owed their brilliant colour to a salt of copper. **1908** C. H. SENN *Dict. Foods* 109 *Petit fours*, F., is but the generic name for all kinds of very small fancy cakes usually highly decorated with fancy icing, crystallised fruits, and bon-bons. **1928** F. HURST *President is Born* xxxix. 392 Crystallized ginger. **1936** AUDEN & ISHERWOOD *Ascent of F6* I. iii. 50 Drinks and eats little but is fond of crystallized apricots. **1965** HUTTON & BODE *Simple Sweetmaking* ix. 70 *Crystallized Fruits.* The aim in crystallizing fruits is to replace some of the water in the fruit with a strong sugar solution. **1970** A. PARKER *Cooking for Christmas* I. 56 Young stem ginger for dessert comes preserved in syrup..; or an alternative is good crystallized ginger, in boxes or tins.

crystallizer ('krɪstəlaɪzə(r)). [f. as prec. + -ER[1].] One who or that which crystallizes; *spec.* an apparatus for crystallizing.

1600 TOURNEUR *Transf. Metam.* Ded., Thou Christalizer of their Castalie. **1870** DASENT *Ann. Eventful Life* I. 22 Boilers, condensers, pumps, and crystallizers.

crystallizing ('krɪstəlaɪzɪŋ), *vbl. sb.* [f. as prec. + -ING[1].] The action of the verb CRYSTALLIZE. Also *attrib.*, as ***crystallizing water***.

1670 W. SIMPSON *Hydrol. Ess.* 68 [It] contributes much towards the chrystallizing of fresh alom. **1794** in *Phil. Trans.* LXXXIV. 423 It discovers no crystallizing water. **1819** G. SAMOUELLE *Entomol. Compend.* 337 Circumstances affecting the crystallizing process.

'crystallizing, *ppl. a.* [f. as prec. + -ING[2].] That crystallizes (*trans.* and *intr.*).

1665 HOOKE *Microgr.* 86 Dissolutions and Coagulations of several crystallizing Salts. **1860** TYNDALL *Glac.* II. xxiv. 353 To be suspended in the middle of the crystallizing solution. **1883** H. DRUMMOND *Nat. Law in Spir. W.* (ed. 8) p. ix, The same crystallising touch is needed in Religion.

crystallo-, combining form of Gr. κρύσταλλος crystal, used in derivatives and compounds: ˌ**crystallo'blastic** *a.* [*ad. G. kristalloblastisch* (F. Becke 1903, in *Compt. Rend. Congr. Géol. Internat.* (1904) II. 563), f. Gr. βλαστικ-ός budding] (see quots.). ˌ**cry-stallo-ce'ramic** *a.*, pertaining to a method of incrusting a medallion of clay with glass. **'crystallo-ceramie** = *cameo-incrustation* (see CAMEO b); also, glassware of this kind. **cry'stalloclast** *nonce-wd.* [cf. *iconoclast*], one who breaks crystals. **'crystallo-en'graving**, a method of making intaglio designs upon glass by means of casting. **'crystallogram** (or **cry'stallo-**), a photographic record of the X-ray diffraction pattern presented by a crystal, hence of its structure. **'crystallo-'granular** *a.*, composed of minute crystalline grains. **'crystallo-mag'netic** *a.*, pertaining to the magnetic properties of crystals and crystallized bodies, as shown by a kind of polarity directly related to the crystalline axes of minerals. **cry'stallotype**, a photographic picture on glass; also *attrib.*

1913 C. K. LEITH *Struct. Geol.* (1914) 77 There is, in the schists, relative perfection of crystal forms, dependent on the character of the minerals... This mineral form and arrangement in schists is the 'crystalloblastic' structure of Milch and Grubenmann. **1939** A. JOHANNSEN *Descr. Petrogr.* (ed. 2) I. 207 *Crystaloblastic* [sic], a crystalline texture due to metamorphic recrystallization. A characteristic of this texture is that the essential constituents are simultaneous crystallizations and are not formed in sequence, so that each may be found as inclusions in all the others. **1960** TURNER & VERHOOGEN *Ign. & Metamorph. Petrol.* (ed. 2) xxii. 592 Fabrics resulting from this latter process are called crystalloblastic, a term introduced by Becke to cover structures of the crystalline schists but nowadays generally extended to include also fabrics of like origin and character in rocks resulting from contact or metasomatic metamorphism. **1870** *Eng. Mech.* 7 Jan. 409/2 Another kind of ornamental manufacture is what is termed the crystallo-ceramic, or glass incrustation. **1821** A. PELLATT (*title*) Memoir on the origin, progress, and improvement of glass manufactures: including an account of the patent crystallo ceramie, or, glass incrustations. **1849** —— *Curiosities of Glass Making* 29 A patent was, some years since, taken out by the author..for ornamental incrustation, called 'Crystallo-Ceramie'... By this process, ornaments of any description—arms, ciphers, portraits, and landscapes of any variety of colour—are enclosed within the glass, so as to become chemically imperishable. **1960** *Times* 12 Nov. 9/3 Collectors group crystallo ceramie into five well-defined classes. **1942** *Electronic Engin.* XV. 188 From the crystallogram it is possible to gain much useful information such as the crystal size and the preferred or random orientation of the crystals. **1837** WHEWELL *Hist. Induct. Sc.* III. xv. ii. 205 Innovators in crystallography, who may properly be called crystalloclasts. **1873** WATTS *Fownes' Chem.* 446 The sodium salt is crystallo-granular. **1883** HEDDLE in *Encycl. Brit.* XVI. 377 Crystallomagnetic action. **1853** in *Proc. Amer. Phil. Soc.* V. 312 Mr. Justice offered for inspection..a 'Crystallotype' of the Moon.

crystallod: see OD[2].

crystallo'genesis. [f. CRYSTALLO- + Gr. γένεσις birth, origination.] The origination or natural formation of crystals (as a department of scientific investigation). So **crystallo'genic** *a.* [see -GEN, -GENIC], crystal-forming, producing crystallization. **crystallo'genical** *a.*, relating to the formation of crystals. **crysta'llogeny** (-'lɒdʒɪnɪ), the production or formation of crystals (scientifically considered).

1879 RUTLEY *Stud. Rocks* x. 161 A key to the important subject of crystallogenesis. **1837** DANA *Min.* (1844) 71 What is this crystallogenic attraction? *Ibid.* 71 Crystallogeny or the formation of crystals may be treated under two heads. **1881** *Nature* XXIII. 398 Between these two kinds of crystallogenic action there are many gradations.

crystallographer (krɪstə'lɒgrəfə(r)). [f. CRYSTALLOGRAPHY: see -GRAPHER.] One who studies crystallography.

1804 *Phil. Trans.* XCIV. 63 A mineralogist and crystallographer. **1878** GURNEY *Crystallogr.* 8 [A crystal] is bounded by flat surfaces..called by crystallographers its faces.

crystallographic (ˌkrɪstələʊ'græfɪk), *a.* [f. as prec.: see -GRAPHIC.]

1. Of or pertaining to crystallography.

1804 *Edin. Rev.* III. 497 The important consequences of Haüy's crystallographic discoveries. **1868** DANA *Min.* Introd. 26 The crystallographic symbols used in this work are essentially those of Naumann.

2. Of or belonging to crystals (as scientifically studied); = CRYSTALLIC.

1857 WHEWELL *Hist. Induct. Sc.* II. 329 The crystallographic axis. **1869** PHILLIPS *Vesuv.* x. 290 The three minerals have nearly the same crystallographic angles.

So **crystallo'graphical** *a.*, dealing with crystallography; = prec. **crystallo'graphically** *adv.*, in relation to crystallography. †**crysta'llographist** = CRYSTALLOGRAPHER.

1801 CHENEVIX in *Phil. Trans.* XCI. 195 The crystallographical arrangement, adopted in the preceding Paper. **1806** *Edin. Rev.* VIII. 78 Excellent crystallographical papers. **1831** BREWSTER *Optics* xxix. §147. 247, I have found this both crystallographically..and optically. **1850** DAUBENY *Atom. Th.* xii. (ed. 2) 417 Two minerals chemically the same, although crystallographically different. **1796** KIRWAN *Min.* I. 446 The late excellent crystallographist, Mr. Romé de Lisle.

crystallography (krɪstə'lɒgrəfɪ). [ad. mod.L. *crystallographia*, f. Gr. κρύσταλλος CRYSTAL + -γραφία writing, description: see -GRAPHY.

Used in Latin by M. A. Cappeller *Prodromus Crystallographiæ*, Lucerne 1723, in French by Romé de Lisle, *Essai de Cristallographie*, 1772.]

That branch of physical science which treats of the structure of crystals (CRYSTAL 9), and their systematic classification; a treatise on this subject.

1802 BOURNON in *Phil. Trans.* XCII. 239 Crystallography also offers some difficulties with respect to this stone. **1861** W. POLE in *Macm. Mag.* III. 186/1 Dr. Wollaston, celebrated as almost the originator of the science of crystallography.

†**cry'stallogy.** *Obs. rare.* [app. f. Gr. κρύσταλ(λος) crystal + -λογια, after *mineralogy*: cf. CRYSTALLOLOGY.] = prec. Hence †**cry'stallogist** = CRYSTALLOGRAPHER.

1811 PINKERTON *Petral.* II. 60 The important and interesting study of Crystallography, or Chrystallogy. *Ibid.* II. Introd. 5 The ingenious crystallogist Romé de Lisle. **1856** KANE *Arct. Expl.* II. xiv. 152, I have named it Cape Forbes, after the eminent crystallogist.

crystalloid ('krɪstəlɔɪd), *a.* and *sb.* [f. Gr. κρύσταλλ-ος crystal + -OID.]

A. *adj.* Crystal-like, of crystalline form or character, *esp.* as contrasted with COLLOID (*a.* 2).

1862 H. SPENCER *First Princ.* II. xiii. §103 Organic matter has the peculiarity that its molecules are aggregated into the colloid and not into the crystalloid arrangement. **1878** GURNEY *Crystallogr.* 29 In crystalloid forms occurring in nature the linear dimensions are subject to no known law.

B. *sb.*

1. A crystalloid or crystalline body or substance, as distinct from a COLLOID (*sb.* 2).

Crystalloids have, in solution, the power (which colloids have not) of passing easily through membranes.

1861 T. GRAHAM in *Phil. Trans.* (1862) 183 Opposed to the colloidal is the crystalline condition. Substances affecting the latter form will be classed as crystalloids. **1878** T. BRYANT *Pract. Surg.* I. 10 As freely as a colloid is penetrated by a crystalloid.

2. A protoplasmic body resembling a crystal in form, occurring in certain vegetable cells.

1875 BENNETT & DYER *Sachs' Bot.* 50 The term Crystalloids [was] proposed by Nägeli..Crystalloids containing colouring matters are found in the petals and fruits.

crysta'lloidal, *a.* [f. prec. + -AL[1].] Of, pertaining to, or of the nature of a crystalloid.

1861 T. GRAHAM in *Phil. Trans.* 184 The colloidal is, in fact, a dynamical state of matter, the crystalloidal being the statical condition. **1876** BARTHOLOW *Mat. Med.* (1879) 414 The active substance, being crystalloidal, diffuses into the blood with facility.

crystallology (krɪstə'lɒlədʒɪ). [mod. f. Gr. κρύσταλλος crystal + -λογια: see -LOGY. In mod.F. *cristallologie* (Littré).] The scientific study of crystals and crystallization: including crystallography and crystallogeny.

a **1864** WEBSTER cites DANA.

crystallomancy ('krɪstələʊˌmænsɪ). [f. as prec. + -MANCY.] Divination by means of a crystal.

1613 PURCHAS *Pilgrimage* IV. v. 310 Crystallomancie, in Crystall. **1652** GAULE *Magastrom.* 165. **1855** SMEDLEY *Occult Sci.* 322 Crystallomancy may be understood to include every variety of divination by means of transparent bodies.

crystallometry (krɪstə'lɒmɪtrɪ). [f. as prec. + -METRY.] The measuring of the angles of crystals, as a department of crystallography.

1837 WHEWELL *Hist. Induct. Sc.* III. xv. ii. 203 Crystallometry was clearly recognised as an authorized test of the difference of substances which nearly resemble each other.

†**'crystallurgy.** *Obs.* [Cf. *metallurgy*.] = CRYSTALLIZATION.

1823 in CRABB [whence in later Dicts.].

crystally ('krɪstəlɪ), *adv.* [f. CRYSTAL *a.* + -LY[2].] After the manner of crystal or crystals.

1859 *Chamb. Jrnl.* XI. 96 Crystally clear is the voice. **1860** *All Year Round* No. 42. 364 Mastic resembles gum Arabic; it is crystally cracked.

'crystalworts. *Bot.* A name given by Lindley to the *Ricciaceæ*, a natural order of liverworts, found in warm and temperate regions.

crystobalite, var. CRISTOBALITE.

crystoleum (krɪ'stəʊlɪːəm). [f. CRYST(AL + L. *oleum* oil.] The name given to a process, in vogue about 1883, for transferring oil paintings or photographs to glass.

1883 *L'pool Daily Post* 28 June, Specimens of crystoleum painting. **1884** *Girl's Own Paper* Jan. 190/1 To how great an extent crystoleum has been practised, a glance at shop windows and a visit to exhibitions will testify.

csardas ('tʃɑːdɑːʃ, 'zɑːdəs). Also **czardas.** [a. Hungarian *csárdás*, f. *csárda* inn.] A Hungarian national dance.

1860 *Players* I. 114 Having made herself thoroughly mistress of the 'Czardas', the national dance of Hungary. **1883** 'OUIDA' *Wanda* vi, They ended their dances with the Hungarian czardas. **1886** W. J. TUCKER *E. Europe* 217 The bewildering postures and maddening antics of the Csárdás. **1888** E. GERARD *Land beyond Forest* II. 245 Whenever the csardas comes to an end there is a violent clapping of hands to make the music resume. **1944** W. APEL *Harvard Dict. Mus.* 198/1 *Czardas*, a Hungarian dance, usually consisting of a slow, pathetic introduction called *lassu*, and a rapid and wild dance called *friss* or *friska*. F. Liszt's Hungarian Rhapsody no. 2 is a well-known example. *Ibid.* 343/2 The Czardas..is said to be a 19th-century revival of the old verbunko.

ctenidial (tɪ'nɪdɪəl), *a. Zool.* [f. next + -AL[1].] Of or pertaining to a ctenidium.

1888 ROLLESTON & JACKSON *Anim. Life* 130 The original (ctenidial) axis of the gill.

‖**ctenidium** (tɪ'nɪdɪəm). *Zool.* [mod.L., a. Gr. κτενίδιον, dim. of κτεν- (κτείς) a comb.] Each of the respiratory organs or gills of *Mollusca*, consisting of an axis with a series of processes on each side like the teeth of a comb.

1883 RAY LANKESTER in *Encycl. Brit.* XVI. 636/1 (*Mollusca*) These are the ctenidia or gill-combs. Usually.. they play the part of gills, but since in many Molluscs (Lamellibranchs) their function is not mainly respiratory.. it is well..to give them a non-physiological name such as that here proposed. **1888** ROLLESTON & JACKSON *Anim. Life* 450 In the majority of Gastropoda the primitive left ctenidium is aborted.

cteno-, combining form of Greek κτείς, κτενό-ς a comb, used in the formation of the scientific words below, also of others of less importance, as **ctenobranch**, a ctenobranchiate animal; **cteno'branchia, -branchi'ata**, a family of Mollusca, also called *Pectinibranchiata*; **cteno'branchiate** *a.*, having pectinate gills. **'ctenodont** *a.*, having ctenoid teeth.

1872 NICHOLSON *Palæont.* 327 Dentition ctenodont.

ctenocyst ('tiːnəʊsɪst). *Zool.* [f. Gr. κτενο- see above, here taken as short for *ctenophora* + κύστις bladder, CYST.] The vesicle, containing clear fluid and otoliths, which constitutes the organ of sense (probably of hearing) in the *Ctenophora*.

1861 J. R. GREENE *Man. Anim. Kingd., Cœlent.* 145 The 'apical canals'..run directly downwards and outwards on either side of the ctenocyst. **1882** in *Syd. Soc. Lex.*

ctenoid ('tiːnɔɪd), *a. Zool.* [ad. Gr. κτενοειδής comb-shaped: see -OID.]

1. Resembling a comb; having marginal projections like the teeth of a comb; pectinate; applied to the scales and teeth of certain fishes.

1872 NICHOLSON *Palæont.* 307 Ctenoid scales..consisting of thin horny plates, but having their posterior margins fringed with spines, or cut into comb-like projections.

2. Belonging to the *Ctenoidei*, an order of fishes in Agassiz's classification, containing those with ctenoid scales. Also as *sb.* A ctenoid fish. (Now disused.)

1847 ANSTED *Anc. World* x. 246 Two orders of Fishes.. the Ctenoids and Cycloids. **1851** RICHARDSON *Geol.* viii. 285 Four fifths of the fishes now living belong to the cycloid and ctenoid orders.

Hence **cte'noidean** *a.* and *sb.* = CTENOID 2.

1837 W. BUCKLAND *Geol.* I. 270 The Ctenoïdians have their scales jagged or pectinated, like the teeth of a comb.

‖**Ctenophora** (tɪ'nɒfərə), *sb. pl. Zool.* [mod.L., neuter pl. (sc. *animalia*) of *ctenophorus*, a. Gr. type *κτενοφορος, f. κτενο- comb + -φορος bearing.] A division of animals, formerly considered as an order of *Acalepha*, and now made a class of the CŒLENTERATA.

The present view is that they are highly specialized derivatives of the *Hydromedusæ*. They are marine animals of pellucid gelatinous substance and more or less spheroidal shape, swimming freely in the sea by means of peculiar fringed or ciliated locomotive organs (*ctenophores*), and having a localized sense-organ (*ctenocyst*). Among the best known genera are *Beroe* and *Cydippe*.

1855 GOSSE *Marine Zool.* 41. **1878** BELL *Gegenbauer's Comp. Anat.* 100. **1888** ROLLESTON & JACKSON *Anim. Life* 721 The Ctenophora are transparent, pelagic, and are widely distributed.

Hence **cte'nophoral** *a.*, of or pertaining to the Ctenophora, or to their characteristic locomotive organs, or parts in connexion with them. **cte'nophoran** *a.*, of or belonging to the class Ctenophora; *sb.* a member of this class. **'ctenophore** ('tiːnəʊfɔə(r)), (*a*) each of the eight meridionally arranged bands or rows of plates, bearing fringes like the teeth of a comb, which constitute the locomotive organs of the Ctenophora; (*b*) a member of the Ctenophora, a Ctenophoran. **cteno'phoric, cte'nophorous** *a.* = CTENOPHORAL.

1861 J. R. GREENE *Man. Anim. Kingd., Cœlent.* 169 Along the opposite sides of each ctenophoral canal. **1888** ROLLESTON & JACKSON *Anim. Life* 721 All movement [in Ctenophora] is carried out by the ctenophoral plates. **1877** HUXLEY *Anat. Invert.* iii. 173 The essential peculiarities of a Ctenophoran. **1888** ROLLESTON & JACKSON *Anim. Life* 578 *note*, The Ctenophoran characters of certain Polyclad *Turbellaria*. **1882** *Syd. Soc. Lex.*, *Ctenophore*. **1884** tr. *Claus' Zool.* I. 211 The Ctenophor type has fundamentally the form of a sphere. **1889** *Athenæum* 27 July 133/2 No figures are given of alcyonarians, ctenophores, [or of] any echinoderm save the star-fish. **1883** *Century Mag.* Sept. 734/1 Observations on the ctenophoric jelly-fishes.

cu, obs. f. COW *sb.*[1], CUE.

‖**cuadrilla** (kwa'drɪlja). [Sp.: see QUADRILLE *sb.*[2]] A group or company; *spec.* the troupe or following of a matador.

1841 G. BORROW *Zincali* II. viii. 354, I alone once robbed a cuadrilla of twenty Gallégos, who were returning to their own country, after cutting the harvests of Castile. **1893** CHAPMAN & BUCK *Wild Spain* v. 67 The *Espada*, or Matador, receives on the day from £120 to £200, including the services of his cuadrilla or troupe, which consists of two picadors, three banderilleros, and a cachetero. **1898** *Daily News* 11 Aug. 7/1 The crowd, blaming the bull, instead of the toreador and his cuadrilla, insisted on that animal being killed. **1932** HEMINGWAY *Death in Aft.* iii. 26 Each matador ..has a cuadrilla, or team, of from five to six men who are paid by him and work under his orders. **1934** [see BANDERILLERO]. **1967** *Economist* 25 Nov. 846/1 They were judged, as members of the *cuadrilla* (armed band), to be jointly responsible for all its acts.

‖**cuartel** (kwɑː'tɛl). Also **quartel.** [Sp.] A military barracks.

1832 W. B. DEWEES *Lett. from Texas* (1852) 142 Seven hundred Mexicans were at the quartel or barracks. **1890** *Outing* (U.S.) Oct. 8/1, I saw you, too, at the *cuartel* at Tucson. **1941** STEINBECK & RICKETTS *Sea of Cortez* (1958) 26 We imagined being held in some mud *cuartel*. **1967** K. GILES *Death in Diamonds* ii. 37 The patrolman..took O'Connors to the *cuartel*.

cub (kʌb), *sb.*[1] Also 6–7 **cubb(e.** [Origin unknown.

It has been compared with a rare Old Irish word *cuib* dog, but no historical connexion has been traced.]

1. *orig.* A young fox.

1530 PALSGR. 211/1 *Cubbe*, a yong foxe. **1552** HULOET, Cubbe or yonge ffoxe, *vulpecula*. **1575** TURBERV. *Venerie* 181 When you have taken the old foxes or badgerdes, and that there is nothing left in the earth but the yong cubbes. **1648** *Hunting of Fox* 13 His skin..when he is a young Cubbe is usually of a darker colour. **1880** *Times* 2 Nov. 4/6 No cub is he, but a full-brushed, high conditioned, dog-fox.

2. a. By extension: The young of the bear and of other wild beasts; also of the whale.

For the young of the bear, lion, etc. the earlier word was *whelp*, as in all versions of the Bible from Wyclif to 1611.

1596 SHAKS. *Merch. V.* II. i. 29 Plucke the yong sucking Cubs from the she Beare. **1683** BURNET tr. *More's Utopia* (1684) 13 The old Crow loves his Young, and the Ape his Cubs. *a* **1687** WALLER (J.), Two mighty whales..One as a mountain vast, and with her came A cub. **1774** GOLDSM. *Nat. Hist.* (1776) II. 334 The lion, or tyger, have seldom above two cubs at a litter. **1823** SCORESBY *Jrnl.* 148 The smallest animals [whales] of the species, mere cubs or 'suckers'. **1829** SCOTT *Anne of G.* ii, With the fury of a bear which had been robbed of her cubs.

b. *transf.*

1769 GRAY *Jrnl. in Lakes* Wks. 1884 I. 253 Passed by the side of Skiddaw, and its cub called Latterig.

c. *Cub*, a junior member of the Scout Association (see SCOUT *sb.*[4] 2 c). In full ***Cub Scout***, (formerly) ***Wolf Cub***.

1922 A. POYSER (*title*) The Cub Song Book. **1923** *Daily Mail* 11 June 16 Boy Scouts and Cubs furnished a guard of honour. **1964** M. KELLY *March to Gallows* xiii. 165, I shan't slip a wicked potion in it... Cubs' honour.

3. *fig.* **a.** An undeveloped, uncouth, unpolished youth.

Compared to the young of the bear, which was fabled to be born in a shapeless condition, and afterwards licked into shape by the mother.

1601 SHAKS. *Twel. N.* v. i. 167 O thou dissembling Cub: what wilt thou be When time hath sow'd a grizzle on thy case? **1687** CONGREVE *Old Bach.* IV. viii, A country squire, with the equipage of a wife and two daughters..But, oh gad! two such unlicked cubs! **1723** STEELE *Consc. Lovers* I. i, Like a bashful, great, awkward cub as you were. **1855** THACKERAY *Newcomes* I. 64 He thinks it necessary to be civil to the young cub. **1884** HUNTER & WHYTE *My Ducats* iv. 62, I know the young cubs you'll have to teach.

b. An apprentice or beginner; *spec.* an apprentice pilot on a steamboat. orig. *U.S.*

[**1840** *Ninawah* (Peru, Ill.) *Gaz.* 14 May 2/3 Awaiting the arrival of 'a cub' (a young speculator).] **1875** 'MARK TWAIN' in *Atlantic Monthly* May 567/1 The pilot not on watch takes his 'cub' or steersman..and goes out in the yawl. *Ibid.* 568/2 Nothing delights a cub so much as an opportunity to go out sounding. **1895** KIPLING *Land & Sea T.* (1923) 72 I'll take him as my cub, for there's no denying he's a resourceful lad. **1966** *New Statesman* 30 Dec. 956/1 Every cub knows that the first rule of reporting is: never show your story to your subjects before it's on the street.

†**4.** A name formerly given at St. Thomas's Hospital, London, to the surgeon's assistant. (The name 'dresser' was substituted in 1738.)

1698 *St. Thomas's Hosp. Rec.* (MS.) 18 June, That no Surgeons cubs or persons of that nature do keep their hatts on before the Physicians or Surgeons of the house. **1702** *Ibid.* 12 Feb., Orders for Cubbs. That no Surgeon have more than three at one time.

5. *Comb.*, as ***cub-bear, -fox***, (sense 2 c) ***cub-master, -mistress***; (sense 3 b) ***cub-engineer, -pilot, -reporter***; †**cub-drawn** *a.*, drawn (or ? sucked dry) by its cubs; **cub-hunting**, hunting young foxes at the beginning of the season; also **cub-hunt** *sb.* and *v.*

1834 H. BRACKENRIDGE *Recoll.* vii. 79 Some would rather pass for cub bears than be disappointed in their endeavours to attract attention. **1605** SHAKS. *Lear* III. i. 12 This night, wherein the cub-drawn bear would couch. **1875** 'MARK TWAIN' in *Atlantic Monthly* Jan 71/1 They..learned to disappear when the ruthless 'cub'-engineer approached. **1684** T. GODDARD *Plato's Demon* 237 A little Cubb Fox. **1858** FROUDE *Hist. Eng.* III. 121 Entertaining a party of friends for cub-hunting. **1870** BLAINE *Encycl. Rural Sports* 489 It is not common to cub hunt in the country intended for the winter practice. *Ibid.* A September cub hunt. **1921** *Daily Colonist* (Victoria, B.C.) 25 Mar. 9/1 To run a troop and pack requires a certain amount of money, which it is hardly fair to ask the individual Scoutmasters and Cubmasters to find. **1927** *Daily Mail* 12 July 10/4 A Hastings Rover Cub-master. **1927** *Daily Tel.* 21 June 3/2 A child who had fallen into a mill stream..was rescued by a local cubmistress. **1970** J. WAINWRIGHT *Prynter's Devil* vii. 160 Shut up, if you can't do anything but make noises like an outraged cub-mistress. **1859** 'MARK TWAIN' in *Univ. Missouri Stud.* (1938) XIII. 57/2 Our friend Sergeant Fathom, one of the oldest cub pilots on the river. **1875** —— in *Atlantic Monthly* Feb. 217/1 (*heading*) A 'cub' pilot's experience; or, learning the river. **1899** J. L. WILLIAMS in *Scribner's Mag.* XXV. 277 (*title*) The cub reporter and the king of Spain. **1908** A. RUHL *Other Americans* ii. 9 The mere gringo feels like a cub reporter at the office of a campaign committee. **1925** E. WALLACE *King by Night* xli. 183 Bobby was a cub reporter on my newspaper in Sacramento.

cub (kʌb), *sb.*[2] Chiefly *dial.* Also 6–7 **cubb(e.** [Of uncertain history, but to be compared with some LG. words: EFr. *kübbing, kübben* in same sense as this word, LG. *kübbung, kübje* a shed or lean-to for cattle, EFr. *kübbe, küb*, Du. *kub*, weir-basket or weel for fish (cf. Dornkaat Koolmann, and Grimm, s.v. *koben*): the latter is cognate with OE. *cofa*, COVE, but in sense closely agrees with this word.]

a. A stall, pen, or shed for cattle; also, a coop or hutch. **b.** A crib for fodder; a chest, bin, or other receptacle.

1546 *Confut. N. Shaxton* H vj b (T.), The anchors also, and charter-monks, vowed they not to die in theyr houses? And why are they not turned out of theyr cubbes, if vowes may not be broken? **1634** *Althorp MS.* in Simpkinson *Washingtons* (1860) App. p. lxvii, Mending posts and rayles about the deer house and the long cubb. *a* **1644** LAUD *Acct. Chancellorship* 132 (T.) The great leidger-book of the statutes is to be placed in archivis among the university charters, and not in any cub of the library. **1675** T. TULLY *Let. Baxter* 9 You are pleas'd..to put me..in the Cubb with divers mean and contemptible Malefactours. **1789** W. MARSHALL *Gloucestershire* I. 231 They have their fill of hay given them..in cribs—provincially 'cubs'—of different forms and descriptions. **18..** LANDOR (W.), I would rather have such..in cub or kennel than in my closet or at my table. **1870** *Eng. Mech.* 21 Jan. 447/3 In this hearth are two apertures leading into the 'Cubs'..which are used for receiving the ore, when ready to be drawn out. **1879** MISS JACKSON *Shropshire Word-bk.*, *Cub*, (1) a chest used in stables to hold corn for the horses. (2) a boarded partition in a granary to store corn..(4) a pen for poultry or rabbits.

cub (kʌb), *v.*[1] [f. CUB *sb.*[1] Cf. *whelp* vb.]

1. *trans.* and *intr.* To bring forth cubs.

1755 in JOHNSON. **1843** MARRYAT *M. Violet* xliv. 369 *note*, It [the puma] will seldom attack unless when cubbing. **1864** *Moral Statist. Glasgow* 299 When the tigress cubs a lamb, when the vulture breeds a dove.

2. *to cub it*: to live as a cub.

3. *intr.* = *cub-hunt v.* s.v. CUB *sb.*[1] 5. Chiefly as *pres. pple.* Cf. CUBBING *vbl. sb.*

1926 *Glasgow Herald* 21 Sept. 7/2 We were cubbing on the high ground above Anstruther. **1931** *Daily Express* 14 Oct. 1/5 They were out cubbing yesterday.

cub (kʌb), *v.*[2] *Obs.* exc. *dial.* [f. CUB *sb.*[2]] *trans.* To confine as in a 'cub'; to coop *up*.

1621 BURTON *Anat. Mel.* I. ii. IV. v, What misery..must it needs bring to him..to be cubbed vp vpon a sudden. **1629** MABBE tr. *Fonseca's Devout Contempl.* 46 David's souldiers ..would faine haue set vpon Saul, when they had him cubb'd vp in the caue. **1693** DRYDEN *Persius' Sat.* v, Cubb'd in a cabbin, on a mattrass laid. **1791** *Gent. Mag.* LXI. II. 809 It is the fashion..for all the English to be cubbed up in the Fauxbourg St. Germain. **1882** *W. Worcester Gloss.*, *Cub*, to confine in small space. *Cubbed-up*, bent, crumpled.

Cuba[1] ('kjuːbə). [The name of a large island in the W. Indies, also called Havana.] A cigar made of tobacco grown in Cuba.

1837 DICKENS *Pickw.* xxix, He..emitted a fragrant odour of full-flavoured Cubas.

†**'cuba**[2]. *Obs.* [? L. *cubā* lie down.] 'A game at cards call'd otherwise laugh and lay down' (Bailey (folio) 1730–6).

cubage ('kjuːbɪdʒ). [f. CUBE *sb.*[1] or + -AGE. Cf. F. *cubage*.] The determination of the cubic content of a solid; the cubic content thus determined.

1840 T. A. TROLLOPE *Summ. in Brittany* II. 87 It has been calculated by the cubage of it to weigh 195,740 pounds. **1885** *Athenæum* 12 Sept. 340/1 The experiments with Dr. Ranke's bronze skull, tending to settle the vexed question of the best method of cubage.

†**cubal** ('kjuːbəl), *a. Obs. rare*[−1]. [f. L. *cubus* CUBE + -AL[1].] = CUBIC *a.* 1

1657 TOMLINSON *Renou's Disp.* 132 Either equilaterally cubal, or drawn out into an unequal angle.

Cuba libre (ˈkjuːbə ˈliːbreɪ). [Amer. Sp., lit. 'free Cuba'.] A long drink containing lime juice and rum (see also quot. 1898).

1898 *Harper's Weekly* 20 Aug. 813/1 We..rode through the swamp, sometimes drinking a little 'Cuba libre' (water and brown sugar). **1937** HEMINGWAY *To have & have Not* III. vii. 133 'What's the lady drinking?'..'A Cuba Libre.' **1963** D. CORY *Hammerhead* v. 85 She had taken full advantage of a round half-dozen of Cuba Libres. **1964** *House & Garden* Nov. 106/2 *Cuba Libre.* Shake one measure of Bacardi rum with the juice of half a lime or lemon. Pour into a tall glass with ice and top up with iced Coca-Cola.

Cuban (ˈkjuːbən), *a.* and *sb.* [See -AN.] **A.** *adj.* Of or pertaining to Cuba. **B.** *sb.* A native or inhabitant of Cuba.

Cuban heel, a medium high, comparatively straight heel; so ***Cuban-heeled*** adj. Also (both forms) with small initial.

1829 *Foreign Q. Rev.* III. 414 The dependence of the Cuban proprietors on usurious merchants..is as dreadful as in other colonies. **1850** R. B. KIMBALL (*title*) Cuba and the Cubans; comprising a History of the Island. **1874** *Chambers's Encycl.* III. 349/2 The Cuban sugar-trade. *Ibid.* 350/1 'Cuba for the Cubans', is the watchword of the creoles. **1877** *Encycl. Brit.* VI. 679/1 Great sympathy had long been shown for the Cubans by the people of the United States. *Ibid.*, The yearly campaigns up to the present time have shown that in the eastern interior the Cuban patriots are practically invincible. **1885** R. L. & F. STEVENSON *Dynamiter* 144 Story of the Fair Cuban. **1908** *Sears, Roebuck Catal.* 813/1 This Gunmetal Blucher Oxford has..light flexible soles, high Cuban heels and large eyelets. **1926** *Contemp. Rev.* Aug. 180 Among the mass of the Cuban peasants, the Cuban politician..strikes a responsive chord. **1936** 'J. TEY' *Shilling for Candles* vii. 86 She held up a foot and exhibited her very modest cuban heel. **1940** N. MARSH *Surfeit of Lampreys* (1941) xvii. 263 Which of those ladies wore cuban-heeled shoes? **1959** 'F. NEWTON' *Jazz Scene* iv. 71 The fashion for mixed Cuban-jazz music.

cubangle (ˈkjuːbæŋg(ə)l). *Math.* [f. CUBE + ANGLE.] The solid angle of a cube (or analogous solid) formed by three edges meeting at right angles to one another.

1889 in *Cent. Dict.*

cubanite (ˈkjuːbənaɪt). *Min.* [f. *cuban* (so named in 1843) + -ITE.] A native sulphide of iron and copper, found first in Cuba.

1868 DANA *Min.* 65.

Cubanize (ˈkjuːbənaɪz), *v.* Also **-ise.** [See -IZE.] *trans.* To claim a right of protection or partial control over (a weaker but independent state), as the United States is alleged to have done with regard to Cuba. So **ˌCubaniˈzation.**

1922 *Q. Rev.* July 151 The various Yankee associations whose ultimate aim is the attraction of Mexico within the political orbit of the United States, and its 'Cubanisation' by treaty. **1924** in J. A. Hammerton *Countries of the World* xv. 1525/1 Among Cuba's other claims to fame may be placed the fact that its political status has originated a new verb—to Cubanise... It is a quasi-protectorate of America and the word was invented to express this relation.

cubard, obs. form of CUPBOARD.

†**cuˈbation**[1]. *Obs.*$^{-0}$ [ad. L. *cubātiōn-em*, n. of action f. *cubāre* to recline.] The action of lying down.

1727 in BAILEY vol. II. Hence in JOHNSON, etc.

cubation[2] (kjuːˈbeɪʃən). *rare.* [n. of action from mod.L. *cubāre* to cube (used or assumed): see -ATION.] = CUBATURE.

1727–51 CHAMBERS *Cycl.*, *Cubature* or *Cubation*, of a solid. **1887** *Q. Rev.* Apr. 441 He [Hobbes] had collected into one volume his quadrature of the circle, cubation of the sphere, and duplication of the cube.

cubatory (ˈkjuːbətərɪ), *a.* and *sb.* *rare*$^{-0}$. [a. L. type **cubātōri-us*, *-um* (cf. *cubātor* one who reclines).] **A.** *adj.* Recumbent.

1755 in JOHNSON. Hence in mod. Dicts.

B. *sb.* A dormitory.

1730–6 BAILEY, *Cubatory*, a dormiter or dormitory.

cubature (ˈkjuːbətjʊə(r)). [f. mod.L. **cubāre* to cube, after *quadrature*. Cf. F. *cubature.*] The determination of the cubic content of a solid.

1679 COLLINS in Rigaud *Corr. Sci. Men* (1841) I. 142 In order to the quadrature of these figures and the cubature of their solids. **1816** *Edin. Rev.* XXVII. 96 The cubature and complanation of solids. **1877** B. WILLIAMSON *Integral Calc.* (ed. 2) ix. §168 The cube..is..the measure of all solids, as the square is the measure of all areas. Hence the finding the volume of a solid is called its cubature.

cubb(e, obs. f. COB *sb.*[1] (5 a), CUB.

cubbard, -erd, -ert, obs. ff. CUPBOARD.

cubbed (kʌbd), *ppl. a. poet. rare*$^{-1}$. [f. CUB *sb.*[1] + -ED[2].] With a cub or cubs.

1889 TENNYSON *Demeter & Perseph.* I. 54, I envied human wives, and nested birds, Yea, the cubb'd lioness.

†**cubbel.** *Obs. rare*$^{-1}$. Something fastened to a beast as a clog.

a **1225** *Ancr. R.* 140 And teide uor þui ane clot of heui eorðe to hire, ase me deð ane cubbel to þe swine þet is to recchinde, & to ringinde abuten.

cubbing (ˈkʌbɪŋ), *vbl. sb.* [f. CUB *sb.*[1] + -ING[1].] = CUB-HUNTING (see CUB *sb.*[1] 5).

1882 *Society* 21 Oct. 18/1 The young hot-blooded youth from Oxford..does not care much for cubbing. **1890** *Daily News* 3 Nov. 5/3 The dry autumn has been unfavourable to 'cubbing'.

cubbish (ˈkʌbɪʃ), *a.* [f. CUB *sb.*[1] + -ISH.] Resembling a cub; awkward, uncouth, unpolished.

1819 SCOTT *Let.* 3 Oct. in *Lockhart*, He was shy and cubbish, and would not [come]. **1888** BURGON *Lives 12 Gd. Men* I. iii. 338 The most awkward and cubbish..of the youths present.

Hence **ˈcubbishly** *adv.*, **ˈcubbishness.**

1828 *Blackw. Mag.* XXIV. 212 One would think a gentleman might shake hands with a familiar friend without any symptoms of cubbishness. **1883** J. W. SHERER *At Home & in India* 85 He cubbishly returned it.

cubboard, -ord, obs. ff. CUPBOARD.

†**ˈcubbridge head.** *Obs. Naut.* Also cubridge-, couperidge-, copperidge-. Also COBRIDGE-HEAD. A partition or bulkhead across the forecastle and the half-deck of a ship.

1622 R. HAWKINS *Voy. S. Sea* (1847) 218 What with our cubridge heads, one answering the other..it was impossible to take us. **1627** CAPT. SMITH *Seaman's Gram.* ii. 11 [Those bulkheads] which doth make close the fore-castle, and the halfe Decke, the Mariners call the Cubbridge heads, wherein are placed murtherers [guns], and abaft Falcons.. to cleare the Decks fore and aft. *a* **1642** SIR W. MONSON *Naval Tracts* III. (1704) 346/1 The Couperidge-Head. *Ibid.* 357/1 With a Half Deck, Fore-Castle and Copperidge-heads.

cubby (ˈkʌbɪ). *local.* [Related to CUB *sb.*[2], or to the LG. words there referred to.]

1. = CUBBY-HOLE, -HOUSE.

1868 *Congress. Globe* 2 June 2762/3 [Many of the national banks] keep a little cubby of an office, loan no money,..and yet draw interest on their circulation. **1887** *Harper's Bazaar* 1 Oct. 675 The odds and ends relegated to this cubby [the lumber closet]. **1888** *W. Somerset Word-bk.*, *Cubby*, *Cubby-hole*, an out-of-the-way snuggery, such as children are fond of creeping into: a hiding-place.

2. In Orkney and Shetland: A straw basket.

1876 D. GORRIE *Summ. & Winters in Orkneys* i. 13 Pockponies went ambling along under the equal-poised weight of pendent cubbies. **1887** *Jamieson's Dict. Suppl.*, *Cubbie*, a small cassie or basket, often made of heather.

Hence **ˈcubby-hole, ˈcubby-house,** (*a*) a nursery or children's name for a snug, cosy place; a little house built by children in play; (*b*) a very small and confined room or closet.

1842 AKERMAN *Wiltsh. Gloss.*, *Cubby-hole*, a snug place. **1853** KANE *Grinnell Exp.* xxvii. (1856) 226 One little fellow ..scampered back again..to his cubby-hole on the deck. **1880** *New Virginians* II. 122 There was a kind of cubby-house in the hay-shed, where the hay had been cut out. **1881** *Leicestersh. Gloss.*, *Cubby-house* and *Cubby-hutch*, a hutch or coop for rabbits or other small animals. **1884** *Century Mag.* XXIX. 45/1 Cubby holes, dark cellars, uninspected closets.

cubdom (ˈkʌbdəm). *nonce-wd.* [f. CUB *sb.*[1] + -DOM.] The state of being a cub.

1892 *Cornh. Mag.* Dec. 562 He is..a little cubbish—has, in spite of his age, never quite grown out of cubdom.

cube (kjuːb), *sb.*[1] [a. F. *cube* (14th c. in Littré) ad. late L. *cubus*, a. Gr. κύβος a cube, *orig.* a die for playing with.]

1. a. *Geom.* One of the five regular solids; a solid figure contained by six equal squares and eight rectangular solid angles; a regular hexahedron.

[**1398** TREVISA *Barth. De P.R.* XIX. cxxvii. (1495) 928 Suche a fygure is callyd Cubus.] **1551** RECORDE *Cast. Knowl.* (1556) 156 [see CUBICLY]. **1570** BILLINGSLEY *Euclid* XI. def. xxi. 318 A Cube is a solide or bodely figure contayned vnder sixe equall squares. **1692** BENTLEY *Boyle Lect.* ii. 58 Spheres, or Cubes, or Pyramids, or Cones. **1753** HOGARTH *Anal. Beauty* 9 The most plain and regular forms, such as cubes and spheres. **1884** tr. *Lotze's Logic* 229 As the side of a cube increases, its volume must also continuously increase, without any alteration in its shape.

b. A material body of this form; a cubical block of anything. e.g. of tea, sugar. Also *attrib.*

1626 BACON *Sylva* §99 Take..a square Vessel of iron, in form of a Cube..put it into a Cube of Wood. **1863** FAWCETT *Pol. Econ.* III. v. 342 The Chinese use pressed cubes of tea. **1897** *Sears, Roebuck Catal.* 17/3 Sugar..Cubes. **1916** *Daily Colonist* (Victoria, B.C.) 8 July 11/3 The vessel's cargo consists of 110 tons of corn, 50 tons of bean coffee, 1,000 cases of cube sugar, [etc.]. **1935** *Discovery* Aug. 240/1 Mr. Benn's host never went on an expedition without a large carton of cubes, which he handed out generously to those Mongolians whose tents they visited.

c. An extremely conventional or conservative person (cf. SQUARE *sb.*). So **Cubesville** (after SQUARESVILLE), a group or set of such persons. *slang.*

1959 J. OSBORNE *Paul Slickey* II. viii, He's strictly from Cubesville. **1960** WENTWORTH & FLEXNER *Dict. Amer. Slang* 133/2 *Cube*, a super 'square';..an ultraconservative; a thorough bore. **1961** *Woman* 11 Mar. 5/1 No need to feel cubesville (that's *worse* than being a square) if you don't follow Kookie patter; even many Americans reckon it odd! **1963** *Sunday Times* 8 Sept. 29/3 As one who left school in July, I feel qualified to write of current oddities mentioned by 'Old Squares' (cubes in teenage slanguage). **1963** *Telegraph* (Brisbane) 24 May 17/2 Square itself is old hat. Too many adults cottoned on..the phrase and proclaimed 'I'm a square' in self defence. You'll simply be A Cube. **1968** 'G. BAGBY' *Corpse Candle* x. 133 When I sang it to him ..he told me I was a complete fool. Daisy Bell was for the cubes.

2. *Arith.* and *Alg.* The product formed by multiplying any quantity into its square; the third power *of* a quantity.

1557 RECORDE *Whetst.* C iv, When I saie twoo tymes twoo, twise, maketh 8. that number is a sounde number: and is named a Cube. **1646** SIR T. BROWNE *Pseud. Ep.* IV. xii. 219 By perfect and sphericall numbers, by the square and cube of 7 and 9 and 12. *a* **1721** KEILL *Maupertuis' Diss.* (1734) 21 The periodical Times of the several Planets, are in proportion to the square Roots of the Cubes of their distances from the Sun. **1838** DE MORGAN *Ess. Probab.* 63 The sum of all the squares of numbers is nearly one third of the cube of the last number.

3. a. *attrib.* (= CUBIC *a.* 2), and in *Comb.*, as ***cube foot***; †**cube-bone** = CUBOID bone; **cube-number**, one that is the cube of an integer; **cube-ore**, a name for PHARMACOSIDERITE; **cube powder**, gunpowder made in large cubical grains; **cube root**, that number of which the given number is the cube; **cube-spar**, a name for ANHYDRITE.

1570 BILLINGSLEY *Euclid* VII. def. xx. 187 A cube number is..that which is contayned vnder three equall numbers. **1615** CROOKE *Body of Man* 1007 The heele is articulated into a sinus of the Cube-bone. **1696** PHILLIPS, *Cube Root.* **1751** HALFPENNY *Designs Chinese Bridges* II. 8, 1040 Cube Feet of Timber. **1804** R. JAMESON *Char. Min.* I. 571 Cube Spar. *Ibid.* II. 345 Cube-Ore. **1827** HUTTON *Course Math.* I. 8, $^3\surd 5$, or $5^{\frac{1}{3}}$, denotes the cube root of the number 5.

b. Sometimes used after a measure expressing the length of the edge of a cube; e.g. 6 ***feet cube*** = of cubical form, and measuring 6 ft. in each direction, *i.e.* containing 6 × 6 × 6 or 216 cubic feet.

1707 S. CLARKE *Third Defence* (1712) 13 The Magnitude of a foot cube of Matter..is made up of Inches cube. **1776** G. TEMPLE *Building in Water* 94 If the Pit was a Mile Cube. **1849** DANA *Geol.* ii. (1850) 74 Some of these were six feet cube.

cube (ˈkuːbeɪ), *sb.*[2] [Amer. Sp. *cubé* (also used).] One of several South American plants of the genus *Lonchocarpus*, having roots which contain rotenone, used as an insecticide.

1924 *Bull. U.S. Dept. Agric.* no. 1201. 6 In 1920, while collecting fishes in Peru, Dr. W. R. Allen procured a supply of the dried roots of 'cube'. **1930** *Sci. Amer.* Nov. 391 The cube plant now grows in a part of South America where the climate is similar to that of the Malay States. **1940** H. J. HOLMAN *Surv. Insecticide Mat.* II. 46 The bulk of the cube root and powder at present exported from Para and Manaos in Brazil is said to be derived from this species [sc. *Lonchocarpus urucu*]. **1960** GUNTHER & JEPPSON *Mod. Insecticides* xii. 197 The name cubé is employed in South America to refer to the principal native species of *Lonchocarpus*, *L. nicou* and *L. utilis*, which were used for poisoning fish, and it has now been adopted in commerce to describe roots of any *Lonchocarpus* species which also display pronounced insecticidal properties.

cube (kjuːb), *v.* [corresponds to F. *cuber* (1554 in Hatzfeld) and prob. mod.L. *cubāre*, f. L. *cubus* CUBE.]

1. *Arith.* and *Alg.* To raise (a quantity) to the third power; to find the cube of.

1588 LUCAS *Colloq. Arte Shooting* 62, I did cube those foure ynches and the Cube thereof was 64. **1765–93** BLACKSTONE *Comm.* I. (ed. 12) 275 Superficial measures are derived by squaring those of length; and measures of capacity by cubing them. **1827** HUTTON *Course Math.* I. 8, 8^3, denotes that the number 8 is to be cubed.

2. *Mensuration.* To measure or compute the cubic content of.

1668 *Phil. Trans.* III. 686 He Cubeth or measureth either of the Segments of a Parabolical Conoid cut..parallel to the Axis. **1883** *Pall Mall G.* 22 Dec. 1/2, I have counted the inmates, cubed the rooms.

3. To pave with cubes or cubical blocks.

1887 *Daily News* 22 Oct. 2/4 They declined to cube the roadway beyond the statutory 18 inches outside their tram-lines.

4. To cut into small cubes.

1947 *Home Institute Cook Book* (N.Y.) 23 *Cube*, to cut into small cubes or solids of six equal square sides. **1951** *Good Housek. Home Encycl.* 354/1 Slice or cube and serve hot with melted butter. **1960** A. WESKER *Kitchen* 17 Cube stale bread for onion soup.

cubeb (ˈkjuːbɛb). Forms: 4 cucubes, 4–5 qui-, quybib(e, -yb(e, 6 -ibbe, 5–6 cubibe, -ube, 7 -ub, 6–7 -ebe, 7– cubeb. [a. Fr. *cubèbe* (14th c. in Littré) = Pr., Sp., It. and med.L. *cubēba*, ad. Arab. *kabābah*. In OF. also *quibibes* (in W. de Biblesworth), *quybybes*, *cucubes* (in MSS. of Mandeville, 14th c.), whence the ME. variants.]

The berry of a climbing shrub *Piper Cubeba* or *Cubeba officinalis*, a native of Java and the adjacent islands; it resembles a grain of pepper, and has a pungent spicy flavour, and is used in medicine and cookery. (Usually in pl. *cubebs*, which in pharmacy is sometimes construed as a collect. sing.) ***African cubebs***: the fruit of an allied African species, *Piper clusii.*

c **1300** *K. Alis.* 6796 Theo gilofre, quybibe, and mace. *c* **1305** *Land of Cokaygne* 78 in *E.E.P.* (1862) 158 Of cucubes þer n'is no lakke. *c* **1314** *Rembrun* v, Clowes, quibibes, gren de Paris. *c* **1400** MAUNDEV. 50 The Fruyt, the whiche is as

Quybybes, thei clepen Abebissam [Fr. *le fruit qest come quibibes* (v.r. *cucubes, cubes, quybybes*)]. *c* **1440** *Promp. Parv.* 421/1 Quybybe, spyce, *quiparum.* **1555** EDEN *Decades* 238 Cububes which growe in the Ilande of Iaua. **1579** LANGHAM *Gard. Health* (1633) 175 Cubebs strengthen a weake and windy stomach. **1605** TIMME *Quersit.* III. 172 Take.. cubebs, cardamony..of eache one ounce and a half. **1830** LINDLEY *Nat. Syst. Bot.* 174 The Cubebs of the shops..are the dried fruit of Piper cubeba. **1875** H. C. WOOD *Therap.* (1879) 504 In some respects, cubebs..resembles black pepper in its effects.

b. *attrib.*, as ***cubeb pepper*** (= prec.), ***cubeb tree.***

1693 *Phil. Trans* XVII. 619 The Cubeb-Tree..from Bengal. **1860** PIESSE *Lab. Chem. Wonders* 106 Cubeb pepper used in medicine.

Hence **cu'bebene**, the chief constituent of oil of cubebs; **cu'bebic acid**, a resinous acid obtained from cubebs; hence **cu'bebate**, a salt of this acid; **cu'bebin**, a crystalline substance existing in cubebs.

1876 HARLEY *Mat. Med.* 436 Hydrate of cubebene or camphor of cubebs. **1875** H. C. WOOD *Therap.* (1879) 505 Ten grammes of the cubebate of magnesium. **1838** T. THOMSON *Chem. Org. Bodies* 896 A peculiar substance, to which he has given the name of cubebin.

cubert, obs. form of CUPBOARD.

cubhood ('kʌbhʊd). [f. CUB *sb.*[1] + -HOOD.] The state or condition of a cub or young animal. Also *transf.* and *fig.*

1842 MRS. GORE in *Tait's Mag.* IX. 569 An appetite that rarely extends beyond the first fortnight of escape from cubhood to ensignhood. **1860** WYNTER *Curios. Civiliz.* 95 They [a mastiff and two lions] were brought up together from cubhood. **1870** HUXLEY *Lay Serm.* xi. (1874) 243 The shaping of the earth from the nebulous cubhood of its youth ..to its present form.

cubi- ('kjuːbɪ), before a vowel **cub-** (kjuːb), combining form of L. *cubus* CUBE, used in some mathematical terms, as †**cubi-cubic** *a.*, in ***cubi-cubic number***, the ninth power of a number, or the cube of the cube; in mod. use denoting 'of the third degree, cubic', as ***cubi-cone, -contravariant, -covariant, cubinvariant***, a cone, etc. of the third degree. (Cf. CUBO-.)

1557 RECORDE *Whetst.* R iij b, .10,077,696. is a Cubicubike number, and his firste Cubike roote is .216. **1662** HOBBES *Seven Prob.* Wks. 1845 VII. 67 Though there be some numbers called plane..others quadrato-cubic, others cubi-cubic. **1885** SALMON *Higher Algebra* Index 262 §254 The cubinvariant of the Hessian.

cubibe, obs. form of CUBEB.

cubic ('kjuːbɪk), *a.* and *sb.* [a. F. *cubique* (Oresme, 14th c.), ad. L. *cubicus*, a. Gr. κυβικός, f. κύβος CUBE.]

A. *adj.* **1. a.** Of the form of a cube; cubical.

1551 RECORDE *Pathw. Knowl.* I. Defin., A dye, whiche is called a cubike bodie by geometricians. **1622** PEACHAM *Compl. Gentl.* ix. (1634) 76 If they would double the Altar in Delos, which was of cubique forme. **1710** *Lond. Gaz.* No. 4691/4 The said Sword [has] the Pummel of a Cubick form. **1874** tr. *Lommel's Light* 56 A cubic vessel the sides of which are made of glass.

b. *Min.* Applied to certain minerals which crystallize in cubes or similar forms; as ***cubic alum***, alum-stone or ALUNITE; ***cubic nitre***, sodium nitrate.

1782 WITHERING in *Phil. Trans.* LXXII. 336 Cubic nitre. **1791** HAMILTON *Berthollet's Dyeing* I. I. III. ii. 254 A dissertation on cubic alum. **1877** WATTS *Dict. Chem.* IV. 105 Nitrate of sodium crystallises in obtuse rhombohedrons, which on cursory inspection have very much the aspect of cubes; hence the name *cubic saltpetre*.

c. *Crystallography.* Another name for the Isometric system, in which the three axes are equal and mutually at right angles; the cube being a typical form of the system.

1878 GURNEY *Crystallogr.* 37 Crystals possessing this highest possible degree of symmetry are said to belong to the Cubic or Tesseral System.

2. *Mensuration.* Of three dimensions; solid; relating to solid content; *esp.* used with a unit of length, to express the content or volume of a cube whose edge is that unit, as a ***cubic foot.***

1660 BOYLE *New Exp. Phys. Mech.* xvii. 116 We may.. define, either in weight or cubick measures the Cylinder of Quick-silver. **1751** LABELYE *Westm. Br.* 87 The two Middle Piers..contain full 3000 cubic Feet. **1812–6** PLAYFAIR *Nat. Phil.* (1819) I. 13 The weight of a cubic inch of water. **1869** E. A. PARKES *Pract. Hygiene* (ed. 3) 125 For sick persons the cubic space should be more than for healthy persons.

3. *Arith., Alg.*, etc. Relating to or involving the cube or third power of a quantity; of three dimensions, of the third degree.

As †***cubic number*** = CUBE number; †***cubic root*** = CUBE root; ***cubic equation***, an equation of the third degree; ***cubic curve***, a curve represented by an equation of the third degree.

1551 RECORDE *Pathw. Knowl.* II. Pref., Extraction of rootes both square and cubike. **1594** BLUNDEVIL *Exerc.* I. xxvi, (ed. 7) 59 A Table containing both the square numbers and Cubique numbers of every Root. **1727–51** CHAMBERS *Cycl.*, *Cubic equation* is an equation wherein the unknown quantity is of three dimensions. *Ibid.* s.v. *Curve*, One [curve] commonly called the *cubic parabola*. **1885** WATSON & BURBURY *Math. Th. Electr. & Magn.* I. 179 The system leads to a cubic equation in ϵ.

B. *sb.* (ellipt. use of the adj.). **1.** *Math.* **a.** A cubic expression or equation. **b.** A cubic curve.

1799 WILSON in *Phil. Trans.* LXXXIX. 301 The rest produce cubics, or cubic-formed sixth powers. **1806** ROBERTSON *Ibid.* XCVI. 310 A cubic, or an equation of three dimensions. **1882** in *Athenæum* 15 Apr. 479/3 On Polygons circumscribed about a Cuspidal Cubic.

2. A cubist painting. *rare.*

1924 GALSWORTHY *White Monkey* I. ii. 14 The cubic called 'Still Life'.

cubica ('kjuːbɪkə). [Sp.] A very fine unglazed shalloon.

1835 BOOTH *Analyt. Eng. Dict.* s.v. *Shalloon* (Draper's Dict.), [It] has the Spanish name of Cubica. It is chiefly exported to Catholic countries to be made into gowns for the ecclesiastics and..several orders of Friars. A stouter sort of Cubicas are sometimes called Says.

cubical ('kjuːbɪkəl), *a.* [f. prec. + -AL[1].]

1. Of or pertaining to a cube; of the form of a cube, cube-shaped. (Now more usual than *cubic* in this sense.) ***cubical powder*** = cube powder; see CUBE *sb.*[1] 3.

1592 R. D. *Hypnerotomachia* 70 b, In the lowest Cubicall Figure..were ingrauen Greeke letters. **1669** STURMY *Mariner's Mag.* I. B iv, How to measure a Cubical vessel. **1794** SULLIVAN *View Nat.* I. 308 The small grains of sea salt and of lead are cubical. **1817** KEATINGE *Trav.* I. 203 Houses ..mostly of cubical forms. **1882** VINES *Sachs' Bot.* 103 A nearly cubical piece of a long epidermal cell.

2. *Mensuration.* = CUBIC *a.* 2. (Now *Obs.* in *cubical foot* and the like; and less common than *cubic* in other applications.)

1571 DIGGES *Pantom.* III. iv. Q iij, So many cubicall feete is in the hollowe vessell. **1660** WILLSFORD *Scales Comm.* 197 Each of these Segments contains 50 cubical yards of earth. **1794** G. ADAMS *Nat. & Exp. Philos.* I. xi. 440 Multiply by 1728, the number of cubical inches in a cubical foot. **1854** J. SCOFFERN in *Orr's Circ. Sc.* Chem. 183, 100 cubical inches. **1871** B. STEWART *Heat* 39 To determine the cubical dilatation of a solid.

3. *Arith., Alg.*, etc. = CUBIC *a.* 3. *Obs.* exc. in names of certain cubic curves, as ***cubical parabola, hyperbola***, etc.

1571 DIGGES *Pantom.* III. ix. R ij, The roote cubicall of your Quotiente is the side of the lesser Cone or Pyramis. **1646** SIR T. BROWNE *Pseud. Ep.* IV. xii. 209 Quadrate and cubicall numbers. **1727–51** CHAMBERS *Cycl.* s.v. *Parabola*, If $a^2x = y^3$; they call it a *cubical paraboloid.* **1873** B. WILLIAMSON *Diff. Calc.* (ed. 2) xviii. §252 The curve $y^2 = x^2(x-a)$..is a cubical parabola having a conjugate point.

†**B.** *sb.* = CUBIC *sb. Obs.*

1676 BAKER in Rigaud *Corr. Sci. Men* (1841) II. 13 All cubicals being reducible..to three equations.

'cubically, *adv.* [f. CUBICAL + -LY[2].] In a cubical manner; to the third power or cube; in the form of a cube or cubes.

1571 DIGGES *Pantom.* III. xiii. S j b, Augment the diameter of the wine vessell cubically, that is to say, by hys owne square. **1653** H. MORE *Conject. Cabbal.* (1662) 164 Such is sixty-four..made..by multiplying four cubically. **1855** J. R. LEIFCHILD *Cornwall* 61 Rocks rising cubically. **1856** *Phil. Trans. R. Soc.* CXLVI. 488 Cubically and spherically isotropic bodies.

'cubicalness. *rare.* [f. as prec. + -NESS.] The state or quality of being cubical; also *fig.*

1707 S. CLARKE *Third Defence* (1712) 34 Circularity.. Squareness..and Cubicalness. **1892** W. W. FENN *Bible in Theol.* 15 They see them as solid, in their cubicalness.

cubicite ('kjuːbɪsaɪt). *Min.* Also -zite. [f. CUBIC + -ITE; in Ger. *kubizit.*] A name for ANALCITE.

1826 EMMONS *Min.* 214 Cubicite. **1829** *Nat. Philos., Polaris. of Light* xi. 39 (U.K.S.) The remarkable mineral called Analcime, or Cubizite.

cubicity (kjuː'bɪsɪtɪ). *rare.* [f. CUBIC + -ITY.] The quality of being cubic.

1881 *Nature* XXIII. 398 The cubicity of the first system.

cubicle ('kjuːbɪk(ə)l). [ad. L. *cubicul-um* bedchamber, f. *cubāre* to recline.]

1. A bedchamber: in the general sense *obs.* since the 16th c., but re-introduced in modern use, *esp.* in English public schools, for one of the series of small separate sleeping chambers, which now often take the place of an undivided dormitory. Hence *gen.* any small partitioned space; *spec.* a carrel in a library.

1483 CAXTON *Gold. Leg.* 72/1, I was delyueryd of a chyld in my cubycle. **1494** FABYAN *Chron.* II. xl. 28 He called theym one by one..into his secrete cubicle or chambre. **1513** BRADSHAW *St. Werburge* I. 5, I rose vp shortly fro my cubycle preparat aboute mydnyght. **1858** *Sat. Rev.* 6 Nov. 449/1 The dormitory was a large chamber divided into about a dozen cubicles, or small sleeping apartments, by wooden partitions and doors which rose within a few feet of the ceiling. **1926** *Bull. Amer. Libr. Assoc.* Oct. 297 Seminars, cubicles, and private studies will be provided for ..advanced students, and visiting scholars. **1938** K. M. B. CROSS *Mod. Public Baths* 61 Dressing cubicles are not required in these changing rooms, where their use is confined to children. **1960** H. LITTLEWOOD *Learning to Swim* ii. 19 Go to your cubicle or the changing room and make sure that you dry yourself thoroughly. **1961** T. LANDAU *Encycl. Librarianship* (ed. 2) 69/1 *Carrel*... Also called cubicle or stall. **1962** A. NISBETT *Technique Sound Studio* 246 *Control cubicle*, the soundproof room equipped with control desk. **1963** *Times* 22 Apr. 2/6 No one seems to know whether cubicles originated in England or America, and the cows don't care, because cubicles are the last word in cow comfort... Some of the cleanest cows to be seen these days..are those in cubicle installations. **1971** *Hampshire Gaz.* (Northampton, Mass.) 19 Feb. 9/4 It adorns the cubicle next to the one marked 'Men'.

attrib. **1891** *Daily News* 11 Nov. 2/7 In the Victoria Home both the dormitory system and the cubicle system had been introduced.

2. *Electr. Engineering.* A chamber or compartment to hold a switch-gear apparatus.

1911 J. F. C. SNELL *Power House Design* 347 The oil-break switches are contained within glazed brick cubicles. *Ibid.* 349 The operating gallery and cubicle gallery in the Bahia Blanca power house. **1927** *Daily Tel.* 14 Mar. 4 Switch-gear cells and cubicles constructed of moulded stone. **1930** [see ARMOUR-CLAD *ppl. a.*]. **1968** F. KERTESZ *Lang. Nuclear Sci.* (Oak Ridge Nat. Lab. TM 2367) 18 *Cubicle* referred to the power supply and control center of an individual calutron.

†**cubicly**, *adv. Obs. rare.* In 6 cubikely. [f. CUBIC + -LY[2].] = CUBICALLY.

1551 RECORDE *Cast. Knowl.* (1556) 156 The cubes do beare the lyke rate cubikly multiplied, as if the sydes be as two to one. **1557** —— *Whetst.* O ij, I multiplie .8..Cubikely, and it maketh .512.

†**cu'bicular**, *sb. Obs.* Also 5–7 -er, -air, -are. [ad. OF. *cubiculaire*, ad. L. *cubiculārius* (a. and sb.) CUBICULARY, f. *cubiculum* bedchamber; see -AR[2].] An attendant in a bedchamber; a groom of the bedchamber; a chamberlain. Chiefly *Sc.*

c **1425** WYNTOUN *Cron.* VI. vi. 24 Hyr Cubiculare By hyr lay, and gat a Barne. **1483** CAXTON *Gold. Leg.* 82/2 The lord comanded hys cubyculyers that she [Judith] shold goo and come at her playsir. *a* **1560** ROLLAND *Crt. Venus* IV. 573 Sensualitie..Quhilk to Venus was richt cheif Cubiculair. *a* **1639** SPOTTISWOOD *Hist. Ch. Scot.* V. (1677) 236 Monsieur Verac, Cubiculare to the French King. **1873** BURTON *Hist. Scot.* V. lx. 299 With the zealots of the church on one side and the 'cubiculars' of the court on the other.

cubicular (kjuː'bɪkjʊlə(r)), *a.* [ad. L. *cubiculāris*, f. *cubiculum* CUBICLE.] Of or belonging to a bedchamber.

1611 COTGR., *Cubiculaire*, cubicular, belonging to the bedchamber. *c* **1645** HOWELL *Lett.* I. VI. xxxii, For his privat cubicular devotions. *Ibid.* IV. xvi. (1892) 583 Being the inseparable Cubicular Companion. **1768** *Life & Advent. Sir B. Sapskull* I. 127 Cubicular devotion.

†**cu'biculary**, *a.* and *sb. Obs.* [ad. L. *cubiculārius*: see prec. and -ARY.]

A. *sb.* = CUBICULAR *sb.*

1382 WYCLIF *Judith* xii. 6 He comaundede to his cubicularies [Vulg. *cubiculariis*], that, as it pleside to hir, she shulde gon out, and comen in.

B. *adj.* = CUBICULAR *a.*

1646 SIR T. BROWNE *Pseud. Ep.* V. vi. 241 That custome by degrees changed their cubiculary beds into discubitory.

cubicule ('kjuːbɪkjuːl). A variant of CUBICLE.

1887 J. M. WILSON *Ess. & Addresses* 36 Neat cubicules and spotless dimity.

‖**cu'biculo.** *Obs.*[−1] [Either a humorous use of Latin, from the phrase *in cubiculo*, or affected use of It. *cubiculo.*] = CUBICULUM, bedchamber.

1601 SHAKS. *Twel. N.* III. ii. 56 *And.* Where shall I finde you? *To.* Wee'l call thee at the Cubiculo: Go.

†**cu'biculous**, *a. Obs.* [f. next + -OUS.] = CUBICULAR *a. rare* and *pedantic.*

1715 *Pancirollus' Rerum Mem.* I. IV. x. 186 Those cubiculous Pallets, whereon we repose..in the Night.

‖**cubiculum** (kjuː'bɪkjʊləm). Pl. -a. [L. = sleeping-chamber, f. *cubāre* to lie down.]

A sleeping-chamber. (Only jocose in modern use.) In *Archæol.*, a burial-chamber in the Catacombs; also, a chapel or oratory attached to a church, *esp.* in a crypt.

1832 GELL *Pompeiana* I. viii. 154 That sort of cubiculum or chamber. **1852** MRS. STOWE *Uncle Tom's C.* xxi. 157, 'I stole up to Tom's cubiculum there, over the stables.' **1879** SIR G. SCOTT *Lect. Archit.* II. 40 This nave had arcades opening into either aisles, or into *cubicula* or oratories.

cubiform ('kjuːbɪfɔːm), *a.* [f. L. *cubus*: see CUBI- + -FORM.] Of the form of a cube, cube-shaped.

1730–6 in BAILEY (folio); thence in JOHNSON. **1881** W. B. CARPENTER *Microscope* (ed. 6) 353 The genus *Amphitetras*.. is chiefly characterized by the cubiform shape of its frustules.

†**'cubify**, *v. Obs. rare. trans.* = CUBE *v.* I.

1676 BAKER in Rigaud *Corr. Sci. Men* (1841) II. 3 Finding out..the four proportionals, and then cubifying them.

Cubism ('kjuːbɪz(ə)m). [ad. F. *cubisme*, f. *cube* CUBE *sb.*] An important early twentieth-century revolutionary pictorial movement arising out of the rejection of traditional Western single-viewpoint perspective: in its first 'analytical' stages characterized by simple geometric forms which soon gave way to further complexes of interlocking semi-transparent planes. In its second major or 'synthetic' phase, flat abstract coloured shapes were assembled and clarified in such a way as to achieve a revisionary significance. Hence **'Cubist** [F. *cubiste*], an artist who adopts one of the styles of Cubism;

also *attrib.* and as *adj.* Also **cu'bistic** *a.*, **cu'bistically** *adv.*

'The word "Cubism"..dates from 1908 and was pronounced for the first time, according to M. Léonce Rosenberg, by a member of the Hanging Committee of the Salon des Indépendants. As a canvas by Georges Braque was being carried by, this person exclaimed, "*Encore des Cubes! assez de cubisme!*" A journalist seized on the *mot* and spread it abroad, and the painter concerned, together with his associates, accepted the nickname and confessed themselves Cubists' (Rutter *Evol. Mod. Art* 80).

1911 *Illustr. Lond. News* 21 Oct. 648/1 Paris is perturbed by the Cubism and the Cubists of the Salon d'Automne. **1911** *Lit. Digest* (N.Y.) 18 Nov. 914/1 The cubists take the blocks of the pavement as their medium for interpreting the external world. **1913** tr. *Gleizes & Metzinger's Cubism* 16 To understand Cézanne is to foresee Cubism. **1914** A. J. EDDY *Cubists & Post-Impress.* 72 Cubism is simply a systematic use of planes. **1915** W. H. WRIGHT *Mod. Painting* 187 Those whose criterion is prettiness are naturally attracted to Whistlerian and Cubistic modes. **1917** W. J. LOCKE *Red Planet* x. 113 All their talk was of Hauptmann and Sudermann..and in art—Heaven save the mark—the Cubist school. **1920** R. FRY *Vision & Design* 186 It is interesting to consider his Cubist period, since Marchand's reaction to Cubism is typical of his nature. **1924** GALSWORTHY *White Monkey* II. ii. 133 [Painter to model] 'No, I shouldn't be treating you cubistically.' **1928** —— *Swan Song* III. xiii. 317, I remember the first shows in London of those post-impressionists and early Cubist chaps. **1936** A. H. BARR *Cubism & Abstract Art* 30 Cubism in the early days developed under the mixed influence of Negro Sculpture and Cézanne. **1948** [see ABSTRACTION 7]. **1966** J. GRIFFIN tr. *Fry's Cubism* 9 Cubism first posed, in works of the highest artistic quality, many of the fundamental questions that were to preoccupy artists during the first half of the twentieth century. **1970** *Oxf. Compan. Art* 293/2 Part of the object of the Cubists was to represent solidity and volume in a two-dimensional plane. *Ibid.*, Cubism is the outcome of intellectualized rather than spontaneous vision.

transf. **1914** A. J. EDDY *Cubists & Post-Impress.* 64 A form of dramatic representation that is essentially Cubist, Futurist, and Orphist in its expression. **1920** A. HUXLEY *Let.* 4 Mar. (1969) 182 Paris shd be amusing: I was there in January and had an entertaining time among the cubists of literature. **1926** W. J. LOCKE *Old Bridge* vi. 91 The.. German tourist and his cubistically attired wife. **1927** W. S. VINES *Movements* 3 Mr. Blunden is a case in point, this critic claiming him for the Georgians, while that one will allege that cubistic symptoms have characterised, if not marred, his later work. **1927** *Observer* 6 Mar. 21/3 A few [ladies' coats] display cubistic ideas, amusing to study in detail.

cubit ('kjuːbɪt). Forms: 4- cubit; also 4-7 cubite, (4 cupyde, cupet), 5 cubete, (cobyte), 5-6 cubyt(e, cubet(te, (7 cubide). [ad. L *cubitum* the elbow, the distance from the elbow to the finger-tips, belonging to *cubit-* ppl. stem of *cubāre*, *-cumbĕre*, to lie down, recline.

The form *cubite* occurs in OF. for the measure, but the living repr. of the L. *cubitus* is F. *coude*, OF. *coute* elbow = Pr. *code*, *coide*, Sp. *codo*, It. *cubito*.]

†**1.** The part of the arm from the elbow downward; the forearm. **b.** The ulna, one of the two bones of the forearm. (In quot. 1398 applied to both the ulna and the radius.) *Obs.*

1398 TREVISA *Barth. De P.R.* v. xxvii. (1495) 136 The arme is made of two bones, one aboue that hyghte the ouer cubyte, and the other beneth that hyghte the nether cubyte. **1483** *Cath. Angl.* 85 A Cubit, *lacertus.* **1634** T. JOHNSON tr. *Parey's Chirurg.* VI. xxvi. (1678) 147 The cubit is composed of two bones, the one of which we call the Radius or Wand, the other we properly call the Cubit, or Ell. **1713** CHESELDEN *Anat.* III. viii. (1726) 202 The muscles that bend and extend the cubit. **1847** SOUTH tr. *Chelius' Syst. Surg.* I. 559 Fracture of the cubit is always consequent to direct violence.

¶By literalism of translation: see quots.

1388 WYCLIF *Jer.* xxxviii. 12 Putte thou elde clothis.. vndur the cubit of thin hondis [Vulg. *sub cubito manuum tuarum; Heb.* under the joints of thy hands] and on the cordis. **1609** BIBLE (Douay) *Ibid.*, Under the cubite of thine armes.

†**c.** Sometimes app. = the elbow. *Obs.*

1544 PHAER *Pestilence* (1553) P iij b, On the muscule of the right arme, vnder the cubite, on the parte where as the pulse lieth. **1624** GEE *Foot out of Snare* 43 A fire from heauen consumed the hands and armes to his cubits. **1882** *Syd. Soc. Lex.*, *Cubit*, the ulna. Also, the elbow.

†**d.** *Zool.* The corresponding part of the fore leg of quadrupeds; **e.** *Entom.* Applied to one of the veins or ribs of an insect's wing.

c **1720** W. GIBSON *Farrier's Guide* I. vi. (1738) 91 The next bone, call'd the Cubit, or Leg-bone. **1774** GOLDSM. *Nat. Hist.* II. 337 In the fore feet, or rather hands, all the arm and the cubit are hid under the skin.

2. An ancient measure of length derived from the forearm; varying at different times and places, but usually about 18-22 inches. *Obs.* exc. *Hist.*

It is the *cubitus* of the Romans = Gr. πῆχυς, Heb. *ammah*, all which words meant primarily the forearm. The Roman cubit was 17·4 inches; the Egyptian 20·64 inches.

c **1325** *E.E. Allit. P.* B. 315 þre hundred of cupydez þou holde to þe lenþe. **1382** WYCLIF *Matt.* vi. 27 Who of ȝou thenkinge may putte to [*v.r.* adde] to his stature oo cubite? **1481** CAXTON *Myrr.* II. v. 69 There dwelleth peple that..ar but ii cubites hye..This peple is callyd pygmans. **1555** EDEN *Decades* 92 Hit scarsely riseth at any tyme a cubet aboue the bankes. **1640** WILKINS *New Planet* viii. (1707) 239 In one Minute it should scarce descend the Space of a Cubit. **1837** THIRLWALL *Greece* IV. xxxiii. 287 A model of a galley three cubits long in ivory and gold. **1875** JOWETT *Plato* (ed. 2) III. 304 He is four cubits high.

3. *attrib.* and *Comb.*, as *cubit-bone*, *-length*, *-rule* (cf. *foot-rule*); *cubic-long* adj.; **cubit arm** (*Her.*), 'an arm couped at the elbow' (Cussans *Handbk. Her.* 115).

a **1400-50** *Alexander* 3908 Wild berys..With ilka tenefull tothe..A cubete lenth. *a* **1700** DRYDEN *Ovid's Met.* xii. (R.), But Theseus, with a club of harden'd oak, The cubit-bone of the bold centaur broke. **1847** LANDOR *Hellenics* II, In ancient letters, cubit-long. **1848** C. C. CLIFFORD *Aristophanes' Frogs* 26 Yard-measures too they'll bring and cubit-rules.

cubital ('kjuːbɪtəl), *a.* [ad.L. *cubitālis*, f. *cubitus* cubit, elbow.]

1. Of the length of a cubit.

c **1420** *Pallad. on Husb.* IV. 431 And cubital let make her longitude. **1646** SIR T. BROWNE *Pseud. Ep.* IV. xi. 207 The towers..being so high, that unto men below they [the watchmen] appeared in a cubitall stature. **1867** *Ecclesiologist* 223 Lines chiselled in cubital letters on its frieze.

2. *Anat.* Pertaining to the forearm, or the ulna.

1611 COTGR. s.v. *Artere*, The cubitall arterie, a branch of th' *Axillaire.* **1802** PALEY *Nat. Theol.* (1804) 127 The inferior cubital nerves.

b. *Zool.* Pertaining to the corresponding part in animals, or to the cubit of an insect's wing.

1828 STARK *Elem. Nat. Hist.* II. 338 Genus *Cinips*..upper wings with one radial triangular cell, and two or three cubital ones. **1874** COUES *Birds N.W.* 703 Cubital edge of fore-arm rather darker than other upper parts.

'cubited, *a. rare*$^{-1}$. In parasynthetic comb., as *twelve-cubited*, *i.e.* twelve cubits long or high.

1616 SHELDON *Miracles Antichrist* 303 (T.) The twelve-cubited man, as Jacobus a Voragine measureth his length.

cubito- ('kjuːbɪtəʊ), used as combining form of L. *cubitus*, in anatomical adjs., in sense 'relating to the ulna and some other part'; as ***cubito-carpal***, ***-cutaneous***, ***-digital***, ***-metacarpal***, ***-palmar***, ***-radial***.

†**'cubiture.** *Obs.*$^{-0}$ [ad. L. *cubitūra*, n. of action f. *cubāre* to lie down.] 'A lying down' (Blount *Glossogr.* 1656).

cubitus ('kjuːbɪtəs). *Ent.* [L.: see CUBIT.]

†**1.** *Obs.* (See quot.)

1826 KIRBY & SPENCE *Entomol.* III. 369 *Cubitus*, the fourth and elongated joint [in the first pair of legs in Hexapods], answering to the Tibia in the legs.

2. = CUBIT 1 e. Hence **'cubital** *a.*, **cubito-**, combining form.

1895 J. H. & A. B. COMSTOCK *Man. Study Insects* iii. 64 The principal veins of the wing—are termed..the costa,..the subcosta,..the cubitus, [etc.]. **1898** *Amer. Nat.* XXXII. 88 The fifth principal vein is the cubitus... Between the cubitus and the anal margin there are typically three veins. *Ibid.*, The two groups of wing-tracheæ thus formed may be designated as the costo-radial group and the cubito-anal group. *Ibid.* 234 The medio-cubital cross-vein. This is a cross-vein extending from media to cubitus. **1918** J. H. COMSTOCK *Wings of Insects* xxvi. 390 The third and last of the branched veins in flies is the cubitus. **1957** RICHARDS & DAVIES *Imms's Textbk. Ent.* (ed. 9) I. 45 The cubitus.. divides into two main branches, the first cubitus..being convex and the second cubitus..concave. **1964** R. M. & J. W. FOX *Introd. Compar. Ent.* iv. 117 A complete cubital system is present in only a few insects... Posterior to the cubitus is a variable number of veins.

cubizite: see CUBICITE.

cubless ('kʌblɪs), *a.* [f. CUB *sb.*[1] + -LESS.] Without or bereft of cubs.

1821 BYRON *Juan* III. lviii, The cubless tigress in her jungle raging. **1854** SYD. DOBELL *Balder* iv. 26 An orphan fawn That ran beside the cubless lioness.

cubo- ('kjuːbəʊ), before a vowel sometimes cub- (kjuːb), combining form from Gr. κύβος die, CUBE: as in †**cubo-cube** [Gr. κυβόκυβος], a name for the sixth power of a quantity, or the cube multiplied by itself; so †**cubo-'cubic**; †**cubo-cubo-cube**, the ninth power; **cubo-'cuneiform** (*Anat.*), relating to the cuboid and cuneiform bones = CUNEOCUBOID; also in *Solid Geom.* and *Crystallography*, denoting a solid which combines the forms of a cube and another solid, as **cubo-octa'hedron** (*cuboctahedron*), a solid of fourteen faces formed by cutting off the corners of a cube, so as to add eight triangular faces corresponding to those of an octahedron, or by similarly modifying an octahedron in the direction of a cube; sometimes restricted to the middle or critical case in which the square faces are reduced to smaller squares; so **cubo-octa'hedral** *a.*, **cubo-dodeca'hedron, -al.**

1696 in PHILLIPS, *Cubocubic.* **1706** —— *Cubo-Cube*..the sixth power of any Number. **1727-51** CHAMBERS *Cycl.*, *Cubo-cubus*, the term whereby Diophantus, Vieta, etc. distinguish the sixth power. **1796** HUTTON *Math. Dict.*, *Cubo-cube*, the 6th power. *Cubo-cubo-cube*, the 9th power. **1805-17** R. JAMESON *Char. Min.* (ed. 3) 203 A crystal is said to be cubo-dodecahedral, cubo-octahedral, cubo-tetrahedral, when it contains a combination of the two forms indicated by these terms. **1868** DANA *Min.* Introd. 22 (Crystallography) Some of the simpler isometric forms..a cube..combination of cube and dodecahedron..cubo-octahedron. **1876** *Quain's Anat.* (ed. 8) I. 178 Cubo-cuneiform Articulation.

Cubo-Futurism (ˌkjuːbəʊ'fjuːtjʊərɪz(ə)m). [ad. Russ. *kubo-futurizm* (1914): see CUBISM and FUTURISM.] An early 20th-century movement among Russian painters, characterized by works treating the subjects of peasant art in the abstract geometrical manner of Cubism.

1936 A. H. BARR *Cubism & Abstract Art* 120 Cubism, Rayonism, Suprematism, Non-Objectivism, Cubo-Futurism, Constructivism had been born and, in some cases, had died. **1962** C. GRAY *Great Experiment* iv. 86 'Cubo-Futurism' is a happier term to describe this Russian movement, alike painting and literary, whose dual development is impossible to separate, and this is the term which I have used to describe work of post-1910, Post-Primitivist, in Russian painting. **1981** *Oxf. Compan. 20th-Cent. Art* 346/2 With the organization of planes and volumes becoming more prominent and systematic while the importance of the subject diminished pictorially, Malevich achieved the personal interpretation of Analytic Cubism, with some suggestions of Futurism, which he called Cubo-Futurism. **1982** A. LIEVEN tr. *L. A. Zhadova's Malevich* i. 16 'Cubo-Futurism' as a general and widely-accepted label gained currency at a time when both critics and general public lumped together the pictures of the Cubists and the poems of the Futurists as equally incomprehensible.

Hence **Cubo-'Futurist** *a.* and *sb.*

1962 C. GRAY *Great Experiment* v. 132 *The Woodcutter* of 1911 is Malevich's first mature Cubo-Futurist work. *Ibid.* vi. 182 The circle of the Moscow Cubo-Futurists. **1969** GLOWACKI-PRUS & MCMILLIN tr. *Malevich's Ess. on Art 1915-1933* II. 89, I think that we should..create an intermediate 'Cubo-futurist' category, which has at the basis of its formation only the sickle-shape formula. **1969** V. MARKOV *Russ. Futurism* iv. 119 Shershenevich remarks in his book, 'In one lecture, they were called "cubo-futurists", and the name stuck.' **1974** *Encycl. Brit. Macropædia* XIX. 480/1 In 1912 Malevich exhibited his first 'cubo-futurist' works, in which the figures were reduced to dynamic coloured blocks. **1981** *Oxf. Compan. 20th-Cent. Art* 138/2 Some historians..have used the term 'Cubo-Futurist' to describe this primitivist reaction generally, far though it often is from either Cubism or Futurism.

cuboid ('kjuːbɔɪd), *a.* and *sb.* [mod. ad. Gr. κυβοειδής cube-like: in mod.L. *cuboīdes*, F. *cuboïde*.]

A. *adj.* Resembling a cube; of a form approximating to that of a cube; cuboidal; *spec.* in ***cuboid bone*** (*os cuboides*), one of the bones of the foot, between the calcaneum and the fourth and fifth metatarsal bones.

[**1706** in PHILLIPS, *Cuboides*, the seventh Bone of the Tarsus of the Foot.] **1829** J. BELL *Anat. Hum. Body* (ed. 7) 73 The place and effect of the cuboid bone is very curious. **1854** BADHAM *Halieut.* 147 Fish..characterized by sharp projecting cheeks, and cuboid heads.

B. *sb.* **1.** *Anat.* Short for *cuboid bone*: see CUBO-.

1839 TODD *Cycl. Anat.* II. 340/1 Bounded on the outside by the cuboid. **1881** MIVART *Cat* 113 The Calcaneum articulates with the..cuboid in front.

2. A cuboidal block or lump.

1883 *Midland Echo* 5 Apr. 3/1 He purchased..two cuboids of nitro-glycerine.

3. *Geom.* A solid resembling a cube, with the rectangular faces not all equal; a rectangular parallelepiped.

1890 R. B. HAYWARD *Elem. Solid Geom.* 78 Cuboids..on the same base are to one another as their heights. *Note.* The need of some short word in the place of the polysyllabic 'rectangular parallelepiped' has been long felt. I have coined the work 'cuboid'.

cuboidal (kjuː'bɔɪdəl), *a.* [f. as prec. + -AL[1].]

1. Having a form resembling or approximating to that of a cube.

1803 *Naval Chron.* X. 199 Chrystals of cuboidal pyrites. **1876** PAGE *Adv. Text Bk. Geol.* v. 93 Certain granites break up in large square-like blocks—a structure which is styled tabular or cuboidal.

2. *Anat.* Of or belonging to the cuboid bone.

1866 HUXLEY in Laing *Preh. Rem. Caithn.* 146 The calcaneum..from the lower edge of the cuboidal facet to the extreme end of the calcaneal process measures 2·55.

cuboite ('kjuːbəʊaɪt). *Min.* [mod. f. CUBO- + -ITE; in Ger. *kuboit.*] = CUBICITE.

1850 DANA *Min.* 311.

'cubomancy. *rare*$^{-0}$. [See CUBO- and -MANCY.] Divination by throwing of dice.

In mod. Dicts.

cubship ('kʌbʃɪp). *nonce-wd.* [f. CUB *sb.*[1] + -SHIP.] The estate or personality of a 'cub' or unformed youth.

1881 *Cheq. Career* 173 We walked aft and observed his cubship.

cubub(e, obs. form of CUBEB.

cuca, cucaine, cucainization, etc., variants of COCA, etc.

1876 BARTHOLOW *Mat. Med.* (1879) 336. **1886** *Brit. Med. Jrnl.* Mar. 592/2.

cuchand, cuche: see COUCHANT, COUCH.

cuchanel, -eneale, -ineel, etc., obs. ff. COCHINEAL.

†**cuchil.** *Sc. Obs. rare.* A grove.

1513 DOUGLAS *Æneis* VIII. x. 10 Ane thik aik wod and skuggy firris stout Belappis all the sayd cuchil about. *Ibid.* IX. iii. 20 Apon the top of Gargarus..Thayr grew a fyr wod ..Thys was my cuchill and my hallowit schaw.

† **cuck**, *v.*[1] *Obs.* In 5 also cukkyn. [Cf. Icel. *kúka* cacare; *kúkr* merda; but the *u* is short in Eng.] *intr.* To void excrement. Cf. CACK. Hence **'cucker**; **'cucking** *vbl. sb.*; also *attrib.*

c **1440** *Promp. Parv.* 143 Esyn or cukkyn..or voydyn as man at priuy place [H. cuckyn, P. kackyn], *stercoriso, merdo, egero. Ibid.* 106 Cukkynge, or pysynge vesselle, *scaphium. a* **1605** MONTGOMERIE *Flyting w. Polwart* 87 Where I cuckied. *Ibid.* 735 Closet mucker, house cucker. **1606** *Choice, Chance, &c.* (1881) 69 Hatcht out of a Cucker broode.

† **cuck**, *v.*[2] *Obs.* [Back-formation from CUCKING-STOOL.] *trans.* To punish by setting in the cucking-stool.

1611 MIDDLETON & DEKKER *Roaring Girl* v. ii, Follow the law, and you can cuck me, spare not. **1648** *Manchester Court Leet Rec.* (1887) IV. 25 Mary Kempe..Convicted for a Comon Scould and should have beene Cuckt by the last Constables..The said Mary Kempe [to be] Cookt accordinglie. **16..** *Roxb. Ballads* (1874) II. 54 Oh such a scold would be cuckt.

cuck (kʊk), *v.*[3] *dial.* To utter the note of the cuckoo; = COOK *v.*[2] Hence **'cucking** *vbl. sb.*

a **1693** URQUHART *Rabelais* III. xiii. 106 The..cucking of Cuckows, bumling of Bees. **18..** *Northumbrld. Rime* in Swainson *Prov. Names Birds* 111 The cuckoo comes of mid March And cucks of mid Aperill.

cuck, *v.*[4] *dial.* Also cook. [Cf. CHUCK.] To throw, cast, chuck. Hence **'cuck-ball**, a kind of rounders.

1787 GROSE *Prov. Gloss.*, *Cook*, to throw. 'Cook me that ball.' Glou. **1788** W. HUTTON *Bosworth Field* Introd. (1813) 17 In his father's house..he cuckt his ball..with the same delight as other lads. **1881** *Leicester Gloss.*, *Cuck*, to throw; also to jerk, lurch. 'Cuck us the ball'; 'The carriage cucks about so'. **1888** *Sheffield Gloss.*, *Cuck-ball*, a game at ball.

† **cuck**, *sb. Obs.* Short for CUCKOLD.

1707 E. WARD *Hud. Rediv.* (1715) I. xv, Not the Horn-Plague, but something worse, Had drove the frighted Cucks from thence.

† **'cuckally**, *a. Obs.* Corruption of CUCKOLDLY or CUCKOLDY.

1589 *Rare Tri. Love & Fort.* IV. in Hazl. *Dodsley* VI. 200 O cuckally luck! O heavy chance, O!

cucking-stool ('kʌkɪŋ-stuːl). *Obs.* exc. *Hist.* Forms: 4 coking-, 4- cucking-, 6 cukkyng-, cuckyng-, cooking-; also (by association with CUCKQUEAN) 6 coqueen-, 7 cockqueane-stool. [app. f. CUCK *v.*[1] + STOOL; cf. CUCK-STOOL. Called in the Chester Domesday (I. 262 b) *cathedra stercoris* (Way, *Promp. Parv.*). So named from one of its common forms, which was perhaps the original.]

An instrument of punishment formerly in use for scolds, disorderly women, fraudulent tradespeople, etc., consisting of a chair (sometimes in the form of a close-stool), in which the offender was fastened and exposed to the jeers of the bystanders, or conveyed to a pond or river and ducked.

For full account of its history, see Dr. T. N. Brushfield's *Obsolete Punishments*, II. *The Cucking Stool*, in *Jrnl. of Archit., Archæol., & Hist. Soc. of Chester*, VI. 203 (1857-9).

[**1215-70** in Borlase *Hist. Cornwall* I. 303 (*transl.*) Brawling women..undergo the punishment of the 'Coking Stole'.] *c* **1308** *Sat. People Kildare* 100 in *E.E.P.* (1862) 155 Brewesters..beþ i-war of þe coking-stole, þe lak is dep and hori. *c* **1325** *Poem Times Edw. II*, 477 in *Pol. Songs* (Camden) 345 The pilory and the cucking-stol beth i-mad for noht. **1511-2** *Act 3 Hen. VIII*, c. 6 §1 To be sett upon the pillorie or the Cukkyngstole Man or Woman as the case shall requyre. **1534** in Boys *Coll. Hist. Sandwich* 684 [Two women] to be placed in the coqueen stool, and dipped to the chin. **1577** HARRISON *England* II. xi. (1877) I. 228 Scolds are ducked upon cuckingstooles in the water. **1633** in Rushw. *Hist. Coll.* (1721) III. II. App. 57 She was committed..to be duck'd in a Cucking-Stool at Holborn-Dike. *a* **1680** BUTLER *Rem.* (1759) I. 217 When Pudding-Wives were launcht in cockquean Stools For falling foul on Oyster-women's Schools. **1769** BLACKSTONE *Comm.* IV. 169 She..shall..be placed in a certain engine of correction called the trebucket, castigatory, or cucking stool..now it is frequently corrupted into ducking stool. **1825** SCOTT *Betrothed* ix, Beware the cucking-stool.

cuckle, dial. var of COCKLE *sb.*[1]

cuckle *v.*, obs. variant of COCKLE *v.*[3]

a **1652** BROME *Eng. Moor* I. iii. Wks. 1873 II. 16 Ile so restore thee 'gain with Cawdels and Cock-broths, So cuckle the up to-morrow.

cuckle, cuckling, dial. vars. of CACKLE, etc.

1715 tr. *D'Anoi's Wks.* 501 Peacocks..their Cuckling might be heard two Leagues off. **1884** *Cheshire Gloss.*, s.v., A hen is said to cuckle when she tells us she has laid an egg.

cuckle-stool, cockle-stool, corruption of CUCKING-STOOL.

1592 in *Corporation Acc. Congleton* (Brushfield in *Jrnl. Chester Arch. Soc.* 1861 VI. 221) Paid for amending the Cockle-stool. **1598** *Ibid.* Paid for mending the Cockling stool. **1653** *Ibid.* 224 Paid..for repairing the Cuckle-stool.

† **'cucknel.** *Obs. rare*[−1]. [Cf. COCKNEL.] The Titling, *Anthus Pratensis.*

1655 MOUFET & BENNET *Health's Improv.* (1746) 191 The Titling, Cucknel, or unfortunate Nurse (for the Cuckow ever lays her Egg in the Titling's Nest).

cuckolane, obs. var. COCKALANE 1, a lampoon.

cuckold ('kʌkəld), *sb.*[1] Forms: 3 cukeweld, 4-5 coke-, 4 koke-, cocke-, couke-, kukwold(e, 5 cok-, cukewalde, 5-6 cok-, cocold(e, 6 cock-, coke-, cowck-, cuckold(e, cucquold, cuckould, (cockhole, cookcold), 6-7 cuckhold, (7 coockould, cucculd, cuckhole, cuckot), 6- cuckold. [ME. *cukeweld, cokewold* (3 syllables), adaptation of an OF. word which appears in 1463 as *cucuault*, pointing to an earlier **cucuald*, f. OF. *cucu* cuckoo (in 15-17 c. *cocu*, 16-17th c. *coucou*, cuckoo and cuckold; mod.F. *coucou* cuckoo, *cocu* cuckold, also, dialectally, cuckoo), with the appellative and pejorative suffix *-ald*, *-auld*, *-ault*, *-aud* = It. *-aldo*, f. Ger. *-wald*: see Diez, *Gramm. Lang. Rom.* (1874) II. 346. (The Sw. dial. *kukkuvall* is from F.; mod.Icel. *kokkáll* from English.)

Another OF. synonym was *coucuol*, *couquiol*, with dimin. ending, app. from Prov.: cf. OPr. *coguiol*, mod.Pr. *cougüieu*, *couquieu*, *couguou*, cuckoo and cuckold. The current F. equivalent is the simple form *cocu*. The origin of the sense is supposed to be found in the cuckoo's habit of laying its egg in another bird's nest; in Ger., *gauch* and *kuckuk*, and in Pr., *cogotz*, were applied to the adulterer as well as the husband of the adulteress, and Littré cites an assertion of the same double use in French; in English, where *cuckold* has never been the name of the bird, we do not find it applied to the adulterer.]

1. A derisive name for the husband of an unfaithful wife.

a **1250** *Owl & Night.* 1544 Heo nah iweld, þa heo hine makie cukeweld. **1362** LANGL. *P. Pl.* A. IV. 140 Hose wilneþ hire to wyue..Bote he beo A Cokewold I-kore, cut of boþe myn Eres. *c* **1386** CHAUCER *Miller's Prol.* 44 Leue brother Osewold, Who hath no wyf, he is no Cokewold [*v.r.* coukekukwold]. *c* **1425** *Voc.* in Wr.-Wülcker 651/29 *Hic ninarius*, cokwalde. *c* **1440** *Gesta Rom.* xcii. 421 (Add. MS.) Thy false monke hathe a-way my wife, and made me a Cokewolde. **1483** *Cath. Angl.* 85 To make Cukewalde [A. Cwkwalde], *curucare.* **1562** J. HEYWOOD *Prov. & Epigr.* (1867) 105 Is thy husband a cockold. **1590** SPENSER *F.Q.* III. x. 11 Without regard..of husband old, Whom she hath vow'd to dub a fayre cucquold. **1650** WELDON *Crt. Jas. I*, 111 Hee was..a Cuckold, having a very pretty wench to his Wife. **1728** YOUNG *Love Fame* i. Wks. (1757) 81 And the brib'd cuckold..glories in his gilded horn. **1845** FORD *Handbk. Spain* I. 46 The Spaniards in the sixteenth century mounted unrepining cuckolds..on asses.

b. *attrib.*

1718 LADY M. W. MONTAGUE *Lett.* lviii. II. 93 A beaten wife and cuckold swain Had jointly cursed the marriage chain. **1789** BURNS '*Oh, Willie brewed*', Who first shall rise to gang awa A cuckold coward loon is he.

2. A book-name of the American cow-bird, *Molothrus ater*, a member of a genus of birds which, like the cuckoo, lay their eggs in other birds' nests. (*Century Dict.*)

3. Short for *cuckold-fish*: see 4.

4. *Comb.* † **cuckold-fish**, a fish with horn-like projections, prob. the cow-fish (*Ostracion quadricorne*); † **cuckold-fly** (see quot.); **cuckold-maker**, 'one that makes a practice of corrupting wives' (J.); so *cuckold-making*; † **cuckold's chorister**, the cuckoo; † **Cuckold's haven, point**, a point on the Thames, below Greenwich; formerly used allusively; † **cuckoldshire** (*humorous*) cuckoldom; † **cuckold's-increase**, a W. Indian leguminous plant, *Vigna unguiculata*; **cuckold's-knot, neck**, a knot or loop made in a rope by crossing it over itself and seizing or binding it together with a cord at the point of crossing; † **cuckold's-row** (*humorous*), cuckoldom; **cuckold-tree**, an American Acacia, *A. cornigera*.

1757 B. MARTIN *Misc. Corr.* II. 544 The *Piscis bicornis*, vulgarly called the *Cuckold-Fish. **1750** G. HUGHES *Barbadoes* 83 *Cuckold Fly..is of the Beetle kind, of about half an inch long, and of a dark-red colour. **1580** BARET *Alv.* C 1726 A *cuckould maker, *mœchus.* **1682** SOUTHERNE *Loyal Brother* II. i, *Soldier.* And I am a cuckold-maker. **1681** OTWAY *Soldier's Fort.* III. i, A bloody *Cuckold-making Scoundrel. **1749** FIELDING *Tom Jones* XI. x, Young gentlemen who profess the art of Cuckold-making. **1592** GREENE *Upst. Courtier* (1871) 6 When the *Cuckold's chorister began to bewray April-Gentlemen with his never changed notes. **1606** DAY *Ile of Guls* (N.), A young girle, married to an old man, doth [long] to run her husband ashore at *Cuckolds haven. *c* **1537** *Thersites* in Hazl. *Dodsley* I. 424 All the court of conscience in *Cuckoldshire. **1756** P. BROWNE *Jamaica* 292 *Cuckold's-Increase. This plant is cultivated in all parts of Jamaica, and the pulse generally made use of at every gentleman's table. **1847-78** HALLIWELL, **Cuckold's-knot*, a noose tied so that the ends point lengthways. **1846** YOUNG *Naut. Dict.*, **Cuckold's neck*, a knot by which a rope is secured to a spar, the two parts of the rope crossing each other and being seized together. **1757** *Poor Robin* (N.), If you are minded for to wed..Let her be..chaste..Lest if at *Cuckolds point you land, etc. *a* **1500** *Cokwolds Daunce* 197 in Hazl. *E.P. Poetry* I. 46, I may dance in the *cokwold row. **1668** L'ESTRANGE *Vis. Quevedo* (1708) 69 Many a brave Fellow lives in Cuckold's-Row. **1815** J. DONN *Hortus Cantab.* 327 *Mimosa cornigera*, *Cuckold-tree. S. America.

† **'cuckold**, *sb.*[2] *Obs.* Variant of COCKLE.

1. = COCKLE[1] 3, the burdock.

1698 SIR R. SOUTHWELL in *Phil. Trans.* XX. 89 What they call Cuckold-Burs, which stick on the Cloths. **1821** T. NUTTALL *Trav. Arkansa* ii. 58 The cornfields, at this season of the year, are so over-run with cuckold-burrs (*Xanthium Strumarium*)..as to prove extremely troublesome to woollen clothes.

2. = COCKLE[2], the shell-fish.

1782 P. H. BRUCE *Mem.* XII. 424 Their shell-fish are..wilkes, cuckolds, craw-fish, lobsters, crabs.

cuckold ('kʌkəld), *v.* [f. CUCKOLD *sb.*[1]]

1. *trans.* To make a cuckold of; to dishonour (a husband) by adultery; said **a.** of a paramour; **b.** of a wife.

a. 1589 WARNER *Alb. Eng.* VI. xxx, Few will judge, I winne, If it shall come in question, that to cockhole [**1612** cuckhole] him were sinne. **1598** SHAKS. *Merry W.* III. v. 138. **1687** SETTLE *Refl. Dryden* 89 An insolent Fellow that he fears Cuckolds him. *a* **1754** FIELDING *New Way to Keep* Wks. 1775 II. 171 It will be believed that I intended to cuckold your uncle.

b. 1604 SHAKS. *Oth.* IV. i. 211 *Oth.* I will chop her into Messes: Cuckold me? *Iago.* Oh, 'tis foule in her. **1710** HEARNE *Collect.* (Oxf. Hist. Soc.) III. 20 A Wife who takes care to have him cuckol'd every day. **1822** T. TAYLOR *Apuleius* 194 We heard a pleasant narration about a poor man being cuckolded by his wife.

† **2.** *fig.* To cheat, trick. *Obs.*

1644-7 CLEVELAND *Char. Lond. Diurn.* 5 This is..hee, that Cuckolds the Generall in his Commission: for he stalkes with Essex, and shoots under his belly.

† **'cuckoldage.** *Obs. nonce-wd.* [See -AGE.] The position of a cuckold, cuckoldom.

1676 WYCHERLEY *Plain-Dealer* Ep. Ded., How many old Dotards [have you preserved] from cuckoldage.

† **'cuckoldize**, *v. Obs. rare.* [f. CUCKOLD *sb.*[1] + -IZE.] *trans.* To make a cuckold.

1681 DRYDEN *Abs. & Achit.* II. 339 Can dry bones live, or skeletons produce The vital warmth of cuckoldizing juice?

† **'cuckoldly**, *a. Obs.* [f. as prec. + -LY[1].] Having the character or qualities of a cuckold; often a mere term of reviling or abuse.

1594 GREENE *Looking Glass* (1598) H ij a, Nay, sir, he was a cuckoldly diuell, for hee had hornes on his head. **1598** SHAKS. *Merry W.* II. ii. 281 Hang him (poore Cuckoldly knaue). **1698** VANBRUGH *Prov. Wife* V. ii, You cuckoldly drunken sot you! **1709** *Brit. Apollo* II. 3/2 My Cuckoldly Jacket. *a* **1734** NORTH *Lives* III. 66 Was it not a cuckoldly world from the beginning; and shall it not be so still?

cuckoldom ('kʌkəldəm). [f. as prec. + -DOM.]

1. The state or position of a cuckold.

1678 DRYDEN *Limberham* V. i, He takes Pains enough o'conscience for his Cuckoldom; and, by my Troth, has earn'd it fairly. **1708** *Brit. Apollo* No. 27. 2/2 Horns should be the Badge of Cuckholdom. **1813** *Examiner* 22 Feb. 123/2 Cuckoldom has been a good joke from time immemorial.

† **2.** = CUCKOLDRY 1. *Obs.*

1680 DRYDEN *Span. Friar* (J.), She is thinking on nothing but her colonel, and conspiring cuckoldom against me. **1711** ADDISON *Spect.* No. 16 ¶3 It is not my Design to be a Publisher of Intrigues and Cuckoldoms. **1756-82** J. WARTON *Ess. Pope* (1782) I. v. 282 To recommend cuckoldom, and palliate adultery, is their usual intent.

cuckoldry ('kʌkəldrɪ). [f. as prec. + -RY.]

1. The dishonouring of a husband by adultery with or on the part of his wife.

1529 S. FISH *Supplic. Beggars* 6 That cuckoldrie and baudrie shulde reigne ouer all emong your subiectes. **1603** FLORIO *Montaigne* II. xii. (1632) 298 Cuckoldries..procured by the Gods against seely mortall men. **1679** in Maidment *Sc. Pasquils* (1868) 248 Let websters preach, and ladies teach The art of cuckoldrie. **1825** LAMB *Elia*, *Pop. Fallacies*, How would certain topics, as aldermanity, cuckoldry, have sounded to a Terentian auditory?

† **2.** A company of cuckolds. *Obs.*

1538 BALE *Thre Lawes* 228 By the masse, I the defye, With thy whole cuckoldrye.

† **3.** The position of a cuckold; cuckoldom. *Obs.*

1612 *Pasquils Night-Cap* (1877) 117 To shew that hornes belong to Cuckoldrie. **1685** COTTON tr. *Montaigne* I. 484, I know some who consentingly have acquired both profit and advancement from cuckoldry.

cuckoldy ('kʌkəldɪ), *a. Obs.* or *arch.* [f. as prec. + -Y.] = CUCKOLDLY.

1618 FIELD *Amends for Ladies* II. i. in Hazl. *Dodsley* XI. 110 If it had been somebody else, I would have called him cuckoldy slave. **1673** SHADWELL *Epsom Wells* IV, I'll tear your eyes out..you cuckoldy villain! **1823** SCOTT *Peveril* vi, I warrant..that the cuckoldy Roundhead ate enough of our fat beef yesterday. **1826** —— *Woodst.* i, Blessed by the old cuckoldy priest of Godstow. **1829** LAMB *Let.* 27 Feb., No lighter texture than their steel did the cuckoldy blacksmith frame to catch Mrs. Vulcan and the Captain in.

cuckoo ('kʊkuː), *sb.* Forms: 3 cuccu, 4 coccou, cockou, 4-5 cukkow, cokkow, (5 cocow, co-, kockowe, cucko, cauko, kukkowe, 5-6 cuckowe, 6 cocowe, cokowe, -oue, koko, kookoo, cokow, coockow; *Sc.* gukkow, gukgo guk-guk; 6-7 cuckoe, 7 cukcow, cockow, (cocoe), 5-9 cuckow, 7- cuckoo. [Identical with F. *coucou* (12-15th c. *cucu*), imitating the cry of the bird.

The OE. name was *ȝéac*, rare ME. *ȝeke*, cognate with Ger. *gauch*, ON. *gaukr*, whence Sc. and north Eng. GOWK. In many languages a tendency has been shown from time to time to abandon inherited forms of this bird's name, which, even though originally echoic, have under the operation of phonetic changes gradually ceased to be so, in order to go back anew to the call of the bird. Thus, since the 15th c. *gauch* has in Ger. been superseded by *kuckuk*, from LG. *kukuk*, MDu. *cucûc*, Du. *koekoek*, a form founded upon the call; and this in some Ger. dialects has given way to the entirely imitative *kuku, guckgu, gúgku, kuckú* (see Grimm). Cf. Gr. κόκκυξ, cuckoo, beside κόκκυ the call; med.Gr. κοῦκος, mod.Gr. κοῦκο the bird. The L. was *cuculus* (cf. Skr. *kôkilas*) and *cucūlus*, whence It. *cu'culo*, Pr. *cogul*; also in late L. (and ? Plautus) *cucus*, whence Sp., Pg., and It. dial. *cuco*. The Fr. *cucu, coucou* was not the representative of any L. form, but taken anew from the call of the bird itself; ME *cuccu* might also be directly echoic, but being found only after the Norman conquest, it was prob. influenced by French example, though the annual lessons given by the bird have prevented the phonetic changes which the word would normally have undergone. In Scotch the stress is as in OF. on the second syllable (ku'ku:). With the 16th c. Sc. forms in *guk-* cf. Bavarian *gucku*, and various early variants of German *kuckuk*, as *gucguc, guckkug*, etc.]

1. a. A bird, *Cuculus canorus*, well known by the call of the male during mating time, of which the name is an imitation. ***cuckoo's note*** (*fig.*): repetition of the same words.

It is a migratory bird, arriving in the British Islands in April, and hence welcomed as the 'harbinger of spring'; it does not hatch its own offspring, but deposits its eggs in the nests of small birds, as the hedge-sparrow, water-wagtail, yellow-hammer, and others; to this peculiarity many allusions occur: cf. also CUCKOLD.

c **1240** *Cuckoo Song*, Sumer is icumen in..murie sing cuccu! Cuccu! cuccu! Wel singes þu cuccu; ne swik þu nauer nu. **1340** *Ayenb.* 22 Þe yelpere is þe cockou þet ne kan naȝt zinge bote of him-zelue. *c* **1381** CHAUCER *Parl. Foules* 358 Ther was..the cokkow [*v.r.* cucko, cuckow, kukkowe, cuccow] most onkynde. **14..** *Nominale* in Wr.-Wülcker 702 *Hic cuculus*, cauko. *c* **1475** *Pict. Voc.* ibid. 762 A cocow. **1513** DOUGLAS *Æneis* XII. Prol. 241 The gukgo [**1553** gukkow] galis, and so quytteris the quaill. **1529** MORE *Dyaloge* I. Wks. 132/1 No more meruailous is a koko than a cock. **1594** SPENSER *Amoretti* xix, The merry Cuckow, messenger of Spring. **1605** SHAKS. *Lear* I. iv. 235 You know Nunckle, the Hedge-Sparrow fed the Cuckoo so long, that it's had it head bit off by it young. **1649** BLITHE *Eng. Improv. Impr.* ii. (1653) 14 He..may as well make a hedge to keep in the Cuckow. **1728-46** THOMSON *Spring* 578 From the first note the hollow cuckoo sings, The symphony of Spring. **1749** WESLEY in *Wks.* 1872 X. 28 Sir, I must come in again with my cuckoo's note,—The proof! Where is the proof! **1804** WORDSW. *To the Cuckoo* i, O Cuckoo! shall I call thee Bird, Or but a wandering Voice? **1841-44** EMERSON *Ess., Over-Soul* Wks. (Bohn) I. 111 Yonder masterful cuckoo Crowds every egg out of the nest..except its own.

b. The family name of the *Cuculidæ*, of which the common cuckoo is the type; the various genera and species are known as ***crested cuckoo, lark-heeled, spur-heeled***, or ***pheasant cuckoo***, etc.; also the ***tree, yellow-billed***, and ***hook-billed cuckoos, ground cuckoos***, and ***gregarious cuckoos***, American types of the family.

1797 P. WAKEFIELD *Mental Improv.* (1801) I. 115 It is a species of cuckow. **1813** BINGLEY *Zool.* II. 118 The different species of cuckoos are scattered through the four quarters of the globe. **1837** SWAINSON in *Penny Cycl.* VIII. 207/1, I have no doubt that the great length of tail possessed by nearly all the cuckoos is given to them as a sort of balance. **1861** SWINHOE *N. China Camp.* 16 You hear the soft notes of the striated cuckoo.

2. The note of the bird, or an imitation of it.

c **1240** [see 1]. **1562** J. HEYWOOD *Prov. & Epigr.* (1867) 216 In Apryll the Koocoo can syng hir song by rote..At fyrst, kooco, kooco, syng styll can she do. **1549** *Compl. Scot.* vi. 39 The titlene followit the goilk, ande gart hyr sing guk guk. **1588** SHAKS. *L.L.L.* v. ii. 911 Cuckow, Cuckow: O word of feare, Vnpleasing to a married eare. **1856** CAPERN *Poems* (ed. 2) 92 Cuckoo, cuckoo, singing mellow, Ever when the fields are yellow.

3. Applied to a person; *esp.* in reference to the bird's monotonous call, or its habit of laying its eggs in the nests of other birds; also = fool, 'gowk'. Now usu. *slang* for 'a silly person'.

1581 J. BELL *Haddon's Answ. Osor.* 59 b, This lesson you learned of your Cowled Coockowes, to braule alwayes with bare names. **1596** SHAKS. *1 Hen. IV*, II. iv. 387 A Horsebacke (ye Cuckoe), but a foot hee will not budge a foot. **1609** *Ev. Woman in Hum.* II. i. in Bullen *O. Pl.* IV, An excellent Cuckoo, hee keepes his note in winter. **1612** *Pasquils Night-Cap* (1877) 75 What Cuckoe laid this egge within your nest. **1823** SCOTT *Peveril* xxiii, The cuckoo I travel with..he also has his uses. **1872** O. W. HOLMES *Poet Breakf.-t.* i. 12 We Americans are all cuckoos,—we make our homes in the nests of other birds. **1889** J. K. JEROME *Three Men in Boat* x. 152 Give us a hand here, can't you, you cuckoo; standing there like a stuffed mummy. **1921** H. C. WITWER *Leather Pushers* i. 4 On account of this cuckoo forgettin' he was a box fighter,..we lose five other bouts. **1924** GALSWORTHY *White Monkey* I. ix. 77 'Don't worry, we'll dig up the just-right cuckoos, somehow.' 'A Chinese Minister would be perfect,' mused Fleur.

†**4.** *Gardening.* See quot.; = F. *coucou*. *Obs.*

1693 EVELYN *De La Quint. Compl. Gard.* II. 158 We must take exact care to pluck all the Cuckows among them, that is, those Strawberry plants that blossom much without knitting.

5. (Usually in *pl.*) The local name of several spring flowers, as the Cuckoo-flower *Cardamine pratensis*, the *Orchis mascula* and *O. Morio*, the common Blue-bell *Scilla nutans*, the Ragged Robin, etc. Cf. Britten and Holland *Plant Names.*

1878 MRS. H. WOOD *Pomeroy Ab.* (ed. 3) 56 The long, deep-pink flowers that children call cookoos.

6. A species of fish; also called *cuckoo-fish, -wrasse. local.*

1848 C. A. JOHNS *Week at Lizard* 230 One species [*Labrus variegatus*]..is called by the fishermen a cuckoo, and is probably the 'striped wrasse' of authors.

‖**7.** = F. *coucou*, a small coach running from Paris to the suburbs.

1821 W. IRVING in *Life & Lett.* (1864) II. ii. 46 Took a place in a cuckoo to St. Cloud.

8. *attrib.* **a.** Of or pertaining to the cuckoo.

1627 P. FLETCHER *Locusts* II. xxxiv, There layd they cuckoe eggs, and hatch't their brood unblest. **1742** YOUNG *Nt. Th.* iii. 375 The cuckow-seasons sing The same dull note to such as nothing prize. **1802** BINGLEY *Anim. Biog.* (1813) II. 118 Of the Cuckoo tribe in general.

b. Resembling, or suggestive of, the cuckoo and its uniformly repeated call.

1650 T. B[AYLEY] *Worcester's Apoph.* 78 Not a little angry with this Redmans cukcow play. **1797** MRS. A. M. BENNETT *Beggar Girl* (1813) III. 159 The hundred thousand rix-dollars were the cuckoo song with Christiana. **1831** CAPT. BERKELEY in *Ho. Com.* 5 July, The cuckoo note..of 'the Bill, the whole Bill, and nothing but the Bill'. **1858** *Sat. Rev.* 6 Nov. 438/1 The cuckoo cry that party is extinct. **1859** HELPS *Friends in C.* Ser. II. I. viii. 238 Tired of hearing this cuckoo exclamation.

9. *Comb.*, as ***cuckoo-bird; cuckoo-echoing*** adj. (poet.); ***cuckoo-like*** adj. and adv.; **cuckoo-ale**, 'ale drunk out of doors to welcome the cuckoo's return' (Halliwell); **cuckoo-ball**, 'a light ball made of party-coloured rags, for young children' (Forby); **cuckoo-bee**, a genus of bees which deposit their eggs in the nests of other bees; †**cuckoo-bone**, the coccyx; **cuckoo('s)bread**, the Wood-sorrel; also the Lady's Smock; **cuckoo-dove**, a genus of doves of the East Indies and Australia; **cuckoo-feeder**, a form of feeder in the bellows of an organ; **cuckoo-fish**, see 6 above; also the boar-fish; **cuckoo fowl** (see quot.); **cuckoo('s)fool, maid(en, mate**, the Wryneck, which arrives at or about the same time as the cuckoo; **cuckoo-froth**, = CUCKOO-SPIT²; **cuckoo-gilliflower**, the Ragged Robin, *Lychnis Flos-cuculi*; **cuckoo-grass**, the Field-Rush, *Luzula campestris*, flowering in spring; **cuckoo gurnard**, a fish, *Trigla cuculus*, which emits a sound resembling the cuckoo's call when taken out of the water; **cuckoo-lamb**, a lamb born between April and June; **cuckoo('s)-maid**, (*a*) = *cuckoo-fool*; (*b*) in Hereford, the Red-backed Shrike; **cuckoo-orchis**, *Orchis mascula*; **cuckoo-point** = CUCKOO-PINT; **cuckoo-ray**, a fish, a species of ray; **cuckoo scab** *Austral.* and *N.Z.*, a skin disease of sheep; **cuckoo's-eye**, *Geranium Robertianum* and *Veronica chamœdryo*; **cuckoo-shell**, a local name of the whelk; **cuckoo('s)shoe**, Dog Violet; **cuckoo-shrike**, the Caterpillar-catcher; **cuckoo's mate** = *cukoo('s)-maid* (*a*); †**cuckoo-spell**, name suggested by Puttenham for the rhetorical figure *Epizeuxis*; **cuckoo-wrasse**, see 6 above.

1839 TODD *Cycl. Anat.* II. 930/2 In the *cuckoo-bee..there are..four imperfectly developed spines. **1598** SHAKS. *Merry W.* II. i. 127 Ere sommer comes, or *Cuckoo-birds do sing. **1668** CULPEPPER & COLE *Barthol. Anat.* IV. xv. 351 Os Coccygis the *Cockow-bone, so called from the shape it hath of a Cuckows-bill. **1516** *Gt. Herbal* I. (1529) C vj b, Alleluya is an herbe called *cuckowes brede. **1578** LYTE *Dodoens* I. xl. 58 The leaues of Cuckowbread, sower Tryfoly, or Alleluya. **1776** WITHERING *Brit. Plants* (1796) II. 431 Yellow-flowered Cuckowbread. **1879** G. M. HOPKINS *Poems* (1918) 41 *Cuckoo-echoing, bell-swarmèd, lark-charmèd. **1661** LOVELL *Hist. Anim. & Min.* Introd., The Mullet, swallow fish, *cuckow-fish. **1884** J. C. BREVOORT in G. B. Goode *Fisheries & Fishing Industries U.S.* I. 257 When freshly taken from the water they grunt quite loudly, whence their popular name of Grunter, or Cuckoo-fish. **1850** D. J. BROWNE *Amer. Poultry Yard* 56 The '*cuckoo fowl'..was so called from its barred plumage, resembling the breast of the cuckoo. **1872** *Proc. Berw. Nat. Club* VI. 386 *Cuckoo-froth, which is secreted by the little frogskip insect. **1578** LYTE *Dodoens* II. vii. 157 It is called..Wilde Williams, Marshe gillofers, and *Cockow gillofers. **1749** W. ELLIS *Shepherd's Guide* 73 All lambs yeaned in April or May are called with us, in Hertfordsire, the *cuckoo lambs, because they fall in cuckoo time. **1570** B. GOOGE *Pop. Kingd.* III. 40 Or *coocoolike continually, one kinde of musique sing. **1601** BP. W. BARLOW *Defence* 95 This Cuckow-like Palinodie of Councels, Doctours, and Church. **1832** G. DOWNES *Lett. Cont. Countries* I. 183 He had two English words, 'very good! very good!' which, cuckoo-like, he was constantly reiterating. **1865** *Cornh. Mag.* July 36 In the North the wryneck is called the '*cuckoo-maiden', because its song foretells the cuckoo's approach. **1597** GERARDE *Herbal* I. xcix. §6. 159 Called male Foole stones, and *Cuckow Orchis. **1941** BAKER *Dict. Austral. Slang* 21 **Cuckoo scab*, a skin disease on sheep on the back of the head and ears. **1951** L. G. D. ACLAND *Early Canterbury Runs* 372 *Cuckoo scab*, a skin disease sheep get at the back of their heads and on their ears. I have only noticed it among merinos and in the back country. **1877** OUIDA *Puck* xxi. 234 The sunny azure of the little *cuckoo's-eye flowers. [**1802** G. MONTAGU *Ornith. Dict.* II, s.v. Wryneck, Appearing at the same time with the Cuckow, it has been termed that bird's servant or attendant.] **1831** G. MONTAGU *Ornith. Dict.* (ed. 2) 123 *Cuckoo's mate.—A name for the Wryneck. **1898** C. M. YONGE *John Keble's Parishes* xvi. 202 Wryneck..or Cuckoo's mate, squeaks all round the woods..just as the cuckoo comes. **1955** D. A. BANNERMAN *Birds Brit. Isles* IV. 119 The approximate dates of its [*sc.* the wryneck's] arrival in Britain, where it is commonly known as 'the cuckoo's mate', have already been given. **1589** PUTTENHAM *Eng. Poesie* III. xix. (Arb.) 211 We might very properly, in our vulgar and for pleasure call him the *cuckowspell. **1865** J. C. WILCOCKS *Sea Fisherman* (1875) 122 The Cook or *Cuckoo-Wrasse, of which the blue marks are very beautiful.

cuckoo ('kʊku:), *v.* [f. prec.]

1. *intr.* To utter the call of the cuckoo, or an imitation of it.

1620 ROWLANDS *Nt. Raven* 4 Nor with your hopping cage birds sing, Nor cuckow it about the spring. **1656** W. D. tr. *Comenius' Gate Lat. Unl.* §142. 43 The Cuckoe which bewrayeth herself by cuckoing. **1879** BARING-GOULD *Germany* II. 310 Clocks..some that strike, some that cuckoo.

2. *trans.* To repeat incessantly and without variation.

1648 *Cuckows Nest* in *Harl. Misc.* 1745 V. 552 These always..cuckow forth one Tune, No King, no King. **1822** *Blackw. Mag.* XII. 633 He cuckooed the old song of reduction. **1857** E. FITZGERALD *Lett.* (1889) I. 251 Their Religion and Philosophy..always seems to me cuckooed over like a borrowed thing.

3. To push out from the nest like a cuckoo.

1870 W. THORNBURY *Tour Eng.* I. i. 19 The government had an eye on him, and soon cuckooed him out by passing a bill to prevent clergymen being representatives in parliament.

cuckoo ('kʊku:), *a. slang* (orig. *U.S.*). [f. the sb.] Crazy, out of one's wits.

1918 *Wine, Women & War* (1926) 75 Wish my daughter would grow up like that... [fn.] Seen her since. Certainly must have been cuckoo! **1923** WODEHOUSE *Inimit. Jeeves* xvii. 241 He pottered about the room for a bit, babbling at intervals. The boy seemed cuckoo. **1928** *Collier's* 29 Dec. 28/1 When everything..failed to reduce Jack's bulk, I was nearly cuckoo with rage and fear. **1955** M. GILBERT *Sky High* vi. 76 Never asked for references?.. She must be cuckoo.

cuckoo-bud. A name of some plant.

Shakspere has been variously supposed to refer to the buttercup, marsh-marigold, and cowslip; Clare perhaps meant an Orchis, or the Cuckoo-pint in bud.

1588 SHAKS. *L.L.L.* v. ii. 906 When Dasies pied, and Violets blew, And Cuckow-buds of yellow hew: And Ladie-smockes all siluer white, Do paint the Medowes with delight. **1821** CLARE *Vill. Minstr.* I. 137 'Neath the weaving thorn, Where the pouch'd-lipp'd cuckoo-bud From its snug retreat was torn. *Ibid.* II. 133 Full many a blue-bell flower and cuckoo-bud.

cuckoo-clock. A clock in which the hours are announced by an imitation of the call of the cuckoo produced by mechanism.

1789 COWPER *Lett.* 5 June, You must buy for me..a cuckoo clock. **1862** KINGSLEY *Water Bab.* ii, A cuckoo clock in the corner, which began shouting as soon as Tom appeared.

'cuckoo-,flower. A name given to various wild flowers which are in bloom when the cuckoo is heard. **a.** The Lady's Smock, *Cardamine pratensis*, a cruciferous plant common in meadows.

1578 LYTE *Dodoens* v. lx. 625 Called..in Englishe, the lesser Watercresse, and Coccow flowers. **1772-84** COOK *Voy.* (1790) I. 40 Scurvy-grass..resembles the English Cuckoo flower, or lady's smock. **1833** TENNYSON *Poems* 38 Each quaintly-folded cuckoopint And silver-paly cuckoo flower.

b. The Ragged Robin, *Lychnis Flos-cuculi.*

1629 PARKINSON *Paradisi in Sole* xxxviii. 256 Some call them in English Crowflowers, and Cuckowe flowers, and some call the double hereof, The Faire Maide of France. **1777** LIGHTFOOT *Flora Scot.* I. 239 Meadow Pinks, Wild Williams, Cuckow Flower, or Ragged Robbins. **1861** MISS PRATT *Flower. Pl.* I. 227.

c. Also applied locally to *Orchis mascula* and *O. Morio*; Red Campion, *Lychnis diurna*; Greater Stitchwort, *Stellaria Holostea*; the Cuckoo-pint; Wood Sorrel; Wild Hyacinth, and others. See Britten and Holland *Plant Names.*

1605 SHAKS. *Lear* IV. iv. 4 With Hardokes, Hemlocke, Nettles, Cuckoo flowres, Darnell, and all the idle weedes that grow In our sustaining Corne. **1802** WORDSW. *Foresight*, Here are daisies..Pansies, and the cuckoo-flower. **1820** CLARE *Rural Life* (ed. 3) 208 Where peep the gaping, speckled cuckoo-flowers. **1865** *Cornh. Mag.* July 34 The orchis is his 'cuckoo-flower,' because it blossoms when the cuckoo is first heard.

'cuckoo-fly. A name given to various species of hymenopterous insects belonging to the *Ichneumonidæ* and *Chrysididæ*, which deposit their eggs in the larvæ or the nests of other insects.

1868 WOOD *Homes without H.* xxv. 481 Then there are the Cuckoo Flies..which are parasitic, feeding on the larvae of other insects. **1889** E. A. ORMEROD *Injur. Insects* (1890) 126 Hop Cuckoo Fly is sometimes very troublesome in Hop-gardens.

'cuckooish, *a.* [See -ISH.] Cuckoo-like.

1605 CHAPMAN *All Fools* III. i, Now, sir, for these cuckooish songs of yours, of cuckolds, horns, grafting, and such-like.

cuckoo-land, short for CLOUD-CUCKOO-LAND. Hence *cuckoo-lander.*

1916 A. HUXLEY *Burning Wheel* 49 For still in Cuckoo-Land they're labouring, With hopes undamped and undiscouraged hearts. *Ibid.* 50 And Cuckoo-Landers not a few shall prove. **1958** *Observer* 28 Sept. 17/1, I am afraid that your paper..is living in a cuckoo-land. Have you no idea what ordinary Cockney people..feel about this mass invasion [of coloured people]?

cuckoo-pint ('kʊku:,pɪnt). [Shortened from next.] The wild or common Arum, *A. maculatum*, or Wake-robin.

1551 TURNER *Herbal* I. (1568) D vj b, Coccowpynt called also in Englyshe rampe or Aron. **1656** RIDGLEY *Pract. Physick* 299 Root of Cuckoe-pint, half a dram. **1762** B. STILLINGFLEET *Econ. Nature* Misc. Tracts 76 There is a kind of cuckow-pint in New-France, that if you break a branch of it, will afford you a pint of excellent water. **1874** T. HARDY *Madding Crowd* I. 239 The odd cuckoo-pint—like an apoplectic saint in a niche of malachite.

† **'cuckoo-,pintle.** *Obs.* [Named from the form of the spadix.] = prec.

c **1450** *Voc.* in Wr.-Wülcker 588 *Jarus*, cokkupyntel, calvysfote. **1597** GERARDE *Herbal* I. lxv. (1598) 90 Wake Robin or Aron..Plinies cowkowpintle. **1635** BROME *Sparagus Garden* III. xi. Wks. 1873 III. 174 S'daggers three pound for a few Cuckoe pintles. **1682** *Hist. Chocolate* in *Harl. Misc* I. 534 They would have thrown away their wake-robins and their cuckow-pointles.

cuckoo's meat, cuckoo-meat. Wood-sorrel, *Oxalis Acetosella*, which flowers at the time the cuckoo is heard; also called *gowk's-meat*.

1516 *Gt. Herbal* Contents ch. l, Alleluya, wood sorell or cocowes meate. **1538** TURNER *Libellus*, Cuckowes meat, *Oxys*. **1578** LYTE *Dodoens* IV. xliii. 503 This herbe is called in..English Wood-sorel..Cockowes meate. **1853** G. JOHNSTON *Nat. Hist. E. Bord.* 50. **1860** H. MARRYAT *Jutland* I. v. 74 The forest is carpeted with the green trefoil leaves of the '*giögemad*' or cuckoo's meat.

b. Locally applied, in error, to Robert's Geranium, *G. Robertianum*; Greater Stitchwort, *Stellaria Holostea*; and Sour Dock, *Rumex Acetosella*.

† **'cuckoo-,spit**[1]. *Obs.* [f. SPIT, a slender bar.] = CUCKOO-PINT.

c **1450** *Alphita* (Anecd. Oxon.) 21 Barba aaron..cokkowe-spitte. **1587** MASCALL *Govt. Cattle* (1627) 267 With the iuyce of cuckospit, and salt, and stubwort mixt, and rub it therewith.

'cuckoo-,spit[2]. [f. SPIT, expectoration; the popular belief being that the matter was spit out by the cuckoo; cf. Germ. *kuckukspeichel*, Du. *koekoeksspog*, etc.]

1. A frothy secretion exuded by certain insects, in which their larvæ lie enveloped on the leaves, axils, etc. of plants; the insect chiefly producing it in Great Britain is the Frog-hopper, *Aphrophora spumaris*, or ***cuckoo-spit insect***.

1592 GREENE *Upst. Courtier* (1871) 7 Loyal lauender..full of Cuckoo spits. **1753** CHAMBERS *Cycl. Supp.*, *Froth spit*, or *cuckow spit*..very common in the spring, and first months of the summer, on the leaves of certain plants. **1857** LIVINGSTONE *Trav.* xxi. 415 While still in the pupa state it is called cuckoo-spit, from the mass of froth in which it envelopes itself.

2. Applied locally to the Lady's Smock, etc.

1876 *Jrnl. Hortic.* 4 May 355 (in Britten & Holl.) In the north of England the plant is known only by the name of cuckoo-spit..no doubt, from the fact of almost every flower-stem having deposited upon it a frothy patch..in which is enveloped a pale green insect.

'cuckoo-,spittle. = prec. (sense 1).

1646 SIR T. BROWNE *Pseud. Ep.* v. iii. 237 It..is..delivered by many, that Cicades are bred out of Cuccow spittle or Woodseare. **1664** POWER *Exp. Philos.* I. 28 That spumeous froth or dew which here in the North we call Cuckow-Spittle, and, in the South, Woodsear. **1884** *Mehalah* xiii. 185 If on a May morning you rub your eyes with cuckoo spittle, you see the fairies.

† **'cuckquean,** *sb. Obs.* Forms: 6 cook-, 6–7 cock-, cuc-, 7 cuck(e-; also 6 cut-, 7 quot-. [f. stem of *cuck-old* + QUEAN.] A female cuckold.

1562 J. HEYWOOD *Prov. & Epigr.* (1867) 62 Ye make hir a cookqueane. **1565** GOLDING *Ovid's Met.* VI. (1593) 146 Queene Progne was a cutqueane made by meanes of her. **1614** *Sco. Venus* (1876) 39 That hast made her a quotqueane shamefully. **1615** HEYWOOD *Foure Prentises* Wks. 1874 II. 216 Hee'd make his wife a Cucke-queane. *a* **1652** BROME *City Wit* IV. i, To bee made Cuckqueane by such a Cockscombe. **1922** JOYCE *Ulysses* 15 A wandering crone..their common cuckquean.

Hence † **'cuckquean** *v. trans.*, to make a cuckquean of.

1592 WARNER *Alb. Eng.* VIII. xli. (1612) 199 Came I from France..to be Cuckquean'd heere? *a* **1652** BROME *Mad Couple* III. i, You can doe him no wrong..to cuckold him, for assure your selfe hee cuckqueans you.

cuckquean-, coqueen-stool: see CUCKING-STOOL.

cuck-shaws, var. of KICKSHAWS, for F. *quelque chose*, something; things unnamed.

1623 WEBSTER *Devil's Law Case* II. i, Cuckshaws, that beget Such monsters without fundaments.

† **cuck-stool.** *Obs.* Forms: 4–5 cok-, kuk-, 5 cuc-, 5–6 cuk-, coke-, 5–7 cuck-, cook(e-, 6–7 cock-, and stule, stole, stool(e, etc.; also 5 cuxtole. [See CUCKING-STOOL.]

1. = CUCKING-STOOL.

1200–15 in WHITTAKER *Hist. Richmondshire* II. 422 Faciet meliorem finem quem poterit, vel ibit ad Cuckestolam. *c* **1320** *Poem on Times Edw. II* (Percy Soc.) lxxii, The pelery and the cok-stol. *c* **1400** *Burgh Laws* lxiii. in *Sc. Stat.* I. 345 Gif scho makis evil ale..scho sall gif..viiis. or..be put on þe kukstule. **1423** *Leet Bk. Coventry* (in *Promp. Parv.* 107) Cokestowle made apon Chelsmore grene to punysche skolders and chidders, as yᵉ law will. *c* **1440** *Promp. Parv.* 106/2 Cukstole, for flyterys, or schyderys [*v.r.* cukstolle, cucstool]. **1576** in E. Peacock *N.W. Linc. Gloss.*, Euery woman that is a scould shall..be sett vpon the cockstoll and be thrise ducked in the water. *a* **1625** FLETCHER *Woman's Prize* III. i, We'll ship 'em out in cuck-stools; there they'll sail..till they discover The happy islands of obedience. **1659** in PICTON *L'pool Munic. Rec.* (1883) I. 229. That a new Cooke Stoole bee made. **1768–9** in Kelly *Anc. Rec. Leicester* 48 Paid Mr. Elliott for a Cuckstool, by order of Hall £2. [**1884** HOLLAND *Cheshire Gloss.*, A street in Macclesfield is called Cuckstool Pit Hill.]

¶ **2.** Erroneously taken for the pillory.

1722–30 RAMSAY *Fables, Twa Cut-purses*, The tane..clam the high cookstool, And put his head and baith his hands Through holes where the ill-doer stands.

cucquean, var. of CUCKQUEAN *Obs.*

† **'cucubate,** *v. Obs.*[−0] [f. L. *cūcubāre*, in same sense.]

1623 COCKERAM, *Cucubate*, to cry like an Owle. **1656** in BLOUNT *Glossogr.*

cucube, form of CUBEB. *Obs.*

cu'culiform, *a. rare.* [ad. mod.L. *cucūliformis*, f. L. *cucūlus* cuckoo: see -FORM.] Cuckoo-like in form or structure; applied to a large division of picarian birds, called by Huxley *Coccygomorphæ*.

'cuculine, *a.* [ad. mod.Zool. L. *cucūlīnus*, f. *cucūlus* cuckoo.] Pertaining or related to the cuckoo; applied to a group of birds related to the cuckoos; also to the cuckoo-bees.

cucullate ('kju:kʌleɪt, kju:'kʌleɪt), *a. Bot.* and *Zool.* [ad. late L. *cucullātus*, f. *cucullus* hood: see -ATE[2] 2.] Hooded; shaped like a hood or cowl.

1794 MARTYN *Rousseau's Bot.* xxvi. 407 The nectary or horn is cucul[l] ate or cowl-shaped. **1845** LINDLEY *Sch. Bot.* v. (1858) 53 Petals distinct, cucullate, or convolute.

Hence **'cucullately** *adv.*

1846 DANA *Zooph.* (1848) 413 Fronds cucullately infolded with one another at base.

cucullated ('kju:kʌleɪtɪd), *ppl. a.* [f. as prec. + -ED.]

1. Cowled, hooded.

1737 OZELL *Rabelais* IV. 239 Cucullated Gentry. **1860** HOOK *Lives Abps.* I. vii. 369 He returned a monk, cucullated, as it was called.

2. *Zool.* and *Bot.* Covered as with a hood or cowl; cowl-shaped; cucullate.

1646 SIR T. BROWNE *Pseud. Ep.* v. iii. 236 They are differently cucullated or capuched upon the heade and back. **1725** SLOANE *Jamaica* II. 99 The flowers..small, galericulated, or cucullated. **1826** KIRBY & SP. *Entomol.* (1828) III. xxxv. 612 In the cucullated species the wing covers are entirely membranous.

† **cuculle.** *Obs.* [In 15th c. *cu'culle*, in 17th *'cucule*: ad. L. *cucullus* hood, cowl.] A hood or cowl of a monk.

c **1420** *Pallad. on Husb.* I. 1166, Eke lether cotes us to were honest is, So thair cuculle aboute oure brolles were. **1533** SIR S. VAUGHAN in Froude *Hist. Eng.* (1856) II. 188 The clokys & cucullys that he sent him out of England. **1677** OWEN *Epigrams Engl.* (Nares), Of Cotta lately made a monk. Cotta perplex'd with 's wife a cucule bought.

Hence † **cuculled** *a.*, cowled, hooded.

c **1550** BALE *K. Johan* (Camden) 93 Exyle thys monster..With..His cuculled vermyne that unto all myschiefe wakes.

cuculliform (kju:'kʌlɪfɔ:m), *a.* [f. L. *cucullus* cowl + -FORM.] Cowl-shaped, hood-shaped.

1835 LINDLEY *Introd. Bot.* (1848) I. 300 The cuculliform pitcher of plants.

cucullo: see CUCUYO.

cucumber ('kju:kʌmbə(r)). Forms: 4–8 cucumer, 5 cocumber, 6 cocomer, (?) concummer, cocomber, cucumbre, 6–8 coucumber, cowcumber, cowcomber, 7 cowcummer, 6– cucumber. [In Wyclif's form *cucumer*, app. directly from L.; in *cocomber*, *cucumber*, etc., a. obs. F. *cocombre* (in 13th c. *coucombre*, now *concombre*) = Pr. *cogombre*, It. *cocomero*, early ad. L. *cucumer-em* (nom. *cucumis*) cucumber.

The spelling *cowcumber* prevailed in the 17th and beg. of 18th c.; its associated pronunciation ('kaʊkʌmbə(r)) was still that recognized by Walker; but Smart 1836 says 'no well-taught person, except of the old school, now says *cow-cumber*..although any other pronunciation..would have been pedantic some thirty years ago'.]

1. A creeping plant, *Cucumis sativus* (N.O. *Cucurbitaceæ*), a native of southern Asia, from ancient times cultivated for its fruit: see 2.

1382 WYCLIF *Baruch* vi. 69 Where cucumeris, *that ben bitter herbis*, waxen. **1398** TREVISA *Barth. de P.R.* XVII. xliv. (Tollem. MS.) Cucumer..is an herbe, of þe whiche Isidor spekeþ. **1551** TURNER *Herbal* I. (1568) M iv b, The fruyte of the cucumbre is for the most part yelow and long. **1584** R. SCOT *Discov. Witchcr.* XIII. viii. 246 The cowcumber loveth water. **1630** J. LEVETT *Ord. Bees* (1634) 57 Wormwood, Woad, wilde Cucumers, Mayweed. **1688** R. HOLME *Armoury* II. 103/2 [Of] Cowcumber, or Cucumber, the branch traileth on the ground. **1713** *Phil. Trans.* XXVIII. 229 The Juice of the Leaves of Cowcomber bruised. **1846** J. BAXTER *Libr. Pract. Agric.* (ed. 4) I. 181 The cucumber is a tender annual, introduced into this country in 1573, from the East Indies.

2. a. The long fleshy fruit of this plant, commonly eaten (cut into thin slices) as a cooling salad, and when young used for pickling (see GHERKIN).

c **1400** *Lanfranc's Cirurg.* 275 Of erbis he schal ete fenel..melones, cucumeris. **1535** COVERDALE *2 Kings* iv. 39 Then went there one in to the felde..& gathered wylde Cucumbers. **1582** N. LICHEFIELD tr. *Castanheda's Conq. E. Ind.* 61 a, [They] brought to sell many gourds and cowcombers. **1646** SIR T. BROWNE *Pseud. Ep.* VII. i. 339 Resembling..in taste a Melon or Cowcumber. **1697** DRYDEN *Virg. Georg.* IV. 182 Cucumers along the Surface creep, With crooked Bodies, and with Bellies deep. **1732** ARBUTHNOT *Rules of Diet.* I. 248 The Juice of Cucumbers is too cold for some Stomachs. **1860** DELAMER *Kitch. Gard.* (1861) 115 In England the first cucumbers fetch high prices.

b. Phr. ***cool*** (†***cold***) ***as a cucumber*** (humorous): perfectly 'cool' or self-possessed; showing no excitement or disturbance of feeling. Hence ***cucumber-cool***.

a **1732** GAY *Poems, New Song on New Similies* iii, I..cool as a cucumber could see The rest of womankind. **1760** GRAY *Lett.* Wks. 1884 III. 47 It was dry as a stick, hard as a stone, and cold as a cucumber. **1838** DE QUINCEY *Greek Lit.* Wks. 1890 X. 318 Thucydides..is as cool as a cucumber upon every act of atrocity. **1851** D. JERROLD (*title*), Cool as a Cucumber. **1955** AUDEN *Shield of Achilles* iii. 75 In his New Jerusalem even chefs will be cucumber-cool machine minders.

c. *slang.* Used with some obscure reference to a tailor. Hence ***cucumber time, season***: see quots.

a **1700** B. E. *Dict. Cant. Crew*, *Cucumbers*, Taylers. *Cucumber-time*, Taylers Holiday, when they have leave to Play, and Cucumbers are in Season. **1720** *Roxb. Ball.* (1891) VII. 471 Here a scratch, there a stitch, And sing Cucumber, Cucumber ho! *a* **1777** FOOTE *Sir J. Jollup* in Hone *Every-day Bk.* II. 848 This cross-legg'd cabbage-eating son of a cucumber. **1865** *Pall Mall G.* 4 Sept. 16/2 Tailors could not be expected to earn much money 'in cucumber season'..'Because when cucumbers are in, the gentry are out of town'.

3. a. Applied to other plants allied to or in some way resembling the common cucumber: as **bitter cucumber**, the Colocynth, *Citrullus Colocynthis*; **Indian cucumber** = *cucumber-root* (see 4); **one-seeded, single-seeded,** or **star cucumber**, the genus *Sicyos*; **serpent** or **snake cucumber**, *Trichosanthes colubrina* and *T. anguina*, also *Cucumis flexuosus* (from the appearance of the fruit); **spirting** or **squirting cucumber**, *Ecbalium agreste* (formerly called *Momordica Elaterium*), the fruit of which when ripe separates from the stalk, and expels the seeds and pulp with considerable force.

1548 TURNER *Names of Herbes* 32 *Cucumis sylvestris*..maye be called in englyshe wylde cucummer or leapyng cucumer. **1578** LYTE *Dodoens* III. xl. 372 Of the wilde spirting Cucumbre..This Cucumber is called..in Englishe Wilde Cucumber, or leaping Cucumber. **1811** A. T. THOMSON *Lond. Disp.* (1818) 143 The Pulp of Coloquintida, or Bitter Cucumber. **1866** *Treas. Bot.* 1168 *Trichosanthes colubrina*, the Serpent Cucumber or Viper Gourd, is so called from the remarkable snake-like appearance of its fruits, which are frequently six or more feet long, and at first striped with different shades of green.

b. Short for *cucumber-tree* (U.S.). Also *attrib.*

1797 F. BAILY *Tour N. Amer.* (1856) 178 Elm, oak, cucumber, and other trees. **1835** A. PARKER *Trip to West* 47 The timber consists of the various kinds of oak,..cucumber, [etc.]. **1904** 'O. HENRY' *Cabbages & Kings* x. 161 Johnny Atwood..prated feebly of cool water to be had in the cucumber-wood pumps of Dalesburg.

4. *attrib.* and *Comb.*, as ***cucumber-bed, -frame, sandwich, -seed, -slicer***, etc.; **cucumber-beetle, -bug, flea beetle** *U.S.* (see quots.); **cucumber mosaic**, one of a group of virus diseases that attack cucumbers and related plants; **cucumber-root**, (*a*) the root of the cucumber; (*b*) the plant *Medeola virginica* (N.O. *Trilliaceæ*), from the taste of its rhizomes; **cucumber-shin** (see quots. 1807, 1849); **cucumber-tree**, (*a*) *Magnolia acuminata* and other American species, the fruits of which resemble small cucumbers; (*b*) *Averrhoa Bilimbi*, an East Indian tree with an acid fruit resembling a small cucumber and used for pickling.

1826 MISS MITFORD *Village* Ser. II. (1863) 387 He..made a very decent cucumber-bed in mine host's garden. **1841** T. W. HARRIS *Insects of Massachusetts* 101 These striped cucumber-beetles..notorious..for their attacks upon the leaves of the cucumber and squash. **1948** *Ada* (Okla.) *Even. News* 2 July 4/4 A powerful insecticide that will kill such stubborn pests as Cucumber Beetles. **1838** *Mass. Zool. Surv. Rep.* 100 The cucumber-bug..is called *Galeruca vittata*. At first sight it appears much like the potato-insect. **1807** W. IRVING *Salmag.* (1824) 79 His shins had the true cucumber curve. **1877** *Rep. Vermont Board Agric.* IV. 154 The Cucumber Flea Beetle,..a little black beetle.., sometimes attacks the raspberry. **1782** COWPER *Let. to J. Hill* 31 Jan., A man..whose chief occupation..is to walk ten times in a day from the fire-side to his cucumber frame and back again. **1934** WODEHOUSE *Right Ho, Jeeves* xx. 251 It sounded as if Carnera had jumped off the top of the Eiffel Tower on to a cucumber frame. **1916** S. P. DOOLITTLE in *Phytopathology* VI. 145 The cucumber mosaic disease shows most markedly on the fruits, the first sign being a yellowish mottling near the stem end. *Ibid.* Plate V (*caption*) Cucumber mosaic. **1923** W. F. BEWLEY *Dis. Glasshouse Plants* vii. 144 (*heading*) Symptoms of Cucumber Mosaic Disease. **1935** *Jrnl. Min. Agric.* XLII. 338 These three diseases [*sc.* green-mottle mosaic, yellow mosaic, yellow-mottle mosaic], collectively known as 'cucumber mosaic', are widespread. **1950** *N.Z. Jrnl. Agric.* Feb. 157/3 Cucumber mosaic..is a virus disease which may cause serious losses in cucumbers, marrows, pumpkins, and squashes. Symptoms consist of stunting of the plants and mosaic mottling of the foliage. *c* **1420** *Pallad. on Husb.* I. 981 Thi seedes with cocumber rootes grounde Lete stepe. **1896** E. TURNER *Little Larrikin* xv. 171 The fates chose that he should be allotted to find a cucumber sandwich for his hostess's sister-in-law. **1899** WILDE *Importance of being Earnest* I. 5 Why all these cups? Why cucumber sandwiches? Why such reckless extravagance in one so young? **1967** *Listener* 23 Mar. 398/1 The kind of smile and soft tone of voice you would connect with cucumber sandwiches and a vicarage lawn. **1607** TOPSELL *Four-f. Beasts* (1673) 202 Three-and-thirty grains of cowcumber seed. **1849–52** TODD *Cycl. Anat.* IV. 1332/1 That peculiar curved form of the bones of the leg [in Negroes] which gives rise to what is popularly designated as the 'cucumber shin'. **1884** *Health Exhib. Catal.* 110/2 Cucumber Slicers. **1785** JEFFERSON *Notes on Virginia* 65 Cucumber-tree. Magnolia acuminata. **1806** T. JEFFERSON *Writ.* (1830) IV. 63 Can you send me some cones or seeds of the cucumber tree?

cucumiform (kjuːˈkjuːmɪfɔːm), *a. rare.*—⁰ [f. L. *cucumis* cucumber + -FORM.] Of the shape of a cucumber.

1826 KIRBY & SPENCE *Entomol.* IV. xlvi. 265 Cucumiform (Cucumiformis). Cucumber-shaped. **1838** *Penny Cycl.* XII. 270/2 The *Cucumiform Holothuriæ*, whose body is but little elongated, more or less fusiform, pentagonal, with tentaculiform suckers. **1860** WORCESTER cites MAUNDER.

‖**ˈcucupha.** *Obs.* Also cucufa. [med.L.; a deriv. or reduplicated form of *cufa*, *cufia* COIF. In F. *cucuphe*.] In old pharmacy: A cap with spices quilted in it, worn for certain nervous disorders of the head.

1656 RIDGLEY *Pract. Physick* 173 A *Cucupha* is common for the wounds and contusions of the Head. **1657** TOMLINSON *Renou's Disp.* 209 A convenient cucufa must be adapted to the head like a cap. **1665** G. HARVEY *Advice agst. Plague* xiv. 20 The brain should likewise be shielded with a *cucupha*, or spice cap.

†**cucurbit**¹ (kjuːˈkɜːbɪt). *Obs.* Forms: 4 concurbite, cocurbite, 4–9 cucurbite, 6–9 cucurbit. [a. F. *cucurbite*, ad. L. *cucurbita* a gourd, also a cupping-glass, in med. or mod.L., as in F. and Eng. (The living F. descendant of late L. *curbita* is *courde*, changed in mod.F. to *courge*, GOURD.)]

1. A vessel or retort, originally gourd-shaped, used in distillation and other chemical (or alchemical) processes, or for keeping liquids, etc., in; forming the lower part of an alembic.

c **1386** CHAUCER *Can. Yeom. Prol. & T.* 241 Cucurbites [*v.r.* concurbites, cocurbites] and Alambikes eek. **1576** BAKER *Jewell of Health* 8 The same substance closed uppe in a Cucurbite or Glasse bodie. **1660** BOYLE *New Exp. Phys. Mech.* Digress. 368 To distill Liquors out of tall Cucurbits. **1794** G. ADAMS *Nat. & Exp. Philos.* II. xiii. 22 The alembic consists of two pieces, a boiler or cucurbit, and a covering called a capital or head. **1823** J. BADCOCK *Dom. Amusem.* 25 Other substances..are..charred in cylinders or cucurbits.

2. A cupping-glass.

1541 R. COPLAND *Galyen's Terap.* 2 Eiij, The sayd medycament draweth to it from all the body in yᵉ maner as cucurbyte and ventose doth the excrementes and superfluytees.

3. *Comb.*, as *cucurbit-glass*.

1664 EVELYN *Kal. Hort.* (1729) 209 Setting the new-invented Cucurbit-Glasses of Beer mingled with Honey to entice Wasps, Flies, etc.

cucurbit². [mod. ad. L. *cucurbita* gourd. (In the sense 'gourd' L. *curbita* was already adopted in OE. in the form *cyrfet*.)] A cucurbitaceous plant; a gourd.

1866 *Treas. Bot.* 358 *Cucurbitaceæ*..Cucurbits, the Cucumber and Gourd family. **1880** F. W. BURBIDGE *Gard. Sun* 81 We saw a pretty white-flowered cucurbit growing over bushes here and there.

cucurbitaceous (kjuːˌkɜːbɪˈteɪʃəs), *a. Bot.* [f. mod.L. *Cucurbitaceæ*, f. *cucurbita*: see -ACEOUS.] Belonging to the Natural Order *Cucurbitaceæ*, comprising trailing or climbing plants with fleshy fruits, as the Gourd, Cucumber, Melon, etc.

1853 TH. ROSS *Humboldt's Trav.* III. xxvi. 114 This air, at once hot and humid..nourishes those vegetable reservoirs, the cucurbitaceous plants. **1880** C. & F. DARWIN *Movem. Pl.* 104 One Cucurbitaceous genus.

cucurbital (kjuːˈkɜːbɪtəl), *a. Bot.* [f. L. *cucurbita* gourd + -AL¹.] Epithet of one of Lindley's alliances, including the *Cucurbitaceæ* and allied natural orders.

1866 *Treas. Bot.* 358 *Cucurbitaceæ*..A natural order of polypetalous and gamopetalous calycifloral dicotyledons, characterising Lindley's cucurbital alliance.

cucurbitin (kjuːˈkɜːbɪtɪn). *Zool.* [ad. L. *cucurbitinus* pertaining to or like a gourd, f. *cucurbita*. In F. *cucurbitin*, *-ain*.] A name for each separated segment or proglottis of a tapeworm, from its resemblance to the seed of a gourd.

[**1398** TREVISA *Barth. De P.R.* VII. xlix. (1495) 262 Wormes that ben nourisshed..in the nether grete bowelles hyghte Ascarides and Cucurbitini, for they ben lyke to the seedes of gourdes.] **1861** HULME tr. *Moquin-Tandon* II. VII. xiii. 400 The successive transformations which the *Tænia communis* undergoes..The fourth stage is that of the Cucurbitins, or separated segments.

cucurbitine (kjuːˈkɜːbɪtaɪn, -ɪn), *a.* [See prec.] Gourd-like: applied to a tape-worm: see prec.

1843 SIR T. WATSON *Lect. Physic* (1871) II. 621 They..have somewhat the appearance of the seeds of cucumbers or gourds; and..for that reason, are sometimes called *cucurbitine* worms.

†**cucurbitive,** *a. Obs.* Erroneous f. of prec.

1757 T. BIRCH *Hist. Royal Soc.* IV. 138 A barber..who for many years past voided pieces of the cucurbitive worm.

†**cuˈcurbittel.** *Obs. rare.* = next.

1605 TIMME *Quersit.* II. v. 123 The feces..must be put into diuers smal cucurbits..Then again pour into euery cucurbittel another spirit of wine.

†**cuˈcurbitule.** *Obs. rare.* [ad. L. *cucurbitula*, dim. of *cucurbita* gourd.] A small cucurbit; a cupping-glass.

1541 R. COPLAND *Galyen's Terap.* 2 Dij, All those medycamentes drawe vnto them from all the body lyke vnto the cucurbitule, that is to say ventose or boxyng.

†**cuˈcuriate,** *v. Obs.*—⁰ [f. L. *cūcūrīre*.]

1623 COCKERAM, *Cucuriate*, to crow like a Cock.

‖**cucuy, cucuyo** (kuːˈkuːɪ, kuːˈkuːjəʊ). Also 6 cucuio, 9 cocuyo, *erron.* cucullo; 9– cucujo. [Sp. *cucuyo*, adaptation of a Haitian or other native American name.] The West Indian firefly (*Pyrophorus noctilucus*), an elaterid beetle which emits brilliant phosphorescent light from spots on the body.

1591 SYLVESTER *Du Bartas* I. v. 794 New-Spain's Cucuio, in his forehead brings Two burning Lamps, two underneath his wings. **1647** W. BROWNE *Polexander* I. 97 These little Cucuyes..mingle their living lights with the obscuritie of this Dungeon. **1692** COLES, *Cucuye*, a bird in Hispaniola, with eyes under the wings, shining in the night. **1706** PHILLIPS (ed. Kersey), *Cucuyos*, a king of Fly in America, which gives such a Lustre in the Night that one may..write and read by the Light of it. **18..** LYDIA M. CHILD *Fountain of Beauty*, The cucullo and the lantern-fly stood at her side. **1836** W. E. SHUCKARD tr. *Burmeister's Man. Ent.* III. 491 Among the natives, all these insects are called *Cucujos* or *Cucujii*. **1842** THOREAU *Excursions* (1863) 60 Launch forth like a cucullo into the night. **1874** *Science Record* 485 The brilliant radiance of the cocuyo is emitted from its ventral region. **1952** E. N. HARVEY *Bioluminescence* xiii. 461 Almost every traveler to the Caribbean region has mentioned luminous elaterids, which Spaniards call 'cucujo', and the French, 'taupin'.

cud (kʌd), *sb.* Forms: 1 cwidu, cwudu, cudu, 2–5 cude, (4–5 kude), 3–5 code, (4–5 kode), 4–5 cod(de, quede, 4–7 cudde, (5–6 kudde), 4–8 quide, 7 cood, 8–9 *dial.* quid, 9 *dial.* queed, keed, 4– cud. [OE. *cwidu* (*cweodu*, *cwudu*, *cudu*) neut., gen. *cwidues*. App. radically identical with OHG. *chuti*, *quiti* glue, glutinous substance; stem *kwed-*, cf. Skr. *jatu* resin; in ablaut relation with ON. *kvāða*, Sw. *kåda* resin, ME. CODE².]

1. a. The food which a ruminating animal brings back into its mouth from its first stomach, and chews at leisure. Usually in *to chew the cud*.

c **1000** ÆLFRIC *Saints' Lives* (Skeat) xxv. 46 þa clænan nytenu þe heora cudu ceowað. *c* **1200** ORMIN 1237 & oxe chewweþþ þær he gaþ Hiss cūde. *a* **1300** *Cursor M.* 1958 (Cott.) O beist has clouen fote in tua An chewand cude [*v.r.* code], ȝee ete o þaa. **1382** WYCLIF *Deut.* xiv. 6 All beest that in two partis deuydith the clee and chewith code [**1388** quide]. *c* **1440** *Promp. Parv.* 85 Cudde of bestys chewynge [**1499** cod], *rumen*. **1587** MASCALL *Govt. Cattle* (1627) 40 A handfull of the hearbe called Cud-wort, which they..conueigh..into the beasts mouth to swallow, that hath lost his quide. **1591** SPENSER *Virg. Gnat* 144 The whiles his flock their chawed cuds do eate. **1736** PEGGE *Kenticisms*, *Quid*, the cud. **1852** N. HAWTHORNE *Blithedale Rom.* xxiv, They began grazing and chewing their cuds. **1880** *Antrim Gloss.*, *Keed*, cud. **1888** *W. Somerset Word-bk.*, *Queed*, cud. Always so pronounced.

b. *fig. to chew the cud*: to recall and reflect meditatively on things said, done, or suffered; to ruminate: see CHEW *v.* 4 b.

2. Any substance used by men to keep in the mouth and chew. In OE. *hwít cwidu*, *cudu*, mastic. Now a dial. form of QUID (of tobacco).

c **1000** *Sax. Leechd.* II. 66 Hwit cwudu. *Ibid.* 182 Mid hwites cwidues duste. **1828** WEBSTER, *Cud*..2. A portion of tobacco held in the mouth and chewed. **1880** *W. Cornwall Gloss.*, *Cud*, a quid of tobacco.

†**3.** See quots. (? An error: not in Johnson.)

1706 PHILLIPS (ed. Kersey), *Cud*, the inner part of the Throat in Beasts. **1721** in BAILEY. **1828** WEBSTER, *Cud*, the inside of the mouth or throat of a beast that chews the cud.

4. *Comb.*, as *cud-chewing* ppl. a.; †**cud-bream** (see quot.); **cud-chewer**, a ruminant animal.

1591 SYLVESTER *Du Bartas* I. v. 314 The delicate, cud-chewing Golden-eye. **1655** MOUFET & BENNET *Health's Improv.* (1746) 268 There is a kind of Bream called *Scarus ruminans*, which we call a Cud-bream, because his Lips are ever wagging like a Cow chawing the Cud. **1800** HURDIS *Fav. Village* 205 The cud-chewing cow. **1927** HALDANE & HUXLEY *Anim. Biol.* iv. 112 In cud-chewers like the cow and sheep.

†**cud,** *v. Obs. rare.* [f. the sb.] *trans.* To chew as cud, ruminate upon.

1569 CROWLEY *Soph. Dr. Watson* i. 127 Cudding the holy scriptures with a spiritual tooth [transl. *spirituali dente ruminans scripturas*]. **1966** *New Statesman* 1 Apr. 473/1 Cows..Cudding, watching, and knowing.

cudbear (ˈkʌdbɛə(r)). Also 8 cut-. [A name devised from his own Christian name by Dr. Cuthbert Gordon (who obtained a patent for this powder).]

1. A purple or violet powder, used for dyeing, prepared from various species of lichens, esp. *Lecanora tartarea*.

1771 *Phil. Trans.* LXI. 129 Dutch litmus, orchel, cudbear..dye silk and wool of a yellow colour. **1794** *Statist. Acc. Scot.* XII. 113 The cudbear manufacture carried on here was begun in 1777. **1870** J. W. SLATER *Manual of Colours* 61 Cudbear is used for dyeing ruby and maroon shades, as well as a variety of browns.

2. The lichen *Lecanora tartarea*.

1766 *Ann. Reg.* 117 Gathering Scotch Cutbear. **1861** H. MACMILLAN *Footnotes fr. Nature* 116 The most useful and best known of our native dye-lichens is the rock-moss or cudbear (*Lecanora tartarea*).

cudde, obs. f. COD *sb.*¹, CUD.

cudde, obs. pa. t. of KYTHE *v.*, to make known.

cuddee, obs. form of CUDDY.

cuddell, a fish, var. of CUTTLE.

cudden (ˈkʌd(ə)n). Also cuddin(g.

†**1.** A born fool, a dolt. *Obs.*

1673 WYCHERLEY *Gentl. Dancing-Master* IV. i, Lord! that people should be such arrant cuddens! **1698** *Def. Dram. Poetry* 80 The Fools we may divide into three Classes, viz. the Cudden, the Cully and the Fop. The Cudden a Fool of God Almighties making. **1700** DRYDEN *Fables, Cymon & Iph.* 179 The slavering cudden, propped upon his staff. **1719** D'URFEY *Pills* V. 309 Jack-puddings, for Cuddens.

2. *local.* A name for: **a.** The coal-fish [Gael. *cudainn*]; **b.** ? The char.

1791 *Ayrsh. Statist. Acc.* III. 589 (Jam.) In both loch and river [Doon] there are..cuddings, or charr. **1836** YARRELL *Brit. Fishes* (1841) II. 251 Among the Scotch islands the Coalfish is called Sillock..Harbin, Cudden, Sethe [etc.]. **1848** *Life Normandy* (1863) I. 283 It was some time before I knew that stainloch, grey-fish, seath, cudding, and poddly, were all one fish at different ages.

cuddicke, -ikie: see CUDDY¹.

cuddie: see CUDDY.

cuddle (ˈkʌd(ə)l), *v.* [A dialectal or nursery word of uncertain derivation.

Possibly a derivative of COUTH *a.* in the sense 'snug, cosy': cf. *fondle* from *fond* adj. An original **couthle* might become *cuddle*, as in ME. *fiðele*, *fithel*, now FIDDLE, the vowel being also shortened before the consonant group. (Close connexion with the ME. *cudde*, *cupped*, pa.t. of *cuðen*, KYTHE, 'to make known, *refl.* to make themselves known, become friends together', is not tenable, because *u* was here = *ü*, OE. *y*, as seen in Ormin's spelling *kipped*.) Another suggestion is that it is related to Du. *kudden* 'coire, convenire, congregari, aggregari' (Kilian), f. *kudde* flock, herd:—OLG. **kuddi* = OHG. *chutti*. Further evidence as to its early use is wanted, there being at present known only one doubtful example before 1700.]

1. *trans.* To press or draw close within the arms, so as to make warm and 'cosy'; to hug or embrace affectionately, to fondle; also *absol.*

c **1520** *Song* in *Rel. Ant.* I. 239 Cudlyng of my cowe. **1719** D'URFEY *Pills* III. 28 'Twas playing with her at Cuddle my Cuddy. **1789** BURNS *2 Ep. Davie* ii, Till bairns' bairns kindly cuddle Your auld gray hairs. *a* **1825** FORBY *Voc. E. Anglia*, *Cuddle*, to hug and fondle. **1825** BROCKETT *N.C. Words*, *Cuddle*, to embrace, to squeeze, to hug. **1863** KINGSLEY *Water Bab.* v. 219 Little boys..who have kind mammas to cuddle them.

fig. **1851** THACKERAY *Eng. Hum.* i. (1876) 148 Temple seems..to have been coaxed, and warmed, and cuddled by the people round about him. *Ibid.* ii. 193 Cuddling to his heart the compliment which his literary majesty had paid him.

b. *to cuddle up*: to arrange comfortably.

1743 H. WALPOLE *Lett. H. Mann* (1834) I. lxxxiv. 296 Mamie herself could not have cuddled up an affair for his Sovereign Lady better.

c. *to cuddle out of*: to coax or wheedle out of.

1808 C. KIRKPATRICK SHARPE *Corr.* (1888) I. 336 To cuddle his mother out of her money.

2. *intr.* To lie close and snug; to nestle in to another person, to cling close together for warmth or comfort. (Often with extension; see quots.)

1711 E. WARD *Quix.* I. 158 Who would in Spite of Wedlock Run To Cuddle with the Emp'rour's Son. **1718** PRIOR *The Dove* 55 She [a partridge] cuddles low behind the brake. **1727** SOMERVILLE *Fab.* xi. (R.), They bill'd, they chirp'd all day, They cuddled close all night. **1888** *W. Somerset Word-bk.*, Two children lying very close together in bed would be said to be *cuddled together*. Again, chickens are said to *cuddle in* under the hen.

b. To curl oneself up in going to sleep; hence, to lie down to sleep. (Also *refl.*)

1822 GALT *Sir A. Wylie* I. x. 76 Whar am I to cuddle. **1847** ALB. SMITH *Chr. Tadpole* vii. (1879) 65 Many a shining-coated insect cuddled itself up within the little tents thus made. **1888** ELIZ. B. CUSTER *Tenting on Plains*, He [a tame beaver] cuddles up under my gown, or on my arm, and goes to sleep.

c. *fig.*

1810 T. JEFFERSON *Writ.* (1830) IV. 146 The nest of office being too small for all of them to cuddle into at once. **1864** LOVELL *Fireside Trav.* 287 A pretty little village, cuddled down among the hills.

Hence ˈ**cuddling** *vbl. sb.*

1880 WEBB *Goethe's Faust* IV. xvii. 232 The kissing and cuddling that went on!

cuddle (ˈkʌd(ə)l), *sb.* [f. prec. vb.] **1.** A hug or embrace.

1825 *Song* in Brockett *N.C. Words* s.v., So then, wiv a kiss and a cuddle, These lovers they bent their ways heym. **1870** R. B. BROUGH *Marston Lynch* xxix. 309 Instead of a rebuke ..he received only a tight cuddle round the neck.

2. *Comb.* **cuddle seat** (see quot.); **cuddle skirt**, a skirt made of thick, soft material.

1947 *Britannica Bk. of Yr. 1946* 840/2 *Cuddle seat*, a contrivance for carrying small children, consisting of a seat hung from a strap slung over the shoulder. It was introduced by Australian war brides. **1958** J. CANNAN *And be a Villain* i. 8 She had put on her new oatmeal 'cuddle' skirt. **1961** *Sunday Express* 5 Mar. 11 Wool and cashmere cuddle-skirt.

cuddleable (ˈkʌd(ə)ləb(ə)l), *a.* *colloq.* [See -ABLE.] = CUDDLESOME *a.*

1928 E. WALLACE *Again the Three Just Men* 32 The Lord has given you kissable lips and a cuddleable body. **1928** *Daily Express* 18 May 11/1, I do not want a brainless doll, but I would like a jolly, lovable, cuddleable woman.

cuddle-me-to-you: see CULL *v.*[2] b.

cuddlesome (ˈkʌd(ə)lsəm), *a.* [See -SOME.] Meet to be cuddled.

1876 BESANT & RICE *Gold. Butterfly* xxxv. 269 She was slender, and if one may so speak of a Peeress, she was cuddlesome! **1893** *Ardrossan & Saltcoats Herald* 1 Sept. 3 The crowd of cuddlesome darlings in nice frocks. **1923** *Daily Mail* 27 Feb. 7 A rattlesnake has produced a family of thirty babies. There is nothing of cuddlesome, infant softness about these tenfold triplets. **1965** F. RAPHAEL *Darling* xviii. 83 The soft toys were cuddlesome as anything. **1970** *Homes & Gardens* June 65/1 There were cuddlesome lion cubs and strokeable deer.

cuddly (ˈkʌd(ə)lɪ), *a.* [f. as prec. + -Y.] Given to cuddling; such as invites cuddling; = CUDDLESOME *a.*

1863 KINGSLEY *Water Bab.* v, She was the most..cuddly creature who ever nursed a baby. **1915** GALSWORTHY *Freelands* xxxvi, She laid her face beside his on the pillow... It made everything seem cuddly and warm. **1922** D. H. LAWRENCE *England, my England* (1924) 55 He put his arm round her and drew her a little nearer to him, in a very warm and cuddly manner. **1923** *Daily Mail* 16 Mar. 14 Cuddly toys appeal to babies. **1927** WODEHOUSE *Small Bach.* i. §1. 6 'Are you trying to convey the idea that she is short and stout?' 'Oh, no, sir, not stout. Just nice and plump. What I should describe as cuddly.' **1963** *Sunday Express* 3 Mar. 15/4 A child became seriously ill after sucking mothballs which can be used to stuff a cuddly toy.

†**cuddy**[1], **cudeigh.** *Irel.* and *Scotl. Obs.* In 6 **cuidichie, cuddeehih, cuddeich; cuddicke, -ikie.** [Corruption of Irish *cuid oidhche* (of which Spenser's *cuddeehih* was an approximate representation), lit. 'evening portion'.]

1. *orig.* A supper and night's entertainment due to the lord from his tenant.

1450 *Stat. Ireland, Act 28 Hen. VI*, c. 1 The Captaines of the same Marchours..doe gather and bring with them.. both men and women..to night suppers called Cuddies, upon the said tenants and husbands. **1577-95** *Descr. Isles Scotl.* (in Skene *Celtic Scotl.* III. App. 429) By thair Cuidichies, that is feisting thair master when he pleases to cum in the cuntrie, ilk ane thair nicht or twa nichtes about. **1586** HOOKER *Girald. Ireland* in *Holinshed* II. 23/2 That no lords..shall extort or take anie coine and liuerie, cosheries, nor cuddies, nor anie other like custome from thenseforth. **1596** SPENSER *State Irel.* Wks. (Globe) 623/2 The sayd Irish Lord is ..cutt of from his customarye services..as Cuddeehih [*v.r.* Cuddie], Cosshirh, Bonaught, Shragh, Sorehim, and such like. **1892** COCHRAN PATRICK *Mediæv. Scotl.* vi. 81 When systematically due..the custom of cuddikie..was restricted to four meals four times in the year to the Chief and his followers.

2. Hence, a rent or present in lieu of this; a present, a douceur, 'a gift, a bribe' (Jam.).

15.. *Lease* in C. Innes *Sk. Early Sc. Hist.* (1861) 385 A sufficient cuddeich [which I believe means a present given in token of vassalage]. **1728** RAMSAY *Last Sp. Miser* xvii, Double pawns With a cudeigh, and ten per cent., Lay in my hands. **1811** AITON *Agric. Surv. Ayrshire* Gloss. 691 *Cudeigh*, bribe. **1892** COCHRAN PATRICK *Mediæv. Scotl.* i. 9 In the Western Islands this rent was called the 'Cuddicke', and is mentioned late on in the fifteenth century.

cuddy[2] (ˈkʌdɪ). Also 7 cuddie, 8 cuddee. [Of uncertain origin. Yule and Burnell disclaim an Oriental origin; they compare 16th c. Du. *kaiûte*, mod.Du. *kajuit*, used in same sense.]

1. *Naut.* **a.** A room or cabin in a large ship abaft and under the round-house, in which the officers and cabin-passengers take their meals.

In 18th c. 'a sort of cabin or cook-room in the fore-part or near the stern of a lighter or barge' (Falconer); the small cabin of a boat.

1660 PEPYS *Diary* 14 May, My Lord went up in his nightgown into the cuddy, to see how to dispose thereof for himself. **1725** DUDLEY in *Phil. Trans.* XXXIII. 264 Another [boat] has had the Stem, or Stern-post..cut off smooth above the Cuddee. **1844** *Regul. & Ord. Army* 365 If the quarter-deck be carried, the Men on Guard are to retire to the Cuddy. **1845** STOCQUELER *Handbk. Brit. India* (1854) 88 She has a magnificent saloon, or cuddy, where 100 persons can dine with comfort in cool weather.

b. *spec.* The captain's cabin.

1917 'TAFFRAIL' *Sub* 109 Breakfast with the skipper was better than breakfast in the gunroom. There were no tinned salmon fishcakes and watery porridge in the 'cuddy'.

2. A small room, closet, or cupboard. (Cf. CUBBY.)

1793 T. JEFFERSON *Writ.* (1859) IV. 74 We must give him from four to six or eight dollars a week for cuddies without a bed. **1873** MISS BRADDON *L. Davoren* I. ii. Prol., Dreaming he was in his cuddy at Battersea, supping upon his beloved sausages. **1885** H. C. MCCOOK *Tenants of Old Farm* 119 A constant personal inspection of all one's house, especially of the cuddies and corners.

3. *attrib.*, as ***cuddy door, roof, table.***

1848 THACKERAY *Van. Fair* lvii, The youngsters among the passengers..used to draw out Sedley at the cuddy-table. **1861** R. E. SCORESBY-JACKSON *Life W. Scoresby* xv. 318 He took up his position on the cuddy-roof.

Hence ˈ**cuddyful.**

1841 MACAULAY *Ess. W. Hastings* (1854) 654 Every ship.. that arrived from Madras..brought a cuddy full of his admirers. **1883** *Spectator* 22 Sept. 1208 A cuddyful of kings.

cuddy[3] (ˈkʌdɪ). Chiefly *Sc.* Also **cuddie.** [Of uncertain derivation: the senses here grouped may be distinct in origin: sense 2 is perh. from Gaelic.

In sense 1, a word of the same homely status in Scotch as *donkey* is in English, for which written evidence begins only in the 18th c. It has been plausibly conjectured to be the same word as *Cuddy*, a familiar diminutive of *Cuthbert* in some parts of the north. Cf. the analogous application of *Neddy, Dicky*, to an ass; but unlike these, *cuddy* has, now at least, no conscious connexion with the proper name, being, like *donkey*, simply a common noun. The Gypsy origin conjectured by Jamieson has no basis in fact; there is no name for the donkey common to the Rommany dialects, and the Scottish Gypsy term is *eizel* from German.]

1. a. A donkey. (Also ***cuddy ass.***)

1714-15 *Jacobite Songs* (1819) 83, *The Riding Mare* iv, Then hey the ass, the dainty ass..And mony ane will get a bite Or cuddy gangs awa. **1807** HOGG *Mountain Bard* 174 (Jam.) Wi' joy we'll mount our cuddy asses. **1815** SCOTT *Guy M.* iii, 'He's nae gentleman..wad grudge..the thristles by the road-side for a bit cuddy.' **1862** SMILES *Engineers* III. 65 Many a time have I ridden straight into the house, mounted on my cuddy.

b. *fig.* A stupid fellow, an 'ass'.

a **1845** HOOD *Kilmansegg, Fancy Ball*, To exhibit a six-legged calf To a boothful of country Cuddies. **1885** RUNCIMAN *Skippers & Sh.* 127 You're not going to make a cuddy of me.

c. A (small) horse. Chiefly *dial.* and *Austral.*

c **1930** in R. Ward *Penguin Bk. Austral. Ballads* (1964) 201 A..stockman..Apostrophized his bloody cuddy. **1944** [see CURL *v.*[1] 1 c]. **1945** BAKER *Austral. Lang.* iii. 71 *Cuddy*, [is] used in North English dialect for a donkey. In Australia we use it for a small, solidly built horse. **1969** C. GEESON *Northumberland & Durham Word Bk.* 72 *Cuddy*, a name for an ass or a small horse.

2. A name for the young of the coal-fish or seath; = CUDDEN 2. [Gael. *cudaig, cudainn.*]

1775 JOHNSON *West. Isl.* Wks. X. 406 The cuddy is a fish ..not much bigger than a gudgeon, but is of great use in these islands. **1865** J. C. WILCOCKS *Sea Fisherman* (1875) 105 Immense numbers of young Coal-fish are taken..in the Scotch lochs under the name of Cuddies. **1883** W. BLACK *Four MacNicols* iii, 'Cuddies' is the familiar name in those parts for young saithe.

3. A local name for the hedge-sparrow or 'dunnock', and for the moor-hen.

1802 G. MONTAGU *Ornith. Dict.* (1833) 188 Moorhen.. Cuddy. **1868** ATKINSON *Cleveland Gloss.*, *Cuddy*, the hedge-sparrow.

4. *Mech.* (See quots.)

1852 S. C. BREES *Gloss. Pract. Archit.* 129 *Cuddy*, a three-legged stand, forming a fulcrum upon which a long pole is placed, and which is used as a spring lever. **1874** KNIGHT *Dict. Mech.*, *Cuddy*, a lever mounted on a tripod for lifting stones, leveling up railroad-ties, etc.

5. *Comb.* **cuddy-legs** (see quot.).

1880-4 F. DAY *Fishes Gt. Brit.* II. 209 Cuddy legs, a large herring.

†**cude.** *Sc. Obs.* Also 6 **cuide.** [Corresponds regularly to ME. *code* (CODE[3]), the two pointing to an OE. **cód*: but this is not found.] A chrism-cloth; = CODE *sb.*[3]

[*c* **1420** *code*; **1483** *cud*: see CODE[3].] *a* **1455** HOLLAND *Houlate* 978 Thy cude, thy claithis, nor thi cost, cummis nocht of the. **1513-75** *Diurn. Occurrents* (1833) 103 The salt fatt be the erle of Eglingtoun, the cude be the lord Sympill. **1552** LYNDESAY *Monarche* 5997 Allace for ws! it had bene gude, We had bene smorit in our cude.

cudeigh: see CUDDY[1].

cudgel (ˈkʌdʒəl), *sb.* Forms: 1 **cycgel, kycgel, kicgel,** 3 **kuggel,** 6 **cogell, coogell, quodgell,** 6–7 **cogil(l, cudgell,** 7 **coggell, cuggel, cudgil,** 6— **cudgel.** [OE. *cycgel, kicgel*, of which the OTeut. type would be **kuggilo-*; but nothing is known of it in the cognate langs. Original *y* has become *ŭ*, as in *blush, clutch, much.*]

1. A short thick stick used as a weapon; a club.

c **897** ÆLFRED *Gregory's Past.* xl. 297 Ðæt hie mid ðæm kycglum [*Cott.* kyclum] hiera worda [*verborum jacula*] onȝean hiera ierre worpiȝen. *a* **899** —— tr. *August. Soliloq.* in Paul & Br. Beitr. IV. 110 [Ic] gaderode me þonne kigclas and stuþan sceaftas. *a* **1225** *Ancr. R.* 292 Mid te holie rode steaue, þet him is loðest kuggel, leie on þe deouel dogge. **1566** in W. H. TURNER *Select. Rec. Oxford* 252 This deponent had a lytell cogell. **1598** SHAKS. *Merry W.* IV. ii. 87 Heauen guide him to thy husbands cudgell: and the diuell guide his cudgell afterwards. **1618** ROWLANDS *Night-Raven* (1620) 29 Tom with his cudgell, well bebasts his bones. **1662** J. BARGRAVE *Pope Alex. III* (1867) 121 I saw..a coggell of wood hanging in a small rope. **1727** SWIFT *Gulliver* II. vi. 146, I prepared two round sticks about the bigness of common cudgels. **1836** MARRYAT *Japhet* lxxix, Saluting him with several blows on his head with his cudgel.

b. in *pl.* Short for: A contest with cudgels; = CUDGEL-PLAY.

1630 *R. Johnson's Kingd. & Commw.* 27 One of our lusty ploughmen..would at fisty-cuffes or cudgels soundly beclowt a Hollander. **1663** *Flagellum; or O. Cromwell* (ed. 2) 8 Players at Foot-ball, Cudgels, or any other boysterous sport. **1712** ADDISON *Spect.* No. 434 ¶2 They learned to Box and play at Cudgels. **1800** WINDHAM *Speeches Parl.* (1812) I. 335 If a set of poor men..prefer a game of cudgels. **1819** *Reading Mercury* 24 May, A good hat to be played for at cudgels.

2. *fig.*, esp. in phr. ***to take up the cudgels***: to engage in a vigorous contest or debate (*for, in defence of, on behalf of*). So † ***to give up*** or ***cross the cudgels***: 'to forbear the contest, from the practice of cudgel-players to lay one over the other' (J.).

1654 WHITLOCK *Zootomia* 233 [Writers] taking up the Cudgels on one side or other. *a* **1661** FULLER *Worthies* (1840) III. 309 Mr. Chillingworth..took up the cudgels against him. **1678** BUTLER *Hud.* III. ii. 40 Which forc'd the stubborn'st for the Cause To cross the cudgels to the laws. **1691** tr. *Emilianne's Frauds Romish Monks* 414 Tho' I did not immediately give up the Cudgels. *a* **1704** L'ESTRANGE (J.), To contend..and then either to cross the cudgels, or to be baffled in the conclusion. **1851** THACKERAY *Eng. Hum.* v, He had..wielded for years the cudgels of controversy. **1869** TROLLOPE *He Knew* i. (1878) 5 His wife had taken up the cudgels for her friend.

3. *Comb.*, as ***cudgel-cracking, -proof*** adj. See also CUDGEL-PLAY, -PLAYER, -PLAYING.

1620 *Swetnam Arraign'd* (1880) 10 A Master..of the magnanimous Method of Cudgell-cracking. **1663** BUTLER *Hud.* I. i. 306 His Doublet was of sturdy Buff, And though not Sword, yet Cudgel-proof. **1774** JOEL COLLIER *Mus. Trav.* (1775) 75 A skin which must be cudgel-proof.

cudgel, *v.* [f. prec. sb.]

1. *trans.* To beat or thrash with a cudgel.

1596 SHAKS. *1 Hen. IV*, III. iii. 159 He call'd you Iacke, and said hee would cudgell you. **1679** WOOD *Life* (Oxf. Hist. Soc.) II. 473 John Dryeden the poet..was about 8 at night soundly cudgell'd by 3 men. **1855** MACAULAY *Hist. Eng.* III. 221 Sometimes he was knocked down: sometimes he was cudgelled.

b. *fig.*

1602 SHAKS. *Ham.* V. i. 63 Cudgell thy brains no more about it. **1679-1714** BURNET *Hist. Ref.*, To terrify the court of Rome, and cudgel the Pope into a compliance with what he desired. **1849** THACKERAY *Pendennis* xv, When a gentleman is cudgelling his brain to find any rhyme for sorrow besides borrow and to-morrow. **1827** DE QUINCEY *China* Wks. 1871 XVI. 254 Luckily we have..cudgelled them out of this hellish doctrine.

2. *intr.* To play cudgels *for*: see CUDGEL *sb.* 1 b.

1840 THACKERAY *Catherine* xii, Monsieur Figue gives a hat to be cudgelled for.

cudgelled (ˈkʌdʒəld), *ppl. a.* [f. prec. sb. and vb. + -ED.] Beaten with a cudgel; †produced by cudgelling (*obs.*).

1599 SHAKS. *Hen. V*, V. i. 93 And patches will I get vnto these cudgeld scarres. **1797** BURKE *Regic. Peace* iii. Wks. VIII. 308 His..cudgelled Ministry, cudgelled by English and by French.

†**b.** Having trimming, etc., laid on thickly and heavily. *Obs.* (*humorous*).

1598 E. GILPIN *Skial.* (1878) 21 He weares a Jerkin cudgeld with gold lace. **1630** J. TAYLOR (Water-P.) *Wks.* (N.), An Irish footman with a jacket cudgeld down the shoulders and skirts with yellow or orange tawny lace.

ˌ**cudgeˈlee.** *nonce-wd.* [f. CUDGEL *v.* + -EE.] One who is cudgelled.

1806 FESSENDEN *Democr.* I. 118 *note*, The gentleman, who in that encounter had the honor to be the cudgellee.

cudgeller (ˈkʌdʒələ(r)). [f. as prec. + -ER[1].] One who cudgels; one who plays cudgels.

1580 HOLLYBAND *Treas. Fr. Tong*, *Vn donneur de Bastonnades*, a cudgeller. **1642** MILTON *Apol. Smect.* (1851) 267 Often lyable to a night-walking cudgeller. **1811** *Sporting Mag.* XXXVIII. 161 Cudgellers, wrestlers, back-sword players.

cudgelling (ˈkʌdʒəlɪŋ), *vbl. sb.* [-ING[1].] The action of the verb CUDGEL: **a.** Beating with a cudgel; **b.** Cudgel-playing.

1606 SHAKS. *Tr. & Cr.* III. iii. 249 Proud of an heroicall cudgelling. **1663** COWLEY *Cutter of Coleman St.* V. xiii, There should ha' been a Beating, a lusty Cudgeling. **1787** MAD. D'ARBLAY *Diary* 10 Feb., For what were you most famous at School?.. Cudgelling, sir. **1827** DE QUINCEY *Murder* Wks. IV. 21 A man deserved a cudgelling for writing 'Leviathan'. *a* **1839** PRAED *Poems* (1864) II. 50 Fearless he risks that cranium thick At cudgelling and singlestick.

ˈ**cudgel-ˌplay.** [lit. *play of cudgels.*] The playing or wielding of cudgels; the art of combat with cudgels; a contest with cudgels.

1636 T. RANDALL in *Ann. Dubrensia* (1877) 19 What is the Barriers, but a Courtly way Of our more downe-right sport the Cudgell-play? **1682** H. MORE *Annot. Glanvill's Lux Orient.* 191 No small fools at the use of the Staff or Cudgil-play. **1712** ARBUTHNOT *John Bull* I. ii, Immense riches, which he used to squander away at back-sword, quarter-staff, and cudgel-play.

Hence **'cudgel-,player, 'cudgel-,playing.**

1711 BUDGELL *Spect.* No. 161 ¶3 A Ring of Cudgel-Players, who were breaking one another's Heads. **1717** LADY M. W. MONTAGUE *Lett.* xxxiv. I. 122 As natural to them as cudgel playing or football to our British swains. **1826** SCOTT in *Croker Papers* (1884) I. xi. 318 When I was a cudgel player, a sport at which I was once an ugly customer. **1859** SMILES *Self-Help* 62 Drew.. while at Cawsand.. won a prize for cudgel-playing.

cudgerie ('kʌdʒəriː). Also cugerie. The native name in Australia of the trees *Hernandia bivalvis* (see quot. 1886) and *Flindersia schottiana*, a large rain-forest tree with light-coloured wood.

1884 A. NILSON *Timber Trees N.S.W.* 135 Cugerie. Flindersia australis. **1886** F. M. BAILEY *Queensland Woods* 67 *Hernandia*, Linn *H. Bivalvis*, Benth. *Flora Austr.*, 'Cudgerie' or Greasenut. A tall tree with a smooth bark... The kernel [of the fruit] contains 64.8 per cent. of oil. **1901** —— *Queensland Flora* IV. 1316 Cudgerie or Grease-nut... Involucel enclosing the fruit.. divided nearly to the base into 2 valves.

cudle, a fish, var. of CUTTLE.

† **Cuds.** *Obs.* A deformation of the word *God's*, in oaths and exclamations; cf. CODS, COTS. Also Cudso, Cudsho (cf. COTSO).

1599 MIDDLETON & ROWLEY *Old Law* IV. i, Cud so, Gnotho, I'll not tarry so long. **1607** MIDDLETON *Michaelmas Term* II. iii, Cuds me! I'm undone. *a* **1627** —— *No Wit* v. ii, Cuds bodkins! **1663** T. KILLIGREW *Parson's Wedding* I. ii, Cud's body, they're twigs of the old rod.. that whipped us so lately. **1711** SWIFT *Jrnl. to Stella* 1 July, Cudsho, the next letter to Presto will be dated from Wexford.

cudweed ('kʌdwiːd). [f. CUD *sb.*: the plant being administered to cattle that had lost their cud.] The common name for the genus *Gnaphalium* of composite plants, having chaffy scales surrounding the flower-heads; originally proper to *G. sylvaticum*; extended to other plants, of allied genera, or similar appearance.

1548 TURNER *Names of Herbes* 25 *Centunculus*.. maye be called in englishe Chafweede, it is called in Yorke shyre cudweede. **1597** GERARDE *Herbal* II. cxcv. 515 English Cudweed hath sundrie slender and vpright stalks. **1688** R. HOLME *Armoury* II. 76/1 The Cotton Weed or Cud-Weed. **1854** S. THOMSON *Wild Fl.* III. (ed. 4) 248 The little silvery-looking cudweeds, or *Gnaphaliums*. **1879** PRIOR *Plant-n.*, Sea-Cudweed, *Diotis maritima*. **1884** MILLER *Plant-n.*, American Cud-weed, *Antennaria margaritacea*. Golden C., *Pterocaulon virgatum*.

† **'cudwort.** *Obs.* Also quide-. = prec.

1548 TURNER *Names of Herbes* 83 *Cartafilago*.. is called in english Cudwurt, or Chafewurte. **1587** MASCALL *Govt. Cattle* (1627) 40 Some doe take a handfull of the hearbe called Cud-wort.. & so conueigh it into the beasts mouth to swallow, that hath lost his quide. **1611** COTGR., *Herbe à cotton*, Cudwort, Chaffweed, Cudweed. **1725** BRADLEY *Fam. Dict.*, *Quide*; an Evil that likewise affects Sheep; to cure which take Quidewort, which grows amongst Corn.

cue (kjuː), *sb.*[1] Forms: 5 cu, 5-7 q, 6 qu, que, kue, kewe, 6- cue.

1. The name of the letter Q, q.v.

1755 JOHNSON, Q.. The name of the letter is *cue*, from *queue*, French, tail; its form being that of an O with a tail. [An entirely erroneous guess.]

† **2. a.** The sum of half a farthing, formerly denoted in College accounts by the letter *q*, originally for *quadrans*. *Obs.* (Cf. CEE.)

c **1440** *Promp. Parv.* 106 Cu, halfe a farthynge, or q, *calcus*.. *minutum*. *c* **1510** BARCLAY *Mirr. Gd. Manners* (1570) B ij, All these.. are scantly worth a kue. **1526** SKELTON *Magnyf.* 36 Not worthe a cue. **1542** RECORDE *Gr. Artes* (1575) 29 A kewe the viij part of a penny. **1600** HOLLAND *Livy* LV. Epit. 1241 A small peece of silver of three halfepence farthing cue. **1617** MINSHEU *Ductor*, *Cue*, halfe a farthing, so called because they set down in the Battling or Butterie Bookes in Oxford and Cambridge the letter q. for halfe a farthing, and in Oxford when they make that Cue or q. a farthing, they say, Cap my q. and make it a farthing thus q̊.

† **b.** *transf.* A term formerly current in the Universities for a certain small quantity of bread; also extended by some writers to beer: cf. CEE.

1603 *Patient Grissil* (Shaks. Soc.) 9 Eight to a neck of mutton—is not that your commons?—and a cue of bread. **1605** *1st Pt. Jeronimo* in Hazl. *Dodsley* IV. 367 Hast thou worn Gowns in the university.. ate cues, drunk cees? **1640** GLAPTHORNE *Wit in Const.* I, You're not now Amongst your cues at Cambridge. **1670** EACHARD *Cont. Clergy* 26 (N.) He never drank above size q of Helicon. **1831** P. WINGATE in B. Peirce *Hist. Harvard Univ.* (1833) 219 We were allowed at dinner a cue of beer, which was a half-pint.

† **c.** *fig.* A little, 'a little bit'.

1654 GAYTON *Pleas. Notes* III. x. 141 Cardenio is rais'd a Cue above the Don.

cue (kjuː), *sb.*[2] Forms: 6 kew, ku, quew, 6-7 q, quue, 6-8 que, 7 Q, qu, kue, 6- cue. [Origin uncertain.

It has been taken as = F. *queue* tail (see next), on the ground that it is the tail or ending of the preceding speech; but no such use of *queue* has ever obtained in French (where the *cue* is called *réplique*), and no literal sense of *queue* or *cue* leading up to this appears in 16th c. English. On the other hand, in 16th and early 17th c. it is found written *Q*, *q*, *q.*, or *qu*, and it was explained by 17th c. writers as a contraction for some Latin word (sc. *qualis*, *quando*), said to have been used to mark in actors' copies of plays, the points at which they were to begin. But no evidence confirming this has been found.

1625 MINSHEU *Ductor*, s. *lit. Q*, A *qu*, a terme vsed among Stage-plaiers, à Lat. *Qualis*, i. at what manner of word the Actors are to beginne to speake one after another hath done his speech. **1633** C. BUTLER *Eng. Gram.*, Q, a note of entrance for actors, because it is the first letter of *quando*, when, showing when to enter and speak.]

I. 1. a. *Theatr.* The concluding word or words of a speech in a play, serving as a signal or direction to another actor to enter, or begin his speech.

1553 in Strype *Eccl. Mem.* III. App. xi. 31 Amen must be answered to the thanksgevyng not as to a mans q in a playe. **1590** SHAKS. *Mids. N.* v. i. 186 Curst be thy stones for thus deceiuing mee.. *Deceiuing me* is Thisbies cue; she is to enter, and I am to spy her through the vvall. **1736** FIELDING *Pasquin* II. i, That I might use him like a dog! *Promp.*.. Where is this servant? Why don't you mind your cue? *Serv.* O, ay, dog's my cue. **1882** *Daily Tel.* 7 Dec., The prompter was away.. and the 'cues' were not properly given. **1884** G. MOORE *Mummer's Wife* (1887) 121 'Cue for the soldier's entrance', shouted the prompter.

b. *Mus.* A direction to enable a singer or player to come in at the right time after a long rest: see quot.

1880 GROVE *Dict. Mus.* I. 423 A few notes of some other part immediately preceding the entrance of his own are.. printed small in the stave as a guide; and this is called a cue.

c. *Cinemat.*, *Broadcasting.* A signal for action to begin or end (see quots.). Also *attrib.* Also *spec.*, a mark on a film serving as a signal or direction to a film editor or projectionist.

1932 *Techn. Descr. Broadcasting House* (B.B.C.) 76/1 In certain announcing rooms.. a cue light is installed, so that the announcer may.. give a cue to, say, the conductor of an orchestra to commence. **1940** *Chambers's Techn. Dict.* 214/2 *Cue* (*Cinematography*), an indication, visual or aural, for action or speech on the part of someone, during continuity. **1948** *Brit. Stand. 1492* 6 The motor cue shall consist of circular opaque marks with transparent outlines... The change-over cue shall consist of 4 frames. **1962** A. NISBETT *Technique Sound Studio* vi. 109 All BBC studios are equipped with green cue lights. *Ibid.* 110 For talks, etc. cue lights are also used to help regulate the timing and pace of the programmes.

d. A facility for playing a video or audio recording during a fast forward wind, so that it can be stopped when a desired point in it is reached; ***cue and review***, this facility combined with a similar one for fast rewind.

1978 *Detroit Free Press* 5 Mar. A18/5 (Advt.), Features automatic tape shut-off, cue and review keys, [etc.]. **1982** *Daily Tel.* 30 July 3/6 (Advt.), Looks terrific—sounds even better. Cue/review. Mute switch. **1984** *Listener* 3 May 20/2 (Advt.), The 615 VHS video has the facility to record up to 4 hours on an E-240 cassette, picture search functions like cue, review, freeze frame, and 9 function wired remote control. **1985** *Electronics Week* 7 Jan. 9 The unit features instant replay or cue on the black and white picture tube of its electronic viewfinder or on a standard color monitor TV. **1985** *Which?* Feb. 74/2 Fast picture search (sometimes called shuttle search or cue and review) is provided on all home video recorders: it plays the tape.. at from four to 12 times normal speed.

2. *fig.* **a.** A sign or intimation when to speak or act; a hint or guiding suggestion how to act, etc.

1565 CALFHILL *Answ. to Martiall* 94 b, For he shut in one before, of purpose, to open it when hys quew came. **1594** SHAKS. *Rich. III*, III. iv. 27 Had you not come vpon your Q my Lord, William Lord Hastings had pronounc'd your part. **1602** —— *Ham.* II. ii. 587 What would he doe, Had he the Motiue and the Cue for passion That I haue? **1622** MABBE tr. *Aleman's Guzman d' Alf.* (1630) 51 Herevpon my Companion taking his Q. It is not (quoth he) any lacke of.. hanging in the aire. **1722** DE FOE *Col. Jack* (1840) 197 My merchant gave me my cue, and by his direction I answered. *a* **1734** NORTH *Exam.* II. iv. §119 (1740) 293 Who was.. to take his Ques from her, and to move and do as she inclined him. **1863** WHYTE MELVILLE *Gladiators* II. 268 His comrades kept behind him, taking their cue from his conduct.

† **b.** A hint of what is coming, a premonition.

1647 H. VAUGHAN *Son-dayes* iii, A taste of Heav'n on earth; the pledge and Cue Of a full feast.

c. A stimulus or signal to perception, articulation, or other physiological response.

1931 *Brit. Jrnl. Psychol.* Apr. 342 The sensory cue of the image on the retina. **1940** *Ibid.* Jan. 228 Tactile and labyrinthine 'cues' may come to be interpreted by the blind with the characteristic immediacy which we associate with visual apprehension. **1956** *Language* XXXII. 274 (*title*) Acoustic cues for nasal consonants. **1963** *Amer. Speech* XXXVIII. 73 Since listeners identify members of minimal pairs with the aid of contextual cues, stress placement has no functional role. **1966** *Listener* 6 Oct. 503/1 This business of olfactory cues, as they are called, has been recognized in mammals too.. but.. overlooked in man.

3. The part assigned one to play at a particular juncture; the proper or politic course to take.

1581 T. HOWELL *Deuises* (1879) 194 Take heede therfore, and kepe each Cue so right, That Heauen for hyre vnto thy lotte may light. **1598** SHAKS. *Merry W.* III. iii. 39 Mistris Page, remember you your Qu. *Mist. Pag.* I warrant thee, if I do not act it, hisse me. **1605** —— *Lear* I. ii. 147 Pat: he comes.. my Cue is villanous Melancholly. **1605** *Tryall Chev.* III. ii. in Bullen *O. Pl.* III. 308 It is thy q. to enter. *a* **1650** MAY *Satir. Puppy* (1657) 23 It was their Qu' now to fly.. which they did with exquisite dissimulation. **1741** RICHARDSON *Pamela* III. 312 You're the Countess of C——'s youngest Daughter Jenny—That's your Cue. **1868** E. EDWARDS *Raleigh* I. x. 175 His cue would naturally be.. to magnify the difficulties of the enterprise.

4. Humour, disposition, mood, frame of mind (proper to any action).

1565 GOLDING *Ovid's Met.* IX. (1593) 228 [He] did not watch Convenient time, in merrie kew at leasure him to catch. **1567** DRANT *Horace Epist.* II. ii. H v, Ech personage in his righte Quue take heede that thou dost frame. **1607** WALKINGTON *Opt. Glass* 21 Men of greater size are seldome i' the right cue. **1752** J. NEWTON *Lett. to Wife* 31 Oct., I should lay the paper aside till I were in a better cue. **1756** TOLDERVY *Two Orphans* I. 69 The 'squire being out of the cue, as he called it, for eating. **1851** HAWTHORNE *Ho. Sev. Gables* xix. (1883) 348 Nobody was in the cue to dance.

5. *Comb.*, as ***cue-call, -fellow, list, sheet.*** **cue-bid** *sb.* and *v. trans.* and *intr.*, **cue-bidder, -bidding** *Contract Bridge* (see quots.); **cue card** (orig. *U.S.*) = *idiot card* s.v. IDIOT *sb.* 4.

1932 G. G. J. WALSHE *Contract Bridge* I. 29 When a suit has been agreed upon between the two partners bids in other suits show features... These bids (Cue bids) are especially valuable. **1963** *Times* 5 June 16/3 He.. refused either to cue-bid or to raise either of my suits. **1932** G. G. J. WALSHE *Contract Bridge* III. 106 The following hands.. will illustrate the methods of the Cue-bidder. *Ibid.*, The original bidder should not.. initiate Cue-bidding without control of the first lead of three suits. **1933** E. CULBERTSON *Contract Bridge Blue Bk.* xviii. 269 The 'cue-bidding' methods which concentrate mainly on showing Aces. **1881** ROSSETTI *Ballads & Sonnets, Sooth-say* vii, In the life-drama's stern cue-call, A friend's a part well-prized by all. **1954** D. C. PHILLIPS et al. *Introduction to Radio & Television* vii. 178 Lettering, photographic copy, or illustrative material.. could consist of 'credits' for the director, cast, and crew, or still photos, cue cards, [etc.]. **1961** [see *idiot board* s.v. IDIOT *sb.* 4]. **1977** *Time Out* 17 June 16/4 On top of this there are more camera scripts to type up and cue cards all of which add to the bulk of work performed by the PA. **1603** HARSNET *Pop. Impost.* 19 He could.. relate (as other his Cue-fellows have done) how hee came to that facility in his part, who were his prompters [etc.]. **1927** *Melody Maker* Sept. 937/3 The present campaign for a better cue list for the provincial or smaller orchestra. *Ibid.* 937/1 The bogey of the Cue Sheet or Suggestion List. **1959** W. S. SHARPS *Dict. Cinemat.* 88/1 *Cue sheet*, the complete schedule of cues for a film production. **1962** A. NISBETT *Technique Sound Studio* vi. 106 A constant check is kept on timing, using either a script or for unscripted programmes, a timed cue-sheet.

cue (kjuː), *sb.*[3] [Variant of QUEUE, a. mod.F. *queue*, in OF. *cue*, *coe*, *keue*, = Pr. *coa*, *coda*, It. *coda*:—L. *cauda* tail]

1. A long roll or plait of hair worn hanging down behind like a tail, from the head or from a wig; a pigtail. Also spelt QUEUE.

1731 CIBBER *Epil.* to *G. Lillo's Lond. Merchant*, The Cit, the Wit, the Rake cocked up in Cue. **1772-84** COOK *Voy.* IV. III. vi. (R.), Those cues or locks.. look like a parcel of small strings hanging down from the crown of their heads. **1843** LEVER *J. Hinton* xxxvi. (1878) 251 The scrupulous exactitude of his powdered cue.

2. The long straight tapering rod of wood tipped with leather, with which the balls are struck in billiards and similar games.

[According to Littré the *queue* was originally the small end of the tapering stick then called the *billard*.]

1749 in B. MARTIN *Dict.* **1779** J. DEW *Billiards* in *Hoyle's Games Impr.* 247 If the Leader follows his Ball with either Mace or Cue past the middle Hole, it is no Lead. **1844** ALB. SMITH *Mr. Ledbury* xxxviii. (1886) 118 He knocked down a large cue that was lying against the billiard-table. **1856** CRAWLEY *Billiards* (1859) 7 The best cues are made plain, of well-seasoned ash.

3. The tail (of an animal). *humorous use.*

1867 LOWELL *Biglow P.* Ser. II. 80 Your [frog's] cues are an anachronism.

4. 'A support for a lance, a lance-rest' (*Imperial Dict.*).

5. *Comb.* (from sense 2), as ***cue-ball, -tip***; **cue-butt** (see quot.); **cue-rack**, a rack for holding billiard cues.

1873 BENNETT & CAVENDISH *Billiards* 26 Cue-tips are made of two pieces of leather cemented together. *Ibid.* 27 The cue-butt or quarter-butt is larger in diameter than the cue, about 5 feet long, and leathered at the bottom. **1881** H. W. COLLENDER *Mod. Billiards* I. 36 The cue-ball is that with which the play is made. **1935** *Encycl. Sports* 82/2 *Cue ball*, ball belonging to the person who is at the table.

cue (kjuː), *sb.*[4] Colloq. abbrev. of CUCUMBER.

1935 *Daily Tel.* 7 June 21/3 'Toms' and 'Cues'. Home-grown tomatoes and cucumbers are in splendid condition. **1963** *Ibid.* 17 Dec. 10/2 (*heading*) 'Tommies and Cues'.

cue (kjuː), *v.*[1] [f. CUE *sb.*[3]] *trans.* To form or twist (the hair) into a cue; to furnish with a cue. Hence **cued** *ppl. a.*[1]

1772-84 COOK *Voy.* IV. III. vi. (R.), They separate it [their hair] into small locks which they woold or cue round with the rind of a slender plant. **1775-83** THACHER *Mil. Jrnl.* (1823) 230 A genteel cued wig. **1824** SCOTT *St. Ronan's* iii, Winterblossom.. wore his hair cued, and dressed with powder.

cue (kjuː), *v.*[2] [f. CUE *sb.*[2]] *trans.* **a.** To provide or furnish with a cue. Also const. *in*, and *fig.* So **cued** *ppl. a.*[2]

1928 *Melody Maker* Feb. 197/2 The 1st alto had melody cued-in. **1937** *Printers' Ink Monthly* Apr. 50/3 *Cue someone*, to give a signal indicating 'proceed with the pre-arranged routine'. **1957** R. MANEY *Fanfare* vii. 95 Stimulated by the martinis, and cued by questions, I volunteered a lot of suggestions. **1959** *Times* 19 Nov. 16/5 He knew the music in the sense that he was able to dispense with the scores and cue his players from memory. **1961** *Listener* 20 Apr. 683/2 Not being cued by the State Department's press officers that this was indeed mighty stuff. **1962** *Ibid.* 4 Oct. 537/3 This scaffolding.. served its purpose which was to introduce

Esterhazy and to cue in his *apologia pro vita sua.* **1962** *Amer. Speech* XXXVII. 227 Velarized or emphatic stops are cued by frequency lowering of second formant. **1964** T. RATTIGAN *Heart to Heart* in *Coll. Plays* III. 426 Super captions. Cue announcer. *Ibid.*, Take out caption. Cue David. **1966** S. JACKMAN *Davidson Affair* ii. 17, I..saw the floor-manager's hand drop to cue me in, and turned to face the camera. **1970** *Radio Times* 30 Apr. 10/2, I want to explain in the programme that we've just heard from our Washington correspondent, and then cue you in live.

b. *spec.* To make an indicatory mark on (a film negative or a recording) (see CUE *sb.*² 1 c).

1938 G. H. SEWELL *Amat. Film-making* iv. 47 The amateur is advised to..'cue' the negative. **1958** *N.Z. Listener* 26 Sept. 9/1 Discs are easier to cue and edit if the programme is complicated and needed in a hurry.

c. *trans.* and *intr.* To position (the pick-up arm, stylus, etc., of a record-player) over or at the desired track of the record. Also *transf.* of pre-recorded tapes, etc.

1958 J. TALL *Techniques of Magnetic Recording* xii. 231 There are two ways to prepare a program of this nature. One way is to 'cue' the master tape, either visually or aurally, so that it is stopped at the proper point, after the cue. **1960**, etc. [implied at CUEING *vbl. sb.*]. **1975** G. J. KING *Audio Handbk.* viii. 198 A record place cueing indicator is included and it is also possible to cue in accurately to any place on the record by servocontrol. **1976** *Gramophone* Feb. 1406/2 Only then can I confidently line up the stylus over a given band on the record and cue it exactly. **1984** *N.Y. Times* 12 July C22/3 Radio-engineers cueing music in broadcast studios.

cue-ball, *a.* *rare*⁻¹. 'Piebald; skewbald' (Davies).

1869 BLACKMORE *Lorna D.* xxxix, A gentleman on a cue-ball horse.

‖**cueca** ('kweka). [Amer. Sp., f. *zamacueca*, a S. Amer. Indian song and dance.] A South American dance.

1912 J. MASEFIELD in *English Rev.* Oct. 383 And girls in black mantillas fit to make a Poor seaman frantic when they dance the cueca. **1917** E. HAGUE *Spanish-Amer. Folk-Songs* 103 (*title*) Cueca or Zamacueca (from Chile). **1928** *Daily Express* 14 Sept. 4 The cueca, like the tango, comes from South America. It is the national dance of Chili. **1960** *Times* 22 Jan. 13/7 He himself danced the *cueca* in Buenos Aires.

cueing ('kjuːɪŋ), *vbl. sb.* [f. CUE *v.*² + -ING¹.] The action of positioning the pick-up arm of a record-player: see sense c of the vb.; also, a device or facility for doing this. Chiefly *attrib.*, as ***cueing device***, ***system***, etc.

1958 J. TALL *Techniques of Magnetic Recording* xi. 209 Another cueing method uses visible markings on the dialogue or main piece. **1960** *High Fidelity Mag.* July 36/1 The recent appearance of certain cuing [sic] devices to aid the less nimble-fingered turntable owner bears this out. **1967** *Pop. Electronics* July 22/2 The new 'Dual' Model 1015 automatic turntable..shares with the more expensive models..a versatile cueing system. **1971** *Ibid.* July 22 It incorporates an AM/FM tuner..a 4-speed automatic turntable with cueing, anti-skate control, [etc.]. **1973** G. DAVEY *Fun with Hi-Fi* v. 34 These arms now have cueing devices for placing the pick-up at any spot on the record. **1976** *Gramophone* May 1836/3 The rate of lowering and raising (cueing) of the pickup arm..can be adjusted. **1984** *N.Y. Times* 8 July II. 19/2 Those with CD players unequipped with index cueing have no way to leap about within a CD except with fast-forward or reverse.

cueist ('kjuːɪst). [f. CUE *sb.*³ + -IST.] One skilled in the use of a cue: an appellation of a billiard-player.

1870 A. STEINMETZ *Gaming Table* II. 153 The extraordinary performances of some of the first-class cueists. **1891** *Doncaster Chron.* 2 Jan. 5/6 The cueist showed wonderful manipulation.

cueless ('kjuːlɪs), *a.* *rare*⁻¹. [See -LESS.] Without a cue or pigtail.

1830 CARLYLE *Richter* Misc. Ess. (1888) III. 27 Bare-necked, cueless.

‖**cuenca** ('kwɛŋkə). [Sp., bowl, socket.] Used *attrib.* of the decoration of tiles: ornamented with sunken patterns surrounded by a raised outline.

[**1911** *Encycl. Brit.* XXVI. 973/1 About 1550..there arose the method *de cuenca* in which the parts of the design to receive different coloured enamels were stamped, slightly concave.., their edges alone being left in relief. **1925** B. RACKHAM in *Hannover's Pott. & Porc.* I. 550 *De cuenca* ('cell') tiles, the term..was invented as a designation by J. Gestoso y Perez, author of *Historia de los barros vidriados Sevillanos*, 1903.] **1939** A. LANE *Guide to Tiles* vii. 59 Patterns were sunk in the soft surface of the tile..in this ..*cuenca* (hollow) technique. **1960** R. G. HAGGAR *Conc. Encycl. Contin. Pott.* 477/1 Ceiling tiles were extensively made in Spain from the sixteenth century with coloured glazes in the *cuenca* technique.

'cue-owl. A name applied to the Scops-owl (*Scops Giu*), common on the shores of the Mediterranean, and a summer visitant to Britain.

[Howard Saunders *Manual Brit. Birds* (1888) 298 says 'To my ear its cry is a clear metallic ringing *ki-ou*—whence the Italian names *chiù, ciù*.']

1855 BROWNING *Andrea del Sarto*, The Cue-owls speak the name we call them by. **1856** MRS. BROWNING *Aur. Leigh* VIII. (1882) 324 The cue-owls from the cypresses Of the Poggio called.

‖**cuerda seca** (kwɛrda seka). [Sp., lit. 'dry cord'.] (See quot. 1960.)

1911 *Encycl. Brit.* XXVI. 973/1 The tediousness of the process gave rise, about 1450, to what is known as the *cuerda seca* (or 'dry cord') method, in which narrow fillets at the edges of the separating interlacings were first stamped upon the tile itself and filled with clay and manganese; these being fired (thus forming a 'dry cord' or line) formed shallow compartments which were in turn filled with coloured enamel. **1939** *Burlington Mag.* Oct. 156/1 Tile-work glazed in the so-called *cuerda seca* technique. **1960** R. G. HAGGAR *Conc. Encycl. Contin. Pott.* 121/2 *Cuerda seca*, 'dry cord': a technique employed by Spanish tile makers in which lines were drawn upon the tile in a purple pigment mixed with a greasy substance which effectually separated the colours filled in on either sides of them, and disappeared during the firing process.

‖**cuerpo.** *Obs.* Forms: 7 cuerpo, quirpo, 7–8 querpo. [Sp. *cuerpo* body:—L. *corpus*.]

1. Only in phrase ***in cuerpo***: without the cloak or upper garment, so as to show the shape of the body; in undress; also *fig.*; sometimes *humorously*, without clothing, naked.

a **1625** FLETCHER *Love's Cure* II. i, Boy: my Cloake and Rapier; it fits not a Gentleman of my ranck to walk the streets *in Querpo.* **1654** H. L'ESTRANGE *Chas. I* (1655) 72 Out came the Lieutenant with his suit of Gallants, all armed in cuerpo. **1691** WOOD *Ath. Oxon.* II. 556 He..under-valued his office by going in quirpo like a young Scholar. **1740** WARBURTON *Div. Legat.* v. Wks. V. 217 He..strips Moses of his mission and leaves him to cool, in querpo, under his civil character. **1748** SMOLLETT *Rod. Rand.* x, The drummer, who had given his only shirt to be washed, appeared *in cuerpo.*

2. *attrib.* and *Comb.*

1644–7 CLEVELAND *Char. Lond. Diurn.* 3 A zealous Botcher in Morefields..contriving some Quirpo-cut of Church-Government. **1741** RICHARDSON *Pamela* lxxxiv, These smart, well-dressing, querpo fellows.

cuesta ('kwɛsta). [Sp. *cuesta* slope:—L. *costa* (see COAST *sb.*).] A gentle slope or inclined plain, esp. one that ends in a steep drop; a hill or ridge with one face steep and the opposite side gently sloping. Orig. local U.S.; adopted in the second sense as a term in *Physical Geogr.* (see quots.).

1818 in *Amer. State Papers* (*For. Relat.*) (1834) IV. 298 A high ridge or mountain surrounds them all; and a cuesta.. more or less rugged and precipitous. **1854** W. L. HERNDON *Amazon* I. 96 The road..ascends a steep and rugged '*cuesta*'. **1896** *Nat. Geogr. Mag.* VII. 294 The plains belong to four great topographic categories, which in the rich Spanish nomenclature of the region may be termed *mesas*, *bolsons*, *plazas*, and *cuestas* (including *bajadas*)... *Cuestas* and *bajadas* are inclined plains, which can also be classed as declivities. **1899** W. M. DAVIS in *Proc. Geol. Assoc. Lond.* (1900) XVI. 76 The outer slope is so gentle that its inclination is hardly noticeable. Such an upland may be called a 'cuesta'. *Ibid.* 77 Finding no name in use for the forms here considered, I have..advocated the general adoption of the term cuesta... By the same natural extension of the original meaning that makes mesa apply to the whole of a tabular elevation, instead of only to its upper surface, cuesta may be made to apply to the entire body of the unsymmetrical linear elevation that is characteristic of certain denuded coastal plains. **1901** *Jrnl. School Geogr.* Oct. 295 This is just at the cuesta-like escarpment. **1939** *Geogr. Jrnl.* XCIV. 414 The Chiltern Hills are a simple chalk cuesta. **1941** C. A. COTTON *Landscape Developed by Erosion* x. 94 Homoclinal ridges grade into *cuestas*, which are developed on escarpment-forming strata of very gentle inclination. **1963** D. W. & E. E. HUMPHRIES tr. *Termier's Erosion & Sedimentation* iii. 66 It is sometimes difficult to distinguish these cliffs from nonmarine cuestas. **1970** R. J. SMALL *Study of Landforms* iii. 75 The most important landforms of such scarp-and-vale scenery are, of course, the cuestas themselves.

cuff (kʌf), *sb.*¹ Forms: 4 coffe, 4–7 cuffe, 6 cuyffe, 7 kuff, 7– cuff. [ME. *coffe*, *cuffe*, of uncertain origin.

The word has some similarity of form to ML. *cuphia*, *cuffia*, in OE. *cuffie*, cap, head-covering, F. *coiffe*, COIF; but no connexion of sense appears.]

†**1.** A mitten or glove. *Obs.*

1362 LANGL. *P. Pl.* A. VII. 56 He caste on his clopes, i-clouted and i-hole, His cokeres and his coffus, for colde of his nayles. *c* **1440** *Promp. Parv.* 106 Cuffe, glove, or meteyne, *mitta* (J. *ciroteca*). **1467** *Nottingham Rec.* II. 262 Unum par chirotecarum vocatarum cuffes de velwet.

2. a. An ornamental part at the bottom of a sleeve, consisting of a fold of the sleeve itself turned back, a band of linen, lace, etc. sewed on, or the like; also, the corresponding part of a shirt-sleeve, or a separate band of linen or other material worn round the wrist so as to appear under the sleeve.

1522 *Test. Ebor.* (Surtees) V. 154 My velvett jacket, to make his childer patlettes and cuyffes. **1594** NASHE *Unfort. Trav.* 15 Cleane shirts and cuffes. *a* **1613** OVERBURY *A Wife* (1638) 162 He never weares Cuffes. **1684** WILDING in *Collect.* (Oxf. Hist. Soc.) I. 259 For a pair of Kuffs. **1768** STERNE *Sent. Journ.*, *Remise Door*, She laid her hand upon the cuff of my coat. **1838** DICKENS *O. Twist* ii, Oliver firmly grasping his [Mr. Bumble's] gold-laced cuff. **1861** WYNTER *Soc. Bees* 153 He turned up his cuffs like an expert chemical lecturer.

b. That part of a long glove or gauntlet which covers the wrist or part of the arm.

1860 J. HEWITT *Anc. Armour* II. *Descr. Engravings* p. vii, The sollerets and the cuffs of the gauntlets.

c. Colloq. phrases: ***off the cuff*** (as if from notes made on the shirt-cuff) orig. *U.S.*, extempore, on the spur of the moment, unrehearsed; also *attrib.* (with hyphens); ***on the cuff***, (*a*) orig. *U.S.*, on credit; (*b*) *N.Z.*, beyond what is appropriate or conventional; excessive (phr. ***a bit on the cuff*** perh. infl. by rhyming collocation ***a bit rough***); ***to shoot one's cuffs***, see SHOOT *v.*

1938 *New York Panorama* (*Federal Writers' Project, N.Y.*) vi. 157 *Double talk* is created by mixing plausible-sounding gibberish into ordinary conversation, the speaker keeping a straight face or *dead pan* and enumerating casually or *off the cuff*. **1941** *Time* (Air Exp. Ed.) 4 Aug. 1/1 Talking off the cuff to a group of civilian-defense volunteers he made them a little homily. **1944** *Penguin New Writing* XX. 130 In that scene, shot off the cuff in a shockingly bad light, there leapt out of the screen..something of the real human guts and dignity. **1948** *Economist* 3 July 17/2 Mr. Truman's off-the-cuff comment. **1960** *News Chron.* 6 July 7/7 He was infuriated by Mr. Macmillan's refusal to give off-the-cuff answers.

1927 K. NICHOLSON *Barker* 149 *On the cuff*, a charged account. **1938** F. D. SHARPE *Sharpe of Flying Squad* 332 *On the cuff*, payment deferred. **1945** B. MACDONALD *Egg & I* (1947) xi. 135 Money was not important at all. All business was transacted on the cuff.

1942 in Webber & Colvin *Johnny Enzed in Middle East* (1946) 8 A bit on the cuff, that sort of thing. **1944** J. H. FULLARTON *Troop Target* xi. 85 That's a bit on the cuff, Dig.

d. The turn-up on a trouser leg. Chiefly *U.S.*

1911 *T. Eaton & Co. Catal.* Spring & Summer 117 Trousers have belt loops, cuff bottoms and full width. **1917** *Ibid.* Fall & Winter 369 Trousers have five pockets, belt loops and finished with cuff. **1931** W. FAULKNER *Sanctuary* vi. 52 Scraping at his trouser-cuffs. **1947** *Book Nine* (Caxton Press, N.Z.) 23 He tapped [the cigarette] ash into his trouser cuff. **1968** *Observer* 10 Mar. 25/5 A technique which guarantees there won't be glass fragments (identifiable by spectrography) in the cuffs of the thief's trousers. **1969** *Catal. J.C. Penney* Fall & Winter 561 Slacks... Rugged corduroy fabric. Belt loops and cuffs.

3. A fetter for the wrist, a HANDCUFF.

1663 BUTLER *Hud.* I. II. 1093 Promises that yoke The Conqueror, are quickly broke, Like Sampson's Cuffs. **1861** THACKERAY *Round. Papers, On being found out* (1876) 132 Mr. Bardolph..puts out his hands to the little steel cuffs, and walks away quite meekly.

4. *attrib.* and *Comb.* ***cuff-edge***, ***-link(s)***.

1883 A. DOBSON *Old World Idylls* 17 The shoulder-knot that slept within her cuff-box. **1684** *Lond. Gaz.* No. 1981/4 A Cuff Button with a Diamond of about ten grains. **1922** JOYCE *Ulysses* 7 Across the threadbare cuffedge he saw the sea hailed as a great sweet mother. **1897** *Sears, Roebuck Catal.* 425 Solid gold Cuff Links, plain polished and raised ornamentation. **1915** 'BARTIMEUS' *Tall Ship* iv. 75 This liberal display of fine linen and flashing cuff-links. **1970** A. CAMERON et al. *Computers & O.E. Concordances* 39 We had slugs made for print chains and finally made cuff links out of the slugs. **1971** *N.Y. Times* 21 Feb. 40 (Advt.), Boutique cufflink collection in swivel lucite top cases. **1677** WOOD *Life* (Oxf. Hist. Soc.) II. 389 For cuff strings, 8*d.*

cuff (kʌf), *sb.*² [Goes with CUFF *v.*¹ (q.v.).]

1. A blow with the fist, or with the open hand; a buffet. Cf. *fisticuff*.

1570 LEVINS *Manip.* 183/37 A cuffe, *colaphus.* **1596** SHAKS. *Tam. Shr.* III. ii. 165 This mad-brain'd bridegroome tooke him suche a cuffe, That downe fell Priest and booke. **1635** N. R. *Camden's Hist. Eliz.* IV. 493 She..gave him a cuffe on the ear. **1712** ADDISON *Spect.* No. 433 ¶6 Their publick Debates were generally managed with Kicks and Cuffs. **1879** *Cassell's Techn. Educ.* IV. 62/1 Many a cuff did the foreman..give him for absenting himself.

b. Phr. ***at cuffs***: at blows, fighting; ***to go*** or ***fall to cuffs***.

1602 SHAKS. *Ham.* II. ii. 373 Vnlesse the Poet and the Player went to Cuffes in the Question. **1669** *Lond. Gaz.* No. 386/4 The Contest grew so high, that they began to deside the dispute at Cuffs. **1683** *Autobiog. Sir J. Bramston* 140 Macedo..fell to cuffs with a Frenchman. **1711** SWIFT *Lett.* (1767) III. 175 He was at cuffs with a brother footman. **1720** *Humourist* 54 Mutatius is generally at Cuffs with himself. *a* **1839** PRAED *Poems* (1864) II. 225 And there were kings who never went To cuffs for half-a-crown.

2. *transf.* A blow or stroke of any kind.

1610 *Mirr. Mag.* 619 (T.) The billows rude..Cuff after cuff, the earth's green banks did batter. **1778** MAD. D'ARBLAY *Diary* 23 Aug., In getting out of the coach, she had given her cap some unlucky cuff. **1872** BLACKIE *Lays Highl.* 34 Granite battlements that..stiffly bear the cuffs and buffet of the strong-armed blast.

cuff, *sb.*³ *slang.* [Cf. CUFFIN, CHUFF¹.] A contemptuous term for an old man; *esp.* a miserly old fellow.

1616 R. C. *Times' Whistle* IV. 1255 Some rich cuffe. *a* **1700** B. E. *Dict. Cant. Crew*, A pleasant Old Cuff, a frolicksom old Fellow. **1725** BAILEY *Erasm. Colloq.* (1877) 371 (D.) *Gi.* I boarded with Antronius. *Ja.* What with that rich old cuff? **1760** COLMAN *Polly Honeycombe* iii, Ten to one the old cuff may not stay with her.

cuff, *sb.*⁴ A variant (of Scottish origin) of SCUFF, SCRUFF, in ***cuff of the neck***, 'the fleshy part of the neck behind' (Jam.); also the coat collar.

1740 in *Inverness Cour.* 29 Dec. 1883. 3/1 Mr. M.'s wife was drawn backwards by the cuff of the neck. **1823** GALT *R. Gilhaize* I. 81 (Jam.) Her husband..seizing his Grace by the cuff of the neck, swung him away from her with.. vehemence. *a* **1873** LYTTON *Ken. Chillingly* IV. x, I took him ..by the cuff of the neck. **1876** SMILES *Sc. Natur.* ii. (ed. 4) 29 She took hold of her son by the cuff of the neck.

Cuff, *sb.*⁵ *U.S.* Abbrev. of CUFFEE.

1755 J. HEMPSTEAD *Diary* (1901) 656 An Indian freewoman wife to Mr. Tilley's Negro Cuff died. **1814** H. M. BRACKENRIDGE *Views of Louisiana* 211 They chased a she bear into a hollow tree... The chopping was renewed; madam Cuff again appeared, and was saluted as before.

1855 WHITMAN *Leaves of Grass* (1860) 29 Growing among black folks as among white, Kanuck, Tuckahoe, Congressman, Cuff.

cuff (kʌf), *v.*¹ [Of uncertain origin: cf. G. Rogues' cant *kuffen* to thrash ('perh. of Hebraic origin', Sievers); also Sw. *kuffa* to thrust, push.]

1. *trans.* To strike with the fist, or with the open hand; to buffet.

1530 PALSGR. 502/2, I cuffe one, I pomell hym about the heed, *Je torche.* **1570** LEVINS *Manip.* 184/3 To cuffe, *colaphizare.* **1591** SHAKS. *1 Hen. VI*, I. iii. 48 Priest, beware your Beard, I meane to tugge it, and to cuffe you soundly. **1676** D'URFEY *Mad. Fickle* v. ii, Sirra you shall be hufft and cufft, and flip'd and kick'd. **1781** MAD. D'ARBLAY *Diary* 25 Aug., I think a man deserves to be cuffed for saying any lady will marry him. **1872** W. BLACK *Adv. Phaeton* iv. 42 She ran out..and cuffed the boys' ears.

b. *transf.* To beat, strike, buffet.

c **1611** CHAPMAN *Iliad* xv. 575 Like a wave..that..down doth come And cuff a ship. *a* **1649** DRUMM. OF HAWTH. *Poems* Wks. (1711) 43 The angry winds not ay Do cuff the roaring deep. **1855** TENNYSON *Maud* I. vi. i, The budded peaks of the wood..Caught and cuff'd by the gale.

†**c.** To vanquish in fight, 'beat', 'lick'. *Obs.*

a **1653** G. DANIEL *Idyll* i. 32 The fabled Monsters, wᶜʰ Sʳ Bevis oft Vanquisht in fight, and our Sᵗ George has Cufft. **1769** JOHNSON 26 Oct. in *Boswell*, I'll take you five children from London, who shall cuff five Highland children.

†**2.** Of birds: To strike or buffet with the wings, as in fighting. (Also *absol.*) *Obs.*

1621 G. SANDYS *Ovid's Met.* XIII. 270 [They] Their opposites with beake and tallons rend; Cuffe with their wings. **1647** N. BACON *Disc. Govt. Eng.* lvii. 171 He hawked at all manner of game..till at length being well cuft and plumed, he was fain to yoke his lawless will under the Grand Charter. **1682** OTWAY *Venice Pres.* II. ii. **1687** DRYDEN *Hind & P.* III. 1224 The Pigeons..with their quills..cuffed the tender chickens from their food. **1725** POPE *Odyss* II. 179 They [two eagles] cuff, they tear; their cheeks and necks they rend.

3. *absol.* or *intr.* To deal or exchange blows; to fight, scuffle.

1611 [see CUFFLE]. **1675** COTTON *Poet. Wks.* (1765) 223 I'll cuff with thee for twenty Pound. *Ibid.* 224 To prate, And cuff it out at Billingsgate. **1693** DRYDEN *Juv.* (J.), While the peers cuff to make the rabble sport. **1812** *Sporting Mag.* XXXIX. 153 All those who choose..in a ring with him to cuff. **1886** J. K. JEROME *Idle Thoughts* (ed. 58) 128 Shrill-voiced women cuff, and curse, and nag.

4. *trans.* To discuss, talk *over* (a tale, matter); also, to tell (a tale). *dial.*

1746 P. LOCK *Exmoor Scolding* (1879) 56 Oll vor..cuffing a tale. **1854** A. E. BAKER *Northants Words* I. 165 The personal appearance and behaviour of Miss H —— was cuffed over at the ball. **1867** W. F. ROCK *Jim an' Nell* (1896) cx, Let's cuff another tale. **1891** R. P. CHOPE *Dial. Hartland* 39 *Cuff over*, to talk over, discuss. 'Let's ha' a pipe an' cuff it auver.'

Hence **'cuffing** *vbl. sb.* and *ppl. a.* (In quot. 1609 *fig.* = contending, opposing.)

1609 JAS. I *Sp. at Whitehall* in *Harl. Misc.* I. 12 There are divers crosse and cuffing statutes, and some are penned as they may be taken in divers, yea, contrary sences. *a* **1680** BUTLER *Rem.* (1759) II. 32 In Cuffing, all Blows are aimed at the Face. **1741** RICHARDSON *Pamela* II. 257, I have but just escaped a good Cuffing. **1886** BURTON *Arab. Nts.* I. 325 Give her a sound cuffing.

cuff (kʌf), *v.*² *rare.* [f. CUFF *sb.*¹] *trans.* To put cuffs on; to handcuff; see CUFF *sb.*¹ 3.

1693 LUTTRELL *Brief Rel.* (1857) III. 1 He was cuff'd and shackled with irons, and committed to Newgate. **1851** SIR F. PALGRAVE *Norm. & Eng.* I. 555 Taken prisoner, cuffed and stripped.

cuffed (kʌft), *a.* [f. CUFF *sb.*¹ + -ED².] Having cuffs: in parasynthetic comb., as ***double-cuffed.***

1558 *Inv.* in *Lanc. & Chesh. Wills* (1857) 178 On shurt, double cuffed, and edged with silver lace. **1951** V. NABOKOV *Speak, Memory* xv. 234 Cuffed hands of wood nailed to boles in the old parks of curative resorts pointed in the direction whence came a subdued thumping of bandstand music. **1960** T. HUGHES *Lupercal* 36 Only a plump, cuffed citizen Gets enough quiet to hear God speak.

Cuffee, Cuffy ('kʌfɪ). *U.S. colloq.* Also with lower-case initial. [A personal name formerly common among Negroes.] **a.** A Negro; also used as a generic name. **b.** A black bear.

1713 S. SEWALL *Diary* (1879) II. 386, I press'd him, and came away with some hope; obliged Cuffee to call for him. **1824** J. DODDRIDGE *Notes* 21 When the bear approached him, he sprang out and hallooed at him; but cuffee..jumped at him with mouth wide open. **1837** *Southern Lit. Messenger* III. 86 The song ceased, and the cuffee advanced in silence. **1844** 'J. SLICK' *High Life N.Y.* I. 74 Jest as I was a thinking this, the cuffy come into the room. **1862** 'ARTEMUS WARD' *His Bk.* (1865) 61 Praps I'm bearin down too hard upon Cuffy. **1959** A. SALKEY *Quality of Violence* iv. 65 A friend to Boss-man and *cuffee.*

cuffer¹ ('kʌfə(r)). [f. CUFF *v.*¹ + -ER¹.] One who cuffs; a boxer, fighter.

1662 GUNNING *Lent Fast* 173 That we..be [not] as such cuffers who fight as it were with their shadow. **1675** HOBBES *Odyssey* XI. 287 Pollux good Cuffer, Castor Cavalier. **1705** STANHOPE *Paraphr.* II. 213, I, like those Wrestlers and Cuffers, fight in very good earnest.

†**b.** *humorously.* The fist. *Obs.*

1694 ECHARD *Plautus* 18 *Mercury* (Holding up his Fist). Rogue, look to yourself. *Socia.* You may act, Sir, as you please, as long as you are so plaguely arm'd with those Cuffers.

cuffer². *dial.* or *slang.* Also **cuffa.** [f. CUFF *v.*¹ 4 + -ER¹.] A yarn or story.

1887 J. FARRELL *How He Died* 65 You made me start to pitch you this most interesting cuffer. **1895** P. H. EMERSON *Marsh Leaves* 156 He'll spin up a rare cuffa along with old Jenks. **1899** F. T. BULLEN *Idylls Sea* xxv. 219 The time-honoured 'cuffer' or yarn was going its soothing round. **1923** *Blackw. Mag.* May 661/1 There's plenty of cuffers, as they're called, about mermaids, phantom ships, dripping corpses, and such like.

cuffin ('kʌfɪn). *Thieves' cant.* Also 6 **cuffen**, 7 **cuffing.** [? connected with CUFF *sb.*³] A man, fellow; chap; = COVE *sb.*² ***queer cuffin***: a churlish fellow; also, a justice.

1567 HARMAN *Caveat* 86 Yonder dwelleth a quyere cuffen ..Yonder dwelleth a hoggeshe and choyrlyshe man. **1609** DEKKER *Lanthorn & Candle-lt.* Wks. 1884-5 III. 196 The word Coue, or Cofe, or Cuffin, signifies a Man, a Fellow. **1641** BROME *Jov. Crew* II. Wks. 1873 III. 389 We are assaulted by a quire Cuffin. *a* **1700** B. E. *Dict. Cant. Crew*, *Queere-cuffin*, a Justice of Peace; also a Churl. **1818** SCOTT *Hrt. Midl.* xxv, 'He knows my gybe as well as the jark of e'er a queer cuffin in England.' **1829** LYTTON *Disowned* 4 'What ho, my bob cuffins,' cried the gipsy guide, 'I have brought you a gentry cove.'

†**'cuffle**, *v. Obs. rare*⁻¹. ? = SCUFFLE.

1596 SPENSER *F.Q.* IV. iv. 29 Most cuffling [**1611** cuffing] close, now chacing to and fro.

'cuffless, *a.* [See -LESS.] **1.** Without cuffs.

1873 MISS BRADDON *Str. & Pilgr.* iii. 64, I should go cuffless and collarless.

2. Of trousers: without turn-ups. Chiefly *U.S.* (Cf. CUFF *sb.*¹ 2 d.)

1957 J. FRAME *Owls do Cry* xxxvii. 167 An attendant with black suit and cuffless trousers. **1958** B. MALAMUD *Magic Barrel* (1960) 76 A green suit with cuffless trousers.

cuffoye, variant of CAFFOY.

1678 *Lond. Gaz.* No. 1278/4.

Cufic, var. of KUFIC *a.*

cufuffle, var. CURFUFFLE.

cui- in Sc. forms; see CO-, COO-, CU-.

‖**cui bono** (kwiː 'bəʊnəʊ, 'bɒnəʊ; formerly kaɪ 'bəʊnəʊ). A Latin phrase, properly *cui bono est*, *fuit*, etc., meaning 'To whom [is or was it] for a benefit?' *i.e.* 'Who profits (or has profited) by it?' attributed by Cicero to a certain Lucius Cassius (*Pro Roscio Amer.* xxx): popularly but erroneously taken in English to mean 'To what use or good purpose?'; hence, sometimes *subst.* The question of the practical advantage of anything; practical utility as a principle.

1604 BP. ANDREWES *Serm.* E j b (T.), For, what of all this? what good? *cui bono?* **1621-51** BURTON *Anat. Mel.* I. ii. IV. vii. (1676) 102/2 To build an house without pins, make a rope of sand, to what end? *cui bono?* **1836** J. F. DAVIS *Chinese* II. 272 (Stanford) The Chinese always estimate such matters by their intermediate and apparent *cui bono.* **1847** DE QUINCEY *Secr. Soc.* i. Wks. 1890 VII. 178 The point on which our irreconcilability was greatest respected the *cui bono* (the ultimate purpose) of this alleged conspiracy.

b. *adj.* or *attrib.* Of or relating to the question *cui bono?*; sometimes = utilitarian.

a **1734** NORTH *Exam.* I. iii. §130 (1740) 207 All which Matters..amount..to a Dæmonstration of the Sort I may term *cui bono.* **1791** BOSWELL *Johnson* (1848) 690/2 Dr. Shaw ..used to say, 'I hate a *cui bono* man'. **1873** H. SPENCER *Stud. Sociol.* iii. 69 Are there any who utter the *cui bono* criticism?

c. *vb.* To put the question *cui bono?* in regard to (anything); to question the utility of.

1837 LYTTON *E. Maltrav.* VIII. i, An ambition, which seemed..to *cui bono* the objects of worldly distinction.

cuich-grass, obs. f. QUITCH-: cf. COUCH *sb.*²

cuif, var. Sc. spelling of COOF, fool.

cuinage, cuynage, obs. forms of COINAGE. As applied to tin, in English Law Books, it means the official stamping of the blocks; = COINAGE 4.

[An erroneous explanation by Cowell (1607) was corrected in Blount's *Law Dictionary* 1670, but, having been copied by Johnson, is still repeated in modern Dictionaries.]

cuinye, -ie, var. of CUNYE *Sc.*, coin.

cuir, obs. Sc. form of CHOIR, CURE.

cuirass (kwɪ'ræs, kjuː'ræs), *sb.* Forms: α. 5 curas, -esse, quyras, 5-7 curace, 6-7 curase, cuirace, -rasse, cuyrasse, 7 curasse, 7- cuirass; β. 6 cuyratz, 6-7 curats, 7 curets, cuirats; γ. 6-7 curet, -e, curat, -e, 6 curiet, curret, -ette, 7 cuiret. [In the forms *curas*, *quyras*, *curace*, *cuirasse*, a. F. *cuirasse* (1418 in Hatzfeld), f. *cuir* leather, after Pr. *coirassa*, It. *corazza*, Sp. *coraza*:—L. *coriācea* adj. (fem.) leathern, f. *corium* leather; the med.L. *corācium*, *corātium*, cuirass, is from the mod. langs. The original OF. name was *cuiriée* (later *quirie*):—L. type **coriāta*, whence ME. *quirie*, *quirre.* In 16th c. a frequent Eng. form was *curats*, *cuirats*, app. under the influence of It. *curazza*: cf. MLG. *koritz*, ODa. *körritz*, *kyrritz*, etc. This being, from its final *s*, treated as a plural, gave the mutilated singular *curat*, *curate*, etc., common 1560-1650. The stress was then on the first syllable, but was subsequently under F. influence shifted to the second: Bailey 1730 has *cui'rass.*]

1. A piece of armour for the body (originally of leather); *spec.* a piece reaching down to the waist, and consisting of a breast-plate and a back-plate, buckled or otherwise fastened together; still worn by some European regiments of cavalry.

The breastplate alone was sometimes called a cuirass, or the two pieces combined were called (***a pair of***) ***cuirasses***, and the breast-plate a ***half-cuirass.*** The word has also been used in a general sense for all kinds of ancient close-fitting defensive coverings for the body, made of leather, metal, or other material.

α. Form *cuirass* (*curas*, etc.), pl. *cuirasses* († *curas*).

1464 *Mann. & Househ. Exp.* 195 And my mastyr lent hym a payr of smale curas wyth gardys and vumbarde. *c* **1489** CAXTON *Sonnes of Aymon* ix. 241 He smote Gerarde thrughe the quyras. **1495** *Act 11 Hen. VII*, c. 64 Preamb., Armours Defensives, as..Billes Hauberts Curesses. **1548** HALL *Chron.* 12 One company had the..border of the curace all gylte. **1598** BARRET *Theor. Warres* v. ii. 141 The Man at Armes..with his cuyrasses of proofe. **1618** BOLTON *Florus* IV. ii. 281 A golden curace, or brest-plate. **1678** tr. *Gaya's Arms of War* 44 The Cuirass is Musket-proof. **1756-7** tr. *Keysler's Trav.* (1760) IV. 289 The armour of the horse-guards with half-cuirasses. **1820** SCOTT *Monast.* xxxv, The troopers..armed with cuirass and back-plate. **1846** *Hist. Rec. Life Guards* 215 On this day (1821) the Household Brigade first appeared in Cuirasses, which it has since worn.

†β. Form *curats*, *cuirats*, etc.

1591 HARINGTON *Orl. Fur.* XXIII. cvi, He casts away his curats and his shield. **1598** CHAPMAN *Iliad* III. 343 The curets that Lycaon wore. **1611** COTGR., *Cuirasse*, a Cuirats. **1627** *Lisander & Cal.* III. 55 Just betweene his arme and the curats. **1647** W. BROWNE tr. *Polexander* II. 216 Hee made his cuirates fly in a thousand pieces.

†γ. This form treated as *pl.*, with a sing. *curat*, etc.

1552 HULOET, *Curet*, breast-plate or stomager. **1555** EDEN *Decades* 98 Eyther bresteplates or curettes of golde. **1596** SPENSER *F.Q.* v. viii. 34 Through his curat it did glyde. *a* **1625** BOYS *Wks.* (1629) 533 Paul here makes no mention of a backe Curate for a Christian souldier. **1627** DRAYTON *Agincourt* 46 Their Curates are vnriuetted with blowes.

†**2.** *pl.* Soldiers wearing cuirasses. *Obs.*

1598 BARRET *Theor. Warres* v. ii. 143 Accompanied with Lances, or cuyrats on horsebacke, I meane armed petranels or pistoliers.

3. *transf.* **a.** The breast-plate of the Jewish high-priest.

1836 KEBLE in *Lyra Apost.* (1849) 169 The mystic cuirass gleams no more, In answer from the Holy One.

b. A close-fitting (sleeveless) bodice, often stiffened with metal trimmings or embroidery, worn by women.

1883 *Standard* 3 Aug. 3/1 A dark brown [dress] with a cuirass of gold lace. **1889** *John Bull* 2 Mar. 150/2 Mrs. C.'s dress was of white silk, with tablier and cuirass bodice embroidered in pearls.

4. *fig.* **a.** Applied to the buckler or any hard protective covering of an animal.

b. *transf.* The armour-plate protection of the sides of a ship, etc.

1598 SYLVESTER *Du Bartas* I. vi. (1641) 51/1 Th' hast armed some [creatures]..with thick Cuirets, some with scaly Necks. **1860** *Engineer* 16 Nov. 316/2 Whitworth's gun may punch a hole in the iron cuirass of these ships. **1888** ROLLESTON & JACKSON *Anim. Life* 831 A very distinct cuticle, either a dorsal thickened cuirass, a bivalved cuirass, or rings of plates.

c. In full ***cuirasse band.*** A band made of linen pressed in layers to protect a cycle tyre.

1906 *Daily Chron.* 28 Nov. 9/2 The winter and tropical tyre..consists of a smooth vulcanised cover, with cuirasse band put on top by hand. **1907** *Ibid.* 12 Oct. 9/4 The Paris cuirasse band... Unlike the Sphinx, the cuirasse becomes an integral part of the tyre, being attached inside the cover.

5. In full ***cuirass respirator.*** An apparatus covering the chest and providing artificial respiration.

1939 *Rep. Med. Res. Council Breathing Machines* 16 The Burstall jacket respirator (1938)..consists of a one-piece aluminium cuirass to enclose the trunk..from the neck to the waist-line... The London County Council cuirass respirator (1938) has been designed..to overcome many of the disadvantages of the original Burstall cuirass. **1955** *Times* 13 May 6/3 A cuirass respirator..which allows the 'iron lung' to be dispensed with after the first few weeks of poliomyelitis. The patient has full use of his limbs and the breathing cycle is maintained by a small pump standing by the bed. **1959** *Times* 25 Sept. 8/5 Later demonstrations included the working of the R.A.F. portable version of an iron lung—the Monaghan cuirass—which is smaller and lighter and allows more mobility than the ground equipment.

cuirass (kwɪ'ræs, kjuː'ræs), *v.* [f. prec. sb.] *trans.* To cover or protect with, or as with a cuirass; to furnish (a ship) with armour-plating.

1863 G. T. LOWTH *Wand. West. France* 326 There were two frigates on the stocks, one..of wood..to be cuirassed. **1880** BROWNING *Dram. Idylls, Clive* 50 His scalemail's warty iron cuirasses a crocodile. **1881** *Daily News* 10 Mar. 5/1 Black silk dresses are cuirassed with an armour of jet.

cui'rassed, *ppl. a.* [f. CUIRASS *sb.* + -ED.]

1. Furnished with or wearing a cuirass; also *fig.*

1727–51 CHAMBERS *Cycl.* s.v. *Cuirasse*, A good part of the German calvary are cuirassed. **1852** MOIR *Portrait of Scott* Poet. Wks. II. 258 The cuirassed warrior, stern and high. **1854** H. MILLER *Footpr. Creat.* iii. (1874) 23 Remains of a large cuirassed fish.

2. Of ships, etc.: Armour-plated.

1864 *Daily Tel.* 12 Oct., The invention of cuirassed vessels. **1870** *Standard* 12 Dec., Cuirassed locomotives were ready on the Orleans line with guns to support.

cuirassier (kwɪrəˈsɪə(r), kjʊə-). In (6 coritser), 7 **cuiraisier, -asseer, -azeer, curaseer, -asheer, -useer, -iazier, -(s)sier, coriassier,** 8 **curiasser,** 9 **cuirasseur, -sieur.** [a. F. *cuirassier*, f. *cuirasse*: introduced in 17th c., and applied to the heavy cavalry in the Civil Wars. *Coritser* for LG. *koritzer* (= early mod.G. *kürisser*), occurs 1551 as an alien word in a document abstracted by Strype.]

1. A horse soldier wearing a cuirass.

The proper name of a certain type of heavy cavalry in European armies. The name is not now used in the British army, though some of the regiments of Guards correspond in equipment.

[**1551** in Strype *Eccl. Mem.* II. 258 Sixteen horsemen and two coritsers.] **1625** MARKHAM *Souldiers Accid.* 41 The first and principall Troope of horsemen .. are now called Cuirassiers or Pistolliers. **1664** POWER *Exp. Philos.* I. 2 Armed Cap-a-pe like a Curiazier in warr. **1671** MILTON *P.R.* III. 328 Cuirassiers all in steel for standing fight. **1702** W. J. *Bruyn's Voy. Levant* ii. 6 Many Troopers, Curiassers, armed Switz. **1801** *Sporting Mag.* XVII. 135 Exercising his regiment of cuirasseurs. **1824** MACAULAY *Naseby*, Our cuirassiers have burst on the ranks of the accurst. **1874** GREEN *Short Hist.* x. 811 The victorious horsemen were crushed in their turn by the French cuirassiers.

b. *fig.* and *transf.*

1658 ROWLAND *Moufet's Theat. Ins.* Ep. Ded., The Fleas that are Curasheers, and their back stiffe with bristles. **1727** POPE & ARBUTHNOT *Art of Sinking* 108 Call an army of angels, angelic cuirassiers.

¶ **2.** (*erroneously*). A cuirass. *Obs.*

1622 PEACHAM *Compl. Gent.* (1661) 162 His Curuseers to be of gold, his robe blew and silver, his buskins of gold. *Ibid.* 165 The Roman Emperours habit was this: their curuseers yellow embroidered with silver.

cuirats, cuiret, obs. ff. CUIRASS.

‖**cuir-bouilli** (kwir bu(l)ji). Forms: 4–5 **quir-, quyr- boilly, -boily, -boyly, -boile, -boyl(l)e, quere-boly, qwyrbolle, coerbuille, -boyle,** 6 *Sc.* **cur-, corbulȝe.** [F., *lit.* 'boiled leather.']

Leather boiled or soaked in hot water, and, when soft, moulded or pressed into any required form; on becoming dry and hard it retains the form given to it, and offers considerable resistance to cuts, blows, etc.

The word was in common English use from 14th to 16th c., after which it is not found till modern times, when it appears as borrowed from modern French.

1375 BARBOUR *Bruce* XII. 22 On his basnet hye he bar Ane hat off qwyrbolle. *c* **1386** CHAUCER *Sir Thopas* 164 Hise Iambeux were of quyrboilly [*v.r.* quereboly]. *c* **1400** MAUNDEV. (Roxb.) xxvi. 123 Þai hafe platez made of coerbuille. **1413** LYDG. *Pilgr. Sowle* IV. xxx. (1483) 80 A feyned hede formed of playstred clothe other of coerboyle. **1513** DOUGLAS *Æneis* V. vii. 77 Thair harnes .. thaim semyt for to be Of curbulȝe corvyne sevin gret oxin hydis. **1880** C. G. LELAND *Minor Arts* i. 1 Solid or pressed work, known as cuir bouilli, in which leather .. after having been boiled and macerated, or rendered perfectly soft, is moulded, stamped, or otherwise worked into form.

‖**cuir ciselé** (kwir siz(ə)le). [Fr., chiselled leather.] Used *attrib.* of a form of decoration on book-bindings in which a design is cut into the leather by means of a pointed tool.

1933 *Library* Mar. 337 (*title*) Some cuir-ciselé book-bindings in English libraries. **1938** *Times Lit. Suppl.* 12 Nov. 732/2 One [blind-stamped binding] is from southern Spain, dating from about 1480, with a *cuir ciselé* design.

cuire, obs. Sc. form of CURE.

cuirie, var. of *quiry*, obs. aphetic form of EQUERRY, royal stables, stud.

c **1565** LINDESAY (Pitscottie) *Chron. Scot.* 159 (Jam.) The King .. caused his Mr. Stabler to pass to his cuirie, where his great horse were. **1601** HOLLAND *Pliny* II. 327 The Empresse Poppæa had her cuirie of she Asses in her traine .. onely to wash and bath her body in their milke.

Cuisenaire rod (kwiːzəˈnɛə(r)). Also **Cuisenaire's rod.** One of a set of wooden rods of different length and colour according to the number they represent, invented by the Belgian educationalist Georges *Cuisenaire* as an aid in the teaching of arithmetic to children.

1954 CUISENAIRE & GATTEGNO *Numbers in Colour* p. vi, For the child engaged in work with Cuisenaire's rods, the monotonous and uncertain feeling that is associated with counting is transformed into an exciting, intense experience of the active intellectual mind. **1962** *Listener* 5 Apr. 593/2 Dr. Dienes's structural games are widely used, as are the Cuisenaire rods and the original apparatus devised by Stern. **1965** in P. Jennings *Living Village* (1968) 208 Children are introduced to number work by using Cuisenaire Rods. Each child has a box of ten compartments with wooden rods of different colours and lengths. Each colour stands for a number of units, and the rods increase in length from one unit to ten units.

cuisine (kwiːˈziːn). [F. *cuisine* kitchen, = Pr. *cozina*, It. *cucina*:—L. *coquina*, *cocina*, f. *coquĕre* to cook.] Kitchen; culinary department or establishment; manner or style of cooking; kitchen arrangements.

[*a* **1483** *Liber Niger* in *Househ. Ord.* (1790) 32 One messe grosse de kusyn.] **1786** HAN. MORE *Florio* 657 (Stanford) Great Goddess of the French Cuisine. **1817** KEATINGE *Trav.* I. 204 Fish and fowls, highly seasoned, according to the Moorish cuisine, with saffron. **1871** NAPHEYS *Prev. & Cure Dis.* III. ix. 956 Those innocent arts of the cuisine, which render food pleasant.

Hence **cuiˈsinic** *a. nonce-wd.*, pertaining to the cuisine; **cuiˈsinier** [F.], a (French) cook.

1848 *Fraser's Mag.* XXXVIII. 134 With his cuisinic knowledge he has so annoyed the members. **1859** LANG *Wand. India* 23 Amongst the most skilful of cuisiniers.

‖**cuisine bourgeoise** (kɥizin burʒwaz). [Fr.] Plain home cooking; chiefly applied to French food. Also *fig.*

1951 E. DAVID *French Country Cooking* 170 Duck cooked with turnips is one of the classic dishes of the French Cuisine Bourgeoise. **1965** *Economist* 3 July 13/2 The immediate result of M. Defferre's crockery coming to bits in his hands is to leave General de Gaulle more than ever in charge of France's *cuisine bourgeoise*. **1969** *Guardian* 30 Aug. 3/2 French cooking has two branches, haute cuisine and the cuisine bourgeoise.

cuisse, cuish (kwɪs, kwɪʃ). Forms: *pl.* 4 **quysseaux, -ewes,** 5 **cusseis, cussues, qwysshewes,** 5–7 **cushies,** 7 **cushes,** 6–9 **cuisses,** 8–9 **cuishes;** *sing.* 5 **cusshewe, cusché,** 7 **cush,** 9 **cuish.** [In 14th c. *quyssewes*, *cuissues*, a. OF. *cuisseaux*, *cuisiaux*, pl. of *cuissel* = It. *cosciale*, L. *coxāle*, f. L. *coxa* hip, It. *coscia*, F. *cuisse* thigh. In Eng. the *-ewes*, *-ues* of the plural being reduced to *-ies*, and at length to *-es*, the latter has been confounded with the plural ending in *fish-es*, etc., and a singular *cuish*, *cuisse* formed. The etymological sing. would be *quissel*, or *quissew*.]

pl. Armour for protecting the front part of the thighs; in *sing.* a thigh-piece.

[**1314** SIR R. DE CLIFFORD in *Hist. Lett. & Pap. North Reg.* (Rolls 1873) 227 Vij. pair de trappes .. ix. pair de quisseus.] *c* **1330** R. BRUNNE *Chron. Wace* (Rolls) 10027 Arthur .. was armed fynly wel Wyþ .. Doublet & quysseaux. *c* **1340** *Gaw. & Gr. Knt.* 578 Queme quyssewes .. coyntlych closed His thik þrawen þyȝez. **1423** *Test. Ebor.* (Surtees) III. 73 Pro uno pare de qwysshewes de mayle, pro defensione crurium. *c* **1425** WYNTOUN *Cron.* VIII. xxxii. 46 Hys Cusche Laynere brak in twa. **1590** SIR J. SMYTH *Disc. Weapons* 3 If he had that day worne his cuisses, the bullet had not broken his thigh bone. **1596** SHAKS. *1 Hen. IV*, IV. i. 105, I saw young Harry with his Beuer on, His Cushes on his thighes. **1602** WARNER *Alb. Eng.* XII. lxix. (1612) 291 The Taishes, Cushies, and the Graues. **1622** F. MARKHAM *Bk. War* IV. viii. 151 They shocke close together, and as it were ioyne Cush to Cush. **1697** DRYDEN *Virgil* Ded., How came the cuisses to be worse tempered than the rest of his armour. **1718** POPE *Iliad* III. 411 The purple cuishes clasp his thighs around. **1814** SCOTT *Ld. of Isles* VI. xxxiii, Helm, cuish, and breastplate stream'd with gore. **1881** PALGRAVE *Vis. Eng.* 136 Sidney struck onward, his cuisses thrown off.

Hence †**cuishard** [F. *cuissard*], **cuisset, cuissot** [F. 13th c.], in same sense. Cf. also CUSSAN.

1598 BARRET *Theor. Warres* Gloss. 250 *Cuisset*, is the armings of a horseman, for his thigh vnto the knees. **1678** tr. *Gaya's Arms of War* 44 Cuissots or Thigh-pieces. **1632** J. HAYWARD tr. *Biondi's Eromena* 145 He bore him a thrust under the vauntplate, between the two cuyshard pieces. **1830** E. HAWKINS *Anglo-Fr. Coinage* 110 Part of his cuissarts appears.

cuisshyn, obs. form of CUSHION.

†**cuit, cute.** *Obs.* Also 6 **cuyte, cuite,** 8 **cutt.** [a. F. *cuit*:—L. *coctus* cooked, boiled, pa. pple. of *cuire*:—L. *coquĕre*. In sense 2, perh. repr. F. *cuite* sb. a boiling, a boil.]

1. Orig. *adj.* in ***wine cuit***, subsequently used *absol.*: New wine boiled down to a certain thickness and sweetened.

c **1460** J. RUSSELL *Bk. Nurture* 118 The namys of swete wynes y wold þat ye them knewe .. wyne Cute. **1574** HYLL *Ord. Bees* xviii, The sweet lycour named Cuyte. **1598** FLORIO, *Vin cotto*, a kinde of sodden wine which we call cute, to put into other wines, to make them keepe the longer. **1601** HOLLAND *Pliny* XXII. xiii. 121 Nettleseed taken in wine cuit as a drinke openeth the matrice. **1615** MARKHAM *Eng. Housew.* II. iv. (1668) 116 If it be Spanish Cute, two gallons will go further than five gallons of Candy Cute. **1703** *Art & Myst. Vintners* 33 Two Gallons of Cutt to every Butt so that it be Spanish Cutt. **1756** *Dict. Trade & Commerce*, *Wine Cuit*, or boiled wine .. by that means still retains its native sweetness.

2. Boiling or seething; a boil.

c **1460** J. RUSSELL *Bk. Nurture* 138 Sugre of iij. cute white hoot & moyst in his propurte. *Ibid.* 159 Gynger of iij. cute.

cuit, var. of COOT² *Sc.*, ankle.

'**cuitchour,** obs. Sc. form of COUCHER² I.

1535 LYNDESAY *Satyre* 2605 Sir, I compleine vpon the idill men .. Iugglers, Iestars, and idill cuitchours.

cuiter (ˈkytə(r)), *v. Sc.* Also **cuter, kuter.** *trans.* To attend to with kindly assiduity; to minister to; to coddle.

1795 BURNS *Deuk's dang our my Daddie* iv, I've seen the day you buttered my brose And cuitered me late and early. **1847** *Ballads & Songs of Ayrshire* Ser. I. 118 O sae kin'ly 's she cuiter'd the weans.

cuith, var. of COOTH, coal-fish.

cuittikin: see CUTIKIN, gaiter.

cuittle (ˈkyt(ə)l), *v. Sc.*

1. *trans.* To curry, wheedle, coax.

c **1565** LINDESAY (Pitscottie) *Chron. Scot.* 97 (Jam.) Thir words were spoken by the Chancellor, purposely to cause .. all the lave .. to follow, and come in the Kings will, and thought to have cutled them off that way. **1816** SCOTT *Old Mort.* xxviii, This Mrs. Dennison, was trying to cuittle favour wi' Tam Rand. **1818** —— *Br. Lamm.* xiv, Sir William .. wad sune cuitle another out o' somebody else. **1820** —— *Abbot* xvi, The Protestant .. cuittles us with the liberty of conscience.

2. To tickle. (? for *kittle*.)

a **1790** A. MACDONALD in Scott *Wav.* xi, And many a weary cast I made To cuittle the moor-fowl's tail.

cuivré (ˈkwiːvreɪ), *a. Mus.* [Fr., pa. pple. of *cuivrer* to play with a brassy tone, f. *cuivre*, pop.L. **copreum*, sb. use of neuter of L. *cupreus* of copper.] Brassy; used as a direction to play a brass instrument with a harsh, blaring timbre. Also *absol.*

[**1927** *Grove's Dict. Mus.* (ed. 3) I. 767/1 *Cuivré*, the French term for indicating stopped notes on the horn.] **1931** G. JACOB *Orchestral Technique* iii. 32 The horn .. is also capable of the most savage attack when roused, the stridency of which is enhanced (though the power actually reduced) by 'stopping' the bell with the hand or a metal mute and blowing hard. The former effect, known as the 'cuivré' is indicated by a cross. **1938** *Oxf. Compan. Mus.* 243/2 *Cuivré*. .. The term is found occasionally in music for brass instruments, especially the horn.

cuk-: see also CUCK-.

cuke (kjuːk). Colloq. abbrev. of CUCUMBER.

1903 *Postcard in Merriam-Webster files* 1 Aug., Received to-day and sold. 3 Boxes Cukes $2.12½. M. Homburger. **1949** O. NASH *Versus* 96 Who coined these words that strike me numb? .. The cuke, the glad, the lope, the mum. **1960** J. SYMONS *Prog. Crime* xiv. 88 You know what he's like, cool as a cuke.

cuke, obs. form of COOK.

†**cuker.** *Obs. rare*⁻¹. Some part of a woman's dress.

c **1460** *Towneley Myst.* 312 The shrew .. is hornyd like a kowe .. The cuker hynges so side now, furrid with a cat skyn.

cul, obs. form of CULL.

-cula: see -CULUS.

†**culb, culbe.** *Obs. rare.* [a. MHG. *kulb(e*, var. of *kolbe*, in same sense.] A retort.

1683 PETTUS *Fleta Min.* I. (1686) 146 Let it boil over the Coal-fire in a little Culbe or boule. *Ibid.* 171 Put it into a sound well luted glass Boule or Culb.

Culbertson (ˈkʌlbətsən). The name of Ely *Culbertson* (d. 1955), an American authority on contract bridge, used chiefly ***attrib.*** and ***ellipt.*** of a system of bidding at contract bridge.

1929 *Bridge World* I. 40, I have been using what is known as the Culbertson System of bidding. **1931** A. WOOLLCOTT *Let.* 22 July (1946) iv. 79, I was gone only three months, but in that time .. everybody had taken up Culbertson. **1932** *Times Lit. Suppl.* 12 May 349/3 Bidding based on the Culbertson principles. **1959** *Listener* 2 July 38/1 The Culbertson Four-Five No Trump convention. *Ibid.* 38/2 Culbertson bidders.

culbut, *v. rare.* [An anglicized adaptation of F. *culbuter*, f. *cul* back, fundament + *buter* to butt, to strike abruptly.] To overturn backwards, throw any one on his back; to drive back in disorder.

a **1693** URQUHART *Rabelais* III. xxvi. 219 Not .. permitted to culbut. **1832** *Blackw. Mag.* XXXII. 545 The generals .. had led or left them to be culbuted by the French. **1842** *Ibid.* LI. 630 A British battalion .. driving him over hill and dale, culbuted in the most exemplary manner.

culch, cultch (kʌltʃ). *local.* Also **culsh.** [Possibly a. OF. *culche* (mod.F. *couche*) couch, bed, layer, stratum, etc.; but the late appearance of the word leaves this uncertain.]

1. *gen.* Rubbish, refuse. (South of Engl., and U.S.)

1736 J. LEWIS *Hist. Thanet* Gloss., *Culch*, lumber, stuff. **1736** PEGGE *Kenticisms*, *Culch*, rags, bits of thread, and the like, such as mantua-makers litter a room with .. it means, I find too, any rubbish. **1888** ELWORTHY *W. Somerset Word-bk.*, *Culch*, broken crockery, oyster shells, and the usual siftings from an ash-pit. **1891** *Jrnl. Amer. Folk-lore* No. 13 This word, when applied to human beings, has a secondary sense of disgust. 'He's a mean old culch!' The epithet is the worst which can be used. *Mod.* (*Essex*), Culsh may be shot here.

2. *spec.* The mass of stones, old shells, and other hard material, of which an oyster-bed is formed.

1667 SPRAT *Hist. R. Soc.* 307 The Spat cleaves to Stones, old Oyster-shells, pieces of Wood, and such like things, at the bottom of the Sea, which they call Cultch. **1774** E. JACOB *Faversham* 83 A dredge full of Cutch instead of oysters. **1863** C. R. MARKHAM in *Intell. Observ.* IV. 424 Paved with stones, old shells, and any other hard substances..so as to form a bed for the oysters, which would be choked in soft mud. This material is called culch. **1891** W. K. BROOKS *Oyster* 103 Oyster shells..form the most available cultch, and are most generally used.

culching, cultching ('kʌltʃɪŋ), *vbl. sb.* [f. CULCH, CULTCH.] The practice of strewing an oyster-bed with culch. Also *attrib.*

1894 *Westm. Gaz.* 3 Apr. 5/3 A Burnham cultching boat. **1904** *Nature* 17 Mar. 466/1 The process known as 'culching', that is, scattering the floor of the bed with rock, loose coral, and so on, to afford the necessary anchorage for the byssus of the young oyster.

culd, obs. f. *could*: see CAN *v.*[1]

Culdean (kʌl'diːən), *a.* [f. next + -AN.] Belonging to the Culdees.

1807 G. CHALMERS *Caledonia* I. III. viii. 434 *note*, The Culdean monks. **1887** J. A. WYLIE *Hist. Sc. Nation* II. xxvi. 353 That ancient Culdean father.

Culdee ('kʌldiː), *sb.* and *a.* Also 5 **Kylde,** 6 **Kilde,** 7 **Culdey.** [In OIr. *céle dé* (mod.Ir. *céile dé*), found in the 8th c. in the sense of 'anchorite'; from *céle* associate, fellow, spouse, sometimes servant, vassal, liegeman, tenant + *dé* of God. In early Scottish records latinized in pl. *keledei, kelledei, keldei*; rendered by Wyntoun *kylde.* By Hector Boece written *Culdei* to suit the derivation *cultores Dei*, whence the *Culdees* of later vernacular writers.

The primary sense of *céle dé* was perh. *socius Dei*, as an appellation of a solitary who forsook the society of men to hold intercourse with heaven alone; Dr. Reeves (*Culdees of the British Isles*, 1864) takes it as an Irish translation of the early Christian appellation *servus Dei*, servant or slave of God, applied to monks; Skene (*Celtic Scotland* II. II. vi) thinks *céle dé* a kind of Irish adaptation or imitation of the term *deicola*, God-worshipper, applied from the 4th c. to religious recluses or anchorites in the east. One of the later Latinized adaptations was *Colidei*, evidently = *Deicolæ*, and the explanation *cultor Dei* appears to have been traditional in the time of Boece.]

A. *sb.* A member of an ancient Scoto-Irish religious order, found from the eighth century onwards.

The name appears to have been first given to solitary recluses; these were afterwards associated into communities of anchorites or hermits, and finally brought under the canonical rule along with the secular clergy, 'until at length the name became almost synonymous with that of secular canon'. (See REEVES *British Culdees*, and SKENE *Celtic Scotland* II. II. vi.)

[**1144–50** *Donation of Monastery of Lochlewyn* (Reeves 130–1) 1 Et cum vestimentis ecclesiasticis, quæ ipsi Chelede habuerunt. *c* **1170** *Charter of Wm. the Lion* (Reeves 119) 293 Episcopis et Keldeis de ecclesia de Brechin. **1178–98** *Charter of Bp. Turpin* (Reeves 119) Testibus.. Bricio priore de Brechin, Gillefali Kelde..Mathalan Kelde, Mackbeth Maywen.] *c* **1425** WYNTOUN *Cron.* (ed. Laing) VI. 722 Kyng he sessyd for to be, And in Sanctandrewys a Kylde. **1526** HECTOR BOECE *Scot. Hist.* VI. lf. 92 b, Ut sacerdotes omnes ad nostra pene tempora, vulgo Culdei, i.e. cultores Dei sine discrimine vocitarentur. *Ibid.* lf. 99 a, Dei cultores, Culdei prisca nostra vulgari lingua dicti. **1549** MONRO *Tour W. Isles* 3 (*Misc. Scotica* II. 113) The priest and the philosophers called in Latine Druides, in English Culdeis and Kildeis, that is worshippers of God..quhilks were the first teachers of religion in Albion. **1596** DALRYMPLE tr. *Leslie's Hist. Scot.* III. xxxiv, Notable men of learneng and religione, called in our vulgar language *Culdei.* **1789** PINKERTON *Enq. Hist. Scot.* (1814) II. 272 The Culdees thus united in themselves the distinction of monks and of secular clergy. **1872** E. W. ROBERTSON *Hist. Ess.* 123 The Secular canons, or culdees, of Durham. **1880** SKENE *Celtic Scotl.* II. 226 It is not till after the expulsion of the Columban monks from the kingdom of the Picts, in the beginning of the eighth century, that the name of Culdee appears.

¶ The name was long ascribed in error to the earlier Columban monks of the 6th and 7th century, and it is still popularly but erroneously associated with the Church of Iona.

1693 *Apol. Clergy Scot.* 52. **1796** MORSE *Amer. Geog.* II. 155. **1867** D. BLACK *Hist. Brechin* I. 4.

B. *adj.* Of or pertaining to the Culdees.

1880 SKENE *Celtic Scotl.* II. 337 We see it [Dunkeld] first as a Culdee church, founded shortly before the accession of the Scottish kings to the Pictish throne.

‖**cul-de-four** (kydfur, often kyl də fuː(r)). *Arch.* Pl. culs-de-four. [F. = furnace bottom, oven bottom.] (See quots.)

1727–51 CHAMBERS *Cycl.*, *Cul de four*, a sort of low, spherical vault, oven-like. *Cul de four of a niche* denotes the arched roof of a niche on a circular plan. **1876** GWILT *Archit. Gloss.*, *Cul de four*, a low vault spherically formed on a circular or oval plan. An oven-shaped vault.

‖**cul-de-lampe** (kydlɑ̃p, often kyl də lɑ̃ːp). Pl. culs-de-lampe. [F. = lamp-bottom: the shape of the ornament suggesting the bottom of an ancient lamp.]

1. *Arch.* An ornamental support of inverted conical form; a pendant of the same form.

1727–51 CHAMBERS *Cycl.*, *Cul de lamp*, a French term.. applied in architecture to several decorations, both of masonry and joinery, used, in vaults and ceilings, to finish the bottom of works, and wreathed somewhat in manner of a testudo. **1833** J. DALLAWAY *Disc. Archit. Eng.*, &c. 94 (Stanford) The roof has several pendents (*culs de lampe*).

2. *Printing.* An ornament used to fill up a blank space in a page, as at the end of a chapter when the matter stops short of the bottom.

1818 SCOTT *Br. Lamm.* i, An ornamented and illustrated edition, with heads, vignettes, and *culs de lampe.*

‖**cul-de-sac** ('kʌldəsæk; formerly as Fr., kydsak, often kyl də sæk). Pl. culs-de-sac. [F. = sack-bottom, bag-bottom.]

1. *Anat.* A vessel, tube, sac, etc. open only at one end, as the cæcum or 'blind gut'; the closed extremity of such a vessel, etc.

1738 *Med. Ess. & Observ.* (ed. 2) IV. 92 An Infundibuliform Cul de Sac or Thimble-like cavity. **1809** BRODIE in *Phil. Trans.* XCIX. 163 The œsophagus.. terminated in a cul-de-sac. **1841–71** T. R. JONES *Anim. Kingd.* (ed. 4) 878 In many Ruminants..a cul de sac occupies the commencement of the vascular bulb of the urethra.

2. A street, lane, or passage closed at one end, a blind alley; a place having no outlet except by the entrance; in *Milit.* use, said of the position of an army hemmed in on all sides except behind. Also *fig.*

1800 A. PAGET *Let.* 10 May in *Paget Papers* (1896) I. 201 This [*i.e.* Palermo] is such a *cul de sac* that it would (be) ridiculous to attempt sending you any news. **1819** WELLINGTON in Gurw. *Desp.* IV. 518 The bridges..being irreparable, they would be in a *cul de sac.* **1828** SCOTT *Jrnl.* (1890) II. 163 Coming home, an Irish coachman drove us into a *cul de sac*, near Battersea Bridge. **1872** BAKER *Nile Tribut.* ix. 143 The herds of game found themselves driven into a *cul-de-sac.* **1885** A. DOBSON *At Sign of Lyre* 30 You tried the *cul-de-sac* of Thought; The *montagne Russe* of Pleasure. **1955** *Sci. Amer.* July 96/1 It has enlisted great talent in what appears to be the 'most hopeless cul-de-sac in the novel's history'. **1955** *Times* 23 July 6/3 The Constitution would then be a sham and a cul de sac, not a bridge to self-government later. **1968** *Listener* 25 July 105/1 My concentration then upon something which was past, something that could never be recovered, was a sort of cul-de-sac.

3. *fig.* 'An inconclusive argument.'

In some mod. Dicts.

†**cule.** *Obs.* Also 3 cul, 4 cuyl. [a. F. *cul* bottom, fundament of the body, anus:—L. *cūlus.*] The rump; a buttock.

c **1220** *Bestiary* 741 in *O.E. Misc.* 23 Of ðo ðe he wile he nimeð ðe cul And fet him wel. *c* **1325** *Coer de L.* 1822 'Away dogs with your taile!..Men schal threste in your cuyl!' **1480** CAXTON *Ovid's Met.* XIV. iii, The cule or buttoks. **1528** ROY *Rede me* (Arb.) 56 Then foloweth my lorde on his mule Trapped with golde vnder her cule. **1543** in Bp. Hutchinson *Witchcraft* (1718) 31 She told her Neighbours it would make the Cule of the Maid divide into Two Parts. **1825** JAMIESON, *Cules*, s.pl. Buttocks (Lat. *nates*).

-cule, *suffix*, corresp. to F. *-cule*, ad. L. *-culus, -cula, -culum*, dim. suffix of all three genders: see -CULUS. In living words, the suffix underwent various phonetic changes in becoming French; e.g. *articulus, orteil; auricula, oreille; cuniculus, conil; masculus, masle, mâle*; but it remained as *-cle* after persisting consonants, as in *avunculus, oncle; cooperculum, couvercle.* After the latter, some words of learned origin were fashioned in *-cle*; e.g. *article*; but in modern times the L. ending has been usually adapted in F. as *-cule*, as *corcule, cornicule, corpuscule.* In English, both endings *-cle* and *-cule* are found, as *corpuscle, corpuscule, crepuscle, crepuscule, animalcule*, formerly also *animalcle, floscule, versicle*, etc. The L. endings *-culus, -culum* are sometimes retained unchanged: see -CULUS. The ending *-cule*, with connecting vowel *i*, is sometimes employed, after L. analogies, to form contemptuous diminutives, as *poeticule*: cf. *criticule.*

culerage: see CULRAGE.

†**culet**[1]. *Obs.* Also cullet(t, colyet, coliet, culiet, cullet, culett(e. [a. OF. *cueillete, coillete, cuillete*, a semi-popular ad. L. *collecta* collection, assessment, collection of dues.] A sum collected from a number of persons chargeable; an assessment, a rate: **a.** *Oxford Univ.* A fee formerly paid by every graduate to the bedel of his faculty, as a recompense for attendance at disputations, lectures, etc. It was collected by the bedel once a year, and was called in Latin *cumulatio.*

1550 *MS. note* in *Liber. Antiq. Bedellorum* (Bodl. Libr. Rawl. 662 fol. 134 b) Chargys of a bachyllar of dewynytte beyng no componder; hys cullet muste be pey[d] yerly. **1602** in Clark *Reg. Univ. Oxon.* (1887) II. i. 221 He is to pay two years' culett beforehand. **1866** ROGERS *Agric. & Pr.* I. v. 123. **1873** *Athenæum* 5 Oct. 442/1.

b. An assessment of parochial dues.

The quotations refer to 'culets' paid by the chapelry of Ulpha to the Parish of Millom, of which it formed a part.

1764 *Churchw. Acct.-bk. Ulpha, Millom, Cumberland* May 5 By a list of four Coliets being one guinea each as follows. **1768** *Ibid.* June 16 By a list of three Culiets and one third £3 9*s.* 6*d.* **1771** *Ibid.* Apr. 28 By a list of four Colyets, one half, one seventh £4 13*s.* 10*d.* **1814** *Ibid.* 5 Aug.

culet[2] ('kjuːlɪt). [a. OF. *culet*, dim. of F. *cul* bottom: cf. F. *culasse*, the term actually used. The form COLLET was app. a corruption due to confusion with COLLET *sb.*[1]]

1. The horizontal face or plane forming the bottom of a diamond when cut as a brilliant.

1678 *Lond. Gaz.* No. 1330/4 A Laske, Indian-cut..under the Collet of the thicker side a little round hole. **1874** WESTROPP *Precious Stones* 4 In a brilliant the culet is the base, and should be two-thirds below the girdle.

2. A part of ancient armour, consisting of overlapping plates, protecting the hinder part of the body below the waist.

1834 PLANCHÉ *Brit. Costume* 287 The lancier was to wear a close casque or head-piece, culessets, culets, or guarde de reins.

†**cu'leuvre.** *Obs. rare.* [a. OF. *culuevre*, in mod.F. *couleuvre*:—L. *colubra* snake.] A snake.

1481 CAXTON *Myrr.* II. vi. 76 The olyfaunt..doubteth & fereth the wesell and the culeuure.

‖**culex** ('kjuːlɛks). [L. gnat.] A gnat; in *Entom.* the genus containing gnats and mosquitoes.

1483 CAXTON *Gold. Leg.* 380/1 What is the cause that culex whiche is a lytel beest hath vi feet & two wynges. **1828** STARK *Elem. Nat. Hist.* II. 227 The Culices, whose larvæ are destined to live and find their subsistence in water, drop their ova on its surface. **1876** DUHRING *Dis. Skin* 600 Culex, or Mosquito is not infrequently the source of considerable irritation upon the skin.

‖**culgee** (kʌl'giː). *Anglo-Ind.* ? *Obs.* Also 8 **kulgie.** [a. Urdū *kalghī*, ad. Pers. *kalagī*, orig. *kalakī*, of or pertaining to a festive or martial gathering, whence as sb. in the following senses. (J. T. Platts.)]

†**1.** A rich figured silk worn as a turban or sash, or otherwise, on a festive occasion; hence, a figured Indian silk formerly imported into England. *Obs.*

1688 *Lond. Gaz.* No. 2312/4 To carry 147 Pieces of Culgees, East-India Taffataes, or clouded Silks. **1696** J. F. *Merchants Wareho.* 6 There is two sorts of Indian Silk called Culgees, the one is Satten, the other is Taffety, they are stained with all sorts of colours..they are much used for Handkerchiefs, and for Lining of Beds, and for Gowns for both Men and Women. **17..** in J. Ashton *Soc. Life Q. Anne* (1882) I. 75 'Stole out of the house of John Barnes..a Culgee quilt.'

2. 'A jewelled plume surmounting the *sirpesh* (*sarpēch*) or aigrette upon the turban' (Yule).

1715 in J. T. Wheeler *Madras in Olden Time* (1861) II. 246 (Y.) A vest and culgee set with precious stones. **1786** *Tippoo's Lett.* 263 (Y.) Three Kulgies, three Surpaishes.. have been despatched to you in a casket. **1832** HERKLOTS tr. *Customs of Moosalm.* App. x. *Kulgee*..a phoenix-feather, fixed into the turban, having generally a pearl fastened to the end of it. Worn only by kings and the great.

culice, -isse, obs. ff. CULLIS.

culicicide ('kjuːlɪsɪsaɪd). Also culicide ('kjuːlɪsaɪd). [f. L. *culex, culicis* gnat: see -CIDE 1.] An insecticide for destroying gnats and mosquitoes; also **ˌculici'cidal, culi'cidal** *adjs.*

1899 *Brit. Med. Jrnl.* II. 683/1 The authors made the following classification of culicidal substances: 1. Substances which kill the eggs. [Etc.] **1900** C. CHRISTY *Mosquitos & Malaria* vii. 47 Culicicidal Substances... The substances which kill the mosquito itself may be divided into odours, fumes, and gases. **1900** J. J. EYRE tr. *Celli's Malaria* II. 205 The most efficient culicide is tobacco smoke. **1901** *Practitioner* Mar. 263 By fumigating the rooms occasionally with some such culicicide as the dried flowers of the chrysanthemum. **1949** M. F. BOYD *Malariology* II. lv. 1203 Carbolic acid crystals and gum camphor, equal parts, were melted together and volatilized by heat. This mixture has been referred to as Mimm's culicide.

culicid ('kjuːlɪsɪd, kjuː'lɪsɪd), *a.* and *sb. Ent.* Also Culicid. [f. mod.L. family name *Culicidæ*, f. generic name CULEX: see -ID[3].] **A.** *adj.* Of or pertaining to the dipteran family Culicidæ, which comprises the mosquitoes. **B.** *sb.* A culicid insect; a mosquito.

1901 F. V. THEOBALD *Monogr. Culicidae* I. 24 (*heading*) Structure of Culicid larvae. **1907** E. G. MITCHELL *Mosquito Life* ii. 34 The Culicids, at first suckers of plant juices, learned the taste of animal blood. **1912** L. O. HOWARD et al. *Mosquitoes N. & Central Amer.* I. 150 *Anopheles* has been found feeding upon the dead bodies of other culicid larvæ. **1977** J. COHEN *Reproduction* x. 180 The culicids (mosquitoes) hatch as long-bodied larvae.

culiciform ('kjuːlɪsɪfɔːm), *a. rare*—[0]. [ad. L. type **culiciform-is*, f. *culex, culicem* gnat; in F. *culiciforme*: see -FORM.] Gnat-shaped, gnat-like.

1828 in WEBSTER. **1847** in CRAIG.

culicifuge ('kjuːlɪsɪfjuːdʒ). [f. as CULICICIDE + -FUGE.] A substance applied to the body or to clothing in order to keep gnats and mosquitoes away; so **ˌculici'fugal** *a.*

1894 GOULD *Dict. Med.* 343/2 *Culicifuge*, an agent that prevents the biting of mosquitoes; as oil of pennyroyal. **1900** J. J. EYRE tr. *Celli's Malaria* II. 212 A person can use culicifugal odours or scents on his body and clothing. **1946** P. F. RUSSELL et al. *Pract. Malariology* xxv. 518 Many chemicals have been recommended as culicifuges to be applied to the skin to repel mosquitoes from biting.

culicine ('kjuːlɪsaɪn, -iːn), *sb.* and *a. Ent.* [ad. mod.L. *Culicini* or *Culicinæ*, f. *culex*, *culicis* gnat: see -INE^1.] A mosquito belonging to the tribe Culicini of the sub-family Culicinæ; of or pertaining to a member of this group.

1911 A. ALCOCK *Ent. Medical Officers* iii. 61 Theobald, making the Culicines a separate family, has divided them into ten groups. **1921** G. H. CARPENTER *Insect Transf.* 198 Less abundant in these countries than the Culicine gnats are the Anophelines. **1923** H. M. LEFROY *Ent.* 419 The Anophelines hang parallel to the surface..but the Culicines hang at an angle. **1929** R. MATHESON *Mosquitoes N. Amer.* 36 The species of Culicine mosquitoes have widely varying larval habits. **1964** H. OLDROYD *Nat. Hist. Flies* vii. 78 Any reference to 'mosquitoes' in what follows may be taken as applying to both tribes, unless it is qualified by the adjectives anopheline or culicine.

culinarian (kjuːlɪ'nɛərɪən), *a. rare.* [f. L. *culīnāri-us* CULINARY + -AN.] Of or pertaining to a kitchen; = CULINARY 1.

1615 SIR E. HOBY *Curry-combe* v. 223 What are the Doctrines..are they not Culinarian Theorems? **1828** *Blackw. Mag.* XXIV. 350 What an air of dignity he might have thrown over the culinarian roof.

'culinarily, *adv. rare.* [f. CULINARY + -LY^2.] In a culinary respect; with regard to cookery.

1837 *Fraser's Mag.* XVI. 660 Culinarily and fairly, because the animal..furnishes us with beef-steak, sirloin, buttock. **1892** *Black & White* 25 June 802/1 The dishes.. culinarily..are so original.

culinarious (kjuːlɪ'nɛərɪəs), *a. rare.* [f. L. *culīnāri-us* CULINARY + -OUS.] = CULINARY 2.

1838 *Fraser's Mag.* XVII. 64 Art culinareous. **1848** THACKERAY *Contrib. to Punch* Wks. 1886 XXIV. 199, I.. request that the Soyer Professorship of Culinarious Science be established without loss of time.

culinary ('kjuːlɪnərɪ, 'kʌ-), *a.* [ad. L. *culīnāri-us*, f. *culīna* kitchen. In F. *culinaire* (Cotgr.).]

1. Of or pertaining to a kitchen; kitchen-.

1638 WILKINS *New World* iii. (1707) 30 Culinary and Elementary Fire are of different kinds. **1669** GALE *Crt. Gentiles* I. III. x. 105 Culinarie Rhetoric, such as is in use amongst Trencher-Knights. **1775** ADAIR *Amer. Ind.* 405 They reckon it unlawful..to extinguish even the culinary fire with water. **1856** MISS MULOCK *J. Halifax* (ed. 17) 93 A very culinary goddess.

2. Of or pertaining to cookery.

1651 BIGGS *New Disp.* ¶272 Culinary prescriptions. **1784** COWPER *Task* I. 125 The palate undepraved By culinary arts. **1858** HAWTHORNE *Fr. & It. Jrnls.* (1872) I. 60 Never keep any fire, except for culinary purposes.

b. Of vegetables: Fit for cooking.

1796 MORSE *Amer. Geog.* I. 386 All kinds of culinary roots and plants. **1846** J. BAXTER *Libr. Pract. Agric.* (ed. 4) I. 148 One of our most common and useful culinary vegetables.

'culiver, erroneous form of CALIVER.

1754 T. PRINCE *Ann. New Eng.* II. in Arb. *Garner* II. 594 He discharges his culliver towards the place. **1864** A. BISSET *Omitted Chap. Hist. Eng.* vi. 365 Breast-plates pistol and culiver proof.

cull, *sb.*^{1} *dial.* Also 5 cole. The fish called Bull-head or Miller's Thumb.

a **1490** BOTONER *Itin.* (Nasmith 1778) 291 Homines possunt piscare..de colys vocat. Myller-thombys. *Ibid.* 358 Yn Wye-water sunt..cullys. **1847–78** HALLIWELL, *Cull*, the bull-head. *Glouc.*

cull (kʌl), *sb.*^{2} *slang* and *dial.* [perh. abbreviation of CULLY.] A dupe, silly fellow, simpleton, fool; a man, fellow, chap.

1698 *In Vino Veritas* 25 How prettily we top upon those Rum Culls called Gentlemen. **1749** FIELDING *Tom Jones* VIII. xii, A way to empty the pocket of a queer cull. *a* **1764** LLOYD *On Rhyme* Poet. Wks. 1774 II. 107 The hen-peck'd culls of vixen wives. **1839** H. AINSWORTH *Jack Sheppard* (1889) 14 (Farmer) Capital trick of the cull in the cloak to make another person's brain stand the brunt for his own.

cull (kʌl), *sb.*^{3} [f. CULL *v.*^{1}]

1. The act or product of culling; a selection.

a **1618** SYLVESTER *Bethulia's Rescue* IV. 383 Some curious Cull Of Croton Dames so choicely Beautifull. **1643** SIR J. SPELMAN *Case of Affairs* 17 This man..presents the world with a cull of all the irregular times of our unfortunate Princes. **1692** R. L'ESTRANGE *Josephus' Antiq.* XII. ii. (1733) 303 To make a Cull out of your several Tribes, of six Elders out of each Tribe. **1958** *Times* 20 May 4/3 An annual cull should be carried out..to limit further increases in the grey seal population. **1968** *Times Lit. Suppl.* 30 May 559/4 A list of the words and phrases I'd found, which may be of interest as showing an average daily cull from an intelligent newspaper.

2. *Farming.* An animal drafted from the flock as being inferior or too old for breeding; usually fattened for the market. Also, a bird drafted as inferior; and *fig.* Cf. CULLING *vbl. sb.*^{1} 2. (Usually in *pl.*)

The use in quot. 1791 is peculiar.

1791 YOUNG *Ann. Agric.* XVI. 493 The Burford ewes are ..culled every year; the oldest are fattened and the ram given to the culls, to answer the purpose of westerns. **1809** *Nat. Hist.* in *Ann. Reg.* 801/2 We have our lamb fairs..our shearling fairs, our fairs for culls. **1858** *Jrnl. R. Agric. Soc.* XIX. I. 39, 20 fat cows..the culls of their herds. **1880** *Blackw. Mag.* Apr. 463 They were 'culls', that is sheep drafted out of other flocks for some fault or on account of age. **1919** H. L. WILSON *Ma Pettengill* viii. 253 It made him feel like a social cull or an outcast, or something. **1950** *N.Z. Jrnl. Agric.* Oct. 359/1 Many culls are unhealthy or diseased and are a potential danger to all other birds with which they come into contact.

attrib. **1793** YOUNG *Ann. Agric.* XIX. 148 Cull ewes, generally..called draught ewes. **1879** *Cassell's Techn. Educ.* IV. 322/1 The purchasing of 'cull' or old ewes from some good breeder.

3. chiefly *pl.* and *attrib.* **a.** *N. Amer.* 'Any refuse stuff; as, in bakeries, rolls not properly baked' (Webster 'Refuse timber, from which the best part has been culled out' (Webster 1864). Also ***cull lumber.*** **b.** *U.S.* 'Any refuse stuff; as, in bakeries, rolls not properly baked' (Webster *Supp.* 1881).

1829 J. MACTAGGART *Three Yrs. Canada* I. 245 The refuse wood is called *culls*, and brings an inferior price. **1867** *Trans. Ill. Agric. Soc. 1865–66* VI. 647 Culls are a quality manufactured from winding, worm-eaten, shaky or dry-rot timber, badly manufactured, or less than sixteen (16) inches in length. **1873** *Wisconsin Rep.* XXIX. 593 About 90,000 feet was not good merchantable lumber, but was what is called culls. **1897** F. C. MOORE *How to Build* ii. 23 The 'cull' lumber should be put in the closets, storerooms, and upper or attic rooms. **1953** *Brit. Commonw. Forest Terminol.* I. 35 *Cull*, (*a*) an inferior plant rejected from nursery stock, (*b*) trees or logs that are of merchantable size but are rendered unmerchantable by defects. **1969** L. G. SORDEN *Lumberjack Lingo* 30 *Cull*, rejected logs having little or no value.

c. Fruit rejected as being of inferior quality. (See also *E.D.D.*) Also *attrib.*

1937 *Nature* 7 Aug. 222/1 The utilization of farm wastes and by-products is being investigated; already cull citrus fruits in California are being processed for producing citric acid, citrus oils and pectin. **1951** *New Biol.* X. 56 Malformed and scarred apples were discarded, and it became a matter of moment to reduce the proportion of 'culls' or waste. **1962** *Times* 31 Mar. 9/7 Some cull apples go, at a low price, into cider manufacture.

cull (kʌl), *v.*^{1} Also 4 cole, 5–7 culle, 6–7 cul. [a. OF. *cuillir* and *-er*, later *cueillir*, in imperative *cuille, coille, cueille* (køʎ), to collect, gather, take, select, etc. = Pr. *coillir, cuelhir, culhir*, Cat. *cullir*, Sp. *coger*, Pg. *colher*, It. *cogliere*:—L. *colligĕre*, pres. indic. *colligo*, which became subsequently *colgo, coglio*, and was conjugated in different parts of the Romanic domain with *-ĕre* (It.), *-ēre* (Sp. and Pg.), *-īre* (Pr. and F.), *-āre* (F.). The word was frequent in ME. in the form *coil* (see COIL *v.*^{1}, and cf. COIL *v.*^{3}) for the OF. form *coillir*; *cull* appears in the 15th c., and may represent the F. stem *cuell-, cueill-*: cf. ME. *puple* for F. *pueple, peuple*. Cf. also ME. CUYL, to collect.]

1. *trans.* To choose from a number or quantity; to select, pick. Now most frequently used of making a literary selection. *cull out*: to pick out, select (*arch.*).

c **1330** R. BRUNNE *Chron. Wace* (Rolls) 2731 Sex hundred of hyse he colede out, þat proued were, hardy & stout. *c* **1440** *Promp. Parv.* 107 Cullyn' owte, *segrego, lego, separo.* **1494** FABYAN *Chron.* VII. 239 The auctours so rawe, and so ferre to culle. **1566** PAINTER *Pal. Pleas.* I. Pref. 9 Certaine have I culled out of the Decamerone of..Boccaccio. *a* **1593** H. SMITH *Serm.* (1622) 338 To cull out of all the people, those which had best courage. **1669** WORLIDGE *Syst. Agric.* (1681) 60 It is no small advantage to pick or cull out the best Seed. **1727** A. HAMILTON *New Acc. E. Ind.* I. viii. 82 This Villian was culled out to be sacrificed to the just Resentment of the People. **1807** CRABBE *Village* II. 159 Words aptly culled, and meanings well exprest. **1877** H. A. PAGE *De Quincey* I. vi. 111 From various notes of later dates we cull the following.

2. To gather, pick, pluck (flowers, fruits, etc.).

1634 MILTON *Comus* 255 The Sirens three Culling their potent herbs. **1743–6** SHENSTONE *Elegies* iv, Then Elegance Shall cull fresh flowrets for Ophelia's tomb. **1840** BARHAM *Ingol. Leg., Leech of Folkest.* (1877) 373 A sprig of mountain ash culled by moonlight. **1880** OUIDA *Moths* I. 12 The strawberries just culled.

fig. **1805** WORDSW. *Prelude* XIII. 131 Where I could..cull Knowledge that step by step might lead me on.

3. *transf.* To subject to the process of selection; to select or gather the choice things or parts from.

1713 STEELE *Guardian* No. 171 ¶3, I shall always pick and cull the Pantry for him. **1821** A. FISHER *Jrnl. Arct. Reg.* 230, I thought that, by attempting to cull it [a subject] I might omit some circumstances that deserved to be mentioned. **1881** *Gard. Chron.* No. 417. 823 The ground is culled at intervals of three, four, or five years.

4. a. To pick out (livestock, etc.) according to their quality. Also *absol.*

The earliest examples are Austral. and N.Z. but the word is now widely used in Britain and elsewhere.

1889 WILLIAMS & REEVES *Colonial Couplets* 9 I'd far sooner choose To be writing to you, than be culling the ewes. **1927** M. M. BENNETT *Christison* xii. 125 Christison used to cull on clearly defined lines. At first coarse calves were culled. **1929** 'M. B. ELDERSHAW' *House is Built* i. 10 There were a few lean, dejected cattle, the best of them having been culled out hours before [by buyers]. **1950** *N.Z. Jrnl. Agric.* Apr. 387/3 All ewes on this farm, which are crossbred sheep, are culled for quality and not for age. **1968** J. GORDON *Beagle Guide* 170 *Cull*, to eliminate unwanted hounds. **1969** *Listener* 27 Mar. 439/3 The battery boys 'cull' (or liquidate) their hens when they've laid for about a year. **1970** *Kenya Farmer* Feb. 15/2 A bigger cow..will..fetch a higher price at culling.

b. *spec.* To select and kill (wild animals or birds), usu. in order to improve the stock or reduce the population.

1934 *Evening Post* (Wellington, N.Z.) 12 Apr. 10/4 With the object of determining the best method of culling deer in the Tararuas..the sum of £10 was granted by the Wellington Acclimatisation Society last night. **1963** E. ROBINS *Africa's Wild Life* xxvi. 212 One should cull at least 50% of one's herd annually. **1964** [implied at CULLING *vbl. sb.* 1 b]. **1978** *Orcadian* 31 Aug. 1/2 Lord Cranbrook..said that 10,000-plus [seal] pups had been culled in the last ten years. **1979** S. FLINT *Let Seals Live!* i. 20 It always appeared to me that the..Nature Conservancy Council had been coerced into appearing to back the decision to cull when its unpopularity became evident.

5. *Forestry.* (See quots.) *N. Amer.*

1904 S. E. WHITE *Blazed Trail Stories* 49 A log is culled, or thrown out, when..it will not make good timber. **1905** *Forestry Bureau Bull.* (U.S.) No. 61, 9 *Cull*, to take out of a forest by selection a portion of the trees. **1953** *Brit. Commonw. Forest Terminol.* I. 35 *To cull*, (*a*) to reject inferior plants from nursery stock, (*b*) to deduct the effective portion of a merchantable log or piece of timber from the gross volume in scaling or measuring timber. (Canada.) **1953** H. L. EDLIN *Forester's Handbk.* iv. 59 Once raised, the stocks should be culled—that is, any obviously stunted, misshapen or diseased specimens should be thrown aside.

† **cull,** *v.*^{2} *Obs.* or *dial.* Also 6 kull. [Var. of COLL *v.*^{1}] *trans.* To fondle in the arms, hug.

a **1564** BECON *Jewel of Joy* Wks. (1844) 443 To kiss and kull him as his dear darling. **1580** LYLY *Euphues* (Arb.) 215 Least making a wanton of my first..I should..kill it by cullyng it. **1601** WEEVER *Mirr. Mart.* D iv, He..Hugges, culles, and clippes him in his aged armes. **1659** RUSHW. *Hist. Coll.* I. 535 Oh! how they could hug and cull it.

b. cull-me-to-you, rural name of the pansy.

1597 GERARDE *Herbal* II. ccxcix. §4. 704 Harts ease, Pansies, Liue in Idlenes, Cull me to you, and three faces in a hood. **1814** L. HUNT *Feast of Poets, Cuddle-me-to-you*, which seems to have been altered by some nice apprehension into the less vivacious request of Cull-me-to-you.

cull(e, early form of KILL.

cullace, -asse, -aze, obs. ff. CULLIS.

cullambine, cullander, obs. ff. COLUMBINE, COLANDER.

culled (kʌld), *ppl. a.* [f. CULL *v.*^{1} + -ED^1.] Chosen, picked, selected; gathered, plucked; *spec.* of sheep: Draught (cf. CULL *sb.*^{3} 2).

1588 SHAKS. *L.L.L.* IV. iii. 234 Of all complexions the cul'd soueraignty Doe meet as at a faire in her faire cheeke. **1665** MANLEY *Grotius' Low C. Warres* 397 Culled men out of Breda. **1707** COLLIER *Refl. Ridic.* 78 Cull'd Words and Paraphrases. **1801** *Med. Jrnl.* V. 277 A nosegay of culled flowers. **1811** *Ann. Reg.* 1809. 801 Fed upon the flesh of the culled sheep.

culleis, -ess, cullen: see CULLIS, CULLION.

Cullen: see COLOGNE. ***Cullen plates:*** see quot.

1890 *Daily News* 21 Oct. 5/2 The durable material is an alloy of copper and zinc, called Cullen plates, from Cologne, the old seat of the manufacture.

cullender: see COLANDER.

culler ('kʌlə(r)). Also 5 culyur, 6 cullyar. [f. CULL *v.*^{1} + -ER^1. In 2 the suffix was perh. -ARD.]

1. a. One who culls, selects, or gathers.

1483 *Cath. Angl.* 86 A Culyur, *collector.* **1611** COTGR., *Cueilleur*..a picker, chuser, or culler. **1809** SYD. SMITH *Ess.* Wks. 1867 I. 178 A mere culler of simples. **1883** E. PENNELL-ELMHIRST *Cream Leicestersh.* 255 The busiest of cullers drained dry of even his November stories.

b. (See quots.)

1849 *Rep. Comm. Patents: Agric.* (U.S.) 322 When the tobacco is taken down, the 'cullers' take each plant and pull off the defective and trashy ground and worm-eaten leaves. **1881** E. INGERSOLL *Oyster-Industry* 243 *Culler*, one who picks over oysters, or *culls* out the worthless and smaller ones. **1953** *Times Lit. Suppl.* 20 Mar. 194/5 Mr. Thomson describes his every-day duties and experiences as a 'culler' employed by the Government of New Zealand to shoot destructive deer. **1969** L. G. SORDEN *Lumberjack Lingo* 30 *Culler*, man who quickly graded and sorted, by picking out the culls or rejects, lumber being cut at the mill.

c. *local.* (See quot.)

1906 J. HOCKADAY in *Vict. Hist. Cornwall* I. 521/2 Many comparatively rough blocks [of slate-rock] are refused by the contract men, and these are passed on to men and boys called cullers, who are paid a fixed price, and make as much out of them as they can.

† **2.** *Farming.* (See quots.) Cf. CULL *sb.*^{3} 2.

1538 ELYOT *Bibl., Reieculæ, uel reijculæ oues*, sheepe drawen out of the folde for aege or syckenesse, kebbers, crones, or cullyars. **1617** MINSHEU *Duct. Ling., Cullers.* **1721** BAILEY, *Cullers*, the worst sort of sheep, or those which are left of a flock when the best are picked out. *C[ountry Word].*

culler, obs. form of COLOUR.

cullery ('kʌlərɪ). *local.* [a. F. *cueillerie* action or product of collecting, f. *cueillir* to collect.] The name in Carlisle of a customary tenure of small copyhold tenements held from the Corporation at an annual rental. Also *attrib.*, as ***cullery tenure, tenant, rent***, etc.

See Nanson in *Trans. Cumbrld. & Westm. Antiq. Soc.* (1883) VI. II. 305 'On the customary Tenure at Carlisle called Cullery Tenure'.

1600 *Carlisle Audit-bk.* (Nanson), Item the rent of the cullerie or pettye farmes of the cittye. **1673** *Cullery Admittance Bks.*, Secundum consuetudinem vocatam coulerie. **1708** *Audit-bk.*, A Rentall of the Rentes belonging to the Corporation of Carlisle called Cullerie Rentes, as they are collected in the year one thousand seven hundred and eight. **1883** NANSON (as above) 309 It is clear that the term cullery rents in its widest signification included any small annual rents due to the Corporation.

cullet ('kʌlɪt). *Glass-making.* [A later form of COLLET *sb.*[1] 4; the name being extended from the 'necks' formed in glass-blowing to all refuse and broken glass melted over again to make inferior glass.] Broken or refuse glass with which the crucibles are replenished.

1817 C. ATTWOOD *Specif. of Patent* No. 4148 Cullet, or old or broken or waste glass. **1875** URE *Dict. Arts* II. 655 The pot is now ready for receiving the topping of cullet, which is broken pieces of window-glass to the amount of 3 or 4 cwts.

†**culli'bility.** *Obs.* Also -ability. [In form from CULLIBLE (of which, however, early instances have not yet been found).] The quality of being cullible; gullibility.

1728 SWIFT *Lett. to Pope* 16 July, Providence never designed him to be above two and twenty, by his thoughtlessness and cullibility. **1768** STERNE *Sent. Journ.* II. *Case of Conscience*, If there is not a fund of honest cullability in man so much the worse. **1807** OPIE *Lect. Art* iii. (1848) 308 Innocent cullibility on one part, and brutality and cunning on the other. **1837** *New Monthly Mag.* XLIX. 7 The coal-mines of Great Britain may possibly be some day exhausted, but its cullability never.

†'**cullible,** *a. Obs.* [This adj., which is presupposed in the derivative *cullibility* (known 1728), would normally be derived from a verb *cull*; but none such is recorded; cf. however CULL *sb.*[2], CULLY *v.*[2] *Gullible, gullibility*, from GULL *v.*, appear much later than *cullibility*.] Easily made a 'cull' or fool of; gullible.

1811 SHELLEY *Let.* 12 Jan. (1964) I. 45 Because men are & have been cullible, I see no reason why they shd. always continue so. **1822** HAZLITT *Table-t., Spirit of Partizanship* (1852) 276 These are lax and cullible in their notions of political warfare.

cullice, *v.*, to beat: see CULLIS.

cullinder, obs. form of COLANDER.

culling ('kʌlɪŋ), *vbl. sb.*[1] [f. CULL *v.*[1] + -ING[1].]

1. a. The action of selecting or picking.

c **1440** *Promp. Parv.* 107 Cullynge, or owte schesynge, *separacio, segregacio.* **1663** *Flagellum, or O. Cromwell* (1672) 70 The House being thus purged, as they called it..the remaining Juncto of his Culling..passed an Ordinance for Tryal of the King. **1878** NEWCOMB *Pop. Astron.* II. v. 225 This culling-out is called Selective Absorption.

b. The action of the verb (sense 4).

1938 *Times* 14 Feb. 20/1 Losses incurred through death and culling are commonly in the region of 30 per cent. **1958** *Times* 1 Nov. 9/4 Litters are bred on more sparing lines than formerly, which means that there are fewer surplus hounds, and the job of 'culling' or drafting is all the more difficult. **1964** C. WILLOCK *Enormous Zoo* vi. 102 The experimental shooting of hippo—culling is the polite conservation term for it—had begun. **1978** *Orcadian* 31 Aug. 1/2 There was no British firm that could take on the two-year contract for the culling work. **1986** *Daily Tel.* 28 Apr. 11/8 In staghunting and deer culling, the sex of the prey is selected carefully.

2. *concr.* The proceeds or residue of culling; a selection; *pl.* portions drafted out.

1692 A. WALKER *Acc. Icon Basilike* 32 (L.) That the Lord Fairfax would take anything out of the cabinet, and send up the cullings to the parliament. **1780** BRODHEAD in Sparks *Corr. Amer. Rev.* (1853) II. 449 The remaining Continentals are the cullings of our troops, and I cannot promise anything clever from them. **1865** *Reader* 5 Aug. 144/3 A passage like the following reads more like a culling from the Oxford 'Lives of the Saints'.

3. *Farming.* See quots. and cf. CULL *sb.*[3] 2, CULLER 2. Also *attrib.*

1611 COTGR., *Brebis de rebut*, an old or diseased sheepe thats not worth keeping; wee call such a one, a drape, or culling. **1627** DRAYTON *Nymphidia* vi. 1496 (L.) My cullings I put off, or for the chapman feed. **1652** S. CLARKE *Lives* (1677) 334 To leave the cullen sheep in a hard condition. *a* **1796** VANCOUVER in A. Young *Ess. Agric.* (1813) II. 284 An assemblage of the refuse stock, and cullings of the adjacent ..counties. **1879** MISS JACKSON *Shropshire Word-bk.*, *Cullings*, the residue, as of a flock of fatted sheep, of which the best have been picked out.

4. *Comb.* **culling-iron**, a long-handled slender hammer, with which the mature oysters are separated from the object on which they have been deposited.

1891 *Scribner's Mag.* Oct. 482.

†'**culling,** *vbl. sb.*[2] *Obs.* or *dial.* [f. CULL *v.*[2]] Embracing, 'cuddling'.

1490 CAXTON *Eneydos* xviii. 69 By oure kyssynge and swete cullynge. **1601** HOLLAND *Pliny* I. 231 Such a culling and hugging of them they keep.

Cullins earth: see CULLEN, COLOGNE.

cullion ('kʌljən), Forms: 4 coillon, coylon, culyon, 4–5 colyoun, -on, coyllon, 6 colion, collion, -an, coulion, coillen, 7 cullian, culion, cullyen, cullen, 6–9 cullion. [a. F. *couillon* = Pr. *colho*, Sp. *cojon*, It. *coglione*, Romanic deriv. of L. *cōleus, culleus* bag, testicle, a. Gr. κόλεος sheath.]

†**1.** A testicle. *Obs.*

c **1386** CHAUCER *Pard. T.* 624, I wolde I hadde thy coillons [*v.r.* coylons, colyounnys, coyllons, culyons] in myn hond. **1481** CAXTON *Reynard* (Arb.) 22 His ryght colyon or balock stone. **1578** LYTE *Dodoens* II. lvi. 218 His rootes..are like to a payre of stones or Cullions. **1611** COTGR., *Animelles*, the stones, cods, or cullions of Lambes, etc. **1737** OZELL *Rabelais* II. xiv. 110.

†**2.** As a term of contempt: A base, despicable, or vile fellow; a rascal. *Obs.* Cf. F. *coïon, coyon* (Cotgr.).

15.. *Peebles to Play*, Where is yon cullion knave? **1575** J. STILL *Gammer Gurton* v. ii, It was that crafty cullion Hodge. **1593** SHAKS. *2 Hen. VI*, I. iii. 43 Away, base Cullions. **1617** COLLINS *Def. Bp. Ely* 553 Thou shalt be censured for a cullian and a wretch. *a* **1652** BROME *City Wit* IV. ii, Thou Cullion, could not thine own cellar serve thee, but thou must be sneaking into Court butteries? **1843** LYTTON *Last Bar.* I. xi, Out on ye, cullions and bezonians!

†**3.** *Fortif.* 'That part of a bulwarke which engineers call the pome, the gard, the shoulder or eares to couer the casamats' (Florio 1611, s.v. *Orecchione*).

1589 IVE *Fortif.* 12 Which cullion or orechion may be made longer and shorter according to the will of the workman.

4. *pl.* A popular name of plants of the genus *Orchis* (or allied genera), from the form of the tubers or 'roots'.

1611 COTGR., *Couillon de chien*, Dogs-stones, Dogs cullions. **1640** PARKINSON *Theat. Bot.* ix. 1341 Satyrion and Orchis. Cullions or Stones. *Ibid.* xiii. 1354 Sweete Cullions. **1776** J. LEE *Introd. Bot.* (ed. 3) 330 Soldier's Cullions, Orchis. **1879** PRIOR *Plant-n.* (ed. 3) 60.

b. The paired tubers of Orchis.

1688 R. HOLME *Armoury* II. 115/1 Cullions, or Stone-roots [are] round roots, whether single, double, or trebble. **1721** in BAILEY; and in later Dicts.

5. *Comb.*, as ***cullion-like*** adj. (sense 2); †**cullion-head** (*Fortif.*).

1591 HARINGTON *Orl. Fur.* XXV. xxv, For what could be more cullenlike or base? **1601** DEACON & WALKER *Spirits & Divels* To Rdr. 10 To desist from those cullion-like courses. **1656** BLOUNT *Glossogr.*, *Cullion-head*, see *Bastian*.

¶ Used by confusion for *cullin* = CULLING.

c **1640** J. SMYTH *Lives Berkeleys* (1883) I. 156 The eldest of the sheep were drawne out as Cullions. [Cf. quot. **1652** s.v. CULLING[1] 3, and **1887** *S. Cheshire Gloss.*, *Cullins*, the worst sheep of a flock.]

†'**cullionly,** *a. Obs.* [f. CULLION 2 + -LY[1].] Like a cullion; rascally, base, despicable.

1605 SHAKS. *Lear* II. ii. 36 You whoreson Cullyenly Barber-monger, draw. **1645** MILTON *Colast.* (1851) 368 His cullionly paraphrase on St. Paul. **1822** SCOTT *Nigel* xii, He would be held a cullionly niggard.

†'**cullionry.** *Obs.* In 7 cullionnerie, cullionrie. [f. as prec. + -RY, -ERY.] The behaviour of a cullion; base rascally conduct.

1611 COTGR., *Coyonnerie*, base roguerie, cowardise, cullionnerie. **1648** R. BAILLIE *Lett. & Jrnls.* (1841) III. 36 Argyle's enemies had..burdened him, among many slanders, with that of cowardice and cullionrie.

cullis ('kʌlɪs), *sb.*[1] Now *rare*. Forms: 5 colys, kolys, culys, colysshe, 5–6 colice, 5–7 coleys(e, culice, 6 colesse, collesse, -yse, culleis, -ace, -ys, -cooliz, 6–7 cullice, -ess(e, 6–8 cullise, 7 collice, cullisse, -ies, -asse, -aze, culisse, coolisse, coollis, 6– cullis. [a. OF. *coleïs* (13th c., later *couleïs, coulis*), subst. use of *coleïs*:—L. type **cōlātīcius*, f. *cōlāre* to strain, flow through, glide, etc.]

A strong broth, made of meat, fowl, etc., boiled and strained; used especially as a nourishing food for sick persons. 'Beef-tea' is a well-known form.

c **1420** *Liber Cocorum* 20 For a kolys þe brawne take of sothun henne or chekyne [etc.]. *c* **1460** J. RUSSELL *Bk. Nurture* 824 Colice of pike, shrympus or perche. **1543** TRAHERON *Vigo's Chirurg.* IX. 228 If the pacient be weake.. ye shall gyve hym the coleys of a yonge capon. **1584** LYLY *Campaspe* III. v, He that melteth in a consumption is to be recured by colices, not conceits. **1662** H. STUBBE *Ind. Nectar* vii. 165 The meat, out of which all the strength is Boil'd or Pressed in Jellies and Cullices. **1796** MRS. GLASSE *Cookery* Pref. 1 Use for a cullis, a leg of veal and a ham. **1853** SOYER *Pantroph.* 76 Take onions..thicken with cullis, oil, and wine.

†**b.** *transf.* and *fig.* (In quot. 1719 app. = a sound beating; cf. quot. 1625 and CULLIS *v.*).

1580 LYLY *Euphues* (Arb.) 356 Expecting thy Letter eyther as a Cullise to preserue, or as a sworde to destroy. **1608** MIDDLETON *Fam. Love* III. ii, Get a cullis to your capacity, a restorative to your reason. *a* **1625** FLETCHER *Nice Valour* III. i, He has beat me e'en to a Cullis. **1719** D'URFEY *Pills* II. 112 A Cullise for the Back too.

cullis ('kʌlɪs), *sb.*[2] *Arch.* Also killis, killesse. [a. F. *coulisse* furrow, groove, gutter, etc., subst. use of fem. of *coulis* adj.: see prec. and COULISSE.] A gutter, groove, or channel. Also *attrib.*, as ***cullis roof*** (see quot. 1875).

1838 BRITTON *Dict. Archit.* 216 *Cullis*, a gutter in a roof; a groove or channel. **1849** *Jrnl. R. Agric. Soc.* X. I. 178 Placed in a barn or ricked in some exposed part with cullis roof, where it will keep dry. **1875** PARKER *Concise Gloss. Archit.*, *Killesse*, also *Cullis, Coulisse* (Fr.), a gutter, groove, or channel..This term is in some districts corruptly applied to a hipped roof by country carpenters, who speak of a killessed or cullidged roof. A dormer window is also sometimes called a killesse or cullidge window.

¶ See also KILLESSE, -ESE.

†'**cullis,** *v. Obs. rare.* [f. CULLIS *sb.*[1] (b).] *trans.* To 'beat to a jelly', beat severely.

1632 CHAPMAN & SHIRLEY *Ball* IV. ii, Quit thy father..or Ile cullice thee With a battoun.

cullisance, -sen, -son, -zan, obs. corruptions of COGNIZANCE ('kɒnɪzəns), a badge, etc.

1599 B. JONSON *Ev. Man out of Hum.* I. i, I'll keep men .. and I'll give coats..but I lack a cullisen. **1609** —— *Case is Altered* IV. iv, But what badge shall we give, what cullison? **1611** *Tarlton's Jests* (1844) 12 Clapping my Lord Shandoyes cullisance upon my sleeve. **1618** DEKKER *Owles Alm.* 36 A blew coat without a Cullizan.

cullom-, cullum-: see COL-.

cullum, var. COOLUNG.

cullurune, var. CULROUN, *Obs. Sc.*

cully ('kʌlɪ), *sb. slang* or *colloq.* Now *rare*. [Orig. slang or rogues' cant, of uncertain origin.

Connexion has been suggested with CULLION or its Ital. cognate *coglione* 'a noddie, a foole, a patch, a dolt; a cuglion, a gull, a meacocke' (Florio). Leland thinks it of Gypsy origin, comparing Sp. Gypsy *chulai* man, Turkish Gypsy *khulai* gentleman.]

1. One who is cheated or imposed upon (*e.g.* by a sharper, strumpet, etc.); a dupe, gull; one easily deceived or taken in; a silly fellow, simpleton. (Much in use in the 17th c.)

1664 BUTLER *Hud.* II. ii. 781 Women, that.. Brought in.. Their Husbands Cullies, and Sweet-hearts. **1687** SEDLEY *Bellamira* I. i, I'll..shew her I am not such a cully as she takes me for. *a* **1720** J. HUGHES in *Duncombe's Lett.* (1773) III. App. xxxvii, The wit is always the cully of the heart. **1751** SMOLLETT *Per. Pic.* (1779) II. lvi. 147 The French syren was baulked in her design upon her English cully. **1833** CARLYLE *Misc.* (1872) V. 89 Cullies, the easy cushion on which Knaves and Knavesses repose, have at all times existed. **1881** SWINBURNE in *Fortn. Rev.* Feb. 133 The whimper of a cheated cully.

attrib. **1678** BUTLER *Hud.* III. *Heroic. Epist.* 168 Why should you..B'allow'd to put all tricks upon Our Cully-Sex, and we use none? **1702** DE FOE *Reform. Manners* I. 308 The Cully Merchant.

2. A man, fellow; a companion, mate.

1676 *Warn. for Housekeepers* 5 If the cully nap us. **1861** MAYHEW *Lond. Lab.* (ed. 2) III. 57 (Hoppe) The showman inside the frame says..'Culley, how are you getting on?' **1888** *New York Mercury* (Farmer, *Americanisms*), What's yer hurry, cully?

†'**cully,** *v.*[1] *Obs. rare*[−1]. [app. related to CULL *v.*[2]: cf. CULYE.] = CULL *v.*[2]

1576 *Tyde Tarryeth no Man*, Ione is pleasaunt, to kisse, and to cully.

†**cully,** *v.*[2] *Obs.* [f. CULLY *sb.* Cf. It. *coglionare*, 'to cosin, to cog, to foist, to deceiue' (Florio).] *trans.* To make a fool of, deceive, cheat, take in.

1676 *Life of Muggleton* in *Harl. Misc.* I. 610 Having for some time being cullied out of his money. **1699** POMFRET *Poems, Divine Attributes*, Tricks to cully fools. **1702** POPE *Wife of Bath* 161 Heaven gave to woman the peculiar grace To spin, to weep, and cully human race. **1768** *Woman of Honour* I. 150 Being..cullied by drabs whom their footmen might disdain.

cullyandre, cullyar, cullyen, obs. ff. COLANDER, CULLER, CULLION.

†**cullyism** ('kʌlɪɪz(ə)m). *Obs. nonce-wd.* [f. CULLY *sb.* + -ISM.] The condition of a cully.

1712 STEELE *Spect.* No. 486 ¶2 Instances of eminent Cullyism.

culm[1] (kʌlm). In 5–6 culme, 7 colme. [The same word as COOM *sb.*[1], pointing to a ME. *culm, colm*. Connexion with *col*, COAL, suggests itself, and is strengthened by the synonymy of ME. *bicolmen, bicollen*, the former a deriv. of *colm, culm*, the latter of *colwen*, from *col*, COAL: cf. BECOOM (BE- 6 a) COLLOW, COLLY. But the actual analysis of the word is obscure.]

1. Soot, smut. *Obs.* exc. *Sc.*; = COOM *sb.*[1] I.

c **1440** *Promp. Parv.* 108 Culme of smeke, *fuligo.* **1565** GOLDING *Ovid's Met.* II. (1593) 34 Againe the culme and smouldring smoke did wrap him round about. **1658** PHILLIPS, *Culm*, smoak or soot. Hence in KERSEY, BAILEY, etc. [in both noted as *Obs.*]. **1847–8** H. MILLER *First Impr.* iv. (1857) 48 A mud-coloured atmosphere of smoke and culm. **1861** CLINGTON *Frank O'Donnell* 171 My face and body all covered with culm..made him take me for the devil.

2. Coal-dust, small or refuse coal, slack.

[**1348** in *Nottingham Rec.* I. 144 Praedictam dimidiam partem minerae carbonum marinorum et culmorum.] **1603** OWEN *Pembrokeshire* (1891) 70 In this kill first is made a fier of Coales or rather colme which is but the duste of the coales. *Ibid.* 91 A smaler Ridle with which they drawe smale coales for the smythes from the colme which is in deede but verie dust, which serveth for lyme burninge. **1703** *Lond. Gaz.* No. 3892/1 An Act for continuing the Duties upon Coles, Culm, and Cynders [= Coke]. **1770–4** A. HUNTER *Georg. Ess.* (1803) III. 149 Culm, or small refuse coal. **1799** KIRWAN *Geol. Ess.* 298 At Whitehaven, under a bed of common clay ..a bed of natural clayey carbon or culm of 3 fathom is found. **1882** *Brit. Q. Rev.* Jan. 87, 4*s.* per ton for culm, or coal-dust.

b. Hence, *spec.* applied to the slack of anthracite or stone-coal, from the Welsh collieries, which was in common use for burning lime and drying malt.

1736 BAILEY *Househ. Dict.* 397. **1756** BP. POCOCKE *Trav.* (1889) II. 188 The coals here [Tenby]..run into culm, which they work up with clay, and make it into balls; it is very good fuel. **1769** *De Foe's Tour Gt. Brit.* II. 366 The County of Pembroke abounds particularly in that Sort of Coal called *Stone Coal*, the small Pieces of which are stiled *Culm.* **1806** MARTIN in *Phil. Trans.* XCVI. 344. **1849** *Jrnl. R. Agric. Soc.* X. I. 149 Culm is the dust of the stone-coal, and is prepared for burning by being mixed with clay or mud from the shore. **1883** A. WILLIAMS *Min. Resources U.S.* 31 A mixture of anthracite slack, or 'culm', with bituminous coal. **1888** ELWORTHY *W. Somerset Word-bk.*, *Culm*, the slack of non-bituminous or anthracite coal is known by no other name.

c. By extension, sometimes employed as a synonym of anthracite, or of one of its varieties, the slaty glance coal. Also in pl. *culms*, like *coals*.

1742 *Lond. & Country Brew.* I. (ed. 4) 8 There is another Sort, by some wrongly called Coak, and rightly named Culm or Welch-coal, from Swanzey in Pembrokeshire, being of a hard stony Substance, in small Bits..and will burn without Smoak. **1841** *Fossil Fuel*, etc. (ed. 2) 336 Varieties of Anthracite (2) The slaty glance-coal..This is the anthracite so abundant in the United States; the culm* of our Welsh collieries. *(*Note.* This is a brittle crumbling anthracite.) **1846** MᶜCULLOCH *Acc. Brit. Empire* (1854) I. 77 The coal.. on the western side being chiefly stone coal or culm, and on the eastern side, bituminous coking coal.

3. *Geol.* (More fully ***culm measures*** or ***series.***) A name given by some geologists to a series of shales, sandstones, etc. containing, in places, thin beds of impure anthracite, which represent the Carboniferous series in North Devon; also to strata supposed to be the analogues of these elsewhere.

The Culm series is generally considered to be contemporary with the Carboniferous limestone, but is much less rich in marine remains. It is extensively developed along the borders of Austria, Poland, and Russia; and includes the *calp* of Ireland.

[**1807** VANCOUVER *Agric. Devon* (1813) 54 Some years since a vein of culm appearing near the surface on the parish of Chittlehampton.] **1836** SEDGWICK & MURCHISON in *Brit. Assoc. Rep.* (1837) V. (*title*) A classification of..Rocks..of Devonshire..On the true position of the Culm Deposits. **1837** —— *Trans. Geol. Soc.* V. 670 The base of the culm series. *Ibid. Note*, The undoubted culm-measures. **1839** DE LA BECHE *Rep. Geol. Cornwall*, etc. 124 Anthracite, or culm, occurs in a few beds, of very variable thickness, between Greenacliff..and..Chittlehampton..The culm itself seems the result of irregular accumulations of vegetable matter intermingled with mud and sand. **1882** GEIKIE *Text-bk. Geol.* VI. iv. §2. 748.

†**4.** Applied (? in error) to coke; cf. quot. 1742 in 2 c. *Obs.*

1727 BRADLEY *Fam. Dict.* s.v. *Brewing*, Dry it leisurely with Pit-coal, char'd, called in some places coak and in others Culm. [Anthracite is a natural coke.]

†**5.** *attrib.* and *Comb.*, as ***culm-dealer***, ***-pit***, etc.

1755 *Gentl. Mag.* XXV. 447 There is also a culm pit, which was worked for fuel a few years ago. **1854** *Illust. Lond. News* 5 Aug. 118/3 Occupations of the People. Culm-dealer.

culm[2] (kʌlm). *Bot.* [ad. L. *culm-us* stalk, stem (*esp.* of grain).] The stem of a plant; *esp.* the jointed and usually hollow stalk of grasses.

1657 *Phys. Dict.*, *Culms*, stalks. **1794** MARTYN *Rousseau's Bot.* xiii. 139 Meadow Fescue..has a culm two feet high. **1854** HOOKER *Himal. Jrnls.* I. iii. 70 A kind of reed work formed of long culms of Saccharum.

Hence **culm** *v. intr.*, to form a culm; **culmed** *ppl. a.*, having a culm.

1860 MAYNE REID in *Chamb. Jrnl.* XIV. I The young maize..is rapidly culming upward. *a* **1862** THOREAU *Excursions, Autumnal Tints* (1863) 223 A very tall and slender-culmed grass.

†**culm**[3]. *Obs. rare.* Also 6 culme. [Shortened f. CULMEN.] The highest point, summit, culminating point.

1587 *Misfort. Arthur* III. iv. in Hazl. *Dodsley* IV. 313 Who strives to stand..On giddy top and culm of slippery court. **1600** HAKLUYT *Voy.* (1810) III. 194 The mountaines are.. seldome uncovered of snow, in their culme and highest tops. **1821** *Tales of my Landlord* (New Ser.), *Witch of Glas Llyn* II. 146 Three times will they be raised against his life. At the third his star will have reached its culm.

culm[4], var. COME *sb.*[2]

1940 in *Chambers's Techn. Dict.* 215/1. **1953** *Word for Word* (*Whitbread & Co.*) 17/1 *Culms* (or Coombes), the rootlets which are sieved from the malt at the end of the malting process; they are used for poultry and cattle food.

†**culmas, culmez, culmische.** *Sc. Obs.* Some kind of weapon, or rural implement used as a weapon.

1513 DOUGLAS *Æneis* XI. xiii. 72 He held in til his hand A rural club or culmas insteid of brand. **1535** STEWART *Cron. Scot.* II. 432 Sum with ane culmische clevin to the belt.

‖**culmen** ('kʌlmɛn). [L. *culmen*, contr. f. *columen* top, summit, roof-ridge, etc.]

1. *gen.* The top or summit; *fig.* the height, acme, culminating point.

1647 CRASHAW *Poems* 129 Chronology and history bear No other culmen than the double art Astronomy, geography impart. **1665** SIR T. HERBERT *Trav.* (1677) 227 At the culmen or top was a Chappel. *a* **1734** NORTH *Exam.* I. iii. §40 (1740) 145 The Culmen of this Historian's Art and Invention. **1856** DOBELL *Eng. in Time of War*, That top and culmen exquisite Whereto the slanting seasons meet. **1928** C. T. ONIONS in *Times* 19 Apr. 10/7 The Oxford English Dictionary is the culmen [of a series of lexicons].

2. *Ornith.* The upper ridge of a bird's bill.

1833 R. MUDIE *Brit. Birds* (1841) II. 34 Their bills being more curved in the culmen. **1874** COUES *Birds N.W.* 45 The bill..slender..with the culmen concave near the base.

3. *Anat.* 'The superior vermiform process of the cerebellum' (*Syd. Soc. Lex.* 1882).

cul'micolous, *a.* [f. L. *culmus* CULM[2] + *-cola* dwelling + -OUS.] 'Living on straw or the stems of graminaceous plants' (*Syd. Soc. Lex.* 1882). Said of some fungi.

culmiferous (kʌl'mɪfərəs), *a.*[1] *Geol.* [f. CULM[1] + -(I)FEROUS, after *carboniferous.*] Containing or producing culm or impure anthracite.

1837 SEDGWICK & MURCHISON in *Trans. Geol. Soc.* V. 670 In North Devon, the beds of the highest group..pass regularly under the base of the culmiferous rocks. *Ibid.* 664 The culmiferous series. **1841** TRIMMER *Pract. Geol.* 209 The culmiferous rocks of Devonshire.

cul'miferous, *a.*[2] *Bot.* [ad. L. type **culmifer* (f. *culmus* CULM[2] + *-fer* bearing) + -OUS.] Of grasses: Having a jointed hollow stalk.

1704 RAY in Harris *Lex. Techn.*, *Plants* §23 *Culmiferous Plants* are such as have a smooth hollow jointed Stalk, with one long sharp-pointed Leaf at each Joint. **1707** SLOANE *Jamaica* I. 102 Herbs..which are culmiferous, are divided into those with large seeds, or Corns, and those with lesser seeds, called Grasses. **1862** BEVERIDGE *Hist. India* II. IV. v. 156 Among culmiferous plants the first place belongs to rice.

culmigenous (-'ɪdʒɪnəs), *a. rare.* [f. as prec. + *-gen-us* born, bearing + -OUS.] 'Produced or growing on straw' (*Syd. Soc. Lex.* 1882).

'culminal, *a. rare.* [f. L. *culmen*, stem *culmin-* (see above) + -AL[1].] Of or pertaining to the culmen or summit; apical.

1889 in *Century Dict.*

culminant ('kʌlmɪnənt), *a.* (and *sb.*). [ad. late L. *culminānt-em*, pr. pple. of *culmināre* to CULMINATE. Cf. mod.F. *culminant.*]

A. *adj.* **1.** Of a heavenly body: That has reached its greatest altitude, that is on the meridian; hence *fig.* that is at its greatest height.

1605 CAMDEN *Rem.* (1637) 358 The whole constellation of Ariadnes crowne, culminant in her nativity. **1658** WILLSFORD *Natures Secrets* 35 When any Star is upon the Meridian, it is said to be culminant; and..is then of most force to that place. **1684** *Observator* No. 129 In the very Lust and Vigour of the Phanatical Conspiracy, when Oates was Culminant. **1824** COLERIDGE in *Lit. Rem.* (1836) II. 411 The superstition of the letter was then culminant. **1875** BLACKMORE *A. Lorraine* I. vii. 41 A softer and more genial star was culminant one evening.

2. Reaching the greatest height, forming the summit or highest point, topmost.

1849 DANA *Geol.* vii. (1850) 420 Islands are but the culminant peaks of mountains. **1854** HOOKER *Himal. Jrnls.* I. i. 22 The culminant rocks are very dry.

†**B.** *sb.* A culminant star (in quot. *fig.*). *Obs.*

1654 WHITLOCK *Zootomia* 288 The..Culminant in a Princes favour, takes all the Honour from the Lord of his Ascending.

culminate ('kʌlmɪneɪt), *v.* [f. late L. *culmi-nāt-*, ppl. stem of *culmināre*, f. *culmen*, *culmin-* (see above); see -ATE, and cf. mod.F. *culminer.*]

1. *intr. Astron.* Of a heavenly body: To reach its greatest altitude, to be on the meridian.

1647 LILLY *Chr. Astrol.* clvi. 649 If the Luminary culminate. **1667** MILTON *P.L.* III. 617 All Sun-shine, as when his Beams at Noon Culminate from th' Æquator. **1879** LOCKYER *Elem. Astron.* iv. 158 To find the time at which any star culminates, or passes the meridian.

2. *gen.* To reach its highest point or summit, as a mountain-chain, etc.; to rise to an apex or summit. Const. *in.*

1665 [see CULMINATING *ppl. a.*]. *a* **1770** C. SMART *Hop Garden* I. (R.), While above Th' embow'ring branches culminate, and form A walk impervious to the sun. **1833** MARRYAT *P. Simple* xv, At which distance the enormous waves culminated and fell with the report of thunder. **1869** RAWLINSON *Anc. Hist.* 16 The mountain system [of Armenia] culminates in Ararat.

3. *fig.* (Chiefly from 1.) To reach its acme, or highest development. Const. *in, to.*

a **1662** HEYLIN *Life of Laud* (1668) 155 Being once in the Ascendent, [he] presumed that he should culminate before his time. **1837** CARLYLE *Fr. Rev.* I. I. i. 3 Thus D'Aiguillon rose again and culminated. **1854** EMERSON *Lett. & Soc. Aims, Eloquence* Wks. (Bohn) III. 195 All the genius ran in that direction, until it culminated in Shakspeare. **1855** MOTLEY *Dutch Rep.* II. v. (1866) 233 The uneasiness, the terror, the wrath of the people, seemed rapidly culminating to a crisis. **1875** HELPS *Anim. & Mast.* viii. 195 There are times when Art seems to culminate and then to descend. **1878** HUXLEY *Physiogr.* 196 These disturbances culminated in the great eruption of A.D. 79.

4. *trans.* To bring (a thing) to its highest point, to form the summit of; to crown.

1659 R. EEDES *Christ's Exaltation* 35 That's the altitude, the very apex that culminates a believer's happiness. **1675** OGILBY *Brit.* Ded., May the same Influences tend to the Culminating all other Arts. **1896** EARL OF ROSEBERY in *Westm. Gaz.* 12 Sept. 5/1 This brings to a head and culminates all the nameless massacres in Asia Minor. **1904** *Illustrated Bee* (Omaha) 25 Sept., A romance extending over several years was culminated. **1927** *Daily Express* 25 Apr. 1/5 They decided that an immediate ceremony would culminate their childhood romance.

'culminate, *a.* [ad. late L. *culmināt-us*, pa. pple. of *culmināre*: see prec.] 'Growing upward, as distinguished from a lateral growth; applied to the growth of corals' (Dana).

1864 in WEBSTER.

'culminating ('kʌlmɪneɪtɪŋ), *vbl. sb.* [f. CULMINATE *v.* + -ING[1].] The action of reaching the highest point; culmination. Often *attrib.*, as in ***culminating point***, point of culmination.

1726 tr. *Gregory's Astron.* I. 265 The same Index will likewise shew the culminating, rising or setting of a given Star. **1850** GLADSTONE *Glean.* V. clxvii. 270 The culminating point of the Supremacy was in the reign of Edward VI.

'culminating, *ppl. a.* [-ING[2].] That culminates; that attains to the greatest elevation.

1662 EVELYN *Chalcogr.* 106 The culminating, or declining sun. **1665** SIR T. HERBERT *Trav.* (1677) 202 The most culminating pyco or top [of Ararat]. **1727** PITT *Horace's Odes* I. xxii. (R.), Where I may view without a shade The culminating sun. **1853** KANE *Grinnell Exp.* xix. (1856) 142 The culminating peak of the northern abutment.

b. *fig.*

1654 WHITLOCK *Zootomia* 260 There is..no culminating Writer..so lofty as out of the reach of Imitation. **1853** RUSKIN *Stones Ven.* II. vi, The Gothic schools exhibited that love [of variety] in culminating energy.

culmination (kʌlmɪ'neɪʃən). [n. of action from CULMINATE *v.*; cf. F. *culmination.*]

1. The attainment by a heavenly body of its greatest altitude; the act of reaching the meridian.

lower or ***upper culmination***: the attainment of least or greatest altitude on any day.

1633 GELLIBRAND in T. James *Voy.* R iij, At the instant of the Moones Culmination or Mediation of Heauen. **1788** SMEATON in *Phil. Trans.* LXXIX. 2 Adjustment..to answer the culmination of any of the heavenly bodies. **1856** KANE *Arct. Expl.* I. viii. 79 The sun's lower culmination, if such a term can be applied to his midnight depression.

2. *fig.* The attainment of the highest point, or state of being at the height; *concr.* that in which anything culminates, the crown or consummation.

1657 FARINGDON *Serm.* 429 (T.) We..wonder how that which in its putting forth was a flower, should in its growth and culmination become a thistle. **1844** EMERSON *Lect. Yng. Amer.* Wks. (Bohn) II. 296 The uprise and culmination of the new..power of Commerce. **1865** LECKY *Ration.* (1878) I. 253 This fresco may be regarded as the culmination of the movement.

3. The raising of the level of the land on either side of a river by allowing flood-water to deposit silt on it. [Cf. It. *colmare* vb.]

1838 F. MACERONI *Mem.* II. 62 The process of culmination is particularly successful if practised high up a river much liable to winter floods.

4. *Geol.* **a.** (Also ***culmination of pitch.***) A part of a fold, esp. a nappe, where the strata were at their highest before they were eroded. **b.** An axis of a system of folds joining the highest parts of successive folds.

1927 L. W. COLLET *Struct. Alps* II. i. 27 Windows generally originate..on culminations of pitch. *Ibid.*, The windows of the Lower Engadine and of the Tauern are due to culminations of the substratum. **1942** M. P. BILLINGS *Struct. Geol.* iii. 49 Culminations and depressions trend essentially at right angles to the trend of the folds; the folds plunge away from culminations toward depressions. **1944** A. HOLMES *Princ. Phys. Geol.* xviii. 392 The nappes..are found to undulate up and down in an alternating succession of broad culminations and depressions. **1965** *Ibid.* (ed. 2) xxx. 1157 (*caption*) Mt. Blanc (15,782 feet) the highest culmination of the Hercynian massifs. **1966** *McGraw-Hill Encycl. Sci. & Technol.* XIII. 408/1 In the culminations, where the higher strata have been removed by erosion, the structure of the lower strata may be seen in the deep valleys.

'culmy, *a.* Also 4 colmie, -omy. [f. CULM[1] + -Y.]

†**1.** Blackened or begrimed with soot: = COOMY.

a **1300** *K. Horn* 1082 He lokede him a-bute Wiþ his colmie snute. **1377** LANGL. *P. Pl.* B. XIII. 356 Thanne pacience parceyued of poyntes [of] his cote, Was colmy [*v.r.* culmy, colomy] þorw coueityse and vnkynde desyrynge.

2. Of the nature of or abounding in culm, as ***culmy beds*** or ***deposits.***

†**cu'lorum.** *Obs.* [Known only in Langland; according to Herbert Coleridge (*Trans. Philol. Soc.* 1860) probably the last syllables of *in sæcula sæculorum* 'for ever and ever', the concluding words of the *Gloria Patri*; Mätzner suggests a corruption of L. *corollarium* COROLLARY.] The conclusion, corollary, or 'moral'.

1362 LANGL. *P. Pl.* A. III. 264 Þe Culorum of þis clause [*B. and C.* cas] kepe I not to schewe. **1377** *Ibid.* B. x. 409 Þe culorum of þis clause curatoures is to mene. **1399** —— *Rich. Redeles* Prol. 72 And constrewe ich clause with þe culorum. *Ibid.* IV. 61 No blame serued..Ho so toke good kepe to þe culorum.

‖**culot** (kylo). [F., dim. of *cul*: see above.]

†**a.** A stand for a crucible in the furnace. †**b.** The heavy mass which falls to the bottom of a crucible. **c.** A little cup of sheet-iron inserted into the hollow base of the Minié and other

projectiles, so as to be driven into the ball and enlarge its diameter, when fired.

1683 SALMON *Doron Med.* I. 317 Place a Crucible upon a Culot in the middle of a Hearth-place in a Wind Furnace. **1727** BRADLEY *Fam. Dict.* s.v. *Essence*, Separate the Dross from the Culot in the Bottom. **1854** CAPT. NORTON in *Mech. Mag.* LXII. 38 For putting an iron cup or culôt into the hollow base of this shot.

culotte (kjuːˈlɒt, ‖kylɔt). [Fr., = knee-breeches; cf. SANSCULOTTE.]

1. Knee-breeches; also *culotte courte*. (Rare in Eng. use.)

1842 BARHAM *Ingol. Leg.* II. 11 Ripping the lace from his coat, And from what, I suppose, I must call his *culotte*. **1848** THACKERAY *Van. Fair* xlv. 408 She said that it was only the thorough-bred gentleman that could wear the Court suit with advantage: it was only your men of ancient race whom the *culotte courte* became. **1877** *Encycl. Brit.* VI. 472/2 Towards the beginning of the 17th century, the high hose.. were transformed into 'culottes', which were full and open at the knees. **1952** *Granta* 29 Nov. 6/1 We may hire the appropriate wigs and culottes from London costumiers.

2. (Usually in *pl.*). A divided skirt. Also *attrib.*

1911 in C. W. Cunnington *Eng. Women's Clothing* (1952) iii. 105 Satin culottes, 10/6. **1927** *Delineator* Mar. 15 The culotte skirt, which originally made its début as a novelty, is translated this spring into practical fashions. **1939** A. KEITH *Land below Wind* ix. 148, I was still fastening my culottes, into which I had hastily jumped. **1939** M. B. PICKEN *Lang. Fashion* 40/3 *Culotte*, informal trouser-like garment having leg portions that are full and fall together to simulate a skirt. Worn as sports skirt. **1960** *Harper's Bazaar* July 55 A daring revival from the thirties—the culotte.. wide pyjama-legged culottes. **1966** *Vogue* Dec. 87 Beautiful culotte dress. **1967** *Guardian* 5 Aug. 5/1 Culotte skirts.. and culotte dresses abound.

3. The soft hair or feather on the back of the forelegs of a dog.

1928 in *Funk's Stand. Dict.* **1948** C. L. B. HUBBARD *Dogs in Britain* 462 *Culotte*, the fringes of soft hair on the backs of the fore-legs of Pomeranians. **1968** H. HARMAR *Chihuahua Guide* 235 *Culotte*, the feathery tail on the back of the forelegs of the Pekingese, Pomeranian and Schipperke.

culottic (kjuːˈlɒtɪk), *a. nonce-wd.* [f. F. *culotte* breeches + -IC after SANSCULOTTIC.] Wearing breeches, respectable, as opposed to *sansculottic*. So **cuˈlottism**.

1837 CARLYLE *Fr. Rev.* II. VI. iii, Young Patriotism, Culottic and Sansculottic, rushes forward emulous. *Ibid.* III. v. ii, Let the guilty tremble therefore, and the suspect, and the rich, and in a word all manner of Culottic men. *Ibid.* III. VII. i, Sansculottism.. having now got deep enough, is to perish in a new singular system of Culottism and arrangement. *Ibid.* III. VII. vi, Garnitures, formulas, culottisms of what sort soever.

culp, obs. Sc. form of CUP.

†**culp(e**. *Obs.* Also 4–5 cope, coupe, 5–6 coulpe. [a. OF. *coulpe* (*colpe*, *culpe*, *coupe*, *cope*), f. L. *culpa* fault, blame.

After the Fr. word had regularly become *coupe*, the *l* was restored from Latin, and was at length pronounced.]

Guilt, sin, fault, blame.

[**1292** BRITTON I. xxix. §3 Par sa coupe ou par sa negligence.] **1377** LANGL. *P. Pl.* B. v. 305 And kaires hym to-kirke-ward his coupe to schewe. *c* **1386** CHAUCER *Pars. T.* ¶261 Baptisme.. which bynymeþ vs þe culpe. **1483** CAXTON *G. de la Tour* I vj, Sayeng that she had no culpe of this dede. *c* **1489** —— *Blanchardyn* xxii. 74 Thourgh the coulpe of a knyght. **1513** HEN. VIII in Strype *Eccl. Mem.* I. App. iii. 6 We do not impute the culp and blame thereof in any person. **1549** *Compl. Scot.* xvii. 155 The coulpe of our synnis. **1601** Q. ELIZ. in *Harl. Misc.* (Malh.) II. 354, I hope God will not lay their culps to my charge.

culpability (kʌlpəˈbɪlɪtɪ). [f. next + -ITY. So mod.F. *culpabilité*, instead of OF. *coupableté*.] The quality of being culpable.

1675 BAXTER *Cath. Theol.* II. II. 30[It] may be said that God indeed is some cause of that, without culpability. **1791** BOSWELL *Johnson* 2 Apr. an. 1779, Amongst various acts of culpability he mentioned evil-speaking. **1875** JOWETT *Plato* (ed. 2) V. 138 The degree of culpability depends on the presence or absence of intention.

culpable (ˈkʌlpəb(ə)l), *a.* (and *sb.*). Forms: 4–5 coupable, (4 -abile, -aple, cupabil, 4–5 cowpable), 4–5 culpabil(l, 4–6 coulpable, 4– culpable. [ME. *coupable*, a. OF. *coupable* (*cop-*, *coulpable*, *culpable*, etc.) guilty:—L. *culpābil-is* blameworthy, f. *culpa* fault, blame. The OF. was regularly reduced to *coupable* in 13th c., but was frequently written *culpable* after L. in 14th c., *coulpable* in 16th c.; the latinized form has in Eng. been established both in spelling and pronunciation.]

1. Guilty, criminal; deserving punishment or condemnation. *Obs.* (or blended with sense 2.)

1303 R. BRUNNE *Handl. Synne* 1331 3yf þou.. Fordost pore mannys sustynaunce þat aftyrwarde he may nat lyve þou art coupable. **1377** LANGL. *P. Pl.* B. XVII. 300 Any creature þat is coupable afor a kynges iustice. **1483** CAXTON *Cato* E j b, How be it that they ben gylty and culpable. **1573** BP. OF PETERBORO in Ellis *Orig. Lett.* II. 196 III. 35 If thei be able justelie.. to finde him culpable. **1661** BRAMHALL *Just Vind.* ii. 22 Meer Schisme.. a culpable rupture or breach of the Catholick communion. **1778** BP. LOWTH *Isaiah* Notes (ed. 12) 343 The inflictor of the punishment may perhaps be as culpable as the sufferer. **1844** THIRLWALL *Greece* VIII. lxii. 151 He was considered at Thebes as culpable.

b. Const. *of*, †*in* (an offence, sin, wrong, etc.).

a **1340** HAMPOLE *Psalter* xxxiv. 13 þai wild haf made me culpabil of syn. *c* **1380** WYCLIF *Wks.* (1880) 312 We ben coupable in þis synne. **1428** *Surtees Misc.* (1890) 8 He was gylty and coulpabyll of all yᵉ trespasse. **1545** BRINKLOW *Compl.* iii. (1874) 14 What can the pore wyfe.. do witthall, being not culpable in the cryme? **1653** H. COGAN tr. *Pinto's Trav.* lvi. 220 They had found themselves culpable of gluttony. **1839** JAMES *Louis XIV*, I. 222 The greatest crime of which a man could render himself culpable.

†**c.** *culpable of* (*punishment, death, judgement*, etc.): deserving, liable to. Also, *culpable to be judged*, etc. (see first quot.).

c **1380** WYCLIF *Serm.* Sel. Wks. I. 16 Sich is coupable aȝens God to be jugid to helle. *Ibid.*, þat man, as Crist seiþ, is coupable of þe fier of helle. *c* **1450** *Mirour Saluacioun* 4570 He is of the deth coupable. **1557** N. T. (Genev.) *Matt.* v. 21 Whosoeuer killeth, shal be culpable of iudgement. **1612** T. TAYLOR *Comm. Titus* i. 7 Culpable of iudgement. **1612** W. SCLATER *Minister's Portion* 45 [Which] makes the offender culpable of death.

2. Deserving blame or censure, blameworthy.

[*c* **1386** CHAUCER *Melib.* ¶575 þe lawe saith þat he is coupable þat entremettith him or mellith him with such þing as aperteyneþ not vnto him.] **1613** R. C. *Table Alph.* (ed. 3), *Culpable*, blame-worthy, guiltie. **1651** HOBBES *Leviath.* I. viii. 33 What circumstances make an action laudable, or culpable. **1789** BELSHAM *Ess.* I. i. 7 Those inclinations.. they know to be highly culpable and unworthy. **1875** J. CURTIS *Hist. Eng.* 146 With great and culpable disregard to the public weal.

b. Artistically faulty or censurable. *rare.*

1768 W. GILPIN *Ess. Prints* 2 It [a print] may have an agreeable effect as a whole, and yet be very culpable in its parts. **1851** [see CULPABLENESS].

†**B.** *sb.* A guilty person, a culprit. *Obs.* [So F. *coupable*.]

1480 *Robt. Devyll* 720 in Hazl. *E.P.P.* I. 247 Euery vnthryftye culpable. **1483** CAXTON *Gold. Leg.* 411/3 He punysshed the culpables. **1651** tr. *De las-Coveras' Hist. Don Fenise* 209 If he could discover the infamous culpable. *a* **1734** NORTH *Lives* (1808) II. 246 (D.) Those only who were the culpables.

culpableness (ˈkʌlpəb(ə)lnɪs). In 4 coupabilnesse. [f. prec. + -NESS.] The quality or fact of being culpable: culpability.

c **1380** WYCLIF *Wks.* (1880) 335 Coupabilnesse of synne. **1648** W. MOUNTAGUE *Devout Ess.* 145 (T.) My culpablenes in those particulars. **1694** KETTLEWELL *Comp. Persecuted* 79 By any culpableness or unadvisedness of my own carriage. **1851** RUSKIN *Stones Ven.* III. i. §40. 26 To show the culpableness.. of our common modes of decoration by painted imitation of various woods or marbles.

ˈ**culpably**, *adv.* [f. as prec. + -LY.] In a culpable or blameworthy manner; to a culpable degree.

16.. JER. TAYLOR (J.), If we perform this duty pitifully and culpably. **1791** BOSWELL *Johnson* 25 June an. 1763 Culpably injurious to the merit of that bard. **1855** MACAULAY *Hist. Eng.* IV. 567 Culpably wanting in filial piety.

†ˈ**culpate**, *v. Obs. rare*⁻¹. [f. L. *culpāt-*, ppl. stem of *culpāre* to blame, f. *culpa* fault, blame.] *trans.* To blame, find fault with.

1548 HALL *Chron.* (1809) 422 They did.. much more culpate and blame his prevy Councellers.

So †**culˈpation**, 'a blaming, a finding fault' (Bailey vol. II. 1727).

ˈ**culpatory**, *a. rare.* [f. as prec. + -ORY.] Tending to or expressing blame.

1762–71 H. WALPOLE *Vertue's Anecd. Paint.* (1786) V. Postscript, If adjectives in *osus*, as famosus, &c. were not most commonly used by Latian authors in a culpatory sense. **1801** W. TAYLOR in *Monthly Mag.* XII. 588 Eloquent culpatory diatribes.

†**culpe**, *v. Obs. rare.* [a. OF. *colper*, *couper* to cut: see COUP *v.*², COPE *v.*²] *trans.* To cut, slice. (Cf. CULPON *v.*)

c **1430** *Two Cookery-bks.* 48 Take gode fat Ele, & culpe hym.

†ˈ**culpon**, *sb. Obs.* Forms: 4–5 culpoun, coulpon, 4– culpon, (5 colpon, 6 culpown, -in, -yn; *Sc.* 6–7 cowpon, coupon, 9 coopin. [a. OF. *colpon*, *coulpon*, *copon*, now *coupon*, cutting, cut, slice, piece, portion, f. *colper*, *coper*, *couper* to cut. The same word has been adopted from mod.Fr. in a special sense as COUPON.]

A piece cut off, a cutting; a portion, strip, slice, bit, shred.

c **1386** CHAUCER *Prol.* 679 This Pardoner hadde heer as yelow as wex.. But thynne it lay by colpons [*v.r.* culpouns] oon and oon. *c* **1400** *Ywaine & Gaw.* 642 Al to peces thai hewed thair sheldes, The culpons flegh out in the feldes. *c* **1450** *Two Cookery-bks.* 89 Take eles.. and choppe hem in faire colpons. **1548** HALL *Chron.* (1809) 635 Velvet embroudered with sundery knottes and culpyns of golde. **1563** WINȜET *Four Scoir Thre Quest.* §5 *margin*, Quhen thai cleik fra ws twa coupounis of our crede, tyme is to speik. **1590** BRUCE *Serm. Sacr.* B viij a, Suppose thou get a cowpon of him [thy sauior] in the sacrament, that cowpon wald do thee na good. **1825** JAMIESON, *Cowpon*.. in *pl.*, shatters, shivers: pronounced *coopins*.

†ˈ**culpon**, *v. Obs.* Also 6 coulpen, 7 *Sc.* coupon. [f. CULPON *sb.*]

1. *trans.* To cut into pieces, cut up, slice.

14.. *Anc. Cookery* 467 Take eles culponde and clene wasshen. **1513** *Bk. Keruynge* in *Babees Bk.* (1868) 265 Termes of a Keruer.. culpon that troute. **1567** DRANT *Horace's Ep.* II. i. F viij, He that did crowse and culpon once Hydra of hellish spyte. **1606** BIRNIE *Kirk-Buriall* (1833) 16 Superstition is lyke some serpents, that though they be couponed in many cuttes, yet they can keepe some lyfe in all.

2. To ornament or trim with strips or patches of a different-coloured material; sometimes, perhaps, to border with pieces of alternate colouring: see Godefroy, s.v. *componné*, *couponné*.

1577–87 HOLINSHED *Chron.* III. 820/1 The trappers of the coursers were mantell harnesse coulpened. *Ibid.* 858/1 A chemere, of cloath of silver, culponed with cloath of gold, of damaske, cantell wise.

culpose (kʌlˈpəʊs), *a. Roman Law.* [f. L. *culpa* fault of negligence or remissness + -OSE, after *dolose* (L. *dolōsus*).] Characterized by *culpa* or (criminal) negligence.

1832 AUSTIN *Jurispr.* (1879) II. 1103 Generally an act of forbearance or omission which is merely culpose (or not dolose) is not a crime or public delict. **1875** POSTE *Gaius* I. Comm. (ed. 2) 153 Not of dolose or intentional delicts, but only of culpose delicts, i.e. committed from negligence.

culprit (ˈkʌlprɪt). [Known (as a word) only from 1678. According to the legal tradition, found in print shortly after 1700, *culprit* was not originally a word, but a fortuitous or ignorant running together of two words (the fusion being made possible by the abbreviated writing of legal records), viz. Anglo-Fr. *culpable* or L. *culpabilis* 'guilty', abbreviated *cul.*, and *prit* or *prist* = OF. *prest* 'ready'. It is supposed that when the prisoner had pleaded 'Not guilty', the Clerk of the Crown replied with '*Culpable*: *prest d'averrer nostre bille*,', i.e. '*Guilty*: [and I am] *ready* to aver our indictment' ; that this reply was noted on the roll in the form *cul. prist, etc.*; and that, at a later time, after the disuse of law French, this formula was mistaken for an appellation addressed to the accused. (See note at end of this article.)]

1. *Law.* Used only in the formula 'Culprit, How will you be tried?' formerly said by the Clerk of the Crown to a prisoner indicted for high treason or felony, on his pleading 'Not guilty'.

Its first recorded use is in the Trial of the Earl of Pembroke for murder in 1678: it does not occur in the Trial of the Regicides 1662, nor in the various State Trials of 1663, 1664, 1669. Its original force was formally to join issue with the defendant's plea of 'Not guilty', and to demand trial and judgement; but this was perhaps forgotten in 1678.

1678 *State Trials* (1810) VI. 1320/2 (*Earl of Pembroke*) *Clerk of Crown.* Are you guilty, or not guilty? *Earl.* Not guilty. *Cl. of Cr.* Culprit, how will you be tryed? *Earl.* By my Peers. *Cl. of Cr.* God send you a good deliverance. **1683** *Tryal A. Sidney* (1684) 6. **1752** LOUTHIAN *Process Scotl.* 197 If the Prisoner answer not guilty, the Clerk saith, Culprist*, [(i.e.) *Culpabilis es, paratus sum verificare*] How wilt thou be tried?—and the Prisoner must answer,—By God and the Country.—Clerk saith, God send thee a good Deliverance.

2. Hence assumed to mean, Prisoner at the bar; he who is arraigned for a crime or offence; the accused.

1700 DRYDEN *Wife of Bath's T.* 273 Then first the culprit answered to his name. **1718** PRIOR *Solomon* Pref., An author is in the condition of a culprit: the public are his judges. **1832** W. IRVING *Alhambra* II. 197 'Well, culprit', said the governor.. 'What have you to say for yourself?' **1841** MACAULAY *W. Hastings* Ess. (1854) 649/2 But neither the culprit nor his advocates attracted so much notice as the accusers.

3. An offender, one guilty of a fault or offence.

[A change of sense, app. due to popular etymology, the word being referred directly to L. *culpa* fault, offence.]

1769 *Junius Lett.* xxii. 100 He had not rendered himself a culprit, too ignominious to sit in parliament. **1822** BYRON *Werner* III. iv, The fled Hungarian, Who seems the culprit. **1890** M. HOLROYD *Mem. G.E. Corrie* ii. 11 He.. always took care.. to send away the offender feeling himself to be a culprit not a martyr.

4. *attrib.*

1750 WHITEHEAD *Roman Father* Epil. (R.), Like other culprit youths, he wanted grace.

[*Note.* The legal tradition as to the origin of *culprit* is thus given:

1717 BLOUNT *Law Dict.* (ed. 3), *Culprit* is compounded of two words, *i.e.* *Cul* and *Prit*, viz. *Cul*, which is the Abbreviation of *Culpabilis*, and is a Reply of a proper Officer in the behalf of the King, affirming the Party to be guilty after he hath pleaded Not Guilty, without which the Issue is not joined: The other word *Prit* is derived from the French word *Prest*, *i.e.* ready; and 'tis as much as to say, That he is ready to prove the Party guilty. See also **1729–72** JACOB *New Law Dict.* s.v. **1765–8** BLACKSTONE *Comm.* IV. xxvi, and note thereon by CHRISTIAN (ed. 1795, p. 340). Also **1841–5** STEPHENS *Comm.* VI. xvii. (1883) 407.

This explanation is in accordance with the fact that the formula *prest* (*prist*) is of constant occurrence in mediæval procedure, to signify that the parties are ready to go to judgement on a point of law, or to trial on an issue of fact: see the old Year-books *passim*; e.g. *Year-book 35 Edw. I* (Rolls) 451 '*Herle.* La pasture de Strepham tut une e nent severe; prest. *Passeley.* Issi severe qe vous ne devez comuner outre les boundes, etc. prest. *Bereford* [Justice]. Vous estes a issue', etc. The force of *prest* further appears in *Year-bk. Michaelmas 12 Edw. III*, Plea 15 'Le defendant dit.. qe les blees furent sciez et emporte[z]; prest, etc.', where another MS. for 'prest, etc.' reads 'et demanda jugement'. Moreover *non cul prist* actually appears as an abbreviated form. In the *Liber Assisarum*, anno 22° Edw. I., placitum 41, we find in the report (*Livre des Assises*, 1679, p. 94) "*Bank.* Il semble que vous luy fistes tresp'.. Pur que r[espo]nd[ez]. *Richm.* [for *Defendant*] De rien culpable, prest daverrer nostre bill", etc. This, in Brooke's *Abridgement* (1568) fol. 7, Section *Accion sur le case*, Plea 78, is thus cited: "*Banke Justic.* Vous luy fist tort.. p' q' rñd'. *Richm.* non cul prist, etc.".]

‖**culrach, -reach** ('kʊlreːx). *Sc. Law. Obs.* Also **colrach, collerauch, -rayth, -reth, coleraith, culreauch.** [app. f. Ir. and Gael. *cul* back + *reachd* law, statute, ordinance.] A surety given to a court from which a cause is removed to another court, to be escheated if full justice is not rendered in the latter court. Required especially when a cause was removed to the court of a lord of regality.

c **1400** *Quoniam Attach.* viii. §4 Demittet ibidem vnum culrach scilicet vnum plegium quod plena lex tenebitur parti in curia domini sui. **1518** in Balfour *Practicks* (1754) 407 (Jam.) Offerand to that effect caution of Collerauch. **1571** in Pitcairn *Crim. Trials Scot.* I. 23 Comperit P.L. Knycht, Stewart within the said Regalitie, and desyrit the s[d] Mr. Robert to be replegeit from the s[d] Justice Court as duelland within the samin boundis; and offerit cautioune of Collerayth, as accordis. **1609** SKENE *Reg. Maj.* 107 He aught to leaue ane borgh, that is called Culreauch, behinde him in that Court, out of the quhilk the defender is borrowed. **1641** *Acts Chas. I*, V. 627 (Jam.) To give and find cautioun *de Collereth* for administratioun of justice. **1700** in R. CHAMBERS *Dom. Ann. Scotl.* anno 1700, Demanding surrender of the two Browns, to be tried in the court of his regality, within whose bounds they had lived, and offering a *culreach* or pledge for them. **1861** *Ibid.* 236 The system of culreach or repledgiation is one of great antiquity in Scotland, but last heard of in the Highlands.

†'**culrage, culerage.** *Obs.* Forms: 4 colerage, 5 culra(t)che, -rayge, curiage, 6 curaige, -agie, (7 kill-ridge), 5–7 culrage, 6–7 culerage. [a. OF. *culrage*, mod.F. *curage*, f. *cul* 'anus' + *rage* rage, rabies, 'from his operation and effect when it is used in those parts' (Gerarde): cf. the Eng. name ARSESMART.] An obsolete name of the plant Water-pepper (*Polygonum Hydropiper*).

a **1387** *Sinon. Barthol.* (Anecd. Oxon.) 33 *Persicaria minor*, colerage. *c* **1420** *Pallad. on Husb.* I. 1016 And curiage, and gladiol the longe. *c* **1440** *Promp. Parv.* 108 Culrache, smerthole, herbe [H., P. culratche], *persiccaria.* **14..** *Voc.* in Wr.-Wülcker 602/21 *Persicaria*, culrage. **1578** LYTE *Dodoens* v. lxvii. 632 This herbe is called.. in English Water pepper.. and of some Curagie. **1611** COTGR., *Curage*, the hearbe Water-pepper, Arse-smart, Kill-ridge, or culerage.

†'**culroun, culrun.** *Sc. Obs.* Also culroin, cullurune. [perh. a corruption of CULLION.] A base fellow, a rascal: an opprobrious appellation.

1513 DOUGLAS *Æneis* VIII. Prol. 43 The cadgear.. Calland the colȝear ane knaif and culroun full queyr. **1540** in Knox *Hist. Ref.* Wks. 1846 I. 75 Be Thomas your brother at command, A cullurune kythed throw many a land. *a* **1568** *Bannatyne Poems, Sons exylit throw Pryd* 27 For hichtines the culroin dois misken His awin maister.

culsh, var. of CULCH.

cult (kʌlt), *sb.* [ad. L. *cultus* worship (f. *colĕre* to attend to, cultivate, respect, etc.), and its F. adaptation *culte* (1611 Cotgr.). Used in 17th c. (? from Latin), and then rarely till the middle of the 19th, when often spelt *culte* as in French.]

†**1.** Worship; reverential homage rendered to a divine being or beings. *Obs.* (exc. as in sense 2).

1617 COLLINS *Def. Bp. Ely* II. ix. 371 You tell vs most absurdly of a diuine cult.. for so cult you are, or so quilted in your tearmes. *Ibid.* 380 You.. referre it to the cult that you so foolishly talked of. **1657–83** EVELYN *Hist. Relig.* (1850) II. 39 God, abolishing the cult of Gentile idols. **1683** D.A. *Art Converse* 92 That Sovereign Cult due to God only.

2. a. A particular form or system of religious worship; *esp.* in reference to its external rites and ceremonies.

1679 PENN *Addr. Prot.* II. App. 245 Let not every circumstantial difference or Variety of Cult be Nick-named a new Religion. **1699** SHAFTESB. *Charac., Inq. conc. Virtue* I. III. §2 In the Cult or Worship of such a Deity. **1850** GLADSTONE *Homer* II. 211 While she [Proserpine] has a cult or worship on earth, he [Aidoneus] apparently has none. **1859** L. OLIPHANT *China & Japan* I. xii. 242 They are devoted in their attentions to the objects of their *culte.* **1874** MAHAFFY *Soc. Life Gr.* xi. 350 The cult of Aphrodite.

b. Now freq. used *attrib.* by writers on cultic ritual and the archæology of primitive cults.

1901 A. J. EVANS *Mycen. Tree & Pillar Cult* 25 Aniconic Cult Images. *Ibid.* 77 Cult Scenes relating to a Warrior God and his Consort. **1903** *Folk-lore* Sept. 264 The image of the patron deity, usually a simple copy of the cult statue. *Ibid.* 269 Inscriptions found at various cult-centres. **1904** *Hastings's Dict. Bible* V. 118/1 The female Divinity must be represented by the female animal, in order to carry out the mythological tale or the cult-act. **1906** D. G. HOGARTH in *Proc. Brit. Acad. 1905–6* 375 Small objects dedicated in that temple, among which are several cult-figurines of the Goddess. **1928** PEAKE & FLEURE *Steppe & Sown* 104 Already in Early Minoan times the double axe had become, not only a symbol of authority, but a cult object. *a* **1930** D. H. LAWRENCE *Apocalypse* (1931) vii. 117 Cult-lore was the wisdom of the old races. **1950** H. L. LORIMER *Homer & Monum.* vi. 349 The earliest cult-image of the goddess. **1950** *Scott. Jrnl. Theol.* III. 368 The rôle of the king in the great cult-drama at the beginning of every new year. **1957** *Antiquity & Survival* II. 167/1 Near it a cult mask, made of clay, was still lying on the floor... In a further room, we discovered a unique cult-standard.. made of bronze, with a tang to fasten it to a pole.

3. *transf.* Devotion or homage to a particular person or thing, now *esp.* as paid by a body of professed adherents or admirers.

1711 SHAFTESB. *Charac.* III. i. (1737) I. 281 Convinc'd of the Reality of a better Self, and of the Cult or Homage which is due to It. **1829** A. W. FONBLANQUE *England Under 7 Admin.* (1837) I. 238 These cults are generally to be found in the same house. **1879** *Q. Rev.* Apr. 368 The cult of beauty as the most vivid image of Truth. **1889** *John Bull* 2 Mar. 141/2 An evidence of the decay of the Wordsworth cult.

†**cult,** *a. Obs. nonce-wd.* [ad. L. *cult-us*, pa. pple. of *colĕre* to cultivate.] Cultivated, cultured.

1617 [see CULT *sb.* 1].

cultar, obs. form of COULTER.

cultch, var. of CULCH.

cultching: see CULCHING *vbl. sb.*

†**cultel.** *Obs.*—[0] [OF. *cultel* (12th c.):—L. *cultellus* knife, dim. of *culter* knife, share.] 'A long knife carried by a knight's attendant, hence called *cultellarius*' (Fairholt).

†**cultelere,** *a. Obs.* [a. OF. *cultelaire, -ere*, ad. med.L *cultellāris* (see next).] = next.

1541 R. COPLAND *Guydon's Quest. Chirurg.* (1579) 50 Which and how many be there of actual cauters?.. The first is called Cultelere (of Cousteau) that is a knyfe.

†'**cultellary,** *a. Obs.* [ad. med.L. *cultellāris* of or belonging to a knife, f. *cultellus* knife: see -ARY.] Having the form of a knife.

[*c* **1400** *Lanfranc's Cirurg.* 200 þou schalt make bitwixe þe fyngris cauteriis þat ben clepid cauterium cultellare. *Ibid.* 307 The .v. cauterie is maad in þis maner & is swiþe comoun & is clepid cultellare.] **1684** tr. *Bonet's Merc. Compit.* XII. 388 The exulcerated and painful Wen.. he cut.. off with a cultellary Cautery.

†'**cultellated,** *a. Obs.* [f. L. *cultellāt-us*, pa. pple. of *cultellāre* to make like a knife, f. *cultellus* knife.] Having a sharp edge like a knife.

1657 TOMLINSON *Renou's Disp.* 297 It produces long.. hard cultellated leaves.

†**culte'llation.** *Obs.* [a. F. *cultellation*, f. L. *cultellus* knife.] An operation in land-measuring to ascertain the horizontal area of a sloping or uneven surface: the measuring line is held horizontally above the surface and a weighted 'arrow' (originally a knife) dropped to stick in the ground at a point vertically beneath its extremity.

1727–51 in CHAMBERS *Cycl.*

cultellus (kʌl'tɛləs). *Ent.* Pl. cultelli (-aɪ). [L., dim. of *culter* knife.] Each of the lancet-like mandibles of blood-sucking Diptera.

1899 D. SHARP in *Cambr. Nat. Hist.* VI. vii. 443 Cultelli (mandibles of other anatomists). **1937** J. R. DE LA TORRE-BUENO *Gloss. Ent.* 70 *Cultellus* (pl., cultelli), one of the blade-like lancets in piercing flies; the mandibles of some authors.

culter, obs. and dial. form of COULTER.

cultic ('kʌltɪk), *a.* [f. CULT *sb.* + -IC, perh. after G. *kultisch.*] Of or pertaining to a religious cult.

1898 PERITZ in *Jrnl. Biblical Lit.* XVII. 117 Whether as divinity, devotee, or cultic official, woman shares cultic duties with man. **1925** G. B. GRAY *Sacrifice in O.T.* 193 Though of course women reckoned their descent from Levi, they did not exercise the special cultic Levitical service. **1925** J. E. MCFADYEN in A. S. Peake *People & Bk.* 216 Gunkel maintains that, though they [*sc.* the psalms] originated in poetry composed for the cult, most of them no longer presuppose any cultic action. **1965** C. L. WRENN in Bessinger & Creed *Medieval & Linguistic Stud.* 42 The runes must be explored in the light of evidences.. that may have cultic significance.

Hence '**cultically** *adv.*, in a cultic manner.

1953 *Scott. Jrnl. Theol.* VI. 343 By their Christological formulas they turn [Christ] into an idol to be cultically worshipped.

cultish ('kʌltɪʃ), *a.* [f. CULT *sb.* + -ISH; cf. G. *kultisch.*] Of, pertaining to, or resembling a cult, *esp.* one regarded as eccentric or unorthodox. Hence '**cultishness**.

1926 *Scribner's* Feb. 2 He takes the 'cultish' and high-brow qualities out. **1948** K. DAVIS *Human Soc.* (1959) xx. 576 Chiropractic and naturopathy, offshoots of osteopathy, though much more backward and cultish. **1948** *Time* 16 Feb. 72 The Foursquare Church is doing its best to evolve from cultishness. **1959** *Guardian* 16 Oct. 10/3 Many will sympathise with Dr. Fromm's outspoken criticisms of the cultishness of the psychoanalytic movement. **1965** W. LAMB *Posture & Gesture* viii. 106 They all had their development in Central Europe during the 1920s and 30s and are liable now to look cultish and dated.

cultism ('kʌltɪz(ə)m). [In sense 1, a. Sp. *cultismo*, F. *cultisme*, f. Sp. *culto* polished, elegant (:—L. *cultus* cultivated): see -ISM; Góngora gave the appellation *estilo culto* to his style of writing; in sense 2, f. CULT *sb.* + -ISM.]

1. A kind of affected elegance of style which prevailed in Spanish literature in the end of the 16th and beginning of the 17th c.; also called *Góngorism* after the poet Góngora. So '**cultist,** a writer affecting cultism.

1839 *Blackw. Mag.* XLVI. 718 Francesco de Roxas, a celebrated cultist in style. **1870** LOWELL *Study Wind.* 391 The school of the cultists. **1887** MOREL-FATIO in *Encycl. Brit.* XXII. 360 The cultism of Góngora, the artifice of which lies solely in the choice and arrangement of words.

2. The spirit, system, or practice of a cult or a cultic activity. So '**cultist,** a person practising cultism; **cul'tistic** *a.*

1917 C. R. PAYNE tr. *Pfister's Psych. Method* II. xvi. 453 For the evangelical pastor, the aim in question is not a cultistic servitude for the confessional as a means of supernatural grace, but an ethical.. purification purpose. **1933** *Fortune* Aug. 47/3 But the cultist will often go to preposterous lengths. **1934** WEBSTER, Cultism. **1949** R. K. MERTON *Social Theory & Struct.* (1951) xii. 314 Cultism, informal cliques.. these and other techniques may be used for self-aggrandizement. **1955** KEEPNEWS & GRAUER *Pict. Hist. Jazz.* xix. 243 Bop did have its share of dubious quirks and of inferior musicians and cultism. **1957** P. WORSLEY *Trumpet shall Sound* x. 214 The Kukuaik movement on Karkar Island began as an orthodox independent Christian body and later turned towards Cargo cultism. **1962** *Sunday Express* 25 Feb. 13/2 The police were sent.. after 68 members of the super-race cult.. The cultists massed on a beach. **1970** *Daily Tel.* 23 Oct. 4 A deranged group of cultists calling itself the 'People of the Free Universe' and threatening death to anyone 'misusing the natural environment'.

cultivable ('kʌltɪvəb(ə)l), *a.* [f. F. *cultivable* (13–14th c. in Hatzfeld), f. *cultiver* to CULTIVATE: see -BLE] Capable of being cultivated.

1682 WHELER *Journ. Greece* VI. 437 Cultivable Ground. **1796** MORSE *Amer. Geog.* I. 535 A mountainous, broken, yet cultivable country. **1813** W. TAYLOR in *Monthly Mag.* XXXV. 425 A fruit exclusively cultivable in hot countries. **1863** RUSKIN *Munera P.* (1880) 112 Faculties.. cultivable.. by education.

Hence ,**cultiva'bility,** cultivable quality.

1881 *Chicago Advance* 8 Sept. 568 The wonderful cultivability of this pastoral art. **1890** *Graphic* 11 Oct. 416 This has.. diminished the cultivability of the soil.

†'**cultivage.** *Obs.* [a. obs. F. *cultivage* tillage (Cotgr.), f. *cultiver.*] Tillage, husbandry.

1632 LITHGOW *Trav.* IV. (1682) 161 Unwilling to be industrious in Arts, traffick, or cultivage. *Ibid.* VIII. 357 The Countrey void of Villages, Rivers, or Cultivage.

cultivar ('kʌltɪvɑː(r)). *Hort.* [f. CULTIV(ATED *ppl. a.* + VAR(IETY 6 b.] A variety that has arisen in cultivation. Also *attrib.*

1923 L. H. BAILEY in *Gentes Herbarum* I. III. 113, I now propose another name, cultivar, for a botanical variety, or for a race subordinate to species, that has originated and persisted under cultivation. **1953** *Rep. 13th Internat. Hort. Congress* 1952 50 The Code provides.. that the term 'cultivar' (abbreviated as cv.) be applied to those special forms which have originated or are maintained only in cultivation. *Ibid.* 51 When revival of the earliest published cultivar-name would cause confusion, it is to be listed as a synonym. **1961** *New Statesman* 19 May 808/2 What happened to tulips, roses, daffodils, is now happening to lilium. Relatively few species are brought together from remote places, crossed and recrossed, and give rise to thousands of cultivars. **1970** R. GORER *Devel. Garden Flowers* 19, I have also followed the practice of using the term cultivar (abbreviated as cv.) to indicate variation that has arisen as a result of cultivation.

cultivatable ('kʌltɪ,veɪtəb(ə)l), *a.* Also **cultivateable.** [f. CULTIVATE + -ABLE.] = CULTIVABLE. Hence **cultivata'bility** (*rare*).

1847 in CRAIG. **1853** *Jrnl. R. Agric. Soc.* XIV. I. 42 On the cultivatable land the work of drainage is going on. **1880** F. W. BURBIDGE *Gardens of Sun* vi. 116, 1,738 acres are supposed to be cultivatable. **1886** *Chicago Advance* 23 Dec. 823 The human cultivatibility of the savage Indian.

cultivate ('kʌltɪveɪt), *v.* [f. *cultīvāt-*, ppl. stem of late (and med.)L. *cultīvāre* to till, (in It. *coltivare*, Pr. *coltivar*, *cultivar*, F. *cultiver*, OF. and dial. *coutiver*), f. late L. *cultīvus* (*cultīva terra*), characterized by being tilled, f. *cultus*, pa. pple. of *colĕre* to till, cultivate, take care of. For the form cf. *captivate.* In earlier use we had CULTIVE *v.*]

I. *lit.* **1. a.** *trans.* To bestow labour and attention upon (land) in order to the raising of crops; to till; to improve and render fertile by husbandry.

1620–55 [see CULTIVATING *vbl. sb.*]. **1656** BLOUNT *Glossogr., Cultivate*, to plow or Till. **1681** OTWAY *Soldier's Fort.* V. i, 'Tis a great pity so good a husbandman as you should want a farm to cultivate. **1719** DE FOE *Crusoe* II. xiii, A Country infinitely populous, but miserably cultivated. **1796** MORSE *Amer. Geog.* II. 551 Most of the rivers of Bengal .. have their banks cultivated with rice. **1838** THIRLWALL *Greece* II. 321 The Athenians returned to cultivate their fields. **1872** YEATS *Techn. Hist. Comm.* 63 Gardens were cultivated by the ancient Greeks.

b. *techn.* To break up (ground) with a CULTIVATOR (sense 3).

1846 *Jrnl. R. Agric. Soc.* VII. II. 288 The stubble was ploughed, and in the spring of 1842 it was manured and grubbed, or 'cultivated', and sown with mangold-wurzel.

2. a. To bestow labour and attention upon (a plant) so as to promote its growth; to produce or raise by tillage. Also *transf.* of fish, etc.

1697 DRYDEN *Virg. Georg.* IV. 193 Pot-herbs..cultivated with his daily Care. 1707 *Curios. in Husb. & Gard.* 4 The Plants that Adam took Pleasure to cultivate there. 1862 *Cornh. Mag.* V. 197 All the species of fish usually cultivated in the country. 1871 R. W. DALE *Commandm.* ix. 231 A rose, however you cultivate it, remains a rose.

b. *Biol.* = CULTURE *v.* c.

1888 *Ann. Bot.* II. 373 The spores, cultivated in suitabel media, give rise..to a copiously branched and septate mycelium. 1891 G. S. WOODHEAD *Bacteria* x. 195 The bacilli, when obtained pure, and cultivated in fluid, grew out into very long threads. 1910 *Jrnl. Amer. Med. Assoc.* 15 Oct. 1381/1 Adult tissues and organs of mammals can be cultivated outside of the animal body. 1924 T. S. P. STRANGEWAYS *Tissue Culture in Rel. Growth* i. 11 The tissues of such an embryo can be readily cultivated, even if removed as much as fourteen days after the death of the animal. 1926 *Proc. R. Soc.* B.C. 273 If the undifferentiated limb-bud of the embryonic Fowl was cultivated *in vitro*, it underwent a considerable amount of progressive development. 1953 *Sci. Progress* XLI. 212 In organ culture, complete rudiments or fragments of organs are cultivated. 1963 PENSO & BALDUCCI *Tissue Cultures in Biol. Res.* vi. 145 Blood cells that can be most easily cultivated are macrophages or monocytes.

II. *fig.* **3.** To improve and develop by education or training (a person, his mind, manners, faculties); to refine, to culture.

1681–6 J. SCOTT *Chr. Life* (1747) III. 377 To cultivate its [a child's] Manners with good Precepts and Counsels. 1713 ADDISON *Cato* I, To cultivate the wild licentious savage With wisdom, discipline, and liberal arts. 1779 BURKE *Corr.* (1844) II. 273, I have endeavoured so to cultivate my mind, that [etc.]. 1831 SIR. J. SINCLAIR *Corr.* II. 348 To learn every thing to cultivate the spirit.

4. To promote the growth of, devote oneself to the advancement or development of (an art, science, sentiment, etc.); to foster.

1662 EVELYN *Chalcogr.* A iij, That great..designe..of cultivating the Sciences, and advancing of usefull knowledge. *Ibid.* 32 Ye that love vertue and cultivate the sciences. 1694 tr. Milton's *Lett. State* Sept. an. 1652, How firmly we are resolv'd to cultivate..that friendship which is between your serenity and this republic. 1747 BUTLER *Serm.* Wks. 1874 II. 302 Let us be the more careful to cultivate inward religion. 1760 GOLDSM. *Cit. W.* cxvi, Though it cannot plant morals in the human breast, it cultivates them when there.

5. a. To devote one's attention to, to prosecute, follow, practise, cherish (any art, science, sentiment, habit, or pursuit, esp. with the object of acquiring it, or improving oneself in it).

1749 FIELDING *Tom Jones* III. ii, [They] cultivate the same superstition with the Bannians in India. 1756 C. LUCAS *Ess. Waters* I. Pref., Let us cultivate our own excellent language. 1862 SIR B. BRODIE *Psychol. Inq.* II. v. 167 The higher mathematics are absolutely necessary to those who cultivate ..astronomy. 1863 MRS. C. CLARKE *Shaks. Char.* v. 123 As a soldier, he cultivates bluntness.

b. Phrases. ***to cultivate the acquaintance, friendship***, or ***good opinion of, relations with.*** (These connect 4 and 5.)

1699 BENTLEY *Phal.* 276 He had ix entire years to cultivate a Friendship with Themistocles. 1748 RICHARDSON *Clarissa* (1811) I. ii. 10 He was more solicitous to cultivate her mamma's good opinion, than hers. 1791 BOSWELL *Johnson* an. 1753, He cultivated his acquaintance. 1818 JAS. MILL *Brit. India* II. v. iv. 472 A desire to cultivate the friendship of the English. 1888 W. R. CARLES *Life in Corea* i. 7 Mr. Mayers..did his utmost..to cultivate some relations with the people and officials.

c. Hence (*ellipt.*) ***to cultivate a person***: to bestow attention upon him with a view to intimacy or favour; to court the acquaintance or friendship of.

1707 COLLIER *Refl. Ridic.* 215 The Great honour him, cultivate him, respect him, court him. 1796 BURKE *Lett. Noble Lord* Wks. VIII. 64, I loved and cultivated him accordingly. 1870 DISRAELI *Lothair* xxxvi. 186, I..felt that he was a person I should like to cultivate. 1889 *Cornh. Mag.* Feb., *The County* iv, I shall cultivate Sir Joseph.

†**d.** *intr.* Const. *with. Obs.*

1772 MAD. D'ARBLAY *Early Diary* (1889) I. 169 If my father was disposed to cultivate with the world, what a delightful acquaintance he might have!

cultivated (ˈkʌltɪveɪtɛd), *ppl. a.* [f. prec.]

1. Of land: Subjected to cultivation; tilled. Of plants: Produced or improved by cultivation.

1797 BEWICK *Brit. Birds* (1847) I. 94 It is frequently seen in cultivated grounds. 1858 HAWTHORNE *Fr. & It. Jrnls.* I. 193 Flowering shrubs, and all manner of cultivated beauty. *Mod.* The plant was described from a cultivated specimen.

2. *fig.* Of persons, their minds, faculties, etc.: Improved by education or training; refined, cultured. Of the voice or utterance: indicating refinement in its user.

1665 GLANVILL *Sceps. Sci.* 81 In the latter and less cultivated ages. 1781 GIBBON *Decl. & F.* III. 189 A cultivated understanding, a copious fancy. 1863 GEO. ELIOT *Romola* II. xxi, The most cultivated men in the most cultivated of Italian cities. 1883 G. LLOYD *Ebb & Flow* I. 24 His cultivated tastes. 1908 *Westm. Gaz.* 2 Jan. 8/1 The prisoner is a well set-up and well-dressed man with a cultivated voice.

'cultivating, *vbl. sb.* [-ING[1].] The action of the verb CULTIVATE; cultivation.

1620–55 I. JONES *Stone-Heng* (1725) 6 The cultivating and manuring of Lands. 1668 WILKINS *Real Char.* Ep. to Rdr., The Cultivating of that part of Learning.

'cultivating, *ppl. a.* [-ING[2].] That cultivates; engaged in tillage.

1806 SURR *Winter in Lond.* (ed. 3) I. 108 The close-cropt grass..showed the hand of cultivating care. 1884 *Athenæum* 12 Jan. 48/2 The condition of the cultivating classes. 1891 *Educat. Rev.* I. 140 The instruction..is in no wise so broad or cultivating as the corresponding study beyond the ocean.

cultivation (kʌltɪˈveɪʃən). [a. F. *cultivation* (16th c.), n. of action from *cultiver*: see CULTIVE *v.* and -ATION.]

1. a. The tilling of land; tillage, husbandry. Also *attrib.*, as ***cultivation field, system***; **cultivation bank, terrace,** a bank or terrace formed either naturally or artificially on a cultivated hillside; a lynchet; **cultivation mark** *Archæol.*, a mark on the soil caused by cultivation in an earlier period; **cultivation paddock**, the part of an Australian farming estate used for the raising of crops.

1725 DE FOE *Voy. round World* (1840) 278 Soil..capable of cultivations and improvements. 1746–7 HERVEY *Medit.* (1818) 144 By industry and cultivation, this neat spot is an image of Eden. 1857 RUSKIN *Pol. Econ. Art* 17 The cultivation of a farm. 1869 DILKE *Greater Brit.* II. 116 The amount of land under cultivation.

attrib. 1923 *Geogr. Jrnl.* May 356 Hitherto I have used this word [*sc.* lynchet] to describe the cultivation-banks of the Celtic system. 1893 F. ADAMS *New Egypt* 94 An open space in the desert, beyond the cultivation fields. 1924 MAWER & STENTON *Introd. Surv. Eng. Place-Names* viii. 156 Air photographs..reveal..trackways and cultivation-marks which would otherwise be overlooked. 1853 ST. JULIAN & SILVESTER *Prod. N.S.W.* IV. 170 Few stations of any magnitude are without their 'cultivation paddocks'. 1902 *Westm. Gaz.* 13 Dec. 2/1 Posy..went over the fence into the cultivation paddock. 1923 *Geogr. Jrnl.* May 347, I think.. that the date 650 B.C. is probably within a century or two of the date when the Celtic cultivation-system was inaugurated. 1911 *Antiquary* VII. 416/1 Within the camp, on the southern slope of the hill-crest, there exists a series of broad cultivation terraces. 1951 *Field Archæol.* (*Ordnance Survey*) (ed. 3) 62 Each of these strips was separated from its neighbours by a 'balk' of untilled land, and if the common field so divided lay on the slope of a hill a cultivation terrace or 'lynchet' formed on the lower boundary of each in the course of time.

†**b.** Improvement (of land); increase of fertility. *Obs. rare.*

1793 SMEATON *Edystone L.* §206 The first shower of rain would turn it all to stone, without affording any sensible cultivation to the land.

2. a. The bestowing of labour and care upon a plant, so as to develop and improve its qualities: the raising of (a crop) by tillage.

1719 DE FOE *Crusoe* I. vii, I saw several Sugar Canes, but wild, and for want of Cultivation, imperfect. 1813 SIR H. DAVY *Agric. Chem.* (1814) 257 The seeds of plants, exalted by cultivation, always furnish large and improved Varieties. 1871 R. W. DALE *Commandm.* ix. 231 You cannot change a rose into a pear tree by cultivation. *Mod.* Land devoted to the cultivation of wheat.

b. *transf.* The production or raising of a 'crop' of any kind (as of oysters, microscopic organisms, etc.); also *concr.* the product of such cultivation (of bacteria, etc.); = CULTURE *sb.* 3 b, c. Also *attrib.* and *Comb.*, as ***cultivation experiment, fluid.*** In wider use (cf. CULTURE *sb.* 3 c).

1884 KLEIN *Micro-Organisms* (1886) 159 Twenty days cultivation of blood-bacilli at 42° to 43° C. does not always yield attenuated virus. *Ibid.* 26 Test-tubes which are to receive cultivation-fluids. 1886 E. M. CROOKSHANK *Bacteriology* 69 In a glass beaker..place the tube containing the cultivation. 1910 *Jrnl. Amer. Med. Assoc.* 15 Oct. 1379/2 (*heading*) Cultivation of adult tissues and organs outside of the body. 1926 *Proc. R. Soc.* B.C. 279 After the 17th day of cultivation the eyes undergo no further development and usually begin to degenerate. 1959 *Chambers's Encycl.* XIII. 653/2 Under certain conditions of cultivation the normal organization of the explanted tissue can be preserved and.. it may undergo a remarkable degree of histological and even anatomical development. 1965 WHITE & GROVE *Proc. Internat. Conf. Plant Tissue Culture* 20 The initial pH of the nutrient media is important for the cultivation of excised roots.

3. *fig.* **a.** The devoting of special attention or study to the development of, or to progress in (a branch of knowledge, a person's acquaintance, etc.).

a 1700 DRYDEN (J.), A cultivation of learning. 1780 HARRIS *Philol. Enq.* Wks. (1841) 463 The cultivation of every liberal accomplishment. 1877 TYNDALL in *Daily News* 2 Oct. 2/4 The cultivation of right relations with his fellow men.

b. The bestowing of special attention upon a person for the sake of gaining his favour. *rare.*

1793 T. TAYLOR *Sallust* xiv. 70 [The gods] become angry with the guilty, but are rendered propitious by proper cultivation.

4. The developing, fostering, or improving (of the mind, faculties, etc.) by education and training; the condition of being cultivated; culture, refinement.

a 1716 SOUTH *Serm.* VI. xi. (R.), Use and cultivation of reason. 1826 DISRAELI *Viv. Grey* II. i, An enthusiastic advocate for the cultivation of the mind, he was an equally ardent supporter of the cultivation of the body. 1869 LECKY *Europ. Mor.* I. i. 88 Increased cultivation almost always produces..fastidiousness.

cultivative (ˈkʌltɪveɪtɪv), *a. rare.* [f. CULTIVATE (or its med.L. base) + -IVE.] Tending or pertaining to cultivation.

1863 *Jrnl. R. Agric. Soc.* XXIV. I. 242 Manuring and other cultivative processes.

cultivator (ˈkʌltɪveɪtə(r)). Also 8 -er. [n. of action in L. form f. med.L. *cultīvāre* to CULTIVATE, prob. after F. *cultivateur* (15th c. in Hatzfeld).]

1. One who tills the ground, or cultivates a particular plant or crop; a tiller, husbandman, farmer, agriculturist.

1665 BOYLE *Occas. Refl., Occas. Medit.* IV. iii. 62 The Divine Son of the great γεωργὸς [*margin* That is, Cultivator of the Ground]. *a* 1691 BOYLE (J.), Some cultivators of clover-grass. 1792 A. YOUNG *Trav. France* 490 An English cultivator, at the head of a sheep farm of three or four thousand acres. 1815 ELPHINSTONE *Acc. Caubul* (1842) I. 389 There are five classes of cultivators in Afghaunistaun.

2. *fig.* **a.** One who cultivates an art, science, etc.

1711 SHAFTESB. *Charac.* (1737) III. 239 A cultivater or supporter of arts or letters. 1774 PENNANT *Tour Scot. in* 1772. 181 A restorer and cultivator of religion after the Egyptian manner. 1846 WRIGHT *Ess. Mid. Ages* I. v. 176 The great cultivators of science and letters.

b. One who, or that which, develops or improves (the mind, etc.) by education and training.

1868 MILL in *Even. Star* 10 July, To give people an interest..in the management of their own affairs was the grand cultivator of mankind. 1886 MORLEY *Pop. Culture, Crit. Misc.* III. 32 The observant cultivator of his own understanding.

3. An agricultural implement for breaking up or loosening the ground, and uprooting weeds between the drills of crops.

1759 tr. *Duhamel's Husb.* II. i. (1762) 126 My alleys were plowed again with the cultivator. 1849 *Mech. Mag.* L. 176 Dr. Newington's hand row hoe and cultivator. 1857 R. TOMES *Amer. in Japan* i. 23 An American 'cultivator'.. which simple plough..drawn by a single horse, accomplished as much as the labour of fifty men, according to the usual method of cultivating the vine with a hoe.

cultivatory (ˈkʌltɪvətərɪ), *a. rare.* [f. CULTIVATE *v.* (or its med.L. base) + -ORY.] Of the nature of or pertaining to cultivation.

1854 *Blackw. Mag.* LXXVI. 656 A certain cultivatory process. 1888 *New York Dispatch* Sept., Here the cultivatory work ends and the manufacturing begins.

†**'cultive,** *v. Obs.* Also 5 -yue, 6 -ife. [a. F. *cultiver* (12–13th c. in Godef.), ad. late L. *cultīvāre* to CULTIVATE. (In OF. the word had also a semi-popular form *coutiver*.)] *trans.* = CULTIVATE. Hence †**'cultiving** *vbl. sb.*, cultivation.

1483 CAXTON *Esope* 145 The labourer..made alle his ground to be cultyued and ered. 1483 —— *Cato* E iij, The cultyuyng and eeryng of the erthe. 1546 *St. Papers Hen. VIII*, XI. 181 To cultife the land. 1614 RALEIGH *Hist. World* I. 27 Whichsoever he tooke pleasure to plant and cultive. 1635 J. HAYWARD tr. *Biondi's Ban. Virgin* 120 Cultiving the seeds of the other Arabian odours.

†**'cultive,** *a. Obs. rare.* [ad. late L. *cultīvus*, f. *cultus* tilled: cf. OF. *teres cultives* arable lands (1270 in Godef.).] Under tillage, cultivated.

1611 MUNDAY *Briefe Chron.* 249 To work in those rough fields, as yet not cultive.

cultor, obs. form of COULTER.

cultorist (ˈkʌltərɪst). [ad. Sp. *cultorista*, in F. *cultoriste*] = CULTIST.

1860 FARRAR *Orig. Lang.* 144 After the beautiful period of Spanish literature come Gongora and his cultorists.

cultrate (ˈkʌltrət), *a. Nat. Hist.* [ad. L. *cultrātus*, f. *culter*, *cultr-* knife, share: see -ATE[2] 2.] Formed like a knife or coulter; having a sharp edge like a knife.

1856–8 W. CLARK *Van der Hoeven's Zool.* I. 387 Borer.. included in a bivalve sheath, compressed, cultrate. *Ibid.* II. 378 Bill cultrate.

'cultrated, *a. Nat. Hist.* = prec.

1797 BEWICK *Brit. Birds* (1805) I. 67 The bill is strong.. the edges are thin, and sharp or cultrated.

cultre, obs. form of COULTER.

cultriform (ˈkʌltrɪfɔːm), *a. Nat. Hist.* [mod. f. L. type *cultriformis*, f. *cultr-* knife: see -FORM.] Shaped like a knife or coulter.

1826 KIRBY & SP. *Entomol.* (1828) IV. 162 The saw of some saw-flies is cultriform. 1846 DANA *Zooph.* (1848) 169 Cultriform lamellæ.

cultrirostral (kʌltrɪˈrɒstrəl), *a. Zool.* [f. L. *cultr-* knife, share + *rostrum* beak + -AL[1]. In F. *cultrirostre*.] Having a bill shaped like a knife or coulter, as certain grallatorial birds (the heron, stork, etc.).

In mod. Dicts.

cul'trivorous, *a. rare.* [f. as prec. + -VOROUS.] Swallowing or pretending to swallow knives.

1846 WORCESTER cites DUNGLISON.

cultual (ˈkʌltjuːəl), *a.* [ad. F. *cultuel*, f. L. *cultus* CULTUS.] Of or pertaining to a cult or organized religious worship.

1906 *Westm. Gaz.* 17 Dec. 2/3 Catholic Cultual Associations. 1912 F. VON HÜGEL *Eternal Life* 163 There is nothing necessarily superstitious in..Cultual Acts.

culturable ('kʌltjʊərəb(ə)l), *a.* [f. CULTURE *v.* + -ABLE.] Capable of culture or cultivation; cultivable. (*lit.* and *fig.*)

1796 W. MARSHALL *W. England* I. 59 The..more easily culturable parts, being converted to the purposes of husbandry. **1883** *Spectator* 12 May 606/2 The faculty of musical apprehension, is, apparently, the most culturable of all. **1889** *Ibid.* 7 Dec., A rich country..with limitless culturable or mineral land.

cultural ('kʌltjʊərəl), *a.* [f. L. *cultūra* tillage, culture + -AL[1]. So in mod.F.]

1. Relating to the culture of plants, or of fish, etc.

1868 J. SCOTT (*title*), The orchardist, or a cultural and descriptive catalogue of fruit trees. **1883** *Pall Mall G.* 2 June Supp., Fish Cultural Apparatus in operation.

2. Relating to culture of the mind, manners, etc.

1875 WHITNEY *Life Lang.* 307 A mere incident of social life and of cultural growth. **1890** *Jrnl. Education* 1 Nov. 631/2 Nobody denies..the cultural value of Greek and Roman history.

3. Relating to civilization, esp. that of a particular country at a particular period; ***cultural anthropology***, the branch of anthropology that is predominantly concerned with the cultural, as opposed to the physical, aspects of the evolution of man; ***cultural attaché***, an embassy official whose function is to promote cultural relations between his country and the country in which he is staying; ***cultural diplomacy***, the furthering of international relations by cultural exchange; the act of publicizing and exhibiting examples of one's national culture abroad; ***cultural revolution***, a cultural and social movement in Communist China, begun in 1965, which sought to combat 'revisionism' and restore the original purity of Maoist doctrine; also *transf.*

1875 W. D. WHITNEY *Life Lang.* 172 All these widely-sundered tribes of men, found at the dawn of history in every variety of cultural condition. **1884** *Science* IV. 21/2 In its cultural development, China stands wholly for itself. **1898** *Daily News* 30 Aug. 5/1 The gigantic cultural problems awaiting solution in the Russian Empire. **1909** *Westm. Gaz.* 22 Apr. 5/2 The Professor [Doerpsfeld] says the excavations reveal several distinct cultural deposits. **1909** A. H. KEANE *Central & S. Amer.* (ed. 2) I. 48 The southern extremity of the cultural zone. **1921** E. SAPIR *Language* x. 221 How do the peoples of the given area divide themselves as cultural beings? what are the outstanding 'cultural areas'? **1923** A. L. KROEBER *Anthropol.* 6 Here..is the cause of the seeming preoccupation of social or cultural anthropology with ancient and savage and exotic and extinct peoples. **1934** H. C. WARREN *Dict. Psychol.* 66/1 *Cultural lag*, slowness in adapting institutions or cultural habits to new or changing conditions or situations; the condition which ensues when certain elements of culture change more slowly than other elements. **1937** *Times* 31 Aug. 11/2 There is a proposal..that three 'cultural attachés' should be appointed to the more important embassies and consulates in foreign countries. **1938** R. G. COLLINGWOOD *Princ. Art.* xi. 242 The groupings recognized by physical anthropology do not coincide with those of cultural anthropology. **1939** V. G. CHILDE *Dawn Europ. Civ.* (ed. 3) vii. 92 Though the temporary nature of the settlements excludes..stratigraphical chronology, the cultural sequence is well established. **1959** R. H. THAYER in *U.S. Dept. of State Bull.* 31 Aug. 310/2 Today we have, in the forefront of the implementation of our foreign policy, 'cultural diplomacy', to my mind the most important means of bringing complete mutual understanding between peoples. **1966** *Economist* 20 Aug. 709/1 Lin Piao..has loyally used the army as a guinea-pig for the 'cultural revolution' dose of salts with which Mao is now purging the whole country. **1967** *Guardian* 16 May 1/3 Chinese leadership..has certainly been prepared to accept serious economic and political losses..for the sake of the 'cultural revolution'. **1967** *Economist* 21 Oct. 274/1 They support Syria's 'cultural revolution' (the regime has just taken over control of its mainly religious private schools). **1968** *Africa Today* XV. 8 (*title*) Cultural diplomacy in African writing. **1970** E. MCGIRR *Death pays Wages* ii. 43 He got the Cultural Attaché to translate that for him. **1986** *Financial Times* 3 Mar. 20/5 The Council states frankly: 'The challenge begins at home in trying to win recognition for the relevance of cultural diplomacy to Britain's influence and prosperity.'

4. *Biol.* Relating to the culture of micro-organisms, tissues, etc. (see CULTURE *sb.* 3 c).

1900 *Jrnl. Exper. Med.* V. 259 The bacillus recovered by us from our several autopsies always showed the same cultural characters. **1969** S. T. LYLES *Biol. Microorganisms* v. 103 Cultural methods will depend both on the organism studied and the purpose for which the study is made.

'culturally, *adv.* [f. prec. + -LY] In relation to culture; *spec.* with reference to a particular form of culture or civilization.

1889 *Temple Bar Mag.* June 87 Each is an advance culturally and artistically on that below. **1921** R. A. S. MACALISTER *Text-bk. Europ. Archæol.* I. v. 120 Communities may be culturally classified as hunters, pastors, and agriculturists, according to the means whereby the majority of their members obtain their livelihood. **1921** E. SAPIR *Language* x. 228 Culturally identical with [the Hupa Indians] are the neighboring Yurok and Karok.

2. *Biol.* With reference to culture or a culture (sense 3 c).

1893 *Daily Tel.* 29 Sept. 4/6 A fatal case..is officially described as 'culturally indistinguishable from true cholera'. **1906** *Practitioner* Nov. 635 Culturally, it possesses no features by means of which it may be readily distinguished from other diplo- or streptococci. **1908** *Ibid.* Jan. 68 Ruppell found that there was a striking resemblance between the non-virulent strains of meningococci and ordinary gonococci, morphologically, culturally, and as regards their immunising power against virulent meningococci.

†**'culturate**, *v. Obs. rare.* [f. F. *culturer* CULTURE *v.* + -ATE[3].] *trans.* To bring under culture, cultivate.

1631 CAPT. SMITH *Advt. Planters* iv. 10 More [land] to spare than all the natives of those Countries can use and culturate.

†**cultu'ration.** *Obs. rare.* [n. of action f. prec.: see -ATION.] Cultivation, culture.

1606 BRYSKETT *Civ. Life* 4 The culturation and manuring of the same.

culture ('kʌltjʊə(r)), *sb.* [a. F. *culture* (in OF. *couture*), ad. L. *cultūra* cultivation, tending, in Christian authors, worship, f. ppl. stem of *colĕre*: see CULT.]

†**1.** Worship; reverential homage. *Obs. rare.*

1483 CAXTON *Gold. Leg.* 81/1 Whan they departe fro the culture and honour of theyr god.

2. a. The action or practice of cultivating the soil; tillage, husbandry; = CULTIVATION 1.

c **1420** *Pallad. on Husb.* I. 21 In places there thou wilt have the culture. **1613** R. C. *Table Alph.* (ed. 3) *Culture*, husbandry, tilling. **1665-9** BOYLE *Occas. Refl.* (1675) 320 Such a..plot of his Eden..gratefully crowns his Culture..with chaplets of Flowers. **1707** *Curios. in Husb. & Gard.* 3 Man was..imploy'd in the Culture of the Garden. **1806** *Gazetteer Scot.* (ed. 3) 296 The soil is clay, and difficult of culture. **1866** ROGERS *Agric. & Prices* I. 11 The same kinds of grain..are sown..and the same mode of culture is adopted.

†**b.** Cultivated condition. *Obs.*

1538 STARKEY *England* I. i. 12 The erth..by..dylygent labur..ys brought to maruelous culture and fertylite.

†**c.** *concr.* A piece of tilled land; a cultivated field. *Obs.*

1557 *MS. Indenture* 30 June, [Conveying] a culture of land called the flatte, in Brantingham, Yks. **1560** WHITEHORNE *Arte of Warre* (1573) 27b, Euery culture where bee Vines and other trees lettes the horses. **1757** DYER *Fleece* (R.), From their tenements..proceeds the caravan Through lively spreading cultures, pastures green.

3. a. The cultivating or rearing of a plant or crop; = CULTIVATION 2.

1626 BACON *Sylva* §402 These..were slower than the ordinary Wheat..and this Culture did rather retard than advance. **1697** DRYDEN *Virg. Georg.* I. 78 The Culture suiting to the sev'ral Kinds Of Seeds and Plants. **1750** JOHNSON *Rambler* No. 33 ¶2 The fruits, which without culture fell ripe into their hands. **1856** EMERSON *Eng. Traits, Ability* Wks. (Bohn) II. 42 [England] is too far north for the culture of the vine. **1887** *Pall Mall G.* 15 Oct. 11/2 There are eighty acres devoted to bulb culture.

b. *transf.* The rearing or raising of certain animals, such as fish, oysters, bees, etc., or of natural products such as silk. ***culture pearl*** = ***cultured pearl.***

1796 MORSE *Amer. Geog.* I. 679 The culture of silk. **1862** *Cornh. Mag.* V. 201 The dredgers at Whitstable have so far adopted oyster culture. **1886** *Pall Mall G.* 23 Sept. 6/2 In the interests of bee-culture, and in the search of improved races of bees. **1921** *Current Hist.* July 623/1 Jewelers in London have been greatly perturbed over a new type of [Japanese] 'culture' pearls which is said to be so perfect that it cannot be distinguished from the natural article. **1937** *Discovery* Mar 87/1 X-ray photographs of culture pearls. **1963** *Times* 12 Mar. (Austral. Suppl.) p. v/7 Culture-pearl farms.

c. The artificial development of microscopic organisms, *esp.* bacteria, in specially prepared media; *concr.* the product of such culture; a growth or crop of artificially developed bacteria, etc. Also applied to the similar growth of plant and animal cells and tissues, and of whole organs or fragments of them. Also in *Comb.*, as ***culture-fluid***, ***-tube***, etc.; **culture medium**, a substance, solid or liquid, in or on which micro-organisms, tissues, etc., are cultured.

1880 G. M. STERNBERG tr. *Magnin's Bacteria* II. i. 113 Cohn, in order..to get rid of the moulds,..employed the following culture-fluid. **1884** KLEIN *Micro-Organisms* (1886) 94 When cultures of this bacterium are kept for some time..their virulence becomes diminished. *Ibid.* 39 A series of new culture-tubes. *Ibid.*, A culture-fluid..that contains ..various species of organisms. **1885** C. S. DOLLEY *Technol. Bacteria Invest.* I. ii. 59 Sterilizing the culture medium is accomplished ordinarily by the use of heat sufficient to kill all germs. **1890** *Jrnl. Chem. Soc.* LVII. 487 Experiments upon the culture of excised barley embryos on nutrient liquids. **1910** A. CARREL in *Jrnl. Amer. Med. Assoc.* 15 Oct. 1379/2 The plasmatic media were inoculated with many tissues or organs, of which all were found to multiply or grow. The cultures of the different tissues—as we shall call them—contain common characteristics. **1914** *Jrnl. Exper. Med.* XIX. 398 (*heading*) The effect of dilution of plasma medium on the growth and fat accumulation of cells in tissue cultures. **1938** R. C. PARKER *Methods Tissue Culture* xvi. 208 The method of tissue culture has also served as a direct means of studying the further development of complex structures and organ rudiments. **1939** F. A. KNOTT *Clin. Bacteriol.* ii. 19 The culture medium chosen depends upon the variety of bacterium sought. **1953** *Sci. Progr.* XLI. 212 Earle and his collaborators..have devised methods for obtaining mass cultures of unorganised tissue from an initial cell suspension or a single cell. **1960** L. PICKEN *Organization of Cells* iii. 83 The presence of minute amounts of penicillin in the culture medium leads to the production of various abnormal forms of bacteria. **1965** WHITE & GROVE *Proc. Internat. Conf. Plant Tissue Culture* 9 Experiments with excised roots as organ cultures. *Ibid.* 28 Sterile seedlings of tomato..were grown in 50 ml of the inorganic solution of the standard root culture medium. **1970** tr. G. Le Douarin in J. A. Thomas *Organ Culture* ii. 17 The patella of a 9-day chick embryo developed cartilage after 3 days of culture.

†**d.** The training of the human body. *Obs.*

1628 HOBBES *Thucyd.* I. vi, Amongst whom [the Lacedaemonians]..especially in the culture of their bodies, the nobility observed the most equality with the commons. **1793** BEDDOES *Let. Darwin* 60 To suppose the organization of man equally susceptible of improvement from culture with that of various animals and vegetables.

4. *fig.* The cultivating or development (of the mind, faculties, manners, etc.); improvement or refinement by education and training.

c **1510** MORE *Picus* Wks. 14 To the culture and profit of theyr myndes. *a* **1633** LENNARD tr. *Charron's Wisd.* (1658) 174 Necessary for the culture of good manners. **1651** HOBBES *Leviath.* II. xxxi. 189 The education of Children [is called] a Culture of their mindes. **1752** JOHNSON *Rambler* No. 189 ¶12 She..neglected the culture of [her] understanding. **1848** MACAULAY *Hist. Eng.* II. 55 The precise point to which intellectual culture can be carried. **1865** DALE *Jew. Temp.* xiv. (1877) 155 The Jewish system was intended for the culture of the religious life of the Jews.

5. a. *absol.* The training, development, and refinement of mind, tastes, and manners; the condition of being thus trained and refined; the intellectual side of civilization.

1805 WORDSW. *Prelude* XIII. 197 Where grace Of culture hath been utterly unknown. **1837** EMERSON *Jrnl.* 24 Nov. (1910) IV. 371 It seems to me that the circumstances of man are historically somewhat better here and now than ever,—that more freedom exists for Culture. **1849** J. A. FROUDE *Nemesis of Faith* x. 85 The end of all culture is, that we may be able to sustain ourselves in a spiritual atmosphere as the birds do in the air. **1855** J. CONINGTON *Academical Study of Latin* (1872) I. 212 That part of our culture which we have not worked out for ourselves, or received from contemporary nations, we owe almost wholly to Rome, and to Greece only through Rome. **1860** MOTLEY *Netherl.* (1868) I. ii. 47 His culture was not extensive. **1869** M. ARNOLD (*title*) Culture and anarchy. *Ibid.* ii. 49 The great men of culture are those who have had a passion..for carrying from one end of society to the other, the best knowledge, the best ideas of their time. **1871** GEO. ELIOT *Middlem.* I. ix. 137 He wants to go abroad again..[for] the vague purpose of what he calls culture, preparation for he knows not what. **1876** M. ARNOLD *Lit. & Dogma* xiii, Culture, the acquainting ourselves with the best that has been known and said in the world. **1889** JESSOPP *Coming of Friars* iii. 131 Some few of the larger..monasteries..[were] centres of culture. *a* **1893** *Mod.* A man of considerable culture. **1916** E. WHARTON *Xingu* i. 3 Mrs. Ballinger is one of the ladies who pursue Culture in bands, as though it were dangerous to meet alone. **1939** tr. H. Johst in C. Leiser *Nazi Nuggets* 83 When I hear the word 'culture' I slip back the safety-catch of my revolver. **1940** K. MANNHEIM *Man & Society* II. ii. 85 The crisis of culture in liberal-democratic society is due, in the first place, to the fact that the social processes, which previously favoured the development of the creative élites, now have the opposite effect. **1948** T. S. ELIOT *Notes Def. Culture* ii. 41 Culture is not merely the sum of several activities, but a *way of life*. *Ibid.* 42 Group culture ..has never been co-extensive with class. *Ibid.* 43 The primary channel of transmission of culture is the family.

¶ With distortion of spelling to indicate affected or vulgar pronunciation.

1931 *Atlantic Monthly* Feb. 149/2 They believe in 'cultchah'. **1959** *Listener* 15 Jan. 128/2 *Italian Bouquet, an Epicurean Tour of Italy*..an American hotchpotch of culcher and food.

b. (with *a* and *pl.*) A particular form or type of intellectual development. Also, the civilization, customs, artistic achievements, etc., of a people, esp. at a certain stage of its development or history. (In many contexts, esp. in Sociology, it is not possible to separate this sense from sense 5 a.)

1867 FREEMAN *Norm. Conq.* (1876) I. iv. 150 A language and culture which was wholly alien to them. **1871** E. B. TYLOR (*title*) Primitive culture. **1891** *Spectator* 27 June, Speaking all languages, knowing all cultures, living amongst all races. **1903** C. LUMHOLTZ *Unknown Mexico* I. 117 A thrifty people whose stage of culture was that of the Pueblo Indians of to-day. **1921** R. A. S. MACALISTER *Text-bk. Europ. Archæol.* I. iv. 99 A language associated with a superior culture has always a tendency to swamp languages that have not such an advantage. **1921** E. SAPIR *Language* x. 222 Historians and anthropologists find that races, languages, and cultures are not distributed in parallel fashion. **1942** BLOCH & TRAGER *Outl. Ling. Analysis* 5 The activities of a society—that is, of its members—constitute its culture... Language, then, is not only an element of culture itself; it is the basis for all cultural activities. **1948** T. S. ELIOT *Notes Def. Culture* i. 28 The culture with which primitive Christianity came into contact..was itself a religious culture in decline. *Ibid.* v. 93 A careful fostering [by Russia in its satellites] of local 'culture', culture in the reduced sense of the word, as everything that is picturesque, harmless and separable from politics such as language and literature, local arts and customs. **1953** A. K. C. OTTAWAY *Education & Society* i. 8 A single word to express 'the whole life of a community' is a special use of the word 'culture', which has been developed by the social anthropologists. **1954** S. PIGGOTT *Neolithic Cultures* v. 123 Probably the word culture should be employed to define the collective and tangible outcome (pot-making, house-planning, tomb-building) of the material and spiritual traditions of a group of people. **1963** *Brit. Jrnl. Sociol.* XIV. 21 By 'culture' is meant the whole complex of learned behaviour, the traditions and techniques and the material possessions, the language and other symbolism, of some body of people.

c. Phr. ***the two cultures***: see quot. 1956.

1956 C. P. SNOW in *New Statesman* 6 Oct. 413/1 The separation between the two cultures has been getting deeper under our eyes; there is now precious little communication between them... The traditional culture..is, of course, mainly literary..the scientific culture is expansive, not restrictive. **1959** —— *Two Cultures & Sci. Revol.* 16 Those in the two cultures can't talk to each other..very little of twentieth-century science has been assimilated into twentieth-century art. **1961** *Listener* 16 Nov. 809/1 The lack of communication between scientists and non-scientists, which has been so much discussed recently in terms of 'the two cultures'. **1967** 'W. HAGGARD' *Conspirators* ii. 14 He could explain things to laymen simply, despising ill-digested chatter about two cultures.

d. *attrib.* and *Comb.*, as ***culture-condition, -instinct, -monger***, etc.; ***culture-loving*** ppl. adj.; **culture shock**: see SHOCK *sb.*[3] 4 d; **culture vulture**, a rhyming collocation indicating a person who is voracious for culture.

1889 G. B. SHAW *London Music* (1937) 201 The race of culture humbugs. **1897** MARY KINGSLEY *W. Africa* 28 The present culture-condition of West Africa. *Ibid.* Pref. p. ix, Your superior culture-instincts may militate against your enjoying West Africa. **1905** *Daily Chron.* 15 June 3/1 The culture-loving Catholic Gael. **1909** *Westm. Gaz.* 2 Jan. 11/2 A modernised, constitutional, culture-loving Turkish State. **1931** A. HUXLEY *Music at Night* 226 Most professional intellectuals will approve of culture-snobbery (even while intensely disliking most individual culture-snobs). **1933** *Amer. Jrnl. Sociol.* XXXIX. 301 (*title*) The bureaucratic culture pattern and political revolution. **1938** DYLAN THOMAS *Let.* 23 Mar. (1966) 190 Advanced writing..sells very well over there [America], they're such culture-snobs. **1939** 'M. INNES' *Stop Press* III. iii. 376 You couldn't have a more persistent culture-hound. **1947** in Wentworth & Flexner *Dict. Amer. Slang* (1960) 134/2 Everybody can't be a culture vulture. *a* **1953** DYLAN THOMAS *Quite Early One Morning* (1954) 67 See the garrulous others, also, gabbing and garlanded from one nest of culture-vultures to another. **1955** *20th Cent.* June 536 An attack on contemporary 'Culture'-mongers. **1960** KOESTLER *Lotus & Robot* 279 Literacy, culture-hunger and leisure-time are increasing even more rapidly than the birth-rate. **1964** *Amer. Speech* XXXIX. 46 The Caribs were very great travelers, and their words became culture words, words found in all the Indian languages on the Caribbean Sea. *Ibid.* 50 These pirates could have made a culture word of *America*. **1966** L. J. COHEN *Diversity of Meaning* i. 15 We also have the notion of a culture-word or culture-sentence, as when a historian of ideas is concerned with the meaning of the word 'mass' in seventeenth-century physics.

Also *spec.* in *Anthropol.* and *Sociol.* (In some contexts the meaning shades into an attrib. use of sense 5.)

1901 *Contemp. Rev.* Mar. 455 The ancient 'culture-heroine'. **1903** *Daily Chron.* 11 June 3/1 The hero-tales and culture-legends of the prehistoric period of the Hebrews. **1907** A. C. HADDON in N. W. Thomas *Anthropol. Ess.* 183 The death dances were introduced into the Western Islands by two culture heroes from New Guinea. **1921** E. SAPIR *Language* x. 223 That a group of languages need not in the least correspond to a racial group or a culture area is easily demonstrated. **1922** D. H. LAWRENCE *Fantasia of Unconscious* xi. 203 The woman is now the responsible party, the law-giver, the culture-bearer. **1931** H. J. ROSE tr. *W. Schmidt's Orig. & Growth Relig.* v. xiv. 221 Leo Frobenius, a pupil of Ratzel, enlarged..the doctrine of 'culture-circles' (or 'spheres', *Kulturkreise*). **1933** *Downside Rev.* LI. 185 Russia is a culture-complex in itself, and Russia's problem is not ours. **1936** *Mind* XLV. 294 In the modern world, with its ever-increasing facilities for culture-contacts, a world-culture is in process of formation. **1945** *Mind* LIV. 78 The culture-hero has a vague complex status, part man, part demi-god. **1948** T. S. ELIOT *Notes Def. Culture* iv. 70 Since..the scattering of Jews amongst peoples holding the Christian Faith, it may have been unfortunate..that the culture-contact between them has had to be within those neutral zones of culture in which religion could be ignored. **1949** M. MEAD in M. Fortes *Social Structure* 27 Teacher, physician, nurse..each in turn represents some different form of culture conflict. **1951** R. FIRTH *Elem. Social Organiz.* iii. 81 Terms such as 'culture-contact'..were introduced to express the way in which new patterns of behaviour or types of relationship were acquired and incorporated into a primitive system. *Ibid.* 109 He is culture-bound in his desires as well as his activities. **1953** *Proc. Prehist. Soc.* XIX. 41 (*title*) The prehistoric culture-sequence in the Maltese Archipelago. **1957** *Burlington Mag.* Nov. 246/2 A theory of culture-circles whereby societies are classified as hunting, food-gathering, harvesting and horticultural. **1960** *Listener* 18 Aug. 244/1 The people of the host country appear to lack the normal conventions of social behaviour or to have a different and apparently illogical system... Most Europeans in Africa withdraw into their own community, and quickly equate their own way of doing things with their own superior material culture... This reaction..has been called 'culture shock'. **1962** D. HARDEN *Phoenicians* i. 24 To pick out what is Egyptian and Mesopotamian among finds and culture-traits in Phoenicia is not nearly so hard. *Ibid.* ii. 25 Their position on the land-route between the two great culture-areas of antiquity laid them open to constant political domination and cultural influences from each. **1969** *Listener* 30 Jan. 155/2 There was a curious naivety..in the frank description of how destructive, physically and socially, the culture-contacts with these remote peoples could be.

6. The prosecution with special attention or study *of* any subject or pursuit; = CULTIVATION 3. (*rare.*)

1876 BANCROFT *Hist. U.S.* I. Introd., An earnest culture of the arts of peace.

culture ('kʌltjʊə(r)), *v.* [a. F. *culture-r* (15th c.), f. *culture*: see prec.] *trans.* To subject to culture, to cultivate: **a.** *lit.* (the soil, plants.) Now chiefly *poetic.* Now *rare.*

1510 *Caxton's Chron. Eng.* IV. F v a/1, 2000 plowmen..for to culture the lande. **1555** EDEN *Decades* 29 The Region was inhabyted and well cultured. **1634** SIR T. HERBERT *Trav.* 3 They cultured the earth with hornes of Goats and Oxen. **1735** THOMSON *Liberty* II. 162 In Countries cultur'd high: In ornamented Towns, where Order reigns. **1809** WIFFEN *Aonian Hours* (1820) 51 The lovely maid..Culturing roses with her spade. **1844** DE QUINCEY *Logic Pol. Econ.* 142 *note*, The capital being gone which should have cultured the estates. **1855-61** [see CULTURED 1].

b. *fig.* (arts, the mind, persons, etc.) Now *rare.*

1776 S. J. PRATT *Pupil Pleas.* II. 89 Our minds are not all formed or cultured alike. **1808** J. BARLOW *Columb.* IX. 498 And if, while all their arts around them shine, They culture more the solid than the fine. **1863** MARY HOWITT *F. Bremer's Greece* I. i. 13 A race and a city which they have contributed to culture in the noblest sense of the word.

c. *Biol.* To maintain (bacteria or other micro-organisms, tissues, organs, etc.) under artificial conditions in a suitable nutrient medium so that they can multiply, grow, or develop.

1908 *Practitioner* Sept. 463 The ovary and tube (unopened) were despatched..with a request to see what organism could be cultured, and to make a vaccine. **1934** HUXLEY & DE BEER *Elem. Exper. Embryol.* vii. 209 Fibroblasts of the fowl have been cultured *in vitro* for over 20 years..and show unchanged characters and an unchanged rate of growth. **1962** C. V. HARDING et al. in A. Pirie *Lens Metabolism Rel. Cataract* 460 The lens had been cultured for two days in 199 with 23% rabbit serum ultrafiltrate. **1971** *Nature* 16 Apr. 472/2 We decided to isolate and culture the bacteria. *Ibid.* 474/1 A technique for culturing green organisms such as filamentous algae and moss protonema on an agar substrate.

culture, obs. form of COULTER.

cultured ('kʌltjʊəd), *ppl. a.* [f. CULTURE *v.* and *sb.* + -ED.] Cultivated.

1. *lit.* **a.** of soil or plants. (Chiefly *poetic.*)

1743-6 SHENSTONE *Elegies* xxv, Our cultur'd vales. **1855** MACAULAY *Hist. Eng.* III. 655 The cultured fields and the stately mansions of the Seine. **1861** MRS. NORTON *Lady La G.* (1862) 102 Cultured shrubs and flowers together blent.

b. Developed under controlled natural conditions, esp. ***cultured pearl***. Cf. CULTURE *sb.* 3 b.

1921 *Current Hist.* July 623/2 It is quite impossible to tell the natural pearl from the cultured pearl. **1930** *Pop. Sci.* Dec. 45/3 Like 'natural' pearls, the cultured product can be dissolved in acids. **1940** *Chem. Abstr.* XXXIV. 4700 An x-ray study of aragonite in natural and cultured pearls.

2. *fig.* Improved by education and training; characterized by intellectual culture; refined.

[**1764** GOLDSM. *Trav.* 236 The gentler morals, such as play Thro' life's more cultur'd walks.] **1777** *Gamblers* 5 Young Pollio's cultur'd muse. **1860** TYNDALL *Glac.* I. i. 7 A cultured man of science. **1865** WHITTIER *Snow-bound* 521 Rebuking with her cultured phrase Our homeliness of words and ways.

¶ With distortion of spelling to indicate affected or vulgar pronunciation.

1929 GALSWORTHY *Exiled* 1, Quate! 'Ow culchad! Hairs and grices! **1940** H. G. WELLS *Babes in Darkling Wood* IV. i. 324 He likes treading out music with a pianola, for example, to the great disdain of the culchad Trotsky.

'cultureless, *a. rare.* [See -LESS.] Without culture, uncultivated (*lit.* and *fig.*).

1826 CAMPBELL *Poems, 'Ye field flowers'*, Earth's cultureless buds, to my heart ye were dear. **1891** E. PEACOCK *N. Brendon* I. 124 The cultureless multitude. **1941** 'G. ORWELL' *Lion & Unicorn* I. vi. 54 A rather restless, cultureless life, centring round tinned food, *Picture Post*, the radio, and the internal combustion engine. **1948** —— *Coll. Ess.* (1968) IV. 457 A genuinely classless society, which Mr. [T. S.] Eliot assumes would be a cultureless society.

'culturer. *rare.* [f. CULTURE *v.* + -ER[1].] One who cultures or cultivates.

1880 OUIDA *Moths* ix. 117 The culturers of human nature are less wise, and they sow poison.

'culturism. *nonce-wd.* [f. CULTURE *sb.* + -ISM.] Systematic devotion to culture.

1886 D. S. GREGORY in *Homilet. Rev.* Dec. 469 Spencerism and general culturism and perfectionism.

culturist ('kʌltjʊərɪst). [f. as prec. + -IST.]

1. One professionally engaged in the culture of plants, fish, or other natural products.

1828 (*title*) Culturist. **1846** Cox in *Jrnl. R. Agric. Soc.* VII. II. 494 Well known to every practical culturist. **1883** *Fisheries Exhib. Catal.* (ed. 4) 97 The naturalist and fish culturist.

2. An advocate or devotee of culture.

1870 J. C. SHAIRP *Culture & Relig.* (1878) 7 The Culturists..by which term I mean not those who esteem culture..but those..who recommend it as the one panacea for all the ills of humanity. **1889** *Harper's Mag.* May 936/1 Adventists, socialists, spiritualists, culturists.

culturology (kʌltjʊə'rɒlədʒɪ). *Social Anthropology. U.S.* [ad. G. *kulturologie* (W. Ostwald *Philos. d. Werte* (1913) xiii. 286); cf. CULTURE *sb.* 5 a, b, -OLOGY.] The science or study of (a) culture. Hence **culturo'logical** *a.*, of or pertaining to culturology; **cultu'rologist**, a student of culturology.

1939 L. A. WHITE in *Amer. Anthropologist* XLI. 571 Application of the viewpoint and principles of the philosophy of evolution is as essential to the solution of many problems in culturology as it is in biology or physics. **1949** *Antiquity* XXIII. 55 What White calls the 'culturological' approach. **1956** F. B. STEINER *Taboo* i. 17, I am not referring to American culturology. **1957** *Contrib. Indian Sociol.* I. 50 The culturologist may feel at ease but the sociologist is at a loss.

‖**cultus** ('kʌltəs). [a. L. *cultus* (*u-* stem) cultivation, tending, culture, adoration, f. ppl. stem of *colĕre*: see CULT.]

†**1.** Worship; = CULT *sb.* 1. *Obs.*

1640 *Canterb. Self-Convict.* 49 To give to it [the altar] any religious worship, any cultus..any adoration, they do detest it, as palpable idolatrie.

2. An organized system of religious worship or ceremonial; also *transf.*; = CULT *sb.* 2, 3.

1838 EMERSON *Addr. Cambridge, Mass.* Wks. (Bohn) II. 194 As the Cultus, or established worship of the civilized world, it has great historical interest. **1846** DE QUINCEY *Christianity as Org. Pol. Movem.* Wks. XII. 253 There was a *cultus*, or ceremonial worship: *that* constituted the sum-total of religion in the idea of a Pagan. **1865** PUSEY *Truth Eng. Ch.* 181 That portion of the Roman Church, which is most devoted to the cultus of the Blessed Virgin.

cultus-cod ('kʌltəs,kɒd). [Chinook *cultus* 'of little worth', G. B. Goode.] A chiroid fish (*Ophiodon elongatus*), an important article of food on the Pacific coast of North America.

1884 *Rep. U.S. Fishery Commission* 267. **1888** G. B. GOODE *Amer. Fishes* 270 The Cultus Cod is universally called 'Cod-fish' where the true cod is unknown. About Puget Sound the English call it 'Ling'.

culur, obs. form of COLOUR.

-culus, -cula, -culum, a L. dim. suffix of all three genders, as in *fasci-culus* little fascis or bundle, *auri-cula* little ear, *opus-culum* small work. For the phonetic representatives of these, and their adapted forms in *-cle*, -CULE, see the latter. A considerable number of the Latin words are retained unchanged in technical or learned use, as *calculus, fasciculus, Ranunculus, Auricula*, esp. of those in *-culum*, as *curriculum, operculum, opusculum, vasculum, vinculum*, etc.

culvard: see CULVERT *a.*

culver[1] ('kʌlvə(r)). Forms: 1-2 **culfre**, 1 **culufre, culefre, culfer**, 3 **cullfre, culure, kulure, colfre**, 3-4 **coluere**, 4 **colure, coluyr**, 4-6 **culuer(e, coluer, -ver**, 5 **colvyr, -uour, couluour, culuor, -uyr, -uour, -vour, (col(l)er, collour)**, 4- **culver.** [OE. *culfre* wk. fem. (and ? *culfer* str. fem.), not known in the other Teut. langs. By Grimm thought to be derived from L. *columba*; but even if we take *culufre* as an earlier form (in which we are hardly justified), it is not easy to connect this phonetically with the L. word. The thoroughly popular standing of the name is also against its adoption from Latin.]

1. A dove, a pigeon; now the name of the wood-pigeon in the south and east of England.

c **825** *Vesp. Psalter* liv. 7 [lv. 6] Hwelc seleð me fiðru swe swe culfran & ic fliȝu & ȝerestu. *a* **1000** *Cædmon's Gen.* 1465 (Gr.) Wæs culufre of cofan sended. *c* **1000** ÆLFRIC *Voc.* in Wr.-Wülcker 131 *Columba*, culfer. *c* **1175** *Lamb. Hom.* 95 On culfre onlicnesse..wes godes gast isceawed. *c* **1200** ORMIN 1254 Cullfre iss milde, & meoc, & swet..& fedeþþ oþerr cullfress bridd. **1297** R. GLOUC. (1724) 190 Foure wyte colfren. **1398** TREVISA *Barth. de P.R.* XII. vi. (Tollem. MS.), In Egypte and in Siria a coluer is tauȝte to bere lettres and to be messangeres oute of on prouynce into anoþer. *Ibid.* XII. vii. (1495) 418 Wylde colouores. *c* **1420** *Chron. Vilod.* 484 Þe colleron þ[t] he was wond to kepe and fede. **1540-1** ELYOT *Image Gov.* 15 Egges of wilde foule and culvers. **1595** SPENSER *Sonn.* lxxxix, The Culuer on the bared bough Sits mourning. *a* **1617** HIERON *Wks.* (1620) II. 469 Now, a doue, a culuer, is a bird that loues salt exceedingly. **1728-46** THOMSON *Spring* 452 Whence, borne on liquid wing, The sounding culver shoots. **1830** TENNYSON *Poems* 81 The culvers mourn All the livelong day. **1868** BROWNING *Ring & Bk.* XII. 479 The lark, the thrush, the culver too.

†**b.** ? A vessel shaped like a dove. *Obs.* (Cf. COLUMBINE *sb.*[2] 4).

1500 *Churchw. Acc. St. Dunstan's, Canterb.* 27 A culver off latyn to ber frank-and-cense in. **1596** *Churchw. Acc. Kirton-in-Lindsey* in *Proc. Soc. Antiq.* 14 Apr. (1864), Payd John Leverett for mending the culver.

c. *fig.* An appellation of tender affection.

a **1225** *Ancr. R.* 98 Cum to me, mi leofmon, mi kulure. *c* **1340** [see CULVER-HOUSE]. **1382** WYCLIF *Song Sol.* vi. 8 Oon is my culuer, my parfit. **1491** CAXTON *Vitas Patr.* (W. de W. 1495) I. xl. 61 b/1 She herde oure lorde whiche callyd her sayenge: Come to me my spowse, my culuer or douue.

2. *Comb.*, as †***culver-dove, -dung***; ***culver-like*** adj.; †**culver-bird**, a young pigeon; **culver-headed** *a.* (*dial.*), soft-headed, stupid (Forby); †**culver-hole**, a dove-cote, pigeon-hole; †**culverwort** = COLUMBINE. Also CULVER-FOOT, -HOUSE, -TAIL.

1382 WYCLIF *Lev.* v. 7 Offre he two turturs, or two *culuer bryddis. **1567** DRANT *Horace's Epist.* x. D vij, The *culuer-doues of auncient league The trewest twaine that bee. **1581** LAMBARDE *Eiren.* IV. iv. (1602) 437 If any Tanner..haue vsed any other, then Lime, *Culuerdung, Hendung, cold Water..and Okenbarke. **1565-73** COOPER *Thesaurus*, *Alveolus*, a *culuer hole, or a place made of woode for culuers. **1581** J. BELL *Haddon's Answ. Osor.* 130 Angelike chastitie, *culverlike simplicitie. **1597** GERARDE *Herbal* App. to Table, *Culverwort is Columbine.

†**'culver**[2]. *rare*$^{-1}$. Used for CULVERIN (perh. by confusion with prec.).

1805 SCOTT *Last Minstr.* IV. xx, Falcon and culver, on each tower, Stood prompt their deadly hail to shower.

† 'culverfoot. *Herb. Obs.* Dove's-foot, a small species of wild Geranium.

c **1450** *Voc.* in Wr.-Wülcker 612/40 *Sparagus*, Colverfot. *c* **1450** *Alphita* (Anecd. Oxon.) 140 Pes Columbinus.. culverfot [*printed* clauerfot]. **1585** LUPTON *Thous. Notable Th.* IX. § 15 If the Fistula be outward, put into it the juice of Culverfoot, for it healeth it. **1879** PICKERING *Chron. Hist. Plants* 718.

† 'culver-house. *Obs.* A pigeon-house, a dove-cote. Also *fig.*

1340 *Ayenb.* 142 þet is þet coluerhous huerinne resteþ and him deþ þe colure oure lhord. *c* **1420** *Pallad. on Husb.* I. 554 Under thi colverhous in alle the brede Make mewes tweyne. **1587** HARMAR tr. *Beza's Serm.* 279 (T.) Yet was this poor culverhouse sorer shaken. **1624** GEE *Foot out of Snare* 21 Who think the time is come, to pull downe our Culver-house, our little Church. **1796** W. MARSHALL *W. England* Gloss., *Culver-house*, pigeon-house or dove-cot. **1887** R. S. FERGUSON in *Archæol. Jrnl.* June 105 An almost forgotten dovecot or 'culverhouse', as such are called in the south.

culverin ('kʌlvərın). Also 6 coulvering, culuerene, -rijn, 6–7 culvering, 7 colverin, 6–9 culverine. [a. F. *coulevrine* (*c* 1400 in Hatzfeld) = It. and med.L. *colubrina*, f. F. *couleuvre*, It. *colubro* snake: cf. L. *colubrīnus* of the nature of a snake. Names of reptiles were frequently applied to early cannon.]

1. The name of a gun and cannon formerly in use: **a.** *orig.* A small fire-arm, a kind of hand-gun. **b.** In later times, a large cannon, very long in proportion to its bore.

The length of the ordinary culverin ranged from 10 to 13 ft., the diameter of its bore from 5 to 5½ inches, and the weight of shot from 17 to 20 lbs. *bastard culverin*, bore 4 in., shot about 7 lbs.; *demi-culverin* or *culverin-moyen*, bore 4½ in., shot about 10 lbs.: see DEMI-CULVERIN.

a. [**1466** *Inv. Fastolf's Goods* in *Paston Lett.* No. 979 III. 441 In artilleria, videlicet Colubrinas librillas diversorum magnitudinum.] **1489** *Ld. Treas. Acc. Scotl.* I. 122 To Qwariour.. to pass to Stirling, to get Culuerinis to bring to the felde. *a* **1572** KNOX *Hist. Ref.* Wks. 1846 I. 221 A certane French man delivred a coulvering to George Tod, Scottisman, to be stocked. **1821** SCOTT *Kenilw.* xv, He found the gate of Say's Court defended by men with culverins. **1864** KIRK *Chas. Bold* I. II. ii. 491 Armed with.. Culverins—a name then applied not, as at a later period, to a species of cannon, but to a rude kind of musket. **1874** BOUTELL *Arms & Arm.* xi. 219.

b. **1515** in Pitcairn *Crim. Trials Scot.* I. 260* Twa culuering-myance, gun-stanis, gun-powdir, and certane hacbuschis. **1549** *Compl. Scot.* vi. 41 Gunnaris.. mak reddy ȝour cannons, culuerene moyens, culuerene bastardis.. culverenis, and hail schot. **1622** R. HAWKINS *Voy. S. Sea* (1847) 214 The saker, the demy-colverin, the colverin, and demi-cannon (being peeces that reach much further point blanke then the cannon). **1687** CONGREVE *Old Bach.* II. ii, O I am calm, Sir; calm as a discharged culverin. **1750** CARTE *Hist. Eng.* II. 714 Wounded in the ancle by a shot from a culverine. **1843** H. AINSWORTH *Tower of London* (1864) 58 He.. crouched beneath the carriage of a culverin.

c. *fig.*

1619 FLETCHER *M. Thomas* II. ii, Do you make me carrier Of your confound-mee's, and your culverings [volleys of oaths]?

2. *attrib.* and *Comb.*, as *culverin-bore*, *-shot*, etc.

1590 SIR J. SMYTH *Disc. Weapons* 12 The Enemies.. will descharge Cannon, Culverin and Saker shot. **1634–5** BRERETON *Trav.* (1844) 165 Six iron demiculverin drakes, four whole culverin drakes. **1640** YORKE *Union Hon.* 64 They lay within Culvering Shot. **1667** SIR R. MORAY in *Phil. Trans.* II. 475 A Gun to be prepared of Culverin-Bore.

culverineer (ˌkʌlvərı'nıə(r)). Also -er. [f. prec. + -EER¹, -ER.] A soldier armed with a culverin (hand-gun); a gunner in charge of a culverin (cannon).

1568 *Reg. Secr. Sig.* lib. xxxiv. fol. 84 To convoy.. þame away with þair armour effeirand for coluerinaris on fute. **1849** J. GRANT *Kirkaldy of Gr.* ix. 85 The culverineers wore a habergeon with sleeves. **1881** GREENER *Gun* 37 One man (the culveriner) levelled and held the weapon during discharge.

'culverkeys. [f. CULVER dove + KEY.]

1. A popular name of various plants, the flowers of which suggest a bunch of keys. **a.** In 17th c. writers, and still in Somersetshire, etc., the wild Hyacinth or Blue-bell, *Scilla nutans*.

(Commentators on Dennys and Walton have wrongly guessed Columbine, Meadow Cranesbill, *Orchis mascula*.)

a **1613** J. DENNYS *Secr. Angl.* I. in Arb. *Garner* I. 157 Pale ganderglass and azure culverkeys. **1653** WALTON *Angler* xi. 214, I could.. see here a Boy gathering Lillies and Lady-smocks, and there a Girle cropping Culverkeys and Cowslips. **1873** *Jrnl. Horticulture* 1 May 350/2 The Culverkey is well known in Somersetshire, and applies to the Bluebell (*Hyacinthus non-scriptus*). In Oxfordshire and Essex the same flower is sometimes called Culvers.

b. The Cowslip. (In some parts said to be the Oxlip; but cowslip and oxlip are confounded dialectally.)

1736 PEGGE *Kenticisms, Culverkeys*, cowslips. **1873** *Jrnl. Horticulture* 1 May 350/2 The term Culverkeys is in general use among all the poorer classes of this neighbourhood [Ashford], and is applied to the Cowslip (*Primula veris*).. Culverkey wine is a much-admired beverage. **1878–86** BRITTEN & HOLLAND citing *Field* 26 June 1876, *Coverkeys* or *Covey-keys*, the Oxlip—not the true *Primula elatior*, but the plant known as *P. variabilis.* Kent. **1887** *Kentish Gloss.*, *Culver key*, the cowslip.

c. In Clare, app. a pale-flowered species of Vetch, ? *Vicia sepium* or *V. sylvatica.*

1835 CLARE *Rural Muse* 68 Here I in cutting nosegays would delight, The lambtoe tuft, the paler culverkey.

2. The seedpods of the ash, ash-keys. *dial.*

1790 GROSE *Provinc. Gloss.* (Britt. & Holl.). **1851** G. JOHNSTON *Flora of Berw.*

culver's-physic, -root. [f. proper name of a Dr. Culver.] A species of Speedwell, *Veronica virginica*, found in the eastern parts of North America, Siberia, etc., the root of which is used in medicine as an emeto-cathartic.

1858 HOGG *Veget. Kingd.* 567 *Veronica virginica* is a native of the United States, and is there called Culver's Physic. **1866** *Treas. Bot.*, *Culver's root* or *Culver's physic*, American names for *Veronica virginica.*

† **'culvert**, *a. Obs.* Also 4 culvart, -vard; and see COLWARD. [a. OF. *culvert*, *colvert*, late L. *collībertus* fellow-freedman, in Middle Ages a serf, villain, one whose condition was intermediate between slavery and freedom, but nearer the former; hence, *adj.* abject, wretched, villainous, vile, infamous, etc.] Infamous, villainous, treacherous.

a **1225** *Ancr. R.* 96 No wouhleche nis so culuert ase is o pleinte wis. *a* **1300** *Floriz & Bl.* 329 þe porter is culuert and felun. *c* **1325** *Chron. Eng.* 788 in Ritson *Met. Rom.* II. 303 The King hede a stiward, That was fel ant culvard.

culvert ('kʌlvət), *sb.* [A recent word of obscure origin.

It has been conjectured to be a corruption of F. *couloir*, in Cotgr. also *coulouëre*, 'a channel, gutter, or any such hollow, along which melted things are to run', f. *couler* to flow. But points of connexion between the Fr. and Eng. words, in form and sense, are wanting. On the other hand some think 'culvert' an Eng. dialect word, taken into technical use at the epoch of canal-making. No connexion with *covert* has been traced.]

A channel, conduit, or tunneled drain of masonry or brick-work conveying a stream of water across beneath a canal, railway embankment, or road; also applied to an arched or barrel-shaped drain or sewer.

Used from *c* 1770 in connexion with canal construction; thence extended to railways, highways, town-drainage, etc. In connexion with railways and highways, it is sometimes disputed whether a particular structure is a 'culvert' or a 'bridge'. The essential purpose of a *bridge*, however, is to carry a road at a desired height over a river and its channel, a chasm, or the like; that of a *culvert* to afford a passage for a small crossing stream under the embankment of a railway or highway, or beneath a road where the configuration of the surface does not require a bridge. Locally, the term 'culvert' is often limited to a barrel drain, bricks shaped for which are known as *culvert-bricks*. See *Notes & Queries*, 8th Ser. III. 248, 377.

1773 *Chron.* in *Ann. Reg.* 97, 40 locks, 114 cart-bridges, 9 foot-bridges, and 120 culverts or aqueducts, including those magnificent ones over the rivers Dove and Trent. **1785** *Dudley & Birm. Canal Act* (25 Geo. III, c. 87 § 6), The said Company.. shall.. make and support good and sufficient Culverts and Aqueducts to convey the same [streams].. in the several and respective courses in which they have hitherto run. **1788** *Deritend Bridge Act* (28 Geo. III, c. 70 § 7), To cause a Culvert to be made of the diameter of six feet at the least. **1801** *Croydon Canal Act* (41 Geo. III, c. 127 § 95). **1804** REES *Cycl.* s.v. *Canal*, The construction of culverts or drains under a canal, for conveying away water from the upper to the lower side of a canal. **1837** WHISHAW *Anal. Railways* 271 *Culvert*, a large drain either of brick or stone used in railways for passing brooks and streams under the embankments. **1840** —— *Railways Gt. Brit.* 426 The largest culvert carries the Claxton brook under the embankment.

b. Applied to an underground channel in which electric cables or mains are laid; also called a *conduit.*

1889 *Daily News* 12 Oct. 6/1 Mr. Crompton's culverts are .. narrow and shallow tunnels lined with brick work. The St. James's Company's cast-iron troughs may be fairly described as portable culverts. They.. are an impregnable protection for the copper cables inside them. **1893** *Electr. Engineer* 12 May vii, Systems of copper strip laid in culverts.

Hence **'culvert** *v.*, to provide or lay with culverts.

1889 *Daily News* 12 Oct. 6/1 The culverting of Clubland [for electric lighting] has been an exceptionally difficult operation. **1890** BOLDREWOOD *Colonial Reformer* I. 121 The streets were aligned, metalled, and culverted.

'culvertage. *Feudal Law.* [a. OF. *culvertage*, f. *culvert* (see CULVERT *a.*) + -AGE. Cf. med.L. *culvertagium* in Du Cange.] The position of a *culvert*, villainage; forfeiture and degradation to the position of a villain or serf.

1613–8 DANIEL *Coll. Hist. Eng.* (1626) 116 King John.. summoning likewise all Earles, Barons.. to defend him.. vnder paine of Culuertage, and perpetuall seruitude. **1700** TYRRELL *Hist. Eng.* II. 753 The Reproach of *Culvertage*.. seems to have been.. not only a Penalty, but also a Term of Reproach for Cowardize. **1757** BURKE *Abridgm. Eng. Hist.* Wks. X. 519 The king of France.. summoned all his vassals, under the penalty of felony, and the opprobrious name of Culvertage.. to attend in this expedition. **1823–6** LINGARD *Hist. Eng.* (ed. 4) III. 31 *note*, Culvertage.. The culprit was liable by law to the forfeiture of all property, and perpetual servitude.

† **'culver-tail.** *Carpentry. Obs.* = DOVETAIL.

1616 BULLOKAR, *Culuertaile*, a strong kind of building by fastening boards or tymber with artificiall joynts so firmely togither that they cannot fall asunder. **1639** HORN & ROBOTHAM *Gate Lang. Unl.* xlviii. § 530 The Joyner.. joyneth them close with culver-tailes. **1703** T. N. *City & C. Purchaser* 125. **1806** GREGORY *Dict. Arts & Sc.* I. 469.

Hence **'culvertail** *v.*; **'culvertailed** *ppl. a.*; **'culvertailing** *vbl. sb.*

1627 CAPT. SMITH *Seaman's Gram.* ii. 7 Culuertailed.. as the Carling ends are fixed in the beames. **1727** BAILEY vol. II, *Culver-tailing.* **1775** ASH, *Culvertail*, to fasten one piece of timber into another, by tenon in the form of a dove's tail.

† **'culvertship.** *Obs. rare*$^{-1}$. [f. CULVERT *a.* + -SHIP.] Villainy, treachery, perfidy.

a **1225** *Ancr. R.* 294 Ure Louerd.. brouhte so to grunde his kointe kuluertschipe & his prude strencðe.

culverwort, columbine: see CULVER¹ 2.

'culye, culȝe, *v. Sc.* ? *Obs.* Also 6 cuilȝe. [app. the same as CULLY *v.*¹, and like it related to CULL *v.*²; but the form seems to represent F. *cueillir*: cf. Sc. *assalȝe*, *assailȝe*, F. *assaillir.*] To cherish, coax, draw forth by coaxing or flattery.

1513 DOUGLAS *Æneis* I. x. 27 Now him withaldis the Phenitiane Dido, And cuilȝeis him with slekit wordis sle. *Ibid.* VIII. x. 86 Scho [the she-wolf].. can thaim culȝe baith. *a* **1605** MONTGOMERIE *Misc. Poems, Invect. agst. Fortune*, Sho causles culȝies, and but falt defames. **1862** HISLOP *Prov. Scot.* 160 Ower narrow counting culyes no kindness.

Hence † **'culyour.**

1510 in Pitcairn *Crim. Trials Scot.* I. *66 Item, gif þair be ony Culȝouris, nycht-walkaris, or Sorneris?

culyon, culyur, obs. ff. CULLION, CULLER.

culys, obs. form of CULLIS.

‖ **cum** (kʌm). Latin preposition, meaning 'with, together with', used in English in local names of combined parishes or benefices, as *Chorlton-cum-Hardy*, *Stow-cum-Quy*, where it originated in Latin documents. Also in several much-used Latin phrases, as ***cum grano salis*** (or familiarly ***cum grano***), lit. 'with a grain of salt,' *i.e.* with some caution or reserve; ***cum privilegio*** (***ad imprimendum solum***) with privilege (of sole printing); and in expressions, technical or humorous, imitating these, e.g. ***cum dividend*** (***cum div.***) relating to the sale or transfer of stock or shares together with the dividend about to be paid on them. Freq. used as a combining word to indicate a dual nature or function.

1589 *Hay any Work* 42 Many bookes.. had *cum priuilegio*, and yet were neuer authorized. **1653** BAXTER *Chr. Concord* 64, I know this speech must be understood *cum grano salis.* **1871** J. C. YOUNG *Mem. C. M. Young* I. iv. 125 (Stanford) He greatly preferred coffee cum chicory to coffee pure and simply. **1871–3** TROLLOPE *Eustace Diamonds* (1873) I. xiii. 173 The Belgrave-cum-Pimlico life. **1877** R. GIFFEN *Stock Exch. Securities* 59 The price quickly rising from 125 cum div. early in July, to 136 ex div. in September. *a* **1893** *Mod.* All he says must be received *cum grano.* **1913** KIPLING *Diversity of Creatures* (1917) 172 Easy motor-bike-*cum*-side-car trips round London. **1939** O. LANCASTER *Homes Sweet Homes* 44 The fervent mediaevalism.. developed a philosophic-cum-economic tinge. **1959** *Manch. Guardian* 3 July 5/6 Three short.. dinner-cum-cocktail dresses. **1959** *Viewpoint* July 33 The atmosphere of laboratory-cum-workshop.

cum, obs. form of COME *v.*, *pa. pple.*, *sb.*²

cumacean (kjuː'meıʃ(ı)ən), *a. Zool.* [f. mod.L. *Cumacea* (see def.), f. *Cuma* genus of crustaceans, f. Gr. *Κῦμα* (see CYME).] Of or pertaining to the Cumacea, an order of small sessile-eyed crustaceans resembling prawns, with a hard brittle carapace. Also as *sb.*

1879 *Ann. & Mag. Nat. Hist.* III. 56 *Diastylis Josephinæ* .. appears to be the commonest Cumacean inhabiting the deep waters between Faröe and Shetland. **1887** G. O. SARS in *Challenger Rep., Zool.* XIX. II. 4 Perhaps even some of the palæozoic forms placed among the Phyllocarida may have formed a direct transition to the Cumacean type. **1900** —— *Crustacea of Norway* III. p. v, The Cumacean fauna of Norway. **1902** *Encycl. Brit.* XXX. 479/2 According to Sars, the Sympoda (or Cumaceans), in spite of their sessile eyes, have closer affinities with the stalk-eyed orders. **1952** F. R. ALLISON in *Scottish Naturalist* LXIV. 40 Most planktonic animals, including.. cumaceans.. recorded in the fulmar's diet, have a vertical diurnal migration which brings them into the surface waters at night.

Cumæan (kjuː'miːən), *a.* and *sb.* [f. *Cumæ* (L. *Cūmæ*, Gr. *Κύμη*), an ancient city on the Italian coast near Naples, founded by the Greeks in the 8th cent. B.C. + -AN.] **A.** *adj.* Of or pertaining to Cumæ, esp. famous for the Sibyl mentioned by Virgil in the 'Æneid'. **B.** *sb.* A native or inhabitant of Cumæ.

1731 J. TRAPP *Works Virgil* II. 347 Have you been led thro' the Cumæan Cave, And heard th 'impatient Maid divinely rave? **1803** C. WILMOT *Let.* 6 Mar. (1920) 168 Aeneas.. landed at the Cumaean shore a little way from the Lake Avernus. **1870** BREWER *Dict. Phr. & Fable* 819/1 The Cumæan sibyl was the conductor of Virgil to the infernal regions. **1931** D. RANDALL-MACIVER *Gk. Cities in Italy & Sicily* i. 6 The Cumaeans, says Pausanias, showed a small stone urn in the cemetery of Apollo which they said contained her [*sc.* the Sibyl's] bones. **1968** *Encycl. Brit.* VI. 889/1 The *antrum* (cave) famous in legend as the seat of the oracle of the Cumaean Sibyl.

cumarin, var. of COUMARIN.

cumarone, var. COUMARONE.

cumate ('kjuːmət). *Chem.* [f. CUM-IC + -ATE[4].] A salt of cumic acid.

1873 WATTS *Fownes' Chem.* 791.

†**cu'matic, -ical**, *a. Obs.* [f. Gr. κῦματ- wave, after L. *cūmātilis* sea-coloured, blue,]

1622 PEACHAM *Compl. Gent.* (1661) 155 Cumatical colour, *i.e.* blew. **1623** COCKERAM *Eng. Dict.* I, *Cumaticall-colour. Ibid.* II, Blew Colour, *Cumaticke.* **1775** ASH, *Cumatical.*

cumbecephalic, bad form of CYMBOCEPHALIC.

1866 LAING & HUXLEY *Preh. Rem. Caithn.* 128 The long-headed, or 'cumbecephalic' inhabitants of Scotland.

cumbent ('kʌmbənt), *a.* [ad. L. *-cumbent-em*, pr. pple. of *-cumbĕre* to lie down, used only in comp., *accumbĕre, recumbĕre*, etc.] Lying down, in a reclining position: *esp.* of figures in statuary.

1644 EVELYN *Diary* 12 Nov., Cumbent figures of marble. **1670–98** LASSELS *Voy. Italy* I. 129 It represents..St. Joseph in a cumbent posture. **1757** DYER *Fleece* I. 84 Too cold the grassy mantle..For cumbent sheep. **1849** ROCK *Ch. Fathers* II. 162 *note*, The very interesting cumbent figure found..in Rochester Cathedral.

cumber ('kʌmbə(r)), *sb.* Forms: 4 **kumbre**, 5 **komber, cumbyre**, 6 **combre**, 6–7 **comber**, *Sc.* **cummer**, (**-ar, -yr**), 6– **cumber**. [Used early in 14th c. in sense 1; but not common till 16th, and then at first chiefly Scotch, where it is also spelt *cummer*. The date, form, and sense, are all consistent with its being either a derivative of CUMBER *v.*, or a shortened form of ENCUMBER *sb.* But sense 2 strikingly coincides with Ger. *kummer*, MHG. (from *c* 1200) *kumber*, MLG. *kummer*, Du. *kommer*.

OF. had only *combre* fem. in the sense 'heap of felled trees, stones, or the like' (Godef.), corresponding to med.L. *combra* 'a mound or mole in a river for the sake of catching fish' (Du Cange), and akin to Merovingian L. *cumbrus*, pl. *cumbri, combri* 'barriers of felled trees' (Du C.), whence med.L. *incumbrāre*, F. *encombrer*, to ENCUMBER. Cf. also Pg. *combro* 'a heap of earth'. In the Meroving. L. *cumbrus*, Diez (s.v. *Colmo* saw a barbaric form, through **cumblus*, of L. *cumulus* heap: so also Littré, Scheler, Brachet, s.v. *Encombre*. But the question of the actual origin of *cumbrus*, and its relation to the Ger. *kummer* and its family, is a difficult one, which has been much investigated and discussed: see Grimm, Kluge, Franck, Doornkaat-Koolmann.]

†**1.** The condition of being cumbered; overthrow, destruction, rout. *Obs.*

1303 R. BRUNNE *Handl. Synne* 12516 Alle þe folk wyþ oute numbre, All broȝt y hem to kumbre. *a* **1400** —— *Chron.* (Rolls) 15474 (Petyt MS.) Elfrik for to bring to komber.

†**2.** Trouble, distress, embarrassment, inconvenience. *Obs.* or *arch.*

1500–20 DUNBAR *Devorit with Dreme* i, Sic hunger, sic cowartis, and sic cumber, Within this land was nevir hard nor sene. **1536** BELLENDEN *Cron. Scot.* (1821) II. 312 Solicitude or grit cummer. **1547** COVERDALE *Old Faith* iii. C j a, Vpon the woman he layed combre sorow and payne. **1552** LYNDESAY *Monarche* 5143 Thay depart frome cair and cummer, Frome trubyll, trauell, sturt, and stryfe. **1560** in E. Lodge *Illustr. Brit. Hist.* (1791) I. 337 Not..w[th]out yo[r] great combre and travayle. **1682** N. O. *Boileau's Lutrin* IV. 280 What Gains Shall answer all this Cumber, all these pains? **1719** D'URFEY *Pills* V. 147 Yet Ise possess more happiness, And he had more of Cumber. **1876** MORRIS *Sigurd* II. 129 Till a man from their seed be arisen to deal with the cumber and wrong.

†**b.** Sometimes attributed to the agent: The action of troubling or embarrassing. *Obs.*

1563 RANDOLPH in Robertson *Hist. Scot.* (1759) II. App. 15 That we may be void of their Comber. **1603** *Philotus* cxxxii, God..Conserue me fra thy cummer. *a* **1651** CALDERWOOD *Hist. Kirk* (1843) II. 523 Let these childer want the heads, which sall..make you quite of their cummer, (*quia mortui non mordent*). **1828** SCOTT *F.M. Perth* xvi, So the Fair City is quit of him and his cumber.

3. That which cumbers, incommodes, or hinders, by its weight, unwieldiness, or obstructive nature; a hindrance, obstruction, encumbrance, burden (*lit.* and *fig.*) Often contrasted with a 'help'.

c **1425** WYNTOUN *Cron.* V. xii. 1128 Hys Fadrys Landis of Herytage Fell til hym..All swylk Cumbyre he forsuke, And til haly lyf hym tuke. **1594** CAREW *Tasso* (1881) 119 Their horse and Camels heauy burdened, Amidst the way a grieuous cumber meet. **1611** COTGR. s.v. *Manteau*, A cloke is but a comber in faire weather. *a* **1639** W. WHATELEY *Prototypes* II. xxvi. (1640) 61 Jacob behaved not himselfe so as to be a cumber and burden to the family, but was helpfull to it. **1644** EVELYN *Mem.* (1857) I. 61 The stools and other cumber are removed when the assembly rises. **1756** J. WOOLMAN *Jrnl.* iii. (1840) 31 To live more free from outward cumbers. **1892** *Cornh. Mag.* Apr. 428 [He] led us outside, up over a cumber of limestone rocks.

†**b.** That which causes trouble or inconvenience; a trouble. *Obs.*

1589 NASHE *Anat. Absurd.* 40 So delighted to heare themselues, that they are a cumber to the eares of all other. **1664** EVELYN *Sylva* (1776) 411 What is reputed a curse and a cumber in some places is esteemed the ornament and blessing of another.

4. The action or quality of encumbering, or fact of being encumbered; hindrance, embarrassment, obstruction, encumbrance; cumbrousness.

a **1618** RALEIGH (J.), The greatest ships..are of marvellous charge and fearful cumber. **1664** EVELYN *Sylva*, Where some..[trees] were planted single in the Park without cumber, they spread above fourscore foot. **1786** *Phil. Trans.* LXXVI. 24 We shall..get rid of $\frac{11}{12}$ths of the..weight; and consequently of much cumber, unhandiness, and derangement. **1851** RUSKIN *Stones Ven.* (1881) I. Pref. 6 Of other prefatory matter..the reader shall be spared the cumber.

†**5.** Occupation with business to an inconvenient or burdensome degree; pressure of business; (with *pl.*) affairs that occupy and trouble one. *Obs.* or *arch.*

[**1653** A. WILSON *Jas. I*, 278 Free and at ease from comber and noise of Business.] **1669** PENN *No Cross* xiii. § 7 As if Cumber, not Retirement; and Gain, not Content, were the Duty and Comfort of a Christian. **1688** SANDILANDS *Salut. Endeared Love* 29 Taken up with the choaking Cares and Cumbers of this present Life. **1849** J. STERLING in *Fraser's Mag.* XXXIX. 178 A trader hoarding bullion in his trunk Will make small profit, though he 'scape from cumber.

cumber ('kʌmbə(r)), *v.* Forms: 3– **cumber**; also 3–7 **comber**, 4–5 **combur, comer**, 4–6 **combre, cumbre**, *Sc.* **cummer**, 5 **combir, cumbir, cumbyre, cummere, comyr**, *Sc.* **cummyr** (*pa. t.* **cumryt**). [*Cumber* vb. is known from *c* 1300. Its early derivatives *cumberment, cumbrance, cumbrous* (14th c. at least) all suppose for it a French derivation: cf. the parallel series under ENCUMBER, and its weakened form ACCUMBER, also OF. *encombrer, -ment, encombrance, encombros, -eus.*

Except in one doubtful instance, Godefroy cites OF. *combrer* only in the sense of *covrer* 'to lay hold of, seize, take', which does not account for the ME. uses of *cumber*. He has no examples of *combrance, combrement*, and only one (16th c.) example of *combreux*. Hence it would be more satisfactory to regard the English words as aphetic forms of the *encumber, acumber* types, but for their appearing earlier than these. The etymological history being unsettled, the order of the senses, and the precise meaning in many cases, is doubtful.]

†**1.** *trans.* To overwhelm, overthrow, rout, destroy. *Obs.*

1303 R. BRUNNE *Handl. Synne* 7465 Seuene maner synnes ..þe whych cumbren men on many folde. *c* **1330** —— *Chron.* (Rolls) 12356 Arthur bar on hym wyþ his launce To combren hym, als of chaunce. —— *Ibid.* 15474 Cadwan seide he wolde passe Humber, Elfrik to struye & to comber. *c* **1325** *E.E. Allit P.* B. 901 Cayre tid of þis kythe er combred þou worthe. **1375** BARBOUR *Bruce* VI. 429 [Douglas] cummerit thaim sua, That weill nane eschapit. *a* **1400–50** *Alexander* 1471 Alexander is at hand, and will vs all cumbre. **15..** *Lord of Learne* 416 in Furniv. *Percy Folio* I. 197 They ..cutten all his ioynts in sunder, & burnte him eke vpon a hyll; I-wis thé did him curstlye cumber.

†**b.** *pass.* To be overwhelmed and held fast, as in a slough. *Obs.* (Cf. Chaucer C.T. Prol. 508 'acombred [*v.r.* encombred] in the myre'.)

a **1300** *Cursor M.* 26514 (Cott.) If þou comberd be in sin. **1362** LANGL. *P. Pl.* A. I. 170 þei beoþ cumbred in care and cunnen not out-crepe. *c* **1440** *York Myst.* xxvi. 171 þou arte combered in curstnesse. **1460** in *Pol. Rel. & L. Poems* (1866) 84 þer was she combred yn a carefulle case.

†**c.** *intr.* (for *refl.*) in same sense. *Obs.*

? *a* **1400** *Chester Pl.* i. 219, I comber, I canker, I kindle in care, I sinke in sorrow.

†**2.** To harass, distress, trouble. *Obs.* (exc. with mixture of sense 4: to incommode, bother).

a **1300** *Cursor M.* 8018 (Cott.) Es nathing þat mai him cumber. *c* **1440** *York Myst.* xxxiv. 211 Ther quenes vs comeres with þer clakke. **1535** COVERDALE *1 Kings* xxi. 5 What is ye matter, that thy sprete is so combred? **1611** BIBLE *Luke* x. 40 Martha was cumbred about much seruing. **1666** COLLINS in Rigaud *Corr. Sci. Men* (1841) II. 462 To cumber you with some later thoughts of my own. **1820** SCOTT *Abbot* xv, I cumber you no longer with my presence. **1852** DICKENS *Bleak Ho.* xxvii, I disgrace nobody and cumber nobody.

†**b.** To confound or trouble the mind or senses; to perplex, puzzle. *Obs.*

c **1350** *Will. Palerne* 4047 þe king in þat carful þouȝt was cumbred ful long. **1398** TREVISA *Barth. De P.R.* III. xvii. (Tollem. MS.), Yf þe þinge þat is sen meueþ to swyftely þe syȝte is combrid. **1535** COVERDALE *Acts* x. 17 Whyle Peter was combred in him selfe what maner of vision this shulde be. **1616** R. C. *Times' Whistle* VI. 2871 To bring't about it my conceit doth cumber.

3. To hamper, embarrass, hinder, get or be in the way of (persons, their movements, etc.).

1375 BARBOUR *Bruce* VI. 141 Bot his hors, that wes born doune, Cummerit thaim the vpgang to ta. *c* **1470** HENRY *Wallace* I. 229 The press was thik, and cummerit thaim full fast. **1529** RASTELL *Pastyme, Hist. Brit.* (1811) 249 Every Frencheman combryd other. **1653** HOLCROFT *Procopius* II. 38 Their arming..combers their foot, then whom the Moors will be much the swifter. **1681** W. ROBERTSON *Phraseol. Gen.* (1693) 344 To *comber*, or incomber and entangle one. **1878** BROWNING *La Saisiaz* 4 Body shall cumber Soul-flight no more.

4. To occupy obstructively, or inconveniently; to block up or fill with what hinders freedom of motion or action; to burden, load.

c **1394** *P. Pl. Crede* 765 Comeren her stomakes wiþ curious drynkes. *c* **1430** *Syr Gener.* (Roxb.) 1332 Thou combrest the hous here. **1534** TINDALE *Luke* xiii. 7 Cut it doune: why combreth it the grounde? **1624** CAPT. SMITH *Virginia* IV. 128 Our ship..being so cumbred with the Passengers prouisions. **1707** FUNNELL *Voy.* (1729) 22 The Captain alledging that he would not cumber up his ship. **1874** S. COX *Pilgr. Ps.* v. 108 Streets cumbered with charred embers. **1885** *Law Times* LXXIX. 153/1 The unwieldy mass of case-law which now cumbers every practitioner's shelves.

5. *fig.* (of prec. senses).

c **1400** *Destr. Troy* 11774 To be cumbrid with couetous. **1493** *Festyvall* (W. de W. 1515) 116 b, The people were so combred with the synne of mawmetry. **1577** *Test. 12 Patriarchs* (1604) 101 When the mind is cumbred with disdain, the Lord departeth from it. **1581** J. BELL *Haddon's Answ. Osor.* 487 How can any such thought..comber your braines, as to beleve you shalbe able..so to bewitch the Queenes highnesse? **1585** ABP. SANDYS *Serm.* (1841) 142 Much authority is cumbered with many cares. **1676** RAY *Corr.* (1848) 123 Which I thought not fit to cumber the book with. **1813** SCOTT *Trierm.* II. x, Cares, that cumber royal sway. **1864** BOWEN *Logic* v. 133 [It] would..cumber and lengthen the sentence unnecessarily.

†**6.** To benumb, stiffen with cold, etc. *Obs.* Cf. CUMBLE *v.*

c **1325** *Metr. Hom.* 129 His sergant that cumbered was Wit parlesi. **1398** TREVISA *Barth. De P.R.* III. xxi. (1495) 68 As whan the fyngres ben combred and croked for grete colde. **1483** [see CUMBERED 1]. **1825–79** JAMIESON, *Cumber*, adj., benumbed. In this sense the hands are said to be cumber'd, *West Loth.*

†**7.** *pa. pple.* Of a hawk: Constipated. *Obs.* (= ENCUMBER 7.)

1486 *Bk. St. Albans* C iv b, A medecine for an hauke combred in the bowillis.

8. *Comb.*, as †**cumber-field**, a name for the Common Knotgrass (*Polygonum aviculare*), a troublesome weed in cornfields (in Bulleyn *Book of Simples* (1562) lf. 32); †**cumber-house**, one that cumbers or inconveniently occupies a house. Also CUMBER-GROUND, -WORLD.

1540 ELYOT *Image Gou.* (1556) 94 b, Semblablie shall I be unto hir an unpleasaunte cumbrehouse.

cumberance, -aunce, var. CUMBRANCE.

cumberband, -bund, var. CUMMERBUND.

cumbered ('kʌmbəd), *ppl. a.* [f. CUMBER *v.*]

†**1. a.** Cf. CUMBER *v.* 1 b. **b.** Benumbed; cf. CUMBER *v.* 6.

c **1430** *Chev. Assigne* 71 'A kowarde of kynde', quod she '& combred wrecche!' *c* **1430** *Hymns Virg.* (1867) 53 A combrid wretche in cowardise. *c* **1460** *Towneley Myst.* 266 Combred cowardes I you calle. **1483** *Cath. Angl.* 86 Cumbyrd (A. *Cummerd*); vbi Clumsyd.

2. Encumbered; hindered, hampered, occupied obstructively, etc.: see the verb.

1590 SPENSER *F.Q.* I. viii. 10 Whiles he strove his combred clubbe to quight Out of the earth. **1623** COCKERAM, *Cumbred*, let, hindred. **1684** BUNYAN *Pilgr.* II. 150 We are full of Hurry, in Fair time. 'Tis hard keeping our Hearts and Spirits in any good Order, when we are in a cumbred Condition. **1848** M. ARNOLD *Poems, Bacchanalia*, On the cumber'd plain.

cumberer ('kʌmbərə(r)). [f. CUMBER *v.* + -ER[1].] One who or that which cumbers: see the verb.

c **1450** *Guy Warw.* (C.) 2152 The ryche emperowre Raynere Wottyth not of thys comberere. *a* **1572** KNOX *Hist. Ref.* Wks. 1846 I. 73 Cumerars and quellars of Christes Kirk. **1746** HARVEY *Flower Garden* (1818) 97 Not one species among all this variety of herbs is a cumberer of the ground. **1831** SCOTT *Cast. Dang.* i, Grey rocks, huge cumberers of the soil.

'cumber-ground. [CUMBER *v.* 8.] A thing or (esp.) person that uselessly cumbers the ground; a useless or unprofitable occupant of a position. (See Luke xiii. 7.)

1657 M. LAWRENCE *Use & Practice of Faith* 143 Meer cumber-grounds. **1720** THORESBY *Diary* II. 304 An useless unprofitable cumber-ground. **1821** CLARE *Vill. Minstr.* II. 82 Where all the cumber-grounds of life resort.

'cumbering, *vbl. sb.* [f. CUMBER *v.* + -ING[1].] The action of the verb CUMBER; †trouble, distress (*obs.*); hindrance, encumbrance, embarrassment.

1303 R. BRUNNE *Handl. Synne* 2195 Hyt may þe brynge to more cumbryng. *a* **1340** HAMPOLE *Psalter* ciii. [civ.] 21 Merk kumbryng of hert.

'cumbering, *ppl. a.* [-ING[2].] That cumbers.

1682 CREECH tr. *Lucretius* (1683) 182 They forc't the cumbring Wood to narrow bounds. **1839** MRS. HEMANS *Poems, Our Daily Paths*, And weigh our burdened spirits down with the cumbering dust of the earth.

Cumberland ('kʌmbələnd). **1.** The name of the English county used *attrib.* to designate a piquant sauce served esp. with cold meat.

1878 'SHORT' *Dinners at Home* 146 Cumberland Sauce for Game (Cold)... Cumberland Sauce (Hot). **1922** F. HAMILTON *P.J.* i. 22 We shall be able to offer you a tolerably good supper, and I will not forget your favourite Cumberland sauce. **1959** *House & Garden* Dec.-Jan. 36/2 Cold spiced beef, ham, chicken or turkey, accompanied by ..Cumberland sauce.

2. Used to designate the manner of cutting up a pig's carcase in which the ham is cut away and cured separately. ? *Obs.*

1905 W. H. SIMMONDS *Practical Grocer* III. 103 It pays to sell the ham separately and convert the rest of the side into 'Cumberland cut' bacon or 'Irish rolls'. **1907** *Yesterday's Shopping* (1969) 20/2 Hams... Cumberland.

'cumberless, *a.* [f. CUMBER *sb.* + -LESS.] Without cumber or encumbrance; unencumbered.

1581 MARBECK *Bk. of Notes* 64 That he might be the more readie and comberlesse to preach the Gospell. **1644** QUARLES *Barnabas & B.* 69 May sit and suck the sweetness of their cumberless estates. **1807** Hogg *Sky Lark*, Bird of the wilderness, Blithesome and cumberless.

ˈcumberment. Now *rare* or *Obs.* [f. cumber *v.* + -ment.]

1. †**a.** Trouble, distress (*obs.*); †**b.** Perplexity, confusion (*obs.*); **c.** Hindrance, embarrassment, entanglement.

c **1300** *K. Alis.* 472 Of powere To kepe hire fro comburment. **1426** Audelay *Poems* 21 Castis awai covetyse that is cause of cumberment. *c* **1430** *Hymns Virg.* (1867) 56 Kepe he him from þe deuelis combirment. **1597** S. Daniel *Civ. Wars* vi. viii, As they stand in desperat comberment Environd round with horror, blood, and shame. **1599** —— *Musophilus* Wks. (1717) 391 Craft (wrapt still in many Comberments) With all her Cunning thrives not.

2. That which cumbers; an encumbrance.

1840 *Blackw. Mag.* XLVIII. 492 'Will you not take off your coat?'..this elegant cumberment of the body.

cumbersome (ˈkʌmbəsəm), *a.* [f. cumber *v.* + -some.]

†**1.** Of places or ways: Obstructing and impeding motion or progress; full of obstruction; troublesome to pass or get through. *Obs.*

1375 Barbour *Bruce* xiii. 351 Bannokburne, that sa cummyrsum was Of slyk, and depnes for till pas. **1555** *Fardle Facions* ii. xi. 246 Pioners..to make the waye, wher the place is combresome. **1563** Golding *Cæsar* (1565) 120 The Britons call it a Towne, when thei have fortified a combersome wood with a dich, and a rampyre. **1681** Cotton *Wonders of Peake* 55 Though the way be cumbersom, and rough.

†**2.** Causing trouble, annoyance, or inconvenience; full of trouble; troublesome; wearisome, oppressive. *Obs.* exc. *dial.*

1535 Stewart *Cron. Scot.* III. 105 Thair names..So cummersum tha ar to put in verss. **1573** Tusser *Husb.* (1878) 19 A cumbersome Landlord is husbandmans rod. **1621–51** Burton *Anat. Mel.* i. ii. iii. x. 111 Cumbersome days..slow, dull and heavy times. **1663** Gerbier *Counsel* 99 A Portch proves often cumbersome, being the receptacle of foul creatures. **1876** Holland *Sev. Oaks* xii. 167 'It would be sort o cumbersome to tell her.' **1862** Hislop *Prov. Scot.* 38 Better unkind than ower cumbersome.

3. Of material objects: Troublesome from bulk or heaviness; unwieldy, clumsy.

1594 Blundevil *Exerc.* vi. Pref. (ed. 7) 596 The Globe is combersome and not portable. **1616** Surfl. & Markh. *Country Farme* 390 This tree..is not so combersome as to keepe away the Sunne and the wind. **1671** Milton *P.R.* iii. 400 That cumbersome Luggage of war. **1716** Addison *Drummer* ii. i, Help me off with this cumbersome Cloak. **1849** E. E. Napier *Excurs. S. Africa* II. 2 At last..the cumbersome waggons gradually got under weigh. **1865** Dickens *Mut. Fr.* i. xv, The cumbersome old table with twisted legs.

fig. **1660** H. More *Myst. Godl.* To Rdr. 17 A vast heap of humane Inventions, useless and cumbersome Ceremonies. **1768** Beattie *Minstr.* ii. lix, With cumbersome, tho' pompous show. **1870** Lubbock *Orig. Civiliz.* ii. (1875) 43 Very cumbersome mode of assisting the memory.

Hence **ˈcumbersomely** *adv.*; also **ˈcumbersomeness.**

1571 Golding *Calvin on Ps.* lxxiv. 16 Although they be troubled through the combersomnes of men. **1611** Cotgr., *Molestément*, troublesomely, offensively, combersomely. **1678** Cudworth *Intell. Syst.* i. iii. Digr. §9 (Contents) Human art acts upon the matter without, cumbersomely or moliminously. **1785** Roy in *Phil. Trans.* LXXV. 430 The cumbersomeness of its weight appeared..objectionable. **1880** *Scribn. Mag.* Feb. 504 The log fence..belonged to the same period of plentifulness, even cumbersomeness, of timber.

†**ˈcumber-world.** *Obs.* [cumber *v.* 8.] A person or thing that uselessly encumbers the world.

c **1374** Chaucer *Troylus* iv. 279, I combre world, that may of no thynge serue. *a* **1420** Hoccleve *De Reg. Princ.* 2091 That combreworlde that my maister slow. **1593** Drayton *Eclogues* ii. 25 A cumber-World, yet in the World am left.

†**ˈcumble,** *sb. Obs.* [ad. F. *comble*:—L. *cumulum* heap, heap over and above a measure, summit, apex, crown, etc.]

1. Heap, accumulation. *rare.*

1694 Burthogge *Reason* 276 That cumble of Accidents, External, Internal.

2. Highest point, apex, culmination. (A Gallicism affected by Howell.)

1640 Howell *Dodona's Grove* 42 For a cumble of all felicity. *c* **1645** —— *Lett.* iii. xxxi, In Philip the seconds time the Spanish Monarchy came to its highest cumble. **1650** —— *Cotgrave's Fr. Eng. Dict.* Ep. Ded., This word Souverain..hath rais'd it self to that cumble of greatnes that it is now applied only to the King.

†**ˈcumble,** *v. Obs.* exc. *dial.* Also **comble,** and in pa. pple. **comelid.** [a. Fr. *comble-r* to load:—L. *cumulāre*: see acumble. Cf. cumber in same sense.] *trans.* To oppress, deprive of power; *esp.* to stiffen or benumb with cold.

1388 Wyclif *Isa.* xxxv. 3 Coumforte ȝe comelid [*v. rr.* clumsid, cumblid] hondes [*manus dissolutas*]. *c* **1440** *Promp. Parv.* 88 Comelyd, for colde, *eviratus*. *a* **1825** Forby *Voc. E. Anglia*, *Cumbled*..oppressed, cramped, stiffened with cold. *Cumbly-cold, adj.* stiff, and benumbed with cold. Intensely cold, if applied to weather.

b. *intr.* To be or become benumbed.

c **1280** *Old Age* in *E.E.P.* (1862) 149, I snurpe, i snobbe, i sneipe on snovte, þroȝ kund i comble an kelde.

Hence **ˈcumbled** *ppl. a.*, **ˈcumbledness.**

c **1440** *Promp. Parv.* 89 Comelydnesse, *eviracio*.

‖**cumbly, cumly** (ˈkʌmlɪ). Forms: 7 combly, camlee, 8 comley, kummul, cumly, 9 camly, cumbly, kumlee. [Hind. *kamlī*:—Skr. *kambala*.] A blanket, a coarse woollen cloth.

1673 Fryer *Acc. E. India & P.* 54 (Y.) The Natives.. wrapping themselves in a Combly or Hair-Cloth. **1696** Ovington *Voy. Suratt* 455 (Y.) Camlees, which are a sort of Hair Coat made in Persia. **1781** *Prison Expenses of Hon. J. Lindsay* in *Lives of Lindsays* (1849) III. (Y.) One comley as a covering. **1798** G. Forster *Trav.* I. 194 (Y.) A large black Kummul, or blanket. **1842** Bischoff *Woollen Manuf.* II. 319 The common sheep of the plains of India, with a coarse fleece..from which the kumlees or coarse blankets are manufactured. **1885** *Macm. Mag.* Nov. 77/2 Rough country blankets, or cumblies, striped in black and white.

†**ˈcumbrance.** *Obs.* Also comber-, combr-, -ance, -aunce, etc. [f. cumber *v.* + -ance: cf. accumbrance, encumbrance.]

1. The action of 'cumbering'; ? overcoming, vanquishing: or ? entanglement, temptation.

1303 R. Brunne *Handl. Synne* 1019 To many on comyþ þarfore evyl þurghe cumberaunce of þe devyl. *c* **1420** *Metr. St. Kath.* (Halliw.) 18 Thou have them fro the fendys comberauns! **1493** *Festivall* (1515) 33 To kepe them from combraunce of the fende that they falle not in to deedly synne.

2. The action of troubling or harassing; trouble, distress, annoyance.

c **1325** *E.E. Allit. P.* B. 4 Kark & combraunce huge. **1377** Langl. *P. Pl.* B. xviii. 265 Care and combraunce is comen to vs alle. *c* **1440** *Promp. Parv.* 89 Comerawnce, *vexacio*. *c* **1489** Caxton *Sonnes of Aymon* i. 19 To waraunt thee.. from evyl and from any combraunce. **1535** Stewart *Cron. Scot.* I. 429 Drewedes with bibill, bell and buik..Witht cruell cursing and with cummerance Thair wareit hes rycht rudlie the Romans. **1568** Grafton *Chron.* II. 81 There is no felicitie..which is not darkened with some clowde of combrance and adversitie. **1639** Fuller *Holy War* v. xix. (1840) 275 The army will be very heterogeneous..which must needs occasion much cumbrance.

b. Trouble of mind; perplexity.

c **1460** J. Russell *Bk. Nurture* 1086 A merchalle is put oft tymes in gret comberaunce For som lordes þat ar of blod royalle & litelle of lyvelode per chaunce, And some of gret lyvelode & no blode royalle. **1561** T. Norton *Calvin's Inst.* i. 37 As it is very hard to know, so doth it bring more businesse and comberance to some wittes than is expedient.

c. A cause of trouble or annoyance; a trouble.

1377 Langl. *P. Pl.* B. xii. 46 Catel and kynde witte [**1393** C. xiii. 245 So couetise of catel] was combraunce to hem alle. **1570** T. Norton tr. *Nowel's Catech.* (1853) 178 The incommodities and cumbrances that light upon us in this life. **1657** Tomlinson *Renou's Disp.* 145 Lest they take detriment from the aforesaid cumbrances.

3. The action of hindering, encumbering, or burdening, or state of being hindered, etc.; hindrance, burden, encumbrance.

1535 Coverdale *Deut.* i. 12 How can I alone beare soche combraunce, and charge, and stryfe amonge you? **1603** Drayton *Bar. Wars* (R.), T' avoid the cumbrance of each hindering doubt. **1621** Ainsworth *Annot. Pentat.* Deut. i. 12 By your cumbrance, understand, the cumbrance that commeth unto me by you.

b. That which encumbers; an encumbrance.

1644 J. Fary *Gods Severity* (1645) 26 A fruitlesse Christian is a very burthen and cumbrance to the place hee lives in. **1664** Evelyn *Sylva* (1679) 5 In transplanting, and removing cumbrances. **1671** Milton *P.R.* ii. 454 Extol not Riches then..The wise man's cumbrance if not snare.

Cumbrian (ˈkʌmbrɪən), *a.* and *sb.* [f. med.L. *Cumbria*, f. W. *Cymry*:—prehist. W. **kombrogi*, pl. of **kombrogos* lit. fellow countryman (W. *bro*:—**mrog-* region).] **A.** *adj.* **1.** Belonging to the ancient British kingdom of Cumbria, which included Cumberland. **2.** Belonging to Cumberland, or its system of rocks; also, more widely, belonging to the Lake District and its fells. **B.** *sb.* **1.** A native of the ancient British kingdom of Cumbria. **2.** A native or inhabitant of Cumberland.

1747 T. Carte *Gen. Hist. Eng.* I. iii. 211 Feuds and quarrels between particular chieftains and their clans were not the only grievance under which the Cumbrian and Straeth-cluyd Britains laboured. *Ibid.* 212 Whether Rydderch imagined, that he was any obstruction to the Cumbrians returning to their former allegiance. **1779** A. Butler *Lives Saints* (ed. 2) I. 140 Among the Straith-Cluid Britons, and the Cumbrians, the latter inhabiting the country from the Picts wall, to the Ribble in Lancashire. *Ibid.*, The Cumbrians..were protected by Urien, lord of Rheged. **1780** T. West *Guide Lakes Cumb.*, etc. (ed. 2) 6 The travelled visitor of the Cumbrian lakes. **1833–4** J. Phillips in *Encycl. Metrop.* (1845) VI. 584/2 The analogous arches of limestone, which begird the primary district of the Cumbrian lakes. **1837** *Penny Cycl.* VIII. 223/2 The Cumbrians have been undeservedly said to be litigious. *Ibid.*, Cumbrian peasantry have various festive meetings, called the *kirn*, or harvest-home, sheep-shearing, merry nights, and upshots. **1882** *Encycl. Brit.* XIV. 40/1 Kentigern,..the restorer of Christianity among the Cumbrians. **1901** A. G. Bradley *Lake District* 4 The simple dalesman,..canny Cumbrian as he is. **1902** W. G. Collingwood *Lake Counties* i. ii. 38 There have been many Cumbrian poets, most of them, like Wordsworth at Grasmere, cottage folk. **1902** W. P. Haskett-Smith in *Ibid.* ii. vi. 259 Leaving out Langdale, which runs down into Westmorland, there are five purely Cumbrian dales. **1963** *Times* 25 Feb. 11/7 While the Cumbrian fight their battles with energy, there is a strong community spirit.

Cumbric (ˈkʌmbrɪk). [f. med.L. *Cumbria* (see prec.) + -ic.] The former Celtic language of Cumbria. Also *attrib.* or as *adj.*

1953 K. Jackson *Lang. & Hist. Early Brit.* i. i. 6 We shall occasionally employ *Primitive Cumbric* (Pr. Cum.) for the Brittonic dialect of Cumberland, Westmorland, northern Lancashire, and south-west Scotland. **1954** —— in. N. K. Chadwick *Stud. Early Brit. Hist.* 67 By Western British I mean the ancestor of Welsh and probably of the Celtic language of Cumbria, called Cumbric here, which seems to have agreed with Welsh in the main. **1967** *Peeblesshire* (R. Comm. Anc. Monuments Scotland) I. 3 The inhabitants.. were responsible for the Brittonic or 'Cumbric' place-names of the region. **1970** B. M. H. Strang *Hist. Eng.* v. 283 The far north-west was brought under English rule in 1092, but it would be foolish to assume that all use of Cumbric immediately ceased.

cumbrous (ˈkʌmbrəs), *a.* Forms: 4–7 cumberous, (8 cumb'rous), 4 *Sc.* cumrouss, 5 comberus, -ose, comborous, comerus, comorows, cumbrusse, 5–6 comerous, 5–7 comberous, combrous, 6 commerous(e, cummerouse, coumbreous, 5– cumbrous. [f. cumber *sb.* + -ous: cf. obs. F. *combreux* (Palsgr.).]

†**1.** Presenting obstruction; difficult of passage or access; = cumbersome 1. *Obs.*

1375 Barbour *Bruce* x. 25 Ane montane..So cumrouss, and eke so stay, That it wes hard to pas that way. **1495** *Will of Shaa* (Somerset Ho.), Noyous & comberus high weyes. **1551** Recorde *Pathw. Knowl.* To Rdr., The way muste needes be comberous, wher none hathe gone before. **1600** Holland *Livy* xxi. xxv. 407 The rough, comberous, and unpassable forests [*saltu invio atque impedito*]. **1613** W. Browne *Brit. Past.* ii. iv, Among the combrous brakes. **1861** Lytton & Fane *Tannhäuser* 107 Now o'er the cumbrous hills began to creep A thin and watery light.

†**2.** Causing trouble, distress, or annoyance; full of trouble or care; troublesome; harassing; wearisome, oppressive; = cumbersome 2. *Obs.*

c **1400** Maundev. (1839) xxvii. 272 Many oþer marueyles ben þere, þat it were to combrous and to long to putten it in scripture of bokes. **1447** Bokenham *Seyntys* (Roxb.) 134 A dysshese she had ful comerous. **1590** Recorde, etc. *Gr. Artes* 291, I shall have a cumbrous worke to do. **1590** Spenser *F.Q.* i. i. 23 A cloud of cumbrous gnattes doe him molest. **1667** Milton *P.L.* xi. 549 How I may be quit, Fairest and easiest, of this cumbrous charge.

3. Troublesome from bulk or heaviness; burdensome, unwieldy, clumsy; = cumbersome 3.

a **1400** *Pistel of Susan* 224 Vr copus weore cumberous, and cundelet vs care. **1494** Fabyan *Chron.* vii. 610 The other [ordenaunce] that were heuy & cumbrusse, he lefte behynde hym. **1555** Eden *Decades* 361 Certeyne lyttle clockes..the whiche..are not comberous to be caryed abowt. **1718** Pope *Iliad* v. 314, I hate the cumbrous chariot's slow advance. **1813** Scott *Rokeby* v. iv, Armour..Cumbrous of size, uncouth to sight. **1875** Jevons *Money* (1878) 144 A currency $15\frac{1}{2}$ times as heavy and cumbrous.

b. *fig.*

1751 Johnson *Rambler* No. 179 ¶11 Throwing off those cumbrous ornaments of learning. **1835** Arnold *Let.* in Stanley *Life & Corr.* (1844) I. vii. 424 To correct the style where it is cumbrous or incorrect. **1877** Geikie *Christ* lii. (1879) 624 The cumbrous machinery of rite and ceremony.

cumbrously (ˈkʌmbrəslɪ), *adv.* [f. prec. + -ly[2].] In a cumbrous, troublesome, or burdensome manner: see the adj.

1401 *Pol. Poems* (Rolls) II. 104 Multipliyng of so many freris, whiche encresen combrouseli. **1548** Udall, etc. *Erasm. Par.* Pref. 19 To be coumbreously entangled as it were. **1875** Whitney *Life Lang.* x. 180 Rejecting both these titles as cumbrously long.

cumbrousness (ˈkʌmbrəsnɪs). [f. as prec. + -ness.] The quality of being cumbrous, troublesome, burdensome, or unwieldy.

1557 *Sarum Primer* Pij, Make me..sadde and sober without comberousnes. **1858** J. Martineau *Studies Christianity* 39 The cumbrousness of ceremonies. **1879** *Cassell's Techn. Educ.* IV. 323/1 The weight and cumbrousness of the apparatus required.

cumdach (ˈkuːdəx). [ad. Ir. *cumhdach*, f. MIr. *cumdach*, f. OIr. *cumtach*.] An ornamental book-casket.

1887 M. Stokes *Early Chr. Art in Ireland* iv. 89 The first cumdach we read of..was made for the 'Book of Durrow', by the king of Ireland, Flann Sinna..who reigned between the years 877 and 916. **1908** *Daily Chron.* 30 Mar. 3/3 It is marvellous that any of those old manuscripts escaped the destructive raids of plundering Danes and Normans, especially as the cumdach, or cover, meant to preserve them from other injuries, was generally enriched with silver or gold, and sometimes inlaid with precious stones or enamels. **1960** G. A. Glaister *Gloss. Book* 93/1 *Cumdach*, a jewelled and elaborately decorated box used in late 9th-century Ireland for keeping manuscript books.

cume-ceil, obs. f. coom-ceil: see coom *sb.*[2] 4.

cumel-: see comel-.

cumeling, obs. form of comeling.

c **1640** J. Smyth *Lives Berkeleys* (1883) I. 334 All such Estrays and Cumelings..found upon the Abbots demesnes.

cumene (ˈkjuːmiːn). *Chem.* [f. L. *cumīnum* cumin + -ene.] A hydrocarbon, C_9H_{12}, found in Roman cumin oil: it is a colourless strongly refracting oil, allied to Benzene. So **cumic** (ˈkjuːmɪk) *a.*, of or derived from cumin, as in *cumic acid* $C_{10}H_{12}O_2$, *cumic aldehyde*, etc. ˈ**cumidine**, a base homologous with toluidine, formed by the action of ammonium sulphide on nitrocumene. **cuˈminic** *a.*, of or derived from cumene; = *cumic*. **cumole** = *cumene*. ˈ**cumyl**, the acid organic radical, $C_{10}H_{11}O$, of Cumic acid, homologous with Benzoyl; hence ˈ*cumylamide*, ˈ*cumylene*, *cuˈmylic*, ˈ*cumylide*, etc.

1863–72 WATTS *Dict. Chem.* II. 173 *Cumene.* Cumol. Hydride of Cumenyl. *Ibid.* 174 Cumene is insoluble in water. **1873** —— *Fownes' Chem.* 818 Cumic Acid is produced by oxidation of cuminol or cumic aldehyde, one of the constituents of oil of cumin. **1850** DAUBENY *Atom. Th.* viii. (ed. 2) 243 A substance called cumidine, lately discovered by Mr. Nicholson in the oil of caraways. **1847** TURNER *Elem. Chem.* 1077 The addition of an acid causes the cuminic acid to separate. **1863–72** WATTS *Dict. Chem.* II. 178 *Cuminic acid*..is produced by the oxidation of the oxygenated oil (hydride of cumyl) contained in essence of cumin. *Ibid.* II. 182 Cumyl in the free state, or Cumylide of Cumyl..is an oily liquid, heavier than water. **1873** —— *Fownes' Chem.* 791 Cymyl Alcohol is also called Cumylic Alcohol.

cumerar, obs. form of CUMBERER.

cumin, cummin (ˈkʌmɪn). Forms: 1 **kymen, cymen, -yn,** 2 **cumin (y),** 4–7 **comyn, -e,** 5–6 **cummyn,** 5–7 **comen,** 6 **comeyn, commine, -men, -myn,** 7 **comin(e, cum(m)ine,** 7–9 **commin,** (8–9 **cumming**), 6– **cum(m)in.** [OE. *cymen* (:—*cumin*), a. L. *cumīn-um* (*cym-*), a. Gr. κύμῑνον. Cf. OHG. *chumin, cumin,* also *chumil* (MHG. *kümel,* Ger. *kümmel*), Sw. *kummin,* Da. *kummen.* The word has also come down in the Romanic langs., It. *cumino, comino,* Sp., Pg. *comino,* OF. *cumin, comin.* ME. *cumin, comin* was either from Fr. (like MDu. *comijn,* Du. *komijn*), or altered from OE. *cymen* after Fr. The Gr. κύμῑνον is supposed to have been a foreign word, cognate in origin with the Semitic names, Heb. *kammôn,* Arab. *kammûn,* and their cognates.]

1. An umbelliferous plant (*Cummin Cyminum*) resembling fennel: cultivated in the Levant for its fruit or seed, which possesses aromatic and carminative qualities; also called *common, garden,* or *Roman cumin.*

oil of cumin: the essential oil of cumin seed, consisting of three hydrocarbons, cymene, cymol, and cuminol.

c **897** K. ÆLFRED *Gregory's Past.* lvii. 439 ȝe tioȝoðiað eowre mintan & eowerne dile & eowerne kymen. *c* **1000** *Ags. Gosp.* Matt. xxiii. 23 Cymen [*v.r.* cymyn; **1160** *Hatton Gosp.* cumin]. *c* **1300** *K. Alis.* 6797 Gynger, comyn gaven odour grace. **1382** WYCLIF *Isa.* xxviii. 25 He shal sowe the sed gith, and the comyn sprengen. **1398** TREVISA *Barth. De P.R.* XVII. xxxviii. (1495) 625 Comyn..is a seed wyth good smell and wyth pale colour. *c* **1420** *Liber Cocorum* (1862) 8 Fors hit with galyngale and gode gyngere, With canel and comyn alle in fere. *c* **1440** *Promp. Parv.* 89 Comyn, seede (*Ciminum,* P.). **1561** HOLLYBUSH *Hom. Apoth.* 5 b, Commen stiped in vinegre. **1736** BAILEY *Househ. Dict.* 228 Cummin is accounted good for the stomach. **1847** EMERSON *Poems, Sphinx* Wks. (Bohn) I. 398 Rue, myrrh, and cummin for the Sphinx—Her muddy eyes to clear. **1875** MANNING *Mission H. Ghost* xi. 309 The Pharisees..gave tithes of mint, anise, and commin.

b. *fig.* in allusion to *Matt.* xxiii. 23.

1741–1841 [see ANISE 2]. **1741** WATTS *Improv. Mind* xiv. §8 (1801) 111 The mint, anise and cumming, the gestures and vestures and fringes of religion. **1892** *Edin. Rev.* Apr. 419 The anise and cummin of a great archæological question, passed, as it were, through the Homeric sieve.

2. With qualifications applied to other plants: as, **Armenian** or **mountain cumin**, the Caraway, *Carum Carui*; **black cumin**, a ranunculaceous plant, *Nigella sativa*, cultivated in Eastern countries for its black, acrid, and aromatic seeds; **royal cumin**, Ammi or Bishop's-weed; **sweet cumin**, the Anise, *Pimpinella Anisum*; **wild cumin**, (*a*) the wild variety of cumin; †(*b*) the wild Nigella; (*c*) an umbelliferous plant, *Lagœcia cuminoides.*

1578 LYTE *Dodoens* II. xciv. 274 The wilde Comyn..hath a brittle stalke. **1614** MARKHAM *Cheap Husb.* I. *Table of Hard Words,* Ameos, Comin royal, is a Herb of some called Bulwort, Bishops-weed, or Herb-william. **1712** tr. *Pomet's Hist. Drugs* I. 3 Ethiopian-Cummin is a Plant which has Leaves like Dill. **1885** BIBLE (R.V.) *Isa.* xxviii. 25 Doth the plowman..not cast abroad the fitches [*marg.* black cummin (*Nigella sativa*)].

3. *attrib.* and *Comb.*, as *cumin cheese, oil, seed,* etc.; **cumin-splitting** *a.*, skin-flint, niggardly [cf. L. *cuminisector*, Gr. κυμινο-πρίστης].

1530 PALSGR. 207/1 Commyn sede, *comyn.* **1605** BACON *Adv. Learn.* I. vii. 35 A carver or divider of Comine seed which is one of the least seedes. *a* **1613** OVERBURY *A Wife* (1638) 96 His wife is the Cummin seed of his Dove-house. *a* **1628** F. GREVILLE *Sidney* (1652) 122 Like a true cutter of Cumine seeds. **1754** GILLIES *Hist. Coll.* I. 406, 28 Cumin cheeses were to be sent us from Leyden. **1822** T. MITCHELL *Aristoph.* II. 304 A sneaking, pitiful, cummin-splitting fellow. **1866** *Treas. Bot.* 360/1 The cumin seeds or fruits are the produce of *Cuminum Cyminum.* **1873** WATTS *Fownes' Chem.* 767 A hydrocarbon, called cumene..exists ready-formed in Roman cumin-oil.

cumli(e, -ly, -ling, obs. ff. COMELY, -LING.

cumly, var. CUMBLY, blanket.

cumm-: see COMM-.

cummer, kimmer (ˈkʌmə(r), ˈkɪmə(r)). *Sc.* Forms: 4 **commare,** 6 **cummar, comere,** 7 **comer,** 6– **cummer,** 8– **kimmer.** [a. F. *commère* (= Pr. *comaire,* Sp. and It. *comadre*):—late L. *commāter* (Laws of Lombards), f. *com-* together with + *māter* mother.]

1. A godmother, in her relationship to the other god-parents and the parents of the child; a commother.

1303 R. BRUNNE *Handl. Synne* 986 Þou man or womman, be nat so wylde To holde to þe bysshope þyn owne chylde, For ȝyf þou do, þou art commare To hym þat hyt gat or bare. **1566** in *Diurnal of Occurrents* (1833) 102 To nominat ane woman in Scotland to be cummar to our soueranis to the bapteising of our prince thair sone. *a* **1670** SPALDING *Troub. Chas. I* (1792) II. 105 (Jam.) An honest burgess of Aberdeen caused bring to the kirk a bairn..to be baptised..and conveened his gossips and comers, as the custom is. **1730** in Chambers *Dom. Ann. Scot.* III. 572 Towards the end of the week, all the friends are asked to what was called the Cummers' Feast.

2. A female companion or intimate; a gossip.

1500–20 DUNBAR *Rycht Airlie on Ask Weddinsday* 2 Drynkand the wyne satt cumeris tway. *Ibid.* 11 'My fair, sweit cummer' quod the tuder. **1644** BAILLIE in Z. Boyd *Zion's Flowers* (1855) Introd. 34, I thank my cummer your wife heartily. **1658** R. FRANCK in A. McKay *Hist. Kilmarnock* 7 Their wives are sociable comers. **1790** *Scots Songs* II. 7 My kimmer and I lay down to sleep. **1820** SCOTT *Monast.* viii, A special cummer of my ain.

3. A woman, a female; familiarly applied, like 'fellow' to a man. With various local specific applications, *e.g.* young woman, lass, girl, witch, wise-woman, midwife, etc.

17.. *Humble Beggar* in Herd *Collect.* (1776) II. 29 (Jam.) Vow, kimmer, and how do ye? **1745** *Song,* What's a' the steer, kimmer? **1785** BURNS *2nd Ep. to Lapraik* x, Fortune..the kittle kimmer. **1806** TRAIN *Poetical Reveries* 89 (Jam.) She in travail was..No kindly kimmer nigh there was To mitigate her pain. **1818** SCOTT *Br. Lamm.* xxiii, 'That's a fresh and full-grown hemlock..mony a cummer lang syne wad hae sought nae better horse to flee..through mist and moonlight.' **1821** *Blackw. Mag.* Jan. 402 (Jam.) It's a bonnie sight to see so mony stark youths and strapping kimmers streaking themselves sae eydently to the harvest darke. **1875** F. I. SCUDAMORE *Day Dreams* 13 In presence of the good cummers of Newhaven.

‖**cummerbund** (ˈkʌməbʌnd). *Anglo-Ind.* Forms: 7 **combar-, commer-,** 8 **cumber-,** 8–9 **cummerband,** 9 **cummer-, kummerbund.** [Urdū and Pers. *kamar-band,* i.e. loin-band.] A sash or girdle worn round the waist; a waist-belt.

1616 R. COCKS *Diary* (Hakl. Soc. 1883) I. 147 (Y.) A sample of gallie pottes..chint bramport, and combarbands, with the prices. **1687** *Lond. Gaz.* No. 2269/2, 234 pieces of Commerbands with Gold Flowers. **1792** *Hist.* in *Ann. Reg.* 193 Uniform turbans and cumber-bands. *c* **1813** MRS. SHERWOOD *Ayah & Lady* ix. 53 Shumsheer had a cummerbund, of rose-coloured muslin. **1869** E. A. PARKES *Pract. Hygiene* (ed. 3) 410 The necessity of cholera belts or kummerbunds is avoided.

cummerous, obs. form of CUMBROUS.

cummin, cumming: see CUMIN.

cummin, -un, -yn, obs. ff. COME *pa. pple.*

ˈ**cumming.** *Sc.* Also 6 **cumyeone, cymming, kymmond.** [? Related to COOMB[1], senses 2, 4, in Sc. *cum, kim* (Gael. *cuman* is prob. from Lowland Sc.).] **a.** In *Brewing.* 'A large oblong vessel, of a square form, about a foot or eighteen inches deep, used for receiving what works over from the masking-fat or barrel. *Loth.*' **b.** 'A small tub or wooden vessel. *Angus, Fife.*' (Jamieson 1825.)

1538 *Aberdeen Reg.* V. 16 (Jam.) Ane flasche fat, ane fysche fat, ane cumyeone. *Ibid.,* Ane gryte kymmond. **1566** *Inv. R. Wardr. etc.* (1815) 174 (Jam.) Tua gyle fattes..ane cumming. *c* **1575** BALFOUR *Practicks* 234 (Jam.) The air sall have..ane masking-fat..ane cymming, ane laid-gallon, ane wort disch. **1825** JAMIESON, *Kimmen, kymmond,* a large shallow tub used in brew-houses. *Upp. Clydes.*

ˈ**cummock.** *Sc.* Variant of CAMMOCK: 'A short staff with a crooked head' (Jam.).

1786 BURNS *On Scott. Bard gone to W. India* vii, To tremble under fortune's cummock.

cumnawnte, obs. form of COVENANT.

cumole: see under CUMENE.

cump-: see COMP-.

cumquat. Former spelling of KUMQUAT.

cumrade, obs. form of COMRADE.

†ˈ**cumray**, *v.* *Sc. Obs.* [app. a by-form of CUMBER; but the form is unexplained.] = CUMBER *v.* 1, to overwhelm, rout.

c **1425** WYNTOUN *Cron.* IX. viii. 41 In schort tyme all þat Rowte wes Swa cumrayid, þat þare bade na man. —— *Ibid.* VIII. xvi. 105; VIII. xi. 20. **1513** DOUGLAS *Æneis* V. x. 70 Fast athir sort gan vthiris rout cumray.

cumrouss, -ryt, obs. ff. CUMBROUS, CUMBERED.

cumse, var. of COMSE *v. Obs.*, commence.

cumseiled, obs. form of *coom-ceiled*: see COOM *sb.*[2] 4.

1699 *Ayr Presbyt. Rec.* in Rogers *Social Life in Scotl.* (1886) III. 400 Cumseiled, with window cases and boards, glasses, partition walls, and all that is necessary.

‖**cumshaw** (ˈkʌmʃɔː). Also **kumshaw.** [According to Giles, the Amoy pronunciation, *kam-siā,* of the Chinese words *kan* to be grateful, *hsieh* thanks = 'grateful thanks', a phrase of thanks used by beggars.] In the Chinese ports: A present or gratuity; a baksheesh.

1839 H. MALCOM *Trav.* II. Gloss., *Cum-shaw,* a present. At Canton, custom has made some cumshaws matter of right. **1885** *Where Chineses Drive* 163 Baldpate..had the exceeding coolness to ask for a cumshaw as they left.

Hence ˈ**cumshaw** *v.*, to make a present to.

†**cum-ˈtwang.** An obsolete term of contempt.

1599 NASHE *Lenten Stuffe* 3 Those graybeard huddle-duddles and crusty cum-twangs were stroke with such stinging remorse.

cumulant (ˈkjuːmjʊlənt). *Math.* [ad. L. *cumulānt-em,* pr. pple. of *cumulāre.*] 'The denominator of the simple algebraical fraction which expresses the value of an improper continued fraction.' Sylvester in *Phil. Trans.* (1853) I. 543.

cumular (ˈkjuːmjʊlə(r)), *a.* [ad. L. *cumulār-is,* f. *cumulus* heap, CUMULUS.] = CUMULOUS.

1837 [see CIRRO-CUMULAR]. **1892** *Ardrossan Her.* 10 June 5 The dark masses of cumular cloud overhead.

cumulate (ˈkjuːmjʊlət), *a.* [ad. L. *cumulāt-us,* pa. pple. of *cumulāre*: see next.] Formed or gathered into a heap; heaped up; massed.

1535 STEWART *Cron. Scot.* I. 118 Ane carne of stonis togither cumulat. **1633** T. ADAMS *Exp. 2 Peter* i. 2 A cumulate or heaped fulness, when it overflows the continent. **1846** DANA *Zooph.* (1848) 391 Their cumulate mode of budding. **1871** EARLE *Philol. Eng. Tongue* §655 Short sentences are prevalent in our language..But we can use the cumulate construction when needed.

cumulate (ˈkjuːmjʊleɪt), *v.* [f. L. *cumulāt-,* ppl. stem of *cumulāre* to heap, f. *cumul-us* a heap, the conical crown of a heaped measure.]

1. a. *trans.* To gather in a heap; to heap up; to pile up, collect, amass, accumulate. Also *fig.*

1534 WHITINTON *Tullyes Offices* I. (1540) 50 We must use that language..which is knowen to us, leest..we cumulatynge in greke wordes maye of very ryght be laughed to scorne. **1541** BARNES *Wks.* (1573) 340/1 Let all these makers of new Gods cumilate themselues togither on a heape. **1612–20** SHELTON *Quix.* IV. vi. (T.) All the extremes of worth and beauty that were cumulated in Camila. **1695** WOODWARD *Nat. Hist. Earth* VI. (1723) 283 Mighty sholes of Shells..cumulated in many Places Heap upon Heap. **1850** J. H. NEWMAN *Diffic. Anglic.* 29 It is often a mistake, in controversy, to cumulate reasons, etc.

b. *Legal.* To combine (a number of actions, defences, etc.) into one; cf. CUMULATION 3.

A Civil Law term still used in Louisiana. (*Cent. Dict.*)

c. *intr.* To accumulate.

1865 DICKENS *Mut. Fr.* II. v, As Fledgeby's affronts cumulated.

2. a. *trans.* To add over and above, to combine *with* something additional.

1640 G. WATTS tr. *Bacon's Adv. Learn.* 384 Which cumulates the evill of Indignation to the evill of suspicion. **1868** E. EDWARDS *Raleigh* I. xxiv. 571 Philip..allowed him to cumulate the councillorship with the corregidorship. **1885** *Sat. Rev.* 28 Nov. 704 Circumstances..have cumulated the function of investigator with that of instructor or adviser.

b. To combine (the entries of an index, catalogue, etc.) in successive issues.

1905 *Readers' Guide Period. Lit.* I. p. vii, The monthly numbers were cumulated, and quarterly and annual volumes were issued. **1931** A. ESDAILE *Man. Bibliogr.* 301 The *English Catalogue* appears annually, and is 'cumulated' every five years. **1965** *Amer. N. & Q.* Mar. 106/2 Monthly issues..will be cumulated every third month.

3. To put the crown or summit to. *Obs.* or *arch.*

1660 GAUDEN *Brounrig* 30 To wicked men their table is a snare, their prosperity cumulates their misery. **1672** MARVELL *Reh. Transp.* I. 308 To cumulate all this happiness, they had this new Law against the Fanaticks. **1860** PUSEY *Min. Proph.* 565 God restores to the penitent all his lost graces..and cumulates them with the fresh grace, whereby He converts him.

†**4.** To heap, load, pile *with. Obs.*

1563–87 FOXE *A. & M.* (1684) I. 6/1 Emperours, Kings, and Princes, plucking from their own, did rather cumulate the Church with superfluities.

Hence ˈ**cumulating** *vbl. sb.* and *ppl. a.*

1637 GILLESPIE *Eng. Pop. Cerem.* II. iv. 20 The cumulating of Ceremonies in the auncient Church. **1885** *Fraser's Mag.* LI. 5 A cumulating pile of crimes, of negligences and of blunders.

cumulated (ˈkjuːmjʊleɪtɪd), *ppl. a.* [f. prec.]

1. Heaped up, accumulated.

1642 BP. REYNOLDS *Israel's Petit.* Ded. 3 United and cumulated mercies. **1926** *Brit. Weekly* 2 Sept. 452/4 The cumulated common sense of the Anglo-Saxon mind.

2. *spec.* Of clouds: Formed into cumuli.

1817 SOUTHEY *Let.* 28 May, They [the Alps] have precisely the appearance of white cumulated clouds. **1853** PHILLIPS *Rivers Yorksh.* v. 164 Great masses of cumulated cloud.

3. (See prec., sense 2 b.)

1905 *(title)* Readers' guide to periodical literature (cumulated). **1938** L. M. HARROD *Librarians' Gloss.* 53 Cumulated book catalogue. **1959** *Indian Nat. Bibliogr. 1958* p. v, All these errors have been corrected in the Cumulated Volume.

cumulately (ˈkjuːmjʊlətlɪ), *adv.* [f. CUMULATE *a.*] In a cumulate manner, by cumulation.

1846 DANA *Zooph.* (1848) 637 The stems lengthen cumulately by gemmation.

cumulation (kjuːmjʊˈleɪʃən). [n. of action f. L. *cumulāre*: see CUMULATE.]

1. The action of heaping up or collecting in masses; an instance of such action; also, a gathered mass, a heap; accumulation, gathering. Chiefly *fig.*

1616 BULLOKAR, *Cumulation*, a heaping up, or increasing. **1625** SHIRLEY *Love-tricks* III. v, I.. wish you all cumulations of prosperity. **1794** PALEY *Evid.* I. II. i §4 This proof.. is properly a cumulation of evidence, by no means a naked or solitary record. **1868** LOWELL *Shakesp. Once More* Prose Wks. 1890 III. 42 It is by suggestion, not cumulation, that profound impressions are made upon the imagination. **1892** *Contemp. Rev.* May 711 This will depend.. on the quality of the particles which form the cumulation.

†**2.** In *English Univ.* = ACCUMULATION 3. *Obs.*

1641 LAUD *Hist. Chancellorsh. Oxf.* 17 (T.) For cumulation, I must needs profess, I never liked it. And it supposes, of and in itself, an unnecessary delay of the first degree, or a needless haste of the second.

3. *Civil Law.* The combination or joining of two or more actions or defences in a single proceeding. Used in Louisiana, and formerly in Scotland.

1645 *State Trials, Sir Rob. Spotiswood* (R.), The defender denies any such custom; but, by the contrary, defences have severally, and without cumulation, been proponed and discussed, as in Ochiltry's process. **1889** in *Cent. Dict.* for Louisiana.

cumulatist (ˈkjuːmjʊlətɪst). *rare.* [f. CUMULATE *v.* + -IST.] One who accumulates.

a **1846** *Christian Observer* cited in WORCESTER.

cumulative (ˈkjuːmjʊlətɪv), *a.* [f. L. *cumulāt-*, ppl. stem of *cumulāre* (see CUMULATE) + -IVE. Cf. mod.F. *cumulatif, -ive.*]

†**1.** Such as is formed by accumulation or heaping on (as opposed to organic growth). *Obs.*

1605 BACON *Adv. Learn.* II. v. §1 As for knowledge which man receiveth by teaching, it is cumulative and not original; as in a water that besides his own spring-head is fed with other springs and streams.

2. a. Constituted by or arising from accumulation, or the accession of successive portions or particulars; acquiring or increasing in force or cogency by successive additions, as ***cumulative argument, evidence, force.***

1668 *Liberty of Conscience the Magistrates Interest* 4 He.. has not only the common tye of a Subject upon him, for his protection as a man, but the cumulative obligation, and thanks to pay for his Indulgence. *a* **1676** HALE *Hist. Placit. Cor.* xiv. (T.) Among many cumulative treasons charged upon the late earl of Strafford. **1823** KEBLE *Serm.* ii. (1848) 37 The argument from the authority of implicit believers is cumulative: i.e. a fresh argument is added every time a new instance is observed of a man's finding his happiness in Christianity. **1841-4** EMERSON *Ess., Self-reliance* Wks. (Bohn) I. 25 Always scorn appearances, and you always may. The force of character is cumulative. **1849** MURCHISON *Siluria* xx. 500 We have.. cumulative evidence to prove the wide-spread diffusion of the same types. **1868** FREEMAN *Norm. Conq.* (1876) II. ix. 432 There are several circumstances which have together a kind of cumulative force.

b. ***cumulative medicine.***

1876 W. BEGBIE *Bk. Med. Inform. & Advice* App. 251 Digitalis is what is called a cumulative medicine: its effects are sometimes not immediately produced; but each successive dose remaining in the system, these may be seen even after the medicine is discontinued.

c. ***cumulative error.***

1887 *Encycl. Brit.* XXII. 707/2 [*Surveying.*] Cumulative error, not eliminable by circuiting, may be caused when there is much northing or southing.. in the direction of the line. **1920** W. N. THOMAS *Surveying* 509 *Cumulative errors* are those which tend always in the same direction, *i.e.* either to make the apparent measurements always too large or always too small... Cumulative errors are directly proportional to the number of observations. **1957** KENDALL & BUCKLAND *Dict. Statistical Terms* 74 *Cumulative error*, an error which, in the course of the cumulation of a set of observations, does not tend to zero.

3. *Sc. Law.* Of jurisdiction: Concurrent, as opposed to *privative* or exclusive.

1746-7 *Act 20 Geo. II*, c. 43 §27 The jurisdiction hereby reserved to such Corporation.. shall be.. taken to be cumulative only. **1754** ERSKINE *Princ. Sc. Law* I. ii. §6 Jurisdiction is either privative or cumulative.. *Cumulative*, otherwise called *concurrent*, is that which may be exercised by any of two or more courts in the same cause.

4. That tends to accumulate.

1873 H. SPENCER *Stud. Sociol.* xiii. 324 Certain actions which go on in the first are cumulative, instead of being, as in the second dissipative.

5. ***cumulative vote,*** or ***system of voting***: a system of voting, where there are several representatives, in which each voter has as many votes as there are representatives, and may accumulate them upon one candidate or distribute them over any number of candidates; a system introduced in connexion with the School Board elections in Great Britain.

1853 J. S. MILL *Lett.* (1910) I. 173 One very strong recommendation of the plan of cumulative votes occurs to me. **1880** MCCARTHY *Own Times* IV. lix. 294 The School Boards.. the principle of the cumulative vote was tested for the first time in their elections. **1886** MORLEY *W.R. Greg* Crit. Misc. III. 255 Lord Grey's prescription.. consisted of the following ingredients:—the cumulative vote; not fewer than three seats to each constituency, etc.

cumulatively (ˈkjuːmjʊlətɪvlɪ), *adv.* [f. prec. + -LY[2].] In a cumulative manner.

1644 MAXWELL *Prerog. Chr. Kings* i. 8 This power is transferred onely cumulatively. **1660** BOND *Scut. Reg.* 70 Puritans and other Sectaries.. pretend that the Government originally proceedeth, and habitually resideth in the people, but is cumulatively and communicatively derived from them, unto the king, and therefore the people.. resuming the Collated power into their own hands again, may transfer it to any other whom they please. **1827** HARE *Guesses* (1859) 46 It.. does not proceed cumulatively and step by step. **1887** LOWELL *Old Eng. Dramatists* (1892) 13 A national consciousness, made.. cumulatively operative by the existence.. of a national capital.

cumulativeness (ˈkjuːmjʊlətɪvnɪs). [f. as prec. + -NESS.] Cumulative quality or character.

1872 *Contemp. Rev.* XX. 619 This cumulativeness of knowledge is a result of the principle of its relativity. **1889** *Theological Monthly* Jan. 49 A certain cumulativeness of style.. culminating in a grand finale of enthusiasm.

cumulato- (kjuːmjuːˈleɪtəʊ-), combining form from L. *cumulātus* CUMULATE, in sense 'cumulately-', 'cumulate and——', as in, e.g., ***cumulato-fasciculate***, bunched or fasciculate, with aggregation of the fascicles.

1846 DANA *Zooph.* (1848) 383 Cumulato-fasciculate, polyps long turbinate. *Ibid.* Gloss., *Cumulato-ramose.* Branches lengthening by buds at apex, the new polyps being successively the terminal.

†ˈ**cumulator.** *Obs.* [agent-n. from L. *cumulāre.*] One who accumulates.

1799 *Morning Chron.* in *Spirit Pub. Jrnls.* (1800) III. 45 Some of them lately fell into the hands of the cumulators.

cumulescent (kjuːmjʊˈlɛsənt), *a.* [f. CUMULUS: see -ESCENT.] Forming into cumulus.

1818 B. O'REILLY *Greenland* 34 Cloud becoming cumulescent.

cumulet (ˈkjuːmjʊlɪt). A high-flying variety of fancy pigeon.

1876 *Bazaar, Exchange & Mart* 12 Jan. 74/3 Pair splendid white eyed cumulets. **1910** A. H. OSMAN *Pigeon Bk.* xii. 131 During the past few years a breed that has been taken up with considerable keenness by exhibitors is the Cumulet. **1965** W. M. LEVI *Encycl. Pigeon Breeds* 596 The Flying Cumulet is one of the ancestors of the Racing Homer and of the Tipper.

cumuliform (ˈkjuːmjʊlɪfɔːm), *a.* [f. L. *cumul-us* + -FORM.] Having the form of cumulus.

1885 *Athenæum* 21 Feb. 254/1 The author [Mr. D. W. Barker] recommends that there should be two simple divisions of clouds, viz., 'stratiform' and 'cumuliform'.

ˈ**cumulo-**, combining form of CUMULUS, used in naming cloud-forms which combine the cumulus with other types: *e.g.* ˌ**cumulo-**ˈ**nimbus**, ˌ**cumulo-**ˈ**stratus**, ˌ**cumulo-cirro-**ˈ**stratus**: see quots.

1803 L. HOWARD *Modif. Clouds* (1865) 4 *Cumulo-stratus*, the Cirro-stratus blended with the Cumulus, and either appearing intermixed with the heaps of the latter or super-adding a wide-spread structure to its base. *Cumulo-cirro-stratus* vel *Nimbus*, the Rain cloud. A cloud, or system of clouds from which rain is falling. It is a horizontal sheet, above which the Cirrus spreads while the Cumulus enters it laterally and from beneath. **1815** T. FORSTER *Atmos. Phenom.* 150 The cumulostratus being a state of the clouds going on to become nimbus. **1856** SCOFFERN & LOWE *Pract. Meteorol.* 55 *Cumulo-stratus*.. chiefly appears towards night in dry windy weather, and is of a leaden colour. **1887** *Leisure Hour* 570/2 Similar cumulus and cumulo-nimbus forms range in latitude from London to near Cape Horn. **1928** D. BRUNT *Meteorol.* iii, Cumulo-nimbus is the thunder-cloud. It frequently takes the form of towers or anvils. **1970** D. FRANCIS *Rat Race* iii. 39 Great heaps of cumulo-nimbus cloud were boiling up.

†**cumuˈlose**, *a. Obs.*[—0] [f. L. type **cumulōs-us*, f. *cumulus*: see -OSE.] Full of heaps or of cumuli.

1727 BAILEY vol. II, *Cumulose*, full of Heaps. **1730-6** —— (folio). Hence in mod. Dicts.

cumulous (ˈkjuːmjʊləs), *a.* [f. next + -OUS.] Heap-like; of the nature of cumulus clouds.

1815 [see CIRRO-CUMULOUS]. **1851** NICHOL *Archit. Heav.* 141 Rising.. like a vast cumulous cloud! **1854** SYD. DOBELL *Balder* vii. 41 The big spent clouds that.. Each upon each lay cumulous. **1887** JESSOPP *Arcady* 135 The clouds have gathered in Arcady's horizon—they are there cumulous and dark.

‖**cumulus** (ˈkjuːmjʊləs). Pl. cumuli. [L. *cumulus* a heap, etc.]

1. A heap, pile; an accumulation, gathering; the conical top of a heaped measure, hence the consummating mass.

1659 HAMMOND *On Ps.* xxxiii. 7 It riseth into a cumulus. **1867** MANNING *Eng. & Christendom* 76 My faith terminates no longer in a cumulus of probabilities gathered from the past. **1882** FARRAR *Early Chr.* II. 213 When we read the Jewish annals of these years we never seem to have reached the cumulus of horrors.

2. *Meteor.* One of the simple forms of clouds, consisting of rounded masses heaped upon each other and resting on a nearly horizontal base. Frequent in the summer sky, where it often presents the appearance of snowy mountain-masses.

1803 L. HOWARD *Modif. Clouds* (1865) 2-3 It may be allowable to introduce a Methodical nomenclature, applicable.. to the Modifications of Cloud.. Cumulus, convex or conical heaps, increasing upward from a horizontal base. **1820** SCORESBY *Acc. Arctic Reg.* I. 419 The grandeur of the cumulus or thunder-cloud is never seen, unless it be on the land. **1846** RUSKIN *Mod. Paint.* I. II. III. iii. §6 In the lower cumuli.. the groups are not like balloons or bubbles, but like towers or mountains.

attrib. **1851** NICHOL *Archit. Heavens* 48 The cumulus cloud predominates. **1892** VERNON LEE in *Contemp. Rev.* Mag. 666 Over the sea the wind had built a bridge.. of white cumulus marble.

3. *Anat.* A thickened portion of the granular lining of the Graafian follicle in which the ovum is embedded; the *Discus proligerus.*

1882 in *Syd. Soc. Lex.*

cumyeone, brewer's vessel: see CUMMING *Sc.*

cun, cunne, *v. Obs.* (or ? *dial.*) [OE. *cunnian*, *-ode*, wk. vb., = OS. *-cunnôn* in *gicunnon* to learn to know:—OTeut. type **kunnojan*, deriv. of *kunnan* to know (see CAN). Cf. the parallel deriv. forms, Gothic *ga-kunnan, kunnaida*, to learn to know, and OHG. *chunnên*, MHG. *kunnen* to learn to know, investigate, try, test. See also *cunner*, CONNER, ALE-CONNER, and CON *v.*]

In OE.: To learn to know, inquire into, explore, investigate; whence **a.** To have experience of, prove, test, try, make trial of (in OE. with genitive, in ME. sometimes with *of*); to taste. *Obs.* or ? *dial.*

Beowulf 1021 þær ȝit wada cunnedon. *c* **888** K. ÆLFRED *Boeth.* v. §3 Mot ic nu cunnian hwon þinne fæstrædnesse? *a* **1000** *Crist* 1418 (Gr.) Uncuþne eard cunnnian. *a* **1000** *Sal. & Sat.* 227 (Gr.) Cunnað dryhtnes meahta. *c* **1200** ORMIN 834 Ne wollde het næfre cunnenn. *a* **1225** *Ancr. R.* 114 He dude his deorewurðe muð þerto, & smeihte ant cunnede þerof. **1597** MONTGOMERIE *Cherrie & Slae* 646 They sall not than the Cherrie cun, That wald not enterpryse. ['Still used in this sense in Dumfr.' (Jamieson 1808).]

†**b.** To try *to do* something. *Obs.*

c **1175** *Lamb. Hom.* 151 Summe to kunnen if heo mihten him mid sunne undernime. *c* **1200** *Trin. Coll. Hom.* 87 Swiche hertes.. cunneð gif he mai þer inne herbergen. *c* **1200** ORMIN 12137 He wollde cunnen swa To brinngenn inn hiss herrte Erþlike þingess lufe & lusst. *a* **1225** *St. Marher.* 13 Heom.. þet cunnið to beon cleane.

c. To get to know, to study or learn: see CON *v.*[1] sense 3, of which examples spelt *cun, cunne*, come down nearly to 1600. In these there was probably a blending of the verbs *cunnan*, CAN, with this verb.

1425-1580 [see CON *v.*[1] 3]. **1668** MAYNWARING *Compl. Physitian* 67 He sits down and cuns his Lesson.

cun: see CAN *v.*[1] and [2], CON *v.*[1] and [2].

cun (kyn), obs. form of KIN.

Cuna (ˈkuːnə). Also **Kuna**. **a.** The name of a Central American Indian people of the isthmus of Panama; a member of this people. **b.** The Chibchan language of this people. Also *attrib.*

1868 *Jrnl. R. Geogr. Soc.* XXXVIII. 92 The Cunas have established themselves on the shores of the Gulf of Uraba. *Ibid.*, Every traveller is heard speaking of the 'Indians' of the Tuyra villages, whereas only Spanish is spoken therein, the Cuna and Darien dialects being totally unknown. **1911** THOMAS & SWANTON *Indian Lang. Mexico & Central Amer.* 96 With Cuna end the languages of isthmian America on the south, the next language (Choco) being included geographically in the continent of South America. **1934** L. E. E. JOYCE *Introd. L. Wafer's New Voy. & Descr. Isthmus of Amer.* p. xvi, 'Huaka', the word still used by modern Cuna for 'stranger', with an inimical implication. **1946** *Internat. Jrnl. Amer. Ling.* XII. 187/2 The Cuna noun neither distinguishes between different genders, nor between animate and inanimate categories. **1964** E. A. NIDA *Toward Sci. Transl.* v. 94 Cuna.. not only has many metaphors but admits new ones readily. **1972** *Times* 10 June 12/1 In the case of the Cuna.. most of the tribe migrated in the nineteenth century to the San Blas islands.. where they.. have an element of autonomy. **1976** *Scotsman* (Weekend Suppl.) 20 Nov. 1/3 It was manned by Charlie Smith, our first Cuna Indian. Like most of his tribe, he was short and stocky, with powerful chest, shoulders and arms, but with curiously thin legs. **1985** *New Yorker* 14 Jan. 78/2 The Kuna of Panama are among a very few tribal groups who have adapted themselves energetically to modern ways while maintaining their cultural identity.

†ˈ**cunables**, *sb. pl. Obs. rare*[—1]. [Adaptation of next: cf. INCUNABLES.] A cradle.

1547 BOORDE *Introd. Knowl.* 208 King Henry the sixt.. being in his cunables, and an infant.

‖**cunabula** (kjuːˈnæbjʊlə), *sb. pl.* [L. *cūnābula* (neut. pl.) cradle, earliest abode. Cf. INCUNABULA.]

1. A cradle; *fig.* the place where anything is nurtured in its beginnings, the earliest abode.
1789 GILB. WHITE *Selborne* I. xx. 176 The swallow and house-martin.. raising and securely fixing crusts or shells of loam as cunabula for their young. **1864** WEBSTER s.v., The cunabula of the human race.

2. Applied to the extant copies of the earliest printed books; = INCUNABULA.
1846 WORCESTER cites *Athenæum*.

cunabular (kjuːˈnæbjʊlə(r)), *a.* [f. L. *cūnābula* (see prec.) + -AR.] Of or pertaining to the cradle or earliest abode.
In mod. Dicts.

cunage, obs. form of COINAGE.

Cunarder (kjuːˈnɑːdə(r)). A Cunard steamer; one of a line of steam-ships between Liverpool and New York.
This line of steamers was founded by Sir Samuel Cunard, of Halifax, N.S., in conjunction with others.
1850 *Knickerbocker* XXXVI. 574 The 'Cunarders'. **1874** 'MARK TWAIN' & C. D. WARNER *Gilded Age* lv. 494 He pointed out where the Cunarders lay when in port. **1881** *Century Mag.* XXIII. 184/1 The great Cunarder.. drew towards us. **1882** *Athenæum* 16 Dec. 806/2 On June 4th, 1840.. a year before the Britannia, the first Cunarder, sailed from Liverpool. **1890** *Times* 30 Dec. 7/4 The arrival of a Cunarder in the Mersey.

cunctation (kʌŋkˈteɪʃən). [ad. L. *cunctātiōn-em*, n. of action f. *cunctārī* to delay.] The action of delaying; delay, tardy action.
1585 PARSONS *Chr. Exerc.* II. i. 195 [He] was ioyned to mee in my good purpose.. without any troublesome cunctation. **1648** HERRICK *Hesper.*, *Delay*, Break off delay, since we but read of one That ever prosper'd by cunctation. **1865** CARLYLE *Fredk. Gt.* V. XIV. ii. 163 Fleury's cunctations were disgusting to the ardent mind. **1867** —— *Remin.* II. 69 After some three years' sad cunctation.

cunctatious (kʌŋkˈteɪʃəs), *a. rare.* [f. prec.: see -TIOUS.] Addicted to delaying, prone to delay.
1865 CARLYLE *Fredk. Gt.* V. xv. i. 271 Noailles being always cunctatious in time of crisis.

cunctative (ˈkʌŋktətɪv), *a. rare.* [f. L. *cunctāt-*, ppl. stem of *cunctārī* (see above) + -IVE.] = prec.
1617 BACON *Sp. Chancery* Wks. XIII. 189, I confess I have somewhat of the cunctative. **1860** MOTLEY *Netherl.* I. ii. 54 'Fabius' [Philip II].. that cunctative Roman.

‖**cunctator** (kʌŋkˈteɪtə(r)). [L., agent-n. f. *cunctārī* to delay.] One who acts tardily, a delayer. Hence **cuncˈtatorship** (*nonce-wd.*).
1654 HAMMOND *Fundamentals* Wks. I. 494 (R.) Being unwilling to discourage such cunctators, [they] always keep them in good hope. **1883** *Sat. Rev.* 25 Aug. 229/1 The part of Cunctator has often.. been played by weak Governments. **1865** CARLYLE *Fredk. Gt.* VIII. XIX. i. 111 Cunctatorship is not now the trade needed; there is nothing to be made of playing Fabius-Cunctator.

cunctatory (ˈkʌŋktətərɪ), *a. rare.* [f. prec.: see -ORY.] Disposed to delay.
1864 CARLYLE *Fredk. Gt.* XII. ix, He gets these requisites and is still cunctatory.

cunctipotent (kʌŋkˈtɪpətənt), *a. rare.* In 5 conctypotent. [ad. late. L. *cunctipotent-em*, f. *cunctus* all + *potens*, *potent-em* powerful (after the classical *omnipotens*).] All-powerful, omnipotent.
c **1485** *Digby Myst.* (1882) II. 596 Ihesu Almyghty.. kyng conctypotent of heuyn glory. **1727** in BAILEY vol. II. **1775** in ASH. **1858** NEALE *Bernard de M.* 31 O true peculiar vision Of God cunctipotent.

†**cuncˈtitenent**, *a. Obs. rare.* [f. L. *cunct-us* all + *tenēns*, *tenēnt-* holding; cf. prec.] Holding or possessing all things.
1727 in BAILEY vol. II. **1775** in ASH.

cund, var. of COND *v.*, to direct a ship.

cunde (-y-), obs. form of KIND.

cundel, cundle (-y-), obs. form of KINDLE *v.*

cundeth, -did, -dit(e, -duit(e, -dyth(e, -dyt(e, obs. ff. CONDUIT, CONDUCT *sb.*

cundum, var. CONDOM.

‖**cundurango** (kʌnduːˈræŋgəʊ). Also con-. [Native Peruvian, f. *cundur*, *cuntur* eagle, condor + *ango* vine.] A Peruvian climbing shrub *Gonolobus Cundurango*, the bark of which was introduced into therapeutic use in 1871. According to the Sydenham Society's Lexicon, ten or twelve different barks have been included under this name, the kind first used being that of *Pseusmagennetus equatoriensis*.
1871 *N. Yk. Druggist's Circular* (in *Pharm. Jrnl.* 18 Nov. 405) The Cundurango or Condor vine.. is a climbing vine resembling much in its habits the grape-vine of our own forests. **1871** *Lancet* II. 621 Condurango. **1872** *Pharmac. Jrnl.* 27 Apr. 861 In Ecuador it is the condor which employs, as an antidote to the venom of serpents, the leaves of a species of Gonolobus, called for this reason *cundur-angu*, or the vine of the condor. **1877** tr. *Ziemssen's Cyclop. Med.* VII. 252 The latest remedy suggested is the Cundurango bark.

cundy, cundie, north Eng. and Sc. dial. form of CONDUIT, a covered drain or culvert.

cune, obs. form of COIN.

cuneal (ˈkjuːnɪəl), *a.* ? *Obs.* [f. med. or mod.L. *cuneālis* (in *os cuneāle* cuneal bone), f. L. *cune-us* wedge.] Wedge-shaped, cuneiform.
1578 BANISTER *Hist. Man* I. 10 The seuenth bone of the head called the Cuneall bone. **1611** COTGR., *Os basilaire*, the Nape, or Necke-bone.. some call it the cuneall bone. **1727** in BAILEY vol. II. **1755** in JOHNSON. **1813** HOGG *Queen's Wake* 228 The ganza waved his cuneal way, With yellow oar, and quoif of green.

cuneate (ˈkjuːnɪət), *a.* [ad. L. *cuneāt-us* wedge-shaped, f. *cuneāre* to make wedge-shaped, f. *cuneus* wedge.] Made in the form of a wedge, wedge-shaped, as ***cuneate leaf***, a leaf with a truncated end, tapering gradually to the stipule.
1810 *Asiatic Res.* XI. 343 Lip obovate-cuneate. **1860** TYAS *Wild Fl.* 73 The leaves of the stem are cuneate. **1884** E. J. LOWE in *Times* 8 Dec. 10 The shape [of the meteor] was circular in front, and cuneate behind (bluntly conical).

b. *Comb.*, as ***cuneate-tailed*** adj.; also adverbially prefixed to another adj., as ***cuneate-lanceolate***.
1870 HOOKER *Stud. Flora* 347 Leaves narrowly cuneate-obovate or -lanceolate. **1881** M. G. WATKINS in *Acad.* 27 Aug. 163/1 The cuneate-tailed gull.

Hence **ˈcuneately** *adv.*, in the form of a wedge, wedge-wise.

cuneated (ˈkjuːnɪeɪtɪd), *ppl. a.* [f. as prec. + -ED.] = prec.
1727 in BAILEY vol. II. **1785** LIGHTFOOT in *Phil. Trans.* LXXV. 11 The tail is two inches long, slightly cuneated. **1828** STARK *Elem. Nat. Hist.* I. 201 The Magpie.. tail lengthened and cuneated.

cuneatic (kjuːnɪˈætɪk), *a.* [f. L. *cuneāt-us* CUNEATE + -IC. Cf. *hieratic*.] = CUNEATE, CUNEIFORM *a.*
1851 LAYARD *Pop. Acc. Discov. Nineveh* Introd. xi, The epithets of cuneiform, cuneatic, arrow-headed.. have been assigned to it. **1874** SAYCE in *Bibl. Arch. Soc. Trans.* III. 465 At the beginning of cuneatic decipherment.

cuneator (ˈkjuːnɪeɪtə(r)). [med.L. equivalent of OF. *coigneur* coiner: cf. L. *cuneāre* to make wedge-shaped.] (See quot.)
1883 *Encycl. Brit.* XVI. 480/2 The office of cuneator was one of great importance at a time [14th c.] when there existed a multiplicity of mints, since he had the sole charge of all the dies used not only at the mint in the Tower of London but also in the provinces.

cuneiform (kjuːˈniːɪfɔːm, ˈkjuːnɪɪ-), *a.* and *sb.* Also 7–9 cuneo-, 7 **cuneform**, 9 **cuniform** (ˈkjuːnɪfɔːm). [f. L. *cune-us* wedge + -FORM; cf. mod.L. *cuneiform-is*, F. *cunéiforme* (in Anatomy, 16th c. Paré).]

A. *adj.*

1. Having the form of a wedge, wedge-shaped. ***cuneiform bone*** (in *Anat.*): (*a*) one of the bones of the carpus; (*b*) each of three bones of the second row of the tarsus, called *internal*, *middle*, and *external*; (*c*) a name for the sphenoid bone of the skull. ***cuneiform cartilages*** or ***tubercles***: the cartilages of Wrisberg.
1677 PLOT *Oxfordsh.* 268 The stones are all cuneoform. **1681** tr. *Willis' Rem. Med. Wks.* Vocab., Cuneform, wedglike or in form of a wedg: a bone so shap'd. **1741** MONRO *Anat. Bones* (ed. 3) 101 The external Surface is mostly convex, except at the cuneiform Apophyse. **1797** BEWICK *Brit. Birds* (1847) I. 138 The tail is cuniform and rather long. **1840** G. ELLIS *Anat.* 28 The cuneiform process of the sphenoid bone. **1850** LEITCH *Müller's Anc. Art* §168 The art of arching by means of cuneiform stones.

2. *spec.* Applied to the characters of the ancient inscriptions of Persia, Assyria, etc., composed of wedge-shaped or arrow-headed elements; and hence to the inscriptions or records themselves.
1818 W. TAYLOR in *Monthly Rev.* LXXXV. 486 The cuneiform character is so simple in its component parts, that it.. consists only of two elements, the wedge and the rectangle. **1829** J. KENRICK in *Philos. Mag.* May 327 Beyond the limits of Persia more than one monument has been found with cuneiform inscriptions. **1869** F. W. NEWMAN *Misc.* 56 A cuneoform text from Assyria. **1876** BIRCH *Rede Lect. Egypt* 39 The recently discovered Assyrian annals in the cuneiform character.

b. *transf.* Relating to, or conversant with, the cuneiform writing and inscriptions.
1862 RAWLINSON *Anc. Mon.* I. v. 330 Cuneiform scholars. **1874** DEUTSCH *Rem.* 309 The vast importance of cuneiform studies.

B. *sb.* **1.** *Anat.* = *cuneiform bone* in A. 1.
1854 R. OWEN in *Circ. Sc.* (*c*1865) II. 78/2 The external cuneiform is the largest of the second series of tarsals.

2. The cuneiform character, cuneiform writing.
1862 *Sat. Rev.* 8 Feb. 162 He [Sir G. C. Lewis] doubts the whole Egyptian chronology,.. thinks the Babylonian annals an imposition, and does not even condescend to mention cuneiform and its decipherers. **1874** DEUTSCH *Rem.* 309 There are three principal kinds of cuneiform.

Hence **cuneiformist**, a student of cuneiform writing.
1884 W. M. RAMSAY in *Athenæum* 27 Dec. 865/2 As to the Hittites in Northern Syria, of course we.. must accept the verdict of cuneiformists and Egyptologists.

cuneo- (ˈkjuːnɪəʊ), combining form of L. *cuneus* a wedge, used in *Anat.*, as **cuneo-ˈcuboid** *a.*, relating to the cuneiform and the cuboid bones; **cuneo-ˈscaphoid** *a.*, relating to the cuneiform and the scaphoid bones.
1836–9 TODD *Cycl. Anat.* II. 343/1 The cuneo-scaphoid articulation.

cunestable, obs. form of CONSTABLE.

‖**cunette** (kjuːˈnɛt). *Fort.* Also 7 cunett. [a. F. *cunette* (1642 in Oudin), a. It. *cunetta* (1611 in Florio) in same sense. This is said by Hatzfeld and Darmesteter to be an aphæretic form of *lacunetta* (dim. of *lacuna* lagoon, ditch, etc.), the *la-* being confounded with the definite article. According to Th. Corneille *lacunette* was the original form in French also.]

A trench sunk along the middle of the dry ditch or moat, serving as a drain, and as an obstacle to the passage of the enemy, or to prevent mining.
1688 J. S. *Fortification* III, I also make a Cunett in my great Moat. **1721** in BAILEY. **1763** *Chron.* in *Ann. Reg.* 112/2 The cunette of Dunkirk is entirely filled up, excepting a trifling part, for which there was no earth. **1828–40** NAPIER *Penins. War* XVI. v. (Rtldg.) II. 350 A *cunette*, or second ditch, had been dug at the bottom of the great ditch.

cunfort, obs. form of COMFORT.

cunge, cungy, obs. form of CONGEE.

cunger, -ur, -yr, obs. ff. CONGER[1].

†**ˈcunicle.** *Obs. rare.* [ad. L. *cunīcul-us* rabbit, underground burrow or passage: in 16th c. F. *cunicule.*] A hole, cave, or passage under ground.
1657 TOMLINSON *Renou's Disp.* 422 Whose cunicles contain not any flint or other stone. **1658–96** PHILLIPS *Cunicle*, (lat.) a Mine or Hole under ground.

cuˈnicular, *a.*[1] [ad. L. *cunīculār-is*, f. *cunīculus*: see prec.]

†**1.** Rabbit-like, living in burrows under ground.
1759 B. MARTIN *Nat. Hist. Eng.* II. 235 The Troglydites, or cunicular Men described by Dr. Brown, that lived not like Men but Rabbits.

2. Of or pertaining to underground passages: see CUNICULUS.
1890 SMITH, etc. *Dict. Gr. & Rom. Antiq.* I. 573 The 'cunicular' drainage of Latium and Southern Etruria belongs rather to the pre-historic antiquities of Italy than to classical times. The subject.. has recently been investigated by Italians desirous of restoring to the Campagna its ancient fertility.

†**cuˈnicular**, *a.*[2] *Obs.* [f. L. *cūnæ* cradle: as if through a dim. *cuniculæ*.] Of or pertaining to the cradle or to infancy.
1676 *Acc. Lodowick Muggleton* in *Harl. Misc.* (Malh.) I. 610 (D.) They might have observed, even in his cunicular days.. an obstinate, dissentious, and opposive spirit.

cuniculate (kjuːˈnɪkjʊlət), *a. Bot.* [f. L. *cunīcul-us* underground passage + -ATE.] 'Traversed by a long passage, open at one end, as the peduncle of *Tropæolum*' (*Treas. Bot.* 1866).

†**cuˈniculine.** *Mil. Obs. rare*$^{-1}$. [f. L. *cunīcul-us* (see prec.) + -INE.] An engine used in mining.
1569 J. SA[NFORD] tr. *Agrippa's Van. Artes* xxii. 33 b, Yᵉ engins called Rams, Testudines, Cuniculines [L. *cuniculi*], Catapultes, Scorpions.

†**cunicuˈlose**, *a. Obs.*$^{-0}$ [ad. L. *cunīculōs-us*: see next.]
1727–31 BAILEY vol. II, *Cuniculose*, full of coneys or coney burroughs. **1775** ASH, *Cuniculose*, stocked with rabbits.

†**cuˈniculous**, *a. Obs.* [ad. L. *cunīculōs-us* abounding in caves, f. *cunīculus* burrow, underground hole: see -OUS, and cf. F. *cuniculeux* (16th c. in Paré, *ulcères cuniculeuses*).]

Full of holes and windings, like a rabbit-warren; also, full of rabbits.
1634 T. JOHNSON *Parey's Chirurg.* XIII. viii. (1678) 312 If the Ulcer be cuniculous or full of windings. *Ibid.* 486 Fistula's may be judged cuniculous, and running into many turnings and windings. **1656** BLOUNT *Glossogr.*, *Cuniculous* .. full of holes or mines under the ground, full of Conies. **1721** BAILEY, *Cuniculous*, full of Cony-burroughs.

‖**cuniculus** (kjuːˈnɪkjʊləs). Pl. -uli. [L. *cunīculus* rabbit, burrow, underground passage.]

1. A burrow, underground passage, or mine; in *Roman Archæol.* applied to the ancient 'cunicular' drains of Latium and Southern Etruria.
1670 E. BROWN in *Phil. Trans.* V. 1196 The water.. falls no lower.. passeth away through a Cuniculus made on purpose, through which both this and the other water.. do run out together at the foot of an Hill. **1693** RAY *Three Disc.* ii. (1713) 267 (Stanf.) Forced to seek Passage where it finds least Resistance through the lateral Cuniculi.

2. *Path.* The burrow of the itch-insect.
1882 in *Syd. Soc. Lex.*

cunig, cunin, obs. ff. CONY.

cuningar, -hare, Sc. var. of CONYGER *Obs.*, rabbit-warren.

cunit ('kju:nɪt). *Timber Industry.* Also **cunet.** [f. C III (= a hundred) + UNIT.] (See quot. 1956.)
1953 *Brit. Commonw. Forest Terminol.* I. 36 *Cunet, cunit,* a unit of stacked wood containing 100 cu. ft. of solid volume within the outside dimensions of the stack. **1956** *N.Z. Timber Jrnl.* Oct. 54/2 *Cunet* or *cunit,* a unit of stacked wood containing 100 cu. ft. of solid volume within the outside dimensions of the stack... Also known as Cubic unit. **1956** in N. K. WALLIS *Austral. Timber Handbk.* 348.

cunjevoi ('kʌndʒɪvɔɪ). *Austral.* [Native name.] **1.** The popular name for the green arum or spoon lily, *Alocasia macrorrhiza.*
1889 J. H. MAIDEN *Useful Native Plants Austral.* 165 *Colocasia macrorrhiza..Alocasia macrorrhiza..*'Pitchu' of the aboriginals of the Burnett River, Queensland; 'Cunjevoi' of those of South Queensland. **1930** *Bulletin* (Sydney) 12 Nov. 26/3 The cunjevoi..grows in dense clumps on river banks and in moist brush forests of eastern and tropical Australia. **1964** *Mod. Encycl. Austral. & N.Z.* 290/1 *Cunjevoi* or *Spoon lily*... Its bulbs (normally poisonous) were cooked in a special way and eaten by aborigines. **1965** *Austral. Encycl.* I. 221/1 One of the commonest Australian species is the cunjevoi,..whose large fleshy rhizomes extend for several feet over the surface of the ground.
2. (Also **-boi, -boy.**) A common ascidian, the sea-squirt (see quots.). Abbrev. **cunjie.**
[**1821** S. LEIGH in W. S. Ramson *Austral. Eng.* (1966) 121 *Conguwa,* a kind of living fungus, which at certain Seasons they detach from the Rocks on the Sea Shore.] **1911** A. E. MACK *Bush Days* 109 Down at the sea's edge grew the cunjeboy, brown and red, upon the rocks. **1925** *Illustr. Austral Encycl.* I. 342/1 *Cunjevoi,* popular name of a polyp (*Cynthia praeputialis*) common on the Australian coasts. It is often used as a bait for fishing. **1945** *Sun* (Sydney) 15 May, The organism known to local fishermen as congeboy, cungevoi, or congevoi. **1960** W. J. DAKIN et. al. *Austral. Seashores* (rev. ed.) xviii. 341 The cunjevoi itself..prefers the outermost rocks facing the ocean. **1965** *Austral. Encycl.* I. 274/2 *Pyura stolonifera* (cunjevoi) is occasionally used as bait but is never marketed as such. *Ibid.* III. 145/2 *Cunjevoi,*.. the name used in New South Wales for the ascidian or sea-squirt. *Ibid.*, A simple ascidian of the cunjevoi type may also be seen growing on wharf-piles or other harbour installations. **1966** BAKER *Austral. Lang.* (ed. 2) xiv. 302 *Cunjie,* a cunjevoi, used for bait.

cunnand, obs. form of CUNNING *a.*

cunndyȝt, obs. form of CONDUCT *sb.*

cunne, obs. f. CAN *v.*[1], CON *v.*[1], CAN *v.*[2], CUN.

cunne, (-y-) obs. form of KIN.

cunner ('kʌnə(r)). Also **conner, connor.** [In the form *conner,* prob. an application of CONNER[3], CONDER of a ship or of herring-boats.]
The name of two fishes of the family *Labridæ* or Wrasses: **a.** The Gilt-head (*Crenilabrus melops*), found on the British coasts. **b.** The Blue Perch or Burgall (*Ctenolabrus adspersus*), found on the Atlantic coast of North America, from Newfoundland to Delaware Bay.
1602 CAREW *Cornwall* 34b, They lay also certaine Weelyes in the Sea for taking of Cunners, which therethrough are termed Cunner-pots. **1620** J. MASON *Newfound-land* 5 Flounders, Crabbes, Cunners, Catfish. **1836** YARRELL *Brit. Fishes* I. 325 The Gilt-Head, Connor, Golden Maid. *Crenilabrus melops* (Cuv.). **1839** *Penny Cycl.* XIII. 261 *Crenilabrus Tinca,* Flem., called the 'Gilt-head', 'Connor,' etc., is found on many parts of our coast. **1852** HAWTHORNE *Amer. Note-Bks.* (1883) 417, I have been fishing for cunners off the rocks. **1865** S. TENNEY *Zool.* 340.

cunner, obs. form of CONNER[1], tester.

cunnerye, rabbit-warren: see CONYGER.

cunney, cunnie, obs. ff. CONY.

cunnilingus (,kʌnɪ'lɪŋgəs). [a. L. *cunnilingus* one who licks the vulva, f. *cunnus* female pudenda + *-lingus* (*lingere* to lick).] Oral stimulation of the vulva or clitoris. Also **'cunnilingue** *v. trans.* and *intr.*, to practise cunnilingus (on).
1887 L. C. SMITHERS tr. *Forberg's Man. Class. Erotology* v. 122 A man who is in the habit of putting out his tongue for the obscene act of cunnilinging. **1897** HAVELOCK ELLIS *Stud. Psychol. Sex.* I. iv. 98 The extreme gratification is *cunnilinctus,*..sometimes called sapphism. **1905** *Ibid.* IV. 21 *Cunnilingus* was a very familiar manifestation in classic times;..it tends to be especially prevalent at all periods of high civilization. **1965** *New Statesman* 26 Mar. 492/3 Cunnilingus, in which the tongue is used. **1969** G. LEGMAN *Rationale of Dirty Joke* viii. 566 A man comes home and finds the vicar cunnilinguing his wife. **1970** *Guardian* 6 Mar. 8/1 'The Beard'—a late night play at the Royal Court which shocked many..because of the mock display of cunnilingus in the last scene.

cunning ('kʌnɪŋ), *sb.* Forms: 4–5 **kunning(e, -yng(e, konning, -yng(e, konyng,** 4–6 **cunnyng(e, conning, -yng(e, coninge, -yng(e,** 5 **kunyng,** (6 **cooninng, coonning, counninge, -ynge),** 5– **cunning.** [Verbal sb. from CAN *v.*[1] (inf. OE. *cunnan,* ME. *cunnen, connen*) in its earlier sense 'to know', hence orig. = L. *scientia, sapientia.* Not recorded in OE. (which had however *oncunning* accusation, from the deriv. *oncunnan* to accuse), but like the cognate CUNNING *a.*, common since the 14th c.]
†**1.** Knowledge; learning, erudition. *Obs.*
1340 HAMPOLE *Pr. Consc.* 2350 Clerkes of grete cunnyng. *Ibid.* 7207 'Flos Sciencie' þat es on Ynglys 'þe flour of konyng'. *c* **1449** PECOCK *Repr.* Prol. 2 Manie han zeel..but not aftir Kunnyng. *c* **1475** *Rauf Coilȝear* 93 The Carll had Cunning weill quhair the gait lay. **1535** JOYE *Apol. Tindale* 50 We be puft up with coninge. **1559** MORWYNG *Evonym.* Pref., Ready to communicate..any cunning I had. **1571** CAMPION *Hist. Irel.* ix. (1633) 27 The Barbarians highly honoured him for his cunning in all languages. *a* **1670** HACKET *Abp. Williams* I. (1692) 13 He that would try his cunning in history when he was old.
†**2.** The capacity or faculty of knowing; wit, wisdom, intelligence. *Obs.*
1340 *Ayenb.* 115 One yefþe of þe holy gost þet is y-cleped þe yefþe of connynge. **1407** W. THORPE in *Exam.*, I..believe that all these three Persons are euen in power and in cunning, and in might. ? **1507** *Communyc.* (W. de W.) A ij, I made the also lyke unto me And gaue the connynge and free wyll. **1514** BARCLAY *Cyt. & Uplondyshm.* (Percy Soc.) p. lxvii, They have scantly the cunning of a snite. **1532** SIR T. MORE *Debell. Salem* Wks. (1557) 1008/1 Great vertues, and great gifts of God, as chastitie, liberalitie.. temperaunce, cunning.
3. Knowledge how to do a thing; ability, skill, expertness, dexterity, cleverness. (Formerly the prevailing sense; now only a literary archaism.)
c **1374** CHAUCER *Troylus* v. 866 Cryseyde..Als ferforthe as she konnynge hadde or myght, Answerde hym. *c* **1400** *Lanfranc's Cirurg.* 347 But for to medle medicyns in þis maner þer mote be miche kunnynge for to proporcioune hem. *c* **1500** *Nottingham Rec.* III. 447 The oath of the Common Councell. Ye shall well and truly, to your cunning and power [etc.]. **1577** HANMER *Anc. Eccl. Hist.* (1619) 15 Grievously diseased..incurable by Man's Cunning. **1611** BIBLE *Ps.* cxxxvii. 5 Let my right hand forget her cunning. **1743** *Lond. & Country Brew.* II. (ed. 2) 140 If such Brewers happen right..it is more by Chance, than Cunning. **1807** WORDSW. *White Doe of Ryl.* I. 94 High-ribbed vault..With perfect cunning framed. **1865** RAWLINSON *Anc. Mon.* III. v. 384 As nature's cunning arranges lines in the rainbow.
†**b.** *transf.* An application of skill; an ingenious device or means (quot. 1527). *Obs.*
1526 *Pilgr. Perf.* (W. de W. 1531) 142 Whiche settyng of stones..[is] ferre greater connynge than is yᵉ hewynge of stones. **1527** ANDREW *Brunswyke's Distyll. Waters* I vj, The same water is a very good connyng for to make the face clere and fayre. **1684** R. H. *Sch. Recreat.* 83 The first..Cunning to be observed in Bowling, is the right chusing your Bowl.
†**4.** A branch of knowledge or of skilled work; a science or art, a craft. In early times often = occult art, magic. *Obs.*
c **1325** *E.E. Allit. P.* B. 1611 Baltazar..þat now is demed Danyel of derne coninges. **1340–70** *Alisaunder* 716 þis King with his conning kithes his werkes With wiles of witchcraft. *c* **1400** *Three Kings Cologne* 14 þey haue maistris..to teche hem þat cunnyng of astronomye. *c* **1449** PECOCK *Repr.* 49 Sadelarie and talarie ben ij dyuerse facultees and kunninges. **1539** in *Vicary's Anat.* (1888) App. iii. 158 Lycens to exercyse hys connyng withyn the libertyes of London. **1592** WEST *1st Pt. Symbol.* § 1 A, Symbolæography is an Art or cunning rightly to fourme and make written Instruments.
5. Now usually in bad sense: Skill employed in a secret or underhand manner, or for purposes of deceit; skilful deceit, craft, artifice. (Cf. CRAFT 4.) **b.** As a personal quality: Disposition to use one's skill in an underhand way; skilfulness in deceiving, craftiness, artfulness.
1583 STANYHURST *Æneis* II. (Arb.) 45 Soom practis or oother Heere lurcks of coonning: trust not this treacherus ensigne. **1595** SHAKS. *John* IV. i. 54 Nay, you may thinke my loue was craftie loue, And call it cunning. **1612** BACON *Ess., Cunning* (Arb.) 434 We take Cunning for a sinister or crooked Wisedome. **1659** B. HARRIS *Parival's Iron Age* 182 A piece of cunning, whereby he had couzened many. *a* **1718** W. PENN *Maxims* Wks. 1726 I. 828 Cunning borders very near upon Knavery. **1842** MISS MITFORD in L'Estrange *Life* III. ix. 142 The perfection of cunning is to conceal its own quality. **1856** EMERSON *Eng. Traits, Truth* Wks. (Bohn) II. 52 Nature has endowed some animals with cunning, as a compensation for strength withheld.

cunning ('kʌnɪŋ), *a.* Forms: 4– **cunning;** also 4–5 **konyng,** (*north.*) **cunnand, connand, conand(e, -aunde,** 4–6 **kunnyng(e, -ing, konnyng, connyng(e, conyng(e, -inge,** 5–6 **cuning, cunnyng(e,** 5–7 **conning,** 6 **connninge.** [Orig. type *cunnende, pres. pple. of CAN *v.*[1] (inf. OE. *cunnan,* ME. *cunnen, connen*), in its earlier sense 'to know'; hence *orig.* = 'knowing'. Not found in OE., but in regular use from 14th c. both in the northern form *cunnand,* and the midl. and south. *cunning, connyng.* The derivative *conandscipe* occurs in *Cursor Mundi,* Cotton MS.]
†**1. a.** Possessing knowledge or learning, learned; versed *in* (†*of*) a subject. *Obs.*
c **1325** *Metr. Hom.* 93 He wil that they..be cunnand in his seruise. *c* **1350** *Will. Palerne* 4810 [þei] were hold.. konyngest of kurtesie, and kowden fairest speke. *c* **1394** *P. Pl. Crede* 378 Als as he were a connynge Clerke. *c* **1449** PECOCK *Repr.* III. x. 335 Myche kunnynger and better leerned. *c* **1450** *Merlin* 17 The Iuges seiden he moste be connynge of moche thynge. **1526** TINDALE *Matt.* xiii. 52 Every scrybe which is coninge vnto the kyngdom of heven. **1667** H. MORE *Div. Dial.* I. x. (1713) 19, I perceive you are cunninger than I in that Philosophy. [**1876** FREEMAN *Norm. Conq.* V. xxiii. 128 Flambard and the other cunning clerks of the King's Chapel.]
b. *transf.* Of things: Characterized by or full of knowledge or learning, learned.
1519 *Interl. Four Elem.* in Hazl. *Dodsley* I. 7 If cunning Latin books were translate Into English. **1534** TINDALE *1 Cor.* ii. 13 Which thinges also we speake, not in the connynge wordes of mannes wysdome, but with the connynge wordes of the holy goost. **1630** DAVENANT *Just Italian* Wks. (1673) 445 Stones of the cunningst soil.
2. a. Possessing practical knowledge or skill; able, skilful, expert, dexterous, clever. (Formerly the prevailing sense; now only a literary archaism.)
1382 WYCLIF *1 Sam.* xvi. 18 The sone of Ysaye Bethlemyte, kunnynge to harpe. **1389** in *Eng. Gilds* (1870) 46 An Aldirman able and konyng to reulen and gouern þe company. **1535** COVERDALE *1 Kings* Contents ch. v, Hiram ..sendeth Salomon connynge craftesmen to buylde the Temple. **1601** SHAKS. *Twel. N.* III. iv. 312 And [= if] I thought he had beene valiant, and so cunning in Fence. **1690** LOCKE *Govt.* II. xix, The tools of Cunninger workmen. **1718** PRIOR *To C'tess of Exeter* 37 While Luke his Skill exprest, A cunning Angel came, and drew the rest. **1843** PRESCOTT *Mexico* V. vii. (1864) 322 Most cunning in the management of their weapons.
b. *transf.* Showing skill or expertness; skilfully contrived or executed; skilful, ingenious.
1423 JAS. I. *Kingis Q.* xcvii, Fair-calling, hir vschere, That coude his office doon in connyng wise. **1535** COVERDALE *2 Chron.* ii. 14 To carue all maner of thinges, and to make what connynge thinge so euer is geuen him. **1587** TURBERV. *Trag. T.* (1837) 133 The cook..made a cunning messe Of meate thereof. **1611** BIBLE *Ex.* xxxix. 8 He made the brestplate of cunning worke. **1699** DAMPIER *Voy.* II. II. 68 They have a peculiar and wonderful cunning way of building..Their Nests hang down two or three Feet from the twigs. **1842** TENNYSON *Vision of Sin* IV. xxxi, Joints of cunning workmanship.
†**3.** *spec.* Possessing magical knowledge or skill: in ***cunning man, cunning woman,*** a fortune-teller, conjurer, 'wise man', 'wise woman', wizard or witch. (Also hyphened ***cunning-man.***) *Obs.* (or ? *dial.*)
[*c* **1350** *Will. Palerne* 653 Ful conyng was sche and coynt, and couþe fele þinges, Of charmes and of chauntemens to schewe harde castis.] **1593** SHAKS. *2 Hen. VI.* IV. i. 34 A cunning man did calculate my birth, And told me that by Water I should dye. **1609** B. JONSON *Sil. Wom.* II. i, Going in disguise to that conjurer and this cunning woman. **1712** ADDISON *Spect.* No. 505 ¶4 How many Wizards, Gypsies, and Cunning-Men. **1797** *Sporting Mag.* X. 273 The wife.. went to a cunning woman to discover the thief. **1807** SOUTHEY *Espriella's Lett.* II. 342 A Cunning-Man, or a Cunning-Woman, as they are termed, is to be found near every town.
4. Possessing keen intelligence, wit, or insight; knowing, clever.
1671 J. WEBSTER *Metallogr.* vi. 106 Wiser heads, and cunninger wits. **1710** PHILIPS *Pastorals* ii. 55 Against ill Luck all cunning Foresight fails. **1766** GOLDSM. *Vic. W.* xix, Your groom rides your horses because he is a cunninger animal than they. **1856** EMERSON *Eng. Traits, Wealth* Wks. (Bohn) II. 73 [These] provisions..have exercised the cunningest heads in a profession which never admits a fool.
5. a. In bad sense: Skilful in compassing one's ends by covert means; clever in circumventing; crafty, artful, guileful, sly. (The prevailing modern sense.)
[**1590** SPENSER *F.Q.* II. i. 1 That conning Architect of cancred guyle.] **1599** SHAKS. *Hen. V,* II. ii. 111 Whatsoeuer cunning fiend it was That wrought upon thee. **1611** —— *Cymb.* I. iv. 100. **1653** H. COGAN tr. *Pinto's Trav.* xvi. 54 Like cunning thieves, desiring that the prey..should not escape out of their hands. **1752** JOHNSON *Rambler* No. 193 ¶1 The cunning will have recourse to stratagem, and the powerful to violence. **1841** ELPHINSTONE *Hist. Ind.* II. 173 He was not naturally either cunning or cruel. **1864** KINGSLEY *Rom. & Teut.* iii. (1875) 73 The stronger, if not the cunninger of the two.
b. Of things: Showing or characterized by craftiness; crafty.
1590 SPENSER *F.Q.* I. iii. 17 Then he by conning sleights in at the window crept. **1611** BIBLE *Eph.* iv. 14 By the sleight of men, and cunning craftinesse, whereby they lye in waite to deceiue. **1840** DICKENS *Old C. Shop* iii, His black eyes were restless, sly, and cunning. **1872** E. PEACOCK *Mabel Heron* I. iii. 49 If I didn't know your cunning ways.
6. *U.S. colloq.* Quaintly interesting or pretty, attractive, taking; as having attributed to it the qualities described in sense 2b, or (as said of young children) in 4 or 5. (Cf. CANNY 9.)
1844 'J. SLICK' *High Life N.Y.* I. 220 'Why, that pair,' sez she,..a burying her hands..down in the pocket of her cunning apron. **1844** DICKENS *Mart. Chuz.* xvii. 216 Tea and coffee arrived (with sweet preserves, and cunning teacakes in its train). **1854** MRS. STOWE *Sunny Mem.* I. 161 My eye had been caught by some cunning little tubs and pails in a window. **1885** G. ALLEN *Babylon* i, Ain't it a cunning little egg? **1887** *Century Mag.* Nov. 43 As a child, she had been called 'cunning' in the popular American use of the word when applied to children; that is to say, piquantly interesting. **1888** *The Lady* 25 Oct. 374/3 'Cunning' little shelves for small bits of pottery.

'cunning, *vbl. sb.* Directing the helm: see under CON *v.*[2]
1659 D. PELL *Improv. Sea* 418 The Helmsman..minded not the cunning of the ship.

cunning, obs. form of CONY, rabbit.

cunningaire, var. CONYGER, rabbit-warren.

†'**cunninghede.** *Obs. rare.* In 5 connyng-. [f. CUNNING + *-hede*, -HEAD.] = CUNNINGNESS 1.

c **1475** *Partenay* 5 Barayne is my soule, fauting connynghede.

cunningly ('kʌnɪŋlɪ), *adv.* Forms: see CUNNING *a.* [-LY[2].] In a cunning manner.

1. With skill, knowledge, or wisdom; wisely, cleverly, knowingly. *Obs.* or *arch.*

In early quots. often = 'with good breeding, politely'. *c* **1375** *Sc. Leg. Saints, Theodera* 402 Hyme ful connandly scho gret. *c* **1385** CHAUCER *L.G.W.* 1485 *Hypsip. & Medea,* Fful cunnyngely these lordes two he grette. *c* **1400** *Destr. Troy* 838 Iason carpes to the kyng, cunnyngly he said. **1413** LYDG. *Pilgr. Sowle* IV. xxxviii. (1859) 63 He salewed hyr goodly, and she welcomed hym ful connyngly, as she wel couthe. *c* **1425** WYNTOUN *Cron.* v. xii. 275 Hucheown.. In-til his gest hystoriale Has tretyd þis mar cunnandly. *c* **1460** *Towneley Myst.* 160 This barne.. That carps thus conandly. **1519** *Interl. Four Elem.* in Hazl. *Dodsley* I. 37 He hath expound cunningly Divers points of cosmography. **1592** R. D. *Hypnerotomachia* 91 Which thoughts were bewraied by my countenance.. which she cunningly perceiuing [etc.]. **1870** MORRIS *Earthly Par.* II. III. 341 Two wise men.. who can Talk cunningly about the ways of man.

2. With skilful art. (Now a literary archaism.)

? *a* **1400** *Chester Pl.* (Shaks. Soc.) I. 114 He so cuninglye this worcke caste. **1555** EDEN *Decades* 31 Chayers and stooles.. very cooningely wrowght. **1682** MILTON *Hist. Mosc.* ii. (1851) 483 They shoot wondrous cunningly: thir Arrow heads are sharpned Stones. **1836–48** B. D. WALSH *Aristoph., Clouds* I. iv, Cunningly-wrought halls. **1883** LD. R. GOWER *My Remin.* II. xxi. 52 Inigo Jones.. decorated the front of Kirby.. in cunningly carved stone.

3. With knowledge employed to conceal facts or designs, or to deceive or circumvent; craftily, artfully. (The current sense.)

1603 KNOLLES *Hist. Turks* (1621) 48 So cunningly had he under the vaile of pietie, shadowed his most execrable treacherie. **1622** R. HAWKINS *Voy. S. Sea* (1847) 104 The cuninglier to colour their greatest disorders and robberies. **1719** D'URFEY *Pills* IV. 201 Women are.. cunningly Coy. **1856** KANE *Arct. Expl.* I. xi. 124 Your lash.. is apt to.. fasten itself cunningly round bits of ice. **1867** DEUTSCH *Rem.* (1874) 8 He saw the cunningly-laid trap.

'**cunningness.** [f. as prec. + -NESS.] The quality of being cunning or knowing.

†**1.** Knowingness; skilfulness, skill, cleverness; something requiring skill; = CUNNING *sb.* 2, 3, 4.

1375 BARBOUR *Bruce* III. 712 It wes gret cunnannes to kep Thar takill in-till sic A thrang. *a* **1400** *Relig. Pieces fr. Thornton MS.* (1867) 12 Worldely mene.. þat castes þaire conaundenes.. vn-to couetyse. *c* **1400** *Lanfranc's Cirurg.* 121 Konyngnesse of þe leche. **1609** DOULAND *Ornith. Microl.* 67 Thou.. hast.. in singing a graceful cunningnesse. **1755** *Connoisseur* No. 70 ¶10 For all your learning, and policy, and cunningness, and judgment.

2. Craftiness, slyness, artfulness; = CUNNING *sb.* 5.

a **1625** FLETCHER *Woman's Prize* IV. ii, Such a drench of balderdash, Such a strange carded cunningness. **1654** COKAINE *Dianea* I. 69 With all candidnesse.. or else with a cunningness. **1702** W. J. *Bruyn's Voy. Levant* xl. 157 The Cunningness of Apes and Falcons. **1727** in BAILEY vol. II.; and in mod. Dicts. **1965** *Listener* 18 Mar. 420/2 His work.. lacks the nudging cunningness of some 'art' photographers.

†'**cunningship.** *Obs.* In 3 (*north.*) conandscipe. [See CUNNING *a.* and -SHIP.] Knowledge.

a **1300** *Cursor M.* 29206 (Cott.) þe gift o wijt, of vnderstanding, o consail, strenght, o gode dreding, o conandscipe, and o pite.

cunnundrum, obs. form of CONUNDRUM.

cunny ('kʌnɪ). *slang.* [Prob. dim. of CUNT; but cf. CONY *sb.* 5 b.] = CUNT 1.

1720 D'URFEY *Pills* VI. 197 All my Delight is a Cunny in the Night, When she turns up her silver Hair. **1865** E. SELLON *New Epicurean* (1875) 11, I frigged and kissed their fragrant cunnies. **1879–80** *Pearl* (1970) 216 Your private parts, or cunny, Should not be let for money. **1891** FARMER & HENLEY *Slang* II. 230 *Cunny-haunted,*.. lecherous. **1922** F. HARRIS *My Life & Loves* I. x. 208 She had limbs like a Greek statue and her triangle of brown hair lay in little silky curls on her belly and then—the sweetest little cunny in the world.

cunny, -yng, obs. forms of CONY, rabbit.

cunopic (kju:'nɒpɪk), *a. nonce-wd.* [f. Gr. κυνώπης the dog-eyed, the shameless.] = CYNOPIC.

1838 *Fraser's Mag.* XVIII. 671 The roystering, rubicund, cunopic cutter of rumps of beef and briskets.

cunstable, -bulle, -bylle, obs. ff. CONSTABLE.

†**cunster.** *Sc. Obs.* In 6 quenster. [Parallel formation to *cunner*, CONNER[1], with suffix -STER.] = CONNER[1], ale-conner.

1535 *Aberd. Reg.* V. 16 And that the officiaris pas oukly with thair cunstaris throu the quarteris. **1551** *Crt. Rec.* in Cramond *Annals Banff* (1891) I. 28 Aill.. fundin gud and sufficient be the quensters. **1628** *Ibid.* I. 60 The Provost, Bailies and Council choose four persons as Cunsters and Visitors of ale, beer and bread. **1676** *Ibid.* I. 156 The goodnes of the aill to be tyrit be cunsteris.

cunt (kʌnt). [ME. *cunte, count(e)*, corresponding to ON. *kunta* (Norw., Sw. dial. *kunta*, Da. dial. *kunte*), OFris., MLG., MDu. *kunte*:—Gmc. **kuntōn* wk. fem.; ulterior relations uncertain.] **1.** The female external genital organs. Cf. QUAINT *sb.*

Its currency is restricted in the manner of other taboo-words: see the small-type note s.v. FUCK *v.*

[*c* **1230** in Ekwall *Street-Names of City of London* (1954) 165 Gropecuntelane.] *a* **1325** *Prov. Hendyng* (Camb. Gg. I. 1) st. 42 Yeue þi cunte to cunnig and craue affetir wedding. *c* **1400** *Lanfranc's Cirurg.* 172/12 In wymmen þe necke of þe bladdre is schort, & is maad fast to the cunte. *c* **1425** *Castle of Perseverance* (1904) 1193 Mankynde, my leue lemman, I my cunte þou schalt crepe. **1552** LYNDESAY *Satyre* Procl. 144 First lat me lok thy cunt, Syne lat me keip the key. *a* **1585** POLWART *Flyting with Montgomerie* (1910) 817 Kis þe cunt of ane kow. *c* **1650** in Hales & Furnivall *Percy's Folio MS.* (1867) 99 Vp start the Crabfish, & catcht her by the Cunt. **1743** WALPOLE *Little Peggy* in *Corr.* (1961) XXX. 309 Distended cunts with alum shall be braced. *c* **1800** BURNS *Merry Muses* (1911) 66 For ilka hair upon her c—t, Was worth a royal ransom. *c* **1888–94** *My Secret Life* VII. 161, I sicken with desire, pine for unseen, unknown cunts. **1934** H. MILLER *Tropic of Cancer* (1935) 15 O Tania, where now is that warm cunt of yours? **1956** S. BECKETT *Malone Dies* 24 His young wife had abandoned all hope of bringing him to heel, by means of her cunt, that trump card of young wives. *transf.* and *fig.* *a* **1680** LD. ROCHESTER *Poems on Several Occasions* (1950) 28 Her Hand, her Foot, her very look's a Cunt. **1922** JOYCE *Ulysses* 61 The grey sunken cunt of the world. **1928** D. H. LAWRENCE *Lady Chatterley* xvi. 296 If your sister there comes ter me for a bit o' cunt an' tenderness, she knows what she's after.

2. Applied to a person, esp. a woman, as a term of vulgar abuse.

1929 F. MANNING *Middle Parts of Fortune* I. viii. 159 What's the cunt want to come down 'ere buggering us about for, 'aven't we done enough bloody work in th' week? **1932** 'G. ORWELL' *Coll. Essays* (1968) I. 88 Tell him he's a cunt from me. **1934** H. MILLER *Tropic of Cancer* (1935) 28 Two cunts sail in—Americans. **1956** S. BECKETT *Malone Dies* 99 They think they can confuse me... Proper cunts whoever they are. **1965** V. HENRIQUES *Face I Had* 69 'What d'you think you're doing, you silly cunt?' the driver shouts at her.

3. *Comb.*

1680 ANON. in *Rochester's Poems on Several Occasions* (1950) 36 Fam'd through the World, for the C--nt-mending Trade. **1868** *Index Expurgatorius of Martial* 32 A satire on Baeticus, who was a priest of Cybele, and a cunt-sucker. **1891** FARMER *Slang* II. 230/2 *Cunt-struck*, enamoured of women. **1923** MANCHON *Le Slang* 97 *Cunt-hat*,.. chapeau de feutre. **1965** F. SARGESON *Memoirs of Peon*, ii. 28 We were all helplessly and hopelessly c... struck, a vulgar but forcibly accurate expression.

cunt-: see CONT-, COUNT-.

cunye, cunzie ('kʏnji:, 'kʏnɪ), *sb. Sc.* Also cun-, cuin-, -ȝe, -ȝee, -ȝey, -ȝhe, -ȝie, -ȝye, -yee, -yie; conȝe, -ȝie, counye, cownye, cwnyhe, coynyhe, coinȝie, coignie. [15th c. Sc. *cunȝe*, repr. OF. *cuigne* var. of *coin*, COIN.]

†**1.** = COIN *sb.* 1 or 2: Corner or corner-stone.

1375 BARBOUR *Bruce* XVIII. 304 Richt till the Cunȝhe of the wall. **1387** *St. Giles Charters* (1859) p. x, Xii hewyn stonys, astlayr and coynyhe. **1645** *Fenwick Session Rec.* in Edgar *Old Ch. Life in Scot.* 16 *note*, That no furmes be placed about the cuinȝies.

†**2.** A coining-house, a mint; = COIN *sb.* 4. *Obs.*

1489 *Sc. Acts Jas. IV* §17 (1597) The silver warke.. quhilk is brocht to the cuinȝie. *a* **1572** KNOX *Hist. Ref.* Wks. 1846 I. 453 It was thocht expedient that a cunȝe should be erected.

3. Coin, money; = COIN *sb.* 6.

c **1375** *Sc. Leg. Saints, Jacobus* 734 Of þaire conȝe.. pennyse thretty. **1482** in Pinkerton *Scot.* App. I. 503 Thar was blak cunye in the realm, strikkin and ordinyt be King James the Thred, half-pennys, and threepenny pennys.. of coppir. **1513** DOUGLAS *Æneis* VIII. Prol. 97 Sum trachour crynis the cunȝe. **1513–75** *Diurn. Occurrents* (Bannatyne Club) 120 Ane proclamatioun twching the new cuinyee. **1552** ABP. HAMILTON *Catech.* 98 Thai that strykis cownye of unlauchful mettall [*margin*, Strykaris of unlauchful connyey]. **1600** *Sc. Acts 16 Jas. VI*, c. 9 Great scairsitie of Cunyie. **1724** RAMSAY *Tea-t. Misc.* (1733) I. 105 When cunzie is scanty.

4. *Comb.* †**cunye-house**, coining-house, mint.

1513–75 *Diurn. Occurrents* (Bannatyne Club) 53 Tuke.. the Quenis irnis of the cunyehous. **1600** *Sc. Acts 16 Jas. VI*, c. 9 Anent the hame-bringing of Bulyeon for furnishing of the Cunye-house. **1637–50** Row *Hist. Kirk* (1842) p. xvii, I culd get no money out of the conze-house. *a* **1657** BALFOUR *Ann. Scot.* (1824–5) II. 2 Naper, Laird of Merchistone, generall of the cunzie housse.

†**cunye,** *v. Sc. Obs.* Forms: see the sb. [f. prec.] *trans.* To coin. Hence '**cunyed** *ppl. a.*

c **1425** WYNTOUN *Cron.* VII. v. 168 This Henry fyrst kyng of Ingland.. ordanyd.. Hys mone to be cwynhede rownd. **1475** *Sc. Acts Jas. III*, §65 (1597) All cuinȝied money. **1549** *Compl. Scot.* xiii. 109 Gold and siluyr, cunȝeit & oncunȝet. **1588** A. KING tr. *Canisius' Catech.* 8, 3. Gif thai bring in or cause coignie any false money.

cunyng, obs. form of CONY, rabbit.

†'**cunyour.** *Sc. Obs.* [a. OF. *coignour, quoingneur* coiner of money.] = COINER 1.

1455 *Sc. Acts Jas. II*, §59 (1597) That the cuinȝioures.. nouther cuinȝie Demy.. nor ȝit sex-penny-groates. **1469** *Sc. Acts Jas. III*, §40 (1597) Black money, stricken and prented be his Cuinzieoures. **1500–20** DUNBAR *Demonstr. to King* 11 Cunȝours, Carvouris, & Carpentaris.

cunze, cunzie: see CUNYE.

cuoshen, obs. form of CUSHION.

cup (kʌp), *sb.* Forms: α. 1–7 cuppe, (4–5 kuppe), 4–7 cupp, 6– cup, (6 *Sc.* culp(p). β. 3–5 cupe, 3–6 coupe, 4–5 cowpe, 6 *Sc.* coup, cowp. γ. 3–5 coppe, 4–5 cope, (5 coop, 6 coope). [OE. *cuppe* wk. fem., supposed to be ad. late L. *cuppa*, the source of It. *coppa* (close *o*), Pr., Sp., Pg. *copa*, OF. *cope, cupe, coupe*, rarely *coppe*, mod.F. *coupe* drinking-vessel, cup.

L. *cuppa* is generally held to be a differentiated form of *cūpa*, tub, cask, vat, which survives in F. *cuve*, Pr., Sp., Pg. *cuba* tub, etc. But beside *cuppe* in ME., are found two forms *coupe* (*cowpe*) and *coppe*, with the variants *cupe, cope, coope.* Of these *coupe* (*cowpe*) directly represents OF. *coupe*; *cupe* prob. represents the earlier OF. spelling of the same word, but may be merely a variant of *cuppe*. The status of *coppe* is not so clear: it may also represent OF. *cope* (sometimes *coppe*), or it may be due to mixture of *cuppe* and OE. *copp*: see COP *sb.*[1]; in the form *coppes* it is impossible to distinguish between the pl. of *copp* and that of *coppe*. The rare forms *cope, coope*, prob. represent OF. *cope*. Nearly all these by-forms of the word became obs. before 1500; only *cuppe* survives in mod. English *cup*.]

I. A drinking-vessel, or something resembling it.

1. A small open vessel for liquids, usually of hemispherical or hemi-spheroidal shape, with or without a handle; a drinking-vessel. The common form of cup (*e.g.* a tea-cup or coffee-cup) has no stem; but the larger and more ornamental forms (*e.g.* a wine-cup or chalice) may have a stem and foot, as also a lid or cover; in such case *cup* is sometimes applied specifically to the concave part that receives the liquid.

α. **cuppe, cupp, cup.** (Sc. culp, culpp, belongs perh. to β.)

c **1000** ÆLFRIC *Voc.* in Wr.-Wülcker 122/37 *Caupus vel obba*, cuppe. *c* **1000** *Sax. Leechd.* II. 290 Nime þonne ane cuppan, do an lytel wearmes wætres on innan. *c* **1205** LAY. 14996 Heo þa cuppe [*later t.* bolle] bitahte þan kinge. *c* **1250** *Gen. & Ex.* 2318 ȝure on haueð is cuppe stolen. *a* **1300** *Cursor M.* 13402 (Cott.) þai fild a cupp [*v.r.* cope, 2 *MSS.* cuppe] þan son in hast. *c* **1380** WYCLIF *Sel. Wks.* III. 157 Monkes haf grete kuppes. *c* **1440** *Promp. Parv.* 109 Cuppe, *ciphus, patera, cuppa.* **1477** EARL RIVERS (Caxton) *Dictes* 70, I haue putte.. wyn in my cuppe. **1542** *Inventories* (1815) 74 (Jam.) Item, twa culpis gilt.. Item, twa culppis with thair coveris gilt. **1583** STANYHURST *Aeneis* II. (Arb.) 68 Massiue gould cups. **1597** SHAKS. *2 Hen. IV*, v. iii. 56 Fill the Cuppe.. Ile pledge you a mile to the bottome. **1667** MILTON *P.L.* v. 444 Mean while at Table Eve.. thir flowing cups With pleasant liquors crown'd. **1770** GOLDSM. *Des. Vill.* 250 Nor the coy maid.. Shall kiss the cup to pass it to the rest. **1842** TENNYSON *Vision of Sin* IV. ix, Fill the cup, and fill the can. **1872** E. PEACOCK *Mabel Heron* I. viii. 136 He half filled a leather cup he carried in his pocket.

β. **cupe, coupe, cowpe.**

c **1275** LAY. 24612 Mid gildene coupe [*earlier t.* bolle]. *a* **1300** *Cursor M.* 4858 (Cott.) A siluer cupe [3 *later MSS.* coupe]. *a* **1300** *Ibid.* 7728 (Cott.) A cupe [F. cuppe, G. & T. coupe] he tok and a sper. [Cf. OF. *Rois* 104 pristrent la lance e la cupe ki fud al chief Saül.] *c* **1325** *E.E. Allit. P.* B. 1458 Couered cowpes foul clene, as casteles arayed. **1393** LANGL. *P. Pl.* C. IV. 23 Coupes of clene gold and coppes of seluer. *c* **1440** *Promp. Parv.* 99 Cowpe, or pece, *crater* (*cuppa*, P.). *c* **1450** *Merlin* 67 The kynge hadde a riche cowpe of goolde.

γ. **coppe** (**cope, coop**): cf. COP *sb.*[1]

c **1290** *S. Eng. Leg.* 41/258 A coppe of seluer. *a* **1300** *Cursor M.* 13402 (Gött.) þai fild a cope [C. cupp, F. cuppe] sone in hast. **1340** *Ayenb.* 30 And brekþ potes and coppes. *c* **1386** CHAUCER *Frankl. T.* 214 With outen coppe [4 *MSS.* cuppe] he drank al his penaunce. *a* **1450** *Voc.* in Wr.-Wülcker 626/9 *Ciphus*, coop. **1483** *Cath. Angl.* 75 A Coppe, *ciphus* [= *scyphus*], condus. *c* **1500** *Yng. Children's Bk.* 106 in *Babees Bk.* (1868) 23 Wype thi mouthe when þou wyll drinke, Lest it foule thi copys brinke.

2. *spec.* **a.** The CHALICE in which the wine is administered at the Communion. (See also sense 8 b.)

[**1382** WYCLIF *Matt.* xxvi. 27 And he takynge the cuppe dede thankyngis and ȝaue to hem.] *c* **1449** PECOCK *Repr.* II. x. 203 The eukarist.. is born in a coupe ordeyned therto. **1547–8** *Ordre of Commvnion* 17 The first Cuppe or Chalice. **1662** *Bk. Com. Prayer, Communion*, Here he is to take the cup into his hand. **1890** J. HUNTER *Devotional Services, Communion*, Then shall the Minister say.. when he delivereth the cup: Drink this in remembrance of Christ.

b. An ornamental cup or other vessel offered as a prize for a race or athletic contest.

c **1640** [SHIRLEY] *Capt. Underwit* III. iii. in Bullen *O. Pl.* (1883) II. 368 Does the race hold at Newmarket for the Cup? **1777** SHERIDAN *Sch. Scand.* III. iii, All the family race cups and corporation bowls! **1837** DICKENS *Pickw.* xxxix, Think you're vinning a cup, Sir. **1885** *Pall Mall G.* 4 Apr. 4/2 The competition for the Challenge Cup.

3. *Surg.* **a.** A vessel used for cupping; a cupping-glass. **b.** A vessel holding a definite quantity (usually four ounces), used to receive the blood in blood-letting.

1617 MOSAN tr. *Wirtzung's Physick* 27 To remoue headach the cups are fixed on the legs. *a* **1735** ARBUTHNOT (J.), Hippocrates tells you, that in applying of cups, the scarification ought to be made with crooked instruments. **1792** H. MUNRO *Th. & Pract. Mod. Surg.* (1800) 15 As soon as the wound is made by these [lancets], a cup, exhausted of its atmospheric air, applied over the orifices, makes them bleed freely. **1889** *Chambers' Encycl.* III. 618 Of old the cups were either small horns.. or glasses of various shapes.

4. A natural organ or formation having the form of a drinking-cup; *e.g.* the rounded cavity or socket of certain bones, as the shoulder-blade and hip-bone; the cup-shaped hardened involucrum (cupule) of an acorn (*acorn-cup*); the calyx of a flower, also the blossom itself when cup-shaped; a cup-shaped organ in certain Fungi, or on the suckers of certain Molluscs; a depression in the skin forming a rudimentary eye in certain lower animals (also ***eye-cup*** or ***cup-eye***).

1545 RAYNOLD *Byrth Mankynde* 81 Take..the cuppes of acornes. **1548–77** VICARY *Anat.* vii. (1888) 48 The.. shoulder-blade..in the vpper part it is round, in whose roundnes is a concauitie, which is called yᵉ boxe or coope of the shoulder. **1590** SHAKS. *Mids. N.* II. i. 31 All their Elues ..Creepe into Acorne cups and hide them there. **1615** CROOKE *Body of Man* 849 The Cup of the Hippe. **1707** *Curios. in Husb. & Gard.* 45 The Cup is that which infolds the Leaves and the Heart of a Flower, while it is yet in Bud. **1743–6** SHENSTONE *Elegies* viii. 38 The cowslip's golden cup no more I see. **1866** *Treas. Bot.* 870 *Peziza*..The hymenium lines the cavity of a fleshy membranous or waxy cup. **1888** ROLLESTON & JACKSON *Anim. Life* 456 The suckers of the *Decapoda* are stalked, and the cup has a marginal horny ring. **1900** F. A BATHER in E. R. Lankester *Treat. Zool.* III. 30 Each cup is coated at its base with pigment. **1927** *Glasgow Herald* 9 July 4 In some of the sea-worms..we start with diagrammatically simple 'cup-eyes', ..and gradually pass to very elaborate 'cup-eyes'. *Ibid.*, A minute optic skin-cup. **1929** *Encycl. Brit.* XX. 628/2 Eye-spots are found in Medusae, starfishes, and some Annelid worms... The first step..is the sinking of the eye-spot into a pit-like depression, thus forming an eye-cup (optic cup). *Ibid.*, The cells situated at the back of the cup. **1940** PARKER & HASWELL *Text-bk. Zool.* (ed. 6) I. 249 [Phylum Platyhelminthes.] When most highly developed the eye..is still of very simple structure, consisting of a cup formed of one or more pigment-cells having sensory cells in close relation to it with processes (nerve-fibres) passing to the brain.

5. A rounded cavity, small hollow, or depression in the surface of the ground or of a rock. *spec.* in *Golf*: see quot. 1887.

1868 HOLME LEE *B. Godfrey* i. 7 The church..stood in a cup of the hillside. **1887** JAMIESON *Supp.*, *Cup*, a term in golfing applied to a small cavity or hole in the course, prob. made by the stroke of a previous player. **1887** SIR W. G. SIMPSON *Art of Golf* 133 Beware of a cup, however small. **1889** *Chambers' Encycl.* III. 618 Cup-markings on rocks..of two varieties—circular cavities or 'cups' pure and simple, and cups surrounded by circles.

6. a. *techn.* Applied to various cup-shaped contrivances; see quots.

c **1850** *Rudim. Navig.* (Weale) 113 *Cup*, A solid piece of cast iron let into the step of the capstan, and in which the iron spindle at the heel of the capstan works. **1874** KNIGHT *Dict. Mech.*, *Cup*. 4. One of a series of little domes attached to a boiler-plate and serving to extend the fire-surface. **1884** F. J. BRITTEN *Watch & Clockm.* 99 There are two varieties of cups—'saucer' and 'balance-wheel'—the former, shaped like a saucer, is generally of gold, and is used in three-quarter plate watches.

b. *Painting.*

1768 W. GILPIN *Ess. Prints* 223 The heavier part of the foliage (the *cup*, as the landskip-painter calls it) is always near the middle: the out-side branches..are light and airy.

c. That part of a brassière which is shaped to contain or support one of the breasts. Also *attrib.* and *Comb.*

1938 'E. QUEEN' *Four of Hearts* (1939) ix. 129 She didn't have to wear a cup-form brassière. **1957** *Housewife* Sept. 104 Thinnest foam rubber curved in the cups..achieves a natural line by gently contouring the bosom itself. **1959** *Ibid.* June 28 Marquisette cup section underlined lace. *Ibid.*, A perfect contour bustline..B and C cups. **1959** *News Chron.* 13 July 6/3 Cup fittings are based on the difference between underbust and full bust measurements. **1970** *Times* 16 June 7/6 The prettiest and the most alluring and flattering bathing suits are halter-necked with a vertiginous ..plunge in the front and very soft, unsupported cups.

7. *Astron.* The constellation CRATER *sb.*

1551 RECORDE *Cast. Knowl.* (1556) 269 The Cuppe standeth on the Hydres backe. **1579** SPENSER *Sheph. Cal.* July 19 The Sonne..Making his way betweene the Cuppe, and golden Diademe. **1868** LOCKYER *Heavens* (ed. 3) 326.

II. Transferred and figurative uses.

8. a. A cup with the liquor it contains; the drink taken in a cup; a cupful. LOVING-CUP (q.v.), a cup of wine, etc. passed from hand to hand round a company. Also *ellipt.* (In quots. 1952 and 1969, ellipt. in sense 12 b (ii).)

1382 WYCLIF *Matt.* x. 42 Who euer ȝiueth drynke to oon of these leste a cuppe of cold water oonly. **1588** A. KING tr. *Canisius' Catech.* 171 b, Quhasaeuer sal giv ony of thais small ains ane coup of watter to drink onelie. **1601** SHAKS. *Twel. N.* I. iii. 85 O knight, thou lack'st a cup of Canarie. **1660** PEPYS *Diary* 28 Sept., I did send for a cup of tee (a China drink) of which I never had drank before. *c* **1760** *Mother Goose's Melody* (1785) 19 Take a cup and drink it up, Then call your Neighbours in. **1784** COWPER *Task* IV. 39 The cups That cheer but not inebriate, wait on each. [See CHEER *v.* 5 c.] **1839** THIRLWALL *Greece* VI. xlviii. 145 A cup of poison had been prepared for him. **1847** C. M. YONGE in *Mag. for the Young* Sept. 189 There is the kettle..all ready for tea!..Won't you sit down and have a cup, Amy? **1849** MRS. CARLYLE *Lett.* II. 44 Each of these gentlemen drank four cups of tea. **1952** A. WILSON *Hemlock & After* I. iii. 51 Anyway, none of it would be your cup, darling. **1969** J. ELLIOT *Duel* I. iii. 68 He enjoys his little Royal Society dinners... Not my cup.

b. *spec.* The wine taken at the Communion. (Cf. 2 a.)

[**1382** WYCLIF *1 Cor.* xi. 26 How ofte euere ȝe schulen ete this breed, and schulen drynke the cuppe.] **1597** HOOKER *Eccl. Pol.* v. lxvii. §5 The bread and cup are his body and blood for that they are so to us. **1681–6** J. SCOTT *Chr. Life* (1747) III. 307 To communicate with them..in this one Baptism, and one eucharistical Bread and Cup. **1884** J. CANDLISH *Sacraments* 91 The wine is described merely as 'the cup', 'the fruit of the vine'.

c. *transf.* Drink; that which one drinks.

1719 YOUNG *Busiris* v. i, Weeds are their food, their cup the muddy Nile.

9. *fig.* Chiefly in the sense (derived from various passages of Scripture): Something to be partaken of, endured or enjoyed; an experience, portion, lot (painful or pleasurable, more commonly the former). Cf. CHALICE 1 b.

a **1340** HAMPOLE *Psalter* x. 7 He calles þaire pynes a cope, for ilk dampned man sall drynk of þe sorow of hell. *Ibid.* xv. 5 He is cope of all my delite & ioy. **1526** *Pilgr. Perf.* (W. de W. 1531) 134 b, To drynke the cuppe of sorowe. **1534** TINDALE *Matt.* xx. 22 Are ye able to drynke of the cuppe that I shall drynke of? **1605** SHAKS. *Lear* v. iii. 304 All Foes [shall taste] The cup of their deseruings. **1611** BIBLE *Ps.* xvi. 5, xxiii. 5, etc. **1732** POPE *Ess. Man* II. 288 In folly's cup still laughs the bubble, joy. **1833** MRS. BROWNING *Prom. Bound* Poems 1850 I. 156, I quaff the full cup of a present doom. **1875** FARRAR *Silence & V.* ii. 40 Filling to the brim the cup of his iniquity. **1879** FROUDE *Cæsar* xviii. 293 To drink the bitterest cup of humiliation.

10. *pl.* The drinking of intoxicating liquor; potations, drunken revelry. ***in one's cups***: †(*a*) while drinking, during a drinking-bout (also †***amidst***, †***among***, †***at***, ***over one's cups***); (*b*) in a state of intoxication, 'in liquor'.

1406 HOCCLEVE *La Male Regle* 165 For in the cuppe seelden fownden is, þat any wight his neigheburgh commendith. **1551** ROBINSON tr. *More's Utop.* (Arb.) 26 Amonge their cuppes they geue iudgement of the wittes of writers. **1611** BIBLE *1 Esdras* iii. 22 And when they are in their cups, they forget their loue both to friends and brethren. **1667** MILTON *P.L.* XI. 718 Thence from Cups to civil Broiles. **1712** ARBUTHNOT *John Bull* II. iv, She used to come home in her cups, and break the china. **1828** BENTHAM *Let. to Sir F. Burdett* Wks. 1843 X. 592, I hear you are got among the Tories, and that you said once you were one of them: you must have been in your cups. **1842** J. H. NEWMAN *Par. Serm.* (ed. 2) V. ii. 22 They..discuss points of doctrine ..even..over their cups. **1861** THACKERAY *Four Georges* i. (1876) 19 The jolly Prince..loving his cups and his ease.

11. A name for various beverages consisting of wine sweetened and flavoured with various ingredients and usually iced; as ***claret-cup***, etc.

1773 GOLDSM. *Stoops to Conq.* II, Here's a cup, Sir..I have prepared it with my own hands, and I believe you'll own the ingredients are tolerable. **1818** R. RUSH *Crt. of London* (1833) 151 Sir Henry recommended me to a glass of what I supposed wine..but he called it King's cup. **1833** *New Monthly Mag.* XXXVII. 193 *footn.*, A foaming tankard of cup. *Note.* Cup is a mixture of beer, wine, lemon, sugar, and spice. **1884** *Pall Mall G.* 16 Feb. 5/1 Who..could produce bottles of 'old Johannisberg' for a guest and make them into cup.

III. 12. a. Proverbs and Phrases. (See also sense 10.) ***between*** (or ***betwixt***) ***the cup and the lip***: while a thing is yet in hand and on the very point of being achieved. (Now usually ***there's many a slip between***, etc.) †***such cup, such cover***, also †***such a cup, such a cruse***: implying similarity between two persons related in some way. †***cup and can***: constant or familiar associates (the can being the large vessel from which the cup is filled). ***a cup too low***: see quots.

1539 TAVERNER *Erasm. Prov.* (1552) 16 Manye thynges fall betweene yᵉ cuppe and the mouth. **1549** LATIMER *5th Serm. bef. Edw. VI* (Arb.) 143 Such a cup, suche a cruse. She would not depart from hir oun. **1550** BALE *Apol.* 132 As for your doctours..they are lyke your selfe, as the adage goeth, suche cuppe suche cover. **1562** J. HEYWOOD *Prov. & Epigr.* (1867) 49 As cup and can could holde. *a* **1700** B. E. *Dict. Cant. Crew.*, *A Cup too low*, when any of the Company are mute or pensive. **1729** SWIFT *Libel on Dr. Delany*, You and he are Cup and Cann. **1777** SHERIDAN *Trip Scarb.* I. ii, If the devil don't step between the cup and the lip. **1801** *Spirit Pub. Jrnls.* (1802) V. 305 He must..be cup and can with sextons and grave-diggers. **1864** H. AINSWORTH *John Law* Prol. x. (1881) 54 You're a cup too low. A glass of claret will make you feel more cheerful. **1887** T. A. TROLLOPE *What I remember* I. xii. 256 A whole series of slips between the cup and the lip!

b. ***cup of tea*** (colloq. phr.): (i) used of a person.

1908 W. DE MORGAN *Somehow Good* xvi. 159 'It's simply impossible to help liking him.' To which Sally replied, borrowing an expression from Ann the housemaid, that Fenwick was a cup of tea. It was metaphorical and descriptive of invigoration. *a* **1909** in Ware *Passing Eng.* (1909) 101/1 Oh, don't yer though. You are a nice strong cup o' tea. **1939** N. MARSH *Overture to Death* xi. 120 Miss Prentice..seems to be a very unpleasant cup of tea. *Ibid.* xxiv. 279 She was a cranky old cup of tea. **1940** A. CHRISTIE *One, Two, Buckle my Shoe* 123 Sounds quite like that old cup of tea who came to see Mrs. Chapman.

(ii) ***one's cup of tea***: what interests or suits one.

1932 N. MITFORD *Christmas Pudding* xiv. 211 I'm not at all sure I wouldn't rather marry Aunt Loudie. She's even more my cup of tea in many ways. **1933** P. FLEMING *Brazilian Adventure* I. iii. 31 The desire to benefit the community is never their principal motive...They do it because they want to. It suits them; it is their cup of tea. **1936** AUDEN & ISHERWOOD *Ascent of F6* II. iii. 96, I had an aunt who loved a plant—But you're my cup of tea! **1937** N. COWARD *Pres. Indic.* III. v. 121 Broadway by night seemed to be my cup of tea entirely. **1948** 'J. TEY' *Franchise Affair* v. 54 Probably she *isn't* your cup of tea...You have always preferred them a little stupid, and blond. **1965** M. SPARK *Mandelbaum Gate* v. 141 Freddy had stood in the doorway of the dark Orthodox chapel and, regarding the heavy-laden altar and the exotic clusters of coloured lamps hung round it, said, 'It's not really my cup of tea, you know.'

(iii) ***a different cup of tea*** (and similar expressions): something of an altogether different kind.

1940 N. MITFORD *Pigeon Pie* xiii. 215 A Fred racked with ideals, and in the grip of Federal Union, was quite a different cup of tea from the old, happy-go-lucky Fred. **1946** 'S. RUSSELL' *To Bed with Grand Music* i. 20 London in wartime ..is a very different cup of tea from Winchester. **1957** *Listener* 5 Dec. 954/1 The outwitted villain..is quite another cup of tea.

13. *attrib.* and *Comb.* **a.** General combinations, as ***cup-augury***, ***-maker***, ***-marking***; ***cup-eyed***, ***-headed***, ***-like***, ***-marked***, ***-shaped*** adjs.

1879 FARRAR *St. Paul* (1883) 251 To presage his fate by a sort of *cup-augury involved in examining the grounds of coffee. **1922** T. HARDY *Late Lyrics* 33 *Cup-eyed care and doubt. **1889** G. FINDLAY *Eng. Railway* 46 The spikes [to fasten the chair to the sleeper] are *cup-headed. **1835–6** TODD *Cycl. Anat.* I. 114/2 The bodies of the vertebrae terminate in two *cup-like cavities. **1864** TENNYSON *En. Ard.* 9 A hazelwood..in a cuplike hollow of the down. **14..** *Nominale* in Wr.-Wülcker 686/22 *Hic cipharius*, a *cop-maker. **1591** PERCIVALL *Sp. Dict.*, *Cubero*, a cup maker. **1889** *Chambers' Encycl.* III. 618 *Cup-marking on rocks and *cup-marked stones belong to a peculiar class of archaic sculpturings. **1845** *Athenæum* 22 Feb. 199 *Cup-shaped bodies.

b. *esp.* in reference to social drinking or drunkenness (cf. sense 10): as ***cup-acquaintance***, ***-caper***, ***-conqueror***, ***-friendship***, ***-god***, ***-mate***, ***-tossing***.

1596 BP. W. BARLOW *Three Serm.* i. 13 Til that same Cup-challenging profession came into our land. *Ibid.* iii. 119 Wine..swilled by challenging Cupmates. **1599** *Soliman & Persida* v. in Hazl. *Dodsley* V. 363 Where is tipsy Alexander, that great cup-conqueror? **1608** D. F. *Ess. Pol. & Mor.* 83 Cup-friendship, is of too brittle and glassie a substance to continue long. **1749** FIELDING *Tom Jones* XVIII. v, Only his cup acquaintance. **1842** S. C. HALL *Ireland* II. 270 She was perfect mistress of the art of cup-tossing.

c. In sense 2 b, as ***cup-taker***, ***-transaction***; **cup-day**, a day on which a race is run for a cup; **cup horse**, a horse that runs for a cup; **cup-tie**, a 'tie' (*i.e.* match or contest between the victors in previous contests) played for a cup; hence **cup-tied** *a.* *Assoc. Football*, of a player: ineligible to play in cup-ties for the remainder of a season through having already played for another club in the current season's competition.

1860 MRS. GASKELL *Let.* 27 Aug. (1966) 631 It was Cup Day at Ascot. **1862** *London Society* II. 98 We travelled [to Ascot] on the Cup day..'The latest prices' of the Cup horses. **1879** BLACK *White Wings* xvii, The master of one of the Cup takers [a yacht]. **1894** *Daily News* 26 Feb. 5/1 Those mighty cup-fighters, the Blackburn Rovers. **1895** *Ibid.* 21 Feb. 5/5 The Wednesday men are noted cup-tie fighters. **1901** *Westm. Gaz.* 22 Apr. 7/3 A typical 'cup-fighting' team. **1902** *Encycl. Brit.* XXIX. 329/2 The expression 'a cup-horse' is understood to imply an animal capable of distinguishing himself over a long distance at even weights against the best opponents. **1905** *Daily Chron.* 14 Apr. 8/1 A special brand of play known as 'the Cup-tie game'. *Ibid.* 25 Dec. 3/4 Old Internationals and Cup-final players. **1908** *Pearson's Weekly* 5 Mar. Suppl. p. iii/3 We're playing a cup-tie! **1910** *Westm. Gaz.* 14 Mar. 14/2 The cup-holders were defeated in their first match. **1963** *Times* 10 Jan. 3/4 The.. good humoured indulgence afforded Hospital cup-ties. **1968** *Listener* 23 May 681/3 There is something wrong with a game when one of its outstanding young exponents, the new Cup-winners' goalkeeper with Under-23 honours, says about it a few weeks before the Cup Final: 'The worst time of the week for me is between three o'clock and twenty to five every Saturday afternoon.' **1970** *Times* 20 Nov. 18/2 Wakeling, being cup-tied after playing for Corinthian-Casuals, will be missed in midfield, and Richards will probably replace him. **1976** *Eastern Even. News* (Norwich) 29 Nov. 14/8 Jimmy Greenhoff, Manchester United's £120,000 buy from Stoke City, is cup-tied and will not be eligible to play against Everton.

d. Special combs. **cup-and-cone**, (*a*) see quot. 1881; (*b*) *Metall.*, designating a fracture in which one surface of the metal consists of a raised rim enclosing a flat central portion into which the other surface fits; **cup-and-ring**, designation of a type of marks found cut in megalithic monuments, consisting of a circular depression surrounded by concentric rings; **cup-and-saucer** *a.*, designation of a naturalistic style in the late nineteenth-century theatre, introduced by T. W. Robertson; **cup-and-saucer limpet**, collectors' name of the molluscous genus *Calyptræa*; †**cup-band**, 'a brace of metal on which masers and handled cups were hung' (Riley *Liber Albus*); **cup-cake** orig. *U.S.*, a cake baked from ingredients measured by the cupful, or baked in a small (freq. paper) cup; **cup-coral** (see CORAL *sb.*[1] 1 b); **cup-custard**, fluid custard served in glass cups; **cup-defect**, the fault in timber of being CUP-SHAKEN; **cup-flower**, a name for *Scyphanthus elegans*, a S. American plant with yellow cup-shaped flowers; **cup-fungus**, any discomycetous fungus having a cup-shaped ascocarp; cf. *cup-mushroom*; **cup-gall**, a cup-shaped gall or excrescence found on oak-leaves; †**cup-glass** = CUPPING-GLASS (in Bullokar, 1616); **cup-grease**, a kind of semi-solid lubricant; **cup-guard**, a cup-shaped sword-guard; **cup-head**, a hemispherical head to a bolt; hence **cup-headed**, *a.*; **cup-hilted** *a.*, having a cup-guard on the hilt; **cup hook**, a hook which is screwed into a wall, shelf, cupboard, etc., and used for hanging up cups, etc.; **cup-leather** (see quots.); †**cup-leech**, one addicted to his cups; **cup-lichen** = cup-moss a. (in Prior, 1879); **cup-man**, a man addicted to cups, a reveller; **cup-mark, -marking**, a shallow cup-like depression found cut in rocks or stone monuments (see 5); also **cup-marked** *a.*; **cup-mouthpiece** (see quot.); **cup-mushroom**, 'a name for various species of *Peziza*' (Britten and Holland); **cup mute**, a kind of mute for a trumpet or trombone; so ***cup-muted*** adj.; **cup-plant** *U.S.*, *Silphium perfoliatum* of N. America; **cup-plate**, see quot. 1891; †**cup-rite**, a libation; **cup-rose**, dial. var. of cop-rose; **cup-sculpture** = *cup-marking*; **cup-seed**, a N. American plant, *Calycocarpum Lyoni* (in Miller, 1884), having seeds hollowed out on one side like a cup; **cup-shrimp** (see quot.); **cup-sponge**, a kind of sponge shaped like a cup; **cup-sprung** *a.*, having the hip-joint dislocated; †**cup-stool**; **cup-valve**, see quot.; †**cup-waiter**, one who serves liquor at a meal or feast. See cup-and-ball, cup-bearer, -moss, -shot.

1881 Raymond *Mining Gloss.*, *Cup-and-cone. A machine for charging a shaft-furnace, consisting of an iron hopper with a large central opening, which is closed by a cone or bell, pulled up into it from below. **1925** Cup-and-cone fracture [see cuppy *a.* c]. **1967** A. K. Osborne *Encycl. Iron & Steel Industry* (ed. 2) 99/2 *Cup-and-cone*... A type of fracture occurring in tensile test pieces from steels possessing reasonable ductility, and containing no local abnormality where the necking occurs. **1867** J. Y. Simpson *Arch. Sculpt.* 2 *Cup and ring cuttings. **1875** C. Maclagan *Hill Forts* Index, Cup and Ring Sculpturings. *Ibid.* 41 On one monolith..are some 'cup and ring markings'. **1900** *Daily News* 11 Oct. 6/1 A rude dial at West Kirby looks like an example of 'cup and ring stones'. **1919** *Proc. Soc. Antiq. Scot.* LIII. 23 The cup- and ring-marked stone which was found near this spot. **1963** S. Piggott in Foster & Alcock *Culture & Environment* iv. 64 The cup-and-ring carvings of Galicia have again been brought into relationship with those of Ireland. **1881** *Times* 27 Dec. 3/5 It [*sc.* Albery's *Two Roses*] has more than the merit, though it has hardly met with the popularity of the '*cup and saucer' comedies of the late Mr. T. W. Robertson. **1892** W. Archer in G. B. Shaw *Prefaces* (1934) 667/2 The scheme of a twaddling cup-and-saucer comedy. **1933** G. B. Shaw in *Shaw on Theatre* (1958) 222 The stuffiness of the London cup-and-saucer theatre. **13..** in *Liber Albus* 609 *Cuppebonde. **1483** *Cath. Angl.* 75 A Copbande, *cru[s]ta.* **1828** E. Leslie *Receipts* 61 *Cup Cake. **1886** *Harper's Mag.* Dec. 134/2 Cousin Carry with her eternal cup-cake. **1887** M. E. Wilkins *Humble Romance* 271 Mis' Steele made some cup-cake to-day... She put a cup of butter and two whole cups of sugar in it. **1907** *Mrs. Beeton's All about Cookery* (new ed.) 216/2 Cup Cakes, Plain (American Recipe)..3 level cupfuls of flour, 1 cupful of sugar, ½ a cupful of butter, 1 cupful of milk... Bake in shallow tins or small cups. **1911** E. Ferber *Dawn O'Hara* viii. 109 There were little round cup cakes made of almond paste that melts in the mouth. **1957** J. Braine *Room at Top* viii. 82 The cakes were fresh..meringues, éclairs, chocolate cup-cakes. **1853** *San Francisco Whig* 28 July 1/4 (Advt.), *Cup Custard. **1862** 'G. Hamilton' *Country Living & Thinking* 72 We had cup-custards at the close of our breakfast that morning. **1867** Mrs. Whitney *L. Goldthwaite* x. 223 Cup-custards, even, disappeared,—cups and all. **1875** Laslett *Timber Trees* 32 The *cup-defect occurs in perfectly sound and healthy-looking trees. **1910** *Encycl. Brit.* XI. 341/2 Owing to the shape of the fruit-body many of these forms are known as *cup-fungi, the cup or apothecium often attaining a large size. **1960** R. W. G. Dennis (*title*) British cup fungi and their allies. **1966** F. H. Brightman *Oxf. Bk. Flowerless Plants* 150 The *Pezizales* or Cup Fungi have a spore-producing layer which develops within a more-or-less shallow cup. **1753** Chambers *Cycl. Supp.*, **Cup-galls*..a kind of galls found on the leaves of the oak, and some other trees. [**1845** Lindley *Veg. Kingd.* 32 The cup shaped galls, so common in Oak leaves.] **1900** Archbutt & Deeley *Lubrication & Lubricants* v. 122 '*Cup' greases are usually thickened with soap from either horse fat, cottonseed oil, or rape oil, saponified with lime. **1935** *Oil & Gas Jrnl.* 14 Nov. 66/2 Large quantities of soft cup greases..are still used for chassis lubrication. **1951** *Good Housek. Home Encycl.* 187/1 The groove of the frame should be freed..of earth and rust, and packed with..cup-grease. **1929** *Encycl. Brit.* III. 827/2 The *cup-head or coach-bolt. **1895** *Montgomery Ward Catal.* 400/1 Brass *Cup Hooks, Size ⅝ in. ¾ in. ⅞ in. 1 in. **1925** *Black. Mag.* Jan. 5/1 He put his pipe to rest in a cup-hook screwed at an angle in the window jamb. **1970** R. Jeffries *Dead Man's Bluff* xix. 180 A weight had been suspended by running string through a cup hook. **1889** *Cent. Dict.*, **Cup-leather*, a piece of leather fastened around the plunger or bucket of a pump. For a bucket it is sleeve-shaped, and for a plunger it is made with a solid bottom. **1904** Goodchild & Tweney *Technol. & Sci. Dict.* 143/1 *Cup leather*, a leather ring, produced by forcing a flat ring of leather into a mould. **1930** *Engineering* 25 July 95/3 They have rams..and..glands with triple cup leathers. **1593** R. Harvey *Philad.* 52 Cheryn was a drunkard, a *cupleache. **1834** Lytton *Pompeii* ii. iii, Oh, a friend of mine! a brother *cupman, a quiet dog..said Burbo. **1884** *Proc. Soc. Antiq. Scot.* XVIII. 110 Edge of Rock with *Cup-marks. **1919** *Ibid.* LIII. 22 The fracture on one side cuts across a cup-mark. **1867** *Ibid.* (1870) VII. 270 A Kist, with a *cup-marked Cover. **1875** C. Maclagan *Hill Forts* 45 The cup-marked stone figured on Plate XI. **1935** *Proc. Prehist. Soc.* I. 150 At either end of this are standing stones, one of which is cup-marked. **1867** J. Y. Simpson *Arch. Sculpt.* 7 In the centres of the remaining six series of circles there are no *cup-markings. **1877** W. Greenwell *Brit. Barrows* 341 A square piece of the same stone..which has a circular pit or cup-marking on each face. **1911** *Encycl. Brit.* XVIII. 947/1 **Cup-Mouthpieces.*—Brass wind instruments are played by means of cup or funnel-shaped mouthpieces, generally made of silver... The shallower the cup the more suitable it is for producing the higher harmonics. **1769** J. Wallis *Nat. Hist. Northumb.* I. viii. 305 Small, sessile, white, proliferous *Cup-Mushrome. **1955** L. Feather *Encycl. Jazz* ii. 64 A variety of mutes, including..*cup..mutes. **1961** A. Berkman *Singer's Gloss* 61 *Cup mute*, a cone-like mute with an added metal or fibre cup which reduces the volume considerably, producing a fine, pleasing tone. **1967** *Crescendo* May 8/2 'Boss Bambino' has bossa nova rhythm and cup-muted trombone. **1846** A. Wood *Class-bk. Bot.* (ed. 2) 336 *Silphium perfoliatum.* *Cup-plant. **1870** *Amer. Naturalist* IV. 580 Another species of the same genus, called the cup plant (*Silphium perfoliatum*)..is common in the moist ravines. **1968** Peterson & McKenny *Field Guide to Wildflowers* 184 Cup-plant, *Silphium perfoliatum.* **1674** *Lond. Gaz.* No. 863/4 Stoln..Ten Pottage Plates, Three *Cup Plates, Two Sawcers. **1891** *Scribn. Mag.* Sept. 353/1 Seven saucers, and ten 'cup-plates'. By cup-plates I mean the little flat saucers in which our grandmothers placed their tea-cups when they poured their tea into the deeper saucers to cool. **1583** Stanyhurst *Æneis* iv. (Arb.) 102 Iuppiter almighty, whom men Maurusian..with *cuprit's magnifye dulye. **1911** W. T. Calman *Life of Crustacea* 245 A smaller species..(*Leander squilla*), and another very similar species ..*L. adspersus*,..are said to be sold on some parts of the English coast as '*Cup Shrimps'. **1741** *Compl. Fam. Piece* iii. 483 For a Lameness in a Cow or Bullock, or when they are Shoulder-pitched, or *Cup-sprung. **1567** *Wills & Inv. N.C.* (Surtees) 272 One flanders chist, one litle *cupstole, one chare. **1850** Weale *Dict. Terms*, **Cup-valve*, for a steam-engine. **1874** Knight *Dict. Mech.*, *Cup-valve*. (*Steam-engine.*) *a.* A cup-shaped or conical valve, which is guided by a stem to and from its flaring seat. *b.* A form of balance-valve which opens simultaneously on top and sides. *c.* A valve formed by an inverted cup over the end of a pipe or opening. **1611** Speed *Hist. Gt. Brit.* ix. xiii. (R.), The maior to attend in his own person as chiefe *cup-waiter..to serve the king in a cup of gold.

cup (kʌp), *v.* [f. cup *sb.*]

1. *Surg.* (*trans.*) To apply a cupping-glass to; to bleed by means of a cupping-glass. Also *absol.*

1482 *Monk of Evesham* (Arb.) 32 As a mannys flesh is wont to blede whenne hit is cuppid. **1607** Topsell *Four-f. Beasts* (1673) 335 Set a cupping-glasse thereon, and cup it. **1695** Congreve *Love for L.* i. ii, A beau in a bagnio, cupping for a complexion. **1757** Franklin *Let.* Wks. 1887 II. 522 They cupped me on the back of the head. **1829** Scott *Jrnl.* (1890) II. 294 Dr. Ross ordered me to be cupped.

†**2. a.** To supply with cups, *i.e.* with liquor; to make drunk, intoxicate. *Obs. rare.*

1606 Shaks. *Ant. & Cl.* ii. vii. 124 Cup vs till the world go round. **1630** J. Taylor (Water P.) *Wks.* (N.), Well entertain'd I was, and halfe well cup'd.

b. *intr.* To indulge in 'cups'; to drink deep.

c **1625** T. Adams *Wks.* (1861) I. 484 The former is not more thirsty after his cupping than the latter is hungry after his devouring. **1649–1868** [see cupping 2].

3. a. *trans.* To receive, place, or take as in a cup.

1838 J. Struthers *Poetic Tales* 138 The dew-drop cupped in the cowslip. **1879** J. D. Long *Æneid* viii. 85 He reverently in his hollow hands Cups water from the stream. **1940** Dylan Thomas *Portr. Artist* 117, I cupped a match to let them see my face in a dramatic shadow.

c. *Golf.* To lodge (the ball) in a 'cup' or depression of the ground. (See cup *sb.* 5.) Usu. as *pa. pple.* or *ppl. adj.*

1896 W. Park *Golf* 95 A cupped ball gives room for playing one of the finest strokes in golf. **1905** H. Vardon *Compl. Golfer* 81 When the ball is really badly cupped. **1909** *Westm. Gaz.* 11 May 12/2 The cleek is only for use when the ball lies cupped.

4. a. *intr.* To form a cup; to be or become cup-shaped.

1830 Withering *Brit. Plants* (ed. 7) II. 368 Mr. Woodward suggests..that the umbels not cupping is owing to their small size. **1851** *Beck's Florist*, New Dahlias..petals smooth, and gently cupping to the centre.

b. *Golf.* 'To mark or break (the ground) with the club when striking the ball; also, to strike (the ground) with the club when driving a ball' (Jam. *Supp.*). Cf. cup *sb.* 5.

5. *trans.* To make concave or cup-shaped; to form into a cup.

1909 G. Stratton-Porter *Girl of Limberlost* xv. 299 'Are you afraid she is going?' Elnora asked. 'If you are, cup your other hand over her for shelter.' **1911** *Encycl. Brit.* XXVII. 39/2 Power presses for working sheet-metal articles include those for cutting out the blanks, termed cutting-out or blanking presses, and those for cupping or drawing the flat blank into shape. **1954** Xan Fielding *Hide & Seek* 228 The despatcher..cupped his hand to my ear and shouted.

cupalo, obs. form of cupola.

cup and ball, cup-and-ball.

1. A toy consisting of a cup at the end of a stem to which a ball is attached by a string, the object being to toss the ball and catch it in the cup or on the spike end of the stem. Also the game played with this. = bilboquet 2.

1760 Goldsm. *Cit. W.* lxxxix, Indolence..tosses the cup-and-ball with infantine folly. **1799** Southey *Amatory Poems* Sonn. i, She held a Cup and Ball of ivory white. **1836** T. Hook *G. Gurney* III. 131 Where sat Mrs. Nubley, alone, on a sofa, playing at cup-and-ball.

2. *attrib.* Of a joint or bones: = *ball and socket*; see ball *sb.*[1] 19.

1854 R. Owen in *Circ. Sc.* (*c*1865) II. 57/2 The cup-and-ball vertebræ in batrachian larvæ.

cup-bearer (ˈkʌpˌbɛərə(r)). One who carries a cup; an officer of a king's or nobleman's household who served his master with wine.

1483 *Cath. Angl.* 75 A Copberer, *ciphigerulus.* **1509–10** *Act 1 Hen. VIII*, c. 14 Esquyers for the Kynges body hys Cuppe berers Carvours and Sewers. **1611** Bible *Neh.* i. 11. **1875** Jowett *Plato* (ed. 2) III. 263 The cup-bearer carries round wine which he draws..and pours into the cups.

cupboard (ˈkʌbəd), *sb.* Forms: 4–6 cup-, cop-, (5 cuppe-, 5–6 cope-, 6 coup-), -bord(e, -bourd(e, -burd(e; 6–7 cupboord, -boarde, 7– -board. Also 5 cowborde, 6 couborde, cowbard, cobord, -erde, cobbourd, -arde, cuppord(e, cubboorde, 6–7 cubbord(e, -ard(e, 7 -erd, -ert, 7–8 -oard, 7 cupbard, -bert. [A combination of cup or cop (or both) and board. In ME. *cop-* is frequent in northern sources, *cuppe-* and *coup-* rare, *cup-* most frequent, even at a time when the independent word was regularly spelt *cuppe*. By the 16th c. the second element was phonetically obscured, and the *p* of *cup-* sunk in the following *b*, as in the existing pronunciation, which is indicated by a multitude of more or less phonetical spellings of the *cubberd, cubbert* type, often crossed by etymological reminiscences. Since the 18th c. the analytical spelling has prevailed.]

†**1.** A 'board' or table to place cups and other vessels, etc. on; a piece of furniture for the display of plate; a sideboard, buffet. (See also court-cupboard.) *Obs.*

c **1325** *E.E. Allit. P.* B. 1440 Couered mony a cup-borde with cloþes ful quite. *c* **1380** *Antecrist* in Todd *3 Treat. Wyclif* 150 Loke Cristis copborde. ? *a* **1400** *Morte Arth.* 206 The kyngez cope-borde was closed in silver. *c* **1440** *Promp. Parv.* 109 Cupburde, *abacus.* **1483** *Cath. Angl.* 75 A Copburde, *abacus.* **1503** *Will* in *Ripon Ch. Acts* 296 Unum copebord sculptum. **1530** Palsgr. 211/2 Cup borde of plate or to sette plate upon, *buffet.* **1555** Eden *Decades* 68 The cobbarde bysyde owr dyninge table. **1591** Harington *Orl. Fur.* xxv. xlix. (1634) 201 One onely lampe upon the cubbard burning. **1592** Greene *Def. Conny Catch.* iii. 10 Her mistress..set all her plate on the cubboorde for shewe. **1663** Gerbier *Counsel* 30 A Candlestick on a Cubbert. **1708** Motteux *Rabelais* iv. lxiv, The Officers..got ready the Tables and Cupboards, laid the Cloth.

†**b.** *transf.* A set of vessels displayed upon a sideboard; a service of plate. *Obs.*

1522 Skelton *Why not to Court* 898 Your cupbord that was, Is tourned to glasse, From sylvere to brasse. **1551** *Acts Privy Council Eng.* (1891) N.S. III. 288 An other like couborde of the value of m[lli]; an other cubborde of viij[cli]. **1579–80** North *Plutarch* (1676) 219 All the whole cubboord of Plate of Gold and Silver. *c* **1645** Howell *Lett.* (1650) II. 40 She desires you to send her a compleat cupboard of the best christall glasses. **1698** Sir T. Morgan *Progr.* in *Select. Harl. Misc.* (1793) 391 His majesty of France had never the kindness to send him his cupboard of plate.

2. A closet or a cabinet (often placed in a corner of a room or a recess in the wall) with shelves, for keeping cups, dishes, etc., provisions ready for use, or anything which it is desired to keep safely, as books or valuables.

1530 Palsgr. 211/2 Cupborde to putte meate in, *dressover.* **1579** Tomson *Calvin's Serm. Tim.* 104/2 If he haue a cofer, or cupbord, there will he keep it [money] fast locked. **1627** Capt. Smith *Seaman's Gram.* ii. 12 Lockers to put any thing in, as in little Cupberts. **1662** Greenhalgh in Ellis *Orig. Lett.* ii. 309 IV. 13 At the east end of the Synagogue standeth a closet, like a very high cupboard, which they call the Ark. **1736** *Swift's Lett.* (1766) II. 243 If a friend happen to come late, [he] will take care to lock up a scrap for him in the cupboard. **1851** *Illust. Lond. News* 8 Feb. 98 The cupboard was breadless. **1874** Micklethwaite *Mod. Par. Churches* 161 A cupboard with shelves for music-books.

b. ***skeleton in the cupboard***: see skeleton.

3. *transf.* Food, provisions; *esp.* in phr. ***to cry cupboard***, to crave for food, feel hungry. ? *Obs.*

c **1665** *Roxb. Ball.* VI. 529 And all for the love of the cubbard. **1681** W. Robertson *Phraseol. Gen.* (1693) 412 My belly cries cupboard. **1768–74** Tucker *Lt. Nat.* (1852) I. 60 Should his head ache, or his stomach cry cupboard. **1855** Kingsley *Westw. Ho!* (1889) 25/2 So now away home, my inside cries cupboard.

4. *attrib.* and *Comb.* **a.** Pertaining or relating to a cupboard, as (in sense 1) †***cupboard banker*** (see banker[1]), †***cupboard cloth***; (in sense 2), ***cupboard door***; **cupboard love**, love insincerely professed or displayed for the sake of what one can get by it (cf. sense 3, quot. 1665); so ***cupboard lover, faith***; †**cupboard-man**, one of an order of disputants in the Inns of Court: so called from their using the cupboard in the hall as a tribune (Douthwaite *Gray's Inn* (1886) 81).

b. Of the form or nature of a cupboard, as ***cupboard library***.

1463 *Bury Wills* (1850) 25 With tablys, trestelys, *cuppe-burd bankers. **1480** *Wardr. Acc. Edw. IV* (1830) 124, iij rede *cupborde clothes of rede worsted. **1640** *Vestry Bks.* (Surtees) 303 For mendinge the *cubert doore in the vesterre. **1862** Ruskin *Munera P.* (1880) 64 That the cupboard door may have a firm lock to it. **1882** Edna Lyall *Donovan* x, No *cupboard faith for him. **1845** R. W. Hamilton *Pop. Educ.* v. (ed. 2) 102 In his little *cupboard library. **1757** *Poor Robin* (N.), A *cupboard love is seldom true. **1874** Dasent *Tales from Fjeld* 184 To have such a *cupboard lover. *c* **1625** Whitelocke *Lib. Fam.* (Camden) 62 In August 1618 being on of the *cubberdmen of the

Middle Temple, I went up to argue at the reading. **1660** *Vind. of Reading of E. Bagshaw held in Middle Temple* 16 My Obligations..to my Cubbardmen, to the Gentlemen of the Bar and under.

cupboard (ˈkʌbəd), *v. rare.* [f. prec. sb.] *trans.* To place, shut up, or keep in or as in a cupboard.

1565 *Darius* (1860) 53 He..With the woman also coberdith his lyfe He regardeth neither father nor mother, and al for his wife. **1607** SHAKS. *Cor.* I. i. 103 The Belly.. idle and vnactiue, Still cubbording the Viand. *a* **1658** CLEVELAND *Hue & Cry* ii, When Kings are cup-boarded like Cheese, Sights to be seen for pence a piece.

ˈ**cupboardy,** *a. nonce-wd.* Cupboard-like.

1877 MISS BRADDON *Weavers & Weft* III. 163 Her funny little cupboardy room.

cupe, obs. form of COOP *sb.*[1], basket.

cupel (ˈkjuːpəl), *sb.* Also 7–8 coppel, cuppel, (7 copel(l, coppell, -ill, -le). [a. F. *coupelle* (15th c.), med.L. *cūpella*, dim. of *cūpa* cask, to which the current form is adjusted.]

1. A small flat circular porous vessel, with a shallow depression in the middle, made of pounded bone-ash pressed into shape by a mould, and used in assaying gold or silver with lead. Also the similarly-shaped 'test' or movable hearth of the reverberatory furnace in which silver is separated from lead by cupellation.

1605 TIMME *Quersit.* I. xvi. 82 Euery goldsmith and mintman..know how to disperase..such mettals into smoake with their cupels. **1611** COTGR., *Coupelle*, a Coppell; the little Ashen pot, or vessell. **1626** BACON *Sylva* §799 As wee see in the Stuffe, whereof Coppells are made..Upon which Fire worketh not. **1678** *Phil. Trans.* XII. 955 It was..first Refined with Lead upon a Copel, for separation of any Copper that might be in it. **1759** B. MARTIN *Nat. Hist. Eng.* II. 232 A large Coppel, where the Lead is now made. **1791** LANE in *Phil. Trans.* LXXXI. 224 The contents of each paper were placed in separate cupels, under a muffle. **1862** *Lond. Rev.* 23 Aug. 175 The argentiferous lead..is then submitted to the process of cupellation. This operation is performed in a reverberatory furnace, on the hearth of which is placed the cupel, which is of an oval form about 4 feet long and 2½ feet broad.

b. *fig.* (Cf. TEST.)

1673 O. WALKER *Educ.* (1677) 52 Suffering is the great trial and cupel of gallant spirits. **1847** DISRAELI *Tancred* II. i, Money is to be the cupel of their worth.

2. *attrib.* and *Comb.*, as ***cupel-furnace, -mould***; †**cupel-ashes,** †**cupel-dust,** ashes and dust used in purifying metals.

a **1626** BACON (J.), It may be also tried by incorporating powder of steel, or copple-dust. **1683** PETTUS *Fleta Min.* I. (1686) 9 There must first be a smooth fire-place, and upon that Copell-Ashes are to be laid the breadth or thickness of a finger. **1800** tr. *Lagrange's Chem.* I. 28 It is employed as a cuppel-furnace by means of a small semicircular aperture. **1875** URE *Dict. Arts* III. 822 The cupels are formed in a cupel-mould made of cast steel.

cupel (ˈkjuːpəl), *v.* For forms see the sb. [f. prec. sb.; cf. F. *coupell-er*, f. *coupelle*: see prec.] *trans.* To assay or refine in a cupel; to subject to cupellation.

1644 [see CUPELLING]. **1666** BOYLE *Orig. Formes & Qual.*, Good Gold having for a certain tryal been cuppel'd with a great deal of Lead. **1754** *Phil. Trans.* XLVIII. 683 A mixture of platina and lead was cupelled. **1863** F. J. RICKARD *Mining Journ. Across Andes* 267 The pigs of argentiferous lead are next cupelled twice, and afterwards refined in a small bone ash test.

Hence ˈ**cupelled** *ppl. a.*

1754 LEWIS in *Phil. Trans.* XLVIII. 685 Upon examining the cupelled matters hydrostatically.

cupellate (ˈkjuːpəleɪt), *v. rare.* [f. as prec. + -ATE[3].] = prec.

18.. DR. THOMSON in *Nat. Encycl.* I. 397 Amalgam of gold..cupellated.

cupellation (kjuːpəˈleɪʃən). Also 8 copp-, cupp-. [f. CUPEL *v.* + -ATION, after F. *coupellation.*] The process of assaying or refining the precious metals in a cupel; the separation of silver from argentiferous lead, on a large scale, on a cupel.

a **1691** [see CUPELLING b]. **1750** *Phil. Trans.* XLVI. 586 That Gold and Silver may be purified from all heterogeneous Substances by Coppellation. **1880** *Sat. Rev.* 20 Mar. 385 Mr. Crookes suggests that thallium might be used instead of lead for the cupellation of silver.

cupelling (ˈkjuːpəlɪŋ), *vbl. sb.* [f. CUPEL *v.* + -ING[1].] = CUPELLATION.

1644 DIGBY *Nat. Bodies* x. (1657) 102 In the coppelling of a fixed metal. *a* **1691** BOYLE *Wks.* III. 453 (R.) The quick melting down of ores, and cupelling of them.

b. *attrib.* and *Comb.*, as ***cupelling-fire, -furnace.***

a **1691** BOYLE *Wks.* III. 713 (R.) We kept it there in a cupelling-fire about three hours (having occasion to continue the cupellation so long for other trials). **1822** IMISON *Sc. & Art* II. 113 The mixed metal is put into a dish called a cupel..and placed in a cupelling furnace.

cupelo, obs. form of CUPOLA.

cupferron (ˈkʌpfɛrən, ˈkjuːp-). *Chem.* [G. (O. Baudisch 1909, in *Chem. Zeitung* XXXIII. 1298), f. L. *cup-rum* copper + *ferr-um* iron + *-on.*] A brownish-yellow crystalline compound, $C_6H_5N(NO)ONH_4$, used as a quantitative precipitant for iron, titanium, zirconium, and certain other metals in acid solution and formerly as a reagent for copper.

1910 *Chem. Abstr.* IV. 557 *Cupferron*..forms complex salts with Cu and Fe, and may be used in the quantitative separation of Cu and Fe from nearly all other metals. **1939** *Thorpe's Dict. Appl. Chem.* III. 335/1 Nitroso-β-phenylhydroxylamine (cupferron) furnishes insoluble red and white complexes with ferric and cupric salts respectively. **1963** SKOOG & WEST *Fund. Anal. Chem.* ix. 195 The ammonium salt of phenylnitrosohydroxylamine, better known as cupferron, is a somewhat more selective organic reagent.

cupful (ˈkʌpfʊl). Pl. cupfuls. [f. CUP *sb.* + -FUL.] As much as fills a cup.

?*a* **1400** *Morte Arth.* 3379 Scho..Kaughte up a coppefulle. **1800** tr. *Lagrange's Chem.* I. 302 The dose employed is about an ounce in two cupfuls of broth. **1834** MRS. CARLYLE *Lett.* I. 6 A cupful of porridge, a few spoonfuls of tea.

Cuphic, var. of KUFIC.

Cupid (ˈkjuːpɪd). In 4–6 Cupide, -yde; also Cupido, -ydo. [ad. L. *Cupīdo*, personification of *cupīdo* desire, love (see 2 below), f. *cupĕre* to desire. Cf. OF. *Cupido* (mod.F. *Cupidon*). F. has had *cupide* adj. = L. *cupidus* from 15th c.]

1. a. In Roman Mythology, the god of love, son of Mercury and Venus, identified with the Greek Eros. Also in *pl.* (after L. *Cupīdines*, Gr. Ἔρωτες). Hence, a representation of the god; a beautiful young boy.

to look for Cupids in the eyes: cf. BABY 3.

c **1381** CHAUCER *Parl. Foules* 652, I wol noght serve Venus ne Cupyde [*rime* betyde]. *c* **1384** —— *H. Fame* I. 137 Hir dowves and dan Cupido, Hir blinde sone. **1548** HALL *Chron.* 194 b, Heated with the darte of Cupido. **1592** R. D. *Hypnerotomachia* 97 The violent force of Cupids artillerie. **1611** SHAKS. *Cymb.* II. iv. 89 Her Andirons..were two winking Cupids Of Siluer. **1612** DRAYTON *Polyolb.* II. (1753) 862 (N.) The Naiads..braid his verdant locks, While in their crystal eyes he doth for Cupids look. **1710** POPE *Windsor For.* 297 In the same shades the Cupids tun'd his lyre. **1713** *Guardian* No. 103 Venus stood by him..with numberless cupids on all sides of her. **1848** DICKENS *Dombey* v, Is he not a Cupid, Sir?

b. ***Cupid's bow,*** designation of a shape or outline resembling the double-curved bow of Cupid. ***Cupid's dart,*** (*a*) the popular name for a variety of *Catananche*; CUPIDONE; (*b*) (also ***Cupid's arrows***) (see quots. 1884, 1910).

[**1858** LYTTON *What will he do with It?* III. VI. vi. 165 Evil passions had destroyed the outline of the once beautiful lips, arched as a Cupid's bow.] **1875** T. SEATON *Fret Cutting* 139 It gives the lip that shape called Cupid's Bow. **1884** E. W. STREETER *Precious Stones & Gems* (ed. 4) 292/3 The brilliant hair-brown needles of Rutile, penetrating the crystal in all directions, impart a curious appearance to the stone, and such specimens are often cut for brooches, under the name of Flèches d'Amour, or 'Cupid's arrows', or 'Venus's Hair-Stone'. **1904** B'NESS VON HUTTEN *Pam* IV. viii, He's a sweetly pretty youth..with a cupid's-bow mouth. **1910** *Encycl. Brit.* XII. 272/1 This form of the mineral [göthite] has long been known as onegite, and the crystals enclosing it are cut for ornamental purposes under the name of 'Cupid's darts' (*flèches d'amour*). **1910–11** H. CESCINSKY *Eng. Furnit. 18th Cent.* II. 246 Figs. 249 and 250 are instructive in exhibiting the evolution of the true 'Cupid's bow' top rail. **1929** J. L. HODSON *Grey Dawn* I. i, Big brown eyes, cupid's bow mouth and broad forehead. **1930** L. H. & E. Z. BAILEY *Hortus* 127/1 Catananche. Cupids-Dart... Herbaceous annuals and perennials with narrow leaves borne near base of stem and longstalked blue or yellow heads. **1935** E. J. SALISBURY *Living Garden* viii. 127 The dry grassy banks of southern Europe have given us Cupid's Dart (*Catananche coerulea*).. brought to this country at the end of the sixteenth century. **1938** 'J. BELL' *Port of London Murders* ix. 167 She touched up her mouth, curving the cupid's bow well above the natural contour of her upper lip. **1962** R. WEBSTER *Gems* I. x. 163 When the enclosed crystals are long hair-like needles of red or golden-coloured rutile the material is called rutilated quartz... Other more popular names such as 'Venus hair stone', 'Cupid's darts' and 'Flèches d'amour' are applied to the material. **1969** *Gloss. Terms Dentistry (B.S.I.)* 44 *'Cupid's bow' operation*, a procedure to re-adjust the vermilion border..of the upper lip into the classical Cupid's bow conformation.

†**2.** Love, desire. [L. *cupīdo.*] *Obs. rare*[−1].

c **1420** *Pallad. on Husb.* I. 624 The cok confesseth emynent cupide When he his gemmy tail begynneth splay.

3. *Comb.* †**Cupid-struck,** smitten with love.

1653 W. HARVEY *Anatom. Exerc.* 17.

cupidinous (kjuːˈpɪdɪnəs), *a. rare.* [ad. L. type **cupidinōs-us*, f. *cupīdo*, *cupīdin-is* desire: see -OUS.] **a.** Full of desire or cupidity; **b.** (*nonce-use*) Lustful, amorous.

1656 BLOUNT *Glossogr.*, *Cupidinous, Cupidous*, covetous, desirous, greedy. **1859** G. MEREDITH *R. Feverel* xxxv, Your extremely cupidinous behaviour.

cupidity (kjuːˈpɪdɪtɪ). [a. F. *cupidité*, ad. L. *cupiditāt-em* passionate desire, f. *cupidus* eagerly desirous.]

1. *gen.* Ardent desire, inordinate longing or lust; covetousness. Const. †*of, for. arch.*

1547 BOORDE *Brev. Health* 110 Cupiditie of worldly substance or goodes. **1548** HALL *Chron.* Hen. VII an. 11 (R.) That tyraunt blynded..with the cupiditie of rulynge and soueraigntie. **1566** PAINTER *Pal. Pleas.* I. 57 Men whiche be giuen to cupiditie of gouernement, honor, and glorie. **1648** MOUNTAGUE *Devout Ess.* xiii. §6 (R.) The serpent..thus sharpens the curiosity while he suggesteth the cupidity. **1755** JOHNSON, *Cupidity*, concupiscence; unlawful or unreasonable longing. **1809–10** COLERIDGE *Friend* (ed. 3) III. 96 The cupidity for dissipation and sensual pleasure in all ranks.

b. (with *pl.*) An inordinate desire or appetite. *arch.*

1542 UDALL *Erasm. Apophth.* I. 85 a, These cupiditees by philosophie to ouercome, in a more honest and ioyly thyng. **1598** BARCKLEY *Felic. Man* (1631) 506 Immoderate desires and cupidities. **1623** WODROEPHE *Marrow Fr. Tongue* 216 (T.) All sorts of cupidities do hinder us to know the word of God. **1754** RICHARDSON *Grandison* (1812) VI. 179 (D.) She calls her idle flame love—a cupidity which only was a something she knew not what to make of. **1859** G. BUSH *Doctrines & Disclosures of Swedenborg* 52 This spirit has appetites, cupidities, desires, affections.

2. *spec.* Inordinate desire to appropriate wealth or possessions; greed of gain.

1436 *Pol. Poems* (Rolls) II. 184 Allas, cupidité! That they that have here lyves put in drede Schal be sone oute of wynnynge, al for mede. *a* **1797** BURKE (Webster 1828), No property is secure when it becomes large enough to tempt the cupidity of indigent power. **1818** JAS. MILL *Brit. India* II. V. i. 326 The country of the Rohillas was an object of cupidity to both. **1872** YEATS *Growth Comm.* 23 Their riches only excited the cupidity of a hardier race.

‖ˈ**Cupidon.** [F. = CUPID.] A 'beau' or 'Adonis'.

1824 BYRON *Juan* XV. xii, A Cupidon broke loose.

cupidone (ˈkjuːpɪdəʊn). [= prec.] Florist's name of a herbaceous border-plant, *Catananche cærulea.*

1866 in *Treas. Bot.* **1889** ROBINSON *Eng. Flower-garden* 312.

ˈ**cupidous,** *a. rare*[−0]. [f. L. *cupid-us* desirous + -OUS.] Full of cupidity.

1656 in BLOUNT *Glossogr.* [see CUPIDINOUS].

cupilo, -low, obs. or dial. forms of CUPOLA.

ˈ**cupiscence** (*nonce-wd.*), short for CONCUPISCENCE. So ˈ**cupiscent** *a.*

1692 D'URFEY *Pills* (1719) V. 2 Thou..could have quench'd thy Cupiscence.

cuple, obs. and dial. form of COUPLE.

cupless (ˈkʌplɪs), *a. rare.* [f. CUP *sb.* + -LESS.] Without a cup.

1806 J. GRAHAME *Birds Scot.* 34 Five cupless acorns.

cuplet (ˈkʌplɪt). *nonce-wd.* A little cup.

1886 BURTON *Arab. Nts.* I. 45 A golden cuplet hung round her neck.

†ˈ**cupmeal,** *adv. Obs. rare.* [f. CUP *sb.* + -MEAL :—OE. *mǽlum*: cf. *piecemeal.*] Cup by cup; a cupful at a time.

1362 LANGL. *P. Pl.* A. v. 139 Whon hit com in cuppemel [*v.r.* cop-mele, cuppemale, B. cupmel, B. & C. coppe-mel].

ˈ**cup-moss. a.** A lichen, *Scyphophorus pyxidatus* or *Cladonia pyxidata*, having cup-shaped processes arising from the thallus. **b.** Locally applied to the CUDBEAR, *Lecanora tartarea*, from its cup-shaped fructification.

1597 GERARDE *Herbal* III. clvii. 1371 *Muscus Pyxidatos*, which I have englished Cup Mosse, or Chalice Mosse. **1718** QUINCY *Compl. Disp.* 227 Cup Moss..with some other Mosses have been mightily in vogue amongst the good Wives for their children's Coughs. **1794** DONALDSON *Agric. Surv. Banffshire* 60 (Jam.) A species of moss named *cud bear* or *cup moss.* *a* **1835** MRS. HEMANS *Summer's Call* Poems (1875) 544 Where the fairy cup-moss lies.

cupola (ˈkjuːpələ), *sb.* Forms: 6– cupola; also 7 coupolo, -ola, -ulo, cupula, -elo, -ilow, cuppola, -olo, -alo, 7–8 (9 *dial.*) cupolo, -alo, -ulo, -ilo. [a. It. *cupola* (also *cuppola*, *cuppula* in Florio), whence also F. *coupole*; ad. L. *cūpula* little cask, small vault, dim. of *cūpa* cask, tun: cf. also It. *cupo* hollow, concave.]

1. a. *Arch.* A rounded vault or dome forming the roof of any building or part of a building, or supported upon columns over a tomb, etc.; *esp.* applied to the pointed or bulbous domes of Saracenic architecture. Often *spec.*: A diminutive dome rising above a roof; a dome-like lantern or skylight; in practical Architecture, the ceiling of a dome. Also *spec.* the dome of the building in which the French Academy meets (*la coupole de l'Institut*).

1549 THOMAS *Hist. Italie* 137 b, Ouer the queere is an whole vaulte called Cupola, facioned like the halfe of an egge. **1615** G. SANDYS *Trav.* 161 Out of the Temple there arise two ample coupulos. *Ibid.* 166 This Round is couered with a Cupolo. **1662** GERBIER *Princ.* 13 A Noble Paire of Staires should have a Cupelo, and no Windowes on the sides. **1670–98** LASSELS *Voy. Italy* I. 188 On the top of it [the Domo of Florence] stands mounted a fair Cupola (or Tholus) made by Brunelleschi. **1682** WHELER *Journ. Greece* I. 75 The Mosques..have their high Cupuloes covered with Lead. **1716** *Protestant Mercury* 7 Aug. 6 The Dome or Cupilo of the Cathedral of St. Paul's. **1716–18** LADY M. W. MONTAGUE *Lett.* I. xxxviii. 153 The roof of the cloisters divided into several cupolas or domes. **1730–6** BAILEY (folio), *Cupolo* [in 1731 vol. II *Cupulo*]. **1793** SMEATON *Edystone L.* §66 In the very top of the lantern, that is, in the cupola. **1821** BYRON *Juan* IV. civ, A little cupola, more neat than solemn, Protects his dust. **1867** FREEMAN *Norm. Conq.* (1876) I. vi. 478 Beneath the spreading cupolas of a Byzantine basilica. **1879** *Cassell's Techn. Educ.* IV. 300/1 The word *dome* is applied to the external part of the spherical..roof, and *cupola* to the internal part. **1900** *Westm. Gaz.* 21 June 1/3 It is only by a majority of one that M. Hervieu is called 'under the cupola'. **1920** *Edin. Rev.* Oct. 276 These guardians of the Cupola. *Ibid.* 279 On the 20th of March 1919, M. René Boylesve..was received under the Cupola by the poet, M. Henri de Regnier.

b. The revolving dome of an observatory.

1831 BREWSTER *Newton* (1855) I. xiii. 369 The practical astronomer has but to look through the cleft in his revolving cupola.

c. *transf.*

1652 BENLOWES *Theoph.* XII. v. 220 Escuriall Tour's that seem Heav'ns Cupulas. **1711** ADDISON *Spect.* No. 98 ¶5 [Nature] seems to have designed the Head as the Cupola to the most glorious of her Works. **1865** LUBBOCK *Preh. Times* xii. (1869) 398 The immense cupola of ice which is known to exist round the South Pole.

2. *Mech.* (In full ***cupola-furnace***.) A furnace for melting metals for casting; so called from a cupola or dome leading to the chimney, which is now frequently absent. Also, a furnace for heating shot to be fired at inflammable objects.

Now called at Sheffield, etc. *cupelow*, *cupilo*: cf. mod.F. *cubilot*, app. from English workmen.

1716 *Lond. Gaz.* No. 5425/9 The Lease for the Cupilo, or Copper-Works, at Lower Redbrooke. **1845** STOCQUELER *Handbk. Brit. India* (1854) 175 The casting or smelting-house, furnished with cupola blast-furnaces for the smelting of iron. **1861** *Times* 23 July, Cupolas for melting the iron for filling Martin's liquid shells.. The cupola consists of a cylindrical shell of wrought-iron, lined with fire-brick, having a blast fan attached. **1885** *Law Times' Rep.* LII. 738/1 They had erected a number of cupola and other furnaces.

3. An armour-plated revolving dome to protect mounted guns on an iron-clad ship; a turret. Hence ***cupola-ship***, ***cupola vessel***.

1862 *Ann. Reg.* 100 He had caused experiments to be made with Captain Coles's cupola. *Ibid.* 106 A cupola vessel to carry great guns. **1873** *Brit. Q. Rev.* Jan., We refer to the construction and trial [in 1861] of the first 'cupola', or 'shield', intended to protect guns mounted, with the shield, on a revolving turn-table.

4. In *Anat.*, *Zool.*, etc. A dome-like organ or process; *esp.* the arched dome-shaped summit of the cochlea of the ear.

1829 BELL *Anat. and Physiol. Human Body* (ed. 7) III. 174 When we cut away the cupola or apex of the cochlea. **1865** GOSSE *Land & Sea* (1874) 156 *Polycystina.* A prevailing type of form is a sort of dome or cupola, with an apical prolongation of spine.

5. *Geol.* A small dome-shaped projection on a batholith.

1911 R. A. DALY in *Proc. Amer. Acad. Arts & Sci.* XLVII. 69 Plutonic Cupolas... The juvenile gases tend to accumulate in any cupola-like irregularities in the roof. *Ibid.* 70 Round intrusive bosses or small stocks are characteristic cupola forms on large batholiths... It is evident that every such cupola increases as well as localizes the danger of true volcanic action. **1914** —— *Igneous Rocks & their Origin* vi. 102 These projections of the igneous mass have been called 'cupolas', after the analogous relation of an artificial cupola to the building of which it is a part. Many stocks are cupolas on batholiths. **1954** M. P. BILLINGS *Struct. Geol.* (ed. 2) xix. 319 Cupolas are isolated plutonic bodies that presumably connect downward with the main batholith.

6. *attrib.* and *Comb.*, as ***cupola-painter***, etc.; ***cupola-capped***, ***-roofed*** adjs.; ***cupola-wise*** adv.; **cupola-furnace** (see 2); **cupola-ship** (see 3).

1754 STRYPE *Stow's Surv.* II. IV. vii. 112/2 Having a fine Porch ascended by steps and covered at the Top Cupulowise. **1710** *Tatler* No. 153 ¶1 The famous Cupola-Painter of those Times. **1816** KEATINGE *Trav.* (1817) I. 205 A white building, with a cupola roof. **1862** H. MARRYAT *Year in Sweden* I. 282 Two lofty cupola-capped towers.

cupola ('kju:pələ), *v.* [f. prec. sb.] *trans.* To furnish or construct with a cupola. Hence **'cupolaed**, **'cupola'd** *ppl. a.*

1615 Coupled [see COUPLED ¶ at end]. **1644** EVELYN *Diary* 22 Oct., Another rich ebony Cabinet cupola'd with a tortoise-shell. *a* **1657** LOVELACE *Poems* (1864) 209 Now hast thou..made Thyself a fame that's cupula'd. **1673** RAY *Journ. Low C.* (1738) I. 246 Round rooms or halls cupulo'd. **1837** DISRAELI *Venetia* v. i, The hallowed form of some cupolaed convent. **1881** TALMAGE in *N.Y. Witness* 13 Apr., The old structure will be..raised, and cupolaed, and enlarged. **1886** SHORTHOUSE *Sir Percival* iii, The low cupolaed arch.

cupolar ('kju:pələ(r)), *a. rare.* [f. CUPOLA *sb.* + -AR[1].] Of the nature of a cupola, cupola-like.

1869 A. W. WARD tr. *Curtius' Hist. Greece* II. III. iii. 558 A new kind of cupolar covering for the opening made in the middle of the roof.

'cupolated, *a. rare.* [f. CUPOLA *sb.* + -ATE + -ED.] Built with a cupola.

1645 EVELYN *Mem.* (1857) I. 161 They shewed us Virgil's sepulchre..in form of a small rotunda or cupolated column. **1924** *Contemp. Rev.* Jan. 78 Their carbuncled, cupolated tops.

cuppa ('kʌpə). A form, freq. in modern times, of *cup o'*. Also used *ellipt.* for *cup o' tea. colloq.*

1925 WODEHOUSE *Sam the Sudden* vi. 42 Come and have a cuppa coffee. **1934** N. MARSH *Man lay Dead* xii. 211 Taking a strong cuppa at six-thirty in their shirt sleeves. **1942** E. LANGLEY *Pea Pickers* 78 At Seymour he got out and begged us to have a 'little cuppa tea and a sangwidge, miss'. **1949** S. GIBBONS *Conf. at Cold Comfort Farm* iii. 39 Come whoam, come whoam, you piece o' dirt. We've no more business here, and I lusts for me cuppa. **1959** 'A. GILBERT' *Death takes a Wife* ix. 119 Sit down and have a cuppa. **1968** M. RICHLER *Cocksure* viii. 46 'Good morning,' Joyce said. 'Coffee?' 'If it's no trouble I'd prefer a cuppa.' **1970** G. GREER *Female Eunuch* 117 Barbara Castle dealt with [it] by the disgusting expedient of having a cuppa with the women and talking it over heart to heart.

cupped (kʌpt), *a.* [f. CUP *sb.* and *v.* + -ED.]

1. Formed or hollowed out like a cup, cup-shaped.

1796 WITHERING *Brit. Plants* II. 291 [*Daucus maritimus*] Umbels white, convex, not cupped when in seed. **1817** KEATS *Sleep & Poetry* 255 Nibble the little cupped flowers. **1835-6** TODD *Cycl. Anat.* I. 419/2 The buffed layer [in blood] sometimes assumes a cupped form. **1881** BROADHOUSE *Mus. Acoustics* 233 Instruments with cupped mouth-pieces. **1882** *The Garden* 30 Sept. 289/1 A full sized flower..with petals beautifully cupped.

2. Lying as if in a cup.

1929 W. FAULKNER *Sartoris* I. ii. 44 He repeated above the cupped match. **1946** DYLAN THOMAS *Deaths & Entrances* 30 And the bird descended On a bread white hill over the cupped farm.

†**cuppeity.** *Obs. nonce-wd.* Also 6 cuppytee. [f. CUP *sb.*] Used to render κυαθότης, 'a word coined by Plato to express the abstract nature of a cup, cuphood' (Liddell and Scott).

1542 UDALL *Erasm. Apophth.* I. 124 b, Witte and reason.. with whiche are perceiued..the tableitees and the cuppytees. **1655-60** STANLEY *Hist. Philos.* (1701) 287/1 Plato discoursing concerning Ideas and naming τραπεζότητα, and κυαθότητα, as if he should say Tableity and Cuppeity, he said, I see, Plato, the Table and the Cup, but not the Tableity and Cuppeity.

cupper[1] ('kʌpə(r)). [f. CUP *sb.* and *v.* + -ER[1].]

†**1.** = CUP-BEARER. *Obs.*

14.. *Voc.* in Wr.-Wülcker 572/46 *Cipharius*, an^ce^ a cuppere, or a dysshere. *c* **1566** in R. Chambers *Life Jas. I* (1830) I. i. 30 To the Queenis Majesty the Earl of Huntlie was Carver, the Earl of Cassillis cupper. **1652** EARL MONM. tr. *Bentivoglio's Relat.* 58 The Carvers, Cuppers, and Suers.

2. One who performs the operation of cupping: see CUP *v.* 1, CUPPING 1.

1812 *London Direct.*, Atkinson, J., Cupper. **1848** THACKERAY *Van. Fair* lxi, The bleeders and cuppers come.

cupper[2]. *Oxford University slang.* [f. CUP *sb.* + -ER[6].] A series of intercollegiate matches played in competition for a cup. Freq. in pl.

1900 *Oxford Mag.* 31 Oct. 52/2 In the Cuppers we are drawn to play against New College. **1903** *Ibid.* 11 Feb. 214/1 Hockey.—.. We are drawn against Magdalen in the second round of the 'Cupper'. **1928** *Observer* 18 Mar. 13/4 The final of 'the rugger cupper'. **1937** C. DAY LEWIS *Starting Point* 37 Next week I've got to go into training for Cuppers. **1961** *Times* 8 Mar. 18/1 The Oxford University Rugby cuppers final.

cuppil(le, obs. form of COUPLE.

cuppiness ('kʌpɪnɪs). *Metall.* [f. CUPPY *a.* c + -NESS.] The state or condition of being cuppy (see CUPPY *a.* c).

1927 *Jrnl. Iron & Steel Inst.* CXV. 453 It may be contended that this 'cuppiness' can be somewhat obviated by taking very light drafts. **1932** E. GREGORY *Metall.* ii. 54 Axial segregation gives rise to the formation of internal flaws and 'cuppiness' in wire-drawing. **1949** R. T. ROLFE *Dict. Metall.* (ed. 2) 65 Cuppiness or cupping...is due to excessive cold working before further annealing, the exterior skin..being..enabled to withstand a much greater deformation than the unsupported interior metal, in which failure first occurs.

cupping ('kʌpɪŋ), *vbl. sb.* [f. CUP *v.* + -ING[1].]

1. *Surg.* The operation of drawing blood by scarifying the skin and applying a 'cup' or cupping-glass the air in which is rarefied by heat or otherwise. (Also called distinctively ***wet cupping***.) ***dry cupping***: the application of a cupping-glass without scarification, as a counter-irritant.

1519 HORMAN *Vulg.* 40 Some do cures..with launsynge ..boxynge, and cuppynge. **1732** ARBUTHNOT *Rules of Diet* 311 Of such sort is dry Cupping. **1886** H. VAN LAUN *Gil Blas* II. VII. xvi. 430 This..he attributed..to the cuppings which he had had the honour of applying.

2. The drinking of intoxicating liquor; a drinking-bout. *arch.* Cf. CUP *sb.* 10, *v.* 2.

c **1625** [see CUP *v.* 2 b]. **1649** *Maid's Petition* 3 To which stream of iniquity we may be a convenient stop, to dam up the[i]re overflowing cupping. **1868** BROWNING *Ring & Bk.* IV. 293 No more wilfulness and waste, Cuppings, carousings.

3. a. The formation of a cup or concavity; a concavity thus formed. *spec.* in *Metall.*, the process of forming a depression in sheet metal by forcing a plunger into it when it is laced over a die, used either to fabricate articles or as a test of the ductility of the metal; so ***cupping test***.

1893 in *N.E.D.* **1921** *Jrnl. Inst. Metals* XXV. 441 A ductility testing machine is described in which the direct pressure necessary to distort the material is measured. The pressure to cause the cupping is weighed directly by means of a confined liquid and a gauge. **1927** *Jrnl. Iron & Steel Inst.* CXV. 926 (*title*) A cupping test for determining qualities of thin metal sheets. **1964** GREGORY & SIMONS *Steel Working Processes* v. 130 Cupping is applied to such parts as containers, brake drums, dishes, pans, trays, beakers, etc.

b. *Metall.* Cuppiness; also, the flaws present in cuppy wire.

1925 A. T. ADAM *Wire-Drawing* x. 199 Two examples of segregation, one in a thick mild steel bar and the other in a wire, both of which resulted in cupping, may be given. **1949** [see prec.]. **1952** *Jrnl. Iron & Steel Inst.* CLXX. 223/1 The rupturing of the segregate bands is analagous [*sic*] to the well-known 'cupping' in segregated cold-drawn wire. **1968** R. N. PARKINS *Mech. Treatm. Metals* iv. 245 If too large a reduction is attempted, the wire may break or develop internal cracks associated with localized necking and referred to as cupping.

4. *attrib.* and *Comb.*, as (in sense 1) ***cupping-apparatus***, ***-horn***, ***-instrument***, ***-vessel***; CUPPING-GLASS; (in sense 2) †**cupping-house**, a drinking-house, tavern.

c **1616** T. ADAMS *Wks.* (1861) I. 277 A cupping-house, a vaulting-house, a gaming-house, share their means, lives, souls. **1858** O. W. HOLMES *Aut. Breakf.-t.* iv. (1891) 72 They [the legs] are sucked up by two cupping vessels. **1874** KNIGHT *Dict. Mech.* I. 659/1 Ancient cupping-horns, similar to those used through the East at the present time.. Cupping-instruments are described by Hippocrates.

'cupping-glass. [f. prec.] A glass vessel or 'cup' with an open mouth to be applied to the skin in the operation of cupping: see CUPPING 1.

1545 RAYNOLD *Byrth of Mankynde* H h vij, Cupping glasses, set vpon or vnder the brestes. *a* **1625** BEAUM. & FL. *Bloody Brother* IV. ii, Still at their books, they will not be pulled off; They stick like cupping-glasses. **1658** ROWLAND *Moufet's Theat. Ins.* 1054 The part affected must be cut.. and the poyson drawn forth with Cupping-glasses. **1811** A. T. THOMSON *Lond. Disp.* (1818) 199 Leeches..are applied ..to places where cupping-glasses cannot be applied.

cupple, cuppul, -ylle, obs. forms of COUPLE.

cuppola, -olo, obs. forms of CUPOLA.

cuppord(e, obs. form of CUPBOARD.

cuppy ('kʌpɪ), *a. rare.* [f. CUP *sb.* + -Y.]

a. Concave like a cup. **b.** Full of 'cups' (see CUP *sb.* 5). ***cuppy lie*** *Golf*, the position of a ball when it lies in a 'cup' or shallow depression. Said also of the ball.

1882 *Garden* 10 June 399/2 Delicate little Peach-coloured cuppy flowers. [**1886** H. HUTCHINSON *Hints Game Golf* 32 If it [*sc.* the ball] lie 'cuppy', a jerking stroke will be necessary.] **1892** *Sport. & Dram. News* 9 Apr. 152/3 Rain.. much needed, as the lies are now very 'cuppy' in places. **1901** W. J. TRAVIS *Pract. Golf* (1903) iv. 46 It is better to.. play each shot the same way—except in the case of a very cuppy lie. **1922** WODEHOUSE *Clicking of Cuthbert* 88 Mortimer..found his ball in a nasty cuppy lie.

c. *Metall.* Of drawn metal, esp. wire: having internal cavities that lead to a cup-and-cone fracture under sufficient tensile stress.

1925 A. T. ADAM *Wire-Drawing* x. 197 'Cuppy' wire—*i.e.* wire which breaks either in drawing or in bending with a very distinct 'cup and cone' fracture. **1927** *Jrnl. Iron & Steel Inst.* CXV. 470 He desired to ask the author whether internal cuppy fractures were not liable to be produced by wrong manipulation in the drawing. **1958** A. D. MERRIMAN *Dict. Metall.* 52/1 *Cuppy wire*... Wire which, though apparently sound, shows on a longitudinal section a series of well-developed internal fractures which open to the surface under bending stresses.

cuppy, *a. Her.*: see VAIRY-CUPPY.

cupra'mmonia. Also erron. **cupra-ammonia.** [f. as next + AMMONIA.] A solution containing a cuprammonium salt; a cuprammonium solution.

1862 H. WATTS tr. *Gmelin's Hand-bk. Chem.* XV. 143 The solution of cellulose in cuprammonia is precipitated by a large quantity of water. **1927** M. H. AVRAM *Rayon Industry* 497 The cupra-ammonia cellulose process.

cuprammonium (kju:prə'məʊnɪəm). Also erron. **cupra-ammonium.** [f. L. *cupr-um* copper + AMMONIUM.] A complex ion of copper and ammonia, $Cu(NH_3)_4^{++}$, obtained in solution by adding excess ammonium hydroxide to a solution of a cupric salt; it forms deep blue aqueous solutions which dissolve cellulose and are used industrially, esp. in the manufacture of some man-made fibres. So ***cuprammonium process***, ***rayon***, ***silk***, etc. Also used *ellipt.* for *cuprammonium solution.*

1862 H. WATTS tr. *Gmelin's Hand-bk. Chem.* XV. 142 Cotton immersed in aqueous biphosphate of cuprammonium becomes first gelatinous, then slippery, and forms an almost transparent gummy liquid. **1888** CROSS & BEVAN *Paper-Making* xvi. 217 The cuprammonium solution. **1907** ROSCOE & SCHORLEMMER *Treat. Chem.* (ed. 4) II. 435 This dissolves to a deep pure blue liquid containing cuprammonium sulphate, $CuSO_4, 4NH_3, H_2O$, which was first described by Stisser in 1693 as an *arcanum epilecticum* and afterwards termed *cuprum ammoniacale*. **1921** T. WOODHOUSE tr. *Foltzer's Artif. Silk* 29 Despeissis Artificial Silk (Cuprammonium Process). *Ibid.* 36 Cuprammonium Solution..is a solution of copper oxide in ammonia. It is a blue liquid known to chemists as Schweitzer's reagent. **1925** *Good Housekeeping* Apr. 142/2 Cuprammonium silk. **1927** M. H. AVRAM *Rayon Industry* 192 The cupra-ammonium solution of cellulose. *Ibid.* 497 Cupra-ammonium Rayon. **1939** *Thorpe's Dict. Appl. Chem.* (ed. 4) III. 355/1 'Schweizer's reagent' or cuprammonium..has the property of dissolving cellulose (cotton wool, linen, filter paper, etc.). **1960** WOOD & HOLLIDAY *Inorg. Chem.* xiv. 347 The deep blue solution of cuprammonium sulphate deposits crystals

..of composition, $Cu(NH_3)_4SO_4.H_2O$. **1964** N. G. CLARK *Mod. Org. Chem.* xvi. 333 One commercial process, giving Cuprammonium Rayon, exploits the ability of an aqueous ammoniacal copper salt solution to dissolve cellulose.

†**cuprane.** *Chem. Obs.* [See -ANE 2 a.] Sir H. Davy's name for cuprous chloride (Cu_2Cl_2). So **cupranea**, for cupric chloride ($CuCl_2$).
1812 SIR H. DAVY *Chem. Philos.* 418 Cuprane is converted into cupranea by being heated in chlorine.

cuprate (ˈkjuːprət). *Chem.* [f. L. *cupr-um* copper + -ATE.] A salt of cupric acid.
1854 J. SCOFFERN in *Orr's Circ. Sc.* Chem. 489 Cuprate of potash.

cuprea (ˈkjuːpriːə). [L., fem. of *cupreus* CUPREOUS *a.*] Used *attrib.* in ***cuprea bark***, the coppery-red bark of the S. American tree *Remijia pedunculata* (and other species), one of the sources of quinine.
[**1882** *Jrnl. Chem. Soc.* XLI. 66 The singular bark described by Dr. Flückiger as *China Cuprea*.] **1884** *Pharm. Jrnl.* 23 Aug. 141/1 The alkaloid of cuprea bark. **1889** G. S. BOULGER *Uses of Plants* II. 100 *Remijia Purdieana*, Willd., and *R. pedunculata*, Trian., from Colombia, have of late years been imported in enormous quantities as sources of quinine etc., under the name of Cuprea Bark. **1939** [see CUPREINE]. **1970** W. SOLOMON in S. W. Pelletier *Chem. Alkaloids* xi. 325 It is doubtful in this connection whether Cuprea bark (*Remijia pedunculata*), which was the sole natural source of cupreine, is now obtainable.

cupreine (ˈkjuːpriːɪn). *Chem.* [f. CUPREA + -INE[5].] A cinchona alkaloid, $C_{19}H_{22}N_2O_2$, contained in cuprea bark.
1884 PAUL & COWNLEY in *Pharm. Jrnl.* 20 Sept. 222/1 This latter alkaloid is susceptible of being split into two other alkaloids, one of them being..quinine..the other an alkaloid.. to which we will provisionally give the name of 'cupreine'. **1886** *Encycl. Brit.* XX. 185/1 Homoquinine has been shown..to be decomposed on treatment with caustic soda into quinine and a new alkaloid, cupreine. **1939** *Thorpe's Dict. Appl. Chem.* (ed. 4) III. 160/2 Cupreine.. occurs together with other cinchona alkaloids..in the so-called 'Cuprea bark'..which is no longer collected commercially. **1966** *McGraw-Hill Encycl. Sci. & Technol.* XI. 193/2 The cinchona alkaloids..are quinoline derivatives; in quinine and quinidine, R = CH_3O; in cinchonine, R = H; and in cupreine, R = OH.

cupreo-, combining form of CUPREOUS, coppery in colour.
1847 HARDY in *Proc. Berw. Nat. Club* II. 251 Abdomen.. irridescent cupreo-versicolorous. *Ibid.* 253 Abdomen.. more or less cupreo-violaceous irridescent.

cupreous (ˈkjuːpriːəs), *a.* [f. L. *cupre-us* of copper (f. *cupr-um* copper) + -OUS.]
1. Of copper; of the nature of copper; consisting of or containing copper.
1666 BOYLE *Orig. Formes & Qual.*, A Cupreous Resin. **1693** SLARE in *Phil. Trans.* XVII. 900 Such Particles as are of a Cupreous Nature. **1807** T. THOMSON *Chem.* (ed. 3) II. 398 Boracic acid and cupreous salts tinge it green. **1857** SCOFFERN *Useful Metals* 530 Wicklow..has long been celebrated for its cupreous deposits.
2. Resembling copper; copper-coloured.
1804 *Phil. Trans.* XCIV. 316 It is most frequently of the colour of bronze, passing to a pale cupreous-red. **1849** THOREAU *Week Concord Riv.* Saturday 32 This bright cupreous dolphin.

cupreˈssineous, *a. Bot.* [f. mod.L. *Cupressineæ* + -OUS.] Of or belonging to the Cypress tribe, *Cupressineæ*, of the Nat. Ord. *Coniferæ*.
1881 *Nature* XXIV. 106 Between this and the next section ..if cupressineous at all.

cupressite (ˈkjuːprɪsaɪt). *Palæont.* [f. L. *cupress-us* cypress + -ITE.] A coniferous fossil plant supposed to be allied to the cypress.

cupric (ˈkjuːprɪk), *a. Chem.* [f. L. *cupr-um* copper + -IC.] Containing copper in chemical combination; applied to compounds in which copper combines as a dyad, as ***cupric chloride***, $CuCl_2$.
1799 SIR H. DAVY in Beddoes *Contrib. Phys. & Med. Knowledge* 184 Cupric phosoxyd. **1854** J. SCOFFERN in *Orr's Circ. Sc.* Chem. 489 Cupric acid..has not been isolated.

cupriferous (kjuːˈprɪfərəs), *a.* [f. as prec. + -FEROUS.] Yielding copper.
1784 KIRWAN *Min.* (1796) II. 109 Cupriferous native silver. *c* **1830** DE LA BECHE *Elem. Geol.* (L.), The whole cupriferous district of North Wales. **1879** *Cassell's Techn. Educ.* IV. 225/1 Arsenical or cupriferous pyrites.

cuprite (ˈkjuːpraɪt). *Min.* [f. L. *cupr-um* copper + -ITE.] Native red oxide of copper (a valuable ore).
1850 DANA *Min.* 517. **1869** PHILLIPS *Vesuv.* x. 282.

cupro- (kjuːprəʊ), before a vowel also **cupr-**, used as combining form of L. *cuprum* COPPER, in *Chem.* and *Min.*, as ***cuprammonium, cupro-sulphate***; **cuproˈmagnesite**, a hydrous sulphate of copper and magnesium (Dana, 1875); ˌ**cupro-ˈnickel**, an alloy of copper and nickel; **cupro-ˈplumbite**, a native sulphide of copper and lead (Dana, 1850); **cuproˈscheelite**, native tungstate of copper and calcium; **cupro-ˈtungstite**, native tungstate of copper (Dana, 1875); etc.
1905 *Kynoch Jrnl.* Jan.-Mar. 18 The bullet is sheathed with a cupro-nickel envelope. **1922** *Encycl. Brit.* XXX. 135/2 This jacket is made from cupro-nickel which.. contains from 80% to 85% copper and from 15% to 20% nickel. **1948** M. LASKI *Tory Heaven* xii. 172 A golden sovereign..changed into four cupro-nickel half-crowns. **1962** *Metal Industry* CI. 102/1 The term cupro-nickel is now more widely applied to any copper-nickel alloy containing less than about 50 per cent of nickel.

cuproid (ˈkjuːprɔɪd). *Cryst.* [f. L. *cupr-um* copper + -OID. So called by Haidinger, because the form occurs in the mineral Tetrahedrite, a sulphide of copper and antimony.] A solid contained under twelve equal triangles, formed by erecting a pyramid on each of the triangular faces of a tetrahedron.
1864 WEBSTER cites DANA.

cuproso- (kjuːˈprəʊsəʊ), *Chem.*, combining form of mod.L. *cuprōsus* CUPROUS.
1863-72 WATTS *Dict. Chem.* II. 55 Aqueous cuproso-cupric Chloride. **1873** —— *Fownes' Chem.* 399 The important ore, called copper-pyrites, is a cuproso-ferric sulphide.

cuprous (ˈkjuːprəs), *a.* [f. L. *cupr-um* copper + -OUS.] **a.** = CUPREOUS. **b.** In *Chem.*, applied to compounds in which copper combines as a monad, as ***cuprous chloride*** Cu_2Cl_2.
1669 W. SIMPSON *Hydrol. Chym.* 29 The *Aqua fortis*, precipitating upon the cuprous plates. **1811** A. T. THOMSON *Lond. Disp.* (1818) 149 Sugar is the antidote of cuprous poisons. **1869** ROSCOE *Elem. Chem.* 264 The ore is repeatedly roasted, in order partially to convert the cuprous sulphide into oxide.

ˈ**cup-shake.** A separation or opening between two of the concentric layers of timber. So ˈ**cup-shaken,** ˈ**cup-shaky** *a.* Cf. *cup-defect* (CUP *sb.* 13 d).
a **1793** G. WHITE *Observ. Vegetables* in *Hist. Selborne* App. (1877) I. 421 The wood [chestnut] is very shakey, and towards the heart cup-shakey, that is to say apt to separate in round pieces like cups. **1807** VANCOUVER *Agric. Devon* (1813) 286 *note*, Such of the yew as was not cup or wind shaken, was cut into plank. **1875** LASLETT *Timber Trees* 31 The cup-shake. This shake..is most frequently met with near the roots of trees.

†**cup-shot,** *a. Obs.* [f. CUP *sb.* + SHOT *pa. pple.*] Overcome with liquor, intoxicated.
a **1593** H. SMITH *Serm.* (1624) 62 To excuse Noah because hee was an old man, and therefore might soone bee taken cup-shot. **1608** *2nd Pt. Def. Ministers' Reasons for Refusal of Subscription* 164 Ridiculous, as a cupshott man that spake to his owne shadowe. **1639** FULLER *Holy War* III. xvi. 135. *a* **1700** B. E. *Dict. Cant. Crew*, *Cup-shot*, drunk.

†**cup-shotten,** *a. Obs.* = prec., being the earlier form.
c **1330** R. BRUNNE *Chron. Wace* (Rolls) 7560 Als þey were ..wel cuppe-schoten, knyght & kyng. **1529** MORE *Dyaloge* I. xxiii. Wks. 153 If a maide be suffred to ronne on the brydle, or be cup shotten, or wax to prowde. **1603** FLORIO *Montaigne* III. xiii. (1632) 624 Store of wine had made his companions cuppe-shotten. *a* **1693** URQUHART *Rabelais* III. xxxviii. 318 Cupshotten and swilling fool.

†**cupˈstantial,** *a. nonce-wd.* A humorous perversion of *substantial*, intended to suggest 'drunken': cf. CUP *sb.* 10.
1583 STUBBES *Anat. Abus.* II. (1882) 65 These be cupstantiall reasons and well seasoned arguments.

cupula: see CUPULE, CUPOLA.

cupular (ˈkjuːpjʊlə(r)), *a.* [f. L. *cūpula* + -AR. Cf. F. *cupulaire* (1798 in Bulliard *Dict. de Botan.*).]
1. *Bot.* Shaped like a cupule.
1870 HOOKER *Stud. Flora* 80 Ilicineæ..funicle often cupular. *Ibid.* 83 Calyx of the male campanulate, female cupular.
2. ***cupular cautery***, 'a cup-shaped cautery, formerly used for destroying portions of the skin of the head in epilepsy and other diseases' (*Syd. Soc. Lex.*).

cupulate (ˈkjuːpjʊlət), *a. Bot.* [f. as prec. + -ATE.] Shaped like a cupule; furnished with or bearing a cupule.
1835 LINDLEY *Introd. Bot.* (1848) I. 163 In figure they are ..occasionally cupulate. **1857** BERKELEY *Cryptog. Bot.* §301 The change from the cupulate to the clavate form.

cupule (ˈkjuːpjuːl). [ad. L. *cūpula*, dim. of *cūpa* cask, tub, (later) cup; cf. F. *cupule* (1798 Bulliard *Dict. de Botan.*). In botany the L. form ˈ*cupula* is also used.]
1. *Bot.* A cup-shaped involucre consisting of bracts cohering by their bases, as in the oak, beech, and hazel. Also, a cup-like receptacle found in such fungi as *Peziza*.
1830 LINDLEY *Nat. Syst. Bot.* 248 An external additional envelope called the cupula. **1845** —— *Sch. Bot.* vii. (1858) 117 The cupule..in common language, is called *husk* in the Filbert, Chesnut, and Beech, and *cup* in the Oak. **1859** TODD *Cycl. Anat.* V. 228/2 The receptacles or cupules in which thecæ are produced.
2. *Zool.* A small cup-shaped organ, as the sucking-disc of the cuttle-fish and of certain aquatic beetles.
1826 KIRBY & SP. *Entomol.* (1828) IV. 179 Caps or cupules surmounted by a tendon.
3. A small cup-shaped depression on a surface.
1883 H. A. NEWTON in *Encycl. Brit.* XVI. 112 (*Meteors*) The surfaces very often have small cup-like cavities, sometimes several inches in diameter, sometimes like deep imprints in a plastic mass made by the ends of the fingers, and sometimes still smaller. These 'cupules'..may be regarded as a characteristic of meteorites..The air pressed hard against it burns it unequally, forming cupules over its surface.

cupuliferous (kjuːpjuːˈlɪfərəs), *a. Bot.* [f. L. *cūpula* CUPULE + -FEROUS.] Bearing a cupule or cupules; belonging to the N.O. *Cupuliferæ*, including the oak, beech, hazel, etc.
1847 in CRAIG.

cupuliform (ˈkjuːpjuːlɪfɔːm), *a. Bot.* [f. as prec. + -FORM.] Shaped like a cupule.
In mod. Dicts.

cupulo, obs. form of CUPOLA.

cupyde, obs. bad form of CUBIT.

cur (kɜː(r)). Forms: (3 **kur-dogge**), 4-6 **kurre**, 4-7 **curre**, 7-8 **curr**, 5- **cur**. [ME. *curre* corresponds to MDu. *corre* 'canis villaticus, domesticus' (Kilian), Sw. and Norw. (widely-spread) dial. *kurre*, *korre* 'dog', etc. The latter is generally associated with the onomatopœic verb ON. *kurra* to murmur, grumble, Sw. *kurra* to grumble, rumble, snarl, Da. *kurre* to coo, Ger. obs. and dial. *kurren* to growl, grumble, murmur, coo, cf. *gurren* to coo, MHG. *gürren* to bray as an ass. The primary sense appears thus to have been 'growling or snarling beast'. But no corresponding verb appears in Eng., so that ME. *kurre* was prob. introduced from some continental source. The combination *kur-dogge* is met with considerably earlier than the simple *kurre*, *cur*. Senses 2 and 3 are possibly independent echoic formations.]
1. A dog: now always depreciative or contemptuous; a worthless, low-bred, or snappish dog. Formerly (and still sometimes dialectally) applied without depreciation, *esp.* to a watch-dog or shepherd's dog.
a **1225** [see CUR-DOG in c]. *c* **1385** CHAUCER *L.G.W.* Prol. 396 The lyoun..Hym deynyth nat to wreke hym on a flye, As doth a curre or ellis a-nothir beste. *c* **1400** *Destr. Troy* 1972 Brittonet þi body into bare qwarters, And caste vnto curres as caren to ete. **1486** *Bk. St. Albans* F vj b, A Cowardnes of curris. **1579** SPENSER *Sheph. Cal.* Sept. 182 Neuer had shepheard so kene a kurre. **1598** MANWOOD *Forest Lawes* xvi. §6 (1615) 112 b, The Mastiues, and such like curres, that are of the Mastiue kinde. **1602** *2nd Pt. Return fr. Parnass.* II. v. (Arb.) 30 Dunghill dogges, trindle tailes, prick-eard curres. **1684** R. H. *Sch. Recreat.* 13 The most Staunch and best Hunting Hounds; (all babling and flying Curs being left at home). **1697** DRYDEN *Virg. Georg.* III. 536 The Shepherd last appears, And with him..his trusty Cur. **1710** PHILIPS *Pastorals* iv. 119 Then send our Curs to gather up the Sheep. **1712** ARBUTHNOT *John Bull* III. App. i, I am hunted away..by every barking cur about the house. **1837** W. IRVING *Capt. Bonneville* II. 208 These dogs ..were of more use than the beggarly curs of cities. **1884** *Cheshire Gloss.*, *Cur*, a good, sharp watchdog. The word does not refer, in the least, to low breeding.
b. *fig.* As a term of contempt: a surly, ill-bred, low, or cowardly fellow.
1590 SHAKS. *Mids. N.* III. ii. 65 Out dog, out cur, thou driu'st me past the bounds of maidens patience. **1607** —— *Cor.* I. i. 172 What would you have, you Curres, That like nor Peace, nor Warre? **1711** ADDISON *Spect.* No. 57 ¶3, I have heard her, in her Wrath, call a substantial Tradesman a Lousy Cur. **1870** BRYANT *Iliad* I. VIII. 263 That I may drive away These curs, brought hither by an evil fate.
c. *Comb.* **cur-dog** in prec. senses.
So ***cur-bitch, -fox, -tyke***; †**cur-fish**, the Dog-fish. Also ***cur-like*** adj.
a **1225** *Ancr. R.* 290 þes dogge of helle..þe fule kur dogge. *c* **1450** *Voc.* in Wr.-Wülcker 562/23 *Agerarius*, a curdogge. **1494** FABYAN *Chron.* VII. ccxxxi. 263 A mastife or great curre dogge. **1591** SPENSER *M. Hubberd* 294 This Curdog..will serue, my sheepe to gather. **1617** FLETCHER *Mad Lover* III. ii, Coward go with thy caitiff soul, thou cur-dog! **1727** HALL in *Phil. Trans.* XXXV. 309 We got three Curr-Dogs. **1859** W. COLLINS *Q. of Hearts* (1875) 24 One of the largest and ugliest cur-dogs in England barking at her heels.
1611 COTGR., *Mastine*, A Mastiue, or Curre bitch. **1663** EARL OF LAUDERDALE in *L. Papers* I. 175, I care not three skips of a Curre tyke what can be said or done against me. **1706** PHILLIPS (ed. Kersey), *Currish*, curr-like, doggish, churlish. **1774** GOLDSM. *Nat. Hist.* (1776) III. 332 The greyhound fox..The mastiff fox..The cur fox is the least and most common.
†**2.** A fish: the Elleck or Red Gurnard, *Trigla cuculus*.
1589 RIDER *Eng.-Lat. Dict.* (1617) E e viij, Fishes. A curre fish, *Cuculus*. **1598** FLORIO, *Capo*..a fish called a cur, a gull, a bulhead, or a millers thumbe. **1661** LOVELL *Hist. Anim. & Min.* 194 Curre is a sweet fish, but not the best, it hath much flesh, white, hard and dry. **1753** in CHAMBERS *Cycl. Supp.*
3. A species of duck: the Golden-eye, *Clangula glaucion. dial.*

1621–51 BURTON *Anat. Mel.* I. ii. II. i. 67 Teals, Curs, Sheldrakes..that come hither in winter. 1841 J. T. HEWLETT *Parish Clerk* III. 8 Harry drew his attention to a solitary cur—a species of duck more easily approachable than the others. 1885 SWAINSON *Prov. Names Birds* 161 Golden-eye..Curre. From the bird's croaking cry.

cur, obs. f. CURE; var. of CURRE.

curability (kjʊərəˈbɪlɪtɪ). [f. CURABLE: cf. mod.F. *curabilité*.] The quality of being curable.

1807–26 S. COOPER *First Lines Surg.* (ed. 5) 222 The curability of every kind of ulcer. 1861 F. H. RAMADGE (*title*), The Curability of Consumption.

curable (ˈkjʊərəb(ə)l), *a.* [ad. L. *cūrābilis*, f. *cūrāre* to cure: perh. through F. *curable* (14th c. in Littré).]

1. Capable of being cured; *fig.* amendable, remediable.

1398 TREVISA *Barth. De P.R.* VII. lviii. (1495) 272 In xl dayes it is curable. *c* 1400 *Lanfranc's Cirurg.* 185 Ulcera.. summe ben curable & summe ben incurable. *c* 1460 *Play Sacram.* 31 He can telle yf yow be curable. 1592 W. PERKINS *Cases Consc.* (1619) 159 Enemies of God and his truth, are also of two sorts, either Curable or Incurable. 1709 STEELE *Tatler* No. 107 ¶2 Evils are much more curable in their Beginnings. 1822 HAZLITT *Table-t., Spir. Partizanship*, Of that they are curable like any occasional disorder.

†**2.** Disposed to cure; able to cure. *Obs.*

1483 CAXTON *Gold. Leg.* 315/3 My brother Fyre be thow to me in this houre debonayre and curable. 1584 WHETSTONE *Mirror* Ep. A iij b, A Physition..may applie a curable Medicine for a hidden Disease. 1615 G. SANDYS *Trav.* III. 174 (D.) The water..retaining a curable vertue against all diseases.

Hence †ˈ**curableness**, curability.

a 1691 BOYLE *Wks.* II. 110 (R.) The arguments..for the curableness of all diseases, are not very cogent. 1727 in BAILEY vol. II.

‖**curaçao, curaçoa** (kjʊərəˈsəʊ). [The name of an island (a Dutch dependency) in the Caribbean sea, near the coast of Venezuela. *Curaçao* is the Spanish (and so Dutch and French) spelling; *curaçoa* a very frequent mis-spelling in English.] A liqueur consisting of spirits flavoured with the peel of bitter oranges, and sweetened.

So called either because first received from the island of Curaçao, or because Curaçao oranges were used in its preparation.

[1810 R. J. THORNTON *Family Herbal* 658 The unripe fruit dried, are called Curaçoa oranges.] 1813 MOORE *Postbag* (L.), And it pleased me to think at a house that you know Were such good mutton cutlets and strong curaçoa. 1848 THACKERAY *Van. Fair* xi, She took curaçao with her coffee.

curaçao bird: see CURASSOW.

curacy (ˈkjʊərəsɪ). [f. CURATE: see -ACY.]

1. The office or position of a curate; the benefice of a perpetual curate.

1682 PRIDEAUX *Lett.* (Camden) 130 A very good curacy of yᵉ college, at Tring in Buckinghamshire..becomeing void. 1719 SWIFT *To Young Clergyman*, If they be very fortunate [they] arrive in time to a curacy in town. 1836 *Penny Cycl.* VI. 487/1 The living is a perpetual curacy. 1872 E. PEACOCK *Mabel Heron* I. iv. 66 He had held a curacy in Yorkshire.

†**2.** The office of a curator or guardian, curatorship. *Obs. rare*$^{-1}$.

a 1734 NORTH *Exam.* II. iv. §57 (1740) 260 The republican Party concluded such Issue must come to the Crown young, and then they had a Game de integro, by Way of Curacy and Protectorship.

curag(e, obs. form of COURAGE.

curaige, -agie, obs. forms of CULRAGE.

curaiows, curale, curan, obs. ff. COURAGEOUS, CORAL, CURRANT.

‖**curare** (kjuːˈrɑːriː). Also curara, -ri. [A corruption of the native name (wuˈrɑli or wuˈrɑri) also written *wourali, woorari, ourali, ourari, wourara*, etc., in the lang. of the Macusi Indians of Guiana, a Carib dialect. The consonant of the last syllable varies between *l* and *r*. In F. *curare*. (The initial *c* is said to represent a click or catch in the native pronunciation.) See OURALI, WOURALI.]

A blackish-brown resinous bitter substance, obtained as an extract from *Strychnos toxifera*, and other plants of tropical South America; used by the Indians to poison their arrows.

When introduced into the blood it acts as a powerful poison, arresting the action of the motor nerves; used largely in physiological experiments.

1777 ROBERTSON *Hist. Amer.* IV. (1778) I. 328 A poison in which they dip the arrows employed in hunting..the chief ingredient in which is the juice extracted from the root of the curare, a species of withe. 1836 MACGILLIVRAY tr. *Humboldt's Trav.* xix. 274 The curare..like the venom of serpents..only acts when introduced directly into the blood. 1875 H. C. WOOD *Therap.* (1879) 186 Animals quieted by curari. 1883 *Contemp. Rev.* June 793 A moral curare..paralysing will and emotion.

curarine (ˈkjʊərəraɪn). *Chem.* [f. prec. + -INE; cf. F. *curarine*.] A bitter poisonous alkaloid, $C_{10}H_{15}N$, obtained from curare.

1863–72 WATTS *Dict. Chem.* II. 186 The physiological action of curarine appears to be the same as that of curara. 1869 ROSCOE *Elem. Chem.* 431.

curarize (ˈkjʊərəraɪz), *v.* [f. CURAR-E + -IZE.] To administer curare to (an animal), *esp.* in a physiological experiment, in order to destroy the motor functions of the nervous system. Hence **ˈcurarized** *ppl. a.*, **curariˈzation**.

1875 H. C. WOOD *Therap.* (1879) 185 Curarized animals poisoned by hydrocyanic acid. *Ibid.* 201 Prevented by curarization and artificial respiration. 1892 *Pall Mall G.* 22 Oct. 2/1 A medical man had told her that the animals would be curarized in such experiments.

curas(e, -rasse, -raseer, -sheer, obs. ff. CUIRASS, -IER.

curassow (ˈkjʊərəsəʊ). Forms: 7 corrosou, -so, -reso, 8 curasso, -raçoa, 8–9 curassao, 9 -sow. [A phonetic spelling of the name of the island *Curaçao* (kuːraˈsɑːu).] One of a family of gallinaceous birds found in Central and South America; they have a general resemblance to the turkey, and several species are domesticated.

The most common species, to which the name *corrosou* or *Curaçao-bird* was originally applied, is the Crested Curassow, *Crax alector*, of a greenish-black colour with a white crest; the Galeated Curassow or Cushew-bird, *Pauxis galeata*, has a large bony protuberance on the upper part of the bill.

1685 L. WAFER *Voy.* (1729) 334 The Corrosou is a large black land-bird, heavy and big as a turkey-hen. 1699 DAMPIER *Voy.* II. II. 67 The Correso..The Cock has a Crown of black Feathers on his Head, and appears very stately. 1837 *Penny Cycl.* VIII. 129/2. 1847 CARPENTER *Zool.* §430 The Crested Curassow is one of the most common Birds of Guiana. 1852 TH. ROSS *Humboldt's Trav.* II. xviii. 162 The cries of the Curassao..and other gallinaceous birds.

attrib. 1756 P. BROWNE *Jamaica* (1779) 470 The Curaçoa Bird. 1863 BATES *Nat. Amazon* ix. (1864) 262 We were amused at the excessive..tameness of a fine Mutum or Curassow turkey.

curat, -e, obs. forms of CUIRASS.

curatage (ˈkjʊərətɪdʒ). [f. CURATE + -AGE.]

†**1.** The office of a curator or guardian; provision of curators or guardians. *Obs.*

1759 *State Papers* in *Ann. Reg.* 255/2 The appointment of the tutelage and curatage for the King, during his minority.

2. Sometimes applied to the house or residence provided for a curate. [After *vicarage*.]

1879 *Standard* 31 July (*Births*), At The Curatage, Biddenden, Staplehurst, Kent. 1893 CROCKFORD *Clerical Directory* Pref. 13 A very few clergymen date their letters from 'The Curatage'..It can only be in very exceptional cases that the house inhabited by a Curate can have the very slightest claim for any sort of name..analogous to that of a vicarage or rectory; and even then it may be questioned whether..it should not be 'Parsonage'.

curate (ˈkjʊərət). Also 4–8 curat, 4–5 curet(t, 6 currat, curatte. [ad. med.L. *cūrātus*, in It. *curato*, F. *curé* (13th c. in Littré). The med.L. and It. are originally adjs. 'of, belonging to, or having a cure or charge', whence as sb. 'one who has a cure or ecclesiastical charge'.]

1. One entrusted with the cure of souls; a spiritual pastor. †**a.** *gen.* Any ecclesiastic (including a bishop, etc.) who has the spiritual charge of a body of laymen. †**b.** A clergyman who has the spiritual charge of a parish (or parochial district); the parson of a parish.

(Now only as an archaism or etymological use.)

c 1340 HAMPOLE *Prose Tr.* (1866) 24 The thride liffe.. longith to men of holi-chirch, as to prelates and to oþer Curatis, the which han cure and souerante ouer othir men forto teche and reule hem. *c* 1350 in Horstmann *Alteng. Leg.* (1881) 51 Saint Peter..was chosen pape of Rome And chief curate of Cristendome. *c* 1382 WYCLIF *Sel. Wks.* III. 518 Not oonly simple prestis and curatis but also sovereyne curatis as bisshopis. *a* 1483 *Liber Niger* in *Househ. Ord.* (1790) 49 Also this Deane is curate and confessour of all this houshold. 1493 in Wadley *Bristol Wills* (1886) 171 (Will of layman), To my Curate, vicar of the saide Church, iiij mesures of wode. 1531 *Dial. on Laws Eng.* II. lv. (1638) 175 Variance began to rise betweene Curats and their Parishioners. 1545 *Primer Hen. VIII, Litany*, Send down upon our bishops and curates..the healthful spirit of thy grace. 1634 CANNE *Necess. Separ.* (1849) 32 Whosoever taketh upon him..to be a curate of souls, parson, bishop, or what other spiritual pastor soever. 1727 SWIFT *Modest Proposal*, To..pay tithes against their conscience to an episcopal curate. 1886 *Guardian* 3 Mar. 321/3 As a preacher, or parochial organizer, or a curate of souls. 1886 *Church Q. Rev.* XXII. 298 In immediate subordination..to the chief curate of the parish, or to the bishop only.

c. *Sc. Hist.* Applied to the episcopal incumbents of the Scottish parishes from 1662 to 1688.

1706 A. SHIELDS *Enq. Church Commun.* Pref. 3 Others could not join in hearing the Curates. 1855 MACAULAY *Hist. Eng.* III. 251 About two hundred curates—so the episcopal priests were called—were expelled.

d. Applied to parish-priests abroad; a French *curé*, Italian *curato*, Spanish *cura*, etc.

c 1650 BRATHWAIT *Barnabees Jrnl.* III. (1818) 141 Thence to Gastile..I drunk stingo With a butcher and Domingo Th' Curat. 1724 DE FOE *Mem. Cavalier* (1840) 6 In our journey to Paris [we met] an old priest..near a little village whereof he was curate. 1801 *Med. Jrnl.* V. 351 In the neighbourhood of Vienna..in the village Brunnam Gebizg: the respectable curate of that parish, etc.

2. a. A clergyman engaged for a stipend or salary, and licensed by the bishop of the diocese to perform ministerial duties in the parish as a deputy or assistant of the incumbent; an assistant to a parish priest.

This use of the word is peculiar to the Church of England and to the R.C. Church in Ireland, where assistants to the parish priests are also so called. It appears to have originated in the application of the name *curate* to the clergyman *in actual charge* of a parish of which the benefice was held by a non-resident clergyman, the head of a college, etc., and to have been thence extended to the deputy of an aged and infirm incumbent, and so gradually to any deputy or assistant of the beneficed clergyman, more fully described as a ***stipendiary*** or ***assistant curate***. This is now the ordinary popular application of *curate*. A clergyman appointed by the bishop to take charge of a parish or chapelry during the incapacity or suspension of the incumbent is called a ***curate-in-charge***. The incumbent of the chapel or church of an ecclesiastical district, forming part of an ancient parish, appointed by the patron and licensed by the bishop is a ***perpetual curate***; these now rank as vicars.

1557 *Indenture of Advowson of Garsington*, And that also the said president [of Trinity Coll., Oxf.] being parson of the said Rectorie [of Garsington] shall likewise for euer at his own proper charge fynde one sufficient Catholike and hable Curat to serve in the said Rectorye and parishe churche. 1587 *Petit.* in Fuller *Ch. Hist.* IX. vii. §1 No Non-resident having already a license or Faculty may enjoy it, unless he depute an able Curate, that may weekly preach and catechize. 1597 HOOKER *Eccl. Pol.* v. lxxx. §2 When a Minister doth serue as a stipendarie Curate. 1614 T. ADAMS *Devil's Banquet* 322 Let vs not take and keepe liuings of an hundred, or two hundred pound a yeare, and allow a poore Curate (to supply the voluntary negligence of our non-residence) eight, or..ten pounds yeerely. 1709 STEELE & SWIFT *Tatler* No. 71 ¶5 Our Vicar..when his Curate.. preaches in the Afternoon..sleeps sotting in the Desk on a Hissock. 1796 *Hull Advertiser* 24 Sept. 3/2 A clergyman has for several years officiated as assistant curate at a very cheap rate. 1844 J. T. HEWLETT *Parsons & W.* xi, The poor perpetual-curate, or sub-vicar. 1883 G. LLOYD *Ebb & Flow* I. 24 Some over-worked curate or sister of mercy. 1892 BLOMFIELD *Hist. Heyford* 51 These three acolytes in succession were curates-in-charge of the parish.

b. ***curate's egg***: taken as a type of something of mixed character (good and bad).

Originating in a story of a meek curate who, having been given a stale egg by his episcopal host, stated that 'parts of it' were 'excellent' (*Punch* 9 Nov. 1895, p. 222).

1905 *Minister's Gazette of Fashion* Aug. 141/1 The past spring and summer season has seen much fluctuation. Like the curate's egg, it has been excellent in parts. 1962 *Oxf. Mag.* 22 Nov. 91/1 All the same it is a curate's egg of a book. While the whole may be somewhat stale and addled, it would be unfair not to acknowledge the merits of some of its parts.

†**3.** One who has a charge; a curator, overseer. *Obs.*

1483 CAXTON *Gold. Leg.* 271/3 What reward yelded the tyrauntes to their curate. 1621 MOLLE *Camerar. Liv. Libr.* III. 197 He caused them [soldiers] all to be hang'd on a tree hard by the castle, and their curat higher than all the rest. 1660 HEXHAM, *Heym-raedt*, the Curates or Overseers of Bancks and Dikes, that the Sea or Water-floods breakes not in.

4. *attrib.* (in quot. *fig.*)

1651 CLEVELAND *Poems* 10 But left the Sun her curate light.

5. a. *jocular.* A small poker (see quot.).

1891 *N. & Q.* 7th Ser. XII. 206/2 A 'curate' is a small auxiliary poker with a steel point, intended for use, in contradistinction to the elaborate fire brasses, which are only kept for show.

b. A cake-stand with two or more tiers. Also called ***curate's comfort, delight, friend***.

1914 G. B. SHAW *Fanny's First Play* III. p. 216 He places the tray on the table. He then goes out for the curate... Juggins returns with the cakes. 1934 M. HARRISON *Weep for Lycidas* I. 152 There were two of those curious stands, known as 'curate's delights', full of cakes. 1937 N. COWARD *Pres. Indic.* v. iii. 180 There..were spread tea-tables ..'Curate's Comforts', and large bowls of strawberries and cream. 1968 M. ALLINGHAM *Cargo of Eagles* xv. 163 A three tier 'curate's friend' cake stand.

6. In Ireland, a spirit-grocer's assistant.

1909 M. HAYDEN & HARTOG in *Fortn. Rev.* Apr. 781 'Curate'..is the assistant to a 'spirit grocer', such as most grocers are in Ireland. 1914 JOYCE *Dubliners* 184 These two gentlemen and one of the curates carried him up the stairs and laid him down again on the floor of the bar.

Hence (chiefly *nonce-wds.*) **ˈcuratess**, the wife of a curate. **cuˈratial** *a.*, having the position of a curate. **cuˈratic, -ical** *a.*, of or pertaining to a curate. **ˈcuratize** *v.*, to act as a curate. **ˈcuratoˌcult, curaˈtolatry**, worship of a curate or curates.

1861 TROLLOPE *Barchester T.* xxi. (D.) A very lowly curate I might perhaps essay to rule; but a curatess would be sure to get the better of me. 1889 G. M. FENN *Cure of Souls* 48 What a charming little curatess she would make! 1886 *Church Rev.* 9 Apr. 180, I now offer to..your curatial readers..Dr. Hayman's table. 1882 *Graphic* 4 Feb. 98 If the curatic period were merely a brief apprenticeship. 1877 LADY WOOD *Sheen's Foreman* I. 239 'The tithe pig's tail' had never tickled his curatical nose. 1801 C. K. SHARPE *Lett.* (1888) I. 103 Her spouse is in the church, and at present curatizing. 1871 *Temple Bar Mag.* Nov. 541 Curatolatry is a light sporadic disorder which spreads a little at certain seasons.

curatel ('kjʊərətɛl). *Roman Law.* [ad. med.L. *cūrātēla*, f. *cūrātus*, *cūrātor*: cf. *tūtēla*. In F. *curatelle*, Ger. *kuratel.*] The position of being under the guardianship of a curator.

1875 POSTE *Gaius* I. Comm. (ed. 2) 119 Wardship and curatel are only incapacities of disposition.

†'**curateship.** *Obs.* [f. CURATE + -SHIP.]

1. The office or position of a curate; a curacy.

1598 FLORIO, *Pieua*, a vicarage, a curatship, a parsonage. **1603** *Const. & Canons Eccl.* §33 Except..he be..admitted ..to some Benefice or Curateship. **1684** tr. *Agrippa's Van. Artes* lxiv. 209 He hath..two Benefices, one Curateship of twenty Crowns, another Priory of forty. **1861** PERRY *Hist. Ch. Eng.* I. xv. 576 In Lincolnshire..there are many miserably poor vicarages and curateships.

2. The personality of a curate. *nonce-use.*

17.. SWIFT *Poems, Parson's Case*, Should fortune shift the scene, And make thy curateship a dean.

3. Curatorship.

1855 LORENZ tr. *Van der Keessel's Sel. Theses* ccccxxi, Wards and others who are under guardianship or curateship.

†**cu'rating**, *vbl. sb.*[1] *Obs.* In *curating-books*, shelf-lists of books in the Bodleian Library, used by its Curators to verify the contents of the shelves.

1705 HEARNE *Collect.* 8 Nov. I. 68 The Curating Books. **1712** *Ibid.* III. 304 Nor can I find by the Curating Book y[t] there ever was.

curating ('kjʊərətɪŋ), *vbl. sb.*[2] [-ING[1].] Acting as curate; performing the duties of a curate.

1831 W. COBBETT *Two-penny Trash* Jan. 159 Non-residence, or stipendiary curating. **1907** E. H. BEGBIE *Vigil* ii. 23, I am to commence vicar. No curating. *Ibid.* v. 68 You have begun curating for me already.

†**cu'ration.** *Obs.* In 4-5 -cioun(e, -cyoun, 4-6 -cion, -cyon. [ME., a. OF. *curacion*, ad. L. *cūrātiōn-em*, n. of action f. *cūrāre* to CURE.]

1. The action of curing; healing, cure.

c **1374** CHAUCER *Troylus* I. 735 þat of þi wo is no curacioun. **1483** CAXTON *Gold. Leg.* 303/1 In medycynal curacion and helynge. **1543** TRAHERON *Vigo's Chirurg.* II. iv. 21 In the curation of a choleryke Aposteme. **1646** SIR T. BROWNE *Pseud. Ep.* II. iii. 74 The method also of curation lately delivered by Daniel Beckherus. **1677** GALE *Crt. Gentiles* II. IV. 143 The curation of the soul from its sin.

2. Curatorship, guardianship.

1769 C. LEE in *G. Colman's Posth. Lett.* (1820) 94 That.. I should have saddled you with the curation of my affairs. **1774** BP. HALLIFAX *Anal. Rom. Law* (1795) 18 History of Curation from its beginning.

curative ('kjʊərətɪv), *a.* (*sb.*). [a. F. *curatif*, *-ive* (15th c.), f. L. *cūrāt-*, ppl. stem of *cūrāre* to CURE: see -IVE.]

I. 1. Of or pertaining to the curing of disease or the healing of wounds.

1533 ELYOT *Cast. Helthe* (1541) 60 b, The part curatiue, whiche treateth of healynge of sycknes. **1541** R. COPLAND *Galyen's Terap.* 2 H iij, Alway the curatyfe indicacions are correspondent to y[e] nombre of y[e] affections and dyseases. **1671** SALMON *Syn. Med.* III. xiii. 349 The Curative part of Medicine. **1800** *Med. Jrnl.* III. 395 Those who have practised the Curative Art in that City. **1878** C. STANFORD *Symb. Christ* viii. 206 Christ's curative miracles.

2. a. Having the tendency or power to cure disease; promoting cure.

1644 BULWER *Chirol.* 147 The conveyance and application of that curative vertue. **1704** F. FULLER *Med. Gymn.* (1711) 4 Consideration of it only as it may prove Curative, not as Palliative. **1865** LIVINGSTONE *Zambesi* ii. 60 This sleeping is curative of what may be incipient sunstroke. **1881** J. SIMON in *Nature* No. 616. 370 Curative medicine.

b. *fig.* Remedial, corrective.

1661 *Origen's Opin.* in *Phenix* (1721) I. 82 All Punishment is curative. **1686** HORNECK *Crucif. Jesus* xix. 542 All afflictions and judgments of this life are curative. **1880** C. H. PEARSON in *Victorian Rev.* 2 Feb. 538 Men..ask whether the plébiscite is to be curative or preventive.

II. as *sb.* A remedial medicine or agent.

1857 D. E. E. BRAMAN *Inform. Texas* i. 15, I place great confidence in the frequent outward use of cold water, as a preventive and curative.

Hence '**curatively** *adv.*; '**curativeness.**

1862 in *Pall Mall G.* 13 Jan. (1885) 4/2 It has shown itself to be curatively deterrent and reformatory. **1875** *Contemp. Rev.* XXV. 303 An element of genuine curativeness. **1879** M. ARNOLD *Irish Cathol.* Mixed Ess. 115 Conscious not of their vain disfigurements of the Christian religion, but of its genuine curativeness.

curator (kjʊ'reɪtə(r), 'kjʊərətə(r)). Forms: 4 curatour, 5 couratour, curature, 5-6 -oure, 6- curator. [Partly a. AF. *curatour* = F. *-ateur* (13th c. in Godefroy Supp.), ad. L. *cūrātor*, *-ōrem*, overseer, guardian, agent-n. f. *cūrāre* (see CURE); partly directly from Latin. The former derivation gave the pronunciation '*curator* in senses 1 and 2; the latter gave *cu'rator*.] One who has the care or charge of a person or thing.

I. Senses derived through AF. *curatour*.

1. One appointed as guardian of the affairs of a person legally unfit to conduct them himself, as a minor, lunatic, etc.; used in *Roman Law*, esp. for the guardian of a minor after the age of tutelage; hence a current term in *Scotch Law*.

1413 LYDG. *Pilgr. Sowle* IV. xxxviii. (1859) 64 They leden the kynge at theyr owne lust, ryght as tutours, and couratours. **1463** *Aberdeen Burgh Rec.* 12 July (Jam. Suppl.), Henry of Culan..of lauchful aige, out of tutoury and has chosine til his curat[our]is to gowerne him. **1555** *Sc. Act Mary* (1597) §35 Quhen onie Minor passis the ȝeires of his Tutorie, and desiris Curatoures. **1590** SWINBURNE *Testaments* 102 b, When he is of the age of 14. yeeres..the minor maie then..choose a curator, either the same person that was tutor or some other. *a* **1649** DRUMM. OF HAWTH. *Hist. Jas. V*, Wks. (1711) 86 A quarrel..arising between the curators of the laird of Langton, and one of his uncles. **1651** HOBBES *Leviath.* I. xvi. 82 Mad-men that have no use of Reason, may be Personated by Guardians, or Curators. **1753** W. STEWART in *Scots Mag.* Mar. 132/2 He is tutor and curator..to several orphans. **1848** WHARTON *Law Lex.* 281/2 In England, the guardian performs the offices both of a tutor and a curator, under the Roman law. **1891** *Pall Mall G.* 12 Nov. 6/1 The Dukes of Fife and Westminster as curators for the Duke of Sutherland's younger sons, oppose the petition.

†**2.** One who has the cure of souls; = CURATE 1.

1362 LANGL. *P. Pl.* A. I. 169 Curatours þat schulden kepe hem clene of heore bodies þei beoþ cumbred in care. **1377** *Ibid.* B. xx. 279 For persones and parish prestes þat shulde þe peple shryue, Ben curatoures called to knowe and to hele, Alle þat ben her parisshiens. *c* **1425** WYNTOUN *Cron.* VII. vi. 29 He wald..Mak for þis man swa gret prayere, As if he had bene his curature. *c* **1450** MYRC 11 Wharefore þou preste curatoure, ȝef þou plese thy sauyoure.

II. Modern senses, from L. *curator*.

3. *gen.* A person who has charge; a manager, overseer, steward.

1632 LITHGOW *Trav.* IX. (1682) 364 The Oven producing at one time three or four hundred living Chickens..for the Hatcher or Curator, is only Recompenced according to the living numbers. **1691** T. H[ALE] *Acc. New Invent.* 34 They who.. are by the Crown made..Curators of the Health and Safety of its Ships. **1755** *Gentl. Mag.* XXV. 495 The orthography might be in some measure altered by the curator of the impression. **1862** RUSKIN *Munera P.* (1880) 29 The real state of men of property being, too commonly, that of curators, not possessors, of wealth.

4. *spec.* in *Universities.* **a.** In some foreign universities: A member of a board (or an individual official) having the general superintendence of the whole university, and the power to select or nominate professors. **b.** In the University of Oxford: A member of one of the committees or boards having the charge of various portions of University property, as the Curators of the University Chest, of the Bodleian Library, etc. So at Durham. **c.** In the Scottish Universities: A member of the body charged with the election of a number of the professors.

a. 1691 WOOD *Ath. Oxon.* I. 406 The curators of that University [Leyden] gave him an yearly stipend. **1727-51** CHAMBERS *Cycl.* s.v., The curators are chosen by the states of each province: the university of Leyden has three; the burghermasters of the city have a fourth. **1834** SIR W. HAMILTON *Discuss.* 358 The curator [at Pisa] was charged with the general superintendence of student and professor; and whatever directly or indirectly concerned the well-being of the University, was within his sphere. **1840** *Penny Cycl.* XVIII. 322/1 An excellent system of public education ..was introduced by the university of Vilna under the superintendence of its curator Prince Adam Czartoryski. **b. 1693** *Oxford Act* II. 11 Next the Curators [of the Theatre] must take care No breach of Peace be suffer'd there. **1710** in H. Bedford *Vind. Ch. Eng.* 172 The Curators in their Annual Visitation of the Library. **1893** *Oxford Univ. Cal.*, Curators of the Bodleian Library..Curators of the Indian Institute..Curators of the Park, etc. **c. 1858** *Universities of Scotl. Act* (21-2 *Vict.* c. 83 §13) The Right of Nomination or Presentation to the Office of Principal and to all Professorships in the University of Edinburgh..exercised by the Town Council of Edinburgh ..shall be transferred..to..Seven Curators.

5. The officer in charge of a museum, gallery of art, library, or the like; a keeper, custodian.

In many cases the official title of the chief keeper.

1661 EVELYN *Diary* 19 July, In which [diving-bell] our curator continued half an hour under water. **1667** *Phil. Trans.* II. 486 The Curator of the Royal Society. **1767** HUNTER *Ibid.* LVIII. 42 The Curators of the British Musæum. **1837** LOCKHART *Scott* vii, In June 1795 he was appointed one of the Curators of the Advocate's library. **1889** *Whitaker's Almanack* 160 Museum of Practical Geology..Curator, Registrar and Librarian.

6. A designation of public officers of various kinds under the Roman Empire.

1728 H. HERBERT tr. *Fleury's Eccl. Hist.* II. 16 Callidius Gratianus who was Curator in the year 314. **1841** W. SPALDING *Italy & It. Isl.* I. 103 The city was..divided into fourteen regions, each of which had two police superintendents, called Curators.

curatorial (kjʊərə'tɔərɪəl), *a.* [f. L. *cūrātōri-us* (f. *cūrātōr-em* curator) + -AL[1].] Of or pertaining to a curator.

1754 ERSKINE *Princ. Sc. Law* (1809) 65 They may authenticate tutorial and curatorial inventories. **1834** SIR W. HAMILTON *Discuss.* (1852) 362 On the curatorial system likewise was established the excellence of the classical schools of Holland. *a* **1854** E. FORBES in Wilson & Geikie *Mem.* xi. 353 My revenues, professorial and curatorial, being as yet small.

curatorship (kjʊ'reɪtəʃɪp). [f. CURATOR + -SHIP.] The office or position of a curator.

1590 SWINBURNE *Testaments* 246 If the names be artificiall, not naturall, as to use proctorship, for curatorship. **1726** AYLIFFE *Parergon* 186 They..are exempted..from Guardianships, Curatorships and the like. **1861** WILSON & GEIKIE *Mem. E. Forbes* xi. 351 His acceptance of the Curatorship of the Zoological Society.

curatory ('kjʊərətərɪ), *sb.* [ad. L. *cūrātōria* guardianship, f. *cūrātor*: see above.]

1. The office or charge of a curator; curatorship; chiefly in *Roman* and *Sc. Law.*

1560 *Bk. Discipl. Ch. Scot.* (1621) 46 That the Rector..be exempted from..any other charge..such as tutorie, curatorie, executorie, and the like. **1672** *Sc. Acts Chas. II*, c. 2 Gifts of Tutory or Curatory. **1862** DALZEL *Hist. Edin. Univ.* I. 243, My curatory of the library distracts me. **1880** MUIRHEAD *Gaius* I. §142 Some are under tutory or curatory, and others under neither of those guardianships.

2. A college of curators in a foreign university.

1834 SIR W. HAMILTON *Discuss.* (1852) 360 The most illustrious scholars in the curatory [of Leyden].

'**curatory**, *a.* [ad. L. *cūrātōri-us*, f. *cūrātor*; in mod. use referred to *cūrāre*, *cūrāt-* to CURE.] Of or pertaining to curing or healing; curative.

1644 BULWER *Chirol.* 148 The curetorie miracles..The exorcists..used this curatorie adjunct. **1681** tr. *Willis' Rem. Med. Wks.* Vocab., *Therapeutick*, the curatory art of medicine. **1854** *Blackw. Mag.* LXXVI. 309 The ordinary curatory process.

curatrix (kjʊ'reɪtrɪks). [L. *cūrātrix*, fem. of *cūrātor* guardian, etc., in F. *curatrice.* Cudworth uses it in a sense taken from the medical sense of *cūrāre* to CURE.]

†**1.** A female healer or curer. *Obs. nonce-wd.*

1678 CUDWORTH *Intell. Syst.* 167 That Nature of Hippocrates, that is the Curatrix of Diseases.

2. A female curator or guardian.

1846 in WORCESTER; whence in later Dicts.

curats, obs. form of CUIRASS.

†**curature.** *Obs.*—[1] [a. OF. *curature*, or ad. L. *cūrātūra* (f. *cūrāre*: see CURE *v.*).]

= CURATORSHIP.

1605 RALEIGH *Introd. Hist. Eng.* (1693) 31 Philip..King of France, was a Child..and..was under the Curature of Baudovin Earl of Flanders. **1730-6** BAILEY (folio), *Curature*, care in ordering or managing any thing.

curature, obs. form of CURATOR.

curb (kɜːb), *sb.* Forms: 5-7 corbe, curbe, 6-7 courbe, 7 courb, corb, kurbe, 7- curb (*dial.* 6-7 crubb(e, 9 crub); also *β.* (chiefly in senses 8-13) 7 kerbe, 7-9 kirb, 9 kerb. See also CRUB. [The senses here placed all derive ultimately from F. *courbe* adj. (= Pr. *corb*, Sp., Pg., It. *curvo*):—L. *curvus* bent, crooked, or from F. *courber*:—L. *curvāre*: see CURB *v.*[1] But their immediate etymological history presents differences, and Branches I and II might be treated as distinct words. Branch I appears only in Eng., and seems to be a derivative from CURB *v.*[1], in the sense 'that which *curbs* or bends the horse's neck'; it seems to be the source of CURB *v.*[2], under the influence of which again some of the senses under Branch III have arisen. Branch II contains a variety of senses found under F. *courbe*, subst. use of *courbe* adj. Branch III appears also to have originated in F. *courbe* in the sense of a curved or arched piece of timber, iron, etc. used for structural purposes; but the sense appears to have been gradually modified after CURB *v.*[2], so as to involve more and more the sense of a restraining or confining border. In this group the word is often spelt KERB, which is at present established in sense 12. Cf. KENNEL.]

I. 1. A chain or strap passing under the lower jaw of a horse, and fastened to the upper ends of the branches of the bit; used chiefly for checking an unruly horse.

The reins being attached to the lower ends of the branches of the bit, leverage is obtained for forcing the chain against the jaw of the horse.

1477 EARL RIVERS (Caxton) *Dictes* 52 If he yeue him [a strong hors] not a strong bitte with a corbe, he shal neuer con gouerne him. **1530** PALSGR. 209/1 Courbe for a bridell, *gourmette.* **1590** SPENSER *F.Q.* I. i. 1 His angry steede did chide his foming bitt, As much disdayning to the curbe to yield. **1684** R. H. *Sch. Recreat.* 24 A plain watering Chain, Cheek large, and the Kirb, thick round and big. **1782** COWPER *Gilpin* xxii, That trot became a gallop soon In spite of curb and rein. **1835** W. IRVING *Tour Prairies* 180 This fine young animal..reduced to..pass his life under the harness and the curb.

2. *fig.* Anything that curbs or restrains; a check, restraint.

1613 SYLVESTER *Microcosmogr.* Wks. 800 Service is to the Lofty minde A Curb, a Spur to th' abiect Hinde. **1632** J. HAYWARD tr. *Biondi's Eromena* 112 So checkt was his forwardnesse with the curbe of bashfulnesse. **1720** OZELL *Vertot's Rom. Rep.* I. VII. 417 A Dictator, whose Authority might be a Curb upon the Cabals and Intrigues of the Tribunes. **1854-6** PATMORE *Angel in Ho.* I. II. ix, In what rough sort he chid his wife For want of curb upon her tongue. **1871** G. MEREDITH *H. Richmond* xxxiv. (1889) 352 My temper was beginning to chafe at the curb.

3. *Electric Telegr.* A method of signalling through a long cable, by sending a powerful signal followed by one or more weak signals of opposite sign, the effect of which is to 'curb' or prevent the main signal from lingering in the cable; a signal transmitted in this way. Only in *Comb.*, as ***curb-key***, ***curb sender*** (an instrument for transmitting signals in this way); ***curb-sending***, ***-signal***.

1867 CULLEY *Handbk. Pract. Telegr.* (ed. 2) 247 Arrangements..for discharging a cable rapidly, and for equalising the effect of dashes and dots; the most effective of which is the curb key. **1877** *Jrnl. Soc. Telegr. Eng.* V. 213 The object of the automatic curb-sender is to diminish the retardation of signals in long cables. **1877** *Telegraphic Jrnl.* 1 Feb. 27 This system of using two currents, one to produce the signal and the other..to neutralize..the residual effect of the first, is what is known as Curb-Sending. *Ibid.*, Trials have been made..to send curb-signals by means of a hand-key.

II. Corresp. to F. *courbe* sb. in various senses.

4. A hard swelling on the hock or other part of a horse's leg; the disease characterized by these.

1523 FITZHERB. *Husb.* § 107 A courbe is an yll sorance, and maketh a horse to halte sore, and appereth vppon the hynder legges..vnder the camborell place. **1616** SURFL. & MARKH. *Country Farme* 145 *margin*, The courbe, or a long swelling beneath the elbow of the hough. **1695** *Lond. Gaz.* No. 3132/4 One brown Gelding..a Curb on his near Hock. **1741** *Compl. Fam. Piece* III. 458 For the Curb, you must leave out the Mercury. **1844** *Regul. & Ord. Army* 380 The Horses..show no tendency to Curb or Spavin.

†**5.** A curve, an arc. [F. *courbe.*] *Obs. rare.*

1601 HOLLAND *Pliny* I. 118 The very coasts of this streight Bosphorus..boweth and windeth like a curb to Mœotis. **1759** tr. *Montaigne* III. iii. 51 The form of my study is round ..so that the curb presents me with a view of all my books.

6. A mould or template by which to mark out curved work. (Sometimes spelt *kerb.*)

1792 P. NICHOLSON *Carpenter's New Guide* (1801) 21 The ceiling wants to be hollowed out..I shall..show the method of making a curb for that purpose..A curve being traced round the points of intersection, will give the form of the curb. **1859** DONALDSON & GLEN *Specifications* 582 The Carpenter is to..provide all kerbs and trammels for tanks and vaults.

†**7.** *Thieves' cant.* A hook. *Obs.*

1591 [see CURBER 2].

III. An enclosing framework or border: in the first place, the curved border of something round, but eventually applied also to things straight.

The name appears to have originally connoted the *curved outline* merely, and to have gradually taken more and more from the sense of CURB *v.*², until this became the characteristic notion, and that of curvature entirely disappeared. Also spelt *kerb* (†*kirb*).

8. a. A frame or 'coaming' round the top of a well (to which the lids or covers are fastened).

1511 *MS. Acc. St. John's Hosp. Canterb.*, Payd for mendyng off a boket off sen johnys welle *jd*..for a stapylle & a hooke *jd*..for..ij corbys ijs iiij*d*. **1512** *Ibid.*, For mendyng off þe corbe of a bowt þe welle. **1610** *Ibid.*, For caryng of the courb of the well to Ivy leane. **1807** HUTTON *Course Math.* II. 252 A carpenter is to put an oaken curb to a round well, at 8*d*. per foot square: the breadth of the curb is to be 7½ inches, and the diameter within 3½ feet. **1839** SIR C. FELLOWS *Trav. Asia Minor* (1852) 18 The mouths or curbs of the wells are formed of the capitals of extremely fine Corinthian pillars.

b. A framing round the top of a brewer's copper; **c.** An aperture in a floor or roof to support a trap-door or sky-light.

1664 EVELYN *Sylva* I. iv. § 15 [Elm] scarce has any superior for kerbs of coppers. **1743** *Lond. & Country Brew.* III. (ed. 2) 211 Fastening his two wooden Doors just above the Curb of the Copper. **1852–61** *Archit. Publ. Soc. Dict.* s.v. *Curb*, The name curb is also given..to the frame of..a skylight. **1859** DONALDSON & GLEN *Specifications* 566 The top being prepared to receive the continuous kerb for the grating. *Ibid.* 578 The floor grating to the Hall is to be fitted with a curb of York stone..rebated on the top edge for the grating.

9. A circular plate or cylindrical ring of timber or iron round the edge of any circular structure (usually to hold it firmly together).

a. A circular or other curvilinear wall-plate at the springing of a dome.

b. A cylindrical ring around the 'eye' of a dome or similar structure, into which the ribs are framed (sometimes supporting a lantern or cupola).

c. The 'race-plate' on the top of the fixed portion of a windmill, on which travel the rollers of the cap as it rotates; also, the circular plate or ring at the base of the cap of a windmill, carrying the rollers.

1733 F. PRICE *Brit. Carpenter* (1753) 28 The kirb, on which stands a lanthorn, or cupola. **1793** SMEATON *Edystone L.* § 48 One Kirb or circle of compass timber at each floor. **1820** TREDGOLD *Carpentry* (1853) 219 The brick dome..of St. Mark, at Venice..was built upon a curb of larch timber ..intended to resist the tendency which a dome has to spread outwards at the base. **1857** J. WALKER *Specif. Whitby High Lantern*, The curb at the top for receiving the ends of the rafters is to consist of a ring of gun-metal. **1885** A. R. WOLFF *Windmill* 64 The cap, or head, of the mill..is made of timber..with a circular curb at the lower part, which revolves upon the one attached to the body of the mill..The rollers..are attached to the upper curb, and revolve against the..lower one.

10. A cylindrical ring of timber, iron, etc. forming the base on which the brickwork of a shaft or well is constructed.

This 'curb' may be built into the crown of the arch of a tunnel, as in the case of a ventilating shaft (cf. 9 b); or it may, as in the construction of a mine-shaft, descend with the steening which it bears, as the excavation proceeds.

1811 FAREY *Derbyshire* I. 327 A curb, or flat ring of sound oak or elm is laid on the bottom, on which the stones or bricks are built to the top. The sinking is then begun within this curb. **1838** F. W. SIMMS *Public Wks. Gt. Brit.* 32 The brickwork shall rest upon a cast-iron curb, fitting into the crown of the arch of the tunnel, forming a level base for the shaft to rest upon. **1844** —— *Tunnelling* 46 The sinking was attempted by means of a barrel (or drum) curb, which upon being undermined descended by its own weight and that of the brickwork (which was constructed upon the curb). *Ibid.* 109 The shaft..can be securely connected with the crown of the tunnel, by means of a curb of brick or cast iron.

11. a. A raised margin or edging around an oast, to confine the hops; also round a bed in a garden or hothouse, or round a hearth, to serve as a fender.

1731–7 MILLER *Gard. Dict.* s.v. *Lupulus*, The Hops must be spread even upon the Oast a Foot thick or more, if the Depth of the Curb will allow it. **1881** *Gard. Chron.* No. 412. 655 The curbs are filled with a nice lot of plants. **1882** *Worc. Exhib. Catal.* iii. 3 Polished brass curb.

b. An inclined circular plate placed round the edge of a soap or salt kettle to prevent the contents from boiling over.

1874 in KNIGHT *Dict. Mech.*

12. a. A margin of stone or other strong material protecting the outer edge of a side-walk and separating it from the roadway on which horses and vehicles travel. In this sense the spelling is now usu. *curb* in U.S., *kerb* in U.K.

1836 *Libr. Entert. Knowl., Pompeii* (ed. 4) I. 91 These curbs [in woodcut, marked 'kirb']..separate the foot pavement from the road. **1861** SMILES *Engineers* II. 29 In fixing the kerbs along the London footpaths. **1882** *Nature* XXV. 517 The idea is to make the curb of the pavement in the form of an iron box.

transf. **1867** HOWELLS *Ital. Journ.* 124 Leaning on the curb of the precipitous rock.

b. The body of curbstone brokers. *U.S.*

1903 *Nation* (N.Y.) 4 June 446 The Stock Exchange and the 'curb'..gave..plain evidence what their opinion was.

13. In various other technical senses, some of which are difficult to classify.

a. *Archit.*, *Building*, etc. An edge or 'nosing', as e.g. to a step; also a raised band (not sufficiently high to be a 'dwarf wall') to receive the lower ends of the palisades or railings of an enclosure or partition; a breast-wall or retaining-wall to hold up a bank of earth; one of the plates forming the top of the sides of a green-house: the lower of the two planes forming the slope of a curb- or mansard-roof; 'the flashing of lead over the curb-plate to a curb-roof'; 'the woodwork forming the arris of a plaster-work groin' (*Archit. Publ. Soc. Dict.*); also applied to a 'crib' or cage to contain concrete until hardened, as in a foundation.

b. The cylindrical casing within which a vortex-turbine wheel revolves; also the curved guide encompassing part of the periphery of a breast-wheel or scoop-wheel to confine and direct the water against its buckets or floats.

†**c.** A 'stilling' or stand in a brewery to support a cask, etc. *Obs.*

1819 P. NICHOLSON *Archit. Dict.* I. 308 *Curb* for Brick Steps, a timber nosing..not only to prevent the steps from wearing, but also from being dislocated. **1852–61** *Archit. Publ. Soc. Dict.* s.v., The edge, to a brick or tile step, is also called a *curb*, even if it be merely a stone or timber nosing. *Ibid.*, Where wrought iron railing bars set close are let into it..a cast iron curb is now much used. *Ibid.*, The plane, *a b* [of the roof] is popularly called the *curb.* **1859** DONALDSON & GLEN *Specifications* 619 Kerb part of the tower roof is to be covered with 6 lb. lead..the surface of the kerbs is to be turned up against the cheeks of the dormers.

1825 FOSBROKE *Encycl. Antiq.* I. 364 Ancient brew-houses had troughs of lead set on the ground, or on courbes.

†**14.** Of uncertain meaning. *Obs.*

1495 *Will of Sir R. Porter* (Somerset Ho.), I bequeith to the church of Conway a furnesse and a Curbe of lede to hill [= cover, roof] the church with. **1527** *Lanc. Wills* (Chetham Soc.) 36 Item I beqweth..a grett pott off brasse and my corbes of leyde a grat of hyron. Item a broche of yron.

IV. 15. *attrib.* and *Comb.* **curb-bit**, **-bridle**, a bit (or bridle) with a curb; **curb-chain**, a chain acting as a curb; **curb-hook**, 'a hook which the curb is hitched to' (Felton *Carriages* Gloss.); **curb-key**, **-sender**, **-signal** (see 3); **curb-market**, **-price**, **-stocks** *U.S.* (cf. CURB-STONE b and KERB *sb.*); **curb-pin** (see quot. 1874); **curb service** *N. Amer.*, service by a shop, etc., to customers in cars at the street curb. Also CURB-PLATE, -ROOF, -STONE.

1688 R. HOLME *Armoury* III. 305/2 Mr. Morgan calls..a Bit or Snaffle..Curbs or *Curb Bits. **1710** *Lond. Gaz.* No. 4698/4 A white Bridle, with a very light Kirb Bit. **1847** YOUATT *Horse* i. 15 To the Romans may be attributed the invention of the curb-bit. **1677** *Lond. Gaz.* No. 1163/4 A green velvet Saddle..and a *curb Bridle. **1795** WOLCOTT (P. Pindar) *Pindariana* Wks. 1812 IV. 213 For those passions make a strong Curb-bridle. **1833** J. HOLLAND *Manuf. Metal* II. 312 This rise in the bit is made to press hard against the roof of the horse's mouth, at the same time that the *curb chain closely presses the chin. **1900** S. A. NELSON *ABC of Wall St.* 10 The *curb market, with its swarm of brokers. **1914** *N.Y. Herald* 17 Nov. 6/4 Prices again strong in curb market. **1874** KNIGHT *Dict. Mech.*, *Curb-pins, the pins on the lever of a watch-regulator which embrace the hair-spring of the balance and regulate its vibrations. **1884** F. J. BRITTEN *Watch & Clockm.* 106 A balance spring uncontrolled by curb pins. **1930** *San Antonio* (Texas) *Light* 31 Jan., Closing *Curb Prices. **1931** *Kansas City Star* 25 Aug., The hoppers sit on the curb in front of the drug store, honk and attack the *curb service boys when they come out. **1938** *Archit. Rev.* LXXXIV. 137 (*caption*) A curb-service restaurant in Washington, D.C. **1962** *Canadian Jrnl. Linguistics* VII. 73 A culture pattern based on the automobile, with its motels, filling stations, and curb-service. **1915** *World's Work* (N.Y.) Oct. 641 Unlisted (*Curb) Stocks.

†**curb**, *v.*¹ *Obs. rare.* [A later spelling of COURBE *v.*, a. F. *courber* to bend, prob. influenced in form by CURB *v.*², and by CURVE, when this was coming in from Latin.]

1. *trans.* To bend, bow, curve. See also CURBED *ppl. a.*¹

1430 [see COURBE *v.* 2]. **1662** H. MORE *Philos. Writ.* Pref. Gen. (1712) 15 [The Spirit of Nature] curbs the matter of the Sun into rounds of figure, which would otherwise be oblong.

2. *intr.* To bend, bow, cringe.

1377 [see COURBE *v.* 1]. **1602** SHAKS. *Ham.* III. iv. 155 [see COURBE *v.* 1: *mod. edd.* curb]. *a* **1649** DRUMM. OF HAWTH. *Cypress Grove* Wks. (1711) 121 Bodies languishing and curbing. **1808** J. BARLOW *Columb.* VI. 26 [They] bow the knee And curb, well pleased, O Cruelty, to thee.

curb (kɜːb), *v.*² [In Branch I, dating back to 16th c., app. f. CURB *sb.* 1; Branch II is much later, f. CURB *sb.* 12.]

I. 1. *trans.* To put a curb on (a horse); to restrain or control with a curb.

1530 PALSGR. 500/1, I courbe a horse, I fasten the courbe under his chynne. **1667** MILTON *P.L.* XI. 643 Part wield thir Arms, part courb the foaming Steed. **1878** M. A. BROWN *Nadeschda* 25 Curbing his fiery steed..with foaming bit.

2. *fig.* To restrain, check, keep in check.

1588 J. UDALL *Diotrephes* (Arb.) 10 Bridles to curbe them that kicke at their lordlines. **1607** SHAKS. *Cor.* III. i. 39 To curbe the will of the Nobilitie. *a* **1631** DONNE *Paradoxes* (1652) 25 To curbe our naturall appetites. **1726** *Adv. Capt. R. Boyle* 106 She begg'd me to curb my transport, for fear of being overheard. **1848** MACAULAY *Hist. Eng.* I. 217 To curb the power of France.

†**b.** Const. *of*, *from*. *Obs.*

1593 SHAKS. *Rich. II*, I. i. 54 The faire reuerence of your Highnesse curbes mee, From giuing reines and spurres to my free speech. **1596** —— *Merch. V.* IV. i. 217 Curbe this cruell diuell of his will. **1719** W. WOOD *Surv. Trade* 297 To curb or restrain our own Subjects from their natural Rights.

II. 3. To furnish or defend with a curb or curb-stone. (In the latter case commonly *kerb.*)

1861 *Sunderland Times* 21 Sept., That the footpath behind Cumberland-terrace be flagged and kerbed. **1874** KNIGHT *Dict. Mech.* s.v. *Curb*, In sinking wells by sections which are curbed before another section is excavated. *Ibid.*, The well at Southampton was..curbed in this way. **1878** *N. Amer. Rev.* CXXVII. 441 Curbed, lighted, sewered, and repaved.

III. †**4.** *Thieves' cant.* (See CURBER 2.) [Perhaps a distinct word.] *Obs.*

a **1592** GREENE *Theeves falling out* in *Harl. Misc.* VIII. 389 (D.) Though you can foyst, nip, prig, lift, curbe, and use the black art.

curbable (ˈkɜːbəb(ə)l), *a.* [f. CURB *v.*² + -ABLE.] That can be curbed or restrained.

1775 in ASH *Suppl.*; and in mod. Dicts.

curbash: see KOORBASH.

†**curbed**, *ppl. a.*¹ Also courbed. [f. CURB *v.*¹] Bent, bowed, curved.

[*c* **1430** LYDG. *Bochas* I. xx. (1554) 36 b, Thing yᵗ is courbyd or wrong..To make it seme as it went vpright. *c* **1450** *Merlin* 261 Longe and courbed, and brode sholderes and leene for age.] **1541** R. COPLAND *Guydon's Quest. Chirurg.*, The lyuer..is of fygure as of the moone, curbed towarde the rybbes. **1603** HOLLAND *Plutarch's Mor.* 678 (R.) By crooked and curbed lines. **1646** G. DANIEL *Poems* Wks. 1878 I. 50 Her haire vndrest, Like Adders on her Curbed Shoulders falls. **1691** RAY *Creation* II. (1704) 231 Though the Course of the Sun be curbed towards the Tropicks.

curbed (kɜːbd), *ppl. a.*² [f. CURB *sb.* and *v.*²]

1. Furnished with or having a curb.

1675 *Lond. Gaz.* No. 975/4 An old curbed Bridle. **1695** *Ibid.* 3048/4 Kirb'd Bridle. **1847** YOUATT *Horse* i. 10 The severe and often cruel curbed-bit.

b. *curbed roof* = CURB-ROOF.

1866 *Intell. Observ.* No. 57. 178 Zinc-work on the curbed roofs.

2. *fig.* Restrained, checked.

1597 SHAKS. *2 Hen. IV*, IV. v. 131 The Fift Harry, from curb'd License pluckes The muzzle of restraint. **1862** LD. BROUGHAM *Brit. Const.* xi. 157 Stephen..owed his curbed authority to the constant rebellion of his Barons.

curber (ˈkɜːbə(r)). Also 6 courber, 7 curbar. [f. CURB *v.*² + -ER¹.]

1. One who or that which curbs, or restrains.

1610 HEALEY *St. Aug. Citie of God* 45 Carthage..the greatest curber and terror of the Roman weale-publike. **1737** L. CLARKE *Hist. Bible* VIII. (1740) 568 Great curbers of their passions. *a* **1849** J. C. MANGAN *Poems* (1859) 37 The instructress of maidens And curber of boys.

†**2.** *Thieves' cant.* (See quot. 1591.) *Obs.* [Perhaps a distinct word.]

1591 GREENE *2nd Pt. Conny-catch.* (1592) 24 The Courber, which the common people call the Hooker, is he that with a Curb (as they tearm it) or hook, doth pul out of a window any loose linnen cloth, apparell, or..other houshold stuffe. **1602** ROWLANDS *Greene's Ghost* (1860) 41 A hooker, whom Conicatching English cals Curbar.

†**'curbing,** *vbl. sb.*[1] *Obs.* [f. CURB *v.*[1]] Curving, curvature.

1601 HOLLAND *Pliny* II. 315 The curbing or crookednesse of the ridge-bone.

curbing ('kɜːbɪŋ), *vbl. sb.*[2] [f. CURB *v.*[2]]

1. The action of the verb CURB; checking.

1661 FELTHAM *Resolves* II. lvii. 306 The curbings and the stroaks of Adversity. **1846** D. KING *Lord's Supper* iv. 102 The partial curbing of vicious lusts.

2. a. The furnishing of a side-walk, etc. with a curb. **b.** *concr.* The stones collectively forming a curb. (In this sense commonly spelt *kerbing.*)

1838 J. HALL *Notes Western States* viii. 106 After removing the rich soil, a stratum of hard clay presents itself, then gravel, and then another layer of clay, all of which are so compact as to require no curbing. **1869** *Daily News* 2 Feb., The granite kerbing on the sea wall. **1892** *Times* 14 Mar. 3/2 No paving, curbing, or channelling has been done to..the road.

†**3.** *Thieves' cant.* (Cf. CURBER 2.) *Obs.* [Perhaps a distinct word.]

1591 GREENE *Disc. Coosnage* (1859) 53 The nature of the Lift, the Black art, and the Curbing law, which is the Filchers and theeves that come into houses..or picklocks, or hookers at windowes.

'curbing, *ppl. a.* [f. CURB *v.*[2]] That curbs; restraining.

1719 D'URFEY *Pills* (1872) VI. 319 Who from thinking are free, That curbing Disease i' the Mind. **1794** SULLIVAN *View Nat.* IV. 66 'To say..that religion is not a curbing motive, because it does not always restrain, is' [etc.].

†**'curble.** *Obs.* Also 6-7 **kirble.** [Derivative of CURB, app. diminutive in form.]

1. = CURB *sb.* 1. Also *attrib.*

1598 FLORIO, *Guancetto*, a little claspe or kirble hooke about a horses bit. **1614** MARKHAM *Cheap Husb.* I. ii. (1668) 24 The kirble shall be thick, round, and large, hanging loosely upon his nether lip.

2. = CURB *sb.* 8.

?**1780** *Five Wonders of World* 6 Hoops in women's petticoats almost as big as a well's curble.

'curbless, *a. rare.* [f. CURB *sb.* + -LESS.] Without curb or restraint.

1813 T. BUSBY tr. *Lucretius* III. 322 The curbless rage inflames his savage blood. **1848** C. BRONTE *J. Eyre* ix, A torrent, turbid and curbless.

'curb-plate. [CURB *sb.* 8, 9.] A curvilinear wall-plate at the springing of a dome, etc.; = CURB 9 a, b; also, the plate or frame round the mouth of a well, etc.; the horizontal timber at the junction of the upper and lower slopes of a curb-roof.

1819 P. NICHOLSON *Archit. Dict.* I. 308 The wall-plate of a circular or elliptically ribbed dome, is termed a *curb-plate*, as also the horizontal rib at the top, on which the vertical ribs terminate. **1860** J. NEWLANDS *Carpenter & Joiner's Assist.* 257 *Curb-plate*..the circular frame of a well.

'curb-roof. [CURB *sb.*] A roof of which each face has two slopes, the lower one steeper than the upper; a mansard-roof.

1733 F. PRICE *Brit. Carpenter* (1753) 18, B is called a kirb roof, and is much in use, on account of its giving so much room withinside. **1820** TREDGOLD *Carpentry* (1853) 95 It appears to have been with a view of lessening..height that the Mansard or curb roof was invented. **1879** D. J. HILL *Bryant* 143 A spacious..mansion..with a curb-roof, antique dormer windows.

curb-sender: see CURB *sb.* 3.

'curb-stone, kerb-stone. Also kirb-stone. One of the stones forming a curb, *esp.* at the edge of a side-path; hence, the stone edge of a side-path.

1791 *Act 31 Geo. III* c. 65 §124 Curb Stone from Eleven to Thirteen Inches wide and from Five to Seven Inches thick. **1806-7** J. BERESFORD *Miseries Hum. Life* (1826) XVIII. iii. 132 The two side-spaces from the wall to the kirb-stone. **1850** KINGSLEY *Alt. Locke* v, You goes and lies on the kerb-stone. **1862** ANSTED *Channel Isl.* I. iv. (ed. 2) 66 Black Guernsey granite for macadamised paving and curb stones.

b. *attrib.*, as **curb-stone broker** (*U.S.*), a broker, not a member of the stock exchange, who transacts business in the streets; also **curbstone agent, operator.**

1848 W. ARMSTRONG *Stocks* 7 This class comprehends.. all those petty operators and non-descripts, who have neither a local habitation or scarcely, a name, that are dignified by the title of curb-stone brokers. **1860** in BARTLETT *Dict. Amer.* **1861** *Knickerbocker* LVII. 635 All sorts of brokers, from the leading houses down to the curbstone 'operator'. **1862** R. B. KIMBALL *Undercurrents* (1868) 321 It is rather a habit with the Curbstone operator when he gets severely winged, to go into the cigar business. **1884** *Cent. Mag.* Aug. 629/2 Peddling 'privileges' to small speculators through curb-stone agents. **1886** *Pall Mall G.* 28 May 14/1 Both of these men are kerbstone brokers.

curbulȝe, obs. Sc. form of CUIR-BOUILLI.

curby ('kɜːbɪ), *a.* [f. CURB *sb.* + -Y.] Liable to be affected with curb (see CURB *sb.* 4). Hence **'curbily** *adv.*

1841 MEESON & WELSBY *Reports* VIII. 132 The term 'curby hocks' indicated a peculiar form of the hock, which was considered as rendering the horse more liable to throw out a curb. **1875** 'STONEHENGE' *Brit. Sports* II. VI. 564 Curby hocks are also hereditary, and should be avoided. **1892** *Sport. & Dram. News* 21 May 360/1 That off hock..was always rather 'curbily' inclined.

curce, obs. form of CURSE.

curch (kɜːtʃ). *Sc.* Forms: 5 **kerche, (courchie),** 5-6 **courch(e, curche, (6 cowrtche), 7 kerch, (8 kirch, 9 kertch), 7- curch.** [An erroneous singular of *curches*, repr. OF. *couvrechés, -chiés*, pl. of *couvrechef*: see COVERCHIEF, KERCHIEF.]

A covering for the head; a kerchief; 'a square piece of linen used in former times by women, instead of a cap or mutch' (Jamieson).

1447 BOKENHAM *Seyntys* (Roxb.) 285 She hyr wolde arayin ful porely..and..Up on hyr hede leyn a foule kerche. **1457** *Sc. Acts Jas. II*, c. 71 On theer heads short curches.. Courchies of theer awin making. *c* **1470** HENRY *Wallace* I. 241 A soudly courche our hed and nek leit fall. **15..** *Peebles to Play*, Ane said, 'My curches are not press'd'. **1530** *Inv.* in *Nugæ Derelictæ* (1880) x. 9 Item xxi neipkins and brest cowrtchis. Itm thre nek cowrtchis. **1698** M. MARTIN *Voy. Kilda* (1749) 50 The Kerch, or Head-dress worn by herself. **1810** SCOTT *Lady of L.* III. v. *note*, The snood was exchanged for the curch, toy, or coif, when a Scottish lass passed, by marriage, into the matron state. **1854** MRS. OLIPHANT *Magd. Hepburn* I. 150 An old woman with long grey locks escaping from her curch. **1900** A. CARMICHAEL *Carmina Gadelica* I. p. xxv, On the morning after the marriage the mother of the bride..placed the 'breid tri chearnach', three-cornered kertch, on the head of the bride before she rose from her bed. *Ibid.*, The feast of the 'bord breid', kertch table, was almost as great as the feast of the marriage table.

curchee, -ie, -y, obs. forms of CURTSY.

curchef, -chyfe, obs. forms of KERCHIEF.

‖**Curculio** (kɜːˈkjuːlɪəʊ). *Entom.* [a. L. *curculio, -ōnem* corn-weevil.] A Linnæan genus of Beetles, containing the Weevils. Now applied especially to the common fruit-weevils, which are very destructive to plums.

1756 P. BROWNE *Jamaica* (1779) 429 The streaked shining Curculio. *Ibid.* 430 Curculio..This insect is very destructive to flour as well as to most sorts of grain. **1860** EMERSON *Cond. Life, Fate* Wks. (Bohn) II. 327 Such an one has curculios, borers, knife-worms. **1882** *Garden* 25 Mar. 191/3 The Curculio has made the cultivation of the Plum impossible in Eastern America.

Hence **cur,culio'nideous** *a*, belonging to the *Curculionidæ* or weevil-family. **cur'culionist,** a specialist in the study of the *Curculionidæ.*

1881 *Athenæum* No. 2827. 904 A curculionideous larva, found feeding in the bulbs of lilies. **1874** MIVART in *Contemp. Rev.* XXIV. 362 That this naturalist is a Carabidist, and that a Curculionist.

‖**curcuma** ('kɜːkjuːmə). Also in anglicized form **curcume.** [med. or mod.L. ad. Arab. *kurkum* saffron, turmeric: see CROCUS.] **a.** *Bot.* A genus of *Zingiberaceæ* consisting of plants with perennial tuberous roots, furnishing various commercial substances, as zedoary, East Indian arrowroot, mango-ginger, turmeric, etc. **b.** The substance called Turmeric, prepared from the tubers of *C. longa*, and used as an ingredient in curry powder, as a chemical test for alkalis, and for medicinal and other purposes. *attrib.*, as **curcuma paper,** turmeric paper used as a chemical test.

1617 MOSAN tr. *Wirtzung's Pract. Physicke* 2nd Table, Turmericke, *Cyperus Indicus*, the Apothecaries call it Curcuma. **1633** GERARDE *Herbal* I. xxvii. 34. **1712** tr. *Pomet's Hist. Drugs* I. 35 The Curcuma of the Shops is a small Root, about the Size of that of Ginger. **1800** *Med. Jrnl.* III. 84 The liquor becomes alkaline, and reddens paper prepared with curcuma. *c* **1865** *Circ. Sc.* I. 351/2 In China, tea is frequently coloured with curcume. **1885** H. O. FORBES *Nat. Wandr. E. Archip.* 196 Rice yellowed with curcuma powder.

Hence **'curcumin,** *Chem.*, the colouring matter of turmeric.

1850 PEREIRA *Mat. Med.* II. I. 1125 Curcumin..is obtained..by digesting the alcoholic extract of turmeric in ether. **1875** J. ATTFIELD *Chem.* (ed. 6) 531 Turmeric..owes its yellow colour to curcumin, a resinous matter.

curd (kɜːd), *sb.* Forms: α. 4-5 **crodde,** (5 **crod(e),** 4-6 **crudd(e,** (5 **cruyde,** 5-6 **crude),** 5- *north. dial.* **crud;** β. 5-6 **curde, curdd(e,** 6 **courd,** 5- **curd.** [ME. *crud* (also *crod*) is found first in 14th c.; the form *curd* is known from 15th c. The metathesis *ru* = *ur* implies that the word is older, and may possibly go back to OE.; but its earlier history and derivation are unknown.

No similar word is known in Teutonic or Romanic; hence the source has been sought in Celtic: Irish has *cruth, gruth, groth*, Gaelic *gruth* curds, but it is not certain what relation (if any) the Celtic words hold to the English.]

1. a. The coagulated substance formed from milk by the action of acids, either naturally as when milk is left to itself, or artificially by the addition of rennet, etc.; made into cheese or eaten as food. (Often in *pl.*)

1362 LANGL. *P. Pl.* A. VII. 269 Twey grene cheeses, and a fewe cruddes and crayme. *c* **1420** *Liber Cocorum* 13 Styr hit wele..Tyl hit be gedered on crud harde. **14..** *Voc.* in Wr.-Wülcker 590/45 *Juncata*..Juncade, *sive* a crudde ymade yn ryshes. *Ibid.* 661/14 *Hoc coagulum*, crodde. **1549** *Compl. Scot.* vi. 42 Thai maid grit cheir of..curdis and quhaye. **1578** LYTE *Dodoens* VI. xlvi. 719 It melteth the clustered crudde, or milke that is come to a crudde. **1611** SHAKS. *Wint. T.* IV. iv. 161 Good sooth she is The Queene of Curds and Creame. **1626** BACON *Sylva* §385 Milk..is..a Compound Body of Cream, Cruds, and Whey. **1788** [see REAM *sb.*[2] 1 a]. **1846** J. BAXTER *Libr. Pract. Agric.* (ed. 4) I. 197 This acid.. transforms the milk into a curd. **1856** MRS. CARLYLE *Lett.* II. 294 Betty, who will have curds and cream waiting for me. **1887** J. SERVICE *Life & Recoll. Dr. Duguid* I. ix. 54 There were nae mair deidly engagements noo than the attack on.. curds and cream.

fig. **1735** POPE *Prol. Sat.* 306 Sporus, that mere white curd of Ass's milk? **1883** *Harper's Mag.* Mar. 574/1 That caused Mrs. Claxton's cloudy suspicion..to settle into an absolute curd of sourness.

†**b.** ? The curdled milk in the stomach of a young sucking animal, or the gastric juice of the same, used for rennet. *Obs.*

c **1420** *Pallad. on Husb.* VI. 141 The mylk is crodded now to chese With crudde of kidde, or lambe, other of calf. **1551** TURNER *Herbal* I. (1568) Bij a, The cruddes found in a kyddes maw, or an hyndecalfes maw. **1601** HOLLAND *Pliny* II. 331 The cruds or rennet of an horse fole maw, called by some Hippace. **1661** LOVELL *Hist. Anim. & Min.* 24 The curd [of the calf] hath the same vertue as that of a Hare, Kid, or Lamb.

2. a. *transf.* Any substance of similar consistency or appearance.

1811 A. T. THOMSON *Lond. Disp.* (1818) 605 Sulphuric ether and compound spirit of ether precipitate a thick, white, tenacious curd.

b. The fatty substance found between the flakes of flesh in boiled salmon, cf. CURDY 3.

1828 SIR H. DAVY *Salmonia* 98 To find a reason for the effect of crimping and cold in preserving the curd of fish. **1863** WOOD *Illust. Nat. Hist.* III. 327 If it [the salmon] be cooked within an hour or two after being taken from the water, a fatty substance, termed the 'curd', is found between the flakes of flesh.

c. The edible 'head' of such brassicas as cauliflower and broccoli.

1916 W. F. ROWLES *Food Garden* xi. 201 We may expect to cut the curds at the end of April. **1950** *N.Z. Jrnl. Agric.* Feb. 154/1 Most cauliflower crops..benefit from a side dressing applied shortly before the curd begins to form. **1951** *Good Housek. Home Encycl.* 393/2 It [*sc.* the cauliflower] has a compact white head (i.e. flowers, often called the curd). **1969** D. BARTRUM *From Garden to Kitchen* 29 Broccoli, with their white, solid flower-heads (curds) are like a small cauliflower but a much hardier vegetable.

3. *attrib.* and *Comb.*, as ***curd-cake, puff*** (confections made with curds); ***curd-like*** adj.; **curd-breaker, -crusher, -cutter, -mill,** apparatus for crushing or cutting up cheese-curd in order to facilitate the separation of the whey; **curd soap,** a white soap made with tallow and soda.

1706 *Closet of Rarities* (N.), To make *curd-cakes.—Take a pint of curds [etc.]. **1805** SOUTHEY *Madoc in W.* xiv, Cheese Of *curd-like whiteness. **1846** J. BAXTER *Libr. Pract. Agric.* (ed. 4) I. 158 Cauliflowers..of a delicate white curd-like appearance. **1879** *Cassell's Techn. Educ.* IV. 247/2 Break the curd into pieces..by means of a *curd-mill. **1769** MRS. RAFFALD *Eng. Housekpr.* (1778) 261 To make *Curd Puffs. **1794** *Hull Advertiser* 20 Sept. 4/1 Yellow Soap 60s.—*Curd 70s. **1875** URE *Dict. Arts* III. 850 The white..tallow soap of the London manufacturers, called curd soap.

curd (kɜːd), *v.* Forms: see the sb. [f. prec.]

1. a. *trans.* To make into curd; to coagulate, congeal; = CURDLE *v.* 1.

1382 WYCLIF *Job* x. 10 Whether not..as chese thou hast crudded me? *c* **1420** *Pallad. on Husb.* VI. 141 Alle fresshe the mylk is crodded now to chese. **1563** T. GALE *Antidot.* II. 36 This oile..courdeth milke by and by. **1602** SHAKS. *Ham.* I. v. 69 It doth posset And curd, like Aygre droppings into Milke, The thin and wholsome blood. **1610** HOLLAND *Camden's Brit.* I. 601 The feat of crudding it [milk] to a pleasant tartnesse. **1823** *New Monthly Mag.* IX. 166/2 So acrid..that they curd milk.

†**b.** To curdle (blood). *Obs. rare.*

1601 SHAKS. *All's Well* I. iii. 155 Dos it curd thy blood To say I am thy mother?

2. *intr.* To become or form curd; to coagulate, congeal; = CURDLE *v.* 3.

1398 TREVISA *Barth. de P.R.* XVI. vii. (1495) 555 Quycke syluer cruddeth not by itself kyndly wythout brymstone. *Ibid.* XIX. lxxvi. (1495) 906 Mylke rennyth and curdyth.. and the wheye is departyd therfro. *c* **1430** *Two Cookery-bks.* 17 Styre it tylle it crodde. **1578** LYTE *Dodoens* VI. xlvi. 719 The iuyce of Figges turneth milke and causeth it to crudde. **1598** *Epulario* K iij, Heat it vntill the Cheese curd.

fig. **1589** *Pappe w. Hatchet* (1844) 29 A Lemman will make his conscience curd like a Posset. **1887** G. M. HOPKINS *Poems* (1918) 65 His thew That onewhere curded, onewhere sucked or sank.

3. *trans.* To render curdy, cover as with curd.

1654 GAYTON *Pleas. Notes* II. i. 33 Two chaf'd Boars, or blowne Mastiffs, whose rage had curded one anothers chops.

Hence **'curding** *vbl. sb.* and *ppl. a.*

1398 TREVISA *Barth. De P.R.* XVII. clxviii. (1495) 712 Whete sod wyth juys of rewe dissoluyth..rennyng and kurdyng of mylke. **1727** C. THRELKELD *Stirpes Hibern.* E ij, In crudding of Milk it may occupy the place of Ches-lope. **1742** *Lond. & Country Brew.* I. (ed. 4) 76 Those harsh, curding Well-waters that many drink of.

curded ('kɜːdɪd), *ppl. a.* Also 5–9 crudded. [f. CURD *v.* and *sb.* + -ED.]

1. Formed into curd, or into a curd-like mass; coagulated, congealed.

c **1440** *Promp. Parv.* 105 Cruddyd, *coagulatus.* **1563** T. GALE *Antidot.* II. 36 If one drope of it..be put into a pynte of mylke, it shall forthwith become courded. **1578** BANISTER *Hist. Man* v. 75 A heape of crudded bloud. **1659** D. PELL *Improv. Sea* 333 The Seas..lye all upon a bubling froth, and curded foam. **1813** J. C. HOBHOUSE *Journey* 33 Curded goat's milk. **1820** SHELLEY *Witch Atl.* lv, She would often climb The steepest ladder of the crudded rock.

2. Of salmon: Having curd (see CURD *sb.* 2 b).

1865 J. G. BERTRAM *Harvest of Sea* (1873) 44 [They] do not like the Dutch salmon so well as their own fine curded fish.

curdiness ('kɜːdɪnɪs). [f. CURDY *a.* + -NESS.] The state or quality of being curdy. (Of fish: see CURD *sb.* 2 b.)

1824 *Blackw. Mag.* XVI. 340 Nothing can then exceed the beautiful curdiness of his texture. **1828** SIR H. DAVY *Salmonia* 98 The albumen is coagulated, and the curdiness [of the salmon] preserved.

curdle ('kɜːd(ə)l), *v.* Also 6–7 crudle, 7–8 (9 *dial.*) cruddle. [Frequentative of CURD *v.*]

1. *trans.* To form (milk) into curd; to turn (any liquid) into a soft solid substance like curd; to coagulate, clot, congeal.

1590–6 [see CURDLED 1, 1 c.]. **1601** HOLLAND *Pliny* XXIII. vii, It wil cruddle milk as wel as rennet. **1611** BIBLE *Job* x. 10 Hast thou not powred me out as milke, and cruddled me like cheese? **1742** *Lond. & Country Brew.* I. (ed. 4) 40 The Wort also will be curdled, and broke into small Particles. **1875** URE *Dict. Arts* I. 767 All acids curdle milk.

b. *to curdle the blood*: usually *fig.* said of the effect of cold, horror, etc. upon a person.

1602 MARSTON *Ant. & Mel.* II. Wks. 1856 I. 26 O how impatience..cruddles thick my blood, with boiling rage! *a* **1674** CLARENDON *Hist. Reb.* XVI. (1704) III. 559 Being now awaken'd by this Alarm..and his flegm a little curdled, he begun to think himself in danger. **1760** C. JOHNSTON *Chrysal* (1822) I. 14 An holy horror curdled all my blood. **1891** BARING-GOULD *In Troub. Land* v. 63 The glacial bise sweeps over the face of the desert, curdling the blood.

2. *transf.* and *fig.*

1627–47 FELTHAM *Resolves* (ed. 7) 154 We are curdled to the fashion of a life by time and set successions. **1794** G. ADAMS *Nat. & Exp. Philos.* I. vi. 210 The surface of the water is fretted and curdled into the finest waves by the undulations of the air. **1816** BYRON *Dream* i, A thought, A slumbering thought..curdles a long life into one hour. **1821** CLARE *Vill. Minstr.* II. 203 So beauty curdles envy's look on thee.

3. *intr.* To become or form curd; to coagulate.

1601 HOLLAND *Pliny* I. 348 The milk..will not cruddle. **1653** H. MORE *Conject. Cabbal.* (1713) 190 How this Primordial Water..should ever coagulate or cruddle into that consistency. **1774** GOLDSM. *Nat. Hist.* (1776) III. 56 The milk of the goat is..not so apt to curdle upon the stomach as that of the cow. **1853** SOYER *Pantroph.* 90 Mint prevented milk from curdling.

b. Of the blood. (Now usually *fig.*)

1611 BEAUM. & FL. *King & no King* I. i, See now my blood cruddles at this! **1668** CULPEPPER & COLE *Barthol. Anat., Manual* I. i. 302 Extravenated Blood..curdles and putrefies. **1784** COWPER *Task* VI. 514 The blood thrills and curdles at the thought. *a* **1845** BARHAM *Ingol. Leg.* (1877) 183 It makes the blood curdle with fear.

c. *transf.* and *fig.*

1818 BYRON *Mazeppa* xviii, An icy sickness curdling o'er My heart. **1860** TYNDALL *Glac.* I. ii. 22 The adjacent atmosphere..curdled up into visible fog.

curdle ('kɜːd(ə)l), *sb. rare.* [f. prec. vb.] The act or product of curdling; †a curd (*obs.*).

a **1593** H. SMITH *Serm.* (1622) 444 There is a kind of downe or curdle upon Wisedom. **1611** COTGR., *Mattes,* curds, or curdles. **1821** CLARE *Vill. Minstr.* I. 30 Tracing the ..winding fountains to their infant bed, Marking each curdle boil and boil away. **1933** D. L. SAYERS *Murder must Advertise* iv. 65 What disgusting stuff cauliflower could be —a curdle of cabbage!

curdled ('kɜːd(ə)ld), *ppl. a.* [f. as prec. + -ED.]

1. Formed into curd; coagulated, congealed, clotted.

1596 SPENSER *Astroph.* 152 With crudled blood and filthie gore deformed. **1676** J. BEAUMONT in *Phil. Trans.* XI. 733 Fill'd with a milky crudeled substance. **1819** SHELLEY *Cyclops* 129 Store of curdled cheese. **1828** SCOTT *F.M. Perth* xxiii, The curdled wounds gave no sign of blood.

b. *fig.* of the blood, etc.

1697 DRYDEN *Virg. Æneid* II. 766, I felt my crudled Blood congeal with Fear. **1815** BYRON *Parisina* xiv, As ice were in her curdled blood.

c. *transf.* and *fig.*

1590 SPENSER *F.Q.* I. vii. 6 Till crudled cold his corage gan assayle. **1602** MARSTON *Ant. & Mel.* I. i. Wks. 1856 I. 16 Crudl'd fogges masked even darknesse brow. **1685** H. MORE *Some Cursory Refl.* 10 This cold and crudled Infidelity. **1821** CLARE *Vill. Minstr.* II. 93 O'er the water crink'd the curdled wave. **1850** KINGSLEY *Alt. Locke* xxviii, Dark curdled clouds..swept on.

2. Of a lens: (see quot.)

1832 PORTER *Porcelain & Gl.* 245 When this fault [imperfect polishing] exists in a degree so exaggerated as to be visible to the naked eye, the lens is said to be *curdled.*

curdler ('kɜːdlə(r)). [f. as prec. + -ER.] **1.** That which curdles or coagulates.

1837 *Penny Cycl.* VII. 13/2 The most natural curdler of milk..is the gastric juice of the stomach of a sucking calf.

2. A story, etc., that curdles the blood (cf. CURDLE *v.* 3 b).

1886 BAUMANN *Londinismen* 36/1 *Curdler,*..blood-freezer. **1966** *Listener* 21 July 103/3 [A play] too complicated to be a real curdler.

curdless ('kɜːdlɪs), *a.* Destitute of curd.

1846 in WORCESTER.

curdling ('kɜːdlɪŋ), *vbl. sb.* [-ING[1].] The action of the vb. CURDLE; also *concr.*

1611 FLORIO, *Quagliata,* a curdling or congealing. **1620** VENNER *Via Recta* vii. 154 They inhibit the crudling of milke in the stomacke. **1851** NICHOL *Archit. Heav.* 107 Nebulosities..having within them *curdlings,* as they seem at first, separate massive clusters.

'curdling, *ppl. a.* [-ING[2].] That curdles.

1. *trans.* (In quots. = blood-curdling.)

1821 SHELLEY *Prometh. Unb.* II. iii, Under the curdling winds. **1863** WHYTE MELVILLE *Gladiators* I. 364 A curdling horror that weighed down the limbs like lead.

2. *intr.*

1699 GARTH *Dispens.* 15 A while his curdling Blood forgot to glide. **1886** R. C. LESLIE *Sea-painter's Log* 110 Here and there a..wave..breaks into curdling foam.

curdly ('kɜːdlɪ), *a.* [f. CURDLE *v.* + -Y.] Apt to curdle; of a curdled nature or appearance.

1689 G. HARVEY *Curing Dis. by Expect.* vi. 38 Milk..in many [is] very corruptible, coagulable or curdly. **1799** G. SMITH *Laboratory* I. 179 If you find the amalgam begin to be curdly. **1820** A. COOPER *Surg. Ess.* 232 The curdly substance mixed with pus is discharged.

cur dog, cur-dog: see CUR.

curdy ('kɜːdɪ), *a.* Also 6–7 cruddy, -ie. [f. CURD *sb.* + -Y.]

1. Full of curds.

1528 PAYNELL *Salerne's Regim.* 2 Olde chese, or verye cruddye chese. **1574** NEWTON *Health Mag.* 32 The thick and curdy Milke..commonly called Beastings. **1882** MRS. CHAMBERLAIN *W. Worcs. Words* 8 *Cruddy,* curdled; full of curds.

2. Full of curd-like coagulations; resembling curded milk; curd-like in consistency or appearance.

1509 HAWES *Past. Pleas.* (Percy Soc.) 4 In the..cruddy firmament. **1590** SPENSER *F.Q.* I. v. 29 His cruell woundes with cruddy bloud congeald. **1597** SHAKS. *2 Hen. IV*, IV. iii. 106 (Qo.) A good sherris sacke..ascendes mee into the braine, dries me there all the foolish and dull and crudy [*Fo.* cruddie] vapors which enuirone it. **1678** *Phil. Trans.* XII. 950 Making it [tin] thick and cruddy, that is, not so ductile, as otherwise. **1797** PEARSON *ibid.* LXXXVIII. 24 The precipitate did not render solution of hard soap at all curdy. **1875** H. C. WOOD *Therap.* (1879) 46 A white curdy precipitate. **1887** BARING-GOULD *Gaverocks* I. xvi. 233 The moon passed behind a white curdy cloud. **1937** E. J. LABARRE *Dict. Paper* 65/1 *Cruddy paper,* i.e. mottled.

3. Of salmon, etc.: Full of curd (see CURD *sb.* 2 b).

1603 OWEN *Pembrokeshire* (1891) 118 There they [the Salmon] are found newe, fresh, fatte and cruddye. *Ibid.* 125 A cruddye matter like creame about the fishe [oysters]. **1859** LEVER *Davenport Dunn* xxxvi, His curdiest salmon declined, his wonderful 'south-down' sent away scarcely tasted. **1892** H. G. HUTCHINSON *Fairway Island* i, We'll eat this [salmon] that had the tide-lice on him. He'll be fine and curdy.

†**curdy,** *v. Obs. rare*[−1]. [f. prec. adj.] *trans.* To make curd-like, to congeal. (But perh. in quot. *curdied* is a misprint for *curdled.*)

1607 SHAKS. *Cor.* V. iii. 66 Chaste as the Isicle That's curdied by the Frost from purest Snow.

cure (kjʊə(r)), *sb.*[1] Also 5–6 cuyr, 6–7 *Sc.* cuir(e, 6 cur. [a. OF. *cure* care (11th c.; also in mod. dial.):—L. *cūra* care.]

I. Care, charge; spiritual charge.

†**1. a.** Care, heed, concern. *to have* (*take, do,* etc.) *no cure of* (*a thing*): not to care for or regard it.

c **1300** *K. Alis.* 4016 For his lord, nymeth god cure, He dude his lif in aventure. *c* **1385** CHAUCER *L.G.W.* Prol. 152 Construeth that as yow lyst, I do no cure. *Ibid.* 1143 *Dido,* I make of yt no cure. *c* **1450** HENRYSON *Mor. Fab.* 5 To get his denner set was all his cure. **1535** STEWART *Cron. Scot.* II. 391 Quhilk labourit hes..With diligence and all the cuir he ma. *a* **1541** WYATT *Poems, Request to Cupid,* The solemne oathe, wherof she takes no cure, Broken she hath. *a* **1605** MONTGOMERIE *Natur passis Nuriture* 46 Of his oun kynd he took no cure.

†**b.** *to do one's* (*busy*) *cure*: to give one's care or attention to some piece of work; to apply oneself diligently (*to* effect something). *Obs.*

c **1340** *Cursor M.* 1726 (Trin.) Noe..ȝaf wriȝtes her mesure And him self dude his cure. *c* **1420** *Pallad. on Husb.* III. 654 And now cerfoil..doo thi cure To sowe in fatte and moist ydounged soil. **1430** LYDG. *Chron. Troy* I. iii, If I see thou do thy besy cure This hyghe empryse for to bryng aboute. **1509** BARCLAY *Shyp of Folys* A ij a, I doo my besy cure for to kepe them honestly frome poudre and dust. **1556** LAUDER *Tractate* 233 Bot trewlie thay suld do thare cure.

†**2.** Care, anxiety, trouble. *Obs.*

a **1340** HAMPOLE *Psalter* cxviii. 31 He despisis þe curys & þe noyes of þis life. **1513** DOUGLAS *Æneis* I. i. 60 Lo how greit cure, quhat travel, pane, and dowte. **15..** *Knt. of Curtesy* 82 Alas, Into this cure who hath you brought?

†**3.** Charge, care (committed to or laid upon any one); a duty, office, function. *Obs.* (exc. as in 4.)

c **1300** *Beket* 837 And [he] quath the quit al clenliche [of] eche other cure [*Laud MS.* wike] ther. **1398** TREVISA *Barth. De P.R.* XIX. cxxxiv. (1495) 944 Pan..hathe cure of shepe and of shepeherdes. **1513** BRADSHAW *St. Werburge* I. 2350 Temporall cures and busynesse worldly. **1555** EDEN *Decades* 38 The women..haue also the cure of tyllage of the grounde. **1641** MILTON *Ch. Govt.* Pref., The Church hath in her immediate cure those inner parts and affections of the mind. [**1848** MACAULAY *Hist. Eng.* I. 57 Cranmer had declared..that God had immediately committed to Christian princes the whole cure of all their subjects.]

4. *Eccl.* **a.** The spiritual charge or oversight of parishioners or lay people; the office or function of a CURATE. Commonly in phrase *cure of souls.*

c **1340** HAMPOLE *Prose Tr.* 25 Holy Bisshopis..which had cure of mennes soules. **1377** LANGL. *P. Pl.* B. Prol. 88 Bischopes and bachelers..þat han cure vnder criste. **1490** CAXTON *How to Die* 15 Euery persone hauyng the cure of soules. **1540** *Act 32 Hen. VIII*, c. 44 The persons and curates of the sayd .v. parishe churches..shall be dyscharged of the cure of the said inhabitantes. **1552** *Bk. Com. Prayer, Ordering of Priests,* So that you may teach the people committed to your cure and charge. **1642** JER. TAYLOR *Episc.* (1647) 309 The Bishops of every province must know that their Metropolitan-Bishop does take cure of all the province. **1776** ADAM SMITH *W.N.* V. i. (1869) II. 395 What is called the cure of souls, or the ecclesiastical jurisdiction in the parish. **1868** M. PATTISON *Academ. Org.* v. 134 Earning an income by tuition or by parochial cure.

b. (with *a* and *pl.*) A parish or other sphere of spiritual ministration; a 'charge'.

? **1483** CAXTON *Vocab.* 21 b, For to gete A cure of fre chapell. **1531** *Dial. Laws Eng.* II. xxxvi. (1638) 127 Then may the Ordinary set in a deputy to serve the Cure. **1552** *Bk. Com. Prayer, Ordering of Priests,* To use both public and private monitions..as well to the sick as to the whole, within your cures. **1660** R. COKE *Power & Subj.* 202 To the end the Cure may not be destitute of a Pastor. **1766** GOLDSM. *Vic. W.* iii, A small cure was offered me. **1855** MACAULAY *Hist. Eng.* III. 252 A proclamation..that..the clergy of the Established Church should be suffered to reside on their cures without molestation. **1882** PEBODY *Eng. Journalism* xi. 78 He held..a cure of souls in Essex.

II. Medical or remedial treatment.

†**5. a.** The medical treatment of a disease, or of a patient. *Obs.*

1393 GOWER *Conf.* III. 49 And lich unto Pithagoras Of surgery he knew the cures. *c* **1400** *Lanfranc's Cirurg.* 124 þei seyn þat mo men ben heelid bi þis maner cure þan dien. **1513** BRADSHAW *St. Werburge* II. 865 Wofully cruciat with peynes hiduous, Passyng mannes cure it for to amende. **1607–12** BACON *Ess. Seditions* (Arb.) 402 The Cure must answeare to the particuler disease. **1722** DE FOE *Plague* (1756) 49 The said Chirurgeons are to be sequestred from all other Cures, and kept only to this Disease. **1725** —— *Voy. round World* (1840) 339 All the while they were under cure.

b. A particular method or course of treatment directed towards the recovery of a patient, as in *water-cure, milk-cure,* etc.

[**1704** F. FULLER *Med. Gymn.* (1711) 54 The Cold Bath.. a severe Method of Cure.] **1842** LONGF. in *Life* (1891) I. xxiii. 427 There are about sixty persons here [Marienberg], going through what is called the water-cure. *c* **1860** MRS. GATTY *Aunt Judy's Tales* (1863) 29 An unlimited and fatal application of the cold-water cure. **1866** A. FLINT *Princ. Med.* (1880) 214 In order to carry out effectually the 'milk cure',..milk..should be taken largely. **1884** *Pall Mall G.* 6 Sept. 3/1 The prayer-cure, faith-cure, touch-cure.

6. a. Successful medical treatment; the action or process of healing a wound, a disease, or a sick person; restoration to health. Also *fig.*

1393 GOWER *Conf.* III. 338 Of maister Cerimon the leche And of the cure, which he dede. *c* **1400** *Lanfranc's Cirurg.* 97 For to remeve causes þat letten þe cure of olde woundes. **1588** SHAKS. *L.L.L.* v. ii. 28 Past care, is still past cure. **1596** DRAYTON *Legends* iii. 177 It was no cure, unlesse he could provide Meanes to prevent the danger to ensue. **1611** BIBLE *Luke* xiii. 32, I cast out deuils, and I doe cures. **1774** GOLDSM. *Nat. Hist.* (1776) III. 362 Its bite is very difficult of cure. **1789** W. BUCHAN *Dom. Med.* (ed. 11) 483 Mankind are extremely fond of every thing that promises a sudden or miraculous cure. **1860** TYNDALL *Glac.* I. xxiii. 162 The conditions were not favourable to the cure of a cold. **1891** *Messenger of Sacred Heart* Oct. 312 His cure..cannot be explained by the use of any remedies known to science.

†**b.** *out of* (*all*) *cure*: beyond remedy; past help. *Obs.*

c **1374** CHAUCER *Troylus* v. 713 And þus despeired out of alle cure She ladde here lyf, þis woful creature. **1393** GOWER *Conf.* II. 60, I..am, as who saith, out of cure For ought that I can say or do.

†**c.** Amendment, rectifying. *Obs. rare.*

1675 tr. *Camden's Hist. Eliz.* To Rdr., The Translation.. was..so out of order..that..it was thought convenient, by comparing it with the Original, to doe something towards the Cure of it.

7. A means of healing; a remedy; a thing, action, or process that restores health. Often *fig.*

1613 SHAKS. *Hen. VIII*, I. iv. 33 For my little Cure, Let me alone. **1667** MILTON *P.L.* IX. 776 Here grows the Cure of all, this Fruit Divine. **1776** TOPLADY *Hymn, 'Rock of Ages',* Let the water and the blood..Be of sin the double cure. **1825** A. CALDCLEUGH *Trav. S. Amer.* II. xv. 109 The most certain cure is to send those attacked from the elevated spot as soon as possible. **1875** JOWETT *Plato* (ed. 2) I. 11 A cure for the headache.

8. †**a.** One under medical treatment, a patient. *Obs.* **b.** A person who has been cured. *rare.*

1579 LYLY *Euphues* (Arb.) 67, I wil follow thy counsel, and become thy cure, desiring thee to be as wise in ministring thy Phisick, as I haue bene willing to putte my lyfe into thy handes. **1591** R. TURNBULL *Exp. Jas.* 121 A physitian bidding his cure and pacient to waxe strong. **1837** *Pall Mall G.* 11 Jan. 4/1 Convalescents or cures of Alpine parching..apostrophize tenderly their 'beloved Davos'.

9. The curing or preserving of fish, pork, etc. Also, a catch of fish so treated.

1743 *Lond. & Country Brew.* II. (ed. 2) 122 That the Wort may have also its Cure as well as the Hop. **1757** W. THOMPSON *R.N. Advoc.* 36 For the Performance of which Method of Cure [salting pork]. **1883** A. SHEA *Newfoundland* 7 The cure of the fish requires much care and judgment... The best cure is effected when the weather is variable. **1902** *Encycl. Brit.* XXXI. 143 The fish caught round the Newfoundland coast are generally of good quality, but the Labrador cure..is often very inferior. **1911** 'VIKING' *Art of Fishcuring* xiv. 67 When salting the fish in the tubs it would not be advisable to put one day's fish down upon the top of the previous day's cure. **1957** *Fish Marketing in W. Europe* (O.E.E.C.) ii. 41 The demand for salted herring was declining, and..the consumer was showing more interest in soft cures, such as pickled, marinated and smoked.

10. [After F. *cure*, G. *kur*, *cur* (see KURSAAL).] A period of residence at a health-resort, under medical regimen, in order to restore or benefit one's health. Also *Comb.*, as ***cure-guest*** (= G. *kurgast*), ***-seeker***.

1887 *Time* Oct. 420 The month's 'cure' at Carlsbad. **1898** *Daily News* 22 July 5/1 One of the speakers was an old cure servant. **1905** *Westm. Gaz.* 11 Sept. 10/2 The number of cure-guests registered [at Carlsbad]. **1906** *Ibid.* 27 Aug. 8/1 Cure-seekers at Homburg. **1908** T. P. O'CONNOR *Campbell-Bannerman* 123 He rarely took the cure [at Marienbad]. *Ibid.*, The severe waters which the other cure-guests were taking. **1921** D. H. LAWRENCE *Let.* ? 8 May (1962) II. 653, I..can't sit supping for ever at these inside Baden-Baden cure-springs. **1955** *Times* 5 July 8/4 [He] has left Berlin on his annual leave for an undisclosed destination 'to take a cure'. **1967** E. S. TURNER *Taking Cure* 9 Taking the cure was usually a quest for healing waters.

11. The process of vulcanizing rubber (see also quot. 1923) or of hardening or curing plastic; also (with qualifying adj.), the degree of hardness produced.

1902 C. O. WEBER *Chem. India Rubber* ix. 301 The pigments and other colouring matters contained in the india rubber...contain some impurity which is responsible for their discoloration, or perhaps the 'cure' has been too prolonged or carried out at too high a temperature. **1907** H. L. TERRY *India-rubber* 32 Fine Para rubber..varies slightly in its properties and price according as it is 'Up-river hard cure' or 'Island soft cure'. **1908** H. A. WICKHAM *Parà Rubber* 24 Extraction and cure of the rubber *latex*. *Ibid.* 29 The antiseptic smoke-cure. **1909** *Westm. Gaz.* 9 Nov. 12/1 Fine Hard Cure Para Rubber. **1922** H. E. SIMMONS *Rubber Manuf.* viii. 48/2 This variation in rate of cure or vulcanizing capacity. *Ibid.* 98/1 There are two general methods of vulcanization, namely, what is known as the 'cold cure' and the 'hot cure vulcanization'. **1923** B. D. W. LUFF *Chem. Rubber* 19 In works practice, and indeed in technical literature, the term 'cure' is frequently employed instead of 'vulcanisation'. While this has the merit of brevity, it is unfortunately used also to denote the 'smoking' of wild or cultivated rubber in the course of its preparation. *Ibid.* 136 Hydrochloric acid gives a rubber having a slower rate of cure. *Ibid.* 137 The effect of alum in retarding the cure of the rubber. **1943** SIMONDS & ELLIS *Handbk. Plastics* iii. 136 The state of cure of a laminated material can be determined with some degree of success by a water-absorption test. **1947** R. L. WAKEMAN *Chem. Commercial Plastics* xxvi. 786 Where concentrations of catalyst in the order of 1 per cent are used, heating to 175–260 °F effects cure after several hours. **1961** L. R. MERNAGH in W. J. S. Naunton *Appl. Sci. Rubber* xii. 1062 Hot-air cures may be divided into open-air cures at atmospheric pressure and oven cures.

12. *attrib.* and *Comb.*, as †**cure-bearer**, one who bears or has the care of something; so **cure-master**; *esp.* one who superintends the curing of herrings; **cure-passing** *a.*, past remedy, incurable.

1545 *Aberdeen Reg.* V. 19 (Jam.) Maister & cuir berar of the townis artailyere and graytht thairof. *c* **1611** CHAPMAN *Iliad* XXII. 27 Cure-passing fevers then Come shaking down into the joints of miserable men. **1622** MISSELDEN *Free Trade* 47 Men of good quality..termed Curemasters. **1733** P. LINDSAY *Interest Scot.* 201 The riding Officer, appointed ..for overseeing the Curing of Herrings..with one Cure-master..at least, to assist him. **1892** C. PATRICK *Mediæv. Scot.* vii. 132 They should be first passed by the Cure Masters of Fish.

†**cure**, *sb.*[2] *Obs.* [An early phonetic variant of COVER; see CURE *v.*[2]] = COVER *sb.*

1502 *Bury Wills* (1850) 92, I beqwethe to..William Coote ..myne syluer salt wyth yᵉ cure, and Alys Coote the other wᵗoute the cure. **1567** *Test. K. Henrie Stewart* in *Scot. Poems 16th C.* II. 262 As the woirme, that workis under cuire At lenth the tre consumis. *a* **1572** KNOX *Hist. Ref.* Wks. I. 461 Thei must neidis reteyre in a verray narrow cure.

†**cure**, *sb.*[3] *Obs.* [ME. *curé*, app. a variant of *curie*, CURY; in 1460 it is rimed with *sure*, perh. by confusion with CURE *sb.*[1]] = CURY.

a **1400–50** *Alexander* 4275 Haue we no cures of courte, ne na cointe sewes. *c* **1420** *Liber Cocorum* 1 Of craft..that men callis cure [*rime* degre]. *Ibid.* 5 Now slyȝtes of cure wylle I preche. *c* **1460** J. RUSSELL *Bk. Nurture* 375 To know þe kervynge of fische and flesche after cockes cure [*rime* sure].

†**cure**, *sb.*[4] *Obs.* [Early southern ME. *cüre*:—OE. *cyre*.] Choice.

c **1000** in Thorpe's *Hom.* I. 112 God forȝeaf him aȝenne cyre. *c* **1205** LAY. 6171 And æfter cure heo him ȝeuen þreo hundred ȝisles. *Ibid.* 8077 Ten þusend monen þet wes þe bezste cure Of al Brut-londe. *a* **1300** *K. Horn* (Ritson) 1446 The ship bigon to sture With wynd god of cure.

cure (kjʊə(r)), *sb.*[5] *slang.* [app. an abbreviation of *curious* or *curiosity*: cf. *curio*.

It appears to have obtained vogue largely from a Music Hall song with the chorus 'The cure, the cure, the perfect cure' (with play on CURE *sb.*), popular in 1862.]

An odd or eccentric person; a funny fellow.

1856 *Punch* XXXI. 201 (Farmer), Punch has no mission to repeat The Slang he hears along the street..But as it's likely to endure, He asks a question, 'What's a cure?' **1889** *Monthly Packet* Christmas No., *Abigail* v. 108 'You *are* a cure of a girl!' was Mrs. Bowden's neat way of expressing her surprise.

cure (kjʊə(r)), *v.*[1] [a. F. *cure-r* (in OF. to take care of, to clean):—L. *cūrāre* to care for, take care of, cure, f. *cūra* care.]

I. †**1. a.** *trans.* To take care of; to care for, regard. **b.** *intr.* To take trouble; to take care.

1382 WYCLIF *Acts* viii. 2 Forsoth men dredeful curiden [Vulg. *curaverunt*] or birieden Stheuene. —— *Tit.* iii. 8 That thei that bileuen to God, curen, or do bisynesse, for to be bifore in goode werkis. *c* **1420** *Pallad. on Husb.* III. 844 In hilles is to cure To set hem on the Southe if thai shall ure. **1603** *Philotus* lxxxv, Of all thy kin curit not the greif. *a* **1618** SYLVESTER *Job Triumphant* III. 386 Whose ragged Fathers I refus'd to keep My Shepheard's Curs, much more to cure my sheep. **1623** A. TAYLOR *Christ's Mercy*, I cur'd and cur'd for all that were in woe.

†**2.** *trans.* (and *absol.*) To take charge of the spiritual interests of (a parish, etc.). *Obs.*

1377 LANGL. *P. Pl.* B. xx. 323 The Frere..hyed faste To a lord for a lettre, leue to haue to curen, As a curatour he were. *c* **1400** *Rom. Rose* 6845, I walke soules for to cure. **1581** J. BELL *Haddon's Answ. Osor.* 314 Sithence this Bishop is carefull and diligent in curyng his owne charge.

II. †**3.** *trans.* To treat surgically or medically with the purpose of healing (a disease, or a patient). *Obs.*

1398 TREVISA *Barth. De P.R.* II. v. (1495) 32 Angels ben callyd Leches and Physicyens for they cure and heele soules. *c* **1400** *Lanfranc's Cirurg.* 94 For & he [the cankre] be curid, þat is to seie kutt or I-brent, þei perischen þe sunnere. **1530** PALSGR. 504 *Je cure* is I cure or helpe as a surgyen dothe. **1592** WEST *1st Pt. Symbol.* §102 B, If..the said H. shal.. refuse any longer to be dressed or cured by yᵉ said F. of the said infirmitie.

4. a. To heal, restore to health (a sick person *of* a disease). Also *fig.*

1382 WYCLIF *Luke* viii. 43 Sum womman..which hadde spendid al hir catel in to lechis, nether myȝte be curid of ony. **1388** —— *2 Kings* v. 3 The prophete schulde haue curid hym of the lepre which he hath. *c* **1440** *Promp. Parv.* 110 Curyn', or heelyn' of seekenesse..*Sano, curo.* **1538** STARKEY *England* II. ii. 185 Nature hyrselfe curyth the patyent. **1611** BIBLE *Luke* vii. 21 Hee cured many of their infirmities. **1803** *Med. Jrnl.* IX. 548 The cold application was of great use.. and she was soon cured. **1883** G. LLOYD *Ebb & Flow* II. 160 To be cured of a troublesome complaint.

fig. *c* **1530** *Pol. Rel. & L. Poems* (1866) 36 Thow shalte nevyr be curyd if thowe oonys knowe the cryme of thyne owne true wyfe. **1600** SHAKS. *A.Y.L.* III. ii. 441 *Ros.* And thus I cur'd him [of love]..*Orl.* I would not be cured, youth. **1752** A. MURPHY *Gray's-Inn Jrnl.* No. 14 ¶2 This has cured me from attempting any sport of that kind. **1758** JOHNSON *Idler* No. 2 ¶1 Disappointment seldom cures us of expectation. **1832** W. IRVING *Alhambra* II. 148 Time cured him of his grief.

†**b.** *transf.* To repair, make good (anything damaged). *Obs.*

1382 WYCLIF *1 Kings* xviii. 30 He curede the auter of the Lord, that was destruyed. *a* **1656** USSHER *Ann.* vi. (1658) 264 And there he cured such of his ships as had..been bruised.

5. a. To heal (a disease or wound); *fig.* to remedy, rectify, remove (an evil of any kind).

14.. *Circumcision* in *Tundale's Vis.* (1843) 91 Hyt cureth sores, hyt heleth every wownd. **1526** *Pilgr. Perf.* (W. de W. 1531) 9 b, The whiche cureth, releueth & heleth all defautes. **1610** SHAKS. *Temp.* I. ii. 106 Your tale, Sir, would cure deafenesse. **1665** GLANVILL *Sceps. Sci.* 50 Deep search discovers more ignorance than it cures. **1708** MOTTEUX *Rabelais* v. xvi, Well, quoth Fryar John..what can't be cur'd must be endur'd. **1791** BURKE *Corr.* (1844) III. 357 To cure the evils brought on by vice and folly. **1872** E. PEACOCK *Mabel Heron* I. ix. 166 He had been successful in curing more than one smoky chimney. *Mod.* The question whether pulmonary consumption can be cured.

b. *absol.* or *intr.* To effect a cure; often in ***kill or cure*** (see KILL *v.* 7 e).

1593 SHAKS. *2 Hen. VI.* v. i. 99 Whose Smile and Frowne, like to Achilles Speare Is able with the change, to kill and cure. **1764–1875** [see KILL *v.* 7 e]. **1787** COWPER *Stanzas Bill Mortality* I. 27 No Med'cine, though it often cure, Can always baulk the Tomb. **1908** *Smart Set* Sept. 82/1 Buttermilk is good for it... Warranted to cure in thirty days or money refunded.

†**6.** *intr.* (for *refl.*) To be cured, get well again. *Obs. rare.*

1592 SHAKS. *Rom. & Jul.* I. ii. 49 One desparate greefe cures with anothers languish. *a* **1774** GOLDSM. tr. *Scarron's Com. Rom.* I. 179 Saldagne's wounds were in the fair way of curing. **1791** GIBBON *Lett.* Misc. Wks. 1796 I. 232, I must either cure or die.

7. a. To prepare for keeping, by salting, drying, etc.; to preserve (meat, fish, fruit, tobacco, etc.).

1665 HOOKE *Microgr.* 161 What their way is of dressing or curing Sponges..I cannot learn. **1711** *Act 9 Anne* in *Lond. Gaz.* No. 4874/1 Hops..brought to be cured and bagged at such Ousts. **1719** DE FOE *Crusoe* (1840) I. ix. 152, I had grapes enough..to have cured into raisins. **1745** *De Foe's Eng. Tradesman* xxvi. (1841) I. 258 Herrings cured red from Yarmouth. **1788** T. JEFFERSON *Writings* (1859) II. 443 The beef cured and packed by them. **1832** HT. MARTINEAU *Weal & Woe* i. 2 A warehouse..where salt for curing the fish.. was stored.

b. *intr.* (for *refl.*) To be or become cured.

1668 STUBBE in *Phil. Trans.* III. 705 In Jamaica the Sugar cures faster in ten days, than in six months in Barbadoes. **1719** DE FOE *Crusoe* (1840) I. vii. 119 They [grapes] might cure and dry in the sun. **1887** *West Shore Mag.* (Brit. Columbia) 451 The bunch grass cures on the roots, as it stands, and remains as hay until..the spring.

†**8.** To clear (land), as for a crop. *Obs.*

1719 DE FOE *Crusoe* (1840) I. xvii. 295 We had gotten as much Land cured and trimmed up, as we sowed 22 Bushels of Barley on. **1722** —— *Col. Jack* (1840) 168, I had a large quantity of land cured, that is, freed from timber.

9. *intr.* To reside for some time at a health-resort, following a regimen for the benefit of one's health. See CURE *sb.*[1] 10.

1902 *Westm. Gaz.* 22 Aug. 2/1 Those who have come up to 'cure' at Davos. **1905** *Ibid.* 9 June 10/1 They 'cured' together on the balcony, and rowed together on the lake.

10. a. *trans.* To vulcanize (rubber); also, to harden (plastic) or otherwise improve physical properties during manufacture by chemical treatment.

1853 C. GOODYEAR *Gum-Elastic* I. vii. 102 Among many experiments for drying and curing the gum,..the inventor was much elated with the result of one. **1881** *Encycl. Brit.* XII. 841/2 The calendered sheets are generally cured between folds of wet cloth. **1902** C. O. WEBER *Chem. India Rubber* ix. 299 'Dry heat cured' water-proof fabrics. *Ibid.*, 'Cold cured' cloth. **1907** H. L. TERRY *India-rubber* 79 Goods cured by Dry Heat..are less likely to be damaged by copper than those which are cold cured. **1908** H. A. WICKHAM *Parà Rubber* 29 The standard rubber known in commerce as 'fine Parà' is smoke-cured. *Ibid.* 32 The weight of the cured rubber should approximate very nearly that of the *latex* used. **1922** H. E. SIMMONS *Rubber Manuf.* viii. 48/2 They cured all of their samples at a temperature of 140 °C. **1947** R. L. WAKEMAN *Chem. Commercial Plastics* xxvi. 782 Furfuryl alcohol can be reacted with formaldehyde to yield a viscous mass which can be cured to a thermoset composition by application of heat. **1961** D. W. HUKE *Introd. Natural & Synthetic Rubbers* v. 82 The early synthetic rubbers were much more difficult to cure than natural rubber. **1964** OLEESKY & MOHR *Handbk. Reinforced Plastics* i. 8 The resin is fully cured and has become an infusible solid.

b. *intr.* To become vulcanized, undergo vulcanization or curing.

1922 H. E. SIMMONS *Rubber Manuf.* viii. 48/2 A rubber which cures an hour and forty-five minutes more quickly than plain or smoked sheets. *Ibid.* 49/1 A rapid curing rubber. **1923** B. D. W. LUFF *Chem. Rubber* 136 Sulphuric acid gives a slow-curing rubber if used in slight excess. **1961** D. W. HUKE *Introd. Natural & Synthetic Rubbers* v. 83 With sulphur and accelerators present the compounded rubber may start to cure while being processed.

11. *trans.* To harden (concrete).

1918 HOOL & JOHNSON *Concrete Engineers' Handbk.* ii. 156 Where products are cured in this way, it is necessary that racks or cars be used. *Ibid.* 158 The curing rooms usually open into the molding department as conveniently as possible to the machines supplying the greatest number of products to be cured. **1921** HATT & VOSS *Concrete Work* II. 175 Demonstrate the relative strength of concrete when cured in the hot sun, in dry air, and in wet sand. *Ibid.* 179 The stone must be cured under a wet cloth. **1953** *Archit. Rev.* CXIII. 85 If these connections are grouted, the whole erection is held up while this is being poured and cured. **1970** *Fremdsprachen* 44 We took great care in curing the concrete, believing that by preventing escape of water from the slab, drying shrinkage would be very small.

†**cure**, *v.*[2] *Obs.* [A phonetically reduced form of ME. *cuure*, COVER, the *v* being vocalized or elided, as in *o'er*, *e'er*; cf. *skiver*, *skewer*.] *trans.* To cover; to conceal; to protect.

a **1400** *Cov. Myst.* (Shaks. Soc.) 392 Diveris clowdys eche of us was sodeynely curyng. *c* **1430** LYDG. *Chron. Troy* I. 2870 But, o allas! how sone he ouer-caste His heste, his feith, with whiche he was assured, And hadde his fraude with flaterie y-cured. *c* **1440** *Promp. Parv.* 110 Curyn', or hyllyn' (W. cueuren), *operio, cooperio, tego.*

†**cure**, *v.*[3] *Obs. rare.* [Cf. CURE *sb.*[4], and obs. conjugation of CHOOSE.] *trans.* To choose.

a **1225** *Leg. Kath.* 1870 Þu most nede..an of þes twa curen and cheosen.

cure, var. of COVER *v.*[2], to recover.

‖**curé** (kyre). In 6 curee. [F., ad. med.L. *cūrātus*: see CURATE.] A parish priest in France or a French-speaking land.

1655 SIR E. NICHOLAS in *N. Papers* (Camden) II. 345 The most plausible curees heere in the Towne and great Jansenists. **1662** J. DAVIES *Voy. Ambass.* (1669) 422 The Curé or Parson of the Parish, came one day to my Quarters. **1871** MORLEY *Voltaire* (1886) 341 One must stand well with the curé, be he knave or dunce.

'cure-ˌall. Something that cures all diseases; a universal remedy, panacea. Also *fig.*

1870 LOWELL *Cathedral* Poet. Wks. (1879) 452 Expect.. A wondrous cure-all in equality. **1871** NAPHEYS *Prev. & Cure Dis.* III. iv. 741 It has been vaunted as a cure-all.

b. As a name for various plants: see quots. (Cf. *all-heal*.)

1793 NEMNICH (cited in Britten & Holland *Plant-n.*), Cure-all, *Geum rivale*. **1882** *Syd. Soc. Lex.*, Cure-all, the *Geum virginianum* and the *Œnothera biennis*.

cured (kjʊəd), *ppl. a.*[1] [f. CURE *v.*[1] and *sb.*[1]]

1. In senses corresponding to those of the verb; *esp.* in sense 7: Preserved by salting, drying, etc.

1715 M. DAVIES *Ath. Brit.* I. 276 The Gratitude of the Cur'd Patient. **1836** *Penny Cycl.* V. 239 Salted meat and cured fish. **1884** *Times* (Weekly ed.) 31 Oct. 7/4 Mild cured butter.

†**2.** [f. the sb.] Having cure of souls. [F. *curé*.]

1393 GOWER *Conf.* I. Prol. 10 For dignite ne for provende Or cured or withoute cure.

†**cured**, *ppl. a.*[2] *Obs.* [f. CURE *v.*[2]] Covered, having a cover.

1463 *Bury Wills* (Camden) 42 My browne cuppe of erthe curyd. *c* **1480** *Paston Lett.* No. 852 III. 271 A standyng coppe curid gilt..a nother standyng cupp cuerid gilt.

cureless ('kjʊəlɪs), *a.* [See -LESS.] Without cure or remedy; incurable, irremediable.

a **1541** WYATT *To his vnkind loue*, In depe wide wound, the dedly stroke doth turne: To cureles skarre. **1579** LYLY *Euphues* (Arb.) 181 Then is thy case almost curelesse. **1655** THETFORD *Perf. Horseman* 34 Many good horses are left cureless of these two gross unsufferable faults. **1718** POPE *Iliad* XVIII. 99 This cureless grief. **1880** MCCARTHY *Own Times* IV. 63 He proclaimed to England that her ancient system must fall into cureless ruin.

Hence '**curelessly** *adv.*, incurably.

1852 ROBERTSON *Serm.* Ser. III. xii. 154 Fatally, radically, curelessly wrong.

curelessness ('kjʊəlɪsnɪs). The quality or condition of being cureless.

1892 KIPLING & BALESTIER *Naulahka* xiii, Her heart torn with the curelessness of it all.

curer ('kjʊərə(r)). [f. CURE *v.*[1] + -ER[1].]

1. One who or that which cures or heals.

1581 T. ROGERS *St. Aug. Praiers* ix. (1597) 45 Thou purger of wickednes and curer of wounds. **1598** SHAKS. *Merry W.* II. iii. 39 He is a curer of soules, and you a curer of bodies. **1775** ADAIR *Amer. Ind.* 438 The curers of ailments. **1845** *Jrnl. R. Agric. Soc.* VI. II. 548 Panaceas.. put forth as checkers or curers of the disease.

2. One whose employment it is to cure fish, etc.

1791 NEWTE *Tour Eng. & Scot.* 103 There is room enough for the cooper and curer to perform their operations all under cover. **1814–15** *Act 55 Geo. III*, c. 94 §20 If the curer of such herrings shall not deliver such account thereof. **1864** *Reader* 23 Jan. 99 Curers crowd to buy the fish.

curesse, curet(e, curets, obs. ff. CUIRASS.

Curetonian (kjʊə'təʊnɪən), *a.* and *sb.* Designation of the Syriac version of the Gospels discovered by the Rev. William *Cureton*, and edited by him from the MS. in 1858.

1861 SCRIVENER *Introd. Crit. N.T.* 236 The Curetonian Syriac. *Ibid.* 237 Such cases..are common to the Curetonian with the Peshito. **1904** F. C. BURKITT (*title*) Evangelion Da-Mepharreshe: The Curetonian Version of the Four Gospels. *Ibid.* II. 17 Where the photograph clearly agreed with the Curetonian against the Peshitta.

curettage (kjʊ'rɛtɑːʒ). *Surg.* [Fr.: see CURETTE and -AGE.] The application of the curette; scraping or cleaning by means of a curette.

1897 *St. Thomas's Hosp. Rep.* New Ser. XXV. 84 Various supplementary measures have been added to the curettage. **1908** *Practitioner* Feb. 180 No more than a curettage of the growth was attempted. **1964** L. MARTIN *Clin. Endocrinol.* (ed. 4) viii. 252 But curettage is seldom desirable in adolescents in whom the condition usually rectifies itself spontaneously. **1965** J. POLLITT *Depression & its Treatment* v. 72 Powerful analgesics or premedication may be urgently required should threatened or incomplete abortion occur, or a dilatation and curettage be needed as a result.

curette (kjʊə'rɛt). *Surg.* [a. F. *curette*, f. *curer* in sense 'to clear, cleanse', applied to various industrial tools as well as in the surgical use.] A small surgical instrument like a scoop, used in removing a cataract from the eye, wax from the ear, granulations, dried mucus, etc., from the throat, uterine cavity, bladder, etc. Also, a suction-instrument used in the removal of a soft cataract.

1753 SHARP in *Phil. Trans.* XLVIII. 325, I then passed the curette (a little scoop) through the pupil. **1758** J. S. *Le Dran's Observ. Surg.* (1772) 259, I took off a Quantity of incrustated Gravel with the *Currette*. **1869** WELLS *Diseases of Eye* 253 The convexity of the curette is to be placed against the edge of the cornea.

Hence **cu'rette** *v.*, to scrape with a curette; **cu'retting** *vbl. sb.*

1888 *Brit. Med. Jrnl.* 11 Feb. 288 My present practice is to curette in every case of disease affecting..the uterine mucous membrane. **1890** BRAITHWAITE *Retrosp. Med.* CII. 108 Antiseptic curetting in Endometritis (Puerperal).

curettement (kjʊ'rɛtmənt). *Surg.* [See CURETTAGE and -MENT.] = CURETTAGE.

1908 *Practitioner* Dec. 787 The right ovary had been removed elsewhere five years ago, at which time curettement had also been done.

curf (kɜːf). *local.* Also **carf, kerf.** [var. f. CARF, KERF.] A cherty limestone found in one of the strata of the Portland beds of stone.

1839 *Civil Engin. & Arch. Jrnl.* II. 375/2 A middle or curf bed occurs only in the southernmost of the quarries. **1893** *Spon's Mechanic's Own Bk.* (ed. 4) 564 Then..the Bastard-Roach, Kerf, or Curf is reached. **1936** *Discovery* Mar. 76/2 Between the 'Whit Bed' and 'Base Bed' there is an irregular deposit of curf and flint, locally called 'Pericott'.

curfew ('kɜːfjuː). Forms: α. (3 coeverfu), 4 corfu, -feu, 4–7 corfew, curfewe, 5 curfu, 5–6 courfeu(e, curpheue, 6–7 curfue, 7 curphew, 8 corfeu, -fue, -phew, curfeu, 5– curfew; β. 4 corfour, 5–6 curfur, 6 courfyre, curfoyr, 7 curfure, -phour; 6 curfle. Also (etymological restorations) 7 couvrefeu, coverfeu, -few. [a. AF. *coeverfu*, = OF. *cuevre-fu, queuvre-feu, covre-feu* (13th c.), f. *couvre*, imper. of *couvrir* to cover + *feu* fire: cf. the med.L. names *ignitegium, pyritegium*, from *tegĕre* to cover. The corrupt forms in *-four, -fur*, etc. appear to be of phonetic origin, though in some cases associated with *fire*.]

1. a. A regulation in force in mediæval Europe by which at a fixed hour in the evening, indicated by the ringing of a bell, fires were to be covered over or extinguished; also, the hour of evening when this signal was given, and the bell rung for the purpose. Also *transf.* and *fig.* **b.** Hence, the practice of ringing a bell at a fixed hour in the evening, usually eight or nine o'clock, continued after the original purpose was obsolete, and often used as a signal in connexion with various municipal or communal regulations; the practice of ringing the evening bell still survives in many towns. In extended use: a restriction imposed upon the movements of the inhabitants of an area for a specified period.

The primary purpose of the curfew appears to have been the prevention of conflagrations arising from domestic fires left unextinguished at night. The earliest English quotations make no reference to the original sense of the word; the *curfew* being already in 13th c. merely a name for the ringing of the evening bell, and the time so marked.

[**1285** *Stat. London* Stat. I. 102 Apres Coeverfu personé a Seint Martyn le graunt.] *c* **1320** *Seuyn Sag.* (W.) 1429 Than was the lawe in Rome toun, That, whether lord or garsoun That after Corfu be founde rominde, Faste men scholden hem nimen and binde. *c* **1386** [see 3]. *c* **1400** *Leges Quat. Burgorum* lxxxi. in *Sc. Acts* I. 349 [He] sal gang til his wache wyth twa wapnys at þe ryngyng of þe courfeu. *c* **1440** *Promp. Parv.* 110/2 Curfu, *ignitegium*. **1495** in Arnolde *Chron.* (1811) 90 Yf ther bee any Parishe Clarke yᵗ ringyth curfew after the curfue be ronge at Bowe chirche. **1530** PALSGR. 210/1 *Courfewe*, a ryngyng of belles towarde evenyng. **1570** LEVINS *Manip.* 190 Curfle, *operitio ignis*. **1561** BP. PARKHURST *Injunctions*, If they doo ring at the buriall of the deade, noone or Curpheue. **1570** *Burgh Rec. Peebles* 324 (Sc. Burgh Rec. Soc.) To regne xij houris, vj houris, and courfyre nychtlie. **1608** *Merry Devil Edm.* in Hazl. *Dodsley* X. 251 Well, 'tis nine o'clock, 'tis time to ring curfew. **1610** SHAKS. *Temp.* v. i. 40. **1632** MILTON *Penseroso* 74 Oft on a plat of rising ground, I hear the far-off curfew sound. **1750** GRAY *Elegy* i, The Curfew tolls the knell of parting day. **1825** COBBETT *Rur. Rides* (1830) I. 317, I got to this place about half an hour after the ringing of the eight o'clock bell, or Curfew. **1850** LYELL *2nd Visit U.S.* II. 43 Every evening, at nine o'clock, a great bell, or curfew, tolls in the market-place of Montgomery, after which no coloured man is permitted to be abroad without a pass. **1922** JOYCE *Ulysses* 414 When the curfew rings for you. **1929** D. H. LAWRENCE *Pansies* 103 The curfew of our great day..the tocsin of this our civilisation. **1939** *Punch* 18 Oct. 435/1 The attempt..to get a nine o'clock curfew imposed on members of the Women's Land Army in training..to prevent them going out with soldiers. **1964** *Ann. Reg. 1963* 309 The new Prime Minister..imposed a dusk-to-dawn curfew in Jerusalem. **1970** D. STUART *Very Sheltered Life* 70 There was an immediate curfew. Everyone had to be off the streets.

¶ The statement that the curfew was introduced into England by William the Conqueror as a measure of political repression has been current since the 16th century, but rests on no early historical evidence. See Freeman *Norm. Conq.* (1875) III. 185 as to what 'seems to be the origin of the famous and misrepresented curfew'.

1568 GRAFTON *Chron.* II. 9. **1647** N. BACON *Disc. Govt. Eng.* I. lvi. (1739) 102 It is affirmed, that the Normans did impose a new custom called Coverfeu. **1743–6** SHENSTONE *Elegies* xv, So droop'd, I ween, each Britons breast of old When the dull curfew spoke their freedom fled. **1769** BLACKSTONE *Comm.* IV. 412.

†**c.** Applied also to the ringing of a bell at a fixed hour in the morning. *Obs.*

1592 SHAKS. *Rom. & Jul.* IV. iv. 4 Come, stir, stir, stir, The second Cocke hath Crow'd, The Curphew Bell hath rung, 'tis three a clocke. **1673** in *L'pool Munic. Rec.* (1883) I. 342 Ring Curphew all the yeare long at 4 a clock in the morning and eight at a night. **1704** *Ibid.* II. 83 Ringing Curfew Bell at four of yᵉ clock in yᵉ morning, and eight at night.

2. A cover for a fire; a fire-plate, a cover-fire.

a **1626** BACON (J.), For pans, pots, curfews, counters and the like. **1779** *Gentl. Mag.* XLIX. 406 He had gotten a piece of household furniture of copper, which he was pleased to call a curfew..F. G...has described it as a curfew, from its use of suddenly putting out a fire. **1837** [see COVER-FIRE].

3. *attrib.* and *Comb.*, as *curfew-knoll, -law, -note, -order, -time.*

c **1386** CHAUCER *Miller's T.* 459 The dede sleepe..Fil on this carpenter..Aboute corfew tyme [*v.r.* corfeu, curfewe]. **1778** W. PEARCE *Haunts Shaks.* 12 At curfew-time lull'd by the lone village bell. **1814** WORDSW. *Excursion* VIII. 172 The curfew-knoll That spake the Norman Conqueror's stern behest. **1818** SCOTT *Hrt. Midl.* xxvii, That sleep should have visited his eyes after such a curfew-note, was impossible. **1897** J. BRYCE *Impr. S. Afr.* xxi. 447 Cape Colony has a so-called 'curfew law', requiring natives who are out of doors after dark to be provided with a pass. **1931** *Daily Express* 16 Oct. 11/3 The curfew order of the university is that no cars may be used after nine without leave.

4. curfew-bell. (See sense 1.) Also *fig.*

c **1320** *Seuyn Sag.* (W.) 1497 Corfour belle ringge gan. **1509** *Bury Wills* (1850) 112, I gyve toward yᵉ ryngers charge off the gret belle in Seynt Mary Chirche, callyd corfew belle. **1597–8** BP. HALL *Sat.* III. iv. 15 But a new rope, to ring the couure-feu bell. *a* **1649** DRUMM. OF HAWTH. *Consid. Parl.* Wks. (1711) 187 That there shall be cover-feu bells rung.. after the ringing of which no man shall be found upon the streets. **1702** C. MATHER *Magn. Chr.* III. III. (1852) 542 He ..would ring a loud courfeu bell wherever he saw the fires of animosity. **1839** KEIGHTLEY *Hist. Eng.* I. 103 A law of police which directed all fires to be put out at the tolling of a bell called Curfew bell, is by later chroniclers ascribed to Wm. the Conqueror, but without any countenance from the early writers.

cur'fuffle, *v. Sc.* [Deriv. of a simple FUFFLE *v.* to disorder: the first syllable is perh. Gaelic *car* twist, bend, turn about; used in combination in *car-fhocal* quibble, prevarication, *car-shùil* rolling eye, *car-tuaitheal* wrong turn: cf. the Lowland Sc. *curcuddoch, curdoo, curgloff, curjute, curmurring, curnoited*, in which the prefix seems to have the sense of L. *dis-*.] *trans.* To put into a state of disorder; to ruffle.

1583 R. S. *Leg. Bp. St. Androis* in *Sempill Ballates* (1872) 215 His ruffe curfufled about his craig. **1768** ROSS *Helenore* 81 (Jam.) Ye ken where Dick curfuffled a' her hair.

cur'fuffle, *sb. Sc.* Also **carfuffle, cafuffle**, etc. [f. prec. vb.

Now widely used as a colloquialism in the forms GEFUFFLE and (esp.) KERFUFFLE.]

Disorder, flurry, agitation.

1813 G. BRUCE *Poems* 65 An' Jeanie's kirtle, aye sae neat, Gat there a sad carfuffle. **1816** SCOTT *Antiq.* xx, Monkbarns in an unco carfuffle. *Ibid.* xxix, Troth, my lord maun be turned feel outright..and he puts himself into sic a curfuffle for ony thing ye could bring him, Edie. **1823** MISSES CORBETT *Petticoat Tales* I. 333 (Jam.) Ye need na put yoursel into ony carfuffle about the matter. **1953** *John o' London's* 3 July 602/3 The word cafuffle is still in general use in her part of Scotland..as a noun meaning a state of confusion. **1955** C. S. LEWIS *Surprised by Joy* vii. 114, I could put up with any amount of monotony far more patiently than even the smallest disturbance, bother, bustle, or what the Scotch call *kurfuffle*. **1960** K. MARTIN *Matter of Time* 187 The girl next door and her boy friend are having a wee cafoufle in the garden. **1961** *Radio Times* 14 Dec. 3/2 You remember the cafuffle there was when the Ministry of Transport introduced their ten-year test for cars. **1971** *Times* 9 Jan. 16/4 Since the predictable pre-April curfuffle, there has been the predictable summer and autumn hush.

curfur(e: see CURFEW.

‖**curia** ('kjʊərɪə). [L. *cūria*, in sense 1.]

1. *Antiq.* **a.** One of the ten divisions into which each of the three ancient Roman tribes were divided; hence used of the divisions in other ancient cities. **b.** The building belonging to a Roman curia, serving primarily as its place of worship. **c.** The senate-house at Rome. **d.** A title given to the senate of ancient Italian towns, as distinguished from that of Rome.

1600 HOLLAND *Livy* v. 209 Camillus should be called back again out of exile by a Ward-leet, or the suffrages of the Curiæ. **1626** MASSINGER *Rom. Actor* I. i, Lets to the curia, And, though unwillingly, give our suffrages, Before we are compell'd. **1656** J. HARRINGTON *Oceana* 76 (Jod.) The people..are first divided into thirty curias, or parishes. **1852** GROTE *Greece* II. lxxxi. X. 549 There is reason for believing that the genuine Carthaginian citizens were distributed into 3 tribes, 30 curiæ, and 300 gentes.

2. A court of justice, counsel, or administration; used *esp.* of the royal and other courts of the feudal organization.

In mediæval L., *curia* was the word regularly employed to render F. *cour*, COURT, and it is so used by modern historians, esp. in *Curia regis*, the King's Curia, or King's Court, of the Norman kings of England.

[*c* **1178** GLANVILLE I Hic incipit liber primus de placitis quae pertinent ad curiam regis.]

1706 PHILLIPS (ed. Kersey) s.v., In our Common Law, *Curia* signifies a Court of Judicature. **1861** PEARSON *Early & Mid. Ages Eng.* 414 Historically, the court of exchequer ..was developed out of the curia, or great court of the king's tenants-in-chief. **1874** STUBBS *Const. Hist.* I. xi. 377 Whereas, under William the Conqueror and William Rufus the term *Curia* generally..refers to the solemn courts held thrice a year or on particular summons, at which all tenants-in-chief were supposed to attend, from the reign of Henry I we have distinct traces of a judicial system, a supreme court of justice called the Curia Regis, presided over by the king or justiciars. **1890** *Guardian* 28 May 868/1 The Archbishop of Canterbury..without a curia, without traditions, without committees of experts and theologians..is going to settle.. some most difficult points.

3. *spec. the Curia*: the Papal court.

'In the stricter sense, the authorities which administer the Papal Primacy; in a wider acceptation it embraces all the authorities and functionaries forming the immediate entourage or Court of the Pope' (*Cath. Dict.*).

1840 S. AUSTIN *Ranke's Hist. Popes* (1847) I. 237 (Stanford) Still more important to the curia was the second article, concerning the plurality of benefices. **1878** STUBBS *Const. Hist.* III. xix. 352 It was a curious coincidence that the great breach between England and Rome should be the result of a litigation in a matrimonial suit, one of the few points in which the Curia had continued to exercise any real jurisdiction.

4. *Hist.* **a.** Each of four electoral bodies in the Austrian constitution of 1861. **b.** Each of three bodies, representing respectively the nobles, knights, and towns, into which the members of the estates of Bohemia were divided in 1446.

1907 *Westm. Gaz.* 28 May 2/1 How false was the idea given by the old Curia Parliament of what were the feelings and the aspirations of the people of Austria. **1908** *Ibid.* 16 Jan. 2/1 He wished to see Bohemia divided into curias—Germans being governed by a German, and Czechs by a Czech curia. **1910** *Encycl. Brit.* III. 26/1 (Austria). *Ibid.* IV. 126/2 (Bohemia).

curial (ˈkjʊərɪəl), *a.* and *sb.* [a. F. *curial*, *-ale* adj., *curiale* sb., ad. L. *cūriāl-is*, f. *cūria*.]

A. *adj.*

†**1.** Of or pertaining to a royal court; having the manners befitting a court; courtly. *Obs.*

1478 *Liber Niger* in *Househ. Ord.* (1790) 45 And other fourmes curiall after the booke of urbanitie. **1484** CAXTON *Curiall* 1 The lyf Curiall whyche thou desirest. *Ibid.* 3 The maner of the peple curyall or courtly. **1520** *St. Papers Hen. VIII*, II. 56 To..fall to more curiall, discrete, and clenly order, than ever they used before. **1560** ROLLAND *Crt. Venus* I. 793 And to my sisteris, and Ladyis curiall.

2. Of or pertaining to a curia: **a.** of an ancient Roman or an Italian curia; **b.** of a judicial, administrative, or other court; **c.** of the papal Curia.

1677 *Govt. Venice* 280 The Vicar of the Podestat, or some other Curial Officer, is permitted to go in their stead. **1864** A. J. HORWOOD *Year Bks. 32–3 Edw. I*, Introd. 19 *note*, In the celebrated Pinenden plea..there is no appearance of curial formalities being observed. **1882** *Sat. Rev.* 18 Mar. 323 The present Pope, so far as he is left untrammelled by the exigencies of conventional or curial etiquette.

B. *sb.*

†**1.** A member of a court; a courtier. *Obs.*

1447 BOKENHAM *Seyntys* (Roxb.) 77 Thou maryd shal bene..To sum curyal of ryht gret dignite.

2. A member of an ancient Roman or an Italian curia.

1677 *Govt. Venice* 280 If the Curial should become a Councellor, the Assistance..would degenerate into Counsel. **1861** J. G. SHEPPARD *Fall Rome* viii. 415 Each municipality was made responsible in the person of its curials, or chief officers..for its own amount of taxation. **1873** G. W. KITCHIN *Hist. France* I. vi. I. 52 The curials (or members of the civil municipality) lost their authority.

†**3.** A treatise on the Court. *Obs.*

The title given to the treatise or letter of Alain Chartier translated by Caxton.

1484 CAXTON *Curiall* 6 Thus endeth the Curial made by Maystre Alain Charretier. Translated thus in Englysshe by Wylliam Caxton. **1822** K. DIGBY *Broadst. Hon.* (1846) 327 What wisdom is in this sentence of Alain Chartier in his Curial!

curialism (ˈkjʊərɪəlɪz(ə)m). [f. CURIAL *a.* + -ISM.] A curial or courtly system: *esp.* applied to the policy or system of the papal Curia; Vaticanism.

1870 *Church Rev.* 13 Aug. 499/2 Curialism, a word come into use during the past week [i.e. in reference to the Vatican Council]. **1891** *Speaker* 2 May 530/2 Though curialism did prevail [at the Vatican Council], some sense of the older Catholicism has revived.

curialist (ˈkjʊərɪəlɪst). [f. as prec. + -IST; cf. F. *curialiste*, Cotgr.] A member of the papal Curia; a supporter of its policy or authority.

1847 BUCH tr. *Hagenbach's Hist. Doctr.* II. 456 In the Roman Catholic Church a controversy was carried on between the Curialists and Episcopalians. **1870** *Contemp. Rev.* XIII. 12 A veteran curialist assured Dr. Mejer that he could discern no principle at all in the manner of transacting business at Rome.

curialistic (kjʊərɪəˈlɪstɪk), *a.* [f. prec. + -IC.] Of or pertaining to curialists or curialism.

1870 *Lett. on [Vatican] Council*, by 'Quirinus' 116 Proclaimed, through the curialistic Cardinal Bonnechose. **1872** W. H. JERVIS *Gallican Ch.* Pref. 11 Those views of the monarchical constitution of the Church..which characterize the ultra-Catholic or Curialistic school.

†**curiˈality.** *Obs.* [ad. OF. *curialité*, med.L. *cūriālitās*, from *cūriālis* CURIAL.]

a. What pertains to a court. **b.** Courtliness. **c.** = COURTESY 3 and 4.

a **1626** BACON *Advice to Sir G. Villiers* (R.), I come to the last of those things which I propounded, which is, the Court and Curiality. **1633** T. ADAMS *Exp. 2 Peter* i. 2 Either through curiosity or curiality, Christian Salutations are thought gross. **1641** HEYLIN *Help to Hist.* (1671) 340 [The title of Earl Marshal] was only given them then by the courtesie or curiality of England. **1671** F. PHILLIPS *Reg. Necess.* 426 The said Earl..was not stiled the Kings Cousin ..a Curiality, with which the more antient and less Frenchified times were unacquainted. **1861** W. BELL *Dict. Law Scot.*, Courtesy or Curiality.

curiara (kuːrɪˈɑːrə). The native name in Venezuela and Colombia for a dug-out canoe.

1910 'H. J. MOZANS' *Up the Orinoco* 174 The curiara is smaller than the bongo or falca. **1910** M. B. & C. W. BEEBE *Our Search* 12 A network of narrow channels..allowed us to explore the far interior in our shallow curiara or dug-out. **1927** *Chambers's Jrnl.* 290/1 Their curiaras are very strong and carefully made.

curiate (ˈkjʊərɪət), *a.* [ad. L. *cūriāt-us* adj., f. *cūria*.] Of or pertaining to the curiæ.

1886 *Encycl. Brit.* XX. 732/1 In Cicero's time there were still curies, curial festivals, and curiate assemblies.

curie (ˈkjʊəriː, ‖kyri). [Named in honour of Pierre *Curie* (1859–1906), co-discoverer of radium.] **1.** Orig., a quantity of radon (radon 222, radium emanation) in radioactive equilibrium with one gramme of radium; later extended to denote an equivalent quantity of any of the decay products of radium. Later, a unit of radioactivity equal to $3{\cdot}7 \times 10^{10}$ disintegrations per second, freq. used *loosely* as a unit of quantity of any radioactive substance in which there is this degree of radioactivity. Cf. BECQUEREL 2.

1910 RUTHERFORD in *Nature* 6 Oct. 430/2 It was suggested that the name Curie, in honour of the late Prof. Curie, should..be employed for a quantity of radium or of the emanation... The name Curie should be used as a new unit to express the quantity or mass of radium emanation in equilibrium with one gram of radium (element). **1931** M. CURIE et al. *Rep. Internat. Radium-Standards Committee* in *Rev. Mod. Physics* III. 432 It is recommended that the use of the term curie be extended to include the equilibrium quantity of any decay product of radium. **1954** *Brit. Jrnl. Radiol.* XXVII. 243/2 Amount of radioactive material shall be expressed in curies (c). The accepted definition of the curie is:—The curie is a unit of radioactivity defined as the quantity of any radioactive nuclide in which the number of disintegrations per second is $3{\cdot}700 \times 10^{10}$. With this definition the curie is independent of the disintegration rate of radium. **1955** *Sci. Amer.* July 50/3 The most powerful modern atomic bomb should release no more than 10 billion curies. **1963** JERRARD & MCNEILL *Dict. Sci. Units* 37 The curie is too large for normal laboratory work where the radioactivity is generally of the order of millicuries. **1968** *Radiation Quantities & Units* (Internat. Commission on Radiation Units & Measurements) 6 In accordance with the former definition of the curie as a unit of quantity of a radioactive nuclide, it was customary and correct to say: 'Y curies of ^{32}P were administered...' It is still permissible to make such statements rather than use the longer form which is now correct: 'A quantity of ^{32}P was administered whose activity was Y curies.' **1970** *Sci. Jrnl.* Aug. 43/1 A single 1000 MWe reactor will therefore accumulate in its fuel many thousands of millions of curies of fission products.

2. curie point or **temperature**, a temperature at which the type of magnetism exhibited by a substance changes; *spec.* that at which a ferromagnetic substance, on being heated, loses its ferromagnetism and becomes paramagnetic; also, an analogous temperature for a ferroelectric substance, at which it either loses its ferroelectricity or becomes ferroelectric.

1911 *Physical Rev.* XXXIII. 269 Weiss states that the 'Curie point' for cobalt is probably in the neighborhood of 1110° C. **1919** *Chem. Abstr.* XIII. 951 At about 1280° Fe undergoes a transformation with respect to its magnetic properties and this is referred to here as the Curie or A4 point. **1925** *Jrnl. Iron & Steel Inst.* CXII. 267 It will be observed that the line of magnetic transformation (the Curie points) in the γ-phase approaches the α to γ transformation curve. **1957** *Encycl. Brit.* XIV. 650/1 The temperature at which any ferromagnetic material loses its magnetism is known as the Curie point; it is 770 °C. for iron and 358 °C. for cobalt. **1960** *McGraw-Hill Encycl. Sci. & Technol.* III. 623/2 The transition between ferrimagnetism and paramagnetism is also marked by a Curie temperature. **1967** *Electronics* 6 Mar. 24/1 (Advt.), High skin temperatures demand an antenna with a high Curie point coupled with low loss characteristics at high frequencies. **1968** CONDON & ODISHAW *Handbk. Physics* (ed. 2) IV. vii. 119 The ferroelectric range of Rochelle salt is very narrow and that of the phosphates and arsenates is limited to low temperatures. Both crystal types..are piezoelectric above the Curie point.

curiet, obs. form of CUIRASS.

curing (ˈkjʊərɪŋ), *vbl. sb.* [-ING[1].] The action of the verb CURE.

1. Healing, cure.

1382 WYCLIF *Jer.* xiv. 19 Tyme of curing [1388 heeling]. **1588** J. READ *Compend. Method* 60 b, Trie all other remedies before he proceede to these sharpe kind of curinges. **1595** SHAKS. *John* III. iv. 112 Before the curing of a strong disease. **1891** tr. *De La Saussaye's Sc. Relig.* xxix. 258 The curing of sickness.

2. a. The process of preparing (fish, etc.) for keeping, by salting, drying or other means.

1672 [see 3]. **1791** *Trans. Soc. Encourag. Arts* IX. 174 Some observations on the curing of coffee. **1884** *Manch. Exam.* 25 Feb. 5/3 Efforts to encourage the growth and curing of tobacco.

b. The process of rendering a substance harder or more durable (cf. CURE *v.*[1] 10, 11).

1853 C. GOODYEAR *Gum-Elastic* I. x. 165 (*heading*) Curing or tanning, commonly known as the acid gas process. **1881** *Encycl. Brit.* XII. 841/1 After which the true vulcanization, or 'curing' as it is termed, can be brought about in the usual way. **1918** HOOL & JOHNSON *Concrete Engineers' Handbk.* ii. 156 Conditions for curing must be such that the product will not be rapidly dried. **1921** HATT & VOSS *Concrete Work* I. viii. 180 The process of keeping the product damp is called curing. It is done by sprinkling, immersion, and by the use of steam. **1930** *Engineering* 25 July 97/3 The sustained pressure during the curing process [of rubber]. **1964** OLEESKY & MOHR *Handbk. Reinforced Plastics* i. 8 Thermosetting plastics..become increasingly infusable on heating. They undergo a chemical change which is not reversible. This reaction is called polymerization or curing.

3. *attrib.* and *Comb.*, as (sense 1) ***curing-stone***; (sense 2) ***curing-room, -stand, -yard***; **curing-house**, a building where curing is carried on; *spec.* 'the building on a sugar estate (in the West Indies) where the hogsheads of newly potted sugar are placed to harden and drain off the molasses' (Simmonds *Dict. Trade*, 1858).

1629 in Chambers *Dom. Ann. Scot.* II. 31 She..had sent to the Laird of Lee to borrow his curing-stone for their cattle. **1672** W. HUGHES *Amer. Physician* 33 Athwart the end of the Sugar-house, or Curing-house (as they term it). **1791** NEWTE *Tour Eng. & Scot.* 100 For the benefit of the Fisheries, public wharfs, store-houses, and curing-houses, should be constructed upon a moderate scale at first. **1862** *Macm. Mag.* Oct. 511 The owners of boats at Wick engage to fish for particular curers, who have curing-stands there. **1878** *Rep. Vermont Board Agric.* 79 In connection with..the manufacturing room was the curing room. **1933** B. SILLIMAN *Man. Sugar Cane* 46 The line of the floor.. deviates only six inches in the curing rooms.

curing, var. of COVERING[2]. *Obs.*, recovery.

c **1440** *Promp. Parv.* 111 Curynge, or recurynge of sekenesse, *convalescencia*.

curio (ˈkjʊərɪəʊ). [A familiar abbreviation of *curiosity*.] **a.** An object of art, piece of bric-à-brac, etc., valued as a curiosity or rarity; a curiosity; more particularly applied to articles of this kind from China, Japan, and the far East.

1851 H. MELVILLE *Whale* iii. 20 A lot of 'balmed New Zealand heads, great curios you know. **1861** SWINHOE *N. China Camp.* 299 Everybody had some rare curios to show me, asking me their worth.

b. *Comb.*, as ***curio-buying, -hunter, -maniac, -shop***.

1886 *Pall Mall G.* 13 Jan. 4/1 As a baby is moved to put everything it sees into its mouth, so the curiomaniac seeks to make everything within the limits of the craze his own. **1887** GUILLEMARD *Cruise 'Marchesa'* I. 41 To the curio-hunter the Liu-kiu Islands are a most unprofitable ground. **1888** *Pall Mall G.* 19 Sept. 2/1 By a first-class Japanese curio-dealer..you are only shown one thing at a time. **1920** M. BEERBOHM *Let.* 18 May (1964) 245 Your visits to the curio-shops. **1970** V. MCKENNA *Some of my Friends have Tails* 77 We had to film a scene in a curio shop—the type that sells objects made from skin and ivory and leather.

curioˈlogic, *a.* and *sb.* [A bad adaptation of Gr. κῡριολογικ-ός (of which the normal Eng. repr. is *cyriologic*) 'speaking literally' (f. κύριος regular, proper, etc. + λόγος speech, -λογια speaking), applied by Clemens Alexandrinus to hieroglyphics consisting of simple pictures, as opposed to συμβολικός symbolic.]

A. *adj.* Of or pertaining to that form of hieroglyphic writing in which objects are represented by pictures, and not by symbolic characters.

1669 GALE *Crt. Gentiles* I. I. xi. 64 The last and most perfect [mode of discourse and writing] is Hieroglyphic, whereof one is Curiologic, the other Symbolic. **1760** *Antiq.* in *Ann. Reg.* 156/2 The proper or curiologic character expressed the sun by a figure representing that luminary. **1816** J. GILCHRIST *Philos. Etym.* 27 The kind of hieroglyphics which the Egyptians very properly named Curiologic.

B. *sb.* Representation by picture-writing.

1816 J. GILCHRIST *Philos. Etym.* 33 Men were led on step by step from hieroglyphics or picture-writing, to curiologics, an abridged form of the former. **1864** R. F. BURTON *Dahome* I. 206 In this land the umbrella is a rude kind of curiologics, faintly resembling European blazonry.

So **curioˈlogical** *a.* = prec., **curioˈlogically** *adv.* **curiˈology** *nonce-wd.*, representation by curiologic symbols.

1740 WARBURTON *Div. Legat.* IV. iv. iii, Hieroglyphics were written curiologically and symbolically. **1814** *Edin. Rev.* Nov. 147 Those hieroglyphics in which part of a material object is put for the whole are called curiological. **1816** J. GILCHRIST *Philos. Etym.* 32 The same system of curiology must have prevailed at a very early period. **1862** H. SPENCER *First Princ.* (1870) 349 The kuriological or imitative [form].

†**ˈcurion.** *Obs. rare*[−1]. [a. F. *curion*, or ad. L. *cūrio*, *-ōnem*, f. CURIA.] The priest of an ancient Roman curia.

1624 A. DARCIE *Birth of Heresies* xii. 51 Because the ancient Curions and Sacrificers were cut and shauen.

‖**curiosa** (kjʊərɪˈəʊsə), *sb. pl.* [neut. pl. of L. *cūriōsus* (see CURIOUS *a.*).] Curiosities, oddities; *spec.* erotic or pornographic books (cf. CURIOUS *a.* 16 b).

1883 *Sat. Rev.* 17 Mar. 350/2 Indicating at the end of his preface such miscellaneous *curiosa* as may be found in the mighty volume ensuing. **1920** M. SECKER *Let.* Jan. in C. Mackenzie *Life & Times* (1966) V. 169 No bookseller would buy a single copy of the Rainbow even with my imprint unless he dealt in 'curiosa'. **1947** N. MARSH *Final Curtain* ix. 143 She's not..the type to pore over literary curiosa unless ..they were curious in the specialised sense. **1959** J. THURBER *Years with Ross* iv. 68 Nash was a keen collector of human curiosa. **1970** E. MCGIRR *Death pays Wages* ii. 43 Somebody told the old chap that the British Museum Reading Room has a huge collection of *curiosa*.

‖**curiosa felicitas** (kjʊərɪˈəʊsə fɛˈlɪsɪtæs). [L. (Petronius *Sat.* cxviii), lit. 'careful felicity'.] A studied felicity of expression.

1752 CHESTERFIELD *Let.* 16 Mar. (1774) II. 229 The delicacy and *curiosa felicitas* of that poet [*sc.* Horace]. **1817** COLERIDGE *Biog. Lit.* II. xxii. 168 The frequent curiosa felicitas of his [*sc.* Wordsworth's] diction. **1886** F. HARRISON *Choice of Books* I. iii. 61 Tennyson..has..a *curiosa felicitas* of phrase. **1908** L. JOHNSON in Yeats & Johnson *Poetry & Ireland* 22 The singular charm, the *curiosa felicitas*, of Celtic style. **1933** R. TUVE *Seasons & Months* iii. 79 The 'Curiosa Felicitas' which produces such 'handsom Turns and apt Expressions'.

curiosity (kjʊərɪˈɒsɪtɪ). Forms: 4–5 cory-, curiouste, 5 curyouste(e, -oste, coriouste, curiowstee, (curyste); also 4–6 curiosite, 5 cury-, curiosite(e, -syte(e, -sytye, 6 curiositye, (kewriosyte), 6–7 curiositie, 6– -ty. [a. OF. *curioseté* (AngloFr. *curiousetė*), ad. L. *cūriōsitātem*, f. *cūriōs-us*: see CURIOUS and -TY. Subsequently conformed more closely to the Latin, both in French as *curiosité*, and in Eng. as *curiositie*, *-ity*.]

I. As a personal attribute.

†**1.** Carefulness, the application of care or attention. *Obs.*

c **1430** *Freemasonry* 32 He that lernede best.. And passud hys felows yn curyste. *a* **1568** Ascham *Scholem.* II. (Arb.) 87 Cæs. Commentaries are to be read with all curiositie. *a* **1619** Fotherby *Atheom.* I. iv. §1 (1622) 20 They which haue marked, with very great curiositie, the memorable things of euery Countrie. **1747** Gould *Eng. Ants* 56 A little Curiosity in Observation will easily remove so plain an Error.

†**2.** Careful attention to detail; scrupulousness; exactness, accuracy. *Obs.*

c **1391** Chaucer *Astrol.* II. §14 *heading*, To knowe the degree of the sonne by thy riet, for a maner curiosite. **1559** Scot in Strype *Ann. Ref.* I. App. x. 28 If they be.. examyned agaїne and agaїne, this curiositie will never come to any end. **1577** B. Googe *Heresbach's Husb.* I. (1586) 9 Everie one will not suffer such curiositie as they require in yᵉ placing of a house. **1630** Sanderson *Serm.* (1681) II. 281 The Curiosity that Men use in Weighing Gold or precious Quintessences for Medicine. **1694** *Acc. Sev. Late Voy.* (1711) p. xxiii, To take the most exact account of all the Coasts.. and to report them at their return with all possible Curiosity.

†**3.** Proficiency attained by careful application; skill, cleverness, ingenuity. *Obs.*

1603 Knolles *Hist. Turks* (1621) 353 Beside her incomparable beautie.. adorned also with all that curiositie could devise. **1664** Power *Exp. Philos.* I. 58 If our Dioptics could attain to that curiosity as to grind us such Glasses.. we might hazard at last the discovery of Spiritualities themselves. **1676** Shadwell *Virtuoso* 11, You will arrive at that curiosity in this watery science [swimming], that not a frog breathing will exceed you. **1742** Leoni *Palladio's Archit.* I. 10 Sumptuous Buildings, which requir'd more Curiosity. **1760–72** tr. *Juan & Ulloa's Voy.* (ed. 3) I. III. ii. 113 Many expert pilots, and other persons of curiosity who have employed their attention on it.

†**4.** Care or attention carried to excess or unduly bestowed upon matters of inferior moment. **a.** Undue niceness or fastidiousness as to food, clothing, matters of taste and behaviour. *Obs.*

c **1386** Chaucer *Pars. T.* ⁋755 The ferthe is, curiosite [*v.r.* coriouste] with gret entent to make and apparayle his mete. *c* **1450** *St. Cuthbert* (Surtees) 2148 Common clething als he vsed, All' curyouste he refused. *c* **1510** Barclay *Mirr. Gd. Manners* (1570) Fj, Though I forbid thee proude curiositie Yet do I not counsell nor moue thee to rudenes. **1531** Elyot *Gov.* III. xxii, The curiositie and wanton appetite of Heliogabalus. **1601** Cornwallyes *Ess.* II. xxviii. (1631) 23 We of these latter times full of a nice curiosity, mislike all the performances of our fore-fathers. **1672** Cave *Prim. Chr.* II. iv. (1673) 68 A vicious curiosity about meats and drinks. **1766** Fordyce *Serm. Yng. Wom.* (ed. 4) I. ii. 59 In affairs of this kind, it is but just to allow to women a degree of curiosity and care.

†**b.** Unduly minute or subtle treatment; nicety, subtlety. *Obs.*

1605 Bacon *Adv. Learn.* I. iv. §6 (1873) 32 This same unprofitable subtility or curiosity is of two sorts. **1620** Markham *Farew. Husb.* II. xix. (1668) 103 Besides many other Seeds, which would.. shew but too much curiosity to repeat. **1680** Burnet *Rochester* (1692) 106 The opposition of Hereticks anciently occasioned too much Curiosity among the fathers.

5. Desire to know or learn: †**a.** In a blamable sense: The disposition to inquire too minutely into anything; undue or inquisitive desire to know or learn. *Obs.*

c **1380** Wyclif *Serm.* Sel. Wks. I. 227 Bi þis answere moun we se how curiouste of science or unskilful coveitise of cunnynge, is to dampne. **1388** —— *Num.* iv. 20 Othere men se not bi ony curiouste tho thingis that ben in the seyntuarie ..ellis thei schulen die. **1526** *Pilgr. Perf.* (W. de W. 1531) 2 That ye neuer by way of curiosite be besy to attempte ony persone therin. **1604** Hieron *Wks.* I. 488 It is curiositie to enquire into that which God hath concealed. **1675** Brooks *Gold. Key* Wks. 1867 V. 142 Curiosity is the spiritual adultery of the soul. Curiosity is spiritual drunkenness. **1756** Burke *Vind. Nat. Soc.* Wks. 1842 I. 5 You feared, that the curiosity of this search might endanger the ruin of the whole fabrick.

b. In a neutral or good sense: The desire or inclination to know or learn about anything, *esp.* what is novel or strange; a feeling of interest leading one to inquire about anything.

1613 Salkeld *Treat. Angels* 43 But peradventure some may with.. just curiositie demaund, how then shall wee know. **1632** J. Hayward tr. *Biondi's Eromena* 12 A noble and solid curiosity of knowing things in their beginnings. **1647** Clarendon *Hist. Reb.* II. (1843) 44/2 There was so little curiosity.. in the country to know any thing of Scotland.. that, etc. **1665** Sir T. Herbert *Trav.* (1677) 382 In curiosity I put some of the wood into my mouth and chewed it. **1707** *Curios. in Husb. & Gard.* 337 A Plant, which he resuscitated in the presence of any, whose Curiosities brought them to see it. **1725** De Foe *Voy. round World* (1840) 253 He had perhaps at first raised this curiosity in me. **1853** C. Bronte *Villette* xiv, Your curiosity is roused at last. **1875** Jowett *Plato* (ed. 2) I. 393 Nor had you any curiosity to know other states or their laws.

c. Inquisitiveness in reference to trifles or matters which do not concern one.

1577 Northbrooke *Dicing* (1843) 95 What was the cause why Dina was rauished? was it not hir curiositie? **1603** Holland *Plutarch's Mor.* 134 Curiositie, which I take to be a desire to know the faults and imperfections in other men. **1836** Hor. Smith *Tin Trump.* (1876) 113 Curiosity—looking over other people's affairs and overlooking our own. **1887** T. Fowler *Princ. Morals* II. i. 44 Curiosity.. is usually employed to denote the habit of inquisitiveness as to trifles, and especially as to the private affairs of one's neighbours.

†**6.** Scientific or artistic interest; the quality of a curioso or virtuoso; connoisseurship. *Obs.*

1661 Evelyn *Diary* (1827) II. 175, I dined at Mr. Palmer's in Gray's Inn, whose curiosity excell'd in clocks. **1694** Molesworth *Acct. Sweden* 47 This.. qualifies them more for a Life of Labour and Fatigue, than of Art and Curiosity. **1779–81** Johnson *L.P., Addison* Wks. III. 73 Mr. Locker.. was eminent for curiosity and literature.

†**7.** A pursuit in which any one takes an interest, or for which he has a fancy; a hobby. *Obs.*

1646 Sir T. Browne *Pseud. Ep.* I. v, Had their curiosities been sedentary. **1653** Walton *Angler* Ep. Ded. 4 This pleasant curiositie of Fish and Fishing.. has been thought worthy the pens and practices of divers in other Nations. *a* **1661** Fuller *Worthies* (1840) III. 487 Fertilizing of barren ground may be termed a charitable curiosity employing many poor people therein.

†**8.** A desire to make trial or experience of anything novel; trifling interest or desire; a fancy, a whim. *Obs.*

1605 Jas. I *Gunp. Plot* in *Harl. Misc.* (Malh.) III. 13 [Parliament] is no place for particular men to utter there their private conceipts, nor for satisfaction of their curiosities. **1663** *Flagellum; or O. Cromwell* (ed. 2) 7 He was placed in Sydney Colledge, more to satisfie his Fathers curiosity and desire, than out of any hopes of Completing him in his Studies. **1672** Cave *Prim. Chr.* I. x. (1673) 295 A curiosity in many in those times of being baptized in Jordan. *a* **1718** Penn *Tracts* Wks. 1726 I. 499 He wholly denied his Wife the Curiosity of changing of but one Piece of foreign Gold.

II. As a quality of things.

†**9.** Careful or elaborate workmanship; perfection of construction; elaborateness, elegance; artistic character. *Obs.*

c **1380** Wyclif *Wks.* (1880) 8 3if þei drawen þe peple in þe holiday by coryouste of gaye wyndownes. **1393** Gower *Conf.* III. 383, I.. axe.. that my boke be nought refused.. For lack of curiosite. **1483** Caxton *Gold. Leg.* 72/3 To wryte the curiosyte and werke of the temple.. passeth my connynge to expresse. **1509** Hawes *Past. Pleas.* XXVII. lviii, Betrapped fayre and gaye Wyth shyning trappers of curiositie. **1584** Burghley *Let.* in Fuller *Ch. Hist.* IX. v. §9 An instrument of 24 Articles of great length and curiosity, formed in a Romish stile. **1665** Hooke *Microgr.* 163 You can hardly look on the scales of any Fish, but you may discover abundance of curiosity and beautifying. **1673** *Lady's Call.* I. v. ⁋53. 49 Because they are loth.. to abate any thing of the curiosity of their dress. **1697** Collier *Ess. Mor. Subj.* II. (1709) 90 The Regularity of Motion, visible in the great variety and Curiosity of Bodies.

†**10.** Careful accuracy of construction; nicety, delicacy. *Obs.*

1593 Fale *Dialling* A iij, The making of the Horologicall Cylindre, and the Ring.. we have presently omitted, partly for their curiosity in cutting and delineation. **1662** Evelyn *Chalcog.* Pref. (1769) 35 This art.. is arrived to the utmost curiosity and accurateness. **1664** Power *Exp. Philos.* III. 170 How many ticklish Curiosities, and nice Circumstances there are to perform this Experiment exactly. **1703** Moxon *Mech. Exerc.* 21 The chiefest Curiosity in the making.. Hinges is, 1. That the Pin-hole be exactly round.. 2. That the Joints are let exactly into one another. **1807** Southey *Espriella's Lett.* I. 154 An idea of the curiosity with which these things are constructed.

11. The quality of being curious or interesting from novelty or strangeness; curiousness.

1597 Morley *Introd. Mus.* 105 This I thought good to shew you, not for anie curiositie which is in it, but [etc.]. **1660** Sharrock *Vegetables* Ep. Ded., The operations themselves.. are devoid of curiosity. **1686** R. Berkeley in *Evelyn's Mem.* (1857) III. 283 From thence we went the next day to Rotterdam, where the curiosity of the place detained us three days. **1774** T. Jefferson *Autobiog.* Wks. 1859 I. App. 124 The distance between these, and the instructions actually adopted, is of some curiosity. **1858** Hawthorne *Fr. & It. Jrnls.* II. 96 The curiosity of which was overlaid by their multitude.

III. A matter or thing that has this quality.

†**12.** A curious question or matter of investigation; a nicety of argument; a subtlety. *Obs.*

c **1380** Wyclif *Wks.* (1880) 6 3if þei.. traveilen not in holy writt but veyn pleies and corioustees. **1586** T. B. *La Primaud. Fr. Acad.* I. 152 Their subtilties and bold curiosities, who have sought to plucke.. out of heaven the secrets hid from the angels. **1597** Hooker *Eccl. Pol.* v. xiii. (1611) 206 These nice curiosities are not worthie the labour which wee bestow to answere them. *a* **1631** Donne *Serm.* 367 Troubling the peace of the Church, with impertinent and inextricable curiosities. **1641** Milton *Ch. Govt.* II. (1851) 145 Not to make verbal curiosities the end. **1678** Owen *Mind of God* v. 144 A wrangling science filled with niceties, subtilties, curiosities, futilous termes of Art. **1700** Astry tr. *Saavedra-Faxardo* I. 198 The Books which contain'd idle Curiosities were burnt.

†**b.** A curious or ingenious art, experiment, etc.

1605 Camden *Rem.* (1637) 243 Divers curious men.. by the falling of a ring Magically prepared.. judged that one Theodorus should succeede in the Empire.. By like curiosities it was found that Odo should succeede. **1626** Bacon *Sylva* §431 There hath been practised also a curiosity, to set a Tree upon the North side of a Wall [etc.]. *a* **1635** Naunton *Fragm. Reg.* (Arb.) 36 They note him to have had certain curiosities, and secret wayes of intelligence above the rest.

†**13.** A matter upon which undue care is bestowed; a vanity, nicety, refinement. *Obs.*

c **1400** *Apol. Loll.* 108 þat he wast himsilf and his goodis, and oþer mennis, in lustis, and in oþer veyn curiositeis. **1474** Caxton *Chesse* IV. iii. (1860) K v b, Therfore ought the good women fle the curiositees and places where they myght falle in blame. *a* **1536** Tindale *Wks.* 238 (R) Yᵉ greater nomber receaue the wordes for a newnesse and curiositie (as they say). **1617** Moryson *Itin.* III. I. ii. 35 This fashion, and the like curiosities, I would haue an Englishman to leaue when he returns out of Italy. **1643** Burroughes *Exp. Hosea* ii. (1652) 180 When we are in danger to be stripped of all, it is not time then to stand about curiosities and niceties. **1705** Stanhope *Paraphr.* I. 97 Useless Curiosities, and such as tend to adorn, but not at all to amend the Man.

†**14.** A curious detail, feature, or trait. *Obs.*

1653 H. More *Antid. Ath.* II. xii. (1712) 79 The Eye.. is so exquisitely framed.. that not the least curiosity can be added. **1665** Hooke *Microgr.* 47 Moscovy-glass, or *Lapis specularis*, is a Body that seems to have as many Curiosities in its Fabrick as any common Mineral I have met with. **1747** Gould *Eng. Ants* 17 Pliny informs us that the Ants of his Country are wont to bury their Dead, which is a Curiosity not imitated by ours in England.

15. An object of interest; any object valued as curious, rare, or strange.

c **1645** Howell *Lett.* I. I. xviii, Amongst other Curiosities which he pleased to shew me up and down Paris. **1664** Evelyn *Kal. Hort.* (1729) 201 The Narcissus of Japan.. that nice Curiosity. **1665** Boyle *Occas. Refl.* (1845) 361 *heading*, Upon the sight of a Branch of Corral among a great Prince's Collection of Curiosities. **1710** Hearne *Collect.* (Oxf. Hist. Soc.) III. 39 These Pyxides or Boxes are mention'd as great curiosities. **1770** Kuckhan in *Phil. Trans.* LX. 302 Collecting natural curiosities of the insect, bird, and beast kinds. **1869** Semmes *Advent. Afloat* II. 695 The cargo, consisting mostly of light Japanese goods, lacker-ware, and curiosities.

†**b.** *collect.* = Curious things. *Obs.*

1786 W. Gilpin *Obs. Pict. Beauty* I. p. xxii, The bowels of the earth, containing such amazing stores of curiosity.

c. Applied to a person who is 'queer' in his appearance, habits, etc.; cf. *oddity*.

1873 *Slang Dict.*, *Cure*, an odd person; a contemptuous term, abridged from *curiosity*, which was formerly the favourite expression.

16. *Comb.*, as ***curiosity-dealer***, ***-monger***; **curiosity-shop**, a shop where curiosities are bought and sold.

1789 Wolcott (P. Pindar) *Subj. for Painters* Wks. 1812 II. 182 Made frequent Curiosity-campaigns. **1818** Hazlitt *Eng. Poets* v. (1870) 128 A museum or curiosity-shop. **1840** Dickens (*title*), Old Curiosity Shop. *Ibid.* i, The curiosity-dealer's warehouse. **1860** *All Year Round* No. 74. 569 One —a notable curiosity-monger.

‖**curioso** (kjʊərɪ'əʊsəʊ). *arch.* Pl. -i, -os. [a. It. *curioso* (kuri'oso) a curious person.] In 17th c., usually one who is curious in matters of science and art; **b.** later, an admirer or collector of curiosities; a connoisseur, virtuoso.

1658–72 Wood *Life* 24 July 1658, Dr. John Wilkins, warden of Wadham Coll., the greatest curioso of his time. **1710** London & Wise *Compl. Gard.* (1719) 40 The most judicious sort of Curioso's. **1727** S. Switzer *Pract. Gardiner* II. xiii. 99 Those curioso's who divide herbs into four degrees of heat, and four degrees of cold. **1806** Surr *Winter in Lond.* I. 216 [The books] remained stationary on the shelves, except to the *curiosi*.

curious ('kjʊərɪəs), *a.* Forms: 4–5 coryous, -ious, curiuse, -yus, 4–6 curiouse, -yous, 5 corius, -iouse, -yowse, curiouss, -iowse, -ose, -yws, -yose, 5–6 curyouse, -ius, 6 courious, 4– curious. [a. OF. *curius* (*Ch. de Rol.*, 11th c.) = Pr. *curios*, Sp. and It. *curioso*:—L. *cūriōs-us* used only subjectively 'full of care or pains, careful, assiduous, inquisitive'; French has also the objective sense in 14th c. (*robes curieuses*).]

A word which has been used from time to time with many shades of meaning; the only senses now really current are 5, 16, and (in some applications) 9.

I. As a subjective quality of persons.

†**1. a.** Bestowing care or pains; careful; studious, attentive. *Obs.*

c **1386** Chaucer *Shipman's T.* 243 My deere wif, I the byseeke.. For to kepe oure good be curious. **1494** Fabyan *Chron.* VI. clx. 152 He shold take hym vnto his cure, and be to hym as curyous as he wolde be vnto his owne chylde. *c* **1500** *Melusine* 109 Melusyne was full curyous and besy to make al thinges redy. **1580** Sidney *Arcadia* v. 457 But the curious servant of Philanax forbade him the entry. **1650** Jer. Taylor *Holy Living* i. §1 He that is curious of his time, will not easily be unready and unfurnished. **1721** R. Bradley *Wks. Nat.* 20 The French Gardeners.. are.. very curious to observe, that no broken part of a mushroom be left. **1779–81** Johnson *L.P., Cowley* Wks. II. 38 They were not always strictly curious, whether the opinions.. were true.

†**b.** Anxious, concerned, solicitous. *Obs.*

c **1400** *Rom. Rose* 1052 Many a traitour envious, That ben ful busie and curious For to dispraise, and to blame. **1513** More in Grafton *Chron.* II. 783 Amongest them that were more amorous of her bodie, then curious of her soule. **1611** Shaks. *Cymb.* I. vi. 191 And I am something curious.. To haue them in safe stowage. *a* **1697** Strathspey *Let.* in *Aubrey's Misc.* 212 Being curious for nothing but the Verity.

†**2.** Careful as to the standard of excellence; difficult to satisfy; particular; nice, fastidious. *Obs.* **a.** *esp.* in food, clothing, matters of taste.

c **1380** Wyclif *Sel. Wks.* III. 205 Take meete and drinke in mesure, ne to costli ne to licorouse, and be not to corious þeraboute. **1489** Caxton *Faytes of A.* I. vii. 17 Not curyous of mygnotes, folyetes ne of iewellis. **1579** Lyly *Euphues* (Arb.) 118 Be not curious to curle thy haire. *a* **1592** H.

SMITH *Serm.* (1866) II. 329 Christ was not curious in his diet. **1605** CAMDEN *Rem.* (1637) 285 There was one that was very curious in keeping of his beard. **1781** GIBBON *Decl. & F.* II. 45 They soon became..curious in their diet and apparel. **1821** SCOTT *Kenilw.* iii, In arranging which [the hair] men at that time..were very nice and curious.

†**b.** *generally.* Particular; cautious. *Obs.*

a **1533** LD. BERNERS *Gold. Bk. M. Aurel.* (1546) H ii, Wise among wyse men, as it is couenable for a curiouse prynce to be. **1596** SHAKS. *Tam. Shr.* IV. iv. 36 For curious I cannot be with you, Signior Baptista. **1617** MORYSON *Itin.* I. III. iii. 252 The Italians, in regard of their clime, are very curious to receive strangers in a time of plague. **1662** GERBIER *Princ.* 15 Builders ought also to be very curious and carefull in the choice of the place to Build a Seat on. **1692** LOCKE *Educ.* §92 In this Choice be as curious, as you would be in that of a Wife for him. **1772** BURKE *Corr.* (1844) I. 375 Men of integrity are curious, sometimes too curious, in the choice of means.

†**c.** Particular about details, or as to manner of action. *Obs.*

1570 B. GOOGE *Pop. Kingd.* Ded. Q. Eliz., Wherein I haue the lesse beene curious, bycause it was chiefly made for the benifite of the common and simpler sorte. **1655** GURNALL *Chr. in Arm.* II. 243 What is the Gospel of all this? but that God is very curious in his worship. **1697** DAMPIER *Voy.* (1698) I. A iij b, I have not been curious as to the spelling of the Names of Places, Plants, Fruits, Animals. **1743** *Lond. & Country Brew.* III. (ed. 2) 195 The Alewives..are most of them as curious in their brewing it [White Ale] as the Dairy-woman in making her Butter.

†**3. a.** Careful or nice in observation or investigation, accurate. *Obs.*

1642 FULLER *Holy & Prof. St.* II. xxi. 137 Having in his whole voyage, though a curious searcher after the time, lost one day. **1764** HARMER *Observ.* XXI. xi. 88 Ascertained by some curious and accurate person. **1816** SINGER *Hist. Cards* i. 10 It is to be desired that some curious orientalist may think the subject worthy an attentive enquiry.

b. Said of the eye, ear, etc.

1592 SHAKS. *Rom. & Jul.* I. iv. 31 What curious eye doth quote deformities? **1684** R. H. *School of Recreation* 9 The little Beagle..is of exceeding Cunning, and curious Scent in Hunting. **1699** BENTLEY *Phal.* 208 The difference..is very small, and such as might escape even a curious Eye in so dim an Inscription. *a* **1713** ELLWOOD *Autobiog.* (1714) 135 Having a curious Ear, he understood by my Tone, when I understood what I read.

†**4.** Ingenious, skilful, clever, expert. *Obs.*

1375 BARBOUR *Bruce* X. 359 A crafty man and a curiouss. *c* **1400** *Destr. Troy* 11677 A tre, But no clerke is so corious to ken vs the nome. **1582** T. WATSON *Cent. Loue* Ep. Ded., The curious pensill of Apelles. **1651** FULLER *Abel Rediv., Junius* (1867) II. 185 A curious limner was employed to draw his picture to the life. **1715** J. RICHARDSON *Th. Painting* 28 A curious Mechanick's Hand must be exquisite. **1762–71** H. WALPOLE *Vertue's Anecd. Paint.* (1786) III. 252 That neat and curious painter Vander Heyden.

5. a. Desirous of seeing or knowing; eager to learn; inquisitive. Often with condemnatory connotation: Desirous of knowing what one has no right to know, or what does not concern one, prying. (The current subjective sense.)

a **1340** HAMPOLE *Psalter* cxxxvi. 3 þei are curiouse & wold witt þat þei are nouȝt worthi till. **1375** BARBOUR *Bruce* IV. 687 Bot feill folk ar sa curiouss, And to witt thingis covatouss. *c* **1384** CHAUCER *H. Fame* I. 29 That somme man is to curiouse In studye. **1526** *Pilgr. Perf.* (W. de W. 1531) 18 b, How no persone sholde be curyous in askyng questyons concernynge the secretes of god. **1653** H. COGAN tr. *Pinto's Trav.* xliv. 172 He was a man very curious, and much inclined to hear of novelties, and rare things. **1754** RICHARDSON *Grandison* (1781) I. xiii. 72 Those branches of science which..serve for amusement to inquisitive and curious minds. **1833** HT. MARTINEAU *Brooke Farm* x. 116 Two or three neighbours..were curious to know what he had seen abroad. **1873** HALE *In His Name* vi. 64 Crowded with curious idlers.

†**b.** Minute in inquiry or discrimination, subtle.

a **1585** ABP. SANDYS *Serm.* (1841) 116 The quiddities of too curious schoolmen.

†**c.** Devoting attention to occult art. *Obs.*

1549 UDALL, etc. *Erasm. Par. Eph.* Argt., That Citie was full of Curiouse menne, and suche as were geuen to magicall artes. **1578** TIMME *Caluine on Gen.* 35 Certaine courious persons abuse this place to colour their vaine prognostications. **1614** BP. HALL *Recoll. Treat.* 137 Curious men, that consulte with starres, and spirits, for their destinies.

d. Of actions, etc.: Prompted by curiosity.

1840 DICKENS *Old C. Shop* i, Every now and then she stole a curious look at my face as if to make quite sure that I was not deceiving her. **1876** BLACKIE *Songs Relig. & Life* 191 Live, and make no curious comment.

†**6. a.** Taking the interest of a connoisseur in any branch of art; skilled as a connoisseur or virtuoso. Const. *of, in* and *infin. Obs.*

1577 B. GOOGE *Heresbach's Husb.* IV. (1586) 170 b, Yet of many curious and fine fellowes, for their rarenesse and daintinesse, they [pheasants] are brought up, and kept. **1644** EVELYN *Mem.* (1857) I. 69 Monsieur Morine..one of the most skilful and curious persons in France for his rare collection of shells, flowers, and insects. **1693** —— *De la Quint. Compl. Gard.* I. 24 Gentlemen that are Curious in Gard'ning. **1734** tr. *Rollin's Anc. Hist.* (1827) VII. XVII. §8. 238 He was exceedingly curious in pictures and designs by great masters. **1751** JOHNSON *Rambler* No. 177 ¶5 A select company of curious men, who met once a week to exhilarate their studies, and compare their acquisitions. Every one of these virtuosos, etc. **1792** *Copper-Plate Mag.* No. 6 The bishop's family being curious botanists.

b. In this sense often absolutely in pl.

1634 SIR T. HERBERT *Trav.* 115 Her Caravans lodge exceeds her Mosque, yet neither, of power to beget admiration with the curious. **1708** J. CHAMBERLAYNE *St. Gt. Brit.* I. III. ii. (1743) 158 There are several Specimens yet remaining in the Cabinets of the Curious. **1768** W. GILPIN *Ess. Prints* 241 A few impressions had been taken from the plate in its first state, which sell among the curious for ten times the price. **1838–9** HALLAM *Hist. Lit.* II. ii. II. §59 The curious in bibliography are conversant with other versions and editions of the sixteenth century.

II. As an objective quality of things, etc.

†**7. a.** Made with care or art; skilfully, elaborately or beautifully wrought. *Obs.*

c **1384** CHAUCER *H. Fame* I. 125 Moo curiouse portreytures..then I sawgh euer. ? *a* **1400** *Morte Arth.* 61 Thare a citee he sette..with curious walles. *c* **1450** *St. Cuthbert* (Surtees) 7848 A bischop staff was preciouse, And in makyng full curiouse. **1579** LYLY *Euphues* (Arb.) 54 Doth not experience teach vs, that in the most curious Sepulcher are enclosed rotten bones? **1611** BIBLE *Ex.* xxviii. 27 The curious girdle of the Ephod. **1653** H. MORE *Antid. Ath.* II. ix. (1712) 67 Made themselves such curious and safe Nests in Bushes and Trees. **1703** MOXON *Mech. Exerc.* 21 If your Work be intended to be curious, the true Square-filing the Upper-side..is a great Ornament. **1760–72** tr. *Juan & Ulloa's Voy.* (ed. 3) I. IV. ix. 182 [Boats]..of a more curious and elegant construction.

†**b.** Of food, clothing, etc.: Exquisitely prepared, dainty, delicate, *recherché. Obs.* or *arch.*

c **1325** *E.E. Allit. P.* B. 1353 In þe clernes of his concubines & curious wedez. *c* **1394** *P. Pl. Crede* 765 And comeren her stomakes With curiuse drynkes. **1514** BARCLAY *Cyt. & Uplondyshm.* (Percy) p. lxvi, I aske no palace nor lodging curious. **1593** SHAKS. *3 Hen. VI*, II. v. 53 His Viands sparkling in a Golden Cup, His bodie couched in a curious bed. **1615** J. STEPHENS *Satyr. Ess.* A vij b, The inviter.. cannot well provide..One dish so curious, as may please each tast. **1702** C. MATHER *Magn. Chr.* III. I. i. (1852) 276 He made a careful, though not curious, diet serve him. **1865** SWINBURNE *Poems & Ball., Leper* 6, I served her wine and curious meat.

†**8.** Carefully worked out or prepared; elaborate. *Obs.*

1561 T. NORTON *Calvin's Inst.* II. 145 Y^e obiections are not so strong that they nede a curious confutation. **1573** G. HARVEY *Letter-bk.* (Camden) 44 Not to look after ani set or curious epistle. **1614** BP. HALL *Recoll. Treat.* 839 Persecuted with most curious torments. **1674** BREVINT *Saul at Endor* 363 Served with the curiousest Music.

9. Of actions, investigations, etc.: Characterized by special care, careful, accurate, minute.

1526 *Pilgr. Perf.* (W. de W. 1531) 142 b, Stones quadrat or squared, polysshed & dressed after the moost curyous maner. *a* **1534** LD. BERNERS *Gold. Bk. M. Aurel.* (1546) G viii b, He made curious diligence to searche out all the players. **1652** NEEDHAM tr. *Selden's Mare Cl.* 168 It did not sufficiently appear..without a more curious examination. **1667** *Observ. Burning London* in *Select. Harl. Misc.* (1793) 446 A more curious and earnest inquiry of the truth. **1859** DISRAELI *Sp.* in *Times* 22 July, A subject, which demands the most curious investigation. **1866** ARGYLE *Reign Law* vii. (1871) 340 Many years of curious enquiry and of laborious contrivance.

†**10.** Characterized by minute inquiry or treatment: **a.** Unduly minute or inquisitive. *Obs.*

c **1340** HAMPOLE *Prose Tr.* (1866) 3 The name of Ihesu.. dos a-waye coryous and vayne ocupacyons fra vs. **1535** COVERDALE *Job* xxxv. 15 Nether hath he pleasure in curious and depe inquisicions. **1577** VAUTROUILLIER *Luther on Ep. Gal.* 16 We must abstaine from ye curious searching of Gods maiestie. **1654** FULLER *Two Serm.* 63 [This question] is curious for man to enquire and impossible to determine. **1742** YOUNG *Nt. Th.* ix. 1853 'Tis not the curious, but the pious path, That leads me to my point.

†**b.** Intricate, abstruse, subtle. *Obs.*

c **1391** CHAUCER *Astrol.* Prol. 2 That curio[u]s enditing & hard sentence is ful heuy atones for swich a child to lerne. **1538** STARKEY *England* I. iv. 137 The maner of syngyng.. was not so curyouse as hyt ys now. **1563** FULKE *Meteors* (1640) 70 b, A Mathematicall reason..more curious, than can be understood of the common sort. **1613** J. SALKELD *Treat. Angels* 335 Amongst other very curious questions which Theodoretus upon Genesis propoundeth, one is this. **1664** POWER *Exp. Philos.* Pref. 10 In these narrow Engines [microscopic animals] there is more curious Mathematics.

†**c.** Recondite, occult. *Obs.*

1382 WYCLIF *Acts* xix. 19 Manye of hem that sueden curiouse thingis brouȝten to gidere bookis, and brennyden hem bifore alle men. *c* **1386** CHAUCER *Frankl. T.* 392 As yonge clerkes that been lykerous To reden Artes that been curious..a book he say Of Magyk natureel. **1611** BIBLE *Acts* xix. 19. **1619** SIR A. GORGES tr. *Bacon's De Sap. Vet.* 95 Unlawfull and curious arts of what kind soever.

†**11.** Minutely accurate, exact, precise. *Obs.*

1614 SELDEN *Titles Hon.* II. i. §43 Your curious learning and judgment may correct where I have erred. **1665** HOOKE *Microgr.* 2 The Points of the most curious Mathematical Instruments. **1672** PETTY *Pol. Anat.* Pref., Curious Dissections cannot be made without variety of proper Instruments. **1764** DUNN in *Phil. Trans.* LIV. 115, I set my watch exactly by the clocks; captain Bentincke and captain Holland were present with curious watches. **1825** CARLYLE *Schiller* II. (1845) 57 Formed upon a strict and curious standard.

†**12.** Of materials: Fine, delicate. *Obs.*

1665 HOOKE *Microgr.* 4 Even the most curious Powder that can be made use of..must consist of..rough particles. *Ibid.* 5 The finest Lawn..so curious that the threads were scarce discernable by the naked eye. **1669** A. BROWNE *Ars Pict.* (1675) 87 Draw the lines of the Eyelids..with a pencil somewhat more curious and sharp then before.

†**13.** Of or pertaining to the exercise of care, skill, or ingenuity; skilled, skilful. *Obs.* (Cf. 4.)

1681 CHETHAM *Angler's Vade-m.* Pref., It is not fine, curious, and skilful Angling, that destroys the breed of Fish. *a* **1687** PETTY *Pol. Arith.* i. (1691) 33 As Trades and curious Arts increase; so the Trade of Husbandry will decrease. **1776** ADAM SMITH *W.N.* I. xi. (1869) I. 163 He decides, like a true lover of all curious cultivation, in favour of the vineyard.

†**14.** Without explicit reference to workmanship: Exquisite, choice, excellent, fine (in beauty, flavour, or other good quality). *Obs.* or *dial.* (Cf. mod. use of *nice.*)

c **1420** *Avow. Arth.* lii, Maydyns..curtase and curiowse Forsothe in bed lay. **1535** STEWART *Cron. Scot.* II. 17 He gat on hir ane sone callit Fergus, In all this warld wes nane mair curious. **1638** SIR T. HERBERT *Trav.* 297 The Orenges..are ..of so curious a relish, as affects the eater beyond measure. *Ibid.* 354 Cloath'd with sweet grasse, long and curious. **1665** PEPYS *Diary* 24 Sept., A very calm, curious morning. **1667** PRIMATT *City & C. Build.* 10 Salisbury Plain, and divers other places of champion ground in England, which are very famous for curious air. **1697** DAMPIER *Voy.* (1698) I. xv. 436 We filled all our Water at a curious Brook close by us. **1725** BRADLEY *Fam. Dict.* s.v. *Vinegar*, In about thirty or forty Days it will be curious Vinegar. **1742** *Phil. Trans.* XLII. 148 (In Suffolk) She said..if her Butter was not curious, she eat dry Bread. **1816** J. PICKERING *Voc. U.S., Curious*..is often heard in New England among the common farmers, in the sense of 'excellent', or 'peculiarly excellent'; as in ..'These are curious apples'; 'this is curious cider'.

†**15.** Calling forth feelings of interest; interesting, noteworthy. *Obs.* or *arch.*

1682 BURNET *Rights Princes* iv. 135 The curiousest Remains of former Ages that are extant. **1759** SIR J. REYNOLDS *Idler* No. 76 ¶5 It is curious to observe, that, etc. **1793** SMEATON *Edystone L.* §56 [It] would have been not only curious, but useful, had it been handed down to us. **1816** KEATINGE *Trav.* (1817) II. 80 It would be very curious to be able to ascertain where and how the scaffolding was obtained for such a work.

16. a. Deserving or exciting attention on account of its novelty or peculiarity; exciting curiosity; somewhat surprising, strange, singular, odd; queer. (The ordinary current objective sense.)

1715 J. RICHARDSON *Th. Painting* 100 This is very Particular, and Curious. **1719** —— *Sc. Connoisseur* 204 What is Rare, and Curious without any Other consideration we Naturally take Pleasure in. **1769** BURKE *Observ. Late State Nation* Wks. 1842 I. 101 A most curious reason, truly! **1807** CRABBE *Par. Reg.* III. 509 No curious shell, rare plant, or brilliant spar, Inticed our traveller. **1869** DILKE *Greater Brit.* II. 163 Seated in the piazza..I had before me a curious scene. **1888** BRYCE *Amer. Commw.* III. xc. 251, I give here a few of the novel or curious provisions of the Constitution of California of 1789.

b. Used as a euphemistic description of erotic or pornographic works.

1877 'PISANUS FRAXI' (*title*) Index librorum prohibitorum: being notes bio-biblio-icono-graphical and critical, on curious and uncommon books. **1925** A. HUXLEY *Those Barren Leaves* I. v. 55 The publications of the Purity League figure invariably under the heading 'Curious' in the booksellers' catalogues. **1934** H. G. WELLS *Exper. Autobiogr.* II. viii. 529 That redoubtable suppressed *Life and Loves* of his..which is sought after by collectors of 'curious' books. **1947** [see CURIOSA]. **1970** I. MONTAGU *Youngest Son* 240 My voracious approach to literature included the pages in the bookseller's catalogue labelled 'Erotica' or 'Curious', and I have yet to see an atom of evidence that pornography ever did anyone any harm.

c. Phr. ***curiouser and curiouser***, more and more curious; increasingly strange.

1865 'L. CARROLL' *Alice in Wonderland* ii. 15 'Curiouser and curiouser!' cried Alice (she was so much surprised, that for the moment she quite forgot how to speak good English). **1931** D. L. SAYERS *Five Red Herrings* xv. 167 'I formed the opinion..that Mr. Gowan had..not departed from Kirkcudbright on the Monday evening..but that he had remained concealed in his own house.'..'Curiouser and curiouser,' said Wimsey. **1939** M. ALLINGHAM *Mr. Campion & Others* I. ix. 203 'Perhaps it wasn't empty then?' 'In that case it's curiouser and curiouser.' **1970** *Guardian* 31 Dec. 8/1 The ways of film companies become curiouser and curiouser.

†**17.** Such as interests the curioso or connoisseur. *Obs.*

1665 BOYLE *Occas. Refl.* (1669) 359 The number of fine things that make up this curious collection. **1719** J. RICHARDSON *Sc. Connoisseur* 45 Pictures, Drawings, Prints, Statues, Intaglias, and the like Curious Works of Art. **1731–7** MILLER *Gard. Dict.* s.v. *Iris*, They are generally banish'd from very curious Gardens, and are proper only for large Gardens. **1768** W. GILPIN *Ess. Prints* 145 In curious collections we meet with a few of Cuyps etchings.

III. †**18.** quasi-*adv.* Curiously. *Obs.*

1593 SHAKS. *Lucr.* 1300 This is too curious-good, this blunt and ill. *a* **1644** QUARLES 11 *Pious Medit.* (1717) 64 They were not wise enough, and yet too wise; Too curious wise. **1687** CONGREVE *Old Batch.* IV. xvii, 'Tis most curious fine weather. **1791** COWPER *Odyss.* XXI. 460 Within the hall, let none look curious forth. **1834** J. H. NEWMAN *Lett.* (1891) II. 39 Curious enough, Rose writes down to praise it.

Hence †'**curious** *v.*, *nonce-wd.* (*intr.*), to work curiously or artistically.

1606 SYLVESTER *Du Bartas* II. iv. II. (1641) 212/2 A great cornaline; Where some rare Artist (curiousing upon't) Hath deeply cut Times triple-formed Front.

curiously ('kjʊərɪəslɪ), *adv.* [f. prec. + -LY².] In a curious manner.

1. Carefully, attentively, *arch.*

1382 WYCLIF *Eccl.* ix. 1 Alle these thingus I tretede in myn herte, that I vndirstonde curyously. *c* **1400** MAUNDEV. (1839) vi. 66 Whiche Sepultures the Sarazines kepen fulle curyously. **1483** CAXTON *Gold. Leg.* 430/2 Kepyng hymself ryght curyously fro the..world. **1670** WALTON *Lives* I. 19 [She] had been curiously and plentifully educated. **1682** SCARLETT *Exchanges* 37 He must curiously observe, if the first and second Advice agree, or not. **1743** *Lond. & Country Brew.* IV. (ed. 2) 322 If they [Welch Coal] are curiously burnt, they gingle like common Cinders. **1871** TENNYSON

Idylls, Last Tourn. 90 Take thou my churl, and tend him curiously.

2. Inquisitively; pryingly.

1382 WYCLIF *2 Thess.* iii. 11 Summe among ȝou.. no thing worchinge, but doynge curiously [**1611** are busi-bodies]. **1869** SEMMES *Advent. Afloat* II. 716 Crowds gathered to look curiously upon her. **1886** BESANT *Children of Gibeon* II. xxxi, Lady Mildred listened and watched him curiously, as if trying to read something unexpressed.

3. With careful art, skilfully, elaborately, exquisitely, cunningly. *arch.*

1340 *Ayenb.* 176 Leuedis þet zuo curiouseliche agrayþeþ hire heaueden mid preciouse agrayþinges. *c* **1380** *Antecrist* in Todd 3 *Treat. Wyclif* 128 Wiþ silver vessel þei ben servyd curiously. *c* **1386** CHAUCER *Frankl. T.* 181 Craft of mannes hand so curiously Arrayed hadde this gardyn. **1570** T. NORTON tr. *Nowel's Catech.* (1853) 197 That we seek not and gather together curiously dainty things for banqueting. **1673** RAY *Journ. Low C.* 20 The Steeple of S. Maries Church is.. Curiously built and carved. **1711** HEARNE *Collect.* (Oxf. Hist. Soc.) III. 283 The Pontifical most curiously illuminated. **1809–12** MAR. EDGEWORTH *Madame de Fleury* x, Her curiously wrought ivory toys. **1875** E. WHITE *Life in Christ* IV. xxiv. (1876) 408 It is of far more importance.. to preserve the body for ever than to clothe it curiously now.

†**b.** By art; artificially. *Obs. rare.*

1615 J. STEPHENS *Satyr. Ess.* (ed. 2) 51 Things curiously Created, differ as much from thinges begotten, as the first Man from birth, and artificiall bodies from mans issue.

4. With minute accuracy, minutely, critically, fastidiously, nicely, delicately. *arch.*

1561 DAUS tr. *Bullinger on Apoc.* (1573) 91 b, I suppose we neede not to reason any curiouslyer hereof at this present. **1586** THYNNE in *Holinshed* II. 405 Curiouslie carping at my barrennes in writing. **1607–12** BACON *Ess. Studies* (Arb.) 8 To be read but not curiously. **1703** MOXON *Mech. Exerc.* 118 Joiners work more curiously, and observe the Rules more exactly, than Carpenters need do. **1823** SCOTT *Peveril* xv, You should enquire into these matters a little more curiously. **1871** BLACKIE *Four Phases* i. 85 As if a man should curiously describe the cylinders and the pistons and the wheels, etc.

†**5.** 'Nicely', finely, excellently, handsomely, beautifully. *Obs.*

1548 HALL *Chron.* 197 b, Richely trapped, and curiouslye armed. **1647** LILLY *Chr. Astrol.* clxxxi. 756 The second wife is.. curiously handsome. **1665** SIR T. HERBERT *Trav.* (1677) 233 A Viol full of intoxicating Wine, which both looked and relished curiously. **1670** NARBOROUGH *Jrnl.* in *Sev. Late Voy.* I. (1711) 67 The Leaves of the Trees are like green Birch-tree Leaves, curiously sweet. **1725** BRADLEY *Fam. Dict.* s.v. *Syllabub*, Let it stand two or three hours, till it settles, and it will eat curiously.

6. In a way that excites interest or surprise; remarkably, strangely, oddly; queerly.

1665 HOOKE *Microgr.* 91 An infinite variety of curiously figur'd Snow. **1797** BEWICK *Brit. Birds* (1847) I. 164 The entrance was long, and curiously arched over with the stems of dried grass. **1870** LOWELL *Among my Bks.* Ser. II. (1873) 161 Verses.. curiously prophetic of the maturer man. **1875** JEVONS *Money* (1878) 128 Curiously enough no modern government thought of employing a well-chosen bronze for small money.

'curious-'minded, *a.* [CURIOUS *a.*] Having a curious or inquisitive or strange mind.

1928 T. E. LAWRENCE *Lett.* (1938) 599 He'd not likely kill an unarmed, solitary man (Arabs are very curious-minded). **1930** M. MEAD *Growing up in New Guinea* i. 1 One of the most fascinating studies open to the curious minded. **1954** J. R. R. TOLKIEN *Fellowship of Ring* 62 The most inquisitive and curious-minded of that family.

curiousness ('kjʊərɪəsnɪs). [f. as CURIOUSLY *adv.* + -NESS.]

1. The quality or condition of being subjectively curious: †**a.** Carefulness; diligence; skilfulness; scrupulosity; fastidiousness. *Obs.*

c **1440** *York Myst.* xxix. 31 Of þe coriousnesse of þat karle þer is carping. **1528** TINDALE *Parab. Wicked Mammon* Wks. I. 58 Be diligent therefore that thou be not deceived with curiousness. **1555** EDEN *Decades* 136 Not theyr ignoraunce and slothfulnes but pernicious curiousnes. **1561** T. HOBY tr. *Castiglione's Courtyer* I. Eiij b, To reprehend hys curyousnesse in hys workes. **1628** WITHER *Brit. Rememb.* VI. 1937 They dresse Their bodies, with such tedious curiousnesse. **1692** DRYDEN *St. Evremont's Ess.* 35 He joined the Curiousness of Negotiations to the Science of War. *a* **1698** TEMPLE *Ess. Gardening* Wks. 1731 I. 176 Much Curiousness or Care, to introduce the Fruits of Foreign Climates.

b. Inquisitiveness: often as a fault; = CURIOSITY 5.

1561 T. NORTON *Calvin's Inst.* III. 302 Yᵉ curiousnesse of men.. which can by no stoppes be restrained from wandring into forbidden compasses. *a* **1640** SIR W. ALEXANDER *Hours* I. lxii. (T.), Ah! curiousness, first cause of all our ill. **1794** MRS. RADCLIFFE *Myst. Udolpho* xx, We had all a little more curiousness than you had. **1859** TENNYSON *Vivien* 362 Howsoe'er In children a great curiousness be well, Who have to learn themselves and all the world. **1866** J. H. NEWMAN *Gerontius* iii, I fain would know.. were it but meet to ask, And not a curiousness.

2. The quality of being objectively curious: †**a.** Beauty; elaborateness; exquisiteness. **b.** Strangeness, novelty, oddness.

c **1386** CHAUCER *Pars. T.* ¶372 (Harl.) In greet preciousnes of vessel & in curiousnesse of vessel and of mynstralcye. **1550** LATIMER *Last. Serm. bef. Edw. VI*, Wks. I. 222 In this sermon of Jonas is no great curiousnes, no great clerkliness. **1610** GUILLIM *Heraldry* II. i. (1660) 50 The curiousness and excellency of their workmanship. **1674** N. FAIRFAX *Bulk & Selv.* 193 The unutterable curiousness of its [the world's] frame and workmanship. **1862** *Parthenon* 26 July 401 The bindings.. are remarkable both for their curiousness, beauty, and fine preservation. **1874** HELPS *Soc. Press.* iii. 35 The appreciation of rarity and curiousness.

curiouste, curius(e, etc., obs. forms of CURIOSITY, CURIOUS, etc.

-curist (ˌkjʊərɪst). As the second element of compounds such as ***mind-curist, sure-curist*** (= one who dabbles in mind-cure, etc.).

1889 in *Cent. Dict.* **1907** *Practitioner* Apr. 580 Whether the engineer calls himself Christian Scientist, or Mind Curist, or Hypnotist, matters nothing.

curite ('kjʊəraɪt). *Min.* [a. F. *curite* (A. Schoep 1921, in *Compt. Rend.* CLXXIII. 1186), f. the name of Pierre *Curie* (see CURIE) + -ITE[1].] An orange-red hydrated oxide of lead and uranium.

1922 *Nature* 12 Jan. 63/1 The mineral was found at Kasolo, Belgian Congo, and occurs along with curite and chalcolite. **1938** R. W. LAWSON tr. *Hevesy & Paneth's Man. Radioactivity* (ed. 2) xv. 150 The mineral curite.. contains no trace of ordinary lead. **1958** C. FRONDEL in *Bull. U.S. Geol. Surv.* No. 1064. 95 Curite is a secondary mineral formed with other hydrated uranyl or lead-uranyl oxides by the alteration of uraninite. The lead of the mineral seems to be radiogenic and derived from the uraninite.

curium ('kjʊərɪəm). [mod.L., f. the name of Pierre *Curie* (see CURIE) and his wife Marie (1867–1934): see -IUM.] An artificially produced, highly radioactive metallic element of the actinide series, formed when plutonium 239 is bombarded with alpha particles and when americium 241 is bombarded with neutrons. Symbol Cm, atomic number 96.

1946 G. T. SEABORG in *Chem. & Engin. News* 10 May 1197/3 For element 96, containing seven 5f electrons, we suggest 'curium', symbol Cm, after Pierre and Marie Curie. **1957** *Oxf. Mail* 9 Sept. 1/7 Curium is 1,000 times more active than ordinary plutonium, which is generally regarded as hazardous. **1964** *Times* 21 Dec. 6/6 The United States Patent Office has issued a patent for a new element, called curium, to Dr. Glenn Seaborg. *Ibid.*, Curium is believed to have valuable properties for space travel.

†**'curkle,** *v. nonce-wd. Obs.* [App. imitative.] To cry as a quail.

a **1693** URQUHART *Rabelais* III. xiii. 107 Curring of Pigeons .. curkling of Quails.

curl (kɜːl), *sb.* [f. CURL *v.*[1]: cf. *twist, wrinkle.* Cf. also Du. *krul*, MDu. *krulle, krolle*, MLG. *krul*, LG. *krulle*, MHG. *krolle, krol*, mod.Ger. dial. *krolle* curl, lock of hair, ON. *krul*, Norw. *krull*, Da. *krölle*; which seem to be derived immediately from the adj.: see CRULL.]

1. A lock of hair of a spiral or convolute form; a ringlet.

Applied indifferently to a flat spiral like the mainspring of a watch, a cork-screw-like form (helix), or anything intermediate to or approaching these forms.

1602 SHAKS. *Ham.* III. iv. 56 Hyperions curles, the front of Ioue himselfe. **1665** SIR T. HERBERT *Trav.* (1677) 132 Their hair was long and dangling in curls. **1711** ADDISON *Spect.* No. 102 ¶7 To.. adjust a Curl of Hair. **1856** MISS MULOCK *J. Halifax* ii, He tossed back his curls, and looked smiling out through the window.

2. Anything of a similar spiral or incurved shape; a coil, wreath, convolution, undulation.

1615 CHAPMAN *Odyss.* XXIII. (R.), [An oar] which breakes The waues in curles. *a* **1634** RANDOLPH *Poems* (1638) 12 About each limbe he hurles His wanton body into numerous curles. **1676** GREW *Anat. Plants* IV. I. i. §11 The several Labels of a Groundsel-Leaf are all laid in a Back-Curl. **1774** T. TWINING in *Recreat. & Stud.* (1882) 30 Purcell, with all his old curls and twiddles, is perfection to him. **1832** G. DOWNES *Lett. Cont. Countries* I. 387 Here and there were curls of smoke.

3. a. The action of curling, or state of being curled. Phr. *in curl, out of curl*: said of hair which is kept curled, or which has gone straight. Also fig., as in ***to go out of curl***: to lose one's activity and 'vim', to become limp.

1665 SIR T. HERBERT *Trav.* (1677) 188 In calm weather.. the water is pacifique and without the least visible curl or wrinkle. **1699** DAMPIER *Voy.* II. III. iv. 27 It [the breeze] comes in a fine, small, black Curle upon the Water. **1793** *Trans. Soc. Encourag. Arts* (ed. 2) IV. 47 The waves.. spend their fury in a gentle curl up the slope. **1835** WHITTIER *Hunters of Men* iii, Hunting the black man, whose sin Is the curl of his hair and the hue of his skin! *a* **1893** *Mod.* To keep the hair in curl. **1913** D. H. LAWRENCE *Sons & Lovers* i. 10 Tha'rt not long in taking the curl out of me. **1924** GALSWORTHY *White Monkey* I. ix, 'If *you* got pneumonia,' he said, 'I should go clean out of curl.' **1964** E. MCCARTHY *Frankly Feminine* 52 A 'perm-set'.. will stay in curl for around eight weeks.

b. ***curl of the lip***: a slight elevation or bending of the upper lip, expressive of scorn or disgust.

1813 BYRON *Corsair* I. x, The lip's least curl, the lightest paleness.. speak alone Of deeper passions. **1857** H. SPENCER *Orig. Music* Ess. 1891 II. 402 Disgust [is shown] by a curl of the lip.

c. *Angling.* An eddy in a stream; also a ripple on the surface of water caused by the wind.

1766 BOWLKER *Univ. Angler* 132 Throw.. into holes and curls of the water, for there the best fish commonly lie. **1834** MEDWIN *Angler in Wales* I. 47 See, the fish are rising.. I think I can reach the curl yonder. **1855** KINGSLEY *Glaucus* (1878) 19 The breeze has come on, and there has been half-an-hour's lively fishing curl.

d. *Cricket.* The action of the verb (see CURL *v.*[1] 9); *spec.* = BREAK *sb.*[1] 5, SPIN *sb.*[1] 2 c.

1833 J. NYREN *Young Cricketer's Tutor* 98 They had such a peculiar curl that they would grind his fingers against the bat. **1867** G. H. SELKIRK *Guide to Cricket-ground* vi. 91 Cover point must be careful to allow for the 'curl' after grounding. **1871** *Baily's Mag.* June 168 His bowling.. being straight.. with a nice curl from the leg across the wicket. **1888** A. G. STEEL in Steel & Lyttelton *Cricket* iii. 170 In 1878 there was another.. slow bowler named Allan.. His bowling had a considerable amount of spin, but.. the most extraordinary thing connected with it was the inward curl in the air towards the body of the batsman.

e. *Math.* The vector product (written curl F or $\nabla \times$ F) of the operator ∇ (see DEL) with some given vector F; it gives a measure of the 'vorticity' or rotation at each point in the vector field F.

1873 J. C. MAXWELL *Electr. & Magnetism* I. 28 To interpret the vector part of $\nabla\sigma$.. let us examine the vector $\sigma - \sigma_0$ near the point *P*. It will appear as in the figure.., this vector being arranged on the whole tangentially in the direction opposite to the hands of a watch. I propose (with great diffidence) to call the vector part of $\nabla\sigma$ the curl, or the version of σ at the point *P*. **1882** O. HEAVISIDE in *Electrician* 18 Nov. 8/1 When one vector or directed quantity, B, is related to another vector, C, so that the line-integral of B *round* any closed curve equals the integral of C *through* the curve, the vector C is called the curl of the vector B. **1911** *Encycl. Brit.* XXVII. 964/1 If A represent the magnetic force at any point of an electro-magnetic field, the vector (∇A) will represent the electric current. In the general case it is called the curl, or the rotation, of A. **1943** MARGENAU & MURPHY *Math. Physics & Chem.* iv. 148 The curl of the linear velocity of any point of a rigid body equals twice the angular velocity. **1965** J. B. MARION *Princ. Vector Anal.* ii. 83 A paddlewheel placed in a fluid will remain stationary.. where curl v = 0. A field which everywhere has a vanishing curl is called an irrotational field. *Ibid.*, Both the divergence and the curl are encountered frequently in hydrodynamics and in electromagnetic theory but only infrequently in the mechanics of particles.

f. In surfing: see quot. 1962.

1962 T. MASTERS *Surfing made Easy* 64 *Curl*, the curved top of a breaking wave. **1965** FARRELLY & MCGREGOR *This Surfing Life* iv. 43 The semi-hollow wave.. allows you to pick up speed in the top half, and when it breaks you can move down to the botton half and ride underneath the curl, free of the white water. **1968** W. WARWICK *Surfriding in N.Z.* 10/3 Paddle towards the peak and as it becomes critical turn your board, and come back with the curl.

4. a. A disease of potatoes, in which the shoots are curled up and imperfectly developed; a disease of other plants, in which the leaves are curled up.

1790 *Trans. Soc. Encourag. Arts* VIII. 29 The [potato] crops.. have.. grown up sound and good, and free from Curl. **1832** *Veg. Subst. Food* 148 The curl first made its appearance in this country in.. 1764, in Lancashire. **1866** *Treas. Bot.* 363 *Curl*, a formidable disease in potatoes, referrible to Chlorosis, in which the tubers produce deformed curled shoots.. which are never perfectly developed. **1882** *Garden* 25 Feb. 133/2 Curl.. occurs when the Roses have been occupying the ground for a very long period.

b. A potato affected with this disease.

1791 *Trans. Soc. Encourag. Arts* IX. 61 Why some Curls appear in a crop that has been carefully managed.

5. *Comb.*, as ***curl-crested, -faced, -headed*** adjs.; ***curl-tuft***; **curl-cloth,** a kind of woollen cloth with a curly surface; **curl-cloud,** = CIRRUS 4.

1591 PERCIVALL *Sp. Dict.*, *Crespo*, curle headed. **1611** SPEED *Hist. Gt. Brit.* VI. xxi. 108 Long bearded, curle-headed. **1611** COTGR., *Volute*.. the writhen circle, or curle-tuft that.. sticks out of the chapter of a piller, etc. **1612** DRAYTON *Poly-olb.* xiv. 227 The curle-fac't bull. **1695** LD. PRESTON *Boethius* I. 7 And raise the curle-headed Wave. **1817** *Blackw. Mag.* I. 637/2 The sky was full of cirrus or curlcloud. **1885** *Daily News* 6 Oct. 3/2 The new astrakhan.. is used for coats and jackets.. It is sometimes called curl cloth.

curl (kɜːl), *v.*[1] Also 5 croul, 5–6 kurl, 6 courl, 6–7 curle; see also CURLED. [The early instances are of the pa. pple., which also occurs in the 14th c. in the forms *crolled, crulled*; these forms attach the vb. to the earlier adj. *croll*, CRULL, curly, which goes back to 1300, and corresponds to similar words in Fris., MDu., and MG. In these langs. also there is a derivative verb: Ger. *krollen, kröllen*, LG., Du., EFris. *krullen* to curl.]

I. *trans.* **1. a.** To bend round, wind, or twist into ringlets, as the hair.

[**1380** see CURLED.] **1447** BOKENHAM *Seyntys* (Roxb.) 142 A chyld apperyd.. Barefoot and wyth heer kurlyd semely. **1493** *Festivall* (W. de W. 1515) 164 Therfore (ye women).. haue not your visage popped ne your here pulled or crouled. **1570** LEVINS *Manip.* 191/4 To curle, *crispare*. **1634** SIR T. HERBERT *Trav.* 20 They curle their haire and are proud of it. **1848** THACKERAY *Lett.* 12 Aug., He curls his hair in the most killing manner. **1891** *Truth* 10 Dec. 1240/2 Black cocks' feathers, curled, formed the collar.

b. *Phr.* ***to curl*** (a person's) ***hair***: to horrify, to frighten. *colloq.*

1949 'P. WENTWORTH' *Spotlight* xix. 119 And anything like the language—.. I give you my word it was enough to curl your hair. **1958** *Ann. Reg.* 1957 186 Mr. Humphrey said that, unless the Government stopped taking so much out of the economy, there would be 'a depression that will curl your hair'.

c. ***to curl the mo***, to succeed brilliantly, to win. So ***curl- (kurl-) the-mo, curl-a-mo***, etc., attrib. phrs., excellent, outstanding. *Austral. slang.*

1941 BAKER *Dict. Austral. Slang* 42 *Kurl*, good, excellent. Also, 'kurl-a-mo'. **1944** *Truth* (Sydney) 13 Feb. 4/3

Breasley saw Kintore donkey-lick a field of youngsters in the Federal Stakes, and had salt rubbed into his wound when the Lewis cuddy Valour curled the mo in the Bond Handicap. **1945** BAKER *Austral. Lang.* vi. 126 *Curl-the-mo* was apparently first used to denote the self-satisfaction of a man who twirled the ends of his flowing moustache. It was then applied to anything meriting approval, was shortened to *curl*... A popular song 'Curl-the-Mo, Uncle Joe'—written in praise of Joseph Stalin, who has a large moustache. **1953** —— *Australia Speaks* iv. 97 There is not infrequent mention in the sporting columns of newspapers of *curl the mo mazuma*.. a way of saying a lot of money. **1963** *Sunday Mirror* (Sydney) 20 Jan. 43/2 Gili, with Mulley apparently 'curling the mo' was possied behind them for his challenge. **1969** *Coast to Coast 1967–68* 86 He.. lifts one of the brimming pilsener glasses: 'Come an' get it! It's curl-a-mo chico. Lead in the old pencil.'

†2. To furnish or adorn with curls or ringlets; also *fig.* *Obs.*

1590 SPENSER *F.Q.* I. v. 34 His [Cerberus'] three deformed heads.. Curled with thousand adders. **1633** G. HERBERT *Temple, Jordan* i, Curling with metaphors a plain intention. **1667** MILTON *P.L.* x. 560 The snakie locks That curld Megæra.

3. a. To bend, twist, or coil up into a spiral or incurved shape; to make curls or undulations upon (a surface); to ripple (water). Often with *up*.

1562 TURNER *Baths* 11 Vntill the sicke man perceyue the endes of his fingers to be kurled or wrinkled. **1597** SHAKS. *2 Hen. IV*, III. i. 23 The Windes, Who take the Ruffian Billowes by the top, Curling their monstrous heads. **1667** MILTON *P.L.* IX. 517 So varied hee [the serpent], and of his tortuous Traine Curld many a wanton wreath. **1715–20** POPE *Iliad* VII. 72 Soft zephyrs curling the wide watery main. **1814** SCOTT *Ld. of Isles* III. xxviii, The morning breeze the lake had curl'd. **1818** *Parl. Deb.* 1016 Those leaves have been sometimes curled by a vitriolic preparation, and coloured for Green tea with verdigrise. **1861** HUGHES *Tom Brown at Oxf.* iii. (1889) 23 Jack [the dog] ..curled himself up on the sofa.

b. *to curl the lip*: to bend or raise the upper lip slightly on one side, as an expression of contempt or scorn.

1816 SCOTT *Old Mort.* xii, His lip was now compressed.. now curled slightly upward. **1847** JAMES *J. Marston Hall* viii, A bitter smile curled the lip of the President.

II. *intr.* 4. Of hair: To form curls or ringlets. In colloq. use: cf. sense 1 b.

1530 PALSGR. 504/2 Se howe his heare curleth nowe that it is newe wasshed. **1662** J. DAVIES *Voy. Ambass.* 74 It is the heat of the Sun that burns the skin, and makes the haire curle. **1810** SCOTT *Lady of L.* II. xxv, His flaxen hair.. Curled closely round his bonnet blue. **1842** BISCHOFF *Woollen Manuf.* II. 301 The finer the fleece naturally is, the more readily it curls. **1887** W. S. GILBERT *Ruddigore* I. 16 When he's excited he uses language that would make your hair curl. **1890** *Monthly Packet* Christmas no., 118 I'll choose a place that will make your hair curl to think of. **1963** V. H. GIELGUD *Goggle-box Affair* iii. 31 The amount of overtime she and Miss Plain worked.. would have made the T.U.C.'s hair curl.

5. a. To take a spiral or incurved form or posture.

1694 *Acc. Sev. Late Voy.* II. (1711) 32 In stormy Weather little Waves curl on the top of the great ones. **1700** DRYDEN *Pal. & Arc.* III. 318 When yielded she lay curling in thy arms. **1796** WITHERING *Brit. Plants* IV. 33 Leaves.. brownish green, curling when dry. **1861** HOLLAND *Less. Life* iii. 40 Cat and kittens will.. curl up in some dark corner. **1875** DARWIN *Insectiv. Pl.* ix. 218 The tentacles began to curl inwards.

b. Of the lip: cf. 3 b.

1813 SCOTT *Rokeby* I. viii, The full-drawn lip that upward curled. **1837** LYTTON *E. Maltrav.* 57 Ernest's lip curled slightly, for his pride was touched.

c. Of potatoes: To become affected with curl: see CURL *sb.* 4.

1793 *Trans. Soc. Encourag. Arts* (ed. 2) IV. 97 A very fine table Potatoe that never curls.

d. *to curl up* (*Sporting*): to give up as dead-beat, to collapse.

1891 *Daily News* 12 June 3/2 At the half-distance Le Nord looked like winning easily; but he curled up in the last few strides. **1892** *Pall Mall G.* 15 Mar. 3/1 The latter college rather 'curled up', as the phrase goes, when once their opponents got the lead.

e. *fig.* To shrink or writhe with horror, shame, etc.; esp. const. *up*.

1913 GALSWORTHY *Fugitive* III. i, It's.. feeling people.. dislike your being there... I curl up all the time. **1923** E. WALLACE *Capt. Souls* xlv. 248 So it got you, huh? I couldn't understand how a fellow like you could see it without curling up! **1940** WODEHOUSE *Quick Service* i. 14 I'm going to call at his office and look him in the eye.. and watch him curl up at the edges. **1960** *Sunday Times* 22 May 17/6 He cheerfully admits to things which would make a good New Statesman-ite curl at the edges. **1967** S. KNIGHT *Window on Shanghai* xii. 57 When I think what some parts of Shanghai must have been like *before* liberation, it makes me curl up!

f. Const. *up*. To lie or sit with the knees drawn up comfortably; to settle down to sleep in this way.

1910 R. BROOKE in *Gownsman* 14 Oct. 9/2 Curled up like some crumpled, lonely flower-petal. **1935** J. STEINBECK *Tortilla Flat* xiv. 238 Most of the time Big Joe simply curled up like a dog, and slept in his clothes. **1964** MRS. L. B. JOHNSON *White House Diary* 15 Jan. (1970) 50 Next followed a little time to curl up in front of the fire in my bedroom and talk to Luci. **1967** O. WYND *Walk Softly* i. 1 It was my plan to take a sleeping pill and curl up. **1986** P. BARKER *Century's Daughter* xiv. 224 She was curled up on the floor, so intent on the book she didn't hear Liza come in.

†6. To twist about, writhe. *Obs.*

a **1637** B. JONSON *Fall of Mortimer* I. i. 23 The very thinking it Would make.. some politic tradesman Curl with the caution of a constable! **1664** *Floddan F.* iii. 27 A Cock curling as he would crow.

7. To move in spiral convolutions or undulations.

1791 MRS. RADCLIFFE *Rom. Forest* (1820) I. 135 The damp vapours curled round him. **1821** CLARE *Vill. Minstr.* I. 208 Brooks curl o'er their sandy bed. **1845** DARWIN *Voy. Nat.* xiv. (1879) 296 Volumes of smoke were curling upwards.

8. *Sc.* To play at CURLING q.v.

1715 PENNECUIK *Author's Answ.* Poems 59 To Curle on the Ice does greatly please Being a manly Scotish Exercise. *Mod.* A piece of water on which they curl in winter.

9. *Cricket.* a. *intr.* Of the ball: to turn in after pitching; also, to turn in its flight before pitching. b. *trans.* Of the bowler: to cause (the ball) to curve in the air.

1833 J. NYREN *Young Cricketer's Tutor* 69 Delivering his ball straight to the wicket, it curled in, and missed the Duke's leg-stump by a hair's-breadth. **1888** STEEL & LYTTELTON *Cricket* ii. 54 Apart from breaking or curling, the ball may shoot or bump. **1900** P. F. WARNER *Cricket in Many Climes* 83 He makes the ball curl in the air. **1904** *Westm. Gaz.* 21 May 3/1 When he first came to England,.. he had that 'curl-in-the-air ball' to a very marked degree. *Ibid.*, Trott shone as a baseball player, and it is to this that he owed his power of curling a ball.

†**curl**, *v.*[2] *Obs. rare*[−1]. [Echoic: cf. CURR *v.*] *intr.* To purr, as a cat.

c **1532** DEWES *Introd. Fr.* in Palsgr. 947 To curle as a catte, *gruler.*

ˈ**curldoddy.** *Sc.* Also curly-doddy. [f. CURL or CURLY + DODDY, that which has a rounded head.] A popular name of various plants with rounded flower heads: a. of species of Wild Scabious; b. of species of trefoil or clover, esp. *Trifolium medium*; c. of the Ribwort Plantain (*Plantago lanceolata*); d. of curled cabbage (Jamieson).

1500–20 DUNBAR *In Secreit Place* 297 Quod he, 'My claver, and my curldodie'. **15..** *Interl. laying of Gaist* in Scott *Border Minstr.* (1810) I. p. clx, With thre heidis of curle doddy. **1806** P. NEILL *Tour Orkn. & Shetl.* 41 (Jam.) *Trifolium medium*.. known in Orkney and in various parts of Scotland by the whimsical name of Red Curldoddy; and *Trifolium repens*, called White Curldoddy. **1847** in R. Chambers *Pop. Rhymes Scot.* (ed. 3) 204 Children thus address the stalk and flower of the scabious or devil's-bit ..'Curly doddy, do my biddin', Soop my house, and shool my midden''.

curled (kɜːld, *poet.* ˈkɜːlɪd), *ppl. a.* Forms: α. 4 crollid, 5 crulled, 6 crouled; β. 5 curlyd, 6 corlde, 6–7 curld, 6– curled. [f. CURL *v.* and *sb.* + -ED. (No other part of the vb. is found so early.)]

1. Formed into curls or ringlets, as hair.

c **1380** *Sir Ferumb.* 1354 þat other wyþ þe crollid her.. þat ys Berard. *c* **1440** *Promp. Parv.* 111 Curlyd, as here, *crispus.* **1496** *Dives & Paup.* (W. de W.) I. viii. 39/1 They be paynted with crulled here. **1553** EDEN *Treat. Newe Ind.* (Arb.) 23 The heare of theyr heades is merueylouslye corlde. **1590** SPENSER *F.Q.* I. iv. 14 Some frounce their curled heare in courtly guise. **1774** GOLDSM. *Nat. Hist.* (1776) II. 88 So curled hair is generally regarded among us as a beauty. **1842** BISCHOFF *Woollen Manuf.* II. 296 The wool.. short and somewhat curled.

2. Having or adorned with curls or ringlets; curly. Also *fig.*

1590 SPENSER *F.Q.* III. viii. 7 Her curled head. **1604** SHAKS. *Oth.* I. ii. 68 The wealthy curled Deareling of our Nation. **1692** O. WALKER *Greek & Rom. Hist. Illustr.* 291 He was not so curled, nor so flat nosed. **1791** COWPER *Odyss.* XIX. 307 His visage swarthy, curl'd His poll. **1841–4** EMERSON *Ess., Nature* Wks. (Bohn) I. 229 The smoothest curled courtier in the boudoirs of a palace.

3. a. Bent into or towards a spiral form; disposed in more or less spiral convolutions.

1577 B. GOOGE *Heresbach's Husb.* II. (1586) 109 The knobbes [of the maple].. hath the fairer and the more courled graine. **1611** HEYWOOD *Gold. Age* I. Wks. 1874 III. 5 Made Neptunes Trident calme the curled waues. **1875** DARWIN *Insectiv. Pl.* iv. 72 The pedicels of these glands were spirally curled. **1881** BESANT & RICE *Chapl. of Fleet* I. viii, Old men.. lay with curled-up limbs, shaking with cold.

b. Of leaves: Having a much waved edge or surface. *transf.* Of plants: Having curled leaves.

1626 BACON *Sylva* §651 Plants that have curled Leaves, do all abound with moisture. **1796** WITHERING *Brit. Plants* III. 360 Leaves slender, curled. **1861** MISS PRATT *Flower. Pl.* III. 261 A variety of this herb.. called Curled Tansy. **1882** VINES *Sachs' Bot.* 924 The Savoy with its curled blistered leaves. *Mod.* A row of Curled Parsley.

c. Of wood: having a wavy or curly grain. Chiefly in ***curled maple*** (see MAPLE 2).

1778 in *Pennsylvania Archives* (1907) 6th Ser. XII. 860 A Curl'd maple Teatable. **1813** H. MUHLENBERG *Catal. Plants* 84 (*Alnus undulata* or *crispata*) Waved alder or curled alder. **1855** *Trans. Mich. Agric. Soc.* VI. 528 Much of this [maple] timber is curled and some bird's-eyed. **1911** *Encycl. Brit.* XVII. 664/2 The most constant use of curled maple is for the stocks of fowling-pieces and rifles.

4. Of potatoes: Affected with CURL (*sb.* 4).

1788 *Trans. Soc. Encourag. Arts* VI. p. xiii, That disease in Potatoes, called the curled Potatoe. **1796** *Hull Advertiser* 3 Sept. 2/2 That fatal disease so incident to.. the Potatoe, known by the appellation of the 'Curled Top'. **1845** *Jrnl. R. Agric. Soc.* VI. I. 164 Curled potatoes ripen early, some weeks before the healthy plants.

5. *Comb.*, as ***curled-horned*** adj.; †**curled-head,** †**curled-pate** *adjs.*, curly-headed.

1607 SHAKS. *Timon* IV. iii. 160 Make curld' pate Ruffians bald. *c* **1611** CHAPMAN *Iliad* II. 380 The curl'd head Greeks. **1826** COBBETT *Rur. Rides* (1885) II. 193 Fine curled-horned and long-tailed ewes.

Hence ˈ**curledness,** curled state or quality.

1530 PALSGR. 211/2 Curlydnesse of ones heer, *crespure.* **1615** CROOKE *Body of Man* 68 The haires.. do vary in.. length and shortnesse, streightnesse and curledness.

curler (ˈkɜːlə(r)). [f. CURL *v.* + -ER[1].]

1. One who curls (hair, etc.); an appliance for curling the hair.

1748 SMOLLETT *Rod. Rand.* (1812) I. 58 You pitiful trencher-scraping pimping curler. **1882** *Echo* 31 Jan. 4/5 Advt., Ostrich Feather Curler wanted. **1887** *Sci. Amer.* 9 July 26 A hair or mustache curler has been patented.

2. A player at the game of curling.

1638 R. BAILLIE *Lett. & Jrnls.* (1841–2) I. 163 He was a curler on the ice on the Sabbath day. **1785** BURNS *Vision* i, The sun had clos'd the winter day, The curlers quat their roarin play. **1864** A. MᶜKAY *Hist. Kilmarnock* 115 The curlers of one quarter of the town would frequently challenge.. those of another.

†ˈ**curlet**[1]. Obs. var. of COVERLET. Cf. CURE *v.*[2] = cover.

1493 *Act. Dom. Conc.* 315 (Jam.) Twa fedder beddis, a doble curlet of sey.

curlet[2] (ˈkɜːlɪt). *rare.* [f. CURL *sb.* + -ET[1].] A little curl or ringlet.

1803 MOORE *Odes of Anacreon* xx. *note*, And every curlet was a tie, A chain by Beauty twined. **1818** *Blackw. Mag.* II. 516 Around thy brow Unharmed the curlets play.

curlew (ˈkɜːl(j)uː). Forms: α. 4 curlu, -leeu, corlue, corolu, kurlu, 4–5 corlew(e, 4–6 curlewe, 4–7 curlue, 5 kyrlewe, corelewe, 7 courlieu, 7–8 curliew, 7– 9 curlieu, 8 kerlew, 4– curlew; also β. 4 cor-, curlure, 5 curlowyr. [Identical with OF. *courlieus* (13th c. in Hatzfeld), *corlys* (16th c. in Littré), *courlis, corlis, corlieu* (Cotgr.), mod.F. *courlieu, courlis*, in F. dial. *querlu, kerlu, corlu, corleru*; cf. also med.L. (*a* 1250) *corlivus*, It. *chiurlo.* The French name is held by etymologists to be an imitation of the cry of the bird; but if so, it was apparently assimilated to the word *corliu* (11th c.), *courlieu, curleu, corli* courier, messenger, deriv. of *courir* to run. Found in verse with stress *cur'lew* in 15th and 19th c.]

1. A grallatorial bird of the genus *Numenius* (family *Scolopacidæ*), with a long slender curved bill; *esp.* the common European species *N. arquatus* (called in Scotland *whaup*).

1377 LANGL. *P. Pl.* B. XIV. 43 Fissch to lyue in þe flode ..þe corlue by kynde of þe eyre. *a* **1440** *Sir Degrev.* 1406 Fatt conyngus and newe, ffesauntus and corelewe. **1555** EDEN *Decades* 119 A great curlewe as bygge as a storke came flying to the gouernours shippe. **1616** SURFL. & MARKH. *Country Farme* 78 The Woodcocke and Curlew, and other birds haunting the Water and Riuers. **1719** DE FOE *Crusoe* I. 233 A Pigeon or a Curlieu. **1810** SCOTT *Lady of L.* v. ix, Wild as the scream of the curlieu. **1842** TENNYSON *Locksley Hall* 3 'Tis the place, and all around it, as of old, the curlews call.

†2. Used (*esp.* in the Bible) to translate L. *coturnix*, Gr. ὄρτυξ, a quail. *Obs.*

a **1340** HAMPOLE *Psalter* civ. 38 þai asked & þe curlu come [**1382** WYCLIF, ther kam a kurlu (*v.r.* curlew, corlure); Vulgate, *venit coturnix*]. **1387** TREVISA *Higden* (Rolls) I. 309 þe same Delon hatte Ortygia; for ortigie, (þat beeþ coturnicies, curlewes,) beeþ þerynne greet plente. *c* **1475** *Pict. Voc.* in Wr.-Wülcker 762/3 *Hic conturnix*, curlowyr. **1508** FISHER *Wks.* (1876) 186 Curlewes, or quayles.

3. Applied in comb. or with qualification to other grallatorial birds, as **curlew-jack, curlew knot,** the Whimbrel, a small species of curlew, *Numenius phæops*; **curlew sandpiper, pigmy curlew,** *Tringa subarquata*; **stone curlew,** a name for the Norfolk plover (*Œdicnemus scolopax*), and also for the whimbrel.

1605 in *Archæol.* XIII. 341 These Foules bee nowe in seasone. Bustarde.. Widgeon, Curlewiake. **1678** RAY *Willughby's Ornith.* III. v. xiv. 306 The Stone-Curlew.. The Throat, Neck [etc.].. like that of a Curlew: whence they of Norfolk call it, the Stone-Curlew. **1766** PENNANT *Zool.* (1768) II. 379 From a similarity of colors to the curlew, it [Norfolk Plover] is there called the stone curlew. *Ibid.* s.v. *Whimbrel*, It.. visit[s] the neighborhood of Spalding (where it is called the *Curlew knot*) in vast flocks in April. **1789** G. WHITE *Selborne* xv. (1853) 63, I wonder that the stone curlew should be mentioned by the writers as a rare bird. **1885** SWAINSON *Prov. Names Birds* 179, 194.

4. *Comb.* **curlew-berry,** a name given in Labrador to the Crowberry (*Empetrum nigrum*).

curlicue (ˈkɜːlɪkjuː), *sb.* Also carlicue, curly-cue, curleycue. [f. CURLY + CUE, either = F. *queue* tail, or the letter Q in its script form *2*.] a. A fantastic curl or twist.

1844 'J. SLICK' *High Life N.Y.* II. xxii. 54, I writ out my name.. and handed it over, curlecues and all. *Ibid.* xxvii. 155 We made a curlecue round both the ships. **1858** *Home Jrnl.* 24 July (Farmer), Architects have a wonderful predilection for all manner of curlycues and breaks in your roof. **1872** KINGSLEY *Madam How & Lady Why* v. 117 Sand and gravel.. arranged in.. waves, and festoons, and curlicues. **1891** ATKINSON *Moorland Parish* 176 A frolicsome letter S, with a curlicue at each termination. **1898** *Literature* 17 Sept. 263/2 In Canada.. the English-speaking country people.. often used the word.. to signify a trifle or a thing of little value—e.g. 'I don't care a carlicue.' 'It is not worth a carlicue.'

b. *to cut up curlicues* (or *carlicues*): to cut capers. (Common in U.S.).

18.. *McClintock's Tales* (Bartlett), I..cut a curlycue with my right foot. **1840** C. F. HOFFMAN *Greyslaer* II. x. 27, I soon saw, by the way in which the white man's track doubled and doubled again..that the fellow could not be cutting such carlicues for nothing. **1848** BARTLETT *Dict. Amer.* Add., *Carlacue*, a caper or boyish trick. 'To cut up carlacues', is a common expression, equivalent to 'cutting up didoes'. Used in New York.

'curlicue, *v.* [f. the sb.] *trans.* and *intr.* To bend elaborately or fantastically. Also *transf.* and *fig.* Chiefly in **'curlicued** *ppl. a.*

1844 'J. SLICK' *High Life N.Y.* I. i. 11 A kind of picket fence made out of iron, all *curlecued* over on the sides. *Ibid.* II. xxii. 66 Then her arms went curlecueing over her head. **1947** E. KAZAN *Notebk. for Streetcar Named Desire* in Cole & Chinoy *Directing the Play* (1953) 297 Blanche is a social type, an emblem of a dying civilization, making its last curlicued and romantic exit. **1963** *Punch* 25 Sept. 456/2 The pink curlicued cupolas.

curlie-wurlie, curly-wurly ('kɜːlɪ'wɜːlɪ). [A reduplicated extension of CURLY; perhaps with some reference in the second part to *whirl*, in Sc. *whurl*.] A fantastically curled ornament.

a **1772** WILKIE in Lockhart *Scott* l, I thought the beauty of architecture consisted in curlie wurlies, but now I find it consists in symmetry and proportion. **1818** SCOTT *Rob Roy* xix, Ah! it's a brave kirk—nane o' yere whigmaleeries and curliwurlies and open-steek hems about it. **1883** *Century Mag.* Sept. 722/2 Its leaves are slit in half and provided with æsthetical curly-wurlies.

'cur-like, *a.* Like or after the nature of a cur.

1627 P. FLETCHER *Locusts* IV. xii, See where proud Dandal chain'd..lies cur-like under boord. **1742** FIELDING *J. Andrews* III. vii, The gentlemen of curlike dispostion.

curliness ('kɜːlɪnɪs). [f. CURLY + -NESS.] The state or quality of being curly.

1818 TODD, *Curliness*, the state of any thing curled. A modern word. **1863** GEO. ELIOT *Romola* II. i, Her brown hair, rough from curliness.

curling ('kɜːlɪŋ), *vbl. sb.*[1] [f. CURL *v.*[1] + -ING[1].]

1. The action of the verb CURL, q.v.; a curl, twist, undulation.

1440 *Promp. Parv.* 111/1 Curlynge of here, *crispitudo.* **1626** BACON *Sylva* §651 Curling on the Sides; as in Lettuce and young Cabbage. **1656** *Artif. Handsom.* 63 The curlings of Ladies haire. **1703** MOXON *Mech. Exerc.* 111 You will find a..Curling on that place upon the stuff.

2. A game played on the ice (on a curling-pond, or other smooth frozen surface) in which large rounded stones (see CURLING-STONE) are hurled along a defined space called the *rink* towards a mark called the *tee.* The game has undergone considerable developments in Scotland since the 17th c., and has now been introduced elsewhere, where climatic conditions are favourable.

It appears in its earlier form to have been akin to Quoits, but has now more analogy with Bowls, with modifications consequent upon the situation. A game similar to it in its early form appears in Flanders *a* 1600; Kilian has *kluyten kalluyten*, 'ludere massis siue globis glaciatis; certare discis in æquore glaciato', to play a match with quoits on a smooth surface of ice. The name appears to describe the motion given to the stone. In Flemish the name *krullebol* (curl-bowl) is given, apparently from its motion, to the wooden bowl with which a somewhat similar game *bolspel* is played in an alley.

1620 [See CURLING-STONE]. **1684** in Fountainhall *Decis. Lords of Council* (1759) I. 328 He was playing at the curling with Riddel of Haining. **1693** WALLACE *Descr. Orkney* 10 Copinsha..in which..are to be found in great plentie excellent stones for the game called Curling. [Hence in *Camden's Brit.* ed. 1695.] **1796** MORSE *Amer. Geog.* II. 154 The diversion of Curling is.. peculiar to the Scots. It is performed upon ice, with large flat stones. **1890** J. KERR *Hist. Curling* ii. 27-8 Curling, when first practised, appears to have been a kind of quoiting on the ice..*Coiting, kuting*, or *quoiting*, was for a long time the word in common use to describe the game, and in some districts it is still applied to it.

3. *attrib.* and *Comb.* **a.** Relating to or used for curling the hair, as ***curling-bodkin, -paper, -pin, -tongs***; CURLING-IRON.

1610 GUILLIM *Heraldry* IV. viii. (1611) 206 Combes, glasses, Head-brushes, curling-bodkings, &c. **1909** in A. Adburgham *Shops & Shopping* (1964) xxiii. 273 Curling Pins. **1763** *Boston Post-Boy* 12 Dec., Curling Tongs. **1816** SCOTT *Antiquary* I. x. 228, I hae the curling-tongs here to gie it a bit turn ower the brow. **1840** THACKERAY in *Fraser's Mag.* XXII. 410/1 Mr. Fitch..gave a twist of the curling-tongs to his beard. **1868** HOLME LEE *B. Godfrey* li. 289 Turtell snatched up a pair of cold curling tongs.

b. Of or pertaining to the game of curling, as ***curling-club, -house, -match, -pond, -rink***; CURLING-STONE.

1814 *Sporting Mag.* XLIII. 193 A curling match took place upon the ice. **1833** [see BEAR *v.*[1] 11 b]. **1864** A. MCKAY *Hist. Kilmarnock* 116 [It] was sometimes converted into a curling-pond. **1890** J. KERR *Hist. Curling* 375 Order in the curling-house is a proof that the club is well managed. **1926** *Daily Colonist* (Victoria, B.C.) 10 Jan. 6/5 The Portage annual bonspiel will commence on..February 16 according to the..committee of the Portage curling rink.

†**'curling,** *vbl. sb.*[2] *Obs.* Also **kurl-**. [Echoic: cf. GURL *v.*] Rumbling in the bowels.

1398 TREVISA *Barth. De P.R.* XVII. clxviii. (1495) 712 Fresshe and newe whete..bredyth ache in the sydes: hurlynge and kurlynge [*rugitum*]. *Ibid.* XIX. liv. 895 Rawe hony..bredyth curlynge and swellyng in the wombe.

'curling, *ppl. a.* [-ING[2].] That curls; see the verb.

1632 LITHGOW *Trav.* VII. (1682) 314 Flocks of flying Fishes, scudding upon the curling Waves. **1700** DRYDEN *Pal. & Arc.* III. 181 The curling smoke mounts heavy from the fires. **1782** COWPER *Gilpin* 69 Each bottle had a curling ear. **1849** DICKENS *B. Rudge* xxxi, The sun..flung across the curling mist bright bars of gold.

Hence **'curlingly** *adv.*

1611 COTGR., *Crespément*, crispingly, frizlingly, curlingly. **1828** MISS MITFORD *Village* Ser. III. (1863) 490 The smoke from whose chimneys sailed curlingly amongst [the trees].

'curling-iron. [CURLING *vbl. sb.*[1]] An iron instrument for curling the hair, which is heated and the hair then twined round it.

1632 SHERWOOD *Eng.-Fr. Dict.*, A curling iron, *fer à frisotter.* **1752** RICHARDSON *Let.* in Mrs. Barbauld *Life* (1804) III. 34 That careless girl..set herself in a blaze with her torturing curling irons. **1844** DICKENS *Mart. Chuz.* xxxviii, A small fire for the convenience of heating curling-irons.

'curling-stone. [CURLING *vbl. sb.*[1] 2.] The stone with which the game of curling is played.

It was in the 17th c. a quoit-like natural stone (channel-stone) of from 5 to 20 lbs., with hollows made for the thumb and fingers; in the 18th c. a heavy natural boulder of 50 to 120 lbs., with smooth base having an iron or wooden handle inserted; it is now a cheese-shaped stone of not more than 36 inches in circumference, or 50 pounds weight, with an iron handle on the upper surface.

1620 H. ADAMSON *Muses Threnodie* (1638) Inventorie p. x, His hats, his hoods, his bels, his bones, His allay bowles, and curling stones. **1891** BARRIE *Lit. Minister* I. xi. 188, I could hear the roar of curling stones at Bathie-bog.

curl-leaf. [CURL *sb.* or *v.*] = CURL *sb.* 4.

1886 *Harper's Mag.* July 283/1 Foreign varieties and their hybrids are sometimes afflicted with the curl leaf.

curlless ('kɜːllɪs), *a.* [f. CURL *sb.* + -LESS.] Without curls.

1861 *Temple Bar Mag.* IV. 138 Raven-black and curlless hair. **1892** *Black & White* 19 Mar. 383/2 Curlless ostrich feathers.

curlock, curlick, local variants of CHARLOCK.

curlowyr, obs. var. CURLEW.

'curl-paper. A piece of soft paper with which the hair is twisted up for some time, so as to give it a curl when the paper is taken out.

a **1817** ANNA LEFROY in Jane Austen *Volume the Third* (1951) 130 In the Dressing room..he had the..satisfaction of picking up a curl paper. **1826** MOORE *Amatory Colloquy* in *Morn. Chron.*, Those soft *billet-doux*..Will serve but to keep Mrs. Coutts in curl-papers. **1852** DICKENS *Bleak Ho.* xxii, With her head in a perfect beehive of curl-papers and nightcap. **1924** C. MACKENZIE *Old Men of Sea* xix. 325 Ciggyrettes! Oh dear!.. I did once have a try at chewing ciggyrettes, but I reckon I might as well have started in chewing curl-papers. **1966** —— *Paper Lives* xv. 203 'Do any women still put their hair in curl-papers? I thought they used these metallic things.'.. 'I recall..seeing our housemaid with her hair covered in curl-papers.'

Hence **'curl-papered** *a.*, having the hair in curl-papers.

1867 *Bk. Humorous Poetry* 324 Wife curl-paper'd, slipshod, unwash'd and undress'd.

'curl-pate. a. A curly head. **b.** A curly-headed person.

1605 CAMDEN *Rem., Surnames* (R.), Compare the Roman names that seeme so stately..what is Crispus but curle-pate. **1615** J. STEPHENS *Satyr. Ess.* (ed. 2) 214 He thinks to have a curle-pate is to have a visible wit. **1789** M. MADAN tr. *Persius* (1795) 17 The exercises of an hundred curl-pates.

'curl-ˌpated, *a.* Having a curly head of hair; curly-headed.

1594 CAREW *Huarte's Exam. Wits* (1616) 188 Why the men of Æthyopia..are commonly curle-pated and flat nosed. **1742** JARVIS *Quix.* I. III. xxvi, A little curl-pated Moor. **1841** MACAULAY *W. Hastings* Ess. (1854) 595/1 The curl-pated minions of James the First.

curlure, obs. var. CURLEW.

curly ('kɜːlɪ), *a.* [f. CURL *sb.* + -Y.]

1. Of hair: Disposed in curls or ringlets.

1772-84 COOK *Voy.* IV. III. vi. (R.), Growing to a tolerable length, and very crisp and curly. **1818** TODD, *Curly*, inclining to curl; falling into ringlets. **1884** F. M. CRAWFORD *Rom. Singer* I. 47 Running his fingers through his curly hair.

2. Having or adorned with curls; having curled hair.

1827 G. HIGGINS *Celtic Druids* 65 Budda with his flat black face and curly head. **1859** DISRAELI in *Hansard* Ser. III. CLIV. 127 When we are juvenile and curly.

3. a. Of a curled form; wavy, undulating; of plants, having curled leaves. ***curly maple*** (see CURLED *ppl. a.* 3 c).

1795 SOUTHEY *Joan of Arc* VIII. 304 So rolls the swelling sea Its curly billows. **1814** BYRON *Corsair* III. xviii, The boats are darting o'er the curly bay. *a* **1845** HOOD *Fairy Tale* vii, Cabbages and curly kale. **1909** G. STRATTON-PORTER *Girl of Limberlost* xi. 218 In an expressed crate was a fine curly-maple dressing table. **1942** C. WEYGANDT *Plenty of Pennsylvania* 29 Curly maple is hard to come by.

b. *Cricket.* Curling (see CURL *v.*[1] 9 a).

1868 J. LILLYWHITE *Cricketers' Comp.* 54 Mr. Jupp.. played Southerton's 'curly' deliveries with consummate skill.

4. Of potatoes: Affected with CURL (*sb.* 4).

1791 *Trans. Soc. Encourag. Arts* IX. 63 A curly crop of Potatoes.

5. *Comb.*, as ***curly-brimmed, -coated, -haired, -headed, -pated***, etc. adjs.; **curly-pate**, a curly headed person.

1795 *Fate of Sedley* I. 59 A curly-poled nymph from Otaheite. **1827** G. HIGGINS *Celtic Druids* 162 The flat-faced, curly-headed Budda. **1848** DICKENS *Dombey* iv, A..merry boy..fair-faced, bright-eyed, and curly-haired. **1862** *Fraser's Mag.* 4 Yellow curly-pated children. **1868** BROWNING *Ring & Bk.* VIII. 3 Seven and one's eight, old curly-pate! **1885** *Bazaar* 30 Mar. 1260/2 Jet black curly-coated retriever dog. **1890** CONAN DOYLE *Firm of Girdlestone* xviii. 142 Curly-brimmed hat. **1953** 'N. BLAKE' *Dreadful Hollow* 203 Both wore dark overcoats and those curly-brimmed Homburg hats.

†**'curly-'murly,** *sb.* and *a. Obs.* [A playful reduplication: cf. CURLIE-WURLIE.] **a.** *sb.* A fantastic curl or twist. **b.** *adj.* Characterized by fantastic curls.

1727-8 MRS. DELANY *Life & Corr.* (1861) I. 159 The curly murly fashion of the hair is not much worn now. **1756** *Ibid.* III. 403 Lappets in all sorts of curli murlis.

curly-wurly ('kɜːlɪˌwɜːlɪ), *a. dial.* and *colloq.* [See CURLIE-WURLIE *sb.*] Twisting and curling.

1853 W. CADENHEAD *Flights of Fancy* 187 Wi' a' their curly-wurly stanes. **1907** N. MUNRO *Daft Days* xix, The dusting of the stair-rauls and the parlour beltings—the curly-wurly places, as she called them.

curmudgel, var. CURMUDGEON (app. for rime).

1675 COTTON *Burlesque upon Burl.* Wks. (1765) 185 Would one Be so ungrateful a Curmudgel To steal away his Age's Cudgel?

curmudgeon (kɜː'mʌdʒən). Forms: 6- curmudgeon; also 6 -mudgen, 6-7 cormogeon, -gion, 7 cormoggian, -mudgeon, curmudgion, -muggion, -mudgin, curr-mudgin, curre-megient, 8 cur-mudgeon. See also CORMULLION. [Derivation unknown: see below.]

'An avaricious churlish fellow; a miser, a niggard' (J.).

1577 STANYHURST *Descr. Irel.* 102/2 in *Holinshed*, Such a clownish Curmudgen. **1593** NASHE *Christ's T.* 85 b, Our English Cormogeons, they haue breasts, but giue no suck. **1604** T. WRIGHT *Passions* v. 289 Why do covetous cormogions distill the best substance of their braines to get riches. **1626** W. SCLATER *Exp. 2 Thess.* (1629) 270 Curre-megients, who scarcely know any other sentence of Scripture, yet..haue this of Paul in their mouthes; worke for your liuing. **1656** EARL MONM. *Advt. fr. Parnass.* 387 Certain greedy curmuggions, who value not the leaving of a good name behind them to posterity. **1705** HICKERINGILL *Priest-cr.* I. (1721) 8 If..the rich Curmudgeon..do not open his Purse wide. **1824** W. IRVING *T. Trav.* I. 254, I had a rich uncle..a penurious accumulating curmudgeon. **1860** WHYTE MELVILLE *Holmby House* 377 A thankless old curmudgeon.

The occurrence in Holland's *Livy*, 1600, of CORNMUDGIN (q.v.) has led to a suggestion that this was the original form, with the meaning 'concealer or hoarder of corn', *mudgin* being associated with ME. *much-en, mich-en* to pilfer, steal, or *muchier*, Norman form of OF. *mucier, musser* to conceal, hide away. But examination of the evidence shows that *curmudgeon* was in use a quarter of a century before Holland's date, and that *cornmudgin* is apparently merely a nonce-word of Holland's, a play upon *corn* and *curmudgeon.* The suggestion that the first syllable is *cur*, the dog, is perhaps worthy of note; but that of Dr. Johnson's 'unknown correspondent', *cœur méchant* for F. *méchant cœur*, 'evil or malicious heart', is noticeable only as an ingenious specimen of pre-scientific 'etymology', and as having been retailed by Ash in the form, 'from the French *cœur* unknown, and *mechant* a correspondent'!

cur'mudgeonly, *a.* [f. prec. + -LY[1].] Of the nature of, or characteristic of, a curmudgeon; miserly, niggardly, churlish.

1590 R. W. *3 Lords & 3 Ladies Lond.* in Hazl. *Dodsley* VI. 380, I care not for him [Wealth], curmudgeonly swad. **1594** NASHE *Terrors of Nt.* E iij, Come a woing to them in the likenes of a cooper or a curmogionly purchaser. **1776** FOOTE *Bankrupt* I. Wks. 1799 II. 99 These curmudgeonly cits regard no ties, no obligations. **1886** *Sat. Rev.* 19 June 845/1 The curmudgeonly jealousy and Trade-Unionism of some practitioners.

So **cur'mudgeonly** *adv.* (*rare.*)

1879 G. MEREDITH *Egoist* xxxvi, She vowed it was done curmudgeonly to vex her.

cur'mur, *v.* [Echoic.] To make a low murmuring or purring sound.

1831 *Blackw. Mag.* XXIX. 701 They two [cats] sit curmurring, forgetful of mice and milk, of all but love.

curmurring (kɜː'mʌrɪŋ), *vbl. sb. Sc.* [f. prec.] A low rumbling, growling, or murmuring sound.

1785 BURNS *Death & Dr. Hornbook* xxvii, Some curmurring in his guts. **1816** SCOTT *Old Mort.* viii, A glass of brandy to three glasses of wine prevents the curmurring in the stomach.

curn, *sb. north.* and *Sc.* [? Related to CURN *v.*]

†**1.** *pl.* Grain, corn-crops. *Obs.*

c **1340** *Cursor M.* 7158 (Trin.) To her tailes fire he bond ..þourȝe þe felde he made hem fle And so her curnes dud he brenne.

2. *Sc.* A grain.

1474 *Act. Audit.* 35 (Jam.) Of ilk chalder the thrid kurne. *c* **1540** LYNDESAY *Kitteis Conf.* 90 Curnis of meil, and luffillis of Malt. **1759** FOUNTAINHALL *Decis. Lords of Council* I. 334 (Jam.) The seed, which is excepted from the multure; this is the 4th pickle or curne. **1824** SCOTT *Redgauntlet* ch. xiii, If there be a drap mair lemon or a curn less sugar than just suits you. **1881** 'J. STRATHESK' *Bits fr. Blink Bonny* (1882) 137, I boil'd their meal and put a curn o' spice in't.

b. *transf.* A small number or quantity; a few.

1785 *Jrnl. from Lond. to Portsm.* 8 (Jam.), I saw a curn of camla-like fellows wi' them. **1787** W. TAYLOR *Scots Poems* 72 (Jam.), I frae the neuk fresh coals an' sticks, An' i' the chimly cast a curn. **1820** *St. Kathleen* IV. 143 (Jam.), Only a curn bubbles brak on the tap. **1847** H. MILLER *Geol. Bass Rock* 109 Yonder's a curn o' rough hills. **1891** A. MATTHEWS *Poems & Songs* 54 Among a curn claikin' wives.

curn, *v.* Early form of KERN, to form grains, to granulate.

1297 R. GLOUC. (1724) 490 Tho grene corn in somer ssolde curne. **1393** LANGL. *P. Pl.* C. XIII. 180 Shal neuer spir springen vp ne spik on strawe curne [*v.r.* kerne, kurne].

curnall, curnell, obs. ff. CORONAL, KERNEL.

curney ('kʌrnɪ), *sb. Sc.* [dim. f. CURN *sb.* 2 b.] A company, lot.

1823 SCOTT *Quentin D.* xxxi, The whole curney of them is gone.

curnock ('kɜːnək). *local.* Also 5 **carnok,** 8 **carnock,** 6–7 **cornock,** 7 **cornook.** [App. another form of CRANNOCK, *crennoc*, one or the other being due to metathesis of *r*.

Perhaps of Welsh origin; the Welsh form being *crynog*, which, according to Silvan Evans, may be for **cyrnog* conical heap, from *cwrn* cone. A parallel form *cyrnen*, conical heap, is common in many parts of Wales. This change of **cyrnog, crynog* in Welsh would, if certain, account for the *carn-, curn-,* and *cran-, cren-, cryn-* forms in Eng. The Welsh *crynog* appears to be known as a measure only in Glamorganshire and part of Monmouthshire.]

An obsolete (or nearly obsolete) dry measure formerly used in the West of England, from Cheshire to Somersetshire, and in parts of South Wales.

Its capacity varied according to place and commodity; for corn it was usually 4 bushels = a 'coomb'; for wheat sometimes 3 bushels. For coal and lime, it varied locally; in Glamorganshire in 1815, from 10 to 12 or 15 bushels (Davies *Agric. of S. Wales* II. 172), and the Cheshire *crenneke* or *crynoke* of salt in the 16th c. appears to have been at least as much.

1479 *Office of Mayor of Bristol* in *Eng. Gilds* (1870) 426 That every sak [of colys] be tryed & provid to be & holde a carnok. **1509** *Will of R. Jamys* (Somerset Ho.), Quatour modios frumenti de mensura de Chepstow, anglice *a Cornock*. **1638** PENKETHMAN *Artach.* D ij, A Cornook conteineth 256 Pounds. **1688** R. HOLME *Armoury* III. 260/2 A Cornock is 2 strikes or 4 Bushels. **1708** J. CHAMBERLAYNE *St. Gt. Brit.* I. III. ii. (1743) 157 Four bushels [make] the Comb or Curnock. **1727** W. MATHER *Yng. Man's Comp.* 198, 4 Bushels a Comb, or Curnock, 2 Curnocks a Quarter. **1727** BRADLEY *Fam. Dict.* s.v. *Dry Measure*. **1863** MORTON *Cycl. Agric.* 1123–7 (in *O.C. & F. Words* 170), *Curnock* (*Worcestershire*), of barley or oats, 4 bushels; of wheat, 9 score 10 lbs. = 3 bushels.

curny ('kʌrnɪ), *a. Sc.* [f. CURN *sb.* + -Y[1].] Consisting of grains, granular.

1808–24 JAMIESON, Meal is said to be *curny*, when the grains of it are large, or when it is not ground very small. **1816** SCOTT *Old Mort.* xx, Wheat-flour..[is] far frae being sae hearty or kindly to a Scotchman's stomach as the curney aitmeal is.

curour, obs. form of COURIER *sb.*

curpen, -in, -on, Sc. var. CROUPON.

curpheue, -ew, -our, obs. forms of CURFEW.

'curple. *Sc.* Also 5 courpale, 6 curpall, 7 -ell. [Phonetic corruption of *curper*, CRUPPER.]

1. A crupper.

1498 in *Ld. Treas. Acc. Scot.* I. 388 Ane courpale..and thre girthis to the samyn sadill. **1535** STEWART *Cron. Scot.* III. 300 Vpoun ane hors..Without saidill, curpall, tre, or brydill. **1584** J. CARMICHAEL in *Wodr. Soc. Misc.* (1844) 432 I'm afraid that John Durie has cracked his curple, at least his mouth is closed. **1675** CUNNINGHAM (of Craigend) *Diary* (1887) 51 To a new Curpell to my maill pillion.

2. *transf.* The rump, posteriors.

1787 BURNS *Answ. Guidwife Wauchope-ho.*, I'd be mair vauntie o' my hap, Douce hingin' owre my curple, Than.. proud imperial purple.

curr (kɜː(r), kʌrr), *v.* [Echoic: cf. Da. *kurren* to coo, to whirr, and the verbs mentioned under CUR.] To make a low murmuring sound, like the cooing of a dove or purring of a cat. Hence **'curring** *vbl. sb.* and *ppl. a.*

1677 N. COX *Gent. Recreat.* iii. 57 When you have so tamed them [Nightingales] that they begin to Cur and Sweet with chearfulness, and record softly to themselves. *a* **1693** URQUHART *Rabelais* III. xiii. 107 The..curring of Pigeons.. curkling of Quails. **1798** WORDSW. *Idiot Boy* xxi, The owlets hoot, the owlets curr. **1855** G. DONALD in *Whistle-binkie* (1890) II. 87 Cheetie, Cheetie pussie..by fireside curring, Sang contented purring. **1860** THOMAS in *Zoologist* X. 3651 [The note of the fern-owl] resembled..the whirring, rapid rotation of a wheel..the sounds intermixed with curring and croaking notes.

curr, *sb.* [Echoic: cf. prec.] A curring sound.

1867 *Blackw. Mag.* Feb. 148 They'll send the stanes spinnin Wi a whirr and a curr till they sit round the tee.

‖**currach, -agh** ('kʌrə, 'kʊrəx). Forms: 5–6 currok, 7 -ogh, (carrogh(e), 8 corrach, 8–9 courach, 9 corach, corrack, 7– corragh, curragh. [Ir. *curach* boat, little ship; also *corrach* boat, coracle; cf. Welsh *corwg*, also *corwgl, cwrwgl* CORACLE; these point to an OCelt. **kuruk-os, *kurok-os* boat. (The spelling *carrogh* in Camden and his citers is prob. only a misprint.)]

A small boat made of wickerwork covered with hides, used from ancient times in Scotland and Ireland; a coracle.

c **1450** *St. Cuthbert* (Surtees) 779 þai called þat bate a currok. **1536** BELLENDEN *Cron. Scot.* (1821) I. p. lix, Ane bait of ane bull hid, bound with na thing bot wandis. This bait is callit ane currok; with the quhilk thay fische salmond ..thay beir it to ony place, on thair bak. **1610** HOLLAND *Camden's Brit.* I. 107 Their carroghes, wherein they passed over the Sciticke vale. **1683** *Brit. Spec.* 144 The Scots likewise out of their Carroghs or Leather vessels..landing in whole Swarms. **1747** CARTE *Hist. Eng.* I. 156 Their wicker boats, covered with hides, and called corraghs. **1828** C. CROKER *Fairy Leg. S. Irel.* II. 53 *Corragh* or *currugh* is a small boat used by the fishermen of that part. **1884** *Graphic* 4 Oct. 353/2 We embarked at an early hour in a 'corrack' at Dugort.

currack, -ock ('kʌrək). *Sc.* Also currach, -och. [Cf. Gaelic *curran* 'paniers slung on horses for carrying bulky loads, as hay, corn' (Macleod). The terminations *-an* and *-ag* are both diminutive, as is also -OCK in Eng. and Sc.] *pl.* A pair of open wooden or wicker frames slung pannier-wise on each side of a horse, for carrying a load of corn, hay, or other bulky stuff. Cf. *crooks*: CROOK *sb.* 9.

1792 *Statist. Acc. Scot.* IV. 395 The fuel was carried in creels and the corns in curracks. **1793** W. ANDERSON *Piper of Peebles* in C. Rogers *Soc. Life Scot.* I. vi. 218 Coops and carts were unco rare An' creels and currocks boot to sair [i.e. behoved to serve]. **1880** GORDON *Bk. Chron. Keith* 443 A load of plants slung over the horse's back in the 'Currach' style. **1892** *Blackw. Mag.* Oct. 479 Panniers or curochs were laid across the pony's back.

currage, obs. form of COURAGE.

curragh ('kʌrəx, 'kʌrə). *Ireland* and *Isle of Man.* [Ir. *corrach* marsh, Manx *curragh* moor, bog, fen.] Marshy waste ground; *spec.* the proper name of the level stretch of open ground in Co. Kildare, famous for its racecourse and military camp.

1664 in *Lex Scripta Isle of Man* (1819) 144 Digg and take away Timber in and out of the Curraughes on the North Side. **1894** HALL CAINE *Manxman* VI. i, The bog-bane to the rushy curragh, say I, Nancy. **1908** —— in *M.A.P.* XX. 362 A widower living alone in some little mud cottage on the curragh.

currajong, var. KURRAJONG.

curral, obs. form of CORAL.

currant ('kʌrənt). Forms: α. 4 (raysons of) Coraunte, 5 (reysyns, etc. of) Corance, -awnce -auns, -ence, -ent, -ons, -ouns, 5–6 -aunce, 6 -ans, -ens, 6–7 (raisins of) Corinth. β. *Pl.* (or *collective*): 6 coraunce, corints, currents, 6–7 -ance, -antes, corans, corantes, (corinthes), 6–8 currans, 7 -ence, -ains, -ands, corants, -ents, -ins, corrans, -ands, -ants, (7–9 corinths), 6– currants. *Sing.* 6 coren, 7 corin, coran, curren, current, 7–8 curran, (corinth, 8 curan), 7– currant. [Orig. *raisins of Corauntz*, AF. *raisins de Corauntz*, = F. *raisins de Corinthe* raisins of Corinth; reduced before 1500 to *corauntz, coraunce*, whence the later *corantes, currants*, and *corans, currence, currans* (found in literature to *c* 1750, and still *dial.*). Some of the 16th c. herbalists restored the original form *Corinth*, which has been affected by some writers down to the 19th c.]

1. The raisin or dried fruit prepared from a dwarf seedless variety of grape, grown in the Levant; much used in cookery and confectionery. (Familiarly distinguished from 2 as ***grocers'*** or ***shop currants***.)

† α. *raisins of Corauntz, Corinth*, etc. *Obs.*

[**1334** in Rogers *Agric. & Prices* II. 545 Raisins de Corauntz.] ? *c* **1390** *Form of Cury* in Warner *Antiq. Culin.* 6 Lat it seeth togedre with powdor-fort of gynger..with raysons of Coraunte. **1463** *Mann. & Househ. Exp.* 217 Item, ffor vj. li. reysonys off corawnce, xviij. d. **1471** MARG. PASTON *Lett.* No. 681 III. 25 Sende me word qwat price a *li.* of..reysonys of Corons. **1562** BULLEYN *Bk. Compounds* 27 a, Take..of Raisons of Corans picked. **1578** LYTE *Dodoens* v. lxxxi. 652 The smal Raysens which are commonly called Corantes, but more rightly Raysens of Corinthe. **1620** VENNER *Via Recta* vii. 122 The small Raisins of Corinth, which we commonly call Currants.

β. *corauntz, currence, currants, currant*, etc.

a **1502** in Arnolde *Chron.* (1811) 234 Coraunce, at i. d'. ob'. **1540** *Act 32 Hen. VIII*, c. 14 Item for a butte of currantes, iii.s. iiii.d. **1578** [see α]. **1599** HAKLUYT *Voy.* II. 165 The plant that beareth the coren. **1611** SHAKS. *Wint. T.* IV. iii. 40 Three pound of Sugar, fiue pound of Currence, Rice. **1628** tr. *Camden's Hist. Eliz.* II. (1688) 235 Grapes of Corinth or Currants. **1655** MOUFET & BENNET *Health's Improv.* (1746) 205 A Prune, a Raisin, or a Curran. **1725** POPE *Odyss.* XIII. 293 *note*, The chief riches of the island [Zant] consist in Corinths. **1747** WESLEY *Prim. Physick* (1762) 50 Breakfast..on Water gruel with Currants. **1748** MRS. S. HARRISON *House-kpr.'s Pocket-Bk.* i. (ed. 4) 2, I suppose you have Currans, Raisons, and Sugars. **1811** PINKERTON *Petral.* II. 115 A plumb-pudding, composed of flour with raisins and corinths. **1859** THACKERAY *Virgin.* xxxiii, Had I not best go out and order raisins and corinths for the wedding-cake? **1860** MRS. HARVEY *Cruise Claymore* 271 Of late years the currant has been much more extensively grown in the neighbourhood of Corinth.

2. a. Transferred to the small round berry of certain species of *Ribes* (*R. nigrum, R. rubrum*) called Black and Red Currants. (The White Currant is a variety of the Red.)

These shrubs, natives of Northern Europe, were introduced into English cultivation some time before 1578, when they are mentioned by Lyte as the Black and Red 'Beyond sea Gooseberry'. They were vulgarly believed at first to be the source of the Levantine currant; Lyte calls them 'Bastarde Currant', and both Gerarde and Parkinson protested against the error of calling them 'currants'.

1578 LYTE *Dodoens* VI. xx. 683 The first kinde is called ..*Ribes rubrum*; in English Redde Gooseberries, Bastard Corinthes. **1629** PARKINSON *Paradisus Terr.* 558 Those berries..usually called red currans are not those currans.. that are sold at the Grocers. **1671** GREW *Anat. Plants* I. v. § 12 Goosberries and Currans. **1677** —— *Anat. Fruits* iv. § 6 A White Corin, without taking off the Skin, sheweth not unpleasantly how the Seeds are fastned. **1708** J. PHILIPS *Cyder* II. 61 Now will the Corinths, now the rasps supply Delicious draughts. **1799** tr. *H. Meister's Lett.* 181 Tartlets of raspberries, currants, and gooseberries. **1872** OLIVER *Elem. Bot.* II. 178 Black and Red Currants belong to the same genus as Gooseberry.

b. The shrub which produces this fruit (more fully ***currant-bush, currant-tree***); also other shrubs of the same genus, as the Flowering Currant, *R. sanguineum*, a native of North America, cultivated for its deep crimson flowers.

1665–76 RAY *Flora* 223 Corinthes or currans, as they are vulgarly called, are plants well known. **1783** JOHNSON 18 Apr. in *Boswell*, I would plant a great many currants; the fruit is good. **1866** *Treas. Bot.* 982 *R[ibes] sanguineum*, the Red-flowered Currant, a native of North America, is.. frequently grown in our gardens for ornamental purposes.

3. Applied to various shrubs having fruit (usually edible) resembling that of *Ribes*.

1866 *Treas. Bot.* 363 Australian Currant, *Leucopogon Richei*. Indian C., an American name for *Symphoricarpus vulgaris*. Native C., of Tasmania, a name applied to some species of *Coprosma*. *Ibid.* 674 *Leptomeria Billardieri* is a pretty broom-like shrub..producing greenish-red berries, which are called Native Currants in New South Wales and Victoria; they have a pleasant acid taste..The fruit of another species, *L. acerba*, is also called Currants in Australia. **1884** MILLER *Plant-n.*, W. Indian Currant, *Jacquinia armillaris, Beureria havanensis*, and *B. succulenta*. .. Indian Currant-bush, of Tropical America, the genera *Miconia* and *Clidemia*.

4. *attrib.* and *Comb.*, as (sense 1) ***currant-bun, -cake, -grape, loaf, -vine***; (sense 2) ***currant-bush*** (see also 3), ***-jelly, -tree, -wine***; **currant-borer, -clearwing,** the clearwing moth *Ægeria tipuliformis* and its larva; **currant-gall,** a small round gall, like an unripe currant, formed on the male flowers and leaves of the oak by the insect *Spathegaster baccarum*; **currant-moth,** a kind of moth that infests currant-bushes, the Magpie-moth; **currant-shrub,** a shrub or acid drink made from currants; **currant-worm,** a larva that infests currant-bushes.

1867 *Amer. Naturalist* June 223 The *currant-borer moth (*Trochilium tipuliforme*) darts about the leaves on hot sunny days. **1961** R. SOUTH *Moths Brit. Isles* (ed. 4) II. 344 This species seems to have been introduced into North America, where its caterpillar is known as the 'currant borer'. **1788** PICKEN *Poems* 13 (Jam.), Whangs o' *curran-buns an' cheese. **1890** *Spectator* 19 Apr. 532/1 Currant-buns and plum-puddings. **1813** J. FORBES *Orient. Mem.* II. xxv. 405 The cotton shrub..in verdure resembles the *currant-bush. **1605** B. JONSON *Volpone* v. iv, Ha you ne're a *curren-but to leape into? **1681** T. JORDAN *London's Joy* in Heath *Grocers' Comp.* (1869) 545, I have dwelt in a Tub..But ne're taught in a Currant-Butt before. **1868** WOOD *Homes without H.* xxv. 492 These are popularly called *Currant-galls, because they look very much like bunches of currants. **1682** WHELER *Journ. Greece* I. 32 We had a present sent to us of Figs, Filberds, and *Currant-grapes. **1731–7** MILLER *Gard. Dict.* (ed. 3) s.v. *Vitis*, The Corinth Grape, vulgarly called the Currant Grape: Is an early Ripener. **1922** W. G. R. FRANCILLON *Good Cookery* (ed. 2) xxi. 385 **Currant loaf*... Cream the yeast. Add some of the milk... Beat in the butter, sugar, fruits and egg. **1933** L. G. D. ACLAND in *Press* (Christchurch, N.Z.) 16 Sept. 15/7 *Brownie*. Bread baked with currants and sugar..called..now, usually, currant loaf. **1858–9** HUMPHREYS *Genera Brit. Moths, Abraxas Grossulariata*, The large Magpie, or *Currant Moth. **1856** *Englishw. Dom. Mag.* IV. 94 How to make *Currant Shrub. **1649** *Surv. Manor Wimbledon* in *Archæol.* X. 424 (D.) The borders of which grass plots are *coran trees. **1731** MEDLEY *Kolben's Cape G. Hope* II. 263 The Stem and Leaves of these shrubs are much like those of Corinth trees. **1877** *Encycl. Brit.* VI. 715/1 In the Ionian Islands the *currant-vine is grown on the sides of the lower hills. *a* **1648** DIGBY *Closet Open.* (1669) 113 *Currants-Wine, take a pound of the best currants. **1850** C. M. YONGE *Langley School* xxvii. 249 They each had a glass of currant wine. **1867** *Amer. Naturalist* June 222 The *Abraxas? ribearia* of Fitch, the well-known *Currant-worm, defoliates whole rows of currant bushes. 1886 *Harper's Mag.* Aug. 447 The natural history of the currant worm and moth.

currant, obs. form of COURANTE, CURRENT.

currant jelly. [CURRANT 4.] A preserve made of the strained juice of boiled currants heated and mixed with sugar in a preserving-pan. Also *fig.* Also *attrib.*, as ***currant-jelly dog***, a harrier.

1747 MRS. GLASSE *Cookery* 145 To make Curran Jelly. Strip the Currants from the Stalks, put them in a Stone Jar [etc.]. 1762 W. GELLEROY *Lond. Cook* 303 To make Currant Jelly. 1831 *Athenæum* 31 Dec. 852/1 Swallowing the bitter powder of instruction by enclosing it in the currant jelly of amusement. 1851 *Illustr. Lond. News* 11 Jan. 27/3 Those agents of woodcraft, called, in flippant parlance, 'currant-jelly dogs'. 1869 L. M. ALCOTT *Good Wives* (1871) v. 47 Fired with a housewifely wish to see her store-room stocked with home-made preserves, she undertook to put up her own currant jelly. [1923 H. COX *Dogs & I* xvii. 145 Those which are contemptuously termed 'Red Currant Jelly Dogs' ..are composed either of Beagle Harriers or..dwarf Foxhounds.]

curranto, var. of CORANTO.

1634 SIR T. HERBERT *Trav.* (1638) 75 Without regarding ought save Cupids Currantoes. 1957 SANCROFT *Mod. Policies* in D'Oyly *Life* II. 261 You hear so much of a curranto in the application.

'curranty, *a.* [See -Y[1].] Full of currants.

1876 M. E. BRADDON *J. Haggard's Dau.* ix, Certain rockcakes, seedy and curranty.

currawong ('kʌrəwɒŋ). *Austral.* [Aboriginal.] The native name in Australia for a bird of the genus *Strepera* (see quot. 1926).

1926 *Austral. Encycl.* II. 19/2 Birds of the other genus, Strepera, are variously known as bell-magpies or black magpies, as well as by the aboriginal name of 'currawong' in New South Wales and Queensland. 1936 F. D. DAVISON *Children of Dark People* 5 Currawongs and willy wagtails flitted among the bushes. 1964 *Telegraph* (Brisbane) 4 Mar. 3/5 Jock was a currawong—a type of magpie—and he sounded off just after dawn every day. 1970 *Southerly* XXX. 8 In season the currawongs in the camphor-laurels cry like tin-shears.

†**curre.** *Obs.* [a. OF. *curre* (*corre, courre*):—L. *currus* chariot.] A chariot.

1483 CAXTON *Gold. Leg.* 72/2 His cartes chares and curres.

curre, obs. f. and var. of CUR.

†**'currence.** *Obs. rare.* [ad. L. type *currentia, f. *current-em*, pr. pple. of *currĕre* to run: see -ENCE. Cf. obs. F. *courance.*] = CURRENCY.

1651 M. BACON *Disc. Govt. Eng.* II. vii. (1739) 44 For the fuller currence of the Money. 1854 *Fraser's Mag.* XLIX. 6 The time..will..not have been lost, if it only strips the argument of all sentimentalism and false currence.

currency ('kʌrənsı). [f. as prec. + -ENCY.]

†**1. a.** The fact or condition of flowing, flow; course; *concr.* a current, stream. *Obs. rare.*

1657 HOWELL *Londinop.* 18 To preserve the currency of the stream. 1698 TYSON in *Phil. Trans.* XX. 135 To shew the Currency of their *Canalis* here. 1758 BINNELL *Descr. Thames* 11 The Currency runs..with such Force, as to render the Navigation thereof imperfect.

†**b.** 'Fluency; readiness of utterance; easiness of pronunciation' (J.). *Obs.*

c. Running, rapid motion. (*nonce-use.*)

1841 L. HUNT *Seer* II. (1864) 69 We are truly in a state of transition,—of currency rather [in a coach].

2. The course (of time); the time during which anything is current.

1726 AYLIFFE *Parergon* 196 The Currency of Time to establish a Custom, ought to be with a Continuando from the beginning to the end of the Term. 1822–56 DE QUINCEY *Confess.* Wks. 1862 I. 288 She might be in the currency of her eighth year. 1846 MCCULLOCH *Acc. Brit. Empire* (1854) I. 465 During the entire currency of the lease. 1850 *Tait's Mag.* XVII. 4/1 Must his exclusion run only during the currency of other parts of his sentence?

3. Of money: The fact or quality of being current or passing from man to man as a medium of exchange; circulation. Also *fig.*

1699 LOCKE *2nd Reply to Bp. of Worcester* (R.), 'Tis the receiving of them by others, their very passing, that gives them their authority and currency. 1722 *Lond. Gaz.* No. 6078/2 All such of the said Bills..lose their Currency. 1729 POPE *Dunc.* I. 23 *note*, The papers of Drapier against the currency of Wood's copper coin in Ireland. 1862 RUSKIN *Munera P.* (1880) 15 The laws of currency and exchange.

4. a. That which is current as a medium of exchange; the circulating medium (whether coins or notes); the money of a country in actual use.

1729 FRANKLIN *Ess.* Wks. 1840 II. 270 Money..by being coined is made a currency. 1776 ADAM SMITH *W.N.* II. ii. (1869) I. 328 The paper currencies of North America. 1861 GOSCHEN *For. Exch.* 58 If there is a large paper currency side by side with the gold. 1866 CRUMP *Banking* vii. 154 The currencies of two countries..being dissimilar.

fig. 1806–7 J. BERESFORD *Miseries Hum. Life* (1826) III. v, General Miseries—the common currency of human existence. 1879 ESCOTT *England* II. 425 Their mischievous influences upon the moral currency.

b. *spec.* Applied to a current medium of exchange when differing in value from the money of account; e.g. the former currency and banco of Hamburg (see BANCO), the depreciated paper currency of various countries, and the local shillings and pence, of less value than sterling money formerly used in various British colonies.

1755 JOHNSON, *Currency*..6. The papers stamped in the English colonies by authority, and passing for money. 1776 ADAM SMITH *W.N.* I. viii. (1869) I. 73 In the province of New York common labourers earn three shillings and sixpence currency. 1872 *Japanese in Amer.* 201 Paper money ..is also called currency.

c. Formerly a name for native-born Australians, as distinguished from *sterling*, or English-born. Also *attrib.* and as *adj.*

1827 P. CUNNINGHAM *N.S. Wales* II. xxi. 53 Our Currency lads and lasses are a fine interesting race. 1828 *Ibid.* (ed. 3) 48 The Currencies grow up tall and slender, like the Americans. 1837 J. D. LANG *N.S. Wales* I. 220 Contests ..between the colonial youth and natives of England, or, to use the phrase of the colony, between currency and sterling. 1878 *Punch* 10 Aug. 60/1 We currency-folk have..been able to absorb your convict refuse without contamination from its criminal leaven. 1892 LENTZNER *Australian Word-bk.* 19 *Currency*, persons born in Australia, natives of England being termed 'sterling'. 1894 W. C. DAWE (*title*) The confessions of a currency girl. 1899 *Macm. Mag.* June 127/1 The boys when questioned would say: 'I'm not English; I'm Currency.' 1953 *Landfall* VII. 173 She spoke the King's English like a currency lass.

5. The fact or quality of being current, prevalent, or generally reported and accepted among mankind; prevalence, vogue; *esp.* of ideas, reports, etc.

1722 *Lond. Gaz.* No. 6077/2 The Currency of the ordinary Distempers. 1798 FERRIAR *Cert. Varieties Man* 213 The story..seems to have gained currency. 1840 CARLYLE *Heroes* (1858) 321 Johnson's Writings, which once had such currency and celebrity, are now as it were disowned by the young generation. 1862 H. SPENCER *First Princ.* II. iv. §53 The currency of this belief continues.

6. *attrib.* and *Comb.* (mostly in senses 3 and 4) as ***currency crank, restriction***; **currency note**, paper money used as currency, esp. the £1 and 10*s.* notes first issued by the Treasury for circulation as legal tender during the war of 1914–18; a treasury note.

1931 H. G. WELLS *Work, Wealth & Happiness of Mankind* (1932) ix. 363 General discussion [on currency] has been further burked by dubbing anyone who raised the question, a 'Currency Crank'. 1944 G. B. SHAW *Everybody's Political What's What* xi. 84 The Currency Crank is a nuisance in every movement for social reform. 1816 KEATINGE *Trav.* (1817) II. 178 Currency-money here has depreciated..a full third. 1885 *Pall Mall G.* 9 June 5 America..has shown itself able to do strange things in the way of currency-mongering. 1891 J. L. KIPLING *Beast & Man in India* v. 105 A currency note for a thousand rupees. 1914 *Proclamation* 3 Feb. in *Jrnl. Inst. Bankers* (1915) XXXVI. 113 Payment for the order at its face value in coins or currency notes. 1920 *Discovery* May 145/1 Our over-issues of currency notes. 1922 *Encycl. Brit.* XXXI. 969/2 The 1914 Act..allowed an issue of £1 and 10*s.* currency notes by the Treasury. 1866 CRUMP *Banking* viii. 160 The great advantage of coined money for currency purposes. 1849 MISS MULOCK *Ogilvies* 17 He is..particularly well read on the currency question. 1967 'R. SIMONS' *Taxed to Death* ix. 151 Several printed forms about currency restrictions.

current ('kʌrənt), *a.* Forms: 4–6 corant(e, coraunt, 6 corrant, 4–8 currant, 5–6 curraunt, 6– current. [ME. *corant, currant*, a. OF. *corant, curant* (from 16th c. *courant*) running, pres. pple. of *courir*, OF. *corre*:—L. *currĕre* to run. The spelling of the Eng. word as *currant* (very common in 16th c.) gradually led to its complete conformation to L. *current-em.*]

1. a. Running; flowing. (Now *rare.*)

*c*1300 *K. Alis* 3461 With him cam..mony faire juster corant. 1393 GOWER *Conf.* III. 96 Like to the currant fire, that renneth Upon a corde. 1523 FITZHERB. *Husb.* §128 Se that there be no water standynge..but that it be alwaye currant and rennynge. 1596 DAVIES *Orchestra* lxix, Those current travases, That on a triple dactyl foot do run Close by the ground. 1651 T. BARKER *Art of Angling* (1653) 10 They will go currant down the River. 1667 MILTON *P.L.* VII. 67 The current streame. 1756 AMORY *Buncle* (1770) I. 265 The water was current through the pond. 1830 W. PHILLIPS *Mt. Sinai* I. 597 The current spring.

†**b.** ***current ship***: see quot. *Obs.*

1555 EDEN *Decades* 120 The lyghtest shyp which maye bee a passinger betwene them: that lyke as we vse poste horses by lande so may they by this current shippe in shorte space certifie the Lieuetenaunt of suche thynges as shall chaunce.

†**c.** *Her.* = COURANT *a. Obs.*

1610 GUILLIM *Heraldry* III. xv. (1660) 176 He beareth.. three Unicornes in Pale, Current. 1681 T. JORDAN *London's Joy* in Heath *Grocers' Comp.* (1869) 542 Argent, three Greyhounds Currant Arm'd and Collard, Gules.

†**d.** Having a fall or inclination; sloping. *Obs.* (Cf. CURRENT *sb.* 3.)

1523 FITZHERB. *Husb.* §128 To make them euen somwat dyscendynge or currant one waye or other. 1530 PALSGR. 441 This water avoydeth nat well; by lykelyhod the goutter is nat courrant.

e. Of handwriting: 'Running', cursive.

1891 E. MAUNDE THOMPSON in *Classical Rev.* Nov. 418/2 Ought our descendants then to infer that we knew nothing of a current hand?

2. *fig.* Smoothly flowing; running easily and swiftly; fluent. (Now *rare.*)

1586 J. HOOKER *Girald. Irel.* in *Holinshed* II. 97 Mistrusting..that all went not currant. 1589 PUTTENHAM *Eng. Poesie* I. iv. (Arb.) 24 Speech by meeter..is more currant and slipper upon the tongue. 1659 HAMMOND *On Ps.* vii. 4 Thus the sense is perspicuous and current. 1709 STRYPE *Ann. Ref.* I. ii. 67 April 18. The Bill..was read the first time. Apr. 19. Read the second time..Apr. 20. Read the third time, and passed the House. So current it seems this bill went. 1818 BYRON *Juan* I. cc. (*MS. reading*), Other incidents..Which shall be specified..in current rhyme.

3. a. Running in time; in course of passing; in progress. Often used *ellipt.*, as in ***the 10th current*** (abbreviated *curt.*), *i.e.* the 10th day of the current month. **b.** Belonging to the current week, month, or other period of time.

1608 HIERON *Defence* III. 131 There was not any long time current and past wherein it has been observed and made usuall. *c*1645 HOWELL *Lett.* (1650) II. 7, I had yours of the tenth current. 1664 H. MORE *Myst. Iniq.* 477 [It] does not imply the time fully run out, but that the last part thereof must then be current. 1708 J. CHAMBERLAYNE *St. Gt. Brit.* I. III. i. (1743) 142 None is to be ordained..Deacon till he is at least twenty-three current. 1734 BERKELEY *Let.* 17 Mar. Wks. IV. 218, I paid the curates for the current year. 1780 BURKE *Sp. Econom. Reform* Wks. 1842 I. 230 No tax is raised for the current services. 1858 HERSCHEL *Outlines Astron.* xviii. §927 A date..always expresses the day or year current and not elapsed. 1862 RUSKIN *Munera P.* (1880) 46 To enlarge his current expenses. 1868 DICKENS *Lett.* (1880) II. 387 We must call the current number for that date the Christmas number.

c. ***current account***, an account kept by a customer at a bank to meet his current expenses; ***current affairs, events***, those in progress, those belonging to the present time; ***current cost accounting***, a method of accounting in which assets are valued on the basis of their replacement cost and increases in their value as a result of inflation are excluded from calculations of profit; ***current goods*** (see quot. 1948).

1846 DICKENS *Pict. Italy* 66 A means of establishing a current account with Heaven, on which to draw..for future bad actions. 1875 H. FISHER *Opening*, etc. *Spec. Banking Accts.* 1 The opening, working, and closing of certain classes of Current and Deposit Accounts. 1899 *Westm. Gaz.* 1 Sept. 6/3 It is the depositor, rather than the current-account customer, who is victimised by this custom. 1951 R. W. JONES *Thomson's Dict. Banking* (ed. 10) 206/1 A current or running account is the active account on which cheques are drawn and to which credits are paid. 1920 BEERBOHM *And Even Now* 60 Swinburne did, from time to time, take public notice of current affairs. 1955 'C. BROWN' *Lost Girls* x. 111 We began each afternoon's session with a 'current affairs' talk. 1957 *B.B.C. Handbk.* 102 Up-to-date information on current affairs. 1975 *Rep. Inflation Accounting Comm.* (F. E. P. Sandilands) i. 3 in *Parl. Papers 1974–75* VII. 411 We recommend that a system to be known as *Current Cost Accounting should be developed. 1977 *Courier-Mail* (Brisbane) 2 Mar. 2/6 Current cost accounting, a system which takes account of inflation, is called inflation accounting in the United States. 1984 HITCHING & STONE *Understand Accounting!* vii. 85 We shall be turning our attention to the question of 'value', and to current cost accounting. 1850 *Harper's Mag.* June 122 (*headline*) Monthly record of current events. 1920 S. LEWIS *Main Street* ix. 107 The Thanatopsis Club..have some of the *best* ..current-events discussions. 1936 *Discovery* Nov. 355/2 The distinction between capital goods and current goods is ..one of the most important in the whole of economics. 1948 G. CROWTHER *Outl. Money* (ed. 2) v. 129 Every year the community produces a certain total of goods and services; some of them are for immediate consumption, the rest are goods whose value will last beyond the immediate present. These two categories can be called current goods and durable goods. All services are naturally current goods.

4. Of money: Passing from hand to hand; in circulation; in general use as a medium of exchange.

1481 CAXTON *Myrr.* III. xiv. 167 In the begynnynge of the Regne of Kynge Edward..was no monoye curraunt in englond but pens and halfpens and ferthynges. 1535 COVERDALE *Gen.* xxiii. 16 Currant money amonge marchauntes [WYCLIF preued comune money]. 1611 CORYAT *Crudities* 286 The currantest money of all both in Venice itselfe and in the whole Venetian Signiory. 1630 *R. Johnson's Kingd. & Commw.* 501 In Kataia a coine is currant, made of the blacke rinde of a certaine tree. 1781 GIBBON *Decl. & F.* II. 66 Of the current coin of the empire. 1872 YEATS *Growth Comm.* 33 Pieces of leather impressed with the government mark and passing current like our bank-notes.

= Locally current. (Cf. CURRENCY 4 b.)

1593 in *Muniments of Irvine* (1890) I. 79 The Burrow meillis..to be payit in Stirlling money..ar resavit in current money to our greit hurt.

†**5.** Having the quality of current coin; sterling, genuine, authentic: opposed to *counterfeit. Obs.*

1579 LYLY *Euphues* (Arb.) 73 Though others seem counterfeit in their deeds..Euphues will be alwayes currant in his dealings. 1599 *Warn. Faire Women* II. 1555 To put your love unto the touch, to try If it be currant, or but counterfait. 1611 COTGR., *A Preuve de marteau*, sound, currant, good, right stuffe. 1634 W. TIRWHYT tr. *Balzac's Lett.* 67 If the report which passeth be current. 1639 HORN & ROB. *Gate Lang. Unl.* ix. §85 With a touch-stone we try metals, whether they be good (currant) or counterfeit. 1744 HARRIS *Three Treat.* III. I. (1765) 141 Do we not try [a piece of Metal]..by the Test, before we take it for Current?

6. Generally reported or known; in general circulation; in general use, prevalent.

1563 *Mirr. Mag., J. Shore* xxiv, What I sayd was currant every where. 1625 BACON *Ess.* Ep. Ded., I doe now publish my Essayes; which, of all my other workes, haue beene most currant. 1631 J. PORY in Ellis *Orig. Lett.* II. 271 III. 267 It is current in every mans mouth that the Kings journey into Scotland is putt off. 1775 BURKE *Corr.* (1844) II. 40, I find it very current that parliament will meet in October. 1855 MACAULAY *Hist. Eng.* IV. 549 The stories which were current about both Seymour and the Speaker.

7. Generally accepted; established by common consent; in vogue. Often with mixture of sense 3: Accepted or in vogue at the time in question.

1593 BILSON *Govt. Christ's Ch.* 169 If laie Elders had bene currant in Gregories time. **1665** GLANVILL *Sceps. Sci.* 78 The current Theology of Europe. **1666** DRYDEN *Ann. Mirab.* Pref., A word which is not current English. **1713** BERKELEY *Hylas & P.* ii. Wks. 1871 I. 309 The current proper signification attached to a common name in any language. **1831** SIR J. SINCLAIR *Corr.* II. 187 The commerce of Holland greatly depends on the current interest. **1884** H. SPENCER in *Contemp. Rev.* XLVI. 46 Current utilitarian speculation.. shows inadequate consciousness of natural causation.

8. Phr. ***to pass, go,*** or ***run current*** (senses 5–7): to be in circulation or in common use; to be generally related, reported, or accepted; to be received as genuine. (Formerly ***to pass*** or ***go for current.***)

1596 HARINGTON *Metam. Ajax* (1814) 12 And so now it passeth current to be spoken and written Ajax. **1600** ABP. ABBOT *Exp. Jonah* 3 Which opinion hath gone so currant, that.. some of the new writers haue accepted it for a truth. **1605** CAMDEN *Rem.* (1637) 16 But most true this may seeme which runneth currant every where. **1611** BIBLE *Transl. Pref.* 4 Why the Translation of the Seuentie was allowed to passe for currant. **1618** BOLTON *Florus* III. iii. (1636) 168 That invincible rage and furious onset, which goes current with the Barbarous for true valour. **1629** J. ROUSE *Diary* 46 It went for currant that the Spanyards had killed the French and Dutch. **1725** DE FOE *Voy. round World* (1840) 210 It went current among the seamen that the Spanish Doctor was an Englishman. **1727** A. HAMILTON *New Acc. E. Ind.* I. xxi. 250 Their Language [Portuguese] goes current along most of the Sea-coast. **1828** MACAULAY *Hallam* Ess. I. 54 If such arguments are to pass current it will be easy to prove [etc.].

current (ˈkʌrənt), *sb.* Forms: 4 curraunt, 6–7 currant, 6– current. [a. OF. *corant, curant,* sb. use of *courant* adj.: see prec., with which this is in its orthographical history identical.]

1. That which runs or flows, a stream; *spec.* a portion of a body of water, or of air, etc. moving in a definite direction.

c **1380** WYCLIF *Serm.* Sel. Wks. I. 186 Men þat knowen þe worchinge of þe elementis.. and worchiþ woundir bi craft in mevynge of currauntis. **1595** SHAKS. *John* II. i. 441 Two such siluer currents when they ioyne Do glorifie the bankes that bound them in. **1665** HOOKE *Microgr.* 212 A small current of blood, which came directly from its snout, and past into its belly. **1727** SWIFT *Gulliver* III. iv. 205 A.. mill turned by a current from a large river. **1863** A. C. RAMSAY *Phys. Geog.* i. (1878) 10 Great ocean currents such as the Gulf Stream.

2. a. The action or condition of flowing; flow, flux (of a river, etc.); usually in reference to its force or velocity.

1555 EDEN *Decades* 353 Where the currant setteth alwayes to the eastwarde. **1683** BURNET tr. *More's Utopia* (1684) 65 There is no great Current in the Bay. **1769** *De Foe's Tour Gt. Brit.* III. 57 [The River Trent] comes down from the Hills with a violent Current into the flat Country. **1832** W. IRVING *Alhambra* I. 25, I came to a river with high banks and deep rapid current. **1863** MARY HOWITT *F. Bremer's Greece* II. xiv. 90 The well-known phenomenon of the changing current in the Straits [of Euripus].

†**b.** The course of a river or other flowing body. *Obs.*

1696 WHISTON *Th. Earth* II. (1722) 119 The rise and currents of Rivers are not always the same now as before the Flood. **1753** HANWAY *Trav.* (1762) I. III. xxvi. 111 The peasants diverted the current of the flame, and saved their villages. **1799** J. ROBERTSON *Agric. Perth* 25 The Earn is a more rapid river than the Forth, has a longer current.

3. The inclination or 'fall' given to a gutter, roof, etc. to let the water run off.

1582 in W. H. Turner *Select. Rec. Oxford* 423 No.. persons shall make their pavements higher then an other, but that hit may have a reasonable currant. **1699** in *Col. Rec. Pennsylv.* I. 559 Neglect of Levelling the streets and ordering the Currents yrof. **1703** T. N. *City & C. Purchaser* 161 Take care that the Gutter.. lie.. in such a Position that it may have a good Current. **1823** P. NICHOLSON *Pract. Build.* 407 All sheet lead is laid with a current to keep it dry. **1874** KNIGHT *Dict. Mech.* s.v., Gutters usually have a current of ¼ inch to the foot.

†**4.** Circulation (of money), currency. *Obs.*

1586 T. B. *La Primaud. Fr. Acad.* I. 635 This privie councell.. taketh order for the currant and finenes of money. **1651** N. BACON *Disc. Govt. Eng.* II. vii. (1739) 44 The regulating of the Mint, and the current of Money. **1691** tr. *Emilianne's Frauds Romish Monks* 91 They find a plentiful current of Devotional-Mony.

5. *fig.* The course of time or of events; the main course.

1586 J. HOOKER *Girald. Irel.* in *Holinshed* II. 136/1 That place was not possessed of the like in manie currents of yeares. **1602** MARSTON *Ant. & Mel.* v. Wks. 1856 I. 66 My joyes passion.. choakes the current of my speach. **1721** STRYPE *Eccl. Mem.* I. 19 More perhaps will be said of him in the current of these memorials. **1788** PRIESTLEY *Lect. Hist.* III. xiii. 106 Without some such general comprehension, as we may call it, of the whole current of time. **1817** CHALMERS *Astron. Disc.* iii. (1852) 77 The whole current of my restless and ever-changing history. **1868** FREEMAN *Norm. Conq.* (1876) II. x. 519 One more tale will bring us back directly to the current of our story.

6. a. Course or progress in a defined direction; tendency, tenor, drift (of opinions, writings, etc.).

1595 SHAKS. *John* II. i. 335 Say, shall the currant of our right rome on. **1607** HIERON *Wks.* I. 370 This is.. plaine and obuious out of the very current of the words. **1692** LOCKE *Toleration* III. x, In your first Paper, as the whole Current of it would make one believe. **1782** PRIESTLEY *Corrupt. Chr.* I. I. 76 The current of men's opinions having.. set that way. **1888** BRYCE *Amer. Commw.* I. xii. 152 [These] words.. express the whole current of modern feeling.

†**b.** The tendency or drift of the common opinion, practice, etc., of a body of persons. *Obs.*

1613 J. SALKELD *Treat. Angels* 218 Against this opinion is the common current of all Doctors and Fathers. **1650** R. HOLLINGWORTH *Exerc. conc. Usurped Powers* 17 The current of the people or community I am of is to be followed. **1738** SWIFT *Pol. Conv.* xxxii, Affecting Singularity, against the general Current and Fashion of all about them. **1863** *Sat. Rev.* XV. 583/1 The current of modern American authorities is in complete accordance with this view.

7. a. *Electr.* The name given to the apparent transmission or 'flow' of electric force through a conducting body: introduced in connexion with the theory that electrical phenomena are due to a fluid (or fluids) which moves in actual 'streams'; now the common term for the phenomenon, without reference to any theory.

An electric current is according to its nature called *alternating* or *continuous, intermittent, pulsatory,* or *undulatory.*

1747 *Gentl. Mag.* XVII. 141 The frequent exciting such currents of ethereal fire in bed-chambers. **1752** FRANKLIN *Let.* Wks. 1887 II. 253 Perhaps the *auroræ boreales* are currents of this fluid in its own region, above our atmosphere. **1842** GROVE *Corr. Phys. Forces* 48 From the manner in which the peculiar force called electricity is seemingly transmitted through certain bodies.. the term current is commonly used to denote its apparent progress. **1871** TYNDALL *Fragm. Sc.* (ed. 6) I. x. 306 Faraday.. illustrated the laws of these induced currents. **1881** W. L. CARPENTER *Energy in Nature* 153 Dynamo machines.. that supply alternating currents, i.e. currents alternately in opposite directions. *Mod. Advt.* The [Electric Lighting] Company are prepared to supply current within the district named.

b. *transf.* Applied to the transmission of nerve-force along a nerve.

1855 BAIN *Senses & Int.* I. ii. §18 A current of nervous stimulus.. derived from the [spinal] cord to the muscles.

8. *attrib.* and *Comb.* **a.** In relation to currents of water, air, and the like, as ***current-drifted***; **current-bedding**, the bedding of geological strata in a sloping direction caused by deposition in a current of water; **current-fender**, a structure to ward off the current from a bank, etc., which it threatens to undermine; **current-gauge, current-meter**, an apparatus made for measuring the flow of liquids through a channel; (see also quot. 1868); **current-mill**, a mill driven by a current-wheel; **current-wheel**, a wheel driven by a natural current of water. **b.** Of or pertaining to an electrical current; as ***current-breaker, -collector, -meter, -regulator, -weigher,*** etc.

1891 *Jrnl. Derbyshire Archæol. Soc.* XIII. 35 The direction of the dip of planes of *current-bedding. **1856** KANE *Arct. Expl.* I. xvii. 206 A *current-drifted cask. **1874** KNIGHT *Dict. Mech.* 661 The dynamometer *current-gage of Woltmann, 1790, is a light water-wheel operated by the current. **1868** W. D. HASKOLL *Land & Marine Surveying* xi. 170 The *current meter is useful also to ascertain the velocity of under currents. **1874** KNIGHT *Dict. Mech.* 661 The *current-wheel is perhaps the first application of the force of water in motion to driving machinery.

1866 R. M. FERGUSON *Electr.* (1870) 185 A contrivance for this purpose is called a rheotome or *current-break. **1962** CORSON & LORRAIN *Introd. Electromagn. Fields* v. 179 A *current-carrying conductor. **1884** F. KROHN tr. *Glaser de Cew's Mag.- & Dyn.-Electr. Mach.* 207 The *current closers and interrupters. **1889** *Pall Mall G.* 16 Mar. 3/3 This *current collector, which is connected with the motor placed between the wheels underneath the floor of the car, moves in the conduit beneath the rail. **1884** F. KROHN tr. *Glaser de Cew's Mag.- & Dyn.-Electr. Mach.* 272 The *current-energised rotating helix. **1962** SIMPSON & RICHARDS *Junction Transistors* xiii. 295 The more usual practice is to define the feedback, solely by the way it is derived, as 'voltage' (parallel) or '*current' (series) feedback. **1964** R. F. FICCHI *Electr. Interference* x. 210 A *current-limiting device in neutral circuits. **1879** G. PRESCOTT *Sp. Telephone* 16 When the latter acts, it does so in obedience to *current pulsations. **1862** *Catal. Internat. Exhib.* II. XIII. 13 As these instruments have no break pieces or *current reversers they cannot get out of order. **1888** BOTTONE *Electr. Instr. Making* (1894) 192 The current reverser for the Wheatstone single needle telegraph. **1881** MAXWELL *Electr. & Magn.* I. 380 A stratum of a conductor contained between two consecutive surfaces of flow.. is called a *Current-Sheet. **1946** *Nature* 13 July 54/2 A system which gives the constant line voltage required for *current-using devices. **1881** MAXWELL *Electr. & Magn.* II. 341 The suspended coil in Dr. Joule's *current-weigher is horizontal and capable of vertical motion.

†**ˈcurrent**, *v. Obs. rare.* Also 7 currant. [f. CURRENT *a.*] *trans.* To render current, give currency or acceptance to.

1602 MARSTON *Ant. & Mel.* Induct. 27 The uneven scale, that currants all thinges by the outwarde stamp of opinion. **1607** —— *What You Will* II. i. 295 Faith, so, so.. As 't please opinion to current it.

‖**currente calamo** (kəˈrɛnteɪ ˈkæləməʊ), *adv. phr.* [L., lit. 'with the pen running on'.] Extempore; without deliberation or hesitation.

The actual phr. is not recorded in cl. L.

1776 W. MASON *Let.* 25 Mar. in *Walpole's Corr.* (1955) XXVIII. 254 What I here send you was written yesterday *currente calamo.* **1857** TROLLOPE *Barchester T.* II. xiii. 258 His letter.. was written, *currente calamo,* with very little trouble. **1915** W. J. LOCKE *Jaffery* ix. 112 Then to work, and in another three months, *currente calamo,* the book would be written.

ˈcurrented, *ppl. a.* [f. CURRENT *sb.* + -ED².] Having a current.

1650 HOWELL *Masaniello* I. 43 A strong currented River.

currentless (ˈkʌrəntlɪs), *a.* [f. CURRENT *sb.* + -LESS.] Having no current.

1860 GOSSE *Rom. Nat. Hist.* 191 We reached a spot where the river expanded, and formed a currentless basin. **1886** J. M. CAULFEILD *Seamanship Notes* 5 An anchorage, which is more or less currentless.

currently (ˈkʌrəntlɪ), *adv.* [f. CURRENT *a.*]

1. In the manner of a flowing stream; with easy rapid movement; smoothly, fluently, readily. Now *rare.*

1586 W. WEBBE *Eng. Poetrie* (Arb.) 68 The English wordes.. wyll become any one of ye most accustomed sortes of Latine or Greeke verses meetely, and run thereon somewhat currantly. **1598** GRENEWEY *Tacitus' Ann.* XV. i. (1622) 223 Neither went things currantly with him.. the siege tooke no effect. **1636** FEATLY *Clavis Myst.* lxx. 900 The spouts will not runne currantly, if we pump not deep. **1649** BLITHE *Eng. Improv. Impr.* (1653) 71 To pare old Trenches .. whose Edges will grow so thick with Grass, that thou canst not get thy water to pass currently. **1768** *Woman of Honor* I. 131 Lady Harriet.. very currently took her share of the intended presents. **1768–74** TUCKER *Lt. Nat.* (1852) I. 58 While he holds the reins we roll smoothly and currently along. **1802** PALEY *Nat. Theol.* ix. (1819) 122 How currently does the work proceed! **1844** LINGARD *Anglo-Sax. Ch.* (1858) II. xi. 187 Able to read in public currently and correctly.

2. In current use, practice, opinion, belief, report, or acceptance; generally, commonly among mankind, popularly; now, at the present time.

1580 NORTH *Plutarch* (1676) 320 Songs and Ballads.. currantly Sung in every place. **1646** SIR T. BROWNE *Pseud. Ep.* III. xxiii. 167 Many.. which beare that name, and currently passe among us. **1719** J. RICHARDSON *Sc. Connoisseur* 89 A Story which passes very currently. **1850** PRESCOTT *Peru* II. 337 He.. was detained at home, as currently reported, by illness. **1868** ROGERS *Pol. Econ.* i. (1876) 5 The view currently taken. **1947** J. HAYWARD *Prose Lit. since 1939* II. 20 The same writer.. is currently writing a section of the secret history of the war. **1969** A. GLYN *Dragon Variation* vi. 187 These were probably the two most exciting and original games [of postal chess] he was currently playing. **1971** *Daily Tel.* 8 June 10/3 They are currently to be seen at the Hampstead Theatre Club.

†**3.** With a common current or direction of evidence, opinion, etc. *Obs.*

1594 HOOKER *Eccl. Pol.* Pref. (J.), Which maketh the simple and ignorant to think they even see how the word of God runneth currently on your side. **1658** BAXTER *Saving Faith* §3. 15 In which you know how currantly the schoolmen.. are against you.

ˈcurrentness. Now *rare* or *Obs.* [f. as prec. + -NESS.] The quality of being current.

†**1.** Fluency, easy flow (of language, etc.). *Obs.*

1586 W. WEBBE *Eng. Poetrie* (Arb.) 51 The English tongue lacketh neyther variety nor currantnesse of phrase. **1656** J. SERGEANT tr. *T. White's Peripat. Inst.* Transl. Addr., Her Interpreter.. should speak all languages; at least to that fair degree of currentnesse, as [etc.].

2. The fact of being current or in circulation; currency; the genuine quality that entitles coin, etc. to pass current (*obs.*).

1583 STOCKER *Hist. Civ. Warres Lowe C.* II. 42 a, The currauntnesse of the Coyne. **1611** COTGR., *Mise*.. the currantnesse, or goodnesse of coyne. **1658** BP. REYNOLDS *Lord's Supper* xvi, As prayer is animated by the Death of Christ (which alone is that character that addes currantness to them).

curreour, currer, obs. forms of COURIER *sb.*

curret, -ette, obs. forms of CUIRASS.

†**curreter, -etter.** *Obs.* [a. 16th c. F. *courratier,* now *courtier,* OF. *coretier, coratier,* in Pr. *corratier,* Sp. *corredor,* broker, prob. f. *correr,* L. *currĕre* to run (Darmesteter). (The phonology opposes derivation from L. *cūrāre.*)] A broker.

1580 HOLLYBAND *Treas. Fr. Tong, Vn courretier.. qui moyenne & va & vient d'vne partie à l'autre, pour faire quelque marché,* a curretter, a broaker. [**1847** in HALLIWELL.]

curreye, var. CONREY *Obs.*, equipment, etc.

curricle (ˈkʌrɪk(ə)l). [ad. L. *curricul-um* running, course, also (race-)chariot, f. *curr-ĕre* to run.]

†**1.** A course, running. (In quot. 1682 taken as *dim.*, a short course.) *Obs.*

1682 SIR T. BROWNE *Chr. Mor.* (1756) 124 Upon a curricle in this world depends a long course of the next. **1710** T. FULLER *Pharm. Extemp.* 271 The Remedy.. is convey'd .. by the Curricle of the Blood into the Tracheal Ducts.

2. A light two-wheeled carriage, usually drawn by two horses abreast.

1752 H. WALPOLE *Let.* 5 Aug. (1903) III. 114 These mountains, where the young gentlemen are forced to drive their curricles with a pair of oxen. **1756–7** tr. *Keysler's Trav.* (1760) IV. 367 A curricle which is put in motion by the person who sits in it, by turning round a single wheel placed in the front. **1769** *Chron.* in *Ann. Reg.* 125/2 A man of 70 much intoxicated . . rolled against the wheel of their curricle. **1794** W. Felton *Carriages* (1801) II. 95 Curricles . . are . . a superior kind of two-wheeled carriage. **1802** *Projects* in *Ann. Reg.* 773/2 In curricles, single horse chaises, or other carriages. **1888** Burgon *Lives 12 Gd. Men* II. xii. 386 He made these periodical journeys . . in a kind of open curricle.

3. *Comb.*, as ***curricle-builder***; *attrib.*, as ***curricle artillery, fire-engine, gun*** (= mounted on a light two-wheeled carriage for rapid movement).

1786 Sir H. Croft *Abbey of Kilkhampton* 107 Coach-builders, curricle-builders. **1802** *Naval Chron.* VIII. 173 Brass guns on curricle carriages. **1807** Southey in *Q. Rev.* II. 126 Two pieces of curricle artillery. **1878-81** E. Matheson *Aid Bk.* (1889) 579 Curricle fire-engines . . may be advantageously fitted with shafts for with one horse.

Hence **'curricle** *v.*; †**curri'cleer**, one who drives a curricle. *nonce-wds.*

1857 Carlyle *Misc.* IV. 98 (D.) Who is this that comes curricling through the level yellow sunlight, like one of respectability keeping his gig? **1794** *Sporting Mag.* IV. 58 The dashing curricle-eers of the day. **1803** *Pic Nic* No. 5 (1806) I. 177 Our tonish navigators and curricleers.

curricular (kəˈrɪkjʊlə(r)), *a. rare.* [f. L. *curricul-um* (see prec.) + -ar.] Of or pertaining to driving or to carriages.

1798 *Spirit Pub. Jrnls.* (1799) II. 186 Gigs, buggies, whiskies, and other implements of curricular motion. **1870** *Temple Bar Mag.* XXIX. 193 Their heroes go to the drive in a tandem with outriders; but, notwithstanding this strange confusion of curricular arrangements [etc.]. **1881** *Standard* 12 Apr., The four-in-hand is, as it were, the curricular unit. If a man can manage a Coach and four . . he can do anything in the way of driving.

‖**curriculum** (kəˈrɪkjʊləm). Pl. -ula. [L., = course, career (*lit.* and *fig.*): see above.] A course; *spec.* a regular course of study or training, as at a school or university. (The recognized term in the Scottish Univerities.) **curriculum vitæ**, the course of one's life; a brief account of one's career.

1633 *Munimenta Univ. Glasg.* (1854) III. 379 Finito anni curriculo discessurum. **1643** *Ibid.* II. 317 Curriculum quinque annorum. **1824** J. Russell *Tour Germ.* (1828) I. iii. 134 When the [German] student has finished his *curriculum*, and leaves the university. **1829** *Glasg. Univ. Cal.* 39 The *curriculum* of students who mean to take degrees in Surgery to be three years. **1870** Rolleston *Anim. Life* Introd. 84 The completion of the entire curriculum of metamorphosis. **1888** Burgon *Lives 12 Gd. Men* II. ix. 201 Butler's immortal Work has . . been elbowed out from the Oxford curriculum. **1902** *New Internat. Encycl.* III. 21/2 Anciently biography was more of a mere *curriculum vitæ* than it is now. **1939** 'M. Innes' *Stop Press* II. iv. 269, I don't know much about Benton's *curriculum vitæ*. . He must have an orthodox . . academic record. **1941** Koestler *Scum of Earth* 59 His superiors . . knew all about my professional travels from the *curriculum vitae* in their files, written by myself. **1954** *New Yorker* 25 Dec. 18/2 As for Mr. Lapidus's *curriculum vitae*, he was born in Russia fifty-two years ago, grew up in Brooklyn, graduated from the Columbia School of Architecture in 1927, and took a job with the well-known firm of Warren & Wetmore. **1971** *Time* 22 Mar. 14/2 Eddie's *curriculum vitae* . . has been served up in plentiful quantity in the press.

curried (ˈkʌrɪd), *ppl. a.*[1] [f. curry *v.*[1] + -ed.] Rubbed down with a comb; dressed; drubbed.

a **1553** Udall *Royster D.* I. iii. (Arb.) 22 The worste is but a curried cote.

'curried, *ppl. a.*[2] [f. curry *sb.*[2] and *v.*[3] + -ed.] Prepared with curry or curry-powder.

1855 Eliza Acton *Mod. Cookery* (1863) 302 Curried Oysters. **1882** B. M. Croker *Proper Pride* I. v. 95 Fish cutlets, curried fowl, tarts, and cream.

[**curriedew, -dow, curridow.** Error based on a misreading of *curreiden* (see quot. *c* 1400 s.v. curry *v.*[1] 4 b).

1561 *Chaucer's Wks.* Ggg vi/2 Tho curreideu glosours. **1617** Minsheu *Ductor*, *Curriedew*, in. Chaucer signifieth *Currie-fauour*, or *Flatter*. **1658** Phillips, *Curriedow*, a curry-favour or flatterer. **1721** Bailey, *Curridow*, a Curry-favour or Flatterer. *O*[*ld*].]

currier[1] (ˈkʌrɪə(r)). Forms: 4 curiour, 4-6 coriour, curryour, 4-7 corier, 5 coryowre, coryer, correher, coureour, curriour, 5-6 coryer, -ar, coryour, 6 corrier, curryar, courrar, currer, 6-7 coriar, 6- currier. [In sense 1, ME. *corier*, *coryer*, a. OF. *corier*, *coryer*:—L. *coriārius*, tanner, currier, f. *corium* hide, leather. The forms in *-our*, as *coureour*, are assimilated to, or directly from, F. *courroyeur*, in Palsgrave *couraieur*, OF. *conreeur* (13th c.) currier, f. *conreer*, in Cotgr. *courroyer*, now *corroyer* to curry, whence senses 2, 3. A confusion between the two words appears already in OF. where we find *coroier*, *couroier* as variants of *coriier*, in which the *oi* is due to *corroyer*, *corroyeur*.]

1. One whose trade is the dressing and colouring of leather after it is tanned.

In the earlier quots. confused with *tanner*; but the two trades were quite distinct and legally incompatible in 1488.

c **1380** Wyclif *Wks.* (1880) 471 Seynt petre dwelte in a corieris hous. **1382** —— *Acts* ix. 43 Many dayes he dwellide in Joppe, at Symound, sum coriour, or tawier [**1388** a curiour; Vulg. *Simonem quemdam coriarium*]. *Ibid.* x. 6 [*v.r.* curryour]. *c* **1440** *Promp. Parv.* 93 Coryowre, *coriarius*, *cerdo*. **1474** Caxton *Chesse* III. iii. 77 Coupers, coryers, tawyers, skynners. **1488** *Act 1 Hen. VII*, c. 5 §2 That no Tanner whiles he occupieth the mistere of a Tanner . . use the mistere of a Coriour nor blak no leder to be put to sale. *c* **1515** *Cocke Lorell's B.* (Percy Soc.) 1 The nexte that came was a coryar And a cobeler, his brother. **1576** Gascoigne *Steele Gl.* (Arb.) 79 When Tanners are with Corriers wel agreede. **1583** Stubbes *Anat. Abus.* II. (1882) 36 The tanners, makers, curriers, and dressers of the same [leather]. **1639** [see curry *v.*[1] 2]. **1697** Dryden *Virg. Georg.* III. 833 Useless to the Currier were their Hides. **1846** McCulloch *Acc. Brit. Empire* (1854) I. 761 The trade of a coach currier is hardly carried on anywhere except in the metropolis. **1854** Lowell *Cambr. 30 Years Ago* Wks. 1890 I. 70 A currier's shop, where . . men were always beating skins.

2. One who curries horses, etc.

1562 J. Heywood *Prov. & Epigr.* (1867) 134 When short hors and short coriers doo meete. **1786** tr. *Beckford's Vathek* (1834) 39 A currier of camels.

3. One who curries favour.

1515 Barclay *Egloges* i. A iv/2 Flatterers and lyers, curriers of fafell.

†**'currier**[2]. *Obs.* Also 6 curriar, corriar, corier, 6-7 curriour, 7 courriour. [By some assumed to be identical with currier[1]; others suggest that it may be from F. *coureur*, light horseman, scout, skirmisher (see courier *sb.* 2); but evidence is wanting.]

1. An early kind of fire-arm: see quot. 1834.

1557-8 Ld. Wentworth *Let. to Q. Mary* (on siege of Calais) in Hardwick *State Papers* (1778), The enemies . . with their curriors (which assuredly shot very great bullets and carry far). **1575** Churchyard *Chippes* (1817) 105 Their corriars were more woorth Then double tolde, the peeces that wee brought. **1599** Hakluyt *Voy.* II. II. 61 He caused his bases, curriers, and harquebusses to be shot off. **1659** Howell *Vocab.* §6 Smaller guns, as courriours, harquebusses, muskets. **1834** *Penny Cycl.* II. 373/2 The *Currier*, or *currier of war* . . of the same calibre and strength as the arquebus, but with a longer barrel.

2. A man armed with a currier.

1577-87 Holinshed *Chron.* III. 1215/1 Heerewith a companie of curriours and caliuers were put forward. **1581** Styward *Mart. Discipl.* I. 44 The Caleuers or Coriers. Such must haue either of them a good and sufficient peece.

currier, -or, obs. forms of courier *sb.*

curriery (ˈkʌrɪərɪ). [f. currier[1]: cf. OF. *corroierie*.] The trade or occupation of a currier; the place where the trade of a currier is carried on.

In mod. Dicts.

currish (ˈkɜːrɪʃ), *a.* Also 5 **kurressh**, 6 **courrissh.** [f. cur + -ish.]

1. Of, relating to, or resembling a cur.

1565-73 Cooper *Thesaurus*, *Caninus*, doggish, currish. **1591** Harington *Orl. Fur.* vi. lxiv. (1634) 46 One of these . . Doth utter barking words with currish sound. **1607** Topsell *Four-f. Beasts* (1673) 139 The Dogs of a Mungrel or Currish kinde. **1709** *Lond. Gaz.* No. 4545/4 An English Spaniel Dog . . his Ears Currish. *c* **1875** Sir R. Christison *Autobiog.* (1885) I. 248 Rabies is rare here . . though dogs both of good breeds and currish are extremely numerous.

2. *fig.* Like a cur in nature; snappish, snarling, quarrelsome; mean-spirited, base, ignoble.

c **1460** in *Pol. Rel. & L. Poems* (1866) 65 A kurresshe herte, a mouthe þat is curteise, Ful wele ye wote thei be not accordyng. **1547** Recorde *Jud. Ur.* A iij, Those currish stomakes, which can do nothyng but barke and brall. **1596** Shaks. *Merch. V.* IV. i. 292 To change this currish Iew. **1614** T. Adams *Devil's Banquet* 286 His snarling and currish inuectiues. **1705** Stanhope *Paraphr.* III. 275 Quarrelsome and currish People that bark and snarl at one another. **1820** Byron tr. *Morgante Maggiore* xxxiv, Currish renegade! **1888** J. Payn *Myst. Mirbridge* II. xiii, His currish nature prompted him to strike where no blow would be returned.

currishly (ˈkɜːrɪʃlɪ), *adv.* [f. prec. + -ly[2].] In a currish manner.

1519 Horman *Vulg.* 128 Thou . . oughtest nat to holde courrisshly ageynst thy maister. **1576** Fleming *Panopl. Epist.* 370 Goodwil and courteous interteinment currishly recompenced. *a* **1632** T. Taylor *God's Judgem.* I. I. x. (1642) 26 Whereat the Emperour being netled . . used him most currishly. **1884** Symonds *Shaks. Predecessors* xiv. 574 Gabriel Harvey . . currishly vented his spleen against the dead man in a clumsy satire.

currishness (ˈkɜːrɪʃnɪs). [f. as prec. + -ness.] Currish condition or quality.

1542 Udall *Erasm. Apophth.* 68 b *marg.*, Thei [Cynics] did with their foule mouthes represente the curryshenesse of doggues. **1627-77** Feltham *Resolves* II. lxix. (R.), Diogenes . . by his currishness got him the name of dog. **1824** Galt *Rothelan* I. II. vi. 199 The natural currishness of their temperament.

curror, -our(e, -owre, -ur, obs. ff. courier *sb.*

†**'curry,** *sb.*[1] *Obs. rare.* In 5 curray. [a. F. *corroi* 13th c. (AngloFr. **corrai*), OF. also *conroi*, *conrei*, etc., with the primary sense 'preparation': see conrey, and curry *v.*[1]] The currying or dressing of leather.

c **1430** Lydg. *Bochas* II. xiii. (1554) 52 a, A skin wrought by good curray.

curry (ˈkʌrɪ), *sb.*[2] Forms: (6 carriel, 7 carree), 8 carrye, curree, kerry, 8- currie, curry. [a. Tamil *kari* sauce, relish for rice, Canarese *karil*, whence Pg. *caril*, and earlier Eng. and Fr. forms; mod.F. is *cari*.]

1. a. A preparation of meat, fish, fruit, or vegetables, cooked with a quantity of bruised spices and turmeric, and used as a relish or flavouring, *esp.* for dishes composed of or served with rice. Hence, *a curry* = a dish or stew (of rice, meat, etc.) flavoured with this preparation (or with curry-powder).

1598 W. Phillips *Linschoten* 88 (Y.) Most of their fish is eaten with rice, which they seeth in broth, which they put upon the rice, and is somewhat soure . . but it tasteth well, and is called Carriel. **1681** R. Knox *Hist. Ceylon* 12 They . . boyl them [fruits] to make Carrees, to use the Portuguez word, that is somewhat to eat with and relish their Rice. **1747** *Art of Cookery* 52 To make a Currey the Indian way. **1766** Grose *Voy. E. Indies* (1772) I. 150 (Y.) The currees are infinitely various, being a sort of fricacees to eat with rice, made of any animals or vegetables. **1848** Thackeray *Lett.*, If you can come to dinner, there's a curry. **1891** Sharman *Fam. Cookery* 16 Pour the curry on the dish with the rice.

b. *attrib.* and *Comb.*, as ***curry-sauce, -stuff***; **curry-leaf tree**, a name for *Bergera Königii*, the aromatic leaves of which are used to flavour curries; **curry-paste, -powder**, preparations of turmeric and strong spices, for making curried dishes.

1855 E. Acton *Mod. Cookery* (rev. ed.) i. 45 A large tablespoonful of Captain White's currie-paste. **1906** Mrs. Beeton *Bk. Househ. Managem.* xvi. 450 Add the stock, curry-paste, sliced apple. **1810** R. J. Thornton *Family Herbal* 12 Turmeric . . a principal ingredient in the composition of curry-powder. **1883** Mrs. Bishop in *Leisure Ho.* 146/1 Curry is at each meal, but it is not made with curry powder. **1845** E. Acton *Mod. Cookery* viii. 201 Currie sauce, highly onioned, is frequently served. **1948** *Good Housek. Cookery Bk.* 280 Curry sauce . . is much improved by the addition of 1 tbsp. cream immediately before use. **1860** Tennent *Ceylon* I. 463 (Y.) Plots of esculents and curry-stuffs of every variety, onions, chillies, yams [etc.].

2. *to give* (a person) ***curry***: see quot. 1941. *Austral. slang.*

1941 Baker *Dict. Austral. Slang* 21 *To give someone curry*, to abuse, reprove, express anger at a person. **1944** *Coast to Coast 1943* 113 I'd like him not to be writing! Wouldn't I give him curry! *Ibid.* 124 I'm going to give those old tarts a bit of curry to-night, Ron. **1945** Baker *Austral. Lang.* vi. 120 A man who attacks another is said . . *to give him curry* or *curried hell.*

†**'curry, currie,** *sb.*[3] *Obs.* or *arch.* Also 6 curee, curie. [a. F. *curée*, in 14-15th c. *cuirée*, f. *cuir* hide, corresponding to a L. type **coriāta* lit. hide-ful, skin-ful, the entrails of the deer being given to the hounds on the skin: see Littré, and Notes to *Sir Tristrem* (1886) l. 474. Cf. quarry.]

The portions of an animal slain in the chase that were given to the hounds; the cutting up and disembowelling of the game; *transf.* any prey thrown to the hounds to be torn in pieces, or seized and torn in pieces by wild beasts: see quarry.

c **1500** *Melusine* xix. 99 þe herte . . was hadde out of the watre and the curee made & gyue to the houndes as custome is to doo. **1600** *Gowrie's Consp.* in *Select. Harl. Misc.* (1793) 192 His maiestie not staying vppon the curie of the deir, as his vse is. *c* **1611** Chapman *Iliad* XVI. 145 A den of wolves . . New come from currie of a stag. *Ibid.* XVI. 693 Two fierce kings of beasts, oppos'd in strife about a hind Slain on the forehead of a hill, both sharp and hungry set, And to the currie never came but like two deaths they met. **1830** R. Chambers *Life Jas. I*, I. ix. 247 It was James's practice to superintend the curry or dissection of the deer. [**1859** Helps *Friends in C.* Ser. II. II. vi. 134 A bill is thrown before the house as the curée to the hounds; and it is torn to pieces by everybody.]

†**'curry,** *sb.*[4] App. an error for carry *sb.* 1.

a **1682** Sir T. Browne *Tracts* i. (1684) 11 Whereof one would lade a Curry or small Cart.

curry (ˈkʌrɪ), *v.*[1] Forms: 3 (?) courey, 4-7 cory, corry, 5-6 cury, 5 corroye, coraye, corey, (core), curray, (*pa. t. pl.* curreiden), couray, 6 courye, -ie, currey, 6-7 courrie, -y, currie, 4- curry. [a. OF. *correie-r*, *coree-r*, orig. *conreder*, *conreer*, *cunreer*, *conraer*, *conraier* to put in order, prepare, arrange, dispose, equip, apparel, curry a horse; in Palsgr. and Cotgr. *courroyer*, mod.F. *corroyer* to curry leather, = Pr. *conrear* to arrange, to entertain, It. *corredare* to equip, furnish, deck out, fit out (a bride or a ship):—early Rom. **conrēdāre* to prepare, make ready, etc.: see conrey.

In OF. the diphthong *ei*, *oi*, in the second syllable, belongs originally only to the stressed forms, whence it has been extended to all. The 16th c. form *courroyer* seems to have been assimilated to *courroye*, *courroie*:—L. *corrigia* thong, leather strap.]

1. *trans.* To rub down or dress (a horse, ass, etc.) with a comb.

c **1290** *S. Eng. Leg.* I. 61/251 And selde heo [an ass] is i-coureyd [? i-conreyd] wel. **1398** Trevisa *Barth. De P.R.* XVIII. xli. (1495) 802 The colte is not . . coryed wyth an horse combe. *c* **1430** Lydg. *Min. Poems* (1840) 53 (Mätzner) Lik as he wold coraye his maystres hors. **1562** J. Heywood *Prov. & Epigr.* (1867) 19 A short horse is soone corryd. **1576** Turberv. *Venerie* 31 It may suffize to rubbe and courrie the hounde three times in a weeke. **1589** *Pappe w. Hatchet* 3 Who would currie an Asse with an Iuorie combe? **1617**

MARKHAM *Caval.* III. 21 First let your groom vncloath him, then currie, rubbe, picke, and dresse him. **1725** BRADLEY *Fam. Dict.* s.v. *Travelling Horse*, Ever where the Horse's hair is thinnest there curry the gentlest. **1839–40** W. IRVING *Wolfert's R.* (1855) 175 Her hide is daily curried and brushed.

b. Applied to persons.

1589 PUTTENHAM *Eng. Poesie* III. xxiii. (Arb.) 273 Thou art that fine, foolish.. Alexander that tendest to nothing but to combe and cury thy haire. **1596** NASHE *Saffron Walden* 107 Currying and smudging and pranking himselfe. **1733** CHEYNE *Eng. Malady* II. xii. §3 (1734) 243 The Parts affected.. being first well curried with a Flesh-Brush. **1806–7** J. BERESFORD *Miseries Hum. Life* xx. (1826) 251 She curries with towels The Chamber-maid's bowels.

c. *fig.*: To tickle, scrape, scratch, claw, etc.

1598 E. GILPIN *Skial.* (1878) 59 We shall be curried with the brislie phrases And prick-song termes he hath premeditate. **1607** DEKKER *Westw. Hoe* v. Wks. 1873 II. 352 You shall go on fidling.. curry your instruments: play and away. **1655** FULLER *Hist. Camb.* (1840) 151 Indeed, with his learned lectures, he.. curried the lazy hides, of many an idle and ignorant friar.

2. To dress (tanned leather) by soaking, scraping, paring, beating, colouring, etc.

14.. *Chalmerlan Air* c. 22 (Jam.) Item, thai wirk it [lethir] or it be courait. *c* **1440** *Promp. Parv.* 110 Currayyn ledyr .. *corradio.* **1490** CAXTON *Eneydos* vii. 30 The hide of an oxe whiche [she] dyd doo corroye well. **1503–4** *Act 19 Hen. VII*, c. 19 Preamb., Upon peyne of forfeitur of every hyde by hym so corryed. **1601** HOLLAND *Pliny* II. 171 Those skins which are to be courried and dressed. **1639** *Sc. Acts, Chas. I* (1870) V. App. 610/1 Edward Spencer Corier, craving libertie to buy hydis.. and vent the same being Coried. **1714** *Fr. Bk. of Rates* 142 All Leather, tanned or curried, coming from Foreign Parts. **1826** SCOTT *Woodst.* xxxi, I made the deer's hide be curried and dressed by a tanner.

†**b.** To work iron in the forge. *Obs.* [F. *corroyer du fer.*]

1703 MOXON *Mech. Exerc.* 58 Spanish-steel.. sometimes proves very unsound, as not being well curried, that is well wrought.

3. *transf.* To beat or thrash one's hide for him, give a drubbing to. Also *fig.*

1526 SKELTON *Magnyf.* 1641 For myrth I have hym coryed, beten and blyst. **1530** PALSGR. 504/2 She hath curryed hym with a good staffe. **1580** BARET *Alv.* C. 1799 He hath well curried thy cote. **1621** FLETCHER *Isl. Princess* IV. ii, I have seen him Curry a fellow's carcass handsomely. **1719** D'URFEY *Pills* V. 227 This is the great Sir Francis Vere, That so the Spaniards curry'd. **1809** W. IRVING *Knickerb.* (1861) 220 He swore.. that.. he would curry his hide till he made him run out of it.

†**4.** *fig.* To 'stroke down' (a person) with flattery or blandishment. *Obs.*

c **1394** *P. Pl. Crede* 365 Whou þey curry kinges & her back claweþ.

†**b.** *intr.* or *absol.* To employ flattery or blandishment, so as to cajole or win favour: cf. next.

c **1400** *Test. Love* I. (1560) 280 b/1 Tho curreiden glosours, tho welcomeden flatterers. **1575** *Brieff Disc. Troubl. at Franckford* (1642) 167 Such as.. can cap it, can cope it, and curry for advantage. **1597** SHAKS. *2 Hen. IV*, v. i. 81 I would currie with Maister Shallow. **1830** A. W. FONBLANQUE *Eng. under Seven Admin.* (1837) II. 51 His Grace meant he was currying to the Duke of Newcastle.

5. †**a.** *to curry favel*: to use insincere flattery, or unworthy compliance with the humour of another, in order to gain personal advantage. (Cf. CURRY-FAVEL below.)

[OF. *estriller fauvel* (*fauveau, fauvain*, also *torcher fauvel*) to curry the chestnut horse, hence, to employ deceit or hypocrisy, to gloze; cf. FAVEL.]

c **1400** *Beryn* 362 She toke hym by the swere, As þouȝe she had lernyd cury fauel of som olde ffrere. *a* **1420** HOCCLEVE *De Reg. Princ.* 189 The knyght or squier.. but he hide The trouthe and cory favelle, he not the ner is His lordes grace. **1426** AUDELAY *Poems* (Percy Soc.) 26 Loke thou core not favel ne be no flaterer. *c* **1561** UNDERHILL *Narr. Reform.* (Camden Soc.) 159 Accordynge to the olde provearbe.. He thatt wylle in courte abyde Must cory favelle bake and syde, for souche gett moste gayne. **1570** T. WILSON *Demosthenes* 77 While they tell you a faire tale and curry fauell with you. **1603** KNOLLES *Hist. Turks* (1610) 108 Her pickthanke favourits, who to curry Favell, spared not [etc.].

b. Later, this phrase was transformed into *to curry favour*: to seek to win favour, or ingratiate oneself *with* another, by officious courtesy or unworthy complaisance.

c **1510** BARCLAY *Mirr. Gd. Manners* (1570) F vj, Flatter not as do some, With none curry fauour. **1557** N. T. (Genev.) *Matt.* viii. 20 *note*, He thoght by this meanes to courry fauour with the worlde. **1691** WOOD *Ath. Oxon.* II. 470 [It] was then by him published to curry favour with the Royalists. **1848** MACAULAY *Hist. Eng.* II. 250 A set of bravos who.. attempted to curry favour with the government by affronting members of the opposition. **1865** LIVINGSTONE *Zambesi* xxiii. 472 Gossiping traders who seek to curry their favour.

†**c.** Hence occas. in other phrases of kindred meaning, as ***to curry acquaintance, good will, applause, friends, pardon.***

1571 CAMPION *Hist. Ireland* (1809) 162 He curryed acquaintance and friendship with meere Irish enemyes. **1587** FLEMING *Contn. Holinshed* III. 1303/2 He.. seeketh all waies he could to currie the bishops good will. **1630** SYMMER *Rest Weary* i. A. iv. b, The proud and ambitious man.. curryes the applause of the world with all his might. *a* **1745** SWIFT *Poems, Dan Jackson's Reply*, 'Tis true indeed, to curry friends, You seem to praise to make amends. **18..** COLERIDGE *Lit. Rem.* (1838) III. 250 Currying pardon for his past liberalism by charging.. himself with the guilt of falsehood.

†**curry**, *v.*[2] *Obs.* [perh. derived from *currier*, common 16–18th c. form of *courier*, as if to ride post, to post. Cf. SCURRY.] *intr.* To ride or run with haste or rapidity; to scurry.

1608 CHAPMAN *Byron's Conspir.* v. Plays 1873 II. 245, I am not hee that can.. by midnight leape my horse, curry seauen miles [etc.]. **1630** J. TAYLOR (Water-P.) *Discov. by Sea* Wks. II. 21/1 We with our Wherry.. Along the christall Thames did cut and curry. **1676** MARVELL *Mr. Smirke* 34 A Sermon is soon curryed over.

curry (ˈkʌrɪ), *v.*[3] [f. CURRY *sb.*[2]] *trans.* To flavour or prepare with curry or curry-powder.

1839 *Britannia* 12 May, The culinary skill by which.. Lord John Russell curried unfortunate Lord Morpeth into the yellow resemblance of a statesman. **1855** [see CURRIED].

ˈ**curry-comb**, *sb.* [f. CURRY *v.*[1]] A comb or instrument of metal used for currying horses, etc.

1573 TUSSER *Husb.* (1878) 35 A currie-combe, mainecombe, and whip for a Jade. **1618** FLETCHER *Loyal Subject* I. iii, The devil with a curry-comb Scratch 'em, and scrub 'em. **1714** in *Phil. Trans.* XXIX. 49 Rubbing and currying.. with a Currycomb and Brush. **1882** H. LANSDELL *Through Siberia* I. 137 Siberian post-horses are sorry objects to look at.. A curry-comb probably never touches their coats.

b. *attrib.* and *Comb.*

1634 HEYWOOD & BROME *Lanc. Witches* II. Wks. 1874 IV. 201, I have.. then halfe a score mile to ride by curriecombe time, i' the morning. **1768** GOLDSM. *Good-n. Man* I, Old Ruggins, the curry-comb maker.

ˈ**curry-comb**, ˈ**currycomb**, *v.* [f. prec. sb.] *trans.* To rub down or groom with a curry-comb; to curry. Also *transf.* and *fig.*: see CURRY *v.*

1708 MOTTEUX *Rabelais* v. vii. (1737) 26 The Groom.. ordered one of his Underlings to.. curricomb him with a Cudgel. **1809** SCOTT in *C. K. Sharpe's Corr.* (1888) I. 366, I would willingly embrace your offer of curry-combing Miss Owenson. **1839** *Times* 13 Sept., They do not believe a priest can currycomb off their sins. **1842** MRS. GORE *Fascin.* 42 The principal clerk.. became suddenly as serious as an ass that is being currycombed.

Hence ˈ**curry-comber**.

1889 RAWLINSON *Anc. Egypt* ii. (ed. 4) 32 The Apis bull .. had his train of attendant priests.. his grooms and curry-combers.

†ˈ**curry-favel(l**. *Obs.* [See CURRY *v.*[1] 5 a.] One who solicits favour by flattery or complaisance.

1515 *State Papers* II. 15 (N.) All the curryfavel, that be next of the deputye is secrete counsayll, dare not.. shewe hym the greate jupardye.. of his soule. **1530** PALSGR. 211/2 Curryfavell, a flatterar, *estrille faueav.* **1589** PUTTENHAM *Eng. Poesie* III. xxiv. (Arb.) 299 Sometimes a creeper, and a curry fauell with his superiors.

b. (See quot.)

1589 PUTTENHAM *Eng. Poesie* III. xvii. (Arb.) 195 If such moderation of words tend to flattery, or soothing, or excusing, it is by the figure *Paradiastole*, which therfore nothing improperly we call the Curry-fauell, as when we make the best of a bad thing.

†ˈ**curry-favour**. *Obs.* [See CURRY *v.*[1] 5 b.]

1. = prec.

1577 HOLINSHED *Chron.* II. 144 A number of prodigal currie favours, who by flatterie set him aloft. **1586** A. DAY *Eng. Secretary* II. (1625) 116 Men infected with this basenesse of condition, being.. Curri-favours of the world. **1658** PHILLIPS, *Curriedow*, a curry-favour, or flatterer.

2. The action of currying favour with others.

1581 MULCASTER *Positions* cxliii. (1887) 276 We.. yeilde to curtesie more, then euen the verie patrones of curtesie do, for all their curifauour.

So †ˈ**curry-favourer** = prec. 1.

1563 NOWEL *Serm. bef. Queen* (1853) 225 Their subjects, servants, curry-favourers, and others, will follow.

currying (ˈkʌrɪɪŋ), *vbl. sb.* [f. CURRY *v.*[1]]

1. The action of rubbing down with a curry-comb.

1577 B. GOOGE *Heresbach's Husb.* III. (1586) 120 In curriyng of them we must begin at the head and the necke. **1634** HEYWOOD & BROME *Lanc. Witches* IV. Wks. 1874 IV. 224 The Beast.. hath cost you more the currying, then all the Combs in your Stable are worth.

b. *Comb.* **currying-glove**, a glove with a rough surface used for currying horses.

2. The process of dressing tanned hides.

1481–90 *Howard Househ. Bks.* (Roxb.) 198 To Cordener for coreyyng of a barkyd hyde iiij. d. **1532–3** *Act 24 Hen. VIII*, c. 1 An acte concernynge true tanninge and coriynge of lether. **1870** YEATS *Nat. Hist. Comm.* 295 Tanned leather often undergoes the further operation of currying.

b. *fig.* Drubbing, thrashing.

1807 W. IRVING *Salmagundi* (1824) 6 Nor will the gentlemen.. escape our currying.

curry-leaf, -powder: see CURRY *sb.*[2] 1 b.

currymaul (*Herb.*), variant of CARMELE.

1791 NEWTE *Tour Eng. & Scot.* 414 A species of liquorice called currymaul.

curs, obs. form of COURSE, CURSE.

cursal (ˈkɜːsəl), *a.* [ad. med.L. *cursālis*, f. *cursus* course: see -AL[1].] Of or belonging to a course; applied to certain canons of St. Asaph's and prebendaries of St. David's Cathedral in Wales.

According to some, because originally their prebends were annually changed by course or rotation: Jones & Freeman *Hist. St. David's* 313. Others would refer it to the '*Cursus*, officium Ecclesiasticum, seu series Orationum, Psalmorum, Hymnorum, et cæterarum precationum, quæ quotidie in Ecclesia decantatur' (Du Cange).

1872 M. E. C. WALCOTT *Sacristy* II. 84 The preachers of Canterbury and cursal Canons of S. Asaph. **1878** CLERGY LIST, *Cathedral Establishments*, St. Davids; Prebendaries: 1st Cursal The Queen.

†ˈ**cursant**, *a. Her. Obs.* [ad. L. *cursānt-em*, pr. pple. of *cursāre* to run: cf. COURSE *v.*] Running, coursing.

1572 BOSSEWELL *Armorie* II. 55 b, Three Greyhoundes cursante.

†**cursarary**, *a. Obs. rare.* [app. f. *cursare*, CORSAIR + -ARY.] Of or pertaining to corsairs.

1632 LITHGOW *Trav.* ix. 385 It serueth them for.. a great defence in time of cursarary inuasions.

cursare, -aro, -ary, obs. forms of CORSAIR.

curse (kɜːs), *sb.* Forms: 1–4 curs, 4–5 kors, 4–6 curss(e, 5 curce, 5– curse. [Late OE. *curs*, of unknown origin; no word of similar form and sense is known in Teutonic, Romanic, or Celtic. (Of connexion with *cross*, which has been suggested, there is no trace.)]

In its various uses the opposite of *blessing*.

1. a. An utterance consigning, or supposed or intended to consign, (a person or thing) to spiritual and temporal evil, the vengeance of the deity, the blasting of malignant fate, etc. It may be uttered by the deity, or by persons supposed to speak in his name, or to be listened to by him.

10.. *Charter of Leofric* in *Cod. Dipl.* IV. 72 Hæbbe he her on ðisse life Goddes curs. [Cf. Earle *Land Charters & Sax. Doc.* 252, 253, etc.] *a* **1050** *Liber Scintill.* lvi. (1889) 174 Bletsung fæder fæstnað hus bearna, curs soðlice moder awyrtwalað trymmincge. *c* **1125** *O.E. Chron.* (Laud MS). an. 656 Leidon þa Godes curs and ealre halȝane curs and al Cristene folces. *c* **1290** *S. Eng. Leg.* I. 287/314 He ȝaf alle godes curs and his. *a* **1300** *Vox & Wolf* 201 in Hazl. *E.P.P.* I. 64 Ich habbe widewene kors Therefore ich fare the wors. **1398** TREVISA *Barth. De P.R.* VI. xiv. (1495) 199 The faders curse greuyth the chyldren. **1594** SHAKS. *Rich. III*, I. iii. 240 Thus haue you breath'd your Curse against your self. **1615** J. STEPHENS *Satyr. Ess.* (ed. 2) 376 Her prayers and Amen, be a charme and a curse. **1780** COWPER *Table Talk* 467 God's curse can cast away ten thousand sail! **1798** COLERIDGE *Anc. Mariner* IV. ix, An orphan's curse would drag to Hell A spirit from on high. **1829** HOOD *Eugene Aram* xii, He told how murderers walk'd the earth Beneath the curse of Cain.

b. *spec.* A formal ecclesiastical censure or anathema; a sentence of excommunication.

a **1050** in Thorpe *Anc. Laws* II. 318 Bisceopum ȝebyreð þæt hi æfre on ænine man curs ne settan, butan hy nyde scylan. *c* **1386** CHAUCER *Prol.* 655 Have noon Awe In swich caas of the Ercedekenes curs. *c* **1440** *Promp. Parv.* 111 Curce, *excommunicatio, anathema.* **1577–87** HOLINSHED *Chron.* III. 936/1 At the suit of the ladie Katharine Dowager, a cursse was sent from the pope, which curssed both the king and the realme. *a* **1763** SHENSTONE *Ess.* 176 If any one's curse can effect damnation, it is not that of the pope, but that of the poor. **1849** WHITTIER *Voices of Freedom, Charter-breakers* iii, The waiting crowd.. Stood to hear the priest rehearse, In God's name, the Church's curse.

2. a. Without implication of the effect: The uttering of a malediction with invocation or adjuration of the deity; a profane oath, an imprecation.

a **1050** *Liber Scintill.* v. (1889) 24 Na aȝyldende yfel for yfele oþþe curs for curse [*maledictum pro maledicto*], ac þer toȝeanes bletsiȝende. *c* **1200** *Trin. Coll. Hom.* 163 Ðe defles sed is.. hoker and scorn.. curs and leasinges. **1590** SHAKS. *Mids. N.* I. i. 196, I giue him curses, yet he giues me loue. **1732** POPE *Ep. Bathurst* 273 Despairing quacks with curses fled the place. **1835** WHITTIER *Hunters of Men* iv, The curse of the sinner and prayer of the saint. **1870** E. PEACOCK *Ralf Skirl.* III. 96 Some curses followed.

b. Used in pl. as an imprecation, expressing irritation or frustration; esp. (histrionically or as a stage-aside) ***curses, foiled again!***

1885 MUSKERRY & JOURDAIN *Khartoum!* viii. 49 Ha! they're here. Ah, curses! **1926** 'S. STEELE' (*title*) Curses, what a night! A nonsensical satire on the mellerdrammer. **1932** J. CORBETT *Vampire of Skies* ii. 29 He happened to be free at the moment — the Yard knew that (curses!) — and his holidays were due in a fortnight. **1967** GERNHARD & HOLLER *Snoopy versus Red Baron* (*song*) 4 He flew into the sky to seek revenge, but the Baron shot him down. Curses, foiled again! **1973** S. ALLEN *Curses!* 119 If you haven't learned anything from this book then, 'Curses! May you be foiled again and again and again!' *c* **1977** V. R. CHEATHAM *Skits & Spoofs for Young Actors* p. v, The Tortoise and the Hare Hit the Road. .. Meet Dr. Frankenstein... Curses! Foiled Again! **1986** R. CLAIBORNE *Saying what You Mean* 197 'Curses!' the baffled villain snarled.

¶ In such phrases as ***not worth a curse, not to care a curse***, the expression possibly comes down from the ME. *not worth a kerse, kers, cres*: see CRESS 2.

But historical connexion between the two is not evidenced, there being an interval of more than 300 years between the examples of the ME. and the modern phrase; and *damn* (cf. CARE *v.* 4 a) occurs as early as *curse*, so that the coincidence may be merely accidental.

1763 T. JEFFERSON *Let.* Writings 1892 I. 346, I do not conceive that any thing can happen.. which you would give a curse to know. **1813** MOORE *Post-bag* ii. 93 For, as to wives, a Grand Signor Need never care one curse about them! **1826** *Blackw. Mag.* XIX. 357/1 The Chapter on Naval Inventions is not worth a curse. **1827** SCOTT *Jrnl.* (1890) II. 43 He will not care a curse for what outward show he has lost.

3. a. An object of cursing or execration; an accursed thing or person.

1382 WYCLIF *Gal.* iii. 13 Crist.. maad for vs curs, that is, sacrifice for curs. **1582** N. T. (Rhem.) *Gal.* iii. 13 Christ.. being made a curse for vs. **1611** BIBLE *Jer.* xxvi. 6, I..wil make this city a curse to all the nations. **1654** tr. *Scudery's Curia Pol.* 168 Bajazet..who is the curse and execration of all the world. **1838** LYTTON *Leila* I. vi, Thy name is a curse in Israel.

b. = CUSS *sb.* 2.

1790 [see RANTIPOLE *sb.* 1]. **1854** B. YOUNG in *Jrnl. Discourses* I. 83 We have known Gladden Bishop for more than twenty years, and know him to be a poor, dirty curse. *Ibid.* 169 Why don't you do it, you poor miserable curses?

c. An angler's name for a very small gnat or midge.

1889 F. M. HALFORD *Dry-fly Fishing* vi. 116 'Curses', or black midges or gnats. **1899** *19th Cent.* Jan. 122 The monstrously minute 'curse'.

4. a. The evil inflicted by divine (or supernatural) power in response to an imprecation, or in the way of retributive punishment.

1382 WYCLIF *Dan.* ix. 11 And al Yrael braken the lawe.. and cursse droppide on vs. **1587** GOLDING *De Mornay* Ep. Ded. 3 He turned the reproch of his crosse into glorie, and the cursse therof into a blessing. **1590** SPENSER *F.Q.* I. ii. 18 'Curse on that Cross,' (quoth then the Sarazin). **1713** ADDISON *Cato* I. ii, Curse on the stripling! how he apes his sire. **1852** MRS. STOWE *Uncle Tom's C.* v. 28 This is God's curse on slavery! a bitter, a bitter, most accursed thing!

b. A great evil (regarded more or less vaguely as inflicted or resting upon a person, community, etc.); a thing which blights or blasts; a blasting affliction, a bane.

1591 SHAKS. *Two Gent.* v. iv. 43 Oh 'tis the curse in Loue ..When women cannot loue, where they're belou'd. **1595** —— *John* IV. ii. 208 It is the curse of Kings, to be attended By slaues, that take their humors for a warrant. **1669** WORLIDGE *Syst. Agric.* x. §1 (1681) 210 The only natural Remedies against this sometimes heavy Curse [mildew]. **1789** W. BUCHAN *Dom. Med.* (ed. 11) 81 Many people look upon the necessity man is under of earning his bread by labour, as a curse. **1846** KINGSLEY *Lett.* (1878) I. 141 The curse of our generation is that so few of us deeply believe anything. **1870** *Pall Mall Budget* 29 Oct. 19/1 Very ill with that curse of his trade the painter's colic.

c. *curse of Scotland*: a name given to the nine of diamonds in a pack of cards.

Origin of the name doubtful. A not unlikely suggestion is that the card was so called from resembling the armorial bearings of Dalrymple, Lord Stair, nine lozenges on a saltire, the number and shape of the spots being identical, and their arrangement sufficiently similar. The first Earl of Stair was the object of much execration, especially from the adherents of the Stuarts, for his share in sanctioning the Massacre of Glencoe in 1692, and subsequently for the influential part played by him in bringing about the Union with England in 1707. An opponent says he was 'at the bottom of the Union', and 'so he may be styled the Judas of the Country'.

1715–47 J. HOUSTON *Mem.* 92 [Lord Justice-Clerk Ormistone] became universally hated in Scotland, where they called him the Curse of Scotland; and when the ladies were at cards playing the Nine of Diamonds (commonly called the Curse of Scotland), they called it the Justice Clerk. **1791** *Gentl. Mag.* 141 The nine of diamonds [is called] the Curse of Scotland, because every ninth monarch of that nation was a bad King to his subjects. **1810** *Sporting Mag.* XXXVI. 75 There is the curse of Scotland, plague take that nine of diamonds. **1893** *Daily News* 21 Feb. 4/8 A problem which has long puzzled antiquaries. Why is the Nine of Diamonds called the Curse of Scotland?

d. *the curse*: menstruation. *colloq.*

1930 J. DOS PASSOS *42nd Parallel* 147 She was afraid her period was coming on. She'd only had the curse a few times yet. **1933** 'E. A. ROBERTSON' *Ordinary Families* vi. 115 Ill luck..had added a premature last straw to my load of misery: I had the curse. **1960** *Woman's Own* 19 Mar. 15/1, I always think it such a pity when girls..call it 'the curse'. **1969** G. GREENE *Travels with my Aunt* xii. 120, I forgot the damn pill and I haven't had the curse for six weeks.

5. *attrib.* and *Comb.*, as *curse-blasted*, *-loving*, *-scarred*, *-worthy* adjs.; **curse-roll**, a list of anathemas; **curse-mete**, app. formed after the erroneous *help-meet* for *help meet* or the modern *help-mate*; **curse-word** = *cuss-word* (CUSS *sb.* 3).

1836 G. S. FABER *Answ. Husenbeth* 34 After the manner of his curse-loving Church. **1844** MRS. BROWNING *Drama of Exile*, I..Who yesterday was helpmate and delight Unto mine Adam, am to-day the grief And curse-mete for him. **1855** BAILEY *Mystic* 127 With ominous and curseworthy glory. **1856** R. A. VAUGHAN *Mystics* (1860) I. 180, I shall have a list longer than the curse-roll of the Pope. **1897** R. M. STUART *Simpkinsville* vii. 225 The popular after-dinner 'curse word story' of the cloth would never have been tolerated in Simpkinsville.

curse (kɜːs), *v.* Forms: 1 cursian, 2–3 cursen, (3–4 kurse, 4 curce), 4–5 cors, (5 cruss), 5–6 cursse, 4– curse. [Goes with CURSE *sb.*, from which, in its OE. form *curs*, the vb. *cursian* was probably immediately derived.]

Generally the opposite of *to bless* in its various uses.

1. *trans.* To utter against (persons or things) words which consign, or are intended or supposed to consign, them to evil spiritual or temporal, as the wrath of God or the malignity of fate; to damn. **a.** Said of the deity or supernatural power.

c **1200** *Trin. Coll. Hom.* 11 Cursed be þe man þe leueð upen hwate. *Ibid.* 181 Þo godes muð cursede eorðe. **1426** AUDELAY *Poems* 2 Murthyr, theft, and avoutre..bene cursyd in heven on hye. **1611** BIBLE *Numb.* xxiii. 8 How shall I curse, whom God hath not cursed? **1761** STERNE *Trist. Shandy* III. xi, May the Father who created man, curse him ..May St. Michael, the advocate of holy souls, curse him. **1821** BYRON *Cain* I. i. 522 O Cain! This spirit [Lucifer] curseth us.

b. Said of persons claiming to speak in the divine name, *esp.* officers of the church: To pronounce a formal curse against, to anathematize, excommunicate, consign to perdition.

a **1154** *O.E. Chron.* (Laud MS.) an. 1137 §4 Þe biscopes & lered men heom cursede æure. *Ibid.* an. 1140, Þe biscop of Wincestre..cursede alle þe men. *a* **1300** *Cursor M.* 17109 (Gött.) Curced in kirc þan sal þai be wid candil, boke, and bell. **1387** TREVISA *Higden* (Rolls) V. 309 [The pope Anastasius] cursede þe emperour. *c* **1400** MAUNDEV. (Roxb.) ix. 36 Machomete cursez all þase þat drinkez wyne. *c* **1440** *Promp. Parv.* 111 Cursyn', *excommunico*, *anathematizo*, *cateziso*. **1568** GRAFTON *Chron.* II. 119 This yere the men of Caithnes in Scotland burned their bishop, because he curssed them for not paiyng of their Tithes. **1611** BIBLE *Numb.* xxii. 6 Come now therefore, I pray thee, curse mee this people, for they are too mightie for mee. **1782** PRIESTLEY *Corrupt. Chr.* I. i. 7 The Jews..cursed them in a solemn manner three times. **1849** WHITTIER *Voices of Freedom*, *Curse of Charter-breakers* ix, Since that stoled and mitred band Cursed the tyrants of their land. **1875** JOWETT *Plato* (ed. 2) V. 79 Those who alienate either house or lot shall be cursed by priests.

2. a. Hence (without implication of the effect): To imprecate or invoke divine vengeance or evil fate upon; to denounce with adjuration of the divine name; to pour maledictions upon; to swear at. Also const. *for*.

c **1200** ORMIN 5050 ʒiff þatt tu currsesst aniȝ mann & hatesst himm wiþþ herrte. *c* **1300** *St. Brandan* 550 Ich mai cursi the tyme that ich ibore was. *c* **1325** *E.E. Allit. P.* B. 1583 He corsed his clerkes & calde hem chorles. *c* **1475** *Partenay* 2851 Full often crussing the hour and the day That thes wordes scapid or mouthed he. **1579** SPENSER *Sheph. Cal.* Jan. 49 A thousand sithes I curse that carefull hower. **1603** KNOLLES *Hist. Turks* (1621) 52 The citizens..cursing the tyrant to the devill. **1715** DE FOE *Fam. Instruct.* I. v. (1841) I. 109, I heard my brother damn the coachman, and curse the maids. **1859** TENNYSON *Guinevere* 529, I did not come to curse thee, Guinevere. **1871** MORLEY *Voltaire* (1886) 163 Voltaire..never knew more German than was needed to curse a postilion. **1922** H. WALPOLE *Cathedral* II. iv. 229 He cursed Foster for a meddling, cantankerous fanatic.

†**b.** with *obj. clause*. *Obs. rare.*

c **1500** *Maid Emlyn* in *Anc. Poet. Tracts* 27 He cursed that he came thyder. **1638** FORD *Fancies* III. iii, The time will come..When he..Will curse he train'd me hither.

c. In imprecations (with no subject expressed): = DAMN, CONFOUND.

1761 STERNE *Tristr. Shandy* III. x, Curse the fellow..I am undone for this bout. **1877** H. SMART *Play or Pay* iv. (1878) 71 'Curse the whist!' he muttered; 'what a fool I was to meddle with it!' **1881** *Scribn. Mag.* XXI. 269/2 'Curse it! why do you treat me so?'

3. To speak impiously against, to rail profanely at (the deity, fate, destiny, etc.); to blaspheme.

c **1050** *Spelman's Psalms* xxxvi[i]. 22 (C. MS.) Forðam þe bletsiende him yrfweardiað eorðan, yfelcweþende [C. cursiynde] soðlice hine forweorðað. **1388** WYCLIF *Job* ii. 9 His wijf seide to hym..Curse thou God, and die. **1590** SPENSER *F.Q.* I. i. 37 He..cursed heven; and spake reprochful shame Of highest God. **1611** BIBLE *Isa.* viii. 21 They shall fret themselues, and curse their King, and their God. **1697** DRYDEN *Virg. Georg.* III. 774 The Clown, who, cursing Providence, repines. **1732** POPE *Ep. Bathurst* 402 And sad Sir Balaam curses God and dies.

4. *absol.* or *intr.* To utter curses; to swear profanely in anger or irritation.

c **1230** *Ancr. R.* 198 Þe þet swereð greate oðes, oðer bitterliche kurseð. *c* **1350** *Will. Palerne* 1977 He..gan to kurse fast; 'Where dwelle ȝe, a deuel wai, ȝe damiseles, so long?' *c* **1450** *St. Cuthbert* (Surtees) 1169 It es mare manhede..to ..beseke god þair bote to bene, þan outhir for to curse or scorne. **1525** LD. BERNERS *Froiss.* II. liii. [lii.] 190 When they saw theyr goodes taken and spente away..they cursed bytwene theyr tethe, sayenge, go into Englande or to the deuyll. **1535** COVERDALE *Matt.* xxvi. 74 Then beganne he to curse and to sweare. **1667** DRYDEN *Wild Gallant* IV. i, I drink not, I curse not, I cheat not; they are unnecessary vices. **1819** SHELLEY *Cenci* III. i. 314 He..came to upbraid and curse, Mocking our poverty. **1892** D. C. MURRAY *Bob Martin's Lit. Girl* I. 13 Coming into collision with some unseen piece of furniture [he] cursed quietly to himself.

5. *trans.* To afflict with such evils or calamities as are the consequences or indications of divine wrath or the malignancy of fate; to blast. *to be cursed with*: to be afflicted with by divine decree, by destiny, or by one's evil fate.

1382 WYCLIF *Deut.* xxviii. 16, 17 Cursid thow shalt be in citee, cursed in feeld; cursid thy bern, and cursid thi relikis. **1592** SHAKS. *Ven. & Ad.* 945 The Destinies will curse thee for this stroke. **1611** BIBLE *Gen.* xii. 3, I will blesse them that blesse thee, and curse him, that curseth thee. **1727–38** GAY *Fables* I. viii. 13 With this plague she's rightly curst. **1781** COWPER *Truth* 182 To..curse the desert with a tenfold dearth. **1805** SCOTT *Last Minstr.* IV. xiv. Sure some fell fiend has cursed our line, That coward should e'er be son of mine! **1880** J. COOK *Boston Lectures, Heredity* x, He was temporarily a drunkard, and God cursed him, through that law of initial heredity. *Mod.* To be cursed with a bad temper, a drunken wife, etc.

cursed, curst (ˈkɜːsɪd, kɜːst), *ppl. a.* Also 4 cursd, curced, -id, cursud, 4–5 cursede, -id, corsed, -id, 4–6 curste, 5 curset, -it, -yd, 5–6 curssed. [f. CURSE *v.* + -ED[1].]

1. That has had a curse pronounced or invoked upon him or it; excommunicated, anathematized; under a curse, blasted with a curse.

a **1300** *Cursor M.* 29332 (Cott.) Qua communs wit cursd man, þat was noght ar, es cursd þan. **1393** LANGL. *P. Pl.* C. XXII. 419 The countrey is þe corsedour þer cardinales comeþ ynne. **1483** *Cath. Angl.* 87 Cursed, *anathematizatus*. **1593** SHAKS. *Rich. II*, IV. i. 147 The wofullest Diuision..That euer fell vpon this cursed Earth. **1611** BIBLE *Matt.* xxv. 41 Depart from me, ye cursed. **1723** GAY *Captives* II. (1772) 41 Shun'd like a pestilence, a curst informer! **1800** WORDSW. *Hart-Leap Well* II. vii, But something ails it now; the spot is curst. **1862** RUSKIN *Munera P.* (1880) 92 The cursed figtree, which has leaves but no fruit.

2. Deserving a curse; damnable, execrable, heinously wicked.

a **1300** *Cursor M.* 1106 (Gött.) To haue done suilk a curced dede. **1388** WYCLIF *Ecclus.* x. 9 No thing is cursidere than an auerouse man. *c* **1400** *Melayne* 310 Appon the cursede Sarazens for to werre. *a* **1592** H. SMITH *Wks.* (1867) II. 34 Who would have said..that the chosen people should become the cursedest upon the earth? **1609** HOLLAND *Amm. Marcell.* XVII. i. 79 Carefull withall, least the cursed foules of the aire [*diræ volucres*] should devoure the bodies. **1667** MILTON *P.L.* I. 388 And with cursed things His holy Rites and solemn Feasts profan'd. **1715** DE FOE *Fam. Instruct.* I. v. (1841) I. 99 The cursed roots from whence this bitter fruit grows up. **1765** H. WALPOLE *Otranto* iv, 'Dare to proceed in thy curst purpose of a divorce..and here I lance her anathema at thy head.'

3. Used intensively in expression of hatred, dislike, vexation, etc.: Execrable, detestable, abominable, 'damned', 'confounded'.

c **1386** CHAUCER *Sompn. Prol.* 43 God save yow alle, save this cursed Frere. **1576** FLEMING *Panopl. Epist.* 39 It was his hard lucke and curssed chaunce. **1664** EVELYN *Kal. Hort.* (1729) 209 Earwigs..are cursed Devourers. **1738** SWIFT *Pol. Conversat.* 22, I have cut my Thumb with this cursed Knife. **1819** BYRON *Juan* II. clii, One's early valet's cursed knock. **1876** E. JENKINS *Blot on Queen's Head* 24 'What a cursed piece of buffoonery!'

b. Used adverbially; sometimes merely emphatic. (Cf. *damned*, *deuced*.)

1719 J. RICHARDSON *Sc. Connoisseur* 116 Our Grandsires they were Papists, Our Fathers Oliverians, Their Bearns 'tis said are Atheists, Ours must be Cursed Queer Ones. **1778** WOLCOTT (P. Pindar) *Ep. Reviewers* Wks. 1812 I. 7 What they disapprove is cursed simple. **1845** FORD *Handbk. Spain* I. 30 They prefer cursed bad wine to holy water.

4. (Usually spelt *curst*.) **a.** Of persons (or their dispositions, tongues, etc.): Malignant; perversely disagreeable or cross; cantankerous, shrewish, virulent. *Obs.* or *arch.* (also *dial.*)

c **1400** MAUNDEV. (1839) viii. 89 This Heroude was over moche cursed & cruelle. **1550** COVERDALE *Spir. Perle* xv, His [Socrates'] curst and shrewd wife. **1578** *Chr. Prayers in Priv. Prayers* (1851) 498 When thou didst deal mildly and gently with me, I became the curster. **1596** SHAKS. *Tam. Shr.* III. ii. 156 Curster than she, why 'tis impossible. **1609** ROWLANDS *Knaue of Clubbes* 44 One plague That vext him ..was his wiues curst tongue. **1642** LAUD *Wks.* (1853) III. 461 They were glad that I gave him so short and so cursed an answer. **1711** SHAFTESB. *Charac.* (1737) II. II. I. §2. 84 Any Nature thorowly savage, curst, and inveterate. **1836** J. DOWNE *Mountain Decam.* I. 218, I have told that lie..why are ye so curst now as to want me to tell it o'er again? **1879–81** MISS JACKSON *Shropsh. Word-bk.* s.v., ''E's a little curst chap.'

†**b.** Of men or beasts: Fierce, savage, vicious.

c **1400** *Song Roland* 486 Corsabran, the curssid, kenyst in halle. **1567** MAPLET *Gr. Forest* 82 To straungers he [the dog] is eger and curst. **1576** TURBERV. *Venerie* 184 Terryers..are muche curster. **1599** SHAKS. *Much Ado* II. i. 25 It is said, God sends a curst Cow short hornes. **1623** BINGHAM *Xenophon* 101 Dogges, that are curst, men vse to tie vp in the day, and let loose in the night. **1644** BULWER *Chirol.* 130 Bridling is like unto curst and fierce bulls. **1727** BRADLEY *Fam. Dict.* s.v. *Bandog*, [It] should be chosen..not too curst nor too gentle of disposition.

†**c.** *fig.* Of hair: Rough, bristly. Of a sore: Malignant, irritable. *Obs.*

1565–73 COOPER *Thesaurus*, *Cæsaries horrida*, a cursed head. **1579** GOSSON *Sch. Abuse* (Arb.) 21 As curst sores with often touching waxe angry.

d. *Comb.*, as *curst-heartedness*, malignity of disposition, wickedness of heart.

1571 GOLDING *Calvin on Ps.* li. 19 Although they fome not out their cursthartednesse openly. **1633** T. ADAMS *Exp. 2 Peter* ii. 10 A tumour of curst-heartedness.

†ˈ**cursedhede.** *Obs.* [-HEAD.] Cursedness, execrable wickedness.

a **1300** *Cursor M.* 6544 (Gött.) And þar-wid forþermare he ȝede, For to se þair curcedhede. **1382** WYCLIF *Lev.* xviii. 27 (MSS. B, D, E, F, H) Alle forsothe thes cursydhedes [*v.r.* cursidnessis, **1388** abhomynacions] diden the tiliers of the erthe that weren bifore ȝow.

†ˈ**cursedhood.** *Obs.* [-HOOD.] Cursedness; *concr.* accursed thing (tr. L. *anathema*).

1382 WYCLIF *1 Chron.* ii. 7 The sones of Zamri..that.. synnede in the theft of cursedhode.

cursedly (ˈkɜːsɪdlɪ), *adv.* Also curstly. [f. CURSED + -LY[2].]

1. In a cursed manner; in a way deserving a curse; wickedly, abominably.

c **1386** CHAUCER *Monk's T.* 239 Thou that..heriest false goddes cursedly. *c* **1489** CAXTON *Sonnes of Aymon* x. 257 Whan bayerd sawe he was so curstly dealed wythall. **1549** CHEKE *Hurt Sedit.* (1641) 61 They judge cursedly the good to bee bad. **1679** BEDLOE *Popish Plot* 1 None more cursedly ingenious in inventing.. methods of doing mischief.

2. Used as an intensive with strong expression of reprobation or dislike: In a cursed manner, execrably, detestably, 'damnably', 'confoundedly'.

1570 DEE *Math. Pref.* 20 To be curstly affrayed of his owne shaddow. **1663** T. PORTER *Witty Combat* II. iii, Why, so thou art, insufferably, cursedly drunk. **1751** SMOLLETT *Per. Pic.* (1779) II. xlix. 106 Cursedly down in the mouth. **1826** DISRAELI *Viv. Grey* v. xv, They voted her ladyship cursedly satirical. **1861** HUGHES *Tom Brown at Oxf.* vi, I can't see why you should be so cursedly particular.

†**3.** Malignantly; with perverse ill-temper; crossly, severely, harshly, virulently.

1430 LYDG. *Chron. Troy* III. xxv, Guido.. hath delite to speake cursedly Alway of women. **1480** CAXTON *Chron. Eng.* ccxxvi. 232 His procuratours.. cursedly and ful slowly serued hym at his nede. **1590** MARLOWE *Edw. II*, v. ii. 64 To make him fret the more, Speak curstly to him. **1646** PAGITT *Heresiogr.* (ed. 3) 74 Father Browne, who would curstly correct his old wife. **1650** H. MORE in *Enthus. Triumph.* (1656) 106 You.. bark and scold.. more cursedly and bitterly then any Butter-quean.

cursedness (ˈkɜːsɛdnɪs). Also curstness. [f. CURSED + -NESS.]

1. The condition of being cursed or under a curse; damnation; misery. †**b.** *pl.* Miseries, misfortunes (*obs. rare*).

1303 R. BRUNNE *Handl. Synne* 7228 Woo to þo þat erly.. haunte þe tauerne.. Cursednes hem folowyþ at þe endyng. **1483** CAXTON *Gold. Leg.* 275/3 To haue soo many cursidnesses or ylle happes. **1579** TOMSON *Calvin's Serm. Tim.* 334/2 Them that were slaues to Sathan, and ouer the eares in the deepe bottomelesse pitte of cursednesse. **1651-3** JER. TAYLOR *Serm. for Year* I. xi. 142 The Poet describes the cursednesse of their posterity. **1836-9** DICKENS *Sk. Boz* (1850) 265/1 Mr. Watkins Tottle had long lived in a state of single blessedness, as bachelors say, or single cursedness, as spinsters think. **1875** T. HILL *True Order Studies* 140 If you would.. know the reality and cursedness of sin.

†**2.** The condition of being execrably wicked; abominable wickedness. **b.** (with *a* and *pl.*) An act or practice of wickedness. *Obs.*

a **1300** *Cursor M.* 1575 (Gött.) Þair cursednes was noght vnkid. *c* **1386** CHAUCER *Pard. T.* 310 Ydel sweryng is a cursednes. **1474** CAXTON *Chesse* 30 In moche cursidnes and wickednes. **1549-62** STERNHOLD & H. *Ps.* x. 7 His mouth is full of cursednes. *a* **1639** W. WHATELEY *Prototypes* II. xxvi. (1640) 75 By walking in a way of cursednesse.

†**3.** An accursed thing, 'abomination'. *Obs. rare.*

c **1550** CHEKE *Matt.* xxiv. 15 When ie se ye cursednes of desolation, which was spooken of bi daniel ye propheet, standing in an holi place.

4. (Usually *curstness.*) Malignancy or perversity of disposition, ill temper, crabbedness; fierceness, savageness; virulence (of poison). *Obs.* or *arch.*

c **1386** CHAUCER *Merch. Prol.* 27 As I.. Koude tellen of my wyues cursednesse. *c* **1430** LYDG. *Min. Poems* (Percy Soc.) 167 He that is to every man contrary, And he that bostithe of his cursidnesse. **1589** PUTTENHAM *Eng. Poesie* III. xix. (Arb.) 209 With spitefull speach, curstnesse and crueltie. **1600** HOLLAND *Livy* XXVII. xxxiv. 654 As the curstnesse and rigor of parents, is to be mollified by patience. **1633** T. ADAMS *Exp. 2 Peter* i. 18 Profane persons swear, as dogs bark, not ever for curstness, but for custom. **1634** T. JOHNSON *Parey's Chirurg.* XXI. xix. (1678) 474 The Basilisk far exceeds all Kinds of Serpents in the curstness of its poison. **1870** RAMSAY *Remin.* (ed. 18) p. xxvi, 'Curstness' (or crabbedness) of man's nature.

cur'see. *nonce-wd.* [-EE.] One who is cursed.

1829 CARLYLE *Misc.* (1872) II. 112 Which curse being strengthened by a sin of very old standing in the family of the cursee.

cursee, obs. form of CURTSY.

curseful (ˈkɜːsfʊl), *a. rare.* [f. CURSE *sb.* + -FUL.] Fraught with a curse or curses.

1382 WYCLIF *Ecclus.* x. 7 Hateful.. is pride; and cursful alle wickidnessis of Jentiles. **1832** *Blackw. Mag.* XXXI. 306 Those curseful events that have made me the wretch I am. **1871** FRANCES R. HAVERGAL *Ministry of Song* (1881) 109 Whose love shone forth upon the curseful tree.

Hence †**'cursefully** [printed *curstfully*] *adv.*, accursedly.

1606 MARSTON *Fawne* IV. Wks. 1856 II. 78 Was not thou most curstfully madd?

curselarie: see CURSORARY.

†**'cursement.** *Obs. rare.* In 4 corsement. [f. CURSE *v.* + -MENT.] Cursing, malediction.

1393 LANGL. *P. Pl.* C. VII. 65 Hus cloþes were of corsement and of kene wordes. [Cf. *Psalm* cix. 18.]

'cursen, -son, dial. f. CHRISTEN *a.* and *v.*

1602 MARSTON *Ant. & Mel.* III. Wks. 1856 I. 38 For all this cursond world. **1606** DAY *Ile of Guls* II. iv, Well, god a mercy of all cursen soules. **1613** BEAUM. & FL. *Coxcomb* II. ii, As I am a cursten'd whore. *Ibid.* IV. iii, *Nan.* Are they cursen'd? *Madge.* No, they call them infidels. **1851** *Cumbrld. Gloss.*, *Cursen*, to christen.

cursenary: see CURSORARY.

curser (ˈkɜːsə(r)). [f. CURSE *v.* + -ER^1^.] One who curses; one who utters a curse or malediction; a profane swearer.

1303 R. BRUNNE *Handl. Synne* 1300 Cursers alle here lyve Shall neuere haue grace for to þryve. **1548** CRANMER *Catech.* 23 These more then deuylish swerers, banners, and cursers. **1635** COWLEY *Davideis* I. 933 Thy Cursers, Jacob, shall twice cursed be. *c* **1750** J. NELSON *Jrnl.* (1836) 133 Such cursers and swearers as could hardly be matched out of hell. **1850** CLOUGH *Dipsychus* I. v. 72 Which is worst, To be the curser or the curst. **1855** MOTLEY *Dutch Rep.* (1858) 63 So speaking, the curser was wont to blow out two waxen torches .. and with this practical illustration the anathema was complete.

curser, cursey, obs. ff. COURSER, CURTSY.

curship (ˈkɜːʃɪp). [f. CUR + -SHIP.] The estate or personality of a cur: used as a mock title.

1663 BUTLER *Hud.* I. ii. 959 How durst th', I say, oppose thy Curship 'Gainst Arms, Authority, and Worship? **1765** WOLCOTT (P. Pindar) *Ode IV to R.A.'s* Wks. 1812 I. 87 The Lord have mercy on your Curship's skin.

cursie, obs. form of CURTSY.

cursing (ˈkɜːsɪŋ), *vbl. sb.* [-ING^1^.]

1. The utterance of words which consign to spiritual and temporal evil, the vengeance of the deity, the malign influence of fate, etc.; malediction, imprecation, damning.

c **950** *Lindisf. Gosp.* Luke xx. 47 Ðas onfoæð cursung mara [*Rushw.* Ðæt mara *vel* mast cursunge; Vulg. *damnationem majorem*]. **1388** WYCLIF *Dan.* ix. 11 And cursyng, and wlatyng which is writun in the book of Moises.. droppide on vs. **1535** COVERDALE *Mal.* iv. 6 That I come not, and smyte the earth with cursynge. **1552** ABP. HAMILTON *Catech.* (1884) 32 The malesonis waryingis or cursingis quhilk God.. schoris to the transgressouris.

†**b.** *concr.* The condition or place of damnation or perdition; hell. *Obs.*

c **950** *Lindisf. Gosp.* Matt. v. 29 Ðon all lichoma ðin ȝesendad beð in tintergo *vel* in cursung. *Ibid.* x. 28.

2. The formal pronunciation of an ecclesiastical curse or anathema; excommunication.

?*c* **1120** *Charter Pope Agatho* (dated 680) in *Cod. Dipl.* V. 30 Hwa swa hit breket ealre biscope cursunge and eal cristene folces he hafe. Amen. *c* **1200** *Trin. Coll. Hom.* 11 No bissop ne mai him chastien ne mid forbode, ne mid scrifte, ne mid cursinge. *a* **1300** *Cursor M.* 29482 (Cott.) Cursing twa-fald es, þe tan es mare, þe toþer lesse. *c* **1330** R. BRUNNE *Chron.* (1810) 130 Whan Thomas it wist, he did mak a cursyng. Roger he cursed first, þat corouned þe ȝong kyng. **1470-85** MALORY *Arthur* I. iii, That they shold to london come by Cristmas vpon payne of cursynge. **1530** PALSGR. 211 Cursyng.. *excommunication.* **1568** GRAFTON *Chron.* II. 35 Forbidden upon paine of curssing. **1872** ELLACOMBE *Ch. Bells Devon* vii. 139 Early in the twelfth century.. William of Winchester, by the authority of Celestine II.. brought in the use of cursing with bell, book, and candle.

3. Imprecation of evil; the profane use of imprecations in hatred or evil temper; blasphemy.

c **1050** *Spelman's Psalms* cviii. 16 (C. MS.) & he lufode wyrȝednysse [C. cursunge] & heo cume him, & he nolde bletsunga & heo bið afyrsad from him. *a* **1240** *Lofsong* in *Cott. Hom.* 205 Wreððe.. cursunge, bac bitunge. **1303** R. BRUNNE *Handl. Synne* 9116 Þy cursyng now sene hyt ys Wyþ veniaunce on þy owne flesshe. **1611** BIBLE *Ps.* lix. 12 For cursing and lying which they speake. *a* **1648** LD. HERBERT *Life* (1886) 215 He had heard that the King was much given to cursing. **1736** BERKELEY *Disc.* Wks. III. 427 It is no common blasphemy.. it is not simple cursing and swearing. **1847** EMERSON *Repr. Men* Wks. I. 343 He will indulge himself with a little cursing and swearing.

'cursing, *ppl. a.* [-ING^2^.] That curses.

1599 SHAKS. *Much Ado* v. i. 212 And you be a cursing hypocrite once, you must be lookt to. **1892** WATSON *G. Gilfillan* iv. 97 The meagre hand of contented or cursing penury.

cursitate (ˈkɜːsɪteɪt), *v. rare.* [f. L. *cursitāre* to run to and fro, freq. of *cursāre*, freq. of *currĕre* to run.] *intr.* To run hither and thither.

1867 BUSHNELL *Mor. Uses Dark Th.* 175 A flitting, cursitating, ghostly appearance.

†**cursi'tation.** *Obs.* [ad. L. *cursitātiōn-em*, n. of action f. *cursitāre*: see prec.] A running or going hither and thither, perambulation.

1630 LORD *Banian* 63 The Bridegroome.. with all the children in the Towne.. make their cursitation round about the most publicke streets.. with Trumpets and kettle-drummes. **1683** CAVE *Ecclesiastici* Introd. 31 In their wild cursitations up and down the streets.

cursitor (ˈkɜːsɪtə(r)). *Obs.* exc. *Hist.* Forms: 6 cursetor, coursetour, -iter, 6-7 -itor, cursitour, 7 -iter, 6- cursitor. [a. Anglo-Fr. *coursetour*, ad. med.L. *cursitor* (Ordericus Vitalis) = *cursor* runner. (App. formed to have the same relation to *cursor*, that *cursitāre* has to *cursāre*.) But the exact derivation in sense 1 is obscure.]

1. One of twenty-four officers or clerks of the Court of Chancery, whose office it was to make out all original writs *de cursu*, i.e. of common official course or routine, each for the particular shire or shires for which he was appointed.

The office was abolished in 1835.

1523 *Act 14-15 Hen. VIII*, c. 8 As well the coursetours and other clerkes, as the sixe clerkes of the said Chauncery. **1641** *Termes de la Ley* 96 Cursiter is an officer or Clerke belonging to the Chancerie.. They are called Clerkes of the Course in the oath of Clerkes of the Chancery. *a* **1655** BP. G. GOODMAN *Crt. Jas. I*, I. 280, I have heard that the cursitor's office of Yorkshire hath been sold for £1,300. **1703** LUTTRELL *Brief Rel.* (1857) V. 308 Mr. Gillingham, cursitor of Monmouth and Hereford, is dead. **1767** *Antiq. Durham Abbey, Descr. Bishoprick* 133 Court of Chancery [Durham], Mr. Thomas Hugall, Cursitor and Examiner.

†**b.** A secretary. *Obs.*

1762 tr. *Busching's Syst. Geog.* I. 80 The.. Lay Inspector .. has one or two Secretaries or Cursitors under him.

†**2.** A running messenger, courier; also *fig.* *Obs.*

1571 HANMER *Chron. Irel.* (1633) 84 [He] sent Scoutes, Cursitors, Messengers.. over the whole land. **1609** HOLLAND *Amm. Marcell.* XXVIII. iii. 337 Their office was this, by running.. to be cursitours to and fro. **1646** FULLER *Wounded Consc.* (1841) 282 The spirits, those cursitors betwixt soul and body. *a* **1661** —— *Worthies* III. 101 Dromedaries.. are the Cursitors for travell for the Eastern Country.

†**3.** One who wanders about the country; a vagabond, tramp. *Obs.*

1567 HARMAN (*title*), A Caueat or Warening, for commen cursetors vulgarely called Vagabones. **1581** MULCASTER *Positions* xxxvii. (1887) 156 Common coursiters, which post about still to suruey all scholes, and neuer staie in one. **1688** R. HOLME *Armoury* II. iii. §68. 167/2 Cursitors or Vagabonds. **1725** *New Cant. Dict.*, *Cursitors*, the Forty-second Order of Vagabonds.

4. cursitor baron. The junior or puisne baron of the Exchequer, a subordinate member of the court who attended to matters 'of course' on the revenue side. The office was abolished in 1856.

1642 VERNON *Consid. Exchequer* 33 The.. Cursitor Baron being so called because he is chosen most usually out of some of the best experienced Clerkes of the two Remembrancers, or Clerke of the Pipes Office, and is to informe the Bench and the Kings learned Counsell.. what the course of the Exchequer is for the preservation of the same. **1689** LUTTRELL *Brief Rel.* (1857) I. 557 Mr. Bradbury, of the Middle Temple, was lately sworn cursitor baron of the exchequer. **1830** PRICE *Law of Exchequer* 77 The Cursitor Baron, or, as he is sometimes called, the Fifth or Puisne Baron of the Court of Exchequer.. has no judicial authority in the Court of Exchequer as a Court of Law.

†**cursitory,** *a. Obs. rare.* [See prec., and -ORY.] = CURSORY. **cursitorily** *adv.*, cursorily.

1632 LE GRYS tr. *Paterculus* 306 Hee that in the cursitory way of this so contracted a worke, dares take upon him [etc.]. **1628** —— tr. *Barclay's Argenis* 214 Having therefore cursitorily reuiewed her face.. I.. desired her to tell me who she was.

cursive (ˈkɜːsɪv), *a.* (*sb.*) [ad. med.L. *cursīv-us*, f. *curs-* ppl. stem of *currĕre* to run: see -IVE. Cf. Du Cange s.v. *Scriptura.* In mod.F. *cursif, -ive* (1797 in Hatzfeld).] Of writing: Written with a running hand, so that the characters are rapidly formed without raising the pen, and in consequence have their angles rounded, and separate strokes joined, and at length become slanted. In ancient manuscripts the cursive style, showing some of these characteristics, is distinguished from the more formal uncial writing.

1784 in W. FRY *New Vocab.* **1827** G. S. FABER *Sacr. Cal. Proph.* (1844) III. 164 The gradual invention and.. general use of the cursive greek character. **1837-9** HALLAM *Hist. Lit.* I. I. §56 The complex system of abbreviations which rendered the cursive handwriting almost as operose.. as the more stiff characters of older manuscripts. **1881** WESTCOTT & HORT *Grk. N.T.* Introd. §102 The Cursive MSS. range from the ninth to the sixteenth centuries.

B. *sb.* A cursive character or manuscript.

1861 SCRIVENER *Introd. N.T.* ii. (1874) 40 Colbert. 2844 or 33 of the Gospels, 'the Queen of the cursives', as it has been called. **1881** WESTCOTT & HORT *Grk. N.T.* Introd. §98 The Greek MSS. of the New Testament are divided into two classes.. Uncials and Cursives, according as they are written in capital or minuscule characters.

cursively (ˈkɜːsɪvlɪ), *adv. rare.* [f. prec. + -LY^2^.]

†**1.** In continuous course or succession. *Obs.*

1603 KNOLLES *Hist. Turks* (1621) 1380 This.. empire.. hath.. beene alwaies hereditarie, from grandfather to father, from father to sonne, and so cursively in that maner.

2. In cursive characters.

1833 G. S. FABER *Recapit. Apostasy* 86 The name uncially expressed ΑΠΟϹΤΑΤΗϹ, or cursively expressed ἀποστάτης. **1885** E. M. THOMPSON in *Encycl. Brit.* XVIII. 149/1 Facsimiles of the cursively written papyri.

'cursiveness. *rare.* [f. as prec. + -NESS.] The quality of being cursive.

c **1820** G. S. FABER *Eight Dissert.* (1845) II. 14 The cursiveness of Ezra's hebrew character. **1833** —— *Recapit. Apostasy* 88 An additional attempt was made to increase the cursiveness of the cursive character.

curskyn, var. CRUSKYN *Obs.*, vessel for liquids.

Cursmas, dial. form of CHRISTMAS.

curson, var. CURSEN, dial. form of CHRISTEN.

cursor (ˈkɜːsə(r)). [a. L. *cursor* runner, agent-n. from *currĕre*, *curs-* to run: cf. COURSER.

The Latin word occurs in the title of 'Þe tretis þat men cals *Cursor Mundi*' (Gött. MS.), 'The Cursur o the world' (Cott. MS), of which it is said, l. 267,

Cursur [*v.r.* Cursor, Coarsur] o werld man oght it call,
For almost it ouer-rennes all.]

†**1.** A runner, running messenger. *Obs.*

[*a* **1300**: see above.] **1566** T. STAPLETON *Ret. Untr. Jewel* III. 125 He went apace like a Cursor that telleth good news. *a* **1632** T. TAYLOR *God's Judgem.* II. iv. (1642) 53 He also kept cursors and messengers.. to ride abroad.

2. a. A part of a mathematical, astronomical, or surveying instrument, which slides backwards and forwards.

1594 BLUNDEVIL *Exerc.* VII. xii. (ed. 7) 666 Every one of these Transames or Cursours must be cut with a square hole ..so as they may be made to run iust upon the staffe to and fro. **1641** W. GASCOIGNE in Rigaud *Corr. Sci. Men* (1841) I. 43 The lowest part of the cross is jointed, to separate it from the cursor on the ruler. **1736** R. NEVE *City & C. Purchaser*, *Cursor*, a little brass Ruler representing the Horizon: a Label. **1793** WOLLASTON in *Phil. Trans.* LXXXIII. 139 The cursor, or moveable wire, in the micrometer-microscopes. **1874** in KNIGHT *Dict. Mech.*

b. A distinctive symbol on a VDU display (e.g. a flashing underline or rectangle) that indicates the position at which the next character will appear or the next action will take effect, and which is usu. under keyboard control.

1967 STOTZ & CHEEK *Low-Cost Graphic Display for Computer Time-Sharing Console* (MIT Technical Memo.) 13 For graphical input, one would like to be able to move a pointer or 'cursor' over a stored picture and yet not store the image of the cursor. *Ibid.*, The cursor on the screen 'follows' the motion of the 'mouse'. **1972** L. W. JAMES in J. F. Slater *Computer-Aided Typesetting* 78/1 The cursor..can be moved vertically a line at a time or horizontally a character at a time to indicate the positions where we wish to make changes in the text. **1983** *Austral. Personal Computer* Aug. 141/3 It can set the cursor to be visible or invisible, blinking or steady, block or underline. **1983** *Times* 16 Aug. 16/6 Once the cursor has located the correct screen character a button on the mouse is pressed to execute the command. **1985** P. LAURIE *Databases* i. 13 In a word processor, for instance, Control F might mean move the cursor forward one character.

‖**3.** In mediæval universities, a bachelor of theology giving the courses of lectures upon the Bible which formed one of the necessary preliminaries to the doctorate.

4. Special Comb.: **cursor (control) key**, any of a set of keys on a VDU keyboard for controlling the movement of a cursor on the screen.

1979 A. CAKIR et al. *VDT Man.* i. 19 The cursor control keys are usually located in a separate block..on one side of the main keyset. **1981** *Electronics* 8 Sept. 115 (*caption*) The cursor keys, right of center, provide menu parameters. **1984** *Which Micro?* Dec. 20/3 With the cursor key cluster on the right, the Plus 4 looks very like an MSX computer. **1985** *Personal Computer World* Feb. 145/2 The MZ-800..has an identical 69-key keyboard which features a standard qwerty layout, five function keys and a cluster of cursor control keys. **1986** *Your Computer* Oct. 36/1 Using the cursor keys or a joystick, you can create your shape and then rotate, invert or produce a mirror image of it before saving it in the program files.

†ˈ**cursorary**, *a. Obs. rare.* = CURSORY.

The reading of the 3rd Quarto (followed by Pope, and by most modern editors), for which Quartos 1 and 2 have *cursenary* and the First Folio *curselarie*: cf. CURSITORY.

SHAKS. *Hen. V*, v. ii. 77 (Qo. 3, 1619) We haue but with a Cursorary eye Ore-view'd them.

cursore, obs. form of CORSAIR, COURSER.

‖**Cursores** (kɜːˈsɔəriːz), *sb. pl. Ornith.* [L. pl. of *cursor* runner: see above.] The name given by De Blainville, 1815–22, to an order of birds, containing the ostrich and its allies, which are incapable of flight, but are mostly swift runners. It corresponds to Merrem's division *Ratitæ*.

1828 STARK *Elem. Nat. Hist.* I. 283 Birds. Order XII.—Cursores. **1847** CARPENTER *Zool.* §440 Of all the Cursores, the Apteryx of New Zealand appears to be the one which is most completely destitute of wings, and which departs most widely from the general type of the class of Birds.

cursorial (kɜːˈsɔərɪəl). *a. Zool.* [f. L. *cursōri-us* running (taken in reference to CURSORES) + -AL[1].] Adapted, or having limbs adapted, for running; *spec.* applied to certain birds (*Cursores*), orthopterous insects (*Cursoria*), and crustaceans.

1836 TODD *Cycl. Anat.* I. 283/2 The sternum of the Cursorial Birds presents few affinities of structure to that of the rest of the class. **1855** OWEN *Skel. & Teeth* 25 The prehensile or cursorial limb of the denizen of dry land.

cursorily (ˈkɜːsərɪlɪ), *adv.* [f. CURSORY *a.* + -LY[2]. The L. *cursōriē* was in early use.] In a cursory manner; in passing; hastily; without attention to details.

[**1549** LATIMER *3rd Serm. bef. Edw. VI* (Arb.) 78, I wyll runne it ouer *cursorie*, rypping a lytle the matter.] **1565** JEWEL *Def. Apol.* (1611) 128 Thus cursorily to passe it ouer. **1603** HOLLAND *Plutarch's Mor.* 1315 Cursarily and by the way to annexe hereto such things as cary some probability. **1685** BOYLE *Effects of Mot.* Advt. 2 While he cursorily read over the Tract. **1756** C. LUCAS *Ess. Waters* III. 23, I have already cursorily mentioned some of the products. **1804** YOUNG in *Phil. Trans.* XCV. 84 Principles which he has but cursorily investigated. **1861** GOSCHEN *For. Exch.* 20 An allusion was cursorily made to the expenditure in travelling.

ˈ**cursoriness.** [f. as prec. + -NESS.] Cursory quality; hastiness or slightness (of examination or treatment).

1727 in BAILEY vol. II. **1885** F. HALL in *N. Y. Nation* XLI. 240/3 The subject of which has been despatched with uncritical cursoriness.

cursorious (kɜːˈsɔərɪəs), *a.* [f. L. *cursōri-us* + -OUS: see CURSORY.] Adapted for running: said of the legs of coleopterous insects.

†ˈ**cursoriwise**, *adv. Obs.*—[0] [Short for *in cursory wise*: see next.] In a cursory manner.

1598 FLORIO, *Alla fuggita*, by the way, cursoriwise. **1659** TORRIANO, *Pér córso*, runningly, cursorie-wise.

cursory (ˈkɜːsərɪ), *a.* Also 7 **cursorie**, **cursary**. [ad. L. *cursōri-us* of or pertaining to a runner or a race, f. *cursōr-em* runner: in OF. *corsoire*, *cursoire*.]

1. Running or passing rapidly over a thing or subject, so as to take no note of details; hasty, hurried, passing.

1601 DENT *Pathw. Heauen* 277 Cursory saying of a few praiers a little before death, auaileth not. **1661** J. STEPHENS *Procurations* 128, I had only a cursory view of it, and that by chance. **1766** GOLDSM. *Vic. W.* xviii, A traveller who stopped to take a cursory refreshment. **1857** KEBLE *Eucharist. Adorat.* 37 Obvious to the most cursory reader of the Gospel. **1866** ROGERS *Agric. & Prices* I. iii. 60 A cursory inspection shews that these statements are untrustworthy.

†**2.** Moving about, travelling. *Obs. rare.*

1606 *Proc. agst. Garnet* F (T.), Father Cresswell, legier jesuit in Spain; father Baldwin, legier in Flaunders..besides their cursorie men, as Gerrard, etc. **1610** ROWLANDS *Martin Mark-all* 24 Their houses are made cursary like our Coaches with foure wheeles that may be drawne from place to place. **1650** FULLER *Pisgah* II. IV. ii. 21 Those Tribes dwelt in their Tents..in a cursory condition, only grazing their Cattel during the season.

3. *Entom.* Adapted for running; = CURSORIOUS.

4. In mediæval universities: **a.** ***cursory lectures***: lectures of a less formal and exhaustive character delivered, especially by bachelors, as additional to the 'ordinary' lectures of the authorized teachers in a faculty, and at hours not reserved for these prescribed lectures.

[The name would appear to have been first given to the lectures delivered by bachelors as part of the *cursus* prescribed for the licence, but to have been afterwards extended to all 'extraordinary' lectures.]

1841 G. PEACOCK *Stat. Univ. Camb.* p. xliv. *note* 1. **1894** RASHDALL *Med. Universities* vi. §4. 426 The 'cursory' lectures of Paris are the 'extraordinary' lectures of Bologna. *Ibid.* 427 Vacation cursory lectures might be given at any hour. *Ibid.* It is probable that the term 'cursory' came to suggest also the more rapid and less formal manner of going over a book usually adopted at these times.

b. ***cursory bachelor***: (in modern writers) a bachelor who gave cursory lectures.

cursour(e, obs. form of CORSAIR, COURSER.

curst, *a.*: see CURSED.

†ˈ**curstable.** *Arch. Obs.* [f. COURSE + TABLE.] 'A course of stones with mouldings cut on them to form a string course' (Parker *Gloss.* 1850).

1278 *Bursar's Acc. Merton Coll.* (Parker), Pro x pedibus de curstable.

ˈ**cursten**, var. CURSEN, dial. form of CHRISTEN.

curstfully: see CURSEFULLY.

curstly, -ness: see CURSEDLY, CURSEDNESS.

‖**cursus** (ˈkɜːsəs). [L. *cursus* course, f. *currĕre* to run.] The Latin word for COURSE; occasionally used in mediæval or technical senses, as **a.** A race-course, running-ground, or drive; also used *spec.* of a type of neolithic monument (see quot. 1963); **b.** A stated order of daily prayer; a ritual, or form of celebration; **c.** An academic course or curriculum.

1740 STUKELEY *Stonehenge* viii. 35 The western branch.. continues curving along the bottom of the hill, till it meets, what I call, the *cursus*. *Ibid.* ix. 41 About half a mile north of Stonehenge, across the first valley, is the *cursus* or *hippodrom*, which I discovered, August 6, 1723. **1838** MRS. BRAY *Trad. Devonsh.* I. 164 For what purpose this avenue or cursus was used. **1865** MCLAUCHLAN *Early Sc. Church* xiv. 188 Whether they made use of any peculiar cursus or liturgy. **1875** MCCOSH *Sc. Philos.* xi. 94 The University Commissioners appointed in 1643 a Cursus for Aberdeen. **1883** *Athenæum* 17 Mar. 348/3 The line would have cut through the avenue and the cursus of Stonehenge. **1951** *Field Archæol.* (*Ordnance Survey*) (ed. 3) 18 Another feature which is now regarded as part of the henge complex is the extremely elongated earthwork of the type originally called a 'cursus' by Stukeley..because he believed that they were designed as racecourses. **1963** E. S. WOOD *Field Guide to Archaeol.* II. 138 A class of still enigmatic neolithic monuments are the cursūs... These are long parallel banks with outside ditches, with squared or curved ends, running across country often for long distances.

d. The regular varying cadences which mark the end of sentences and phrases, esp. in Greek and Latin prose.

1904 H. A. WILSON in *Jrnl. Theol. Stud.* V. 387 Prof. E. Norden has traced the use of the 'cursus' in Classical writers, Greek as well as Latin. **1910** *Encycl. Brit.* VIII. 304/1 The *cursus* or prose rhythm of the pontifical chancery of the 11th and 12th centuries. **1910** A. C. CLARK (*title*) The cursus in mediaeval and vulgar Latin. **1959** H. J. ROSE *Outl. Class. Lit.* vi. 188 Three rhythms found their way..into medieval Latin prose..where naturally accented syllables took the place of long ones. Hence the three 'runs' (*cursus*) as they were called.

cursy, obs. form of CURTSY.

curt (kɜːt), *a.* [ad. L. *curt-us* cut or broken short, mutilated, abridged, which became in late L. and Romanic the ordinary word for 'short': It., Sp. *corto*, Pr. *cort*, F. *court*.

The Latin adj. was app. adopted at an early date in Ger., giving OS. and OFris. *curt* (MDu. *cort*, Du., MLG., and LG. *kort*, whence also mod.Icel. *korta*, Sw. and Da. *kort*), OHG. *kurt*, *kurz* (MHG. and mod.Ger. *kurz*), where the word has taken the place of an original Teut. **skurt-*, in OHG. *scurz*, in OE. *scort*, *sceort*, SHORT. But the latter was retained in English.]

1. Short in linear dimension; shortened.

1665 SIR T. HERBERT *Trav.* (1677) 295 In more temperate climes hair is curt. **1840** LYTTON *Pilgr. of Rhine* xix, Thy limbs are crooked and curt. **1862** MERIVALE *Rom. Emp.* (1865) III. xxviii. 297 Plancus..enacted the part of the sea-god Glaucus in curt cerulean vestments.

b. of things immaterial, modes of action, etc.

1664 H. MORE *Myst. Iniq.* 351 For which curt reckoning Grotius has no excuse. **1675** TRAHERNE *Chr. Ethics* xx. 318 That vertue so curt and narrow, which we thought to be infinite. *a* **1677** BARROW *Serm.* (1687) I. xviii. 258 The most curt and compendious way of bringing about dishonest or dishonourable designs. **1874** REYNOLDS *John Bapt.* ii. 89 An angelic Spirit makes a more curt and much easier use than we can do of the functions of matter in its most ethereal form.

2. Of words, sentences, style, etc.: Concise, brief, condensed, terse; short to a fault.

1630 B. JONSON *New Inn* III. i, What's his name? *Fly.* Old Peck. *Tip.* Maestro de campo, Peck! his name is curt, A monosyllable, but commands the horse well. **1645** MILTON *Tetrach.* (1851) 177 The obscure and curt Ebraisms that follow. **1791** BOSWELL *Johnson* (1887) III. 274 He could put together only curt frittered fragments of his own. **1814** D'ISRAELI *Amen. Lit.* (1867) 132 Their Saxon-English is nearly monosyllabic, and their phraseology curt. **1866** ROGERS *Agric. & Prices* I. iii. 61 The dry and curt language of a petition in parliament.

b. So brief as to be wanting in courtesy or suavity.

1831 DISRAELI *Yng. Duke* v. vii. (L.), 'Ah! I know what you are going to say', observed the gentleman in a curt, gruffish voice, 'It is all nonsense.' **1863** GEO. ELIOT *Romola* (1880) I. Introd. 9 He might have been a little less defiant and curt, though, to Lorenzo de' Medici.

†**curt**, *v. Obs.* [f. L. *curt-āre* to cut short, shorten, mutilate, f. *curtus* short.] *trans.* To cut short, shorten.

a **1618** SYLVESTER *Mem. Mortalitie* I. xciii, Curting thy life, hee takes thy Card away.

Hence †ˈ**curted** *ppl. a.*, shortened, curtailed, curt.

1568 NORTH tr. *Gueuara's Diall Pr.* IV. viii. 129 a, To see a foolish courtier weare..a litel curted cape. **1581** SIDNEY *Astr. & Stella* xcii, Be your words made, good Sir, of Indian ware, That you allow me them by so small rate? Or do you curtted Spartanes imitate? **1610** GUILLIM *Heraldry* IV. xiv. (1611) 229 The old Britans..were wont to weare a short and broad Sword; so did the Spartanes also, whom..their Enemies mocked for so curted a weapon.

curt., cur[t]. An abbreviation of CURRENT *a.*, esp. in such phrases as the 10th curt., *i.e.* of the current month.

curt, curtace, obs. ff. COURT, COURTEOUS.

curtail (kɜːˈteɪl), *v.* Forms: 6–7 curtal(l, -toll, 6 curteyl, 7 curtel, cur-, cour-, curt-tail, 6– curtail. [Originally *curtal(l*, f. CURTAL *a.*, and still stressed on the first syllable by Johnson 1773. But already in the 16th c. the second syllable began to be associated with the word *tail* (cf. sense 1), and perhaps by some in the 17th and 18th c. with F. *tailler* to cut, whence the spelling *cur-tail*, *curt-tail*, *curtail*, and the current pronunciation, given without qualification by Walker 1791.]

†**1.** To make a curtal of by docking the tail; to dock. *Obs.*

1577 B. GOOGE *Heresbach's Husb.* II. (1586) 115 b, Hys tayle is..a great commoditie to him to beate away flies: yet some delight to have them curtailed, specially if they be broade buttockt. **1601** HOLLAND *Pliny* II. 363 The ashes also of an hardy-shrewes taile; provided alwaies, that the shrew were let go aliue, so soone as she was curt-tailed. **1611** COTGR., *Escouer*, to curtall, or cut off the taile.

2. To cut short in linear dimension; to shorten by cutting off a part.

1580 LYLY *Euphues* (Arb.) 326 Thou hast rackte me, and curtalde me, sometimes I was too long, sometimes to[o] shorte. **1596** NASHE *Saffron Walden* 19 If it be too long, thou hast a combe and a paire of scissers to curtall it. **1607** ROWLANDS *Famous Hist.* 38 And Estellard I cur-tail'd by the knees. **1674** S. VINCENT *Gallant's Acad.* 39 Let the three Huswively Spinsters of Destiny rather curtal the thred of thy life. **1787** 'G. GAMBADO' *Acad. Horsemen* (1809) 27, I.. firmly believe, that ten men are hanged for every inch curtailed in a Judge's wig. **1827** STEUART *Planter's G.* (1828) 71 To lop and deface them..and..to curtail the roots.

b. As applied to *sentences*, *verses*, *lines*, *letters*, and the like, the sense leads on to 3.

1553 T. WILSON *Rhet.* (1580) 169 Some againe will be so short, and in suche wise curtall their sentences. **1599** THYNNE *Animadv.* (1865) 64 Whiche wordes are curteyled for the verse his cause. **1605** CAMDEN *Rem.* 21 Neither do we or the Welsh so curtall Latine, that we make all therein Monosyllables. **1766** H. WALPOLE *Lett. Conc. Rousseau* iv. 153 You have suffered my letter to be curtailed.

3. To shorten in duration or extent; to cut down; to abbreviate, abridge, diminish, or reduce, in extent or amount.

1589 *Pasquil's Return* D b, With what face dares anie politique..curtoll the maintenance of the Church? **1591** LYLY *Endym.* v. ii, I will by peece-meele curtall my affections towards Dipsas. **1611** SHAKS. *Cymb.* II. i. 12 When a Gentleman is dispos'd to sweare: it is not for any standers by to curtall his oathes. **1663** BUTLER *Hud.* I. iii. 597 Yet I'd be loth my Days to curtal [*rime* mortal]. **1781** GOUV. MORRIS in Sparks *Life & Writ.* (1832) I. 234 Greatly to cur-tail salaries is a false economy. **1843** MRS. CARLYLE *Lett.* I. 195 His family's slumbers were probably curtailed. **1856** FROUDE *Hist. Eng.* I. iii. 244 The jurisdiction of the spiritual courts was not immediately curtailed.

4. *to curtail* (*a person*, etc.) *of*: to dock him of some part of his property, to deprive or rob him of something that he has enjoyed or has a right to. So *to curtail in*, to shorten in respect of.

1581 LAMBARD *Eiren.* III. iv. (1586) 369 Not altogether beheading them [Statutes] of their preambles, Nor any whit curtailing them of their wordes. **1594** SHAKS. *Rich. III*, I. i. 18, I, that am curtail'd of this faire Proportion. **1642** ROGERS *Naaman* 396 How doe we curtall him of his ordinary dues. *a* **1719** ADDISON (J.), Fact..had taken a wrong name, having curtailed it of three letters; for that his name was not Fact but Faction. **1830** D'ISRAELI *Chas. I*, III. vi. 114 His beard curtailed of ancient dimensions, he wore peaked. **1856** DOVE *Logic Chr. Faith* v. i. §2. 279 God is there..curtailed in no attribute.

†**5.** To cut *off* short, lop off. *Obs.*

1594 LODGE *Wounds Civ. War* IV. in Hazl. *Dodsley* VII. 172 Go, curtal off that neck with present stroke.

†**cur'tail**, *sb. Obs.* [f. CURTAIL *v.*] The act of curtailing, curtailment.

1797 E. M. LOMAX *Philanthrope* 19 Fancying myself present..at this office of curtail or extension.

curtail, obs. form of CURTAL *sb.* and *a.*

curtailed (kɜː'teɪld), *ppl. a.* Also 6–7 curtalled, etc. [f. CURTAIL *v.* and CURTAL *sb.* + -ED.]

1. Made a curtal; having the tail docked or cut off.

1591 FLORIO *Sec. Fruites* 43 Another [horse] broken winded, curtald, lame, blinde, foundred. **1603** HOLLAND *Plutarch's Mor.* 419 My curtailed dog. **1610** FLETCHER *Faithf. Shepherdess* To Rdr., With cur-tailed dogs in strings. **1870** SWINBURNE *Ess. & Stud.* (1875) 101 The yelp of curtailed foxes in every generation is the same.

†**b.** *transf.* Shaped at the end as if cut off short.

1575 GASCOIGNE *Wks.* (1587) 154 A curtolde slipper and a short silke hose. **1592** GREENE *Def. Conny Catch.* (1859) 33 A..peake pendent, either sharpe..or curtold lyke the broad ende of a Moule spade. **1601** HOLLAND *Pliny* II. 218 The smallest roots of Ellebor, such as be..curtelled, and not sharp pointed in the bottom.

2. Cut short; shortened, abridged; diminished in length, extent, power, privilege.

1561 T. NORTON *Calvin's Inst.* III. 217 But let vs heare their curtalled argumentes. *c* **1620** S. SMITH *Serm.* (1866) I. 156 With the curtailed skirts of David's ambassadors [cf. 2 Sam. x. 4]. **1641** MILTON *Reform.* I. (1851) 13 They must mew their feathers, and their pounces, and make but curt-tail'd Bishops of them. **1879** LUBBOCK *Addr. Pol. & Educ.* x. 205 According to the most curtailed chronology.

†**3.** ? Short-skirted: cf. CURTAL 3 d. *Obs.*

1624 FLETCHER *Wife for Month* II. vi, They are curtall'd queanes in hired clothes.

Hence **cur'tailedly** *adv.*, shortly, abbreviatedly.

1658 W. BURTON *Itin. Anton.* 167 The name thereof.. perhaps..was written curtail'dly.

cur'tailer. [f. CURTAIL *v.* + -ER.] One who curtails, shortens, abridges.

1724 WATERLAND *Athan. Creed* x. 141 That the Latins had not been interpolators of the creed, but that the Greeks had been curtailers. **1813** SHELLEY *Q. Mab* Note viii, Disease and war, those sweeping curtailers of population.

cur'tailing, *vbl. sb.* Also 6–7 curtalling, 7 curtling. [-ING[1].] The action of the verb CURTAIL; shortening, abridging.

1586 A. DAY *Eng. Secretary* I. (1625) 3 When..with too much curtalling our arguments..wee abbreviate..our Epistles. **1591** PERCIVALL *Sp. Dict.*, *Derrabadura*, curtalling, *caudæ truncatio.* **1610** MARKHAM *Masterp.* II. clix. 468 Now for the manner of curtalling of horses, it is in this sort. **1650** FULLER *Pisgah* III. i. 315 The curtling of Jerusalem into Solyma. *c* **1720** W. GIBSON *Farrier's Guide* II. lviii. (1738) 217. **1737** SWIFT *Letter* 23 July, Against the corruption of English..with abominable curtailings and quaint modernisms. **1775** SHERIDAN *Rivals* Pref., I profited by his judgment and experience in the curtailing of it.

curtailment (kɜː'teɪlmənt). [f. CURTAIL *v.* + -MENT.] The action of curtailing, shortening, diminishing; abridgement.

1794 G. ADAMS *Nat. & Exp. Philos.* I. p. ix, A curtailment of a few repetitions. **1830** MACKINTOSH *Eth. Philos.* Wks. 1846 I. 44 A curtailment of gratification. **1878** MORLEY *Diderot* I. 167 The copies were returned to their owners with some petty curtailments.

'curtail-step. Also 8 curtal-. [Origin uncertain: *curtal* adj., and *cur tail*, have both been suggested.] The lowest step (or steps) of a stair, having the outer end carried round in the form of a scroll.

1736 B. LANGLEY *Anc. Masonry* 389 The first, or Curtal-step. **1819** in P. NICHOLSON *Archit. Dict.* 716. **1852–61** *Archit. Publ. Soc. Dict.* s.v. *Curtail*, The newel generally stands upon a curtail step..Curtail steps..are employed in handsome staircases.

curtain ('kɜːtɪn, -t(ə)n), *sb.*[1] Forms: 4–6 cortyn(e, -eyn(e, courtyn(e, -ein(e, -ayn, curtyn(e, -ein(e, -eyn(e, -ayn(e, 4–7 courtin(e, curten, -ine, 4–8 cortine, curtin, (4 couertine, 5 quirtayn, 5–6 courting), 6 cortaine, -ayne, (curteynge, cowrtyng), 6–8 courtain(e, 7–8 curtaine, 4, 7– curtain. [ME. *cortine, curtine*, a. OF. *cortine, courtine* in same sense = Sp. and It. *cortina*:—L. *cortīna*, in Vulgate (*Exod.* xxvi. 1, etc.) a curtain. The connexion of this with classical L. *cortīna* round vessel, cauldron, round cavity, vault, arch, circle, is obscure, and the etymology uncertain: see Körting *Lat.-Roman, Wbch.* s.v.]

1. a. A piece of cloth or similar material suspended by the top so as to admit of being withdrawn sideways, and serving as a screen or hanging for purposes of use or ornament; e.g. to enclose a bed (the earliest English use), to separate one part of a room from another, to regulate the admission of light at a window, to prevent draught at a door or other opening, etc.

[*a* **1186** ROBERT OF TORIGNI *Chron.* (Rolls) 292 Cortinæ illæ circa lectum conjugis suæ.] *a* **1300** *Cursor M.* 11240 (Cott.) Was þar na pride o couerled, chamber curtin [*v.r.* curten, -ain, -eyn] ne tapit. *c* **1320** *Sir Beues* 3217 A couertine on raile tre, For noman scholde on his bed ise. *c* **1340** *Gaw. & Gr. Knt.* 854 þer beddyng watz noble, Of cortynes of clene sylk, wyth cler golde hemmez. **1413** LYDG. *Pilgr. Sowle* I. iv. (1483) 4 By ouer drawynge of a grete corteyne. *c* **1475** *Rauf Coilȝear* 267 Ane burely bed..Closit with Courtingis, and cumlie cled. **1552** HULOET, Curtayne aboute a hall. **1587** GOLDING *De Mornay* xxxiv. 545 The Veile or Courtaine of the Temple did rend a sunder. **1605** B. JONSON *Volpone* v. ii, I'le get vp, Behind the cortine, on a stoole, and harken. **1674** BREVINT *Saul at Endor* 167 A great Cortin, that hanged before our Ladies Image. **1704** *Lond. Gaz.* No. 4033/4 Lost..3 Damask Window-Curtains. **1712** BUDGELL *Spect.* No. 313 ¶ 16 There is a Curtain which used to be drawn across the Room. **1827** O. W. ROBERTS *Centr. Amer.* 78 Under the necessity of using mosquito curtains.

b. *to draw the curtain*: (*a*) to draw it back or aside, so as to discover what is behind; (*b*) to draw it forward in front of an object, so as to cover or conceal it. Also *fig.*

1509 BARCLAY *Shyp of Folys* 14, I drawe the curtyns to shewe my bokes then. **1597** SHAKS. *2 Hen. IV*, I. i. 72 Such a man, so faint, so spiritlesse..Drew Priams Curtaine, in the dead of night. **1657** *Lust's Dominion* I. i. (*Stage Direct.*), Eleazar, sitting on a chair, suddenly draws the curtain. **1709** ADDISON *Tatler* No. 19 ¶ 3, I started up and drew my Curtains to look if any one was near me. **1820** HAZLITT *Lect. Dram. Lit.* 4, I shall..try to 'draw the curtain of Time, and shew the picture of Genius'.

1509 HAWES *Past. Pleas.* Introd. vi, To drawe a curtayne I dare not to presume, Nor hyde my matter with a misty smoke. **1605** SHAKS. *Lear* III. vi. 89 Make no noise, make no noise, draw the Curtaines. **1728–46** THOMSON *Spring* 980 While Evening draws her crimson curtains round.

†**c.** Applied in the Bible to the skins or pieces of cloth with which a tent or tabernacle was hung; the canvas of a tent.

1382 WYCLIF *Ex.* xxvi. 1 The tabernacle forsothe thow shalt make thus; ten curteyns [Vulg. *decem cortinas*]. **1535** COVERDALE *2 Sam.* vii. 2 The Arke of God dwelleth amonge the curtaynes [Vulg. *in medio pellium*]. **1611** BIBLE *Hab.* iii. 7 The curtaines of the land of Midian did tremble.

d. Applied variously to hanging pieces of cloth or fabric: as, a veil, an overhanging shade of a bonnet, an ensign. *curtain of mail*: the piece of chain-mail hanging from the edge of a helmet of the Saracen type; the camail.

1541 ELYOT *Image Gou.* 21 Your predecessors..wold not be seen of the people but seldome, and oftentymes with a courteine before theyr visage. **1599** SHAKS. *Hen. V*, IV. ii. 41 Their ragged Curtaines poorely are let loose, And our Ayre shakes them passing scornefully. **1788** E. SHERIDAN *Jrnl.* (1960) 138 Bonnets I see most generally worn and some with very deep Curtains, The Bonnet itself is small. **1861** C. M. YONGE *Stokesley Secret* ii. 31 Her lilac-spotted sun-bonnet ..with a huge curtain serving for a tippet. **1889** *Century Mag.* Dec. 260/2 When our grandmothers had curtains to their bonnets.

e. *pl.* A wrinkled effect resembling a draped curtain on a painted or varnished surface. *colloq.*

1922 M. TOCH *How to paint Permanent Pictures* 79 A very heavy-bodied Linseed Oil,..was so viscous that it flowed down..and formed 'curtains', and teardrops. **1951** R. MAYER *Artist's Handbk.* iii. 136 *Streamlines.* The surface defect resembling drops of water running down a window pane is variously known by painters and paint technicians as frilling, curtains, runs, or tears. **1958** *Listener* 28 Aug. 323/1 Just flow them [*sc.* jelly paints] on a little more generously. .. You are not likely to have any trouble with runs or 'curtains'.

2. a. In a theatre, etc.: The screen separating the stage from the auditorium, which is drawn up at the beginning and dropped at the end of the play or of a separate act. *to call* (*an actor*) *before the curtain*: to summon him to appear after the curtain falls to mark one's appreciation of his performance. Also in various phrases used *fig.*, *to drop* or *raise the curtain*, to end or begin an action; *the curtain falls, drops*, or *rises*, etc.

1599 [see 7]. *a* **1649** DRUMM. OF HAWTH. *Cypress Grove* Wks. (1711) 125 Every one cometh there to act his part of this tragi-comedy, called life, which done, the courtain is drawn, and he removing is said to dy. **1677** [see b]. **1709** STEELE *Tatler* No. 193 ¶ 3, I have..been bred up behind the Curtain, and been a Prompter from the Time of the Restoration. **1752** YOUNG *Brothers* v. i, No; death lets fall The curtain, and divides our loves for ever. **1768** GOLDSM. *Good-n. Man* IV, *Cro.* Perhaps this very moment the tragedy is beginning. *Mrs. Cro.* Then let us reserve our distress till the rising of the curtain. **1811** BYRON *Hints from Hor.* 216 The hands of all Applaud in thunder at the curtain's fall. **1888** *Pall Mall G.* 13 Sept. 5/1 Macready..as Richard III., was the first actor to be summoned before the curtain at Covent Garden.

b. *behind the curtain*: 'behind the scenes', away from the public view.

1677 GILPIN *Dæmonol.* (1867) 130 To put us in mind who it is that is at work behind the curtain, when we see such things acted upon the stage. **1682** *Enq. Elect. Sheriffs* 26 Some behind the curtain had undoubtedly laid the project. **1763** LD. BARRINGTON in Ellis *Orig. Lett.* II. 449 IV. 461 Lord Bute..declares he will not be Minister behind the Curtain, but give up business entirely. **1818** JAS. MILL *Brit. India* II. v. viii. 631 The circumstances, however, which constituted the real nature of the transaction were only behind the curtain.

c. In various ellipt. or allusive uses: (i) = *curtain-call*; (ii) the finale of a play, act, or scene; also *transf.*; (iii) = *curtain-fall.*

1884 *Referee* 31 Aug. 3/3 *Written in Sand* was well received, and Broughton had to 'take a curtain'. **1885** *Ibid.* 15 Mar. 7/3 It is singular, considering how excellently French dramatists write, that they so frequently fail in getting a good 'curtain'. **1895** G. B. SHAW *Our Theatres in Nineties* (1932) I. 165 The doggerel tags before the final curtain. **1897** E. TERRY *Let.* 19 June in *E. T. & Shaw* (1931) 219 The last week I've dragged myself through that long long part, and toppled down when it was Curtain on Thursday night. **1917** R. FIRBANK *Caprice* xii. 102 The other afternoon I 'offered my services' and obtained three curtains at a gala matinée. **1919** WODEHOUSE *My Man Jeeves* 146 Curtain of act one on hero..kidnapping the child. **1928** *Evening News* 7 Aug. 7/3 There were ten curtains after the second act and an enthusiastic reception when the curtain fell. **1928** *Daily Tel.* 4 Dec. 9/1 'Sapper' gives a decidedly original curtain to his dramatic murder tale 'The Hidden Witness'. **1965** *Listener* 9 Sept. 393/1 A lyrical outpouring, leading to a most effective curtain.

d. In *pl.* (also occas. in *sing.*), the end (cf. sense 2 c (iii)). *slang.*

1912 D. LOWRIE *Life in Prison* vii. 82 There ain't much dope here now, an' it's curtains t' get nailed with it. **1918** WODEHOUSE *Piccadilly Jim* xi. 114 'What's wrong?' 'Curtains!.. I've been fired.' **1937** C. DAY LEWIS *Starting Point* II. i. 135, I rather fancy potassium cyanide. You just chew a piece, and quick curtain. **1940** N. MONKS *Squadrons Up!* 213 Once he gets the enemy lined up in that ring, it is curtains for the enemy. **1956** WALLIS & BLAIR *Thunder Above* (1959) xii. 131 If the Party ever got on to it..it would be curtains for Kurt.

e. *curtain up*: the beginning of a performance.

1942 E. S. L. ROBINSON *Curtain Up* 9 The call-boy makes his rounds rapping like Fate at each dressing-room door... 'Curtain up.' **1968** *Guardian* 19 Feb. 6/1 Curtain-up is a month away. **1969** 'S. TROY' *Swift to its Close* vi. 90 What are you going to do till curtain-up?

3. a. *transf.* and *fig.* Anything that covers or hides.

1430 LYDG. *Chron. Troy* I. v, Under curtyn and veyle of honeste Is closed chaunge and mutabilitye. **1610** SHAKS. *Temp.* I. ii. 407 The fringed Curtaines of thine eye aduance, And say what thou see'st yond. **1796** H. HUNTER tr. *St. Pierre's Stud. Nat.* (1799) III. 141 The moon appeared.. enveloped with a cloudy curtain. **1855** BAIN *Senses & Int.* II. ii. §2 The circular curtain called the *iris.* **1858** LONGF. *Birds of Passage, Jewish Cemetery* ii, The trees..o'er their sleep wave their broad curtains.

b. *Mil.* (In full *curtain of fire, curtain fire.*) A concentration of rapid and continuous artillery or machine-gun fire, etc., on a designated line or area, to prevent the advance or retreat of enemy troops, or to clear the way for the combatant's advance. Also, a concentration of fire to block the progress of aircraft.

1916 'BOYD CABLE' *Action Front* 114 Shells began to batter at their parapet, and to prepare a curtain of fire along their front. **1920** D. A. MACALISTER *Field Gunnery* (ed. 4) vii. 157 During an attack..the batteries, acting in concert, establish the 'curtain of fire' or 'barrage'. **1922** *Encycl. Brit.* XXX. 98/2 The idea also was evolved of barrage fire, a curtain of bursting shell to be put up in the path of the raiders. **1943** T. HORSLEY *Find, Fix & Strike* 92 We..began our glide through the curtain of lead towards the inner harbour.

c. Short for *iron curtain* (see IRON *sb.*[1]); also with capital initial. Also used in similar metaphors, esp. implying restriction of information.

1945 *Sunday Empire News* 21 Oct. 2/2 (*heading*) A curtain across Europe. **1946** *Spectator* 13 Sept. 257/2 The Russians ..would admit their 'iron curtain', but pointed out that there was also the Anglo-U.S. 'uranium curtain'. **1949** [see BAMBOO *sb.* 2]. **1950** M. PETERSON (*title*) Both sides of the Curtain. **1953** *School & Society* LXXVIII. 129 (*title*) The language curtain. **1955** *Times* 21 July 6/4 The reaction at G.H.Q. East Africa has been to tighten even further its own security curtain. **1970** 'W. HAGGARD' *Hardliners* iv. 37 A foreigner from behind the Curtain.

4. a. *Fortif.* The plain wall of a fortified place; the part of the wall which connects two bastions, towers, gates, or similar structures. *complement of the curtain*: see COMPLEMENT.

1569 STOCKER tr. *Diod. Sic.* I. iv. 9 The towne was well manned..and the curten of suche heigth and thicknes that the besieged with great ease became victors. **1571** DIGGES *Pantom.* I. xxv. H b, Laders that shall reache from the brym of the ditch or edge of the counterscarfe, to the top of the wal or curtein. **1670** COTTON *Espernon* I. III. 113 They..pass'd within forty paces of the Courtine which play'd upon them all the while. **1759** STERNE *Tr. Shandy* II. xii, The curtain, Sir, is the word we use in fortification, for that part of the wall.. which lies between the two bastions. **1871** *Daily News* 7 Feb., There is a small breach in the curtain of the southern front.

b. *Archit.* A plain enclosing wall not supporting a roof.

1633 J. DONE *Hist. Septuagint* 61 About the same [the temple] is a girt of three Curtaines of Wals raysed in the Ayre, to the height [etc.]. **1865** W. G. PALGRAVE *Arabia* I. 76 A large semicircular curtain.. built roughly and unsymmetrically with rubble and coarse blocks. **1879** SIR G. SCOTT *Lect. Archit.* I. 59 The wall, in fact (where the system [of attaching buttresses] was carried to its extreme limits), became a mere curtain.

5. *Nat. Hist.* **a.** In mushrooms or fungi, the *velum partiale*, a marginal veil hanging from the pileus as a shreddy membrane. **b.** In bivalve molluscs, the inner pendent margin of the mantle.

1796 WITHERING *Brit. Plants* (ed. 3) IV. 155 When very young some woolly fibres connect the pileus to the stem in place of a curtain. **1846** *Proc. Berw. Nat. Club* II. 175 Profusely covered over its pileus, curtain, and stem, with a yellowish powder. **1854** WOODWARD *Mollusca* (1856) 260 Animal (of meleagrina) with mantle-lobes united at one point by the gills, their margins fringed and furnished with a pendent curtain; curtains fringed in the branchial region.

6. *techn.* **a.** A partition in the leaden chamber in which sulphurous acid is converted into sulphuric acid. **b.** The piece of leather which overlaps the parting of a portmanteau, trunk, etc. **c.** In some locks, a circular plate revolving round the keyhole, which closes it up when any instrument is introduced in an attempt to pick the lock.

1874 in KNIGHT *Dict. Mech.* **1875** URE *Dict. Arts* III. 958 These leaden chambers are sometimes divided into 3 or 4 compartments by leaden curtains placed in them.. These curtains serve to detain the vapours, and cause them to advance in a gradual manner through the chamber.

d. A contrivance consisting of wooden slats which can be rolled up: *spec.* one of a number of these used to form a dam or weir. Also *attrib.*, as ***curtain-dam, -valve, -weir.***

1895 *Montgomery Ward Catal.* 608/3 Low Curtain Office Desk... Has lap joint, dust and knife proof curtain. **1903** THOMAS & WATT *Improvem. Rivers* viii. 244 Curtain Dams. .. The Caméré curtain.. consists of narrow horizontal strips of wood, hinged together, and capable of being rolled up by a chain. *Ibid.* 253 The space between the two rows [of shutters] was then filled with water by opening curtain-valves. **1927** E. WEYMANN *Dams* 586 The curtains are suspended from hooks on the face of the frames. **1929** *Encycl. Brit.* XXIII. 489/1 The curtain weir... In it wooden curtains that can be rolled up from the bottom were substituted for the needles in the Poirée weir.

7. *attrib.* **a.** Pertaining to a curtain or curtains.

1599 MARSTON *Sco. Villanie* III. xi. 226 What ere he saies Is warranted by Curtaine plaudities. **1881** *Daily News* 23 Aug. 3/6 In the curtain department an increased business is being done.. many curtain machines are still well employed. **1885** *Century Mag.* XXIX. 553/2 A long curtain-calico gown.

†**b.** Done behind the curtains; secret, hidden.

1660 HICKERINGILL *Jamaica* (1661) 69 We thunder fear, A toy to th' Curtain-whisper in the Ear. **1673** JANEWAY *Heaven on E.* (1847) 135 He knew.. our most secret workings, our closet curtain-business.

8. *Comb.*, as ***curtain-cord, -lifter; curtain-like*** adj.; **curtain-angle**, the angle formed at a bastion, etc., where the curtain begins; **curtain-call**, a call by an audience for an actor or actors to take a bow after the fall of the curtain (see 2); †**curtain-coach**, a coach with curtains in the window-spaces; **curtain-fall**, the fall of the curtain at the end of an act or scene; the situation or tableau when the curtain falls; also *fig.*; **curtain hook**, any of a number of hooks that may be attached to a curtain in order to hook it on to curtain rings or to a curtain rail; **curtain line**, the last line of a play, act, or scene; also *transf.*; **curtain-paper** (see quot.); **curtain-pole**, = *curtain-rod*; **curtain rail** = *curtain-rod*; **curtain-raiser** (orig. *slang*), a short opening piece performed before the principal play of the evening (cf. *lever de rideau*); also *transf.*; **curtain-ring**, one of the rings by which a curtain is hung on the curtain rod, and which slide on the rod when the curtain is drawn; **curtain rise**, the rise of the curtain at the beginning of an act or scene; **curtain-rod**, the horizontal rod from which a curtain is suspended; **curtain wall**, (*a*) see sense 4 b; (*b*) see quot. 1901; also ***curtain walling***; hence ***curtain-walled*** adj. Also CURTAIN-LECTURE, -SERMON.

1884 'F. LESLIE' *Let.* 15 July in W. T. Vincent *Recoll. F.L.* (1893) I. x. 176 You will find a room specially adapted for rehearsing *curtain calls. **1919** WODEHOUSE *Damsel in Distress* xii. 144 He felt a wave of stage-fright such as he had only once experienced before in his life—on the occasion when he had been young enough to take a curtain-call on a first-night. **1706** *Lond. Gaz.* No. 4224/3 Three Hackney Glass Coaches.. and a very good *Curtain Coach to carry 6 People. **1523** FITZHERB. *Husb.* §58 Take a smalle *curteyne corde, and bynde it harde aboute the beastes necke. **1863** A. D. WHITNEY *Faith Gartney's Girlh.* xvii, She drew the curtain-cord to let in the first sunbeam. **1939** T. S. ELIOT *Old Possum's Pract. Cats* 14 The curtain-cord she likes to wind. **1900** T. E. PEMBERTON *Kendals* ix. 276 He must be forgiven and at *curtain-fall live happily ever after. **1909** *Daily Chron.* 26 Jan. 5/6 'A Merry Christmas!' he shouts light-heartedly at curtain-fall. **1962** *Times* 27 Nov. 14/7 Within the confines of curtain-rise and curtain-fall. *c* **1505** *Curtain hook [see *curtain rod*]. **1898** C. S. PEEL *New Home* xiv. 237 Curtain-hooks.. should be button-holed on with waxed thread. **1982** H. O'LEARY *Curtains & Blinds* i. 16 Curtain hooks are attached to the curtain heading and then inserted through runners or gliders on the curtain track. **1939** D. L. SAYERS *In Teeth of Evidence* 200 'I will rest on my laurels'—that was a beautiful *curtain line you gave him there. **1959** *Listener* 31 Dec. 1171/2 Conversations [in a novel] end with brave, ringing curtain lines. **1858** SIMMONDS *Dict. Trade*, **Curtain-paper*, a peculiar kind of paper-hangings made in the Western States of America.. used as substitutes for roller blinds by a large class of people. **1874** KNIGHT *Dict. Mech.*, *Curtain-paper*, a heavy paper, printed and otherwise ornamented, for window-shades. **1865** GEO. ELIOT *Ess.* (1884) 206 Unctuous personages.. who soar above the *curtain-poles without any broomstick. **1908** *Sears, Roebuck Catal.* 880/1 Heavy brass curtain pole rings. **1924** *Cabinet Maker* 5 July Suppl. p. xlv. (Advt.), The [Arthur Clay] ball bearing *curtain rail. **1982** H. O'LEARY *Curtains & Blinds* i. 15 (*heading*) Curtain tracks and rails. **1886** *Birm. Wkly. Mercury* 23 Oct. 5 The slight opening pieces, or '*curtain raisers' as they are profanely styled.. are often hurried through amid much confusion. **1892** *Leeds Mercury* 1 Apr. 5/3 A new piece.. put on as a curtain-raiser for 'Lady Windermere's Fan'. **1940** *War Illustr.* 26 Jan. 24 What has happened to date is the curtain-raiser to that aerial blitzkrieg which is still part of the stock-in-trade of the Nazi boasters. **1955** *Times* 27 July 2/6 There was a curtain raiser earlier this month when the case was put that the proposed scheme was ultra vires. **1969** *Australian* 24 May 36/6 The three Australian selectors.. will watch Sydney Seconds.. in the curtain-raiser before focusing on the main game. **1905** *Daily Chron.* 11 Feb. 6/2 Miss Tree sings, at *curtain-rise, to very charming purpose. **1962** Curtain-rise [see *curtain-fall*]. **1483** *Act 1 Rich. III*, c. 12 §2 No Merchant Stranger.. shall bring into this Realm.. Hanging Lavers, *Curtain-rings, Cards for Wooll. **1719** D'URFEY *Pills* (1872) III. 123 I'll rattle his Curtain-rings every Night. *c* **1505** *Churchw. Acc. St. Dunstan's, Canterbury*, For *curten roddis and hookys. **1792** WOLCOTT (P. Pindar) *Ode to Margate Hoy* Wks. 1812 III. 65 With fingers.. loaded much like Curtain-rods with Rings. **1853** TURNER *Dom. Archit.* III. II. vii. 226 A *curtain wall connecting it. **1879** SIR G. SCOTT *Lect. Archit.* I. 250 As buttresses increased in projection, greater and greater openings in the curtain wall were ventured on. **1901** R. STURGIS *Dict. Archit. & Building* 731/1 **Curtain wall.* In modern construction, most often a thin subordinate wall between two piers or other supporting members; the curtain being primarily a filling and having no share—or but little—in the support of other portions of the structure. Thus, in skeleton construction, curtain walls are built between each two encased columns and.. on a girder at each floor level. **1930** *Engineering* 1 Aug. 131/3 The curtain wall[of the Welland Ship Canal] is 3 ft. 6 in. thick and set back 10 ft. 6 in. from the upstream face. **1950** *Archit. Rev.* CVII. 221 On the ground (banking floor) these curtain walls are of glass blocks to give the maximum light without permitting passers-by to see inside. **1952** *Ibid.* CXII. 392 'Curtain wall' is a recent American term for a form of rigid skin walling. It is basically an extension of sheet cladding to cover wider spans... In a more developed form it includes the growing practice, particularly on slab blocks, of covering a complete elevation with subsidiary framing holding both cladding and windows. **1959** *Listener* 3 Dec. 976/2 *Curtain-walled office-blocks. **1958** *Archit. Rev.* Jan. 7 The increasing use of *curtain walling and similar systems. **1963** *Listener* 28 Feb. 371/1 Curtain walling has made it possible to turn the whole facade into a huge shiny texture. *Ibid.* 371/2 Curtain walling is being used to create simple geometric form at the expense of the spaces behind.

curtain, *sb.*[2] Variant of COURTIN.

1853 *Jrnl. R. Agric. Soc.* XIV. II. 316 The cattle are kept in open curtains with shedding, each curtain containing from 8 to 12 animals.

'curtain, *v.* [f. CURTAIN *sb.*[1]]

1. To furnish, surround, cover, adorn, with a curtain or curtains.

c **1300** *K. Alis.* 1028 With samytes, and baudekyns, Weore cortined the gardynes. *c* **1340** *Gaw. & Gr. Knt.* 1181 G. þe god mon, in gay bed lygez.. Vnder couertour ful clere, cortyned aboute. **1605** [see CURTAINED]. *c* **1611** CHAPMAN *Iliad* v. 199 Eleven fair chariots stay.. Curtain'd and arrast under foot. **1828** SCOTT *Tapestried Chamber*, The tapestry hangings, which.. curtained the walls of the little chamber.

b. *transf.* and *fig.* To cover, conceal, veil, protect, shut *off*, as with a curtain.

c **1430** LYDG. *Bochas* VIII. xxiv, Some skyes donne Myght percase curtayne his beames clere. **1588** SHAKS. *Tit. A.* II. iii. 24 When with a happy storme they were surpris'd, And Curtain'd with a Counsaile-keeping Caue. **1607** WALKINGTON *Opt. Glass* ii. (1664) 22 Curtained, and over-shadowed with a palpable darkness. **1861** GEO. ELIOT *Silas M.* 95 A supreme immediate longing that curtained off all futurity—the longing to lie down and sleep.

Hence **'curtained** *ppl. a.*, **'curtaining** *vbl. sb.* (spec. *colloq.* in *Painting*, the formation of 'curtains': see CURTAIN *sb.*[1] 1 e and *ppl. a.*

1605 SHAKS. *Macb.* II. i. 51 Wicked Dreames abuse The Curtain'd sleepe. **1820** KEATS *Lamia* II. 18 Near to a curtaining Whose airy texture, from a golden string, Floated into the room. **1836** DICKENS *Sk. Boz* (1877) 2 The churchwardens.. duly installed in their curtained pews. **1883** *Harper's Mag.* Jan. 196/1 A sudden escape from curtaining oak branches brought us full upon the summit. **1940** in *Chambers's Techn. Dict.* 217/1. **1953** in *Gloss. Paint. Terms* (*B.S.I*) II.

'curtain-'lecture. 'A reproof given by a wife to her husband in bed' (Johnson).

1633 T. ADAMS *Exp. 2 Peter* ii. 5 Often have you heard how much a superstitious wife, by her curtain lectures, hath wrought upon her Christian husband. **1660** HICKERINGILL *Jamaica* (1661) 85, I am not awed.. with the dreadfull Catechisme of a Curtain Lecture. **1710** ADDISON *Tatler* No. 243 ¶4 He was then lying under the Discipline of a Curtain-Lecture. **1846** D. JERROLD (*title*), Mrs. Caudle's Curtain-lectures. **1851** THACKERAY *Eng. Hum.* iii. (1876) 233 As confidential as a curtain-lecture.

Hence ,**curtain-'lecture** *v.*

1859 G. MEREDITH *R. Feverel* iii, No curtain-lecturing with a pipe.

'curtainless, *a.* Without a curtain.

1822 ELIZA NATHAN *Langreath* III. 387 The curtainless casement. **1863** MISS BRADDON *J. Marchmont* I. ii. 29 The pale wintry sunshine, creeping in at the curtainless window.

†**'curtain-'sermon.** *Obs.* = CURTAIN-LECTURE.

1611 SPEED *Hist. Gt. Brit.* IX. xv. §44 The Curtaine-Sermons nightly enlarged vpon the same Text. **1621–51** BURTON *Anat. Mel.* III. iii. IV. ii. 629. **1631** R. H. *Arraignm. Whole Creature* xv. §2. 255 He heares Curtaine.. Sermons, ere the Morning.

curtais(e, -aisi, obs. ff. COURTEOUS, COURTESY.

†**curtal** ('kɜːtəl), *sb.* and *a.* *Obs.* exc. *Hist.* (or *arch.*). Forms: see the senses. [In 16th c. also *courtault*, *curtald*, a. 15th c. F. *courtault*, *-auld*, now *courtaud*:—OF. *cortald*, *curtald*; cf. It. *cortalda* short bombard, pot gun, *cortaldo petriero* a short perrier; a derivative of Romanic *corto*, F. *court*, 'short', with suffix *-aldo*, *-ald*, *-alt*, *-aud*, of Teutonic origin: cf. Diez *Gram.* III. I. i. 3. French has the various senses 'short or dumpy man', 'docked horse or dog', 'short piece of artillery', 'short bassoon', which have been at various times, and more or less independently, taken into English.]

A. as *sb.* **I.** 6 **courtault, -tall, -tal,** 6–7 **cortall, curtall,** (6 **curtell, -tole, -tayle,** 6–7 **-toll, -taile,** 6–8 **-tail**), 6– **curtal.**

1. A horse with its tail cut short or docked (and sometimes the ears cropped); app. sometimes a horse of a particular breed or small size, with which this practice was usual. Cf. COCKTAIL *sb.*

1530 PALSGR. 68 *Covrtavlt*, a courtall, a horse. *Ibid.* 506/1, I wyll cutte of my horse tayle and make hym a courtault. **1564–78** BULLEYN *Dial. agst. Pest.* (1888) 80 You can make a stoned horse a geldyng, and a longe taile a courtall. **1577–87** HOLINSHED *Chron.* III. 1056/2 Mounted on a curtaile. **1610** MARKHAM *Masterp.* (1636) 539 Of the making of Curtals, or cutting off of the tailes of Horses. **1611** COTGR., *Double courtaut*, a strong curtall; or, a horse of a middle size betweene th' ordinarie curtall, and horse of seruice. **1620** E. BLOUNT *Horæ Subs.* 36 They.. thence vpon their Curtoe.. goe to the Tauerne. **1653** H. COGAN tr. *Pinto's Trav.* xxxix. 156 Six pages apparelled in his livery mounted on white Curtals.

2. *transf.* and *fig.* **a.** Any animal that has lost its tail. **b.** Anything docked, or cut short.

1607 TOPSELL *Serpents* (1608) 696 Certain [serpents].. whose bodies of an equal.. thicknesse, so as they appear without tails; being for that purpose called 'Decurtati', Curtails. **1669** *Address Yng. Gentry Eng.* 80 There remains nothing of it but the shade of a great name, the empty curtail of its faint eccho. **1866** LOWELL *Biglow P.* Introd., Consider what a poor curtal we have made of Ocean. There was something of his heave and expanse in o-ce-an.

3. Applied to persons: **a.** with fig. reference to sense 1: One whose ears are cropped.

1592 GREENE *Upst. Courtier* in *Harl. Misc.* (Malh.) II. 235, I am made a curtall, for the pillory.. hath eaten off both my eares.

b. *cant.* A rogue who wears a short cloak.

(In quot. 1725 differently explained.)

1561 AWDELAY *Frat. Vacab.* 4 A Curtall is much like to the Upright man.. He useth commonly to go with a short cloke, like to grey Friers. **1567** HARMAN *Caveat* 37 There bee of these Roges Curtales, wearinge shorte clokes. *a* **1700** B. E. *Dict. Cant. Crew*, *Curtals*, the Eleventh Rank of the Canting Crew. **1725** *New Cant. Dict.*, *Curtails*.. so called from their Practice to cut off Pieces of Silk, Cloth, Linen or Stuff, that were hung out at the Shop-Windows of Mercers, etc... Also a Species of Cut-purses.

c. A term of derision or opprobrium. [Direct connexion with F. *courtaud* 'short or dumpy person' is doubtful.]

1578 WHETSTONE *Promos & Cass.* I. iv. (N.), Were you born in a myll, curtole, that you prate so hye. **1581** J. BELL *Haddon's Answ. Osor.* 201 b, That this creeppled curtoll of Osorius may stand upright upon his legges. *c* **1612** BEAUM & FL. *Thierry* I. i, Your old and honor'd Mistress, you tyr'd curtals, Suffers for your base sins.

d. A drab. [Perhaps referring to short skirts.]

1611 COTGR., *Caignardiere*, a hedge-whore, lazie queane, lowsie trull, filthie curtall, Doxie, Morte. **1706** PHILLIPS (ed. Kersey), *Curtail*, a Drab, or nasty Slut.

II. 6 **courtault, curtald, cortoute,** 6–7 **curtall,** 7 **cortal;** *pl.* 6–7 **curtaux, -tawes, -towes.**

4. a. A kind of cannon with a comparatively short barrel, in use in the 16th and 17th c. The ***demi-*** or ***half***, and ***double curtall*** were smaller and larger varieties.

a **1509** RAMSAY *Let. to Hen. VII* in Pinkerton *Hist. Scot.* II. 440 (Jam.), ij great curtaldis that war send out of France. **1530** PALSGR. 448/1 They bended agaynst the castell ten courtaultes and fyftene serpentynes. **1548** HALL *Chron.* (1809) 671 Bombards Curtawes and demy Curtaux. *Ibid.*

680 One pece of ordinaunce called a Curtall. *Ibid.* 693 Double Curtalls. **1629** *Shertogenbosh* 36 The Enemies did shoot aboue 110 shot with halfe Curtowes. **1664** *Flodden F.* ii. 18 Culverings and Cortals great, And double Canons two or three.

b. ***curtal-sonnet*** (see quot.).

a **1889** G. M. HOPKINS *Poems* (1918) Pref. 6, Nos. 13 and 22 are Curtal-Sonnets, that is they are constructed in proportions resembling those of the sonnet proper, namely 6 + 4 instead of 8 + 6, with however a halfline tailpiece (so that the equation is rather $\frac{12}{2} + \frac{9}{2} = \frac{21}{2} = 10\frac{1}{2}$.

III. 6 curtoll, 7–8 courtel, 8 curtail, -till, curtal, (8–9 courtaud, -aut).

5. An obsolete musical instrument, a kind of bassoon; also an organ-stop of similar quality of tone; also ***double curtal***.

1582 BATMAN *Upon Barthol.* 423/1 *marg.*, The common bleting musicke is yᵉ Drone, Hobius, and Curtoll. **168..** *Let.* in Hawkins *Hist. Mus.* (1776) V. 355 Then Mr. Harris challenged Father Smith to make additional stops..these were the Vox-humane, the Cremona or Violin stop, the double Courtel or base Flute. **1706** E. WARD *Hud. Rediv.* (1707) II. v. 24 With Voice as hoarse as double Curtal. **1776** HAWKINS *Hist. Mus.* IV. ix. 139 An instrument, called, by reason of its shortness, the Courtaut. **1888** STAINER & BARRETT *Mus. Terms, Courtaut, Cortaud, Corthal,* an ancient instrument of the bassoon kind.

B. *attrib.* or *adj.* Also 6–7 curtall, -toll.

1. Of horses: Having the tail docked; made a curtal.

1576 *Inv.* in *Ripon Ch. Acts* 377 A curtall nagge. **1578** in W. H. Turner *Select Rec. Oxford* 396 One grey trotting curtoll mare. **1632** *Thomas of Reading* in Thoms *Prose Rom.* (1858) I. 146 If he ware a long taile, he would make him curtall. *c* **1640** J. SMYTH *Lives Berkeleys* (1883) I. 208 A Dun Curtall horse with a white head and black mane.

2. Of dogs: Having the tail cut short or cut off.

1590 SHAKS. *Com. Err.* III. ii. 151, I thinke..she had transform'd me to a Curtull dog, and made me turne i'th wheele. **1599** *Pass. Pilgr.* 273 My curtail dog, that wont to have play'd, Plays not at all, but seems afraid. *a* **1663** *R. Hood & Curtal Fryer* xxxiv. in Child *Ballads* (1888) III. v. 125/2 The curtal dogs, so taught they were, They kept their arrows in their mouth.

3. Shortened, short in linear dimension.

1590 GREENE *Orl. Fur.* (1599) 45 What has thou mard my sword? The pummel's well, the blade is curtall short. **1605** CAMDEN *Rem.* (1657) 195 A new round curtall weed which they called a cloak. **1630** J. TAYLOR (Water-P.) *Vertue of a Tayle* Wks. II. 128/2 He notes the curtall cannes halfe fild with froth.

4. Abridged, curtailed; brief, scant, curt.

1579 FULKE *Refut. Rastel* 750 There needeth none other creed..but onely this short curtall creed. **1579** TOMSON *Calvin's Serm. Tim.* 623/1 Wee muste not take this so short and curtall a passage for a life. **1649** MILTON *Eikon.* Wks. 1738 I. 410 Matters of this moment..not to be..determin'd here by Essays and curtal Aphorisms. *a* **1661** HOLYDAY *Juvenal* 255 A thankless countrey's curtal love.

5. Of the nature of a curtal or drab: see A. 3 d.

1595 GOSSON *Quippes Upst. Gentlewom.* 278 Next, curtaile flurt, as ranke as beast.

6. ***curtal friar***: app. a friar with a short frock; cf. A. 3 b, quot. 1561, B. 3 , quot. 1605.

Applied in ballads to the friar (Tuck) who plays a part in some Robin Hood stories, called also 'cutted friar'. Hence, as a vague archaism, in Scott. [The conjecture that *curtal* here means *curtilanus*, as 'having the care and keeping of the *curtile* or vegetable garden', is inadmissible.]

c **1610** *Ballad* (Pepysian Libr. I. No. 37), The famous Battelle betweene Robin Hood and the Curtall Fryer. *a* **1663** *R. Hood & Curtal Fryer* vi. in Child *Ballads* (1888) III. v. 124/1 There lives a curtal frier in Fountains Abby Will beat both him and thee. *Ibid.* xiii. *ibid.* 124/2 Carry me over the water, thou curtal frier. **1820** SCOTT *Ivanhoe* xxxii, Now, sirs, who hath seen our chaplain? where is our curtal Friar? *Ibid.*, Curtal Priest..thou hast been at wet mass this morning. **1888** F. J. CHILD *Ballads* III. v. No. 117 A curtal, or cutted friar, called Friar Tuck.

curtal, -all, obs. forms of CURTAIL *v.*

† **'curtal-ax, -axe.** *Obs.* exc. *Hist.* (or *arch.*). Forms: 6–7 curtleax(e, 6 curtilax, 6–7 courtelax(e, curtelax(e, 7 curt-, courtlax, curtelaxe, courtle-axe, cortelax, 6–9 curtle-ax(e, curtle axe, 8– curtal-axe. [A much perverted form of the word CUTLASS *sb.* (in 16th c. *coutelas, coutelase, cuttleass,* etc.), through the intermediate perversions *cut(t)le-ax,* and *curtelas, courtelace,* CURTELACE, the peculiarities of which it combines. The form *curtal-ax,* with its variants, was so distinct from *cutlass,* that it acquired a kind of permanent standing, the identification of the final part with AXE, *axe,* being favoured by the use of the weapon in delivering slashing blows.]

A short broad cutting sword, a CUTLASS *sb.*; any heavy slashing sword. (Apparently sometimes taken by persons unfamiliar with the weapon for some kind of battle-axe. Cf. Spenser's CURTAXE.)

1579–80 NORTH *Plutarch* (1676) 798 His Father..drew out his Curtleax and wounded him. **1590** LODGE *Euphues Gold. Leg.* Pref., Hewn down by a soldier with his curtle axe. **1600** SHAKS. *A.Y.L.* I. iii. 119 A gallant curtelax vpon my thigh. **1610** GUILLIM *Heraldry* III. xxi. (1660) 229 A Fawcheon or Court-lax to slash and wound his Enemy. **1665** G. HAVERS *P. della Valle's Trav. E. India* 109 A short and very broad Sword like a Cortelax. **1813** SCOTT *Triermain* III. xiii, A weighty curtal-axe he bare. **1874** MOTLEY *Barneveld* I. viii. 334 Swinging the sharpest curtal-axes.

† **'curtalize,** *v. Obs.* [f. CURTAL + -IZE.] = CURTAIL.

1622 WITHER *Philar.* Postscr., Do they think that I will.. Mayme or Curtolize my free Invention Because Fooles weary are of their attention. **1638** BASTWICK *Brief Relation* 12 To curtolize a Romans eares, like a Curre. **1655** FULLER *Ch. Hist.* XI. vii. §64 How unworthy it was to curtallize his Eares.

curtall, obs. form of CURTAL, CURTAIL.

† **'curtan.** *Obs.* Also cortan, curtane. [Anglicized from next.] A broad, pointless sword.

1697 DAMPIER *Voy.* (1698) I. xiv. 400 She had about 40 men all armed with Cortans, or broad Swords. **1699** *Ibid.* II. I. iv. 80 The Executioner being provided with a large Curtane or Backsword..at one stroke he severs the head from the body.

‖ **curtana** (kɜːˈtɑːnə, -ˈeɪnə). Also 3 curtein, 7 curteyn, -teine, CURTAN. [The AF. form *curtein* is identical with OF. *cortain, courtain,* the name of the sword of Roland, so called, according to the *Karlamagnus-saga,* because it broke a little at the point, when thrust into a block or *perron* of steel (Gaston Paris, *Charlem.* 370, and see Godefroy). The word is an extended derivative of L. *curtus,* Rom. *corto,* OF. *cort, curt* shortened, short: cf. *certain* from L. *certus,* and, for the sense, CURTAL *a.* 3, *curted,* quot. 1610 (s.v. CURT *v.*). The Anglo-L. form *curtana* appears to be an adj. feminine, agreeing with *spatha, spada,* sword.]

The pointless sword borne before the kings of England at their coronation; emblematically considered the sword of mercy; also called the sword of King Edward the Confessor.

In the Coronation procession *Curtana* is borne in the front rank of the regalia, supported to the right and the left by two pointed swords, the sword of justice, and the third sword, all three being drawn; they are followed by Garter King of Arms, the Lord Great Chamberlain, and the Sword of State borne in its scabbard; then follow the Sceptre, St. Edward's Crown, and the Orb, borne abreast; then the Paten and the Chalice abreast, immediately in front of the Sovereign.

a **1259** MATTHEW PARIS (*Coron. Hen. III*), Comite Cestriæ gladium S. Edwardi qui curtein dicitur ante regem bajulante. **1308** *Rot. Claus. 1st Edw. II* (in *Rymer*), Et gladium qui vocatur curtana portavit Comes Lancastriæ. **1377** *Officia in Coronationem* (Maskell *Mon. Rit.* II. 73), Deinde sequentur tres comites gladios gestantes induti serico, comes quidem Cestriæ..portabit gladium qui vocatur curtana. **1483** *Wardr. Acc. 1 Rich. III*, iij swerdes whereof oon with a flat poynt, called curtana. **1607** COWELL *Interpr.*, Curteyn was the name of King Edward the sainct his sword, which is the first sword that is carried before the kings..at their coronation. **1685** *Acct. Coronation* in *Lond. Gaz.* No. 2028/1 The Sword of State, the Sword Curtana, and the two pointed Swords, together with the Gold Spurs, were presented to His Majesty, and laid on a Table before Him. **1687** DRYDEN *Hind & P.* II. 419 When Curtana will not do the deed, You lay that pointless clergy-weapon by, And to the laws, your sword of justice, fly. **1700** TYRRELL *Hist. Eng.* II. 892 The Earl of Chester..carried the Sword of St. Edward, called *Curteine,* before the King. **1702** C. FIENNES *Diary* (1888) 254, 3 other Lords following wᵗʰ yᵉ sword of justice, yᵉ Curtana sword of mercy, and another poynted sword. **1820** A. TAYLOR *Glory of Regality* 71 The principal sword which is borne before our kings at their coronation is the sword of Mercy called *Curtana.*

curtas(e, -asi(e, obs. forms of COURTEOUS, COURTESY.

curtast, obs. superl. of COURTEOUS.

curtate (ˈkɜːteɪt), *a. Geom.* and *Astron.* [ad. L. *curtāt-us,* f. *curtāre* to cut short: see CURT *v.*]

1. Shortened, reduced; applied to a line projected orthographically upon a plane. ***curtate distance***: the distance of a planet or comet from the sun or earth, projected upon the plane of the ecliptic. ***curtate cycloid***: see CYCLOID.

1676 HALLEY in Rigaud *Corr. Sci. Men* (1841) I. 239 As cosine of inclination to radius, so SP, the curtate distance, to the true distance of the planet from the sun. **1726** [see CURTATION 2]. **1833** HERSCHEL *Astron.* viii. 275. **1893** J. R. HARRIS *Stichometry* 18 The lines represent respectively a somewhat curtate half-hexameter and a similarly divided iambic trimeter.

2. *Economics* and *Statistics.* Shortened or limited according to some formula or rule; *esp.* counting or calculated for the number of full years in a period, to the exclusion of the odd fraction of a year.

1875 *Encycl. Brit.* II. 78 This formula gives the average number of *complete* years that persons of the given age will live..and makes no allowance for the portion of the year in which death occurs. The expectation thus found is called the curtate expectation. **1927** BOWLEY & STAMP *Nat. Income, 1924* 21 When the averages of these curtate groups are taken, that for women is often higher than for men. **1927** B. C. HOSKINS *Insur. Lexicon* 134 If payments cease with the last payment preceding the death, the annuity is said to be 'non-apportionable', or 'without proportion', or 'curtate'. **1957** KENDALL & BUCKLAND *Dict. Statistical Terms* 75 If an assurance matures in 3 years 9 months, the curtate duration is 3 years.

† **'curtated,** *ppl. a.* [f. as prec. + -ED.] = prec.

1749 B. MARTIN *Dict., Curtation,* the difference between the distance of a planet from the sun and a curtated distance.

cur'tation. [n. of action from L. *curtāre* to shorten.]

† **1.** *Alch.* The shorter process for transmuting metals into gold. *Obs.*

1584 R. SCOT *Discov. Witchcr.* XIV. v. 301 In this art there are two waies, the one called longation, the other curtation. **1606** BRETON *Ourania* Song K iij a, Perilous is the way of Curtation. **1699** R. L'ESTRANGE *Colloq. Erasm.* (1711) 217 Vouchsafe to instruct me in the blessed way of Curtation.

2. *Astron.* The difference between the true and the curtate distance of a planet from the sun.

1706 PHILLIPS (ed. Kersey), *Curtation of a Planet,* is a little part cut off from the Line of its Interval, or Distance from the Sun. **1726** tr. *Gregory's Astron.* I. 467 The Curtation, which being substracted from the Distance of the Planet from the Sun in its own Orbit..leaves the Curtate Distance of the Planet from the Sun.

'curtatively, *adv. rare.* [f. CURTATE + -IVE + -LY.] In a shortened or clipt manner.

1826 G. S. FABER *Diff. Romanism* (1853) 326 *note,* Through this dexterous alternation of quoting and suppressing..Ambrose, as thus curtatively exhibited, appears [etc.].

† **'curtaxe.** *Obs. rare*⁻¹. An alteration of CURTAL-AXE, probably with a supposed derivation from *curt* short, and *axe.*

1596 SPENSER *F.Q.* IV. ii. 42 With curtaxe used Diamond to smite, And Triamond to handle speare and shield, But speare and curtaxe both usd Priamond in field.

curtays(e, -eis(e, obs. forms of COURTEOUS.

curtby, -eby, -epy, vars. of COURTEPY *Obs.*

curtchie, obs. form of COURTESY, CURTSY.

curted: see CURT *v.*

curtein, -teyn: see CURTANA.

† **'curtel.** *Obs.* Also curtell(e, -tle, -til, -tyl(l. [ME. southern form of KIRTLE.]

1. = KIRTLE q.v.

2. Used by Trevisa to translate L. *tunica,* as a coat of an artery, and of the eye, and retained in this sense in the later versions of Bartholomew.

1398 TREVISA *Barth. de P.R.* III. xvii. (Tollem. MS.), þe smale curtyles and humouris of þe ye. *Ibid.* IV. vii, þe harde curtels of þe arteries. *Ibid.* XVII. lxxv, It is defendid..as it were with many curtils and cotes [*pluribus tuniculis*]. **1582** BATMAN *on Barthol.* v. iv. 38 The eye is made of tenne things. Of seauen smal curtils, and three humours.

† **curtelace.** *Obs.* Also 6 curtilace, 7 curtelas, -lasse, courtelace, courtlace, courtlas, curtlas. [A variant of *coutelace,* 16th c. F. *coutelas.* It is doubtful whether the *r* represents an earlier *l* (*coultelas,* cf. It. *coltellaccio*), or arises from phonetic corruption, or popular etymology.] A kind of short cutting sword; a cutlass.

1555 *Fardle Facions* II. vii. 160 Thei cary in their warres ..a curtilace. **1598** SYLVESTER *Du Bartas* II. i. I. (1641) 86/1 There springs the Shrub 3 foot above the grass, Which fears the keen edge of the Curtelace. **1611** COTGR., *Coutelas,* a Cuttelas, courtelas, or short sword. **1653** H. COGAN tr. *Pinto's Trav.* xv. 46 They sent him a Courtelas of great value. **1677** W. HUBBARD *Narrative* 127 One Davis his Serjeant cut the Bow-string with his Courtlace.

† **curtelain.** *Obs. rare.* [perh. repr. a med.L. **curtilānus* like *hortulānus.*] ? A gardener; the monk in charge of the garden of a monastery.

a **1300** *Cursor M.* 27240 (Cott.) In scrift..þe preist agh spere al wit resun..o monk, curtelain, or aduocate.

curtelax(e, obs. forms of CURTAL-AXE.

curteous, etc.: see COURTEOUS, etc.

curteynge, obs. form of CURTAIN.

Curt-hose (ˈkɜːthəʊz). [OF. *curte-hose* short boot, from OF. *hose, huese, hoese, house, heuse,* boot, in mod.Picard *heuse* a boot coming up to the knee, med.L. *hosa*; of Teutonic origin: cf. OHG. *hosa,* MLG. *hose,* MDu. *hoze,* Du. *hoos,* OE. *hose,* covering for the leg (and foot); see HOSE.] Short-boot, -legging, or -greave: a surname given to Robert, eldest son of William the Conqueror; the med.L. was *Curta ocrea.*

[*a* **1143** W. MALMESBURY *Gest. Reg.* IV. §389 (1840) II. 607 Genitore..dicente, 'Per resurrectionem Dei! probus erit Robelinus Curta Ocrea'. Hoc enim erat ejus cognomen, quod esset exiguus.] **12..** *Chron. de Mailros* (*Rerum Angl. Script. Vet.* (1684) I. 160), Rodbertus Curtehose guerram contra patrem suum movit. **1350–70** *Eulogium Hist.* (1863) III. v. ci. 40 Robertus Courthoese. **1460** CAPGRAVE *Chron.* (Rolls) 130 He..beqwathe..to Robert, clepid Curthose, the duchi of Normandie. **1839** KEIGHTLEY *Hist. Eng.* I. 97 Robert named Gambeson or 'Curthose' from the shortness of his legs.

† **curti-cone.** *Obs.* [f. L. *curt-us* short + CONE.] A truncated cone.

1706 PHILLIPS (ed. Kersey) s.v. *Truncated,* A Truncated Cone or the Frustum of that Body is sometimes call'd a

Curti-Cone. **1721** BAILEY, *Curti-Cone*, a Cone whose Top is cut off by a Plane parallel to its Basis. So later Dicts.

curtil, obs. form of KIRTLE.

curtilage (ˈkɜːtɪlɪdʒ). Also 4–5 (9) courte-, 5–6 curty-, 5–7 curte-, 6 corte-, 7 courtilage; 5 curt-, cortlage, 7 court-lodge, 7–9 courtledge, 9 courtlage, -lege. [a. AngloF. *curtilage*, OF. *cor-*, *courtillage* (med.L. *cor-*, *curtilagium*), f. *cortil*, *courtil* little court or garth, = Pr. *cortil*, It. *cortile*, med.L. *cortile*, *curtile* court, yard; f. *cortis*, *curtis*, It. *corte*, Pr. *cort*, OF. *cort*, *curt*, COURT; the suffix is the Romanic -AGE, as in *village*, etc. Popular etymology in 17th c. saw in it a compound of *court*, as *court-lodge*, *-ledge*, etc.]

A small court, yard, garth, or piece of ground attached to a dwelling-house, and forming one enclosure with it, or so regarded by the law; the area attached to and containing a dwelling-house and its out-buildings. Now mostly a legal or formal term, but in popular use in the south-west, where it is pronounced, and often written, *courtledge*.

[**1206** *Rotuli Chartarum* 163/1 Unum mesagium cum curtillag[io]. **1292** BRITTON III. vii. §5 Des gardins, curtilages, columbers, et des autres issues de eynz la court.] *c* **1330** *Owayn Miles* 32 This is our courtelage, And our castel tour. **1434** *E.E. Wills* (1882) 99 All my mesuage, with the curtylage and all the appurtenance. **1523** FITZHERB. *Surv.* 1 b, A curtylage is a lytell croft or court, or place of easment to put in catell for a tyme, or to ley in woode, cole, or tymbre, or suche other thynges necessary for housholde. **1586** J. HOOKER *Girald. Irel.* in *Holinshed* II. 174/1 He had gotten in within the iron doore or gate of the courtlodge all his men. **1613** SIR H. FINCH *Law* (1636) 158 And for his Winde-mill necessary increase of court or Court-lodge. **1649** PRYNNE *Demurrer to Jews' Remitter* 36 They may buy houses and curtelages. **1769** BLACKSTONE *Comm.* IV. 225 The capital house protects and privileges all it's branches and appurtenants, if within the curtilage or homestall. **1807** VANCOUVER *Agric. Devon* (1813) 211 Passing through the courtlege or farm-yards. **1855** KINGSLEY *Westw. Ho* xiv. (D.), At the back, a rambling courtledge of barns and walls. **1882** ELTON *Orig. Eng. Hist.* 190 Where several houses had been built within the enclosure or curtilage of one homestead.

†**b.** Tillage of a croft or kitchen-garden. *Obs.*

c **1430** LYDG. *Bochas* VIII. vi. (1554) 180 b, Dioclesian.. Left his craft of deluing and cortlage.

†ˈ**curtilate**, *v.* *Obs.*$^{-1}$ [f. CURTAL, app. after *mutilate*.] *trans.* To curtail.

1665 J. WEBB *Stone-Heng* (1725) 53 Mr. Jones cannot properly be said to have curtilated the Text.

†ˈ**curtiler.** *Obs. rare*$^{-1}$. [a. OF. *cortiller*, *courtillier*, f. *courtil*: see CURTILAGE.]

A gardener.

a **1300** *Vox & Wolf* 272 in *Rel. Ant.* II. 278 This ilke frere heyte Ailmer, He wes hoere maister curtiler. .... in SPELMAN *Gloss.* (1664) s.v. *Curtillum*, 'MS. quidam codex priscus *Hortulanos* interpretatur *curtilers*.'

curtin(e, obs. form of CURTAIN.

†**curti'pendulous**, *a.* *Obs.* [f. L. *curt-us* short + PENDULOUS *a.*] Hanging by a short stem.

1657 TOMLINSON *Renou's Disp.* 370 Fruits..which have no lignous pills, as all curtipendulous Apples.

curtis, -issie, obs. ff. COURTEOUS, COURTESY.

curtisaine, -san, -zan, obs. ff. COURTESAN.

curtlax, curtle-ax(e: see CURTAL-AXE.

curtling, obs. form of CURTAILING.

curtly (ˈkɜːtlɪ), *adv.* [f. CURT *a.* + -LY[2].] In a curt manner; †shortly, tersely (*obs.*).

1654 GAYTON *Pleas. Notes* IV. xv. 252 Mr. Licenciat.. hath curtly, succinctly, and concisely..epitomiz'd the long story. **1866** GEO. ELIOT *F. Holt* xxxv, 'Sit down', he said, curtly. **1874** GREEN *Short Hist.* iv. 201 A direct demand.. to nominate the great officers of state had been curtly rejected.

curtness (ˈkɜːtnɪs). [f. CURT *a.* + -NESS.] The quality of being curt.

1762 KAMES *Elem. Crit.* II. 130 (L.) The sense must be curtailed..to make it square with the curtness of the melody. **1882** OUIDA *Maremma* I. 94 She spoke with curtness.

curtoe: see CURTAL I.

curtois, -oys(e, -oyus, obs. ff. COURTEOUS.

curtol(l, obs. ff. CURTAL *sb.* and CURTAIL *v.*

curtsy, curtsey (ˈkɜːtsɪ), *sb.* Forms: α. See COURTESY. β. 6 curtsye, 6–7 -sie, 7 courtsie, curt'sie, 8 court'sie, court'sy, curt'sy, 8–9 courtsey, 6– curtsy, curtsey. γ. 6–7 curtchie, 7 courchie, 6–8 curchie. δ. 6–7 cursie, -sey, 7 -sy, -see, 8 coursey. [A variant of COURTESY, reduced to two syllables, and then sometimes altered to *curtchie*, *cursie*.]

1. = COURTESY in various senses (*esp.* 1 c, 6, 7).

1575 CHURCHYARD *Chippes* (1817) 111 Our enmyes now became more circumspect And curtsie made so nere our camp to come.

†**2.** The customary expression of respect by action or gesture; = COURTESY 8.

α. **1513**, etc. [see COURTESY 8].

β. *a* **1553** UDALL *Royster D.* III. iii. (Arb.) 48 To come behind, and make curtsie. **1599** SHAKS. *Much Ado* II. i. 56 It is my cosens dutie to make curtsie.

γ. **1587** CHURCHYARD *Worth. Wales* (1876) 79 Will curchie make.

δ. **1546** *St. Papers Hen. VIII*, XI. 13 We receyved many curseys of them that offered. **1580** LYLY *Euphues* 275 Thankes and cursie made to each other, we went to the fire.

3. An obeisance; now applied to a feminine movement of respect or salutation, made by bending the knees and lowering the body. Commonly ***to make, drop a curtsy***.

α. **1575** LANEHAM *Lett.* (1871) 42 At this, the minstrell made a pauz & a curtezy, for *Primus passus.* **1583** HOLLYBAND *Campo di Fior* 57 Put of thy cappe boye. Make a fine curtesie, Bowe thy right knee..As it hath bene taught thee. **1665** SIR C. LYTTELTON in *Hatton Corr.* (1878) 47 She was dressd in a vest, and, instead of courtesies, made leggs and bows. **1679** *Trials White & Other Jesuits* 79 She says she saw his Face, and made him a Curtesie. **1710** STEELE *Tatler* No. 253 ¶2 The whole female Jury paid their Respects by a low Courtesie. **1747** CHESTERF. *Lett.* I. cxxv. 334 At Vienna men always make courtesies, instead of bows, to the Emperor. **1866** G. MACDONALD *Ann. Q. Neighb.* vi. (1878) 72 [She] dropped such a disdainful courtesy.

β. **1681** OTWAY *Soldier's Fort.* IV. i, Make me a Curt'sy and give me a kiss now. **1700** DRYDEN *Fables, Wife of Bath's T.* 228 One only hag remained And drop'd an awkward court'sie to the Knight. **1859** GEO. ELIOT *A. Bede* 72 Hetty dropped the prettiest little curtsy. **1861** HUGHES *Tom Brown at Oxf.* xviii. (1889) 171 The sound of light footsteps..made her turn round and drop a curtsey.

γ. **1616** LANE *Sqr.'s Tale* 571 With a crooked curtchie, wried aright, Goglinge bothe eies, sayd, 'At your service dight'. *c* **1685** *Bagford Ballads* (1876) 53 The Hostess, the Cousin, and Servant..Made Courchies. **1719** D'URFEY *Pills* (1872) I. 353 Why, set thy face, and thy best Curchy make. **1786** BURNS *Holy Fair* iii, An' wi' a curchie low did stoop, As soon as e'er she saw me.

δ. **1594** *Sec. Pt. Contention* (1843) 155 The match is made, she seales it with a cursie. **1694** R. L'ESTRANGE *Fables* cccx. (1714) 325 She very Civilly dropt him a Cursie. **1705** HICKERINGILL *Priest-cr.* II. Pref. A iv. b, I hope..the Women will make me a Coursey.

†**4.** A 'mannerly' or moderate quantity, a small quantity. *Obs.*

α. **1530**, etc. [see COURTESY 10].

β. **1528** PAYNELL *Salerne's Regim.* R, The figges.. myngled with a curtsy of the water that they were sodde in. *Ibid.*, With the water shulde be mixed a litell curtsy of vineger. **1584** R. SCOT *Discov. Witchcr.* v. viii. 84 If anie woman had..borrowed a curtsie of Seasing.

γ. **1571** GOLDING *Calvin on Ps.* lxxii. 16 But a little cursie of wheate (namely, but as much as a man can holde in the palme of his hand). **1592** WARNER *Alb. Eng.* VII. xxxvii. (1612) 178 The Owle..feasteth in her house The Swallow with a cursee of her then disgorged wheat.

5. *attrib.* and *Comb.*

1591 SYLVESTER *Du Bartas* I. iii. 1060 Great Scipio, sated wth fain'd curtsy-capping, With Court-Eclipses. **1603** BRETON *Dignitie & Indign. Man* 196, I am no capper nor curtsie man.

curtsy, curtsey (ˈkɜːtsɪ), *v.* [f. prec. sb.]

1. *intr.* To make a curtsy; to do reverence *to*; now, like the sb., said only of women.

a **1553** UDALL *Royster D.* I. iv. (Arb.) 26 Curtsie whooresons, douke you, and crouche at euery worde. **1567** *Triall Treas.* (1850) 14 Curchy, lob, curchy downe to the grounde. **1592** SHAKS. *Rom. & Jul.* II. iv. 58 *Mer.* Such a case as yours constrains a man to bow in the hams. *Rom.* Meaning to cursie. **1672** *Westminster Drollery* II. 80 And every Girle did curchy, Curchy, curchy on the Grasse. **1712** STEELE *Spect.* No. 284 ¶6 She was all the while curtsying to Sir Anthony. **1804** JANE AUSTEN *Watsons* (1879) 323 Emma curtsied, the gentleman bowed. **1866** GEO. ELIOT *F. Holt* (1868) 26 She liked to be curtsied and bowed to by all the congregation.

β. **1741** RICHARDSON *Pamela* (1824) I. vi. 20, I curtesied to him, and to Mrs. Jervis for her good word. **1752** CHESTERF. *Lett.* III. cclxxxix. 323 It is respectful to bow to the King of England..it is the rule to courtesy to the Emperor. **1845** S. C. HALL *Whiteboy* v. 45 Mistress M. entered, curtesied down to the ground, etc.

b. With advb. extension.

1824 BYRON *Juan* XVI. ci, Ladies rose, And curtsying off, as curtsies country dame, Retired. **1849** MISS MULOCK *Ogilvies* xvi, As she curtseyed herself out.

c. *transf.* and *fig.*

1588 SHAKS. *Tit. A.* v. iii. 74 Shee whom mightie kingdomes cursie too. **1599** —— *Hen. V*, v. ii. 293 O Kate, nice Customes cursie to great Kings. **1840** DICKENS *Barn. Rudge* x, The plump pigeons..were skimming and curtseying about it. **1887** LOWELL *Democr.* 142 He had fancied that the laws of the universe would curtsy to the resolves of the National Convention.

2. *trans.* To make a curtsy to.

1566 DRANT *Horace's Sat.* I. ix. (R.), To leade him home, to curtsey him, and cap him when he stayes. *a* **1592** H. SMITH *Serm.* (1622) 207 How would they cap me, and coursie me? **1654** GAYTON *Pleas. Notes* I. iii. 13 The Ladies ..curtesied him.

b. To give or express by curtsying.

1775 SHERIDAN *Rivals* Epil., She smiles preferment, or she frowns disgrace, Curtsies a pension here—there nods a place. **1798** JANE AUSTEN *Northang. Ab.* (1833) II. vii. 145 She courtesied her acquiescence.

Hence ˈ**curtsying** *vbl. sb.* and *ppl. a.*

1668 WILKINS *Real Char.* 327 Curcheeing, Genuflexion. **1714** MANDEVILLE *Fab. Bees* (1725) I. 38 The first rude essays of curt'sying. **1870** *Daily News* 16 Apr., Curtseying maidens and obsequious hinds, anxious to do honour to the man.

curtus, -uus, -yse, obs. forms of COURTEOUS.

‖**curucui** (kʊərʊˈkuːɪ). *Ornith.* Also couroucou, couroucoui. [The native name, of echoic origin, in Brazil and Guiana: in mod.F. *couroucou*.] A bird (*Trogon curucui*) found in Brazil and other parts of South America.

1678 RAY *Willoughby's Ornith.* 140 The Brazilian *Curucui* of Marggrave. It is a very elegant and beautiful bird. **1781** LATHAM *Hist. Birds* I. 545 Couroucou. **1785** W. F. MARTYN *Dict. Nat. Hist.*, *Curucui*, a bird of the wood-pecker kind, found in Brazil. **1815** J. F. STEPHENS *Zool.* ix. 4. **1885** LADY BRASSEY *The Trades* 118 The specimens included..parrots, paroquets, couroucoui, pigeons.

curule (ˈkjʊər(j)uːl), *a.* [ad. L. *curūl-is*, *currūlis*, supposed to be f. *curru-s* chariot. F. *curule*.]

1. *Rom. Antiq.* ***curule chair***: a chair or seat inlaid with ivory and shaped like a camp-stool with curved legs, used by the highest magistrates of Rome.

1695 LD. PRESTON *Boeth.* II. 54 When thou sawest them in the Court placed in their Curule Seats. **1781** GIBBON *Decl. & F.* II. xxxvi. 349 The curule chair was successively filled by eleven of the most illustrious senators. **1877** GEIKIE *Christ* lxii. 758 The ivory curule chair of the procurator.

2. Privileged to sit in a curule chair; as ***curule magistrate***, ***curule*** ÆDILE (q.v.).

1600 HOLLAND *Livy* x. xxxiii. 376 In the time of his curule Aedileship. **1838** ARNOLD *Hist. Rome* I. xvi. 343 Every curule magistracy was supposed to convey something of kingly and therefore of sacred dignity. **1880** MUIRHEAD *Gaius* I. §6 *note*, The curule aediles were first created at the same time as the urban praetor.

3. *transf.* Pertaining to any high civic dignity or office, as that of a magistrate or mayor.

1663 BUTLER *Hud.* I. i. 715 We that are merely mounted higher Than Constables in Curule Wit. **1818** SCOTT *Hrt. Midl.* xii, A wealthy burgher, who might one day..hold the curule chair itself. **1882** W. B. WEEDEN *Soc. Law Labor* 124 The way of the good apprentice..to the..curule seat.

curvable (ˈkɜːvəb(ə)l), *a.* *rare.* [f. CURVE *v.* + -ABLE: cf. L. *curvābilis*.] Capable of being curved or bent.

1868 HELPS *Realmah* vii. (1876) 137 Everything about the human body should be loose, flowing, soft, and curvable.

curvaceous (kɜːˈveɪʃəs), *a.* *colloq.* (orig. *U.S.*). [f. CURV(E *sb.* + -ACEOUS.] Curving, full of curves; *spec.* of a well-rounded female figure.

1936 *Screen Book Mag.* Feb. 61 The curvaceous lady [*sc.* Mae West] receives from Paramount just as many dollars per week for her scenario work as she receives for her acting. **1959** *N.Z. Listener* 21 Aug. 8/1 Legs that are strong, and curvaceous, and graceful, and a pleasure to the eye! **1959** H. HOBSON *Mission House Murder* xviii. 119 Sharon; lissome and curvaceous in a revealing leopard-spotted bikini. **1965** *New Statesman* 30 Apr. 693/1 Curvaceous red paint marks ..seemed to indicate a vague and unrealised intention to paint a female nude. **1970** *Interior Design* Dec. 759 (*caption*) A curvaceous upholstered armchair.

ˈ**curval**, *a.* *Her.* = next.

ˈ**curvant**, *a.* *Her.* [ad. L. *curvānt-em*, pr. pple. of *curvāre* to CURVE.] Curving.

1830 ROBSON *Brit. Her.* Gloss., *Curval* or *Curvant*, Curved or bowed.

ˈ**curvate**, *a.* *rare.*$^{-0}$ [ad. L. *curvāt-us* bent, pa. pple. of *curvāre*.] = next.

1864 in WEBSTER.

curvated (ˈkɜːveɪtɪd), *a.* *rare.* [f. as prec. + -ED.] Curved; of a curved form.

1727 BAILEY vol. II, *Curvated*, bended. **1802** CORRY *Mem. A. Berkeley* 71 The vast..moorlands of Stanmore reared their rugged curvated summits.

curvation (kɜːˈveɪʃən). [ad. L. *curvātiōn-em*, n. of action from *curvāre*.] Curving, bending.

1656 tr. *Hobbes' Elem. Philos.* (1839) 195 The bending or curvation of a strait line into the circumference of a circle. **1659** PEARSON *Creed* (1839) 393 The inclination and curvation of our limbs. **1721** R. BRADLEY *Wks. Nat.* 150 It swims about by Curvations, appearing like the figure of an S. **1862** *Morn. Star* 19 June, A self-adjusting carriage wheel, adapted to any curvation or line of railway.

curvative (ˈkɜːvətɪv), *a.* *Bot. rare.* [f. *curvāt-*, ppl. stem of *curvāre*: see -IVE.] See quots.

1856 HENSLOW *Dict. Bot. Terms*, *Curvative*..in vernation and estivation, where the separate parts are scarcely folded but have the margins merely curved a little. **1866** *Treas. Bot.* 364 *Curvative*, when the margins are slightly turned up or down, without any sensible bending inwards.

curvature (ˈkɜːvətjʊə(r)). [ad. L. *curvātūra* bending, f. *curvāre*, *curvāt-* to bend: see -URE.]

1. a. The action of curving or bending; the fact, quality, or manner of being curved; curved form; (with *pl.*) a particular instance of this.

In *Pathol.* esp. of the spine, of which there are two sorts, ***angular*** or ***Pott's curvature***, and ***lateral curvature***.

1665 HOOKE *Microgr.* 236 Attributed to the Curvature of the visual Ray..through so differingly Dense a Medium. **1753** HOGARTH *Anal. Beauty* 2 A line..of that peculiar curvature. **1800** *Med. Jrnl.* IV. 271 Pains are not even perceived..in curvatures of the back-bone. **1840** R. LISTON *Elem. Surg.* (ed. 2) II. 547 When curvature commences there is very generally more or less weakness of the limbs. **1875**

Bennett & Dyer *Sachs' Bot.* III. iv. 706 Sudden curvature of growing shoots from a blow or concussion. *Ibid.* 707 The permanent curvature which remains..or the *Curvature of Concussion*, is the result of a lengthening of the convex and a simultaneous contraction of the concave side.

b. *Geom.* The amount or rate of deviation (of a curve) from a straight line, or (of a curved surface) from a plane.

circle of curvature: the circle which osculates a curve at any point, and serves to measure the curvature of the curve at that point. ***centre of c.***, ***radius of c.***: the centre and radius of the circle of curvature. ***chord of c.*** (see quot. 1875). ***double curvature***: that of a curve which twists so as not to lie in one plane, *e.g.* the curve of a screw.

1710 J. Harris *Lex. Techn.*, *Curvature of a Line*, is the peculiar manner of its bending or Flexure, whereby it becomes a Curve of such peculiar Properties..The Curvatures of different Circles are to one another Reciprocally as their Radii. **1796** Hutton *Math. Dict.*, *Curve of a Double Curvature*, is such a curve as has not all its parts in the same plane. **1807** —— *Course Math.* II. 320 The radius of a circle which has the same curvature with the curve at any given point, is the radius of curvature at that point. **1866** *Chamb. Jrnl.* XXVIII. 271 The axles of the locomotive are directed towards the centre of curvature of the railway. **1875** Todhunter *Diff. Calc.* xxiv. §320 If a straight line be drawn from any point of a curve in any direction, the portion of this straight line which is intercepted by the circle of curvature at the assumed point is called the *chord of curvature*. **1879** Thomson & Tait *Nat. Phil.* I. I. v, The direction of motion changes from point to point, and the rate of this change, per unit of length of the curve..is called the *curvature*.

c. A generalization of the notion of curvature applied to a space or manifold of four (or more) dimensions, first made in the theory of non-Euclidean geometry and further developed by Einstein in the general theory of relativity; the property of not being Euclidean or 'flat'. So ***curvature of space-time***, etc.

1873 W. K. Clifford tr. Riemann in *Nature* 8 May 36/2 If we assume independence of bodies from position, and therefore ascribe to space constant curvature, it must necessarily be finite provided this curvature has ever so small a positive value. **1910** *Encycl. Brit.* XI. 727/2 Riemann's work contains two fundamental conceptions, that of a manifold and that of the measure of curvature of a continuous manifold. **1916** *Monthly Notices R. Astr. Soc.* LXXVI. 707 The mathematical interpretation of G is the *curvature* of the four-dimensional system of reference. **1920** A. S. Eddington *Space Time & Gravit.* x. 158 We thus get the idea that space-time may have an essential curvature on a great scale independent of the small hummocks due to recognised matter. **1920** R. W. Lawson tr. *Einstein's Relativity: Special & General Theory* 127 Half of this deflection is produced by the Newtonian field of attraction of the sun, and the other half by the geometrical modification ('curvature') of space caused by the sun. **1959** Spitz & Gaynor *Dict. Astron.* 399 The curvature of space existing in the vicinity of a massive body, like the sun, affects the course of a ray of light. **1966** Taylor & Wheeler *Spacetime Physics* iii. 175 The existence of this curvature destroys the possibility of describing motion with respect to a single ideal Euclidean reference frame that pervades all space. **1971** *Sci. Amer.* May 22/3 A gravitational-radiation detector built on this principle should be capable of measuring the gravitational waves (and hence the curvature of space-time) predicted by relativity theory.

2. *concr.* A curved portion of anything; a curve.

1603 Holland *Plutarch's Mor.* 1312 The said *Sistrum* being in the upper part round, the curvature and *Absis* thereof comprehendeth foure things. **1686** Goad *Celest. Bodies* III. ii. 409 [It] makes the Lofty Curvature of the Celestial Arch to ring. **1800** *Med. Jrnl.* III. 168 The second curvature of the duodenum was partly torn. **1881** J. Russell *Haigs* 3 A magnificent curvature of the river Tweed.

Hence **'curvature** *v. intr.*, to curve, bend. **'curvatured** *a.*, having curvature, curved (*rare*).

a **1810** Tannahill *Poems* (1846) 28 Our tiny hero.. Ascends the hair's curvatur'd side. **1812** J. J. Henry *Camp. agst. Quebec* 175 We came to the main passage, which curvatured down the hill.

curve (kɜːv), *a.* and *sb.* [ad. L. *curv-us* bending, bent, curved, crooked.]

A. *adj.* Curved. Now *rare.*

1571 Digges *Pantom.* II. xiii. Niij b, Suche playne Superficies as are enuironed with curue lynes. **1665** *Phil. Trans.* I. 107 The Tail is Curve. **1716** Cheyne *Philos. Princ. Relig.* I. 95 Partly terminated with plain, and partly with curve surfaces. **1755** Amory *Mem.* (1769) II. 156 On which are fastened curve pieces of wood. *c* **1865** Brougham Introd. Disc. in *Circ. Sc.* I. p. xi, The Earth moves round the Sun in the same curve line.

B. *sb.* (Short for *curve-line*, etc.: cf. F. *courbe* = *ligne courbe*.)

1. a. *Geom.* A curved line: a locus which may be conceived to be traced by a moving point, the direction of whose motion continuously changes or deviates from a straight line. (In *Higher Geometry*, extended to include the straight line.)

algebraic curve: a curve expressed by an equation containing only algebraic functions, i.e. such as involve only addition, multiplication, involution, and their converses; of which kind are the various conic sections: opposed to ***transcendental*** (or ***mechanical***) ***curve***, one which can be expressed only by an equation involving higher functions, as the catenary, cycloid, etc. ***curve of probability***: a transcendental curve representing the probabilities of recurrences of an event. ***curve of pursuit***: the curve traced by a point moving with constant velocity, whose motion is directed at each instant towards another point which also moves with constant velocity (usually in a straight line). ***curve of sines***: a curve in which the abscissa is proportional to some quantity and the ordinate to the sine of that quantity; so also ***curve of cosines, tangents***, etc. See also anaclastic, catenary, caustic, cubic, exponential, etc. etc.

1696 Whiston *Th. Earth* I. 22 All Bodies..which revolve in Curves..are attracted..continually towards that Point or Center. **1706** H. Ditton *Fluxions* 221 That Curve to which this Property agrees, must be the Curve of swiftest Descent. **1751** Chambers *Cycl.*, *Radial curves*, is a denomination given by some authors to curves of the spiral kind, whose ordinates..all terminate in the centre of the including circle, and appear like so many *radii*..whence the name. **1871** Tait & Steele *Dynamics of a Particle* (ed. 3) i. §32 Illustrations..are to be found in what are called *Curves of Pursuit*. These questions arose from the consideration of the path taken by a dog who in following his master always directs his course towards him. **1875** Jevons *Money* (1878) 138 The curve..shows the course of variation of the standard of value. **1882** Minchin *Unipl. Kinemat.* 38 What curve do the chalk marks make in the rolling body? Evidently..a circle..What curve do the chalk marks make on the fixed plane? Evidently a right line.

†**b.** A curved surface. *Obs.*

1728 tr. *Newton's Opt. Lect.* 173 The Refraction of a Ray by a Curve is the same, as by a Plane touching the Curve in the Point of Refraction.

c. *Physics, Statistics*, etc. A graph or line drawn from point to point so as to represent diagrammatically a continuous variation of a quantity, either with time or with respect to some other quantity.

1854 *Amer. Jrnl. Sci. & Arts* 2nd Ser. XVII. 423 The same general law gives the intensity of the induced magnetism as a function of the exciting force... The curves which represent the law of induction for diamagnetic substances are surrounded..by the curves for magnetic substances. **1874** *Proc. R. Soc.* XXII. 27 There will be three curves—one expressing the relation between temperature and pressure for gas with liquid, another expressing that for gas with solid, and another expressing that for liquid with solid. **1884** *Pharmaceut. Jrnl. & Trans.* 26 July 77/2 The object of these curves was to show clearly some of the most important factors in the growth of crops. **1886** F. Galton in *Jrnl. Anthropol. Inst.* XV. 263 Section of surface parallel to *XY* is a true curve of frequency. **1899** Temperature curve [see Temperature 10]. **1909** K. Pearson *Problem Pract. Eugenics* 11 The curve for all possibly reproductive wives is amply verified by the curve for young wives. **1911** W. E. Dalby in *Rep. Brit. Assoc. 1910* 695 The curves of mileage, passengers carried, and goods carried increase regularly with the increase of capital. **1940** R. S. Woodworth *Psychol.* (ed. 12) 62 If we outline the shape of the distribution by a line joining the tops of adjacent columns we have the distribution curve. **1958** *Times Rev. Industry* Apr. 81/2 In the..Community industries the curve of annual steel production increase is flattening out. **1959** *Listener* 13 Aug. 237/2 The population curve has slowed down.

2. A curved form, outline, etc.; a curved thing or portion of a thing. *spec.* the curving line of the female figure; usu. in *pl.*

1728 Pope *Dunc.* II. 172 It rose, and labour'd to a curve at most. **1750** Franklin *Experiments* Wks. 1887 II. 203 Take a wire bent in the form of a C, with a stick of wax fixed to the outside of the curve to hold it by. **1783** P. Pott *Chirurg. Wks.* III. 407 A smart blow, or a violent strain had immediately preceded the appearance of the curve [of the spine]. **1856** Kane *Arct. Expl.* II. xi. 112 Etah is on the northeastern curve of Hartstene Bay. **1862** *Harper's Mag.* June 45/1 The full round shape hid half its voluptuous curves in the shade of the dark-green riding-suit. **1906** *Dress* Nov. 26/2 Where the figure of the client is naturally too flat to meet this present demand for curves, the corsetière is apt to add a few little pinked-out silken frills. **1929** Wodehouse *Mr. Mulliner Speaking* i. 9, I can remember the days..when every other girl you met stood about six feet two in her dancing-shoes and had as many curves as a Scenic Railway. **1931** A. Christie *Sittaford Myst.* i. 8 What was the good of a woman if she didn't look like a woman? Papers said curves were coming back. About time, too. **1963** van Praagh & Brinson *Choreogr. Art* 174 The emancipated modern woman is athletic, well-groomed and chic with good proportions and fewer curves than in earlier periods.

3. (See quot.)

1874 Knight *Dict. Mech.*, *Curve*, a draftsman's instrument having one or a variety of curves of various characters..Some are constructed for specific purposes, such as *shipwright's curves, radii-curves*, etc.

4. *Baseball.* 'The course of a ball so pitched that it does not pass in a straight line from the pitcher to the catcher, but makes a deflection in the air other than the ordinary one caused by the force of gravity' (*Cent. Dict.*). Also *attrib.* and *fig.*

1879 *De Witt's Baseball Guide* 24 The great difficulty in curve pitching is to obtain the required command of the ball. **1887** *Outing* (U.S.) May 98/1 Assertions were rife in all quarters that the curve was a fallacy. **1912** C. Mathewson *Pitching* 14 Big League ball-players recognize only two kinds of pitched balls—the curve and the straight one. **1960** H. Seymour *Baseball* xxiii. 278 Fooling him with a curve on the outside. **1970** W. Smith *Gold Mine* xxxv. 92 Are we going to sit back and let them have a free run? No, sir! We are going to throw down our own curve ball!

5. *pl.* Round brackets; parentheses. *U.S.*

1928 M. H. Weseen *Crowell's Dict. Eng. Gram.* 169 *Curves.* This term is sometimes used to denote parenthesis marks ( ). **1961** R. B. Long *Sentence & Parts* xx. 475 Curves are usable to inclose quite clearly what occurs where commas would be confusing and dashes a little strong.

C. *Comb.*, as **curve-billed** (epithet of a N. American thrush); **curve-fitting**, the determination of the equation of the curve which, subject to any conditions such as the possible number of parameters, most closely represents the points on a graph or describes most accurately the relation between the variables they represent; †**curve-lined** *a.*, composed of curved lines, curvilinear; **curve-plotting**, the graphic representation of a curve in a plan or diagram by means of points marked on co-ordinates; **curve-ruler** (see quot.); **curve-veined** *a.* (of leaves), having veins diverging from the midrib and converging towards the margin.

1881 *Amer. Naturalist* XV. 217 The *curve-billed thrush (*H[arporhynchus] curvirostris*). **1902** *Biometrika* I. 266 Half the difficulty of curve-fitting..lies in the choice of a suitable curve. **1924** *Proc. Nat. Acad. Sci.* X. 79 (*heading*) The development of a frequency function and some comments [on] *curve fitting. **1930** *Meteorol. Gloss.* (ed. 2) 51 Two main types of problems arise in connexion with curve fitting. We may either require to represent a variable quantity as a function of some independent variable such as time,..by drawing a curve to represent the functional relationship, or we may require to represent the frequency of occurrence of different values of a quantity,..by means of a curve whose formula must be obtained. **1970** *Computers & Humanities* IV. 343 Through use of a curve-fitting technique, high-order polynomial expressions relating pitch to time (rhythm) are generated for each incipit. **1677** Plot *Oxfordsh.* 288 Innumerable sorts of *Curve-lined figures. *c* **1865** Brougham Introd. Disc. in *Circ. Sc.* I. p. vi, There are *curve-lined* figures as well as straight. **1905** Ashe & Keiley *Electr. Railways* 6 *Curve plotting is accomplished by means of a series of perpendicular and parallel lines.. termed coördinates. **1945** *Jrnl. Franklin Inst.* CCXL. 278 Curve-plotting output units. **1879** T. Baker *Land & Eng. Surv.* 159 Railway *Curve-rulers are a series of arcs of circles of various radii..used for projecting railway curves on parliamentary maps. **1866** *Treas. Bot.* 364 *Curvinerved*, **Curve-veined*, the same as Convergentinervose. **1870** Bentley *Botany* 147.

curve (kɜːv), *v.* [ad. L. *curvā-re* to crook, f. *curv-us* crooked, curve *a.* Cf. F. *courber.*]

1. *trans.* To bend so as to form a curve; to cause to take a curved form; to inflect.

1669 Holder *Elem. Speech* (L.), The tongue is drawn back and curved. **1791** Cowper *Iliad* IV. 145 When the horn was curved to a wide arch. **1855** Tennyson *Maud* I. xiii, Curving a contumelious lip.

2. *intr.* To have or assume a curved form.

1594 [see curving *vbl. sb.*]. **1748** Richardson *Clarissa* Wks. 1883 VI. 141 He [Boreas] puffed away most vehemently; and often made the poor fellow curve and stagger. **1855** Tennyson *The Brook* 182 And out again I curve and flow To join the brimming river. **1875** Darwin *Insectiv. Pl.* ii. 37 The tentacles curve inwards.

3. *trans. Baseball.* To throw or pitch (a ball) with a curve (see curve *sb.* 4).

[**1856** *Spirit of Times* 6 Dec. 229/1 It is questionable.. whether his style of pitching is most successful, many believing a slow ball curving near the bat, to be the most effective.] **1878** *De Witt's Baseball Guide* 35 With a view of settling the vexed question as to whether a pitcher can or cannot curve a ball, practical experiments were made. **1960** H. Seymour *Baseball* xvi. 177 The pitcher..dominated the game merely because he could curve a ball.

curved (kɜːvd, -ɪd), *ppl. a.* [f. curve *v.*] **a.** Bent or formed into a curve; bending; deviating from the straight (or plane) form continuously, *i.e.* without angles. (It has partly taken the place of curve *a.*)

1710 J. Clarke *Rohault's Nat. Phil.* (1729) I. 83 The Motion will be made in a Line differently curved. **1797** Bewick *Brit. Birds* (1847) I. 111 The claws are curved and short. **1818** Shelley *Lines Euganean Hills*, From the curved horizon's bound. **1869** Tyndall *Notes on Light* §79 Reflexion from Curved Surfaces.

b. ***curved fire***, gun-fire with an angle of elevation or departure exceeding that of direct fire.

The angle is variously specified: see quots.

1879 [see indirect *a.*]. **1883** G. Mackinlay *Text Bk. Gunnery* 162 Indirect or curved fire. Fire from guns, with reduced charges, and from howitzers and mortars, at all angles of elevation not exceeding 15°. **1897** *Text Bk. Gunnery* (*War Office*) (ed. 3) II. iv. 249 When the curvature of the trajectory becomes considerable, as in High Angle and Curved Fire. **1907** O. M. Lissak *Ordn. & Gunnery* 358 Direct Fire is with high velocities, and angles of elevation not exceeding 20 degrees. Curved Fire is with low velocities, and angles of elevation not exceeding 30 degrees. **1917** W. H. Tschappat *Ordn. & Gunnery* 426 For convenience of discussion curved fire will be considered as firings with elevations between 15° and 40° and high-angle fire as firings with elevations above 40°. **1920** D. A. Macalister *Field Gunnery* (ed. 4) i. 19 *Curved Fire.*—Where the angle of elevation is not above 30°.

c. In *Baseball* (see curve *v.* 3).

1905 *Chicago Daily News* 17 July 4/1 His curved ball was breaking much better for him too.

Hence **'curvedly** *adv.*, in a curved manner; **'curvedness**, state of being curved. (*rare.*)

1676 Wiseman *Surg.* VII. i. (R.), A curvedness, which may be reduced to a fracture. **1805** Luccock *Nat. Wool* 152 That the wool..possess..such a degree of curvedness. **1880** Watson in *Jrnl. Linn. Soc.* XV. No. 82. 109 Lines.. curvedly radiating.

curveless ('kɜːvlɪs), *a.* [f. curve *sb.* + -less.] Without a curve.

1885 B. Harte *Maruja* i, Her straight, curveless mouth. **1890** *Illust. Lond. News* 11 Oct. 466/2 The curveless, cornerless, inevitable 'thoroughfare' lengthening out before him.

'curvesome, *a.* [-some[1].] = curvaceous *a.*

1935 *N.Y. Even. Jrnl.* 7 May, Six burleycue lassies who daily peel off enveloping garments..to disclose their curvesome charms. **1938** M. BRINIG *May Flavin* iii. 289 She was fairly tall and had a curvesome figure, and this was the best thing about her. **1940** *Time* 8 July 49/1 Mazeppa, traditionally played by a curvesome female.

curvet ('kɜːvɪt, kɜː'vɛt), *sb.* Forms: α. 6 curuetto, 7 corvetto, coruetti, curvetty; β. 6 *pl.* cooruez, 7 coruet, corvet, corveit, 7–9 curvett, 7– curvet. [ad. It. *corvetta*, dim. of *corvo*, *corva*, now *curvo* bent, arched:—L. *curvus*. Cf. Sp. *corveta*, F. *courbette*. Originally stressed on the final, but now very generally on the first syllable: so altered by Todd 1818 from Johnson's *cur'vet*.]

In the *manège*: A leap of a horse in which the fore-legs are raised together and equally advanced, and the hind-legs raised with a spring before the fore-legs reach the ground. (Often used more or less vaguely of any leaping or frisking motion; cf. CARACOL.)

1575 LANEHAM *Let.* (1871) 25 To see..the cooragioous attempts..the daungeroous cooruez, the feers encoounterz. **1589** *Pasquill's Counter-c.* 3 O how my Palfrey fetcht me uppe the Curuetto. **1601** SHAKS. *All's Well* II. iii. 299 The bound and high curuet Of Marses fierie steed. **1614** MARKHAM *Cheap Husb.* I. ii. (1668) 27 When your horse can bound perfectly, then you shall teach him the Corvet. **1751** JOHNSON *Rambler* No. 163 ¶7 As a sportsman delights the squires..with the curvets of his horse. **1852** KINGSLEY *Andromeda* 300 As..some colt..at last, in pride of obedience Answers the heel with a curvet.

fig. **1645** MILTON *Colast.* Wks. (1851) 353 Hee must needs first shew us a curvett of his madnes.

curvet (kɜː'vɛt, 'kɜːvɪt), *v.* Also 6 coruet, 7 corvet, -bet, curuette, -ete, -eat. Inflected cur'vetted, -ing, and 'curveted, -ing. [ad. It. *corvettare* 'to corvet or praunce', f. *corvetta* CURVET *sb.* Originally always stressed on the final, but now very generally (though less so than the sb.) on the first syllable. Todd has '*curvet* for the sb., *cur'vet* for the vb.; Webster 1828, Smart 1836, have '*curvet* for vb. as well as sb.]

1. *intr.* Of a horse: To execute a curvet, leap in a curvet. Said also of the horseman.

1592 SHAKS. *Ven. & Ad.* 279 Anon he rears upright, corvets and leaps. **1682** SHADWELL *Medal* 4 The sprightly Horse y' have seen, Praunce, and curvet, with pleasure to the sight. **1695** MOTTEUX *St. Olon's Morocco* 8 He took a fancy..to Curvet in his Gardens on a fiery Horse. **1768–74** TUCKER *Lt. Nat.* (1852) II. 445 He may let him sometimes prance and caper and curvet. **1805** SCOTT *Last Minstr.* IV. xxi, Forced him, with chastened fire, to prance, And, high curvetting, slow advance. *a* **1839** PRAED *Poems* (1864) II. 423 Looking for her as he curvets by. **1866** R. M. BALLANTYNE *Shifting Winds* vi. (1881) 60 [The] fresh and mettlesome steeds curveted and pranced.

b. *trans.* To cause to curvet.

1613 WOTTON in *Reliq. Wotton.* (1672) 419 Sir R. Drury ..corbeteth his Horse before the King's window.

2. *transf.* To leap about, frisk: also *fig.*

1600 SHAKS. *A.Y.L.* III. ii. 258 Cry holla to the tongue, I prethee: it curuettes vnseasonably. **1649** G. DANIEL *Trinarch. Hen. V*, xiv, As were the yeare Beat in a Plott, and Dayes were Curvetting [*rime* king]. **1860** J. P. KENNEDY *Swallow B.* iii. 40 A mischievous imp, who curvets about the house.

'curveter. *nonce-wd.* [f. CURVET *v.* + -ER[1].] A curvetting horse.

1841 C. LEVER *C. O'Malley* xxxiii. 176 The management of your arching necked curveter.

curveting ('kɜːvɪtɪŋ), **curvetting** (kɜː'vɛtɪŋ), *vbl. sb.* [-ING[1].] The action of the verb CURVET, q.v.

1784 tr. *Beckford's Vathek* (1868) 55 The unwieldy curvetting of these poor beasts. **1801** STRUTT *Sports & Past.* III. v. 203 Imitating the curvetings and motions of a horse. **1840** BARHAM *Ingol. Leg.*, *Witches' Frolic*, Such lofty curvetting And grand pirouetting.

'curveting, cur'vetting, *ppl. a.* [-ING[2].] That curvets: see the verb.

1599 MARSTON *Sco. Villanie* III. xi. 228 His very intellect Is naught but a curuetting Sommerset. **1750** WESLEY *Wks.* (1872) II. 185 A fine curvetting horse. **1848** MACAULAY *Hist. Eng.* II. 490 Rushed through the drawn swords and curvetting horses. **1878** M. A. BROWN *Nadeschda* 25 On his curveting charger's back.

curvi- ('kɜːvɪ-), combining form of L. *curv-us* curved; chiefly in adjectives used in *Nat. Hist.* (of many of which analogous forms are used in modern French), as **curvi'caudate** [L. *cauda* tail; in mod.F. *curvicaude*], having a curved tail. **curvi'costate** [L. *costa* rib], 'marked with small bent ribs' (Webster 1864). **curvi'dentate** [L. *dent-em* tooth], having curved teeth. **curvi'foliate** [L. *folium* leaf], 'having leaves bent back' (Webster). **'curviform** [see -FORM], of a curved shape. **curvi'nervate, curvi'nerved,** = *curve-veined* (see CURVE *a.* and *sb.* C). **curvi'rostral** [L. *rostrum* beak], having a curved beak. **curvi'serial**, forming a series disposed in a curve (of leaves on a stem).

1880 GRAY *Struct. Bot.* iii. §4. 92 Curvinerved, when nerves curve in their course, as in the leaves of Funkia. **1870** BENTLEY *Bot.* 140 No leaf can be placed precisely in a straight line over any preceding leaf, but disposed in an infinite curve, and hence called curviserial.

†**'curvify,** *v. Obs.* [f. L. *curv-us* curved + -FY.] **a.** *intr.* To become curved or crooked. **b.** *trans.* To make curved, bend; to curl (hair).

1599 A. M. tr. *Gabelhouer's Bk. Physicke* 111/1 When any mans Backe beginneth to curvifye or wax croockede. **1623** COCKERAM II, To make Crooked, *curuefie*.

curvi'linead. [f. CURVI- + *līnea* line + -AD.]

1826 J. ALDERSON in *Trans. Soc. Arts* XLIV. 151 A mathematical instrument of my invention called a curvilinead, wherewith to describe regular curve lines. **1842** in G. FRANCIS *Dict. Arts.*

curvilineal (kɜːvɪ'lɪnɪəl), *a.* [f. CURVI- + L. *līneālis* lineal.] = next. Hence **curvi'linealness.**

1656 HOBBES *Six Lessons* Wks. 1845 VII. 259 Curvilineal angles. *a* **1746** MACLAURIN *Newton's Philos. Disc.* III. ii. (R.), The curvilineal motion of the moon in her orbit. **1768** LANDEN in *Phil. Trans.* LVIII. 174 The computation of curvilineal areas. **1831** BREWSTER *Nat. Magic* vi. (1833) 133 Describing a kind of curvilineal path.

1727 BAILEY vol. II, *Curvilinealness*, the Consisting of crooked Lines.

curvilinear (kɜːvɪ'lɪnɪə(r)), *a.* (*sb.*) [f. CURVI- + L. *līnea* line, *līneār-is* linear.] Consisting of, or contained by, a curved line or lines; having the form of a curved line. (Opposed to *rectilinear*, and in Gothic Archit. to *perpendicular*, as applied to window-tracery.)

1710 BERKELEY *Princ. Hum. Knowl.* Introd. §10 Neither swift nor slow, curvilinear nor rectilinear. *a* **1746** MACLAURIN *Newton's Philos. Disc.* III. iii. (R.), All the curvilinear motions in the solar system. **1843** RUSKIN *Mod. Paint.* I. II. III. iii. §6 The minor contours..are..beautifully curvilinear. **1865** TYLOR *Early Hist. Mankind* viii. 195 Scrapers with curvilinear edges.

Hence **curviline'arity; curvi'linearly** *adv.*

1847 CRAIG, *Curvilinearity*, the state of being curvilinear. **1824** LANDOR *Imag. Conv.* (1846) I. 183 Rectilinearly, curvilinearly, and perpendicularly. **1872** COHEN *Dis. Throat* 51 Another fold..stretching curvilinearly backwards.

So †**curvi'lineary,** †**curvi'lineous** [cf. F. *curviligne*, †*courbeligne*] *adjs.* = CURVILINEAR.

1706 PHILLIPS (ed. Kersey), *Curvilineal* or *Curvilineary* (in *Geom.*), crooked-lined. **1721** in BAILEY. **1692** RAY *Dissol. World* 115 Curvilineous concretions of Salts.

curving ('kɜːvɪŋ), *vbl. sb.* [-ING[1].] The action of the verb CURVE; bending, flexure, curvature. Also *fig.*

1594 NORDEN *Spec. Brit., Essex* 11 The Roding..after manifolde curuings, it maketh way vnder Wodforde bridge. **1748** RICHARDSON *Clarissa* Wks. 1883 V. 335 Curvings from the plain simple truth. **1882** VINES *Sachs' Bot.* 905 The curving of the [antheridium]..indicates that fertilisation does not usually take place between the contiguous organs.

'curving, *ppl. a.* [-ING[2].] That curves.

1762 FALCONER *Shipwr.* III. (1818) 106 Watch the curving prow. **1878** MACLEAR *Celts* iii. (1879) 31 The curving shores of Provence and Narbonne.

'curvingly, *adv.* [-LY[2].] In a curving manner.

1923 *Weekly Dispatch* 13 May 7 Decorated with blue and white stripes that ran out curvingly, somewhat in swastika fashion. **1938** E. THOMPSON *Youngest Disciple* i. 9 It was a valley cut deep in the mountains, as by a scimitar, not straight but curvingly.

curvital ('kɜːvɪtəl), *a. Geom.* [a. mod.F. *curvital*, f. *curvité* curvity + -AL[1].] Of or pertaining to curvity or curvature. ***curvital function***, a function expressing the length of the perpendicular from a fixed point of a curve upon the normal at a variable point, in terms of the length of the arc from the fixed to the variable point.

1886 CARR *Synopsis Math.* Index C 60.

†**'curvity.** *Obs.* [ad. L. *curvitās* (or a. F. *curvité*, Oresme 14th c.), f. *curvus* curved, crooked.]

1. Curved or bent quality or state; curvature; a curved portion of anything, a curve.

1547 BOORDE *Brev. Health* cviii. 41 A backe the which may have many infirmities, as debylytie, and wekenes, curvytie and gybbositie. **1656** HOBBES *Six Lessons* Wks. 1845 VII. 253 The rectitude or curvity of the lines. **1705** *Phil. Trans.* XXV. 2062 The divers flexures and curvities of the Serpent. **1715** MACHIN in Rigaud *Corr. Sci. Men* (1841) I. 269 [I] have added a rule for finding the curvity. **1831** BREWSTER *Newton* (1855) I. iii. 42 According to their more or less curvity.

2. *fig.* Moral obliquity, crookedness of conduct.

1616 BRENT tr. *Sarpi's Counc. Trent* (1676) 166 The whole nature of man..remained crooked; not by the curvity of Adam, but by his own. **1675** BAXTER *Cath. Theol.* I. III. 82 That there is as much positivity of Relation in disobedience as in obedience, in curvity as in rectitude. **1678** GALE *Crt. Gentiles* III. 136 That God be the motor..of the action.. but not of the obliquitie or curvitie in acting.

'curvograph. [f. CURVE (or L. *curvus*) + -GRAPH.] An instrument for describing curves.

1817 W. WARCUP in *Trans. Soc. Arts* XXXV. 109 An instrument of my invention for describing curve lines, which I purpose calling the *curvograph*. **1874** KNIGHT *Dict. Mech.*, *Curvograph*, an instrument for drawing a curve without reference to the center.

curvometer (kɜː'vɒmɪtə(r)). [f. CURVE *sb.* + -OMETER.] An instrument for measuring the length of a curve.

1902 *Encycl. Brit.* XXX. 578/1 More complicated curvometers or kartometers have been devised.

curvous ('kɜːvəs), *a. rare.* [f. CURVE *sb.* + -OUS, on L. type **curvōs-us*.] Curved; crooked.

1674 BLOUNT *Glossogr.* (ed. 4), *Curvous*, crooked, bowed, uneven. *c* **1825** BEDDOES *Poems*, *Apotheosis* 99 Around the curvous atmosphere Of my own real existence I revolve.

curvy ('kɜːvɪ), *a.* [-Y[1].] Having a curve or curves; full of curves, marked with curves. *Comb.*, as ***curvy-brimmed*** adj.

1902 *Westm. Gaz.* 23 Oct. 3/2 The collar and the quaint curvy applications on the skirt should be of guipure lace. **1965** G. MCINNES *Road to Gundagai* xii. 204 Men in curvy-brimmed top hats.

cur'whibble. ? *dial.* [app. connected with *whybibble* given by Forby as 'a whimsey, idle fancy, silly scruple, etc.' With the first syllable cf. CURFUFFLE, and *carwitchet*, CARRIWITCHET.] ? A whimsical or nonsensical contrivance; also *attrib.*

1842 S. LOVER *Handy Andy* x. 99 Don't the English catch their fish..with a long rough stick, and a little curwhibble of a bone at the end of it? **1887** H. KNOLLYS *Sk. Life Japan* 114 Workmen..laboriously cutting, with little, clumsy, curwibble hooks, the crop, handful by handful.

cur'willet. *dial.* [From the cry of the bird.] A local name for the Sanderling (*Calidris arenaria*), a bird of the snipe family.

1674 RAY *Coll. Words* 90 The Sanderling or Curwillet, so called about Pensans. **1678** RAY *Willughby's Ornith.* 303. **1804** BEWICK *Brit. Birds* II. 1 Sanderling, Towillee, or Curwillet. **1885** SWAINSON *Brit. Birds* 195 *Curwillet*, Cornwall, a name given to the Sanderling from its cry.

†**'cury**[1]. *Obs.* Also 4 **kewery.** [a. OF. *keuerie*, *queuerie*, *queurie* (14th c.), cookery, kitchen, f. *keu*, *queu*, *coeu*:—L. *coquus*, *cocus* cook: see -ERY.] **a.** Cookery. (Also the 'concoction' of substances in alchemy.) **b.** Cooked food; a dish.

1387 TREVISA *Higden* (Rolls) I. 405 They conne ete and be mury Wiþ oute grete kewery. [CAXTON cury, Higden *coquorum artificia*]. ? *c* **1390** (*title*), Form of Cury. ? *a* **1400** *Morte Arth.* 1063 Here es cury un-clene, carle, be my trowthe. *c* **1460** J. RUSSELL *Bk. Nurture* 506 Cookes with þeire newe conceytes..Many new curies..þey are contryvynge & Fyndynge. **1513** DOUGLAS *Æneis* VIII. Prol. 95 Throw cury of the quentassens.

cury[2]. *rare.* = L. *curia*.

1886 [See CURIATE].

curyal, -ose, obs. forms of CURIAL, CURIOUS.

euryd, curys, obs. forms of *cured*, *cures*.

cus, obs. form of KISS.

cusche, cuschet, obs. ff. CUISSE, CUSHAT.

cuschoun, obs. form of CUSHION.

Cusco-bark. Also Cuzco-. A kind of cinchona bark, obtained from Cuzco in Lower Peru. Also called **Cusco-china.**

Hence **Cusco-cinchonine, 'Cusconine, Cu'sconidine,** alkaloids obtained from Cusco-bark.

1879 WATTS *Dict. Chem.* 3rd Suppl. I. 495–7.

‖**cuscus**[1] ('kʊskʊs). Also 7 **cuskus.** [The same word as COUSCOUS, the dish so called being originally made of this grain. In F. *couscou*, in 18th c. *cuzcuz*, *cousse-couche*, *couche-couche*.] The grain of the African Millet, *Holcus spicatus* Linn., *Penicillaria spicata* Willd., a cereal indigenous to Africa, where it has constituted from the earliest times an important article of food.

1625 PURCHAS *Pilgrims* II. VIII. XI. 1368 Their bread is made of this *Coaua*, which is a kind of blacke Wheate, and *Cuscus* a small white Seed like Millet in Biskany. **1629** CAPT. SMITH *Trav. & Adv.* xiii. 25 Cuskus. **1634** SIR T. HERBERT *Trav.* (1638) 23 (*Madagascar*), You shall have in exchange.. Barley, Rice and Cuscus, with what fruit you like. *Ibid.* 28 The Ile [Mohelia] inricht us with..Buffols..Rice, Pease, Cuscus, Honey. **1852** W. F. DANIELL in *Pharmac. Jrnl.* XI. 395 It constitutes the *kouskous* of the Joloffs and Moorish nations, the *dra* and *bishna* of Tripoli.

‖**cuscus**[2] ('kʌskʌs). Also **kuss-kuss, cuss cuss, kuskos, cuscuss.** [ad. Pers. and Urdū *khas khas* the sweet-scented root of the grass in question.] The long fibrous aromatic root of an Indian grass, *Andropogon muricatus*, used for making fans, screens, ornamental baskets, etc. Hence ***cuscus-grass, cuscus-root.***

1810 T. WILLIAMSON *E. India Vade M.* I. 235 (Y.) The Kuss-Kuss..when fresh, is rather fragrant, though the scent is somewhat terraceous. **1862** MRS. SPEID *Last Years Ind.* 72 The root of a sweet smelling grass, the cuscus. *attrib.* **1889** *Blackw. Mag.* Aug. 247 A large cuscus mat.

‖**cuscus**³ (ˈkʌskʌs). [mod.L. from the native name; see COUSCOUS².] A genus of marsupial quadrupeds found in New Guinea.

1662 J. DAVIES *Mandelslo's Trav. E. Ind.* 165 There is in this Island a kind of beasts they call *Cusos*, that keeps constantly in trees, living on nothing but fruit. They resemble our Rabbets. **1880** D'ALBERTIS *N. Guinea* I. 407 On the branch of a tall tree we may perhaps see a cuscus slowly creeping along. **1889** H. H. ROMILLY *Verandah N. Guinea* 69 The opossums and cuscus tribe taste strongly of gum leaves on which they feed.

cuscus, -cus(s)u, -cosoo, vars. of COUSCOUS¹.

cusec. Abbreviation, used in Engineering, etc., of '*cu*bic foot per *sec*ond'.

1913 THOMAS & WATT *Improvem. Rivers* (ed. 2) I. i. 46 The abbreviation 'second-feet' which is frequently used in America instead of 'cubic feet per second', has the equivalent of 'cusecs' among the Anglo-Indian engineers. **1915** C. E. HOUSDEN *Is Venus Inhabited?* 37 We should need a continuous flow of 20,000,000 cusecs. **1960** *Times* 25 July 11/6 A rise in river-flow from three cusecs in dry weather to 55,000 in wet.

†**cuser,** aphetic f. ACCUSER.

1589 WARNER *Alb. Eng.* VI. xxx. (1612) 151 More honest than her Cuser.

cush (kʊʃ), colloq. shortening of CUSHION *sb.*, esp. in sense 3 c.

1895 A. ROBERTS *Adv.* ix. 111 The red was under the cush. Alias hesitated at which ball to play. **1905** *Westm. Gaz.* 21 Oct. 4/1 It is like watching a game of billiards with wooden cushes and beechwood balls. **1947** D. DAVIN *Gorse blooms Pale* 97 And these bottoms and legs bouncing through the room. Cushioned against reality. It cannoned off their cush. **1965** 'A. HALL' *Berlin Memorandum* viii. 83, I was placed in a slow drift for a right-angle..and brought the nose round full-lock with the kerb for a cush.

cush, *v.*, var. *cosh* (see COSH *sb.*³). Hence ˈ**cusher.**

1923 F. L. PACKARD *Four Stragglers* I. ii, 'A bit of a "cushing" expedition, was it?'..'Just the usual bash on the head with a neddy.' *Ibid.* II. iv, That was the method of the 'cusher'.

cushag (ˈkʊʃəg). *dial.* Also -og. [Manx *cuishag vooar*, lit. 'big stalk'.] The common ragwort, *Senecio jacobæa*.

1887 HALL CAINE *Deemster* xxiv, There's gold on the cushags yet. **1894** —— *Manxman* II. xxii, Philip plucked the cushag. **1900** *Westm. Gaz.* 1 Oct. 2/3 The term 'weeds' is defined as including thistles, cushags, and common docks.

cushat (ˈkʌʃət). Chiefly *Sc.* and *north. dial.* Forms: 1 cúscute, -scote, -sceote, 5 cowscott, -schote, 6 cowschet, kowschot, 6–7 coushot, 7, 9 cowshot, 8 cowshut, 8–9 cooscot, 9 cowscot; 6 cuschet, 8– cushat, 9 *dial.* cushie, cusha. [OE. *cúscute*, *-scote*, *-sceote* (wk. fem.) has no cognates in the other Teutonic langs., and its etymology is obscure. The element *scote*, *scute* is app. a deriv. of *scéotan* (weak grade *scut-*, *scot-*) to shoot, and may mean 'shooter, darter': cf. *sceotan* in Ælfric's *Colloquy*, glossed *tructos* 'trouts', app. in reference to their rapid darting motion; also cf. OHG. *scozza* str. f., shoot (of a plant). For the first part, *cú* cow offers no likely sense, and Prof. Skeat suggests that we may here have an echo of the bird's call = modern *coo*: this is doubtful. Others have taken the first part as OE. *cúsc* chaste, modest, pure; but the rest of the word then remains unexplained.] The wood-pigeon or ring-dove.

a **700** *Epinal Gloss.* 829 *Palumbes*, cuscutan [*Erfurt* cuscotae, *Corpus* cuscote]. *c* **1000** *Voc.* in Wr.-Wülcker 260/7 *Pudumba*, cusceote. **10**.. *Ibid.* 286/2 *Palumba*, cuscote, *uel* wuduculfre. **14**.. *Ibid.* 702/34 *Palumbus*, cowscott. **1483** *Cath. Angl.* 79 Cowschote, *palumbus*. **1513** DOUGLAS *Æneis* XII. Prol. 237 The cowschet [*v.r.* kowschot] crowdis and pirkis on the rys. **1653** URQUHART *Rabelais* I. xxxvii, Some dozens of queests, coushots, ringdoves and wood-culvers. **1788** MARSHALL *Yorksh.* Gloss., *Cooscot*, a wood-pigeon. **1781** J. HUTTON *Tour to Caves* Gloss., *Cowshut*, a wild pigeon. **1792** BURNS *Bess & Spinning-wheel* iii, On lofty aiks the cushats wail. **1813** SCOTT *Rokeby* III. x, He heard the Cushat's murmur hoarse. **1866** *Cornh. Mag.* Aug. 224 The building cushats cooed and cooed.

b. So ***cushat-dove*** (Sc. *cusha-dow*, *cushie-doo*).

1805 SCOTT *Last Minstr.* II. xxxiv, Fair Margaret, through the hazel grove, Flew like the startled cushat-dove. **1886** SIDEY *Mistura Curiosa* 103 The Cushie doo That croodles late at e'en.

cushaw (kəˈʃɔː, ˈkʌʃɔː). *U.S.* Also cashaw. [perh. Algonquin.] A winter crookneck squash, or a variety of this.

1588 T. HARRIOT *Briefe & True Rep. of Virginia* sig. c4ᵛ, *Coscushaw*, some of our company tooke to bee that kinde of roote which the Spaniards in the West Indies call *Cassauy*. **1698** G. THOMAS *Pennsylvania* 21 Cucumbers, Coshaws, Artichokes. **1705** R. BEVERLEY *Hist. Virginia* II. iv. 27 Their Cushaws are a kind of Pompion, of a bluish green Colour, streaked with White, when they are fit for Use. **1868** W. N. WHITE *Gardening for South* 214 The best variety [of squash] for family use is the Cashaw, a long, cylindrical, curved variety. **1924** J. W. RAINE *Land of Saddle-Bags* 28, I asked an old man why he preferred 'cushaws' (a large crook-neck squash) to pumpkins.

cush-cush (ˈkʊʃkʊʃ). [Native name.] A species of yam, *Dioscorea trifida*, native to South America and cultivated for its edible tubers.

1871 KINGSLEY *At Last* ii. 49 Great roots of yam and cush-cush. *Ibid.* 72 Wild cush-cush roots. **1929** NICHOLLS & HOLLAND *Textbk. Trop. Agric.* (ed. 2) xv. 446 Cush-cush Yam of Trinidad or Yampi of Jamaica (*Dioscorea trifida*, Linn.). **1960** *Guardian* 8 Jan. 4/7 The 'couscouche' yam, the cush-cush of the British West Indies..are often made into fritters. **1969** *Oxf. Bk. Food Plants* 182/1 All [yams] are of Old World origin except the cush-cush yam *Dioscorea trifida* which is native to America.

cushes, -ies: see CUISSE.

ˈ**cushew-bird.** Also cashew bird. [So called from the likeness of the blue knot on its forehead to the *cashew-nut*.] A West Indian name of the Galeated Curassow (*Pauxis galeata*).

1758 G. EDWARDS *Gleanings Nat. Hist.* II. lxxv. 182 The Cushew-Bird takes its name from the knob over its bill, which in shape much resembles an American nut called Cushew. **1852** TH. ROSS tr. *Humboldt's Trav.* II. xviii. 172 The curassaos and cashew-birds.

cushie, cushie-doo: see CUSHAT.

cushinet, obs. form of CUSHIONET.

Cushing's syndrome (ˈkʊʃɪŋ). *Med.* [f. the name of Harvey Williams *Cushing* (1869–1939), American surgeon, who described the condition in 1932.] A syndrome of hypertension, obesity, metabolic disorders, etc., caused by hypersecretion of hormones by the adrenal cortex. **Cushing's disease,** Cushing's syndrome accompanied and caused by an adenoma of the basophil cells of the pituitary gland.

1934 *Proc. R. Soc. Med.* XXVII. 397 He regarded the case ..as a typical one of Cushing's syndrome. **1936** H. D. ROLLESTON *Endocrine Organs* iii. 104 (*heading*) Cushing's syndrome. Synonym: pituitary basophilism. **1937** *Index-catal. Surgeon-General's Office* 4th Ser. II. 130/2 (*heading*) Basophilism, pituitary (Cushing's disease). **1962** J. HOWKINS *Shaw's Textbk. Gynæcol.* (ed. 8) xviii. 447 *Cushing's disease* must be distinguished from Cushing's syndrome. Cushing's disease is due perhaps to a basophil adenoma of the anterior pituitary which leads to hyperfunction of the suprarenal cortex. The main symptoms and signs are those due to a disorder of the suprarenal which are now referred to under the term Cushing's syndrome. **1964** L. MARTIN *Clin. Endocrinol.* (ed. 4) i. 32 It is generally accepted that the symptoms of Cushing's syndrome result ultimately from adrenocortical overactivity. *Ibid.*, The basophil adenoma..is only present in about 50 per cent of cases of Cushing's syndrome.

cushion (ˈkʊʃən), *sb.* Forms: α. 4 cuyschun, cuȝshen, 4–6 cuyssh-, cuissh-, -in, -en, -un, -yn, etc.; 4–7 quishin, qui-, quy-, qwi-, qwy-, (quyi-), -ss-, -ssh-, -ssch-, -sch-, -sh-, (szh-), -in, -yn, -en, -ene, -an, -on, -un, -ion, -yon, -ing, -ynge, etc.; 6 quesion, 8 quishing; 4–5 whyss-, whyssh-, whish-, wyssh-, -in, -yne, -ene, etc., etc. β. 4–6 cusshyn, -on, -en, -ion, -eyn, -on; 5 cusch-, cosch-, cossh-, kussh-, kossch-, cos-, -yn(e, -en, -oun, -one, -yon, -ing, cowssing, etc.; 6–7 cush-en, -in, -yn, -ian, -eon, -ing, etc., (6 cussin, cochen, kushen; 7 cuoshen, coussin, -ion); 6– cushion. (Nearly 70 forms occur.) [Of this word ME. had two types, α. *cuisshin, quishin* (north. *whishin*), a. OF. *coissin*, later *coessin, cuissin* (13–15th c. in Littré); and β. *cusshyn, cushin*, a. F. *coussin* (14th c.)—earlier *cussin* (12th c. in Hatzf.); in both languages the latter type is the surviving one. OF. *coissin* was = Fr. *coissin*, Cat. *coixi*, Sp. *coxin, cojin*, It. *coscino, cuscino*:—L. type *coxinum*, f. *coxa* hip, thigh: cf. L. *cubitāl* elbow-cushion, f. *cubitus* elbow. (See P. Meyer in *Romania* 1892, 87).

The history of the form *coussin*, with which *cushion* goes, is more obscure. Hatzfeld suggests that it is an altered variant of *coissin*, influenced by OF. *coute* quilt:—L. *culcita* quilt, cushion. T. A. Jenkins in *Mod. Lang. Notes*, May 1893, argues for its being:—late L. **culticinum*, for **culcitinum*, a conjectured deriv. of *culcita*; in which case *coissin* and *coussin* would be distinct words without etymological connexion: this their history makes improbable.]

1. a. A case of cloth, silk, etc. stuffed with some soft elastic material, used to give support or ease to the body in sitting, reclining, or kneeling.

α. *c* **1340** *Gaw. & Gr. Knt.* 877 Whyssynes vpon quelde-poyntes, þa[t] koynt wer boþe. [**1361** *Will of Edw. Blk. Prince* in Nichols *Royall Wills* (1780) 74 Curtyns, quissyns, traversyn.] *c* **1374** CHAUCER *Troylus* II. 1229 And doun she sette here by hym..vp-on a quysshon [*v.r.* cuisshyn] gold y-bete. **1388** WYCLIF *1 Sam.* v. 9 Seetis of skynnes, ethir cuyschuns. *a* **1400** *Isumbras* 579 Bryng a chayere and a qwyschene. **1418** *E.E. Wills* (1882) 36 Vj reof quisshens of worsted. **1530** PALSGR. 211/2 Cuysshen, *coessyn*. **1547** in Strype *Eccl. Mem.* II. App. A. 293 Ther was a carpet and quission laid..for the chief mourner. **1601** HOLLAND *Pliny* XIX. iv, Beautified with green quishins. **1615** CROOKE *Body of Man* 74 It serueth vs instead of a quishion.

β. **1382** WYCLIF *Ezek.* xiii. 18 Woo to hem that sewen togider cusshens [**1388** cuschens] vndir eche cubit of hoond. *c* **1440** *Promp. Parv.* 94 Coschyne, *sedile*. *Ibid.* 111 Cuschone [**1499** PYNSON cusshyn], *cuscina*. **1470–85** MALORY *Arthur* XIX. xi, And there was layd a cusshyn of gold that he shold knele vpon. *c* **1530** LD. BERNERS *Arth. Lyt. Bryt.* (1814) 151 They set them downe on cosshyns of sylke. **1577–87** HOLINSHED *Chron.* III. 800/1 With cushins of fine gold. **1601** SHAKS. *Jul. C.* IV. iii. 243 Ile haue them sleepe on Cushions in my Tent. **1678** R. L'ESTRANGE *Seneca's Mor.* (1702) 52 A Soldier lent you his Cloak for a Cushing. *a* **1732** GAY *Mad Dog* (R.), A prude, at morn and evening prayer, Had worn her velvet cushion bare. **1883** G. LLOYD *Ebb & Flow* II. 103 A space on the tiny lawn where rugs and cushions were spread out.

b. That set on the book-board of a pulpit, etc., to suppport the bible or other book; cf. ***cushion-cuffer, -thumper*** in 11.

1615 *Vestry Bks.* (Surtees) 69 One clothe and one quission of black vellure for the pulpett. **1709** STEELE & SWIFT *Tatler* No. 70 ¶4 Neither is banging a Cushion, Oratory. **1719** SWIFT *To Yng. Clergyman*, You will observe some clergymen with their heads held down..within an inch of the cushion. **1872** E. PEACOCK *Mabel Heron* I. ix. 151 To mend a rent in the cushion of the reading-desk.

c. The seat of a judge or ruler. Cf. WOOLSACK.

1659 B. HARRIS *Parival's Iron Age* 82 Maurice..having changed the Magistrates in many Towns..the Arminians were fain to leave the cushion against their wills. *a* **1734** NORTH *Lives* (1826) I. 130 The Court of Common Pleas had been outwitted by the Kings Bench, till his Lordship came upon the cushion. **1844** H. H. WILSON *Brit. India* II. 415 Bhawani Sing..was placed upon his cushion of sovereignty by the assistant to the Political Agent in Malwa.

d. *fig.*; also as an emblem of ease and luxury.

1589 *Pappe w. Hatchet* B iv, The diuell take al, if truth find not as many soft cushions to leane on, as trecherie. **1607** SHAKS. *Cor.* IV. vii. 43 Not moouing From th' Caske to th' Cushion. **1652** A. ROSS *Hist. World* Pref. 1 Idlenesse..the Devils Cushion, as the Fathers call it. **1785** COWPER *Wks.* (1837) XV. 174 At last [I] have placed myself much at my ease upon the cushion of this one resolution. **1833** CARLYLE *Misc.* (1872) V. 89 Cullies, the easy cushion on which Knaves and Knavesses repose.

2. *transf.* **a.** Applied to anything resembling or acting as a cushion.

1813 SCOTT *Triermain* I. viii, The silver-moss and lichen twined..A cushion fit for age. **1860** MAURY *Phys. Geog. Sea* i. 19 Protected from..the violence of its waves by cushions of still water. **1882** VINES *Sachs' Bot.* 220 A circular leaf-bearing cushion. **1954** *Economist* 30 Oct. 411/1 Tea shares are a tricky market; numerous small companies whose shares seldom change hands make it impossible for the stock jobbers to hold any cushion of stock. **1955** *Times* 6 July 5/5 Mr. Eric Fletcher..moved an amendment to enable a plaintiff to be entitled to costs on High Court scale when he recovered a sum of £250 or more. He said the introduction of this 'cushion' was essential to justice. **1965** *Listener* 17 June 886/2 Part of their training was to find themselves jobs and hold them with no ecclesiastical cushion to fall back on.

†**b.** A swelling simulating pregnancy: sometimes called ***Queen Mary's cushion***, after Mary Tudor. (Perhaps sometimes an actual cushion or pad.) *Obs.*

1597 SHAKS. *2 Hen. IV*, V. iv. 16 But I would the Fruite of her Wombe might miscarry. *Officer.* If it do, you shall haue a dozen of Cushions againe, you haue but eleuen now. **1649** MILTON *Eikon.* iii. (1851) 356 And thus his pregnant motives are at last prov'd nothing but a Tympany, or a Queen Maries Cushion. **1689** *Let. fr. the Pope* in *Harl. Misc.* (Malh.) I. 370 (D.) That a King..should praise (or rather mock) God for a child, whilst his Queen had only conceived a pillow, and was brought to bed of a cushion..This was the old contrivance of another Mary-Queen. **1694** S. JOHNSON *Notes Past. Let. Bp. Burnet* I. 37 His Wife went fourty Weeks with a Cushion.

3. a. In various specific and technical applications: as, the 'pillow' used in making bone-lace; a receptacle for pins, a PIN-CUSHION; †an ink-pad for inking a seal, die, etc. (*obs.*); a flat leathern bag filled with pounce, used by engravers to support the plate; the elastic leathern pad on which gold-leaf is spread and cut with the palette-knife; the rubber of an electrical machine.

1574 HELLOWES *Gueuara's Fam. Ep.* (1577) 316 To see her ..take her cushin for bone lace, or her rocke to spinne. **1607** SHAKS. *Cor.* II. i. 98 Your Beards deserue not so honourable a graue, as to stuffe a Botchers Cushion. **1735** *Dict. Polygraph.* s.v. *Engraving*, The *Graving cushion* is a roundish, but flattish leather bag filled with sand to lay the plate upon, on which it may be turn'd easily any way at pleasure. **1768–74** TUCKER *Lt. Nat.* (1852) I. 93 Like those cushions your gossips stick with pins in hearts, lozenges, and various forms, against a lying-in. **1776** *Trial of Nundocomar* 43/2 He dipt his seal on the cushion and sealed the bond. **1832** *Nat. Philos., Electric.* iii. §57. 15 (Useful Knowl. Soc.) The earlier electricians contented themselves with using the hand as a rubber, till a cushion was introduced for that purpose by Professor Winkler. **1837** WHITTOCK *Bk. Trades* (1842) 117 (*Carver & Gilder*), With one hand he holds the cushion, which is merely a flat board covered with soft leather. *Ibid.* 214 (*Engraver*), The sand-bag, or cushion..is used for laying the copper plate upon. **1866** *Joyce's Sci. Dial.* 492 (*Electrical Machine*) The cushion or rubber is fixed on a glass pillar.

b. A pad worn by women under the hair; a pad or bustle worn beneath the skirt of a woman's dress.

1774 *Westm. Mag.* II. 424 We are sorry to find the Ladies returning..to the long-exploded mode of dressing their hair with the borrowed aid of the Cushion. **1806** LADY DOUGLAS in *Examiner* 15 March 1813, 173/1 She wore a cushion behind. **1860** FAIRHOLT *Costume* (ed. 2) 476 The hair was arranged over a cushion formed of wool, and covered with silk.

c. The elastic rim or lining of the inner side of a billiard-table or bagatelle board, from which the balls rebound.

1778 C. JONES *Hoyle's Games Impr.* 193 The Adversary is obliged to play Bricole from the opposite Cushion. **1837** D.

WALKER *Games & Sports* 89 There are likewise two small cushions placed against the sides. **1853** C. BEDE *Verdant Green* xii, A game of billiards on a wooden table that had no cushions. **1856** CRAWLEY *Billiards* (1859) 5 The cushions are now almost universally made of Vulcanised India-rubber, though..old players say that the stroke is more certain from the old stuffed list cushions.

d. *Mech.* A body of steam (or air) left in the cylinder of a steam-engine (or air-engine) to act as an elastic buffer to the piston. Also, a body of air which supports an aircraft, hovercraft, etc.

1848 *Pract. Mech. Jrnl.* I. 78 A cushion of steam is interposed to partially sustain the force of the blow [in a steam hammer]. **1891** RANKINE *Steam Engine* 364 The volume of the cushion air when it is under the greatest pressure [in an air engine]. **1928** *New Republic* 15 Aug. 331/1 When the plane catches itself on a cushion of air at the end of a plunge, you feel heavy. **1960**, etc. [see *air-cushion* s.v. AIR *sb.*[1] B. II]. **1967** *Gloss. Terms Air-Cushion Vehicles* (*B.S.I.*) 5 *Cushion*, a volume of air under pressure enclosed between the bottom of an ACV and the supporting surface by rigid structure, curtains, skirts or any combination thereof.

e. A sweetmeat in the shape of a cushion.

1906 E. NESBIT *Railway Children* ix. 190 I'll give you some peppermint cushions for the little ones. **1921** L. THORPE *Bonbons & Simple Sugar Sweets* 49 Satin Cushions... With a pair of scissors cut the mixture into small cushions and leave them until quite firm. **1970** J. AIKEN *Embroidered Sunset* v. 89 Bars of coconut candy, mounds of chocolate drops, of peppermint cushions.

4. In a horse, pig, etc.: **a.** The fleshy part of the buttock. **b.** The fibro-fatty frog in the interior of a horse's hoof; also the coronet or fibrous pad extending round the upper part of the foot, immediately above, and united to the hoof.

1710 *Lond. Gaz.* No. 4777/4 Both of them formerly cut with I.G. on the Cushion. **1712** *Ibid.* No. 4858/4 A black Spot on each Quishing. **1722** *Ibid.* No. 6079/9. **1892** W. FREAM *Elem. Agric.* xix. (ed. 4) 344 Outside these structures are two fibro-cartilages, one on each side, united behind and below by the plantar cushion..The coronary cushion. *Mod.* A cut of bacon off the cushion.

5. a. *Ent.* The little pad or cushion-like process of an insect's foot; a pulvillus. **b.** *Bot.* The enlargement at, or just below, the point of attachment of some leaves; a pulvinus; also a dense mass of foliage such as is formed by some saxifrages and stonecrops.

1828 STARK *Elem. Nat. Hist.* II. 285 A distinct cushion; antennæ of nine joints. **1870** HOOKER *Stud. Flora* 137 *Sedum acre*..Tufts or cushions 3–10 in. diam.

6. *Arch.* = COUSSINET, q.v.

1852 BREES *Gloss. Pract. Archit.* 133 *Cushion*, or *Coussinet*, a stone lying on the top of a pier supporting an arch.

†**7.** A drinking-vessel. *Obs.*

1594 *Taming of Shrew* I I, Why, Tapster, I say, Fils a fresh cushen heere! *c* **1618** FLETCHER *Q. Corinth* II. iv, Quissions ye Knaves! (Enter drawers with Quissions).

8. (*Our*) *Lady's Cushion*, a name for several plants, esp. *Armeria maritima*.

1578 LYTE *Dodoens* IV. l. 509 Some call it [Thrift] in Englishe our Ladies quishion.

9. *Cycling.* Short for *cushion-tire*.

1891 *Pall Mall G.* 17 Sept. 1/1 Twenty-one starters, five using pneumatic tyres, two cushions, all the rest solids.

10. *Phrases.* †**a.** *to miss the cushion*: to miss the mark; to make a mistake, err. *Obs.*

c **1525** SKELTON *Col. Cloute* 998 And whan he weneth to syt Yet may he mysse the quysshyon. **1535** JOYE *Apol. Tindale* 48 Yet hath he missed the kushen in many placis. **1571** HANMER *Chron. Irel.* (1623) 168 He was elected Archbishop of St. Davids, but at Rome he was out bid, by him that had more money, and missed the Cushin. **1593** DRAYTON *Eclogues* viii. 80 Thy Wits doe erre and misse the Cushion quite. **1608** HIERON *Defence* II. 157 He hath missed the cushen and sitteth bare. **1609** HOBY *Let. to Mr. T.H.* 45 They may misse the cushion in the analogie of the place.

†**b.** *beside* (or *wide of*) *the cushion*: away from the main purpose or argument, beside the mark; erroneously or mistakenly. *Obs.*

1576 FLEMING *Panopl. Epist.* Bjb, Thou leanest beside the cushing. **1581** J. BELL *Haddon's Answ. Osor.* 78 He raungeth abroad to originall sinne altogether besides the cushian. **1598** R. BERNARD tr. *Terence* (1607) 230 Thou art beside the cushin [L. *erras*]. **1690** W. WALKER *Idiom. Anglo-Lat.* 517 He is wide of the cushion. *a* **1783** H. BROOKE *Female Officer* I. xiii, The man did not speak much beside the cushion of common sense.

†**c.** *to set* or *put beside* (or *besides*) *the cushion*: to turn (any one) out of his place or position; to depose, set aside; to deprive or disappoint of an office or dignity. *Obs.*

1562 J. HEYWOOD *Prov. & Epigr.* (1867) 80, I may set you besyde the cushyn yit. **1587** FLEMING *Contn. Holinshed* III. 1305/1 To put enimitie betweene the king and hir; and to set hir besides the cushion. *a* **1624** BP. M. SMITH *Serm.* 188 Sometimes putting them besides the cushion, and placing others in their roome. **1663** SPALDING *Troub. Chas. I* (1792) I. 291 (Jam.) The master of Forbes' regiment was.. discharged..Thus is he set beside the cushion.

11. *attrib.* and *Comb.*, as *cushion-canvas*, *-cover*, *-layer*, *-stuffer*; *cushion-footed*, *-like*, *-shaped* adjs.; **cushion capital** *Arch.* (see quots.); †**cushion-cuffer** = *cushion-thumper*; †**cushion-lord** (see quot.); **cushion-pink**, a name for Thrift (*Armeria maritima*); **cushion plant**, a plant that grows in a dense cushion-like tuft (cf. sense 5 b above); **cushion-rafter**, an auxiliary rafter beneath and parallel to a principal rafter, a principal brace; **cushion-rest** in *Billiards* (see quot.); **cushion-rider**, an early name for a hovercraft type of vehicle supported by a 'cushion' of air; so *cushion-riding* vbl. sb. and ppl. a.; **cushion-scale**, a common scale-insect, very injurious to orange and other trees; **cushion-star**, a fossil star-fish of the genus *Goniaster*; **cushion-stitch**, a flat embroidery stitch used to fill in backgrounds in old needlework, *esp.* in Church embroidery; **cushion-thumper**, a preacher who indulges in violent action; **cushion-tire**, a bicycle tire made of india-rubber tubing stuffed with shreds of india-rubber; hence *cushion-tired ppl. a.*; **cushion-work** in *Embroidery* (see quot.). Also CUSHION-CLOTH, -DANCE.

1611 COTGR., *Gaze*, *Cushion Canuas; the thinne Canuas that serues women for a ground vnto their Cushions, or Purse-worke, &c. **1835** WHEWELL *Archit. Notes* 55 *Cushion capitals..consist of large cubical masses projecting considerably over the shaft of the column, and rounded off at the lower corners. **1842–76** GWILT *Encycl. Archit.* Gloss., *Cushion Capital*, a capital used in Romanesque and early Mediæval architecture, resembling a cushion pressed down by a weight. It is also a cap consisting of a cube rounded off at its lower angles, largely used in the Norman period. **1881** C. C. HARRISON *Woman's Handiwork* I. 61 The *cushion-cover..has a ground of royal purple velvet. **1960** I. JEFFERIES *Dignity & Purity* xii. 183 She carried on enthusing about cushion covers. **1683** E. HOOKER *Pref. Ep. Pordage's Mystic Div.* 36 Our impertinently idl Pulpit-praters, or..too busily laborious *Cushion-Cuffers. **1865** *Reader* 12 Aug. 175/3 A smooth and velvety tiger.. Supple and *cushion-footed. **1679** *Trials of Green & Berry* 64 Mrs. Warrier..being *Cushion-layer in the Chappel. **1647** H. MORE *Song of Soul* I. II. lix, Soft mosse..Whose velvet hue and verdure *cushion-like did show. **1951** S. SPENDER *World within World* 258 Fields enclosed by *cushion-like hedges. **1847–78** HALLIWELL, **Cushion-lord*, a lord made by favour, and not for good service to the state; hence, an effeminate person. **1863** PRIOR *Plant-n.*, **Cushion-pink*, from its dense tufted growth. **1903** W. R. FISHER tr. *Schimper's Plant-geogr.* III. iv. 705 The type of *cushion-plants..is represented in the alpine region of mountains of higher latitudes in both hemispheres..by a multitude of forms. **1911** *Encycl. Brit.* XXI. 764/1 In 'cushion plants' the leaves are very small, very close together, and the low habit is protective against winds. **1819** P. NICHOLSON *Archit. Dict.* 652 Sometimes called *principal braces*, and sometimes **cushion rafters.* **1873** BENNETT & CAVENDISH *Billiards* 28 **Cushion-rests* are rests, shaped to fit over the face of the cushion. **1959** *Times* 13 Aug. 10/2 This year's Farnborough flying display will feature..a '*cushion-rider'. **1961** *Spectator* 14 July 53 A cushion-rider can be lifted vertically and then driven over the ground at speeds which reach into the take-off speeds of ordinary jet aircraft. **1960** *Aeroplane* XCIX. 771/1 Doubtless it has other applications and ideas for *cushion-riding craft in mind. **1961** *Spectator* 14 July 53 A transition between cushion-riding and ordinary aerofoil lift. **1886** *Rep. Comm. Agric. Washington U.S.* 466 The Cottony *Cushion-scale is found only in California, Australia, South Africa and New Zealand. **1843** FORBES in *Proc. Berw. Nat. Club* II. 80 Orange-yellow..with crimson-red, are the usual hues of the *cushion-stars. **1880** L. HIGGIN *Handbk. Embroidery* v. 47 *Cushion Stitches are taken..so as to leave all the silk and crewel on the surface. **1886** *Daily News* 14 Dec. 7/6 Billiard *cushion stuffer wanted. **1876** ROCK *Text. Fabr.* viii. 81 Done in cross and tent stitch, or the '*cushion style'. *a* **1643** W. CARTWRIGHT *Ordinary* III. v, Thou violent *cushion-thumper, hold thy tongue. **1891** *Cyclist* 25 Feb. 164 *Cushion Tyres are getting quite fashionable here. **1891** *Wheeling* 4 Mar. 436 We rode 40 miles on a *cushion-tyred Cremorne. **1845** *Ecclesiologist* IV. 98 The [gold] threads are laid upon the linen, and fastened down at intervals with silk. This method is called *cushion-work.

cushion ('kʊʃən), *v.* [f. prec. sb.]

1. a. *trans.* To furnish with a cushion or cushions.

1820 W. IRVING *Sketch-Bk., Country Church* (1865) 124 The congregation..sat in pews, sumptuously lined and cushioned.

transf. **1890** *Illust. Lond. News* Christm. No. 11/1 An eyot cushioned with luxurious grass.

b. To pad or protect as with cushions. Also *fig.*

1836–9 TODD *Cycl. Anat.* II. 158/1 [The] surfaces [of the scapula] are cushioned with muscles. **1863** GEO. ELIOT *Romola* II. xxxi, No persuasive blandness could cushion him against the shock. **1958** *Times* 23 Jan. 7/2 Aircraft firms should diversify their activities so that their other work could cushion the fluctuations in aircraft requirements. **1962** *Listener* 19 Apr. 672/1 The trouble he has been at..to take action now to cushion the economy against a recession.

2. To rest, seat, or set (a person or thing) upon a cushion; to support, or prop *up* with cushions.

1735–8 BOLINGBROKE *On Parties* xii. (R.), Instead of inhabiting palaces, and being cushioned up in thrones. **1847–8** H. MILLER *First Impr.* iv. (1859) 150 The eye never slides off the landscape, but cushions itself upon it with a sense of security and repose. **1860** PUSEY *Min. Proph.* 183 Propped and cushioned up on both sides.

3. *fig.* To suppress (anything) quietly; to take no notice of it.

1818 BP. J. MILNER in Husenbeth *Life* 350 The South and West thought it prudent to cushion it. **1835** *Tait's Mag.* II. 273 The book..has been much less talked of than it deserves to be. We trust there is no desire in certain circles to cushion it. **1849** C. BRONTE *Shirley* xxviii, There my courage failed: I preferred to cushion the matter. **1887** *Pall Mall G.* 23 Aug. 1/1 The way in which complaints are cushioned in official quarters is startling.

4. *Billiards.* **a.** To place or leave (a ball) close to, or resting against, the cushion. **b.** *intr.* (In U.S.) To make the ball hit the cushion before cannoning or after contact with one of the balls. *Cent. Dict.*

5. To deaden the stroke of (the piston) by a cushion of steam; to form into a cushion of steam.

1850 [see CUSHIONING]. **1891** RANKINE *Steam Engine* 420 The quantity of steam confined or 'cushioned' is just sufficient to fill the clearance at the initial pressure.

Hence '**cushioning** *vbl. sb.* (*spec.* in *Mech.*: see quots. and cf. CUSHION *sb.* 3 d.)

1850 *Pract. Mech. Jrnl.* III. 104 This cushioning of the pistons, and the gradual restraining of the momentum. **1887** J. A. EWING in *Encycl. Brit.* XXII. 501/2 (*Steam-engine*), Admission before the end of the back stroke..together with the compression of steam left in the cylinder when the exhaust port closes, produces the mechanical effect of cushioning.

†'**cushion-cloth.** *Obs.* App. 'a cushion case or covering' (Nares).

a **1577** GASCOIGNE *Ferd. Jeronimi* Wks. (1587) 269 Hee would leaue eyther in the bed, or in hyr cushencloth, or by hyr looking-glasse..a peece of money. **1611** COTGR., *Desabiller*, a Ladies cushion-cloth. **1626** MIDDLETON *Women beware W.* III. i, Why is there not a cushion-cloth of drawn-work, Or some fair cut-work pinn'd up in my bed-chamber? **1705** *London Ladies Dressing Room* (N.), Three night-gowns of the richest stuff; Four cushion-cloaths are scarce enough.

'**cushion-dance.** A round dance, formerly danced at weddings, in which the women and men alternately knelt on a cushion to be kissed.

1607 HEYWOOD *Woman kilde* Wks. 1874 II. 97, I that haue ere now deseru'd a cushion, call for the cushion dance. **1621** BURTON *Anat. Mel.* II. ii. VI. iv. **1698** *The Dancing Master* 7 Joan Sanderson or the Cushion Dance, an old Round Dance. [Described in full.] **1767** W. HANBURY *Charities Ch. Langton* 86 The Cushion Dance..seemed to be his greatest favourite. **1870** BROUGH *Marston Lynch* ii. 6 There was to be a mistletoe, and the cushion-dance.

cushioned ('kʊʃənd), *ppl. a.* [f. CUSHION *sb.* and *v.* + -ED.]

1. a. Furnished or fitted with a cushion or cushions.

1839 J. L. STEPHENS *Trav. Greece, etc.* 65/1, I had a large cushioned seat of the diligence to myself. **1877** W. THOMSON *Voy. Challenger* I. i. 21 The top of the locker is cushioned, and serves for a lounge.

b. *transf.* Cf. sense 6 below.

1861 W. F. COLLIER *Hist. Eng. Lit.* 400 Grass-cushioned crags. **1863** *Possib. of Creation* 235 The cushioned, spreading feet [of the camel]. **1960** *New Statesman* 30 Jan. 146/1 An earth-to-moon flight with a cushioned landing on the moon and return flight to the earth.

c. Padded. See CUSHION *sb.* 3 b.

1777 COLMAN *Epil. Sheridan's Sch. Scandal*, Farewell the plumèd head, the cushion'd tête. **1807–8** W. IRVING *Salmag.* (1824) 32 Our ladies..When bishop'd, and cushion'd, and hoop'd to the chin.

d. *Cycling.* Furnished with cushion-tires.

1891 *Wheeling* 11 Mar. 453 The best plan..is that..of making forks wide enough for either pneumatic or cushioned wheels.

e. *fig.* Of the voice: soft and smooth, velvety.

1909 *Daily Chron.* 20 Jan. 5/6 Complaining for two hours against fate in that cushioned voice of hers. **1920** GALSWORTHY *In Chancery* II. xiii, There was comfort in her cushioned voice.

2. a. Seated on, or propped up with cushions.

1818 HAZLITT *Eng. Poets* v. (1870) 116 The in-door quiet and cushioned ease. **1877** BLACKIE *Wise Men* 274 A languid life And cushioned soft recumbency.

b. *fig.* Comfortable; protected.

a **1941** V. WOOLF *Captain's Death Bed* (1950) 32 A luxurious, educated, cushioned career for life.

3. *Arch.* *cushioned capital* = *cushion capital*, (see CUSHION *sb.* 11.)

? **1754** GRAY *Norman Archit.* Wks. 1884 I. 298 The capitals of the piers..have great variety in their forms; the square, the octagon, the cushioned, or swelling beneath.

4. *Bot.* Cushion-shaped, pulvinate.

1832 LINDLEY *Introd. Bot.* IV. Gloss. 374 *Cushioned* (*pulvinatus*), convex and rather flattened; seldom used.

5. *Billiards.* Placed close to the cushion. Said also of the player whose ball is so placed.

1770 J. LOVE *Cricket* 5 Or when the Ball, close cushion'd, slides askew, And to the op'ning Pocket runs, a Cou.

6. Of air: made into a 'cushion'.

1935 *Times* 4 Mar. 11/3 It has been held that lift rapidly decreases when the helicopter moves above the area of cushioned air created where the down-wash from the screws strikes the earth.

†'**cushionet.** *Obs.* Also 6 quysshenet, cushnet, 7 cushinet, -onet, coshionet. [a. F. *coussinet* (in 16–17th c. also *coissinet*), dim. of *coissin*, *coussin* cushion: see -ET[1].] A little cushion; a pin-cushion.

1542 *Will of Jane Fitzwilliam* (Somerset Ho.), Quysshenet. **1592** GREENE *Disput.* 33 If he layd those slippes on her cushnet. **1611** COTGR., *Espinglier*..a Pinpillow or cushinet to sticke pinnes on. **1647** H. MORE *Song of Soul* I. II. lxxvi, Closer set With sharp distinctions than a cushionet With pins and needles. **1721** BAILEY *Cushinet*, a little Cushion.

'**cushioning,** *ppl. a.* [f. CUSHION *v.* + -ING[2].] Forming a cushion.

1887 TOURGÉE *Button's Inn* 304 The soft..snow..may have formed a cushioning mass saving him from instant death.

cushionless (ˈkʊʃənlɪs), *a.* [f. CUSHION *sb.* + -LESS.] Without a cushion or cushions.

1837 HAWTHORNE *Twice Told T.* (1851) I. vi. 96 Rows of long cushionless benches. **1866** GEO. ELIOT *F. Holt* (1868) 52 His cushion-less arm-chair.

cushiony (ˈkʊʃənɪ), *a.* [f. CUSHION *sb.* + -Y.] Resembling a cushion in shape, softness, etc. *fig.* Easy, comfortable, 'soft'. Cf. CUSHY *a.*

1839–47 TODD *Cycl. Anat.* III. 908/1 The soft cushiony end of the nose. **1866** FLINT *Princ. Med.* (1880) 245 The emphysematous portions.. have a soft, cushiony feel. **1908** *Daily Chron.* 25 Feb. 4/4 A lot of them have rare cushiony jobs.

Cushite (ˈkʌʃaɪt), *a.* and *sb.* Also **Kushite.** [f. *Cush*, name of an ancient country in the Nile valley + -ITE.] **A.** *adj.* Pertaining or relating to an ancient people of eastern Africa, south of Egypt. **B.** *sb.* A member of this people; a sub-family of the Afro-Asian family of languages; also called **Cushitic, Kushitic** (kʌˈʃɪtɪk).

1836 N. MORREN tr. *Rosenmüller's Bibl. Geogr. Central Asia* I. ii. 80 A Cushite was the same as 'a man of colour'. *Ibid.* 82 Each nation placed its Cushites or Æthiopians to the south.. as known to them. **1846** *Cycl. Bibl. Lit.* I. 503/1 The name Cush was applied to tracts of country both in Arabia and Africa —.. on the very probable supposition that the descendants of the primitive Cushite tribes, who had settled in the former country, emigrated across the Red Sea to the latter region of the earth. *Ibid.* 504/1 Part of the Cushite population immigrated to Africa. **1883** R. N. CUST *Sk. Mod. Lang. Africa* I. 126 Lepsius recognizes them as the modern representatives of the Kushites of the Old Testament, the Ethiopians of Herodotus. **1910** *Encycl. Brit.* XII. 894/1 All these Cushitic languages, extending from Egypt to the equator, are separated by Reinisch as Lower Cushitic from the High Cushitic group, *i.e.* the many dialects spoken by tribes dwelling in the Abyssinian highlands. **1933** BLOOMFIELD *Language* iv. 67 The fourth branch of Semitic-Hamitic is Cushite, south of Egypt; it includes a number of languages, among them Somali and Galla. **1939** L. H. GRAY *Found. Lang.* 366 The Kushitic sub-division occupies part of the western coast of the Red Sea. **1954** PEI & GAYNOR *Dict. Linguistics* 117 *Kushitic*, a branch of the Hamitic sub-family of the Semito-Hamitic family of languages; it consists of a great many vernaculars, the principal ones being Somali and Galla. **1961** A. J. ARKELL in R. Oliver *Dawn Afr. Hist.* 10 The Cushites clashed with.. Assyria. *Ibid.*, The pharaoh sacked the old Cushite capital of Napata. **1970** NEW ENG. BIBLE *Jeremiah* xxxviii. 7 Ebedmelech the Cushite, a eunuch.

cushla, var. ACUSHLA.

1928 'BRENT OF BIN BIN' *Up Country* xiv. 243 And sure, Cushla-ma-chree, if you can't stand me I'll up and go away.

cushy (ˈkʊʃɪ), *a. colloq.* Also **cushey.** [Anglo-Ind., f. Hind. *khūsh* pleasant.] Of a post, job, etc.: easy, comfortable, 'soft'. Of a wound: not dangerous or serious.

1915 D. O. BARNETT *Lett.* 44 The billets here are very good.. and we have rooms to ourselves... It's all very cushey and nice. **1916** *Blackw. Mag.* Jan. 91/2 I've got a cushy wound. **1916** *Daily Mail* 1 Nov., He's got a cushy job. **1917** P. GIBBS *Battles of Somme* 146 All our men who have had the luck to get a 'cushie wound'. **1928** E. WAUGH *Decl. & F.* I. iii, I was sent to Ireland on a pretty cushy job connected with postal service. **1938** AUDEN & ISHERWOOD *On the Frontier* III. i, There're too many healthy young men slacking in cushy staff jobs! **1957** *Listener* 26 Dec. 1066/2 It was not a particularly cushy job and two of our men were killed in action. **1970** A. SILLITOE *Start in Life* 285 You were always on the lookout for a cushy billet. **1971** *Time* 18 Jan. 30/3 Something is not quite right even at the state's cushiest 'correctional facilities' (bureaucratese for prisons), some of which could pass for prep schools.

Hence **ˈcushiness**, the state or condition of being 'cushy'.

1930 S. SASSOON *Mem. Infantry Officer* ix. 268 There were times when I felt perversely indignant at the 'cushiness' of my convalescent existence.

cusin, -ing, obs. forms of COUSIN.

cusing, aphetic form of ACCUSING. Cf. CUSER.

c **1470** HENRY *Wallace* VI. 400 Him selff began a sair cusyng to mak.

cusk (kʌsk). A local name for two different fishes of the cod tribe: **a.** In Great Britain, the Torsk, *Brosmius vulgaris.* **b.** In U.S., the Burbot, *Lota maculosa.*

1624 CAPT. SMITH *Virginia* VI. 216 Cuske or small Ling, Sharke, Mackarell. **1867** WHITTIER *Tent on Beach* xxi, Tough and dried As a lean cusk from Labrador. **1884** *Stubbs' Merc. Circular* 194/2 The total catch of ground fish, including cod, haddock, hake, pollock, and cusk.

†**cuskin, -yn.** *Obs.* App. a variant of *curskyn*, CRUSKYN.

1526 *Will of T. Hustwayte* (Somerset Ho.), Oon of my siluer pottes called a Cuskyn. **1585** HIGGINS tr. *Junius' Nomenclator* 232 (Halliw.) Any kinde of pot to drink in: a cup: a cuskin. **1721** BAILEY, *Cuskin*, an ivory cup.

cusp (kʌsp). [ad. L. *cuspis, cuspid-em* point.]

1. *Astrol.* The beginning or entrance of a 'house'.

1585 LUPTON *Thous. Notable Th.* (1675) 165 Whosoever hath any fixed Star of the first Honour or Magnitude.. in the Degree of their Cuspe, of the tenth House. **1647** LILLY *Chr. Astrol.* iv. 33 The Cusp or very entrance of any house, or first beginning. **1651** CULPEPPER *Astrol. Judgem. Dis.* (1658) 47 In this figure Capricorn is upon the cuspe of the ascendent. **1815** SCOTT *Guy M.* iii, Houses of heaven, with their cusps, hours, and minutes; *Almuten, Almochoden, Anabibazon, Catabibazon.* **1856** VAUGHAN *Mystics* II. 51 Reckoning the cusps and hours of the houses of heaven!

2. *gen.* A point, pointed end, apex, peak; an ornament of a pointed form.

1647 H. MORE *Song of Soul* II. App. lxvii, The Cuspe of the Cone. **1847** SIR H. TAYLOR *Minor Poems* Wks. 1864 III. 232 And mid the loftiest [mountains] we could well discern One that was shining in a cusp of snow. **1876** ROCK *Text. Fabr.* vi. 59 Stopped with graceful cusps and artichokes.

†**b.** *erroneously*: Top, surface.

1658 R. FRANCK *North. Mem.* (1821) 61 That bush, whose slender branches wantonly dangle sporting themselves on the cusp of the water.

3. *Astron.* Each of the pointed extremities or 'horns' of the crescent moon (or of Mercury and Venus); also of the sun when partially eclipsed.

1676 HALLEY in Rigaud *Corr. Sci. Men* (1841) I. 229, 70 degrees from the northern cusp [of the moon], then something obtuse. **1764** *Phil. Trans.* LIV. 106 About the middle of the eclipse, the air was very clear, and the cusps well defined. **1793** HERSCHEL in *Phil. Trans.* LXXXIII. 202 One cusp of Venus appearing pointed, and the other blunt.

4. *Geom.* A point at which two branches of a curve meet and stop, with a common tangent; or at which the moving point describing the curve has its motion exactly reversed. Called also *spinode* or *stationary point.* (Also applied to an analogous point on a curved surface.)

1758 I. LYONS *Treat. Fluxions* vii. §191. 142 A point of Reflection or Cusp. **1857** WHEWELL *Hist. Induct. Sc.* II. 362 The peculiar inflected form of the wave surface, which has what is called a cusp. **1875** TODHUNTER *Diff. Calc.* (ed. 7) xxii. §301 If the two branches lie on opposite sides of the common tangent, the cusp is said to be of the first species; if on the same side, the cusp is said to be of the second species.. Cusps of the first species have been called 'keratoid' cusps, and of the second 'rhamphoid cusps'.

5. *Arch.* Each of the projecting points between the small arcs or 'foils' in Gothic tracery, arches, etc.

1813 SIR J. HALL *Ess. Gothic Archit.* 32 In all the concave bends of the stone-work, a small pointed ornament occurs, which is very common in Gothic windows.. I have ventured to apply to it [the name] of *cusp*, by which mathematicians denote a figure of this sort. **1845** *Ecclesiologist* IV. 20 Ball-flowers, mouldings, feathered cusps, and other decorative detail.

6. *Anat.* **a.** A projection or protuberance upon the crown of a tooth: cf. CUSPIDATE. **b.** Any pointed projection or extremity, as of the valves of the heart.

1849–52 TODD *Cycl. Anat.* IV. 921/1 The four principal cusps.. are more pointed and prolonged than in Man. **1872** MIVART *Elem. Anat.* vii. (1873) 252 The sixth and seventh teeth of the lower jaw are called true molars. Each bears five cusps. **1878** T. BRYANT *Pract. Surg.* I. 301 The valve cusps being unable to meet and close the canal.

7. *Bot.* A pointed end of any organ; *esp.* a sharp rigid point of a leaf.

1870 HOOKER *Stud. Flora* 319 Leaves opposite hastate-deltoid with horizontal cusps. *Ibid.* 328 *Euphorbia amygdaloides*.. cusps of glands converging.

cuspadore: see CUSPIDOR.

‖**Cuˈsparia.** *Bot.* [f. native name *Cuspare.*] A genus of trees, now usually called *Galipea*, species of which yield the *Angustura* or *Cusparia* bark used as a tonic; also = CUSPARIN.

1852 TH. ROSS *Humboldt's Trav.* I. vi. 213 *note*, The Cuspare of Angostura, known in America under the name of Orinoco bark. **1876** W. BEGBIE *Bk. Med. Inform.* App. 251 *Cusparia*, a useful tonic in convalescence from diarrhœa and dysentery.

Hence **ˈcusparin** (*Chem.*), a crystalline substance obtained from Angustura bark.

1824 R. PHILLIPS tr. *Pharm. Lond.* (1836) 191 It is stated by Saladin that the virtue of Cusparia resides in a peculiar neutral substance which he calls Cusparin. **1879** WATTS *Dict. Chem.* VIII. 87.

cuspate (ˈkʌspeɪt), *a.* [f. CUSP + -ATE.] Shaped like a cusp.

1896 F. P. GULLIVER in *Bull. Geol. Soc. Amer.* VII. 401 In this paper will be considered those forelands which present a more or less sharply pointed form, whose two sides are bounded by shore curves... These are called cuspate forelands. **1941** *Proc. Prehist. Soc.* VII. 6 The forecourt walls may be.. convex, when the forecourt is cuspate, cusp-shaped or heart-shaped. **1952** F. P. SHEPARD in *Bull. Amer. Assoc. Petr. Geol.* XXXVI. 1911 Prominent points or horns found extending into the bays and lagoons inside many barriers. These may be referred to as 'cuspate spits'.

cuspated (ˈkʌspeɪtɪd), *a. Arch.* [Erroneously f. CUSP: the etymological derivative is *cuspidated.*] Furnished with a cusp or cusps.

1848 RICKMAN *Archit.* 134 Windows.. with circles in the head, sometimes.. cuspated. **1865** *Gentl. Mag.* CXXXV. I. 413 These early cuspated windows are as ugly as possible.

cusped (kʌspt), *a.* [f. CUSP + -ED.]

1. Having a cusp or cusps.

1822 IMISON *Sc. & Art* I. 425 The appearance of our moon when she is cusped or horned. **1853** RUSKIN *Stones Ven.* II. vi, A cusped round arch, perfectly pure and simple. **1879** SALMON *Higher Plane Curves* §214 To the cusped class also belongs the Cissoid of Diocles.

2. Of the form of a cusp.

1883 *Scribn. Mag.* III. 427 This cusped junction displays the qualities of the curves at their meeting most conspicuously.

cuspid (ˈkʌspɪd), *sb.* and *a.* [ad. F. *cuspide* or L. *cuspid-em*: see CUSP.]

A. *sb.* †**1.** *Geom.* = CUSP 4. *Obs.*

1743 *Phil. Trans.* XLII. 334 Points of contrary Flexure and Cuspids.

2. A cusped or cuspidate tooth.

1878 L. P. MEREDITH *Teeth* 47 The incisors are called often.. the 'front teeth'; the upper cuspids, canine and 'eye teeth'.

B. *adj.* = CUSPIDATE. (*Syd. Soc. Lex.* 1882.)

cuspidal (ˈkʌspɪdəl), *a.* [f. L. *cuspid-em* + -AL[1].]

†**1.** Belonging to the apex (of a cone). *Obs.*

1647 H. MORE *Song of Soul* Notes 160/1 The cuspidall particles of the Cone.

2. *Geom.* Having, relating to, or of the nature of, a cusp: see CUSP 4.

1874 SALMON *Geom. three Dimens.* §305 The locus of points where two consecutive generators of a developable intersect is a curve.. which is called the *cuspidal edge* of that developable. **1879** —— *Higher Plane Curves* §209 Cuspidal cubics.

3. Of teeth: = CUSPIDATE.

1867 BUSHNELL *Mor. Uses Dark Th.* 274 Cuspidal teeth.

cuspidate (ˈkʌspɪdət), *a.* [ad. mod.L. *cuspidāt-us*, f. *cuspid-em* CUSP. In mod.F. *cuspidé.*]

Having a cusp or sharp point. *spec.* **a.** *Bot.* Of leaves: Ending in a rigid point or spine. **b.** Applied to the canine teeth, each of which ends in a single point; a name first given by J. Hunter.

1692 tr. *Blancard's Phys. Dict.* (1693) 157/1 *Parasentesis*.. a Perforation of the Chest and Abdomen through a cuspidate Channel. [**1771** J. HUNTER *Nat. Hist. Teeth* Wks. 1835 II. 21, I choose to divide them [teeth] into the four following classes viz. *Incisores*, commonly called fore teeth; *Cuspidati*, vulgarly called canine; *Bicuspides*, or the first two grinders; and *Molares*, or the last three teeth.] **1835** LINDLEY *Introd. Bot.* (1848) II. 356 *Cuspidate*, tapering gradually to a rigid point. It is also used sometimes to express abruptly acuminate. **1848** DANA *Zooph.* 485 Long cuspidate branches. **1882** *Syd. Soc. Lex.*, *Cuspidate teeth*, the canine teeth, so called from their shape.

†**cuspidate,** *v. Obs.*$^{-0}$ [f. L. *cuspidāre* to point: see -ATE[3].] *trans.* To sharpen to a point.

1623 COCKERAM, *Cuspedate*, to sharpen. **1656** in BLOUNT *Glossogr.* **1721** in BAILEY.

cuspidated (ˈkʌspɪdeɪtɪd), *a.* [f. as prec. + -ED.] Having a cusp or cusps; = CUSPIDATE *a.*

1668 WILKINS *Real Char.* 331 Cuspidated nayle, peg, pin. **1731–7** MILLER *Gard. Dict.*, *Cuspidated* Plants.. are such Plants, the Leaves of which are pointed like a Spear. **1827** J. JOPLING in *Mech. Mag.* VIII. 263 [The pencil] will describe an evolute, which is an infinite cuspidated line. **1883** *Athenæum* 15 Dec. 782/3 The.. cuspidated pediment, and finial of the Sion organ.

cuspiˈdation. *Arch.* [n. of action f. L. *cuspidāre*: see prec.] Decoration with cusps; cusping.

1848 RICKMAN *Archit.* App. 57 The feathering or cuspidation of arches in tracery. **1890** *Athenæum* 11 Oct. 489/1 One of the.. characteristics of the Early English doorways in Gottland is the frequency of cuspidation in the heads and down the sides of those openings.

cuspidine (ˈkʌspɪdaɪn). *Min.* [f. L. *cuspid-em* spear-point, cusp + -INE.] A fluo-silicate of calcium from Vesuvius occurring in pale rosy spear-shaped crystals.

1882 DANA *Min.* App. iii. 33 Cuspidine.

cuspidor, -ore (ˈkʌspɪdɔː(r), -əə(r)). *U.S.* Also 8 **cuspadore.** [a. Pg. *cuspidor* spitter, f. *cuspir* to spit, deriv. of L. *conspuĕre.*] A spittoon.

1779 FORREST *Voy. N. Guinea* 235 Before each person was placed a large brass salver, a black earthen pot of water, and a brass cuspadore. **1871** *Specif. Heath's Patent* No. 1858 Improvements in Cuspidores. **1892** HOWELLS *Mercy* 10 Nickel-plated cuspidors.

cusping (ˈkʌspɪŋ), *sb. Arch.* [f. CUSP + -ING: cf. *coving, roofing*, etc.] A formation consisting of cusps; cusp-work.

1860 G. E. STREET in *Archæol. Cant.* III. 124 The cusping was let into a groove. **1870** F. R. WILSON *Ch. Lindisf.* 101 It has five lights, the cuspings of which.. are early.

‖**cuspis** (ˈkʌspɪs). Pl. **cuspides** (-ɪdiːz). [L.] = CUSP, q.v., in various senses.

1646 SIR T. BROWNE *Pseud. Ep.* 60 [The magnetized] Needle.. will obvert or turne aside its lyllie or North point, and conforme its cuspis or South extreme unto the andiron. **1647** H. MORE *Song of Soul* II. App. vii, The Cuspis of the Cone. **1794** MARTYN *Rousseau's Bot.* xxxi. 475 Vallisneria has a cuspis on each petal.

cuss, cusse (y), obs. forms of KISS.

cuss (kʌs), *sb. U.S. colloq.* or *slang.* [In its origin a vulgar pronunciation or attenuation of *curse*; but in sense 2 often used without consciousness of the origin, and perhaps with the notion that it is short for *customer.*]

1. An execration, etc.; see CURSE *sb.*

1848 LOWELL *Biglow P.* ix, Them Rank infidels that go agin the Scriptur'l cus o' Shem. **1865** 'ARTEMUS WARD' *His Book* 115 Not keering a tinker's cuss.

2. Applied to persons, in the way of slight reproach or contempt, or merely humorously with no definite meaning; also to animals.

1775 *Narraganset Hist. Reg.* (1885) III. 263 A man that.. was noted for a damn cuss. **1848** LOWELL *Biglow P.* ii, The everlastin' cus he stuck his one-pronged pitchfork in me. **1866** *Ibid.* 2nd Ser. Introd., *Cuss*, a sneaking, ill-natured fellow. **1883** P. ROBINSON in *Harper's Mag.* Oct. 706/2 The 'horned toad' is distinctly an 'amoosin cuss'. **1883** *Century Mag.* XXVI. 285 The concern is run by a lot of cusses who have failed in various branches of literature themselves.

3. *Comb.*, as **cuss-word**, a profane expletive.

1872 'MARK TWAIN' *Innoc. at Home* 20 (Farmer) He didn't give a continental for anybody. Beg your pardon, friend, for coming so near saying a cuss-word. **1888** *Detroit Free Press* 15 Sept. (Farmer), He.. never asked us for a chew of tobacco.. or a free puff.. and he didn't use cuss-words.

cuss, *v.* orig. *U.S.* **a.** Vulgar pronunciation or attenuation of CURSE *v.*

1815 D. HUMPHREYS *Yankey in Eng.* 104 *Cuss*, curse. **1841** DICKENS *Barn. Rudge* xxxi. 116 Am I to thank thee, Fortun', or to cuss thee — which? **1841** THACKERAY *Gt. Hoggarty Diamond* (1849) xi. 143 Have him in.. for, cuss me, I like to see a rogue. **1848** LOWELL *Biglow P.* iv, Their masters can cuss 'em an' kick 'em. *Ibid.* ix, I wish I may be cust. **1849** THACKERAY *Pendennis* I. xiii. 115 Dammin and cussin up stairs and down stairs. **1861** *Sat. Rev.* 7 Dec. 583 This is why people like Major Pendennis go cussing up stairs and down stairs, as his valet described that hero doing.

b. With *out.* (See quot. 1881.)

1881 *N.Y. Times* 18 Dec. in *N. & Q.* (1882) 6th Ser. V. 65/1 *Cuss out*, to subdue by overwhelming severity of tongue. 'He cussed that fellow out', *i.e.*, he annihilated him verbally. **1901** S. E. WHITE *Westerners* xvi. 134 Clearly he could not 'cuss out' the delinquents as they deserved.

†**'cussan.** *Obs. rare.* [app. a. OF. *cuisson*, f. *cuisse* thigh.] *pl.* = CUISSES, thigh-plates.

c **1475** *Rauf Coilȝear* 472 His Cussanis cumlie schynand full clear.

cuss-cuss, var. KAS-KAS.

cussed ('kʌsɪd), *a.* orig. *U.S.* Vulgar pronunciation of CURSED. *spec.* obstinate, pig-headed. So **'cussedly** *adv.*

1846 D. CORCORAN *Pickings* 10, I never keeps low company, and you is so cussedly vulgar. **1848** LOWELL *Biglow P.* ii, A Yung feller of our town that wuz cussed fool enuff to [etc.]. **1864** TROLLOPE *Can you forgive Her?* I. xvii. 133 It's the cussidest place in all creation. **1882** *Three in Norway* x. 77 It was a thoroughly cussēd morning. **1888** *Gd. Words* 470 You see stranger.. Uncle Sam don't care a dime for you and me being robbed, but it's a cussedly different thing, touching the mails. **1952** A. GRIMBLE *Pattern of Isl.* 149, I should of course have made up my mind in all decency then to find the place for myself... But I was cussed. **1959** *Economist* 21 Feb. 661/1 Blindly and cussedly anti-farmer.

cussedness ('kʌsɪdnɪs). *colloq.* or *slang.* (orig. *U.S.*). Malignity, perversity of disposition, cantankerousness, 'contrariness'.

1866 LOWELL *Biglow P.* Introd., *Cussedness*, meaning wickedness, malignity. **1881** J. HAWTHORNE *Fort. Fool* I. xxxiv, What has been termed by some philosophers the natural cussedness of things. **1888** BRYCE *Amer. Commw.* I. 360 Owing to the inherent disputatiousness and perversity (what the Americans call 'cussedness') of bodies of men. **1904** *Daily Chron.* 9 Sept. 3/2 The kind of man.. who out of sheer 'cussedness'.. would succeed where a dozen others would fail. **1905** E. M. FORSTER *Where Angels fear to Tread* v. 153 He could understand pure cussedness, but it did not seem to be that. **1922** JOYCE *Ulysses* 605 He put it down to sheer cussedness. **1931** E. O'NEILL *Mourning becomes Electra* I. IV. 90, I guess there's bitterness inside me—my own cussedness, maybe.

cusseis, cussues: see CUISSE.

cussen, obs. form of COZEN.

cusser, var. COURSER² 2, stallion.

1815 SCOTT *Guy M.* xi, For ye ken a fie man and a cusser fearsna the deil.

†**cust¹.** *Obs.* Forms: 1 cyst, 3- cust (y). [In form identical with OE. *cyst* choice, excellence, virtue, etc. from *custi-* = OS. *cust* (MDu. *cust*, Du. *kust*), OHG. *chust*, (Goth. *ga-kusts*):—OTeut. **kusti-z* fem. abstr., f. *kus-* weak grade of *keusan* to taste, prove, choose.

Parallel masc. forms are Gothic *kustu-s*, and ON. *kostr*: see COST *sb.*¹ Found only in OE. and early southern ME.: its Midland and mod.Eng. form would have been *kyst, kist.* But in the midl. dialect its place was supplied by COST *sb.*¹ from Norse, to which also *cust* seems to have been entirely conformed in sense, so that it may be viewed simply as the southern form of *cost.*]

1. Choice, action or faculty of choosing.

a **1000** *Cædmon's Gen.* 1919 (Gr.) Ic ðe cyst abead. *c* **1000** *Ags. Ps.* lxiv. 4 (Thorpe) Se þe hine ece God cystum ȝeceoseð.

2. Quality, character, manner, way; = COST *sb.*¹

c **1205** LAY. 12020 Heo i-cneowen wel a þan wolcne þas wederes custes. *Ibid.* 20324 Swa nauere na mon nuste Of Baldulfes custe [*c* **1275** Of Baldolf his custes]. *a* **1250** *Owl & Night.* 9 And eiþer seide of oþres custe þat alre worste þat hi wuste. *Ibid.* 1398 Sum arist of þe flesches luste, And sum of þe gostes custe. *a* **1250** *Prov. Alfred* 252 in *O.E. Misc.* 119 Ac leorne hire custe [*a* **1275** Her þu hire costes cuþe].

†**cust².** *Sc. Obs.* Also cuist, coyst. [Derivation unknown: its abbreviation from *custroun* has been suggested, but the spelling seems to indicate Sc. (ø, y), repr. ME. *ō*, which is a different vowel.] A base, low fellow; a custroun.

a **1500** *Colkelbie Sow* I. 406 (Jam.) Ilk knave, and ilk cust, Comprysit Horlore Hust. **1535** *Aberdeen Reg.* V. 15 (Jam.) Calling him coyst carll & commound theyf, & vther vyil wordis. *a* **1605** MONTGOMERIE *Flyting* 13 We mell thou sall yell, little cultron cuist.

custage, var. COSTAGE *Obs.*, cost, expense.

custard ('kʌstəd). [app. a perverted form of CRUSTADE, with which it is connected by the forms *crustarde* and *custad(e.* The fashion of the thing appears to have altered about 1600.]

1. †**a.** Formerly, a kind of open pie containing pieces of meat or fruit covered with a preparation of broth or milk, thickened with eggs, sweetened, and seasoned with spices, etc. = CRUSTADE. **b.** Now, a dish made with eggs beaten up and mixed with milk to a stiff consistency, sweetened, and baked; also a similar preparation served in a liquid form.

[*c* **1390** *Crustarde*: see CRUSTADE.] *c* **1450** *Two Cookery-bks.* 74 Custarde.. Custard lumbarde [Recipes identical with those on pp. 50, 51, for Crustade and Crustade lumbard]. *c* **1460** J. RUSSELL *Bk. Nurture* 802 Bakemete, or Custade Costable, when eggis & crayme be geson. **1530** PALSGR. 211/2 Custarde, *dariolle* ['*Darioles*, small pasties filled with flesh, hearbes, and spices, mingled, and minced together' (Cotgr.)]. *a* **1592** GREENE *Jas. IV* (1861) 208 Cut it me like the battlements Of a custard, full of round holes. **1628** EARLE *Microcosm., Cook* (Arb.) 47 Quaking Tarts, and quiuering Custards, and such milke sop Dishes. **1665** *Phil. Trans.* I. 118 White like the white of a Custard. **1688** R. HOLME *Armoury* (in *Babees Bk.* (1868) 211), *Custard*, open Pies, or without lids, filled with Eggs and Milk; called also Egg-Pie. **1740** SOMERVILLE *Hobbinol* iii. (1749) 158 The Custard's jelly'd Flood. **1864** MRS. CARLYLE *Lett.* III. 231 To take always the new milk and the custard at twelve. **1887** R. N. CAREY *Uncle Max* xv. 114 [Her] custards and flaky crust were famed in the village.

2. *attrib.* and *Comb.* **a.** = Custard-like, as †*custard-cap*, †*-crown*, †*-pate*; **b.** *custard cup*, *pudding*; *custard-crammed* adj.; †**custard-coffin**, the 'coffin' or crust of a 'custard'; **custard-cups**, a local name (Shropshire) for the Willow-herb, *Epilobium hirsutum* (cf. *codlins-and-cream*); **custard pie**, a pie containing custard; commonly used as a missile in broad comedy, hence used *attrib.* or allusively to denote comedy of this type; **custard powder**, a preparation in powder form for making custard by mixing it with milk; **custard tree**, the tree bearing the custard-apple.

1676 D'URFEY *Mad. Fickle* I. i, You shall drink Bumpers out of your *Custard-Cap you Rogue. **1596** SHAKS. *Tam. Shr.* IV. iii. 82 It is [a] paltrie cap, A *custard coffen, a bauble, a silken pie. **1671** F. PHILLIPS *Reg. Necess.* 373 Not to bear Offices in their Parishes or *Custard-cram'd Companies. **1599** NASHE *Lenten Stuffe* (1871) 29 The houses here have not such flat *custard-crowns at the top, as they have [at Cadiz]. **1825** *Columbian Centinel* 5 Jan. 3/5 (Advt.), Dishes, Tureens, *Custard Cups. **1843** DICKENS *Christmas Carol* iii. 95 A custard-cup without a handle. *a* **1625** BEAUM. & FL. *Bloody Bro.* III. ii, Do you hear? You *Custard Pate, we go to't for high Treason. **1832** L. M. CHILD *Frugal Housewife* 68 It is a general rule to put eight eggs to a quart of milk, in making *custard pies. **1920** S. LEWIS *Main Street* xvi. 198 Mr. Schnarken slipped a piece of custard pie into the clergyman's rear pocket. **1933** *Punch* 29 Nov. 609/3 [The show] is wanting in straight-cut wit, and it falls back too often on custard-pie. **1940** GRAVES & HODGE *Long Week-End* ix. 133 Charlie Chaplin.. won enormous popularity.. with his custard-pie comedies. **1852** H. BEASLEY *Druggist's Gen. Receipt Bk.* (ed. 2) 268 *Custard Powder consists of sago meal, coloured with turmeric, and flavoured. **1951** *Good Housek. Home Encycl.* 433/2 Mock custards.. can be made with cornflour or with the various proprietary custard powders on the market. **1728** E. SMITH *Compleat Housewife* 95 To make a *Custard Pudding. **1769** MRS. RAFFALD *Eng. Housekpr.* (1778) 169 A boiled Custard Pudding. **1787** WOLCOTT (P. Pindar) *Ode upon Ode* Wks. 1794 I. 382 Rich as.. custard pudding at a city feast. **1808** T. ASHE *Trav.* x. 85 [Custard Island abounds] with the papaw, which is vulgarly known by the name of the Custard tree.

Hence **'custardly, 'custardy** *adjs.*, of the nature of or resembling custard.

1870 J. ORTON *Andes & Amazons* xix. (1877) 290 The rind.. incloses a rich custardly pulp. *Ibid.* II. xxxviii. 510 A rich custardy pulp. **1901** G. MEREDITH *Let.* 31 Dec. (1912) II. 522 The Madeira apples were custardy and curious. **1961** M. BEADLE *These Ruins are Inhabited* (1963) iii. 39 Dinner.. ends with something custardy.

'custard-apple. [f. prec.] The fruit of *Anona reticulata*, a native of S. America and the West Indies, introduced in 16th c. into the East Indies; it has a dark brown rind, and a yellowish pulp resembling custard in appearance and flavour. (Also called *bullock's heart.*) **b.** The tree itself.

1657 LIGON *Barbadoes* (1673) 11 Every one a dish of fruit.. the first was Millions, Plantines the second, the third Bonanos.. the sixth the Custard Apple. **1703** DAMPIER *Voy.* III. 33 Full of a white soft Pulp, sweet and very pleasant, and most resembling a Custard of any thing.. From whence probably it is called a Custard-Apple by our English. **1869** WALMSLEY *Ruined Cities Zulu Land* I. 115 Like the custard-apple of the Madras Presidency, black, rough, and repulsive-looking outside, and a white, delicious custard inside.

custardmonger, obs. form of COSTERMONGER.

custe, obs. pa. t. of KISS *v.*

†**custi** (y), *a. Obs.* In 1 cystiȝ, 3 kisstiȝ (*Orm.*). [OE. *cystiȝ* = OHG. *chustig*, MHG. *kustig*, f. OE. *cyst* = OHG. *chust*, *kust*, in sense of excellence, munificence.] Liberal, munificent.

c **897** K. ÆLFRED *Gregory's Past.* xx. 148 Ðæt he sie cystiȝ and mildheort. *c* **1200** ORMIN 4698 þiss mahhte.. makeþþ þe full kisstiȝ mann Off whattse Godd te leneþþ. *c* **1275** LAY. 4075 He was of ȝeftes custi.

Hence **'custinesse**, liberality.

c **1175** *Lamb. Hom.* 105 *Largitas*, þet is custinesse on englisc.

†**custil(e, costile.** *Obs.* Also custell. [a. OF. *coustille*, 15th c. in Godefroy.] A two-edged dagger or large knife.

c **1475** *Partenay* 1722 Of Army peple seing grett fuson, With Custiles and Gisarmes many on. *Ibid.* 4334 Gaffray hym smote vppon the hanche.. Wyth a costile which in hys sleffe gan hold. *Ibid.* 5853 That fine good custell.. that.. gan hold Brandes the good knyght. **1479** *Office Mayor of Bristol* in *Eng. Gilds* 427 With no Glaythes, speerys, longe swerdys, longe daggers, custils, nother Basȝelardes.

custock. Sc. form of CASTOCK, cabbage-stalk.

1785 BURNS *Halloween* v. *a* **1810** TANNAHILL *Poems* (1846) 80 A heart not worth a custock. **1871** C. GIBBON *Lack of Gold* x, Here's a fine custock.

custode¹. [In ME. a. OF. *custode* (12th c. in Littré), ad. L. *custos*, *custōd-em* keeper, custodian: cf. It. *custode*, also Pr. *custodi*, Sp. *custodio*, from Rom. type *custōdius.* This has long been obsolete, but the word has been re-introduced in recent times from Italian.] One who has the custody of anything; a guardian, custodian:

†**a.** in ME. (kʊ'stoːd). *Obs.*

c **1380** WYCLIF *Wks.* (1880) 43 þe chesynge of his successour be maad of mynistris prouincial and custodis. *c* **1470** HARDYNG *Chron.* CCXXI. vii, And of his soonne Henry he made custode Thomas Beauford, his vncle.

b. in modern use, a. It. *custode* (kus'tode), pl. *-odi*, custodian.

[**1832** GELL *Pompeiana* II. xi. 4 If the *custodi* can be believed.] **1860** HAWTHORNE *Marb. Faun* vii, The old custodes knew her well. **1881** RUSKIN *Bible in Amiens* IV. 1, I love too many cathedrals—though I have never had the happiness of being custode of even one.

Hence †**custodery, custodrie**, office of a custode, custodianship.

c **1380** WYCLIF *Wks.* (1880) 43 þe mynystris & custodis may.. in þe same ȝeer in here custodries onys clepe to-gidre here breþeren to chapitre.

†**cu'stode².** *Obs.* [a. F. *custode* fem., ad. L. *custōdia* CUSTODY.] = CUSTODIAL *sb.*

1653 H. COGAN tr. *Pinto's Trav.* lvi. 218 In this Procession were.. also the rich Custodes of their Idols.. They that carryed them were clothed in yellow.

custodee (kʌstə'diː). [f. stem of L. *custōd-em*, *custody*, etc. + -EE, after *trustee.*] A person entrusted with the custody of anything.

1812 M. EDGEWORTH *Tales Fashionable Life* V. 221 Sir Terence O'Fay's exploits in evading duns,.. tricking *custodees.* **1832** AUSTIN *Jurispr.* (1879) I. xxv. 487 The possession of the custodee ought to be deemed the possession of the owner. **1836** C. FORSTER *Life Bp. Jebb* iii. (ed. 2) 203 The friend of Dr. Townson, and custodee of his papers.

custodial (kʌ'stəʊdɪəl), *a.* and *sb.* [f. L. *custōdia* CUSTODY + -AL¹.]

A. *adj.* **1.** Relating to custody or guardianship.

1772 *Letter to Bp. Rochester* 2 (R.) The custodial charges and government [of a church]. **1841** *L'pool. Jrnl.* 4 Dec., After much learned argument as to the custodial relations of illegitimate children. **1887** *Scribn. Mag.* II. 147 Custodial duties.

2. Special collocation. *custodial sentence*, a judicial sentence requiring an offender to be held in custody (esp. in prison or at a detention centre), as opp. to a fine, community service, etc.

1953 *Tentative Draft of Revision of Rules Courts of N.J.* (Supreme Court New Jersey) 142 In all *custodial sentences the prisoner shall receive credit on the term imposed for any time he may have served in custody between his arrest and the imposition of sentence. **1965** *Criminal Law Rev.* Nov. 657 A fresh proposal for the custodial training of adults.. (a) All custodial sentences of less than six months to be abolished, since no effective training is thought possible in this length of time. **1971** R. CROSS *Punishment, Prison & Public* IV. 187 The courts should be empowered to pass fixed-term custodial sentences on young offenders between the ages of seventeen and twenty-one. **1986** *Church Times* 24 Oct. 11/1 What are prisons *for*? What do we expect from them? How do we handle long-term custodial sentences?

B. *sb.* A vessel for preserving sacred objects, as the host, relics, etc. (Cf. F. *custode.*)

1860 READE *Cloister & H.* lxii. (D.), The priest.. then took the custodial, and showed the patient the *Corpus Domini* within. **1887** HUTCHINSON tr. *Viresalingam's Fortune's Wheel* 65 Harisastri picked up his custodial and withdrew.

cu'stodiam. *Irish Law.* Also erron. -ium. [L. *custodiam* custody, from the phraseology of the grant.] A grant by the Exchequer (for three years) of lands, etc., in possession of the Crown.

1662 EARL ORRERY *State Lett.* (1743) I. 82 These lands, which come out of the custodium at April next. **1686** R. PARR *Life of Ussher* 26 A Person of Quality.. who had newly obtained the Custodium of the Temporalities of that See. **1787** *Minor* 270 Fresh custodiums, detainers, and executions were issued without number. **1801** MAR. EDGEWORTH *Castle Rackrent* (1886) 41 He takes him out a custodiam on all the denominations.

attrib. **1848** WHARTON *Law Lex.*, *Custodiam lease*, a grant from the Crown under the Exchequer seal, by which the custody of lands, etc., seised in the King's hands, is demised or committed to some person as custodee or lessee thereof.

custodian (kʌˈstəʊdɪən). [f. as prec. + -AN.] One who has the custody of a thing or person; a guardian, keeper.

[Not in TODD 1818, WEBSTER 1828, or CRAIG 1847.]

1781 in *Sel. Papers Twining Fam.* (1887) 58 The custodian of the galleries. **1836** DICKENS *Sk. Boz* (ed. 3) II. 205 To act as custodian of the person of the supposed lunatic. **1872** BAGEHOT *Physics & Pol.* (1876) 28 The close oligarchy, the patriciate..recognised as the authorised custodian of the fixed law.

Hence **cu'stodianship**, the office of a custodian.

1858 *Sat. Rev.* VI. 550/1 Loading the library table and increasing the responsibility of Mr. Miller's custodianship. **1883** *Times* 1 June 4 The public should contribute to..a well-organized custodianship for such treasures.

†**cu'stodient**, *a. Obs. rare*⁻¹. [ad. L. *custōdient-em*, pr. pple. of *custōdīre* to guard.] Guarding, protecting.

1657 JEANES in Heber's *Jer. Taylor* (1839) I. 63 The custodient grace of God.

custodier (kʌˈstəʊdɪə(r)). Also 5 costodyer, 9 custodiar. [f. L. *custōdia* custody + -ER.] One who has the custody of anything; a custodian. Now esp. Scotch.

c **1470** HARDING *Chron.* LXXVIII. i, My knightes..My landes helpe, custodye[r]s of my crowne. *c* **1485** *Digby Myst.* (1882) II. 628 Now euery costodyer kepe well hys wall. **1820** SCOTT *Abbot* xix, He had become..the custodier, as the Scottish phrase went, of some important state secret. **1839** *Morn. Herald* in *Spirit Metrop. Conserv. Press* (1840) I. 151 Custodiar to the Bank of England's treasure. **1892** LD. HANNEN in *Law Rep.* App. Cases 165 The appellant..is bound..to live in the bank house as custodier of the whole premises.

†**'custodite**, *v. Obs. rare*⁻¹. [f. L. *custōdīt-*, ppl. stem of *custōdīre* to guard, f. *custōd-em* guardian.] *trans.* To guard, protect.

1657 TOMLINSON *Renou's Disp.* 341 The athenian matrons ..the better to custodite their chastity.

custodrie: see CUSTODERY under CUSTODE.

custody (ˈkʌstədɪ). Also 5-6 -dye, 5-7 -die, 7 costodie. [ad. L. *custōdia* guarding, keeping, f. *custos, custōd-em* guardian, keeper: see -Y.]

1. Safe keeping, protection, defence; charge, care, guardianship. Const. *of* the thing guarded, or *of* the person guarding it.

1491 *Act 7 Hen. VII*, c. 3 There to rest as your Tresour in the Custodie of the seid Chief Officer. **1513** MORE in Grafton *Chron.* II. 772 Both..for a while to be in the custody of their mother. **1555** EDEN *Decades* 54 Leauynge the custodye of the fortresse with a certeyne noble gentelman. *a* **1626** BACON (J.), There was prepared a fleet of thirty ships for the custody of the narrow seas. **1652** SIR E. NICHOLAS in *N. Papers* (Camden) I. 320 When he shall have the custody of the Great Seal. **1704** *Lond. Gaz.* No. 4048/4 She [a mare] was seen..in custody of a Man. **1781** GIBBON *Decl. & F.* III. lxiv. 609 The custody of the passes was neglected. **1891** *Law Times* XC. 462/1 Where the court refuses a parent the custody of his child.

2. The keeping of the officers of justice (for some presumed offence against the law); confinement, imprisonment, durance.

[**1590** SHAKS. *Com. Err.* I. i. 156 Iaylor, take him to thy custodie.] **1611** CORYAT *Crudities* 4 He shall be apprehended by some Souldiers..and committed to safe custody til he hath paid some fee for his ransome. **1665** MANLEY *Grotius' Low C. Warres* 129 He had..committed him to hard and close Custody, more out of suspition, than for any Crimes. **1727** SWIFT *What passed in London*, That so ..honest a man should be ordered into custody. **1802** M. EDGEWORTH *Moral T.* (1816) I. xv. 120 The constables.. appeared. T. R. was taken into custody. **1888** MORLEY *Burke* 61 The messenger of the serjeant-at-arms attempted to take one of them into custody in his own shop in the city.

†**3.** The office of a keeper; guardianship. *Obs.*

1609 BIBLE (Douay) *Num.* viii. 26 Thus shalt thou dispose to the Levites in their custodies. **1611** SPEED *Hist. Gt. Brit.* IX. ix. 30 Who gaue away..such Honours, Custodies, and Dignities, as were vacant. **1613** SIR H. FINCH *Law* (1636) 286 Custodies of Woods, Parks, Forrests, Chases.

†**4.** A case for keeping a thing in. *Obs. rare.*

1483 CAXTON *Gold. Leg.* 240/3 His bookes whiche had [not] a custodye [*nullum habentes conservatorium*] fyl in the water.

5. *attrib.*

a **1625** COPE in Gutch *Coll. Cur.* I. 122 Custody Lands, anciently termed the Crown Lands, answered in the Pipe.

custom (ˈkʌstəm), *sb.* Forms: 2-7 custume, custome, (3 kustume), 3-7 costome, (4 -toum, -tum, kostome), 4-7 custum, costom, (5 customme, costeme, 5-6 costume, 6 coustome, 4- custom. [a. OF. *custume, costume* 11-12th c. (later *coustume*, now *coutume*) from Romanic **costumne*:—L. **costūmen*, substituted for **costudne*:—L. *consuētūdinem*. In other Romanic forms, Pr. *costum*, It. and Pg. *costume*, Sp. *costumbre*, masc., there is change of gender after sbs. in *-ūmen*; while Pr. *costuma, cosdumna*, It. *costuma*, f. med.L. *coustuma*, show retention of gender with assimilation of the ending to *-a* nouns. COSTUME is another form of the same word, of recent adoption from It., through Fr.]

1. a. A habitual or usual practice; common way of acting; usage, fashion, habit (either of an individual or of a community).

c **1200** *Trin. Coll. Hom.* 75 Bereȝe us wið alle iuele customes. *Ibid.* 89 It is custume þat ech chirchsocne goð þis dai a procession. *c* **1340** HAMPOLE *Psalter* xxi. 16 As hundes folus ther custom in berkyng & bitynge. *c* **1350** *Will. Palerne* 2010 On þat knew þe kostome of þe cuntre of grece. *c* **1450** tr. *T. à Kempis' Imit.* I. xiv, Olde custom is harde to breke. **1526** *Pilgr. Perf.* (W. de W. 1531) 162 b, Let vs not come to yᵉ chirche by vse & custome, as the oxe to his stalle. **1576** FLEMING *Panopl. Epist.* B iij, Other fourmes of salutations are also in custome. **1602** SHAKS. *Ham.* I. iv. 15 It is a Custome More honour'd in the breach, then the obseruance. **1683** EVELYN *Diary* 12 Feb., Much offended at the novel costome of burying every one within the body of the Church. **1713** BERKELEY *Hylas & Phil.* II. Wks. I. 309 Common custom is the standard of propriety in language. **1732** —— *Alciphr.* v. §12 The general manners and customs of those people. **1719** YOUNG *Revenge* IV. i, I went into the garden, As is my custom. **1833** HT. MARTINEAU *Briery Creek* iii. 46 The settlers..followed the old custom..of holding their market on a Saturday. **1859** MILL *Liberty* 126 The despotism of custom is everywhere the standing hindrance to human advancement.

b. The practising of anything habitually; the being or becoming accustomed.

1526 *Pilgr. Perf.* (W. de W. 1531) 78 Whan a synner commeth to the custome of synne, than he falleth to contempte. **1534** WHITINTON *Tullyes Offices* I. (1540) 27 Custome and practyse must be vsed, that we may be as good accompters of our offyces. **1608** BP. HALL *Char. Virtues & V.* II. 94 Custome of sinne hath wrought this senslesnesse. **1867** JEAN INGELOW *Dreams that came true* vii, Custom makes all things easy.

†**c.** *of custom*: according to custom, usually, as usual; also *adjectivally*, usual, customary. *Obs.*

c **1400** *Lanfranc's Cirurg.* 124 A man þat usiþ of custum sich a maner dietynge. **1556** *Chron. Gr. Friars* (Camden) 74 It hathe bene of ane olde costome that sent Gorge shulde be kepte holy day. **1576** FLEMING *Panopl. Epist.* 111 For some things there be which of custome I shake off. **1688** EVELYN *Mem.* (1857) II. 296, 29th Nov. I went to the Royal Society. We..dined together as of custom.

†**d.** *custom of women* (med.L. *consuetudo*): menstruation. *Obs.*

1611 BIBLE *Gen.* xxxi. 35 The custome of women is vpon mee. **1705** BOSMAN *Guinea* 210 When the Custom of Women is upon the Female Sex, they are..esteemed unclean.

e. Applied to specific usages of particular peoples; *e.g.* the periodical massacres in Dahome.

1820 *Q. Rev.* XXII. 296 Dahomeans do not make war to make slaves, but to make prisoners to kill at the Customs. **1881** *Standard* 12 Nov. 5/1 The Ashantis, like the Dahomeyans, have their 'customs' or periodical executions.

2. *Law.* An established usage which by long continuance has acquired the force of a law or right, *esp.* the established usage of a particular locality, trade, society, or the like.

In French history applied to the special usages of different provinces and districts which had grown into a local body of law, as the *custom of Normandy, of Paris*, etc.

c **1400** *Test. Love* III. (1560) 293 b/1 Custome is of commen usage by length of time used, and custome nat write is usage. **1523** FITZHERB. *Surv.* 4 Oxganges, rentes, or suche other customes as the tenauntes vse. *a* **1626** BACON *Max. & Uses Com. Law* (1635) 37 Having..gained a custome by use of occupying their lands, they now are called coppy holders. **1680** MORDEN *Geog. Rect.* (1685) 22 The Common Law of England is a Collection of the General Common Custom, and Usages of the Kingdom. **1726** AYLIFFE *Parergon* 195 A Statute has the express Consent of the People, whereas a Custom has only their tacit agreement to it. **1767** BLACKSTONE *Comm.* II. 98 Declaring, that the will of the lord was to be interpreted by the custom of the manor. **1769** *De Foe's Tour Gt. Brit.* II. 409 Stafford..This Town retains the antient Custom of Borough English. **1818** CRUISE *Digest.* (ed. 2) I. 360 Every species of waste..not warranted by the custom of the manor. **1884** KIRK *Chas. Bold* I. II. ii. 500 The 'customs' of Liége—that is to say its constitution and its laws—were..forever abrogated.

†**3.** Customary service due by feudal tenants to their lord; customary rent paid in kind or in money; any customary tax or tribute paid to a lord or ruler. *Obs.* in actual use.

c **1330** R. BRUNNE *Chron.* (1810) 111 Ne costom no seruise of þing þat he forgaf. *c* **1450** *St. Cuthbert* (Surtees) 7984 The monkes possessiouns made he Fra all seruice and customes fre. **1523** FITZHERB. *Surv.* Prol., What rentes, customes, and seruice he ought to haue of them [the tenants]. **1535** COVERDALE *Ezra* iv. 13 Then shal not they geue tribute, toll, and yearly custome. **1632** LITHGOW *Trav.* IV. (1682) 152 He disannulled all the exactions..upon his tributary Christian subjects; and cancelled the custom or tythe of their male children. **1641** *Termes de la Ley* 97 Custome is also used.. for such services as Tenants of a Manor owe unto their Lord. *c* **1730** BURT *Lett. N. Scotl.* (1818) II. 52 Their rent is chiefly paid in kind..such as barley, oatmeal, and what they call customs, as sheep, lambs, poultry, butter, &c.

4. a. Tribute, toll, impost, or duty, levied by the lord or local authority upon commodities on their way to market; *esp.* that levied in the name of the king or sovereign authority upon merchandise exported from or imported into his dominions; now levied only upon imports from foreign countries. ***the Customs***: the duties levied upon imports as a branch of the public revenue; the department of the Civil Service employed in levying these duties. (Now rarely in singular, and never with *a*.)

In this sense the OE. name was *toll* (Ger. *zoll*); *consuetudo* occurs in Magna Carta, *custuma* in med.L. passim. In early times the customs were distinguished as ***magna custuma***, 'the great custom', levied upon exports and imports, and ***parva custuma***, 'the little custom', levied upon goods taken to market within the realm.

[*c* **1325** *Iter Camerarii* i. (Sc. Statutes), Braxiatores, carnifices, custumarios magne et parue custume. *15th c. Sc. transl.* Breustaris, fleschewaris, custumaris alswel of greit custom as of small custum.] *c* **1400** MAUNDEV. (Roxb.) xvi. 75 Þe emperour takez mare of þat citee [Tabreez] to customez of marchandise þan þe riccest Cristen king..may dispend. *c* **1440** *Promp. Parv.* 111 Custum, kyngys dute, *custuma.* **1483** *Act 1 Rich. III*, c. 8 Pream., Paying less Custume for the Lokkys then for the hole wollyn Flese. **1534** TINDALE *Matt.* ix. 9 He sawe a man syt a receyuinge of custome, named Mathew. **1581** MARBECK *Bk. of Notes* 271 Customes are these which are paide of Merchaundises, and of those things which are either carried out or brought in. **1609** SKENE *Reg. Maj.* 152 Custumers of the litill custum (that is, of gudes cumand to the market). **1669-70** MARVELL *Corr.* cxl. Wks. II. 311 Setting a high custom upon all forain Corn. **1710** SWIFT *Jrnl. Stella* Oct. 10 §19 The handkerchiefs will be put in some friend's pocket, not to pay custom. **1766** C. LEADBETTER *Royal Gauger* (ed. 6) II. ix. 333 The Commissioners of the Customs are to pay into the Exchequer the remaining Part of the Produce of such Seizure made by the Officers of the Customs. **1838-42** ARNOLD *Hist. Rome* (1846) III. xliii. 114 Collectors of customs and port duties. **1863** H. COX *Instit.* I. ix. 196 Among the permanent taxes, the most considerable are the customs..and the excise duty.

b. ***customs*** (freq. without article), the area at a seaport, airport, etc., where goods, luggage, and other items are examined and customs duties levied.

1921 C. CROW *Travelers' Handbk. China* (ed. 3) 8 Travelers should note that..if goods other than personal effects are taken out of the country it is necessary to pass them through the customs before they can be accepted by the shipping companies. **1932** G. GREENE *Stamboul Train* I. i. 7 He was the first through customs. **1966** T. FRISBY *There's Girl in my Soup* III. 48 How on earth did you have the nerve to bring all those [cigarettes] through the customs. **1971** V. ELIOT in T. S. Eliot *Waste Land* Draft p. x, He asked Quinn to send a clerk to meet Eliot at the dock and see him through customs. **1984** M. HANSSEN *E for Additives* 8 Although it is not very obvious when you go through Customs, a stated objective of the European Economic Community..is to harmonize laws.

5. The practice of customarily resorting to a particular shop, place of entertainment, etc. to make purchases or give orders; business patronage or support.

1596 SHAKS. *Tam. Shr.* IV. iii. 99 Go hop me ouer euery kennell home, For you shall hop without my custome sir. **1664** PEPYS *Diary* 31 Mar., A tailor, whom I have presented my custom. **1669** BUNYAN *Holy Citie* 17 What wonderful custom the Church of God at this day shall have among all sorts of People, for her Heavenly Treasures. **1729** SWIFT *Modest Proposal*, This food would likewise bring great Custom to taverns. **1833** HT. MARTINEAU *Brooke Farm* vii. 88 They ran in debt to the grocer till he refused their custom. **1893** *Law Times* XCV. 5/2 Other persons who had been customers discontinued their custom.

6. a. *attrib.* and *Comb.*, as (sense 1) ***custom-generated, -governed*** adjs.; (sense 2-3) ***custom law, -service***; (sense 4) ***custom-collector, -gatherer; customs duties, laws, officer, official, union***, etc.; CUSTOM-HOUSE; (sense 5) ***custom-shrunk*** adj., ***-work***; **custom-built, -made** *adjs.*, built or made to order or to measure; so **custom-build** *v. trans.*; †**custom-day**, ? a day on which a customary service is rendered by a tenant; **custom-free** *a.*, free from custom, toll, or tribute; free from custom duty; **custom-mill**, (*a*) a mill belonging to a feudal proprietor at which his tenants are obliged to grind their corn, paying 'custom' for the accommodation; (*b*) a mill that grinds for customers; **custom-office** = CUSTOM-HOUSE; †**custom-sick** *a.*, morbidly subject to custom or habit; **custom smelter** *U.S.*, a smelter who treats rock or ore for customers.

1960 *Design* 29 Feb., A willingness to accept a new situation and to *custom build the standards for it. **1925** *Art & Publicity* 36 (Advt.), *Custom-built exclusiveness without excessive cost. **1955** T. STERLING *Evil of Day* vii. 77 A custom built Rolls Royce cloud. **1957** M. SHARP *Eye of Love* iii. 33 His good custom-built suit. *c* **1688-9** in Maidment *Sc. Pasquils* (1868) 263 Our new kings vicegerent ..More fit to be a factor or *custome collector. **1518** *Rental Bk.* in *Trans. Kilkenny Archæol. Soc.* Ser. II. IV. 123 A *custom day on every howse to ripp bind & drawe. **1845** McCULLOCH *Taxation* II. v. (1852) 234 *Customs duties existed in England previously to the Conquest. **1878** JEVONS *Prim. Pol. Econ.* 128 The customs duties levied upon wine, spirits, tobacco..when they are imported. *a* **1680** BUTLER *Rem.* (1759) I. 80 To take up a Degree, With all the Learning to it, *Custom-free. **1810** in *Risdon's Surv. Devon* App. 17 Towns..free from Tax and Toll, such as we..call Custom-free. **1656** TRAPP *Comm. Luke* iii. 12 These [publicans] were toll-takers, *custom-gatherers for the Romans. **1630** *R. Johnson's Kingd. & Commw.* 71 The..*Custome law, that (by the particular custome of Manors and Towns) lands should be divided by the custome of Gavel kinde. **1855** *Chicago Weekly Times* 16 Jan. 1/2 [There] may be found a large and splendid assortment of *custom made boots and shoes. **1959** *Observer* 8 Mar. 15/5 Because of the peculiar idiosyncrasies of faces they [*sc.* spectacle frames] often need to be custom-made. **1703** *Lond. Gaz.* No. 3898/4 The Manor and Royalty of Bovey-Tracy, with the Fairs, Markets, and *Custom Mills. **1888** Eissler *Metal. Gold* 33 At custom-mills the quartz is delivered in wagons. **1844** H. H. Wilson *Brit. India* I. 25 The Company's *custom-offices on the opposite bank. **1676** Phillips *Purch. Pattern* 2 What *Custom-service hath been done of old By those who formerly the same did hold. **1603** Shaks. *Meas. for M.* i. ii. 85 What with the gallowes, and what with pouerty, I am *Custom-shrunke. **1634** W. Wood *New Eng. Prosp.* ii. iv, They are not a little phantasticall or *custom-sick in this particular. **1880** G. T. Ingham *Digging Gold* 268 There is at Galena a small *custom smelter. **1963** *Times* 22 Apr. (Zinc Suppl.) p. ii/1 The custom smelters (smelters without their own mines). **1705** in *15th Rep. Hist. MSS. Commission* (1897) App. vi. 11 The Justices of the Peace are to assist the *customs-officers. **1923** D. H. Lawrence *Birds, Beasts & Flowers* 29 But here, even a *customs-official is still vulnerable. **1903** 'Vigilans sed Æquus' *German Ambitions* iv. 55 The Hague *Courant*, which advocated a *Customs Union with Germany. **1956** *Planning* XXII. 224 Three small nations—Belgium, the Netherlands, and Luxemburg—have formed Benelux, a customs union for nearly everything except agricultural products. **1884** *N.Y. Herald* 27 Oct. 746 Wanted—tailoress on first class *custom work.

b. *attrib.* passing into *adj.* Designating articles made to measure or to order, or places where such articles are made, or people producing work of this kind; = bespoke *ppl. a.* Also *fig.* Hence as advb., in combs., as ***custom-fitted***, ***-mixed***, ***-tailored*** adjs. Cf. *custom-built*, *-made* above. Chiefly *U.S.*

1830 *Williams's N.-Y. Ann. Reg.* 163 There are no manufactories of cotton or woollen but such as are used for custom work. **1851** C. Cist *Sk. Cincinnati* 175 Fine and coarse work for foreign markets, and custom work for home consumption. *Ibid.* 176 Two-thirds of these [shoes] at least, are made here, wholesale, or at custom shops. **1895** *Montgomery Ward Catal.* 269/3 For higher priced clothing, we refer you to our custom tailoring department, where we make clothing to order in any size and style desired. **1903** *N.Y. Times* 26 Sept. 6 (Advt.), Custom tailors charge for suits like these $35. **1905** *Washington Star* 24 Nov. 5 (Advt.), Double or Single-Breasted Sacks, as perfect-fitting as the finest custom garments. **1943** J. P. Marquand *So Little Time* (1944) iv. 31 He made Jeffrey conscious of his own custom-tailored suit, of the shine on his brown low shoes and the crease in his trousers. **1955** T. Sterling *Evil of Day* xxi. 207 He had designed the murder for one woman and no other. It was a perfect custom fit. **1957** W. H. Whyte *Organization Man* xxiii. 299 A small area with 'custom' houses. **1959** *Sunday Express* 1 Feb. 19/4 His custom-tailored suit. **1961** M. Beadle *These Ruins are Inhabited* (1963) iv. 51 An awesome superstructure of custom-fitted plugs and adaptors. **1964** *Punch* 23 Sept. 456/3 Custom-mixed after-shave lotion. **1968** *Listener* 12 Sept. 331/1 The custom cars, whose flamboyant shapes are public property while their mechanical niceties are reserved for the initiated.

†**custom** ('kʌstəm), *v. Obs.* or *arch.* [a. OF. *costumer*, *coustumer*, f. *costume*, *coustume* custom.]

1. *trans.* To render (a thing) customary or usual, to practise habitually; usually *pass.* to be customary or usual; = accustom 1.

1394 *Proclam.* in *York Myst.* Introd. 34 Yat yai come furth in array and in ye manere as it has been vsed and customed before yis time. **1483** *Cath. Angl.* 87 To Custome or to make Custome, *guadiare, ritare, jnguadiare.* *c* **1500** *Melusine* xxi. 114 The patrons made theire recommendacions to god as customed it is. **1626** W. Sclater *Expos. 2 Thess.* (1629) 175 Let him iterate it, of intolerable it becomes graue onely..custome it, it proues.. insensible.

2. To accustom, habituate (oneself or another).

c **1510** Barclay *Mirr. Gd. Manners* (1570) G ij, Nor custome not thy selfe to boste. **1580** Hollyband *Treas. Fr. Tong*, *Accoustumer*, to custome, to enure. *s'Accoustumer*, to vse, to custome himselfe. **1633** J. Done *Hist. Septuagint* 92 Those that custome and acost themselves with men Wise and Prudent. **1855** Singleton *Virgil* I. 73 Custom thyself to be invoked by vows.

b. *pass.* To be accustomed, wont, or used (*to do* something).

1483 Caxton *G. de la Tour* cxxxviii. 195 Yf he be custommed to doo euylle. *a* **1533** Ld. Berners *Huon* cxxv. 456 The trybute that is coustomyd to be payed in this cityе. **1561** Hollybush *Hom. Apoth.* 29 a, He is costumed to eat unnaturall and unkinde meates. **1674** *Govt. Tongue* ix. §15 (1684) 154 As a horse [turns]..into that inn to which he is customed.

c. *intr.* (in same sense as b). *rare.*

c **1430** *Pilgr. Lyf Manhode* i. cxxix. (1869) 68, I hadde not customed to be armed. **1596** Spenser *F.Q.* v. ii. 7 On a Bridge he custometh to fight.

3. *trans.* To pay duty or toll on; to pass through the custom-house.

1494 *Act 11 Hen. VII*, c. 13 Every Mare so shipped ere they be customed. *c* **1592** Marlowe *Jew of Malta* i. 1, Thy ships are safe..the merchants..haue sent me to know whether yourself will come and custom them. **1599** Hakluyt *Voy.* II. 238 When they have customed their goods. **1609** Skene *Reg. Maj.* 152 They search not the shippes, for wooll, or gudes not custumed. **1720** *Lond. Gaz.* No. 5851/3 If any Person shall Custom any Goods of any Stranger..whereby the King loseth his Custom.

b. To levy duty or toll upon. *rare.*

1611 Heywood *Golden Age* iv. i, We custom them, And they enrich our coffers.

4. To bestow one's custom on; to deal with (a person) or at (a shop); to frequent as a customer.

1605 Bacon *Adv. Learn.* ii. xiii. §7. 52 If a shoemaker should haue no shooes in his shoppe, but onely worke, as hee is bespoken, hee should bee weakely customed. **1639** Mayne *City Match* ii. v, We..custom'd your house And help'd away your victuals. **1681** P. Rycaut *Critick* 121 When they perceived the Shop so well customed by the famous Themistocles.

customable ('kʌstəməb(ə)l), *a.* Also 4–6 **custum(m)able**, 5 **-abil**, **-eable**, **customabylle**, **-mable**, **custymabil**, 6 **costomable**. [a. OF. *cust-*, *cost-*, *coustumable*, f. *custume*, *coustumer*, custom *sb.* and *v.*: see -able.]

†**1.** Of things or actions: According to custom; customary, usual. *Obs.*

1388 Wyclif *Numb.* xxix. 6 With customable [**1382** woned] fletynge offryngis. **1460** Capgrave *Chron.* 34 Whanne Nylus, the grete ryver, had..descendid into his customable mesure. **1532** More *Confut. Tindale* Wks. 389/1 After hys custumable fashion. **1571** Golding *Calvin on Ps.* xlix. 5 It was a customable matter in those dayes to sing Psalmes to the harp. **1663** *Aron-bimn.* 65 It is so natural, so customable to us, we have no sense or feeling of it.

†**b.** Depending upon established custom; = customary 4. *Obs.*

1580 Lyly *Euphues* (Arb.) 438 The regiment that they haue dependeth vppon statute lawe..Then vpon common law..Then vpon customable law.

†**c.** as *adv.* = customably. *Obs.*

1303 R. Brunne *Handl. Synne* 3768 Þys synne [of cursing] ys nat dampnable But hyt be seyde custummable. **1567** R. Mulcaster *Fortescue's De Laud. Leg.* (1672) 121 b, In the common bench there are customable v. Justices, or six at the most. **1661** Morgan *Sph. Gentry* iv. iii. 47 The one sort customable wearing their hood on the left shoulder.

†**2.** Of persons: **a.** Accustomed (*to*), wont (*to do* a thing); **b.** (with agent-noun) Habitual. *Obs.*

1303 R. Brunne *Handl. Synne* 2014 Ȝyf thou be custumable þar to, þou synnest gretly. **1430** Lydg. *Chron. Troy* iv. xxxii, He was aye customable..for to be vengeable. *c* **1449** Pecock *Repr.* (Rolls) II. iii. xix. 414 King Saul was a wickid customable synner. **1575** Coverdale (*title*), A Christian Exhortacion unto customable Swearers.

3. Liable to custom or duty; dutiable. *rare.*

1529 *Oath of Comptroller of Customs* in Thynne *Animadv.* (1865) Notes 131 The thinges customeable which shall cum to the saide porte. **1597** Skene *Sc. Acts* Table s.v. *Customers*, Customable gudes may nocht be caried foorth of the Realme. **1763** *Act 3 Geo. III*, c. 22 Any Ship..laden with customable or prohibited Goods. **1893** *Times* 17 June 13/5 A return has been presented to the House of Commons of the duty on 'Customable' goods..removed, duty paid, from Great Britain to Ireland.

Hence †'**customableness**.

1388 Wyclif *Ecclus.* xx. 28 Betere is a theef than the customablenesse of a man, a leesynmongere. **1583** Golding *Calvin on Deut.* clvii. 971 The customablenesse of sicknesses. **1730–6** Bailey (folio), *Customableness*, customariness, liableness to pay custom.

†'**customably**, *adv. Obs.* [f. prec. + -ly[2].] According to custom, as a matter of custom; habitually, usually, customarily.

1303 R. Brunne *Handl. Synne* 2697 Ȝyf þey synne custummably Yn þe hope of hys mercy. *c* **1430** *Pilgr. Lyf Manhode* i. cxxviii. (1869) 67 This targe..whiche the kyng Salomon bar sum tyme customableche. **1485** Caxton *Chas. Gt.* 118 Gyue almesse to þe poure peple largely and customably. **1548–9** (Mar.) *Bk. Com. Prayer* 133 b, Whensoeuer the people be customably assembled to pray in the churche. **1697** *View Penal Laws* 257 Where the Inhabitants have not customably used to river or wash their Sheep.

†'**customage**. *Obs. rare.* [a. OF. *coustumage*, f. *coustumer*: see custom *v.* and -age.] Levying or payment of custom.

1632 Rowley *Woman never Vext* i. i, When she returns laden with merchandise, And safe deliver'd with our customage.

customal, *sb.*: see custumal.

†'**customal**, *a. Obs. rare.* [ad. OF. *costumel* customary: see custom *sb.* and -al[1].] Customary, usual, habitual.

1401 *Pol. Poems* (Rolls) II. 71 Thou usist thi customale condicion, thou has so lerned to lye thou kanst not leve werk.

†'**customance**, '**custumance**. *Obs.* [a. OF. *cost-*, *coustumance*, f. *cost-*, *coustumer* to custom + -ance.]

1. Customary practice; custom, habit.

c **1386** Chaucer *Monk's T.* 521 This Nero hadde eek a custumance In youthe agein his maister for to ryse. **1393** Gower *Conf.* II. 164 Of his comun custumaunce. **1483** Caxton *Gold. Leg.* 307/4 Ledde..fro the cyte of Sodome that is to wete fro the custommaunce of Synne. **1528** Paynel *Salerne's Regim.* 1 Breakynge from customable vse hurteth greuously: for customance is an other nature.

2. Customary gathering; frequenting. *rare.*

1513–75 *Diurn. Occurrents* (1833) 340 At the croce of Edinburgh quhair maist custumance of peipill war.

customarily ('kʌstəmərılı), *adv.* [f. customary *a.* + -ly[2].] In a customary manner; usually, habitually; as a matter of custom.

a **1612** Donne *Βιαθανατος* (1644) 187 Naturally and customarily men thought it good to dye so. **1660** T. Gouge *Chr. Direct.* iii. (1831) 33 They are uttered customarily in a way of form, merely from the teeth outward. **1720** *Lond. Gaz.* No. 5826/1 The Nobility met as customarily. **1859** Mill *Liberty* i. (1865) 5/2 There seems to be no principle by which the propriety..of government interference is customarily tested.

'**customariness**. [f. next + -ness.]

1. The quality of being customary or habitual.

1660 Boyle *Seraph. Love* xviii. (1700) 111 By the customariness of their being possessed, they prove less conspicuous. **1663–4** Marvell *Corr.* Wks. 1872–5 II. 132 Out of the customariness of that expression. **1836** Sir H. Taylor *Statesman* vi. 41 The customariness of many metaphorical uses of words makes us unconscious of their metaphor. **1890** *Spectator* 4 Jan., This customariness of our well-being..partly explains optimism.

†**b.** Perfunctoriness or formality arising from habitual performance. *Obs.*

a **1640** J. Ball *Power of Godliness* (1657) 158 Discontent and hypocrisie, and customariness in good duties. **1646** T. Horton *Sinne's Discov.* 4 Our prayers are so full of coldnesse..and our fastings so full of customariness. **1653** Baxter *Peace Consc.* 119 Their.. dulness and customariness in duty.

2. A being accustomed or used to a thing. *rare.*

1864 Hawthorne *Dr. Grimshawe's Secret* xi, Still dim.. but our eyes..have gained an acquaintance, a customariness, with the medium.

customary ('kʌstəmərı), *a.* Also 6 **-rye**, 6–7 **-rie**, 7 **costomary**. [ad. med.L. *custumārius*, *-omārius*, repr. L. *consuētūdinārius*, f. *consuētūdinem*: see custom and -ary.]

1. According to custom; commonly used or practised; usual, habitual, accustomed, wonted.

1607 Shaks. *Cor.* ii. iii. 93, I haue heere the Customarie Gowne. **1645** Rutherford *Tryal & Tri. Faith* (1845) 116 Customary running lengtheneth the breath. **1705** Stanhope *Paraphr.* III. 525 The utter Insensibility..of the.. Conscience, which customary sinning introduces. **1712** W. Rogers *Voy.* 33 Such Weather is customary as we draw near the Line. **1838** Lytton *Alice* 43 Recovering his customary self-possession. **1863** Geo. Eliot *Romola* i. xx, It was customary to have very long troops of kindred and friends at the..betrothal.

†**b.** *transf.* of persons. *Obs.* (Cf. *habitual.*)

1796 Pegge *Anonym.* (1809) 189 It falls not within the compass of my remembrance, that a customary Dram-drinker ever left it off.

2. Established by or depending on custom.

1660 Willsford *Scales Comm.* 36 The customary measure of any place being known..to find how much it will make by a greater or a lesser measure of another place. **1875** Jowett *Plato* (ed. 2) III. 161 The family was a religious and customary institution binding the members together.

†**3.** Perfunctory or mechanical from habitual performance. *Obs.*

1654 Whitlock *Zootomia* 349 In her devotions, she is serious, not Customary. [**1670** Clarendon *Contempl. on Ps.* Tracts (1727) 712 There is a customary recital of prayers, and as customary an unconcernment in them.]

4. *Law.* **a.** Liable, subject to, or under customs or dues of various kinds, as ***customary tenants*** (med.L. *custumarii*), ***tenure***, ***lands***, etc. But in later usage this has come to be taken as: Holding or held by custom (*e.g.* of the manor). **b.** Relating to, depending on, or established by custom as contrasted with general law.

customary mill = custom mill: see custom 6.

1523 Fitzherb. *Surv.* Prol., Than may the lorde..haue parfyte knowledge..who is his freholders, copye holders, customarye tenaunte, or tenaunt at his wyll. *Ibid.* 15 They ..ought to haue a customarie role, wherin is euery mannes lande contayned, and what rent, customes, and seruyces euery man ought to pay and do. **1577** Harrison *England* ii. ix. (1877) i. 202 Customarie law consisteth of certeine laudable customes vsed in some priuat countrie. **1592** West *1st Pt. Symbol.* §103 C, The said customarie lands and tenements. **1620** J. Wilkinson *Coroners & Sherifes* 145 If any customarie tenant or copiholder hold two parcels of land by herriot service. **1709** *Lond. Gaz.* No. 4505/4 The several Manors of Bovey-Tracey [etc.]..with the Market and Fairs of Bovey-Tracey aforesaid, and the Customary Mills there. **1789** Bentham *Princ. Legisl.* xix. §28 The laws..may subsist either in the form of statute or in that of customary law. **1858** Ld. St. Leonards *Handy Bk. Prop. Law* xx. 151 Property of every description, including copyhold and customary lands. **1880** *Times* 9 Aug. 3/5 A custom had existed, which had now become a part of the customary estate, that the customary tenants should win and get the minerals under their own tenements.

c. ***customary court***: formerly in England, a manorial court which exercised jurisdiction over the copyhold tenants of the manor, and administered the custom of the manor as contrasted with the common law. It is distinguished from the court baron which exercised a jurisdiction over freeholders. ***customary holder***, a customary tenant; so ***customary-hold***.

1523 Fitzherb. *Surv.* xviii. (1539) 39 Copye holder, Customary holder. **1628** Coke *On Litt.* 58 a, A customary Court, and that doth concerne Copiholders, and therein the Lord or his Steward is the Judge. Now as there can be no Court baron without freeholders, so there cannot bee this kind of customary Court without Copiholders or Customary holders. **1844** Williams *Real Prop.* (1877) 225 Any freehold, copyhold or customary-hold property. **1876** K. E. Digby *Real Property* v. §6. 256.

†**5.** Of the nature of customs-duty or tribute.

1677 Sir T. Herbert *Trav.* 43 Toll gatherers..ready to search and exact a customary Tribute for the Mogul.

6. as *sb.* A customary ceremony.

1756 S. Richardson *Corresp.* (1804) III. 231 The little parting customaries are not to be mentioned.

customary ('kʌstəmərı), **custumary** ('kʌstjuːmərı), *sb.* [ad. med.L. *custumārius*, *-ārium*, representing OF. *coustumier*, L.

consuētūdinārius, *-ārium*, subst. uses of the adj.: see prec.]

1. *Law.* A written collection of customs (see CUSTOM *sb.* 2); a book or document setting forth the customs of a manor, city, province, etc.

1604 in *Eng. Gilds* (1870) 432 The Costomary of the mannor of Tettenhall regis. *a* **1618** RALEIGH in Gutch *Coll. Cur.* I. 64 By the customary of Bretaigne the Lords have aids towards the marrying of their daughters. **1818** HALLAM *Mid. Ages* (1841) I. i. 133 The earliest written customary in France is that of Bearn. **1885** *Law Times' Rep.* LIII. 503/1 Although such custom was not contained in any of the customaries of the manor.

b. *transf.* The customs of a country, etc. collectively, even though not reduced to writing.

1796 BURKE *Regic. Peace* i. Wks. VIII. 182 The whole of the polity and economy of every country in Europe..was drawn from the old Germanick or Gothick custumary. **1859** DASENT *Pop. Tales fr. Norse* Introd. xi., The codes of the Lombards, Franks, and Goths were not mere savage, brutal customaries.

2. *Eccl.* A treatise containing the ritual and ceremonial usages of a religious house, order, college; = CONSUETUDINARY *sb.*

1882 J. W. LEGG *Notes Hist. Liturg. Colours* 43 Richard de Ware was Abbot of Westminster from 1258 to 1283, and caused a custumary to be written.

†**customed** (ˈkʌstəmd, *poet.* ˈkʌstəmɪd), *ppl. a. Obs.* or *arch.* [f. CUSTOM + -ED.]

1. Accustomed, usual, customary; established by custom.

1382 WYCLIF *Ex.* v. 18 ȝe shulen ȝelde the customyd noumbre of tilys. **1483** CAXTON *Gold. Leg.* 428/2 On esterday aboue his customed pytaunce he ete two egges. **1595** SHAKS. *John* III. iv. 155 No common winde, no customed euent, But they will..call them Meteors, prodigies, and signes. **1649** BLITHE *Eng. Improv. Impr.* (1653) 95 Let not passion nor old customed corrupted Will prevail. **1750** GRAY *Elegy* xxviii, One morn I miss'd him on the custom'd hill. **1872** G. MACDONALD *Wilf. Cumb.* I. xiii. 207 The invitation to dance, a customed observance at Moldwarp Hall.

2. Of merchandise: Charged with duty, or on which duty has been paid.

1604 E. GRIMSTONE tr. *Acosta's Hist. Indies* 225 Siluer that was marked and customed. **1611** COTGR., *Gabellé*.. Customed for; on which an Impost is layed. **1621** BOLTON *Stat. Irel.* 44 (*12 Edw. IV*) He or they so..carrying hydes, or any other staple merchandises into Scotland, not customed, shall forfeit [etc.].

3. Frequented or patronized by customers.

1594 PLAT *Jewell-ho.* III. 66 A house well customed. **1611** RICH *Honest. Age* (1844) 39 An ill customed shoppe. **1703** LD. ORRERY *As you find it* II. ii, I have more invitations.. than the best-custom'd Lawyer has Clients.

†ˈ**customer**, *a. Obs.* [a. OF. *costumier*, *coustumier* customary, accustomed, wonted = Pr. *costumier*, *cosdumnier*, med.L. *costumārius* :—Rom. **costumnario* for L. *consuētūdinārius*: see CUSTOM- and -ER.]

Accustomed, wont.

1303 R. BRUNNE *Handl. Synne* 8807 Who so euer þarto ys custummer. **1393** GOWER *Conf.* I. 224 If thou were ever Custumere To fals semblaunt in any wise. *c* **1400** *Rom. Rose* 4939 Youthe, his chamberere That to done yvelle is custommere. *c* **1450** *Knt. de la Tour* (1868) 134 The good lady was custumer to herburghe the holy profites.

customer (ˈkʌstəmə(r)), *sb.* Forms: 5 custummere, costomer, 5–7 custumer, 6 customar, custymer, customyer, 7 custumier, 5– customer. [In senses 1 and 2, and in 6, a. late AngloFr. *custumer*, med.L. *custumārius* = *consuētūdinārius*: see Du Cange. In other senses the word appears to be an Eng. formation upon CUSTOM.]

†**1.** One who acquires ownership by long use or possession; a customary holder. *Obs.*

c **1440** *Promp. Parv.* 111 Custummere, *custumarius*, *usucaptor*.

†**2.** An official who collects customs or dues; a custom-house officer. *Obs.*

[See CUSTOM *sb.* 4 a 1st quot.] **1448** *Act 27 Hen. VI*, c. 2 Chescun Custumer Countrollour Sercheour & Surveiour. *a* **1483** *Liber Niger Edw. IV* in *Househ. Ord.* 27 Corouners, custumers, countrollers, serchers. **1486** *Act 3 Hen. VII*, c. 8 The Customer or Comptroller of the same Port. **1509** BARCLAY *Ship of Fooles* (1570) 11 He shall be made a common Customer..of Lin, Callis, or of Deepe. **1548** UDALL etc. *Erasm. Par. Mark* ii. 22 Sitting at the receipt of custome, for he was a publicane or customer. **1609** [see CUSTOM *sb.* 4 a]. **1651** BEDELL in *Fuller's Abel Rediv.*, *Erasmus* (1867) I. 74 All the gold he brought with him.. except five pounds, was seized..by the customers [at Dover]. **1748** *St. James's Evening Post* No. 5982 Lord Petersham..to be Customer, Collector, etc., in the Port of Dublin.

3. a. 'One who frequents any place of sale for the sake of purchasing' (J.); one who customarily purchases from a particular tradesman; a buyer, purchaser. (The chief current sense.) Also *attrib.*

c **1480** in *Eng. Gilds* (1870) 317 To wᵗ-draw from yoʳ M., ne from no brother of þᵉ craft, any of ther costomers. **1523** FITZHERB. *Husb.* §119, I saye to my customers, and those that bye any horses of me. **1592** GREENE *3rd Pt. Connycatch.* 33 His shop very well frequented with Customers. **1611** SHAKS. *Wint. T.* IV. iv. 192 No Milliner can so fit his customers with Gloues. **1745** DE FOE *Eng. Tradesman* (1841) I. viii. 59 Parcels fit to fill their shops, and invite their customers. **1832** *Chambers's Jrnl.* I. 276/4 When customer work failed, he was fain to work a piece upon speculation. **1834** MEDWIN *Angler in Wales* I. 222 The alehouse..had neither customers nor host. **1863** FAWCETT *Pol. Econ.* II. x. (1876) 259. **1955** J. G. DAVIS *Dict. Dairying* (ed. 2) 98 Though the cost of these seals is comparatively high they have an established 'customer-appeal'. **1964** *Times Rev. Industry* Feb. 19/2 The costs of customer placation (warranty costs, the costs of preventive and corrective service and maintenance, and the cost of maintaining spares stocks) must be added. **1969** *Jane's Freight Containers 1968–69* 416/1 The increase in distant-market customer-confidence.

b. In extended use: an applicant or client.

1896 *Westm. Gaz.* 5 Dec. 4/2 A. R. Downer is the latest 'customer' for Bredin. He last night telegraphed.. expressing his willingness to run the new professional 350 yards for £50 a side.

†**4. a.** A person with whom one has dealings; a familiar associate or companion (*of* some one). *Obs.* (passing into sense 5).

1548 HALL *Chron.* 153 The wagoner came to the gate, called the porter..The porter (whiche wel knew the voice of his customer). **1562** T. HEYWOOD *Prov. & Epigr.* (1867) 81 To his accustomed customers he gat. **1590** SHAKS. *Com. Err.* IV. iv. 63 You Minion you, are these your Customers? **1621** BP. MOUNTAGU *Diatribæ* 2 Lazy ignorance, or patient idlenesse, the common customers of the clergy.

†**b.** A common woman, prostitute. *Obs.*

1601 SHAKS. *All's Well* V. iii. 287, I thinke thee now some common Customer. **1604** —— *Oth.* IV. i. 123, I marry her! What? a customer!

5. *colloq.* A person to have to do with; usually with some qualifying adjective, as *ugly*, *awkward*, *queer*, *rum*, etc.: 'chap', 'fellow'. Also used of animals.

1589 R. HARVEY *Pl. Perc.* (1590) 11 False witnes..is taken vp now for a custome of one lewd Customer. **1652** HEYLIN *Cosmogr.* To Rdr., Such a Countrey-customer I did meet with one. **1818** SCOTT *Hrt. Midl.* xxviii, An thou meetest with ugly customers o' the road. **1837** DICKENS *Pickw.* ii, Queer customers those monks. *Ibid.* xx, A precious seedy-looking customer. **1854** R. S. SURTEES *Handley Cross* xxxiv. 268 A light-coloured fox beat him so often as to acquire the name of the 'old customer'. **1863** *Spring Lapl.* 185 Certainly, a bull elk is an awkward customer when brought to bay. **1899** *Westm. Gaz.* 15 Feb. 9/2 Almost immediately a fox went away, and he proved to be a real customer.

†**6.** = CUSTOMARY *sb.*, CUSTUMAL *sb. Obs.*

1614 SELDEN *Titles Hon.* 331 That *aide de Rançon* (as it is calld in the Custumier of Normandie). **1771** *Antiq. Sarisb.* 29 From the Grand Customer of Normandy we learn, that Bordage was a base tenure.

ˈ**customerless**, *a. nonce-wd.* [f. prec. + -LESS.] Without a customer.

1859 SALA *Gas-light & D.* vii, For years the railway tavern stood..deserted-looking, customerless.

†ˈ**customership.** *Obs.* [f. CUSTOMER 2 + -SHIP.] The office of a collector of customs.

1487 *Act 3 Hen. VII*, c. 7 The said..Office of Customership, Comptroller or Searcher. **1591** PERCIVALL *Sp. Dict.*, *Almoxarifadgo*, the customership, custome. **1652** WADSWORTH tr. *Sandoval's Civ. Wars Spain* 216 Profitable rights, as..Subsidies, Customerships.

custom-house (ˈkʌstəmhaʊs). [CUSTOM 4.]

1. A house or office at which custom is collected; *esp.* a government office situated at a place of import or export, as a seaport, at which customs are levied on goods imported or exported. **b.** *transf.* The office of the establishment or department which has the management of the customs.

a **1490** BOTONER *Itin.* (Nasmith 1778) 167 Transeundo per le custom-hous usque per le condyt. **1548** UDALL, etc. *Erasm. Par. Matt.* ix. (R.), As he passed by the custome-house, he espyed sitting there a certayne publicane, called Matthewe. **1604** DEKKER *Honest Wh.* Wks. 1873 II. 141 My men are all at Custome-house vnloding Wares. **1661** COWLEY *Disc. Govt. O. Cromwell* Wks. 1710 II. 659 How much we have gotten by it, let the Custom-house and Exchange inform you. **1712** BUDGELL *Spect.* No. 277 ¶3 Its Cargo was seized on by the Officers of the Custom-house. **1803** SOUTHEY *Eng. Eclogues* ix, He..Swore no false oaths, except at the custom-house. **1840** DICKENS *Old C. Shop* iv, Smoked his smuggled cigars under the very nose of the Custom-House.

2. *attrib.*, as ***custom-house oath***, ***officer***, ***station***.

1725 DE FOE *Voy. round World* (1840) 101 Agreeing with the custom-house officer for a small matter. **1748** OVERAL in Whiston *Mem.* 411 A Custom-House Oath is become a proverbial Expression, for a Thing not to be reguarded. **1856** EMERSON *Eng. Traits, Religion* Wks. (Bohn) II. 101 The modes of initiation are more damaging than custom-house oaths.

Hence **custom-houser** (*nonce-wd.*), a custom-house officer.

1865 CARLYLE *Fredk. Gt.* XXI. ii, Caitiff of a Custom-houser.

†ˈ**customing**, *vbl. sb. Obs. rare.* [f. CUSTOM *v.* 3 + -ING¹.] (See quot.)

1611 COTGR., *Gabellage*, a customing; an imposing or paying of custome.

customization (ˌkʌstəmaɪˈzeɪʃən). [f. CUSTOMIZE *v.* + -ATION.] The action or result of customizing; creation or adaptation (of something) according to the customer's requirements.

1975 *Physics Bull.* May 227/1 Complete units can be built to different designs for various requirements, allowing a certain degree of 'customization'. **1979** *Personal Computer World* Nov. 79/2 Obviously no two companies are exactly the same so some customisation is always going to be needed. **1982** *Times* 2 Nov. 18/8 Today's business user is faced with two main problems..: software, which with less than 20 per cent customisation, will best suit his needs [etc.].

ˈ**customize**, *v.* orig. *U.S.* [f. CUSTOM *sb.* 5 + -IZE.] *trans.* To make to order or to measure; to model or alter according to individual requirements. So ˈ**customized** *ppl. a.*, ˈ**customizing** *vbl. sb.*

1934 H. L. MENCKEN in *Words* Nov. 5/2 Obviously American..are such curious forms as..*to customize*. **1960** *Times* 14 Sept. 12/7 In the shops [in the U.S.], too, much time is saved with such contractions as 'Customized Drapes' which really reads much more dashingly than 'Curtains made to customers' specifications'. **1963** *Engineering* 31 May 740/1 A new and more economical means of obtaining a Grand Tourer was devised by 'customizing' an ordinary production sports car. **1965** *New Society* 2 Dec. 5/3 Not bigger and better engines—but more gadgets, more comfort, more customising. **1967** *Electronics* 6 Mar. 22/1 (Advt.), The high cost of 'customizing' is eliminated. **1970** *Daily Tel.* 26 Jan. 11/3 The cult of 'customised' transport—cars and motorcycles sculpted and plastered to express the personal fantasies of their owners.

ˈ**customless**, *a. nonce-wd.* [f. CUSTOM *sb.* 5 + -LESS.] Lacking custom.

1838 *New Monthly Mag.* LIV. 537 The aspect of Bond-street with its customless tradesmen.

†ˈ**customly**, *adv. Obs.* [f. CUSTOM *sb.* + -LY².] As a matter of custom, habitually.

1481 CAXTON *Myrr.* III. xxi. 181 Who that customly doth gladly the good werkes. **1549** COVERDALE *Erasm. Par. 1 Pet.* II. 15 Salute you euery one other with a kysse, not after the sorte that is geuen more customely than hartely. **1556** J. OLDE tr. *Gualter's Antichrist* iv. 128 b, We haue customly vsed to serue God..by a farre other maner.

‖**custos** (ˈkʌstɒs). *Obs.* (exc. as Latin.) [L. *custos*. Formerly treated as Eng. with pl. *custoses*: now consciously Latin, with pl. *custodes*.]

1. A keeper, guardian, warden, custodian.

1465 *Mercers' Rec.* in Blades *Life Caxton* 150 John lambert, John Warde, John Baker, John Alburgh, Custoses. **1523** LD. BERNERS *Froiss.* Pref. 1 The vertue of history.. hath to her custos and kepar, it (that is to say, tyme), whiche consumeth the other writynges. **1568** GRAFTON *Chron.* II. 158 The king..made Stephen Edworth Constable of the Tower, and Custos of the Citie of London. **1635** PAGITT *Christianogr.* 197 In the absence and minority of the Kings ..divers Clergymen have beene Custosses or Viceroyes of the Kingdome. **1855** THACKERAY *Newcomes* I. 166 The senior pupil and Custos of the room. **1878** STUBBS *Const. Hist.* III. xviii. 112 On the 21st [April 1430] Gloucester was appointed lieutenant and custos of the kingdom.

2. In certain Latin titles retained more or less in general use.

†***custos brevium*** ('Keeper of the briefs'): an officer in the Courts of King's Bench and Common Pleas, who had the custody of writs, warrants, and other documents.

custos rotulorum: the principal Justice of the peace in a county, who has the custody of the rolls and records of the sessions of the peace.

custos sigilli: the Keeper of the Seal.

1542–3 *Act 34–35 Hen. VIII*, c. 27 §53 There shall be.. one custos rotulorum in euery of the sayd twelue shires. **1654** *View Regul. Chancery* 49 The Custos brevium in the Court of Common-Pleas which hath been an office usually granted by Letters-Patent from before the Reign of Edw. I. **1696** LUTTRELL *Brief Rel.* (1857) II. 202 Mr. Fowkes, who hath the custos brevium office in the Kings bench court. **1862** LD. BROUGHAM *Brit. Const.* xvii. 274 The Lord Lieutenant, or rather the Custos Rotulorum in each county.

ˈ**custosship.** [f. prec. + -SHIP.] The office of custos.

1641 PRYNNE *Antip.* 186 Thomas de Corbridge.. bestowed..[the] Custoseship of the Parish of Saint Sepulcher on one Gilbert Segrave. **1866** *Daily News* 12 Feb. 5/6 Neither the dignity of the viceroyalty nor that of the Kingston Custosship has been..enhanced..by Gordon's capture.

†**custrel** (ˈkʌstrəl). *Obs.* exc. *Hist.* Also 6 coustrell, 6–7 costrel(l, costerel. See also COISTREL. [Coincides in meaning with OF. *coustillier*, *-illeur*, lit. a soldier armed with a *coustille* (see CUSTILE), hence, 'an esquire of the bodie, an armour-bearer vnto a knight, the seruant of a man at armes; also, a groome of a stable' (Cotgr.). But the regular Eng. repr. of this would be *custeler*, *custler*, and it is not easy to account for the metathesis of this to *custrel*. The secondary sense 'knave, base fellow' (commoner in the variant *coistrel*) is not found with Fr. *coustillier*, and seems to have arisen from association with CUSTRON.]

1. An attendant on a knight or man-at-arms.

1492 in Rymer *Fœdera* (1710) XII. 478 Every of theim havyng with him his Custrell and his Page. **1495** HEN. VII in Ellis *Orig. Lett.* I. II. I. 21 To make as many speres with their custrelles and di.lances..as ye can furnisshe. **1548** HALL *Chron.* (1809) 512 The Kyng ordeined 50 gentlemenne to bee speres, euery of theim to haue an Archer a Demilaunce and a Custrell. *a* **1577** SIR T. SMITH *Commw.*

Eng. I. xix. (1609) 26 They [Esquires] were at the first Costerels or the bearers of the Armes of Lords or Knights. **1613–18** DANIEL *Coll. Hist. Eng.* (1626) 93 Brabansons (which were certayne Mercenaries commonly called the Routs or Costerels). **1830** JAMES *Darnley* xi. 50/2 Now promoted to the dignity of custrel, or shield-bearer.

2. A term of reproach: Knave, base fellow. See COISTREL 2.

1581–1783 [see COISTREL]. **1608** SHAKS. *Per.* IV. vi. 176 Thou art the damned doorkeeper to every custerel [*printed* cusherel, *Globe* coistrel], that comes enquiring for his Tib.

custrel, var. of COSTREL[1], *Obs.*

†**'custreling, coustrelyng.** *Obs.* [dim. of CUSTREL: see -ING.] Lad, groom, 'knave'.

a **1553** UDALL *Royster D.* I. iv. (Arb.) 29 Oh, your coustrelyng Bore the lanterne a fielde so before the gozelyng.

†**'custron.** *Obs.* Forms: 4 quystron, qwistron, 4–6 quystroun(e, 5 quisteroun, quysteroun, (?) qwistoune, custrun, 6 coystrowne; *Sc.* custron, 6–7 -oun, 7 -one. [a. OF. *coistron, coestron, quistron, coitron*, in nom. case *questres, quaistre*, scullion:—late L. *cocistrōnem*, nom. *cocistro* 'tabernarius' (Papias).]

1. A scullion, a kitchen-knave; hence a boy or lad of low birth, base-born fellow, 'cad', vagabond.

c **1300** *K. Alis.* 2511 Ther n'as knave, no quystron, That he no hadde god waryson. *a* **1400** *Octouian* 154 Sche seyth a boy lothly of face, A quysteroun . . And seyde: 'Hark, thou cokes knaue'. *a* **1400–50** *Alexander* 3303 Lo! so þe quele of qwistrunnes [*printed* qwistrumnes] my qualite has changid! *c* **1400** *Rom. Rose* 886 This God of Love of his fasoun Was lyke no knave, ne quystroun. *a* **1529** SKELTON (*title*), Agaynste a comely coystrowne, that curyowsly chawntyd, and curryshly cowntred. —— *Howe douty D. Albany* 171 Suche a foule coystrowne. **1530** LYNDESAY *Test. Papyngo* 390 Pandaris, pykthankis, custronis, and clatteraris Loupis vp frome laddis, sine lychtis amang lardis. *a* **1605** POLWART in Montgomerie *Flyting* 128 Vile vagabound . . Custroun!

2. = CUSTREL I.

1494 FABYAN *Chron.* VII. 503 The sperys to haue for them and theyr custrun euery day halfe a floreyn.

custum, -e, etc., obs. forms of CUSTOM, etc.

custumal ('kʌstjuːməl), **customal** ('kʌstəməl), *sb. Law.* [from med.L. *liber custumalis*: see next.] A written collection or abstract of the customs of a manor, city, province, etc.; = CUSTOMARY *sb.*

1570–6 LAMBARDE *Peramb. Kent* (1826) 110 A Latine Custumall of the towne of Hyde. **1741** T. ROBINSON *Gavelkind* iii. 35 Set forth in the Custumal of those Manors. **1771** *Gent. Mag.* XLI. 351 The Customall of the Cinque Ports. **1875** MAINE *Hist. Inst.* i. 6 The Custumals or manuals of feudal rules plentiful in French legal literature. **1882** *Athenæum* 8 Apr. 441/3 The 'Customes of Yardley Hastings', in 1607 . . is not . . a manor customal, but . . an account, taken on the oaths of old men, of the ecclesiastical customs of the parish.

'custumal, *a.* [ad. med.L. *cos-, custumālis*, corresponding to OF. *costumel*, f. Rom. and med.L. *costuma*, OF. *costume* CUSTOM: see -AL[1].] Having to do with the customs of a city, etc.

1889 SIR J. MONCKTON in *Pall Mall G.* 5 Oct. 6/3, I find in the records no note of deviation from the usual custom, and as the custumal officer of the Corporation I should feel bound to advise against it.

†**'custumhede.** *Obs. rare.* [f. CUSTOM *sb.* + -HEAD.] Customary practice, custom, habit.

c **1340** *Cursor M.* 29139 (Cotton Galba) þe first in thoght, þat oþer in dede, þe thrid in syn of custumhede.

cusyn, -yng, obs. forms of COUSIN.

'cusyng, aphetic f. *accusing*. (Cf. CUSER.)

c **1470** HENRY *Wallace* VI. 400 Began a sair cusyng to mak.

cut (kʌt), *sb.*[1] Also cutt, -e. [Origin and original sense uncertain.

This has been usually regarded as merely a special use of CUT *sb.*[2] (under which it is still treated in recent dictionaries); but to this identification two considerations are opposed. First, *cut* 'the act or result of cutting' is (like such verbal derivatives generally) a word only of Modern English, known from the 16th c., while *cut* 'lot' goes back before 1300, standing quite alone without any sense of CUT *sb.*[2] to explain or support it. Secondly, in ME., in the verb CUT and its pa. pple., the forms *kyt, kit, ket* are of constant occurrence, but no such spellings are found for this word, only *cut, cutt* (*cutte*). The latter circumstance opposes also any such suggestion as that *cut* 'lot' is an absolute use of the pa. pple. meaning 'the cut stick or straw', 'the cut or marked thing drawn', a use which would besides be very difficult to admit at so early a date. There is no cognate word, and no derivative from any word meaning 'cutting', used in the other Teutonic languages; in these the word LOT, with its cognates, is the native term. It is evident that *drawing cuts* has been from the 13th c. a more popular form of sortilege, or a more popular and colloquial expression for it, than 'casting lots'. Welsh has *cwt* 'a little piece, a cut, a gobbet, a lot' (Silvan Evans); *cwt* lot occurs in Salesbury's transl. of the Bible, 1520; and the word has in Welsh the derivatives *cwtws* lot, lottery-ticket, share, *cwtysyn* lot, ticket; but it may be from English.]

1. = LOT: in the phrase ***draw cuts***, originally ***draw*** (or ***lay***) ***cut***, applied to a ready way of casting lots, by the chance drawing of sticks or straws of unequal length.

The simplest and most usual way is to take as many bits of straw, stick, or the like, as there are persons concerned, one of these bits being *shorter* (or it may be *longer*) than the others; these being held so that one end only is exposed, each person draws one of the bits for himself, and he who chances to draw the bit differing in length is the person to whom the lot falls. In later use each bit is called *a cut*, but in earlier use the decisive bit appears as the 'cut'.

α. To draw (lay) *cut*.

a **1300** *Cursor M.* 16699 (Cott.) A-bute his kirtel drou þai cutt. *a* **1340** HAMPOLE *Psalter* xxi. 18 On my clathe þai laid kut. *c* **1386** CHAUCER *Pard. T.* 465–7, I rede, that cut among us alle We drawe, and let se wher the cut wil falle; And he that hath the cut, with herte blithe Schal renne to the toun. *c* **1440** *York Myst.* xxxv. 293, I rede we drawe cutte for þis coote. *Ibid.* 295 The schorte cutte schall wynne. **1483** *Cath. Angl.* 88 To drawe Cutte, *sortiri.* **1533** MORE *Apol.* xxxvii. Wks. 903/1 Let them draw cut betwene them.

β. To draw *cuts*.

1450–1530 *Myrr. our Ladye* p. lviii, They drew cuttes amonge them whiche of theym shulde be kyllyd. **1530** PALSGR. 526/2, I drawe lottes, or drawe cuttes, as folkes do for sporte, *je joue au court festu* [short straw]. **1580** SIDNEY *Arcadia* (1613) 154 My daughter Mopsa . . may draw cuts, and the shortest cut speake first. **1590** SHAKS. *Com. Err.* v. i. 422. **1600** *Maides Metam.* IV. in Bullen *O. Pl.* I. 149 Whether shall begin his note? Draw cuttes . . content; the longest shall begin. **1641** BROME *Jov. Crew* III. Wks. 1873 III. 405, I am pussell'd in the choice. Would some sworne Brother . . were here to draw a Cut with me. **1653** WALTON *Angler* 75, I think it is best to draw cuts and avoid contention . . Look, the shortest Cut fals to Coridon. *a* **1745** SWIFT *Direct. Servants*, Who is to stay at home is to be determined by short and long cuts. **1855** KINGSLEY *Westw. Ho* (1861) 300 We three will draw cuts for the honour of going with him.

†**b.** The drawing or casting of lots: †***with*** or ***by cut***, by lot. *Obs.*

12.. *Leges quat. Burgorum* liv. (Sc. Stat.), Et sciendum est quod stallangiator nullo tempore potest habere loth cut neque cavyl de aliquo mercimonio cum burgense. *a* **1340** HAMPOLE *Psalter* xv. 6 Strengis . . fell as wiþ kut. **1513** DOUGLAS *Æneis* I. viii. 27 Be cut or cavil that pleid sone partid was. **1535** STEWART *Cron. Scot.* (1858) I. 39 Be cut and cavill than till his part fell he.

†**2.** (One's) lot, fate, fortune; fate or fortune as a ruler of events. *Obs.*

a **1340** HAMPOLE *Psalter* xxx. 18 In þi hend [are] my kuttes. **1423** JAS. I *Kingis Q.* cxlv, Hir that has the cuttis two In hand, both of ȝour wele and of ȝour wo. *c* **1450** *St. Cuthbert* 1367 To þe couent he him putt In religioun to prove his cutt. *Ibid.* 6743 To England felle a sary cutt. **1513** DOUGLAS *Æneis* I. iii. 76 Quhilk is by cutt gevin me to bair in hand. **1530** PALSGR. 211/2 Cutte or lotte, *sort.* **1635** PAGITT *Christianogr.* I. (1646) 206 You see . . how fortunate a cut those Gods have given us, whom wee robbed.

cut (kʌt), *sb.*[2] [In branches I–V f. CUT *v.*; in VI elliptical use of the pa. pple.; in VIII the word may be distinct, since the phrase occurs about or before 1400, while the sb. otherwise appears only in the 16th c.]

I. Act of cutting. **1.** *lit.*

1808 COBBETT *Pol. Reg.* 25 June 997 The speech is all whet and no cut. It is merely flummery. **1841** MRS. LOUDON *Ladies' Comp. Flower Gard.* (ed. 9) 81 The shoot should be cut off with what gardeners call a clean cut.

2. a. A stroke or blow with a sharp-edged instrument, as a knife, sword, etc.

1601 SHAKS. *Jul. C.* III. ii. 187 Through this, the wel-beloued Brutus stabb'd . . This was the most vnkindest cut of all. **1719** DE FOE *Crusoe* (1840) II. iv. 68 Seeing him give the fellow a barbarous cut with the hatchet. **1889** FROUDE *Chiefs of Dunboy* v. 55 His face . . had been disfigured by a sabre cut.

b. *Fencing* and *Sword exercise.* A slashing blow or stroke given with the edge of the weapon (distinguished from a *thrust* given with the point).

1592 G. HARVEY *Pierce's Super.* 140 Cuttes, slashes and foines. **1833** *Regul. Instr. Cavalry* I. 148 Each 'Cut' has its 'Guard'. **1840** DICKENS *Old C. Shop* II. i, The broadsword exercise with all the cuts and guards complete.

c. ***cut and thrust***: (*a*) as *sb.*, the act of cutting and thrusting; hand-to-hand struggle; (*b*) as *adj.* (the words being hyphened), adapted for both cutting and thrusting; addicted to or connected with cutting and thrusting; also *fig.*; (*c*) *ellipt.* = cut-and-thrust sword.

1760 STERNE *Tr. Shandy* III. iv. 15 Pell mell, helter skelter, ding dong, cut and thrust . . have they been trimming it [*sc.* a jerkin] for me. **1840** THACKERAY *Catherine* i, He-devils, sword and pistol, cut and thrust, pell-mell came tumbling into the redoubt! **1843** LYTTON *Last Bar.* I. iii, Thanks, but I leave cut and thrust to the gentles. **1846** GROTE *Greece* (1862) I. ii. 63 The cut and thrust of actual life.

1763 *Brit. Mag.* IV. 301 My sword with a cut-and-thrust blade. **1820** SCOTT *Abbot* iv, The word *sword* comprehended all descriptions, whether back-sword or basket-hilt, cut-and-thrust or rapier. **1838** DICKENS *Nich. Nick.* ix, That . . scowl with which the cut-and-thrust counts, in melodramatic performances, inform each other they will meet again. **1875** JOWETT *Plato* (ed. 2) II. 421 The short cut and thrust method of Socrates.

3. a. A sharp stroke or blow with a whip, cane, etc.

1725 *New Cant. Dict.*, I took him a Cut cross the Shoulders. **1787** 'G. GAMBADO' *Acad. Horsemen* (1809) 36 A good smart cut over his [the horse's] right cheek and eye. **1833** HT. MARTINEAU *Manch. Strike* iii. 29 A cut across the knuckles with his riding-whip. **1886** BURTON *Arab. Nts.* (Abr. ed.) I. 296 He sentenced him to receive an hundred cuts with the scourge.

b. *pl.* Corporal punishment, esp. of schoolchildren. *Austral.* and *N.Z. slang.*

1915 *Bulletin* (Sydney) 28 Oct. 47/1 'Six cuts yer give him,' roared the whiskers . . . The stick emphasized the last remark by a rapid descent on the meek one's shoulders. **1938** P. LAWLOR *House of Templemore* xi. 123 'Urry or yer'l git th' cuts. **1945** F. SARGESON *When Wind Blows* ii. 14 [You] would get the cuts for sure. **1963** D. ADSETT *Magpie Sings* 57 If anyone was careless enough to use the wrong peg, their coat, hat and bag could be thrown to the floor without fear of getting the cuts.

4. *fig.* An act whereby the feelings are deeply wounded, as a sarcasm, an act of unkindness, etc.; a severe disaster or misfortune; a blow, shock.

1568 C. WATSON *Polyb.* 65 a, The Romans . . acknowledged this their simple cutte and sore repulse. **1606** SHAKS. *Ant. & Cl.* I. ii. 173. **1635** R. BOLTON *Comf. Affl. Consc.* iii. 15 A most cruel cut to a troubled conscience. **1766** *Goody Two-Shoes* II. vii. (1881) 136 This was a Cut to a Man of his imperious Disposition. **1889** E. BAGSHAW *Advent Pastoral* 17 Contemptuous cuts and disparaging words.

5. An excision or omission of a part.

1604 MIDDLETON *Father Hubbard's T.* Wks. (1886) VIII. 77 He must venture . . to the Bankside, where he must sit out the breaking-up of a comedy, or the first cut of a tragedy. **1779** SHERIDAN *Critic* II. ii, Hey day! here's a cut! What, are all the mutual protestations out? **1880** *Sat. Rev.* 1 May 568 The piece . . will perhaps have a still better effect if the cuts which we have suggested are made.

6. The act of 'cutting down'; a reduction in rates or prices; also, a reduction in wages, supplies, services, etc. orig. *U.S.*

1881 *Chicago Times* 17 June, Supplemented by a still further 'cut' of two cents. **1888** *Times* 13 Nov. 5/1 (Philadelphia) Stocks declined to-day because of a radical cut in the freight rates between Chicago and the sea-board. **1921** *Daily Herald* 29 Apr. 1/4 The L.C.C. do not contemplate any immediate cuts in their tramway service. **1946** *Daily Tel.* 27 Mar., A statement of unusual gloom emanated from the Food Ministry . . prophesying a fresh 'cut' in the soap and margarine rations. **1968** R. HARRIS *Nice Girl's Story* ii. 14 The gas . . flickered blue and cold. 'There's some kind of a cut, I think . . .' **1971** *Daily Tel.* 18 Feb. 15/2 It is still not known how much next year's cut of 10,000 in the total of 180,000 assisted passages . . will affect candidates from Britain.

7. The act of 'cutting' by a horse: see CUT *v.* 27: the part of the leg injured by cutting.

1688 *Lond. Gaz.* No. 2376/4 A brown Gelding . . cuts on the Speedy cut of both his Fore-Legs. **1865** YOUATT *Horse* xvi. (1872) 371 The inside of the leg, immediately under the knee . . is subject to injury from what is termed the *speedy cut*.

8. *Card-playing.* The act of cutting a pack of cards; the card obtained by cutting. †***new cut***: name of some game at cards (*obs.*).

1598 FLORIO, *Trinca*, a game at cards called swig or new cut. **1728** SWIFT *Jrnl. Mod. Lady*, The deal, the shuffle, and the cut. **1860** CRAWLEY *Handy Bk. Games* 324 Should a card be exposed, there must be a fresh cut, the dealer having the option of shuffling them before the next cut. Not fewer than four cards are considered a cut.

9. A step in dancing: see CUT *v.* 30.

1676 ETHEREDGE *Man of Mode* v. ii, No one woman is worth the loss of a cut in a caper. **1751** SMOLLETT *Per. Pic.* xiv, Performed sundry new cuts with his feet. **1842** DICKENS *Amer. Notes* (1850) 62/2 Single shuffle, double shuffle, cut and cross-cut. **1892** MRS. H. WARD *D. Grieve* viii, David stopped his cut and shuffle.

10. A particular stroke in various games with balls: **a.** *Cricket.* The stroke described s.v. CUT *v.* 31 a. **b.** *Lawn Tennis.* The stroke described s.v. CUT *v.* 31 b; also the 'screw' put on the ball by this stroke. **c.** *Croquet.* A stroke in which a ball is driven away obliquely by another ball. **d.** *Rackets.* A ball served so that it strikes upon or below the 'cut-line', which is a fault.

1833 *Gentl. Mag.* July 44/2 Beldham was great in every hit, but his peculiar glory was the cut. **1855** STONEHENGE *Brit. Sports* (1868) 568 The main difference is between the perpendicular cut to leg and the horizontal one to off side. **1874** J. D. HEATH *Croquet Player* 33 More force will be required to send a ball a given distance by a cut, than when it is rushed in a straight line. **1874** *Field* 15 Aug., Good balls always bound, except when they have that cut on which W. H. E. evidently dislikes. **1878** JULIAN MARSHALL *Lawn Tennis* 37 The cut will also be found very useful in the service. **1888** STEEL & LYTTELTON *Cricket* (Badm. Libr.) 61–2 The real genuine cut goes to the left side of point . . When the player is well in . . he very often makes . . a clean cut; that is to say, he hits with a bat quite horizontal to the ball, and not over it.

11. *Gun Manuf.* Each of the various processes through which the several limbs of the gun pass.

1881 GREENER *Gun* 270 In some arms upwards of 1,000 separate cuts have to be made to complete each gun, to say nothing of drilling the various holes.

12. *colloq.* **a.** The act of 'cutting' or refusing to recognize an acquaintance.

1798 [see CUTTEE]. **1829** *Anniversary, Travelled Monkey* 133 That look which London calls a cut, Our traveller on his cousin put. **1848** THACKERAY *Bk. Snobs* ii. (D.), We met and gave each other the cut direct that night. **1862** MERIVALE *Rom. Emp.* (1865) V. xliv. 268 The *Cut*, the last resource of sullenness and shyness is, I believe, a strictly English institution.

b. Intentional absence from or deliberate omission to attend (an event). Cf. CUT *v.* 33 c.

1851 B. H. HALL *College Words* 90 *Cut*, an omission of a recitation. **1856** *Ibid.* (ed. 2) 147 *Cuts.* When a class [at Bowdoin College] for any reason become dissatisfied with one of the Faculty, they absent themselves from his recitation, as an expression of their feelings. **1915** *Dialect*

Notes IV. 233 *Cut*, unexcused absence from class. **1919** W. T. Grenfell *Labrador Doctor* (1920) ii. 22 Attendance at chapel was compulsory, and no 'cuts' were allowed.

13. (See quot.)

1879 *Scribner's Mag.* XIX. 327/1 Often in storms a strong swift current runs along the coast between the outer bar and the shore, called by the surfmen the 'set' or 'cut'.

†**14.** *Irish Hist.* A levy of money, a tax, an impost: cf. cut *v.* 35. *Obs.*

1634–5 *Stat. Ireland* (1765) II. 169 To that end doe make cuts, levies and plotments upon themselves to pay them.

15. *Cinemat.* A quick transition from one shot to the next (see also quot. 1940). Cf. cut *v.* 21 e.

1933 I. Dalrymple in A. Brunel *Filmcraft* 174 Don't ignore the stunt or effect cut. **1933** M. Hankinson *Ibid.* 225 A cut is always made between the second and third sprocket-holes of a frame..on the action and parallel on the track..because..the ordinary joining machine loses two sprocket-holes on each bit of film it joins. **1940** *Chambers's Techn. Dict.* 217/2 *Cut*, the junction between one strip of continuous film of motion-picture and the next. **1944** S. Cole *Film Editing* 10 In similar circumstances such a cut would be acceptable even without any sound at all. **1959** *Viewpoint* July 19 A straight 'cut' instead of the conventional 'fade' helped to achieve a startling visual jerk. **1961** G. Millerson *Telev. Production* 298 The cut is the simplest transition—an immediate change from one shot to the next.

II. 16. a. A passage, course, or way straight across; *esp.* as opposed to going round a corner or by a circuitous route. Also *concr.*, and *fig.*

1577–87 Harrison *Descr. Brit.* ii. 3 in *Holinshed*, The shortest and most usuall cut that we have out of our Iland to the Maine is from Dover..unto Calice. **1581** Savile *Tacitus' Hist.* i. xxxi. (1591) 19 Tired and sick with so long a cut [*longa navigatione*]. **1600** Holland *Livy* xxxii. xxiii. 824 Whence the passage over to Corinth is a cut [*trajectus*] almost of seven miles. **1637** Heywood *Dial.* xv. Wks. 1874 VI. 233 So long a cut Must I take pains to waft thee. **1831** A. Fonblanque *Eng. under 7 Administ.* (1837) II. 174 The cut across the fields is shut up. **1883** Parker *Tyne Childe* 273 One of those rhetoricians who would take any cut to a climax.

b. *esp.* in ***short cut***, a crossing that shortens the distance. *abstr.* and *concr.*, *lit.* and *fig.*

1589 Greene *Menaphon* (Arb.) 70 He..hauing the winde fauourable, made a short cut. *c* **1590** Marlowe *Faust.* iii. 52 The shortest cut for conjuring Is stoutly to abjure the Trinity. **1601** Holland *Pliny* I. 63 The shortest cut into Greece. **1658** W. Burton *Itin. Anton.* 114 The way is not alwaies by the shortest cut. **1866** Argyll *Reign Law* vii. (ed. 4) 363 There are no short cuts in Nature. **1888** Burgon *Lives 12 Gd. Men* II. xi. 311 A short cut across the fields..was made for the convenience of the inhabitants.

c. Also ***near cut***. (Still common in *Sc.*)

1614 Bp. Hall *Recoll. Treat.* 1115 Hee..now leades them the nearest cut to Jericho. **1673** E. Brown *Trav. Germ.* (1677) 2 The nearest cut out of England into Holland is from Laistoffe Point to Gravesandt. **1783** Ainsworth *Lat. Dict.* (Morell) iv. s.v. *Anaxagoras*, There is a near cut to heaven from every place. **1801** Gabrielli *Myst. Husb.* II. 135 He set forward, taking, for expedition, all the nearest cuts. **1803** Maria Vanzee *Fate* 42 The old man..had arrived before me, by a nearer cut in the wood.

III. 17. a. The shape to which, or style in which a thing is cut; fashion, shape (of clothes, hair, etc.). *spec.* Short for *hair-cut*, used esp. with defining word.

1579 Lyly *Euphues* (Arb.) 152 With costly attyre of the newe cut. **1600** Shaks. *A.Y.L.* ii. vii. 155 With eyes seuere, and beard of formall cut. *c* **1684** *Frost of 1683–4.* 19 The cuts were diamond, the substance ice. **1703** Moxon *Mech. Exerc.* 15 You see how the Files of several Cuts succeed each other. **1751** Johnson *Rambler* No. 138 ¶5 Wearing a gown always of the same cut and colour. **1805** *Naval Chron.* XV. 125 From the cut of her sails an enemy. **1883** S. C. Hall *Retrospect* II. 187 A broad-brimmed hat and coat of Quakerish cut. **1951** N. Marsh *Opening Night* iv. 90 I'm a shoulder-length natural ash-blonde and I've had to have an urchin cut and go black. **1953** *Encycl. Brit. Bk. of Yr.* 639/2 Fashion produced the Pony-Tail and the Poodle-Cut, two hairstyles for women. **1960** *Sunday Express* 14 Aug. 12/4 The short cut..was *made* for me. *Ibid.* 23 Oct. 14/3 One guinea for a 'cut'.

b. *fig.* Fashion, style, make.

1590 Nashe *Pasquil's Apol.* i. C ij b, A right cutte of the worde, without gigges or fancies. **1602–3** Manningham in *Eng. Illust. Mag.* Mar. (1884) 368/2 A young gallant, but of a short cutt. **1628** Prynne *Love-lockes* 25 Others of the common ranke and cut. **1741** Richardson *Pamela* (1824) I. 171 My good mother was one of this old fashioned cut. **1856** Mrs. Carlyle *Lett.* II. 307 These Londoners are all of the cut of this woman.

c. ***the cut of one's jib***: one's general appearance or look. *slang*, orig. nautical: see jib.

1823 Southey in *Life & Corr.* V. 144 Their likeability, which depends something upon the cut of their jib. **1833** Marryat *P. Simple* ii, I see you're a sailor by the cut of your jib. **1881** R. Buchanan *God & Man* ii. iii, I like the cut of your jib less than ever.

18. Phrase. ***a cut above*** (some person or thing): a degree or stage above. *colloq.*

[**1797** Lamb *Lett.* (1888) I. 78 There is much abstruse science in it above my cut.] **1818** Scott *Hrt. Midl.* xvi, Robertson is rather a cut abune me. **1842** Marryat *Percival Keene* i, She was..a cut above the housekeeper in the still-room. **1891** L. B. Walford *Mischief of Monica* xi, The girl herself is a cut below par.

IV. The result, effect, or product of cutting.

19. An opening in a surface made by a sharp-edged instrument, an incision; a wound made by cutting, a gash.

1530 Palsgr. 211/2 Cutte, a wounde, *covppevre.* **1557** N. T. (Genev.) *Matt.* ix. 16 The cutte is made worse. **1618** N. Field *Amends for Ladies* iii. iv, How came they by such cuts and slashes? **1719** De Foe *Crusoe* (1840) II. ix. 215 Two or three of the men had cuts in their backs and thighs. **1830** Cooper *Dict. Surgery* (ed. 6) 1269 When the wound is a common cut, the sides of the division ought to be brought in contact.

20. An incision made in the edge of a garment, etc., for ornament; a slash; a natural indentation, as in the edge of a leaf.

1563 *Homilies* ii. *Excess of Apparel* (1859) 313 While one spendeth his patrimony upon pounces and cuts. **1578** Lyte *Dodoens* ii. lxxxiii. 261 Sauing that euery little leafe his cuttes are a great deale narrower. **1599** Shaks. *Much Ado* iii. iv. 19 Cloth a gold and cuts, and lac'd with siluer. **1641** Milton *Ch. Govt.* vi. (1851) 126 She might go jagg'd in as many cuts and slashes as she pleas'd. **1719** De Foe *Crusoe* (1840) II. xiii. 277 The habit..with..cuts and slashes almost on every side.

21. A passage or channel: **a.** An artificial watercourse cut or dug out; a channel, canal, cutting. (In common use in the Fen district in England.)

1548 *Petit. of Sandwich* in Boys *Sandwich* (1792) 735 To authorize the said mayor..and inhabitants..to cut out, newe erect and make one newe cutt into their said haven. **1570** *Act 13 Eliz.* c. 18 Preamb., The Leading and Passage of the said Water, thorough such a..Cut, as may serve for the Navigation of Barges. **1603** Knolles *Hist. Turks* (1638) 89 Invironed with a nauigable ditch or cut. **1696** *Phil. Trans.* XIX. 344 Through these Fens run great Cuts or Dreyns. **1803** G. Rose *Diaries* (1860) II. 20 To make a..navigable cut from the Red Sea to the Nile. **1893** *Act 36–7 Vict.* c. 71 §58 Any watercourse, mill race, cut, leat, or other channel for conveying water..from any river.

†**b.** A natural narrow opening or passage by water; a channel or strait.

1598 Grenewey *Tacitus' Ann.* v. ii. (1622) 119 Hastening ouer the Toronæan and Thermean cut, and passing by Eubœa. **1610** Holland *Camden's Brit.* ii. 203 Mona whereof Cæsar maketh mention, in the mids of the Cut..betweene Britaine and Ireland. **1642** Fuller *Holy & Prof. St.* ii. viii. 77 As it were but a narrow cut to ferry over. **1678** tr. *Gaya's Art of War* ii. 102 The Castle of Salses, on the Cut of the Sea.

c. A creek or inlet. Now *local.*

1630 *R. Johnson's Kingd. & Commw.* 456 The Country is full of cuts and inlets from this River. **1727** *Beverley Beck Act* 1 A Creek or Cut, commonly called Beverley Beck. **1890** M. Townsend *U.S.* 137 *Cut*, used on the eastern shore of Florida as synonymous with inlet.

d. A passage cut as a roadway through a rock, wood, dense part of a city, etc.; a railway cutting.

1730 Sir H. Sloane in *Phil. Trans.* XXXVI. 261 Having again continued our Journey under Ground in the Salt-work, we then found ourselves in the Cuts. **1789** *Ess. Shooting* (1791) 300 The sportsman may..watch at some opening, or cut which runs through the wood. **1881** *Chicago Times* 12 Mar., The snow is six feet in the cuts. **1881** *Scribner's Mag.* XXII. 528/2 On the left are cuts and tunnels.

e. *Theatr.* A narrow longitudinal opening, cut in the flooring of the stage, by which scenes are moved up and down.

1859 Sala *Gas-light & D.* ii. 23 On this frame the scene to be painted is placed; and..worked up and down the cut as the painter may require. **1881** L. Wagner *Pantomimes* 55 The visitor will discern what are called the cuts in the flooring of the stage..When required these cuts are opened..for the passage of the scenes to be sent up.

22. a. A design cut or engraved upon wood, copper, or steel; the impression from this; an engraving, a plate. Now restricted to engravings on wood (see woodcut), those on metal being called *plates.*

1646 Sir T. Browne *Pseud. Ep.* 258 Set forth in the Icons or Cuts of Martyrs by Cevallerius. **1662** Evelyn *Chalcogr.* 23 The Invention of Copper-cuts, and their Impressions. *Ibid.* 84 With some other cuts in wood known by his mark..All those excellent Wood Cuts. **1695** *Lond. Gaz.* No. 3131/3 The Cutts of the University..richly bound, and Printed in Folio at the Theatre. **1710** Hearne *Collect.* (Oxf. Hist. Soc.) III. 17 The wooden Cutts of the actors. **1781** Crabbe *Library* Wks. 1834 II. 39 Bibles, with cuts and comments. **1824** J. Johnson *Typogr.* I. 253 The cuts to this edition are better executed. **1885** *Mag. of Art* Sept. 449/1 A glance at our first two cuts will give an idea of their position.

b. A gramophone record or recording. Cf. cut *v.* 23 d. orig. *U.S.*

1949 *Music Libr. Assoc. Notes* Dec. 42 A recording artist *cuts* a master and the recording executive may reject the *cut.* **1962** A. Nisbett *Technique Sound Studio* 247 *Cut*,..one of several separately recorded bands..on a disc. **1970** *New Yorker* 12 Dec. 182/2 These two cuts, along with..'Little Sadie', showed promise of saying something interesting.

†**23.** A carving. *Obs. rare.*

1658 *Hist. Q. Christina* 264 The Church of St. Francis..with noble statues, embossed works, and infinite cuts of Greeke marble.

V. A piece cut off.

24. a. A piece of anything cut off; *esp.* of meat, a slice.

1591 Percivall *Sp. Dict.*, *Tajada*, a cut of flesh, a slice of bread. **1641** Peacham *Worth of Penny* in Arb. *Garner* VI. 265 The worst and first cut, as of boiled beef. **1737** Johnson in *Boswell*, I had a cut of meat for sixpence, and bread for a penny. **1864** D. G. Mitchell *Sev. Stor.* 52 Perhaps we can take a cut off the same joint.

†**b.** A slice of meat as a slight meal. Cf. *cold cuts. U.S. Obs.*

1770 Washington *Diary* 9 June (1925) I. 383 Had a cold cut at Mrs. Campbell's. **1773** *Ibid.* 21 Feb. II. 102 [They] call here, but would not stay dinner, taking a Cut before it. **1816** U. Brown *Jrnl.* 24 Sept. in *Maryland Hist. Mag.* (1916) XI. 230 At last comes to an Orniary [*sc.* Ordinary], fed & took a cut. **1827** *Cincinnati Enquirer* 15 Aug. 2/5 A cold cut at Utica.

c. A number of sheep or cattle cut out from the flock or herd. *U.S.*, *Austral.*, and *N.Z.*

1888 Roosevelt in *Century Mag.* Apr. 860/2 As the animals of a brand are cut out they are received and held apart by some rider detailed for the purpose, who is said to be 'holding the cut'. **1907** S. E. White *Arizona Nights* i. vi. 112 The round-up Captain appointed two men to hold the cow-and-calf cut, and two more to hold the steer cut. **1933** E. Jones *Autobiogr. Early Settler* xxi. 93 [They] took a small cut of twenty or thirty sheep up to the river. **1953** B. Stronach *Musterer on Molesworth* x. 68 At last we got a small cut of our mob [of cattle] over [the bridge] and the rest was easy.

d. *slang.* Share (of profit, etc.); commission; = rake-off. orig. *U.S.*

1918 H. C. Witwer *Baseball to Boches* ix. 363 If you get nailed we'll give your wife a cut of our winnin's! **1940** Wodehouse *Quick Service* xii. 101, I don't mind giving Howard Steptoe his cut, but..five hundred pounds has got to be earmarked for me. **1957** W. H. Whyte *Organization Man* 282 The real money would come from..the company's cut..of every dollar spent in the shopping center. **1970** *New York* III. 30 Nov. 28/3 The net proceeds of a $2 million stock offering after the underwriter had taken his cut.

25. A piece of cloth of definite length cut from a warp.

1753 Hanway *Trav.* (1762) I. iii. xxvii. 113 The present..consisting of several cuts of fine cloth. **1891** *Labour Commission* Gloss., *Cuts*, sometimes called 'ends', are pieces of cloth of a certain length (generally of or about 100 yards) cut from a warp.

26. A certain quantity of yarn; properly containing 120 rounds of the legal reel, and 91 inches long. (*Sc.* and *north. Engl.*)

1632 *N. Riding Rec.* (1885) III. ii. 194 Two women for stealing 30 cuttes of linen yarn. **1726** *Ibid.* VIII. 174 Linen yarne..must be 'good and full tale of six score threads to the cutt'. **1791** *Statist. Acc. Roxburghsh.* (*Galashiels*) II. 308 (Jam.) A stone of the finest [wool]..will yield 32 slips of yarn, each containing 12 cuts, and each cut being 120 rounds of the legal reel. **1840** Mar. Edgeworth *Parent's Assistant* (1854) 341 Mary spun nine cuts a day besides doing all that was to be done in the house.

27. The quantity cut (of a nautral product, *esp.* timber). Chiefly *U.S.*

1805 R. W. Dickson *Pract. Agric.* (1807) II. 360 A medium crop for the first cut. **1878** *Lumberman's Gaz.* 16 Mar., The cut of this year exceeded the cut of last year by at least 20 per cent. **1890** *Times* 22 Sept. 4/2 The cut of violet clovers in France is not likely to be large.

28. (See quot. 1890.) Also, a portion of a field cut, or intended for cutting, at one time. *U.S.*

1765 Washington *Diary* 6 Nov. (1925) I. 216 Finishd sowing Wheat at the Mill—viz 19 Bushls. in ye large cut within the Post and Rail fence and 6 B. in ye small cut. **1770** *Ibid.* 14 Sept. 399 Morris at Doeg Run began to sow his third Cut of Wheat. **1855** G. N. Jones *Florida Plant. Rec.* (1927) 132 The Cotton in the lower most cut of prelow will avrige knee high, the next two cutes will not avrige quit wast high. **1890** *Dialect Notes* (Boston), *Kentucky words* ii. 64 *Cut*, with tobacco raisers..a portion of a tobacco field. 'Did you finish worming that cut you were on?'

VI. Substantive uses of the pa. pple.

†**29.** 'A familiar expression for a common or labouring horse' (Nares). *Obs.* [It is doubtful whether the sense is 'cut-tail horse' or 'gelding'.]

1526 Skelton *Magnyf.* 296 In fayth, I set not by the worlde two Dauncaster cuttys. **1577** Whetstone *Remembr. Gascoigne* in *Steel Gl.* (Arb.) 24 The Colliers cut, the Courtiars Steed will tire. **1596** Shaks. *1 Hen. IV*, ii. i. 6, I prethee Tom, beate Cuts Saddle..the poore Iade is wrung in the withers. **1612** *Two Noble K.* iii. iv, He's buy me a white cut, forth for to ride.

†**30.** A term of absue, applied to a man or woman. *Obs.* or *dial.*

[Perh. from prec. sense: with *Call me cut*, cf. Falstaff's 'call me horse' in *1 Hen. IV*, ii. iv. 215. As applied to a woman, app. more opprobrious: cf. cutty.]

c **1490** H. Medwall *Nature*, If thou se hym not take hys owne way Call me cut when thou metest me another day. **1575** J. Still *Gamm. Gurton* v. ii, That lying cut is lost, that she is not swinged and beaten. **1601** Shaks. *Twel. N.* ii. iii. 203 If thou hast her not i' the end, call me Cut. **1605** *Lond. Prodigal* C ij b, And I doe not meete him, chill giue you leaue to call me cut. **1725** *New Cant. Dict.*, A *Cut* in some Northern Counties..signifies a Strumpet. **1820** Scott *Abbot* xix, 'You shall call me cutt if I do go down', said Adam.

†**31. a.** *Gunnery.* A short cannon of any calibre.

1672 *Compleat Gunner* i. vii. 9 Bastard Pieces are shorter chases..and are therefore called Cuts of the same nature of the Piece they agree with in the bore; as those of Demi-Culverin bore, are called Demi-Culverin Cuts, etc.

b. *Gaming.* (*pl.*) = Cut dice; dice made of irregular shape for cheating. *Obs.*

1711 Puckle *Club* 21 *note*, At dice they have the doctors, the fulloms, loaded dice, flats, bars, cuts.

†**32.** A kind of blanket: see quot. *Obs.*

1677 Plot *Nat. Hist. Oxfordshire* 279 Of their best tail wooll they make the blankets of 6 quarters broad, commonly called cuts, which serve Sea-men for their Hammocs.

33. *pl.* Persons who have 'cut' each other, *i.e.* renounced each other's acquaintance. *colloq.*

1871 *Daily News* 13 Feb., Bismarck and 'our Fritz', are very nearly what schoolboys call 'cuts.' **1880** *Times* 21 Sept. 4/1 People who leave Southampton the best of friends and arrive in Bombay dead cuts.

VII. †**34.** *Falconry.* (Of uncertain history. See quot.)

1611 Cotgr., *Cousteau*.. the principall feather in a Hawkes wing, tearmed by our Faulkoners (in short-winged Hawkes) the Cut, or Cuttie.

VIII. †**35.** Phrase. ***to keep one's cut, keep cut***: a phrase of obscure origin, meaning something like: 'To keep one's distance, be coy or reserved'. Most of the later occurrences appear to refer to Skelton's *Phyllyp Sparrowe*, or at least to have the same origin. *Obs.*

[The variant *fend cut* suggests a fencing phrase: but there is the great difficulty, referred to above, of the early date of the phrase, which makes it doubtful whether it really belongs to this word; and its place here must be considered as merely provisional.]

? *a* **1400** *Cov. Myst., Woman taken in Adultery* 148 Com forth, thou sloveyn! com forthe, thou slutte! We xal the teche with carys colde, A lytyl bettyr to kepe thi kutte. **1421–2** Hoccleve *Dial.* 789 If..some of hem thee ther-of vpbreide, Thow [Hoccleve] shalt be bisy ynow..Thy kut to keepe. *a* **1529** Skelton *P. Sparowe* 118 It wold syt on a stole And lerned after my scole For to kepe his cut, With, Phyllyp, *kepe youre cut.* *a* **1577** Gascoigne *Praise P. Sparrow* Wks. (1587) 285 As if you say but *fend cut* Phip, Lord, how the peat will turne and skip. **1581** Sidney *Astr. & Stella* lxxxiii, Good brother Philip..craftily you seem'd your cut to keepe, As though that faire soft hand did you great wrong. *a* **1627** Middleton *More Dissemblers* I. iv, O that a boy should so keep cut with his mother, and be given to dissembling. **1632** Brome *North. Lasse* III. ii, And Philip 'twas my Sparrow..Chirp it would, And hop, and fly to fist, Keepe cut, as 'twere a Vsurers Gold, And bill me when I list. *a* **1652** —— *New Acad.* IV. i, But look how she turnes and keeps cut like my Sparrow.

IX. 36. *Comb.*, **a.** with advbs., as **cut-down**, a reduction in wages (cf. cut *v.* 54); see also cut-in, cut-off, cut-out, cut-up; **b.** †**cut-beaten** *a.*, beaten with cuts or strokes of a whip, etc.; **cut-heal**, name for a species of valerian; **cut-line** *Rackets*, (*a*) a line painted on the front wall about the height of 9 ft. 6 in. from the floor, above which the ball must be served; (*b*) (see quot. 1912); (*c*) descriptive wording below an illustration; **cut-looker** (*Weaving*), see quot.; **cut-mark** (*Weaving*), see quot.; **cut-over**, a sharp cut or stroke over the legs, etc. (cf. cut *v.* 58 c); †**cut-painted** *a.*, adorned with cuts or gashes, tattooed; **cut-side**, the side of a canal or of a railway cutting; **cut-through**, an act of cutting through; *spec.* in *Rugby Football* (Webster, 1934); cf. cut *v.* 18 b.

1634 S. R. *Noble Soldier* II. i, I'de make thee roare And weare *cut-beaten-sattyn. **1888** *Boston* (Mass.) *Jrnl.* 30 July 2/3 Strike against a *cut-down. **1892** in *N.Y. Nation* 11 Aug. 100/3 No cut-down in wages. **1863** Prior *Plant-n.*, **Cut-heal*, the valerian. **1878–86** Britten & Holland *Plant-n., Cut-heal, Valeriana officinalis* according to Prior, but more likely *V. pyrenaica.* **1883** *Encycl. Brit.* XX. 210/1 Another white line across the front wall, termed the '*cut line', because the in-player, when serving, must first make the ball rebound from the front wall above this line. **1912** M. Drake *Eng. Glass-painting* 183 The panes composing it [*sc.* the panel] should be laid in their places on a sheet of paper and their outlines traced by a pencil run round their edges. This sheet of paper will serve the glazier as a 'cut-line' drawing when the panels are handed to him for re-leading. **1923** —— *Doom Window* xxv. 290 Cartoons began to be completed, and Reinecke and Sophie now made the cut-line drawings. **1938** L. M. Harrod *Librarians' Gloss.* 54 *Cut line*, matter appearing below an illustration. More often called a 'caption'. **1964** H. Waugh *Missing Man* xi. 48 Betty Moore's picture ran two columns wide on the front pages with the cutlines describing her as the 'widowed beauty'. **1891** *Labour Commission* Gloss., **Cut-looker*, the person who examines and is held responsible for the work produced by the weaver. A *cut* or piece means a given length of calico. **1874** Knight *Dict. Mech.*, **Cut-mark*, a mark made upon a set of warp-threads before placing on the warp-beam of the loom, to mark off a certain definite length. **1874** Dasent *Half a Life* I. 155 The marks of kicks and *cuts over at hockey. **1611** Speed *Hist. Gt. Brit.* 1239 They couered their *Cut-painted bodies with Garments. **1870** *Birm. Town Crier* IX. No. 13. 8/1 Walk along the *cutside, and chuck pebbles over the summit bridge. **1960** *Times* 28 Dec. 4/4 Leicester were in trouble again after a *cut-through by Jeeps. **1962** *Ibid.* 2 Mar. 4/2 There was a fast, weaving cut-through by Watkins.

cut (kʌt), *v.* Forms: 3 cute, 4 kot, kuytte, 4–5 kut, kutt(e, kytt(e, kitt(e, 5 kette, cytte, 5–6 kyt, kit, 5–7 cutt(e, 6– cut. *Pa. t.* α. 3–5 cutt(e, 4– cut; also 4 kut, kit, citte, 4–5 kutte, kytte, kitte, 5 kyt; β. 4 kittide, kottede, 5 cutted, (*pl.*) kuttiden, 6 *Sc.* cuttit. *Pa. pple.* α. 4 kit, kitt(e, ikett, 4–5 kut, kutt(e, y-kyt(t, 4–6 cutte, 4–7 cutt, 5 y-kitt, ykette, 5–6 kyt, 5– cut; β. 4 kytted, kittid, 4–6 cuttid, 4–7 (9 *dial.*) cutted, 5 cuttyd, -ede, 6 *Sc.* cuttit. [Found in end of 13th c., and in common use since the 14th c., being the proper word for the action in question, for which OE. used *snīðan*, *ceorfan*. The phonology is doubtful; the early variants *cutte, kitte, kette*, with pa. pple. *cut, kyt, kit, kett*, are parallel to the early variants of shut, OE. *scyttan*, and point to **cyttan, kytten* (from **cutian*) as the original form, an earlier *y* (y), having here, as in *shut* and other words, given later *u* (now ʌ). The word is not recorded in OE. (nor in any WGer. dialect), and there is no corresponding verb in Romanic. Mod. Norwegian *kutte* = *skjære* to cut (chiefly used by sailors) is certainly adopted from English; but a verb *kåta*, (*kutå*) = *skära, hugga* to cut, is widely diffused in Swedish dialects, and app. an old word, from an OTeut. stem **kut-*, **kot-*, which is probably the source also of the Eng. vb., whatever the intermediate history of the latter.

A conjectured derivation of *cut* from Welsh *cwta* 'short' is in the opinion of Prof. Rhŷs quite untenable. Neither *cwta* nor any of its derivatives have any relation whatever to the use of a knife or other cutting instrument; while the South Wales *cwt* = cut, gash, e.g. in the hand, is a mere adoption of the Eng. sb.]

I. To make incision in or into.

1. a. *trans.* To penetrate with an edged instrument which severs the continuity of the substance; to wound or injure with a sharp-edged instrument; to make incision in; to gash, slash.

c **1275** Lay. 30581 He cutte [**1205** nom] his owe þeh.. þar of he makede breade [= roast]. *c* **1330** *Arth. & Merl.* 392 Ther was mani throte y-kitt. **1382** Wyclif *Isa.* xxxvii. 1 He kutte [**1388** to rente] his clothis, and wrappid is with a sac. *c* **1430** *Pilgr. Lyf Manhode* (1869) 122 At the laste he kitte his owen throte. **1502** Arnolde *Chron.* (1811) 165 Kyt it wyth a knyf and late it be opened. **1526** *Pilgr. Perf.* (W. de W. 1531) 278 Cutte me, burne me, launce me. **1634** Sir T. Herbert *Trav.* 196 The ordinary tricke of cutting and slashing their skin. **1694** Congreve *Double Dealer* I. v, Cut a diamond with a diamond. **1779** *Gentl. Mag.* XLIX. 466 No lives were lost in the riot, though one or two of the country people were cut. **1830** Cooper *Dict. Surgery* (ed. 6) 826 He [Cheselden] cut another part of the bladder. **1885** *Truth* 11 June 921/1 A detective..cut the boy's head open by knocking it against a lamp-post. *Mod.* Who has cut the table-cloth?

b. Predicated also of the edged instrument or material (a knife, glass, etc.); also *transf.* of keen cold wind, frost, or the like.

1738 Swift *Pol. Conversat.* iii. 198 Sharp's the Word with her; Diamonds cut Diamonds.

2. *absol.* or *intr.* **a.** To make incision. With various preps. as *in, through*, etc., or adv. or adj. complement.

1596 Shaks. *Merch. V.* IV. i. 280 For if the Iew do cut but deepe enough, Ile pay it instantly, with all my heart. **1664** Evelyn *Kal. Hort.* (1729) 190 Cut close to the Stem. **1830** Cooper *Dict. Surgery* (ed. 6) 825 Cheselden thought it unnecessary to cut on the groove of the staff. **1833** A. Fonblanque *Eng. under 7 Administ.* (1837) II. 319 [The late Parliament] excised the cancer, and it did not cut deep enough. **1861** Mill *Utilit.* (1862) 84 Any attempt on their part to cut finer.

b. Said of the instrument; also *transf.* and *fig.* ***to cut both*** (or ***two***) ***ways***, to have a double or mixed effect; to have both favourable and unfavourable aspects or implications.

c **1400** *Lanfranc's Cirurg.* 32 (MS. B.) Cold matere streyneþ, drye matere kutteþ. *Ibid.* 127 (MS. A.), & þis schave schal kutte on þe side þat foldiþ ynward & it schal be blunt on þe oon side þat is outward. **1605** Hickeringill *Priest-cr.* II. Pref. A iij b, Fame, like a two-edg'd Sword, does cut both ways. *a* **1633** G. Herbert *Jacula Prudentum*, The tongue is not steel, yet it cuts. **1732** Berkeley *Alciphr.* VI. §8 Edged tools are in general designed to cut. **1830** Gen. P. Thompson *Exerc.* (1842) I. 290 Whether the razor did or did not cut well. **1854** J. C. Rutter *Let.* 23 May in M. Lutyens *Millais & Ruskins* (1967) 192 What you state about the Woman's Brain..might cut both ways..might not the irritant arise from want of consummation? **1866** [see double-edged *a.*]. **1935** *Discovery* Oct. 313/1 Clever arguments cut two ways.

c. With complement (prep., adv., or adj.).

1713 Addison *Cato* I. vi, Tormenting thought! it cuts into my soul. **1809** Cobbett *Pol. Reg.* 25 Mar. 421 The argument ..cuts deeper against him than for him. **1888** Rider Haggard *Col. Quaritch* I. i. 7 The bullet cut through his enemy.

d. *intr.* in *passive* sense. To suffer incision, admit of being cut: see 13.

3. To strike sharply with a whip, a thin stick or the like; to lash. Also said of the whip, etc. *trans.* and *absol.*

1607 Dekker & Webster *Westw. Hoe* v. i, I cut hym ouer the thumbes thus. **1765** *Ann. Reg.* 278 In rugged ways, the reins and steeds Alone the skilful driver heeds, Nor stays to cut behind. **1872** Black *Adv. Phaeton* xix. 275 He cut at.. the hedges with his stick. **1877** H. Smart *Play or Pay* i. 19 Fetch me a pair of spurs and a whip that will cut.

4. *Fencing*, etc. (*intr.*) To make a cut or slashing stroke: see cut *sb.*[2] 2 b.

1833 *Regul. Instr. Cavalry* I. 141 Recovering the sword ready to cut to the rear. *Ibid.* 142 Raise the hand prepared to cut 'One'. *Mod.* One of the dragoons cut at him.

5. *fig.* (*trans.*). To wound deeply the feelings of; to distress greatly. Now chiefly in phr. ***to cut to the heart.*** (Cf. *cut up* 60 h; cutting *ppl. a.*)

1582 N. T. (Rhem.) *Acts* v. 33 When they had heard these things, it cut them to the hart. *c* **1680** Beveridge *Serm.* (1729) II. 4 Every word in it will cut them to the heart. **1688** S. Penton *Guardian's Instr.* 75 Never..upbraid him with his Follies before Strangers; this may cut him too much, and never be forgotten. **1782** Miss Burney *Cecilia* III. viii, He says something so sorrowful that it cuts us to the soul! **1805** Lamb *Lett.* (1888) I. 220, I have been very much cut about it indeed. **1871** Carlyle in *Mrs. Carlyle's Lett.* III. 243 Often enough had it cut me to the heart, to think what she was suffering.

†**6.** *fig.* To rebuke severely, to upbraid. *Obs.*

1737 Whiston *Josephus' Antiq.* II. vi. §8 Reubel also was large in cutting them upon this occasion.

II. To make incision through.

7. a. *trans.* To divide into two or more parts with a sharp-edged instrument; to sever. Used simply of cord, string, and the like, and of bread, wood, or other articles cut for use. Const. *in two* (†*a-two*), *asunder*, etc.; *in, into parts* or *pieces*; also with adj. complement. Cf. *cut up, cut down.*

c **1300** *K. Alis.* 2709 Mony hed atwo y-kyt. *c* **1340** *Cursor M.* 8875 (Fairf.) Wiþ ax he walde haue kut hit [the tree] þan. *Ibid.* 16554 (Trin.), & cut þis tre in two. **1387** Trevisa *Higden* (Rolls) I. 165 Sche..kutte þe hyde into a þong þat was ful long and ful smal. *c* **1430** *Freemasonry* (1844) 735 (Mätz.) Kette thy bred al at thy mete Rigth as hyt may be ther yete. *c* **1430** *Two Cookery-bks.* 21 Take clowes and kutte hem. *c* **1489** Caxton *Sonnes of Aymon* i. 56 He cutted hym asonder. *a* **1541** Wyatt *Poems* (1861) 135 With his fatal knife the thread for to kit. **1653** H. Cogan tr. *Pinto's Trav.* xix. 67 Cutting her cables..and sailing away with all the speed he could. **1855** Macaulay *Hist. Eng.* IV. 371 The Dutch way of cutting and eating asparagus.

b. *fig.* To sever, divide (a connexion, association, etc.).

1625 Bacon *Ess., Friendship* (Arb.) 173 It [Friendship] redoubleth Ioyes, and cutteth Griefes in Halfes. **1668** Dryden *Evening's Love* IV. iii, 'Tis well there was no love betwixt us; for they [your scissars] had been too dull to cut it. **1876** E. Jenkins *Blot on Queen's Head* 13 The innkeeper ..is a fool if he suddenly cuts the associations which endear it to all his customers.

c. ***to cut to*** (or ***in***) ***pieces***: (*fig.*) to rout in battle with great slaughter.

1632 J. Hayward tr. *Biondi's Eromena* 79 The foote were cut all to pieces. **1781** Gibbon *Decl. & F.* III. 235 [He] surprised and cut in pieces, a considerable body of Goths. **1838** Thirlwall *Greece* II. 347 The Theban cavalry.. suddenly fell upon them, cut to pieces six hundred, and drove them into the hills.

d. *slang.* To divide or share (spoils, profits, etc.); to receive (a share). Also *intr.* Cf. cut *sb.*[2] 24 d.

1928 E. Wallace *Again 3 Just Men* x. 216 It was wicked ..that anybody should have so much money if he could not 'cut' his share. **1932** —— *When Gangs Came* xxviii. 278 'The other fellows' had refused to 'cut'.

8. a. *spec.* To carve (meat); also *absol.*

1601 Shaks. *Twel. N.* I. iii. 130 *And.* Faith, I can cut a caper. *To.* And I can cut the Mutton too't. **1738** Swift *Pol. Conversat.* ii. 121 Don't cut like a Mother-in-Law, but send me a large Slice. **1888** Rider Haggard *Col. Quaritch* x, Ida allowed Mr. Quest to cut her some cold boiled beef.

b. (*slang* or *colloq.*) ***to cut it too fat***: to 'come it strong', overdo a thing.

1836–9 Dickens *Sk. Boz* 54 Gentlemen in alarming waist-coats and steel watch-guards..'cutting it uncommon fat'. **1854** W. G. Curtis *Potiphar Papers* 131 (Bartlett) But to have a philosopher of the Sennaar school show you why you are [uncomfortable], is cutting it rather too fat.

c. ***to cut fine***: see fine *a.* 7 g.

9. a. To make a narrow opening through (a dyke, etc.), or through the bank of (a canal), so as to let the water escape.

1590 [see cutting *vbl. sb.* 1]. **1677** *Lond. Gaz.* No. 1232/3 Report said the French..had cut the Canal. **1710** *Ibid.* 4582/1 Orders are..given for cutting the Scarpe at Bioche.. in order to draw off the Water..into the adjacent Marshes. **1831** Palmerston in Bulwer *Life* II. ix. 117 *note*, This extensive inundation was carried into effect by cutting the great sea-dykes.

b. *Mining.* To intersect (a vein of ore).

1778 W. Pryce *Min. Cornub.* 319 *Cut*, to intersect a vein, branch, or lode by driving horizontally or sinking perpendicularly. **1881** in Raymond *Mining Gloss.*

c. with *through.*

1883 *Manch. Guardian* 15 Oct. 5/7 To shorten the course of the river..by cutting through the neck of the low land opposite Greenwich.

d. ***to cut and cover***: to plough so that the furrow-slice is turned over on an unploughed strip. *U.S.*

1839 [see 61 below]. **1861** *Trans. Ill. Agric. Soc.* IV. 111 Mr. Mills is not in favor of any implement that 'cuts and covers'. Col. Harris.. says that cutting and covering is practiced by some of the Scioto farmers.

10. To break up, reduce, or dissolve the viscidity of (a liquid, phlegm, etc.).

1578 Lyte *Dodoens* II. lxxv. 248 The same..cutteth or severeth the grosse humors. **1657** W. Coles *Adam in Eden* lxxv, Hyssop..cutteth and breaketh tough Phlegme. **1698** Petiver in *Phil. Trans.* XX. 333 The Root..taken in Water corrects and cuts tough Phleagm. **1743** *Lond. & Country Brew.* IV. (ed. 2) 305 It will cut and cure a Butt of ropy Beer.

11. To separate the leaves of (a book) by cutting through the folds of the sheets with a paper knife. (Properly ***to cut open.***)

1786 Mad. D'Arblay *Diary* 2 Aug., The Queen had given me a new collection of German books..to cut open for her. **1848** Thackeray *Lett.* 28 July, I thought I would begin to cut open a book I had bought. *Mod.* This book is not cut. I have cut a few leaves at the beginning.

12. a. To divide with an edged instrument, as an axe, saw, sickle, etc. (a natural growth) for the purpose of taking the part detached; to reap (corn), mow (grass), hew (timber), etc.

This passes into branch III.

c **1300** *Havelok* 942 Al that euere shulden he nytte, Al he drow, and al he citte. *c* **1400** Maundev. (1839) xv. 168 Whan it is ripe..than men kytten hem. **1419** in *Surtees Misc.* (1890) 14 Thay that has taken tham to ferme..sall kytte the herbage. **1512** *Act 4 Hen. VIII*, c. 1 §4 It [shall] be laufull ..to cutte and to hew heth in any mannes grounde. **1611** Bible *2 Chron.* ii. 8 Thy servants can skill to cut timber in Lebanon. **1817** W. Selwyn *Law Nisi Prius* (ed. 4) II. 1218 Until it [the crop] was cut and carried away.

b. The object may be unexpressed, or may be the ground on which the crop grows.

1789 *Trans. Soc. Encourag. Arts* II. 73, I cut one perch of ground..the produce of which weighed five hundred and one pounds. 1876 Saunders *Lion in Path* i, The more distant meadows are cut. 1892 *Sporting & Dram. News* 14 May 328/2 The mowers have commenced 'cutting' at the earliest streak of daylight.

13. a. *intr.* (in *pass.* sense). To suffer incision, to get cut; to admit of being cut; to turn out of a specified quality on being cut.

1560 *Nice Wanton* in Hazl. *Dodsley* II. 172, I will make your knave's flesh cut. 1751 Chambers *Cycl.*, Alabaster cuts very smooth and easy. 1642 Fuller *Holy & Prof. State* III. xxiii. 218 None could come near to feel his estate; it might therefore cut fatter in his purse. 1834 Medwin *Angler in Wales* II. 138 The trout..cut red. 1839 De Quincey *Casuist. Roman Meals* Wks. 1863 III. 264 Who would think that a nonentity could cut into so many somethings? 1882 Nares *Seamanship* (ed. 6) 157 Chain..is not so liable to cut against rocks. *Mod.* The cloth does not cut to advantage.

b. To yield when cut or shorn (as sheep). Also of land, to yield as a crop.

With advb. complement passing into simple object.

1754 *Essex Inst. Hist. Coll.* XLIII. 90 The Pasturing good ..and cuts enough to keep all the stock. 1840 J. Buel *Farmer's Comp.* (ed. 2) 211 One acre of good grass will cut three tons of hay, or keep a cow... Four acres of lean, poor grass will cut little more..than three tons of hay. 1854 *Jrnl. R. Agric. Soc.* XV. I. 228 The Hampshiredowns..cut a heavier fleece than the Southdowns. 1858 *Ibid.* XIX. I. 59 The half-breds cut less wool than the Shropshire Downs. 1872 *Rep. Vermont Board Agric.* 351 It would cut only hay enough to winter four cattle. 1923 R. D. Paine *Comr. Rolling Ocean* x. 169, I quit the sea for a spell to run my own place—she cuts thirty ton o' hay.

III. To separate or detach with an edged tool.

14. a. *trans.* To separate or remove by cutting; to sever from the main body; to lop off. With const. *from* or equivalent prep., or advb. complement, as *adrift*; also frequently ***cut away, cut off, cut out.***

† *to cut a purse*: to steal it by cutting it from the girdle to which it was suspended.

a1300 *E.E. Psalter* cxviii. 39 Cute mine up-braidinge [Wyclif 1382 Kut of my repref, 1388 Kitte awey my schenschip]. 1340 Hampole *Pr. Consc.* 3715 Þe lymes þat er cutted fra þe body. 1393 Gower *Conf.* II. 347 Till he the mannes purs have kut. 1432–50 tr. *Higden* (Rolls) III. 473 Thauȝhe Alexander kytte [*absciderit*] myne hede he may not sle my sawle. c1450 *Mirour Saluacioun* 2603 All the braunches of the tree shuld be kitted. 1585 in Ellis *Orig. Lett.* I. 216 II. 297 There, was a schole howse sett upp to learne younge boyes to cutt purses. 1632 J. Lee *Short Surv. Sweden* 84 Cut out of his mothers wombe. 1694 *Acc. Sev. Late Voy.* II. (1711) 173 So cut the Fat from it by pieces. 1745 P. Thomas *Jrnl. Anson's Voy.* 175 We were obliged.. to cut the Raft adrift. 1842 Gen. P. Thompson *Exerc.* VI. 413 Halfpenny-worths of bread cut off the loaf.

†b. = *cut off* (56b). *Obs.*

1583 Stocker *Hist. Civ. Warres Lowe C.* I. 72b, Hee made also a bridge ouer the Maze, that he myght..cut the enemie from victuals. 1789 *Triumphs of Fortitude* II. 63 We cannot be cut from the privileges..of friendship.

c. *transf.* = 57d. *U.S.*

1903 A. Adams *Log Cowboy* ii. 13 Flood had the first pick, and cut twelve bays and browns.

IV. To pass through as in cutting.

15. a. *trans.* To divide, separate, pierce, intersect, run into or through: expressing relative position, not motion. Also *intr.* with *through*, etc. and *to cut across* (fig.).

1432–50 tr. *Higden* (Rolls) II. 47 And from that hit [Watling strete] kyttethe ouer [*transcindit*] Seuerne nye to Worcestre. c1590 Marlowe *Faust.* Wks. (Rtldg.) 91/2 Just through the midst runs flowing Tiber's stream With winding banks that cut it in two parts. 1665 Sir T. Herbert *Trav.* (1677) 31 Places very hot..in regard the Æquinoctial cuts them. 1811 Pinkerton *Petral.* I. 314 Serpentine mountains, which it [steatite] cuts through in small, perpendicular, or rake veins. 18.. Whittier *Norembega* vii, Yon spire..That cuts the evening sky. 1885 *Law Rep.* 14 Q. Bench Div. 919 The old part of the path which the line had cut across. 1927 Carr-Saunders & Jones *Soc. Struct. Eng. & Wales* 83 But these other associations cut across industrial, occupational, and income classifications. 1960 R. Davies *Voice from Attic* 38 We exist as a class which cuts across all classes.

b. *Geom.* Of a line (or surface): To pass through or across, to cross (a line or surface), intersect.

1570 Billingsley *Euclid* I. xxiii. 33 The two pointes, where the circumference of the circle cutteth the lines. 1660 Barrow *Euclid* III. Def. ii, The right line *FG* cuts the circle *FED*. 1746 *Tom Thumb's Trav. Eng.* 114 Most of the Streets ..cut one another at Right Angles. 1862 Todhunter *Elem. Euclid* I. xv, If two straight lines cut one another, the vertical, or opposite, angles shall be equal.

16. †a. To cross (a line): expressing motion. *Obs.*

1634 Sir T. Herbert *Trav.* 11 The last of May after a storme wee cut the Tropique of Capricorne. 1642 Fuller *Holy & Prof. St.* II. xxi. 136 Then cutting the Line, they view the face of that heaven which earth hideth from us.

b. To come across, strike, hit upon (a path, etc.). esp. *U.S.* with *trail*. Also *ellipt.*

1892 *Field* 23 Jan. 119/1 At length we cut our spoor again, and hunted it along carefully and slowly. 1899 T. Hall *Tales* 19 One of his men dashes breathlessly in..with the exciting report that he has cut the raiders' trail. 1903 A. Adams *Log Cowboy* vii. 90 If you have no authority to cut this trail then you don't cut this herd. *Ibid.*, They were merely cutting (trail cutting) in the interest of the immediate locality.

17. *intr.* To cross, to pass straight through or across; esp. ***cut over, cut across*** (adv. or prep.).

1551 *Acts Privy Council Eng.* III. 320 The Marishall.. woll passe by lande to Dovour, and from thens cutt over to Bulloigne. 1570–6 Lambarde *Peramb. Kent* (1826) 236 Thus have I walked about this whole Diocese: now therefore let me cutte over to Watlingstreete. 1581 Marbeck *Bk. of Notes* 163 Except the ships cut and take course even justlie betweene both, they hardlie scape drowning. 1600 Holland *Livy* xxviii. ii. 669b, Before that he cut over the streights of Gibraltar to Gades. 1610 Guillim *Heraldry* III. ii. (1660) 107 Cutting through the Magellanike Straits..he encompassed the whole world. 1823 *New Monthly Mag.* VIII. 500 A few of the most active cut across to the shallows. 1858 R. S. Surtees *Ask Mamma* xiv. 47 They cut across the deer studded park.

18. a. *trans.* To pass sharply through, cleave (the air, the water).

1576 Fleming *Panopl. Epist.* 423 Shippes..cut the waves as they are furthered with a merrie winde. 1596 Spenser *Hymn, Heav. Love* 69 With nimble wings to cut the skies. 1696 Tate & Brady *Ps.* viii. 8 The Fish that cuts the Seas. 1709 Watts *Hymn, 'Awake, our Souls'* v, Swift as an Eagle cuts the air. 1870 Bryant *Iliad* I. II. 74 In his beaked galleys, swift to cut the sea.

b. *intr.* with *through*.

1606 Shaks. *Tr. & Cr.* I. iii. 40 Behold The strong ribb'd Barke through liquid Moutaines cut. 1694 *Acc. Sev. Late Voy.* II. (1711) 33 This same noise the Ships make likewise when they cut through the Sea. 1728 Pope *Dunc.* I. 182 And pond'rous slugs cut swiftly thro' the sky. 1848 Thackeray *Lett.* 28 July, The ship cutting through the water at fifteen miles an hour.

19. *slang* or *colloq.* (*intr.*) a. To run away, make off, 'be off'. Also ***to cut it.*** (See also *cut and run* 41.) Originally with *away*, *off*.

1590 Spenser *F.Q.* II. vi. 5 It [a boat] cut away upon the yielding wave. 1591 Sylvester *Du Bartas* I. i. Wks. (Grosart) 841 (D.), I fear to faint if (at the first) too fast I cut away, and make too hasty haste. 1664 Cotton *Scarron.* IV. Poet. Wks. (1765) 90 Put on the wings that used to bear ye, And cut away to Carthage quickly. 1834 Dickens *Sk. Boz* (1836) 1st Ser. I. 92 The linen-draper cut off..leaving the landlord his compliments and the key. 1844 *P. Parley's Ann.* V. 140 The door of her prison was opened, and the turnkey told her that she might 'cut'. 1848 Dickens *Dombey* xv. 156 Mr. Toodle..tapped her on the back; and said..'Polly! cut away!' 1858 Trollope *Dr. Thorne* ix, Now, my lady, do cut it, cut at once. c1867 T. W. Robertson *Caste* I. 7, I did get leave, and I did cut away; and while away, I was miserable. 1882 *Macm. Mag.* XLVI. 443, I looked out of the tail of my eye, to see what she was doing, but she'd cut. 1932 A. J. Worrall *Eng. Idioms* 67 The prefect told the small boy to cut off.

b. Hence, To move sharply, to run rapidly. With various advbs. and preps. Also with *along*, *out*. ***to cut round*** (U.S. colloq.): to make a display; to act in a lively, gay fashion.

1797 B. Hawkins *Lett.* (1916) 126 He was driving a wagon at the time he was taken, and they cut out and took the horses with him. 1833 S. Smith *Major Downing* 139 What made us cut back so quick from Concord? 1834 D. Crockett *Life* 63, I saw a little woman streaking it along through the woods like all wrath, and so I cut on too. *Ibid.* 65, I took my eldest brother..and cut out to her father's house to get her. a1852 F. M. Whitcher *Widow Bedott P.* (1856) 91 They say she cut round and hollered and laffed and tried to be wonderful interestin'. 1857 Hughes *Tom Brown* II. iii, We all cut up-stairs after the Doctor. a1859 in Bartlett *Dict. Amer.*, Instead of sticking to me as she used to do, she got to cuttin' round with all the young fellows, just as if she cared nothin' about me no more. 1864 Dickens *Mut. Fr.* I. II. viii. 240 I'll cut back and ask for leave. 1873 Black *Pr. Thule* xiv. 219 And now the carriage cut round the corner. 1878 'Stonehenge' *Brit. Sports* I. I. vii. §10. 109 The rabbits..cut in and out of the rides or runs. 1879 F. R. Stockton *Rudder Grange* viii. 86 [The dog] was only cuttin' round because he was so glad to get loose. 1902 E. Nesbit *Five Children & It* ix. 237 You'll be late for your grub!.. Then cut along home. 1932 A. J. Worrall *Eng. Idioms* 68, I told him to cut out and buy some tea. 1949 'M. Innes' *Journeying Boy* ii. 25 'And now you'd better cut along.' Captain Cox was a great believer in the moral effects of abrupt dismissals on the young. 1958 T. Williams *Orpheus Descending* III. 88 *Lady.* So you're—cutting out, are you? *Val.* My gear's all packed. I'm catchin' the southbound bus.

c. To get up *behind* a vehicle. *U.S.*

1848 *Popular Songs* 36 Another calls out 'cut behind'. 1860 O. W. Holmes *Prof. Breakf.-t.* viii. 171 Here is a boy that loves to..chalk doorsteps, 'cut behind' anything on wheels or runners [etc.].

V. To shorten or reduce by cutting.

20. *trans.* To shorten or reduce by cutting off a portion; to trim, clip, shear; to prune.

a1300 *Cursor M.* 7240 (Gött.) Quilis he slep scho cutt his her. c1385 Chaucer *L.G.W.* 973 *Dido*, Hire clothis cutte were un-to the kne. c1420 *Pallad. on Husb.* I. 127 To kytte a vyne is thinges iij to attende. c1440 *Promp. Parv.* 111 Cutte vynes, *puto*. 1665–72 Wood *Life* (Oxf. Hist. Soc.) II. 69 To my barber for cutting my haire, 6*d*. 1878 Morley *Diderot* I. 136 Diderot and his colleagues are cutting their wings for a flight to posterity.

21. a. *fig.* To curtail, abridge, shorten, reduce; to shorten (a play, etc.) by omitting portions; = *cut short, cut down*.

1413 Lydg. *Pilgr. Sowle* II. xliii. (1859) 49 Glosynge, cuttynge, kouerynge, and cloutynge the lawe of Crystes gospel. 1585 Jas. I. *Ess. Poesie* (Arb.) 55 Maist kyndis of versis quhilks are not cuttit or brokin. 1865 *Pall Mall G.* 24 July 11/1 In 'cutting' an opera it is not to be supposed that any two persons will agree as to what ought to be left out. 1888 *Standard* 14 May, The market has begun to cut rates again.

b. *imp.* (*slang*) = *cut out* (see 57a below). Colloq. phr. ***cut the cackle*** (see cackle *sb.* 3a).

1859 Hotten *Dict. Slang* 28 *Cut*,..to cease doing anything. *Ibid.*, *Cut that*, be quiet, or stop. a1871 T. W. Robertson *Caste* I. 6 *Geo.* Well, then, eighteen months ago — *Haw.* Oh, cut that; you told me all about that. 1907 E. S. Field *Six-Cylinder Courtship* 54 'My dear fellow—' I began. 'Cut it!' he commanded. 1919 F. Hurst *Humoresque* 314 Come on, Herm, cut the comedy. It's time we were getting across to our hotel.

c. To outdo, excel. Cf. senses 54e and 57f below. Chiefly *U.S.* in modern use (see quot. 1952).

1884 *Referee* 13 Apr. 1/4 George's performance..is hardly likely to be disturbed for a long time to come, unless he cuts it himself. 1897 *Penrith Obs.* 21 Dec. (E.D.D.), He went thirteen feet t'first lowp, but I cut him bi' three inch. 1952 B. Ulanov *Hist. Jazz* (1958) xxv. 351 'Cut' also means to best a soloist or band in competition.

d. ***to cut a corner*** or ***corners***: to pass round a corner or corners as closely as possible; *fig.*, to pursue an economical or easy but hazardous course of action; to act in an unorthodox manner to save time; also, to act illegally.

1869 'Mark Twain' *Innoc. Abr.* (1870) xxiii. 171 He cuts a corner so closely now and then..that I feel myself 'scrooching', as the children say. 1894 Kipling *Day's Work* (1898) 303 It was at this point that he began to cut corners. 1909 M. Diver *Candles in Wind* 57 Her husband's tendency to 'cut corners' when confronted with awkward facts. 1915 *The Cape* I. xx. 38 They turn out of side-streets at high speed, and cut corners in a dangerous manner. 1957 W. H. Whyte *Organization Man* 292 A disciplining force that helped them resist the temptation to cut corners. 1966 'S. Ransome' *Hidden Hour* xii. 149 He could cut a sharp corner without letting it bother his conscience. 1966 'S. Woods' *Enter Certain Murderers* ii. 41 If Dad had cut any corners, I think I'd have known about it.

e. (*Cinemat., Radio.*) *trans.* To edit (a film, etc.). Also *intr.*, to make a quick transition from one shot *to* the next. *imp.* A signal to stop.

1913 [implied in 52c]. 1916 E. W. Sargent *Technique Photoplay* (ed. 3) 184 You can cut to some single person who overlooks the crime and later tells the story. 1937 *Amer. Speech* XII. 100 *Cut* is used by [radio] production men as an imperative to halt a rehearsal. 1938 *Times* 7 Jan. 13/6 In front of the [television] producer sit the sound engineer controlling total output, and the sound mixer selecting and cutting it. 1947 D. Lean in O. Blakeston *Working for Films* 29 The scene should be cut like this. 1953 K. Reisz *Technique Film Editing* III. xiv. 240 We cut to a closer shot of Pip. 1959 *Elizabethan* June 26/1 When the director wants to stop the camera he calls out 'Cut'. 1960 N. Kneale *Quatermass & Pit* I. 11 Cut—to the excavation. *Ibid.* 12 Cut —to where a spadeful of clay is being swung down from the truck.

f. *trans.* and *intr.* To cut out (see 57r below).

1938 Hemingway *Fifth Column* (1939) III. ii. 88 Cut those lights! 1957 *Granta* 9 Mar. 19/1 Then I would lie down on my back watching them, hoping their engines wouldn't cut just then. 1958 'N. Shute' *Rainbow & Rose* i. 34, I gave her a little throttle..and then cut it as she rolled on to the grass. 1970 D. MacKenzie *Kyle Contract* (1971) 12 He drove into his carport and cut the motor.

22. a. *Dyeing.* To reduce (a colour) to a softer shade.

1862 O'Neill *Dict. Calico Printing* 149/2 The colours are cut or reduced by passing the pieces in warm water containing very acid oxymuriate of tin.

b. To dilute or adulterate. Chiefly *U.S.*

1930 J. P. Burke in *Amer. Mercury* Dec. 455/1 We don't cut hooch any more. 1938 *Amer. Speech* XIII. 190/2 Other types of narcotics are cut. 1954 *Encounter* July 27/2 My wife ..had a cup of coffee cut with bourbon ready for me. 1955 *Times* 9 Aug. 6/1 Most of the wine..when mixed or 'cut' with Algerian wine, provides a good deal of the ordinary *vin courant*. 1966 *Guardian* 31 Aug. 11/6 When I was 13 I knew how much quinine and sugar water you needed to cut heroin and sell it. 1967 *Boston Globe* 21 May 23/4 Use bleach which has been cut with water and spread on the counter tops.

VI. To shape, fashion, form, or make by cutting.

23. a. To make or form by cutting (*e.g.* a statue, engraving, seal, jewel, etc.), to sculpture or carve (a statue or image), to engrave (a plate, seal, etc.), to fashion (a stone or jewel), to shape (garments, utensils, etc.).

15.. *Ballad on Money* in Halliwell *Nugae Poet.* 48 Craftysmen that be in every cyte..Sum cutte, sum shave, sume knoke, sum grave, Only money to wynne. 1596 Shaks. *Merch. V.* I. i. 84 Why should a man..Sit like his Grandsire, cut in Alablaster? 1623 B. Jonson *On Shaks. Portrait in 1st Folio*, This Figure, that thou here seest put, It was for gentle Shakespeare cut. 1634 Sir T. Herbert *Trav.* 146 Their Boots are well sewed, but ill cut. 1662 Evelyn *Chalcogr.* 69 We have seen some few things cut in Wood by..Hans Holbein the Dane. 1709 Steele *Tatler* No. 142 ¶5 His Seals are..exquisitely well cut. *Ibid.* No. 166 ¶2 He knows perfectly well when a Coat is well cut. 1874 Boutell *Arms & Arm.* x. 196 It was escalloped, or cut into some rich openwork pattern. 1887 *Westm. Rev.* June 340 Pointed piles, evidently cut by a metal instrument.

†b. *fig.* To make ready, prepare, plan; = *cut out* 57l. *Obs.*

c1645 Howell *Lett.*, Cut him work to do.

c. *pa. pple.* Formed, fashioned, shaped (as if by cutting).

c1511 *1st Eng. Bk. Amer.* (Arb.) Introd. 32/2 His wingis kyt like a rasour. 1850 L. Hunt *Autobiog.* II. x. 21 His skull was sharply cut and fine. 1883 S. C. Hall *Retrospect* II. 218 His features were finely cut [etc.].

d. *Sound Recording.* To record; to make (a record). orig. *U.S.*

1937 *Printers' Ink Monthly* Apr. 50/3 *Cut a disk*, to make a recording. 1948 *Newsweek* 19 July 38/2 Bernard Baruch cut a record of 'Yankee Doodle'. 1958 M. White in P.

Gammond *Decca Bk. Jazz* xviii. 221 The recording studios, where a number of very fine sides indeed were cut. **1962** *Melody Maker* 7 July 2 She cut five titles which will be released as part of the sound-track album of her film.

24. a. To hollow out, excavate (a hole, channel, canal, road, etc.).

1634 Sir T. Herbert *Trav.* 87 A streame cut through the Coronian Mountaine. **1665** *Ibid.* (1677) 36 From Suez.. where several attempts have been made to cut such a Sluice or Channel as should give Ships a navigable and free passage from the Mediterranean thither. **1682** Lithgow *Trav.* x. 479 Cutting in the middle Circle a devalling Hole. **1772** T. Simpson *Vermin-Killer* 2 Their holes..made round as if cut with an auger. **1798** in *Spirit Pub. Jrnls.* (1799) II. 43 The canal which is now cutting across the Isthmus of Suez. **1878** Markham *Gt. Frozen Sea* xxii. (1880) 278 The men being employed in cutting a road through the hummocks. **1887** *Spectator* 28 May 723/2 We do not see how the canals are to be cut.

b. *to cut one's way, a passage*: to advance by cutting through obstructions.

1599 Shaks. *Hen. V*, II. ii. 16 The powres we beare with vs Will cut their passage through the force of France. **1665** Sir T. Herbert *Trav.* (1677) 34 The Ships cut their way slowly. **1848** Macaulay *Hist. Eng.* I. 600 He cut his way gallantly through them, and came off safe.

25. To perform or execute (an action, gesture, or display of a grotesque, striking, or notable kind): chiefly in certain established phrases, as *to cut* a caper, a dash, a figure, a joke, a voluntary, for which see these substantives. Also, *to cut an antic, a curvet, a flourish*; *to cut faces*, to make grimaces, distort the features.

1601 [see caper *sb.*[2] 1 b].
1664 Cotton *Scarron.* iv. (1807) 68 Wilt thou cut faces evermore For husband dead as nail in door? **1688** Shadwell *Sqr. Alsatia* I. i, He shall cut a sham or banter with the best wit or poet of 'em all. **1768–74** Tucker *Lt. Nat.* (1852) I. 431 Like the twitchings we sometimes feel in our limbs, or habits men get of cutting faces. **1811** W. Irving *Life & Lett.* (1864) I. xvii. 262, I cut one of my best opera flourishes. **1835** —— *Tour Prairies* xxii, Two of us..saw a fellow..cutting queer antics. **1830** *Fraser's Mag.* I. 457 [They] cut a curvet in the air.

VII. Special senses, elliptical, contextual, or technical.

26. *Surg.* **a.** To castrate.

1465 *Mann. & Househ. Exp.* 313 Paid for xvij. kokerelles to make capons of.. Item, for the kyttynge of them. **1577** B. Googe *Heresbach's Husb.* III. (1586) 150 b, The Bore Pigges they cutte when they were sixe monethes olde. *a* **1643** W. Cartwright *Ordinary* I. ii, The great Turk..did command I should be forthwith cut. **1865** *Jrnl. R. Agric. Soc.* Ser. II. V. II. 253 The lamb is stronger for being cut late.

b. To make an incision in the bladder for extraction of stone; also *absol.* to perform lithotomy.

1566 Securis *Detection* A iij, I will not cut those that haue the stone. **1603** Florio *Montaigne* (1632) 433 A Gentleman in Paris was not long since cut of the stone. **1615** Crooke *Body of Man* Pref., That they should not cut any man for the Stone. **1782** H. Watson in *Med. Commun.* I. 92 The patients cut in our hospitals. **1830** Cooper *Dict. Surgery* (ed. 6) 825 *Lithotomy*, Mr. Cheselden never resumed his second manner of cutting.

†**c.** To circumcise. *Obs. rare.*

1634 Sir T. Herbert Trav. (1638) 236 Such an apostat rascall..is cut and marked for a Mahometan.

27. Of horses: *intr.* To strike or bruise the inside of the fetlock with the shoe or hoof of the opposite foot.

1660 Fisher *Rusticks Alarm* Wks. (1679) 139 See..how he..interferes, and cuts one Leg against another, and is not sensible of it. **1675** *Lond. Gaz.* No. 1028/4 The other a bright bay..trots and gallops only, cuts a little behind. **1727–51** Chambers *Cycl.*, *Cutting*, in the manage, is when the horse's feet interfere. **1865** Youatt *Horse* xvi. (1872) 380 Some horses will cut only when they are fatigued or lame and old; many colts will cut before they arrive at their full strength.

28. *Naut.* (*absol.*) To cut the cable (in order to get quickly under way). See also *cut and run* 41.

1707 *Lond. Gaz.* No. 4378/3 The Enemy had escaped, having..cut and tow'd out. **1743** C. Knowles in *Naval Chron.* (1799) I. 107, I made the signal to cut. **1780** Ld. Rodney *Let.* in *New Ann. Reg.* 42 Ready at a moment's warning to cut or slip in order to pursue or engage the enemy.

29. *Card-playing.* (*trans.* and *intr.*) To divide (a pack of cards); *spec.* to do so at random into two or more parts in order to determine the deal, prevent cheating in dealing, etc. Also, to divide cards as a means of selecting one's partner, and *transf.*

1532 *Dice Play* (Percy Soc.) 33 At trump..cutting at the neck is a great vantage, so is cutting by a bum card (finely) under & over. *c* **1592** Marlowe *Mass. Paris* I. ii, Thou hast all the cards within thy hands, To shuffle or cut. **1654** Whitlock *Zootomia* 425 Shufling and cutting ones selfe a Fortune in this scambling World. **1674** Cotton *Compl. Gamester* in Singer *Hist. Cards* 342 Having shuffled the cards, the adversary cuts them. **1750** Hoyle *Whist* (ed. 10) 159 [Rule] xv. You are to cut two Cards at the least. **1793** *Sporting Mag.* I. 27 The person who cuts the lowest, is entitled to the deal. **1824** *Hist. Gambling* 58 Dick stated that he could cut any card he chose at any time. **1878** H. H. Gibbs *Ombre* 19 His left-hand player then cuts to him, lifting and also leaving at the least three cards. **1880** H. C. Adams *College Days at Oxford* 52 They cut for partners. **1937** A. Thirkell *Summer Half* i. 28 While they cut for partners, while they dealt,..his mind was in a turmoil. **1938** C. Morgan *Flashing Stream* III. 221 Cut for drinks... (*They throw dice on a table.*) **1958** H. Phillips *Penguin Hoyle* 4 Before each rubber those taking part 'cut' for partners and choice of seats.

30. *Dancing.* (*intr.*) To spring from the ground, and, while in the air, to twiddle the feet one in front of the other alternately with great rapidity.

1603 Florio *Montaigne* 228 (T.) Dances, wherein are divers changes, cuttings, turnings, and agitations of the body. **1760** C. Johnston *Chrysal* (1822) I. 232 One of them had shewn greater agility and cut higher than any one. **1836–9** Dickens *Sk. Boz*, Out went the boots, first on one side then on the other, then cutting, then shuffling. **1844** —— *Christm. Carol* (1885) 26 Fezziwig 'cut'—cut so deftly, that he appeared to wink with his legs, and came upon his feet again without a stagger.

31. In various games: **a.** *Cricket. trans.* and *intr.* To hit a length ball, a little wide of the off stump, with a bat held quite, or nearly, horizontal, by which the ball is driven to the left side of point. Also, of a cricket ball: to turn sharply after pitching; of a bowler: to make (the ball) turn sharply after pitching. **b.** *Lawn Tennis. trans.* and *intr.* To strike the ball sharply with the racket held at an angle, or with a downward motion, so as to make it revolve, by which it tends to shoot with a very slight rise on striking the ground. **c.** *Croquet. trans.* To drive (a ball) away obliquely by a stroke from another ball. Also *intr.*

1816 W. Lambert *Instr. & Rules Cricket* 15 Aided by a turn or motion of the wrist, the Ball may be made to cut or twist, after it has grounded. **1833** J. Nyren *Young Cricketer's Tutor* 31, I do not remember to have seen Lambert cut at a ball with the bat held horizontally. *Ibid.* 65 Peter Steward..could cut the balls very hard at the point of the bat. [**1840** Nyren *Cricketer's Guide* 21 Beldham would cut at such a ball with a horizontal bat.] **1851** J. Pycroft *Cricket Field* vii. 150 Harry Walker, Robinson, and Saunders were the three great Cutters; and they all cut very late. **1857** Hughes *Tom Brown* II. viii, Johnson..bowls a ball almost wide to the off; the batter steps out and cuts it beautifully to where cover-point is standing very deep. **1888** Steele & Littleton *Cricket* (Badm. Libr.) ii. 62 We have never seen Shrewsbury..cut in any other way. **1960** I. Peebles *Bowler's Turn* 67 Geary and Macaulay cut and spun the ball at a sharp pace.

b. 1875 'Stonehenge' *Brit. Sports* (ed. 12) III. I. v. 691/2 The ball after contact with the ground has a tendency to shoot with a very slight rise in comparison with a ball that is not cut. *Ibid.*, If the ball is purely cut, stand well back from it.

c. 1874 J. D. Heath *Croquet-Player* 33 If the ball is to be 'cut' to the left, the right side of it must be struck. *Ibid.*, Considerable practice will be required before the player can cut perfectly. **1966** J. W. Solomon *Croquet* 95 To cut the rush to one side or the other, was for a long time to me a matter of luck.

32. *Painting.* **a.** *trans.* (See quot. 1727.) **b.** *intr.* Of a colour: To show itself obtrusively, stand out strongly.

1727–51 Chambers *Cycl.*, *Cutting*, in painting, the laying one strong lively colour over another, without any shade or softening.—The cutting of colours has always a disagreeable effect. *c* **1816** Fuseli *Lect. Art* viii. (1848) 508 Those that cut and come forward, first,—and those which more or less partake of the surrounding medium, in various degrees of distance.

33. *colloq.* **a.** *trans.* To break off acquaintance or connexion with (a person); also (as a single act) to affect not to see or know (a person) on meeting or passing him. Often emphasized by *dead.*

1634 S. R. *Noble Soldier* II. i, Why shud a Souldier..Be cut thus by..a Courtier? **1786** G. Colman in *Europ. Mag.* IX. 370 Some bow, some nod, some cut him. **1796** Jane Austen *Sense & Sens.* xliv. (D.), He had cut me ever since my marriage. **1822** Hazlitt *Table-t.* II. viii. 188 *To cut an acquaintance*..has hardly yet escaped out of the limits of slang phraseology. **1826** Disraeli *Viv. Grey* I. iv, Any fellow voluntarily conversing with an usher was to be cut dead by the whole school. **1887** F. S. Russell *Earl of Peterborough* II. vii. 230 He met Bolingbroke..and..cut the ex-Minister dead.

†**b.** *intr.* To break off acquaintance or connexion with. *Obs.*

1782 in Mad. D'Arblay *Early Diary* (1889) II. 305 Mr. Poor and the Fits' have cut, which I regret, but poor man nobody likes him. **1808** Southey *Lett.* (1856) II. 110 For more than a year Scott has cut with the 'Edinburgh Review'. **1825** *New Monthly Mag.* XIV. 180 I've cut dead with Lucy Drummond, so you may be perfectly easy in that affair.

c. *trans.* To renounce, give up, absent oneself from, avoid (a thing).

1791 'G. Gambado' *Ann. Horsem.* x. (1809) 109, I shall cut riding entirely. **1794** *Gentl. Mag.* Dec. 1085/1, I was told of men..who..*cut* chapel, *cut* gates, *cut* lectures, *cut* hall, *cut* examinations, [etc.]. *c* **1814** in Whibley *In Cap & Gown* (1890) 104 Bid him not set me an imposition For cutting his lectures this morning at eight. **1835** E. Caswall *Art of Pluck* (Oxford ed. 6) 37 He that cutteth chapel often. **1861** Hughes *Tom Brown at Oxf.* vii. (1889) 59, I would cut the whole concern to-morrow. **1930** W. S. Maugham *Cakes & Ale* iv. 49 She was prepared to cut an engagement in London.

34. To finish. *N.Z. slang.*

1945 J. Henderson *Gunner Inglorious* xvi. 134 Let's cut the lot. **1947** 'A. P. Gaskell' *Big Game* 41 Is the beer all cut? **1952** G. Wilson *Julien Ware* xxxiv. 241 Here, drink it down. We must cut this bottle tonight.

†**35.** *Irish Hist.* (*trans.*) To levy (a tax, etc.). Also *absol.* [Ir. *gearraim sraid*: cf. F. *tailler.*]

1596 Spenser *State Irel.* 87 Cutting upon every portion of land a reasonable rent. **1610** Davies *2nd Let. Earl Salisb.* (1787) 280 He..had power to cut upon all the inhabitants, high, or low, as pleased him. **1612** —— *Why Ireland, etc.* 126, I may cut the erick upon the country.

†**36.** *Thieves' cant.* To speak, talk, say. (*trans.* and *intr.*) *Obs.*

c **1500** *Maid Emlyn* in *Anc. Poet. Tracts* (Percy Soc.) 17 Than wolde she mete, With her lemman swete, And cutte with hym. **1567** Harman *Caveat* 84 *To cutte bene whydds*, to speake or geue good wordes.. *To cutte*, to saye. **1725** in *New Cant. Dict.*, *To Cut*, to Speak. **1815** Scott *Guy M.* xxviii, Meg..has some queer ways, and often cuts queer words.

†**37.** *intr.* ? To shape one's discourse, trim, try not to commit oneself. *Obs.*

1672–3 Marvell *Reh. Transp.* I. 114 He cuts indeed and faulters in this discourse, which is no good sign. **1710** E. Ward *Brit. Hud.* 74 Some Crafty Zealots cut and wheadl'd, And lying vow'd they never meddl'd.

VIII. *Phrases.*

38. *to cut a feather*: †**a.** To make fine distinctions, 'split hairs'. *Obs.*

a **1633** Austin *Medit.* (1635) 169 Nor seeke..with nice distinctions, to cut a Feather [with the Schoolemen]. **1684** T. Goddard *Plato's Demon* 317 Men who..have not the skill to cut a feather.

b. *Naut.* Of a ship: To make the water foam before her.

1627 Capt. Smith *Seaman's Gram.* ii. 10 If the Bow be too broad, she will seldome..cut a feather, that is, to make a fome before her. **1867** Smyth *Sailor's Word-bk.*, *To cut a Feather*, when a ship has so sharp a bow that she makes the spray feather in cleaving it.

39. *to cut a tooth, one's teeth*: to have them appear through the gums; also *fig.* to become knowing, attain to discretion; so *cut one's eye-teeth.*

1677 Lady Hatton in *Hatton Corr.* (1878) 148 Poor little Susana is very ill about her teeth. I hope in God they will not be long before they be cut. **1694** Congreve *Double Dealer* II. iv, Like a child that was cutting his teeth. *a* **1735** Arbuthnot (J.), When the teeth are ready to cut. **1860** Reade *Cloister & H.* xxx, He and I were born the same year, but he cut his teeth long before me. **1869** Princess Alice *Mem.* (1884) 220 Baby..is now cutting his fifth tooth, which is all but through.

40. *to cut and carve*: see carve *v.* 11. *to cut and contrive*: to practise economy so as to keep one's expenses within one's means. *to cut and dry*: to render cut and dried: see cut *ppl. a.*

1854 Dickens *Hard Times* I. ii, A mighty man at cutting and drying. **1876** Geo. Eliot *Dan. Der.* I. iii, I am obliged to cut and contrive. **1883** H. Drummond *Nat. Law in Spir. W.* (ed. 8) 360 You cannot cut and dry truth. **1888** J. Payn *Myst. Mirbridge* xiv, Cutting and contriving to make both ends meet.

41. *to cut and run* (*Naut.*): see quot. 1794; (*slang* or *colloq.*) to make off promptly, hurry off. Also as *attrib. phr.*

1704 *Boston News-Let.* 12 June 2/2 Cap. Vaughn rode by said Ship, but cut & run. **1794** *Rigging & Seamanship* II. 248* *To Cut and run*, to cut the cable and make sail instantly, without waiting to weigh anchor. **1821** Byron *Let. to Murray* 7 Feb., Greek and Turkish craft..were obliged to 'cut and run' before the wind. **1861** Dickens *Gt. Expect.* v, I'd give a shilling if they had cut and run. **1909** *Daily Chron.* 23 Oct. 9/1 If it is the cut-and-run mood that has conquered she goes home. **1945** *Hutchinson's Pict. Hist. War* 27 Sept. 1944–13 Mar. 1945 54 We anticipated a cut-and-run operation by a force consisting of two or three battleships and a couple of carriers.

42. *to cut loose*: **a.** *trans.* To loosen or set free by cutting that which fastens or confines; **b.** *intr.* To sever oneself, free oneself, escape.

1828 Scott *Tales Grandfather* Ser. I. xxv, Dacre's quarters were attacked, and his horses all cut loose. **1852** Mrs. Stowe *Uncle Tom's C.* vii. 41 In leaving the only home she had ever known, and cutting loose from the protection of a friend whom she loved and revered. **1889** A. E. Barr *Feet of Clay* xv. 301, I will cut loose from every entanglement.

c. To begin to act freely; to start off; to commence an attack; to let oneself go. *U.S.*

1900 Ade *More Fables in Slang* (1902) 182 She would approach the Piano timidly and sort of Trifle with it for a while, and say they would have to make Allowances, and then she would Cut Loose and worry the whole Block. **1901** S. E. White *Westerners* xviii. 157 You just ought to see him when he cuts loose. **1910** W. M. Raine *B. O'Connor* 244 It was York shot Reilly, after Cork had cut loose at him. **1918** E. M. Roberts *Flying Fighter* 66 My lorry had been seen, however. As I was taking it round a corner the Huns cut loose and caused me to go down that road as fast as the motor would take me. **1923** R. D. Paine *Comr. Rolling Ocean* xi. 196 He just now cut loose with 'Goodness gracious..I should call this the deuce of a mess'. **1941** H. L. Mencken *Newspaper Days* (1942) xi. 184 When he got down his first dozen mugs..he cut loose with an exultant yodel.

†*to cut scores*: to settle accounts (*with*): see score *sb. Obs.*

43. *to cut short*: (*trans.*) **a.** to shorten by cutting off a part or parts; to abridge, curtail. *lit.* and *fig.* (Sometimes to *cut shorter.*)

1545 Brinklow *Compl.* 21 Cut shorter your processe. **1548** Hall *Chron.* 202 He was taken and..cut shorter by the hedde. **1611** Bible *2 Kings* x. 32 In those dayes the Lord began to cut Israel short [*margin*, Hebr. to cut off the ends]. **1664** H. More *Apol.* 507, I must..cut my skirts as short as I can, that they sit not upon them. **1781** Mad. D'Arblay *Diary* 25 Aug., That gentleman..cut the matter very short, and would not talk upon it at all. **1868** Freeman *Norm. Conq.* (1876) II. viii. 293 William cuts the whole story very short. **1875** Jowett *Plato* (ed. 2) I. 149, I will ask you to cut your answers shorter.

b. To curtail, abridge, or restrict (any one) in his privileges, means, etc.

1586 A. DAY *Eng. Secretary* II. (1625) 29 Your Lordships ..cut me yet thirtie pound shorter. **1653** WALTON *Angler* 156 Because I cut you short in that, I will commute for it, by telling you that that was told me for a secret. **1672** H. MORE *Brief Reply* 302 You..unjustly take upon you to cut us short of Salvation. **1755** JOHNSON, *To cut short*, to abridge: as, the soldiers were cut short of their pay. **1799** NELSON in Nicolas *Disp.* VII. p. cxciii, I am cut short enough by having no other emolument.

c. To bring to a sudden end, break off, put a stop to abruptly. **d.** To interrupt abruptly; to stop, 'pull up' (a speaker).

1593 SHAKS. *2 Hen. VI*, III. i. 81 The welfare of vs all Hangs on the cutting short that fraudfull man. **1611** BIBLE *Rom.* ix. 28 He will finish the worke, and cut it short in righteousnesse. **1697** DRYDEN *Virg. Æneid* (J.), More he would have said, But the stern heroe turn'd aside his head, And cut him short. **1713** BERKELEY *Hylas & P.* I. Wks. 1871 I. 294 It would probably have cut short your discourse. **1855** MACAULAY *Hist. Eng.* IV. 232 But the Admiral..cut him short. 'I do not wish to hear anything on that subject.' **1873** BLACK *Pr. Thule* xiv. 222 Her speculations..were cut short by the entrance of her husband.

e. *intr.* To stop short, be brief.

1691 tr. *Emilianne's Obs. Journ. Naples* 184, I was oblig'd to cut short, and tell her [etc.]. **1726** J. M. tr. *Trag. Hist. Chev. de Vaudray* 116 To cut short..we broke up.

44. ***to cut one's stick*** (slang): to take one's departure, be off, go. Also *to cut one's lucky*.

1825 *Blackw. Mag.* XVIII. 42/1 He..has cut his stick mayhap until we sail. **1840** DICKENS *Old C. Shop* xl, I'm afraid I must cut my stick. **1844** W. H. MAXWELL *Sports & Adv. Scot.* iii. 47, I am glad you 'cut your lucky'.

45. ***to cut the coat according to the cloth***: to adapt oneself to circumstances, keep within the limits of one's means (see CLOTH *sb.* 10). So also †*to cut one's cloth according to one's calling.*

1562 J. HEYWOOD *Prov. & Epigr.* (1867) 16, I shall Cut my cote after my cloth. **1597** HOOKER *Eccl. Pol.* v. lxxviii. §13 To teach them how they should cut their coats. **1622** FLETCHER *Beggar's Bush* IV. i, Keep yourself right and even cut your cloth, sir, According to your calling. **1867** *Homeward Mail* 16 Nov. 953/2 Times are changed, and..we must, to use the homely metaphor, 'cut our coat according to our cloth'.

†**46.** ***to cut sail, one's sail***: see quot. 1692. ?*Obs.*

1569 *Hawkins' 2nd Voy. W. Ind.* in Arber *Garner* V. 88 At which departing, in cutting of the foresail, a marvellous misfortune happened to one of the Officers. **1582** N. LICHEFIELD tr. *Castanheda's Discov. E. Ind.* 71 a, The whole Fleete, hauing wayed, did then begin to cut and spread their sayles with a great pleasure. **1692** in *Capt. Smith's Seaman's Gram.* I. xvi. 76 *Cut the Sail*, that is unfurl it, and let it fall down. **1721** in BAILEY.

47. ***to cut the throat of***: (*fig.*) to destroy, ruin, injure irretrievably.

1637 R. HUMPHREY tr. *St. Ambrose* Pref., This cuts the throat of that misconceived opinion. **1692** BP. OF ELY *Answ. Touchstone* 10 This, which cuts the throat of the Roman Cause. **1824** LEICESTER STANHOPE *Greece in 1824*. 15 Generals..who cut their own throats by word of command. **1867** FROUDE *Short Stud.* (ed. 2) 114 They..believed that Elizabeth was cutting her own throat.

48. ***to cut it (too) fat***: see 8 b.

49. ***to cut to pieces***: see 7 c.

50. ***to cut the comb of***: to lower the pride of: see COMB. ***to cut the gold*** (Archery): see GOLD. ***to cut the grass under***, or ***the ground from under, a person's feet***: see GRASS, GROUND. ***to cut the hair***: to split hairs: see HAIR. ***to cut the knot***: see KNOT. ***to cut the round***: see ROUND. ***to cut the volt***: see VOLT, etc. ***to cut didoes*** (DIDO[2]), ***dirt*** (DIRT *sb.* 6 d), ***eyes***, ***(no) ice***, ***the painter*** (PAINTER[2] 2 b), ***a splurge***, ***a swath*** (SWATH[1] 3 c), ***to waste*** (WASTE *sb.* 10 d): see the sbs. For ***cut one's loss(es)***, ***cut prices***, see LOSS *sb.*[1], PRICE *sb.*

IX. In comb. with adverbs.

51. cut about. a. *trans.* To damage or disfigure by random cutting and chipping of the surface. Chiefly *pass.*

1874 DASENT *Half a Life* II. 119 The most precious monuments of the Abbey..how cut about and mutilated they are!

b. *intr.* To run or dart about: see 19 b.

cut adrift: see 14. **cut asunder**: see 7.

52. cut away.

a. *trans.* To cut so as to take or clear away, to remove by cutting.

c **1320** *Seuyn. Sag.* 604 (W.) And his bowes awai i-kett. *c* **1440** *Promp. Parv.* 111 Cuttyyn' a-way, *abscindo, amputo.* *c* **1450** *St. Cuthbert* (Surtees) 4229 Some bad þe bolnyng cutt away. **1688** R. HOLME *Armoury* III. 399/2 Used to draw up the Cataract off the sight of the eye while it is cuting away. **1886** BESANT *Childr. Gibeon* 107, I will cut away the dead leaves.

†**b.** *fig.* To take away, remove forcibly; to stop the supply of, cut off. *Obs.*

1382 WYCLIF *2 Cor.* xi. 12, I kitte awey the occasioun of hem. *c* **1450** tr. *De Imitatione* I. xx, He þat wolde kutte awey al maner of veyne besines. **1562** N. WINȜET *Cert. Tractates* i. Wks. 1888 I. 10 All errour and abuse being cuttit away. **1707** FREIND *Peterborow's Cond. Sp.* 251 Yesterday they cut away the Water of a Mill in this Town.

c. *intr.* To go on cutting continuously or without cessation: see AWAY 7.

53. cut back.

a. *trans.* To prune by cutting off the shoots close back to the main stem or stock.

1871 SHIRLEY HIBBERD *Amateur's Fl. Garden* 210 Early in March cut back all the shoots.

b. To plough the second time, across or at right angles to the first furrow; = CROSS-PLOUGH.

1858 *Jrnl. R. Agric. Soc.* XIX. I. 65 The ordinary method ..was for the farmer in the autumn to plough down the field ..in the spring he had it cut back.

c. *Cinemat.* To return to a previous scene by repeating a portion of that scene. (See CUT-BACK *sb.* 2.) Also *trans.*

1913 E. W. SARGENT *Technique Photoplay* (ed. 2) 91 The same device may be used to get rid of a dinner scene... We cut-back to some other action. **1916** *Ibid.* (ed. 3) 194 It is well to remember..that not all plays may be cut back. **1959** HALAS & MANVELL *Technique Film Animation* 337 Cut back so many frames..and these frames are shot again.

d. *trans.* To reduce or decrease (expenditure, etc.). Also *intr.*

1943 *Sat. Even. Post* 6 Nov. 112 If the Army cuts back a program, it will not need the steel for some other program. **1953** *Manch. Guardian Weekly* 7 May 3 Western Europe was cutting back its defence programme. **1958** *Engineering* 4 Apr. 433/1 Industry is continuing to cut back markedly on capital spending plans. **1965** *Listener* 2 Sept. 334/1 Germany, another country whose aid budget had been built up impressively by the early nineteen-sixties, has recently cut it back. **1971** *Daily Tel.* 14 Jan. 2/7 A spokesman for ICI said that recruitment of Ph.D. students had been cut back.

e. *intr.* In *Surfing*, to turn one's surf-board back towards the breaking part of a wave.

1963 *Surfing Yearbk.* 41/1 *Cutting back*, when a rider is getting too far ahead of the curl, and has to change his direction to get in a better position relative to the wave. **1969** *Observer* 3 Aug. 35/1 He can 'cutback', turning the board back toward the breaking wave.

54. cut down.

a. *trans.* To cut so as to bring or throw down; cause to fall by cutting; to fell.

1382 WYCLIF *Matt.* iii. 10 Euery tree..shal be kitt [**1388** kit] doun. *a* **1400–50** *Alexander* 2850 To cutte down..Bowis of buskis and of braunches. **1534** TINDALE *Matt.* xxi. 8 Other cut doune braunches from the trees. **1611** BIBLE *Deut.* vii. 5 Ye shall destroy their altars..and cut downe their groues. **1784** *Gentl. Mag.* LIV. II. 643 A hill contiguous is cutting down. **1884** J. HATTON *Irving's Impr. Amer.* II. v. 86 A ship laden with corn was cut down and sunk by floating ice. **1952** *Oxf. Jun. Encycl.* VI. 174/1 As the old trees are cut down, seedlings spring up naturally to replace them.

b. To let fall or take down (the body of one who has been hanged) by cutting the rope.

1547 BOORDE *Introd. Knowl.* xxxii. (1870) 203 Whosoeuer that is hanged by-yonde see, shall neuer be cutte nor pulled downe. **1563–87** FOXE *A. & M.* (1631) III. xii. App. 1023/2 He being hanged till he was halfe dead, was cut downe and stripped. **1883** GARDINER *Hist. Eng.* 1603–42 I. vii. 282 The King having given orders that he should not be cut down until he was dead.

c. To lay low or kill with the sword or the like.

1821 BYRON *Sardan.* II. i. 166 Soldiers, hew down the rebel!..Cut him down. **1874** GREEN *Short Hist.* iii. 154 The Welsh..were cut ruthlessly down in the cornfields.

†**d.** *fig.* To put a stop to. *Obs. rare.*

1577 NORTHBROOKE *Dicing* (1843) 177 That the magistrates and rulers may..cut downe this wicked vice that it may be no more vsed.

e. To take the lead of decisively in a race or run; to surpass, get the better of.

1713 ADDISON *Ct. Tariff* (J.), So great is his natural eloquence, that he cuts down the finest orator, and destroys the best contrived argument. **1865** SURTEES *Facey Romford's Hounds* 156 (Illustration) Captain Spurrier 'cut down' by Romford.

f. *Naut.* (See quot. 1769.)

1769 FALCONER *Dict. Marine, Raser un vaisseau*, to cut down a ship, or take off part of her upper works, as the poop, quarter-deck, or fore-castle, in order to lighten her, when she becomes old and feeble. **1805** *Naval Chron.* XIII. 174 The..Indiaman..had been cut down.

g. To reduce, abridge, retrench, curtail, *esp.* a speech, expenses, wages. Also *intr.*, freq. with *on.*

1857 LEVER *Fort. Glencore* viii, A system of..cutting down every one's demand to the measure of their own pockets. **1885** DUNCKLEY in *Manch. Weekly Times* 6 June 5/5 Only one London newspaper attempts to give the speeches in full, the rest cut them down unmercifully. **1886** BARING-GOULD *Court Royal* I. ix. 144 Expenses ought to be cut down in every way. **1939** H. W. HORWILL *Anglo-Amer. Interpreter* 54, I am cutting down on my meat. **1945** E. BOWEN *Demon Lover* 90, I got my hundred [cigarettes] this morning... I can't seem to cut down, somehow. Mary, have you cut down? **1962** A. NISBETT *Technique Sound Studio* xii. 220 Methods of cutting down on the labour have been suggested.

h. ***to cut down to size***: to reduce to suitable dimensions; *fig.* to reduce to a true or proper level of importance.

1821 M. WILMOT *Let.* 20 Mar. (1935) 100 We..*cut down* silk stockings to Cat's size. **1904** G. B. SHAW *Lett. to G. Barker* 6 Dec. (1956) 45 The theme is a huge one; and it cant be cut down to Court size. **1927** HEMINGWAY *Men without Women* (1928) 33 He wheeled his horse..towards..the far side of the ring where the bull would come out... 'Pic him, Manos,' he said. 'Cut him down to size for me.' **1959** *Listener* 2 July 12/2 We are in danger of forgetting our place, of getting ideas above our station. It is good to have Mr. Graves to cut us down to size. **1959** *Guardian* 17 Sept. 18/1 Production and distribution of films has been cut down to size and other interests have been greatly extended. **1969** J. DRUMMOND *People in Glass House* xxxvi. 140 You've had thirty good years, perhaps it's time you were cut down to size.

55. cut in.

a. *trans.* To carve or engrave in intaglio.

1883 *Act 36 & 37 Vict.* c. 85 §3 Her official number..shall be cut in on her mainbeam.

b. *Whale-fishery.* To cut up (a whale) so as to remove the blubber.

1839 T. BEALE *Nat. Hist. Sperm Whale* 185 As soon as possible after the whale has been killed, it is brought alongside the ship to be cut in, by means of instruments which are called 'spades'. **1840** F. D. BENNETT *Whaling Voy.* II. 208 The next proceeding of the whaler is to 'cut in', or remove the blubber. *Ibid.* 210 From three to five hours are required to 'cut in' an ordinary school whale.

c. *intr.* To penetrate or enter sharply or abruptly; *esp.* so as to make a way for oneself or occupy a position between others. In later use also, to drive a motor-vehicle between two others which are passing each other in opposite directions; more recently, to drive a motor vehicle, cycle, etc., past another and move sharply in front of the overtaken vehicle. Also *transf.*

1612 DRAYTON *Poly-olb.* i. 3 Neptune cutting in, a cantle forth doth take. **1630** *R. Johnson's Kingd. & Commw.* 117 A huge arme of the Sea, which cutting in betweene the Land by the West, watreth Cornwall on the right hand, and Wales on the left. **1799** in Owen *Wellesley's Desp.* 114 The enemy having cut in between them and Seedasere. **1820** *Kaleidoscope* 25 July 29/2 Amid the din Of drunken coachmen *cutting in.* **1856** WHYTE MELVILLE *Kate Cov.* iii, After much 'cutting in', and shaving of wheels and lashing of horses. **1925** *Don'ts for Motorists* 100 How to avoid accidents... Don't 'cut in'. **1926** *Weekly Disp.* 5 Sept. 1/1 He is supposed to have been reported for cutting in at the second and eleventh tees. **1931** *Highway Code* 10 Your reluctance to stop dead may tempt you to 'cut in' by threading your way between other vehicles. This is a frequent source of accidents. **1954** *Ibid.* 8 Never cut in, that is, do not pull in sharply in front of a moving vehicle which you have just overtaken. **1955** R. BANNISTER *First Four Minutes* 21, I was unguarded against the man outside me who was cutting in.

d. To interpose or interrupt abruptly in conversation or the like; to strike in. So ***cut into*** for ***cut in to.*** *spec.* To have one's name added to a lady's dancing programme; also (orig. *U.S.*), to supersede a partner during a dance.

1830 GALT *Lawrie T.* v. viii, When Mr. Van Haarlem had finished his compliments, then Mr. Breagle cut in. **1857** G. A. LAWRENCE *Guy Livingstone* vi. 47 Keeping all her after-supper waltzes for him religiously, though half the men in town were trying to cut in. **1859** FARRAR *J. Home* vi, 'I say, Home', cut in Kennedy hastily, 'shall I go?' **1890** R. F. D. PALGRAVE *O. Cromwell* xiii. 288 The Royalists had only to wait, ready to cut in when the Levellers had done the work. *c* **1890** R. KIPLING *Phantom 'Rickshaw*, etc. (ed. 3) 74 It will save you cutting into my talk. **1896** ADE *Artie* x. 91 He did n't want no one else to cut in. **1919** *Ladies' Home Jrnl.* Sept. 169 All the men want to cut in when she dances. **1920** F. SCOTT FITZGERALD *This Side Paradise* (1921) I. ii. 70 The dance began... Boys cut in on Isabelle every few feet.

e. *Card-playing.* To join in a game (of whist) by taking the place of a player ***cutting out*** q.v.

1760 C. JOHNSTON *Chrysal* (1822) I. 277 When the rubber was finished, my mistress was asked to cut in. **1763** *Brit. Mag.* IV. 542 Instead of cutting in to a party of whist, they play the rubbers by rotation. **1870** *Mod. Hoyle* 6 Players cutting in take the chairs of players cutting out.

f. To receive a share (of profits, booty, etc.); also *trans.* (orig. *U.S.*), to give (a person) a share; freq. with *on. slang.*

1890 R. D. BLACKMORE *Kit & Kitty* III. xiv. 192 The brothers..smiled a sour smile, as much as to say,—'You don't cut in for any of it.' **1924** R. LARDNER *How to write Short Stories* (1926) 335 They'll cut you in on the big money. **1930** I. GOLDBERG *Tin Pan Alley* 210 For plugging certain numbers these leaders collect—'cut in'—on payments and royalties. **1950** G. GREENE *Third Man* xiv. 122 Were you going to cut me in on the spoils?

g. *trans.* To connect (an electric circuit, etc.). Also *intr.* of a motor.

1910 [see sense 57 r].

h. *trans.* To insert (a scene) into a film sequence. Also *transf.*

1928 *Film Weekly* 29 Oct. 17/3 These shots I cut in with other and varied material. **1934** C. LAMBERT *Music Ho!* iv. 262 A picture of the mother crying was 'cut in' with a picture of a dripping kitchen tap. **1947** D. LEAN in O. Blakeston *Working for Films* 29 Now where would you cut in the close-up of the banana-skin? **1962** A. NISBETT *Technique Sound Studio* ii. 43 Special [sound] effects are cut in as required. *Ibid.* vii. 128 We may wish to edit music..to cut in a retake.

56. cut off.

a. *trans.* To cut so as to take off; to detach by cutting (something material).

to cut off a corner: see CORNER *sb.*[1] 2 b.

c **1380** WYCLIF *Sel. Wks.* I. 401 Ȝif þi hond or þi foot sclaundir þee, kitte it of, and caste it fro þee. **1526** *Pilgr. Perf.* (W. de W. 1531) 177 b, Though thou cut of my heed. **1634** SIR T. HERBERT *Trav.* 119 To have their noses and eares cut off. **1664** EVELYN *Kal. Hort.* (1729) 196 Cutting off the dead Wood. **1864** TENNYSON *Enoch Arden* 895 This hair is his: she cut it off and gave it.

b. To remove, take away, sever, strike off (something immaterial).

1581 J. BELL *Haddon's Answ. Osor.* 98 b, When as I doe cut of so much of myne owne right unto you. **1601** SHAKS. *Jul. C.* III. i. 101 Why he that cuts off twenty yeares of life, Cuts off so many yeares of fearing death. *a* **1700** DRYDEN (J.), No vowel can be cut off before another, when we cannot sink the pronunciation of it. **1792** COKE & MOORE *Life J. Wesley* I. (ed. 2) 4 Determined..at a single blow to cut off from the established Church every Minister of honesty and conscience.

c. To bring to an end suddenly or abruptly; to put a stop to; to break off, cut short. ***to cut off an entail***: see ENTAIL *sb.*² 1.

1576 FLEMING *Panopl. Epist.* 17, I had rather cut off all old acquaintance with him. **1611** BIBLE *Lam.* iii. 53 They haue cut off my life in the dungeon. **1635** STAFFORD *Femall Glory* (1860) 51 Obedience calls upon me to cut off..this digression. **1647** W. BROWNE tr. *Polexander* II. 73 Zabaim, cutting him off, bade him answer succinctly. **1865** MRS. RIDDELL *World in Church* xxvii. 303 You wish to cut off the entail. **1878** BOSW. SMITH *Carthage* 285 [These things] cut off all hopes of a reconciliation.

d. To put to death (suddenly or prematurely), to bring to an untimely end.

c **1565** LINDESAY (Pitscottie) *Cron. Scot.* (1728) 16 If the Earl of Douglas..had been cutted off suddenly. **1611** BIBLE *1 Sam.* xx. 15 When the Lord hath cut off the enemies of Dauid. **1712** ADDISON *Spect.* No. 483 ⁋2 Why such an one was cut off in the flower of his youth. **1888** BURGON *Lives 12 Gd. Men* II. x. 239 His father was cut off at the age of twenty-five.

†**e.** To shorten, cut short. *Obs. rare.*

1607 DEKKER & WEBSTER *Westw. Hoe* v. Wks. 1873 II. 362 The story of vs both shall bee as good as an olde wiues tale, to cut off our way to London.

f. To intercept, stop the passage or supply of.

1569 STOCKER tr. *Diod. Sic.* I. iv. 9 Leosthenes seeing that he could not by force winne the towne, straightwaies cut of their victuals. **1780** COXE *Russ. Disc.* 198 The Chinese.. found means to cut off several straggling parties of Russians. **1818** JAS. MILL *Brit. India* II. v. v. 495 [They] cut off several vehicles of baggage. **1836–9** DICKENS *Sk. Boz, The Streets* iii, At last the company's man came to cut off the water. **1879** MISS YONGE *Cameos* Ser. IV. iii. 29 War..would cut off their wool from the Flemish looms.

g. To interrupt, stop (communication, passage, etc.); to render impossible by interposing an insurmountable obstacle.

1599 B. JONSON *Ev. Man out of Hum.* II. iii, 'Slight, our presence has cut off the conuoy of the iest. **1653** H. COGAN tr. *Pinto's Trav.* vii. 19 He cut off his way, and stopt him from passing further. **1776** N. WOODHULL in Sparks *Corr. Amer. Rev.* (1853) I. 260 Cutting off the communication between the army in town and country. **1823** J. D. HUNTER *Captiv. N. Amer.* 52 We attempted to cut off their retreat. **1845** LEVER *O'Donoghue* (1862) 352, I have sent a strong party..to cut off their advance.

h. To exclude from access, intercourse, view, etc.; to shut out; to debar. *spec.* To deprive of communication by telephone or telegraph; to disconnect (a telephone).

1576 FLEMING *Panopl. Epist.* 405 You might alledge.. some other impediment which cut you off from keeping company. **1709** BERKELEY *Th. Vision* §77 The wall interposing cuts off all that prospect of sea and land. **1857** W. COLLINS *Dead Secret* III. i. (1861) 66 The first cottage.. which was cut off from other houses by a wall all round it. **1859** JEPHSON *Brittany* vi. 76 Declaring a man a leper, and cutting him off from social intercourse. **1891** E. S. ELLIS *Check 2134* v. 38 The company can't afford to be cut off this way. **1932** D. WHIPPLE *Greenbanks* viii. 91 The telephone had its merits after all; Ambrose could be cut off. **1940** AUDEN *Another Time* 91 Stop all the clocks, cut off the telephone.

i. ***to cut off with a shilling***: to disinherit by bequeathing a shilling (the bequest being a proof that the disinheritance was designed).

[**1710** ADDISON *Tatler* No. 216 ⁋15 My eldest Son John.. I do disinherit and wholly cut off from any Part of this my Personal Estate, by giving him a single Cockle Shell.] **1834** HOOD *Tylney Hall* (1840) 268 Vowing..to cut him off with a shilling. **1861** GEO. ELIOT *Silas M.* iii, I might get you turned out of house and home, and cut off with a shilling.

57. cut out.

a. *trans.* To cut so as to take out; to excise, extract, or extirpate by cutting (something material). Freq. *fig.* in recent colloq. use: to stop doing or using (something); to leave off, do without, omit, drop: esp. in imper. phr. ***cut it out.***

c **1400** MAUNDEV. (Roxb.) xix. 88 With þat knyf he cuttez out a pece of his flesch. *c* **1483** CAXTON *Vocab.* 20 He can cutte out the stone. **1662** EVELYN *Chalcogr.* 9 With the Burine one cuts the peece all at once out of the plate. **1707** HEARNE *Collect.* 31 Oct., He found the Leaves..cut out. **1711** ADDISON *Spect.* No. 23 ⁋4 The Pope..ordered his Tongue to be cut out. **1840** LISTON *Elem. Surgery* I. (ed. 2) 215 The affected parts..should be cut out. **1903** ADE *People you Know* 82 Cut it out! **1905** 'H. MCHUGH' *You can search Me* i. 27 I've been speculating again after faithfully promising her to cut out all the guessing contests. So cut out the yesterday gag. *a* **1910** 'O. HENRY' *Sixes & Sevens* (1916) xviii. 209 To be frank with you, Whatsup, I've cut out the dope. **1914** G. ATHERTON *Perch of Devil* I. 137 If it were more the primal instinct..so much the worse, the more reason to 'cut it out'. **1923** R. D. PAINE *Comr. Rolling Ocean* vi. 110 Will you cut out the booze while you are ashore in Jamaica? **1933** AUDEN *Poems* (ed. 2) 52 Its no use raising a shout. No, Honey, you can cut that right out. **1937** R. STOUT *Red Box* iv. 54 Llewellyn..was expostulating: 'Now, Dad, cut it out,—now listen a minute.' **1939** D. L. SAYERS *In Teeth of Evidence* 202 'The great man himself. London's rising dramatist.'.. 'Cut it out,' said Scales. **1970** M. GUYBON tr. *Solzhenitsyn's First Circle* xlix. 366 'Cut it out!' said Pryanchikov, struggling violently. ' I'm sick of prosecutors and trials.'

b. To remove, excise, omit (a portion of a literary work, etc.).

1736 FIELDING *Pasquin* I, I wish you could cut the ghost out, sir. **1779** SHERIDAN *Critic* II. ii, Sir, the performers have cut it out. **1886** SALMON *Introd. N.T.* xviii. 380 The parts which it is proposed to cut out are indissolubly connected with those which are left behind. **1891** MAUDE *Merciful Divorce* 117 Before I cut you out of my will.

c. To surprise and carry off (a ship) from a harbour, etc., by getting between her and the shore.

1748 *Anson's Voy.* II. iii. 141 How impossible it would prove, either to board or to cut out any vessel protected by a force posted on shore within pistol-shot. **1781** MAD. D'ARBLAY *Lett.* Jan., After..cutting a few ships out of Torbay. **1882** STEVENSON *Fam. Stud. Men & Bks.* 162 He could not swoop into a parlour and, in the naval phrase, 'cut out' a human being from that dreary port.

d. *U.S.*, *Australia* and *N.Z.* To detach or separate (an animal) from the herd.

1862 E. R. CHUDLEIGH *Diary* 13 Feb. (1950) i. 28 On the run all day cutting out bullocks we succeeded in yarding about 60. **1867** J. T. THOMSON *Rambles with Philosopher* xxvi. 149 We scampered away to the pasture grounds of his cattle, in order to cut out one of the mob for slaughter. **1869** *Overland Monthly* III. 126 Another rides in, selects a stray brand and 'cuts it out', by chasing it out with his horse. **1885** *Pall Mall G.* 20 Mar. 3/2 The two best hands will go in and 'cut out' the cattle that bear the brand of their employers. **1887** *Scribner's Mag.* II. 508 *Cut out*, to separate an animal from the herd.

†**e.** To exclude, debar (*from*); = *cut off*. *Obs.*

1729 BUTLER *Serm.* Wks. 1874 II. 47 They in a manner cut themselves out from all advantage of conversation.

f. To get in front of a rival so as to intervene between him and success, or take the first place from him; to out-do, supplant in preference.

A driver or rider who 'cuts in', cuts out some one else.

16.. DRYDEN in Birch *Milton's Wks.* 1738 I. 48 This man [Milton] cuts us all out, and the Antients too. **1845** LD. HOUGHTON in *Life* (1891) I. 355 The King of the French has lent all the Crown jewels to the duchess, so she will quite cut our Queen out. **1848** THACKERAY *Bk. Snobs* (1881) 220 He cut out all the other suitors of the duchess.

g. To deprive, do out *of*.

1815 SCOTT *Guy M.* ii, The apprizer..cut the family out of another monstrous cantle of their remaining property. **1860** S. L. WINDSOR *Ethica* iii. 136 Cutting him out of his annual butt of sack.

†**h.** To divide for distribution. *Obs.*

1633 D. ROGERS *Treat. Sacraments* I. 142 By vertue of Christ cut out and divided to thee.

i. To excavate, carve out; to form by excavation or carving.

1548 [see CUT *sb.*² 21]. *a* **1648** LD. HERBERT *Life* (1886) 102 The whole forest..was cut out into long walks every way. **1659** D. PELL *Improv. Sea* 159 To what end the Lord did cut out all those Harbours, Creeks, Chanels. **1726** SHELVOCKE *Voy. round World* (1757) 165 [They] saw the word Magee.. and Capt. John cut out under it, upon a tree.

j. To fashion or shape by cutting (out of a piece).

1551 T. WILSON *Logike* (1580) 42 b, Although one have clothe, yet can he not have the use of it, except the Tailer cut it out. **1696** J. F. *Merchant's Ware-ho.* 38 How to cut out a Shift out of two Ells of Holland. **1891** E. PEACOCK *N. Brendon* II. 108 She..could cut out men's shirts. *Ibid.* 110 She could cut out much better than the ladies themselves.

k. *fig.* To form, fashion, shape, to carve out.

1593 SHAKS. *Rich. II*, II. iii. 144 To..Be his owne Caruer, and cut out his way, To find out Right with Wrongs. **1611** — *Wint. T.* IV. iv. 393 By th' patterne of mine owne thoughts, I cut out The puritie of his. **1802** MAR. EDGEWORTH *Moral T.* (1816) I. xx. 190 You..expect every ..man to be just cut out upon the pattern of..Henry. **1842** S. LOVER *Handy Andy* xix. 174, I thought it was manners to cut out my behaviour on your pattern.

l. *fig.* To plan; to prepare (*work* to be done). Phr. ***to have (all) one's work cut out***: see WORK *sb.* 30.

1619 *Relat. betw. Eng. & Germ.* Ser. II. (Camden) 68 How they may by..ill affected subjects cutt us out newe worke in Ireland and Scotland. **1754** A. MURPHY *Gray's-Inn Jrnl.* No. 98 ⁋5 The excessive Officiousness of the female World in cutting out Matches. **1795** BURKE *Regic. Peace* IV. ad fin. Wks. IX. 126 They will cut out work for one another, and France will cut out work for them all. **1866** CARLYLE *Inaug. Addr.* 174 The most unhappy of all men is the man..who has got no work cut out for him in the world.

m. (*a*) To form or fashion by nature (*for* a particular purpose). (Usually in *pa. pple.*)

1645 J. BOND *Occasus Occid.* 61 It was a Country by scituation..cut out for safety. **1708** DR. SMITH in Hearne *Collect.* 23 Dec., You seeme as it were to bee cut out for those studyes. *a* **1715** BURNET *Own Times* (1766) I. 401 He was not cut out for a Court. **1874** BURNAND *My Time* xiv. 115 She was cut out for a clergyman's wife.

†(*b*) To fix upon (*for* a purpose). *Obs.*

1667 PEPYS *Diary* 2 Sept., They told me both that they had long cut me out for Secretary to the Duke of York.

†**n.** ***to cut it out***: to flaunt, make a show, cut a dash. *Obs.*

1619 J. DYKE *Counter poyson* (1620) 39 They must flaunt, and cut it out in apparell, furniture [etc.]. **1679** G. R. tr. *Boyatuau's Theat. World* II. 149 Cutting it out in their Silks, Perfumes, and Embroideries.

o. *intr.* To admit of being cut out into shape.

1829 *Bone Manure, Rep. Doncaster Comm.* 31 The whole [manure]..will cut out like a jelly. **1850** *Jrnl. R. Agric. Soc.* XI. I. 139 Hay never cuts out so well as when it has been stacked from the field as fast as made.

p. *intr.* (orig. *passive*) *Card-playing.* To come out of or be excluded from a game (of whist) by cutting an unfavourable card; done in order to allow another player or players to *cut in*.

1771 T. HULL *Sir W. Harrington* (1797) II. 216 My Lord and I, happening to be cut out at the same time at whist. **1780** MAD. D'ARBLAY *Diary* June, Mrs. G——, having cut out at cards..approached us. **1810** *Sporting Mag.* XXXVI. 122 With the same pleasure that a gentleman who has cut out returns to a rubber. **1870** *Mod. Hoyle* 5 (*Whist*) The fifth and sixth players..have the right to cut into the game when a rubber has been completed by the first four players. This operation is effected by two players cutting out. *Cutting out* ..the players cut and the highest go out, whether two or one.

q. To finish shearing. Also in extended use: *trans.*, to finish; *intr.*, to come to an end. *Austral.* and *N.Z.*

1890 *Melbourne Argus* 20 Sept. 13/6 When the stations 'cut out', as the term for finishing is. **1896** H. LAWSON *In Days when World was Wide* (1900) 47 The cheque was spent that the shearer earned, and the sheds were all cut out. **1919** W. H. DOWNING *Digger Dial.* 18 *Cut-out* (vb.), cease. *a* **1925** F. S. ANTHONY *Follow Call* (1936) xiii. 156 I've never been able to save a cent since I cut out the roll I made with you. **1925** R. REES *Lake of Enchantment* vi. 94 If they could 'cut out' (or in other words get all their shearing over) by the end of the week. **1933** *Bulletin* (Sydney) 31 May 38/3 Tomorrow they would cut out the last of the sheep and the men would be paid off. **1941** BAKER *Dict. Austral. Slang* 21 *To cut out*,..to complete any task. **1948** *Landfall* II. 123 After the flax cut out and the mill moved on. **1959** H. P. TRITTON *Time means Tucker* iv. 29/1 The last sheep was shorn, the bell rang, the whistle blew and Charlton was cut out. **1963** A. LUBBOCK *Austral. Roundabout* 157 The great mines in Victoria..began to cut out..but the miners often remained in the district.

r. *trans.* To disconnect or switch off (an electric circuit, etc.). Also *intr.*, to switch off; to cease operating.

1910 *Chambers's Jrnl.* May 350/1 By means of a switch near the keyboard the organist can cut the motor in and out as desired. **1912** *Ibid.* Aug. 556/2 The dynamo is cut out automatically. **1917** *Blackw. Mag.* May 804/1 We continued in a westerly direction, with one cylinder still cutting out. **1924** A. W. JUDGE et al. *Mod. Motor Cars* III. 75 Which causes the hammer to vibrate and to cut-out the battery circuit. **1926** H. H. U. CROSS *Electric Lighting* (ed. 4) 264 When the gears are fully enmeshed, the electro-magnet is.. cut out by a disconnecting switch. **1928** *Motor Manual* (ed. 27) 110 When the dynamo speed falls below a certain minimum the device cuts out or opens the charging circuit. **1930** *Daily Express* 16 Aug. 5/5 When aero engines were much more liable to cut out and force one down in isolated places. **1935** *Jrnl. R. Aeronaut. Soc.* XXXIX. 472 There is a danger of the engine cutting out during take-off.

58. cut over.

a. *intr.* To run or pass across: see 17.

1551–1570 [see 17].

b. *trans.* To cut down the trees or bushes growing over (an area); to pass over cutting.

1789 *Trans. Soc. Encourag. Arts* I. 171 By the time the whole four acres had been cut over. **1889** W. SCHLICH *Man. Forestry* I. 10 The trees consist of stool shoots or root suckers which are cut over periodically.

c. To strike a person sharply over some part of the body with a weapon or missile; mostly *passive*: e.g. to be struck over the legs at hockey, to be struck or hurt by the ball at cricket; to be wounded.

1867 *J. Lillywhite's Cricketers' Compan.* 12 You will.. prevent yourself from being cut over in that part which takes all the batting out of you. **1874** DASENT *Half a Life* I. 122 [At hockey] Now mind you look out..or you'll be cut over. **1890** R. KIPLING *Wee Willie Winkie* 66 If he lives, he writes Home that he has been 'potted', 'sniped' , 'chipped', or 'cut over'. **1893** *Cricket Field* 29 July 304 He was cut over twice in rapid succession owing to inequalities in the ground, and inaccuracies in the bowlers.

d. To cut down, throw over with a slashing blow.

1884 J. COLBORNE *Hicks Pasha* 153 The officer cut over the first with a blow on his neck.

59. cut under. To cut out by underselling. *colloq.*

1859 BARTLETT *Dict. Amer.* (ed. 2), *To cut under*, to undersell in price. New York. **1874** MAYHEW *London Char.* 469 (Farmer) The spirit of competition on the part of the masters—the same universal desire to cut under.

60. cut up.

a. *trans.* To cut so as to take or get up; to root up by cutting; also *fig.*

1602 MARSTON *Ant. & Mel.* IV. Wks. 1856 I. 45 Rootes, rootes? alas, they are seeded, new cut up. **1611** BIBLE *Job* xxx. 4 Who cut vp mallowes by the bushes. **1690** LOCKE *Govt.* I. xi, This doctrine cuts up all government by the roots. **1767** BLACKSTONE *Comm.* II. 15 The law has therefore wisely cut up the root of dissension. **1839** *Morning Herald* 28 Aug., The gum trade..is nearly cut up by the roots.

b. To cut in pieces; to divide into parts by cutting, to carve; to cut open.

1580 BARET *Alv.* C 1876 Cut vp: or winne these partriges. **1611** MIDDLETON & DEKKER *Roaring Girl* III. ii, No wild fowl to cut up but mine! **1847** MARRYAT *Childr. N. Forest* iii, Now I'll cut up the onions, for they will make your eyes water. **1885** *Illust. Lond. News* 10 Oct. 362 Every lady and gentleman was instructed how to cut up a turkey, capon or bustard.

c. *fig.* To divide into parts, destroy the continuity of; to destroy or mar irretrievably.

1813 LEIGH HUNT in *Examiner* 19 Apr. 242/2 His night's sleep had been cut up. **1817** FARADAY in B. Jones *Life & Lett.* (1870) I. 248 My time is just now so closely cut up. **1864** BURTON *Scot. Abr.* I. iii. 123 They will very soon cut up and destroy all we have in this country.

d. To overcome with great slaughter, 'cut to pieces': see 7 c.

1803 WELLINGTON in Owen *Wellesley's Desp.* 787 A parcel of stragglers cut up our wounded. **1821** BLACKER *Mahratta War* I. ix. 155 *note*, The body of cavalry..employed to cut up the column of infantry.

e. To cut, hack, or gash the surface of irregularly; to damage by or as by cutting.

a **1592** H. SMITH *Serm.* (1622) 301 Like the plough, which cutteth up the ground that it may receive the seed. **1765**

STERNE *Tr. Shandy* VIII. xx, The roads, which were terribly cut up. **1827** HONE *Every-day Bk.* II. 104 The ice was much cut up. **1859** *All Year Round* No. 13. 306 The ground was..much cut up between wickets.

†**f.** To whip up, to incite with the whip. *Obs.*

1756-66 AMORY *Buncle* (1770) II. 24 My horse was as good..and I cut him up, and pricked him over the turf.

g. *fig.* To censure, criticize, or review with destructive severity.

1760 GOLDSM. *Cit. W.* xx, The book-answerers..when they have cut up some respectable name. **1782** MISS BURNEY *Cecilia* VII. v. 'May be..it's out of bashfulness: perhaps he thinks we shall cut him up.' **1784** R. BAGE *Barham Downs* II. 228 The conversation fell naturally..upon Miss Whittaker's affair, and Lord Winterbottom was cut up.. without mercy. **1860** SALA *Lady Chesterf.* 55 [The reviewer] savagely cutting up people's books or pictures.

h. To wound deeply the feelings of; to distress greatly. (Usually in *pass.*)

1844 DICKENS *Christmas Carol* i, Scrooge was not so dreadfully cut up by the sad event. **1876** F. E. TROLLOPE *Charming Fellow* II. ix. 127, I believe he was dreadfully cut up at my going away.

†**i.** *to cut up short*: to cut short, interrupt.

1607 HIERON *Wks.* I. 197 Shee, beeing..something a shrewd-tongued woman, by and by cut Him vp short.

j. To share (plunder), to divide. *slang.*

[**1779** R. CUMBERLAND *Wheel of Fort.* IV. iii. (Farmer). A gentleman who trusts to servants in his absence is sure to be cut up.] **1879** *Macm. Mag.* XL. 505 (Farmer) We had between sixty and seventy quid to cut up.

k. *intr.* To admit of being cut up or divided, to turn out as to amount of fortune; properly a butcher's phrase; said of a person after his death. *slang.*

1782 MISS BURNEY *Cecilia* V. ix, Pray, how does he cut up? What has he left behind him? **1792** GIBBON *Misc. Wks.* I. (1814) 366 Geneva would cut up as fat as most towns in Europe. *a* **1797** BURKE (T.), The only question..of their legislative butchers, will be, how he cuts up? **1831** DISRAELI *Yng. Duke* IV. vii, 'You think him rich?' 'Oh, he will cut up very large,' said the Baron. **1848** THACKERAY *Bk. Snobs* vii, The old banker died in course of time, and..'cut up' prodigiously well.

l. *to cut up rough, rusty, savage*, etc.: (*intr.*) to become angry or quarrelsome. *colloq.*

1837 DICKENS *Pickw.* xlii, I may say I von't pay, and cut up rough. **1849** THACKERAY *Pendennis* l, Hang it! you cut up quite savage. **1873** BLACK *Pr. Thule* vii. 101 'Now, Ingram ..don't cut up rough about it.'

m. To cut a dash; show off; to behave (in a specified way); to behave badly or indecorously. *U.S. colloq.*

1787 *Generous Attachment* I. 89 A couple of plough boys.. would do, when properly dressed, and cut it up..as well as the best. **1859** H. W. BEECHER *Notes fr. Plymouth Pulpit*, I believe I never did cut up so bad any one week as I did that week. **1861** LOWELL *Biglow P.* Ser. II. i, It ain't no use to argerfy ner try to cut up frisky. **1888** HOWELLS *Likely Story* in *Harper's Mag.* Dec. 26 If you dare to touch them, I'll ring for Jane, and then she'll see you cutting up.

n. *Sporting slang.* To 'behave' (*badly*, etc.) in a race or competition.

1883 *Scotsman* 11 July 18/1 He cut up badly and can have no chance for the Cup. **1883** *Illustr. Lond. News* 12 May 463/2 (Farmer) Export again cut up wretchedly in the Burwell Stakes.

o. *trans.* With *caper, shines*, etc.: to behave in a mischievous or frolicsome manner. *U.S.*

1775 in *Narrag. Hist. Reg.* III. 263 A man that was in company there the evening before that cut up a caper. **1846** D. CORCORAN *Pickings* 28 He vas cutting up all kinds of extra shines.. like these here theatric fellers. **1847** [see *monkey-shines* (MONKEY *sb.*)]. *a* **1848** *Knickerbocker* (Bartlett), A wild bull of the prairies was cutting up shines at no great distance, tearing up the sod with hoofs and horns. **1851** [see DIDO[2]]. **1903** A. D. MCFAUL *Ike Glidden* ii. 11 It was not Ike that cut up the mischief this time. **1945** S. LEWIS *C. Timberlane* (1946) xvii. 102 People recognizing you and staring at you cutting up monkey-shines!

p. To conduct or manage (a contest) fraudulently. *Sporting slang.*

1923 *Daily Mail* 16 Jan. 7 Georges Carpentier, M. Descamps, his manager, and M. Hellers, the manager of the coloured boxer Siki, have been acquitted by the French Boxing Federation of having arranged and 'cut up' the fight in which Siki was declared victor. **1923** *Weekly Disp.* 13 May 7, I read in newspapers now that more than half the races under National Hunt rules are cut up, and that jockeys and trainers are out to rob the public.

q. *intr.* Of the surface of the ground: to become broken up irregularly.

1891 W. G. GRACE *Cricket* iii. 70 Snow had fallen during the day, and the wicket cut up badly. **1909** *Moa Flat Estate* 36 Six-ton loads went through..before the roads 'cut up' and would not bear traffic.

r. *to cut up (old) touches*: to gossip or reminisce. *U.S. slang.*

1931 D. RUNYON *Guys & Dolls* (1932) viii. 180 They are cutting up old touches. *Ibid.* xiii. 281 Having a drink together..and..cutting up old touches of the time when they run with the Hudson Dusters together. **1941** *New Yorker* 1 Nov. 27/3 He and Dutch would get together and cut up touches.

s. To cut in front of (another vehicle or its driver), esp. causing it to brake or take other evasive action; to pass recklessly or illegally. *colloq.*

1939 H. HODGE *Cab, Sir?* xv. 219 To 'cut a man up' means much the same as the more official driving term 'cutting in'. **1975** *Observer* 11 May 1/4 They drove up the inside of a line of traffic waiting to turn right into Ley Road. One of the vehicles they 'cut up' turned out to be a 'nondescript' (unmarked) police van.

X. Phraseological expressions and combinations containing the verb-stem.

61. cut-and-come-again. *sb. phr.* **a.** The act or faculty of cutting (from a joint of meat, etc.) and of returning to help oneself as often as one likes; hence, unfailing supply, abundance; also *fig.* or *attrib.* **b.** A variety of kale.

1738 SWIFT *Pol. Conversat.* iii. 121, I vow, 'tis a noble sirloyn. Ay; here's cut and come again, Miss. **1827** S. P. in Hone *Every-day Bk.* II. 54 A ham..is a cut-and-come-again dish, ready at hand. **1841** THACKERAY *Gt. Hoggarty Diamond* iv, Always happy to see a friend in our plain way, —pale sherry, old port, and cut and come again. **1861** SALA *Dutch Pict.* xv. 241 You cut your steak off hot from the living animal, on the cut and come again principle. **1886** F. T. ELWORTHY *W. Somerset Word-Bk.* 177 *Cut and come again*, a very prolific variety of kale or winter greens; much grown in cottage gardens. **1959** *Listener* 21 May 911/1 Here is a delicious way to cook cut-and-come-again (or cottage kale).

62. cut-and-cover. **a.** *Agric.* A method of ploughing in which the furrow-slice is turned over on an unploughed strip (see sense 9d above). *U.S.* **b.** *Engineering.* A method of constructing a tunnel by making a cutting in which the brickwork lining is built and then covered in: employed with advantage when the depth below the surface is comparatively small.

1839 J. BUEL *Farmer's Comp.* xiii. 113 The cut-and-cover practice is still worse as it leaves..two thirds of the soil, undisturbed by the plough. **1877** *Rep. Vermont Board Agric.* IV. 93 The old Dutch wooden plow..[was] used among the stumps and roots of the newish lands, with the plowman's ideal of cut and cover. **1892** *Daily News* 2 Nov. 2/8 Certain portions of this work..could be much better and more cheaply executed by the method of cut-and-cover. *Ibid.* 22 Nov. 3/1 Excavating what is technically called the 'cut and cover' portion of the work—the portion of the tunnel, that is to say..cut out, arched over, and covered in again.

63. cut-and-fill: the process or result of removing material from a place and depositing it near by (see quots.); also as vb.

1904 CHAMBERLIN & SALISBURY *Geol.* (1905) I. iii. 183 This is cut-and-fill. The sediment eroded from the curve which is concave toward the stream is shifted down-stream, while that deposited in the curve which is convex toward the stream is brought down from above. **1934** WEBSTER, *Cut and fill*, to construct, as a stadium, by using material excavated from the center to form walls. **1940** *Chambers's Techn. Dict.* 218/1 *Cut-and-fill*, a term used to describe any cross-section of highway or railroad earthworks which is partly in cutting and partly in embankment. **1965** G. J. WILLIAMS *Econ. Geol. N.Z.* vii. 80/1 The existence of current-bedding, imbricate arrangement of pebbles, cut-and-fill bedding, and scour channels.

64. *cut and thrust*: see CUT *sb.*[2] 2c.

65. *Comb.* **a.** with object noun, = 'that which or he who cuts...' as *cut-air, -beard, -caper, -girdle, -nose*; CUTPURSE, CUTTHROAT, CUTWATER; **b.** = '...used to cut, cutting', as *cut-whip*, CUT-GRASS.

a **1661** HOLYDAY *Juvenal* 266 A cut-purse..is by Plautus ..called..a cut-girdle. **1665** HOOKE *Microgr.* 174 The biggest stem of all the wing, and may be properly enough call'd the cut-air. *a* **1678** MARVELL *Poems, Brit. & Raleigh*, And Commons' votes shall cut-nose guards disband. **1693** SHADWELL *Volunteers* I. ii, Her sense and breeding is fit for none but a cutcaper. **1767** S. PATERSON *Another Trav.* I. 39 Not one..greasy, lying, tale-bearing..newsmonger cut-beard is to be found. **1887** *Pall Mall G.* 5 Aug. 3/1 A light, thin, supple whalebone cut whip.

cut (kʌt), *ppl. a.* [Pa. pple. of CUT *v.*]

1. a. Gashed or wounded with a sharp-edged instrument; having an incision made in it.

c **1665** MRS. HUTCHINSON *Mem. Col. Hutchinson* (1838) 47/1 To bind up a cut finger. **1889** F. TREVES *Man. Surgery* (ed. 6) II. xi. 473 The ordinary cut throat of the suicide or homicide.

b. *esp.* Of clothes, etc.: Having the edges or other parts purposely indented or slashed, for ornament or as a fashion.

1480 CAXTON *Chron. Eng.* ccxxvi. 233 Short clothes and streyte wastyd dagged and kyt, and on euery syde slatered. **1528** TINDALE *Parable Wicked Mammon* Wks. I. 103 In a visor, in a disguised garment, and a cut shoe. **1573** G. HARVEY *Letter-bk.* (Camden) 6 His kut dublets. *a* **1627** MIDDLETON *Mayor of Q.* v. i, You'd both need wear cut clothes. **1678** *Lond. Gaz.* No. 1273/4 Another Apron laced with cut and slash Lace.

c. Of leaves and other natural objects: Having the margins deeply indented and divided.

1565-73 COOPER *Thesaurus, Alcea*..marsh mallow: or cut mallow. **1591** PERCIVALL *Sp. Dict., Malvavisco salvage* cut mallowes. **1796** WITHERING *Brit. Plants* IV. 38 Leaves small, cut, hoary. **1867** BABINGTON *Man. Brit. Bot.* (ed. 6) 160 Ovate cut or pinnatifid leaflets.

2. a. That has been subjected to cutting; affected or modified by cutting.

1588 SHAKS. *Tit. A.* II. i. 87 Easie it is Of a cut loafe to steale a shiue we know. **1803** *Sporting Mag.* XXI. 326 *Cut-cards*..cards..having the good cards..all cut shorter, and the bad ones cut something narrower. **1881** *Daily News* 1 Sept. 3/3 In the Bank of England..buyers having now to choose between..Napoleons and German 20 marks at 76*s.* 6½*d.*, and cut sovereigns at 77*s.* 10½*d.* **1892** *Pall Mall G.* 5 Aug. 3/1 Cut cloth is canvas painted, from which the carpenters cut away all portions which are not touched with paint.

b. Of money: see *cut-money* (12a below). *U.S.*

1844 in C. Cist *Cincinnati Misc.* (1845) I. 6/1 As late as 1806..the business house in Philadelphia in which I was apprentice, received over one hundred pounds of cut silver.

3. a. Formed, shaped, fashioned, or made by cutting; having the surface shaped or ornamented by grinding and polishing, as *cut glass*; also (*transf.*, *colloq.*) an affected expression or mode of speech; also (with hyphen) *attrib.* *cut velvet*: velvet having the pile cut so as to form patterns. †*cut river*: a canal.

1677 YARRANTON *Eng. Improv.* 7 By making Cut Rivers Navigable in all places where Art can possibly effect it. **1717** BERKELEY *Tour in Italy* Wks. IV. 515 The gardens..have fine cut walks. **1800** M. SYMES *Acct. Embassy to Ava* xvi. 382 A handsome girandole of cut glass. **1802** C. WILMOT *Let.* 3 Jan. in T. U. Sadleir *Irish Peer* (1920) 22 The Room lighted by a handsome cut glass Lustre. **1816** KEATINGE *Trav.* (1817) II. 81 The masonry is, as usual with the Romans, stratified in alternate courses of cut-stone and brick-work. **1840** THACKERAY *Catherine* viii, The cut-velvet breeches. **1845** C. KNIGHT *Capital & Labour* 169 Cut-glass is now comparatively..cheap. **1874** KNIGHT *Dict. Mech.*, *Cut-nail*, a nail cut from a nail-plate, in contradistinction to one forged from a nail-rod. **1875** MRS. STOWE *We & Neighbors* xxxii. 303, I arranged it in my high cut-glass dish and covered it with foamy billow of whites of eggs. **1945** DYLAN THOMAS *Let.* 30 July (1966) 282 A position or positions—cut-glass for job or jobs. **1957** *Granta* 9 Mar. 20/1 All I can remember now is a cut-glass decanter stopper. **1962** *John o' London's* 24 May 507/2 An impeccable cut-glass accent. **1966** 'L. LANE' *ABZ of Scouse* 96 She talks cut glass.

b. *cut bank*: see quot. 1932. *N. Amer.*

1819 *N. Amer. Rev.* VIII. 11 The Nottoway at Cut Bank Bridge. **1837** S. CUMMINGS *Western Pilot* 66 You pass close by this cut bank of the bar. **1884** 'MARK TWAIN' *Huck. Finn* xv. 127 In about a minute I come a-booming down on a cut bank with..big trees on it... That cut bank was an island. **1897** *Medicine Hat* (Alberta) *News* 28 Jan. 1/6 The horse on which he was riding went over the cut bank near the iron bridge. **1932** *Dialect Notes* VI. 228 Cut-bank. This word (variously spelled *cutbank*, *cut-bank*, and *cut bank*) is often used for the outer bank at the bend of a stream, the bank which the stream cuts into, leaving the opposite side flat. **1968** R. M. PATTERSON *Finlay's River* 26 On the right bank of the Parsnip [River] there is a high cutbank, a sand-and-gravel cliff.

c. *cut paper*, paper cut into a desired shape, usually for decorative purposes. Also (with hyphen) *attrib.*

1847 E. BRONTË *Wuthering Heights* I. xiii. 323 A fireplace hung with cut paper dropping to pieces. **1891** KIPLING *Light that Failed* (1900) 9 The boy who..had decorated Amomma's horns with cut-paper ham-frills. **1962** *Times* 31 May 16/4 The marvellous cut-paper experiments in pure colour which are far more familiar in America than here. **1967** E. SHORT *Embroidery & Fabric Collage* i. 28 When working out designs in cut paper.

4. Divided into pieces by cutting.

c **1440** *Promp. Parv.* 111 Cutte a-sundere, *scissus.* **1659** LOVELACE *Poems* (1864) 166 Then let me be Thy cut anatomie. **1840** F. D. BENNETT *Whaling Voy.* II. 85 Enclosing the cut leaf in the delicate husk of the Indian-corn. **1847-78** HALLIWELL *Cut-meat*, hay; fodder; chaff cut into short lengths. *North. Mod.* A heap of cut fire-wood.

5. a. Severed or detached by cutting; lopped off.

c **1380** WYCLIF *Serm.* Sel. Wks. I. 167 A kitt braunche. **1845** *Florist's Jrnl.* 13 The unhealthiness attributed to cut flowers, when introduced into..sleeping-rooms. **1878** EMERSON in *N. Amer. Rev.* CXXVI. 405 A show of cut flowers.

b. *cut and laid*, of a hedge: see LAY *v.*[1] 6b. Also *ellipt.*, a hedge made in this manner.

1919 MASEFIELD *Reynard* II. 73 Robin made Pip [*sc.* his horse] go crash through the cut and laid. **1927** *Daily Express* 31 Oct. 9 Neat-cropped grass fields split by 'cut and laid' fences.

6. a. Shortened, lessened, or reduced by, or as by cutting; curtailed; cut down. Of prices, etc.: reduced (orig. *U.S.*). Hence **cut-price, -rate** *adjs.*, having, or offered at, reduced prices; also *fig.*

1646 CRASHAW *Steps to Temple* 54 Short-cut lives of murder'd infants. **1881** *Chicago Times* 12 Mar., The New York Central..has been meeting the cut rate made via Baltimore. **1884** *Pall Mall G.* 1 Oct. 5/2 Parliament will accept..the cutting of the coupon, but the guarantee of the cut coupon—that is altogether another affair. *a* **1889** *Boston Jrnl.* (Farmer), The plain people who enjoy a spectacular, musical, and dramatic season at cut rates. **1897** *Sears, Roebuck Catal.* 684 No wholesale house can meet our cut prices. **1904** *Westm. Gaz.* 27 May 10/2 The policy of the 'cut-rate' may continue. **1904** *Daily Chron.* 15 June 7/3 One out of every eighty of the cut-rate arrivals was ordered back to Europe. **1910** *Sat. Even. Post* 10 Sept. 76/2 Tricky cut-price operators..selling below living prices. **1930** R. SIMMAT *Personal Salesmanship* 85 If a salesman once..gives a cut price he will..be always expected to give a cut price. **1934** J. B. PRIESTLEY *English Journey* 17 A number of blatant cut-price shops, their windows crammed with goods, mostly inferior and dubious, and loud with placards. **1958** *New Statesman* 30 Aug. 238/3 Their decision to offer unsecured personal advances at, in effect, cut-rates. **1963** A. ROSS *Australia 63* 19 M.C.C.'s batsmen were offered only cut-price bowling, and they savaged it accordingly. **1964** *Daily Tel.* 18 Jan. 8/2 Giving the consumer more of a choice between 'quality' and cut-rate shopping.

b. Diluted; adulterated. (Cf. CUT *v.* 22b.) Chiefly *U.S.*

1938 H. ASBURY *Sucker's Progr.* 343 Suckers..paid exorbitant prices for cut and adulterated liquor. **1969** D. BAGLEY *Spoilers* vi. 180 'This is morphine.' 'Cut or uncut?' asked Follet. 'It's pure—or as pure as you can make the stuff in a slum like this.'

7. Castrated.

1624 *Nero* IV. i. (1888) 56 Your cut-boy Sporus. *Mod.* A cut horse.

8. *slang.* Drunk, intoxicated.

1673 R. HEAD *Canting Acad.* 171 He is flaw'd, fluster'd, Cup shot, cut in the leg or back. *a* **1700** B. E. *Dict. Cant. Crew, Cut,* Drunk; *Deep Cut.. Cut in the Leg or Back,* very drunk. **1760** C. JOHNSTON *Chrysal* (1822) I. 134 Your excellency was a little cut, but you broke up much the strongest of the company. **1823** LOCKHART *Reg. Dalton* I. vii. (1842) 36 I'm sure we had not much more than a bottle apiece.. I was not cut. **1848** THACKERAY *B. Snobs* xlviii, I was so cut last night.

† **9.** ***cut and long tail***: *lit.* horses or dogs with cut tails and with long tails; hence *fig.* all sorts of people. *Obs.*

1575 LANEHAM *Let.* (1871) 25 The rest of the band.. tag and rag, cut & long tail. **1579** FULWELL *Ars Adulandi* I, Yea, even their very dogs, Rug, Rig, and Risbie, yea, cut and long-taile, they shall be welcome. **1598** SHAKS. *Merry W.* III. iv. 47, I that I will, come cut and long-taile, vnder the degree of a 'Squire. **1698** VANBRUGH *Æsop.* IV. ii, Your worship has six coach-horses (cut and long-tail,) two runners, half-a-dozen hunters. **1699** FARQUHAR *Const. Couple* II. iv, I whipped all the whores, cut and long tail, out of the parish.

10. a. ***cut and dried*** (also ***cut and dry***): originally referring to herbs in the herbalists' shops, as contrasted with growing herbs; hence, *fig.* ready-made and void of freshness and spontaneity; also, ready shaped according to *a priori* formal notions. (Usually of language, ideas, schemes or the like.)

1710 J. B. *Let. to Sacheverell* 13 Your Sermon was ready Cut and Dry'd. **1730** SWIFT *Poems, Betty the Grizette,* Sets of Phrases, cut and dry, Evermore thy Tongue supply. **1796** WOLCOTT (P. Pindar) *A Satire* Wks. 1812 III. 408 Phrases ready cut and dried. **1883** *St. James' Gaz.* 1 Dec. 3/1 A Socialist, but a Socialist who has no cut-and-dry scheme of Socialism. **1887** JESSOPP *Arcady* vii. 191 Quite enough to scatter my cut and dried theories to the winds.

b. *ellipt.* as sb. (*cut and dry*) = cut and dried tobacco, etc.

1725 RAMSAY *Gent. Sheph.* II. i, Ye've coft a pund o cut and dry. *a* **1735** ARBUTHNOT *Misc. Wks.* (1751) II. 123 Isaac extolls her out of a Quartern of Cut and Dry every day she lives.

c. Hence ***cut-and-driedness***. *nonce-wd.*

1882 SAINTSBURY *Short Hist. French Lit.* Interchapter iv. 504 The reduction of.. important departments in literature to a condition of cut-and-driedness which has no parallel in history.

11. With adverbs: see CUT *v.* 51–60. See also CUT-AWAY, CUT-OUT, CUT-UNDER.

1743 W. ELLIS *Mod. Husb.* Oct. v. 147 The great Importance of curing cut down Wheat in the Field, is.. known to the meanest Rustic. **1809** *Naval Chron.* XXII. 90 The *Regulus,* a cut down 44. **1823** G. S. FABER *Dispensations* (1849) II. 104 Like a cut-down plant. **1861** DICKENS *Gt. Expect.* xxxv, A cut-up plum-cake. **1874** KNIGHT *Dict. Mech., Cut-in Notes* (Printing), notes which occupy spaces taken out of the text, whose lines are shortened to give room therefor. **1932** W. FAULKNER *Light in August* (1952) vii. 143 The small figure in cutdown underwear. **1941** J. CARY *House of Children* iii. 10 Wild hordes of mountain children in their father's cut-down trousers. **1949** F. MACLEAN *Eastern Approaches* II. iii. 200 A new, cut-down Ford station waggon.

12. *Comb.*, **a.** qualifying a sb., as **cut cloth, drop** (see quot. 1961); † **cut-fowl** = insect; **cut-money** *U.S.* (see quot. 1822); **cut-rock** (see quot. 1837); **cut-rope** *Naut.*, = PAINTER[2]; **cut sheet (rubber)**, rubber cut into sheets from a pressed block; **b.** similar combinations used attrib., as ***cut-finger***, ***-flower***, ***-glass*** (see 3 a), ***-leaf***, ***-paper*** (see 3 c), ***-pile***, ***-steel***, ***-tail*** (also = 'cut-tail dog'); **cut-card**, applied to a type of relief decoration on silverware, etc., in which a thin sheet of metal is cut ornamentally and soldered to the surface; **c.** parasynthetic derivatives of these as ***cut-fingered***, ***-leaved***, ***-lugged*** (Sc. = crop-eared), ***-nosed*** (= slit-nosed), ***-tailed***, etc. See also CUT-LIPS, CUT-WAIST, etc.

1920 *Catal. Eng. Silversmiths' Work* (V. & A. Mus.) 18 Another method of decoration was that known as '*cut-card' work, the decoration being cut out from a separate sheet of metal. **1939** *Oxoniensia* IV. 201 A candle-cup, of 1672, with fine 'cut-card' decoration. **1956** G. TAYLOR *Silver* v. 135 The Parisian goldsmiths.. effected a monumental elegance ..due to an admirable harmony... Perhaps the most attractive.. is cut-card work, a term used to describe flat patterns of sheet metal applied to the body of the object to be decorated. **1969** R. MAYER *Dict. Art Terms & Techniques* 103 *Cut-card work,* a decorative technique in metalwork in which a design cut out of a sheet of metal is superimposed on the surface of an object of the same metal, usually around a protuberance such as a handle or a finial. Cut-card work is used almost exclusively for silver. **1884** J. HATTON *Irving's Imp. Amer.* I. vii. 165 The well-known Hampton Court cloth [in 'Charles I'] was so perfect.. that it was regarded as a *cut cloth, with 'raking' and water-pieces. **1933** P. GODFREY *Back-Stage* xi. 143 The drop-scenes, cut-cloths, and borders.. became as obsolete as the 'aside' in acting. **1961** BOWMAN & BALL *Theatre Lang.* 89 *Cut cloth, cut-cloth,* a British term for a cut drop. **1961** BOWMAN & BALL *Theatre Lang.* 90 **Cut drop,* a drop painted and then cut out so that the spectator sees a scene formed not only by this drop but also by whatever is placed behind it. **1883** JEFFERIES *Nature near London* 44 [They] call the foliage of the knotted figwort *cutfinger leaves, as they are believed to assist the cure of a cut or sore. **1591** NASHE *Introd. Sidney's Astr. & Stella,* 'Tis as good to go in *cut-fingered pumps as cork shoes, if one wear Cornish diamonds on his toes. **1902** *Westm. Gaz.* 4 Apr. 8/1 The *cut-flower trade. **1970** W. E. SHEWELL-COOPER *Cut Flowers for House* i. 9 The keen cut-flower gardener should expect to have blooms and foliage from his garden from March to October at least. **1587** GOLDING *De Mornay* ix. 124 Smal things, as Woorms, *Cutfoules, and such other. **1897** G. B. SUDWORTH *Arborescent Flora U.S.* 261 *Robinia pseudacacia dissecta..* *Cutleaf Locust. **1923** E. F. WYATT *Invis. Gods* 16 Mountain ash and cut-leaf birch flickered their light foliage. **1731** P. MILLER *Gard. Dict.* I. s.v. *Lilac,* Lilac, with cut Leaves, falsely call'd, The *Cut-leav'd Persian Jasmine... The Cut-leav'd Sort.. having its older Leaves deeply cut in. **1870** HOOKER *Stud. Flora* 174 The 'Cut-leaved Elder'. **1814** SCOTT *Wav.* xxx, Ye *cut-lugged, graning carles! **1809** in W. Littell *Statute Law of Kentucky* (1814) IV. 45 To pay *cut money into the public treasury. **1822** J. WOODS *Eng. Prairie* 230 We found change at these towns very scarce; what there was, was mostly cut-money; that is, when change is wanted they often cut dollars, half-dollars, and quarter-dollars, into smaller pieces with an ax or chisel. **1824** W. N. BLANE *Excursion* 257, I was obliged to cut a silver dollar, into quarters, and even into eighths; a practice so common in the Western States, that the cut-money as it was called, was the only change that could be had in Missouri. **1591** PERCIVALL *Sp. Dict., Desnarigado,* *cut nosed. **1880** SIR E. REED *Japan* II. 223 Silk and *cut-pile fabrics. **1837** W. IRVING *Capt. Bonneville* II. 200 All these basaltic channels are called *cut rocks by the trappers. **1851** MAYNE REID *Scalp Hunt.* xxxi, We found the path strewed with loose cut-rock. **1909** *Westm. Gaz.* 3 July 2/2 The *cut-rope [painter] of an old boat is apt to be very rotten. *Ibid.* 21 Aug. 2/2 Benjie ran into the water for the cut-rope. **1900** *Cut sheet [see SHEET *sb.*[1] 9 c]. **1907** H. L. TERRY *India-Rubber* xii. 161 Cut sheet rubber. **1748** SMOLLETT *R. Random* II. xliv. 79 A fourth [sword] *cut steel inlaid with gold. **1896** *Westm. Gaz.* 10 Dec. 3/2 A cut-steel buckle. **1925** W. DE LA MARE *Connoisseur* (1926) 334 The cut-steel brooch of coloured gems. **1530** PALSGR. 211/2 *Cuttayled beest, *queve courte.* **1627** DRAYTON *Agincourt, etc.* 143 His gamesome cut-tayld Curre. *Ibid.* 152 Whistles Cut-tayle from his play. **1712** *Lond. Gaz.* No. 4997/4 A Bay Mare.. cut Tail'd.

† **cu'taceous**, *a. Obs. rare.* [f. L. *cut-is* hide, skin: see -ACEOUS.] Of the nature of skin.

1649 BULWER *Pathomyot.* II. ix. 212 You may rightly call them either cutaceous Muscles, or a Musculous skin.

cu'taneal, *a.* [f. as next + -AL[1].] = CUTANEOUS.

1650 GENTILIS *Consid.* 210 Cutaneall diseases. **1882** in *Syd. Soc. Lex.*

† **cu'tanean**, *a. Obs. rare.* [f. as CUTANEOUS + -AN.] = CUTANEOUS.

1601 HOLLAND *Pliny* II. 268 Spots and pimples arising vpon the skin.. cutanean specks and blemishes. *Ibid.* II. 529 To represse shingles & such cutanean wild-fires.

cutaneo- (kjuːˈteɪniːəʊ), combining form of next.

1885 LANDOIS & STERLING *Hum. Physiol.* II. 611 In the crocodile the glands open under the margins of the cutaneo-osseous scales.

cutaneous (kjuːˈteɪnɪəs), *a.* Also 7 -ious. [f. mod. or med.L. *cutāne-us* (f. *cut-is* the skin) + -OUS. Cf. F. *cutané* (1721 in Hatzf.).] Of, pertaining to, or affecting, the cutis or skin.

1578 BANISTER *Hist. Man* VIII. 110 The cutaneous distribution of nerues. **1683** ROBINSON in *Ray's Corr.* (1848) 137 In cutaneous diseases. **1744** BERKELEY *Siris* §4 Cutaneous eruptions and ulcers. **1845** DARWIN *Voy. Nat.* v. 97 These reptiles possess great powers of cutaneous absorption.

b. *fig.* = External, superficial.

1742 YOUNG *Nt. Th.* VIII. 455 All the distinctions of this little life Are quite cutaneous, foreign to the man. **1853** READE *Chr. Johnstone* i. (1853) 15 Cutaneous disorders, such as love.

† **cutany**, *a. Obs.* [a. F. *cutané.*] = prec.

1615 CROOKE *Body of Man* 851 The cutany veynes or veynes of the skinne. **1727** A. HAMILTON *New Acc. E. Ind.* I. v. 41 It appears between the Cutany and outward Skin.

'cut-away, *a.* (*sb.*) [f. CUT *pa. pple.* + AWAY.]

1. a. Of a coat: Having the skirt cut back from the waist in a slope or curve, as contrasted with a frock-coat.

1841 J. T. HEWLETT *Parish Clerk* II. 251 From the pocket of his clerical cut-away coat. **1869** E. A. PARKES *Pract. Hygiene* (ed. 3) 414 The tunic.. a great improvement over the old cut-away coatee.

b. *ellipt.* as *sb.* A cut-away coat.

1849 *Theatr. Programme* 23 July 58 A nondescript coat something between a Newmarket 'cut-away' and a shooting jacket. **1857** HUGHES *Tom Brown* I. vi, A fifth-form boy, clad in a green cut-away, with brass buttons and cord trousers. **1887** *Edin Rev.* Oct. 334 A frock coat or even a 'cutaway' may be worn.

2. Applied to a model or drawing of a piece of apparatus, etc., in which part is cut away so as to reveal the interior.

1946 W. L. BEAUCHAMP et al. *Everyday Problems in Science* 653 (*caption*) A cutaway view of the clutch and the transmission gears of an automobile. **1959** *Motor Man.* (ed. 36) v. 110 This cutaway drawing.. shows the internal construction of the Hydrosteer control valve unit.

3. *Cinemat.* As *sb.*, the process of making a quick transition to another scene. (Cf. CUT *v.* 21 e.) Also *attrib.*

1951 G. H. SEWELL *Amat. Film-Making* (ed. 2) x. 100 Between the items of a procession you cut away to various shots of the spectators in the crowd... When you are taking the original scenes you must remember to take some cut-away material as well. **1953** REISZ *Technique Film Editing* i. 26 The suspense.. achieved by devices like the quick cut-away to shot 37. **1962** *Listener* 15 Mar. 486/3 We had to have cut-aways to the [television] camera operators laughing just to show they thought the item funny too. **1970** *New Yorker* 19 Sept. 103/1 In a cutaway shot so placed that it pierces your heart, the old man's eyes glitter.

'cut-back, cutback, *sb.* [f. CUT *v.* 53.]

1. *Hort.* A plant which has been pruned by cutting off shoots close back to the main stem.

1897 *Garden* 21 Aug. 141 The 'cutbacks' [*sc.* young vines] planted in March. **1920** *19th Cent.* July 173 Too often they [*sc.* roseries] consist of little more than serried rows of 'cutbacks'. **1966** *Gloss. Landscape Work* (B.S.I.) IV. 19 *Cut back,* a tree or shrub which has been cut back to induce strong growth and subsequently grown on for one or more years.

2. *Cinemat.* A scene which is a return to a previous action.

1913 E. W. SARGENT *Technique Photoplay* (ed. 2) 90 Originally the cut-back was used to close up a gap in the action, to obviate the actual showing of a crime [etc.]. **1916** *Ibid.* (ed. 3) 360 *Cut-back,* one or more returns to a previous action, either to avoid the showing of prohibited action, to raise the effect through contrast or to quicken the action. **1927** *Sunday Times* 27 Feb. 6/4 In the last ten minutes a 'cut-back' occurs, and the quarrel and killing are reconstructed. *Ibid.* 15 May 10/5 The discovery of the 'close-up' and the 'cut-back' has always been accredited to Griffith.

3. A conglomerate product, as bitumen that has been thinned by the addition of lighter oils.

1936 *Jrnl. R. Aeronaut. Soc* XL. 547 A layer of sound deadening cement (a conglomerate of asphaltum, lead oxide, cork and rubber, called 'cut back' by the automobile trade). **1940** *Chambers's Techn. Dict.* 218/1 *Cut backs,* blends of asphaltic bitumen with various solvents, for use at comparatively low temperatures for road surfacing.

4. A reduction in expenditure, production, etc. orig. *U.S.*

1943 *Iron Age* 6 May 152 More than 90 per cent of prime contractors holding Army ordnance contracts are now operating.. below capacity because of recent cut-backs in ordnance contracts. **1952** *Manch. Guardian Weekly* 10 Jan. 3 How to get more raw materials to Britain without causing such cutbacks in American civilian production. **1957** *Economist* 28 Sept. 1009/1 The swingeing cutbacks recently inflicted on China's economic plan. **1965** *New Statesman* 30 Apr. 673/2 Even if the 20 per cent cutback some have forecast did actually take place in their sector, this would probably mean a loss of not much more than 15,000 houses.

5. *Surfing.* The turning of the surf-board back towards the wave. Cf. CUT *v.* 53 e.

1965 J. POLLARD *Surfrider* ii. 19 Swing back into the wave while riding it and you do a 'cut-back'. **1970** *Surf* I. x. 9/2 Will also ease up tail pressure in turns and cutbacks.

cutch[1] (kʌtʃ). [ad. Malay *kachu* (Canarese *kāchu, kācchu*) catechu. The name occurs in Portuguese authors of 16th c. as *cacho,* and in 17–18th c. Eng. writers as *cacha, cotch.* See CATECHU.] The commercial name of the catechu obtained from *Acacia Catechu,* used in tanning, etc.

[**1617** COCKS *Diary* (1883) I. 294 (Y.), 7 hhds. drugs cacha; 5 hampers pochok.] **1759** in *Oriental Repert.* I. 109 (Y.) Hortal and Cotch, Earth-oil, and Wood-oil. **1805** HATCHETT in *Phil. Trans.* XCV. 288 Twenty grains of the common cutch or catechu. **1865** J. G. BERTRAM *Harvest of Sea* (1873) 179 Boilers bubble with the brown *catechu,* locally called 'cutch', used as a preservative for the nets and sails.

b. *attrib.*, as ***cutch tree***.

1888 *Times* 22 Oct. 13/5 The *Acacia catechu,* or cutch tree, is found in large forests.. The wood is chipped, boiled, and the cutch thus extracted.

cutch[2] (kʌtʃ). *Gold-beating.* [app. ad. F. *caucher* in same sense, f. *caucher* to press down, *orig.* to tread:—L. *calcāre.*] A pile of vellum (or parchment paper) leaves, between which laminæ of gold-leaf are placed to be beaten.

1879 *Cassell's Techn. Educ.* IV. 172/1.

cutch, var. of COUCH *sb.*[2] (*Triticum repens*).

‖**cutcha** (ˈkʌtʃə), *a.* (*sb.*) *Anglo-Indian colloq.* Also **kacha, kutcha.** [a. Hindī *kachchā* raw, crude, unripe, uncooked.] Imperfect, slight, temporary, makeshift (opp. to *pucka,* solid, substantial, permanent, etc.). As *sb.* = Sun-dried brick, dried mud, as a material.

1834 *Baboo* I. xi. 181 (Stanf.) An old low bungalow, of kutcha, or mud-work. **1861** *Daily Tel.* 7 Oct., They [targets] were constructed of kutcha, or sun-dried bricks, a material as hard as stone. **1863** LD. ELGIN *Lett. & Jrnls.* (1872) 432 (Y.) Where they cannot get a *pucka* railway they take a *kutcha* one instead. **1886** YULE & BURNELL *Anglo-Indian Gloss.* s.v., A *cutcha* brick is a sundried brick. A *pucka* brick is a properly kiln-burnt brick.. A *cutcha* appointment is acting or temporary. A *pucka* appointment is permanent. **1920** *Blackw. Mag.* Oct. 921/1 My friend transported me over three extra miles of 'kacha' road. **1975** *Bangladesh Times* 20 July 2/5 A good number of kacha houses were damaged.

cutchenele, -ineale, -aneale, etc.: obs. forms of COCHINEAL.

cutcher (in *Paper-making*) = COUCHER[3].

‖**cutcherry** (kəˈtʃɛrɪ), **cutchery** (ˈkʌtʃərɪ). *Anglo-Indian.* Also 7 cichery, queshery, 8 cutcheree, -ie, kuchurry, 8–9 **kutchery**, 9 kutcheri, kucheree, 20 kach(ch)eri. [a. Hindī *kachahri, kacherī,* hall or chamber of audience, hence, court for administration of business, office, town-house. The first pronunciation above is used in Northern India, the second at Madras.]

1. An office of administration, a court-house. Also the business office of an indigo-planter, etc.

1610 HAWKINS in Purchas *Pilgrims* (1625) I. 439 (Y.) The Cichery or Court of Rolls, where the King's Viseer sits every morning some three houres. **1698** FRYER *Acc. E. India & P.* 261 (Y.) The Royal Exchange or Queshery. **1763** VERELST in *Phil. Trans.* LIII. 266 The great Cutcherry there, with brick walls. **1818** JAS. MILL *Brit. India* II. IV. i. 9 The [broker].. fixes upon a habitation, which he calls his cutchery. **1848** THACKERAY *Van. Fair* lvii, The prodigious labours of cutcherry. **1903** *Oxf. Mag.* 11 Feb. 208/1 The Kachcheri.. is the centre of official life in the province. **1926** *United Free Ch. Miss. Rec.* Sept. 391/2, I can't have the Kacheri turned into a pawnshop.

attrib. **1771** *Gentl. Mag.* XLI. 403 We had 100 people employed upon the Cutcherry List. **1913** L. WOOLF *Village in Jungle* vii. 179 He was standing..frightened, on the Kachcheri verandah.

†**2.** A division or brigade of infantry. *Obs.*

1799 HARRIS in Owen *Wellesley's Desp.* 119 A cutcherie or Brigade of Infantry was pushed forward.

cutcherry, obs. var. KEDGEREE (*Anglo-Ind.*).

cutchion, abbreviated form of ESCUTCHEON.

1632 LITHGOW *Trav.* x. (1682) 477 Whose Cutchions cleave so fast to Top and side, Portends to me, his Arms shall ever bide.

cutchy, var. of COACHEE, COACHY, coachman.

1602 *2nd Pt. Return fr. Parnass.* III. iv. (Arb.) 44 Or Ile dismount thee [Phœbus] from thy radiant coach, And make thee a poore Cutchy here on earth.

cute (kjuːt), *a. colloq.* Also 'cute. [Aphetic form of ACUTE *a.* 7.]

1. Acute, clever, keen-witted, sharp, shrewd.

1731 BAILEY vol. II, *Cute*, sharp, quick-witted. **1756** TOLDERVY *Two Orphans* II. 39 'You may think as you please,' said parson Drill; 'but I take him to be a very cute one'. **1777** in MAD. D'ARBLAY *Early Diary* (1889) II. 279, I didn't pity the man for having such a cute answer made him. **1840** DICKENS *Barn. Rudge* (1849) 26/1 'He will be a 'cute man yet', resumed the locksmith. **1848** LOWELL *Biglow P.* Poems 1890 II. 47 Aint it cute to see a Yankee Take sech everlastin' pains [etc.]?

2. (orig. *U.S. colloq.* and *School-boy slang.*) Used of things in same way as CUNNING *a.* 6. Now in general colloq. use, applied to people as well as things, with the sense 'attractive, pretty, charming'; also, 'attractive in a mannered way'.

1834 C. A. DAVIS *Lett. J. Downing* 214 I'm goin' to show you about as cute a thing as you've seen in many a day. **1857** 'PORTE CRAYON' *Virginia Illustr.* ii. 166 'What cute little socks!' said the woman. **1868** G. E. HUGHES in T. Hughes *Mem. Brother* (1873) 155 His study is awfully 'cute (= 'tidy and full of knick-knacks'). **1879** F. R. STOCKTON *Rudder Grange* vi. 61 [The flat] was so cute, so complete. **1880** A. A. HAYES *New Colorado* (1881) vii. 97 The way that Smart Aleck hollered when we swung round some of them 'cute' curves. **1900** *Daily News* 15 Nov. 6/5 A small and compact wooden house, what the Americans would call 'cute'. **1908** *Daily Chron.* 21 Apr. 3/3 American visitors who are used to wide rectangular streets are delightfully bewildered when I take them through sinuous byeways and tortuous alleys. They proclaim it 'just too cute and lovely'. **1941** A. HUXLEY *Grey Eminence* ii. 18 The tiny boy..looking almost indecently 'cute' in his claret-coloured doublet and starched ruff. **1945** —— *Time must have Stop* vii. 77 A French accent so strong, so indecently 'cute', so reminiscent of the naughty-naughty twitterings of a Parisian miss on the English musical comedy stage. **1960** P. MORTIMER *Sat. Lunch with Brownings* 92 She's ever so cute—blue eyes. **1966** *Amer. Speech* XLI. 285 The style also gets cute at times, as when he writes that such adjectives as *washable* and *non-shrinkable* are 'among the most..not-to-be-got-along-withoutable adjectives'.

†**cute**, *sb. Obs. rare*$^{-1}$. A cur.

1622 DRAYTON *Poly-olb.* xxiii. 340 Forc'd by some yelping cute to give the greyhounds view. [*Margin* A curre.]

cute, variant of CUIT *Obs.*, boiled wine, etc.

cute, obs. or Sc. form of COOT.

cuteler, -ellar, -ellerie, obs. ff. CUTLER, -ERY.

cutely ('kjuːtlɪ), *adv. colloq.* Also 'cutely. [Aphetic f. ACUTELY: see CUTE *a.*] In a cute manner, acutely.

1762 FOOTE *Orator* I. Wks. 1796 I. 194, I did speechify once at a vestry..and came off cutely enough. **1864** *Louie's Last Term* (N.Y.) 79 So he pricked up his ears, and said cutely [etc.].

cuteness ('kjuːtnɪs). *colloq.* Also 'cuteness. [Aphetic f. ACUTENESS: see CUTE *a.*] The quality of being cute.

1768 GOLDSM. *Good-n. Man* II, Who could have thought so innocent a face could cover so much cuteness! **1807-8** W. IRVING *Salmag.* iv. (1860) 88 All that quaintness, cuteness, and clumsiness, for which he is remarkable. **1845** *Knickerbocker* Aug. (Bartlett), He had a pair of bright, twinkling eyes, that gave an air of extreme cuteness to his physiognomy. **1872** H. M STANLEY *How I found Livingstone* xii. 464 Very fine people and singularly remarkable for commercial "cuteness' and sagacity. **1903** *Booklovers Mag.* Dec. (Advt.), The illustration gives but a faint idea of the beauty and cuteness of the calendar itself.

cut-grass. [f. CUT *v.* 65: *lit.* 'grass that cuts'.] A genus of grasses, *Leersia*, esp. the species *L. oryzoides*, the range of which extends as far north as the south of England.

1840 BIGELOW *Flora* (Bartlett *Dict. Amer.*), *Cut-grass*..a species of grass, with leaves exceedingly rough backward, so as to cut the hands if drawn across them. **1849** BROMFIELD in *Phytologist* III. 683 Cut-grass..[is] remarkable for.. extreme asperity, which even makes some precaution requisite to avoid cutting the hand, an accident that is said to befal the women employed in weeding it out of the rice-fields in Lombardy.

cuth, var. of COOTH, coal-fish; obs. pa. t. and pple. of CAN: see also COUTH.

Cuthbert[1] ('kʌθbət). The apostle of Northumbria. Hence

1. (St.) Cuthbert's beads. A popular name, originating on Holy Island and the Northumbrian coast, for the detached and perforated joints of encrinites there found. Cf. Scott, *Marmion* II. xvi,

St. Cuthbert sits, and toils to frame
The sea-born beads that bear his name.

1697 *Phil. Trans.* XXVII. 467 The same place afforded also some variety of Fossil Shells, and plenty of Cuthbert's Beads. **1792** *Gentl. Mag.* LXII. I. 130 St. Cuthbert's beads ..are a species of *entrochi* picked up among the rocks [of Lindisfarne] by the children, who sell them to travellers. **1831** J. HODGSON in J. Raine *Mem.* (1858) II. 222.

2. (St.) Cuthbert's duck. Also **Cuthbert duck.** The eider duck, which breeds on the Farn Islands, and figures in the legend of St. Cuthbert.

[*c* **1165** REGINALDUS *Libellus*, etc. (Surtees 1835) 62 Aves illæ Beati Cuthberti specialiter nominantur.] **1674** RAY *Coll. Words, Water Fowl* 96 The Cuthbert-Duck: *Anas S. Cuthberti*, building only on the Farn Islands upon the Coast of Northumberland. **1845** YARRELL *Brit. Birds* (ed. 2) III. 300 The Eider Duck is also called St. Cuthbert's Duck. **1849** EYRE *St. Cuthbert* 44 n., The eider or Cuthbert duck arrives at its full growth at the fourth year.

Hence † **Cuthbert down**, eider-down.

1397 *Status Officij Feretrarij* (Soc. Antiq. MS.), Item ij parva pulvinaria quorum j est de Cuthbert doun.

Cuthbert[2]. A slang name for a man who deliberately avoids military service; esp. in the war of 1914–18, one who did so by securing a post in a Government office or the Civil Service; a conscientious objector.

1917 *Evening News* 25 Jan. [in a cartoon by 'Poy']. **1919** *Mr. Punch's Hist. Gt. War* 225 As a set-off to the anti-'Cuthbert' campaign in the Press the War Cabinet has ..declared that 'the whole Empire owes the Civil Service a lasting debt of gratitude'. **1933** J. CARY *Amer. Visitor* xvi. 182 All you Cuthberts are fit for is to dodge responsibility at the cost of other people's lives. **1935** A. J. CRONIN *Stars look Down* II. xii. 372 Not good enough for you, eh? Not fancy enough for Cuthbert?

cuthe, early form of KYTHE.

cuticle ('kjuːtɪk(ə)l). Also 7 -cule. [ad. L. *cutīcula*, dim. of *cutis* the skin. Boyle has *cuticule* (quot. 1685 below), which is the form in Fr.]

1. a. The EPIDERMIS or scarf-skin of the body.

1615 CROOKE *Body of Man* 61 The Scarfe-skin or Cuticle being voide of sense itselfe. *Ibid.* 70 The Cuticle, which the Greekes call Epidermis, because it runnes vppon the surface of the true skinne. **1685** BOYLE *Enq. Notion Nat.* 200 The Cuticule or Scarf-skin. **1704** F. FULLER *Med. Gymn.* (1711) 37 Let us consider how we can separate the Cuticle from the true Cutis. **1836** TODD *Cycl. Anat.* I. 102/2 The cuticle of these animals [i.e. amphibia] is frequently shed.

b. Applied to other superficial skins or integuments; *e.g.* the transparent membrane which envelopes annelids.

1661 LOVELL *Hist. Anim. & Min.* Introd., Under it [the tongue of serpents] is a cuticle, which like a vesicle covereth the teeth. **1872** HUXLEY *Phys.* xii. 278 The shaft of a hair of the head consists of a central pith..of a cortical substance surrounding this..and of an outer cuticle. **1888** ROLLESTON & JACKSON *Anim. Life* 198 The cuticle [of the earthworm] is thin, transparent, and variable in thickness in different regions of the body.

c. The cell-wall of Infusoria.

d. The dead skin at the base of a finger-nail or toe-nail. Also *attrib.*

1907 *Yesterday's Shopping* (1969) 538/1 Cuticle knife, ivory handle. *Ibid.* 538/2 Cuticle scissors... Cuticle cream for softening the skin at base of nail. **1919** *Ladies' Home Jrnl.* Jan. 67/2 Cutex, the Cuticle Remover, comes in 35c, 65c and $1.25 bottles. **1962** *Woman* 1 Dec. 9/2 Every night, take care of your cuticles. *Ibid.*, Apply cuticle cream. **1966** *Vogue* Nov. 61/2 Everything needed for a manicure..cuticle remover, orange stick, emery board.

2. *Bot.* Formerly, the primary integumentary tissue or epidermis; now, a superficial film formed of the cutinized outer layers of the superficial walls of the epidermal cells.

The later usage was introduced by Ad. Brongniart (*Ann. des Sci. Nat.*, Ser. 2, I. 65). It appears in Eng. in Henfrey's transl. of von Mohl's *Vegetable Cell* 1852, p. 34.

1671 GREW *Anat. Plants* I. ii. §2 That extreme thin Cuticle which is spread over the Lobes of the Seed. **1807** J. E. SMITH *Phys. Bot.* 19 The cuticle is formed so as to accommodate itself..to the natural growth of the plant. **1858** CARPENTER *Veg. Phys.* §1 The presence of a kind of skin or cuticle, which envelops the whole. **1884** BOWER & SCOTT *De Bary's Phaner.* 29 Epidermis, outer skin, is the name given to the layer of cells which is covered by and produces the cuticle.

†**3.** *transf.* 'A thin skin formed on the surface of any liquor' (J.); a film or thin coating.

1657 G. STARKEY *Helmont's Vind.* 314 This [salt] being boyled to a Cuticle will shoot like to any other Salt. **1664** POWER *Exp. Philos.* I. 34 Without breaking thorow the tender cuticle and film of so brittle and thin a substance [an air-bubble]. **1704** NEWTON *Optics* (J.), When any saline liquor is evaporated to cuticle, and let cool, the salt concretes in regular figures.

‖**cuticula** (kjuːˈtɪkjʊlə). [L.: see prec.]

1. = CUTICLE 1, 2; now *esp.* of certain lower organisms.

1621 BURTON *Anat. Mel.* I. i. II. iii, The skinne couers the rest, and hath Cuticulam or a little skinne vnder it. **1718** J. CHAMBERLAYNE *Relig. Philos.* (1730) I. iv. §14 The Cuticula, or upper Skin. **1880** HUXLEY *Crayfish* iv. 175 The tough, outer coat, which has been termed the *cuticula*.

†**2.** = CUTICLE 3. *Obs.*

1662 R. MATHEW *Unl. Alch.* §113. 184 Let it vapor away til thou see it covered wit a Cutecula, or thin scum.

cuticular (kjuːˈtɪkjʊlə(r)), *a.* [f. CUTICULA + -AR. Cf. F. *cuticulaire.*] Of or pertaining to a cuticle; of the nature of, or resembling, cuticle.

1578 BANISTER *Hist. Man* VII. 94 The cuticular construction of the auricle. **1677** PLOT *Oxfordsh.* 39 Much used in cuticular Diseases. **1708** J. KEILL *Anim. Secretion* 74 The Orifices of..the cuticular Glands. **1830** LINDLEY *Nat. Syst. Bot.* 1 The presence of flowers..and of cuticular stomata. **1880** HUXLEY *Crayfish* i. 33 The cuticular skeleton of the crayfish.

cu,ticulari'zation. [f. next + -ATION.] The action or process of forming into cuticle.

1875 BENNETT & DYER tr. *Sachs' Bot.* 209 The cuticularisation of the outer layers never advances far inwards, the cuticle generally remaining thin. **1881** *Jrnl. Microsc. Sc.* 25 The cuticularisation of the walls of the bundle sheath.

cuticularize (kjuːˈtɪkjʊləraɪz), *v.* [f. CUTICULAR + -IZE.] *trans.* To make cuticular; to form into cuticle. Hence **cu'ticularized** *ppl. a.*

1875 BENNETT & DYER tr. *Sachs' Bot.* 34 The cuticularised layer becomes actually separated from the non-cuticularised shell. **1881** *Jrnl. Microsc. Sc.* Jan. 20 An epidermal layer with cuticularised outer walls.

cutie ('kjuːtɪ). *slang* (orig. *U.S.*). Also **cutey.** [f. CUTE *a.* + -IE.] A cute person; esp. an attractive young woman. (In quot. 1768 the sense is 'a superficially clever person'.)

1768 in A. Hare *Georgian Theatre in Wessex* (1958) iv. 72 Let shallow Cuties, who, in Love with Sound, Care not a Pin if Action's never found. **1917** D. G. PHILLIPS *S. Lenox* II. viii. 204 It was the bartender. 'Evening, cutie,' he said. 'What'll you have?' 'Some rye whiskey,' replied Susan. **1923** R. D. PAINE *Comr. Rolling Ocean* viii. 130 Her friends thought she was a cutey for turning the trick. **1927** 'J. BARBICAN' *Confess. Rum-Runner* xiv. 149 He goes about with a high-stepping cutie who's ace-high on the face and figure. **1927** *Daily Express* 5 Dec. 13 His sweetheart, a 'cabaret cutie'. **1945** W. PLOMER *Dorking Thigh* 20 Just like a young cutie Between the wars.

cutification (kjuːtɪfɪˈkeɪʃən). [n. of action from CUTIFY: see -FICATION.] Formation of cutis or skin; also transplantation of cuticle for the promotion of cicatrization (*Syd. Soc. Lex.*).

1878 T. BRYANT *Pract. Surg.* I. 47 Bands of skin..which, during recovery, will become the centres of cutification.

cutify ('kjuːtɪfaɪ), *v.* [f. L. type **cutificāre*, f. *cutis* skin: see -FY.] *intr.* To form skin.

1890 in *Cent. Dict.*

cutigeral (kjuːˈtɪdʒərəl), *a.* [f. L. type **cutiger* (f. *-ger* bearing) + -AL[1].] Carrying or bearing skin.

1882 *Syd. Soc. Lex.*, *Cutigeral cavity*, a circular depression in the upper border of the hoof of the horse, into which the coronary cushion is received.

cutikin ('kʏtɪkɪn). *Sc.* Also **cuttikin, cuittikin, cuitican.** [f. *cuit, cute*, COOT[2], ancle, with dim. suffix.] A gaiter, a spatterdash.

1816 SCOTT *Antiq.* xi, As he exchanged his slippers for a pair of stout walking shoes, with *cutikins*, as he called them, of black cloth. **1833** MOIR *Mansie Wauch* vi. (1849) 32 A cuttikin of corduroy, deficient in the instep.

cutin ('kjuːtɪn). *Bot.* [f. CUT-IS + -IN.] The cellulose body forming the cuticle of plants, CUTOSE.

1863-72 WATTS *Dict. Chem.* II. 186. **1884** BOWER & SCOTT *De Bary's Phaner.* 74 Cutin..resists rotting far longer than cellulose.

cut-in, *sb.* [See CUT *v.* 55.]

1. An act of cutting in: in senses of the verb (seeCUT *v.* 55).

1883 *Referee* 17 June 7/4 (Farmer), I am anxious to have a cut in and get a big advertisement for nothing. **1898** *Westm. Gaz.* 21 June 9/2 Herminius himself, with all his weight, is likely to have a cut in for the same race. **1920** F. SCOTT FITZGERALD *This Side of Paradise* (1921) I. ii. 62 The cut-in system at dances. **1931** I. L. REEVES *Ol' Rum River* 182 Others within the organization will think they are entitled to a cut-in should the brewery attempt at any time to make anything other than near-beer. **1939** *Chatelaine* May 35/3 When I see a 'debbie' who never dances more than halfway round the ballroom without a cut-in, I make this mental note:..she'll soon be among the 'young marrieds'. **1953** *Time* 23 Feb., It was a world where..*cut-ins* (giving a performer a share of a song's profits)..were standing operating procedure. **1958** *Listener* 6 Nov. 731/1 He's still going to get to the petrol pump by a neat cut-in.

2. *Cinemat.* A 'leader' inserted into a film sequence. In full *cut-in leader.* Also, an interposed scene.

1913 E. W. SARGENT *Technique Photoplay* (ed. 2) ii. 15 All other leaders have been between scenes, but this is right in the middle, so it is known as a '*cut-in leader*', because it is cut into the scene. *Ibid.* vii. 50 The quoted leader is handy, but it should not be used too much, and there is a growing tendency to use two and even three cut-in leaders in one scene. A straight leader and one cut-in is about the limit. A leader or a cut-in, but not both should suffice. **1921** LESCARBOURA *Cinema Handbk.* 21 *Cut-in*, anything inserted in a scene which breaks its continuity. **1953** K. REISZ *Technique Film Editing* ii. 190 The cut-in of the crowd.. was necessary to indicate the passage of time while the horses file out of the paddock. **1961** G. MILLERSON *Telev. Production* 302 The cut-in provides shock treatment. A cut-in to a field of thistles would be a dynamic introduction to a programme on 'The Weed Menace'.

3. A device for starting an engine by completing the electric circuit.

1921 *Motor Electrical Man.* viii. 109 In some switch-boxes the automatic cut-in and cut-out for the charging circuit is fitted. **1924** A. W. JUDGE et al. *Mod. Motor Cars* III. 74 A more common form of cut-in is that depending upon electro-magnetic action. *Ibid.* 76 There are many other forms of electrical, thermostatic, and mechanical 'cut-out' and 'cut-in' devices for the battery-dynamo and battery-ignition circuits.

'cutinize, *v.* [f. CUTIN + -IZE.] = CUTICULARIZE. Hence **cutini'zation**.

1890 in *Cent. Dict.*

‖**cutis** ('kju:tɪs). [L. = the skin.]

1. *Anat.* The true skin or derma of the body, underlying the epidermis or cuticle.

1603 B. JONSON *Sejanus* II. i, And then prepare a bath To cleanse and clear the cutis. **1623** MASSINGER *Bondman* IV. iv, Your ten-crown amber possets, good to smooth The cutis, as you call it. **1748** HARTLEY *Observ. Man* I. ii. 117 The thinness of the Cutis, and the Softness and thinness of the Cuticle. **1878** T. BRYANT *Pract. Surg.* I. 119 A tubercle in its early stage feels to the finger like a foreign body introduced into the cutis.

2. *Bot.* The peridium of certain fungi.

cuti'sector. [f. L. *cuti-s* skin + *sector* a cutter.] A knife used in making thin sections for microscopy.

1874 in KNIGHT *Dict. Mech.*

cutitis (kju:'taɪtɪs). *Path.* [f. CUT-IS + -ITIS.] Inflammation of the skin.

1857 in DUNGLISON *Dict. Med. Science.*

cutization. [f. L. *cutis* skin + -IZE + -ATION.] 'The alteration of structure, drying, thickening, and hardening, which takes place in a mucous membrane, when exposed to the air and to friction' (*Syd. Soc. Lex.* 1882).

cutlass ('kʌtləs), *sb.* Forms: 6 coutelace, 7 coutelas, cuttelas, cuttleass, 8 cutlace, 7- cutlass. Also *corruptly* β. 7 cutleax, cuttleaxe, cotellax; γ. 8- cutlash. [a. F. *coutelas*, augm. of *couteau* (*coutel*) knife; cognate with It. *coltellaccio*: Lat. type **cultellāceum*. The original *coutel-as*, *coutel-ace*, has undergone many perversions in English under the influence of popular etymology, which has transformed the first part into *cuttle*, *curtal*, *curtle*, *curt*, *cut*, and the second into *ax*, *axe*. A later change has made *cutlass* into *cut-lash*. The forms *cuttle-ax* and *cut-lash* are included here; see CURTELACE, CURTAL-AXE, CURT-AXE, in their alphabetical places.]

1. A short sword with a flat wide slightly curved blade, adapted more for cutting than for thrusting; now *esp.* the sword with which sailors are armed.

α. **1594** KYD *Cornelio* I. in Hazl. *Dodsley* V. 189 Arm'd with his blood-besmeared keen coute-lace. **1603** KNOLLES *Hist. Turks* (1621) 1333 A Cuttelas verie curiously wrought, and inricht with stone. **1633** T. JAMES *Voy.* 67 The boyes with Cuttleasses, must cut boughes. **1678** tr. *Gaya's Arms of War* 32 A kind of Cutlass, which they called Cinacis, and in English Cimeter. **1719** DE FOE *Crusoe* (1840) I. xvii. 300 A great cutlass (as the seamen call it) or sword. **1825** WATERTON *Wand. S. Amer.* I. i. 92 With a cutlass to sever the small bush-ropes. **1868** *Regul. & Ord. Army* ¶ 1299 The sailors armed with cutlasses are to proceed to the hatchways.

β. [**1598** FLORIO, *Coltellaccio*, a curtelax or chopping knife.] **1611** —— A cutleax, a hanger. Also a chopping knife, a great knife. **1630** J. TAYLOR (Water-P.) *Laugh & be fat* Wks. II. 79/1 The bloudy cutthroat cuttleaxe of swaggering Mars. **1647** N. BACON *Disc. Govt. Eng.* I. lxxi. (1739) 194 Either a Cotellax, or such-like Weapon.

γ. **1704** *Collect. Voy.* (Church.) III. 779/1 Men arm'd with Cutlashes. **1725** POPE *Odyss.* XIV. 87 Of two, his cutlash launch'd the spouting blood. **1757** SMOLLETT *Reprisals* II. viii, A good cutlash in my hand. **1867** SMYTH *Sailor's Word-bk.*, *Cutlas*.. the small-handed swords supplied to the navy, the *cutlash* of Jack.

2. *Comb.*, *cutlass-blade*, etc.; *cutlass-proof* adj.; **cutlass-fish**, a name of a species of fish, the Silvery hair-tail, so called from its shape.

1711 E. WARD *Quix.* I. 26 That he conceiv'd 'twas Cutlace proof. **1827** O. W. ROBERTS *Centr. Amer.* 300 The Indians constantly require.. moscheates, or cutlass blades. **1884** G. B. GOODE *Nat. Hist. Aquatic Anim.* 335 The name 'Cutlass-fish', which is current for the same species [sc. *Trichiurus lepturus*] in the British West Indies. **1963** P. H. GREENWOOD *Norman's Hist. Fishes* (ed. 2) ii. 14 At the other extreme are fishes with long bodies, which may be.. very much compressed, as in the ..Cutlass-fishes.

Hence **'cutlass** *v. nonce-wd.*, to hew with a cutlass; **'cutlassed** *ppl. a.*, furnished with cutlasses.

1890 *Harper's Mag.* Feb. 413/1 He will cutlass his way through forest to the summit of peaks to find particular herbs. **1839** *Morn. Herald* 11 July, The nucleus of a cutlassed gendarmerie.

cutle, obs. form of CUITTLE.

cutler ('kʌtlə(r)). Forms: 5 coteler(e, cotteler, cut(t)eller, (cultelere), 5-6 cuteler, 6 cotelar, cuttelar, cutellar, cutlar, 5- cutler. [a. F. *coutelier*:—L. type *cultellāri-us*, f. *cultellus*, OF. *coutel* knife.] One who makes, deals in, or repairs knives and similar cutting utensils.

c **1400** *Beryn* 2297 The Cotelere.. that made the same knyff. *c* **1430** LYDG. *Hors Shepe & G.* 130 Dagars wrought by the cutlers. **1538** LELAND *Itin.* V. 108 Ther be many Smithes and Cuttelars in Halamshire. **1592** GREENE *3rd Pt. Conny-catch.* 23 One.. came vnto a poore Cutler to haue a Cuttle made. **1647** CLARENDON *Hist. Reb.* I. §53 An ordinary knife, which he bought of a common cutler for a shilling. **1723** *Lond. Gaz.* 6196/9 Edward Birch, late of Birmingham .. Short-Cutler. **1884** *Harper's Mag.* June 81/2 Technically [at Sheffield] the cutler is the man who puts the knife together.

Hence **'cutleress**, **'cutler-woman**, a female cutler.

c **1765** FLLOYD *Tartarian T.* (1785) 48/1 The cutleress was ready to die. *Ibid.* 45/1 The sequins the cutler-woman promised me.

cutlery ('kʌtlərɪ). In 5 cutellerie. [a. OF. *coutelerie* (mod.F. *coutellerie*) cutler's art, cutlery, f. *coutelier* CUTLER: see -ERY.]

a. The art or trade of the cutler. b. *collect.* Articles made or sold by cutlers, as knives, scissors, etc. Also *attrib.*

c **1449** PECOCK *Repr.* I. x. 50 As thou3 therfore sporiorie and cutellerie entermeeneden and enterfereden with gold smyth craft.. The al hool craft of cutleri. **1624** in *Harper's Mag.* (1884) June 72/2 The makers of knives, sickles, shears, scissors, and other cutlery wares. **1792** A. YOUNG *Trav. France* 49 There is a considerable cutlery manufacture. **1846** MᶜCULLOCH *Acc. Brit. Empire* (1854) I. 599 The manufacture of hardware and cutlery at Birmingham, Sheffield, &c.

cutlet ('kʌtlɪt). Also 8 costelet(te, (9 côtelette). [a. F. *côtelette* (formerly *costelette*, whence 18th c. Eng. form), double dim. of *coste*, *côte* (dim. *costele*) rib. The mod.Eng. spelling suggests that it is a dim. of *cut*. In *menus* the French form is frequently used.] A small piece of meat, generally mutton or veal, in the former case usually cut off the ribs, *esp.* the smaller ones near the neck, used for broiling, frying, etc.

1706 PHILLIPS (ed. Kersey), *Cutlets*, a Term in Cookery, a dainty Dish made of the short Ribs of a Neck of Mutton. **1727** BRADLEY *Fam. Dict.* s.v. *Filets*, Another Way to order Slices of Veal or Cutlets. *a* **1734** NORTH *Lives* I. 95 He desired the company of some.. friends to join in a costelet and a sallad at Chattelin's. **1796** MRS. GLASSE *Cookery* v. 45 Take a leg of lamb, cut it in thin cutlets across the grain. **1886** G. ALLEN *Maimie's Sake* x, See that she.. has a nice cutlet and a glass of hock.

'cutling, *sb.*[1] [? f. CUT *v.*] A name applied to groats (husked oat-grains), or to coarse oatmeal.

1688 R. HOLME *Armoury* III. 317/1 Groats, or Cutlings (are) Oats husked. **1847-78** HALLIWELL, *Cutlins*, oatmeal grits. *North.* **1858** SIMMONDS *Dict. Trade*, *Cutlings*, a name for groats, bruised oat seeds freed of the pericarp, used for gruel, porridge, etc.

'cutling, *sb.*[2] *rare.* [f. CUT *sb.* + -LING] A small piece cut off.

1834 *Drakard's Stamford News* 4 Nov., Propagating apple trees.. by small cutlings.

'cutling ('kʌtlɪŋ), *vbl. sb. dial.* [f. as if from a verb *to cutle*; cf. also CUTTLE *sb.*[2], a knife.

The verb is in common use in south of Scotland in sense 'to grind or sharpen knives', etc., *e.g.* 'to send a razor to be cutled'.]

The business or occupation of a cutler, the making of cutlery. Also *attrib.*

1645 MILTON *Colast.* Wks. (1851) 357 That the men of Toledo.. were excellent at cutling. *c* **1765** FLLOYD *Tartarian T.* (1785) 42/2 Not satisfied with his cutling-trade alone. *a* **1804** MATHER *Songs* (1862) 66 (*Sheffield Gloss.*), When he wrought at cutling, mere twelves made him sick. **1839** in Bywater *Sheffield Dial.* (1877) 40 Cum all yo cutlin heroes.. All yo wot works at flat-backs.

cut-lips ('kʌtlɪps). [That which is distinguished by cut or abrupt lips.] The popular name of two American fishes: a. *Exoglossum maxilingua*; b. The hare-lipped Sucker, *Quassilabia lacera.*

1880 GÜNTHER *Fishes* 596 From the fresh waters of North America.. *Exoglossum* (the 'Stone Toter' or 'Cut-lips'.)

cut-off ('kʌt'ɒf, *attrib.* 'kʌtɒf), *sb.* [CUT *v.* 56.]

1. An act of cutting off or portion cut off.

1741 RICHARDSON *Pamela* II. 151 This, though, was a great Cut-off; a whole Week out of ten Days. **1954** J. SOUTHWARD *Mod. Printing* (ed. 7) II. xv. 212 Cut off is the amount [*sc.* of paper] severed from the webs to form individual copies of an edition.

2. a. A new and shorter passage cut by a river through a bend; sometimes also applied to the crescent-shaped lake formed by the remains of the old channel when cut off from the new by silting. Also, a lateral channel dug across a bend in a river (also *attrib.*). orig. *U.S.*

1773 *Acts Gen. Assembly Georgia* (1881) 300 To make any such cut off as shall be thought necessary from River to River. *Ibid.*, In such Cuts off and Clearing. **1817** S. R. BROWN *Western Gaz.* 222 It is about four miles across the several branches of the Pascagola.. intersected by bayous and cut-offs. **1830** LYELL *Princ. Geol.* I. 186 At one spot called the 'grand cut off', vessels now pass from one point to another in half a mile, to a distance which it formerly required twenty miles to reach. **1874** in N. H. Bishop *Voy. Paper Canoe* (1878) 223 If you take to the cut-offs, you may get into.. interior bayous, from which you will never emerge. **1913** THOMAS & WATT *Improvem. Rivers* (ed. 2) I. 27 When a bend has become almost a complete curve, the river breaks through the intervening neck of land and forms a cut-off. *Ibid.* II. 337 The entire river was dammed at or near the upper part of a sharp bend, and a cut-off or lateral canal was dug across the bend from the pool thus formed. *Ibid.* 367 Cut-off walls resting on the river-bed. **1937** WOOLDRIDGE & MORGAN *Physical Basis Geogr.* xii. 173 The abandoned loops form 'cut-offs', 'ox-bows' or 'mortlakes' which, in time, become silted up.

b. A piece of road or railway which cuts off or saves a bend; a short cut, cross-cut.

1806 Z. M. PIKE *Jrnl.* 28 Jan. in *Sources Mississ.* (1810) I. 64 Observed Mr. Grant's trackes going through it; found his mark of a cut off, (agreed on between us) took it, and proceeded very well. **1818** *Boston Weekly Messenger* 23 July (Th.), They pointed [it] out to him as being a nigh cut-off to the high road. **1881** *Chicago Times* 14 May, The Company is.. building a cut-off six miles in length near Omaha. **1908** *Westm. Gaz.* 31 Dec. 3/1 The Great Western's Ashendon to Aynho 'cut-off', which will provide that company with a new route to Birmingham, nineteen miles shorter than its existing one. **1924** W. M. RAINE *Troubled Waters* iii. 29 Evidently she was taking the cut-off back to the ranch, unaware that the bridge had been washed out by the freshet. **1947** J. STEINBECK *Wayward Bus* i. 6 Those who came over the cut-off from San Juan de la Cruz.

3. a. An interruption or stopping of a continuance or flow. Also *attrib.*

1881 T. STEVENSON in *Nature* XXIII. 560 Difficulty.. of effecting a sharp cut-off on a particular bearing. **1956** *Kenyon Rev.* XVIII. 417 Abrupt voice cutoff. **1966** M. A. K. HALLIDAY in C. E. Bazell *In Memory of J. R. Firth* 152 Lexis seems to require the recognition merely of linear co-occurrence together with some measure of significant proximity, either a scale or at least a cut-off point. **1970** *Globe & Mail* (Toronto) 25 Sept. B10/2 The cutoff day for commitments in the current quarter is Wednesday. **1971** *Times* 23 Jan. 18/1 It is used here as a cut-off point between the poor and the rest of the community.

b. *spec. Steam-engine.* An arrangement by which the admission of steam to the cylinder is cut off when the piston has travelled part of the stroke, so that the steam during the remainder of the stroke works expansively; a contrivance for effecting this purpose. Also *attrib.*

1849 FAIRBAIRN in *Mec. Mag.* LI. 258 The space between the cut-off valve and the working cylinder. **1850** *Pract. Mech. Jrnl.* III. 29 All the requirements of an accurate self-regulating cut-off. **1891** *Engineer* 18 Sept. LXII. 229 This valve gear has an unusually large range of cut-off.

c. Applied to various mechanical contrivances for stopping the flow of a liquid, cutting off or closing a connexion, and the like.

1874 KNIGHT *Dict. Mech.*, *Cut-off*.. 2. a valve or gate in a spout, to stop discharge.. 3. a device in a rain-water spout to send the falling water in either of two directions. **1886** *Pall Mall G.* 26 Mar. 12/1 Cut-off for hydraulic and other engines.

d. *fig.*

1859 SAXE *Poems, Early Rising* ii, Who first invented.. That artificial cut-off—Early Rising.

e. In a magazine rifle, a device which prevents the feeding of cartridges from the magazine into the chamber, and enables the rifle to be used as a single-loader.

1890 *Times* 6 Dec. 15/4 The cut-off is a strong and simple arrangement for bringing the magazine into action or for cutting it off. **1898** *Daily News* 9 May 3/1 Magazine Cut-off. **1904** *Westm. Gaz.* 9 Dec. 7/2 As the Navy considered that a cut-off was necessary this.. is fitted to all naval rifles. **1919** 'BOYD CABLE' *Old Contemptibles* ix. 141 In a twinkling every man.. had his rifle muzzle over the parapet, and his fingers busy with magazine and cut-off.

f. An automatic safety device for shutting off light, esp. the light of a cinema-projector.

1906 *Daily Chron.* 28 June 2/7 Automatic cut-off devices. **1917** C. N. BENNETT *Guide to Kinematography* ix. 146 Before the condenser.. is a safety device called the hand light cut-off. **1923** F. A. TALBOT *Moving Pictures* ix. 119 The 'cut-off', an automatic safety shutter, mounted between the lamp and the film, which falls to intercept the light when the machine is at rest.

g. Chiefly *Electr.* A marked increase in the attenuation (or decrease in the amplification) of an oscillation when its frequency reaches some value, esp. of an alternating current or voltage by a filter, waveguide, etc.; usu. *attrib.*, as *cut-off frequency*, *point.*

1926 FRANKLIN & TERMAN *Transmission Line Theory* v. 141 This frequency is called the cut-off frequency of the high-pass filter, for it marks the transition from pass to attenuated frequencies. **1930** *Bell System Techn. Jrnl.* IX. III. 483 The cutoff points are taken as those at which the attenuation reaches a value 10 db greater than that at 1,000 cycles. **1930** *Discovery* Dec. 398/2 The directional filter offers very little attenuation to frequencies on one side of a certain frequency (cut-off frequency). **1959** *Chambers's Encycl.* XII. 735/1 The capacitative reactance of the air chamber in front of the diaphragm tends to raise the frequency at which this occurs, but results in a much sharper cut off at still higher frequencies. **1970** D. F. SHAW *Introd. Electronics* (ed. 2) xii. 272 The current gain of a transistor falls off at high frequencies... This frequency dependence is expressed accurately by the expression $\alpha_f = \alpha_0/(1 + jf/f_\alpha)$ where..f_α is called the alpha cut-off frequency.

cut-off, ('kʌt'ɒf), *a.* [See CUT *v.* 56.] **1.** = CUT-AWAY.

1840 *Ann. Reg.* 8 Dressed in a cut-off green coat with brass buttons.

2. Shut out, excluded, remote (see CUT *v.* 56 h). Hence **cut-offness**, the state or condition of being cut off.

1894 M. DYAN *All in Man's Keeping* I. xii. 203 Would he never lose this cut-off feeling, this awful ache for comradeship? **1927** D. H. LAWRENCE *Let.* 3 Aug. (1962) II. 993 Our being cut off..is our ailment... I wish I saw a little clearer how you get over the cut-offness. **1939** J. CARY *Mr. Johnson* 92 The poorer, more cut-off people do not want roads. **1960** *Encounter* XV. 73 The cut-off-ness of the modern 'intellectual man' from the world.

cutose (kjuː'təʊs). *Chem.* [f. CUT-IS + -OSE.] One of the cellulose bodies: the hyaline substance which forms the cuticle or cuticular layers of plants. Also called *cutin*.

1881 WATTS *Dict. Chem.* VIII. 2097 *Cutose* constitutes the fine transparent membrane which covers the exposed parts of vegetables. **1885** *Athenæum* 7 Feb. 188/1 *Cutose*, the substance which covers and protects the aërial organs of plants.

cut-out (kʌt'aʊt, 'kʌtaʊt), *sb.* [CUT *v.* 57.]

1. a. *Electr. Engin.* A contrivance for automatically cutting lamps, motors, or other electrical appliances out of circuit, when the current supplied to them reaches a point at which it is undesirable to work.

One of the commonest kinds is a *fuse* or *fusible cut-out*, a short piece of metal in circuit which melts when the current attains an unsafe magnitude. There are also other kinds, mostly electro-magnetic in their form, which may be made to act with an increase, a decrease, or a change in direction of current. The name was formerly sometimes applied to a short-circuiting switch on a telegraph circuit.

1874 in KNIGHT *Dict. Mech.* **1887** SPONS *Househ. Management* (1887) 95 Cut-outs or safety valves, are essential to the security of a house. **1888** *Rules & Regul. Teleg. Eng. & Electricians* 23 All circuits should be protected with cut-outs. —— 24 Where fusible cut-outs are used, etc. **1893** *Verity & Sons' Compend.* 34 Automatic magnetic cut-out.

b. In an internal-combustion engine, a valve through which exhaust gases can escape without passing through the silencer.

1905 *Motor Cycle* 2 Jan. 6 An exhaust cut-out. **1906** *Daily Chron.* 17 July 3/3 Nothing is easier than to have a 'cut-out' in the exhaust pipe, worked by a wire from the steering column, and so produce this noise and eliminate the back pressure whenever you wish. **1907** *Public Opinion* 17 May 628/2 The attention of the Committee of the Royal Automobile Club has been called to the increase in the use of sirens and exhaust cut-outs by certain motorists. **1926** T. E. LAWRENCE *Seven Pillars* (1935) VIII. xciv. 521 The cars, with closed cut-out, would..carry the trenches by surprise.

2. a. The space formed by a piece or section being cut out (as of a floor). *U.S.*

1851 A. O. HALL *Manhattaner in New Orleans* v. 30 Above the bar and post-office (the former..looked down upon through a wide cut-out in the floor) are the..reading-rooms of the merchants.

b. A railway or canal cutting. *U.S.*

1898 *Engineering Mag.* XVI. 116/1 The dredge by which the cut-outs were excavated and embankments constructed.

c. A figure cut out (or designed for cutting out) of paper, cloth, cardboard, wood, etc.; *spec.* in *Theatr.* (see quot. 1961). Also *fig.*

1905 CALKINS & HOLDEN *Art of Mod. Advertising* 10 The grocer must be supplied with attractive counter slips, 'hangers', window-cards, 'cut-outs', posters and other forms of lithographed matter. **1920** E. G. LUTZ *Animated Cartoons* 84 This model, specifically spoken of as a 'cut-out', is pushed over the background under the camera and photographed. **1923** *Daily Mail* 1 Mar. 6 (Advt.), The famous Polly Pratt cut-outs for the kiddies. **1927** E. G. LUTZ *Motion-Pict. Cameraman* 169 A series of cut-outs for a continued action. **1927** *Daily Express* 27 Sept. 5/2 Cut-outs are all the rage—cut-outs in wood and in cardboard painted. **1927** *Ladies' Home Jrnl.* Dec. 68/3 It would be easy enough to adapt for the purpose the various animal cut-outs and illustrations. **1927** *Home Notes* 17 Dec. 863/2 Embroidered Appliqué and Making Directions Supplied with Each Cut-Out. **1949** *Here & Now* (N.Z.) Oct. 14/2 The stage size is the same every night—props are at a minimum, and such customary essentials as drapes..and cut-outs are eliminated. **1956** *Essays in Criticism* VI. 372 The character of Harcourt, which the author has simply left as a cardboard cut-out. **1959** J. MASTERS *Fandango Rock* 328 The upper row of the Moorish arches made the familiar pattern of cut-outs in brown-red paper against a backdrop of blue. **1961** BOWMAN & BALL *Theatre Lang.* 90 *Cut out, cut-out, cutout*, a small flat, usually of profile board, cut to simulate trees, rocks, etc... Hence *cut-out scenery*. **1971** B. CALLISON *Plague of Sailors* 15 The mountain was still a jet black two-dimensional cut-out.

3. a. An act of cutting out cattle from the herd. *U.S.*

1874 J. G. MCCOY *Cattle Trade* 81 In the beginning of the cut-out, a few gentle cows or working oxen are driven a short space from the round-up and held, to form a nucleus, to which those cut out gather. **1907** C. E. MULFORD *Bar-20* xi. 120 In this contest Hopalong Cassidy led his nearest rival, Red Connors,..by twenty cut-outs. **1920** —— *J. Nelson* xxiii. 254 Sam saw no use of collecting infants only to have them turned loose at the cut-out.

b. A place where cut-out animals are collected.

1920 J. M. HUNTER *Trail Drivers of Texas* 98 Our camp was the catch and cut-out for all the other horses.

c. The finish of shearing, end of shearing-time; completion of the shearing of a specified group of sheep (e.g. the rams) or of a particular flock, etc. *Austral.* and *N.Z.*

1900 H. LAWSON *Over Sliprails* 33 It was within a couple of days of cut-out, so I told Mitchell—who was shearing—that I'd camp up the Billabong and wait for him. **1922** C. G. TURNER *Happy Wanderer* 143 A 'cut-out'—the finishing of a line of sheep or of the shed itself. **1926** J. DEVANNY *Butcher Shop* vii. 73 Another two days would have seen the cut out. **1959** H. P. TRITTON *Time means Tucker* iv. 34/1 At the cut-out, when we were at the office getting our cheques.

4. A person acting as middle-man, esp. in espionage. *slang.*

1963 J. JOESTEN *They call it Intelligence* I. i. 44 A very important figure in espionage is the 'cutout'. This is a trusted middleman. **1966** M. R. D. FOOT *SOE in France* iv. 94 A cut-out..is a means of establishing contact between two agents which..affords the minimum for the enemy security services to bite on. One agent passes a message in a simple code to the cut-out... The cut-out holds the message till approached by the next agent down the line. **1969** E. AMBLER *Intercom Conspiracy* (1970) ii. 45 Through our cut-out I have made an offer for the shares.

cut-out, *a.* [See CUT *v.* 57 j and CUT *ppl. a.* 11.] Formed by cutting out a piece of paper, cloth, cardboard, etc.; of or pertaining to the piece cut out. Cf. CUT-OUT *sb.* 2 c.

1799 G. SMITH *Laboratory* I. 40 Behind the cut-out letters is pasted oil paper. **1873** *Young Englishwoman* Apr. 202/2 Make a deep flounce..and set this under the cut-out place. **1886** KIPLING *Plain Tales* (1888) 88 Mrs. Hauksbee was expecting some cut-out pattern things in flimsy paper. **1898** *Westm. Gaz.* 4 June 7/2 The slate-coloured cut-out frames, on which the prints are mounted. **1927** E. G. LUTZ *Motion-Pict. Cameraman* 162 Cut-out figures photographed in sequence. **1929** *Publishers' Circular* 22 June 73 Attractive cut-out figures, in full colours. **1970** *New York* III. 7 Dec. 61/2 The Tom Thumb finger-puppet theater with cut-out figures.

cut-over, *a.* and *sb.* [See CUT *v.* 58 and CUT *ppl. a.* 11.] **A.** *adj.* Cleared of timber by cutting. orig. *U.S.*

1899 *Westm. Gaz.* 6 Jan. 10/2 At least 90 per cent. of the cut-over lands [on the Pacific coast] are of absolutely no value for agricultural purposes. **1911** H. QUICK *Yellowstone N.* xii. 338 The solitary guest which is the only thing that brings the haunch to the spit in the Minnesota cut-over forest. **1946** *Nature* 13 July 71/2 Experiments carried out in certain marked strips of cut-over forest to ascertain the results of allowing the areas to lie fallow for a varying period of years.

B. *sb.* **1.** *Fencing.* An offensive disengage executed over the opponent's blade.

1897 *Encycl. Sport* I. 389/1 To elude quarte made with the hand very low, riposte with a cut-over thus. **1969** T. PARKER *Twisting Lane* 111 Going forward he made the first attack: a fast lunge and cut-over in Quarte.

2. An area on which the timber has been cut. *U.S. rare.*

1922 H. TITUS *Timber* vi. 60 If we had known we could have gone north..into the hardwood cutover and made a go of it.

cutpurse, cut-purse ('kʌtpɜːs). [CUT *v.* 65.] 'One who steals by the method of cutting purses, a common practice when men wore their purses at their girdles' (J.); hence, a pickpocket, thief, robber; also *fig.*

1362 LANGL. *P. Pl.* A. VI. 118 'Bi Crist', quaþ a Cuttepors [B. v. 639 cutpurs, C. VIII. 283 kitte-pors] 'I haue no kun þere'. **1530** PALSGR. 505/2 His eares be cutte of, it is a signe he hath ben a cut purse. **1587** GOLDING *De Mornay* xii. 176 How often hast thou seene the Cutpurse hanged with the purse about his necke? **1611** SHAKS. *Wint. T.* IV. iv. 686. **1668** R. L'ESTRANGE *Vis. Quev.* (1708) 74 A crowd of Cut-Purses, running full speed from their own ears. **1709** STEELE *Tatler* No. 25 ¶ 11, I approached him as if I knew him a Cut-purse. **1824** W. IRVING *T. Trav.* II. 244 Measures were taken to arrest this cut-purse of the ocean.

attrib. **1597** SHAKS. *2 Hen. IV*, II. iv. 137 Away you Cut-purse Rascall, you filthy Bung, away. **1884** *Pall Mall G.* 19 Sept. 1/2 Incapable of that cut-purse policy.

Hence † '**cutpursing** *vbl. sb.*, cutting of purses.

1499 *Promp. Parv.* 111 (Pynson) Cut pursinge, *burcidium*. **1579** J. JONES *Preserv. Bodie & Soul* I. xv. 28 This..is farre worse than coosining, cut pursing, or roging.

† **Cuts**[1]. *Obs.* [Cf. COTS.] A deformation of *God's*.

1671 *Welch Trav.* 193 in Hazl. *E.P.P.* IV. 337 Cuts plutteranails! was tell a lie, hur found it as hur went. **1707** E. WARD *Hud. Rediv.* II. ii, Cuts Bobs, says Frisk, my Brains grow addl'd. **1719** D'URFEY *Pills* V. 64 Cuts-plutter-a-nails, quoth Taffy.

cuts[2], **cutts.** *local.* [prob. plural of CUT *sb.* in some application, the plural referring to the two pairs of wheels, 'a pair of *cuts*'.] (See quots.)

1847–78 HALLIWELL, *Cuts*, a timber-carriage. *Linc.* **1877** *N.W. Linc. Gloss.*, *Cuts*..for conveying timber. It consists of two pairs of wheels with a long pole as a coupling between them, so as to place them far apart. **1886** *S.W. Linc. Gloss.* s.v., He was fined for using a pair of cutts on the highway without having his name painted thereon.

† **cut-scratch.** *Obs.* A kind of short wig: see SCRATCH.

1753 A. MURPHY *Gray's-Inn Jrnl.* No. 30 Without any other Qualification than that of a Cut-Scratch. *Ibid.* No. 57 We can now boast as many Cut-Scratches as any Seminary in the City.

† **cutt.** *Obs.* (See quots.)

1706 PHILLIPS (ed. Kersey), *Cutts*, a sort of flat-bottom'd Boats, formerly us'd in the Channel for Transporting Horses. **1775** ASH, *Cutt.* **1867** SMYTH *Sailor's Word-bk.*, *Cutts*, flat-bottomed horse-ferry boats of a former day.

cuttable ('kʌtəb(ə)l), *a.* [f. CUT *v.* + -ABLE.] Capable of being cut.

c **1449** PECOCK *Repr.* II. iv. 160 The Yuel therbi coming is ..kutteable awey bi good and thrifti bisynes therto sett. **1743** *Maxwell's Trans. Soc. Impr. Agric. Scot.* 204 (Jam.) All the cuttable grass of the nearest field.

cuttanee ('kʌtəniː). Also 7 cottony. [Urdū and Pers. *kattānī*, f. Arab. *kattān* flax.] Fine linen from the East Indies.

1622 COCKS *Diary* (1883) I. 179 (Stanf.), 2 handkerchefs Rumall cottony. **1696** OVINGTON *Voy. Suratt* 218 (Y.) Rich Silks, such as Atlasses, Cuttanees, Sooseys. **1721** C. KING *Brit. Merch.* I. 298 Crevats with Gold and Silver.. Cuttanees with Gold..Callicoes. **1813** MILBURN *Orient. Comm.* (Y.) (*List of Calcutta piece-goods*), Cuttannees.

† **cutted** ('kʌtɪd), *ppl. a. Obs.* or *dial.* [An earlier form of the pa. pple. of CUT *v.*, retained for some time in adjective use.] = CUT *ppl. a.*

1. Wounded, mutilated, etc., by cutting; castrated; carved, sculptured, engraved, etc.

1438 *E.E. Wills* (1882) 111 My cuttyd hors. **1521** *Test. Ebor.* (Surtees) V. 129 A sylver spoyne with cuttid starttis. *a* **1649** DRUMM. OF HAWTH. *Poems* Wks. (1711) 35/2 Where cutted carcasses quick members reel. **1830** GALT *Lawrie T.* I. ii. (1869) 5 The cutted fingers of the shearers.

2. Cut short; curtailed; ending abruptly.

c **1386** CHAUCER *Pars. T.* ¶ 348 The horrible disordinat scantnesse of clothyng, as been thise kuttid sloppes or haynselyns. *c* **1394** *P. Pl. Crede* 434 His wijf walked him wiþ.. In a cutted cote, cutted full heyȝe. **1562** TURNER *Herbal* II. 62 b, The Nardus of the mountayn..hathe a short eare and cutted. **1607** TOPSELL *Four-f. Beasts* (1673) 555 A silver pillar, with a short or cutted point.

b. Wearing short skirts. *cutted friar*: = *curtal friar*: see CURTAL B 6.

c **1460** J. RUSSELL *Bk. Nurture* 305 These Cuttid galauntes with theire codware; þat is an vngoodly gise. **16..** *R. Hood & Fryer Tucke* iii. in Child *Ballads* (1888) III. 123 'I'le never eate nor drinke', Robin Hood sa[id], 'Till I that cutted friar see'.

3. Contracted in expression; abbreviated, concise.

1565–73 COOPER *Thesaurus*, *Circuncisæ et breues orationes* .. Cutted, and short sentences, or orations. **1569** J. SANFORD tr. *Agrippa's Van. Artes* 10 b, If he had not broken the weightnesse of woordes with cutted sentences. **1581** J. BELL *Haddon's Answ. Osor.* 198 His cutted Sillogisme. **1589** PUTTENHAM *Eng. Poesie* III. xix. (Arb.) 222 This figure for pleasure may be called in our vulgar the cutted comma, for that there cannot be a shorter diuision then at euery words end.

b. Short to rudeness; curt, snappish.

1530 [see CUTTEDLY]. **1600** HOLLAND *Livy* x. xxiii. 376 Whereupon, there began some short and cutted shrewd words to be dealt betweene. *a* **1627** MIDDLETON *Women beware W.* III. i, She's grown so cutted, there's no speaking to her. **1746** *Exmoor Scolding* (E.D.S.), Ye rearing, snapping, tedious, cutted Snibblenose. **1880** *E. Cornwall Gloss.*, *Cuttit*, sharp in reply; pert; impudent.

Hence † '**cuttedly** *adv.*, shortly, concisely, abruptly, curtly; † **cuttedness.**

1530 PALSGR. 835/1 Cuttedly, frowardly, *cauesne*. **1548** UDALL, etc. *Erasm. Par.* Pref. 18 a, Can not be reported, but both coldely and also cuttedly. *a* **1662** BAILLIE *Lett.* (1775) I. 104 (Jam.) The moderater, cuttedly (as the man naturally hath a little choler), answered, That, etc. **1622** MABBE tr. *Aleman's Guzman D'Alf.* I. 136 The man that would liue long must not be too short [in temper and speech]. This cuttednesse hath cut off many a mans life before his time.

cuttee (kʌ'tiː). [See -EE.] One who is cut socially. See CUT *v.* 33.

1798 *Monthly Mag.* in *Spirit Pub. Jrnls.* (1799) II. 382 The cutter either walked smartly by, pretending not to see the cuttee; or, if he wished to make the cut more complete, looked him full in the face. **1821** P. EGAN *Life in London* II. v. 301 The '*cut direct*' comes with the *severity* of a paralytic stroke on the feeling of the poor *cuttee*. **1859** *Habits of Gd. Society* ix. 277 It does the cutter as much injury as the cuttee.

cutter ('kʌtə(r)), *sb.*[1] [f. CUT *v.* + -ER[1].]

1. a. One who cuts; one who shapes things by cutting: the name of operatives in many subordinate branches of industry.

1483 *Cath. Angl.* 88 A Cutter, *scissor*. **1485** *Nottingham Rec.* III. 240 Gevyn in ale to þe cutters of the pole jd. **1530** PALSGR. 211/2 Cutter of throtes, *coupeur de gorges*. **1685** BOYLE *Effects of Mot.* ii. 12 An experienced cutter of Gems. **1881** *Porcelain Works Worcester* 8 The transferrers, who place the prints on the wares; and the cutters, who prepare the paper for them.

b. With adverbs, as *cutter-down*, *-off*, *-out* (also *spec.* in *U.S.*, *Austral.*, and *N.Z.* one who separates cattle from a herd: see CUT *v.* 57 d), etc. *cutter-in*, (*a*) in *Whale-fishery*, one who cuts up a whale so as to remove the blubber (cf. CUT *v.* 55 b); (*b*) a motorist who cuts in between or in front of vehicles (cf. CUT *v.* 55 c).

1600 SHAKS. *A.Y.L.* I. ii. 53 The cutter off of natures witte. **1611** COTGR., *Avalleur*, a..feller, cutter downe. **1824** MISS MITFORD *Village* Ser. I. (1863) 114 She was accomplished in all the arts of the needle..a capital cutter-out. **1843** E. DIEFFENBACH *N.Z.* I. ii. 51 [The tongue] is a monopoly of the 'tonguer' or 'cutter-in'. **1886** BURTON *Arab. Nts.* (abr. ed.) I. 99 Fifty horsemen..cutters-off of the highway, wild as wild Arabs. **1910** C. E. MULFORD *Hopalong Cassidy* iii. 28 Each of the cutters-out rode after some calf. **1920** —— *J. Nelson* xxv. 259 There was only one pair of ropers..and only three cutters-out. **1928** *Daily Express* 5 June 9/1 The cutters-in, and the speed-at-any-price merchants who spoil travelling. *Ibid.* 26 June 10/2 The cutter-in and the speeder-up..are the causes of..accidents. **1940** E. C. STUDHOLME *Te Waimate* (1954) xvi. 136 The 'cutter-out' rode through [the cattle], and after spotting the beast he wanted, would follow it out to the edge of the mob.

c. In many combinations, as ***fustian-***, ***stone-***, ***wood-cutter***, etc.: see these words.

2. *spec.* †**a.** A hair-cutter. *Obs.*

c **1425** *Voc.* in Wr.-Wülcker 652/8 *Hic tonsor*, cuttere. *Hic rasor*, a shawere. **1624** HEYWOOD *Captives* III. ii, I sought the villadge through and cold find neare a cutter.

b. A carver, sculptor, engraver.

1572 BOSSEWELL *Armorie* II. 25b, Payntors, cutters, grauers, glasiers, and embrodurers. **1615** G. SANDYS *Trav.* 105 In this Hippopatom the cutter chose rather to follow then reforme an error. **1880** WARREN *Book-plates* xii. 126 Naming Durer as its designer, but not as its cutter upon the wood-block.

c. †(*a*) A tailor. *Obs.* (*b*) Now, The person employed in a tailoring or similar establishment to take the measures and cut out the cloth.

1599 MINSHEU *Sp. Dict.*, *Claravoya*, iags or cuts in garments, such as cutters inuent for gentle-women. **1668** R. L'ESTRANGE *Vis. Quev.*, Another called himself a Cutter: We ask'd him whether in Wood or Stone? Neither, said he, but in Cloth and Stuff (Anglicè a Taylor). **1885** *Law Times* LXXX. 8/1 Employed by..a tailor in Regent-street, as a cutter and fitter of wearing apparel.

d. One who cuts or castrates animals.

1562 LEIGH *Armorie* (1597) 53 This my Bore is chast, for my cutter hath cut him. **1603** *Canterbury Marriage Licences* (MS.), Anthony Latenden of Wittersham, horse cutter. **1705** *Lond. Gaz.* No. 4182/4 He..is by Trade a Cutter of Pigs. **1888** in ELWORTHY *W. Somerset Word-bk.*

e. *Cinemat.* One who cuts or edits a film (see CUT *v.* 21 e). Also ***film-cutter***.

1921 D. BOUGHEY *Film Industry* vii. 65 So interwoven are the functions of the editor, or cutter..that the two must work in perfect harmony. **1928** *Sunday Express* 18 Mar. 4/3 In America the film-cutter is a man with a sub-editorial mind developed to the *n*th degree, and film-cutting..is one of the highest paid professions. **1961** K. REISZ *Technique Film Editing* (ed. 9) ii. 185 In a newsreel unit the man in charge is generally referred to as the Editor, and the man who does the actual assembling in the cutting room, the Cutter. **1966** *Listener* 17 Mar. 383/2 That shows how much you owe to the cutter and the director when it comes to the screen.

†**3. a.** One over-ready to resort to weapons; a bully, bravo; also, a cutthroat, highway-robber. *Obs.*

1568 GRAFTON *Chron.* II. 85 He..gathered together a companye of Roysters and Cutters, and practised robberyes. **1581** PETTIE *Guazzo's Civ. Conv.* III. (1586) 135b, Like these cutters, and hackers, who will take the wall of men, and picke quarrells. **1607** R. C. tr. *H. Stephen's World of Wonders* 95 A theefe, or rather a cutter by the high way. *a* **1734** NORTH *Lives* II. 57 His infirmities were passion, in which he would swear like a cutter [etc.]. **1826** SCOTT *Woodst.* xxvii, I see, sir, you understand cutter's law—when one tall fellow has coin, another must not be thirsty.

†**b.** Applied to some riotous weavers in 1769.

1769 *Chron.* in *Ann. Reg.* 124/1 The new body of cutters, that have made a fresh disturbance in the neighbourhood of Spital-fields, are handkerchief-weavers. *Ibid.* 132/2 Fifty weavers, commonly called cutters, all masked, assembled..in Hoxton-square. **1770** *Monthly Rev.* 77 Two of the Spitalsfields rioters, or cutters, were sentenced to be hanged.

4. a. That which cuts; an implement or tool for cutting; the cutting part of a machine, etc.

Used in a number of specific applications in various trades, and in numerous combinations, as ***chaff-cutter***, ***disc-cutter***, ***turnip-cutter***, etc.

1631 *Star Chamb. Cases* (Camden) 84 He provided rules and cutters for making of farthings. **1686** PLOT *Staffordsh.* 163 Another Workman takes them [iron bars] whilst hot, and puts them through the Cutters. **1788** *Trans. Soc. Encourag. Arts* VI. 200 In cutting small Wheels, Nuts, or Pinions, the Cutter must go in between the Chaps. **1833** J. HOLLAND *Manuf. Metal* II. 60 Giving rotatory motion to a circular horizontal cutter. **1859** *Handbk. Turning* 65 Slide the cutter towards the edge of the work by turning the screw of the slide rest.

†**b.** One of the front or cutting teeth; an incisor.

1579 J. JONES *Preserv. Bodie & Soule* I. xxi. 40 Whereof eight [teeth] be cutters, foure biters, and twentie grinders. **1668** CULPEPPER & COLE *Barthol. Anat., Manual* IV. xii. 348 In Man they [the teeth] are of a threefold figure: Cutters, Dog-teeth, and Grinders. **1691** RAY *Creation* (J.), The cutters [are] before, that they may be ready to cut off a morsel..to be transmitted to the grinders.

c. *Sound Recording.* A tool which cuts a groove in a recording medium. In full ***cutter stylus***.

1908 *Jrnl. R. Soc. Arts* LVI. 642/1 With a 12 inch disc, when the cutter is ½ inch from the edge, it will in one revolution describe a line on the record of a length approximately equal to the circumference of a circle of 11 inches diameter. **1962** A. NISBETT *Technique Sound Studio* iv. 87 The hot-stylus method..helps to smooth the wall as the cutter moves on. *Ibid.* 88 The cutter stylus ploughs its way through the surface of a disc.

5. a. One who or that which cuts, in various transferred senses of the verb (see the quots.); one who cuts an acquaintance; a cutting remark, etc.

1579–80 NORTH *Plutarch* (1676) 625 See, the cutter of my words riseth. **1656** RIDGLEY *Pract. Physick* 232 Then apply a Repeller, as Oyl of Roses, with which mingle cutters, or Vinegar. **1691** T. BROWNE *Mr. Bays Changing Relig.* (ed. 2) 15 This is a cutter, by my faith Mr. Bays, it lashes somewhere with a vengeance. **1781** SMEATHMAN in *Phil. Trans.* LXXI. 179 *note*, Not only all his cloaths were destroyed by white Ants or Cutters, but his papers also. **1798** [see CUTTEE]. **1835** *Fraser's Mag.* XII. 145, I never cut any one..and have, indeed, a very considerable contempt for all cutters. **1882** *Knowledge* No. 19. 409/2 The cards are not shuffled between the cuts, so that the cutter, if he fails the first time, has a rather better chance next time.

b. *Cricket.* (*a*) A batsman who 'cuts' the ball (see CUT *v.* 31 a) or who is adept at making this stroke. (*b*) A ball that turns sharply after pitching (see CUT *v.* 31 a).

1851 J. PYCROFT *Cricket Field* vii. 148 The balls may be regularly rising: in this case every one would like to see a good cutter at the wicket. **1955** *Times* 15 July 3/3 Palmer..is a particularly effective driver and cutter. **1960** I. A. R. PEEBLES *Bowler's Turn* 40 By way of variation he bowled a cutter. **1966** E. R. DEXTER *Ted Dexter Declares* ii. 21 They gave me a bit of bowling and I started with medium-pace swingers and off cutters.

6. *Mining.* A crack or fissure intersecting the bedding or lines of stratification; the cleavage of slate (usually in *pl.*); a crack in a crystal or precious stone. *dial.*

1756 MRS. CALDERWOOD *Jrnl.* (1884) 15 A soft sandy stone, so open in the cutters, and so loose, that the ground above it can have very little moisture. **1785** HUTTON in *Trans. R. Soc. Edin.* (1788) I. 259 A stratum of porous sandstone does not abound so much with veins and cutters as a similar stratum of marble. **1799** J. ROBERTSON *Agric. Perth* 34 Slates..of a muddy brown complexion along the cutters. **1865** PAGE *Geol. Terms*, *Cutters*, a quarryman's term for any narrow crack or fissure that cuts or crosses the strata; hence 'backs and cutters' for what is known to geologists as the jointed structure.

7. a. A superior quality of brick, which can be cut and rubbed, called also *cutting brick*; used for arches of doorways and windows, quoins, etc.

1842 GWILT *Archit.* (1876) 526 The finest marl stocks..are technically called firsts, or cutters..There is also a red cutting brick, whose texture is similar to the malm cutter, which must not be confounded with the red stock. **1881** *Every man his own Mechanic* §1152 The bricks are sorted into classes known as cutters..picked stocks, etc.

b. An animal yielding an inferior grade of meat. orig. *U.S.*

1905 *Chicago Daily News* 3 July 7/7 Canners and cutters were rather slow, as packers did not care to secure them. **1916** *Yorkshire Post* 23 Feb. 10/6 Pigs continue to rise in value, 6[d] extra per score being charged for cutters and sows. **1958** *Times* 1 July p. iii/4 Any line of demarcation between porkers and the rather heavier 'cutters' (near bacon weights) has practically disappeared. **1971** *Daily Hampshire Gaz.* (Northampton, Mass.) 12 Feb. 5/5 Prices per cwt. were:..24 cutters, up to $21.90.

8. *Comb.*, chiefly belonging to sense 4, as ***cutter-block***, ***-frame***, ***-screw***, ***-stock***, various parts of cutting-machines or cutting-tools; **cutter-bar**, (*a*) a bar in which cutting-tools are so fastened as to serve for circular cutting, as in a machine for boring the inside of cylinders; (*b*) the bar in a mowing or reaping machine that bears the knives; **cutter-dredge**, **-dredger**, a river-dredge fitted with knives; **cutter-grinder**, an implement for sharpening the cutters of reaping machines, etc.; **cutter-head**, the revolving head of a tool with cutters or sharpened edges; **cutter-loader**, a machine that cuts coal from a coal-face and loads it on a conveyor; **cutter-wheel**, a wheel serving for cutting.

1831 HOLLAND *Manuf. Metal* I. 217 If we suppose the cutter, or rather the cutter-frame to move upon a pivot. **1833** *Ibid.* II. 130 This cutter-block is constructed to slide upon the hollow cast iron shaft..a metal stopper inside connected with the cutter-head by pins. **1862** *Chambers' Encycl.* s.v. *Cork*, Cutter-wheels and other suitable machines are brought to bear on the revolving cork. **1873** J. RICHARDS *Wood-working Factories* 80 Cutter-screws and bolts should be made of the very best refined iron. **1913** THOMAS & WATT *Improvem. Rivers* (ed. 2) I. 100 The cutter dredge,..in which the material is loosened by a series of knives shaped so that they will not clog, fastened to a shaft and revolving close to the end of the suction pipe. **1940** *Chambers's Techn. Dict.* 218/2 *Cutter dredger*, a dredger of the sand-pump or suction type. **1948** *Something Done* (*Central Office of Information*) 19/2 Besides the Meco-Moore, two other British cutter-loaders are now in the advanced experimental stage.

cutter ('kʌtə(r)), *sb.*[2] *Naut.* [app. a specific use of CUTTER *sb.*[1] Some think it refers to CUT *v.*, comparing the early use of RUNNER for a small fast vessel used as a dispatch boat, etc.; others would refer it more especially to the build, whereby it is, in Johnson's words, 'a nimble boat that cuts the water'. The conjecture that it is possibly a corruption of CATUR is inadmissible.]

1. A boat, belonging to a ship of war, shorter and in proportion broader than the barge or pinnace, fitted for rowing and sailing, and used for carrying light stores, passengers, etc.

1745 P. THOMAS *Jrnl. Anson's Voy.* 284, I have seen and heard six Times more Confusion..and Hurry in hoisting out one Cutter (or small Boat). **1748** *Anson's Voy.* II. xiii. 276 The inconsiderable size of a Cutter belonging to a sixty gun ship, (being only an open boat about twenty-two feet in length). **1784** *Cook's 3rd Voy.* (1790) VI. 2227 Two sailors ..went off with a six-oared cutter. *c* **1860** H. STUART *Seaman's Catech.* 9 Cutters are used as despatch boats and for light work, such as answering signals, rowing guard, picking up a man overboard, or to assist in towing.

2. A small, single-masted vessel, clinker- or carvel-built, furnished with a straight running bowsprit, and rigged much like a sloop, carrying a fore-and-aft main-sail, gaff-top-sail, stay-foresail, and jib; a style of building and rigging now much used in yachts.

According to an old French engraving of a naval action in 1779, and *Rigging & Seamanship* 1794, vol. I. *last plate*, the cutters of that time were rigged like the half of an old schooner, with square topsails.

revenue cutter (formerly ***custom-house cutter***): a cutter-built vessel employed by the customs authorities for the prevention of smuggling, etc.; in *U.S.* applied to all vessels employed in this service whether steamers or sailing vessels; hence ***revenue cutter service***, etc.

1762 CAPT. EVERITT in *Naval Chron.* XIII. 30 Let the *Lurcher* Cutter attend the Boats. **1769** FALCONER *Dict. Marine* (1789), *Cutter*, a small vessel commonly navigated in the channel of England; it is furnished with one mast, and rigged as a *sloop*. Many of these vessels are used on an illicit trade, and others employed by the Government to seize them. **1799** *Naval Chron.* I. 441 The Hind Revenue Cutter. **1806** A. DUNCAN *Nelson* 14 The Rambler cutter was..engaged..with a French cutter. **1892** *Whitaker's Alm.* 606/1 In the first-class division, Mr. John Jameson's cutter, Iverna, built in 1890, headed the winning list.

3. *transf.* A small light sledge or sleigh for one or two persons. *Canada* and *U.S.*

1803 'C. CAUSTIC' *Poet. Petition against Tractorising Trumpery* 37 Then condescend to be my crony, And guide my wild Parnassian pony, Till our aerial cutter runs Athwart 'a wilderness of suns'! **1836** *Backwoods of Canada* 207 The usual equipages for travelling are the double sleigh..and cutter; the two former are drawn by two horses abreast, but the latter..has but one. **1857** B. TAYLOR *North. Trav.* xv. 155 The sleighing was superb. How I longed for a dashing American cutter, with a span of fast horses. **1887** *Cornh. Mag.* Mar. 261 The dainty Canadian 'cutter', with its..curved..runners.

4. *Comb.*, as ***cutter-built***, ***-rigged***, adjs.; **cutter-brig**, 'a vessel with square sails, a fore-and-aft main-sail, and a jigger-mast with a smaller one' (Smyth); formerly ***brig cutter***; **cutter-gig**, a boat of a size between a cutter and a gig; **cutter-yacht**, a yacht built and rigged like a cutter.

[**1799** *Naval Chron.* I. 255 They were met by a brig cutter.] *Ibid.* I. 261 The Perseverance [is] cutter-rigged. **1803** *Ibid.* X. 333 The squadron has sent in the..brig *l'Aiguille*..cutter built. **1805** *Ibid.* XIV. 340 Two large French Cutter Brigs ran alongside. *c* **1850** *Rudim. Navig.* (Weale) 101 In the Royal Navy, when cutter-built vessels are thus rigged, they are called Cutter Brigs. **1885** LADY BRASSEY *The Trades* 309 We passed the bishop's smart little cutter-yacht.

cutter, *sb.*[3] Corruption or error for GUTTER.

1731 BAILEY, *Cutters*, the little Streaks in the Beam of a Deer.

'cutter, *v.* *north. dial.* [app. cognate with G. dial. *kuttern* to coo like a dove, also applied to various other sounds; Sw. *qvittra* to chirp; cf. also ON. *kvitta* to rumour. But the Eng. word may be directly echoic, with iterative form: cf. *whitter*, *whatter*, *chatter*, *mutter*.]

1. *intr.* **a.** To whisper; to talk privately and confidentially. **b.** To coo like a pigeon.

1781 J. HUTTON *Tour Caves* Gloss., *Cutter*, to whisper. **1803** R. ANDERSON *Cumbrld. Ball.* 66 I' the pantry the sweethearters cutter'd sae soft. **1855** ROBINSON *Whitby Gloss.*, *Cuttering*, talking low. 'They sat hottering and cuttering over the fire.' **1869** *Lonsdale Gloss.*, *Cutter*, to whisper. *Cutterin*, cooing like a pigeon. **1878** *Cumbrld. Gloss.*, *Cutter*, to whisper or talk softly.

2. To fondle, make much of. [Cf. CUITER.]

1746 COLLIER (Tim Bobbin) *View Lanc. Dial.* (1862) Introd. 36, I dunnaw meeon heaw fok harbort'n't or cuttern't o'er thee. **1787** GROSE *Prov. Gloss.*, *Cutter*, to fondle, or make much of, as a hen or goose of her young. **1825** in BROCKETT *N. Country Gloss.*

cutthroat, cut-throat ('kʌtθrəʊt). [See CUT *v.* 65.]

1. a. One who cuts throats; a ruffian who murders or does deeds of violence; a murderer or assassin by profession.

1535 STEWART *Cron. Scot.* II. 449 Thir cankerit cut-throttis of crudelitie. **1694** tr. *Milton's Lett. State* May an. 1658, Those sanctifi'd Cut-throats. **1793** *Ld. Auckland's Corr.* III. 109 A corps franc, raised on the frontiers of Hungary..I never saw such a set of desperate cut-throats. **1889** FROUDE *Chiefs Dunboy* xxv. 380, I am a soldier, sir, and not a cut-throat.

b. *transf.* and *fig.*

1583 BABINGTON *Commandm.* x. (1637) 93 It is the very tryed cut-throat of all amity, friendship, etc. **1600** SURFLET *Countrie Farme* VII. xxix. 855 There is no greater a cut-throte to dogs than the wild bore. **1878** W. BLACK *Goldsmith* xii. 102 A paid libeller and cut-throat of public reputations.

c. Used *attrib.* or *ellipt.* of several games of chance, esp. of a three-handed card game in which one or more players score individually rather than in partnership. orig. *U.S.*

1823 I. HOLMES *Acct. U.S.* 353, I have seen at least twenty boys surrounding a billiard table, playing at a sort of game of chance they call cut-throat. **1868** *All Year Round* 31 Oct. 489/2 It is not uncommon, therefore, to see merchants (especially American) having a social game of 'cut-throat monte', 'eucre', or 'poker', with piles of gold before them. **1870** J. C. DUVAL *Big-foot Wallace* 247 As soon as I can learn to play poker and cut-throat loo. **1904** E. A. TENNANT *ABC of Bridge* (ed. 4) 100 Cut-Throat Bridge. Though the above is the simplest way of playing three-handed Bridge, Cut-Throat has great attractions for some people. **1932** E. WAUGH *Black Mischief* vii. 257 Anstruther, Legge and William were playing cut-throat bridge.

d. Used *attrib.* or *absol.* of a razor consisting of a blade set in a handle, as distinguished from a safety-razor.

1932 D. L. SAYERS *Have His Carcase* i. 18 At the cost of a slight cut on her finger, she drew up an open cut-throat razor. **1957** J. FRAME *Owls do Cry* 75 The old lather-up and the strop and the cut-throat razor for him. **1959** *Sunday Times* 22 Feb. 29/3 The advent of the safety-razor.. happily put an end to my first clumsy essays with the open cut-throat.

†**2.** A kind of fire-arm; cf. *murderer*. *Obs.*

1566 in Thomson *Invent.* (1815) 169 (Jam.) Item, sex cutthrottis of irne with their mekis. **1567** *Sempill Ballads* (1872) 2 Cunning of crosbow cutthrot and culuering.

†**3.** A dark lantern. *Obs.*

1783 BAILEY, *Cut-throat*, also a kind of lantern. **1825** JAMIESON, *Cut-throat*, a dark lantern or bowet.. so constructed that the light may be completely obscured, when.. necessary for the perpetration of any criminal act.

4. The Mustang grape of Texas, having an acrid taste.

Century Dict. refers to *Sportsman's Gazetteer*.

5. a. More fully **cut-throat finch**: a bird-fancier's name for *Amadina fasciata*, the Red-collared Bengaly of Swainson, a small West African bird, the male of which has a red mark round the throat.

[Here *cut* is the pa. pple. qualifying *throat*.]

1872 *Revised List Vertebr. Anim. Zool. Gard.* 137 Cut-throat Finch. **1873** *Spectator* 22 Feb. 240/1 Here are 'Cut-throats', the male with a murderous red mark round his soft neck, the female without it. **1891** *Bazaar* 20 Feb., Cut-throats, silver bills, waxbills.. spice birds, Java sparrows.

b. In full *cut-throat trout*: see quots.

1891 *Cent. Dict.*, *Cutthroat trout*, the Rocky Mountain brook-trout. **1897** *Outing* (U.S.) XXX. 163/2 The father of all the Pacific trout, the black-spotted or 'Cut-throat' (*Salmo mykiss*) with the scarlet splotch on his lower jaw. **1946** *Mazama* Dec. 33/2 Steelhead trout and sea-run cut-throat trout provide capital sport for fishermen.

6. *attrib.* That is, or has the character of, a cutthroat or assassin; of or pertaining to cutthroats; murderous, ruffianly. Also *transf.*

Cut-throat Lane, a frequent local appellation of a lonely lane.

1567 DRANT *Hor. Epist.* vi. Dij, A cut throte rutterkin. **1596** SHAKS. *Merch. V.* I. iii. 112 You call me misbeleeuer, cut-throate dog. **1706** PHILLIPS (ed. Kersey), *Cut-Throat Place*, an Inn or Tavern, where People are exacted upon. **1848** W. ARMSTRONG *Stocks* 31 [Harlem rail road stock] is generally considered to be most essentially a 'cut-throat stock'. **1874** DASENT *Half a Life* II. 110 A cut-throat lonely place. **1881** *Bradstreet's* 16 Apr. 237/4 The three great objects.. are.. to avoid cut-throat competition. **1886** *Pall Mall G.* 24 Nov. 12/1 Cut-throat competition is not for gentlemen. **1903** *Westm. Gaz.* 17 Jan. 3/1 The wide valley of the Po, where, in nine months of the year, the cut-throat *tramontana* is a frequent visitant. **1914** W. B. YEATS *Responsibilities* 35 A cloud blown from the cut-throat north. **1938** E. WAUGH *Scoop* I. v, It's going to be a tough assignment from all I hear. Cut-throat competition.

7. *Comb.*, as *cutthroat-like* adj.

1611 COTGR., *Meurtrierement*, murtherously, cruelly, cut-throat-like.

Hence (*nonce-wds.*) **'cut-throat** *v. trans.*, to cut the throat of. **'cut-throatry, -ery**, practice proper to a cutthroat. **'cut-throatish, 'cut-throaty** *adjs.*, pertaining or proper to a cut-throat.

a **1625** BEAUMONT & FL. *Laws of Candy* IV. ii, Money.. Is now a god on earth. It.. Bribes Justice, cut-throats Honour. **1606** *Wily Beguiled* in Hazl. *Dodsley* IX. 229 For to let my house before my lease be out, is cut-throatery. **1870** *Echo* 15 Dec., They look more cut-throatish than ever. **1660** R. COKE *Justice Vind.* 32 If God made man.. as he [Mr. Hobbs] saies, in such a cut-throatty condition.

cutting ('kʌtɪŋ), *vbl. sb.* [-ING[1].]

1. a. The action of the verb CUT, in various senses.

1398 TREVISA *Barth. De P.R.* XVII. ii. (1495) 597 Wythout kyttynge or keruynge. *c* **1400** *Lanfranc's Cirurg.* 150 It is necessarie a surgian to make hise kuttyngis & hise brennyngis bi lenkþe of þe necke. **1590** WEBBE *Trav.* 21 There we staide to see the cutting or parting of the Riuer of Nilo.. vpon the 25 of August. **1691** tr. *Emilianne's Frauds Romish Monks* 27 Some gests and cutting of Faces, wherein they oblige the Company to imitate them. **1692** BENTLEY *Boyle Lect.* 63 This shuffling and cutting with atoms. **1700** T. BROWN tr. *Fresny's Amusem.* 60 Those who live by Cutting of Purses. **1827** in W. Denison *Sk. Players* (1846) 39 There would be comparatively no cutting to the point or slip. **1856** MISS BIRD *Englishw. in Amer.* 41 That extreme of civilisation vulgarly called 'cutting' is common. **1884** HON. I. BLIGH in *Lillywhite's Cricket Annual* 5 His cutting and off-driving alike masterly.

b. The action of cutting down prices or underselling; also *attrib.*, as *cutting line, work*. (*colloq.*)

1851 MAYHEW *Lond. Labour*, There is great competition in the trade, and much of what is called 'cutting', or one tradesman underselling another. *Ibid.* (1861) III. 425/1 A man started as a grocer in the same street, in the 'cutting' line, and I had to compete with him. **1892** *Pall Mall G.* 15 Mar. 2/1 This cutting work—competition gone mad I call it—is really a gigantic conspiracy against labour.

c. The separating of cattle from a herd; cf. CUT *v.* 57 d. Also *attrib. U.S.* and *Austral.*

1887 F. FRANCIS *Saddle & Moccasin* (Lentzner), I had been furnished with a trained cutting pony, reported to be one of the best in the valley. **1892** LENTZNER *Austral. Wd.-bk.* 19 *Cutting*, separating cattle from a herd and lassoing them.

d. *Cinemat.* The action of CUT *v.* 21 e. Also in *Sound Recording*.

1921 A. C. LESCARBOURA *Cinema Handbk.* (1922) 21 *Cutting*, editing a picture by elimination of useless or unacceptable film. **1936** A. ASQUITH in C. Brahms *Footnotes to Ballet* vi. 244 Photographing the same scene from different positions and changing them in the cutting. **1958** *Listener* 6 Nov. 752/2 The success of the total effect was due to the cutting and assemblage of the recordings under the composer's care.

†**2.** An intersection; also a section. *Obs.*

1598 BARRET *Theor. Warres* v. i. 125 These two straight lines shall come to be cut, in the which cutting shall the Angle of the Bulwarke be. **1726** tr. *Gregory's Astron.* I. 327 The Arcs of the cutting contain'd between two Parallels are equal.

3. a. *concr.* A piece cut off; *esp.* a shred made in preparing or trimming an object for use.

1382 WYCLIF *1 Kings* xi. 31 And he seith to Jeroboam, Tak to thee ten kyttyngis. **1432-50** tr. *Higden* (Rolls) II. 449 Codrus.. berenge as kyttenges of trees in his necke. **1626** BACON *Sylva* §667 The burning also of the cuttings of Vines, and casting them upon Land, doth much good. **1812** J. SMYTH *Pract. Customs* (1821) 110, 550 lbs. Cuttings of Losh Hides, value 3*d.* per lb. **1825** LAMB *Refl. Pillory*, Dirty cuttings from the shambles at three-ha'pence a pound.

b. A quantity that may be cut.

1902 S. E. WHITE *Blazed Trail* xxvii. 191 'Its a fine country,' went on Thorpe so everyone could hear, 'with a great cutting of white pine.' **1957** *Brit. Commonw. Forest Terminol.* 55 *Cutting*, the amount of timber.. that can be cut from sawn timber.

4. *spec.* **a.** A small shoot or branch bearing leaf-buds cut off a plant, and used for propagation.

1664 EVELYN *Kal. Hort.* (1729) 222 Figs.. will be propagated by their Suckers, Cuttings, and Layers. **1727** BRADLEY *Fam. Dict.* s.v. *Fierides*, The Cuttings being planted in a natural Bed of Earth. **1881** DELAMER *Fl. Gard.* 76 The shrubby *Calceolarias*.. are readily propagated by cuttings.

b. A paragraph or short article cut out of a newspaper, etc.

1856 *N. & Q.* 2nd Ser. I. 292, I am desirous of mounting a collection of newspaper cuttings. **1866** *Athenæum* 24 Nov. 687/1 Hardly more comical than the following 'cutting' from the *Boston Gazette*.

5. *Irish Hist.* The levying of a tax or impost; tailage.

1596 SPENSER *State Irel.* Wks. (1862) 506/2 The Tanist hath.. certaine cuttings and spendings upon all the inhabitants under the Lord. **1607** DAVIES *Lett. Earl Salisb.* i. (1787) 222 Affirming that the Irish cutting was an usurpation and a wrong. **1612** —— *Why Ireland* (1787) 127 These chiefries.. did consist chiefly in cuttings and cosheries, and other Irish exactions. **1633** T. STAFFORD *Pac. Hib.* ii. (1821) 232.

6. A figure produced by cutting; a carving, etc.

1787 MAD. D'ARBLAY *Diary* Sept., She gave me a cutting of my dearest Mrs. Delany.. exquisitely resembling her fine venerable countenance. **1852** MOTLEY *Corr.* (1889) I. v. 139 Curious cuttings in wood and alabaster.

7. *Mining.* (See quots.)

1874 KNIGHT *Dict. Mech.* 668 *Cutting*, a poor quality of ore mixed with that which is better. *Ibid.* 669 *Cuttings*, the larger and lighter refuse which is detained by the sieve in the hotching tub, or hutch.

8. An open, trench-like excavation through a piece of ground that rises above the level of a canal, railway, or road which has to be taken across it.

1836 *Hull & Selby Railw. Act* 6 To construct.. arches, cuttings and fences. **1838** SIMMS *Public Wks. Gt. Brit.* 62 The railway is carried through this cutting. **1878** HUXLEY *Physiogr.* 23 Some good geological sections may be seen in railway cuttings.

9. With adverbs. Also *attrib.* **a.** *cutting away.*

c **1380** WYCLIF *Serm.* Sel. Wks. I. 335 þis kitting awei is clepid circumcisioun.

b. *cutting down. spec. cutting-down line* (Ship-building): a curved line forming the upper side of the floor-timbers at the middle-line, continued to the stem and stern over the dead-woods, and representing the curve on which the keelson lies; *cutting-down*, the curve or surface which this line represents.

1469 *Bury Wills* (Camden) 46 Wythout any dystruccyon or kyttynge down of treis. **1769** FALCONER *Dict. Marine* (1789), *Cutting-down line*, a curved line used by shipwrights in the delineation of ships. *c* **1850** *Rudim. Navig.* (Weale) 113 The cutting-down line is intended to represent, on the Sheer Draught, the limit of the depth of every floor-timber at the middle-line, and also the height of the upper part of the dead-wood afore and abaft. *Ibid.* 124 They are bolted.. to the cutting-down of the knee. *Ibid.* 142 They must be deeper in the throat or at the cutting-down.

c. *cutting-in*: (*a*) See CUT *v.* 55 c.

1856 [see CUT *v.* 55 c]. **1925** *Don'ts for Motorists* 55 Cutting in is another evil practice. **1960** *News Chron.* 7 June 1/2 Bad overtaking and cutting-in—normal faults of holiday drivers.

(*b*) See CUT *v.* 55 d.

1920 F. SCOTT FITZGERALD *This Side Paradise* (1921) I. ii. 74 The reassured beaux and the eternal cutting in. **1928** *Daily Express* 14 Dec. 19 The American practice known as 'cutting-in'.. consists.. of any man who wishes to dance tapping the shoulder of another man who is already dancing and abducting his partner.

(*c*) The action of starting an engine by some device which closes the circuit. Also used of the engine itself, and *attrib.*

1924 A. W. JUDGE et al. *Mod. Motor Cars* III. 74 When the dynamo speed is low, the spring holds the contacts apart, but as soon as the 'cutting-in' speed is attained [etc.]. **1928** *Motor Manual* (ed. 27) 110 A dynamo has what is termed a definite 'cutting-in' speed, which means that at, say, 400 revolutions per minute, it begins to generate effective current, which, by the action of a device known as the cut-out, connects the dynamo to the battery and charges it.

d. *cutting-out*: (*a*) See CUT *v.* 57 j. Also *attrib.*, as *cutting-out scissors*, large scissors for cutting patterns from fabric.

1819 M. WILMOT *Let.* 21 Dec. (1935) 47 [My] pink dress which you were at the cutting out of. **1840** MARRYAT *Poor Jack* xxxii, Virginia.. superintended the cutting-out department. **1873** *Young Englishwoman* Mar. 147/2 Cutting-out scissors, small scissors, and button-hole scissors. **1930** *Times Educ. Suppl.* 24 May 238/4 Well qualified.. in Practical Needlework, with Cutting-out. **1936** R. LEHMANN *Weather in Streets* I. ii. 40 Pins in her mouth, the cutting-out scissors in her hand.

(*b*) = sense 1 c.

1874 J. G. MCCOY *Cattle Trade* v. 81 Whilst from six to ten cow boys hold the herd together the ranchman with one or two assistants separate such as are suitable. This process is termed 'cutting out'. **1877** R. E. STRAHORN *Hand-bk. Wyoming* 35 Our artist has given a very fair representation of the 'cutting out' scene. **1884** W. SHEPHERD *Prairie Exper.* 34 This cutting-out goes on all the day long. **1890** 'R. BOLDREWOOD' *Squatter's Dream* ii. 13 He's the best cutting-out horse. **1910** W. M. RAINE *B. O'Connor* 75 I'm running this cutting-out expedition. **1920** C. E. MULFORD *J. Nelson* xxv. 255 Selecting from their best cutting-out animals, saddles were hastily changed, [etc.].

e. *cutting-up*: (*a*) The action of CUT *v.* 60; *spec.* boisterous, frolicsome, or silly behaviour. (*U.S.*)

1687 CONGREVE *Old Bach.* IV. ii, A delicious melon.. only waits thy cutting up! **1812** SOUTHEY *Omniana* I. 83 Before the butcher's phrase 'cutting up' was supposed to be synonymous with criticizing. **1843** 'R. CARLTON' *New Purchase* II. 209 Cutting up.. consists in cracking nuts and jokes—racing one another and slamming doors—in upsetting chairs, and even kicking up carpets! **1883** J. A. MACON *Uncle Gabe Tucker* 162 De perlicemen nebber would 'a' let John de Baptis' do any sich cuttin'-up as dat.

(*b*) *Founding.* (See quot.)

1888 J. G. HORNER *Dict. Mech. Engin.* 101 *Cutting-up*, the gashing of the broken edges or faces of a sand mould preparatory to adding fresh sand for mending-up.

10. *attrib.* and *Comb.*, as *cutting line, work* (see 1 b); *cutting place*, etc.; *esp.* in names of tools, etc. used in the process of cutting, as *cutting-board, -burnisher, -compass, cylinder, -edge* (also fig.), *-engine, file, -gauge, -hook, -knife, -machine, -mill, -nipper, -plane, -plate, -plier, -press, -punch, -spade, -table, -tool*, etc.; (sense 1 d) *cutting-bench, -print*; **cutting-bed** (*Microscopy*), a part of a microtome on which the cutting knife slides; **cutting-bill**, a bill for cutting wood; **cutting-box**, †(*a*) ? a chaff- or straw-cutter; (*b*) a receptacle for the diamond dust in diamond-cutting; **cutting-brick** = CUTTER *sb.*[1] 7; **cutting compound** = *cutting oil* (see also quot. 1963); **cutting contest** orig. *U.S.*, an informal competition of jazz musicians; **cutting horse** *U.S.*, a horse trained in separating cattle from a herd (cf. CUT *v.* 57 d); **cutting-house**, a house where the cutting of clothing materials, meat, or other substances is done; **cutting oil**, a preparation for the lubrication and cooling of the tool and the piece of metal being cut or worked in various machining operations; **cutting pony** *U.S.*, a pony trained in separating cattle from a herd (cf. CUT *v.* 57 d); **cutting-pot**, a pot used for the planting of cuttings; **cutting-room**, (*a*) a room where the cutting of clothing materials, meat, etc. is done; †(*b*) a room where surgical operations are performed; (*c*) a room where a film is cut or edited (see CUT *v.* 21 e); **cutting service** (*Lawn Tennis*), a service in which the player cuts the ball; **cutting session** orig. *U.S.* = *cutting contest*; **cutting-shoe**, a shoe specially constructed for horses which cut or interfere (see CUT *v.* 27); **cutting stick**, a strip of wood or other material which receives the edge of the knife in the cutting cylinder of a paper-cutting machine as it severs each sheet; **cutting stylus** = CUTTER *sb.*[1] 4 c.

1881 W. B. CARPENTER *Microscope* (ed. 6) v. 229 The circular *cutting-bed, instead of being fixed on the upper end of the cylinder, is made to *screw* upon it. **1936** P. ROTHA *Documentary Film* ii. 77 Nothing photographed, or recorded on to celluloid, has meaning until it comes to the *cutting-bench. **1601** HOLLAND *Pliny* I. 536 Able to beare the *cutting-bill. **1771** *Phil. Trans.* LXI. 161 Other sorts [of trees] bear the woodman's cutting-bill more kindly. **1825**

HONE *Everyday Bk.* I. 1081 It..furnishes shoemakers with their *cutting-boards. **1744** W. ELLIS *Mod. Husb.* Jan. vii. 69 The Chaffcutter's Way was, to..put them upon some Cavings of Wheat..that he first placed at the Bottom of the long *Cutting-box. **1778** H. HERBERT *Mil. Equitation* 136 Every troop ought to have a cutting-box..and one man constantly employed..in chopping hay, straw, &c. **1816** J. SMITH *Panorama Sc. & Art* I. 187 The finest kind of marl and red bricks are called *cutting bricks. **1874** KNIGHT *Dict. Mech.*, **Cutting-compass*, a compass, one of whose legs is a cutter, to make washers, wads, and circular disks of paper for other uses. **1910** *Metall. & Chem. Engin.* May 293/1 They mixed a small amount..with their *cutting compound and..the tool did not blunt nearly so rapidly as before. **1963** R. F. WEBB *Motorists' Dict.* 71 *Cutting compound*, an abrasive paste used for smoothing the paintwork of a car before the final polishing. **1946** MEZZROW & WOLFE *Really Blues* 372 **Cutting contest*, competitive get-together of performers. **1969** *Listener* 13 Mar. 358/3 Not to mention cutting contests in jazz, *Eisteddfodau*, and the choral and brass-band competitions which flourish in Northern industrial towns. **1909** *Daily Chron.* 11 June 7/5 Each colour is rolled out in long sheets, and passes through separate rollers upon which what is known as a '*cutting cylinder' is rotating continuously, one to each colour. **1929** *Encycl. Brit.* XIV. 166/2 In this process the scratched material is rolled into a continuous sheet, and led..under a revolving 'cutting cylinder'. **1964** *Gloss. Letterpress Rotary Print. Terms (B.S.I.)* 23 *Cutting cylinder*, the cylinder that holds the knives that cut the web into individual lengths or sheets. **1825** LOUDON *Encycl. Agric.* §501 It resembles a large..shovel, strongly prepared with iron on the *cutting edge. **1831** *Mech. Mag.* 23 July 334 The cutting-edges must be parallel to each other. **1909** A. BERGET *Conquest of Air* II. v. 212 Angle of cutting edge, 7 degrees. **1927** CARR-SAUNDERS & JONES *Soc. Struct. Eng. & Wales* 207 No one supposes that it is possible to put a sharp cutting-edge on a leaden blade. **1966** *Rep. Comm. Inquiry Univ. Oxf.* I. 56 There is a cutting edge to our recommendation that Oxford should..remain of medium size. **1825** J. NICHOLSON *Operat. Mechanic* 495 If both wheels are cut in the *cutting-engine by the same cutter. **1601** HOLLAND *Pliny* I. 530 Some good husbands..with a *cutting hook (turning the edge vpward) fetch vp the eies budding out beneath. **1881** G. W. ROMSPERT *Western Echo* 177 Each firm has particular horses trained for this business, and they are called '*cutting horses'. **1937** *Dial. Notes* VI. 618 A *cutting* horse is one especially trained to separate..a single animal from a whole herd. (I have seen one 'cutting' horse who could 'cut' a hen from a big flock of chickens.) **1660** PEPYS *Diary* 10 Mar., In the morning went to my father's, whom I took in his *cutting house. **1925** F. WALTON *Linoleum* 48 An octagonal cylinder, arranged with a number of *cutting knives. **1876** *Encycl. Brit.* IV. 43/2 A rotary *cutting-machine or 'ripper'. **1891** CHASE & CLOW *Stories of Industry* II. 43 The cutting-machine or shearing engine..shears the nap off close, leaving a smooth face to the cloth. **1917** J. R. BATTLE *Lubricating Engin. Handbk.* 300 The usual soluble *cutting oil is made of a combination of oils..and is designed to permit its being mixed with varying amounts of water to form a stable cutting emulsion. **1955** *Oxf. Jun. Encycl.* VIII. 248/2 Today there are various brands of cutting oils, most of which are mixtures of mineral oil, soaps, and an emulsifying chemical which makes the oils mix readily with water. These keep the tool and work-piece cool during the cutting operations, and so prevent excessive wear and distortion of the work. **1664** EVELYN *Sylva* (1776) 500 At the Kerf, or *cutting place near the root. **1684** *Lond. Gaz.* No. 1949/4 He hath rubbed the Hair in the cutting place behind. **1876** PREECE & SIVEWRIGHT *Telegraphy* 195 The *cutting-plate itself is in the form of a screw, and thus acts both as a drill and cutting-plate. **1887** F. FRANCIS *Saddle & Mocassin* (Lentzner), I had been furnished with a trained *cutting pony. **1902** A. MACGOWAN *Last Word* 435 A lady that's been as able as any cowboy on the range..to manage anything, from a cuttin' pony as fine as silk, to the meanest buckin' bronc. **1953** K. REISZ *Technique Film Editing* 279 **Cutting-print*, the particular positive print which the editor assembles and on which he works. **1892** E. P. DIXON (Hull) *Seed Catalogue* 30 A great acquisition for *cutting purposes. **1708** *New View Lond.* II. 763/2 The *Cutting Room..where they cut for the stone. **1840** DICKENS *M. Humphrey* iv. 101 A young hairdresser..had..a floor-clothed cuttin'-room upstairs. **1902** *Daily Chron.* 25 Oct. 7/6 At the rear is a cutting-room, where meat is cut up. **1918** R. WAGNER *Film Folk* vi. 273 The cutting room of a studio is the slaughterhouse of vain ambition. **1936** 'J. TEY' *Shilling for Candles* ii. 23 Treating me like bits on the cutting-room floor. **1936** *Words* Oct. 6/1 Cutting room terms are especially exotic. **1959** *Guardian* 9 Nov. 5/7 The young technicians..crowded into the cutting-room to watch some ..experimental commercials. **1874** *Field* 8 Aug., Far better than a game run off by a *cutting service. **1959** *Jazz Review* May 12/1 A wild *cutting session was in progress and sitting around the piano were twenty or thirty musicians. **1711** *Lond. Gaz.* No. 4832/4 [A horse] shod with *cutting Shoes turn'd up the inside Web. **1888** WILSON & GREY *Mod. Printing Mach.* III. xxvi. 431 Small cutting machines are frequently turned by hand... *Cutting-sticks, which fit into the table immediately under the knife, are generally made of hard wood. **1926** *Wireless World* 15 Sept. 399/2 This megaphone concentrated the sound waves on to a mechanical diaphragm to which was connected a *cutting stylus resting on a revolving disc of soft wax. **1883** *Harper's Mag.* Feb. 443/2, I caught the young ragamuffin up on one of the *cutting-tables dancing.

'cutting, *ppl. a.* [-ING².]

1. That cuts, in various senses of the verb.

c **1400** *Destr. Troy* 12802 A kene spere, cuttyng before. *c* **1530** LD. BERNERS *Arth. Lyt. Bryt.* (1814) 43 Full of cutting and sharpe rockes. **1620** VENNER *Via Recta* vii. 109 It is of a cooling, cutting, and penetrating faculty. **1696** *Lond. Gaz.* No. 3247/4 Two Swords, one..with a full cutting Blade. **1703** MOXON *Mech. Exerc.* 215 Their Edge Tools..are also of a different shape..towards the cutting end. **1885** H. C. MCCOOK *Tenants Old Farm* 240 Several large colonies of cutting-ants.

b. Of wind, weather, etc.

1798 SOUTHEY *Eng. Eclogues* iv, 'Tis cutting keen! I smart at every breath. **1821** SHELLEY *Prometh. Unb.* 270 In Lightning and cutting hail. **1834** HT. MARTINEAU *Farrers* i. 1 Perhaps you don't know..what a cutting wind it is.

c. That cuts down prices or undersells. *colloq.*

1851 MAYHEW *Lond. Labour* II. 262 (Hoppe), Those employers who seek to reduce the prices of a trade are known technologically as 'cutting employers'. *Ibid.* (1861) III. 425/2 By that time other 'cutting' shops were opened. **1884** *Christian World* 12 June 443/4 An employer of the cutting sort would..say 'Now, we must produce this article for a shilling less'.

2. That acutely wounds the mind or feelings.

1583 STANYHURST *Æneis* IV. (Arb.) 111 Dido the poore Princesse gauld with such destenye cutting, Crau's mortal passadge. **1652** STAPYLTON *Herodian* XIV. 115 Their cutting quips and wonted jeering. **1754** RICHARDSON *Grandison* IV. iv. 31 You said cutting things! Very cutting things. *a* **1796** H. VENN in *Compl. Duty Man, Mem.* (1841) 18 The cutting affliction of losing you. **1849** C. BRONTE *Shirley* ix. 123 He can say the driest, most cutting things in the quietest of tones.

†**3.** That is a 'cutter' or swaggering blade. *Obs.*

1589 R. HARVEY *Pl. Perc.* (1860) 3 Cutting Hufsnufs Roisters. *c* **1590** GREENE *Fr. Bacon* v. 19 Wherefore have I such a company of cutting knaves to wait upon me. **1592** —— *Disput.* 28 Brave youthfull Gentlemen and cutting companions. [**1821** SCOTT *Kenilw.* xix, The cutting mercer of Abingdon..dashing Master Goldthred.]

'cutting grass. [CUTTING *ppl. a.*] **1.** Any of several grasses or sedges of Australia and New Zealand having sharp-edged leaves or stems, esp. *Gahnia psittacorum*.

1831 HOVELL & HUME *Journey of Discovery to Port Phillip 1824–25* 61 They had the misfortune to encounter that species of long grass, which is known in the colony by the name of the 'cutting grass'. **1858** T. MCCOMBIE *Hist. Victoria* i. 8 Long grass, known as cutting-grass, between four and five feet high, the blade an inch and a half broad, the edges exquisitely sharp. **1894** *Age* 19 Oct. 5/8 (Morris), 'Cutting grass' is the technical term for a hard, tough grass about eight or ten inches high, three-edged like a bayonet, which stock cannot eat because in their efforts to bite it off it cuts their mouths. **1968** G. R. COCHRANE et al. *Flowers & Plants of Victoria* 16/2 The leaves of many sedges will often cause deep cuts, and they are commonly referred to as sword grass or cutting grass.

2. = *cane-rat* (CANE *sb.*¹ 10).

1934 *Times Educ. Suppl.* 31 Mar. p. iv/3 The Curator of Mammals was recently informed that some 'cutting grass' were being sent as a gift from West Africa... On arrival, they turned out to be three young great cane rats, or 'ground hogs'. **1960** *Times* 29 Sept. (Nigeria Suppl.) p. xxi/6 Roast cutting-grass.

cuttingly ('kʌtɪŋlɪ), *adv.* [f. CUTTING *ppl. a.* + -LY².] In a cutting manner, as so as to cut; sharply, acutely.

1611 FLORIO, *Alla recisa*, cuttingly, hackingly. **1649** ROBERTS *Clavis Bibl.* 404 Doth he reprove sin? how cuttingly and piercingly doth he describe it? **1805** SOUTHEY *Madoc in Azt.* xi, His struggles now But bind more close and cuttingly the band. **1871** CARLYLE in *Mrs. C.'s Lett.* III. 293 The thought is cuttingly painful while I live.

cuttle ('kʌt(ə)l), *sb.*¹ Forms: 1 cudele, 5 codull(e, cotul(l, 6–7 cuttell, (7 cudle, cuttel, cuddell, 9 *dial.* coodle, cuddle), 6– cuttle; also 6 scuttel, 7–8 SCUTTLE. [OE. *cudele*, also in OLow-Frankish, *c* 1100 (Grimm); of unknown derivation. The original form survives in the dialectal *cuddle*, *coodle*; *cuttle* appeared about 1500. Cf. Ger. *kuttel-fisch*, perh. from English.]

A cephalopod of the genus *Sepia* or family *Sepiidæ*, esp. the common cuttlefish, *Sepia officinalis*, also called *ink-fish* from its power of ejecting a black fluid from a bag or sac, so as to darken the water and conceal itself from pursuit. Thence the name is extended to other decapod, and sometimes even to octopod, cephalopods.

c **1000** *Suppl. Ælfric's Voc.* in Wr.-Wülcker 181 *Sepia*, cudele, *uel* wasescite. *c* **1490** *Promp. Parv.* 96 (K.H.) Cotul, fisshe [PYNSON cotull or codull, fisshe], *cepia*. **1538** ELYOT *Biblioth.*, *Sepia*, a fyshe callyd a Cuttell. **1597–8** BP. HALL *Sat.* IV. i. 41 The craftie Cuttle lieth sure In the blacke cloude of his thicke vomiture. **1623** WHITBOURNE *Newfoundland* 94 The Squid, which is something like the Cuddell. **1658** WILLSFORD *Natures Secrets* 135 Cuttles with their many legs swimming on the top of the water..do presage a storm. **1883** JEFFERIES *Story of my Heart* iii. 58 The ghastly cuttles. **1880** *W. Cornwall Gloss.*, *Cuddle*, *coodle*, a cuttle-fish.

β. Now usually called **cuttle-fish**.

1591 PERCIVALL *Sp. Dict.*, *Xibia*, a cuttle fish, *sepia*. **1615** CROOKE *Body of Man* 24 So the Cuttle-fish..powreth forth a blacke humor, and in that clowd she escapeth. **1766** SMOLLETT *Trav.* 166 The sepie or cuttle-fish, of which the people in this Country make delicate Ragout. **1873** DAWSON *Earth & Man* iv. 69 The highest of the Mollusca, represented in our seas by the cuttle-fishes.

†**b.** Used allusively in reference to the animal's habit of darkening the water when alarmed. *Obs.*

1555 RIDLEY *Declar. Lord's Supper* Wks. (Parker Soc.) 36 They will not cease to go about to play the cuttles, and to cast their colours over them. *a* **1556** CRANMER *Wks.* I. 75 Note well here, reader, how the cuttle cometh in with his dark colours.

2. *attrib.* and *Comb.* (of *cuttle* and *cuttle-fish*), as ***cuttle shell***, CUTTLE-BONE; ***cuttle-fish tribe***.

1802 BINGLEY *Anim. Biog.* (1813) III. 429 Of the sepia, or cuttle-fish tribe. **1812** J. SMYTH *Pract. Customs* (1821) 80 Cuttle shells or bones, produced by the Sepia or Cuttle-Fish. **1889** *Pall Mall G.* 4 Dec. 2/2 To enter into a dispute ..with such a cuttle-fish controversialist. **1891** R. KIPLING *City Dreadf. Nt.* 18 Is he trying to run a motion through under cover of a cloud of words, essaying the well-known 'cuttle-fish trick' of the West?

†**cuttle,** *sb.*² *Obs.* [app. a. OF. *coutel* (mod.F. *couteau*):—L. *cultellum* knife. Cf. COUTEL. The OF. form in *-el* was however obsolete before *cuttle* appears in Eng.] A knife. Also *fig.*

1546 BALE *Eng. Votaries* II. (1550) 14 b, Dysmembrynge hymselfe with a sharpe cuttle in her presence. **1592** GREENE *3rd Pt. Conny-catch.* 23 One..came vnto a poore Cutler to haue a Cuttle made vnto his owne minde. **1661** K. W. *Conf. Charact. Pragmatick Pulpit-filler* (1860) 83 The blunt and notcht cuttles of their wit.

b. *transf.* or ? = CUTTER¹ 3.

1597 SHAKS. *2 Hen. IV*, II. iv. 139 Away you Cut-purse Rascall, you filthy Bung, away..Ile thrust my Knife in your mouldie Chappes, if you play the sawcie Cuttle with me.

c. *Comb.*, as **cuttle-bung**, a knife used for cutting purses; **cuttle-haft**, a popular name of the Yellow Flag, *Iris Pseudacorus*.

1591 GREENE *Disc. Coosnage* (1592) 13 In Figging Law, the knife [is called] the Cuttle boung. **1599** NASHE *Lenten Stuffe* (1871) 84 He..the fisherman..unsheathed his cuttle-bong, and..dismembered him. **1610** ROWLANDS *Martin Mark-all, A Cuttle bung*, a knife to cut a purse. **1688** R. HOLME *Armoury* II. 100/1 Some call..Flag..Sword-point, or Edge-Tool; and others Cuttle-haft.

cuttle, *sb.*³ *local.* [?] A layer of cloth when the finished piece is folded.

1541 *Act 33 Hen. VIII*, c. 3 The said clothes..shall be folded either in pleights, or cuttelle, as the clothes of all other Countries of this Realme commonly haue beene vsed. **1885** *Yorkshire Wool-Trade Terms*, *Cuttle*, the layers of cloth in the finished piece. The width of the cuttle varies according to the requirements of the market for which the cloth is intended, but is generally twenty inches.

Hence **'cuttle** *v.*¹, to fold cloth so as to lay it in 'cuttles' or pleats.

1883 *Almondbury & Huddersf. Gloss.* 34 *Cuttle*, to fold cloth in the following manner. First, a small portion is doubled, then another upon it (not round it), and so on until it is all doubled up; finally wrap the end, left first or last, round all. The reasons for adopting this mode are, that the cloth is supposed to keep best; it is easier to unfold for show purposes; it piles best.

†**'cuttle,** *v.*² *rare.* [? related to CUTTER *v.*]

1746 H. WALPOLE *Lett. H. Mann* 15 Sept., Recollecting how you used to cuttle over a bit of politics with the old Marquis, I set myself to be wondrous civil to Marquis Folco. **1878** *Cumbrld. Gloss.*, *Cuttle* (North), to chat or gossip.

'cuttle-bone. The internal shell of the cuttle-fish, a light, cellular, calcareous body of an elongated oval form enclosed in the substance of the mantle; formerly used in medicine as an antacid and absorbent, and now for pounce, as a polishing material, etc.

1547 SALESBURY *Welsh Dict.*, *Bron alarch*, Scuttel bone. **1575** TURBERV. *Faulconrie* 273 The powder of a cuttell bone. **1656** RIDGLEY *Pract. Physick* 152 Driness of the Tongue is cured with scraping of cuttle bone. **1836** TODD *Cycl. Anat.* I. 546/1 The..Cuttle-bone..formerly figured in the Materia Medica as an antacid. **1841** *Penny Cycl.* XXI. 373/1 The *cuttle-bone*, as it is erroneously termed, consists of various membranes hardened by carbonate of lime, without the smallest mixture of phosphate.

cuttle-fish: see CUTTLE *sb.*¹

cuttoe ('kʌtəʊ). *Obs.* exc. *U.S.* [A 17th c. ad. F. *couteau* knife: see COUTEAU.] = COUTEAU.

1678 *Lond. Gaz.* No. 1286/4 Also a Cuttoe Sword, with a hollow ground back Blade. **1685** *Ibid.* No. 2017/8 Two Silver hilted Swords, one with a single Shell Cuttoe Hilt cut in the Shell with a silver Gilt Wire Handle, and a plain Cuttoe Blade. **1851** S. JUDD *Margaret* ii. (1871) 9 There were no suits of knives and forks, and the family helped themselves on wooden plates with cuttoes.

'cuttoo. *Carriage-building.* (See quot.)

1794 W. FELTON *Carriages* (1801) I. 48 At the two ends of this timber are left projections, called cuttoos, which cover the top or back end of the wheels, to shelter the axle-tree arms from the dirt, which would otherwise get in behind the wheels, and clog them. *Ibid.* I. 50 The fore axle-tree-bed..has also cuttoos on the ends the same as the hind bed has. *Ibid.* Gloss., *Curtuers* or *Cuttos*.

cutts, var. of CUTS².

cutty ('kʌtɪ), *a.* and *sb.* [f. CUT *v.*] **A.** *adj.*

1. Cut short, curtailed, so abnormally short as to appear to have been cut, *esp.* in certain connexions, as ***cutty knife***, ***cutty pipe*** (humorously ***cutty gun***), ***cutty spoon***, ***cutty sark***, etc. (in which the two words are often unnecessarily hyphened). *Sc.* and *north. dial.*

17.. *Old Song, Andro, etc.* (Jam.), But wha cam in to heese our hope, But Andro, wi' his cutty-gun? **1790** BURNS *Tam O'Shanter* 171 Her cutty sark, o' Paisley harn..In longitude tho' sorely scanty. **1810** CROMEK *Rem. Nithsdale Song* 208 (Jam.) He gae to me a cuttie knife, And bade me keep it as my life. **1816** SCOTT *Old Mort.* Introd., The man of cutty-spoon and ladle saw his trade interrupted. **1855** THACKERAY *Newcomes* xxiii, Allowed to use his cutty-pipe. **1878** *Cumbrld. Gloss.*, *Cutty*, short.

†**2.** In Engraving (see quot.). *Obs.*

1660 *Albert Durer Revived* 5 Let nothing be done hard, sharp, or cutty.

3. 'Testy, hasty, short of temper' (Jamieson). *Sc.*

4. *Comb.* **cutty-brown**, a dock-tailed brown horse; **cutty-stoup**, 'a pewter vessel holding the eighth part of a chopin or quart' (Jamieson).

a **1776** in Herd *Songs* (1776) II 220 (Jam.), I scoured awa to Edinborow-town, And my cutty-brown together. **17..** *Song* (Jam.), The cuttie-stoup bit hauds a soup, Gae fetch the Hawick gill, O.

5. Capable of cutting, sharp. *spec.* (*N.Z.*) **cutty grass** (also **cuttigrass**) = CUTTING GRASS I.

1903 KIPLING in *Windsor Mag.* Sept. 364/1 We'll draw fine, freehand, tribal patterns on their backs with the cutty edges of mussel-shells. **1910** L. COCKAYNE *N.Z. Plants* vii. 109 Here is also the home of the sedge family, to which the so-called 'cutty-grasses' belong. **1920** J. MANDER *Story of N.Z. River* ii. 29 Among the rushes and cuttigrass. **1927** W. H. GUTHRIE-SMITH *Birds of Water, Wood & Waste* (ed. 2) 162 The nest is planted deep..in the heart of a bunch of cutty grass. **1957** *Landfall* XI. 213 The cutty grass sawed at her dress.

B. *sb.* **1. a.** Short for *cutty spoon.* (*Sc.*)

17.. *Earl Lithgow* xlix. in Child *Ballads* IV. (1886) 470/1 Bring to me my horn cutties, That I was best used wi. **1768** ROSS *Helenore* 116 (Jam.) The green-horn cutties rattling in her lap. **1776** in Ramsay *Sc. Prov.* 44 (Jam.) It is better to sup with a cutty than want a spoon.

b. Short for *cutty pipe.*

1776 in Ramsay *Sc. Prov.* Wks. 1818. III. 185 I'm nae sae scant o'clean pipes as to blaw wi' a brunt cutty. **1859** *Macm. Mag.* Nov. 74 Either as long clay or as cutty. **1888** M. ROBERTSON *Lombard St. Myst.* xv, Knocking the ashes of his cutty on the floor.

2. a. 'A short stump of a girl. *Dumfriesshire*' (Jamieson). **b.** A term of reprobation for a testy, or naughty girl or woman; but often used playfully.

1816 SCOTT *Old Mort.* x, He's gaun to be merried to Meg Murdieson, ill-faur'd cuttie as she is. **1830** GALT *Lawrie T.* VII. xi. (1849) 351 The cutty of a servant lass said..with a smile that Miss Beeny was at home. **1891** BARRIE *Lit. Minister* I. viii. 131 To gie her her due, she's cracky, and as for her being a cuttie, you've said so yoursel.

3. A familiar local appellation of some animals: **a.** The wren; also *cutty-quean, -wren.* **b.** The Black Guillemot (*Uria Grylle*). **c.** The hare.

a **1776** in Herd *Sc. Songs* (1776) II. 167 (Jam.) Go, pack ye out at my chamber door, Ye little cutty-quean. *a* **1808** FLEMING *Tour in Arran* (Jam.), On the passage I observed several Black Guillemots..which the boatmen called cutties. **1819** *Edin. Mag.* July 507 (Jam.) Common Hare.—Maukin, Cuttie. **1875** PARISH *Sussex Gloss., Cutty*, a wren; also called a *kitty.* **1883** *Hampsh. Gloss., Cuttran, Cutty*, a wren. *Cutty* is the commoner term.

cutty-stool. *Sc.* [CUTTY *a.*]

1. A low stool.

1820 SCOTT *Monast.* iv, Hitching her seat of honour..a little nearer to the cuttie-stool on which Tibb was seated. **1832-53** *Whistle-binkie* (Sc. Songs) Ser. III. 120, I grieve to see ye sit Sae laigh upon your cutty stool In sic a dorty fit!

2. Formerly, in Scotland, a particular seat in a church, where offenders against chastity, or other delinquents, had to sit during the time of divine service and receive a public rebuke from the minister; the stool of repentance. Also *fig.*

a **1774** FERGUSSON *Farmer's Ingle* Poems (1845) 37 Marion for a bastard son Upon the cutty stool was forced to ride. **1791** NEWTE *Tour Eng. & Scot.* 251 In most of the kirks there is a small gallery..painted black, placed in an elevated situation, near the roof of the church, which they call the cutty-stool, and on which offenders against chastity are forced to sit. **1818** KEATS *Life & Lett.* I. 170 If he does I must sit on the cutty-stool all next winter. **1871** C. GIBBON *Lack of Gold* viii, To sit in penance on the cutty-stool.

cut-under. *U.S.* More fully *cut-under buggy*; a vehicle having the body cut out so as to allow the front wheels to pass under in turning.

1887 A. HAYES *Jesuit's Ring* 61, I have chartered a cut-under. Jump in.

cut-up, *sb.* [CUT *v.* 60; in sense 2 from the ppl. adj.] **1. a.** An act of cutting up.

1782 MISS BURNEY *Cecilia* IX. i, 'Why indeed, sir,' said Hobson, 'I can't but say it was rather a cut-up.' **1878** M. C. JACKSON *Chaperon's Cares* xi, It will be a fearful cut-up for the Hartopp girls.

b. orig. *U.S.* (*a*) The act of making practical or verbal jokes; clowning. *rare.* (*b*) A person who 'cuts up' or capers (see CUT *v.* 60 m and o). Also *attrib.*

1843 'R. CARLTON' *New Purchase* II. 209 Art and tact..are requisite for the cut-up... If the affair is not done up to the point—it is teasing; if beyond—it is horse-play. *Ibid.*, The cut-ups were usually in wet weather. **1882** I. M. RITTENHOUSE *Maud* (1939) iii. 91 He and the Menagers are the greatest friends imaginable and such cut-ups. **1911** R. W. CHAMBERS *Common Law* v. 157 Jests emanating from the boarding-house cut-up—a blonde young man with rah-rah hair and a brier pipe. **1923** R. D. PAINE *Comr. Rolling Ocean* viii. 129 As a college cut-up he was the star comedian of the campus. **1936** WODEHOUSE *Laughing Gas* x. 107 Anything for a laugh is your motto. Well, good night, old cut-up. **1960** B. KEATON *Wonderf. World of Slapstick* (1967) 122 We cutups and cute kids only had one bad moment. **1969** *Listener* 16 Jan. 87/2 We have to take his word for most of what we're told in the book's final section; for the cut-ups and the rave-ups, for that wild weekend with 'Ronnie' Laing.

2. A kind of hosiery (see quot. 1892).

1845 *Encycl. Metrop.* VIII. 749/1, 6,000 frames making cut-ups, &c., produce 1,960,000 dozens. **1892** *Labour Commission* Gloss., *Cut-ups*, articles made upon steam round-about machines, sometimes in long straight pieces, which are cut up with scissors into the shape of stockings, shirts, or pants, and sewn together by a machine. **1893** *Westm. Gaz.* 10 Mar. 6/3 'Cut-ups' are an inferior class of hosiery turned out by the machine in long straight lengths.

† **'cut-waist.** *Obs.* An insect, *esp.* one with the division between thorax and abdomen deeply cut.

1607 TOPSELL *Serpents* (1653) 659 Wilde Hornets..live in the hollow trunks or cavities of trees, there keeping themselves close all the Winter long, as other Cut-wasts do. *Ibid.* 779 The Butter-fly, or any other Cut-waste.

So **'cut-waisted** *ppl. a.*

1577 HARRISON *England* III. vi. (1878) II. 36 The cut wasted (for so I English the word *Insecta*) are the hornets, waspes, bees, and such like. **1607** TOPSELL *Serpents* (1608) 638 A Bee is a cut-wasted living creature.

cutwal, -waul: see KOTWAL, Indian police officer.

cutwater, cut-water ('kʌt,wɔːtə(r)).

1. The knee of the head of a ship, etc., which serves to divide the water before it reaches the bow; also, the forward edge of the stem or prow.

1644 J. WINTHROP *Hist. New Engl.* (1853) II. 239 It struck against the head of a bolt in the cut-water of the Dartmouth ship, and went no further. **1712** W. ROGERS *Voy.* 218 Her Rudder and Cut-water were eaten to pieces. **1789** G. VASSA *Life* (1792) 102 She struck our ship with her cutwater. **1853** KANE *Grinnell Exp.* I. (1856) 477 Stretching from end to end, and shielded at the stem and stern by cutwaters of bone. **1866** R. M. BALLANTYNE *Shifting Winds* xiii. (1881) 132 The steamer..sent the cutwater crashing through bulwark, plank, and beam.

2. The wedge-shaped end of the pier of a bridge which serves to divide the current, break up masses of ice, etc., flowing against the pier.

1776 G. SEMPLE *Building in Water* 100 Brace your Cut-water Pile with temporary Braces. *Ibid.* 101 The Cut-water in the first projecting Course of the Pier.

3. An American sea-fowl, the Skimmer, *Rhynchops nigra*, allied to the terns.

1732 MORTIMER in *Phil. Trans.* XXXVII. 449 *Larus major rostro inæquali.* The Cut-Water. They probably take their English Name from their commonly flying close to the Water, from the Surface whereof they seem to scoop up some Food with the under Part of their Bill, which is much longer than the upper. **1787** LATHAM *Hist. Birds* App. I. 269 The head preponderates for some distance, when the bill is seen to cut the water; hence the name of Cut-water. **1844** DE KAY *Zool. N.Y.* II. 297 The..Cut-water..reaches our coast from tropical America in May.

'cut-weed. 'A name applied to various marine Algæ, as *Fucus vesiculosus*, *F. serratus*, and *Laminaria digitata*' (Britten and Holl.).

† **'cutwith, 'cutwithy.** *Obs.* exc. *dial.* Forms: 5 **cutwythy**, 6 **-wydy**, 7 **-withy**, 9 **-widdie, -wuddie.** [f. CUT *ppl. a.* + WITH, WITHY twig.] The cross-bar or similar fastening at the end of the beam of a plough or harrow to which the gear of the draught animals is attached.

1565 *Richmond. Wills* (Surtees) 179, ij coulters, ij paire cutwydyes, j. horse draughte. **1624** *N. Riding Rec.* (1885) III. II. 201 An Acklam labourer presented for stealing two yron cutwithies. **1823** TENNANT *Card. Beaton* 114 (Jam.) Couters, and barrow-trams, an' cudwuddies. **1825** JAMIESON, *Cutwiddies*, the links which join the swingletrees to the threiptree in a plough. *Clydes.* **1863** MORTON *Cycl. Agric.* Gloss., *Cutwith* (Heref.), the bar of the plough to which the traces are attached.

'cut-work, 'cutwork.

1. *gen.* Work produced by cutting or carving.

1662 EVELYN *Chalcogr.* 6 Those who wrought any of these hollow cut-works, were by some call'd Cavatores, and Graphatores. **1832** MISS MITFORD *Village* (1863) 509 The Valentine..a raised group of roses and heart's-ease, executed on a kind of paper cut-work. **1877** *N.W. Linc. Gloss., Cutwork*, (1) open-work carving.

2. a. The embroidery with elaborately cut-out edges in vogue towards the close of the 14th c. **b.** A kind of openwork embroidery or lace worn in the latter part of the 16th and in the 17th c. **c.** Appliqué work, in which the pattern is cut out and sewed upon the ground.

1470 HARDING *Chron.* CXCIII. iii, Cut werke was greate both in court and tounes, Bothe in menes hoddis and also in their gounes. **1576** GASCOIGNE *Steel Gl.* (Arb.) 71 Baudkin, broydrie, cutworks, nor conceits. **1621-51** BURTON *Anat. Mel.* II. ii. IV, Women..haue curious needle-workes, cut-workes, bone-lace, &c. to busie themselues about. **1698** *Lond. Gaz.* No. 3373/3 An Act for rendring the Laws more Effectual, for Preventing the Importation of Foreign Bone-lace, Loom-lace, Needle-work, Point, and Cut-work. **1869** MRS. PALLISER *Lace* i. 5 There is preserved in the Cathedral at Prague an altar-cloth of embroidery and cutwork worked by Anne of Bohemia, queen of Richard II. **1876** ROCK *Text. Fabr.* 88 When anything..is wrought by itself upon a separate piece of silk or canvas and afterwards sewed on to the vestment..it comes to be known as cut-work.

attrib. **1599** B. JONSON *Ev. Man out of Hum.* IV. iv, Six purls of an Italian cut-work band I wore. **1624** MASSINGER *Parl. Love* II. i, An Italian cutwork smock. **1820** SCOTT *Monast.* xvi, Three cut-work shirts with falling bands.

† **3.** Flower-beds elaborately cut into patterns of which the details are outlined in turf. Much in vogue about 1700. *Obs.*

1693 EVELYN *De la Quint. Compl. Gard.*, Dict., *Cutworks*, are Flower Plots, or Grass plot consisting of several pieces cut into various pleasing figures answering one another, like cut work, made by Women. **1712** J. JAMES tr. *Le Blond's Gardening* 34 Parterres of Cut-work..differ from the others, in that all the Parts which compose them should be cut with Symmetry. **1727** BRADLEY *Fam. Dict.* s.v. *Flower*, It must be always observ'd that Ranunculus's and Tulips be put apart, in particular Cut-works, and in separate Beds.

† **4.** Work in cutting, hacking, or slashing. *Obs.*

1620 FLETCHER *Chances* II. iii, If he cut here, I'll find him cut-work.

5. In *Printing.* Woodcut-work, i.e. the printing of work containing cuts or illustrations. [f. CUT *sb.*[2] 21.]

'cutworm. A caterpillar which cuts off by the surface of the ground the young plants of cabbage, melons, maize, etc.; *esp.* in *U.S.*, the larvæ of species of *Agrotis*, a genus of moths.

1808-79 JAMIESON, *Cutworm*, a small white grub, which destroys coleworts and other vegetables of this kind, by cutting through the stem near the roots. **1817-8** COBBETT *Resid. U.S.* (1822) 187 No patching after the cut-worm, or brown grub. **1883** *Cassell's Nat. Hist.* vi. 30 Perhaps the most formidable of all [caterpillars] are those called 'cutworms' in America, which live beneath the surface of the ground, and eat through the roots of plants.

† **cut'zooks.** *Obs.* = COTZOOKS, GADZOOKS.

1719 D'URFEY *Pills* III. 42 At last Cutzooks, he made such sport.

cuuaunt, cuunand, obs. ff. COVENANT.

cuuel, -staf, obs. ff. COWL, -STAFF.

‖ **cuve.** *Obs.* [F. *cuve*:—L. *cūpa.*] A cask, vat.

14.. *Voc.* in Wr.-Wülcker 577/22 *Cuva*, a cuve or a vaat. **1630** *R. Johnson's Kingd. & Commw.* 175 Wine, one million two hundred thousand Cuves. **1673** O. WALKER *Educ.* I. ix. 95 As the wine which pleaseth in the cuve must be drunk in the must.

‖ **cuvée** (kyve). [Fr., lit. 'vatful' (*cuve*, see CUVE).] The contents of a vat of wine; a particular blend or batch of wine.

1833 C. REDDING *Mod. Wines* iv. 68 *Cuvée*, the contents either of a cellar or vat at the vintage. **1883** *19th Cent.* Sept. (Advt.) (Stanford), Perrier Jouet's..Extra Dry [Champagne] Reserved Cuvee. **1911** *Encycl. Brit.* XXVIII. 724/1 These vattings, and indeed all blendings of any particular batch of wines, are termed *cuvées.* **1920** G. SAINTSBURY *Notes Cellar-Bk.* vi. 99 Some of the great shippers used to send out wines cheaper than their official *cuvées.* **1939** E. AMBLER *Mask of Dimitrios* xiv. 301 The wine must be champagne..it must be a vintage *cuvée.* **1968** *Vogue* Dec. 40/2 Even the great *Cuvée* could not wash away the lump in my throat.

‖ **cuvette** *sb.*[1] (ky'vɛt). [Fr., dim. of *cuve* (see above); applied to various basins: the use in Fortification shows some confusion (perhaps graphic) with *cunette.*]

1. *Fort.* = CUNETTE.

1678 tr. *Gaya's Art of War* II. 115 *Cuvette*, a little Ditch made in the middle of the great Foss. **1704** in HARRIS *Lex. Tech.* **1706** in PHILLIPS. **1721** in BAILEY. **1761** STERNE *Tr. Shandy* III. xxiv, Trim's foot getting into the cuvette, he tumbled full against the bridge too.

2. An ornamental shallow dish or basin for holding water, etc.

1706 PHILLIPS (ed. Kersey), *Cuvet*, (*Fr.*) a kind of Dish of an Oval Form. *Cuvette*, a Cistern for a Dining-room. **1725** BRADLEY *Fam. Dict.* s.v. *Oils*, Putting the Cuvets on a Silver Dish, with a Silver Ladle therein, with which every one of the Guests may take out some Soop, when the Oil is set on the Table. **1887** tr. *Sachs' Lect. Physiol. Plants* 305 Glass vessels with parallel walls, and as large as possible (so called Cuvettes), were filled with the solutions, and fixed something like windows.

3. *Glass-making.* A large clay basin or crucible used in making plate glass (see quot. 1875).

1832 G. R. PORTER *Porcelain & Gl.* 199 The other crucibles, which are smaller, are called cuvettes. **1875** URE *Dict. Arts* II. 662 The *cuvettes* receive the melted glass..and decant it out on the table to be rolled into a plate.

4. *Geol.* (See quot. 1929.)

1907 *Daily Chron.* 28 Oct. 3/3 The sand dunes and cuvettes round Lake Chad. **1910** *Encycl. Brit.* X. 598/1 There are 'short-synclines', '*brachysynclinaux*' or 'cuvettes'. **1929** L. J. WILLS *Physiogr. Evol. Britain* II. vi. 79 *Cuvette* is a convenient term for a basin in which sedimentation is going on..as distinct from a tectonic basin due to folding of pre-existing rocks.

[**cuvette.** *sb.*[2] A spoon-like instrument used in extracting a cataract. Error for CURETTE. 1849 in CRAIG; hence in some later Dicts.]

Cuvierian (kjuːvɪ'ɪərɪən), *a.* [f. *Cuvier* (see below) + -IAN.] Of, pertaining to, or named after the French naturalist Georges Cuvier (1769-1832); characteristic of his methods or system of classification.

Cuvierian ducts, two short transverse venous ducts in the vertebrate fœtus and in fishes which return the blood from the cardinal veins to the sinus venosus of the heart; the common cardinal veins. ***Cuvierian organs*** (see quot. 1897).

1856 *Chambers's Jrnl.* 27 Sept. 207/2 A Cuvierian examination of the various articles. **1870** G. ROLLESTON *Forms Anim. Life* 146 It has been said that the 'Cuvierian organs', certain structures of..doubtful function attached to the stem of the respiratory tree or inserted upon the cloaca, are wanting in all Cucumariae with unequal tentacles. *Ibid.* 262 (*index*) Cuvierian ducts. **1897** PARKER & HASWELL *Zool.* I. ix. 394 In the Holothurians..the 'Cuvierian organs' are simple filiform glandular tubes.. connected with the cloaca. **1905** H. S. PRATT *Vertebr. Zoöl.* 52 Joining each end of the transverse sinus venosus is a large and conspicuous duct or sinus called the Cuvierian duct.

1962 D. NICHOLS *Echinoderms* vi. 81 In aspidochirotes there are two groups of special defensive cuvierian organs branching from the bases of the respiratory trees. **1964** W. COLEMAN *G. Cuvier Zoologist* iii. 50 The second Cuvierian anatomical rule, the subordination of characters, may be considered as the epitome of the hierarchical arrangement of functions and therefore of organs.

cuvy. *local.* The name given in the Orkneys to a large sea-weed, *Laminaria digitata.*
1841 HARVEY *Phycol. Brit.* I. Table 338. **1866** CLOUSTON in *Treas. Bot.* 365 The Cuvy growing so far out in the sea.

cuvyn(e, cuwyn(e, obs. Sc. forms of COVIN.

cuward, obs. form of COWARD.

cuy-: see CUI-, COI-.

†**cuyl,** *v. Obs. rare.* [a. F. *cueill-ir, cuill-ir*:—L. *colligĕre* to collect. Cf. COIL *v.*[1], CULL *v.*[1]] To collect.
c **1380** WYCLIF *Wks.* (1880) 433 þei ben cuylid pens of pore men.

cuyl(l, var. CULE *Obs.*, fundament; obs. f. KILL.

cuynde, obs. form of KIND.

cuyr, obs. form of CURE *sb.*[1]

cuyschun, -sshen, cuȝshen, obs. ff. CUSHION.

cuz. [Abbrev. of COUSIN.]
1. Also **cuzze, cuze.** Obs. var. of COZ q.v.
2. (See quot.)
1730–1800 BAILEY, *Cuz*, a name or title among Printers, given to one who submits to the Performance of some jocular Ceremonies; after which, and a drinking Bout, he is intitled to some peculiar Privileges in the Chapel or Printing-House.

Cuzco-bark, -china: see CUSCO-.

cuzen, obs. form of COUSIN.

cw-, OE. and early ME spelling of QU-: as *cwath, cweth,* obs. forms of QUOTH. Also early Sc. spelling of CU- (*cou-*): as *cwld, cwnnand, cwnyhe* (= *cunye*), etc.

†**cweise.** *Obs. rare.* [a. ON. *kveisa* whitlow, boil.] A sore or boil.
a **1225** *Ancr. R.* 328 þeos kointe harloz þet scheaweð forð hore gutefestre & hore vlowinde cweisen.

cwm (kuːm). *Geol.* [Welsh *cwm* (cf. COOMB[2]).] A valley; in *Phys. Geogr.*, a bowl-shaped hollow partly enclosed by steep walls lying at the head of a valley or on a mountain slope and formed originally by a glacier; a cirque.
1853 MRS. GASKELL *Ruth* I. vii. 170 Some 'Cwm', or hollow. **1882** GEIKIE *Text-bk. Geol.* III. II. ii. 407 Several hundred feet below, in the corrie or cwm at the bottom, lies the re-cemented glacier. **1933** *Geogr. Jrnl.* LXXXII. 202 The snow-patches are cwm-ice masses occupying deep scallops in an elevated position of the old erosion-surface. **1936** *Nature* 19 Dec. 1041/2 Its glaciers..widened their heads into cwms and gave to the basin its only fiord. **1951** *Times* 27 Nov. 5/7 While 'cwm' may occur..purely as a place-name..technically the word is restricted to the huge cauldron-shaped hollows found high up on heavily glaciated slopes. **1953** J. HUNT *Ascent of Everest* ii. 14 When Mallory saw it..in 1921, he named it the 'Western Cwm'. **1957** G. E. HUTCHINSON *Treat. Limnol.* I. i. 59 Such amphitheaters are called *cirques* in the French-speaking parts of the Alps, *Kars* in the German-speaking regions, *cwms* in Wales, and *corries* in Scotland. All four terms have achieved some degree of international usage, but the first seems to have been the most widely employed.

cwoint(e, obs. form of QUAINT.

cwsynes, obs. Sc. form of COUSINESS.

cwt., abbreviated symbol of HUNDREDWEIGHT (*c* standing for L. *centum* hundred, and *wt.* for *weight*). Formerly also c. or C. alone.

cy, cye, OE. pl. of cow.

-cy, suffix of sbs., originating in L. *-cia, -tia,* Gr. *-κια, -κεια, -τια,-τεια,* in which the abstract ending *-ia* (-Y) follows another formative element. Occurring chiefly in the combined forms -ACY, -ANCY, -ENCY, -CRACY, -MANCY, q.v. Also in *prophecy,* Gr. *προφητεία,* f. *προφήτης* prophet; *policy,* Gr. *πολιτεία,* f. *πολίτης* citizen, -polite, *secrecy* f. *secret.* In words in *-acy* from L. *-ātia,* and those in *-ncy,* the *c* represents an original *t* before *i,* which became *c* often in late L. and in French, e.g. L. *infantia,* late L. also *infancia,* F. *enfance, infancy.* Hence abstracts in *-ncy* arise out of adjs. or sbs. in *-nt,* expressing the quality of an adjective (*fluent, fluency*), or the estate or position of an agent or officer (*agent, agency*). But by proximity of sound, *-cy* is extended from sbs. in *-nt* to some in *-n,* e.g. *chaplain-cy, captain-cy, alderman-cy* (after *incumbency, lieutenancy, adjutancy*), and *-cy* being thus treated as an independent suffix = *ship,* is extended to other words as *colonel-cy,* and is even added to words in *-t* (instead of being substituted for the *-t*), as in *bankrupt-cy* (for which the regular etymological form is *bankrupcy*), *idiot-cy* variant of *idiocy* (Gr. *ἰδιωτεία*), *baronet-cy, brevet-cy, cornet-cy* (as against *secret, secrecy*).

cya-, shortened form of CYANO-, in the names of some chemical compounds, as **cy'amelide,** a white crystalline substance polymeric with cyanic acid, called also *insoluble cyanuric acid.* **cyame'luric acid,** a white crystalline powder formed from mellone by the action of alkalis at boiling heat; a salt of this is a **cyame'lurate. cy'aphenine,** a substance polymeric with phenyl cyanide.
1850 DAUBENY *Atom. Th.* vii. (ed. 2) 183 Hydrated cyanic acid..decomposes spontaneously into cyamelide, a white porcelain looking solid, insoluble in water.

'cyamid. *Zool.* A crustacean of the family *Cyamidæ*; a whale-louse.

cyamoid ('saɪəmɔɪd), *a. rare.*—[0] [f. Gr. *κύαμ-ος* bean + -OID.] 'Resembling a small bean' (*Syd. Soc. Lex.* 1882).

cyan ('saɪən). = CYAN-BLUE.
1889 in *Cent. Dict.* **1957** R. W. G. HUNT *Reprod. Colour* iv. 37 The colours of the dyes used are cyan, magenta, and yellow. **1964** *Observer* 22 Nov. 23/1 Pinkish lights would make the picture greenish-blue or cyan, the engineers' word for sickly green.

cyan-. **1.** Combining form of Gr. *κύανος* and *κυάνεος* 'dark-blue' before a vowel: see following words, and CYANO-, also CYAN-BLUE.
2. *Chem.* = CYANO- 2, used as combining form of CYANOGEN before a vowel, and in names of cyanogen compounds and derivatives, as in CYANAMIDE, CYANATE, CYANIC, CYANIDE *sb.*, etc. Also **cyan'hydric** *a.* = hydrocyanic. **cya'nuramide,** an organic base polymeric with cyanamide; also called melamine. **cya'nurate,** a salt of **cya'nuric** [URIC], or **cyanu'renic** acid, an acid polymeric with cyanic acid, obtained by heating dry urea in a flask; it is inodorous and not poisonous. **cya'nylic** [-YL] *acid,* an acid isomeric with cyanuric acid; a salt of this is a **cy'anylate.** Also *cyanacetate, cyanethine,* etc.
1838 T. THOMSON *Chem. Org. Bodies* 208 *Cyanuric acid.* This acid..has been described in the *Chemistry of Inorganic Bodies* (vol. ii. p. 227), under the name of *cyanic acid. Ibid.* 211 Cyanilic acid was discovered by M. Liebig in 1833. **1869** ROSCOE *Elem. Chem.* 369 Obtained synthetically by the action of potash upon ethyl cyanacetate. **1877** WATTS *Fownes' Chem.* II. 97 Cyanuric acid is changed by a very high temperature into cyanic acid.

cyanamide (saɪ'ænəmaɪd). *Chem.* [f. CYAN- 2 + AMIDE.]The amide of cyanogen CN_2H_2, a white crystalline body; also, a salt of this compound, in which one or both of the hydrogen atoms are replaced by another element or radical; *spec.* = calcium cyanamide ($CaCn_2$), used as a fertilizer and as a source of other nitrogen compounds. *cyanamide process,* the production of calcium cyanamide by the reaction between calcium carbide (CaC_2) and nitrogen at a high temperature.
1838 T. THOMSON *Chem. Org. Bodies* 781 If we sprinkle ammonia on crystallized chloride of cyanogen, and heat gently, it loses its crystalline aspect, and is reduced to a white powder..This substance is *cyanamide.* **1897** *Jrnl. Chem. Soc.* LXXI. I. 460 Among the products of the change..we get sodium cyanide and sodium cyanamide, $C(NNa)_2$. **1914** J. KNOX *Fixation Atmosph. Nitrogen* 88 The metallic cyanamides are derivatives of cyanamide, H_2CN_2. **1922** PARTINGTON & PARKER *Nitrogen Industry* 188 The second important method of nitrogen fixation—viz., the cyanamide process. **1926** J. F. CROWLEY in E. Fyleman tr. *Waeser's Atmosph. Nitr. Industry* I. p. xiv, Cyanamide has been found to be a useful fertiliser for particular soils. **1965** P. A. S. SMITH *Chem. Open-Chain Org. Nitrogen Compounds* I. vi. 251 Substituted cyanamides are for the most part named by simply adding the name of the substituent, as 'methylcyanamide'. *Ibid.* 253 Heavy metal cyanamides, however, have solubilities similar to sulfides and acetylides.

cyanate ('saɪəneɪt). *Chem.* [f. CYAN- 2 + -ATE.] A salt of cyanic acid.
1845–6 G. DAY tr. *Simon's Anim. Chem.* I. 50 Urea may also be obtained..by the decomposition of certain cyanates.

cyan-blue. [f. Gr. *κύαν-ος* or *κυάν-εος* (see below).] A greenish-blue colour, lying between green and blue in the spectrum.
1879 ROOD *Chromatics* vii. 81 The lake itself displays a wonderfully intense cyan-blue colour. **1880** *Nature* XXI. 426 The cyan-blue region lying between green and blue.

‖**cyanea** (saɪ'eɪniːə). [fem. of L. *cyaneus,* Gr. *κυάνεος* dark blue.] A genus of jelly-fishes. Hence **cy'aneid,** a jelly-fish of this family.
1883 C. F. HOLDER in *Harper's Mag.* Jan. 181/2 The cyaneas tint the sea with a greenish light.

cyanean (saɪ'eɪniːən), *a. rare.* [f. L. *cyane-us* (see prec.) + -AN.] Of an azure colour.
1846 WORCESTER cites PENNANT.

cyaneous (saɪ'eɪniːəs), *a. rare.* [f. as prec. + -OUS.] Deep blue, azure.
1688 R. HOLME *Armoury* II. 311/2 Cyaneous [is] a bright blue, an azure colour. **1843** HUMPHREYS *Brit. Moths* I. 30 The fringe..of a cyaneous colour.

cya'nescent, *a.* [f.L. *cyane-us* after *albescent,* etc.] Inclining to cyaneous; of a dark bluish colour.
1882 in *Syd. Soc. Lex.*

cyanhydric, cyanilic: see CYAN- 2.

‖**cya'nia.** [mod.L.] A synonym of CYANOSIS.
1834 GOOD *Study Med.* (ed. 4) II. 667.

cyanic (saɪ'ænɪk), *a.* [f. CYAN- 2 + -IC.]
1. *Chem.* Of cyanogen, containing cyanogen in composition. ***cyanic acid,*** a colourless, pungent, volatile, unstable liquid (CNHO). ***cyanic ethers,*** the cyanates of the alcohol radicals.
1832 CHRISTISON *Poisons* xxviii. (ed. 2) 663 Cyanic and Cyanous acids are not poisonous. **1869** ROSCOE *Elem. Chem.* 378 Cyanic acid itself cannot be prepared in the free state from its salts.
2. Blue, azure; **a.** in *Path.*, of a diseased condition of the skin, etc.; **b.** in *Bot.*, one of the two series into which Candolle divided the colours of flowers (the other being *xanthic* = yellow).
1849–52 TODD *Cycl. Anat.* IV. 1455/2 A soldier..attracted particular attention on account of the cyanic colour of his sclerotica. **1879** *Edin. Rev.* CL. 382 Some whites belong to the xanthic, and some to the cyanic, group of colours.

cyanicide (saɪ'ænɪsaɪd). *Metallurgy.* [f. CYAN(IDE + -CIDE 1.] Any substance present in an ore or in tailings which consumes the cyanide in the solution used for cyaniding gold or silver, so reducing its effectiveness as a solvent for those metals.
1894 *Jrnl. Soc. Chem. Industry* 31 Oct. 951/2 To overcome the cyanide-destroying qualities of the acid or iron salts present it is necessary to have recourse to neutralisation.., with or without a preliminary water washing to remove such soluble 'cyanicides' as may be present. **1904** JULIAN & SMART *Cyaniding* xxviii. 202 The principal cyanicide remaining in the Rand concentrates is the basic ferric sulphate. **1936** J. V. N. DORR *Cyanidation Gold & Silver Ores* ix. 152 If precious-metal ores contain cyanicides, which preclude the use of cyanidation, flotation may be the only solution. **1966** *McGraw-Hill Encycl. Sci. & Technol.* VI. 233/1 Sulfides of copper, iron, antimony, and arsenic (cyanicides)..consume cyanide and oxygen, thus causing poor gold recoveries.

,cyani'dation. *Metallurgy.* [f. CYANIDE *v.*: see -ATION.] The process of cyaniding gold or silver ores; the extraction of these metals from their ores by means of the cyanide process.
1896 *N. Amer. Rev.* Apr. 479 The development of certain wet processes, cyanidation..has supplemented the work. **1915** T. K. ROSE *Metall. Gold* (ed. 6) xiii. 281 The roasting of gold ores as a preliminary to chlorination or cyanidation. **1936** [see CYANICIDE]. **1959** J. NEWTON *Extractive Metall.* vii. 431 Cyanidation is the most important for recovering gold, but it is often used in conjunction with other processes.

cyanide ('saɪənaɪd), *sb. Chem.* [f. CYAN- 2 + -IDE.] **a.** A simple compound of cyanogen with a metal or an organic radical, as ***potassium cyanide*** (KCy), an extremely poisonous crystalline solid.
1826 HENRY *Elem. Chem.* I. 458 Cyanide of Iodine. *c* **1865** G. GORE in *Circ. Sc.* I. 226/1 The cyanide produced by the fusion of the ferro-cyanide of potassium alone..is termed 'black cyanide'.
b. *attrib.* ***cyanide gauze,*** a gauze rendered antiseptic by impregnation with a cyanide, used in dressing wounds; ***cyanide hardening,*** case-hardening of iron or steel by the cyanide process; ***cyanide process,*** (*a*) a method of extracting gold and silver from ores by treatment with a dilute solution of sodium or calcium cyanide (or, formerly, potassium cyanide); (*b*) the fixation of atmospheric nitrogen by chemical reaction at high temperatures so as to form alkali cyanides or other cyanogen derivatives; (*c*) a process for case-hardening iron or steel by immersing it in molten cyanide and then quenching it in water or oil.
1895 *Arnold & Sons' Catal. Surg. Instr.* 726 Double Zinc-Cyanide Gauze. **1913** A. BENNETT *Regent* ii. §4 He did nothing but cover up the place with a bit of cyanide gauze. **1925** R. W. G. HINGSTON in E. F. Norton *Fight for Everest: 1924* III. vi. 350 The following equipment is required:..Cyanide gauze, 2 lb. **1921** *Jrnl. Iron & Steel Inst.* CIII. 435 Cyanide Hardening Due to Nitrogen... Steel case-hardened in cyanide contains much nitrogenised material, and nitrogen is believed to exert an appreciable influence on the properties of steel so treated. **1928** *Ibid.* CXVIII. 365 General practice in cyanide hardening is discussed, and reference is made to the Shimer process for case hardening and the cyanogen gas process. **1890** J. S. MACARTHUR in *Jrnl. Soc. Chem. Industry* 31 Mar. 270/1 By the cyanide process, ores containing lead, zinc, or earthy carbonates which cannot be worked to profit by chlorination, may be as ..profitably treated as any other. **1926** E. FYLEMAN tr.

Waeser's Atmosph. Nitr. Industry 486 (*heading*) The cyanide processes. **1940** R. H. Heyer *Engin. Physical Metall.* x. 341 The speed, low cost,..and cleanliness of the hardened surface make the cyanide process readily adaptable to production heat treatment. **1945** D. M. Liddell *Handbk. Nonferrous Metall.* (ed. 2) II. xi. 294 Outside of smelting and refining, the present-day metallurgy of gold and silver may be summarized under three heads: mechanical methods.., amalgamation, and the cyanide process. **1959** *Chambers's Encycl.* VI. 413/2 The cyanide process was developed by J. S. Macarthur and R. W. and W. Forrest of Glasgow and used at Johannesburg in 1890.

'cyanide, *v. Metallurgy.* [f. the sb.] *trans.* To treat with a cyanide. **a.** To treat (ores of gold or silver) with a dilute cyanide solution as part of the cyanide process for extracting the metal. **b.** To immerse (iron or steel) in molten cyanide in order to case-harden it. Hence **'cyanided** *ppl. a.*; **'cyanider; 'cyaniding** *vbl. sb.*

a. 1894 *N. Brit. Daily Mail* 30 July 5 Cyaniding syndicates. **1895** M. Eissler *Cyanide Process* 39 The cost of cyaniding was as follows. **1896** *Daily News* 10 Dec. 2/7, 2,666 tons cyanided, producing 352 ozs. **1900** J. Park *Cyanide Process* 124 The many worries which the use of cyanide entails on even the successful cyanider. **1945** D. M. Liddell *Handbk. Nonferrous Metall.* (ed. 2) II. xi. 294 Chlorination of gold and hyposulphite leaching of silver ores were practically superseded by cyaniding by the year 1900. **1959** J. Newton *Extractive Metall.* vii. 431 Flotation may be used to produce concentrates that can be cyanided or amalgamated. **1965** G. J. Williams *Econ. Geol. N.Z.* viii. 109/2 In the late 1890's interest revived in the hope that the ore could be cyanided. **b. 1921** *Jrnl. Iron & Steel Inst.* CIII. 435 After annealing the cyanided bar is still hard to file. **1940** R. H. Heyer *Engin. Physical Metall.* x. 348 In certain carburizing and cyaniding processes nitrogen is introduced into the steel in addition to the carbon. **1966** *McGraw-Hill Encycl. Sci. & Technol.* XIII. 313/2 Both carburizing steels and medium carbon steels..are often cyanided.

cyanidin (saɪˈænɪdɪn). *Chem.* [a. G. *cyanidin* (Willstätter and Everest 1913, in *Ann. d. Chemie* CDI. 204), f. CYAN- + -IDIN.] An anthocyanidin (usu. isolated as the chloride, $C_{15}H_{11}O_6Cl$) which in combination with various sugars constitutes many of the most important natural anthocyanin plant pigments.

1914 *Chem. Abstr.* VIII. 336 A violet sol[utio]n..is hydrolyzed..giving 2 mol[ecule]s glucose and cyanidin chloride, $C_{16}H_{13}O_7Cl$. *Ibid.* 3422 If quercetin be reduced at 35° instead of at 0°, a small quant[ity] (0·5–4·0%) of cyanidin is formed. **1939** *Thorpe's Dict. Appl. Chem.* (ed. 4) III. 512/1 Cyanidin is the most common and widely distributed of the anthocyan pigments of plants, and occurs naturally in the form of various glycosides. **1966** J. B. Harborne in T. Swain *Compar. Phytochem.* xvi. 283 The fifth [*Plumbago* species], *Plumbago rosea*, is very distinct, having glycosides of kaempferol, quercetin, pelargonidin, cyanidin and delphinidin in its petals.

cyanin (ˈsaɪənɪn). *Chem.* [f. CYAN- 1 + -IN.] The blue colouring matter of certain flowers, as the violet and corn-flower.

1863–72 Watts *Dict. Chem.* II. 274 Red flowers are said also to owe their colour to the presence of cyanin reddened by a free acid.

cyanine (ˈsaɪənaɪn). *Chem.* [f. CYAN- 1 + -INE.] **1.** A blue dye-stuff prepared from chinoline with amyl iodide, used in calico-printing.

1872 Watts *Dict. Chem.* VI. 431.

2. ***cyanine blue***: the name of a permanent blue pigment, a compound of cobalt and Prussian blue.

1886 *Pall Mall G.* 13 Sept. 13/2 (Water-colours unchanged by light) Cyanine blue, Prussian blue, Cobalt, etc.

cyanite (ˈsaɪənaɪt). *Min.* Also **kyanite**. [f. as prec. + -ITE.] **1.** A native silicate of aluminium, usually blue.

1794 Kirwan *Min.* I. 209 Cyanite of Werner. **1811** Pinkerton *Petral.* I. 125 The kyanite of Werner. **1852** Th. Ross *Humboldt's Trav.* I. v. 195 We detached..a fragment of cyanite from a block of splintered and milky quartz.

2. (See quot.).

1884 *Health Exhib. Catal.* 36/1 *Cyanite*, a Fire-proof priming for Paint, Varnish, &c.

cyanize (ˈsaɪənaɪz), *v. Chem.* [f. CYAN- 2 + -IZE.] *trans.* To convert into a cyanide, esp. as part of a process for fixing nitrogen. Hence **'cyanized** *ppl. a.*, **'cyanizing** *vbl. sb.*, **ˌcyaniˈzation**.

1881 *Chem. News* 29 Aug. 106/1 Cyanised Camphor... This compound, in alcoholic solution, is partly resolved into hydrocyanic and camphic acids. **1890** *Ibid.* 15 Aug. 82/1 The process consisted of passing the gas from a coal fire through large vertical cylinders..filled with a mixture of wood charcoal and potash... The cyanised charcoal was withdrawn at the bottom of the cylinder and dropped into..water containing powdered spathic iron ore in suspension, by which the cyanides were converted into ferrocyanides or prussiates. **1926** E. Fyleman tr. *Waeser's Atmosph. Nitr. Industry* 499 In order to determine whether pure nitrogen is necessary for cyanisation. *Ibid.* 501 The cyanising apparatus. *Ibid.*, The cyanised briquettes contained 19 per cent. of sodium cyanide. *Ibid.* 507 Mond cyanises briquettes of barium carbonate and charcoal in a ring furnace.

cyano- (before a vowel or *h* usually **cyan-**).

1. Used as combining form of Gr. κύανος a dark-blue mineral, κυάνεος *adj.* dark-blue, in scientific terms, in sense 'dark-blue', 'azure', as **cyano'chalcite** *Min.* [Gr. χαλκός copper], a blue silicate of copper (1872 in Dana). **cyano'chlorous** *a.* [Gr. χλωρός yellowish-green], bluish green (*Syd. Soc. Lex.*). **cya'nochroite** *Min.* [Gr. χροιά colour], a blue hydrous sulphate of copper and potassium (1868 in Dana); also called **'cyanochrome** (1857 in Shepard *Min.*). **'cyanolite** *Min.* [see -LITE], a bluish mineral consisting largely of silica (1861 in Bristow's *Gloss.* 102). **cya'nopathy** *Path.* [Gr. -πάθεια, f. πάθος suffering] = CYANOSIS (1857 in Dunglison); so **cyano'pathic** *a.* **cya'notrichite** *Min.* [Gr. θρίξ, τριχ-, hair], a blue fibrous sulphate of copper and aluminium (Dana 1854).

1890 *Daily News* 11 Dec. 3/5 His appearance was cyanopathic, his eyes were inflamed.

2. *Chem.* (= CYAN- 2): Of or containing cyanogen; in the names of cyanogen compounds, as **cyanobenzine**, benzonitril or phenyl cyanide. **cy'anodide**, obs. synonym of CYANIDE *sb.* **cyanonaphthalene**, naphthyl cyanide, etc.

ˌcyanocoˈbalamin. *Biochem.* [f. CYANO- + COBALAMIN.] Vitamin B_{12}.

1950 [see COBALAMIN]. **1961** *Lancet* 26 Aug. 482/2 It seems probable that the pharmacopœial term 'vitamin B 12', at present restricted..to cyanocobalamin, will soon have to be extended to include also hydroxocobalamin. **1962** *New Scientist* 15 Feb. 390/2 A by-product of the streptomycin fermentation is cyanocobalamin (vitamin B_{12}), an important constituent of liver extract, used in treating pernicious anaemia.

cyanogen (saɪˈænədʒɛn). *Chem.* [ad. F. *cyanogène*, f. Gr. κύανος a dark-blue mineral + -GEN, named (by Gay-Lussac, who isolated it in 1815) from its entering into the composition of Prussian blue.] A compound radical consisting of one atom of nitrogen and one of carbon (symbol CN or Cy). In the form of ***di-cyanogen*** (C_2N_2), it is a colourless gas, highly poisonous, with a strong odour like that of prussic acid. It exists in a great number of compounds, the cyanides, cyanates, cyanurets, etc.

1826 Henry *Elem. Chem.* I. 451 The vapour, collected over mercury, proved to be pure cyanogen. **1855** Bain *Senses & Int.* II. ii. §8 An evolution of the unwholesome and suffocating gas, cyanogen.

cyanogenic (saɪənəʊˈdʒɛnɪk), *a. Biochem.* [f. CYANO- + -GENIC.] Capable of producing (hydrogen) cyanide; containing a cyanogen group in the molecule. Also **cyanogeˈnetic** *a.*

1902 *Phil. Trans. R. Soc.* A. CXCIX. 409 Besides lotusin and dhurrin,..only one other cyanogenetic glucoside is definitely known. **1957** W. M. Hailey *Afr. Survey 1956* xii. 826 The root of the bitter variety contains cyanogenetic glucoside which develops hydrocyanic acid. **1961** Webster, Cyanogenic. **1968** M. Pyke *Food & Society* viii. 114 Hydrangeas contain cyanogenic glycosides, and..the *Journal of the American Medical Association* described the painful symptoms suffered by a horse which ate a potted hydrangea. **1979** R. D. Montgomery in Vinken & Bruyn *Handbk. Clin. Neurol.* XXXVI. xx. 515/1 The presence of cyanogenetic glucosides may have a defensive role in protecting the plant against invasion by insects or possibly from grazing by animals. **1985** *Arch. Biochem. & Biophysics* CCXLIII. 361 (*heading*) Isolation and characterization of two cyanogenic β-glucosidases from flax seeds.

Hence **cyanoˈgenesis**, cyanogenic property.

1939 *Jrnl. Genetics* XXXVIII. 357 (*heading*) Genetics of cyanogenesis in white clover. **1985** *Compar. Biochem. & Physiol.* B. LXXXII. 747/2 Cyanogenesis in all species may have been derived from a common cyanogenic protoheliconian ancestor.

cyanometer (saɪəˈnɒmɪtə(r)). [f. CYANO- 1 + -METER, after F. *cyanomètre* (1791 in Hatzfeld).] An instrument for measuring the intensity of the blue of the sky.

1829 *Nat. Philos., Optics* xviii. 65 (Useful Knowl. Soc.) In order to measure this intensity, M. Saussure contrived an instrument called a Cyanometer. **1852** Th. Ross *Humboldt's Trav.* I. ii. 84 We beheld with admiration the azure colour of the sky. Its intensity at the zenith appeared to correspond to 41° of the cyanometer.

Hence **cyano'metric** *a.*; also **cya'nometry**, measurement of the intensity of the blue of the sky.

1853 *Pharmac. Jrnl.* XII. 499 A New Cyanometric Process..founded upon the reaction of iodine upon the cyanides. **1885** *Encycl. Brit.* XVIII. 481 Peltier's other papers..are devoted in great part to atmospheric electricity, waterspouts, cyanometry and polarization of sky-light.

cyanose¹ (ˈsaɪənəʊs). *Path.* [Cf. F. *cyanose.*] = CYANOSIS.

1834 J. Forbes *Lænnec's Dis. Chest* (ed. 4) 575 A violet or blueish colour of the skin..named by several authors the *blue jaundice*, the *blue disease*, or *cyanose*.

Hence **'cyanosed** *ppl. a.*, 'afflicted with, or having the appearance of, cyanosis' (*Syd. Soc. Lex.*).

1857 Dunglison *Med. Lex.* s.v. *Cyanopathy*, A child affected with blueness is said to be *cyanosed*. **1876** tr. *Ziemssen's Cycl. Med.* IV. 635 In severe cases, even the hands and feet become cyanosed.

cyanose² (ˈsaɪənəʊs). *Min.* Also **cyanosite** (saɪˈænəsə(ɪ)t). [f. Gr. κύανος dark-blue mineral.] A synonym of CHALCANTHITE.

1844 Alger *W. Phillips' Min.* 495 Blue vitriol, Cyanose. **1854** Dana *Min.* 380 Cyanosite [rejected by him in 1868 ed.]. **1869** Phillips *Vesuv.* x. 285 Cyanose—Sulphate of Copper—occurs sparingly on surfaces of lava.

‖**cyanosis** (saɪəˈnəʊsɪs). *Path.* [a. Gr. κυάνωσις dark-blue colour, f. κύανος a dark-blue mineral; see -OSIS.] Blueness or lividness of the skin owing to the circulation of imperfectly oxygenated blood (*esp.* as caused by congenital malformation of the heart); blue disease, blue jaundice.

1834 Good *Study Med.* (ed. 4) II. 669 *note*, Obstruction..may likewise bring on Cyania, or as it is more frequently named Cyanosis. **1851** S. Judd *Margaret* II. ii. (1871) 193 His love for me produces a cyanosis. **1876** tr. *Wagner's Gen. Pathol.* 336 Constant cyanosis of the mucous membranes.

cy'anosite (*Min.*): see CYANOSE².

cyanotic (saɪəˈnɒtɪk), *a. Path.* [f. CYANOSIS: see -OTIC and cf. F. *cyanotique.*] Pertaining to, or of the nature of cyanosis; affected with cyanosis.

1852 tr. *Rokitansky's Path. Anat.* IV. II. 246 Cyanotic symptoms. **1866** A. Flint *Princ. Med.* (1880) 246 This..may give rise to a cyanotic hue. **1875** B. W. Richardson *Dis. Mod. Life* 34 All through their lives, cyanotic persons are disabled from taking active exertion.

cyanotype (saɪˈænətaɪp). [f. CYANO- + -TYPE.] A photographic process in which paper sensitized by a cyanide is employed; a picture or print obtained by this process: see quot. Also *attrib.*

1842 Herschel in *Phil. Trans.* CXXXII. 210 *Cyanotype.* If a nomenclature of this kind be admitted..the whole class of processes in which cyanogen in its combinations with iron performs a leading part, and in which the resulting pictures are blue, may be designated by this epithet. The varieties of cyanotype processes seem to be innumerable.

†**'cyanous,** *a. Chem. Obs.* [f. CYAN- 2 + -OUS: = F. *cyaneux.*] In ***cyanous acid***, 'the name originally given by Serullas to cyanic acid, on the supposition that it contained only half as much oxygen as the acid then called *cyanic*, but now *cyanuric* acid' (Watts *Dict. Chem.* II. 286).

1832 [see CYANIC 1].

cya'nurate, -uric, etc.: see CYAN- 2.

cyanuret (saɪˈænjʊərɛt). *Chem.* [f. CYAN- 2 + -URET.] = CYANIDE *sb.*

1827 Faraday *Chem. Manip.* xvi. 417 The part containing the cyanuret is therefore to be heated. **1854** in *Orr's Circ. Sc.* Chem. 440 The cyanurets, or cyanides, of iron.

cyanurin (saɪəˈnjʊərɪn). Also **-urine, -ourine.** [f. CYAN- 1 + URINE.] A blue deposit sometimes found pathologically in urine.

1845 tr. *Simon's Anim. Chem.* I. 45. **1858** Thudichum *Urine* 4 The blue colour may be due to cyanurine (uroglaucine).

cyanylic, etc.: see CYAN- 2.

‖**cyar** (ˈsaɪɑː(r)). *Anat.* [a. Gr. κύαρ eye of a needle, orifice of the ear.] The orifice of the internal ear.

1823 in Crabb; and in mod. Dicts.

†**'cyath.** *Obs.* Also 6 **cyathe, ciath(e, cyat, ciat.** [a. F. *cyathe* (in 15th c. *ciate*), ad. L. *cyathus*: see CYATHUS.] = CYATHUS 1.

1544 Phaer *Regim. Lyfe* (1553) I iv b, The dose of it is one ciath or a little cup ful. **1601** Holland *Pliny* XXI. xxx, It must anon be swallowed down in a cyath of water. **1631** Massinger *Emp. of East* IV. iv, With a little cyath or quantity of my potable elixir.

cyathiform (ˈsaɪəθɪfɔːm), *a.* [f. CYATH-US + -(I)FORM: cf. F. *cyathiforme.*] Shaped like a cup a little widened at the top. (Chiefly in *Bot.*)

1776 J. Lee *Introd. Bot.* 245 *Ciathiform*, shaped like a Drinking-Glass. **1794** Martyn *Rousseau's Bot.* xxii. 316 Bignonia has a cyathiform calyx, narrow at bottom and spreading wide at top. **1835** *Penny Cycl.* III. 535/2 They [Doric pillars] are fluted and tapering, with a large cyathiform capital. **1846** Dana *Zooph.* (1848) 140 When fully expanded, the disk is cyathiform.

cyathoid (ˈsaɪəθɔɪd). *a.* [f. CYATH-US + -OID: cf. F. *cyathoïde*; Gr. had κυαθώδης.] Resembling a cup or drinking-glass.

1882 in *Syd. Soc. Lex.*

cyatholith (saɪˈæθəlɪθ). *Biol.* [f. CYATHUS + -LITH.] A kind of coccolith resembling two cups placed base to base.

1875 Carpenter *Microsc. & Rev.* §367 Two distinct types are recognizable among the Coccoliths, which Prof. Huxley has designated respectively *discoliths* and *cyatholiths*. *Ibid.* §409 When viewed sideways or obliquely..the cyatholiths are found to have a form somewhat resembling that of a shirt-stud.

cyathophylloid (ˌsaɪəθəʊˈfɪlɔɪd), *a.* and *sb.* [f. mod.L. *Cyathophyllum* (f. Gr. κύαθος cup + φύλλον leaf) + -OID.]

A. *adj.* Akin to the fossil cup-corals of the genus *Cyathophyllum.*

1862 DANA *Man. Geol.* II. 374 Cyathophylloid corals. **1879** GEIKIE in *Encycl. Brit.* X. 345 Corals (cyathophylloid forms..) abound, especially in the Corniferous Limestone.

B. *sb.* A coral of this family, a cup-coral.

1872 DANA *Corals* i. 21 The Cyathophylloids were the earliest of polyps and the most abundant in Paleozoic time.

cyathozooid (saɪəθəʊˈzəʊɔɪd). *Zool.* [f. Gr. κύαθο-ς CYATHUS + ZOOID.] An abortive first stage of the embryo of certain compound ascidians, which becomes by gemmation the foundation of a colony.

1877 HUXLEY *Anat. Inv. Anim.* x. 617 The result [of yelk-division] is the formation of an elongated flattened blastoderm which occupies one pole of the egg, and is converted into what I termed the *cyathozooid,* which is..a sort of rudimentary ascidian. **1888** ROLLESTON & JACKSON *Anim. Life* 446 The germinal disc in *Pyrosoma* developes in the posterior region into a transitory Cyathozooid.

‖**cyathus** (ˈsaɪəθəs). Pl. cyathi (-θaɪ). [a. L. *cyathus,* a. Gr. κύαθος wine-cup, measure.]

1. a. *Greek* and *Roman Antiq.*: A cup or ladle used for drawing wine out of the CRATER *sb.* or mixing-bowl; also, a measure (both dry and liquid) = about $\frac{1}{12}$ of a pint. Also **kyathos. b.** *Med.* Used in prescriptions for a wine-glass. (Abbreviated *cyath.*)

1398 TREVISA *Barth. De P.R.* XIX. cxxviii. (1495) 932 The weyght Ciatus conteyneth 7. dragmes. **1658** ROWLAND *Mouf. Theat. Ins.* 1104 In three cyathi of water they will break inward Impostumes. **1768–74** TUCKER *Lt. Nat.* (1852) I. 464 Hyle bears no greater proportion therein to soul than the drops in a cyathus to the waters of the ocean. **1854** BADHAM *Halieut.* 522 The cyathus..was of as uncertain dimensions as our modern wine-glass, which is the medical cyathus, and a fair equivalent. **1889** *Cent. Dict.,* Kyathos. **1935** RICHTER & MILNE *Shapes & Names Athenian Vases* 30 *Kyathos*... Ladle in the form of a cup with foot and long upward curving handle. **1948** A. LANE *Greek Pott.* ii. 9 The *kyathos* or ladle for dipping the mixture off into jugs. **1960** R. G. HAGGAR *Conc. Encycl. Cont. Pott. & Porc.* 211/1 *Kyathos*—ladle;..*Oenochoe*—jug for wine; *Kylix*—shallow stem cup.

2. *Bot.* ‘The cup-like body which contains propagula or the reproductive bodies of *Marchantia*’ (*Treas. Bot.* 1866).

cyatica, -yca, obs. forms of SCIATICA.

cyb(be, obs. form of SIB.

cybernation (saɪbəˈneɪʃən). [f. CYBERN(ETICS *sb. pl.* + -ATION.] The theory, practice, or condition of control by machines. Hence (as a back-formation) **ˈcybernate** *v. trans.,* to control in this manner; **ˈcybernated** *ppl. a.*

1962 D. MICHAEL (*title*) Cybernation: the silent conquest. **1962** *Punch* 7 Feb. 231/2 Cybernation..is becoming a dirty word in America. **1962** *Catholic Gaz.* Nov. 320/1 (*heading*) The cybernated society. *Ibid.,* When the machines are controlled by the computers human operators become unnecessary and the society is cybernated... Many jobs have been partially or completely cybernated. **1963** J. A. T. ROBINSON *Honest to God* vii. 139 All the drives of modern secular society, whether collectivized or cybernated. **1969** *Northwest* (Sunday Oregonian Mag.) 14 Dec. 18/1 The major problems of the day—cybernation, the revolution in human rights and the threats of growing militarism.

cybernetics (saɪbəˈnɛtɪks). [f. Gr. κυβερνήτης steersman, f. κυβερνᾶν to steer (see GOVERN *v.*) + -ICS.] The theory or study of communication and control in living organisms or machines. Hence (as back-formation) **cyberˈnetic** *a.,* pertaining or relating to cybernetics. So **cyberneˈtician, cyberˈneticist,** one who is skilled in cybernetics.

Used in Fr. form *cybernétique* (= the art of governing) by A.-M. Ampère *Essai sur la Philos. des Sciences,* 1834.

1948 N. WIENER *Cybernetics* 19 We have decided to call the entire field of control and communication theory, whether in the machine or in the animal, by the name Cybernetics. **1951** *Jrnl. R. Aeronaut. Soc.* Oct. 624/2 All these machines represent developments in that part of what has been called the cybernetic revolution which is gradually taking over those operations in the fields of numbers, quantities, and data that are strictly clerical or mechanical. **1952** *Science News* XXIII. 77 The cyberneticists approach the problem of neural activity from a purely functional angle, and seek to model the activity of the brain as a whole on the electronic devices of modern communications systems and servo-mechanisms. **1958** *Listener* 18 Sept. 413 The claim of cybernetics is that we can treat organisms *as if* they were machines, in the sense that the same methods of synthesis and analysis can be applied to both. **1959** *Times* 11 May 6/6 Cybernetics is the study of man in relation to his particular job or machine with special reference to mental processes and control mechanisms. **1961** *Times Lit. Suppl.* 6 Jan. 2/4 It is all right for cyberneticians to make machines like men. **1961** J. WILSON *Reason & Morals* ii. 113 If men are machines, at least their behaviour suggests that they are cybernetic or self-regulating machines. **1962** *Listener* 1 Nov. 718/1 Cyberneticians, as the people who practise cybernetics now appear to call themselves, can build a larynx with which an injured man can speak. *Ibid.* 718/2 In education, too, cybernetics begins to intrude as electronic teaching machines make good the lack of human teachers. **1968** *Brit. Med. Bull.* XXIV. 197/2 The integration of cells, organs, and systems..appears to be done on a cybernetic basis with feed-back processes..clearly interwoven at all levels. **1970** *Nature* 12 Sept. 1167/1 The cyberneticist's approach to the concepts of psychology is not, however, in evidence here.

cyborg (ˈsaɪbɔːg). [Blend of CYB(ERNETIC *a.* and ORG(ANISM.] A person whose physical tolerances or capabilities are extended beyond normal human limitations by a machine or other external agency that modifies the body's functioning; an integrated man-machine system.

1960 *N.Y. Times* 22 May 31/1 A cyborg is essentially a man-machine system in which the control mechanisms of the human portion are modified externally by drugs or regulatory devices so that the being can live in an environment different from the normal one. **1960** CLYNES & KLINE in *Astronautics* Sept. 27/1 For the exogenously extended organizational complex functioning as an integrated homeostatic system unconsciously, we propose the term ‘Cyborg’. The Cyborg deliberately incorporates exogenous components extending the self-regulatory control function of the organism in order to adapt it to new environments. **1966** C. M. CADE *Other Worlds than Ours* x. 218 The ‘Cyborg’—which is the name..for animal-machine combinations—seems to be the man of the future. **1970** A. TOFFLER *Future Shock* ix. 185 Advanced fusions of man and machine—called ‘Cyborgs’—are closer than most people suspect. **1976** *Physics Bull.* June 266/1 There is a fundamental limit to the mass for a given rate of information processing... Perhaps even the most advanced cyborgs stop far short of this theoretical limit. **1984** M. AMIS *Money* 308, I am a robot, I am an android, I am a cyborg, I am a skinjob.

†**cybory.** *Obs.* [In form repr. L. *ciborium,* F. *ciboire*: see CIBORIUM; but in sense repr. κιβώτιον chest, ark.] The ark of the Jewish tabernacle.

1483 CAXTON *G. de la Tour* G iij, Before the arch or cybory wherin was the holy bred of the manna.

cybotaxis (saɪbəʊˈtæksɪs). *Physics.* [f. Gr. κύβος CUBE + τάξις arrangement.] An arrangement of molecules in a liquid (see quot. 1927). Hence **cyboˈtactic** *a.,* of or pertaining to cybotaxis.

1927 G. W. STEWART & R. M. MORROW in *Physical Rev.* XXX. 233 The present paper..interprets the space array..not as caused by fragmentary crystals, but by a type of molecular arrangement wherein there is combined mobility of the component molecules and yet a recognizable space array. To this state is given the name ‘cybotaxis’, which means ‘space-arrangement’. The adjective is ‘cybotactic’. A new word is necessary in order to distinguish this state from that called ‘crystalline’. **1941** *Nature* 22 Nov. 617/1 There are..two main types of conception of liquid structure..(1) group and (2) statistical conceptions... The most elegant development of the group type of conception is Stewart's theory of ‘cybotaxis’. In this the groups are considered to be of transitory nature, continually forming and disappearing. **1948** *Sci. News* VIII. 96 Their views fit in well with Stewart's theory that liquids have a ‘cybotactic’ structure, viz., that there are small aggregates of molecules arranged as they would be in a crystalline particle.

cyc- in obs. forms: see CIC-.

cycad (ˈsaɪkəd). *Bot.* [ad mod.L. generic name *Cycas, -adis,* a. supposed Gr. κύκας found in old edd. of Theophrastus, but now known to be a scribal error for κόϊκας acc. pl. of κόϊξ, the Egyptian doum-palm: see Liddell and Scott.]

A plant of the genus *Cycas* which gives its name to the *Cycadaceæ,* a natural order of Gymnosperms, related to the *Conifers,* but in appearance resembling palms, and having affinity with tree-ferns.

1845 LINDLEY *Veg. Kingd.* (1853) 224 The near relation of conifers and cycads. **1883** *Sunday Mag.* 547/1 Her Majesty planted in the gardens..a splendid Chinese cycad.

cycadaceous (sɪkəˈdeɪʃəs), *a. Bot.* [f. mod.L. *Cycadāceæ*: see prec. and -ACEOUS.] Of or belonging to the N.O. *Cycadaceæ,* or cycads.

1837 *Penny Cycl.* VIII. 248 A Cycadaceous stem partakes in structure of the peculiarities of both Exogens and Endogens. **1876** PAGE *Adv. Text Bk. Geol.* xvii. 327 Cycadaceous plants likewise flourish on the Australian continent.

cyˈcadeous, *a. Bot.* [f. mod.L. *Cycade-æ* = *Cycadaceæ* (see prec.) + -OUS.] = prec.

1847 ANSTED *Anc. World* ix. 198 The ancient shores..clothed with cycadeous vegetation. **1851** RICHARDSON *Geol.* (1855) 169 Such a specimen is to be referred to some coniferous or cycadeous plant.

cycadiform (sɪˈkædɪfɔːm), *a.* [See CYCAD and -FORM.] Resembling the cycads in form.

cycadite (ˈsɪkədaɪt). *Palæont.* [f. as prec. + -ITE.] A fossil cycad.

18.. BUCKLAND, Our fossil cycadites allied..to existing Cycadeæ. **1885** J. PHILLIPS *Man. Geol.* (ed. Etheridge) II. 354.

cycamore, obs. form of SYCAMORE.

cyche, cychory, obs. ff. CHICH, CHICORY.

1651 BIGGS *New Disp.* ¶80 Opium and cychory.

cyclad (ˈsɪkləd). *Zool.* [ad. mod.L. *Cyclas, -adis* the typical genus: see CYCLAS.] A mollusc of the genus *Cyclas* or family *Cycladidæ,* comprising numerous fresh-water species.

1866 TATE *Brit. Mollusks* ii. 36 The shell of *Cyclas lacustris* contrasts with those of other Cyclads in its sub-rhombic form.

Cycladic (sɪˈklædɪk), *a.* [f. L. *Cyclades* pl., a. Gr. Κυκλάδες (νῆσοι islands) + -IC.] Of or pertaining to the Cyclades, a group of islands in the Aegean, lying in a circle round Delos; *spec.* designating, or pertaining to, the prehistoric civilization of these islands. Also *absol.*

1915 H. R. HALL *Ægean Archæol.* ii. 24 It has become a misnomer to call the island culture by a name connecting it in any way with the ‘Mycenæan’. The word ‘Cycladic’ is now used, as the chief discoveries of this early stage of Greek civilisation have been made in the Cyclades. **1920** *Discovery* June 178/2 ‘Cycladic’..is sometimes substituted for ‘Minoan’ when one speaks exclusively of the island sites outside of Crete. **1921** *Brit. Museum Return* 60 Large beaked jug of later Cycladic style..From Melos or Thera. **1927** PEAKE & FLEURE *Priests & Kings* 113 These [sub-periods] have been named in the same way, ranging from Early Cycladic I to Late Cycladic III. **1957** V. G. CHILDE *Dawn Europ. Civilization* (ed. 6) iv. 49 While it has been customary to assign most cemeteries to the Early Cycladic period (before 2000 B.C.), Åberg has shown that some graves must be Middle or even Late Cycladic.

cyclamate (ˈsɪkləmeɪt, ˈsaɪkləmeɪt). [f. *cyclo*hexylsulph*amate,* f. CYCLO- + HEXYL + *sulphamate,* f. *sulpham(ic* (f. SULPH- + AM(IDE + -IC) + -ATE[4].] A salt of cyclohexylsulphamic acid, $C_6H_{11}{\cdot}NH{\cdot}SO_3H$, esp. the sodium and calcium salts, which have been used as artificial sweetening agents. So **ˈcyclamated** *a.,* containing a cyclamate, having had a cyclamate added.

1951 *Jrnl. Amer. Pharm. Assoc.* (Sci. ed.) XL. 1 (*heading*) Studies on cyclamate sodium (Sucaryl sodium), a new noncaloric sweetening agent. **1965** *Observer* 17 Oct. 33/1 The use of cyclamate as an ‘artificial sweetener’. *Ibid.,* Cyclamates fed to rats at levels of 5 per cent or 10 per cent of the diet reduced their rate of growth. **1969** *Daily Tel.* 21 Nov. 8/2 The decision to withdraw the ban was the result of the recommendation by a special scientific panel convened to determine the best way of making cyclamated products readily available to diabetics. **1970** *New Scientist* 1 Jan. 21/1 The cyclamate issue..is certainly stimulating research into ways of satisfying Man's sweet tooth. *Ibid.,* Cyclamates are only 30 times sweeter than sucrose and saccharin 300 times sweeter.

cyclamen (ˈsɪkləmɛn). Also (6 ciclamin), 7 **cyclamine, siclamine,** (8 **ciclament**). [med. and mod.L. *cyclamen,* L. *cyclamīnos* or *-on,* Gr. κυκλάμινος (also κυκλαμίς), ? f. κύκλ-ος circle, with reference to the shape of the bulbous root.]

a. A genus of *Primulaceæ,* belonging to Southern Europe, cultivated for their handsome early-blooming flowers; the fleshy root-stocks are greedily sought after by swine, whence the name SOWBREAD. **b.** A plant of this genus.

c **1550** LLOYD *Treas. Health* (1585) N ij, Yᵉ rote of Ciclamin. **1578** LYTE *Dodoens* III. xi. 329 Of Sowbread.. There be two sortes of Cyclamen, as Dioscorides writeth. **1727** BRADLEY *Fam. Dict.* s.v. *Cyclamen,* The way of planting Cyclamens, is to put their Bulbs two Inches deep in the Ground. **1830** LINDLEY *Nat. Syst. Bot.* 226 The root of Cyclamen is famous for its acridity; yet this is the principal food of the wild boars of Sicily. **1856** EMERSON *Eng. Traits, First visit to Eng.* Wks. (Bohn) II. 3 He praised the beautiful cyclamen which grows all about Florence.

c. The shade of colour characteristic of the red or pink cyclamen flower.

1923 *Daily Mail* 29 Jan. 1 In shades of Powder Blue.. Cyclamen,..Flamingo, Pink. **1926** *Spectator* 24 Apr. 750/2 Sleeveless cardigan, in various shades of cyclamen, rose marie and saxe. **1960** *Harper's Bazaar* Aug. 80/2 Cyclamen rayon satin.

cyclamin (ˈsɪkləmɪn). *Chem.* [f. prec. + -IN.] A poisonous principle extracted from the tubers of Cyclamen; it is a non-azotized glucoside.

1842 E. TURNER *Elem. Chem.* (ed. 7) III. 1123 Cyclamine. **1863–72** WATTS *Dict. Chem.* II. 294–5 Cyclamin.

cyclane (ˈsaɪkleɪn). *Chem.* [f. CYCL(IC *a.* 7 or CYCL(O- + -ANE.] Any saturated cyclic hydrocarbon.

1932 *Brit. Chem. Abstr.* 559/2 (*heading*) Raman spectra of cyclanes... Raman spectra of *cyclo*-propane, -pentane, -hexane, -heptane, and -octane and their Me derivatives show great similarity. **1939** *Thorpe's Dict. Appl. Chem.* (ed. 4) III. 532/1 They [*sc.* cyclenes] can..readily be derived from various simple derivatives of the saturated cyclic hydrocarbons (cyclanes).

cyclar (ˈsaɪklə(r)), *a. rare.* [f. CYCLE + -AR.] Of or pertaining to a cycle; = CYCLIC.

1768 HORSEFALL in *Phil. Trans.* LVIII. 102 *D* and *E* are the cyclar numbers, and *d* and *e* are the *anno domini* numbers. **1837** *Fraser's Mag.* XVI. 632 The cyclar system of that ingenious nation [Egypt].

cyclarthrodial (sɪkləˈθrəʊdɪəl), *a. Anat.* [f. Gr. κύκλ-ος circle + ἀρθρωδία articulation + -AL[1].] Of, or of the nature of, a cyclarthrosis.

‖**cyclarthrosis** (sɪkləˈθrəʊsɪs). *Anat.* [mod.L., f. Gr. κύκλ-ος circle + ἄρθρωσις articulation.] A circular or rotatory articulation, as that of the radius with the ulna.

‖**cyclas** ('sɪkləs). *Hist.* [L. *cyclas*, a. Gr. κυκλάς a woman's garment with a border all round it.] A tightly-fitting upper garment or tunic worn by women from ancient times; also sometimes by men, *esp.* the tunic or surcoat made shorter in front than behind, worn by knights over their armour in the 14th century.

1860 Fairholt *Costume* 97 The lady wears a long gown, over which is a *cyclas*, or tightly-fitting upper-tunic. **1868** Cussans *Her.* i. 32 Prince John Plantagenet.. is represented ..as wearing a Cyclas, which reaches below the knees behind, and to the lower part of the thighs in front, being open at the sides as far as the hips. **1883** M. E. Haweis in *Contemp. Rev.* Sept. 425 Judith of Bohemia wore a cyclas worked with gold, in 1083.

¶ Identified or confused with ciclatoun q.v.; see also Du Cange s.v. *Cyclas*.

1834 Planché *Brit. Costume* 95 A rich stuff manufactured in the Cyclades, and therefore called *cyclas* or *ciclaton*, gave its name to a garment like a dalmatica or super-tunic worn by both sexes. **1876** Rock *Text. Fabr.* iv. 27.

cycle ('saɪk(ə)l), *sb.* Also 4, 7 cicle, 5 cikil. [a. F. *cycle* or ad. L. *cycl-us*, a. Gr. κύκλος circle.]

I. 1. *Astron.* A circle or orbit in the heavens.

1631 Brathwait *Whimzies* 13 Horizons, Hemispheares.. Astrolabes, Cycles, Epicycles, are his usuall dialect. **1667** Milton *P. L.* viii. 84 How gird the Sphear With Centric and Eccentric scribl'd o're, Cycle and Epicycle, Orb in Orb. *fig.* **1831** Carlyle *Sart. Res.* iii. viii, What infinitely larger Cycle (of Causes) our little Epicycle revolves on.

2. a. A recurrent period of a definite number of years adopted for purposes of chronology. (See quot. 1788.)

cycle of indiction: see indiction.
Metonic or *lunar cycle*: a cycle of 19 years, established by the Greek astronomer Meton, and used for determining the date of Easter.
solar cycle: a period of 28 years, at the end of which the days of the week (according to the Julian Calendar) recur on the same days of the month.

1387 Trevisa *Higden* (Rolls) VII. 271 The dissonaunce of þe cicles of Dionise the lesse ageyne the trawthe of gospelles. **1398** —— *Barth. De P.R.* ix. iv. (1495) 349 The Cycle and course of the mone conteyneth twelue comyn yeres and seuen yeres Embolismalis. *c* **1425** Wyntoun *Cron.* ix. xxiii. 5 Ðe cikil of our Salvatioune Ðat is þe Annuntiatiowne. **1646** Sir T. Browne *Pseud. Ep.* iv. xii. 211 Of months, of years, Olympiades, Lustres, Indictions, Cycles, Jubilies, &c. **1656** Blount *Glossogr.* s.v., This revolution is called the Cycle of the Sun, taking name from Sunday, the letter whereof (called therefore Dominical) it appoints for every yeer. **1788** Priestley *Lect. Hist.* iii. xiv. 111 The greatest difficulty in chronology has been to accommodate the two methods of computing time by the course of the moon and that of the sun to each other.. This gave birth to many *cycles* in use among the ancients. **1844** Lingard *Anglo-Sax. Ch.* (1858) I. i. 47 The Roman church, about the middle of the sixth century, adopted a new cycle, which had been lately composed by Dionysius Exiguus... But the British churches ..continued to use the ancient cycle.

b. *gen.* A period in which a certain round of events or phenomena is completed, recurring in the same order in succeeding periods of the same length.

1662 Petty *Taxes* 24 The cycle within which dearths and plenties make their revolution. **1795** Burke *On Scarcity* Wks. VII. 379 Wages..bear a full proportion..to the medium of provision during the last bad cycle of twenty years. **1836** J. H. Newman in *Lyra Apost.* (1849) 185 The world has cycles in its course, when all That once has been, is acted o'er again. **1867** Freeman *Norm. Conq.* (1876) I. iii. 96 One of those curious cycles which so often come round in human affairs.

c. A long indefinite period of time; an age.

1842 Tennyson *Locksley Hall* 184 Better fifty years of Europe than a cycle of Cathay. **1851** Mayne Reid *Scalp Hunt.* xix, After many years—ages, centuries, cycles perhaps.

3. a. A recurrent round or course (of successive events, phenomena, etc.); a regular order or succession in which things recur; a round or series which returns upon itself.

1664 Evelyn *Kal. Hort.* (J.), To present our gardeners with a complete cycle of what is requisite to be done throughout every month of the year. **1691** Wood *Ath. Oxon.* II. 824 The Caroline Cycle [for the election of Proctors] being still kept back a year. **1861** M. Pattison *Ess.* (1889) I. 47 A committee of nine members, in which every Hanse town was in its turn represented, according to a fixed cycle. **1875** Lyell *Princ. Geol.* II. iii. xxxvii. 329 The whole cycle of changes returns into itself, just as do the metamorphoses of an insect.

b. *Physics*, etc. A recurring series of operations or states, *spec.* in internal combustion engines. Also, short for ***cycles per second*** (abbrev. C.P.S., cps., c/s), the unit of frequency of an oscillation (as an alternating current, a sound wave, etc.).

a **1884** Knight *Dict. Mech.* Suppl. 382/2 The complete cycle of motions in the Otto engine is accomplished only by two complete revolutions of the working shaft, or four strokes of the piston. **1887** *Encycl. Brit.* XXII. 479/2 Generally in heat-engines the working substance returns periodically to the same state of temperature, pressure, volume, and physical condition. When this has occurred the substance is said to have passed through a complete cycle of operations. **1893** T. O'C. Sloane *Standard Electr. Dict.* 175 *Cycle of alternation*, a full period of alternation of an alternating current. It begins properly at the zero line, goes to a maximum value in one sense and returns to zero, goes to maximum in the other sense and returns to zero. **1920** *Whittaker's Electr. Engineer's Pocket-Bk.* (ed. 4) 348 In the early days, when electricity was used only for lighting, frequencies round about 100 cycles were usual. **1929** A. F. Collins *Aviation* 148 After the power stroke is completed three more strokes must take place before there is another explosion stroke and, hence, another power stroke. Then the series of strokes, or cycle, as it is called, begins all over again, and this is what is meant by a four-stroke cycle engine. **1940** *Chambers's Techn. Dict.* 206/1 C.P.S., cps., c/s, abbrevs. for *cycles per second*, the usual measure of frequency. **1944** A. Wood *Physics of Music* iv. 42 The lowest frequencies used in the orchestra are those of the double bass and the bass tuba, which lie between 60 and 80 cycles per second... Tones of male speech embrace a range of from 120 to 8000 c.p.s. **1959** *Consumer Rep.* (N.Y.) Sept. 452/2 Only one [tweeter] provided adequate and relatively uniform power in the high-frequency range to beyond 20,000 cps. **1965** *Electronics Weekly* 10 Mar. 22/5 It operates from a standard single phase 50 c/s supply. **1967** *Electronics* 6 Mar. 325/1 Markus continues to use 'cycles per second' instead of 'hertz'.

c. Geol. ***cycle of erosion, sedimentation*** (see quots.).

1904 Chamberlin & Salisbury *Geol.* (1905) I. iii. 78 It has now been seen that by whatever method erosion by running water proceeds..the final result of subaërial erosion must be the production of a base-level... The time involved in the reduction of a land area to base-level is a cycle of erosion. **1921** L. D. Stamp in *Geol. Mag.* LVIII. 109 A 'cycle of sedimentation' comprises the deposits of a complete oscillation of the basin, each oscillation including a positive phase of marine invasion and a negative phase of regression. **1960** —— *Britain's Struct. & Scenery* (ed. 5) vii. 70 As the cycle of erosion progresses..features which are due to varying resistance of the rocks..gradually become eliminated as the surface is reduced to a monotonous level.. plain.

4. *gen.* A round, course, or period through which anything runs in order to its completion; a single complete period or series of successive events, etc.

1821 Shelley *Adonais* xxvii, Or hadst thou waited the full cycle, when Thy spirit should have filled its crescent sphere. **1845–6** Trench *Huls. Lect.* Ser. i. iv. 66 The cycle of God's teaching is complete. **1869** J. Martineau *Ess.* II. 230 Doctrines which have run their cycle.

5. A complete set or series; a circle, a round.

1662 Evelyn *Chalcogr.* Bb, To compile, and publish a Compleat Cycle and Hystory of Trades. **1678** Wood *Life* (Oxf. Hist. Soc.) II. 401 Vide the printed cycle for names of collectors and how many admitted. **1829** Scott *Demonol.* iv. 121 [He] figures among a cycle of champions. *a* **1836** Godwin *Ess.* (1873) 217 The most intolerable sentence in the whole cycle of religious morality.

6. *spec.* A series of poems or prose romances, collected round or relating to a central event or epoch of mythic history and forming a continuous narrative; as the ***Arthurian cycle***. Also *transf.*

Originally used in the ***Epic cycle*** [Gr. ὁ (ἐπικὸς) κύκλος], the series of epic poems written by later poets (*Cyclic poets*) to complete Homer, and presenting (with the Iliad and Odyssey) a continuous history of the Trojan war and of all the heroes engaged in it.

1835 Thirlwall *Greece* I. vi. 248 They..formed the basis or nucleus of the epic cycle. **1837** *Penny Cycl.* IX. 470/1 Those cycles of metrical romances which have for their subjects the exploits of Alexander the Great, King Arthur, and other heroes. **1870** Swinburne *Ess. & Stud.* (1875) 66 The marvellous opening cycle of twenty-eight sonnets. **1873** H. Morley *First Sk. Eng. Lit.* 61 The cycle of the Charlemagne romances..those of the Arthurian cycle. **1874** H. R. Reynolds *John Bapt.* i. §6. 56 The mythopoeic faculty has not engendered a cycle of miracles around the simple story.

7. *Med.* [L. *cyclus*.] With the 'methodic' physicians: A course of remedies, hygienic and medicinal, continued during a fixed series of days.

1882 *Syd. Soc. Lex.* s.v. *Cyclus*, Cælius Aurelianus distinguished three kinds of cycles or periods..The cycle was resumed several times if needed.

8. *Bot.* A complete turn of the spire recognized in the theory of spiral leaf-arrangement.

1857 Henfrey *Bot.* 41 The series of leaves included by the spiral line in passing from the first leaf to that which stands directly above it is called a *cycle*.

9. *Zool.* In corals, a set of septa of equal length.

1877 Huxley *Anat. Inv. Anim.* iii. 164 The septa in the adult *Hexacoralla*..of the same lengths are members of one 'cycle'; and the cycles are numbered according to the lengths of the septa, the longest being counted as the first. In the young, six equal septa constitute the first cycle.

10. *Math.* **a.** *Geom.* A closed path in a cyclic or multiply-connected region. **b.** (See quot. 1893.)

1881 Maxwell *Electr. & Magn.* I. 16 Every new line completes a loop or closed path, or, as we shall call it, a cycle. **1893** Forsyth *Theory of Functions* 593 In the theory of Substitution-Groups the set of homologous corners of a given region is called a cycle.

II. 11. [An abbreviation, familiar and conveniently inclusive, of *bicycle* and *tricycle*; but Gr. κύκλος 'circle' also meant 'wheel'.] A bicycle, tricycle, or other machine of the kind.

[**1870** *Nat. Hist. Bicycles* in *Belgravia* Feb. 443 Another idea for a monocycle (which, by the way, might be called a 'cycle' at once, for shortness).] **1881** *Pall Mall G.* 23 June 10/2 The 'spider wheel'..marks the commencement of the present era of 'cycles. **1882** *Standard* 1 May 3/7 To tax 'Cycles' for the benefit of those who have carriages.

12. *attrib.* and *Comb.* (chiefly in sense 11), as ***cycle-battery, -horn, -man, -racing, -scout, -shop, -track***, etc.; **cycle-car**, a light motor-driven vehicle with three (rarely four) wheels; **cycle-clip** = *bicycle-clip*; **cycleway**, a path or lane for the (usu. exclusive) use of bicycles; cf. *bikeway* s.v. bike *sb.*² 2 b.

1887 *Spectator* 17 Sept. 1244 We may see the time when *cycle-batteries will be a feature of every army. **1913** (*title*) The autocycle, side car and *cycle car user. **1914** *Morn. Post* 9 Feb. 5 A Cyclecar Paperchase. **1954** 'N. Shute' *Slide Rule* 12 A little car built of motor bicycle components, then known as a cyclecar. **1939–40** *Army & Navy Stores Catal.* p. xxxi/1 *Cycle clips. **1955** P. Larkin *Less Deceived* 28 Hatless, I take off My cycle-clips in awkward reverence. **1891** *Bicycling News* 141 Bells and *cycle-horns. **1887** *Globe* 19 Apr., '*Cycleman' is the latest name for the 'Uhlan on wheels'. **1922** Joyce *Ulysses* 153 Rover *cycleshop. **1916** —— *Portrait of Artist* iv. 182 Some jesuits were walking round the *cycletrack. **1936** *Min. Transport Circ. 454* (*Roads*) 2 Separate cycle tracks will often be justified solely on the grounds of public safety. **1963** *Ann. Reg. 1962* 449 Extensive use was made of cycle tracks and pedestrian footpaths for segregating traffic about other parts of the town. **1899** *Sci. Amer.* 13 May 296/3 Mr. Horace M. Dobbins, of Pasadena, organized what is known as the 'California *Cycleway Company'. **1963** *Times* 13 Dec. 15/4 Professor Buchanan might well consider again some adaptation of the Stevenage 'cycleways' experiment. **1972** *Oxford Times* 27 Oct. 3 Cycleways could be introduced in many parts of Oxford. **1983** M. W. Jones *Snickelways of York* 10/2 The York City Council bestowed upon the street the status of *cycleway*.

cycle ('saɪk(ə)l), *v.* [f. prec. sb. Cf. Gr. κυκλεῖν to go round and round.]

1. *intr.* To move or revolve in cycles; to pass through cycles.

1842 Tennyson *Two Voices* 348 It may be that no life is found, Which only to one engine bound Falls off, but cycles always round. **1859** Darwin *Orig. Spec.* xiv. 490 Whilst this planet has gone cycling on according to the fixed law of gravity.

2. To ride a bicycle or tricycle, to travel by cycle.

1883 [see cycling *vbl. sb.*]. **1891** *Cycl. Tour. Club Gaz.* Dec. 340 On landing at Dieppe [he] would cycle or train, according to the state of the weather.

cycle, obs. form of shekel, sickle.

cycled ('saɪk(ə)ld), *ppl. a.* [f. cycle + -ed.] Characterized by or consisting of cycles.

1850 Tennyson *In Mem.* lxxxv. 28 All knowledge that the sons of flesh Shall gather in the cycled times.

cycledom ('saɪk(ə)ldəm). *nonce-wd.* [f. cycle *sb.* 11 + -dom.] The domain or 'world' of cycles and their riders.

1890 B. W. Richardson in *Asclepiad* VII. 24 In the world of cycledom. **1892** *Standard* 18 Mar. 6/4 Neither do we intend usurping the part of protectors to Italian cycledom.

cycler ('saɪklə(r)). [f. cycle *v.* 2 + -er.] One who rides a bicycle or tricycle.

1884 *Springfield Wheelmen's Gaz.* Nov. 105/2 Over 5000 were mounted cyclers. **1888** J. Pennell in *Pall Mall G.* 25 Oct. 5 From the standpoint of a touring cycler.

cyclery ('saɪklərɪ). *N. Amer.* [f. cycle *sb.* 11 + -ery.] A bicycle shop.

1897 *Trans-Mississippian* (Council Bluffs, Iowa) 20 Apr. (Advt.), Council Bluffs Cyclery. **1899** J. F. Fraser *Round World on Wheel* xxxvii. 484 There is a cyclery—that's an American word—where machines are hired out at a shilling an hour. **1901** *Daily Colonist* (Victoria, B.C.) 1 Oct. 8/2 (Advt.), The stock, tools, etc. of the B.C. Cyclery & Supply Co. **1936** Mencken *Amer. Lang.* (ed. 4) 176 In Pasadena, Calif.,..there is a *hattery*, in South Pasadena a *cyclery*.

cyclette (saɪ'klɛt). [Fr.: see -ette.] A small (motor) bicycle.

1898 *Daily News* 15 Nov. 7/6 The one-mile motor cyclette race. **1923** *Daily Mail* 28 Feb. 6 The Paris-Nice Trial. How the motor cyclettes fared under strenuous conditions.

cyclian ('sɪklɪən), *a. rare.* [f. Gr. κύκλι-ος circular, cyclic + -an.] = cyclic 2, 3.

1699 Bentley *Phal.* Wks. 1836 I. 341 The chorus belonging to the dithyramb was not called a *tragic*, but *cyclian* chorus. **1840** tr. *Müller's Hist. Lit. Greece* xiv. 204 In the time of Aristophanes, the expressions 'dithyrambic poet' and 'teacher of cyclian choruses' (κυκλιοδιδάσκαλος) were nearly synonymous. **1847** Leitch tr. *Müller's Anc. Art* §415 The Cyclian poets, who formed the introduction and continuation to the Iliad.

cyclic ('saɪklɪk, 'sɪ-), *a.* [a. F. *cyclique* (16th c. in Hatzfeld), or ad. L. *cyclic-us*, a. Gr. κυκλικός moving in a circle, cyclic, f. κύκλος cycle.]

1. a. Of or pertaining to a cycle or cycles; of the nature of a cycle; revolving or recurring in cycles.

1794 Sullivan *View Nat.* II. 226 The order he [Moses] has given his narrative is..conformable to the cyclic ideas of the people he lived amongst. **1840** Mrs. Browning *Drama of Exile*, While all the cyclic heavens about me spun. **1879** Proctor *Pleas. Ways Sc.* ii. 31 Cyclic associations between solar and terrestrial phenomena.

b. Belonging to a definite chronological cycle.

1838 Arnold *Hist. Rome* I. xvii. 368 *note*, Twenty cyclic years, of ten months each. **1850** C. P. Brown (*title*), Cyclic Tables of Chronology of the history of the Telugu and Kannadi countries (Madras).

c. Characterized by recurrence in cycles.

1885 F. W. Pary in *Lancet* 17 Oct. 706 These cases..have a cyclic character belonging to them, and hence my adoption of the term Cyclic Albuminuria. **1886** *Braithwaite's Retrosp. Med.* XCIII. 219 A Physiological cyclic change. **1888**

FAGGE *Princ. & Pract. Med.* (ed. 2) II. 600 ' Cyclic albuminuria', by which is denoted the recurrence of traces of albumen in the urine at more or less regular intervals.

d. *Aeronaut.* ***cyclic pitch control***, a method of controlling the direction or motion of a helicopter by varying the angle of the rotor blades during each cycle of rotation. So *cyclic pitch lever, stick*.

1944 H. F. GREGORY *Helicopter* (1948) xiv. 164 The first and probably the most common [method of controlling helicopters]..is called cyclic pitch control. What it means is the change of pitch of a blade..as the blade moves in its cycle of rotation. **1959** F. D. ADAMS *Aeronaut. Dict.* 55/2 *Cyclic pitch stick*, a control stick for cyclic pitch control. **1962** *Flight Internat.* LXXXI. 865/2 According to the position of a pendulous 'cyclic-pitch' lever, the complete rotor disc and resulting lift vector can be tilted to control the flight path.

2. a. Of or belonging to a cycle of mythic and heroic story: see CYCLE *sb.* 6. ***Cyclic poet***: one of the writers of the 'Epic cycle'.

a **1822** SHELLEY *Def. Poetry* Prose Wks. 1888 II. 20 They are the episodes of that cyclic poem written by Time upon the memories of men. **1840** tr. *Müller's Hist. Lit. Greece* vi. 64 This class of [later] epic poets is called the *Cyclic*, from their constant endeavour to connect their poems with those of Homer, so that the whole should form a great cycle. **1868** GLADSTONE *Juv. Mundi* i. (1870) 11 The Cyclic Poems, which aimed at completing the circle of events with which they deal.

b. *transf.* Belonging to the cycle of current Greek tradition which underlies the Synoptic Gospels, as distinguished from what is peculiar to a single Synoptist.

1851 WESTCOTT *Introd. Gospels* iv. (ed. 5) 225 In all the cases of Cyclic quotations parallels occur in the other Synoptic Gospels agreeing (as St. Matthew) with the LXX.

3. ***cyclic chorus*** [Gr. κύκλιος χορός] in *Gr. Antiq.*: the dithyrambic chorus, which was danced in a ring round the altar of Dionysus.

1846 WORCESTER, *Cyclic*..noting a kind of verse or chorus, cyclical. *Beck.*

4. *Bot.* Of a flower: Having its parts arranged in whorls.

1875 BENNETT & DYER *Sachs' Bot.* 565 In the great majority of Dicotyledons the parts of the flower are arranged in whorls, or the flowers are *cyclic*; only in a comparatively small number of families..are all or some of them arranged spirally (*acyclic* or *hemicyclic*).

5. *Math.* Of or pertaining to a circle or cycle. *spec.* ***cyclic axis*** (of a cone of the second order): a line through the vertex perpendicular to the circular section of the cone. (**1852** BOOTH.) ***cyclic constant***: the constant by which a many-valued function is increased after describing a non-evanescible circuit or cycle in a cyclic region. (**1881** MAXWELL *Electr. & Magn.* I. 18.) ***cyclic planes*** (of a cone of the second order): the two planes through one of the axes which are parallel to the circular section of the cone. (**1874** SALMON *Analyt. Geom. Three Dim.* 194.) Sometimes used of any circular sections. ***cyclic quadrilateral***: one inscribable in a circle. (**1888** CASEY *Plane Trigonometry* 184.) ***cyclic region***: a region or domain within which a closed line can be drawn in such a manner that it cannot shrink indefinitely without passing out of the region.

6. *Gr. Prosody.* Of a dactyl or anapæst: Occupying in scansion only three 'times' instead of four; applied to dactyls which interchange, not (as in Hexameters) with spondees, but with trochees.

1844 BECK & FELTON tr. *Munk's Metres* 102 The cyclic anapæsts, so called, are analogous to the irrational dactyls. **1879** L. CAMPBELL *Sophocles* I. Pref. 44 According to a doubtful theory the dactyls in logaoedic verse are each of them equivalent in time to a trochee, much as a triplet may be occasionally introduced in ordinary music without altering the time. Such a foot is called a 'lyrical' or 'cyclic' dactyl (ποὺς κύκλιος).

7. *Org. Chem.* Of a compound: having a molecular structure containing one or more 'closed chains' or rings of atoms; also, of or pertaining to such compounds. See also ALICYCLIC, CARBO-CYCLIC, HETEROCYCLIC, *isocyclic* (s.v. ISO-) adjs.

1898 *Jrnl. Chem. Soc.* LXXIV. I. 637 It is extremely difficult to separate benzene from cyclic hydrocarbons boiling at a much lower temperature. **1913** *Bloxam's Chem.* (ed. 10) 544 The cyclic or closed-chain series. **1923** T. H. POPE tr. *Molinari's Org. Chem.* II. 616 Cyclic compounds. **1937** *Thorpe's Dict. Appl. Chem.* (ed. 4) I. 33/2 Cyclic acetals, of use in perfumery and as industrial solvents, are made by condensing dihydric alcohols with unsubstituted araliphatic aldehydes. **1961** L. F. & M. FIESER *Adv. Org. Chem.* ii. 51 The hydrocarbon is indeed known, and since it has the same number of carbon atoms as propane but is cyclic it is called cyclopropane.

cyclical (ˈsaɪklɪkəl, ˈsɪ-). *a.* [f. as prec. + -AL[1].]

1. Of a line: Returning into itself so as to form a closed curve. *rare.*

1817 COLERIDGE *Biog. Lit.* 122 [The point] must flow back again on itself; that is, there arises a cyclical line which does inclose a space.

b. Of a letter: Circular, encyclical. *rare.*

1879 FARRAR *St. Paul* I. 434 The genuineness of this cyclical letter is evinced by its extreme naturalness.

2. = CYCLIC 1.

a **1834** COLERIDGE (W.), Time, cyclical time, was their abstraction of the Deity. **1837** SIR F. PALGRAVE *Merch. & Friar* iii. (1844) 78 Modes of thought, not cyclical, but successive. **1854** MOSELEY *Astron.* lxxix. (ed. 4) 219 The changes of the planetary orbits must return in certain cyclical periods. **1861** E. SMITH (*title*), Health and Disease, as influenced by the Daily, Seasonal, and other Cyclical Changes in the Human System.

b. Belonging to a definite chronological cycle.

1838 ARNOLD *Hist. Rome* I. xviii. 382 The truce..was to last only for forty cyclical years of ten months each. **1875** JOWETT *Plato* (ed. 2) III. 579 Plato also speaks of an 'annus magnus' or cyclical year.

3. = CYCLIC 2.

1841 DE QUINCEY *Homer* Wks. VI. 293 The many epic and cyclical poems which arose during post-Homeric ages. **1873** SYMONDS *Grk. Poets* vii. (1877) 203 The cyclical poets.

4. *Bot.* **a.** Rolled up circularly, as the embryos of many seeds. **b.** Arranged in whorls, verticillate; hence *transf.* in *Zool.*

1866 in *Treas. Bot.* **1870** HOOKER *Stud. Flora* 36 Wartcress..embryo in some species cyclical. **1881** W. B. CARPENTER *Microscope* 546 We find in the nautiloid spire a tendency to pass..into the cyclical mode of growth.

5. ***cyclical number***: (see quot.).

1875 JOWETT *Plato* (ed. 2) III. 113 A perfect or cyclical number, i.e. a number in which the sum of the divisors equals the whole.

cyclically (ˈsaɪklɪkəlɪ, ˈsɪ-), *adv.* [f. CYCLICAL *a.* + -LY[2].] In a cyclic or cyclical way; in cycles.

1882 *Proc. R. Soc.* XXXIV. 40 When any cyclic change of I is made to take place by varying H cyclically. **1895** *Athenæum* 1 June 710/1 Mr. Burstall commenced the reading of a paper 'On the Measurement of a Cyclically Varying Temperature'. **1939** *New Republic* 27 Sept. 210 Employment in this area has been decreased by thousands, not as a result of recession but in addition to the thousands of men cyclically displaced. **1961** P. J. DAVIS *Lore of Large Numbers* 60 A decimal whose digits recur cyclically must be a fraction.

cyclicism (ˈsɪklɪsɪz(ə)m). [f. CYCLIC + -ISM.] The quality of being cyclic; cyclic condition.

1857 GOSSE *Creation* 367 The principle of prochronic development obtains wherever we are able to test it; that is wherever another principle, that of cyclicism, exists.

cyclicotomy (sɪklɪˈkɒtəmɪ). *Surg.* [f. Gr. κυκλικό-ς circular + -τομια a cutting.] Division of the ciliary body.

1882 in *Syd. Soc. Lex.*

cyclide (ˈsaɪklɪd, ˈsɪklaɪd). *Geom.* [a. F. *cyclide*, f. CYCLE.] 'The envelope of a sphere whose centre moves on a fixed quadric, and which cuts a fixed sphere orthogonally' (Salmon).

1874 SALMON *Analyt. Geom. Three Dim.* 496. **1881** H. HART in *Athenæum* 23 Apr. 563/2 On the Five Focal Quadrics of a Cyclide.

cycling, *vbl. sb.* and *ppl. a.* [f. CYCLE *v.*] **a.** The action or activity of riding a bicycle etc.; that rides a bicycle etc.

1883 B. W. RICHARDSON *Cycling* in *Longm. Mag.* Oct. 593 To the human family the art of cycling is the bestowal of a new faculty. *Ibid.* 595 The choicest representatives of cycling circles.

b. ***cycling lizard***, a kind of lizard found in Australia (see quots.).

1937 *Discovery* May 137/1 The Racehorse or Cycling Lizard..runs at an incredible speed..and the movement of the back legs bears a remarkable resemblance to the motion of a cyclist. **1955** A. J. ROSS *Australia 55* 46 The 'cycling' lizard, whose leg motions resemble the pedalling action of a man on a bicycle,..of which the Commonwealth Railway brochure speaks so enticingly.

cyclism (ˈsaɪklɪz(ə)m). *nonce-wd.* [f. CYCLE *sb.* + -ISM.] The practice of the cyclist; the use of bicycles or tricycles as a means of progression.

1890 *Sat. Rev.* 2 Aug. 136/1 Military cyclism..only asks for..fair trial.

cyclist (ˈsaɪklɪst). [f. as prec. + -IST.] One who rides a cycle or practises cycling.

1882 *Pall Mall G.* 25 Sept. 3 The cyclists of London. **1887** *Times* 9 Apr. 5/4, I passed a group of Lieutenant-Colonel Savile's military cyclists.

attrib. **1884** C. DICKENS jun. *Dict. Lond.* 37/2 The Cyclist Touring Club. **1887** *Times* 8 Apr. 4/1 There will be an extensive reconnaissance carried out by the Cyclist Corps to the north-east of Canterbury.

2. One who reckons by a cycle or cycles; one who recognizes cycles in the course of phenomena, etc.

Hence **cyˈclistic** *a.*

1882 *Bazaar, Exch. & Mart* 15 Feb. 175 Readers with cyclistic tendencies.

‖**cyclitis** (sɪˈklaɪtɪs). *Path.* [f. Gr. κύκλ-ος circle + -ITIS.] Inflammation of the ciliary body.

1861 BUMSTEAD *Ven. Dis.* (1879) 718 Inflammations of the ciliary body, or cyclitis.

cyclize (ˈsaɪklaɪz), *v. Org. Chem.* [f. CYCL(IC *a.* 7 + -IZE.] *trans.* To make (a compound) cyclic (CYCLIC *a.* 7); *intr.* to undergo cyclization, become cyclic. So **cycliˈzation**, the rearrangement of the atoms in a molecule to form one or more 'closed chains' or rings: **ˈcyclized** *ppl. a.*

1909 *Chem. News* 16 July 24/2 The cyclisation of ketone acids always occurs at one of the carbon atoms near the ketone function. Cyclic chains containing C_5 and C_6 are most easily formed. **1933** *Jrnl. Chem. Soc.* II. 1111 The cyclisation of aromatic compounds in which a cyclic system forms part of an unsaturated side chain. **1934** WEBSTER, *Cyclize* v.t. **1936** *Nature* 7 Mar. 411/2 Open 'cyclised' polypeptides. **1942** G. EGLOFF et al. *Isomerization of Pure Hydrocarbons* vi. 170 1,1,3,3-Tetraphenylbutene cyclized at 215° in the presence of 'Floridin'. *Ibid.* vi. 171 The other form, when treated in the same manner, cyclized into 1-benzyl-2, 3-diphenylindane. **1949** H. W. FLOREY et al. *Antibiotics* II. xxviii. 958 Attempts to cyclize this compound. **1954** *Archit. Rev.* CXV. 356/1 Cyclized (or isomerized) rubber is mostly used for paints which are required to withstand steam and condensation and is thus most commonly used in kitchens and bathrooms. **1967** M. E. HALE *Biol. Lichens* viii. 117 A similar pathway, but with reduction instead of cyclization, could explain the synthesis of fatty acids.

cyclo- (saɪkləʊ, sɪkləʊ). **1.** Combining form of Gr. κύκλος circle (see CYCLE), occurring in many technical terms; *e.g.* **cycloˈbranchian**, a mollusc belonging to the sub-order Cyclobranchia; **cycloˈbranchiate** *a.* [Gr. βράγχια gills], having gills circularly arranged; applied to a suborder of gastropodous molluscs (*Cyclobranchia, -branchiata*); also said of the gills; **cycloˈcentric** *a.* (see quot.); **cycloceˈphalian, -lic** *a.*; **cycloˈcephalus** [κεφαλή head] (see quots.); **cycloˈclinal** *a. Geol.* [cf. ANTICLINAL], sloping in all directions from a central point; = QUAQUAVERSAL; **cycloˈcœlic** *a.* [κοιλία intestines], having the intestines coiled: said of birds; opposed to *orthocœlic*; **cycloˈgangliate, -ated** *a. Zool.*, having circularly-arranged ganglia; **ˈcyclogen** *Bot.* [-γενης born, produced], a plant having woody tissue disposed in concentric circles; = EXOGEN; so **cyˈclogenous** *a.* (*Syd. Soc. Lex.*); **cycloˈgiro, -gyro** [cf. AUTOGIRO], see quots.; **ˈcyclogram** [-GRAM], the figure produced by a cyclograph; **ˈcyclograph** [-γραφος writer], (*a*) an instrument for tracing circular arcs; (*b*) *Electr.* (see quots.); hence **cycloˈgraphic** *a.*; **cyˈclographer**, a writer of a cycle (of legends, etc.); **ˈcyclolith** [λίθος stone, after *monolith*, etc.], a name given by some archæologists to a prehistoric stone circle; **ˌcyclomorˈphosis** *Biol.* [ad. G. *cyclomorphose* (R. Lauterborn 1904, in *Verh. Naturh.-Med. Ver., Heidelberg* VII. 614), occas. used in English], the phenomenon in certain organisms, esp. planktonic animals, of undergoing recurrent seasonal changes in form; **cycloˈneurous, -ˈose** *a. Zool.*, having the nervous axis circularly arranged, as in the *Radiata*; **cycloˈplegia** *Path.* [Gr. πληγή stroke], paralysis of the ciliary muscle; hence **cycloˈplegic** *a.*, producing cycloplegia; *sb.* a cycloplegic agent; **cyˈclopterous** *a.* [πτερόν wing], round-winged, round-finned; **cycloˈrrhaphous** *a. Ent.* [f. mod.L *Cyclorapha, Cyclorrhapha* (F. Brauer *Monographie der Oestriden* (1863) 34), Gr. ῥαφή seam (ῥάπτειν to sew)], of or pertaining to the Cyclorrhapha, a division of dipterous insects in which the adult emerges from the puparium through a circular seam; distinguished from ORTHORRHAPHOUS *a.*; **ˈcycloscope** [-σκοπος viewing], (*a*) an apparatus for measuring the velocity of revolution, by means of a revolving ruled cylinder, viewed through an aperture partially closed by a tuning-fork vibrating at a known rate; (*b*) an instrument for setting out railway curves; **cycloˈspermous** *a. Bot.* [σπέρμα seed], having the embryo coiled about the central albumen; **cycloˈsporin** *Pharm.* [mod.L. *poly-sporum*, specific epithet of the fungus producing it, f. *spora* SPORE], a cyclic undecapeptide produced by a fungus and used as an immunosuppressive drug to prevent the rejection of grafts and transplants; also ***cyclosporin A***; **cyˈclostomate, -ˈstomatous, -stomous** *a.* [στόμα mouth], having a round sucking mouth, as a lamprey, or a circular aperture of the shell, as some gastropods; also belonging to a certain division of the Polyzoa (*Cyclostomata*), having the cellmouth not guarded by an operculum or process; **ˈcyclostome** *a.* = *cyclostomous*; *sb.* a cyclostomous fish, as the lamprey; a cyclostomous gastropod; **cycloˈstrophic** *a. Meteorol.* [see STROPHE], designating the force acting on a wind as a result of the curvature of its path, and also a (hypothetical) wind in which this force exactly balances that arising from the horizontal pressure gradient; **cycloˈsystem**, the circular system or arrangement of the pores in some *Hydrocorallina* (Millepores. etc.); **ˈcyclothem** *Geol.* [Gr. θέμα something laid down (see THEME)], see quot. 1932; **ˈcyclothyme** *a.* and *sb.* = *cyclothymic*; **cycloˈthymia** *Psychiatry* [Gr. θυμός mind, temper], a condition marked by cyclic alternations of mood from exhilaration to depression with a tendency, when aggravated, to manic-depression; hence **cyclo'thymic** *a.* and *sb.*, (a person) affected with this; (cf. CYCLOID *sb.* 3).

1837 *Penny Cycl.* VIII. 248/2 *Cyclobranchians. **1839** *Ibid.* XIII. 485/1 With regard to the marine species [of Limacineans], which Cuvier has approximated to these, M. de Blainville observes that they constitute his genus *Peronia* in his order of Cyclobranchians. **1836-39** TODD *Cycl. Anat.* II. 388/1 In the *Cyclobranchiate order. **1854** WOODWARD *Mollusca* (1856) 154 The cyclobranchiate gill of Patella. **1882** *Syd. Soc. Lex.*, **Cyclocentric*, a term applied to those coiled shells which have the starting-point of the spiral at a little distance from the centre, so that the first whorl runs around it. *Ibid.*, **Cyclocephalic*, having the characters of a *Cyclocephalus*. Also, applied to the form of the head of an hydrocephalic person. *Ibid.*, **Cyclocephalus*, a monster having two contiguous eyes, or a double eye in the median line. **1876** PAGE *Adv. Text-Bk. Geol.* iv. 84 Periclinal, *cycloclinal or quaquaversal..that is dipping in every direction. **1836-9** TODD *Cycl. Anat.* II. 412/2 The ..*cyclogangliate..divisions of the animal kingdom. *Ibid.* 392/2 The nervous system of the Gasteropoda..the most perfect form of the..cyclo-gangliated type. **1933** *Nat. Advis. Comm., Techn. Rep. 474* (Nomencl. Aeronaut.) 12/2 **Cyclogiro*, a type of rotor plane whose support in the air is normally derived from airfoils mechanically rotated about an axis perpendicular to the plane of symmetry of an aircraft, the angle of attack of the airfoils being always less than the angle at which the airfoils stall. **1931** S. R. ROGET *Dict. Electr. Terms* (ed. 2) 77/1 **Cyclogram*, a record obtained from a cyclograph. **1946** *Electronic Engin.* XVIII. 378 The Lissajous figure is perhaps the most important type of cyclogram display. **1823** P. NICHOLSON *Pract. Build.* 562 The *Cyclograph is an instrument for drawing arcs of circles. **1931** S. R. ROGET *Dict. Electr. Terms* (ed. 2) 77/1 *Cyclograph*, a name sometimes given to an instrument with an optical or electron-jet 'pointer' moving in two dimensions under control respectively of different variables. **1940** *Chambers's Techn. Dict.* 220/1 *Cyclograph*, an instrument in which a beam of light or cathode rays is made to move under the action of two controlling forces at right-angles to each other, thereby producing a closed figure (cyclogram) on the screen. **1841-4** C. ANTHON *Class. Dict.* 353 Dionysius, the *cyclographer, makes Circe the daughter of Æëtes. **1933** R. A. W. WATT et al. *Applications Cathode Ray Oscillograph* i. 3 Braun also introduced the *cyclographic method of using the tube. **1940** *Chambers's Techn. Dict.* 220/1 **Cyclogyro*, a rotorcraft depending for its lift on power-driven rotors rotating on horizontal axes. **1926** C. WESENBERG-LUND in *K. Dansk. Videnskab. Skr.* (*Natur. & Math.*) 8th Ser. XI. 127 The *cyclomorphose [in *Daphnia cucullata*] has been thoroughly studied in many lakes. **1930** *Ibid.* 9th Ser. II. 37 In the seasonal variations or cyclomorphoses Lauterborn saw accommodations to variations in the external medium. *Ibid.* 38 The *cyclomorphosis is a process of senility. **1939** *Q. Rev. Biol.* XIV. 137/1 The phenomenon of cyclomorphosis among plankton organisms is particularly well exemplified in fresh-water Cladocera, especially in the group *Daphnia cucullata* and *D. longispina*. **1961** S. C. KENDEIGH *Animal Ecol.* vi. 60/1 An interesting phenomenon is cyclomorphosis, a seasonal change in body form that develops in many plankton organisms. **1835-6** TODD *Cycl. Anat.* I. 107/2 An organization..more complex than that of the *cycloneurose classes. **1902** *Jrnl. Amer. Med. Assoc.* XXXVIII. 1136/2 Difficulty in accommodating for hyoscin commenced in fifteen to eighteen minutes, and there was complete *cycloplegia in thirty to forty-eight minutes. *Ibid.* 1135/2 (*heading*) Comparative values of *cycloplegics... Atropin has been the chief reliance of ophthalmologists as a cycloplegic. *Ibid.* 1137/1 Tests possess sufficient accuracy to enable us to select the best out of the candidates for cycloplegic honors, namely hyoscin hydrobromate. **1956** *Nature* 17 Mar. 523/2 Variable..disturbances of vision, due to cycloplegic and mydriatic actions. **1957** *Encycl. Brit.* XXIII. 213/1 The use of cycloplegics (a kind of eye drops) is a conventional clinical method which attempts to determine the intrinsic relation of lens systems to length of eyeball when the accommodation is relaxed. **1889** *Cent. Dict.*, *Cyclorhaphous. **1901** G. H. VERRALL *Brit. Flies* VIII. 11 Cyclorrhaphous flies of not at all a leathery texture. **1961** J. E. COLLIN *Brit. Flies* VI. 1 It is now more usual to ..adopt as the two main divisions the Nematocera and Brachycera with the latter subdivided into the Orthorrhaphous- and Cyclorrhaphous-Brachycera. **1866** *Engineer* 415 The *Cycloscope. **1976** *Helv. Chim. Acta* LIX. 1480 *Cyclosporin A is a cyclic undecapeptide $C_{62}H_{111}N_{11}O_{12}$ which may be isolated from *Trichoderma polysporum*. **1979** *Daily Tel.* 5 Sept. 8/3 The new drug Cyclosporin A..makes it possible to hope for more transplants for children who are endangered by the standard treatment against organ rejection. **1984** *Listener* 23 Aug. 4/3 The advent of a new drug to prevent rejection of transplanted organs—cyclosporin—has already led to improvements in survival in adult heart-transplant patients. **1839-47** TODD *Cycl. Anat.* III. 966/2 In the *cyclostomatous Fishes..the skeleton is of still more simple structure. **1835** KIRBY *Hab. & Inst. Anim.* II. xxi. 390 The *Cyclostomes or suckers, with regard to their skeletons, are the most imperfect of all the Vertebrates. **1854** BADHAM *Halieut.* 440 Our little cyclostome..the lamprey. **1855** H. SPENCER *Princ. Psychol.* §8 The cyclostome Fishes. **1826** KIRBY & SP. *Entomol.* xlvii. (1828) IV. 427 Some of the *cyclostomous fishes..are supposed to connect the fishes with the *Annulosa*. **1916** *Cyclostrophic [see GEOSTROPHIC *a.*]. **1959** R. E. HUSCHKE *Gloss. Meteorol.* 151 The cyclostrophic wind can be an approximation to the real wind in the atmosphere only near the equator..or in cases of very great wind speed and curvature of the path. **1932** WANLESS & WELLER in *Bull. Geol. Soc. Amer.* XLIII. 1003 The word '*cyclothem' is..proposed to designate a series of beds deposited during a single sedimentary cycle of the type that prevailed during the Pennsylvanian period. **1957** *Encyl. Brit.* IV. 844/1 Coals are more important than limestones in identifying cyclothems because most cyclothems include only one coal whereas two or more limestones may occur. **1925** W. J. H. SPROTT tr. *Kretschmer's Physique & Char.* xii. 208 We call the members of that large constitution-class, from which the schizophrenes are recruited, 'schizothymes', and those that correspond to the circular psychotics are called '*cyclothymes'. **1932** *Brit. Jrnl. Psychol.* Jan. 236 The mean age of the cyclothyme group is greater than that of the schizothyme. **1951** *John o'London's* 9 Nov. 724/3 Dickens was undoubtedly a cyclothyme. **1921** GLUECK & LIND tr. *A. Adler's Neurot. Constit.* 187 Dementia præcox, paranoia and *cyclothymia. **1929** P. MAIRET tr. *A. Adler's Probl. Neurosis* 27 A cyclothymia beginning late in life. **1925** W. J. H. SPROTT tr. *Kretschmer's Physique & Char.* xiv. 259 Among *cyclothymic temperaments a certain mood-disposition usually goes with a certain psychic tempo. *Ibid.*, Cyclothymic psychomotility is distinguished by the natural quality of reaction and bodily movement which is now quick, now slow. **1926** W. MCDOUGALL *Outl. Abnormal Psychol.* 353 Most of us..are liable to mild alternations of this kind, moods of 'excitement' and of depression... When the liability to such alternations is well marked, the personality is said to be of the cyclothymic type. *Ibid.* 356 Cyclo-thymics, in whom periods of energetic euphoria alternate with despondent impotence. **1965** J. POLLITT *Depression & its Treatment* iv. 59 In cyclothymic subjects, and those who have suffered from manic episodes, a large dose continued too long may produce hypomanic features.

2. *Org. Chem.* Also *ital.* (see quot. 1958). A prefix used in forming the names of some cyclic compounds.

1894 G. M'GOWAN tr. *Bernthsen's Text-bk. Org. Chem.* (ed. 2) xv. 323 Their 'official names' are Cyclo-propane, Cyclo-butane, etc. **1900** E. F. SMITH tr. *von Richter's Org. Chem.* (ed. 3) II. 17 In accordance with the decision of the Geneva Conference, they take the name of the normal hydrocarbons with like carbon content, and add to the same the prefix 'cyclo'—e.g., cycloparaffins. **1904** *Jrnl. Chem. Soc.* LXXXVI. I. 413 It was not found possible to eliminate nitrogen from this compound and so obtain a *cyclo*octane derivative. **1911** *Encycl. Brit.* XXII. 31/1 Cyclo-hexanol, $C_6H_{11}OH$, is produced by the reduction of the corresponding ketone. **1925** A. W. JUDGE *Automobile Engines* i. 10 A mixture of 20 parts benzole and 80 parts cyclohexane will enable an engine to be run at 200 lb. per sq. in. compression pressure. **1944** L. F. & M. FIESER *Org. Chem.* 49 Cycloparaffins (cycloalkanes) bear a close resemblance to the paraffins. **1952** *Sci. News Let.* 24 Dec. 412/1 A new mold chemical, cycloserine, was..reported promising against tuberculosis. **1955** *Electronic Engin.* XXVII. 513 A special solvent, the main constituent of which is cyclohexanone. **1955** H. WELCH et al. in *Antibiotic Med.* (N.Y.) I. 72 Cycloserine is the generic name for a new antibiotic produced by *Streptomyces orchidaceus*. **1957** *Nomencl. Org. Chem.* (I.U.P.A.C.) (1958) 18 The names of saturated monocyclic hydrocarbons (with no side chains) are formed by attaching the prefix 'cyclo' to the name of the acyclic saturated unbranched hydrocarbon with the same number of carbon atoms. **1958** PACKER & VAUGHAN *Mod. Approach to Org. Chem.* ii. 40 They are called *cyclo*-alkanes or *cyclo*-paraffins and are named correspondingly, e.g. *cyclo*-pentane, *cyclo*-hexane. *Ibid.*, In American practice italics are not used for the cyclo, e.g. cyclopentane. **1963** *New Scientist* 9 May 321/2 The photochemical process that Japanese chemists recently developed for converting cyclohexane into caprolactam—which is used in the manufacture of nylon 6—is now in full scale production.

cyclo-cross ('saɪkləkrɒs). [f. CYCLE *sb.* 11 + *cross* as in CROSS-COUNTRY *a.*] Cross-country bicycle racing.

1953 *Cycle Sport Ann.* 63 Winter winds..offer a challenge to the enthusiasm of the Cyclo-Cross expert. **1963** *Times* 4 Feb. 20 The national cyclo-cross championship.

cyclode ('saɪkləʊd, 'sɪk-). *Math.* [f. Gr. κύκλος circle + ὁδός path.] A name introduced by Prof. Sylvester, 1869, for the involute of any order to a circle. See INVOLUTE.

1869 SYLVESTER in *Proc. Lond. Math. Soc.* II. 137-160 A Cyclode is the continued [n^{th}] involute of a circle.

cyclodialysis (saɪkləʊdaɪ'ælɪsɪs). *Surg.* [ad. G. *cyklodialyse* (Heine 1905, in *Deutsche Med. Woch.* 25 May 824/2), f. Gr. κύκλο-ς any circular body, eye + διάλυσις separating (see DIALYSIS).] An operation for relieving the tension of the eyeball in cases of glaucoma (see quot. 1964).

1908 W. L. PYLE tr. *Meller's Ophthalmic Surg.* xv. 204 Cyclodialysis, though able to diminish the intra-ocular pressure, cannot be called preferable or even equal to iridectomy. **1961** *Lancet* 22 July 166/2 A localised cyclodialysis plus air injection. **1964** S. DUKE-ELDER *Parsons' Dis. Eye* (ed. 14) xxi. 310 A communication between the anterior chamber and the suprachoroidal space, which also may lower the tension by cutting off some of the blood supply to the ciliary body, comprises the operation of cyclodialysis.

cycloid ('saɪklɔɪd, 'sɪk-), *sb.* (*a.*) [See next.] **1.** *Math.* **a.** The curve traced in space by a point in the circumference (or on a radius) of a circle as the circle rolls along a straight line.

The ***common cycloid*** is that traced by a point in the circumference of the circle, and has cusps where this point meets the straight line; that traced by a point within the circle is a ***prolate cycloid*** (with inflexions); by a point without the circle, a ***curtate cycloid*** (with loops).

1661 BOYLE *Spring of Air* (1682) 101 Each point will by this compound motion describe on the plain..a perfect cycloid. **1727** SWIFT *Gulliver, Voy. Laputa* ii, A pudding [cut] into a cycloid. **1812-6** PLAYFAIR *Nat. Phil.* (1819) I. 135 The line in which a heavy body descends in the least time from one given point to another..is an arch of a cycloid ..Hence the cycloid is called the *line of swiftest descent*.

b. ***companion to the cycloid***: the curve formed by successive positions of the point of intersection of a horizontal line drawn through a fixed point in the circumference of the rolling circle with a vertical line through its point of contact with the (horizontal) line on which it rolls.

1857 WHEWELL *Hist. Induct. Sc.* II. 244 The curve must be of the nature of that which is called the companion to the cycloid.

2. *Zool.* A cycloid fish: see next.

1847 ANSTED *Anc. World* x. 246 Two orders of Fishes.. the Ctenoids and Cycloids.

3. *Psychiatry.* A person characterized by a tendency to alternate between exhilaration and depression. Also *attrib.* or as *adj.*

1925 W. J. H. SPROTT tr. *Kretschmer's Physique & Char.* xi. 127 In an adverse situation the cycloid is either sorrowful or hot-headed, but he is never in the very least nervous. **1927** HENDERSON & GILLESPIE *Text-Bk. Psychiatry* ix. 190 The 'syntonic' or 'cycloid' personality, in which, if mental illness develops, it tends to be of the manic-depressive kind. **1929** F. H. GARRISON *Hist. Med.* (ed. 4) 679 Cycloids are cheerful, temperamental, well adjusted to the business world, but liable to sudden alternations of exhilaration and depression. **1943** H. READ *Educ. through Art* iv. 76 The 'depressive cycloid' temperament is certainly our old friend the melancholic humour.

'cycloid, *a.* [ad. Gr. κυκλοειδής, κυκλώδης circular: see CYCLE and -OID.] Resembling a circle; *spec.* in *Zool.* **a.** Of a somewhat circular form, with concentric striations; applied to the scales of certain fishes. **b.** Belonging to the *Cycloidei*, or order of fishes with cycloid scales.

1847 ANSTED *Anc. World* iv. 62 The remaining two groups [of Fishes] are called respectively Ctenoid..and Cycloid.. from the shape and structure of the scale. **1851** RICHARDSON *Geol.* (1855) 283 Nearly all the cycloid genera..are extinct. **1872** NICHOLSON *Palæont.* 326 Scales cycloid or rhomboid.

cycloidal (saɪ'klɔɪdəl, sɪk-), *a.* [f. as prec. + -AL[1].] **1.** *Geom.*, etc. Of, pertaining to, or of the form of a cycloid.

cycloidal engine: an instrument used in engraving an 'engine-turned design' upon the plates for bank-notes, etc., as a precaution against counterfeiting; the graver-point having a motion compounded of translation and rotation. ***cycloidal paddle***: a name erroneously given to a paddle-wheel in which each float is divided longitudinally into several strips in a slightly retreating order, *en echelon*, so as to lessen the concussion and make the resistance more uniform (Knight). ***cycloidal pendulum***: a pendulum constructed to swing in a cycloid, so as to be perfectly isochronous.

1704 J. HARRIS *Lex. Techn.* s.v. *Cycloid*, The space within this Curve and the Subtense..is called the Cycloidal Space. **1830** KATER & LARDNER *Mech.* xi. 159 Availing himself of this property of the curve, Huygens constructed his cycloidal pendulum. **1884** F. J. BRITTEN *Watch & Clockm.* 122 The upper part of the pendulum is a double cord hanging between two cycloidal cheeks to give a cycloidal path to the bob.

2. *Zool.* = CYCLOID *a.* a.

1872 NICHOLSON *Palæont.* 326 The scales..are cycloidal in shape, and are arranged in an imbricate manner.

Hence **cy'cloidally** *adv.*, in the form of a cycloid.

1727 CHAMBERS *Cycl.* s.v. *Phonicks*, A smooth wall.. arched..cycloidally or elliptically.

cy'cloidean, *a.* and *sb. Zool.* Also **-ian.** [f. mod.L. *cycloide-us* (f. Gr. κυκλοειδής CYCLOID) + -AN.] **A.** *adj.* Belonging to the cycloid fishes. **B.** *sb.* A cycloid fish.

1837 BUCKLAND *Geol.* I. 270 The Herring and Salmon are examples of Cycloidians.

†cy'cloidical, *a. Obs.* = CYCLOIDAL 1.

1793 SIR G. SHUCKBURGH in *Phil. Trans.* LXXXIII. 88 The spring, by which the pendulum is suspended..so constructed as to produce cycloidical arcs of vibration.

cyclomatic (saɪkləʊ'mætɪk), *a.* [f. Gr. κύκλωμα, -ματ-, anything rounded or made circular, a wheel + -IC.] Of or pertaining to cycles.

1881 MAXWELL *Electr. & Magn.* I. 16 The existence of cycles is called cyclosis, and the numbers of cycles in a diagram is called its cyclomatic number.

cyclometer (saɪ'klɒmɪtə(r)). [f. Gr. κύκλο-ς circle + μέτρον measure, -μετρος, -μετρης measuring.]

1. An instrument for measuring circular arcs.

1815 W. ADAMSON (*title*), An Universal Principle for Dividing the Circle..by a new Instrument called the Cyclometer. **1880** C. & F. DARWIN *Movem. Pl.* 93 The black lines on the hypocotyls..became distinctly curved, but in very various degrees (namely, with radii between 20 and 80 mm. on Sachs' cyclometer).

2. An apparatus attached to the wheel of a vehicle, *esp.* of a cycle, for registering the distance traversed.

1880 *Scribn. Mag.* Feb. 496 The cyclometers registered thirty-five miles. **1883** B. W. RICHARDSON *Cycling* in *Longm. Mag.* Oct. 604 By means of their cyclometers they [cyclists] could correct..errors respecting distances which the 'signposts' almost invariably make.

3. *humorously.* A 'circle-squarer'.

1866 DE MORGAN in *Athenæum* 27 Oct. 534/2 Cyclometers have their several styles of wit.

cyclometry (saɪ'klɒmɪtrɪ). [f. as prec.: see -METRY.] Measurement of circles; 'circle-squaring'.

1656 in BLOUNT *Glossogr.* **1656** WALLIS *Correct. of Hobbes* 116 (T.), I must tell you, that Sir H. Savile had confuted Joseph Scaliger's cyclometry. **1866** DE MORGAN in *Athenæum* 27 Oct. 535/1 A friend of mine..will spend a thousand pounds..in black and white cyclometry.

Hence **cyclo'metric, -al**, *a.*, of or relating to cyclometry.

1838 HALLIWELL *Brief Acct. S. Morland* 27 Morland's Cyclometrical treatise.

cyclonal (saɪ'kləʊnəl), *a. rare.* [f. CYCLONE + -AL[1].] Of or pertaining to a CYCLONE (1 c).

1881 C. ABBE in *Smithsonian Rep.* 295 The cyclonal curvature of the wind orbit is accompanied by a stronger gradient..than is the anticyclonal curvature.

cyclone ('saɪkləʊn). [f. Gr. κύκλος circle (or κυκλῶν moving in a circle, whirling round): see quot. 1848.

Piddington's account of his formation of the word is vague; the sense he assigns suggests that the Gr. word he meant was κύκλωμα, which means *inter alia* 'the coil of a serpent'; hence *cyclome* occurs as an early variant.]

1. a. *gen.* A name introduced in 1848 by H. Piddington, as a general term for all storms or atmospheric disturbances in which the wind has a circular or whirling course.

1848 H. PIDDINGTON *Sailor's Horn-bk. 8 Winds.* Class II. (Hurricane Storms..Whirlwinds..African Tornado.. Water Spouts..Samiel, Simoom), I suggest..that we might, for all this last class of circular or highly curved winds, adopt the term 'Cyclone' from the Greek κυκλως (which signifies amongst other things the coil of a snake) as ..expressing sufficiently the tendency to circular motion in these meteors. *Ibid.* 176 Throughout the preceding parts the word Cyclone has been, as proposed..added after the words in common use to express circular-blowing winds. In this part I propose to use it alone.

b. *spec.* A hurricane or tornado of limited diameter and destructive violence.

1856 KANE *Arct. Expl.* II. xxii. 220 One of the most fearful gales I have ever experienced. It had the character and the force of a cyclome. **1857** S. P. HALL in *Merc. Marine Mag.* (1858) V. 10 This season has been..prolific in typhoons or cyclones. **1893** *Daily News* 27 May 6/8 A severe cyclone has been raging for the last three days at the head of the Bay of Bengal.

c. *Meteorol.* A system of winds rotating around a centre of minimum barometric pressure, the centre and whole system having itself also a motion of translation, which is sometimes arrested, when the cyclone becomes for a time stationary. Cf. ANTICYCLONE. (Such a system often extends over many thousands of square miles.)

As to the differences between this and b, see A. BUCHAN in *Encycl. Brit.* XVI. 129.

1875 A. BUCHAN in *Encycl. Brit.* III. 33 Areas of low pressure or Cyclones..A cyclone which passed over north-western Europe on the morning of 2d November, 1863. **1881** R. H. SCOTT in *Gd. Words* July 454 Barometrical depressions or cyclones. **1887** *Daily News* 13 Oct. 5/1 There was..a twofold reason for northerly winds—the anticyclone off the west of Ireland and the cyclone over the flats of Holland.

d. *transf.* Applied to a violent rotatory storm in the sun's atmosphere.

1868 LOCKYER *Heavens* (ed. 3) 53 Immense cyclones pass over the surface of the Sun with fearful rapidity, as is rendered evident by the form and changes of certain spots.

e. Used (freq. *attrib.*) of a machine in which a flow of gas or liquid is used to remove or separate solids, usu. by centrifugal force.

1898 *Daily News* 8 Feb. 3/5 The 'cyclone'—a great grey tube with ramifications to all the machines that saw or chip wood... A forced draught carries the chips through the.. tube to the boiler house. **1930** *Engineering* 22 Aug. 221/3 The cyclone filter consisted of a cylindrical vessel fitted with tangential air inlets near the top..and a conical bottom for the reception and discharge of the deposited dust. **1962** *Gloss. Coal Preparation (B.S.I.)* 17 *Cyclone classifier*, a device for classification by centrifugal means of fine particles suspended in water. **1967** *Gloss. Materials Handling (B.S.I.)* III. 6 *Cyclone*, a device imparting a rotary motion to the fluid stream thereby causing the entrained particles to be separated by centrifugal force and gravity.

2. *Comb.* **cyclone cellar** *U.S.*, a cellar intended to give shelter during a cyclone; also *fig.* **cyclone-pit**, 'on the prairies and plains of the western United States, a pit or underground room made for refuge from a tornado or cyclone' (*Cent. Dict.*).

1887 E. CUSTER *Tenting on Plains* (1889) 652 Those women who take refuge..in their cyclone-cellar. **1904** G. H. LORIMER *Old Gorgon Graham* 125 This was one of those holy moments..when an outsider wants to pull his tongue back into its cyclone cellar. **1929** *Monthly Weather Rev.* (U.S. Weather Bur.) LVII. 338/1 People had seen the tornado approaching and had taken to storm caves—the well known 'cyclone cellars' of the West—and basements, where they were safe. **1946** *Reader's Digest* Mar. 135/1 In the winter it was snug and cozy, and in summer-time as cool and nice as our cyclone cellar.

cyclonic (saɪ'klɒnɪk), *a.* [f. prec. + -IC.] Of, pertaining to, or of the nature of, a cyclone.

1860 ADM. FITZ-ROY in *Merc. Marine Mag.* VII. 226 A similar continuous circulation, or cyclonic commotion. **1868** LOCKYER *Heavens* 54 A [sun] spot of the normal character, by no means cyclonic. **1880** *Times* 27 Sept. 5/12 A small cyclonic vortex had formed in the Bay of Bengal.

So **cy'clonical** *a.* = prec. **cy'clonically** *adv.*, after the manner of a cyclone. **'cyclonist, cyclo'nologist**, one who studies cyclones. **cyclo'nology**, the study of cyclones.

1881 J. G. JEFFREYS in *Nature* XXIII. 300 A cyclonical storm. **1884** *Nature* XXX. 305 Towards and around this depression the winds blow cyclonically. **1882** E. D. ARCHIBALD *ibid.* XXVI. 31 The general incurvature of the winds in a cyclone, which was formerly altogether denied by the cyclonists—so-called—Reid and Piddington. **1860** MAURY *Phys. Geog. Sea* xix. §789 The cyclonologists do not locate their storms in such high latitudes. **1860** ADM. FITZ-ROY in *Merc. Marine Mag.* VII. 355 Any person acquainted with cyclonology.

cyclonish ('saɪkləʊnɪʃ), *a.* Somewhat cyclonic (*fig.*).

1884 *Harper's Bazaar* in *Advance* (Chicago) 1 Jan. (1885), Giving the door a cyclonish bang. **1893** *Nation* (N.Y.) 15 July 32/2 She is altogether of the 'breezy', indeed cyclonish, western type—a good tempered girl with no end of go.

cyclonite ('saɪklənaɪt). *Chem.* [f. *cyclo*-trimethylenetri*nitramine*.] A colourless crystalline substance, $(CH_2{\cdot}N{\cdot}NO_2)_3$, used as a high explosive; also called RDX.

1923 *Chem. Abstr.* XVII. 2051 A description is given of the characteristics of..cyclonite..for use as 'booster'. **1939** *Thorpe's Dict. Appl. Chem.* (ed. 4) III. 535/2 Cyclonite.. was first described under the name 'Hexogen' in 1899 by G. F. Henning. **1948** *Times* 10 Jan. 4/2 Cyclonite..has approximately the strength of dynamite. **1951** KIRK & OTHMER *Encycl. Chem. Technol.* VI. 40 Cyclonite, therefore, may be considered at least the equal if not the superior of any other solid bursting-charge explosive available on a production basis. **1966** MILLAR & SPRINGALL *Sidgwick's Org. Chem. Nitrogen* (ed. 3) xviii. 599 The very powerful military high explosive Cyclonite or RDX..was first prepared by the action of nitric acid (99 per cent) on hexamine.

Cyclop: see CYCLOPS.

cyclopædia, -pedia (saɪkləʊ'piːdɪə). Also in Anglicized forms, 7 **cyclopædy, -pedy.** [A shortening or modification of ENCYCLOPÆDIA (itself due to an erroneous Greek reading), perh. intended to convey more obviously the ostensible sense 'circle of learning', from Gr. κύκλος circle + παιδεία education, a branch of learning.]

†**1.** The circle of learning; the whole body of arts and sciences; = ENCYCLOPÆDIA 1. *Obs.*

1636 H. BLOUNT *Voy. Levant* (1637) 85 This Cyclopædia hath beene observed to runne from East to West: Thus have most Civilities, and Sciences come..from the Indian Gymnosophists into Egypt, from thence into Greece, so into Italy. *a* **1661** FULLER *Worthies* II. (1662) 289 Nor yet was it a work of the Cyclopedy of Arts. **1676** HOBBES *Iliad* Pref. (1686) 8 The whole Learning of his time (which the Greeks call *Cyclopedia*).

2. A book containing extensive information on all branches of knowledge, or on all the branches of some particular art, science, etc.; usually arranged alphabetically; = ENCYCLOPÆDIA 2, 3.

1728 CHAMBERS *(title)*, Cyclopædia, or General Dictionary of Arts and Sciences. **1738** W. BOWYER in Nichols *Lit. Anecd. 18th C.* (1812) V. 659 While the second edition of Chambers's Cyclopædia was in the press I went to the author and begged leave to add a single syllable to his magnificent work, and that for Cyclopædia he would write *Encyclopædia*..I urged that Vossius had observed in his book *de Vitiis Sermonis* that 'Cyclopædia was used by some authors, but Encyclopædia by the best'. **1878** MORLEY *Diderot* I. 118 He first suggested the idea of a cyclopædia on a fuller plan.

cyclopædiac (saɪkləʊ'piːdɪæk). *a. rare.* [f. prec. + -AC.] Of or pertaining to a cyclopædia; dealing with all branches of knowledge.

1877 S. CHEETHAM in *Academy* 14 Apr. 311 Isidore..the best-known cyclopædiac writer of that time.

cyclopædic, -pedic (saɪkləʊ'piːdɪk), *a.* [Irregularly formed on *cyclopædia*: see prec. The element *-pædic* would properly represent Gr. παιδικός childish.] Pertaining to or of the nature of a cyclopædia.

a **1843** in SOUTHEY (F. Hall). **1869** J. H. PEPPER *(title)*, Cyclopædic Science Simplified. **1876** *N. Amer. Rev.* 224 Dr. Rees, of Cyclopaedic memory.

Hence **cyclo'pædically** *adv.*, in a cyclopædic manner; like a cyclopædia.

1888 *Harper's Mag.* 9 Nov. 929/2 Ubiquitous in business hours, and cyclopædically ready of response to any requisition.

'cyclopædize, *v.* [See -IZE.] *trans.* To bring together or arrange in systematic form.

1860 *Sat. Rev.* X. 85/2 That stage of intellectual progress which cyclopædizes its information.

cyclope ('saɪkləʊp), *a. rare*[−1]. [a. F. *cyclope* CYCLOPS.] Resembling a Cyclops; one-eyed, or using one eye.

1868 O. W. HOLMES *Poems, To C. G. Ehrenberg*, Even as the patient watchers of the night,—The cyclope gleaners of the fruitful skies.

Cyclopean, -ian (saɪkləʊ'piːən, saɪ'kləʊpɪən), *a.* [f. L. *Cyclōpē-us*, a. Gr. Κυκλώπειος, and *Cyclōpius*, a. Gr. Κυκλώπιος, f. Κύκλωπες the builders of the walls of Mycenæ, pl. of Κύκλωψ a Cyclops, a one-eyed giant of ancient mythology.]

1. a. Belonging to or resembling the Cyclopes; monstrous, gigantic, huge; single, or large and round, like the one eye of a Cyclops.

1641 SYMONDS *Serm. bef. Ho. Com.* C iv b, To redeem from the Cyclopean power that which is the glory of Christ. **1725** POPE *Odyss.* IX. 422 Such as th' unbless'd Cyclopean climes produce. **1762** FALCONER *Shipwr.* III. 293 Then, forged by Cyclopean art, appear'd Thunders. **1858** LARDNER *Hand-bk. Nat. Phil.* 7 Press by which the Britannia tubular bridge was erected..The weight and bulk of this cyclopean engine were in accordance with its vast mechanical power. **1878** NEWCOMB *Pop. Astron.* II. i. 139 We may liken the telescope to a 'Cyclopean eye'.

b. (See CYCLOPIA.)

2. *Antiq.* Applied to an ancient style of masonry in which the stones are of immense size and more or less irregular shape; found in Greece, Italy, and elsewhere, and anciently fabled to be the work of a gigantic Thracian race called Cyclopes from their king Cyclops. Now applied also to similar ancient work in other regions.

1822 M. WILMOT *Jrnl.* 26 Mar. in *More Lett.* (1935) 158 Fondi: remarkable for its gate, its Ciclopean wall, its tower. **1835** THIRLWALL *Greece* I. ii. 61 The huge structures.. commonly described by the epithet Cyclopean. *Ibid.* 62 The most unsightly Cyclopian wall. **1845** PETRIE *Round Towers Irel.* 169 A style of masonry perfectly Cyclopean.

'cyclopede. An adapted form of CYCLOPÆDIA.

1774 WARTON *Hist. Poetry* xxxvi. (1840) III. 12 Peter Lombard's scholastic cyclopede of divinity, called the Sentences. **1817** HOBHOUSE in Smiles *John Murray* II. 460 The work should be done like a cyclopede dictionary.

cyclophobia (*nonce-wd.*): see -PHOBIA.

cyclophosphamide (saɪkləʊ'fɒsfəmaɪd). *Pharm.* [f. CYCLO- + PHOSPH- (in *phosphoric acid*) + AMIDE.] A fine white crystalline powder used as a cytotoxic drug in the treatment of tumours and some kinds of leukæmia, and usu. given intravenously or orally; 2-[di-(2-chloroethyl)-amino-]-1-oxa-3-aza-2-phosphacyclohexane 2-oxide, $C_7H_{15}Cl_2N_2O_2P$.

1960 *Brit. Med. Jrnl.* 24 Dec. 1837/1 We report our experiences in the treatment of Hodgkins's disease and other tumours of lymphoreticular tissue with a cyclic nitrogen mustard phosphamide ester, cyclophosphamide. **1963** *Times* 16 Feb. 5/4 A drug, cyclophosphamide,..killed some of the cells thought to be responsible for rejecting foreign tissue such as the newly grafted kidney. **1966** *Lancet* 24 Dec. 1382/1 Cyclophosphamide was tried, unsuccessfully, in one patient, but this drug is known to be antagonised by dapsone. **1967** *Martindale's Extra Pharmacopoeia* (ed. 25) 818/2 The most troublesome side-effect of cyclophosphamide therapy is alopecia. **1969** *Nature* 1 Feb. 468/2 Cyclophosphamide shows promise as a method of removing the wool from sheep chemically. **1970** *Sci. Jrnl.* Mar. 63/1 Modern drugs such as methotrexate and cyclophosphamide are extremely valuable in the treatment of many cancers and especially leukaemias.

cyclopia (saɪ'kləʊpɪə). *Zool.* and *Path.* Also in anglicized form **cyclopy.** [f. Gr. κύκλωψ Cyclops: see below.] (See quot. 1882.) Hence **cy'clopian** *a.*

1839–47 TODD *Cycl. Anat.* III. 738 Cyclopian monsters. **1849–52** *Ibid.* IV. 967/1 Want of the under jaw often coexists with Cyclopia. **1862** *Chambers' Encycl.* s.v. *Deformities*, Cyclopy, when both the eyes run into one. **1882** *Syd. Soc. Lex.*, *Cyclopia*, a kind of monstrosity consisting in the fusion of two eyes into one place in the middle of the forehead, like the Cyclops. It is a normal condition of some Crustacea.

Cyclopian, var. of CYCLOPEAN.

Cyclopic (saɪ'klɒpɪk), *a.*[1] [ad. Gr. κυκλωπικ-ός.] Belonging to or resembling a Cyclops; monstrous; Cyclopean.

1633 W. STRUTHER *True Happines* 55 This is nothing but the old blinde cyclopick superarrogancie. **1667** WATERHOUSE *Fire Lond.* 68 Which it took into its Cyclopique arms, and crumbled into ashes. **1692** SIR T. P. BLOUNT *Ess.* 46 Some Cyclopick Monster, which eats and drinks the Flesh and Blood of Mankind.

cy'clopic, *a.*[2] *Chem.* [f. botanical name *Cyclopia* + -IC.] (See quot.) So **'cyclopine**, an alkaloid obtained from *Cyclopia*.

1879 WATTS *Dict. Chem.* VII. 418 *Cyclopic acid*, an acid obtained from *Cyclopia Vogelii*, a plant used in Africa for the preparation of tea..The cyclopic acid is deposited in the form of a yellow powder.

†**Cy'clopical**, *a. Obs.* [f. as CYCLOPIC + -AL[1].] = CYCLOPIC *a.*[1]

1583 STUBBES *Anat. Abus.* (1836) 75 Their hautie stomackes, and more than Cyclopical countenaunces. **1653** URQUHART *Rabelais* II. xxvi, Armed..with Cyclopical annuils.

Hence **Cy'clopically** *adv.*, in a Cyclopic manner, as by a Cyclops.

1868 LOWELL *Poems, Winter Even. Hymn to Fire* vi, Upon the anvils of the brain..cyclopically wrought By the fast-throbbing hammer of the poet's thought.

†**'Cyclopism.** *Obs. rare*[−1]. [f. CYCLOPS + -ISM.] Practice characteristic of a Cyclops.

1617 COLLINS *Def. Bp. Ely* II. x. 413 Vnles you wil be so wood now, as to adde brutish Vbiquitisme, to your barbarous Cyclopisme.

cyclopite ('sɪkləʊpaɪt, 'saɪ-). *Min.* [f. L. *Cyclōpi-us* (*Cyclopia saxa*) + -ITE.] A variety of

ANORTHITE, found in the Cyclopean islands near Sicily.

1811 PINKERTON *Petral.* II. 499 The analcimes of Haüy, which he proposes to call cyclopites, because they were first found in the rocks of the Cyclops. **1868** DANA *Min.* 340 Cyclopite occurs in white transparent glassy crystals.

cyclopoid (ˈsɪkləʊpɔɪd, ˈsaɪ-), *a.* and *sb. Zool.* [f. mod.L. *Cyclops* (in Zoology) + -OID.]

A. *adj.* Belonging to, or resembling the family *Cyclopidæ* of Copepods, of which the genus *Cyclops* is the type. **B.** *sb.* One of the *Cyclopidæ*.

1852 DANA *Crust.* II. 1309 In one section, that most closely Cyclopoid, the eight natatory legs have the ordinary form. *Ibid* 1408 They have usually an articulated abdomen, furcate at extremity, like the Cyclopoids.

‖**Cyclops** (ˈsaɪklɒps). Also Cyclop. Pl. Cyclopes (saɪˈkləʊpiːz); also **Cyclops, Cyclopses.** [a. L. *Cyclōps, -ōpem*, a. Gr. Κύκλωψ lit. 'round-eyed', f. κυκλο-ς circle + -ὤψ eye. In It. and Sp. *Ciclope*, Pg. and F. *Cyclope*, whence Eng. *Cyclop.*]

1. One of a race of one-eyed giants in ancient Greek mythology, who forged thunderbolts for Zeus. Hence often used allusively.

α. sing. *Cyclops*, pl. *Cyclopes*; but the latter in early use may be like F. *Cyclopes*, pl. of *Cyclope*.

1513 DOUGLAS *Æneis* III. x. 39 A huge peple we se Of Ciclopes cum hurland to the port. **1561** T. NORTON *Calvin's Inst.* I. 7 Vnlesse the Epicureans like the Giauntes Cyclopes would..make warre against God. **1645** MILTON *Tetrach.* (1851) 234 Such an obdurat Cyclops, to have but one eye for this text. **1802** WORDSW. *Daisy* iv, A little cyclops, with one eye Staring to threaten and defy. **1883** LIDDELL & SCOTT *Gr. Lex.* (ed. 7) s.v., In Hesiod *Theogony* 140, we find three Cyclopes..who forged the thunderbolts for Zeus.

β. sing. *Cyclop*, pl. *Cyclops*. [F. *Cyclope, -s.*]

1592 R. D. *Hypnerotomachia* 3 b, Achemenides being afraide of the horrible Cyclops. **1602** SHAKS. *Ham.* II. ii. 511. **1697** DRYDEN *Virg. Georg.* IV. 245 The Cyclops, at th' Almighty Nod, New Thunder hasten for their angry God. **1725** POPE *Odyss.* IX. 473 The Cyclops all that round him dwell. *Ibid.* 484 The Cyclop from his den replies. **1819** SHELLEY *Cyclops* 111 Cyclops, who live in caverns, not in houses. **1855** MACAULAY *Hist.* IV. xix. 321 In front of the helmet was a huge glass eye like that of a cyclop.

γ. pl. *Cyclopses*.

1681 RYCAUT *Critick* 206 What shall I say of so many Cyclopses? **1819** SHELLEY *Cyclops* 25 The one-eyed children of the Ocean God, The man-destroying Cyclopses.

2. *Zool.* A genus of small fresh-water copepods, having an eye (apparently single, but really double) situated in the middle of the front of the head.

1849–52 TODD *Cycl. Anat.* IV. 967/1 The metamorphosis of the eyes in..Cyclops. **1860** GOSSE *Rom. Nat. Hist.* 63 Tiny cyprides and cyclopes disporting in the umbrageous groves of their world.

3. *attrib.* and *Comb.* (Cf. CYCLOPE *a.*)

1682 DRYDEN *Medal* 226 Then, Cyclop like, in humane Flesh to deal. **1687** *Third Coll. Poems, A Warning* (1689) 29/1 His Cyclop Priests will make you truckle under. **1803** SARRETT *New Pict. London* 177 A Cyclops pig..because it has only one eye..placed in the middle of the forehead.

cyclopy: see CYCLOPIA.

cyclorama (saɪkləˈrɑːmə). [mod.f. Gr. κύκλος circle + ὅραμα spectacle.] **1.** A picture of a landscape or scene arranged on the inside of a cylindrical surface, the spectator standing in the middle.

1840 *Penny Cycl.* XVII. 191 The panorama forms the surface of a hollow cylinder..(whence it is..called..cyclorama). **1849** (*title*), Description of the Royal Cyclorama..Regents Park, opened in 1848. **1888** *Pall Mall G.* 25 June 11/1 The cyclorama [of Niagara] which has 'fetched' all London.

2. *Theatr.* A large backcloth or wall, freq. curved, at the back of a stage, used esp. to represent the sky.

1915 H. K. MODERWELL *Theatre To-Day* ii. 52 The 'skydrops'..have been replaced..by an invention that makes a natural landscape possible. This is the 'Horizont', which we may name for the purpose a cyclorama. **1930** *Observer* 18 May 11/2 The stage will have unique features, including an artificial horizon or cyclorama. **1957** *Oxf. Compan. Theatre* (ed. 2) 173 The cyclorama is, in essence, a curved wall, or section of a dome, built at the back of the stage, and demanding one quality—an absolutely unbroken surface. **1958** W. T. O'DEA *Social Hist. Lighting* vii. 166 In 1902 the first attempts were made to produce coloured sky effects by coloured light only, the 'cyclorama' being installed by Mariano Fortuny at the Scala Opera House in Milan. The cyclorama, which is a smooth, light-coloured surface the full height and width of the stage, can also be used for optical projection of scenery and effects, but it must not be in the path of any illumination other than that deliberately cast upon it.

Hence **cycloˈramic** *a.*

1886 *Appleton's Ann. Cycl.* 278 (in *Cent. Dict.*) The laws of cycloramic perspective.

ˈcyclorn. = *cycle-horn*: see CYCLE *sb.* 12.

1891 *Wheeling* 4 Mar. 426 With an eldritch screech from his cyclorn. **1891** *Cycl. Tour. Club Gaz.* Aug. 200/1 The croak of a cyclorn warns him.

cyclosis (saɪˈkləʊsɪs). [a. Gr. κύκλωσις encircling, f. κυκλό-ειν to encircle, to move in a circle.]

1. *Biol.* A term (proposed by C. H. Schultz in 1831) for the circulation of latex (milky juice) in the vessels of plants; also applied to the circulation of protoplasm in certain cells.

1835 LINDLEY *Introd. Bot.* (1848) II. 336 The phenomenon of cyclosis consists of a motion of fluid called latex. **1882** *Jrnl. Quekett Microsc. Club* Ser. II. No. I. 28 The phenomenon of cyclosis as seen in many hairs.

2. *Math.* The occurrence of cycles; see CYCLE 10.

1881 [see CYCLOMATIC]. **1885** WATSON & BURBURY *Math. Th. Electr. & Magn.* I. 6 The correction for cyclosis.

cyclostylar (saɪkləʊˈstaɪlə(r)), *a. Arch.* [f. Gr. κύκλος + στῦλος pillar, column + -AR.] (See quot.)

1850 WEALE *Dict. Terms*, *Cyclostylar*, relating to a structure composed of a circular range of columns without a core; with a core, the range would be a peristyle.

cyclostyle (ˈsaɪkləʊstaɪl), *sb.* [f. Gr. κύκλος circle, wheel + STYLE, L. *stilus*.] Name of an apparatus for printing copies of writing.

It consists of a pen with a small toothed wheel at the point which cuts minute holes in specially prepared paper tightly stretched over a zinc plate; this paper is then used as a stencil-plate from which copies are printed. Hence ***cyclostyle apparatus, ink, pen***, etc.

1883 *Knowledge* 16 Feb. *Advt.*, The Cyclostyle. **1887** *Chicago Advance* 19 May 306/1 She..prints it herself with the cyclostyle. **1892** *Pall Mall G.* 17 June 6/1 This is probably the last specimen of a cyclostyle-printed journal which will see the light in Mashonaland.

ˈcyclostyle, *v.* [f. the sb.] *trans.* To print (copies) by cyclostyle. Hence **ˈcyclostyled** *ppl. a.*

1897 *Westm. Gaz.* 3 July 2/3 Note the gradual rise from the cyclostyled circular to the printed appeal. **1928** *Daily Express* 5 Mar. 2/3 No candidate can be directly boosted by name in any matter printed, typed, or cyclostyled. **1957** *Times* 19 Aug. 2/7 The inquirer's first carefree letter to manufacturers will be answered by a flood of shiny prospectuses and cyclostyled price lists.

cyˈclotomy. [f. Gr. κύκλος circle + -τομια cutting. In sense 1 rendering Ger. *kreistheilung*.]

1. *Math.* The problem of the division of a circle into a given number of equal parts (Sylvester).

1879 SYLVESTER in *Amer. Jrnl. Math.* 380 Bachmann's work, as it seems to me, gives proof, that Cyclotomy is to be regarded not as an incidental application, but as the natural and inherent centre and core of the arithmetic of the future. **1892** MATHEWS *Theory of Numbers* I. 184.

2. *Ophthalmic Surg.* (See quot.)

1889 BERRY *Dis. Eye* vii. 222 Division of the ciliary muscle, or cyclotomy.

Hence **cycloˈtomic** *a.*, as in ***cyclotomic functions***.

1879 SYLVESTER in *Amer. Jrnl. Math.* 357 The species of cyclotomic..functions of which the cubic function above written is an example.

cyclotron (ˈsaɪklətrɒn). [f. CYCLO- + -TRON.] An apparatus for accelerating charged atomic particles by subjecting them repeatedly to a (usu. horizontal) electric field as they revolve in orbits of increasing diameter in a constant (usu. vertical) magnetic field.

1935 E. O. LAWRENCE et al. in *Physical Rev.* XLVIII. 495/2 An apparatus of the type developed by Lawrence and Livingston was used to produce a beam of high speed deuterons... Since we shall have many occasions in the future to refer to this apparatus, we feel that it should have a name. The term 'magnetic resonance accelerator' is suggested... The word 'cyclotron', of obvious derivation, has come to be used as a sort of laboratory slang for the magnetic device. **1936** *Discovery* June 193/1 Princeton University is..developing its high voltage apparatus by the installation of a cyclotron, which has proved the most satisfactory means of procuring the high-speed ions necessary for the study of nuclear transformations. **1942** *Endeavour* I. 40/1 The cyclotron..consists essentially of a large electromagnet with circular pole pieces, between which is fixed a shallow cylindrical vacuum-tight metal chamber. **1951** *Sci. News* XXII. 58 The cyclotron derives directly from the linear accelerator. The great length and numerous electrodes of the linear accelerator can be avoided if the particles are made to move in a spiral path by a magnetic field. **1966** [see DEE *sb.* 2]. **1969** AUDEN *City without Walls* 97 The High Priests of telescopes and cyclotrons Keep making pronouncements.

‖**cyclus** (ˈsɪkləs, ˈsaɪkləs). [L., a. Gr. κύκλος CYCLE.] = CYCLE 6; also a series of pictures representing romantic or historical cycle.

1810 H. WEBER *Metr. Rom.* I. Introd. 69 A..third cyclus of romance, no less extensive than that of Arthur and of Charlemagne. **1837–9** HALLAM *Hist. Lit.* (1847) I. iv. §65. 305 That legendary cyclus of heroic song. **1838** BARONESS BUNSEN in Hare *Life* I. xi. 482 Hesse's designs for a cyclus representing the conversion of Germany to Christianity.

cycnean, cygnean (sɪkˈniːən, sɪg-), *a. rare.* [f. L. *cycnēus, cygnēus*, = Gr. κύκνειος, f. *cycnus, cygnus* swan.] Of or pertaining to a swan; swan's.

1610 J. MELVIL *Diary* (1842) 720 The moderatoris cygnean songe. **1840** MILMAN *Hist. Chr.* II. II. iv. 62 His last, if we may borrow the expression, his cycnean voice, dwelt on a brief exhortation to mutual charity.

cycorie, -y, obs. forms of CHICORY.

ˈcycular, *a.* [An illiterate formation from CYCLE, after *vehicular* (f. *vehicul-um*): cf. BICYCULAR.] Pertaining to cycles or cycling.

1891 *Cyclist* 25 Feb. 142 Entirely in touch with matters cycular. **1892** *Strand Mag.* July 33/2 The high-water mark of cycular invention.

cyd, var. of SIDE *a. Obs.*, hanging low.

cyder, var. of CIDER.

Cyderach, var. of CIDERAGE, *Obs.*

1579 LANGHAM *Gard. Health* (1633) 37 Cyderach..apply it to greene or fresh wounds.

‖**Cydippe** (saɪˈdɪpiː). *Zool.* [mod.L., a. Gr. Κυδίππη proper name of a Nereid.] A typical genus of Ctenophora, of which one beautiful species, *C. pilosa*, is common in the British Seas. Hence **cyˈdippian** *a.*; **cyˈdippid**, a ctenophoran of the family of Cydippe.

1835–6 TODD *Cycl. Anat.* I. 39/1. **1846** PATTERSON *Zool.* 39 We took a dead Cydippe, and..exposed it to the sun. **1855** GOSSE *Marine Zool.* I. 39 The *Beroes* and *Cydippes*..look like tiny melons of glass, down whose bodies run bands or meridian-lines of paddles. **1860** AGASSIZ *Nat. Hist. U.S.* III. 184, I merely infer its Cydippian relationship from the position of the tentacles. **1888** ROLLESTON & JACKSON *Anim. Life* 721 The larva is at first a Cydippid-form.

†**cydon.** *Obs. rare.* [f. L. *cydōnia* (sc. *mala*) quinces, quince, from *Cydōnia*, Κυδωνία a town of Crete. (In L. also *cotōnia, cotōnea*, whence Pr. *codoing*, F. *coing*, OF. pl. *coins*, Eng. *quince*.)] Quince. Hence †**cyˈdoniate** *v.*, to treat with juice of quinces. **ˈcydonin**, mucilage of quince seeds.

1643 J. STEER tr. *Exp. Chyrurg.* vi. 26 Adde..the musilage of Cydon seeds a little. **1684** tr. *Bonet's Merc. Compit.* XIX. 743 The tincture of Steel pomated or cydoniated. **1853** PEREIRA *Elem. Mat. Med.* (ed. 3) II. II. 1814 Cydonin (peculiar gum of Quince Seed). **1882** *Syd. Soc. Lex.*, *Cydonin*..forming the chief part of the secondary membrane of the epidermis of the seed.

cyen, cyence: see SCION.

cyerge, cyete, obs. forms of CIERGE, CITY.

cyesiology (saiːsɪˈɒlədʒɪ). [f. Gr. κύησις conception, pregnancy + -(O)LOGY.] That branch of physiology which treats of pregnancy.

1846 WORCESTER cites DUNGLISON. **1882** in *Syd. Soc. Lex.*

cyfer, cyffre, cyfre, obs. forms of CIPHER *sb.*

cyft, cygh, obs. forms of SIFT, SIGH.

ˈcygnean, *a.*: see CYCNEAN.

cygneous (ˈsɪgniːəs), *a.* [f. L. *cygn-us* swan: cf. L. *cycnēus, cygnēus* of a swan.] Swan-like; in *Bryology*, curved like a swan's neck.

1880 R. BRAITHWAITE *Brit. Moss-Flora* I. 192 *Phascum curvicolle*..perichætium rufous-purple, oval with a short apiculus, on a pale cygneous pedicel.

cygnet (ˈsɪgnɪt). Forms: 5 **sygnett, syngnett**, 5–7 **signett**, 6 **singnett**, 6–7 **signet**, 6–8 **cignet**, 7 **cygnette**, 7– **cygnet.** [A dim., of Eng. or (?) Anglo-Fr. formation, of F. *cygne* or L. *cygnus* swan. OF. had the dim. *cignel, cigneau* (Godef.).

F. *cygne* is found in end of 14th c., but the ordinary OF. form was *cine*, earlier *cisne, cinne*. *Cisne* appears to be cognate with Sp. *cisne*, and OIt. *cecino* swan, which Romanic scholars derive from L. *cicinus* = *cycnus*, a. Gr. κύκνος swan. L. *cycnus* appears to have split into two types: **cicinus*, found in Plautus (and app. in late popular Latin), whence the Romanic forms, and *cygnus*, which was long the accepted form in later MSS. and texts. Under the influence of the latter OF. *cine* became *cygne* (cf. mod. It. *cigno*).]

1. A young swan. In *Her.* see quot. 1825.

c **1430** *Two Cookery-bks.* 57 Conuiuium domini Henrici Regis quarti, In coronacione sua apud Westmonasterium..Grаund chare. Syngnettys. **1481–90** *Howard Househ. Bks.* (Roxb.) 281 That brout venison and ij. signetts to my Lady. **1562** BULLEYN *Bk. Simples* (1579) 78 The Signets bee better than the old Swannes. **1591** SHAKS. *1 Hen. VI*, v. iii. 56 So doth the Swan her downie Signets saue. **1616** R. C. *Times' Whistle* vii. 2938 Her skin sleek sattin or the cygnettes brest. **1634** *Althorp MS.* in Simpkinson *Washingtons* xv, For 1 dozen of signetts. **1707** FLEETWOOD *Chron. Prec.* (1745) 86 For 8 Cignets or young Swans. **1825** W. BERRY *Encycl. Herald.* I, *Cygnet*..properly, a young swan, but *swans* borne in coat-armour are frequently blazoned *cygnets*. **1856** KANE *Arct. Expl.* I. xxxi. 424 It now rejoices in a drapery as grey as a cygnet's breast.

2. *Comb.*, as ***cygnet-down***; **cygnet-royal** (*Her.*), see quot.

1795 WOLCOTT (P. Pindar) *Liberty's Last Squeak* Wks. 1812 III. 423 Lone silence..Her shoes of cygnet-down shall lend. **1847** H. GOUGH *Gloss. Heraldry*, *Cygnet royal*, a swan gorged with a ducal coronet, having a chain affixed thereunto and reflexed over its back.

cykory, -ie, obs. ff. CHICORY.

cykylle, cykyr: see SICKLE, SICKER.

cyl-, in various words = SIL-.

cyle, see CEIL, CHILL.

cylens, see SILENCE.

cylere, see CYLLOUR, CELURE.

cylinder ('sɪlɪndə(r)), *sb.* Also 6-7 cylindre, 7 cilinder, sillinder. [ad. L. *cylindrus* cylinder, roller, a. Gr. κύλινδρος roller, deriv. of κυλίνδ- ειν to roll. Cf. 16th c. F. *cilindre, cylindre.* There was an earlier form CHILINDRE (in sense 3) in ME. and OF.]

I. 1. a. *Geom.* A solid figure of which the two ends are equal and parallel circles, and the intervening curved surface is such as would be traced out by a straight line moving parallel to itself with its ends in the circumferences of these circles.

If the direction of this straight line be perpendicular to the planes of the circles, the figure is a ***right cylinder***; if not, an ***oblique cylinder***.

1570 BILLINGSLEY *Euclid* XI. Def. xviii. 318 A cylinder is a solide or bodely figure which is made, when one of the sides of a rectangle parallelogramme, abiding fixed, the parallelogramme is moued about. **1579-80** NORTH *Plutarch* (1676) 263 The proportion between the Cylinder..and the sphere or globe contained in the same. **1647** H. MORE *Insomn. Philos.* ix, A duskish Cylindre through infinite space It did project. **1727** SWIFT *Gulliver* III. ii. 186 Cut our bread into cones, cylinders. **1879** *Cassell's Techn. Educ.* II. 100 A cylinder is a solid body of the character of a prism, but its ends are circles.

b. In *mod. Geom.*, the solid generated by a straight line moving always parallel to itself and describing any fixed curve (not necessarily a circle).

1877 B. WILLIAMSON *Int. Calc.* (ed. 2) ix. §168 When the base..is a closed curve of any form..the surface generated is called a *cylinder. Ibid.* ix. Ex. 12 The axis of a right circular cylinder.

2. a. Any body or object of cylindrical form (either solid or hollow); in quot. 1661 applied to a cylindrical jewel worn in the ear. ***axial cylinder*** = *axis-cylinder*: see AXIS; ***renal*** or ***urinary cylinder*** = renal or urinary cast: see CAST 30 c.

1641 HOBBES *Lett.* Wks. 1845 VII. 457 Such matter as the cylinder is made of. *a* **1661** HOLYDAY *Juvenal* 21 Wed and be mute. Thy silence and his fear With rich cylinders then shall grace thine ear. **1807** J. E. SMITH *Phys. Bot.* 35 The cylinder of bark was found lined with layers of new wood. **1879** CALDERWOOD *Mind & Br.* 44 The axial cylinder of each nerve being surrounded by medullary matter.

b. A cylindrical container, *spec.* one for liquefied or compressed gas.

1791 HAMILTON *Berthollet's Dyeing* II. II. III. iii. 177, I poured the decoctions into glass cylinders. **1889** S. S. WALLIAN tr. *J. N. Demarquay's Ess. on Medical Pneumatol.* vi. 245 Carbon dioxide...may also be had in all the larger cities, compressed in iron cylinders. **1904** [see *gas-cylinder* s.v. GAS *sb.*[1] 7]. **1935** [see BUTANE]. **1969** *Sears Catal.* 760/1 Deluxe stove... (Cylinders not incl.)... Economy camp stove. Includes two disposable propane cylinders. **1977** J. BOWYER *Central Heating* ii. 13 The cylinder is often in an airing cupboard.

c. A cylindrical record for a phonograph. Also *attrib.*

1891 'MARK TWAIN' *Let.* 28 Feb. (1920) 297 Ask them on what terms they will rent me a phonograph for 3 months and furnish me cylinders enough to carry 75,000 words. **1893** *Harper's Mag.* Jan. 214/2 It's just a phonograph... It don't seem to be exactly in order. Perhaps the cylinder's got dry. **1907** *Pearson's Mag.* Jan. (Advt.), You cannot get the best results from any talking machine without using Columbia Disc or Cyclinder Records. **1956** R. GELATT *Fabulous Phonograph* ii. 17 Edison cylinders could be shaved and used over and over again while gramophone cylinders had to be discarded much more quickly. **1967** *Amer. N. & Q.* Sept. 15/1 Booth's wax cylinder recording of Othello's speech to the Senate.

†3. A kind of portable sun-dial; = CHILINDRE.

1593 FALE *Dialling* A iij b, The making of the Horologicall Cylindre.

4. a. A cylindrical or somewhat barrel-shaped stone, pierced longitudinally for suspension from the wrist, used as a seal by the Babylonians and Assyrians, and incised with figures, symbols, and cuneiform (or occasionally Aramaic) characters. **b.** A barrel-shaped, hollow object of baked clay, usually of considerable size, covered with cuneiform writing and buried under the foundations of Babylonian and Assyrian temples.

1851 LAYARD *Pop. Acc. Discov. Nineveh* Introd., A few cylinders and gems..from Assyria and Babylonia. **1857** LOFTUS *Chaldæa & Susiana* 130 This discovery at Múgeyer convinced him that the commemorative cylinders of the founders were always deposited at the corners of Babylonian edifices.

II. In *Mechanics.*

5. Applied more or less specifically to many cylindrical parts of machines, etc. (with reference either to the internal chamber or external surface); a revolving roller in a lock.

e.g. The bore of a gun barrel, the part of a revolver which contains the chambers for the cartridges; the barrel of a pump in which the piston works; the glass barrel of an electrical machine; a cylindrical revolving part in a loom, or a carding machine; a revolving roller in a lock, etc.

1571 DIGGES *Pantom.* I. xxx. K, Hauing respecte to the length of the peece, waighte of the Bullet..proportion of the concaue Cylinders. **1660** BOYLE *New Exp. Phys. Mech.* Proem 13 The Pump consists of four parts, a hollow Cylindre, a Sucker, a handle..and a Valve. **1669** STURMY *Mariner's Mag.* v. xii. 58 If the mouth of the Piece be grown wider then the rest of the Cylinder within by often shooting. **1706** PHILLIPS (ed. Kersey), *Charged Cylinder*..that part which receives the Charge of Powder and Shot.. *Vacant Cylinder*, that part of the Hollow which remains empty, when the Gun is Charg'd. **1819** *Rees's Cycl.* XXI. Sig. G g 4v/2 The whole mechanism of the lock, consisting of an interior cylinder or barrel..with its appendages. **1851** *Illustr. London News* 6 Sept. 275/1 On his fifth visit, he had succeeded in..turning the cylinder a quarter round..when the instrument..slipped... He then had to readjust the cylinder..and on the day on which he did so..opened the lock. **1875** URE *Dict. Arts* II. 392 Colt's revolvers..If the hammer be lowered in the pin, the cylinder is prevented from revolving. **1894** [see *cylinder lock* (sense 9 b below)]. **1957** *Encycl. Brit.* XIV. 269/2 The cylinder..or the part in which the key operates, consists of an outer barrel which is fixed to the door and a cylindrical plug which is rotated by the key. **1972** *How Things Work* I. 234 Another..type of cylinder lock is the disc tumbler lock, in which the locking action is provided..by movable discs which lock the cylinder.

6. The cylindrical chamber in which the steam (or other fluid) acts upon the piston. By extension, applied to the corresponding chamber of rotary engines which is sometimes of an annular form. ***to function*** (or ***click, hit, operate***, etc.) ***on all*** (or ***four, six***, etc.) ***cylinders***, of an internal-combustion engine: to be working at full power; hence *fig.*, to function properly, to be in good form; so ***to miss on all*** (or ***four***, etc.) ***cylinders***, to be working badly, to be in bad condition.

1697 PAPIN in *Phil. Trans.* XIX. 483 He proposes the..turning a small Surface of Water into Vapour, by Fire applied to the bottom of the Cylinder that contains it, which Vapour forces up the Plug in the Cylinder. **1751** BLAKE in *Phil. Trans.* XLVII. 200 The best Proportions for Steam engine Cylinders. **1782** *Specif. Watt's Patent* No. 1321. 3 The said piston is suspended by a rod..capable of sliding through a hole in the cover of the cylinder. **1830** J. MILLINGTON *Mech. Philos.* 417 Newcomen's engine was the first in which a truly bored cylinder with a well-fitting piston was employed. **1893** *Engineer* LXXV. 574 That will depend on the total amount of work done in the cylinder by expansion. **1912** C. MATHEWSON *Pitching in a Pinch* xii. 269 So the best infielder takes time to fit into the infield of a Big League club and have it hit on all four cylinders again. **1917** 'CONTACT' *Airman's Outings* 72 The needle on the rev.-counter quivered to the left as the revolutions dropped, and the engine missed on first one, then two cylinders. **1932** WODEHOUSE *Hot Water* ii. 38 He had tended..to undernourish his spiritual self. He had given it the short end, and it was missing, he knew, on several cylinders. *Ibid.* xv. 245 His smiling face, taken in conjunction with the bottle of wine which he carried, conveyed to Gordon Carlisle the definite picture of a libertine operating on all six cylinders. **1936** —— *Laughing Gas* xxi. 228 The old *preux chevalier* spirit was functioning on all six cylinders. **1951** M. MCLUHAN *Mech. Bride* 96/1 A sure sign that you are clicking on all cylinders. **1958** *Spectator* 22 Aug. 249/3 Only when he [*sc.* an actor] allows himself to play deliberately on all cylinders does he stage a dazzling display. **1960** [see BACK-LINE, BACKLINE].

7. *Printing.* **a.** The engraved hollow metal roller used in printing calico, etc. **b.** A similar roller used in letter-press printing for inking the type (now *inking-roller*), pressing the paper against the type, or carrying the type or printing surface.

1764 *Specif. Fryer's Patent* No. 810 (*Calico Printing*) The invention is performed by means of engraved copper cylinders. **1790** *Specif. Nicholson's Patent* No. 1748. 8 A is the printing cylinder covered with woollen cloth, and B is the inking cylinder with its distributing rollers. **1818** *Specif. Cowper's Patent* No. 4194. 2 Conveying the..paper from one printing cylinder to another. **1858** *Specif. Applegath's Patent* No. 372 Comparatively few printing rollers can be arranged round the cylinder carrying the type.

8. *Watchmaking.* The cylindrical recess on the verge of the balance in a horizontal escapement.

1765 MUDGE *Thoughts on Improv. Watches* (1772) 23 Making the cylinder of harder materials..would be an advantage. **1773** HATTON *Clock & Watch Work* 197 The tooth [of the balance wheel] ought to act at right angles to a line which would touch the cylinder. **1883** BECKETT *Clocks & Watches* 320 In the best watches the cylinder is made of a ruby.

9. *attrib.* and *Comb.* **† a.** simple *attrib.* or as *adj.* Cylindrical. *Obs.*

1621-51 BURTON *Anat. Mel.* I. iii. III. 211 Concave and Cylinder glasses [= mirrors]. **1669** STURMY *Mariner's Mag.* I. Biv, How to measure a Cylinder Vessel.

b. *Comb.*, as ***cylinder block*** (see 6), ***card*** (see 5), ***gun*** (see 5), ***head*** (see 6), ***machine, -plug, saw, seal*** (see 4 a), ***stove***, etc.; ***cylinder-like*** adj.; **cylinder-axis** = axis-cylinder (see AXIS[1]); **cylinder-bore**, (*a*) *sb.* a gun of which the bore is cylindrical or of uniform diameter; so ***cylinder-bored***; (*b*) *vb.* to make with a cylindrical bore; **cylinder-cock**, a cock at the end of the cylinder in a steam-engine to allow water of condensation to escape; **cylinder-cover**, the steam-tight lid at the end of a steam-cylinder; **cylinder-desk**, a writing-desk having a curved revolving top which can be pushed back or drawn forward and locked; **cylinder-engine** (see quot.); **cylinder-epithelium**, epithelium consisting of cylindrical cells; **cylinder-escapement**, a form of watch escapement (also called *horizontal escapement*), invented by Tompion in 1695, or later by Graham; **cylinder-gauge**, (*a*) a tool for giving the size of the opening in the cylinder of an escapement; (*b*) a gauge for testing the diameter of projectiles for rifled ordnance; also a carefully turned iron cylinder used to gauge the accuracy of the finished bore of a gun (Farrow, *Mil. Dict.* New York 1885); (*c*) a steam-gauge attached to the cylinder of an engine; **cylinder-glass**, sheet glass, made by blowing glass into the form of a cylinder which is then cut open and flattened; **cylinder lock**, a lock (esp. a door-lock) in which a pin tumbler mechanism is contained inside a cylinder barrel; **cylinder-paper-machine**, a paper-making machine in which the pulp is taken up by a wirecloth-covered cylinder, instead of the flat wire-cloth used in the Fourdrinier machine; **cylinder-press** (U.S.), **-printing-machine**, a machine in which a cylinder is used either for carrying the type or giving the impression; **cylinder-watch**, a watch with a cylinder or horizontal escapement.

1882 *Syd. Soc. Lex.*, *Cylinder-axis, Purkinje's term for the central or axial part of a nerve tubule. **1923** H. R. RICARDO *Internal Combustion Engine* II. vi. 142 When the induction system is cast in the *cylinder block the whole of its internal surface is rough. **1881** GREENER *Gun* 189 *Cylinder-bored guns. **1812** *Deb. Congress* 12 June (1853) 2188 In the year 1762 *cylinder cards were first made use of by Mr. Peel. **1827** FAREY *Steam Eng.* 372 The *cylinder-cover must be lifted up whenever the piston is packed. **1891** RANKINE *Steam Eng.* 481 The cylinder cover has in it a stuffing box for the passage of the piston rod. **1874** KNIGHT *Dict. Mech.*, **Cylinder-engine*, a paper-machine in which the pulp is taken up on a cylinder and delivered in a continuous sheet to the dryers. **1886** H. SPENCER in *19th Cent.* May 763 A mucous membrane of the kind covered by *cylinder-epithelium. **1807** T. YOUNG *Nat. Philos.* II. 695 *Cylinder 'scapement. **1893** *Horological Jrnl.* July 165 Tompion undoubtedly patented the cylinder escapement in 1695. **1884** F. J. BRITTEN *Watch & Clockm.* 76 [A] *Cylinder Gauge..[is] a steel plate having two tapered slits. **1892** *Treat. Ammunition* (War Depmt.) 314 *note*, The cylinder gauge has the advantage of detecting an excentric stud, which could not be found by ring gauges. **1851** *Rep. Juries of Exhibition* 526 It was not until the year 1832 that the manufacture of *cylinder or sheet glass was introduced into this country. **1892** W. W. GREENER *Breech-Loader* 141 An old or true *cylinder gun will not..put three pellets into a pigeon thirty yards distant. **1884** 'MARK TWAIN' *Huck. Finn* xxxii. 332 We blowed out a *cylinder-head. **1895** KIPLING *Land & Sea Tales* (1923) 205 Cylinder-head blown off. **1688** R. HOLME *Armoury* III. 319/1 Provided it be of length *Cilender like. **1878** *Specifications of Patents* (U.S. Patent Office) 19 Feb. 637/1 A new Improvement In *Cylinder-Locks. **1894** *Official Gaz.* (U.S. Patent Office) 14 Aug. 893/1 Cylinder lock. Johannes T. Pedersen, New York, N.Y...a locking plate having a sliding movement on the forked lever, a rotatable cylinder, [etc.]. **1926** G. H. CHUBB *Locks & Lockmaking* iv. 54 Although many firms in this and other countries now make cylinder locks with pin tumbler mechanism, the credit for producing a modern lock in that form belongs to the Yales. **1982** *Inventions that changed World* 154 This cylinder lock was cheap to produce. **1860** W. BLACKWOOD *Let.* 28 Mar. in *Geo. Eliot's Lett.* (1954) III. 284 We have got the new *cylinder machine working perfectly. **1867** *Printers' Register* June 138 Davis and Primrose, Manufacturers of..Single Cylinder Machines. **1962** F. T. DAY *Introd. Paper* iv. 44 A popular name for the M.G. [machine glazed] or cylinder machine is the 'Yankee'. **1886** BRITTEN *Watch & Clockm.* 90 **Cylinder-plugs*, plugs fitting into the top and bottom of the cylinder..at the extremities of which the pivots are formed. **1859** *Printer* (N.Y.) II. 30 Messrs. Hoe have long been pre-eminent in the manufacture of *cylinder presses. **1851** *Rep. Juries of Exhibition* 198 *Cylinder printing machines are exhibited by Messrs. Napier. **1851** C. CIST *Cincinnati* 181 They are..fed to a *cylinder saw, which cuts them into staves of the proper thickness and curve. **1887** *Scribner's Mag.* Jan. 80 The earliest printing-press was a seal, and the *cylinder-seal may be said to have been an archaic rotary press. **1922** *Guide Babylonian & Assyrian Antiq.* (*Brit. Mus.*) (ed. 3) 82 Cylinder seal..of Syrian type. **1927** PEAKE & FLEURE *Priests & Kings* 64 Some of the Egyptians used mace-heads and cylinder-seals almost exactly similar to those found somewhat later in Mesopotamia. **1898** E. N. WESTCOTT *David Harum* 162 The proximity of wet boots and garments to the big *cylinder stove. **1765** MUDGE *Thoughts on Improv. Watches* (1772) 22 The *cylinder watch..is a fine invention. **1885** D. GLASGOW *Watch & Clock Making* 133 In the best Geneva-made cylinder watches the escape wheel is made small.

'cylinder, *v.* [f. prec. sb.] *trans.* To act upon with a cylinder, to press under a cylinder.

1887 *Brit. Merc. Gaz.* 15 June 34/1 Occasionally they are cylindered to give them a polish.

cylindered ('sɪlɪndəd), *ppl. a.* [See -ED[2].] Having a cylinder or cylinders (of a specified number or type).

1899 *Daily News* 14 Sept. 7/5 The engine..is one of Mr. Drummond's latest type of four-wheel-coupled inside cylindered express locomotives. **1908** *Westm. Gaz.* 14 May 4/2 As a hill-climber the Argyll, with its 120 by 140 cylindered engine, has great claims. **1934** A. W. JUDGE *Automobile & Aircraft Engines* (ed. 3) i. 20 Variation in the mixture strength in the different cylinders in the multi-cylindered engines. **1952** H. WEBSTER *Railway Motive Power* iv. 71 This was an inside cylindered engine of tractive effort 12,808 lb.

cylin'draceo-. Used in *Zool.* as combining form of CYLINDRACEOUS *a.*

1822 J. PARKINSON *Outl. Oryctol.* 195 A straight cylindraceo-tubular operculated shell. **1887** W. PHILLIPS *Brit. Discomycetes* 161 Asci cylindraceo-clavate.

cylin'draceous, *a.* [Corresponds to mod.F. *cylindracé*, and prob. to a mod.L. **cylindrāceus*, f. *cylindrus*: see CYLINDER *sb.* and -ACEOUS.] Of the form of or resembling a cylinder; cylindrical.

1676 H. MORE *Rem. on 2 late Disc.* 31. **1686** PLOT *Staffordsh.* 221 Several cylindraceous cavities..running parallel with the grain of the wood. **1839** *Proc. Berw. Nat. Club* I. 197 Body enclosed in an elongated cylindraceous sac. **1856-8** W. CLARK *Van der Hoeven's Zool.* I. 231 *Lumbricus* .. Body cylindraceous.

†**cy'lindral,** *a. Obs.* [f. L. *cylindr-us* CYLINDER *sb.* + -AL[1].] = CYLINDRICAL.

a **1711** KEN *Hymns Evang.* Wks. 1721 I. 5 Twice three cylindral Thunder-bolts for bits.

‖**cylindrenchyma** (sɪlɪn'drɛŋkɪmə). *Bot.* Also in anglicized form **cylindrenchym.** [f. Gr. κύλινδρ-ος CYLINDER *sb.* + ἔγχυμα infusion.] Tissue consisting of cylindrical cells.

1835 LINDLEY *Introd. Bot.* (1848) II. 149 The cylindrenchym of the stigma. **1866** *Treas. Bot.*, *Cylindrenchyma*, cylindrical cellular tissue, such as that of *Conferva*, of many hairs, etc.

†**cy'lindriac,** *a. Obs.* = CYLINDRIC.

1612 STURTEVANT *Metallica* (1854) 67 Round Cylindriack timber, as also other Square timber.

cylindric (sɪ'lɪndrɪk), *a.* [ad. mod.L. *cylindric-us*, a. Gr. κυλινδρικός, f. κύλινδρος CYLINDER *sb.*: see -IC. So F. *cylindrique* (1596 in Hatzf.).] Having the form of a cylinder, cylindrical.

1688 R. HOLME *Armoury* III. 357/1 A long round Iron Cilindrick socket. **1870** HOOKER *Stud. Flora* 200 *Anthemis nobilis*..disk-flowers cylindric.

b. With other adjectives, denoting a combination of the cylindric and some other form; frequent in *Bot.*, as ***cylindric-campanulate, -fusiform, -oblong, -ovoid, -subulate.***

1870 HOOKER *Stud. Flora* 216 *Crepis taraxifolia*.. involucre cylindric-campanulate. *Ibid.* 432 *Agrostis australis* ..Panicle large, 1-3 in., cylindric-fusiform.

cylindrical (sɪ'lɪndrɪkəl), *a.* [as prec. + -AL[1].]

1. Of the form of a cylinder.

cylindrical epithelium = cylinder or columnar epithelium. ***cylindrical eye***: an astigmatic eye. ***cylindrical lens***: a lens of the form of a cylinder, or of which one or both surfaces are portions of cylindrical surfaces. ***cylindrical vault***: 'one in the shape of the segment of a cylinder' (Gwilt).

1646 SIR T. BROWNE *Pseud. Ep.* III. i. 106 The grosse and somewhat Cylindricall composure of the legs. **1660** BOYLE *New Exp. Phys.-Mech.* Proem 13 The Cylindrical cavity. **1831** BREWSTER *Optics* xxxiii. §163. 275 Particles of hail, some..globular and others cylindrical.

2. Of, pertaining, or relating to a cylinder.

cylindrical projection: a form of projection (in maps, etc.) in which part of a spherical surface is projected upon the surface of a cylinder, which is then unrolled into a plane. (Cf. *conical projection.*) ***cylindrical machine***: a cylinder (printing) machine.

1656 BLOUNT *Glossogr.*, *Cylindrical*, pertaining to, or like a Cylinder. **1862** *Rep. of Juries, Exhibition* 1862 XXVIII. C 4 The French cylindrical machines are very excellent. **1866** PROCTOR *Handbk. Stars 38 note*, Mercator's projection is an instance of cylindrical projection, but on a principle altogether distinct.

Hence **cy'lindrically** *adv.*; **cy'lindricalness.**

1656 J. SERGEANT tr. *White's Peripat. Inst.* 84 It distends these fibres, and..makes them enwrap one another, as it were, cylindrically, like a bark. **1766** LANE in *Phil. Trans.* LVII. 452 The pillar of the Electrometer, made of wood, bored cylindrically about ⅜ of its length. **1727** BAILEY vol. II, *Cylindricalness*, the being of a cylindrical Form.

cylindricity (sɪlɪn'drɪsɪtɪ). *rare*[−0]. [f. CYLINDRIC + -ITY.] Cylindrical quality or form.

1846 WORCESTER cites MAUNDER.

cy'lindrico-, = CYLINDRIC b.

1846 DANA *Zooph.* (1848) 129 Of a cylindrico-hemispherical form.

cy'lindricule. *rare.* [see -CULE.] A small cylinder or cylindrical body.

1855 OWEN *Anat. Vert.* (L.), Each twin-corpuscle is surrounded by a circle of cylindricules.

cylindriform (sɪ'lɪndrɪfɔːm), *a.* [f. L. *cylindrus* CYLINDER *sb.* + -FORM: in mod.F. *cylindriforme.*] Of the form of a cylinder; cylindrical.

1870 ROLLESTON *Anim. Life* 80 They differ also in being.. cylindriform. **1877** tr. *Ziemssen's Cycl. Med.* XV. 76 Cylindriform casts..that arise from the renal tubules.

cylindrite (sɪ'lɪndraɪt). *Min.* Also kyl-. [ad. G. *kylindrit* (A. Frenzel 1893, in *N. Jahrb. Min.* II. II. 125), f. Gr. κύλινδρ-ος CYLINDER (see quot. 1893) + -ITE[1].] A blackish-grey sulphide of lead, antimony, and tin, known only from Bolivia.

1893 *Jrnl. Chem. Soc.* LXIV. II. 576 At the Santa Cruz mine at Poopô, in Bolivia, a new mineral has been discovered. This the author has named kylindrite from the cylindrical form in which it occurs. **1896** A. H. CHESTER *Dict. Min.*, Kylindrite. **1929** H. A. MIERS *Mineralogy* (ed. 2) II. vii. 399 Among other sulpho-salts may be mentioned.. cylindrite, the representative of a small but curious class of compounds containing tin together with lead, antimony, and sulphur. **1968** EMBREY & PHEMISTER tr. *Kostov's Mineralogy* 183 Cylindrite is found as cylindrical forms.. and occurs in the Bolivian mines in paragenesis with franckeïte, pyrite, and sphalerite.

cylindro- (sɪ'lɪndrəʊ), combining form of Gr. κύλινδρος CYLINDER *sb.*, used in many recent combinations, as **cy'lindro-ce'phalic** *a.* [Gr. κεφαλή head], having a head of cylindrical or elongated shape. **cy'lindro-'conic, -'conical** *a.*, of cylindrical form with one end conical; so **cy'lindro-co'noidal** *a.* **cy'lindro-cy'lindric, -al** *a. Arch.*, formed by the intersection of two cylinders. **cylindro'metric** *a.*, relating to the measurement of cylinders. **cy'lindro-o'gival** *a.*, (of a shot) having a cylindrical body and ogival head.

1878 BARTLEY tr. *Topinard's Anthrop.* v. 177 *Cylindro-cephalic*, elongated cylindrical skull. **1858** GREENER *Gunnery* 141 Cut a bullet of an elongated form—cylindro-conical if wished. **1876** GROSS *Dis. Bladder* 313 Wounds inflicted by cylindro-conoidal projectiles. **1823** P. NICHOLSON *Pract. Build.* 110 Cylindro-cylindric arches, or Welsh groins.

cylindroid ('sɪlɪndrɔɪd), *sb.* [mod. ad. Gr. κυλινδρο-ειδής cylinder-like: see -OID.]

1. A figure resembling a cylinder; *spec.* one on an elliptical base, an elliptic cylinder.

1663 DARY in Rigaud *Corr. Sci. Men* (1841) I. 99, I call them cylindroids (by which I mean) a solid contained under three surfaces. **1704** J. HARRIS *Lex Techn.*, *Cylindroid*, is a Solid Figure with Elliptical Bases, parallel, and alike situated. **1879** SIR G. G. SCOTT *Lect. Archit.* I. 239 That the vaulting surfaces should be portions of cylinders or regular cylindroids.

2. A conoidal cubic surface of fundamental importance in the theory of screws and complexes.

1871 BALL *Theory of Screws* in *Trans. R. Irish Acad.* 13 Nov.

cylindroid (sɪ'lɪndrɔɪd, 'sɪlɪndrɔɪd), *a.* [f. as prec.] Resembling a cylinder; somewhat cylindrical in form.

1839-47 TODD *Cycl. Anat.* III. 627/1 A cylindroid body. **1847-9** *Ibid.* IV. 499/1 The bodies of the spermatozoa are.. frequently..cylindroid.

cylindroidal (sɪlɪn'drɔɪdəl), *a.* [f. as prec. + -AL[1].] Of the form of a cylindroid; also = prec.

1844 WHEWELL in Todhunter *Acct. W.'s Works* (1876) II. 324 Cylindroidal surfaces. **1849-52** TODD *Cycl. Anat.* IV. 1521/1 The cylindroidal form which the arm acquires.

‖**cylindroma** (sɪlɪn'drəʊmə). *Path.* [corresp. to a Gr. type *κυλίνδρωμα n. of result, f. κυλινδρόειν to roll.] A name applied by Billroth to a certain kind of tumour, characterized among other peculiarities by the arrangement of its cells in cylinders of varying thickness.

1876 tr. *Wagner's Gen. Pathol.* 333 Mucous metamorphosis occurs..in cylindroma and cancer.

‖**cylix** ('sɪlɪks). *Gr. Antiq.* Also **kylix.** [Gr. κύλιξ.] A shallow cup with tall stem; a tazza.

1850 LEITCH *Müller's Anc. Art* §367. 460 A cylix with Prometheus reconciled on the bottom. **1885** *Athenæum* 634/3 A black-figured cylix of the potter Nicosthenes.

cylke, cyllable, etc.: see SILK, SYLLABLE, etc.

†**cyll.** *Obs.* [a. F. *ciel* in sense 'canopy': cf. CEIL *v.* and *sb.*] A canopy.

a **1552** LELAND *Collect.* (1774) IV. 295 In it was a Cyll of Cloth of gold; bot the King was not under for that sam Day.

Cy'llenian, *a.* [f. L. *Cyllēni-us* (f. *Cyllēne*, a mountain, the birthplace of Mercury) + -AN.] Of Mercury: ***Cyllenian art***, thieving.

1738 *Comm. Sense* (1739) II. 277 Although the Cyllenian Art did not flourish, etc.

†**'cyllerie.** *Obs.* [f. CYLL: see -ERY.] Drapery forming a canopy.

1592 R. D. *Hypnerotomachia* 11 Capitels..wrought with a waved shell worke, and cyllerie or draperie.

cyllowre, cylour, -ure, var. of CELURE *Obs.*, ceiling, canopy. So **cylured** *a.*, ceiled, canopied.

c **1440** *Promp. Parv.* 77 Cyllowre (P. cylere), *celatura*. —— Cylured (*v. rr.* -uryd, -ered), *celatus*.

cylte, cyluer, obs. forms of SILT, SILVER.

‖**cyma** ('saɪmə). Also 6 **syma,** 6-9 **sima,** 7-8 **scima,** 8-9 **cima.** [mod.L., a. Gr. κῦμα anything swollen, a billow, a wave, a waved or ogee moulding, the young sprout of a cabbage (in which sense also L. *cȳma*, whence the botanical use).]

1. *Arch.* A moulding of the cornice, the outline of which consists of a concave and a convex line; an ogee.

cyma recta: a moulding concave in its upper part, and convex in its lower part. ***cyma reversa*** (rarely ***inversa***): a moulding convex in its upper part, and concave in its lower part.

1563 SHUTE *Archit.* C i b, 4 partes geue also to Sima reuersa. *Ibid.* C iij b, That second parte which remayneth of the Modulus ye shall geue vnto Syma. **1703** MOXON *Mech. Exerc.* 267 Scima reversa..Scima recta, or Ogee. **1726** LEONI *Alberti's Archit.* II. 34 b, A Cima inversa of the breadth of two minutes. **1761** *Brit. Mag.* II. 642 The true cima, or cimaise. **1850** LEITCH *Müller's Anc. Art* §249. 258 A base of several plinths and cymas.

2. *Bot.* = CYME 1 and 2.

1706 PHILLIPS (ed. Kersey), *Cyma*..the young Sprout of Coleworts, or other Herbs; a little Shoot, or Branch: But it is more especially taken by Herbalists for the top of any Plant. **1775** LIGHTFOOT *Flora Scotica* (1792) I. 236 The cyma, or little umbel which terminates the branches.

cymagraph ('saɪməgrɑːf, -æ-). [f. prec. + Gr. -γραφος writing, a writer.

Erroneously formed: the combining forms of Gr. κῦμα being κυματο-, κυμο-, *cymato-*, *cymo-*.]

An instrument for copying or tracing the contour of profiles and mouldings.

1837 *Athenæum* 11 Mar. 179 A paper..from the Rev. R. Willis descriptive of a new instrument invented by him for tracing profiles and mouldings, and which he called the Symagraph. **1842** R. WILLIS in *Civ. Eng. & Arch. Jrnl.* V. 219 (*title*) Description of the Cymagraph for copying mouldings. **1889** *Athenæum* 19 Jan. 90/1 The mouldings have been taken full size with the cymagraph.

Hence **'cyma-,** prop. **cymograph** *v. nonce-wd.*

1844 G. PEACOCK *Address Brit. Assoc.* p. xliv, Carefully reduced and tabulated, and their mean results *cymographed* or projected in curves.

‖**cymaise** (sɪ'meɪz). *Arch. Obs.* Also **cymace, cymaize, cimaise.** [F. *cymaise*, ad. L. *cymatium*: see below.] = CYMA, CYMATIUM.

1656 BLOUNT *Glossogr.*, *Cymace*..a ledge or outward member in Architecture, fashioned somewhat like a Roman S, and termed a Wave or Ogee. **1726** LEONI *Alberti's Archit.* II. 32 a, The cymaize being any list that is at the top of any member. *Ibid.* 35 a, The heads of the Mutules are cut perpendicular, with a cymaise over them. **1761** *Brit. Mag.* II. 642 The true cima, or cimaise, imitated in ornaments.

cymar (sɪ'mɑː(r)). Also 7-9 **simarre,** (7 **semeare**), 8-9 **simar, symar:** see SIMARRE. [ad. F. *simarre* (OF. *chamarre*): see CHIMER[1], SIMARRE.]

1. A robe or loose light garment for women; *esp.* an under garment, a chemise.

Used somewhat vaguely in poetry and fiction.

[**1641** *Ariana* 201 A Persian simarre or mantle.] **1697** DRYDEN *Virgil, Æneid* IV. 196 A flow'r'd Cymarr with Golden Fringe, she wore. **1700** —— *Cymon & Iphig.* 100 Her body shaded with a slight cymarr. **1824** WIFFEN *Tasso* VI. xci, Whilst young Erminia laid her vests aside..And to her flowered cymar disrobed complete. **1825** SCOTT *Talism.* iii, Disrobed of all clothing saving a cymar of white silk. *a* **1839** PRAED *Poems* (1864) II. 22, I ask not what the vapours are That veil thee like a white cymar.

2. = CHIMER: *spec.* that of a bishop.

1673 BP. PARKER *Repr. Reh. Transp.* 499 (T.) Vests, perukes, tunicks, cimarrs. **1762** HUME *Hist. Eng.* II. xl. 380 The episcopal habit, the cymarre and rochette. **1868** MILMAN *St. Paul's* xi. 266 Bishop Grindal preached..in his rochet and cymar.

cymatium (sɪ'mætɪəm, -'eɪʃ(ɪ)əm). *Arch.* Also 6-7 **cimatium,** 8 **scimatium,** 9 **-ion.** [L. *cȳmatium* an ogee, an Ionic volute, a. Gr. κυμάτιον, dim. of κῦμα wave, billow, CYMA.] = CYMA.

1563 SHUTE *Archit.* C j b, Coronix..you shall deuid into .4. partes. geue one part vnto Cimatium vnder Corona..the fourth part which remaineth, geue vnto Cymatium ouer Corona. **1663** GERBIER *Counsel* (1664) 32 The Cimatium, the list of the Cimatium. **1703** MOXON *Mech. Exerc.* 267 Scima reversa, or Scimatium. **1850** LEITCH *Müller's Anc. Art* §274. 304 The contrast between the Doric and Lesbian cymatium. **1880** J. H. MIDDLETON in *Academy* 21 Aug. 141/1 One of the cornices has been replaced by another one with different dentils and cymatium.

cymatolite (sɪ'mætəʊlaɪt). *Min.* [f. Gr. κῦμα, κυματ- wave + -LITE.] A mineral found continuous with spodumene in white masses with delicate wavy fibrous structure.

1868 DANA *Min.* 456.

cymbal ('sɪmbəl). Forms: 1 **cim-, cymbal,** 4-6 **symbal,** 5 **cym-, symbale, cimbelle,** 6 **cimbal,** 6-7 **cymball,** 4- **cymbal.** [ad. L. *cymbalum*, a. Gr. κύμβαλον, deriv. of κύμβη hollow of a vessel, cup. In OE. directly from L.; in ME. partly through OF. *cymble*, in 15th c. *cymbale*, the latter a learned adaptation of the L. word.]

1. a. One of a pair of concave plates of brass or bronze, which are struck together to produce a sharp ringing sound. Also used singly and struck with a drumstick or the like.

Till late in the 18th c. apparently known only as the name of ancient and foreign instruments of the type described (esp. as mentioned in the Bible).

c **825** *Vesp. Psalter* cl. 5 Herȝað hine in cymbalan bel hleoðriendum herȝað in cimbalan wynsumnisse. *c* **1000** *Sax. Leechd.* III. 202 Cimbalan oððe psalteras oððe strengas. *c* **1325** *E.E. Allit. P.* B. 1415 Symbales & sonetez sware þe noyse. **1382** WYCLIF *1 Cor.* xiii. 1, I am maad as bras sownnynge, or a symbal [**1388** cymbal] tynkynge. **1398** TREVISA *Barth. De P.R.* XIX. cxlii. (1495) 946 Cymbales.. ben smytte togider and sowneth and ryngeth. **1535** COVERDALE *Ps.* cl. 3 Prayse him in the cymbals and daunse. **1553** EDEN *Treat. Newe Ind.* (Arb.) 14 A great noyse of cimbals, drumslades, timbrelles, shames..and diuerse other musical instrumentes. **1607** SHAKS. *Cor.* v. iv. 53 The Trumpets, Sackbuts, Psalteries, and Fifes, Tabors, and

Symboles, and the showting Romans. **1629** MILTON *Christ's Nativity* 208 In vain with cymbals' ring They call the grisly king. **1795** SOUTHEY *Occas. Pieces* ii, It is the funeral march .. Hark! from the blacken'd cymbal that dead tone! *a* **1839** PRAED *Poems* II. 331 Hark to the cymbal, and the bellowing drum! **1934** E. LITTLE *Mod. Rhythmic Drumming* 17 The cymbal should be struck with that part of the stick at a point about half-way between the fingers and the tip. **1959** WESTRUP & HARRISON *Collins Mus. Encycl.* 174 There are also two ways of using a single cymbal: (a) hitting it with a stick, hard or soft, in the manner of a gong, (b) performing a roll on it with timpani or side-drum sticks. **1961** J. BLADES in A. Baines *Mus. Instruments* xiv. 340 In modern works in general, an additional cymbal suspended on a stand .. is necessary.

b. *fig.* (with reference to *1 Cor.* xiii. 1).

1874 HELPS *Soc. Press.* xv. 217, I often wonder at the sort of passionate delight which Milverton, and people like him, have in the tinkling of cymbals.

2. Formerly applied loosely or ignorantly to other musical instruments.

1727–51 CHAMBERS *Cycl.* s.v., The modern cymbal is a paltry instrument, chiefly in use among vagrants, gypsies, etc. It consists of steel wire, in a triangular form, whereon are passed five rings, which are touched and shifted along the triangle with an iron rod held in the left hand. **1745** J. G. COOPER *Power Harmony* I. (R.), Let but the tuneful rod On brazen Cymbal strike. **1851** MAYHEW *Lond. Labour* III. 160 It took me just five months to learn the—cymbal, if you please—the hurdy-gurdy ain't it's right name.

3. A kind of stop on an organ.

1852 SEIDEL *Organ* 174 In large organs the great organ often contains both a mixture and a cymbal, the latter with more ranks than the former. **1876** HILES *Catech. Organ* x. (1878) 76 *Cymbel*, the most acute of the Mixture stops, and formed exclusively of octaves.

4. A sort of spongy cake or doughnut. *U.S. local.*

1860 in WORCESTER. **1867** O. W. HOLMES *Guardian Angel* xix, The genteel form of doughnut called in the native dialect *cymbal*.. which graced the board with its plastic forms.

5. *attrib.* and *Comb.*, as ***cymbal-beating***, ***-player***, ***-tinkler***; †**cymbal doctor**, a teacher who gives forth an empty sound (cf. *1 Cor.* xiii. 1).

1649 MILTON *Eikon.* viii. (1851) 395 How much he was the Disciple of those Cymbal Doctors. **1837** CARLYLE *Fr. Rev.* I. VII. xi. 351 Roman triumphs and ovations, Cabiric cymbal-beatings. **1889** FURNIVALL in *Pall Mall G.* 14 Dec. 2/1 Some talk and writing of a certain cymbal-tinkler being a greater poet .. than Browning.

Hence (chiefly *nonce-wds.*) **'cymbal** *v.*, to play on cymbals; **'cymbaled** *ppl. a.*, (*a*) furnished with cymbals; (*b*) produced or accompanied by cymbals; **'cymballing** *vbl. sb.*, playing on cymbals. **cymba'leer, -lier** [F. *cymbalier*], a cymbalist. Also **cym'balics**, music produced by cymbals. **'cymbaline** *a.*, cymbal-like. **'cymbalist, 'cymballer**, a player on the cymbals.

c **1340** *Cursor M.* 13140 (Trin.) Before þe kyng in his palaise .. She cymbaled tomblyng wiþalle. **1864** CARLYLE *Fredk. Gt.* XII. ix, With pomp and professional cymballing. **1847** TENNYSON *Princess* v. 500 Among the statues, statuelike, Between a cymbal'd Miriam and a Jael. **1861** LYTTON & FANE *Tannhäuser* 22 Cymbal'd music. **1836** F. MAHONEY *Rel. Father Prout, Songs of France* iv. (1859) 309 Now come the cymbaleers. **1859** SALA *Tw. round Clock* (1861) 279 Brassy screeds, and tinkling cymbalics. **1878** E. JENKINS *Haverholme* 224 The cymbaline clatter of the Turcophile Gazette. **1656** BLOUNT *Glossogr.*, *Cymbalist*, he that plays on the Cymbals. **1803** *Med. Jrnl.* X. 349 One of the Duke of York's black cymbalists. *c* **1878** *Oxford Bible-Helps* 239 David appointed Asaph chief of the cymbalists. **1879** E. ARNOLD *Lt. Asia* (1883) 47 A chosen band Of nautch girls, cup-bearers, and cymballers.

‖**cymbalo** ('sɪmbələʊ). [ad. It. *cembalo*, *cimbalo*, repr. L. *cymbalum* CYMBAL, but applied to the dulcimer, Magyar *czimbalom* (*cymbalom*), Polish *cymbaly*.] The dulcimer, a kind of stringed instrument in which the strings are struck by small hammers held in the hands; the prototype of the pianoforte. It has lately become known in England as used in the music of Hungarian bands.

1879 HIPKINS in Grove I. 300/1 *Cembalo* or *Cimbalo*.. a dulcimer, an old European name of which, with unimportant phonetic variations, was Cymbal. According to Mr. Carl Engel this ancient instrument is at the present day called *cymbaly* by the Poles, and *cymbalom* by the Magyars. **1889** *Pall Mall G.* 16 May 6/1 Mdme. Schulz .. played her cymbalo, with which the Hungarian band have of late years familiarized us. It is a system of wires stretched over a sounding-board and struck with wands.

‖**'cymbalon** = CYMBAL.

1824 WIFFEN *Tasso* I. lxxi, The mingled voice profound Of trumpet, tambour, horn, and cymbalon.

cymbidium (sɪm'bɪdɪəm). *Bot.* [mod.L. (O. Swartz 1799, in *Nova Acta R. Soc. Scient. Upsala* VI. 70), f. Gr. κύμβη cup.] A tropical orchid of the genus so named, with a hollow recess in the lip of the flower.

1815 *Curtis's Bot. Mag.* XLII. 1751 (*heading*) Sword-leaved Cymbidium. **1895** *Daily News* 21 Mar. 2/5 There were three or four large groups that inlcuded .. cymbideums. **1911** C. A. HARRISON *Orchids for Amateurs* xx. 71 Cymbidiums do not like being disturbed more than can be helped. **1930** T. W. BRISCOE *Orchids for Amateurs* vii. 114 Cymbidiums are strong growers. **1959** *Times* 2 May 9/3 If one has a greenhouse that can be kept just free of frost, cymbidiums will grow perfectly well. **1962** *Amateur Gardening* 31 Mar. 19/1 A good deal of the colour naturally came from the cymbidiums.

cymbiform ('sɪmbɪfɔːm), *a. Anat.*, *Bot.*, etc. [f. Latin type **cymbiformis*, from *cymba* boat: see -FORM.] Boat-shaped.

[**1706** PHILLIPS (ed. Kersey), *Naviculare Os* (in *Anat.*), otherwise call'd *Cymbiforme*.] **1836** *Penny Cycl.* V. 252/2 (*Botanical Terms*), *Cymbiform*, having the form of a boat. **1870** HOOKER *Stud. Flora* 387 *Tofieldia*.. seeds many .. cymbiform. **1882** *Syd. Soc. Lex.*, *Cymbiform bone*, the os naviculare, a bone of the tarsus.

cymblin(g, cymling, see SIMLIN.

cymbocephalic (ˌsɪmbəʊsɪ'fælɪk), *a.* (*erron.* **cymbe-, kumbe-.**) [f. Gr. κύμβη boat + κεφαλή head + -IC.] Having a skull long and narrow, and, as viewed from above, somewhat boat-shaped.

1861 *Sat. Rev.* 7 Sept. 253 This peculiar boat-shaped or cymbe-cephalic skull. **1878** BARTLEY *Topinard's Anthrop.* v. 177 Cymbocephalic, Kumbecephalic.

cyme[1] (saɪm). Also 8 **cime.** [a. F. *cime*, *cyme*, in the sense 'top, summit' (12th c. in Hatzf.):—pop. L. *cima* = L. *cyma* (see above); in the Bot. sense an 18th c. adaptation of the ancient L.]

†**1.** (*cime.*) A 'head' (of unexpanded leaves, etc.). *Obs. rare.*

1725 BRADLEY *Fam. Dict.* s.v. *Sallet*, The Buds and tender Cime of Nettles by some eaten raw, by others boiled.

2. *Bot.* (*cyme.*) A species of inflorescence wherein the primary axis bears a single terminal flower which develops first, the system being continued by axes of secondary and higher orders which develop successively in like manner; a centrifugal or definite inflorescence: opposed to RACEME. Applied *esp.* to compound inflorescences of this type forming a more or less flat head.

1794 MARTYN *Rousseau's Bot.* v. 55 The arrangement of the flowers in the elder is called a cyme. **1854** S. THOMSON *Wild Fl.* III. (ed. 4) 250 The meadow-sweet, with its crowded cymes.

3. *Arch.* = CYMA.

1877 BLACKMORE *Erema* III. xlvii. 106 This is what we call a cyme-joint, a cohesion of two curved surfaces.

cyme[2] (Shaks. *Macb.* v. iii. 55, 1st Folio), supposed to be an error for *cynne*, SENNA.

1605 SHAKS. *Macb.* v. iii. 55 What Rubarb, Cyme, or what Purgatiue drugge Would scowre these English hence.

'cymelet. [See -LET.] A small or diminutive cyme, a cymule.

cymene ('saɪmiːn). *Chem.* [f. Gr. κύμινον CUMIN + -ENE.] A hydrocarbon, $C_{10}H_{14}$, discovered in 1840 in the volatile oil of Roman cumin, and in other plants. So a series of compounds, parallel to those under CUMENE: **cymic** ('sɪmɪk) *a.*, of or pertaining to the radical cymene and its compounds, as in ***cymic phenol***, etc. **'cymidine**, a base, $C_{10}H_{15}N$. **'cymol** = *cymene*. **'cymyl**, the organic radical $C_{10}H_{13}$ of cymene, etc. Hence ***'cymyla'mine***, ***cy'mylic***, etc.

1863–72 WATTS *Dict. Chem.* II. 295–6 *Cymene* or *Cymol*.. Colourless strongly refracting liquid, having a very agreeable odour of lemons. **1879** *Ibid.* VII. 421 *Cymic Disulphide*.. is formed by oxidation of cymic mercaptan. **1863–72** *Ibid.* II. 298 *Cymylic Alcohol* $C_{10}H_{14}O$. Hydrate of Cymyl. Cuminic Alcohol .. Colourless liquid, having a very faint .. aromatic odour, and a sharp spicy taste.

cyment, obs. form of CEMENT.

cymetery, -itier, -itory, obs. ff. CEMETERY.

cymic, cymidine: see CYMENE.

cymiferous (saɪ'mɪfərəs), *a.* Bearing cymes.

1847 in CRAIG, and in later Dicts.

cymitar, -er, obs. forms of SCIMITAR.

'cymling: see SIMLIN, a kind of squash.

1796 MORSE *Amer. Geog.* I. 192 Cymlings (*Cucurbita verrucosa*).

cymming, brewer's vessel: see CUMMING *Sc.*

cymnel(l, obs. form of SIMNEL.

ˌcymobotry'ose, *a.* [f. L. *cȳma* CYME + BOTRYOSE.] 'Applied to cymes arranged in a racemose manner' (*Syd. Soc. Lex.*).

cymogene ('saɪməʊdʒiːn). [f. *cymo-* deriv. of CYMENE + -GENE, as in F. *oxygène*, etc.] 'A gaseous substance, consisting chiefly of butane, given off during the distillation of crude paraffin, used condensed by pressure for the production of extreme cold by evaporation' (*Syd. Soc. Lex.* 1882).

1886 *Harper's Mag.* Jan. 248 The next product [of Petroleum] is known as 'Cymogene'.

cymograph: see CYMA-.

cymoid ('saɪmɔɪd), *a.* [f. CYMA + -OID.] Resembling a cyma.

1815 T. FORSTER *Atmos. Phenom.* 145 Before storms a feature of cirrostratus appears, of a cymoid figure, like some architectural ornaments. *Ibid.* 193 The curious cymoid feature .. is not merely alternate bars, but the bars are curiously curved. **1846** in WORCESTER, and in later Dicts.

cymol: see CYMENE.

cymophane ('saɪməʊfeɪn). *Min.* [f. Gr. κυμο-, comb. form of κῦμα wave + -φανης -showing.] A synonym of CHRYSOBERYL.

1804 *Fourcroy's Chem.* II. 406. **1850–6** O. W. HOLMES *Poems*, *Mysterious Illness* 80, Her white arm, that wore a twisted chain Clasped with an opal-sheeny cymophane.

Hence **cymophanous** (saɪ'mɒfənəs) *a.*, 'having a wavy, floating light; opalescent; chatoyant' (Webster 1864).

cymoscope ('saɪməskəʊp). *Electr.* (*Disused.*) [See CYMA and -SCOPE.] A wave-detecting device used in wireless telegraphy; any device that serves as a detector of electromagnetic waves.

1906 J. A. FLEMING *Princ. Electric Wave Telegraphy* vi. 353 It seems desirable to possess a term .. which shall connote all the forms of electric wave-detecting device, and the word *cymoscope* has been suggested by the author. **1924** *Harmsworth's Wireless Encycl.* 639/1 One of the earliest forms of cymoscope to be used was the Hertz tuned loop.

cymose (saɪ'məʊs), *a. Bot.* [ad. L. *cȳmōs-us*, f. *cȳma*: see -OSE.] Bearing cymes, cymiferous; of the nature of a cyme; arranged in a cyme. (Of an inflorescence = *centrifugal* or *definite*; opposed to *racemose.*)

1807 J. E. SMITH *Phys. Bot.* 311 In the cymose plants. **1872** OLIVER *Elem. Bot.* I. vii. 83 Forms of inflorescence in which the peduncle, or axis, itself terminates in a flower are termed *definite* or *cymose*.

Hence **cy'mosely** *adv.*, in the manner of a cyme.

1870 HOOKER *St. Flora* 242 Flowers .. cymosely panicled.

cymotrichous (saɪ'mɒtrɪkəs), *a. Anthrop.* [f. Gr. κῦμα wave (see CYMA) + τριχ-, θρίξ hair + -OUS.] Having wavy hair. Hence **cy'motrichy**, wavy-hairedness.

1909 A. C. HADDON *Races of Man* 3 These three varieties [of hair] are now termed leiotrichous, cymotrichous, and ulotrichous. **1924** *Ibid.* (ed. 2) 5 *Cymotrichy*, or smooth, wavy and curly hair. *Ibid.* 6 Some cymotrichous peoples have very hairy bodies. **1936** *Antiquity* X. 244 Three sorts of hair—woolly, wavy and straight—are carefully distinguished... They would indicate that ulotrichy, cymotrichy, and leiotrichy were simultaneously present.

cymous ('saɪməs), *a. rare*$^{-0}$. [ad. L. *cȳmōs-us*, f. *cȳma*, corresp. to F. *cymeux*, *-euse*.] = CYMOSE.

In mod. Dicts.

cymphan, obs. form of SYMPHONY.

†**cymphe.** *Obs.* [ad. F. *cymbe*, ad. L. *cymbium*, a. Gr. κυμβίον small cup.]

1490 CAXTON *Eneydos* v. (1890) 22 Eneas ordeyned to take many cymphes that ben vessels ordeyned for to make suche sacrifyce.

cympyl(le, obs. form of SIMPLE.

Cymric ('kɪmrɪk), *a.* [f. Welsh *Cymru* Wales, *Cymry* the Welsh, pl. of *Cymro*, prob. repr. ancient *Combrox* compatriot (cf. *Allobrox* men of another country).] Of or pertaining to the Welsh people and language.

[**1688** R. HOLME *Armoury* III. 415/2 The Alphabet of the ancient Cymra's or Britains. **1656** BLOUNT *Glossogr.*, *Cymraecan* (from the Br. *Cymraeg* i. Welsh) Cambrian. **1833** SOUTHEY *Nav. Hist. Eng.* I. 1 The Cambrians, or, more properly, the Cymry.] **1839** KEIGHTLEY *Hist. Eng.* I. 78 Beneath them were the Cymric princes.

cymule ('saɪmjuːl). *Bot.* [f. Latin type **cȳmula*, dim. of *cȳma* CYME.] A small cyme. Hence **cymu'lose** *a.*

1880 GRAY *Struct. Bot.* v. 151 One of these very simple cymes, by itself or as a part of a larger cyme, may be called a Cymule.

cymyl: see CYMENE.

cymytery, obs. form of CEMETERY.

cyn-: see CIN-, SIN-.

‖**cynanche** (sɪ'næŋkiː). *Path.* [L., a. Gr. κυνάγχη, f. κυν- dog- + ἄγχειν to strangle, throttle: cf. QUINSY.] A name for diseases of the throat, characterized by inflammation, swelling, and difficulty of breathing or swallowing; *esp.* QUINSY.

1706 PHILLIPS (ed. Kersey), *Cynanche*, the Squinancy, or Quinsey .. This Disease is so call'd because it often happens to Dogs and Wolves. **1830** LINDLEY *Nat. Syst. Bot.* 241 Prescribed by the native practitioners of India in cynanche.

cynanthropy (sɪ'nænθrəpɪ). *Path.* [mod. f. Gr. κυνάνθρωπος lit. dog-man: in F. *cynanthropie*.] A species of madness in which a man imagines himself to be a dog.

1594 T. B. *La Primaud. Fr. Acad.* II. 266 There are some that behaue themselues like dogges and wolues..because they thinke they are transformed into those kinde of beasts, by..that malady, which is..named by the Græcians cynanthropie and lycanthropie. **1656** in BLOUNT *Glossogr.*, *Cynanthropie.* **1755** in JOHNSON.

cynaraceous (sɪnəˈreɪʃəs), *a. Bot.* [f. mod.L. *Cynaraceæ*, f. *Cynara* artichoke: see CYNAREOUS and -ACEOUS.] Belonging to the order *Cynaraceæ* proposed by Lindley, identical with the suborder *Cynaroideæ* or *Cynarocephalæ* of Composite plants, including the thistles, artichoke, burdock, etc.

1847 in CRAIG.

cynarctomachy (sɪnɑːkˈtɒməkɪ). *nonce-wd.* [f. Gr. κυν- dog- + ἄρκτος bear + -μαχια fighting.] Fighting of dogs and bears; bear-baiting.

1663 BUTLER *Hud.* I. i. 752 That some occult Design doth ly In bloudy Cynarctomachy.

cynareous (sɪˈnɛəriːəs), *a. Bot.* [f. mod.L. *Cynareæ*, f. *Cynara* artichoke, a. Gr. κυνάρα taken as = κινάρα artichoke.] = CYNARACEOUS.

1846 LINDLEY *Veg. Kingd.* 707 In general the Cynareous genera are characterised by intense bitterness.

cynaroid (ˈsɪnərɔɪd), *a. Bot.* [f. mod.L. *Cynara* (see prec.) + -OID.] Allied to the artichoke; CYNARACEOUS.

1882 G. ALLEN *Colours of Flowers* ii. 51 The second, or cynaroid tribe, is that of the thistle-heads.

cynder, -dyr, obs. forms of CINDER.

cyne, obs. form of SIGN.

†**cyne-** (kʏnə-, kɪnə-), in OE. = royal; occurring in many compounds, as *cynehelm* crown, *cynestól* throne, some of which are retained as technical terms by modern historians; *e.g.* **cynebót** (BOOT *sb.*[1] 9), the king's boot, compensation paid to the people for the murder of the king.

a **1000** in Thorpe *O.E. Laws* I. 186 Gebiraþ seo cynebot ðam leodum. **1872** E. W. ROBERTSON *Hist. Ess.* 208 'Blessed to king, and raised to his cynestole by Archbishop Eanbald.' **1874** STUBBS *Const. Hist.* §59 A fine of equal amount [to the king's *wergild*], the *cynebot*, was at the same time due to his people.

[**cyne,** erroneous for *cyve*, CIVY.]

cynegetic (sɪniːˈdʒɛtɪk), *a.* (*sb.*). *rare.* [mod. ad. Gr. κυνηγετικ-ός pertaining to the chase, f. κυνηγέτης huntsman, f. κυν- dog + ἡγέτης leader. In F. *cynégétique.*] **A.** *adj.* Relating to the chase.

1716 M. DAVIES *Athen. Brit.* III. *Diss. Physic* 2 Our Modern Practitioners..understand as little of them, as they do of the Geoponick, Hieracosophick, or Cynogetick Physicks. **1838** W. H. DRUMMOND *Rights Anim.* v. 36 To indulge their cynegetic propensities in the fox chase. **1887** *Times* 3 Oct. 6/1 A Cynegetic Exhibition, including weapons and appliances used in the chase.

B. *sb. pl.* **cynegetics**: hunting, the chase.

1646 SIR T. BROWNE *Pseud. Ep.* I. viii. 32 There are extant of his in Greeke, foure bookes of Cynegeticks or venation. **1887** *St. Bernards* xv. 178 Dr. Octavius Puffemup.. Member of the Royal Institution of Cynegetics.

†**cyner.** *Obs.* [ad. L. *ciner-em.*] Ashes, cinders.

c **1420** *Pallad. on Husb.* XII. 366 A yespon alto grounde of cyner.

cynew, obs. form of SINEW.

cynghanedd (kəŋˈhanɛð). *Prosody.* [Welsh.] An intricate system of alliteration and rhyme in Welsh poetry.

1849 T. STEPHENS *Lit. of Kymry* iv. 490 The rhythmical consonancy, termed *Cynghanedd*, was introduced at that time [*sc.* late 14th century], and has ever since formed an essential feature in Kymric poetry. [**1878** G. M. HOPKINS *Let.* 5 Oct. (1935) 15 Certain chimes suggested by the Welsh poetry I had been reading (what they call *cynghanedd*).] **1886** —— *Let.* 6 Oct. (1938) 222 His employment of the Welsh *cynghanedd* or chime I do not look on as quite successful. **1962** *Times* 31 Jan. (Surv. Wales) p. x/5 *Cynghanedd*, that complicated system of consonantal correspondencies and internal rhyme.

cynic (ˈsɪnɪk), *a.* and *sb.* Also 6 cinike, 6–7 cinick(e, cynicke, -ike, -ique, 6–8 cynick, (7 cinnick(e, cynnick). [ad. L. *cynic-us* (perh. in part through F.; cf. *cinicque*, 1521 in Hatzf.), a. Gr. κυνικός dog-like, currish, churlish, Cynic, f. κύων, κυν-ός dog: see -IC.

In the appellation of the Cynic philosophers there was prob. an original reference to the κυνόσαργες, a gymnasium where Antisthenes taught; but popular use took it simply in the sense 'dog-like, currish', so that κύων 'dog' became a nickname for 'Cynic'.]

A. *adj.* **1.** (With capital initial.) Belonging to or characteristic of the sect of philosophers called Cynics: see B. 1.

1634 MILTON *Comus* 708 O foolishness of men! that.. fetch their precepts from the Cynic tub, Praising the lean and sallow Abstinence! **1846** TRENCH *Mirac.* iii. (1862) 145 The Cynic philosopher. **1868** tr. *Zeller's Socrates* 247 The Cynic philosophy claims to be the genuine teaching of Socrates.

2. Having the qualities of a cynic (see B. 2); pertaining to a cynic; cynical.

1597 *Pilgr. Parnass.* IV. 468, I am not such a peece of Cinicke earthe That I neglect sweete beauties deitie. **1676** GLANVILL *Seas. Refl.* 136 No sullen or Cynick humours, but the complaint of all mankind. **1811** W. R. SPENCER *Poems* 51 Cold Cynic censurers. **1851** DISRAELI *Life Ld. G. Bentinck* (1852) 12 The cynic smile..the signal of a contempt which he was too haughty to express.

3. *cynic year* or *period*: the *canicular cycle* of the ancient Egyptians; see CANICULAR 3.

1607 TOPSELL *Four-f. Beasts* (1673) 112 That Egyptian Cynick Year which is accomplished but once in 1460 years. **1837** *Fraser's Mag.* XVI. 632 This erratic period of 1461 years became the great regulating cycle of the Egyptian calendar, under the name of the cynic or canicular period.

4. *cynic spasm*: see quot. 1882.

1684 tr. *Bonet's Merc. Compit.* XIV. 474 A Cynick Spasm came upon him. **1882** *Syd. Soc. Lex.*, *Cynic spasm*, a convulsive contraction of the facial muscles of one side..so that the teeth are shown in the manner of an angry dog.

B. *sb.*

1. (With capital initial.) One of a sect of philosophers in ancient Greece, founded by Antisthenes, a pupil of Socrates, who were marked by an ostentatious contempt for ease, wealth, and the enjoyments of life; the most famous was Diogenes, a pupil of Antisthenes, who carried the principles of the sect to an extreme of asceticism.

1547–64 BAULDWIN *Mor. Philos.* (Palfr.) I. xix, He fel straight to the sect of the cinikes, and became Diogenes scholer. **1642** HOWELL *For. Trav.* (Arb.) 15 Like the Cynique shut up alwaye in a Tub. **1751** J. BROWN *Shaftesb. Charac.* 174 All the old philosophers, from the elegant Plato walking on his rich carpets, to the unbred cynic snarling in his tub. **1868** tr. *Zeller's Socrates* 256 To the Cynic nothing is good but virtue, nothing bad but vice.

2. A person disposed to rail or find fault; now usually: One who shows a disposition to disbelieve in the sincerity or goodness of human motives and actions, and is wont to express this by sneers and sarcasms; a sneering fault-finder.

1596 *Edward III*, II. i, Age is a cynic, not a flatterer. **1599** B. JONSON *Ev. Man out of Hum.* II. ii, Thou art such another Cynique now, a man had need walke uprightly before thee. **1632** HEYWOOD *Iron Age* I. I. Wks. 1874 III. 281 Peace Cinicke, barke not dogge. **1782** COWPER *Progr. Err.* 175 Blame, cynic, if you can, quadrille or ball. **1866** ALGER *Solit. Nat. & Man* II. 63 The cynic, who admires and enjoys nothing, despises and censures everything. **1879** G. MEREDITH *Egoist* vii. (1889) 60 Cynics are only happy in making the world as barren to others as they have made it for themselves.

cynical (ˈsɪnɪkəl), *a.* [f. as prec. + -AL[1].]

1. Resembling the Cynic philosophers in contempt of pleasure, churlishness, or disposition to find fault; characteristic of a cynic; surly, currish, misanthropic, captious; now *esp.* disposed to disbelieve in human sincerity or goodness; sneering.

1588 GREENE *Pandosto* (1607) 24 Canst thou not loue? Commeth this Cynicall passion of prone desires, or peeuish frowardnes? **1615** J. STEPHENS *Satyr. Ess.* (ed. 2) 43 They seeke..To be accounted sharpe and Cynicall. **1670** P. HENRY *Diaries & Lett.* (1882) 225 In lodging, diet, apparel, cynical below the calling of a Gospel minister. **1814** D'ISRAELI *Quarrels Auth.* (1867) 440 Our cynical Hobbes had no respect for his species. **1875** FARRAR *Silence & V.* iii. 65 A cynical journalism which sneered at every belief.

†**2.** Belonging to the sect of Cynic philosophers; = CYNIC *a.* 1. *Obs. rare.*

1675 OTWAY *Alcibiades* 33 Let the Cynical fool call pleasure a toy.

3. With etymological allusion: Relating to a dog; dog-like.

1616 BULLOKAR, *Cynicall*, doggish. *c* **1645** HOWELL *Lett.* (1650) III. 27 Besides this Cinicall, ther is a kind of Wolvish humor hath seizd upon most of this peeple. **1869** SIR G. BOWYER in *Times* Sept., Writing..in 'ecclesiastical Latin' (to which a more cynical name might be given).

cynically (ˈsɪnɪkəlɪ), *adv.* [f. prec. + -LY[2].] In a cynical way; after the manner of a cynic.

1605 BACON *Adv. Learn.* II. xxi. §9 Fraudes..and vices.. handled..rather in a Satyre and Cinicaly, then seriously and wisely. **1614** BP. HALL *Recoll. Treat.* 501 Not Cynically unsociable. **1789** MRS. PIOZZI *Journ. France* I. 82 I was.. feeling..cynically disposed. **1856** THACKERAY *Christmas Bks.* (1872) 43 Our street from the little nook..whence I and a fellow lodger..cynically observe it.

ˈ**cynicalness.** *rare*$^{-0}$. [f. as prec. + -NESS.] Cynical quality or character.

1727 BAILEY vol. II, *Cynicalness*, Churlishness, Moroseness. In mod. Dicts.

cynicism (ˈsɪnɪsɪz(ə)m). [f. CYNIC + -ISM. Cf. CYNISM.]

1. (*with capital C.*) The philosophy of the Cynics: see CYNIC B. 1.

1672 SIR T. BROWNE *Lett. Friend* xxiv. (1881) 143 Yet his sober contempt of the world wrought no Democritism or Cynicism, no laughing or snarling at it. **1868** tr. *Zeller's Socrates* 268 The leading thought of Cynicism is the self-sufficiency of virtue.

2. Cynical disposition, character, or quality.

1672 [see 1]. **1847** LYTTON *Lucretia* (1853) 152 The cynicism of his measured vice. **1881** P. BROOKS *Candle of Lord* 150 The bitter cynicism of the newspaper satirist.

b. An instance of cynicism; a cynical utterance.

1891 *Spectator* 20 June 847/1 That he had uttered his dangerous cynicisms.

ˌ**cynicoˈcratical,** *a.* [See CYNIC and -CRAT.] Of or pertaining to a ruling body of cynics.

1881 L. A. TOLLEMACHE in *Jrnl. Educ.* Oct. 225 Power.. in the hands of a Cynicocratical Conclave.

†**cyniph,** *Obs.*: see CINIPHES.

1607 TOPSELL *Serpents* (1653) 763 Among the Cyniph plagues, this still shall bear the bell. *a* **1631** DONNE *Ess.* (1651) 183 When they attempted to make Cyniphs.

‖**Cynips** (ˈsɪnɪps). *Entom.* [mod.L.; according to Darmsteter, formed by Linnæus from Gr. κυν- dog + ἴψ a kind of cynips, or insect that eats vine-buds, etc. (Others have thought it an alteration of late L. *ciniphes, sciniphes*, in Vulgate, *Exod.* viii. 16, rendering Gr. σκνίφες.) Also mod.F. *cynips.*]

The typical genus of the gall-flies, hymenopterous insects which puncture plants in order to deposit their eggs, and thus produce galls or gall-nuts.

Hence ˈ**cynipid**, an insect of the *Cynipidæ*, or family allied to *Cynips*. **cyniˈpidean, cyniˈpideous, cyˈnipidous** *adjs.*, of or pertaining to the *Cynipidæ* or gall-flies.

1777 LIGHTFOOT *Flora Scotica* II. 583 Excrescencies occasioned by a small insect called *Cynips.* **1884** *Athenæum* 15 Nov. 628/1 Oak-galls produced by cynipidean insects.

cynism (ˈsɪnɪz(ə)m). *rare.* [a. F. *cynisme*, late L. *cynismus*, Gr. κυνισμός Cynicism, f. κύων, κυν- dog, Cynic: see -ISM.] = CYNICISM.

1833 THIRLWALL in *Philol. Mus.* II. 540 The cynism of Antisthenes. **1837** *Blackw. Mag.* XLII. 395 Principles..of licentiousness and moral cynism in literature. **1854** tr. *Lamartine's Celebr. Char.* II. 49 From some unintelligible cynism in language.

cynke, obs. form of SINK.

cynnaber, cynne, obs. ff. CINNABAR, SIN-.

cyno-. a. Gr. κυνο-, combining form of κύων (κυν-) dog; occurring in Greek in many compounds, partly adopted and largely imitated in modern technical terms and nonce-words, as ***cyno-geneˈalogist, cyno-phreˈnology***; also ˈ**cynoclept** [Gr. κλέπτης thief; cf. κυνοκλόπος dog-stealing], a dog-stealer; **cyˈnography** [F. *cynographie*], a writing or treatise on dogs; **cynoˈlogical** *a.*, of or pertaining to cynology; **cyˈnologist**, one who is versed in cynology; **cyˈnology**, natural history of dogs; **cyˈnophilist** [F. *cynophile*; f. Gr. φίλος loving], a lover of dogs; **cynoˈphobia** [Gr. φόβος panic fear], aversion to and dread of dogs; **cyˈnopodous** *a.* [Gr. ποδ- foot], dog-footed, having feet with non-retractile claws; **cyˈnorrhodon** [so F.; f. Gr. ῥόδον rose], dog-rose, wild-rose.

1863 H. KINGSLEY *A. Elliot* xxiv. (1865) 223 He was the greatest..cynoclept, or dog-dealer, in England. **1839** *New Monthly Mag.* LVI. 63 Your good cynogenealogist will trace out..the pedigree of any particular race. **1962** *Times Lit. Suppl.* 7 Sept. 662/2 They set up a 'Cynological Institute' in ..Prague [in 1911]. **1926** A. HUXLEY *Essays New & Old* 201 No cynological philosopher has arisen to denounce the abject degeneracy of the Irish terrier. **1948** C. L. B. HUBBARD *Dogs in Brit.* iii. 17 A foundation upon which cynologists might work out the origin of breeds. **1878** BARTLEY tr. *Topinard's Anthrop.* Introd. 9 Cynology being the natural history of the dog. **1890** G. FLEMING in *19th Cent.* Mar. 505 Consider the perpetual abolition of the diabolical muzzle, ye cynophilists. **1879** M. D. CONWAY *Demonol.* I. II. v. 136 The wild notion of Goethe, joined with his cynophobia. **1706** PHILLIPS (ed. Kersey), *Cynorrhodon*, the wild Rose, or Sweet-brier Rose. **1744** ARMSTRONG *Preserv. Health* I. 278 Where the cynorhodon with the rose For fragrance vies. **1817** N. DRAKE *Shaks.* II. 81 The colour of the cynorhodon, or canker-rose.

cynocephalic (sɪnəʊ-, saɪnəʊsɪˈfælɪk), *a.* [f. as next + -IC.] = CYNOCEPHALOUS.

1887 B. HEAD *Hist. Numorum* 723 Hermes..holding.. caduceus and cynocephalic ape.

cynoˈcephalist. [f. as next + -IST.] = CYNOCEPHALUS.

1656 BLOUNT *Glossogr.*, *Cynocephalist*, a beast like an Ape, but having the face of a dog: a Babion. **1837** WHEELWRIGHT tr. *Aristophanes* I. 312 Contend'st thou with a cynocephalist?

cynocephalous (sɪnəʊ-, saɪnəʊˈsɛfələs), *a.* [f. next + -OUS.] Pertaining to or of the nature of a cynocephalus; dog-headed.

1831 MRS. GORE in *Fraser's Mag.* IV. 13 The cynocephalous species. **1889** RAWLINSON *Phœnicia* 227 A huge baboon or cynocephalous ape.

‖**cynocephalus** (sɪnəʊ-, saɪnəʊˈsɛfələs). Pl. -i. Also 5–7 anglicized **cynocephale.** [L., a. Gr. κυνοκέφαλος dog-headed, the dog-faced baboon,

f. κυνο- dog- + κεφαλή head. In mod.F. *cynocéphale*.]

1. One of a fabled race of men with dogs' heads.

c **1400** MAUNDEV. (Roxb.) xxi. 97 Men and wymmen of þat ile hase heuedes lyke hundes; and þai er called Cynocephales. **1650** BULWER *Anthropomet.* 7 It may be the Cynocephali were but men with such heads, discovered by some Grecian. **1816** G. S. FABER *Orig. Pagan Idol.* II. 479 The cynocephali or dog-headed priests of..Anubis.

2. A kind of ape having a head like that of a dog; the Dog-faced Baboon. In *Zool.* taken as the name of the genus.

1601 HOLLAND *Pliny* I. 157 They..liue of the milke of certain beasts that we cal Cynocephales, hauing heads and snouts like dogs. *Ibid.* I. 232 Apes that be headed and long snouted like dogs, and thereof called Cynocephali. **1607** TOPSELL *Four-f. Beasts* (1673) 6 The shape of their snout like a cynocephale. **1774** GOLDSM. *Nat. Hist.* (1776) IV. 207 The last of the ape kind is the Cynocephalus. **1876** BIRCH *Rede Lect. Egypt* 27 Their fauna, comprising the cynocephalus and the camelopard.

† **'cynogloss.** *rare.* [a. F. *cynoglosse* (Paré 16th c.), ad. L. *cynoglossum*, Gr. κυνόγλωσσον, f. κυνο- dog- + γλῶσσα tongue.] The plant *Cynoglossum* or Hound's-tongue.

1704 F. FULLER *Med. Gymn.* (1718) 93 Another Plant, the Cynogloss..seems not unlikely to be of use.

cynoid ('sɪnɔɪd), *a.* [ad. Gr. κυνοειδής dog-like, canine, f. κυνο- dog.] Dog-like, allied in form to the dog; belonging to the *Cynoidea* or canine division of the *Carnivora*.

cynomome, obs. form of CINNAMON.

cynomorphic (sɪnəʊ-, saɪnəʊ'mɔːfɪk), *a.* [Ultimately f. Gr. κυνόμορφος, f. κυνο- dog- + μορφή form. Cf. mod.F. *cynomorphe* dog-shaped.]

1. *Zool.* Belonging to the division *Cynomorpha* of catarrhine monkeys.

2. (*nonce-use*, app. after *anthropomorphic*.) Relating to a dog's ideas and ways of looking at things. So **cyno'morphism**.

1892 L. ROBINSON in *Contemp. Rev.* Sept. 360 An instance of the operation of the cynomorphic idea can be seen in the behaviour of a dog when a bone is given to him. *Ibid.* 359 There is, affecting the dog's point of view, almost undoubtedly such a thing as cynomorphism.

cynoper, obs. form of CINNABAR.

cynopic (sɪn-, saɪ'nɒpɪk), *a. nonce-wd.* [f. Gr. κυνώπης dog-eyed, shameless (f. κυνο- dog- + ὤψ, ὠπ- eye, face) + -IC.] Dog-faced, shameless.

1854 BADHAM *Halieut.* 416 This canicula..is equal to the gigantic white shark in *cynopic* impudence and rapacity.

cynosural (sɪnə-, saɪnə'sjʊərəl), *a.* [f. next + -AL[1].] Relating to or of the nature of a cynosure.

1855 KINGSLEY *Westw. Ho!* 17/2 That cynosural triad [of poets]. **1885** HUXLEY in *Times* 9 June 10 To preserve the statue in its cynosural position in this entrance-hall.

cynosure ('sɪnəʊ-, 'saɪnəʊsjə(r), -zjʊə(r)). Also 6–7 in Lat. form. [a. F. *cynosure* (16th c.), ad. L. *cynosūra*, a. Gr. κυνόσουρα dog's tail, Ursa Minor.]

1. The northern constellation *Ursa Minor*, which contains in its tail the Pole-star; also applied to the Pole-star itself.

1596 FITZ-GEFFRAY *Sir F. Drake* (1881) 14 Cynosure, whose praise the sea-man sings. **1612** DAVIES *Why Ireland, etc.* (1787) 199 The circuit of the Cinosura about the pole. **1627** MAY *Lucan* III. (1631) 239 These Ships..the Cynosure Guides straight along the sea. **1792** D. LLOYD *Voy. Life* IV. 72 The stedfast Cynosure renown'd at sea.

2. *fig.* **a.** Something that serves for guidance or direction; a 'guiding star'.

1596 FITZ-GEFFRAY *Sir F. Drake* (1881) 33 The Cynosura of the purest thought, Faire Helicé, by whom the heart is taught. **1649** BP. HALL *Cases Consc.* (1650) 9 For the guidance of our either caution or liberty..the onely Cynosure is our Charity. **1691** WOOD *Ath. Oxon.* I. 18 He hath written, The Rudiments of Grammar..the Cynosura for many of our best Grammarians. **1809** MRS. WEST *Mother* (1810) 225 Thy victor-flag Flames like a steady cynosure.

b. Something that attracts attention by its brilliancy or beauty; a centre of attraction, interest, or admiration.

[**1599** *Broughton's Lett.* viii. 26 You Cynosura and Lucifer of nations, the stupor and admiration of the world.] **1601** BP. W. BARLOW *Serm. Paules Crosse* 64 Himselfe..the Cynosure of their affections. **1632** MILTON *L'Allegro* 77 Some beauty..The Cynosure of neighbouring eyes. **1837** CARLYLE *Fr. Rev.* I. II. i, The fair young Queen..the cynosure of all eyes. **1870** DISRAELI *Lothair* lxxxiii. 445 Before another year elapses Rome will be the cynosure of the world.

cynque, cynter: obs. ff. of CINQUE, CINTRE.

Cynthia ('sɪnθɪə). [L. *Cynthia* (*dea*), the Cynthian goddess, *i.e.* Artemis or Diana, said to have been born on Mount Cynthus; hence the Moon.] A poetic name for the Moon personified as a goddess. Hence **'Cynthian**, of the Moon.

1632 MILTON *Penseroso* 59 While Cynthia checks her dragon yoke. **1680** OTWAY *Caius Marius* IV. i, The reflection of pale Cynthia's Brightness. **1814** BYRON *Lara* II. xxiv, When Cynthia's light almost gave way to morn. **1632** LITHGOW *Trav.* VII. 318 Nylus increaseth..when the Sunne..warming with his vigorous face, the Septentrion sides of these Cynthian Mountaynes.

cynurenic (sɪnjʊ'rɛnɪk), *a. Chem.* Also **kyn-**. [f. Gr. κυν- dog + οὖρ-ον urine.] In ***cynurenic acid***, a crystalline substance occurring in the urine of the dog. Called also **cy'nuric** ***acid***.

1860 in *New Syd. Soc. Year-bk.* 100. **1868–82** in WATTS.

cyon, obs. form of SCION.

cyparesse (Spenser): see CYPRESS[1].

cyperaceous (sɪpə'reɪʃəs), *a. Bot.* [f. Bot. L. *Cyperāceæ*, f. *Cyperus*: see -ACEOUS.] Belonging to the *Cyperaceæ* or Sedges.

1852 TH. ROSS *Humboldt's Trav.* I. vi. 217 Cyperaceous and gramineous plants.

So **cy'peroid** *a.*, allied in structure to a Cyperus.

cype'rographer. *nonce-wd.* [CYPERUS.] A writer on sedges. So **cype'rologist**.

1881 BENTHAM in *Jrnl. Linn. Soc.* XVIII. 361 This essay seems not to have fallen into the hands of any subsequent Cyperographers.

cypers, obs. form of CYPRESS.

‖**Cyperus** (saɪ'pɪərəs, 'saɪpərəs). *Bot.* [L. *cypērus, -os*, a kind of rush, a. Gr. κύπειρος, κύπερος (Herod.), an aromatic marsh-plant.] A large genus of endogenous plants, giving its name to the N.O. *Cyperaceæ*. About 700 species are described; *C. longus* is the Sweet Cyperus, or English Galingale, having aromatic and astringent roots.

1597 GERARDE *Herbal* I. ix. (1633) 13 Cyperus Grasse hath roots somewhat like Cyperus. **1658** SIR T. BROWNE *Gard. Cyrus* iv, Why Fenny waters afford the hottest and sweetest plants as Calamus, Cyperus and Crowfoot. **1837** HOWITT *Rur. Life* IV. i. (1862) 312 Lo! cyperus decks the ground.

cyphac, var. SIPHAC, the peritonæum.

cyphel ('saɪfəl). [? ad. Gr. κύφελλα *pl.* the hollows of the ears, clouds of mist: see next.]

1. Formerly a name for the Houseleek (*Sempervivum*); now a book-name for *Cherleria sedoides*.

1674–91 RAY *N.C. Words* 133 *Cyphel*, Houseleek. **1787** WITHERING *Bot. Arrangem.* (ed. 2) I. 462 *Cherleria sedoides*..Cyphel. **1883** G. ALLEN *Mountain Tulip* in *Longm. Mag.*, The Scottish asphodel, the mossy cyphel.

2. Adapted form of CYPHELLA.

‖**cyphella** (saɪ'fɛlə). *Bot.* Pl. **-æ**. [mod.L., ad. Gr. κύφελλα (plural) the hollows of the ears.]

1. A cup-like depression on the under surface of the thallus of some lichens.

1857 BERKELEY *Cryptog. Bot.* §452.

2. Generic name of some hymenomycetous fungi.

cypher, var. CIPHER *sb.*

cyphon, obs. f. SIPHON.

cyphonism ('saɪfənɪz(ə)m). *Gr. Antiq.* [ad. Gr. κυφωνισμός, punishment by the κύφων, crooked piece of wood, bent yoke of a plough, a sort of pillory, f. κυφός bent, crooked.] Punishment by the κύφων, a sort of pillory in which slaves or criminals were fastened by the neck (Liddell and Scott).

For notions formerly held about it see quot. 1848.

1727–51 in CHAMBERS *Cycl.* **1848** WHARTON *Law Lex.*, *Cyphonism*..some suppose to have been the smearing of the body with honey, and exposing the person to flies, wasps, etc. But the author of the notes on Hesychius says..that it ..signifies that kind of punishment still used by the Chinese, called..the wooden collar, by which the neck of the malefactor is bent or weighed downward.

‖**cy'phosis.** *Path.* Also **kyphosis**. [mod.L., a. Gr. κύφωσις, humpbacked condition, f. κυφός bent, hunch-backed.] Backward curvature of the spine; hump-back. Hence **cy'photic** *a.*, hump-backed (*Syd. Soc. Lex.*).

1847 SOUTH tr. *Chelius' Surg.* II. 164 The *lordosis* is most easy, the *cyphosis* the most difficult of cure. **1876** *Wagner's Gen. Pathol.* 13 Kyphosis. **1878** T. BRYANT *Pract. Surg.* I. 277. **1889** TREVES *Man. Surg.* II. 338 In the confirmed kyphotic curve of old age treatment is of little avail.

‖**Cypræa** (saɪ'priːə). *Zool.* Also **cyprea**. [mod.L. f. *Cypria* a name of Venus: cf. *Venus-shell, Artemis*, and other names of conchology.] The extensive genus of gastropods containing the cowries. Hence **cy'præid**, a gastropod of the cowrie family, *Cypræidæ*. **cy'præiform**, **cy'præoid** *adjs.*, resembling or allied to the cowries.

1822 J. PARKINSON *Outl. Oryctol.* 153 *Cypræa*, an ovate and vaulted univalve. **1834** C. M. YONGE *Let.* 4 July in C. Coleridge *C.M.Y.* (1903) iv. 123, I send..Jane a *cyprea*. **1913** B. B. WOODWARD *Life of Mollusca* vi. 97 The young Cowry shell (*Cypræa*) has a thin, sharp lip.

† **'cypre.** *Obs.* Also **cypyr, -ur, cipre, -er.** [ad. L. *cyprus*, a. Gr. κύπρος (from Κύπρος Cyprus), the henna plant. The L. form also occurs.]

1. The henna-shrub (*Lawsonia alba* or *inermis*), with fragrant white flowers, found in the Levant.

1382 WYCLIF *Song Sol.* i. 13 The clustre of cipre tree [**1611** camphire]. **1398** TREVISA *Barth. De P.R.* XVII. xxv. (1495) 618 The Cypre is a tree in Egypte lyke to Oliue in leues. **1558** WARDE tr. *Alexis' Secr.* II. 50 b, Take..Damaske roses..Bengewyn, Cypre Alexandrine. [**1748** *Phil. Trans.* 566 The Cyprus grows..as a Shrub of ten or fifteen Feet in Height, and has very much the Appearance of Privet.]

¶ **2.** Used by confusion for CYPRESS[1].

a **1440** *Sir Eglam.* 277 Cypur treys were growyn owte. **14**.. *Voc.* in Wr.-Wülcker 716/41 *Hec cipressus*, a cypyrtre. **1583** STANYHURST *Aeneis* II. (Arb.) 66 A ciper by the churche seat abydeth. **1632** LITHGOW *Trav.* 63 Cypre-trees.

‖ **'cypres** ('siːpreː). [Late Anglo Fr. = F. *si près* so near, as near.] *Law.* As near as practicable: applied to a process in equity by which, in the case of trusts or charities, when a literal execution of the testator's intention becomes impossible, it is executed as nearly as possible, according to the general purpose. (Used as *adv.*, *sb.*, and *adj.*)

c **1481** LITTLETON *Tenures* §352 En ceo cas si l'baron deuy, viuant la feme, deuant ascun estate en le taile fait a eux, &c. donques doit le feoffee per la ley faire estate a la feme cy pres le condition, et auxy cy pres lentent de la condition que il poit faire. [**1628** COKE *On Litt.* 219 In this case if the husband dyeth liuing the wife before an estate in taile made vnto them, &c. then ought the feoffee by the law to make an estate to the wife as neere the condition, and also as neere to the entent of the condition as he may make it.] **1802** VESEY *Reports* VII. 42 The question..is, whether the gift fails on account of the death of the trustee; or, whether the doctrine of *cy pres* takes place; and whether the Court sees its way sufficiently to execute what was the general intention. **1872** J. A. HESSEY *Mor. Difficulties Bible* v. 112 A cypres or approximate administration of a trust is admissible. **1885** VAUGHAN HAWKINS in *Law Rep.* 29 Ch. Div. 562 The general intention of the testator..will be carried out *cy-près*.

b. *fig.* An approximation.

1850 *Tait's Mag.* XVII. 769/2 The variety of metres introduced is as happy a *cy-pres* as the language admits of.

cypress[1] ('saɪprɛs). Forms: 4 **ciprese, cypris, sypres,** 4–5 **cipris,** 4–7 **cipres, cypres,** 5 **cipriss, -ys, cyprys, syprees, -ese, cupresse,** 5–6 **cipresse,** 5–7 **cypresse,** 6 **cipreis, cyparesse, syprys, cypers,** (6–7 **cipers,** 7–8 *erron.* **ci-, cyprus**), 8 **cipress,** 4, 7– **cypress.** [ME. *cipres, cypres*, etc., a. OF. *ciprès* (12th c.), *cypres* (= Pr. *cypres*, It. *cipresso*), ad. late L. *cypressus* (Vulgate, Isidore, etc.), ad. Gr. κυπάρισσος cypress. The earlier L. adaptation of the word was *cupressus*; the later *cypressus* and rare *cyparissus* were refashioned after Gr. The current Eng. *cypress* is assimilated to the late L. form.]

1. a. A well-known coniferous tree, *Cupressus sempervirens*, a native of Persia and the Levant, extensively cultivated in Western Asia and Southern Europe, with hard durable wood and dense dark foliage; often regarded as symbolic of mourning (see c). Hence, the English name of the genus.

a **1300** *Cursor M.* 1377 (Cott.) Cedre, ciprese [*v.r.* cipres, cipris], and pine. *a* **1400** *Pistill of Susan* 69 Þe sauyne and sypres, selcouþ to sene. **1513** DOUGLAS *Æneis* III. x. 47 The cipres berand hych thair bewis. **1551** TURNER *Herbal* I. (1568) N iij b, The lefe of Cypres neuer falleth, but is euer grene. **1616** BULLOKAR, *Cypresse*, a tree..very tall and slender, the tymber whereof is yellowish and of a pleasant smell. **1797** MRS. RADCLIFFE *Italian* vi, A garden, shaded with avenues of melancholy cypress. **1872** OLIVER *Elem. Bot.* 247 The wood of Cypress..is almost imperishable; the gates of Constantinople made of this wood lasted 1,100 years.

b. The wood of this tree.

a **1300** *Cursor M.* 8007 (Gött.) Þu sal find þa wandis þare, Of cydyr, pyne, and of cypress. *c* **1386** CHAUCER *Sir Thopas* 170 His spere was of fine cipres. **1474** J. PASTON *Lett.* No. 739 III. 110 My wryghtyng box of syprese. **1504** *Bury Wills* (1850) 98 My coffyr of syprys. **1621** LADY M. WROTH *Urania* 261 Into a coffer of Ciprus..he shut it vp. **1673** *Phil. Trans.* VIII. 6015 Another sort of wood, called Cypress..better than any Pine for Masts.

c. The branches or sprigs of the tree, used at funerals, or as a symbol of mourning. Also *fig.*

1590 SPENSER *F.Q.* II. i. 60 The great earthes wombe they open to the sky, And with sad Cypresse seemely it embrace. **1591** —— *Daphn.* lxxvi, Vouchsafe to deck the same [a hearse] with Cyparesse. **1695** PRIOR *Ode after Queen's Death* v, Let the King dismiss his Woes..And take the Cypress from his Brows. **1761** STERNE *Tr. Shandy* III. lxxv, 'Tis one thing for a soldier to gather laurels,—and 'tis another to scatter cypress. **1850** TENNYSON *In Mem.* LXXXIV. iv, But that remorseless iron hour Made cypress of her orange flower.

2. a. Applied to various trees or shrubs allied to the true cypress, as **African c.**, the genus *Widdringtonia* (Miller *Plant-n.*); **bald, black,** or **deciduous c.**, *Taxodium distichum*; **embossed c.**, the Chinese genus *Glyptostrobus*; **Japanese c.**, the genus *Retinospora*; **swamp c.**, the genus *Chamæcyparis* (Miller).

1794 MARTYN *Rousseau's Bot.* xxviii. 447 Deciduous Cypress has the leaves in two ranks, and spreading; it is a native of America. **1866** *Treas. Bot.* 967 *Retinospora*.. *R. obtusa*, the Japanese Cypress.. very fine forest tree, eighty or more feet high.

b. Applied to various plants taken to resemble the cypress-tree, as **broom c.**, *Kochia scoparia*; **dwarf c.**, **heath c.**, names proposed by Turner for *Lycopodium alpinum*; **field c.**, *Ajuga Chamæpitys*; **garden c.**, (*a*) in Gerarde, *Artemisia maritima*; (*b*) in Lyte, *Santolina Chamæcyparissus*; **standing c.**, *Gilia coronopifolia*; **summer c.**, *Kochia scoparia*.

[*c* **1000** *Sax Leechd.* I. 116 Genim þa ylcan wyrte & cypressum, & dracentsan & huniȝ.] **1548** TURNER *Names of Herbes* 25 Chamaecyparissus.. maye be called in englishe heath Cypres, because it groweth amonge heath, or dwarfe Cypres. **1578** LYTE *Dodoens* I. xviii. 28 Called.. in English .. Ground Pyne, Herbe Iue, Forget me not, and field Cypres. *Ibid.* xix. 29 Some call it in English Lauender Cotton, and som Garden Cypres. **1878–86** BRITTEN & HOLLAND *Plant-n.*, Cypress.. 2. *Tamarix gallica.—Cornw.*

3. *attrib.* **a.** Of cypress or cypress-wood. **b.** Resembling the foliage or shade of a cypress; cypress-like; dark, gloomy, funereal.

1596 SHAKS. *Tam. Shr.* II. i. 353 In Iuory cofers I haue stuft my crownes: In Cypres chests my arras counterpoints. **1597** *Lanc. Wills* II. 228 A Cypresse chest standing in the like parlour. **1659** T. PECKE *Parnassi Puerp.* 67 Great was Macedo; but the Stagyrite, As much out shin'd; as bright Day, Cypress Night. **1870** *Athenæum* 19 Nov. 665 Plenty of cypress sentimentality in Kensal Green.

4. *Comb.*, as *cypress-arbour*, *-bough*, *-bud*, *-cone*, *-grove*, *-leaf*, *-shade*, *-spire*, *-swamp*, *-timber*, *-tree*, *-wood*, *-wreath*; *cypress-crowned*, *cypress-like* adjs.; **cypress-apple**, the fruit or cone of the cypress; **cypress-knee**, a large woody tumour occurring on the roots of *Taxodium* (*Treas. Bot.*); **cypress-moss**, the Alpine or Savin Club-moss (*Lycopodium alpinum*); also the moss *Hypnum cupressiforme*; †**cypress-nut**, the roundish fruit or cone of the cypress; **cypress pine** *Austral.*, a tree of the genus *Callitris*; **cypress-spurge**, *Euphorbium Cyparissias* (called by Lyte *cypress tithymal*); **cypress-vine**, a name of several American species of *Ipomæa*, convolvulaceous climbing plants.

1712 J. JAMES tr. *Le Blond's Gardening* 148 Its Fruit, call'd the *Cypress-Apple. **1883** A. DOBSON *Old World Idylls, Dead Letter* I. vi, And still the *cypress-arbour showed The same umbrageous hollow. **1720** GAY *Poems* (1745) II. 152 Black *Cypress boughs their drooping heads adorn. **1829** PRAED *Poems* (1865) I. 359 Pale, *cypress-crowned. **1812** BYRON *Ch. Har.* II. xxxviii, The pale crescent sparkles.. Through many a *cypress grove. **1889** *Science* XIII. 176/2 Processes.. sufficiently developed to be classed in importance with the *cypress knees. **1640** PARKINSON *Theat. Bot.*, *Cypress-moss, *Lycopodium alpinum*. **1769** J. WALLIS *Nat. Hist. Northumberland* I. viii. 282 Creeping Cypress-Moss, or Heath-Moss is frequent on Cheviot. **1847** LEICHHARDT *Jrnl.* i. 13 It was covered with *cypress-pine, and an Acacia. **1885** *Spons' Mech. Own Bk.* 131 Cypress pine (*Callitris columellaris*) is a plentiful tree in Queensland. **1936** F. CLUNE *Roaming round Darling* ix. 76 Box-trees and cypress-pines in plenty. **1967** A. M. BLOMBERY *Guide Native Austral. Plants* III. 108 Cupressaceae. A family.. including the well-known native *Callitris* (Cypress Pine). **1707** *Curios. in Husb. & Gard.* 154 The Wood-Spurge, the *Cipress-Spurge, and the Mirtle Spurge. **1578** LYTE *Dodoens* III. xxix. 359 The fifth kinde called *Cypres Tithymal. **1535** COVERDALE *Ecclus.* xxiv. 13 As a *Cypers tre vpon the mount Hermon. **1818** SHELLEY *Rev. Islam* v. liv. 5 The banquet.. Was spread beneath many a dark cypress tree. **1861** MISS E. A. BEAUFORT *Egypt. Sepulchr.* II. xxiv. 324 A very fine hall.. with a ceiling of *cypress wood.

†**'cypress**[2]. *Obs.* [A corruption of L. *cyperus*, *cyperos*, app. confounded with CYPRESS[1].] The Sweet Cyperus or Galingale.

c **1430** *Two Cookery-bks.* 21 Vyaund de cyprys bastarde.. take whyte Gyngere, and Galyngale, and Canel fayre y-mynced. **1549** *Compl. Scot.* vi. 67, I sau cipresses, that is gude for the fluxis of the bellye. **1607** TOPSELL *Four-f. Beasts* (1673) 143 Against tikes, lice, and fleas, anoint the dog with bitter almonds.. or roots of maple, or cipers. **1712** tr. *Pomet's Hist. Drugs* I. 35 Long Cypress.. is a knotty Root. **1799** C. SMITH *Laboratory* II. 400 Add one drachm of the powder of cypress.

b. *Comb.*, as *cypress-powder*, *cypress-root*.

1634 W. TIRWHYT tr. *Balzac's Lett.* 99 Enjoyning me never to goe to the Warres, but when Muskets are charged with Cypres-powder. **1652** URQUHART *Jewel* Wks. (1834) 229 Like another Sejanus, with a periwig daubed with Cypres powder. **1790** W. WOODVILLE *Med. Bot.* I. 75 *note*, The root [of *Arum maculatum*] is used by the French to wash the skin with.. under the name of Cypress Powder. **1879** PRIOR *Plant-n.* 61 Cypress-root, or Sweet Cypress.. a plant the aromatic roots of which are known as English galingale, *Cyperus longus*.

†**'cypress**[3]. *Obs.* or *dial.* Forms: 5–7 cipres, 6–9 cyprus, 6–7 cypres, cy-, cipresse, 7 cipress, 7–cypress; also 5 (cipre), cipyrs, 6 sipers, sipars, (cyrpe), 6–7 sypers, sipres, 7 sypress, sipris. [prob. f. OF. *Cipre*, *Cypre*, the island of Cyprus, from which, in and after the Crusading times, various fabrics were brought: see Aldis Wright, note to Shaks. *Twelfth Night* III. i. 119.]

1. A name of several textile fabrics originally imported from or through Cyprus: **a.** A cloth of gold or other valuable material.

[*c* **1400** *Inv.* in Sir F. Palgrave *Kal. & Invent. Treas.* III. 358 Primerement, xxv draps d'or de diverses suytes dount iiii. de Cipre les autres de Lukes.] **14..** LANGL. *P. Pl.* B. xv. 224 (MS. O.) Clenlich yclopéd in cipres [MS. C. cipyrs; B. purpre] and in tartaryne. *a* **1440** *Sir Degrev.* 1482 The scochenus of many knyȝt Of gold and cyprus was i-dyȝt.

b. A valuable quality of satin, called more fully *satin of Cypres*, *satin Cypres*.

1533 in Weaver *Wells Wills* (1890) 27 A Sondays gowne of blak lyned with sattyn of sypers. **1548** HALL *Chron.* (1809) 599 Long and large garmentes of blewe Satten panned with Sipres, poudered with spangles of bullion golde. **1552–3** *Inv. Ch. Goods, Staff.* in *Ann. Litchfield* IV. 39 On redde vestement of saten sipars with all things to hitt. **1603** *Draperies sold at Norwich*, in *38th Rep. Keeper Public Rec.* 444 Fustyans of Naples.. Paris clothes.. sattins of Cipres, Spanish sattins.

c. *esp.* (= *cypress lawn*) A light transparent material resembling cobweb lawn or crape; like the latter it was, when black, much used for habiliments of mourning.

[**1398** *Test. Ebor.* I. 240 Unum [velum] de cypres. **1402** *Ibid.* I. 289, ij flameola de cipres.] **1577** EDEN & WILLES *Hist. Trav.* 260 With two Oxe hornes, as it were, made of fine cypres hangyng downe about theyr eares. **1594** NASHE *Unfort. Trav.* 84 A hundred pages in sutes of white cipresse. **1611** SHAKS. *Wint. T.* IV. iv. 221 Lawne as white as driuen Snow, Cypresse blacke as ere was Crow. **1616** B. JONSON *Epigr.* lxxiii, One half drawn In solemn cyprus, th' other cobweb lawn. **1678** PHILLIPS, *Cipress*, a fine curled Stuff, part Silk, part Hair, of a Cobweb thinness, of which Hoods for Women are made. **1721** *Lond. Gaz.* No. 5930/1 Officers wearing Mourning-Scarfs of Cypress. **1722** *Ibid.* No. 6084/4 The Colours furled and wrapped in Cypress. [**1820** SCOTT *Monast.* xviii, The murrey-coloured double-piled Genoa velvet, puffed out with ciprus.]

transf. **1718** WARDER *True Amazons* (ed. 2) 3 Having four Wings.. with strong Fibres round and cross them, to strengthen the fine Cypress of which they are framed.

2. A piece of cypress used as a kerchief for the neck or head, as a band for the hat, etc., in sign of mourning, and the like.

1530 PALSGR. 205/2 Cypres for a womans necke, *crespe*. *c* **1540** *Four P.P.* in Hazl. *Dodsley* I. 350 Sipers, swathbands, ribbons, and sleeve-laces. **1601** SHAKS. *Twel. N.* III. i. 131 A Cipresse, not a bosome, Hides my heart. **1609** DEKKER *Gvlls Horne-bk.*, Him that wears a trebled cyprus about his hat. **1611** FLORIO, *Velaregli*, shadowes, vailes, Launes, Scarfes, Sipres or Bonegraces that women vse to weare. *a* **1717** PARNELL *Night-Piece on Death* 72 Why then thy flowing sable stoles, Deep pendant cypress, mourning poles.

3. *attrib.* (or *adj.*). **a.** Of cypress.

1530 PALSGR. 173 *Crespine*, a cypres lynyn clothe. **1607** W. S. *Puritan* Stage Direct., Enter the widow Plus, Frances, Mary, Sir Godfrey, and Edmond, all in mourning; the latter in a cyprus hat. **1632** MILTON *Penseroso* 35 Sable stole of cypress lawn. **1678** J. PHILLIPS *Tavernier's Trav. Persia* I. 10 The Travellers are wont to wear black Cypress Hoods.. over their Faces.

b. Resembling cypress in texture; gauze-like.

1598 SYLVESTER *Du Bartas* I. vii. (1641) 64/2 The Spider .. neat and nimbly her new web she weaves.. Open, lest else th' ungentle Winds should tear Her Cipres Tent. **1713** WARDER *True Amazons* (ed. 2) 30 Not only Bees, but all other Creatures having a Cypress wing.

c. Dark grey with darker markings; hence *cyprus-cat*, a variety of tabby cat (*local*).

1857 WRIGHT *Prov. Dict.*, *Cypress-cat*, a tabby-cat, *East*. **1879** LUBBOCK *Fauna of Norfolk* 7 An immense cat of a cypress colour. **1887** *N. & Q.* 7th Ser. IV. 289/1 While discussing the merits of a new kitten recently with a lady from Norwich, she described its colour as 'Cyprus'—dark grey, with black stripes and markings.

cypressed ('saɪprɪst), *a.* [f. CYPRESS[1] + -ED[2].] Planted or adorned with cypresses.

1850 SIR A. DE VERE *Pict. Sk.* II. 248 The citied hills, the cypressed vales. **1861** THORNBURY *Turner* (1862) I. 222 On the Cypressed Hill.

Cyprian ('sɪprɪən), *a.* and *sb.* Also 7 Ciprian. [f. L. *Cyprius* of Cyprus + -AN. In F. *cyprien*.]

A. *adj.* **1.** Belonging to Cyprus, an island in the eastern Mediterranean, famous in ancient times for the worship of Aphrodite or Venus.

1627 MASSINGER *Gt. Dk. Florence* v. ii, By all the vows which lovers offer at The Cyprian goddess' altars. *c* **1673** *Roxb. Ball.* VI. 112 A stranger unto Love am I.. The Ciprian Boy shall not destroy My freedome and my Reason.

2. *transf.* Licentious, lewd; in 18–19th c. applied to prostitutes.

1599 MARSTON *Sco. Villanie* I. iii. 184 Consuming all the yeare In Cyprian dalliance. **1782** WOLCOTT (P. Pindar) *Ode to R.A's.* ix. Wks. I. 35 A Damsel of the Cyprian class. **1859** *Sat. Rev.* VIII. 71/1 The Cyprian patrol which occupies our streets in force every night.

B. *sb.* An inhabitant or native of Cyprus, a Cypriote; hence *transf.* A licentious or profligate person; in later use *spec.* a prostitute.

1598 MARSTON *Pygmal.* ii. 145 See how he paceth like a Ciprian. **1819** J. H. VAUX *Mem.* I. 72 A very interesting young Cyprian whom I.. attended to her apartments. **1829** *Sun* 17 Sept. 4/4 A cyprian of the lowest grade. **1843** tr. *Custine's Empire of Czar* III. 84 The expenses of these poor cyprians were not diminished in the same proportion as their gains.

Cyprianic (sɪprɪ'ænɪk), *a.* [ad. mod.L. *Cyprianicus*, f. *Cypriānus*.] Of, pertaining to, or characteristic of St. Cyprian (Thascius Cæcilius Cyprianus), bishop of Carthage, martyred A.D. 258.

1695 J. SAGE (*title*) The Principles of the Cyprianic Age. **1696** G. RULE (*title*) The Cyprianick Bishop examined and found not to be diocesan, nor to have superior power to a parish minister, or presbyterian moderator. *a* **1861** W. CUNNINGHAM *Hist. Theology* Wks. (1863) I. 164 The Cyprianic bishop was very different from the modern one. **1916** J. R. HARRIS *Testimonies* I. viii. 77 We have an almost contemporary witness for the Cyprianic text. *Ibid.* xiv. 127 Justin starts with the first chapter of the Cyprianic Christology. **1920** *Christian World* 19 Aug. 8/4 We need for the recovery of Christian unity a man of Cyprianic grasp, though not of Cyprian's opinions. **1945** G. DIX *Shape of Liturgy* v. 116 The 'Cyprianic' doctrine of the sacrifice came to prevail in the West.

cyprid ('saɪprɪd). *Zool.* An ostracod crustacean of the family Cyprididæ (see CYPRIS).

1913 H. M. CADELL *Story of Forth* i. 8 Other shale seams are almost entirely composed of minute entomostraca or cyprids.

cypriferous (saɪ'prɪfərəs), *a.* *Geol.* [f. mod. Zool. L. *Cypris* (from L. *Cypris* a name of Venus) + -FEROUS.] Abounding in fossil shells of the genus *Cypris* of freshwater crustaceans.

1833 LYELL *Pr. Geol.* III. 233 Green cypriferous marls.

†**cyprine**, *a.*[1] *Obs.*[—0] [Erroneous formation. L. *cyprinum*, Gr. κύπρινον are deriv. of *Cyprus* CYPRE, the henna plant.]

1656 BLOUNT *Glossogr.*, *Cyprine*.. of or belonging to the Cypress-Tree. [Hence in ASH 1775 and mod. Dicts.]

cyprine ('sɪpraɪn, -ɪn), *a.*[2] *Ichth.* [ad. L. *cyprīnus*, a. Gr. κυπρῖνος carp.] Belonging to the carp genus *Cyprīnus*, or the carp family, *Cyprinidæ*.

1828 in WEBSTER; whence in mod. Dicts.

cyprine ('sɪpraɪn), *sb.* *Min.* [mod. f. L. *cyprius* of COPPER q.v.] A blue variety of VESUVIANITE supposed to contain copper.

1823 PHILLIPS *Min.* 262 Cyprine.

cyprinid (sɪ'praɪnɪd). *Ichth.* [f. mod.L. *Cyprīnidæ*, the family of fresh-water fishes of which the carp, *cyprīnus*, is the type.] A fish of the carp family. So **cy'priniform** *a.*, carp-like in structure.

cyprinodont (sɪ'praɪnəʊdɒnt). *Ichth.* [f. as mod.L. generic name *Cyprinodon*, from L. *cyprīnus* carp + Gr. ὀδοντ- tooth.]

A. *sb.* A malacopterygious fish of the family *Cyprinodontidæ*, of which the typical genus is *Cyprinodon*; they differ from the cyprinids in having the jaws more projecting and toothed.

1857 AGASSIZ *Nat. Hist. U.S.* I. 48 Among fishes.. the Cyprinodonts, the Chætodonts. **1887** C. C. ABBOTT *Waste-Land Wand.* vi. 166 The many-barred cyprinodont that throngs every stream from Maine to Florida.

B. *adj.* Of or belonging to this family.

Hence **cyprino'dontid**, **-'dontoid** *a.*, of or allied to the Cyprinodonts.

cyprinoid (sɪ'praɪnɔɪd), *a.* and *sb.* *Ichth.* [f. L. *cyprīnus* carp + -OID.]

A. *adj.* Resembling or allied to the carp; belonging to the division *Cyprinoidea* of fishes, comprising the *Cyprinidæ* and other families.

1859 TODD *Cycl. Anat.* V. 287 In the cyprinoid families. **1876** BENEDEN *Anim. Parasites* 9 A cyprinoid fish.

B. *sb.* A fish belonging to the *Cyprinoidea*.

1849–52 TODD *Cycl. Anat.* IV. 1146/2 The vascular tissue .. on the palate of the Cyprinoids. **1878** BELL *Gegenbauer's Comp. Anat.* 525 In the Cyprinoids the mucous membrane .. is interwoven with.. muscular fibres.

Hence **cypri'noidean** *a.* and *sb.*

Cypriot ('sɪprɪɒt), **Cypriote** ('sɪprɪəʊt), *a.* and *sb.* [ad. Gr. Κυπριώτης, f. Κύπρος Cyprus. Cf. CYPRIAN.] **A.** *adj.* Belonging to Cyprus. **B.** *sb.* A native or inhabitant of Cyprus; the Greek dialect (ancient or modern) of Cyprus.

1599 HAKLUYT *Voy.* II. I. 309, I was credibly informed by a Cipriot a marchant of good wealth. **1639** FULLER *Hist. Holy Warre* v. xxix. 278 Take their names as I find them in the Catalogue of Stephen a Cypriot. **1750** *Universal Mag.* July 4/1 For a while he triumphed over the Tyrians, Sidonians, and Cypriots. **1797** R. HERON *Collect. Voy. & Trav.* 198 St. Spiridion, the Cypriot. **1837** *Penny Cycl.* VIII. 261/2 Almost every house has a garden, of which the Cypriotes are very fond. **1878** *Murray's Handbk. Trav. Turkey in Asia* (ed. 4) 179/1 The Inscriptions found.. in Cyprus are in three languages: 1. Cypriote. *Ibid.* 182/1 Androcles.. was present in the Cypriote fleet which supported Alexander. **1920** J. A. ROBERTSON *Hidden Rom. N.T.* i. 20 The wealthy Cypriote Mnason, who entertained Paul. **1920** G. E. BUCKLE *Disraeli* VI. 300 The occupation of Cyprus ensured the fair treatment of the Cypriot Greeks. **1920** *Q. Rev.* July 38 This Cypriote School, with its grand Græco-Oriental seriousness, had many ramifications, one of which, the Palyrene.. lasted down to the third century A.D. **1927** *Times* (weekly ed.) 25 Aug. 208/3 The Cypriots in Egypt. **1955** *Times* 6 May 4/3 The House was entitled to know what progress had been made in the discussions with Cypriots about their constitutional future.

cypri'pedin. *Med.* [f. F. *cypripède* = Bot. L. *Cypripedium* Lady's slipper (Linnæus *Gen. Pl.*

1015), app. a corruption of *Cypripodium*, f. Gr. Κύπρις Aphrodite + ποδίς shoe, πόδιον little foot.]

A brown powder prepared from the roots of *Cypripedium pubescens*, a North American orchid; used as an antispasmodic.

1863-72 in WATTS *Dict. Chem.* II. 300.

cypripedium (sɪprɪ'piːdɪəm). *Bot.* [mod.L. (Linnæus *Systema Naturæ* (1735)), f. Gr. Κύπρις Aphrodite + πέδιλον slipper, in reference to the inflated pouch formed by the labellum; cf. CYPRIPEDIN.] A member of the large genus of orchids so named. Cf. LADY'S SLIPPER I.

1775 T. BLAIKIE *Diary Scotch Gardener* 4 June (1931) 37 In those woods grow great plenty of the *Cepredium*. **1813** *Curtis's Bot. Mag.* XXXVIII. 1569 In the Cypripediums which we have before figured.. the two lower external petals are united together. **1873** *Young Englishwoman* Aug. 395/2 *Cypripedium*, or Slipper plant. **1890** W. WATSON *Orchids* xxviii. 155 When Cypripediums show signs of bad health, they should be at once shaken free of soil. **1902** *Westm. Gaz.* 31 Dec. 10/1 Cypripedium orchids. **1904** R. J. FARRER *Garden Asia* 250 On the shelving banks of grass in open places [grows] the cypripedium. **1938** T. HAY *Plants for Connoisseur* 47 The hardy terrestrial Cypripediums have long been highly esteemed for the border or rock garden. **1962** *Amateur Gardening* 14 Oct. 6/3 There are a number of cypripediums suitable for cool house conditions.

‖**Cypris** ('saɪprɪs). *Zool.* [mod.L., a. Gr. Κύπρις Aphrodite. (Names of Venus are applied to many shells.)] A genus of minute fresh-water crustacea, having the body enclosed in a delicate bivalve shell.

1832 LYELL *Princ. Geol.* II. 275 This cypris inhabits the lakes and ponds of England, where it is not uncommon. **1860** GOSSE *Rom. Nat. Hist.* 63 Tiny cyprides and cyclopes disporting in the umbrageous groves of their world.

cyproid ('saɪprɔɪd). *Zool.* [f. prec. + -OID.] A crustacean allied to the Cypris.

1852 DANA *Crust.* II. 1407 Species of Cyproids.

cyprus, cyprus-lawn: see CYPRESS³.

cyprus (*Bot.*): see CYPRE.

cyprusite ('saɪprəsaɪt). *Min.* [f. *Cyprus* + -ITE.] A sulphate of iron occurring in Cyprus.

1882 DANA *Min.* App. iii. 33 *Cyprusite.* [Named 1881.]

cyprys, obs. form of CYPRESS¹.

‖**Cypsela** ('sɪpsɪlə). *Bot.* [mod.Lat., ad. Gr. κυψέλη hollow vessel, chest, box.] A kind of dry one-seeded fruit; an achene with an adnate calyx, as in the *Compositæ*.

1870 BENTLEY *Bot.* 313 The Cypsela differs in nothing essential from the achænium, except in being inferior and of a compound nature. **1880** GRAY *Struct. Bot.* vii. §2. 295 An akene with adnate calyx has been termed a Cypsela.

cypseline ('sɪpsɪlaɪn), *a. Zool.* [f. L. *cypselus*, a. Gr. κύψελος the swift.] Of the family *Cypselidæ* or genus *Cypselus* of birds, comprising the Swifts.

1874 WOOD *Nat. Hist.* 287 The Swifts, technically called the 'Cypselinæ', or Cypseline birds.

So **'cypseliform, 'cypseloid, cypselo'morphic** *adjs.*, having the form or structure of a Swift; belonging to Huxley's group *Cypselimorphæ*.

cypselous ('sɪpsɪləs), *a. Bot.* [f. CYPSELA + -OUS.] Of the nature of a CYPSELA.

1878 MASTERS *Henfrey's Bot.* 292 The involucre, the cypselous fruit, and the pappus.

Cyrcean, obs. form of CIRCEAN.

1609 DOWNAM *Chr. Liberty* 95 The Cyrcean cup of the Libertines.. transformeth Christianisme into Epicurisme.

cyrcle, cyrcuite, etc.: see CIRCLE, etc.

cyre, obs. form of SIR, SIRE.

cyred, obs. form of CERED *ppl. a.*

1558-80 W. WARDE tr. *Alexis' Secr.* I. I. 14 b, A Violl well stopped with waxe and cyred clothe.

Cyrenaic (saɪrɪ'neːɪk), *a.* and *sb.* [ad. L. *Cȳrēnaic-us*, a Gr. Κυρηναϊκός, f. Κυρήνη Cyrene, a Greek colony in Africa. In mod.F. *Cyrénaïque.*]

A. *adj.* Belonging to the school of the Socratic philosopher Aristippus of Cyrene, whose doctrine was one of practical hedonism.

1641 MILTON *Ch. Govt.* II. (1851) 179 Not Epicurus, nor Aristippus with all his Cyrenaick rout. **1845** MAURICE *Mor. & Met. Philos.* in *Encycl. Metrop.* 585/1 The Cyrenaic doctrine.. terminated in Epicurism.

B. *sb.* A Cyrenaic philosopher; a follower of Aristippus.

1586 T. B. *La Primaud. Fr. Acad.* I. 222 Aristippus and all the Cyrinaiks. **1753** L. M. tr. *Du Bosq's Accomplish'd Woman* I. 200 [Aristippus] by birth a Cyrenian; from whence his followers were call'd Cyrenaics. **1889** *Athenæum* 2 Nov. 592/1 Even the Cyrenaics upheld a certain standard of personal dignity.

Hence **Cyre'naicism**, the doctrine of Aristippus.

Cyrenaican (saɪrɪ'neɪkən), *a.* [f. as CYRENAIC *a.* + -AN.] Of or pertaining to the region of Cyrenaica in north Africa, or its people. Also as *sb.*

1607 TOPSELL *Four-f. Beasts* 548 There are more kinds of mice in the Cyrenaican region. **1942** 'M. HOME' *House of Shade* v. 80 Suppose he had taken on the character of a Cyrenaican or a Tripolitanian from some southern oasis. **1963** I. W. ZARTMAN *Govt. & Pol. N. Afr.* (1964) v. 97 There is also a Cyrenaican Workers' Federation, but there is no nation-wide union. **1969** J. WRIGHT *Libya* xii. 133 The Cyrenaicans lost heavily during tough fighting in the spring of 1914.

Cyre'nean, Cy'renian *a.* = CYRENAIC.

1882 *Contemp. Rev.* Aug. 214 This reads like an avowal of Epicureanism or of the more selfish philosophy of pleasure known as Cyrenaicism. **1828** *Edin. Rev.* XLVIII. 221 A peculiar school of philosophy, known over the lettered world by the title of the Cyrenean. **1847** CRAIG, *Cyrenian.*

Cyrillic (sɪ'rɪlɪk), *a.* [f. the proper name *Cyril* (*Cyrill-us*) + -IC. In mod.F. *cyrillique.*] Applied to the alphabet employed by the Slavonic peoples of the Eastern Church, the invention of which is attributed to St. Cyril in the 9th century. The Cyrillic is distinguished from another ancient Slavonic alphabet, the Glagolitic (q.v.).

1842 *Penny Cycl.* XXII. 104/2 The use of the Cyrillic letters.. remained in full vigour among those [Slavonians] who belonged to the Eastern Church. *Ibid.* 127/1 The Servians.. make use of the Cyrillic alphabet. **1856** [see ROUMAN *sb.* 2]. **1881** *Academy* 26 Mar. 226 The Slaves, when they became converts to Christianity, framed two alphabets, the Cyrillic and the Glagolitic. **1884** *Sat. Rev.* 7 June 761/1 The Russian Government.. had already forbidden the printing of Lithuanian texts in any but the Cyrillic character.

cyring, obs. form of SYRINGE.

cyriologic (sɪrɪəʊ'lɒdʒɪk), *a.* In 7 kyrio-. The analogical form of CURIOLOGIC. So **cyrio'logical**.

1655-60 STANLEY *Hist. Philos.* (1701) 350/1 In the Kyriologick way, to express the Sun, they make a Circle; the Moon, a Crescent. **1824** JOHNSON *Typographia* II. 434 *Cyriological Hieroglyphics*, in which the figures were taken in a proper sense; as the image of a man was placed for a man. **1828** WEBSTER, *Cyriologic*, relating or pertaining to capital letters. [An error, reprinted in later Dicts.]

cyrographer, obs. form of CHIROGRAPHER.

cyrto- (sɜːtəʊ-), repr. Gr. κυρτο- from κυρτός curved, arched. In some recent technical terms, as **cyrto'ceratite** *Palæont.*, a fossil cephalopod of the genus *Cyrtoceras*, having the shell incurved or bent like a horn. So **cyrtocera'titic, cyr'toceran** *adjs.*; **cyrto'ceratid**, a member of the family containing *Cyrtoceras*. **'cyrtograph**, an instrument for the same purpose as the cyrtometer (*Syd. Soc. Lex.*). **'cyrtoid**, *a.*, resembling a hump or swelling on the back (*Syd. Soc. Lex.*). **'cyrtolite** *Min.*, a variety of zircon with the pyramidal planes convex (Dana). **cyr'tometer** [F. *cyrtomètre*], an instrument for measuring and recording the curves of the chest; also (***Wilson's C.***) for measurement of the head; whence **cyrto'metric** *a.*, **cyr'tometry**. **'cyrtostyle**, a circular portico projecting from the front or other part of a building (Webster, 1864).

1867 *Amer. Jrnl. Sc.* Ser. II. XLIV. 224 Before the blow-pipe cyrtolite glows brilliantly. **1870** S. GEE *Auscultation & Perc.* ii. 10 The Cyrtometer. **1879** KHORY *Princ. Med.* 45 When the outlines are drawn on paper by the help of the cyrtometer. **1885** *Lancet* 26 Sept., A cyrtometric tracing taken of the chest about the nipple level.

cyrurgien, -erie, early ff. CHIRURGEON, etc.

cysars, -ers, -ors, -ours, obs. ff. SCISSORS.

cyse, cyser, obs. forms of SIZE, CIDER.

cysme, obs. form of SCHISM.

cyst (sɪst). Also 8 cist. [ad. mod.L. *cystis* (in earlier use: see CYSTIS): in mod.F. *kyste.*]

1. *Biol.* A thin-walled hollow organ or cavity in an animal body (or plant) containing a liquid secretion; a bladder, sac, vesicle.

c **1720** W. GIBSON *Farrier's Dispens.* ii. I. (1734) 36 Under their [vipers'] tongue is a little Cyst or bag where the poison is deposited. **1796** MORSE *Amer. Geog.* I. 228 The Ink or Cuttle fish.. is furnished with a cyst of black liquor. **1866** *Treas. Bot.*, *Cyst*.. the hollow spaces in parenchyma in which oily matter collects, as in the rind of the orange.

2. *Path.* A closed cavity or sac of a morbid or abnormal character, containing liquid or semi-solid matter.

1731-1800 BAILEY, *Cist*.. a Tumour where the obstructed Matter collects as in a Bag. **1807-26** S. COOPER *First Lines Surg.* (ed. 5) 25 In abscesses of long standing, the cysts are often of very considerable thickness.

fig. **1884** *Jaunt in a Junk* 71 As it were, form an indelible cyst of penal associations round the very idea.

b. *spec.* The sac enclosing a hydatid, or larval form of a species of *Tænia* or tape-worm, found parasitic in man and various other animals. (Cf. ACEPHALOCYST.)

1713 CHESELDEN *Anat.* (1726) 181 The liver full of hydatids, and cysts of hydatids adhering to it. **1888** ROLLESTON & JACKSON *Anim. Life* 231 The cyst in which the *Cysticercus* lies is formed by the irritated tissues of its host.

3. *Biol.* and *Cryptogamic Bot.* A cell or cavity containing reproductive bodies, embryos, etc.; *e.g.* the spore-case of certain fungi.

1857 BERKELEY *Cryptog. Bot.* 134 Müller informs us that in *C. tuberculosa*, he has repeatedly seen two kinds of cysts, one scarlet, and constituting antheridia, the other larger and at length producing spores. **1867** J. HOGG *Microsc.* II. i. 263 They occasionally develop an enveloping cyst and thus become encysted zoospores.

4. *Comb.*, as ***cyst-fluid, -wall, -worm***; also ***cyst-like*** a.

1836-39 TODD *Cycl. Anat.* II. 220/2 Cyst-like tumours. **1847-9** *Ibid.* IV. 95/2 Atrophy of the renal textures dependent on cyst-formation. **1871** HOLMES *Syst. Surg.* (ed. 2) V. 917 The cyst-worms of one animal give rise to tape-worms in another and *vice-versa.*

cyst, obs. form of CIST.

cyst-, combining form of Gr. κύστις, CYST before vowels (cf. CYSTI-, CYSTO-): as **cy'stalgia** [F. *cystalgie*; Gr. ἄλγος pain] *Path.*, pain in the bladder, *esp.* of a spasmodic character. **cy'stectasy** [Gr. ἔκτασις extension: see ECTASIS], dilatation of the bladder; *spec.* a form of lithotomy in which the neck of the bladder is dilated so as to allow of the removal of the stone. **'cystelminth** [Gr. ἕλμινς, ἑλμινθ- worm], a cystic worm. **cy'stenchyma, cy'stenchyme** [Gr. ἔγχυμα infusion], a kind of connective tissue occurring in some sponges, and presenting analogies to the parenchyma of plants; hence **cysten'chymatous** *a.* **cysthe'patic** *a.* (*Anat.*) [F. *cysthépatique*: see HEPATIC], applied to ducts supposed to pass directly from the liver to the gall-bladder.

1887 SOLLAS *Sponges* in *Encycl. Brit.* XXII. 419 A tissue, *cystenchyme*, which in some respects resembles certain forms of vegetable parenchyme, occurs in some sponges. *Ibid.*, Cystenchyme very commonly forms a layer just below the skin of some *Geodinidæ*, particularly of *Pachymatisma*. **1678** PHILLIPS, *Cystepatick Arterie.* **1839-47** TODD *Cycl. Anat.* III. 176/1 Among the Chelonia the gall-bladder.. receives its secretion through.. cysthepatic ducts.

cy'stectomy. *Surg.* [f. CYST + -ECTOMY.] Surgical removal of either the gall-bladder or all or part of the urinary bladder, or of a cyst.

1891 C. W. M. MOULLIN *Surgery* Index, Cystectomy. **1896** J. G. SMITH *Abdom. Surg.* (ed. 5) II. ix. 961 Weir of New York records three cases of partial cystectomy. In one he removed a triangular portion of the bladder measuring 2½ inches on the sides. **1962** *Lancet* 19 May 1048/2 Total cystectomy was necessary. **1967** S. BOYARSKY *Neurogenic Bladder* xxvi. 203/2 Three patients continued to have chronic cystitis with copious drainage of purulent material from the urethra. Cystectomy was performed in all 3 after attempts at local therapy with anti-bacterial irrigations.

cysted ('sɪstɪd), *a. rare.* [f. CYST + -ED.] Enclosed in a cyst, encysted.

1755 in JOHNSON (*Cisted*); hence in later Dicts.

cysteine ('sɪstiːɪn, 'sɪstiːaɪn). *Biochem.* Also -ein. [ad. G. *cysteïn* (E. Baumann 1882, in *Zietschr. f. physiol. Chem.* VIII. 302), f. CYST(INE + -EINE.] An amino-acid, $HS{\cdot}CH_2{\cdot}CH(NH_2){\cdot}COOH$, which is a reduction product of cystine and a constituent of glutathione and many proteins.

1884 *Jrnl. Chem. Soc.* XLVI. A. 1382 Cystine and Cysteïne... The hydrochloride of the new base cysteïne is obtained by evaporating the filtrate. **1923** *Nature* 24 Feb. 274/1 The reduction of methylene blue by the sulphydryl compounds, reduced glutathione, cystein, and thioglycollic acid, is an autocatalytic reaction. **1961** *Lancet* 8 July 87/2 Two cysteine molecules readily give up their hydrogen atoms.. to reunite as cystine. **1970** R. W. MCGILVERY *Biochem.* xvii. 382 Cystine enters metabolism as cysteine.

cyster, cysterne, obs. ff. SISTER, CISTERN.

cysti- (sɪstɪ), combining form of Gr. κύστις, CYST; in many modern technical words: as **cy'sticolous** *a.* [L. *-colus* inhabiting], inhabiting a cyst. **cy'stiferous** *a.* [L. *-fer* bearing], bearing or producing cysts. **'cystiform** *a.*, of the form of a bladder or cyst. **cy'stigerous** *a.* [L. *-ger* bearing], bearing or containing cysts. **cysti'rrhœa** [F. *cystirrhée*] = *cystorrhœa* (see CYSTO-). **'cystitome** [F. *cystitome*; Gr. -τομος cutting], an instrument for cutting open the capsule of the crystalline lens.

1885 *Athenæum* 11 Apr. 474/2 The cysticolous Myzostomida. These parasites inhabit cysts.. which.. are malformations of the tissues of the host produced by the irritation. **1836-39** TODD *Cycl. Anat.* II. 407/2 The Cystiform Entozoa. **1885** W. ROBERTS *Urin. & Renal Dis.* (ed. 4) II. i. 239 Dense fibrous tissue, containing many large cystiform spaces. **1870** HOLMES *Syst. Surg.* I. 511 Cystic or cystigerous growths. **1830** S. COOPER *Dict. Pract. Surg.* 373 Cystitome.

cystic ('sɪstɪk), *a.* [a. F. *cystique* (Paré 16th c.), ad. mod.L. *cysticus*, f. Gr. type *κυστικός, f. κύστις: see CYST and -IC.]

1. *Anat.* Pertaining to or connected with the gall-bladder: as ***cystic artery, duct***.

1634 T. JOHNSON *Parey's Chirurg.* 111 The cysticke twins from the gate veine [of the liver]. *a* **1735** ARBUTHNOT (J.), The bile is of two sorts; the cystick..or the hepatick. **1831** R. KNOX *Cloquet's Anat.* 702 The cystic artery..sends a very considerable twig between the liver and gall-bladder.

2. Pertaining to the urinary bladder.

1881 MIVART *Cat* 186 The depression in which the bladder lies is called the cystic fissure.

b. ***cystic oxide***: = CYSTINE. ***cystic calculus***, a urinary calculus containing cystine; so ***cystic urine***.

1810 *Edin. Rev.* XVII. 166 Dr. Wollaston proposes to name it the cystic oxide. **1834** GOOD *Study Med.* IV. 407 The Cystic Calculus has a crystalline appearance. **1839–47** TODD *Cycl. Anat.* III. 805/2 Cystic Oxide is wholly dissipated by heat.

3. a. *Path.* Of the nature of a cyst; characterized by formation of cysts, containing cysts (CYST 2).

1713 R. RUSSELL in *Phil. Trans.* XXVIII. 277, I separated a Cystick Tumour. **1877** ROBERTS *Handbk. Med.* I. 30 Ovarian dropsy..is a cystic disease of the ovary.

b. ***cystic fibrosis***: = *mucoviscidosis* s.v. MUCO-.

1938 *Amer. Jrnl. Dis. Children* LVI. 344 (*heading*) Cystic fibrosis of the pancreas and its relation to celiac disease. **1959** *Jrnl. Amer. Med. Assoc.* 5 Sept. 1/1 The primary defect in cystic fibrosis is a dysfunction of the exocrine glands. **1985** *N.Y. Times* 9 Jan. C10/6 Nosebleeds are sometimes a sign of a serious underlying condition, such as high blood pressure in older adults or cystic fibrosis in young children.

4. Enclosed or living in a cyst, as a hydatid.

1859 TODD *Cycl. Anat.* V. 25/2 The Cystic Entozoa. **1877** HUXLEY *Inv. Anim.* iv. 211 In this condition the animal is what is termed a Cystic worm, or bladder-worm.

‖**cysticercus** (sɪstɪ'sɜːkəs). *Zool.* Pl. -ci (-saɪ). [mod.L., f. Gr. κύστις bladder + κέρκος tail. F. *cysticerque*.] The scolex or larva of a tape-worm in its encysted state; a hydatid.

1841–71 T. R. JONES *Anim. Kingd.* (ed. 4) 152 The discovery that the cystiform Entozoa, *Cœnurus* and *Cysticercus*.. are merely the *Scoleces* of ordinary Tape worms. **1875** H. WALTON *Dis. Eye* 24 The cysticercus, the ..larval state of the..pork tape-worm, gains access to the human body by being swallowed in an earlier larval condition.

Hence **cysti'cercal** *a.*, **cysti'cercoid** *a.* and *sb.*, **cysticer'coidal** *a.*

1858 COPLAND *Dict. Pract. Med.* III. II. 1385 A portion of the *Tæniæ* pass through a true cysticercal (bladder-worm) stage. *Ibid.*, True *Cysticerci* occur only in warm-blooded animals..and cysticercoid forms principally in cold-blooded animals. **1877** HUXLEY *Anat. Inv. Anim.* iv. 212 The dog devours the louse, and the Cysticercoid becomes a *Tænia cucumerina* in his intestine.

cysticle ('sɪstɪk(ə)l). [dim. of CYST after L. type **cysticula*: see -CULE.] A small cyst: applied by Owen to an organ, supposed to be that of hearing, in some *Acalephæ*.

1855 OWEN *Anat. Inv. Anim* ix. 169 The part, for which, from its characteristic constancy..I have proposed the definite term of 'cysticle'. *Ibid.* 170 In some Acalephæ the cysticles are not complicated with pigment-cells.

cysticotomy (sɪstɪ'kɒtəmɪ). *Surg.* [f. CYSTIC (in *cystic duct*) + -TOMY.] Incision into the cystic duct.

1900 in DORLAND *Med. Dict.* **1901** W. W. SEYMOUR tr. *Kehr's Gallstone Dis.* II. 135 After 190 conservative gall-bladder operations (among them 37 cysticotomies..) I have lost..only 3 patients. **1908** *Practitioner* Dec. 826 A stone was extracted after the incision of the cystic duct (Cysticotomy). **1938** M. THOREK *Mod. Surg. Technic* III. xxxv. 1606 Cysticotomy. This operation consists of opening the cystic duct followed by immediate repair. The operation is only of historical interest.

cystid ('sɪstɪd). [f. mod.L. *cystis* CYST + -ID.]

1. *Geol.* A member of the order *Cystidea* or *Cystoidea* of fossil echinoderms; a cystidean.

1862 DANA *Man. Geol.* 162 The Cystids are the most anomalous of Radiates. **1877** LE CONTE *Elem. Geol.* (1879) 299 Stemmed Echinoderms or Crinoids, may be divided into three families, viz.: 1. Crinids, 2. Cystids, 3. Blastids.

2. *Zool.* 'The sac-like ciliated embryo of some of the *Polyzoa*' (*Syd. Soc. Lex.*).

1877 HUXLEY *Anat. Inv. Anim.* viii. 459 From one end of this cystid, one or more polypides are developed from thickenings of the wall of the sac.

cystidean (sɪ'stɪdiːən). *Geol.* [f. mod.L. *cystidea*, f. *cystis*: see CYST and -ID.] = CYSTID 1.

1862 DANA *Man. Geol.* 398 Cystideans..became extinct in the beginning of the Devonian. **1876** PAGE *Adv. Text-Bk. Geol.* xii. 207 So may a cystidean..be considered a sea-urchin attached to the bottom by a similar jointed column.

‖**cy'stidium.** *Bot.* Pl. -ia. [mod.L., repr. Gr. type *κυστίδιον, dim. of κύστις bladder: in mod.F. *cystidion*: sometimes anglicized *cystide*.]

1. Link's name for a 1-celled, indehiscent, superior, membranous, apocarpous fruit; = utriculus.

2. One of the projecting cells originating among the basidia of hymenomycetous fungi, and supposed to be sterile basidia.

1858 CARPENTER *Veg. Phys.* §778 These..*cystidia* have been supposed to have the nature of antheridia; but this is uncertain. **1881** *Gard. Chron.* No. 403. 369 Cystidia are distinctly hyaline and glutinous bodies.

cystine ('sɪstaɪn). *Chem.* Also -in. [mod. f. Gr. κύστις bladder + -INE.] An organic base, $C_3NHO_7SO_2$, a yellowish crystalline substance, found in a rare kind of urinary calculus.

1843 JONES in *Trans. Med.-Chirurg. Soc.* XXVI. 110 The layers exterior to this nucleus contained no cystine.

attrib. **1853** G. BIRD *Urin. Deposits* (ed. 4) vii. 187 The specific gravity of cystine urine is generally below the average. **1885** W. ROBERTS *Urin. & Renal Dis.* (ed. 4) I. iii. 89 The following case of cystine calculus..occurred in the Manchester Infirmary.

Hence **cysti'nuria**, the condition of body in which cystine is found in the urine.

1853 G. BIRD *Urin. Deposits* vii. 193. **1963** *Lancet* 19 Jan. 127/1 In patients with cystinuria, lysine and arginine are poorly absorbed from the jejunum and ileum.

‖**cystis** ('sɪstɪs). *Obs.* Also 6 **chistis**. [med. or mod.L., a. Gr. κύστις bladder.] = CYST.

1543 TRAHERON *Vigo's Chirurg.* II. v. 39 Thys caustyue Medicyne hathe strengthe, to breake the node..euen to the chistis or purse. **1646** SIR T. BROWNE *Pseud. Ep.* 110 The humour [is] contained..in a vesicle or little bladder, though some affirme it hath no cystis or bag at all. **1758** *Le Dran's Observ. Surg.* (1771) 249 The Cystis of the Hydrocele.

cystitic (sɪ'stɪtɪk), *a.* *Path.* [f. CYSTIT(IS + -IC.] Affected with cystitis.

1910 *Practitioner* July 44 Distended cystitic bladder gave way.

cystitis (sɪ'staɪtɪs). *Path.* [f. CYSTIS + -ITIS. F. *cystite*.] Inflammation of the bladder.

1776–83 W. CULLEN *First Lines* §431 (1827) II. 83 The Cystitis, or inflammation of the bladder. **1878** T. BRYANT *Pract. Surg.* (1879) II. 60 Cystitis is a common consequence of stone, prostatic disease, stricture, or gonorrhœa.

cysto- (sɪstəʊ), combining form of Gr. κύστη = κύστις bladder, cyst, usually in reference to the urinary bladder; as in **cystobu'bonocele** [see BUBONOCELE], hernia of the bladder through the inguinal opening; **'cystocele** [F. *cystocèle*; Gr. κήλη tumour, CELE], hernia of the bladder; **'cystocyte** [-CYTE], one of the large and cyst-like cells of cystenchyma in sponges; **cy'stogenous** [-GENOUS], producinng cysts, cystiferous; **cy'stometer**, any instrument for measuring pressure and volume within the bladder; **cysto'metrogram** [Gr. μέτρον measure], a diagram showing the relationship between bladder pressure and volume as it fills; **cy'stometry**, the measurement of the pressure and volume within the bladder; the study of the bladder by means of such measurements; so **cysto'metric** *a.*; **cysto'morphous** [Gr. μορφή form], having the form of a cyst, cyst-like; **'cystoplast** (*Biol.*) [Gr. πλαστός formed, moulded], a cell having a cell-wall; **cysto'plastic** *a.* (*Surg.*), belonging to cystoplasty; **'cystoplasty** [F. *cystoplastie*], an operation for repair of the bladder, as in the case of vesico-vaginal fistula; **cysto'plegic** *a.*, relating to *cystoplegia* or paralysis of the bladder; **cysto'rrhœa** [Gr. ῥοία flow, flux], a flow of mucus from the bladder, vesical catarrh; **'cystoscope** [Gr. -σκοπος viewing], *sb.* an instrument for examining the interior of the bladder; *v.* to examine (the bladder) with this instrument; **cysto'scopic** *a.*, relating to or performed with the cystoscope; **cy'stoscopy** [Gr. σκοπιά lookout, watch], examination of the bladder with a cystoscope, **cy'stostomy** [Gr. στόμα mouth], the formation of an opening into the bladder by incision; **'cystospasm**, spasm of the bladder; **cysto'spastic** *a.*, relating to cystospasm; **'cystotome** [so in F.: Gr. -τομος cutting], an instrument for the operation of cystotomy; also an instrument for lacerating the capsule of the crystalline lens in the operation for cataract; **cy'stotomy** [Gr. -τομια cutting], cutting into the bladder for extraction of a stone or other purpose.

1860 MAYNE *Expos. Lex.* 254 **Cystobubonocele*..a rare kind of Hernia, in which the urinary bladder protrudes through the inguinal opening. **1811** in R. HOOPER *Med. Dict.*, **Cystocele.* **1876** GROSS *Dis. Bladder* 343 The bladder is liable to protrude from the pelvic cavity, constituting what is denominated a cystocele. **1927** D. K. ROSE in *Jrnl. Amer. Med. Assoc.* 15 Jan. 151/2, I have devised an instrument called a *cystometer. **1933** *Brain* LVI. 185 The volume-pressure curve as measured by the Rose cystometer, and used to estimate disturbances of vesical innervation. **1964** G. W. LEADBETTER in J. F. Glenn *Diagnostic Urol.* vii. 135 One of three cystometers may be used: (a) water column manometer, (b) Lewis electric recording cystometer, or (c) strain gauge with an electronic recorder. **1927** *Jrnl. Urol.* XVII. 493 *Cystometric curve is quite similar to one obtained after giving a sacral anaesthetic. **1964** G. W. LEADBETTER in J. F. Glenn *Diagnostic Urol.* vii. 133 Cystometric study is essential to diagnosis and management in patients who have evidence of neurologic disease. **1936** *New England Jrnl. Med.* 26 Mar. 617/1 In an attempt to arrive at a better method of treating urinary bladders paralyzed as the result of spinal cord injuries, it was soon demonstrated that *cystometrograms were essential. **1976** *Lancet* 4 Dec. 1221/1 During the acute stage a cystometrogram showed a flaccid insensitive bladder. **1959** *Danish Med. Bull.* VI. 194/1 *Cystometry, the measurement of intravesical pressure at various fillings of the bladder and during micturition, appears to have been effected exclusively by means of a catheter inserted through the urethra... We have worked out a new technique..using a polyethylene catheter inserted percutaneously into the bladder. **1977** *Lancet* 13 Aug. 335/2 Simple cystometry with a central-venous-pressure set can..be done in all hospitals and might help to delineate that group of patients who, although presenting with stress incontinence, in reality suffer from detrusor instability. **1984** *Brit. Med. Jrnl.* 9 June 1720/2 Cystometry has been used to study bladder function for over 100 years. **1876** GROSS *Dis. Bladder* 43 Catarrh of the bladder, technically denominated *cystorrhœa. **1889** FENWICK in *Brit. Med. Jrnl.* 6 July, Since the introduction of the incandescent-lamp *cystoscope. **1893** *Ibid.* 10 June 1209 In nearly every case of tumour which I have cystoscoped. **1889** FENWICK in *Brit. Med. Jrnl.* 1 Apr. 49/3 On *cystoscopic examination. **1910** *Practitioner* Mar. 378 As a general rule the operation of cholecystectomy shows a higher mortality than the cholecystostomy, but in Rimann's statistics the reverse is the case (cystectomy 3·4 per cent. and *cystostomy 14·3 per cent.). **1908** *Practitioner* Sept. 434 *Cystoscopy is of great use in determining the character of the fluid issuing from each ureter. **1909** *Ibid.* Nov. 664 Cytoscopy and ureteral catheterization are necessary. **1938** *Nature* 24 Sept. 555/1 The radiological methods include.. cystoscopy. **1847** SOUTH tr. *Chelius' Surg.* II. 594 The operator now grasps the *cystotome with his right hand. **1869** WELLS *Diseases of Eye* 237 For flap extraction I prefer Graefe's cystotome. **1721** BAILEY, **Cystotomy*, the cutting of the Bladder. **1888** *Pall Mall G.* 19 Sept. 6/2 General Salomon..underwent the operation of cystotomy yesterday.

cystocarp ('sɪstəʊkɑːp). *Bot.* [f. CYSTO- + Gr. καρπός fruit.] The sexual fruit of the *Florideæ*, a group of *Algæ*; also called CRYPTOCARP. Hence **cysto'carpic** *a.*

1875 BENNETT & DYER tr. *Sachs' Bot.* 213 The receptacle, here termed the Cystocarp. *Ibid.* 235 The cystocarps consist of branches formed of only one or two cells. **1889** *Athenæum* 14 Dec. 826 The specimen exhibited [*Gracilaria divergens*] possessed tetrasporic and cystocarpic fruits.

cystoid ('sɪstɔɪd), *a.* and *sb.* [mod. f. Gr. κύστις bladder, CYST + -OID: in mod.F. *cystoïde*.]

A. *adj.* **1.** *Path.* Of the nature of a cyst.

1871 HOLMES *Syst. Surg.* (ed. 2) V. 256 Cystoid formations. **1874** JONES & SIEV. *Pathol. Anat.* 155 Cystoid Tumours.

2. *Geol.* Belonging to the order *Cystoidea* of fossil echinoderms: see CYSTID.

1876 PAGE *Adv. Text-Bk. Geol.* xiii. 224 Among the echinoderms a few crinoid and cystoid forms.

B. *sb.* *Path.* A cystoid formation; = CYST 2.

1872 THOMAS *Dis. Women* 648 The cystoids of the ovary.

Hence **cy'stoidean** *a.* = CYSTOID *a.* 2; *sb.* A member of the *Cystoidea*.

cystolith ('sɪstəʊlɪθ). [CYSTO- + Gr. λίθ-ος stone.]

1. *Bot.* A club-shaped stratified outgrowth of the walls of some cells, containing minute crystals of calcium carbonate.

1857 HENFREY *Elem. Bot.* 503 Crystals..accumulated on a clavate process..called cystolithes. **1875** BENNETT *Sachs' Bot.* 64 Masses of cellulose..known as Cystoliths.

2. *Path.* 'Stone or calculus of the bladder' (*Syd. Soc. Lex.*). Hence **cysto'lithic** *a.* [in F. *cystolithique*], relating to stone in the bladder.

1846 WORCESTER cites DUNGLISON (*Cystolithic*).

‖**cystoma** (sɪ'stəʊmə). *Path.* Pl. cystomata. [mod. f. Gr. κύστις CYST + *-ōma* forming nouns of product.]

a. A tumour containing cysts; a cystic tumour. **b.** A cyst or cystic tumour which is a new development, as distinguished from one in which the sac is a natural formation (*Syd. Soc. Lex.*).

1872 PEASLEE *Ovar. Tumours* 30 All ovarian cystomata contain several..cysts at the beginning. **1876** *Wagner's Gen. Pathol.* 504 A small portion of cysts are new formations; properly so-called cystomata.

cy'stomatous *a.*, of the nature of a cystoma.

1876 *Wagner's Gen. Pathol.* 475 A cystomatous adenoma of the pituitary body of the size of a walnut was observed.

cystose (sɪ'stəʊs), *a.* *rare*$^{-0}$. [f. L. type **cystōsus*: see CYST and -OSE.] Containing, or resembling, a cyst; cystic.

1864 in WEBSTER.

cystous ('sɪstəs), *a.* *rare*$^{-0}$. [f. CYST + -OUS: cf. mod.F. *cysteux*.] = prec.

1857 in DUNGLISON. **1882** *Syd. Soc. Lex.*, Cystous, same as *Cystic*.

cytarin, cytern(e, obs. ff. *cittern*, CITHERN.

cytase ('saɪteɪs, -z). *Biochem.* [f. CYT(O- + -ASE.] Any of various enzymes found in some plant seeds which hydrolyse the hemicellulose constituents of cell walls and were formerly thought to dissolve the whole cell wall. Hence **cytasic** (saɪ'teɪzɪk) *a.*

1895 W. JAGO *Bread-making* 123 The enzyme, which thus dissolves the parenchymatous cell-walls of the endosperm, has received the name Cytase. Cytase is secreted by the embryo during germination. **1899** J. R. GREEN *Soluble Ferments* vii. 88 The existence of cytase has not been known for many years, our acquaintance with it dating back only to 1886, when it was discovered by De Bary. *Ibid.* xxi. 371 *Bacillus mesentericus vulgatus* has been shown to be possessed of diastasic, inverting, cytasic, and peptonising power. **1938** E. C. MILLER *Plant Physiol.* (ed. 2) xi. 802 The cytases are destroyed at a temperature of 60°C. or above. **1956** *New Biol.* XXI. 12 The secretion of enzymes (cytases) attacking the cell walls of the endosperm. **1962** HOWARTH & WARNE *Lowson's Textbk. Bot.* (ed. 13) ii. 32 When the seeds. e.g. of lupin and date, germinate, an enzyme, cytase, hydrolyses the hemicellulose, forming sugars.

cytaster ('saɪtæstə(r)). *Biol.* [a. G. *cytaster* (W. Flemming *Zellsubstanz* (1882) 379), f. as prec. + ASTER 4.] **a.** = ASTER 4. **b.** An aster-like structure which may be present in or induced in the cell when the nucleus is not dividing.

1892 A. A. CROZIER *Dict. Bot. Terms* 50/2 *Cytaster*, a series of achromatic rays extending from each pole of the nucleus in karyokinesis into the cytoplasm. **1901** E. B. WILSON in *Arch. f. Entwickelungsmechanik* XII. 541 In these eggs the first stage is..followed by the appearance of a variable number of vague clear spots in the cytoplasm which ..become surrounded with radiating lines of granules and finally assume the form of asters. These, which are obviously identical with Morgan's 'artificial astrospheres', may be called cytasters, in contradistinction to the nuclear asters that are connected with the nucleus. **1925** —— *Cell* (ed. 3) 1129 *Cytaster*... An aster not associated with chromosomes; commonly employed as equivalent to 'accessory aster' or supernumerary aster. **1952** A. HUGHES *Mitotic Cycle* iv. 108 Cytasters induced in activated *Echinarachnius* eggs were examined. **1960** L. PICKEN *Organization of Cells* vii. 254 Any part of the cytoplasm can participate in the formation of scattered cytasters and of the normal amphiaster.

-cyte (saɪt). *Biol.* [ad. Gr. κύτ-ος hollow, receptacle.] Frequent in composition with the sense 'cell', as in *collencyte, cystocyte, leucocyte,* etc.

cyte, -zane, -ein, -yn, obs. ff. CITY, CITIZEN.

cytharist, cyther: see CITH-, CIDER.

cythen: see SIE *v. Obs.*, to strain.

Cytherean (sɪθə'riːən), *a.* and *sb.* [f. L. *Cytherēa* = Gr. Κυθέρεια a name of Aphrodite or Venus, from Κύθηρα Cythera, Cerigo.] **A.** *adj.*

1. Pertaining to Venus; also *transf.* (cf. B).

1866 *Elgin Cathedral Guide* 45 A Cytheraean temple under State supervision and protection.

2. Pertaining to the planet Venus.

1885 CLERKE *Pop. Hist. Astron.* 284 Three distinct atmospheres—the solar, terrestrial, and cytherean—combine to deform outlines.

B. *sb.* A votaress of Venus; a prostitute attached to a heathen temple in India; also generally.

1751 *Beau-philosopher* 238 The Baron..obliged him..to tack about to some other Cytherean. **1807** J. JOHNSON *Orient. Voy.* 96 The contaminated embrace of a modern Cytherean.

cythero'mania. [f. as prec. + MANIA.] Nymphomania.

1874 in DUNGLISON. **1884** in *Syd. Soc. Lex.*

cythole, cythren, var. CITOLE, CITHERN *Obs.*

cytidine ('saɪtɪdiːn). *Biochem.* [ad. G. *cytidin* (P. A. Levene and W. A. Jacobs 1910, in *Ber. d. Deut. Chem. Ges.* 3152), f. as CYTASTER + -IDINE.] A nucleoside, $C_9H_{13}N_5O_5$, composed of cytosine and ribose and obtained by the hydrolysis of ribonucleic acid.

1911 *Jrnl. Chem. Soc.* C. I. 96 On partial hydrolysis of nucleic acid with ammonia, cytidine, $C_9H_{13}O_5N_3$, is obtained. **1958** *Oxf. Univ. Gaz.* 23 Apr. 894 An investigation into the metabolism of cytidine nucleotides, with special reference to cytidine diphosphate polyols.

cytisine ('sɪtɪsaɪn). *Chem.* [mod. f. next + -INE.] A poisonous alkaloid, $C_{20}H_{23}N_3O$, extracted from the ripe seeds of the Laburnum, *C. Laburnum*, and other species of *Cytisus*.

1830 LINDLEY *N.S. Bot.* 91 The seeds of the Laburnum are poisonous; they contain a principle called Cytisine. *attrib.* **1878** tr. *Ziemssen's Cycl. Med.* XVII. 825 Cytisine poisoning.

‖**cytisus** ('sɪtɪsəs). *Bot.* [L., a Gr. κύτισος a shrubby leguminous plant.] **a.** A shrubby plant mentioned by the Greek and Roman writers, as useful for fodder; now identified with the Shrubby Medic, *Medicago arborea*. **b.** *Bot.* Adopted by Linnæus as the name of a genus of leguminous shrubs and trees, including the common Broom (though this has by many been made the type of a separate genus), the Laburnum, and other species, one of which (*C. racemosus*), a well-known early flowering greenhouse and window plant with a profusion of yellow flowers, is the *Cytisus* of florists.

By early writers the name was often applied to other shrubby leguminous plants.

1548 TURNER *Names of Herbes*, Cytisus groweth plentuously in mount Appennine..I haue not sene it in Englande. Cytisus may be called in englishe tre trifoly. **1578** LYTE *Dodoens* VI. lxi, Cytisus is a shrubbe or bush with leaues, not muche vnlyke Fenugreke, or Sene; the flowers be faire and yellow, almost like to Broome flowers. *a* **1729** CONGREVE *Ovid's Art of Love* (T.), There tamarisks with thick-leav'd box are found, And cytisus and garden-pines abound. **1794** MARTYN *Rousseau's Bot.* xxv. 362 Evergreen Cytisus has the flowers coming out singly from the side of the stalk. **1855** SINGLETON *Virgil* I. 8 No [more] my goats.. the blooming cytisus..shall you browse. **1892** *Star* 14 May 1/7 Marguerites..wave gaily above rows of drooping cytisus and hanging grass.

cytitis (sɪ'taɪtɪs). [mod. f. Gr. κύτος skin + -ITIS.] 'Inflammation of the skin' (*Syd. Soc. Lex.*).

cytlyng, obs. form of KITLING.

cyto-, combining form of Gr. κύτος hollow, receptacle, etc., taken in modern formations with the meaning 'cell' (cf. -CYTE), and used in many biological terms: as CYTOBLAST, etc.: see below. **cyto'chemist,** one who studies cytochemistry; **cyto'chemistry,** the chemistry of cells; *spec.* a branch of biochemistry using microscopical techniques for this study; hence **cyto'chemical** *a.*, pertaining to cytochemistry; **cyto'coccus** [Gr. κόκκος berry], Haeckel's term for the nucleus of a *Cytula* or impregnated ovum; **ˌcytodiag'nosis,** diagnosis by examining the cell-contents of effusions into the serous cavities of the body (Dorland 1903); **cy'togamont,** an organism in the process of cytogamy; **cy'togamy,** (*a*) the fusion of cells; conjugation, syngamy; (*b*) a kind of reproduction that sometimes occurs in *Paramecium* and some other ciliated Protozoa, in which two organisms undergo autogamy while in contact with each other but without any exchange of nuclear material; hence **cy'togamous** *a.*, undergoing cytogamy; **cyto'genesis,** the generation or production of cells; **cyto'genic, cy'togenous** *adjs.*, producing cells, or characterized by the formation of cells; **cy'togeny** = *cytogenesis*; **cytolysin** (saɪ'tɒlɪsɪn, saɪtəʊ'laɪsɪn) [see LYSIN], a substance that causes cytolysis; **cy'tolysis,** the dissolution of cells; hence **cyto'lytic** *a.*; **cytomor'phosis,** the series of morphological changes undergone by cells during their life; **cyto'pathic, cytopatho'genic** *adjs.*, of, pertaining to, or producing damage to cells; **cytopa'thologist,** one who studies cytopathology; **cytopa'thology,** the pathology of cells; **'cytoplasm,** the substance forming the essential constituent of cells, protoplasm; *spec.* the protoplasm of a cell as distinguished from the nucleus; **cyto'plasmic** *a.*, pertaining to or consisting of cytoplasm; **'cytoplast,** the body or unit of protoplasm contained in a cell (cf. BIOPLAST); **'cytopyge** [Gr. πυγή rump], the excretory opening or anus of a unicellular animal; **'cytostome** [Gr. στόμα mouth], the absorbent opening or mouth of a unicellular animal; **cy'tostomous** *a.*, pertaining to the cytostome; **cyto'toxic** *a.*, toxic to cells; of or pertaining to a cytotoxin; **cyto'toxin,** any substance having a toxic effect on cells; **cy'totrophy** (see quot.); **cyto'tropism** = *cytotrophy*; **cyto'zoa** *sb. pl.* (*Zool.*), [Gr. ζῷον animal], a synonym of the *Sporozoa* or *Gregarinida*; **'cytozyme** (see quots.).

1940 CASPERSSON & SCHULTZ in *Proc. Nat. Acad. Sci.* XXVI. 507 At the centre of the discussion was the nucleolus, which in its staining properties resembled some of the cytoplasmic components, and in some cases appeared ..to be extruded into the cytoplasm. With the recent advances in *cytochemical technique, these problems can be studied more critically. **1946** *Nature* 21 Dec. 917/1 (*heading*) Establishment of Cytochemical Techniques... It might be feared that his remarks will leave the *cytochemist with a gloomy feeling. [**1899** A. GRAF in *Nova Acta Acad. Leopoldino-Carolinæ* LXXII. 280 Cytochemie.] **1905** GOULD *Med. Dict.* Suppl. 204/1 **Cytochemistry*, the chemistry of living cells. **1960** *Times* 26 May 3/2 Honours graduate required for the cyto-chemistry section of the Division of Pathology. **1962** *Sci. Survey* XI. 185 Another way of exploring the function of structures within cells is to establish their nature by combining electron microscopy with cell chemistry (cytochemistry). **1908** *Practitioner* Oct. 621 The method of *cytodiagnosis..usually gives satisfactory results, especially in the case of pleural exudates. **1965** tr. *Smolka & Soost's Outl. & Atlas Gynaecol. Cytodiagnosis* 3 The development of fundamental cytology and cytodiagnosis in other medical fields has been furthered by the work of the American Society of Cytology. **1939** R. WICHTERMAN in *Nature* 15 July 123/1 *Cytogamous paramecia, which are considerably smaller than typical vegetative ones, are very insecurely attached to each other at their anterior ends at the beginning of the process... The micro-nucleus of each cytogamont leaves its place near the macro-nucleus and then gradually increases in size. **1900** B. D. JACKSON *Gloss. Bot. Terms* 71/1 **Cytogamy*, the union of cells. **1906** M. HARTOG in *Camb. Nat. Hist.* I. i. 33 This process [*sc.* syngamy] is called also 'conjugation' or 'cytogamy'. **1939** R. WICHTERMAN in *Nature* 15 July 123/1, I am therefore proposing a new term, *cytogamy*, for this phenomenon as distinct from autogamy in single individuals and true conjugation involving a nuclear transfer in joined pairs. **1961** MACKINNON & HAWES *Introd. Study Protozoa* iv. 292 The life-cycle of *Paramecium* is complicated. It consists of periods of growth interrupted by binary fission, which is its only means of multiplication, and periodic recourse to the curious sexual processes of conjugation, autogamy, and cytogamy. **1859** TODD *Cycl. Anat.* V. 140/1 The blastodermic cells are produced by a process of *cytogenesis. **1876** *Wagner's Gen. Pathol.* 439 *Cytogenic tissue consists of a vascular fibrous framework and of cells. **1874** JONES & SIEV. *Pathol. Anat.* 153 *Cytogenous connective-tissue is met with in other organs. **1905** *Jrnl. Path. & Bacteriol.* X. 111 The *cytolysins contained in [snake] venom. **1937** *Times Lit. Suppl.* 6 Mar. 173/2 Prominent among the mobile agents for defence found in the blood stream are the cytolysins. **1907** *Brit. Med. Jrnl.* 20 Apr. 923/1 There seems to be some toxic condition produced which overcomes natural resistance, resulting in *cytolysis. **1946** *Nature* 21 Dec. 917/2 It is therefore necessary to kill the cell fragments, to remove diffusion difficulties by thorough cytolysis. **1904** *Keene's Bath Journal* 28 May 5/5 The '*cytolytic' milk of a cow has been tried. **1910** *Practitioner* Feb. 199 The virulence of the cocci was evidenced..by the cytolytic findings. **1908** C. S. MINOT (*title*) The problem of age, growth, and death; a study of *cytomorphosis. **1968** BLOOM & FAWCETT *Textbk. Histol.* (ed. 9) ix. 219/1 The cartilage cells in a center of ossification undergo a regular sequence of changes referred to as the cytomorphosis of the cartilage cells. **1961** *Lancet* 29 July 248/2 A..degeneration of the embryonic cells, a cytopathic effect. **1956** *New Gould Med. Dict.* (ed. 2) 313/2 *Cytopathogenic. **1959** *Brit. Jrnl. Exper. Path.* XL. 61 Experiments..to isolate cytopathogenic agents from sarcoidotic lesions. **1962** *Lancet* 26 May 1109/1 Cytopathogenic effects in tissue-cultures of sarcoid skin which are reminiscent of changes that might be associated with a virus. **1962** *Times* 26 June 3/2 A newly-created post of *Cyto-pathologist. **1936** STEDMAN *Med. Dict.* (ed. 13) 281/2 **Cytopathology*, cellular pathology; morbid changes occurring in cells. **1957** *Encycl. Brit.* XV. 204/2 A major development of cytopathology is the study of 'new growths', among which cancer takes a leading place. **1874** BARKER tr. *Frey's Histol.* 66 This primordial cell-substance is known at the present day by the name protoplasm. It has also received from Beale, Kölliker, and Dujardin respectively the names bioplasm, *cytoplasm, and sarcode. **1889** VINES in *Nature* 24 Oct. 624 The embryo is developed from the whole of the nucleus and more or less of the cytoplasm of the ovum. **1889** *Cent. Dict.*, *Cytoplasmic. **1920** L. DONCASTER *Study of Cytology* vii. 91 (*heading*) The cytoplasmic structures in spermatogenesis and oogenesis. **1952** G. H. BOURNE et al. *Cytology & Cell Physiol.* (ed. 2) i. 51 Phase-contrast microscopy reveals the presence of numerous cytoplasmic inclusions in the living cell. **1968** H. HARRIS *Nucleus & Cytoplasm* i. 8 The expression of the genetic information is effected by means of cytoplasmic regulatory mechanisms. **1891** M. HARTOG in *Nature* XLIV. 484/1 The union of cells, *cytoplast to cytoplast. **1888** ROLLESTON & JACKSON *Anim. Life* 833 Infusoria..A mouth or cytostome with an oral tube, and an anal spot or *cytopyge, are absent only in the endoparasitic Opalinidae. **1907** *Practitioner* Aug. 191 The result of *cytotoxic activity. **1943** Cytotoxic [see ANTIRETICULAR *a.*]. **1961** *New Scientist* 19 Oct. 186/1 The so-called cytotoxic drugs used in the treatment of cancer. **1969** *Ibid.* 3 Apr. 30/3 There also seems to be a direct cytotoxic effect on the malignant cells. **1902** *Science* 2 May 697/2 In that they are destructive for the specific cells through which they have been produced, they are termed '*cytotoxins'. **1915** *Practitioner* Jan. 171 (*title*) Pituitary insufficiency and a pituitary antiserum or cytotoxin. **1964** M. HARRIS *Cell Culture & Somatic Variation* viii. 462 The possiblity that cytotoxins and hemagglutins may be actually the same isoantibodies, demonstrated merely by two different techniques. **1901** G. N. CALKINS *Protozoa* 217 The phenomena of *cytotrophy, or the mutual attraction of two or more cells. **1909** *Cent. Dict.* Suppl., *Cytotropism. **1938** J. R. CARPENTER *Ecol. Gloss.* 76 *Cytotropism*, the coming together of cells of a frog's eggs in stage of early cleavage when artificially broken apart. **1885** RAY LANKESTER in *Encycl. Brit.* XIX. 852 The falciform young..penetrates a cell of some tissue of its host and there undergoes the first stages of its growth (hence called *Cytozoa*). **1927** HALDANE & HUXLEY *Anim. Biol.* viii. 166 A waxy substance called *cytozyme produced by the breaking-up of cells. **1958** HARTMANN & GUENTHER tr. *Morawitz's Chem. Blood Coagulation* iv. 68 Fuld called the active 'zymoplastic agent' of the cells 'cytozyme', while I have referred to it as 'thrombokinase'.

cytoblast ('saɪtəʊblɑːst, -æ-). *Biol.* [mod. f. (by Schleiden) CYTO- + -BLAST germ. F. *cytoblaste.*] The protoplasmic nucleus of a cell, regarded as the germinal spot from which its development proceeds.

A term introduced by Schleiden (*a* 1840) on the hypothesis that it was the germ from which the cell springs.

1842 BALY tr. *Müller's Physiol.* I. 47 In some cases the cytoblasts seem to be permanent. **1870** BENTLEY *Bot.* 26 Almost all young cells contain one or more bodies called Nuclei or Cytoblasts.

cytoblastema (saɪtəʊblæ'stiːmə). *Biol.* [f. as prec. (by Schleiden) + BLASTEMA protoplasm. F. *cytoblastème.*] A name for the protoplasm from which the cell is produced.

1842 BALY tr. *Müller's Physiol.* II. 1643 Schwann has observed their development in the exterior of other cells in a structureless substance, the cytoblastema. **1882** GILBURT in *Jrnl. Quekett Microsc. Club* Ser. II. No. I. 31 The substance in which the cells arose was named cell-germinating material or cytoblastema.

Hence **cytobla'stemal, cytobla'stematous, cytobla'stemic, cytobla'stemous** *adjs.*

1859 TODD *Cycl. Anat.* V. 770 Cytoblastemal formations.

cytochrome ('saɪtəʊkrəʊm). [f. CYTO- + Gr. χρῶμα colour.] **1.** (See quot.)

1900 DORLAND *Med. Dict.*, *Cytochrome*, a nerve-cell having an ill-developed cell-body, in which the stained nucleus appears to be completely surrounded, and does not exceed in size the nucleus of a neuroglia-cell or a leukocyte.

2. Any of several closely related compounds, present in the cells of most aerobic organisms, which play an important part in cell respiration and consist of an iron-containing porphyrin attached to a protein; together they constitute the *cytochrome system*.

1925 D. KEILIN in *Proc. R. Soc.* B. XCVIII. 314 There is ample evidence that this pigment is not a simple compound, but a complex formed of three distinct haemochromogen compounds, the nature of which is not yet completely elucidated. I propose therefore to describe it under the name of *Cytochrome*, signifying merely 'cellular pigment'. **1948** *New Biol.* V. 126 Oxygen of the atmosphere enters the metabolism of the cell by combining with cytochrome, which then hands it on to other substances. **1953** FRUTON & SIMMONDS *Gen. Biochem.* xiv. 339 Cytochrome a_1 and a_2 were observed spectroscopically in certain bacteria that lack cytochrome a. **1957** *Endeavour* Oct. 196/1 [Lundegårdh's] suggestion.. was that the cytochrome system, which carries electrons from the substrates of the respiration system to molecular oxygen at the surface of the cell, might function as a carrier of anions towards the centre of the cell. **1965** BELL & COOMBE tr. *Strasburger's Textbk. Bot.* (new ed.) II. i. 282 An electron is transferred from the hydrogen to the cytochrome *c*, making its trivalent iron again divalent. **1969** *Times* 29 Apr. 13/1 Human cytochrome C is identical to the equivalent molecule in chimpanzees in all of its 104 units. **1970** AMBROSE & EASTY *Cell Biol.* vii. 228 Chlorophyll, haemoglobin, and the cytochromes all contain a common cyclic structure, called a porphyrin. **1970** *New Scientist* 16 July 119/1 Cytochrome c is a key molecule in the final stages of the 'burning' of foodstuffs for the provision of energy in living cells.

cytode ('saɪtəʊd). *Biol.* [f. as CYTOBLASTEMA with ending -ODE[1], repr. Gr. -ωδης, -οειδης, -like, -form.]

1. A microscopic non-nucleated unicellular mass of protoplasm, the lowest form in which life is exhibited. (A term proposed by Haeckel in 1866.)

1879 tr. *Haeckel's Evol. Man* I. vi. 130 Cytods: living, independent existences which consist merely of an atom of plasm. **1882** GILBURT in *Jrnl. Quekett Microsc. Club* Ser. II. No. I. 21 A cell is a little mass of protoplasm, inside which lies a nucleus; while a cytode is a little mass of protoplasm without a nucleus.

2. 'Also applied to the lymph and lymphoid cells; called also *Leucocytes*' (*Syd. Soc. Lex.*).

cytogenetics (saɪtəʊdʒɪ'nɛtɪks), *sb. pl. Biol.* [f. CYTO- + *genetics* (s.v. GENETIC *sb.*).] The study of cytology and genetics in relation to each other; *esp.* the study of the behaviour and properties of chromosomes as the constituents of cells that determine the hereditary properties of an organism. So **cytoge'netic, cytoge'netical** *adjs.*, of or pertaining to cytogenetics; **cytoge'netically** *adv.*; **cytoge'neticist**, one who studies or pursues cytogenetics.

1931 E. B. BABCOCK in *Amer. Nat.* LXV. 5 (*heading*) Cytogenetics and the species concept. *Ibid.* 7 Many such forms have been described as species and their hybrid nature has been discovered later by cytogenetic investigation. **1946** *Nature* 5 Oct. 461/2 The cell types of explanted tissues are cytogenetically fixed: they breed true to histological type. **1951** M. J. D. WHITE in L. C. Dunn *Genetics in 20th Cent.* xvi. 362 The cytogenetical investigations of the future. **1957** *New Biol.* XXIV. 31 To the cyto-geneticist the foraminifera present a range of material.. rivalling the ciliates in diversity. **1960** *Times* 1 July 2/4 Cytogeneticist required for work in a clinical Cytogenetics group. **1970** *Watsonia* VIII. 1 Papers on the cytogenetics and experimental taxonomy of British plants. **1970** *Nature* 20 June 1177/2 Twenty infants ..in whom the diagnosis of Down's syndrome had been confirmed cytogenetically were studied. *Ibid.* 19 Sept. 1271/1 During the past decade extensive cytogenetical studies have been carried out on man's normal chromosomes and chromosome variants.

cytoid ('saɪtɔɪd), *a. Biol.* [f. as CYTODE + -OID.] Of the nature of a cell; cell-like. Also *sb.*

1870 ROLLESTON *Anim. Life* Introd. 17 *note*, No morphological unit, nor even any cell-like or 'cytoid' body, can have been at work. *Ibid.* 18 Chauveau's experiments.. shew that in the absence, if not of certain animal cells, still of certain animal 'cytoids' or 'leucocytes', the vaccine poison is inoperative. **1882** *Syd. Soc. Lex.*, *Cytoid corpuscles*, Henle's term for Leucocytes.

cytokinin (saɪtəʊ'kaɪnɪn). *Biochem.* [f. CYTO- + KININ.] Any of numerous compounds which are present as growth regulators in higher plants and which promote cell division, inhibit ageing, and act with auxins to control the growth and development of the plant.

1965 E. MAEDA in *Plant & Cell Physiol.* VI. 653 (*heading*) Inhibition of lamina inclination by cytokinin in excised rice leaves. **1966** *Science* CLII. 726/3 Cytokinins occur in seeds, and they have a role in early stages of embryo growth and germination. **1968** *New Scientist* 5 Sept. 503/1 The cytokinins.. are necessary for leaves to remain green and healthy. **1970** STREET & ÖPIK *Physiol. Flowering Plants* xi. 232 The sepals (and sometimes also the petals) synthesize auxin, gibberellin and cytokinin and export these hormones to the developing fruit.

cytole, cytrin, -yn(e, -on: see CIT-.

cytology (saɪ'tɒlədʒɪ). *Biol.* [f. CYTO- + -LOGY.] The study of the cells of organisms; ***exfoliative cytology***, the examination of cells that have been shed by an internal or external surface of the body as a means of detecting and identifying any tumours that may be present.

1889 *Athenæum* 4 May 571/2 The questions of variation, heredity, cytology, &c. **1911** *Encycl. Brit.* XXI. 765/1 The elementary unit of plant structure.. is the cell... Upon our knowledge of its minute structure or cytology, combined with a study of its physiological activities, depends the ultimate solution of all the important problems of nutrition, ..variation, sex and reproduction. **1928** E. B. WILSON *Cell* (ed. 3) 17 The present work has been written by a student of embryology and cytology, with especial reference to the cell considered as the physical basis of heredity and development. **1949** *Ann. Internal Med.* XXXI. 661 (*heading*) A survey of the actualities and potentialities of exfoliative cytology in cancer diagnosis. **1952** C. P. BLACKER *Eugenics* x. 234 The second province of science (cytology) on which genetics is founded is concerned with the internal structure of the cell, especially of its nucleus. **1970** PASSMORE & ROBSON *Compan. Med. Stud.* II. xxviii. 9/1 While exfoliative cytology is a useful screening technique, a definitive diagnosis should be confirmed by more reliable means, such as biopsy, whenever possible.

Hence **cyto'logic** (chiefly *U.S.*), **-'logical** *adjs.*, of or pertaining to cytology; also, in or on cells; **cyto'logically** *adv.*, from the point of view of cytology; **cy'tologist**, one who studies cells.

1895 *Ann. Bot.* IX. 505 Boveri and with him many other cytologists believe that they [*sc.* the centrosomes] do actively direct and control the process of nuclear division. **1896** E. B. WILSON *Cell* ii. 70 A consideration of the forces at work in mitotic division.. leads us into one of the most debatable fields of cytological inquiry. **1908** *Practitioner* Apr. 525 The infected region.. should be bacteriologically and cytologically examined. **1922** R. C. PUNNETT *Mendelism* (ed. 6) 116 The cytologists have not provided us with any evidence of sex-chromosomes in plants. **1942** *Jrnl. Technical Methods* XXII. 75 Cytologic studies with the electron microscope. **1952** G. H. BOURNE *Cytol. & Cell Physiol.* (ed. 2) ix. 406 Apart from their capacity to induce malignancy, these agents have one cytological action in common. They are all capable of bringing about aberrations of mitosis. **1952** *Proc. Soc. Exper. Biol. & Med.* LXXIX. 252 (*heading*) Cytologic changes in rat adenohypophysis following administration of adrenocorticotrophin or cortisone. **1970** *Nature* 12 Sept. 1109/2 They are characterized cytologically by the presence of nucleoli of unequal size in most cells.

cytosine ('saɪtəʊsaɪn, -iːn). *Biochem.* [ad. G. *cytosin* (A. Kossel and A. Neumann 1894, in *Ber. d. Deut. Chem. Ges.* XXVII. II. 2219), f. CYT(O- + -OS(E[2] + -INE[5].] A crystalline pyrimidine base, $C_4H_5N_3O$, which is one of the constituents of nucleic acids and occurs in double-stranded DNA paired with the purine base guanine.

1894 *Jrnl. Chem. Soc.* LXVI. I. 631 Hydrolysis of nucleïc acids... Cytosine, $C_{21}H_{30}N_{16}O_4 + 5H_2O$, is precipitated. **1954** *New Biol.* XVI. 15 In desoxyribose nucleic acid the purine is either adenine or guanine, the pyrimidine either cytosine or thymine. **1955** *Sci. Amer.* Oct. 70/3 DNA is a long-chain molecule constructed from four comparatively simple chemical units: adenine, thymine, guanine and cytosine. **1969** *Times* 8 Dec. 12/2 One possibility is that the cytosine arabinoside.. destroys the normal cells in bone marrow.

cytotaxonomy (ˌsaɪtəʊtæk'sɒnəmɪ). *Biol.* [f. CYTO(LOGY + TAXONOMY.] **a.** Taxonomic classification of organisms using evidence from cytological investigation, esp. studies of chromosomes. **b.** The description of a particular organism or group of organisms, using this method. Hence **ˌcytotaxo'nomic** *a.*, **ˌcytota'xonomist**.

1930 *Biol. Abstr.* IV. Index, Cytotaxonomy. **1937** *Amer. Jrnl. Bot.* XXIV. 126/1 The cyto-taxonomy of section Telephium of *Sedum* is discussed in the present paper. **1942** *K. Fysiogr. Sällsk. Lund Forhändl.* XII. 58 (*title*) Cytotaxonomic studies on boreal plants. **1954** A. LÖVE in *Rapp. 8me Congr. Int. Bot.* IX/X. 61 Cytotaxonomists.. are able to deduce considerable understanding of the relationship of genera and even families from the study of chromosomes themselves. *Ibid.* 66 Cytotaxonomy is a very young branch of science, and its methods are still in a state of rapid development. **1964** DAVIS & HEYWOOD *Princ. Angiosperm Taxon.* vi. 193 Cytotaxonomy is the discipline which seeks to study variation and explain variational discontinuities and relationships in terms of cytology. **1971** *Watsonia* VIII. 286 A cytotaxonomic study of the collective species *Lamiastrum galeobdolon* in England and Wales showed two subspecies with different ploidy levels.

cytte, obs. f. CITY; var. SITE *Obs.*, sorrow.

cyttenere, var. of CITINER *Obs.*, citizen.

cyttern, obs. form of *cittern*, CITHERN.

cyttyn, cytuat, obs. ff. SIT, SITUATE.

‖**cytula** ('sɪtjʊlə). *Biol.* [mod.L., dim. f. CYTE, Gr. κύτος taken as = cell.] The parent cell of an organism; an impregnated ovum.

1879 tr. *Haeckel's Evol. Man* II. xvi. 55 After the cytula has originated, by the re-formation of a cell-kernel, from the morula, the parent-cell breaks up, by repeated division, into numerous cells.

Hence **'cytuloplasm**, the protoplasmic substance of a cytula.

cyul, cyule. Modern literary adaptations of *cyula*, latinized form in Gildas and Nennius of OE. *céol, ciol:—ciul*, KEEL, boat, sailing vessel.

[*c* **525** GILDAS *De Excidio Brit.* xxiii, Tribus, ut lingua ejus [gentis] exprimitur cyulis, nostra lingua longis navibus. *c* **620** NENNIUS *Eulog. Brit.* xxviii, Tres chiulæ.. in quibus erant Hors et Hengist. Cf. *OE. Chron.* (Laud MS.) an. 449 Hi þa coman on þrim ceolum hider to Brytene.] **1610** HOLLAND *Camden's Brit.* (1637) 128 (D.) Embarqu'd in forty cyules or pinnaces, and sailing about the Picts' coasts. *Ibid.* II. 66 (D.) In every ciule thirtie wives. **1876** SKENE *Celtic Scot.* I. I. iii. 146 Three cyuls came from Germany.

cyve, obs. form of CHIVE, SIEVE.

cyy-: see SI-.

cyyn: see SIE *v. Obs.*

‖**czako**, [Polish spelling of Magyar *csáko* = ('tʃɑko).] = CHACO, SHAKO.

1891 *Daily News* 26 Dec. 3/7 From the sides of the cart dangled their swords and czakos.

czar (tsɑː(r)) [Russ. *tsar'*], formerly the usual spelling of TSAR, q.v. for etymology and history.

czarate: see TSARATE.

czardas: see CSARDAS.

czardom: see TSARDOM.

czarevitch, czarewich: see TSAREVICH.

czarevna: see TSAREVNA.

czarian: see TSARIAN *a.*

czaric: see TSARIC *a.*

czaricide: see TSARICIDE.

†**'czarin.** *Obs.* [a. Germ. *czarin, zarin*; f. *czar, zar*, with the German suffix *-in* of *kaiserin, königin, fürstin*, etc.] = CZARINA, CZARITZA.

1716 *Long. Gaz.* No. 5497/2 The Czarin.. intends.. to follow the Czar to Holland.

czarina: see TSARINA.

czarish: see TSARISH *a.*

czarism: see TSARISM.

czaritza: see TSARITSA.

czarship: see TSARSHIP .

Czech, Czekh (tʃɛk, tʃɛx), *sb.* and *a.* Also **Tshekh.** [Boh. *Čech*, Pol. *Czech.*] The native name of the Bohemian people; Bohemian; the language of this people. Also = CZECHOSLOVAKIAN *sb.* and *a.* Hence **'Czechian, 'Czechic, 'Czechish** *adjs.*

1841 PRICHARD *Phys. Hist. Mankind* (ed. 3) III. 416 The Moravians are nearly akin to the Tschechi or Bohemians. **1850** LATHAM *Varieties of Man* 539 Native name Tshekh (Czech). **1852** —— *Ethnol. Europe* 241 Both populations are Tshekh speaking the Tshekh language. **1866** ENGEL *Nat. Mus.* vii. 265 The national dances of the Czechs. **1879** *Encycl. Brit.* VIII. 701/2 Czech, or Tsekh, is the national language of Bohemia, and is also largely spoken in Moravia and north-western Hungary. **1883** *Nation* XXXVI. 546 To reunite.. Bohemia, Moravia, and Austrian Silesia into one Czechic realm. **1884** *Brit. & For. Evang. Rev.* Oct. 618 Church historians both German and Czechish. **1938** *Times* 24 May 12/5 My figure of 14,000 Czechs in Germany, which includes not only Czech-speakers but also bilinguals, does not refer to the small Czech-speaking proportion of the 186,000 Czechoslovak nationals resident in Germany. *Ibid.* 4 Oct. 7/1 Guarantees to the Czechs... His Majesty's Government would be prepared.. to join in an international guarantee of the new boundaries of Czechoslovakia. **1957**

Encycl. Brit. VI. 951/2 The native home of the Czechs today lies in the Czechoslovak republic..in the western parts of which..they are the dominating and almost the sole population.

Czechize ('tʃɛkaɪz), *v.* [f. CZECH + -IZE.] *trans.* To make Czech in character, language, etc. So **Czechi'zation.**

1920 *Glasgow Herald* 21 Sept. 8 If Magyarisation was bad, Czechisation is little better. **1927** *Contemp. Rev.* Feb. 173 Efforts to 'Czechise' place-names and to impose the Czech language. **1938** *Times* 26 Aug. 10/1 Increasing Czechization of industries and railways. **1941** A. J. P. TAYLOR *Habsburg Monarchy* xi. 179 Ruthenes and Slovaks can be polonised and magyarised—but *Germans* can't be czechised.

Czechoslovak (tʃɛkəʊ'sləʊvæk), *sb.* and *a.*

A. *sb.* A native or inhabitant of Czechoslovakia. **B.** *adj.* Of or pertaining to Czechoslovakia or its inhabitants.

1917 L. B. NAMIER *(title)* The Czecho-Slovaks. An oppressed nationality. **1920** POKORNÝ & SELVER *(title)* The Czechoslovak Republic, its economical, industrial and cultural resources. **1929** *(title)* An anthology of Czechoslovak literature, selected and translated..by P. Selver. **1938, 1957** [see CZECH *sb.* and *a.*].

Czechoslovakian (tʃɛkəʊsləʊ'vækɪən), *sb.* and *a.* = prec. Also, the language of this people.

1920 *Glasgow Herald* 7 Oct. 5 The efforts made by the Czechoslovakian Government towards the furtherance of peace. *Ibid.*, The debt of gratitude of Czechoslovakians towards the Allies. **1930** A. BENNETT *Imperial Palace* lxxi. 600 While they spoke in English they were thinking in French..or Czecho-Slovakian. **1952** E. F. DAVIES *Illyrian Venture* xi. 218 This was Checko, a big, good-looking Czechoslovakian pilot in the R.A.F.

D

D (diː), the fourth letter of the Roman alphabet, corresponding in position and power to the Phœnician and Hebrew *Daleth*, and Greek *Delta*, *Δ*, whence also its form was derived by rounding one angle of the triangular form. It represents the sonant dental mute, or point-voice stop consonant, which in English is alveolar rather than dental. The plural has been written D's, Ds, de's.

The phonetic value of D in English is constant, except that in past participles the earlier full spelling *-ed* is retained where the pronunciation after a breath-consonant is now *t*, as in *looked, dipped, fished, passed*. The spelling *-ed* is now even extended to words in which OE. had *t*, as in *wished, puffed, kissed*, OE. *wyscte, pyfte, cyste*.

c **1000** ÆLFRIC *Gram.* iii. (Z.) 6 *B, c, d, g, p, t*, ȝeendiað on *e*. **1673** WYCHERLEY *Gentl. Dancing-Master* v. i, His desperate deadly daunting dagger:—there are your d's for you! **1726** LEONI *Alberti's Archit.* I. 67b, The Walls..of Memphis [were] built in the shape of a D. **1879** MISS BRADDON *Vixen* III. 168 This..must end in darkness, desolation, despair—everything dreadful beginning with *d*.

2. a. Used in reference to the shape of the letter, as ***D block, D-front, D link, D trap, D valve***, etc.; ***D-shaped, D-fronted*** adjs. See also DEE.

1794 *Rigging & Seamanship* I. 156 *D-Blocks* are lumps of oak in the shape of a D..bolted to the ship's side, in the channels. **1827** FAREY *Steam Eng.* 707 Sliding valves.. called D valves. **1849** E. E. NAPIER *Excurs. S. Africa* I. 161 The saddle..should be abundantly studded..with iron loops: or as they are—from their shape—termed in Colonial phraseology, D's. [See DEE *sb.*] *Ibid.* 163 Append to one of the D's of the said saddle, a leathern bottle. **1883** W. S. GRESLEY *Gloss. Coal-m.* 72 *D link*, a flat iron bar attached to chains, and suspended from a hemp rope to a windlass at surface. It is a loop in which one man is lowered and raised in an engine-pit. **1890** W. J. GORDON *Foundry* 135 A closed crucible with a D-shaped opening in one of its sides. **1892** T. B. F. EMERSON *Epid. Pneumonia* 11 The catch-pit was covered in by a D trap. **1895** *Westm. Gaz.* 22 Nov. 5/3 D-shaped and oval tubes. **1908** *Ibid.* 16 Nov. 4/2 A D-front limousine. *Ibid.* 19 Nov. 5/2 A 'D'-fronted landaulette.

b. *Billiards*, etc. A semi-circle marked on the baulk side of the baulk-line from within which a player must strike the cue-ball when in hand; the area bounded by this semi-circle.

1873 J. BENNETT *Billiards* ii. 18 The diameter of the D varies from 21 in. on championship tables to 23 in. on ordinary tables. **1904** J. P. MANNOCK *Billiards Expounded* I. ii. 53 What I want you to do is, following your losing hazard in the corner pocket, to then take your ball to the D, and play in again off the red from there. ? **1968** *Billiards & Snooker* ('Know the Game' Ser.) 12/1 A player, whenever 'in hand' ..must play out of the 'D' from some point within it. **1981** G. BRANDRETH *Everyman's Indoor Games* 240 On the baulk line there is a semi-circle known as the 'D'.

3. Used euphemistically for *damn* (often printed d——), etc. Cf. DEE *v.*

1861 DICKENS *Gt. Expect.* xi, He flung out in his violent way, and said, with a D, 'Then do as you like'. **1877** GILBERT *Com. Opera, H.M.S. Pinafore* 1, Though 'bother it' I may Occasionally say, I never use a big, big D——.

II. 1. a. Used like the other letters of the alphabet to denote serial order, with the value of *fourth*; applied, *e.g.*, to the fourth quire or sheet of a book, a group or section in classification, etc.

1886 *Oxford Univ. Statutes* (1890) 109 The examination in the above-mentioned Group D shall be under the direction of the Board of the Faculty of Theology.

b. In typical or hypothetical examples of any argumentation, D is put for a fourth person or thing. (Cf. A, II. 4.)

1858 KINGSLEY *Let. to J. Ludlow* in *Life* xvii. (1879) II. 78 How worthless opinions of the Press are. For if A, B, C, D, flatly contradict each other, one or more must be wrong, eh? **1864** BOWEN *Logic* 208 If A is B, C is D. **1887** *Times* (Weekly Ed.) 21 Oct. 3/2 This or that understanding between Mr. A, Mr. B, Mr. C, and Mr. D.

c. ***D-layer, -region***: the lowest stratum of the ionosphere, occurring between 25 and 50 miles above the earth's surface, below the Heaviside or E-layer.

1930 APPLETON & RATCLIFFE in *Proc. R. Soc.* A. CXXVIII. 155 We therefore attribute the result of the small variation of the reflection coefficient with distance, to the influence of an absorbing zone (D region) of ionisation situated below the region (E region) in which the main bending takes place. *Ibid.*, Rays which travel to the more distant receiving stations have a longer path through the D region. **1935** *Nature* 8 June 953/2 Besides these two main regions [F and E], the existence of a so-called D or absorbing layer has been suggested. *Ibid.*, The appearance of echoes from the D layer is closely connected with the weakening of echoes from the E layer. **1955** *Sci. Amer.* Sept. 128/2 The lowest stratum of the ionosphere is called the D layer. Its electron density has not been measured accurately but is known to be low, because the layer does not reflect radio waves of one megacycle per second or higher frequency. **1968** G. M. B. DOBSON *Explor. Atmos.* (ed. 2) viii. 151 These radio waves will be absorbed as they come down through the *D* region.

2. *spec.* in *Music*. The name of the second note of the 'natural' major scale. (In Italy and France called *re.*) Also, the scale or key which has that note for its tonic.

1596 SHAKS. *Tam. Shr.* III. i. 77 *D sol re*, one Cliffe, two notes haue I. **1880** GROVE *Dict. Mus.* II. 269/2 A Concerto of Bach in D minor.

3. In *Algebra*: see A, II. 5. In the higher mathematics, *d* is the sign of differentiation, and *D* of derivation; *D* is also used to denote the deficiency of a curve.

1852 SALMON *Higher Plane Curves* ii. (1879) 30 We call the deficiency of a curve the number D, by which its number of double points is short of the maximum. **1873** B. WILLIAMSON *Diff. Calc.* (ed. 2) §5 When the increment is supposed infinitely small, it is called a *differential*, and represented by *dx*.

4. ***D notice***, short for *Defence notice* (see quot. 1967). Hence ***D list***, a list of D notices currently in force.

The Services, Press and Broadcasting Committee was set up in 1912 as the 'Admiralty, War Office and Press Committee'. Its main function is to give guidance to the press, etc., about matters which, in the interests of national security, should not be publicly disclosed.

1940 GRAVES & HODGE *Long Week-End* xxvi. 450 The Prime Minister authorized a 'D' notice to be sent round to the newspapers, warning them not to print it. **1961** *Times* 12 May 20/4 Mr. Lipton..asked the Prime Minister which Minister was responsible for preparing the D-list... *Mr. Macmillan*—Ministerial responsibility for D-notices rests on the Minister responsible for the subject covered by the notice. **1964** 'C. E. MAINE' *Never let Up* v. 41 No names were mentioned... The story had probably been put out with a 'D' notice, which meant that editors were asked to toe the security line. **1967** *Rep. Comm. Privy Counsellors* (Cmnd. 3309) 1, A 'D' notice is a formal letter of warning or request, signed by the Secretary of a Committee known as the Services, Press and Broadcasting Committee, and addressed to newspaper editors, to news editors in sound broadcasting and television, [etc.]... Their purpose is to request a ban on the publication of certain subjects, indicated in the notices, which bear upon defence or national security.

III. Abbreviations, etc.

1. *d* stands for L. *denarius* and so for 'penny', 'pence'; as 1*d.* = one penny, £. *s. d.* = pounds, shillings and pence. †Formerly also, *d.* = one half (L. *dimidium*, also contracted *di., dim.*); D. = dollar (in *U.S.*; now $).

1387 *E.E. Wills* 2 Y be-quethe to the werkes of poulys vj s. viij d. **1488** *Nottingham Rec.* III. 269 For d. a quarter of pepur. *c* **1500** *Debate Carpenter's Tools* in Halliwell *Nugae Poet.* 15 Fore some dey he wyll vij.[d] drynke. **1588** SHAKS. *L.L.L.* III. i. 140 What's the price of this yncle? i.d. **1791** JEFFERSON in *Harper's Mag.* (1885) Mar. 535/1 A pound of tea..costs 2 D. **1866** CRUMP *Banking* 233 Pence or halfpence are not legal tender for more than 12*d.*, or farthings for more than 6*d.*

2. D, the sign for 500 in Roman numerals, as MDCCCXCIII = 1893. [Understood to be the half of CIↃ, earlier form of M = 1,000.]

(Formerly occasionally written D[c].)

1459 *Inv.* in *Paston Lett.* I 469 Summa, DCCCC lxv. unces. *Ibid.* 471 Summa, D[c] unces. **1569** GRAFTON *Chron.* 16 This Thurston obteyned the rule of the Abbey againe for the price of D. pound.

3. (Abbreviations cited here with full stops are frequently used without them.) **a. D.** = various proper names, as Daniel, David; **D**, 'in the *Complete Book*, means dead or deserted' (Adm. Smyth); **D.**, Deputy; **D.**, detective (*slang*); **D.**, Dictionary; **D.**, dimensional, as ***3-D, 3 D***, three-dimensional; **D.**, Distinguished; **D.**, District; **D.** = Doctor (in *academical degrees*, as a Lat. word following, and as English preceding, other initials), as ***D.D.*** (*Divinitatis Doctor*), Doctor of Divinity, ***LL.D.*** (*Legum Doctor*), Doctor of Laws, ***M.D.*** Doctor of Medicine, ***Ph.D.***, Doctor of Philosophy, ***D.C.L.***, Doctor of Civil Law, ***D.Lit., Lit.D.***, Doctor of Literature, ***D.Phil.***, Doctor of Philosophy, ***D.Sc.***, Doctor of Science; †**D.** = Duke; ***d*** (in dental formulæ) = deciduous, as ***dc.***, deciduous canine, ***di.***, deciduous incisor; **d.**, decent, esp. in *jolly d.*; †**d.** = degree (of angular measure); **d.**, ***d.*** (usually before a date) = died; **d** or **D** (*Anat.*) = dorsal; **d.** (in a ship's log) = drizzling; **D.A.**, Dictionary of Americanisms; **D.A.**, District Attorney (*U.S.*); **D.A.**, duck's arse (style of haircut); **D.A.A.G.**, Deputy Assistant Adjutant General; **D.A.E.**, Dictionary of American English; **D.A.G.**, Deputy Adjutant General; **D. and C.**, dilatation and curettage; **D. and P., d and p**, developing and printing; **D.A.Q.M.G.**, Deputy Assistant Quarter Master General; **db.**, decibel; **D.B.E.**, Dame Commander of the British Empire (established 1917); **DBMS**, database management system; **DBS**, direct-broadcast satellite; direct broadcasting by satellite; **D.B.S.T.**, Double British Summer Time; **dbx** [f. *db* = decibel + *x* = expander], a proprietary designation for devices aimed at increasing the dynamic range of reproduced sound; **D.C.** (*Music*) = DA CAPO (q.v.); **D.C., d.c.**, direct current; **D.C.**, District Commissioner; **D.C.M.**, Distinguished Conduct Medal (established 1862); **d.d., D.D.** (L., *dono dedit*) gave as a gift; **d.d.d., D.D.D.** (L. *dat, dicat, dedicat*) gives, devotes, and dedicates; **D.E.W.**, distant early warning; so ***Dew line*** (see quot. 1956); **D.F.**, direction(al) finding; **D.F.C., D.F.M.**, Distinguished Flying Cross, Medal (established 1918); **D.G.** = L. *Dei gratia*, by the grace of God, *Deo gratias*, thanks to God; **D.I.**, Defence Intelligence; **D.I.Y.**: see DO-IT-YOURSELF; **D.J.**, dinner jacket; **D.J.**, disc jockey; **D.L.**, Deputy Lieutenant; **D.M., D-mark**, Deutsche mark; **D.M.Z.**, demilitarized zone; **D.N.A.**, de(s)oxyribonucleic acid (q.v.); **D.N.B.**, Dictionary of National Biography; **D.O.**, District Officer; **D.O.A.**, dead on arrival (at a hospital, etc.); **DOE**, Department of the Environment; **DOM** (*slang*), dirty old man; **DOS** (*Computing*) = *disc operating system* s.v. DISC *sb.* 8f, usu. with pronunc. (dɒs); **D.O.S.T.**, Dictionary of the Older Scottish Tongue; **D.P.**, displaced person; **D.P.P.**, Director of Public Prosecutions; **D.S.C.**, Distinguished Service Cross (established 1914); **D.S.I.R.**, Department of Scientific and Industrial Research; **D.S.M.**, Distinguished Service Medal (established 1914); **D.S.O.**, Distinguished Service Order (established 1886); **D.T.**, vulgar abbrev. of *delirium tremens*; **D.T.L.** (*Shooting*), down-the-line; **D.V.** = L. *Deo volente*, God willing; **D.Z.**, dropping zone. See also (as main entries) D-DAY, D.D.T., DORA, D.T.

1949 N. SPAIN *Poison for Teacher* I. i. 19 Jolly *d. of you to ask us. **1960** N. FAIRBROTHER *Cheerful Day* II. vi. 166, I *say*. Jolly *d.* It's *exactly* what I want. **1635** J. WELLS *Sciogr.* 4 Let 60 *d. of the chorde, be equal to 30 d. of the Sines. **1869** R. P. WHITWORTH *Comic Guide to Dunedin* 27 These.. are gentlemen who give their talents and time to the paternal government for a certain modicum [*sic*] of payment, and are known as *D.s. **1879** 'T. FREDUR' *Sk. Shady Places* ii. 16, I have a few friends among the D's (detectives), who give me the job to watch a house occasionally. **1916** J. B. COOPER *Coo-oo-ee* vii. 84 'The "D" started askin' wot's wot didn't he?' asked Sam. **1938** F. D. SHARPE *Sharpe of Flying Squad* xvi. 184 They [*sc.* crooks] very often know that a man is a 'D', as they call us, without being aware of his identity, because of the fact that he happens to be on the lookout. **1953** A. COOKE in *Manch. Guardian Weekly* 27 Aug. 7/2 One big studio has done a Technicolor 3-*D movie of 'Kiss Me, Kate' which..has the effect of whisking the audience into the most privileged seat in a live theatre. **1954** *Ann. Reg.* *1953* 381 The true 3-D films, involving left and right-eyed vision and the use of polarizing spectacles. **1969** *Listener* 4 Sept. 310/1 Now imagine that instead of the 3-D flesh and blood we are all composed of, we were 2-D people entirely confined to this 2-D world, the surface of the Earth, rather like flatfish. **1606** COKE in *True & Perf. Relat.* Tjb, A Doctor of fiue *Dd, as Dissimulation, Deposing of Princes ..Destruction. **1630** WADSWORTH *Pilgr.* vii. 64 This North was created *D.D. in Paris. **1710** SACHEVERELL *Sp. on Impeach.* 51 This argues a scandalous Ignorance..in a D.D. **1870** LOWELL *Study Wind.* (1886) 62 His cousin, the *Ph.D. **1872** O. W. HOLMES *Poet Breakf.-t.* v. (1885) 119 The D.D.'s used to be the leaders. **1895** *Edin. Univ. Cal.* *1895–96* 136 Degree of *D.Phil. Graduates who have taken the degree of Master of Arts in any Scottish University..in Mental Philosophy..may offer themselves for the degree of Doctor of Philosophy (D.Phil.) in the same University after the expiry of five years. **1906** W. JOHNSTON *Graduates Univ. Aberdeen* p. xii, *D.Phil.*, Doctor of Philosophy. *Ibid.* p. xv, *Ph.D.*, Doctor of Philosophy. This form of contraction is used to distinguish the degree when obtained from a Continental University. *Cf.* D.Phil., which is the British form. **1938** *Times* 3 Feb. 14/2 A thesis on South African history, which brought him the degree of D.Phil. at Oxford. **1601** R. JOHNSON *Kingd. & Commw.* (1603) 75 Betwixt the Emp. then living and the last *D. [= Duke] great gelosies underhand. **1934** WEBSTER, *D.A., District Attorney. **1959** *Times Lit. Suppl.* 30 Jan. 55/4 The author had worked at the House of Refuge (a very tough New York reformatory) and the New York Parental School (for truants) before he went to the D.A.'s office. **1951** *Sunday Pictorial* 29 Oct. (*caption*) The *D.A. [haircut], so called because of its remarkable resemblance to a duck's rear. **1961** M. DICKENS *Heart of London* IV. 381 His hair, which was swept back in the popular D.A. hair-cut into a little drake's tail at the back. **1899** *Westm. Gaz.* 8 Nov. 2/1 Calling into consultation..the

*D.A.A.G. for Topography. **1960** *Blakiston's Illustr. Pocket Med. Dict.* (ed. 2) 187 *D and C. Short for dilatation of the cervix *and* curettage of the uterus. **1968** J. Fleming *Kill or Cure* i. 17 You ask him to perform an instant D. and C. on a young girl. **1924** *Brit. Jrnl. Photographic Alm.* 333 The appliances used in a..*D and P (developing and printing) establishment. **1971** *Interactive Bibliographic Search* 204 *DBMS are often referred to as generalized data base management systems. **1983** [see *database management system* s.v. database 2]. **1983** *Your Computer* (Austral.) July 20/1 dBase II..is the most popular micro DBMS. **1981** *Microwaves* Feb. 15/1 A direct-broadcast satellite (*DBS) will be beaming three separate channels of national programming into American homes within five years. **1984** *Listener* 8 Mar. 5/2 Japan has already launched a DBS satellite. **1986** *Stage & Television Today* 7 Aug. 17/1 ITN has put together a schedule for DBS operators. **1945** *Daily Express* 5 May 1/2 All enemy forces..have surrendered to the 21st Army Group, effective 08.00 hours *D.B.S.T. tomorrow. **1975** *Stereo Rev.* (U.S.) June 93 (Advt.), The *dbx 117 Dynamic Range Enhancer Noise Reduction Unit restores up to 20 db of the dynamics missing from records, tapes, and FM broadcasts. **1975** *Official Gaz.* (U.S. Patent Office) 11 Nov. TM178/2 DBX Inc., Waltham, Mass...*dbx* for companders and parts thereof for recording systems... First use as early as Apr. 9, 1971. **1977** *Rolling Stone* 24 Mar. 79/2 Basically, the dbx 'compander' compresses the wide dynamic range of live music to fit within the bounds of even moderately priced cassette tape decks. **1986** *Making Music* Apr. 34/4 Personal Multitrack Recorder..offers..switchable dbx over fixed Dolby B noise reduction. **1898** E. J. Houston *Electr. Words* (ed. 4) 735/1 *D.C., a contraction for direct current. **1924** *Times Trade & Engin. Suppl.* 29 Nov. 249/1 Recent developments at the Treforest power station included the installation of the Highfield transverter apparatus, enabling the transmission of d.c. at a high pressure over long distances. **1960** *Oxf. Univ. Gaz.* 19 Feb 743/1 A variety of other samples, soils, British multiple coin-moulds, and Roman pewter, was also analysed by the d.c. arc method. *a* **1912** W. T. Rogers *Dict. Abbrev.* (1913) 53/1 **D.C.*, District Commissioner. **1950** 'N. Shute' *Town like Alice* ii. 39 The truck halted at the D.C.'s office and the subaltern went inside. **1914** *Daily Express* 10 Nov. 6/3 Our fellows were extraordinarily brave, and I think several of them should get the *D.C.M. **1955** *D.E.W. [see distant *a.* 8]. **1956** W. A. Heflin *U.S. Air Force Dict.* 165/1 *Dew line*, a line of radar stations at about the 70th parallel on the North American continent, financed by the American government but undertaken in cooperation with the Canadian government. **1957** P. Frank *Seven Days to Never* ii. 53 The DEW line—the Distant Early Warning radar and interceptor net stretching from Alaska to Greenland. **1920** *Year Bk. Wireless Telegr.* 946 If the ship is equipped with *D.F. apparatus every wireless station becomes a beacon on which a bearing can be taken. **1940** C. Gardner *A.A.S.F.* 66 They'd managed to get Fécamp radio station shut down, so that German aircraft could no longer take D.F. bearings from it. **1919** *London Gaz.* 5 Dec. 15050/1 It is ordained that the award of the Distinguished Flying Cross shall entitle the recipient to have the initials *D.F.C. appended to his name. *Ibid.*, The award of the Distinguished Flying Medal shall entitle the recipient to have the initials *D.F.M. appended to his name. *a* **1866** Keble *Lett. Spir. Counsel* (1870) 186 My dear wife (*D.G.) bore up well through the nursing. **1964** *Observer* 12 July 36/6 According to the *Security Gazette*, the Secret Service, MI5, is now known as *DI5. **1966** J. Porter *Sour Cream* ii. 20 We had several lectures from a languid D.I.5 man. **1967** J. Gardner *Madrigal* viii. 230 This Madrigal was young, slim and immaculate in a smoke-grey *DJ with black silk lapels. **1961** A. Berkman *Singers' Gloss. Show Business Jargon* 19 *D.J.*,..disk jockey. **1965** *Daily Tel.* 19 July 17/4 The BBC is plainly fascinated by the phenomenon of the disc jockey, now abbreviated to DJ. **1960** *Amer. Speech* XXXV. 261 Some thousands of American troops defending the *DMZ or Demilitarized Zone between North and South Korea. **1968** *Globe & Mail* (Toronto) 17 Feb. 4/3 The appearance of Communist tanks along the eastern end of the DMZ above Con Thien. **1903** E. Gosse *Let.* 15 Jan. in E.E. Charteris *Life & Lett.* (1931) xix. 287 To see if anything has been overlooked by the **D.N.B.* **1930** *N. & Q.* 11 Oct. 257/2 Corrigendum for the D.N.B. **1954** G. Durrell *Bafut Beagles* iii. 60 Sometimes I get palaver with the *D.O., an' dat de tire me most of all. **1958** *Times* 6 Sept. 8/6 Even in these progressive times when authority is fast being transferred into African hands, the D.O., often under a new name and guise, and with new functions, may still be the administrative Jack-of-all-Trades, still tour his District, and still review cases in the Native Courts. **1958** T. Flint *Emergency Treatment* (ed. 2) 9 Cases in which a spark of life is suspected..should not be classified as '*D.O.A.'. **1972** *Times* 12 Apr. p. v, The *DOE—as it has come to be called—swallowed..three other independent and quite powerful ministries: Transport, Public Building and Works and Housing and Local Government. **1959** W. Camp *Ruling Passion* xii. 85 Poor Shirley, she thought, Harry is going to become a prize *D.O.M. **1972** B. Rodgers *Queens' Vernacular* 64 DOMs should know better than to come to the tubs and fuck it up for the rest of us. **1967**, etc. *DOS [see *disc operating system* s.v. disc sb. 8f]. **1977** *Chicago Tribune* 2 Oct. XII. 49/8 (Advt.), Our modest size EDP department presently working on IBM DOS system, is scheduled to grow substantially. **1984** Gore & Stubbe *Computers & Information Syst.* (ed. 2) viii. 173 An example of a widely used DOS is the CP/M operating system. **1986** M. L. Harris *Introd. Data Processing* (ed. 3) ix. 199 Placing DOS on a floppy disk rather than in ROM means that it can be updated quite easily without having to make physical changes to the computer. **1945** *Picture Post* 15 Sept. 18, I saw an exercise in the registration of *D.P.s. **1942** Partridge *Dict. Abbrev.* 34/2 **D.P.P.*, Director of Public Prosecutions. **1958** *Spectator* 27 June 827/1 What instruction, if any, I would give to the DPP should Archbishop Makarios visit this country. **1970** *It* 12–25 Feb. 19/1 With the large increase in crimes of violence and offences against property the time of the police and the DPP would have been better employed, in my submission, in those directions. **1917** *Flying* 19 Sept. 140/2 The first co-operative Research Association to be established under the auspices of the *D.S.I.R. will probably be for cotton. **1964** *Guardian* 29 July 14/1 (*heading*) Tories plan a science shake-up. DSIR to disappear. **1887** *Times* 21 May 15/3 Brevet Major Archibald Hunter, *D.S.O., from Supernumerary Captain, to be Captain. **1901** 'M. Gray' *Four-Leaved Clover* i, He's got a D.S.O. You've got to deserve a D.S.O., mind you, before you get it. *a* **1917** E. A. Mackintosh *War, the Liberator* (1918) 100 If you want a D.S.O. Or a small M.C. or so Don't go crawling rashly out When there's nobody about. **1930** *N. & Q.* 4 Oct. 245/2 There was a good sprinkling of D.S.O.'s and O.B.E.'s. **1954** *Shooting Times* 15 Jan. 41/3 Three Counties *D.T.L. Championship. **1972** *Ibid.* 27 May 9/1 Down-the-Line shooters take some stick, these days. But the average DTL competitor seems to take a greater pride in his appearance than do many sporting shooters. **1843** C. Brontë *Let.* 1 Aug. in Mrs. Gaskell *Life C. Brontë* (1857) I. xii. 296, I will continue to stay (*D.V.) some months longer. **1873** H. Spencer *Study Sociol.* ii. 30 The 'D.V.' of a missionary-meeting placard. **1918** D.V. [see apotropaic *a.*]. **1954** X. Fielding tr. *Boulle's Bridge on River Kwai* (1956) IV. viii. 181 A second team was dropped on to a *D.Z. some distance away.

b. *d* or *D* (*Physics, Chem.*) = diffuse: originally used to designate one of the four main series in atomic spectra, but now more frequently applied to electronic orbitals, states, etc., possessing two units of angular momentum.

1890 J. R. Rydberg in *Phil. Mag.* XXIX. 335 K (D_1, 4) denotes the fourth line of the first diffuse series of the spectrum of potassium. **1922** A. Fowler *Rep. Series in Line Spectra* iii. 15 Three of the chief series were recognised..namely..Principal, Diffuse, Sharp... Rydberg's names..are conveniently abbreviated to *P,D,S.* **1955** Richtmyer & Kennard *Introd. Mod. Physics* (ed. 5) vii. 245 The use by spectroscopists of the mysterious letters *S,P,D,F*..to represent various values of *L. Ibid.*, The lowest *D* level. **1965** Phillips & Williams *Inorg. Chem.* I. iv. 102 The withdrawal of the *d* electrons from the valence shell.

c. *Particle Physics.* [See note s.v. S 15.] *d* is the symbol of the down quark (see down *a.* 5).

1964, etc. [see S 15]. **1981** D. H. Perkins in J. H. Mulvey *Nature of Matter* iv. 77 The proton is (uud) and the neutron (ddu). **1983** *Sci. Amer.* July 106/1 An alternative is for the *b* to emit a Z^0, transforming the *b* into an *s* or a *d*.

-d, formative of *pa. pple.* as in *heard, paid, dead*: see -ed *suffix*.

da (dɑː). Nursery and homely abbrev. of dada. Also *dial.*

1851 Lady Duff Gordon *Let.* in *Three Gener. Englishwomen* (1888) II. 216 Whether Da and my mother will stay at Weybridge, I know not. *Ibid.* 217 Da is gloomy, I fear 'tis his normal state. **1875** W. Alexander *Sks. Life Ain Folk* 184 Da promis't to tak' me in o' 's bosie. **1922** Joyce *Ulysses* 70 Waiting outside pubs to bring da home. **1936** 'N. Blake' *Thou Shell of Death* xiii. 232 Miss Judith grew up to be..the apple of her da's eye.

da, obs. form of daw, day, doe.

dab (dæb), *sb.*[1] In 3–4 dabbe. [f. dab *v.*[1], both being found c. 1300.]

1. a. A blow of somewhat sharp and abrupt character. **b.** A blow from a bird's beak, or with the corner or point of anything which scarcely or only slightly penetrates; a thrust as if aiming to strike or stab; an aimed blow. **c.** *dial.* A slight blow with the back of the hand or the like, a box, a slap.

1300 *K. Alis.* 2306 Philot him gaf anothir dabbe, That in the scheld the gysarme Bylefte hongyng, and eke the arme. *Ibid.* 2794 They laughte dedly dabbe. *Ibid.* 7304 Bytweone you delith hit with dabbe, And with spere, and sweordis dunt. **1706** Phillips (ed. Kersey), *Dab*..also a light blow on the Chaps, or box on the Ear. **1731** Swift *Mem. Capt. Creichton* Wks. 1768 XI. 161, I gave him a dab in the mouth with my broken sword, which very much hurt him. **1748** Smollett *Rod. Rand.* (1812) I. 69 Giving us several dabs with its beak. **1865** Dickens *Mut. Fr.* II. xi, Making two dabs at him in the air with her needle. **1875** A. R. Hope *My School-boy Fr.* 125 She made furious dabs at him. **1879** Miss Jackson *Shropsh. Word-bk.*, *Dab*, a slight blow, generally with the back of the hand. [So in *N.W. Linc.* and *Cheshire Gloss.*]

d. *fig.* (cf. *rap, poke, thrust.*)

1705 in Perry *Hist. Coll. Amer. Col. Ch.* I. 160 Here's another dab upon Gov[r] Nicholson. **1748** Richardson *Clarissa* (1811) II. xx. 140 At our alighting, I gave him another dab. **1820** *Blackw. Mag.* VI. 391 'Tis now an age..Since we have had a dab at any body.

2. A gentle blow or tap with a soft substance, which is pressed slightly on the object and then quickly withdrawn; a stroke with a dabber.

1755 in Johnson.

3. a. A flattish mass of some soft or moist substance dabbed or dropped on anything.

1749 in Doran *Mann & Manners* (1876) I. xiii. 293 Putting a large dab of hot wax under the arms. **1768–74** Tucker *Lt. Nat.* (1852) II. 596 We..garnish the rims of our dishes with dabs of chewed greens. **1779** Mad. D'Arblay *Diary* 3 Nov., How can two or three dabs of paint ever be worth such a sum as that? **1874** Mrs. H. Wood *Mast. Greylands* iii. 32 Fifteen dishes he wanted for his dinner, if he wanted one. And all of 'em dabs and messes.

b. *pl.* Fingerprints. *slang.*

1926 N. Lucas *London & its Criminals* i. 7 The finger-print system is without doubt the crooks' greatest enemy... The verifying of their 'dabs' soon brings their dossier to court. **1947** N. Marsh *Final Curtain* xvii. 263 Bailey's gone over it [*sc.* a tin] for dabs. **1957** K. Farrer *Gownsman's Gallows* xxii. 183 You'll get his photo and dabs by airmail today.

4. *fig.* Applied slightingly to (*a*) a small or trifling amount, as of money given; (*b*) a slight effort of the pen, etc.

1729 Mrs. Delany *Life & Corr.* I. 453, I had your hasty dab as you call it..your dabs are of more worth to me than folios of letters from any one else. **1735** Hervey *Mem.* II. 13, 3200*l.* ever since he was King, besides several little dabs of money. **1762** H. Walpole *Lett. H. Mann* (1833) II. 337 (D.) A new dab called *Anecdotes of Polite Literature.* **1788** Mad. D'Arblay *Lett.* 29 Jan., I actually asked for this dab of preferment.

5. a. A wet or dirty clout. **b.** A pinafore. *dial.*

1714 Swift *Hue & Cry*, Reckon with my Washerwoman; making her allow for old Shirts, Socks, Dabbs and Markees, which she bought of me. **1721** Bailey, *Dab*..a dirty clout. **1837** Thackeray *Yellowplush* i, Wet dabs of dishclouts flapped in your face. **1877** *N.W. Linc. Gloss.*, *Dab*, a child's pinafore.

6. Applied to persons: **a.** An untidy woman, a drab. **b.** A small child, a chit.

1730–6 Bailey (folio), *Dab*..also a word of Contempt for a Woman. **1797** Mrs. Bennett *Beggar Girl* (1813) I. 91 It [Betty] is such an engaging, good-hearted little dab. **1879** Miss Jackson *Shropshire Word-bk.*, *Dab*, an untidy, thriftless woman. [So *Cheshire Gloss.*] **1833** Sir F. Head *Bubbles of Brunnen*, A little bare-headed, bare-footed dab of a child. **1864** Capern *Devon Provinc.*, *Dab*, a chit.

7. See quots.

1758 Dyche *Dict.*, *Dab*..likewise a mangled piece of fat meat goes by this name. **1836** Dickens *Sk. Boz* (1877) 38 Dabs of dingy bacon.

8. *pl.* The refuse or sediment of sugar.

1858 Simmonds *Dict. Trade*, *Dabs*, refuse foots of sugar. **1881** *Daily News* 7 Sept. 3/4 Barbadoes dabs, 20s. to 21s... Grenada dabs, 17s. to 19s. 6d.

9. *Type-founding.* See quots.

1874 Knight *Dict. Mech.*, *Dab*, an impression in typemetal of a die in course of sinking. **1889** T. B. Reed (*in letter*), The common process of producing cast ornaments for printing before the introduction of electrotyping was known in English type-foundries as 'dabbing'. The original woodblock is dropped sharply into a bed of molten lead on the point of cooling. A mould or matrix of the design is thus produced. To produce replicas of the design, the operator strikes this matrix into lead. The result is a 'cast' or 'dab' in relief, which when mounted can be used to print along with type.

10. A printer's dabber.

1861 W. F. Collier *Hist. Eng. Lit.* 75 The worker of the press has found the..dabbers..unfit for use..He sits down with raw sheep-skin and carded wool, to stuff the balls and tie it round the handle of the dab.

11. *Comb.*, as ***dab-pot***; **dab cricket**, a children's pencil-and-paper game based on cricket; †**dab-stone**, a game with stones; cf. *dabbers* and *dib-stone*; **dab-wash** (*dial.*), a wash of a few small articles, as distinct from the usual household wash; hence ***dab-wash*** vb.

1938 L. MacNeice *I crossed Minch* vii. 98 While reviewing a novel, Mr. Mackenzie had played *dab cricket...He explained to me his system... Consonants mean one; vowels mean two,..a double consonant following a double consonant means that the next man is out for nought. **1946** B. Marshall *George Brown's Schooldays* 115 He was going to continue his game of dab cricket. **1876** Browning *Pacchiarotto* 410 Stick thou, Son, to paint-brush and *dab-pot! **1652** J. Donne *Ep. Ded.* in *Donne's Paradoxes*, Lelius and Scipio are presented to us as playing at *Dabstone before they fought against Hanniball. *a* **1812** Malone in Todd s.v. *Dab*, *Dab-wash. **1863** Mrs. Gaskell *Sylvia's L.* vi, Having had what is called in the district a 'dab-wash' of a few articles, forgotten on the regular day. **1881** Richardson in *Gd. Words* 51 A few clothes that had just gone through a 'dab-wash'.

¶ **12.** *dab* is frequently written instead of daub = rough mortar, clay used in plastering, esp. in ***wattle and dab*** (*daub*).

1839 Loudon *Encycl. Arch.* 840 Instead of brick nagging for partitions, cob is used for filling in the framework..This sort of work is called rab and dab. **1881** Miss Braddon *Asphodel* vi. 70 Cottages, with walls of wattle and dab.

dab (dæb), *sb.*[2] [Etymology unknown: cf. however dab *sb.*[1] 3.] A species of small flat-fish, *Pleuronectes limanda*, nearly resembling the flounder, common on the sandy parts of the British coast; also used as a 'street term for small flat fish of any kind' (*Slang Dict.*).

1577 Harrison *England* III. iii. (1878) II. 20 The plaice, the but, the turbut, dorreie, dab, &c. **1620** Venner *Via Recta* iv. 72 The Dabbe or little Plaice is of the same nature. **1778** Pennant *Tour in Wales* (1883) I. 29 Dabs visit us in November. **1851** Mayhew *Lond. Labour* I. 165 The fish fried by street dealers is known as 'plaice dabs' and 'sole dabs', which are merely plaice and soles, 'dab' being a common word for any flat fish. **1886** R. C. Leslie *Sea-painter's Log* x. 193 A dab or plaice soon getting pale-coloured when lying upon a white surface.

b. *Comb.*, as **dab-darter**, one who spears flat-fish; **dab-fish**, flat-fish.

1883 G. C. Davies *Norfolk Broads* xxvi. (1884) 203 In the deeper water the dab-darters are often hard at work..the 'dart'..is like the head of a large rake with the teeth set vertically. **1876** Robinson *Whitby Gloss.*, *Dab-fish*, all kinds of flat fish.

dab (dæb), *sb.*[3] [Appears before 1700; frequently referred to as school slang: origin unknown.

Conjectures have been offered as to its being a corruption of *adept*, and of *dapper*, but without any other evidence than appears in the general likeness and use of the words. It is possible that it is a derivative of dab *v.*]

One skilful or proficient *at* (†*of, in*) anything; an expert, an adept.

1691 *Athenian Mercury* IV. No. 3 Qu. 8 [Love is] such a Dab at his Bow and Arrows. *a* **1700** B. E. *Dict. Cant. Crew*, *Dab*, expert, exquisite in Roguery..*He is a Dab at it*, He is well vers'd in it. **1711** *Vind. Sacheverell* 83 The Dr. is charg'd with being a great Dab, as the Boys say, for he plays on Sundays. *a* **1754** Fielding *Ess. Conversation* Wks. (1840)

642 (To fetch a phrase from school..) great dabs of this kind of facetiousness. **1759** GOLDSM. *Bee* No. 1 A third [writer] is a dab at an index. **1845** THACKERAY *Punch in the East* iv, I wish to show I am a dab in history. **1874** HELPS *Soc. Press.* v. (1875) 69, I am 'a dab', as we used to say at Eton, at suggesting subjects for essays.

b. *attrib.* or *Comb.*, as ***dab hand.***

1828 *Craven Dialect*, *Dab-hand*, expert at any thing. **1870** MISS BRIDGMAN *Ro. Lynne* II. iii. 67 He was a dab hand at water-colours. [The comb. occurs in many dialect glossaries from *Lonsdale* and *Holderness* to *W. Somerset.*]

dab, *sb.*[4] *slang.* A bed.

1812 *Sporting Mag.* XXXIX. 16 Those who had been accustomed to a downy dab. **1812** J. H. VAUX *Flash Dict.*, *Dab*, a bed. **1823** W. T. MONCRIEFF *Tom & Jerry* III. iii. (Farmer), Vhen ve've had the liquor, ve'll..all go to our dabs.

dab (dæb), *v.*[1] In 4 dabben, 6 dabbe. Inflected **dabbed, dabbing.** [This and the accompanying sb. DAB[1] appear about 1300; there is nothing similar in OE.

Middle and early modern Dutch had a verb *dabben*, according to Oudemans, 'to pinch, knead, fumble, dabble': cf. Ger. *tappen* to grope, fumble (with the hands, as in the dark); but it is not clear that there is any connexion between this and the English word. Rather does the latter appear to be of independent onomatopœic origin, being, primarily, the expression of the mechanical action in question by analogous oral action, including (but only in a secondary way) the representation of the sound. Cf. DUB *v.*, which in some of its senses appears to be of kindred formation.]

I. To strike, peck, stick, etc.

1. *trans.* To strike somewhat sharply and abruptly. (The ME. sense is not quite clear.) **b.** To strike so as slightly to pierce or indent; to peck as a bird with its bill; to pick the surface of a stone (see quot. 1876); to stick or thrust. Now chiefly *Sc.* **c.** in mod. dial. To strike with a slight blow, as with the back of the hand. † ***to dab nebs***: to kiss.

a **1307** *Pol. Songs* (Camden) 192 This Frenshe come to Flaundres..The Flemmisshe hem dabbeth o the het bare. **1532** MORE *Confut. Tindale* Wks. 551/1 The pricke of the fleshe, to dabbe him in the necke. **1630** DEKKER *2nd Pt. Hon. Whore* IV. ii, Let me alone for dabbing them o' th' neck. **1730–6** BAILEY (folio), *Dab*, to cuff or bang; to slap or strike. **17..** in Jamieson *Pop. Ball. & Songs* (1806) I. 87 (Jam.) The thorn that dabs I'll cut it down, Though fair the rose may be. **1786** *Yng. Coalman's Courtship* (ed. 20) 5 You may..dab nebs wi' her now an' then. **1876** GWILT *Archit. Gloss.*, *Dabbing*, *Daubing*..working the face of a stone..with a pick-shaped tool..so as to form a series of minute holes. **1885** RUNCIMAN *Skippers & Sh.* 82 One chap dabbed his sticker through my arm here. **1887** *Cheshire Gloss.*, *Dab*, to give a slight blow to. 'Dost want dabbin i' th' maith' [= mouth].

d. *intr.* Of a bird: To peck with the bill. **e.** To aim *at* in order to strike, as in playing at marbles, or throwing a stone at a bird, etc. *Sc.*

1805 J. NICOL *Poems* I. 43 (Jam.) Weel daubit, Robin! there's some mair, Beath groats an' barley, dinna spare. **1826** WILSON *Noct. Ambr.* Wks. 1855 I. 25 Chuckies.. dabbing at daigh and drummock. *Mod. Sc.* If you go near the nest, the hen will dab at you. Which marble shall I dab at? Some boys dabbing at a cat on the roof of the shed.

2. To strike or cause to strike (usually with something soft and of broadish surface) so as to exert a slight momentary pressure, and then withdraw quickly. The object may be **a.** the brush, dabber, etc. used; **b.** the moist or sticky substance applied; **c.** the surface to which it is applied.

a. 1592 NASHE *P. Penilesse* (ed. 2) 13 b, A Painter..needs no more but wet his pencill, and dab it on their cheekes, and he shall haue vermillion and white enough. **1823** J. BADCOCK *Dom. Amusem.* 143 A common printer's ball..is now to be dabbed on the whole surface. **1863** TYNDALL *Heat* viii. §313, I dip my brush..and dab it against the paper.

b. 1562 TURNER *Herbal* II. 31 a, Laser..is dabbed about the styngynges of scorpiones with oyle well menged or tempered. **1750** E. SMITH *Compl. Housewife* 352 Dab it on with a fine rag. **1833** HT. MARTINEAU *Tale of Tyne* i. 8 One who dabs brick-clay into a mould. **1853** READE *Chr. Johnstone* 109 [It] dabbed glue on his gauzy wings.

c. 1747 WESLEY *Prim. Physic* (1762) 63 Dip a soft rag in dead small Beer, new Milk warm, and dabb each eye, a dozen times gently. **17..** S. SHARP (J.), A sore should never be wiped by drawing a piece of tow or rag over it, but only by dabbing it with fine lint. **1879** *Newspaper*, If the bleeding be too copious, dab the part with a rag wetted with creasote.

d. *spec.* in *Printing*, *Etching*, etc.: To strike or pat with a dabber for various purposes, as *e.g.* in order to spread colour evenly over a surface.

1759 MRS. DELANY *Life & Corr.* (1861) III. 573, I found one painting and another dabbing. **1799** G. SMITH *Laboratory* I. 339 The interstices may be dabbed over with the tincture of that colour which you would have for the general ground-work. **1832** G. R. PORTER *Porcelain & Gl.* 300 Holding the brush perpendicular to the glass, every part of the latter must be dabbed so that the surface will be dimmed by the oil. **1874** KNIGHT *Dict. Mech.* I. 673/1 The insinuation [in stereotyping] of the damp paper into the interstices of the letters by dabbing the back of the paper with a hair brush.

3. To set or put down with a sharp, abrupt motion (cf. to *stick down*); to throw or fling down in a rough, careless, untidy manner.

1772 G. WASHINGTON in *Mag. Amer. Hist.* May (1884) 71 They [clothes] will be..dabbed about, in every hole and corner. **1877** *Holderness Gloss.*, *Dab*, *Dab-doon*..to fling down with violence. **1884** *Chester Gloss.*, *Dab*, to set things down carelessly, not in their right place.

II. Specific senses of doubtful history, or indirect connexion with prec.

†**4.** *Fishing.* To fish by dipping the bait gently and lightly in the water; to dap, dib. *Obs.*

1676 COTTON *Angler* II. v. 295 This way of fishing we call daping, dabbing, or dibbing.

5. To dibble. *dial.*

1787 W. MARSHALL *East Norf.* Gloss., *Dabbing*, dibbling. **1847** in HALLIWELL.

6. *Type-founding.* To produce a 'dab' in the process of making matrices, etc.

1889 [see DAB *sb.*[1] 9].

†**7.** ? To deceive, jape. *Obs.*

1616 R. C. *Times' Whistle* vi. 2402 Like the parish bull he serves them still And dabbes their husbandes clean against their will.

8. A modification of DAUB *v.*, to plaster.

1577 *Ludlow Churchw. Acc.* (Camden) 164 Item, to Humfreis for dabinge the churche house..vj d. **1730** A. GORDON *Maffei's Amphith.* 272 The Steps are..dabbed over with Lime and Mortar. *Ibid.* 374 Those who in various ways transform and dab over those parts of the Building. **1855** BROWNING *Grammarian's Funeral* 72 Fancy the fabric Quite, ere you build..Ere mortar dab brick!

Hence **dabbed** (dæbd) *ppl. a.*, **'dabbing** *vbl. sb.* and *ppl. a.*

1885 *W. Rhind's Trade Circular*, A beautiful smooth ground, which..will stand the acid bath better than any dabbed ground. **1843** *Penny Cycl.* XXVII. 577/2 The wound itself does not require..washing and sponging and dabbing. **1874** KNIGHT *Dict. Mech.*, *Dabbing-machine*, the machine employed in casting large metal type.

†**dab,** *v.*[2] *Obs.* [Cf. DABBY and DABBLE.] ? To be wet and dabbled, to hang like wet clothes.

1558 PHAER *Æneid* VI. (R.), I creping held with crokid hands the mountaynes toppe, Encombrid in my clothes that dabbing down from me did droppe.

dab, *adv.* [The verb-stem or sb. used elliptically.] With a dab, or sudden contact.

1608 ARMIN *Nest Ninn.* 2 He dropt downe..as heauy as if a leaden plummet..had fallen on the earth dab. **1884** RUSKIN in *Pall Mall G.* 10 Dec. 11/1 One who sharpens his pencil point, instead of seizing his biggest brush and going dab at the mountains with splotches of colour.

dabber ('dæbə(r)). [f. DAB *v.*[1] + -ER[1].]

1. One who or that which dabs. **b.** *spec.* A rounded mass of some elastic material, enclosed in leather or silk, used to apply ink, colour, etc., evenly to a surface; employed in printing from type, wood-blocks, or engraved plates, in painting on china, etc.; in *Printing* = BALL *sb.*[1] 13. **c.** A brush used in stereotyping for pressing the damped paper into the interstices of the type, or for various purposes in gilding, photography, etc.

c **1790** *Artist's Assistant Mech. Sc.* 193 The ground..is to be laid on thinly and dabbed all over with the dabber. **1799** G. SMITH *Laboratory* II. 419 Have ready a dabber made of a round piece of white glove leather..filled with cotton, or wool, and tied close into a ball. **1821** CRAIG *Lect. Drawing* vii. 397 Taking the dabber, on which some portion of the etching ground has been left. **1854** tr. *Lamartine's Celebr. Char.* II. 333 Dabbers to spread the ink on the letters. **1870** *Eng. Mech.* 28 Jan. 487 (*Gilding*), Go over gently with a dabber [brush].

2. (See quot.)

1881 *Oxfordsh. Gloss.* Supp., *Dabbers*, a game played by children with small round flint stones. *Dabber*, a stone with which the game of Dabbers is played.

dabbity ('dæbɪtɪ). *Sc.* [f. DAB *sb.*[1] (cf. 3, 4); cf. southern dial. *dabbit* (E.D.D.), small quantity.] A chimney-piece ornament.

1923 J. A. FLEMING *Sc. Pottery* i. 28 On the East Coast of Scotland the fisherfolk are famous for their gallery of 'wallie' dogs, lions, parrots, cats, etc. The Aberdonians call them 'dabbities'. **1961** *Times* 8 Apr. 11/6 'Chimney ornaments'. To the Scottish potter they were 'dabbities'.

dabble ('dæb(ə)l), *v.* [Appears late in 16th c. Agrees in form, and in sense 2, with Du. *dabbelen*, var. of *dabben*, expl. by Plantijn as 'pattrouiller, ou patteler de mains' to dabble with the feet or hands, *met de voet int slijck dabbelen*, 'trepiner des piedz en la fange', to trample with the feet in the mud. In form Du. *dabbelen* is the frequentative of *dabben*: the relation of *dabble* and *dab* in Eng. is less clear.]

1. *trans.* To wet by splashing, as in running through a puddle or wading about in shallow water, or by pressing against wet shrubs, or the like; to move anything to and fro in water; hence to wet in a casual way; to disfigure or soil with splashes of any liquid; to bespatter, besprinkle, bedabble. Said of the personal agent, or the liquid medium.

1557 TUSSER 100 *Points Husb.* xxvii, Set bauen alone, lay the bowghes from the blockes: the drier, the les maidens dablith their dockes [skirts behind]. **1594** SHAKS. *Rich. III*, I. iv. 54 A Shadow like an Angell, with bright hayre Dabbel'd in blood. **1604** MIDDLETON *Witch* II. iii. 3 We must take heed we ride through all the puddles..that your safeguard there May be most probably dabbled. *a* **1656** USSHER *Ann.* vi. (1658) 570 The Country being woody they were daily dabled with the fall of snow from the trees. **1676** WISEMAN *Surg.* (J.), I scarified, and dabbled the wound with oil of turpentine. **1860** GEN. P. THOMPSON *Audi Alt.* III. cxxi. 66 The men who are dabbling the Queen's robe in blood. **1887** T. A. TROLLOPE *What I remember* II. v. 85, I dabbled a handkerchief in a neighbouring fountain for her to wash her streaked face.

b. *causal.*

1847 TENNYSON *Princess* III. 297 Or in the..holy secrets of this microcosm, Dabbling a shameless hand.

2. *intr.* To move (with feet or hands, or the bill) in shallow water, liquid mud, etc., so as to cause some splashing; to play about in shallow water, to paddle.

1611 COTGR., *Patouiller*..to padle, or dable in with the feet. **1626** J. PORY in Ellis *Orig. Lett.* I. 331 They..made her to dable in the durte on a foul morning from Somersett House to St. James. *a* **1661** FULLER *Worthies* (1840) III. 135 Ducklings, which..naturally delight to dabble in the water. **1789** WORDSW. *Evening Walk*, Where the duck dabbles 'mid the rustling sedge. **1821** CLARE *Vill. Minstr.* II. 118 The long wet pasture grass she dabbles through. **1858** FROUDE *Hist. Eng.* III. xvii. 488 The minister who..had stooped to dabble in these muddy waters of intrigue.

3. *fig.* To employ oneself in a dilettante way *in* (any business or pursuit) without going deeply or seriously into it; to work off and on *at*, as a matter of whim or fancy. Const. *in* (*with*, *at*, etc.).

1625 B. JONSON *Staple of N.* II. i, Let him still dabble in poetry. **1676** MARVELL *Mr. Smirke* 14 Some Youngster that had been Dabbling amongst the Socinian Writers. **1768–74** TUCKER *Lt. Nat.* (1852) I. 120 One of those sources of disputation which must not be dabbled with: we must drink deep, or had better not taste at all. **1792** T. JEFFERSON *Writ.* (1830) IV. 465 Examining how far their own members..had been dabbling in stocks. **1840** DICKENS *Old C. Shop* xxviii, It's the delight of my life to have dabbled in poetry. **1879** G. MACDONALD *P. Faber* III. i. 14 The man who dabbles at saving the world by science, education, hygeian and other economics.

†**b.** To meddle, tamper *with*; to interfere *in.*

1660 R. COKE *Justice Vind.* 7 He has bound himself up from dabling with the Grounds of Obedience and Government. *a* **1732** ATTERBURY *To Pope* (J.), You, I think, have been dabbling here and there with the text. **1776** PAINE *Com. Sense, Addr. Quakers* (1791) 80 Dabbling in matters, which the professed quietude of your principles instruct you not to meddle with. **1794** SIR F. M. EDEN in *Ld. Auckland's Corr.* (1862) III. 238 As he loves to be dabbling, he may perhaps go.

†**4.** To move up and down in a playful, trifling manner, like one dabbling in water. *Obs.*

a **1688** VILLIERS (Dk. Buckhm.) *Poems* (1775) 169 I'll dabble up and down, and take the air.

'dabble, *sb.* [f. prec. verb.] The act of dabbling; that which dabbles.

1871 R. ELLIS *Catullus* lxiii. 7 While still the gory dabble did anew the soil pollute.

'dabbled, *ppl. a.* [f. DABBLE *v.* + -ED.] Wetted by splashing; casually or irregularly wetted; stained or soiled with water, blood, mud, etc.

1591 SYLVESTER *Du Bartas* I. iv. 397 The lively Liquor God With dabbled heels hath swelling clusters trod. **1727** SWIFT *Poems, City Shower*, Rising with dabbled wings. **1887** STEVENSON *Underwoods* I. ix. 18 The maiden jewels of the rain Sit in your dabbled locks again.

'dabblement. *nonce-wd.* [See -MENT.] Dabbling (in semi-concrete sense).

1866 CARLYLE *Remin.* (1881) II. 236, I..alas, was met by a foul dabblement of paint oozing downstairs.

dabbler ('dæblə(r)). [f. DABBLE *v.* + -ER[1].]

1. One who dabbles, *esp.* in any business or pursuit.

1611 COTGR., *Patouillard*, a padler, dabler, slabberer; one that tramples with his feet in plashes of durtie water. *a* **1625** FLETCHER *Elder Bro.* II. ii, A little unbaked poetry Such as the dabblers of our time contrive. **1768–74** TUCKER *Lt. Nat.* (1852) I. 7 Your dabblers in metaphysics are the most dangerous creatures breathing. **1869** FREEMAN *Norm. Conq.* (1876) III. xi. 72 A dabbler in arts and sciences.

†**2.** (See quot.) *Obs.*

1611 COTGR., *Papefif*, the maine course; that part of the maine-sayle whereto the bonnets, or dablers be fastened.

'dabblesome, *a. nonce-wd.* [See -SOME.] Given to dabbling.

1866 BLACKMORE *Cradock Nowell* liii. (1883) 370 Dabblesome interferences with ancient institutions.

dabbling ('dæblɪŋ), *vbl. sb.* [-ING[1].] The action of the verb DABBLE; an instance or result of such action.

1677 HUBBARD *Narrative* 109 Many of the rest were sorely wounded, as appeared by the dabbling of the Bushes with blood. **1712** SWIFT *Jrnl. Stella* 19 Dec., We are full of snow and dabbling. **1856** FROUDE *Hist. Eng.* (1858) I. iv. 361 Some further paltry dabbling was also attempted with the phraseology. **1884** *Chr. Treasury* Feb. 92/1 The disconnected dabblings of..untrained forgers.

'dabbling, *ppl. a.* [-ING[2].] That dabbles.

1661 LOVELL *Hist. Anim. & Min.* 518 In dabbleing weather and autumne. **1816** J. GILCHRIST *Philos. Etym.* 178 Superficial, dabbling authors. *a* **1845** HOOD *Mermaid of Margate* xii, A scaly tail, of a dolphin's growth, In the dabbling brine did soak.

Hence **'dabblingly** *adv.*

1811 W. TAYLOR in *Monthly Rev.* LXV. 134 The first number is written by the editor, and treats dabblingly of 'dabblers'.

dabby ('dæbɪ), *a.* [f. DAB *v.*², DAB *sb.*¹ 5.] Damp, moist: (of clothes) wet and clinging to the body; flabby; flaccid.

1581 J. STUDLEY *Seneca's Medea* 131 b, When the stormy southerne winde with dankish dabby face Of hoary winter sendeth out the gushing showres apace. **1812** *Sporting Mag.* XL. 167 All very greasy, blousy, dabby, dusty, salt-watery, and so on. *a* **1825** FORBY *Voc. E. Anglia, Dabby*, moist, and somewhat adhesive; sticking to the skin like wet linen. **1844** J. T. HEWLETT *Parsons & W.* v, Your.. overalls, which hang dabby and flabby about your legs. *a* **1845** HOOD *Domestic Asides* iv, I should have loved to kiss her so,—(A flabby, dabby babby!).

dabchick ('dæbtʃɪk). Forms: α. 6 **dapchicke, dopchicken**, 6–7 **dopchick(e**; β. 7 **dip-chicke**, 9 **dibchick**; γ. 6 **dobchickin**, 7–8 **dobchick**; δ. 7–9 **dab-chick**, 8– **dabchick**. [The early forms *dap-*, *dop-chick*, with the later *dip-chick*, and synonym DOPPER, appear to connect the first part of the word with the ablaut stem *deup*, *dup-*, *dop-* of DIP, DEEP; but the forms in *dob-*, *dab-*, seem to be associated with some senses of DAB *v.*]

The Little Grebe, *Podiceps minor*, a small water-bird, found in rivers and other fresh waters, and noted for its diving; in *U.S.* the name is applied to another species of Grebe, *Podilymbus podiceps*.

α. **1575** TURBERV. *Faulconrie* 150 Small fowle, as the dapchicke, or suche like. **1583** GOLDING *Calvin on Deut.* xc. 552 The Swanne the Cormorant the pellicane, the Dopchicken the storke. **1615** CHAPMAN *Odyss.* xv. 636 She.. Shot dead the woman, who into the pump Like to a dop-chick dived. **1732** MORTIMER in *Phil. Trans.* XXXVII. 449 *Podicipes minor rostro vario*, The Pied Bill Dopchick. **1888** *W. Somerset Word-bk.*, Dapchick. (Always.)

β. **1602** CAREW *Cornwall* 35 a, The Dip-chicke (so named of his diving and littlenesse). **1827** T. ATTWOOD in C. M. Wakefield *Life* viii. (1885) 109, I am glad Bosco has got the dibchicks.

γ. **15..** *Parl. Byrdes* 88 in Hazl. *E.P.P.* III. 171 The Cote, the Dobchick, and the water Hen. **1598** FLORIO, *Piombrino* .. a bird called a kingsfisher. Some take it for a dobchickin. **1670** NARBOROUGH *Jrnl.* in *Acc. Sev. Late Voy.* I. (1694) 59 White-breasted Divers, and Dobchicks. **1678** RAY *Willughby's Ornith.* 340 The Didapper, or Dipper, or Dobchick, or small Doucker. **1766** PENNANT *Zool.* (1768) II. 397. **1796** MORSE *Amer. Geog.* I. 214 Dobchick.

δ. **1610** [see c]. **1728** POPE *Dunc.* II. 63 As when a dab-chick waddles thro' the copse, On feet and wings, and flies, and wades, and hops. **1789** G. WHITE *Selborne* (1853) II. xli. 273 Dabchicks and coots fly erect. **1870** THORNBURY *Tour Eng.* I. i. 7 Brentford again dived, to reappear suddenly, like a dab chick on the surface of history.

b. *dial.* Applied to the Moor-hen or Water-hen.

1877 *N.W. Linc. Gloss., Dab-chick*, the water-hen. **1879** *Shropsh. Word-bk., Dab-chick*, the Water-hen.

c. *fig.* Of a girl.

1610 B. JONSON *Alch.* IV. ii, 'Fore God, She is a delicate Dab-chick! I must have her.

¶ Ash's explanation 'A chicken newly hatched' (to which the *Century Dictionary* refers the quot. from Pope in **a** δ) is merely an amusing blunder.

dabitis ('dæbɪtɪs). *Logic.* [L., = you will give.] The mnemonic term for that indirect mood of the first figure of syllogisms in which the major premiss is universal and affirmative, and the minor premiss and conclusion are particular and affirmative.

1599 BLUNDEVIL *Logike* 121 Celantes: Dabitis: Fapesmo: Frisesomorum. **1685** tr. *Arnauld & Nicole's Logic* viii. 35 These five modes are generally denoted by these words, Baralipton, Celantes, Dabitis, Fapesmo, Frisemorum. **1849** H. L. MANSEL *Artis Logicæ Rudimenta* 65 The five indirect moods of the first figure were called Baralip, Celantes, Dabitis, Fapesmo, Frisesmo.

†**dablet**, *Obs.* In 4 **deblet**, 7 *Sc.* **dablet, daiblet.** [a. OF. *deablot* (14th c. Godefr.), dim. of *deable*, *diable* DEVIL.] A little devil, an imp.

c **1380** WYCLIF *Serm.* Sel. Wks. II. 328 Þe fend moveþ þes debletis to fere Cristene men fro treuþe. *a* **1605** MONTGOMERIE *Flyting* 379 When the Weird Sisters had this voted, all in an voyce, The deid of [the] dablet. *Ibid.* 515 For the din of thir daiblets raisd all the deils.

‖**daboya** (də'bɔɪə, 'dɑːbəʊjɑː, 'dæb-). Also **daboia.** [Hindī *daboyā* that lies hid, the lurker, f. *dabnā* to lurk.] The large viper of the East Indies.

1872 W. AITKIN *Sci. & Pract. Med.* (ed. 6) I. 387 A horse bitten by a daboia. **1889** *Century Mag.* Aug. 505 Among the vipers the daboya is entitled to rank as a poisoner close to the cobra.

dabster ('dæbstə(r)). [In sense 1 f. DAB *sb.*³: see -STER.]

1. One skilled at anything; an expert or dab. Chiefly *dial.*

1708 *Brit. Apollo* No. 93. 3/2 Ye Dabsters at Rhime. **1770–86** P. SKELTON *Wks.* V. 203 The right dabsters at a sly, or a dry joke. **1824** *Hist. Gaming* 29 Her.. luck at play (for she was a dabster). **1842** AKERMAN *Wiltshire Gloss., Dabster*, a proficient. **1888** *Berksh. Gloss., Dabster*, one who excels greatly. [So in many dialect Glossaries.]

2. Applied depreciatively: cf. DAUBSTER, DABBLER.

1871 BROWNING *Pr. Hohenst.* 389 Lines Which every dabster felt in duty bound To signalize his power of pen and ink By adding to a plan once plain enough. **1892** *Idler* Sept. 203, I am a very indifferent amateur, a slouchy dabster, a mere artistic sarcasm.

‖**dabuh.** [Arab. *ḍabuʿ* hyæna = Heb. *tsābūaʿ* Jer. xii. 9.] The Arab name of the Striped Hyæna, retained by some early naturalists.

1600 J. PORY tr. *Leo's Africa* II. 342 Of the Beast called Dabuh.. It.. will rake the carkeises of men out of their graves, and will devour them. **1607** TOPSELL *Four-f. Beasts* 439 The second kind of hyena, called Papio or Dabuh.

dab-wash: see DAB *sb.*¹ 11.

‖**da capo** (da 'kapo). *Mus.* [It. *da* from *capo* head, beginning.] A direction at the end of a piece of music to repeat from the beginning; the end of the repeat being usually marked with a pause or the word *Fine.* (Abbreviated *D.C.*) Also *fig.*

1724 *Short Explic. For. Wds. in Mus. Bks.* (Stanf.), *Da capo*, or by way of Abbreviation D.C. **1740** DYCHE & PARDON, *D.C.* in Musick signifies *Da Capo*, that is, give or play the whole or some particular part of an air again. **1855** THACKERAY *Newcomes* i, And then will wake Morrow and the eyes that look on it; and so *da capo*.

Hence **da capo** *v.* (*nonce-wd.*), to repeat (music).

1764 *Poetry* in *Ann. Reg.* 240 Say, will my song, *da capo'd* o'er, *Piano* soft, *Andante* roar. **1803** in *Spir. Pub. Jrnls.* (1804) VII. 21 Thus you may da capo this musical entré.

dacca, dacha, varr. DAGGA¹.

dace (deɪs). Also 5 **darce, darse**, 6 **dase.** [ME. *darse*, etc., a. OF. *darz*, *dars*, nom. (and pl.) of *dart*, from 15th c. *dard* DART, dace: cf. Cotgr., '*Dard*, a Dart; also, a Dace or Dare fish'; so called from its darting motion: cf. DARE.]

1. A small fresh-water cyprinoid fish, *Leuciscus vulgaris*.

c **1430** *Two Cookery-bks.* 20 Take Dace, Troutys, and Roche. *c* **1460** J. RUSSELL *Bk. Nurture* 575 Perche, rooche, darce. **1496** *Bk. St. Alban's, Fishing* (1810) 36 Another [bayte] for darse & roche & bleke. **1538** LELAND *Itin.* V. 90 Bremes, Pikes, Tenches, Perches and Daces. **1655** MOUFET & BENNET *Health's Improv.* (1746) 271 Daces or Darts, or Dares, be of a sweet Taste, a soft Flesh and good Nourishment. **1802** BINGLEY *Anim. Biog.* (1813) III. 84 Dace afford great amusement to the angler. **1833** LAMB *Elia, Old Margate Hoy*, With no more relish for the sea, than a pond-perch or a dace might be supposed to have.

b. *U.S.* Applied locally to other fishes resembling or allied to this: as the genus *Rhinichthys*, and the redfin, *Minnilus cornutus*. (*Cent. Dict.*)

2. *Comb.*, as *dace-like*.

1838 LYTTON *Alice* VI. iv, Stopping Mr. Douce's little.. dace-like mouth.

‖**dacey** ('deɪsɪ). *Anglo-Ind.* [ad. Hindī *dēsī*, f. *dēs* country.] Of or belonging to the country (i.e. India), native; = COUNTRY 13 b, as in ***dacey-cotton, silk, manufacture***, etc.

1876 L. P. BROCKETT *Silk-weaving* i. 13 (*Cent. Dict.*).

‖**dacha** ('dætʃə). Also **datcha, datsha.** Pl. **da(t)chas, datche.** [Russ. *dácha*, orig. 'grant (of land)', f. *dat'* to give.] In Russia, a small house or villa for summer use, in the country near a town.

1896 *Edin. Rev.* Jan. 83 Russian officials run down to their *datchas*, or country houses. **1905** *Daily Chron.* 9 Sept. 4/5, I was privileged to visit one of these datche and to dine with the family. **1926** *Blackw. Mag.* Sept. 302/2 Colonel Napier .. had a dacha for the summer just outside the town. **1929** *Times* 14 Nov. 13/2 The settlers of German descent.. are at present precariously housed in the 'Datchas', or summer chalets of the Moscow countryside. **1950** KOESTLER in R. H. S. Crossman *God that Failed* 66 Two-room flats.. not to mention motor-cars and summer *datshas*. **1955** *Times* 8 Aug. 5/1 His principal guests—at a summer dacha 60 miles from Moscow.. were the ambassadors and ministers accredited to the Soviet Government. **1971** *Guardian* 21 Jan. 3/3 Mr Krushchev.. in the country dacha to which he had retired.

dachs ('dæks). Colloq. abbrev. (*sing.* and *pl.*) of DACHSHUND.

1886 G. MEREDITH *Let.* 24 July (1970) II. 821 The dog.. is the dearest little Dachs. **1892** B. POTTER *Jrnl.* 25 Oct. (1966) 291 The Duchess's *Dinah* is dead... The surviving dachs was noisy. **1960** M. SHARP *Something Light* viii. 77 *Some* sort of dog... We settled on dachs because they're so easy.

‖**dachshund** ('dakshʊnd). Also in partly anglicized form **dachs-hound.** [Ger. = badger-dog.] One of a German breed of short-legged long-bodied dogs, used to draw badgers; a badger-dog.

c **1881** M. ARNOLD *Later Poems, Poor Matthias*, Max, a dachshound without blot. **1888** MRS. H. WARD *R. Elsmere* (1890) 285 The sleek dachshund.. sat blinking beside its mistress.

dachsie ('dæksɪ). Also **dachsy, daxie.** Colloq. abbrev. of DACHSHUND. Cf. DACHS.

1899 *Daily News* 28 Oct. 7/5 They (like Daxies again) delight in playing tricks. **1900** *Ibid.* 22 Dec. 6/3 Coercion distinctly disagreeing with daxies! **1961** PARTRIDGE *Dict. Slang* Suppl. 1056/2 *Dachsie* (or *-sy*), a dachshund: domestic coll.: C. 20. **1967** 'A. BLAISDELL' *Something Wrong* (1968) ii. 19 He saw some dogs—poodles, dachsies.

Dacian ('deɪʃ(ɪ)ən), *a.* and *sb.* Also 8 **Dacic.** [f. *Dacia* (see below) + -AN.] **A.** *adj.* Of or pertaining to Dacia, an ancient country of south-eastern Europe, or its people, or their language. **B.** *sb.* **1.** A member of this people. **2.** The language of this people.

a **1666** EVELYN *Diary* 26 Feb. an. 1645 (1955) II. 378 We came to the Forum Trajanum where his Culumna stands yet intire, wrough[t] with admirable Bass-relievo & comprehending the Dacian War. *a* **1773** A. BUTLER *Moveable Feasts* (1774) III. 134 The most illustrious Roman Conquerors often took Names.. from Countries which they had subdued.. as the African,.. the Germanic, Dacic, &c. **1776** GIBBON *Decl. & F.* I. i. 5 The Dacians, the most warlike of men, who dwelt beyond the Danube. **1818** BYRON *Ch. Har.* IV. cxli, *There* were his young barbarians all at play, *There* was their Dacian Mother—he, their sire, Butcher'd to make a Roman holiday. **1837** *Penny Cycl.* VIII. 281/2 Domitian celebrated his pretended exploits against the Dacians by assuming the title Dacicus. **1847** *Howitt's Jrnl.* 12 June 325/2 A sentence or two will enable the reader to compare the modern Dacian with the ancient Roman. *Ibid.* 326/1 The adoption of the Cyrillian alphabet had the effect of carrying away.. the association of Dacian words from their Latin sources. **1861** MAX MÜLLER *Lect. Sci. Lang.* IV. 116 We possess fragments of Dacian speech in the botanical names collected by Dioskorides. **1877** *Encycl. Brit.* VI. 758/2 He advanced to the Dacian capital. *Ibid.*, The Dacians come forward as one of the most powerful enemies of Rome. **1948** *Oxf. Jun. Encycl.* I. 413/1 Later began a series of invasions by Goths, Tartars, Huns and Magyars.., all of whom left their mark on the Dacian people. **1959** *Chambers's Encycl.* XII. 51/2 The remote ancestors of the Rumanians were the Dacians who inhabited lands north and south of the Lower Danube.

dacite ('deɪsaɪt). *Geol.* [Named 1863 from Dacia, the Roman province including Transylvania + -ITE.] A name for varieties of greenstone or trachyte rock containing quartz.

[**1878** LAWRENCE *Cotta's Rocks Class.* 185 Stache has given the name of Dacit to a quartzose trachyte.] **1879** RUTLEY *Stud. Rocks* xii. 235 The chemical composition of the dacites varies considerably.

dacity ('dæsɪtɪ). *dial.* Also (s.w.) **docity.** [An aphetic form of *audacity*: so in local dialects *dacious*.] Capacity, ability; activity, energy.

1636 W. SAMPSON *Vow Breaker* v, I have plai'd a Major in my time with as good dacity as e're a hobby-Horse on 'em all. **1746** *Exmoor Scolding* (1879) 209 Tha hast no Stroil ner Docity, no Vittiness in enny keendest Theng. **1855** ROBINSON *Whitby Gloss., Dacity*, fitness, capacity, suitable address in a matter.

dacka, var. DAGGA¹.

dacker, daiker ('dækə(r), 'deɪkər), *v. Sc.* and *north. dial.* Also **daker.** [app., in sense 1, the same as MFlem. *daeckeren* 'volitare, motari, mobilitari; et vibrare, coruscare' (Kilian, 1599). But sense 7 is not clearly connected with the others, and may be a separate word.]

I. 1. *intr.* To shake to and fro, waver, totter, stagger. *Eng. dial.*

1668 SKINNER *Etym.* (1671), *Dacker*, vox in argo Lincoln. usitata: significat autem Vacillare, Nutare. **1674** RAY *N.C. Words* 13 *Dacker*, to waver, stagger or totter, a word used in Lincolnshire. **1876** *Whitby Gloss., Daikering*.. also quavering with the limbs; 'a daikering sort of a body', a paralysed person. **1877–89** *N.W. Linc. Gloss.* (ed. 2), *Dacker*, to waver, to shake fitfully.. 'I could see the chimla dacker ivry gust that came'.

2. To walk totteringly as from feebleness or infirmity; to toddle; to go about slowly, idly or carelessly; to saunter, dander.

1818 SCOTT *Rob Roy* xxiii, Gin ye'll.. just daiker up the gate with this Sassenach. —— *Hrt. Midl.* viii, Wha wad hae thought o' his daikering out this length? **1825** JAMIESON, *Dacker, daiker*.. (7) To go about in a feeble or infirm state. *Ettrick Forest.* **1851** *Cumbrld. Gloss., Dakerin*, walking carelessly.

3. To work in an irregular or pottering way.

1703 THORESBY *Let. to Ray* (E.D.S.), *Daker*, to work for hire after the common days work is over, at 2*d*. an hour. **1808** JAMIESON, *Dacker, daker, daiker*.. 3. To toil as in job work, to labour.. 5. To be engaged about any piece of work in which one does not make great exertion; to be slightly employed.

4. *fig.* To remain or hang on in a state of irresolution; to vacillate, equivocate, waver; be irregular in one's ways. Also, to have relapses in sickness.

1818 SCOTT *Rob Roy* vi, Sae I e'en daiker on with the family frae year's end to year's end. **1877** in *N.W. Linc. Gloss.*, 'I knew he was liein', he dacker'd.. in his talk.'

5. To truck, to traffic (*Lothian*).

'It properly signifies to deal in a piddling and loose sort of way; as allied in sense to E. *higgle*' (Jamieson).

6. To have dealings, engage, grapple *with*.

1785 *Poems Buchan Dialect* 10 (Jam.), I dacker'd wi' him by mysel'. **1882** in Edwards *Mod. Sc. Poets* Ser. IV. 193 'Twere well wi folk they oft would think Afore they daiker long wi drink.

II. 7. To search (*intr.* and *trans.*).

1634 *Burgh Rec.* in Cramond *Ann. Banff.* (1893) II. 251 The bailyie, haiffing causit searche, seik, and dacker the duelling housis. **1717** *Kirk Session Rec.* in Gordon *Chron. Keith* (1880) 90 Warrant for dackering for the said meal.

1768 Ross *Helenore* 91 (Jam.) To dacker for her as for robbed gear.

‖**dacoit** (də'kɔɪt), *sb.* Also **dakoit, decoit.** [Hindī *ḍakait*, orig. *ḍākait*, f. *ḍākā* gang-robbery, f. Skr. *dashṭaka* compressed, crowded.]

A member of a class of robbers in India and Burmah, who plunder in armed bands.

Also applied to pirates who formerly infested the Ganges between Calcutta and Burhampore; see quot. 1810.

1810 T. Williamson *E. India Vade M.* II. 396 (Y.) Decoits, or water-robbers. **1844** H. H. Wilson *Brit. India* I. 399 The Dakoits did not commonly proceed to murder; but they perpetrated atrocious cruelties. **1888** *Pall Mall G.* 1 Feb. 3/2 The whole of Lower Burmah was ravaged by bands of dacoits, who defied and defeated the local authorities and robbed whole villages.

Hence **da'coit** *v.*, to plunder as a dacoit; **da'coitage, da'coiting**, the practice of a dacoit, dacoity; **dacoi'tee**, one robbed by a dacoit.

1886 *Athenæum* 1 May 578 The only choice left him is that of dacoiting or of being dacoited. **1890** *Times* 26 Dec. 3/1, 2000 rupees and other property belonging to them were dacoited. **1887** *New York Examiner* 12 May (*Cent. Dict.*), We may expect soon to hear that Dacoitage has begun with as much vigor as ever. **1887** *Edin. Rev.* Apr. 499 It may be a pleasanter game to play the dacoit than the dacoitee. **1885** *Manch. Courier* 16 Dec., It is stated that dacoiting..has taken place at Bhamo.

‖**dacoity** (də'kɔɪtɪ). Also **de-, dacoitee, -ie.** [a. Hindī *ḍakaitī*, abstr. sb. f. *ḍakait.*]

The system of robbery practised by the dacoits; gang-robbery; an act of robbery with violence committed by an armed band (now, according to the Indian penal code, of not less than five men).

1818 Jas. Mill *Brit. India* (1840) V. 466 (Y.) The crime of dacoity (that is, robbery by gangs). **1845** Stocqueler *Handbk. Brit. India* (1854) 223 Not less than one hundred Dacoities..are annually reported. **1891** *Times* 12 Jan. 5/2 A dacoity did occur..and property was carried off.

¶ Erroneously for dacoit.

1849 E. E. Napier *Excurs. S. Africa* II. 7 Once the property of a renowned Decoitee, or river-pirate.

dacre, obs. form of dicker (of hides).

Dacron ('dækrɒn, 'deɪ-). Also **dacron.** [Invented name; cf. nylon, Orlon.] The proprietary name for polyethylene terephthalate used as a textile fibre. Cf. Terylene.

1951 *Du Pont Mag.* June–July 31/1 Du Pont has adopted the trade-mark 'Dacron' for its new textile fiber, originally called Fiber V. **1951** *Official Gaz.* (U.S. Patent Office) 13 Nov. 336/2 E. I. du Pont de Nemours and Company... *Dacron.* For synthetic polyester fibers for generalized use in the industrial arts. **1952** [see Acrilan]. **1952** *Trade Marks Jrnl.* 17 Sept. 867/2 *Dacron*... Woven and knitted piece goods, all included in Class 24 and made from synthetic materials in the form of fibres, filaments, yarns or threads. E. I. Du Pont de Nemours and Company. **1957** P. Wildeblood *Main Chance* ii. 36 His smiling teeth looked as expensively synthetic as his orlon shirt and dacron suit and nylon socks. **1958** [see Terylene]. **1962** A. Huxley *Island* ix. 134 A Whisper-Pink Bra in Dacron and Pima Cotton. **1969** B. Malamud *Pictures of Fidelman* i. 11 A dacron shirt and set of cotton-dacron underwear, good for quick and easy washing for the traveller. **1978** A. Welch *Bk. Airsports* i. 11/1 (*caption*) A hang glider is constructed from aluminium tube and Terylene (Dacron) sail fabric. **1978** J. A. Michener *Chesapeake* xiii. 835 The intense heat of the gasoline fire had melted some of the dacron lines into blobs of expensive goo.

dacryd ('dækrɪd). *Bot.* [f. mod.L. *Dacrydium*, a. Gr. δακρύδιον, dim. of δάκρυ tear, in allusion to resinous drops exuded by these trees.] A tree or shrub of genus *Dacrydium*, allied to the Yew.

1846 Lindley *Veg. Kingd.* 228 In New Zealand the Dacryds are sometimes no bigger than Mosses.

dacryo-, combining form of Gr. δάκρυον tear, as in ˌ**dacryoade'nalgia** [ad. G. *dacryoadenalgie* (J. A. Schmidt *Über die Krankheiten des Thränenorgans* (1803) I. ii. 117)], pain in a lachrymal gland; ˌ**dacryoade'nitis,** inflammation of a lachrymal gland; ˌ**dacryocy'stitis**, inflammation of a tear-sac.

1848 Dunglison *Med. Lex.* (ed. 7) 250/1 Dacryoadenalgia, Dacryoadenitis. *Ibid.* 250/2 Dacryocystitis. **1887** *Buck's Handbk. Med. Sci.* IV. 366/2 Neuralgia of the gland has also been observed, and the name 'dacryo-adenalgia' was given to it. *Ibid.*, Dacryo-adenitis, or inflammation of the lachrymal gland, is another affection which is seldom encountered. *Ibid.* 369/1 Acute dacryo-cystitis, or abscess of the sac, as it is termed, is a serious malady. **1908** *Practitioner* Feb. 288 Acute and chronic dachryocystitis [*sic*] are usually associated with epiphora. **1952** M. E. Florey *Clinical Appl. Antibiotics* xv. 458 A few results of the treatment of dacryocystitis have been recorded, but as the condition was usually chronic, distortion of the ducts often prevented chemotherapy alone from effecting a cure. **1964** S. Duke-Elder *Parsons' Dis. Eye* (ed. 14) xxxii. 512 Dacryo-adenitis occurs occasionally in general infections (mumps, influenza, etc.), sometimes leading to suppuration.

dacryolin ('dækrɪəʊlɪn). *Chem.* [mod. f. Gr. δάκρυ tear + -ol + -in.] The form of albumin found in the tears.

1875 A. Flint *Physiol. Man.* V. 145 The albumen..is called by some authors, lachrymine..or dacryoline. **1882** *Syd. Soc. Lex.*, *Dacryolin*..is converted by slow evaporation into a yellow insoluble substance.

dacryolith, -lite ('dækrɪəʊlɪθ, -laɪt). *Path.* [f. as prec. + λίθος stone.] A calculus or concretion occurring in the lacrymal passages.

1847–9 Todd *Cycl. Anat.* IV. 82/1 Calculous formations in the lacrymal organs..may be known by the generic name dacryolith. **1875** H. Walton *Dis. Eye* 1009 Conjunctival dacryoliths have been described. **1882** *Syd. Soc. Lex.*, *Dacryolith*, same as *Dacryolite.*

‖**dacry'oma.** *Path.* [f. as prec. after such sbs. as *carcinoma.*] An impervious state of one or both of the puncta lachrymalia, preventing the tears from passing into the lachrymal sac.

1830 in S. Cooper *Dict. Surg.* 373. **1857** in Dunglison.

dacryon ('dækrɪɒn). *Anat.* [a. F. *dacryon* (P. Broca 1875, in *Bull. Soc. d'Anthropol. Paris* 2nd Ser. X. 361), a. Gr. δάκρυον tear.] In the cranium, the point of juncture of the lachrymal and frontal bones with the frontal process of the maxillary bone.

1878 R. Bartley tr. *Topinard's Anthropol.* I. i. 35 At the point where the posterior border of the ascending process joins the frontal and the os unguis, is the..dacryon. **1951** *Cunningham's Text-bk. Anat.* (ed. 9) 160 The upper end of the suture between the two bones is called the dacryon. **1959** *Chambers's Encycl.* I. 460/1 [Anthropometry.] The ophryon is now obsolete and the asterion, dacryon and inion are likewise falling into disuse.

‖'**dacryops.** *Path.* [f. as dacryoma + ὤψ eye, face.] **a.** An affection of the eyelid: a clear cyst due to distension of one of the lachrymal ducts. **b.** A watery eye.

1857 in Dunglison. **1859** Hulke in *Opthalm. Hosp. Repts.* I. 287.

dactalomancy, error for dactyliomancy.

†'**dactile.** *Obs.* [? f. dactyl *sb.*] ? *v. intr.* To run quickly and nimbly. (If not a misprint for *ductile* adj., as treated by Gifford, or for *tactile.*)

a **1637** B. Jonson *Mortimer's Fall*, Thy form doth feast mine eye, thy voice mine ear..And softness of thy skin my very touch, As if I felt it dactile through my blood.

dactyl ('dæktɪl), *sb.* Also 5 -ylle, 5–6 -ile, 6 -il, -ill, 7–9 -yle. [ad. (perh. through F. *dactyle*) L. *dactylus*, a. Gr. δάκτυλος, a finger, a date, a dactyl (from its 3 joints).]

†**1.** The fruit of the date-palm; a date. *Obs.*

[**1398** Trevisa *Barth. De P.R.* xvii. cxvi. (1495) 678 The frute of the palme is callyd *Dactulus.*] **1483** *Cath. Angl.* 88 A Dactylle fute (fruytt A.), *dactilis.* **1541** R. Copland *Guydon's Formularye* X iij b, Powdre of dactiles. **1644** Bulwer *Chirol.* A iij, Thus while the gratefull Age offer whole springs Of Palme, my zeale an humble Dactyle brings. **1656** in Blount *Glossogr.*

2. *Prosody.* A metrical foot consisting of a long syllable followed by two short (or, in modern verse, of an accented syllable and two unaccented).

c **1420** *Wyclif Bible, Job* Prol. (1850) II. 671 Vers of sixe feet, rennende with dactile and sponde feet. **1581** Sidney *Apol. Poetrie* (Arb.) 71 The French..hath not one word, that hath his accent in..*Antepenultima*, and little more hath the Spanish: and therefore, verie gracelesly may they vse Dactiles. **1589** Puttenham *Eng. Poesie* ii. xiv. (Arb.) 140 This distique..standing all vpon perfect dactils. **1670** Eachard *Cont. Clergy* 13 If..upon the first scanning, he knows a sponde from a dactyl..A forward boy! cries the school-master. **1779** Burney in *Phil. Trans.* LXIX. 196 If he discovers a partiality for any particular measure, it is for dactyls of one long and two short notes. **1838–9** Hallam *Hist. Lit.* ii. v. §92 The first foot of each verse is generally a dactyle. **1848** Macaulay *Hist. Eng.* I. 30.

3. A mollusc, the piddock (*Pholas dactylus*).

1802 Bingley *Anim. Biog.* (1813) III. 442 The Dactyle Pholas.

4. a. A finger or toe. **b.** = dactylopodite. **c.** A part of the pretarsus of an insect.

1889 *Cent. Dict.*, *Dactyl*, a digit, whether of the hand or foot. **1946** *Nature* 9 Nov. 668/2 In ecdysis, any available rough surface is used to anchor the dactyl-claws of the walking legs. **1960** T. H. Waterman *Physiol. Crustacea* I. xvii. 564 In this crab autotomy never results after injury to the dactyl, the most distal segment of a walking leg.

†'**dactylar**, *a. Obs. rare.* [f. L. type *dactylār-is*, f. *dactyl-us*: see prec.] Pertaining to a dactyl; dactylic.

[*c* **1400** *Lanfranc's Cirurg.* 307 The .vj. is cleped dactilare for it is schape as it were þe stoon of a date.] **1828** in Webster.

†**dacty'let.** *Obs. nonce-wd.* [f. dactyl + -et[1], dim. suffix.] A little dactyl.

1597 Bp. Hall *Sat.* i. vi. 14 How handsomely besets Dull spondees with the English dactilets.

dactylic (dæk'tɪlɪk), *a.* and *sb.* [ad. L. *dactylic-us*, a. Gr. δακτυλικός, f. δάκτυλος: see -ic.]

A. *adj.* Of, pertaining to, or of the nature of, a dactyl; consisting of or characterized by dactyls.

1589 Puttenham *Eng. Poesie* ii. (Arb.) 130 That which Stanihurst first tooke in hand by his exameters dactilicke and spondaicke in the translation of Virgills Eneidos. **1751** Johnson *Rambler* 94 ⁋9 The power of the spondaick and dactylick harmony. **1853** Lowell *Moosehead Jrnl.* Prose Wks. 1890 I. 11 The dactylic beat of the horses' hoofs. **1871** *Publ. Sch. Lat. Gram.* §225 The Dactylic Hexameter occupies as large a space in Latin poetry as all other Verses together.

B. *sb.* A dactylic verse.

1795 Southey (*title*), The Soldier's Wife. Dactylics. **1797** Canning & Gifford *Parody* in *Anti-jacobin* No. 6 Ne'er talk of ears again! look at thy spelling-book; Dactylics, call'st thou 'em?—'God help thee, silly one!' **1872** M. Collins *Two Plunges* I. v. 103 She got hold of a blind poet..and made him tell the story in dactylics.

dactylically (dæk'tɪlɪkəlɪ), *adv. Prosody.* [f. dactylic *a.*: see -ly[2].] With a dactylic rhythm.

1891 Stevenson *Vailima Lett.* (1895) 85 'Ulufanua the isle of the sea', read that verse dactylically and you get the beat.

dactylio-, combining form of Gr. δακτύλιος finger-ring [f. δάκτυλος finger: see dactyl], as in **dac'tylioglyph** [Gr. δακτυλιογλύφ-ος], an engraver of gems for finger-rings; also, according to Brande, 'the inscription of the name of the artist on a gem'; hence **dacˌtylio'glyphic** *a.*; **dactyli'oglyphist** = *dactylioglyph*; **dactyli'oglyphy** [Gr. δακτυλιογλυφία], the art of engraving gems (Webster 1864). **dactyli'ographer**, one who describes finger-rings, engraved seals, etc.; hence **dacˌtylio'graphic** *a.*; **dactyli'ography**, the description of finger-rings, 'the science of gem-engraving' (Brande); **dactyli'ology**, the study of finger-rings.

1850 Leitch *Müller's Anc. Art* §131. 109 The luxury of ring-wearing..raised the art of the dactylioglyphist to the height which it was capable of attaining. **1872** C. W. King *Antique Gems & Rings* Index, *Dactyliology.*

dactyliomancy (dæk'tɪlɪəʊˌmænsɪ). *erron.* dactylo-. [f. Gr. δακτύλιος finger-ring + -mancy.] Divination by means of a finger-ring.

(For methods see E. B. Tylor, *Prim. Culture* I. 115.)

1613 Purchas *Pilgrimage* I. iv. v. 310 Dactyliomancie was a divination with Rings. **1652** Gaule *Magastrom.* 165 Dactylomancy. **1871** Tylor *Prim. Cult.* I. 115 These mystic arts..are rude forms of the classical dactyliomancy. **1877** W. Jones *Finger-ring L.* 112 Another method of practising Dactylomancy.

†'**dactylist.** *Obs. rare.* [f. dactyl + -ist.] A writer of dactylic verse.

1785 Warton *Pref. Milton's Min. Poems* (T.), May is certainly a sonorous dactylist.

‖**dactylitis** (dæktɪ'laɪtɪs). *Path.* Inflammation of a finger or toe. Hence **dactylitic** (-'ɪtɪk) *a.*, pertaining to dactylitis.

1861 Bumstead *Ven. Dis.* (1879) 671 This affection..was formerly called syphilitic panaris. We use the term dactylitis. *Ibid.* 772 Dactylitic swellings.

dactylo- ('dæktɪləʊ, dæktɪ'lɒ), combining form of Gr. δάκτυλος finger, as in ˌ**dactylo'deiktous** *a.* (*nonce-wd.*) [Gr. δακτυλόδεικτος], pointed at with the finger; '**dactylogram** [Gr. γράμμα letter], a finger-print; **dacty'lographer** [graph(y + -er[1]], one who takes or studies finger-prints (in quots. 1926 and 1931 the sense is 'typist'); **dacty'lography** = dactylology; **dacty'lonomy** [-nomy], the art of counting on the fingers; **dacty'lopodite** (*Zool.*), [Gr. ποδ- foot], the terminal joint of a limb in Crustacea; '**dactyloˌpore** (see quot.); hence **dactylo'poric** *a.*; **dacty'lopterous** *a.*, having the characters of the genus *Dactylopterus* of fishes, in which the pectoral fins are greatly enlarged and wing-like; so **dacty'lopteroid** *a.*; **dacty'loscopy** [Gr. σκοπιά seeing], the examination of finger-prints; hence ˌ**dactylo'scopic** *a.*; ˌ**dactylo'zooid, -'zoid**, a mouthless cylindrical zooid in some Hydrozoa.

1721 Bailey, *Dactylonomy*, the Art of Numbering on the Fingers. **1852** *Times* 27 May 5/6 Oxford must..be represented in politics..by an universally dactylodeiktous personage. **1870** Rolleston *Anim. Life* 92 Appendages which are known as the 'propodite' and 'dactylopodite'. **1880** Huxley *Crayfish* iv. 219 The dactylopodites of the two posterior thoracic limbs. **1882** *Syd. Soc. Lex.*, *Dactylopore*, a name given to the pores in the corallum of Hydrocorallinæ, from which the dactylozoids protrude. **1884** J. C. Gordon *Deaf Mutes* in *Amer. Annals* Apr. (1885) 128 *note*, A much simpler system of 'dactylography' based upon the Dalgarno alphabet. **1888** Rolleston & Jackson *Anim. Life* 758 The hydranth is sometimes modified for special functions, and the following must be regarded as polymorphic forms of it.. The *Dactylozooid*, a mouthless hydranth, modified for solely defensive and offensive purposes. Such zooids are universal among *Hydrocorallina.* **1908** *Boston Transcript* 10 Oct., An interesting illustration of the practical value of the science of dactyloscopy. **1910** *Let. to J. A. H. Murray* 5 Mar., The dactyloscopic records of the Boston Police Department. **1913** Dorland *Med. Dict.* (ed. 7), *Dactylogram*, a finger-print taken for purposes of identification. **1921** *Discovery* Oct. 259/1 You would not find two dactylograms alike, says Galton,..if you were to examine a series of 64,000,000. *Ibid.* [Poroscopy] is infinitely more fruitful in results than the one known by the name of dactyloscopy. *Ibid.* 259/2 In all cases of dactyloscopic analysis. **1926** F. M. Ford *A Man could stand Up* I. ii. 36 A dactylographer of respectability. **1931** H. G. Wells *Work, Wealth & Happiness of Mankind* (1932) xii. 567 There would be stenographers and dactylographers swiftly available. **1935** *Discovery* Sept. 261/1 The print of a finger can be definitely characterised by the dactylographer. **1936** BENTLEY & ALLEN *Trent's Own Case* x. 122 Looking at these well-marked prints of a finger and thumb, he had no more than a vague recollection of the dactyloscopic terms to be used in describing them. **1970** *Reader's Digest* Dec. 207 In 1910, few policemen believed in dactyloscopy, the examination of fingerprints.

dactyloid ('dæktɪlɔɪd), *a. rare*⁻⁰. [ad. Gr. δακτυλοειδής finger-like: see -OID.] Resembling a finger.

1882 in *Syd. Soc. Lex.*

dactylology (dæktɪ'lɒlədʒɪ). Also 7 **dactylologie.** [f. Gr. δάκτυλος finger + -λογια discourse: see -LOGY.] 'Finger-speech'; the art of 'speaking' or communicating ideas by signs made with the fingers, as in the deaf-and-dumb alphabet. (Formerly CHIROLOGY.)

1656 BLOUNT *Glossogr.*, *Dactylogie*..finger-talk, speech made with the fingers. **1680** DALGARNO *Deaf & Dumb Man's Tutor* Introd., Cheirology, or dactylology..is interpretation by the transient motions of the fingers. **1860** *Guardian* 24 Oct. 927/1 The ceremony was performed in the finger language, or, as it is grandiloquently termed, dactylology. **1885** G. MEREDITH *Diana* II. xii. 303 They pressed hands at parting..not for the ordinary dactylology of lovers, but in sign of the treaty of amity.

dactylose (dæktɪ'ləʊs), *a. rare*⁻⁰. [f. DACTYL (or its source) + -OSE.] 'Having fingers, or finger-shaped' (*Syd. Soc. Lex.*).

dad (dæd), *sb.*[1] *colloq.* Also 6–7 **dadd(e.** [Occurs from the 16th c. (or possibly 15th c.), in representations of rustic, humble, or childish speech, in which it may of course have been in use much earlier, though it is not given in the *Promptorium* or *Catholicon*, where words of this class occur.

Of the actual origin we have no evidence: but the forms *dada*, *tata*, meaning 'father', originating in infantile or childish speech, occur independently in many languages. It has been assumed that our word is taken from Welsh *tad*, mutated *dad*, but this is very doubtful; the Welsh is itself merely a word of the same class, which has displaced the original Celtic word for 'father' = Ir. *athair*.]

1. A childish or familiar word for father: originally ranking with *mam* for mother, but now less typically childish. Cf. DADDY.

?*a* **1500** *Chester Pl.* (Shaks. Soc.) I. 43 *Cayme.* I will.. Speake with my dadde and mam also..Mamme and dadd, reste you well! [Of uncertain date: the MS. is only of 1592. Harl. MS. of 1607 reads (ii. 678) 'sire and dam', (ii. 681) 'father and mother'.] **1553** WILSON *Rhet.* 31 Bryngyng forthe a faire child unto you..suche a one as shall call you dad with his swete lispyng wordes. **1590** GREENE *Never too late* (1600) 53 The boy sayes, Mam, where is my Dad, when will he come home? **1595** SHAKS. *John* II. i. 467 Since I first cal'd my brothers father Dad. **1625** GILL *Sacr. Philos.* I. 95, I have not read so farre in heraldry, as to tell you who was his Dad, nor of what house his mother came. **1708** MRS. CENTLIVRE *Busie Body* I. i, An Uncle who..tho' he made me his Heir, left Dad my Guardian. **1816** 'QUIZ' *Grand Master* I. Argt., Leaving his dad and mam in tears. **1886** BESANT *Childr. of Gibeon* II. viii, Poor old dad!

fig. **1608** T. MORTON *Pream. Encounter* 93 It is better to be a lad then (that I may so say) a dad in falshood. **1682** N. O. *Boileau's Lutrin* I. 222 For he was Dad of all the singing Tribe. **1828** *Craven Gloss.*, *Dad* is also used for one that excels in any thing, but chiefly in a bad sense. 'He 'st dad of au for mischief'.

2. Used as a form of address to a person, not necessarily elderly, other than one's own father. *colloq.* (esp. in Jazz talk).

1959 J. C. HOLMES *Horn* 128 Here, dad, have a brew while I get these boys set up. **1960** *Time & Tide* 24 Dec. 1599/1, I think 77 *Sunset Strip* is real zoolie, dad. **1966** *Melody Maker* 30 July 8/3 Take that bit where everybody was called Dad... Altoist Bruce Turner..even called his wife 'dad'.

dad, *sb.*[2] *Sc.* and *north. dial.* Also **daud, dawd.** [f. DAD *v.*]

1. A firm and shaking blow, a knock or thump (*e.g.* on the back of a man or beast, or on any body with dull resonance).

1718 RAMSAY *Christ's Kirk* III. xiii, He..Play'd dad, and dang the bark Aff's shins that day. **1789** D. DAVIDSON *Seasons* 15 (Jam.) Whoe'er did slight him gat a daud. **1827** J. WILSON *Noct. Ambr.* Wks. (1855) I. 277 The snaw was.. giein them sair flaffs and dads on their faces.

2. A large piece knocked off, a 'thumping' piece, a lump (of bread or other solid matter).

1785 BURNS *Holy Fair* xxiii, Cheese an' bread..dealt about in..dawds that day. **1837** R. NICOLL *Poems* (1843) 89 Dauds o' counsel ye would gie. **1849** in Robson *Bards of Tyne* 77 Lumps o' beef, an' dads o' duff. **1879** *Cumbrld. Gloss.* Suppl., *Daud*, a flake of snow.

dad, *sb.*[3] A deformation of *God*, in asseverations: now *dial.* or *U.S.* (Cf. ADAD, BEDAD; also DOD.)

1678 OTWAY *Friendship in F.* III. i, But by Dad he's pure company. **1681** N. N. *Rome's Follies* 30 Say'd thou so, Neighbour? dad, you have very much reviv'd my heart. **1834** W. A. CARRUTHERS *Kentuckian in N.Y.* I. 216 I'll be dad shamed if it ain't all cowardice. **1842** S. LOVER *Handy Andy* iii, By dad! Andy, you've made a mistake this time that I'll forgive you. **1884** 'C. E. CRADDOCK' *Tenn. Mts.* I. 45 Dad-burn that..idle poultry. *Ibid.* III. 141 That dad-burned scoundrel. **1884** 'MARK TWAIN' *Huck. Finn* xxxiv. 354 It's de dad-blame' witches. **1890** *Dialect Notes* (Boston U.S.), *Kentucky Words* II. 64 *Dad, dod*, for *God*, in certain curses..'Dad drat your hide'. **1901** W. H. HARBEN *Westerfelt* xiv. 195 'Don't act so dadratted foolish,' he said. *Ibid.* xxii. 300 Yes, dad burn it; you know she loves you. **1911** R. D. SAUNDERS *Col. Todhunter* vi. 84 I'll be dadblamed if I know what's goin to come of it all some day! **1927** *Hollis St. Theatre Progr.* (U.S.) 19 Sept., But who'd think where buildings are tall Business could be so dad-burned bum? **1944** T. D. CLARK *Pills, Petticoats & Plows* 156 There was a sentiment that 'a dad-blamed hog and a dad-gummed cow were the most aggravating things that ever made tracks on a piece of cotton land'. **1968** *Word Study* Feb. 7/2 'Darn it', 'dad gum it', 'heck'.

dad, daud (dæd, dad), *v. Sc.* and *north. dial.* [Onomatopœic; expressing orally the action in question, and its abrupt and somewhat dulled sound. The occasional Sc. spelling *daud* does not imply a long vowel, but merely the low back wide (ɑ), often approaching (ɔ).]

1. *trans.* To strike with a blow that shakes or sends a shock through; to knock, beat; to shake with knocking or beating.

a **1572** KNOX *Hist. Ref.* Wks. 1846 I. 260 One took him [the 'idole'] by the heillis, and dadding his head to the calsay, left Dagon without head or handis. **1715** RAMSAY *Christ's Kirk* II. iii, Then took his bannet to the bent And daddit aff the glar. **1722** —— *Three Bonnets* IV, This said, he dadded to the yate. **1816** J. WILSON *Noct. Ambr.* Wks. 1855 I. 138 Twa stout young fellows daudin ane anither about..wi' their neives. **1833** MOIR *Mansie Wauch* xvii. (1849) 113 Dadding the end of his staff on the ground. **1849** CARLYLE *Let.* in Froude *Life* II. 11 Nervous system all 'dadded about' by coach travel.

2. *intr.*

1719 RAMSAY *2nd Answ. Hamilton* iv, Dad down a grouf, and tak a drink. **1865** MRS. CARLYLE *Lett.* III. 258 The shock it was to me to find..all those weak, wretched letters ..'dadding about' [knocking about] in the dining-room.

dada[1] ('dædə, də'dɑː). Also **dadda, da-da.** [Cf. DAD *sb.*[1]] A child's word for father; cf. *papa.* (In some parts pronounced *da'da*, like *pa'pa*, and used instead of that word.)

1688 *3rd Coll. Poems, Loyal Litany* xvi, Or if the Smock and Dada fails, Adopt a Brat of Neddy Hayles. **1689** FARQUHAR *Love & Bottle* I, Poor child! he's as like his own dadda as if he were spit out of his mouth. **1775** MAD. D'ARBLAY *Early Diary* (1889) II. 117 Dear Dada, I have this moment received your letter. **1842** in Robson *Bards of Tyne* (1863) 227 A, U, A, my bonny bairn..A, U, A—thou suin may learn To say dada se canny. **1866** MISS YONGE *Prince & Page* iii. 52 The child still cried for her da-da.

Dada[2] ('dada). [Fr. (*être sur son dada*, ride one's hobby-horse); title of a review which appeared at Zürich first in 1916, founded by Tzara (a Rumanian poet), Arp (an Alsatian German artist), and Huelsenbeck (a German poet).] Applied to an international movement in art and literature, characterized by a repudiation of traditional conventions and reason, and intended to outrage and scandalize. Hence **'Dadaism**, the theory or practice of this movement. So **'Dadaist(e** *sb.* and *a.*, **Dada'istic, Dada'istical** *adjs.* (Also with lower-case initials.)

1920 A. HUXLEY *Let.* 4 May (1969) 184 The three I have mentioned are almost wholly dada in style and sympathy. *Ibid.*, Most of the dadaist publications issue from a press named Au Sans Pareil. **1920** *Athenæum* 13 Aug. 221/2 The movement 'Dada'..has its headquarters in Paris, and its principal promoters are Francis Picabia and Tristan Tzara, neither of whom is of French nationality. *Ibid.*, Mr. Dent defines Dadaism as being a 'whole-heartedly æsthetic movement', in contradistinction to 'papaism' and 'nanaism'. *Ibid.* 222/2 [Guillaume Apollinaire's] most advanced, most nearly dadaistical poetry. **1920** *Times Lit. Suppl.* 2 Sept. 569/3 M. Mille still believes in *bon sens*, clarity and humour as valuable assets in art, a belief which has got him into serious trouble with the Dadaistes. **1920** *Glasgow Herald* 27 Nov. 6 Maeterlinck in his early days wrote verse not easily distinguishable from the work of the Dadaist. *Ibid.*, Dada means nothing... We gather some idea of the Dada position. **1923** A. HUXLEY *On Margin* 43 Dadaist literature always reminds me a little of..the inconsequent music of water. **1927** G. MURRAY *Class. Tradition* ix. 254 Does this mean that the words are only sounds and the poem a collection of sounds? That is clearly nonsense—a form of nonsense that is admired in certain French coteries, and is called 'dadaism'. **1934** C. DAY LEWIS *Hope for Poetry* 83 'Any work of art that can be understood is the product of a journalist' (Dada Manifesto). *Ibid.* 86 That was in fact the position that the Dadaists took up. 'Art is a private matter: the artist does it for himself.' **1935** D. GASCOYNE *Short Survey Surrealism* 25 The Dada spirit was something shared by a number of extreme individualists of various nationalities, all of whom were in revolt against the whole of the epoch in which they lived. **1947** A. E. BALAKIAN *Lit. Orig. Surrealism* 141 If the Dadaists sought to place themselves beyond the control of Beauty and its rules, it was because of their inner consciousness of something greater. **1956** C. GIEDON-WELCKER *Contemp. Sculpture* p. xiv, Dadaism created a metaphysic of banality by discovering the plastic vitality that emanates from nameless or unnoticed things. **1965** *Economist* 18 Sept. 1197/2 During the past year there has been an underground film festival featuring the latest 8 mm dadaistic experiment. **1965** H. RICHTER *Dada* 113 The idea of putting people in a position to exploit their mental and physical energies in a spirit of unbounded optimism and faith in themselves—this was the idea behind the wild and exuberant antics of Dada.

†**da da**, *int. Obs.* [app. of nursery origin; but the history is unknown.] A childish and familiar expression for 'Good-bye!'; the earlier form of TA-TA.

1681 OTWAY *Soldier's Fort.* III. i, Well, da, da, da.. prithee don't be troubled, da, da. **1733** *Hampton Court Misc.* 10 *Wife*..Da, Da, Monster [exit laughing]. *Husb.* Farewel, Tormentor.

†**'dadder**, *v. Obs.* exc. *dial.* In 5 dadir. [Cf. DODDER, DIDDER, DITHER: the form is that of a frequentative, as in *patter*, *shiver*, *totter*, etc.: but the etymology of the stem *dad-*, *did-*, *dod-*, is obscure; cf. DADE.] *intr.* To quake, tremble.

1483 *Cath. Angl.* 88/1 To Dadir, *frigucio.* **15..** *Hye Way to Spyttil Hous* 118 in Hazl. *E.P.P.* IV. 28 Boyes, gyrles, and luskysh strong knaues, Dydderyng and dadderyng, leaning on their staues. **1570** LEVINS *Manip.* 77/47 To Dadder, *trepidare.* **1878** *Cumbrld. Gloss.*, *Dadder*, *Didder*, *Dodder*, to shiver; to tremble.

Hence **dadder-**, **dodder-grass**, *Briza media.*

1878 *Cumbrld. Gloss.*, *Dadder grass*, *Dotherin grass*, quaking grass.

daddie, var. of DADDY.

daddle ('dæd(ə)l), *sb. dial.* The hand or fist.

1785 in GROSE *Dict. Vulg. Tongue.* **1812** *Sporting Mag.* XXXIX. 47 His daddles he us'd with such skill and dexterity. **1827** SCOTT *Two Drovers* ii, 'Adzooks!' exclaimed the bailiff—'sure..men forget the use of their daddles'. **1881** MISS JACKSON *Shropshire Word-bk.* Suppl. s.v., 'Tip us yer daddle' is an invitation to shake hands.

'daddle, *v.*[1] *dial.* [app. f. same root as DADDER, with dim. ending -LE: cf. *toddle.*] *intr.* To walk totteringly or unsteadily, like a child; to be slow in motion or action; to dawdle, saunter, trifle. Cf. DAIDLE, DAWDLE.

1787 GROSE *Prov. Gloss.*, *Daddle*, to walk unsteadily like a child; to waddle. **1825** BROCKETT *North C. Wds.*, *Daddle*, to walk unsteadily, to saunter or trifle. **1878** *Cumbrld. Gloss.*, *Daddle*, to walk or work slowly; to trifle. **1881** MISS JACKSON *Shropshire Word-bk.* Suppl., *Daddle*, to trifle; to loiter; to dawdle.

'daddle, *v.*[2] *dial.* = DIDDLE.

1886 STEVENSON *Treasure Isl.* I. iii. 21 'I'll trick them again ..I'll shake out another reef, matey, and daddle 'em again.'

daddock ('dædək). *dial.* Also 7 **dadocke.** [Stem *dad-* of uncertain etymology; but cf. DODDER: the suffix appears to be dim. -OCK, as in *bullock*, *hillock.*] Rotten or decayed wood; also †*daddock-wood.*

a **1624** BP. M. SMITH *Serm.* (1632) 106 How long would it be before you could..make mortar of sand, or make a piece of dadocke-wood to flame? **1674** BLOUNT *Glossogr.* (ed. 4), *Daddock*, when the heart or body of a Tree is throughly rotten, it is called *Daddock*, *quasi*, *dead Oak.* **1787** GROSE *Prov. Gloss.*, *Daddock*, rotten wood, touch-wood. *Glouc.* **1845** S. JUDD *Margaret* II. i, The great red daddocks lay in the green pastures where they had lain year after year, crumbling away. **1884** *Upton-on-Severn Gloss.*, *Daddock*, decayed wood, touchwood.

Hence **'daddocky** *a.*, decayed, rotten.

1825 BRITTON *Beaut. Wiltshire*, *Daddicky*, dry, decayed. **1884** *Upton-on-Severn Gloss.*, *Daddocky*, flimsy, unsubstantial, soft with decay.

daddy ('dædɪ). Also 6 **daddye**, 6–8 **dady**, 8–9 **daddie.** [dim. of DAD *sb.*[1]: see -Y.] **1.** *colloq.* **a.** A diminutive and endearing form of DAD, father.

?*a* **1500** *Chester Pl.* (Shaks. Soc.) I. 38 As my daddye hath taughte yt me, I will fulfill his lore. [MS. of 1592: Harl. MS. reads 'father'.] *a* **1529** SKELTON *Image Ipocr.* 158 Now God save these dadyes And all ther yong babyes. **1552** HULOET, Dadde or daddy, as infantes cal their fathers. **1673** R. LEIGH *Transproser Reh.* 8 Every Nurse can readily point to Daddy's Eyes. **1794** J. WOLCOTT (P. Pindar) *Rowl. for Oliver* Wks. II. 413 So [I] ask'd my daddy's leave to study Painting. **1880** MISS BRADDON *Just as I am* xl, She could not believe that there was a fault in daddy.

b. *irreverently.*

1749 CHESTERF. *Lett.* II. cxciii. 220 All day long afraid of old Daddy in England. **1892** *Spectator* 24 Dec. 927/2 In other respects, he is an Old Daddy!

c. = DOYEN 2.

1925 *New Yorker* 11 July 11 The Daddy of Sunday Painters. **1959** *Times* 26 Nov. 16/1 At full-back Uren, who must have been the daddy of the entire party, started falteringly.

2. Various slang uses (see quots.).

1859 HOTTEN *Slang Dict.*, *Daddy*, the stage manager.—*Theatr.* **1860** *Ibid.* [*adds*] *Daddy*, the person who gives away the bride at weddings. **1864** *Ibid.*, At mock raffles, lotteries, &c., the Daddy is an accomplice, most commonly the getter up of the swindle, and in all cases the person that has been previously arranged to win the prize. **1874** *Ibid.*, *Daddy*, the old man in charge—generally an aged pauper—at casual wards. **1886** *Graphic* 10 Apr. 399/2 The manager himself is sometimes known as the 'gorger', and 'daddy' is the stage-manager. **1901** 'M. FRANKLIN' *My Brilliant Career* xxi. 183 Joe Archer told me you ran into a clothes-line on race-night, and ever since then mother has kept up a daddy of a fuss about ours. *Ibid.* xxii. 194, I never felt such a daddy of a thirst on me before. **1941** BAKER *Dict. Austral. Slang* 22 *The daddy of them all*, the most notable or expert, the largest. **1962** *Woman* 31 Mar. 18/3 He [an Australian] had had his share of knockbacks. Including a daddy of a one from Belle herself. **1969** W. GARNER *Us or Them War* iv. 42 You graduate from taking little chances to taking big ones. This one was the daddy of 'em all.

3. Used in Jazz slang as a form of address. Also more generally applied to an older person, and (*U.S. slang*), a lover. Cf. DAD *sb.*[1] 2; *sugar daddy.*

1926 C. VAN VECHTEN *Nigger Heaven* 285 *Daddy*, husband or lover. **1927** *Jrnl. Abnormal & Social Psychol.*

XXII. 15 Come on, daddy, let's have some fun. **1935** WODEHOUSE *Blandings Castle* xi. 244 A two-timing daddy. **1948** *New Yorker* 3 July 28 The bebop people have a language of their own. They call each other Pops, Daddy, and Dick. **1957** J. KEROUAC *On Road* (1958) I. vii. 44 A waitress..slightly hung-up on a few sexual difficulties which..I think you can manage, you fine gone daddy you. **1960** *Time & Tide* 24 Dec. 1599/1 He calls his colleagues the detectives, 'daddy', his clothes he refers to as 'threads'. **1962** *Amer. Speech* XXXVII. 34 This suggests to me that possibly the word *daddy*, meaning 'a male lover', may be a 'pure' Americanism. *Ibid.* 35 *Daddy* has a history beginning much earlier than 1935 as a term meaning simply 'lover' in Negro songs and blues. **1970** H. WAUGH *Finish me Off* (1971) 133 He wasn't pimping for her... He's my daddy and he plays it for five other girls.

Hence **'daddyism** *nonce-wd.*, the characteristics of an 'old daddy' (cf. sense b above); in *U.S.* boast of or respect for ancestry.

1871 KATE FIELD in *Harper's Bazaar* Aug. (Farmer), 'His grandfather was a distinguished man.' 'Was he?' replied the man of Chicago. 'That's of no account with us. There's less daddyism here than any part of the United States. What's he himself?' **1892** *Spectator* 24 Dec. 927/2 If this great truth had broken upon Carlyle's biographer, how much daddyism had we been spared!

,daddy-'long-legs. [From its very long slender legs.] **a.** A popular name for the CRANE-FLY. (Called also *father-* and *Harry-long-legs*.) **b.** A name for Arachnids or spiders of similar appearance, such as those of the genus *Phalangium*.

a **1814** DIBDIN *Quanki Fongo* in *Univ. Songster* II. 58/1 Old daddy longlegs, when he drank his congo. **1840** WESTWOOD tr. *Cuvier's Anim. Kingd.* 619 These insects are well known under the names of *Daddy long-legs, Tailors*, &c. **1884** F. J. LLOYD *Science Agric.* 279 Next to the wireworm the crane fly or daddy-longlegs..is probably most hurtful.

'daddy-o. Colloq. var. DADDY (various senses).

1949 *Music Libr. Assoc. Notes* Dec. 42 Daddy-o, friend, buddy. Originated with Negro musicians. **1952** R. ELLISON *Invisible Man* xxiii. 366 A group of zoot-suiters greeted me in passing. 'Hey, now, daddy-o,' they called. **1959** C. MACINNES *Absolute Beginners* I. i. 18 Oh yes it can, daddy-o. **1959** E. AMBLER *Passage of Arms* iv. 107 You Americans give away billions of dollars... Because big daddy-o wants to be loved. **1960** *Time & Tide* 24 Dec. 1599/3 The walls are crazy,..And the scene uncool for you, Daddy-o. **1963** 'A. GARVE' *Sea Monks* iii. 101 What you goin' to do..when you finished it, Daddy-O? *Ibid.*, D'you reckon we oughter let Daddy-O 'ave a tool like that? **1969** N. COHN *AWopBopaLooBop* (1970) vi. 56 Who calls the English teacher daddy-o?

dade (deɪd), *v. Obs.* exc. *dial.* Also *dial.* dad, dawd. [perh. the same as the root of DADDER.]

1. *intr.* To move slowly or with uncertain steps, to toddle, like a child just learning to walk.

1612 DRAYTON *Poly-olb.* i. 8 Which nourisht and bred up ..No sooner taught to dade, but from their mother trip. *Ibid.* xiv, But eas'ly from her source as Isis gently dades.

2. *trans.* To lead and support (one who totters, *esp.* a child learning to walk). Also *fig.*

1598 DRAYTON *Heroic. Ep.* xxi. 108 The little children when they learne to goe, By painefull Mothers daded to and fro. **1603** HOLLAND *Plutarch's Mor.* 18 A guide..to stay and dade them when they learned to go. *Ibid.* 399 Such he ought to enforme, to direct, to dade and leade by the hand. **1859** E. WAUGH *Lanc. Songs* 72 (*Lanc. Gloss.*), Dost think thae could doff me an' dad me to bed? **1879** MISS JACKSON *Shropshire Word-bk.*, *Dade*, to lead children when learning to walk. **1881** *Leicestershire Gloss.*, *Dade*, to help to walk..'I shouldn' ha' got home, if they hadn' daded me along'.

Hence **'dading** *vbl. sb.*, as in † *dading-sleeves, -strings* (dial.), leading-strings.

1675 TEONGE *Diary* (1825) 13 His sonn..with his mayd to leade him by his dading sleeves. **1865** BEN BRIERLEY *Irkdale* I. 259 He's nobbut like a chilt in its dadins. **1879** MISS JACKSON *Shropshire Word-bk.*, *Dading-strings*, by which a child is held up when learning to walk.

† **dade**, *sb. Obs.* Name of some wading bird.

1686 *Loyal Garland* xx. ii, There's neither swallow, dove, nor dade, Can soar more high, or deeper wade.

dade, early form of DEED.

'dadless, *a. rare*$^{-1}$. [f. DAD *sb.*[1] + -LESS.] Fatherless.

1606 WARNER *Alb. Eng.* XIV. xci. 369 So many dadlesse Babes.

dado ('deɪdəʊ). *Arch.* [a. It. *dado* die, cube (= Pr. *dat*, OF. *det, dé*):—L. *datum*: see DIE.]

1. The block or cube, with plane faces, forming the body of a pedestal, between the base mouldings and the cornice; the die.

1664 EVELYN tr. *Freart's Archit.* 124 [The Pedestal] is likewise called Truncus the Trunk.. also Abacus, Dado, Zocco, &c. **1688** R. HOLME *Armoury* III. 102/1 Dado or Dye is a flat in a Cornice or Pedestal. **1816** J. SMITH *Panorama Sc. & Art* I. 171 Each central portion, as dado of pedestal, shaft of column. **1820** T. CROMWELL *Excurs. Ireland* ii. 81 The dado of the pedestal, above the entablature.

2. The finishing of wood running along the lower part of the walls of a room, made to represent a continuous pedestal; strictly applied only to the flat surface between the plinth and the capping. Hence, **b.** Any lining, painting, or papering of the lower part of an interior wall, of a different material or colour from that of the upper part.

1787 *Builder's Price-Bk.* 39 Dado. ¾ inch dado, level, skirted, and caped. **1794** *Ibid.* 41 Whole deal dove-tailed dado and keyed. **1837** *Penny Cycl.* VIII. 284/2 The dado employed in the interiors of buildings is a continuous pedestal..constructed of wood, and is usually about the height of a chair-back. Its present use is to protect the stucco-work or paper of the walls. **1854** *Ecclesiologist* XV. 357 A dado of oak-panelling. **1858** *Household Words* No. 456. 66 (The Alhambra) The dados, or low wainscotings, are of square glazed tiles, which form a glittering breast-high coat of mail.

b. 1877 BLACK *Green Past.* xl. (1878) 323 Oh, by the way, Lady Sylvia, how did your dado of Indian matting look? **1879** MISS BRADDON *Vixen* III. 249 Mabel insisted upon having..a sage-green wall with a chocolate *dado*—did you ever hear of a *dado*?—in the new morning-room.

3. *attrib.*, as *dado-moulding*.

1837 *Penny Cycl.* VIII. 284 A cornice or dado moulding surmounting the die. **1852-61** *Archit. Publ. Soc. Dict.* s.v., The capping or surbase, sometimes called the dado molding.

dadoed ('deɪdəʊd), *ppl. a.* [f. DADO *sb.* + -ED.] Furnished with a dado.

1881 MISS BRADDON *Asph.* xiv. 159 The old oak-dadoed drawing-room. **1890** *Pall Mall G.* 13 Aug. 2/3 A pretty morning-room..with dadoed walls.

dae, Sc. form of DOE.

† **'Dædal**, *sb. Obs.* In 7 Dædale, Dedal(l. [ad. L. DÆDAL-US: see below. Cf. F. *Dédale* maze.]

1. An anglicized form of the proper name Dædalus; a skilful artificer or fabricator like Dædalus.

[**1619** H. HUTTON *Foll. Anat.* A v a (Stanford), My lame-legd Muse..Yet doth aspire with Dedall's wings.] *c* **1630** DRUMM. OF HAWTH. *Poems* Wks. (1711) 18 The Silk-worm of Love. A Dædale of my death.

2. A maze or labyrinth.

1699 EVELYN *Acetaria* (1729) 119 Groves, Labyrinths, Dedals..Close-Walks..and other Relievo's of Topiary and Hortulan architecture.

dædal ('di:dəl), *a.* Chiefly *poetical.* Also 6-7 (9) dædale, 7 dedall, 7-9 dedal. [ad. L. *dædal-us*, a. Gr. δαίδαλος skilful, cunningly wrought, variegated, etc.: see prec.]

1. Skilful, cunning to invent or fashion.

1590 SPENSER *F.Q.* III. Prol. ii, All were it Zeuxis or Praxiteles, His dædale hand would faile and greatly faynt. *c* **1630** DRUMM. OF HAWTH. *Poems* Wks. (1711) 36 Out-run the wind-out-running dædale hare. **1828** *Blackw. Mag.* XXIV. 346 Here the dashing Blind Harry the Harper had hung up his dædal harp. **1872** BLACKIE *Lays Highl.* 33 By the dædal hand of Titan Nature piled.

2. Displaying artistic cunning or fertility of invention; maze-like; = DÆDALIAN I.

c **1630** DRUMM. OF HAWTH. *Poems* Wks. (1711) 42 Ye, who with curious numbers, sweetest art, Frame dedal nets our beauty to surprize. **1746** J. WARTON *Ode* iii. (R.), Here ancient art her dædal fancies play'd In the quaint mazes of the crisped roof. **1836** LANDOR *Pericles & A.* Wks. 1846 II. 372 The dedal dance is spun and woven.

3. Of the earth, etc.; 'Manifold in works'; hence, varied, variously adorned.

A vague poetic use after Lucretius (I. 7 'dædala tellus'; v. 234 'natura dædala rerum').

1596 SPENSER *F.Q.* IV. x. 45 Then doth the dædale earth throw forth to thee Out of her fruitfull lap abondant flowres. **1745** T. WARTON *Pleas. Melanch.* 248 What dædal landscapes smile! **1817** WORDSW. *Sequel to 'Beggars'*, For whose free range the dædal earth Was filled with animated toys. **1834** D'ISRAELI *Rev. Epick* I. xv, The dædal faith of the old world had died. **1864** SKEAT *Uhland's Poems* 28 With what dædal fulness Thy beds their blossoms shew!

† **4.** ? Mazy, labyrinthine; ? changeful. *Obs.*

1818 KEATS *Endym.* IV. 459 Search my most hidden breast! By truth's own tongue, I have no dædale heart!

† **5.** *Bot.* = DÆDALEOUS, DÆDALOUS. *Obs.*

1793 T. MARTYN *Lang. of Bot.*, *Dædaleum folium*, a Dædal leaf.

dæ'daleous, *a. Bot.* [f. as next + -OUS.]

1835 LINDLEY *Introd. Bot.* (1848) II. 357 *Dædaleous*; when the point has a large circuit, but is truncated and rugged.

Dædalian, -ean (di:'deɪlɪən), *a.* Also De-. [f. L. *Dædalĕ-us* relating to Dædalus, Gr. δαιδάλεος cunningly wrought + -AN; or f. *Dædal-us* + -IAN.]

1. Of or after the style of Dædalus; skilful, ingenious, formed with art; resembling the labyrinth of Dædalus, intricate, maze-like.

1607 WALKINGTON *Opt. Glass* 111 The Dædalian.. Labyrinths wherein hee takes his turnes. *a* **1634** CHAPMAN (W.), Our bodies decked in our dædalian arms. **1757** J. BROWN in *Pope's Wks.* 1757 III. p. xv. (Stanford), Dædalian arguments but few can trace. **1776** ADAM SMITH *W.N.* II. ii. (1869) I. 322 Suspended upon the Daedalian wings of paper money. **1880** *Contemp. Rev.* XXXVII. 475 *note*, Beauty of contrivance, adaptation, or mechanism..we have called Daedalian beauty.

1636 *Raleigh's Tubus Hist.* Pref. B, Contrived by a Dædalean Hand. **1697** J. SERGEANT *Solid Philos.* 41 To please the Dædalean Fancies of the ingenious Contrivers. **1850** CARLYLE *Latter-d. Pamph.* iii. 14 Such creatures, like moles, are safe only underground, and their engineerings there become very dædalean. **1854** BADHAM *Halieut.* 512 Unable to wind his way through the Dædalean mazes of a modern bill of fare.

† **2.** = DÆDAL *a.* 3. *Obs.*

1598 SYLVESTER *Du Bartas* II. ii. *Arke* 425 In various sort Dedalian Nature seems her to disport.

3. (See quot.)

1848 WORNUM *Lect. Painting* 351 *note*, The black vases, or those with the black figures (skiagrams) or the stained reddish-yellow terra cotta, are the most ancient..The style of design of these black figures has been termed the Egyptian or Dædalian style.

Dædalic ('di:dəlɪk), *a. Archæol.* Also Dedalic. [f. as DÆDALIAN *a.* + -IC.] Designating a Greek sculptural style of the 7th century B.C., done in clay, metal, and stone, mainly in Dorian areas.

1931 H. PAYNE *Necrocorinthia* xvi. 233 This is no place for a history of Daedalic sculpture. **1936** R. J. H. JENKINS *Dedalica* I. ii. 10 The term 'Dedalic' so used is not entirely a term of convenience, for the monuments in question are closely bound to each other stylistically, and represent unquestionably the Creto-Peloponnesian or Dorian sculptural tradition of the seventh century, when Dedalus was apparently active in the districts. **1962** R. W. HUTCHINSON *Prehist. Crete* xii. 340 Archaeologists have come to employ the term 'Dedalic' of the sculptural style characteristic of, though not confined to, Doric-speaking cities [in Crete] in the eighth and early seventh centuries B.C. *Ibid.* 342 The new Dedalic style affected not only figurines of clay or bronze and jewellery, but also had a notable effect on..the making of *pithoi* or large stone jars with moulded ornaments.

Dædalist ('di:dəlɪst). *nonce-wd.* [See -IST.] An imitator of Dædalus.

1713 ADDISON *Guardian* No. 112 ¶3, I have fully considered the project of these our modern Dædalists, and am resolved so far to discourage it, as to prevent any person from flying in my time.

† **'dædalize**, *v. Obs. nonce-wd.* [f. DÆDAL *a.* + -IZE.] *trans.* To make intricate or maze-like.

a **1618** SYLVESTER *Du Bartas, Lacrymæ* 89 Wee Lawyers then, who dedalizing Law, And deading Conscience, like the Horse-leach drawe.

dædalous ('di:dələs), *a. Bot.* Also dedalous. [f. L. *dædal-us* cunningly-wrought + -OUS.]

Of leaves: 'Having a margin with various windings and turnings; of a beautiful and delicate texture' (Webster 1828, citing Martyn, and Lee).

‖ **Dædalus** ('di:dələs). See also DÆDAL *sb.* [L., a. Gr. Δαίδαλος 'the cunning one', name of the workman who constructed the Cretan labyrinth, and made wings for himself and his son Icarus.] A skilful or cunning artificer (like Dædalus).

c **1630** DRUMM. OF HAWTH. *Poems* Wks. (1711) 50 Gone is my sparrow..A Dedalus he was to catch a fly. **1631** HEYWOOD *Eng. Eliz.* (1641) 123 Gardiner was the onely Dedalus and inventour of the engine.

dæl, early form of DEAL.

dæmon, dæmonic, etc.: see DEMON[1], etc.

daer-stock ('dɑ:eɪrstɒk). *Irish Antiq.* [f. MIr. *dáer*, OIr. *dóir, dóer* base, ignoble, unfree, servile, mod.Ir. *daor* captive, condemned, guilty + STOCK.] Stock or cattle belonging to the landlord of which the tenant or vassal has the use; used *attrib.* in ***daer-stock tenant, tenancy***.

1875 MAINE *Hist. Inst.* vi. 159 The Daer-stock tenant had unquestionably parted with some portion of his freedom. *Ibid.*, The relation between vassal and chief called Daer-stock tenancy.

dæsman, var. of DESMAN.

dafadar, daffadar, variant forms of DUFFADAR.

daff (dɑ:f, -æ-), *sb. Obs.* exc. *north. dial.* Also 4-5 daf, 4-6 daffe. [Etymology uncertain: cf. DAFT.

It has been conjecturally referred to ON. *dauf* deaf, dull, savourless, which survives in Sc. *dowf, douf* dull, spiritless, but this is phonetically inadmissible.]

One deficient in sense or in proper spirit; a simpleton, a fool; a coward.

c **1325** *Poem Times Edw. II*, 99 in *Pol. Songs* (Camden) 328 If the parsoun have a prest of a clene lyf..Shal comen a daffe and putte him out..That can noht a ferthing worth of god. **1362** LANGL. *P. Pl.* A. I. 129 'þou dotest daffe' quaþ heo 'Dulle are þi wittes.' *c* **1386** CHAUCER *Reeve's T.* 288 And when this Iape is tald another day I sal been halde a daf, a cokenay. *c* **1440** *Promp. Parv.* 111/2 Daffe, or dastard, or he þat spekythe not yn tyme, *oridurus*. **1587** HARRISON *England* II. ii. (1877) I. 58 Certes it [Landaffe] is a poore bishoprike ..the late incumbent thereof being called for..in open court made answer: The daffe is here, but the land is gone'. **1616** BULLOKAR, *Daffe*, a dastard. **1876** *Whitby Gloss.*, *Daff*, a half-wit; a coward.

daff (dɑ:f, -æ-), *v.*[1] Chiefly *Sc.* [f. DAFF *sb.*

Cf. the dial. *daffle* to become stupid, grow imbecile; also to dumbfounder, confuse the faculties; *daffly* imbecile, stupid from failure of the faculties. *Whitby Gloss.*]

1. *intr.* To play the fool; to make sport, toy, dally, talk or behave sportively.

1535 STEWART *Cron. Scot.* III. 342 Quhat do ȝe now? I se ȝe do bot daf. *a* **1605** POLWART *Flyting w. Montg.* 662 Dastard, thou daffes, that with such divilrie mels. **1813** PICKEN *Poems* I. 175 (Jam.) Come yont the green an' daff wi' me, My charming dainty Davy. **1876** *Whitby Gloss.*, *Daff*, to chat in a daudling way; to loiter. Also to falter in memory; 'beginning to daff'. **1886** STEVENSON *Kidnapped* iv. 30 Gentlemen daffing at their wine.

†**2.** *trans.* To daunt. *north. dial. Obs.*

1674 RAY *N.C. Words* 13 *Daffe*, to Daunt.

daff (dɑːf, -æ-), *v.*[2] [A variant of DOFF to do off, put off.

(Johnson, misunderstanding the pa. t., as in quot. 1596, made the present stem *daft*.)]

†**1.** *trans.* To put off (as clothes); to throw off, divest oneself of. *Obs.*

1597 SHAKS. *Lover's Compl.* 297 There my white stole of chastity I daff'd. **1606** —— *Ant. & Cl.* IV. iv. 13 He that vnbuckles this, till we do please To daft [= daff't] for our Repose, shall heare a storme.

2. To put or turn aside, to thrust aside; *esp.* in the Shaksperian phrase ***to daff the world aside*** (= to bid or make it get out of one's way), and imitations of this (sometimes vaguely or erroneously applied).

1596 SHAKS. *1 Hen. IV*, IV. i. 96 The..Mad-Cap, Prince of Wales, And his Cumrades, that daft the World aside, And bid it passe. **1599** —— *Much Ado* v. i. 78 *Claud.* Away, I will not haue to do with you. *Leo.* Canst thou so daffe me? **1599** —— *Pass. Pilgr.* 183 She bade good night, that kept my rest away; And daff'd me to a cabin hang'd with care. **1601** WEEVER *Mirr. Mart.* A vij, We daft the world with time ourselues beguiled. **1820** KEATS *Lamia* II. 160 Some knotty problem, that had daft His patient thought. **1880** GOLDW. SMITH in *Atl. Monthly* No. 268. 202 We have no right to daff a pessimist's argument aside merely because [etc.]. **1884** *Sat. Rev.* 14 June 787/1 Its pleasant fashion of daffing the world aside.

†**b.** To put off (with an excuse, etc.). *Obs.*

1604 SHAKS. *Oth.* IV. ii. 176 Euery day thou dafts [*v.r.* doffest] me with some deuise Iago.

daff (dæf). Colloq. abbrev. of DAFFODIL.

1915 C. MACKENZIE *Guy & Pauline* vi. 307 'We shall have all the daffs gone before we know where we are,' said the Rector. **1934** D. L. SAYERS *Nine Tailors* II. i. 69 You want a few more daffs. on the decani side, Mrs. Venables.

daffadowndilly, daffydowndilly. Also daffe-. [A playful expansion of DAFFO-DILLY.] A daffodil; used at first in the generic sense. Still a widespread popular name of the Yellow Daffodil, under the dialect forms ***daffadown-, -doon-, daffidown-, daffodowndilly.***

1573 TUSSER *Husb.* xliii. (1878) 95 Herbes, branches, and flowers, for windowes and pots..7 Daffadondillies. **1579** SPENSER *Sheph. Cal.* Apr. 140 Strowe mee the grounde with daffadowndillies. **1708** MOTTEUX *Rabelais* IV. li, Their Hair ..stuck with Roses, Gilly-flowers..Daffidown-dillies. **1840** BARHAM *Ingol. Leg.*, *Barney Maguire* ii, With roses and lillies, and daffy-down-dillies.

2. A shrub: prob. the Mezereon, which is still so called in Yorkshire 'from the slight similarity of the Greek name *Daphne* with *Daffodil*' (Britten and Holland).

1591 PERCIVALL *Sp. Dict.*, *Adelfa*, a daffadoundilly, or rather rose bay tree, *Rhododaphne.* **1611** FLORIO, *Oleándro*, the weede Oleander. Also a Daffadounedillie.

daffing ('dɑːfɪŋ, -æ-), *vbl. sb.* [f. DAFF *v.*[1] + -ING[1].]

1. Fooling, folly; sportive behaviour or talk; frolicking, toying, merriment.

1535 STEWART *Cron. Scot.* I. 449 Into sic daffing putting ȝour delyte, As brutell beist that followis appetyte. **1686** G. STUART *Joco-ser. Disc.* 39 You would have burst your heart with laughing To've seen the gang so full of daffing. **1787** BURNS *Twa Dogs* 43 Until wi' daffin weary grown, Upon a knowe they sat them down. **1823** LOCKHART *Reg. Dalton* VII. v. (1842) 416 They're young folk; daffin's natural to them. **1886** STEVENSON *Kidnapped* xxiii. 232 It was all daffing; it's all nonsense.

2. Mental derangement, insanity.

a **1614** J. MELVILL *MS.* 58 (Jam.) There he falls into a phrenzie and daffine which keeped him to his death. **1857** DUNGLISON *Dict. Med.* 274 *Daffing*, insanity.

daffingly ('dæfɪŋlɪ), *adv.* [f. *daffing*, pres. pple. of DAFF *v.*[1] + -LY[2].] Sportively.

1902 D. S. MELDRUM *Conquest of Charlotte* III. xix, 'Ah! he's married: that's crucial,' I said, daffingly. **1907** J. H. MCCARTHY *Needles & Pins* xx, 'I should have taken a great fancy to you,' he answered daffingly, 'if I had been a free man when we met.'

'**daffish,** *a. Obs.* exc. *north. dial.* [f. DAFF *sb.* + -ISH.] Spiritless; stupid.

1470–85 MALORY *Arthur* IX. xlii, This is but a daffyssh knyght. [**1869** *Lonsdale Gloss.*, *Daffish*, shy, modest.]

daffle ('dæf(ə)l), *v. dial.* or *colloq.* [f. DAFF *v.*[1] + -LE.] *intr.* To become silly, daft, or faltering; to act stupidly or inanely.

1796 W. H. MARSHALL *Rur. Econ. Yorks.* (ed. 2) II. 315 'He daffles', he wanders, or falters in his speech or conversation. **1853** R. S. SURTEES *Sponge's Sp. Tour* xxxvi, If your old man is done daffling with your draft, I should like to have the pick of it.

daffodil ('dæfədɪl). Also 6 daffodyll, 6–7 daffo-, daffadill, 7–8 daffadil. (9 daffodel): see also DAFFODILLY, and DAFFADOWNDILLY. [A variant of AFFODILL, q.v. The initial *d* has not been satisfactorily accounted for.

It has been variously suggested as due to childish or playful distortion, as in *Ted* for *Edward*, *tante* for *aunt*; to union of the article *th'* (cf. COTGR., *Affrodille*, *Th' Affodill*, and north. Eng. *t' affadil*); to final *d* of *and*, in (e.g.) 'fennell an-*d affodil*'; to union of the Dutch or Flemish article, as *de affodil* = the affodil; and to Fr. prep. *d'* as in *fleur d'aphrodille*. It is noteworthy that as in Eng. the word has gained a letter, in 16th c. Fr. it sometimes lost one: Littré (s.v. *asphodèle*) quotes from De Serres (16th c.), 'Des racines *d' afrodille*', and also 'Decoction de lapace, *de frodilles*'. A third form *daffrodille* is quite conceivable.

Affodill and its popular variants *daffodil, daffadilly*, were originally and properly the Asphodel; then by popular misconception, due apparently to the application to both plants, at their first introduction to England, of the fanciful name *Laus tibi* (see Turner *Libellus* B 3 b), it was applied, especially in the popular variations, to species of Narcissus, etc. Botanists, after resisting this misapplication, compromised the matter by retaining *affodil* for the Asphodel, and accepting the more popular *daffodil* for Narcissus. Finally *affodil* was 'rectified' to *asfodyl* and *asphodel*, and *daffodil* restricted in popular use to the Yellow Narcissus or Yellow Daffodil of Eng. fields and gardens.]

†**1.** The same as AFFODILL; the genus *Asphodelus* (formerly including some allied plants). *Obs.*

[**1538** see AFFODILL.] **1548** TURNER *Names of Herbes* s.v. *Albucus*, Asphodillus groweth..in gardines in Anwerp, it maye be named in englishe whyte affodil or duche daffodil. **1567** MAPLET *Gr. Forest* 40 Daffadill, some call Anthericon, the Romanes Kings spare. **1578** LYTE *Dodoens* v. lxxix. 649 This herbe [*Asphodelus* in 3 species] is called..in English also Affodyl, and Daffodyll. **1607** TOPSELL *Four-f. Beasts* (1673) 304 Asphodelus (englished by some *daffadil*).

†**2.** The genus *Narcissus*, of which it is the common Eng. name in the Catalogue of Gerarde's Garden 1599, where twelve *Daffodils* or Narcissuses are distinguished, the ***white daffodil*** being the common White Narcissus or Poet's Lily (*N. poeticus*) of Eng. gardens, the 'White Lily' of Scotland; the ***yellow daffodil*** (*N. pseudo-Narcissus*) the plant to which the name is now restricted.

1548 TURNER *Names of Herbes* (E.D.S.) 10 This that we take for daffodil is a kinde of Narcissus. **1578** LYTE *Dodoens* II. l. 211 These pleasant flowers are called..in Englishe Narcissus, white Daffodill, and Primerose pierelesse [In Lyte's own annotated copy in the Brit. Mus. Libr. he has written over the figure of *N. poeticus* on p. 210 'White primrose pyerles, Laus tibi, and of some Daffodille']. **1597** GERARDE *Herbal* I. lxxxiv. 111 The double white Daffodill of Constantinople [*N. orientalis*] was sent into England vnto the right Honorable the Lord Treasurer, among other bulbed flowers. **1629** PARKINSON *Paradisi in Sole* iv. (1656) 8 Many idle and ignorant Gardiners..do call some of these Daffodils Narcisses, when as all know that know any Latine, that Narcissus is the Latine name, and Daffodil the English of one and the same thing.

3. Now restricted to *Narcissus pseudo-Narcissus* (also called Lent Lily), found wild in various parts of England and cultivated as an early spring flower.

[**1562** TURNER *Herbal* II. 62 a, Our comen daffadil is one kynde of Narcissus.] **1592** GREENE *Upst. Courtier* (1871) 2 The yellow daffodil, a flower fit for jealous dotterels. **1611** SHAKS. *Wint. T.* IV. iii. 1 When Daffadils begin to peere, With heigh the Doxy ouer the dale. **1648** HERRICK *Hesper.*, *To Daffadils*, Faire Daffadills, we weep to see You haste away so soone. **1746–7** HERVEY *Medit.* (1818) 129 Who emboldens the daffodil..to trust her flowering gold with inclement and treacherous skies? **1855** TENNYSON *Maud* III. 6 When the face of night is fair on the dewy downs, And the shining daffodil dies.

4. ***chequered daffodil***: the Fritillary or Snake's head, *Fritillaria Meleagris*. Still known as the *daffodil* in Hants. (Britten and Holland).

1597 GERARDE *Herbal* I. lxxxix, The checquered Daffodil or Jinny hen floure..chequered most strangely. **1599** —— *Catal.*, *Frittillaria*, Checkerd Daffodill.

5. The colour of the daffodil; a pale yellow. Also *attrib.* or as *adj.*

1855 TENNYSON *Maud* I. XXII. ii, On a bed of daffodil sky. **1884** *Pall Mall G.* 21 Sept. 1/2 A belt of daffodil in the east announced the approach of dawn. **1886** *St. Stephen's Rev.* 13 Mar. 14/1 A primrose, a daffodil, or an orange-coloured gown.

daffodilly, daffadilly ('dæfədɪlɪ), *sb.* [f. prec.: perh. influenced by *lily*.] The same as DAFFODIL: a poetic (and dialect) form.

1538 [see AFFODILL]. **1579** SPENSER *Sheph. Cal.* Jan. 22 Thy sommer prowde, with Daffadillies dight. **1593** DRAYTON *Eclogues* iii. 81 See that there be store of Lillyes, (Call'd of Shepheards Daffadillyes). **1637** MILTON *Lycidas* 150 Bid amaranthus all his beauty shed, And daffadillies fill their cups with tears. **1847** MARY HOWITT *Ballads* 7 He cut the leaves of the snow-drop down, And tied up the daffodilly.

'**daffodilly,** *a. rare.* [f. DAFFODIL + -Y.] Full of or furnished with daffodils.

1892 *Temple Bar Mag.* Sept. 125 An exceedingly unpretentious, yet palm-y and daffodill-y drawing-room.

Daffy ('dæfɪ), *sb.*[1] Also daff(e)y. [The name of Thomas Daffy, an English clergyman of the seventeenth century.] Orig. in ***Daffy's elixir***, a medicine given to infants, 'tinctura sennæ composita' (Dunglison), to which gin was commonly added; hence, a slang name for gin itself.

1680 *The True News: or, Mercurius Anglicus* no. 33 10–13 Mar. [2]/2 Whereas divers Persons have lately exposed to sale a counterfeit Drink called Elixir Salutis, the true Drink of that Name, having been long since published by Mr. Anthony Daffy, (and generally known by the name of Daffy's Elixir Salutis), [etc.]. **1681** [see ELIXIR *sb.* 2 b]. *c* **1711** C. MORDAUNT *Let.* in Lady Hamilton *Mordaunts* (1965) iv. 79 Daphios Elixir for Chollick. **1768–74** [see ELIXIR *sb.* 2 b]. **1776** *Hibernian Jrnl.* 8–10 Apr. 179/3 (Advt.), Daffy's Elixir, just imported. **1821** *The Fancy* I. 304 While carrying on his new vocation as publican, Jack did not deny himself the use of drops of Daffy. **1828** *Sporting Mag.* XXI. 435 His predilection for daffey of late years grew upon him. **1838** DICKENS *O. Twist* I. ii. 15 [A little gin] to put into the blessed infants' Daffy. **1846** *Swell's Night Guide* 58, I takes the swell into the tape shop, took our daffies..and planted Flabby Bet on him. **1857** TROLLOPE *Barchester T.* xxiii, Not got a coral—how can you expect that he should cut his teeth? Have you got Daffy's Elixir? **1861** A. HALLIDAY in Mayhew *Lond. Labour* Extra vol. (1862) 430/2 When I goes in where they are a havin' their daffies—that's drops o' gin, sir. **1871** *London Figaro* 15 Apr. 10/2 [If the baby] should bawl persistently,..he would..bathe it in Mrs. Winslow's syrup, and thoroughly dose it with 'Daffy'. **1882** *Punch* 29 Apr. 193/2 A good many of them..had been partaking freely of *daffy*. **1967** E. BURTON *Georgians at Home* vi. 226 They [*sc.* Ward's pills] could hardly have done more harm or good than the snake-root and brandy.., Daffy's Elixir, usquebaugh, [etc.].

daffy ('dæfɪ), *sb.*[2] *colloq.* (orig. *dial.*). Abbreviated form of DAFFODILLY. So '**daffying** *sb.* (see quot. 1871).

1777 M. CUTLER in W. P. & J. P. Cutler *Life & Corr. M. Cutler* (1888) I. 63 Planted out in my borders in a great alley ..early and late Daffies, and Peonies. **1871** *Leisure Hour* 25 Mar. 184/1 Another of our rustic treats..was going to gather daffodils... In Herefordshire this little festival was called Daffying. **1878** W. DICKINSON *Gloss. Cumberland* 25/1 *Daffy-doon-dilly, Daffy*, the daffodil. **1925** *Sunday at Home* June 536/2 Little winds just rose on purpose to stir the daffies. **1928** *Daily Express* 28 Mar. 3/3 This has been a bad season for 'daffies' owing to a recent spell of frost in Cornwall.

daffy ('dæfɪ), *a. dial.* or *slang.* [f. DAFF *sb.*, *v.*[1]; cf. DAFFLE *v.*] = DAFT *a.*

1884 R. LAWSON *Upton-on-Severn Words* 14 *Daffy*, simple, soft. **1896** ADE *Artie* iii. 24 She'd make anybody daffy. **1902** *Munsey's Mag.* XXII. 491/2, I want to know what this new affair is. If I'm daffy, there's the reason. **1908** C. E. MULFORD *Orphan* xiv. 180 Old man Gordon was daffy on education, which is a good thing to be daffy over. **1922** *19th Cent.* Feb. 270 Guess the poor old devil's gone daffy. **1923** R. D. PAINE *Comr. Rolling Ocean* xv. 258 England was daffy over spy stories during the war. **1941** *Penguin New Writing* II. 87 Your eyes are all staring and aching..and they burn like hell. And it drives you nigh on daffy. **1959** I. & P. OPIE *Lore & Lang. Schoolchildren* x. 179 A person who is 'wanting in the upper storey' is..daffy. **1968** *Guardian* 28 Feb. 8/3 One of those charming fusions of the daffy benevolence of youth with the guilelessness of middle aged PROs.

daft (dɑːft, -æ-), *a.* Now chiefly *Sc.* and *north.* [In early ME. *daffte*, corresp. to OE. *ȝedæfte* mild, gentle, meek:—OTeut. **gadaftjo-z*, f. *gadafti* vbl. sb. from stem *dab-*, in Gothic *gadaban* to become, be fit, OE. pa. pple. *ȝedafen* becoming, fit, suitable. The *æ* here is app. for umlaut *ę* before *ft*, *st*, which explains the two-fold ME. development *daft* and *deft*. The primary meaning of the adj. must have been 'becoming, fit'; cf. the adv. *ȝedæftlíce* fitly, suitably, seasonably, and the vb. *ȝedæftan* to make fit or ready, to prepare; from 'fit, ready, apt' came the general later sense of *deft*; from 'becoming, *decens*' as said of persons, came that of 'meek, mild, innocent', and from 'innocent, inoffensive' app. that of 'irrational' said of beasts, and of 'silly, foolish, deficient in sense' as said of persons: cf. a common sense of 'innocent', and the sense-history of SILLY. See also DEFT.

DAFF, 'a fool,' is found *c* 1325; its relationship to *daft* is uncertain; if originally distinct, it may have contributed to the development of the sense 'foolish' here.]

†**1.** Mild, gentle, meek, humble. *Obs.*

c **1000** *Ags. Gosp.* Matt. xxi. 5 Nu þin cyning þe cymð to þe ȝedæfte. *c* **1200** ORMIN 2175 Shammfasst, and daffte, and sedefull. *Ibid.* 4610 And meoc, and daffte, and sedefull.

2. Silly, foolish, stupid. Cf. INNOCENT, SILLY.

a. Said of beasts.

c **1325** *Body & Soul* 302 in *Map's Poems* 343 Ne wuste what was good or il, But as a beest, doumbe and daft. *c* **1450** HENRYSON *Mor. Fab.* 81 Who sayes ane sheepe is daft, they lie of it.

b. Of persons: Wanting in intelligence, stupid, foolish.

c **1450** *St. Cuthbert* (Surtees) 443 Bot to make it I am daft, For I can noȝt of potter craft. **1535** LYNDESAY *Satyre* 2008 Thou art the daftest fuill that ever I saw. **1570** LEVINS *Manip.* 9/33 Dafte, doltishe, *stupidus.* **1637–50** ROW *Hist. Kirk* (1842) 462 Cast away these daft conceits, and..take you seriouslie to your booke and studies. **1674** RAY *N.C. Words* 13 *Daft*, stupid, blockish, daunted, a verbo Daffe. **1855** ROBINSON *Whitby Gloss.*, *Daft*, dull of apprehension.

3. Of unsound mind, crazy, insane, mad.

1536 BELLENDEN *Cron. Scot.* (1821) I. viii, He that was trublit with the falling evil, or fallin daft or wod. **1540** *Ld. Treas. Accts. Scot.*, Makand him Curatour to P.N. quhilk is daft, and hes na wit to gyde him selff. **1816** SCOTT *Old Mort.* vii, 'The woman would drive ony reasonable being daft.' **1829** ARNOLD *Let.* in Stanley *Life & Corr.* (1844) I. v. 254, I hope you will not think I ought to..adjourn to the next asylum for daft people. **1880** R. G. WHITE *Every-Day Eng.* 122 We have preserved our common sense, and have not gone clean daft.

4. Thoughtless or giddy in one's mirth; madly gay or frolicsome. ***daft days***: the days of merriment at Christmas.

c **1575** *Dial. betw. Clerk & Courtier* (Jam.), Quhen ye your selfis ar daft and young. **1768** Ross *Helenore* 117 (Jam.) Awa, she says, Whaever's daft to day, it setsna you. **1787** Burns *Twa Dogs* 155 In a frolic daft. *a* **1774** Fergusson *Poems* (1789) II. 10 (*title*) The Daft Days. **1816** Scott *Antiq.* xxi, 'Ay, ay—they were daft days thae—but they were a' vanity and waur.' **1832–53** *Whistle-binkie* (Sc. Songs) Ser. III. 81 At Yule, when the daft-days are fairly set in, A ploy without him wadna be worth a pin.

†**5.** = deft, skilful. *Obs.*

?*a* **1500** *Chester Pl.* (Shaks. Soc.) 134 (MS. 1592) For semlye he was and wounder dafte [MS. Harl. (1607) 2124 wondrous defte].

Hence †**dafteliʒk, daffteleʒʒc** [ON. *-leikr* suffix of action or condition], gentleness, meekness. **'daftie** (*colloq.*), a daft person. **'daftish** *a.*, somewhat daft. **'daftlike** *a.*, having an appearance of folly or craziness. **'daftly** *adv.*, †(*a*) mildly, meekly (*obs.*); (*b*) foolishly. **'daftness**, foolishness, madness.

c **1200** Ormin 2188 Forr kaggerrleʒʒc shall don þatt ʒho Shall daffteleʒʒc forrwerrpenn. **1872** C. Gibbon *For the King* i, The daftie still maintained his position. **1825** Jamieson, *Daftish*, in some degree deranged. **1855** Robinson *Whitby Gloss.*, A daftish dizzy sort of a body. **1725** Ramsay *Gent. Sheph.* iv. i, 'Tis sae daftlike. **1816** Scott *Antiq.* iv, Never think you..that his honour..would hae done sic a daft-like thing. *c* **1200** Ormin 1215 And haʒherrlike ledesst te And dafftelike and faʒʒre. **1724** Ramsay *Tea-t. Misc.* (1733) I. 34 We daftly thought to row in rowth. **1552** Abp. Hamilton *Catech.* 151 The word of the crosse semis to be daftnes and folie to thame that perischis.

daft, pa. t. of daff *v.*[2]

dag (dæg), *sb.*[1] In 4–5 dagge. [Of uncertain origin: the same senses are partly expressed by tag.]

†**1.** A pendant pointed portion of anything; one of the pointed or laciniated divisions made by deeply slashing or cutting the lower margin of a cloak, gown, or other garment, as was done for ornament in the 15th c. *Obs.*

1399 Langl. *Rich. Redeles* 193 Dryue out þe dagges and all þe duche cotis. *c* **1440** *Promp. Parv.* 111 Dagge of clothe, *fractillus.* **1617** Minsheu *Ductor*, Dagge or ragge of cloth.

†**2.** A tag or aglet of a lace, shoe-latchet, or the like; = aglet 1, 2. *Obs.*

c **1400** *Rom. Rose* 7262 Grey clothis..fretted fulle of tatarwagges [= dags, *sense* 1] And high shoos knopped with dagges. **1616** Bullokar, *Dagges*, latchets cut out of leather.

3. a. One of the locks of wool clotted with dirt about the hinder parts of a sheep; a 'clag'; = dagging, dag-lock.

[The relationship of this to the prec. senses, and to dag *v.*[1], is not clear.]

1731 Bailey, *Dagges*..the Skirts of a Fleece cut off. **1887** *Kentish Gloss.*, *Dag*, a lock of wool that hangs at the tail of a sheep and draggles in the dirt. *Dag-wool*, refuse wool; cut off in trimming the sheep.

b. *Comb.* **dag-boy, -cutter, -man, -pick** *v.*, **-picker** (see quots.). *Austral.* and *N.Z.*

1913 A. I. Carr *Country Work & Life in N.Z.* vi. 15 The dag cutter..has a seat handy and with a pair of shears cuts off all the wool he can, which he throws into another bin. **1933** *Bulletin* (Sydney) 8 Feb. 21, I work and whistle on my own..Dag-pickin' all day long. **1933** L. G. D. Acland in *Press* (Christchurch, N.Z.) 7 Oct. 15/7 The dags are afterwards gone through by a dag-picker or dag-boy, who cuts out any wool worth saving. **1958** *New Statesman* 23 Aug. 218/3 They were given jobs as..dag-men, which implied following around any one of 20,000 sheep and snipping off dung. **1965** [see dagger *sb.*[2] b].

4. A 'character', an extraordinary person, a 'tough' but amusing person (see also quot. 1941). *Austral.* and *N.Z. slang.*

1916 *Anzac Book* 47 Yes; 'Enessy was a dag if ever there was one! **1931** V. Palmer *Separate Lives* 222 Chook chuckled suddenly...'Ain't he a dag?' **1940** F. Sargeson *Man & Wife* (1944) 64 Struth he was a dag, Bill was. **1941** Baker *Dict. Austral. Slang* 22 Dag, an amusing or eccentric person. Whence, *dag* adj., good, excellent: *a dag at*, expert at. **1945** *N.Z. Geographer* I. 35 He was a tough old dag, and no mistake. **1949** E. de Mauny *Huntsman in Career* i. 33 Scotty's a bit of a dag, isn't he? **1970** D. M. Davin *Not Here, Not Now* II. ix. 115 Gerald seemed to have become a bit of a dag since the old days.

†**dag**, *sb.*[2] *Obs.* [Derivation unknown.

Referred by some to F. *dague* a dagger; but no trace has been found of any connexion between the two words.]

1. A kind of heavy pistol or hand-gun formerly in use.

1561 *Diurn. Occurrents* (Bannatyne Club) 66 Thay..schot furth at the said servandis ane dag. **1587** Harrison *England* II. xvi. (1877) I. 283 To ride with a case of dags at his sadle bow. **1598** Barckley *Felic. Man* (1631) 252 Because the dagge being overcharged brake..he draweth his dagger to stabbe him. **1602** Warner *Albion's Eng.* IX. xliv. (1612) 211 By wars, wiles, witchcrafts, daggers, dags. **1642** Laud *Wks.* (1853) III. 461, I heard a great crack, as loud as the report of a small dag. **1725** *New Cant. Dict.*, *Dag*, a Gun. **1849** Grant *Kirkaldy of G.* xxiv. 283 The captain rushed upon Lennox and shot him through the back with a dag. **1881** Greener *Gun* 61 A chiselled Italian dagg manufactured by one of the Comminazzo family about 1650.

2. *attrib.* and *Comb.*

a **1568** *Def. Crissell Sandelandis* 53 in *Sempill Ballates* (1872) 234 Snapwark, adew, fra dagmen dow nocht stand. **1587** Fleming *Contn. Holinshed* III. 1409/2 The dag was bought..of one Adrian Mulan a dag-maker dwelling in east Smithfield. **1589** R. Harvey *Pl. Perc.* (1860) 33 A Dag case may be as good now and then as a case of Dags. **1721** Wodrow *Hist. Ch. Scot.* (1829) II. II. ix. 250 Alexander Logan, Dagmaker in Leith Wynd.

[The sense 'dagger' given by Johnson (without quotation), and repeated in later dictionaries (in *Century Dict.* with erroneous quotation), appears to be a mere mistake, due to misapprehension of the frequent 16–17th c. collocation 'dag and dagger' in descriptions of personal accoutrement. Sense 3 in *Century Dict.* 'a stab or thrust with a dagger', is a blunder due to misreading of Minsheu.]

dag (dæg), *sb.*[3] [a. F. *dague* dagger, also the first horn of a young stag, and in some technical senses. Sense 2 is not found in French.]

1. The simple straight pointed horn of a young stag.

1859 Todd *Cycl. Anat.* V. 517/2 These processes acquire in the second year the form of..dags. **1861** Hulme tr. *Moquin-Tandon* II. III. 181 At first the new horns [of the stag] are simple protuberances, and are known by the name of 'dags'.

2. A pointed piece of metal, etc.; a pin or bolt.

1727 Bradley *Fam. Dict.* s.v. *Bridge*, You must so joint the Timber, as..to resemble an Arch of Stone..the Joints ought to be..strongly shut together with Cramps and Dags of Iron. **1805** R. W. Dickson *Pract. Agric.* (1807) II. 598 The upper pair [of rollers] being stuck with coggs and dags.

3. *dial.* (See quots.)

a. 1863 Barnes *Dorset Dialect*, *Dag*, a small projecting stump of a branch.

b. 1880 *W. Cornwall Gloss.*, *Dag*, a mining tool; an axe.

dag (dæg), *sb.*[4] *dial.* [app. of Norse origin: cf. ON. *dögg*, gen. *daggar*, pl. *daggir*, dew, Swed. *dagg* (Norw. *dogg*, Da. *dug*) = Goth. **daggwa-*, OTeut. **dauwo-*, OLG. *dauw*, OE. *deaw*, dew.]

1. Dew.

1674–91 Ray *S. & E.C. Words* 95 *Dag*, Dew upon the Grass. **1876** *S. Warwicksh. Gloss.*, *Dag*, dew. 'There's been a nice flop of dag.'

2. a. A thin or gentle rain. **b.** A wet fog, a mist. **c.** A heavy shower (*Ayrshire*).

1808 in Jamieson. **1825** Brockett *N.C. Words*, *Dag*, a drizzling rain.

dag (dæg), *sb.*[5] *dial.* or *slang.* [perh. altered from darg (one's) task.] A feat of skill; chiefly *pl.*, esp. in *doing dags* (see quots.).

1879 *N. & Q.* 5th Ser. XII. 128/1 'I'll do you (or your) dags.'—An expression used by children of young, and sometimes of older, growth, meaning, 'I'll do something that you cannot do.' **1886** F. T. Elworthy *W. Som. Word-Bk.* s.v., To 'set a dag' is to perform some feat in such a way as to challenge imitation... There's a dag for you—do it if you can. **1886** *Fun* (Farmer), He was very fond of what, in schoolboy days, we used to call doing dags. **1898** *Daily News* 4 Oct. 6/3 What does your entertainment principally consist of?.. Doing 'dags' to make the people laugh. **1902** *Windsor Mag.* June 114/1 Wearing it in your hat shows that you don't funk me. It's doing my dags to touch you.

dag, *v.*[1] [Connected with dag *sb.*[1] The senses have no connexion with each other.]

†**1.** *trans.* To cut the edge of (a garment) into long pointed jags; to slash, vandyke. *Obs.*

c **1386** Chaucer *Pars. T.* ¶344 Costlewe furring in here gownes..so moche daggyng of scheris. *Ibid.* ¶347 Suche pounsed and daggid clothing. **1393** Langl. *P. Pl.* XXIII. 143 Let dagge hus cloþes. *c* **1440** *Promp. Parv.* 112 Daggyn, *fractillo.* **1480** Caxton *Chron. Eng.* ccxxvi. 233 Short clothes and streyte wastyd dagged and kyt. **1523** Skelton *Garl. Laurel* 630 Raggid and daggid & cunnyngly cut.

2. a. To clog with dirt, bemire, daggle, bedraggle. *Obs.* exc. *dial.* (Cf. dag *sb.*[1] 3.)

1484 Caxton *Æsop* III. xvii, Al to-fowled and dagged. *a* **1529** Skelton *El. Rummyng* 123 Wyth theyr heles dagged, Theyr kyrtelles all to-iagged. **1530** Palsgr. 445/2 Indede, damoysell, you be dagged..*vous estes crottée.* **1611** Cotgr. s.v. *Archediacre, Crotte en Archediacre*, dagd vp to the hard heeles (for so were the Archdeacons in old time euer woont to be, by reason of their frequent..Visitations). *a* **1661** Holyday *Juvenal* 136 Vexing the baths with his dagg'd rout. **1869** *Lonsdale Gloss.*, *Dag*..(2) To trail or dirty in the mire, to bedaub, to daggle. **1879** Miss Jackson *Shropsh. Word-bk.*, *Dag*..to trail in the wet or dirt.

b. *intr.* To daggle or trail in the dirt or wet.

1869 *Lonsdale Gloss.*, *Dag* v. i. **1880** *W. Cornwall Gloss.* s.v. *Dagging*, 'That tree is dagging with fruit.' 'Her dress is dagging in the mud.'

3. *Farming.* To cut off the 'dags' or locks of dirty wool from (sheep); the usual word in Australia and N.Z. (Cf. dag *sb.*[1] 3.)

1706 Phillips (ed. Kersey), *To Dag sheep*, to cut off the Skirts of the Fleece. **1887** *Kentish Gloss.*, *Dag*, to remove the dags or clots of wool, dirt, etc. from between the hind legs of sheep. **1889** Williams & Reeves *Colonial Couplets* 9 Dagging the hoggets, or drafting the rams. **1923** W. Perry *Sheep Farming in N.Z.* vi. 73 The ewes should also be dagged..before turning the rams in. **1965** J. S. Gunn *Terminology Shearing Industry* I. 20 *Dag*, wool mixed with dung, dirt, or other rubbish, hanging from the sheep. To 'dag' is to remove this wool with 'dagging shears'.

†**dag**, *v.*[2] *Obs.* [Related to F. *dague* dagger (13th c. in Littré): cf. also 16th c. F. *daguer* to strike with a *dague* or dagger; but the latter is not the source of the Eng. verb. See also dagger.]

trans. To pierce or stab, with or as with a pointed weapon.

?*a* **1400** *Morte Arth.* 2102 Dartes the Duche-mene daltene aȝaynes, With derfe dynttez of dede, daggesthurghe scheldez. *Ibid.* 3750 Derfe dynttys they dalte with daggande sperys. **1639** Horn & Rob. *Gate Lang. Unl.* lxiv. §668 Remorse..pierceth and daggeth guilty persons with the anguish of a galled conscience. **1794** A. Gallatin in J. A. Stevens *Life* iv. (1884) 95 One Ross of Lancaster..half drew a dagger he wore..and swore any man who uttered such sentiments ought to be dagged.

†**dag**, *v.*[3] *Obs.* [f. dag *sb.*[2]] *trans.* and *intr.* To shoot with a dag or hand-gun.

a **1572** Knox *Hist. Ref.* Wks. (1846) I. 87 Thei schote spearis and dagged arrowis, whare the cumpanyes war thikest. *c* **1580** J. Hooker *Life Sir P. Carew*, They soe dagged at these loopes, that sundrye of theyme within were slayne.

dag (dæg), *v.*[4] *dial.* [app. of Norse origin: cf. dag *sb.*[4] and ON. *döggva*, Swed. *dagga* to bedew. See also deg.]

1. *trans.* To sprinkle, to wet with sprinkling.

1855 Robinson *Whitby Gloss.*, *Dag*, to sprinkle with water. **1877** *Holderness Gloss.*, *Dag*, to sprinkle. 'Dag cawsey afoor thoo sweeps it!' **1879** Miss Jackson *Shropsh. Word-bk.*, *Dag*, to sprinkle clothes with water preparatory to mangling or ironing.

2. *intr.* To drizzle.

1825 Brockett *N.C. Words*, *Dag*, to drizzle.

dagar, -ard, -are, obs. forms of dagger.

dageraad ('dægə,rɑːd, -,rɑːt, ‖'dɑx-, 'dag-). *S. Afr.* Also **daggerhead, daggerheart.** [Afrikaans, f. Du. *dageraad* daybreak, the name of the fish being supposed to refer to its brilliant colouring.] The brilliantly coloured sea-fish *Chrysoblephus cristiceps* (family Sparidæ).

Derivation via Du. *dorade*, ad. Sp. and Pg. *dorado* dorado (Boshoff & Nienaber *Afrikaanse Etim.*, 1967) does not account for the phonology of the S. Afr. word.

1853 L. Pappe *Edible Fishes Cape Gd. Hope* 20 *Pagrus laniarius*..(*Dageraad*)..Strong conical teeth in the upper jaw, which..project from the mouth..those of the lower jaw much smaller. The whole fish is of a dark rose-colour. ..Lower jaw white; iris silvery; length 12 inches. **1906** *East London Dispatch* 3 July 3/3 This fish was probably what is known as a 'daggerhead' (pagrus laniarius). **1913** Pettman *Africanderisms* 135 *Dageraad*, *Pagrus laticeps*...is sometimes corrupted into Daggerhead, Daggerheart, etc. **1953** F. Robb *Sea Hunters* viii. 122 Then we'll go inshore and fish daggerheads and soldiers. **1957** S. Schoeman *Strike!* iii. 40 The dageraad is also called daggerhead along the Pondoland and Natal Coast.

‖**dagesh, daghesh** ('dɑːgɛʃ), *sb. Heb. Gram.* [med.Heb *dāghēsh*, f. Syriac *d'ghash* to prick.] A point or dot placed within a Hebrew letter, denoting either that it is doubled (*dagesh forte*), or that it is not aspirated (*dagesh lene*).

1591 Percivall *Sp. Dict.* Bj, *B*..very often..is sounded like the Hebrew ב when it is in the middest of a word without daggesh. **1749** B. Martin *Dict. Introd. Eng. Tongue* 9 If any of the aspirated letters has the point (call'd Dagesh) in them, they are then pronounced without the H. **1834** A. Willis *Hebr. Gram.* 5 A point is sometimes inserted in the middle of a consonant affecting the pronunciation, and called Dagesh or Mappik.

Hence **'dagesh** *v. trans.*, to mark with a dagesh. Also **'dagessate** *v.*, **'dagessate, -ated** *pa. pple.*

1751 Wesley *Wks.* (1872) XIV. 156 In some Verbs..the middle Radical is dageshed. **1871** Bolton tr. *Delitzsch's Psalms* II. 259 *note*, The dageshing of the opening mute of the following word.

dagga[1] ('dægə, ‖'daxa). *S. Afr.* Also **dacca, dacha, dacka, dakha, dak(k)a.** [Afrikaans, f. Hottentot *dachab.*] A name for hemp, *Cannabis sativa*, used as a narcotic. Also applied to any indigenous plant of the genus *Leonotis*, called wild dagga, which is similarly used. Also *attrib.* and *Comb.*

[**1668** O. Dapper *Kaffrarie* in I. Schapera *Early Cape Hottentots* (1933) 40 Zekeren krachtigen wortel, dien zy *dacha* noemen.] **1670** J. Ogilby *Africa* 583 A powerful Root, which they call *Dacha*; sometimes eating it, otherwhiles mingling it with Water to drink; either of which ways taken, causeth Ebriety. **1785** G. Forster tr. *Sparrman's Voy.* (1786) I. 145 *Bucku* (*diosma*) and wild *dacka* (*phlomis leonurus*) which are known both by the colonists and the Hottentots to be as efficacious as they are common. **1796** tr. *Le Vaillant's New Travels* III. 267 The people wished for tobacco and dacca (the leaves of hemp). **1822** W. J. Burchell *Trav. Interior S. Afr.* I. 366 The common hemp, called *dakka*, was here raised..as presents to the Bushmen, who smoke it instead of tobacco. **1835** J. W. D. Moodie *Ten Yrs. S. Afr.* I. 41 Many of these people [*sc.* Hottentots] have..a pernicious habit of smoking a plant called 'dacha'... The 'dacha rookers' are held in great contempt by the tobacco smokers of their nation. **1894** C. H. Donovan *With Wilson in Matabeleland* vii. 140 It is exceedingly entertaining to watch these boys 'dakha-smoking'. **1910** J. Buchan *Prester John* vii. 119 He must have been a *dacha*-smoker, for he coughed hideously. **1912** *East London Dispatch* 28 June 9/6 The red Dagga, or 'Mfincafincane', of the Kaffirs. **1921** *Blackw. Mag.* Jan. 110/2 They are..much addicted to smoking a drug which is known as 'daka'. **1939** *Times Lit. Suppl.* 9 Sept. 531/3 Marihuana, otherwise..ganja, dagga, and about a hundred other names. **1950** *Cape Times* 19 Sept. 12/7 Prison sentences for dagga smokers. **1953** P. Lanham *Blanket Boy's Moon* vi. 131 There is..a huge trade carried on in South Africa in the growing, smuggling and peddling of dagga. **1969** *Sci. Jrnl.* Sept. 38/1 Some preparations of the [Cannabis] plant, like the *ganja* of India, are more intoxicating than marihuana... Others, like Indian *bhang*, Moroccan *kif*, and South African *dagga*, are nearly equivalent to marihuana.

dagga[2] ('dɑːgə). *S. Afr.* Also **daager, dagher, dargha.** [f. Zulu and Xhosa *daka* mud, clay, mortar.] A kind of mortar made of mud and cow-dung, often mixed with ox-blood. Hence as *vb.*, to smear with dagga.

1878 H. A. ROCHE *On Trek in Transvaal* xii. 251 A Kafir came to 'daager' or smear our floors. **1880** H. M. PRICHARD *Friends & Foes* 282 Kafir women..smear the walls and floor with 'dargha'. **1893** BLENNERHASSETT & SLEEMAN *Adv. Mashonaland* 32 We had heard..that 'daghering' and 'smearing' would be essential parts of our work. **1896** H. L. TANGYE *In New S. Afr.* v. 326 This lends some colour to the theory that the inhabitants adapted themselves..to the practice of the country and lived in dagher huts. **1899** W. H. BROWN *On S. Afr. Frontier* 63 The houses were built of 'dagga' (mud), brick, and corrugated iron. **1905** *Blackw. Mag.* Mar. 389/1 The room was floored with dagga—anthill earth brought to a high stage of hardness and mahogany-like polish by frequent dressings of bullock's blood and kraal manure. **1936** P. M. CLARK *Autobiogr. Old Drifter* vii. 92 A hut constructed of dagga—that is, ant-heap mixed with cowdung.

'daggar. *dial.* 'An old term for a dog-fish' (Smyth, *Sailor's Word-bk.* 1867).

a **1728** KENNETT cited by HALLIWELL.

† **dagged,** *ppl. a.*[1] *Obs.* [f. DAG *v.*[1]]

1. Of a garment: Having the margin cut into long pointed projections; jagged, slashed.

c **1386** [see DAG *v.*[1] 1]. *c* **1430** LYDG. *Min. Poems* (Percy Soc.) 200 Undir hire daygyd hood of green. **1523** [see DAG *v.*[1] 1]. [**1884** *Pall Mall G.* '*Extra*' 24 July 28/2 The costume is all dagged and slashed into the shape of leaves and flowers.]

2. Clogged with dirt, daggled.

1484, *a* **1529**, **1661** [see DAG *v.*[1] 2].

dagged, *ppl. a.*[2] *Obs.* exc. *dial.* [f. DAG *v.*[4]] Wet with dew, drizzling rain, or a sprinkling of anything. **b.** *slang.* Drunk.

a **1605** MONTGOMERIE *Sonn.* lxviii. 11 My Bee's aloft, and daggit full of skill: It getts corn drink, sen Grissall toke the bed. **1745** FRANKLIN *Drinker's Dict.* Wks. 1887 II. 23 He's dagg'd. **1847–78** HALLIWELL, *Dagged*, tipsy. *North.*

dagger ('dægə(r)), *sb.*[1] Forms: 4– **dagger**; also 4–5 **daggere**, *Sc.* **dagare**, 5 **daggare**, 5–6 **dager**, **dagar**, **daggar**, 6 **dagard**. [Related to F. *dague* (Sp., It. *daga*) dagger, and to DAG *v.*[2]

No such form is known in Old French. Med.L. shows *daggarius, -arium, -erius, -ardum* (see Du Cange), app. from English, so that the form *dagger* appears to be really of English formation (? f. DAG *v.*[2], of which however only later instances are known). If the form *daggard* could be assumed as the original, the word might be an augmentative in *-ard* of F. *dague*; but, though *extracto cultello daggardo* occurs in Walsingham, 15th c. (Du Cange), the forms *daggarium* and *dagger* are of earlier appearance and better supported.]

1. a. A short stout edged and pointed weapon, like a small sword, used for thrusting and stabbing.

[*a* **1375** *Fragm. Vetusta* xxiv. in *Sc. Acts* (1844) I. 388 Habeat equum, hauberkion, capilium de ferro, ensem, et cultellum qui dicitur *dagare*. *Ibid.* Habeat archum et sagittas, et daggarium et cultellum.] *c* **1386** CHAUCER *Prol.* 113 He baar..on that oother syde a gay daggere[*rime* spere]. —— *Pard. T.* 502 And with thy daggere [*so* 4 *MSS.*, 3 dagger] looke thou do the same. **1440** *Promp. Parv.* 111 Daggare, to steke wythe men, *pugio*. **1463** *Paston Lett.* No. 466 II. 126 The same dager he slewe hym with. **1535** *Bury Wills* (1850) 127 Wt my dagard. **1601** SHAKS. *Jul. C.* III. ii. 157, I feare I wrong the Honourable men, Whose Daggers haue stabb'd Cæsar. **1605** —— *Macb.* I. iii. 33 Is this a Dagger which I see before me? **1719** YOUNG *Busiris* IV. i, Loose thy hold, Or I will plant my dagger in thy breast. **1866** KINGSLEY *Hereward* iii. 88 'You have a dagger in your hand!' said he.

† **b.** *ale dagger, alehouse dagger*: see ALE, B. II. *dagger of lath*: the weapon worn by the 'Vice' in the old 'Moralities'. *Obs.*

1592 NASHE *P. Penilesse* (Shaks. Soc.) 40 All you that will not..weare ale-house daggers at your backes. **1596** SHAKS. *1 Hen. IV*, II. iv. 151 A Kings Sonne? If I do not beate thee out of thy Kingdome with a dagger of Lath..Ile neuer weare haire on my face more. **1601** —— *Twel. N.* IV. ii. 136 Like to the old vice..Who with dagger of lath, in his rage and his wrath, Cries ah ha, to the diuell.

2. Phr. *daggers' drawing* (fig.): the commencement of open hostilities. *at* (or *to*) *daggers' drawing*, now *at daggers drawn*: on (or to) the point of fighting or quarrelling; in a state of open hostility. Also (rarely) *at daggers' points*.

at daggers drawn is found in 1668, but becomes usual only in 19th c.

1553 GRIMALDE *Cicero's Offices* 12 a, They..among themselues are wont to bee at daggers drawing. **1576** FLEMING *Panopl. Epist.* 267 That countrie was at defiaunce and daggers drawing with the lande of Græcia. **1652** J. WADSWORTH tr. *Sandoval's Civ. Wars Sp.* 19 The Grandees of the Court were com almost to daggers drawing. **1668** R. L'ESTRANGE *Vis. Quev.* (1708) 214 Upon this Point, were they at Daggers-drawn with the Emperor. *a* **1735** SWIFT *Drapier's Lett.* vii, A quarrel in a tavern, where all were at daggers-drawing. **1801** MAR. EDGEWORTH *Castle Rackrent*, Three ladies..talked of for his second wife, all at daggers drawn with each other. **1837** LADY L. STUART in *Lady M. W. Montagu's Lett.* (1893) I. 104 Both these ladies inherited such..imperial spirit, as to..insure daggers drawing as soon as it should find..opportunity to display itself. **1847** MRS. SHERWOOD *Lady of Manor* III. xviii. 36 You will be at daggers-drawing..with every order..of persons in the town. **1855** DICKENS *Dorrit* (Househ. ed.) 395/1 Five minutes hence we may be at daggers' points. **1870** R. B. BROUGH *Marston Lynch* xxiv. 257 Was Marston still at daggers drawn with his rich uncle?

3. *fig.* **a.** Something that wounds or afflicts grievously.

1596 SHAKS. *Merch. V.* III. i. 115 Thou stick'st a dagger in me, I shall neuer see my gold againe. **1605** —— *Macb.* II. iii. 45 Where we are there's Daggers in mens Smiles. **1704** STEELE *Lying Lover* II, This was to me Daggers. **1800** MRS. HERVEY *Mourtray Fam.* III. 240 Every word he spoke was a dagger to her heart.

b. *to speak* or *look daggers*: to speak so as to wound, to speak or look fiercely, savagely, or angrily.

1602 SHAKS. *Ham.* III. ii. 414, I will speake Daggers to her, but vse none. **1622** MASS. & DEKKER *Virg. Mart.* IV. i, And do thine eyes shoot daggers at that man That brings thee health? **1833** MARRYAT *P. Simple* lii, Lord Privilege..looked daggers at me. **1839** H. AINSWORTH *Jack Shep.* iv, A glance..which was meant to speak daggers.

† **4.** *fig.* (*contempt.*) A bravo, braggadocio. *Obs.*

1597 *1st Pt. Return fr. Parnass.* I. i. 289 Soothe upp this..ingrosser of cringers..this great hilted dagger! *Ibid.* IV. i. 1236 This bracchidochio..this meere rapier and dagger.

† **5.** A bayonet. (See BAYONET *sb.* 1, 2.) *Obs.*

1688 CAPT. J. S. *Art of War* 27 Draw your Daggers. Fix them in your Musquet.

6. a. The upright piece of wood nailed to the bars in the middle of a rail or gate. **b.** *Naut.* (See quot.)

1641 BEST *Farm. Bks.* (Surtees) 15 A dagger, which goeth straight downe the middle of the spelles, and is nayled to each spell. *c* **1850** *Rudim. Navig.* (Weale) 113 *Dagger*, a piece of timber that faces on to the poppets of the bilge-ways, and crosses them diagonally, to keep them together. The plank that secures the heads of the poppets is called the dagger-plank. The word 'dagger' seems to apply to anything that stands diagonally or aslant.

c. = DOG-SHORE.

1838 *Civil Engin. & Arch. Jrnl.* I. 384/2 At 11 o'clock the dagger was knocked down, and the beautiful vessel..glided majestically into the river. **1896** *Strand Mag.* XII. 325 Being simultaneously released..these weights instantly fall, and..bring down the daggers, thus removing all obstacle to the passage of the ship down the ways.

† **7.** The horn of a young stag; = DAG *sb.*[3] 1. *Obs.*

1616 SURFL. & MARKH. *Country Farme* 684 The second yeare they haue their first hornes, which are called daggers.

8. *Printing.* A mark resembling a dagger (†), used for marginal references, etc.: also called *obelisk*. *double dagger*: a mark having each end like the hilt of a dagger (‡), similarly used.

1706 PHILLIPS (ed. Kersey), *Dagger*..a..Mark in Printing..(†). **1770** *Hist. Printing* 259 The Obelisk, or long Cross, erroneously called the single Dagger..The Double Dagger. **1862** ANSTED *Channel Isl.* II. viii. (ed. 2) 166 Those that are certainly not indigenous being indicated by a little dagger (†) placed before the name.

9. A collector's name of moths of the genus *Acronycta* having a black dagger-like or ψ-like mark near the anal angle of the fore wings.

1832 J. RENNIE *Conspectus Butterf. & Moths* 79 The *Dark Dagger* appears in June. **1862** E. NEWMAN *Brit. Moths* 249, I do not know why this insect [*Acronycta tridens*] is called the 'Dark Dagger': it is no darker than the 'Gray Dagger' [*A. Psi*].

10. *pl.* Applied locally to various plants with long sword-like leaves, as Sword-grass (*Poa aquatica*), Water-flag (*Iris Pseudacorus*), etc.

1847–78 HALLIWELL, *Daggers*, sword-grass. *Somerset.* **1882** *Devonsh. Plant-n.* (E.D.S.), *Daggers*, *Iris Pseudacorus*, and *I. fœtidissima*. The name evidently has reference to the sword-like flags or leaves.

† **11.** The name of a celebrated tavern in Holborn *c* 1600 (Nares); hence *attrib.* as in *dagger-ale*, *-frumety*, *-pie*. *Obs.*

1576 GASCOIGNE *Diet Droonkardes* (N.), But we must have March beere, dooble dooble beere, dagger-ale, Rhenish. **1602** DEKKER *Satiromastix* in Hawkins *Orig. Eng. Drama* III. 115 (N.) Good den, good coosen..When shall we eat another Dagger-pie. **1610** B. JONSON *Alch.* I. i, My lawyer's clerk, I lighted on last night, In Holborn, at the Dagger. *Ibid.* v. ii, Her grace would have you eat no more Woolsack pies, Nor Dagger frumety.

12. *Comb.*, as *dagger-blade*, *-hilt*, *-stab*, *-work*; *dagger-like*, *-proof* adjs.; † **dagger-ale** (see 11); † **dagger-cheap** *a.*, very cheap, 'dirt-cheap'; † **dagger-frumety** (see 11); **dagger-grass**, ? = sword-grass (see 10); **dagger-knee** (*Naut.*), see quot.; † **dagger-man**, a man who carries a dagger, a bravo; † **dagger-money**, 'a sum of money formerly paid to the justices of assize on the northern circuit to provide arms against marauders' (Ogilvie); † **dagger-pie** (see 11); **dagger-piece** (*Naut.*) = sense 6 b; **dagger-plank** (*Naut.*), see quot. under 6 b; **dagger-plant**, a plant of the genus *Yucca*, also called *Adam's needle*, having sharp-edged and pointed leaves; **dagger-wood** (*Naut.*) = sense 6 b.

1562 *Act 5 Eliz.* c. 7 §3 *Dagger-blades, Handles, Scabbards. **1592** BP. ANDREWES *Serm. Christ's Tempt.* vi. (1843) V. 546 We set our wares at a very easy price, he [the devil] may buy us even *dagger-cheap, as we say. **1834** MEDWIN *Angler in Wales* I. 262 These tracks were sometimes lost in high *dagger-grass. **1676** GREW *Anat. Plants* Lect. IV. ii. §18 Crystals..figur'd crossways like a *Dagger-Hilt. *c* **1850** *Rudim. Navig.* (Weale) 114 Any straight hanging knees, not perpendicular to the side of the beam, are in general termed *dagger-knees. **1603** SHAKS. *Meas. for M.* IV. iii. 16 Mr Starue-Lackey the Rapier and *dagger man. **1867** SMYTH *Sailor's Word-bk.*, **Dagger-piece*, or *Dagger-wood*, a timber or plank that faces on to the poppets of the bilge-ways, and crosses them diagonally, to keep them together. **1866** *Treas. Bot.*, *Dagger plant, a name for *Yucca*. **1885** LADY BRASSEY *The Trades* 220 The road was bordered by hedges of cactus and dagger-plants. **1892** BARING-GOULD *Roar of Sea* II. xxix. 141 Miss Travisa..cast a glance at her niece like a *dagger-stab. **1890** MICHAEL FIELD *Tragic Mary* I. i. 7, I never saw such *dagger-work..As that which pierced him. Six and fifty wounds!

'dagger, *sb.*[2] *Austral.* and *N.Z.* [f. DAG *sb.*[1] 3 + -ER.] **a.** *pl.* (See quot. 1945.)

1878 G. H. GIBSON *Southerly Busters* 179 I'm able for to shear 'em clean, And level as a die; But I prefers to 'tommy-hawk', And make the 'daggers' fly. **1945** BAKER *Austral. Lang.* iii. 64 Handshears are known as daggers, jingling johnnies.

b. (See quot. 1965.)

1889 WILLIAMS & REEVES *Colonial Couplets* 28 He could do anything, he swore..Would take what came,..Be 'brander', 'rouse-about', or 'dagger'. **1952** *Arena* XXXI. 4 The dogs, the roussies and penners-up and daggers. **1965** J. S. GUNN *Terminology Shearing Industry* I. 21 In earlier times, but not often to-day, shedhands known as 'daggers' and 'dag boys' were given the job of 'dag picking' or recovering wool from the dags.

'dagger, *v.* [f. DAGGER *sb.*[1]]

1. *trans.* To stab with a dagger.

1658 R. FRANCK *North. Mem.* (1821) 36 When Democrasians dagger the crown. **1806** *Naval Chron.* XV. 453 Rackstraw was daggered, and died immediately. **18..** A. SUTHERLAND *Tales of Pilgrim, Brigand of Loire*, He was in no danger of being daggered.

2. *Printing.* To mark with a dagger (†).

1875 FURNIVALL in *Thynne's Animadv.* Introd. 37 *note*, The dishes chang'd in the list are daggerd.

Hence **'daggering** *vbl. sb.*, stabbing with a dagger; *ppl. a.*, stabbing, fatal.

1694 WESTMACOTT *Script. Herb.* (1695) 214 Every Month produces sad and fatal Instances of its [Brandy's] daggering force. **1830** *Blackw. Mag.* XXVII. 55 The screaming and daggering and death-rattling.

daggered ('dægəd), *a.* [f. DAGGER + -ED.]

1. Armed with a dagger.

c **1400** MAUNDEV. (1839) xii. 137 Now swerded, now daggered, and in alle manere gyses. **1794** COLERIDGE *Relig. Musings*, The dagger'd Envy. *c* **1830** BEDDOES *Poems, Boding Dreams*, A daggered hand beside the bed.

2. Stabbed or wounded with a dagger.

1604 DEKKER *Hon. Whore* Wks. II. 38 How many Gallants have drunke healths to me, Out of their dagger'd armes.

3. *Printing.* Marked with a dagger.

daggerhead, daggerheart: see DAGERAAD.

daggeswayne, var. DAGSWAIN *Obs.*

daggett ('dægɪt). Also **degote**, **degutt**. [ad. Russ. *dëgot'* tar.] A dark tar obtained by the distillation of the bark of the European white birch, and used in the preparation of Russia leather, and formerly as a local application for diseases of the skin.

1861 *Chambers's Encycl.* II. 104/1 [The birch] yields also the B[irch] Tar, or *Degutt*. [**1875** *Encycl. Brit.* III. 698/1 An empyreumatic oil, called *diogott* in Russia.] **1890** BILLINGS *Nat. Med. Dict.*, *Daggett*, birch-tar. **1900** DORLAND *Med. Dict.*, *Degote*, tarry oil of white birch. **1935** *Discovery* Oct. 299/2 Birch bark..by destructive distillation, yields an empyreumatic oil, known as Oil of Birch Tar, Dagget [etc.].

dagging ('dægɪŋ), *vbl. sb.* Now *dial.* [f. DAG *v.*[1] + -ING[1].] The action of the verb DAG; clogging with dirt, *esp.* of the wool about the hinder parts of a sheep; *spec.* in Austral. and N.Z., the operation of cutting off the 'dags' or locks of dirty wool from (sheep); in *pl.* (*concr.*) = DAG-LOCKS.

1547 SALESBURY *Welsh Dict.*, *Dibyl*, daggyng. **1587** MASCALL *Govt. Cattle* (1627) 197 Keeping them from cold in Winter, dagging in Summer. **1890** F. T. ELWORTHY (*in letter*), In Kent these clots of dung which are apt to..stick to the wool around the tails of sheep, with the wool attached, are called 'daggings'. **1898** H. B. VOGEL *Maori Maid* xix. 147 When the docking, and dagging, and cutting comes. **1915** J. R. MACDONALD *N.Z. Sheepfarming* xl. 120 Cleanliness, by way of proper dipping, dagging, and crutching are good preventive aids [against blowfly]. **1934** T. WOOD *Cobbers* viii. 99 Dagging, in polite terms, is the removal, by shears, of wool which is matted on the thighs by excreta.

daggle ('dæg(ə)l), *v.* Also 6 **daggyll**, 6–7 **dagle**. [Frequentative of DAG *v.*[1] sense 2: associated in its sense-development with DABBLE and DRAGGLE and perhaps with DAG *v.*[4]]

1. *trans.* To clog with wet mud; to wet and soil a garment, etc., by trailing it through mud or wet grass.

1530 PALSGR. 594/1 You shall daggyll your clothes, *vous crotterez voz habillemens*. **1560** ROLLAND *Crt. Venus* II. 566 Daglit in weit richt claggit was his weid. **1611** COTGR., *Crotter*..to dagle, bedurtie. **1660** T. GOUGE *Chr. Directions* xv. (1831) 85 As a long coat is in greater danger to be daggled than a short one. **1825** BROCKETT *N.C. Words*, *Daggle*..to bemire.

b. In later use, chiefly said of the effect of wet: To wet by splashing or sprinkling. See DAG *v.*[4]

1805 SCOTT *Last Minst.* I. xxix, The warrior's very plume ..Was daggled by the dashing spray. **1862** MISS YONGE *Countess Kate* viii. (1880) 81 The pretty soft feather had been daggled in the wet.

2. To drag or trail about (through the mire).

1681 OTWAY *Soldier's Fort.* v. i, After you have been daggling yourself abroad for prey..you come sneaking hither for a crust, do you? 1822 SCOTT *Nigel* viii, I have been daggled to and fro the whole day.

3. *intr.* To walk in a slovenly way (through mud or mire); to drag or trail about. Cf. DRAGGLE.

1705 VANBRUGH *Confed.* I. ii, Then, like a dutiful son, you may daggle about with your mother, and sell paint. 1735 POPE *Prol. Sat.* 225, I ne'er..like a puppy daggled through the town To fetch and carry sing-song up and down. 1869 *Lonsdale Gloss., Daggle* v. i., to trail in the dirt. 1876 *Whitby Gloss.* s.v. *Daggling*, 'Trailing and daggling', said of a person walking in a shower.

† **'daggle**, *sb. Obs. rare.* [f. prec. vb.] A clot or spot of wet mud, as on a daggled garment.

1591 PERCIVALL *Sp. Dict., Carpas*, daggles of durt, spots of durt.

daggled ('dæg(ə)ld), *ppl. a.* [f. DAGGLE *v.* + -ED[1].] Having the skirts clogged or splashed with dirt or wet; bespattered, bemired.

1607 *Barley-Breake* (1877) 21 What..dagled mayd with payle. 1638 *Songs Costume* (Percy Soc.) 140 Fringe with gold your daggl'd tails. 1727 SWIFT *Poems, City Shower*, To shops in crowds the daggled females fly. 1742 MRS. DELANY *Life & Corr.* (1861) II. 193 Caught in a smart shower of rain, [[we] came home in a fine daggled condition.

b. *Comb.* † **daggled-tail** *a.* = DAGGLE-TAILED.

1708 SWIFT *Agst. Abol. Christianity*, Shocked at the sight of so many daggled-tail parsons.

daggle-tail ('dæg(ə)lteɪl), *sb. Obs.* exc. *dial.* A person (*esp.* a woman) whose garments are bemired by being trailed over wet ground; an untidy woman, slut, slattern. Now DRAGGLE-TAIL.

1577–87 HOLINSHED *Chron.* III. 1098/2 Vpon their ioining with the queens soldiors, the one part could not be discerned from the other, but onelie by the mire and durt.. which stacke vpon their garments..wherefore the crie on the queenes part..was; Downe with the daggle tailes. 1674–91 RAY *S. & E. C. Words* 95, *Daggle-tail*..a Woman that hath dabbled her Coats with Dew, Wet or Dirt. 1881 *Leicestersh. Gloss., Daggle-tail*, a slut..'Doll Daggle-teel'.

daggle-tailed ('dæg(ə)lteɪld), *a. Obs.* exc. *dial.* Having the skirts splashed by being trailed over wet ground; untidy, slatternly. (Usually of a woman.) Now DRAGGLE-TAILED.

1573 G. HARVEY *Letter-bk.* (Camden) 125 A nobeler witt Then that daggiltayld skitt. 1824 SCOTT *St. Ronan's* xxxiii, To make love to..some daggletailed soubrette.

daggling ('dæglɪŋ), *vbl. sb.* [-ING[1].] **a.** The action of the verb DAGGLE, q.v. † **b.** *concr.* = DAGGING (*obs.*).

1580 HOLLYBAND *Treas. Fr. Tong, Crottes*, daglings. 1650 FULLER *Pisgah* IV. vi. 100 To prevent the dangling down, and dagling of so long garments.

'daggling, *ppl. a.* [-ING[2].] That daggles: see the verb.

1562 PHAER *Æneid.* VIII. Z iij b, A she wolfe downe was layed, and next her dugs two goodly twins, Two daggling sucking boies. 1611 COTGR., *Crottes*, durt, filth, mire; dagling stuffe, etc. 1705 VANBRUGH *Confed.* I. ii, Who is this good woman, Flippanta?..An old daggling cheat, who hobbles about..to bubble the ladies of their money.

'daggly, *a. dial.* [f. DAGGLE + -Y.]

1869 *Lonsdale Gloss., Daggly*, wet, showery. 1887 *S. Cheshire Gloss., Daggly*, wet, dewy. 'It was daggly i' th' mornin'.'

daggy ('dægɪ), *a. N.Z.* [f. DAG *sb.*[1] 3 + -Y[1].] Of a sheep or wool: clotted with dags.

1923 W. PERRY *Sheep Farming in N.Z.* vi. 75 The ewes will be very daggy by the lambing season. 1940 G. MEEK in A. E. Woodhouse *N.Z. Farm & Station Verse* (1950) 153 A truck of daggy wool. 1950 *N.Z. Jrnl. Agric.* Oct. 310 One daggy sheep can stain quite a few clean sheep when penning up is in progress.

daggysweyne, var. DAGSWAIN, *Obs.*

dagh(e, obs. form of DOUGH.

dagher: see DAGGA[2].

daghesh, daghyng: see DAGESH, DAWING.

Daghestan, Dagestan (dɑːgə'stɑːn). The name of a region of the eastern Caucasus, used *attrib.* and *ellipt.* of locally made rugs with geometric designs.

1904 W. D. ELLWANGER *Oriental Rug* vi. 61 The Daghestan rugs of Caucasia are only second in importance to those from Persian looms. 1913 W. A. HAWLEY *Oriental Rugs* xi. 199 The rugs which acquired the trade name of Daghestans are different from almost all other Caucasian pieces. 1931 A. U. DILLEY *Oriental Rugs* Pl. 51 (*caption*) Border motive became the property of Daghestan and Shirvan rugs.

dag-lock. [f. DAG *sb.*[1] 3 + LOCK.] *pl.* Locks of wool clotted with dirt about the hinder parts of a sheep.

1623 *Althorp MS.* in Simpkinson *Washingtons* (1860) p. xlv, To 12 women..2 daies washing dag-loakes. 1724 *Lond. Gaz.* No. 6264/2 Frauds..are..committed..by winding in Fleeces, Locks, Tail-Locks, Sheer-Locks, Dagg-Locks. 1799 W. PITT in *Commun. Board Agric.* II. 464 A very small proportion of breechings or daglocks. 1805 LUCCOCK *Nat. Wool* 223 The bundles contained..a quantity of dag-locks, of wool from dead sheep. 1881 *Leicestersh. Gloss., Dag-locks*, the long locks of wool about a sheep which *dag* in the dirt when the animal lies down, etc.

dagman: see DAG *sb.*[2] 2.

Dago ('deɪgəʊ). *slang* (orig. *U.S.*). Also **dago** [Supposed to be a corruption of *Diego* a Spanish equivalent of James: applied as a generic proper name to Spaniards.] **1.** A name originally given in the south-western section of the United States to a man of Spanish parentage; now extended to include Spaniards, Portuguese, and Italians in general, or as a disparaging term for any foreigner. Also *attrib.*

[1723 BUMSTEAD in *New England Hist. & Gen. Reg.* (1861) XV. 199 The negro Dago hanged for fiering Mr Powell's house.] 1832 E. C. WINES *Two Years in Navy* (1833) I. vi. 145 These *Dagos* [of Minorca], as they are pleasantly called by our people, were always a great pest. 1858 *Knickerbocker* Jan. 7 And so, Bill, you served as a ingineer with these ere blamed dagos, you say. 1882 W. A. BAILLIE-GROHMAN *Camps in Rockies* 372, I waited until a lot of Dago emigrants passed. 1888 *American* 18 July (Farmer), The shrimps..are caught by Dagos. 1890 *N.Y. Nation* (25 Sept.) LI. 237/1 Mr. Reed makes no effort to conceal his contempt for this proposition to trade with a lot of 'Dagoes', as he calls them. 1899 *Westm. Gaz.* 11 Dec. 3/2 Whilst licensed pilots take to drink, And Dago crews to prayer. 1902 [see CHIN *sb.*[1] 1 e]. 1904 T. ROOSEVELT *Let.* 2 Sept. in H. F. Pringle *T. Roosevelt* (1931) 294 It will show these Dagos that they will have to behave decently. 1909 H. G. WELLS *Tono-Bungay* III. iv. 406 'E's a foreigner... That's what E is—a *Dago*! 1911 C. E. W. BEAN '*Dreadnought' of Darling* xxiv. 212 'Afghan' in the West is about as wide as 'Dago' on the coast. 1932 [see ADJECTIVAL *a.* b]. 1934 N. MARSH *Man lay Dead* iii. 51 'Such indiscretion has doubtless been suitably chastised,' remarked the Russian... Charles Rankin..slipped his arm through Nigel's. 'Not a very delicious gentleman, that dago,' he said loudly. 1940 N. MITFORD *Pigeon Pie* iii. 41 There are Chinks and Japs and Fuzzy Wuzzies and Ice Creamers and Dagos, and so on. 1968 *Listener* 19 Dec. 819/2 England should have won. All that stopped us was that the dagos [*sc.* Paraguayans] got more goals than us.

2. The Spanish or Italian language.

1900 *Dialect Notes* II. 31 *Dago*, the Italian language. 1901 "H. McHugh' *John Henry* 32 She said she was svelte. I suppose that's Dago for a shine. 1923 MRS. M. WATTS *Luther Nichols* 119 They were eternally being enjoined to say it in French, say it in German, say it in dago!

3. dago red, cheap red wine, esp. Italian. *U.S.*

1906 AITKEN & HILTON *Hist. Earthquake San Francisco* vi. 120 Casks of wine (real 'Dago red'). 1910 E. A. WALCOTT *Open Door* xii. 146 You know I'm..pleased when the meal can be washed down only with diluted 'dago red'. 1963 *Freedomways* III. III. 410 Bad niggers stopped their drinking Dago red. 1966 J. DOS PASSOS *Best Times* iii. 83 As we poured down the dago red he would become mischievous.

‖**dagoba** ('dɑːgəʊbə). [ad. Singhalese *dāgaba*:—Pālī *dhātugabbho*:—Skr. *dhātu-garbha* relic-receptacle (Yule). Also adopted as *dhagope, daghope, dhagob, dagop*, from the form of the name in the Mōgadhī dialect of south Behār.]

In Buddhist countries, a *tope* or dome-shaped monumental structure containing relics of Buddha or of some Buddhist saint.

1806 SALT *Caves of Salsette* in *Trans. Lit. Soc. Bombay* (1819) I. 47 (Y.) In this irregular excavation are left two dhagopes, or solid masses of stone bearing the form of a cupola. 1855 YULE *Mission to Ava* (1858) 35 (Y.) The bluff knob-like dome of the Ceylon dagobas. 1892 *Pall Mall G.* 28 Sept. 6/1 Mdme. Blavatsky's dagoba is to be built of pink sandstone from Rajpootanah.

† **'dagon**[1]. *Obs.* Also **dagoun**. [? related to DAG *sb.*[1]] A piece (of cloth).

c 1386 CHAUCER *Sompn. Tale* 43 Or gif us..A dagoun of your blanket, leeve dame. 1486 *Bk. St. Albans* B v a, Take a dagon or pece of Rough blanket vnshorn.

‖**Dagon**[2] ('deɪgən). [a. L. *Dagon*, a. Gr. *Δαγών*, a. Heb. *dāgōn* 'little fish, dear little fish', f. *dāg* fish.]

The national deity of the ancient Philistines; represented with the head, chest, and arms of a man, and the tail of a fish. **b.** *transf.* An idol, or object of idolatrous devotion.

1382 WYCLIF *Judg.* xvi. 23 The princis of Philistiens camen to gidre in oon, for to offre oostis of greet worship to Dagon, her god. *a* 1572 [see DAD *v.* 1]. 1667 MILTON *P.L.* I. 462 Dagon his Name, Sea Monster, upward Man And downward Fish. 1677 GILPIN *Dæmonol.* (1867) 440 Though the Roman synagogue join force to subtlety in the advancement of their dagon. 1868 STANLEY *Script. Portr.* 89 The head was deposited (probably at Ashdod) in the temple of Dagon.

c. A term of reproach to a man.

1500–20 DUNBAR *Flyting* 66 ȝe, dagone, dowbart. [Cf. DOGONE in *Tua Mariit Wemen* 457.]

Hence **'Dagonals** *sb. pl. nonce-wd.* (after *bacchanal*), rites or orgies in honour of Dagon.

1614 T. ADAMS *Devil's Banquet* 5 A Banket worse then Jobs childrens; or the Dagonals, of the Philistins; (like the Bacchanals of the Moenades).

† **'dagswain.** *Obs.* Forms: 5 dagswaynne, daggysweyne, 6 daggeswayne, -swanne, dagswayne, -swain. [Etymology obscure: the first part has been associated with DAG *sb.*[1] (cf. description in quot. 1519): cf. also DAGON[1].] A coarse coverlet of rough shaggy material.

? *a* 1400 *Morte Arth.* 3610 Dubbyde with dagswaynnes dowblede they seme. *c* 1440 *Promp. Parv.* 112 Daggysweyne, *lodix.* 1519 HORMAN *Vulg.* 167 b, My bedde is couered with a daggeswayne: and a quylte..Some dagswaynys haue longe thrummys and iaggz on bothe sydes: some but on one. 1547 BOORDE *Introd. Knowl.* v. (1870) 139 Symple rayment doth serue us full well; Wyth dagswaynes and roudges we be content. 1577 HARRISON *England* II. xii. (1877) I. 240 Our fathers..and we..haue lien full oft vpon straw pallets..vnder couerlets made of dagswain..or hop-harlots (I vse their owne termes).

'dag-tailed, *a.* [f. DAG *sb.*[1]] Having the wool about the tail clotted with dirt. (Cf. DAG *sb.*[1] 3, DAG-LOCK.)

1597–8 BP. HALL *Sat.* v. i. 116 To see the dunged foldes of dag-tayled sheepe.

dague, var. of DAG *sb.*[3]

Daguerrean (də'gɛrɪən), *a.* Also **Daguerreian, Daguerryan.** [See DAGUERREOTYPE.] Pertaining to Daguerre or the daguerreotype; photographic.

1843 J. EGERTON tr. *Lerebours's Treat. Photogr.* IV. xxv. 164 The Daguerreian phenomena. *Ibid.* 166 On the formation of the Daguerreian images. 1844 *Yale Lit. Mag.* IX. 381 His imitative bump is certainly 'large'—so large, in fact, that it becomes almost Daguerryan in its workings, in that its productions only want an appearance of life and health to counterfeit the original. 1851 C. CIST *Cincinnati* 161 Daguerrean rooms. 1878 W. ABNEY *Treat. Photogr.* ix. 63 The method of developing the Daguerrean image. *Ibid.* xxxiii. 264 Both of these eminent physicists employed the Daguerrean process with the greatest success in these researches. 1889 *Anthony's Photogr. Bull.* II. 5 A full fledged daguerrean artist.

daguerreotype (də'gɛrəʊtaɪp), *sb.* Also **daguerrotype.** [a. F. *daguerréotype*, f. *Daguerre* name of the inventor + TYPE.]

1. One of the earliest photographic processes, first published by Daguerre of Paris in 1839, in which the impression was taken upon a silver plate sensitized by iodine, and then developed by exposure to the vapour of mercury. † **b.** The apparatus used for this process (*obs.*). **c.** A portrait produced by this process.

1839 *Athenæum* 26 Jan. 69 The newly invented machine, which is to be called the Daguerotype. 1839 E. FITZGERALD *Lett.* I. 53 Perhaps you are not civilized enough to know what Daguerreotype is. 1849 THACKERAY *Lett.* 14 Sept., I am going..to give you a daguerreotype of myself. 1875 *Vogel's Chem. Light* ii. 14 The little pictures that were called daguerreotypes from their inventor.

† **2.** *fig.* An exact representation or description. *Obs.* (since the daguerreotype itself has yielded to improved photographic processes).

1850 WHIPPLE *Ess. & Rev.* II. 351 The masquerade at Ranelagh, and the scene at Vauxhall..are daguerreotypes of manners. 1866 DOOLITTLE (*title*), Social Life of the Chinese: a Daguerreotype of Daily Life in China.

3. *attrib.*

1841 CARLYLE *Misc.* (1872) VI. 212 Contemporary Daguerreotype delineator. 1845 *Athenæum* 22 Feb. 202 Daguerréotype plates. 1858 J. MARTINEAU *Stud. Chr.* 234 From which it must be copied, with daguerreotype exactitude, into every disciple's mind.

da'guerreotype, *v.* [f. prec. sb.]

1. *trans.* To photograph by the daguerreotype process.

1849 C. BRONTE *Shirley* vii. 80 A head, that daguerreotyped in that attitude..would have been lovely. 1867–77 G. F. CHAMBERS *Astron.* VII. vii. 707 The sensitive silver compounds used in Daguerreotyping.

† **2.** *fig.* To represent or describe with minute exactitude. *Obs.*

1839 E. FITZGERALD *Lett.* (1889) I. 53 All Daguerreotyped into the mind's eye. 1861 J. G. SHEPPARD *Fall Rome* xiii. 706 That daguerreotyping power which he possesses beyond any

So **da'guerreotyper**, = *daguerreotypist*. **daguerreo'typic** (-'tɪpɪk), **-'typical** *adjs.*, relating to the daguerreotype process. **da'guerreotypism** (*nonce-wd.*), minute exactness as of a daguerreotype. **da'guerreotypy** (-taɪpɪ), the daguerreotype process, the art of taking daguerreotypes. **da'guerreotypist** (-taɪpɪst), a photographer who uses this.

1864 WEBSTER, *Daguerreotyper.* 1840 THACKERAY *Crit. Rev.* Wks. 1886 XXIII. 156 Mr. Maclise has a daguerréotypic eye. 1854 J. SCOFFERN in *Orr's Circ. Sc.* Chem. 91 The language of Daguerreotypic art. 1840 *Fraser's Mag.* XXI. 729 Painted with a daguerréotypical minuteness. 1846 RUSKIN *Mod. Paint.* I. II. I. vii. §30 He professes nothing but coloured Daguerreotypeism. 1841 EMERSON *Lect., Times* Wks. (Bohn) II. 251 Whilst the Daguerreotypist, with camera-obscura and silver plate, begins now to traverse the land. 1853 *Chamb. Jrnl.* XX. 79 There is something new in daguerreotypy.

dah (dɑː), *sb.*[1] Also **dao, dha, dhao.** [Burmese.] A short heavy sword, used also as a knife, especially in Burma; also *attrib.*

1832 J. BELL *Syst. Geogr.* IV. 588 A short sword called *dah*, having a blade of about a foot and a half in length. 1839 H. MALCOM *Trav. S.-E. Asia* I. II. iii. 247 Their chief tool, and one used for all manner of purposes, from the felling of a tree to the paring of a cucumber, is the dah. The handle is like that of a cleaver, and the blade like a drawing-knife.

1858 C. T. Winter *Six Months Brit. Burmah* xiii. 104 The Burman has few agricultural implements... A cart, plough, dah (or sword-knife), and sickle are about all he requires. **1859** J. W. Palmer *New & Old* 423 The Burmese dropped their..lances and dhars. **1876** Voyle & Stevenson *Milit. Dict.* (ed. 3), *Dhao*, a Burman tool or weapon (half chopper, half sword) used in clearing jungle and in cutting down trees. **1884** *Encycl. Brit.* XVII. 163/2 The only implements of tillage being the *dáo* or hill knife, and a *kodáli* or hoe. **1888** Kipling *Departm. Ditties* (1890) 19 Amid the jungle-grass ..grinned and jabbered Little Boh Hla-oo and cleared the dah-blade from the scabbard. **1920** *Blackw. Mag.* June 834/2 The two men were allowed to come on after they had deposited their guns and *dhas*. **1923** *Ibid.* May 569/2 They ..are armed with..spear and *dao*. *Ibid.* Sept. 304/2 Thrust into his coloured sash were two silver-mounted dahs. **1947** 'N. Shute' *Chequer Board* v. 121 Many of them also wore their dahs, long straight steel blades with clumsy wooden handles.

dah (dɑː), *sb.*[2] Chiefly *U.S.* [Imitative.] In Morse telegraphy, etc.: = dash *sb.*[1] 7 f. Also *transf.* Cf. dit *sb.*[2]

1942 *Tee Emm* (Air Ministry) II. 143 To join the..throng who understand the dits and dahs of Q.D.M.'s and Q.D.R.'s. **1957** J. S. Bruner *Contemp. Approaches to Cognition* 60 One's limited immediate memory span requires one to deal first with the dits and dahs of single letters. **1970** *Southerly* XXX. 126 Beyond the road with its white morse of dahs along the spine..lay the sea. **1977** *Sci. Amer.* Dec. 42/3 The tapes offer a meticulous set of graded dit-dah practice sessions, half an hour each at 5, 7.5, 10 and 13 words per minute.

‖**dahabeeyah, -biah** (dɑːhəˈbiːjə). Also -beeah, -bieh, -beiah. [Arab. *ðahabīyah* lit. 'the golden', f. *ðahab* gold: name of the gilded state barge of the Moslem rulers of Egypt.] A large sailing-boat, used by travellers on the Nile.

1846 I. F. Romer *Pilgrimage Temples of Egypt* I. 109 The Dahabieh and her crew were hired at a daily expense. **1876** *Western Morning News* (Plymouth) 2 Feb. 3/3 Three young English ladies..were sailing up the river in a dahabeah. **1877** A. B. Edwards *Up Nile* Pref. 12 The Dahabeeyah hired by the European traveller, reproduces in all essential features the painted galleys represented in the tombs of the kings. **1890** Sayce in *Trans. Lanc. & Cheshire Antiq. Soc.* VII. 4 Coming down the Nile in a dahabiah. **1905** E. F. Benson *Image in Sand* i, A couple of dayabeahs moored to the bank were a blaze of Syrian awnings. **1916** J. B. Cooper *Coo-oo-ee* xvi. 244 The winding river, glowing with opal fire, and the dahabiehs, that was the Egypt of his dreams. **1936** E. M. Forster *Abinger Harvest* iv. 249 The Sahara where horsemen..are silently riding towards the Nile to intercept the dahabiyeh. **1952** C. P. Blacker *Eugenics* 24 The party travelled in some style in a dahabeyah. **1963** *Times Lit. Suppl.* 11 Jan. 28/2 As his *dahabia* navigates the last of the cataracts.

†**dahet, dathet.** *Obs.* Forms: 3-4 dahet, daþet, (dayet), daþeit, dathait, daþeheit, daiþat, dait, dai. [a. OF. *dahet, dehet*, usually *dehé, dahé, daé, deé*, also *dehait, dahait*; in pl. *dehez, dahez, daez, dehaiz*, 'misfortune, mischief, evil, curse', used only in imprecations.

As to the OF. word, see M. Gaston Paris in *Romania* (1889) 469. He shows it to be distinct from OF. *deshait* evil disposition or condition, sorrow, woe, etc., and suggests the meaning 'God's hate', in primitive Merovingian French **deu hat*. In English, the primary *dahet* is very rare; the usual *daþeit, datheit, dathet* are difficult to account for, unless they represent the OF. phrase *da(h)et ait, daat ait*, or in pl. *dahez, daez, daaz ait*, just as in OF. itself M. Paris explains *dehait, dahait*, from the running together of *dehé ait*. Apparently, the phrase being thus taken for the simple word, the verb had to be added anew, as in OF. *dehait ait!* ME. *daþeit haue!* In Robert of Brunne written *daþet* with dotted *þ*, printed by Hearne as dotted *ẏ*.]

[= OF. *dehet ait, dehait ait.*] **a.** In the construction *dahet have, dathet have*: = May (he, etc.) have misfortune! a mischief, curse, damnation be to...

a **1250** *Owl & Night.* 99 Dahet habbe that ilke best, That fuleth his owe nest. *c* **1290** *S. Eng. Leg.* I. *Beket* 1884 Daþeheit habbe þat so atstonde so folliche. *c* **1320** *Seuyn Sag.* (W.) 2395 Datheit haue thou..Al to loude thou spak thi Latin! *c* **1330** R. Brunne *Chron.* (1810) 143 Daẏet haf his lip, & his nose þerbẏ.

b. without *have* [so OF. *dehait, dahait*]: A curse upon!

c **1290** *S. Eng. Leg.* I. *Beket* 2036 Daþeit alle þat it seide! *c* **1308** *Sat. People Kildare* xiv. in *E.E.P.* (1862) 155 Daþeit ȝur curteisie, ȝe stinkeþ al þe strete. *c* **1330** R. Brunne *Chron.* (1810) 95 A Breton (daẏet his nose) for Roberd þider sent.

c. followed by relative clause [so OF. *daha ait qui, dahait qui*].

c **1300** *Beket* (Percy Soc.) 2072 Daithat hit so sede. *c* **1300** *Havelok* 300 Daþeit hwo it hire yeue. *c* **1300** *Seyn Julian* 202 Dait þat him wolde bymene. *Ibid.* 134 Dai þat wolde..him biseche. *c* **1330** R. Brunne *Chron.* (1810) 167 Daẏet þat þerof rouht, his was alle þe gilt.

¶The following is prob. a mere coincidence: cf. *dash it!* **1875** *Lanc. Gloss.*, *Dathit* (Furness), *interj.* a mild curse on making a mishap.

dahil, var. dayal.

Dahlgren (ˈdɑːlgrɛn). Now *Hist.* [Name of J. A. B. *Dahlgren* (1809-70), U.S. naval officer.] In full *Dahlgren gun*. A cast-iron smoothbore gun invented by Dahlgren in 1856.

1861 *Times* 28 Dec. 6/6 They might..be relying on their new Dahlgren guns. **1862** G. B. McClellan *Disp.* 4 May in T. P. Kettell *Hist. Rebellion* (1865) 252 The rebels abandoned..four nine-inch Dahlgrens. **1867** H. Latham *Black & White* 86 Each [gunboat] was armed with two 15-inch Dahlgrens. **1876** Voyle & Stevenson *Milit. Dict.* (ed. 3) s.v., The Dahlgren 11-inch was once a formidable gun on the seas. **1910** *Sat. Even. Post* 30 July 27/3 They're big fellows—those Dahlgrens and Columbiads.

dahlia (ˈdeɪlɪə, properly ˈdɑːlɪə). [Named 1791 in honour of *Dahl*, a Swedish botanist.]

1. A Genus of Composite plants, natives of Mexico, introduced into Europe in 1789, and commonly cultivated in gardens.

In the wild plant the flowers are 'single' with a dull scarlet ray and yellow disk; in the cultivated forms the varieties of colour are very numerous, and the 'double' varieties are distinguished by the remarkable regularity of their flowers, in which florets of the ray completely cover the disk.

1804 *Curtis's Bot. Mag.* XIX. 762 Of the genus Dahlia there are three species described by Cavanilles. **1840** Hood *Kilmansegg, Her Honeymoon* ix, A double dahlia delights the eye. **1863** Longf. *Wayside Inn, Student's Tale* 182 Among the dahlias in the garden walk.

b. *blue dahlia*: *fig.* something impossible or unattainable (no blue variety of the dahlia having been produced by cultivation).

1880 *Daily News* 17 Dec. 5/4 Whether the colonisation of Gilead be a blue dahlia or not.

2. Name for a particular shade of red.

1846 *Art Union Jrnl.* Jan. 26 Their Mazarine blue, their puce, their dahlia, their Turkey red, or their azure. **1892** *Pall Mall G.* 29 Sept. 1/3 One of the many ugly shades that are to be worn this season is dahlia.

dahlin (ˈdɑːlɪn). *Chem.* [f. dahlia + -in.] A name for inulin from the tubers of the dahlia.

1826 Henry *Elem. Chem.* II. 326 *Dalhine.* This substance was extracted by Layen from the bulbs of the Dalhia. **1882** *Syd. Soc. Lex.*, *Dahlia*..The roots of the several species are eaten when cooked, and supply Dahlin.

dahllite (ˈdɑːlaɪt). *Min.* [ad. G. *dahllit* (Brögger and Bäckström 1888, in *Vet. Akad. Stockh. Oefv.* XLV. 493). f. the names of T. and J. *Dahll*, Norwegian mineralogists: see -ite[1].] A variety of hydroxyapatite containing carbonate.

1890 *Jrnl. Chem. Soc.* LVIII. 714 (*title*) Dahllite, a new Norwegian mineral. *Ibid.*, This new mineral, the only combination of a phosphate and a carbonate yet known, has been named dahllite, in honour of..Tellef and Johann Dahll. **1957** *Encycl. Brit.* II. 93/1 Carbonate-containing apatites related to fluorapatite and hydroxyapatite are known as francolite and dahllite, respectively.

dahn (dɑːn), repr. regional and colloq. pronunc. of down *adv.*, etc.

1849 C. Brontë *Shirley* I. viii. 178 Making the remark.. that it was 'Raight dahn warm for Febewerry'. **1898** J. D. Brayshaw *Slum Silhouettes* 1 Got a scar right dahn 'is fice? Yus, that's 'im. **1951** [see pansy *v.*]. **1971** *Trans. Yorks. Dial. Soc.* XIII. 24 I t'end..t'owd ahse hed to be pooled dahn as one o t'walls war tummelin.

Dahoman (dəˈhəʊmən), *sb.* and *a.* Also **Dahomean, Dahomeyan, Dahomian.** [f. the name of the country *Dahomey* or the tribal name *Dahomeh.*] **A.** *sb.* **1.** A member of the people of the former kingdom of Dahomey, now part of the West African republic of the same name. **2.** The language of this people. **B.** *adj.* Of or pertaining to this state or people.

1793 A. Dalzel *Hist. Dahomy* I. i. 1 The Dahomans were formerly called Foys, and inhabited a small territory, on the north-east part of their present kingdom. *Ibid.* v. 21 The Dahoman Prince received the news of this victory with every possible demonstration of joy. **1820** J. Macleod (*title*) A voyage to Africa; with some account of the manners and customs of the Dahomian people. **1837** *Penny Cycl.* VIII. 285/2 The Dahomans..made their appearance on the coast. *Ibid.*, The captains of these forts..were now prisoners in the Dahoman camp. **1851** F. E. Forbes (*title*) Dahomey and the Dahomans, being the journals of two missions to the King of Dahomey. **1864** R. F. Burton *Mission to Gelele* I. iii. 36 The Ffon, or Dahoman, a dialect of the great Yoruba family, has, ..a G and a Gb, the latter..difficult to articulate. **1877** *Encycl. Brit.* VI. 766/2 The Dahomans have at several times penetrated along the beach towards the east as far as Badagry. **1883** C. A. Moloney *W. Afr. Fisheries* 50 It has been for some time conveniently contrary to the Dahoman fetish to cross water. **1941** *Jrnl. R. Anthropol. Inst.* LXXI. 49/2 Perhaps the Dahomean diviners did not know as much. **1957** *Encycl. Brit.* VI. 978/2 Of this population the majority was constituted by the Dahomeyans or Dahomi (in their own language called Fon or Djedjé). **1959** *Chambers's Encycl.* IV. 349/1 In 1890..French troops were heavily defeated by 9,000 Dahomeans. **1965** R. & D. Morris *Men & Snakes* ii. 27 When a Dahoman caught sight of one of the reptiles, he immediately prostrated himself on the ground.

dai, daiblet: see day, dablet.

dai: see daye.

daid (deɪd), repr. U.S. Black and dial. pronunc. of dead *a.*

1890 *Harper's Mag.* Dec. 112/1, I al'ays layin' out to go back home, but I 'ain' been yit. Dee's mos' all daid b'fo' dis, suh? **1934** C. Carmer *Stars fell on Alabama* iv. iii. 208 Wasn't hardly a time when ole Man Smith wasn't daid to the worl'. **1955** F. O'Connor *Wise Blood* xiv. 230 No, he ain't daid. He's moving. **1970** R. D. Abrahams *Positively Black* vi. 132 Oh, he's probably daid, the house caved in.

daidle (ˈdeɪd(ə)l), *sb. Sc.* A pinafore. Hence **ˈdaidlie, -ey** (diminutive).

17.. *Jacobite Relics* (1819) I. 7 Jenny [shall have] the sark of God For—petticoat, dishclout, and daidle. **1833** Moir *Mansie Wauch* v. (1849) 23, I was a wee chap with a daidley.

daidle (ˈdeɪd(ə)l), *v. Sc.* and *north. dial.* [app. Sc. form of daddle *v.*] *intr.* To move or act slowly or in a slovenly manner; to saunter, loiter. Chiefly in *pres. pple.* = loafing, idling, lazy, slovenly. (Cf. dawdle.)

1808 in Jamieson. **1816** Scott *Old Mort.* xvii, He's but a daidling coward body. *Sc. Proverb*, A primsie damsel makes a daidlin' dame.

daie, obs. form of day.

daigh, Sc. form of dough.

daign, obs. form of deign.

daiker (ˈdeɪkər), *v. Sc.* [? a. F. *décorer* to decorate, adorn.] *trans.* To set in order.

1820 *Blackw. Mag.* Sept. 652 (Jam. s.v. *Daiker*) Say Madge Mackittrick's skill has failed her in daikering out a dead dame's flesh. **1880** Mrs. L. B. Walford *Troubl. Dau.* I. ii. 31 Your room will be daikert by the time it's wanted.

daiker: see dacker.

dail(e, obs. form of dale, deal.

Dail Eireann (dɔɪl ˈɛərən). [Ir. *Dáil Éireann* assembly of Ireland.] The lower house of the Parliament of the Republic of Ireland (before 1922, the Sinn Fein Parliament in Ireland). Also ellipt. **Dail.**

1919 *Times* 21 Jan. 9/4 A committee had been nominated 'to select Irish technical terms for the work of "An Dail Eireann",' the Gaelic appellation of the new Irish Parliament. *Ibid.* 22 Jan. 9/4 The first word in English was spoken when the Dail had been in session for about three-quarters of an hour. **1921** *Punch* 30 Mar. 254/3 The Government should enter into unconditional negotiations with Dail Eireann. **1923** *Contemp. Rev.* Sept. 332 Parliament has been sitting continuously ever since the last Dail elections. **1964** *Ann. Reg. 1963* 280 It was bitterly contested in the Dail.

ˈdailiness. [f. daily *a.* + -ness.] The quality of being daily; daily occurrence, etc.

1607 Hieron *Wks.* I. 135 There are very few duties of religion, but the scripture speaks of the dailines of them. *a* **1670** Hacket *Chr. Consolations* ii. (1840) 19 The dailiness of sin must be bewailed with the dailiness of sorrow. **1898** A. Bennett *Man from North* xix, The drab dailiness of her existence in Carteret Street. **1899** *Academy* 14 Oct. 432/1 That which Mrs. Meynell has well called the 'dailiness' of life. **1906** *Daily Chron.* 22 May 6/6 All necessary implication of dailiness has long disappeared from the word 'journal'. **1906** E. V. Lucas *Wand. in Lond.* i. 9 Perhaps a touch of grime is not unnecessary. Perhaps houses can be too clean for the truest human dailiness. **1935** W. J. Blyton *Country Airs* viii. 74 Our homely, uncouth husbandry, with its divine humilities and dailiness.

daill, obs. Sc. form of dale.

daily (ˈdeɪlɪ), *a.* (*sb.*) Forms: 5-8 **dayly,** 6 **daylie, dailie,** (*Sc.* **dalie**), 6- **daily.** [OE. *dæȝlíc* (in the compounds *twádæȝlíc, préodæȝlíc*, happening once in two or three days) = OHG. *tagalîh, dagalîh*, ON. *dagligr*, an ancient derivative of WGer. *dag*, OE. *dæȝ* day: see -ly[1]. The ordinary OE. word was *dæȝhwamlíc*, in 12th c. *deihwanlich.*]

A. *adj.* **1. a.** Of or belonging to each day; occurring or done every day; issued or published every day (or every week-day).

c **1470** Henry *Wallace* xi. 1291 For dayly mess, and heryng off confessioun. **1526** Tindale *Matt.* vi. 11 Geve vs this daye oure dayly breade. **1553** Eden *Treat. Newe Ind.* (Arb.) 7 Proued..by dayly experience. **1611** Bible *Ex.* v. 13 Fulfill your workes, your dayly taskes. **1711** Hearne *Collect.* (Oxf. Hist. Soc.) III. 153 A Daily paper comes out call'd The Spectator. **1862** Ld. Brougham *Brit. Const.* iv. 62 The daily labour to gain their daily bread.

b. with agent-nouns, as in *daily waiter*, one who waits daily (a title of certain officers of the Royal household). Also *daily girl*, etc.

1568 E. Tilney *Disc. Mariage* Cj, A daylie gamester, a common blasphemer. **1642** *Brass in Weybridge Church* (*N. & Q.* 1 Oct. 1892), Here lieth the body of Humphry Dethick Esq. who was one of his Ma[ts] Gent. Vshers (dayly Waiter). **1715** *Lond. Gaz.* No. 5300/4 Sir William Oldes, to be his Majesty's first Gentleman Usher, Daily Waiter and Black Rod. *a* **1895** *Mod.* A daily visitor to the well. **1921** *Dict. Occup. Terms* (1927) §900 *Daily servant, daily girl*..; a non-resident general servant. **1933** A. Bryant *Pepys: Man in Making* 434/2 Taylor, Pepys' 'daily woman'. **1939** D. L. Sayers *In Teeth of Evidence* 36 The daily woman, Mrs. Crabbe, had been in the house till nearly dinner-time. **1971** *Woman* 13 Feb. 13/2, I gave Mrs. Candy, the daily help, a suit for her daughter.

†**2.** Of the present day; belonging to the present time. *Obs. rare.*

1663 Gerbier *Counsel* 8 Why modern and daily Buildings are so exceedingly Defective.

3. *spec.* **daily breader** *colloq.*, one who earns his own living or 'daily bread'; **daily dozen** *colloq.*, used of physical exercises performed each day on rising (see quot. 1925).

1906 *Westm. Gaz.* 25 Sept. 1/3 In place of the neat villa of the daily-breader..it now journeys between rows of low, monotonous houses. **1930** J. A. R. Marriott *How we Live* i. 8 Most of them live by their own exertions. They are in fact (to use the colloquial but expressive phrase) 'daily breaders'. **1942** N. Streatfeild *Table for Six* 99 There I was catching a tube, a daily breader. **1919** *Red Cross Mag.* Dec. 30/3 It was while engaged in this work that he evolved what he calls his 'short-hand system' of setting-up exercises, or 'the daily dozen'. **1925** *Yale Univ. Obituary Rec.* 1349 Walter [Chauncey] Camp.. devised.. exercises for cabinet officers and civilian personnel in Washington out of which grew the 'Daily Dozen' series, which he introduced in all naval stations and in several aviation and army cantonments. **1936** WODEHOUSE *Laughing Gas* iv. 43 Ann is one of those girls who always look as if they had just stepped out of a cold bath after doing their daily dozen. **1965** W. LAMB *Posture & Gesture* ix. 121 Physical exercises, whether performed privately as a daily dozen, or in a class to the accompaniment of music, may be a pleasant and stimulating way of passing the time.

B. *sb.* (*ellipt.*) **1.** A daily newspaper. (orig. *U.S.*)

[**1823** D. WEBSTER *Priv. Corr.* (1857) I. 333, I am glad to see that you publish, in the Daily [*sc.* the *Boston Daily Advertiser*], your narrative.] **1832** J. K. PAULDING *Westward Ho!* I. xxi. 190 'Make out an estimate of the cost of establishing a paper.' 'A daily, sir?' 'Ay, a daily, if you wish.' *Ibid.* 191 I'll attack them in my Daily. **1846** [see WEEKLY *sb.*]. **1858** *Times* 29 Nov. 6/3 Clever weeklies and less clever dailies. **1881** *Academy* 26 Mar. 234 The foreign correspondent of one of the great dailies. **1933** *Archit. Rev.* LXXIV. 176/2 The women's pages of the popular dailies. **1965** *New Statesman* 30 Apr. 679/1 The national daily he would like is still denied him. *Ibid.*, Two Fleet Street dailies as well as the *Sun* are.. vulnerable.

2. 'Daily bread', food; livelihood.

1906 E. DYSON *Fact'ry 'Ands* xiv. 182 What's er bonzer like you doin' spreadin' sour paste fer yer daily? **1922** JOYCE *Ulysses* 57 Boland's breadvan delivering with trays our daily but she prefers yesterday's loaves.

3. A domestic cleaner or servant who does not live on the premises.

1933 MRS. C. S. PEEL *Life's Enchanted Cup* xix. 261 In my youth there were charwomen but the 'daily' is a new invention. **1953** 'P. WENTWORTH' *Watersplash* v. 31 Mrs. Deacon.. was Miss Blake's daily and a very good cook. **1967** L. MEYNELL *Mauve Front Door* iii. 31 Most 'dailies' I have known have been disastrous. They come late; charge exorbitantly; drop ash all over the place.

4. *pl.* The first prints from cinematographic takes (TAKE *sb.*), rapidly made for film producers or editors.

1934 *Tit-Bits* 31 Mar. 12/2 Every time a scene is successfully 'shot' it is called 'a take'; the whole of the day's 'takes' are then assembled and shown to the producer in a private projection room, but are then known as 'the rushes' or 'the dailies'. **1952** L. ROSS *Picture* (1953) iii. 106, I haven't had a chance to tell you how wonderful I feel the dailies (rushes) are.

daily ('deɪlɪ), *adv.* Forms: 5–7 dayly, (6 *Sc.* dalie, -y), 6 dailie, 6–7 daylie, 7– daily. [f. DAY + -LY[2]. The OE. word was *dæghwamlíce*.] Every day, day by day. Often in a looser sense: Constantly, always, habitually.

c **1440** *York Myst.* xxvi. 9 My desire muste dayly be done. **1526** *Pilgr. Perf.* (W. de W. 1531) 1 b, Wherin.. dayly & hourly I myght loke, as in a myrour. **1635** A. STAFFORD *Fem. Glory* (1869) 79 With bended knees I dayly beseech God. **1712** ADDISON *Spect.* No. 265 ¶6, I am informed that this Fashion spreads daily. **1747** WESLEY *Prim. Physic* (1762) 97 Drink daily half a Pint. **1848** MACAULAY *Hist. Eng.* II. 75 He continued to offer his advice daily, and had the mortification to find it daily rejected. **1885** R. BUCHANAN *Annan Water* v, The public waggonette ran daily between Dumfries and Annanmouth.

'daimen, *a.* *Sc.* Also 9 demmin. [Origin unknown. In Ayrshire pronounced as *'demmin*. (Perh. a pple.: cf. Whitby *daum'd out*, dealt out sparingly.)] 'Rare, occasional' (Jam.).

1785 BURNS *To a Mouse*, A daimen-icker in a thrave 'S a sma' request. **1821** *Edin. Mag.* Apr. 352 (Jam.) At a demmin time I see the Scotchman. [Still in use in Ayrshire, as in 'a daimen ane here and there'.]

daiment, var. DAYMENT, *Obs.*

‖**daimio** ('daɪmjəʊ). [Japanese, f. Chinese *dai* great + *mio*, *myo* name.] The title of the chief territorial nobles of Japan, vassals of the mikado; now abolished.

1839 *Penny Cycl.* XIII. 94/1 The nobility or hereditary governors of the provinces and districts are called *Daimio*, or High-named, and *Siomio*, or Well-named. **1875** *N. Amer. Rev.* CXX. 283 The writer.. has lived in a daimio's capital before, during, and after the abolition of feudalism.

Hence **'daimiate, 'daimioate, 'daimiote,** the territory or office of a daimio.

1870 *Pall Mall G.* 26 Aug. 4 Japanese students.. from all parts of the empire, from the inland daimiotes as well as from the sea-coasts. **1882** *Athenæum* 10 June 730/1 The abolition of the Daimioates has elevated the masses of the people [of Japan] from a state of feudal servitude to the condition of free citizens. **1889** *Ibid.* 6 Apr. 436/1 Old Japanese tenures [of land].. no doubt differed considerably in the different daimiates.

‖**daimon** ('daɪməʊn), a direct transliteration of Gr. δαίμων divinity, one's genius or DEMON[1].

1852 THOREAU *Lett.* (1865) 73 It is the same daimon, here lurking under a human eyelid. **1875** E. C. STEDMAN *Victorian Poets* (1876) 154 The Laureate.. is his own daimon,—the inspirer and controller of his own utterances.

Hence **dai'monic** *a.*, belonging or pertaining to the spirit world; of the nature of a daimon. Cf. DEMONIC *a.* 2.

1903 J. BUCHAN *Afr. Colony* xix. 393 The faults of.. [Cecil Rhodes'] methods.. did not impair that legacy of daimonic force which he left to his countrymen. **1941** R. TURNER *Great Cultural Traditions* I. ii. 92 Early man conceived of the universe as a host of intangible and invisible beings who worked good and evil for man outside of, contrary to, and in spite of physical forces and circumstances... As a view of the organization of the world in which man lives, they may properly be designated the *daimonic universe*. **1957** J. S. HUXLEY *Relig. without Revelation* (rev. ed.) iii. 50 God hypotheses are part of a more general theory, the daimonic theory as it is usefully called, according to which supernatural spiritual beings, good, bad, or indifferent, and of very different degrees of importance, play a part in the affairs of the cosmos. **1978** *Washington Post* 14 Apr. B4/1 The ego has to be very strong. And if the wild forces—the daimonic forces—are too strong, the person may go mad. Hence the closeness of genius to lunacy.

†**dain,** *sb.* *Obs.* Also 5 deyne, dene, 6 daine, dayne, deane. Syncopated from *dedain*, DISDAIN *sb.*

1. Disdain, dislike, distrust.

a **1400–50** *Alexander* 1863 þat ay has deyne [*Dublin MS.* dene] & dispite at dedis of litill. **1591** LYLY *Sappho* v. i. 207 Which striketh a deepe daine of that which wee most desire.

2. The suffering or incurring of disdain; contumely, ignominy, reproach.

?*a* **1500** *MS. St. John's Coll. Oxon.* No. 117 fol. 123 b (in Maskell *Mon. Rit.* III. 356), Thi beginning of thi lif, care and sorwe; thi fo[r]thliving, trauail, and dene, and disese. **15..** *Merline* in *Percy Folio* I. 444 'Nay, certaine,' said the old queane, 'yee may it doe without deane.'

3. Repulsiveness of smell; 'stink, noisome effluvia. Still used in this sense in the west of England' (Nares).

(Quot. 1575 taken in this sense by Nares and Halliwell may belong to 2; 1601 may belong to DAIN *adj.*)

1575 *Mirr. Mag.*, *Cordila*, From bowres of heauenly hewe, to dennes of dayne. **1601** HOLLAND *Pliny* XI. liii, The breath of Lions hath a very strong deane and stinking smell with it [*animae leonis virus grave*]. **1825** BRITTON *Prov. Words in Beauties of Wiltsh.* (E.D.S.), *Dain*, infectious effluvia. **1847–** in HALLIWELL (*Wilts*).

†**dain,** *a.* *Obs.* or *dial. rare.* Also 6 daine, dane. [a. OF. *deigne, Burg. *doigne* = F. *digne* worthy: cf. Chaucer's *deyn* under DIGNE *a.*]

1. Haughty; reserved, distant; repellent. *Sc.*

c **1500** DUNBAR *Tua mariit Wemen* 132 Than am I dangerus and dane and dour of my will. *Ibid.* 253 Thought I dour wes and dane, dispitois and bald. *c* **1540** LYNDESAY *Kitteis Conf.* 6 Bot ȝit ane countenance he bure, Degeist, deuote, daine, and demure.

2. Repulsive, esp. in smell; stinking. Cf. DIGNE *a.*

[**1601** cf. DAIN *sb.* 3.] **1888** *Berkshire Gloss.*, *Dain*, tainted, putrid, bad-smelling.

†**dain,** *v.* *Obs.* Also 5 deyne, 6 dayne. Syncopated form of *dedain*, DISDAIN *v.*

a **1400–50** *Alexander* 4579 Owþir ȝe gesse at ȝe be gods.. Or deynes with oure driȝtins for þat we þam dere hald. **1514** BARCLAY *Cyt. & Uplondyshm.* (Percy Soc.) 6 Youthe dayneth counsayle, scornynge dyscrecyon. *a* **1592** GREENE *Alphonsus* I. Wks. 226/1 She shall have scholars which will dain to be In any other Muse's company. *Ibid.* III. 237/2; IV. 240/1.

dain(e, obs. forms of DEIGN.

†**'dainful,** *a.* *Obs.* Also 6 deignfull. Syncopated form of *dedainful*, DISDAINFUL.

c **1530** H. RHODES *Bk. Nurture* 672 in *Babees Bk.* (1868) 100 A busy tongue makes of his friend oft tymes his daynfull Foe. **1578** T. PROCTOR *Gorg. Gallery* in *Heliconia* I. 91 Cipres well, with dainful chaung of fraight, Gave thee to drinke infected poyson colde. **1600** FAIRFAX *Tasso* IV. lxxxix, Yet tempred so her deignfull lookes alway.

†**daint,** *a.* and *sb.* *Obs.* Also 6 daynt, deint. = DAINTY (of which it appears to be merely a shortened form, or perh. a misreading of the old spelling *dainte*, *deynte*, etc.).

A. *adj.*

1590 SPENSER *F.Q.* I. x. 2 To cherish him with diets daint. *Ibid.* II. xii. 42 Whatever.. may dayntest fantasy aggrate. **1596** *Ibid.* IV. i. 5 Demeanour daint.

B. *sb.*

1633 P. FLETCHER *Pisc. Ecl.*, *The Prize* xxxvii, Excesse or daints my lowly roof maintain not.

Hence †**'daintly** *adv.*, daintily.

1563 SACKVILLE *Mirr. Mag.*, *Induct.* xxxviii, As on the which full dayntlye would he fare. **1591** PERCIVALL *Sp. Dict.*, *Regaladamente*, gentelie, curteouslie, deintlie.

†**'dainteous,** *a.* *Obs.* Forms: α. 4–5 deyn-, dein-, (den-), dayntevous, -vous, (-uos, dentyuous); β. 4–6 deyn-, 6 dayn-, deinteous. [app. orig. *dayntivous*, f. *dayntive* DAINTIVE + -OUS: afterwards altered so as to appear f. *daynte*, DAINTY + -OUS. Cf. BOUNTEOUS, PLENTEOUS.] = DAINTY *a.*

c **1386** CHAUCER *Merch. T.* 470 Ful of instrumentz and of vitaille The moste deyntevous of all Ytaille. **1387** TREVISA *Higden* (Rolls) III. 323 Wiþ gret plente of deynteous mete and drink. ?*a* **1400** *Morte Arth.* 4196 Itt was my derlynge daynteuous, and fulle dere holdene. *c* **1510** BARCLAY *Mirr. Gd. Manners* (1570) D v, The soure sauce is serued before meat deynteous. **1548** UDALL, etc. *Erasm. Par. Matt.* x. 64 This is no daynteouse and delycate profession.

Hence †**'dainteously** *adv.*, daintily.

c **1380** WYCLIF *Sel. Wks.* III. 157 Somme men deynteuously norischen hor body. **1393** LANGL. *P. Pl.* C. IX. 324 Thenne was þis folke feyn and fedde hunger deynteuosliche [*v.r.* denteuous-, deyntifliche]. *a* **1556** CRANMER *Wks.* (Parker Soc.) II. 194 Yet will they.. fare daintiously, and lie softly.

dainteril, var. of DAINTREL *Obs.*, a dainty.

dainteth, -ith ('deɪntɪθ), *sb.* and *a.* Now only *Sc.* Forms: 4–5 dein-, deyn-, dain-, daynteth(e, *rarely* -ith(e, -yth, (also den-, dan-, dayen-, dayne-), 8–9 *Sc.* daintith, -eth. [a. OF. *daintiet*, *deintiet*:—L. *dignitāt-em*, f. *dignus* worthy: see DAINTY *sb.*] **A.** = DAINTY *sb.*

c **1290** *S. Eng. Leg.* I. *Beket* 1190 Heo bi-gan to serui þis holi man and deinteþes [*Percy Soc.* l. 1202 deyntés] to him brouȝte. *a* **1340** HAMPOLE *Psalter* lxxv. 10 With other.. he has litill daynteth to dwell. *c* **1400** *Destr. Troy* 463 Sho hade no deintithe to dele with no deire meite. *c* **1450** *Bk. Curtasye* 527 in *Babees Bk.* (1868) 316 Yf any deyntethe in countré be, þo stuarde schewes hit to þo lorde so fre. *a* **1774** FERGUSSON *Drink Eclogue* Poems (1845) 52 On bien-clad tables.. Bouden wi' a' the daintiths o' the land. **1820** *Blackw. Mag.* VII. 520 Sic daintiths are rare.

†**B.** = DAINTY *a.* *Obs.*

c **1430** LYDG. *Chorle & Byrde* lx, A dunghyll Douke as deyntieth as a Snyte. *c* **1440** *Gesta Rom.* lviii. 374 (Add. MS.) He myght not take of the noble and deynteth metes.

Hence †**'daintethly** *adv.*, †**'daintethness.**

c **1440** *Gesta Rom.* l. 370 (Add. MS.) Riche men.. þat.. etyn and drynkyn deyntethly. *c* **1440** *York Myst.* I. 78 Thi dale, lord, es ay daynetethly delande. **1548** THOMAS *Ital. Gram.*, *Dilicatezza*, daintethnesse, or delicacie.

daintifi'cation. *nonce-wd.* [f. DAINTIFY: see -FICATION.] Daintified condition.

1780 MAD. D'ARBLAY *Diary* Apr., A mighty delicate gentleman.. all daintification in manner, speech, and dress.

†**'daintiful,** *a.* *Obs.* [f. DAINTY *sb.* + -FUL.] = DAINTY *a.*

1393 GOWER *Conf.* I. 28 There is no lust so deintefull. *a* **1400–50** *Alexander* 4274 A dayntefull diete. *c* **1440** *Gesta Rom.* xlvi. 184 (Harl. MS.) How that he made so gret festes, and hadde so deyntefulle metis.

Hence †**'daintifully** *adv.*, daintily.

1393 LANGL. *P. Pl.* C. IX. 324 (MS. G.) þis folke.. fedde hunger deyntfulliche [*v.r.* deynteuosliche, deyntifliche].

daintify ('deɪntɪfaɪ), *v.* *nonce-wd.* [See -FY.] *trans.* To make dainty. Hence **'daintified** *ppl. a.*

1780 MAD. D'ARBLAY *Lett.* July, My father charges me to give you his kindest love, and not to daintify his affection into respects or compliments. **1834** *New Monthly Mag.* XLI. 317 A silken cushion—which.. the daintified animal did not hurt.

daintihood ('deɪntɪhʊd). *rare.* Daintiness.

1780 MAD. D'ARBLAY *Diary* May, Shocking her by too obvious an inferiority in daintihood and *ton*. **1890** *Temple Bar Mag.* Jan. 146 Her youth, her daintihood.

daintily ('deɪntɪlɪ), *adv.* [f. DAINTY *a.* + -LY[2].]

†**1.** Excellently, finely, handsomely, delightfully.

?*a* **1400** *Morte Arth.* 723 Dukkes and duzseperes dayntethely rydes. *c* **1425** WYNTOUN *Cron.* IX. xxvii. 8 Rycht wele arayt and dayntely. **1625** BACON *Ess. Truth* (Arb.) 499 A naked.. day-light, that doth not show the masques.. of the world halfe so Stately, and daintily, as Candlelights. **1640** HOWELL *Dodona's Gr.* 2 There is no Forrest on Earth so daintily watered, with such great navigable Rivers.

2. In a dainty manner; with delicate attention to the palate, personal comfort, etc.

c **1340** *Cursor M.* 3655 (Trin.) Venisoun.. Deyntily diȝte to his pay. *c* **1440** *Gesta Rom.* xxxvi. 145 (Harl. MS.) The fleshe is i-fed deyntili. **1549** LATIMER *2nd Serm. bef. Edw. VI* (Arb.) 52 The rich.. gloton whych fared well and deyntely euery day. **1588** SHAKS. *Tit. A.* v. iii. 61 Baked in that Pie, Whereof their Mother dantily hath fed. **1647** COWLEY *Mistress, Love's Ingratitude* ii, And daintily I nourish'd Thee With Idle Thoughts and Poetry. **17..** BROOME *View Epick Poems* (J.), To sleep well and fare daintily.

3. Delicately, nicely, etc.; elegantly, gracefully, neatly, deftly.

1561 T. NORTON *Calvin's Inst.* III. viii. §1 He was not tenderly & deintily handled. **1592** GREENE *Disput.* 1 You tread so daintily on your typtoes. **1654** TRAPP *Comm. Ps.* xxiii, So daintily hath he struck upon the whole string. **1860** G. H. K. *Vac. Tour.* 117 The daintily tripping roe. **1860** MOTLEY *Netherl.* (1868) vii. 443 The envoy performed his ungracious task as daintily as he could.

†**4.** Rarely, sparingly. *Obs.* (Cf. DAINTY *a.* 2.)

1494 FABYAN *Chron.* VII. ccxxi. 242 To be kept there as a prysoner, where he was so dayntely fed that he dyed for hunger. **1581** SIDNEY *Apol. Poetrie* (Arb.) 65 The Auncients haue one or two examples of Tragy-comedies.. But.. we shall find, that they neuer, or very daintily, match Horn-pypes and Funeralls.

daintiness ('deɪntɪnɪs). [f. DAINTY *a.* + -NESS.] The quality of being dainty.

1. †**a.** The quality of being fine, handsome, delightful, etc. *Obs.* in general sense. **b.** Of food: Choiceness, deliciousness.

1552 HULOET, Deyntines of meates at a banquet, *lautitia*. **1577** B. GOOGE *Heresbach's Husb.* IV. (1586) 167 In daintinesse and goodnesse of meat, the Hennes may compare with.. the goose [etc.]. **1627** HAKEWILL *Apol.* (J.), It was more notorious for the daintiness of the provision which he served in it, than for the massiness of the dish.

2. Delicate beauty, elegance, gracefulness; neatness, deftness.

1580 SIDNEY *Arcadia* I. (1725) 106 Leucippe was of a fine daintiness of beauty. **1669** A. BROWNE *Ars Pict.* (1675) 19 The grossness, slenderness, clownishness, and daintyness of Bodies. **1878** J. W. EBSWORTH *Brathwait's Strappado* Introd. 28 There is poetic grace and daintiness of expression in the charming little lyric. **1884** BLACK *Jud. Shaks.* xxx, The pretty daintinesses of her coaxing.

3. Niceness, fastidiousness, delicacy, scrupulousness (of taste, sensibility, etc.).

1579 TOMSON *Calvin's Serm. Tim.* xxi. 250/2 What greter daintinesse doe we make at blasphemies? **1593** SHAKS. *Rich. II*, v. v. 45 Daintinesse of eare. **1624** WOTTON *Archit.* I, Of sand, Lyme, and clay, Vitruvius hath discoursed without any daintiness. **1892** *Speaker* 3 Sept. 299/1 A certain discrimination, a certain daintiness of choice.

4. Niceness of appetite; fastidiousness with regard to food, personal comfort, etc.; softness.

1530 PALSGR. 212/2 Deyntinesse, *friandise.* **1598** HAKLUYT *Voy.* I. 250 (R.) How iustly may this barbarous and rude Russe condemne the daintinesse and nicenesse of our captaines. **1670** MILTON *Hist. Eng.* v. (1851) 232 The People..learnt..of the Flemish daintiness and softness. **1836** W. IRVING *Astoria* I. 78 What especially irritated the captain was the daintiness of some of his cabin passengers. They were loud in their complaints of the ship's fare.

†**5.** Physical delicacy or tenderness. *Obs.*

1575 TURBERV. *Faulconrie* 229 In these cures of diseases that grow in the eyes there must be great care used..bicause of the dayntinesse of the place.

daintith: see DAINTETH.

†**'daintive**, *sb.* and *a. Obs. rare.* In 6 **deyntyue.** [app. a. Anglo-Fr. **daintif, -ive*, f. *dainté*: cf. OF. *bontif, -ive*, f. *bonté.*] = DAINTY *sb.* and *a.*

13.. [see adv. below]. **1526** *Pilgr. Perf.* (W. de W. 1531) 70 b To taste of his deyntyue delycates. *Ibid.* 71 [He] fedeth vs with the deyntyues of his owne delycate dysshe.

Hence †**'daintively** *adv.* (in 4 *deyntifliche*).

13.. *Cursor M.* 27904 (Cotton Galba) To ȝern metes dayntyuely. **1393** LANGL. *P. Pl.* C. IX. 324 (MS. I) Þis folke ..fedde hunger deyntifliche.

†**'daintrel.** *Obs.* Also 6 **deintrelle**, 7 **dainteril, -trill.** [Cf. OF. *daintier* a tit-bit, a delicacy. The formation is obscure.] A dainty, delicacy.

1575 J. STILL *Gamm. Gurton* II. i, But by thy words, as I them smelled, thy daintrels be not many. **1577** tr. *Bullinger's Decades* (1592) 240 Neither glut thy selfe with present delicates, nor long after deintrelles hard to be come bye. **1615** SIR E. HOBY *Curry-combe* i. 7 These dainterils haue layen so long vpon his hands, that I feare me they are scarce sweete. **1640** BROME *Spar. Garden* III. vii, You say I shall fill my belly with this new Daintrill.

dainty ('deɪntɪ), *sb.* Forms: 3–6 **dein-, deyn-, dain-, daynte, -ee,** (4–5 **dayn-, deyntte**), 4–6 **dein-, deyntie, -y(e,** 4–6 *Sc.* **dante(e,** 6 **-ie,** 5 **dente,** 6 **denty, -ie,** 4–7 **daynty(e, -ie,** 6–7 **daintie, -ye,** 4– **dainty.** [a. OF. *deintié, daintié, dainté* pleasure, tit-bit:—L. *dignitātem* worthiness, worth, beauty, f. *dignus* worthy. The earlier OF. form was in *-et*, whence DAINTETH.]

†**1.** Estimation, honour, favour (in which anything is held); esteem, regard; affection, love.

a **1225** *Ancr. R.* 412 Me let lesse deinte to þinge þet me haueð ofte. *c* **1305** *St. Dunstan* 35 in *E.E.P.* (1862) 35 For deynte þat he hadde of him: he let him sone bringe Bifore þe prince of Engelond. **1375** BARBOUR *Bruce* XIII. 475 Schir eduard..Lufit [him], and held in sic dante. **1377** LANGL. *P. Pl.* B. XI. 47 Of dowel ne dobet no deyntee me ne þouȝte. *c* **1430** LYDG. *Bochas* Prol. 52 These Poetes..Were by olde time had in great deintye With Kinges. **1513** DOUGLAS *Æneis* IV. viii. 28 Sen ȝonne..man, deir sister, the Was wount to cherise, and hald in gret dantie.

†**2.** Liking or fondness *to do* or *see* anything; delight, pleasure, joy. *Obs.*

c **1325** *Song of Yesterday* 5 in *E.E.P.* (1862) 133 Þei haue no deynte forto dele With þinges þat bene deautly made. **1375** BARBOUR *Bruce* XII. 159 Than all ran in-to gret dantee The Erll of Murreff for till se. *c* **1386** CHAUCER *Man of Law's T.* 41 Euery wight hath deyntee to chaffare With hem. *c* **1449** PECOCK *Repr.* I. xiii. 66 The reeding in the Bible.. drawith the reders..fro loue and deinte of the world. **1508** DUNBAR *Twa maryit wemen* 413 Adew dolour, adew! my daynte now begynis. *a* **1529** SKELTON *Bouge of Courte* 337 Trowest thou..That I haue deynte to see thee cherysshed thus?

†**3.** Delightful or choice quality; sumptuousness.

a **1300** *Cursor M.* 3655 (Cott.) Venison þou has him nommen, Wit dainte dight til his be-houe. *c* **1300** *K. Alis.* 7070 They haven seolk, gret plenté, And maken clothis of gret deynté. *c* **1440** *Promp. Parv.* 117/1 Dente (K.H.P. deynte), *lauticia.*

†**4.** Daintiness; fastidiousness. *Obs.*

1590 SPENSER *F.Q.* I. ii. 27 He feining seemely merth, And shee coy lookes: so dainty, they say, maketh derth. **1597** SHAKS. *2 Hen. IV*, IV. i. 198 Note this: the King is wearie Of daintie, and such picking grieuances.

†**5.** *concr.* Anything estimable, choice, fine, pleasing or delightful; hence occas., a luxury, rarity (cf. DAINTY *a.* 2). *Obs.* exc. as in 6.

1340 HAMPOLE *Pr. Consc.* 7850 Þare es plenté of dayntes and delice. *a* **1400–50** *Alexander* 5298 Ware slike a wondire in oure marche of Messedone..It ware a daynte to deme. **1562** J. HEYWOOD *Prov. & Epigr.* (1867) 51 Plenty is no dainty. **1617** RICH *Irish Hubbub* 47 It was a great dainties.. euen amongst their greatest nobility, to see a cloake lined thorow with Veluet. *a* **1661** FULLER *Worthies* (1840) II. 439 [He] made such a vent for Welch cottons, that what he found drugs at home, he left dainties beyond the sea. **1798** FERRIAR *Illustr. Sterne, Eng. Hist.* 227 Those who can only be allured by the dainties of knowledge.

†**b.** As a term of endearment. (Cf. *sweet.*)

1611 B. JONSON *Catiline* II. i, There is a fortune comming Towards you, Daintie.

6. *esp.* Anything pleasing or delicious to the palate; a choice viand, a delicacy.

c **1300** *Beket* 1202 Heo servede this holi man and of deyntes him broȝte. **1393** GOWER *Conf.* II. 255 Tho was there many a deinte fet And set to-fore hem on the bord. *c* **1440** *Promp. Parv.* 117 Delyce, or deyntes, *delicie.* **1576** FLEMING *Panopl. Epist.* 291 Some whet their teethe upon sugred deinties. **1611** BIBLE *Ps.* cxli. 4 Let mee not eate of their dainties. **1794** SOUTHEY *Wat Tyler* III. ii, Your larders hung with dainties. *a* **1839** PRAED *Poems* (1864) i. 305 The cunning caterer still must share The dainties which his toils prepare.

fig. **1393** GOWER *Conf.* III. 26 Suche deinties..Wherof thou takest thin herte food. **1614** BP. HALL *Recoll. Treat.* 59 There be some..to whom sin..is both food and dainties.

†**7.** Phrase. *to make dainty of* (*anything*): to set great store by; hence, to be sparing or chary of; ***to make dainty to do*** (or ***of doing***; also *absol.*), to be chary or loth, to scruple. *Obs.*

1555 WATREMAN *Fardle Facions* I. iii. 37 The moste noble Citrus, wherof the Romaines made greate deintie. **1579** TOMSON *Calvin's Serm. Tim.* ix. 107/1 They will not make daintie of the name of our Lord Jesus Christe, to worke their subtill and mischeevous practises. **1581** SAVILE *Tacitus' Hist.* I. xlvi. (1591) 26 Some..made noe dainty to beare any burden. **1592** SHAKS. *Rom. & Jul.* I. v. 21 Which of you all Will now deny to dance? She that makes dainty, She Ile sweare hath cornes. *a* **1617** HIERON *Wks.* II. 492 Shee ranne home and made no dainties of it; all her neighbours were the better for her store. *a* **1628** PRESTON *New Cov.* (1634) 410 Defer not, make not dainty of applying the promises. **1633** BP. HALL *Hard Texts* Matt. x. 39 Hee that makes so dainty of his life as that..he will not expose it to danger. **1638** FEATLEY *Strict. Lyndom.* II. 122 We have all reason to make great dainties of the noble confession of ..our Romish adversaries. **1649** MILTON *Eikon.* 43 If..he made so dainty and were so loath to bestow [etc.].

†**8.** As an asseveration: ? = By God's dignity, or honour. *Obs.*

1611 TOURNEUR *Ath. Trag.* II. v, S'daintie, I mistooke the place, I miss'd thine eare and hit thy lip.

dainty ('deɪntɪ), *a.* [from prec. sb.]

†**1.** Valuable, fine, handsome; choice, excellent; pleasant, delightful. *Obs.* or *dial.* in general sense.

c **1340** *Gaw. & Gr. Knt.* 1253 To daly with derely your daynte wordez. *c* **1386** CHAUCER *Prol.* 168 Full many a deynte hors hadde he in stable. **1526** TINDALE *Rev.* xviii. 14 All thynges which were deyntie and had in pryce. **1573** TUSSER *Husb.* xxxv. (1878) 81 More daintie the lambe, the more woorth to be sold. **1626** BACON *Sylva* §389 The daintiest Smells of Flowers, are out of those plants, whose Leaves smell not. **1712** STEELE *Spect.* No. 354 ¶1 To hear Country Squires..cry, Madam, this is dainty Weather. **1816** SCOTT *Old Mort.* vi, 'Ay? indeed? a scheme o' yours? that must be a denty ane!' **1855** ROBINSON *Whitby Gloss.*, *Denty* or *Dentyish*, a weather term, genial, cheering.

†**2.** Precious; hence, rare, scarce. *Obs.*

? *a* **1500** *How Plowman lerned Pater-Noster* 28 in Hazl. *E.P.P.* (1864) I. 211 Malte had he plentye; And Martylmas befe to hym was not deyntye. **1578** LYTE *Dodoens* VI. xi. 671 The blacke [whorts] are very common..but the red are dayntie, and founde but in fewe places. **1616** HIERON *Wks.* I. 584 If sermons were dainty..they would be more esteemed. **1677** LADY CHAWORTH in *12th Rep. Hist. MSS. Comm.* App. v. 37 A rare muffe, but judged to be some dainty squirell skin.

3. Pleasing to the palate, choice, delicate.

1382 WYCLIF *Prov.* xxi. 17 Who loueth deynte metis. *c* **1386** CHAUCER *Pard. T.* 58 To gete a glotoun deyntee mete and drinke. **1541** BARNES *Wks.* (1573) 299/1 To eate..costly fishes, and that of the dentiest fashion dressed. **1588** SHAKS. *L.L.L.* I. i. 26 Dainty bits Make rich the ribs. **1627** MILTON *Vac. Exerc.* 14 The daintiest dishes shall be serv'd up last. **1758** JOHNSON *Idler* No. 100 ¶12 Her house is elegant and her table dainty. **1892** STEVENSON *Wrecker* ii, Fine wines and dainty dishes.

4. Of delicate or tender beauty or grace; delicately pretty; made with delicate taste.

c **1400** *Destr. Troy* 3060 Her chyn..With a dympull full derne, daynté to se. **1555** WATREMAN *Fardle Facions* I. v. 77 She is estemed, as a deinty derling, beloued of many. **1579** SPENSER *Sheph. Cal.* June 6 The grassye ground with daintye Daysies dight. **1609** B. JONSON *Sil. Wom.* IV. i, Let your gifts be slight and dainty, rather than precious. *c* **1645** HOWELL *Lett.* I. xxviii. 54 Such a diaphonous pellucid dainty body as you see a Crystall-glasse is. **1877** M. M. GRANT *Sun-Maid* vii, There stood waiting for her the daintiest of little broughams.

5. Of persons, etc.: Possessing or displaying delicate taste, perception, or sensibility; nice, fastidious, particular; sometimes, over-nice.

1576 FLEMING *Panopl. Epist.* 357 Fine fellowes, that bee verie deintie and circumspect in speaking. **1581** LAMBARDE *Eiren.* IV. v. (1588) 497 Sundry other daintie and nice differences doth M. Marrow make. **1591** SHAKS. *1 Hen. VI*, V. iii. 38 No shape but his can please your dainty eye. **1602** —— *Ham.* v. i. 78 The hand of little Imployment hath the daintier sense. **1700** CONGREVE *Way of World* III. xv, I am somewhat dainty in making a resolution—because when I make it I keep it. **1841** LYTTON *Nt. & Morn.* III. ii, You must take me as you take the world, without being over-scrupulous and dainty. **1855** H. REED *Lect. Eng. Lit.* iii. 101 From being too dainty in our choice of words.

†**b.** with *of*: Particular or scrupulous about (anything); careful, chary, or sparing *of. Obs.*

1576 FLEMING *Panopl. Epist.* 251 Friendes..garnished w[t] learning, & not deintie of their travell. **1605** SHAKS. *Macb.* II. iii. 150 Let vs not be daintie of leaue-taking, But shift away. **1642** FULLER *Holy & Prof. St.* v. iii. 367 The devil not being dainty of his company where he finds welcome.

†**c.** with *infin.*: Disinclined or reluctant (*to do*).

1553 B. GILPIN in Strype *Eccl. Mem.* II. xxiii. 440 Such as be dainty to hear the poor. **1612** SIR R. DUDLEY in *Fortesc. Papers* 7 *note*, I will not bee dainty to make you a partie to my designes.

6. Nice or particular as to the quality of food, comforts, etc.; †luxurious.

a **1533** LD. BERNERS *Gold. Bk. M. Aurel.* (1546) K j b, The heart of a woman is deyntee. **1614** BP. HALL *Recoll. Treat.* 85 As..some daintie guest knowing there is so pleasant fare to com. **1683** TRYON *Way to Health* 181 You dainty Dames that are so nice, that you will not endure this pleasant Element to blow upon you. **1855** MOTLEY *Dutch Rep.* III. VI. v. 521 When men were starving they could not afford to be dainty. **1892** STEVENSON *Wrecker* ii, I was born with a dainty tooth and a palate for wine.

†**7.** Delicate (in health or constitution). *Obs.*

1562 BULLEYN *Campoundes* 46 a, Thei maie be giuen to drinke to them that are weake or feable, or as thei call it deintie. **1581** MULCASTER *Positions* xxii. (1887) 94 Whose mother was delicate, daintie, tender, neuer stirring.

8. *quasi-adv.* Daintily. (*rare.*)

1614 BP. HALL *Recoll. Treat.* 726 You quote Scriptures, tho (to your prayse) more dainty indeede then your fellowes. **1671** H. M. tr. *Erasm. Colloq.* 72 If rich men shall fare somewhat dainty. **1873** MISS BROUGHTON *Nancy* III. 144 So exceedingly fair and dainty wrought.

9. *Comb.*, as ***dainty-chapped, -eared, -fingered, -mouthed, -tongued, -toothed*** adjs.

1725 BAILEY *Erasm. Colloq.* (1877) 42 (D.) You *dainty-chapped fellow, you ought to be fed with hay. **1549** LATIMER *3rd Serm. bef. Edw. VI* (Arb.) 90 *marg.*, How tender and *deynety eared men of these days be. **1713** ROWE *Jane Shore* I. i, This tough impracticable Heart Is govern'd by a *dainty-finger'd Girl. **1530** PALSGR. 309/2 *Deynty mouthed, *friant.* *a* **1633** AUSTIN *Medit.* (1635) 233 They are so *daintie-Tongued that their Company is too costly. **1577** tr. *Bullinger Decades* (1592) 154 Let euery young man bee.. not licorish lipped, nor *dainty toothed.

†**dainty** ('deɪntɪ), *v. Obs. rare.* [f. prec. sb. or adj.] *trans.* With *up*: To pamper or indulge with dainties.

1622 H. SYDENHAM *Serm. Sol. Occ.* (1637) 108 So that they would..nourish, not daintie up the body. **1778** MRS. THRALE in *Mad. D'Arblay's Diary* Sept. I. 68 She dainties us up with all the meekness in the world.

Daiquiri, daiquiri ('daɪkɪrɪ, 'dæk-). Also **daquiri.** [f. *Daiquiri*, name of a district in Cuba.] A cocktail containing rum, lime, etc.

1920 F. SCOTT FITZGERALD *This Side of Paradise* (1921) I. iii. 115 Here's the old jitney waiter. If you ask me, I want a double Daiquiri. **1921** J. HERGESHEIMER *San Cristóbal de la Habana* 17 The moment..had arrived for a Daiquiri... I lingered over the frigid mixture of Ron Bacardi, sugar, and a fresh, vivid green lime. **1929** F. SHAY *Drawn from Wood* 181 Daquiri. **1935** *Lady Sysonby's Cook Bk.* 264 Daquiri (*Long drink*). The juice of 1 fresh lime, 1 teaspoonful of sugar. Fill your tumbler with dry crusted ice, and pour over Baccardi rum. Add sprigs of mint on the top. **1958** G. GREENE *Our Man in Havana* v. iv. 228 It was always a daiquiri I used to drink with him. **1967** L. JAMES *Chameleon File* (1968) x. 118 Wilson ordered the frozen Daiquiri which had been invented at La Florida.

dair, dairt, obs. forms of DARE, DART.

dairawe, daired: see DAY-.

‖**dairi** ('daɪriː). Also 7 **dayro.** [Japanese, f. Chinese *dai* great + *ri* within.] In Japan, properly the palace or court of the Mikado: also a respectful mode of speaking of the mikado or emperor.

Hence **dairi-sama**, *lit.* lord of the dairi or palace, an appellation of the Mikado.

1662 J. DAVIES tr. *Mandelslo's Trav. E. Ind.* 184 That great State hath always been govern'd by a Monarch, whom, in their Language they call *Dayro.* **1780** *Phil. Trans.* LXX. App. 7 We were not allowed to see the Dairi, or ecclesiastical emperor.

dairy ('dɛərɪ), *sb.* Forms: 3 **deierie,** 4 **dayerie, dayry,** 5 **deyery, deyry,** 6 **deirie, dary,** *pl.* **deyris, dayres,** 6–7 **deyrie, dayery(e, dery, dayrie, dairie,** 7 **daery, darie, dayry,** 7– **dairy.** [ME. *deierie*, etc., f. *deie, deye*, DEY female servant, dairy-maid + *-erie*, -ERY 2, suffix of Romanic origin. The *dai-ry* is thus the place where the function of the *dey* is performed: cf. *dey-woman, -house.*]

1. a. A room or building in which milk and cream are kept, and made into butter and cheese. **b.** Sometimes in towns the name is assumed by a shop in which milk, cream, etc. are sold.

c **1290** *S. Eng. Leg.* I. 192/14 Hire deierie was euere of chese and botere bar and swiþe lene. *Ibid.*, For þare nas in þe deierie nouȝt adel of none ȝwite. *c* **1386** CHAUCER *Wife's T.* 15 Thropes, beernys, shipnes, dayrys. *c* **1440** *Promp. Parv.* 117 Deyrye, *vaccaria.* **1577** B. GOOGE *Heresbach's Husb.* I. (1586) 3 As my Foldes..or my Dayrie and Fishpondes wyl yeelde. **1621** B. JONSON *Gipsies Metamorph.* Wks. (Rtldg.) 624/1 To Roger or Mary Or Peg of the dairy. **1727–46** THOMSON *Summer* 262 Some [insects] to the house, The fold, and dairy, hungry, bend their flight. **1837** HOWITT *Rur. Life* VI. i. 402 The elegant dairy for the supply of milk and cream, curds and butter.

2. That department of farming, or of a particular farm, which is concerned with the production of milk, butter, and cheese. Hence, sometimes applied to the milch cows on a farm collectively.

c **1386** CHAUCER *Prol.* 597 His lordes scheep, his meet, and his dayerie, His swyn, his hors, his stoor, and his pultrie, Was holly in this reeves governynge. **1673** TEMPLE *Trade in Ireland* Wks. 1773 III. 22 Grounds were turned much in England from breeding either to feeding or dairy. **1779** H.

SWINBURNE *Spain* xxxviii. (R.), The large dairy of cows established here by the present king. **1814** JANE WEST *A. de Lacy* III. 238 The..troopers..drove off our good cow-dairy. **1882** *Somerset Co. Gaz.* 18 Mar., Dairy of 12 or 16 cows to be let. **1888** ELWORTHY *W. Somerset Word-bk.*, *Dairy*, the milking cows belonging to any farm or house.

3. A dairy-farm.

1562 PHAER *Æneid.* IX. A a ij b, Stormy showres and winds about mens deiries houling. **1594** NORDEN *Spec. Brit., Essex* (Camden) 8 In Tendring hundred wher are manie wickes or dayries. *a* **1661** FULLER *Worthies* II. 144 The Goodnesse of the Earth, abounding with Deries and Pasture. **1769** *De Foe's Tour Gt. Brit.* II. 41 All the lower Part of this County ..is full of large feeding Farms, which we call Dairies; and the Cheese they make is excellent.

4. *attrib.* and *Comb.*, as ***dairy-cabin***, ***-country***, ***cow***, ***-damsel***, ***-pail***, ***produce***, ***-society***, ***-ware***, ***-wench***, ***-wife***, ***-work***, etc.; ***dairy-fed*** adj.; **dairy butter**, butter made at a private dairy; **dairy cream**, real cream as distinct from synthetic cream; **dairy factory** chiefly *N.Z.*, a factory with plant for the conversion of milk into butter or cheese; **dairy-farm**, a farm chiefly devoted to the production of milk, butter, and cheese; so **dairy-farmer**, **-farming**; **dairy-grounds**, cow-pastures; **dairy herd**, a herd of milch-cows; **dairy-school**, a technical school for teaching dairy-work or dairy-farming; **dairy shorthorn**, a shorthorn bred primarily to yield milk; **dairy-woman**, a woman who manages a dairy.

1874 *U.S. Dept. Agric. Rep. 1873* 250 During 1873, ..'good *dairy' butter touched 40 cents as its highest extreme. **1797** MRS. RADCLIFFE *Italian* xiii, It was a *dairy-cabin belonging to some shepherds. **1626** BACON *Sylva* §354 Children in *Dayrie Countries doe waxe more tall, than where they feed more upon Bread, and Flesh. **1656** R. VERNEY in M. M. Verney *Mem.* (1894) III. viii. 271, 4 *Dairy Cowes..13 draught Bullocks. *c* **1830** *Farm-Rep. Glouc. Hill-Farm* 17 in *Brit. Husbandry* (1840) III, The twenty heifer-calves are bred to keep up the stock of dairy-cows. **1963** A. CLARKE *Coll. Plays* 291 A thousand Shorthorns and half as many dairy cows Are hers. **1962** L. DEIGHTON *Ipcress File* ii. 19 The notice that told customers not to expect *dairy cream in their pastries. **1970** *Harrod's Summer Food News* (back cover), Fresh dairy cream, fresh eggs, pure sugar, fresh milk, and natural flavourings are used to produce these wonderful ice creams. **1818** SCOTT *Hrt. Midl.* xli, The yet more considerate *dairy-damsel. **1888** J. P. DOWLING *Dairying in Australia* iv. 19 *Dairy Factories—Co-operative and otherwise. **1888** R. M. MCCALLUM *Rep. Dairy Factories in N.Z.* 5, I have inspected a number of the dairy factories in the colony. **1950** *N.Z. Jrnl. Agric.* Jan. 21/3 There are two dairy factories in the area, a butter factory at Wairoa and a cheese factory at Nuhaka. **1959** A. MCLINTOCK *Descr. Atlas N.Z.* 57 Dairy factories are in the main owned cooperatively by the farmers. **1784** J. TWAMLEY *Dairying* 93 There is no branch in Husbandry seems of more importance..than the conducting and managing of *Dairy-farms. **1807** A. YOUNG *Agric. Essex* II. 270 Dairy farms at Bumpstead and Hempstead, with much more grass than arable. **1895** *U.S. Dept. Agric. Yearbk. 1894* 295 The dairy farm should be carefully selected, all the requirements of the business being well considered. **1790** W. H. MARSHALL *Rural Econ. Midl. Counties* I. 354 A *dairy farmer declares, that, one year, he lost forty pounds, by the mismanagement of his dairywoman. **1818** SCOTT *Hrt. Midl.* ix, To employ them as a dairy-farmer, or cowfeeder, as they are called in Scotland. **1906** *Westm. Gaz.* 10 Oct., People often ask why English dairy-farmers have not adopted the co-operative methods. **1831** *Lincoln Herald* 21 Oct. 1/1 For *dairy-fed porkers the price is at 4s to 5s. **1842** S. LOVER *Handy Andy* x, I've seen them in England killing your dairy-fed pork. **1961** *Guardian* 28 Apr. 6/6 An organised..sales programme..for dairy fed meat and poultry. *a* **1618** SYLVESTER *Hymn of Alms* 131 His douns with Sheep, his *daery-grounds wth Neat. **1879** J. P. SHELDON *Dairy Farming* i. 5/2 Whilst a cow is kept in the *dairy herd. **1928** *Daily Express* 3 Feb. 5/2 Instruction is given in the management of small dairy herds. **1818** KEATS *Endym.* I. 44 The *dairy pails Bring home increase of milk. **1530** PALSGR. 212/1 *Dayrie place, *meterie*. **1842** *Ainsworth's Mag.* I. 44 The sale of *dairy produce at the market town. **1930** T. S. ELIOT tr. *St. J. Perse's Anabasis* 59 The Stranger ..honoured with gifts of dairy produce and fruit. **1893** *Queen* 25 Mar. 278/2 They will..establish *dairy schools all over England. **1932** *Discovery* Feb. 58/2 Indeed with the most important of English breeds—the *dairy shorthorn—the quality of calves when they enter the dairy herd seems still largely a matter of chance. **1957** *Encycl. Brit.* V. 47/1 Strains of Shorthorns have been selected for milk and butterfat production, as well as beef, and in the United States are called Milking Shorthorns; in Canada, Dual-Purpose Shorthorns; in England and Australia, Dairy Shorthorns. **1890** *Farmer's Gaz.* 4 Jan. 5/2 The numerous *dairy societies in America. **1727** *Philip Quarll* (1816) 61 Having a store of *dairy ware, he resolved to make a place to keep it in: the kitchen..not being a proper place for cream and milk. **1684** OTWAY *Atheist* v. i, The *Dairy-Wench or Chamber-maid. **1798** BLOOMFIELD *Farmer's Boy, Spring* 251 Suffolk *dairy-wives run mad for cream. **1609** *Ev. Woman in Hum.* i. in Bullen *O. Pl.* IV, I shall goe to court now, and attired like an old *Darie woman. **1841** M. L. HAWTHORNE in *Hawthorne & Wife* (1885) I. 230 Bring us home a box of butter, if your dairy-woman is very nice. **1748** RICHARDSON *Clarissa* (1811) III. ix. 67, I have..admired them in their *dairy-works. **1890** *Farmer's Gaz.* 4 Jan. 5/2 As a specialist in dairy work.

'dairy, *v. rare.* [f. DAIRY *sb.*] *trans.* To keep or feed (cows) for the dairy.

1780 A. YOUNG *Tour Irel.* II. 142 The cattle system is generally dairying Cows. **1805** LUCCOCK *Nat. Wool* 245 Those [lands] of a stiffer quality are employed in the dairying of cows.

'dairy-house. A house or building used as a dairy; = DAIRY *sb.* 1; the house of a dairy-man.

1530 PALSGR. 212/2 Deyrie house, *meterie.* **1616** SURFL. & MARKH. *Country Farme* 16 You shall haue a Dairie-house or small vaulted Roome paued, and lying slope-wise..to serue for the huswifes Dairie. **1741** RICHARDSON *Pamela* III. 101 You'd better see her now-and-then at the Dairy-house or at School.

dairying ('dɛərɪɪŋ). [f. DAIRY *v.* + -ING[1].] The business or management of a dairy; the production of milk and manufacture of butter and cheese; dairy-farming.

1649 BLITHE *Eng. Improv. Impr.* To Rdr., To shew the way of Cow-keeping, Dayrying, or raising most Cheese and Butter. **1893** *Queen* 25 Mar. 478/2 They have the subject of dairying and dairy schools very much at heart.

b. *attrib.*

1784 TWAMLEY *Dairying* 8 In a considerable Dairying Country. **1890** *Times* 22 Feb. 7/3 The improvement and extension of the dairying industry.

dairymaid ('dɛərɪmeɪd). A female servant employed in a dairy.

1599 B. JONSON *Cynthia's Rev.* IV. i, Now I would be an empresse; and by and by a duchess; then a great lady..then a deyrie maide. **1712** ADDISON *Spect.* No. 530 ¶2 He has married a dairy-maid. **1879** J. WRIGHTSON *Dairy Husb.* in *Cassell's Techn. Educ.* IV. 246/2 When the butter falls from side to side in a compact lump the dairy-maid knows that her work approaches completion.

dairyman ('dɛərɪmən). A man who manages, or is employed in, a dairy. **b.** A man engaged in the sale of milk and other dairy produce.

1784 TWAMLEY *Dairying* 58 An object not unworthy a Dairy-man's notice. **1813** L. RICHMOND *(title)*, The Dairy-man's daughter. **1882** *Somerset Co. Gaz.* 18 Mar., Wanted, a steady young man as Dairyman.

dairy-woman: see DAIRY 4.

dais ('deɪɪs, deɪs). Forms: 3–5 **deys**, 3–6 **deis**, 4–5 **des**, 4–6 **dese**, **dece**, **deyse**, **dees**, 5 **deise**, **deesse**, 5–6 **dess(e**, **deas(e**, 6 **deasse**, **dysse**, *Sc.* **deiss**, **deische**, 8–9 *Sc.* **deas**, 4, 8–9 **dais**, 9– **daïs**. Pl. **daises**, **daïses**. [a. OF. *deis* (later *dois*), mod.F. (from Picard dial.) *dais* = Pr. *des*, It. *desco*:—L. *disc-um* (nom. *discus*) quoit, disk, dish, in late L. table.

The sense-development has been 'table, high table (including its platform), the raised end of the hall occupied by the high table and used for other purposes of distinction, the canopy covering this': the latter being only in modern French, and thence in Eng. The word died out in Eng. about 1600, but was retained in Sc. in sense 3; its recent revival, chiefly since 1800, in sense 2, is due to historical and antiquarian writers; it appears in no Eng. dicts. until Worcester 1846, Craig 1847. Always a monosyllable in Fr., and orig. so in Eng.; the disyllabic pronunciation is now the more usual.

1927 in *Amer. Speech* (1929) V. 132 *Dais*—two syllables. **1967** A. C. GIMSON *Everyman's Eng. Pronouncing Dict.* 118/2 *Dais, -es* 'deiis (deis), -iz.]

1. †**a.** A raised table in a hall, at which distinguished persons sat at feasts, etc.; the high table. (Often including the platform on which it was raised: see next sense.) *Obs.* since 1600.

a **1259** MATT. PARIS *Vitae Abbatum S. Alb.* in Walsingham (Rolls) I. 521 Priore prandente ad magnam mensam quam 'Deis' vulgariter appellamus. **1297** R. GLOUC. (Rolls) 11073 Vort hii come vp to þe deis. *a* **1300** *Cursor M.* 12560 (Cott.) Ne brek þair brede, ne tast þair mes, Til he war cummen til þair des. *c* **1350** *Will. Palerne* 4564 þe semli segges were sette in halle, þe real rinkes bi reson at þe heiȝe dese, and alle oþer afterward on þe side benches. *c* **1450** HENRYSON *Mor. Fab.* 10 So that Good-will be caruer at the Dease. *c* **1500** in Arnolde *Chron.* (1811) 241 Syttyng at the hygh dees: My Lord of Ely in the myddes. **1535** STEWART *Cron. Scot.* II. 395 Quhair that he sat into his stait royall, With mony ding lord sittand at his deische. *a* **1575** *Wife lapped in Morrelles Skin* 312 in Hazl. *E.P.P.* IV. 193 The Bride was set at the hye dysse.

†**b.** ***to begin the dais***: to take the chief seat, or preside, at a feast: see BEGIN *v.*[1] 5. Also ***to hold the dais*** in same sense. *Obs.*

1297 R. GLOUC. (Rolls) 7166 He ber þe croune & huld þe deis mid oþer atil also. *c* **1320** *Sir Beues* 2123 þow schelt þis dai be priour And be-ginne oure deis. *c* **1430** *Syr Tryam.* 1636 Quene Margaret began the deyse, Kyng Ardus, wyth owtyn lees, Be hur was he sett. *c* **1440** *Partonope* App. 7210 (Roxb.) Next the Quene he began the deyse.

2. a. The raised platform at one end of a hall for the high table, or for seats of honour, a throne, or the like: often surmounted by a canopy. *Obs.* since *c* 1600, until revived *c* 1800 in historical and subsequently in current use.

In earlier times sometimes app. meaning a bench or seat of honour upon the raised platform: cf. sense 3.

c **1290** *S. Eng. Leg.* I. 361/71 On þe heiȝe deis him sette, mete and drinke he him ȝaf. *c* **1300** *K. Alis.* 1039 Spoused scheo is, and set on deys. *c* **1325** *E.E. Allit. P.* B. 38 He were sette solempnely in a sete ryche, Abof dukes on dece, with dayntys serued. *c* **1386** CHAUCER *Merch. T.* 467 And atte fest sittith he and sche With othir worthy folk upon the deys. *c* **1450** *St. Cuthbert* 3049 He satt doune opon þe dese. **1501** DOUGLAS *Pal. Hon.* II. xlv, Tho I saw our ladyis twa and twa Sittand on deissis. **1513** BRADSHAW *St. Werburge* I. 1625 Ouer the hye desse..Where the sayd thre kynges sate crowned all. **1575** LANEHAM *Let.* (1871) 41 A doouty Dwarf too the vppermost deas Right peartly gan prik, and, kneeling on knee..Said 'hail, syr king'. **1778** PENNANT *Tour in Wales* (1883) I. 13 The great..hall is..furnished with the high *Dais*, or elevated upper end, and its long table for the lord and his jovial companions. **1820** SCOTT *Ivanhoe* iii, For about one quarter of the length of the apartment, the floor was raised by a step, and this space, which was called the dais, was occupied only by the principal members of the family. **1840** ARNOLD *Hist. Rome* II. 459 Like the dais or upper part of our old castle and college halls. **1860** EMERSON *Cond. Life, Behaviour* Wks. (Bohn) II. 386 The grandee took his place on the dais. **1893** F. THOMPSON *Poems* 50 Underneath her azured daïs, Quaffing, as your taintless way is, From a chalice. **1898** H. NEWBOLT *Island Race* 69 The College Eight and their trainer dining aloof, The Dons on the daïs serene. **1907** R. M. BURROWS *Discoveries in Crete* i. 10 At one end of a pillared hall..there is a narrow raised daïs.

b. By extension: The platform of a lecture hall; the raised floor on which the pulpit and communion table stand in some places of worship.

1888 *Nature* 26 Jan. 299/1 As a lecturer he was not brilliant; he appeared shy and nervous when on the dais. **1893** *Newspr.* A Flower Service was held in the church; the pulpit and dais were tastefully decorated.

c. *Freemasonry.* (See quot. 1866.)

1866 *Masonic Eclectic* Sept. 371 *Dais*, the platform or raised floor in the East, on which the presiding officer is seated. **1925** A. HARDINGE *Life H. H. M. Herbert* I. 223 The crippling decisions of the Grand Master and the 'Dais' or board. *Ibid.*, The 'Dais' was consternated at the audacity of so young a brother.

3. In some early examples (chiefly northern) it appears to have the sense 'seat, bench'; so in *Sc.* **a.** 'A long board, seat, or bench, erected against a wall', a settle; also, 'a seat on the outer side of a country house or cottage'. **b.** A seat, bench, or pew in a church. (Jamieson.) ***chamber of dais***: see CHAMBER *sb.* 11.

a **1330** *Syr Degarre* 765 Amidde the halle flore A fir was bet stark and store: He sat adoun upon the dais, And warmed him wel eche wais.

a **1774** FERGUSSON *Farmer's Ingle* (1845) 38 In its auld lerroch yet the deas remains, Where the guidman aft streeks him at his ease. **17..** JAMIESON *Pop. Ball.* (1806) I. 211 (Jam.) The priest afore the altar stood,—The Mer-man he stept o'er ae deas, And he has steppit over three. **1818** SCOTT *Hrt. Midl.* xviii, The old man was seated on the deas, or turf-seat, at the end of his cottage. **1832–53** *Whistle-binkie* (Sc. Songs) Ser. III. 73 Last Sunday, in your faither's dais, I saw thy bloomin' May-morn face. **1872** E. W. ROBERTSON *Hist. Ess.* 107 The chamber of Deese, the best room in the farmhouse of a certain class.

4. *transf.* (from 2) A raised platform or terrace of any kind; *e.g.* in the open air.

1861 N. A. WOODS *Prince of Wales in Canada* 341 A noble and lofty flight of steps—those daises of architecture which ..add..to the grand and imposing effect of lofty façades. **1884** C. ROGERS *Soc. Life Scot.* I. ix. 378 On the slopes of ancient daisses or hill terraces.

5. [after mod.Fr.—not an Eng. sense.] The canopy over a throne or chair of state.

1863 THORNBURY *True as Steel* I. 147 The Bishop.. occupied with bland dignity the chief throne under the dais. **1866** *Village on Cliff* iii, An old daïs of Queen Anne's time still hung over his doorway.

dais, Sc. pl. of DAW, DOE.

daise, obs. form of DAZE.

‖**daisho** ('daɪʃəʊ). [Jap., lit. 'large and small'.] A Japanese set of matched sword and dagger worn at the waist, esp. by a samurai. Cf. KATANA.

1923 H. C. GUNSAULUS *Japanese Sword-Mounts* ii. 31 These two known as the *dai-shō* ('long and short') were the pride of the samurai, who alone were privileged to wear two swords. **1957** *Encycl. Brit.* XXI. 694/1 Among the various kinds of Japanese swords are the *daisho*, a pair of swords, the larger being called a *katana* and the smaller a *wakizashi*. **1973** *Times* 10 Apr. 16/6 A seventeenth-century *daisho*, or pair of blades..made £8,400.

daisied ('deɪzɪd), *a.* Also 7 **dazied**. [f. DAISY *sb.* + -ED[2].] Adorned with or abounding in daisies. (Chiefly *poetic.*)

1611 SHAKS. *Cymb.* IV. ii. 398 Let vs Finde out the prettiest Dazied Plot we can. *c* **1720** GAY *Dione* I. iv, Daisy'd lawns. **1883** *Contemp. Rev.* June 862 Beneath the daisied turf.

daisle, daisterre, obs. ff. DAZZLE, DAY-STAR.

daisy ('deɪzɪ), *sb.* Forms: 1 **dæȝeseȝe**, **-eaȝe**, 3–4 **dayes-eȝe**, **-eghe**, 4 **dayesye**, **-eye**, 4–5 **daysye**, 4–7 **daysie**, **daisie**, (5 *pl.* **dayses**), 5–6 **daysy**, 6 **deysy**, **dasye**, **dasey**, **dayzie**, 6–7 **dasy**, 7 **days-eye**, **dazy**, **-ie**, (*pl.* **dayzes**, *Sc.* **desie**, **deasie**), 7–8 **daizy**, 6– **daisy**. [OE. *dæȝes éaȝe* day's eye, eye of day, in allusion to the appearance of the flower, and to its closing the ray, so as to conceal the yellow disk, in the evening, and opening again in the morning.]

1. a. The common name of *Bellis perennis*, N.O. *Compositæ*, a familiar and favourite flower of the British Isles and Europe generally, having small flat flower-heads with yellow disk and white ray (often tinged with pink), which close in the evening; it grows abundantly on grassy hills, in meadows, by roadsides, etc., and blossoms nearly all the year round; many varieties are cultivated in gardens.

c **1000** ÆLFRIC *Gloss.* in Wr.-Wülcker 135/22 *Consolda*, dæȝeseȝe. *c* **1000** *Sax. Leechd.* III. 292 ȝearwe, and fif-leafe, dæȝeseȝe, and synnfulle. *a* **1310** in Wright *Lyric P.* xiii. 43 Dayes-eȝes in thio dales. *c* **1385** CHAUCER *L.G.W.* Prol. 43 Of al the floures in the mede, Thanne love I most these floures white and rede, Suche as men called daysyes. *Ibid.* 184 Wele by reson men it calle may The dayeseye, or ellis the eye of day. *c* **1450** *Crt. of Love* xv, Depeinted wonderly, With many a thousand daisies, rede as rose, And white also. **1579** SPENSER *Sheph. Cal.* June 6 The grassye ground with daintye Daysies dight. **1588** SHAKS. *L.L.L.* v. ii. 904 Daisies pied and Violets blew. **1625** BACON *Ess. Gardens* (Arb.) 556 For March, There come Violets..The Yellow Daffadill; The Dazie. **1710** ADDISON *Tatler* No. 218 ¶9 Visits to a Spot of Daizies, or a Bank of Violets. **1803** LEYDEN *Scenes of Inf.* I. 291 When evening brings the merry folding hours, And sun-eyed daisies close their winking flowers. **1833** MARRYAT *P. Simple* xxxv, She was as fresh as a daisy. **1861** DELAMER *Fl. Gard.* 81 There are Quilled, Double, and Proliferous or Hen-and-Chicken Daisies.

b. Cf. DAISY-CUTTER 1.

1847 W. IRVING *Life & Lett.* (1864) IV. 28 My horse, now and then cuts daisies with me when I am on his back.

c. Slang phrases: ***under the daisies***, dead and buried; ***to push up daisies, to turn one's toes up to the daisies***, to be in one's grave, to be dead.

1842 BARHAM *Ingol. Leg.* Ser. II. *Babes in the Wood* iv, Be kind to those dear little folks When our toes are turned up to the daisies. **1866** G. MACDONALD *Ann. Q. Neighb.* I. xi. 356, I shall very soon hide [my name] under some daisies. *a* **1918** W. OWEN *Poems* (1963) 65 'Pushing up daisies' is their creed, you know. **1928** S. VINES *Humours Unreconciled* xxi. 268, I think she's drinking herself under the daisies, so to speak. **1938** G. HEYER *Blunt Instrument* xiii. 252 'Where is the wife now?'.. 'Pushing up daisies... Died..a couple of years ago.' **1961** S. CHAPLIN *Day of Sardine* xiii. 245 Everybody goes to hell their own way and by the time you're privileged to be able to help a lost soul he'll be pushin' up daisies. **1970** *Guardian* 30 Dec. 9/6 In ten years time I think I should be pushing up daisies.

2. Applied to other plants with similar flowers or growing in similar situations. **a.** *simply*. In N. America, the Ox-eye Daisy, *Chrysanthemum Leucanthemum* (see b); in Australia, various *Compositæ*, esp. *Vitadenia* and *Brachycome iberidifolia*; in New Zealand, the genus *Lagenophora*. **b.** With qualifications, as **African daisy**, *Athanasia annua*; **blue daisy**, (*a*) the Sea Starwort; (*b*) the genus *Globularia*; **bull d.** = *ox-eye d.*; **butter d.**, locally applied to the Buttercup, and to the Ox-eye Daisy; **Christmas d.**, several species of *Aster*, esp. *A. grandiflorus*; **dog d.** = *ox-eye d.*; **globe d.**, the genus *Globularia*; **great d.**, **horse d.**, **midsummer d.**, **moon d.** = *ox-eye d.*; **marsh d.** = *sea d.*; **Michaelmas d.**, various cultivated species of *Aster* which blossom about Michaelmas; also applied to the wild *Aster Tripolium*; **ox-eye daisy**, *Chrysanthemum Leucanthemum*, a common plant in meadows, with flowers resembling those of the common daisy but much larger, on tall stiff stalks; **sea daisy**, Thrift, *Armeria maritima*. (See *Treas. Bot.*, and Britten & Holland *Eng. Plant-n.*)

a **1387** *Sinon. Barthol.* (Anecd. Oxon.) 16 *Consolida media*, grete dayeseghe. **1578** LYTE *Dodoens* II. xix. 169 There be two kindes of Daysies, the great and the small. *Ibid.* III. xxxiii. 364 Some call it blew Camomil or blew Dasies. **1794** MARTYN *Rousseau's Bot.* xxvi. 396 The Ox-eye Daisy, a plant common among standing grass in meadows. **1838** SCROPE *Deerstalking* 388 Even the highest hills..are scattered over with the sea daisy and other plants. **1861** MISS PRATT *Flower. Pl.* III. 286 (Sea-Starwort)..Country people call it Blue Daisy.

3. A species of sea-anemone (*Actinia bellis*).

1859 LEWES *Sea-side Stud.* Index.

†**4.** As a term of admiration. *Obs.*

c **1485** *Digby Myst.* (1882) III. 515 A dere dewchesse, my daysyys Iee! *a* **1605** MONTGOMERIE *Misc. Poems* (1887) xxxix. 1, Adeu, O desie of delyt.

5. *slang.* (chiefly *U.S.*). A first-rate thing or person; also as *adj.* First-rate, charming.

1757 FOOTE *Author* II. Wks. 1799 I. 148 Oh daisy; that's charming. **1886** MRS. BURNETT *Little Ld. Fauntleroy* xv. (1887) 263 'She's the daisiest gal I ever saw! She's —well she's just a daisy, that's what she is.' **1888** *Denver Republican* May (Farmer), Beyond compare a pugilistic daisy. **1889** *Boston* (Mass.) *Jrnl.* 22 Mar. 2/3 In a new book upon 'Americanisms,' some of the less familiar are..daisy, for anything first-rate.

6. *attrib.* or as *adj.* **a.** Resembling a daisy.

a **1605** MONTGOMERIE *Well of Love* 41 Hir deasie colour, rid and vhyte. **1611** BARKSTED *Hiren* (1876) 83, I sweare by this diuine white daizy-hand. **1854-6** PATMORE *Angel in Ho.* I. II. iv, She Whose daisy eyes had learned to droop.

b. *U.S. slang.* (See sense 5.) Also as *adv.*

1886 [see sense 5]. **1887** F. FRANCIS *Saddle & Mocassin* x. 189 Well, if he can kick anything out of a Government mule, he's a daisy burro. **1892** *Harper's Mag.* Feb. 438/1 A passenger informed on him for having his coat unbuttoned. Daisy passenger, wasn't it? **1902** S. E. WHITE *Blazed Trail* xxxvii. 252 She's my daisy Sunday best-day girl. **1905** R. BEACH *Pardners* (1912) v. 130 The noose sailed up and settled over him fine and daisy. **1927** E. WALLACE *Mixer* i. 14 I'll introduce you to the daisiest night club in town.

7. *Comb.*, as ***daisy-bud, -flower, -head, -lawn, -root; daisy-dappled, -diapered, -dimpled, -dotted, -flowered, -frilled, -like, -painted, -peeping, -powdered, -spangled*** adjs.; **daisy anemone** = sense 3; **daisy-bush**, a New Zealand shrub of the genus *Olearia*; **daisy fleabane** *U.S.*, any of several plants of the genus *Erigeron*; **daisy-leaved** *a.*, having leaves like those of the daisy; **daisy roots** *Rhyming slang*, boots; also *ellipt.*; **daisy-tree** *Austral.* and *N.Z.* (see quots.); **daisy-wheel**, a kind of removable printing unit for typewriters and printers, in which the printing elements are on the sides of arms radiating from a central hub and forming a flat wheel which is automatically rotated to bring a selected character in front of the hammer; also (in full ***daisy-wheel printer*** or ***typewriter***), a machine employing such a unit.

1857 WOOD *Comm. Obj. Sea Shore* vi. 114 A bad-tempered *Daisy Anemone (*Actinia bellis*), which lived in a cave..and did not approve of intrusion. **1596** FITZ-GEFFREY *Sir F. Drake* (1881) 81 The *daysie-diap'red bankes. **1845** HIRST *Poems* 54 Over *daisy-dimpled meadows. **1925** W. J. ARKELL in *Oxf. Poetry* 10 The *daisy-dotted meadow. **1848** A. GRAY *Man. Bot.* 206 *Erigeron annuum*, *Daisy Fleabane. *Ibid.*, Narrow-leaved *E. strigosum*, Daisy Fleabane. **1872** *Rep. Vermont Board Agric.* I. 279 *Erigeron annuum* and *E. strigosum*, Daisy Fleabanes, acrid plants, mingle their coarse stalks quite too freely with the hay from newly seeded land. **1931** W. N. CLUTE *Common Names Plants* 131 'Kiss-me-and-I'll-tell-you' replied an attractive native of the Southern States when asked the name of that plant which people of colder climes know as the daisy fleabane. **1881** WILDE *Poems* 209 Your queen in *daisy-flowered smock. **1924** E. SITWELL *Sleeping Beauty* x. 36 Her *daisy-frilled frock. **1887** SIR W. G. SIMPSON *Art of Golf* 91 One sweeps off *daisy heads with a walking-stick. **1796** WITHERING *Brit. Plants* (ed. 3) III. 577 *Daisie-leaved Lady smock. **1796** T. TOWNSHEND *Poems* 20 The *daisy-painted green. **1929** BLUNDEN *Near & Far* 41 Through spring's *daisy-peeping wonder. **1820** 'JANUS WEATHERCOCK' in *London Mag.* Mar. 287/1 A dark-haired girl, 'amorous of mischief', curled on the *daisy-powdered grass. **1626** BACON *Sylva* §354 Boyling of *Dasie-Roots in Milk. [**1859** HOTTEN *Slang Dict.* 290 *Daisy recroots* (so spelt by my informant of Seven Dials, he means, doubtless, *recruits*), a pair of boots.] **1859** MATSELL *Vocabulum* 24/1 *Daisy-roots*, boots and shoes. **1873** HOTTEN *Slang Dict.* 366 *Daisy roots*, a pair of boots. **1879** *Macm. Mag.* XL. 501/2 I piped three or four pair of daisy-roots (boots). *Ibid.* 503/1 While waiting for my pal I had my daisies cleaned. **1943** *Gen* 25 Sept. 50/1 Your toes is poking out of your daisy-roots. **1813** SHELLEY *Q. Mab* VIII. 82 The *daisy-spangled lawn. **1898** MORRIS *Austral Eng.* 113/1 **Daisy Tree*, two Tasmanian trees, *Astur stellulatus*..and *A. glandulosus*. **1926** J. C. ANDERSEN in *Trans. N.Z. Instit.* LVI. 702/2 *Olearia*: daisy tree, daisy-tree, tree-daisy. **1977** *Office* Mar. 134/2 *Daisy-wheel printing mechanism allows operator to change wheels for a variety of typestyles and sizes. **1979** *New Scientist* 4 Jan. 27/3 'Daisy wheel' printers are now ousting 'golfballs' in word processing systems. **1982** *Observer* 3 Oct. 21 Printers like the daisywheel..produce copy of high enough quality to be used for correspondence. **1983** *Your Computer* (Austral.) Nov. 20/3 The characters reside on the fingers of a plastic or metal wheel, called a daisywheel or thimble, which revolves past a single hammer.

'daisy, *v. rare.* [f. prec. sb.] *trans.* To cover or adorn with daisies.

1767 G. S. CAREY *Hills of Hybla* 8 When fertile nature dasy'd ev'ry hill. **1831** E. TAYLOR *Remembrance* 29 The earth we tread shall be daisied o'er.

daisy chain. **1.** A chain of daisies sewed or fastened together, made by children in play.

1841 LYTTON *Nt. & Morn.* I. ix, I never walk out in the fields, nor make *daisy-chains.

2. *fig.* and *transf.* **a.** (esp. in services' contexts: see quots.).

1856 C. M. YONGE *Daisy Chain* II. xxv. 641 He called her [*sc.* his dead daughter] the first link of his Daisy Chain drawn up out of sight. **1950** V. PENIAKOFF *Private Army* v. 134 We used a device christened the 'daisy chain', made from gun-cotton primers threaded on a five-foot length of prima cord... Five primers went to each daisy chain spaced out and held in place by knots in the cord. **1959** *Times* (Queen in Canada Suppl.) 18 June p. xiii/3 It is connected with Edmonton, Alberta, by..the Northwest Staging Route, a daisy chain of airfields, built during the war between interior Alaska and Canada. **1961** *Flight* LXXX. 996/1 If..four loads are to be dropped in a stick, the first is extracted by a parachute stowed on the floor sill and released by the dropping officer, whilst loads 2, 3 and 4 are extracted by parachutes carried by and released from loads 1, 2 and 3 (this technique is now well known as the 'daisy-chain' system). **1979** *Times* 15 Dec. 3/6 A collision known in Army slang as a 'daisy chain'... One man's parachute 'stole' the air from his comrade's, both canopies deflated and the men plunged..to their deaths. **1986** *Times* 19 Feb. 17/3 Can.. order be brought to the daisy chain market? The daisy chain takes its name from the string of traders who sell or buy from each other on paper a cargo of Brent crude.

b. Sexual activity involving three or more persons. *slang.*

1941 G. LEGMAN in G. W. Henry *Sex Variants* II. 1162 *Daisy-chain*, a spintry; a group of more than two persons —heterosexual, homosexual, or both—linked together in simultaneous sexual intercourse of any kind or combination of kinds... A person participating in a spintry is termed a *daisy-chainer*. **1951** S. LONGSTREET *Pedlocks* II. v. 93 The screened, discreet box at the Comique led to an unbelievably evil circus at the Casino ('Oh, them daisy chains,' said Condon). **1964** [see POT *sb.*[5] 1]. **1972** F. WARNER *Maquettes* 12 *Bride One.* Will you give us a baby? *Groom.* One between two. A Siamese Solomon. *Bride Two.* We call it a daisy-chain sandwich, in the best wife-swapping circles. **1977** E. J. TRIMMER et al. *Visual Dict. Sex* (1978) xvii. 164 In the frantic search for novelty..a group sex activity called the *daisy chain* has been invented.

'daisy-cutter. [*lit.* 'cutter of daisies': see DAISY *sb.* 1 b.]

1. A horse that in trotting lifts its feet only very slightly from the ground.

1791 'G. GAMBADO' *Ann. Horsem.* xvi. (1809) 129, I luckily picked up a Daisy-cutter, by his throwing me down on the smoothest part of the grass. **1847** YOUATT *Horse* iv. 87 The careless daisy-cutter, however pleasant on the turf, should..be avoided. **1867** READE *Griffith Gaunt* (1889) 5 Daisy-cutters were few in those days.

2. *Cricket* and *Baseball.* A ball so bowled or batted as to skim along the surface of the ground.

1857 *Bell's Life* 1 Nov. 7/1 The umpires called play, Grange being again on the defensive to the under-hand 'daisy cutters' of Sadler. **1889** 'MARK TWAIN' *Yankee at Crt. K. Arthur* (Tauchn.) II. 226 I've seen him catch a daisy-cutter in his teeth. **1891** FARMER *Slang Dict.*, *Daisy-cutter*, a ball which travels more than half the 'pitch' along the ground without rising; a 'sneak'. **1963** *Times* 13 June 13/3 The ball that kept low had to be a daisy-cutter although a first-class cricket pitch has surely been sufficiently mown to lose all likeness to a flowery meadow.

So **'daisy-cutting** *vbl. sb.* and *ppl. a.*

1827 HONE *Every-day Bk.* II. 461 Nimble daisy-cutting nags. **1837** T. HOOK *Jack Brag* i, None of your bowling-green, daisy-cutting work for us. **1875** 'STONEHENGE' *Brit. Sports* II. II. i. §3. 502 The..low daisy-cutting form which suits the smooth turf of our race-courses.

dait, obs. form of DATE.

‖**dāk** (dɔːk, dɑːk). *Anglo-Ind.* Also 8- **dawk**, 8 **dog, dock**, 9 **dork, dauk.** [Hindī and Marāthī *ḍāk*, perh. related to Skr. *drāk* quickly.] **a.** Post or transport by relays of men or horses stationed at intervals; a relay of men or horses for carrying mails, etc., or passengers in palanquins.

to travel dāk: to travel in this way. *to lay a dāk*: to arrange for relays of bearers or horses on a route.

1727 [see b]. **1780** H. F. THOMPSON *Intrigues of Nabob* 76 (Y.), I wrote..for permission to visit Calcutta by the Dawks. **1781** *Hicky's Bengal Gaz.* 24 Mar. (Y.), Suffering People to paw over their Neighbour's Letters at the Dock. **1809** VISCOUNT VALENTIA *Trav. India, etc.* (1811) I. ii. 49 My arrangements had been made for quitting Burhampore ..not only had the dawk been laid, but [etc.]. *a* **1826** HEBER *Narr. Journey Ind.* (1828) I. 328 In the line of road I am most likely to follow..I am not certain that any Dâk exists. **1840** E. E. NAPIER *Scenes For. Lands* II. vi. 193 By having bearers posted at stated distances, which is called travelling 'dawk', long journeys are made in a comparatively brief space of time. **1861** HUGHES *Tom Brown at Oxf.* xliv. (D.), After the sea voyage there isn't much above 1000 miles to come by dauk.

b. *attrib.*, as ***dāk-bag, -bearer, choky, journey, traveller***, etc.; **dāk bungalow** (rarely **house**), a house for the accommodation of travellers at a station on a dāk route; **dāk-wallah**, a letter-carrier.

1727 A. HAMILTON *New Acc. E. Ind.* I. 149 (Y.) Those Curriers are called Dog Chouckies. **1796** in Seton-Karr *Select. Calcutta Gaz.* II. 185 The re-establishment of Dawk Bearers upon the new road. *a* **1826** HEBER *Narr. Journey Ind.* (1828) I. 277, I will..bring it safe on to the next dâk-house. **1828** *Asiatic Costumes* 40 The dauk-wala is dispatched from the post-office every day with his bundle of letters. **1853** *Calcutta Rev.* July-Dec. 175 The dâk bungalows, the modern form of the Mogul Serais. **1866** TREVELYAN (*title*), The Dawk Bungalow. *Ibid.* (1869) 98 Too old travellers to expect solitude in a dawk bungalow. **1872** E. BRADDON *Life in India* vii. 260 The arrival at any village of the *dâk-walla* (letter-carrier) with a letter is an event to be remembered and talked of. **1923** *Blackw. Mag.* Nov. 678/2 My old *dâk-wallah*..had scented the battle from afar. **1926** *Ibid.* Nov. 587/1 An 'Urgent' dak bag arrived from the Agency with a letter from Baird. **1928** *Ibid.* Jan. 5/2 The correspondence came to an abrupt stop. Great soggy chunks of silence filled the incoming dâk-bag.

daka, dakha, varr. DAGGA[1].

daker. Also daiker, dakir. [a. OF. *dacre, dakere*, med.L. *dacra*: see DICKER.] Variant of DICKER, a set of ten.

1531 *Aberdeen Burgh Rec.* XIII. 248 The dakir of hidis. **1597** SKENE *De Verb. Sign.* s.v. *Serplaith*, Ten hides makis ane daiker, and twentie daiker makis ane last. **1753** MAITLAND *Hist. Edin.* III. 248 For every Daker of Hides landed at Leith—8 pennies. **1866** ROGERS *Agric. & Prices* I. 171 The dicker or daker was..a measure for hides and gloves.

daker, var. of DACKER.

daker-hen. *dial.* [Connexion has been suggested with DAIKER *v.*, and with Flem. *daeckeren* 'volitare, motari, mobilitare, et coruscare' (Kilian). But no such name appears to be applied to the bird in Flanders.] The Corn-crake or Land-rail.

1552 ELYOT *Bibl.*, *Crex*, a certaine birde, whiche semeth by Aristotle to be that whiche in some places is called a Daker hen. **1678** RAY *Willughby's Ornith.* 170 The Rail or Daker-hen. **1766** PENNANT *Zool.* (1768) II. 387. **1789** G. WHITE *Selborne* (1853) 347 A man brought me a land-rail or daker-hen. **1869** *Lonsdale Gloss.*, *Daker-hen*, the corn-crake.

‖**dakhma** ('dɑːkmə). Also **dokhma.** [Pers.] A tower of silence (see SILENCE *sb.* 2 c).

1865 [see SILENCE *sb.* 2 c]. **1908** *Westm. Gaz.* 4 Aug. 10/1 Neither God is pleased nor the dead are benefited by a showy expenditure on a Dokhma. **1912** H. G. RAWLINSON *Bactria* iii. 40 Alexander promptly ordered the *dakhmas*, or Towers of Silence, to be closed. **1957** *Encycl. Brit.* XXIII.

989/1 The dead..are to be left on the appointed places (*dakhmas*) and exposed to the vultures and wild dogs.

Dakin ('deɪkɪn). The name of H. D. *Dakin* (1880–1952), British chemist, used in the possessive to designate a solution of sodium hypochlorite used as an antiseptic, or a dressing saturated in this fluid.

1920 MARTINDALE & WESTCOTT *Extra Pharmacop.* (ed. 17) I. 56 Dakin's (Stronger) Hypochlorite Solution. **1927** A. J. CLARK *Applied Pharmacol.* (ed. 2) 10 The chief chlorine compounds used for disinfection of the body are: (1) eusol and Dakin's fluid. **1928** EDMUNDS & GUNN *Cushny's Textbk. Pharmacol.* (ed. 10) 160 Dakin's solution is prepared by adding chlorinated lime to a solution of sodium carbonate. **1929** F. A. POTTLE *Stretchers* (1930) 149 Small éclat removed. Dakin dressing. **1963** *Brit. Pharmaceutical Codex* 1198 Surgical solution of chlorinated soda, Dakin's solution. **1964** J. J. WALSH *Understanding Paraplegia* xi. 78 The urinal should be..soaked for two hours in a suitable antiseptic solution such as 16% Dakins [*sic*] Solution.

dakoit, etc.: see DACOIT, etc.

Dakota (də'kəʊtə), *sb.* and *a.* Also **Dacota, Dacotah,** †**Dahcota.** [Dakota (Santee dialect) *dakota*, lit. 'allies'.] **A.** *sb.* **1.** A North American Indian tribe inhabiting the upper Mississippi and Missouri river valleys, speaking a language of the Siouan stock; a member of this people. Also commonly called SIOUX.

[**1804** LEWIS & CLARK *Jrnls.* (1904) I. 132 This Great Nation who the French has given the Nickname of Suouex, Call themselves *Dar co tar*... Those *Dar ca ter's* or Suoux inhabit..the country on the Red river.] **1810** *Ibid.* (1962) 508 As to Sioux Indians..the Indians call themselves Dacota. **1824** W. H. KEATING *Narr.* I. viii. 376 The Dacotas are a large and powerful nation of Indians. **1852** S. R. RIGGS *Gram. & Dict. Dakota Lang.* p. xv, The nation of the Sioux Indians, or Dakotas, as they call themselves, is supposed to number about twenty-five thousand. **1877** L. H. MORGAN *Anc. Soc.* II. ii. 86 In some tribes, as among the Dakotas, the gentes had fallen out. **1948** A. L. KROEBER *Anthropol.* (ed. 2) viii. 322 Among the Dakota each man was free to seek his own 'vision' or inspiration from supernaturals.

2. The language of this people.

1923 A. L. KROEBER *Anthropol.* v. 116 The number of words recorded in Klamath,..is 7,000;..in Dakota, 19,000. **1933** BLOOMFIELD *Lang.* iv. 72 The Siouan family includes many languages, such as Dakota, Teton, Oglala, [etc.].

B. *adj.* Of, pertaining to, or designating this people or their language.

1809 in D. Jackson *Lett. Lewis & Clark Exped.* (1962) 476 A Large Mantle, made of the Buffalow skin, worn by the Scioux, or Soue, Darcota Nation. **1841** J. BELL *Let.* 31 Aug. in J. D. Richardson *Compilation Messages of Presidents* (1897) IV. 62 They are divided into bands..the generic name for the whole being the Dahcota Nation. **1846** C. LANMAN *Summer in Wild.* (1847) 56 Here it was I first saw ..Sioux or Dacotah Indians. **1852** S. R. RIGGS (*title*) Grammar and dictionary of the Dakota language. **1880** *Encycl. Brit.* XII. 831/2 The Dakota or Sioux nation is at present the most powerful of the Indian tribes in North America. **1881** *Harper's Mag.* Feb. 472/1 The story is told by..the author of a grammar and dictionary of the Dakota tongue. **1902** *Encycl. Brit.* XXXIII. 890/1 The Dakota Indians invented a chronological table, or winter count. **1959** E. TUNIS *Indians* 21/2 About thirty different Indian names are listed for the Dakota Indians, and a fair percentage of them can be translated to mean 'cutthroats'.

Hence **Da'kotan, -ian** *sb.* and *adj.*, (an inhabitant) of the Dakota Territory, or of the states of North or South Dakota.

1884 M. D. WOODWARD *Diary* 22 Mar. in *Checkered Yrs.* (1937) 32 The Dakotan of the next generation should be an educated person. **1889** *Cent. Dict.*, Dakotan, *a*...*n*. **1898** *Monthly South Dakotan* I. 5 Here the judge first inculcated the principle of Dakotan jurisprudence. *Ibid.*, One hundred sorrowing Dakotans. **1914** W. H. RIVERS *Kinship & Soc. Organ.* 89 Professor Kroeber does not specify which kinds of grandfather and father-in-law are classed together in Dakotan nomenclature. **1947** *Amer. Speech* XXII. 249 Mr. Bruce Nelson, of Bismarck, N.D., tells me that *Dakotan* now prevails [over *Dakotian*] in both Dakotas. **1861** (*title*) Weekly Dakotian. **1877** L. M. MORGAN *Anc. Soc.* II. vi. 154 (*heading*) Dakotian Tribes. A large number of tribes are included in this great stock of the American aborigines.

Daks (dæks). Also **daks.** [App. f. DA(D *sb.*[1] + *slac*)*ks* (SLACK *sb.*[3] 5).] A proprietary name for a make of clothes, esp. of men's trousers with self-supporting waistband, and subsequently also of suits, jackets, etc.

1933 *Trade Marks Jrnl.* 4 Oct. 1202/2 Daks 543,009. Trousers. S. Simpson, Ltd., 92–100 Stoke Newington Road, London, N.16; Manufacturers. **1938** *Ibid.* 10 Aug. 971/1 Daks 584,941. Suits, being articles of clothing. S. Simpson. **1949** A. WILSON *Wrong Set* 177 In his jade green linen shirt, white silk scarf with green spots and olive green daks, he looked very English intellectual, very Pirates of Penzance. **1959** P. TOWNEND *Died o' Wednesday* vii. 122 The rear door of the car opened slowly and a pair of suède shoes, surmounted by pale green Daks, followed by the man himself, were eased with nonchalant grace on to the dusty road. **1961** P. PORTER *Once Bitten* 19 This new Daks suit, greeny-brown, Oyster-coloured buttons. **1970** *Private Eye* 27 Mar. 16 I've got..a pretty clean pair of *thunderbags* under me daks.

‖**dal** (dɑːl). *Anglo-Ind.* Forms: 7–9 **dol(l,** 9 **dhal(l, dhol(l, dal(l.** [Hindī *dāl* split pulse:—Skr. *dala*, f. *dal* to split.] The pulse obtained from some leguminous plants, chiefly from the Cajan, *Cajanus indicus*, extensively used as an article of food in the East Indies.

1698 FRYER *Acc. E. India* 101 (Y.) At their coming up out of the Water they bestow the largess of Rice or Doll (an Indian Bean). **1727** HAMILTON *New Acc. E. Ind.* I. xiv. 161 Doll and Rice being mingled together and boyled, make Kitcheree, the common Food of the Country. **1866** *Treas. Bot.* 189 *Cajanus indicus*..In India the pulse is called Dhal or Dhol or Urhur, and [is] ranked as third in value among the pulses. **1883** F. M. CRAWFORD *Mr. Isaacs* v. 87 A mouthful of dal to keep his wretched old body alive. **1923** *Nature* 12 May 626/2 The addition of oatmeal and dhall to the British ration.

dal: see DALE, DEAL, DOLE.

‖**Dalai, Dalai-lama:** see LAMA.

‖**dalang** (da'laŋ). [Mal., Javanese, etc.] The central performer who recites the story and manipulates the puppets in Indonesian and Malaysian shadow-play (see also quot. 1817).

1817 T. S. RAFFLES *Hist. Java* I. vii. 335 In general, the *Dálang*, or manager of the entertainment, recites the speeches, while the performers have only to 'suit the action to the word'. **1910** R. J. WILKINSON *Papers on Malay Subjects: Life & Customs* III. 52 The narrator of this tale speaks of himself as *dalang*. **1937** M. COVARRUBIAS *Island of Bali* viii. 237 The *dalang* is an artist and a great spiritual teacher. **1958** H. FORSTER *Flowering Lotus* i. 16 In front of us..sat the *dalang*, the story-teller and manipulator of the puppets. **1976** *Times* 31 Aug. (Malaysia Suppl.) p. iv/5 The puppeteer, called a *dalang*, serves a long apprenticeship and has great skill, speaking the whole of the unwritten dialogue in different voices for up to three hours.

Dalcroze (dæl'krəʊz). The name of É. Jaques-*Dalcroze* (1865–1950), a Swiss exponent of musical education through physical exercises, used *attrib.* and *ellipt.* to designate his system, the movements involved, or an institution where the method is taught. Cf. EURHYTHMIC *a.*

1913 G. B. SHAW *Let.* 30 June in A. Dent *Shaw & Mrs. P. Campbell* (1952) 125 The Dalcroze school at Hellerau.. is very interesting. **1920** D. W. BLACK in B. Russell *Pract. & Theory Bolshevism* I. iv. 65, I saw..some quite wonderful Eurythmic dancing, in particular an interpretation of Grieg's *Tanz in der Halle des Bergkönigs* by the Dalcroze method. **1920** D. H. LAWRENCE *Women in Love* (1921) xiv. 172 'Will you sing while I do Dalcroze?'.. 'While you do —?,' she asked vaguely. 'Dalcroze movements,' said Gudrun. **1964** *New Society* 13 Feb. 16/3 The period 1915–30 was a time for trying out experimental methods: Dalcroze eurythmics, the Winnetka technique, the project method, the Dalton Plan, the Junior Republics, the Montessori system.

dalder, obs. form of DOLLAR.

dale[1] (deɪl). Forms: 1–3 **dæl,** 1–4 **dal,** 3– **dale;** also 3 **deale,** 4 **dalle,** 5 **dall, daile, daylle,** 6 **daill.** [OE. *dæl*, gen. *dæles*, dat. *dæle*, pl. *dalu*, *dalo*, neuter; Com. Teut. = OS. *dal*, OFris. *del*, *deil*, MDu. and Du. *dal*, all neuter, OHG., MHG. *tal*, masc. and n., Ger. *thal* n., LG. *dal*, *dâl*, Goth. *dal* n., ON. *dalr* m. (Sw., Da. *dal*):—OTeut. *dalo-m*, *dalo-z*, of which the root-meaning appears to be 'deep or low place': cf. Goth. *dalaþ* down, *dalaþa* below. As used in ME. the native word appears to have been reinforced from Norse, for it is in the north that the word is a living geographical name.

As to the final *e* in Ormin's *dăle*, see Sachse *Unorganische E im Orrm.* 22. The form *deales* pl. in *Ancren Riwle* is difficult to explain.]

1. A valley. In the northern counties, the usual name of a river-valley between its enclosing ranges of hills or high land. In geographical names, e.g. *Clydesdale*, *Annandale*, *Borrowdale*, *Dovedale*, it extends from Lanarkshire to Derbyshire, and even farther south, but as an appellative it is more or less confined to the district from Cumberland to Yorkshire. In literary English chiefly poetical, and in the phrases ***hill and dale, dale and down.***

c **893** K. ÆLFRED *Oros.* I. iii, þæs dæles se dæl se þæt flod ne grette ys ʒyt to-dæʒ wæstmberende on ælces cynnes blædum. *c* **1200** *Trin. Coll. Hom.* 37 Hwile uppen clives and hwile in þe dales. *c* **1200** ORMIN 9203 Nu sket shall illc an dăle beon all heȝedd upp & filledd. —— *ibid.* 14568, & coude & feld, & dale & dun. *c* **1205** LAY. 26934 Heo comen..in ane dale deope. *a* **1225** *Ancr. R.* 282, I þe deales..þu makest wellen uorto springen. *a* **1300** *Cursor M.* 22532–4 (Cott.) Al þis werld bath dale and dune..þe dals up-rise, þe fells dun fall. *c* **1386** CHAUCER *Sir Thopas* 85 By dale and eek by doune. *c* **1440** *Promp. Parv.* 112 Dale, or vale, *vallis*. *a* **1533** LD. BERNERS *Huon* xxi. 60 They..rode by hylles and dales. **1560–1** *Bk. Discipl. Ch. Scotl.* v. ii. §10 Galloway, Carrick, Niddisdaill, Annanderdaill, with the rest of the Daillis in the West. **1611** BIBLE *Gen.* xiv. 17 The valley of Shaveh, which is the Kings dale [**1885** *R.V.* vale]. **1727–46** THOMSON *Summer* 1271 Where, winded into pleasing solitudes, Runs out the rambling dale. **1806** *Gazetteer Scot.* (ed. 2) 343 *Linlithgowshire*..Its surface is finely diversified with hill and dale. **1820** WORDSW. *Scenery of Lakes* (1822) 62 That part of these Dales which runs up far into the mountains. **1847** TENNYSON *In Mem.* Concl., Till over down and over dale All night the shining vapour sail. **1876** *Whitby Gloss.* 50/2 Around Whitby all the valleys are 'dales'..There are many smaller dales into which the larger are divided. 'Deealheead' is the upper portion of the vale; 'Deeal end' being the lower part.

b. *fig.*

c **1250** *Gen. & Ex.* 19 Ðan man hem telled soðe tale..Of blisses dune, of sorwes dale. *a* **1340** HAMPOLE *Psalter* xxiii. 3 Falland down agayn til þe dale of synn. —— *Pr. Consc.* 1044 Twa worldes..An es þis dale, whar we er wonnand. *a* **1661** FULLER in Spurgeon *Treas. Dav.* Ps. cxxi. 1 Viewing the deep dale of thy own unworthiness.

†**2.** A hole in the ground, a hollow, pit, gulf. Cf. DELL 1. *Obs.*

a **800** *Corpus Gloss.* 274 *Baratrum*, dæl [*Leiden* dal]. *a* **1000** *Cædmon's Gen.* 421 On ðæt deope dæl deofol ʒefeallaþ. *c* **1420** *Pallad. on Husb.* XI. 481 Ther thay stonde a dale Do make, and drenche hem therin. **1489** CAXTON *Faytes of A.* I. xxv. 78 Dyches or dales or euyll pathes.

3. *attrib.* and *Comb.*, as ***dale furze***; **dale-end,** the lower end of a dale; **dale-head,** the head of a dale or valley; **dale-land,** 'the lower and arable ground of a district' (Jamieson); **dale-lander, -man,** 'an inhabitant of the lower ground' (Jam.); **dale-backed** *a.*, hollow in the back (as a horse).

1676 *Lond. Gaz.* No. 1078/4 Lost..a brown bay Nag..a little dale backt. **1807** VANCOUVER *Agric. Devon* (1813) 250 The..dwarf or dale furze blooming in the autumn. **1876** [see sense 1].

dale[2] (deɪl). Also *Sc.* **dail(l.** [The northern phonetic variant of DOLE:—OE. *dál* part, portion, division, allotment, dealing, dole; cf. northern *hale*, *stane* = standard Eng. *whole*, *stone*. Used *esp.* in the following senses; for others see DOLE.]

1. A portion or share of land; *spec.* a share of a common field, or portion of an undivided field indicated by landmarks but not divided off.

c **1241** *Newminster Cartul.* (1878) 87, j acram et j rodam in campo del West in duas mikel dales quas Rob. fil. Stephani et Sywardus quondam tenuerunt. **1531** *Dial. on Laws Eng.* I. xxx. (1638) 53 The grantee suffereth a recovery..by the name of a rent in Dale of a like sum as, etc. **1735** *N. Riding Rec.* IX. 157 All the..closes, inclosures, dales and parcels of arrable land meadow and pasture ground thereto belonging. **1820** WORDSW. *Scenery of Lakes* ii. (1823) 43–4 The arable and meadow land of the vales is possessed in common fields; the several portions being marked out by stones, bushes, or trees; which portions..to this day are called Dales. **1875** *Lanc. Gloss.*, *Dale* [local], an unseparated portion of a field.. often unmarked, or only shown by stakes in the hedge and stones at the corners of the dale. 'A dale of about a quarter of an acre on Black Moss belongs to this farm.'

†**2.** Dealing; having to do with; business. *Sc. Obs.*

c **1375** BARBOUR *Troy-bk.* II. 2839 Cume and ly heire besyde me now, So þat I may haf dale with þe. **1469** *Act. Audit.* 9 (Jam.) He sall hafe na dale nor entermeting tharwith in tyme to cum. **1513** DOUGLAS *Æneis* XII. iv. 161 All to ȝyng wyth sic ane to haue daill [**1553** dale]. **1535** STEWART *Cron. Scot.* III. 302 That he wald get the best part of the daill. **1592** *Sc. Acts Jas. VI* (1814) 544 The successioun proceding of that pretendit mariage or carnall daill.

dale[3] (deɪl). Also 7 **daile,** 8, 9 **dail, (dill).** [Corresponds in sense 1 to LGer. and Du. *daal*; also to F. *dalle*, which is also used for a conduit-tube of wood or metal used in various technical processes, Sp., Pg., It. *dala*, Sp. also *adala*. According to Littré *dalle* in Picard is also a kitchen-sink; and Cotgr. has '*dalle*, a sewer or pit whereinto the washings, dishwater, and other such ordure of houses are conueyed'. See Littré and Diez.]

1. A wooden tube or trough for carrying off water, as from a ship's pump; a pump-dale.

1611 COTGR., *Escoursouër*, the dale of a (ships) pumpe, whereby the water is passed out. **1627** CAPT. SMITH *Seaman's Gram.* ii. 8 The daile is a trough wherein the water doth runne ouer the Deckes. **1800** S. STANDIDGE in *Naval Chron.* III. 472 They pumping the water into a pump dill. *c* **1850** *Rudim. Navig.* (Weale) 139 *Pump dales*, pipes fitted to the cisterns, to convey..water..through the ship's sides.

2. An outlet drain in the Fen district.

1851 *Jrnl. R. Agric. Soc.* XII. II. 304 When those fens were first embanked and drained, narrow tracts, called 'dales', or washes, were left open to the river..Every district, with its frontage of dales, is tolerably well drained.

dale: see DEAL.

dale *v.*, northern form of DOLE *v.*

Dalecarlian (dalɪ'kɑːlɪən), *a.* [f. *Dalecarlia* (see below) + -AN.] Of or pertaining to the province of Dalecarlia (Dalarna) in central Sweden or its inhabitants or their language. Also as *sb.*, a native or inhabitant of Dalecarlia.

1837 *Penny Cycl.* VIII. 290/1 The Dalecarlians are distinguished by their stature, courage, spirit of independence, and frankness of character. **1881** C. C. HARRISON *Woman's Handiwork* I. 95 Quaint Dalecarlian lace of an antique pattern has been brought to America by Swedish peasants immigrating to the far West. **1932** *Antiquity* VI. 429 A late Dalecarlian runic alphabet. **1959** *Times* 10 Jan. 9/6 The Dalecarlian poet Erik Axel Karlfeldt.

daleir, obs. form of DOLLAR.

Dalek ('dɑːlɛk). [Invented word.] A type of robot appearing in 'Dr. Who', a B.B.C. Television science-fiction programme; hence used allusively. Also *attrib.* and *Comb.*

1963 *Radio Times* 26 Dec. 11/1 Dalek voices: Peter Hawkins, David Graham. **1966** *BBC Handbk.* 39 The main activity over the period in this 'merchandising' operation concerned the widely popular Daleks from the ' Dr. Who' series. Some sixty licences for the production of Dalek-inspired articles were issued. **1969** C. HODDER-WILLIAMS *98·4* iv. 49 Under what interesting new law do you propose to enforce this regime? Or have you hired the Daleks? **1971** *Radio Times* 30 Dec. 10/1 Who are the Daleks? Dr. Who's most dangerous enemies, written into his second adventure in 1963 by Terry Nation, who named them after an encyclopaedia volume covering DAL-LEK.

dalesman ('deɪlzmən). [= *dale's man* from DALE[1].] A native or inhabitant of a dale; *esp.* of the dales of Cumberland, Westmorland, Yorkshire, and adjacent northern counties of England.

1769 GRAY *Jrnl. in Lakes* Wks. 1884 I. 257 A little path.. passable to the Dale's-men. **1813** SCOTT *Rokeby* III. ii, In Redesdale his youth had heard Each art her wily dalesmen dared. **1848** MACAULAY *Hist. Eng.* I. 285 Even after the accession of George the Third, the path over the fells from Borrowdale to Ravenglas was still a secret carefully kept by the dalesmen.

So **'dalesfolk, 'dalespeople, 'daleswoman.**

1863 MARY HOWITT *F. Bremer's Greece* I. 224 Our dalesfolk of Mora. **1886** HALL CAINE *Son of Hagar* I. ii, There is a tough bit of Toryism in the grain of these Northern dalesfolk. **1883** F. A. MALLESON *Wordsw. & Duddon* in *Gd. Words,* The dreary wastes of Wrynose, which the dalespeople call Wreyness. **1892** MRS. H. WARD *David Grieve* I. v. 362 Her daleswoman's self-respect could put up with him no longer.

dalf(e, Obs. pa. t. of DELVE.

daliance, dalie, obs. ff. DALLIANCE, DALLY.

Daliesque (,dɑːlɪ'ɛsk), *a.* Also **Dali-esque.** [f. the name of Salvador *Dali*, Spanish painter (born 1904) + -ESQUE.] Resembling the style, or in the manner, of the paintings of Dali; surrealistic.

1941 *Time* 24 Feb. 40/2 A Daliesque-Italian-primitive trifle in which a monkey-like Satan deftly garners three damsels. **1958** *Observer* 26 Jan. 5/5 A patch over one eye on which somebody had painted a Daliesque white eyeball. **1968** *Punch* 24 Apr. 619/2 The present Bond (Lucky James?) seems less dominant—the Dali-esque melting pistol on the jacket may be symbolic.

†**dalk**[1]. *Obs.* [OE. *dalc, dolc,* in ON. *dálkr.*] A pin, brooch, clasp, buckle.

c **1000** ÆLFRIC *Josh.* vii. 21 Ic ȝeseah sumne gildenne dalc on fiftiȝum entsum. *c* **1000** ÆLFRIC *Voc.* in Wr.-Wülcker 152 *Fibula,* preon, uel oferfeng, uel dalc. *a* **1100** *Anglo-Sax. Voc.* ibid. 313/22 *Spinther,* dolc, oððe preon. **1483** *Cath. Angl.* 89 A Dalke (or a tache), *firmaculum, firmatorium, monile.* **1488** *Will* in *Ripon Ch. Acts* 286 Unum portiferium cum a dalk cum ymagine B. Mariæ.

†**dalk**[2], **delk.** *Obs.* exc. *dial.* [? dim. of DALE, DELL: cf. E. Fris. *dölke* small hollow, dimple, dim. of *döle* excavation, hollow: see Kluge *Nominale Stammbild.* 29.] A hole, hollow, depression.

c **1325** *Gloss. W. de Biblesw.* in Wright *Voc.* 146 *Au cool troveret la fosset,* a dalk in the nekke. **1340** HAMPOLE *Pr. Consc.* 6447 For als a dalk es even Imydward þe yholke of þe egge, when it es hard, Ryght swa es helle pitte.. Ymyddes þe erthe. *c* **1420** *Pallad. on Husb.* IV. 607 Or brason scrapes oute of everie dalke Hem scrape. *c* **1440** *Promp. Parv.* 112 Dalke, *vallis.* **1688** R. HOLME *Armoury* II. 85/1 The daulk..is..the Crown, top, or head of an apple, where the blossom is. *a* **1825** FORBY *Voc. E. Anglia, Delk,* a small cavity, in the soil, in the flesh of the body, or in any surface which ought to be quite level.

dalk, in mining: see DAUK.

dall, obs. Sc. spelling of DAW *v.*

dallastype ('dæləstaɪp). [f. proper name *Dallas* + TYPE.] (See quot.)

1875 D. C. DALLAS *Circular,* I have..perfected the method known as Dallastype—a process of Photographic Engraving by which can be produced as Blocks for Surface Printing..copies of Wood-cuts, Type or MS. Matter. **1884** *Academy* 9 Feb. 94 The photographic process known as Dallastype.

†**dalle**[1]. *Obs. rare*[−1]. [app. an infantile word. Cf. DADDLE.] The hand.

c **1460** *Towneley Myst.* (Surtees) 118 Haylle! put furthe thy dalle, I bryng the bot a balle.

‖**dalle**[2] (dal). [Fr., in both senses.

It is probable that the two senses are really distinct words; in sense 2, the F. word is the same as DALE[3]; in sense 1 Hatzfeld suggests connexion with Ger. *diele,* board, DEAL.]

1. A flat slab of stone, marble, or terra cotta, used for flooring; *spec.* an ornamental or coloured slab for pavements in churches, etc.

1855 *Ecclesiologist* XVI. 200 The choir, the chapels..were paved with these dalles.

2. *pl.* The name given (originally by French employés of the Hudson's Bay Company) in the Western U.S. to rapids where the rivers are compressed into long narrow trough-like channels.

1884 *Harper's Mag.* Feb. 364/1 The Columbia River is there∴compressed into 'dalles', or long, narrow, and broken troughs. **1890** M. TOWNSEND *U.S.* 137 The *Dalles* of the Columbia, Oregon; the *Dalles* of the Wisconsin, Minnesota.

Hence **'dallage** [Fr.], flooring with dalles.

1856 *Ecclesiologist* XVII. 57 In the *dallage* the treatment is archaic.

daller, obs. form of DOLLAR.

dalliance ('dælɪəns). Forms: 4–6 **dalyaunce, daliaunce,** 4–7 **daliance,** (5 **-auns, -ans(e),** 5–6 **dalyance,** 6 **dally-, dalliaunce,** 6– **dalliance.** [f. DALLY *v.* + -ANCE: prob. formed in OFr. or AngloFr., though not yet recorded.]

†**1.** Talk, confabulation, converse, chat; usually of a light or familiar kind, but also used of serious conversation or discussion. *Obs.*

c **1340** *Gaw. & Gr. Knt.* 1012 þurȝ her dere dalyaunce of her derne wordez. *c* **1440** *Promp. Parv.* 112 Dalyaunce, *confabulacio, collocucio, colloquium.* **1447** BOKENHAM *Seyntys* (Roxb.) 162 Marthe fyrst met hym [Christ]..And hadde wyth hym a long dalyaunce. **1496** *Dives & Paup.* (W. de W.) VI. xv. 259/1 Redynge & dalyaunce of holy wryt & of holy mennes lyues.

2. Sport, play (with a companion or companions); *esp.* amorous toying or caressing, flirtation; often, in bad sense, wanton toying.

c **1385** CHAUCER *L.G.W.* Prol. 332 (Cambr. MS) For to han with ȝou sum dalyaunce. *c* **1386** —— *Doctor's T.* 66 At festes, reueles, and at daunces, That ben occasiouns of daliaunces. *c* **1400** MAUNDEV. (Roxb.) xxvi. 124 þai schall.. ete and drinke and hafe dalyaunce with wymmen. *a* **1553** UDALL *Royster D.* IV. vi. (Arb.) 70 Dyd not I for the nonce ..Read his letter in a wrong sense for daliance? **1602** SHAKS. *Ham.* I. iii. 50 Whilst like a puft and recklesse Libertine Himselfe the Primrose path of dalliance treads. **1725** POPE *Odyss.* VIII. 348 The lewd dalliance of the queen of love. **1742** FIELDING *J. Andrews* III. vi, He, taking her by the hand, began a dalliance. **1820** SCOTT *Monast.* xxiv, Julian.. went on with his dalliance with his feathered favourite. **1860** MOTLEY *Netherl.* (1868) I. vi. 346 The Earl's courtship of Elizabeth was anything..but a gentle dalliance.

3. Idle or frivolous action, trifling; playing or trifling *with* a matter.

1548 BECON *Solace of Soul* Catechism (1844) 571 In health and prosperity Satan's assaults seem to be but trifles and things of dalliance. **1561** T. NORTON *Calvin's Inst.* III. xii. §1 When they come into the sight of God, such dalliances must auoide, bicause there is..no trifling strife aboute wordes. **1627** F. E. *Hist. Edw. II* (1680) 16 Divine Justice, who admits no dalliance with Oaths. **1641** *Lett.* in Sir J. Temple *Irish Rebell.* II. 47 Now there is no dalliance with them; who ..declare themselves against the State. **1814** WORDSW. *Excursion* I. Wks. (1888) 423/2 Men whose hearts Could hold vain dalliance with the misery Even of the dead. **1843** PRESCOTT *Mexico* (1850) I. 63 He continued to live in idle dalliance.

†**4.** Waste of time in trifling, idle delay. *Obs.*

The first quot. prob. does not belong here: see DELAYANCE.

[*c* **1340** *Cursor M.* 26134 (Fairf.), & for-þink his lange daliaunce [*Cott.* delaiance] þat he for-drawen has his penance.] **1547–64** BAULDWIN *Mor. Philos.* (Palfr.) v. vi, Death deadly woundeth without dread or daliance. **1590** SHAKS. *Com. Err.* IV. i. 59 My businesse cannot brooke this dalliance.

dallier ('dælɪə(r)). Also 6 **dalier.** [f. DALLY *v.* + -ER[1].] One who dallies: see the verb.

1563–87 FOXE *A. & M.* (1596) 1553/2 To bee no dalliers in Gods matters, but to be..earnest. *a* **1568** ASCHAM *Scholem.* I. (Arb.) 85 The greatest makers of loue, the daylie daliers. **1861** GEN. P. THOMPSON in *Bradford Advertiser* 19 Oct. 6/1, 'I will go *so far*', says the dallier with evil; and everybody knows where the dallier comes to.

dallop, var. of DOLLOP *sb.*

dallop, var. DOLLOP *v.*

dally ('dælɪ), *v.* Forms: 4–6 **daly(e, dayly(e,** (5 **dallyn),** 6 **dalie, dallye,** 6–7 **dallie,** 6– **dally.** [a. OF. *dalier* to converse, chat, pass one's time in light social converse, etc.; common in AngloFr.: see Glossary to *Bozon* (ed. P. Meyer). Godef. has an instance of *dallier* trans. to 'chaff'.]

†**1.** *intr.* To talk or converse lightly or idly; to chat. *Obs.*

c **1300** *K. Alis.* 6991 Dysers dalye, reisons craken. *c* **1340** *Gaw. & Gr. Knt.* 1114 þay dronken & daylyeden, & dalten vntyȝtel. *Ibid.* 1253 To daly with derely your daynte wordez. *c* **1440** *Promp. Parv.* 112 Dalyyn or talkyn, *fabulor, confabulor, colloquor.*

2. To act or speak sportively, make sport, amuse oneself; to toy, sport, play *with, esp.* in the way of amorous caresses; to flirt, wanton.

c **1440** *Promp. Parv.* 112 Dallyn, or hallesyn, *amplector.* **1573** G. HARVEY *Letter-bk.* (Camden) 105 Did you never see a flye in yᵉ nighte Dally so longe with yᵉ candle lighte. **1594** SHAKS. *Rich. III,* I. iii. 265 Our Ayerie buildeth in the Cedars top, And dallies with the winde. **1621–51** BURTON *Anat. Mel.* II. ii. IV. 274 Little else..but to dally with their cats. **1685** *Roxb. Ball.* VII. 473, I have a Chamber here of my own, Where we may kiss and dally alone. **1842** TENNYSON *Day Dream, Revival* iv, The chancellor..dallied with his golden chain. **1883** R. NOEL in *Academy* No. 577. 365/3 Leaping lambs and lovers dallying.

b. To play *with* a thing or subject which one does not intend to take seriously; to coquet, flirt, *esp.* with temptation and the like.

1548 UDALL, etc. *Erasm. Par.* Pref. 18 The auncient doctoures..doe in expounyng the allegories, seme oft tymes to playe and dalie with it. **1637** MILTON *Lycidas* 153 For, so to interpose a little ease Let our frail thoughts dally with false surmise. **1642** ROGERS *Naaman* 167 Dally not with her, as Eve with the serpent. **1774** FLETCHER *Fict. & Gen. Creed* viii. Wks. 1795 III. 343 When we dally with temptation. **1780** COWPER *Table-t.* 544 To dally much with subjects mean and low. **1855** PRESCOTT *Philip II,* I. II. xiii. 290 Men ..who..had been led to dally with the revolution in its infancy..now turned coldly away.

3. To trifle *with* a person or thing under the guise of serious action; to play *with* mockingly.

1548 HALL *Chron.* 225 But the Duke of Burgoyne dalied and dissimuled with all parties..gevyng them faire wordes. **1579** TOMSON *Calvin's Serm. Tim.* 440/1 We see a great number yᵗ wold dallie thus with God. **1600** HOLLAND *Livy* II. xxiii. 59 a, Then thought the people..they were mocked and dallied withall [*eludi*]. **1614** BP. HALL *Recoll. Treat.* 697 If wee feared the Lord, durst wee dally with his name? **1706** ADDISON *Rosamond* III. iii, Why will you dally with my pain? **1722** DE FOE *Relig. Courtsh.* I. i. (1840) 17 Why do you trifle and dally so long with a thing of such consequence?

†**b.** *trans. to dally out*: to trifle with, elude.

1548 HALL *Chron.* 146 The matter was wynked at, and dalyed out. **1563–87** FOXE *A. & M.* (1684) I. 173/1 He would suffer no man..to dally out [*eludere*] his laws without condign punishment. **1611** SPEED *Hist. Gt. Brit.* IX. xvii. 112 But Lewis..dallied out Edward with shewes of firme faith, till hee had effected the thing hee went about. **1618** BOLTON *Florus* II. ii, Skill to shift aside Oares, and to dally out the strokes of beake-heads, by yare and ready turning.

4. *intr.* To spend time idly or frivolously; to linger, loiter; to delay.

1538 BALE *Thre Lawes* 241 Ye are disposed to dallye. **1594** WILLOBIE *Avisa* (1605) 28 The poesie..bids you doe, but dallie not. Doe so, sweete heart, and doe not stray, For dangers grow from fond delay. **1600** HEYWOOD *1 Edw. IV,* Wks. 1874 I. 32 We dallied not, but made all haste we could. **1647** R. STAPYLTON *Juvenal* xvi. 285 If, being my debtour, he..stand Dallying to pay me. **1822** W. IRVING *Braceb. Hall* i. 6 Lest when he find me dallying along..he may hurry ahead. **1860** MAURY *Phys. Geog. Sea* xv. §651 One vessel.. dallying in the Doldrums for days.

†**5.** *trans.* To put off or defer by trifling. In earlier use *to dally off*; cf. *dally out* in 3 b. *Obs.*

1574 WHITGIFT *Def. Answ.* i. Wks. (1851) I. 165 This is but a shift to dally off a matter which you cannot answer. **1589** GREENE *Menaphon* (Arb.) 50 Fates and Fortune dallying a dolefull Catastrophe. **1611** SPEED *Hist. Gt. Brit.* IX. xxi. 19 The Councell of Flanders..dallied him off with many Excuses. **1616** *Marlowe's Faust.* Wks. (Rtldg.) 126/1 But wherefore do I dally my revenge? **1633** T. ADAMS *Exp. 2 Peter* ii. 2 Neither dally this execution. **1821** CLARE *Vill. Minstr.* I. 34 Some long, long dallied promise to fulfil.

†**6.** To play or toy with; to influence or move by dalliance. *Obs.*

1597 DANIEL *Civ. Wars* II. xix, Pleas'd with vain shewes, and dallied with delyt. **1627–77** FELTHAM *Resolves* I. xxv. 44 Like a cunning Courtizan, that dallies the Ruffian to undo himself. **1677** GILPIN *Dæmonol.* (1867) 70 Mark Antony by this means became a slave to Cleopatra..and so dallied himself into his ruin.

7. *to dally away*: to consume or spend (time) in dalliance or by dallying.

1685 *Roxb. Ball.* VII. 473 Now when the night was dalli'd away..She 'rose and left me snoring in bed. *c* **1765** FLLOYD *Tartarian T.* (1785) 90/1 They had dallied away a part of the night. **1828** SCOTT *F.M. Perth* viii, He asked them what they meant by dallying away precious time.

Dally ('dælɪ), *a.* and *sb. N.Z. colloq.* [abbrev. DALMATIAN.] Of Dalmatian origin. Also as *sb.*, a native of Dalmatia; a person of Dalmatian parentage.

1940 F. SARGESON *Man & Wife* (1944) 10 Two young Dallies who ran an orchard..had come out from Dalmatia. **1950** O. E. MIDDLETON in D. M. Davin *N.Z. Short Stories* (1953) 411 You can buy an awful lot of Dally plonk for four pounds. **1961** B. CRUMP *Hang on a Minute* 77 Henry..got this dog off an old Dally scrub-cutter. *Ibid.*, A couple of days later they found the Dally dead on the hillside.

dallying ('dælɪɪŋ), *vbl. sb.* [-ING[1].] The action of the verb DALLY, q.v.: toying, trifling, etc.; dalliance.

c **1440** *Promp. Parv.* 112 Dallynge, or halsynge, *amplexus.* **1545** BRINKLOW *Compl.* 53 Cardys, dalyeng with women, dansing, and such like. *c* **1680** BEVERIDGE *Serm.* (1729) I. 470 There is no dallying with Omnipotence. **1828** SCOTT *F.M. Perth* xxxiii, Speak out at once..I am in no humour for dallying. **1889** *Athenæum* 14 Dec. 816/3 The pleasant enough dallying and 'daffing' of her young people.

'dallying, *ppl. a.* [-ING[2].] That dallies; toying, trifling, etc.: see the verb.

1548 HALL *Chron.* 234 b, A Chaplayne mete for such a dalyeng pastyme. **1580** BARET *Alv.* F 662 A flatterer or dallying deceiuer, *adulator.* **1652** CRASHAW *Delights of Muses* Poems 89 A warbling doubt Of dallying sweetness.

Hence **'dallyingly** *adv.*

1550 BALE *Image both Ch.* II. (R.), Wher as he doth but dalliengly perswade, they may enforce and compel. **1563–87** FOXE *A. & M.* (1596) 1459/1 What an arrogant..boy is this [John Bradford], that thus stoutly and dallyinglie behaueth himselfe before the Queenes Counsell? **1637** BASTWICK *Litany* I. 3.

Dalmatian (dæl'meɪʃən), *sb.* and *a.* [f. *Dalmatia*, the name of a region of Yugoslavia on the eastern coast of the Adriatic (formerly an Austrian province), + -AN.] **A.** *sb.* **1.** A native or inhabitant of Dalmatia.

1581 W. ALLEN *Apol. Two Eng. Coll.* iii. f. 29ᵛ He [*sc.* Gregory XIII] hath made one [seminary] for the Dalmatians. **1654** T. BAYLY *End to Controversie* 11 Dalmatians, who immediately after their supper inducing, or mixing, the Heresies of Manchæus with the Catholike Religion, were overthrown, and supplanted by the Turks. **1788** [see SERVIAN *sb.*]. **1911** *Encycl. Brit.* XXIII. 507/2 The Venetians..regained their power over the Dalmatians.

2. *ellipt.* for *Dalmatian dog* below.

1893 H. DALZIEL *Diseases of Dogs* (ed. 3) 58 Dogs that travel much on hard dry roads, as Dalmatians often do. **1959**

Chambers's Encycl. IV. 579/2 The Dalmatian..is large with a white coat covered with black or brown spots.

3. A Romance language formerly spoken by natives of Dalmatia.

1911 *Encycl. Brit.* XXIII. 507/2 Of these nine [Romance] languages, Dalmatian is now extinct. **1933** BLOOMFIELD *Lang.* iv. 61 The Dalmatian is extinct: one of the dialects, Ragusan, died out in the fifteenth century; another, Veliote, survived into the nineteenth. **1954** PEI & GAYNOR *Dict. Linguistics* 52 *Dalmatian*, an extinct Romance language, spoken formerly on the eastern coast of the Adriatic.

B. *adj.* **1.** Of or pertaining to Dalmatia.

a **1680** EVELYN *Diary* June an. 1645 (1955) II. 446 A prospect down the Adriatic as far as Istria & the Dalmatian side. **1813** J. C. EUSTACE *Tour through Italy* I. vii. 163 This wonderful event..is attested by the *ocular* evidence of some Dalmatian peasants. **1936** A. W. CLAPHAM *Romanesque Archit.* iii. 63 That masterpiece of Dalmatian art the west doorway of the cathedral of Trogir (Trau).

2. Dalmatian dog, the spotted coach-dog, sometimes called 'smaller Danish dog'. Also **Dalmatian pointer**, etc.

1810 *Sporting Mag.* XXXVI. 61/2 Portrait of a Dalmatian dog. **1824** BEWICK *Quadrupeds* (ed. 8) 339 The Dalmatian, or Coach Dog..has been erroneously called the Danish Dog ..It is frequently kept in genteel houses, as an elegant attendant on a carriage. **1881**, **1897** [see PLUM PUDDING c].

Dalmatic (dælˈmætɪk), *a.* and *sb.* [The sb. occurs earliest, being a. F. *dalmatique* (15th c. in Littré), ad. L. *dalmatica*, subst. use (sc. *vestis*) of *Dalmaticus* adj. of Dalmatia. (Thence L. *dalmaticātus* attired in a dalmatic.) The adj. is of later adaptation from L.]

A. *adj.* Belonging to Dalmatia, Dalmatian. ***Dalmatic robe***: a dalmatic, or a garment resembling it; so ***Dalmatic vestment***.

1604 E. G. *D'Acosta's Hist. Indies* v. xx. 384 Their habite and robe was a red curtin after the Dalmatike fashion, with tasselles belowe..They were attired in a Dalmatike robe of white wroght with blacke. **1634** SIR T. HERBERT *Trav.* (1638) 38 Their habit, a long coat or vest of white quilted Callico of the Dalmatick sort. **1722** *Lond. Gaz.* No. 6089/3 The King's Regal Mantle, and Dalmatick Vestment. **1804** *Ann. Rev.* II. 83/2 The deacon, standing, in the dalmatic vestment, bears the chalice. **1838** *Rubric Coron. Q. Vict.* in Maskell *Mon. Rit.* (1847) III. 114 Then..the Imperial Mantle, or Dalmatic Robe, of Cloth of Gold, lined or furred with Ermins, is..delivered to the Dean of Westminster, and by him put upon the Queen, standing.

B. *sb.* An ecclesiastical vestment, with a slit on each side of the skirt, and wide sleeves, and marked with two stripes, worn in the Western Church by deacons and bishops on certain occasions. **b.** A similar robe worn by kings and emperors at coronation and other solemnities.

Cf. ISIDORE *Orig.* XIX. xxii. 9 Dalmatica vestis primum in Dalmatia provincia Græciæ texta est, tunica sacerdotalis candida cum clavis ex purpura.

c **1425** WYNTOUN *Cron.* IX. vi. 153 Wyth a prestis vestment hale Wyth twynykil and Dalmatyk. **1483** CAXTON *Gold. Leg.* 350/1 The byere was couerd with a clothe named dalmatyke. **1782** PRIESTLEY *Corrupt. Chr.* II. VIII. 118 Mention is made of Dalmatics for the deacons. **1844** LINGARD *Anglo-Sax. Ch.* (1858) II. ix. 69 The usual episcopal vestments, the amice.. tunic and dalmatic. **1855** BROWNING *Misconceptions* ii, The true bosom..Meet for love's regal dalmatic.

†**Dalˈmatical**, *a. Obs.* = DALMATIC *a.*

1599 THYNNE *Animadv.* (1865) 35 The kinges dalmaticall garmente..was crymsone.

dalo (ˈdɑːləʊ). [Fijian.] = TARO.

1879 *Encycl. Brit.* IX. 156/2 The taro or dalo..is grown in ditches, by streams, or on irrigated ground. **1924** *Countries of World* XIX. 1874/1 The yam and the dalo, for which irrigation is necessary, are the staple roots.

Dalradian (dælˈrɑːdɪən), *a. Geol.* [f. *Dalrad-*, altered form of *Dalriada*, name of an ancient kingdom in Scotland and northern Ireland + -IAN.] Epithet of a series of metamorphosed sedimentary and volcanic rocks found in a belt running north-east from the west coast of Ireland through the southern highlands of Scotland, thought to be of early Cambrian age and in part probably pre-Cambrian; of or characteristic of this series. Also *ellipt.*

1891 A. GEIKIE in *Q. Jrnl. Geol. Soc.* XLVII. 75 It is well known that from the old kingdom of Dalriada, in the north of Ireland, a colony settled in Argyllshire, and gradually acquiring dominion over the whole of Scotland, gave that kingdom its present name. I would therefore propose that the term 'Dalradian' might be adopted..for the crystalline schists of the north of Ireland and centre and south-west of Scotland. (The adjective ought properly to be 'Dalriadan', with the accent on the second syllable; but I feel compelled to alter it into a form more consonant with English habits of pronunciation.) **1903** —— *Text-bk. Geol.* (ed. 4) I. II. ii. 192 The limestones of the Dalradian metamorphic series of Scotland (Islay), which may possibly be pre-Palæozoic. **1910** *Encycl. Brit.* XIV. 744/2 The other metamorphic areas of the north [of Ireland] present even greater difficulties... Hence it is useful to speak of them merely as 'Dalradian'. **1931** GREGORY & BARRETT *Gen. Stratigr.* i. 33 The Lennoxian, along the southern side of the Dalradian, is a band of slates, grits, and fine conglomerates composed of fragments of the Dalradian Schists. **1959** *Chambers's Encycl.* XI. 164/2 The Dalradian Series, which is of considerable thickness, contains a great variety of metamorphosed sediments including quartzites, grits, limestone, slates, phyllites, mica-schists and gneisses. **1962** *Times* 6 Feb. 3/7 His work on structures and metamorphism in the Dalradian of the Scottish Highlands. **1967** D. H. RAYNER *Stratigr. Brit. Isles* iii. 66 This genus is only known from beds of Lower Cambrian age..and the uppermost Dalradian strata are therefore Cambrian, but how much is uncertain.

‖**dal segno** (dal ˈseɲɲo), *adv.* (and *sb.*) *phr. Mus.* [It. *dal* from the + *segno* sign.] = AL SEGNO *phr.* Abbreviated *D.S.* Also as *sb.*

1876 STAINER & BARRETT *Dict. Mus. Terms.* **1944** W. APEL *Harvard Dict. Mus.* 199/2 *Dal segno*.., abbreviated *d.s.*, means repetition, not from the beginning.., but from another place (frequently near the beginning) marked by the sign §. **1959** *Collins Mus. Encycl.* 176/1 *Dal segno*..'from the sign', *i.e.* go back to a point in the music marked by the sign 𝄋. Often abbreviated D.S. **1967** *Crescendo* Feb. 26/2 Can you find the 'go to coda' sign in a hurry? No? Then make it big. Same goes for the *dal segno*—never mind trying to copy the printed one; put a whacking great dollar sign on the part instead. **1979** M. HURD *Oxf. Jun. Compan. Mus.* (ed. 2) 107/2 *Dal segno*... This tells the performer to go back to the place where he sees the sign 𝄋 and repeat the music from that point until he arrives at the word *fine* ('end'), or at a double bar with a pause sign (𝄐) above it.

dalt (dɔːlt). *Sc.* Also **dault.** [ad. Gael. *dalta* in same sense.] A foster-child.

1775 JOHNSON *Western Isl.* Wks. X. 485 When he dismisses his dalt, for that is the name for a fostered child. **1828** SCOTT *F.M. Perth* xxix, It is false of thy father's child ..falsest of my dault!

dalt(e, obs. pa. t. and pple. of DEAL *v.*

Dalton[1] (ˈdɔːltən). The name of the high school (at *Dalton*, Mass., U.S.A.) in which the educational plan so named (devised by Miss Helen Parkhurst) was first adopted in 1920, which consists essentially in dividing up the year's work into monthly 'assignments' which the pupils contract to carry through (with certain preliminary aids) on their own responsibility and with their own discipline. Hence **ˈDaltonize** *v. trans.*, to manage or arrange by this educational method; ˌ**Daltoniˈzation**; **Dalˈtonian** *sb.*[2], an advocate of the method; **ˈDaltonism**[2], the method itself.

1920 *Times Educ. Suppl.* 18 Nov. 605/4 Mr. Ernest Jackman, headmaster of the Dalton High School, writes:—I am glad to answer the questions of various English educators regarding Miss Parkhurst's plan, now to be renamed at her desire, 'The Dalton Plan'. **1922** H. PARKHURST *Educ. on Dalton Plan* ii. 15 The Dalton Laboratory Plan provides that means by diverting his energy to the pursuit and organization of his own studies in his own way. *Ibid.* iv. 40 Demonstrating the superiority of the Dalton Plan from the point of view of economy. **1924** A. J. LYNCH *Individual Work & Dalton Plan* iii. 31 Review provision is made for six laboratories or subject-rooms corresponding with the six subjects that are Daltonised. *Ibid.* 34 The teaching of arithmetic under the Dalton Plan. *Ibid.* 47 Convinced Daltonians recognise at once that assignments are the heart and centre of the plan. *Ibid.* vi. 124 He could find no fault with any other Dalton teacher. **1927** A. HUXLEY *Proper Studies* 117 The first step in the Daltonization of a school consists in the abolition of class rooms and the substitution of specialist rooms. *Ibid.* 125 In a well-run Daltonized school the problem of discipline solves itself. *Ibid.* 133 These ancient seats of learning [*sc.* Oxford and Cambridge] were Daltonized long before Daltonism was invented. **1959** *Chambers's Encycl.* IV. 353/2 In a number of English schools, where a modified Dalton plan is still used, one finds a mixture of class-teaching and of individual assignments. **1964** [see DALCROZE].

dalton[2] (ˈdɔːltən). Also **Dalton.** [f. the name of John *Dalton* (see DALTONIAN *a.* and *sb.*).] A name for the atomic mass unit (see ATOMIC *a.* and *sb.* A. 1), used chiefly in *Biochem.*; freq. used as a dimensionless unit of molecular weight.

1938 C. M. BEADNELL *Dict. Sci. Terms* 65/1 *Dalton*, mass unit, being the 1/16 of mass of O atom. **1967** *New Scientist* 27 Apr. 196/1 The size in molecular weight units was about five million daltons—in other words each molecule of DNA weighed as much as five million atoms of hydrogen. **1969** *Nature* 11 Oct. 150/1 All DNAs were sheared to a single-stranded molecular weight of about 400,000 Daltons by passage through a French pressure cell. **1970** *Ibid.* 28 Nov. 889/2 Thus it would be correct to write..'the molecular mass of protein X is 250,000 [*read* 25,000] daltons'; or 'the relative molecular mass (that is, molecular weight) of protein X is 25,000'... It would, however, be incorrect to say: 'the molecular weight of protein X is 25,000 daltons', for the dalton is a unit of mass, and molecular weight is dimensionless.

Daltonian (dɔːlˈtəʊnɪən), *a.* and *sb.*[1] [f. the name of John *Dalton*, a famous English chemist (1766–1844), who was affected with colour-blindness; see DALTONISM[1].]

A. *adj.* Relating to John Dalton, or the atomic theory first enunciated by him.

1813 *Ann. Philos.* II. 32 (*heading*) On the Daltonian theory of definite proportions in chemical combinations. **1850** DAUBENY *Atom. Th.* iii. (ed. 2) 108 The Daltonian method of notation may still be of use, just as pictorial representation often comes in aid of verbal description. **1962** S. TOULMIN in *Quanta & Reality* 21 With his Periodic Table, Mendeléeff had shown that chemical atoms fell into well-defined families, having resemblances which could not be explained on Daltonian principles alone. **1962** M. P. CROSLAND *Hist. Stud. Lang. Chem.* iii. 264 Even Berzelius.. made use of Daltonian symbols in at least one publication.

B. *sb.* A person affected with colour-blindness.

[First used in Fr., *daltonien.*]

[**1827** P. PREVOST in *Bibl. Univ. Sciences et Arts* XXXV. 321 De ceux qui j'ai coutume d'appeler *daltoniens.*] **1841** E. WARTMANN in *Rep. Brit. Assoc.* II. 40 There are two classes of Daltonians. **1881** *Times* 10 Jan. 4/2 Daltonians of the same nature [not perceiving red].

Daltonism[1] (ˈdɔːltənɪz(ə)m). [ad. F. *daltonisme*, f. as prec.

Introduced by Prof. Pierre Prevost of Geneva, but objected to by English authors on the ground that it associated a great name with a physical defect. See Wartmann's papers on 'Daltonisme' in *Mem. Soc. Phys. de Genève* (1843) X. 273; and (1849) XII. 183.]

A name for colour-blindness; *esp.* inability to distinguish between red and green.

1841 E. WARTMANN in *Rep. Brit. Assoc.* II. 40 An incomplete vision of colours which has been called *Daltonism.* **1855** J. DIXON *Pract. Study Dis. Eye* 261 Of all the unfortunate inventions of pathological nomenclature the word Daltonism..seems to me the worst. **1882** *Nature* 23 Mar. 493 This case of temporary daltonism for red is attributed to the fatigue of the retina for red.

Hence **ˈDaltonist** = DALTONIAN *sb.*[1]

1879 H. T. FINCK in *Macm. Mag.* XLI. 128/2 The authorities last mentioned class those only among the Daltonists who show..that they cannot physically distinguish between certain colours.

dalve, obs. pa. t. of DELVE.

†ˈ**daly**, *sb. Obs.* Also **dayly**; *pl.* **dalies, dalys, daleys.** [Derivation unknown.] A die, or a knuckle-bone used as a die; also a cubical piece of anything, a cube.

c **1440** *Promp. Parv.* 112 Dayly, or pley (K.P. daly), *tessura*, C.F. (*alea, decius*, K.). **1519** HORMAN *Vulg.* xxxii. 280 Men play with III dice: and children with iiij dalies [*astragalis vel talis*]. Cutte this flesh into daleys [*tessellas*].

daly (ˈdeɪlɪ), *a. rare.* ? *Obs.* [f. DALE *sb.*[1] + -Y.] Abounding in dales; of the nature of a dale.

1523 FITZHERB. *Surv.* iii. 3 Groundes that is bothe hylly and dalye. **1606** J. RAYNOLDS *Dolarney's Prim.* (1880) 61 The daly grounds in garments greene were clad.

daly(e, dalyance, obs. ff. DALLY, DALLIANCE.

dam (dæm), *sb.*[1] Forms: 4– **dam**, 4–7 **damme**, 5–6 **dame**, (6 **dampne**, 7 **damn(e, damp, damb)**, 7–8 **damm.** [Common Teut. = OFris. *dam, dom*, MDu. *dam(m)*, MLG. and Du. *dam*, MHG. *tam*, mod.G. *damm* (from LG.), Norse *dammr* (14–15th c.), Sw., Da. *dam.* The earlier existence of the word is proved by the derivative vbs., Goth. *faurdammjan* to stop up, OE. *dęmman*, OFris. *dęmmen*, MHG. *temmen*, Ger. *dämmen*: see DEM *v.*]

1. a. A bank or barrier of earth, masonry, etc., constructed across a stream to obstruct its flow and raise its level, so as to make it available for turning a mill-wheel or for other purposes; a similar work constructed to confine water so as to form a pond or reservoir, or to protect land from being flooded.

c **1440** *Promp. Parv.* 113 Dame, or hye bankys (K. dam or heybanck), *agger.* **1530** PALSGR. 212/1 Damme of a myll, *escluse.* **1626** T. H[AWKINS] *Caussin's Holy Crt.* 525 As a Torrent, which after it hath a long tyme been restrayned, breaketh the forced dammes, and..drowneth the fields. *c* **1630** RISDON *Surv. Devon* (1714) II. 152 Whose House was called Hemeanton, now Weare, by Reason of certain Damps. which we call Weares. **1650** H. BROOKE *Conserv. Health* 93 Banks and Dambs. **1832** TENNYSON *Miller's D.* 99 The sleepy pool above the dam, The Pool beneath it never still. **1841** ELPHINSTONE *Hist. Ind.* II. 71, 50 dams across rivers, to promote irrigation.

b. The barrier constructed in a stream by beavers.

1748 F. SMITH *Voy. Disc. N.-W. Pass.* 139 The Plenty of Water was..owing to its being kept up by Dams, the work of the Beavers; which..had also built a House on the side of this Creek. **1834** MᶜMURTRIE *Cuvier's Anim. Kingd.* 89 Beavers..keep the water at an equal height, by dams composed of branches of trees, mixed with clay and stones. **1875** WHITNEY *Life Lang.* xiv. 290 Building a particular style of shelter, as the beaver its dam.

c. A causeway through fens.

1809 CRABBE *Tales, Lover's Journey*, When next appear'd a dam,—so call the place,—Where lies a road confined in narrow space..on either side Is level fen.

d. *fig.*

1602 MARSTON *Antonio's Rev.* v. iii, The States of Venice Like high-swoln floods drive down the muddie dammes of pent allegeance. **1642** ROGERS *Naaman* 528 To keep up the damme of their owne consciences from breaking in upon them. *a* **1711** KEN *Hymnotheo* Poet. Wks. 1721 III. 138 Thou down the sensual Dam dost throw, Which made me stagnate here below.

2. a. The body of water confined by a dam or embankment. (Now local, Yorkshire, etc.)

c **1325** *E.E. Allit. P.* C. 312 Þy stryuande stremez..In on daschande dam, dryuez me ouer. *a* **1340** HAMPOLE *Psalter* 509 Þe dam of waters [*gurges aquarum*]. **1391** *Selby Cartulary* (Yorks. Archæol. Soc.) I. 4 Indentura..de Stagno vocato le Damme [Selby Dam]. **14..** *Nom.* in Wr.-Wülcker 736/29 *Hoc stangnum*, a dame. *c* **1530** *Remedy of Love* xxxv, Wer..All water ynke in damme or in flood. **1621–51** BURTON *Anat. Mel.* III. iv. I. i. 642 As a damme of water stopt in one place breaks out into another. **1857** D. LIVINGSTONE *Missionary Travels* v. 103 The industry of the Boers augurs well for future formation of dams and tanks. *c* **1869** GATTY *Hunter's Hallamshire* ix. 186 *note*, Several of the smaller dams at Crook's Moor [Sheffield] were filled up in 1839..The large dams are still made use of by the company. **1884** A. K. JOHNSTON *Africa* (ed. 4) xxiv. 391 Wherever there is a homestead, there is generally a water 'dam', with an orchard and garden. **1888** *Sheffield Gloss.*, *Dam*, a piece of water impounded by damming up a stream. **1892** LENTZNER *Australian Word-bk.* 19 *Dam* (up-country), a pond for watering cattle..made by throwing up a bank across a hollow or little gully.

b. In south of Scotland, the stream of water from a weir or pond, which drives a mill; a mill-race; ***tail-dam***, a tail-race. (The *dam* in sense 1 is a 'cauld'.)

3. A flat land from which water is drained off and excluded. *local.*

1629 *S'hertogenbosh* 13 It lyeth as it were in a Myre, hauing on the one side a small moore or damp. **1800** in G. C. Davies *Norfolk Broads* xv. (1884) 107 Tame and meadowed flats, here called dams, between Yarmouth and Norwich, producing turf, peat, furze, flag and sedge.

4. a. *Mining.* A partition of boards, masonry, etc. in a mine to keep out water, fire, or gas. **b.** *Smelting.* (See quot. 1881.) **c.** ***floating dam***: †(*a*) = CAMEL *sb.* 2; (*b*) 'a caisson used instead of gates for a dry-dock' (Smyth *Sailor's Word-bk.*).

1706 *Lond. Gaz.* No. 4262/3 A Machine, termed a Floating-Damm, whereby he is capable of carrying Barges ..over..Shallows. **1881** RAYMOND *Mining Gloss.*, *Dam*.. the wall of refractory material, forming the front of the fore-hearth of a blast furnace. It is built on the inside of a supporting iron plate (dam-plate).

d. A reservoir or tank, as of loam and brick construction, in which metal is collected for heavy castings.

a **1877** KNIGHT *Dict. Mech.* I. 674/2. **1880** *Encycl. Brit.* XIII. 299/2 The tymp arch usually projects a little forward from the earth wall, constituting the 'fore hearth', at the base of the front of which is the dam, a block of stone or mass of firebrick pierced by a vertical cavity..through which the molten pig iron is drawn off from time to time.

e. In full ***rubber dam***. A sheet of soft rubber pierced with one or more holes and fitted in the mouth so as to protect the exposed tooth or teeth from saliva while a filling or other operation is done; also (without an article), rubber in the form used for this purpose. Chiefly *U.S.*

It was invented by S. C. Barnum, of New York, in 1864.

1872 L. P. MEREDITH *Teeth* 117 By the use of the rubber-dam inconvenience and unsuccessful operations may be avoided. **1908** G. E. HUNT in C. N. Johnson *Text-bk. Oper. Dentistry* ix. 146 For operations on the anterior six teeth a triangular shaped piece of dam will be found both efficient and economical. **1927** J. D. H. JAMIESON *Oper. Dentistry* iii. 30 It is used in the form of strips of rubberdam. *Ibid.* 33 Rubberdam is supplied in three grades of thickness. **1940** S. D. TYLMAN *Theory & Pract. Crown & Bridge Prosthesis* xxiii. 284 In those patients whose flow of saliva is copious, much time may be saved by the use of a rubber dam. **1969** R. E. MCDONALD *Dentistry for Child & Adolescent* x. 176/2 A few explanatory words and referral to the rubber dam as a 'raincoat' for the tooth or as a 'Halloween mask' will invariably allay the child's fear.

5. *Comb.*, as ***dam-like*** adj.; **dam-head** (*Sc.*), a weir or cauld on a river for diverting the water into a mill-race; **dam-plate, dam-stone** (see quot. and sense 4b); †**dam-shed** (*Sc.*), 'a portion of land bordering on a dam' (Jam.). See also COFFER-DAM, MILL-DAM.

1540 *Sc. Acts Jas. V.* (1814) 37 The dene of Logy, dame and damsched tharof, and thair pertinentis. **1760** WARK in *Phil. Trans.* LII. 2 Locks and dam-heads might be raised.. by the help of furze. **1776** ADAM SMITH *W.N.* IV. v. (1869) II. 86 As much water must run over the dam-head as if there was no dam at all. **1820** SCOTT *Monast.* v, A stong wear or damhead, running across the river. **1881** RAYMOND *Mining Gloss.*, *Dam-plate*, the plate upon the dam-stone or front stone of the bottom of a blast furnace.

dam (dæm), *sb.*[2] Forms: 3- **dam**, 4-7 **damme**, 6 **dambe**, 6-7 **damm**. [A variant of DAME, also written from 14th c. *damme*, retaining the short sound of F. *a*; originally used in all the senses, but from about the 16th c. differentiated.]

†**1.** = DAME. *Obs.*

1297 R. GLOUC. (Rolls) 11732 Dam Maud þe Mortimer. *a* **1300** *Cursor M.* 2312 (Cott.) Melche, loth, and dam sarra. **1340** HAMPOLE *Pr. Consc.* 1273 Dam fortone..turnes about ay hir whele. *c* **1382** WYCLIF *Pref. Epist.* vi. 67/1 The olde chaterynge damme. *c* **1430** *Hymns Virg.* 3 (Mätz.) þou deintiest damme.

2. A female parent (of animals, now usually of quadrupeds). Correlative to *sire*.

1320 [see DAME 8 b]. **1486** *Bk. St. Albans* E iv a, A fawne sowkyng on his dam. **1523** FITZHERB. *Husb.* §68 A sandy colte..neyther lyke syre nor damme. **1607** TOPSELL *Four-f. Beasts* (1673) 363 The duckling, the first day [can] swim in the water with his dam. **1665** HOOKE *Microgr.* 216, I have observed the young ones of some Spiders have almost kept the same proportion to their Dam. **1697** DRYDEN *Virg. Eclog.* I. 32 So Kids and Whelps their Sires and Dams express. **1774** GOLDSM. *Nat. Hist.* (1776) III. 25 Calves.. taken from the dam in a savage state. **1834** MUDIE *Brit. Birds* (1841) I. 301 And when the dam [robin] leaves her eggs. **1870** BRYANT *Iliad* I. v. 162 Two young lions, nourished by their dam.

†**b.** Phr. ***the devil and his dam***; ***the devil's dam***, applied opprobriously to a woman. *Obs.*

1393 LANGL. *P. Pl.* C. XXI. 284 Rys vp ragamoffyn and reche me alle þe barres, That belial þy bel-syre beot with þy damme. **1538** BALE *Thre Lawes* 1070 The deuyll or hys dam. **1588** SHAKS. *Com. Err.* IV. iii. 51 *Ant.* It is the diuell. *S. Dro.* Nay, she is worse, she is the diuels dam. **1707** J. STEVENS tr. *Quevedo's Com. Wks.* (1709) 350 Such..Sayings are a Discredit to your self. As for instance..the Devil and his Dam. **1783** AINSWORTH *Lat. Dict.* II, *Trivenefica*, a great witch, a devil's dam.

3. = Mother (human): usually in contempt.

a **1547** SURREY *Aeneid* IV. 477 Ne Goddesse was thy dam [*nec tibi Diva parens*]. **1606** *Choice, Chance, etc.* (1881) 66 His Dad a Tinker, and his Dam a Tit. **1611** SHAKS. *Wint. T.* II. iii. 94 This Brat is none of mine..Hence with it, and together with the Dam, Commit them to the fire. **1801** WOLCOTT (P. Pindar) *Tears & Sm.* Wks. 1812 V. 55 And said, that George allowed his dam But thirty pounds a year.

4. *fig.*

c **1540** *Pilgr. T.* in Thynne *Animadv.* App. i. 80 As we be taught of the churche our dam. **1594** BARNFIELD *Aff. Sheph.* II. liv, Ignorance..the Damme of Errour. **1621-51** BURTON *Anat. Mel.* III. iv. I. ii. 648 That high Priest of Rome, the dam of that monstrous and superstitious breed. **1892** R. KIPLING *Barrack-r. Ballads* (ed. 2) 80 What dam of lances brought thee forth to jest..with Death?

5. *Comb.*

1605 SYLVESTER *Du Bartas* II. iii. IV. *Captains* 1237 Dam-Murdering Vipers, Monsters in-humane. **1622** BOYS *Wks.* 936 As the carefull Dam-bird [loves] her unfeathered brood.

dam, *sb.*[3] Chiefly *Sc.* Forms: 6 **damme**, 7 **dame**, 9 **dam**. [a. F. *dame* lady (DAM[2], DAME), the name of each piece in the *jeu de dames* or draughts, *esp.* of the crowned pieces which can move forwards or backwards; in Ger. *dame* (*damenspiel*, *damspiel* draughts), Du. *dam* (*damspel* draughts): cf. DAMBROD.]

Each of the pieces in the game of draughts or checkers (*obs.*); *pl.* the game itself.

App. in early times a piece, pawn, or 'man' in various games. *Dame* is given by Cotgrave 1611 as 'also, a man at Tables or Draughts', and *dames* is the name of Draughts in Rabelais; Florio 1598 has Ital. '*dame*, men to play at tables or chesse with'.

1580 HOLLYBAND *Treas. Fr. Tong*, *Le jeu des Merelles*, the playe of dammes. [COTGR. '*Le Jeu des merelles*, the boyish game called Merills, or fiue-pennie Morris; played here most commonly with stones, but in France with pawnes, or men made of purpose, and tearmed Merelles.'] **1653** URQUHART *Rabelais* 94 (Jam.) There he played at the Dames or draughts. **1814** *Saxon & Gael* I. 94 (Jam.) After playing twa or three games at the dams. **1828** WEBSTER, *Dam*..3. a crowned man in the game of draughts. **1870** RAMSAY *Remin.* vi. (ed. 18) 246 Dams were the pieces with which the game of draughts was played.

†**dam**, *sb.*[4], **damp.** *Obs.* Also 6 **dame**. [a. OF. *dam* (also *dan*, *domp*, *dant*, in nom. *dans*, *danz*):—L. *dominus* lord, used in OF. as a feudal title (ranking between *comte* and *baron*), but commonly prefixed to the name of a person by way of honour.] Lord; as a prefix = Sir, Master. Cf. DAN.

c **1300** *Havelok* 2468 He knew, þe swike dam, Euerildel god was him gram. *c* **1375** *Lay Folks Mass Bk.* (MS. B.) 18 Dam Ieremy [*v.rr.* Dane Ieremi, Saynte Ierome] was his name. **1506** *Bury Wills* (Camden) 108 Dame John Barkyng, pytauncer of the monasterij in Bury.

c **1386** CHAUCER *Nun's Pr. Prol.* 26 (Harl.) Wherfor sir monk, damp Pieres by ȝour name. *c* **1489** CAXTON *Sonnes of Aymon* ix. 199 They met wyth damp Rambault, the free knyght. *Ibid.* ix. 201 Damp bysshop, ye be welcom. *Ibid.* xvi. 382 'Damp emperour', sayd thenne the duke naymes.

dam (dɑːm), *sb.*[5] *Obs.* exc. *Hist.* Also **daum**, **dawm**. [Hind. *dām*.] An Indian copper coin of the value of one fortieth of a rupee.

1781 F. BALFOUR tr. *Forms of Herkern* 39 The sum of twenty one lacks. of dams. **1801** R. PATTON *Asiat. Mon.* 182 A crore of dams. **1871** in E. G. BALFOUR *Cycl. India* (ed. 2) II. 10. **1884** *Encycl. Brit.* XVII. 343/1 The gold coinage and the silver rupee are seldom seen [in Nepal], the ordinary currency consisting of the copper dāms and paisā, and the mōhar or half rupee. **1962** R. A. G. CARSON *Coins* 515 On occasional issues both of Sher Shah and his successor Islam Shah (1545-52) the coins were struck on a square flan. A new denomination, the dam, was struck in copper at a weight of 21·5 gm.

dam (dæm), *v.*[1] Forms: 6-7 **damme**, (**damn**, 7 **dambe**), 7-8 **damm**, 6- **dam**. [f. DAM *sb.*[1]; taking the place of the etymological DEM, OE. *dęmman*, found in early ME. and existing dialects.]

1. *trans.* To furnish with a dam; to obstruct or confine (a stream, or water) by means of a dam. Usually with *up*; also (rarely) with *back*, *out*, etc.

1563 W. FULKE *Meteors* (1640) 57 Wells that have beene dammed up. **1659** B. HARRIS *Parival's Iron Age* 106 He had dammed up the Rivers. **1697** DRYDEN *Virg. Past.* III. 171 Now dam the Ditches and the Floods restrain. **1850** LYELL *2nd Visit U.S.* II. 253 The Mississippi forms long bars of sand, which frequently unite with some part of the coast, so as to dam out the sea and form lagoons. **1867** PARKMAN *Jesuits N. Amer.* xxi. (1875) 314 The beavers had dammed a brook and formed a pond.

2. *transf.* and *fig.* To stop up, block, obstruct; to shut up, confine: **a.** things material.

1553 BRENDE *Q. Curtius* VII. iv. 132 The sand in the plaines is blowen together..wherby the accustomed wayes be damned. **1590** GREENE *Never too late* (1600) 90 Hauing the Ouen the hotter within for that is was damd vp. **1603** FLORIO *Montaigne* I. xxiv. (1632) 61 Lamps dammed with too much oyle. **1652** WADSWORTH tr. *Sandoval's Civ. Wars Spain* 351 Don Hernande..dammed up all the doors but one. **1794** SULLIVAN *View Nat.* I. 347 When a ridge of mountains thus dams the cloud.

b. things immaterial.

1582 BENTLEY *Mon. Matrones* III. 261 Vnthankfulnesse.. dammeth vp the fountaine of thy godlie mercie. **1632** SANDERSON *12 Serm.* 522 He doth also dambe vp the mercy of God by his contempt. **1875** MCLAREN *Serm.* Ser. II. iv. 66 His love [is] too divine for us to dam it back. *a* **1876** G. DAWSON *Improvers of Shaks.*, They dammed up all human energy into two channels—the chapel and the shop.

†**dam**, *v.*[2] *Obs. rare.* [f. DAM *sb.*[2]] To give birth to (young): said of animals.

1577 B. GOOGE *Heresbach's Husb.* III. (1586) 139 Such [lambs] as are afterwarde dammed, are feeble and weake.

dam, var. DAMN.

Dama: see DAMARA.

damacene, -yne, obs. ff. *damascene*, DAMSON.

damage ('dæmɪdʒ), *sb.* Forms: α. 4- **damage**; 5-8 **dammage**. (6 **dampnage**, 6-7 **damnage**, 7 **damadge**). β. 4-7 **dommage**, 5-7 **domage**. [a. OF. *damage* (11th c. in Littré), also *domage*, *daumage*, *demage*, since 15th c. *dommage* = OSp. *domage*, f. OF. *dam*, damage, prejudice, loss (= Pr. *dam*, It. *danno* loss), ad. L. *damnum* loss, hurt, damage + -AGE. Cf. Pr. *damnatge* and It. *dannatico* on L. type **damnāticum*. The ME. form *domage*, *dommage* is after later French; *dam(p)nage* after med.L.].

1. Loss or detriment caused by hurt or injury affecting estate, condition, or circumstances. *arch.*

α. [**1292** BRITTON I. v. §1 En despit et damage de nous et de noster poeple.] **1300** *K. Alis.* 959 The scoumfyt, and the damage, Feol on heom of Cartage. *c* **1386** CHAUCER *Pars. T.* ¶383 As moche to oure damage as to oure profit. **1535** COVERDALE *Luke* ix. 25 Though he wanne the whole worlde and loseth himself or runneth in dammage of himself. **1609** SKENE *Reg. Maj.* 89 The damnage and skaiths, quhilks he hes susteined by the defender, sall be taxed. **1611** BIBLE *Dan.* vi. 2 That..the king should haue no damage. **1778** C. JONES *Hoyle's Games Impr.* 21 You could receive no Damage by playing the King the third Round. **1851** HUSSEY *Papal Power* ii. 86 The corrupting by bribes of the late Legats..to the damage of S. Peter. **1877** J. D. CHAMBERS *Div. Worship* 141 These..Anthems have been wholly omitted, to our great damage.

β. **1481** CAXTON *Myrr.* I. xiv. 45 [It] torneth contrarye to them & to their dommage. **1508** FISHER *Wks.* (1876) 193 The great domage whiche we suffre by the absence of many of them. *a* **1612** DONNE *Βιαθανατος* (1644) 124 If a publique profit recompence my private Domage.

2. a. Injury, harm; *esp.* physical injury to a thing, such as impairs its value or usefulness.

c **1374** CHAUCER *Boeth* I. v. 25 þou hast wepen for þe damage [ed. **1560** dommage] of þi renoune þat is appaired. **1430** LYDG. *Chron. Troy* I. vi, He was enoynted with an oyntment On his body that kept him from damage. *c* **1440** *Promp. Parv.* 113 Damage, or harme, *dampnum*. **1577** tr. *Bullinger's Decades* Introd., He..suffered all the damages of the body. **1637** GILLESPIE *Eng. Pop. Cerem.* II. ix. 50 His answere bringeth great damnage to his owne cause. **1639** T. DE GRAY *Compl. Horsem.* 9 Lest in foling, the colt receive domage. **1719** DE FOE *Crusoe* (1858) 353 She was leaky, and had damage in her hold. **1869** HOOK *Lives Abps.* II. ii. 94 To repair the damage done to the monastery.

b. (with *a* and *pl.*) A loss, an injury.

1470-85 MALORY *Arthur* I. xv, Kyng Lott made grete dool for his dommagis & his felawes. **1577-87** HOLINSHED *Scot. Chron.* 188 The damages & skathes committed by theeues and robbers. **1593** T. WATSON *Tears of Fancie* xxiv. Poems (Arb.) 190 That I..brought faire beauty to so fowle a domage. **1600** J. PORY tr. *Leo's Africa* II. 55 They paid the said owners for all dammages committed. **1771** GOLDSM. *Hist. Eng.* I. 79 Repairing the damages which the kingdom had sustained by war.

†**3. a.** A disadvantage, inconvenience, trouble. **b.** A matter for regret, a misfortune, 'a pity'.

a. **1398** TREVISA *Barth. de P.R.* VI. i. (Tollem. MS.), Age haþ with him many damagis. **1637** R. HUMPHREY tr. *St. Ambrose* i. 15 They hold profit to consist in the goods secular, wee reckon these for dammages. **1721** DE FOE *Col. Jack* (1840) 33 'Tis an unspeakable damage to him for want of his money.

b. *c* **1385** CHAUCER *L.G.W.* 578 *Cleopatra*, And of his deth it was ful gret damage. *c* **1489** CAXTON *Blanchardyn* xxii. 74 It were domage yf suche a lady..sholde perysshe. **1524** *Losse of Rhodes* in Hakluyt *Voy.* II. I. 84 Sir Francis de Frenolz..it was great dammage of his death, for he was a worthy man. **1612** SHELTON *Quix.* I. I. iv. 25 The Damage is..that I have no money here about me.

4. *Law.* (Now always in *pl.*) The value, estimated in money, of something lost or withheld; the sum of money claimed or adjudged to be paid in compensation for loss or injury sustained.

[**1430** *Act 8 Hen. VI*, c. 9 Le pleyntif recovera ses damages au treble vers le defendant. **1538** STARKEY *England* II. ii. 190 The party condemnyd..schold euer be awardyd to pay costys and al other dammage cumyng to hys aduersary by the reson of the vniust sute and vexatyon.] **1542-3** *Act 34-5 Hen. VIII*, c. 27 §36 Actions personall, whereof the dette, and domage amounteth to the summe of fourtie shillinges. **1548** HALL *Chron.* 31 For recoveryng of damages for injuries to them wrongfully done. **1631-2** *Star Chamb. Cases* (Camden) 168 He shall therefore pay 500[li] to the King and 200[li] Dammage to M[r] Deane and make recognition of his fault and wrong. **1767** BLACKSTONE *Comm.* II. 438 When the jury has assessed his damages. **1858** LD. ST. LEONARDS *Handy Bk. Prop. Law* ii. 5 An action..for the recovery of damages for breach of contract.

5. *slang.* Cost, expense. Esp. in phr. ***what's the damage?*** how much is there to pay?

1755 *Connoisseur* No. 68 ¶10 'There', says he, 'there's your damage—thirteen and two-pence.' **1812** BYRON *Wks.* (1832) II. 179, I must pay the damage, and will thank you to tell me the amount of the engraving. **1829** J. HUNTER *Hallamshire Gloss.* 29 'What is the damage?' This expression is equivalent to 'What expence have I incurred?' 'What must I pay?' **1852** MRS. STOWE *Uncle Tom's C.* xiv, What's the damage, as they say in Kentucky..what's to be paid out for this business? **1855** DICKENS *Lett.* I. 409 Excellent stowage for the whole family..Damage for the whole, seven hundred francs a month. **1875** J. G. HOLLAND *Sevenoaks* xxii. 303 What's the damage for the sort o' thing ye're drivin' at this morning? **1888** A. C. GUNTER *Mr. Potter of Texas* xi, 'What's the damage?' 'Damage?' echoes Lubbins, not understanding this Americanism. 'Yes, how much do I owe?'

6. *attrib.* and *Comb.*, as **damage control**, (the exercise of) measures to minimize or control the effect of damage caused by an accident, etc., *esp.* to a ship; also *fig.*; **damage limitation**, the action or process of restricting damage caused by an accident, error, etc., or of attempting to do this, *esp.* in political and military contexts; hence **damage-limiting** *a.*

[**1938** *Engineering* 22 July 116/3 The problem also requires study from a damage stability viewpoint.] **1959** *Chambers's Encycl.* IV. 356/2 *Damage control, the principles by which a certain degree of control may be exercised over the stability and buoyancy of a ship which has received serious underwater damage. **1982** W. SAFIRE in *N.Y. Times Mag.* 26 Sept. 12 Whenever anybody in politics or corporate life goofs.., the people who race to minimize the reaction..are said to be engaged in *damage control.* [**1962** R. S. MCNAMARA in *Vital Speeches* 1 Mar. 297/2 We may be able to use our retaliatory forces to limit damage done to ourselves, and our allies, by knocking out the enemy's bases before he has had time to launch his second salvos.] **1963** *Ibid.* 1 Dec. 116/1 The *damage-limiting capability of our numerically superior forces is, I believe, well worth its incremental cost. **1965** H. KAHN *On Escalation* viii. 153 'Damage limitation' is current jargon for capabilities and tactics that attempt to limit damage if deterrence fails and war breaks out. *Ibid.*, The United States can buy a very important increment in damage-limiting capability. **1977** *Economist* 26 Feb. 22/3 Whitehall is mesmerised by a phrase worthy of the Nixon White House, 'damage limitation' (i.e., aiming for nothing while hoping to give away as little as possible). **1987** *Economist* 17 Jan. 39/3 The damage limitation after the Reykjavik summit, brilliantly managed by the White House staff, went down the plug hole in the flood of post-Iran doubts.

¶ Erroneously for DANGER.

1464 *Plumpton Corr.* (Camden) 13 Now you bee utterly out of his dammage.

'damage, *v.* Forms: see the sb. [a. OF. *damagier, -er, domager,* f. *damage*: see prec. sb.]

1. *trans.* To do or cause damage to; to hurt, harm, injure; now commonly to injure (a thing) so as to lessen or destroy its value.

13.. [see DAMAGING *vbl. sb.*]. **1477** EARL RIVERS (Caxton) *Dictes* 106 A king in his kyngdome may be dommaged and hurte, and specially be fyue thinges. **1548** HALL *Chron.* (1550) 24 The English studied all the waies possible to dammage their enemies: some shot arrowes, some cast stones. **1594** SHAKS. *Rich. III*, IV. ii. 60 To stop all hopes, whose growth may dammage me. *a* **1674** CLARENDON *Hist. Reb.* III. 459 (R.) He..gave him a broadside, with which he ..damaged the ship. **1794** NELSON in Nicolas *Disp.* I. 492 Not any notice having been taken..of my eye being damaged. *a* **1859** MACAULAY *Hist. Eng.* V. 130 He missed no opportunity of thwarting and damaging the Government. **1892** *Laws Times' Rep.* LXVII. 251/1 The *Merchant Prince* ..ran into and damaged the *Catalonia.*

2. *intr.* To suffer damage or injury. *rare.*

1821 CLARE *Vill. Minstr.* I. 37 Her Sunday clothes might damage with the dew.

damageable ('dæmɪdʒəb(ə)l), *a.* For forms cf. DAMAGE *sb.*; also 5 **dommegeable,** 6 **dommagiable, domagable,** 6–7 **damagable.** [a. OF. *damag(e)able, dom-,* causing or bringing damage, f. *damagier*: see prec. and -ABLE.]

†**1.** Causing loss or injury; hurtful, injurious.

1474 CAXTON *Chesse* II. iii. (1860) Cj, The tunges of advocates and men of lawe ben perilous & dommegeable. **1570** DEE *Math. Præf.* 45 Neither by worde, deede, or thought,.. damageable, or iniurious to you. **1604** DEE in Hearne *Collect.* 3 Nov. 1705, That..most grievous and dammageable Sclaunder. **1636** E. DACRES tr. *Machiavel's Disc. Livy* I. 166 Many faults..dommageable to that tyrannie. **1674** *Govt. Tongue* xii. (1684) 164 Immodest talk ..damagable and infectious to the innocence of our neighbors. **1796** BURKE *Regic. Peace* i. Wks. 1802 IV. 437 Before it is clearly known whether the innovation be damageable or not, the judge is competent to issue a prohibition to innovate until the point can be determined.

2. Liable to be damaged.

1755 MAGENS *Insurances* II. 273 If Goods easily damageable be in a Ship. **1881** J. F. KEANE *Six Months in Meccah* vii. 183 Much destruction..to all damageable property.

Hence †**'damageably** *adv.*, injuriously.

1660 HEXHAM, *Kommerlick*..Dammageably, or with Molestation.

†**damage-cleere,** *Law. Obs.* [ad. Anglo-Fr. *damage clers* for *damage des clers,* in med.L. *damna clericorum* 'clerks' costs'.]

A fee formerly paid in the courts of Common Pleas, King's Bench, and Exchequer, in cases where damages were recovered: abolished in 1665.

1665 MARVELL *Corr.* xlviii. Wks. 1872–5 II. 183 There are several other Bills in hand; as..the taking away of Damage cleere.

damaged ('dæmɪdʒd), *ppl. a.* [f. DAMAGE *v.* + -ED[1].] **a.** That has suffered damage; injured (*esp.* physically).

1771 SMOLLETT *Humph. Cl.* 10 July an. 1768, Clinker.. unscrewed the damaged iron. **1891** *Daily News* 23 June 2/3 If any sovereign or half-sovereign is more than three grains below the standard weight, it shall be considered a damaged coin.

b. ***damaged goods***: merchandise that has deteriorated in quality through unsaleability, exposure to the elements, etc. Also *fig.* of persons, esp. implying a woman's loss of virginity (see also quot. 1911).

1809 [see GOOD *sb.* 8 b]. **1815** J. SCOTT *Visit to Paris in 1814* xiii. 264 Damaged goods of every description, were brought out for the Cossack-market. **1841** S. WARREN *Ten Thousand a Year* i, Didn't I feel like damaged goods, just then! **1872** *Porcupine* Aug. 330/3 Everything seemed to be done in some shops to steal money and pass off damaged goods. **1911** J. POLLOCK tr. *Brieux's Damaged Goods* 111, They are not bad cases [of syphilis]; they are simply the damaged goods of our great human cargo. **1936** *Times Lit. Suppl.* 14 Nov. 925/3 When she came home, somewhat damaged goods in the world's eyes, her father was dead. **1952** *Essays in Criticism* II. 176 Donald Farfrae is not aware when he marries her that Lucetta is damaged goods.

damage-feasant. *Law.* Also 7 **-feasaunt, -faisant,** 7–8 **-fesant.** [OF. *damage fesant,* F. *dommage faisant,* doing damage, causing loss.]

Said of a stranger's beasts, etc., found trepassing on a man's ground without his leave, and there doing him damage, as by feeding or otherwise. (Properly *adj. phr.*; also used as *sb.*)

1621 R. BOLTON *Stat. Irel.* 191 (33 Hen. VIII), In any replegiare or second deliverance for rentes, customes, services or for damages feasaunt or other rent or rents. **1681** CHETHAM *Angler's Vade-m.* xl. §18 If I leave my Angle-rod behind in another's ground he may take it Damage feasant. **1714** SCROGGS *Courts-leet* (ed. 3) 73 Any Thing distrained for Damage-feasant cannot be distrained for Rent. **1768** BLACKSTONE *Comm.* III. i. III. 6. **1887** *Edin. Rev.* Jan. 77 The right of distraining animals trespassing as we now say 'damage-feasant'.

†**'dameful,** *a. Obs.* [f. DAMAGE *sb.* + -FUL.] Injurious, hurtful.

c **1449** PECOCK *Repr.* II. viii. 182 It were ful umprofitable and damageful to alle Cristene. **1611** SPEED *Hist. Gt. Brit.* IX. xiii. 107 His warre in Ireland was more dammageful. **1645** T. COLEMAN *Hopes Deferred* 15 These purposes of mischiefe are either issulesse, or damagefull, or dangerous.

damagement ('dæmɪdʒmənt). *rare.* [a. OF. *damagement,* f. *damagier* to DAMAGE.] The action of damaging, or fact of being damaged.

1603 J. DAVIES *Microcosmos* Wks. (1876) 44 (D.) The more vs'd they [pleasures] are excessiuely, The more's the soule and bodie's damagement. **1885** *Pall Mall G.* 20 May 5/1 If war has any *raison d'être* at all, that must lie in the effective damagement of your enemy.

†**damageous,** *a. Obs.* For forms cf. DAMAGE *sb.*; also 5 **damegeous,** 6 **dammagious, -ius.** [a. OF. *damageus, -gious, -jos,* f. *damage*: see DAMAGE *sb.* and -OUS.] Fraught with damage, hurtful, injurious; causing loss or disadvantage.

c **1386** CHAUCER *Pars. T.* ℙ364 Whan þat meynee is felonous and damageous to þe peple. **1474** CAXTON *Chesse* III. vi. (1860) H iij b, What synne is fowler than this synne.. ne more dommageous. **1477** EARL RIVERS (Caxton) *Dictes* 48 Lakking of thy lore is to vs a damegeous thing. **1611** COTGR. s.v. *Vimaires,* Fearefull or dommageous accidents. **1637** HEYWOOD *Royall Ship* 32 All the rauenous and dammageous beasts to be destroyed through his land.

damaging ('dæmɪdʒɪŋ), *vbl. sb.* [-ING[1].] The action of the verb DAMAGE, q.v.

13.. *Childh. Jesus* 1344 (Mätz.) Of þe liones he made a semblingue bifore heom withoute damagingue. **1568** GRAFTON *Chron.* II. 93 The French king..in dammagyng of king Richard, layde siege to the Castell of Aubevyle.

'damaging, *ppl. a.* [-ING[2].] That damages; causing damage or injury, injurious, hurtful.

1856 EMERSON *Eng. Traits, Relig.* Wks. (Bohn) II. 101 The modes of initiation are more damaging than custom-house oaths. **1885** *Athenæum* 5 Sept. 299/2 [The hedgehog's] moral character..is the subject of damaging criticism.

Hence **'damagingly** *adv.*, hurtfully.

1854 KITTO *Bible Illustr.* (1867) VIII. 427 The stroke is usually..inflicted damagingly to the mouth, with the heel of a shoe. **1868** *Daily News* 7 Sept., Mr. McCarthy thinks the defence unassailable. To use it appears very easily and very damagingly assailable.

damaisele, obs. form of DAMSEL.

damalic (də'mælɪk), **damolic** (də'mɒlɪk), *a. Chem.* [f. Gr. δάμαλις, δαμάλη heifer + -IC. The second form is perh. short for *damal-olic.*] In ***damalic*** or ***damolic acid,*** an acid (C_7H_8O) discoverd by Städeler in cows' urine. Hence **'damolate** [-ATE[4]], a salt of damolic acid. **dama'luric** [URIC] ***acid,*** an acid ($C_8H_{10}O_2$) akin to damolic, and of the same origin; its salts are **dama'lurates.**

1858 THUDICHUM *Urine* 343 Damaluric acid produces a precipitate in a solution of basic acetate of lead. **1863–72** WATTS *Dict. Chem.* II. 301 Damaluric and Damolic acids, two volatile acids said to exist in cows' and horses' urine. **1879** *Ibid.* VI. 541 The filtered solution deposits, first crystals of barium damolate, then the damalurate.

‖**daman** ('dæmən). [From the Arabic name *daman isrāil,* sheep or lamb of Israel.] The Syrian rock-badger or 'cony' of Scripture (*Hyrax Syriacus*); the name is also extended to the species found at the Cape (*H. Capensis*).

1738 T. SHAW *Trav. Barb. & Levant.* 336 The Daman Israel is an Animal likewise of Mount Libanus, though common in other places of this Country..We have.. presumptive Proof that this Creature is the Saphan of the Scriptures. **1790** BRUCE *Trav.* I. x. 241, I went ashore here [Cape Mahomet] and shot a small animal among the rocks, called Daman Israel or Israel's Lamb; I do not know why, for it has no resemblance to the sheep kind. **1825** GORE tr. *Blumenbach's Man. Nat. Hist.* iv. 47 The Daman, Cape Hyrax. **1835** KIRBY *Hab. & Inst. Anim.* II. xxiv. 497 The skin..is nearly naked, except in the case of the swine, the daman, the mammoth and some others.

damar: see DAMMAR.

Damara ('dɑːmərə, 'dæ-). Also **Dama** ('dɑːmə). In full ***Hill, Berg,*** or ***Mountain Damara.*** One of a negroid people in the mountainous parts of South-West Africa, who have adopted the language of the Nama Hottentots.

1801 J. BARROW *Trav. S. Afr.* I. vi. 397 The Damaras are obviously the same race of people as the Kaffers. **1880** *Encycl. Brit.* XI. 731/2 *Damaraland,* a region of South-Western Africa..so called from the native race known..to the Cape colonists as Damara (Damra, or Dama). *Ibid.,* 85,000 are Herero proper, 30,000 Hill Damara, 3000 Bushmen. **1884** A. K. JOHNSTON *Africa* (ed. 4) xxvi. 463 These degraded Hill or Berg-Damaras name themselves *Houquain* or 'real men'. **1902** *Encycl. Brit.* XXXII. 736/2 The Bantu..enslaving the Mountain Damaras. **1935** L. G. GREEN *Great Afr. Mysteries* x. 122 The Berg Damaras.. living in the almost inaccessible mountain strongholds of South West Africa. **1947** M. OLDEVIG *Sunny Land* 53 There were also the Dama people, living in the mountains further to the north, who were capable of forging iron weapons—the Hilldamaras or Klipkaffirs of the present day. *Ibid.,* The Damas. **1956** A. G. MCRAE *Hill called Grazing* xii. 126 This derelict appeared to be a Berg Damara, a tribe with hardly any tribal cohesion.

damas, obs. form of DAMASK.

Damascene (dæmə'siːn), *a.* and *sb.* Also 4 **damyssene, -assene,** 4–7 **damasene,** 6–7 **damascen, -sine**: see also DAMSON. [ad. L. *Damascēn-us,* Gr. Δαμασκηνός of Damascus. Cf. Ger. *damascen.*] **A.** *adj.*

1. Of or pertaining to the city of Damascus.

[*c* **1386** CHAUCER *Monk's T.* 17 Loo Adam in the feeld of Damyssene [= *in agro Damasceno*] With goddes owene fynger wroght was he.] **1543** TRAHERON *Virgo's Chirurg.* VI. i. Gloss., Another kynde [of viscum] is called Damascene, and commeth from Damasco. **1611** COTGR. s.v. *Damas, Huile de Damas,* oyle Damascene. **1875** SCRIVENER *Lect. Text N. Test.* 17 About the ninth century, a rough, brown, unsightly paper, made of cotton rags, and sometimes called Damascene from the place where it was invented, crept gradually into use.

2. Of or pertaining to damask, (fabrics), or to the art of damascening metal; as ***damascene work.***

1541 *Ord. 33 Hen. VIII* in Nicholls *Househ. Ord.* (1790) 215 In fine Diaper, In Damasene worke. **1550** in *Athenæum* 21 Oct. (1871) 520/3, 4 damascene buttons were cut off my lord's gown in the privy-chamber. **1880** G. C. M. BIRDWOOD *Industr. Arts India* I. 141 A vast establishment of ..damascene workers, chiefly for ornamenting arms. **1882** CAULFEILD & SAWARD *Dict. Needlework* 139/1 Damascene Lace... The difference between it and Modern Point lace.. consists in the introduction into Damascene of real Honiton sprigs, and the absence of any needle-worked Fillings. **1883** C. C. PERKINS *Ital. Sculpt.* 100 (Stanford) The damascene work and the foliated ornaments..challenge comparison with bronzes of any period.

3. ***damascene plum***: see DAMSON 1 c.

B. *sb.* **1.** A native of Damascus.

1382 WYCLIF *2 Cor.* xi. 32 The cite of Damascenys.

2. Damascene work; formerly applied to damask.

1481–90 *Howard Househ. Bks.* (Roxb.) 285 For brynging of damysens from Colchester. **1553** in Rogers *Agric. & Prices* III. 489/3 [Damascene, 6 ells @3/.]. **1844** *Mech. Mag.* XL. 342 The damascene which appears upon the surface of steel is very various. **1873** DIXON *Two Queens* I. v. i. 233 A Spanish silversmith copied arabesques and damascenes.

3. See DAMSON.

damascene (dæmə'siːn), *v.* Also 9 **-ine.** [f. prec. adj.; cf. DAMASKEEN *v.*] *trans.* **a.** To ornament (metal-work, *esp.* steel) with designs incised in the surface and filled in with gold or silver. **b.** To ornament (steel) with a watered pattern, as in Damascus blades.

1585–1613 [see DAMASKEEN *v.*]. **1848** LYTTON *Harold* III. ii, His arms were damascened with silver. **1880** *Sat. Rev.* No. 1302. 461 Swords beautifully damascened in gold.

c. *transf.* and *fig.*

1878 *Examiner* 2 Mar. 283/1 These essential elements.. are damascened upon a ground of really good story. **1891** G. MEREDITH *One of our Conq.* xix, M. Falarique damascenes his sharpest smile.

damascened (dæmə'siːnd), *ppl. a.* [f. prec. + -ED.] Of steel and other metal-work: **a.** Inlaid with ornamental designs, gold or silver; **b.**

Having the watered pattern of dark lines characteristic of Damascus blades.

1862 J. GRANT *Capt. of Guard* li, The earl's cuirass was of Milan steel, magnificently damascened. **1888** *Athenæum* 17 Mar. 344/3 Swords..with splendid damascened hilts.

c. *transf.*

1879 RUTLEY *Stud. Rocks* xi. 181 *Damascened*.—The author suggests this term as a convenient one by which to describe the structure shown in some obsidians, in which streaks or threads of glass are contorted in a confused manner, which somewhat resembles the markings on Damascus sword-blades, or the damascening on gun-barrels.

damascener (dæmə'siːnə(r)). [f. as prec. + -ER.] One who damascenes metal.

1855 tr. *Labarte's Arts Mid. Ages* x. 361 The damascener and the goldsmith. **1883** *Harper's Mag.* June 57/1 Damasceners..and gun-makers are Mohammedan.

damascening (dæmə'siːnɪŋ), *vbl. sb.* [-ING[1].] The action of the vb. DAMASCENE; also the design or figured surface so produced.

1860 *Cornh. Mag.* No. 3. 271 Delightful arabesques and damascenings. **1880** BIRDWOOD *Ind. Art* I. 163 Damascening is the art of encrusting one metal with another ..in the form of wire, which by undercutting and hammering is thoroughly incorporated with the metal which it is intended to ornament.

Damascus (də'mæskəs). Formerly also in the Ital. form **Damasco**. [L. *Damascus*, Gr. *Δαμασκός*, from Semitic: cf. Heb. *Dammeseq*, Arab. *Dimashq, Dimeshq*; thence Heb. *d'meseq* or *d'mesheq*, transl. 'silken' in Amos iii. 12 (Rev. V.).] An ancient city, the capital of Cœle-Syria, famous for its steel and its silk fabrics. Often used *attrib.*, as ***Damascus blade*** (see quot. 1875), etc.; also *absol.* = Damascus steel, etc.

Damascus iron: a combination of pieces of iron and steel welded together and rolled out, in imitation of the steel of Damascus. *Damascus-twist*: see quot.

a **1625** FLETCHER *Elder Bro.* v. i, A Milan hilt, and a Damasco blade. **1665** SIR T. HERBERT *Trav.* (1677) 149 A Sword not so hooked as the Damasco. **1727-51** CHAMBERS *Cycl.*, *Damascus-steel*..remarkable for its excellent temper. **1830** *Mech. Mag.* XIV. 31 By filing semicircular grooves into both sides of the blade, and again subjecting it to the hammer, a beautiful roset-shaped Damascus is obtained. **1846** GREENER *Sc. Gunnery* 113 On examination of..real Damascus barrels. **1874** KNIGHT *Dict. Mech.* s.v. *Damascus-iron*, The fineness of the Damascus depends upon the number and thickness of the alternations [of iron and steel]. *Ibid.*, *Damacus-twist*, a kind of gun-barrel made of a ribbon of Damascus-iron coiled around a mandrel and welded.

† **dama'see.** *Obs.* Also -ysé, -esé. [A corruption or abbreviation of *damasene* DAMSON: cf. first quot. there.] = DAMSON.

14.. *T. of Erceldoune* 180 (Thornton MS.) Whare frwte was growande gret plentee The date and als the damasee [*v.rr.* damese, damyse]. ? *c* **1475** *Squyr lowe Degre* 36 The date, also the damyse [*rime* larel-tre].

damasin, obs. form of DAMSON.

† **damasine,** *a. Obs.* = DAMASCENE. ***damasine-rose***: = damask rose.

1607 TOPSELL *Four-f. Beasts* (1673) 430 Herbs which smell sweet like musk: as..the damasine-rose.

damask ('dæməsk), *sb.* and *a.* Forms: 4-7 damaske, -asc, 4- damask; also 5 dameske, 5-6 dammask(e, 7 damasque, -ast; *Sc.* 5-6 dammas, -es, -ys, 6 domas, 7 damas, -es. [Prob. originally a. AngloFr. **Damasc* = It. *Damasco*, L. *Damascus* proper name of the city; Littré and Hatzfeld have an OF. *Damas* of 14th c., whence the Sc. forms above. The French text of Mandeville (Roxb. Club) ch. xiv. has *Damasce*.]

I. † **1.** The city of Damascus. *Obs.*

c **1250** *Gen. & Ex.* 761 At damaske is ðe ðridde stede, Quer abram is bigging dede. **1377** LANGL. *P. Pl.* B. xv. 486 So many prelates..Of Nazareth, of Nynyue, of Neptalim, and damaske. *c* **1485** *Digby Myst.* (1882) II. 32 Thorow all dammask and liba. **1539** *Inventories* 49 (Jam.) Tapestryis. —Item, vi pece of the cietie of Dammys.

2. *attrib.* = Made at or brought from Damascus, as ***damask blade, sword***, etc. (see 7 below); ***damask cloth, silk*** (see 3 and 6 below); also the following:

† **damask plum, prune** = DAMSON. *Obs.*

1543 TRAHERON *Vigo's Chirurg.* 268 b/1 (Stanford) Take of reysons..of damaske prunes. **1616** SURFL. & MARKH. *Country Farme* 393 Damaske Plums..are of three sorts, the black, red, and violet colour. **1664** EVELYN *Kal. Hort.* (1729) 210 Plums..Damasc, Denny Damasc.

† **damask powder,** ? a toilet-powder scented with damask roses. *Obs.*

c **1540** [cf. *Damask rose* below]. **1634** *Althorp MS.* in Simpkinson *Washingtons* lxviii, For 4 li of damaske powder for Gooddy Webb. **1637** HEYWOOD *Royall King* IV. Wks. 1874 VI. 70 Now farewell Gun-powder, I must change thee into Damask-powder.

damask rose, a species or variety of rose, supposed to have been originally brought from Damascus.

Apparently, originally the *Rosa gallica* var. *damascena*, a tall shrub with semi-double pink or light-red (rarely white) flowers, cultivated in the East for attar of roses; but this underwent many changes under cultivation in the West, and the name has been very variously applied by English authors. According to Miller (1768) the *monthly rose, striped monthly*, and *York-and-Lancaster*, were supposed to be varieties of the Damask rose. According to Flückiger and Hanbury, *Pharmacographia*, the name is now applied at Mitcham to a variety of *R. gallica* with very deep-coloured flowers.

c **1540** *Recipe* in *Vicary's Anat.* (1886) App. 224 Putt therto half an vnce of fyne pouldre of redde dammaske rosys. **1578** LYTE *Dodoens* VI. i. 655 We cal them in English, Roses of Prouince, and Damaske Roses. *Ibid.* 654 The flowers..be neither redde nor white, but of a mixt colour betwixt red and white, almost carnation colour. **1582** HAKLUYT *Memoranda* in *Voy.* II. i. 165 The Damaske rose [brought in] by Doctour Linaker, King Henry the seuenth and King Henry the eights Physician. **1646** J. HALL *Poems* 45 Damast-roses yet unblown. **1744** *C. Thompson's Trav.* III. 13 Rose-Water made of the Damask Roses which grow here plentifully. **1869** HOLE *Bk. about Roses* xi, The Damask [rose] with its few rich velvety-crimson petals, is a memory, and that is all.

damask violet = DAME'S-VIOLET. (In Ger. *Damastblume*.)

1578 LYTE tr. *Dodoens* 153 In English Damaske violets, Dames violets or Gillofers. **1597** GERARDE *Herball* II. cxvi. 377 Dames Violets is called..in English Damaske Violets [etc.]. **1861** PRATT *Flower. Plants* I. 154.

† **damask water,** rose-water distilled from Damask roses. *Obs.*

[**1306** N. DE TINGEWICK in *Archæol. Jrnl.* XIV. 271 Item pro aqua rosata de Damasco.] **1519** *Four Elements* in Hazl. *Dodsley* I. 44 With damask water made so well, That all the house thereof shall smell, As it were paradise. **1555** EDEN *Decades* 224 The Capitayne sprinkeled the Kynges with damaske water. **1611** COTGR. s.v. *Damas, Eau de Damas*, Damaske, or sweet, water (distilled from all sorts of odoriferous hearbs).

II. As a name of substances originally produced at Damascus.

3. A rich silk fabric woven with elaborate designs and figures, often of a variety of colours.

Also applied to figured materials of silk and wool, silk and cotton, or worsted or cotton only, used for furniture-covering, curtains, etc. 'True damasks are wholly of silk, but the term is now applied to any fabric of wool, linen, or cotton, woven in the manner of the first damasks' (Beck, *Draper's Dict.*).

c **1430** LYDG. *Storie of Thebes* III. vi, Clothes of veluet, Damaske and of golde. **1473** *Paston Lett.* No. 725 III. 91 A newe vestment off whyght damaske ffor a dekyne. **1532-3** *Act. 24 Hen. VIII*, c. 13 No man, vnder the saide estates.. shall..weare any saten, damaske, silke, chamblet, or taffata. **1577** tr. *Bullinger's Decades* II. x. 239 A linnen or wollen garment doeth as well couer and become the bodie, as damaskes and veluets. **1689** *Lond. Gaz.* No. 2425/4, 3 Pieces of Crimson Missena Damasks, of a large Flower, commonly used for Beds, and Hangings of Rooms. *c* **1710** C. FIENNES *Diary* (1888) 290 All ye bed and hangings are of fine damaske made of worsted. **1725** DE FOE *Voy. round World* (1840) 21 A quantity of China damasks, and other wrought silks. **1842** BISCHOFF *Woollen Manuf.* II. 415 The draw-loom..is now used to a very considerable extent in weaving carpets and figured damasks.

b. A twilled linen fabric richly figured in the weaving with designs which show up by opposite reflexions of light from the surface; used chiefly for table-linen.

1542 in Rogers *Agric. & Prices* III. 487/3 Damask diaper 1 yd...2/2. **1624** *Will* in *Ripon Ch. Acts* 364 One suite of damaske..for his table. **1696** J. F. *Merchants' Ware-ho.* 13 Damask..is a very fine sort of..Linnen, and is wrought into several sorts of fine Imagery, and Figures..it is for few uses except for Table-Linnen. **1759** GOLDSM. *Bee* No. 3 He looked at the tablecloth, and praised the figure of the damask. **1877** MRS. FORRESTER *Mignon* I. 23 The table is laid..damask, plate, glass, is perfect.

4. a. Steel manufactured at Damascus; also steel or a combination of iron and steel exhibiting a similar variegated surface: more fully ***damask steel***. **b.** The wavy pattern on the surface of Damascus steel, or of iron and steel welded together and corroded with weak acid.

1603 KNOLLES *Hist. Turks* (1621) 1297 Two knives of damaske, with hafts of jasper. **1844** *Mech. Mag.* XL. 342 All steel which exhibits a surface figured with dark lines, is called damask. **1874** KNIGHT *Dict. Mech. Damask-steel*, a laminated metal of pure iron and steel, of peculiar quality, produced by careful heating, laborious forging, doubling, and twisting. **1881** *Blackw. Mag.* May 567 The curious product called damask-steel possesses both edge and elasticity, and all the great Eastern swords owe to it their celebrity. *Ibid.* 568 He made some swords which would bend till the point touched the hilt, and which would also cut through an iron bar..the same two faculties have never been conjoined in any other steel than damask.

1818 FARADAY *Exp. Res.* xvi. (1820) 59 The damask itself is merely an exhibition of crystallisation. **1844** *Mech. Mag.* XL. 342 Common steel acquires no visible damask by gradual refrigeration.

5. The colour of the damask rose: esp. as seen in the face of a woman.

1600 SHAKS. *A.Y.L.* III. v. 123 There was a pretty rednesse in his lip..'twas iust the difference Betwixt the constant red and mingled Damaske. **1607** —— *Cor.* II. i. 232 The Warre of White and Damaske in Their nicely gawded Cheekes. **1600** FAIRFAX *Tasso* II. xxvi, Her damaske late, now chang'd to purest white. **1820** KEATS *Lamia* I. 116 She ..Blush'd a live damask.

III. *attrib.* and *adj.* from senses under II. But early examples of *damask cloth, blade*, etc., mean literally 'of Damascus', and so belong to 2 above.

6. Made of damask (silk or cloth); furnished with damask.

c **1489** CAXTON *Blanchardyn* xix. (1890) 61 A fayre whyte coueryng of damaske clothe. **1609** B. JONSON *Sil. Woman* III. i, A Damask table cloth, cost me eighteen pound. **1682** *Vestry Bks.* (Surtees) 340 One fair damask linen cloth and a damask napkin. **1755** MRS. DELANY *Let. to Mrs. Dewes* 17 Nov., Lady Anson began the last ball in a green damask sack. **1814** *Hist. Univ. Oxford* II. 261 The dress of the Chancellor is of black damask silk. **1842** TENNYSON *Audley Court* 20 A damask napkin wrought with horse and hound.

7. Made of Damascus steel; having the fine temper and watered surface of Damascus steel.

c **1611** CHAPMAN *Iliad* x. 63 By him his damask curets [ἔντεα ποικίλα] hung. **1632** J. HAYWARD tr. *Biondi's Eromena* 78 The fine edge of his damaske blade. **1820** FARADAY *Exp. Res.* xvi. (1859) 59 The wootz..retains..a damask surface when forged, polished, and acted upon by dilute acid.

8. Of the colour of the damask rose; blush-coloured.

1588 SHAKS. *L.L.L.* v. ii. 296 Faire Ladies..Dismaskt, their damaske sweet commixture showne. **1601** —— *Twel. N.* II. iv. 115 She neuer told her loue, But let concealment like a worme i' th' budde Feede on her damaske cheeke. **1842** TENNYSON *Day Dream* Prol., While, dreaming on your damask cheek, The dewy sister-eyelids lay. **1861** MRS. H. WOOD *East Lynne* xvi, Her pretty cheeks were damask with her mind's excitement.

† **9.** = DAMASKED 3 (? a misprint).

1648 HERRICK *Hesper.*, *Country Life* 42 (MS. version, ed. Hazl. p. 457) The damaske [*v.r.* damaskt] meddowes, and the crawling streames.

IV. 10. *Comb.*, as ***damask-coated, -coloured, -gowned*** ppl. adjs.; ***damask-wise*** adv.; † **damask branch,** a figured pattern like that of damask or damask-work; so † **damask-branched** *ppl. a.*; **damask carpet** (see quot.); **damask loom,** a loom for weaving figured fabrics; **damask steel** (see 4); **damask-stitch** (see quot.); **damask-work,** the veining on Damascus-blades; incised ornamentation inlaid with gold or silver.

1634 PEACHAM *Gentl. Exerc.* I. xiv. 46 Diapering..(in *Damaske branches, and such like)..it chiefly serveth to counterfeit cloath of Gold, Silver, *Damaskbrancht, Velvet, Chamlet, &c., with what branch, and in what fashion you list. **1874** KNIGHT *Dict. Mech.*, **Damask-carpet*..a variety of carpet resembling the Kidderminster in the mode of weaving, but exposing the warp instead of the weft. **1606** DEKKER *Sev. Sins* III. (Arb.) 25 The *damask-coated Cittizen. *a* **1631** DRAYTON *Noah's Flood*, The *damask-colour'd dove..His sundry colour'd feathers. **1861** W. F. COLLIER *Hist. Eng. Lit.* 135 A magnificent array of satin and *damask-gowned priests. **1846** MCCULLOCH *Acc. Brit. Empire* (1854) I. 708 The *damask loom is capable of producing any figure, however complicated. **1882** CAULFEILD & SAWARD *Dict. Needlework*, **Damask Stitch*. A name given to Satin Stitch when worked upon a linen foundation. **1580** HOLLYBAND *Treas. French Tong*, *Tailler quelque chose à la Damasquine*, to cut some thing *damaske wise. **1611** COTGR., *Damasquiner*..to flourish, carue, or ingraue Damaske-wise. **1598** FLORIO, *Damaschino*, *damaske worke vpon blades. **1830** TENNYSON *Recoll. Arab. Nts.* iii, All..The sloping of the moon-lit sward Was damask-work, and deep inlay Of braided blooms unmown.

damask ('dæməsk), *v.* [f. prec. sb. By Milton and Phineas Fletcher stressed *da'mask*.]

1. *trans.* To weave with richly-figured designs.

[**1599**, etc. see DAMASKED 1.] **1706** PHILLIPS (ed. Kersey), *Damask* or *Damasquine*..to imprint the Figures of Flowers on Silk, or Stuff. **1755** JOHNSON, *Damask*, I. to form flowers upon stuffs.

2. = DAMASCENE *v.*

1585 T. WASHINGTON tr. *Nicholay's Voy. Turkie* B. II. xxi. 584 b, A fair basen of Copper damasked. **1653** H. COGAN tr. *Pinto's Voy.* 159 Armed with..Partisans damasked with gold and silver. **1673** RAY *Journ. Low C.* (1738) II. 354 They damask their cymeters with a blewish colour. **1877** W. JONES *Finger-ring L.* 247 The wooden sides were plated with gold, and damasked with gold wire.

3. *transf.* and *fig.* To ornament with or as with a variegated pattern or design; to diaper.

1610 G. FLETCHER *Christ's Vict.*, There pinks eblazed wide And damaskt all the earth. **1633** P. FLETCHER *Purple Isl.* XII. i, Where various flowers damask the fragrant seat. **1667** MILTON *P.L.* IV. 334 As they sat recline On the soft downie Bank damaskt with flours. **1744** SHENSTONE *Song*, 'O'er desert Plains' 5 Tho' my path were damask'd o'er With beauties e'er so fine. **1872** O. W. HOLMES *Poet Breakf. T.* i. (1891) 34 Fair pictures damasked on a vapor's fold.

4. To make red or blush-coloured like a damask-rose.

1863 MRS. MARSH *Heathside Farm* I. 58 Cathie's peach-like cheek was damasked by heat and laughter.

5. To deface or destroy, by stamping or marking with lines and figures.

1673 in *Stationers' Rec.* (1883), Order of Bishop of London to damask 'The Leviathan'. **1678** *Ibid.*, Order of Bishop of London to damask Seditious books seized at Frances Smith's, and to burn in the Company's garden adjoining their Hall the Books not fitt for damasking. **1706** PHILLIPS (ed. Kersey), *Damask* or *Damasquine*, to stamp rude Draughts on waste Paper, etc. **1709** *Act. 8 Ann* c. 21 Such offender or offenders shall forfeit such Book or Books ..to the proprietor or proprietors of the Copy thereof, who shall forthwith damask and make wast Paper of them. **1845** CAMPBELL *Chancellors* (1856) I. 23 The ceremony of breaking or 'damasking' of the old Great Seal consists in the Sovereign giving it a gentle blow with a hammer, after which it is supposed to be broken, and has lost all its virtue.

† **6.** To warm (wine): see quot. 1706. *slang.*

1699 B. E. *Dict. Cant. Crew*, *Damask the Claret*, Put a roasted Orange slasht smoking hot in it. **1706** PHILLIPS (ed. Kersey), *To Damask Wine*, is to warm it a little, in order to take off the edge of the Cold and make it mantle. **1778** CUMBERLAND in *Goldsmith's Wks.* (1881) I. 101 Wilt have it steep'd in Alpine snows, Or damask'd at Silenus' nose?

damasked ('dæməskt), *ppl. a.* [f. prec.]
1. Of silk, fine linen, and other fabrics: Woven with richly-figured designs.
1599 MIDDLETON *Micro-Cynicon* iii. Wks. (1886) VIII. 124 Sitting at table..All covered with damask'd napery. **1607** TOPSELL *Four-f. Beasts* (1673) 206 The outward appearance of the said skin is like to a damaskt garment. **1866** *Pall Mall G.* 24 Oct. 4 The exports in damasked silk.
2. Of steel or other metal; = DAMASCENED.
c **1611** CHAPMAN *Iliad* III. 345 His sword he took, and fasten'd it, All damask'd, underneath his arm. **1631** WEEVER *Anc. Fun. Mon.* 202 The out side was..damasked and embossed with wires of gold. **1820** FARADAY *Exp. Res.* xvi. (1859) 59 It is certainly true that a damasked surface may be produced by welding together wires of iron and steel. **1832** BABBAGE *Econ. Manuf.* xviii. (ed. 3) 167 Barrels of double-barrel guns, twisted and damasked.
3. *transf.* Variegated; diapered.
1648 EARL OF WESTMLD. *Otia Sacra* (1879) 88 The Crimson streaks belace the Damaskt West. **1855** SINGLETON *Virgil* I. 360 Blooming be the gates with damasked wreaths.
4. Having the hue of the damask rose.
c **1600** SHAKS. *Sonn.* cxxx, I haue seene Roses damaskt, red and white, But no such Roses see I in her cheekes. **16..** WOTTON *Farewell to Vanities*, Beauty, th' eye's idol, [is] but a damask'd skin. **1652** BENLOWE *Theoph.* III. xxviii, So Roses damaskt robe, prankt with green ribbons, sents.
5. Furnished or hung with damask.
1861 *Our English Home* 134 The damasked chambers.

† **dama'skeen, -kin,** *a.* and *sb. Obs.* Also 6 -en, -yne. [a. F. *damasquin, -ine* damascene, ad. It. *damaschino*, f. *Damasco*, Damascus.]
A. *adj.* = DAMASCENE *a.*
1551 in Strype *Eccl. Mem.* II. II. ix. 319 Under a baron, no man to wear..any embroidery of gold or silver, or damasken work or goldsmiths work. **1585** T. WASHINGTON tr. *Nicholay's Voy. Turkie* II. xxiii. 62 b, Vessels of gold..faire painted after the Damaskin fashion.
B. *sb.* A Damascus blade.
1562 J. SHUTE *Two Comm.* ii. Ccj a (Stanford), A Scimitar bending lyke vnto a falchion, he was a righte damaskyne. **1625** PURCHAS *Pilgrims* I. IV. i. ¶2. 346 A Damaskeen, or Turkish Sword, richly garnished with Siluer and Gilt. *c* **1645** HOWELL *Lett. Chas. I* (1753) 124 No old Toledo Blades, or Damaskins.

damaskeen (dæmə'ski:n), *v.* In 6 -kane, 6–7 -kine, 8–9 -quine, -keen. [a. F. *damasquiner*, f. *damasquin* adj.: see prec.] = DAMASCENE *v.*
1585 T. WASHINGTON tr. *Nicholay's Voy. Turkie* III. ix. 84 b, A litle hatchet damaskined. **1613** PURCHAS *Pilgrimage* III. xiii. (1626) 315 Cups of fine Corinthian Latten, gilded and damaskined. **1848** LYTTON *Harold* IX. iii, His axe..was so richly gilt and damasquined. **1863** —— *Caxtoniana* I. 152 Only on their hardest steel did the smiths of Milan damaskeen the gracious phantasies.
Hence **dama'skeened** *ppl. a.*, **dama'skeening** *vbl. sb.*
1676 *Phil. Trans.* XI. 715 The Persians are exquisitely skilful in damaskining with Vitriol. **1727–51** CHAMBERS *Cycl.*, *Damaskeening*, the art, or act, of adorning iron, steel, etc. by making incisions therein, and filling them up with gold or silver wire. **1882** *Cornh. Mag.* Feb. 171 His drawn sword with its beautiful damasquined blade.

'damasker. *rare*$^{-1}$. [f. DAMASK *v.* + -ER.] = DAMASCENER.
1621 *Canterbury Marriage Licences* (MS.), Robert Worsley of St. Marys in Sandw'ch, damasker.

damasking ('dæməskɪŋ), *vbl. sb.* [-ING[1].] The action of the verb DAMASK; *esp.* the damascening of metal.
1591 PERCIVALL *Sp. Dict.*, *Atauxía*, damasking of a knife or sword. **1677** J. PHILLIPS *Tavernier's Trav.* v. xii, The Persians are excellent artists at Damasquing with vitriol, or engraving Damask-wise upon Swords. **1881** *Blackw. Mag.* May 567 The art of damasking (which is a very different matter from the damaskeening alluded to just now) has lost its use since swords have ceased their service.
b. *transf.* (In quot. 1660 applied to the natural veining or 'marbling' of wood.)
1611 SPEED *Hist. Gt. Brit.* v. vii. 40 Their painting and damasking of their Bodies. **1660** EVELYN *To Dr. Wilkins* 17 Feb., Above all conspicuous for these workes and damaskings, is the Maple.

damasky ('dæməskɪ), *a.* [f. DAMASK *sb.* + -Y[1].] Of or pertaining to damask (sense 3).
1931 E. BOWEN *Friends & Relations* II. vii. 170 The dark-and-light damasky stripes of the lawn. **1958** W. SANSOM *Cautious Heart* ii. 27 We sat among the well-known damasky walls.

dama'squeenery. *rare*$^{-0}$. [a. F. *damasquinerie*.] The art of damascening; damask-work.
1730–6 BAILEY (folio), *Damasquenery*, Steel work damaskeened, or the Art itself. **1775** ASH, *Damasqueenery*.

‖ **dama'squine** (-'ski:n). = DAMASKEEN *sb.*
1849 in WEALE *Dict. Terms*.

‖ **damassé** (damase), *sb.* and *a.* [F. *damassé* = *linge damassé* Hatzfeld.] A. *sb.* A kind of linen manufactured in Flanders, woven with flowers and figures like damask.
1864 in WEBSTER.
B. *adj.* Woven like damask.
1882 CAULFEILD & SAWARD *Dict. Needlework* 141 *Damassé*, a French term applied to all cloths manufactured after the manner of damask, in every kind of material. **1896** *Godey's Mag.* Apr. 443/2 White damassé mohair.

damassen, -syn, -zeene, -zine, obs. forms of DAMSON.

damassin ('dæməsɪn). [Deriv. of F. *damas*, DAMASK.] 'A species of woven damask with gold and silver flowers' (Brande *Dict. Arts* 1842); see also quot. 1882.
1839 URE *Dict. Arts*, *Damassin* is a kind of damask, with gold and silver flowers, woven in the warp and woof; or occasionally with silk organzine. **1882** BECK *Draper's Dict.*, *Damassin, Damasquitte*, an ingenious modification of brocade invented by the Venetians in the 17th century, which by being subjected after being woven to great pressure between rollers, caused the metal wires which formed part of the fabric to appear in one unbroken and brilliant plate of gold or silver.

damaysele, -elle, obs. forms of DAMSEL.

damb(e, obs. (erron.) form of DAM, DAMN.

dambo ('dæmbəʊ). *Central Africa.* [Mang'anja *dambo* treeless grass-covered plain, open glade in the bush.] A grassy clearing.
1907 *Macm. Mag.* Jan. 194 Large open patches, or *dambos*, covered with fresh green grass and well-watered. **1916** *Cornhill Mag.* Mar. 385 Crossing those 'dambos' in the fierce heat of the day. **1954** *New Biol.* XVII. 13 Wherever the drainage is sufficiently retarded to give grey soils, seasonal water-logging is common and grassy 'dambos' result on the valley flats.

dambonite ('dæmbənaɪt). *Chem.* [f. *dambo* native African name + -ITE.]
A sweet white crystalline substance ($C_4H_8O_3$) found in a kind of caoutchouc obtained from a plant growing near the Gaboon in Western Africa.
[**1861** DU CHAILLU *Equat. Afr.* x. 121 The caoutchouc of Africa is obtained from a vine (called *dambo* by the natives).] **1879** WATTS *Dict. Chem.* VI. 541 The exuded juice, coagulated by exposure to the air, is kneaded into loaves called by the natives *n'dambo*..Dambonite is white, easily soluble in water and in alchohol of ordinary strength, sparingly soluble in absolute alcohol.

dambose ('dæmbəʊs). *Chem.* [f. prec. + -OSE.] A crystallizable sugar ($C_3H_6O_3$) obtained from dambonite.
1879 WATTS *Dict. Chem.* VI. 541 Dambose is a polyatomic alcohol, and dambonite its methylic ether.

dambre: see DAMMAR.

dam-brod, dam-board. *Sc.* [f. DAM *sb.*[3] + BROD[2], BOARD: = Du. *dambord*, Ger., Da. *dambret*, Sw. *dambräde*, the board on which the *dams* or *jeu de dames* is played.] A draught-board. b. *attrib.* Checkered.
1779 *Inv. Goods of D. Steuart, Earl of Buchan* (MS.), 8 Damboard T[able] Cloths. **1826** J. WILSON *Noct. Ambr.* Wks. 1855 I. 124 Baith at gammon and the dambrod. **1870** RAMSAY *Remin.* v. (ed. 18) 113 [She] asked to be shown table-linen, a *dam-brod pattern*.

dame (deɪm). Also 5 *Sc.* deym(e, 5- deme, 9 *north. dial.* deame, deeam. [a. OF. *dame* (11th c. in Littré):—earlier *damme* = Pr. *dama, domna*, It. *donna*:—L. *domina* lady, mistress, fem. of *dominus* lord, master. A variant now differentiated is DAM[2].]
I. Expressing relation or function.
1. A female ruler, superior or head: = 'lady', as fem. of *lord* ('our most gracious Sovereign *Lady*, Queen Victoria'); the superior of a nunnery, an abbess, prioress, etc.; *spec.* the title given to Benedictine nuns who have made their solemn profession (cf. DAN[1], DOM[1]); also, any fully professed nun. Also *fig.* or *transf.*
a **1225** *Ancr. R.* 428 Almihti God..ȝiue ure dame his grace, so lengre so more. *c* **1420** *Chron. Vilod.* 774 When he [= she] was hurr' Abbas and hurr' Dame. *c* **1425** *Hampole's Psalter* Metr. Pref. 24 At a worthy recluse prayer cald dame Merget kyrkby. *c* **1490** *Promp. Parv.* 113 (MS. K) Dame, *domina*. *c* **1590** in *Cath. Rec. Soc. Publ.* (1908) V. 192 Dame Isabel Whitehead an ancient religious woman. **1594** T. B. *La Primaud. Fr. Acad.* II. 440 Reason, which is the principal faculty and power of the soule..is called of them the Queene, Dame, and Mistress. **1667** MILTON *P.L.* IX. 612 Sovran of Creatures, universal Dame. **1677** GALE *Crt. Gentiles* II. III. 139 Zenobia Queen of Arabia and Dame of Antioch. *a* **1700** *Cath. Rec. Soc. Publ.* (1911) IX. 335 She leaving the world went over to the English Benedictine Dames of our Blessed Lady of Consolation. *Ibid.* 339 The R[d] Dames, Dame Magdalena, D. Augustina, D. Maria, and D. Clementia. **1795** in B. N. Ward *Dawn Cath. Revival* (1909) II. xxiii. 82 The three houses of English Dames at Paris. **1867** A. T. DRANE *Chr. Schools* II. iv. 179 Dame Mabel Wafre, abbess of Godstow. **1908** P. NOLAN (*title*) The Irish Dames of Ypres, being a history of the Royal Irish Abbey of Ypres.
2. a. The 'lady' of the house, the mistress of a household, a housewife. Now *archaic* or *dial.* (*my dame* = my wife, my 'missus'), or humorously applied to an aged housewife.
c **1330** R. BRUNNE *Chron. Wace* 15150 At Londone anoþer kyng gan wone..Saberk þan was his name, Dame Rytula highte his dame. *c* **1386** CHAUCER *Shipm. T.* 356, I toke vnto our dame ȝoure wif at home þe same gold aȝein. **1483** *Cath. Angl.* 89 Dame; vbi a huswyfe. **1535** COVERDALE *Isa.* xxiv. 2 The Master as the seruant, the dame like the mayde. **1548–9** (Mar.) *Bk. Com. Prayer, Catechism* Rubr., Fathers, mothers, maisters, and dames. **1593** BILSON *Govt. Christ's Ch.* 58 Every poor woman that hath either maid, or apprentise is called *Dame*: and yet Dame is as much as *Domina* and used to Ladies of greatest account, as Dame Isabel and Madam. **1611** SHAKS. *Wint. T.* IV. iv. 57 Upon This day, she was..Both Dame and Seruant: Welcom'd all, seru'd all. **1741** RICHARDSON *Pamela* III. lvii. 147 The Gentry love both him and my Dame, and the poor People adore them. **1833** CARLYLE in Emerson *Eng. Traits* Wks. (Bohn) II. 7 My dame makes it a rule to give to every son of Adam bread to eat. **1855** ROBINSON *Whitby Gloss.* s.v., *My deeam*, my mistress, my wife. *An aud deeam*: an old woman.
b. *transf.*
1632 MILTON *L'Allegro* 52 The cock..stoutly struts his dames before.
c. A girl; a woman. Chiefly *U.S. slang.*
Also *dial.* (see E.D.D.).
1902 *Commentator* (N.Y.) Jan. 104 Look to de frowsy dames erbout us. **1923** G. H. MCKNIGHT *Eng. Words* iv. 61 In the vocabulary of modern youth, chivalry is dead... A girl is a *jane*, a *dame*, a *moll*, [etc.]. **1928** *Punch* 12 Dec. 666/1 *Skid* is reputed to be a squire of dames ('dame' being apparently the American feminine of 'guy'). **1929** G. MITCHELL *Mystery of Butcher's Shop* xvii. 192 Here was this frightful dame named Bradley coming and invading the place. **1936** A. HUXLEY *Eyeless in Gaza* xxv. 353 Mr. Beavis ..began to describe his researches into modern American slang... 'I might say you had a dame complex, Anthony.' **1962** J. CANNAN *All is Discovered* iii. 77 I've never set eyes on the dame.
d. In modern pantomime, a comic character, that of a middle-aged woman, traditionally played by a man.
1902 in A. E. Wilson *Prime Minister of Mirth* (1956) iii. 53 Mr. Robey is different. To a stage which for years had been inhabited by pantomime 'dames', by the drink comedian, by the lodger and by the lodger's wife he came. **1925** M. W. DISHER *Clowns & Pantomimes* iii. 44 The wife of Noah..is sister to the dame of pantomime. **1933** G. ROBEY *Looking Back on Life* xi. 88 My most important pantomimes..were in the big cities... I was often cast for the Dame. **1946** M. DICKENS *Happy Prisoner* ix. 189 He had been afraid they were going to guy her up like a pantomime dame. **1950** *Oxf. Jun. Encycl.* IX. 273/2 Pantomimes..all have their stock characters—the Fairy Queen, the Demon King, the Clown, the Dame (played by a male comedian). **1961** E. WILLIAMS *George* xxiii. 368 He was like a lively don who spends his vacs playing dame in some witty pantomime.
3. The mistress of a private elementary school for children. (Usually an old woman or widow.) Now almost *Obs.*
a **1649** WINTHROP *New. Eng.* (1826) II. 50 He bewailed.. his disobedience to his parents, his slighting and despising their instructions and the instuctions of his dame. **1850** W. IRVING *Goldsmith* i, Those good old motherly dames, found in every village, who cluck together the whole callow brood ..to teach them their letters.
4. At Eton: A matron who keeps a boarding-house for boys at the school. (Also applied to a man who does the same.)
c **1737** H. WALPOLE *Let. to Montagu* (1857) I. 15 A dame over the way, that has just locked in her boarders. **1825** C. M. WESTMACOTT *Eng. Spy* I. 52 Do you bid the Dames of old Eton appear. **1844** DISRAELI *Coningsby* I. ii, The room in the Dame's house where we first order our own breakfast. **1886** DOWDEN *Life Shelley* I. 22 Hexter..being, not only an Eton writing-master and a 'dame', but also a magistrate of the county.
II. Expressing rank or honour.
5. A form of address originally used to a lady of rank, or a woman of position; the feminine corresponding to *Sire*; = My lady, Madam: gradually extended to women of lower rank, and, after the 16th c., left to these (cf. sense 2, 6 c).
a **1225** *Leg. Kath.* 2080 Hu nu, dame, dotestu? Cwen, acangestu nu? *a* **1300** *Cursor M.* 8349 (Cott.) Dame, I did þe hider call, Als mi wedded wijf of all. *a* **1300** *Floriz & Bl.* 56 Dame, he sede, þis hail is þin. *c* **1386** CHAUCER *Reeve's T.* 36 þer durst no wiȝt clepe hur but dame. *a* **1440** *Sir Eglam.* 871 'Dame,' he seyde to the qwene, 'Mekylle of solas have we sene.' *c* **1462** *Wright's Chaste Wife* 139 Thus seyd the wyfe of the hows, 'Syr, how faryth my swete spouse..?' 'Sertes, dame,' he seyd, 'wele'. *c* **1470** HENRY *Wallace* v. 330 A wedow thar duelt..'Fayr deyme', he said, 'ȝe gat sum meit for me'. **1606** SHAKS. *Ant. & Cl.* IV. iv. 29 Fare thee well Dame, what ere becomes of me, This is a Soldiers Kisse. **1669** PENN *No Cross* x. §5 Now ..men of ordinary Trades in England [are called] Sir, and their Wives, Dame; (which is the legal Title of a Lady), or else Mistress. **1722** DE FOE *Col. Jack* (1840) 90 How much was it, dame?
† 6. a. Prefixed as a title to the name of a lady or woman of rank; = Lady, Mistress, Miss. Now only *fig.* in personifications, as ***Dame Fortune, Dame Nature.***
a **1300** *Cursor M.* 23719 (Cott.) Dame [*v.r.* Dam] fortune turnes þan hir quele. *c* **1305** *Saints' Lives* in *E.E.P.* (1862) 71 Tuei maidenes clene ynou hire douȝtren were also Dame Margerie and dame Alice..Dame Mabille þe gode moder þis children louede ynou. *c* **1386** CHAUCER *Man of Law's T.* 151 The Emperours doghter dame Custance. **1413** LYDG. *Pilgr. Sowle* I. i. (1859) 1 The noble worthy lady dame Misericord. **1500–20** DUNBAR *Lucina Schynnyng* 11 Me thocht Deme Fortoun..Stude me beforne. **1568** GRAFTON *Chron.* II. 119 Alexander king of Scottes maryed dame Jane the sister of king Henry. **1593** [see 2]. **1600** THYNNE *Emblems* xiii, Dame Lais is a puritane. **1669** A. BROWNE *Ars Pict.* (1675) 14 Dame Nature is extremely Various in her Representations.
b. The legal title prefixed to the name and surname of the wife of a knight or baronet, for which *Lady* prefixed to the surname is in common use.
1611 *Patents creating baronets* in Selden *Titles Hon.* II. v. §46 Quod uxores..gaudeant hac appellatione, videlicet

Anglice, *Lady, Madame*, et *Dame* respective, secundum usum loquendi. **1614** *Ibid.* II. ix. §2 By custom..the Ladies that are Knights' wives are in conveyance for the most part stiled Dames, and other Ladies only of greater honor, Ladies; which we see is a title much more frequently given to this sex than Lord to males. **1648** PRYNNE *Plea for Lords* 42 Dame Alice Piers was brought before the lords. **1661** *Protests Lords* I. 19 Sir Edward Powell Knt. and Brt., and Dame Mary his wife. **1793** in J. L. Chester *Westm. Abbey Reg.* (1876) 452 Dame Sidney Hawkins [relict of a knight] died the 18th.

c. Prefixed to the surname of a housewife, an elderly matron or schoolmistress. *arch.* or *dial.*

c **1300** *Havelok* 558 [Grim] bar him hom to hise cleue, And bi-taucte him dame leue [his wife]. **1575** J. STILL *Gamm. Gurton* Prol., Dame Chat her deare gossyp. [Also called 'Goodwife Chat', 'Mother Chat'.] **1791** BOSWELL *Johnson*, He was first taught to read English by Dame Oliver, a widow, who kept a school for young children in Lichfield. *a* **1894** *Chapbook title.* The History of Dame Trot and her Cat.

7. a. The wife or daughter of a lord; a woman of rank, a lady. Now *historical* or *poetic*.

1530 PALSGR. 212/1 Dame, a lady, *dame*. *a* **1562** G. CAVENDISH *Life of Wolsey*, Your..banquette, where was assembled such a number of excellent fair dames. **1590** SHAKS. *Mids. N.* v. i. 298 [Thisbe] the fairest Dame That liu'd, that lou'd, that lik'd, that look'd with cheere. **1606** —— *Tr. & Cr.* I. iii. 282 Hee'l say in Troy..The Grecian Dames are sun-burnt. **1630** WADSWORTH *Pilgr.* vii. 73 They ..intice likewise the young Dames. **1702** POPE *Sappho* 17, No more the Lesbian dames my passion move. **1764** GOLDSM. *Trav.* 251 Dames of ancient days Have led their children through the mirthful maze. **1848** MACAULAY *Hist. Eng.* I. 383 Dames of high rank visited him [Claude Duval] in prison. **1856** MRS. BROWNING *Aur. Leigh* III. 345 She had the low voice of your English dames.

b. A woman in rank next below a lady: the wife of a knight, squire, citizen, yeoman. *arch.* or *dial.*

1574 HELLOWES *Gueuara's Fam. Ep.* (1577) 20 The Ladyes and dames that serue you, and the gallants and Courtiers that attende vppon you. **1752** JOHNSON *Rambler* No. 189 ¶7 The city dame who talks of her visits at great houses, where she happens to know the cook-maid. **1864** CAPERN *Devon Provincialism, Dame*, an appellation bestowed on yeomen's wives.

c. The title of female members of the Primrose League of the same rank as the 'knights'.

1890 G. S. LANE FOX *Primrose League* 13 The members of the League consist of Knights, Dames, and Associates (men and women).

d. The title of women members of the Order of the British Empire; also ***Dame Commander, Dame Grand Cross.***

1917 *Times* 2 June 6/1 The New Order of the British Empire... Degrees of classification for women,..(1) Dame Grand Cross, (2) Dame Commander, (3) Dame Companion. **1930** *Ibid.* 1 Jan. 14 Made a Dame of the Order of the British Empire for her services to aviation.

III. A mother; = DAM *sb.*[2]

†**8.** A mother. *Obs.* **a.** of human beings.

a **1225** *Ancr. R.* 230 Ase þe moder mid hire ȝunge deorlinge vlihð from him..& let hit sitten one, & loken ȝeorne abuten, & cleopien, Dame! dame! & weopen. *c* **1275** in *O.E. Misc.* 190 Hire sire and hire dame þreteþ hire to bete. *c* **1386** CHAUCER *Manciple's T.* 213 Thus taughte me my dame; My sone [etc.]. *c* **1400** *Test. Love* Prol. (1560) 272/1 In such wordes as wee learneden of our dames tongue. ?*c* **1475** *Sqr. lowe Degre* 622 To bydde this chylde go sucke his dame. **1593** SHAKS. *Lucr.* 1477 The sire, the sonne, the dame and daughter die.

b. of animals; = DAM *sb.*[2] 2.

c **1320** R. BRUNNE *Medit.* 286 As chekenes crepyn vndyr þe dame wyng. *c* **1400** MAUNDEV. (1839) xxx. 302 Þei putten forth anon the ȝonge foles and maken hem to nyȝen after hire dames. **1548** UDALL, etc. *Erasm. Par. Matt.* xxi. 100 This she asse is the dame of the fole. **1598** YONG *Diana* 219 Despoyling the harmlesse Nightingale of her deerest pretie ones, and the sorrowfull Dame fluttering vp and downe ouer their heads. **1709** BLAIR in *Phil. Trans.* XXVII. 63 They quit their Dame at 6 Months.

IV. †**9.** The queen at chess. [= F. *dame.*] *Obs. rare.*

1574 HELLOWES *Gueuara's Fam. Ep.* (1584) 231 Somtimes we were wont to play at the chesse..and [I] cannot advise me that you gave me the dame.

V. 10. *Comb.*, as **dame-errant** (*nonce-wd.* after *knight-errant*); **dame-school** (also **dame's school**), an elementary school for children kept by a dame.

1852 MISS YONGE *Cameos* (1877) II. xxxiii. 338 Henry received her with the courtesy due to a distressed *dame-errant. **1821** MAR. EDGEWORTH *Sequel to Rosamond* II. 65 The name of this 'tiny play'..'The *Dame-school Holiday.' **1876** GRANT *Burgh Sch. Scotl.* II. xvi. 527 Dame schools.. have..ceased to exist in Scotland. *a* **1817** JANE AUSTEN *Generous Curate* in *Volume the First* (1954) 73 A twopenny *Dame's School in the village.

dame, obs. f. DAM *sb.*[1] and [4], and DAMN.

‖**dame de compagnie** (dam də kɔ̃paɲi). Also, semi-anglicized **damdecompany**. [Fr.; lit. 'lady of company'.] A paid female companion. Also *transf.*

1784 H. MANN *Let.* 8 Oct. in H. Walpole *Lett.* (1858) VIII. 518 The duchess brought with her, as a *dame de compagnie*, a Frenchwoman. **1821** SHELLEY *Let.* 18 Feb. (1964) II. 265 The situation of *Dame de compagnie* is one indeed in which there is little to be hoped compared with what is to be feared. **1832** *Edin. Rev.* July 481 The female professor, late *dame de compagnie* to La Fayette. **1848** THACKERAY *Van. Fair* xxxiii. 289 Marry a drawing-master's daughter, indeed!—marry a *dame de compagnie*—for she was no better, Briggs. **1885** 'L. MALET' *Col. Enderby's Wife* II. iii, A nice, gentle, little person in grey, who put in an appearance at dinner—*dame de compagnie*, I suppose. **1897** *Sat. Rev.* 5 June 641 'Mees' became a 'damdecompany' to an old Contessa.

‖**dame d'honneur** (dam dɒnœr). [Fr.; lit. 'lady of honour'.] A maid of honour, lady-in-waiting.

1805 C. WILMOT *Let.* 26 Aug. in Londonderry & Hyde *Russ. Jrnls.* (1934) II. 170 My name was given in to the Countess Protassoff, Dame d'Honneur for a presentation. **1848** THACKERAY *Van. Fair* lv. 500 Some said she..had become a *dame d'honneur* to the Queen of Bulgaria. **1900** M. CORELLI *Master Christian* 261 Madame Bozier, who had been her first governess, and who now lived with her, as a sort of dame d'honneur.

damegeous, var. DAMAGEOUS *Obs.*, injurious.

dameisele, damesel(le, obs. ff. DAMSEL.

dames, obs. form of DAMASK.

damesé, var. of DAMASEE *Obs.*, damson.

damesene, obs. form of DAMSON.

dameship ('deɪmʃɪp). *nonce-wd.* [f. DAME *sb.* + -SHIP.] The office or position of a dame.

1837 CARLYLE *Fr. Rev.* I. III. viii, He shall have..a Dameship of the Palace for his niece.

dameson, -yn, obs. forms of DAMSON.

dame's-violet. [A transl. of the Latin name in the old herbalists, *Viola matronalis*, or of its equivalents. The form *damas* or *damask violet* appears to have been a corruption.] A popular name of the common Garden Rocket, *Hesperis matronalis*; by Lyte called also *dame's gilliflower*.

1578 LYTE *Dodoens* II. v. 153 Of Dames violets or Gilofloures..These floures be now called in Latine *Violæ Matronales* [so in TURNER 1562]: in English Damaske violets, Dames violets or Gillofers, and Rogues gillofers; in French *Violettes de Dames*; in base Almaigne Mastbloemen, and after the Latine name they call it Joncfrouwen vilieren, which may be Englished Dames violets. **1597** GERARDE *Herbal* II. cxvi. §1. 376 Dames Violets or Queenes Gilloflowers. **1688** R. HOLME *Armoury* II. 74/1 The double Dame Violet groweth many together in a knot. **1886** *Pall Mall G.* 8 Oct. 5/1 The sweet smell of the purple dame's-violet.

damewort ('deɪmwɜːt). [f. DAME + WORT *sb.*[1]] A book name for the garden rocket, *Hesperis matronalis*; = DAME'S-VIOLET.

1776 WITHERING *Veget. Gt. Brit.* II. 403 Damewort, with a simple upright stem.

damfool ('dæm'fuːl). *colloq.* Also (*jocular*) damphool, -phule. [f. DAMN *a.* + FOOL *sb.*[1]] A 'damned fool' (DAMNED *ppl. a.* 4); a person who behaves stupidly; *transf.*, a foolish thing or affair. Also *attrib.* or as *adj.*, foolish, stupid. Hence **dam'fool** *v. trans.*, to treat as a fool. Also **dam'foolery, dam'foolishness.**

1881 'MARK TWAIN' *Lett. to Publishers* (1967) 135 Send me some of those damphool 'ready letter-writers'. **1882** J. J. JENNINGS *Theatr. & Circus Life* xxviii. 409 All the victim can do is to balance the account by putting experience on the debit side of the ledger and damphoolishness on the other. **1883** G. M. HOPKINS *Let* 28 Jan. (1955) 172 There is a great deal of nonsense about that set, often it sickens one..but still I disapprove of damfooling people. **1886** 'F. ANSTEY' *Fallen Idol* xi. 216 When I open the note I see in Greek characters, and forgif me that I rebeat such words to you at all, but I see written there—'Do not a damfool be!' **1898** 'O. THANET' *Heart of Toil* 100 Was that the damfool way he had talked himself? **1900** KIPLING in *Daily Express* 20 June 4/5 'Fighting heroically' in some damfool trap he's walked into with his eyes open! **1908** G. H. LORIMER *J. Spurlock* iv. 66 The grasshopper isn't the only damphool in the good old summer-time. *Ibid.* xii. 328 It's all damfoolishness. *a* **1909** in J. R. Ware *Passing Eng.* (1909) 103 Now, Hennery, I am going to break you of this damfoolishness, or I will break your neck. **1909** D. H. LAWRENCE *Let.* 8 May (1962) I. 53 She has lost all that damfoolery of faddishness about this, that and the other. **1913** W. J. LOCKE *Stella Maris* ii, It's perhaps the only tremendous thing in my damfool of a life. *a* **1953** DYLAN THOMAS *Quite Early one Morning* (1954) 51 Proclaim their right, as Englishmen, to look at the damfool place however they willynilly will. **1960** *Analog Science Fact/Fiction* Oct. 31/1 This desperate bit of damfoolery.

damicel, obs. form of DAMSEL.

damie ('deɪmɪ). *Sc.* [f. DAME + -IE, -Y dim. suffix.] A diminutive or pet form of DAME.

1789 BURNS *To Dr. Blacklock* v, Ye glaiket, gleesome, dainty damies [the Muses].

damine ('deɪmɪn, -aɪn), *a. Zool.* [f. L. *dama* deer + -INE[1].] Belonging to or resembling the fallow deer, *Dama dama.*

1891 FLOWER & LYDEKKER *Mamm.* 323 Damine group of existing Deer. **1950** G. K. WHITEHEAD *Deer* x. 151 Fallow deer belong to the damine group.

damisel, -en, obs. ff. DAMSEL, DAMSON.

‖**dammar** ('dæmə(r)). Also (? 5 dambre), 7–9 damar, 8–9 dammer. [a. Malay *damar* resin, whence the botanial genus *Dammara* (N.O. *Coniferæ*), the typical species of which, *D. orientalis*, yields the resin in Amboyna and the Moluccas.]

The name of various resins obtained from different trees growing in the East Indies, New Guinea, and New Zealand; *esp.* the cat's-eye resin (*E. India dammar*) from *Dammara orientalis*, used instead of pitch for caulking ships, etc., and the Kauri-gum from *D. australis* of New Zealand; both these are used for making varnish. ***white dammar***, or ***dammar pitch***, is obtained from *Vateria indica*; ***black dammar*** from *Canarium strictum*. (Also ***dammar-gum, dammar-resin, gum dammar***.) Also (in full **dammar pine, dammar tree**), any tree yielding dammar resin.

[*c* **1440** *Secrees* 165 A dragme and a half of good muske, & a dragme of dambre, and þre dragmes of þe tree of aloes.] **1698** FRYER *Acc. E. India & P.* 37 The..Planks are sowed together..and calked with Dammar (a sort of Rosin taken out of the sea). **1727** A. HAMILTON *New Acc. E. Ind.* II. xxxviii. 73 Damar, a Gum that is used for making Pitch and Tar for the Use of Shipping. **1805** *Trans. Soc. Encourag. Arts.* XXIII. 412 Resins..called dammer in India..the produce of various trees. **1829** J. C. LOUDON *Encycl. Plants* 802 This genus [sc. *Agathis*] is formed of the Dammar Pines. **1832** W. ROXBURGH *Flora Indica* (ed. 2) II. 603 In the Bednore country, it is called the Dammar tree by the English, and blossoms during the hot season. **1846** LINDLEY *Veg. Kingd.* 229 Liquid storax is thought to be yielded by the Dammar Pine. **1880** C. R. MARKHAM *Peruv. Bark* 347 The *Canarum strictum*, or black dammer tree. **1892** R. KIPLING *Barrack-r. Ballads* 130 He has taken my bale of dammer and spice I won beyond the seas. **1959** J. C. T. UPHOF *Dict. Economic Plants* 12/1 *Agathis alba* Foxw. (syn. *Dammara alba* Lam.). White Dammar Pine.

‖'**Dammara.** *Bot.* [See prec.] A genus of trees yielding dammar. Also *attrib.*, as ***dammara resin.*** Hence in *Chem.* '**dammaran**, a neutral resin, and **da'mmaric** *acid*, constituents of dammar. '**dammarin**, '**dammarol**, '**dammarone**, '**dammaryl**, chemical derivatives of dammar.

1863–72 WATTS *Dict. Chem.* II. 301 *Dammara resin, Australian*..consists of an acid resin, dammaric acid, and a neutral resin, dammaran.

†'**dammaret.** *Obs.* Also damouret. [ad. F. *dameret* 'an effeminate fondling or fond carpet knight' (Cotgr.); deriv. of *dame* lady.] A ladies' man: 'one that spends his whole time in the entertaining or courting of women' (Cotgr.).

1635 DRUMM. OF HAWTH. *Commend. Verses* to Person's *Varieties*, The Lawyer here may learne Divinity, The Divine, Lawes..The Dammaret respectively to fight, The Duellist to court a Mistresse right. *a* **1649** —— *Fam. Epist.* Wks. (1711) 145 Place me with a damouret..if I praise him in the presence of his mistress, he will be ready to perform like duties to me.

dammas, -aske, obs. forms of DAMASK.

dammasin, obs. form of DAMSON.

damme ('dæmɪ). Also 7 **dammee**, 7–9 **dammy**.

1. *int.* Shortened form of *damn me!* used as a profane imprecation.

c **1645** HOWELL *Lett.* (1650) I. 237 My Lord Powis..said, dammy if ever he come to be King of England, I will turn rebel. **1652** *Total Rout* in *Commw. Ballads* (Percy Soc.) 132 Hee's not a gentleman that wears a sword, And fears to swear dammee at every word. **1791** WOLCOTT (P. Pindar) *Magpie & Robin* Wks. 1812 II. 476 Damme is it you? **1848** THACKERAY *Van. Fair* lv, Tandyman wouldn't pay: no, dammy, he wouldn't pay.

2. as *sb.* **a.** The oath itself, or its utterance.

1775 SHERIDAN *Rivals* III. iv, Let me begin with a damme. **1823** BYRON *Juan* XI. xliii, And yet the British 'Damme's' rather Attic.

†**b.** *transf.* A person addicted to using this oath; a profane swearer. Also †*damme-boy*. *Obs.*

1618 MYNSHUL *Ess. Prison* 45 Though he steale his band of tenne thousand Dam-mees. *a* **1658** CLEVELAND (N.), Punks and dammy-boys. **1662** NEWCOME *Diary* (Chetham Soc.) 52 The ranting dammees of yᵉ nation. **1674** COTTON *Compl. Gamester* in Singer *Hist. Cards* 335 A grand-jury of dammees.

†**3.** *attrib.* or *adj. Obs.*

1660 H. ADIS *Fannaticks Mite* *iij b, That multitude of dammy and debauched Baudy-houses.

damme, obs. form of DAM, DAMN.

dammed (dæmd), *ppl. a.* [f. DAM *v.*[1] + -ED.] Furnished with a dam; obstructed or confined by a dam (usually with *up*).

1664 DRYDEN *Ind. Queen* IV. i, Like dammed-up streams. **1879** ATCHERLEY *Boërland* 97 This race was intended to bring water from a dammed creek. **1899** *Westm. Gaz.* 17 May 8/1 In a dammed-up glacial valley. **1904** W. M. GALLICHAN *Fishing Spain* 115, I made a few casts with the fly over a dammed-up pool. **1946** *Nature* 12 Oct. 527/1 While, however, we have had a partial moratorium on the creations of fundamental science.., we have undoubtedly a new stock of dammed-up ideas.

dammer ('dæmə(r)), *sb.* [f. DAM *v.*[1] + -ER[1].] One who constructs dams.

1816 SCOTT *Antiq.* xxiii, Auld George Glen the dammer and sinker.

†'**dammer**, *v. Obs. rare.* [Cf. Ger. *dämmern* to become dim, to dim.] To make dim or dark.

1610 HOLLAND *Camden's Brit.* (1637) 649 So greate a mercate towne and faire withall that..it dammereth and dimmeth the light in some sort of Radnor.

dammer, var. DAMMAR, resin.

dammes, -ys, obs. Sc. ff. DAMASK.

damming ('dæmɪŋ), *vbl. sb.* [-ING[1].] The action of the verb DAM[1]; obstructing or confining by a dam. (Also with *up*.)

1802 PLAYFAIR *Illustr. Hutton. Th.* 353 The damming up of those rivers. **1861** HUGHES *Tom Brown at Oxf.* XVII. (1889) 162 A small brook..with careful damming is made to turn a mill.

dammisel, obs. form of DAMSEL.

'**dammish**, *v. Sc.* Also **daimish**. [Possibly a variant of DAMAGE; OF. had *damachier* beside *damagier*. But cf. Ger. *dämisch* stupid.]

†**1.** *trans.* To stun, stupefy. *Obs.*

a **1598** ROLLOCK *On the Passion* (1616) 38 (Jam.) As a man who falls downe from an high place..lyes without sense, and is dammished with the fall. **1722** WODROW *Hist. Suff. Ch. Scot.* II. 25 He was perfectly dammished with the stroke.

2. To bruise the surface of (an apple or similar fruit) by a knock.

In south of Scotland (*daimish*).

dammit ('dæmɪt), for *damn it*, esp. used in comparative phrases.

1908 E. WALLACE *Angel Esquire* xii, 'Outside as quick as dammit!' he cried. **1921** WODEHOUSE *Jill the Reckless* i. 31 When I'm alone with Barker—for instance—I'm as chatty as dammit. **1931** F. D. GRIERSON *Mystery in Red* vii. 106 You were as near rude to him as dammit. **1956** A. H. COMPTON *Atomic Quest* iii. 193 Dammit, give it stuff to spare. **1961** *Guardian* 24 Apr. 9/7 The score standing as near as dammit at two. **1971** *Sunday Times* (Colour Suppl.) 21 Feb. 43/3 Whenever I talk about Rizzo and brutality, I have to use the word 'allege', but dammit all, I have so many *facts*, baby, there ain't nothing alleged about it.

dammosen, obs. form of DAMSON.

damn (dæm), *v.* Forms: 3-6 **dampne**, (4 **dempne, damp**), 4-7 **damne**, (5 **dame**, 5-6 **damme**, 5-7 **dam**, 7 **damb**), 7- **damn**. [a. OF. *dampne-r*, *damne-r*, ad. L. *damnāre*, *dampnāre*, orig. to inflict damage or loss upon, to condemn, doom to punishment; taken early into F. in legal and theological use. Cf. Pr. *dampnar*, It. *dannare*.]

†**1. a.** *trans.* To pronounce adverse judgement on, affirm to be guilty; to give judicial sentence against; = CONDEMN 1 (in part), 2. *Obs.*

a **1300** *Cursor M.* 13756 (Cott.), I damp þe not quar-so þou far, But go nu forth and sin na mar. **1382** WYCLIF *John* viii. 10 Womman, wher ben thei that accusiden thee? no man dampnede thee. *c* **1385** CHAUCER *L.G.W.* Prol. 387 It is no maysterye for a lord To dampne a man with-oute answere. **1440** J. SHIRLEY *Dethe K. James* (1818) 23 This same Erle of Athetelles was endited, arreyned, and dampned. **1483** CAXTON *G. de la Tour* N iij, Ye hadde made hym to be dampned and destroyed withoute cause. **1495**, **1551** [see DAMNED 1].

†**b.** To condemn *to* a particular penalty or fate; to doom; = CONDEMN 3, 6. *Obs.*

a **1300** *Cursor M.* 20888 (Gött.) Bat ananias and his wijf For suilk he dampned þaim of lijf. *c* **1320** R. BRUNNE *Medit.* 556 Pylat..dampnede his Lorde to dye on the croys. *c* **1460** *Towneley Myst.* 209 Pylate, do after us, And dam to deth Jesus. **1483** CAXTON *Gold. Leg.* 382/2, ii. thousand peple cristen which had been longe there dampned for to hewe the marble. **1557** *K. Arthur* (Copland) VIII. ii, So she was dampned by the assent of the barons to be brente. **1559** *Mirr. Mag., Tresilian* xvii, I poore Tresilyan..was dampned to the galowes. **1611** SPEED *Hist. Gt. Brit.* VI. xlviii. 168 Let the Edict be dambd to eternal silence. **1734** POPE *Ess. Man* IV. 284 See Cromwell damned to everlasting fame. **1872** BLACKMORE *Maid of Sk.* (1881) 69, I will take it as a separate case, and damn the country in the fees.

2. †**a.** To adjudge and pronounce (a thing, practice, etc.) to be bad; to adjudge or declare forfeited, unfit for use, invalid, or illegal; to denounce or annul authoritatively; to CONDEMN. *Obs.* exc. as in b, or as associated with other senses.

c **1386** CHAUCER *Wife's Prol.* 70 For hadde God comaundid maydenhede, Than had he dampnyd weddyng with the dede. **1387** TREVISA *Higden* (Rolls) VIII. 289 Kyng Edward dampned sodeynliche fals money þat was slyliche i-brouȝt up. **1483** RICH. III in Ellis *Orig. Lett.* III. xlii. I. 105 Damnyng and utterly distroying all the stamps and Irons. **1556** *Chron. Grey Friars* (Camden) 20 And also there [Paul's Cross]..ware many bokes of eryses..damnyd and brent be fore hys face. **1635** PAGITT *Christianogr.* III. (1636) 40 A Councell, in which Image-worshippe was damned. **1676** WYCHERLEY *Pl. Dealer* Prol., And with faint praises one another damn [cf. Pope *Prol. Sat.* 200]. **1700** WELWOOD *Mem.* (ed. 3) 231 All the Charters in the Kingdom were damn'd in the space of a Term or two. **1797** GODWIN *Enquirer* II. vii. 266 We should [not] totally damn a man's character for a few faults. **1868** G. DUFF *Pol. Surv.* 9 An assembly..gathered together for the express purpose of damning modern civilization.

b. *spec.* To condemn (a literary work, usually a play) as a failure; to condemn by public expression of disapproval.

1654 WHITLOCK *Zootomia* 254 We glosse him with Invectives, or damne the whole Book for Erratas. **1696** tr. *Du Mont's Voy. Levant* A vij, The Book must be damn'd for the Clownishness of the Author. **1749** FIELDING *Tom Jones* XIII. xi, A new play, at which two large parties met, the one to damn, and the other to applaud. **1791** BOSWELL *Johnson* an. 1777, A comedy by Mr. Hugh Kelly, which..in the play-house phrase, was damned. **1860** J. P. KENNEDY *W. Wirt* I. xx. 309 The ordeal of facing the authorship of a play that has been damned.

†**c.** Used by Coverdale as a rendering of Heb. *heḥ͏ͤrîm* to devote to destruction. *Obs.*

1535 COVERDALE *Josh.* vi. 18 Howbeit this cite, & all that is therin, shalbe damned vnto the Lorde..Onely bewarre of it that is damned, lest ye damne youre selues (yf ye take ought of it which is damned). *Ibid.* xi. 11 He..smote all the soules that were therin with the edge of the swerde, and damned it..& damned Hasor with fyre.

3. *transf.* To bring condemnation upon; to prove a curse to, be the ruin of.

1477 EARL RIVERS (Caxton) *Dictes* 68 The wikked werkes dampne and distroye the good. **1611** SHAKS. *Cymb.* III. iv. 76 Hence vile Instrument, Thou shalt not damne my hand. **1607** —— *Timon* IV. iii. 165. **1691** T. H[ALE] *New Invent.* p. lxxxiii, He would damn all Patents that damned the River. **1728** YOUNG *Love Fame* iii. (1757) 101 Who borrow much..And damn it with improvements of their own. **1848** LD. G. BENTINCK in *Croker Papers* III. xxv. 165 The Budget has damned the Whig Government in the country. **1893** *Publishers' Circular* 3 June 623/1 Chapman's..remarkable preface..if written by a modern author would at once damn his book.

4. *Theol.* **a.** To doom to eternal punishment in the world to come; to condemn to hell.

c **1325** *Metr. Hom.* 112 Sain Jon hafd gret pite That slic a child suld dampned be. *a* **1340** HAMPOLE *Psalter* i. 6 Wicked sall noght rise..for to deme, bot for to be demed and dampned. **1483** CAXTON *G. de la Tour* E ij, He wold pray god for hym that he myght knowe whether she was dampned or saued. *a* **1533** LD. BERNERS *Huon* xlv. 151 Haue pyte of your owne soule, the whiche shal be dampnyd in hell. **1638** CHILLINGW. *Relig. Prot.* I. ii. §101 You damne all to the fire, and to Hell, that any way differ from you. **1727** SWIFT *To Very Young Lady*, Some people take more pains to be damned, than it would cost them to be saved. **1870** M. CONWAY *Earthw. Pilgr.* xxiii. 270 He had rather be damned with Plato than saved with those who anathematised him.

b. *transf.* To cause or occasion the eternal damnation of.

1340 *Ayenb.* 115 He is manslaȝte and him-zelue damneþ ase zayþ þe wrytinge. **1377** LANGL. *P. Pl.* B. XII. 92 Riȝt so goddes body bretheren but it be worthily taken, Dampneth vs atte daye of dome. *c* **1440** *York Myst.* xlviii. 161 þe dedis þat vs schall dame be-dene. **1547** BAULDWIN *Mor. Philos.* II. iii, The iustice of God and their owne desertes damne them vnto euerlasting death. **1658** *Whole Duty Man* xvi. §1. 127 Some..make it their only comfort, that their enemies will damn themselves by it. *a* **1703** BURKITT *On N.T., Luke* i. 66 'Tis..the contempt and neglect of the sacrament that damns. **1837** J. H. NEWMAN *Par. Serm.* (ed. 2) III. xv. 235 You have the power to damn yourself.

†**c.** In passive sense: = *be damned. Obs. rare.*

1611 BEAUM. & FL. *Philaster* IV. ii, *Cle.* Sir, shall I lie? *King.* Yes, lie and damn, rather than tell me that. **1625** MASSINGER *New Way* II. i, So he serve My purpose, let him hang or damn, I care not.

5. Used profanely (chiefly in optative, and often with no subject expressed) in imprecations and exclamations, expressing emphatic objurgation or reprehension of a person or thing, or sometimes merely an outburst of irritation or impatience. (Now very often printed 'd——n' or 'd——', in pa. pple. 'd——d'.) Also, ***damn** (one's) **eyes!***, used as an abusive expression.

[**1431** JOAN OF ARC in De Barante *Ducs de Bourgogne* vi. 116 Mais, fussent-ils [les anglais] cent mille Goddem de plus qu'à présent, ils n'auront pas ce royaume.] **1589** *Pappe w. Hatchet* (1844) 16 Hang a spawne? drowne it; alls one, damne it! **1605** SHAKS. *Macb.* V. iii. 11 The diuell damne thee blacke, thou cream-fac'd Loone. **1633** T. STAFFORD *Pac. Hib.* vi. (1821) 292 His owne manifold Letters..(full of God damne him). **1709** STEELE *Tatler* No. 13 ¶1 Call the Chairmen: Damn 'em, I warrant they are at the Ale-house already! **1751** SMOLLETT *Per. Pick.* viii, I'll be d——d if ever I cross the back of a horse again. **1761** STERNE *T. Shandy* III. xii. 64 From the great and tremendous oath of William the Conqueror, (*By the splendour of God*) down to the lowest oath of a scavenger, (*Damn your eyes*). **1815** SCOTT *Guy M.* xxxvi, Then take broadswords and be d——d to you. **1836** DICKENS *Let.* 20 Sept. (1965) I. 175, I will see them d——d before I make any further alteration. **1849** THACKERAY *Pendennis* xxvii, D—— it, I love you: I am your old father. **1850** H. MELVILLE *White Jacket* II. xxvi. 170 What man-of-war's-men call a *damn-my-eyes-tar*, that is, a humbug. And many damn-my-eyes humbugs there are in this man-of-war world of ours. **1859** DICKENS *T. two Cities* I. ii, One pull more and you're at the top, and be damned to you. **1906** 'Q' *Mayor of Troy* xi. 151 D——n your eyes, it's *twins*—and both *girls*! **1912** KIPLING *As Easy as A.B.C.* 5 It's refreshing to find any one interested enough in our job to damn our eyes. **1922** JOYCE *Ulysses* 287, I was just passing the time of day with old Troy..and be damned but a bloody sweep came along and he near drove his gear into my eye. **1943** N. BALCHIN *Small Back Room* xiv. 200, I shall have to let go of the other wrench. Damn and blast. **1953** H. MILLER *Plexus* (1963) v. 175 Those things never happen to me. So you peddled candies in the Café Royal? I'll be damned.

6. To imprecate damnation upon; to curse, swear at (using the word 'damn'). Also *absol.*

1624 MASSINGER *Parl. Love* I. v, If you have travelled Italy, and brought home Some remnants of the language, and can..Protest, and swear, and damn. **1665** DRYDEN *Indian Emp.* Epil., Their proper business is to damn the Dutch. **1796** STEDMAN *Surinam* I. vii. 135 Insulted by a row-boat, which damned him, and spoke of the whole crew in the most opprobrious terms. **1848** MACAULAY *Hist. Eng.* (1871) II. xiii. 49 The dragoons..cursing and damning him, themselves, and each other, at every second word.

damn (dæm), *sb.* [f. prec. vb.

(The conjecture that, in sense 2, the word is the Hindī *dām*, *dawm*, an ancient copper coin, of which 1600 went to a rupee (see Yule), is ingenious, but has no basis in fact.)]

1. The utterance of the word 'damn' as a profane imprecation.

1619 FLETCHER *M. Thomas* II. ii, Rack a maids tender ears, with dam's and Devils. **1719** DE FOE *Crusoe* (1850) II. 460 'What! he no hear you curse, swear, speak de great damn?' **1775** SHERIDAN *Rivals* II. i, Ay, ay, the best terms will grow obsolete. Damns have had their day. **1849** THACKERAY *Pendennis* lxvii, How many damns and curses have you given me, along with my wages? **1877** BESANT & RICE *Son of Vulc.* I. xii, That [oath] once discharged, he relapsed..into numerous commonplace damns.

2. Used vaguely (in unconventional speech) in phrases ***not worth a damn, not to care a damn, not to give a damn.*** (Cf. CURSE *sb.* 2¶.)

1760 GOLDSM. *Cit. W.* xlvi, Not that I care three damns what figure I may cut. **1817** BYRON *Diary* Wks. (1846) 423/1 A wrong..system, not worth a damn. **1827** SCOTT *Jrnl.* (1890) II. 22 Boring some one who did not care a d—— about the matter, so to speak. **1849** MACAULAY *Life & Lett.* (1883) II. 257 How they settle the matter I care not, as the Duke [of Wellington] says, one twopenny damn. **1895** J. L. WILLIAMS *Princeton Stories* 165, I don't give a damn for the girl. **1929** *Eugenics Rev.* July 86/2 See the happy moron, He doesn't give a damn. I wish I were a moron. My God! Perhaps I am! **1939** WODEHOUSE *Uncle Fred in Springtime* xviii. 263, I don't give a single, solitary damn. **1959** J. CARY *Captive & Free* i. 13 It was obvious, as one angry young woman remarked, that he didn't give a damn—and so they were enraged.

damn (dæm), *a.* and *adv.* Also **damn'**, **dam'**, **dam**. Clipped form of DAMNED *ppl. a.* (See also DAMFOOL.) ***damn all***: see ALL A. 8 f.

1775 *Narragansett Hist. Reg.* (1885) III. 263 A man that..was noted for a damn cuss. **1776** *Ibid.* (1882) I. 304 You damn old Tory Raskel. **1787** *Mirror* 164 Don't beef and butter go off damn soberly? **1882** in T. M. Healy *Lett. & Leaders* (1928) I. 150 T. P. quoted my answer as 'I'm damn glad'. **1897** C. M. FLANDRAU *Harvard Episodes* 4 You've gone through the whole damn thing yourself. *Ibid.* 218 'But he isn't bad, really bad.' 'No, certainly not; merely a damn fool.' **1901** MERWIN & WEBSTER *Calumet 'K'* iv. 62 My only order was, 'Clear the road—and be damn quick about it'. **1903** KIPLING *Five Nations* 199 I've known a lot o' people ride a dam' sight worse than Piet. **1918** W. J. LOCKE *Rough Road* xviii, It's all dam funny! **1919** H. J. LASKI *Let.* 14 Nov. (1953) I. 221, I won't say that this is the best of all possible worlds; but it's damn near it. **1928** D. L. SAYERS *Bellona Club* iii, If you understand that..you understand a damn' sight more than I do. **1928** E. WALLACE *Again the Three Just Men* 209 It's none of your dam' business. **1929** H. MILES tr. *Morand's Black Magic* iii. 48 A dam' cracker that I don't know ran into me. **1938** S. V. BENÉT *Thirteen O'Clock* 281 Lisa's got her damn-fool side. **1941** N. COWARD *Australia Visited* i. 6 We were in it once and for all and intended to damn well get on with it. **1945** C. S. LEWIS *That Hideous Strength* ix. 228 You're in a dam dangerous position already. **1959** 'O. MILLS' *Stairway to Murder* xiii. 138 It was a damnfool thing to do, and I realise it now. **1966** C. MACKENZIE *Paper Lives* viii. 116 These dam new towns with which the Accommodation people are infesting the countryside. **1970** N. MARSH *When in Rome* 89, I call it a damn poor show. Leaving us high and dry. **1970** D. STUART *Very Sheltered Life* 248 You one of those damn' Yankee reporters?

damn(e, obs. (erron.) form of DAM.

damnability (dæmnə'bɪlɪtɪ). [f. next.] Quality of being damnable; liability to damnation.

1532 MORE *Confut. Tindale* Wks. 438/1 The damnabilitie belonging to the mortall offence. **1648** BP. DUPPA *Angels Rejoic.* 19 It may bring a damnability (as the Schoole speakes), but not damnation. **1845** CARLYLE *Cromwell* I. iv. 72 Which in that time meant temporal and eternal Damnability.

damnable ('dæmnəb(ə)l), *a.* Also 4-6 **dampnable**. [a. F. *damnable*, in 12-13th c. *dampnable*, ad. L. *dam(p)nābilis*, f. *damnāre*: see DAMN.]

†**1.** Worthy of condemnation; to be reprobated; highly reprehensible. *Obs.* (or merged in 2, 4.)

c **1380** WYCLIF *Sel. Wks.* III. 341 Myche more ben þei dampnable þat letten Goddis lawe to shyne. **1509** BARCLAY *Shyp of Folys* 123 Than it [daunsynge] in erth no game is more damnable. **1634** PRYNNE *Documents agst. Prynne* (Camden) 21 For a man to endeavour to defraude the Kinge of this treasure is a most damnable offence. **1841** EMERSON *Lect., Conservative* Wks. (Bohn) II. 268, I observe that there is a jealousy of the newest, and that the seceder from the seceder is as damnable as the pope himself.

†**b.** Liable to judicial condemnation. *Obs. rare.*

c **1460** *Towneley Myst.* 193 Sir Cayphas, bi my wytt, he shuld be dampnabille.

2. Subject to divine condemnation; liable to or worthy of damnation.

1303 R. BRUNNE *Handl. Synne* 3768 þys synne ys nat dampnable But hyt be seyde custummable. *a* **1340** HAMPOLE *Psalter* xvii. 25 þe pynes of dampnabil men. **1532** MORE *Confut. Tindale* Wks. 475/2 The contrarye beliefe pertayneth to the damnacion of our soules, if heresye be damnable. **1614** H. GREENWOOD *Jayle Delivery* 468 O what must poore lamentable damnable I doe to be saved. **1751** SMOLLETT *Per. Pic.* xxxvi, Those enthusiasts who look upon every schism from the established articles of faith as damnable. **1882-3** SCHAFF *Encycl. Relig. Knowl.* II. 1366 Who makes us damnable..of his own will.

†**3.** Causing loss or harm; hurtful, pernicious. *Obs. rare.*

c **1420** *Pallad. on Husb.* I. 181 Yf thi wey be foule, it is dampnable. **1659** B. Harris *Parival's Iron Age* 108 A most damnable Victory to the House of Austria.

†**b.** Causing damnation. *Obs. rare.*

a **1617** Hieron *Serm.* (1634) 185 The mercy of God, if it bee rightly applyed, there is nothing more comfortable; if it be abused.. there is nothing more damnable.

4. As a strong expression of angry dislike (or merely as a strong intensive): Fit to be 'damned'; 'damned', 'confounded'. (Now regarded as vulgar or profane.)

1594 Sir J. Harington in *Nugæ Antiq.* (1804) I. 167, I will write a damnable storie, and put it in goodlie verse, about Lord ——. **1596** Shaks. *1 Hen. IV*, I. ii. 101 O, thou hast damnable iteration. **1606** —— *Tr. & Cr.* V. i. 29 Thou damnable box of enuy thou. **1712** Hearne *Collect.* (Oxf. Hist. Soc.) III. 347 This is a damnable Shame. **1843** Lytton *Last Barons* x. vi, That damnable wizard and his witch child. **1880** Mrs. Forrester *Roy. & V.* II. 143 That blackguard has been telling his damnable lies to you.

†**B.** as *adv.* Damnably, execrably; also as a strong intensive. *Obs.*

1611 Shaks. *Wint. T.* III. ii. 188 That did but shew thee ..inconstant, And damnable ingratefull. **1668** Davenant *Man's the Master* Wks. (1673) 352 She's damnable handsom! **1678** Bunyan *Pilgr.* I. 152 After he went to the iron gate [of Doubting Castle].. but that lock went damnable hard, yet the key did open it. **1712–35** Arbuthnot *John Bull* I. xv. (1755) 29 They are damnable greedy of the pence.

'damnableness. [f. prec. + -ness.] The quality of being damnable.

1638 Chillingw. *Relig. Prot.* Answ. to Pref. §29 The question being of the Damnableness of Error.

damnably ('dæmnəblɪ), *adv.* [f. as prec. + -ly².] In a damnable manner.

†**1.** So as to deserve or incur damnation. *Obs.*

c **1386** Chaucer *Melib.* ¶860 Cursedly and dampnably we han ygilt aȝeinst ȝoure gret lordship. **1522** *Act. 5–6 Edw. VI*, c. 1 §1 A greate nombre of People.. do wilfullye and dampnablye.. abstayne and refuse to come to their Parishe Churches. **1651** C. Cartwright *Cert. Relig.* I. 149 It is granted, that the invisible Church cannot erre damnably. **1768–74** Tucker *Lt. Nat.* (1852) II. 64 He should make himself damnably wicked as fast as he can.

2. In a 'damnable' way, execrably, confoundedly; sometimes merely as a strong intensive. (Now considered vulgar or profane.)

1596 Shaks. *1 Hen. IV*, IV. ii. 14, I haue mis-vs'd the Kings Presse damnably. **1667** Dryden *Wild Gallant* I. i, I was drunk; damnably drunk with ale. **1687** Congreve *Old Bach.* I. i, I find I am damnably in love. *c* **1753** in Hanway *Trav.* (1762) 417, I hate the dutch most damnably. **1843** Dickens *Lett.* (1880) I. 87 The bitterness of hearing those infernally and damnably good old times extolled.

damnage, obs. form of damage.

damnation (dæm'neɪʃən). Also 3–6 dampnacion, -oun, etc. [a. F. *damnation*, in 12th c. *dampnation*, *-acion*, ad. L. *dam(p)nātiōn-em*, n. of action f. *damnāre*: see damn *v.*]

†**1.** The action of condemning, or fact of being condemned (by judicial sentence, etc.); condemnation. *Obs.* exc. as in b.

a **1300** *Cursor M.* 15472 (Cott.) Þis traitur.. þat þus his suete lauerd soght vn-to dampnacion. **1382** Wyclif *Luke* xxiii. 40 Nethir thou dredist God, that thou art in the same dampnacioun? **1534** More *On the Passion* Wks 1276/1 Her offspring.. had not.. fallen in dampnacion of death. **1639** Laud *Wks.* (1849) II. 297 In a council.. Pope Alexander III condemend Peter Lombard of heresy, and he lay under that damnation for thirty and six years.

b. The damning of a play, etc. by publicly expressed disapproval.

1742 Fielding *J. Andrews* III x, Don't lay the damnation of your play to my account. **1880** Lamb *Let. to Manning* 16 Dec., I met him in the lobby immediately after the damnation of the Professor's play. **1806** H. Siddons *Maid, Wife, etc.* II. 147 The fatal cough, well known to authors as the sure forerunner of dramatic damnation.

2. *Theol.* Condemnation to eternal punishment in the world to come; the fact of being damned, or doomed to hell; spiritual ruin; perdition. (Opposed to *salvation.*)

a **1300** *Cursor M.* 16455 (Cott.) Þai ches þaim-self dampnacion.. And brocht vs til saluacion. *c* **1340** Hampole *Prose Tr.* (1866) 7 Sentence of dampnacyone ffelle one me. *c* **1420** *Chron. Vilod.* 193 Þat his sowle was sauyed from dampnacyon. **1541** Barnes *Wks.* (1573) 241/2 Hee woulde haue hell or euerlasting dampnation to hys rewarde. **1616** R. C. *Times Whistle* vi. 2481 Whose concupiscence, Like thine, deservde black helles damnation. **1667** Milton *P.L.* I. 215 That with reiterated crimes he might Heap on himself damnation. **1719** Young *Revenge* v. ii, So Lucifer broke into Paradise, And soon damnation follow'd. **1869** W. P. Mackay *Grace & Truth* (1875) 243 You are, O sinner, on the edge of eternal damnation.

b. Cause or occasion of damnation or ruin; sin incurring or deserving damnation.

1377 Langl. *P. Pl.* B. XII. 89 Goddes body.. is.. deth and dampnacioun to hem þat dyeth yuel. *c* **1386** Chaucer *Wife's T.* 211 'My love?' quod he, 'nay, nay, my dampnacioun'. **1596** Shaks. *Merch. V.* II. vii. 49 'Twere damnation To thinke so base a thought. **1605** —— *Macb.* I. vii. 20 His Vertues Will pleade like Angels, Trumpet-tongu'd against The deepe damnation of his taking off. **1712** Swift *To Dr. Sheridan*, Tell me.. What name for a maid, was the first man's damnation?

3. In profane use: **a.** as an imprecation, or exclamation of emphatic objurgation.

1604 Shaks. *Oth.* III. iii. 396 Death, and damnation, Oh! **1709** Steele *Tatler* No. 137 ¶2 [He] invokes Hell and Damnation at the Breaking of a Glass. **1747** *Gentl. Mag.* XVII. 46 The ensign more than once drank 'Damnation to all Scotchmen!' **1836** Marryat *Midsh. Easy* xii. 39 'Damnation!' cried the master, who was mad with rage.

b. as *adj.* or *adv.* = 'Damned'.

1757 Lloyd *Satyr & Pedlar* Poet. Wks. I. 57 The wit with metaphors makes bold, And tell's you he's *damnation* cold; Perhaps, that metaphor forgot, the self-same wit's *damnation* hot. **1772** *Ann. Reg.* 236 Hail hopeful Cambridge! once did all thy sons O'er tea *damnation* hot, make *damn'd* odd puns. **1843** Marryat *M. Violet* xxxvi, He would have the lives of the damned Frenchman and his damnation horse.

‖**4.** *Roman Law.* [tr. L. *damnātio*, with reference to *damnas* condemned, sentenced, bound to make a gift or contribution.] (See quot.)

1880 Muirhead *Ulpian* xxiv. §11 a, The most advantageous form of legacy is that by damnation. **1880** —— *Gaius* Digest 528 A legacy by damnation.. was one in which the testator imposed an obligation on his heir to give to the legatee the thing bequeathed, and which afforded the latter a personal claim against the heir, but no real right in the object of bequest.

Hence †**dam'nationly** *adv.* = prec. 3 b.

1762 Goldsm. *Life of Nash* (Globe ed.) 549/1, I knew him when he and I were students at Oxford, where we both studied damnationly hard.

damnatory ('dæmnətərɪ), *a.* [ad. L. *damnātōri-us*, f. *damnātōr-em*, agent-n. from *damnāre*: see damn *v.*]

1. Conveying condemnation; condemnatory.

1682 *Case Prot. Eng.* 7 The Sentence.. is not pretended to be damnatory. **1817** Coleridge *Biog. Lit.* II. xxi. 118, I do not arraign the keenness or asperity of its damnatory style. **1884** *Pall Mall G.* 11 Dec. 3/1 No one who knows Dean Burgon will be surprised to find that his view of these changes is entirely damnatory.

b. Occasioning condemnation; damning or ruinous in effect.

1858 J. B. Norton *Topics* 157 It was either a sneer or a most damnatory admission. **1862** W. M. Rossetti in *Fraser's Mag.* July 70 It is a fatal weakness in art, more damnatory by far than even the tendency to ungainliness.

2. *Theol.* Containing or uttering a sentence of damnation; consigning to damnation; damning.

1738 Neal *Hist. Purit.* IV. 617 Athanasius's creed being disliked by reason of the damnatory clauses. **1838** Arnold *Let.* in Stanley *Life & Corr.* (1844) II. viii. 122, I do not believe the damnatory clauses in the Athanasian Creed under any qualification given of them. **1882–3** Schaff *Encycl. Relig. Knowl.* I. 204/2 Nor was the absence of baptism damnatory.

Hence **'damnatorily** *adv.*

1892 J. Barlow *Irish Idylls* iv. 79 Somewhat damnatorily faint praise.

damned (dæmd, *poet.* 'dæmnɪd), *ppl. a.* [f. damn *v.* + -ed¹.]

1. †**a.** Condemned, judicially sentenced. *Obs.*

c **1440** *Promp. Parv.* 113 Dampnyd, *dampnatus.* **1495** *Act 11 Hen. VII*, c. 48 §2 Felons, fugitif, outlawed, convicte and dampned persones. **1551** Robinson tr. *More's Utop.* I. (Arb.) 49 Condempned to be common laborers.. In some partes.. these seruing men (for so be these dampned persons called) do no common worke. **1616** Brent tr. *Sarpi's Hist. Counc. Trent* (1676) 442 To shew what Books did contain damned or Apocryphal Doctrine. **1821** Lamb *Elia* Ser. I. *Witches*, The reveries of the cell-damned murderer.

b. Condemned by publicly expressed disapproval, as a play, etc.: also *transf.* of an author.

1708 Pope *Let. to Cromwell* 10 May, Damnation follows death in other men, But your damn'd Poet lives and writes agen. **1710** *Ibid.* 17 May, I am, it must be own'd.. dead in a poetical Capacity, as a damn'd Author.

2. a. *Theol.* Doomed to or undergoing eternal punishment; condemned or consigned to hell.

1393 Gower *Conf.* I. 189 O dampned man to helle. **1508** Fisher *Wks.* (1876) 20 The dampned spyrytes. **1590** Shaks. *Mids. N.* III. ii. 382 Damned spirits all, That in crosse-waies and flouds haue buriall. **1667** Milton *P.L.* II. 482 For neither do the spirits damn'd Lose all their virtue. **1882** Rossetti *Ballads & Sonn.*, *Rose Mary* II. 43 Full well hath thy treason found its goal, O thou dead body and damnèd soul.

b. *absol.* as *sb. pl.* The souls in hell, 'the lost'.

? **1507** *Communyc.* C ij, The payne.. That dampned haue in hell. **1610** Shaks. *Temp.* I. ii, It was torment To lay upon the damn'd. **1651** Hobbes *Leviath.* III. xxxviii. 242 The place of the Damned. **1827** Pollok *Course T.* v, In dreadful apparition, saw before His vision pass the shadows of the damned.

c. See quot. (Cf. F. *âme damnée.*)

a **1791** Grose *Olio, Grumbler* viii. (1796) 30 Men who attend at the Custom house, under the denomination of Damned Souls, in order, for a certain fee, to sware out any goods whatsoever for the merchants.

†**3.** Lying under, or worthy of, a curse; accursed, damnable, execrable. *Obs.* exc. as in 4, or as a conscious extension of 2.

1563 Nowell in *Liturg. Serv. Q. Eliz.* (1847) 493 Filthy and dampned Mahomet, the deceiver of the world. **1603** Knolles *Hist. Turks* (1621) 48 A damned writing was subscribed by the young emperour her son. **1605** Shaks. *Macb.* V. i. 39 Out damned spot: out I say. **1667** Sir R. Moray in *Lauderdale Papers* (1885) II. lv. 88 There is a Damned book come hither from beyond sea called Naphtali, or the Wrestlings of the Church of Scotland. **1792** Wolcott (P. Pindar) *Ode to Burke* Wks. 1812 III. 35 What Bat-like Demon, with the damn'dest spite, Springs on thy fame. **1871** B. Taylor *Faust* (1875) I. xix. 174 And so, though even God forgive, On earth a damned existence live.

4. a. Used profanely as a strong expression of reprehension or dislike, or as a mere intensive. Now usually printed 'd——d'. In the Southern U.S., a common epithet prefixed to *Yankee.*

1596 Shaks. *Tam. Shr.* V. i. 122 Where is that damned villaine Tranio? **1664** Butler *Hud.* II. ii. 832 And streight another with his Flambeaux, Gave Ralpho's o'er the eyes a damn'd blow. **1749** Fielding *Tom Jones* XVI. ii, It is a d——d lie, I never offered him anything. **1812** *Weekly Reg.* III. 45/1 Take the middle of the road or I'll hew you down, you d'——d Yankee rascal. **1818** H. B. Fearon *Sk. Amer.* 210 His friend.. said that there was 'nothing in America but d——d Yankies and rogues, and that it was not fit for a dog to live in'. **1830** Galt *Lawrie T.* (1849) II. i. 42 The pigs may do their damnedst with me. **1833** H. Barnard *Let.* 30 Apr. in *Maryland Hist. Mag.* (1918) XIII. 361 It is only surpassed by their hatred of the d——d Yankees. **1848** Thackeray *Van. Fair* lv, You would be a d—— fool not to take the place. **1865** *N.Y. Even. Post* 28 Sept. 1/1 They swore to some men of a cavalry patrol camped across the river, that they would shoot the first d——d Yankee who tried to cross the bridge.

b. as *adv.* Damnably.

1757 Lloyd *Satyr & Pedlar* Poet. Wks. I. 57 Damn'd's the superlative degree; Means that alone and nothing more ..Examples we may find enough, Damn'd high, damn'd low, damn'd fine, damn'd stuff. **1768** Foote *Devil on 2 Sticks* I. Wks. 1799 II. 251 How damn'd hot it is! **1848** Thackeray *Van. Fair.* xiii, I believe she's d——d fond of me.

c. Substantival use of superlative in phr. *one's damnedest* (*damndest*): (*a*) the worst one can do, the utmost evil or harm possible; (*b*) one's very best effort (the usual recent sense).

1830 [see damned *ppl. a.* 4 a]. **1846** J. J. Hooper *Adv. Simon Suggs* xii. 144, I.. tried my d——dst, but it wouldn't grind no way. **1891** H. Herman *His Angel* 176 Now do your damnedest at your peril. **1928** S. Vines *Humours Unreconciled* xviii. 237 She.. had done her 'damnedest' to please him. **1932** S. Gibbons *Cold Comfort Farm* xx. 268 Reuben.. gave her thirty pounds with which to do her damndest. **1955** *Times* 31 Aug. 5/3 The frenzy of fanaticism invites choir and orchestra to do their damnedest. **1958** Hayward & Harari tr. *Pasternak's Dr. Zhivago* I. vi. 183 Now, do your damnedest to get hold of a cab.

Hence †**'damnedly** *adv.*

1607 Tourneur *Rev. Trag.* III. vi, *Sup.* Fell it out so accursedly? *Amb.* So damnedly? **1675** R. Head *Art of Wheedling* 186 He mortgages his Soul to the Devil, by swearing damnedly there is not a cleaner piece of Wine between Aldgate and Westminster.

†**damnement, dampne-.** *Obs. rare.* [a. OF. *dam(p)nement*, f. *dam(p)ner.*] Damnation.

1480 Caxton *Ovid's Met.* xv. x, Cleopatra.. shal be.. deceyved of her folysshe empryse unto shame and to dampnement.

damner ('dæmə(r)). [f. damn *v.* + -er¹.] One who damns: see the verb.

1647 *Power of Keys* v. 120 Hindred from being damners of other men. **1695** Hickeringill *Wks.* (1716) I. 337 Fewer Swearers and Cursers and Damners. **1743** Garrick *Lethe* I, I was a great damner [of plays] myself, before I was damn'd. **1852** T. Parker in *Life & Corr.* I. 150 Damnation is of no advantage to the damned, only to the damner.

†**'damnifiable,** *a. Obs. rare.* [f. damnify + -able (here in active sense).] Injurious, hurtful, detrimental.

1604 T. Wright *Passions* I. v. 21 To provide for themselues all those thinges that are profitable, and to avoyde all those things which are damnifieable.

†**dam'nific,** *a. Obs.*⁻⁰ [ad. L. *damnific-us*, obs. F. *damnifique*, f. *damnum* loss, injury + *-ficus* -making, -doing: see -fic.] Causing damage or loss; injurious.

1727 Bailey vol. II, *Damnifick*, that bringeth damage.. endamaging. [Hence in Johnson and mod. Dicts.]

damnification (ˌdæmnɪfɪ'keɪʃən). [n. of action from damnify: see -ation.] The action of damnifying; infliction of injury or loss. (Now only in legal use.)

1628 Donne *Serm. John* xiv. 26 Not onely disestimation in this world, and damnification here, but damnation in the next world. **1798** Dallas *Amer. Law Rep.* II. 167 Putting the obligee in danger of being arrested is a damnification. **1875** Poste *Gaius* IV. Comm. (ed. 2) 623 Grievous damnification (*laesio*) occasioned by some exceptional condition.

damnify ('dæmnɪfaɪ), *v.* Also 6–8 dampn-. [a. OF. *damnifier* (in 14th c. *damnefier*, *dampni-*), ad. L. *damnificāre* (in Itala), to injure, f. *damnific-us* hurtful, injurious: see damnific and -fy.]

1. *trans.* To cause injury, loss, or inconvenience to; to injure, damage, hurt; to inflict injury upon, to wrong. (Very common in 17th c.; now *rare.*) **a.** in estate, condition, or circumstances. (Now chiefly in legal use.)

1512 *Act 4 Hen. VIII*, c. 19 §10 That no persone be.. in any wyse greved or dampnifyed by reason of any certificate ..excepte onely for rate and taxe beforeseid. **1574** Hellowes *Gueuara's Fam. Ep.* (1584) 225 The Judge is more damnified in his fame, than the suiter in his goods. **1614** T. Adams in Spurgeon *Treas. Dav.* Ps. x. 9 A money-man may not be damnified, but he may be damned. **1654** Gayton *Pleas. Notes* IV. ii. 181 Who could damnify her, who had nothing to lose, not so much as credit? **1737** Whiston

Josephus' Antiq. XI. vi. §5 That the King might not be damnified by the loss of the tributes. **1891** *Law Times* XC. 460/2 Induced by a fraudulent prospectus to make contracts whereby he was damnified.

†**b.** To injure physically or bodily. *Obs.*

a **1562** G. CAVENDISH *Wolsey* (1893) 229 The cross.. fallyng uppon Mayster Bonner's hed..whiche was dampnefied by the overthroweng of the crosse. **1612** WOODALL *Surg. Mate* Wks. (1653) 11 You are sure either to break them [the teeth] or to damnifie the jaw bone. **1712** M. ROGERS *Voy.* 300 Their Masts and Rigging being much damnified. **1812** J. SMYTH *Pract. Customs* (1821) 208 Hemp-seed and Lin-seed, bad, mixed, or damnified.

†**c.** To inflict injury upon in war. *Obs.*

1598 BARRET *Theor. Warres* V. i. 123 Forts..placed..in such partes as may most damnifie the enemy. **1653** H. COGAN tr. *Pinto's Trav.* lxiv. 261 The besieged were therewith mightily damnified.

†**2.** With double object: To subject (a person, etc.) to the loss of (so much money or property); to injure to a specified extent. *Obs.*

1578 A. PARCKHURST in Hakluyt *Voy.* III. 134 To grant me leave to stay here so much of their goods as they haue damnified mee. **1631** *Star Chamb. Cases* (Camden) 63 Sr Cornelius hath been damnifyed hereby more than 2000li.. **1721** *St. German's Doctor & Stud.* 188, I think him bound to give restitution..of all that they be damnified by it.

†**3.** To cause the loss of, bring to destruction or ruin. *Obs.*

1612 T. TAYLOR *Comm. Titus* i. 9 Satans kingdome shall be destroyed and damnified. *c* **1645** HOWELL *Lett.* IV. iv. (1892) 561 A most mischievous design that would have damnified not only his own soul, but destroyed the Party against whom it was intended. **1693** LUTTRELL *Brief Rel.* (1857) III. 232 The privateers and other ships were haled a shore within the land, and were damnifyed.

†**4.** *absol.* To do injury. *Obs.*

1621 AINSWORTH *Annot. Pentat.* Ex. xxi. 28 Every living creature which is in the power of man, if it shall damnifie, the owners are bound to pay for it.

†**5.** *intr.* (in passive sense): To become damaged; to spoil. *Obs.*

1712 E. COOKE *Voy. S. Sea* 312 Our Goods..would damnify staying so long.

Hence '**damnified** *ppl. a.*, '**damnifying** *vbl. sb.* and *ppl. a.*

1545 *Act 37 Hen. VIII*, c. 6 §1 A newe..kind of Vice, Displeasure, and dampnifienge of the Kings true Subjects. **1616** SURFL. & MARKH. *Country Farme* 192 They that would haue them [Melons] grow vpon beds, as lesse damnifying. **1690** LOCKE *Govt.* II. ii. §2 The damnified Person has this Power of appropriating to himself the Goods or Service of the Offender. **1780** *Banff Burgh Rec.* in Cramond *Ann. Banff* (1843) II. 233, 1400 pounds of damnified teas. **1893** *Edin. Rev.* July 61 Our author discredits all stories concerning him..which would be damnifying.

damning ('dæmɪŋ), *vbl. sb.* [-ING[1].]

1. The action of the verb DAMN, q.v.; condemnation; damnation.

c **1400** *Apol. Loll.* iii. 17 To tak þe sentence of daming. *Ibid.* xvii. 61 Vndur syn, bondage, nor damping. *c* **1400** *Rom. Rose* 6645 He etith his owne dampnyng. **1707** WYCHERLEY in *Pope's Lett.* (1735) I. 32 'Tis my infallible Pope has, or would redeem me from a poetical Damning.

2. Profane swearing: cf. DAMN *v.* 6.

1679 T. SIDEN *Hist. Sevarites* II. 16 Take heed of swearing, cursing, or damning. **1721** DE FOE *Col. Jack* (1840) 198, I heard a great deal of swearing and damning. **1914** G. B. SHAW *Pygmalion* (1916) II. 131, I dont mind your damning and blasting..but there is a certain word I must ask you not to use.

†**3.** A 'company' of jurors. *Obs.*

1486 *Bk. St. Albans* F vj b, A Dampnyng of Jurrouris.

damning ('dæmɪŋ, 'dæmnɪŋ), *ppl. a.* [-ING[2].]

1. That damns; that brings damnation.

1599 MARSTON *Sco. Villanie* I. iii. 185 To take a damning periured oath. **1795** SOUTHEY *Joan of Arc* III. 508 Such a look..As shall one day, with damning eloquence, Against the oppressor plead! **1803** T. BEDDOES *Hygëia* x. 78 A religion full of damning dogmas. **1882** A. B. BRUCE *Parab. Teaching of Christ* II. viii. (1891) 384 That the supreme virtue is love, and that the damning sin is selfish inhumanity.

†**b.** In passive sense: Incurring damnation. *Obs. rare.* (Cf. DAMN *v.* 4 c.)

1655 GURNALL *Chr. in Arm.* (1669) 283/2 [They] are so cruell to their dying damning souls, that they turn Christ their Physician out of doors.

2. That leads to or occasions condemnation or ruin. (Cf. DAMN *v.* 3.)

1798 COOKE in *Ld. Auckland's Corr.* (1862) III. 421 We took up the two Shears to-day, with damning papers. **1844** DISRAELI *Coningsby* VI. i, Without which..the statesman, the orator, the author, all alike feel the damning consciousness of being charlatans.

3. Addicted to profane swearing.

1667 PEPYS *Diary* 14 June, The most debauched, damning, swearing rogues that ever were in the Navy.

Hence '**damningly** *adv.*, '**damningness**.

1709 CHANDLER *Effort agst. Bigotry* 32 No Party of Protestants is so in the Right..that the other be damningly wrong. **1645** HAMMOND *Pract. Catech.* I. §3. 85 For the emptinesse and damningnesse of them [sins].

‖**damnosa hereditas** (dæm'nəʊsə hɪ'rɛdɪtæs). [L., = 'insolvent inheritance'.] In Law, an unprofitable legacy; now widely applied to any inheritance, tradition, etc., involving more burden than profit.

1848 WHARTON *Law Lex.* 159/1 *Damnosa hæreditas*, a disadvantageous inheritance. **1889** S. ALEXANDER *Moral Order* III. ii. 307 Murder and lying and theft are a *damnosa hereditas* left us from a time when they were legitimate institutions. **1912** J. E. C. FLITCH *Modern Dancing* vii. 98 Lottie Collins left a legacy of style behind her which her successors probably found to be a *damnosa hereditas*. **1931** *Times Lit. Suppl.* 7 May 357/1 He is not himself immune from the effects of a *damnosa hereditas* common to the species. **1935** *Ibid.* 3 Jan. 1/3 He bequeathed his resentment in a Will so complicated..that it threatened..to become the *damnosa hereditas* of *The Times*. **1938** R. G. COLLINGWOOD *Princ. Art* x. 214 Hume did not recognize the difference; and his failure has been a *damnosa hereditas* for all subsequent philosophy. **1955** *Times* 10 May 4/2 The rule that an executor was not compelled to accept a *damnosa hereditas* did not provide a reliable guide.

†**dam'nose**, *a. Obs.*—0 [ad. L. *damnōs-us*: see next.] Hurtful. So †**dam'nosity**, hurtfulness.

1727 BAILEY vol. II.

damnous ('dæmnəs), *a. Law.* [ad. L. *damnōs-us*, f. *damnum* hurt, harm, damage: see -OUS.] Of the nature of a *damnum*, i.e. causing loss or damage of any kind, whether involving a legal wrong (*injury*) or not. Hence '**damnously** *adv.*

1870 SIR J. MELLOR in *Law Rep.* 5 Exch. 249 All the injurious or damnous consequences..resulted from an act done on the land of the owner. **1884** LD. BLACKBURN in *Law Times Rep.* LII. 146/1 They have injuriously, as distinguished from damnously, affected the plaintiff's rights.

damnum ('dæmnəm). *Law.* [L., = hurt, harm, damage.] A loss or wrong: see quot. 1862.

1828 *Reg. Deb. Congress U.S.* IV. I. 424 It is a loss which gives no legal title to indemnity; it is a *damnum*, but a *damnum*, as the law has it, *absque injuria*. **1862** J. W. SMITH *Man. Com. Law* 264 Damnum is such a damage, whether pecuniary or perceptible, or not, as is capable, in legal contemplation, of being estimated by a jury. **1969** R. F. V. HEUSTON *Salmond's Law of Torts* (ed. 15) xx. 719 A person who suffers *damnum* cannot recover compensation on the basis of *injuria* suffered by another.

Damocles ('dæməʊkliːz). [L. from Gr.] Proper name, occurring in the expression *sword of Damocles*, *Damocles' sword*, used by simile of an imminent danger, which may at any moment descend upon one.

Damocles, a flatterer, having extolled the happiness of Dionysius tyrant of Syracuse, was placed by him at a banquet with a sword suspended over his head by a hair, to impress upon him the perilous nature of that happiness.

1747 *Scheme Equip. Men of War* 58 Hanging over our Heads, like Damocles Sword. **1892** *Law Times* XCII. 213/1 Little do directors and their companies know of this sword of Damocles that hangs over them.

Hence **Damo'clean** *a.*, of or as of Damocles (*erron.* **Damoclesian**).

1888 *Voice* (N.Y.) 12 Apr., This curse hangs over their homes, like a Damoclesian sword. **1963** *Times* 13 May 17/1 In particular, the Damoclesian sword of a veto from General de Gaulle hangs over the whole proceedings.

‖**damoiseau** ('dæmɪzoː). *Obs.* or *arch.* [a. OF. *damoiseau*, earlier *damei-*, *dami-*, *damoisel*:—L. *dominicellus*; the masculine corresp. to *damoisel*, DAMSEL.] A young man of gentle birth, not yet made a knight. (Occurring in 15th c. translations from French, and in modern archaists.)

c **1477** CAXTON *Jason* 5 The damoiseau Jason. *c* **1500** *Melusine* 125 Two yong & fayre damoyseaulx brethren ..'Frende', said the damoyselle, 'be they so fayre damoyseaux as ye say?' **1870** MORRIS *Earthly Par.* I. I. 194 So thou, O damoiseau, must wait; Tie up thine horse anigh the gate. **1872** E. W. ROBERTSON *Hist. Ess.* 190 The aspirant for knighthood was supposed to pass his life between 7 and 14 as a page..figuring during the next 7 years as a Damoiseau or Esquire.

damoisel, -elle, etc., obs. forms of DAMSEL.

damolic, see DAMALIC (acid).

damosel, -zel: see DAMSEL.

damosin, -zin, obs. forms of DAMSON.

damouret, var. of DAMMARET.

damourite (də'mʊəraɪt). *Min.* [Named by Delesse 1845 after the F. chemist Damour.] A hydrous potash mica, with pearly lustre, occurring in small yellowish scales.

1846 *Amer. Jrnl. Sc.* Ser. II. I. 120 *Damourite*, a new mineral. **1879** RUTLEY *Stud. Rocks* x. 134 Damourite and Sericite are hydrous potash micas usually occurring in scaly aggregates.

damp (dæmp), *sb.*[1] In 5 domp. [Corresponds with MLG. and mod.Du. and Da. *damp* vapour, steam, smoke, mod.Icel. *dampr* steam, MHG. *dampf*, *tampf*, mod.Ger. *dampf* vapour, steam; cf. also Sw. *damb* dust. The word is not known in the earlier stages of the languages, and its history in Eng. before its appearance in 1480 is unknown; it is difficult to conceive of its having come down from OE. times without appearing in writing. See DAMP *v.*]

†**1. a.** An exhalation, a vapour or gas, of a noxious kind. *Obs.* exc. as in b.

1480 CAXTON *Chron. Eng.* lxxv. 58 After this dragon shal come a goot and ther shal come oute of his nostrel a domp that shal betoken honger and grete deth of peple. **1577** B. GOOGE *Heresbach's Husb.* I. (1586) 8 b, The Fennes and Marshes, in the heate of the yeere, doo send foorth pestilent and deadly dampes. **1586** COGAN *Haven Health* 243 (*The Plague*) All infected in a manner at one instant by reason of a dampe or miste which arose within the Castle yeard. **1606** DEKKER *Sev. Sinnes* VII. (Arb.) 47 What rotten stenches, and contagious damps would strike vp into thy nosthrils? **1662** J. BARGRAVE *Pope Alex. VII* (1867) 121 It [the Catacombs] is a horrid place to go into and dangerous, for fear of damps. **1744** BERKELEY *Siris* §144 In poisonous damps or steams, wherein flame cannot be kindled, as is evident in the Grotto del Cane near Naples. **1774** GOLDSM. *Nat. Hist.* (1776) VIII. 31 Exposed..to the damps and exhalations of the earth. **1824** W. IRVING *T. Trav.* I. 52 The mode of keeping out the damps of ditch-water by burnt brandy.

b. *spec.* in coal mines: (*a*) = CHOKE-DAMP; also called ***black damp***, and ***suffocating damp***. (*b*) = FIRE-DAMP, formerly ***fulminating damp***.

1626 BACON *Sylva* §375 We see Lights will go out in the Damps of Mines. **1665** *Phil. Trans.* I. 44 The Colliers.. retired immediately and saved themselves from the eruptions of the Damp. **1670** W. SIMPSON *Hydrol. Ess.* 97 A sulphureous damp..which by the flame of a candle.. might very probably take fire. **1695** WOODWARD *Nat. Hist. Earth* IV. (1723) 227 One is called the Suffocating, the other the Fulminating Damp. **1774** PENNANT *Tour Scotl. in 1772*, 50 The damp or fiery vapour was conveyed through pipes to the open air, and formed a terrible illumination. *c* **1790** IMISON *Sch. Art* I. 106 Air that has lost its vivifying spirit is called damp..The dreadful effects of damps are known to such as work in mines. **1836** *Scenes of Commerce* 334 The miners..also meet with foul air, called by them the black damp..which suffocates the instant it is inhaled.

fig. *a* **1592** H. SMITH *Wks.* (1866) I. 367 The remembrance of death is like a damp, which puts out all the lights of pleasure. **1642** *Vind. King* i, An open Presse to cleere every imagination which is not stifled in this Dampe.

†**2.** Visible vapour; fog, mist. *Obs.*

(This being usually humid gives rise to the sense of 'moisture' in 3.)

1601 SHAKS. *All's Well* II. i. 166 Ere twice in murke and occidentall dampe Moist Hesperus hath quench'd her sleepy Lampe. **1739** LADY M. W. MONTAGU *Lett.* III. 8, I have lost all my bad symptoms, and am ready to think I could even bear the damps of London. **1742** YOUNG *Nt.-Th.* ii. 688 While rising vapours, and descending shades, With damps and darkness drown the spacious vale. **1808** J. BARLOW *Columb.* III. 654 Thou darkening sky Deepen thy damps, the fiend of death is nigh.

fig. **1625** DONNE *3rd Serm. John* i. 8 Yet there is a damp or a cloud of uncharitableness. **1751** SMOLLETT *Per. Pic.* (1779) III. lxxxi. 182 He hangs like a damp upon society, and may be properly called kill-joy. **1827** POLLOK *Course T.* III, Sin, with cold, consumptive breath, Involved it still in clouds of mortal damp.

3. a. Moisture (diffused through the air as vapour, or through a solid substance, or condensed upon a surface); dampness, humidity. (The ordinary current sense.)

[**1586** COGAN *Haven Health* ccxli, The coldnesse of stones and the dampe of the earth are both verie hurtfull to our bodies.] **1706** PHILLIPS (ed. Kersey), *Damp*, Moisture, Wetness. **1758** JOHNSON *Idler* No. 11 ⁋10 He..may set at defiance the morning mist and the evening damp. **1806** SURR *Winter in Lond.* (ed. 3) III. 66 We keep fires in all the rooms by turns, so that no damp has come to the tapestry. **1838** LYTTON *Alice* I. vi, Mrs. Merton, who was afraid of the damp, preferred staying within. **1875** JEVONS *Money* xi. 129 To corrode by exposure to air or damp.

b. with *pl.* (Usually more concrete in sense.)

[**1577** GOOGE *Heresbach's Husb.* I. (1586) 42 b, Howe so ever the Barne be, you must place it as hie as you may, least ye corne be spoyled with moysture or dampes.] **1721** R. BRADLEY *Wks. Nat.* 166 An Hygrometer in the.. Conservatory, by which we might regulate the over Moisture or Damps in the Air of the House. **1797** MRS. RADCLIFFE *Italian* xxvi, Cold damps which hung upon his forehead betrayed the agony of his mind. **1839** LONGF. *Voices of Nt.*, *L'Envoi.*, Amid the chills and damps Of the vast plain where death encamps. **1858** HAWTHORNE *Fr. & It. Jrnls.* I. 120 Covered with damps, which collected and fell upon us in occasional drops.

c. *slang.* A drink, a 'wetting'. (DAMP *v.* 5 b.)

1837 DICKENS *Pickw.* xxvii, We'll just give ourselves a damp, Sammy.

†**4.** A dazed or stupefied condition; loss of consciousness or vitality, stupor. *Obs.* (Cf. DAMP *v.* 2.)

1542 BECON *David's Harp* 150 b, He was in a trauns, that is to say in a dampe, a stupour, abashement, and soden privacion of sence or fealyng. **1552** HULOET, Traunce or dampe, *ecstasis*. **1667** WOOD *Life* (Oxf. Hist. Soc.) II. 140 [It did] strike him into a damp, and being carried thence in a chaire to his chamber, died the next day. **1667** MILTON *P.L.* XI. 293 Adam by this from the cold sudden damp Recovering, and his scatterd spirits returnd. **1711** *Vind. Sacheverell* 94 He..struck a damp upon W[hig]g[i]sm, and laid it in a State of Death. **1712** ADDISON *Spect.* No. 538 ⁋3, I felt a general Damp and a Faintness all over me.

5. A state of dejection; depression of spirits.

1606 G. W[ODCOCKE] tr. *Justin* 22 a, Their heartes were stricken into a great dampe, and were so discouraged, that [etc.]. **1647** CLARENDON *Hist. Reb.* V. (1702) I. 550 He found a great damp upon the spirit of the Governour. **1692** R. L'ESTRANGE *Josephus' Antiq.* X. xii. (1733) 275 The Dread of this Decree, put all People into a general Damp and Silence. **1760** *Impostors Detected* I. 13 [This] put a sudden damp to their zeal. **1838** PRESCOTT *Ferd. & Is.* (1846) I. ix. 398 This news struck a damp into the hearts of the Castilians. **1840** BROWNING *Sordello* V. 433 This idle damp Befits not.

6. A check, discouragement.

1587 GREENE *Carde of Fancie* Wks. 1882 IV. 59 To driue him more into doleful dumps shee returned him this damp. **1642** CHAS. I *Declar.* 12 Aug. 18 Such a dampe of Trade in the Citie. **1680–90** TEMPLE *Ess. Pop. Discontents* Wks. 1731 I. 268 Some little Damps would be given to that pestilent Humour and general Mistake. **1769** BURKE *Observ. Late State Nation* Wks. 1842 I. 92 Those accidents that cast an occasional damp upon trade. **1832** Ht. Martineau *Life in Wilds* vi. 70 A sudden damp seemed to be cast over all the plans.

7. *Comb.*, as † ***damp-hole*** (sense 1), ***-sheet*** (see quot. 1881); ***damp-proof***, ***-worn*** (sense 3) adjs.; **damp-course**, *prop.* **damp-proof course**, 'a course of some impermeable material laid on the foundation walls of a building a short distance above the level of the outside soil, to prevent the damp from rising up the walls' (Gwilt); **damp-proofed** *ppl. a.*, rendered impervious to damp; **damp-proofing** *vbl. sb.* (also *attrib.*).

1876 *Damp course [see *damp-proof course* below]. **1890** A. Whitlegge *Hygiene* vi. 150 A 'damp-course' must be provided, that is a continuous horizontal course of glazed earthenware, slate, or other impervious material. **1601** Holland *Pliny* I. 41 Which *dampe holes breathing out a deadly aire. **1870** *English Mechanic* XII. 262 **Damp-proof paper.*—Can any of your readers inform me where to obtain paper which will be unaffected by constant damp? **1889** F. E. Gretton *Memory's Harkback* 199 Provided your day be fine, and your shoes damp-proof. **1876** *Encycl. Brit.* IV. 462/2 A *damp-proof course, intended to prevent that rise of damp from the soil in the brickwork... This damp course is formed in various ways, as a layer of asphalt, or asphalt canvas, or some similar material. **1884** *Health Exhib. Catal.* 50/2 Sanitary Stoneware of every description, including.. air-bricks, damp-proof course. **1963** *Gloss. Build. Terms (B.S.I.)* 17 *Damp-proof membrane*, a damp-proof course within a floor or flat roof. **1962** *Times* 3 Dec. (Agric. Suppl.) p. iii/4 A *damp-proofed floor. **1934** H. Hiler *Notes on Technique of Painting* i. 38 Any good *damp-proofing solution, such as shellac dissolved in petrol, etc. **1962** *Listener* 22 Mar. 534/2 You can get heat-resisting, mould-resisting, and damp-proofing paints. **1881** Raymond *Mining Gloss.*, **Damp sheet*, a large sheet, placed as a curtain or partition across a gate-road to stop and turn an air-current. **1852** Dickens *Bleak Ho.* II. xviii. 5 The time and *damp-worn monuments.

damp, *sb.*[2] Variant of dam *sb.*[4]

damp (dæmp), *a.* [f. damp *sb.*[1]]

† **1.** Of the nature of, or belonging to, a 'damp' or noxious exhalation: see damp *sb.*[1] 1. *Obs.*

1634 Milton *Comus* 470 Such are those thick and gloomy shadows damp Oft seen in charnel vaults and sepulchres. **1671** —— *Samson* 8 The air, imprison'd also, close and damp, Unwholesome draught. **1733** Sir J. Lowther *Damp Air in Coal-pit* in *Phil. Trans.* XXXVIII. 112 It is to be observed that this sort of Vapour, or damp Air, will not take Fire except by Flame.

† **2.** Affected with or showing stupefaction or depression of spirits; dazed, stupefied. *Obs.* or *arch.*

1590 Greene *Never too late* Canzone, An object twice as bright, So gorgeous as my senses all were damp [*rime* lamp]. **1667** Milton *P.L.* i. 523 With looks Down cast and damp. *Ibid.* v. 65 Mee damp horror chil'd. **1697** Dryden *Virg. Æneid* vi. 85 The trembling Trojans hear, O're-spread with a damp sweat and holy fear. **1843** J. Martineau *Chr. Life* (1867) 473 Murky doubts and damp short-sightedness. **1855** Thackeray *Newcomes* liv, The dinner was rather a damp entertainment.

3. Slightly wet as with steam, suspended vapour, dew, or mist; holding water in suspension or absorption; moist, humid. (The ordinary current sense.)

1706 Phillips (ed. Kersey), *To Damp*, to make damp, or moist. **1735** Berkeley *Querist* §412 A cold, damp, sordid habitation, in the midst of a bleak country. **1748** F. Smith *Voy. Disc. N.W. Pass.* I. 21 The Weather.. disagreeably damp from the great Wetting of the Fog. **1874** Kingsley *Lett.* (1878) II. 429 We have come out of intense winter into damp spring. *Mod.* A cold caught by sleeping in a damp bed.

4. As quasi-adv. in ***damp-dry*** v. trans. and intr., to dry to the state of being only damp.

1956 *N.Y. Times* 15 Jan. 65 (Advt.), It *automatically* fills, washes, rinses, damp dries, shuts itself off! **1960** *Daily Mail* 9 Feb. 8/8 Incidentally, a spin drier damp dries. **1961** M. Beadle *These Ruins are Inhabited* (1963) iii. 39 If fed a shilling, this latter [*sc.* a gas heater] will yield enough warmth to damp-dry socks draped on the rungs of a chair.

damp (dæmp), *v.* [f. damp *sb.*[1]; frequent from *c* 1550. Ger. *dampfen*, Du. *dampen*, also go back to the 16th c.; in Ger. a causal *dempfen* appears to go back to OHG. (*demphan*:—**dampian*). For *dampped* in *Allit. Poems* B. 989, see dump.]

1. a. *trans.* To affect with 'damp', to stifle, choke, extinguish; to dull, deaden (fire, sound, etc.). Also *fig.*

1564 tr. *Jewel's Apol. Ch. Eng.* iv. (Parker Soc.) 82 Their own matter is damped, and destroyed in the word of God as if it were in poison [*in veneno extingui vident et suffocari*]. **1597** Hooker *Eccl. Pol.* v. lxiii. §2 An euill moral disposition .. dampeth the very light of heauenly illumination. **1626** Bacon *Sylva* §147 All shutting in of Air, where there is no competent Vent, dampeth the Sound. **1637** Shirley *Lady of Pleas.* iv. i, Her phlegm would quench a furnace, and her breath Would damp a musket ball. **1705** Leuwenhoek in *Phil. Trans.* XXV. 2159 If we take a piece of Wood-coal, that has been damp'd or extinguished. **1818** *Blackw. Mag.* II. 528 Having damped his own appetite with a couple of slices. *Mod.* To damp a fire with small coal.

b. *to damp down* (a fire or furnace): to cover or fill it with small coal, ashes, or coke, so as to check combustion and prevent its going out, when not required for some time. Also *fig.*

1869 J. Martineau *Ess.* II. 278 Fire which must not be permitted to damp itself down. **1884** *Pall Mall G.* 20 Feb. 2/1 The notices terminate at the end of the month.. and the furnaces will be damped down. *Ibid.* 28 Aug. 1/1 Mr. Gladstone's speeches may tend to damp down the agitation.

c. *Acoustics, Music*, etc. To stop the vibrations of a string or the like; to furnish (the strings of a pianoforte) with dampers. In wider use: to impose or to act as a resisting influence on (an oscillation or vibration of any kind) so that it is either progressively reduced in amplitude or, if the resistance is sufficiently great, converted into non-oscillatory return to an equilibrium position; also used with the oscillating body as obj. So *to damp out*: to damp, to extinguish by damping. So **damped** *ppl. a.*

1840 *Penny Cycl.* XVIII. 140 A piece of cloth.. to damp or stop the string [in a clavichord]. **1877** *Phil. Mag.* III. 482 The measurement of a resistance according to Weber's method of 'damped vibrations'. **1883** A. J. Hipkins in Grove *Dict. Mus.* III. 636 The higher treble of the piano is not now damped. **1897** Nichols & Franklin *Elem. Physics* III. xv. 168 The vibrations of a heavy, elastic body, such as a tuning fork, are but slightly damped. **1899** *Phil. Trans. R. Soc.* A. CXCII. 247 Any natural vibrations of the suspended system would be rapidly damped out. **1911** *Encycl. Brit.* XX. 348/1 This needle.. must be so damped that when the current is cut off it returns to zero at once without overshooting the mark. **1922** Glazebrook *Dict. Appl. Physics* II. 1040/2 The above methods of detection are appropriate for the reception of damped wave signals but not for continuous wave signals. **1927** E. G. Richardson *Sound* iv. 121 All vibrations of solids of whatever type are damped by internal friction. **1929** E. Mallett *Telegr. & Teleph.* xii. 320 The discharge current is oscillatory and of the 'damped wave' form. **1935** F. J. Camm *Pract. Motorist's Encycl.* 82/2 The leaf-springs of the car's suspension system.. damp-out a large proportion of the road shocks and vibrations suffered by the wheels of the car. **1940** *Illustr. London News* CXCVI. 576, I was very impressed by the springing, which damped-out all but exceptionally bad bumps on the road. **1950** *Engineering* 7 Apr. 397/1 Spring-loaded clamping devices heavily damped by hydraulic means to provide virtually solid clamping. **1957** *Encycl. Brit.* XXIII. 175/1 The low elasticity of the gut causes these high constituents [of the note] to be quickly damped. **1961** Bickley & Talbot *Introd. Theory Vibrating Systems* iv. 37 We consider the typical case of a mass *m* controlled by a spring of stiffness *s* damped by a resistance proportional to the speed.

d. *Magnetism.* To stop the oscillations of a magnetic needle by placing a mass of conducting metal near it.

1879 Thomson & Tait *Nat. Phil.* I. i. §379 The oscillations of a magnetized needle about its position of equilibrium are 'damped' by placing a plate of copper below it.

† **2.** To stifle (the faculties) with noxious 'fumes'; to stupefy, benumb, daze. *Obs.*

1570 Dee *Math. Pref.* 1 The fantasies of those hearers were dampt. **1633** T. Adams *Exp. 2 Pet.* ii. 20 (1865) 559 The lusts of the flesh, like the vapours of a replete stomach rising up and damping the brain. **1716** Bentley *Serm.* xi. 375 We may damp or stifle them [our Faculties] by Sloth and Neglect. **1726** Leoni tr. *Alberti's Archit.* I. 5 a, The Understanding can never be clear, the Spirits being dampt and stupify'd.

3. To deaden to restrain the ardour or energy of; to depress, deject, discourage, check.

a. persons, their spirits, zeal, hopes, etc.

1548 Udall, etc. *Erasm. Par. Matt.* iii. (R.), That.. they that were puffed vp before.. should bee damped, and be brought lowe. **1654** Trapp *Comm. Job* xiii. 15 As that woman of Canaan.. who would not be damped or discouraged with Christs.. silence. **1654** Whitlock *Zootomia* 24 Nor shall their scorne spoyle good purposes, by damping my resolutions. **1748** *Anson's Voy.* i. i. 11 Our hopes of a speedy departure were even now somewhat damped. **1766** Goldsm. *Vic. W.* v, This is the way you always damp my girls and me when we are in spirits. **1821** Clare *Vill. Minstr.* I. 166 Sorrow damps my lays. **1876** J. H. Newman *Hist. Sk.* II. ii. ii. 242 How little his personal troubles had damped his evangelical zeal. **1887** Frith *Autobiog.* I. xxiii. 329 Damped by the indifference of my artist-friends.

b. actions, projects, trade, etc. Now *rare.*

1548 Udall, etc. *Erasm. Par. Luke* xvi. (R.), To dampe y[e] taunting mockes of such persones. **1622** Bacon *Hen. VII*, 75 To stop and dampe Informations upon Penall Lawes, by procuring Informations by collusion. **1689** C. Mather in *Andros Tracts* (1869) 13 The Courses immediately taken to damp and spoyl our Trade. **1787** T. Jefferson *Writ.* (1859) II. 89 To damp that freedom of communication which the resolution of Congress.. was intended to re-establish. **1832** Austin *Jurispr.* (1879) I. vi. 301 If they think.. that a political institution damps production and accumulation.

† **4.** To envelop in fog or mist; also *fig.*

1629 Donne *Serm. Matt.* xi. 6 If my religion did wrap me in a continual cloud.. damp me in a continual vapour, smoke me in a continual sourness.

5. a. To make moist or humid, to wet as steam, vapour, mist, or dew does; to moisten.

1671 R. Bohun *Wind* 14 They [winds from South] damp innen and paper, though never so carefully guarded from the Air. **1789** W. Buchan *Dom. Med.* (ed. 11) 129 That baneful custom said to be practised in many inns, of damping sheets, and pressing them in order to save washing. **1868** Hawthorne *Amer. Note-Bks.* (1879) I. 180 The dew damped the road. **1875** Ure *Dict. Arts* III. 648 The paper used in printing is always damped before being sent to the press, wet paper taking the ink considerably better than dry.

b. *refl.* To take a drink, 'wet one's whistle'. *slang.*

1862 Lowell *Biglow P.* Poems 1890 II. 283 A tent.. Where you could go, ef you wuz dry, an' damp ye in a minute.

6. *Gardening. to damp off* (intr.): Of plants: To rot or go off from damp; to fog off.

1846 Mrs. Loudon *Gardening for Ladies* 90 Cuttings when thus treated are very apt to damp off. **1881** *Gard. Chron.* XVI. 690 See that none of the spikes touch the glass or they may speedily damp off.

damp, obs. var. dam *sb.*[1]; obs. (erron.) form of damn.

dampen ('dæmp(ə)n), *v.* (Now chiefly *U.S.*) [f. damp *a.* + -en, or derivative form of damp *v.*]

1. *trans.* To dull, deaden, diminish the force or ardour of, depress, deject; = damp *v.* 1, 3.

c **1630** Jackson *Creed* vi. i. Wks. VI. 36 By which the fervency of better spirits devotion is so much dampened. **1633** P. Fletcher *Purple Isl.* vii. xxxiii, Himself dampens the smiling day. **1813** W. Irving *Life & Lett.* (1864) I. xviii. 296 The miserable accounts from the frontier dampened in some measure the public zeal. **1824** Landor *Imag. Conv.* vii. Wks. 1846 I. 28 His genius hath been dampened by his adversities. **1885** *Century Mag.* 427/1 This adversity seemed to dampen the ardor of the crew.

2. *Magnetism.* = damp *v.* 1 d.

1879 G. Prescott *Sp. Telephone* 36 The object in using the rubber is to dampen the movement of the disk.

3. To make damp, moisten; = damp *v.* 5.

1827 J. F. Cooper *Red Rover* I. xv. 246 It is seldom that .. he is dampened with salt water. **1885** G. H. Boughton *Sk. Rambles Holland* v. 77 The high tide must somewhat dampen the poor departed [in a churchyard]. **1902** C. C. Munn *Rockhaven* i. 9 We took a handful o' matches, an' dampenin' 'em, rubbed the ends round the eyes.. o' the critter. **1906** H. D. Pittman *Belle of Bluegrass C.* xxi. 302 The heavy dews.. fell upon her, dampening her hair.

4. *intr.* To become dull or damp.

1686 Goad *Celest. Bodies* ii. xi. 305 Fog, close, dampning, windy. **1857** Lowell *Poems, Captive*, Yet he came not, and the stillness Dampened round her like a tomb.

Hence **'dampening** *vbl. sb.* and *ppl. a.*; **'dampener** (*U.S.*), a contrivance for damping linen, etc.; also *fig.*

1814 Byron *Lara* i. xxviii, And o'er his brow the dampening heart-drops threw The sickening iciness of that cold dew. **1836** *New Monthly Mag.* XLVI. 204 The gallantry and beauty of Tuscany sped through the dampening air. **1864** Lowell *Lincoln* Wks. 1890 V. 178 To withstand the inevitable dampening of checks, reverses, delays. **1887** *Sci. Amer.* 26 Mar. 202/2 A seam dampener has been patented.. for use in laundries, etc. **1920** *Glasgow Herald* 5 Nov. 11 Socialism has received a decided dampener.

damper ('dæmpə(r)). [f. damp *v.* + -er.] That which damps, in various senses of the vb.

1. a. Something that damps or depresses the spirits, etc.; also, a person who does the same.

1748 Richardson *Clarissa* Wks. 1883 VII. 282, I very early discharged shame, that cold water damper to an enterprising spirit. **1749** H. Walpole in Hissey *Holiday on Road* (1887) 140 Sussex is a great damper of curiosity. **1818** *Blackw. Mag.* II. 528 Out of sixteen people, five dampers were present. **1822** Hazlitt *Table-t.* Ser. ii. xii. (1869) 248 This is a damper to sanguine and florid temperaments. **1855** Thackeray *Newcomes* xxvi, I feel myself very often an old damper in your company.

b. Something that takes off the edge of appetite.

1804 Mar. Edgeworth *Pop. Tales, Limerick Gloves*, In the kitchen, taking his snack by way of a damper. **1811** Lamb *Edax on Appetite*, I endeavour to make up by a damper, as I call it, at home before I go out.

2. a. A piece of mechanism in a pianoforte for 'damping' or stopping the vibrations of the strings, consisting of a small piece of wood or wire covered with cloth or felt, which rests against the strings corresponding to each key, and is raised or withdrawn from them when the key is pressed down.

1783 *Specif. J. Broadwood's Patent* No. 1379, *b*, *b*, are the dampers, which also is fixt under the strings. **1856** Mrs. C. Clarke tr. *Berlioz' Instrument.* 72 The sign ⊕ indicates that the dampers must be replaced by quitting the pedal.

b. 'The mute of a horn and other brass wind instruments' (Stainer & Barrett *Dict. Mus. Terms*).

c. In an organ: a thumping-board (see thumping *vbl. sb.* b).

1879, 1881 [see thumping *vbl. sb.* b].

3. A metal plate made to turn or slide in a flue or chimney, so as to control the combustion by regulating or stopping the draught.

1788 *Specif. Gardner's Patent* No. 1642 These registers or dampers are enclosed in the chimney. **1791** Beddoes in *Phil. Trans.* LXXXI. 174 He first turned the flame from off the metal, which is done by letting down a damper upon the chimney. **1823** Moore *Fables, Holy Alliance* 86 Those trusty, blind machines.. by a change as odd as cruel, Instead of dampers, served for fuel! **1829** R. Stuart *Anecd. Steam Engines* I. 269 The heat of the furnace under the boiler was rudely regulated in both machines by a damper.

4. a. *Magnetism.* (See quot., and cf. damp *v.* 1 d.)

1881 Maxwell *Electr. & Magn.* II. 344-5 A metallic surface, called a Damper, is sometimes placed near a magnet for the express purpose of damping or deadening its vibrations. We shall therefore speak of this kind of resistance as *Damping.*

b. *Electr. Engin.* One of a set of short-circuited conductors in the pole faces of a synchronous electric motor or generator which resist any tendency of the machine to 'hunt', i.e. oscillate by running alternately faster and slower than the synchronous speed. Also ***damper bar***, ***winding***.

1906 A. RUSSELL *Altern. Curr.* II. 191 In order to prevent phase swinging, Hutin and Leblanc provided the field magnets with 'amortisseurs', or 'dampers', which tend to prevent any relative change between the positions of the magnetic field due to the armature and the field due to the field magnets. **1920** *Whittaker's Electr. Engineer's Pocket-Bk.* (ed. 4) 223 Care must be taken that the damper bars have not the same pitch as the armature slots as this might cause ripples in the c.c. pressure. **1934** WEBSTER, Damper winding. **1964** N. N. HANCOCK *Matrix Analysis of Electr. Machinery* xi. 198 The damper windings of synchronous machines are mechanically simple but electrically complicated devices. *Ibid.* 201 For synchronous motors it may be a wholly false assumption, since high resistance dampers may be used to obtain adequate starting torque.

c. Any device designed to damp mechanical vibrations; *spec.* a shock-absorber on a motor-car.

1929 NEWTON & STEEDS *Motor Vehicle* xxix. 332 Designers..try to reduce the friction [in a laminated spring] to the minimum, and they introduce additional friction when it is required by external devices which are called 'dampers'. **1935** W. K. WILSON *Pract. Soln. Torsional Vibration Probl.* vii. 365 There is a definite setting for every damper at which the maximum reduction of vibration amplitude is obtained. **1952** A. W. JUDGE *Mod. Motor Engineer* (ed. 5) III. iii. 59 In most cases this damping action is improved by the use of dampers or shock absorbers fitted between the axles and the chassis frame. **1958** *Engineering* 7 Mar. 295/1 The car was tried without any suspension dampers at all. **1958** *Chambers's Techn. Dict.* Add. 971/1 Yaw damper suppresses directional oscillations in high-speed aeroplanes, while a roll damper does likewise laterally. **1961** BICKLEY & TALBOT *Introd. Theory Vibrating Systems* x. 122 In many mechanical systems friction is unwanted, and minimized, but in some cases vibration dampers are a feature of the design.

5. Any contrivance for damping or moistening.

e.g. An appliance for moistening the gummed back of postage stamps; one for damping paper for a copying-press, for cleaning slates, etc.

1845 *Mech. Mag.* XLII. 285 Postage stamp, wafer, and label damper. **1854** *Ibid.* LXI. 86 The damper may be left in any position when not in use, as the water will not of itself run out.

6. Chiefly *Austral.* and *N.Z.* A simple kind of unleavened cake or bread made, for the occasion, of flour and water and baked in hot ashes.

1827 P. CUNNINGHAM *Two Years in N.S.W.* II. xxviii. 190 The farm-men usually bake their flour into flat cakes, which they call dampers, and cook these in the ashes. **1833** STURT *Two Exped. S. Australia* II. 203 While drinking their tea and eating their damper. **1843** S. STEPHENS *Let.* 4 Sept. 169 (MS.), Flour, from which I make what we call 'dampers' in a frying pan. **1852** MUNDY *Antipodes* vi. (1855) 149 The Australian bush-bread, a baked unleavened dough, called damper—a damper, sure enough, to the stoutest appetite. **1891** *Melbourne Argus* 7 Nov. 13/5 When you've boiled your billy and cooked your damper you put out the fire and move ..on to camp. **1918** KIPLING *Land & Sea T.* (1923) 96 Wonderful hot cakes called 'dampers'. **1939** J. MULGAN *Man Alone* (1949) xiv. 138 He..then cooked a damper of flour and oatmeal. **1944** W. E. HARNEY *Taboo* (ed. 3) 37 You eat up, old men. I will wait for mine to cool off—hot dampers make me sick. **1964** F. CHICHESTER *Lonely Sea & Sky* 49 In order to bake 'damper', which is unleavened bread, we used to hang the oven high above the log fire and pile hot ashes on the lid.

7. A till, a cash register; a drawer in which cash is kept. *slang.*

1846 R. L. SNOWDEN *Magistrate's Assistant* 344 To rob a till, to pinch a lob: or draw a damper. *Ibid.*, A till, a lob or damper. **1944** D. RUNYON *Runyon à la Carte* (1946) 104 Go over to his hotel..and get the night clerk to open his damper.

8. *Comb.* **a.** in sense 2 a, as ***damper-crank***, ***-rail***, ***-stick***, †***-stop***; **damper-pedal**, that pedal in a pianoforte which raises all the dampers, the 'loud pedal'. **b.** in sense 3, as **damper-regulator**, a contrivance by which the heat of the furnace or the pressure of steam is made to control the damper; **damper weight** (see quot.).

1840 *Penny Cycl.* XVIII. 140 Fig. 2, *e*, Damper stick. *Ibid.* 141 The damper-stop raised the dampers from the strings. *Ibid.*, Fig. 10, *k*, Damper Crank. *Ibid.* 142 Fig. 11, *g*, Damper rail. **1874** KNIGHT *Dict. Mech.* 676 The damper-regulators which act by the pressure of steam are of three or more kinds. **1888** *Lockwood's Dict. Mech. Engin.* 102 *Damper weight*, a weight used to counterbalance that of the damper of a steam boiler in order to render it easy of adjustment.

'dampiness. *rare.* [f. DAMPY *a.* + -NESS.] The state of being 'dampy' or somewhat damp.

1830 *Blackw. Mag.* XXVIII. 886 You know not whether it be rain, snow, or sleet, that drenches your clothes in dampiness.

damping ('dæmpɪŋ), *vbl. sb.* [-ING[1].] **1. a.** The action of the verb DAMP, q.v. Also *attrib.*, as in ***damping-machine***, ***damping-plate*** (= DAMPER 3).

1756 TOLDERVY *Two Orphans* III. 172 The flames, by slight damping, soon became the more violent. **1816** J. SMITH *Panorama Sc. & Art* II. 312 The bottom of the furnace..the holes of the damping plate. **1874** KNIGHT *Dict. Mech.*, *Damping-machine. 1. (Printing.)* A machine for damping sheets of paper previous to printing..2. A machine in which starched goods are moistened previous to running them through the calendering-machine.

b. The action of damping an oscillation or an oscillating body (also ***damping out***: see DAMP *v.* 1 c, d); the resistance to an oscillation; also, the amount of this, as measured by the rate at which the oscillation diminishes in amplitude.

1870 *Phil. Mag.* XXXIX. 435 An oscillatory current.. sustains itself twice as long against the damping action of resistance as a comparatively steady current of the same maximum value. **1874** *Ibid.* XLVII. 296 The damping effect which the multiplier exerts on the swing of the needle. **1877** RAYLEIGH *Theory of Sound* I. iii. 57 The vibrations of a tuning fork properly constructed and mounted are subject to very little damping. **1879** *Encycl. Brit.* X. 51/1 By damping is meant the decrease of the extent of the oscillations of the galvanometer needle arising from the dissipation of energy through the resistance of the air, the action of currents induced in neighbouring metallic circuits, the viscosity of the suspension fibre, and so on. **1881** [see DAMPER 4]. **1883** ATKINSON tr. *Ganot's Physics* (ed. 11) 832 The greater the masses of metal, and the more closely they surround the magnet, the stronger is the damping. **1907** J. ERSKINE-MURRAY *Handbk. Wireless Telegr.* i. 28 Damping or decrease of amplitude is due to two causes—firstly, to dissipation of energy, as heat, in the local circuits; secondly, to radiation. **1912** *Q. Rev.* July 242 The damping-out of oscillations cannot be expected to be as rapid. **1945** *Electronic Engin.* XVII. 455 Resulting in better damping of the receiver diaphragm and consequently suppression of the effects of resonance. **1958** *Van Nostrand's Scientific Encycl.* (ed. 3) 476/2 The metal specimen is vibrated and the rate of damping-out of the vibrations observed. **1967** CONDON & ODISHAW *Handbk. Physics* (ed. 2) II. iii. 22/1 As the magnitude of the damping is increased, the rate of decay of the oscillations becomes greater..until..the motion becomes aperiodic and is said to be critically damped.

2. ***damping off***, the collapse of seedlings or cuttings caused by any of several parasitic fungi and encouraged by excessive moisture in the plant's environment. (Cf. DAMP *v.* 6.)

1899 G. MASSEE *Text-bk. Plant Dis.* 54 The term 'damping off' is applied to a disease of seedlings, characterised by the falling over and dying of the plantlets. **1928** F. T. BROOKS *Plant Dis.* i. 4 Parasitic attack of seedling plants at soil level often causes 'damping off'. **1970** LIEBSCHER & KOEHLER tr. *Fröhlich & Rodewald's Pests & Dis. Tropical Crops* 293 Symptoms of damping-off appear in seedbeds. **1971** *Daily Colonist* (Victoria, B.C.) 13 Mar. 38/4 The dreaded 'damping-off' disease, a soil-borne infection that attacks and rots the stems of small seedling plants just at soil level.

3. *attrib.*, as (sense 1 b) **damping capacity** [tr. G. *dämpfungsfähigkeit* (O. Foeppl 1923)], the ability of a metal or other solid to absorb vibrational energy and dissipate it as heat; **damping coefficient, constant,** or **factor,** any number representing the degree to which an oscillation is damped, usu. defined as the reciprocal of the time in which the amplitude decreases by a factor *e*; **damping winding** = DAMPER 4 b.

1931 *Proc. Amer. Soc. Testing Materials* XXXI. II. 157 Engineering materials..are able to dissipate energy without failure when subjected to cyclic stresses below the fatigue limit... This property is known as 'mechanical hysteresis effect', 'internal friction' (of solids), or '*damping capacity'. The latter nomenclature was proposed by O. Foeppl in 1923, who offered the following definition: 'Damping Capacity' is the amount of work dissipated into heat by a unit volume of the material during a completely reversed cycle of unit stress. This damping capacity is measured in inch-pounds per cubic inch per cycle. **1953** S. P. TIMOSHENKO *Hist. Strength of Materials* xii. 378 The damping capacity of metals and its relation to fatigue strength. **1959** *Chambers's Encycl.* X. 326/2 Damping Capacity..is low in a sonorous metal such as bell-metal, and high in a 'dead' metal like lead. **1906** J. A. FLEMING *Princ. Electr. Wave Telegr.* i. 21 The Napierian logarithm of the ratio of any maximum current or ordinate to the next maximum in the opposite direction multiplied by twice the frequency, gives us the value of the *damping coefficient. **1929** W. E. DALBY *Balancing of Engines* (ed. 4) viii. 259 The damping coefficients derived from the dynamic magnifier are more likely to approximate to the damping of the loaded bridge than damping coefficients determined from the residual oscillations. **1922** F. F. FOWLE *Stand. Handbk. Electr. Engineers* (ed. 5) xxiv. 1963 The *damping constant of a circuit is a measure of the ratio of the dissipative to the reactive component of its admittance or impedance. **1906** J. A. FLEMING *Princ. Electr. Wave Telegr.* iii. 162 The *damping factor *a* is a quantity the dimensions of which are those of the reciprocal of a time, whilst the logarithmic decrement is a mere numeric. **1920** *Whittaker's Electr. Engineer's Pocket-Bk.* (ed. 4) 224 *Damping windings are also fitted on synchronous generators..to damp out pulsations due to variations in the armature ampere-turns.

damping ('dæmpɪŋ), *ppl. a.* [-ING[2].] That damps, in various senses: see DAMP *v.*

1607 WALKINGTON *Opt. Glass* 28 The damping fumes that the Sun elevates from bogges. **1691–8** NORRIS *Pract. Disc.* 151 What a damping Thought must it be for such a Man to consider [etc.]. **1844** DICKENS *Mart. Chuz.* xiii, It was somewhat of a damping circumstance to find the room full of smoke. **1878** M. C. JACKSON *Chaperon's Cares* I. xi. 153 Clarissa's presence generally has a slightly damping effect upon Forster. **1928** S. P. TIMOSHENKO *Vibration Probl. Engin.* i. 22 These damping forces may arise from several different sources, such as air or fluid friction, internal friction of the material of the vibrating body, or friction between sliding surfaces. **1936** W. HEITLER *Quantum Theory of Radiation* i. 34 But because of the damping force the amplitude of the oscillator will decrease. **1958** C. G. WILSON *Electr. & Magn.* v. 137 These oscillations cease when all the energy of the coil is dissipated in overcoming the damping forces present.

dampish ('dæmpɪʃ), *a.* [orig. f. DAMP *sb.*[1] + -ISH (cf. *boyish*): subsequently treated as if f. DAMP *a.*]

†**1.** Of the nature of, or infested with, exhalations or (noxious) vapours; vaporous, foggy, misty. *Obs.*

1577 B. GOOGE *Herebach's Husb.* I. (1586) 8 b, All waters commonly with dampishe vapours in Summer..doo infect both man and beast with pestilence. **1596** SPENSER *Hymn Heav. Beaut.* 165 The darke And dampish aire. —— *F.Q.* IV. viii. 34 The drowzie humour of the dampish night. *a* **1649** DRUMM. OF HAWTH. *Poems* Wks. (1711) 13 His caves and dampish bow'rs.

†**2.** *fig.* **a.** Of stifling or extinguishing nature (cf. DAMP *v.* 1). **b.** ? Stifled, choked. *Obs.*

1603 H. CROSSE *Vertues Commw.* (1878) 123 Lampes.. which with dampish idlenesse are soon put out. **1604** T. M. *Black Bk.* Middleton's Wks. (Bullen) VIII. 33 With a whey-countenance, short stops, and earthen dampish voice, the true counterfeits of a dying cullion.

3. Somewhat damp or moist.

[**1577** GOOGE *Heresbach's Husb.* IV. (1586) 192 b, Set them up in some moist and dampish place.] **1641** BEST *Farm. Bks.* (Surtees) 24 Stone floores are allwayes moist and dampish. **1727** BAILEY vol. II, *Dampish*, something damp or moist or wet. **1803** *Trans. Soc. Encourag. Arts* XXI. 302 Wood placed in dampish situations. **1963** *Times* 23 May 4/4 A dampish pitch and slow outfield at the start.

Hence **'dampishly** *adv.*, **'dampishness.**

1615 MARKHAM *Eng. Housew.* II. iii. (1668) 109 Let them be dampishly moistened with Damask Rose-water. **1617** —— *Caval.* VI. 24 It shall defend him from the colde dampishnes of the earth. **1626** BACON *Sylva* §937 To put a Lay of Chalke between the Bricks, to take away all Dampishnesse. **1727** BAILEY vol. II, *Dampishness*, moistness, wetness. **1906** *Westm. Gaz.* 7 Apr. 2/2 The leading lady solemnly wipes the inside of her glass..and breathes into it—breathes, I fancy, rather dampishly.

damply ('dæmplɪ), *adv. rare.* [f. DAMP *a.* + -LY[2].] In a damp manner.

1887 *American* XIV. 234 The house was damply cold. **1891** C. DUNSTAN *Quita* II. II. v. 115 It was damply, foggily cold.

dampnacion, dampne, etc., obs, ff. DAMNATION, DAMN, etc.

dampnage, obs. form of DAMAGE.

dampness ('dæmpnɪs). [f. DAMP *a.* + -NESS.] The condition or quality of being damp; moistness, humidity; moisture.

1665 MANLEY *Grotius' Low C. Warres* 423 The dampness of the fields. **1687** DRYDEN *Hind. & P.* III. 508 Nor need they fear the dampness of the sky..'Twas only water thrown on sails too dry. **1765** A. DICKSON *Treat. Agric.* (ed. 2) 55 A careful observer, in a night when there is a great dew, will perceive a dampness upon every surface. **1848** THACKERAY *Van. Fair* xxii, The valet..cursing the rain and the dampness of the coachman who was steaming beside him.

dampson, obs. form of DAMSON.

dampy ('dæmpɪ). *a.* [f. DAMP *sb.*[1] + -Y.]

†**1.** Full of, or of the nature of (noisome or gloomy) vapour or mist; foggy. *Obs.*

1600 TOURNEUR *Transp. Metamorph.* v, O see how dampy shewes yond' torche's flame. *Ibid.* lxxx, How like blacke Orcus lookes this dampy cave. **1605** DRAYTON *Man in Moon* 363 The dampy Mist, From earth arising. **1729** SAVAGE *Wanderer* III. 284 Dispers'd, the dark and dampy vapours fly.

fig. a **1627** HAYWARD *Edw. VI* (1630) 141 To dispell any dampie thoughts which the remembrance of his unkle might raise.

b. Of a mine: Infested with 'damps' or noxious gases.

18.. WEALE (cited in *Encycl. Dict.*), When foul gases do not move freely by the ordinary natural ventilation in a colliery, it is said to be dampy.

2. Affected with moisture; somewhat damp.

a **1691** BOYLE *Wks.* VI. 397 (R.) Very dampy vapours about the mouth of the baroscope. **1710** PHILIPS *Pastorals* iii. 42 His beauteous Limbs upon the dampy Clay. **1820** *Blackw. Mag.* VII. 677 The clay-hole you live in, cold, dirty and dampy.

damsax: see DANISH AXE.

damsel ('dæmzəl), **damosel** ('dæmɒzɛl). Forms: α. 3 dameisele, 3–4 damaisele, 4 dammaisele, 3–5 damaysele, 5 -elle; β. 4–6 damesel, -ele, -elle, damysel, -ele, -elle, damisel, -elle, 5 dammisel, *Sc.* damyseill, 6 *Sc.* damicel, -ell; γ. 5–7 damsell, 6– damsel; δ. 4–6 damoysele, -el, damoisele, -el, (9 damoiselle); ε. 6–7 (9) damosel, -elle, damozel(l, -elle, (6 damusel); ζ. 7 dam'zell, 7–8 dam'sel. [Early ME. *dameisele*, *damaisele*, a. OF. *dameisele* (*damisele*) (12th c.), later *damoisele*, *-elle* (the only form in Cotgrave), *demoiselle* (14th c.). The OF. *dameisele* was a new formation from *dame*, instead of the popular *danzele*, *dansele*, *doncele* = Pr. and It. *donzella*, Sp. *doncella*:—late L. **dominicella*, med.L. *domnicella*, *domicella*, dim. of *domina* mistress, lady, fem. of *dominus* lord. (There is a 10th c. F. instance of the learned form *domnizelle*.) In Eng. the middle syllable was reduced from *ei* (*ai*), to *i*, *ĕ*, and finally disappeared. The variant *damoiselle* was introduced in 15th c. from Parisian F. (by Lydgate, Caxton, etc.), and gave rise here to *damosel*, *damozel*, so frequent in 16–17th c., and affected in 19th c. in sense 1. See also DONZEL.]

I. 1. A young unmarried lady; originally one of noble or gentle birth, but gradually extended as a respectful appellation to those of lower rank. Now merged in sense 2; but modern poets and romantic writers (led by Sir W. Scott) have recalled the 16–17th c. *damosel*, *damozel*, to express a more stately notion than is now conveyed by *damsel*.

α. [**1292** BRITTON I. xix. §5 Des enfauntz madles, damaysels et vedues.] *c* **1290** *S. Eng. Leg.* I. 84/37 Þe Iustise bi-heold þat maide..'Dameisele,' he seide, 'ȝwat art þou?' **1297** R. GLOUC. (Rolls) 1492 Þe nobloste damaisele þat was in eni londe. *a* **1450** *Knt. de la Tour* cxx. 166 The yonge damayselle, the whiche the knight hadde refused.

β. **1300–40** *Cursor M.* 3837 (Cott.) Iacob lifted vp þe sten, And spak þan wit þe damisel. *c* **1380** *Sir Ferumb.* 2103 Þan hym spak duk Roland..Tak thys damesele by þe hand as þow louest me. *c* **1386** CHAUCER *Nun's Pr. T.* 50 The fairest hiewed..Was cleped fayre damysel Pertilote. *a* **1440** *Sir Degrev.* 623 To chyrche the gay dammisel Buskede hyr ȝare. *c* **1500** *Lancelot* 2351 Sche had no knycht, sche had no damyseill.

γ. *c* **1400** *Destr. Troy* 7887 A damsell faire, þat bright was of ble, and Breisaid she hight. **1649** MILTON *Eikon.* xxi, The Damsell of Burgundie [the Duchess]. **1711** 'J. DISTAFF' *Char. Don Sacheverellio* 9 [He] took..the very Scrubs of both Sexes for Knights and Damsels. **1848** MACAULAY *Hist. Engl.* I. 586 Damsels of the best families in the town wove colours for the insurgents.

δ. *c* **1400** *Rom. Rose* 1622 These damoysels & bachelers. *c* **1477** CAXTON *Jason* 6 Barounes and knightes, ladies and damoiselles, ete in the halle. **1549** CHALONER *Erasmus on Folly* O iij b, Amonges the damoysels and Madames of the court. **1557** *K. Arthur* (Copland) I. xvii, There came a damoysell..a passyng fayre damisel. [**1841** D'ISRAELI *Amen. Lit.* (1867) 223 Those romances of chivalry..long formed the favourite reading of the noble, the dame and the damoiselle.]

ε. *c* **1300** *K. Alis.* 171 Ladies and damoselis Maken heom redy. **1523** LD. BERNERS *Froiss.* I. ix. 9 All knyghtes ought to ayd to theyr powers all ladyes and damozels. *Ibid.* ccxiii. 264 They rode about the countrey, and vysited the ladies nad dumasels [*elsewhere* damozelles, dammuselles]. **1548** HALL *Chron.* 240 The yonge Princes and Damosell of Burgoyne. **1590** SPENSER *F.Q.* II. i. 19 Th' adventure of the errant damozell. **1615** G. SANDYS *Trav.* 215 Hercules..walking along the shore with a Damosel, whom he loued. **1813** SCOTT *Trierm.* Introd. viii, Of errant knight and damozelle. **1871** ROSSETTI *Blessed Damozel* i, The blessed damozel leaned out From the gold bar of Heaven. **1884** F. M. CRAWFORD *Rom. Singer* I. 256 Your boy wants to marry a noble damosel.

2. A young unmarried woman (without any connotation of rank or respect—sometimes even slightingly); a maid, maiden, girl, country lass.

Since 17th c., archaic and literary or playful; not in ordinary spoken use.

β. *c* **1380** WYCLIF *Wks.* (1880) 9 To geten þe stynkyng loue of damyselis. **1483** *Cath. Angl.* 89 Damesselle..*nimpha.* *a* **1550** *Christis Kirke Gr.* ii, To dans thir damysellis thame dicht, thir lassis licht of laitis. **1558** KNOX *First Blast* (Arb.) 52 Aged fathers and tendre damiselles.

γ. **1535** COVERDALE *Zech.* viii. 5 Yonge boyes and damselles, playnge vpon the stretes. **1687** CONGREVE *Old Bach.* III. vi, Good words, damsel, or I shall ——. **1712** STEELE *Spect.* No. 278 ¶2 You will not deny your Advice to a distressed Damsel. **1832** W. IRVING *Alhambra* II. 139 Awed and abashed in the presence of a simple damsel of fifteen. **1870** DICKENS *E. Drood* viii, The two young men saw the damsels enter the court-yard of the Nuns' House.

ε. **1522** SKELTON *Why not to Court* 209 With Dalyda to mell, That wanton damozell. **1576** *Act 18 Eliz.* c. 7 §1 Of Women, Maids, Wives and Damosels. **1611** BIBLE *Mark* v. 39, 41 The damosell is not dead, but sleepeth..Damosell (I say vnto thee), arise. **1642** ROGERS *Naaman* 7 A poore damosell and captive. **1704** J. PITTS *Acc. Mohammetans* 27 The Father of the Damosel usually makes up the Match.

ζ. **1632** QUARLES *Div. Fancies* III. vii, Dam'sel arise? When death had clos'd her eyes, What power had the Dam'sel to arise? **1718** PRIOR *Solomon* II. 301 And one mad Dam'sel dares dispute my pow'r.

†**3.** A maid in waiting, a female attendant. Originally a young lady of gentle birth, as maid of honour or waiting-woman to a lady of rank; but gradually extended downward. Now *Obs.* exc. as merged in 2.

[**1199** *Rot. Chartarum* 25/2 Beatriciae et Aeliciae domicellis praedictae reginae sororis nostrae.] *c* **1314** *Guy Warw.* (A.) 618 Felice þe feir answerd þo [to her maid], Damisel, sche seyd, whi seistow so? **1377** LANGL. *P. Pl.* B. IX. 12 Dobet is hir damoisele [C. XI. 138 damesele] sire doweles douȝter To serue þis lady lelly. *c* **1489** CAXTON *Blanchardyn* ix. 39 A goode auncyent damoysell whiche dyde norisshe her of her brestys..called her nouryce and maystresse. **1594** CAREW *Huarte's Exam. Wits* x. (1596) 130 He sent his damsels [*ancillas suas*] to call to the Castle. **1649** ROBERTS *Clavis Bibl.* 387 His friends and her Damosels, being the foure speakers. **1664** BUTLER *Hud.* II. i. 98 A slender Young waiting damsel to attend her. **1833** HT. MARTINEAU *Loom & Lugger* II. v. 100 The terrified kitchen damsels.

II. *transf.*

4. A hot iron for warming a bed.

App. a humorous allusion to 1 Kings i. 1–4.

1727–51 CHAMBERS *Cycl.*, *Damsel*, a kind of utensil put in beds, to warm old mens feet withal. It consists of a hot iron inclosed in a hollow cylinder, which is wrapped round with linen cloth..Some call it a *nun.* **1848–9** SOUTHEY *Common-pl. Bk.* IV. 434.

5. A projection on the spindle of a mill-stone for shaking the shoot.

1880 *Antrim & Down Gloss.*, *Damsel*, an iron rod with projecting pins, that shakes the shoot of the hopper in a corn mill. **1880** JEFFERIES *Gt. Estate* 167 Tibbald, of course, had his joke about that part of the [mill] machinery which is called the 'damsel'.

III. 6. *attrib.*, as ***damsel train***, etc. *Comb.* **damsel-errant**, feminine of knight-errant (Scott, after Spenser's 'errant Damozell' in 1 ε); **damsel-fish**, a small brightly-coloured fish of the family Pomacentridæ; **damsel-fly**, the slender dragon-fly *Agrion Virgo*, and kindred species, called in French *demoiselle*.

a **1592** GREENE & LODGE *Looking Glasse* i. (1861) 118 Ile send for all the damosell Queenes..To wait as hand maides to Remelia. **1671** MILTON *Samson* 721 Her harbinger, a damsel train behind. **1725** POPE *Odyss.* XXIII. 46 At his nod the damsel-train descends. **1815** MOORE *Lalla R.*, *Parad. & Peri*, The beautiful blue damsel flies. **1821** SCOTT *Kenilw.* xxv, If any man shall find me playing squire of the body to a damsel-errant. **1840** BROWNING *Sordello* I. 284 Flittered in the cool some azure damsel-fly. **1905** D. S. JORDAN *Guide to Study of Fishes* II. xxii. 381 The *Pomacentridæ*, called rock-pilots or damsel-fishes, are exclusively marine. **1931** J. R. NORMAN *Hist. Fishes* xii. 246 Interesting examples of commensalism occur among the Pomacentrids or Damsel-fishes (*Pomacentridae*) of tropical coral reefs. **1968** J. E. RANDALL *Caribbean Reef Fishes* 189 Many of the damselfishes are highly territorial and pugnacious.

Hence '**damselhood**, the condition or age of a damsel, young-womanhood. '**damselish** *a.*, of or proper to a damsel (*nonce-wds.*).

1867 *Contemp. Rev.* VI. 363 'One of the queene's damselles' is set forth as riding about (certainly in a very damselish way) at random..to find the desired champion. **1880** *Daily News* 1 July, The great majority..had not reached the glory of damselhood; they were simply children.

damson ('dæmz(ə)n). Forms: 4–9 **damascene**, 4–5 **damacene, -yne**, 4 **damesene**, 5 **damesyn, -ys(s)yn**, 5–6 **-asyn**, 6 **dameson, -ysen, -isen, -ozin, dammosen, damasson, -en**, 6–7 **dam(m)asin**, 6–9 **damascen**, 7 **-azine, -azeene, -osin**; 5 **damsyn**, 6 **dampson, damsine, -ing**, 6–7 **damsen**, 7 **-zin**, 7–8 **damsin**, 5– **damson.** [ME. (or ? AngloFr.) *damascene*, ad. L. *Damascēnum* for *Prūnum Damascēnum* plum of Damascus (Isidore XVII. vii. 10 Damascena a Damasco oppido). The various weakenings, *damesene*, *damesen*, *damsen*, *damson*, appear to be all of English development.]

1. A small plum, black or dark purple, the fruit of ***Prunus communis*** or *domestica*, variety *damascena*, which was introduced in very early times into Greece and Italy from Syria.

a **1400** *Pistill of Susan* 89 Þer weore growyng so grene þe Date wiþ þe Damesene. *c* **1400** *Lanfranc's Cirurg.* 192 Take xx. damascenes & xii. figis. *c* **1460** J. RUSSELL *Bk. Nurture* 77 in *Babees Bk.* 122 Serve fastynge, plommys, damsons, cheries. *Ibid.* 668 Damesyns. **1542** BOORDE *Dyetary* xxi. (1870) 285, .vi. or .vii. damysens eaten before dyner, be good to prouoke a mans appetyde. **1573** TUSSER *Husb.* (1878) 76 Damsens, white and black. **1626** BACON *Sylva* §509 In Fruits, the white commonly is meaner, as in Pear-plumbs, Damosins, etc. **1657** R. AUSTEN *Fruit Trees* I. 57 The Damazeene also is an excellent fruit. **1747** MRS. GLASSE *Cookery* xviii. *heading*, To preserve damsons whole. **1750** JOHNSON *Rambler* No. 51 ¶14 The art of scalding damascenes without bursting them. **1818** MRS. SHERWOOD *Fairchild Fam.* (1829) I. xiv. 115 Mrs. Fairchild and Betty boiled up a great many damascenes in sugar. **1866** *Treas. Bot.*, *Prunus institia*, the Bullace..A variety occurs with yellowish fruit, which latter are sold in London as White Damsons.

b. Locally, a distinction is sometimes made between *damson* and *damascene*, the latter being applied to the so-called damson-plum: see c.

1818 TODD *Suppl.*, *Damascene.* This and the damson are distinct sorts of plums: the damascene is the larger of the two, and not at all bitter; the damson is smaller, and has a peculiar bitter or roughness. **1891** *Daily News* 17 Nov. 5/2 In Nottinghamshire there is, it seems, a recognised distinction between 'damsons' or 'damsons' and 'damascenes'..in the Newark County Court..a greengrocer..complained that whereas he had ordered damsons he was supplied with damascenes.

c. ***damson plum***: formerly = *damson*: but now applied to a sub-variety of plum somewhat like the damson: see quot 1892.

1586 COGAN *Haven Health* (1636) 104 The Damasin Plummes are woont to be dried and preserved as figges. **1611** COTGR., *Damaisine*, a Damascene, or Damsen plum. **1770** FOOTE *Lame Lover* III. Wks. 1799 II. 85 It was..the best of plum-trees, it was a damascen plum. **1892** *Daily News* 13 Sept. 3/2 The damson plum..is quite as good for most purposes as the damson, and has not its acridity or roughness.

2. The tree which bears this: also ***damson tree.***

1398 TREVISA *Barth. de P.R.* XVII. cxxxv. (1495) 686 Of plumme tree is many manere of kynde but the Damacene is the beste. **14..** *T. of Erceldoune* 180 (Cambr. MS.) Þe darte and also þe damsyn tre. **1575** *Art of Planting* 11 To set Damsons or Plum trees. **1625** BACON *Ess.*, *Gardens* (Arb.) 556 In Aprill follow..The Dammasin, and Plum-Trees in Blossome. **1860** DELAMER *Kitch. Gard.* 158 In shallow or wet soils it is better to bud [peaches] on plum stocks, such as damsons, St. Juliens, &c.

3. Applied to *Chrysophyllum oliviferum* of the W. Indies (*damson-plum*, quot. 1756); ***bitter*** or ***mountain damson***, a name for *Simaruba amara.*

1756 P. BROWNE *Jamaica* 171 The Damson-plumb..is found wild in many parts of Jamaica. **1811** A. T. THOMSON *Lond. Disp.* (1818) 327 The Simaruba quassia, or mountain damson, as it is called in Jamaica. **1858** R. HOGG *Veg. Kingdom* 224 *Simaruba officinalis*..attains the height of sixty feet, and is called *Bitter Damson*, *Mountain Damson*, and *Slave Wood.*

4. a. *attrib.* or *adj.* Of the colour of the damson. Also ***damson brown.***

1661 LOVELL *Hist. Anim. & Min.* Introd., Partridge, grecian, reddish, cinereous, white, and damascen. **1684** *Lond. Gaz.* No. 1963/4 A Damson brown Mare. **1791** HAMILTON *Berthollet's Dyeing* II. II. VI. iv. 347 Damascene colours, and other shades of browns of the common dye.

b. *attrib.* and *Comb.*, as ***damson dumpling***, etc.; **damson-cheese**, an inspissated conserve of damsons and sugar; **damson-pie, -tart** (*slang*, after *damn*), profane language; **damson-plum** (see 1 c, 3).

1769 MRS. RAFFALD *Eng. Housekpr.* (1778) 183 To make Damson Dumplins. *c* **1803** C. K. SHARPE *New Oxford Guide* ii. in *Mem.* (1888) I. 15 Cakes, ruskins, prunelloes, and sweet damson cheese. **1887** JESSOPP *Arcady* 213 His language is profane from long habit—'given over to damson tart like', as they say in Arcady. **1888** W. BLACK *Strange Adv. House Boat* viii. (Farmer), Even if you were to hear some of the Birmingham lads giving each other a dose of damson-pie..you wouldn't understand a single sentence.

damysé, var. of DAMASEE *Obs.*, damson.

damysel, damysen, obs. ff. DAMSEL, DAMSON.

†**Dan**[1]. *Obs.* Also 4–5 **daun, danz, daunz**, 4–6 **dane**, 5 **dann**; see also *Sc. dene*, DEN. [a. OF. *dan* (also *dant*, *dam*, *damp*, in nom. *dans*, *danz*) = mod.F. *dom*, Pr. *don*, *dompn*, Sp., Pg. *don*, It. *donno*:—L. *dominus* lord. Cf. DAM *sb.*[4]]

An honourable title = Master, Sir: **a.** used in addressing or speaking of members of the religious orders; cf DOM; **b.** applied to distinguished men, knights, scholars, poets, deities, etc.; its modern affected application to poets appears to be after Spenser's 'Dan Chaucer'.

1303 R. BRUNNE *Handl. Synne* 73 Dane Phelyp was mayster þat tyme. *c* **1330** —— *Chron. Wace* (Rolls) 8829 With hem wente daunz Merlyn ffor þo stones to make engyn. **1340** *Ayenb.* 1 Þis boc is dan Michelis of Northgate. *c* **1386** CHAUCER *Monk's Prol.* 41 My lorde the Monk quod he..Wher shal I calle yow my lord daun Iohn, Or daun Thomas, or elles daun Albon? Of what hous be ye? **1393** GOWER *Conf.* III. 86 Lo, thus Danz Aristoteles These thre sciences hath devided. **1483** *Cath. Angl.* 89 A Dan; *sicut monachi vocantur.* **1523** SKELTON *Garl. Laurel* 391 The monke of Bury..Dane Johnn Lydgate. **1587** TURBERV. *Trag. T.* (1837) 9, I undertook Dan Lucans verse. **1596** SPENSER *F.Q.* IV. ii. 32 Dan Chaucer, well of English undefyld. **1714** POPE *Imit. Hor.*, *Sat.* II. vi. 153 Our friend Dan Prior. **1717** PRIOR *Alma* II. 120 Pray thank Dan Pope who told it me. **1832** TENNYSON *Dream Fair Women* 5 Dan Chaucer, the first warbler.

dan[2] (dæn). Also 8 **dann. a.** A small buoy, made of wood or inflated sheepskin, supporting a stout pole which bears a flag by day and lamp by night, used either to mark the position of deep-sea lines, or as a centre round which a steam-trawler is worked.

1687 *Lond. Gaz.* No. 2298/4 They will..forthwith cause to be laid a White Buoy, having a Dann thereupon, till they may be able to erect another Beacon. **1883** *Fisheries Exhib. Catal.* 7 Fleet of Cod Lines..ready for Baiting, with Dans, Dantows, and Anchors complete. **1892** *Whitby Gaz.* 11 Nov. 3/1 The vessel then drifts slowly on until a distance of about two miles separates it from the dan.

b. *attrib.* **dan-buoy**, spec., one marking an area cleared by minesweepers, or indicating the position of sea-mines; **dan-tow**, the rope fastening the dan to the lines or, in steam-trawling, to a small anchor or anchors.

1916 *Chambers's Jrnl.* Oct. 665/2 Dan buoys, seen in the half-light,..are apt to be deceptive. **1943** *H.M.'s Minesweepers* v. 31/2 The Captain..gives him practice in dropping and picking up the dan-buoys which are used to mark the position of mines or the limits of a cleared area. **1962** *Times* 29 May 14/6 We sight the 'dan', or marker, buoys of our pots.

Hence '**danner, 'dan-layer**, a vessel used to lay dans.

1942 J. MASEFIELD *Generation Risen* 44 (*title*) The danlayers. **1943** *H.M.'s Minesweepers* vii. 49/1 Certain ships being detailed to act as dan-layers. **1946** J. IRVING *Royal Navalese* 60 *Danner*, a special vessel, following behind a force of mine-sweepers, which lays Dan-buoys to mark.. the channel as it is swept. **1954** *Jane's Fighting Ships 1954–55* 195 Now rated as..inshore minesweepers..but used mainly as danlayers.

dan[3]. *Coal-mining. local.* A small truck or sledge on which coal is drawn from the workings to the main road or shaft. Hence **dan** *v.*

1852 BRANDE *Dict. Sc.* (ed. 2), *Dans*, small trucks or sledges used in coal mines. **1871** *Trans. Amer. Inst. Mining Eng.* I. 305 The coals were brought along the face to the hill, on a 'dan'..there reloaded and hauled to the shaft. **1879** MISS JACKSON *Shropsh. Word-bk.*, *Dan*, a small tub used for drawing coals from the workings to the main road where the skips are loaded. *Danning* is drawing the coals in the dans, which is done by boys.

Dan[4] (dæn). The name of one of the twelve tribes of Israel and of a town in its territory, taken to represent the northern limit of Israelite settlement in Old Testament times, and used in proverbial phrases to indicate a farthest extremity, esp. in phr. *from Dan to Beersheba*. (Cf. Judges xx. 1, II Samuel xxiv. 2, I Kings iv. 25.)

1738 SWIFT *Polite Conv.* I. 76, I remember, you told me, you had been with her from Dan to Bersheba. **1768** STERNE *Sent. Journ.* I. 85, I pity the man who can travel from Dan to Beersheba, and cry, 'Tis all barren. **1828** SCOTT *Jrnl.* 9 Apr. (1941) 222 The whole saving will not exceed a guinea or two for being cursd and damnd from Dan to Beersheba. **1905** H. G. WELLS *Mod. Utopia* ix. 268 The Utopians distinguished two extremes of this Kinetic class according to the quality of their imaginative preferences, the Dan and Beersheba, as it were, of this division.

dan[5] (dæn). [Japanese.] In Judo, a degree of proficiency; the holder of such a qualification.

1941 M. FELDENKRAIS *Judo* 166 All teachers..are of the first Dan in the beginning of their teaching career. **1954** E. DOMINY *Teach yourself Judo* i. 17 There are six *kyu* grades and ten *dan* grades. The word *kyu* means pupil and *dan* means degree or master. **1958** G. KOIZUMI *Judo* 44 Two third Dans, members of the grading panel, are required to recommend to First Dan. **1968** R. HARRIS *Nice Girl's Story* ii. 16, I often practised my judo. I..was, by this time, a 4th Dan.

Hence **dan-holder**, one who is, or possesses, a dan.

1941 M. FELDENKRAIS *Judo* 167 It is too easy for a higher Dan holder to beat a single opponent so he is opposed to a group. **1956** K. TOMIKI *Judo* i. 8 Of the *dan*-holders those from the 1st to the 5th wear a black belt or sash.

Danaert ('dænət). Also **dannert**. The name of the German inventor of spring steel wire, usually barbed and in a spiral form, used in anti-tank and other forms of defensive warfare. Usu. *attrib.*, as ***dannert wire***.

1945 *Penguin New Writing* XXVI. 31 Pillboxes had already been put up and a dannert wire apron fence encircled the pier arcade. **1948** *Hansard* CCCCXLV. 1535 There is concealed dannert wire in the grass around the camps. **1960** C. FITZGIBBON *When Kissing had to Stop* xi. 200 A score of bell-tents, surrounded by coils of dannert. **1961** *Wire Industry Encycl. Handbk.* 333/1 *Danaert wire*, the circles of barbed wire widely used in wartime for barbed wire entanglements. Also known as concertina wire.

Danaid ('dæneɪɪd). [In Fr. *Danaide*, ad. Gr. *Δαναΐς*, pl. *Δαναΐδες*, the *Danaides* or daughters of Danaus king of Argos, who, having murdered their husbands on the wedding-night, were condemned eternally to pour water into bottomless or sieve-like vessels.]

a. A daughter of Danaus; used *attrib.* in reference to the labour of the Danaides: endless and futile. So **Danaï'dean** *a.*; and **'Danaus** used *attrib.*

a **1628** F. GREVILLE *Sidney* (1652) 62 A Danaus sive of prodigality. **1884** *Century Mag.* Mar. 704 The crew are worn out with their Danaidean task.

b. = DANAINE.

1881 S. H. SCUDDER *Butterflies with Ref. Amer. Forms* 298 Tribe Festivi Fabricius [*Danaides* Boisd.] Danaids. **1892** W. L. DISTANT *Naturalist in Transvaal* 65 The female Hypolimnas being present with the Danaids. **1936** *Discovery* July 212/2 Danaids and various Nymphalids. **1937** H. D. PEILE *Guide Coll. Butterflies of India* 76 The females of this genus [*sc. Pareronia*] appear to be mimics of common blue and black Danaids. **1957** M. A. WYNTER-BLYTH *Butterflies of Indian Region* vi. 63 The Danaids are chiefly a tropical and sub-tropical family.

danaide ('dæneɪaɪd). [a. mod.F. *danaïde* (see prec.): so named in 1813 by a committee of the French Academy of Sciences, to whom it was submitted by the inventor Mannoury d'Ectot, from a fancied analogy to the vessels which the Danaides were required to fill.]

A kind of horizontal water wheel, consisting of a vertical axis to which is attached a conical drum and case, with radial spiral floats; the water is directed against the floats by a chute and escapes at the bottom: also called 'tub-wheel'.

1825 *Mech. Mag.* IV. 41 Description of the Danaide. **1856** CRESY *Encycl. Civ. Eng.* 959 *Danaide*..this machine may be classed among hydraulic wheels.

danaine ('dæneɪɪn), *a.* and *sb.* *Ent.* [ad. mod.L. *Danainæ*, f. generic name DANAIS: see -INE[1].]

A. *adj.* Of or belonging to the subfamily Danainæ of the family Nymphalidæ of butterflies. **B.** *sb.* A member of this subfamily.

1897 E. B. POULTON *Theory Mimicry* in *Hope Rep.* (1901) II. 2 All of them possess a dark tip to the fore wing crossed by a white bar, as in the Danaine butterfly. *Ibid.*, The abundant black-and-white Danaines. **1913** *Oxf. Univ. Gaz.* 4 June 951/2 The rare Danaine butterfly *Amauris ansorgei*. **1930** R. A. FISHER *Natural Selection* vii. 161 This is probably true of many Danaines. **1945** E. B. FORD *Butterflies* v. 96 Professor G. D. Hale Carpenter has seen the male of the African Danaine *Amauris psyttalea* Plötz hover over the female and dust her with the scented powder with which the wing-pocket is filled in this insect. **1957** *Encycl. Brit.* XV. 517/2 The above facts point directly to the conclusion that there is some advantage in mimicking Danaine butterflies.

danais ('dæneɪɪs). [mod.L. (P. A. Latreille 1807, in *Magazin für Insectenkunde* VI. 291), a. Gr. *Δαναΐς*.] A butterfly belonging to the genus so named, now usually included in the genus *Danaus*.

1878 P. ROBINSON *In my Indian Garden* 101 The coppery Danais flitted at ease about the shrubs. **1892** W. L. DISTANT *Naturalist in Transvaal* 65 Birds may..make an experimental dash at a *Danais*.

danaite ('deɪnəaɪt). *Min.* [Named 1833 after J. F. Dana, an American chemist.] A variety of arsenopyrite or mispickel, containing cobalt.

1833 *Amer. Jrnl. Sc.* XXIV. 386 *Danaite*, a new ore of cobalt and iron.

Danakil ('dænəkɪl, də'nɑːkɪl), *sb.* and *a.* Also **Dankali** (dæŋ'kɑːlɪ). [Cushitic.] **A.** *sb.* **a.** A member of a widely spread Hamitic people of north-eastern Ethiopia. **b.** The language of this people. **B.** *adj.* Of or pertaining to this people, their language, or the areas they inhabit.

1875 *Encycl. Brit.* I. 61/1 Abyssinia..may be regarded as ..having..E., the territory of the Danakils. **1885** *Ibid.* XVIII. 778/2 The third or Ethiopic division [of the Hamitic Family] includes as its chief members the Beja or Bishârîn, the Saho, the Dankali..the first two lying along the Red Sea north of Semitic Abyssinia, the others south of it, to the equator. **1902** *Ibid.* XXXII. 703/2 The native population [of French Somaliland] is either of the Danakil or of the Galla race. **1910** *Ibid.* I. 85/2 The Danakil lowlands have a hot, dry climate producing semi-desert conditions. **1934** L. M. NESBITT *Desert & Forest* 11 The territory inhabited by the Danakils is divided into two parts by the frontier separating Abyssinia from Eritrea. **1936** G. B. SHAW *Simpleton of Unexpected Isles* Pref. 4 The Abyssinian Danakil kills a stranger at sight. **1937** —— *Platform & Pulpit* (1962) 283 In Abyssinia a Danakil woman will not marry a man until he proves that he has at least four homicides to his credit. **1961** D. BATES *Fly-switch from Sultan* xviii. 102 Some splendid savages called the Danakil, who hovered around us eyeing our private parts with a predatory eye and a sharp knife. **1969** *Times* 16 Sept. (Somali Republic Suppl.) p. ii/6 Nearly half the population of the territory are Somalis of the Issa ethnic division who overflow into the Somali Republic and into Ethiopia, and the other half are Muslim *Dankalis* (or Afars) who also spread into Ethiopia.

danalite ('deɪnəlaɪt). *Min.* [Named 1866 after J. D. Dana, an American mineralogist: see -LITE.] A silicate of iron, glucinum, etc. with sulphide of zinc, occurring in reddish octahedrons in granite.

1866 *Amer. Jrnl. Sc.* Ser. II. XLII. 72 On Danalite, a new Mineral Species.

danburite ('dænbəraɪt). *Min.* [Named 1839 from Danbury, Ct., U.S., where it occurs.] A boro-silicate of lime, brittle, translucent, and of a yellowish or whitish colour.

1839 *Amer. Jrnl. Sc.* XXXV. 137 Danburite, a new Mineral Species. **1886** ERNI *Min.* 295 The presence of boracic acid in danburite.

dance (dɑːns, -æ-), *sb.* Forms: 4–7 **daunce**, (4–5 **dauns(e**, 5–6 **dawnce**, 6 **dans(s)**, 5– **dance**. [a. OF. *dance*, *danse*, f. the vb. *dancer*, *danser*. So Pr., Cat. *dansa*, Sp. *danza*, Pg. *dança*, *dansa*, It. *danza*; also Ger. *tanz*, Du. *dans*.]

1. A rhythmical skipping and stepping, with regular turnings and movements of the limbs and body, usually to the accompaniment of music; either as an expression of joy, exultation, and the like, or as an amusement or entertainment; the action or an act or round of dancing.

c **1300** *K. Alis.* 6990 Murye they syngyn, and daunces maken. **1303** R. BRUNNE *Handl. Synne* 4684 Daunces, karols, somour games. *c* **1340** *Cursor M.* 7601 (Trin.) In her daunse [*v.r.* dauncing, karol] þis was þe song. *c* **1400** *Rom. Rose* 808 It to me liked right wele, That Courtesie me cleped so, And bade me on the daunce go. **1535** COVERDALE *Ps.* cxlix. 3 Let them prayse his name in the daunce. **1590** SHAKS. *Mids. N.* II. i. 254 Lul'd in these flowers with dances and delight. **1611** BIBLE *Judg.* xxi. 21 If the daughters of Shiloh come out to daunce in daunces. **1667** MILTON *P.L.* v. 619 That day..they spent In song and dance about the sacred Hill. **1730–46** THOMSON *Autumn* 1225 Leaps wildly graceful in the lively dance. **1762–71** H. WALPOLE *Vertue's Anecd. Paint.* (1786) II. 157 The holy family with a dance of Angels..is a capital picture. **1841** LEVER *C. O'Malley* cxviii, Waltzers whirled past in the wild excitement of the dance. *Mod.* Her partner for the next dance.

2. a. A definite succession or arrangement of steps and rhythmical movements constituting one partiticular form or method of dancing.

1393 GOWER *Conf.* III. 365 The hove daunce and the carole. **1521** R. COPLAND (*title*), Maner of Dauncynge of base daunces after the vse of Fraunce. **1599** SHAKS. *Hen. V*, II. iv. 25 If we heard that England Were busied with a Whitson Morris-dance. **1600** J. PORY tr. *Leo's Africa* I. 55 A kind of dance which they use also in Spaine..called The Canaries. **1711** BUDGELL *Spect.* No. 67 ¶2 Pyrrhus.. Inventing the Dance which is called after his Name. **1879** H. N. MOSELEY *Nat. on Challenger* 331 The most interesting dances were a Club Dance and a Fan Dance.

b. A tune or musical composition for regulating the movements of a dance, or composed in a dance rhythm.

1509 HAWES *Past Pleas.* XVI. xix, She commaunded her mynstrelles right anone to play..the gentill daunce. **1597** MORLEY *Introd. Mus.* 180 *Ballete* or daunces..songs, which being song to a dittie may likewise be daunced. **1711** BUDGELL *Spect.* No. 67 ¶9 [He] bid the Fidlers play a Dance called Mol Patley. **1880** GROVE *Dict. Mus.* I. 350/1 His [Chopin's] first..compositions were dances: Polonaises, Mazurkas, and Valses.

3. A social gathering for the purpose of dancing; a dancing party.

c **1385** CHAUCER *L.G.W.* 1269 *Dido*, And waytyn hire at festis and at dauncis. **1790** BURNS *Tam O'Shanter* 178 Ah! little kenn'd thy reverend grannie, That sark she coft for her wee Nannie..Wad ever graced a dance of witches! *a* **1845** BARHAM *Ingold. Leg.*, *Wedding day*, When asked to a party, a dance, or a dinner. *Mod.* Mrs. S. is giving a dance instead of a garden party this year.

4. *transf.* and *fig.*

1751 JOHNSON *Rambler* No. 85 ¶4 The dance of spirits, the bound of vigour..are reserved for him that braces his nerves. **1879** STAINER *Music of Bible* 3 One might say that rhythm is the dance of sound. **1881** *Daily Tel.* 28 Jan., The dance of the waters, especially to windward, was visible for over a mile around.

†**5.** *fig.* Course of action; mode of procedure, play, game. ***to know the old dance***: cf. F. '*elle sçait assez de la vieille danse*, she knowes well enough what belongs to the Game' (Cotgr.).

a **1352** MINOT *Poems* i. 66 At Donde now es done þaire daunce, And wend þai most anoþer way. *Ibid.* v. 14 Sare it þam smerted þat ferd out of France, þare lered Inglis men þam a new daunce. *c* **1386** CHAUCER *Prol.* 476 Of remedies of loue she knew per chaunce For she koude of that Art the olde daunce. **1423** JAS. I. *Kingis Q.* clxxxv, Tham that ar noght entrit inne The dance of lufe. *c* **1449** PECOCK *Repr.* I. xvi. 86 God for his merci and pitee kepe Ynglond, that he come not into lijk daunce. **1513** MORE *Rich. III*, Wks. 53 The lord Stanley and he had departed with diuerse other lordes, and broken all the daunce. **1659** B. HARRIS *Parival's Iron Age* 193 The Emperour..troubled, at this too long and too bloody dance. **1733** WALPOLE in Morley *Life* viii. (1889) 174 This dance..will no further go. I meant well, but..the Act could not be carried into execution without an armed force.

6. Phrases: **a.** ***to begin, lead the dance***; *fig.* to take the lead in any course of action.

c **1325** *Coer de L.* 3739 The damyseles lede daunse. *c* **1374** CHAUCER *Troylus* II. 504 Yet made he þo as fressh a contenaunce, As þough he schulde haue led þe newe daunce. *c* **1380** WYCLIF *Sel. Wks.* II. 360 Crist þat ledip þe daunce of love. **1526** SKELTON *Magnyf.* 1348 Foly foteth it properly, Fansy ledeth the dawnce. **1579** TOMSON *Calvin's Serm. Tim.* 522/2 They must begin the dance to be punished. *a* **1616** BEAUM. & FL. *Cust. Country* II. i, They heard your lordship Was, by the ladies' choice, to lead the dance. **1742** MANN *Let. to H. Walpole* 23 Sept., M. de Gages is now the man who begins the dance.

b. ***to lead***, rarely ***give*** (***a person***) ***a dance***; *fig.* to lead (him) in a wearying, perplexing, or disappointing course; to cause him to undergo exertion or worry with no adequate result.

a **1529** SKELTON *Edw. IV*, 29 She [Fortune] toke me by the hand and led me a daunce. **1599** PORTER *Angry Wom. Abingd.* III. ii, I pray God, they may..both be led a dark dance in the night! **1682** HICKERINGILL *Wks.* (1716) II. 37, I think he has led me a fair dance, I am so tyred. **1700** S. L. tr. *C. Fryke's Voy. E. Ind.* 45 [A monkey] led me such a dance, that I had almost stuck in the Slough. **1798** W. HUTTON *Autobiog.* 65, I should have led them a dance of twenty miles to breakfast at Kidderminster. **1874** ALDRICH *Prud. Palfrey* i. (1885) 12 It was notorious that the late Maria Jane had led Mr. Wiggins something of a dance in this life.

c. ***Dance of Death***: an allegorical representation of Death leading men of all ranks and conditions in the dance to the grave: a very common subject of pictorial representation during the middle ages. Also called ***Dance of Macabre***, F. *danse macabre*: see Littré.

c **1430** LYDG. *Daunce of Machabree* Prol., The which daunce at sainct innocentes Portrayed is with all the surplusage. *Ibid.*, Death fyrst speaketh vnto the Pope, and after to euery degree as foloweth. **1480** *Robt. Devyll* 26 For and we nowe in deathes daunce stode To hell shoulde we go, with horrible vengeaunce. **1494** FABYAN *Chron.* VI. clvi. 145 But deth y[t] is to all persones egall, lastlye tooke hym in his dymme daunce, whan he had ben kyng .xlvii. yeres. **1631** WEEVER *Anc. Fun. Mon.* 378 The dance of Death..the Picture of death leading all estates. **1833** J. DALLAWAY *Archit. Eng.* 137 (Stanford) The Dance of Macabre (Holbein's Dance of Death) was painted on the walls.

d. ***St. Vitus's dance*** = CHOREA, q.v.; also *fig.* Also *St. John's*, *St. Guy's dance*, terms applied to the dancing-mania of the middle ages.

1621 BURTON *Anat. Mel.* I. i. I. iv, *Chorus Sancti Viti*, or S. Vitus Dance..they that are taken with it can do nothing but dance till they be dead, or cured. **1721** BAILEY, *Chorea Santi Viti*, St. Vitus's Dance. **1746** J. ANDREE (*title*), Cases of Epilepsy, Hysteric Fits, and St. Vitus's Dance, with the Process and Cure. **1804** SOUTHEY in H. D. Traill *Coleridge* (1884) 106 His [Coleridge's] mind is in a perpetual St. Vitus's dance—eternal activity without action. **1840** TWEEDIE *Pract. Med.* II. 205 In St. John's dance, as well as in that of St. Vitus..a tympanic state of the abdomen was a frequent symptom.

e. ***dance upon nothing***: an ironical expression for hanging (cf. DANCE *v.* 3 b).

1840 HOOD *Kilmansegg, Her Death* ix, Just as the felon condemned to die..From his gloomy cell in a vision elopes, To caper on sunny greens and slopes, Instead of the dance upon nothing. *a* **1845** —— *An Open Question, note*, If a dance upon Sunday led so inevitably to a dance upon nothing!

7. *attrib.* and *Comb.*, as ***dance-band***, ***-floor***, ***-frock***, ***-leader***, ***-lover***, ***-rhythm***, ***-step***, ***-tune***; ***dance-loving*** adj.; **dance-card**, a card bearing the names of (a woman's) prospective partners at a dance; **dance-director**, the person who, in musical comedies, arranges the dances; **dance-drama**, a rendering through dancing of a dramatic situation; **dance-hall, -house** orig. *U.S.*, a public dancing saloon; **dance hostess,** (*a*) a woman who holds a dance at her house, etc.; (*b*) a dancing-partner (sense *b*, DANCING *vbl. sb.* b); **dance-music**, 'music designed as an accompaniment to dancing; also, music written in dance rhythm though not for dancing purposes' (Grove *Dict. Mus.*); **dance programme** = *dance-card*.

1927 *Melody Maker* Aug. 739/1 It was his boast then that he would have a symphonic *dance band. **1962** J. WAIN *Strike Father Dead* 67 The convention that lays it down that English dance-band singers must put on an American accent. **1895** J. L. WILLIAMS *Princeton Stories* 199 You will here meet several of those whose names you have on your *dance-card, and you may make up your mind whether to remember that fact or not. **1922** JOYCE *Ulysses* 11 Old feather fans, tasselled dancecards, powdered with musk. **1932** WODEHOUSE *Louder & Funnier* 84 The *dance-director is instructed to think up a lot of different business for the first encore. **1924** *New Republic* 26 Nov. 11 Spend a few hours in a New Mexico pueblo at the end of the day of one of their sacred *dance-dramas. **1938** *Encycl. Brit. Bk. of Yr. 1938* 251/2 Dance dramas, marionette shows, musical comedies, [etc.]. **1958** *Times* 13 Aug. 5/3 Darrell's dance-drama *The Prisoners*..was not only topical..but also gripping. **1968** *Jrnl. Mus. Acad. Madras* XXXIX. 1 The dramatic poem of the Composer Nauka Caritram was also produced as a dance-drama. **1928** *Melody Maker* Feb. 171/3 The *dance floor was crowded. **1959** M. SHADBOLT *New Zealanders* 32 There was even a crude dance-floor erected for the night a little back from the beach. **1904** *Westm. Gaz.* 18 Feb. 4/2 An accordion-pleated lace net is one of the prettiest *dance-frocks I have seen for some time. **1858** *Mass. Acts & Resolves* 125 Any person who shall offer to view..any..show, concert, or *dance-hall exhibition of any description shall be punished by a fine. **1891** *Scribner's Mag.* Sept. 276/1 Port Said..abounds in French cafés and dance-halls. **1904** CONRAD *Nostromo* I. viii. 107 From the doors of the dance hall men and women emerged tottering. **1934** T. S. ELIOT *Rock* i. 40 Everythink useful for the people: dance 'alls, picture palaces, swimmin' baths. **1909** *Daily Chron.* 8 July 6/5 Lady Londesborough was one of the chief *dance hostesses last night. **1934** F. B. YOUNG *This Little World* ix. 179 A young woman of a most undesirable class—a 'dance-hostess' (the word was vaguely familiar and unpleasant) in a London night club. **1961** A. WILSON *Old Men at Zoo* ii. 113 She's a dance hostess. **1848** *Western Boatman* (Cincinnati) June 133 That afternoon I wrote a letter to a friend of mine in Natchez, who was a woman that kept a *dance-house. **1875** MRS. STOWE *We & Neighbors* xli. 375 He told me that he was in the constant habit of passing through the dance-houses, and talking with people who kept them. **1889** *Boston* (Mass.) *Jrnl.* 24 Apr. 1/8 To run a dance-house and gambling-den. **1946** G. FOREMAN *Last Trek of Indians* 256 His forsaken wife, Comes-at-Rain, sprang through the window of the dance house. *c* **1440** *Promp. Parv.* 114 *Dawnceledere, *coralles*. **1860** G. H. K. *Vac. Tour.* 152 Very popular..as a means of producing *dance music. **1906** *Dialect Notes* III. 133 Got your *dance-program filled up yet? **1913** C. MACKENZIE *Sinister St.* I. II. i. 149 The dance programme, with Muriel's name fourteen times repeated. **1926** S. T. WARNER *Lolly Willowes* I. 42 A bunch of dance programmes kept for the sake of their little pencils. **1968** D. HOPKINSON *Incense-Tree* iv. 46 Dance programmes were usual—with the names of the dances on one side and space for the names of partners on the other, and a small pink pencil tied on with blue cord. **1880** GROVE *Dict. Mus.* II. s.v. Melody, In the matter of rhythm there are two things which play a part—the rhythmic qualities of language, and *dance rhythms. **1947** A. EINSTEIN *Mus. Romantic Era* xvi. 290 A pathetic recitative changes suddenly into the most impudent dance-rhythm. **1920** S. LEWIS *Main St.* 380 The rude fiddling and banging *dance-steps in the barn. **1936** *Discovery* June 186/2 For the different kinds of spirits [to be exorcised] different dances are held, each with its special dance-steps. **1962** *Times* 26 Apr. 8/1 Ready-made and established dance-steps.

dance (dɑːns, -æ-), *v.* Forms: 4-6 daunse, 4-7 daunce, (5 dawnce, 6 dans(s, danse), 5- dance. [a. OF. *dance-r*, *danse-r* = Pr. *dansar*, Sp. *danzar*, Pg. *dançar*, *dansar*, It. *danzare*.

The origin of the Romanic word is obscure; it is generally held (after Diez) to be an adoption of OHG. *dansôn* to draw, to stretch out, from which is supposed to have arisen the sense 'to form a file or chain in dancing'. From Romanic the word has been taken (back) in the sense 'dance' into German: MHG. *tanzen* (11th c, MDu. *dansen*. (OHG. *dansôn* was a derivative form from *dinsan* = Goth. *þinsan* in *at-þinsan* to draw towards one.)]

1. *intr.* To leap, skip, hop, or glide with measured steps and rhythmical movements of the body, usually to the accompaniment of music, either by oneself, or with a partner or in a set.

c **1300** *K. Alis.* 5213 Mery time it is in May..Maydens so dauncen and thay play. **1388** WYCLIF *2 Sam.* vi. 14 Dauid.. daunside with all strengthis bifor the Lord. **1483** CAXTON *Gold. Leg.* 147/3 He..sente them into the gardyn to daunse & to carolle. **1530** PALSGR. 361 After dynner men avaunced them to daunce eche man with eche woman. **1632** MILTON *L'Allegro* 96 Many a youth and many a maid Dancing in the chequer'd shade. **1712** STEELE *Spect.* No. 466 ¶3 You shall see her dance, or, if you will do her that Honour, dance with her. **1884** MISS BRADDON *Ishmael* ix, I never danced with any one in my life until to-day. I have danced by myself in the yard sometimes when there was an organ.

†**b.** *to dance barefoot*: said of an elder sister when a younger one was married before her. *Obs.*

1596 SHAKS. *Tam. Shr.* II. i. 33 She must haue a husband; I must dance bare-foot on her wedding day, And for your loue to her leade Apes in hell. **1742** MRS. DELANY *Life & Corr.* (1861) II. 188 The eldest daughter was much disappointed that she should dance barefoot, and desired her father to find out a match for her.

c. Of animals taught to perform certain regular movements.

c **1530** *Hickscorner* in Hazl. *Dodsley* I. 184 Then should ye dance as a bear. **1854** WOOD *Anim. Life* 210 The education of most bears seldom aspires beyond teaching the animal to stand on its hind legs, and raise each foot alternately, a performance popularly entitled 'dancing'.

d. *transf.* and *fig.*

c **1430** LYDG. *Bochas* I. viii. (1544) 11 a, Beware afore or ye daunce in the rowe Of such as Fortune hath from her whele ithrow. **1613** SHAKS. *Hen. VIII*, v. iv. 68, I haue some of 'em in *Limbo Patrum*, and there they are like to dance these three dayes.

e. *to dance to* or *after* (*a person's*) *pipe, whistle*, etc.: *fig.* to follow his lead, act after his desire or instigation.

1562 J. HEYWOOD *Prov. & Epigr.* (1867) 61 To daunce after her pipe, I am ny led. **1604** MIDDLETON *Father Hubb. Tales* Wks. 1886 VIII. 65 Till the old devourer..death, had made our landlord dance after his pipe. **1707** NORRIS *Treat. Humility* iii. 98 When a man..dances to the tune of the age wherein he lives. **1823** SCOTT *Peveril* vii, I thought I had the prettiest girl in the Castle dancing after my whistle. **1845** S. AUSTIN *Ranke's Hist. Ref.* I. 523 That most of these councillors..will 'dance to Rome's piping', if they do but see her gold.

2. To leap, skip, spring, or move up and down, with continuously recurring movement, from excitement or strong emotion. Said also of the lively skipping or prancing of animals, and of the heart, the blood in the veins, etc.

c **1325** *E.E. Allit. P.* A. 345 þoȝ þou daunce as any do, Braundysch, & brais þy braþez breme. *c* **1400-50** *Alexander* 2618 For þe dowt of þe dyn daunced stedis. **1526** *Pilgr. Perf.* (W. de W. 1531) 291 Some were constrayned to leape and daunce for ioye. **1553** EDEN *Treat. Newe Ind.* (Arb.) 21 The woman runneth vp and down, daunsing continually like a frantike bodie. **1611** SHAKS. *Wint. T.* I. ii. 110, I haue *Tremor Cordis* on me: my heart daunces, But not for ioy. *a* **1720** SHEFFIELD (Dk. Buckhm.) *Wks.* (1753) I. 160 The blood more lively danc'd within our veins. **1792** S. ROGERS *Pleas. Mem.* I. 142 When the heart danced, and life was in its spring. **1821** LAMB. *Elia, Valentine's Day*, He saw, unseen, the happy girl unfold the Valentine, dance about, clap her hands. **1859** TENNYSON *Enid* 505 Yniol's heart Danced in his bosom, seeing better days.

b. To run, go, or move on with dancing or tripping motion.

1712 ARBUTHNOT *John Bull* I. x, How you have danced the round of all the Courts. **1820** SCOTT *Abbot* xxiv, The moments..danced so rapidly away. *Ibid.* xxxiv, Some sprightly damsel, who thinks to dance through life as through a French galliard. **1872** BLACK *Adv. Phaeton* ii. 20 These boys of twenty-five will dance over the world's edge in pursuit of a theory.

3. Of things inanimate: To bob up and down on the ground, on the surface of water, in the air, etc. Often with personification or figurative reference to gay and sprightly motion.

1563 W. FULKE *Meteors* (1640) 7 b, The flame appeareth to leape or daunce from one part to the other, much like as bals of wild fire daunce up and downe in the water. **1567** DRANT *Horace's Epist.* xviii. F vj, Whilst thy ship doth kepe a flote, ydauncinge on the plaine. **1665** HOOKE *Microgr.* 231 Why the limb of the Sun, Moon, Jupiter..and Venus, appear to move or dance. **1703** MOXON *Mech. Exerc.* 135 Care must be taken that the Bressummers and Girders be not weakned more than needs, lest the whole Floor dance. **1812** H. & J. SMITH *Rej. Addr., Cui bono?* iv, Light as the mote that dauncеth in the beam. **1884** Q. VICTORIA *More Leaves* 138 The little boat rolled and danced.

b. Grimly applied to the movements of the body in or after death by hanging; *to dance upon nothing*, to be hanged.

1837 MAJOR RICHARDSON *Brit. Legion* viii. (ed. 2) 210 To see a fellow-being dancing in air after death, in the manner practised in England. **1839** H. AINSWORTH *Jack Sheppard* xxxi. (Farmer), 'You'll dance upon nothing, presently', rejoined Jonathan, brutally. **1862** CARLYLE *Fredk. Gt.* (1865) III. VIII. iv. 21 This poor soldier, six feet three, your Majesty, is to dance on the top of nothing for a three-halfpenny matter!

4. *trans.* with the name or description of a dance or measure as cognate object.

c **1385** CHAUCER *L.G.W.* Prol. 200 (MS. Gg) Daunsynge aboute this flour an esy pas. **1509** HAWES *Past. Pleas.* XVI. xix, To daunce true mesures without varyaunce. **1599** PORTER *Angry Wom. Abingd.* III. ii, They have danced a galliard at beggars'-bush for it. *a* **1627** MIDDLETON *Chaste Maid* IV. iii, As if they'd dance the sword-dance on the stage. **1762** GOLDSM. *Life of Nash* Wks. 1881 IV. 69 A minuet, danced by two persons. **1844** E. FITZGERALD *Lett.* (1889) I. 142 If you could see the little girl dance the Polka with her sister!

†**b.** *to dance Barnaby*: to dance to a quick movement, move expeditiously. *to dance the Tyburn jig*: to be hanged: cf. 3 b. *Obs.*

1664 COTTON *Scarron.* 15 Bounce cries the Port-hole, out they fly And make the world dance Barnaby. **1664** ETHEREDGE *Com. Revenge* v. ii, Widow, here is music; send for a parson, and we will dance Barnaby within this half hour. **1697** VANBRUGH *Relapse* Epil., Did ever one yet dance the Tyburn jig With a free air, or a well-pawdered wig?

5. *to dance attendance*: to wait (upon a person) with assiduous attention and ready obsequiousness; *orig.* to stand waiting or 'kicking one's heels' in an antechamber. See also ATTENDANCE 5.

1522 SKELTON *Why not to Court* 626 And Syr ye must daunce attendance, And take patient sufferaunce, For my Lords Grace, Hath now no time or space, To speke with you as yet. **1613** SHAKS. *Hen. VIII*, v. ii. 31 To suffer A man of Place..To dance attendance on their Lordships pleasures, And at the dore too, like a Post with Packets. **1675** TRAHERNE *Chr. Ethics* xxv. 380 Few have observed that the sun and moon and stars dance attendance to it [the earth], and cherish it with their influences. **1768** GRAY in *Corr. w. Nicholls* (1843) 75 Here are a pair of your stray shoes, dancing attendance, till you send for them. **1883** GILMOUR *Mongols* xxxi. 362 After dancing attendance on the court for a month or two they receive their dismission.

6. *causal.* **a.** To lead in a dance, cause to dance.

1665 PEPYS *Diary* 11 Oct., Having danced my people as long as I saw fit to sit up, I to bed. **1762** STERNE *Tr. Shandy* VI. ii, When my father had danced his white bear backwards and forwards, through half-a-dozen pages. **1773** GOLDSM. *Stoops to Conq.* I, Though I am obligated to dance a bear, a man may be a gentleman for all that.

b. To move or toss up and down with a dancing jerky motion; to dandle.

WYCLIF *Isa.* lxvi. 12 Vp on the knes men shul daunte [*MS. H. a* **1450** daunsen] ȝou. **1546** HEYWOOD *Proverbs* II. x, In hope..In hir dotyng daies to be daunst on the lappe. **1622** FLETCHER *Sp. Curate* II. i, I have dandled you, and kissed you, and played with you..and danced you. **1681** W. ROBERTSON *Phraseol. Gen.* (1693) 418 To dance a child in one's arms. **1773** MAD. D'ARBLAY *Early Diary* July, It was no sport to me to be danced up and down, and to find the waves..rougher every instant. **1850** TENNYSON *In Mem.* Epil., I, that danced her on my knee.

7. With *compl.*: To remove, put, bring, impel, etc., *off*, *away*, *out*, *in*, etc., by dancing.

a **1633** AUSTIN *Medit.* (1635) 208 So was the blessed head of John..danced off his shoulders by a Harlot. **1787** *Generous Attachment* I. 200, I danced away the recollection of it. **1812** BYRON *Waltz* vii, Her nimble feet danced off another's head. **1862** MERIVALE *Rom. Emp.* (1865) VI. l. 169 That an obscure player..should dance himself into the chamber of the empress. **1880** G. MEREDITH *Trag. Com.* iv. (1892) 29 Like a lady danced off her sense of fixity. *Mod.* I fear he has danced away his chance.

danceable ('dɑːnsəb(ə)l, -æ-), *a. colloq.* [f. DANCE *v.* + -ABLE; cf. F. *dansable.*] Suitable for dancing; fit to dance with.

1860 W. COLLINS *Wom. White* I. vi. 22 A flirtable, danceable, small-talkable creature of the male sex. **1891** *Sat. Rev.* 25 July 123/2 'The Shaking Polka'..is a very bright and danceable specimen.

dancer ('dɑːnsə(r), -æ-). [f. DANCE *v.* + -ER.]

1. a. One who dances; *spec.* one who dances professionally in public.

c **1440** *Promp. Parv.* 114 Dawncere, *tripudiator, tripudiatrix.* **1599** SHAKS. *Much Ado* II. i. 111 God match me with a good dauncer. **1688** *Lond. Gaz.* No. 2318/4 Stage-Plays, Dancers of the Ropes, and other Publick Shews. **1790** BURNS *Tam O'Shanter* 146 The dancers quick and quicker flew. **1858** THACKERAY *Virginians* xxviii, She is a dancer, and..no better or worse than her neighbours.

†**b.** A dancing-master. *Obs.*

1599-16.. MIDDLETON, etc. *Old Law* III. ii, His dancer now came in as I met you. *a* **1627** MIDDLETON *Chaste Maid* I. i, I hold my life you have forgot your dancing: when was the dancer with you?

†**c.** *transf.* A dancing-dog. *Obs.*

1576 FLEMING tr. *Caius' Dogs* in Arb. *Garner* III. 261 The dog called the Dancer..[They] are taught and exercised to dance in measure. **1688** R. HOLME *Armoury* II. 184/1.

2. (*pl.*) A sect of enthusiasts who arose in 1374, chiefly in parts of Flanders, and were noted for their wild dancing; in *Pathol.* those affected with the dancing-mania (*St. Vitus'*, *St. John's dance*, etc.) of the middle ages.

1764 MACLAINE tr. *Mosheim's Ch. Hist.* XIV. II. v. §8 Directly the reverse of this melancholy sect was the merry one of the Dancers, which..arose at Aix-la-Chapelle. **1844** BABINGTON tr. *Hecker's Epidemics Mid. Ages.* i. 88 *note*, According to the Chronicle of Cologne, the St. John's dancers sang during their paroxysms. **1882-3** SCHAFF *Encycl. Relig. Knowl.* I. 602 The sect of the Dancers, who were enthusiasts, first appeared in 1374, on the Lower Rhine, dancing in honor of St. John.

3. = DANDY-ROLLER, q.v.

4. *pl.* Stairs. *slang.*

1671 R. HEAD *Eng. Rogue* I. v. (1874) 52 (Farmer) Track up the dancers, go up the stayres. **1725** in *New Cant. Dict.* **1812** J. H. VAUX *Flash Dict.*, *Dancers*, stairs. **1829** LYTTON *Disowned* 65 Come, track up the dancers, and dowse the glim. **1858** —— *What will he do?* xvi. (D.), Come, my Hebe, track the dancers, that is, go up the stairs.

5. *pl.* A local name for the aurora borealis or northern lights. Also *merry dancers*.

c **1717** *Lett. fr. Mist's Jrnl.* (1722) I. 99 In the North of Scotland..they are seen continually every Summer in the Evening..they call them Dancers. **1727** *Phil. Trans.* XXXV. 304 The Meteor call'd by our Sailors, Merry Dancers, was visible, and very bright. **1863** C. ST. JOHN *Nat. Hist. Moray* 86 April 7th (1847)..we saw a very brilliant aurora borealis, or as they term it here, 'The Merry Dancers'.

6. *slang.* (See quots.)

1864 HOTTEN *Slang Dict.* 117 *Dancer*, or *dancing-master*, a thief who prowls about the roofs of houses, and effects an entrance by attic windows, &c. **1930** E. WALLACE *Lady of Ascot* xiii. 120 There were active young men who called themselves dancers, and whose graft was to get into first-floor flats and get out quickly with such overcoats, wraps, and movables as could be whisked away in half a minute.

dancercise ('dɑːnsəsaɪz, -æ-). orig. *U.S.* Also **dancercize.** [Blend of DANCE *sb.* and EXERCISE *sb.*] Dancing performed as an exercise;

organized physical exercise which incorporates the rhythms of (modern) dance. Also as *v. intr.*

Formerly a proprietary term in the U.S.

1967 D. DRAKE (*title*) Dancercize. *Ibid.* i. 15 Dancercize not only remolds your body, but gives you grace, poise and beauty. **1971** *Official Gaz.* (U.S. Patent Office) 8 June 95 Debbie Drake, New York, N.Y... *Dancercize*... Instructions in dancing and physical conditioning. **1973** *Seventeen* Apr. 118/1 Exercise, dance, yoga..you can combine it all with Dancercise. Jon Devlin, who started the Dancercise Clubs in New York, says, 'My way of dancing and exercising is to use the body's natural motions.' **1982** *Maclean's Mag.* 1 Feb. 61 Witnessing a performance of Les Ballets Jazz de Montréal is much like watching a 'dancercise' class work itself into a quasi-religious lather of shimmying, shaking, jiving, and high-kicking. **1983** *Sunday Tel.* 18 Dec. 17/3 (*heading*) Come dancercising. *Ibid.* 17/4 While 'Dancercise' was a London-based phenomenon in its youth, classes are spreading all over England.

† **danceress.** *Obs.*, exc. as *nonce-wd.* [a. OF. *danceresse, danseresse*, now supplanted by *danseuse*: see -ESS.] A female dancer.

1388 WYCLIF *Ecclus.* ix. 4 Be thou not customable with a daunseresse [**1382** a leperesse or tumbler], neither here thou hir. **1491** CAXTON *Vitas Patr.* (W. de W. 1495) I. xli. 62 b/1 The moost excellent Jonglouresse or Dawncerresse that was in the cytee of Anthyoche. **1633** PRYNNE *Histrio-Mastix* v. viii. 260 What doth a Danceresse doe? She impudently uncovers her head. **1855** *Househ. Words* XI. 57 A cavalier may..offer ..a glass now and then to his danceress.

† **'dancery.** *Obs. rare*$^{-1}$. [a. OF. *danserie*, dancing, ball: see -ERY.] Dancing.

1615 CHAPMAN *Odyss.* VIII. 504 Two, with whom none would strive in dancery.

dancette (dæn'sɛt), *sb.* [app. a modern formation, inferred from next.]

1. *Her.* A fesse with three indentations.

1864 BOUTELL *Heraldry Hist. & Pop.* xiv. §1 (ed. 3) 160 The 'daunces' are equivalent to a group of fusils conjoined in fesse across the shield, which is sometimes blazoned as a 'dancette' or a fesse dancettée.

2. *Arch.* A zigzag or chevron moulding.

1838 BRITTON *Dict. Archit.* 249 The chevron moulding, or dancette. **1876** GWILT *Encycl. Archit.* Gloss.

dancetté, -ee ('dænsɘteɪ, -tɪ), *a. Her.* Also **-ty.** [app. a corruption of F. *danché, denché*, in OF. also *dansié* (:—late L. *denticātus*, f. *dent-* tooth) used in same sense.

Dancetté or *danceté* may have originated in a scribal error for *danché* or *dansié*. OF. had also the phrase *à danses* = *danché*.]

Of a line, the edges of a fesse, etc.: Having large and deeply marked indentations, usually three in number; = DANCY.

1610 GUILLIM *Heraldry* II. iii. (1660) 55 These two last mentioned sorts of Lines viz. Indented and Daunsette are both one..their forme is all one, but in quantity they differ much in that the one is much wider and deeper than the other. **1661** MORGAN *Sph. Gentry* I. ii. 15 Dancette differs from Indented, by reason it consists but of three teeth only. **1864** BOUTELL *Heraldry Hist. & Pop.* xiii. (ed. 3) 115 A chief dancettee. **1882** CUSSANS *Heraldry* ii. 47 The lines by which a shield is divided..may assume any of the following forms ..Indented, Dancetté (but 3 indentations). *Ibid.* iv. 59 Argent; a Bend vert, between Cotises dancetté gules.

dancing ('dɑːnsɪŋ, -æ-), *vbl. sb.* [-ING^1.] **a.** The action of the verb DANCE.

a **1300** *Cursor M.* 7601 (Gött.) In þair dauncing þis was þair sang. *a* **1340** HAMPOLE *Psalter* xxxix. 6 Hoppynge & daunceynge of tumblers & herlotes. **1530** TINDALE *Pract. Prelates* Wks. (1573) 375 As who should say, we payd for all mens daunsing. **1633** P. FLETCHER *Purple Isl.* VII. xxx. 92 With dancings, gifts and songs. **1670** COTTON *Espernon* II. VI. 244 One night that the King had appointed a great Dancing at Court. **1766** FORDYCE *Serm. Yng. Women* (ed. 4) I. vi. 236 What is dancing, in the best sense, but the harmony of motion rendered more palpable? **1855** THACKERAY *Newcomes* xxiv, They had no dancing at Grandmamma's: but she adores dancing.

b. *attrib.* and *Comb.*, as ***dancing-assembly, -chamber, -class, -club, -days, -dress, -floor, -hall, -house, -list, -match, -party, -pipe, -pump, -shoe, -teacher***, etc.; **dancing-malady, -mania, -plague** = CHOREA; **dancing-mistress,** a female teacher of dancing; **dancing-partner,** (*a*) a person with whom one dances; (*b*) (see quot. 1921); † **dancing rapier,** a sword worn only for ornament in dancing; **dancing-room,** a room for dancing; *spec.* one for public dancing. Also DANCING-MASTER, -SCHOOL.

1765 COWPER *Let. to J. Hill* 3 July, Here is a card-assembly, and a *dancing-assembly. *c* **1385** CHAUCER *L.G.W.* 1106 *Dido*, To *daunsyng-chaumberys..This Enyas is led. **1870** MRS. STEPHENS *Married in Haste* xxxi. 172 Constance had never felt..pleasure in departing for her *dancing classes. **1902** 'G. M. MARTIN' *Emmy Lou* 277 'There's to be a *dancing club on Friday evenings,' she explained, 'and I'm invited.' **1918** A. BENNETT *Roll-Call* II. i. 217 They had belonged to two dancing clubs whose members met weekly in the saloons of the great hotels. **1592** SHAKS. *Rom. & Jul.* I. v. 33 Nay sit..For you and I are past our *dauncing daies. **1724** SWIFT *Stella's Birthday*, As when a beauteous nymph decays, We say, she's past her dancing-days. **1843** LONGF. *Sp. Student* II. i, Now bring me..my *dancing dress And my most precious jewels! **1839** —— *Hyperion* III. iii, Used as a *dancing-floor. **1753** GOLDSM. *Let.* Wks. 1881 IV. 474 When a stranger enters the *dancing-hall he sees one end of the room taken up with the ladies. **1818** SCOTT *Hrt. Midl.* ix, Nae frequenter of play-house, or music-house, or *dancing-house. **1871** MRS. STOWE *Pink & White Tyranny* xxi. 263 Her *dancing-list seemed in a fair way to be soon filled up for the evening. **1878** tr. *Ziemssen's Cycl. Med.* XIV. 416 As a pandemic disease, the *dancing-mania died out in the fifteenth century. **1741** RICHARDSON *Pamela* II. 145 All the Ladies could prevail upon my Master for, was a *Dancing-match. **1852** DICKENS *Bleak H.* II. vii, *Dancing-mistress though in her limited ambition she aspired to be. **1920** *World's Pict. News* 27 Feb. 9/2 (*caption*) Gaby..with her famous *dancing partner. **1921** *Dict. Occup. Terms* (1927) §899 *Dancing partner*.., an expert dancer engaged by proprietor or manager of dancing hall or by individual dancer, to act as partner when required and to teach ball-room dancing. **1852** J. REYNOLDS *Pioneer Hist. Illinois* 52 They arrange all things necessary for the *dancing party. **1889** *Kansas Times & Star* 13 Dec., The dancing party given by Mrs. Kirk Armour and her sister, Mrs. Ed Smith, at the Casino last night was the most brilliant social event of the early winter. *c* **1440** *Promp. Parv.* 114 *Dawncynge pype, *carola.* **1847** ALB. SMITH *Chr. Tadpole* xix. (1879) 167 They all wear jackets and trowsers, and trodden out *dancing-pumps. **1788** WOLCOTT (P. Pindar) *Peter's Pension* Wks. 1812 II. 17 T'illume The goodly Company and *Dancing-room. **1836** *Murray's Handbk. N. Germ.* 271 Occupied by low taverns and dancing-rooms. **1709** STEELE *Tatler* No. 180 ¶8 *Dancing-Shoes not exceeding Four Inches Height in the Heel. **1841** J. F. COOPER *Deerslayer* xxiv. 112 His step as lofty as *dancing-teachers and a light heart could make it. **1880** G. W. CABLE *Grandissimes* xliii. 336, I could be..a dancing-teacher.

'dancing, *ppl. a.* [-ING^2.] That dances, in various senses of the verb.

[*c* **1386** CHAUCER *Knt's T.* 1343 What ladies fairest bene or best daunceinge.] **1568** FULWEL *Like Will to Like* in Hazl. *Dodsley* III. 310 Whom have we here? Tom Tumbler, or else some dancing bear? **1583** STUBBES *Anat. Abus.* II. (1882) 33 Their dansing minions, that minse it ful gingerlie. **1697** DRYDEN *Virg. Georg.* I. 506 Chaff with eddy Winds is whirl'd around, And dancing Leaves are lifted from the ground. **1701** DE FOE *True-born Eng.* 8 A Dansing Nation, Fickle and Untrue. **1887** J. BALL *Nat. in S. Amer.* 15 The irregular surface of the little dancing waves.

b. † **dancing-goats** [Lat. *capræ saltantes*], a species of meteor or aurora; **dancing-damsel, -wench, -woman** = DANCING-GIRL.

1563 W. FULKE *Meteors* (1640) 6 b, Of fiery meteors..they have divers names: for they are called burning stubble, torches, dauncing or leaping Goates. *Ibid.* 7 b, Dansing Goats are..as when two torches be seene together, and the flame appeareth to leape or daunce from one part to the other. **1606** G. W[OODCOCKE] tr. *Justin* 42 b, He begat Larissa, a dauncing damsel. **1698** FRYER *Acc. E. India & P.* 160 The Dancing Wenches singing with Bells at their Wrists and Heels. **1810** T. WILLIAMSON *E. India Vade M.* I. 386 (Y.) The dancing-women are of different kinds.

'dancing-girl. [DANCING *ppl. a.*]

1. A girl who dances in public; a female professional dancer; *esp.* in India, a nautch-girl (in Pg. *bailadeira*, BAYADÈRE 1).

1760 GOLDSM. *Cit. W.* xlv, Pleased with the postures as well as the condescension of our dancing girls. **1782** *Ann. Reg.* 43 A company of strolling dancing girls from Surat appeared on a platform. **1842** LONGF. *Sp. Stud.* I. i, A mere dancing-girl, who shows herself Nightly, half-naked, on the stage, for money. **1848** HT. MARTINEAU *East. Life* (1850) 283 There was a booth with dancing-girls, a horrid sight.

2. ***dancing-girls***: a plant, *Mantisia saltatoria*, cultivated in green-houses for the beauty and singularity of its purple and yellow flowers.

1866 *Treas. Bot.* 719/1 Its flowers..present some resemblance to a ballet-dancer; hence the popular name, Dancing Girls, applied to the plant.

dancingly ('dɑːnsɪŋlɪ, -æ-), *adv.* [f. DANCING *ppl. a.* + -LY^2.] In a dancing or capering manner.

1667 H. MORE *Div. Dial.* III. xxxvi. (1713) 283 If you be so dancingly merry. **1892** *Chamb. Jrnl.* 27 Aug. 552/2 A chill gleam..lit dancingly on Miss Mattie's face.

'dancing-,master. [DANCING *vbl. sb.*] A professional teacher of dancing.

1651 (*title*), The English Dancing-Master. **1681** OTWAY *Soldier's Fort.* v. v, Odd, they'll make an old fellow of sixty-five cut a caper like a dancing-master. **1711** ADDISON *Spect.* No. 29 ¶11 The Shepherds..acquit themselves in a Ball better than our English Dancing-Masters. **1860** EMERSON *Cond. Life, Culture* (Bohn) II. 371 In town, he can find the swimming-school, the gymnasium, the dancing-master.

'dancing-school. [f. as prec.] A school for instruction in dancing.

1580 BARET *Alv.* D 118 A daunsing schoole. **1599** SHAKS. *Hen. V*, III. v. 32 They bid vs to the English Dancing-Schooles. **1647** WARD *Simp. Cobler* 9 The Church..will sooner become the Devils dancing-Schoole, then Gods Temple. **1837** HT. MARTINEAU *Soc. Amer.* II. 356 A warning that no young lady who attended dancing-school that winter should be employed.

† **'dancitive,** *a. Obs. nonce-wd.* [f. DANCE *v.*, on the analogy of *sensitive*: cf. *talkative.*] Inclined or given to dancing.

1606 *Sir G. Goosecappe* II. in Bullen *O. Pl.* III. 31 Your Lord is very dancitive me thinkes.

† **dancy,** *a. Her. Obs. rare.* [a. OF. *dansié, danché*:—late L. *denticātus* toothed, f. *dent-*tooth.] Toothed, indented.

1611 COTGR., *Danché*, indented; or (as in termes of blazon) dancy. **1706** PHILLIPS, *Dancette* or *Dancy.*

dand, slang or dial. abbreviation of DANDY.

1886 T. HARDY *Mayor of Cast.* xxvii, Farfrae, being a young dand. **1891** —— *Tess* I. 89 You will never set out.. without dressing up more the dand than that?

dandelion ('dændɪlaɪən). Forms: 6 **dent de lion, dentdelyon, dantdelyon, 6–7 dan-, dantedelyon,** 7 **dent-, dendelion,** 6– **dandelion.** [a. F. *dent de lion*, in med.L. *dens leonis*, 'lion's tooth', from the toothed outline of the leaves.]

1. A well-known Composite plant (*Taraxacum Dens-leonis* or *Leontodon Taraxacum*), abundant in meadows and waste ground throughout Europe, Central and Northern Asia, and North America, with widely toothed leaves, and a large bright yellow flower upon a naked hollow stalk, succeeded by a globular head of pappose seeds; the leaves, stalk, and root contain a bitter milky juice.

1513 DOUGLAS *Æneis* XII. Prol. 119 Seyr downis smaill on dent de lion sprang. **1578** LYTE *Dodoens* V. xvi. 568 Dandelion flowreth in April and August. *Ibid.* 569 The seconde kinde is called..in shoppes *Dens leonis*..in French *Pisse-en-lict*..in Englishe Dandelyon. **1655** HARTLIB *Ref. Silk-worm* 31 They wil also eate the hearb called Dantedelyon. **1692** TRYON *Good House-w.* xxii. (ed. 2) 216 Our Herb called Dandelion (that is in English, Lyons Tooth, because of the similitude of its Leaf). **1732** ARBUTHNOT *Rules of Diet* I. 249 The Juice of the Dandelion is a remedy in intermitting Fevers. **1805** WORDSW. *Vaudracour & Julia*, A tuft of winged seed..from the dandelion's naked stalk..Driven by the autumnal whirlwind. **1872** OLIVER *Elem. Bot.* II. 195 In Dandelion, all the florets are..ligulate and yellow.

2. Applied, with qualifying words, to other Composites: as **autumnal d.,** *Apargia autumnalis*; **blue d.,** a species of lettuce (*Lactuca sonchifolia*) with toothed leaves; **dwarf d.** (U.S.), *Krigia virginica*; **false d.,** 'a branching composite of the southern United States, *Pyrrhopappus Carolinianus*, with dandelion-like heads' (*Cent. Dict.*).

3. *attrib.* and *Comb.*, as ***dandelion flower, plush, seed, wine***; **dandelion-clock** = CLOCK *sb.*^{1} 8; **dandelion coffee,** a beverage prepared from dried dandelion roots; **dandelion greens** *U.S.*, fresh dandelion leaves used as a green food or herb.

1876 *Aunt Judy's Mag.* XIV. 628 He did not ask now why *dandelion clocks go differently with different people. **1925** W. DE LA MARE *Broomsticks* 51 Buttercups and dandelion-clocks and meadow-sweet. **1950** 'P. WOODRUFF' *Island of Chamba* vii. 109 You could blow her away like a dandelion clock in the summer fields. **1852** S. MOODIE *Roughing it in Bush* 89, I met with an account of *dandelion coffee published in the *New York Albion*, given by a Dr. Harrison, of Edinburgh, who earnestly recommended it as an article of general use. **1886** *Harper's Mag.* Sept. 578/2 If you'd asked pleasanter, I should just as soon told you that we use dandelion coffee. **1907** *Yesterday's Shopping* (1969) 518/2 Schweitzer's Dandelion Coffee. **1821** CLARE *Vill. Minstr.* I. 114 The *dandelion flowers. **1887** M. E. WILKINS *Humble Romance* 234 There were..two old women—one.. searching for *dandelion greens among the short young grass. **1889** R. T. COOKE *Steadfast* xvii. 190 Dandelion greens is better 'n a doctor. **1945** *New Yorker* 26 May 60 With the shad came a dish of dandelion greens in a tart sauce. **1963** *New Good Housek. Cookbook* 452/2 Heap chopped, cooked dandelion greens and scallions on tomato slices. **1656** MENNIS & SMITH *Musarum Del, Oberon's Apparel*, His [Oberon's] breeches..lined with *dandelyon plush. **1883** MISS BRADDON *Gold. Calf* vii. 83 As light and airy as that *dandelion seed. **1906** *Mrs. Beeton's Bk. Househ. Managem.* xlix. 1483 **Dandelion wine*..dandelion flowers.. sugar..ginger..lemon..orange..yeast. **1973** B. BROADFOOT *Ten Lost Years* xv. 179 He was laughing when he said it, with a big tumbler of dandelion wine in his hand.

dander ('dændə(r)), *sb.*^{1} *Sc.* [Origin unknown]. A piece of the vitrified refuse of a smith's fire or a furnace; a calcined cinder or piece of slag.

1791 NEWTE *Tour Eng. & Scot.* 230 These [peats] burnt in kiln-pots leave a plate of yetlin amongst the ashes, which the country people call a dander. **1828** SCOTT *F.M. Perth* iii, 'Nay, father,' said the Smith, 'you cannot suppose that Harry Gow cares the value of a smithy-dander for such a cub.' **1828** *Specif. T. Stirling's patent* No. 5685. 3 A layer of dander or the scoriæ obtained from the Carron Ironworks in Scotland. **1888** *Cycl. Tour. Club Gaz.* Mar. 98 1 The horse sprained the fetlock joint in the near forefoot..in consequence of a number of lumps of ashes or 'danders' having been left on the road.

dander ('dændə(r)), *sb.*^{2} [Origin uncertain: app. West Indian or American.] (See quot.) Now commonly DUNDER, q.v.

? *c* **1796** SIR J. DALRYMPLE *Observ. Yeast-cake* 1 The season for working molasses lasts five months, of which three weeks are lost in making up the dander, that is, the ferment.

'dander, *sb.*^{3} = DANDRUFF, q.v.

dander ('dændə(r)), *sb.*^{4} *colloq.* (orig. *U.S.*) and *dial.* [Conjectured by some to be a fig. use of DANDER^3, dandruff, scurf; but possibly fig. of DANDER^2, ferment.] Ruffled or angry temper; in phr. ***to get one's dander up***, etc.

1831 H. J. FINN *Amer. Comic Ann.* 148 A general roar of laughter brought Timmy on his legs. His dander was raised. **1832** SEBA SMITH *Major Downing* 104 My dander began to rise, and I couldn't hold in any longer. **1834** C. A. DAVIS

Lett. J. Downing 34 He was as wrathy as thunder—and when he gets his dander up, it's no joke, I tell you. **1837–40** HALIBURTON *Clockm.* (1862) 31 He was fairly ryled, and got his dander up. **1847** HALLIWELL *Dict. Arch. & Prov. Words* I. 291/2 *Dander*, anger. **1848** LOWELL *Biglow P.* Poems 1890 II. 49 *Wut 'll git your dander riz?* **1849** THACKERAY *Pendennis* xliii, When my dander is up it's the very thing to urge me on. **1861** G. DU MAURIER *Let.* Dec. (1951) 97 If you want to get on you must put the kicking straps on your dander and offend nobody. **1884** *Cheshire Gloss.* s.v., 'I got his dander up' means I put him out of temper. [In Dialect Glossaries of *Cumbrld., Sheffield, Berkshire.*] **1966** *Listener* 17 Mar. 395/1 Precocious manifestos raise the critical dander.

dander ('dændə(r)), *sb.*[5] *Sc.* and *dial.* Also **daunder, dauner.** [f. DANDER *v.*]

1. *Sc.* A stroll, a saunter.

1821 *Joseph the Book-Man* 17 He'd from Edina take a dander To Glasgow. **1883** NASMYTH *Autobiog.* xxi. 379 We had a long dander together through the Old Town.

2. *dial.* A fit of shivering.

1877 in *Holderness Gloss.*

dander ('dændə(r)), *v.* *Sc.* and *dial.* Also **daunder, dauner, dawner.** [A frequentative form like *blunder, wander*. Conjectured by some to be akin to DANDLE: cf. *dadder* and *daddle*.]

1. *intr.* To walk idly or purposelessly; to stroll, saunter. (*Sc.* and *north. dial.*)

a **1600** BUREL in Watson *Collect.* (1706) II. 19 (Jam.) Quhiles wandring, quhiles dandring. **1724** RAMSAY *Tea-t. Misc.* (1733) I. 75 Alane through flow'ry hows I dander. **1808** ANDERSON *Cumbrld. Ball.* 57 The wearied auld fwok dander'd heame. **1830** GALT *Lawrie T.* IX. viii. (1849) 434, I would just dauner about and dwine away. **1856** MRS. CARLYLE *Lett.* II. 288 To see poor Jess Donaldson daundering about, opening drawers and presses. **1889** BARRIE *Window in Thrums* xvi. 153 Hendry dandered in to change his coat deliberately.

2. *dial.* **a.** To 'wander' or 'ramble' in talk, to talk incoherently. **b.** To tremble, to vibrate; applied also to the rolling sound of a drum. In this sense akin to *dunder, dunner*.

a **1724** *Battle of Harlaw* xviii. in *Evergreen* I. 85 The Armies met, the Trumpet sounds, The dandring Drums alloud did touk. **1847–78** HALLIWELL, *Dander*..to talk incoherently. *Chesh.* **1855** ROBINSON *Whitby Gloss.*, *Dander*, to tremble as a house seems to do from the inside when a carriage passes heavily in the street. **1876** *Mid. Yorksh. Gloss.*, 'Thou danders like an old weathercock—hold still with thee.'

Hence '**danderer**, one who 'danders'; '**dandering** *ppl. a.*, that 'danders'.

1821 *Blackw. Mag.* Jan. 407 (Jam.) Thou art but a daunderer a-down the dyke-sides. *a* **1774** FERGUSSON *Poems, Cauler Oysters*, We needna gie a plack For dand'rin mountebank or quack. **1849** MRS. CARYLE *Lett.* II. 85 There are always some 'dandering individuals' dropping in.

dandiacal (dæn'daɪəkəl), *a.* [A Carlylean derivative of DANDY, after *hypochondriacal* and the like.] Of the nature of, or characteristic of, a dandy; dandified.

1831 CARLYLE *Sart. Res.* III. x. (*heading*) The Dandiacal Body..It appears as if this Dandiacal Sect were but a new modification..of that primeval Superstition, Self-worship. **1845** MRS. CARLYLE *Lett.* I. 301 How washed out the beautiful dandiacal face looked. **1886** SALA in *Illustr. Lond. News* 7 Aug 138 Arrayed in the most dandiacal manner.

Dandie Dinmont ('dændɪ 'dɪnmənt). Also shortened to **Dandie.** [Name of a character in Sir Walter Scott's novel *Guy Mannering* (q.v. ch. xxii, 'Dandy Dinmont's Pepper and Mustard terriers', and Note C).] A breed of terrier from the Scottish borders, having short legs, long body, and rough coat. Also *attrib.*

[**1826** SCOTT *Jrnl.* 1 Apr. (1939) 145 Sometimes attending to the humours of two curious little terriers of the Dandie Dinmont breed.] **1848** *Sporting Life* 8 Jan. 246/1 The dog celebrated by Sir Walter Scott as the Pepper and Mustard, or Dandie Dinmont breed. **1859** 'STONEHENGE' *Shot-Gun* 77 The Dandie Dinmont..is an excellent rabbit dog. **1862** J. BROWN *Our Dogs* 29 From this dog descended Davidson (the original Dandie Dinmont) of Hyndlee's breed. **1875** MRS. STOWE *We & Neighbors* i. 7 A rough coated Dandie Dinmont terrier. **1894** R. B. LEE *Mod. Dogs (Terriers)* 287 He has never known one of his Dandies show the 'white feather'. **1925** *Chambers's Jrnl.* 772/1 The two so-called Dandies. **1952** R. LEIGHTON *Complete Bk. Dog* (rev. ed.) 241 When Dandies fight it is a serious matter. **1963** S. M. LAMPSON *Country Life Bk. Dogs* 122 The Dandie Dinmont has the distinction of being the only breed of dog named after a character in fiction.

dandification (ˌdændɪfɪ'keɪʃən). *colloq.* [f. DANDIFY *v.*] The action of dandifying or fact of being dandified; *concr.* a dandified adornment.

1827 *Blackw. Mag.* XXI. 828 There is no dandification about it, no cockneyism. **1856** THACKERAY *Christmas Bks.* (1872) 137 [He] surveys his shining little boots..his gloves and other dandifications with a pleased wonder.

'**dandified,** *ppl. a. colloq.* [f. next + -ED.] Made or adorned in the style of a dandy; foppish.

1826 DISRAELI *Viv. Grey* IV. i, He was dressed..in the most dandified style that you can conceive. **1856** R. A. VAUGHAN *Mystics* (1860) I. VI. i. 150 A rainbow-coloured, dandified puppy, a secretary of the bishop's.

dandify ('dændɪfaɪ), *v. colloq.* Also **dandyfy.** [see -FY.] *trans.* To give the character or style of a dandy to; to make trim or smart like a dandy.

1823 *Mirror* I. 365/2 Dandyfying in the first style for the occasion. **1824** *New Monthly Mag.* XI. 150 The male is dandyfying his plumage. **1859** W. H. GREGORY *Egypt* II. 134 For fear, if smartened up and dandified, he should become the object of envy.

'**dandilly,** *a.* and *sb. Sc.* Also **dandily.** [app. a deriv. of DANDLE *v.*] **A.** *adj.* Petted, spoiled by being made too much of. Jamieson also gives the meaning 'Celebrated'. **B.** *sb.* A pet, a darling.

1500–20 DUNBAR *Schir, ȝit remembir* 62, I wes in ȝowth on nureiss kne, [cald] Dandely, bischop, dandely. **1697** CLELAND *Poems* 76 (Jam.) The fate of some [that] were once Dandillies, Might teach the younger stags and fillies, Not for to trample poor cart-horse. **17..** in R. Jamieson *Pop. Songs* (1806) I. 324 (Jam.) And he has married a dandily wife, She wadna shape, nor yet wad she sew. *a* **1808** ROSS *Songs* 145 (Jam.) The dandilly toast of the parish Is woo'd and married and a'. **1818** SCOTT *Br. Lamm.* xxxiv, Yon dandilly maiden ..a' glistenin' wi' goud and jewels.

dandily, dandiness: see DANDY.

dandiprat ('dændɪpræt). *Obs.* or *arch.* Also 6 **dande-, dandy-, dandipratt(e, danty-, 6–8 dandy-, 7 dantiprat, (dand-prat).** [Etymology unknown; as the sense-development is also uncertain, the senses are here arranged chronologically.]

†**1.** Applied to a small coin, worth three halfpence, current in England in the 16th c. *Obs.*

c **1520** T. NORFOLK in Ellis *Orig. Lett.* Ser. III. 129 I. 381 Suche a Coyne might be devised as were the dandipratts. **1530** PALSGR. 498/2 Coyle out the dandyprattes and Yrisshe pence. **1542** RECORDE *Gr. Artes* (1575) 198 A Dandiprat, worth 3 halfe pens. **1574** HELLOWES *Gueuara's Fam. Ep.* (1577) 253 If they aske an halfpenie for spice, a penie for candels, a dandiprat for an earthen pot. **1605** CAMDEN *Rem.* (1657) 188 K. Henry the 7th stamped a small coine called dandyprats. **1641** PRYNNE *Antip.* 99 A poore Knave, scant worth a dandyprat.

2. A small, insignificant, or contemptible fellow; a dwarf, pygmy. Also *attrib. Obs.* or *arch.*

1556 J. HEYWOOD *Spider & F.* lx. 158 Yet as the giantes pawes pat downe dandipratts, So shall we put downe these dandiprat brag bratts. **1606** SYLVESTER *Du Bartas* II. iv. i. (1641) 195/2 Am I a Dog, thou Dwarfe, thou Dandi-prat? **1659** TORRIANO, *Spithaméi*, pigmeis, or dandy-prats that be but three spans long. **1718** MOTTEUX *Quix.* (1733) I. 211, I saw a little Dandiprat riding about, who, they said, was a hugeous great Lord. **1841** GEN. P. THOMPSON *Exerc.* (1842) VI. 133 The dandiprats of St. Stephen's..took themselves for patricians of old Rome.

b. Said of a young lad, little boy, urchin; rarely (quot. 1638) a young girl. *Obs.* or *arch.*

1583 STANYHURST *Æneis* I. (Arb.) 41 On father Æneas his neck thee dandiprat hangeth. **1638** HEYWOOD *Wise Woman* I. Wks. 1874 V. 284 Her name is Luce. With this Dandiprat, this pretty little Apes face, is yon blunt fellow in love. **1706** ESTCOURT *Fair Examp.* III. i, *Boy*. A Candle, Sir! 'tis broad Daylight yet. *Whims.* What then, you little Dandyprat? **1821** SCOTT *Kenilw.* xxvi, It is even so, my little dandieprat. **1875** CALVERLEY *Fly-Leaves, Cock & Bull*, It's a thing I bought Of a bit of a chit of a boy..'Chop' was my snickering dandiprat's own term.

dandizette (dændɪ'zɛt). Also **dandisette, dandysette, -zette.** [f. DANDY; app. after French words like *grisette*.] A female dandy.

1821 *New Monthly Mag.* I. 409 The city dandy and dandisette. **1825** *Blackw. Mag.* XVII. 336 Lord Foppington was a dandy, and Lady Fanciful a dandyzette. **1890** *Daily News* 16 Sept. 4/7 The humours of the Dandies and the Dandizettes are shown up..in these pleasant pages.

dandle ('dænd(ə)l), *v.* Also 6 **dandil(l, -yll.** [Not known before 16th c. To be compared with It. *dandola*, var. of *dondola*, 'a childes baby [= doll]; also a dandling'; *dandolare*, var. of *dondolare*, 'to dandle the baby' (Florio), to swing, toss, shake to and fro; dally, loiter, idle, play, sport, toy. But actual evidence of the derivation of the Eng. word from the Italian has not been found. Another suggestion is that the word may be cognate with Ger. *tändeln* intr. 'to dawdle, toy, trifle, dally, play, dandle', dim of MHG. *tänden* to make sport (with), play; but no word of this family is known in Old or Mid.Eng., and the sense is not so close to the English as in the Italian word.]

1. *trans.* To move (a child, etc.) lightly up and down in the arms or on the knee. Also *fig.*

1530 PALSGR. 506/2, I dandyll, as a mother or nourryce doth a childe upon their lappe. **1614** BP. HALL *Recoll. Treat.* 804 Your Church, in whose lappe the vilest miscreants are dandled. *c* **1672** WOOD *Life* (Oxf. Hist. Soc.) I. 79 [He] would often take her out of the cradle, dandle her in his armes. **1762** GOLDSM. *Nash* 93 Dandling two of Mr. Wood's children on her knees. **1847** J. WILSON *Chr. North* (1857) I. 146 He sits dandling his child on his knee. **1882** F. P. VERNEY in *Contemp. Rev.* XLII. 961 The nurse took up a child and dandled it kindly.

b. *transf.* To move (anything) up and down playfully in the hand.

a **1678** MARVELL *Poems, Checker Inn*, Thou'lt ken him out by a white wand He dandles always in his hand. **1865** TYLOR *Early Hist. Man.* ii. 20 In the sign..for 'child', the right elbow is dandled upon the left hand.

2. *fig.* To make much of, pet, fondle, pamper.

1575 GASCOIGNE *Pr. Pleas. Kenilw.* Wks. (1587) 12, I would confesse that fortune then, fully freendly dyd me dandle. **1592** WYRLEY *Armorie* 143 She dandles him, and then on him she frowns. **1605** Z. JONES *Loyer's Specters* 16 Which did entertain and dandle him with all manner of delights. **1742** YOUNG *Nt. Th.* i. 315 By blindness thou art blest; By dotage dandled to perpetual smiles. **1881** GOLDWIN SMITH *Lectures & Ess.* 42 No man or nation ever was dandled into greatness.

†**3.** To trifle, play, or toy with. *Obs.*

1569 E. FENTON *Secr. Nature* 66a, Noble men, whome she courted and dandled with such dissimuled sleightes in loue. **1596** SPENSER *State Irel.* Wks. (Globe) 648/1 They doe soe dandle theyr doinges, and dallye in the service to them committed, as yf they would not have the Enemye subdued. **1611** SPEED *Hist. Gt. Brit.* IX. xx. (1632) 970 King Henries Ambassadors..hauing been dandled by the French during these illusiue practises. **1646** J. HALL *Horæ Vac.* 83 Some studies would be hug'd as imployments, others onely dandled as sports.

4. *intr.* To play or toy (*with*). *rare.*

1829 *Westm. Rev.* XI. 207 That sort of dandling with Irish history. **1865** CARLYLE *Fredk. Gt.* VI. XVI. ix. 256 While dandling with the flute.

†**5.** = DANGLE. *Obs.* (? erroneous.)

1614 R. TAILOR *Hog hath lost Pearl* IV. in Hazl. *Dodsley* XI. 480 A holy spring, about encompassed By dandling sycamores and violets. **1656** W. D. tr. *Comenius' Gate Lat. Unl.* § 147 The wild Swan..in his crop, (dandling just below his beak) insatiable. **1687** A. LOVELL tr. *Bergerac's Com. Hist.* I. 33 Having more shaggy Rags dandling about me than the errantest Tatterdemallion.

†**6.** = DANDER I. *Sc. Obs.*

a **1600** BUREL in Watson *Collect.* (1706) II. 39 (Jam.) Euin as the blind man gangs be ges, In houering far behynd, So dois thou dandill in distres.

dandler ('dændlə(r)). [f. DANDLE + -ER[1].] One who dandles: see the verb.

1598 FLORIO, *Trescatore*, a iester, a dallier, a dandler. **1611** COTGR., *Mignardeur*, a luller, dandler, cherisher. **1830** CUNNINGHAM *Brit. Paint.* I. 269 Poor Miss Morris was no dandler of babes.

†'**dandling,** *sb. Obs.* (or *dial.*) [f. DANDLE *v.* + -ING.] A dandled child; a fondling, a pet.

1611 COTGR., *Mignot*, a wanton, feddle, fauorite; a dilling, dandling, darling. **1695** KENNETT *Par. Antiq.* App. 695 Fortune..before made him her dandling. [**1847–78** HALLIWELL, *Dandling*, a fondling child.]

dandling ('dændlɪŋ), *vbl. sb.* [-ING[1].] The action of the verb DANDLE, q.v.

1591 W. WEBB *Let. to R. Wilmott* in *Tancred & Gismund*, Let it run abroade (as many parentes doe their children once past dandling). **1592** SHAKS. *Ven. & Ad.* 562. **1602** MARSTON *Ant. & Mel.* III. Wks. 1856 I. 39 That wanton dandling of your fan. **1836** SIR W. HAMILTON *Discuss.* (1852) 260 [He] has long out-grown the need of any critical dandling.

'**dandling,** *ppl. a.* [-ING[2].] That dandles: see the verb. Hence '**dandlingly** *adv.*

1598 FLORIO, *Vezzosaménte*, wantonly, dandlinglie.

dandruff, dandriff ('dændrəf, -ɪf). Forms: 6 **dandrif, 6–7 -ruffe, -raff(e, 7 -ruf, -riffe, 7– -ruff, -riff;** also **6–7 dandro, 8–9** (esp. *U.S.*) **dander.** [Of unknown origin.

For conjectures, see Wedgwood, Edward Müller, Skeat: nothing satisfactory has been suggested.]

Dead scarf-skin separating in small scales and entangled in the hair; scurf.

1545 RAYNOLD *Byrth Mankynde* IV. vi. (1634) 198 They that haue blacke hayre haue more store of Dandruffe then others. **1601** HOLLAND *Pliny* XX. vi, The iuice of Garlick being taken in drink clenseth the head from dandruffe. **1611** COTGR., *Crasse de la teste*, Dandriff; the skales that fall from the head, etc. in combing. **1730** SWIFT *Poems, Lady's Dressing-Room*, Combs..Fill'd up with Dirt..Sweat, Dandriff, Powder, Lead and Hair. **1866** YOUATT *Horse* xv. 342 The scales which fall off in the shape of dandriff.

β. **1591** PERCIVALL *Sp. Dict.*, *Caspa de cabeça*, Dandro, *Furfures capitis*. **1650** BULWER *Anthropomet.* 53 To breed Lice and Dandro, after the manner of your Irish. **1786** *Sportsman's Dict.* G g viij, Some horses have neither scales, dander, or scabs. *a* **1800** *Spirit of Farmer's Museum* (1801) 278 An infant child..had ever since its birth, been grievously afflicted with a certain disorder in the head, called by the learned, 'the dander, or dandriff'. **1860** J. G. HOLLAND *Miss Gilbert's Career* viii. 131 A young man that.. keeps the dander all off his coat collar..always makes a good husband. **1875** —— *Sevenoaks* v. 65 I've took more nor three quarts o' dander out iv 'is hide. **1876** *Whitby Gloss.*, *Dander*, a slight scurf on the skin.

attrib. **1668** DRYDEN *Evening's Love* IV. iii, There's the dandriff comb you lent me.

Hence '**dandruffy** *a.*, scurfy.

1858 MAYNE REID in *Chamb Jrnl.* IX. 333 A white dandruffy surface was exhibited.

dandy ('dændɪ), *sb.*[1] (and *a.*). [Origin unknown. In use on the Scottish Border in the end of the 18th c.; and about 1813–1819 in vogue in London, for the 'exquisite' or 'swell' of the period.

Perhaps the full form was JACK-A-DANDY, which occurs from 1659, and in 18th c. had a sense which might pass into that of 'dandy'. Connexion with *dandiprat* or with F. *dandin* has been guessed, but without any apparent ground. It is worthy of notice also that *Dandy* = Andrew in Sc. See Rev. C. B. Mount in *N. & Q.* 8th Ser. IV. 81.]

A. *sb.* **I. 1. a.** One who studies above everything to dress elegantly and fashionably; a beau, fop, 'exquisite'.

c **1780** *Sc. Song* (see *N. & Q.* 8th Ser. IV. 81), I've heard my granny crack O' sixty twa years back When there were sic a stock of Dandies O; Oh they gaed to Kirk and Fair, Wi' their ribbons round their hair, And their stumpie drugget coats, quite the Dandy O. **1788** R. GALLOWAY *Poems* (Jam.), They..laugh at ilka dandy at that fair day. **1818** MOORE *Fudge Fam. Paris* i. 48 They've made him a Dandy, A thing, you know, whiskered, great-coated, and laced, Like an hour-glass, exceedingly small in the waist. **1819** ANDERSON *Cumbrld. Ball.* (1823) 148, I..went owre to see Carel Fair; I'd heard monie teales o' thur dandies—Odswinge! how they mek the fwok stare! **1831** CARLYLE *Sart. Res.* III. x, A Dandy is a Clothes-wearing Man, a Man whose trade, office, and existence consists in the wearing of Clothes. **1874** DASENT *Half a Life* II. 65 Like the cabriolets which some dandies still drive.

b. Said of animals and things.

1835 SIR G. STEPHEN *Adv. Search Horse* ii. 18, I mounted many a slug and many another dandy before I again ventured to buy. **1885** RUNCIMAN *Skippers & Sh.* 54 The barque looked a real dandy.

2. *slang* or *colloq.* Anything superlatively fine, neat, or dainty; *esp.* in phr. ***the dandy*** (now usu. ***a dandy***), 'the correct thing', 'the ticket'.

1784 G. COLMAN *Song* in *Two to One*, Her breath is like the rose, and the pretty little mouth Of pretty little Tippet is the Dandy O! **1814** *Apollo* (in *N. & Q.* 6th Ser. IX. 136), For marriage to old maids is the dandy, O. **1822** *Pennsylv. Intelligencer* 3 Dec. (Th.), The reader will suppose this was a dandy of a thing, since it was on writing paper. **1832** W. STEPHENSON *Gateshead Local Poems* 105 A cure for coughs I know, It will prove the dandy. **1837–40** HALIBURTON *Clockm.* (1862) 340 The new railroad will be jist the dandy for you. **1887** *Amer. Angler* XII. 360, I had the largest, the dandy, and was satisfied. **1887** *Harper's Mag.* June 160/1 'Death loves a shining mark', and she hit a dandy when she turned loose on Jim. **1897** S. HALE *Lett.* (1919) 319 Mrs. B. was a dandy, she didn't fuss nor worry. **1919** H. L. WILSON *Ma Pettengill* iv. 111 It was just one punch, though a dandy. **1968** D. HELWIG in R. Weaver *Canad. Short Stories* 2nd Ser. 376 We..sat..waiting for Barrow Man to light his fire. At nine-fifteen he did it. It was a dandy.

II. Technical and other senses; app. transferred applications of prec. to things considered neat, trim, or 'tidy' in form or action.

3. *Naut.* 'A sloop or cutter with a jigger-mast abaft, on which a mizen-lug-sail is set' (Smyth, *Sailor's Word-bk.*). Hence ***dandy-rig***, ***-rigged*** adjs.

1858 *Merc. Marine Mag.* V. 134 Dandy 3, Flats 4. **1880** *Daily News* 12 Nov. 3/7 Busy Bee, fishing dandy, of Lowestoft, struck on a wreck and foundered. **1886** *Times* 2 Jan. 3 The lifeboats..dandy Snowdrop, of Ramsgate..dandy Lady's Page, of Scarborough..dandy Seabird, of Yarmouth, saved vessel and six.

1858 SIMMONDS *Dict. Trade*, *Dandy-rigged-cutter*. **1883** *Fisheries Exhib. Catal.* (ed. 4) 132 An elliptical stern Dandy-rig Fishing-boat. **1891** *Daily News* 15 Dec. 5/6 His smack..dandy-rigged, and of only thirty-seven tons, was again overtaken by a storm.

4. *Naut.* A piece of mechanism, resembling a small capstan, used for hoisting the trawl. Hence **dandy-span**, the handle-bar by which a dandy is worked.

1883 *Fisheries Exhib. Catal.* 10 Bridles, Dandies..Hauling Lines, and Running Gear. *Ibid.* 12 Manilla Bridles..Dandy Span.

5. *dial.* A bantam fowl. (***dandy-cock, dandy-hen.***)

1828 *Craven Dialect*, *Dandy-cock*, a bantam cock, a diminutive species of poultry. **1884** *Cheshire Gloss.*, *Dandy*, a bantam. The sexes are specified as dandy-cock and dandy-hen. **1887** *S. Cheshire Gloss.* 167 'Hey struts abowt like a dandy-cock.'

6. *Irish.* A small jug; a small glass (of whisky).

1838 *Blackw. Mag.* May (Farmer), 'Father Tom and the Pope'. Dimidium cyathi vero apud Metropolitanos Hibernicos dicitur dandy. **1859** *All Year Round* No. 12. 285 Take a dandy—there's no headache in Irish whisky.

7. In various other technical applications; *e.g.* a handy accessory to various machines or structures; a running-out fire for melting pig-iron in tin-plate manufacture; a small false grate fitted for purposes of economy into an ordinary grate or fireplace; a light iron hand-cart used to carry coke to a blast furnace; also short for DANDY-CART, -ROLLER.

1850 MRS. F. TROLLOPE *Petticoat Govt.* 13 She blew a small dandy-ful of shavings and cinders into warmth, for the purpose of causing the water in her diminutive kettle to boil. **1851** *Rep. Juries of Exhibition* 428 A channelled and perforated roller technically called a 'dandy', to remove part of the water from the pulp. **1875** URE *Dict. Arts* III. 490 The two rollers following the dandy..are termed couching-rollers. **1884** W. H. GREENWOOD *Steel & Iron* 276 Price's puddling furnace..consists of a bed or hearth at one end of which is a chamber or dandy in which the pig-iron is first placed for preliminary heating. **1892** [see DANDY-CART].

Hence (*nonce-wds.*) **ˈdandyhood**, the state or style of a dandy. **ˈdandyic** *a.*, dandyish. **ˈdandyize** *v. intr.* to play the dandy. **ˈdandy-jack** *v.*, to play the jack-a-dandy. **ˈdandy-land** [cf. *fairyland*], the (imaginary) land of dandies. **ˈdandyling**, a diminutive or petty dandy.

1823 *New Monthly Mag.* VII. 229 Prank'd out in dandihood withal To the top pitch of fashion's folly. **1832** *Fraser's Mag.* V. 171 Done..not with philosophic, permanent colours, but with mere dandyic ochre and japan. **1830** *Ibid.* II. 200 We have dandyised in our time with the..turbaned exquisites of..Stamboul. **1831** CARLYLE *Sart. Res.* III. x, Those Dandiacal Manicheans, with the host of Dandyising Christians, will form one body. **1887** FENN *Master of Cerem.* xi, 'My, he do go dandy-jacking along the cliff.' **1831** MOORE *Summer Fête* 498 Two Exquisites, a he and she, Just brought from Dandyland, and meant For Fashion's grand Menagerie. **1846** WORCESTER, *Dandyling*, a little dandy; a ridiculous fop. *Qu. Rev.*

B. *attrib.* and *adj.* **1.** Of, belonging to, or characteristic of a dandy or dandies; of the nature of a dandy; affectedly neat, trim, or smart.

1813 BYRON *Let. to Moore* 25 July, The season has closed with a Dandy Ball. **1821** —— *Juan* v. cxliii, Even a Dandy's dandiest chatter. **1824** MISS MITFORD *Village* Ser. I. (1863) 172 The stiff cravat, the pinched-in waist, the dandy-walk. **1848** THACKERAY *Van. Fair* lx, A dandy little hand in a kid-glove. **1887** JESSOPP *Arcady* 194 They..had the dandy youths taught how to ride.

2. a. Fine, splendid, first-rate. *colloq.* (orig. *U.S.*). Freq. in phr. ***fine and dandy***.

1794 *Massachusetts Spy* 27 Aug. (Th.), My uncle Cuthbert blew out a prodigious puff of my dandy tobacco. **1842** W. BAGLEY *Let.* 22 June in N. E. Eliason *Tarheel Talk* (1956) iv. 128, I now have a real dandy suit of clothes & I step about New York just as if I was some great one. **1894** P. L. FORD *Hon. Peter Stirling* (1903) 163 'If I was as big as him,' said one, 'I'd fire all the peelers.' 'Wouldn't that be dandy?' cried another. **1908** C. E. MULFORD *Orphan* vi. 73, I got yore smokin', Orphant!.. Here she is, right side up and fine and dandy! **1910** S. E. WHITE *Rules of Game* I. i, 'How's Mrs. Orde..?' he inquired. 'Mrs. Orde is fine and dandy.' **1926** 'R. CROMPTON' *William—the Conqueror* v. 83 Oh, how *dandy*! **1940** *War Illustr.* 5 Jan. 571/1 The troops had told the Dominions Secretary that the crossing had been 'dandy', and the General told us the same thing. **1940** O. NASH *Face is Familiar* 259 Candy is dandy But liquor is quicker. **1964** WODEHOUSE *Frozen Assets* ii. 31 I'm fine and dandy now, but before I saw you I was feeling extremely blue.

b. As *adv.* Finely, splendidly. *U.S. colloq.*

1908 S. E. WHITE *Riverman* xli. 323 'She's holding strong and dandy,' said Orde.., examining critically the clumps of piles. **1952** in Wentworth & Flexner *Dict. Amer. Slang* (1960) 140/1 She and her husband get along just dandy. **1963** O. NASH *Everyone but Thee & Me* 110 And, should Furnace or freezer act less than dandy, There's always a quaint old handy-man handy.

Hence **ˈdandily** *adv.*, **ˈdandiness**.

1834 *Fraser's Mag.* IX. 147 We were not so dandily dressed. **1825** SOUTHEY *Lett.* (1856) III. 473 The first two numbers..displeased me as much by their dandiness as ——'s does by its blackguardism.

dandy, *sb.*[2] Also **dandy-fever**. [See DENGUE.] The popular name in the West Indies of DENGUE fever, on its first appearance there in 1827.

1828 STEDMAN in *Edin. Med. Jrnl.* XXX. 227 As it was unknown to the faculty, the vulgar, as commonly happens, gave it names of their own; and ridiculous as they may sound, they soon became the only appellations of the new malady. The English negroes in St. Thomas called it the *Dandy Fever*, while the French vulgar called it the *Bouquet*, which again was corrupted into the *Bucket*. —— *ibid.* 239 The contagion was supposed to be brought by a vessel from the coast of Africa which touched at St. Thomas. **1830** FURLONGE *Ibid.* XXXIII. 51 (*title*) A few remarks on the Dandy which prevailed in the West Indies towards the close of 1827 and beginning of 1828. **1869** E. A. PARKES *Pract. Hygiene* (ed. 3) 573 'Dandy fever', or break-bone (Dengue), has prevailed several times. **1880** FAGG & PYE SMITH *Textbk. Med.*, The negroes called the new disease 'Dandy-fever', apparently in ridicule of the attitude and gait of the patient.

‖**dandy, dandi** (ˈdændɪ), *sb.*[3] *Anglo-Ind.* Also **dandee**. [Hindī *ḍanḍī*, deriv. of *ḍanḍ*, *ḍanḍ* staff, oar (Yule).]

1. A boatman of the Ganges.

1685 HEDGES *Diary* 6 Jan. (Y.), Our Dandees (or Boatmen) boyled their rice. **1763** W. HASTINGS in Long *Select. Rec.* (1869) 347 (Y.) They..plundered and seized the Dandies and Mangies' vessel. *c* **1813** MRS. SHERWOOD *Ayah & Lady* ix. 51 To make sport for the dandies, and other people in the boat. **1867** SMYTH *Sailor's Word-bk.*, *Dandies*, rowers of the budgerow boats on the Ganges.

2. (*Dandi.*) A S'aiva mendicant who carries a small wand (F. Hall).

1832 H. H. WILSON in *Asiatic Res.* XVII. 173 The *Dańdi* is distinguished by carrying a small *dań'd*, or wand, with several processes or projections. **1862** BEVERIDGE *Hist. India* II. IV. ii. 74 The Dandis, distinguished by carrying a small *dand* or wand.

3. 'A kind of vehicle used in the Himalaya, consisting of a strong cloth slung like a hammock to a bamboo staff, and carried by two (or more) men [***dandy-wallahs***]' (Yule).

1870 C. F. GORDON CUMMING in *Gd. Words* 135/1 As the darkness closed in, my dandy-wallahs stumbled, so that I had to give up the attempt to use the dandy, and struggle on on foot. **1888** *Times* 2 July 5/2 Major Battye and Captain Urmston joined the rear and placed the wounded man in a dandy.

ˈdandy-brush. [app. f. DANDY *sb.*[1]] A stiff brush used in cleaning horses, made of split whalebone or vegetable fibre, as the stiff root fibres of *Chrysopogon Gryllus*, the Venetian or French Whisk.

1845 *Jrnl. R. Agric. Soc.* VI. I. 77 Then have every bullock well brushed with what is called a dandy-brush (being a brush made with whale-bone, for taking the rough dirt off horses). **1879** MISS BRADDON *Vixen* xxxii. 249 Poor Bates..brushed away more than one silent tear with the back of the dandy-brush.

ˈdandy-cart. A kind of spring-cart, used by milkmen, etc.

1861 RAMSAY *Remin.* Ser. II. 105 May be some o'ye wad be sae kin' as to gie me a cast out in a dandy-cart. **1892** *Melbourne Age* 31 Dec. 10/1 Advt., Milk dandy, good, high wheels, half cost.

dandy-cock, -hen: see DANDY[1] 5.

dandydom (ˈdændɪdəm). [f. DANDY *sb.*[1] + -DOM.] The condition of a dandy; the world of dandies.

c **1850** in *Daily Chron.* (1902) 4 Nov. 3/2 It 'flustered the realms of dandydom'. **1885** *Society in London* 155 A glorified dragoon who has reached the apotheosis of old dandydom. **1899** *Strand Mag.* Mar. 273/2 He was..reduced to a state of dilapidated dandy-dom.

dandy-fever: see DANDY[2].

dandyfunk. *Naut.* [? f. DANDY *sb.*[1] II + FUNK *sb.*[2]] Hard tack soaked in water and baked with fat and molasses.

1883 in *Amer. Speech* (1959) XXXIV. 28 **1902** A. B. LUBBOCK *Round the Horn* iii. 94 Loring..proposed that we should make some dandyfunk for tea. *Ibid.* 95 The dandy-funk..steaming hot, a mixture between a cake and a pudding. **1903** C. PROTHEROE *Life Mercantile Marine* ix. 87 'Dandy-funk' is another dish..the substitution of a little molasses furnishing the excuse for another name. **1931** E. LINKLATER *Juan in America* I. iii. 37 They grew tender over memories of lobscouse and dandy-funk.

ˈdandy-horse. A kind of velocipede, an early form of the bicycle, in which the rider sat on a bar between the two wheels, and propelled himself by pushing the ground with each foot alternately.

1819 J. HODGSON in J. Raine *Mem.* (1857) I. 247 The little boys about London are all getting dandy-horses, for such seems at present the name of the Velocipede. **1892** *Strand Mag.* IV. 30 (*Evolution of Cycle*) Mr. Dennis Johnson..a coachmaker at 75 Long-acre took out a patent for this dandy or hobby-horse in 1818.

dandyish (ˈdændɪɪʃ), *a.* [f. DANDY[1] + -ISH.] Somewhat characteristic of a dandy; foppish.

1826 DISRAELI *Viv. Grey* IV. v, Pacing Bond Street..with an air at once dandyish and heroical. **1883** F. H. BURNETT *Through one Admin.* I. vii. 70 His rather dandyish light overcoat.

dandyishly (ˈdændɪɪʃlɪ), *adv.* [f. DANDYISH + -LY[2].] Like a dandy, in the manner of a dandy.

1868 *Good Words* 1 Nov. 699 Dandyishly dressed in spotless white linen. **1909** H. G. BARKER *Voysey Inheritance* IV. 172 Very dandyishly dressed, he still seems by no means so happy as his clothes might be making him.

dandyism (ˈdændɪɪz(ə)m). [f. as DANDYISH *a.* + -ISM.] The character, style, or manners of a dandy.

1819 *Blackw. Mag.* IV. 565 The affectation of Dandyism on the part of some..of our day. **1883** V. STUART *Egypt* 32 A house..with some attempt at architectural dandyism.

ˈdandy-line. [Cf. DANDY *sb.*[1] 4.] A kind of line used in herring fishing: see quot.

1882 DAY *Fishes Gt. Brit.* 215 The 'dandy-line' is used in herring fishery at Peterhead..A piece of lead about 1½ lb. in weight is attached to a line, which carries at short intervals transverse pieces of whalebone or cane, having unbaited hooks at either end. Herrings are such hungry fish that they fly at the naked hooks, and are easily caught in this manner.

ˈdandy-loom. A name given to a loom invented by William Radcliffe and patented in 1805 by Thomas Johnson.

1823 *Mech. Mag.* I. 45 A hand loom on a new construction has been recently introduced which has received the appellation of the Dandy Loom. **1878** A. BARLOW *Weaving* 245 Radcliffe's loom was long known as the 'Dandy loom'.

ˈdandy-note. A document used in the British Customs for giving the export officer particulars of the bonded goods delivered from a warehouse for shipment at his station.

[The name is generally held, by those who have to do with the matter, to be a corruption of *addenda note*, these documents being of the nature of addenda to the *pricking notes*, used to advise the export officers of bonded goods intended for shipment.]

ˈdandy-ˌroller. *Papermaking.* Also **dandy-roll**. A perforated roller for solidifying the partly-formed web of paper, and for impressing the water mark.

(Patented by John Wilks in 1830, No. 5934, but the word does not occur in his specification.)

1839 *Specif. Joynson's Patent* No. 7977. 2 [The] said roller is commonly known by the name of a dandy roller, a dancer, or a top roller. **1875** URE *Dict. Arts* III. 491 The pulp..receiving any desired marks by means of the dandy-roller. **1879** *Print. Trades Jrnl.* XXVI. 9 Dandy-roll..for producing water-marks on writing papers.

dandysette, -zette: see DANDIZETTE.

dandy-wink. [f. DANDY *sb.*[1] II + WINK *sb.*[2]] A small windlass worked by short fixed levers, e.g. in a fishing-boat.

1883 W. C. RUSSELL *Round Galley Fire* 92 The dandy-wink is manned, the beam secured, and the net is then dragged in over the side.

Dane (deɪn). [Corresponds to Da. *Daner*, ON. *Danir*:—OTeut. *Dani-z* pl., Danes, L. *Dani* pl. The OE. form was *Dęne* pl. (with umlaut), which would have given *Dene* in ME.: cf. OE.

Denemearc in 11th c., later *Denmearc, Denmarc*, in ON. *Danmörk* (:—*marku*), Da. *Dannemark, Danmark*, the Danish mark or country, Denmark.]

1. A native or subject of Denmark; in older usage including all the Northmen who invaded England from the 9th to the 11th c.

901 *O.E. Chron.*, Butan ðam dæle þe under Dena onwalde wæs. *a* **1050** *Ibid.* an. 1018 (Laud MS.) And Dene and Engle wurdon sam mæle æt Oxnaforda. *a* **1300** *Cursor M.* 24771 (Cott.) Harald..þat born was o þe danis [*v.r.* danas, danes] blod. **1483** *Cath. Angl.* 89 A Dan, *dacus, quidam populus.* **1596** SPENSER *State Irel.* Wks. (Globe) 642/2 The others [hills] that are rounde were cast up by the Danes..for they are called Dane-rathes, that is, hills of the Danes. **1602** SHAKS. *Ham.* v. ii. 352, I am more an Antike Roman than a Dane. **1682** EVELYN *Let. to Pepys* 19 Sept., If euer there were a real dominion [of the seas] in the world, the Danes must be yielded to haue had it. **1863** TENNYSON *Welcome to Alexandra*, Saxon and Norman and Dane are we, But all of us Danes in our welcome of thee.

2. Applied to a breed or breeds of dogs.

great Dane (also simply *Dane*): a large, powerful, shorthaired breed of dog, between the mastiff and greyhound types. *lesser Dane*: the Dalmatian, or coach-dog.

[**1750** BUFFON *Hist. Nat.* s.v. *Chien*, Le grand danois.] **1774** GOLDSM. *Nat. Hist.* III. viii. 286 The Bull-dog, as Mr. Buffon supposes, is a breed between the small Dane and the English mastiff. The large Dane is the tallest dog that is generally bred in England. —— *ibid.* 292 The great Dane. **1800** SYDENHAM EDWARDS *Cynogr. Brit.* s.v., A beautiful variety, called the Harlequin Dane, has a finely marbled coat. **1870** BLAINE *Encycl. Rur. Sports* 394 The great Dane is rather pied or patched than spotted..The lesser Dane dog, Dalmatian, or coach dog. **1883** *Great Dane Club Rules* (*Standard of Points*), The Great Dane is not so heavy as the Mastiff, nor should he too nearly approach the Greyhound in type. **1891** *Times* 28 Oct. 11/5 Great Danes have certainly become very popular during the last few years.

3. *attrib.* or as *adj.* = DANISH.

1873 STUBBS *Const. Hist.* I. 199 The amalgamation of the Dane and Angle population began from the moment of the conversion.

dane, obs. form of DAN[1], DEAN.

danebol: see DENNEBOL.

Danebrog: see DANNEBROG.

Danegeld, -gelt (ˈdeɪngɛld, -gɛlt). *Eng. Hist.* Also 4 **Dangilde**, 4–6 **Danegilt, Dane gilt**, 5–7 **Dane ghelte, Daneghelt**, 6 **Dane gelt**, 7 **Danageld**, 7–9 **Danegelt**. [Corresponds to ON. **Danagiald*, in ODa. *Danegjeld*, mod.Da. *Danegæld*, f. *Dana-, Dane-* + *gjald, gjeld*, payment, tribute, corr. to OE. *ȝield, ȝild, ȝeld*, whence ME. *ȝeld, ȝild*, YELD. Cf. med.L. *Danigeldum*.]

An annual tax imposed at the end of the 10th c. or in the 11th c., originally (as is supposed) to provide funds for the protection of England from the Danes, and continued after the Norman Conquest as a land-tax. Also *transf.* and *fig.*

The name is not known to occur in OE., and the actual contemporary notices, beginning with Domesday, are mainly of fiscal character. Bromton (14th c.) calls it 'tallagium datum Danis', apparently identifying it with the *gafol* or tribute paid to the Danes in 991, and on two subsequent occasions, to buy them off. In the so-called 'Laws of Eadweard' (Schmid 496) it is described as an annual tax to hire mercenaries to resist and put down pirates. This might identify it with the *heregyld* 'army-tax' levied by the Danish kings to maintain their army and navy (see *O.E. Chron.* 1039–40), and said to have been afterwards remitted by Edward the Confessor. Mr. Freeman suggests (*Norm. Conq.* II. App. Q) 'that *Denageld* was a popular name of dislike, originally applied to the payments made to buy off the Danes, and thence transferred to these other payments made to Danish and other mercenary troops, from the time of Thurkill onwards'. The Danegeld was levied as a land-tax by the Norman kings; it disappears under that name after 1163, but in fact continued under the name of *tallage*.

[**991** *O.E. Chron.*, On þam ȝeare man ȝerædde þæt man ȝeald ærest gafol Deniscan mannum, for þam mycclan broȝan þe hi worhtan be þam sæ riman.] **1086** *Domesday Bk.* (1816) 336 Stanford..dedit geldum T.R.E. pro. XII. hundrez & dimidio. In exercitu & nauigio & in Danegeld. **1100–35** *Charter to London* in Stubbs *Sel. Ch.* III. 103 Et [cives] sint quieti de schot et de loth, de Danegildo et de murdro. *c* **1250** *Gloss. Law Terms* in *Rel. Ant.* I. 33 Danegeld, *Tailage de Danais.* *c* **1330** R. BRUNNE *Chron.* (1810) 57 Edward him granted..þat neuer þe Dangilde.. Suld be chalanged for man of Danes lond. **1483** CAXTON *Gold. Leg.* 324/2 An ayde was thenne cleped the dane ghelte. **1577** HOLINSHED *Chron.* I. 239 an. 991 This money was called Danegylt or Dane money, and was levyed of the people. Although others take that to be Danegylte, whiche was gyuen unto such Danes as king Egelred afterwards reteyned in his service, to defende the lande from other Danes and enimyes. **1644** MILTON *Areop.* (Arb.) 73 Not he who takes up armes for cote and conduct, and his four nobles of Danegelt. **1756** P. C. WEBB *Short Acc. Danegeld* 2 It was called Danegeld as being originally agreed to be paid to the Danes, and, like many other things, continued to retain the name long after it became appropriated to uses entirely different. **1873** STUBBS *Const. Hist.* I. 105 It may be questioned whether any money taxation properly so called ever existed before the imposition of Danegeld by Ethelred the Unready. *Ibid.* I. 279 The Conqueror..imposed the Danegeld anew. *Ibid.* I. 462 The Danegeld from this very year 1163 ceases to appear as a distinct item of account in the Pipe Rolls. **1911** FLETCHER & KIPLING *School Hist. Eng.* ii. 39 It is always a temptation to an armed and agile nation, To call upon a neighbour and to say:—'We invaded you last night—we are quite prepared to fight, Unless you pay us cash to go away'. And that is called asking for Dane-geld. **1920** *19th Cent.* July 28 A policy dictated by fear should be interpreted in terms of *danegeld* payable by Great Britain to the Moscow Camarilla. **1955** *Times* 18 May 11/5 Amounted to little more than blackmail and the payment of *danegelt*, which has never yet satisfactorily settled any dispute.

dane gun. *W.* and *S. Afr.* Also **Dane gun.** [f. DANE + GUN *sb.* 3.] Any of several kinds of primitive firearms, orig. introduced by Danish traders.

1900 *Daily News* 25 Sept. 8/3 In the village were found 300 Dane guns, 40 rifles, three Martini-Henry carbines. **1901** *Daily Chron.* 31 Aug. 3/4 Three Ashantis, armed with their long dane guns. **1920** *Blackw. Mag.* Mar. 384/2 Every man or boy who could wield a spear or hold a dane gun. **1935** *Geogr. Jrnl.* LXXXV. 126 The dance that followed was accompanied by the firing of dane-guns. **1947** J. STEVENSON-HAMILTON *Wild Life S. Afr.* xv. 103 The native with his Dane gun, or Tower musket.

Dane-law (ˈdeɪnlɔː). Also 1 **Dena laȝu**, 3 **Denelaȝe, Dene lawe**, 6 **Dane lawe**, 8 **Dane-lage**, (**-lege**), 9 **Dane-lagh**. Latinized 2 **Denelaga**, 2–9 **Danelaga**. [OE. *Dęna laȝu* Danes' law, of which *Dane-law* is a modern equivalent.]

1. The Danish law anciently in force over that part of England which was occupied or held by the Danes.

c **1050** *Laws of Edw. & Guthr.* 7 (Bosw.) Gylde lahslihte inne on Dena laȝe and wite mid Englum. *a* **1135** *Leges Hen. I*, vi. 2 (Stubbs *Sel. Chart.* III. 100) Legis etiam Anglicae trina est partitio..alia enim Westsexiae, alia Mircena, alia Denelaga est. *a* **1300** *Shires of Eng.* in *O.E. Misc.* 146 þes .xxxij. schire syndon to delede on þreo lawan. On is west-sexene lawe, oþer Dene lawe, þe þrydde Mercena lawe.. To Dene lawe bilympeþ .xv. schire. **1576** LAMBARDE *Peramb. Kent* (1826) p. xvi, The Dane lawe, West-Saxon lawe, and Merchen lawe: The first of which was brought in by the Danes. **1765** BLACKSTONE *Comm.* (1830) I. Introd. 66 The Dane-Lage, or Danish law, the very name of which speaks its original and composition.

2. Hence, The part of England over which this law prevailed, being the district north-east of Watling Street, ceded by the Treaty of Wedmore, 878, or perhaps the Northumbrian territory in Danish occupation.

This use appears explicitly only in modern historians (chiefly under the barbarous forms *Dane-lage, Dane-lagh*, which are neither Old nor modern English), though founded on ancient passages, such as those of quots. 1050, 1300, in 1. [In Icelandic *lög* 'law' had, according to Vigfusson, the sense 'law-district', '*almost* as a local name' in *Gulaþings-lög, prænda-lög*, etc.]

1837 *Penny Cycl.* VIII. 299/2 The eastern part of England retained long after the name of Danelagh, or Danish law. **1874** GREEN *Short Hist.* i. 50 The Danelagh, as the district occupied by the Danes began to be called. **1877** FREEMAN *Norm. Conq.* (ed. 3) II. 663 Danes in the sense of being inhabitants of the *Denalagu*. **1886** F. YORK POWELL *Hist. Eng. to 1509*, I. vi. 37 He [K. Eadmund] got the whole Danelaw south of Humber into his hands.

† **ˈDane-money.** *Obs.* = DANEGELD.

1563–87 FOXE *A. & M.* (1684) I. 679/1 Without paying of any manner of imposition or Dane-money.

Dane particle (deɪn). *Med.* [Named after D. M. S. *Dane* (b. 1923), English pathologist, who with others reported its discovery (*Lancet* (1970) 4 Apr. 695).] A spherical particle found in the blood of patients with hepatitis B, now recognized as the capsulated form of the virus responsible for the disease.

1971 J. D. ALMEIDA in *Postgrad. Med. Jrnl.* XLVII. 486/2 The particles described by Dane *et al.* (1970) which we shall describe as Dane particles. **1976** *Lancet* 20 Nov. 1123/1 There was a rapid and reproducible fall in the serum levels of Dane-particle-associated D.N.A., D.N.A. polymerase, and core antigen, all of which are thought to be components of the complete hepatitis-B virus particle. **1981** GREENWOOD & WHITTLE *Immunol. of Med. in Tropics* v. 137 Hepatitis B surface antigen occurs in the serum in three forms, spherical particles..filamentous forms and double-shelled particles about 40 nm in diameter. The last structures, known as Dane particles..are thought to be the complete virion.

ˈDanes'-blood. [Of the same origin as DANEWORT, q.v.] A local name for plants abundant on sites noted for the slaughter of Danes.

a. The Danewort or Dwarf Elder.

1607 CAMDEN *Brit.* 326 Ebulum enim quod sanguineis baccis hic [at Bartlow] circumquaque copiose prouenit, non alio nomine quam *Danes-bloud*, id est *Danicum sanguinem*, etiamnum appellitant, ob multitudinem Danorum qui ibidem ceciderunt. **1631** WEEVER *Anc. Fun. Mon.* 707 Danewort, which, with blood-red berries, commeth vp here plenteously, they still call by no other name, then Danes-bloud, of the number of Danes that there were slaine. **1656–85** AUBREY *Nat. Hist. Wilts* (1847) 50 Danes-blood (*ebulus*) about Slaughtonford is plenty. There was heretofore a great fight with the Danes, which made the inhabitants give it that name. **1875** *Gardener's Chron.* IV. 515.

[*Note.*—The berries of this plant are not red, but black or reddish black, yielding a violet dye].

b. Clustered Bell-flower, *Campanula glomerata.*

1861 MISS PRATT *Flower. Pl.* III. 342 The author..found this clustered bell-flower [at Bartlow, Cambs.] largely scattered about these mounds..and was told that it was 'Danes-blood'.

c. The Pasque-flower, *Anemone Pulsatilla.*

So called in East Anglia, Essex, Cambs., Herts. (Britten & Holland.)

ˈDanes'-flower. *local.* = DANES'-BLOOD c.

1878–86 BRITTEN & HOLLAND cite the name from Cambridgeshire.

Daneweed (ˈdeɪnwiːd). [See next.]

† **a.** A local name for *Eryngium campestre. Obs.*

b. = DANEWORT. (Prior *Plant-n.*)

1748 *De Foe's Tour Gt. Brit.* II. 416 (D.) Everything hereabouts is attributed to the Danes, because of the neighbouring Daventry, which they suppose to have been built by them. The road hereabouts..being overgrown with Daneweed [*Eryngium*], they fansy it sprung from the blood of the Danes slain in battle. **1737** W. STUKELEY *Mem.* (Surtees) III. 56 Much daneweed still grows upon the Roman road in Castor fields.

Danewort (ˈdeɪnwɜːt). Forms: 6 **danwoort, danewurt, daine-, daynworte**, 6–7 **danwort, danewoort**, 7– **danewort**. [f. DANE + WORT, in accordance with a popular notion that the plant sprang up in places where Danes slaughtered Englishmen or were slaughtered by them.]

A name for the Dwarf Elder, *Sambucus Ebulus.*

(The name is found in Turner 1538, but only the earlier name Wallwort or Wellewort, OE. *wealwyrt*, is given in *Sinon. Barthol.* of 14th c., and *Alphita* c 1450; Rous also, who died 1491, in relating the legend, has only the name *Walwort*; so that the names *Danewort, Daneweed, Dane's blood*, etc. can hardly have belonged to early tradition. While suggested in part by the abundance of the plant at certain spots historically or traditionally associated with slaughter, there was also an element of fanciful etymology in explaining the Latin name *Ebulus* from *ebullire* to bubble forth, with reference to the flowing of blood. See also WALLWORT.)

a **1491** J. ROSSI [ROUS] *Hist. Reg. Angl.* (1716) 105 Herbam ebule, id est *Walwort*,..quæ ex ebullitione sanguinis humani naturaliter originem trahit. **1538** TURNER *Libellus*, Danwort, *chameacte.* **1551** —— *Herbal* I. (1568) O vj a, Walwurt..named in englyshe also danewurt..hath a spoky or busshy top as elder hath. **1578** LYTE *Dodoens* III. xlv. 380 This herbe is called..in Englishe Walwort, Danewort, and Bloodwort. **1640** PARKINSON *Theatr. Bot.* 210 It is supposed it tooke the name Danewort from the strong purging quality it hath, many times bringing them that use it unto a fluxe, which then we say they are troubled with the Danes. **1861** MISS PRATT *Flower. Pl.* III. 131 Dwarf Elder, or Danewort..is..an herb and not a tree.

dang, *v.* A euphemistic substitute for DAMN.

1793–7 *Spirit Pub. Jrnls.* (1799) I. 146 [Kentish man says] Dang me, if I sometimes know how to answer them. **1802** R. ANDERSON *Cumbrld. Ballads, Barbary Bell*, 'Wey, dang it!' says I, 'but this is nit fair!' **1838** DICKENS *Nich. Nick.* ix, 'Dang my boans and boddy if I stan' this ony longer'. **1884** J. PURVES in *Gd. Words* May 330/2 'Dang me if I can make out what they mean to be at'. **1886** MRS. RANDOLPH *Mostly Fools* II. v. 142 'Danged shady lot'.

dang, pa. t. of DING *v.*; also its dial. equivalent = to drive, push, knock, or dash.

1877 *Holderness Gloss., Dang*, to throw anything with vehemency, or passion. **1878** *Cumbrld. Gloss., Dang*, to push, to strike. **1887** *Cheshire Gloss., Dang*, to dash down or about.

dang, *sb. slang.* [f. DANG *v.*] A damn, cuss.

1906 SOMERVILLE & 'ROSS' *Irish Yesterdays* 113 He wouldn't give a dang for them.

danger (ˈdeɪndʒə(r)), *sb.* Forms: 3–6 **daunger**, 4–5 **daungere, dawnger(e, dangere**, 5 **daungeur, dangeour**, 5–6 **daungeour(e**, 6 **daungier, daengier**, *Sc.* **dangeir, -gier, -geare, denger**, 4– **danger**. [a. OF. *dangier, danger*:—late L. **dominiārium*, deriv. of *dominium* lordship, sovereignty, f. *dominus* lord, master. The sense-development took place in OF.: see Godefroy. For the *a* cf. DAN[1].]

A. *sb.* **1.** † **a.** Power of a lord or master, jurisdiction, dominion; power to dispose of, or to hurt or harm; *esp.* in phr. ***in* (*a person's*) *danger***, within his power or at his mercy; sometimes meaning *spec.* in his debt, or under obligation to him. *Obs.* or *arch.*

a **1225** *Ancr. R.* 356, & þolieð ofte daunger of swuche oðerwhule þet muhte beon ower þrel. **1297** R. GLOUC. (Rolls) 1751 þat he wolde hom al out bringe of þe daunger of rome. *c* **1386** CHAUCER *Prol.* 663 In dawngere had he att his owen gise The ȝonge girles of þe diocise. **1440** J. SHIRLEY *Dethe K. James* (1818) 19 Thou hadest nevyr mercy of lordes ..ne of non other gentilman, that came yn thy dawnger. **1461** *Paston Lett.* No. 399 II. 25, I am gretly yn your danger and dette for my pension. **1556** *Ridley's Wks.* (1843) 101 They put themselves in the danger of King Ahab, saying, 'Behold we have heard that the kings of the house of Israel are pitiful and merciful'. **1596** SHAKS. *Merch. V.* IV. i. 180 You stand within his danger, do you not? **1603** KNOLLES *Hist. Turks* (1621) 408 He..having got him within his danger, cruelly put him to death. *a* **1679** HOBBES *Rhet.* I. xiii. (1681) 33 Persons obnoxious to Injury are..Such as are in our danger. **1825** SCOTT *Betrothed* xxx, If the Constable were once within his danger.

† **b.** Power (of a person, weapon, or missile) to inflict physical injury; reach or range. Also *fig.*

1375 BARBOUR *Bruce* III. 43 To withdraw ws..Till we cum owt off thar daunger. **1523** LD. BERNERS *Froiss.* I. clxii. 199 The archers shotte so holly togyder, that none durst come in their dangers. **1576** NEWTON *Lemnie's Complex.* (1633) 39 Within the levill and danger of this vice, are all they. **1602** SHAKS. *Ham.* I. iii. 35 Keepe within the reare of your Affection; Out of the shot and danger of Desire. **1603** KNOLLES *Hist. Turks* (1621) 679 If he should show himself by troups within the danger of the shot. **1618** LATHAM *2nd Bk. Falconry* (1633) 42 Your Spaniels will hunt..so neere you and your Hawke, as they shall neuer spring any thing out of her danger. **1676** *Doctr. of Devils* 200 This draws the Birds into their Dangers.

†**c.** Power of another as it affects one under it; a state of subjection, bondage, or captivity. *Obs.*

c **1350** *Will. Palerne* 4227 Boute daunger or duresse or any despit elles. *c* **1400** *Destr. Troy* 6584 Troilus was..turnyt furth louse, And don out of daunger for the due tyme. *c* **1420** *Anturs of Arth.* xxv, Thynke one þe dawngere and the dole þat I in duelle [in hell]. **1526** *Pilgr. Perf.* (W. de W. 1531) 4 Free from all captiuite and daunger. **1535** COVERDALE *Isa.* lviii. 6 Till..thou lowse him out of bondage, that is in thy daunger.

†**d.** Liability (to loss, punishment, etc.). ***in danger to*** or ***of***: liable to. *Obs.*

1377 LANGL. *P. Pl.* B. XII. 206 For he þat is ones a thef is euermore in daungere, And as lawe lyketh to lyue or to deye. **1465** *Paston Lett.* No. 508 II. 200 Thei say that I am sufficient to bere the hole daunger. **1526** TINDALE *Pathw. Holy Scrip.* Wks. I. 9 The wretched man (that knoweth himself to be..in danger to death and hell). **1611** BIBLE *Matt.* v. 22 In danger of the iudgment. **1689** WOOD *Life* Aug. 31 (Oxf. Hist. Soc.) A Gent. threatned to bring him into danger.

e. The phrase ***out of debt out of danger*** perh. originally belonged here; but is now taken in sense 4.

1730-6 in BAILEY (folio), s.v. *Debt*. **1804** MAR. EDGEWORTH *Pop. Tales, Out of Debt Out of Danger.*

†**2. a.** Difficulty (made or raised); hesitation, reluctance, chariness, stint, grudging; coyness. ***to make danger*** [OF. *faire dangier* (*de*)]: to make a difficulty (about doing anything). *Obs.*

c **1290** *S. Eng. Leg.* I. 397/155 Sein eustas made gret daunger & natheles ate nende to þe emperour..he gan wende. **1375** BARBOUR *Bruce* v. 283 He but danger till him gais. *c* **1386** CHAUCER *Wife's Prol.* 521 With danger uttren we all our chaffare. *c* **1400** *Rom. Rose* 1147 Gold and silver for to dispend Withouten lacking or daungere. *c* **1440** HYLTON *Scala Perf.* (W. de W. 1494) II. x, And our lorde made fyrste daungeour by cause she was an alyene. *c* **1500** *Melusine* 219 They of Coloyne made grete daunger to lete passe the oost thrughe the Cite at brydge. **1526** DALABER in Foxe *A. & M.* (1583) 1196, I made danger of it a while at first: but afterwarde being perswaded by them..I promised to do as they wold haue me.

b. Untowardness; ungracious, uncompliant, or fractious conduct. *Obs.*

a **1300** *Cursor M.* (Cott.) 6299 Wit þair danger, sir moyses [*v.r.* grucchynge on moyses], Oft þai did him haue malees. *c* **1374** CHAUCER *Anel. & Arc.* 186 Hir daunger made him booþe bowe and beende And as hir lyste made him tourne and wende.

†**3.** A place where one is at the mercy of an enemy; a narrow pass; a strait. *Obs.*

1393 GOWER *Conf.* III. 208 In the daunger of a pas, Through which this tiraunt shulde pas She shope his power to compas. *c* **1440** *Promp. Parv.* 114 Daunger, or grete [PYNSON streyte] passage, *arta via.*

4. a. Liability or exposure to harm or injury; the condition of being exposed to the chance of evil; risk, peril. (Directly from sense 1; see esp. 1 d. Now the main sense.)

c **1489** CAXTON *Sonnes of Aymon* xiv. 352 There is daungeour by cause of the nyghte. *a* **1533** LD. BERNERS *Huon* lxxxii. 253 Esclaramonde saw Huon her housebonde in that daunger. **1552** *Bk. Common Prayer, Communion*, So is the daunger great, if we receyue the same vnworthely. **1620** SHELTON *Quix.* III. xli. 280 'Tis ordinarily said that Delay breeds Danger. **1789** A. DUNCAN *Mariner's Chron.* (1805) IV. 44 The sea running immensely high, it brought them again into great danger. **1822** HAZLITT *Table-t.* I. ix. 187 Danger is a good teacher, and makes apt scholars. **1874** MICKLETHWAITE *Mod. Par. Churches* 186 It is also a source of danger to the building.

b. Const. (*a*) *of* that which is exposed to peril. (Now *rare* or *arch.* exc. with *life*.) (*b*) *of* the evil that threatens or impends. (Now the ordinary const.) †(*c*) *to* with *inf. Obs.*

c **1489** CAXTON *Sonnes of Aymon* xxii. 479 Elles they ben in daungeur of their lives. **1555** EDEN *Decades* Pref. to Rdr. (Arb.) 51 The Moore..possessed a greate parte of Spayne to no smaule daungeoure of the hole Christian Empire. *c* **1676** LADY CHAWORTH in *12th Rep. Hist. MSS. Comm.* App. v. 32 Lord Mohun..was four days in danger of lyfe but now is upon recovery. **1726** LEONI *Alberti's Archit.* II. 105 b, In gravel..there is no danger of finding water. *Mod.* He goes in danger of his life.

1490 CAXTON *Eneydos* vi. 29 In dangeour of myserable deth. **1690** LOCKE *Govt.* II. xiv. §168 This..wise Princes never need come in the Danger of. **1715** J. RICHARDSON *Th. Painting* 128 There was no danger of that in Rafaëlle. **1848** MACAULAY *Hist. Eng.* I. 373 They lost their way..and were in danger of having to pass the night on the plain.

1580 NORTH *Plutarch, Theseus* §35 In danger to die. **1611** BIBLE *Transl. Pref.* 1 Sure to be misconstrued, and in danger to be condemned. **1695** BP. PATRICK *Comm. Gen.* 293 It might have been in danger to have been neglected.

c. *spec.* on *Railways.* Risk in a train's proceeding owing to an obstruction, etc. on the line; the position of a signal indicating this.

1841 *Committee on Railways* Q. 467 You think it would be desirable that on all railways red should indicate danger? **1874** *Proc. Inst. Civ. Eng.* XXXVIII. 149 A signal is said to be 'on', when it is at danger.

5. a. (with *a* and *pl.*) An instance or cause of danger; *pl.* perils, risks.

1538 STARKEY *England* I. ii. 42 Ful of manyfold peryllys and daungerys. **1568** GRAFTON *Chron.* II. 25 To commit themselves unto the daungers of the sea. **1859** HELPS *Friends in C.* Ser. II. I. Addr. to Rdr. 3 Blind to the dangers of their country. **1884** *Times* (Weekly Ed.) 5 Sept. 3/2 Two territorial questions..unsettled..each of which was a positive danger to the peace of Europe.

b. *Naut.* A submerged rock, or the like, causing danger to vessels.

1699 HACKE *Coll. Voy.* iii. 59 At three quarters Ebb, you may see all the Dangers going in..But I would not advise any Man to go in till he has viewed the Harbour at low Water. **1858** *Merc. Marine Mag.* V. 347 It appeared to him to be a detached danger, 6 or 9 feet under the surface. **1875** BEDFORD *Sailor's Pock. Bk.* v. (ed. 2) 137 Buoys painted red and black are placed on detached dangers.

†**6.** Mischief, harm, damage. *Obs.*

c **1400** *Destr. Troy* 146 And he no daunger nor deire for þat dede haue. **1530** PALSGR. 212/1 Daunger on the see, *naufraige*. **1568** GRAFTON *Chron.* II. 277 Then the king of his mere pity..suffered them to passe through his hoste without daunger. **1596** SHAKS. *Merch. V.* IV. i. 38. **1601** —— *Jul. C.* II. i. 17 We put a Sting in him, That at his will he may doe danger with.

†**7.** The lordship over a forest; the rent paid in acknowledgement of this (so OF. *dangier*). 'In the Forest-Law, a duty paid by the Tenants to the Lord for leave to plough and sow in the time of Pannage, or Mast-feeding' (Phillips 1706). *Obs.*

1693 *Phil. Trans.* XVII. 691 He ends this Treatise with an Enumeration of the Quit-rents formerly paid out of the Weald, as *Gavel-swine, Scot-ale, Corredy*, and *Danger*.

†**8.** ***to make danger***: in 17th c. used in sense of L. ***periculum facere***, to make trial or experiment; to venture, 'risk it'. *Obs.*

(Perhaps the phrase in 2 taken in a new sense.)

1618 FLETCHER *Legal Subj.* III. iv, Make danger, Trie what they are, trie. **1621** —— *Wild Goose Chase* I. ii, I shall make danger. *a* **1625** —— *Hum. Lieut.* IV. ii, *Leon.* Art thou so valiant? *Lieut.* Not absolutely so neither—yet I'll make danger, Colonel.

†**B.** ? as *adj.* Dangerous, perilous. *Obs. rare.*

c **1470** HENRY *Wallace* VIII. 202 We ar our ner, sic purpos for to tak; A danger chace thai mycht vpon ws mak.

C. *Comb.*, usually *attrib.* (cf. sense 4), as ***danger-area, -board, -chuckle*** (see quot.), ***-flag, -level, -point, -spot, -whistle, -zone***; ***danger-free, -teaching*** adjs.; **danger angle**, (*a*) *Naut.* the angle enclosed by lines drawn from two known points to a point marking the limit of safe approach to a danger to navigation, so that a ship by steering a course keeping the two known points at a larger or smaller angle will avoid the danger; (*b*) *Gunnery* (see quot. 1918); **danger line**, a line, real or imaginary, representing the division between safety and danger; **danger man**, a player or competitor in a sports contest regarded as posing a serious threat to the opposition; one capable of winning or turning a game; **danger money**, a payment made beyond basic wages for dangerous work; also *fig.*; **danger-signal**, a signal indicating danger; *spec.* on *Railways*, a signal (usually the extended arm of a signal-post painted red, or a red light) indicating an obstruction, etc. ahead.

1892 *Notes on Navigation H.M. Ships* (ed. 3) 13 The use of a *danger angle in passing outlying rocks with land behind should also not be forgotten. **1902** *Encycl. Brit.* XXXI. 109/2 To avoid an unnecessarily wide détour in rounding points and shoals, extensive use is now made of both horizontal and vertical danger angles. *Ibid.*, The vertical danger angle enables similar results to be attained by measuring the vertical angle subtended by a known height. **1918** E. S. FARROW *Dict. Mil. Terms, Danger angle*, the angle which the tangent to the trajectory at the point of splash makes with the plane containing the point of splash and parallel to the horizontal plane through the muzzle of the piece in the firing position. **1929** *Star* 21 Aug. 12/4 The gas leak..which made a portion of New Bridge-street a '*danger area'. **1939** *News Review* 30 Nov. 10 Sandringham is a 'danger area' inasmuch as the East coast..might well be the route taken by German bombers on their way to London. **1955** A. L. ROWSE *Expansion Eliz. Eng.* i. 12 We get flashes of light upon the lurid scene from the comparative security of the towns..which swept like a sickle around the danger-area. **1891** *Cycling* 21 Feb. 86 The local centre is about to erect a *danger-board on Maur Tor Hill. **1859** DARWIN *Orig. Spec.* vii. (1860) 192 If a hen gives the *danger-chuckle. **1862** *Athenæum* 31 May 717 The *danger-flag held out to warn their children off the road. **1640** SHIRLEY *St. Patrick for Irel.* v. iii, And make thy person *danger-free. **1935** *Discovery* Dec. 360/2 A simple timing device will indicate whether this approaches the *danger-level. **1967** *Oxford Computer Explained* 31 *Danger level*, a predetermined level of stock, which when broken requires that any outstanding delivery previously requested be hastened. **1890** *Congress. Rec.* 5 June 5654/2, I believe the good sense of our law-makers will still hold us inside the *danger line of peril. **1892** *Notes on Navigation H.M. Ships* (ed. 3) 8 The five-fathom line on most Admiralty charts is to be considered as a caution or danger line. **1902** *Monthly Weather Rev.* 3/1 The December floods of the Tennessee..continued considerably above the danger lines for the first few days. **1953** L. P. HARTLEY *Go-Between* xiv. 167 Again I was lucky with the Psalms; the Sunday before there had been forty-four verses; this Sunday there were forty-three, seven below the danger line. **1976** *Sunday Mail* (Glasgow) 28 Nov. 44/7 Musselburgh went in at half-time two goals up after Aird had scored from a penalty and *danger man Blackie added another. **1980** *Guardian Weekly* 5 Oct. 24 He had to wait nearly an hour before he knew that his total of 269 would be good enough... Bernhard Langer of Germany, Severiano Ballesteros, Brian Waites and Lee Trevino all loomed as danger men. **1942** W. H. BEVERIDGE *Social Insurance* 39 If an occupation is specially hazardous it should carry remuneration—'*danger money'. But to give danger money only in the form of higher wages, that is to say, only so long as no accident has occurred, is of little value. **1953** B. BOLAND *Return* in J. C. Trewin *Plays of Year* IX. 341 There is nothing on this earth so dangerous as putting out a finger to touch another human being's life... We should get danger-money. **1958** *Economist* 15 Nov. 573/2 It means..adding a new regiment of Naafi volunteers, with their 'danger money', to the British men and women who will have to be protected. **1966** *Punch* 19 Jan. 90/1 It may be that the rage for allowances was originally inspired by the dockers, with their claims for danger money, dirty money,..and all the rest. **1835** J. A. ROEBUCK *Short Rev. Long Session* 11/1 When this excitement reaches *danger-point the Lords will yield. **1897** *Daily News* 22 Apr. 6/3 The Macedonian difficulty, which is the real danger-point. **1910** *Westm. Gaz.* 6 Apr. 2/3 The axle is the danger-point in all heavy vehicles which are run at high speeds. **1933** *Archit. Rev.* LXXIII. p. lviii, Such nosings..are apt to wear smooth..and furnish a danger-point at a critical part of the tread. **1848** *Rep. Railway Commissioners* App. 84 The pointsman had not then turned the *danger signal. **1888** J. SHALLOW *Templars Trials* 71 A danger-signal to Christendom. **1905** *Westm. Gaz.* 4 Oct. 3/2 The *danger-spot in our new Treaty with Japan..is the provision for 'insuring the independence and integrity of the Chinese Empire'. **1939** L. MACNEICE *Autumn Jrnl.* xii. 49 Education ..Trains us to keep the roads nor reconnoitre..the beauty-spots or danger-spots. **1616** LANE *Sqr.'s T.* 120/47 Fames highe *daunger-teachinge schoole. **1872** RUSKIN *Eagle's N.* 61 The *danger-whistle of the engines on the bridge. **1907** *Westm. Gaz.* 5 Feb. 7/3 An alarming fire broke out in the City *danger-zone soon after six o'clock last night. **1925** E. F. NORTON *Fight for Everest: 1924* 58 Anywhere beyond the Base Camp may be considered as the 'danger zone'. **1927** *Observer* 5 June 19/2 The chief new feature [of contract bridge] introduced in America has been what is known as the 'Vulnerable' or 'Danger Zone'. **1928** V. WOOLF in *Times Lit. Suppl.* 19 Jan. 34/1 Let us, as we approach the danger-zone of Hardy's philosophy, be on our guard. **1954** A. J. P. TAYLOR *Struggle for Mastery* xvii. 373 He and his advisers recognized that there was a 'danger-zone', an imaginary period when the British might suspect German designs and destroy her navy before it could hold its own. **1969** *New Yorker* 14 June 44/1 Ashe and Clark Graebner have long since entered the danger zone where any major mistake can mean the loss of the set.

D. Colloq. phr. (***to be***) ***on the danger list***: (to be) dangerously ill (as of a patient in hospital).

1938 S. PUDER (*title*) On the danger list. A case history. **1950** C. MACINNES *To Victors* III. 346, I asked them what they thought of the men on the danger list. **1960** E. H. CLEMENTS *Honey for Marshal* xi. 184 The fellow wasn't on the danger list any more... He could have come up by ambulance. **1970** *Times* 16 Feb. 3/8 Five patients on the danger list were slightly better, the hospital said.

†ˈ**danger**, *v. Obs.* [a. OF. *dangerer*, f. *dangier*, *danger*, DANGER.]

1. To render liable.

a **1400-50** *Alexander* 1176 And all þe trouage..þat he to Darius of dewe was dangird to paye. **1544** *Four Supplic.* (1871) 52 They be compelled to sell theyr landes..or els to daunger them selfe in dette to many. **1633** T. ADAMS *Exp. 2 Peter* ii. 1 If it [libel] be liked, they know the authors; if it be dangered to penalty, it is none of theirs.

2. To bring into or expose to danger; to endanger, imperil, risk.

1470 [see DANGERING]. **1544** BALE *Chron. Sir J. Oldcastell* in *Harl. Misc.* (Malh.) I. 247 They whyche..haue daungered theyr liues for a commonwelthe. **1579** LYLY *Euphues* (Arb.) 133 The heedelesse practiser, which daungereth the patient. **1590** MARLOWE *Edw. II*, v. iii, Therefore, come; dalliance dangereth our lives. **1606** SHAKS. *Ant. & Cl.* I. ii. 199. **1663** PEPYS *Diary* 1 May, My stone-horse was very troublesome, and begun to fight with other horses, to the dangering him and myself.

b. (with *inf.*) To run the risk; to be in danger.

1672-3 MARVELL *Reh. Transp.* II. 238 Should the Legislator persist..he would danger to be left in the field very single.

3. ? To damage, harm, injure. (Cf DANGER *sb.* 6.)

1538 BALE *God's Promises* I. in Hazl. *Dodsley* I. 288 He must needs but fall..And danger himself. **1591** HARINGTON *Orl. Fur.* I. ix, He would..bestow The damsell faire on him that in that fight..should..danger most the Pagans with his might. **1614** MARKHAM *Cheap Husb.* III. i. (1668) 86 The dodder sheep is the best breeder, and his Issue never dangereth the Dam in yeaning.

Hence ˈ**dangered** *ppl. a.*, ˈ**dangering** *vbl. sb.*

a **1400-50** [see 1]. *c* **1470** HENRY *Wallace* VIII. 547 It is my dett to do all that I can To fend our kynrik out off dangeryng. ? *c* **1600** *Distracted Emp.* I. i. in Bullen *O. Pl.* III. 172 A long daungered seaman in a storme. **1612** T. TAYLOR *Comm. Titus* iii. 2 To the present dangering and drowning of both. **1645** QUARLES *Sol. Recant.* 34 Why should thy too much righteousnesse betray Thy danger'd life? **1819** KEATS *Otho* I. i. Poems (1889) 423 This danger'd neck is saved. **1915** *Oxf. Mag.* 21 May 317/1 High Powers that love this dangered folk.

†ˈ**dangerful**, *a. Obs.* [f. DANGER *sb.* + -FUL.] Full of danger, dangerous.

1548 [see DANGERFULLY]. **1607** WALKINGTON *Opt. Glasse* 54 Much eating is also dangerfull for this humour. **1622** PEACHAM *Compl. Gentl.* viii. (1634) 67 The Atlanticke or Western Ocean is most rough and dangerfull. *a* **1708** T. WARD *Eng. Ref.* II. 172 (D.) As Lion, Scorpion, Bear, and Bull, And other things less dangerful.

Hence †ˈ**dangerfully** *adv.*, dangerously.

1548 UDALL, etc. *Erasm. Par. Luke* xi. 107 a, Certain Jewes..whose solles y[e] spirite of Satan did more daungierfully possesse.

dangerless ('deɪndʒəlɪs), *a.* (and *adv.*). Now *rare.* [f. as prec. + -LESS.] Without danger; free from danger.

a **1568** COVERDALE *Carrying Christ's Cross* iii, We..shall be dangerles in such felicite and ioy. **1581** MULCASTER *Positions* xv. (1887) 69 For the better and more daungerlesse performing therof. **1660** S. FISHER *Rusticks Alarm* Wks. (1679) 379 One of his wonted Fits of dangerless fear. **1795** SOUTHEY *Joan of Arc* VIII. 371 Nor dangerless To the English was the fight. **1882** WOOLSON *Anne* 361 It is the long monotony of dangerless days that tries the spirit hardest.

b. as *adv.* Without danger; †without damage or harm (*obs.*).

c **1440** *Generydes* 4567 For all that he skapid daungerles. **1602** WARNER *Alb. Eng.* XI. lxvi. (1612) 281 Howbeit Burrough did therein, not Dangerles, preuaile. **1633** L. ROBERTS *Prelim. V.* to P. Fletcher's *Purple Isl.*, Where all may dangerlesse obtain..cheapest, greatest gain.

Hence **'dangerlessness**, freedom from danger.

1818 COLERIDGE in *Rem.* (1836) I. 133 The dangerlessness—τὸ ἀκίνδυνον.

dangerous ('deɪndʒərəs), *a.* Also 3, 6 **dangerus**, (3 **daungcherous**), 4–6 **daungerous**, (5 **dawngerowse**, 5–6 **daungerouse**. [a. AF. *dangerous* = OF. *dangeros*, *-eus*, mod.F. *dangereux*, f. *danger*: see -OUS.]

†**1.** Difficult or awkward to deal with; haughty, arrogant; rigorous, hard, severe: the opposite of affable. *Obs.*

a **1225** *Ancr. R.* 108 Heo is a grucchild, & ful itowen, dangerus, & erueð for te paien. *c* **1290** *S. Eng. Leg.* I. 280/83 þe pope makede him dauncherous and nolde ensenti þer-to. *c* **1386** CHAUCER *Prol.* 517 He was to synful man nought despitous Ne of his speche daungerous ne digne. *c* **1400** *Rom. Rose* 591 And she to me was nought unmeke, Ne of hir answer daungerous. *Ibid.* 1483 So fiers & daungerous was he, That he nolde graunte hir askyng.

†**b.** Difficult to please; particular, ticklish; fastidious, nice, dainty, delicate. *Obs.*

c **1386** CHAUCER *Melib.* Prol. 21, I wol yow telle a litel thing in prose, That oughte like yow..Or elles certes ye be to daungerous. *c* **1430** *Pilgr. Lyf Manhode* I. cxx. (1869) 63 Of þi mete and of þi drink be þou neuere more daungerous. What þou fyndest take it gladliche. **1568** E. TILNEY *Disc. Mariage* C ij b, Daungerous, and circumspect in matters touching his honesty. *a* **1568** ASCHAM *Scholem.* I. (Arb.) 65 Great shippes require costlie tackling, and also afterward dangerous gouernment. **1577** B. GOOGE *Heresbach's Husb.* I. (1586) 31 The Oate is not daungerous in the choyse of his grounde, but groweth lyke a good fellowe in every place.

†**c.** Reluctant to give, accede or comply; chary of. *Obs.*

c **1386** CHAUCER *Wife's Prol.* 514 For that he Was of his loue daungerous to me. **14..** *Pol. Rel. & L. Poems* 155 If she be dawngerowse, I will hyr pray. **1494** FABYAN *Chron.* clv. 144 And requyryd hym of his comforte and ayde, wherof he was not daungerous. **1556** ROBINSON tr. *More's Utopia* (Arb.) 166 As myne I am nothinge daungerous to imparte, So better to receaue I am readie. **1598** W. PHILLIPS *Linschoten* (1864) 200 They are so dangerous of eating and drinking with other men which are not their Countrimen.

2. Fraught with danger or risk; causing or occasioning danger; perilous, hazardous, risky, unsafe. (The current sense.)

1490 CAXTON *Eneydos* xxi. 78 Atte this tyme whiche is so daungerouse. **1540** *Act 32 Hen. VIII*, c. 19 Some houses be ..redy to fal downe, and therfore dangerus to passe by. **1577** B. GOOGE *Heresbach's Husb.* I. (1586) 40 b, Delay herein is daungerous. **1599** SANDYS *Europæ Spec.* (1632) 148 The daungeroust enemie Spaine had in the world. **1670** MILTON *Hist. Eng.* IV. *Wks.* (1847) 516 They who pray against us.. are our dangerousest Enemies. **1748** SMOLLETT *R. Rand.* xii His wife..seeing her husband in these dangerous circumstances, uttered a dreadful scream. **1779–81** JOHNSON *L.P.*, *Milton* Wks. II. 142 To be of no church is dangerous. **1859** HELPS *Friends in C.* Ser. II. I. ii. 131 In most of the European nations there are dangerous classes, dangerous, because uncared for and uneducated. **1893** SIR J. W. CHITTY in *Law Times' Rep.* LXVIII. 430/1 A most dangerous doctrine.

†**3.** Ready to run into or meet danger; venturesome. *Obs. rare.*

1611 TOURNEUR *Ath. Trag.* IV. ii, And I doubt his life, His spirit is so boldly dangerous. **1642** [see DANGEROUSLY 3].

4. In danger, as from illness; dangerously ill. Now *dial.* and *U.S. colloq.*

a **1616** BEAUM. & FL. *Bonduca* IV. iii, *Reg.* Sure His mind is dangerous. *Drus.* The good gods cure it! **1619** FLETCHER *M. Thomas* II. i, Which will as well restore To health again the affected body..As leave it dangerous. **1620** MELTON *Astrolog.* 14 A Spirit that will fright any disease from the most dangerous and ouer-spent Patient. *a* **1825** FORBY *Voc. E. Anglia*, *Dangerous*, endangered. 'Mr. Smith is sadly-badly; quite dangerous.' **1864** BARNES *Dorset Gloss.*, *Dangerous* in danger. **1884** *Bread-winners* (U.S.) 244 He's dangerous; they don't think he'll live.

†**5.** Hurtful, injurious. *Obs.* (Cf. DANGER *sb.* 6.)

1548 HALLE *Chron.* 17 b, The encounter was sharpe, the fight was dangerous. **1576** FLEMING *Panopl. Epist.* 400 Two vices, very daungerous and noysome among men.

†**6.** as *adv.* Dangerously. *Obs. rare.*

1593 SHAKS. *3 Hen. VI*, I. i. 11 Either slaine or wounded dangerous.

dangerously ('deɪndʒərəslɪ), *adv.* [f. prec. + -LY².] In a dangerous manner.

†**1.** With reserve; shyly; charily. *Obs.*

a **1577** GASCOIGNE *Fable of Ieronimi*, I..alwayes dangerouslye behaued my selfe towards him. **1647** CLARENDON *Hist. Reb.* VII. (1703) II. 304 He was so sottishly and dangerously wary of his own Security..that he would not proceed.

2. In a way involving danger or risk; perilously.

c **1540** *Four P.P.* in Hazl. *Dodsley* I. 372 To die so dangerously, For her soul-health especially. **1603** KNOLLES *Hist. Turkes* (1638) 101 Hee fell dangerously sicke. **1766** GOLDSM. *Vic. W.* xxxi, One of my servants has been wounded dangerously. **1860** TYNDALL *Glaciers* I. §11. 78 The slope..was most dangerously steep.

†**3.** Venturesomely. (Cf. prec. 3.) *Obs. rare.*

1642 MILTON *Apol. Smect.* (1851) 293 A Satyr..ought.. to strike high, and adventure dangerously at the most eminent vices among the greatest persons.

dangerousness ('deɪndʒərəsnɪs). [f. as prec. + -NESS.] The quality of being dangerous.

†**1.** Chariness, grudgingness. *Obs.*

1548 UDALL, etc. *Erasm. Par. Mark* vi. 49 a, It came not of any daungerousnes, or difficultie on his behalf.

2. Perilousness.

1530 PALSGR. 212/1 Dangerousnesse, *dangerevseté*, *dangier.* **1602** CAREW *Cornwall* 1 b, The dangerousnesse of the passages laid them open to priuie inuasions. **1736** CARTE *Ormonde* I. 99 The ill circumstances of his lady's health and the dangerousness of her condition. **1881** J. SIMON in *Nature* No. 616. 372 Experiments which illustrated the dangerousness of sewage-polluted water-supplies.

dangersome ('deɪndʒəsəm), *a. Obs.* exc. *dial.* [f. DANGER *sb.* + -SOME.] Fraught with danger.

1567 MAPLET *Gr. Forest* 96 The sluggish owle hath bene to man Most often daungersome. **1651** *Reliq. Wotton.* 8 The dangersome marks. **1885** *Century Mag.* XXIX. 549/1 How to run in daylight without it being dangersome for Tim.

dangle ('dæŋg(ə)l), *v.* [Appears at end of 16th c.; corresponds to Da. *dangle*, Norw. and Sw. dial. *dangla*, North Fris. *dangeln*, ablaut-derivs. of Da. *dingle*, Norw., Sw., Icel. *dingla* to dangle. In form these seem to belong to the stem *ding-*, *dang-* (DING *v.*), but the connexion of sense is not clear.]

1. *intr.* To hang loosely swaying to and fro.

c **1590** *Sir T. More* (Shaks. Soc. 1844) 46 How long Hath this shagg fleece hung dangling on thy head? **1598** YONG *Diana* 228 Her disshiueled hair..in curled lockes hung dangling about her snow-white forehead. **1633** P. FLETCHER *Pisc. Ecl.* I. vi, Our thinne nets dangling in the winde. **1678** NORRIS *Misc.* (1699) 37 Ripe Apples now hang dangling on the Tree. **1782** COWPER *Gilpin* 132 For all might see the bottle-necks Still dangling at his waist. **1877** BLACK *Green Past.* xxxvi, Mr. Bolitho was seated on a table, his legs dangling in the air.

b. To hang from the gallows; to be hanged.

1678 BUTLER *Hud.* III. i. 641 And men [have] as often dangled for't, And yet will never leave the sport. **1748** SMOLLETT *Rod. Rand.* xxx, Let the rascal be carried back to his confinement. I find he must dangle. **1841** JAMES *Brigand* xxxviii, Set him dangling from the battlements.

2. *trans.* To make (a thing) hang and sway to and fro; to hold or carry (it) suspended loosely.

1612 *Two Noble K.* I. ii. 57 What canon is there That does command my rapier from my hip, To dangle 't in my hand? **1748** SMOLLETT *Rod. Rand.* xlv, I..dangled my cane and adjusted my sword knot. **1808** SCOTT *Marm.* V. xii, The bridegroom stood dangling his bonnet and plume. **1873** SYMONDS *Grk. Poets* x. 314 Lazy fishermen..dangling their rods like figures in Pompeian frescoes.

b. *fig.* To keep (hopes, anticipations, etc.) hanging uncertainly before any one.

1863 KINGLAKE *Crimea* (1877) II. ii. 31 The mighty temptation which seemed to be dangled before him. **1871** FREEMAN *Norm. Conq.* (1876) IV. xviii. 193 The hopes of a royal marriage were again dangled before the eyes of Eadwine.

c. To hang (any one) on a gallows.

1887 W. C. RUSSELL *Frozen Pirate* II. iv. 92 This is evidence to dangle even an honester man than you.

3. *fig.* (*intr.*) To hang *after* or about any one, especially as a loosely attached follower; to follow in a dallying way, without being a formally recognized attendant.

1607 DEKKER *Sir T. Wyatt* Wks. 1873 III. 115 Wyat.. rising thus in armes, with the Kentish men dangling at his taile. **1727** SWIFT *Past. Dial.*, *Marble Hill & Richmond Lodge*, Plump Johnny Gay will now elope; And here no more will dangle Pope. **1734** FIELDING *Univ. Gallant* 1, Pray take her, I dangled after her long enough too. **1760** FOOTE *Minor* I. Wks. 1799 I. 232 The sleek..'prentice us'd to dangle after his mistress, with the great Bible under his arm. *a* **1859** MACAULAY *Hist. Eng.* V. 5 Heirs of noble houses.. dangling after actresses. **1862** MERIVALE *Rom. Emp.* (1865) IV. xxxvii. 271 The exquisites of the day were men who dangled in the train of ladies.

†**b.** To stroll idly, or with lounging steps: cf. 1607, 1760 above. *Obs.*

1778 *Learning at a Loss* II. 76 They quitted, or, to use their own expression, dangled out of the Room.

4. *trans.* To lead about in one's train, or as an appendage.

a **1723** GAY *Distressed Wife* 11, I am not to be dangled about whenever and wherever his odious business calls him.

5. To while *away* or cause to pass in dangling.

1727 BOLINGBROKE in *Swift's Lett.* (1766) II. 77 The noble pretension of dangling away life in an ante-chamber.

6. *Comb.* (of the verb stem) **dangle-berry**, Blue Tangle, *Gaylussacia frondosa*, an American shrub, N.O. *Vacciniaceæ*; **dangle-jack** (see quot.).

1881 *Leicestersh. Gloss.*, *Dangle-jack*, the primitive roasting-jack, generally a stout bit of worsted with a hook at the end, turned by giving it a twist from time to time with the fingers.

'dangle, *sb.* [f. DANGLE *v.*] Act or manner of dangling (*rare*); something that dangles.

1756 *Connoisseur* No. 122 Seeming ravished with the genteel dangle of his sword-knot. **1888** O. CRAWFURD *Sylvia Arden* ii. 21 He lay there in a swound till they got him up the ladder, with just a dangle of life in him. **1903** *Westm. Gaz.* 26 Mar. 8/2 We get dangles in the shops made and ready for our use, fashioned of silk cords and tassels. **1909** *Cent. Dict.* Suppl., *Dangle-money*, an early Chinese bronze coinage, so called from its resemblance to and former use as dangles of a musical instrument. **1909** M. B. SAUNDERS *Litany Lane.* I. ix, A pair of long jet earrings representing funeral urns with cloths over them had replaced the usual golden dangles. **1909** WEBSTER s.v., A dangle of curls. **1937** PARTRIDGE *Dict. Slang* 207/2 *Dangle-parade*, a 'short-arm' inspection: New Zealand soldiers'. **1957** J. KEROUAC *On Road* (1958) I. vii. 44 On the wall was a nude drawing of Dean, enormous dangle and all.

'dangle, *a. rare.* [f. DANGLE *v.*] Dangling.

1600 J. PORY tr. *Leo's Africa* II. 341 A tame beast..having long and dangle eares. **1889** BRAITHWAITE *Retrosp. Med.* C. 241 In many cases the leg is a mere 'dangle limb' of no service whatever.

'dangled, *ppl. a.* [f. DANGLE *v.* + -ED.] Hung dangling, or furnished with dangling appendages.

1593 NASHE *Christ's T.* (1613) 148 For thy flaring frounzed Periwigs, lowe dangled downe with loue-lockes, shalt thou haue thy head side, dangled downe with more Snakes than euer it had hayres. *a* **1688** VILLIERS (Dk. Buckhm.) *Poems* (1775) 141 Nor is it wit that makes the lawyer prize His dangled gown: 'tis knavery in disguise.

danglement ('dæŋg(ə)lmənt). [f. DANGLE *v.* + -MENT.] **1.** Dangling.

1834 BECKFORD *Italy* II. 75 He..passes the flower of his days in this singular species of danglement. **1849** LYTTON *Caxtons* VII. i, The..suspension and danglement of any puddings whatsoever right over his ingle-nook.

2. *concr.* (*pl.*) Dangling appendages. *dial.*

1855 ROBINSON *Whitby Gloss.*, *Danglements*, tassels and such like appendants.

dangler ('dæŋglə(r)). [f. as prec. + -ER¹.]

1. One who dangles; one who hangs or hovers about a woman; a dallying follower.

1727 FIELDING *Love in Sev. Masq.* Wks. 1775 I. 37 The dangler after a woman. **1730–6** BAILEY (folio), *Dangler*, so the Women in Contempt call a Man, who is always hanging after them, but never puts the Question home. **1770** MAD. D'ARBLAY *Early Diary* 10 Jan., 'You see', she cried, 'what a herd of danglers flutter around you.' **1828** CARLYLE *Misc.* (1857) I. 228 Fashionable danglers after literature. **1882** BESANT *All Sorts* xix. 139 Dick Coppin was not..a dangler after girls' apron-strings.

2. A dangling appendage or part.

1731–7 MILLER *Gard. Dict.* (ed. 3) s.v. *Vitis*, You must go over the Vines again..rubbing off all Danglers, as before, and training in the leading Shoots. **1870** MISS BROUGHTON *Red as Rose* iv, The long red pendant to his [a turkey-cock's] nose: I confess to being ignorant as to what function that long flabby dangler has to fulfil.

dangling ('dæŋglɪŋ), *vbl. sb.* [-ING¹.] The action of the verb DANGLE, q.v.; †*concr.* (*pl.*) dangling appendages.

1611 COTGR., *Pendiloches*, jags, danglings, or things that hang danglingly. **1650** FULLER *Pisgah* IV. vi. 100 To prevent the dangling down and dagling of so long garments. **1678** BUTLER *Hud.* III. ii. 202 The Royalists..To leave off Loyalty and Dangling. **1855** SMEDLEY *H. Coverdale* i. 5 I've given up flirting and dangling.

'dangling, *ppl. a.* [-ING².] That dangles.

1593 SHAKS. *Rich. II*, III. iv. 29 Goe binde thou vp yond dangling Apricocks. **1635** QUARLES *Emblems* I. Invoc., Cast off these dangling plummets. **1750** MRS. DELANY *Life & Corr.* (1861) II. 602, I am very happy that I have no dangling neighbours. **1856** MRS. BROWNING *Aur. Leigh* III. 767 Thin dangling locks.

Hence **'danglingly** *adv.*

1611 COTGR., *Pendiller*, to hang danglingly, loosely, or but by halves.

dangly, *a.* [f. DANGL(E *v.* and *sb.* + -Y¹.] = DANGLING *ppl. a.*

1903 *Westm. Gaz.* 1 Jan. 3/1 Then often passementerie motifs dangle from bolero fronts of the short sac kind, for these attractive dangly things are more popular than ever. **1959** C. WILLIAMS *Man in Motion* iv. 47 She was wearing dangly ear-rings.

Danian ('deɪnɪən), *a. Geol.* [ad. F. *Danien* (A. d'Orbigny *Prodrome de Paléont.* (1850) II. 290), f. L. *Dania* Denmark, f. *Danus* DANE: see -IAN.] Epithet of a stratigraphical stage or series (not represented in Britain) lying below the Montian stage, and held variously to be the highest division of the Cretaceous or the lowest of the Tertiary; of or pertaining to this stage or the period during which it was deposited. Also *absol.*

1873 *Q. Jrnl. Geol. Soc.* XXIX. 377 Cretaceous Period. Danian or Waipara Formation... This is the Cretaceo-Tertiary formation of Dr. Hector. *Ibid.* Index, Danian formation of New Zealand. **1882** GEIKIE *Text-bk. Geol.* 823 The uppermost division, or Danian, of the Continental chalk appears to be absent in England, unless its lower portions are represented by some of the uppermost beds of the Norwich Chalk. **1893** P. LAKE tr. *Kayser's Comp. Geol.* 314 In the North of France the succession of the Upper

Cretaceous rocks closely resembles that of England; but still higher zones are represented, and these are united under the term Danian. **1925** *Countries of the World* xxx. 3072/1 A beautiful stone resembling marble is secured from phosphatic beds of Danian Age. **1960** L. D. Stamp *Britain's Struct.* (ed. 5) xii. 139 These strata form..transition beds between the Cretaceous and the Tertiary and are sometimes grouped with the one, sometimes with the other, sometimes separated as the Danian and the Montian. **1969** *Proc. Geol. Soc. Lond.* Aug. 152 The rocks commonly accepted as of Danian age should be included in the Cainozoic. **1971** *Nature* 19 Feb. 553/2 Impoverished Danian faunas are.. often separated by a bedding plane from Cretaceous faunas of similar sedimentary facies.

† **'Danic**, *a. Obs.* [ad. med.L. *Danic-us*, f. *Dania* Denmark.] = Danish.

1613-8 Daniel *Coll. Hist. Eng.* 12 During this Danicq warre. **1692** Ray *Dissol. World* iii. v. (1732) 363 In the Baltick Danick and Holland shores.

Hence **'Danicism**, a Danish idiom or expression.

1881 F. York Powell in *Encycl. Brit.* XII. 628 The intercourse [of Iceland] with Denmark began to leave its mark in loan-words and Danicisms.

Daniell ('dænjəl). [The name of John Frederic *Daniell*, English physicist (1790-1845).] **a.** Used *attrib.* or in the possessive to designate inventions of Daniell or their modifications, as **Daniell('s) battery** or **cell**, a cell in which the cathode is zinc in either dilute sulphuric acid or a solution of zinc sulphate and the anode is copper in a saturated solution of copper sulphate, with the zinc sulphate solution either floating on top of the copper sulphate solution or separated from it by a porous plate; also *Daniell's hygrometer*.

1840 *Phil. Trans. R. Soc.* CXXX. i. 191 Five cells of Professor Daniell's constant battery were charged and connected with the electro-magnetic machine. **1863** E. Atkinson tr. *Ganot's Physics* vi. vi. 269 There are many sources of error in Daniell's hygrometer. *Ibid.* x. i. 609 The current produced by a Daniell's battery is constant for some hours. **1884** F. Krohn tr. *Glaser de Cew's Magn.- & Dyn.-Electr. Mach.* 233 If the instrument were always graduated with a Daniell cell. **1948** Glasstone *Physical Chem.* (ed. 2) xii. 934 In the familiar Daniell cell.. the metallic zinc at the left-hand electrode passes into solution as zinc ions, liberating two electrons. **1955** H. L. Penman *Humidity* iv. 28 Daniell's hygrometer (1827), where the cooling is produced by forced evaporation of ether. **1957** *Encycl. Brit.* III. 216/1 The Daniell cell has an open-circuit voltage of about 1·08.

b. Used *ellipt.* for *Daniell cell*.

1871 *Engl. Mechanic* 430/2 The improved Daniell devised by me. **1878** *Encycl. Brit.* VIII. 93/2 The sawdust Daniell, invented by Sir Wm. Thomson (1858), is very convenient when portability is desired. **1922** Glazebrook *Dict. Appl. Physics* II. 70/2 Kelvin's tray battery, which is a form of gravity Daniell, has been largely used in submarine telegraphy.

Daniglacial (deɪnɪ'gleɪʃɪəl, -ʃəl, -'gleɪsɪəl), *a. Geol.* Also **Dani-glacial**. [f. L. *Dani-a* Denmark + glacial *a.*] Epithet of the first division or 'sub-epoch' of the Late Glacial epoch in north-western Europe, when the ice-sheet of the last glaciation retreated from Denmark and halted near the tip of the Scandinavian peninsula; of or pertaining to this sub-epoch. Also *absol.* Cf. Gothiglacial, Finiglacial *adjs.*

1912 G. De Geer in *Compt. Rend. XI Congr. Géol. Internat. 1910* I. 253 As to the first of the late-glacial sub-epochs, which properly may be called the Dani-glacial one, or that part of the last ice-recession when the ice-border retired from the extreme limit of the last glaciation past Denmark.., its duration is not yet known. **1923** —— *Let.* 3 Nov. in W. J. Sollas *Anc. Hunters* (1924) xiv. 662, I hope it will be possible to date not only the commencement of the Gothi-glacial sub-epoch but of the Dani-glacial as well, and thus to determine the whole time which has elapsed since the maximum of the last glaciation. **1927** Peake & Fleure *Hunters & Artists* i. 6 The first of these lines has been called the Daniglacial moraine, and the second the Gothiglacial, while the space between the two is known as the area of the Daniglacial retreat, and that between the second line and a third to be described is termed the area of the Gothiglacial retreat. **1957** J. K. Charlesworth *Quaternary Era* II. I. 1525 The Daniglacial recession alone may have lasted 10,000-15,000 years. **1960** L. D. Stamp *Britain's Struct.* (ed. 5) xiv. 170 The Dani-Glacial was the period of the ice retreat from Denmark—when ice still covered the whole of Norway and Sweden.

Danish ('deɪnɪʃ), *a.* and *sb.* In OE. **Denisc**; 3-4 **Denshe, Dench, Danshe**; 6 *Sc.* **Dence, Dens, Densch**. Also ME. **Danais, Danoys**, and 6-7 Dansk, q.v. [OE. *Dęnisc*:—OTeut. **danisk-*, whence ON. *Danskr*, f. *Dani-*, *Dęne*, Danes + -ish. Thence ME. *Densh*, etc. In *Danish*, the vowel is changed as in Dane. The ME. *Danais* was immed. from OF. *daneis*, *danoys* (:—L. *Danēnsis*); and the late *Dansk* directly from Danish.]

Of or belonging to the Danes and to Denmark. *subst.* The language of Denmark. ***Danish axe***: a kind of battle-axe with very long blade, and usually without a spike on the back. ***Danish blue*** (***cheese***): see quot. 1948; ***Danish dog***: see Dane. ***Danish embroidery***: see quot. 1882; ***Danish modern***: a modern style of furniture, characterized by simple clear lines, light woods, and lack of carved or painted decoration; ***Danish pastry***: a yeast cake garnished with sugar, spice, nuts, icing, etc.; also *ellipt.*

833 *O.E. Chron.*, þa Denescan ahton wælstowe ȝewald. **845** *Ibid.* [Hi] ȝefuhton æt Pedridan muþan wiþ Deniscne here. **1297** R. Glouc (1724) 299 Atte laste myd a denchax me smot hym to grounde. *c* **1300** *Havelok* 1403 Mi fader was king of denshe lond. *c* **1314** *Guy Warw.* A. 3585 A danisax [*ed.* damsax] he bar on his hond. *c* **1340** *Gaw. & Gr. Knt.* 2223 A felle weppen A denez ax nwe dyȝt. **1398** Trevisa *Barth. de P.R.* xv. lxi. (1495) 510 Frisia..endyth atte Danysshe see. **1500-20** Kennedy *Flyting w. Dunbar* 356 Densmen of Denmark ar of the kingis kyn. **1545** *Aberdeen Reg.* V. 19 (Jam.) Ane densh aix. *a* **1578** *Gude & Godly Ball.* (1868) 159 Inglis prelatis, Duche and Dence For thair abuse ar rutit out. **1602** Shaks. *Ham.* iv. iv. 1 Go Captaine, from me greet the Danish King. **1643** in *Statist. Acc. Moray* V. 16 *note*, Furnished with..halberds, densaixes, or Lochaber aixes. **1774** Goldsm. *Nat. Hist.* III. viii. 284 The Grey Matin Hound..transported to the north, becomes the great Danish dog..The Mastiff..transported into Denmark, becomes the little Danish dog. **1825** Scott *Note* in Jamieson (*Suppl.*) s.v. *Densaixes*, A Danish axe was the proper name of a Lochaber-axe; and from the Danes the Isles-men got them. **1870** Blaine *Encycl. Rur. Sports* 394 The Danish dog is considered as the largest dog known; probably it would be more correct to call it the tallest. **1882** Caulfield & Saward *Dict. Needlework*, *Danish Embroidery*, this is an embroidery on cambric, muslin, or batiste, and is suitable for handkerchief borders, necktie ends, and cap lappets..[Also] a variety of the work only useful for filling in spaces left in Crochet, Tatting, and Embroidery. **1934** Webster, Danish pastry. **1948** *Good Housek. Cookery Bk.* 383 *Danish Blue*, a soft white cheese with a blue mould veining, made in Denmark in imitation of Roquefort. **1948** A. H. Rutt *Home Furnishing* (ed. 2) xiii. 217 Finnish, Norwegian, and Danish Modern employ laminated wood and bentwood effectively. **1950** B. Schulberg *Disenchanted* (1951) v. 50 The waitress ..brought him..Danish pastry and coffee. **1953** R. Fuller *Second Curtain* I think I shall have just a little cheese. They often have Danish blue. **1955** D. Barton *Glorious Life* 27 Their Danish Blue sandwiches and bitter arrived. **1963** 'M. Albrand' *Call from Austria* i. 12 'I could do with another cup of coffee.' 'And a Danish?' **1969** S. Greenlee *Spook who sat by Door* xv. 133 He entered the panelled reception room, decorated in Danish modern. **1970** *New Yorker* 26 Sept. 33/2 She stopped at a delicatessen along the way to pick up a Danish pastry ring. *Ibid.*, When the Danish was finished ..she ran the palms of her hands along the sides of her chair.

† *β.* **Danais, Danoys.**

a **1300** *Cursor M.* 24796 (Cott.) To spek a-bute sum pais, bituix him and þe danais. *c* **1450** *Merlin* 42 The Danoys, that Vortiger hadde brought in to the londe. **1480** Caxton *Chron. Eng.* xci. 73 Kyng Adelbright that was a danoys helde the countie of norfolk and southfolk.

Hence **'Danishry** *Obs.* exc. *Hist.* [cf. *Irishry*, etc.], the people of Danish race (in Britain).

c **1470** Harding *Chron.* cviii. x, Where Alurede had the victorie, And slewe that daye al the Danyshrye. *Ibid.* cxix. xiii, A duke of the Danishrie. **1857** *Fraser's Mag.* LVI. 27 The Danishry rose *en masse*.

Danisk: see Dansk.

Danism[1] ('deɪnɪz(ə)m). [f. Dane + -ism.] A Danish idiom or expression, a Danicism.

1886 *Encycl. Brit.* XXI. 369/2 Many Danisms and a few Suecisms were imported into the language [of Norway].

† **'danism**[2]. *Obs.*—[0] [ad. Gr. δανεισμός money-lending, δανειστής, L. *danista* money-lender, δανειστικός, L. *danīsticus* usurious.] Money-lending on usury. So **'danist, da'nistic** *a.*

1623 Cockeram, *Danisme*, Vsurie. *Danist*, a vsurer. **1656** in Blount *Glossogr.* [who adds] *Danistick*, pertaining to usury. **1692** in Coles. **1775** in Ash. **1848** Wharton *Law Lex.*, *Danism*, the act of lending money on usury.

Danite ('dænaɪt). *Obs.* exc. *Hist.* [f. *Dan*, the name of one of the sons of Jacob and of the tribe of Israel founded by him + -ite[1]. Cf. *Genesis* xlix. 16 and 17.] **1.** A member of the Hebrew tribe of Dan.

1535 Coverdale *Judg.* xiii. 2 There was a man at Zarga, of one of the kynreds of the Danites, named Manoah. **1667** [see Herculean *a.* 2]. **1847** J. Kitto *Cycl. Bibl. Lib.* I. 514/1 The inability of the Danites to expel the Philistines and Amorites. **1968** *Encycl. Brit.* XIII. 119/1 The Levite, however, was persuaded by the Danites migrating northward to accompany them and he became the first priest of the famous sanctuary at Dan.

2. A member of an alleged secret order of Mormons supposed to have arisen in the early days of that sect to act as spies and suppressors of disaffection.

1838 *Test* (Rushville, Ill.) 12 Dec. 3/4 There, Patton, one of the bloodiest of the Danites, directed two of his bands. **1857** *Congress. Globe* 24 Feb. App. 289/3 They suppose that there is a secret society existing there, called Danites, Shanpips, or Destroying Angels. **1882** C. Waite *Adv. Far West* 252 The Danites are expected to act as spies upon the federal officers and other gentiles; to watch the feelings and spirits of the saints, and to report the first indications of disaffection. **1905** *Daily Chron.* 22 June 3/1 The duties of the Danites, or 'avenging angels'. **1948** *Jrnl. Amer. Folk-Lore* Jan.—Mar. 20 See those dreadful Danites how they lynch many lives.

† **dank**, *sb. Obs.* Forms: see adj. [app. f. dank *a.*] **1.** Wetness, humidity, damp.

? *a* **1400** *Morte Arth.* 3751 One þe danke of þe dewe many dede lyggys. **1602** Marston *Antonio's Rev.* Prol., The rawish danke of clumzie winter ramps The fluent summers raine. [Cf. Clumsy.]

2. A wet place, pool, marsh, mere.

1513 Douglas *Æneis* vii. Prol. 60 Bedovin in donkis deyp was every syk. **1560** Rolland *Crt. Venus* i. 2 Eolus out ouir thir rokkis rang, Be donk and daill. **1667** Milton *P.L.* vii. 441 Yet oft they quit The Dank, and rising on stiff Pennons, towre The mid Aereal Skie.

dank (dæŋk), *a.* Forms: 5 **dannke**, 5-7 **danke**, 6 **dancke**, 6- **dank**; also 6 **donk**, 7 **donke**, 8-9 *dial.* **donk**. [The adj. and sb. are known from *c* 1400, the vb. (which we should expect to be formed from the adj.) appears nearly a century earlier; the early quots. for both vb. and adj. refer to dew. The etymology is uncertain.

The only words allied in form, and possibly in sense, are Swedish *dank* 'moist place in a field, marshy spot', Icel. *dökk* (: *-danku-*) pit, pool. These must evidently be separated from the Germanic stem *dink-*, *dank-*, *dunk-*, whence ON. *dökkr* dark, Ger. *dunkel*. There is no original connexion, either of form or sense, between *dank* and *damp*, but in recent times *damp* has acquired the sense of *dank* and largely taken its place.]

† **1.** Wet, watery, wetting: **a.** said of dew, rain, clouds, water, etc. *Obs.*

? *a* **1400** *Morte Arth.* 313 þe dewe þat es dannke, whene þat it doune falles. *c* **1400** *Destr. Troy* 2368 Dropis as dew or a danke rayne. **1513** Douglas *Æneis* iii. ix. 3 Aurora the wak nycht dyd..chays fra hevin with hir dym skyis donk. **1549** *Compl. Scot.* vi. 38 The drops of the fresche deu, quhilk of befor hed maid dikis ande dailis verray donc. **1601** Weever *Mirr. Mart.* B ij, Fruits..Which the danke moisture of the ayre doth cherish.

b. said of marshes, fens, soaking ground, humid tropical forests, and the like.

[**1667** Milton *P.L.* ix. 179 Through each Thicket Danck or Drie.] **1735** Somerville *Chase* i. 340 O'er the dank Marsh, bleak Hill, and sandy Plain. **1799** *Scotland described* (ed. 2) 14 A pool in the midst of a wide, dead, and dank morass. **1851** Sir F. Palgrave *Norm. & Eng.* I. 163 On the dank marshy shores of the oozy Yare. **1857** S. Osborn *Quedah* xxiv. 351 In those dank and hot forests reptiles abound.

2. Damp: with the connotation that this is an injurious or disagreeable quality. **a.** of fog, vapour, the air, weather, etc.

1601 ? Marston *Pasquil & Kath.* v. 70 The euening's raw and danke; I shall take cold. **1757** Dyer *Fleece* i. 365 Dank or frosty days. **1784** Cowper *Task* i. 437 Vapours, dank and clammy. **1822** Hazlitt *Table-t.* Ser. ii. xiv. (1869) 288 A dank, cold mist, encircling all objects. **1860** Tyndall *Glac.* i. v. 41 Dull dank fog choked the valley.

b. of substances or surfaces.

In this sense app. *Obs.* after 1650, exc. in northern dialect; but revived by the romantic writers in end of 18th c.

1573 Tusser *Husb.* xxii. (1878) 60 Dank ling forgot will quickly rot. **1590** Shaks. *Mids. N.* ii. ii. 75 Sleeping sound On the danke and durty ground. **1626** Bacon *Sylva* §352 In a Cellar or Dank room. **1642** Rogers *Naaman* 618 Oh that our powder were not danke. **1787** Grose *Prov. Gloss.*, *Donk*, a little wettish, damp. N[orth]. **1813** Scott *Rokeby* ii. ix, The dank and sable earth receives Its only carpet from the leaves. **1855** Robinson *Whitby Gloss.*, 'As donk as a dungeon.' **1876** Humphreys *Coin-Coll. Man.* xxvi. 400 Pages of vellum that served as knee-rests to the monks on the dank stone pavements.

3. In 19th c., often said of rank grass or weeds growing in damp places. [perh. associated with *rank*.]

1820 Shelley *Sensit. Plant* iii. 55 And thistles, and nettles, and darnels rank, And the dock, and henbane, and hemlock dank. **1827** Keble *Chr. Y. 1st Sunday after Trin.*, Here over shatter'd walls dank weeds are growing. **1863** Geo. Eliot *Romola* i. xviii, That dank luxuriance [of the garden] had begun to penetrate even within the walls of the ..room.

dank (dæŋk), *v. Obs.* exc. *dial.* Forms: 4-5 **donk(e**, 5 **downk(e**, 5-6 **danke**, 6 **dounk**, 7- **dank**, 9 *dial.* **donk**. [See dank *a.*]

† **1.** *trans.* To wet, damp, moisten; originally said of dew, mist, drizzling rain, etc. *Obs.*

a **1310** in Wright *Lyric P.* xiii. 44 Deowes donketh the dounes. *c* **1400** *Destr. Troy* 7997 The droupes, as a dew, dankit his fas. *Ibid.* 9639 A myste..All donkyt the dales with the dym showris. **1552** Lyndesay *Monarche* 6309 The dew now dounkis the rossis redolent. **1634** W. Wood *New Eng. Prosp.* ii. vii, The water having dank't his pistoles.

b. *fig.* To damp (the spirits or aspirations); to depress. Still *dial.*

1555 Abp. Parker *Ps.* viii. I j b, Thy foes to blanke: their threates to danke. *a* **1575** —— *Corr.* 237, I am..not amazed nor danked. **1864** Bamford *Homely Rhymes* 135 (*Lanc. Gloss.*) Put th' Kurn-bill i' the divel's hous 'At it no moor may dank us.

† **2.** *intr.* To become damp. *Obs.*

1590 Sir J. Smyth *Disc. Weapons* 21 The ayre of some moyst weather hath..caused the powder to give and danke.

b. To be a fine rain or mist; to drizzle. *dial.*

1866 *Gentl. Mag.* I. 546 They have a peculiar expression in Lancashire, to convey the description of a hazy showery day: 'it donkes and it dozzles'. **1869** *Lonsdale Gloss.* s.v., 'It donks and it dozzles' = It damps and drizzles.

Hence **'danking** *vbl. sb.* and *ppl. a.*

c **1340** *Gaw. & Gr. Knt.* 519 When þe donkande dewe dropez of the leuez. ? *a* **1400** *Morte Arth.* 3248 Was thare no downkynge of dewe that oghte dere scholde.

Dankali, var. Danakil *sb.* and *a.*

dankish ('dæŋkɪʃ), *a.* [f. dank *sb.* and *a.*]

† **1.** = dank *a.*: wet, humid. *Obs.*

1545 Raynold *Byrth Mankynde* iv. ii. (1634) 187 The earth may be ouer waterish, dankish, or ouerhot and dry. **1545** Ascham *Toxoph.* ii. (Arb.) 118 Take heed also of mistie and dankyshe dayes. **1590** SHAKS. *Com. Err.* v. i. 247 In a darke and dankish vault at home, There left me and my man. **1626** BACON *Sylva* §696 The Moath breedeth upon Cloth.. Especially if..laid up dankish and wet. **1644** NYE *Gunnery* I. (1647) 13 You must suffer the said water to settle..and congeal in a dankish room.

2. Somewhat dank; inclined to be wet or moist.
1727 BAILEY vol. II, *Dankish*, a little Moist or Wet. **1886** *Pall Mall G.* 21 July 6/1 Butts and tubs..stood close packed and cumbersome upon its dankish floor.

Hence **'dankishness**, dankish quality, humidity.
1576 T. NEWTON *Lemnie's Complex.* II. 112 a, A fustie dankishnesse..vnder the skin. **1611** COTGR., *Relant*, mustinesse, fustinesse, ranknesse, dankishnesse. **1630** in J. S. Burn *Hist. Parish Reg. Eng.* (1862) 68 This place is very much subject to dankishness. **1727** BAILEY vol. II, *Dankishness*, moistness.

dankly ('dæŋklɪ), *adv.* [f. DANK *a.* + -LY[2].] In a dank or humid manner.
1818 SHELLEY *Rev. Islam* VI. 4 The dew is rising dankly from the dell. **1870** MISS BROUGHTON *Red as a Rose* xxvii, Upon the broken headstones the lichens flourish dankly.

dankness ('dæŋknɪs). [f. DANK *a.* + -NESS.] The quality of being dank; humidity, dampness.
1601 HOLLAND *Pliny* II. 476 The naturall moisture and dankenesse that commeth from thence. **1651** tr. *Bacon's Life & Death* 5 To save them from the Dankness of the Vault.

danky ('dæŋkɪ), *a.* Also *dial.* donkey, -ky. [f. DANK + -Y[1].] Somewhat dank, dampish.
1796 W. MARSHALL *Midl. Counties* Gloss., *Donkey*, dampish, dank. **1820** MOIR in *Blackw. Mag.* VIII. 176 The sward is dim with moss and danky weeds. **1821** *Ibid.* IX. 271 The owl sends forth her whoop from danky vaults. **1869** *Lonsdale Gl.*, *Donky*, damp, moist, humid: 'a donky day'.

Dann, obs. form of DAN[1].

‖**Dannebrog** ('dænəbrɒg). Also **Dane-**. [Da. *Dan(n)ebrog*, f. *Danne-*, *Dane-*, Danish + *brog* supposed to be ODa. *brog*, breech, cloth.] The Danish national flag; hence, a Danish order of knighthood, founded in 1219, revived in 1671, and regulated by various later statutes; it is sometimes bestowed upon foreigners.
1708 *Lond. Gaz.* No. 4434/2 His Majesty conferred.. three white Ribbons, the Order of Dannebrog on Monsieur Plessen [etc.]. **1714** *Ibid.* No. 5269/2 His..Majesty..made a Promotion of seven Knights of the Order of Dannebrog. **1837** *Penny Cycl.* VIII. 401/2 The orders of knighthood are the order of the Elephant..the Danebrog order, founded in 1219, and now bestowed for eminent services.

dannemorite ('dænəmɒraɪt). *Min.* [Named from Dannemora in Sweden, where found: see -ITE.] A variety of hornblende.
1857 *Amer. Jrnl. Sc.* Ser. II. XXIV. 120 A columnar or fibrous mineral..named Dannemorite.

danner, var. of DANDER *v. Sc.*, to saunter.

dannert: see DANAERT.

'dannocks, *sb. pl. local.* [Forby prefers the form *darnocks*, and says it is a corruption of *Dorneck*, *Dornick*, Flemish name of *Tournai.*] (See quots.)
a **1825** FORBY *Voc. E. Anglia*, *Darnocks, Dannocks*, hedger's gloves. **1854** *N. & Q.* 1st Ser. IX. 273/1 Gloves made of Whit-leather (untanned leather) and used by workmen in cutting and trimming fences are called in this part of Norfolk dannocks. **1883** BECK *Glover* 233 The dannocks, or hedging gloves of labourers in our time.

Dano- ('deɪnəʊ), used as combining form of *Danus* DANE, DANISH, = 'Danish and', as ***Dano-German***, ***-Irish***; **Dano-Norwegian** *sb.* and *a.*, (a modified form) of the Danish language used in Norway after its separation from Denmark, and now one of the two standard languages.
1931 *Times Lit. Suppl.* 19 Feb. 128/2 The Dano-German Münte. **1880** *Encycl. Brit.* XIII. 252/2 The many feuds between the Irish clans in which the Dano-Irish shared. *Ibid.*, During the independence of the Dano-Irish kingdom of Dublin. **1892** J. Y. SARGENT *Gram. Dano-Norwegian Lang.* p. vi, I have given..the Syntax of sentences simple and compound, so far as the Dano-Norwegian idiom differs from the English. **1911** *Encycl. Brit.* XIX. 818/1 The close of 1899 and the beginning of 1900 were occupied by a discussion..as to the adoption of the *landsmaal*..in place of the *rigsmaal* or Dano-Norwegian. **1933** BLOOMFIELD *Lang.* iv. 59 The present-day standard languages [in Scandinavia] are Icelandic, Danish, Dano-Norwegian, Norwegian Landsmaal, and Swedish. *Ibid.* xxvii. 484 The Norwegians modified their standard Danish in the direction of Norwegian speech-forms. This Dano-Norwegian *Riksmaal* ('national language') became the native speech of the educated upper class. **1961** L. F. BROSNAHAN *Sounds of Lang.* ix. 205 The *Riksmål*, which originated in the Dano-Norwegian speech of the educated population of the south-east.

‖**dansant** (dɑ̃sɑ̃), fem. **dansante** (dɑ̃sɑ̃t), *a.* [Fr., pr. pple. of *danser* to DANCE.] Accompanied by dancing, as in ***thé dansant*** (erron. *-ante*), an afternoon entertainment at which there is dancing and tea is served; ***soirée dansante***, an evening party with dancing.
1819 M. WILMOT *Let.* 24 Oct. (1935) 28 Another Eveg there was a *thé danceant* at old Prince Esterhazy's. **1841** *Punch* 28 Aug. 83/2 The elegant *soirées dansantes*, nightly held at the 'Frog and Fiddle'. **1845** *Ibid.* 26 July 52/1 Among the fashionable parties of the season we have observed the frequent announcement of a *Thé Dansante*, or a dancing tea. **1849** THACKERAY *Pendennis* I. vii. 71 What did Lady Snapperton do..at her *déjeuné dansant* after the Bohemian Ball? **1854** —— *Newcomes* xiv, Mrs. Toddle Tompkyns's *soirée dansante* in Belgrave Square. **1858** *Punch* 29 May 214/1 Two medical students..got up an impromptu *Thé Dansante.* **1872** E. BRADDON *Life in India* v. 151 The projection of balls and parties *dansantes.* **1945** J. BETJEMAN *New Bats in Old Belfries* 28 How restful to putt, when the strains of a band Announced a *thé dansant* was on at the Grand. **1971** *Times* 16 June 4/1 In the inelegant heart of London beside Piccadilly Circus it is still possible to go to a thé dansant.

‖**danse du ventre** (dɑ̃s dy vɑ̃tr). [Fr., lit. 'dance of the belly'.] = *belly-dance* (BELLY *sb.* 17).
1893 *National Police Gaz.* (U.S.) 23 Dec. 2/2 The *danse du ventre* has reached New York at last, and has raised quite a storm. **1926** F. M. FORD *A Man could stand Up* II. i. 90 They had watched the Hun do the *danse du ventre!* **1967** G. FALLON *Rendezvous in Rio* xv. 129 She arched her back and started to gyrate her stomach in the fascinating *danse du ventre.*

danse macabre: see MACABRE *a.*

‖**danseur** (dɑ̃sœːr). [Fr., dancer.] A male ballet-dancer. So **danseur noble** [see NOBLE *a.*], the partner of a ballerina.
1828 J. EBERS *Seven Years of King's Theatre* iii. 66 They directed their endeavours towards forming an engagement with Albert, *premier danseur.* **1912** J. E. C. FLITCH *Mod. Dancing* ii. 32 Perhaps the greatest danseur who has ever lived—Gætano Vestris. **1943** K. AMBROSE *Ballet-Lover's Pocket-Bk.* 36 When the attributes of the ideal *danseur* are under discussion, it is first necessary to determine whether one is speaking of the male dancer as a *soloist*, or primarily as a partner to a *ballérina*: a *danseur noble.* **1947** *Ballet Ann.* I. 55 A *danseur noble* and pefect partner in classical adagio. **1959** *Observer* 24 May 19/5 Some of those portly senior *danseurs* were prudently left behind. **1961** *Times* 11 May 18/6 Mr. Royes Fernandez—a true *danseur noble.*

‖**danseuse** (dɑ̃søːz). [Fr., fem. of *danseur* dancer.] A female dancer, a ballet-dancer.
1828 J. EBERS *Seven Years of King's Theatre* iii. 69 A carriage was sent for the accommodation of the *première danseuse.* **1840** A. BUNN *Stage* II. iv. 90 Those charming stanzas addressed to the fair *danseuse.* **1845** *Athenæum* 8 Mar. 236 A *danseuse* to whose notice he had been recommended. **1878** H. S. EDWARDS in Grove *Dict. Mus.* I. 131 Three other danseuses and a befitting number of male dancers.

†**Dansk**, *a.* (*sb.*) *Obs.* Also 6 **Danisk**. [a. Da., Sw., Icel. *Dansk*: see DANISH. Spenser's *Danisk* unites *Dansk* and *Danish.*] = DANISH.
1569 *Wills & Inv. N.C.* (Surtees) 301 A danske chiste that was his sisters. **1596** SPENSER *F.Q.* IV. x. 31 On her head a crowne She wore, much like unto a Danisk hood. **1610** MARKHAM *Masterp.* II. xcvii. 387 Our English [Iron] is best, the Spanish next, and the Danske worst.
b. *sb.* Denmark.
1568 TURNER *Herbal* III. 5 The rootes are now condited in Danske.

‖**'Dansker.** *Obs.* [Da. *Dansker* Dane, f. *Dansk* Danish.] A Dane.
1602 SHAKS. *Ham.* II. i. 7 Enquire me first what Danskers are in Paris.

†**dant**[1]. *Obs.* [Cf. obs. Du. *dante* 'ambubaia, mulier ignava'.] 'A profligate woman' (Halliwell).
a **1529** SKELTON *Elynor Rumm.* 515 In came another dant She had a wide wesant.

dant[2]. *Obs.* or *local.* [Derivation unknown: perh. more than one word.] (See quots.)
1688 R. HOLME *Armoury* II. 24/1 Dants or Sulphury Damps..all proceed from dry and hot slimy Vapours. *Ibid.* III. 97/1 Down, is the Dant, or pure soft airy Feathers which have no Quills. *Ibid.* III. 316/1 The Bolted Meal was put to fall into the Wheel..and the pure Dant, or second sort of Meal to fall into the Ark. **1888** GREENWELL *Coal-trade Terms Northumb. & Durh.*, *Dant*, soft sooty coal found at backs, and at the leaders of hitches and troubles.

dant, -ar, obs. or Sc. forms of DAUNT, -ER.

dante. Also 6 dant, 8–9 danta. [Cf. It. *dante*, 'a kind of great wilde beast in Affrike hauing a very hard skin' (Florio 1598): see ANTE *sb.*[1] In the second sense app. a transferred use of the same word by the Spanish settlers in S. America.]
†**1.** (Also *dant.*) Some African quadruped: the same as ANTE *sb.* q.v. *Obs.*
1600 J. PORY tr. *Leo's Africa* I. 39 Buffles..and Dantes (of whose hard skins they make all their targets) range in heards up and down the woods. *Ibid.* II. 340 The beast called Lant or Dant..in shape resembleth an oxe, saving that he hath smaller legs and comelier horns.
2. (Also *danta.*) The American tapir.
(The early accounts are often exaggerated and erroneous.)
1601 HAKLUYT tr. *Galvano's Discov. World* (1862) 206 Many heards of swine, many dantes. **1712** E. COOKE *Voy. S. Sea* 392 This Country [Verapaz]..has abundance of Lyons, Tygers, and Dantas. **1760–72** tr. *Juan & Ulloa's Voy.* (ed. 3) I. 362 Peru..infested with bastard lions, bears, dantas or grand bestias, (an animal of the bigness of a bullock, and very swift, its colour generally white, and its skin very much valued for making buff leather; in the middle of its head is a horn bending inward). **1796** MORSE *Amer. Geog.* I. 83 American beasts..averse to cold; such are apes, dantes, crocodiles. **1887** W. T. BRIGHAM *Guatemala* 370, I have seen the tracks of the danta (*Tapirus Americanus*) in the Chocon forests.

dante(e, -ie, dantely, obs. ff. DAINTY, -ILY.

Dantean ('dæntiːən), *a.* [See -AN.] Of or relating to Dante or his writings; resembling Dante's style or descriptions. Also *sb.* A student or admirer of Dante.
1785 A. SEWARD *Let.* 25 Aug. (1811) I. 77 The Dantean Angel of Vengeance is diabolically insatiable. *a* **1850** ROSSETTI *Dante & Circ.* I. (1874) 20 Among our Danteans. **1872** C. KING *Mountain Sierra Nev.* ix. 193 It was no small satisfaction to climb out of this Dantean gulf. **1879** J. COOK *Marriage* 93, I do not adopt the Dantean view of the state of the lost in another life.

So **Dantei'ana** [see -ANA]; **'Danteish** *a.* = DANTEAN *a.*; **Dan'tescan** *a.* = DANTEAN *a.*; **Dantesque** *a.* [see -ESQUE] = prec.; **'Dantism**, the branch of study concerned with the works and life of Dante; **'Dantist**, a Dante scholar; **'Dantize** *v.*, to imitate the style of Dante; **Dan'tologist**, one versed in Dantology; **Dan'tology** = DANTISM; **Dan'tophilist**, an admirer of Dante.
1764 *Acct. of Bks.* in *Ann. Reg.* 272/2 Michael Angelo..is not ashamed, in some of his compositions, to *dantize.* **1813** J. FORSYTH *Remarks Excursion Italy* 66 Style..speckled even to affectation with *Dantesque* terms. **1833** *Edin. Rev.* LVII. 417 A poem thoroughly Dantesque. **1834** *Q. Rev.* LI. 23 Mr. Wright's double triplets..sound to our ears as little like the Dantescan harmony as Cary's blank verse. **1844** DISRAELI *Coningsby* IV. xi, 'Too insipid', said the Princess. 'I wish that life were a little more Dantesque.' **1872** LOWELL *Dante* Prose Wks. IV. 147 The veneration of Dantophilists for their master is that of disciples for their saint. **1876** *Encycl. Brit.* V. 291/2 Dantescan commentators and scholars. **1889** W. W. VERNON *Readings on Dante's Purg.* I. Pref., One of the greatest Dantists of his time—the late Duke of Sermoneta. **1903** *Daily Chron.* 7 Jan. 3/3 This.. branch of Dantology. **1910** *N. & Q.* 30 July 83 It is as yet little known to Dantologists. **1922** *Glasgow Herald* 23 Nov. 3 Since Witte's day Dantism has developed into something like an exact science. **1924** *Blackw. Mag.* 7 Jan. 24/1 A Danteish spot..had one redeeming feature. **1924** H. DE SÉLINCOURT *Cricket Match* v. 126 He moved away with a look of deep dejection upon his Dantesque face. **1936** *N. & Q.* CLXXI. 172/2 (*heading*) Danteiana. **1959** *Times Lit. Suppl.* 25 Sept. 548/3 There has been a remarkable flowering of Dantology under such scholars as Pézard, Gilson, [etc.].

danthonia (dæn'θəʊnɪə). *Bot.* [mod.L. (de Candolle & Lamarck *Flore Française* (1805) III. 32), irreg. f. the name of Étienne *Danthoine*, Fr. botanist + -IA[1].] A member of a large genus of tufted perennial pasture grasses so named, chiefly of Australia and New Zealand.
[**1863** *Proc. Calif. Acad. Nat. Sci.* II. 182 *Danthonia Californica* (California Oat Grass)..on borders of cultivated fields near the bay of Oakland. **1870** *Trans. N.Z. Inst.* II. 104 *Danthonia semi-annularis*, a variable grass found in nearly all soils and situations throughout the colony.] **1918** *N.Z. Jrnl. Agric.* 20 Mar. 135 On poor tussock country..the use of danthonia invariably increases the carrying capacity. **1921** H. GUTHRIE-SMITH *Tutira* xix. 167 On hard hill-tops and narrow ridges and knobs, danthonia and micrœlena had grouped themselves in little companies. **1952** A. R. D. FAIRBURN *Three Poems* 59 In time of drought The danthonia shines like a flame. **1955** *Landfall* IX. 108 The paddock of dry danthonia grass.

dantiprat, obs. var. of DANDIPRAT.

danton: see DAUNTON.

Dantonist ('dæntənɪst). [f. the name of *Danton* + -IST.] A follower of Georges Jacques Danton (1759–94), one of the leaders in the French revolution. So **Danto'nesque** *a.*, resembling the style of Danton.
1849 THACKERAY *Pendennis* I. xix. 179 He avowed himself a Dantonist, and asserted that Louis the Sixteenth was served right. **1879** *Encycl. Brit.* IX. 606/2 Two parties..the *Exagérés*, or Hebertists..and the *Modérés*, the Dantonists. **1899** A. H. BEESLY *Danton* 316 The indictment against the Dantonists. **1901** *Daily Chron.* 31 Dec. 3/1 He who had corrected the proofs of the Dantonist appeal for mercy. **1924** *Contemp. Rev.* Apr. 420 He can cut a knot with a phrase of Dantonesque audacity. **1928** *Sunday Express* 10 June 10/5 Camille Desmoulins was one of..the Dantonists.

Dan(t)zig ('dænzɪg, -tsɪg). Name of a city (now Gdańsk) near the mouth of the Vistula and of the district containing that city, used *attrib.* chiefly to designate kinds of timber grown in that district, as ***Dantzig deal, fir, oak.*** **Dantzig beer**, a black syrupy beer made at Dantzig; **Dantzig spruce**, beer made by adding a decoction of the buds or cones of spruce.
a **1592** GREENE *Fr. Bacon* (1594) sig. D3, All the westerne kings That lie alongst the Dansick seas. **1629** J. PARKINSON *Paradisi* II. liii. 524 Of Cowcumbers there are diuers sorts. .. The Dantsicke kinde beareth but small fruit, growing on short branches or runners: the pickled Cowcumbers that are vsually sold are of this kind. **1720** J. STEUART *Letter-Bk.* (1915) 122 Two small caves with best double strong Dantzig waters. **1843** *Ainsworth's Mag.* IV. 327 Having..laughed as frequently at the bottle of transparent 'Dantzic'. **1855** OGILVIE Suppl., Black-beer, or Dantzic. **1862** *Chambers's Encycl.* IV. 334/2 It [*sc.* the Norway spruce fir] is the.. Danzig Deal of the market. **1871** S. T. AVELING *Carpentry & Joinery* 9 The weight of a cubic foot of English oak generally considered seasoned is about 50 lb... Of Dantzic

oak about 48. **1879** *Encycl. Brit.* IX. 223/2 The well-known 'Danzig-spruce' is prepared by adding a decoction of the buds or cones to the wort or saccharine liquor before fermentation. **1889** J. J. WELCH *Text Bk. Naval Archit.* 111 The wood employed [for decks] is generally Dantzic fir. **1945** [see GOLDWASSER].

Danubian (dæ'nju:bɪən), *a.* [f. med.L. *Danubius, Danuvius*, Gr. *Δανούβιος*: see -IAN.] Of or pertaining to, bordering on, the river Danube, or pertaining to the prehistoric cultures of the surrounding region.

Danubian principalities, (Hist.) the principalities of Moldavia and Wallachia, now forming part of Rumania. ***Danubian reed***, the giant reed *Arundo donax*, cultivated in Australia.

1847 *Howitt's Jrnl.* I. 327/2 By these [devices] does Russia tyrannize over the Danubian principalities. **1848** THACKERAY *Van. Fair* lxvi. 600 Tyrolese glove-sellers and Danubian linen-merchants. **1875** *Encycl. Brit.* II. 700/1 The Danubian provinces. **1876** [see SERB *a.*]. **1878** GLADSTONE *Berlin Treaty* 27 The union of the Danubian Principalities. **1909** WEBSTER, Danubian reed. **1927** PEAKE & FLEURE *Priests & Kings* 138 Their civilization, which in many respects resembled that of Thessaly, is known as Danubian. **1941** AUDEN *New Year Let.* I. 26 The dazed uncomprehending stare Of the Danubian despair. **1957** G. CLARK *Archaeol. & Society* (ed. 3) iv. 116 A settlement of 'Danubian' (Neolithic) peasants on a loess patch near Cologne.

Danz, obs. f. DAN[1].

dao, dhao, varr. DAH *sb.*[1]

daou, var. of DHOW.

†**daourite.** *Min.* Also daurite. [Named from Daouria in Siberia, where found.] An obsolete synonym of rubellite or red tourmaline.

1802 BOURNON in *Phil. Trans.* XCII. 316 The tourmalin ..of Siberia, to which the names of *rubellite*, of *daourite*, and of *Siberite*, have been successively given. **1804** R. JAMESON *Min.* I. 130 *Daurite*.

dap (dæp), *sb.*[1] *Obs.* exc. *dial.* [perh. f. DAP *v.*, in which case sense 2 (as held by Halliwell) would be the original.]

1. *pl.* Ways, modes of action; hence *dial.* likeness, image (in ways and appearance).

1583 STANYHURST *Æneis* IV. (Arb.) 110 His daps and sweetening good moods to the soalye [thee solely] were opned. **1622** MABBE tr. *Aleman's Guzman d' Alf.* II. 239 He ..knew the Dapps of the world. **1746** *Exmoor Scolding* 230 (E.D.S.) Tha hast tha very Daps o' thy old Ount Sybyl. **1787** GROSE *Prov. Gloss.*, *Dapse*, likeness. The very dapse of one, the exact likeness in shape and manner. **1888** *W. Somerset Word-bk.*, *Daps*, 1. habits or ways. 2. Likeness; image.

2. A bounce of a ball; a hop of a stone on the water.

1835 (*Said at Rugby School*), He caught the ball first dap. **1847-78** HALLIWELL, *Dap*, a hop, a turn. *West.* **1888** in *West Somerset Word-bk.*

dap (dæp), *sb.*[2] *colloq.* and *dial.* [Perh. f. DAP *v.* 2, in which case a use of DAP *sb.*[1]] *pl.* Rubber-soled shoes; *spec.* (*a*) slippers; (*b*) plimsolls.

1924 *Western Daily Press* (Bristol) 20 Mar. 9/4 Boot-shop windows sometimes display Daps for sale; they are shoes with rubber soles. **1931** BROPHY & PARTRIDGE *Songs & Slang 1914-18* (ed. 3) 299 *Daps*, slippers. Regular Army. **1939** DYLAN THOMAS *Map of Love* 67 The daps and the gaiters were lost forever in the grass. **1974** W. LEEDS *Herefordshire Speech* 58 Daps = plimsolls. (Ross.)

dap (dæp), *v.* Also dape. [Known only from 17th c.: app. a parallel formation to DAB, a lighter or slighter touch being expressed by the final *p*. In its use possibly also associated with DIP. Cf. also DOP.]

1. *intr.* (rarely *trans.*) To fish by letting the bait dip and bob lightly on the water; to dib, dibble.

1653 WALTON *Angler* 70, I have taught him how to catch a Chub with daping a Grashopper. *Ibid.* 118 With these [flies] and a short line..you may dap or dop. **1676** COTTON *Angler* (T.), The stone-fly we dape or dibble with, as with the drake. **1799** G. SMITH *Laboratory* II. 271 The larger trout are to be taken..with a stout rod.. dapping therewith (which term you will find used by eel-fishers) on the surface of the water. **1888** *W. Somerset Word-bk.*, *Dap*..to fish with a rod in a peculiar manner. When the stream is flooded and the water muddy, the bait, whether fly or grub, is kept close to the top of the rod, with only an inch or two of line, and is made to bob up and down very quickly on the surface of the water.

b. *gen.* To dip lightly or suddenly into water.

1886 R. C. LESLIE *Sea-painter's Log* 70 The 'dapping' of the kittywake gulls tell[s] where a shoal of mackerel lies. **1892** H. HUTCHINSON *Fairway Island* 129 In a few hours came a dapping of the lead line.

2. To rebound, bounce; to hop or skip (as a stone along the surface of water).

1851 *Voy. Mauritius* vi. 204 A shot fired over the smooth sea astonished them much, as they watched the ball dapping along the surface. **1880** *Boy's own Bk.* 148 The other player then strikes it..before it has..dapped (i.e. hopped from the ground) more than once.

†**da'patical**, *a.* *Obs.*[−0] [f. late L. *dapātic-us* sumptuous, f. *dap-em* feast: cf. also Gr. *δαπάνη* cost, expense.] Sumptuous, costly.

1623 COCKERAM, *Dapatical meates*, daintie meates. **1656** BLOUNT *Glossogr.*, *Dapatical*, sumptuous, costly, magnificent. **1721** in BAILEY. [Hence in mod. Dicts.]

dapchick(e: see DABCHICK.

dape: see DAP *v.*

Daphnad ('dæfnəd). *Bot.* Lindley's name for plants of the order *Thymelaceæ*, including *Daphne*. So **'Daphnal** ***alliance***, that containing the Daphnads and Laurels.

1847 LINDLEY *Veg. Kingd.* 530. **1876** HARLEY *Mat. Med.* (ed. 6) 448 Daphnal Exogens, apetalous, or polypetalous.

Daphne ('dæfni:). [Gr. *δάφνη* the laurel or bay-tree: in *Mythol.* a nymph fabled to have been metamorphosed into a laurel.]

1. a. The laurel. **b.** in *Bot.* The name of a genus of flowering shrubs containing the Spurge Laurel and Mezereon.

c **1430** LYDG. *Compl. Bl. Knt.* x, I sawe the Daphene closed under rynde, Grene laurer and the holsome pyne. **1634** HABINGTON *Castara* (Arb.) 19 Climbe yonder forked hill, and see if there Ith' barke of every Daphne, not appeare Castara written. **1862** ANSTED *Channel Isl.* IV. xxi. (ed. 2) 497 Daphnes flourish marvellously and remain in flower a long time.

2. *Astron.* The name of the 41st of the Asteroids.

Hence **'Daphnean** *a.* [Gr. *Δαφναῖος*, L. *Daphnæus*], of or pertaining to Daphne; *transf.* of or pertaining to virgin timidity and shyness. †**Daph'neon**, a grove of laurels or bays.

1606 *Sir G. Goosecappe* III. ii. in Bullen *O. Pl.* III, Nor Northren coldnesse nyppe her Daphnean Flower. **1887** T. HARDY *Woodlanders* xl, The Daphnean instinct, exceptionally strong in her as a girl. **1664** EVELYN *Sylva* (1716) 398 They [Bays]..grow upright and would make a noble Daphneon.

‖**Daphnia** ('dæfnɪə). *Zool.* [mod.L. (Müller *Entomostraca*, 1785) f. DAPHNE.] A genus of minute fresh-water entomostracous crustacea; a water-flea. Hence **daphni'aceous** *a.* **'daphniad**, a member of the order containing the water-fleas. **'daphnioid** *a.*, allied in structure to Daphnia; *sb.* a daphniad.

1847 CARPENTER *Zool.* §805 After the third or fourth moulting, the young Daphnia begins to deposit its eggs in the cavity of its back. **1852** DANA *Crust.* II. 1525 No Daphnioids..have been yet reported from the Torrid Zone.

daphnin ('dæfnɪn). *Chem.* [f. DAPHNE + -IN.] A bitter glucoside obtained from two species of Daphne. So **'daphnetin**, a product of the decomposition of daphnin.

1819 CHILDREN *Chem. Anal.* 289 Daphnin is the bitter principle of the daphne alpina. **1847** E. TURNER *Elem. Chem.* (ed. 8) 1165 Daphnine, from the bark of Daphne mezereum and other species. It is crystallizable. **1872** WATTS *Dict. Chem.*, Daphnetin. **1876** HARLEY *Mat. Med.* (ed. 6) 449 Colourless prisms of daphnetin.

†**'daphnomancy.** *Obs.*[−0] [f. Gr. *δάφνη* laurel, DAPHNE + -MANCY.] 'Divination by a Lawrel Tree' (Blount *Glossogr.* 1656).

‖**dapifer** ('dæpɪfə(r)). [L., f. *daps, dapi-* food, feast + *fer-* bearing.] One who brings meat to table; hence, the official title of the steward of a king's or nobleman's household.

1636 BRATHWAIT *Roman Emp.* 308 This Emperour also appointed divers Offices in the Empire, as Chancellor, Dapifer, etc. **1657** REEVE *God's Plea* (T.), Thou art the dapifer of thy palate. **1706** PHILLIPS (ed. Kersey), *Dapifer*, he that carries up a Dish at a Feast, a Server..Afterwards the Title was given to any trusty Servant, especially the chief Steward, or Head Bailiff of an Honour, etc. **1845** C. MACFARLANE *Hist. Eng.* I. 163 The royal cup-bearer or dapifer ordered him to withdraw.

†**dapinate**, *v.* *Obs.*[−0] [f. L. *dapināt-*, ppl. stem of *dapināre* to serve up (food), f. *daps* (cf. prec.).] 'To prouide daintie meates' (Cockeram).

daply, var. of DAPPLY *a.*

†**dapo'caginous**, *a.* *Obs.*

1674 BLOUNT *Glossogr.* (ed. 4), *Dapocaginous* (from the Ital. *dapoco*), that has a little or narrow heart, low-spirited, of little worth.

dapper ('dæpə(r)), *a.* Also 5 dapyr, 6 daper; 6 *erron.* **dappard, -art.** [Not found in OE. or ME. App. adopted in the end of the ME. period from Flemish or other LG. dialect (with modification of sense, perh. ironical or humorous): cf. MDu. *dapper* powerful, strong, stout, energetic, in mod.Du., valiant, brave, bold, MLG. *dapper* heavy, weighty, steady, stout, persevering, undaunted, OHG. *tapfar*, MHG. *tapfer* heavy, weighty, firm, in late MHG. and mod.G., warlike, brave. The sense of ON. *dapr* 'sad, downcast' appears to be developed from that of 'heavy'. Possibly cognate with OSlav. *dobrŭ* good.]

1. Of persons: Neat, trim, smart, spruce in dress or appearance. (Formerly appreciative; now more or less depreciative, with associations of littleness or pettyness; cf. b.)

c **1440** *Promp. Parv.* 113 Dapyr, or praty, *elegans*. *a* **1529** SKELTON *Image Hypocr.* 95 As dapper as any crowe And perte as any pie. **1530** PALSGR. 309/1 Daper, proper, *mignon, godin*. **1594** NASHE *Unfort. Trav.* 1 The dapper Mounsier Pages of the Court. **1648** HERRICK *Hesper.*, *The Temple*, Their many mumbling masse-priests here, And many a dapper chorister. **1673** R. LEIGH *Transproser Reh.* 9 As if the dapper Stripling were to be heir to all the Fathers features. **1749** FIELDING *Tom Jones* I. xi, The idle and childish liking of a girl to a boy..is often fixed on..flowing locks, downy chins, dapper shapes. **1828** SCOTT *F.M. Perth* viii, The spruce and dapper importance of his ordinary appearance. **1861** *Sat. Rev.* Dec. 605 Our dapper curates, who only open their mouths to say 'L'Eglise, c'est moi!' **1885** MISS BRADDON *Wyllard's Weird* I. 89 A good-looking man..well set up, neat without being dapper or priggish.

b. *esp.* Applied to a little person who is trim or smart in his ways and movements: 'little and active, lively without bulk' (J).

1606 *Wily Beguiled* in Hazl. *Dodsley* IX. 229 Pretty Peg ..'Tis the dapp'rest wench that ever danced after a tabor and pipe. **1634** MILTON *Comus* 118 Trip the pert fairies and the dapper elves. **1792** WOLCOTT (P. Pindar) *Ode to Ld. Lonsdale*, Much like great Doctor Johnson..With dapper Jemmy Boswell on his back. **1823** SCOTT *Peveril* xxxv, The clean, tight, dapper little fellow, hath proved an overmatch for his bulky antagonist. **1840** HOOD *Up the Rhine* 66 A smart, dapper, brisk, well-favoured little fellow. **1870** EMERSON *Soc. & Solit.*, *Civilization* Wks. (Bohn) III. 12 We are dapper little busybodies, and run this way and that way superserviceably.

2. *transf.* Of animals and things.

1579 SPENSER *Sheph. Cal.* Oct. 13, The dapper ditties, that I wont devise, To feede youthes fansie. [Gloss., *Dapper*, pretye.] **1589** *Tri. Love & Fort.* IV. in Hazl. *Dodsley* VI. 198 There was a little dappard ass with her. **1592** GREENE *Upst. Courtier* in *Harl. Misc.* (Malh.) II. 218 A little daper flowre like a ground hunnisuckle. **1672** WOOD *Life* (1772) 48 Mounting my dapper nagg, Pegasus. **1704** *Moderat. Displ.* vi. 23 A Dapper Animal, whose Pigmy Size Provokes the Ladies Scorn, and mocks their Eyes. **1802** G. COLMAN *Br. Grins, London Rurality* i, Would-be villas, ranged in dapper pride. **1870** EMERSON *Soc. & Solit.*, *Work & Days* Wks. (Bohn) III. 65 What of this dapper caoutchouc and gutta-percha, which makes water-pipes and stomach-pumps?

†**3.** as *sb.* A dapper fellow. *Obs.*

1709 *Tatler* No. 85 ¶1 A distant Imitation of a forward Fop, and a Resolution to over-top him in his Way, are the distinguishing Marks of a Dapper. *Ibid.* No. 96 ¶4. **1747** W. HORSLEY *Fool* No. 68 The well-dressed Beaus, the Dappers, the Smarts.

4. *Comb.*, as ***dapper-looking***.

1874 BURNAND *My Time* iii. 28 [The] dapper-looking, though common chairs.

'dapperism. *nonce-wd.* [-ISM.] The style, manners, etc. of a dapper person.

1830 CARLYLE *Richter* Misc. (1888) III. 33 A degree of Dapperism and Dilettantism..unexampled in the History of Literature.

dapperling ('dæpəlɪŋ). [f. DAPPER *a.* + -LING: cf. *weakling*.] A little dapper fellow.

1611 COTGR., *Nambot*, a dwarfe; elfe, little staruelimg; a dandiprat, or low dapperling. **1829** CARLYLE *Signs of Times* Misc. (1888) II. 246 An intellectual dapperling of these times. **1881** P. BAYNE in *Lit. World* 14 Jan. 26/1 She loves Anthony, a dapperling in person.

dapperly ('dæpəlɪ), *adv.* [-LY[2].] In a dapper manner; neatly, trimly, sprucely.

1858 LD. MALMESBURY in *Times* 1 Oct. (1884) 4/4 A slight figure..always with spurs and dapperly dressed. **1862** *Temple Bar Mag.* V. 290 Horns set dapperly upon the head.

dapperness ('dæpənɪs). [-NESS.] The quality of being dapper; spruceness, trimness.

1530 PALSGR. 212/1 Dapyrnesse, propernesse, *mignotterie*. **1841** EMERSON *Lect.*, *Man the Reformer* Wks. (Bohn) II. 238 Each requires of the practitioner..a certain dapperness and compliance, an acceptance of customs. **1881** *Athenæum* 12 Feb. 242/2 Dapperness rather than assumed dignity being the chief characteristic.

dapping ('dæpɪŋ), *vbl. sb.* [f. DAP *v.* + -ING[1].] Fishing by a method in which the bait is allowed to dip or bob lightly on the water. So **'dapper**, one who daps; **dap** *sb.*[3], the bait used in dapping; **'dapped** *ppl. a.*, dipped.

1799 E. SMITH *Laboratory* II. 272 The few which you may ..take, by dipping or dapping, will scarcely be eatable. **1867** F. FRANCIS *Angling* (1876) 263 Daping is in some places called 'shade-fishing'. **1908** *Westm. Gaz.* 13 June 11/3 Heavy trout being captured with the natural insect on 'dapping' tackle. **1920** *Glasgow Herald* 17 July 4 A position from which he can lower his 'dap' on to the water without drawing the fishes' attention. *Ibid.*, The floating imitation of the dry-fly fisher or the dapper's living lure. **1928** *Daily Express* 28 July 4/6 The patient 'dapper', who thrusts his rod between the branches of over-hanging foliage and dangles a blue-bottle temptingly at the extremity of a 3x cast. **1933** 'R. CROMPTON' *William—the Rebel* viii. 163 His father..needed all his rods—either for 'dapping' or 'trolling' or 'casting'. **1960** *Times* 3 Dec. 9/4 It also rises freely in the daytime to a dapped grasshopper. **1967** *Daily Mail* 8 July 6/6, I am a beautiful dapper: My daddy-longlegs skimmed the surface of the lake like a corps de ballet. *Ibid.*, Levin, though he lacks the light touch needed for dapping, does..cast as to the manner born.

dapple ('dæp(ə)l), *sb.* Also 6 dappell. [Unless this is the first element in *dapple-grey* (q.v.), it is not known until late in the 16th c., being preceded somewhat by examples of the adj. of the same form, and followed by those of the vb. in the simple tenses; the (? ppl.) adj. *dappled* however appears two centuries earlier. The mutual relations of these and the derivation and etymological development of the whole group are, from the want of data, still uncertain. The primary meaning of *dappled* was 'spotted, specked, blotched', which might arise either from a vb. 'to spot' or a sb. = 'spot, blotch'. A possible connexion is the Icel. *depill* (found in 13th c.) 'spot, dot'; according to Vigfusson 'a dog with spots over the eyes is also called *depill*'. This is app. a dim. of *dapi* pool: cf. mod. Norw. *dape*, *depel* muddy pool, pond, dub; MLG. *dope*, *dobbe*. Thus *dapple* might perhaps originally mean a 'splash', and, hence, a small blotch or speck of colour.]

1. One of many roundish spots or small blotches of colouring by which a surface is diversified.

1580 SIDNEY *Arcadia* II. 271 (R.) As many eyes upon his body, as my gray mare hath dapples. **1611** COTGR., *Place*.. a spot or dapple on a horse. **1868** LOWELL *Let.* 4 Sept. (1894) I. 453, I should like to lie under a tree for a year, with no other industry than to watch the dapples of sunlight on the grass. **1916** D. H. LAWRENCE *Amores* 49 When the yellow dapples Of autumn tell the withered tale again.

2. (Without *pl.*) Spotting, clouding; mottled marking of a surface; dappled condition, dappling.

1591 HORSEY *Trav.* (Hakluyt Soc.) 220 A goodly fare white bull, all spotted over with black naturall dappell. **1648** EARL OF WESTM. *Otia Sacra* (1879) 88 The Crimson streaks belace the Damaskt West.. And cast so fair a Dapple o'r the Skies. **1713** *Lond. Gaz.* No. 5176/4 A Grey Mare.. a little Fleabitten.. on the Dapple behind. **1820** J. HODGSON in J. Raine *Mem.* (1857) I. 291 The whole sky has a harsh and unnatural dapple. *a* **1889** G. M. HOPKINS *Poems* (1918) 52 For earth.. her dapple is at an end.

3. An animal, as a horse or ass, with a mottled coat. [app. subst. use of DAPPLE *a.*]

a **1635** CORBET *Poems* (1807) 16 The king.. rides upon his brave gray dapple. **1733** FIELDING *Quix.* I. i, Thou art just such another squat bag of guts as thy Dapple. *a* **1800** COWPER *Needless Alarm* 115 Be it Dapple's bray, Or be it not, or be it whose it may. **1861** *Times* 8 Oct. 8/1 The pure-blooded dapple, shaking his long ears over that manger.

dapple ('dæp(ə)l), *a.* Also 6 **daple**. [See DAPPLE *sb.*, and DAPPLED. The simple adj. is known *c* 1550: its relation to the sb. and vb. is uncertain. According to analogy, it might be the source of either or both of these; but its date would suggest that it may itself have been worn down from *dappled*, or short for *dapple-grey*.] = DAPPLED.

1551 T. WILSON *Logike* 79 All horses bee not of one colour, but.. some baye, some daple. **1735** SOMERVILLE *Chase* IV. 249 With his Hand Stroke thy soft dapple Sides, as he each Day Visits thy Stall. **1841** LANE *Arab. Nts.* I. 46 There approached them a third sheykh, with a dapple mule.

[*Dapple* cited by Imperial and Century Dicts. from Scott, is an error for *dappled*: see *Guy M.* XXV.]

Hence †'**dappleness**, dappled state.

1611 COTGR., *Pommelure*, plumpenesse, roundnesse; also daplenesse.

dapple ('dæp(ə)l), *v.* Also 7 **daple, dappel**. [The (? ppl.) adj. DAPPLED (q.v.) occurs from the end of the 14th c.; but the simple vb. is first known two centuries later, and might have been inferred from the ppl. adj., or formed directly on the sb. or adj. of same form: see DAPPLE *sb.*]

1. *trans.* To mark or variegate with rounded spots or cloudy patches of different colour or shade.

1599 SHAKS. *Much Ado* V. iii. 27 The gentle day.. Dapples the drowsie east with spots of grey. *c* **1620** FLETCHER & MASS. *Trag. Barnavelt* IV. i. They should have dapled ore yon bay with fome, Sir. *a* **1658** CLEVELAND *Wks.* (1687) 14 The trembling Leaves.. Dappling the Walk with light and shade. **1697** *Phil. Trans.* XIX. 781 A Negro-Boy that is dappel'd in several Places of his Body with White Spots. **1791** COWPER *Odyss.* XX. 427, I see the walls and arches dappled thick With gore. **1799** G. SMITH *Laboratory* I. 320 How to dapple a horse. **1824** MISS MITFORD *Village* Ser. I. (1863) 79 An adjoining meadow, where the sheep are lying, dappling its sloping surface like the small clouds on the summer heaven. **1870** LOWELL *Among my Bks.* Ser. I. (1873) 240 The flickering shadows of forest-leaves dapple the roof of the little porch.

b. *fig.*

1647 WARD *Simp. Cobler* 76 It is in fashion with you to.. dapple your speeches, with new quodled words. **1682** N. O. *Boileau's Lutrin.* I. 41 Discord dappled o're with thousand Crimes.

2. *intr.* To become dappled or speckled.

1678 *Lond. Gaz.* No. 1266/4 An iron gray Gelding, beginning to dapple. **1818** BYRON *Mazeppa* xvi, Methought that mist of dawning gray Would never dapple into day. **1883** D. C. MURRAY *Hearts* I. vi. 138 The green flooring of the dell [began] to dapple with light and shadow.

Hence '**dappling** *vbl. sb.* and *ppl. a.*

1830 WORDSW. *Russian Fugitive* I. ii, In the dappling east Appeared unwelcome dawn. **1870** RUSKIN *Lect. Art* vi. (1875) 172 The dappling of one wood glade with flowers and sunshine. **1883** G. ALLEN in *Knowledge* 3 Aug. 66/1 The.. colour and dappling [of orchids].

'**dapple-bay**, *sb.* [After *dapple-grey*: see BAY *a.*] A dappled bay (horse).

1835 D. BOOTH *Analyt. Dict.* 305 The colours of Horses are various.. There are also Dapple-bays.

dappled ('dæp(ə)ld), *a.* Also 5 **dappeld**, 6 **daplit**, 6–7 **dapled**. [In form, the pa. pple. of DAPPLE *v.*, which however it precedes in recorded use by two centuries. If DAPPLE *sb.* occurred early enough, an adj. from it in *-ed* = 'spotted', would be possible; cf. F. *pommelé*, OF. *pomelé*, dappled, which similarly occurs long before the vb. *pommeler*, and was perh. immediately f. *pommelle*, or OF. *pomel*, dim. of *pomme* apple; also OE. *æppled* in *æpplede gold*, 'formed into apples or balls', from *æppel* sb.]

Marked with roundish spots, patches, or blotches of a different colour or shade; spotted, speckled.

c **1400** MAUNDEV. (Roxb.) xxxi. 142 It [Giraffe] es a faire beste, wele dappled [*Cott. MS.* a best pomelee or spotted, Fr. *une beste techchele*]. *Ibid.* 143 þer er also wilde suyne.. dappeld and spotted [*Cott. MS.* all spotted, Fr. *toutz tecchelez*]. **1535** STEWART *Cron. Scot.* (1858) I. 21 The daplit sky wes lyke the cristell cleir. **1590** SPENSER *F.Q.* II. i. 18 A gray steede.. Whose sides with dapled circles weren dight. **1610** FLETCHER *Faithful Sheph.* II. ii, Only the dappled deer .. Dwells in this fastness. **1632** MILTON *L'Allegro* 41 Till the dappled dawn doth rise. **1718** PRIOR *Poems, The Garland* i, The dappl'd Pink, and blushing Rose. **1860** RUSKIN *Mod. Paint.* V. I. i. §6 Beeches cast their dappled shade. **1868** DARWIN *Anim. & Pl.* I. ii. 55 Horses of every colour.. are all occasionally dappled.

b. *Comb.* ***dappled grey*** = DAPPLE-GREY (horse).

1590 SPENSER *F.Q.* III. vii. 37 Fast flying, on a Courser dapled gray. **1810** SCOTT *Lady of L.* I. xxiii, He saw your steed, a dappled grey. **1842** TENNYSON *Talking O.* 112 Her mother trundled to the gate Behind the dappled grays.

dapple-grey ('dæp(ə)lgreɪ), *a.* (*sb.*) Forms: 4–5 **dappel-, -ul(l-, -il(l-**, 6–7 **daple-**, 5– **dapple-grey, -gray**. [See DAPPLE *sb.*, *a.*, *v.* and GREY.

Since *dapple-grey* occurs nearly two centuries before *dapple* itself is exemplified in any grammatical capacity (the only form known to be of equal age being the ppl. adj. *dappled*), it is difficult to conjecture whence or how the compound was formed. In such combinations, the first element is usually a sb.: e.g. in *apple-grey*, *iron-grey*, *sky-blue*, *snow-white*, etc.; but it is difficult to attach any analogous meaning to 'spot-grey', if we suppose *dapple* here to be the sb. The Germanic languages generally have a combination meaning 'apple-grey': viz. ON. *apalgrár* 'dapple-grey, i.e. apple-grey, having the streaky colour of an apple' (Vigfusson), Sw. *apel-grå*, Norw. *apel-graa*, Da. *abildgraa*, pied, piebald; OHG. *aphelgrâ* 'glaucus' (Grimm), MHG. *apfelgrâ*, Ger. *apfelgrau* 'dapple-grey' (Flügel), 'applied to the apple-round spots which show themselves on grey horses' (Grimm), Du. *appel-graauw* 'dapple-grey'. So F. *pommelé* (f. *pomme* apple) marked with roundish spots (of any colour), *gris-pommelé* grey dappled with darker spots, dapple-grey, *pomely grey* in Chaucer, *C.T. Prol.* 616; with which cf. Russ. *yablochnyĭ* dappled, f. *yabloko* apple; all said esp. of the coats of horses. It is not easy to believe that 'dapple-grey' which renders these words, has no connexion with 'apple-grey', their actual translation; the explanation may be that *dapple-grey* was a mixture of DAPPLED spotted, taken as the sense-equivalent of F. *pommelé*, with *apple-grey* the *formal* representative of Norse *apal-grâ-*, and its Teutonic equivalents. This would account at once for the difficulty in analysing *dapple-* in this combination, and for its presence here before its appearance as an independent word.]

Grey variegated with rounded spots or patches of a darker shade: said of horses.

c **1386** CHAUCER *Sir Thopas* 173 His steede was al dappull gray [*v. rr.* dappel- (3 MSS.), dapull, dapil-, dapple-grey]. **14..** *T. of Erceldoune* I. 41 Hir palfraye was a dappill grayе [*v. rr. Cott.* dappyll, *Lansd.* daply, *Cambr.* dappull gray]. **1577** B. GOOGE *Heresbach's Husb.* III. (1586) 116 The bay, the sorrell, the dunne, the daple gray. **1599** T. M[OUFET] *Silkwormes* 72 How they color change.. Then to an yron, then to a dapple gray. **1664** EVELYN *Sylva* (1679) 29, I read .. That an handful or two of small Oak buttons, mingled with Oats, given to Horses which are black of colour, will in few days eating alter it to a fine Dapple-grey. **1688** R. HOLME *Armoury* II. 154/2 Daple-Gray is a light Gray spotted, or shaded with a deeper Gray. **1722** *Lond. Gaz.* No. 6052/2 The other upon a Dapple-grey Horse. **1805** SCOTT *Last Minstr.* I. xxiv, O swiftly can speed my dapple-grey steed.

transf. **1639** MAYNE *City Match* V. v. in Hazl. *Dodsley* XIII. 307 She has three Children living; one dapple-grey, Half Moor, half English.

b. *absol.* A horse of this colour.

1639 DRUMM. OF HAWTH. *Challenge of Knights Err.* Wks. (1711) 232 Christianus.. mounted on a dapple gray, had his armour sky-coloured.

'**dapply**, *a. rare.* [f. DAPPLE *sb.* + -Y.] = DAPPLE *a.* ***dapply-grey*** = DAPPLE-GREY.

17.. SWIFT *Poems, On Rover*, Make of lineaments divine Daply female spaniels shine. **1744** J. CLARIDGE *Sheph. Banbury's Rules* 5 Clouds small and round, like a dappley-grey with a North-wind.

daps: see DAP *sb.*[1]

dapsone ('dæpsəʊn). *Pharm.* [f. D(I-[2] + A(MINO- + P(HENYL + S(ULPH)ONE in a systematic name (cf. below).] A sulphone given as tablets and by injection in the treatment of leprosy and dermatitis herpetiformis; bis-(4-aminophenyl)sulphone, $(H_2N{\cdot}C_6H_4)_2SO_2$.

1952 *Brit. Pharmaceutical Codex 1949* Suppl. 19 Dapsone is bacteriostatic... It is used in the treatment of lepromatous and tuberculoid leprosy. **1958**, etc. [see PROMIN]. **1968** *New Scientist* 19 Sept. 582/2 A proportion of leprosy patients who have relapsed during treatment with dapsone or thiambutosine carry drug-resistant strains of *M. leprae*. **1983** *Oxf. Textbk. Med.* II. XX. 73/1 Dermatitis herpetiformis... A gluten-free diet rigidly adhered to controls some but not all patients; 70 per cent can omit dapsone after two years of such dieting.

daquiri: see DAIQUIRI.

dar, obs. form of DARE *sb.*[3], DARE *v.*[1]

dar, var. of *þar*, THAR *v.*, need, needs.

darapti (də'ræptaɪ). *Logic.* A mnemonic term designating the first mood of the third figure of syllogisms, in which both premises are universal affirmatives (*a*, *a*), and the conclusion a particular affirmative (*i*).

The initial *d* indicates that the mood may be reduced to *darii* of the first figure; the *p* following the second vowel that there must be conversion *per accidens* of the minor premiss.

1551 T. WILSON *Logike* (1580) 30 The thirde figure.. *Da rap ti.* **1654** Z. COKE *Art Logick* (1657) 136 The third Figure .. The Modes of this Figure are six. Called, *Darapti, Felapton, Disamis, Datisi, Bocardo, Ferison.* **1727–51** CHAMBERS *Cycl.* s.v. *Darapti*.. e.g., *dA*. Every truly religious man is virtuous; *rAp*. Every truly religious man is hated by the world: *tI*. Therefore, some virtuous men are hated by the world. **1827** WHATELY *Logic* (1848) 101 Third, *Darapti*, viz. (dA) Every Y is X; (rAp) Every Y is Z; therefore (tI) some Z is X.

darayne, var. of DERAIGN *Obs.*

darbar: see DURBAR.

Darby ('dɑːbɪ). A southern (not the local) pronunciation of *Derby*, the name of an English town and shire, which was formerly also sometimes so spelt. Hence an English personal surname, and an appellation of various things named after the place or some person of that surname.

1575 LANEHAM *Let.* (1871) 4 Chester.. Darby, and Staffoord. **1654** TRAPP *Comm. Ps.* iii. Introd., Summerset, Nottingham, Darby.

1. ***Father Derby's*** or ***Darby's bands***: app. Some rigid form of bond by which a debtor was bound and put within the power of a money-lender. (It has been suggested that the term was derived from the name of some noted usurer of the 16th c.)

1576 GASCOIGNE *Steele Gl.* (Arb.) 71 To make their coyne, a net to catch yong frye. To binde such babes in father Derbies bands, To stay their steps by statute Staples staffe. **1592** GREENE *Upst. Courtier* in *Harl. Misc.* (Malh.) II. 229 Then hath my broker an usurer at hand.. and he brings the money, but they tie the poore soule in such Darbies bands. **1602** CAREW *Cornwall* 15 b, Hee deliuers him so much ware as shall amount to fortie shillings.. for which thee poore wretch is bound in Darbyes bonds, to deliuer him two hundred waight of Tynne.

2. *pl.* Handcuffs: sometimes also, fetters. *slang.*

1673 R. HEAD *Canting Acad.* 13 Darbies, irons, or Shackles or fetters for Fellons. **1815** SCOTT *Guy M.* xxxiii, 'But the darbies', said Hatteraick, looking upon his fetters. **1889** D. C. MURRAY *Dang. Catspaw* 301 Better get the darbies on him while he's quiet.

†**3.** Ready money. *Obs. slang.*

1682 HICKERINGILL *Wks.* (1716) II. 20 Except they.. down with their Dust, and ready Darby. **1688** SHADWELL *Sqr. Alsatia* I. i, The ready, the Darby. **1692** *Miracles performed by Money* Ep. Ded., Till with Darby's and Smelts thou thy Purse hast well stored. *c* **1712** ESTCOURT *Prunella* I. 4 (Farmer) Come, nimbly lay down Darby; Come, pray sir, don't be tardy. **1785** in GROSE *Dict. Vulg. Tongue.*

4. Short for Derby ale; ale from that town being famous in the 17th c.

[**1614** J. COOKE *Greene's Tu Quoque* in Hazl. *Dodsley* XI. 234, I have sent my daughter this morning as far as Pimlico, to fetch a draught of Derby ale.] *a* **1704** T. BROWN *Wks.* (1760) II. 162 (D.) Can't their Darby go down but with a tune? **1719** D'URFEY *Pills* IV. 103 He.. Did for a.. Draught of Darby call.

5. *Plastering.* A plasterer's tool, consisting of a narrow strip of wood two or three feet long, with two handles at the back, used in 'floating' or levelling a surface of plaster; also applied to a plasterer's trowel with one handle, similarly used: see quot. 1881. (Formerly also *Derby*.)

1819 REES *Cycl.* s.v. *Stucco*, The first coat.. is to be laid on with a trowell, and floated to an even surface with a darby (*i.e.* a handle-float). **1823** P. NICHOLSON *Pract. Build.* 390 The Derby is a two-handed float. **1842** GWILT *Archit.* (1876) 675 The Derby .. is of such a length as to require two men to use it. **1881** *Every Man his own Mechanic* §1379 For laying on fine stuff, and smoothing the finishing surface of a wall, a trowel of peculiar form and make, with the handle springing from and parallel to the blade.. is required.. This trowel is technically called a 'darby'.

6. Darby and Joan. A jocose appellation for an attached husband and wife who are 'all in all to each other', especially in advanced years and in humble life. Hence *dial.*, a pair of china figures, male and female, for the chimney-piece.

Hence **Darby-and-Joan** *v.*, **-Joanish** *a.*; **Darby and Joan club**, a club for elderly men and women.

The *Gentl. Mag.* (1735) V. 153 has under the title 'The joys of love never forgot: a song', a mediocre copy of verses, beginning 'Dear Chloe, while thus beyond measure, You treat me with doubt and disdain', and continuing in the third stanza 'Old Darby, with Joan by his side, You've often regarded with wonder: He's dropsical, she is sore-eyed, Yet they're never happy asunder'. This has usually been considered the source of the names, and various conjectures have been made, both as to the author, and as to the identity of 'Darby and Joan', but with no valid results. It is possible that the names go back to some earlier piece, and as Darby is not a common English surname, it may have originated in a real person. There is also a well-known 19th c. song of the name.

1773 GOLDSM. *Stoops to Conq.* I. i, You may be a Darby, but I'll be no Joan, I promise you. **1857** MRS. MATHEWS *Tea-Table Talk* I. 50 They furnished..a high-life illustration of Derby and Joan. **1869** TROLLOPE *He Knew* xc. (1878) 500 When we travel together we must go Darby and Joan fashion, as man and wife. **1881** MISS BRADDON *Asph.* III. 251 Daphne..sat by Edgar's side in a thoroughly Darby-and-Joanish manner. **1887** *Punch* 18 June 294 Both their Graces were present, Darby-and-Joaning it all over the shop. **1942** *Times* 18 Dec. 2/4 The Darby and Joan Club, which is believed to be the only one of its kind, was opened by Lord Soulbury at 16, Leigham Court Road, Streatham, yesterday. **1967** *Nursing Times* 18 Aug. 1083/3 For the gregarious elderly there are Darby and Joan clubs. **1970** D. CLARK *Deadly Pattern* v. 106 She often sang for the Darby and Joan club.

Darbyism (ˈdɑːbɪɪz(ə)m). [f. the name of Rev. John N. Darby, their first leader.] The principles of a sect of Christians (founded *c* 1830), also called Plymouth Brethren, or of a branch of these called Exclusive Brethren. So **ˈDarbyite**, one who holds these principles.

1876 SPURGEON *Commenting* 62 Good as they are, their Darbyism gives them an unpleasant and unhealthy savour. **1882-3** E. E. WHITEFIELD in Schaff *Encycl. Relig. Knowl.* III. 1856 Plymouth Brethren..upon the European Continent generally named 'Darbyites'. **1890** J. WOOD BROWN *Ital. Campaign* II. ii. 148 Darbyite views.

darce, obs. var. DACE, a fish.

Darcy (ˈdɑːsɪ). [The name of H. P. G. *Darcy* (1803–58), inspector of the Paris waterworks.] **1.** Used *attrib.* and in the possessive to designate concepts arising out of Darcy's work on fluid flow, esp. in **Darcy's law**, a law governing the flow of fluid through a porous medium, according to which the volume flow per unit cross-sectional area is proportional to the pressure gradient divided by the viscosity of the fluid.

1881 *Encycl. Brit.* XII. 493/2 (*heading*) Ganguillet & Kutter's modified Darcy formula. **1931** *Physics* I. 35 In the case of the flow of liquids through porous media..the empirically established law (D'Arcy law [*sic*]) that the velocity is proportional to the pressure gradient has been taken as the basis of the hydrodynamics. **1957** *Nature* 23 Feb. 407/2 The section concerned with underground water devoted most of the sessions to an appreciation of the so-called Darcy's Law and its application and validity over a wide range of ground-water problems. **1972** R. G. KAZMANN *Mod. Hydrol.* (ed. 2) v. 184 It is only in connection with water flow in the vicinity of discharging wells that..the flow is often turbulent, and Darcy's law does not apply.

2. Written **darcy** (pl. **darcys, darcies**). A c.g.s. unit of permeability to fluid flow, being the permeability of a medium that allows a flow of 1 cubic centimetre per second of a liquid of 1 centipoise viscosity under a pressure gradient of 1 atmosphere/centimetre.

1933 R. D. WYCKOFF et al. in *Rev. Sci. Instruments* IV. 395/2 In view of Darcy's fundamental work in establishing the laws of flow for porous media it has seemed appropriate to name the unit of permeability the darcy. **1971** *Bull. Amer. Assoc. Petroleum Geologists* LV. 1694/2 Average porosity is about 34%, and average permeability is in excess of 3 darcys. **1975** G. ANDERSON *Coring* i. 15 The American Petroleum Institute has modified the darcy to standardize its use for the petroleum industry.

Dard (dɑːd), *sb.*[1] and *a.* **A.** *sb.* **a.** A member of any of several peoples of Dardistan, in the extreme north-west of the Indian sub-continent. **b.** Any of the Indo-Aryan languages of these peoples. **B.** *adj.* Of or pertaining to these peoples or their languages.

1873 G. W. LEITNER *Results Tour Dardistan* I. III. p. ii, He might have studied..my Dardu 'Vocabularies and Dialogues'..and then would have been enabled to have *added* something to our knowledge of..the Dard languages. **1875** F. DREW *Jummoo & Kashmir* xix. 442, I think that the Dārd character, at all events of the lower classes, is generally straightforward. *Ibid.* xviii. 422 The existence of the Dārds as a separate race, as well as something of their language, have..been facts within the reach of readers of travels. **1879** *Encycl. Brit.* X. 598/1 The Dards are described as decidedly Aryan in features. **1902** *Ibid.* XXVIII. 729/2 Eleven different languages, which have all been usually classed together under the name Dard. **1920** *Blackw. Mag.* May 620/1 The 'Indians' to whom Herodotus refers are none other than the Dards. *Ibid.*, In Ladakh to this day we find pure Dard settlements.

dard (dɑːd), *sb.*[2] *Bot.* Formerly also **dart.** [Fr., fruit-spur.] (See quots.)

1925 W. R. DYKES tr. *Lorette's System of Pruning* p. xxviii, The dart (*dard*) is an eye which has not grown beyond a certain point and which is surrounded by a rosette of two or three leaves. It is the sign of fruitfulness in the pear. *Ibid.*, In ordinary circumstances, the dart..swells and adds to itself a rosette of leaves, which gradually increase in number from three to five. Continuing to develop, the dart is finally crowned with seven leaves and is then known as a fruit-spur (*lambourde*). **1946** *Ibid.* (ed. 2) 5 We have..adopted the original French spelling of dard and brindille, written in the first English edition dart and brindle—for both the latter have meanings totally unrelated to the objects referred to as dard and brindille. *Ibid.* 24 The dard is a bud which has not grown beyond a certain point [etc.]. **1951** *Dict. Gardening* (R. Hort. Soc.) II. 638/2 *Dard*, a bud on an apple or pear tree... It may develop into shoot if it receives too much sap, but usually with a steady supply of sap..becomes a spur carrying a fruit bud.

dard(e, obs. f. DART, and *dared* (see DARE *v.*).

Dardan (ˈdɑːdən), *a.* and *sb.* [ad. L. *Dardanus*, *Dardanius* (poet.) Trojan.] *adj.* Trojan, of Troy. *sb.* A Trojan. So **Darˈdanian** *a.* and *sb.*; ‖**Darˈdanium** [Pliny *N.H.* XXXIII. iii. 12 *Dardanium*, vel *Dardanum*, sc. aurum, ornamentum aureum], a golden bracelet.

1606 SHAKS. *Tr. & Cr.* Prol. 13 On Dardan Plaines. **1813** BYRON *Br. Abydos* II. iv, Of him who felt the Dardan's arrow. **1818** —— *Ch. Har.* IV. i, The Dardan Shepherd's prize. **1596** SHAKS. *Merch. V.* III. ii. 58 The Dardanian wiues. **1623** COCKERAM, *Dardanean Art*, Witchcraft. **1648** HERRICK *Hesper.*, *To Julia*, About thy wrist the rich Dardanium.

[dardyline-, *sb.*[1] Error for DANDY-LINE.

1889 in *Cent. Dict.* (citing Day *Brit. Fishes*).]

dare (dɛə(r)), *v.*[1] Pa. t. **durst** (dɜːst), **dared** (dɛəd); pa. pple. **dared.** Forms: see below. [One of the interesting group of Teutonic preterite-present verbs, of which the extant present is an original preterite tense: see CAN, DOW, etc. OE. *durran*, pres. *dearr*, *durron*, pa. *dorste*, = OS. *gidurran*, *-dar*, *-durrun*, *-dorsta*, MLG. *doren*, *dar*, *doren*, *dorste*, OFris. *dûra*, (*dûr* or *dor*), *dorste*, OHG. *gi-turran*, *-tar*, *-turrun*, *-torsta*, pa. pple. *gitorran*, MHG. *turren*, *tar*, *turren*, *torste*, subj. *törste*, Goth. *ga-daursan*, *-dars*, *-daursun*, subj. *-daursjau*, *-daursta*: belonging originally to the third ablaut series *ders-*, *dars-*, *durs-*, Aryan *dhers-*, *dhars-*, *dhrs-*: cf. Skr. *dhrsh-*, perf. *dadhārsha*, to be bold, Gr. θαρσ-, θρασ- in θρασύς bold, θαρσεῖν to be bold, OSlav. *drŭzate* to be bold, dare. In ON., the word is wanting, its sense being supplied by the weak verb *þora*. It is also lost in mod.Ger. and Du.; in MDu. it appears to have run together with the verb *dorven*, = OE. *þurfan* to need (see THAR); hence in Du., *durven* is to dare; and Ger. *dürfen* in some of its uses approaches the sense 'dare'. These two verbs have also fallen together under a *d* form in some Frisian dialects; and in ME. there was some confusion between them, *dar* being sometimes written for *thar*, while, on the other hand, *th-* forms (some of them at least from Norse) appear with the sense of *dar*: see A. 9 below.

The original 3rd sing. pres. *he dare*, and pa. t. *durst*, remained undisturbed to the modern period, in which the transitive senses (B. II.) were developed; but early in the 16th c. the new forms *dares*, *dared*, appeared in the south, and are always used in the transitive senses, and now also in the intransitive sense when followed by *to*. In the original construction, followed by the infinitive without *to*, *dare*, *durst* are still in common use (esp. in the negative 'he dare not', 'he durst not'); and most writers prefer 'he dare go', or 'he dares to go', 'to dares go'. The northern dialects generally retain 'he dare, he durst', and writers of northern extraction favour their retention in literary English when followed by the simple infinitive without *to*.]

A. Inflexions.

1. *Pres. Indic.* **a.** *1st sing.* 1 **dear(r,** *north.* **darr,** 1–3 **dear,** 2–4 **der,** 3 *Orm.* **darr,** 3–6 **dar,** 5– **dare,** (*Sc.* 7 **dar,** 8–9 **daur).**

c **950** *Lindisf. Gosp., Jerome's Prol.* ⁋2 þe ich darr huelc hwoego..to eccanne. *c* **1000** ÆLFRIC *Gen.* xliv. 34 Ne dear ic ham faran. *c* **1200** ORMIN 10659 Ne darr i þe nohht fullhtnenn. *c* **1205** LAY. 6639 Ne der ich noht kennen. *a* **1225** *St. Marher.* 16 Speoken i ne dar nawt. *a* **1240** *Ureisun* in *Cott. Hom.* 185 Mi leofman dear ich swa clipien. *c* **1350** *Will. Palerne* 938 Y dar nouȝt for schame. *Ibid.* 2169, I der leye mi lif. *c* **1420** *Avow. Arth.* xxxviii, I dar lay. **1513** MORE in Grafton *Chron.* II. 770, I dare well avowe it. **1605** SHAKS. *Macb.* I. vii. 44 Letting I dare not wait vpon I would. **1711** ADDISON *Spect.* No. 58 ⁋1, I dare promise my self. **1725** RAMSAY *Gent. Sheph.* II. iv, I daurna stay. **18..** [see examples in B].

b. *2nd sing.* 1 **dearst,** (*north.* ***darst),** 2–3 **dærst,** 2–4 **derst,** 3 *Orm.* **darrst,** 3–6 **darst, darryst, daryst,** 4–5 **darist,** 5 **darste,** 5– **darest,** (7 **darst,** 7– **dar'st).** β. **north.** 4–6 **dar,** 4– **dare.**

Beowulf 1059 Gif ðu..dearst..bidan. *c* **1175** *Lamb. Hom.* 27 þu ne derst cumen bi-foren him. *c* **1200** ORMIN 5614 þatt tu Ne darrst nohht Drihhtin wraþþenn. *c* **1205** LAY. 20375 þu ne dærst [*c* **1275** *darst*]..abiden. *c* **1385** CHAUCER *L.G.W.* 1450 *Hypsip. & Medea*, Now daryst thow [*v.r.* darstou] take this viage. *c* **1400** *Rom. Rose* 2532 That thou resoun derst bigynne. *c* **1400** *Lanfranc's Cirurg.* 302 Whanne þou..ne darist not do it. **1470–85** MALORY *Arthur* x. lv, Arte thou a knygte and darste not telle thy name? **1616** R. C. *Times' Whistle* v. 2143 [Thou] darst repaire. **1667** MILTON *P.L.* II. 682 Thou..That dar'st..advance.

β. *a* **1300** *Cursor M.* 5668 (Cott.) How dare [*v.r.* dar] þou sua þi broþer smite! *c* **1470** HENRY *Wallace* III. 361 Quhi, Scot, dar thou nocht preiff? **1578** *Gude & Godlie Ballates* (1868) 116 How dar thow for mercy cry?

c. *3rd sing.* **a.** 1 **dear(r,** *north.* **darr,** 1–3 **dear,** 2–3 **der,** 3 *Orm.* **darr,** 3–6 **dar,** 5– **dare,** (8–9 *Sc.* **daur).** β. 6 **dareth, -yth,** 6– **dares.**

Beowulf 1373 Gif he ȝesecean dear. *c* **1175** *Lamb. Hom.* 111 He his men eisian ne der. *c* **1275** *11 Pains of Hell* 231 in *O.E. Misc.* 153 Ne dar no seynt heom bidde fore. **1340** *Ayenb.* 32 þet ne dar naȝt guo ine þe peþe. **1382** WYCLIF *Rom.* x. 20 Ysaie dar, and seith. *c* **1400** MAUNDEV. (Roxb.) xii. 51 Nere þis see dare na man dwell. **1483** CAXTON *G. de la Tour* F viij, A coueytous herte dar well Saye. **1549** *Compl. Scotl.* 14 3it he dar be sa bold. **1599** SHAKS. *Much Ado* III. i. 74 Who dare tell her so? **1603** —— *Meas. for M.* V. i. 315 The Duke dare No more stretch this finger of mine, then he Dare racke his owne. **1630** DAVENANT *Cruel Bro.* I, A pretty curr! Dare it bite as well as barke? **1816** SCOTT *Antiq.* xxvi, 'Shew me a word my Saunders daur speak, or a turn he daur do.' **1850** TENNYSON *In Mem.* xlviii, Nor dare she trust a larger lay.

β. **1533** J. HEYWOOD *Mery Play betw. Johan, Tib, etc.*, The kokold..for his lyfe daryth not loke hether ward. **1605** SHAKS. *Macb.* I. vii. 46–7, I dare do all that may become a man, Who dares do more, is none. **1697** DRYDEN *Virg. Georg.* III. 418 The fearful Stag dares for his Hind engage. **1798** FRERE & HAMMOND in *Anti-Jacobin* No. 28 (1852) 140 The man who dares to die. **1812** J. WILSON *Isle of Palms* II. 241 Poor wretch! he dares not open his eye. **1856** EMERSON *Eng. Traits, Lit.* Wks. (Bohn) II. 113 No priest dares hint at a Providence which does not respect English utility.

¶ The present *dare* has been carelessly used for the past *dared* or *durst*.

1760 *Impostors Detected* I. 232 He pretended that the marquis dare not appear abroad by day. **1811** A. BELL in Southey *Life* (1844) II. 651 I wish I dare [= durst] put them down among our books. **1847** MARRYAT *Childr. N. Forest* vii, He told me he dare not speak to you on the subject. **1857** KINGSLEY *Two Y. Ago* I. 214 She was silent; for to rouse her tyrant was more than she dare do. *Ibid.* 298 But she went into no trance; she dare not.

2. *Pres Indic. plural.* **a.** 1 **durron(-e),** 2–3 **durre(n,** 3–4 **duren, dorre(n,** 4–5 **durn(-e), dore(n, -un,** 4–5 **dur, dor.** β. 3–6 *north.* **der,** 4–5 **dar,** (5–6 **darne),** 5– **dare,** (*Sc.* 7 **dar,** 8–9 **daur).**

c **900** *Bæda's Hist.* I. xxvii. Resp. 5 (1890) 72 þæt heo nowiht swelces ne durron ȝefremman. *c* **1205** LAY. 25705 þis lond cnihtes ne durren wið him mare na fehten [*c* **1275** ne dorre þis lond cnihtes]. *a* **1225** *Juliana* 47 Hu durre ȝe? *c* **1250** *Gen. & Ex.* 2239 He ne duren ðe weie cumen in. *c* **1290** *S. Eng. Leg.* I. 244/133 þat ne dorre we nouȝt. **1340** *Ayenb.* 38 þet..nolleþ oþer ne dorre riȝt do. **1382** WYCLIF *Gen.* xliv. 26 We dorun [**1388** doren] not se the face of the lord. *c* **1386** CHAUCER *Can. Yeom. Prol.* & *T.* 108 (Harl. MS.) As þay þat dor [*v.r.* dore, dur, dar (3 MSS.), dare] nouȝt schewen her presence. *c* **1400** in *Wyclif's Sel. Wks.* III. 476 Now durne worldly prestis take so grete lordschipe upon hem. *c* **1400** MAUNDEV. (1839) xxvii. 271 Therfore dur not the marchauntes passen there. **1401** *Pol. Poems* (Rolls) II. 107 Privyly as ȝe doren.

β. *a* **1300** *Cursor M.* 17425 (Cott.) þan dar we sai. **1377** LANGL. *P. Pl.* B. Prol. 152 We dar nouȝte wel loke. **1393** *Ibid.* C. IV. 214 Pore men der nat pleyne. *c* **1400** MAUNDEV. (1839) vi. 64 Thei dar wel werre with hem. *c* **1400** *Test. Love* II. (1560) 281/2 Loues servaunts..in no place darne appeare. **15..** *Sir Andrew Barton* in *Surtees Misc.* (1890) 64 To France nor Flanders we der not goe. **1562** WINȜET *Tractates* I. Wks. 1888 I. 4 We dar not contemne. **1581** MULCASTER *Positions* xxxviii. (1887) 168 Ladies who dare write themselues. **1664** EVELYN *Kal. Hort.* (1729) 186 We dare boldly pronounce it. **1861** DICKENS *Gt. Expect.* xxiii, How dare you tell me so?

3. *Pres. Subj.* **a.** *sing.* 1 **dyrre,** 1–5 **durre,** 3–4 **dure,** 4 **derre,** 4–5 **dorre;** *pl.* 1–5 **durren,** 4–5 **durre.** β. 4– **dare,** 5 **dair,** (8–9 *Sc.* **daur).**

Beowulf 2763 (Z.) 1380 Sec ȝif ðu dyrre. *c* **888** K. ÆLFRED *Boeth.* xiv. §1 Hwæðer ðu durre ȝilpan. *c* **1220** *Bestiary* 187 Noȝ[t] wurdi, ðat tu dure loken up. *a* **1250** *Owl & Night.* 1704 Non so kene, That durre abide mine onsene. *c* **1380** *Sir Ferumb.* 451 Com on ȝif þov derre. *c* **1430** *Pilgr. Lyf Manhode* IV. xix, Soo þat she durre no more be so proud. *Ibid.* xxix. 191 If þou dorre entre..þer in.

β. *a* **1340** HAMPOLE *Psalter* xiii. 1 þof a wreche dare thynke god is noght. **1380** [see B. 1 b]. **1526** SKELTON *Magnyf.* 2205 Here is my gloue; take it vp, and thou dare. **1592** DAVIES *Immort. Soul* viii. ii, If we dare to judge our Makers Will. *Mod.* Do it if you dare!

4. *Past Indic.* **a.** *sing.* 1 **dorste,** *north.* **darste,** 2–6 **dorste,** 1–6 **durste,** 3 *Orm.* **durrste,** 4–6 **dorst,** 4– **durst,** (5 **darste, derste, drust,** 5–7 **dirst);** *pl.* 1 **dorston,** 2–5 **dorste(n, durste(n,** (4 **draste),** 4–6 **dorst,** 4– **durst.** β. 6– **dared,** (8–9 *Sc.* **daur'd).**

c **893** K. ÆLFRED *Oros.* IV. xi, Hwæðer he wið Romanum winnan dorste. **918** *O.E. Chron.* (Earle 104), Hie ne dorston þæt land nawer ȝesecan. *a* **1154** *Ibid.* an. 1135 Durste nan man misdon wið oðer on his time. *c* **1175** *Lamb. Hom.* 97 Ða apostlas ne dursten bodian. *c* **1200** ORMIN. 2098 Forrþi durrste he sipþenn Don hise þeowwess takenn Crist. *c* **1200** *Trin. Coll. Hom.* 139 He ne dorste for godes eie forleten. *c* **1250** *Gen. & Ex.* 2593 Durste ȝhe non lengere him forhelen. *a* **1300** *Cursor M.* 2928 (Cott.) þar again durst he not spek. *c* **1300** *Havelok* 1866 But dursten he [= they] newhen him no more. **1340** *Ayenb.* 73 þe raþre..þanne þou dorstest..consenti. *a* **1340** HAMPOLE *Psalter* xxi. 18 His kirtil þe whilke þai durst noght shere. **1380** [see B. 2]. **1393** GOWER *Conf.* II. 174 He his mother derste love. *c* **1440** *Partonope* 1075 And the hethen drust not abyde. *c* **1440** *York Myst.* xxiv. 14 How durst þou stele so stille away! **1535** JOYE *Apol. Tindale* 32 He stretched forth his penne..as farre as he dirst. **1583** HOLLYBAND *Campo di Fior* 219 Wentest thou to see? I durst not. **1641** R. BROOKE *Episc.* 39 As Mercury once spared Jupiter's thunder-bolts which he dirst not steale.

1752 JOHNSON *Rambler* No. 204 ¶11 They durst not speak. **1849** MRS. CARLYLE *Lett.* II. 88, I durst not let myself talk to you at Scotsbrig.

β. c **1590** GREENE *Fr. Bacon* iv. 10 Lovely Eleonor, Who darde for Edwards sake cut through the seas. *Ibid.* iv. 18 She darde to brooke Neptunus haughty pride. **1641** BURROUGHS *Sions Joy* 26 They dared not doe as others did. **1650** FULLER *Pisgah* I. 145 They dared not to stay him. **1790** COWPER *Let. to Mrs. Bodham* 21 Nov., Such as I dared not have given. **1821** SOUTHEY in *Q. Rev.* XXV. 345 He dared not take the crown himself. **1848** DICKENS *Dombey* xxx, Florence hardly dared to raise her eyes. **1864** J. H. NEWMAN *Apologia* 288, I dared not tell why. **1883** FROUDE *Short Stud.* IV. I. iv. 48 Any one who dared to lay hands on him.

5. *Past Subj. sing.* as in *Past Indic. pl.* 1 **dorsten,** 2– as in *Indic.*

a **1000** *Boeth. Metr.* i. 54 Gif hi leodfruman læstan dorsten. *c* **1374** CHAUCER *Troylus* I. 906 Yn loue I dorst [*v.r.* durst] haue sworn. **1377** LANGL. *P. Pl.* B. Prol. 178 Þere ne was ratoun . . þat dorst haue ybounden þe belle aboute þe cattis nekke. **1556** *Aurelio & Isab.* (1608) C viij, What man . . that dorste haue tolde me.

¶ This Past Subj. or Conditional *durst* (= would dare) is often (like the analogous *could, would, should, ought*) used indefinitely of present time.

c **1400–50** *Alexander* 1673 Sire, þis I depely disire, durst I it neuyn. **1606** W. CRASHAW *Rom. Forgeries* 161 Do but promise that you will iudge without partialitie, and I durst make you iudges in this case. **1662** GLANVILL *Lux Orient.* (1682) 83, I confess, I'm so timorous that I durst not follow their example. **1761** STERNE *Tr. Shandy* III. xx, I have no desire, and besides if I had, I durst not. **1793** MRS. INCHBALD *Midn. Hour* II. i, I hear his vessel is just arrived, I durst not leave my house. **1881** *Private Secretary* I. 132 My mother does not drink wine and my father durstn't.

6. *Pres. Inf. α.* 1 ***durran,** 2–5 **durre(n,** 3–4 **dur,** 5 **durn, doren, dorn, dore.** *β.* 5 **daren, -un, darn, (derre),** 5– **dare,** (8–9 *Sc.* **daur).**

a **1300** *Cursor M.* 22603 (Cott.) He a word ne sal dur speke. **1340** HAMPOLE *Pr. Consc.* 4548 Na man sal þam dur biry. *c* **1430** *Pilgr. Lyf. Manhode* I. lxxxi, Þer shulde noon dore resceyue it. *c* **1440** *Promp. Parv.* 114 Darn, or durn (PYNSON darun, daren, or dorn), *audeo.* *c* **1450** LONELICH *Grail* xlii. 538 They scholen not doren lyen. **1481** CAXTON *Reynard* (Arb.) 72 To dore to me doo suche a shame.

β. c **1400** MAUNDEV. (Roxb.) iv. 12 So hardy þat he sall dare ga to hir. **1488** *Cath. Angl.* 89 Dare, *audere, presumere, vsurpare. Ibid.* 97 Derre, *vsurpare, presumere, audere.* **1715** DE FOE *Fam. Instruct.* I. iii. (1841) I. 64 They shall not dare to despise it. **1816** SCOTT *Old Mort.* viii, 'They'll no daur open a door to us.' **1841–4** EMERSON *Ess., Self-Reliance* Wks. (Bohn) I. 35 You cannot hope too much, or dare too much. **1871** MACDUFF *Mem. Patmos* xi. 153 We cannot dare read the times and seasons of prophecy.

7. *Pres. pple.* and *vbl. sb.* 6– **daring.**

1586 A. DAY *Eng. Secretary* II. (1625) 29 None now daring to take the same from you. **1889** *Spectator* 19 Oct., Power . . held on the tenure of daring to do, as well as daring to decide.

8. *Pa. pple. α.* 5 ? **dorren** [cf. OHG. *gitorran*], **dorre;** 6 **dare.** *β.* 6–7, *dial.* 8–9 **durst.** *γ.* 6– **dared.**

α. c **1430** *Pilgr. Lyf Manhode* II. v. (1869) 78 How hast thou dorre be so hardi? *c* **1500** *Melusine* xlix. 324 How one knyght alone had the hardynes to haue dare come.

β. **1509** BARCLAY *Shyp of Folys* (1874) I. 207 They sholde not have durst the peoples vyce to blame. **1605** SYLVESTER *Du Bartas* II. iii. *Law*, But Iochebed would faine (if she had durst) Her deere sonne Moses secretly have nource't. **1665** PEPYS *Diary* (1875–79) III. 315 A hackney-coach, the first I have durst to go in many a day. **1691** tr. *Emilianne's Obs. Journ. Naples* 217 They had not durst so much as to take one step. *Mod. Sc.* If I had durst do it.

γ. **1529** in W. H. Turner *Select. Rec. Oxford* 65 They have dared to break out so audaciously. **1603** SHAKS. *Meas. for M.* II. ii. 91 Those many had not dar'd to doe that euill. **1883** *Daily Tel.* 10 Nov. 4/8 A simple monk had dared to consign a Papal decree to the flames.

9. Forms with initial *þ, th* [partly from Norse *þora, þorði* (Sw. *torde*, Da. *turde*), partly confused with THAR to need]: *Pres. Indic.* 2 *sing.* 3–4 **therstou,** *pl.* 3–4 *we* **thore,** 5 *they* **ther(not);** *Pa. Indic.* 3 **þurte,** 3–4 **therste,** 4 **therst,** 5 **thorst.**

c **1300** *Havelok* 10 Þe wicteste man . . That þurte riden on ani stede. *c* **1300** *St. Brandan* 581 We ne thore oure maister i-seo. *Ibid.* 585 Hou therstou . . bifore him nemne his name? *c* **1300** *Beket* 1550 Hi ne therste aȝe the Kinges wille nomore holde him so. [Also 895, 1156.] *c* **1380** *Sir Ferumb.* 2668 Was þer þan no man þat in wraþþe þerst sen ys fas. **1460** *Lybeaus Disc.* 1155 The four gonne to fle, And thorst naght nyghhe hym nere. **1465** MARG. PASTON in *Paston Lett.* No. 506 II. 195 They say that they thernot take it uppon hem.

B. Signification.

I. *intr.* (Inflected *dare, durst* (also *dares, dared*).)

1. To have boldness or courage (*to do* something); to be so bold as. **a.** followed by *inf.* without *to* (the original const.).

a **1000** [see examples in A. above]. **1154** *O.E. Chron.*, Ne durste nan man don oþer bute god. *a* **1225** *Juliana* 42 Þenne darie we & ne durren neuer cumen biuoren him. *a* **1300** *Cursor M.* 3586 (Cott.) Baldlik þat dar i sai. **14..** [see examples in A. above]. **1568** GRAFTON *Chron.* II. 395 Whatsoever the king did, no man durst speake a worde. **1611** BIBLE *John* xxi. 12 None of the disciples durst aske him, Who art thou? **1743** JOHNSON *Debates in Parlt.* (1787) II. 441 No man dared afterwards . . expose himself to the fury of the people. **1759** H. WALPOLE *Corr.* (ed. 3) III. cccxxxv. 302 Two hundred and sixty-eight Sequins are more than I dare lay out. **1848** MACAULAY *Hist. Eng.* II. 74 Nature has caprices which art dares not imitate. **1862** HISLOP *Sc. Prov.* 5 Ae man may steal a horse where anither daurna look ower the hedge.

b. The *inf.* is often unexpressed.

a **1225** *Ancr. R.* 128, & ȝelpeð of hore god, hwar se heo durren & muwen. *c* **1350** *Will. Palerne* 2040, [I] missaide hire as i durst. *c* **1380** WYCLIF *Serm.* Sel. Wks. I. 222 He mai be martyr if he dair. **1535–83** [see A. 4]. **1652** CULPEPPER *Eng. Physician* (1809) 343, I have delivered it as plain as I durst. **1725** DE FOE *Voy. round World* (1840) 344 [They] brought them as near the place as they durst. **1810** SCOTT *Lady of L.* I. xxi, The will to do, the soul to dare. **1852** MISS YONGE *Cameos* II. xxii. 238 John of Gaunt had favoured the reformer as far as he durst.

c. with *to* and *inf.*

In this construction the 3rd sing. is now *dares* and the pa. t. *dared*; but *durst to* was formerly used. 'None dared to speak', is more emphatic than 'none durst speak'.

c **1555** HARPSFIELD *Divorce Hen. VIII* (1878) 269 The Counsell . . neither durst to abridge or diminish any of them. **1611** BIBLE *Transl. Pref.* 9 It were to be wished, that they had dared to tell it. **1619** BRENT tr. *Sarpi's Counc. Trent* (1676) 35 A Spanish Notary dared to appear publickly in the Rota. **1625** BURGES *Pers. Tithes* 6 No intelligent man durst absolutely to deny any of these Conclusions. **1677** GALE *Crt. Gentiles* II. IV. 5 No one durst to breathe otherwise than according to the Dictates of her Law. **1836** W. IRVING *Astoria* I. 289 No one would dare to desert. **1870** E. PEACOCK *Ralf Skirl.* III. 218 He did not dare to meet his uncle. **1848, 1883** [see A. 4].

2. (*ellipt.*) To dare to go, to venture.

c **1380** *Sir Ferumb.* 3726 Ferrer ne draste þay noȝt for fere. **1660** GAUDEN *Brownrig* 151 There is nothing so audacious which wit unsanctified will not . . dare at in Heaven or Hell. **1697** DRYDEN *Virg. Past.* VI. 6 Apollo . . bade me feed My fatning Flocks, nor dare beyond the Reed.

II. *trans.* (Inflected *dares, dared.*)

3. To dare to undertake or do; to venture upon, have courage for, face.

1631 MAY tr. *Barclay's Mirr. Mindes* II. 135 To dare all things, but nothing too much. **1704** SWIFT *T. Tub* xi, Should some sourer mongrel dare too near an approach. **1827** HEBER *1st Olympic Ode* 145, I will dare the course. **1867** LADY HERBERT *Cradle L.* iii. 110 To teach them fortitude that they might dare all things, and bear all things for their Lord.

4. To dare or venture to meet or expose oneself to, to run the risk of meeting; to meet defiantly, defy (a thing).

1602 SHAKS. *Ham.* IV. v. 133, I dare Damnation . . onely Ile be reveng'd. **1611** HEYWOOD *Gold. Age* I. Wks. 1874 III. 7 A Crown's worth tugging for, and I wil ha't Though in pursute I dare my ominous Fate. **1645** QUARLES *Sol. Recant.* 23 O why should'st thou provoke thy God, and dare His curse upon thy practise? **1701** ROWE *Amb. Step-Moth.* IV. i. 1738 If thou still persist to dare my Power. **1727–38** GAY *Fables* I. xx. 36, I stand resolv'd, and dare the event. **1844** LINGARD *Anglo-Sax. Ch.* (1858) II. xiii. 260 He hesitated not to dare the resentment of the pontiff. **1853** C. BRONTË *Villette* vi, I saw and felt London at last . . I dared the perils of the crossings.

5. a. To challenge or defy (a person).

1580 LYLY *Euphues* (Arb.) 316 An English man . . [cannot] suffer . . to be dared by any. **1589** *Hay any Work* 37 What wisedome is this in you to dare your betters? *c* **1620** Z. BOYD *Zion's Flowers* (1855) 138 A gyant tall, who darr'd him to his face. **1703** ROWE *Ulyss.* I. i. 270 The Slave Who fondly dares us with his vain defiance. **1748** RICHARDSON *Clarissa* (1811) VIII. 395 Woman confiding in and daring woman. **1813** HOGG *Queen's Wake* 190 To range the savage haunts, and dare In his dark home the sullen bear. **1886** *Harper's Mag.* Dec. 105/2 Jabe Pennell begun to hunt him an' dare him. **1908** L. M. MONTGOMERY *Anne of Green Gables* xxiii. 254 All the silly things . . were done . . because the doers thereof were 'dared' to do them. **1969** I. & P. OPIE *Children's Games* ix. 264 Sometimes you're dared to go and tie the wifies' doors together.

b. With various const., *e.g.* to dare (a person) *to do* something, *to* the fight, etc., †to dare *out.*

1590 GREENE *Orl. Fur.* (1861) 92 With haughty menaces To dare me out within my palace gates. **1603** KNOLLES *Hist. Turks* (1638) 148 He would . . meet the Rebell in the heart of Lydia, and there dare him battell. **1606** SHAKS. *Ant. & Cl.* III. xiii. 25, I dare him therefore To lay his gay Comparisons a-part. **1632** RANDOLPH *Jeal. Lovers* v. viii, I dare him to th' encounter. **1672** BAXTER *Bagshaw's Scand.* 11 As children dare one another into the dirt. **1785** BURNS *Halloween* xiv, I daur you try sic sportin. **1847** MARRYAT *Childr. N. Forest* xvii, You wish to dare me to it—well, I won't be dared to anything. **1873** BLACK *Pr. Thule* xxvii. 451 He knew she was daring him to contradict her.

III. dare say. [From sense 1.] **a.** *properly.* To be as bold as to say (because one is prepared to affirm it); to venture to assert or affirm.

a **1300** *Cursor M.* 4509 (Cott.) Bot i dar sai, and god it wat, 'Qua leli luues for-gettes lat'. *c* **1350** *Will. Palerne* 1452, I dar seie & soþliche do proue, sche schal weld at wille more gold þan ȝe siluer. *c* **1460** *Play Sacram.* 316 Neyther mor or lesse Of dokettis good I dar well saye. **1540–54** CROKE 13 *Ps.* (Percy Soc.) 7 My sute is heard . . I dare well saye. **1570–6** LAMBARDE *Peramb. Kent* (1862) 311 No Towne nor Citie is there (I dare say) in this whole Shire comparable . . with this one Fleete. **1614** BP. HALL *Recoll. Treat.* 759 Who devised your Office of Ministery? I dare say, not Christ. **1699** BENTLEY *Phal.* 120 This I dare say is the best and neatest Explication . . and . . I believe it the truest.

b. *transf.* To venture to say (because one thinks it likely); to assume as probable, presume. Almost exclusively in the parenthetic 'I dare say'; rarely in oblique narration, 'he dared say'. (In this use now sometimes written as one word, with stress on the first syllable.)

Some dialects make the past *daresaid, darsayed, dessayed.*

1749 FIELDING *Tom Jones* VII. xii, You give your friend a very good character . . and a very deserved one, I dare say. **1768** STERNE *Sent. Journ.* I. 54 (*The Letter*), La Fleur . . told me he had a letter in his pocket . . which, he durst say, w[d] suit the occasion. **1807** ANNA PORTER *Hungar. Bro.* v, 'Other women have admired you as much . . I dare say' . . 'O! if it's only a "dare say"' cried Demetrius, shrugging up his shoulders. **1853** MRS. CARLYLE *Lett.* II. 221, I daresay you have thought me very neglectful. **1885** SIR C. S. C. BOWEN *Law Rep.* 14 Q.B.D. 872, I daresay the rule was drafted without reference to the practice at common law.

dare (dɛə(r)), *v.*[2] *Obs.* or *dial.* Also 3 **deare,** 4 **dere.** [OE. *darian*, app. in sense 3; to þam scræfe þær þa wiðersacan inne dariað behydde (Ælfric *Saints' Lives* xxiii. 322). Perh. identical with the stem of MDu. and LG. *bedaren* to appease, abate, compose, calm, Flemish *verdaren, verdarien* to astonish, amaze; but the word has not been found in the earlier stages of the Teutonic langs., and the primary signification and sense-development are uncertain.]

I. *intr.*

†**1.** To gaze fixedly or stupidly; to stare as one terrified, amazed, or fascinated. *Obs.*

a **1225** *Leg. Kath.* 2048 Þe keiser . . dearede al adeadet, druicninde & dreori. *a* **1250** *Owl & Night.* 384 Ich mai i-son so wel so on hare, Theȝ ich bi daie sitte an dare. *c* **1350** *Will. Palerne* 4055 Þe king was kast in gret þouȝt; he dared as doted man for þe bestes dedes. **1444** *Pol. Poems* (Rolls) II. 218 The snayl goth lowe doun, Darythe in his shelle, yit may he se no sight. **1526** SKELTON *Magnyf.* 1358, I have an hoby can make larkys to dare. **1530** PALSGR. 506/2, I dare, I prye or loke about me, *je aduise alentour.* What darest thou on this facyon? me thynketh thou woldest catche larkes. **1549** THOMAS *Hist. Italie* 96 The emperour . . constreigned Henry Dandolo . . to stande so longe daryng in an hotte basen, that he lost his sight.

†**2.** *fig.* To be in dismay, tremble with fear, lose heart. dread. *Obs.*

c **1300** *Cursor M.* 21870 (Edin.) For þe se sale rise and rute, mani man sal dere and dute. *c* **1340** *Gaw. & Gr. Knt.* 2258 For drede he wolde not dare. *c* **1440** *York Myst.* xxviii. 2 My flesshe dyderis and daris for doute of my dede. **1513** BRADSHAW *St. Werburge* I. 2654 Dredefully daryinge comen now they be, Theyr wynges traylynge entred into the hall.

†**3.** To lie motionless (generally with the sense of fear), to lie appalled; to crouch. Also *fig.*, esp. in ***droop and dare.*** *Obs.*

c **1220** *Bestiary* 406 Ne stereð ȝe [ðe fox] noȝt of ðe stede . . oc dareð so ȝe ded were. *a* **1225** *Juliana* 42 Þenne darie we & ne durren neuer cumen biuoren him. *c* **1386** CHAUCER *Shipman's T.* 103 Thise wedded men þat lye and dare As in a fourme sit a wery hare. *c* **1420** *Anturs of Arth.* iv, The dere in the dellun Thay droupun and daren. *a* **1450** *Le Morte Arth.* 2575 Knyghtis of kynges blode, That longe wylle not droupe and dare. ? *a* **1500** *Chester Pl.* (Shaks. Soc.) II. 148 (Date of MS. 1592), Builded thinges to grounde shall falle . . And men in graves dare.

†**4.** To be hid, lie hid, lurk. *Obs.*

a **1225** *Leg. Kath.* 1135 Ȝef drihtin, þe darede in ure mennesse, wrahte þeos wundres. **1382** WYCLIF *Mark* vii. 24 And Jhesus . . mighte not dare *or be priuy* [**1388** be hid]. **14..** *Epiph.* in *Tundale's Vis.* 107 The worm . . Dareth full oft and kepeth hym covertly. *c* **1430** LYDG. *Bochas* IV. xvii. (1554) 117 b, Under floures lyke a serpent dare Til be may styng. *c* **1440** HYLTON *Scala Perf.* (W. de W. 1494) I. lxiii, There is moche pryde hydde in the grounde of thyne herte, as the foxe dareth in his denne. *c* **1440** *Promp. Parv.* 113 Daryn, or drowpyn or prively to be hydde, *latito, lateo.*

†**b.** with indirect obj. (dative): To be hid from, escape, be unknown to.

1382 WYCLIF *2 Pet.* iii. 5 It daarith hem [**1388** it is hid fro hem] willinge this thing. *Ibid.* iii. 8 Oo thing daare ȝou not *or be not unknowun.* —— *Acts* xxvi. 26, I deme no thing of these for to dare him.

II. *trans.*

†**5.** To daze, paralyse, or render helpless, with the sight of something; to dazzle and fascinate. ***to dare larks***, to fascinate and daze them, in order to catch them. (Cf. sense 1, quots. 1526–30, and DARING *vbl. sb.*[2]) *Obs.*

1547 HOOPER *Answ. Bp. Winchester's Bk.* Wks. (Parker Soc.) 203 Virtuous councillors, whose eyes cannot be dared with these manifest and open abominations. *a* **1556** CRANMER *Wks.* I. 107 Like unto men that dare larks, which hold up an hoby, that the larks' eyes being ever upon the hoby, should not see the net that is laid on their heads. **1602** WARNER *Alb. Eng.* X. xxxix. (1612) 256 The Spirit that for God himselfe was made, Was dared by the Flesh. **1613** SHAKS. *Hen. VIII*, III. ii. 282 Let his Grace go forward, And dare vs with his Cap, like Larkes. **1621** FLETCHER *Pilgrim* I. i, Some costrell That hovers over her and dares her daily. **1671** TEMPLE *Ess. Const. Empire* Wks. 1731 I. 90 They think France will be dared, and never take Wing, while they see such a Naval Power as ours and the Dutch hovering about all their Coasts. **1860** SALA in *Cornh. Mag.* II. 239 A 'dare' for larks or circular board with pieces of looking-glass inserted, used in sunshiny days, for the purpose of daring or dazing larks from their high soaring flight to within a distance convenient for shooting or netting them.

†**6.** To daunt, terrify, paralyse with fear. Now *dial.*

1611 BEAUM. & FL. *Maid's Trag.* IV. i, For I have done those follies, those mad mischiefs, Would dare a woman. **1627** DRAYTON *Agincourt* 97 Clifford whom no danger yet could dare. **1778** *Gloss. Exmoor Scolding* (ed. 9), *Dere*, to hurry, frighten, or astonish a Child. s.v. *Thir, Dere*, a Word commonly used by Nurses in Devonshire, signifying to frighten or hurry a Child out of his senses. **1864** CAPERN *Devon Provinc.*, *To dare*, to frighten. *He dare'd me*, he surprized me, *I was dare'd*, I was surprized.

Hence **dared** *ppl. a.*

a **1400–50** *Alexander* 3044 Selcuth kniȝtis, Sum darid [*Dubl. MS*, dasyd], sum dede, sum depe wondid. **1563** *Homilies* II. *Idolatry* III. (1859) 252 They desire as wise as the blocks themselves which they stare on, and so fall down as dared larks in that gaze. **1678** DRYDEN *Œdipus* I. i, Then cowered like a dared lark.

dare, *v.*[3] obs. var. DERE., to injure, hurt.

dare (dεə(r)), *sb.*[1] Also 6 **darre.** [f. DARE *v.*[1]]
1. An act of daring or defying; a defiance, challenge. Now *colloq.*
1594 *First Pt. Contention* v, *Card.* Euen when thou darest. *Hu.* Dare. I tell thee Priest, Plantagenets could neuer brooke the dare. **1600** HEYWOOD *2 Edw. IV* Wks. 1874 I. 96 His defiance and his dare to warre. **1606** SHAKS. *Ant. & Cl.* I. ii. 191 Sextus Pompeius Hath giuen the dare to Cæsar. **1688** BUNYAN *Dying Sayings* Wks. 1767 I. 48 Sin is the dare of God's justice. **1892** R. H. DAVIS *Van Bibber* 87, 'I didn't suppose you'd take a dare like that, Van Bibber', said one of the men. **1897** KIPLING *Capt. Cour.* viii. 161 In a minute half the boats were out and bobbing in the cockly swells, but Troop kept the *We're Heres* at work dressing-down. He saw no sense in 'dares'. **1959** I. & P. OPIE *Lore & Lang. Schoolch.* xi. 230 To give themselves guts when accepting a dare.
†**2.** Daring, boldness. Now *rare* or *Obs.*
1595 MARKHAM *Sir R. Grinvile* lxxvii, And yet, then these my darre shall be no lesse. **1596** SHAKS. *1 Hen. IV*, IV. i. 78 It lends.. A larger Dare to your great Enterprize. **1904** H. R. MARTIN *Tillie* 13, I would love to play in the evening if I had the dare.

dare (dεə(r)), *sb.*[2] [f. DARE *v.*[2]] A contrivance for 'daring' or fascinating larks.
1860 SALA *Hogarth* in *Cornh. Mag.* II. 239 *note*, The 'dare' I have seen resembles a cocked hat, or *chapeau bras*, in form, and is studded with bits of looking-glass, not convex, but cut in facets inwards, like the theatrical ornament cast in zinc, and called a 'logie'. The setting is painted bright red, and the facets turn on pivots, and being set in motion by a string attached to the foot, the larks are sufficiently 'dared' and come quite over the fascinating toy. **1888** *Athenæum* 28 Jan. 122/1 The dare for larks, or mirror surrounded by smaller ones, over the mantel-piece, which exercised many commentators [Hogarth's *Distressed Poet*].

†**dare,** *sb.*[3] *Obs.* Also 5 **dar.** [A singular formed on *dars*, OF. *dars, darz*, pl. of *dart, dard* dart, dace. The OF. pl. *dars* and nom. sing. *dars* became in Eng. *darse, darce*, DACE.] = DACE.
[**1314** in *Wardrobe Acc. 8 Edw. II*, 21/12 Dars roches et pik 2s. 8d.] *c* **1475** *Pict. Vocab.* in *Wr.-Wülcker* 763/36 *Hic capita*, a dar. **1622** DRAYTON *Poly-olb.* xxvi, The pretty slender dare, of many call'd the dace. **1708** MOTTEUX *Rabelais* I. iii, As large as a Dare-Fish of Loire. **1740** R. BROOKES *Art of Angling* I. xxiii. 60 The Dace or Dare.. is not unlike a Chub.

†**dare, darre,** *sb.*[4] *Obs.* [Cf. F. *dare*, 'a huge big bellie; also, Dole' (Cotgr.).] ? A portion (or some definite portion).
1528 *Papers of Earls of Cumbrld.* in Whitaker *Hist. Craven* (1812) 308 Item, for herbes five dares.. for yeast, five dares. **1601** F. TATE *Househ. Ord. Edw. II*, §2 (1876) 6 His livere.. shalbe a darre of bredde. *Ibid.* §9 He may take two darres of bred.

dare (= *dar*), **darh,** var. of THAR *v.*, need.

'dare-all. [f. DARE *v.*[1] + ALL: cf. *dare-devil.*] One who or that which dares all; a covering that braves all weather, a 'dread-nought'. Also *attrib.* or as *adj.*
1840 T. HOOK *Fitzherbert* I. xi. 120 Enveloped in mackintoshes, great-coats, dare-alls, boas and oilskins. **1902** *Daily Chron.* 18 Mar. 3/2 Their dare-all Vikings came sailing over the sea to possess themselves of our homes. **1939** 'A. BRIDGE' *Four-Part Setting* iii. 29 This had developed in her.. a dare-all and try-all attitude which didn't really belong to her character. **1942** PARTRIDGE *Usage & Abusage* 97/1 Venturesome journalists and dareall writers should employ them with care and discretion.

dared, *ppl. a.*: see DARE *v.*[2]

dare-devil ('dεə,dεvɪl), *sb.* and *a.* [f. DARE *v.*[1] + DEVIL: cf. *cutthroat, scarecrow.*]
A. *sb.* One ready to dare the devil; one who is recklessly daring.
1794 WOLCOTT (P. Pindar) *Odes to Mr. Paine* ii, I deemed myself a dare-devil in rhime. **1841** LYTTON *Nt & Morn.* (1851) 152 A dangerous, desperate, reckless dare-devil. **1874** GREEN *Short Hist.* x. §1 Robert Clive.. an idle dare-devil of a boy whom his friends had been glad to get rid of.
B. *adj.* Of or pertaining to a dare-devil; recklessly daring.
1832 W. IRVING *Alhambra* II. 193 A certain dare-devil cast of countenance. **1860** MOTLEY *Netherl.* I. 159 Plenty of dare-devil skippers ready to bring cargoes.
Hence **'dare-,devilish** *a.*, **'dare-,devilism, 'dare-,devilry, -deviltry** (U.S.).
1886 *Blackw. Mag.* CXL. 737 His faults were dare-devilism and recklessness. **1859** *Sat. Rev.* VIII. 24/2 The dare-devilry which prompts a respectable girl to make her way into the haunts of vice. **1886** MRS. C. PRAED *Miss Jacobsen's Chance* I. vi. 111 The spice of dare-devilry in him was in piquant contrast to, etc. **1881** *N.Y. Nation* XXXII. 369 No city has for courage and dare-deviltry surpassed Milan.

dare-fish: see DARE *sb.*[3]

†**'dareful,** *a. Obs. rare.* [f. DARE *sb.*[1] or *v.*[1] + -FUL.] Full of daring or defiance.
1605 SHAKS. *Macb.* v. v. 6 We might haue met them darefull, beard to beard. **1614** SYLVESTER *Parl. Vertues Royall* 994 Not by the Prowesse.. Of his owne darefull hand.

darer ('dεərə(r)). [f. DARE *v.*[1] + -ER.] One who dares or ventures; one who challenges or defies.
1614 RALEIGH *Hist. World* II. v. iii. §16. 454 The best, and most fortunate of these Great Darers. **1624** FLETCHER *Rule a Wife* III. v, Another darer come? **1748** RICHARDSON *Clarissa* (1811) V. 348 Women to women, thou knowest, are great darers and incentives. **1884** A. FORBES in *Eng. Illust. Mag.* Dec. 150 Of such men as Cavagnari is our empire of India—a thinker, a doer, a darer.

'daresome, *a. dial.* [See -SOME.] Venturesome, foolhardy.
1854 L. N. COMYN *Atherstone Priory* I. 101, I don't like to see her so careless and daresome-like.

darf, var. of DERF *a. Obs.*, keen, and THARF *v. Obs.*, to need.

darg (dɑːg). *Sc.* and *north. dial.* Also 5 **dawerk, dawark,** 8 **daurk,** 9 **daark, dark, darrak, darroch, dargue, daurg.** [A syncopated form of *daywerk*, or *daywark*, DAYWORK, through the series of forms *dawark*, **da'ark*, *dark, darg*, the latter being now the common form in Scotland.] A day's work, the task of a day; also, a defined quantity or amount of work, or of the product of work, done in a certain time or at a certain rate of payment; a task.
c **1425** WYNTOUN *Chron.* IX. xiv. 44 (Jam.) That duleful dawerk that tyme wes done. **1489** *Act. Audit.* 147 (Jam.) Ffor the spoliatioune of vi dawarkis of hay. **1535** STEWART *Cron. Scot.* II. 596 For that same darg and deid. **1605** in Pitcairn *Crim. Trials Scot.* II. 451 Fourscoir dargis of hay. **1787** BURNS *Auld Farmer's Salut.* xvi, Monie a sair daurk we twa hae wrought. **1794** *Statist. Acc. Scot.* XII. 300 A darg of marl, i.e. as much as could be cast up by the spade in one day. **1818** SCOTT *Hrt. Midl.* xxvi, I have a lang day's darg afore me. **1832-4** DE QUINCEY *Cæsars* Wks. 1862 IX. 51 You did what in Westmoreland they call a good *darroch*. **1851** GREENWELL *Coal-tr. Terms Northumb. & Durh.* 21 *Darg*, a fixed quantity of coal to be worked for a certain price.. the general term in use about Berwick. **1878** *Cumbrld. Gloss.*, *Darrak* (Centre), *dark* (S.W.), *darg* (North C.), day's work. **1875** RUSKIN *Fors Clavigera* VI. 8 Lett. 61 And goes out himself to his day's darg.
Hence **'darg-days,** days of work done in lieu of rent or due to the feudal lord. **'darger, 'darker, 'dargsman,** day labourer. **'darging,** working as a day-labourer.
1803 JAMIESON *Water-Kelpie* iv. in Scott *Minstr. Sc. Bord.*, The darger left his thrift. **1807** J. STAGG *Poems* 64 The laird and dar'ker cheek by chowle, Wad sit and crack of auld lang seyne. **1788** R. GALLOWAY *Poems* 119 (Jam.) Glad to fa' to wark that's killing, To common darguing. **1885** in D. H. Edwards *Mod. Sc. Poets* Ser. VIII. 44 A bargain.. for drainin' or for dargin'. **1845** *Whistle-binkie* Ser. III. (1890) I. 418 Warnin dargsmen to put on their claes.

dargha: see DAGGA[2].

dari, = DURRA, Indian millet or Guinea corn.
1892 *Daily News* 28 June 2/8 Buckwheat, dari, and millet firm. *Ibid.* 27 Oct. 7/4 Linseed, buckwheat, dari, and millet.

darial, dariel(le, var. of DARIOLE *Obs.*, pasty.

daric ('dærɪk). Also 6-7 **daricke, dari(c)que,** 7-9 **darick.** [ad. Gr. Δᾱρεικ-ός (properly and adj. agreeing with στατήρ stater).] A gold coin of ancient Persia, said to have been named from the first Darius. Also a Persian silver coin of the same design, specifically called *siglos.*
1566 PAINTER *Pal. Pleas.* I. 40 The King.. sent to the man.. a cuppe of golde and a thousand darices. **1586** T. B. *La Primaud. Fr. Acad.* 336 Two cups.. full, the one of Dariques of gold, the other of silver Dariques. **1665** SIR T. HERBERT *Trav.* (1677) 243 Timagoras.. had received a bribe of ten thousand Dariques or Sagittaries. **1767** SWINTON in *Phil. Trans.* LVII. 273 *note*, The bow and arrow.. visible.. on a very curious Daric. **1879** H. PHILLIPS *Notes Coins* 5 The Persian Daric, of which an example in silver is shown.

darie, obs. form of DAIRY.

'darii. *Logic.* A mnemonic word designating the third mood of the first figure of syllogisms, in which the major premiss is a universal affirmative (*a*), and the minor premiss and the conclusion particular affirmatives (*i*); thus, All A are B; Some C are A: therefore, Some C are B.
1551 T. WILSON *Logike* (1580) 27 Vnto the firste figure belong fower Modes.. *Barbara, Celarent, Darii, Ferio*.. whereby every Proposition is knowne, either to be universall or particular, affirmative or negative. **1717** PRIOR *Alma* III. 383, I could.. With learned skill, now push, now parry. From Darii to Bocardo vary. **1869** FOWLER *Ded. Logic* (ed. 3) 99 Thus Disamis, when reduced, will become Darii.

daring ('dεərɪŋ), *vbl. sb.*[1] [f. DARE *v.*[1] + -ING[1].] The action of the verb DARE[1]; adventurous courage, boldness, hardihood.
1611 SPEED *Hist. Gt. Brit.* IX. ix. (1632) 596 Incredible darings.. were not wanting. **1651** HOBBES *Leviath.* I. xv. 80 As if not the Cause, but the Degree of daring, made Fortitude. **1874** GREEN *Short Hist.* vii. §6. 406 The whole people had soon caught the self-confidence and daring of their Queen.

†**'daring,** *vbl. sb.*[2] *Obs.* [f. DARE *v.*[2]] The action of the verb DARE[2]; *esp.* the catching of larks by dazing or fascinating them (see DARE *v.*[2] 5).
c **1440** *Promp. Parv.* 113 Darynge, or drowpynge, *licitacio, latitatio.* **1602** CAREW *Cornwall* (1811) 96 Little round nets fastened to a staff, not much unlike that which is used for daring of larks. **1704** *Dict. Rust.*, *Clap-net* and Looking-glass; this is otherwise called Doring or Daring. **1766** PENNANT *Zool.* I. 150 What was called daring of larks.
b. *attrib.* and *Comb.*, as ***daring-glass, -net.***
1590 GREENE *Neuer too late* (1600) 8 They set out their faces as Foulers doe their daring glasses, that the Larkes that soare highest, may stoope soonest. **1616** SURFL. & MARKH. *Country Farme* 712 You.. shall with your horse and Hawke ride about her.. till you come so neere her that you may lay your daring-net over her. **1659** GAUDEN *Tears of Church* 197 New notions.. are many times.. the daring-glasses or decoyes to bring men into the snares of their.. damnable doctrines.

'daring, *ppl. a.*[1] [f. DARE *v.*[1] + -ING[2].]
1. Of persons or their attributes: Bold, adventurous; hardy, audacious.
1582 STANYHURST *Æneis*, etc. (Arb.) 143 A loftye Thrasonical huf snuffe.. in phisnomye daring. **1596** SHAKS. *1 Hen. IV*, v. i. 91, I do not thinke a brauer Gentleman.. More daring, or more bold, is now aliue. **1667** MILTON *P.L.* VI. 129 Half way he met His daring foe. **1758** S. HAYWARD *Serm.* xvii. 539 The daring insolence.. of prophane Sinners. **1855** MACAULAY *Hist. Eng.* IV. 325 Montague, the most daring and inventive of financiers.
2. *transf.* and *fig.*
1617 MIDDLETON & ROWLEY *Fair Quarrel* I. i. 314 To walk unmuffl'd.. Even in the daring'st streets through all the city. *a* **1661** FULLER *Worthies* (1840) III. 202 Witness Wimbleton in this county, a daring structure. **1697** ADDISON *Ess. on Georgics*, The last Georgic has indeed as many metaphors, but not so daring as this. **1876** FREEMAN *Norm. Conq.* V. 39 This daring legal fiction.
†**3.** In quasi-*advb. comb.* with another adj., as ***daring-hardy.*** *Obs.*
1593 SHAKS. *Rich. II*, I. iii. 43 On paine of death, no person be so bold Or daring hardie as to touch the Listes.

'daring, *ppl. a.*[2] *Obs.* Also 4 **dareand.** [f. DARE *v.*[2]] Staring, trembling, or crouching with fear, etc.: see the vb.
1333 MINOR *Poems, Halidon Hill* 39 Now er þai dareand all for drede, þat war bifore so stout and gay. **1611** COTGR., *Blotir*, to.. lye close to the ground, like a daring Larke, or affrighted fowle.

daringly ('dεərɪŋlɪ), *adv.* [f. DARING *ppl. a.*[1] + -LY[2].] In a daring manner.
1605 CHAPMAN, etc. *Eastw. Hoe* I. i. (R.), Prouder hopes which daringly o'erstrike Their place and means. **1771** *Junius Lett.* xliii. 220 The civil rights of the people are daringly invaded. **1848** MACAULAY *Hist. Eng.* II. 533 Men asked.. what impostor had so daringly and so successfully personated his highness.

daringness ('dεərɪŋnɪs). [f. as prec. + -NESS.] Daring quality or character.
1622 MABBE tr. *Aleman's Guzman d'Alf.* II. 70 Full of Daringnesse and of Lying. **1647** CLARENDON *Hist. Reb.* VII. (1703) II. 276 [*Falkland*], The daringness of his Spirit. **1795** COLERIDGE *Plot Discov.* 49 The frequency and daringness of their perjuries. **1880** M. BETHAM-EDWARDS *Forestalled* I. I. ix. 140 The daringness of.. youth.

‖**dariole.** Also 5 **daryol(e, -iolle, -ial, -yal, -eal, -iel(le, -yel.** [a. F. *dariole* (14th c.) a small pasty 'filled with flesh, hearbes, and spices, mingled and minced together' (Cotgr.), now a cream-tart.] Orig., = CUSTARD 1 a. Now, an individual dish of various kinds prepared in a dariole mould; a sweet or savoury custard, soufflée or jelly; ***dariole (mould)***, a very small tin mould shaped like a flower-pot.
? *a* **1400** *Morte Arth.* 199 With darielles endordide, and daynteez ynewe. *c* **1420** *Liber Cocorum* (1862) 38 For darials. Take creme of almonde mylke [etc.]. *c* **1430** *Two Cookery-bks.* 47 Daryoles.—Take wyne & fressche broþe, Clowes, Maces, & Marow.. & put þer-to creme.. & ȝolkys of Eyroun. *Ibid.* 53 Darioles. *c* **1440** *Anc. Cookery* in *Househ. Ord.* (1790) 443 Daryalys. **1664** ETHEREDGE *Com. Revenge* III. iv, I.. did buy a dariole, littel custarde. [**1823** SCOTT *Quentin D.* iv, Ordering confections, *darioles*, and any other light dainties he could think of.] **1846** A. B. SOYER *Gastron. Regen.* 507 *Darioles.* Line (very thinly) a dozen small dariole moulds with paste.. flour.. eggs.. sugar... They will be as light as sugar and eat as delicate. **1890** *Mrs. Beeton's Cookery Bk.* 216/2 Oyster darioles. **1892** T. F. GARRETT *Encycl. Pract. Cookery* I. 516/1 Receipts for.. various Darioles will be found.. the original principle being that of lining a Dariole-mould.. with thin paste and filling up with rich cream, or custard. **1895** *Army & Navy Co-op. Soc. Price List* 15 Sept. 308 Dariols, Plain. Do. Fluted. **1901** *Daily Chron.* 23 Nov. 8/4 Line some dariole moulds thinly with tomato aspic. *Ibid.*, Set a dariole on each slice of tomato. **1903** *Ibid.* 21 Mar. 8/5 Darioles à la Maraschino. **1930** *Daily Mail* 6 June 15/3 Dariole of salmon is made with flaked cooked salmon, set in a mould with aspic jelly, sliced hard-boiled eggs, and shrimps. **1965** *Listener* 16 Sept. 434/2 We then took six individual dariole moulds, the kind used for baking little castle cakes.

Darjeeling (dɑːˈdʒiːlɪŋ). The name of a town and district in Bengal, used attrib. or absol. to designate tea grown there.
1882 *Tea Cycl.* 294/2 A good field for Darjeeling tea will be found to exist in an active competition with China for the supply of Thibet. **1907** F. F. THURSTAN *Few Facts concerning Tea* 5 *Darjeeling*, very flavoury, fine quality, coloury liquor, darkish, well made, tippy leaf; appearance no criterion. **1964** L. DEIGHTON *Funeral in Berlin* i. 10 He poured boiling water on to the Darjeeling. 'You like Darjeeling?' **1967** N. FREELING *Strike Out* 16 Arlette poured out tea.. Darjeeling tea.

dark (dɑːk), *a.* Forms: 1-2 **deorc,** 3 **dearc, derc, dorc, dorck, darc, darck, deork, durc,** 3-6 **derk,** 4 **deorke, durke,** 4-6 **derke, dirk(e, dyrk,** 5 **derck, dyrke, dork,** 4-7 **darke,** 6 **darck, dearcke,** 6- **dark.** [OE. *deorc* (repr. earlier **derk*, with fracture of *e* before *r* + cons.); there is no corresponding adj. in the other Teutonic langs., but the OHG. wk. vb. *tarchanjan, tarhnen, terchinen* to conceal, hide, of which the WGer, form would be *darknjan*, appears to contain the same stem *derk, dark*. In ME. there is a notable variant *therk(e, ðherke, thyrke*, with the rare substitution of initial *þ, th*, for *d*, for which see THERK.]

I. *literal.*

1. a. Characterized by (absolute or relative) absence of light; devoid of or deficient in light; unilluminated; said *esp.* of night.

Beowulf 3584 Niht-helm ȝeswearc deorc ofer dryhtgumum. *c* **1000** *Ags. Ps.* lxxiii[i]. 16 þu dæȝ settest and deorce niht. *a* **1225** *Juliana* 30 Dreihen hire into darc [*v.r.* dorc] hus. *c* **1275** LAY. 7563 Hit were dorcke niþt. *c* **1340** *Cursor M.* 16783 (Trin.) þe day wex derker þen þe nyȝt. **1470–85** MALORY *Arthur* XVI. xvii, Hit was soone derke soo that he myght knowe no man. **1548** HALL *Chron.* 113 A very darke night. **1568** GRAFTON *Chron.* II. 275 The gate was closed, because it was at that time darke. **1697** DRYDEN *Virg. Georg.* IV. 354 Lizards shunning Light, a dark Retreat Have found. **1752** JOHNSON *Rambler* No. 198 ¶10 The room was kept dark. **1861** FLO. NIGHTINGALE *Nursing* 24 People lose their health in a dark house. **1875** J. C. WILCOCKS *Sea Fisherman* 190 They will bite when it is so pitchy dark that you cannot see to bait your hook.

†**b.** A ***dark house*** or ***room*** was formerly considered a proper place of confinement for a madman; hence to ***keep (a person) dark***, to keep him confined in a dark room. *Obs.*

1590 SHAKS. *Com. Err.* IV. iv. 97 Both Man and Master is possest..They must be bound and laide in some darke roome. **1600** —— *A.Y.L.* III. ii. 421 Loue is meerely a madnesse, and..deserues as wel a darke house, and a whip, as madmen do. **1601** —— *All's Well* IV. i. 106 Till then Ile keepe him darke and safely lockt. **1630** MASSINGER *Renegado* IV. i, He..charged me To keep him [a madman] dark, and to admit no visitants. **1687** JEFFERIES in *Magd. Coll.* (Oxf. Hist. Soc.) 61 This man ought to be kept in a dark room. Why do you suffer him without a guardian?

c. Of luminous bodies: Dim; invisible. ***dark moon*** = ***dark of the moon***; † ***dark star*** (see 1594).

a **1123** *O.E. Chron.* an. 1106 Se steorra ætywde innon þæt suðwest he wæs litel ȝeþuht and deorc. **1551** RECORDE *Cast. Knowl.* (1556) 272 They..that be called Cloudy starres: and a lesser sorte yet named Darke starres. **1594** BLUNDEVIL *Exerc.* III. I. xxiii. (ed. 7) 328 Besides these, there be fourteene others [stars], whereof five be called cloudy, and the other darke, because they are not to be seene but of a very quick and sharpe sight. **1653** in Picton *L'pool Munic. Rec.* (1883) I. 192 Two lanthorns..everie night in yᵉ dark moone be sett out at the High Crosse. **1860** BARTLETT *Dict. Amer.*, *Dark moon*, the interval between the old and the new moon.

2. Of clouds, the sky, etc.: Reflecting or transmitting little light; gloomy from lack of light, sombre.

c **1000** *Ags. Ps.* lxviii. [lxix.] 14 Ado me of deope deorces wæteres. *c* **1290** *S. Eng. Leg.* I. 441/365 þat lodlokeste weder þat miȝhte beo..Swart and deork and grislich. *c* **1325** *E.E. Allit. P.* B. 1020 þe derk dede see hit is demed euer more. **1460** CAPGRAVE *Chron.* 152 A wedyr so dirk and so lowd, that men supposed the Cherch should falle. **1658** WILLSFORD *Natures Secrets* 100 Cloudy and dark weather. **1711** ADDISON *Spect.* No. 159 ¶8 Those dark Clouds which cover the Ocean. **1870** C. F. GORDON-CUMMING in *Gd. Words* 133/2 A deep valley, with dark hills on every side.

3. a. Of the ordinary colour of an object: Approaching black in hue.

1382 WYCLIF *Lev.* xiii. 6 If more derker were the lepre, and not waxed in the skynne..it is a scab. *c* **1400** *Lanfranc's Cirurg.* 181 If þe colour of his bodi be derk ouþer blac. **1606** SHAKS. *Tr. & Cr.* I. i. 41 And her haire were not somewhat darker than Helens. **1795** SOUTHEY *Joan of Arc* v. 27 Her dark hair floating on the morning gale. **1800** tr. *Lagrange's Chem.* II. 88 Two liquors, one of which has a dark and almost black colour. **1873** *Act 36–7 Vict.* c. 85 §3 Her name ..shall be marked on her stern, on a dark ground in white or yellow letters.

b. Of the complexion: The opposite of fair.

c **1400** *Rom. Rose* 1009 This ladie called was Beaute..Ne she was derk ne broun, but bright. **1784** COOK *Third Voy.* v. iii. (R.), Their complexion is rather darker than that of the Otaheiteans. **1870** DICKENS *E. Drood* ii, Mr. Jasper is a dark man of some six-and-twenty.

c. Prefixed, as a qualification, to adjectives of colour: Deep in shade, absorbing more light than it reflects; the opposite of *light*. (Usually hyphened with the adj. when the latter is used attributively.)

c **1532** DEWES *Introd. Fr.* in *Palsgr.* 909 The rede darke. **1727–46** THOMSON *Summer* 11 On the dark green grass. **1776** WITHERING *Brit. Plants* (1796) IV. 148 Stem hollow.. dark mouse or almost black below. **1810** SCOTT *Lady of L.* II. xxv, The bound of dark-brown doe. **1846** MᶜCULLOCH *Acc. Brit. Empire* (1854) I. 223 The sheep..many are grey, some black, and a few of a peculiar dark buff colour. **1863** M. L. WHATELY *Ragged Life Egypt* xvii. 163 Clad in the ordinary dark-blue drapery.

II. *fig.*

4. Characterized by absence of moral or spiritual light; evil, wicked; also, in a stronger sense, characterized by a turpitude or wickedness of sombre or unrelieved nature; foul, iniquitous, atrocious.

a **1000** *Satan* 105 (Gr.) Feond seondon reðe, dimme, and deorce. *c* **1000** *Ags. Gosp.* Luke xi. 34 3if þin eaȝe..byð deorc eall þin lichama byð þystre. **1377** LANGL. *P. Pl.* B. XIX. 21 Alle derke deuelles aren adradde to heren it [þe name of ihesus]. **1393** GOWER *Conf.* I. 63 Semende of light they werke The dedes, whiche are inward derke. **1593** SHAKS. *Rich. II*, I. i. 169 My faire name..To darke dishonours vse, thou shalt not haue. *Ibid.* v. ii. 96 Thou fond mad woman Wilt thou conceale this darke Conspiracy? **1663** J. SPENCER *Prodigies* (1665) 335 We shall find these consecrated weapons of infinite more force against the powers of the Dark Kingdom. **1732** POPE *Ep. Bathurst* 28 It [gold] serves what life requires, But, dreadful too, the dark Assassin hires. **1792** MARY WOLLSTONECR. *Rights Wom.* v. 239 Sometimes displaying the light and sometimes the dark side of their character. **1848** MACAULAY *Hist. Eng.* I. 166 Associated in the public mind with the darkest and meanest vices. **1852** MISS YONGE *Cameos* II. xx. 216 A dark tragedy was preparing in the family of King Robert.

5. a. Devoid of that which brightens or cheers; gloomy, cheerless, dismal, sad.

a **1000** *Wanderer* 89 (Gr.) Se ðis deorce lif deope ȝeond-þenceþ. **1592** SHAKS. *Rom. & Jul.* III. v. 36 More darke & darke our woes. **1636** HEYLIN *Sabbath* II. 141 Then the times were at the darkest. **1715** DE FOE *Fam. Instruct.* I. i. (1841) II. 5 We don't see the house is the darker for it. **1818** SHELLEY *Rosalind & Helen* 171 So much of sympathy to borrow As soothed her own dark lot. **1849** ROBERTSON *Serm.* Ser. I. iv. (1866) 76 To look on the dark side of things. **1888** BRYCE *Amer. Comm.* II. xl. 90 The prospect for such an aspirant is a dark one.

b. Of a person's disposition, etc.: Gloomy, sullen, sad.

1596 SHAKS. *Merch. V.* v. i. 87 The motions of his spirit are dull as night And his affections darke as Erebus. **1705** ADDISON *Italy* (J.), Men of dark tempers. **1735** SOMERVILLE *Chase* I. 200 If in dark sullen Mood The glouting Hound refuse his wonted Meal. **1862** CARLYLE *Fredk. Gt.* (1865) III. IX. x. 178 Ah, ah, you are in low spirits, I see. We must dissipate that dark humour.

c. Of the countenance: Clouded with anger or dislike, frowning.

1599 SHAKS. *Ven. & Ad.* 182 Adonis..with a heavy, dark, disliking eye..cries 'Fie, no more of love!' **1821** SHELLEY *Epipsych.* 62 Art thou not..A smile amid dark frowns? **1852** MRS. STOWE *Uncle Tom's C.* iii. 14 The brow of the young man grew dark.

6. a. Obscure in meaning, hard to understand.

c **1320** *Cast. Love* 71 þauh hit on Englisch be dim and derk. *c* **1380** WYCLIF *Serm.* Sel. Wks. I. 105 Men ben blyndid bi derke speche. **1387** TREVISA *Higden* (Rolls) V. 279 His prophesie þat is so derk. **1495** *Act 11 Hen. VII*, c. 8 Which acte..is so obscure derke and diffuse that [etc.]. **1535** COVERDALE *2 Chron.* ix. 1 The quene of rich Arabia.. came..to proue Salomon with darke Sentences. **1559** SCOT in Strype *Ann. Ref.* I. App. x. 30 This matter is..darke, and of great difficultie to be..playnlye discussed. **1626** BACON *Sylva* §103 The Cause is dark, and hath not been rendred by any. **1687** R. L'ESTRANGE *Answ. Dissenter* 44 He's a little Dark in this Paragraph; but the Change of One Word will make him..Clear. **1866** ARGYLL *Reign Law* vi. (1871) 299 These may seem far-fetched illustrations, and of slight value in so dark a subject.

†**b.** Obscure in name or fame; little known or regarded. *Obs.*

c **1374** CHAUCER *Boeth.* III. ix. 83 What demest þou..is þat a dirke þing and nat noble þat is suffisaunt reuerent and myȝty. **1551** TURNER *Herbal* I. Prol. A iij a, I..darker in name, and farr vnder these men in knowledge. **1577–87** HOLINSHED *Chron.* III. 1221/1 She hath made hir councell of poore, darke, beggerlie fellows.

c. Obscure to 'the mind's eye', or to memory; indistinct, indiscernible.

1592 SHAKS. *Ven. & Ad.* 760 If thou destroy them not in dark obscurity. **1610** —— *Temp.* I. ii. 50 What seest thou els In the dark-backward and Abisme of Time? *a* **1800** COWPER *On Biogr. Brit.* 8 Names ignoble, born to be forgot..dark oblivion soon absorbs them all. **1810** SCOTT *Lady of L.* III. i, The verge of dark eternity.

d. *Phonetics.* Of an *l* sound: formed with the tip of the tongue against the teeth-ridge and the rest of the tongue placed as for the articulation of a back vowel. Of a vowel: articulated with the front of the tongue somewhat depressed and the back raised in the direction of the soft palate. Opp. CLEAR *a.* 13 b.

1899 W. RIPPMANN *Elem. Phonetics* 42 When the tongue is raised a little further back we obtain lower, darker sounds ..; when it is raised a little further forward we obtain higher, clearer sounds. **1909** I. F. WILLIAMS *Phonetics for Scottish Students* x. 47 In forming l in English the tip of the tongue is raised to the teeth-ridge, and the part immediately behind the tip is somewhat hollowed. This hollowing makes the English l much darker than the French l, where the part behind the tip is arched. In Scottish the hollowing is much more considerable than in English, and the l still 'darker'. **1918** [see CLEAR *a.* 13 b]. **1942** *Amer. Speech* XVII. Suppl. 27 [ɑ] seems often to be a somewhat 'darker' or more retracted sound than the normal American variety. **1953** *English Studies* XXXIV. 250 To express 'vowel + glide' and not a 'dark' flavour of the following consonants. **1958** A. CARTIANU et al. *Course Mod. Rumanian* 22 English dark *l* in words like: *middle, tell, almost* does not exist in Rumanian.

7. a. Hidden from view or knowledge; concealed, secret. ***to keep dark***: to keep secret (*colloq.*).

1605 SHAKS. *Lear* I. i. 37 We shal expresse our darker purpose..Know, that we haue diuided In three our Kingdome. **1681** CROWNE *Hen. VI*, II. 14 By your passions I read all your natures, Though you at other times can keep 'em dark. **1861** DICKENS *Gt. Expect.* l, He hid himself..kept himself dark. **1888** J. PAYN *Myst. Mirbridge* xxiii, She kept it dark about the young lady who was staying with her.

b. Of a person: Secret; silent as to any matter; reticent, not open, that conceals his thoughts and designs.

1675 OTWAY *Alcibiades* II. i, But use such secrecy as stolen Loves should have, Be dark as the hush'd silence of the grave. **1706** J. LOGAN in *Pa. Hist. Soc. Mem.* X. 145 He is exceedingly dark and hidden, and thoughts work in his mind deeply without communicating. **1738** POPE *Epil Sat.* II. 131 And Lyttelton a dark, designing knave. **1846** PRESCOTT *Ferd. & Isab.* I. ii. 125 The dark, ambiguous character of Ferdinand. **1885** *Century Mag.* XXX. 380/2 Of course, I'll keep as dark about it as possible.

8. Of whom or which nothing is generally known; about whose powers, etc., the public are 'in the dark'.

dark horse (*Racing slang*), a horse about whose racing powers little is known; hence *fig.* a candidate or competitor of whom little is known or heard, but who unexpectedly comes to the front. In *U.S. Politics*, a person not named as a candidate before a convention, who unexpectedly receives the nomination, when the convention has failed to agree upon any of the leading candidates.

1831 DISRAELI *Yng. Duke* v. (Farmer), A dark horse, which had never been thought of..rushed past the grand stand in sweeping triumph. **1860** *Sat. Rev.* IX. 593/1 A Headship..often given by the College conclaves to a man who has judiciously kept himself dark. **1865** *Sketches from Camb.* 36 (Hoppe) Every now and then a dark horse is heard of, who is supposed to have done wonders at some obscure small college. **1884** in *Harper's Mag.* Aug. 472/1 A simultaneous turning toward a 'dark horse'. **1885** BERESF. HOPE in *Pall Mall G.* 19 Mar. 10/1 Two millions of dark men..whose ignorance and stupidity could hardly be grasped. **1888** *Boston* (Mass.) *Jrnl.* 19 June 5/4 That a dark horse is likely to come out of such a complicated situation as this is most probable. **1891** N. GOULD *Double Event* 8 When he won the Regimental Cup with Rioter, a dark horse he had specially reserved to discomfort them. **1893** *Standard* 17 Apr. 6/6 Irish Wake, a 'dark' son of Master Kildare.

9. Not able to see; partially or totally blind; sightless. *Obs.* exc. *dial.*

1382 WYCLIF *Gen.* xlviii. 10 The eyen forsothe of Yrael weren derke for greet eelde, and cleerli he myȝte not se. **14**.. *Stacyons of Rome* 321 in *Pol. Rel. & L. Poems* (1866) 124, I may se now þat ere was derke. **1576** FLEMING *Panopl. Epist.* 242 So farre foorth as my dimme and darke eyesight is able to pearce. **1658** ROWLAND *Mouff. Theat. Ins.* 1098 Some there are, that cure dark sights by reason of a Cataract. **1768** *Chron.* in *Ann. Reg.* 203/1 Mr. Bathom has been totally dark for seven years. **1806** *Med. Jrnl.* XV. 152 His other eye was nearly quite dark. **1875** *Lanc. Gloss.*, *Dark*, blind. 'Help him o'er th' road, poor lad, he's dark.'

10. Void of intellectual light, mentally or spiritually blind; unenlightened, uninformed, destitute of knowledge, ignorant.

See also *dark ages* in 14c.

c **1374** CHAUCER *Boeth.* III. ii. 67 Of whiche men þe corage alwey..seekeþ þe souereyne goode of alle be it so þat it be wiþ a derke memorie. **1513** BRADSHAW *St. Werburge* cclxxxviii. *Balade* i, To be examined by my rudenes all derke. *a* **1668** DENHAM (J.), The age wherein he liv'd was dark. **1667** MILTON *P.L.* I. 22 What in me is dark Illumine, what is low raise and support. **1688** SHADWELL *Sqr. Alsatia* IV, I am not so dark neither; I am sharp, sharp as a needle. **1774** FLETCHER *Hist. Ess.* Wks. 1795 IV. 15 If you oppose his principles..he supposes that you are quite dark. **1837** J. H. NEWMAN *Proph. Office Ch.* 184 Anglican divines will consider him still dark on certain other points of Scripture doctrine.

¶**11.** Sometimes two or more fig. senses are combined. as in ***the Dark Continent*** = Africa. Freq. in *superl.* as an epithet for Africa and hence applied (chiefly joc. or ironically) to other places that are considered remote, uncivilized, etc.

1878 H. M. STANLEY (*title*), Through the Dark Continent. **1890** —— (*title*), Through Darkest Africa. **1891** BOOTH (*title*), In Darkest England, and the way out. **1907** R. DUNN *Shameless Diary of Explorer* 68 He met the missionary in darkest Africa. **1915** L. EINSTEIN *Let.* 14 Mar. in *Holmes–Einstein Lett.* (1964) II. 110 We had an interesting enough journey through darkest Europe to reach here. **1958** *Listener* 4 Dec. 956/2 Television comes to darkest Surrey. **1959** G. D. PAINTER *Marcel Proust* I. xii. 206 The beautiful Marie Nordlinger..had arrived from darkest Manchester to study painting and sculpture in Paris. **1964** C. WILLOCK *Enormous Zoo* i. 6 The Mitumbe hills..jagged, unfriendly and epitomizing darkest Africa. **1968** C. COOPER *Thunder & Lightning Man* ii. 27 They shunted him off to darkest Somerset.

12. Of a theatre, etc.: closed.

1916 *Variety* 27 Oct. 12/1 The Star and Garter theatre, Hyde & Behman's local Columbia Circuit burlesque house, through being dark last week, when 'The London Belles' refused to accept the engagement, lost its share of the probable gross receipts. **1921** *Daily Colonist* (Victoria, B.C.) 30 Oct. 13/3 Last night the picture show was 'dark', and most of those people with families were spending the evening at home. **1953** *Economist* 28 Mar. 853/1 The owner or lessor of the theatre..is likely to cover his expenses.. except in bad times when he has the burden of a 'dark' theatre. *Ibid.* 853/2 It could happen that as many as one-fifth of all the seats in the London theatres were not even on sale, because the theatres were dark.

13. quasi-*adv.* In a dark manner, darkly.

1600 SHAKS. *A.Y.L.* III. v. 39 Beauty..I see no more in you Then without Candle may goe darke to bed. **1821** JOANNA BAILLIE *Met. Leg.*, *Ld. John* xv, Then dark lower'd the baron's eye. **1865** *Sketches from Camb.* 36 A man may choose to run dark, and may astonish his friends in the final contest of the mathematical tripos. [Cf. *dark horse* in 8.]

14. *Comb.* **a.** adverbial, as ***dark-closed, -embrowned, -flowing, -glancing, -rolling, -shut, -working***; **b.** parasynthetic, as ***dark-bosomed, -browed, -coloured, -complexioned, -eyed, -faced, -haired, -hearted*** (hence ***-heartedness***), ***-leaved, -minded, -skinned, -stemmed, -toned, -veiled, veined, -visaged, -winged***, etc.

a. **1594** DANIEL *Cleopatra* Wks. (1718) 278 Thou [Nemesis] from *dark-clos'd Eternity..The World's Disorders dost descry. **1726–46** THOMSON *Winter* 813 Sables, of glossy black; and *dark-embrowned. **1868** LD. HOUGHTON *Select.* 80 The *dark-flowing hours I breast in fear. **1812** BYRON *Ch. Har.* I. lix, Match me those Houries ..With Spain's *dark-glancing daughters. **1931** BLUNDEN

To Themis 22 Dark-glancing onward as he sings and guides. *a* **1835** MRS. HEMANS *Poems, Guerilla Leader's Vow*, Through the *dark-rolling mists they shine. **1853** HICKIE tr. *Aristoph.* (1872) II. 603 O, *dark-shining dusk of night. **1912** W. DE LA MARE *Listeners* 27 Laid in their *dark-shut graves. **1859** TENNYSON *Lancelot & Elaine* 337 The face before her lived, *Dark-splendid. **1590** SHAKS. *Com. Err.* I. ii. 99 *Darke working Sorcerers.

b. **1863** I. WILLIAMS *Baptistery* II. xxvii, *Dark-bosom'd, glorious sea! **1830** TENNYSON *Poems* 87 *Darkbrowed sophist, come not anear. **1845** MRS. NORTON *Child of Islands* (1846) 188 Dark-browed and beautiful he stood. **1952** E. POUND *Personae* 271 Come not anear the darkbrowed sophist. **1768–74** TUCKER *Lt. Nat.* (1852) II. 369 Whether I shall put on..my *dark-coloured suit. **1840** R. H. DANA *Bef. Mast* x. 24 A delicate, *dark-complexioned young woman. **1605** SHAKS. *Lear* II. i. 121 Out of season, thredding *darke ey'd night. **1814** BYRON *Corsair* III. xvii, And now he turned him to that dark'd-eyed slave. **1923** D. H. LAWRENCE *Birds, Beasts & Flowers* 171 They are royalty, *dark-faced royalty, showing the conscious whites of their eyes. **1813** SCOTT *Trierm.* II. xxvii, Slow the *dark-fringed eyelids fall. **1833** J. S. MILL *Let.* 25 Nov. (1910) I. 77 *Dark-haired men with formidable moustaches. **1881** LADY HERBERT *Edith* 2 A bright, dark-haired young lady. **1870** D. G. ROSSETTI *Let.* 15 Mar. (1965) II. 816 Where..the *dark-hearted golden sunflowers shine? **1862** M. HOPKINS *Hawaii* 367 In the time of our *dark-heartedness. **1870** BRYANT *Homer* I. II. 61 Forty *dark-hulled Locrian Barks. **1817** KEATS *Epistle to G. F. Mathew* in *Poems* 55 Where the *dark-leav'd laburnum's drooping clusters Reflect athwart the stream their yellow lustres. **1861** MISS PRATT *Flower. Plants* V. 105 The Dark-leaved Sallow. **1795** SOUTHEY *Joan of Arc* VIII. 618 *Dark-minded man! **1742** YOUNG *Nt. Th.* ii. 344 Quite wingless our desire, In sense *dark-prison'd. *a* **1600** HOOKER *Eccl. Pol.* Pref. §3 The *dark-sighted man is directed by the cleere about things visible. **1701** *Lond. Gaz.* No. 3754/8 Missing.. Elizabeth Benson..dark-brown Hair'd..a little dark sighted. **1885** MABEL COLLINS *Prettiest Woman* ix, The *dark-skinned Russian women had made a hero of him. **1934** *Burlington Mag.* Sept. 132/2 A fine relief in *dark-toned wood. **1935** C. DAY LEWIS *Time to Dance* 32 Over the dark-toned earth. **1634** MILTON *Comus* 129 Goddess of nocturnal sport, *Dark-veiled Cotytto. **1613–39** I. JONES in Leoni *Palladio's Archit.* (1742) II. 50 Light-vein'd Marble ..*dark-vein'd, ditto. **1906** *Daily Chron.* 30 July 6/6 Another *dark-visaged countryman of Reid, a typical specimen of the black Celt. **1925** E., O. & S. SITWELL *Poor Young People* 5 Where now a *dark-winged southern wind soft grieves.

c. Specialized comb. or phrases: **dark ages** (often with capital initials), (*a*) a term sometimes applied to the period of the Middle Ages to mark the intellectual darkness characteristic of the time; often restricted to the early period of the Middle Ages, between the time of the fall of Rome and the appearance of vernacular written documents; (*b*) (freq. in *sing.*) the period between the end of the Bronze Age and the beginning of the archaic age in Greece and other Aegean countries; (*c*) *transf.*, a period of obscurantism or ignorance; *joc.*, an obscure or little regarded period before the present; **dark arches (moth)**, a British noctuid moth of the genus *Xylophasia* (cf. ARCH *sb.* 7); **dark box** (*Photogr.*), a box totally excluding light, used for storing plates, etc.; **dark chamber**, †(*a*) a camera obscura (*obs.*); (*b*) *Photogr.* = *dark-room*; †**dark-closet**, (see quot.); **dark current** *Electr.*, the current that flows in a photoeletric device when there is no light (or any other radiation capable of causing a current) incident on the photosensitive region; **dark-field** = *dark-ground*; **dark glasses**, (*a*) (see quot. 1867); (*b*) spectacles with darkly-tinted lenses; **dark-ground**, applied *attrib.* to denote a type of illumination used in microscopy in which direct light is prevented from reaching the eyepiece and the only light seen is that scattered by the object, which appears as bright against a dark background; hence in *transf.* sense to denote any light-coloured matter on a dark background; **dark-house** (see 1 b); †**dark light** = DEAD-LIGHT 1; **dark night (of the soul)** [tr. Sp. *noche oscura* (St. John of the Cross)], a period of spiritual aridity suffered by a mystic; also *transf.*; **dark-room** (*Photogr.*), a room from which all actinic rays of light are excluded, used by photographers when dealing with their sensitized plates: see also 1 b; **dark slide** (*Photogr.*), the holder for the sensitized plate; **dark smoke** (see quot. 1954); †**dark tent**, a camera obscura; **dark-well**, an arrangement in a microscope for forming a dark background to a transparent object when illuminated from above.

[**1687** BURNET *Trav.* III. 11 There is an infinite number of the Writers of the *darker Ages.] **1730** A. GORDON *Maffei's Amphith.* 398 A Theatre..called so in the dark Ages, when such Names were given at random. **1748** SMOLLETT *R. Random* I. p. iv, In the dark ages of the world, when a man had rendered himself famous for wisdom or valour, his family..represented his character and person as sacred and supernatural. **1834** M. EDGEWORTH *Helen* iv. 46, I must go back..quite to the dark ages, the time when I knew nothing of my daughter's character but by the accidental lights which you afforded me. **1837** HALLAM *Hist. Lit.* I. §5 Gregory I..the chief authority in the dark ages. **1857** BUCKLE *Civiliz.* I. ix. 558 During these, which are rightly called the Dark Ages, the clergy were supreme. **1860** C. M. YONGE *Hopes & Fears* I. x. 370 What was natural science with the one, was natural history with the other. One went deep in systems and classifications, and thrust Linnæus into the dark ages. **1871** GEO. ELIOT *Middlem.* I. ii. 20 We must have Thought: else we shall be landed back in the dark ages. **1876** F. KILVERT *Diary* 4 May (1944) 308 It was built in the Dark Ages of fifty years ago and was simply hideous. **1887** KIPLING *Under Deodars* (1889) 58 Centuries ago—in the Dark Ages, before I met you, dear. **1907** G. MURRAY *Rise of Greek Epic* ii. 29 There lies between the prehistoric palaces of Crete, Troy, or Mycenae, and the civilization which we know as Greek a Dark Age covering at least several centuries. **1915** W. LEAF *Homer & Hist.* i. 34 The answer to the question lies somewhere in what, following Professor Murray, I have called the Dark Ages, the three or four hundred years which precede the first glimmer of authentic history in the eighth century. **1935** (*title*) Map of Britain in the Dark Ages (Ordnance Survey) [p. 5] This map covers that portion of English and Welsh history which falls between the years 410 A.D. and 871 A.D. **1943** F. M. STENTON *Anglo-Saxon Eng.* viii. 267 No other king of the Dark Ages ever set himself, like Alfred, to explore whatever in the literature of Christian antiquity might explain the problems of fate and free will. **1950** H. L. LORIMER *Homer & Monuments* viii. 461 Even in the Dark Age there must have been some degree of communication, as the common features of proto-Geometric culture show. **1952** CHILDE & SIMPSON *Anc. Monuments Scotland* 6 The 'Dark Ages'... Approximately fifth–eleventh centuries A.D. **1953** K. H. JACKSON *Lang. & Hist. Early Brit.* 377 Dark-Age Latin. **1957** G. E. WRIGHT *Bibl. Archaeol.* iv. 56/2 Shortly before 1700 B.C. a dark age settled over Egypt which was to last some one hundred and fifty years. This was caused by the invasion of Asiatics whom the Egyptians called *Hyksos*. **1832** J. RENNIE *Consp. Butterfl. & Moths* 65 The *Dark Arches..appears the end of June and beginning of July. **1921** Dark Arches [see ARCH *sb.* 7]. **1951** COLYER & HAMMOND *Flies Brit. Isles* xxi. 267 *L*[*arvaevora*] *ferox*..has been bred from the Dark Arches Moth. **1958** W. J. STOKOE *Caterp. Moths* (ed. 2) I. 255 *The Dark Arches*, sub-family Agrotinae, Apamea monoglypha, occurring in all parts of the British Isles... It is very variable in its general colouring. **1887** *Brit. Jrnl. Photogr.* 11 Nov. 713/2 Wind them on to rollers to be put into journal bearings in a *dark box. **1860** C. M. YONGE *Hopes & Fears* II. iv. 66 'Where is she?' 'In the *dark chamber, doing a positive of the cathedral.' **1726** LEONI *Designs* 3 b, Ward-robes or Cupboards, which by a new name in the Art are called *Dark-closets. **1914** *Astrophys. Jrnl.* XXXIX. 438 Two spurious currents..are found in the photo-electric cell... The second is what has been called a '*dark current', in the same direction as the light current. **1963** B. FOZARD *Instrumentation Nucl. Reactors* vi. 67 Dark current is the current flowing in the cathode, or in the complete multiplier tube, with no illumination of the cathode. Dark current is due mainly to thermionic emission of electrons from the cathode and the early-stage dynodes. **1865** R. BECK *Achromatic Microscope* 34 In every kind of '*dark-field illumination' the light comes upon the object from below, but at such an oblique angle as never to enter the object-glass direct. **1966** D. G. BRANDON *Mod. Techniques Metallogr.* 16 Features that can be observed by dark field illumination are always faintly visible by direct illumination. .. The same is not true of transparent biological specimens. **1867** SMYTH *Sailor's Word-bk.*, **Dark glasses*, shades fitted to instruments of reflection for preventing the bright rays of the sun from hurting the eye of the observer. **1927** HEMINGWAY *Men without Women* (1928) 187 We were both tired of the sun... You could not sit outside the hut without dark glasses. **1965** R. ERSKINE *Passion Flowers in Business* v. 58 One would see later if dark glasses in the office would be a good thing. **1860** *Q. Jrnl. Microscopical Sci.* VIII. 207 (*heading*) On a *dark-ground illuminator. **1949** H. C. WESTON *Sight, Light & Efficiency* iv. 142 A well-known ophthalmologist recommended dark-ground reading matter for the use of partially-sighted children. **1965** W. J. GARNETT *Freshwater Microscopy* (ed. 2) iii. 55 For the observation of microscopic freshwater life..much more can be achieved by the use of dark-ground illumination. *Ibid.*, It is important with all dark-ground work to use a strong source of light. **1683** *Robin Conscience* 278 in *Songs Lond. Prent.* (Percy) 80 But, when the shop-folk me did spy, They drew their *dark light instantly. **1820** SCORESBY *Acc. Arctic Reg.* II. 452 We..caulked the dark-lights. **1864** D. LEWIS tr. *St. John of the Cross's Wks.* I. 3 The *dark night, through which the soul passes, on its way to the Divine Light. *Ibid.* 57 Faith, the dark night of the soul. **1913** C. MACKENZIE *Sinister St.* I. II. xv. 409 An Half-hour with St. John of the Cross made him ask himself whether this were the dark night of the soul through which he was passing. **1927** J. S. HUXLEY *Relig. without Rev.* iv. 124 The sense of being forsaken... Mystics have called it 'the dark night of the soul', and describe it as an abandonment of the soul by God. **1951** G. GREENE *End of Affair* II. i. 52 What do I know of phrases like 'the dark night' or of prayer? **1970** *Guardian* 22 Dec. 2/4 Governor Nelson Rockefeller..has emerged from the dark night of the soul that afflicts all politicians pondering the supreme sacrifice. **1841** *Specif. Claudet's Patent* No. 9193. 3 [Red light] allows the operator to see how to perform the work without being obliged..to remain in a *dark room. **1852** *Specif. Newton's Patent* No. 179 Apparatus for taking photographic pictures without the use of a dark room. **1883** W. K. BURTON *Mod. Photogr.* (1892) 21 To purchase a 'dark-room lamp' from a photographic apparatus dealer. **1887** *Brit. Jrnl. Photogr.* 11 Nov. 717/1 Professor Stebbing exhibited a metal *dark slide. **1954** *Beaver Committee Rep.* (*Cmd.* 9322), New legislation should prohibit the emission of *dark smoke..from any chimney. .. By 'dark smoke' we mean smoke of density equivalent to, or greater than, shade 2 on the Ringelmann Chart. **1958** *Times* 31 May 3/7 The Clean Air Act 1956 will be fully in force to-morrow, and it will be an offence punishable by fine to emit dark smoke from any chimney in England and Wales. **1706** PHILLIPS (ed. Kersey), **Dark Tent*, a Box made almost like a Desk, with Optick Glasses, to take the Prospect of any Building, Fortification, Landskip, etc. **1867** J. HOGG *Microsc.* I. ii. 83 The use of a set of *dark-wells.

d. *Physics.* **dark lines** = *absorption lines* (ABSORPTION 6); so ***dark-line*** attrib. or as adj.; **dark space**, one or other of two non-luminous regions (the CATHODE or CROOKES or ***first dark space*** and the FARADAY or ***second dark space***) in a vacuum tube traversed by an electric discharge; also ***dark discharge***.

1802 W. H. WOLLASTON in *Phil. Trans.* II. 378 C, the limit of green and blue, is not so clearly marked as the rest; and there are also, on each side of this limit, other distinct dark lines. **1838** M. FARADAY in *Phil. Trans.* I. 138 A purple stream..appeared on the end of the positive rod,..but never joining the negative glow, there being always a short dark space between. *Ibid.* 139 The dark discharge through air..leads to the inquiry, whether the particles of air are.. capable of effecting discharge from one to another without becoming luminous. **1878** *Encycl. Brit.* VIII. 64/1 The dark spaces that sometimes appear in the spark in gas at the atmospheric pressure. *Ibid.*, When the discharge takes place in highly rarefied gas, a dark space of this kind almost always separates the positive from the negative light. *Ibid.*, Pending further investigation, Faraday called it the dark discharge. **1879** *Ibid.* IX. 728/1 The dark lines of the spectrum of sunlight. **1895** S. P. THOMPSON *Elem. Less. Electr. & Magn.* (ed. 2) II. iv. 307 The kathode exhibits a beautiful bluish or violet glow, separated from the conductor by a narrow *dark space*. **1920** Dark space [see *cathode dark space* s.v. CATHODE c]. **1928** W. M. SMART *Sun, Stars & Universe* vi. 83 Certain groups of lines which are known to belong to the arc spectra of the elements concerned..together with their dark-line counterparts in the solar spectrum. **1958** [see *Faraday dark space*].

dark (dɑːk), *sb.* Forms: 4–5 derk(e, 5 dirk, 6 darcke, 6–7 darke, 6–dark. [f. DARK *a.*: cf. the analogy of *light* sb. and adj.]

1. a. Absence of light; dark state or condition; darkness, *esp.* that of night.

dark of the moon: the time near new moon when there is no moonlight: cf. *dark moon* s.v. DARK *a.* 1 c.

a **1300** *K. Horn* 1431 He ladde hure bi þe derke Into his nywe werke. *c* **1450** *Mirour Saluacioun* 1950 To seke crist in the derke with Lanternes and with fire brandes. **1553** T. WILSON *Rhet.* (1580) 160 Gropyng in the darcke. **1598** ROWLANDS *Betraying of Christ* Wks. 54 The Sunne was hid, nights darke approcht apace. **1626** BACON *Sylva* §276 If you come suddenly..out of the Dark into a Glaring Light, the eye is dazeled for a time. **1651** *Hartlib's Legacy* (1655) 160 Gardiners and Husbandmen..talking of the dark of the Moon. **1760** C. JOHNSTON *Chrysal* (1822) III. 116 He dares not to sleep by himself or be a moment alone in the dark. **1801** tr. C. F. DAMBERGER'S *Trav. Africa* 122 If a boy is born ..in the dark of the moon. **1830** TENNYSON *Ode to Memory* iv, To dimple in the dark of rushy coves. **1871** E. EGGLESTON *Hoosier Schoolm.* (1872) x. 87 But it must be rendered in the dark of the moon. **1889** FARMER *Americanisms* 193 *Dark Moon* or *Dark of the Moon*, the period between the moon's change from 'full' to 'new'. Also provincial in England. **1945** TENNESSEE WILLIAMS *Battle of Angels* II. i. 41 In the dark of the moon, beside a broken fence rail in some big rolling meadow.

b. The dark time; night; nightfall.

c **1400** *Destr. Troy* 1079 The derke was done & the day sprange. *a* **1400–50** *Alexander* 4773 It droȝe to þe derke. **1718** LADY M. W. MONTAGUE *Lett.* lii. II. 73 Before we got to the foot of the mountain, which was not till after dark. **1771** E. LONG *Trial of Dog 'Porter'*, One evening after dark. **1833** HT. MARTINEAU *Tale of Tyne* i. 3 He quitted the keel ..just at dark. **1868** MORRIS *Earthly Par.* I. 93 While day and dark, and dark and day went by.

c. A dark place: a place of darkness.

c **1400** *Destr. Troy* 2361 So I wilt in the wod..Till I drogh to a derke, and the dere lost. **1587** *Mirr. Mag., Elstride* ix, Like as you see in darkes, if light appeare Strayght way to that ech man directs his eye. **1706** DE FOE *Jure Div.* I. 8 Above the Skyes they fix'd his blest abode, And from the Darks of Hell fetch'd up the God. **1883** S. LANIER *Eng. Novel* 47 (*Cent. Dict.*) Those small darks which are enclosed by caves and crumbling dungeons.

2. *fig.* (*a leap in the dark*: see LEAP.)

c **1369** CHAUCER *Dethe Blaunche* 609 To derke is turned all my lighte. *a* **1541** WYATT *Penit. Psalms* li. *The Author* iv, Light of Grace that darke of sin did hide.

3. a. Dark colour or shade; *spec.* in *Art.* a part of a picture in shadow, as opposed to a *light*.

1675 A. BROWNE *Ars Pict.* 90 Ever place light against dark, and dark against light. **1715** J. RICHARDSON *Th. Painting* 112 A Picture sometimes consists of a Mass of Light.. sometimes..of a Mass of Dark at the bottom, another Lighter above that. **1821** CRAIG *Lect. Drawing* iii. 153 A light is made brighter by being opposed to a dark. **1855** M. ARNOLD *Poems, Mycerinus* 119 The palm-tree plumes that roof'd With their mild dark his grassy banquet hall. **1860** RUSKIN *Mod. Paint.* V. IX. viii. 287 His lights are not the spots, but his darks.

b. *fig.* A dark spot, a blot.

1637 SHIRLEY *Lady of Pleas.* I. i, Had not the poet been bribed to a modest Expression of your antic gambols in't, Some darks had been discovered.

4. a. The condition of being hidden from view, obscure, or unknown; obscurity. ***in the dark***: in concealment or secrecy.

1628 FELTHAM *Resolves* I. xlii. 127 Vice..ever thinks in this dark, to hide her abhorred foulnesse. **1643** SIR T. BROWNE *Relig. Med.* II. §4, I am in the dark to all the world, and my nearest friends behold me but in a cloud. *a* **1732** ATTERBURY (J.), All he says of himself is, that he is an obscure person; one, I suppose..that is in the dark. **1888** BRYCE *Amer. Commw.* III. xcvi. 342 *note*, Such legislation.. is usually procured in the dark and by questionable means.

†**b.** Obscurity of meaning. *Obs.*

1699 BENTLEY *Phal.* 175 The Threat had something of dark in it.

5. ***in the dark***: in a state of ignorance; without knowledge as regards some particular fact.

1677 W. HUBBARD *Narrative* II. 47 As to what hapned afterward, we are yet much in the dark. **1690** LOCKE *Hum. Und.* II. xxiii. §28 If here again we enquire how this is done, we are equally in the dark. **1782** COWPER *Mutual Forbearance* 9 Sir Humphrey, shooting in the dark, Makes answer quite beside the mark. **1791** BURKE *Corr.* (1844) III. 185, I am entirely in the dark about the designs..of the powers of Europe. **1802** M. EDGEWORTH *Moral T.* (1816) I. xix. 165, I hope you will no longer keep me in the dark. **1876** GLADSTONE in *Contemp. Rev.*, June 2 We seem to be..in the dark on these..questions.

6. *attrib.* and *Comb.* **dark adaptation**, self-adjustment of the eye to reduced intensity of light by means of an increase in the sensitivity of the retina; **dark-adapted** in *passive* and as *ppl. a.*, of an eye in which there is dark adaptation.

1909 E. B. TITCHENER *Text-Bk. Psychol.* I. xviii. 74 The immediate after-effect of general adaptation is always this contrary trend of vision:..if dark-adapted, [you are] now light-sighted. **1909** *Ibid.* xix. 80 When dark-adaptation has gone a certain distance. **1920** Dark adaptation [see ADAPTATION 2 b]. **1922** R. S. WOODWORTH *Psychol.* x. 225 Go into a dark room, and at first all seems black, but by degrees—provided there is a little light filtering into the room—you begin to see, for your retina is becoming dark-adapted. **1934** H. C. WARREN *Dict. Psychol.* 68/2 *Dark-adapted eye*, an eye whose condition has been so modified by the withdrawal of general light stimulation that faint stimuli have become more effective. **1935** *Discovery* May 138/1 This increased sensitiveness of the retina is called Dark-Adaptation. **1946** *Nature* 31 Aug. 303/2 Perhaps it will be possible to find somebody who has more visual purple in the dark-adapted state. **1963** C. D. SIMAK *They walked like Men* ii. 11 By now my eyes had become somewhat dark-adapted and I could make out the formless shape of furniture.

dark (dɑːk), *v. arch.* or *dial.* Forms: 4 durk, 4–6 derke, 4–7 darke, 5–6 dirke, 6 dirk, 6–dark. [f. DARK *a.*]

†**1.** *intr.* To become dark; = DARKEN 1. Of the sun or moon: To suffer eclipse. *Obs.*

[*c* **1050** *Suppl. Ælfric's Voc.* in Wr.-Wülcker 175 *Crepusculum*, tweoneleoht, *uel* deorcung.] *c* **1340** *Cursor M.* 16749 (Trin.) Fro þenne hit derked til þe mone: ouer al the world wide. **1430** LYDG. *Chron. Troy* I. vi, The euening begon for to dirke. **1485** CAXTON *Chas. Gt.* 211 In the same yere the mone derked thre tymes. *a* **1529** SKELTON *Col. Cloute* 196 When the nyght darkes. **1596** H. CLAPHAM *Briefe Bible* II. 172 Sun darks, Starres fall, the Moone doth change her hue. **1606** SHAKS. *Tr. & Cr.* v. viii. 7 With the vaile and darking of the Sunne.

fig. **1400** *Pol. Rel. & L. Poems* (1866) 236 Vnder sleuþe darkit þe loue of holinesse.

†**2.** *trans.* To make dark; = DARKEN 6. *Obs.*

c **1300** *Beket* 1417 Overcast heo is with the clouden.. Whar thurf the churchen of Engelonde idurked beoth echon. **1382** WYCLIF *1 Kings* xviii. 45 Heuenes ben derkid. *c* **1477** CAXTON *Jason* 29 b, The ayer was derked and obscured with the quarels and arowes and stones. *c* **1500** *Not-Browne Mayd* 32 My somers day in lusty may is derked before the none. **1530** PALSGR. 506/2 What thyng hath darked this house..me thynke they have closed up dyvers wyndowes. **1634** MILTON *Comus* 730 The winged air darked with plumes. **1715** RAMSAY *Eclipse of Sun* ii, No cloud may hover in the air, To dark the medium.

b. To cloud, dim, obscure, hide (something luminous).

c **1380** WYCLIF *Sel. Wks.* II. 406 Þe sunne mai be derkkid heter bi fumes þat shal cleer þe erþe. *c* **1489** CAXTON *Blanchardyn* xx. 62 That derked the lyght of the sonne. **1557** *Tottell's Misc.* (Arb.) 269 The golden sunne doth darke ech starre. **1592** CONSTABLE *Sonn.* III. viii, The shadie woods seeme now my sunne to darke. **18..** MRS. BROWNING *Soul's Trav.* 112 Though we wear no visor down To dark our countenance. **1850** —— *Poems* II. 5 The uplands will not let it stay To dark the western sun.

†**3.** To darken in shade or colour. *Obs.*

c **1374** CHAUCER *Boeth.* I. i. 5 The wiche cloþes a derkenes of a forleten and dispised elde had duskid and dirkid. **1573** *Art of Limming* 5 Orpyment may be..darked with Oker de Luke.

†**4.** To darken (the eyes or vision); to blind. *lit.* and *fig. Obs.*

c **1374** CHAUCER *Boeth.* I. i. 7, I of whom þe syȝt plonged in teres was derked. *c* **1450** tr. *De Imitatione* III. xxxviii, In many þe eye of intencion is dirked. **1508** FISHER *Wks.* (1876) 305 Her syght should haue be derked. **1526** *Pilgr. Perf.* (W. de W. 1531) 10 b, He wyll blynde thy reason & derke thy conscyence. **1653** T. WHITFIELD *Treat. Sinf. Men* ix. 40 The Sun..darkes weake eyes.

†**b.** *intr.* To be or become blind. *Obs.*

a **1440** WYCLIF *1 Sam.* iv. 15 [MS. Bodl. 277] Heli..hise iȝen derkeden [*v.r.* dasweden], and he myȝte not se.

5. *fig.* To obscure, eclipse, cloud, dim, sully.

c **1374** CHAUCER *Boeth.* I. iv. 20 Þe wiche dignite, for þei wolde derken it wiþ medelyng of some felonye. *c* **1430** LYDG. *Bochas* I. iv. (1544) 6 b, Process of yeres..hath..Derked their renoune by forgetfulnes. **1559** BP. COX in Strype *Ann. Ref.* I. vi. 100 And shortly [shall] Christ Jesus be utterly forgotten, and darked as much..as in the time of Papistry. **1579** SPENSER *Sheph. Cal.* Feb. 134 Thy wast bignes but cumbers the ground, And dirks the beauty of my blossomes rownd. **1608** SHAKS. *Per.* IV. Prol. 35 Marina gets all praises ..This..darks In Philoten all graceful marks. **1647** H. MORE *Song of Soul* Ded. 4 Nor can ever that thick cloud.. dark the remembrance of your pristine Lustre. **1818** SCOTT *Hrt. of Midl.* xviii, One woman is enough to dark the fairest plot that ever was planned.

†**6.** *intr.* To lie in the dark, to lie hid or unseen.

a **1300** *Cursor M.* 25444 (Cott.) In hope i durk and dare. *c* **1350** *Will. Palerne* 17 Þe child þan darked in his den dernly him one. **1398** TREVISA *Barth. De P.R.* XVII. clii. (1495) 704 Abowte hegges lurkyth and derkyth venemouse wormes. *c* **1400** *Destr. Troy* 13285 Folis..þat heron the melody [of the Sirens]..derkon euon down on a depe slomur. **1447** BOKENHAM *Seyntys* (Roxb.) 218 Darkyng in kavys and gravys.

7. *intr.* To listen privily and insidiously. *dial.*

1781 J. HUTTON *Tour Caves* Gloss., *To dark for betts*, to hearken silently which side the opinion is of. **1825** BROCKETT *N. Country Wds.*, *Dark*, to listen with an insidious attention. **1855** ROBINSON *Whitby Gloss.*, *Dark*, to listen, to pry into. 'They dark and gep for all they can catch.' [Also in Glossaries of *Holderness*, *Mid-Yorks.*, *Cumbrld.*, *Lonsdale*.]

Hence **darked** *ppl. a.*, **darking** *vbl. sb.*

c **1050** [see 1]. *c* **1430** LYDG. *Chron. Troy* Prol., Dyrked age. *a* **1541** WYATT *Compl. Absence of his Love*, My darked pangs of cloudy thoughts.

darken (ˈdɑːk(ə)n), *v.* Forms: 4 derkn-en, darkn-en, derkin, 4–5 durken, 5 dyrkyn, 6 dirken, -in, darcken, 6– darken. [f. DARK *a.*: see -EN *suffix*[5]. Cf. OHG. *tarchanjan* under DARK *a.* Not very common in ME.; in later times it has taken the place of DARK *v.*]

I. *intransitive.*

1. To grow or become dark, said *esp.* of the coming on of night. (Sometimes with *down.*)

a **1300** *Cursor M.* 24414 (Cott.) Þe aier gun durken [*v.r.* to derkin] and to blak. **13..** *Thrush & Night.* 4 in *Relig. Antiq.* I. 241 The dewes darkneth in the dale. **1731** POPE *Ep. Burlington* 80 Behold Villario's ten years' toil complete, His Quincunx darkens, his Espaliers meet..And strength of Shade contends with strength of Light. **1821** SHELLEY *Prometh. Unb.* I. 257 The Heaven Darkens above. **1863** HAWTHORNE *Old Home, London Suburb* (1879) 239, The chill..twilight of an Autumn day darkening down.

b. To become obscure. (With *upon, from.*)

1722 WOLLASTON *Relig. Nat.* ix. 209 When yonder blue regions and all this scene darken upon me and go out. **1848** LYTTON *Harold* I. i, The vision darkens from me.

†**2.** To lie dark, lie concealed; to lurk privily *after*. Cf. DARK *v.* 6. *Obs.*

c **1420** *Anturs of Arth.* v, Alle dyrkyns [*v. rr.* durkene, darkis] the dere, in the dym scoghes. **1508** DUNBAR *Mariit Wem. & Wedo* 9, I drew in derne to the dyk to dirkin eftir myrthis.

3. To become blind. *lit.* and *fig.*

1580 HOLLYBAND *Treas. Fr. Tong* s.v. *Entrecharger*, My sight diminisheth, darkneth, or waxeth darke. **1813** SHELLEY *Q. Mab* 149 Man..Shrank with the plants and darkened with the night.

4. To become dark in shade or colour.

1774 GOLDSM. *Nat. Hist.* (1776) II. 234 The complexions of different countries..darken in proportion to the heat of their climate. **1858** HAWTHORNE *Fr. & It. Jrnls.* II. 39 A bright angel darkening into what looks quite as much like the Devil. **1883** *Hardwick's Photogr. Chem.* (ed. Taylor) 248 Such papers darken in the sun.

5. To grow clouded, gloomy, sad; *esp.* of the countenance: to become clouded with anger or other emotion.

1742 YOUNG *Nt. Th.* viii. 97 Where gay delusion darkens to despair! **1797** MRS. RADCLIFFE *Italian* xii, 'Do you menace me?' replied the brother, his countenance darkening. **1824** SCOTT *Redgauntlet* ch. xvii, His displeasure seemed to increase, his brow darkened. **1850** HAWTHORNE *Scarlet L.* iii, His face darkened with some powerful emotion.

II. *transitive.*

6. To make dark, to deprive of light; to shut out or obstruct the light of. Also *fig.*

1382 WYCLIF *Isa.* xiii. 10 Al to-derkned is the sunne in his rising. *c* **1535** DEWES *Introd. Fr.* (in Palsgr. 951), To darken, *obscurer*. **1555** EDEN *Decades* 245 The heauen is seldome darkened with clowdes. **1613** SHAKS. *Hen. VIII*, I. i. 226 Whose Figure euen this instant Clowd puts on, By Darkning my cleere Sunne. **1667** MILTON *P.L.* I. 501 When Night darkens the Streets. **1768** STERNE *Sent. Journ.* (1775) I. 15 (*Calais*), I perceived that something darken'd the passage more than myself..it was effectually Mons. Dessein. **1847** TENNYSON *Princess* IV. 295 You stood in your own light and darken'd mine. **1862** —— *Idylls* Ded. 17 Like eclipse, Darkening the world. **1864** —— *Aylmer's F.* 416 The tall pines That darken'd all the northward of her Hall. **1874** LOWELL *Agassiz* I. i, The veil that darkened from our sidelong glance The inexorable face.

b. *to darken* (*a person's*) *door* or *doors*: emphatic for to appear on the threshold (as a visitor); usually with negative (expressed or implied).

1729 FRANKLIN *Busy-Body* Wks. 1887 I. 341, I am afraid she would resent it so as never to darken my door again. **1748** RICHARDSON *Clarissa* Wks. 1883 VIII. 237 If ever my sister Clary darkens these doors again, I never will. **1826** *Blackw. Mag.* XIX. 11/1 You are the first minister that ever darkened these doors. **1842** TENNYSON *Dora* 30 You shall pack And never more darken my doors again.

7. To deprive of sight, to make blind; *fig.* to deprive of intellectual or spiritual light.

1548 UDALL, etc. *Erasm. Par. Matt.* iii. 30 That he might obscure and darken all men. **1582** N. T. (Rhem.) *Rom.* i. 21 Their folish hart hath been darkened. **1611** BIBLE *Ps.* lxix. 23 Let their eyes be darkened, that they see not. **1758** S. HAYWARD *Serm.* 41 We shall find the understanding awfully darkned. **1843** CARLYLE *Past & Pr.* (1858) 115 His eyes were somewhat darkened.

8. *fig.* To make dark or obscure in meaning or intelligibility; to destroy the clearness of.

1548–9 (Mar.) *Bk. Com. Prayer*, *Of Cerem.* 35 b, They dyd more confounde, and darken, then declare..Christes benefites. **1611** BIBLE *Job* xxxviii. 2 Who is this that darkeneth counsel by words without knowledge? **1674** ALLEN *Danger Enthus.* 20 You confound things together which are distinct, to the darkning of them in your understandings. **1781** COWPER *Hope* 769 They speak the wisdom of the skies, Which art can only darken and disguise. **1865** KINGSLEY *Herew.* viii, This belief was confused and darkened by a cross-belief.

9. *fig.* To cloud with something evil, painful, or sad; to cast a gloom or shadow over.

1553 T. WILSON *Rhet.* (1580) 119 He..that poisoneth.. and seeketh to obscure and darken his estimation. **1606** SHAKS. *Ant. & Cl.* I. iv. 11 Euils enow to darken all his goodness. **1611** —— *Wint. T.* IV. iv. 41 With these forc'd thoughts, I prethee darken not The Mirth o' th' Feast. **1781** GIBBON *Decl. & F.* III. 96 The fame of the apostles..was darkened by religious fiction. **1829** LYTTON *Disowned* 41 No, I will not darken your fair hopes. **1883** S. C. HALL *Retrospect* II. 138 Domestic affliction..darkened the later years of his life.

†**b.** To deprive (a person) of lustre or renown, to eclipse. *Obs.*

1606 SHAKS. *Ant. & Cl.* III. i. 24 Ambition (The Souldiers vertue) rather makes choice of losse, Then gaine which darkens him. **1607** —— *Cor.* IV. vii. 5 And you are darkned in this action Sir, Euen by your owne.

10. To make dark in shade or colour.

1717 POPE *Eloisa* 168 Her gloomy presence Shades ev'ry flow'r, and darkens ev'ry green. **1821** SHELLEY *Ginevra* 16 The bridal veil Which..darkened her dark locks. **1869** E. A. PARKES *Pract. Hygiene* (ed. 3) 90 Organic matter from the lungs, when drawn through sulphuric acid, darkens it.

darkened (ˈdɑːk(ə)nd), *ppl. a.* [f. prec. + -ED.] Made dark, deprived of light. *lit.* and *fig.*

1733 POPE *Hor. Sat.* II. i. 97 The darken'd room. **1856** DOVE *Logic Chr. Faith* v. i. § 2. 268 Darkened and deluded as I am. **1871** MORLEY *Voltaire* (1886) 241 A generation of cruel and unjust and darkened spirits.

darkener (ˈdɑːk(ə)nə(r)). [-ER.] One who or that which darkens.

1611 COTGR., *Noircisseur*, a blacker..darkener, obscurer. **1630** BRATHWAIT *Eng. Gentlem.* (1641) 5 A great darkener and blemisher of the..beauty of the mind. **1776** G. CAMPBELL *Philos. Rhet.* (1800) I. I. ii. 47 A sophister or darkener of the understanding. **1866** GEO. ELIOT *F. Holt* III. xxxvii. 48 That feminine darkener of counsel.

darkening (ˈdɑːk(ə)nɪŋ), *vbl. sb.* [-ING[1].]

1. The action of making or becoming dark.

1584 *Bagford Coll.* No. 81 lf. 20 A great and totall Eclipse, or darkenyng of the Moone vnto xvi. poyntes. **1677** GILPIN *Dæmonol.* (1867) 348 Necessity can do much to the darkening of the understanding. **1875** DARWIN *Insectiv. Pl.* vii. 144 The..darkening or blackening of the glands.

2. Nightfall, dusk. *Sc.*

1814 SCOTT *Wav.* lxiii, It's near the darkening, sir. **1865** MRS. CARLYLE *Lett.* III. 296 The cock is shut up..from darkening till after our breakfast.

ˈdarkening, *ppl. a.* [-ING[2].] Becoming or making dark.

1725 POPE *Odyss.* IX. 213 A lonely cave..with dark'ning lawrels covered o'er. **1800** HERSCHEL in *Phil. Trans.* XC. 280 To try an application of the darkening apparatus to another part of the telescope. **1873** BLACK *Pr. Thule* 6 Peaks..still darker than the darkening sky.

darkey: see DARKY.

darkfall (ˈdɑːkfɔːl). [f. DARK *sb.* + FALL *sb.*[1]] The coming on of dark; dusk, nightfall.

1897 'O. RHOSCOMYL' *White Rose Arno* 292, I can have fifteen of them here by darkfall. **1929** A. CLARKE *Pilgrimage* 41 At darkfall in a house where nobles throng. **1930** —— *Flame* 34, I hear them coming, For it is darkfall now.

darkful (ˈdɑːkfʊl), *a. rare.* [OE. *deorcfull*, f. *deorc* adj. DARK: see -FUL.] Full of darkness.

a **1050** *Liber Scintill.* lxi. (1889) 187 Eall lichama þin deorcfull byð. **1382** WYCLIF *Matt.* vi. 23 3if thyn eiȝe be weyward, al thi body shal be derkful. *c* **1470** HENRY *Wallace* VIII. 1182 The nycht was myrk, our drayff the dyrkfull chance. **1633** T. ADAMS *Exp. 2 Peter* i. 19 Pagans have a darkful night. **1875** MCCLELLAN *New Test.* 390 The horrible degradation of mankind to a darkful existence.

†**ˈdarkhede, derkhede.** *Obs.* Also durchede. [f. DARK *a.* + *-hede*, -HEAD.] Darkness.

1297 R. GLOUC. (1724) 560 Þoru al þe middelerd derkhede þer was inou. *c* **1300** *St. Brandan* 37 Al o tide of the dai we were in durchede.

darkie, var. DARKY, DARKEY.

darkish (ˈdɑːkɪʃ), *a.* [f. DARK *a.* + -ISH.] Somewhat dark: **a.** through absence of light.

1557 SACKVILLE *Mirr. Mag.*, *Induct.* ii, The dayes more darkishe are. **1659–60** PEPYS *Diary* (1879) I. 56 We drank pretty hard..till it began to be darkish. **1777** HOWARD *Prisons Eng.* (1780) 178 The passages are narrow..and darkish. **1858** GEN. P. THOMPSON *Audi Alt.* II. lxxvi. 29 A state of darkish twilight.

b. in shade or colour.

1398 TREVISA *Barth. De P.R.* XIX. xxiii. (1495) 877 Matere that is dymme and derkysshe and vnpure. **1538** LELAND *Itin.* IV. 124 The..Colour..is of a darkish deepe redde. **1775** ADAIR *Amer. Ind.* 6 Their hair is lank, coarse, and darkish. **1881** C. A. YOUNG *Sun* 197 A scarlet ribbon, with a darkish band across it.

Hence **ˈdarkishness**, darkish quality or state.

1583 GOLDING *Calvin on Deut.* XC. 556 God held them in darkishnes, giuing them but a small tast of his Grace.

ˈdark-ˈlantern. A lantern with a slide or arrangement by which the light can be concealed.

1650 FULLER *Pisgah* IV. iii. 45 The pillar of the cloud, the first and perfect pattern of a dark-lantern. **1680** HICKERINGILL *Meroz* 27 Vaux is Vaux though he carry a Dark-lanthorn and wear a Vizard. **1828** SCOTT *F.M. Perth* v, Simon Glover..now came to the door with a dark-lantern in his hand.

b. *slang.* (See quot.)

a **1700** B. E. *Dict. Cant. Crew*, *A Dark-Lanthorn*, the Servant or Agent that Receives the Bribe (at Court).

darkle (ˈdɑːk(ə)l), *v.* [A modern word, evolved out of the adverb *darkling* analysed as a pple.

Probably some parallelism to *sparkling* has been supposed. See next.]

1. *intr.* To lie darkling; to show itself darkly.

1819 Byron *Juan* II. xlix, The night..darkled o'er the faces pale And the dim desolate deep. **1855** Thackeray *Newcomes* lxxv, The..Founder's Tomb..darkles and shines with the most wonderful shadows and lights. **1885** *Century Mag.* 539 The..fountain..whose statues and bas-reliefs darkled above and around a silent pool.

b. To lie in the dark, conceal oneself.

1864 Thackeray *D. Duval* viii, I remember half-a-dozen men darkling in an alley.

2. To grow dark.

1823 Byron *Juan* VI. ci, Her cheek began to flush, her eyes to sparkle, And her proud brow's blue veins to swell and darkle. **1870** Morris *Earthly Par.* II. III. 330 Cold and grey, And darkling fast, the waste before her lay. **1880** Howells *Undisc. Country* ix. 129 The houses darkled away into the gloom of the country.

b. Of the countenance, etc.: To become dark with anger, scorn, etc.

1800 Moore *Ode to Anacreon* xvii. Note 7 Now with angry scorn you darkle, Now with tender anguish sparkle. **1855** Thackeray *Newcomes* lxvi. (D.), His honest brow darkling as he looked towards me. **1886** *Illust. Lond. News* Summer No. 19/2 Peltzer darkling at him with a wicked grin.

3. *trans.* To render dark or obscure.

1884 [see darkling B. 3]. **1893** *National Observer* 25 Feb. 370/2 The dramatist..whose province it is to darkle and obscure.

'darkless, *a. nonce-wd.* Free from darkness.

1888 *Daily News* 29 Sept. 5/1 In summer time the 'darkless nights' are enchanting.

darkling ('dɑːklɪŋ), *adv.* and *a.* [ME. *darke-ling*, f. dark *a.* + -ling, adverbial formative: cf. *back-ling*, *flat-ling*, *grove-ling*, *half-ling*.]

A. *adv.* In the dark; in darkness. *lit.* and *fig.*

a **1450** *Knt. de la Tour* 21 She wolde not come in mennis chaumbres bi night derkelyng withoute candelle. **1580** Sidney *Arcadia* (1662) 379 He came darkeling into his chamber. **1590** Shaks. *Mids. N.* II. ii. 86 O wilt thou darkling leaue me? **1633** T. Adams *Exp. 2 Peter* ii. 1 Our lamps..at last go out, and leave us darkling. **1667** Milton *P.L.* III. 39 The wakeful Bird Sings darkling, and in shadiest Covert hid Tunes her nocturnal Note. **1712** Steele *Spect.* No. 406 ⁋7 Darkling and tir'd we shall the Marshes tread. **1813** Scott *Rokeby* I. xxvi, Wilfrid is..destined, darkling, to pursue Ambition's maze by Oswald's clue. **1859** Tennyson *Vivien* 732 He..darkling felt the sculptured ornament.

B. *pres. pple.* and *adj.* [the ending being confounded with the *-ing* of participles.]

1. Being, taking place, going on, proceeding, etc. in the dark.

a **1763** Shenstone *Upon Riddles* in Dodsley *Coll. Poems* (1782) V. 64 Ye writers..O spare your darkling labours! **1794** Hurdis *Tears Affect.* 58 Which soars aloft In the first glimpse of morning, and performs A darkling anthem at the gates of Heav'n. **1814** Chalmers *Evid. Chr. Revel.* x. 285 A single word from God..is worth a world of darkling speculations. **1859** G. Meredith *R. Feverel* xx, Here like darkling nightingales they sit. **1863** Mrs. Oliphant *Salem Ch.* xvi. 286 The mother and son hurried on upon their darkling journey.

2. Characterized by darkness; lying in darkness; showing itself darkly; darksome, obscure.

1739 P. Whitehead *Manners* 3 A doleful tenant of the darkling Cell. **1855** M. Arnold *Balder Dead* ii, And by the darkling forest-paths the Gods Follow'd. **1865** Gosse *Land & Sea* (1874) 20 Another..brook that breaks out from its darkling bed beneath dwarf willows.

fig. **1795** G. Wakefield *Reply to Age of Reason, Part II*, 24 To let the sun of your intellect shine out..for the illumination of us darkling mortals. **1813** Scott *Rokeby* VI. xiv, Darkling was the sense; the phrase And language those of other days. **1878** White *Life in Christ* III. xix. 257 Some darkling sensation of pleasure or pain.

3. Darkening; obscuring.

1884 Lowell *Poems, To Holmes*, As many poets with their rhymes Oblivion's darkling dust o'erwhelms.

4. **darkling-beetle**, a black beetle, *Blaps mortisaga*, living in dark places, as cellars, etc.

1816 Kirby & Sp. *Entomol.* (1843) I. 335 Mr. Baker..kept a darkling beetle (*Blaps mortisaga*) alive for three years without food of any kind. **1836-9** Todd *Cycl. Anat.* II. 863/2 The fifth section..includes..the darkling-beetles.

'darkling, *sb.*[1] *nonce-wd.* [See -ling.] A child of darkness; one dark in nature or character.

1773 J. Ross *Fratricide* I. 629 (*MS.*) I'll catch Th' impetuous darkling [i.e. Cain] at his first recoil, And temporize his hatred to my wish! *Ibid.* I. 175 The morning ..brought his darkling to the field.

'darkling, *sb.*[2] [subst. use of darkling *a.*] = dark *sb.*

1903 *Westm. Gaz.* 13 Jan. 2/3 At darkling of the moon. **1909** H. G. Wells *Tono-Bungay* IV. i. 443 She carried some rugs for me through the shrubbery in the darkling. **1923** —— *Men like Gods* I. vii. 112 He..blundered by two couples of lovers who whispered softly in the darkling. **1963** A. Garner *Moon of Gomrath* xiii. 102 Once Anghalac sounds you may not know peace again, not in the sun's circle nor in the darkling of the world.

'darklings, *adv. rare.* [f. darkling *adv.*, with adverbial genitive: cf. *backward*, *-wards*, etc.] In the dark; = darkling *adv.*

a **1656** Bp. Hall *Wks.* (1837-9) VII. 344 (D.) Idle wanton servants, who play and talk out their candle-light, and then go darklings to bed. **1785** Burns *Halloween* xi, To the kiln she goes then, An' darklins grapit for the bauks. **1847** *Tait's Mag.* XIV. 11 A kind of pantomime..done darklings in a lawyer's back shop.

b. *at darklins* is used dialectally.

1870 E. Peacock *Ralf Skirl.* I. 282, I wonder you're not scared to be with her by your sen at darklins.

†**'darklong,** *adv.*, obs. variant of darkling. [Cf. *headlong*, *sidelong*.]

1561 T. Hoby tr. *Castiglione's Courtyer* (1577) M vj a, The two arose and wente to bed darkelong. **1577** Eden & Willes *Hist. Trav.* 258b, Darkelong without al pompe and ceremonies, buryed in a dunghil. **1620** Shelton *Quix.* IV. xiv. 112 Sometimes he went dark-long and without Light.

darkly ('dɑːklɪ), *adv.* [f. dark *a.* + -ly[2]. OE. had *deorclīce*; but the word appears to have been formed anew in ME.] In a dark manner or way. In OE. known only in the *fig.* sense 'darkly in a moral sense, horridly, foully'.

c **1000** *Gloss. Prudent.* 142 *Tetrum*, deorclice.

1. In the dark; in secrecy, secretly.

c **1600** Shaks. *Sonn.* xliii, When I sleep, in dreams they [my eyes] look on thee, And darkly bright are bright in dark directed. **1601** —— *All's Well* IV. iii. 13, I will tell you a thing, but you shall let it dwell darkly with you. **1631** Weever *Anc. Fun. Mon.* 223 Bradwardin lieth buried in the South wall, somewhat darkly. *a* **1845** Hood *Irish Schoolmaster* vi, Tame familiar fowls..sit darkly squatting.

2. With a dark or sombre hue.

1509 Hawes *Past. Pleas.* XLIV. ii, On his noddle darkely flamyng Was set Saturne. **1641** French *Distill.* v. (1651) 139 Melt it not, onely let it darkly glow. **1794** Southey *Sonn.* viii, How darkly o'er yon far-off mountain frowns The gather'd tempest! *a* **1835** Mrs. Hemans *Poems, Modern Greece*, The river's darkly-rolling wave. **1843** Mrs. Browning *To Flush* iii, Darkly brown thy body is.

3. In a gloomy, frowning, ominous manner.

1594 Shaks. *Rich. III*, I. iv. 175 How darkly, and how deadly dost thou speake! **1601** —— *Twel. N.* II. i. 4 My starres shine darkely ouer me. **1814** Byron *Corsair* I. ix, His frown of hatred darkly fell. **1837** Hawthorne *Twice Told T.* (1851) I. v. 76 The men of iron shook their heads and frowned so darkly, that the revellers looked up.

4. In an obscure, vague, or mysterious manner.

1377 Langl. *P. Pl.* B. x. 372 Where dowel is, or dobet derkelich ȝe shewen. *c* **1450** *Merlin* 53, I..will speke..so derkly that they shul not vndirstonde what I sey. **1576** Fleming *Panopl. Epist.* 213 This booke was..written of sett purpose very darkely. **1840** Mrs. Norton *Dream* 151 Darkly-worded spells. **1889** Jessopp *Coming of Friars* i. 3 Because he spoke so darkly, men listened all the more eagerly.

5. With obscure vision; dimly, blindly.

c **1430** *Pilgr. Lyf Manhode* II. lvii. (1869) 98 Sum time thou shalt se me thikkeliche and derkliche. **1526** *Pilgr. Perf.* (W. de W. 1531) 185 In this lyfe we se and knowe god but confusely or derkly, as it were by a glasse. **1732** Pope *Ess. Man* II. 4 A being darkly wise, and rudely great. **1875** Jowett *Plato* (ed. 2) I. 427 Are not we..seeking to discover that which Socrates in a glass darkly foresaw?

'darkly, *a. rare.* [-ly[1]: cf. *sickly*.] Dark-looking, somewhat dark.

1821 Clare *Vill. Minstr.* II. 52 Sweet tiny flower of darkly hue.

'darkmans. *Thieves' cant.* [f. dark *a.*: the second element occurs also in *crackmans* a hedge, *lightmans* the day, etc.] The night.

1567 Harman *Caveat* 85, I couched a hogshead in a Skypper this darkemans. **1611** Dekker *Roaring Girle* Wks. 1873 III. 216 With all whom I'le tumble this next darkmans in the strommel. *a* **1700** B. E. *Dict. Cant. Crew*, *Darkmans-Budge*..one that slides into a House in the Dusk, to let in.. Rogues to rob. **1737** *Bacchus & Venus*, Each Darkmans I pass in an old shady Grove. **1815** Scott *Guy M.* xxviii, Men were men then, and fought other in the open field, and there was nae milling in the darkmans.

darkness ('dɑːknɛs). [OE. *deorcnes*, *-nys*, f. *deorc* dark *a.* + *-nes*, *-nis*, *-nys*, -ness.] The quality or state of being dark.

1. Absence or want of light (total or partial).

a **1050** *De Vitiis* in *Liber Scintill.* (1889) 228 On þyssere swa micelre deorcnysse. *c* **1320** *Cast. Love* 1706 Another peyne they shull have of derknes. *c* **1385** Chaucer *L.G.W.* Prol. 95 (MS. Gg) And clothede was the flour..ffor derknesse of the nyht. *c* **1440** *Promp. Parv.* 121 Dyrkenesse, *obscuritas*. **1508** Fisher *Wks.* (1876) 50 Bytwene the shynynge lyght and black derknes. **1667** Milton *P.L.* I. 63 No light, but rather darkness visible Serv'd only to discover sights of woe. **1860** Tyndall *Glac.* I. xxv. 188 An aperture through which the darkness of the chasm was rendered visible.

2. The quality of being dark in shade or colour.

c **1374** Chaucer *Boeth* I. i. 5 Þe wiche cloþes a darkenes of a forleten and dispised elde had[de] duskid and dirked. **1413** Lydg. *Pilgr. Sowle* II. lix. (1859) 57 The fyre taketh smoke and derkenesse of the mater to whiche he is conioyned. **1818** Shelley *Laon* XII. xxiii. 7 The glossy darkness of her streaming hair. **1856** Ruskin *Mod. Paint.* IV. v. xviii. §3 Darkness mingled with colour gives the delight of its depth and power.

3. Want of sight; blindness.

c **1374** Chaucer *Troylus* IV. 272 Ende I wil as Edippe in derknesse My sorowfull liff. **1568** Turner *Herbal* III. 6 The litle filmes that go over the eyes, wherof darknes doth rise. **1842** Tennyson *Godiva* 70 His eyes, before they had their will, Were shrivell'd into darkness in his head.

4. *fig.* **a.** The want of spiritual or intellectual light; esp. common in biblical imagery.

kingdom, power of darkness: the empire of evil. ***prince of darkness***: Satan.

c **1340** *Cursor M.* 17881 (Trin.) Þo folk in dedly derkenes stad þis grete liȝt made hem glad. **1382** Wyclif *Col.* i. 13 The which delyuerde vs fro the power of derknisses. **1526** *Pilgr. Perf.* (W. de W. 1531) 4 The prynce of derknes..our goostly ennemy the deuyll. **1531** Tindale *Exp. 1 John* 15 All that lyue in ignoraunce are called darknesse. **1654** Whitlock *Zootomia* 140 A second famous Leader under the Prince of Darknesse. **1712** Addison *Spect.* No. 419 ⁋5 The Darkness and Superstition of later Ages. **1766** Fordyce *Serm. Yng. Wom.* (1767) II. viii. 6 The powers of darkness ..concur..in misleading. **1871** Morley *Voltaire* (1886) 229 They [the clergy] were..the incarnation of the average darkness of the hour.

b. Absence of the 'light' of life; death.

1388 Wyclif *Job* x. 21 Befor that Y go..to the derk lond, and hilid with the derkness of deth. **1535** Coverd. *Job* x. 21 To that londe of darcknesse & shadowe of death. **1603** Shaks. *Meas. for M.* III. i. 14 If I must die, I will encounter darknesse as a bride, And hugge it in mine armes. *Mod.* The darkness of the tomb.

5. Gloom of sorrow, trouble, or distress.

c **1645** Howell *Lett.* (1650) I. 142 There is some darkness happened betwixt the two favourites. **1811** Shelley *Bigotry's Victim* iii. 7 The darkness of deepest dismay.

6. A condition or environment which conceals from sight, observation, or knowledge; obscurity; concealment, secrecy.

1382 Wyclif *Matt.* x. 27 That thing that Y say to ȝou in dercnessis, saye ȝee in the liȝt. **1543-4** *Act 35 Hen. VIII*, c. 1 The vaile of darcknes of the vsurped power..of the see and bishoppes of Rome. **1601** Shaks. *Twel. N.* v. i. 156 To vnfold, though lately we intended To keepe in darkenesse, what occasion now Reueales. **1692** E. Walker *Epictetus' Mor.* (1737) 'To the Author', Truth's still in darkness undiscovered. **1869** Freeman *Norm. Conq.* (1876) III. xii. 253, I found the question wrapped in darkness. **1889** J. Corbett *Monk* xiii. 191 This formidable figure that had arisen so suddenly and with such mystery, this man of darkness [Monk].

7. Obscurity of meaning.

1553 T. Wilson *Rhet.* (1580) 165 Poeticall Clerkes.. delightyng muche in their owne darckenesse. *a* **1568** Ascham *Scholem.* (Arb.) 156 The vse of old wordes is not the greatest cause of Salustes roughnes and darknesse. **1666** Boyle *Orig. Formes & Qual.*, Apt to occasion much darknesse and difficulty in our enquiries into the things themselves. *a* **1715** Burnet *Own Time* (1823) I. 279 He preached and prayed often himself, but with so peculiar a darkness.

8. *Phonetics.* The quality of being dark (sense 6 d).

1906 W. Rippman *Sounds of Spoken Eng.* 47 The 'darkness' of the [l] is particularly noticeable when it comes at the end of a word.

†**'darkship.** *Obs. nonce-wd.* [See -ship.] The personality of one who is dark.

1707 E. Ward *Hud. Rediv.* (1715) II. 7 That his Darkship [*i.e.* a devil] was unable To terrify an English Rabble.

darksome ('dɑːksəm), *a.* [f. dark *sb.* + -some: cf. *toilsome*.]

1. Characterized (more or less) by darkness; somewhat dark or gloomy. Now chiefly a poetic synonym of *dark*, of vaguer connotation.

1530 Palsgr. 309/2 Darkesome, *tenebreux*. **1549-62** Sternhold & H. *Ps.* cxxxvi. 9 And Starres that doe appeare To guide the darksome night. **1667** Milton *P.L.* II. 973 By constraint Wandring this darksome desart. **1718** Rowe tr. *Lucan* 357 She seeks the Ship's deep darksome Hold below. **1848** M. Arnold *Sick King Bokhara*, Alone and in a darksome place Under some mulberry-trees I found A little pool.

2. Somewhat dark in shade or colour; sombre.

1615 G. Sandys *Trav.* 73 He hath a little haire on his vpper lip..of a darksom color. **1667** Milton *P.L.* XII. 185 A darksom Cloud of Locusts swarming down. **1807** Wordsw. *White Doe* IV. 56 With pine and cedar spreading wide Their darksome boughs on every side. **1879** Dixon *Windsor* I. i. 2 Darksome clump, and antique tower.

3. *fig.* **a.** Characterized by obscurity of meaning.

1574 tr. *Marlorat's Apocalips* 1 To the Fathers of olde tyme, Daniels vision seemed moste darkesome. **1597-8** Bp. Hall *Sat.* III. Prol., Whose words were short, and darksome was their sense. **1626** Bacon *Sylva* §900 Paracelsus and some darksome authors of Magic. **1838** C. Sumner *Mem. & Lett.* (1878) I. 379 The darksome notes and memoranda which he made on the margin of the volumes he read.

b. Characterized by gloom, sadness, or cheerlessness.

1649 Roberts *Clavis Bibl.* ii. 24 All my darksome doubtings fled away. **1719** D'Urfey *Pills* (1872) IV. 109 It is a darksome Passion. **1828** Carlyle *Misc.* (1857) I. 199 His darksome, drudging childhood and youth. *a* **1845** Hood *Two Swans* iv, In darksome fears They weep and pine away.

c. Morally of dark character.

1880 McCarthy *Own Times* IV. lxvii. 532 Some rather darksome vices..prove their existence in the character.

Hence **'darksomeness**, darkness, obscurity.

1571 Golding *Calvin on Ps.* xviii. 12 Darksomnesse of water. **1583** —— *Calvin on Deut.* xlii. 248 Let vs not charge it [God's truth] with darksomenesse. *a* **1642** Sir W. Monson *Naval Tracts* v. 495/2 The Darksomness of the Night.

darky, darkey ('dɑːkɪ). [f. dark *a.* + -y, dim. and appellative: cf. blacky.]

1. The night. *slang.*

1789 G. Parker *Life's Painter* 124 (Farmer) Bless your eyes and limbs..I don't come here every darkey. **1836** R. Burrowes *Death of Socrates* in *Rel. Father Prout* (1860) 269 Then at darkey we waked him in clover.

2. A dark-lantern. *slang.*

1812 J. H. VAUX *Flash Dict.*, *Darky*, a dark lanthorn. **1838** DICKENS *O. Twist* xxii, 'Crape, keys, centre-bits, darkies —nothing forgotten?' inquired Toby.

3. Also **darkie**. A Black, esp. a Southern U.S. Black (usu. considered patronizing or mildly offensive). Also *attrib. colloq.*

1840 R. H. DANA *Bef. Mast* xxxiii. 129 The darkey tried to butt him. **1883** *Century Mag.* XXVII. 132 The manners of a corn-field darky. **1884** *19th Cent.* Feb. 246 A coffin of curious darkey workmanship. **1848** J. R. LOWELL *Biglow Papers* 1st Ser. 24 I'd an idee that they were built arter the darkie fashion all. *a* **1860** in Bartlett *Dict. Amer.* (ed. 3) 114, I wish de legislatur would set dis darkie free, Oh! what a happy place den de darkie land would be. **1936** *Discovery* Oct. 308/2 The simple words of the darkie mother. **1941** W. A. PERCY *Lanterns on Levee* i. 10 They held Sunday school for their own and the darkies' children. **1957** [see BOOT *sb.*[3] 1 e]. **1971** G. LAMMING in J. Figueroa *Caribbean Voices* I. 20 Often in our green folly We mocked the celluloid display, How darkies south of civilization Clowned their ways to fame. **1983** 'J. LE CARRÉ' *Little Drummer Girl* I. iv. 81 Was it something about not taking on the darkies as conductors?

4. A blind man. *dial.*

1807 J. STAGG *Poems* 144 A darky glaum'd her by the hip.

darl, colloq. abbrev. of DARLING *sb.*[1]

1930 K. S. PRICHARD *Haxby's Circus* xxviii. 329 'Oh, darl, don't you bother,' he begged. 'I hate you to get all het-up.' **1952** J. CLEARY *Sundowners* i. 13 I'm so glad you're built like you are, darl. **1959** C. MACINNES *Absolute Beginners* 16 'Hi, darl,' she said. 'Hi, hon,' I answered. That's how we heard two movie stars address each other at a film we went to ages ago. **1970** J. CLEARY *Helga's Web* iv. 72 'Darl——.' He hadn't called her that for several years: short for *darling*, there had been a time when he had called her nothing else.

darling ('dɑːlɪŋ), *sb.*[1] and *a.* Forms: 1-3 **deorling**, (1 **dior-**, **dir-**, **dyrling**), 1-6 **derling**, (4-6 **derlinge**, **-yng(e)**, 2-4 **durling**, **-yng**, 5-6 **darlyng(e**, 6 **darlinge**, 6- **darling**; also 3 **deoreling**, 3-6 **dereling**, **-yng**, 4-6 **deer(e)ling**, **-yng**, 6-8 **dearling**, (6 **-inge**, **-yng(e)**. [OE. *déorling*, *díerling*, deriv. of *déor* DEAR: see -LING. Thence ME. *dereling*, *derling*, which subseq. became *darling*, as usual with *er* followed by a consonant; but the analytical *dere-ling*, *dear-ling* also continued in partial use till the 18th c. or later, as a dialectal or nonce-form.]

1. A person who is very dear to another; the object of a person's love; one dearly loved. Commonly used as a term of endearing address.

c **888** K. ÆLFRED *Boeth.* xxxix. §10 Se godcunda anweald ʒefriþode his diorlingas [*v.r.* deorlingas]. *c* **897** —— *Gregory's Past.* I. 393 Bi Dauide ðæm Godes dirlinge. *c* **1000** ÆLFRIC *Hom.* (Thorpe) I. 58 (Bosw.) Iohannes se Godspellere, Cristes dyrling. *a* **1200** *Moral Ode* 385 Crist scal one beon inou alle his durlinges. *c* **1350** *Will. Palerne* 1538 Sweting welcome! Mi derworþe derling. **1388** WYCLIF *Song Sol.* i, 13 My derlyng is to me a cluster of cipre tre. ? *a* **1400** *Chester Plays* III. 372 And nowe farewell my darling deere. **1562** J. HEYWOOD *Prov. & Epigr.* (1867) 65 It is better to be An olde mans derlyng, than a yong mans werlyng. **1583** STANYHURST *Æneis* ii. (Arb.) 63 Flee, fle, my sweet darling. **1714** GAY *Sheph. Week* v. 110 While on her Dearling's Bed her Mother sate. **1842** TENNYSON *Gardener's Dau.* 272 The idol of my youth, The darling of my manhood. **1859** —— *Merlin & V.* 395 Answer, darling, answer, no.

†**b.** A favourite, a minion. *Obs.*

c **888** K. ÆLFRED *Boeth.* xxvii. §2 ʒif ðe licode his dysiʒ.. swa wel swa his dysegum deorlingum dyde. *a* **1400-50** *Alexander* 3442 An ald derling of Darius was duke made of pers. **1530** PALSGR. 213/1 Derlyng, a man, *mignon.* **1548** HALL *Chron.* (1809) 219 The Quenes dearlynge William Duke of Suffolke. **1579** J. STUBBES *Gaping Gulf* E viij, The king.. had like to haue marred al, by lauishing out a word hereof to one of hys deerelyngs. *a* **1719** ADDISON (J.), She became the darling of the princess.

c. The favourite in a family, etc.

c **1330** R. BRUNNE *Chron.* (1810) 50 Knoute of his body gate sonnes þre.. Knoute lufed [Harald] best, he was his derlyng. **1675** *Art Contentm.* iv. §9 The most discountenanc'd child oft makes better proof, than the dearling. **1712** ARBUTHNOT *John Bull* III. ii, John was the darling! He had all the good bits.

d. One meet to be much loved, a lovable creature, a 'pet'.

1799 SOUTHEY *King of Crocodiles* II, Six young Princes, darlings all, Were missing. **1863** MISS BRADDON *Eleanor's Vict.* (1878) iii. 23 His duty towards those innocent darlings. **1864** KINGSLEY in *Life* xxi. (1879) II. 173 With every flock of sheep and girls are one or two enormous mastiffs.. They are great darlings, and necessary against bear and wolf.

2. *transf.* and *fig.* **a.** of persons, as ***the darling of the people***, etc.

c **1205** LAY. 6316 Alfred þe king, Englelondes deorling. *Ibid.* 25576 þa spac Angel þe king, Scottene deorling. **1548** UDALL, etc. *Erasm. Par. Luke* Pref. 8 Wantons and derelynges of fortune. **1615** BACON *Adv. Learn.* II. xxiii. §36 Augustus Cæsar.. when he was a dearling of the Senate. **1639** FULLER *Holy War* (1640) 1 A prince so good, that he was styled the Darling of mankind. **1702** *Eng. Theophrast.* 193 Fortune turns.. every thing to the advantage of her Darlings. **1875** STUBBS *Const. Hist.* III. xxi. 508 Henry V was, as he deserved to be, the darling of the nation.

b. of things.

c **1430** *Hymns Virg.* (1867) 25 Loue is goddis owne derlinge. **1577** tr. *Bullinger's Decades* (1592) 303 Where God is, there also is Patience his derling which he nourisheth. **1604** SHAKS. *Oth.* III. iv. 66 Take heede on't, Make it a Darling, like your precious eye. **1750** G. HUGHES *Barbadoes* Pref. 1 Then Oratory became their darling. **1870** EMERSON *Soc. & Solit., Work & Days* Wks. (Bohn) III. 67 Trade, that pride and darling of our Ocean.

†**3.** A name for a variety of apple. *Obs.*

1586 COGAN *Haven Health* (1636) 101 The best Apples.. are Pepins, Costards.. Darlings, and such other.

4. *Comb.*, as ***darling-like*** adj. (*nonce-wd.*).

1873 BROWNING *Red Cott. Nt.-cap* 835 Her figure? somewhat small and darlinglike.

B. *adj.* [attrib. use of *sb.*] **1.** Dearly loved, very dear; best-loved, favourite. **a.** of persons.

[**1509** HAWES *Past. Pleas.* XVI. lxxii, Dyane derlyng pale as any leade.] **1596** SPENSER *F.Q.* IV. Prol. v, Dred infant, Venus dearling dove. **1667** MILTON *P.L.* II. 373 His darling Sons. **1736** W. THOMPSON *Epithalamium* xiv. 9 Our dearling prince. **1819** SHELLEY *Cyclops* 246 My darling little Cyclops. **1849** DICKENS *Dav. Copp.* xxxii, My unchanged love is with my darling child.

b. of things.

c **1600** SHAKS. *Sonn.* xviii. 3 Rough winds do shake the darling buds of May. **1645** FULLER *Good Th. in Bad T.* (1841) 64 To acknowledge my darling faults. **1701** W. WOTTON *Hist. Rome, Marcus* i. 7 Philosophy was his darling Study. **1799** COLERIDGE *Devil's Thoughts* vi, The Devil did grin, for his darling sin Is pride that apes humility. **1848** MACAULAY *Hist. Eng.* I. 101 A few enthusiasts.. were bent on pursuing.. their darling phantom of a republic.

2. Sweetly pretty or charming, 'sweet'. *affected.*

1805 E. CAVANAGH *Let.* 4 Oct. in Londonderry & Hyde *Russ. Jrnls.* (1934) II. 187 We all follow'd them out of doors across a Garden to a *darling* place. **1854** *Punch* Mar. 116 Isn't it the darlingest, sweetest, prettiest, little dear darling darling! Oh! did you ever!! **1858** QUEEN VICTORIA *Let.* 1 Apr. in R. Fulford *Dearest Child* (1964) 84 Darling Beatrice came.. in short clothes with darling little stockings and.. pink satin shoes—really too darling. **1906** *Punch* 21 Mar. 215/1 You have a darling little note-book.. to match your frock. **1908** B. HARRADEN *Interplay* 373 It is perfectly darling of you to have chosen Hughie. **1937** D. ALDIS *Time at Heels* v. 109 Your little boy did so beautifully... He was simply darling. **1952** M. MCCARTHY *Groves of Academe* (1953) i. 14 I've seen them with you in the Co-op, Dr. Mulcahy. They're *darling*. **1970** *New Yorker* 28 Feb. 54/2 Isn't it going to be darling!

Hence (*nonce-wds.*) **'darling** *v. trans.*, to address as 'darling'; **'darlingly** *adv.*; **'darlingness**.

1888 LADY V. SANDARS *Bitter Repent.* III. ii. 25 They still darlinged and deared each other as heretofore, especially in the presence of others. **1873** BROWNING *Red Cott. Nt.-cap* 1600 Writing letters daily, duly read As darlingly she hands them to myself. **1875** —— *Aristoph. Apol.* Wks. XIII. 30 Right they named you.. some rich name.. Kallistion? Phabion for the darlingness? **1942** T. RATTIGAN *Flare Path* II. i. 123 Wonderful the way you stage people darling each other. **1967** *Punch* 19 July 82/2 In the interval she seems to be in every bar and every corridor, darlinging everybody in sight.

'Darling, *sb.*[2] The name of a river in western New South Wales used *attrib.* in the names of certain plants growing in its neighbourhood; also **Darling shower**, a local name for a dust-storm.

1898 MORRIS *Austral Eng.* 115/1 *Darling Pea*, an Australian plant, *Swainsonia galegifolia*. *Ibid.*, *Darling Shower*, a local name.. for a dust storm, caused by cyclonic winds. **1899** *Westm. Gaz.* 20 Feb. 10/1 The Riverina breeds a particularly distressful variety of dust-storm known as 'Darling showers'. **1909** WEBSTER, Darling lily, *Crinum flaccidum*. **1936** A. RUSSELL *Gone Nomad* viii. 65 By this time, owing to the protracted drought, sand-storms or 'Darling showers', as we facetiously called them, had become an almost daily occurrence in the Red Country. **1945** BAKER *Austral. Lang.* iii. 63 *Darling Pea*... One of Australia's poisonous plants; cattle eating it become afflicted with staggers and die: so a man wandering in gait or dazed in appearance is said to be suffering from Darling Pea. *Ibid.* x. 189 Cobar shower, denotes a duststorm. Darling shower, Wilcannia shower, and Bedourie shower are employed similarly. **1963** A. LUBBOCK *Austral. Roundabout* 11 It [*sc.* Patterson's Curse].. does not poison animals, as does the innocuous-sounding Darling Pea.

darlint ('dɑːlɪnt). *dial* and *joc.* = DARLING[1] 1.

1888 KIPLING *Soldiers Three* (1890) 89 She cried loud, poor darlint, bein' mishandled. **1922** JOYCE *Ulysses* 143 Quicker, darlint! **1930** E. POUND *XXX Cantos* x. 43 Siggy, darlint, wd. you not stop making war on insensible objects.

darloch, var. of DORLACH.

darn (dɑːn), *v.*[1] Forms 7-8 **dern**, **dearn**, 7- **darn**; 9 *Sc.* **dern**. [Derivation unknown.

The verb appears about 1600, and becomes at once quite common: it may be that this particular way of repairing a hole or rent was then introduced. The form suggests relationship to DERN (later *darn*) secret, hidden, and its verb *dern*, *darn* to conceal, put out of sight; but satisfactory connecting links between the two have not yet been found. On the other hand the Celtic derivation suggested by Wedgwood is absolutely inadmissible. Welsh *darn* 'piece, fragment' has no association with darning or mending in any way, and the sense 'patch' given by Owen Pughe is correct only in the sense that a 'piece' may be used to patch. The Welsh *darnio hosan* would mean 'to cut a stocking to pieces' (with a knife); 'to darn a stocking' is *creithio hosan*. (D. Silvan Evans, and Prof. Rhŷs.)]

1. a. *trans.* To mend (clothes, etc., *esp.* stockings) by filling-in a hole or rent with yarn or thread interwoven so as to form a kind of texture. (This is done with a *darning-needle*.)

c **1600** *Q. Eliz. Househ. Bk.* in *Househ. Ord.* (1790) 294 The Serjant hath for his fee, all the coverpannes, drinking towells, and other linen clothe.. that are darned. **1603** HOLLAND *Plutarch's Mor.* 783 (R.) For spinning, weaving, derning and drawing up a rent. **1611** COTGR., *Rentraire*.. to draw, dearne, or sow vp a rent in a garment. **1697** *Lond. Gaz.* No. 3303/4 Breeches darned with Worsted at the Knees. **1710** STEELE *Tatler* No. 245 ¶2 Four Pair of Silk-Stockings curiously derned. **1836** MRS. CARLYLE *Lett.* I. 63 The holes in the stair-carpet all darned. **1881** BESANT & RICE *Chapl. of Fleet* II. iii. (1883) 135 His grey stockings were darned with blue worsted.

absol. **1720** GAY *Poems* (1745) I. 233, I can sow plain-work, I can darn and stitch. **1875** *Plain Needlework* 18 The machine is not yet invented which can patch or darn.

fig. **1641** MILTON *Church Govt.* vi. (1851) 128 To dearn up the rents of schisme by calling a councell.

b. To thread one's way in and out between obstacles.

1890 *Blackw. Mag.* No. 897. 9/1 Lithe bodies.. darning themselves out and in of the many-coloured seething crowd.

c. *transf.* To mend (a hole in a wall, road, etc.) by filling-in.

1801 W. BEATTIE *Entertaining & Instruct. Tales* (1813) I. 30 He staps wi' strae ilk navus bore, An' ilka crevice darns. **1850** 'H. HIEOVER' *Pract. Horsemanship* 146 There is a mode of keeping our present roads in order, that I have heard termed 'darning' them: i.e. if a part is seen somewhat lower than the surface, the unbroken pieces of granite are got up to it, and there left to be crushed by the wheels of carriages.

2. To ornament or embroider with darning-stitch.

1882 [see s.v. DARNING *vbl. sb.* 3]. **1900** DAY & BUCKLE *Art in Needlework* 108 The flower stalk is defined by darning the first row in a darker colour. *Ibid.*, The background is darned diaper fashion.

darn, *v.*[2] Perversion of DAMN, in profane use. (Chiefly *U.S.*)

1781 *Pennsylvania Jrnl.* 20 June, In New England prophane swearing.. is so far from polite as to be criminal, and many.. use.. substitutions such as *darn* it, for d—n it. **1809** A. B. LINDSLEY *Love & Friendship* 8 Darn my skin 'f you wouldn't dewe it. **1825** J. K. FAULDING *J. Bull in Amer.* iii. 36 If I don't have him before the justice, darn my soul. **1837-40** HALIBURTON *Clockm.* (1872) 92 Darn it all, it fairly makes my dander rise. **1861** H. KINGSLEY *Ravenshoe* vi. (D.), My boy.. was lost in a typhoon in the China sea; darn they lousy typhoons! **1922** S. LEWIS *Babbitt* v. 51 Darn it, I thought you'd quit this darn smoking! *Ibid.* viii. 119 Every small American town is trying to get population and modern ideals. And darn if a lot of 'em don't put it across! **1968** *Globe & Mail Mag.* (Toronto) 17 Feb. 9/3 'Play, darn it!' he shouted to the open-mouthed pianist.

darn, *sb.*[1] [f. DARN *v.*[1]] The act or result of darning; a hole or rent mended by darning.

1720 *Lond. Gaz.* No. 5868/9, 1.. Muslin Apron, with a large Darn in the Bottom. **1851** *Beck's Florist* 40 Then she'd .. wash my linen, or put a patch here and a darn there. **1879** MISS BIRD *Rocky Mount.* I. 245 One pair of stockings, such a mass of darns that hardly a trace of the original wool remains.

darn, *sb.*[2] *slang* (orig. *U.S.*). [Cf. DARN *adv.* and *a.*] ***by darn***, used as a form of asseveration. Also ***not to care*** (or ***give***) ***a darn***, not to care at all.

1840 C. F. HOFFMAN *Greyslaer* II. iv. 206 But, by darn, the capting's cleared out without speaking to one.. but ourselves. **1850** W. K. NORTHALL *Life & Recoll. Yankee Hill* 119 You may put down all our family... I don't care a darn. **1854** M. J. HOLMES *Tempest & Sunshine* xxiv. 330, I don't care a darn how many Miss Betsy's I git. **1891** M. E. RYAN *Told in Hills* 92, I don't care a darn about the sheep just now. **1920** GALSWORTHY *Foundations* I, *Anne.* Which do you like to be called—John or James? *James.* I don't give a darn. **1957** I. CROSS *God Boy* (1958) i. 8, I would love shooting and kicking out at my enemies, not giving a darn what they try to do to me.

darn, *adv.* and *a. slang* (orig. *U.S.*). [Arbitrary perversion of DAMN *a.* and *adv.*]

A. *adv.* Extremely, intensely.

1789 WEBSTER *Diss. Eng. Lang.* 385 The word (*dern*) is in common use in New England and pronounced *darn.* It has not, however, the sense it had formerly; it is now used as an adverb to qualify an adjective, as *darn sweet*; denoting a great degree of the quality. **1797** D. MACKINTOSH *Rational Ess. Eng. Gram.* 82 We say, dea'rn or da'rn, heark'en, heart', hearth'. **1869** BARNUM *Struggles & Triumphs* (1871) 146 Darn glad to see you, by hokey; I came down here to have lots of fun. **1892** *Century Mag.* June 264 It was a darn good churn too. **1922** S. LEWIS *Babbitt* ii. 18 You're so darn scared of the car that you drive up-hill with the emergency brake on! *Ibid.* v. 64 You're pretty darn near talking socialism! **1969** *New Yorker* 12 Apr. 62/3 We want to make darn sure we get there and back.

B. *adj.* 'Blessed', 'confounded'. Also *absol.*

1840 C. F. HOFFMAN *Greyslaer* III. iv. 141 'Jim, you've done the darn thing agin us to-night, and no mistake' said one. **1899** S. HALE *Lett.* (1919) 348 You know they are all here improving their minds, learning some darn thing or other. **1904** H. R. MARTIN *Tillie* 40 To fill out blanks answerin' to a lot of darn-fool questions 'bout one thing and 'nother. **1924** A. J. SMALL *Frozen Gold* iii. 87 I'm doing my darnest to drive you out of Cedar Falls. **1929** *Melody Maker* Jan. 15/1, I know a darn' sight more about the makings of a piano than I did a month ago.

darn, var. of DERN *a.* and *v.*

dar'nation. Perversion of DAMNATION, in profane use. (Chiefly *U.S.*)

1798 *Aurora* (Philadelphia) 14 Aug. (Thornton, s.v. *Nation*), It seems as if the Irish are as incorrigible as the darnation Bostonians. **1825** S. WOODWORTH *Forest Rose* I. iii, Darnation take the garlic, I say. **1832** [see TARNATION *sb.*]. **1840** *Daily Pennant* (St. Louis) 9 May (Thornton, s.v. *Chip*), It wouldn't take so much.. to make it a darntation sight riz-er. **1878** MRS. STOWE *Poganuc P.* iii. 33 If I didn't hold on to him he'd have us all to the darnation in five minutes. **1924** in *Dialect Notes* V. 265.

darned (dɑːnd), *ppl. a.*[1] [f. DARN *v.*[1]]

1. Mended by darning.

1628 Wither *Brit. Rememb.* v. 1019 Peec'd, and neatly dearned. **1838** Dickens *O. Twist* iv, A suit of thread-bare black, with darned cotton stockings. **1847** Ld. Lindsay *Chr. Art* I. 137 A piece of darned and faded tapestry.

2. Formed, made, or ornamented with darning-stitch.

1881 C. C. Harrison *Woman's Handiwork* I. 86 Italian punto a maglia or darned netting. **1882** Caulfeild & Saward *Dict. Needlework* 145/2 The Darned Embroidery most practised in Europe has been chiefly worked upon cotton. **1895** *Montgomery Ward Catal.* 79/1 Darned or embroidered net, 72 in. **1909** *Westm. Gaz.* 27 Feb. 15/2 The theatre or afternoon dress is of darned filet over satin or cashmere. *Ibid.* 7 Aug. 15/1 Darned net, such as was worn about 1830, or even earlier, looks very well.

darned, *pa. pple., ppl. a.*², and *adv.* Perversion of damned, in profane use. (Chiefly *U.S.*)

1. *pa. pple.*

1808 J. N. Barker *Tears & Smiles* 18 I'll be darned, sir, if I think this is the way. **1844** *John Chawbacon* ii. in Halliwell *Dict.* (1865) I. p. xv, I'll be darn'd if I know. **1847** J. K. Paulding *Bucktails* II. ii. 33 I'll be darned but I guess I've lost my way. **1888** A. C. Gunter *Mr. Potter of Texas* xxii, He sinks back..in amazed astonishment and mutters: 'Wall, I'm darned!'

2. *ppl. a.*

1815 in *Amer. Speech* (1928) III. 231. **1834** C. A. Davis *Lett. J. Downing* 41 'Do you want another report?' 'Not by a darn'd sight,' says he. **1837–40** Haliburton *Clockm.* (1862) 29, I guess they are pretty considerable superfine darned fools. **1891** M. E. Ryan *Told in Hills* 123 She..was the 'darndest, cutest, little customer he ever saw'. **1904** W. H. Smith *Promoters* xviii. 269 Darndest fellow to take things up that way.

b. *absol.*

1844 'J. Slick' *High Life in N.Y.* II. 233 There must al'ers be an eend tu every thing that's sweeter than common, that's the darndest of it. **1907** N. Munro *Daft Days* iv. 31 This is a funny dog... Isn't He the darndest? **1960** *Farmer & Stockbreeder* 8 Mar. 147/1 The public are eating between four and five eggs each week and the Egg Board are doing their darndest to increase this figure still further.

3. *adv.*

1807 L. Beach *Jonathan Postfree* 23 Drove down old Squire Herdy's cattle—darn'd ugly creatures to drive. **1822** Woodworth *Deed of Gift* 45, I have taken a liking to you, 'cause you are so darn'd pretty. **1848** Lowell *Biglow P.* I. xiii, Ef you're arter folks o' gumption, You've a darned long row to hoe. **1888** *Harper's Mag.* July 323/2 In Colorado the man who tells the first story has a darned poor show. **1922** S. Lewis *Babbitt* v. 57 Machine looks brand new now—not that it's so darned old, of course; had it less 'n three years. **1962** J. Ludwig in R. Weaver *First Five Years* 19 By God, she tells herself, this is a darned good face.

darnel ('dɑːnəl). Forms: 4–5 dernel, 5 dernal -eil, darnelle, -ylle, -ail, 6 dernell, (dernolde), 6–7 darnell, -all, 4– darnel. [Occurs also in the Walloon dialect of Rouchy, '*darnelle*, ivraie, *lolium temulentum*'; ulterior history unknown.]

1. A deleterious grass, *Lolium temulentum*, which in some countries grows as a weed among corn.

Known first as the English name for the *lolium* of the Vulgate: see cockle *sb.*¹ 2. The grass is now rare in England, but appears to have been much more common formerly when seed-corn was largely imported from the Mediterranean regions, where the weed abounds. It is now held to be deleterious only when infested by ergot, to which it is particularly liable.

c **1325** *Metr. Hom.* 145 Than com his fa, and seu riht thare Darnel, that es an iuel wede. *c* **1340** *Cursor M.* 1138 (Fairf.) Þi quete darnel [*Cott., Gött.* zizanny, *Trin.* cokul] sal hit be. **1382** Wyclif *Matt.* xiii. 25. *c* **1440** *Promp. Parv.* 119 Dernel, a wede, *zizania, lollium.* **1523** Fitzherb. *Husb.* §20 Dernolde groweth vp streyght lyke an hye grasse, and hath longe sedes on eyther syde the stert. **1572** J. Jones *Bathes Buckstone* 5 b, Some darnell is crept in amongest the good corne. **1605** Shaks. *Lear* IV. iv. 5. **1697** Dryden *Virg. Past.* v. 56 Oats and Darnel choak the rising Corn. **1742** *Lond. & Country Brew.* I. (ed. 4) 10 Darnel is a rampant Weed and grows much among some Barley, especially in the bad Husbandman's Ground. **1799** *Med. Jrnl.* II. 106 Externally applied, darnel is said to produce anodyne properties. **1833** Tennyson *Poems* 3 Then let wise Nature work her will And on my clay her darnels grow.

b. Sometimes used as a book-name of the genus *Lolium.* ***red darnel***: Rye-grass, *L. Perenne.*

1647 Fuller *Good Th. in Worse T.* (1841) 109 There is a kind of darnel, called *lolium murinum.* **1794** Martyn *Rousseau's Bot.* xiii. 143 Lolium or Darnel, has a one-leaved involucre containing one flower only.

2. Loosely 'applied to *Papaver Rhœas,* or some other corn-field poppy' (Britten & Holland).

1612 Drayton *Poly-olb.* xv. (R.), The crimson darnel flower, the blue-bottle and gold.

3. *fig.* Cf. cockle, tares.

1444 *Pol. Poems* (Rolls) II. 216 Nor of thy tounge be nat rekkelees, Uttre nevir no darnel with good corn. **1563–87** Foxe *A. & M.* (1684) III. 501 The destestable darnel of desperation. **1590** H. Barrow *Brief Discov.* 3 [Satan] sowing his darnel of errors and tares of discord amongst them. *a* **1640** J. Ball *Answ. to Can* ii. (1642) 12 A graine of good corne in a great deale of darnell.

attrib. **1868** Lowell *Under Willows* vi, No darnel fancy Might choke one useful blade in Puritan fields.

4. *attrib.*, and *Comb.*, as ***darnel-like*** adj.

1601 Holland *Pliny* II. 144 Darnell floure laid too, with Oxymell, cureth the gout. *c* **1620** Z. Boyd *Zion's Flowers* (1855) 73, I dizzy am as fed with Darnall seede. **1834** *Brit. Husb.* I. 511 *Festuca loliacea*, or darnel-like fescue.

darner ('dɑːnə(r)). [-er.]

1. One who darns.

1611 Cotgr., *Rentraieur*, a Seamster..or Dearner. **1837** Ht. Martineau *Soc. Amer.* III. 149 The humble stocking-darner. **1841** Lane *Arab. Nts.* III. 177 He took [the veil] forth from the shop, and gave it to the darner.

2. a. A darning-needle.

1882 in Caulfield & Saward *Dict. Needlework.* **1966** *Price List* (*Olney Amsden & Sons, Ltd.*) 29 Needles... Sharps, Crewels, Darners, etc.

b. A darning-machine.

1876 J. S. Ingram *Centenn. Exposition* x. 346 The Complete Darner. *Ibid.* 347 The top..could be removed for the insertion of a ball of darning-cotton into the swell of the 'darner'. **1897** *Sears, Roebuck Catal.* 324/1 The Magic Darner is a machine recently invented and patented for mending hosiery, silk, wool or cotton.

c. A darning-ball or similar device.

1895 *Montgomery Ward Catal.* 91/1 Egg Darners, with handle. **1909** *Daily Chron.* 25 May 9/1 Even the embroiderer who does not use a hoop will find it more convenient in working stockings to do the embroidery over a darner. **1966** *Price List* (*Olney Amsden & Sons, Ltd.*) 29 Wood Darner..1/6.

darnex, darnick, obs. forms of dornick¹.

darning ('dɑːnɪŋ), *vbl. sb.* [-ing¹.]

1. a. The action or process of filling up a hole in a fabric with thread or yarn in interwoven stitches; the result of such mending.

1611 Cotgr., *Rentraicture*..a dearning. **1720** *Lond. Gaz.* No. 5868/9, 1 long Muslin Apron..the middle flourished with Sprigs of true Darning. **1882** *Mrs. Raven's Tempt.* I. 211 Charity usually did her darnings and mendings in her own apartment. **1886** B. C. Saward in *Housewife* I. iv. 109/1 To understand grafting, patching, Swiss darning, ladder darning, and corner darning, as well as plain darning.

b. *fig.* (= 'Threading' one's way in and out.)

1881 Mrs. Holman Hunt *Childr. Jerus.* 114 Phœbe.. made her way by a darning process up to..the official dignitary.

c. Embroidering with darning-stitch; also = darning-stitch.

1882 Caulfeild & Saward *Dict. Needlework* 148/1 The embroidery is done in Satin stitch or in plain Darning. **1930** tr. *T. de Dillmont's Encycl. Needlework* 519 Close ground-work of darning and little wheels.

2. Articles darned or to be darned.

Mod. The week's darning lay on the table.

3. *Comb.*, as ***darning-cotton, wool, work***; **darning-ball, -last,** an egg-shaped or spherical piece of wood, ivory or other hard substance, over which a fabric is stretched while being darned; **darning-egg** = *darning-ball*; **darning-machine,** a machine for darning stockings, clothes, etc. (Knight *Dict. Mech.* Suppl. *a* 1884); **darning-needle,** (*a*) a long and stout needle used in darning; (*b*) (see *devil's darning-needle* s.v. devil *sb.* 25 b, c); **darning-stitch,** (*a*) a stitch used in darning which imitates the texture of the fabric darned; (*b*) a straight stitch used in embroidery to make a regular open-work pattern.

1811 Jane Austen *Let.* 18 Apr. (1952) 270 *She* is in want of chimney lights for Tuesday; —— & *I*, of an ounce of darning cotton. **1876** Darning-cotton [see darner 2 b]. **1897** *Sears, Roebuck Catal.* 335/3 Our woman's tool set consists of ..one pinking iron, one darning egg, [etc.]. **1925** E. Glasgow *Barren Ground* III. ii. 410 Dorinda..slipped her darning-egg into one of Nathan's socks. **1956** K. Hulme *Nun's Story* iv. 62 The lean self-abnegating face bent over a darning egg. **1848** Hor. Smith *Idler upon town* 54 This case ..containing two bodkins and a darning needle. **1881** C. C. Harrison *Woman's Handiwork* I. 27 Darning stitch is used to restore old embroideries. **1882** Caulfeild & Saward *Dict. Needlework* 148/2 Fillings for the centre of any designs that are not worked in Satin or Darning stitch. *Ibid.* 149/1 Darn the thick lines up and down in Point de Reprise or plain Darning stitch. **1934** M. Thomas *Dict. Embroidery Stitches* 72 Darning Stitch is really a long running or tacking stitch, the difference being that in darning used for decoration, only one thread of the material is picked up with each stitch. *Ibid.* 73 Darning Stitch..is also used in pattern darning. **1912** A. Bennett *Matador* 61 I've made this bouquet for you... You must excuse it being tied up with darning wool. **1932** D. C. Minter *Mod. Needlecraft* 178/2 Darning wool is better slightly finer than that of which the knitted garment was made. **1711** Shaftesb. *Charac.* (1737) III. 265 The gouty joints and darning-work..by which, complicated periods are so curiously strung, or hook'd on, one to another.

darnix, darnock, obs. forms of dornick¹.

daroga, darogha (də'rəʊgə). *Anglo-Ind.* Also 7 daruga, derega, droga, droger, 7–8 deroga, 8 darouga. [a. Pers. and Urdū *dārōghah*, contr. *drōghah* governor, overseer.] A governor, superintendent, chief officer, head of police or excise. Under the Mongols, the Governor of a province or city, but in later times gradually degraded.

1634 Sir T. Herbert *Trav.* (1638) 132 The Daraguad in person came. **1662** J. Davies tr. *Olearius' Voy. Ambass.* 232 The Baily, or Judge of the City, whom they call Daroga. **1753** Hanway *Trav.* (1762) II. xv. ii. 413 Orders being given to the darougas..not to let any one pass. **1815** Elphinstone *Caubul* (1842) II. 265 The Darogha of the Bazars fixed prices, and superintends weights and measures. **1892** *Daily News* 19 July 7/3 The official..sent it off to Gwalior by a daroga.

darr, obs. form of dare *v.*¹

darraign, -rain(e, -rayne, -rein(e, -reyne, etc., var. of deraign *Obs.*

† **da'rrein,** *a. Old Law.* [a. OF. *darrain, derrein* (still in various F. dialects *dérain, darain*, etc. = F. *dernier*):—late L. **de-retrānus* hinder, f. *de retro* (whence F. *derrière*) behind.]

Last, ultimate, final; = dernier. ***darrein presentment***: the last presentation to an ecclesiastical benefice (as a proof of the right to present): see quot. 1760. ***darrein resort***: = *dernier ressort.*

[**1292** Britton IV. i, De assise de Dreyn Present. *Ibid*, IV. xii. §5 Si le derreyn verdit soit contrarie al premer.] **1555** *Act 1 Mary* 2nd Sess. c. 5 Any writ of assise of darren presentment. **1672** W. de Britaine *Interest Eng. Dutch War* 9 War is the darrein resort of every wise and good Prince. **1760** Burn *Eccl. Law* I. 26 Darrein presentment is a writ which lieth, where a man or his ancestor hath presented a clerk to a church, and afterwards (the church becoming void by the death of the said clerk or otherwise) a stranger presenteth his clerk to the same church, in disturbance of him who had last..presented. **1833** *Act 3–4 Will. IV*, c. 27 §36 And be it further enacted, That no..Writ of Assize of novel disseisin..Darrein-presentment..or Mort d'ancestor ..shall be brought after the Thirty-first Day of December One thousand eight hundred and thirty-four.

darse, obs. var. of dace, a fish.

‖ **darshan** ('dɑːʃən). [ad. Hindi *darśan*, f. Skr. *darśana* view, f. *darś* to see.] The sight of an august or holy personage.

1920 M. K. Gandhi in *Young India* 20 Oct. 3/1 In vain did Mrs. Gandhi and others plead with the crowds for self-control and silence... The answer was that they had come many miles to have *darshan* and *darshan* they must have. **1947** J. P. Chander *Teachings of Mahatma Gandhi* 140 *Darshan.* Love that is satisfied with touching the feet of its hero and making noise at him is likely to become parasitical. **1960** Koestler *Lotus & Robot* I. v. 152 To be in the mere presence of the guru conveys darshan, a spiritual enrichment and an intellectual lesson which need not be conveyed in words. **1962** *Times* 9 Oct. 9/1 Many of these people come simply to have *darshan* of the President. **1964** V. Naipaul *Area of Darkness* x. 251 She gave *darshan*—made an appearance, offered a sight of herself—only on important anniversaries. **1971** *Illustr. Weekly India* 4 Apr. 11/1 A Khatri cannot have *darshan* of the Kul Devi before *dev kaj. Ibid.* 23/2 An old man who only wanted to touch his feet and receive darshan was nearly killed by a lathi.

darst(e, obs. pa. indic. of dare *v.*¹

dart (dɑːt), *sb.* Also 4–6 darte, 7 *Sc.* dairt. [a. OF. *dart*, accus. of *darz, dars.* in 15th c. *dard* = Pr. *dart*, Sp. and It. *dardo.*]

1. a. A pointed missile weapon thrown by the hand; a light spear or javelin; also applied to pointed missiles in general, including arrows, etc.

c **1314** *Guy Warw.* (A.) 3488 Launces, swerdes, and dartes. *c* **1330** R. Brunne *Chron.* (1810) 178 A darte was schot to þem, bot non wist who it schete. *c* **1400** *Destr. Troy* 10548 Parys cast at the kyng..þre darttes. **1535** Coverdale *Prov.* xxvi. 18 As one shuteth deadly arowes and dartes. **1662** J. Davies tr. *Mandelslo's Trav.* II. 156 They use no other Arms than the Dart, (which they cast..dexterously). **1718** Pope *Iliad* IV. 511 The sounding darts in iron tempests flew. **1840** Thirlwall *Greece* VII. 7 After a short siege, he was killed by a dart from an engine.

b. *fig.*

1382 Wyclif *Eph.* vi. 16 The firy dartis of the worste enmye. **1509** Hawes *Past. Pleas.* XLI. i, Deth with his darte arest me sodenly. **1664** Evelyn *Kal. Hort.* (1729) 201 The too parching Darts of the Sun. **1764** Goldsm. *Trav.* 231 Love's and friendship's finely pointed dart. *a* **1839** Praed *Poems* (1864) II. 259 The lightning's vivid dart.

c. *transf.* A kind of eel-spear (see quot. 1883); a needle-shaped piece of caustic used in surgery; †a representation of a dart or arrow used to mark direction on a drawing, etc. (*obs.*); the tongue or spear of flame produced by a blowpipe.

1784 *Specif. Watt's Patent* No. 1432. 9 The direction of motion of these..wheels is shown by the darts. **1816** Accum *Chem. Tests* (1818) 174 Expose it to the flame of a blowpipe dart. **1876** tr. *Ziemssen's Cycl. Med.* IV. 80 Darts of equal parts of iodine and iodide of potassium prepared with dextrine and made as fine as Carlsbad needles, are used.. with success in the treatment of..hypertrophied tonsils. **1883** G. C. Davies *Norfolk Broads* xxxi. (1884) 244 The spear in use on the Ant and Thurne is the dart, and is made with a cross-piece, with barbed spikes set in it like the teeth of a rake.

d. A light pointed missile thrown at a target in the game called *darts.* Also *attrib.* and *Comb.*

1901 *Stationer, Printer*, etc. 1 June 322 Ring Boards. Dart Boards. Parlour Cricket. **1916** H. G. Wells *Mr. Britling* I. v. §11 Dart-throwing and ring-throwing stalls. **1924** B. Gilbert *Bly Market* 18 Coconut Saloons. Shooting Galleries. Dart-Saloons. *Ibid.* 419 Darts, darts, darts, penny a dart. Over 50 wins the prize... No skill needed. **1929** *B'ham Post* 12 Jan., A peculiar thing I noticed was that two darts, such as they use in public-houses, were near the body. **1941** 'G. Orwell' *Lion & Unicorn* 15 A nation of stamp-collectors, pigeon-fanciers..coupon-snippers, darts-players. **1958** *Times* 29 Apr. p. x/4 In the past 30 years darts has become the most important of all public house games. *Ibid.* p. x/5 The darts themselves have changed during the past 20 years, from the comparatively light, wooden-stemmed type with feather flights to a shorter kind with much heavier metal body carrying plastic flights.

2. *Zool.* An organ resembling a dart: *spec.* **a.** The sting of a venomous insect, scorpion, etc., or that part which pierces the skin. **b.** A dart-like organ in some gastropods, having an excitatory function (see *dart-sac* in 8).

1665 HOOKE *Microgr.* 163 The Sting of a Bee..I could most plainly perceive..to contain in it, both a Sword or Dart, and the poisonous liquor that causes the pain. **1768** BEATTIE *Minstr.* I. x, It poisons like a scorpion's dart. **1860** HAWTHORNE *Marb. Faun* xx, His [a demon's] scaly tail, with a poisonous dart at the end of it! **1861** HULME tr. *Moquin-Tandon* II. III. ii. 84 Their [snails'] generative organs.. contain a copulative pouch, the dart enclosed in a sac. **1888** ROLLESTON & JACKSON *Anim. Life* 118. *Ibid.* 481 Some *Pulmonata* and certain species of *Doris* possess a dart, attached in the former to the female, in the latter to the male, duct.

3. *Dress-making.* A seam joining the two edges left by cutting a gore in any stuff.

1884 *Dress Cutting Assoc. Circular*, To sew the Darts (or Breast Plaits) commence at the top, holding both edges even for one inch. **1893** *Weldon's Ladies' Jrnl.* XIV. 252/3 The shape is fitted with hip darts.

4. A name for the snake-like lizards of the genus *Acontias* (formerly supposed to be venomous serpents) from their habit of darting upon their prey; = *dart-serpent*, *-snake* (see 8).

1591 PERCIVALL. *Sp. Dict.*, *Tiro*, a caste, dart, also a serpent called a dart..*Acontias.* **1607** TOPSELL *Serpents* (1608) 696. **1635** SWAN *Spec. M.* (1670) 440 The Dart taketh his name from his swift darting or leaping upon a man to wound and kill him.

†**5. a.** The fish otherwise called DACE or DARE.

1655 MOUFET & BENNET *Health's Improv.* (1746) 271 Daces or Darts, or Dares, be of..good Nourishment.

b. Short for *dart-moth*: see 8.

6. a. [f. the vb.] The act of darting; a sudden rapid motion.

1721 R. BRADLEY *Wks. Nat.* 71 The first Dart they make at any thing. *c* **1850** *Arab. Nts.* (Rtldg.) 306 A bird made a sudden dart from the air upon it. **1867** TROLLOPE *Chron. Barset* II. li. 87 She rose quickly..and prepared herself for a dart at the door.

b. The act of casting a dart or pointed missile; the range within which it may be thrown.

1839 T. BEALE *Sperm Whale* 180 With their harpoons held above their heads ready for the dart. *Ibid.* 182 The whale continuing to descend the moment either of the boats got within dart of him.

7. *slang* (chiefly *Austral.*). Plan, aim, scheme. Also, (one's) fancy or favourite.

1882 *Sydney Slang Dict.* 3 Dart, object of attraction, or enticing thing or event, or a set purpose. **1887** FARRELL *How he died* 20 Whose 'dart' was to appear the justest steward that ever hiked a plate round. **1889** BOLDREWOOD *Robbery under Arms* (1890) 29 The great dart is to keep the young stock away from their mothers until they forget one another. **1890** *Melbourne Argus* 9 Aug. 4/2 When I told them of my 'dart' some were contemptuous. **1895** in Morris *Austral Eng.* (1898) 115 'Fresh strawberries eh!—that's my dart,' says the bushman when he sees the fruit lunch in Collins-street. **1914** JOYCE *Dubliners* 112 Suddenly..he thought of Terry Kelly's pawn-office... That was the dart! Why didn't he think of it sooner?

8. *Comb.*, as ***dart-caster***; ***dart-holding***, ***-shaped***, ***-wounded*** adjs.; **dart-moth**, a moth of the genus *Agrotis*, so called from a mark on the fore wing; **dart-sac**, a hollow structure connected with the generative organs of some gastropods, from which the darts (2 b) are ejected; **dart-serpent**, **dart-snake**, a snake-like lizard of the genus *Acontias* (= DART 4).

1550 NICOLLS *Thucyd.* 118 (R.) A certaine number of slingers and *dart-casters. **1647** H. MORE *Song of Soul* III. lxviii, No fear of Death's *dart-holding hand. **1819** G. SAMOUELLE *Entomol. Compend.* Index, *Dart-moths. **1848** *Proc. Berw. Nat. Club* II. 329 *Agrotis segetum* (the Dart Moth), and *Agrotis exclamationis* (the Heart and Dart Moth). **1870** ROLLESTON *Anim. Life.* 49 A cylindrical hollow muscular organ, the *dart-sac. **1607** TOPSELL *Serpents* (1653) 697 Suddenly there came one of these *Dart-serpents out of the tree, and wounded him. **1745** P. THOMAS *Jrnl. Anson's Voy.* 338 (*C. Good Hope*) The Eye-Serpent..is also call'd sometimes the *Dart-Serpent*, from its darting or shooting himself forward with great swiftness. **1835–6** TODD *Cycl. Anat.* I. 203/1 *Dart-shaped mandibles. **1688** J. CLAYTON in *Phil. Trans.* XVIII. 135 This I think may..be referred to the *Dart-Snakes. **1843** J. DAYMAN tr. *Dante's Inferno* XXIV. 154 Though puffsnake, dartsnake, watersnake, she [Libya] boast. *a* **1400–50** *Alexander* 225 Hire bewte bitis in his brest..as he ware *dart-wondid.

dart (dɑːt), *v.* [f. DART *sb.*: cf. F. *darder* (15th c.) from *dard.*]

†**1.** *trans.* To pierce with a dart or other pointed weapon; to spear, transfix. Also *fig. Obs.*

c **1374** CHAUCER *Troylus* IV. 212 As the wilde bole.. ydarted to the herte. **1557** *Tottell's Misc.* (Arb.) 234 Till death shall darte him for to dye. **1624** CAPT. SMITH *Virginia* II. 32 Staues like vnto Iauelins headed with bone. With these they dart fish swimming in the water. **1632** LITHGOW *Trav.* x. 489 When death..had darted King Iames of matchlesse memory. **1748** RICHARDSON *Clarissa* Wks. 1883 VI. 159 She..darts dead at once even the embryo hopes of an encroaching lover. **1752** BOND in *Phil. Trans.* XLVII. 431 [They] are never sure of darting a whale, till they are within a yard.

2. To throw, cast, shoot (a dart or other missile).

1580 NORTH *Plutarch* (1676) 770 Such other Iauelins as the Romans darted at them. **1662** J. DAVIES tr. *Mandelslo's Trav.* 51 A kind of long headed Pike, which they dart with great exactness. **1770** LANGHORNE *Plutarch* (1879) I. 426/1 He bound it fast to a javelin, and darted it over. **1839** T. BEALE *Sperm Whale* 161 They..sometimes get near enough to dart the harpoon.

3. *transf.* and *fig.* To send forth, or emit, suddenly and sharply; to shoot out; to cast (a glance) quickly and keenly.

1592 SHAKS. *Ven. & Ad.* 196 Thine eye darts forth the fire that burneth me. **1596** —— *Tam. Shr.* v. ii. 137 Dart not scornefull glances from those eies. **1634** SIR T. HERBERT *Trav.* (1638) 171 The Sunne darted his outragious beames so full upon us. **1676** *Phil. Trans.* XI. 680 (*Fire engine*) The water issuing out of the tube that darts it. **1705** BOSMAN *Guinea* (1721) 246 The Camelion..when a Fly comes in his way..darts out his Tongue with utmost Swiftness. **1784** COWPER *Task* II. 720 His gentle eye Grew stern, and darted a severe rebuke. **1835–6** TODD *Cycl. Anat.* I. 272/1 Darting the bill with sudden velocity into the water. **1852** THACKERAY *Esmond* I. viii, Her eyes..darted flashes of anger as she spoke.

4. *intr.* To throw a dart or other missile.

1530 PALSGR. 506/2 These Yrisshe men darte best, or throwe a darte best of all men. **1614** RALEIGH *Hist. World* II. 370 One Laodocus in darting. **1662** J. DAVIES tr. *Olearius' Voy. Ambass.* 72 They pursue her [the whale] and dart two or three times more at her.

5. To move like a dart; to spring or start with a sudden rapid motion; to shoot. Also *fig.*

1619 FLETCHER *False One* II. i, Destructions darting from their looks. **1781** GIBBON *Decl. & F.* III. I. 119 They dart away with the swiftness of the wind. **1794** MRS. RADCLIFFE *Myst. Udolpho* xxvi, A thousand vague fears darted athwart her mind. **1852** MRS. STOWE *Uncle Tom's C.* xiii, 'No, no', said little Ruth, darting up. **1885** *Spectator* 18 July 950/1 A deer darts out of the copse. **1886** RUSKIN *Præterita* I. 296 The road got level again as it darted away towards Geneva.

†**dartars.** *Obs.* Also **darters.** [Corruption of F. *dartre*: see DARTRE.] A disease of sheep: see quots.

1580 *Well of Woman Hill, Aberdeen* A iv a, It perfytlie curis the exteriour scabbis, wyldefyre, darteris, and vther filthines of the skyn. **1587** MASCALL *Govt. Cattle, Sheepe* (1627) 221 There is..a certaine scab that runnes on the chinne which is commonly called of the shepheards the dartars. **1726** *Dict. Rust.* (ed. 3), *Chin-scab*, a Scabby Disease in Sheep..commonly call'd The Darters. **1741** *Compl. Fam. Piece* III. 496 There is a certain Scab on the Chin of Lambs at some Seasons, occasioned by their feeding on Grass covered with Dew; it is called by the Shepherds the Dartars; which will kill a Lamb if not stopt.

darted (ˈdɑːtɪd), *ppl. a.* [f. DART *v.* + -ED[1].]

†**1.** Pierced with, or as with, a dart; punctured.

c **1374** [see DART *v.* 1]. **1622** H. SYDENHAM *Serm. Sol. Occ.* II. (1637) 161 With darted bosomes and imbalmed hearts. **1763** COLLINSON in *Phil. Trans.* LIV. 67 Several darted twigs [i.e. pierced by insects] were..carefully examined, and opened.

2. Thrown or shot as a dart; sent or put forth suddenly and rapidly.

1669 DRYDEN *Tyran. Love* IV. i, A darted Mandate came From that great Will which moves this mighty Frame. **1672** —— *Conq. Gran.* I. i, The darted Cane. *a* **1711** KEN *Edmund* Poet. Wks. 1721 II. 314 Darted Pray'r returns for darted Spight. **1859** TENNYSON *Vivien* 935 With darted spikes and splinters.

darter (ˈdɑːtə(r)). [f. DART *v.* + -ER[1].]

1. a. One who throws or shoots darts; a soldier armed with a dart.

1565–73 COOPER *Thesaurus* s.v. *Certus*, *Iaculis certus*, a sure and cunning darter. **1580** NORTH *Plutarch* (1676) 391 Appointing his Archers and Darters to hurl..their Darts.. to the tops of the Houses. *a* **1656** USSHER *Ann.* (1658) 730 Having a strong guard of darters and slingers. **1820** EDGEWORTH *Mem.* I. 199 He was called Jack the Darter. He threw his darts..to an amazing height. **1849** GROTE *Greece* II. liii. VI. 520 To organise either darters or slingers.

†**b.** A harpooner. *Obs.*

1724 R. FALCONER *Voy.* (1769) 8 The wounded Fish [dolphin] immediately flounces..which the Darter observes, giving him Rope and Play.

2. A person or animal that darts or moves swiftly.

1818 BYRON *Ch. Har.* IV. lxvii, The finny darter with the glittering scales.

†**3.** = DART *sb.* 4, dart-snake. *Obs.*

1607 TOPSELL *Serpents* (1608) 696 Certain [serpents] in Hungary..do leap upon men, as these darters do. **1820** W. TOOKE tr. *Lucian* I. 96 Innumerable asps..darters, cow-suckers and toads.

4. a. English name of the genus *Plotus* or family *Plotidæ* of web-footed birds of the pelican tribe, with long neck and small head, found in parts of tropical Africa and America, and in Australia; so called from their way of darting on their prey.

1825 GORE tr. *Blumenbach's Nat. Hist.* v. 126 *Anhinga*, the Darter. P. ventre albo. **1881** MANVILLE FENN *Off to Wilds* xxx. (1888) 210 That curious water-bird, the darter, swimming with its body nearly submerged, and its long, snaky neck, ready to dart its keen bill with almost lightning rapidity at the tiny fish upon which it fed.

b. *pl.* The order *Jaculatores* in Macgillivray's classification of birds, comprising the kingfishers, bee-eaters, and jacamars; from their habit of darting upon their prey.

5. A name for various fishes; *esp.* the small fresh-water fishes constituting the N. American subfamily *Etheostominæ* of the family *Percidæ*, which dart from their retreats when disturbed.

1842 J. E. DEKAY *Zool. N.Y.* IV. 20 The Tessellated Darter. *Bolesoma tessellatum*... It is usually seen at the bottom of clear springs or streams, lying for a while perfectly still, and then suddenly darts off with great velocity at its prey. This habit has acquired for it the popular name of Darter. **1884** GOODE *Fisheries of U.S.* 417 Darters are found in all fresh waters of the United States east of the Rocky Mountains. **1887** C. C. ABBOTT *Waste-Land Wand.* vii. 210 There was a goodly company of little darters or etheostomoids..all of one species—the common tessellated darter.

darting (ˈdɑːtɪŋ), *vbl. sb.* [-ING[1].] The action of the verb DART, q.v.; throwing or shooting of darts, etc.; rapid movement as of a dart, etc.

1565–73 COOPER *Thesaurus*, *Campus iaculatorius*, a fielde where men exercise darting. **1626** BACON *Sylva* §944 Sudden Glances, and Dartings of the Eye. **1694** *Acc. Sev. Late Voy.* II. (1711) 220 Their Fishing ordinarily is darting, their Darts are long, strongly barbed. **1756** MOUNSEY in *Phil. Trans.* I. 21 Pain on the stomach..with dartings inwardly. **1839** T. BEALE *Sperm Whale* 161 They then make use of the lance either by darting or thrusting.

ˈ**darting,** *ppl. a.* [-ING[2].] That darts (see the verb).

1. *trans.* Shooting darts; shooting or casting forth like a dart.

1606 SHAKS. *Ant. & Cl.* III. i. 1 Now darting Parthya art thou stroke. **1634** MILTON *Comus* 753 Love-darting eyes. *c* **1825** LONGF. *Burial of Minnisink* vii, With darting eye and nostril spread.

2. *intr.* Moving or shooting swiftly like a dart.

1664 EVELYN *Kal. Hort.* (1729) 197 The sudden darting Heat of the Sun. **1859** TENNYSON *Enid* 1318 They vanish'd panic-stricken, like a shoal Of darting fish.

Hence ˈ**dartingly** *adv.*, ˈ**dartingness.**

1674 N. FAIRFAX *Bulk & Selv.* 129 When we give a dartingness to outcasts [i.e. missiles]. **1846** WORCESTER, *Dartingly.*

dartle (ˈdɑːt(ə)l), *v. rare.* [A modern dim. and iterative of DART *v.*: cf. *sparkle.*] To dart or shoot forth repeatedly (*trans.* and *intr.*).

1855 BROWNING *My Star*, My star that dartles the red and the blue. **1893** *Athenæum* 18 Mar. 346/2 He..showed me the chestnut logs which spit and dartle, the birch logs which smoke and moulder.

dartless, *a.* Without a dart.

1769 S. PATERSON *Another Trav.* II. 184.

ˈ**dartman.** A soldier armed with a dart.

1605 SYLVESTER *Du Bartas* II. iii. *Vocation* 304 Without an aime the Dart-man darts his speare. **1838** THIRLWALL *Greece* III. xix. 98 Archers and dartmen.

Dartmoor (ˈdɑːtmʊə(r), -mɔə(r)). Name of a district in Devonshire, applied *attrib.* (also *ellipt.*) to special breeds of ponies and sheep produced there.

1831 YOUATT *Horse* iv. 59 The Dartmoor pony is larger than the Exmoor, and, if possible, uglier. **1837** —— *Sheep* vii. 252 The South Downs never succeeded well on the heath-clad hills of the Dartmoor sheep. **1902** *Encycl. Brit.* XXV. 189/2 Native ponies include those variously known as English, New Forest, Exmoor, Dartmoor. *Ibid.* 194/2 The Dartmoor is a hornless, longwool, white-fleeced sheep. **1906** *Westm. Gaz.* 24 Sept. 8/1 An intelligent Dartmoor, that would follow its master like a dog. **1937** HULL & WHITLOCK *Far-Distant Oxus* i. 24 In the last stall a tiny shaggy Dartmoor butted her with his head. **1955** *Times* 6 July 7/3 Miss Calmady-Hamlyn, of Buckfast, had both male and female champions in the Dartmoor pony classes for the second year running. **1970** *Observer* (Colour Suppl.) 26 Apr. 36/2 Dartmoors look rather like shaggy dogs.

b. Special Combs. **Dartmoor-clip** *v.* [*Dartmoor*, name of the convict prison near Princetown], to cut (a person's) hair very short as for a convict; **Dartmoor crop**, hair so cut; **Dartmoor granite** (see quot.).

1932 KIPLING *Limits & Renewals* 197 He was run round to the barber an' Dartmoor-clipped for wearin' oily and indecent appendages. **1930** E. RAYMOND *Jesting Army* I. i. 11 He was the only officer on the ship with his hair shaved down to his skull in what was known as the 'Dartmoor Crop'. **1904** GOODCHILD & TWENEY *Technol. & Sci. Dict.* 74/2 *Dartmoor Granite*, a greyish granite used in large work —*e.g.* London Bridge.

dartoid (ˈdɑːtɔɪd), *a. Anat.* [mod. f. Gr. δαρτ-ός DARTOS + -OID.] Like or of the nature of the dartos.

1872 F. G. THOMAS *Dis. Women* (ed. 3) 635 The dartoid sacs of the labia majora. **1890** THANE *Ellis' Anat.* (ed. 11) 445 The subcutaneous layer in the scrotum..is named the dartoid tissue.

‖**dartos** (ˈdɑːtɒs). *Anat.* [mod. a. Gr. δαρτός flayed, excoriated, verbal adj. of δείρειν to flay.] The layer of connective and unstriped muscular tissue immediately beneath the skin of the scrotum.

1634 T. JOHNSON *Parey's Chirurg.* 119 The epididymis or dartos. **1875** FLINT *Phys. Man* V. 314 A loose, reddish, contractile tissue, called the dartos, which forms two distinct sacs, one enveloping each testicle.

dartre (ˈdɑːtə(r)). [F. *dartre*, of doubtful etymology: see Diez, Littré, and *Dict. des Sciences Med.* XXV. 648. For an earlier adoption of the word into Eng., see DARTARS.] A vague generic name for various skin diseases, *esp.* herpes; also, a scab or the like formed in such diseases.

1829 BATEMAN *Synops. Cutan. Dis.* (ed. 7) Pref. 15 The dartres..are said to be of seven kinds. **1834** GOOD *Study Med.* (ed. 4) IV. 481 The proper meaning of dartre, or tetter, is herpes. **1843** Sir C. Scudamore *Med. Visit Gräfenberg* 72 Boils and 'dartres' formed near the seat of pain.

dartrous ('dɑːtrəs), *a.* [ad. F. *dartreux*, f. *dartre*: see prec.] Pertaining to or of the nature of dartre: applied to a peculiar diathesis.

1839–47 Todd *Cycl. Anat.* III. 190/2 Dartrous diseases of the skin. **1831** Piffard *Therap. Skin* 126 The rheumic or dartrous diathesis, as it is called in France, is the predisposing cause, I believe, of eczema, psoriasis, and pityriasis.

'dartsman. [f. *dart's.*] = dartman.

1770 J. Ross *Epitaph on Friend* 11 (MS.) Death—dread dartsman!.. May strike thee sudden in life's blooming May.

darvis, darvish, obs. forms of dervish.

Darwin ('dɑːwɪn). The name of Charles *Darwin* (see Darwinian *a.* 2), used *attrib.* (also *ellipt.*) to designate a race of tulips with tall stems and large self-coloured flowers.

1889 F. Darwin *Let.* 13 Apr. in E. H. Krelage *Drie Eeuwen Bloembollenexport* (1946) II. 553 Allow me to thank you for your courteous note in which you tell me of your wish to name after my father a new strain of tulips... I hope I shall see the 'Darwin Tulips' at Paris. **1891** *Gardeners' Chron.* 4 July 10/3 The Darwin Tulips are of Flemish origin. *a* **1916** H. H. Munro *Toys of Peace* (1919) 237 The Darwin tulips haven't survived the fact that most of the cats of the neighbourhood held a parliament in the middle of the tulip bed. **1922** F. M. Ford *Let.* 24 Oct. (1965) 145, 200 Darwin tulips. **1969** Hay & Synge *Dict. Garden Plants* 368/2 The old tulips of the Dutch flower painters.. are usually not so vigorous as the Darwins or Darwin hybrids.

b. Used in the possessive: see Darwinian *a.* 3.

Darwinian (dɑː'wɪnɪən), *a.* (*sb.*) [f. proper name *Darwin* + -ian.]

1. Of or pertaining to Erasmus Darwin (1731–1802), and to his speculations or poetical style.

1794 W. B. Stevens *Jrnl.* 3 June (1965) ii. 161 The lines are truly Darwinian. **1797** Scott *Lett.* (1932) I. 62, I do not for example, think quite so severely of the Darwinian style, as to deem it utterly inconsistent with the Ballad. **1804** *Edin. Rev.* July 297 One objection.. to the Darwinian modulation with which Mr. Sotheby's versification is infected. **1842** Mrs. Browning *Bk. of Poets* Wks. 1890 V. 279 A broad gulf between his [Wordsworth's] descriptive poetry and that of the Darwinian painter-poet school. **1950** H. Darbishire *Wordsworth* i. 17 He is balancing his lines in the Darwinian manner with ornamental epithets.

2. a. Of or pertaining to the celebrated naturalist Charles Darwin (grandson of Erasmus Darwin, 1809–82), and to his scientific views or observations, *esp.* his theory of the evolution of species: see Darwinism 2.

1860 T. H. Huxley in *Westm. Rev.* Apr. 566 The Darwinian hypothesis has the merit of being eminently simple and comprehensible. **1866** K. Stanley *Jrnl.* 22 Aug. in B. & P. Russell *Amberley Papers* (1937) I. 525 It was a very fine address, Darwinean in principle. **1867** (*title*) The Darwinian Theory of the Transmutation of Species. **1881** *Knowledge* 9 Dec. 128/1 The principles which will guide us in the choice of subjects will be Darwinian—to wit, natural selection and the survival of the fittest. **1884** W. S. Gilbert *Princess Ida* 11, Darwinian Man, though well-behaved, At best is only a monkey shaved! **1971** M. S. Howard *Jonathan Cape* 313 The logical conclusions of Darwinian theory had yet to be drawn in simple terms to demonstrate the link between animal behaviour patterns and those of human society.

b. as *sb.* A follower of Charles Darwin; one who accepts the Darwinian theory. (In quot. 1809, the sense is 'a follower of Erasmus Darwin'.)

1809 *Monthly Pantheon* Apr. 262 Hear this, ye.. Darwinians. **1869** A. R. Wallace *Malay Archip.* I. iv. 61 This is.. the first instance known of a 'flying frog', and it is very interesting to Darwinians. **1871** Huxley *Crit. & Addresses* (1873) 251 Mr. Mivart is less of a Darwinian than Mr. Wallace, for he has less faith in the power of natural selection. **1881** *Athenæum* 29 Oct. 566/1 Mr. Balfour is a practical Darwinian. **1915** A. Huxley *Let.* Aug. (1969) 76 Laforgue was also a hearty Darwinian and liked the thought of being a developed beast.

3. Darwinian tubercle, a projection sometimes present on the edge of the human external ear (see quots.), believed by some scientists to be a relic of the pointed ear of quadrupeds; also called ***Darwin's tubercule, Darwin's peak.***

1890 Billings *Med. Dict.*, *Darwinian tubercle*.., eminence on edge of helix of external ear, believed to correspond with end of pointed ear of apes, and therefore considered a vestige. **1920** I. F. & W. D. Henderson *Dict. Sci. Terms* 69/2 *Darwinian tubercle*, the slight prominence on the helix near the point where it bends downwards. **1957** *Encycl. Brit.* VII. 823/2 Round the margin [of the ear] in its upper three-quarters is a rim called helix, in which is often seen a little prominence known as Darwin's tubercle, representing the folded-over apex of a prick-eared ancestor.

Dar'winianism. [f. prec. + -ism.]

†**1.** Imitation of the style of Erasmus Darwin (see prec. 1). *Obs.* (*nonce-use.*)

1804 *Edin. Rev.* July 297 We can substantiate our charge of Darwinianism.

2. The Darwinian theory of evolution; = Darwinism 2; also, a Darwinian idiom or phrase.

1883 E. M. Underdown in *N. & Q.* 13 Oct. 284/2, I know not if any one.. has noticed a literary ancestor, to use a Darwinianism, for that of Francis I after Pavia. **1893** J. H. Stirling (*title*), Darwinianism: Workmen and Work.

Dar'winical, *a.* *rare*⁻⁰. = Darwinian 2. Hence **Dar'winically** *adv.*

1864 Huxley *Lay Serm.* (1870) 334 It is one thing to say, Darwinically, that every detail observed in an animal's structure is of use to it [etc.].

Darwinism ('dɑːwɪnɪz(ə)m). [-ism.]

†**1.** The doctrine or hypothesis of Erasmus Darwin. *Obs.* (*nonce-use.*)

1856 B. W. Richardson *Life T. Sopwith* (1891) 256 Mr. Sopwith described the hypothesis of the development of living things from a primordial centre. That, said Reade, is rank Darwinism. It was the first time I had heard that word used.. it had reference to Erasmus Darwin.

2. The biological theory of Charles Darwin concerning the evolution of species, etc., set forth especially in his works entitled 'The Origin of Species by means of Natural Selection, or the preservation of favoured races in the struggle for life' (1859), and 'The Descent of Man and Selection in relation to Sex' (1871).

1864 T. H. Huxley in *Nat. Hist. Rev.* Oct. 567 What we may term the philosophical position of Darwinism. **1871** *Athenæum* 15 July 84 It is impossible to reconcile the Doctors of the Church with the Doctors of Darwinism. **1876** Ray Lankester tr. *Haeckel's Hist. Creation* I. 1 The scientific theory.. commonly called.. Darwinism, is only a small fragment of a far more comprehensive doctrine. **1889** A. R. Wallace (*title*), Darwinism, An exposition of the theory of Natural Selection with some of its applications.

So **'Darwinist**, a follower of Darwin, a Darwinian. **Darwi'nistic** *a.*, of or pertaining to Darwinism. **'Darwinize** *v.*, to speculate or theorize after the manner of (Erasmus or Charles) Darwin; also *trans.*; so **'Darwinized** *ppl. a.*

1883 *Sci. & Lit. Gossip* I. 79 Interesting to every sincere Darwinist. **1875** tr. *Schmidt's Desc. & Darw.* 292 Decisive in favour of Darwinistic views. **1882** *Athenæum* 27 May 663/2 In connexion with Darwinistic explanations of ends. **1880** *Nature* XXI. 246 Coleridge invented the term 'Darwinising' to express his contempt for the speculations of the elder Darwin. **1886** *Contemp. Rev.* Sept. 435 Darwinizing sociologists. **1920** G. B. Shaw in *Public Opinion* 13 Aug. 160/2 It has restored faith in Providence to a Darwinised world. **1929** Blunden *Nature in Eng. Lit.* 14 The great mind which compares and sifts evidence until a new *De Rerum Natura* darwinizes us.

Darwinite ('dɑːwɪnaɪt), *sb.*¹ (*a.*) [-ite.]

A. *sb.* A follower of Charles Darwin; a Darwinian.

1862 *Illust. Lond. News* XLI. 41/1 Here are Darwinites.. reviving the doctrine of Lord Monboddo that men and monkeys are of the same stock. **1885** *Athenæum* 8 Aug. 171/2 A wave of reaction against what we may term the ultra-Darwinism of the Darwinites.

B. *adj.* = Darwinian 2.

1867 Kingsley *Let.* in *Life* xxii. (1883) 280 Can you tell me where I can find any Darwinite lore about the development of birds?

'darwinite, *sb.*² *Min.* [Named by Forbes 1861 after Chas. Darwin: see -ite.] A synonym of whitneyite.

1861 in Bristow *Gloss. Min.* 104.

dary, obs. form of dairy.

‖**das** (das). Also **dasse.** [Du. *das* = Ger. *dachs*, OHG. *dahs*:—WGer. **þahs*, whence also med.L. *taxus* badger. In sense 1 retained by Caxton in his English version of Reynard; in sense 2 belonging to the Dutch of South Africa.]

†**1.** A badger. *Obs.*

1481 Caxton *Reynard* iv. (Arb.) 7 Tho spack Grymbart the dasse. *Ibid.* xvii. 39 The beres, the foxes, the cattes and the dassen.

2. The daman or rock-badger of the Cape.

1786 Sparrman *Voy. Cape G.H.* 309 Those little animals which.. by the colonists are called dasses or badgers. **1838** W. H. R. Read in *Penny Cycl.* XII. 419 (s.v. *Hyrax*) Its name at the Cape is the Dasse, which is, I believe, the Dutch for a badger. **1884** Wood in *Sunday Mag.* Nov. 719/1 The most successful Das hunter.

†**dasart.** *Obs. rare.* [f. *dase*, daze *v.* + -ard: cf. MDu. *dasaert* (Oudemans), in Kilian *daesaerd* a fool.] A dazed, stupefied, or inert person; a dullard; = dasiberd, dastard 1.

a **1400** *Minor Poems Vernon MS.* 333 Ouur-al maiȝt þou comen and go, Whon a Moppe dasart schal not so.

†**dascan,** *v.* *Sc. Obs.* Also **daskan, dascon.** [perh. for descant.] To ponder, consider.

c **1579** Montgomerie *Navigatioun* 227 They daskand farther:—What if the Quene war deid? *a* **1600** Burel in Watson *Coll. Sc. Poems* II. 45 (Jam.) Than did I dascan with my sell, Quhidder to heuin or unto hell, Thir persouns suld pertene. **1632** Lithgow *Trav.* vii. 328 To dascon this, remarke, when they set land, Some this, some that, doe gesse, this Hill, that Cape.

dase, obs. form of dace, daze.

‖**Dasein** ('dazaɪn). *Philos.* Also 9 **Daseyn.** [G., f. *da* there + *sein* being, a favourite word of Goethe's.] **a.** In Hegelian philosophy: existence, determinate being. **b.** In existentialism, esp. that of Heidegger and Jaspers: human existence, the being of man-in-the-world.

1846 J. D. Morell *Hist. Philos.* II. v. 141 This may appear clearer to the German scholar, if we say in Hegel's language, that *Sein* and *Nichts* form *Daseyn*. **1874** W. Wallace *Logic of Hegel* Proleg. p. clxxx, To bring a thing into *Daseyn* is to give it definite being. **1938** G. Reavey tr. *Berdyaev's Solitude & Society* ii. 56 Heidegger speaks with greater authority of the *Dasein* than of existence itself. **1956** F. Copleston *Contemp. Philos.* x. 160 As an empirical being which is 'there',.. I am *Dasein*, object.

dasel(l, obs. form of dazzle.

dasewe: see daswen *v. Obs.*

dasey, obs. form of daisy *sb.*

dash (dæʃ), *v.*¹ Forms: 3–4 **dasse**, 3–5 **dasche**, 4 **dassche**, 4–6 **dasshe**, 4–7 **dashe**, 6– **dash.** [ME. *daschen, dassen*, found *a* 1300, perh. from Norse: cf. Sw. *daska* to drub, Sw. dial. to slap with open hand, Da. *daske* to beat, strike; but an ON. **daska* is not recorded, and the word is not known in WGer. It may be a comparatively recent onomatopœic word, expressing the action and sound of striking or driving with violence and smashing effect: cf. *clash, crash, bash, pash, smash*, etc. The *trans.* and *intr.* uses are exemplified almost equally early, and there is no definite evidence as to their actual order: cf. dush *v.*]

I. Transitive senses.

1. a. To strike with violence so as to break into fragments; to break in pieces by a violent stroke or collision; to smash. Now generally with complement, as ***to dash to pieces***; but the simple *dash* is still said of the action of wind or rain in beating, bruising, and disfiguring flowers or plants.

1297 R. Glouc. (1724) 51 Þe pykes smyte hem þoru out.. And daschte and a dreynte fourty schippes. *Ibid.* 540 [Thei] with axes thuder come, & that ȝat to hewe, & to dasse. *c* **1330** *Arth. & Merl.* 9051 (Mätz.) The hors chine he dassed a-to. **1387** Trevisa *Higden* (Rolls) III. 63 [He was] al to dasshed so þat no þing of his body myȝte be founde. **1593** Shaks. *2 Hen. VI*, iii. ii. 98 The splitting Rockes.. would not dash me with their ragged sides. **1610** —— *Temp.* i. ii. 8 A braue vessell.. Dash'd all to peeces. **1642** Rogers *Naaman* 142 As if one should with his foote dash a little childs house of oystershels. **1748** *Anson's Voy.* ii. i. 116 He fell amongst the rocks, and was dashed to pieces. **1847** Tennyson *Princ.* v. 132 Altho' we dash'd Your cities into shards with catapults. **1892** Gardiner *Student's Hist. Eng.* 11 The waves had dashed to pieces a large number of his ships. *Mod.* The roses were beautiful, before they were so dashed by the wind and rain.

b. To strike violently against.

(Without implication of smashing.)

1611 Cotgr., *Talemouser*, to cuffe, or dash on the lips. **1624** *Aphor. of State* in *Harl. Misc.* (Malh.) III. 495 With the like thunderbolt, to dash the heads of the sacred Empire. **1776** Gibbon *Decl. & F.* I. xxv. 746 The oars of Theodosius dashed the waves of the Hyperborean ocean. **1843** J. Martineau *Chr. Life* (1866) 349 Like brilliant islands.. vainly dashed by the dark waters of human history.

2. a. To knock, drive, throw, or thrust (*away, down, out*, etc.) with a violent stroke or collision.

c **1290** *S. Eng. Leg.* I. 344/147 And daschte þe tiez [= teeth] out of is heued. *a* **1400–50** *Alexander* 3882 A brand and a briȝt schild bremely he hentis.. Dasches dragons doun. **1592** Shaks. *Rom. & Jul.* iv. iii. 54 Shall I not.. dash out my desperate braines. **1664** H. More *Myst. Iniq.* 268 It [rain] is naturally drunk in, not dash'd in by force. *a* **1700** Dryden (J.), The brushing oars and brazen prow Dash up the sandy waves. **1828** Scott *F.M. Perth* ii, Dashing from him the snake which was about to sting him. **1833** Ht. Martineau *Manch. Strike* x. 112 While she, dashing away her tears, looked for something to do.

†**b.** To drive impetuously *forth* or *out*, cause to rush *together*. *Obs.*

1523 Ld. Berners *Froiss.* I. clvii. 191 Then thenglyshmen dashed forthe their horses after the frenchmen. *Ibid.* I. cccxlii. 538 Lorde Langurant.. couched his speare.. and so dyde Bernarde, and dasshed to their horses. **1577–87** Holinshed *Chron.* III. 922/2 The king.. pulled downe his visar.. and dashed out such a pleasant countenance and cheere, that all.. reioised verie much.

3. To throw, thrust, drive, or impel (something) *against, upon, into* (something else) with a violence that breaks or smashes; to impel (a thing) into violent and destructive contact with something: **a.** a solid body. (Also *fig.*)

1530 Palsgr. 507/1 He dasshed my heed agaynst the postes. **1568** Grafton *Chron.* II. 24 He foorthwith dashed his spurres into his horse and fled. **1614** Raleigh *Hist. World* ii. 376 In so doing he dasheth himself against a notable Text. **1724** R. Falconer *Voy.* (1769) 62 Lest another Wave should dash me against it [the rock]. **1820** Scoresby *Acc. Arctic Reg.* I. 401 A violent storm of wind dashed her.. stern first, against a floe of ice. **1861** Hughes *Tom Brown at Oxf.* vii. (1889) 61 [He] dashed his right fist full against one of the panels.

b. To splash (water or other liquid) violently upon or against something.

1697 Dryden *Virg. Georg.* i. 457 The Waves on heaps are dash'd against the Shoar. **1839** T. Beale *Sperm Whale* 350 Dashing the salt water in our faces.

†**c.** With reversed construction: ***to dash one in the teeth with*** (***something***): to 'cast it in one's teeth'. *Obs.* (Cf. CAST *v.* 65.)

1530 PALSGR. 507/1, I dasshe one in the tethe with a lye or a glosynge tale, *Jembouche*.. What nedest thou to dasshe me in the tethe with the monaye thou haste lente me.

4. a. To bespatter or splash (a thing) *with* anything (*e.g.* water or mud) cast with force or violence upon or against it.

1530 PALSGR. 507/1, I dasshe, I araye with myer, *Je crotte*. Your horse hath all to dasshed me. **1670** MILTON *Hist. Eng.* Wks. VI. (1851) 268 The Sea..came rowling on, and without reverence both wet and dash'd him. **1694** *Acc. Sev. Late Voy.* II. (1711) 166 Some Whales blow Blood to the very last..and these dash the Men in the Long-boats most filthily. **1785** H. WALPOLE *Mod. Gardening* (R.), Vast basins of marble dashed with perpetual cascades. **1875** BEDFORD *Sailor's Pocket Bk.* viii. (1877) 307 The face may be dashed with cold water.

fig. **1621** *Bk. Discipl. Ch. Scot.* Pref., Some will dash you by the odious name of Puritan. **1633** G. HERBERT *Temple, Marie Magd.* iii, Her sinnes did dash Ev'n God himself.

b. To put *out* (fire) by dashing water upon it.

1610 SHAKS. *Temp.* I. ii. 5 But that the Sea..Dashes the fire out. **1844** DICKENS *Mart. Chuz.* xxvii, Rows of fire-buckets for dashing out a conflagration.

c. *pa. pple.* Marked as with splashes.

1578 LYTE *Dodoens* II. xliv. 202 Floures..poudered or dashte with small spottes. **1797–1804** BEWICK *Brit. Birds* (1847) I. 119 The top of the head, the back, and the tail black: the rump is dashed with ash. **1850** TENNYSON *In Mem.* lxxxiii. 11 Deep tulips dash'd with fiery dew. **1873** BLACK *Pr. Thule* xxvii. 452 The sea was dashed with a wild glare of crimson.

5. a. To affect or qualify (anything) *with* an element of a different strain thrown into it; to mingle, temper, qualify, dilute *with* some (usually inferior) admixture. Also *fig.*

1546 *Confut. N. Shaxton* A. iii. (R.), Youre sermons dashed ful of sorowful teares and depe sighinges. **1586** COGAN *Haven Health* cvii. (1636) 108 Boyle them [fruit] againe with sufficient sugar, to dash them with sweet water. **1682** SIR T. BROWNE *Chr. Mor.* (1756) 40 Notable virtues are sometimes dashed with notorious vices. **1684** tr. *Bonet's Merc. Compit.* v. 137 Vinegar..dashed with water..is an Antidote against drunkenness. **1712** ADDISON *Spect.* No. 267 ¶8 To dash the Truth with Fiction. **1843** LEVER *J. Hinton* vi, Dash the lemonade with a little maraschino. **1853** TRENCH *Proverbs* 141 The pleasures of sin..are largely dashed with its pains.

b. *Coal-mining.* To mix (fire-damp) with air till the mixture ceases to be inflammable.

1851 GREENWELL *Coal-trade Terms Northumb. & Durh.* 21 *Dashing Air.*—Mixing air and gas together, until..the mixture ceases to be inflammable.

6. *fig.* To destroy, ruin, confound, bring to nothing, frustrate, spoil (a design, enterprise, hope, etc.): cf. *to smash*. In 16–17th c. the usual word for the rejection of a bill in Parliament, and frequent in various applications; now *Obs.* exc. in ***to dash*** (***any one's***) ***hopes***. (Cf. next.)

1528 *Beggar's Petit. agst. Popery* in *Select. Harl. Misc.* (1793) 153 He shall be excommunicated, and then be all his actions dashed! **1563–87** FOXE *A. & M.* (1596) 169 All the hope of Anselme was dasht. *a* **1577** SIR T. SMITH *Commw. Eng.* (1633) 92 As the cry of yea or no is bigger so the Bill is allowed or dashed. **1627** DRAYTON *Agincourt* 4 A warre with France, must be the way To dash this Bill. *a* **1656** BP. HALL *Rem. Wks.* (1660) 59 Those hopes were no sooner conceived than dasht. **1697** DAMPIER *Voy.* (1698) I. 157 So the design was wholly dashed. **1710** PRIDEAUX *Orig. Tithes* iv. 214 To dash what arguments may be brought from hence. **1840** *Chartist Circular* No. 5. 225 This dashes the bit-by-bit system [of reform]. **1861** PEARSON *Early & Mid. Ages Eng.* 143 Dunstan's hopes were again dashed by the news of Edward's death.

7. a. To cast down, depress; to daunt, dispirit, discourage.

1550 COVERDALE *Spir. Perle* v, How small soever their temptation or plague is, their heart is dashed. **1579** L. TOMSON *Calvin's Serm. Tim.* 466/1 We shalbe all dasht that our prayers do but soare in the ayre. **1604** SHAKS. *Oth.* III. iii. 214, I see, this hath a little dash'd your Spirits. **1676** DRYDEN *Aurengz.* II. i. 524 Why did you speak? you've dash'd my Fancy quite. **1791** COWPER *Odyss.* IX. 295 We, dash'd with terror, heard the growl Of his big voice. **1840** DICKENS *Old C. Shop* xxvi, This discouraging information a little dashed the child. **1891** MISS DOWIE *Girl in Karp.* 167 Somewhat dashed, we went down..to the spot where my horse had fallen with me.

b. To confound, put to shame, abash.

1563–87 FOXE *A. & M.* (1596) 1574/2 Frier Bucknham..was so dashed, that neuer after hee durst peepe out of the pulpit against M. Latimer. **1588** SHAKS. *L.L.L.* v. ii. 585 An honest man, looke you, and soon dasht. **1634** MILTON *Comus* 447 Chaste austerity..that dashed brute violence With sudden adoration and blank awe. **1728** VANBR. & CIB. *Prov. Husb.* II. i, The Girl..has Tongue enough: she woa'nt be dasht. **1766** FORDYCE *Serm. Yng. Wom.* (1767) II. xiii. 246 From her a..look..will dash the boldest offender. **1860** TRENCH *Serm. Westm. Abbey* x. 108 Dashed and abashed as no doubt for a moment she was.

†**c.** Phr. ***to dash*** (***a person***) ***out of countenance*** (***conceit, courage***). *Obs.*

1530 PALSGR. 507/1, I dasshe out of countenaunce or out of conceyte, *Je rens confus*. **1576** FLEMING *Panopl. Epist.* 162 Your deerest friends..damnified, and dashed out of courage. **1598** GRENEWEY *Tacitus' Ann.* III. xiv. (1622) 85 Cause sufficient, to haue dasht the best practised out of matter. **1617** HIERON *Wks.* (1619–20) II. 408 It would dash him quite out of countenance. **1754** RICHARDSON *Grandison* I. xi. 61 In order to dash an opponent out of countenance by getting the laugh instead of the argument on his side.

8. To put *down* on paper, throw *off*, write, or sketch, with hasty and unpremeditated vigour.

1726 WODROW *Corr.* (1843) III. 234 Please dash down anything that is proper for me to help. **1728** POPE *Dunc.* II. 47 Never was dash'd out, at one lucky hit, A fool, so just a copy of a wit. **1771** FOOTE *Maid of B.* Epil. Wks. 1799 II. 201 His ready pen he drew, And dash'd the glowing satire as he flew. **1847** TENNYSON *Princ.* IV. 121 Ourself..into rhythm have dash'd The passion of the prophetess. *Ibid.* v. 414 Then came a postscript dash'd across the rest. **1859** KINGSLEY *Misc.* (1860) II. 15 The impressions of the moment..dashed off with a careless but graceful pen.

9. a. To draw a dash through (writing); to strike *out*, cancel, erase, efface. Now *rare* or *Obs.*

1549–62 STERNHOLD & H. *Ps.* lxix. 29 And dash them cleane out of the booke of hope. **1576** FLEMING *Panopl. Epist.* 80 A faulte in writing is dashed out with a race of the penne. **1581** SIDNEY *Astr. & Stella* l. in Arb. *Garner* I. 528 And now my pen these lines had dashed quite. **1607** TOPSELL *Four-f. Beasts* (1673) 212 Before the snow be melt, and the footings dashed. **1670** WOOD *Life* (Oxf. Hist. Soc.) II. 199 He would correct, alter, dash out or put in what he pleased. **1856** FROUDE *Hist. Eng.* I. 454 She took a pen and dashed out the words.

b. To draw (a pen) vigorously *through* writing so as to erase it.

1780 COWPER *Table T.* 769 To dash the pen through all that you proscribe.

10. To mark with a dash, to underline.

1836 T. HOOK *G. Gurney* I. 17 The infinite pains I took to dash and underline the points. **1871** *Athenæum* 13 May 583 He did so dash his initials at the end of letters.

11. *slang.* or *colloq.* Used as a euphemism for 'damn', or as a kind of veiled imprecation.

1800 T. MORTON *Speed the Plough* II. ii. 28 But dash it, Lady Nelly, what do make thee paint thy vace all over we rud ochre zoo? **1812** H. & J. SMITH *Rej. Addr., G. Barnwell*, Dash my wigs, Quoth he, I would pummel and lam her well. **1844** *John Chawbacon* ii. in Halliwell *Dict.* (1865) I. p. xv, Dash my buttons, Moll—I'll be darn'd if I know. **1852** DICKENS *Bleak Ho.* III. i. 7 Dash it, Tony..you really ought to be careful. **1865** —— *Mut. Fr.* II. viii, Dashed if I know.

II. Intransitive senses.

12. To move, fall, or throw itself with violence or smashing effect; to strike in violent collision *against* (*upon*, etc.) something else.

c **1305** *Saints' Lives* in *E.E.P.* (1862) 80 þat weþer bigan to glide..þer hit gan dasche adoun..Ac in þe norþ half of þe churche..þer ne ful noȝt a reynes drope. *c* **1400** *Melayne* 964 Dede he daschede to the grounde. **1638** BAKER tr. *Balzac's Lett.* II. 43 In my way there are..many stones to dash against. **1694** *Acc. Sev. late Voy.* II. (1711) 168 The Whale..doth strike about with his Tail and Finns, that the Water dasheth up like Dust. **1724** R. FALCONER *Voy.* (1769) 62 The Tempest was very much abated, and the Waves not dashing so often. **1842** TENNYSON *Day-dream, The Revival* ii, And all the long-pent stream of life Dash'd downward in a cataract. **1891** E. PEACOCK *N. Brendon* II. 418 The full force of the Atlantic is dashing on the cliffs.

fig. **1638** D. FEATLEY *Strict. Lyndom.* I. 102 Lyes dash one with the other, and truth breakes out of the mouth of the lyar.

13. a. Of persons: To throw oneself with violence, such as would overthrow obstacles or resistance; to go, run, or rush with sudden impetuosity, or with spirited or brilliant action. Also *fig.* (Const. with var. preps. and advbs.)

c **1300** *K. Alis.* 2837 The gate..up he brak; In to the cité he con dassche. *c* **1330** *Arth. & Merl.* 6293 (Mätz.) Forth dassed the kinġ. *a* **1533** LD. BERNERS *Huon* lviii. 200 Ye sarazyns dasshed in to the prese to haue rescued Huon. **1596** *Pleas. Quippes Upstart Gentlw.* in Hazl. *E.E.P.* IV. 258 Our wantons now in coaches dash, From house to house, from street to street. **1682** DRYDEN *Abs. & Achit.* II. 414 Doeg..Spurred boldly on, and dashed through thick and thin, Through sense and nonsense. **1794** MRS. RADCLIFFE *Myst. Udolpho* xviii, Dashing at the steps below. **1823** BYRON *Juan* VIII. liv, [He] Dash'd on like a spurr'd blood-horse in a race. **1870** MORRIS *Earthly Par.* III. IV. 377 [He] rode on madly..Dashed through the stream and up the other bank. **1886** RUSKIN *Præterita* I. vii. 230 To leave her card on foot at the doors of ladies who dashed up to hers in their barouche. **1892** GARDINER *Student's Hist. Eng.* 11 Cæsar..dashed at his stockade and carried it by storm.

b. Said of action with pen or pencil.

a **1680** ROCHESTER *An Allusion to Horace* (R.), With just bold strokes he dashes here and there, Showing great mastery with little care.

†**14.** To clash. *Obs.*

c **1325** *Coer de L.* 4615 Trumpes blewen, tabours dashen.

15. *colloq.* To make a display, 'cut a dash'; ***dash off, out***, to burst off, come out, with a dash.

1786 *Francis, the Philanthr.* I. 159 Bidding fair to dash out, when he was qualified by manhood and experience. **1800** HELENA WELLS *Const. Neville* III. 68 He intended to dash off as a star of the first magnitude in the circles of fashion. **1806** SURR *Winter in Lond.* (ed. 3) III. 215 That blade dashes most confoundedly..he is a princely fellow, to be sure. **1807–8** W. IRVING *Salmag.* (1824) 290 Every lady..dresses and dashes.

III. 16. *Comb.* **a.** with verb + object, as †**dash-buckler**, a swaggering fellow, swashbuckler; **b.** with the verb-stem used attrib., as **dash-pot**, a contrivance for producing gradual descent in a piece of mechanism or for preventing vibration or sudden motion, consisting of a cylinder or chamber containing liquid in which a piston moves; a hydraulic buffer; **dash-wheel** (see quot. 1874). See also DASH-BOARD.

1567 FENTON *Trag. Disc.* 123 b, A traine of *dashbucklers or squaring tospottes. **1861** *Sci. Amer.* 30 Mar. 196/2 The *'dash pot' which Watt invented to graduate the descent of the puppet valve into its seat. **1874** KNIGHT *Dict. Mech.* 666 s.v. *Cut-off*, To seat them without slamming, the valve-stems are provided with dash-pots. **1878** in J. Dredge *Electr. Illum.* (1885) II. App. p. lxiv, The arm of the lever may be at right angles to the carbon, one end being weighted and the other attached to the core of a solenoid; the core may have a dash-pot action. **1902** *Encycl. Brit.* XXVIII. 86/1 The arc-lamp mechanism is provided with a dash-pot, or contrivance in which a piston moving nearly air-tight in a cylinder prevents sudden jerks in the motion of the mechanism. **1926** *Gloss. Terms Electr. Engin.* (*Brit. Engin. Standards Assoc.*) 50 *Dash-pot*, an appliance for preventing the sudden or oscillatory motion of any moving part of a piece of apparatus, by the friction of air or of a liquid. **1930** *Engineering* 21 Feb. 249/2 The proper function of the piston chamber is, however, that of a dash-pot. **1931** *Flight* 13 Nov. 1131/2 The dashpot is double acting, and there is a powerful check to spring recoil. **1936** *Gloss. Terms Railway Signalling* (*B.S.I.*) 16 *Dash pot*, a cylinder with a piston valve in which the escape of air or liquid is checked by the valve to assist in lessening shock. **1940** *Chambers's Techn. Dict.* 225/1 *Dash pot*, a device for damping out vibration; it consists of a piston attached to the part to be damped, fitting loosely in a cylinder of oil. **1959** *Times Rev. Industry* Mar. 36/1 The variable feed rate for cutting is controlled by a hydraulic dashpot. **1962** *Engineering* 15 June 793/1 The relay trip current setting is adjustable..simply by altering vertically the position of the self-locking dashpots. **1839** URE *Dict. Arts* 226 Put this mixture into the colour trough..and after two days wash in the *dash-wheel. **1874** KNIGHT *Dict. Mech., Dash-wheel.* (*Bleaching.*) A wheel with compartments revolving partially in a cistern, to wash and rinse calico in the piece, by alternately dipping it in the water and then dashing it from side to side of the compartments.

dash, *v.*²: see after DASH *sb.*²

dash (dæʃ), *sb.*¹ Forms: 4 **dasch**, 5–6 **dasshe**, 6 **dasche, dashe**, 6– **dash**. [f. DASH *v.*]

1. A violent blow, stroke, impact, or collision, such as smashes or might smash.

(With quot. 1577 cf. DASH *v.* 2.)

a **1375** *Lay-Folks Mass-Bk.* App. iv. 351 Wiþ his hed he yaf a dasch Aȝeyn þe Marbelston. **1470–85** MALORY *Arthur* x. lxxix, Syr Ector..gaf sire Palomydes suche a dasshe with a swerd. **1577–87** HOLINSHED *Chron.* III. 1153/2 He offered to hir his cloke, which she (putting it backe with hir hand with a good dash) refused. **1690** W. WALKER *Idiomat. Anglo-Lat.* 22 Let me alone, or I will give you a dash on the teeth. **1725** DE FOE *Voy. round World* (1840) 258 The water, falling from a height..and meeting in the passage with many dashes and interruptions. **1727–46** THOMSON *Summer* 1114 The dash of clouds, or irritating war Of fighting winds. **1858** LYTTON *What will he do?* I. v, Whistling..in time to the dash of the oars.

†**2.** *fig.* in phrases ***at*** (***the***) ***first dash, at one*** (or ***a***) ***dash***: cf. *stroke, blow* (F. *coup*). *Obs.*

1550 BALE *Apol.* 37 (R.) He heapeth me in, an whole halfe leafe at a dash, out of Saynt Augustyne. **1591** SHAKS. *1 Hen. VI*, I. ii. 71 She takes vpon her brauely at first dash. **1627** H. LESLY *Serm. bef. Majesty* 4 Wee are not made absolute entire Christians at the first dash. **1681** W. ROBERTSON *Phraseol. Gen.* (1693) 753 What? At first dash so to jear and frump your friend? **1699** W. HACKE *Voy.* II. 9 In..danger, to lose both our Lives and all our substance at one dash. **1710** *Acc. Last Distemp. Tom Whigg* II. 48 Designing to immortalize himself and his Patron at a Dash.

†**3.** *fig.* A sudden blow or stroke that casts down, confounds, depresses, dispirits, etc.; an affliction, discouragement. *Obs.*

1580 *Apol. Prince of Orange* in Phœnix (1721) I. 450 That the Course of his Life be found blessed..without any dash, blow, stumbling. **1629** RUTHERFORD *Lett.* v. (1862) I. 48, I have received many..dashes and heavy strokes, since the Lord called me to the ministry. **1637** *Ibid.* I. 287 The glory of manifested justice in giving of His foes a dash. **1730** T. BOSTON *Mem.* vii. 134 This gave me a sore dash.

4. a. The violent throwing and breaking of water (or other liquid) upon or against anything; a splash; a sudden heavy fall of rain; †*concr.* a portion of water splashed up.

1570 LEVINS 35/5 A dashe, *labes, aspersio*. **1612** T. TAYLOR *Comm. Titus* i. 8 To giue her harbour..till the dash and storme be ouer. **1677** W. HARRIS tr. *Lemery's Chym.* (ed. 3) 602 During the ebullition..a great many little dashes of water do fly about. *a* **1700** B. E. *Dict. Cant. Crew* s.v. *Gust*, We say a *Dash of Rain*, for a sudden, short, impetuous Beat of Rain. **1804** *Med. Jrnl.* XII. 247 Dr. Macneil seems..to think the sponging is better than the dash. **1848** MRS. GASKELL *M. Barton* (1882) 12/1 'He's coming round finely, now he's had a dash of cowd water.'

b. The sound of dashing; esp. the splashing sound of water striking or being struck.

1784 COWPER *Task* I. 186 Music not unlike The dash of Ocean on his winding shore. **1820** SCOTT *Abbot* xxxv, Why did ye not muffle the oars?..the dash must awaken the sentinel.

5. a. A small portion (of colour, etc.) as it were dashed or thrown carelessly upon a surface.

1713 BERKELEY *Ess. in Guardian* v. Wks. III. 161 The rosy dashes of light which adorn the clouds of the morning and evening. **1884** J. T. BENT in *Macm. Mag.* Oct. 426/1 Syra is almost entirely a white town, relieved now and again by a dash of yellow wash.

b. A small quantity (*of* something) thrown into or mingled as a qualifying admixture with something else; an infusion, touch, tinge. Usually *fig.*

1611 SHAKS. *Wint. T.* v. ii. 122 Now (had I not the dash of my former life in me) would Preferment drop on my head. **1678** CUDWORTH *Intell. Syst.* 892 A thing..not sincerely good, but such as hath a great dash or dose of evil blended with it. **1697** DAMPIER *Voy.* (1698) I. 293 It makes most delicate Punch; but it must have a dash of Brandy to hearten it. **1712** ADDISON *Spect.* No. 299 ¶2, I..resolved that my Descendents should have a Dash of good Blood in their Veins. **1820** W. IRVING *Sketch-Bk.* I. 335 There was a dash of eccentricity and enterprize in his character.

†**c.** A slight specimen, a touch; = CAST *sb.* 9. *Obs.*

a **1672** WOOD *Life* (1848) 161 He gave A. W. a dash of his office.

6. A hasty stroke of the pen.

1615 STEPHENS *Satyr. Ess.* (ed. 2) 414 And thus by meere chaunce with a little dash I have drawne the picture of a Pigmey. *a* **1656** BP. HALL *Rem. Wks.* (1660) 310 With one dash to blot it out of the holy Calender. **1691** RAY *Creation* I. (1704) 41 That this was done by the temerarious dashes of an unguided Pen. **1803** MACKINTOSH *Def. Peltier* Wks. 1846 III. 246 Fifty Imperial towns have been erased from the list of independent states, by one dash of the pen.

7. A stroke or line (usually short and straight) made with a pen or the like, or resembling one so made: *spec.* **a.** Such a mark drawn through writing for erasure. **b.** A stroke forming part of a letter or other written or printed character, or used as a flourish in writing. **c.** A horizontal stroke of varying length (-, —, ——) used in writing or printing to mark a pause or break in a sentence, a parenthetic clause, an omission of words or letters or of the intermediate terms of a series, to separate distinct portions of matter, or for other purposes; sometimes implying the use of strong language; hence as a mild substitute for *devil*. **d.** *Mus.* A short vertical mark (') placed above or beneath a note to indicate that it is to be performed *staccato*. **e.** A linear marking, as if made with a pen, on the wings of insects, etc.

1552 HULOET, Dashe or stryke with a penne, *litura*. **1594** BLUNDEVIL *Exerc.* I. iv. (ed. 7) 12 Having cancelled the first figure of the multiplyer, by making a dash thorow it with your Pen. **1607** DEKKER *Westw. Hoe* II. Wks. 1873 II. 297 Marke her dashes, and her strokes, and her breakings, and her bendings. **1612** BRINSLEY *Ludus Lit.* xiii. (1627) 177 Making a dash with a pen under every fault. **1712** ADDISON *Spect.* No. 470 ¶10 The Transcriber, who probably mistook the Dash of the I for a T. **1733** SWIFT *Poems, On Poetry*, In modern wit all printed trash is Set off with num'rous breaks — —and dashes ——. **1824** L. MURRAY *Eng. Gram.* (ed. 5) I. 406 The Dash, though often used improperly..may be introduced with propriety, where the sentence breaks off abruptly..A dash following a stop, denotes that the pause is to be greater than if the stop were alone. **1848** RIMBAULT *First Bk. Piano* 63 The Dash requires a more separate and distinct manner of performance than the Point. **1880** MUIRHEAD *Gaius* Introd. 13 Passages that are illegible in the MS...are indicated by dashes, thus — — —. **1883** LD. R. GOWER *My Remin.* II. xxviii. 259 Who the Dash is this person..and what the Dash does he here? **1899** A. NICHOLAS *Idyl of Wabash* 64 A dreadful thought which if put in print would have contained a dash.

f. One of the two signals (the other being the dot) which in various combinations make up the letters of the Morse alphabet. Also ***dash-and-dot***, more usually ***dot-and-dash*** (DOT *sb.*[1] 8).

1859 T. P. SHAFFNER *Telegr. Man.* 469 Whether the dots, spaces, and dashes be long or short, they should be uniform. **1873** F. JENKIN *Electr. & Magn.* xxii. §4 Morse signals are sent by a simple key... A short depression or mere tap sends the short elementary signal technically called a *dot*; a longer depression sends the second elementary signal technically called a *dash*. **1882** OGILVIE Suppl., *Dash-and-dot*, consisting of dashes and dots; as, the dash-and-dot alphabet. **1916** J. BUCHAN *Greenmantle* xx. 268 The sound was regular and concerted—dot, dash, dot—dash, dot, dot...the longs and shorts of the Morse Code. **1942** *Electronic Engin.* XV. 36 On automatic sending it transmits S.O.S. three times followed by a long dash.

8. A sudden impetuous movement, a rush; a sudden vigorous attack or onset. Also *fig.*

1809 ADM. COCHRANE in *Naval Chron.* XXVI. 164 Our loss in this little dash has..been severe. **1861** HUGHES *Tom Brown at Oxf.* v. (1889) 36 He..made up his mind..to make a dash..for something more than a mere speaking acquaintance. **1885** *Manch. Exam.* 25 Feb. 5/2 The dash was successfully made across the desert to Metammeh.

9. a. Spirited vigour of action; capacity for prompt and vigorous action.

1796 *Mod. Gulliver's Trav.* 50, I began now to suspect I was with sharpers..and correcting my dash, betted cautiously. **1808** WELLINGTON in Gurw. *Desp.* IV. 95 The affair..was occasioned..by the imprudence of the officer, and the dash and eagerness of the men. **1866** LIVINGSTONE *Jrnl.* I. v. 120 In dash and courage they are deficient.

b. ***to do one's dash*** (Austral. colloq.), see quots. 1916 and 1966; ***to have a dash (at)*** (colloq.), to make an attempt.

1916 C. J. DENNIS *Songs Sentimental Bloke* 121 *To do one's dash*, to reach one's Waterloo. **1923** WODEHOUSE *Inimit. Jeeves* iii. 37 The blighter's manner was so cold and unchummy that I bit the bullet and had a dash at being airy. **1930** —— *Very Good, Jeeves!* (1957) vi. 114, I supposed I had better have a dash at it and get it over. **1966** G. W. TURNER *Eng. Lang. Austral. & N.Z.* vii. 152 It is tempting to wonder whether the expression 'he's done his dash' meaning 'he is played out', 'he has done all he can' is connected with the gold-miner's *dashing*.

10. A gay or showy appearance, display, parade: usually in phr. ***to cut a dash***, to make a display (see CUT *v.* 25), in Sc. ***to cast a dash***.

1715 PENNECUIK *Tweeddale* 16 (Jam.) Large orderly terrace-walks, which in their summer verdure cast a bonny dash at a distance. **1771** FOOTE *Maid of B.* I. Wks. 1799 II. 213 The squire does not intend to cut a dash till the spring. *a* **1774** FERGUSSON *Poems* (1789) II. 32-33 (Jam.) Daft gowk, ..Are ye come here..To cast a dash at Reikie's cross? **1842** *P. Parley's Ann.* III. 246 Mrs. Cloff was for cutting a dash, giving large dinner-parties. **1887** *Punch* 12 Mar. 125/1 My wife and girls will wish to cut a dash.

11. *Sporting.* **a.** A race run in one heat. *U.S.* **b.** A sprint. *U.S.*

1836 *Spirit of Times* (N.Y.) 20 Feb. 5/3 Or, I will make two races, for one thousand dollars each, give you fifty yards in a dash of one mile, and one hundred yards in a dash of two miles. **1881** *Standard* 7 Sept. 5/2 They have certainly coined..the word 'dash', to signify a race run in one heat. **1895** *Chicago Tribune* 24 May 11/4 At least three of the rivals likely to meet in the 100-yard dash are said to be capable of tying the intercollegiate record. **1948** *P.C.C. Chron.* (Pasadena, Calif.) 31 Mar. 4/5 Anderson took a third in the open 100 yard dash. **1957** *Encycl. Brit.* XIX. 665/1 Distances up to and including 220 yd. are, in the United States, called dashes.

12. a. = DASH-BOARD I.

1868 *Rep. Comm. Patents 1867* (U.S.) I. 481/2 Carriage Boot..January 15, 1867. The apron is combined with a dash cover. **1874** in KNIGHT *Dict. Mech.* **1893** (used by an Oxford coach-builder in letter). **1911** J. C. LINCOLN *Cap'n Warren's Wards* ii. 15 He says the buggy dash is pretty well scratched up.

b. Now esp. in motor vehicles; = DASHBOARD I b.

1902 KIPLING in *Windsor Mag.* Dec. 13/2 Kysh's hands juggling with the levers behind the discreet backward sloping dash. **1906** *Daily Chron.* 14 Nov. 9/3 The coil and commutator, being fixed on the dash, are always in front of the driver. **1919** *Autocar Handbk.* (ed. 9) 253 A second lamp placed somewhere on the dash. **1929** *Daily Express* 10 Jan. 3/1 The car is fitted with electrical devices with lights on the dashfront to keep the driver informed when anything goes wrong with the lubrication or the ignition. **1944** *Coast to Coast 1943* 163 They got in the truck and by the light from the dash Black read the slip. **1966** M. WOODHOUSE *Tree Frog* xxvii. 205, I fitted the key into the truck's dash and backed off.

13. The DASHER of a churn, esp. the plunger of the old upright or ***dash-churn***; hence ***dash-boards***, the fixed beaters in a barrel-churn.

1796 in *Repert. Arts & Manuf.* (1797) VII. 290 Specification of the Patent granted to Mr. William Raley, of Newbald, in the East Riding of Yorkshire. November 10, 1796... O, the moving dashes or breakers. **1847** in HALLIWELL. **1865** *Harper's Mag.* Mar. 541/2 Last summer Joe bought an old-fashioned dash churn. **1877** in *N.W. Linc. Gloss.* **1963** *Times* 18 May 11/5 *Meadar loinithe* is a plunging or dash churn.

14. *Comb.* **dash-guard**, the metal plate which protects the platform of a tram-car from being splashed by the horses; **dash-lamp**, a carriage lamp fixed in the centre of the dash-board or 'dash'; **dash-light**, a light on the dash-board of a motor vehicle; †**dash-line** = DASH *sb.* 7; **dash-rule** (*Printing*), a 'rule' or strip of metal for printing a dash across a column or page. Also DASH-BOARD.

1684 R. H. *School Recreat.* 120 The dash Lines..above and below, are added only when the Notes ascend above the Staff, or descend below it. **1874** KNIGHT *Dict. Mech.*, *Dash-rule*. **1926** *Catholic Mirror* June 47 'Don't they call this the dash light?' she queried, fingering the little nickel-plated illuminator. **1935** M. EBERHART *Cases of Susan Dare* 285 His mouth tightened in the little glow from the dashlight.

‖**dash**, *sb.*[2] [Corruption of DASHEE, through taking the pl. *dashees* as *dashes*.] A gift, present, gratuity; = DASHEE.

1788 FALCONBRIDGE *Afr. Slave Tr.* 7 The Kings of Bonny ..to whom..they usually make presents (in that country termed dashes). **1867** SMYTH *Sailor's Word-bk.*, *Dash*, the present with which bargains are sealed on the coast of Africa. **1881** *Mem. Geo. Thomson* ix. 119 We called in the head man and gave him a dash proportioned to the kindness with which he had received us.

Hence **dash** *v.*, to give a present to, to 'tip'.

1861 DU CHAILLU *Equat. Afr.* xiii. 191, I..offered to *dash* him (give him some presents). **1881** *Mem. Geo. Thomson* x. 139 The head man had dashed him a hog.

dash, *adv.* [The stem of DASH *v.* used adverbially: cf. *bang*, *crash*, etc.] With a dash: see the various senses of the sb. and vb.

1672 VILLIERS (Dk. Buckhm.) *Rehearsal* III. i. (Arb.) 67 T'other's..at him again, dash with a new conceipt. *a* **1700** DRYDEN (J.), The waters..with a murmuring sound, Dash, dash, upon the ground, To gentle slumbers call. **1787** 'G. GAMBADO' *Acad. Horsemen* (1809) 22 Fall in with a hackney coach, and he [a horse] will carry you slap dash against it. *Mod.* The boat went dash against the rocks.

'**dash-board.** [f. DASH *v.* and *sb.* + BOARD.]

1. a. A board or leathern apron in the front of a vehicle, to prevent mud from being splashed by the heels of the horses upon the interior of the vehicle. Also, movable sides to a cart for the same purpose (Halliwell).

1846 *Rep. Comm. Patents* (U.S.) 81 An improvement in sleighs, principally connected with the dash-board, has been patented this year. **1851** *Gt. Exhib. Catal.* II. 635/1 Adjusting-iron for dash-lamps suitable for sweeps of carriage dash-boards. **1859** LANG *Wand. India* 172 He fell asleep, his feet over the dashboard, and his head resting on my shoulder. **1882** MISS BRADDON *Mnt. Royal* I. iii. 77 If you fasten the reins to the dashboard, you may trust Felix.

b. In motor vehicles, the panel beneath the windscreen on which electrical instruments and controls are mounted. Also in aircraft.

1904 A. B. F. YOUNG *Compl. Motorist* iv. 114 A cooling apparatus has now been fitted behind the bonnet and in front of the dashboard. **1925** W. DEEPING *Sorrell & Son* v. §1 Sorrell remained by the car. He liked the colour of it, and the compact brightness of the dash-board. **1942** *Electronic Engin.* XV. 9 A course meter on the dashboard gives a rough indication of distances.

2. a. The spray-board of a paddle-wheel.

b. In calico printing (see quot.).

1860 URE *Dict. Arts* (ed. 5) II. 7 Dash wheels..were revolving wheels having dash-boards, which are much used in the washing processes necessary in calico printing.

3. *Arch.* A sloping board to carry off rain-water from the face of a wall.

1881 *Every Man his own Mechanic* §1298 A piece of wood attached to the face of the wall at an angle and called a dash-board.

4. In a churn: see DASH *sb.*[1] 13.

dash-buckler: see DASH *v.* III.

dashed (dæʃt), *ppl. a.* [f. DASH *v.* + -ED[1].]

1. Struck violently against or by something; splashed; mingled, tempered, etc.: see the verb.

1646 CRASHAW *Steps to Temple* Poems 53 Torn skulls, and dash'd out brains. **1647** H. MORE *Song of Soul* III. App. lxvii, Their dashèd bodies welter in the weedy scum. **1772** *Town & Country Mag.* 88 Half a dozen glasses of dashed wine. **1879** *Spectator* 6 Sept. 1126/2 Seeing it [the garden] present a more or less dashed appearance.

2. Marked with a dash, underlined.

1859 DARWIN in *Life & Lett.* (1887) II. 154 Your dashed 'induce' gives the idea that Lyell had unfairly urged Murray.

3. *slang* or *colloq.* A euphemism for 'damned' (see DASH *v.* 11). Also *advb.*, deucedly, confoundedly. Hence '**dashedly** *adv.*

1881 W. E. NORRIS *Matrimony* III. 300 A dashed pack of quacks and swindlers. **1888** J. PAYN *Prince of Blood* I. xi. 187 He would find himself dashedly mistaken. **1893** W. S. GILBERT *Utopia* 11, How utterly dashed absurd.

‖'**dashee**, *sb.* Also 8 dasje. [Given by Atkins, 1723, in a List of 'Negrish words' used on the Guinea Coast.] A gift, present, gratuity.

Hence **dashee** *v.*, to bestow a dashee on, to 'tip'.

1705 BOSMAN *Guinea* (1721) 450 After giving them their Dasje or Present, I dealt with them for the Ivory. **1723** J. ATKINS *Voy. Guinea* (1735) 60 The Negrish Language alters a little in sailing..Some Negrish words..*Attee ho*, how do you do? *Dashee*, a Present..*Tossu*, be gone. *Yarra*, sick, etc. *Ibid.* 64 There is a Dashee expected before Ships can wood and water here. *Ibid.* 100 The Fetish..whom they constantly Dashee for Health and Safety. *Ibid.* 169 That Captain..had..dashee'd his Negro Friends to go on board and back it.

dasheen (dæ'ʃiːn). [Origin uncertain.]

A cultivated variety (*Colocasia esculenta*) of the taro.

1899 *West Indian Bull.* I. 131 What is known in Trinidad as 'dasheen', also a *Colocasia*, is not, I think, grown in Jamaica at all. **1910** *U.S. Dept. Agric., Bur. Plant Industry Bull. No.* 164 27 It is not always easy to distinguish between the dasheens and the taros, for some of the dasheens have a tendency to throw sprouts from the tips of the tubers. **1913** W. H. PAGE *Let.* 26 Jan. in B. J. Hendrick *Life of W. H. Page* (1922) I. iv. 128 I'm going to grow dasheens. **1918** *Bull. Dept. Agric. Trinidad* XVII. 29 The name dasheen appears to be a corruption of the French phrase 'de la Chine'. **1953** P. LEIGH FERMOR *Violins of St. Jacques* 88 Living on dasheen and yam and breadfruit they had uprooted from the plantations. **1968** J. W. PURSEGLOVE *Tropical Crops* II. 587 Some..also provide temporary lateral shade, as do *Xanthosoma* spp. (tannias), *Colocasia* spp. (dasheen and eddoes).

†'**dashel.** *Obs.* In 6 dasshel(l. [f. DASH *v.* + -EL[1], -LE instrumental, as in *threshel*, *handle*.] A brush for sprinkling holy water; an aspergillum.

1502 *Will of J. Moore* (Somerset Ho.), A Holy Water pott cum le dashell. **1540** *Inv. of Plate* in Greene *Hist. Worcester* II. App. 5 A holy water tynnell of selver and gylte, and a dasshel to the same, selver and gylte.

dasher ('dæʃə(r)). [-ER[1].]

1. A person who dashes; *spec.* one who 'cuts a dash'; a dashing person; a 'fast' young woman (*colloq.*).

1790 DIBDIN *Sea Songs, Old Cunwell* (Farmer), My Poll, once a dasher, now turned to a nurse. **1802** MAR. EDGEWORTH *Almeria* (1832) 292 She was astonished to find in high life a degree of vulgarity of which her country companions would have been ashamed; but all such things in high life go under the general term of *dashing*. These young ladies were *dashers*. **1807** W. IRVING *Salmag.* (1824) 361 To charter a curricle for a month, and have my cypher put on it, as is done by certain dashers of my acquaintance. **1887** *Pall Mall G.* 23 Nov. 3/2 The fast married woman of fashion..the unmarried dasher of the same species.

2. That which dashes; *spec.* the contrivance for agitating the cream in a churn.

1846 *Rep. Comm. Patents* (U.S.) (1847) 233 What I claim as my invention..is the combination of the vertical dasher with the oscillating dashers. **1848** D. DRAKE *Let.* 7 Jan. in C. D. Drake *Pion. Life Kentucky* (1870) v. 93 The latter stages of the process [of churning], when the butter rises on the dasher. **1853** *Jrnl. R. Agric. Soc.* XIV. I. 74 The old-fashioned barrel-churn, the dashers of which are fixed. **1872** O. W. HOLMES *Poet Breakf.-t.* i. (1885) 26 The empty churn with its idle dasher.

3. = DASH-BOARD I. *U.S.*

1858 O. W. HOLMES *One-hoss Shay*, Boot, top, dasher, from tough old hide. **1859** —— *Prof. Breakf.-t.* i. (1891) 14 By no means..to put their heels through the dasher.

4. Applied to a hunting-cap.

1802 *Sporting Mag.* XX. 314 Two new pair of Cordovan boots..and a black velvet dasher from the cap-maker.

5. A dashing attempt, movement, etc. *colloq.*

1884 *Punch* 18 Oct. 186/1 Drop your curb, pluck up heart, And go at it a dasher!

‖**dashi** (ˈdaʃɪ). [Jap., shortened from *dashi-jiru*, f. *dashi* to draw, extract + *jiru* (*shiru*) juice, broth.] Cooking stock, esp. a fish stock based upon dried bonito and seaweed; a broth made from the dried flesh of the bonito.

1963 H. TANAKA *Pleasures Jap. Cooking* i. 4 *Dashi*, a light, clear fish stock.. is quite indispensable to Japanese cookery. *Ibid.* iii. 58 Dashi is pale amber in color, crystal clear and delicate in flavor. **1969** *Guardian* 16 July 16/4 Dried bonito (*Katsuobashi*).. [is] used to make.. the simplest and lightest of stocks, *dashi*. You make it like tea. **1980** *Washington Post* 4 Dec. E4 He recommends, as an alternative to homemade dashi, the instant dashi, which I have never found without monosodium glutamate in the market.

dashiki (ˈdaʃɪkɪ). Also **dasheki**. [Of W. Afr. origin.] A West African type of shirt, sometimes worn symbolically by U.S. Negroes.

1969 *Observer* 26 Jan. 9/7 The revolution has spread to the Church: Negro ministers often wear *dashikis* or turtle-neck sweaters. **1969** *Sunday Times* 9 Mar. (Colour Suppl.) 40 The Harlem blacks want the dasheki, the short African jacket. **1970** 'J. MORRIS' *Candywine Devel.* xvi. 184 A sleek, oxblood brown singer who was flapping his *dashiki* shirt.

dashing (ˈdæʃɪŋ), *vbl. sb.* [-ING¹.]

1. The action of the verb DASH (q.v.), in various senses.

1580 HOLLYBAND *Treas. Fr. Tong, Heurtement*, a dashing, a striking. **1694** *Acc. Sev. Late Voy.* II. (1711) 47 This Ice becometh very spungy by the dashing of the Sea. **1805** SOUTHEY *Madoc in W.* xvii, The dashing of the oars awaken'd her. **1820** HAZLITT *Lect. Dram. Lit.* 15 The roar and dashing of opinions.

2. Splashing; *concr.* a dash or splash (of mud, etc.); plaster dashed or laid roughly upon a wall; *fig.* aspersion.

1591 PERCIVALL *Sp. Dict.*, *Salpicaduras*, dashings, *conspersiones*. **1598** FLORIO, *Zaccarélle*.. dashings or spots of durt or mire. **1655** FULLER *Ch. Hist.* v. iv. §24 There is no dashing on the credit of the Lady, nor any the least insinuations of inchastity. **1809–12** MAR. EDGEWORTH *Absentee* ix, The dashing was off the walls, no glass in the windows.

3. *colloq.* The action of 'cutting a dash'; showy liveliness in dress, manners, etc.

1802 [see DASHER 1]. **1806** SURR *Winter in Lond.* II. 11 Mere pips of popularity—mere dots of dashing. *a* **1847** MRS. SHERWOOD *Lady of Manor* I. ix. 381 That most tasteless and disgusting style of manners which for some years past has obtained the name of *dashing*; by which term is generally understood all that is ungracious, ungenteel, and repulsive.

4. *Comb.* **dashing-iron**, the iron frame by which the dash-board is fixed to the carriage; **dashing-leather**, a leathern dash-board.

a **1841** HOOK *Martha*, They slipped over the dashing iron between the horses. **1794** W. FELTON *Carriages* (1801) I. 206 A dashing leather is fixed on the fore part of a Carriage, to prevent the dirt splashing against the passenger.

ˈ**dashing**, *ppl. a.* [-ING².]

1. That dashes; that beats violently against something; splashing.

c **1325** *E.E. Allit. P.* C. 312 Þy stryuande stremez.. In on daschande dam, dryuez me ouer. **1628** EARLE *Microcosm.*, *Tauerne* (Arb.) 34 Like a street in a dashing showre. **1839** T. BEALE *Sperm Whale* 391 The howling winds and dashing waves.

2. Characterized by prompt vigour of action; spirited, lively, impetuous.

1796 BP. WATSON *Apol. Bible* 271 Even your dashing Matthew could not be guilty of such a blunder. **1796** BURKE *Lett. noble Ld.* Wks. 1842 II. 267 In the dashing style of some of the old declaimers. **1874** GREEN *Short Hist.* ii. §7. 95 A bold, dashing soldier. **1891** E. PEACOCK *N. Brendon* I. 8 He drove away at a dashing pace.

3. Given to fashionable and striking display in manners and dress; that is a 'dasher'.

1801 MAR. EDGEWORTH *Belinda* xix, Mrs. Freke.. was a dashing, fashionable woman. **1824** W. IRVING *T. Trav.* II. 39 She had two dashing daughters, who dressed as fine as dragons.

b. *transf.* Of things: Fashionably showy; stylish, 'swell'.

1816 J. SCOTT *Vis. Paris* (ed. 5) 75 The dashing colonnade of the Garde Meuble. **1847** DE QUINCEY *Sp. Mil. Nun* vi. (1853) 12 A dashing pair of Wellington trousers.

dashingly (ˈdæʃɪŋlɪ), *adv.* [-LY².] In a dashing manner or style.

1803 CHALMERS *Let.* in *Life* (1851) I. 476 They were determined to go dashingly to work. **1837** HAWTHORNE *Twice Told Tales* (1851) I. xvi. 25 In a smart chaise, a dashingly dressed gentleman and lady. **1870** DASENT *Ann. Eventful Life* (ed. 4) iii. 69 None of that dashingly destructive work.

dashingness (ˈdæʃɪŋnɪs). [f. DASHING *ppl. a.* 3 + -NESS.] The quality of being dashing.

1934 E. BOWEN *Cat Jumps* 94 Her dashingness, curtness, and air of experience. **1943** —— *Seven Winters* 31 Edwardian dashingness.

†ˈ**dashism**. *Obs. nonce-wd.* The character of having dash, or being a 'dasher'.

1788 V. KNOX *Winter Even.* xxviii. (R.), He must fight a duel, before his claim to complete heroism, or dashism, can be universally allowed.

dash-pot, dash-wheel: see DASH *v.* III.

‖**dasht** (dæʃt). [Pers. *dasht* desert, plain without water.] A name in Iran and some other parts of Asia for a desert, esp. a stony desert.

[**1875** *Encycl. Brit.* III. 223/2 The Dasht-Baha-rak is an extensive plain in this district, on which was formerly situated a large city, once the capital of Badakhshan.] **1901** *Mem. Geol. Surv. India* XXXI. 189 These floods, which, no doubt, were more frequent in former times, have spread the pebbles over large areas in the desert, giving rise to the stony plains known by the name of 'dasht'. **1925** *Blackw. Mag.* Mar. 333/2 The coastal belt.. was.. primeval *dasht*—a dismal succession of open mud flats, patches of low tamarisk, pools of bitter water. **1950** W. B. FISHER *Middle East* xiii. 267 Firm sandy or stony stretches in which sand dunes (*rig*) may occur, giving a more 'normal' desert topography similar to that of Arabia or the Sahara. The term *dasht* is applied to this firm desert.

dashy (ˈdæʃɪ), *a.* [f. DASH *v.* and *sb.* + -Y.]

1. Showy, ostentatiously fashionable, stylish; = DASHING *ppl. a.* 3, 3 b. *colloq.*

1822 *Blackw. Mag.* XI. 399 New rugs, with swans and leopards, all so dashy. **1835** *Fraser's Mag.* XII. 186 Dashy suburban congregations.

2. Characterized by hastiness of execution.

1844 LD. BROUGHAM *A. Lunel* III. v. 147 The style was.. somewhat dashy, and here and there a little indistinct.

3. Marked with dashes or strokes. *nonce-use.*

1856 DICKENS *Lett.* (1880) I. 425 Many a hand[writing] have I seen.. some loopy, some dashy, some large, some small.

†**dasiberd**. *Obs.* Also **dasy-, daysy-, dasa-, dose-, dosa-, dossi-, doziberd(e, dosebeirde**. [The better form is prob. *dasyberd* = *dazy-beard*: see DAZY *a.* inert, dull. Mätzner compares LG. *dösbârt*, and the same notion appears in Lowland Sc. *dulbart*, *dulbert* = dull-beard, dullard.] A stupid fellow, dullard, simpleton.

c **1400** *Sowdone Bab.* 1707 Trusse the forth eke, sir Dasaberde. **14..** *Nom.* in Wr.-Wülcker 694/22 *Hic duribuccus*, a dasyberd. **1468** *Medulla Gram.* in *Promp. Parv.* 114 *Duribuccus*, þat neuer openeþ his mouþ, a dasiberde. ? *a* **1500** *Chester Pl.* xii. 5 (MS. of 1592) There is a Doseberd [*v.r.* Dosseberde] I wolde dear, That walkes about wyde-where. *Ibid.* 94 Some other sleight I must espie This Dosaberd [*v.r.* Doziberde] for to destroy.

dasill, dasle, obs. forms of DAZZLE.

dasje, daskand: see DASHEE, DASCAN.

dasometer, bad form for DASYMETER.

dass, Sc. var. of DESS, layer, stratum, ledge.

dasse, var. DAS; obs. form of DASH.

dassel(l, obs. form of DAZZLE.

dassie (ˈdæsɪ, ˈdasɪ). *S. Afr.* Also **dasje, dassi**. [Afrikaans: see DASSY.] **1.** = DAS 2, DASSY.

1814 J. PINKERTON tr. *Thunberg's Acct. Cape of Good Hope* XVI. 129 The uppermost covers himself with the skin of a Dassi (*cavia capensis*), to keep out the cold and bad weather. **1828** J. PHILIP *Res. S. Afr.* I. ii. 27 Their Sonquaas (soldiers).. wander daily in the fields to catch dasjés, jackals, and other animals. **1835** ANDREW SMITH *Diary* 10 July (1940) II. 106 The dassie chews the cud. **1866** J. LEYLAND *Adv. S. Afr.* iii. 118 In these mountains I also saw the Dassi (Hyrax Capensis), or Rock Rabbit of the Cape. **1902** [see sense 2]. **1931** *Times Educ. Suppl.* 22 Aug. iv/3 Hyraxes, known also as 'Dassies', or 'Rock-rabbits', the conies of the Bible. **1946** *Cape Times* 28 Aug. 7/6 Eagles, Cape dassies, the mongoose. **1952** *Ibid.* 22 Nov. 4/6 A whole colony of dassies (rock-rabbits).

2. The sea-fish *Diplodus sargus* (family Sparidæ); black-tail.

1853 L. PAPPE *Edible Fishes Cape G.H.* 22 *Cantharus Emarginatus*.. Dasje.. Rare in Table Bay, but more frequently caught in the several Bays to the East of the Cape. **1902** *Trans. S. Afr. Philos. Soc.* XI. 220 The Dasje might also with a little stretch of the imagination be likened to the rabbit or dassie, from its general shape, and this is the name by which it is known in Cape Town, Hout Bay, and Kalk Bay. **1930** C. L. BIDEN *Sea-Angling Fishes of Cape* xii. 199 Dassie are often caught that when taken from the water are silvery.

dassievanger (ˈdæsɪvæŋə(r), ‖ˈdasifaŋər). *S. Afr.* [Afrikaans, f. prec. + *vanger* catcher.]

Quot. 1867 identifies the bird with the popular name of 1 and the scientific name of 2.

1. The bateleur eagle, *Terathopius ecaudatus*. Cf. BERGHAAN.

1867 [see BERGHAAN]. **1889** H. A. BRYDEN *Kloof & Karoo* 273 A great black mountain eagle. We know him at once for a berghaan (cock of the mountain), or dassie-vanger (coney-eater). **1893** A. NEWTON *Dict. Birds* 132 Dassie-vanger (Coney-catcher), the Dutch name for an Eagle in South Africa, adopted by English residents.

2. A large, black bird of prey with a **Y**-shaped white mark on the rump, *Aquila Verreauxi*, found in S. and N.E. Africa and in Palestine.

1951 *Cape Argus* 20 Oct. (Mag.) 2/4 Most difficult of all birds to shoot, Hoesch found, was the black eagle or dassievanger.

‖ˈ**dassy**. [ad. Du. *dasje*, dim. of *das*, DAS.] The Cape daman, *Hyrax capensis*; = DAS 2.

1846 H. H. METHUEN *Life in Wilderness* iv. 79 A rock-rabbit, or dassy (*Hyrax Capensis*), was shot in the rocks, amongst which these animals always dwell. **1882** MRS. HICKFORD *Lady Trader* 106 A dassy, or rock rabbit.

dastard (ˈdɑːstəd, -æ-), *sb.* and *a.* Also 6 **daster**. [Known only from the 15th c. Notwithstanding its French aspect (cf. *bastard*) it appears to be of Eng. formation. The Promptorium identifies it in sense with *dasiberde*; cf. also *dasart*, of kindred derivation and meaning; these make it probable that the element *dast* is = *dased* dull, stupid, inert, f. *dase*, DAZE; cf. other native formations with the suffix *-ard*, as *dasart*, *drunkard*, *dullard*, *laggard*, *sluggard*.] **A.** *sb.*

†**1.** One inert or dull of wit, a dullard; a sot. *Obs.*

c **1440** *Promp. Parv.* 111 Daffe, or dastard, or he þat spekythe not yn tyme, *oridurus*. *Ibid.* 114 Dastard, or dullarde, *duribuctius* (P. *vel duribuccus*). *c* **1440** *York Myst.* xxxii. 88 What dastardis! wene ye be wiser þan we? **1509** BARCLAY *Shyp of Folys* (1570) 192 These dronken dastardes .. drinke till they be blinde. **1530** PALSGR. 212/1 Dastarde, *estovrdy*, *butarin*. **1552** HULOET, Dastard, *excors*.. *socors*, *vecors*.

2. One who meanly or basely shrinks from danger; a mean, base, or despicable coward; in modern use, *esp.* one who does malicious acts in a cowardly, skulking way, so as not to expose himself to risk.

[**1470–85** MALORY *Arthur* IX. iv, As a foole and a dastard to alle knyghthode.] **1526** SKELTON *Magnyf.* 2220 Thou false harted dastarde, thou dare not abyde. *c* **1537** *Thersites* in Hazl. *Dodsley* I. 395, I shall make the dasters to renne into a bag, To hide them fro me. **1593** SHAKS. *Rich. II*, I. i. 190 Before this out-dar'd dastard. *a* **1661** FULLER *Worthies* (1840) III. 41 He was, though a dwarf, no dastard. **1715** POPE *Iliad* II. 427 And die the dastard first, who dreads to die. **1770** LANGHORNE *Plutarch* (1879) II. 602/2 The greatest dastard and the meanest wretch in the world. **1808** SCOTT *Marm.*, *Lochinvar*, A laggard in love and a dastard in war. **1870** BRYANT *Iliad* I. II. 52 What chief or soldier bears a valiant heart, And who are dastards.

B. *adj.* Characterized by mean shrinking from danger; showing base cowardice; dastardly.

c **1489** CAXTON *Blanchardyn* liv. 219 Casting away his dastard feare. **1592** *Nobody & Someb.* (1878) 292 The dastardst coward in the world. **1602** *2nd Pt. Return fr. Parnass.* III. v. (Arb.) 48 To waile thy haps, argues a dastard minde. **1725** POPE *Odyss.* IV. 447 A soft, inglorious, dastard train. **1866** NEALE *Sequences & Hymns* 125 We fling the dastard question from us!

C. *Comb.*, as ***dastard-like*** adj. or adv.

1835 LYTTON *Rienzi* I. iii, The clients of the Colonna, now pressing, dastard-like, round the disarmed and disabled smith.

†ˈ**dastard**, *v. Obs.* [f. prec.: cf. COWARD *v.*] *trans.* To make a dastard of; to cow, terrify.

1593 NASHE *Christ's T.* (1613) 73 My womanish stomacke hath serued me to that, which your man-like stomackes are dastarded with. **1620** SHELTON *Quix.* III. xxvi. 186 The Scholar was frighted, the Page clean dastarded. **1665** DRYDEN *Ind. Empr.* II. i, I'm weary of this Flesh, which holds us here, And dastards manly Souls with Hope and Fear.

†ˈ**dastardice, -ise**. *Obs.* [f. DASTARD *sb.* + *-ise*, -ICE¹, after COWARDICE.] Mean or base cowardice.

1603 FLORIO *Montaigne* III. v. (1634) 498 His faintnesse, dastardise, and impertinencie. **1748** RICHARDSON *Clarissa* Wks. 1883 VII. 143, I was upbraided with ingratitude, dastardice, and [etc.].

ˈ**dastardize**, *v.* [f. DASTARD *sb.* + -IZE: cf. COWARDIZE (of same age).] = DASTARD *v.*

c **1645** HOWELL *Lett.* (1650) II. 16 To dastardize or cowe your spirits. *a* **1700** DRYDEN (J.), Such things.. As.. would dastardize my courage. **1748** RICHARDSON *Clarissa* (1811) IV. 208 The moment I beheld her, my heart was dastardized. **1841** *Tait's Mag.* 561 To lie.. dastardized in the dust.

dastardliness (ˈdɑːstədlɪnɪs, -æ-). [f. DASTARDLY *a.* + -NESS.] The quality of being dastardly.

†**1.** Inertness or dullness of wit; stupidity. *Obs.*

1553 GRIMALDE *Cicero's Offices* I. (1558) 45 That our appetites obaye reason: and neyther runne before it, nether for slouth or dastardlinesse dragge behind it. **1557** RECORDE *Whetst.* Y iij, But for euery mater to require aied.. it might seme mere dastardlinesse.

2. Mean or base cowardliness.

1561 T. HOBY tr. *Castiglione's Courtyer* I. Civb, Dastardlines or any other reproche. **1612** T. TAYLOR *Comm. Titus* i. 14 Alas, our dasterdlines, and timiditie, that faint before daies of triall. **1684** MANTON *Exp. Lord's Pr.* Wks. 1870 I. 223 Observe Peter's dastardliness.. a question of the damsel's overturns him. **1807** F. WRANGHAM *Serm. Transl Script.* 10 Their proverbial dastardliness of character.

ˈ**dastardling**. *nonce-wd.* [f. DASTARD *sb.* + -LING, dim. suffix.] A contemptible dastard.

1800 COLERIDGE *Piccolom.* IV. iii. 53 Will *he*, that dastardling, have strength enough [etc.]?

dastardly (ˈdɑːstədlɪ, -æ-), *a.* [f. DASTARD *sb.* + -LY¹.]

†**1.** Inert of mind or action; stupid, dull. *Obs.*

1567 MAPLET *Gr. Forest* 96 b, The Owle is called the dastardly Bird: she is of such slouth and sluggishnesse.

2. Like or characteristic of a dastard; showing mean or despicable cowardice.

1576 FLEMING *Panopl. Epist.* 251 A fearefull, cowardly, and dastardly loute. **1603** KNOLLES *Hist. Turks* (1638) 333 Losing courage continually, and daily growing more base and dastardly. **1761** HUME *Hist. Eng.* II. xxix. 157 The Swiss infantry..behaved in a dastardly manner and deserted their post. **1855** MACAULAY *Hist. Eng.* IV. 207 The most dastardly and perfidious form of assassination. **1872** SPURGEON *Treas. Dav.* Ps. lv. 12 III. 19 The slanders of an avowed antagonist are seldom so mean and dastardly as those of a traitor. *Mod.* A dastardly outrage.

† **'dastardly**, *adv. Obs.* [-LY².] Like a dastard; in a cowardly manner.
1552 HULOET, Dastardly, or lyke a dastarde, *pusillanimiter.* *a* **1649** DRUMM. OF HAWTH. *Skiamachia* Wks. (1711) 201 And the brave men of Scotland all the while shall ly still quiet..calling dastardly upon a parliament.

† **'dastardness.** *Obs.* [-NESS.]
1. Inertness of understanding, stupidity, dullness.
1552 HULOET, Dastardnes, *socordia.* **1562** TURNER *Herbal* II. N iij b, By dastardnes and weiknes of mynde.
2. Base cowardice, dastardliness.
1519 HORMAN *Vulg.* 55 He rebuked him of his dastardnes and pekishnes. **1639** FULLER *Holy War* IV. xix. (1840) 211 The dastardness of the Egyptians made these mamalukes more daring.

dastardy ('dɑːstədɪ, -æ-). *arch.* Also 6–7 -ie. [f. DASTARD *sb.* + -Y, after *cowardy*, *bastardy*.] The quality of a dastard; base or mean cowardice.
1588 ALLEN *Admon.* 19 The whole world deriding our effeminate dastardie. **1611** SPEED *Hist. Gt. Brit.* IX. viii. 22 Farre from any suspition of dastardy. *a* **1640** JACKSON *Creed* XI. xxiv. Wks. X. 461 Which did especially aggravate the Israelites dastardy. **1706** COLLIER *Refl. Ridic.* 298 We must bear with those that are above us..without dastardy and baseness. **1850** BLACKIE *Æschylus* II. 168 Why run ye thus ..into the hearts of men Scattering dastardy?

daster, -liness, obs. var. DASTARD, -LINESS.

dastoor, dastur(i, varr. DUSTOOR, DUSTOORY.

† **daswen**, *v. Obs.* Also 4–5 dasewe(n. [Closely related to *dase-n*, to DAZE. The suffix may be as in *herwen*, *harwen*, *harewen*, occurring beside *heriȝen*, *herien*, mod. *harrow* and *harry*, from OE. *herȝian*. The word would thus be a parallel form to **dasiȝen*, **dasien*, from *dasiȝ* adj.: see DAZY.] *intr.* Of the eyes or sight: To be or become dim.
1382 WYCLIF *Deut.* xxxiv. 7 The eyȝe of hym [Moses] daswed not. —— 1 *Sam.* iii. 2 Heli leye in his place, and his eyen daswiden. *c* **1386** CHAUCER *Manciple's Prol.* 31 Thyn eyen daswen eek [*v.rr.* dasewen, dasen, dasoweþe]. *c* **1430** *Hymns Virg.* (1867) 68 Myn iȝen daswen, myn heer is hoore. *c* **1440** *Promp. Parv.* 114 Daswyn' [*printed* Dasmyn'], or messen as eyys (H., P. dasyn, or myssyn as eyne), *caligo.* **1496** *Dives & Paup.* (W. de W.) VIII. xvi. 343 Age.. feblenesse, dasewynge of syght.
b. *pa. pple.*
c **1384** CHAUCER *H. Fame* II. 150 Thou sittest at another booke Tyl fully dasewyd ys thy looke. **14..** HOCCLEVE *To Dk. Bedford* 9 Myn yen hath custumed bysynesse So daswed. **1438** CAXTON *G. de la Tour* F j b, Ye be dasewed and sore dyseased of your syght and wytte.

dasy(e, obs. form of DAISY *sb.*, DAZY.

dasylirion (dæsɪ'lɪrɪən). [mod.L. (J. G. Zuccarini 1838, in *Allgemeine Gartenzeitung* 18 Aug. 258/1), f. Gr. δασύ-ς thick + λείριον lily.] A plant of the liliaceous genus of this name, indigenous to Mexico and the south-western U.S., having white bell-shaped flowers, cultivated as a greenhouse evergreen plant.
[**1858** *Curtis's Bot. Mag.* LXXXIV. tab. 5030 (*heading*) Bearded-leaved Dasylirium. **1866** LINDLEY & MOORE *Treas. Bot.* I. 385/1 *Dasylirion*, a genus of *Bromeliaceæ*, consisting of Mexican plants with short stems, and densely crowded linear leaves which droop gracefully.] **1880** *Encycl. Brit.* XII. 262/1 The Dasylirions have stout woody stems and large heads of narrow leaves. **1933** *Punch* 11 Jan. 45/1, I simply yearn to look a dasylirion in the eye. **1951** *Dict. Gardening* (R. Hort. Soc.) II. 640/1 Dasylirions are excellent plants for subtropical bedding, their gracefully drooping leaves being ornamental at all times. **1963** W. BLUNT *Of Flowers & Village* 29 The dasylirion has leaves as sharp as saws.

dasyll, obs. form of DAZZLE.

dasymeter (dæ'sɪmɪtə(r)). Improperly daso-. [mod. f. Gr. δασύ-ς dense + μέτρον measure.] An instrument for measuring the density of gases.
1872 YEATS *Techn. Hist. Comm.* 404 The manometer, or dasometer, for finding the density or rarity of the atmosphere. **1874** KNIGHT *Dict. Mech.*, *Dasymeter*.. consists of a thin glass globe, which is weighed in the gas and then in an atmosphere of known density.

dasypeltis (dæsɪ'pɛltɪs). [mod.L. (J. G. Wagler *Natürliches System der Amphibien* (1830) IV. 178), f. Gr. δασύ-ς thick + πέλτη small shield.] A small harmless egg-eating snake of the genus of this name found in central and south Africa.
[**1849** A. SMITH *Illustr. Zool. S. Afr. Reptilia* Tab. LXXIII, On discovering that *Anodon* had been employed by conchologists, I adopted *Dasypeltis*, as proposed by Wagler.] **1887** *Encycl. Brit.* XXII. 194/2 A very peculiar genus of snakes, Dasypeltis, represented by three species only, is the type of a separate family. **1927** HALDANE & HUXLEY *Anim. Biol.* xi. 223 The egg-eating snake, Dasypeltis. **1969** A. BELLAIRS *Life of Reptiles* I. iv. 119 Among the selective feeders are the egg-eating colubrids *Dasypeltis* and *Elachistodon*; many snakes are fond of birds' eggs.

dasyphyllous (dæsɪ'fɪləs), *a. Bot.* [f. Gr. δασύ-ς rough, hairy + φύλλ-ον leaf + -OUS.] 'Having hairy or woolly leaves' (*Syd. Soc. Lex.*).

dasypod ('dæsɪpɒd). *Zool.* [f. generic name *Dasypus*, ad. Gr. δασύπους, δασυποδ-, hairy or rough-footed.] Of or pertaining to *Dasypus*, a genus of armadillos; an animal of this genus. Hence **da'sypodid** *sb.*, **da'sypodine** *a.*

‖**Dasyprocta** (dæsɪ'prɒktə). *Zool.* [mod.L., f. Gr. δασύπρωκτ-ος having hairy buttocks (f. δασύ-ς hairy + πρωκτός buttocks).] A genus of South and Central American rodents, the agoutis. Hence **dasy'proctid** *a.* (*sb.*), **dasy'proctine** *a.*
1875 BLAKE *Zool.* 67 Hares are rarest in South America, where their place is occupied by the Cavies and dasyproctine Rodents.

dasypygal (dæsɪ'paɪgəl), *a. Zool.* [mod. f. Gr. δασύπῡγ-ος (f. δασύ-ς hairy + πῡγή rump, buttocks).] Having hairy buttocks, rough-bottomed.
1875 BLAKE *Zool.* 17 The higher dasypygal or anthropoid Apes.

dasyure ('dæsɪ(j)ʊə(r)). *Zool.* [ad. mod.L. *dasyūrus*, f. Gr. δασύ-ς rough, hairy + οὐρά tail.] An animal of the genus *Dasyurus* or subfamily *Dasyurinæ*, comprising the small carnivorous marsupials of Australia and Tasmania, also called 'brush-tailed opossums' or 'native cats'.
1839–47 TODD *Cycl. Anat.* III. 261/2 The Opossums resemble in their dentition the Bandicoots more than the Dasyures. **1881** *Times* 28 Jan. 3/4 The smaller pouched herbivores have their slayers in the 'native devil' (*sarcophilus*), and in the dasyures or native cats.
Hence **dasy'urine** *a. Zool.*, belonging to the subfamily *Dasyurinæ*.
1839–47 TODD *Cycl. Anat.* III. 260/1 In..its hinder feet *Myrmecobius* resembles the Dasyurine family.

DAT (diːeɪ'tiː, dæt), *sb.* Also **dat.** [Acronym f. *digital audio tape* s.v. DIGITAL *a.* 5 b.] Digital audio tape; a recording made in this format.
1985 *New Scientist* 7 Nov. 32/1 DAT makes existing audio cassette recorders obsolete. **1986** *Times* 3 Sept. 23/2 Dats will be a serious threat to the compact disc market. **1987** *Courier-Mail* (Brisbane) 5 Feb. (Blitz Suppl.) 2/1 Unlike compact discs, DAT tapes allow consumers to make their own 'perfect sound' dubbings, raising fears of massive copyright breaches.

dat (dat), *conj.*, *dem. pron.*, *adj.*, etc. Repr. dial. (esp. Ir.), W.I., and U.S. Black pronunc. of *that.*
1688 T. WHARTON *New Song*, Ho, Brother Teague, dost hear de Decree, Lilli Burlero Bullena-la, Dat we shall have a new Debittie, Lilli Burlero Bullena-la. **1792** H. H. BRACKENRIDGE *Mod. Chivalry* II. v. i. 74 Massa say, somebody say, dat de first man was de fite man; but you say, dat de first man was de black a-man. **1801** in M. Johnson *Amer. Advertising, 1800–1900* (1960), All dat goarse [*sc.* coarse] skin. **1880** W. T. DENNISON *Orcadian Sketch-Bk.* 3 He tankid de Lord for gaean' Charlie the kingdom an dat wus tankin him for what he niver deud. **1883** [see *cutting-up* (*a*) s.v. CUTTING *vbl. sb.* 9 e]. **1926** N. N. PUCKETT in A. Dundes *Mother Wit* (1973) 5/2 The Negro..also sings 'I wouldn' marry dat yelluh Nigger gal.' **1939** JOYCE *Finnegans Wake* 379 And be the seem talkin wharabahts hosetanzies, dat sure is sullibrated word! *c* **1960** L. BENNETT in Ramchand & Gray *West Indian Poetry* (1972) 24 A job Dat suit her dignity. **1973** *Sunday Express* (Trinidad & Tobago) 1 Apr. (Suppl.) 12/3 Stop dat ole talk.

dat, obs. form of DAUT *v.*, *Sc.* to fondle.

data ('deɪtə), pl. of DATUM, q.v.

database ('deɪtəbeɪs). Also **data base, data-base.** [f. DATA *sb. pl.* + BASE *sb.*¹] **1.** A structured collection of data held in computer storage; *esp.* one that incorporates software to make it accessible in a variety of ways; *transf.*, any large collection of information.
1962 *Technical Memo.* (System Development Corp., Calif.) TM-WD-16/007/00. i. 5 A 'data base' is a collection of entries containing item information that can vary in its storage media and in the characteristics of its entries and items. **1967** E. R. LANNON in Cox & Grose *Organiz. Bibliogr. Rec. by Computer* IV. 83 The Search area provides a means of querying the data base. **1971** *New Scientist* 4 Mar. 498/1 A database is a generalised collection of data not linked to one set of functional questions. **1972** *Computer Jrnl.* XV. 290/1 Engineering information files set up on disc by Hawker Siddeley Aviation Ltd... form the data base for a fully integrated production control system. **1972** *Science* 3 Nov. 472/1 The data base from which the volumes are compiled is maintained on magnetic tape and is updated weekly. **1973** *Nature* 13 Apr. 485/1, I gave a list of the fifty most cited authors for 1967, using the 1967 SCI as the data base. **1974** *Florida FL Reporter* XIII. 88/2 A number of sociolinguists..gradually moved closer to the creolist position as their data-base expanded. **1981** *IBM Jrnl. Res. & Development* XXV. 505 Around 1964 a new term appeared in the computer literature to denote a new concept. The term was 'data base', and it was coined by workers in military information systems to denote collections of data shared by end-users of time-sharing computer systems. The commercial data processing world ..appropriated 'data base' to denote the data collection which results from consolidating the data requirements of individual applications. **1984** SMITH & BAILEY *Mod. Eng. Legal Syst.* i. 10 It would..cause chaos, even in an age of computerised legal data bases, if every decision on whether a defendant had behaved 'unreasonably'..could potentially be cited. **1985** *Sunday Times* 10 Mar. 80/3 CIR went through its data-base looking for companies interested in investing in new ideas in electronics. **1985** *Ashmolean* IX. 1/1 A museum and its records are one vast database.
2. Special Comb.: **database management**, the organization and manipulation of data in a database; **database management system**, a software package that provides all the functions required for database management; abbrev. *DBMS* s.v. D III. 3; **database manager** = *database management system* above; **database system**, a database together with a database management system.
1964 *Proc. Symposium Development & Managem. Computer-Centered Data Base*, Economic Considerations Relevant to *Data Base Management, V. LaBolle (work session). **1969** in *Communications Assoc. Computing Machinery* (1971) XIV. 318/2 A survey of generalized data base management systems. **1971** [see *DBMS* s.v. D III. 3]. **1983** *Computerworld* 7 Feb. ID-53/1 Data bases and data base management systems (DBMS) were developed to overcome the handicap of file-oriented systems. **1985** *Personal Computer World* Feb. 25/1 (Advt.), Powerful database management and applications generator with optional graphics and development tools. **1975** *Proc. World Conf. Med. Information* I. 335 One general purpose *database manager, available through a commercial time-sharing service, was tested. **1984** *Which Micro?* Dec. 20/2 The four programs..consist of a wordprocessor, a spreadsheet, a data base manager and a business graphics designer. **1962** *Technical Memo* (System Development Corp., Calif.) TM-WD-16/007/00. i. 5 It is necessary to define the characteristics of a data base to the *Data Base System so that when instructed to manipulate data, the system can recognize the format and positioning of item information in the entries. **1980** C. S. FRENCH *Computer Sci.* xl. 300 Data base systems are *possible* with the current hardware available. It is the necessary interface (the data base management system) which needs development.

datable, dateable ('deɪtəb(ə)l), *a.* [f. DATE *v.* + -ABLE.] Capable of being dated.
1837 *Fraser's Mag.* XVI. 401 Dateable contemporary inscriptions. **1884** *Athenæum* 19 Jan. 94/1 The oldest datable Reynolds in the gallery.

datal ('deɪtəl), *a.* [f. L. *datum* DATE + -AL¹.]
a. Of or pertaining to date; chronological. *rare.*
1882 *Bradshaw's Railw. Manual*, The Parliamentary Intelligence..first appears in datal order.
b. Containing or including the date (as of a charter).
1837 T. D. HARDY *Rot. Chart.* 31 The Datal clause in Anglo-Saxon charters generally..precedes the names of the witnesses. *Ibid.* 34 William the Conqueror..also commemorated historical occurrences in his datal clauses. **1858** *Topographer & Genealogist* III. 120 Same seal and datal clause.

datal, dataller: see DAYTALE, DAYTALER.

datary¹ ('deɪtərɪ). [ad. mod.L. *datārius*, It. *datario*, f. L. *dat-um*, It. *dato*, DATE: ancient L. had *datārius* adj. in sense 'to be given away'.]
1. An officer of the Papal Court at Rome, charged with the duty of registering and dating all bulls and other documents issued by the Pope, and representing the Pope in matters relating to grants, dispensations, etc.
1527 KNIGHT in Pocock *Rec. Ref.* I. xxviii. 58 The datary hath clean forsaken the court. **1533** BONNER *Let. to Hen. VIII* in Froude *Hist.* II. 145, I desired the datary to advertise his Holiness that I would speak with him. **1691** W. B. *Hist. Roman Conclave* i. 2 The Datary, the Secretaries, and all such as have in their keeping the Seals of the deceased Pope, are obliged to surrender them. **1825** C. BUTLER *Bk. R.C. Church* 112 The lips of a Roman datary would water at the sight of a bill of an English proctor.
†**2.** An expert in dates; a chronologer. *Obs. rare.*
1655 FULLER *Ch. Hist.* III. v. §7 *Die quinto Elphegi.* I am not Datary enough to understand this. *a* **1661** —— *Worthies* I. (1662) 329 Let me onely be a Datary, to tell the Reader, that this Lord was created Earl of Portland, February 17 [1632].

'datary². [ad. mod.L. *datāria*: see prec.] The office or function of dating Papal bulls and other documents; a branch of the Apostolic Chancery at Rome separately organized in the 13th c. for this and other purposes: see prec.
c **1645** HOWELL *Lett.* (1650) I. 55 Besides the temporal dominions, he hath..the datary or dispatching of bulls. **1667** *Lond. Gaz.* No. 146/1 The next day..the Datary was kept open, and several businesses dispatcht. **1838** J. R. HOPE SCOTT *Let.* in *Mem.* (1884) I. ix. 168 It is supposed to be in the Datary.
b. *attrib.* or *adj.*
1688 BURNET *Lett. Pres. State of Italy* 113 It may bring in more profit into the Datary Court.

datcha, var. DACHA.

date (deɪt), *sb.*¹ [a. OF. *date* (13th c. in Littré), now *datte*:—L. *dactyl-us*, a. Gr. δάκτυλος date, *orig.* finger. The OF. came through intermediate forms **dactele*, *dacte*; cf. Pr. *dáctil*, *dátil*, Sp. *dátil*, OIt. *dattilo* (whence Ger. *dattel*, etc.), mod.It. *dattero*.]

1. a. The fruit of the date-palm (*Phœnix dactylifera*), an oblong drupe, growing in large clusters, with a single hard seed or stone, and sweet pulp; it forms an important article of food in Western Asia and Northern Africa, and is also dried and exported to other countries.

c **1290** *S. Eng. Leg.* I. 380/115 A ȝeord of palm cam in is hond..þe ȝeord was ful of Dates. *c* **1400** *Lanfranc's Cirurg.* 307 It is schape as it were þe stoon of a date. *c* **1400** MAUNDEV. (Roxb.) viii. 30 Palme treesse berand dates. **1553** EDEN *Treat. Newe Ind.* (Arb.) 19 A tree..which bringeth foorth dates lyke vnto the Palme tree. **1655** MOUFET & BENNET *Health's Improv.* (1746) 297 Dates are usually put into stew'd Broths..and restorative Cullices. **1712** tr. *Pomet's Hist. Drugs* I. 136 Dates..serve for the Subsistence of more than an hundred Millions of Souls. **1870** YEATS *Nat. Hist. Comm.* 183 The best dates come to us from Tunis, viâ Marseilles.

b. *slang.* A foolish or comic person, esp. ***soppy date***. (Usu. an affectionate term of abuse.)

1914 W. L. GEORGE *Making of Englishman* III. v. 302 These girls were used to the foreigner... I could fall into gallicisms now, and merely be called a 'date'. **1923** J. MANCHON *Le Slang* 101 *You date!* que tu es drôle! **1935** G. INGRAM *Cockney Cavalcade* iv. 55 A kid like that ought not to talk about love at her age, the soppy little date. **1959** I. & P. OPIE *Lore & Lang. Schoolchildren* iii. 45 They say to him 'You're a soppy date.'

2. The tree which bears dates, the date-palm (*Phœnix dactylifera*). ***wild date***: an Indian species, *P. sylvestris*.

a **1400** *Pistill of Susan* 89 Þer weore growyng so grene þe Date wiþ þe Damesene. ?*c* **1475** *Sqr. lowe Degre* 36 The boxe, the beche, and the larel-tre, The date, also the damysè. **1742** COLLIER *Orient. Ecl.* iv. 51 The date, with snowy blossoms crown'd! **1866** *Treas. Bot.* 878 *P[hœnix] sylvestris*, called the Wild Date, is supposed by some authors to be the parent of the cultivated date.

†**3.** Name of a variety of plum. *Obs.*

1664 EVELYN *Kal. Hort.* (1729) 214 Plums, Imperial, Blue, White Dates.

4. *Comb.*, as ***date-fruit***, ***-grove***, ***-stone***, ***-tree***; **date-bearer**, a date-tree bearing fruit; **date-brandy**, an intoxicating liquor from the fermented sap of the date-tree; **date-disease**, a distemper also called *Aleppo boil*; **date-fever** = DENGUE (see quot.); **date-fish** *U.S.*, a date-shell or piddock; **date-palm** = sense 2; **date-plum**, the fruit of species of *Diospyros* (N.O. *Ebenaceæ*), having a flavour like that of a plum; also the tree itself; **date-shell**, a mollusc of the genus *Lithodomus*, which burrows in stone or rock; so called from its shape; cf. It. *dattero*, *dattilo* 'also a kinde of hard shell fish' (Florio 1598); **date-sugar**, sugar from the sap of the wild date-tree of India; **date-wine**, wine made by fermenting the sap of the *Phœnix dactylifera* and other species.

1880 L. WALLACE *Ben-Hur* 225 The sky palely blue through the groinery of countless *date-bearers. **1827** MAGINN *Red-nosed Lieut.* in *Forget-me-not*, *Date-brandy was not to his taste. **1875** tr. *Ziemssen's Cycl. Med.* II. 508 At Port Said..it [dengue] was epidemic every year at the season of the date-harvest, and thus acquired the name of *date-fever. **1838** *Knickerbocker* XI. 446 Each separate raisin therein embedded, bearing much resemblance to the *date-fish in his rock. **1884** G. B. GOODE *Nat. Hist. Aquatic Anim.* 707 Some cousins (*Zirphæa crispata*, *Platydon cancellatus*, etc.) are esteemed delicacies on the coast of California under the name of 'Date-fish'. **1884** J. COLBORNE *Hicks Pasha* 85 The river..is lined with stately *date-groves. **1837** M. DONOVAN *Dom. Econ.* II. 347 The phœnix dactylifera or *date-palm. **1877** A. B. EDWARDS *Up Nile* iii. 57 A dense, wide-spreading forest of stately date-palms. **1866** *Treas. Bot.* 411 The fruit of the Chinese *Date Plum, *D[iospyros] Kaki*, is as large as an ordinary apple..*D. virginiana* is the Virginian Date Plum or Persimon..The fruit..is an inch or more in diameter. **1882** *Syd. Soc. Lex.*, *Date plum, Indian*, common name for the fruit of the *Diospyros lotus*. **1851** WOODWARD *Mollusca* 266 The '*date-shell' bores into corals, shells, and the hardest limetsone rocks. **1696** AUBREY *Misc.* (1721) 60 Take 6 or 10 *Date-stones, dry..pulverize, and searce them. **1840** *Penny Cycl.* XVIII. 104 *Date-sugar is not so much esteemed in India as that of the cane. *c* **1400** *Rom. Rose* 1364 Fyges, and many a *date tree There wexen. **1535** COVERDALE *Song Sol.* vii. 7 Thy stature is like a date tre. **1601** HOLLAND *Pliny* XIII. iv. (R.), Date-trees love a light and sandie ground. **1852** GROTE *Greece* II. lxix. IX. 47 The soldiers..procured plentiful supplies..of *date-wine.

date (deɪt), *sb.*[2] Also 5–6 *Sc.* dait. [a. F. *date*, OF. also *datte* (13th c. in Littré) = Pr., Sp., It. *data* fem.:—L. *data* fem. sing. (or neuter) of *datus* given. In ancient L., the date of a letter was expressed thus '*Dabam Romæ prid. Kal. Apr.*', i.e. 'I gave or delivered (this) at Rome on the 31st March', for which the later formula was '*Data Romæ*, given at Rome', etc. Hence *data* the first word of the formula was used as a term for the time and place therein stated. Cf. *postscript*, etc.]

1. The specification of the time (and often the place) of execution of a writing or inscription, affixed to it, usually at the end or the beginning.

c **1430** *Stans Puer* 97 in *Babees Bk.* 33 In þis writynge, þouȝ þer be no date. **1512** *Act 4 Hen. VIII*, c. 10 A paire of Indentures..the date wherof is the xij[th] daie of Aprill in the secound yere of your..reigne. **1630** LD. DORCHESTER in Ellis *Orig. Lett.* II. 267 III. 259, I have received your Letters of severall dates. **1712** STEELE *Spect.* No. 320 ¶4 A long Letter bearing Date the fourth Instant. **1817** W. SELWYN *Law Nisi Prius* (ed. 4) II. 883 The policy should be dated.. The insertion of a date may tend to the discovery of fraud. **1837** MACAULAY *Bacon* Ess. 1854 I. 353/2 A public letter which bears date just a month after the admission of Francis Bacon. **1837** *Penny Cycl.* VII. 330 A three-halfpenny piece ..bearing the date of 1599.

2. a. The precise time at which anything takes place or is to take place; the time denoted by the date of a document (in sense 1).

c **1330** R. BRUNNE *Chron.* (1810) 47 Þat tyme he died..þe date was a þousand & sextene mo. **1377** LANGL. *P. Pl.* B. XIII. 269 In þe date of owre dryȝte, in a drye apprile, A þousande and thre hondreth tweis thretty and ten. *c* **1400** MAUNDEV. (Roxb.) iii. 9 Þe date when þis was writen..was ii[m] ȝere before þe incarnacion of Criste. **1607** SHAKS. *Timon* II. i. 22 His days and times are past, And my reliances on his fracted dates Haue smit my credit. **1776** *Trial of Nundocomar* 74/2 When was it?—I only remember the sum: I do not remember the date. **1838** LYTTON *Leila* II. i, That within two weeks of this date thou bringest me..the keys of the city. **1893** *Weekly Notes* 68/2 Up to the date at which he received notice.

b. More vaguely: The time at which something happened or is to happen; season, period.

c **1325** *E.E. Allit. P.* A. 540 Þe date of þe daye þe lorde con knaw. *c* **1400** MAUNDEV. (1839) iii. 18 The Date whan it was leyd in the Erthe. **1639** tr. *Du Bosq's Compl. Woman* II. 32, I would faine know..of what date they would have their Habits. **1647** CLARENDON *Hist. Reb.* I. (1843) 17/1 From these..circumstances..the duke's ruin took its date. **1764** GOLDSM. *Trav.* 133 Not far remov'd the date, When commerce proudly flourish'd through the state. **1828** CARLYLE *Misc.* I. 222 Up to this date Burns was happy.

c. An appointment or engagement at a particular time, freq. with a person of the opposite sex; a social activity engaged in by two persons of opposite sex. Cf. *blind date*. Also *attrib.* *colloq.*

[**1876** G. MEREDITH *Let.* 9 Mar. (1970) I. 512 If you do come I shall celebrate the event and make a date of it.] **1885** E. W. HOWE *Mystery of Locks* 187 If he'll make a date with me, I'll exchange stories with him. **1896** ADE *Artie* vii. 65, I s'pose the other boy's fillin' all my dates? **1900** —— *Fables in Slang* (1902) 138 Her Date Book had to be kept on the Double Entry System. **1903** J. M. FORMAN *Journeys End* iii. 42, I must be going on. I've a date to keep. **1906** 'O. HENRY' *Four Million* 176, I made a date for dinner this evening. **1916** C. J. DENNIS *Songs of Sentimental Bloke* 121 *Date*, an appointment. **1919** W. S. MAUGHAM *Moon & Sixpence* xlvii. 203 He walked away as if he'd remembered he had a date. **1923** A. CHRISTIE *Murder on Links* xxvi. 285 It still worried me that Bella hadn't kept her date with me. **1923** L. J. VANCE *Baroque* xv. 147 I'll give you a ring and make a date. **1928** M. BARING *Comfortless Mem.* iii, Mr. Donne can't come; he's got a date. **1937** W. S. MAUGHAM *Theatre* xxii. 209 He's got a date. Is the young ruffian having an affair with this girl? **1938** WODEHOUSE *Code of Woosters* ix. 206 Before parting, we had made a date for half-past four next day on the same spot. **1949** M. MEAD *Male & Female* xii. 263 The girl in the perfect date-dress. *Ibid.* xiv. 282 The dress that is described as 'date bait'. **1958** *Times* 19 Feb. 3/3 The idea of *The Broken Date*, to give it its English title, is simple.

d. A person of the opposite sex with whom one makes or has made an appointment or engagement. *colloq.* (orig. and chiefly *U.S.*).

1925 *Amer. Speech* I. 102/2 My date was late last evening. **1943** STEINBECK *Once there was War* (1959) 125 On these terraces the soldiers come to sit about and to meet dates. **1951** J. D. SALINGER *Catcher in Rye* vii. 60 Stradlater was in the back, with his date, and I was in the front, with mine. **1959** T. GRIFFITH *Waist-high Culture* (1960) 32 In pairs we crowded into cars, our dates in our laps.

e. *Theatr. colloq.* A theatrical engagement or performance; a place where a performance is given, freq. as part of a tour. Also *transf.*, esp. (*U.S.*) a recording session.

1904 G. V. HOBART *Jim Hickey* vi. 101 God, please, if Danny is booked in Heaven won't You cancel his dates for a while and let him play here with me. **1933** P. GODFREY *Back-Stage* vi. 75 He then discusses the best provincial 'dates' to play before coming to London. *Ibid.* 115 He can book a series of touring dates with unsuccessful theatres. *Ibid.* xvi. 205 Smart watering-places, which in the holidays rank as No. 1 dates. **1936** N. COWARD *To-night at 8.30* I. 92 *Bert.* She nearly got the bird second house. *Lily.* Too refined, I expect. For this date. *Ibid.* 93 This is as good a date as you can get. **1949** L. FEATHER *Inside Be-bop* ii. 16 Charlie's first small-band date, September 15, 1944. **1952** WODEHOUSE *Barmy in Wonderland* i. 17 He proposed to teach it a few simple tricks and get it dates on television.

3. The period to which something ancient belongs; the age (of a thing or person).

c **1325** *E.E. Allit. P.* A. 1039 Vchon in scrypture a name con plye, Of Israel barnez folewande her datez, Þat is to say, as her byrþ whatez. **1576** FLEMING *Panopl. Epist.* 415 This our common wealth, last in date, but first in price. **1699** BP. NICOLSON *To Ralph Thoresby* (T.), The best rules for distinguishing the date of manuscripts. **1832** W. IRVING *Alhambra* I. 50 The Torres Vermejos, or vermilion towers ..are of a date much anterior to the Alhambra. **1864** TENNYSON *Aylmer's F.* 80 When his date Doubled her own. **1869** FREEMAN *Norm. Conq.* (1876) III. xiii. 291 Rich in antiquities of Roman date.

4. The time during which something lasts; period, season; duration; term of life or existence.

13.. *Chron. Eng.* 972 in Ritson *Met. Rom.* II. 310 Thah the sone croune bere The fader hueld is date here. *c* **1386** CHAUCER *Can. Yeom. Prol. & T.* 858 Neuere to thryue were to long a date. *c* **1440** LYDG. *Secrees* 421 So to perseuere and lastyn a long date. *c* **1534** tr. *Pol. Verg. Eng. Hist.* (Camden) I. 153 Miserablie finishinge the date of her dayse. **1667** MILTON *P.L.* XII. 549 Ages of endless date Founded in righteousness. **1676** DRYDEN *Aurengz.* IV. i. 1725 To lengthen out his Date A Day. **1782** COWPER *Lett.* 11 Nov., When the date of youth is once expired. **1890** R. BRIDGES *Shorter Poems* III. vi, Her [a flower's] brief date.

5. The limit, term, or end of a period of time, or of the duration of something. *Obs.* or *arch.*

c **1325** *E.E. Allit. P.* A. 492 Þer is no date of hys godnesse. **1447** BOKENHAM *Seyntys* (Roxb.) 41 Fer in age I am runne and my lyves date Aprochith faste. **1557** *Tottell's Misc.* (Arb.) 129 The dolefull dayes draw slowly to theyr date. *a* **1600** RALEIGH *Poems, Reply to Marlowe* vi, But could youth last, and love still breed, Had joyes no date, nor age no need. *c* **1600** SHAKS. *Sonn.* xiv, Thy end is Truthes and Beauties doome and date. **1712–4** POPE *Rape Lock* III. 171 What Time would spare, from Steel receives its date. **1784** COWPER *Task* v. 529 All has its date below; the fatal hour Was registered in Heaven ere time began.

†**6.** ? A fixed decree. *Obs.* [Cf. med.L. *datum* 'statutum, decretum' (Du Cange).]

c **1470** HENRY *Wallace* II. 195 Is this thi dait, sall thai our cum ilkane? On our kynrent, deyr God, quhen will thow rew? *Ibid.* VI. 97 What is fortoune, quha dryffis the dett so fast? [*v.r.* drawis the dait].

7. Phr. ***out of date*** (attrib. ***out-of-date***): out of season; no longer in vogue or fashion, or suitable to the time; obsolete, antiquated; also *advb.*, as in ***to go out of date***, to become obsolete or old-fashioned. (***brought, written, posted***) ***up to date***: said in book-keeper's phrase of accounts, a journal, ledger, etc.; hence, *fig.* up to the knowledge, requirements, or standard of the time (*colloq.*). ***to date***: to the present time or moment. See also UP TO DATE.

1608 ROWLANDS *Hum. Looking Gl.* 10 Choller is past, my anger's out of date. **1707** COLLIER *Refl. Ridic.* 291 Till she's out of Date for Matrimony. *a* **1734** NORTH *Exam.* III. vi. §13 (1740) 432 With his wire-drawn Slanders and out-of-date Reflections. **1824** MEDWIN *Convers. Byron* (1830) I. 124 Shakespeare's Comedies are quite out of date; many of them are insufferable to read. **1868** FREEMAN *Norm. Conq.* (1876) II. App. 538 An idea which had altogether gone out of date. **1890** DILKE *Probl. Gr. Brit.* I. p. vii, I..tried to bring my volumes up to date. **1893** *Westm. Gaz.* 9 Mar. 6/3 The two gentlemen..who invented the Gaiety burlesque 'up to date' —and gave this detestable phrase to the language. **1936** *Nature* 21 Nov. 888/2 The results to date of the treatment.. of cases of cancer..are detailed. **1940** *War Illustr.* 26 Jan. 24 It may be deduced that what has happened to date is the curtain-raiser to that aerial blitzkrieg. **1947** J. S. HUXLEY *Unesco* i. 16 The highest product of evolution to date. **1969** *Listener* 5 June 806/1 All this adds up to one of Dylan's most beautiful songs to date.

8. *Comb.*, as ***date-stamping***; **date-cancel** *v. trans.*, to cancel by a written or stamped date; **date-letter**, a letter stamped upon gold or silver plate, pottery, etc., denoting the year of manufacture; cf. *date-mark*; **date-line**, a line relating to dates; *spec.* the line in the Pacific Ocean (theoretically coincident with the meridian of 180° from Greenwich) at which the calendar day is reckoned to begin and end, so that at places east and west of it the date differs by one day; also a line, or part of one, giving the date of issue of a newspaper or the date (and usually also place of origin) of a dispatch, letter, etc.; hence *vb.* (usually in pa. pple., ***date-lined***); **date-mark** *sb.*, a mark showing the date; *spec.* a letter stamped upon gold or silver plate, denoting the year of manufacture; hence as *vb.* (*nonce-wd.*), to mark with something that shows the date or age; **date-stamp**, a stamp with adjustable types, used in recording the date of posting or delivery of a letter or parcel, receipting a bill, receiving a book, and the like; also, the impression made by such a stamp; so **date-stamp** *v. trans.*, **date-stamping** *vbl. sb.*

1929–30 *Unemployment Book* 2 *Date-cancel stamps immediately. **1863** W. CHAFFERS (*title*) Hall marks on gold and silver plate, with tables of annual *date letters employed in the principal assay offices of England, Scotland and Ireland. **1935** *Burlington Mag.* June 288/1 Over-stamping on Sheffield-made candlesticks the London date-letter for 1775–6. **1880** *Libr. Univ. Knowl.* VIII. 80 *Date-lines.. occur in the Pacific Ocean between islands that have received dates by eastward, and..by westward communication. **1888** *Missouri Republican* 24 Mar. (Farmer *Americanisms* s.v. *Fake*), The telegraph man, who has edited Mulhatton's yarns before, and knows a fake from a barn-door, by the date line alone. **1892** *N.Y. Nation* 21 Apr. 304/1 He has provided an index, but..so simple a device as the running date-line should not have been neglected. **1922** C. SANDBURG *Slabs of Sunburnt West* 35 Turning among headlines, date lines, funnies, ads. **1942** W. FAULKNER *Go down, Moses* 262 It [*sc.* a press report] was datelined from Joliet, Illinois, this morning. **1944** *Daily Express* 7 Sept. 1/5 A message..datelined Zurich to the German-controlled Scandinavian Telegram Bureau. **1959** *Elizabethan* June 28/1 The date line says Jenin, Thursday. **1970** *New Yorker* 3 Oct. 29/2 A recent article in the *Times*, datelined New Providence, commented that a 'developing crisis..has cast a pall over tourism here'. **1850** *Ecclesiologist* X. 181 It is devoid of distinctive *date-marks, except the vague pointed vaulting. **1890** *Whitaker's Almanack* 636 By the following table of date-marks the age of any piece of plate manufactured in London and assayed at Goldsmiths' Hall may be ascertained. **1891** *Times* 12 Oct. 9/5 Each one [guess] has been date-marked, so to speak, by the peculiar beliefs.. of the time or of the place. **1879** TROLLOPE *John Caldigate*

III. x. 139 They got hold of some young man at the post-office who knew how to fix a *date-stamp with a past date. **1908** *Chambers's Jrnl.* Jan. 102/1 As in cases of delay in transmission or delivery, when the date-stamp shows the cause to be late posting. **1909** *Daily Chron.* 2 July 5/5 Mr. Buxton has undertaken that the date-stamps shall not in future bear the name of the firms. **1928** F. M. FORD *Last Post* vii. 168 Each egg wired to the bottom of its box, waiting till she had time to date-stamp it. **1930** C. WILLIAMS *War in Heaven* iii. 37 From date-stamp to waste-paper basket, from basket to files, from files to telephone Adrian pursued his investigation. **1959** *Clarendonian* Mar. 4 At a later stage two copies of each jacket come from the Bindery; one is date-stamped,.. and is then filed for future reference. **1886** *Pall Mall G.* 12 Aug. 5/2 The *date-stamping apparatus on the counter [of a ticket-office]. **1908** *Chambers's Jrnl.* Jan. 102/1 The first process.. to which letters are subjected is that of date-stamping. **1960** *News. Chron.* 22 Sept. 9/7 A housewife faced a conference of food inspectors.. to demand the date-stamping of all perishable foods.

date (deɪt), *v.* [f. DATE *sb.*²: cf. F. *dater*, Sp. *datar* to date.]

1. *trans.* To affix the date to (a writing, etc.); to furnish or mark with a date. A letter is said to be dated *from* the place of writing named in it.

1433 *E.E. Wills* (1882) 94 Dated, ȝere & day aboveseyd. **1530** PALSGR. 507/1 Bycause you use nat to date them [letters], I wotte nat whyther to sende to you. **1682** SCARLETT *Exchanges* 100 A Bill dated the 30th of January. **1712** STEELE *Spect.* No. 308 ¶5 The following Letter.. dated from York. **1796** JANE AUSTEN *Pride & Prej.* (1833) 172 Elizabeth opened the letter.. It was dated from Rosings at eight o'clock in the morning. **1893** *Law Times* XCV. 33/2 A blank transfer.. neither dated nor executed by the bank nor stamped.

2. a. To ascertain or fix the date or time of (an event, etc.); to refer or assign to a certain date, to reckon as beginning *from* (some time or event). Also, to mark as being of a certain date or period; to render outdated or only briefly fashionable or appealing. Also *intr.*, to bear evidence of its or one's date or period; to be or become old-fashioned or outdated (*colloq.*).

1430 LYDG. *Chron. Troy* Prol., Of theyr death he dateth not the yeare. **1654** WHITLOCK *Zootomia* 297 That the yeare of their Maioralty may date the building, or repaire of some Conduit. **1694** PRIOR *Hymn to Sun* ii, From the blessings they bestow, Our times are dated, and our eras move. **1720** SWIFT *Mod. Education*, I date from this æra the corrupt method of education among us. **1844** LINGARD *Anglo-Sax. Ch.* (1858) II. ix. 52 Every Christian Church which dates its origin from any period before the Reformation. **1865** TYLOR *Early Hist. Man.* v. 91 The art of dating events. **1895** *Westm. Gaz.* 13 Mar. 5/1 Every portion of a picture was 'dated' from every other portion of it. **1896** G. B. SHAW *Our Theatres in Nineties* (1932) II. 168, I have been led into this investigation of 'dating' by the fact that The School for Scandal.. dated very perceptibly last Saturday night at the Lyceum in point of morals. **1901** *Daily Chron.* 17 May 6/6 In the four or five years it has been laid aside it [*sc.* a play] has not 'dated' in the slightest degree. **1911** in C. W. Cunnington *Eng. Women's Clothing* (1952) iii. 104 These hats would.. never date their owners. **1915** H. G. WELLS *Research Magnificent* 9 He had found the word 'Bushido' written with a particularly flourishing capital letter, and twice repeated. 'This was inevitable,' said White... 'And it dates... Yes—this was early.' **1924** *Glasgow Herald* 6 Nov. 8 George Eliot still has her readers,.. but she has begun to 'date' rather decidedly. **1925** *Sat. Rev.* 7 Nov. 1 Younger men say with contemptuous brevity that his views 'date'. **1927** E. BOWEN *Hotel* ix. 103 The ornaments on Mrs. Kerr's dressing-table.. 'dated' her friend for her inevitably. **1928** BELLOC *Convers. w. Angel* xxiv. 198 All the middle and early Victorians are already dating—except Macaulay. **1928** GALSWORTHY *Swan Song* III. xvi. 341 'I respected old Forsyte,' he said to his son... 'He dated, and he couldn't express himself; but there was no humbug about him.' **1932** N. COWARD *Cavalcade* II. iii. 80 'I was in "Mirabelle" then.' .. 'I was taken to see that.'.. '*Taken* to see it, were you! That dates us a bit.' **1951** R. KNOX *Stimuli* i. 4 Nothing.. so dates our generation as this habit of talking about things being dated. **1957** *Times Lit. Suppl.* 20 Dec. 773/4 Almost all the films he discussed just ten short years ago have either badly dated or been forgotten.

b. To reckon chronologically or by dates.

182. BYRON *To C'tess Blessington* iv, My life is not dated by years—There are moments which act as a plough. **1837** DISRAELI *Venetia* II. i, Life is not dated merely by years.

c. *absol.* To count the time, reckon.

a **1742** BENTLEY (J.), Whether we begin the world so many millions of ages ago, or date from the late æra of about six thousand years. **1807** *Med. Jrnl.* XVII. 27 Six full days had ..passed..dating from the time when the eruption appeared.

d. To make or have a 'date' with (see DATE *sb.*² 2 c); *spec.* to do so regularly. Freq. in *pass.* Also *intr.* and with *up*. *colloq.* (orig. *U.S.*).

1902 ADE *Girl Proposition* 70 Before he left that Evening he had himself all dated up for a return engagement. **1903** A. KLEBERG *Slang Fables* 67 She was Dated to a chap with Uncounted wealth. **1917** E. W. LARDNER *Gullible's Travels* iii. 86, I.. dated her up to meet me down-town the next day. **1919** *Saucy Stories* Nov. 57/2 'What about the movies..?' 'All I can hand you is my thanks, I'm dated up!' **1924** *Ibid.* Feb. 30/1 What will.. people.. think when you are dated to show up with Miss Future Wife. **1924** 'W. FABIAN' *Sailors' Wives* iv. 59 Warren Graves wants to date me for the Deuces Wild party Saturday night. **1928** *Collier's* 5 May 36/3 Dat fool gal datin' wid me and wawkin' off wid dat money man. **1938** D. RUNYON *Furthermore* v. 95 These characters keep trying to date up the nurses. **1938** E. BOWEN *Death of Heart* II. vi. 290 I'm afraid I've given you rather a miss... But it's been a thickish week, and I got all dated up. **1947** 'N. SHUTE' *Chequer Board* 62 The white troops found to their concern that every girl was dated up by a negro. **1958** S. ELLIN *Eighth Circle* (1959) II. xvi. 172 'When will I see you again?' 'You can't!' she said in alarm. 'I mean, not this way, as if we were dating or something.' **1970** *New Yorker* 18 July 28/3, I was too busy with other social engagements. I was all dated up with the Greeks.

e. To assign *to* a specified date.

1913 E. T. LEEDS *Archaeol. Anglo-Saxon Settlements* v. 86 This find can be dated by coins to about A.D. 290. **1957** G. BIBBY *Testimony of Spade* xxiii. 371 The discovery.. of swords of the La Tène type together with Roman coins, of which the latest was dated to 54 B.C. **1971** *N. & Q.* CCXVI. 116/1 Both he [*sc.* Jordan] and Luick date the final /iu/ stage to the fifteenth century.

†**3.** To put an end or period to. *Obs.*

1589 GREENE *Menaphon* (Arb.) 25 Alledging how death at the least may date his miserie. **1612** T. TAYLOR *Comm. Titus* iii. 2 The precept is neuer dated, but in full force. *a* **1618** SYLVESTER *Epist.* v. 11 His matchlesse Art, that never age shall date.

†**4.** To assign a time or duration to. *Obs. rare.*

1676 HALE *Contempl.* I. 67 The studies of Policy, Methods of War.. are all dated for the convenience and use of this life.

†**5.** To give (oneself) out as. *Obs. rare.*

1612 CHAPMAN *Widowes T.* Plays 1873 III. 11 A Spartan Lord, dating himselfe our great Viceroies Kinsman.

†**6.** *to date from*: to refer or ascribe to (a particular origin). *Obs. rare.*

1725 N. ROBINSON *Th. Physick* 150 As we have dated the immediate Cause of all Acute Diseases, especially Fevers, from the Contraction of the Solids.

7. *intr.* (for *refl.*). To bear date, be dated; to be written or addressed *from* (a specified place).

a **1850** ROSSETTI *Dante & Circ.* I. (1874) 27 Dante's sonnet probably dates from Ravenna. **1874** DEUTSCH *Rem.* 363 A recent.. edition dates Wilna 1852. *Mod.* The letter dates from London.

8. a. To assign itself or be assigned to a specified time or period; to have its origin, take its rise *from* a particular time or epoch.

a **1828** E. EVERETT (Webster), The Batavian republic dates from the successes of the French arms. **1846** GROTE *Greece* I. i. I. 68 The worship of the Sminthian Apollo dates before the earliest periods of Æolic colonization. **1856** KANE *Arct. Expl.* I. xi. 27 We learned that the house dated back as far as the days of Matthew Stach. **1868** FREEMAN *Norm. Conq.* (1876) II. viii. 177 Two stately parish churches, one of them dating from the days of Norman independence.

b. To rank in point of date or standing *with*.

1827 HOOD *Plea Mids. Fairies* xxviii, For we are very kindly creatures, dating With Nature's charities.

date, obs. form of DAUT *v.* Sc., to fondle.

dateable: see DATABLE.

dated ('deɪtɪd), *ppl. a.* [f. DATE *v.* (and *sb.*²) + -ED.]

1. Marked or inscribed with a date.

1731 POPE *Ep. Burlington* 135 To all their dated Backs he turns you round; These Aldus printed, those Du Süeil has bound. **1881** H. B. WHEATLEY *Cath. Angl.* Pref. p. ix, The Catholicon is specially valuable as a dated Dictionary.

†**2.** Having a fixed date or term. *Obs.*

1586 MARLOWE *1st Pt. Tamburl.* II. vi, The loathsome circle of my dated life. **1592** NASHE *P. Penilesse* (ed. 2) 18 b, That can endow your names with neuer dated glory. **1718** D'URFEY *Grecian Heroine* III. ii. in *New Opera's* (1721) 122 His dated time comes on.

3. Belonging to or characteristic of a particular period; bearing evidence of its (or one's) date or period; old-fashioned, outdated. *colloq.*

1900 F. H. STODDARD *Evol. Eng. Novel* ii. 53 It is a dated society, and it is a dated woman, not the woman of all time. **1926** *Atlantic Monthly* June 769/1 Another newspaper sent out a man who, it happened, was 'dated' in his reportorial training. He.. got the facts. **1944** *Burlington Mag.* Dec. 312/2 It is this meticulous realism which makes his figures appear so peculiarly 'dated'. **1954** KOESTLER *Invis. Writing* I. ii. 28 The orthodox 'proletarian' literature of the 'thirties appears to-day shallow and dated. **1962** *Oxford Mail* 19 Feb. 6/5 Much of the music has a dated air. **1970** *Daily Tel.* 17 Oct. 6/5 A great many I saw at the races were still wearing dated, conventional two-piece outfits—a bit too long, a bit too dowdy.

dateless ('deɪtlɪs), *a.* [-LESS.]

1. a. Without a date, bearing no date, undated.

1644 PRYNNE & WALKER *Fiennes's Trial* 5 A Note.. without name or date, with a datelesse, namelesse Paper inclosed. **1798** W. TAYLOR in *Monthly Rev.* XXVII. 514 A dateless account.. inserted after the edict for its abolition. **1891** *Spectator* 4 Apr., Here is a dateless letter.

b. Free from engagements or appointments. *U. S.*

1923 *N. Y. Tribune* 25 Apr., The young men at Northwestern University have agreed to join the young women of that institution in observing three dateless nights each week. **1944** *Chicago Tribune* 10 Dec. Grafic Mag. 4 Sometimes that mood indigo comes up briefly on a dateless Friday night.

2. Having no limit or fixed term; endless.

1593 SHAKS. *Rich. II*, I. iii. 151 The datelesse limit of thy deere exile. **1624** DARCIE *Birth of Heresies* 108 Thy datelesse fame. **1811** SHELLEY *St. Irvyne* Prose Wks. 1888 I. 219 A dateless and hopeless eternity of horror. **1870** LOWELL *Study Wind.* (1886) 164 Immortal as that dateless substance of the soul.

3. Of indefinite duration in the past; so ancient that its date or age cannot be determined; immemorial.

1794 COLERIDGE *Poems, Relig. Musings*, In the primeval age a dateless while The vacant shepherd wandered with his flock. **1814** WORDSW. *Excursion* VI. Wks. (1888) 493/2 From dateless usage which our peasants hold Of giving welcome to the first of May. **1849** RUSKIN *Sev. Lamps* iii. §4. 66 The dateless hills, which it needed earthquakes to lift, and deluges to mould.

4. *dial.* Out of one's senses, crazed; insensible. Also, foolish, 'clueless'.

a **1686** A. MARTINDALE *Life* (1845) iv. 79 Which he, being almost datelesse for age,.. readily granted. **1848** MRS. GASKELL *M. Barton* II. vi. 98 Poor soul, she's gone dateless, I think, with care, and watching, and over-much trouble. **1854** *N. & Q.* 1st Ser. X. 211/1 'After he hit me o' th' heead I was *dateless*;' that is, I took no note of time. **1863** MRS. GASKELL *Sylvia's L.* II. 263 Mother is gone dateless wi' sorrow. **1867** E. WAUGH *Dead Man's Dinner* 19 (*Lanc. Gloss.*) They.. laid her upo' th' couch cheer, as dateless as a stone. **1961** J. I. M. STEWART *Man who won Pools* v. 58 She'll be pretty dateless, won't she, as the wife of a man with hundreds of thousands of pounds? *Ibid.* xi. 121 He'd been pretty well flourishing a quarter of a million pounds at her like she was a dateless shopgirl.

5. *absol.* Cf. TIMELESS *a.* 2 b.

1894 *Daily News* 17 Sept. 4/6 Its [*sc.* the British Museum's] way of bringing itself.. to date is to approach nearer and nearer to the dateless.

Hence **'datelessly** *adv.*; **'datelessness**, the quality of being dateless; the absence of a fixed limit of time.

1660 T. M. *Hist. Independ.* iv. 91 The Officers of his [Monk's] Army.. agreed.. that the Parliament intended.. to perpetuate the Nations slavery by their datelesness. **1956** K. CLARK *Nude* iv. 117 The standing woman is not so datelessly naturalistic. Her.. complex pose seems to have been derived from an antique relief.

dater ('deɪtə(r)). [-ER¹.] **a.** One who dates. **b.** An apparatus for date-stamping.

1611 COTGR., *Dataire*, a dater of writings.. the dater, or dispatcher, of the Pope's Bulls; an ordinarie Officer in the Court of Rome. **1887** *Richford's Circular*, Perpetual hand daters.

daðe, obs. form of DEATH *sb.*

daþeit, daþet, etc.: see DAHET.

datholite, erron. var. of DATOLITE.

dating ('deɪtɪŋ), *vbl. sb.* [-ING¹.] **a.** The action of the verb DATE, q.v.; *spec.* the act or process of becoming 'dated' (see DATE *v.* 2, DATED *ppl. a.* 3).

1678 *Trials of Ireland, &c.* 19 He was then in London.. as I suppose by the dateing of his Letters. **1891** B. NICHOLSON in *Athenæum* 10 Jan. 61/2 As other datings of his are apparently advanced one year, his dating requires to be inquired into. **1896** [see DATE *v.* 2]. **1936** C. CONNOLLY *Rock Pool* 12 The fault I am most conscious of.. is that of dating. .. In this case my debt is with the nineteen-twenties.

b. *Archæol.* The determination of the age of an object, etc., found in archæological research. Also *attrib.*

1926 *Encycl. Brit.* I. 157/2 It is.. possible .. to lay down a chronological order by the sequence method of dating, based primarily on pottery. **1936** *Discovery* Nov. 362/2 The Bournemouth specimens were found in conditions which give no criterion for dating. **1950** F. E. ZEUNER *Dating Past* (ed. 2) I. 11 Dendrochronology may well become a dating-method in such areas.

c. The act or practice of making or having 'dates' (see DATE *sb.*² 2 c). Also *attrib. colloq.* (orig. *U.S.*).

1939 G. GREENE *Lawless Roads* x. 249 Rating for dating. The famous sub-deb chart for getting along with boys. **1951** M. MCLUHAN *Mech. Bride* 72/2 She has to be so rigorously self-controlled during several years of dating. *Ibid.* 99/1 The precocious dating habits of middle-class children. **1952** W. SPROTT *Social Psychol.* 167 The 'dating' system in America. **1958** H. REILLY *Ding Dong Bell* (1959) viii. 78 He was around yesterday and again today. Rather heavy dating, considering that he and Carol have only known each other a month or so. **1959** *Economist* 30 May 821/2 The Americans are better since.. they have already, at 17, several years of dating experience behind them. **1968** *Globe & Mail* (Toronto) 17 Feb. 53/4 (Advt.), Many more exciting dates, parties, and trips. Dating by computer!

dation ('deɪʃən). [ad. L. *datiōn-em*, n. of action from *dare* to give.] The action of giving. †**a.** *Med.* A dose. **b.** *Civil Law.* A rendering of L. *datio*, F. *dation*, the legal act of giving or conferring, *e.g.* of an office; *esp.* as distinct from *donation*.

1656 BLOUNT *Glossogr.*, *Dation*, a giving, a gift, a dole. **1657** TOMLINSON *Renou's Disp.* 163 That.. quantity of a medicament which is prescibed.. is a Dosis, for Dosis is Dation. —— *Gloss.*, *Dation*, the quantity or dosis of any medicament that is administred to the patient at once. **1889** in *Century Dict.* (in sense b).

‖**Datisca** (də'tɪskə). *Bot.* [mod.L. (Linnæus gives no source).] The name of a genus of monochlamydeous exogens (N.O. *Datiscaceæ*); *D. cannabina*, the Cretan or Bastard Hemp-plant, is indigenous to Nepaul and the Levant; its leaves contain a colouring matter known as *datisca-yellow*, used in dyeing silk, etc. Hence **da'tiscin**, a glucoside, $C_{21}H_{22}O_{12}$, allied to salicin, obtained from the leaves and root of Datisca. **da'tiscetin**, $C_{15}H_{10}O_6$, a crystalline product of the decomposition of datiscin.

1863–72 WATTS *Dict. Chem.* II. 306 The leaves contain a peculiar colouring matter, *datisca-yellow*. *Ibid.* 307 Pure datiscin forms colourless silky needles.. By boiling with strong potash-ley, it is decomposed with formation of datiscetin.

datisi (də'taɪsaɪ). *Logic.* The mnemonic term designating the mood of the third figure of syllogisms in which the major premiss is a universal affirmative (*a*), and the minor premiss and conclusion particular affirmatives (*i*, *i*).

The initial *d* indicates that the mood may be reduced to *darii* of the first figure; the *s* following the second vowel, that this is done by simple conversion of the minor premiss.

1551 T. WILSON *Logike* (1580) 30 The third figure. *Da.* All hipocrites count will workes hie holines. *ti.* Some hipocrites have been Bishoppes. *si.* Therefore some Bishoppes have coumpted will workes hie holinesse. **1654** Z. COKE *Art Logick* (1657) 136 The Modes of this Figure are six. Called, *Darapti, Felapton, Disamis, Datisi, Bocardo, Ferison.* **1864** BOWEN *Logic* vii. 200.

Datism (ˈdeɪtɪz(ə)m). *rare.* [ad. Gr. *Δᾱτισμός* 'a speaking like Datis (the Median commander at Marathon), *i.e.* speaking broken Greek' (Liddell & Scott).] Broken or barbarous speech; a fault in speaking such as would be made by one not fully acquainted with the language.

1617 MINSHEU *Ductor, Datisme*, when by a heape of Synonimaes wee rehearse the same things. **1891** *Sat. Rev.* 14 Nov. 554/2 We can understand that a small Athenian boy should commit a Datism in Latin; but we cannot see why the Roman boy should make a neuter verb transitive.

datival (dəˈtaɪvəl), *a. Gram.* [f. L. *datīv-us* (see next) + -AL[1].] Belonging to the dative case.

1818 *Monthly Mag.* XLVI. 322 Instead of the genitival and datival terminations.

dative (ˈdeɪtɪv), *a.* and *sb.* [ad. L. *datīv-us* of or belonging to giving, f. *dat-us* given; in grammar rendering Gr. δοτική(πτῶσις), from δοτικός of giving nature, f. δοτ-ός given.] **A.** *adj.*

1. *Gram.* The name of that case of nouns in Aryan and some other languages which commonly denotes the indirect or more remote object of the action of a verb, that *to* or *for* whom or which we do a thing, or *to* whom we give a thing.

c **1440** *Gesta Rom.* xci. 416 (Add. MS.) The thrid Falle is datif case, for there are some that are prowde for they mow gyve. **1580** HOLLYBAND *Treas. Fr. Tong*, A.. serueth many times to expresse the Datiue case: as *Je l'ay donne à mon pere*, I gaue it to my father. **1668** WILKINS *Real Char.* 352 The Dative Case is expressed by the Preposition (To). **1879** ROBY *Lat. Gram.* IV. ix. §1130 The Dative case is used in two senses only: (A) It expresses the *indirect object* ..(B) It is used *predicatively* in a quasi-adjectival sense. *Mod.* The pronouns *me, thee, him, her, us, you, them*, which we now use both as direct and indirect objectives, were originally dative forms; the original accusatives are disused.

†**2.** Disposed to give; having the right to give. *Obs. rare.* (In first quot. with play on sense 1.)

14.. *Piers of Fullham* 368 in Hazl. *E.P.P.* II. 15 To knowen folke that ben datyff: Their purches be called ablatif: They haue their ȝen vocatif. **1656** BLOUNT *Glossogr., Dative*, that giveth, or is of power to give.

†**3.** Of the nature of a gift; conferred or bestowed as a gift. (Freq. opposed to *native*.) *Obs.*

1570–6 LAMBARDE *Peramb. Kent* (1826) 453 All Nobilitie and Gentrie is either, Native, or Dative, that is to say, commeth either by Discent, or by Purchase [i.e. acquisition]. **1661** MORGAN *Sph. Gentry* III. iii. 28 The first Native.. the second Dative, being given in rewards.

4. *Law.* **a.** That may be given or disposed of at pleasure; in one's gift. **b.** Of an officer: Appointed so as to be removable at pleasure: opposed to *perpetual*. **c.** *Sc. Law.* Given or appointed by a magistrate or a court of justice, not by a testator or by the mere disposition of law; pertaining to such appointment: as in ***executor dative***, an executor appointed by decree of the commissary when none has been appointed by the deceased, an administrator; ***decree dative***, a decree appointing an executor dative; ***testament dative***, the decree confirming and conferring full title on an executor dative; ***tutor dative***, a tutor appointed by the Court on the failure of tutors-nominate and tutors-at-law; *tutory dative*, the office of a tutor dative. **d.** ***tutor dative***, in *Rom. Law*, one appointed by the testator, as distinguished from ***tutor optive***.

1535–6 *Act 27 Hen. VIII*, c. 28 §15 Pryours or governours datyff & removable from tyme to tyme. **1575** *T. Huntar v. D. Hunter* in Balfour *Practicks* 115 Sum tutoris ar testamentaris, sum tutoris of law, and sum ar tutoris dative. The tutor dative is maid and gevin be the King. **1651** N. BACON *Disc. Govt. Eng.* II. vi. (1739) 29 They shall certify.. whether a Prior be perpetual, or dative. **1726** AYLIFFE *Parergon* 265 Those are term'd Dative Executors who are appointed such by the Judges Decree, as Administrators with us here in England. **1754** ERSKINE *Princ. Sc. Law* (1809) 85 If no tutor of law demands the office, any person ..may apply for a tutory-dative. **1796** (*title*), The Testament Dative, and Inventory of the debts..justly owing to umquhile Robert Burns.. at the time of his decease ..faithfully made out and given up by Jean Armour, widow of the said defunct, and executrix qua relict, decerned to him by decreet dative of the Commissary of Dumfries. **1848** WHARTON *Law Lex., Dative*.. that which may be given or disposed of at will and pleasure. **1861** *Sat. Rev.* 25 May 542 In the fourth year of Henry V, all the dative alien priories were dissolved and granted to the Crown. **1880** MUIRHEAD *Gaius* I. §154 Tutors appointed in a testament by express nomination are called tutors dative; those selected in virtue of a power of option, tutors optive.

B. *sb.* (ellipt. use of the adj.)

1. *Gram.* Short for *dative case*: see A.

1520 WHITINTON *Vulg.* (1527) 11 Somtyme in the stede of genytiue case he wyll haue a datyue. **1751** HARRIS *Hermes* II. iv. (1786) 287 The Dative, as it implies Tendency to, is employed.. to denote the Final Cause. **1861** MAX MÜLLER *Sc. Lang.* vi. 208 The locative may well convey the meaning of the dative.

attrib. **1868** G. STEPHENS *Runic. Mon.* I. 260 Other examples of this.. dative-ending.

†**2.** *Sc. Law.* A decree dative: see A. 4 c. *Obs.*

1564 *Act of Sederunt* 24 July (Jam.), We haif given.. power to our saids Commissaries of Edinburgh, to give datives, and constitute.. executors-datives. **1666** *Instruct. Commissaries* in *Acts Sedt.* 1553–1790 p. 95 If neither nearest of kin, executor or creditor shall desire to be confirmed.. ye shall confirm your procurator fiscal, datives always being duly given thereto before.. After the said datives (but before confirmation).

C. *Comb.* **dative absolute**, in some inflected languages, a construction resembling the Latin ablative absolute, in which a substantive and participle in the dative case form an adverbial clause of time, cause, or coexistence; **dative-accusative** *a.*, having the functions of both the dative and the accusative case; *sb.*, such a grammatical form; **dative-object**, an object governed by the verb and in the dative case; **dative-phrase**, a phrase in which a preposition has a function equivalent to that of a dative case-ending in a language like Latin (cf. *case-phrase*); **dative-verb**, a verb regularly constructed with the dative.

1870 F. A. MARCH *Compar. Gram. Anglo-Saxon* III. 152 *Dative absolute.*— A substantive and participle in the dative may make an adverbial clause of time, cause, or coexistence. **1918** M. CALLAWAY *Syntax Lindisfarne Gospels* i. 14 As before 1889, so in these later discussions, two views as to the dative absolute construction in Gothic are advocated. **1965** B. MITCHELL *Guide to Old English* v. 105 The dative absolute is used in imitation of the Latin absolute, e.g. *gewunnenum sige* 'victory having been gained'. **1933** L. BLOOMFIELD *Lang.* xxiv. 437 Nominative *ye*: dative-accusative *you*. **1940** C. C. FRIES *Amer. Eng. Gram.* 88 The six distinctive dative-accusitive forms of pronouns (me, us, him, them, her, whom). **1959** M. SCHLAUCH *Eng. Lang.* i. 32 Prepositions ceased to 'control' more than one following case (a single form serving as dative-accusative, which for nouns had become identical with the nominative). **1927** E. A. SONNENSCHEIN *Soul of Gram.* 29 In English, in Greek, and occasionally in Latin the dative-object may become the subject... I was shown the way. **1940** C. C. FRIES *Amer. Eng. Gram.* 254 Nouns which formerly stood before the so-called impersonal verbs as dative-objects.. now.. functioned as subjects. **1927** E. A. SONNENSCHEIN *Soul of Gram.* 49 The dative-phrases of French and Spanish are simply developments of dative-phrases found in all periods of Latin. **1804** —— *Gr. Gram.* II. 168 (*heading*) Verbs taking the Dative (Dative Verbs).

datively (ˈdeɪtɪvlɪ), *adv. Gram.* [f. prec. + -LY[2].] In the dative case; as a dative.

1846 MONIER WILLIAMS *Elem. Gram. Sanscrit* ix. 160 Datively Dependent.. those in which the relation of the first word to the last is equivalent to that of a dative. **1886** *Century Mag.* XXXII. 898 The pronoun of the first or second person, used datively.

dativo- (dəˈtaɪvəʊ), combining form of L. *datīvus*, DATIVE, used in adverbial comb. with other adjectives.

1882 F. HALL in *Amer. Jrnl. Philol.* III. 17 Our infinitive, where *to* precedes it, having been generally, of old, dativo-gerundial [*i.e.* of the nature of a dative gerund]. **1930** T. SASAKI *Lang. of R. Bridges' Poetry* 87 Use of the infin. in the dativo-locative function.

‖**dato** (ˈdɑːtəʊ), **datu** (ˈdɑːtuː). Also **datoh, datoo, datto.** [Malay *datu* ruler, chief; *dato'*, *datok* elder, title of respect or distinction; Tagalog *datò* ruling head of clan or tribe.] A landowner or chief in northern Borneo, the Philippine Islands, and some adjacent areas.

[**1820** J. CRAWFURD *Hist. Ind. Archip.* III. VIII. i. 22 Native term for king in Javanese is *Ratu*, which is the same word that is written *Datu* in some other languages. Its literal meaning is grandfather, and by a slight inflection a senior or elder, from which last is taken its figurative meaning, a lord or chief.] **1841** J. BROOKE in E. Hahn *James Brooke* (1953) v. 68 The revenue will be collected by the three Datus, bearing the seal of the governor. **1867** SMYTH *Sailor's Word-bk., Datoo*,.. a Malay term of rank, and four of whom form the council of the sultan of the Malayu Islands. **1897** *Geogr. Jrnl.* Jan. 36 The Galas district is nominally under the charge of the Dato. **1906** *Daily Colonist* (Victoria, B.C.) 13 Jan. 2/4 [In the Philippine Islands] W. J. Bryan yesterday was created a 'Datto' and saluted by fifty pieces of native artillery. **1925** *Chambers's Jrnl.* 46/1 The Malay point of view was well expressed by a certain *Datoh*, or landowner of good birth. **1960** S. RUNCIMAN *White Rajahs* III. iv. 219 The Resident and four Datus were lined up there to greet him.

datolite (ˈdætəʊlaɪt). *Min.* Also erron. **datholite** (*Werner*). [Named by Esmark 1806: irreg. f. initial part of Gr. δατεῖσθαι to divide + -λιθος stone: see -LITE.]

A borosilicate of calcium, occurring in glassy crystals of various colours, in white opaque compact masses, or in botryoidal masses (*botryolite*).

1808 T. ALLAN *Names of Min.* 26 Datholite. **1868** DANA *Min.* 382 Datolite is found in trappean rocks.

‖**dattock** (ˈdætək). [Native name in W. Africa.] The hard mahogany-like wood of a West African tree, *Detarium senegalense*, N.O. *Leguminosæ*; also the tree itself.

1884 MILLER *Plant-n.*, 'Dattock', of W. Tropical Africa.

‖**datum** (ˈdeɪtəm). Pl. **data** (ˈdeɪtə). [L. *datum* given, that which is given, neut. pa. pple. of *dare* to give.] **1. a.** A thing given or granted; something known or assumed as fact, and made the basis of reasoning or calculation; an assumption or premiss from which inferences are drawn.

1646 HAMMOND *Wks.* (1674) I. 248 (Stanf.) From all this heap of *data* it would not follow that it was necessary. **1691** T. H[ALE] *Acc. New Invent.* 128 Out of what Data arises the knowledge. **1737** FIELDING *Hist. Register* Ded., All.. will grant me this datum, that the said.. person is a man of an ordinary capacity. **1777** PRIESTLEY *Matt. & Spir.* (1782) I. xii. 146 We have no data to go upon. **1807** HUTTON *Course Math.* II. 350 The omission of a material datum in the calculation.. namely, the weight of the charge of powder. **1888** BRYCE *Amer. Commw.* III. lxxvi. 9 The historical and scientific data on which the solution.. depends.

b. *Comb.*, as ***datum-feature, -level, -line, -mark, -plane, -point, -year.***

1954 *Defs. Mech. Engin.* (*B.S.I.*) 9 A datum plane, line or point establishes an exact geometrical reference as distinct from the physical reference provided by a datum feature. **1869** R. B. SMYTH *Goldfields Victoria* 609 *Datum Water-Level*, the level at which water was first struck in a shaft sunk on a reef or gutter. **1909** *Daily Chron.* 6 July 5/7 The price is below what one may call the datum level of £6,000. **1957** G. E. HUTCHINSON *Treat. Limnol.* I. ii. 165 The maximum depth will vary slightly with variations in water level, and ideally it should be referred to some independent datum level. **1855** H. SPENCER *Princ. Psychol.* (1872) II. VI. viii, Mountains.. can have their relative heights determined only by reference to some common datum-line, as the level of the sea. **1882** GEIKIE *Text-bk. Geol.* VII. (1885) 925 The lines of stratification may be used as datum-lines to measure approximately the amount of rock which has been worn away. **1954** Datum line [see *datum feature* above]. **1926** *Nat. Hist. Oxf. District* 75 The datum mark of the Thames at Osney is 186 ft. above its outlet at the Nore. **1885** *Science* 19 June 499 The horizontal datum-plane adopted by German craniologists. **1954** Datum plane [see *datum feature* above]. **1912** *Aeroplane* 5 Dec. 570/2 Their duty will be to enable battery commanders to fix 'Datum Points' in the sky. **1933** H. G. WELLS *Shape of Things to Come* IV. §4. 359 The intrinsic quality of this book has been entirely overshadowed by its importance as a datum point in history. **1954** Datum point [see *datum feature* above]. **1940** *Economist* 9 Nov. 581/1 The Treasury's choice of datum years does allow most industries the advantage of retaining part.. of their.. profits.

c. *Philos.* ***datum of consciousness***, etc. (see quots.). Esp. ***datum of sense*** (cf. SENSE-DATUM).

1846 W. HAMILTON *Wks. T. Reid* 749/2 The primary data of consciousness are.. admitted.. to be true. **1856** A. C. FRASER *Ess. Philos.* iv. 212 This notion of the Infinite is in fact an *ultimate datum* of consciousness. **1887** A. SETH *Hegelianism* iv. 118 That elementary statement must be originally made in virtue of.. some immediate *datum* of experience. **1890** W. JAMES *Princ. Psychol.* II. xx. 252 'Can a doubleness, so easily neutralized by our knowledge, ever be a datum of sensation at all?' such an anti-sensationalist might ask. **1890** A. C. FRASER *Locke* 186 Locke thus reduces the entire certain knowledge of sensible things that man is capable of to one's present data of sense, and one's memory of past data. **1895** W. JAMES *Coll. Ess. & Rev.* (1920) 392 For our colleague Ladd,.. the soul.. furthermore performs a unifying *act* on the naturally separate data of sense. **1902** —— *Var. Relig. Exper.* 427 Mystical states merely add a supersensuous meaning to the ordinary outward data of consciousness.

d. *pl.* The quantities, characters, or symbols on which operations are performed by computers and other automatic equipment, and which may be stored or transmitted in the form of electrical signals, records on magnetic tape or punched cards, etc.

1946 *Ann. Computation Lab. Harvard Univ.* I. 11 Two card feeds for supplying the machine with empirical or other data. **1946** *Math. Tables & Other Aids to Computation* II. 97 The [IBM card] reader scans standard punched cards.. and causes data from them to be stored in relays located in the constant transmitter. **1958** GOTLIEB & HUME *High-Speed Data Processing* i. 6 The machine as a whole can be considered to be a device which accepts data and instructions.., stores them.., operates on the data.. and produces results by the output. **1960** E. DELAVENAY *Introd. Machine Transl.* ii. 21 A memory may be used to store data, or to store programme instructions. **1964** *AFIPS Conference Proc.* XXVI. I. 219 Data is transferred to main storage as soon as two bytes are accumulated. **1967** *Times Rev. Industry* July 53/3 Up to 50 types of data can be analysed with one pass through the machine. **1969** P. B. JORDAIN *Condensed Computer Encycl.* 306 Data are recorded on the tape by magnetizing narrow lengthwise stripes (called tracks) in alternating directions. **1970** *Sci. Jrnl.* June 23/3 During each orbit data from the experiment is transmitted from the satellite to Fairbanks in Alaska and from there.. to Oxford for initial processing. **1970** A. CHANDOR et al. *Dict. Computers* 99 Data is sometimes contrasted with information, which is said to result from the processing of data.

2. *pl.* Facts, esp. numerical facts, collected together for reference or information.

1899 W. W. F. PULLEN (*title*) Tables and data for the use of students in engineering laboratories. **1913** (*title*) Handbook of chemistry and physics; a ready-reference book of chemical and physical data. **1923** C. G. CONRADI *Mech. Road Transport* v. 51, I have concluded this chapter with three tables, giving the requisite data pertaining to various solids, liquids and gases.. which may be employed as fuels.

1934 H. B. DWIGHT (*title*) Tables of integrals and other mathematical data. **1946** *Nature* 12 Oct. 519/1 Hexavalent chromium compounds were selected for this study as accurate X-ray and magnetic data for these compounds are available. **1958** MACDUFF & CURRERI *Vibration Control* vii. 165 Most of the data concerning shock and vibration on airplanes are classified. **1971** *Daily Tel.* 28 June 17 Desk research means collecting data from all published sources including government censuses, production figures, import and export statistics,..and trade publications.

3. Used *attrib.* and in *Comb.* in the pl. form, as ***data bank, -handling, -transfer*** vbl. sb., ***transmission***; **data capture** *Computing*, the action or process of entering data into a computer, esp. when it occurs as an accompaniment to a related operation; cf. CAPTURE *sb.* 1 e; **data entry** *Computing*, the action, process, or an act, of entering data into a computer; freq. *attrib.*; **data file** *Computing*, a file containing data (as opposed to a program); **data link**, a telecommunications link over which data are transmitted, usu. to or from a data-processing centre; **data logger**, any instrument for making a recording, either continuously or intermittently, of the successive values of a number of different physical quantities; so **data-logging** *vbl. sb.*; **data processing**, the performance by automatic means of any operations on empirical data, such as classifying or analysing them or carrying out calculations on them; also *transf.*; so **data processor; data protection**, the legal regulation of access to data held in computer storage; **data retrieval** *Computing*, retrieval of data held in computer storage; **data sheet**, a leaflet containing a summary of useful information on some subject; **data structure** *Computing*, the way data is organized in a computer, in so far as it affects the use or modification of the data; also, a collection of data items given a particular structure; **data terminal** *Computing*, a terminal at which a person can enter data into a computer-based system or receive data from one; **data type** *Computing*, a particular kind of data item, as defined by the values it can take or the operations that can be performed on it.

1970 *Daily Tel.* 8 Oct. 9/4 *Data banks containing comprehensive personal files covering criminal records, health records, income tax and so on, would be liable to abuse. **1966** S. BEER *Decision & Control* xv. 384 Mechanical, electrical, photo-electric and electronic means can be used to detect the information sought. A range of..*data-capture devices is already available for the purpose. **1972** *New Scientist* 27 Jan. 207 The credit card holder can be replaced with a document holder or a roll of paper tape, for other data capture purposes. **1978** *Bookseller* 17 June 3196/1 Teleordering could facilitate..data capture at the point of sale. **1984** *Dictionaries* VI. 184 The university had neither the experience nor interest in the initial data capture through manual entering. **1970** C. T. MEADOW *Man-Machine Communication* vii. 194 Here, then, [in library cataloguing] is a truly complex *data entry operation. **1977** *Time* 14 Mar. 1/1 (Advt.), Philips Data Systems products include office computers, small business computers, terminal systems, data-entry systems and mini computers. **1978** W. S. DAVIS *Information Processing Systems* iv. 74 One growing application of CRTs is in data entry... Using a CRT, the terminal operator can enter the data through the keyboard and *directly* into the computer. **1979** *Arizona Daily Star* 5 Aug. (Advt. Section) 1/9 Will operate data entry equipment... Requires equivalence of a high school education, data entry skills and one year of data entry work experience. **1983** G. WIEDERHOLD *Database Design* (ed. 2) v. 260 If an error can be detected while the source of the data is still available, the cost of correction may be only a few times the cost of the original data entry. **1966** C. J. SIPPL *Computer Dict. & Handbk.* (1967) 87/1 A permanent *data file is one in which the data is perpetually subject to being updated... A working data file is a temporary accumulation of data sets which is destroyed after the data has been transferred to another form. **1984** *Which Micro?* Dec. 51 (Advt.), You can store up to 50 different data files per cartridge. **1964** *Language* XL. 214 Human beings are somehow specially designed to do this, with *data-handling ability. **1968** *Brit. Med. Bull.* XXIV. 189/2 The computer is a machine which can perform any data-handling procedure. **1966** *Guardian* 4 May 20/3 *Data links exist now. **1968** *New Scientist* 8 Feb. 312/2 From this central collection point the telephone *data link will connect the various patients to the computer system. **1962** *Aeroplane* CIV. 34/3 A 500-channel *data logger capable of scanning 100 channels per second. **1963** B. FOZARD *Instrumentation Nucl. Reactors* xiii. 157 Instrumentation of a nuclear power reactor is commonly undertaken on a very large scale and incorporates *data-logging equipment. **1954** *Instruments & Automation* Dec. 1916/1 New 'Model CRC 102-A Electronic Computer' and its auxiliary..are designed for ..*data processing. **1956** *Collier's Year Bk.* 105/1 Data processing, in the broadest definition, means the handling of information by arithmetic rules and logic. It is performed by most types of business machines, the simple mechanical adding machines as well as the complex electronic card sorting systems or accounting machines. **1959** *B.S.I. News* Nov. 5/1 Punched cards and tapes used in automatic data processing. **1960** *Times* 22 Jan. 15/5 It..is designed for both mathematical calculations and commercial data-processing. **1966** R. L. GREGORY *Eye & Brain* iv. 46 Some of the data processing for perception takes place in the eye. **1954** *Instruments & Automation* Dec. 1905/1 The most advanced techniques for automatic control of plant, factory, and office operations..were represented..(4) electronic computers and *data processors. **1960** E. DELAVENAY *Introd. Machine Transl.* ii. 19 The big I.B.M. data-processers..are..endowed with high operational speeds. **1975** *Computers & Privacy* (Cmnd. 6353) 9 in *Parl. Papers 1975–76* XX. 245 The Government..will therefore appoint ..a non-statutory body whose function it will be to prepare the way for the setting up of the permanent machinery. This interim body will be referred to here as the *Data Protection Committee. **1980** *Times* 31 July 2/8 Data protection laws are already in force in France, West Germany, Austria, Scandinavia and Luxembourg. **1985** *Library Assoc. Rec.* Feb. 60 *Data Protection: A Guide for Library and Information Management*..provides a comprehensive study of the data protection issue... The Data Protection Act is examined in detail. **1959** *Mod. Uses Logic in Law* Sept. 1 This is the first issue of the newsletter established by the Electronic *Data Retrieval Committee of the American Bar Association at its meeting in Los Angeles on May 26, 1959. **1972** *Computers & Humanities* VII. 8 This system uses synonym dictionaries, hierarchical arrangement of subject identifiers, and statistical and syntactic phrase generation methods for data retrieval on the IBM 7094 and 360/65. **1985** *Oil & Gas Jrnl.* 4 Feb. 66/1 The main computer system controls data retrieval from the production areas through a multi-tasking operating system installed on the main computer. **1898** *Machinery* (N.Y.) June 312/1 Four *data sheets containing information on laying out gear blanks. **1971** *Amateur Photographer* 3 Mar. 31 This, No. 1 in a series of data sheets covering all major facets of photography, provides basic information on the general purpose black-and-white films on the market. **1963** *Communications Assoc. Computing Machinery* VI. 402/1 Harold W. Lawson, Jr.,..delivered at the ACM Conference a paper [called]..The Use of Chain List Matrices for the Analysis of COBOL *Data Structures. **1971** *Ibid.* XIV. 316/2 Data structure is the view of the data as seen by the user of the system and excluding any details of storage techniques used. **1973** C. W. GEAR *Introd. Computer Sci.* vii. 265 The computer program must store the input data in a form that shows the relation between items. In this case the data structure must indicate which reservations a passenger holds and what passengers are booked on each flight. **1980** C. S. FRENCH *Computer Sci.* x. 46 In many situations, sets of data items..way be conveniently arranged into a sequence and referred to by a single identifier... Such an arrangement is a data structure called an array. **1984** J. HILTON *Choosing & using your Home Computer* vi. 146 In a computer's memory there is only data, byte after byte of it. .. Meaning is given to those bytes by the data structure that the central processor imposes. **1959** *Trans. AIEE* LXXVII. 872 (*heading*) SAGE *data terminals. **1965** BENNETT & DAVEY *Data Transmission* vii. 247 (*heading*) Data terminals using amplitude modulation. **1982** *McGraw-Hill Yearbk. Sci. & Technol. 1982–83* 16/2 The installation consists of a central computerized base station and trucks equipped with an FM radio transceiver, a microprocessor data terminal with a liquid crystal or light-emitting diode display screen, [etc.]. **1959** J. JEENEL *Programming for Digital Computers* v. 253 Techniques for *data transfers to and from magnetic disks. **1985** *Personal Computer World* Feb. 192/2 To control this data transfer various protocols exist which ensure a method of recovering data errors, [etc.]. **1946** *Math. Tables & Other Aids to Computation* II. 91 The design of *data-transmission and servo units, the development of codes and related equipment for the rapid set-up of problems, and the conversion of continuous variables..into digital form. **1967** COX & GROSE *Organiz. Bibliogr. Rec. by Computer* II. 23 Each element carried an indication of the type of data it contained, eight different types (0 to 7) being allowed for... Alphabetical data became *data-type 0. **1979** *Personal Computer World* Nov. 74/1 Line 2 introduces a new data type, the character type CHAR which consists of a single letter.., digit or normal keyboard punctuation mark.

¶ Used in pl. form with sing. construction.

1807 W. IRVING *Salmag.* xviii. 366 My grandfather..took a data from his own excellent heart. **1902** A. S. TOMPKINS *Hist. Rec. Rock Co., N.Y.* 46 There is but little data to estimate Indian populations. **1931** H. F. PRINGLE *T. Roosevelt* p. viii, The author has preserved this data. **1955** [see *biomedical* s.v. BIO-]. **1963** *Daily Express* 23 Sept. 3 He took out a patent but some of the data is missing. **1964, 1970** [see 1 d above]. **1965** J. ALLAN *Speaking of Computers* 5 Incidentally, by general usage *data* is now accepted as a singular collective noun. **1971** *Computer Weekly* 13 May 3/1 They have done little to analyse and interpret this data.

‖**Datura** (də'tʃ(j)ʊərə). *Bot.* [mod.L. ad. Hindī *dhatūra*, native name of *D. fastuosa* and *D. Metel*, common Indian species used to stupefy and poison.] A genus of poisonous plants (N.O. *Solanaceæ*), of which *D. Stramonium* is the Strammony or Thorn-apple, supposed to be a native of Western Asia, but now half naturalized over the warmer temperate regions of the world; it is a powerful narcotic.

1662 J. DAVIES tr. *Mandelslo's Trav.* 104 A drug which.. stupefies his senses..The Indians call this herb *Doutro*, *Doutry*, or *Datura*, and the Turks and Persians, *Datula*. **1862** BEVERIDGE *Hist. India* II. IV. iv. 126 From Hindoos was first learned..the benefit of smoking datura in asthma.

attrib. **1883** *Century Mag.* XXVII. 205 Large white datura blossoms.

Hence **da'turine** (also **da'turia**), the poisonous alkaloid found in the Thorn-apple and other species; = ATROPINE.

1832 R. CHRISTISON *Poisons* (ed. 2) 726 A peculiar alkaloid, which has been named Daturine or Daturia.

dau, var. of DAUW.

dau (*Cursor M.* 5108, etc.): see DAWE and DAY.

daub (dɔːb), *v.* Forms: 4–7 **daube, dawbe**, 4–5 **dobe**, 5 **doybe**, 5–6 **doube**, 6–9 **dawb**, 7– **daub**. [a. OF. *daube-r*:—L. *dealbāre* to whiten over, whitewash, plaster, f. *de-* down, etc. + *albāre* to whiten, f. *albus* white. The word had in OF. the senses 'clothe in white, clothe, furnish, whitewash, plaster'; in later F. 'to beat, swinge, lamme' (Cotgr.); cf. *curry, anoint*, etc. All the English uses appear to come through that of 'plaster'.]

1. *trans.* In building, etc.: To coat or cover (a wall or building) *with* a layer of plaster, mortar, clay, or the like; to cover (laths or wattle) with a composition of clay or mud, and straw or hay, so as to form walls. (Cf. DAB *v.* 8.)

c **1325** *E.E. Allit. P.* B. 313 Cleme hit [the ark] with clay comly with-inne, & alle þe endentur dryuen daube withouten. **1382** WYCLIF *Lev.* xiv. 42 With other cley the hows to be dawbid. **1483** *Cath. Angl.* 102 Dobe, *linere, illinere.* **1489** CAXTON *Faytes of A.* II. xxxiv. 145 Thys bastylle muste be aduironned with hirdels aboute and dawbed thykke with erthe and clay thereupon. **1515** BARCLAY *Egloges* iv. (1570) Civ/1 Of his shepecote dawbe the walles round about. **1530** PALSGR. 507/2 Daube up this wall a pace with plaster..I daube with lome that is tempered with heare or strawe. **1605** SHAKS. *Lear* II. ii. 71, I will tread this vnboulted villaine into mortar, and daube the wall of a Iakes with him. *c* **1710** C. FIENNES *Diary* (1888) 169 Little hutts and hovels the poor Live in Like Barnes..daub'd with mud-wall. **1877** *N.W. Linc. Gloss.* 243 *Stud and mud walling*, building without bricks or stones, with posts and wattles, or laths daubed over with road-mud.

absol. **1523** FITZHERB. *Surv.* 37 He shall bothe thacke & daube at his owne cost and charge. **1642** ROGERS *Naaman* 534 He falls to dawbing with untempered mortar.

fig. **1612–5** BP. HALL *Contempl., O.T.* XII. vi, He..is faine to dawbe up a rotten peace with the basest conditions.

2. To plaster, close *up*, cover *over*, coat *with* some sticky or greasy substance, smear.

1597–8 BP. HALL *Sat.* VI. i. (R.), Whose wrinkled furrows ..Are daubed full of Venice chalk. **1614** —— *Recoll. Treat.* 174 Take away this clay from mine eyes, wherewith alas they are so dawbed up. **1658** A. FOX tr. *Wurtz' Surg.* II. xxviii. 190 She had been plaistered and dawbed with Salves a long time. **1719** DE FOE *Crusoe* (1840) II. xv. 309 We daubed him all over..with tar. **1832** LANDER *Adv. Niger* II. viii. 26 The women daub their hair with red clay.

fig. **1784** COWPER *Task* v. 360, I would not be a king to be ..daubed with undiscerning praise.

b. To smear or lay *on* (a moist or sticky substance). Also *fig.*

1646 FULLER *Wounded Consc.* (1841) 289 For comfort daubed on will not stick long upon it. **1750** E. SMITH *Compl. Housewife* 309 With a fine rag daub it often on the face and hands.

c. To bribe, 'grease'. *slang* (Cf. quot. 1876 in DAUB *sb.* 2.)

a **1700** B. E. *Dict. Cant. Crew, Dawbing*, bribing. **1785** GROSE *Dict. Vulg. Tongue*, The cull was scragged [hanged] because he could not dawb.

3. To coat or cover *with* adhering dirt; to soil, bedaub. Also *fig.*

a **1450** *Knt. de la Tour* (1868) 31 Her heles, the whiche is doubed with filthe. **1535** JOYE *Apol. Tindale* 50 Dawbing eche other with dirte and myer. **1651** C. CARTWRIGHT *Cert. Relig.* I. 5 Such..verities, as would have adorned, and not dawb'd the Gospel. **1661** PEPYS *Diary* 30 Sept., Having been very much daubed with dirt, I got a coach and home. **1721** DE FOE *Mem. Cavalier* (1840) 197 The fall plunged me in a puddle..and daubed me. **1768–74** TUCKER *Lt. Nat.* (1852) II. 596 Filthy metal that one could not touch without daubing one's fingers. **1840** DICKENS *Old C. Shop* iii, To daub himself with ink up to the roots of his hair. **1881** BESANT & RICE *Chapl. of Fleet* I. xi. (1883) 89 My name is too deeply daubed with the Fleet mud; it cannot be cleansed.

†**4.** To soil (paper) with ink, or with bad or worthless writing. *Obs.*

1589 *Marprel. Epit.* (1843) 6 When men have a gift in writing, howe easie it is for them to daube paper. *a* **1618** BRADSHAW *Unreas. Separation* (1640) 81 In the proofe of the Assumption he daubs sixe pages. **1792** SOUTHEY *Lett.* (1856) I. 7 The latter loss, to one who daubs so much, is nothing.

5. In painting: To lay on (colours) in a crude or clumsy fashion; to paint coarsely and inartistically. Also *absol.*

1630 [see DAUBED]. **1642** FULLER *Holy & Prof. St.* v. x. 394 A trovell will serve as well as a pencill to daub on such thick course colours. **1695** DRYDEN tr. *Du Fresnoy's Art of Painting* (L.), A lame, imperfect piece, rudely daubed over with too little reflection, and too much haste. **1796** BURKE *Regic. Peace* i. Wks. VIII. 147 The falsehood of the colours which [Walpole] suffered to be daubed over that measure. **1840** HOOD *Up the Rhine* Introd. 4 It had been so often painted, not to say daubed, already. **1867** TROLLOPE *Chron. Barset* II. li. 77 He leaned upon his stick, and daubed away briskly at the background.

†**6.** To cover (the person or dress) *with* finery or ornaments in a coarse, tasteless manner; to bedizen. *Obs.* or *dial.*

a **1592** GREENE & LODGE *Looking Glass* Wks. (Rtldg.) 124/2 My wife's best gown..how handsomely it was daubed with statute-lace. **1639** tr. *Du Bosq's Compl. Woman* II. 32 They dawb their habits with gold lace. **1760** WESLEY *Wks.* (1872) III. 13 A person hugely daubed with gold. **1876** *Whitby Gloss.* s.v., *Daub'd out*, fantastically dressed.

†**7.** *fig.* To cover with a specious exterior; to whitewash, cloak, gloss. *Obs.*

1543 BECON *Agst. Swearing* Early Wks. (1843) 375 Perjury cannot escape unpunished, be it never so secretly handled and craftily daubed. **1594** SHAKS. *Rich. III*, III. v. 29 So smooth he dawb'd his Vice with shew of Vertue. **1678** YOUNG *Serm. at Whitehall* 29 Dec. 31 To dawb and palliate our faults, is but like keeping our selves in the dark. **1683** tr. *Erasmus' Moriæ Enc.* 114 They dawb over their oppression with a submissive flattering carriage. **1785** [see DAUBED].

†**b.** *absol.* or *intr.* To put on a false show; to dissemble so as to give a favourable impression.

c. To pay court with flattery. *Obs.* or *dial.*

1605 SHAKS. *Lear* IV. i. 53 Poore Tom's a cold. I cannot daub it further. **1619** W. WHATELY *God's Husb.* ii. (1622) 52

What auailed it Ananias and Saphira, to dawbe and counterfeit? **1619** W. Sclater *Exp. 1 Thess.* (1630) 288 With such idle distinctions doe they dawbe with conscience. **1650** Baxter *Saints' R.* iii. xiii. (1662) 508 Do not daub with men, and hide from them their misery or danger. *a* **1716** South (J.), Let every one, therefore, attend the sentence of his conscience; for, he may be sure, it will not daub, nor flatter. **1876** *Whitby Gloss., Daubing*..paying court for the sake of advantage. **1877** *Holderness Gloss., Daub*, to flatter, or besmear with false compliment, with the object of gaining some advantage.

daub (dɔːb), *sb.* [f. daub *v.* In some dialects (dɒb, dab), whence the spelling *dab*: cf. dab *sb.*[1] 12.]

1. Material for daubing walls, etc.; plaster, rough mortar; clay or mud mixed with stubble or chaff, used with laths or wattle to form the walls of cottages, huts, etc. Hence ***wattle and daub*** (also *dab*).

1446 *Yatton Churchw. Acc.* (*Somerset Record Soc.* 82), Item for ryses for the dawbes..ij *d.* **1481–90** *Howard Househ. Bks.* (Roxb.) 514 Payd..for bryngyng of dawbe and cley in to the said castell. **1587** *Manch. Crt. Leet Rec.* (1885) II. 18 For yᵉ cariage of any mucke, dunge, dawbe, clay. **1622** R. Hawkins *Voy. S. Sea* (1847) 113 The soyle..which, with water..they make into clay, or a certaine dawbe. **1857** Livingstone *Trav.* xix. 369 Traders' houses..built of wattle and daub. **1876** R. F. Burton *Gorilla L.* II. 22 Heaps of filthy hovels, wattle and daub and dingy thatch. **1884** *Cheshire Gloss.* 279 A raddle and dobe house.

b. Anything that is daubed or smeared on. **c.** *fig.* Insincere compliments, flattery. *dial.*

1602 *Narcissus* 209 (1893) Though with the dawbe of prayse I am loath to lome her. **1693** Dryden *Juvenal's Sat.* vi. (R.), She duely, once a month, renews her face; Mean time, it lies in daub, and hid in grease. **1877** *Holderness Gloss., Daub*, hypocritical affection.

2. An act or instance of daubing.

1669 A. Browne *Ars Pict.* (1675) 82 And with two or three dawbes of your great Pencil, lay it on in an instant. **1721** Kelly *Sc. Prov.* 256 (Jam.) Many a time have I gotten a wipe with a towel; but never a daub with a dishclout before. **1876** *Whitby Gloss., Daub o' t' hand*, a bribe; compensation. 'They got a daub o' t' hand for 't.'

3. A patch or smear of some moist substance, grease, colouring, etc.

1731 Swift *Poems, Beautiful Young Nymph*, [She] must, before she goes to Bed, Rub off the Dawbs of White and Red. **1881** Tylor *Anthropol.* 418 Their bodies painted with black daubs.

4. A coarsely executed, inartistic painting.

1761 Sterne *Tr. Shandy* III. xii, And did you step in, to take a look at the grand picture?..'Tis a melancholy daub, my lord! **1784** Cowper *Task* vi. 285 That he discerns The difference of a Guido from a daub. **1839** Marryat *Diary in Amer.* 1st Ser. I. 292 A large collection of daubs, called portraits of eminent personages. **1880** A. H. Huth *Buckle* I. i. 15 A coarse daub of a picture.

5. *attrib.* or *Comb.*, as ***daub-hole***.

1848 S. Bamford *Early Days* i. (1859) 13 An old timber and daub house. **1875** *Lanc. Gloss., Daub-hoil, daub-hole*, a clay or marl pit.

‖**daube** (dəʊb). Also in anglicized form **daub**. [Fr.] A braised meat (usu. beef) stew with wine, spices, etc. So ***à la daube, en daube***: stewed or braised.

1723 [see à la b]. **1747** H. Glasse *Art of Cookery* ii. 20 Beef *à la Daub.* You may take a Buttock..of Beef, lard it, fry it..put it into a Pot..stew it. **1877** E. S. Dallas *Kettner's Bk. of Table* 371 A stew of fresh-water fish is called a matelote..of beef, a daube. **1927** V. Woolf *To Lighthouse* i. xvi. 125 They were having Mildred's masterpiece—Bœuf en Daube. **1961** *Spectator* 7 July 11 Then came a daube of beef..with an unthickened but short sauce of wine and tomato purée.

daubed (dɔːbd), *ppl. a.* [f. daub *v.* + -ed.] Plastered or coated with clay, paint or sticky matter; *fig.* bedizened, bearing a specious exterior.

c **1325** *E.E. Allit. P.* B. 492 In þat cofer þat watz clay daubed. *c* **1420** *Pallad. on Husb.* i. 785 Hym liketh best a daubed wough. **1581** Pettie *Guazzo's Civ. Conv.* iii. (1586) 125 b, Those dawbed, pargetted, and vermilion died faces. **1598** Marston *Pygmal.* 135 Glittering in dawbed lac'd accoustrements. **1630** Sir S. D'Ewes *Jrnls.* (1783) 67 This daubed piece..the face hath no similitude. **1785** Sarah Fielding *Ophelia* I. xxv, The painted canvas is most innocent; but the daubed hypocrite most criminal.

Daubenton's bat (dəʊbɑ̃tɔ̃z). *Zool.* [f. the name of Louis Jean Marie *Daubenton* (1716–?1800), French naturalist + bat *sb.*[1]] A species of bat, *Myotis daubentoni*, of Europe and parts of Asia.

Orig. named *Vespertilio daubentonii* (1817).

1887 G. H. C. Haigh in *Zoologist* XI. 293 *Vespertilio daubentonii*... The cry of Daubenton's Bat is very weak and shrill, sometimes prolonged into a sort of chatter. **1904** J. G. Millais *Mammals Gr. Brit.* I. 86 Daubenton's Bat. *Myotis Daubentoni*... Daubenton's Bat has not infrequently been confused with Natterer's and the Whiskered Bats; it, however, possesses very much larger feet. **1960** *Times* 14 June 14/7 The Daubenton's bat was usually near the old mill dam.

dauber (ˈdɔːbə(r)). [f. daub *v.* + -er[1]. In sense 1 prob. going back to AFr. *daubour*, in med.L. *daubātor* whitewasher, plasterer.] One who or that which daubs.

†**1.** One who plasters or covers walls with mortar, clay, etc.; a plasterer; one who builds with daub. *Obs.*

[*c* **1300** *Lib. Cust. Edw. I*, I. 99 (Godef.) De plastrers, de daubours, de teulers.] **1382** Wyclif *Isa.* xli. 25 As a daubere, or a pottere to-tredende the lowe erthe. **1398** Trevisa *Barth. De P.R.* xvi. ii. (1495) 553 Claye is tough erthe..and ableth to dyuers werkes of dawbers. **1419** *Liber Albus* (Rolls Ser.) I. 289 Carpenters, masouns, plastrers, daubers, teulers. *c* **1515** *Cocke Lorell's B.* (Percy Soc.) 10 Parys plasterers, daubers, and lyme borners. **1535** Coverdale *2 Kings* xii. 12 To them that buylded and wroughte in the house of the Lorde, namely, to the dawbers and masons. **1601** Cornwallyes *Ess.* xi, Straw, and durt good only for Thatchers, and Dawbers. **1641** Milton *Animadv.* vi. (1851) 240 Yet this Dauber would daub still with his untempered Mortar. **1816** in Peel *Spen Valley* (1893) 288 [A plasterer who] under the sobriquet of Dick Dawber was known far and near. *a* **1825** Forby *Voc. E. Anglia, Dauber*, a builder of walls with clay or mud, mixed with stubble or short straw..In Norfolk it is now difficult to find a good dauber.

†**2.** One who puts a false show on things; a hypocritical flatterer. *Obs.*

1642 Rogers *Naaman* 425 Put case, thou wert under the Ministery of a dawber and flatterer. **1653** Baxter *Meth. Peace Consc.* 388 Meddle not with men-pleasers and daubers. **1692** E. Walker *Epictetus' Mor.* lxxi, If praised, he can despise The fulsome Dawber, and his Flatteries.

3. A coarse or unskilful painter.

1655 Fuller *Ch. Hist.* i. i. §1 They were not Artists in that Mystery..being rather Dawbers then Drawers. **1697** Dryden *Virg.* (1806) II. 150 It hath been copied by so many sign-post daubers. **1751** Smollett *Per. Pic.* (1779) II. xlii. 55 What is the name of the dauber who painted that? **1880** *Manch. Guard.* 31 Dec., They will see..in David Cox something more than a dauber.

4. *U.S.* A species of sand-wasp: from the way in which it daubs mud in forming its nest.

1844 Gosse in *Zoologist* II. 582 The little boys..informed me that these were the nests of dirt-daubers. **1889** in Farmer *Americanisms.*

5. Anything used to daub with; *e.g.* a rag-brush or stump used to put blacking upon boots, where it is spread by the blacking-brush.

6. = dabber 1 b (Ogilvie).

daubery, daubry (ˈdɔːbərɪ, ˈdɔːbrɪ). [f. dauber: see -ery.] The practice of daubing; the specious or coarse work of a dauber.

1546 Bale *Eng. Votaries* i. (1550) 9 To patch up that dauberye of the deuyll, their vowed wyuelesse and husbandles chastite. *Ibid.* 89 Thys dyvinite of yours is but dongyshe daubry. **1598** Shaks. *Merry W.* iv. ii. 186 She works by Charmes, by Spels, by th' Figure, & such dawbry as this is. **1693** W. Freke *Sel. Ess.* xxii. 123 We should have a graceful embroidery, not a daubery in expression. **1830** *Fraser's Mag.* II. 114 He..could colour either side of any question brought before him with gay daubery. **1876** *Whitby Gloss., Daubery*..applause doubtfully deserved; cajolery; the purport of an inflated announcement.

daubing (ˈdɔːbɪŋ), *vbl. sb.* [-ing[1].]

1. The action of the vb. daub in various senses.

chinking and daubing: see chinking *vbl. sb.*[1] 2.

1393 Langl. *P. Pl.* C. ix. 198 Peers..putte hem alle to werke, In daubyng and in deluyng. **1486** *Nottingham Rec.* III. 241 Temperyng of morter, and lattyng and dawbyng at þe hous. **1544** *Churchw. Acc. St. Giles, Reading* 70 To a mason for lathyng [an]d dawbyng iiijᵈ. **1656** *Artif. Handsom.* 115 [They] used such..dawbings of black, red, and white, as wholly changed the very naturall looks. **1658** A. Fox *Wurtz' Surg.* iii. xv. 263 To prevent this swelling..much salving, dawbing, annointing, &c. they have used. **1743** *Lond. & Country Brew.* iii. (ed. 2) 186 Corrupt and foul Puddles, whose ill Scents and nasty Daubings are always ready to affect and damage the Utensils and Worts. **1848** Macaulay *Hist. Eng.* II. 432 *note*, Blackening a character which was black enough without such daubing.

b. The putting a false show on anything (*obs.*); hypocritical flattery.

1655 Sanderson *Serm.* II. Pref., That all court chaplains were parasites, and their preaching little other than daubing. **1681–6** J. Scott *Chr. Life* iii. (1696) 390 God..sees through all the Dawbings and Fucu's of Hypocrisie. **1766** Smollett *Trav.* II. xxix. (Jodr.), Without any daubing at all, I am very sincerely your very affectionate humble servant. **1803** Scott *Let. Miss Seward* in *Lockhart* xi, Such exaggerated daubing as Mr. Hayley has bestowed upon poor Cowper.

c. Painting coarsely or inartistically; hence, a coarsely or badly executed painting.

1654 Whitlock *Zootomia* 491 No such..offensive Sight as Pencill-dawbing. **1680** Otway *Orphan* Ded., Hasty dawbing will but spoil the picture. **1713** Pope *Guardian* No. 78, I knew a painter..make his dawbings to be thought originals by setting them in the smoak. **1752** Foote *Taste* i. Wks. 1799 I. 9 How high did your genius soar? To the daubing diabolical angels for ale-houses. **1870** E. Peacock *Ralf Skirl.* III. 194 Worth a housefull of Verrio's daubings.

2. Material with which anything is daubed; *esp.* mortar or clay used in daubing walls; rough-cast.

1382 Wyclif *Ezek.* xiii. 12 Wher is the dawbynge, that ȝe dawbiden [**1611** the dawbing wherwith ye haue dawbed it]? **1598** Florio, *Empiastro*, a plaister, a daubing. **1650** Bulwer *Anthropomet.* 158 To force and wrong Nature with Birdlime, Chaulk, Dawbing, and such trash. **1726** Leoni *Alberti's Archit.* I. 49 b, They..are not too hasty to lay the second dawbing over this. **1806–7** A. Young *Agric. Essex* (1813) I. 49 The old cottages are generally of clay daubing. *a* **1848** Carlton *New Purchase* I. 61 (Bartlett) The interstices of the log wall were 'chinked'—the chinking being large chips and small slabs..and the daubing, yellow clay..splashed in soft.

b. According to Knight, *Dict. Mech.* (U.S.), a synonym of dubbing for leather.

3. *attrib.* and *Comb.*

1540 *MS. Acc. St. John's Hosp., Canterb.*, For a dawbyng forke *jd.* **1660** Fisher *Rusticks Alarm* Wks. (1679) 473 Such ..shifting and canvesing, and daubing doings in a business of such moment. **1663** Gerbier *Counsel* D j a, The old Norman gotish Lime and Haire-like daubing custome.

ˈdaubing, *ppl. a.* [-ing[2].] That daubs; *esp.* that bedaubs with flattery (*obs.*). Hence **ˈdaubingly** *adv.*, in a daubing manner.

1655 Gurnall *Chr. in Arm.* v. §3 (1669) 84 He hath his daubing Preachers..with their soul-flattering. **1676** Wycherley *Pl. Dealer* i She..hates the lying, masking, daubing world. **1682** S. Pordage *Medal Rev.* Ep. 2 As much to the life, as the pretended Whiggs Heroe most daubingly was lately aimed at, by the Author of the *Medal.* **1719** W. Duncombe in *J. Duncombe's Lett.* (1773) I. 239 The daubing sycophant.

daubreelite (ˈdɒbriːlaɪt). *Min.* [f. as next + -lite.] A black sulphide of chromium, found in meteoric iron.

1892 *Pall Mall G.* 17 Sept. 7/2 The..constituent parts of meteoric iron are..numerous compounds, such as ferrous sulphide (troilite), sulphide of chromium (daubréelite), calcium sulphide (oldhamite).

daubreite (ˈdɒbriːaɪt). *Min.* [Named 1867 after M. *Daubrée*, a French mineralogist: see -ite.] A native oxy-chloride of bismuth.

1876 *Amer. Jrnl. Sc.* Ser. iii. XII. 396.

daubry: see daubery.

daubster (ˈdɔːbstə(r)). [f. daub, dauber: see -ster.] A clumsy painter; a dauber.

1853 Reade *Chr. Johnstone* vi. 63 The young artist laughed the old daubster a merry defiance.

dauby (ˈdɔːbɪ), *a.* [f. daub *sb.* + -y.]

1. Of the nature of or resembling daub; sticky.

1697 Dryden *Virg. Georg.* iv. 54 Th' industrious Kind With dawby Wax and Flow'rs the Chinks have lin'd. **1787** Marshall *Rur. Econ. East Norfolk* Gloss., *Dauby*, clammy, sticky; spoken of land when wet. **1884** *Upton-on-Severn Gloss., Dauby*, damp and sticky; used of bread made from 'grown' wheat.

2. Given to daubing: dirty, etc. (see quots.). *dial.*

1855 Robinson *Whitby Gloss., Dauby*, untidy, dirty. *Dauby folks*, slovenly people in household matters. **1877** *N.W. Linc. Gloss., Dauby*, dirty. 'What a dauby bairn thoo art'. **1877** *Holderness Gloss., Dauby*..(2) feignedly affectionate; (3) gaudily dressed, without taste.

3. Of the nature of a daub.

1829 *Blackw. Mag.* XXVI. 962 The painter's work—be it dawby or divine. **1878** *Mozley's Ess.* I. Introd. 43 A slovenly, and, to use his own expression, dauby style of writing.

daud: see dad *sb.*[2] and *v.*

daudle, var. of dawdle.

dauermodification (ˈdaʊəmɒdɪfɪˈkeɪʃən). *Genetics.* Also ‖**Dauer-, dauermodifikation** (pl. -en). [ad. G. *dauermodifikation* (V. Jollos 1913, in *Biol. Centralbl.* XXXIII. 233), f. *dauer* duration + *modifikation* modification.] A character, usu. one artificially induced in an organism, which is inherited through the cytoplasm and tends to disappear after a few generations.

1938 *Genetica* XX. 126 A transitory change of the plasmatic nature in a basal part of the original individual, which change is not a common modification, neither a plasmatic mutation, because it is inherited in some degree for a few generations, but it disappears in succeeding generations..it may be classified as a case of 'Dauermodifikation' (permanent modifications). **1943** *Hereditas* XXIX. 424 The so-called dauermodifications.. are inherited for some time and then disappear. **1944** *Nature* 5 Aug. 167/1 The carcinogens..induce in plants dauermodifications of limited or unlimited persistence. **1968** M. W. Strickberger *Genetics* xiii. 259 Persistent abnormalities ('dauermodifikationen') can be induced in plants and animals by chemical and environmental treatment and carried for several generations by the female line.

daugh, dauch (dɑx). *Sc. Mining.* [Etymol. uncertain: the form points to an earlier *dalgh, dalȝ*; cf. dauk.] See quots.

1793 Ure *Hist. Rutherglen* 289 *Daugh*, a soft and black substance, chiefly of clay, mica, and what resembles coal-dust. **1807** Headrick *Arran* 217 The dauch which separates the two seams of coal. **1859–65** Page *Geol. Terms, Douk, Dauk*, or *Daugh*, applied in mining to beds or bands of hard, tough clay or clayey admixture; generally without lamination, and more or less compact and homogeneous.

Hence **ˈdauchy** *a.*, of the character of daugh.

1807 Headrick *Arran* 217, 8 or 10 inches of a dauchy till. **1845** *Whistlebinkie* (Sc. Songs) (1890) I. 373 The ice is dauchie.

daughter (ˈdɔːtə(r)). Forms: α. 1 dohtor, -ur, 1–3 dohter, 3–4 douȝter, -ir, 3–5 doȝter, -ir, -ur, 3–6 (9 *dial.*) dowter, 4 dohuter, -ir, -yr, **dowȝghtur, douther, 4–5 doghtir, -ur, douter, 4–5** (8 *Sc.*) doghter, 4–6 doughter (dowghter, 5 **doughtur, dughter, dowtir, -yr, þowȝtur,**

thowghter, 5-6 *Sc.* **dochtir**, 5-9 *Sc.* **dochter**, 6 **doughtour**, *Sc.* **douchter**). β. (6 *dial.* **dahtorr**, **doffter**, 6-7 **dafter**), 6- **daughter** (riming with *after* in *Pilgr. Prog.*, etc.). *Plural*: see below. [A Com. Teutonic and Common Aryan word of relationship, OE. *dohtor* (*-ur*, *-er*) = OFris. *dochter*, OS. *dohtar* (MDu., Du., LG. *dochter*), OHG. *tohter* (MHG. *tohter*, Ger. *tochter*), ON. *dóttir* (:—*dohter*), (Sw., Norw. *dotter*, Da. *datter*), Goth. *dauhtar*:—OTeut. **dohtẽr*; corresp. to pre-Germanic **dhuk'tēr* from original **dhughə'tēr*, whence Skr. *duhitar-*, Zend *duγδar*, Armen. *dustr*, OSlav. *dŭšti*, Lith. *duktė*: cf. also Gr. θυγάτηρ. Generally referred to the verbal root **dhugh-*, Skr. *duh-* to milk.

The normal modern repr. of OE. *dohtor*, ME. *doȝter*, is *doughter* still used in 16th c., and now represented by Sc. *dochter*, *dowchter*, north. Eng. *dowter*. The form *daughter* appeared in the 16th c. (substituted in Cranmer's ed. of the Bible for Tindale's and Coverdale's *doughter*, whence in all later versions, and always in Shakspere and later writers). It appears to be of southern origin, and analogous to the southern phonetic development of *bought*, *sought*, *thought*: a Wells will of 1531 has *dahtorrs*: cf. the mod. Somerset and Devon ('da:tə(r)).

In OE. the dative sing. was *dehter*; genitive *dohtor* (sometimes *dehter*); the uninflected genitive continued in use to the 16th c. The plural shows a variety of forms, viz. OE. *dohtor*, *-ur*, *-er* (like the sing.), *dohtru*, *dohtra*, Northumb. *dohter*, *dohtero*; the first of these app. did not survive the OE. stage; the form in *-u*, *-a*, is represented in early ME. by Layamon's *dohtere*, *dohtre*; but Layamon has also *dohtren*, which survived in S.W. dialect to 1500. Ormin has *dohhtress*, and the later text of Layamon *dohtres*, which is always found in northern ME., and became the standard form. An umlaut plural *deȝter* appears n the West Midland *Alliterative Poems* of 14th c. and the *Troy-book* of *c* 1400; it occurs elsewhere with inflexional endings, *dehtren*, *deȝteres*: cf. *brether*, *brethren*. The unfixedness of the form is seen in this, that the earlier text of Layamon has both *dohtere* and *dohtren*, the later both *dohtren* and *dohtres*; the MSS. of Chaucer also show both *doughtres* and *doughtren*, *Hali Meidenhad* has *dohtren* and *dehtren*, the *Alliterative Poems* *deȝter* and *deȝteres*.

With the OE. plural forms, cf. OFris. *dohtera* and *dohteren*, OHG. *tohter*, *tohterâ*, *tohterûn*, MHG., with umlaut, *töhter*, Ger. *töchter*, LG. *dechter*. The original Teutonic nom. pl. was **dohtriz*, in early Norse runes *dohtriR*, whence regularly Norse *dœtr*, *dœttr*; a corresponding OE. **dœhter*, **dehter* is not found, but the ME. West Midland *deȝter* may be its descendant. The other forms in the various languages are later, and analogical. For OE. *dohtor*, *dohtru*, *-ra*, see the similar forms under BROTHER: it is possible that those in *-ru*, *-ra*, northern *-ero*, are assimilated to *-os*, *-or* stems like *lombru*, *-ra*, *-ero*. ME. *doȝtren*, *deȝtren* exemplify the usual passage of vowel plurals in early southern ME. into the *-en* type, and Ormin's *dohtress* the early ascendancy of *-es* plurals in the north and midlands.]

A. Illustration of the plural forms.

†α. OE. **dohtor, -ur, -er; dohtra, -ru, -ero;** ME. 2-3 **dohtere, -tre.**

c **1000** *Ags. Ps.* xliv. 10 Cyningca dohtor [*filiæ regum*]. *Ibid.* cxliii. 15 Heora dohtru [*filiæ eorum*]. *c* **1000** *Ags. Gosp.* Luke xxiii. 28 Eala dohtra hierusalem [*c* **950** *Lindisf.* dohtero, *c* **975** *Rushw.* dohter, *c* **1160** *Hatton* dohter]. *c* **1205** LAY. 24509 Comen .. þere hehere monnen dohtere.

†β. 4 **deȝter**, 4-5 **deghter.**

c **1325** *E.E. Allit. P.* B. 939 Loth & his lef, hys luflyche deȝter. *c* **1400** *Destr. Troy* 1474 Sonnes .. ffyue .. and þre deghter. *Ibid.* 1489 Of his Deghter by dene .. One Creusa was cald.

†γ. 2 **dochtren**, 3 **dohteren, -tren, doȝtren**, 4 **douh-, douȝ-, doghtren**, 4-5 **doughtren.**

a **1175** *Cott. Hom.* 225 ȝedéir sunen and dochtren. *c* **1205** LAY. 2924 þe king hefde þreo dohtren [*c* **1275** dohtres]. *c* **1230** *Hali Meid.* 41 þu schalt .. teamen dohtren & sunen. **1297** R. GLOUC. (1724) 509 Hor wiues & hor doȝtren. *c* **1320** *Cast. Love* 289 Foure doughtren hedde þe kyng. *c* **1374** CHAUCER *Troylus* IV. Prol. 22 Oye herynes nyghttes doughtren thre. **1480** CAXTON *Chron. Eng.* xiii. 15 Tho ii eldest doughtren wolde not abide till Leyr hir fadre was deede.

†δ. **deghtren**; 3-5 **dehtren**, 5 **deytron.**

c **1230** *Hali Meid.* 19 Alle hise sunnen and alle hise dehtren. **14..** *Chron. Eng.* 543-5 in Ritson *Anc. Metr. Rom.* (1802) II. (Mätz.), Edward hade .. Nine dehtren ant five sones. *c* **1420** *Chron. Vilod.* 367 þe Bysshop .. sayde deytron ycham fulle hevy.

ε. †**dohtres**, †**doughters**, etc.; **daughters.**

c **1200** *Trin. Coll. Hom.* 19 To sunes and to dohtres. *c* **1250** *Gen. & Ex.* 1092 Loth and his doȝtres two. *c* **1300** *Havelok* 717 Hauelok .. And hise two doutres. *c* **1325** *E.E. Allit. P.* B. 814 His two dere doȝterez. *c* **1340** *Cursor M.* 18983 (Fairf.) ȝoure sones and ȝoure douȝtris. *c* **1386** CHAUCER *Nun's Pr. T.* 555 Eek hir doghtres two [*v. rr.* doughtres, douȝters, dowhters, doughteryn]. *c* **1450** *Merlin* 3 He had thre doughters and a sone. **1535** COVERDALE *Acts* ii. 17 Youre sonnes and youre doughters. **1539** CRANMER *ibid.*, Youre sonnes and youre daughters.

†ζ. 4 **deghteres, -tres, deȝteres, deȝtters.**

a **1300** *Cursor M.* 9623 Sir, o þi deghteres am I an. *c* **1325** *E.E. Allit. P.* B. 899 þy wyf & þy wyȝez & þy wlonc deȝtters. *Ibid.* B. 933 His wyf & his wlonk deȝteres.

B. Signification.

1. *prop.* The word expressing the relation of a female to her parents; female child or offspring. The feminine term corresponding to SON.

α. Form *doughter*. *Obs.* exc. *dial.*

c **1000** *Ags. Gosp.* Matt. xx. 37 Se ðe lufað sunu oððe dohtor [*v.r.* dohtur] swyþur þonne me. *c* **1160** *Hatton G.* ibid., Se þe lufeð sune oððe dohter. *c* **1200** *Trin. Coll. Hom.* 197 His seuen sunes and þrie dochtres. *c* **1340** *Cursor M.* 155 (Trin.) Mary also hir douȝter mylde [*v.r.* doghter, douther]. **14..** *Nominale* in Wr.-Wülcker 691/17 *Hic gener*, a dowghter husband. *c* **1449** PECOCK *Repr.* v. iii. 500 Marie .. bare sones and douȝtris after that sche .. bare Crist. **1535** COVERDALE *Ezek.* xvi. 44 Soch a mother, soch a doughter.

Sc. and *dial.* **1609** SKENE *Reg. Maj.* 33 Gif there be moe dochters nor ane, the here age sall be divided amonst them. **1724** RAMSAY *Tea-t. Misc.* (1733) I. 8 I'm come your doghter's love to win. **1793** BURNS *Let. to Cunningham* 3 Mar., Do you know the .. old Highland air called 'The Sutor's Dochter'? **1863** *Tyneside Songs* 24 For he a dowter had.

β. Form *daughter*.

1531 W. BABE in *Wells Wills* (1890) 114 To my to dahtorrs a kow. **1532** T. BUDD *ibid.* (1890) 183 To their eldest dafters. **1539** CRANMER *Matt.* ix. 18 My daughter is even now diseased. **1596** SHAKS. *Tam. Shr.* I. i. 245 So could I 'faith boy, to haue the next wish after, That Lucentio indeede had Baptistas yongest daughter. **1684** BUNYAN *Pilgr.* II. (Hanserd Knollys ed.) 339 Dispondencie, good-man, is coming after, And so also is Much-afraid, his Daughter. **1749** FIELDING *Tom Jones* VI. vii, The misery of all fathers who are so unfortunate as to have daughters. **1847** TENNYSON *Princ.* v. 319 'Boys!' shriek'd the old king, but vainlier than a hen To her false daughters in the pool.

dial. **1864** CAPERN *Devon Provinc.*, *Darter*, daughter. **1837** DICKENS *Pickw.* viii, 'My da'ater.']

2. *transf.* **a.** A female descendant; a female member of a family, race, etc.; a woman in relation to her native country or place. (Cf. CHILD 9.)

c **1000** *Ags. Gosp.* John xii. 15 Ne ondræd þu Siones dohtor. *c* **1160** *Hatton G.* ibid., Ne on-dræd þu þe Syones dohter. **1382** WYCLIF *Judg.* xiv. 1 A woman of the douȝtris of Philistien. —— *Luke* xiii. 16 This douȝtre of Abraham. —— xxiii. 28 Douȝtris of Jerusalem. **1667** MILTON *P.L.* I. 453 The Love-tale Infected Sions daughters with like heat. **1812** BYRON *Ch. Har.* II. lxxxi, Danced on the shore the daughters of the land. **1833** TENNYSON *Lady Clara* i, The daughter of a hundred Earls. **1850** —— *In Mem.* Concl. ii, A daughter of our house. **1855** —— *The Brook* 69 A daughter of our meadows.

b. Used in pl. in the names of various women's societies, as ***Daughters of Liberty*** (Boston, 1769-70), ***Daughters of the American Revolution*** (1890), ***of the Confederacy*** (1894), etc. Also *sing.*, a member of one or other of these societies. *U.S.*

1769 *Boston Gaz.* 16 Oct. 1/3 And as true Daughters of Liberty, they made their Breakfast upon Rye Coffee. **1890** (*title*) Daughters of the American Revolution Constitution and By-Laws. **1894** *Confederate Veteran* II. 180/1 Daughters of the Confederacy are also organized. **1911** R. D. SAUNDERS *Col. Todhunter* i. 4 Working the Daughters of the Confederacy as a political proposition. *Ibid.* 7 Mrs. Todhunter, an ardent Daughter had gone early in the day. **1940** E. FERGUSSON *Our Southwest* 54 All our national and sectional Daughters are there and active, and even more patriotic Daughters of Texas' founders, fighters, signers, or early arrivals. **1962** *Listener* 18 Jan. 125/1 You are fed some dull crap by a sweet bunch of uptown Daughters of the American Revolution.

3. Used as a term of affectionate address to a woman or girl by an older person or one in a superior relation. *Obs.* or *arch.*

c **1000** *Ags. Gosp.* Matt. ix. 22 Gelyf dohtor, þin ȝeleafa þe ȝehælde. *c* **1230** *Hali Meid.* 3 Jher me dohter he seið. **1382** WYCLIF *Matt.* ix. 22 And Jhesus .. saide, Douȝter, haue thou trust; thi faith hath made thee saaf. **1534** TINDALE *ibid.*, Doughter, be of good confort. [So **1535** COVERDALE, **1539** CRANMER, **1557** *Geneva*, **1582** *Rheims*; **1611**, daughter.] **1592** SHAKS. *Rom. & Jul.* IV. i. 39 Are you at leisure, Holy Father, now?.. *Fri.* My leisure serues me, pensiue daughter, now. **1790** COWPER *Odyssey* XXIII. 79 To whom thus Euryclea, nurse belov'd, What word, my daughter, hath escaped thy lips?

4. A girl, maiden, young woman (with no express reference to relationship). *Obs.* or *arch.*

1382 WYCLIF *Song Sol.* ii. 2 As a lilie among thornes, so my leef among douȝtres. **1483** CAXTON *Cato* E viij b, If a doughter drynke of the water .. yf she be a mayde she shal crye. **1611** BIBLE *Prov.* xxxi. 29 Many daughters haue done virtuously, but thou excellest them all. **1818** SHELLEY *Revolt of Islam* VIII. ii. 9 She is some bride, Or daughter of high birth.

5. *fig.* A woman viewed in relation to some one whose spirit she inherits, or to some characteristic, quality, pursuit, or other circumstance. (A Hebraism of Scripture.) (Cf. CHILD 12, 13.)

1382 WYCLIF *Eccl.* xii. 4 And alle the doȝtris of the song shul become doumb. —— *1 Pet.* iii. 6 As Sare obeschide to Abraham .. of whom ȝe ben douȝtres wel doynge. **1738** WESLEY *Wks.* (1872) I. 158 A daughter of affliction came to see me. **1847** TENNYSON *Princ.* IV. 259 Eight daughters of the plough, stronger than men. **1859** in Allibone *Dict. Eng. Lit.* I. 266 We .. claim her [Mrs. Browning] as Shakspere's daughter!

6. *fig.* **a.** Anything (personified as female) considered in relation to its origin or source.

c **1230** *Hali Meid.* 15 Vre wit is godes dohter. **1340** *Ayenb.* 26 Fole ssame .. is .. doȝter of prede. **1667** MILTON *P.L.* IX. 653 God .. left that Command Sole Daughter of his voice. **1728** POPE *Dunc.* I. 12 Dulness .. Daughter of Chaos and eternal Night. **1805** WORDSW. *Ode to Duty* 1 Stern Daughter of the Voice of God! O Duty! **1820** SHELLEY *The Cloud* vi, I am the daughter of earth and water. *Mod.* Italian, the eldest daughter of ancient Latin.

b. Applied to the relation of cities to their metropolis or mother-city; in Scripture to the smaller towns dependent on a chief city.

1535 COVERDALE *Josh.* xv. 47 Asdod with the doughters [**1611** towns] and vyllages therof. *Mod.* Carthage the famous daughter of Tyre.

c. ***Duke of Exeter's daughter***, ***Scavenger's daughter*** [corruption of *Skevington's daughter*] names given to instruments of torture of which the invention is attributed to the Duke of Exeter and Sir W. Skevington, Lieutenant of the Tower of London, respectively. So ***gunner's daughter***, the gun to which seamen were lashed to be flogged. See GUNNER, SCAVENGER.

[**1642** FULLER *Holy & Prof. St.* IV. xiii. 301 A daughter of the Duke of Exeter invented a brake or cruel rack.] *a* **1700** B. E. *Dict. Cant. Crew, Duke of Exeter's Daughter*, a Rack in the Tower of London, to torture and force Confession; supposed to be introduced by him. **1720** *Stow's Surv.* (ed. Strype 1754) I. I. xiv. 66/2 The Brake or rack, commonly called the Duke of Exeter's daughter because he was the deviser of that torture. **1878** J. GAIRDNER *Rich. III*, iv. 125 Being .. a prisoner in the Tower, in the severe embrace of 'the Duke of Exeter's daughter'.

d. *Nuclear Sci.* A nuclide formed by the nuclear disintegration (either spontaneous or induced) of another nuclide. Orig. short for *daughter atom, element*.

1926 [see 7c]. **1933** O. H. BLACKWOOD et al. *Outl. Atomic Physics* xii. 222 At present we cannot tell whether the daughter of radium C'' is identical in all its properties with radium D. **1950** GLASSTONE *Sourcebk. Atomic Energy* v. 119/2 Since the daughter element also disintegrates, it is itself the parent of a daughter. **1956** A. H. COMPTON *Atomic Quest* 89 The average number of 'daughters' that each neutron generates. **1970** *Nature* 25 July 362/2 The decay product of natural uranium, thorium and their daughters.

7. a. *attrib.* and *Comb.* (usually *fig.*), as ***daughter-branch, -bud, -city, -colony, -house, -island, -land, -language, -nation, -state; daughter-like*** adj.

1586 T. B. *La Primaud Fr. Acad.* 510 The rare example of daughter-like pietie. **1614** RALEIGH *Hist. World* II. ix. §1 (R.) A fruitful vine planted by the well side, and spread her daughter-branches along the wall. **1641** MILTON *Reform.* Wks. (1847) 21 This Britannic empire .. with all her daughter-islands about her. *a* **1721** PRIOR *Celia to Damon* 104 And when the parent rose decays and dies .. the daughter-buds arise. **1871** MARCUS DODS tr. *St. Aug. City of God.* I. 107 How, then, could that be a glorious war which a daughter-state waged against its mother? **1878** BOSW. SMITH *Carthage* 5 The Phoenicians alike of the parent country and daughter cities. **1886** ABP. BENSON *Prayer at opening Col. & Ind. Exhib.* May 4, That all the daughter-lands of her Realms and Empire may be knit together in perfect unity. **1901** *National Rev.* Nov. 347 The conduct of these daughter nations during our South African struggle. **1903** *Westm. Gaz.* 3 June 9/3 Everyone was too busy talking about their grand Imperial theories, and the duties of the mother-country, to bother about the dull little domestic facts that are worrying the daughter-land. **1905** *Spectator* 11 Feb. 205/1 The great self-governing daughter-nations. **1937** *Discovery* Aug. 229/2 The silver didrachm .. of the Greek city states was introduced into the daughter-colonies and became the chief coin of Italy for nearly 400 years.

b. *Biol.*, etc. Applied to things having the relation of offspring of the first generation, or resulting from a primary division or segmentation; **daughter-cell** (*Biol.*), one of two or more cells produced by the fission of an original or mother-cell.

1876 *Trans. Clinical Soc.* IX. 137, I cut down upon the tumour so as freely to expose it, and then punctured it, when a quantity of clear water escaped, and with it two or three small daughter cysts. **1876** *Wagner's Gen. Pathol.* 92 The daughter-cells separate after complete division. **1882** VINES *Sach's Bot.* 139 One of the two daughter-cells (the Apical Cell) remains .. similar to the mother-cell. **1900** B. D. JACKSON *Gloss. Bot. Terms* 71/2 *Daughter chromosome*, a secondary chromosome, derived from division of the original. **1900** DORLAND *Med. Dict.* 188/1 *Daughter-cyst*, a small cyst developed from the wall of a larger one. **1924** J. A. THOMSON *Science Old & New* xliv. 257 A non-cellular organism multiplies by division, budding and spore-forming, and its daughter-units separate off. **1937** *Nature* CXL. 759 On this process [*sc.* crossing-over] .. the later reduction in number and segregation to opposite daughter-cells equally depend. **1964** M. HYNES *Med. Bacteriol.* (ed. 8) xxix. 453 Daughter-cysts may be endogenous, *i.e.*, developed within the primary cyst, or exogenous, *i.e.*, buds penetrate the cyst wall and develop externally.

c. (sense 6d) ***daughter atom, element, product.***

1933 O. H. BLACKWOOD et al. *Outl. Atomic Physics* xii. 219 The atomic weight of radium is 226, and the daughter atom should be four units lighter because of the loss of an alpha particle. **1955** *Gloss. Terms Radiology* (*B.S.I.*) 6 The atom containing the original nucleus is sometimes called the parent atom and the resulting atom the decay product or daughter atom. **1926** R. W. LAWSON tr. *Hevesy & Paneth's Man. Radioactivity* viii. 87 A radio-element is in a state of radioactive equilibrium with its disintegration product, when the same number of atoms of the daughter element disintegrate as are formed in the unit of time. **1962** *Newnes Conc. Encycl. Nuclear Energy* 176/2 The decay products of a radioactive element are often referred to as its daughter products.

Hence **'daughterful** *a.* (*nonce-wd.*), full of daughters. **'daughterhood**, (*a*) the condition of being a daughter; (*b*) daughters collectively (cf. *sisterhood*). **'daughterkin** (*nonce-wd.* after Ger. *töchterchen*), little daughter. **'daughterless** *a.*, without a daughter. **'daughterling** (*nonce-wd.*), little daughter. **'daughtership** (*nonce-wd.*), the condition or relation of a daughter.

1830 CARLYLE in *For. Rev. & Cont. Misc.* V. 45 In a daughter-full house. 1835 *Tait's Mag.* II. 101 The motherhood of Great Britain..and the unportioned daughterhood. 1890 J. PULSFORD *Loyalty to Christ* I. 250 Daughter, thou hast lost thy divine daughterhood. 1858 CARLYLE *Fredk. Gt.* II. x. i. 571 His poor little Daughter-kin. 1393 GOWER *Conf.* III. 305 Ye shull for me be doughterles. 1887 *Cornhill Mag.* Oct. 434 Wifeless and daughterless. 1853 C. BRONTE *Villette* xxv. (D.), What am I to do with this daughter or daughterling of mine? 1808 SOUTHEY *Lett.* (1856) II. 65, I shall not condole with you on the daughtership.

ˈdaughter-in-law. [See BROTHER-IN-LAW.]

1. The wife of one's son.

1382 WYCLIF *Ruth* i. 22 Thanne cam Noemy with Ruth Moabite, hir douȝter in lawe. *c*1440 *Promp. Parv.* 129 Doȝtyr in lawe, *nurus.* 1611 BIBLE *Matt.* x. 35 The daughter in law against her mother in law. 1886 BESANT *Childr. Gibeon* II. xxxii, A mother is difficult to please in the matter of daughters-in-law.

2. = STEPDAUGHTER. (Now considered incorrect. Cf. FATHER-IN-LAW 2.)

[1530 PALSGR. 215/1 Doughter in lawe, *belle fille.*] 1841 *Gentl. Mag.* I. 312 Isabella, daughter of the late Lieut. John Raleigh Elwes..and daughter-in-law to J. Brown, M.D.

daughter-law. Now *dial.* = DAUGHTER-IN-LAW.

1526-34 TINDALE *Matt.* x. 25 The doughterlawe ageynst her motherlawe. 1567 TURBERVILLE *Ovid's Epist.* 36 (Halliw.) Thy father would not entertaine In Greece a daughter-lawe. 1888 ELWORTHY *W. Somerset Word-bk.*, *Darter-law*, (always) daughter-in-law.

daughterly (ˈdɔːtəlɪ), *a.* [f. DAUGHTER + -LY[1].] Pertaining to or characteristic of a daughter; such as becomes a daughter; filial.

*a*1535 MORE *Wks.* 1449 (R.) Youre very daughterly dealing. 1562 LEIGH *Armorie* (1597) 96 b, Mooued to knowe their seuerall actions and daughterly loue. 1794 HURDIS *Tears Affect.* 45 To relate..the soft tale Of daughterly affection. 1871 H. B. FORMAN *Our Living Poets* 231 The mere fear lest our wives and daughters should..become less wifely and daughterly.

Hence **ˈdaughterliness.**

1664 H. MORE *Exp. 7 Epist.* B ij b, The Womanishnesse or Daughterlinesse, if I may so speak, of the Church of Rome. 1882 *Argosy* XXXIV. 280 She cared for her with a tender daughterliness.

dauk (dɔːk). *Mining.* Also (*Sc.*) **dalk, dawk,** (*north Eng.*) **dowk.** [The earlier Sc. form was evidently *dalk*, but the north Eng. points to *dolk*: the etymology is obscure; cf. DAUGH.] See quots.

1795 *Statist. Acc. Stirlings.* XV. 329 (Jam.) Below the coal, there is eighteen inches of a stuff, which the workmen term dalk. 1829 SOPWITH *Mines Alston Moor* 108 In Alston the contents of the unproductive parts of veins are chiefly described as dowk and rider. The former is a brown, friable, and soft soil. 1859-65 PAGE *Geol. Terms, Dauk* or *Dawk*, a mining or quarry term for bands and beds of tough, compact, sandy clay. 1873 *Swaledale Gloss.*, *Dowk*, tenacious black clay in a lead vein. 1876 *Mid-Yorks, Gloss.*, *Dowk*, a mine-working of a stiff clayey nature. *Nidderdale.*

dauk, daukin: see DAWK, DAWKIN.

†**dauke.** *Obs. rare.* [ad. L. *daucus, daucum* carrot.] The wild carrot, *Daucus Carota.*

*c*1450 *Alphita* (Anecd. Oxon.) 47 Daucus creticus..gall. dauk. 1688 R. HOLME *Armoury* II. 73/1 The Dauke, or wild Carrot [hath] flower white.

Daulian (ˈdɔːlɪən), *a.* [f. mod.L. *Daulias* used as the generic name of the nightingale (*D. luscinia*), a. Gr. *Δαυλίας* woman of Daulis, Procne, who was changed into a nightingale.] *Daulian bird*, an affected name for the nightingale.

1894 *Daily News* 22 Jan. 5/1 That tiny modest tome [*sc.* Keats's Poems of 1817], a brown Daulian bird in brown paper. 1904 *Westm. Gaz.* 9 June 12/1 Until three years ago the existence of the Daulian birds in Devonshire was strenuously denied. 1909 *Ibid.* 12 May 5/1 Londoners who want to hear the Daulian birds with complete certainty must now journey to Kew or Chingford.

daulk, obs. form of DALK[2].

daulphin, obs. form of DAUPHIN.

dault, var. DALT; obs. pa. pple. of DEAL *v.*

daun, obs. form of DAN[1].

†**daunch,** *a. Obs.* Fastidious.

*c*1460 *Towneley Myst.* xvii. 509 Begyn I to rekyn I thynk alle dysdayn For daunche. 1888 *Sheffield Gloss.*, *Daunch*, adj. fastidious, over nice, squeamish.

dauncherous, obs. form of DANGEROUS.

dauncy (ˈdɔːnsɪ), *a. U.S.* and *dial.* [var. DONSIE *a.*] Sickly; delicate, not robust.

1846 E. W. FARNHAM *Life in Prairie Land* (1847) iv. 39, I shall give her enough to eat and wear, and I dont calculate she'll be very *dauncy* if she gets that. 1874 E. EGGLESTON *Circuit Rider* vi. 61 You look powerful dauncy, said the old man. 1880 W. H. PATTERSON *Antrim & Down Gloss.* 31 *Donsy, Dauncey*, sick, sick-looking. 1891 M. E. RYAN *Pagan of Alleghanies* v. 82 He ain't one o' yer skim-milk, dauncy ones. He's as stout as a young bull. 1912 I. S. COBB *Back Home* 148 He looks sort of dauncy and low in his mind. 1926 E. M. ROBERTS *Time of Man* (1927) iv. 152 Dorine said that he must be sick. 'He looks dauncy,' she said. *Ibid.* x. 377 'Pap he's sick today,' Joe said. 'I see that. He's dauncy all day.'

daunder, dauner, daunger: see DANDER, DANGER.

†**ˈdaunsel,** *v. Obs.* [a. OF. *daunceler, danzeler* to caress, dandle, f. *danzele, dansele* damsel, girl.] To caress, make much of, coax.

1362 LANGL. *P. Pl.* A. XI. 30 Luytel is he loued or leten bi þat such a lessun redeþ, Or daunseled [*v.r.* dauntid] or drawen forþ. 1393 *Ibid.* C. VII. 20 (MS. F.) Demed for her doyngus & daunselde [*other MSS.* excited] many oþure.

daunt (dɔːnt), *v.* Also 4-6 **daunte, dawnt(e,** 4-7 (4-6 *Sc.*) **dant.** [a. OF. *dante-r* (12-14th c. in Littré), var. of *donter* (mod.F. *dompter*) = Pr. *domtar*:—L. *domitāre*, freq. of *domāre* to tame, subdue. (For the *a* of *danter*, cf. DAN *sb.*[1])]

I. †**1.** *trans.* To overcome, subdue, vanquish.

*c*1300 *K. Alis.* 1312 Sone he wol daunte thy maigne! 1375 BARBOUR *Bruce* IV. 602 The lord persy..Dantit suagat all the land. 1391 CHAUCER *Boeth.* IV. vii. 147 Hercules..dawntede þe proude Centauris. 1509 HAWES *Past. Pleas.* IV. xii, He mette an hydeous gyaunt..With his great strokes he did hym daunt. 1549 *Compl. Scot.* i. 21 The riche monarche of rome, quhilk dantit ande subdeuit al the varld? 1610 HOLLAND *Camden's Brit.* (1637) 256 Being now daunted by time, there remaineth an heape of rammell and rubbish, witnessing the ruines thereof.

†**2.** To tame, break in (an animal). *Obs.*

1377 LANGL. *P. Pl.* B. XV. 393 Makometh..Daunted a dowue, and day and nyȝte hir fedde. 1481 CAXTON *Myrr.* II. vi. 72 Bullys whiche..haue hornes that remeue about hym so that noman may tame ne daunte them. 1549 *Compl. Scot.* xvii. 145 Sum of them began to plant treis, sum to dant beystis. 1569 NEWTON *Cicero's Olde Age* 43 a, To daunte fierce horses.

†**3.** *fig.* To bring into subjection, subdue, tame; to hold in subjection, control. *Obs.*

1303 R. BRUNNE *Handl. Synne* 8420 þat þou mayst nat þy flesshe daunte Be not þarfor yn wanhope. *c*1390 CHAUCER *Truth* 13 Daunt thi self that dauntest otheres dede. *c*1425 JAS. I (Scotl.) *Good Counsel* in *Kingis Q.* (1884) 51 Sen word is thrall and thocht is only free, Thow dant thi twnge, that pouer has and may. 1533 GAU *Richt Vay* (1888) 14 Thay quhilk wil nocht suffer god to dant and rewl thayme..efter his halie wil. 1621 BURTON *Anat. Mel.* I. ii. IV. vii. (1651) 163 It daunts whole kingdoms and cities.

†**b.** To cast down, put down, quell. *Obs.*

?*a*1400 *Arthur* 113 He daunted þe proude & hawted þe poure. 1513-75 *Diurn. Occurrents* (1833) 144 To dant the insolence of George erle Huntlie. 1594 G. W. SENIOR *Pref. Verses Spenser's Amoretti*, Dawnting thereby our neighboures auncient pride. 1709 STRYPE *Ann. Ref.* I. xlvii. 511 The secretary in a letter..trusted the Queen's Majesty would proceed here in such sort, as both these mischiefs would be daunted.

4. To abate the courage of, discourage, dispirit; to put in awe, abash; to overcome with fear, intimidate, cause to quail. (The current sense.)

*c*1475 *Rauf Coilȝear* 600, I dreid me, sa he dantit the, thow durst not with him deill. 1568 GRAFTON *Chron.* II. 615 This discomfiture..daunted the hartes of the..Gascons. 1596 SHAKS. *Tam. Shr.* I. ii. 200 Thinke you a little dinne can daunt mine eares? 1614 BP. HALL *Recoll. Treat.* 1063 True Christian fortitude..may be overborne, but it cannot be daunted. 1781 GIBBON *Decl. & F.* II. xxxii. 227 The spirit of their chief was not daunted by misfortune. 1863 GEO. ELIOT *Romola* II. iv, She was not daunted by the practical difficulties in the way.

†**5.** To daze, stupefy. *Obs.* exc. *dial.*

1581 MULCASTER *Positions* xiii. (1887) 62 Such as..haue their senses daunted, either thorough dreaming melancholie, or dulling phleame. 1590 SPENSER *F.Q.* I. i. 18 Much daunted with that dint her sence was dazd. 1847-78 HALLIW., *Daunt*..in the provinces, to stun, to knock down.

†**II. 6.** To dandle, fondle, caress. *Obs.*

1303 R. BRUNNE *Handl. Synne* 4880 þe fadyr..þe chylde dauntede on hys kne. 1382 WYCLIF *Isa.* lxvi. 12 Vp on the knes men shul daunte ȝou. 14.. *Prose Legends* in *Anglia* VIII. 132 Wiþ siche woordes & cosses dauntynge hir body. 1483 *Cath. Angl.* 92 To Dawnte (A. or to cherys), *blanditractare.*

†**b.** *absol.* To toy. *Obs. rare.*

*a*1529 SKELTON *Image Ipocr.* 225 Some daunte and daly..in the blak ally Wheras it ever darke is.

III. 7. *Herring Fishery.* To press salted herrings into the barrel with a 'daunt'.

1733 P. LINDSAY *Interest Scot.* 201 The largest Herrings..repackt by themselves, and sufficiently served with fresh Salt, daunted and well oyled. 1891 *Rep. Deputation Fishery Board Scot. to Continent* 7 No daunting should be used, when the barrel is fully filled up, but it is most desirable on the first filling up.

daunt, *sb.* [f. DAUNT *v.*]

†**1.** The act of daunting; dispiriting, intimidation; a check. *Obs.*

*a*1400 in *Leg. Rood* 139 þe deuel..Mony folk In-to helle he clihte, Til þe crosses dunt ȝaf him a daunt. 1573 TWYNE *Æneid.* XI. Ii iv b, b, O Tyrrhene dastardes still? What daunt within youre hartes doth light? 1640 BP. REYNOLDS *Passions* xxvii. 279 In a sudden daunt and onset of an unexpected evill.

†**2.** Dandling, caress. *Obs.*

*a*1548 *Thrie Priests Peblis* in Pinkerton *Sc. Poems* I. 43 (Jam.) Of me altyme thow gave but lytil tail; Na of me wald have dant nor dail.

3. *Herring Fishery.* A disc of wood, usually made of two barrel heads nailed together cross-wise, used to press down salted herrings in the barrels.

1890 *Regul. Branding Herrings* (*Sc. Fishery Board*) 5 The daunt must be used with all repacked herrings. *Ibid.* 6 The..herrings then left in the barrel..shall be pressed down..steadily and uniformly, by daunt or otherwise.

daunted (ˈdɔːntɪd), *ppl. a.* Also 4-6 *Sc.* **dantit, -yt.** [f. DAUNT *v.* + -ED[1].]

†**1.** Tamed, subdued, brought under control; trained (quot. 1530). *Obs.*

*c*1375 *Sc. Leg. Saints, Jacobus* 350 þe oxine [ȝokkit] to þe wane mekly As þai had bene wel-dantyt ky. 1487 *Sc. Acts Jas. III*, c. 18 Davntit hors depute to werk & nocht to þe sadill. 1530 LYNDESAY *Test. Papyngo* 277 Maisteris of Museik, to recreat thy spreit With dantit voce and plesande Instrument. 1560 ROLLAND *Crt. Venus* Prol. 229 Be dantit refrenatioun, A man may..alter his Inclinatioun.

2. Dispirited; overcome with fear.

1577-87 HOLINSHED *Chron.* I. 176/2 The forepart of his dawnted host. 1771 MRS. GRIFFITH tr. *Viaud's Shipwreck* 143 The daunted look with which he eyed us. 1867 JEAN INGELOW *Poems, Story Doom* VII. 46 The daunted mighty ones kept silent watch.

Hence **ˈdauntedness.**

1660 G. FOX *Salut. to Chas. II*, 6 God struck thy Fathers Party with dauntedness of spirit.

daunten: see DAUNTON *v. Sc.*

daunter (ˈdɔːntə(r)). Also 6 *Sc.* **danter, -ar.** [f. DAUNT *v.* + -ER[1].]

1. One who daunts; †a subduer, vanquisher.

1513 DOUGLAS *Æneis* IV. Prol. 226 Danter of Affrik, Quene fundar of Cartage. 1552 LYNDESAY *Monarche* 4183 The danter of the Romanis pompe and glorye. 1586 WARNER *Alb. Eng.* I. vi. (R.), The danter then of trespassers.

†**2.** A tamer (of horses), horse-breaker. *Obs.*

1513 DOUGLAS *Æneis* VII. iv. 84 Kyng Picus, Dantar of horss. 1549 *Compl. Scot.* xvii. 151 The maist perfyit industreus horse dantars of macedon.

daunting (ˈdɔːntɪŋ), *vbl. sb.* [-ING[1].] The action of the verb DAUNT; vanquishing; taming; caressing; discouragement, intimidation.

*c*1400 *Rom. Rose* 4032 Man may for no dauntyng Make a sperhauke of a bosarde. *c*1440 *Promp. Parv.* 115 Dawntynge, or grete chersynge, *focio.* 1581 MULCASTER *Positions* xli. (1887) 235 It is a great daunting to the best able man. 1654 E. JOHNSON *Wond. Work. Provid.* 117 To the danting of every proud heart.

ˈdaunting, *ppl. a.* [-ING[2].] That daunts: intimidating, etc.; see the verb.

*a*1300 *Cursor M.* 21343 (Cott.) Leon dantand harsk and herd. *c*1585 *Faire Em* III. 1052 As for his menacing and daunting threats. 1677 GILPIN *Demonol.* (1867) 467 A daunting and commanding authority over the consciences of men. 1847 EMERSON *Poems, Monadnoc* Wks. (Bohn) I. 439 Open the daunting map beneath.

Hence **ˈdauntingly** *adv.*, **ˈdauntingness.**

1794 BURNS *M'Pherson's Farewell*, Sae dauntingly gaed he. 1613-18 DANIEL *Coll. Hist. Eng.* 4 (D.) As one who well knew..how the first euents are those which incusse a dauntingnesse or daring.

dauntless (ˈdɔːntlɪs), *a.* [f. DAUNT *v.* (hardly from the *sb.*) + -LESS.] Not to be daunted; fearless, intrepid, bold, undaunted.

1593 SHAKS. *3 Hen. VI*, III. iii. 17 Let thy dauntlesse minde still ride in triumph, Ouer all mischance. 1667 MILTON *P.L.* I. 603 Browes Of dauntless courage. 1761 GRAY *Fatal Sisters* 41 Low the dauntless Earl is laid. 1817 SCOTT (*title*), Harold the Dauntless. 1874 GREEN *Short Hist.* viii. §5. 514 Laud was as dauntless as ever.

Hence **ˈdauntlessly** *adv.*, **ˈdauntlessness.**

1813 SHELLEY *Q. Mab* VII. 196 Therefore I rose, and dauntlessly began My lonely..pilgrimage. 1730-6 BAILEY (folio), *Dauntlesness*, a being without Fear or Discouragement. 1876 BANCROFT *Hist. U.S.* VI. xlviii. 292 Shelby..among the dauntless singled out for dauntlessness.

daunton, danton (ˈdɔːntən), *v. Sc.* Forms: 6-7 **dantoun,** 5-9 **danton,** 7-9 **daunten,** 8-9 **daunton.** [A derivative form of DAUNT *v.*; perh. a mistaken form of *daunten* pres. inf. (in Chaucer, etc.). Always spelt *danton, -oun* in earlier Sc., as *dant* was then regularly used for *daunt.*] = DAUNT *v.*: To subdue, tame, intimidate, etc.

1535 STEWART *Cron. Scot.* II. 8 How the Emprioure Theodocius send ane Armie..to dantoun this foirsaid Octaueus. *a*1572 KNOX *Hist. Ref.* Wks. 1846 I. 371 This wonderouse wark of God..aucht to have dantoned hir furie. 1599 JAS. I *Βασιλ. Δῶρον* III. 121 Use..to ride and danton..couragious horses. 1609 BP. W. BARLOW *Answ. Nameless Cath.* 121 To enforce a grant, or daunten the Prince. 1681 COLVIL *Whigs Supplic.* (1751) 128 Who once at Rome, his pride to danton, His nose saluted with a panton. *c*1794 BURNS *Song, Blude red Rose*, An auld man shall never daunton me. 1837 R. NICOLL *Poems* (1842) 162 Its sadness shall never danton me.

Hence **ˈdauntoned** *ppl. a.*, tamed, broken in.

1597 SKENE *Quon. Attach.* c. 48 §11 Bot it is otherwise of a tame and dantoned horse [*de equo domito*].

daunz, obs. form of DAN[1].

dauphin (ˈdɔːfɪn). *Fr. Hist.* Forms: α. 5-6 **dolphyn,** 6 **dolphyne, dolphine, doulphyn,** 6-8 **dolphin;** β. 5 **daulphyn,** 6-7 **daulphin,** 7- **dauphin.** [a. F. *dauphin* (earlier *daulphin*, in 15th c. also *doffin*) = Pr. *dalfin*:—pop. L. **dalphinus*, for L. *delphin-us* (ad. Gr. *δελφίς* dolphin), whence Sp. *delfin*, It. *delfino.* In earlier use Eng. had *daulphin*, also *dolphyn, -in*, the same as the name of the fish; *dauphin* is after mod.F., since the

17th c. See DOLPHIN.] The title of the eldest son of the King of France, from 1349 to 1830.

Originally a title attached to certain seigneuries: Dauphin of the Viennois, Dauphin of Auvergne. According to Littré, the name Dauphin, borne by the lords of the Viennois, was a proper name *Delphinus* (the same word as the name of the fish), whence the province subject to them was called *Dauphiné*. Humbert III, the last lord of Dauphiné, on ceding the province to Philip of Valois in 1349, made it a condition that the title should be perpetuated by being borne by the eldest son of the French king.

α. Form *daulphin, dauphin.*

1485 CAXTON *Paris & V.* 1 A ryche baron daulphyn and lord of the lond. *a* **1577** SIR T. SMITH *Commw. Eng.* (1633) 44 In France the Kings eldest Sonne hath the title of Daulphin. **1614** SELDEN *Titles Hon.* 172 The sonne and heire apparant of the French King is known to all by the name of *Daulphin.* **1681** NEVILE *Plato Rediv.* 107 The Barons call'd in Lewis the Dauphin. **1871** MORLEY *Voltaire* (1880) 159 To celebrate the marriage of the dauphin.

β. Form *dolphin, dolphyn, doulphyn.* (Rare after 1670.)

1494 FABYAN *Chron.* VII. 500 Kyng Iohn..sent sir Charlys his sone, dolphyn of Vyenne, into Normandy. **1530** PALSGR. 214/2 Doulphyn, the frenche kynges eldest sonne. **1559** *Mirr. Mag., Salisbury* xxiii, Charles the Dolphyn our chief enemy. **1591** SHAKS. *1 Hen. VI*, I. i. 92 The Dolphin Charles is crowned King in Rheimes. **1670** COTTON *Espernon* II. v. 216 The Joy all good Frenchmen were full of, for the Birth of the young Dolphin. **1708** T. WARD *Eng. Ref.* (1716) 140 The Scottish Queen Had to the Dolphin married been.

†**2.** *attrib.* or *adj.* = DELPHIN, q.v. *Obs.*

1705 HEARNE *Collect.* (Oxf. Hist. Soc.) I. 14 The Dauphin Edition of this Author.

Hence †**dauphinage** (*dolphynage*); also **dauphinate**, the rule or jurisdiction of a dauphin (of Viennois).

1494 FABYAN *Chron.* VII. 498 In this yere the dolphyn of Vyen..solde his dolphynage vnto the Frenshe kynge. **1884** J. WOODWARD in *N. & Q.* 16 Aug. 137 The dauphinate of Viennois was then vested in the Crown.

dauphiness ('dɔːfɪnɪs). Forms: α. 6 **dolphines, dolphynesse**, etc.; β. 6 **daulph-**, 7- **dauphiness.** [f. DAUPHIN + -ESS; the F. title is *dauphine.*] The wife of the dauphin.

1548 HALL *Chron.* 230b, The dolphin & his dolphines. *Ibid.* 240b, The Ladye Elizabeth, entiteled Dolphynesse of Vyen. **1596** DANETT tr. *Comines* 202 The Lady Daulphinesse. **1685** *Lond. Gaz.* No. 2048/3 The King accompanied with the Dauphin and Dauphiness. **1712** SWIFT *Jrnl. Stella* 11 Feb., It is very surprising this news to-day, of the dauphin and dauphiness both dying within six days. **1860** FROUDE *Hist. Eng.* VI. 364 The dangerous competition of the Queen of Scots and Dauphiness of France.

daur, Sc. f. DARE.

daurg, var. of DARG *Sc.*

daut, dawt (dɒt), *v.* *Sc.* Also 6-8 **date.** [Etymology unknown.

If *daut, dawt*, is, as it appears to be, the proper form, it ought to represent an original *dalt*: cf. Sc. *faut, maut, saut*, etc.; but the two 16-17th c. examples of *date* from Scotch writers of English make even this doubtful. *Dalt* suggests Gael. *dalta* foster-child; but, though the word appears to be exclusively Scotch, there is no evidence pointing to a Gaelic origin. Connexion with DOTE, *doat* is excluded by the fact that Sc. *au, aw*, does not answer to Eng. *ō* from any source. Cf. also DAUNT *v.* 6.]

trans. To pet, fondle, caress, make much of. Also *absol.*

1500-20 DUNBAR *Petit. Gray Horse* 49, I was nevir dautit into stabell, My lyf hes bene so miserable. **1573** *Commend. Vprichtnes* 228 in *Sat. Poems Ref.* (1891) I. 285 Quha preissis vprichtlie To serue the Lord mon..na wayis dres to daut thame daintelie. *a* **1598** ROLLOCKE *Passion* 491-2 (Jam.) The father will make much of his sonne, and allure him..so the Lord dates and allures us. **1633** W. STRUTHER *True Happiness* 123 Though he datted the Patriarchs by the familiaritie of his divine presence. **1637** RUTHERFORD *Lett.* (1862) I. 461, I am dawted now and then with pieces of Christ's love and comforts. **1786** BURNS *Poet's Welcome to Child* ii, I, fatherly, will kiss and daut thee. **1853** J. MILNE *Jrnl.* in *Life* xiii. (1868) 203 My Lord surely dawts his weak foolish child.

Hence **dauted, dawted** *ppl. a.*, petted, fondled.

1636 RUTHERFORD *Lett.* (1862) I. 193, I am handled as softly and delicately as a dawted child. **1692** *Scot. Presbyt. Eloq.* (1738) 105 Will not a Father take his little dated Davie in his Arms. **1796** MACNEILL *Will & Jean* lvii, The tenderest mither, Fond of ilk dear dauted wean. **1851** *Cumbrld. Gloss.*, *Dawtet*, caressed, fondled.

dautie, dawtie ('dɔːtɪ). *Sc.* Also **dawty.** [f. prec. or its source: but a formation with the dim. and appellative *-ie*, -Y, from a verb, is unusual.] A person caressed or indulged; a darling, pet, favourite.

1676 J. FRASER *Autobiog.* in *Select. Biog.* (Wodrow Soc.) II. 89, I was no dawty. **1727** P. WALKER *Remark. Passages* 122 (Jam.) Giving an account of old Quintin Dick, one of his Dawties. **1823** GALT *Entail* I. xix. 156, 'I hae thought o' that, Girzy, my dawty', said he.

‖**dauw** (daːʊ). Also **dau, dow.** [South African Dutch form of the native name.] A South African species of zebra, *Equus Burchellii*, approaching the quagga in character.

1802 *Sporting Mag.* XX. 140 Two sorts of wild horses, the Dau and the Kwagga. **1847** *Nat. Encycl.* I. 265 The indigenous Pachydermata are..the zebra, the dauw, the quagga.

†**davach, -och.** *Sc. Hist.* In 7 **dawach(e.** [OIr. *dabach, dabhach* vat, tub (perhaps as a corn-measure); cf. the similar uses of *pint, pottle*, and *gallon*, as measures of land in Anglo-Irish. In med.L. *davaca* (erron. *-ata*).

A conjectured derivation from *damh* ox, is erroneous. *Dabach* occurs as a land-measure in the 'Book of Deir'. (*Goidelica* (ed. 2) 217.)]

An ancient Scottish measure of land, consisting in the east of Scotland of 4 ploughgates, each of 8 oxgangs; in the west divided into twenty penny-lands. It is said to have averaged 416 acres, but its extent probably varied with the quality of the land.

1609 SKENE tr. *Quon. Attach.* xxiii. § 11 Provyding that the husband man did haue of him the aucht parte of ane dawache of land [*marg.* of ane oxgait of land], or mair [*unius dauace terre vel plus*]. **1794** *Statist. Acc. Scot.* XIII. 509 There is a davoch of land belonging to this parish. **1797** *Ibid.* XIX. 290 A davoch contains 32 oxen-gates of 13 acres each, or 416 acres of arable land. *c* **1817** HOGG *Tales & Sk.* VI. 269 Heir to seven ploughgates of land, and five half davochs. **1854** C. INNES *Orig. Paroch. Scot.* II. 335 By an ordinance of King John Balliol in 1292 eight davachs of land, including the islands of Egge and Rume, were among the lands then erected into the Sheriffdom of Skey. **1872** E. W. ROBERTSON *Hist. Ess.* 127 Davoch, a large pastoral measure at one time answering to the plough-gate, though in actual extent 4 times as large.

davenport[1] ('dæv(ə)npɔət). Also **devonport.** [Said to be from the maker's name.] A kind of small ornamental writing-table or escritoire fitted with drawers, etc.

(Remembered in 1845.)

1853 *Pract. Mechanic's Jrnl.* VI. 212 This very elegant and convenient desk is similar to an ordinary Devonport. **1875** *Argosy* May 329 At her davenport, pen in hand, sat her ladyship.

attrib. **1883** *Harper's Mag.* Jan. 235/1 An inlaid davenport desk.

Davenport[2]. Used to designate china, earthenware, etc., made by a family of this name at Longport, Staffordshire, between 1793 and 1882.

[**1829** S. SHAW *Hist. Staffs. Potteries* 2 The largest Potteries known, being Wedgewood's, Etruria;.. Davenport's, Longport; Minton's, Stoke.] **1863** W. CHAFFERS *Marks Pott. & Porc.* 124 Davenport Stone China. Staffordshire. Longport. **1872** LADY C. SCHREIBER *Jrnl.* (1911) I. 156 We got nothing but a 'Davenport' plate. **1875** L. TROUBRIDGE *Life amongst Troubridges* (1966) 106 A bowl ..marked with an anchor, this we thought at first was Chelsea, but know since that it is Davenport. **1954** G. SAVAGE *Porcelain* II. viii. 270 Much nineteenth-century Davenport porcelain survives. *Ibid.*, Two Davenport *plaques* painted in the manner of Birkett Foster. **1965** A. CHRISTIE *At Bertram's Hotel* i. 10 The china, if not actually Rockingham and Davenport, looked like it.

Davenport[3]. *N. Amer.* Also **davenport.** [Orig. uncertain: perh. from the maker's name.] A type of large, upholstered couch or sofa which may be convertible into a bed. Freq. *attrib.* Cf. CHESTERFIELD 2.

1897 *Washington Post* 31 Oct. 2/5 (Advt.), Davenport sofa, green color. **1898** *Amer. Cabinet Maker & Upholsterer* 1 Jan. 13/1 Dealers are receiving neatly printed cards reminding them that the entire new line of couches,.. Davenports, Turkish sofas and oriental divans of the Jamestown Lounge Co., will be on exhibition..during January. **1911** *Daily Colonist* (Victoria, B.C.) 22 Apr. 4/4 (Advt.), Davenport sofas, upholstered in Spanish leather, solid quarter cut oak, Early English finish or fumed oak $55. **1957** J. AGEE *Death in Family* II. 242 They slept on the brand-new davenport in the sitting room. **1981** *N.Y. Times Mag.* 21 June 10/2 There used to be a split on *davenport* and *sofa*; now the split is between *sofa* and *couch.*

daver ('deɪvə(r)), *v. dial.* [In I. app. cognate with Du. *daveren* to shake, quake, MLG., LG. *dawern*, a word of frequentative form, of which the root is uncertain. In II. perh. transferred from the same.]

I. *Scotch* and *north Eng. intr.* To move or walk as if dazed or stupefied, to stagger; also to be benumbed. *trans.* To stupefy, stun, benumb.

c **1600** BUREL in Watson *Collect.* ii. (1706) 30 (Jam.) Bot tauren and dauren, Like ane daft doitit fule. **1785** *Jrnl. fr. Lond.* 6 in *Poems Buchan Dial.* (Jam.), We bein wat wou'd soon grow davert to stand..i' the cauld that time o' night. **1796** MACNEILL *Will & Jean* lxiii, See them now—how changed wi' drinking!.. Davered, doited, daized and blinking. **1820** *St. Kathleen* III. 115 (Jam.) 'Here's the bed, man! Whare..are ye davering to?' **1824** E. SWINBURNE in J. Raine *Mem. J. Hodgson* (1858) II. 45, I am somewhat *davered* about the vignettes.

II. *south-west. dial. intr.* To fade, wither. Also *fig.* (In first quot. *causative* or *trans.*)

1621 J. REYNOLDS *God's Revenge agst. Murder* I. v. 154 As if time and age had not power to wither the blossomes of our youth, as the Sunne hath to dauer the freshest Roses and Lillies. **1622** W. YONGE *Diary* 63 [The] hedges..davered as if they had been scorched with lightning. **1654** VILVAIN *Epit. Ess.* VII. 54 My Piety 'gan to daver [L. *labefacta cadebat*]. **1787** GROSE *Prov. Gloss.*, *Daver*, to fade like a flower. *Devon.* **1880** *W. Cornwall Gloss.*, *Daver*, to soil; to fade as a flower.

davered ('deɪvəd), *ppl. a. dial.* [f. DAVER *v.*] Withered, faded, drooping.

1837 M. PALMER *Dialogue Devonshire Dial.* 6 Now, dear soul, her's like a daver'd rose. **1864** CAPERN *Devon Provinc.*, Thy heart is like the daver'd rose.

So **'daverdy** *a. dial.*, dowdy, unkempt.

1906 GALSWORTHY *Man of Property* I. vii. 95 Even in the garden, that sense of things being pokey haunted old Jolyon; the wicker chair creaked under his weight; the garden-beds looked 'daverdy'. *Ibid.* II. iii. 148 That was how he liked 'em, all of a piece, none of your daverdy, scarecrow women! **1924** —— *On Expression* 7 What an expressive variant of the word 'dowdy'..is the word 'daverdy'..! Dowdy suggests the flannel petticoat, the thick, the dusty appearance; daverdy a sea-green, trailing, down-at-heeledness.

Davey: see DAVY[1].

david, obs. form of DAVIT.

Da'vidian. = DAVIDIST.

1885 R. W. DIXON *Hist. Ch. Eng.* III. 472 The rising Davidians, Davists, Georgists, or Family of Love, which.. gave trouble in the reign of Elizabeth.

Davidic (deɪ'vɪdɪk), *a.* [f. personal name *David* + -IC.] Of or pertaining to David as king of Israel, or as the reputed author of the Psalms. Also **Da'vidical** *a.*

[*c* **1000** *Leechdoms* (1866) III. 428 Of ðam dauiticum sealmum.] **1827** COLERIDGE *Table-t.* 10 Mar., I apprehend many of the Psalms to be Davidical only, not David's own compositions. **1865** *Chambers's Encycl.* VII. 819/1 The first [book]..contains the Davidic Jehovistic psalms. **1877** *Encycl. Brit.* VI. 841/2 We cannot well stop short of the admission that the Psalter must contain Davidic psalms. **1883** *Ibid.* XVI. 54/1 Amos foretold the redintegration of the Davidic kingdom. **1918** E. GRUBB *Relig. Experience* 186 The glories of the ancient Davidic monarchy. **1951** R. A. KNOX *Stimuli* vii. 15 The Saviour..to whose coming they looked forward, was to be a national Saviour, a Davidic ruler. **1957** G. E. WRIGHT *Bibl. Archaeol.* ix. 146/1 The southern kingdom, calling itself 'Judah', retained the Davidic dynasty.

'Davidist. [f. personal name *David* + -IST.]

1. One of a fanatical sect founded by David George or Jores, a Dutch Anabaptist of the 16th century. Also ***David-Georgian, -jorian, -jorist.***

1657 BAXTER *Agst. Quakers* 13 Down to the David-Georgians, Wegelians, Familists, and the like of late. **1727-51** CHAMBERS *Cycl*, *Davidists*..a sect of heretics. **1882-3** SCHAFF *Encycl. Relig. Knowl.* II. 1471 The 'David-jorists', and other uproarious Anabaptists.

2. A follower of David of Dinant.

davidsonite ('deɪvɪdsənaɪt). *Min.* [Named 1836 after Dr. Davidson of Aberdeen: see -ITE.] A variety of beryl found near Aberdeen.

1836 T. THOMSON *Min.* I. 247.

[**David's quadrant**, error for *Davis's quadrant*: see QUADRANT and next.]

[**David's staff.** Originally an error of Pietro della Valle's, who gave *Dauidstoff* as the English name of an instrument for taking the altitude of the sun. This was reproduced by his translator, Havers, as *David's Staff*, which was copied by Blount and Phillips, and is repeated in some modern Dicts. So also *David's quadrant* (= BACK-STAFF) in Phillips (ed. 1696), corrected in Kersey's ed. (1706) to *Davis's quadrant*: see QUADRANT *sb.*[1], quot. 1696.

1623 PIETRO DELLA VALLE *Viaggi* Let. i. 22 Mar. (1663) IV. 16 Con diuersi altri strumenti: e con vno in particolare, che mi dissero, da poco tempo in quà, essere stato inventato da vn tal Dauid, che dal suo nome l'haueua chiamato *Dauidstoff*, che in lingua Inglese vale à dir legno di Dauid. **1664** G. HAVERS *translation*, One [instrument] invented by one *David*, and from his name call'd *David's Staff*. **1674** BLOUNT *Glossogr.*, *Davids-staff*, is an instrument in Navigation, consisting of two Triangles united together, one longer then the other, both having their base arched, and between them in the circle of their bases, containing an entire Quadrant of ninety degrees. *Valle's Travels.*]

Davie: see DAVY (JONES).

'daviely, *adv. Sc.* Spiritlessly, listlessly.

1789 BURNS *Elegy on* 1788, Observe the vera nowte an' sheep, How dowf and daviely they creep. **1825** in JAMIESON.

daviesite ('deɪvɪzaɪt). *Min.* [f. the name of Thomas *Davies* (1837-92), British mineralogist: see -ITE[1].] (See quots.)

1889 L. FLETCHER in *Min. Mag.* May 171 Crystals of..an Oxychloride of lead (Daviesite), from Mina Beatriz, Sierra Gorda, Atacama, South America. **1951** in C. PALACHE et al. *Dana's Syst. Min.* (ed. 7) II. 58. **1963** M. H. HEY *Index Min. Species, App.* (ed. 2) 98 Daviesite... Delete..Syn. of hemimorphite.

davina (*Min.*): see DAVYNE.

Davis[1] ('deɪvɪs). The name of Dwight F. *Davis* (1879-1945), Amer. politican, used in ***Davis Cup***: a cup presented by him and played for annually by international lawn tennis teams; also, the contest for this cup.

1901 *Outing* (U.S.) June 320/1 Another challenge has now been received from them..and a second attempt to 'lift' the Davis Cup will be made this season. **1936** 'R. WEST' *Thinking Reed* xi. 374 He would secure front-row seats for the Davis Cup. **1950** *Oxf. Jun. Encycl.* IX. 309/1 In 1900 an American player called Dwight Davis presented the Davis Cup, which is competed for annually by many countries.

Davis[2] ('deɪvɪs). The name of Sir Robert H. *Davis* (1870–1965), used *attrib.* to designate: (*a*) apparatus invented by him to permit escape from a submarine; (*b*) a decompression-chamber for deep-sea diving.

1931 *Hansard* 10 June 1021 Six ratings..escaped from the wreck by means of the Davis submarine escape apparatus. **1936** R. H. DAVIS *Deep Diving* 6 The Davis submersible decompression chamber..was submitted to the Admiralty in 1929. *Ibid.* vi. 113 Divers could not do useful work there [beyond 204 feet] unless means could be found for improving the conditions of their ascent... The problem has now been solved by the invention of the Davis submersible decompression chamber. *Ibid.* xiv. 206 The procedure in case of emergency would be for two men to enter the locks wearing the Davis apparatus..to open the upper hatches and, floating through them, escape to the surface. **1940** E. ELLSBERG *Men under Sea* vii. 89 The Davis 'lung'..has always carried in addition to the chemical cartridge a small oxygen cylinder, from which fresh oxygen can be continuously supplied. *Ibid.* xxii. 305 A diver may work 20 minutes at a depth of 300 feet, come up in a total of 13 minutes' time to 60 feet, where he enters the Davis chamber, and then be hauled aboard. **1947** *Sci. News* IV. 12 The Davis submarine escape apparatus is the simplest form of diving apparatus. It consists simply of a counter-lung with a small oxygen cylinder and soda-lime canister, and a mouth-piece.

'**Davist.** = DAVIDIST.

1885 R. W. DIXON *Hist. Ch. Eng.* III. 201.

davit ('dævɪt, 'deɪvɪt). *Naut.* Forms: 4 **daviot,** 5 **daviott, devette, dyvette,** 7 **dauid, -yd, -ed,** 7– **davit.** [Formerly also *David*, and app. an application of that Christian name, as in the case of other machines and tools. Cf. F. *davier*, the name of several tools, etc., altered from *daviet* (Rabelais) = *Daviet*, dim. of OF. *Davi* David; the tool was still called *david* by joiners in the 17th c. (Hatzfeld and Darmesteter).]

1. a. A curved piece of timber or iron with a roller or sheave at the end, projecting from a ship's bow, and used as a crane to hoist the flukes of the anchor without injuring the side of the vessel; a ***fish-davit***. **b.** One of a pair of cranes on the side or stern of a ship, fitted with sheaves and pulleys for suspending or lowering a boat.

[**1373** in *Norman-Fr. Indenture* in Riley *Lond. Mem.* 370 (*transl.*), 30 *ores*, 1 *daviot*, for the same boat.] **1485** *Naval Accts. Hen. VII* (1896) 40 Daviott for the bote. *Ibid.* 49 Daviottes in the ffore castell. **1495** *Ibid.* 193 Devettes with a shyver of yron. *Ibid.*, Dyvettes with a colke of brasse. **1622** R. HAWKINS *Voy. S. Sea* (1847) 188 His boate fitted with.. tholes, dauyd, windles, and other. **1626** CAPT. SMITH *Accid. Yng. Seamen* 12 The forecastle, or prow..the fish-hooke, a loufe-hooke, and the blocke at the Dauids ende. **1627** —— *Seaman's Gram.* ii. 10 The *Dauid*..is put out betwixt the Cat and the Loufe, and to be remoued when you please. **1691** T. H[ALE] *Acc. New Invent.* 125 Bitts, Catheads and Davits. **1769** FALCONER *Dict. Marine* (1776) s.v., The davit ..is employed to fish the anchor. **1820** SCORESBY *Acc. Arctic Reg.* II. 196 The boats are..suspended from davits or cranes fixed on the sides of the ship. **1875** J. C. WILCOCKS *Sea Fisherman* 48 Crane-davits of galvanised iron, in shape of the ordinary boat-davits.

2. *Comb.* **davit-cast,** a heavy spar used as a crane on board ship; **davit-guy,** a rope used to steady a davit; **davit-roll,** the roller or sheave of a davit; **davit-rope,** the lashing which secures the davit to the shrouds when out of use.

1794 NELSON in Nicolas *Disp.* I. 434 Our *davit-cast unfortunately has broke it's windlass. **1893** R. KIPLING *Many Invent.* 364 Stop, seize and fish, and easy on the *davit-guy. **1793** SMEATON *Edystone L.* §143 A strong hawser..being passed..over the *davit-roll..the anchor and chain were then let down.

davite ('deɪvaɪt). *Min.* [See quot.] A variety of ALUNOGEN or native sulphate of alumina.

1828 MILL in *Brande's Q. Jrnl.* 379, I shall therefore take leave to call it Davite in honor of Sir Humphry Davy.

davoch: see DAVACH.

davreuxite (dəv'rø:zaɪt). *Min.* [Named 1878 after the Belgian chemist Ch. Davreux: see -ITE.] A hydrous silicate of alumina and manganese found in Belguim.

1882 in DANA *Min.* App. iii. 35.

Davy[1] ('deɪvɪ). In full **Davy lamp, Davy's lamp.** [Named after the inventor.] The miner's safety-lamp invented by Sir Humphry Davy, in which the flame is surrounded with wire-gauze, so as to prevent its communication to explosive gases outside the lamp.

1817 FARADAY in B. Jones *Life* I. 214 The great desideratum of a lamp to afford light with safety:..merely to refer to that which alone has been found efficacious, the Davy. **1880** C. M. MASON *Forty Shires* 15 The men find fault with the Davy.

davy[2] ('deɪvɪ). *slang.* A vulgar shortening of AFFIDAVIT, *esp.* in phr. *to take one's davy* (= 'to take one's oath').

1764 O'HARA *Midas* II. iv. (Farmer), And I with my davy will back it, I'll swear. **1785** CAPT. GROSE *Dict. Vulgar Tongue*, I'll take my davy of it. **1871** M. COLLINS *Mrq. & Merch.* I. vi. 210 [They] take their solemn oath and davy that they didn't do it.

Davy Jones ('deɪvɪ 'dʒəʊnz). Also simply **Davy.** In nautical slang: The spirit of the sea; the sailors' devil. ***Davy Jones's*** (or ***Davy's***) ***locker***: the ocean, the deep, *esp.* as the grave of those who perish at sea.

1751 SMOLLETT *Per. Pic.* xiii. (Brewer), This same Davy Jones, according to the mythology of sailors, is the fiend that presides over all the evil spirits of the deep. **1790** DIBDIN *Poor Jack* iii, And if to old Davy I should go, friend Poll, Why you will ne'er hear of me more. *c* **1790** J. WILLOCK *Voy.* 12 The great bugbear of the ocean is Davie Jones..At the crossing of the line..[they call] out that Davie Jones and his wife are coming on board and that every thing must be made ready. **1803** *Naval Chron.* X. 510 The..seamen would have met a watery grave; or, to use a seaman's phrase, gone to Davy Jones's locker. **1839** *Marryat Phant. Ship* xli, I thought you had gone to Davy's locker.

davyne ('deɪvɪn). *Min.* [ad. Ital. *davina*, named 1825 after Sir Humphry Davy.] A variety of nephelite, from Vesuvius.

1826 *Amer. Jrnl. Sc.* XI. 257 Davina (Davyne). **1869** PHILLIPS *Vesuv.* x. 292 Davyne, a hydrous nepheline, is found in cavities of ejected blocks of gray lava on Somma.

davyum ('deɪvɪəm). *Chem.* [Named after Sir Humphry Davy, with termination *-um* as in *platinum*, etc.] The name given by Kern in 1877 to a supposed metal of the platinum group, announced by him as discovered in Russian platinum ore.

1879 WATTS *Dict. Chem.* VIII. 626.

daw (dɔ:), *sb.* Also 5–8 **dawe,** 6–8 *Sc.* **da.** [Known only from the 15th c. (so the compound *ca-daw*, CADDOW): its form points to an OE. **dawe* (:—*da'wā* from *daȝ'wā*), in ablaut relation to OHG. *tâha*, MHG. *tâhe* (Gothic type **dêhwô*, OTeut. **dǣhwā*:—'*dēhwā*). Mod. HG. dialects have *dähi, däche, dacha*; MHG. shows a dim. form *tâhele* (OHG. **tâhala*), mod.G. *dahle*, since 18th c. *dohle*; whence med.L. *tacula*, It. *taccola*.]

1. A small bird of the crow kind (*Corvus monedula*); now commonly called JACKDAW.

1432–50 tr. *Higden* (Rolls) IV. 307 A poor sowter informede a dawe to speke. **1530** PALSGR. 212/1 Dawe, a foule, *corneille*. **1604** DRAYTON *Owle* 188 The theevish Daw, and the dissembling Pye. **1713** SWIFT *Poems, Salamander*, Pyes and daws are often stil'd With christian nick-names like a child. **1851** CARLYLE *Sterling* I. iii. (1872) 14 Old ruinous castles with their ivy and their daws.

2. *fig.* Applied contemptuously to persons. †**a.** A silly fellow, simpleton, noodle, fool. *Obs.*

c **1500** *Yng. Children's Bk.* 140 in *Babees Bk.* (1868) 25 At thi tabull noþer crache ne claw, Than men wylle sey þou arte A daw. **1560** INGELEND *Disob. Child* in Hazl. *Dodsley* II. 285, I never saw One..in so easy a matter..thus play the daw. **1563** *Homilies* II. *Idolatry* III. (1859) 236 O seely, foolish, and dastardly daws. **1608** J. DAY *Law Trickes* I. i, How the daw Scoures ore his rustie phrases.

b. A lazy person, sluggard; **c.** An untidy woman, slut, slattern. *Sc.*

c **1460** *Towneley Myst.* 26 Bot if God help amang I may sit downe daw to ken. **1500–20** DUNBAR *Dance 7 deidly Synnis* 71 Mony slute daw and slepy duddroun. **1513** DOUGLAS *Æneis* XIII. Prol. 184, I will my cunnand kepe, I will nocht be a daw, I will nocht slepe. **1598** FERGUSSON *Sc. Prov.*, A year a nurish, seven year a da. **1768** ROSS *Helenore* 135 (Jam.) But I see that but spinning I'll never be braw, But gae by the name of a dilp or a da. **1862** A. HISLOP *Prov. Scot.* 16 A morning's sleep Is worth a fauld o' sheep To a hudderin-dudderin daw.

d. With reference to the fable of the jay in peacock's plumes.

1731 FIELDING *Mod. Husb.* II. ii, That ever Heav'n shou'd make me father to such a drest up daw!

3. *Comb.*, as †**dawcock,** *lit.* a male jackdaw; *fig.* = sense 2 a; †**dawpate** = sense 2 a.

1556 J. HEYWOOD *Spider & F.* xcii, Where *dawcocks in doctrine have dominacioun. **1861** W. ROBERTSON *Phraseol. Gen.* (1693) 621 Who brought hither this fool in a play; this very daw-cock to lead the dance. *a* **1529** SKELTON *Agst. Garnesche* 94 Lyke a doctor *dawpate. **1562** J. HEYWOOD *Prov. & Epig.* (1867) 187 Thou arte a very dawe pate.

daw obs. form of DEW; see also DAWE, DAY.

†**daw** (dɔ:), *v.*[1] *Obs.* exc. *Sc.* Forms: 1 **daȝian,** 2–3 **daȝen,** 3–5 **dawe(n,** 6– **daw.** [OE. *daȝian*, corresp. to MDu. *daghen*, Du. and LG. *dagen*, OHG. *tagên*, G. *tagen*, to become day, f. WGer. *dag-* DAY. Since the OE. change of *a* to *æ* did not take place in the vb., the latter is *daw*, against the sb. *day*: cf. *draw, dray, saw, say*, etc. In northern dial. sometimes inflected *dew, dawen*, after the strong verbs *blow, snow*, etc. In 16th c. Sc. erroneously spelt *dall* after *fall, fa'*, etc.]

1. *intr.* To dawn. **a.** with *it* as subject.

c **900** *Bæda's Eccl. Hist.* IV. x, Ðonne hit daȝian ongynneþ. *c* **1205** LAY. 1694 A-marwen þo it dawede. *c* **1350** *Will. Palerne* 1791 Til it dawed to day. *c* **1375** *Sc. Leg. Saints, Ninian* 1417 On þe morne, as It dew day. **1470–85** MALORY *Arthur* XVII. ii, Within a whyle it dawyd.

b. with *day* (or *morning*) as subject.

c **1200** *Trin. Coll. Hom.* 103 Ac alse wat swo þe þridde dai dageð. *c* **1375** BARBOUR *Troy-bk.* II. 797 And whene þe day was dawyne lyght. **1393** LANGL. *P. Pl.* C. XXI. 471 Tyl þe day dawede these damseles daunsede. *c* **1475** *Rauf Coilȝear* 365 Vpon the morne airlie, quhen the day dew. **1513** DOUGLAS *Æneis* XIII. Prol. 182 As menstralis playng *The joly day now dawis*. *a* **1605** MONTGOMERIE *Poems, The Night is neir gone* 1 Hay! nou the day dauis. **1612** DRAYTON *Poly-olb.* x. (N.), The other side from whence the morning daws. **1789** BURNS *Happy Trio*, The cock may craw, the day may daw. **1837** R. NICOLL *Poems* (1842) 97 Nor hamewith steers till morning daw.

c. *fig.*

a **1225** *Ancr. R.* 352 Hwon he þet is ower lif daweð and springeð ase þe dawunge efter nihtes þeosternesse. **1377** LANGL. *P. Pl.* B. XVIII. 179 Ioye bygynneth dawe.

2. To recover from a swoon, 'come to'; to awake from sleep; = ADAW *v.*[1] 1.

c **1314** *Guy Warw.* (A.) 558 Adoun he fel a-swounie, & when he gan to dawei [etc.]. **1674–91** RAY *N.C. Words* 19 *To Daw*, in common speech is to awaken: *to be dawed*, to have shaken off sleep, to be fully awakened.

3. *trans.* To rouse or awaken from sleep or a swoon; to revive, 'bring to'; = ADAW *v.* 2.

1470–85 MALORY *Arthur* XI. x, The Quene..felle to the erthe in a dede swoune, and thenne syr Bors took her vp, and dawed her. **1530** PALSGR. 507/2, I dawe from swounyng, *Je reuiue, je resuscite*. **1562** A. BROKE *Romeus & Jul.* in Hazl. *Shaks. Libr.* (1875) I. 179 She thought to breake her slepe.. She thought to daw her now as she had done of olde. **1612** DRAYTON *Poly-olb.* vi. 90 Thinking her to daw Whom they supposed faln in some inchanted swound.

†**daw,** *v.*[2] *Obs. rare.* [f. DAW *sb.*] *intr.* ? To play the 'daw' or fool.

1596 SIR J. SMYTHE in *Lett. Lit. Men* (Camden) 92 That I would..ryde lobbinge and dawinge to rayle at your Lordship.

†**daw,** *v.*[3] *Obs. rare.* [Aphetic f. ADAW *v.*[2], q.v.] *trans.* To daunt, subdue, frighten.

1616 B. JONSON *Devil an Ass* IV. iv, You daw him too much, in troth, Sir. **1664** H. MORE *Myst. Iniq.* 545 External force imprints Truth and Falshood, Superstition and Religion alike upon the dawed spirits of men.

daw (dɔ:), *a.* [Of obscure origin; Ir., Gael. *dath* 'colour' has been suggested.] Of a pale primrose colour, as the eyes of certain game fowl.

1856 W. B. TEGETMEIER *Poultry Bk.* xiii. 100 Black-breasted reds..have a fine long head; daw eyes. *Ibid.*, The required 'daw eye'..is that which resembles the grey eye of a jackdaw. **1873** L. WRIGHT *Bk. Poultry* 277 There never was a Malay with red eyes; they are invariably pearl, yellow, or daw. **1913** W. BATESON *Mendel's Princ. Heredity* (ed. 3) 110 Malay fowls are peculiar in having a pale, yellowish white iris—the 'daw-eye' of fanciers.

dawache: see DAVACH.

dawcock: see DAW *sb.*

dawd, var. of DAD *sb.*[2]

dawdle ('dɔ:d(ə)l), *v.* Also **daudle.** [Not in Bailey; nor in Johnson's Dict. (though used by himself in 1781). It apparently became common about 1775 (at first chiefly in feminine use). Ussher's example (*a* 1656) was prob. local or dialectal. Supposed to be a local variant of DADDLE, but used in a more reprehensory sense, perh. by some association with DAW *sb.* sense 2 b.]

1. *intr.* To idle, waste time; to be sluggish or lazy; to loiter, linger, dally.

a **1656** USSHER *Ann.* vi. (1658) 382 While he stood dawdling was taken short in his undertakings. **1781** JOHNSON 3 June in *Boswell*, If he'll call on me, and dawdle over a dish of tea in an afternoon. **1796** JANE AUSTEN *Pride & Prej.* xx. 97 Mrs. Bennet, having dawdled about in the vestibule to watch for the end of the conference. **1819** SCOTT *Let. to D. Terry* 18 Apr. in *Lockhart*, A propensity which.. the women very expressively call *dawdling*. **1866** RUSKIN *Eth. Dust* v. (1883) 90 You all know when you learn with a will and when you dawdle. **1872** BLACK *Adv. Phaeton* xxii. 307 The rest of us dawdled along the road.

2. quasi-*trans.* (usually with *away*).

1768 MAD. D'ARBLAY *Early Diary* July, I could not..ask for it..and so dawdled and fretted the time away until Tuesday evening. **1873** BROWNING *Red. Cott. Nt.-Cap* 230 Dawdle out my days In exile here at Clairvaux. **1887** *Spectator* 21 May 696/2 To employ with profit many hours that might otherwise be dawdled away.

dawdle ('dɔ:d(ə)l), *sb.* Also 8 daudle. [f. prec.]

1. One who is the personification of dawdling; *esp.* a dawdling girl or woman.

a **1764** LLOYD *Chit-Chat* Poet. Wks. 1774 I. 185 Be quick —why sure the gipsy sleeps! Look how the drawling daudle creeps. **1800** MRS. HERVEY *Mourtray Fam.* III. 141 Mrs. Thornley was rather too much of, what she [Mrs. M.] called, a dawdle, to please her. **1843** F. E. PAGET *Pageant* 118 His wife..was..one of those helpless, indolent dawdles that are fit to be nothing but fine ladies. **1879** BARING-GOULD *Germany* I. 392 The sharp clever boy goes into business, the dunce or dawdle into the army.

2. The act of dawdling.

1813 LADY BURGHERSH *Lett.* (1893) 38 What with dawdles and delays of the German post-boys. **1876** GREEN *Stray Stud.* 70 The evenings are..a dawdle indoors as the day has been a dawdle out.

dawdler ('dɔ:dlə(r)). [-ER[1].] One who dawdles; an idler, loiterer.

1818 TODD, *Dawdle*, or *Dawdler*, a trifler; a dallier; one who proceeds slowly or unskilfully in any business. A low word. **1849** THACKERAY *Pendennis* (1850) I. 280, I have been a boy and a dawdler as yet. **1888** J. PAYN *Myst. Mirbridge* xv,

Your habitual dawdler—the man who never keeps his appointments by any chance.

dawdling ('dɔːdlɪŋ), *vbl. sb.* [-ING[1].] The action of the verb DAWDLE.

1819 [see DAWDLE *v.* 1]. **1849** THACKERAY *Lett.* 13 July, Ryde..would be as nice a place as any..for dawdling, and getting health. **1875** B'NESS BUNSEN in Hare *Life* II. viii. 457 With old age comes dawdling, that is, doing everything too slowly.

'dawdling, *ppl. a.* [-ING[2].] That dawdles; characterized by dawdling.

1773 MAD. D'ARBLAY *Early Diary* 3 May, The mother is a slow, dawdling, sleepy kind of dame. **1782** —— *Diary* 8 Dec., With whom I had a dawdling conversation upon dawdling subjects. **1843** MRS. CARLYLE *Lett.* I. 265 The dreaming, reading, dawdling existence which best suits me.

Hence **'dawdlingly** *adv.*

1860 *Sat. Rev.* IX. 145/1 Some very important Bill which ..has been dawdlingly postponed from day to day.

dawdy, Sc. dial f. DOWDY.

dawe (daue, daw), dawen, dawes, obs. forms or inflexions of DAY. *Dawes* was the early form of the pl. = *days*; *dawen* was originally dative pl., but when reduced to *dawe, daw, daue, dau,* came sometimes to be treated as sing.: see DAY 13 aβ, and 17.

dawen, obs. f. DOWN *sb.*

dawenyng(e, obs. form of DAWNING.

dawerke, obs. form of DAYWORK.

dawg (dɔːg). Colloq. var. DOG *sb.*

1898 J. D. BRAYSHAW *Slum Silhouettes* 125 Ev'ry markit mornin' yer ter be my dawg, ev'ry mornin' till yer like ter chuck it. **1939** O. LANCASTER *Homes Sweet Homes* 60 Beaten copper reminders that a man's best friend is his dawg (beloved of the golf-playing classes). **1966** 'J. HACKSTON' *Father clears Out* 14 The dawg's 'ad 'is ribs stove in.

dawing ('dɔːɪŋ), *vbl. sb. Obs.* exc. *Sc.* Forms: 1 **daȝung,** 3 **dawung,** 4 **daghyng(e,** 3–6 **dawyng,** 4– **dawing,** (5 **dayng,** 7 **dauing,** 8 **dawin**). [OE. *daȝung*, from *daȝian* to become day, to DAW. After 1400, northern and chiefly Scotch, being displaced in Eng. by DAWNING.]

1. Dawn, daybreak; morning twilight.

c **900** tr. *Bæda's Eccl. Hist.* III xix. (xxvii.) 242 þa eode [he] ut in daȝunge of þam huse. *a* **1000** *O.E. Chron.* (Laud MS.) an. 795 Betwux hancred and daȝunge. *a* **1225** *Ancr. R.* 20 Bi nihte ine winter, ine sumer iþe dawunge. **1375** BARBOUR *Bruce* VII. 318 [Thai] Com on thame in the dawyng, Richt as the day begouth to spryng. *c* **1420** *Avow. Arth.* lv, Erly in the dawyng Come thay home from hunting. **1513** DOUGLAS *Æneis* III. viii. 29 The dawing gan..wax reid, And chasit away the sterris. *a* **1605** MONTGOMERIE *Misc. Poems, Solsequium* 40 The dauing of my long desyrit day. *c* **1794** BURNS *As I was a wandering* iii, I could na get sleeping till dawin' for greetin'.

†2. Recovery from swoon, 'coming-to'. *Obs.* (See DAW *v.* 2, 3.)

1530 PALSGR. 212 Dawyng, gettyng of lyfe, *resuscitation.*

†'dawing, *ppl. a. Obs.* exc. *Sc.* Also 4 *north.* **dawande.** [f. DAW *v.*[1] + -ING[2].] Dawning.

c **1325** *E.E. Allit. P.* C. 445 Þe dawande day.

†dawish ('dɔːɪʃ), *a. Obs.* [f. DAW *sb.* + -ISH.] Like or characteristic of a daw; silly, sluttish.

1540 HYRDE tr. *Vives' Instr. Chr. Wom.* (1592) M iij, Dawish, and brainlesse, cruell, and murderers. **1543** BALE *Yet a Course, &c.* 59 (T.) Such dawishe dodypols. **1605** CHAPMAN *All Fools* in *Dodsley* (1780) IV. 167 If he [a jackdaw] fed without his dawish noise He might fare better.

dawk (dɔːk), *sb. dial.* [app. the same as DALK[2].] A hollow in a surface; a depression, furrow, incision.

1703 MOXON *Mech. Exerc.* 66 This Iron..would not make Gutters on the Surface of the Stuff, but (at the most) little hollow dawks. *Ibid.* 82 The Iron of the Fore-plane..makes great Dawks in the Stuff..The Iron..will yet leave some Dawks in the Stuff for the Jointer..to work out.

Hence **dawk** *v.*, to make a hollow or incision in.

1703 MOXON *Mech. Exerc.* 203 The Chissel..might run too fast into the Work, and dawk it. **1847–78** HALLIWELL, *Dauk*, to incise with a jerk, or insert a pointed weapon with rapidity.

dawk, var. of DĀK, DAUK.

'dawkin. *dial.* [? dim. of DAW] **a.** A fool. **b.** A slattern. Hence **'dawkinly** *adv.*, foolishly.

1565 CALFHILL *Answ. Treat. Crosse* (1846) 236 (D.) Then Martiall and Maukin, a dolt with a daukin, might marry together. **1674** RAY *N.C. Words* 13 *Dawgos* or *Dawkin*, a dirty, slattering woman. *c* **1746** COLLIER (Tim Bobbin) *View Lanc. Dial.* Wks. (1862) 52 After looking dawkinly-wise a bit. **1875** *Lanc. Gloss., Dawkin*, a dull, stupid person. *Dawkinly*, stupidly, foolishly.

dawly, obs. form of DOWLY *a.* and *adv.*

dawn (dɔːn), *sb.* [Appears late in 16th c., the earlier equivalents being DAWING, DAWNING. App. f. the verb-stem (see next); cf. *break* in 'break of day' (quoted 1584). ON. had *dagan, dögun* dawn, f. *daga* to dawn, *i dagan, at dagan* at dawn: but, notwithstanding the likeness of form, there is no evidence that this is the original of the Eng. word.]

1. a. The first appearance of light in the sky before sunrise, or the time when it appears; the beginning of daylight; daybreak.

high dawn, dawn appearing above a bank of clouds on the horizon; ***low dawn***, dawn appearing on or close to the horizon.

1599 SHAKS. *Hen. V*, IV. i. 291 Next day after dawne. **1603** —— *Meas. for M.* IV. ii. 226 Come away, it is almost cleere dawne. **1697** DAMPIER *Voy.* I. 498 With such dark black Clouds near the Horizon, that the first glimpse of the Dawn appeared 30 or 40 degrees high..it is a common saying among Sea-men..that a high dawn will have high winds, and a low dawn, small winds. **1778** BP. LOWTH *Transl. Isaiah* xxvi. 19 Thy dew is as the dew of the dawn. **1832** TENNYSON *Death Old Year* ii, He will not see the dawn of day. **1852** MISS YONGE *Cameos* II. viii. 101 The assault had begun at early dawn.

b. An opalescent colour resembling that seen in the sky at dawn.

1894 *Daily News* 11 Apr. 3/1 Palest pink and blue shot silk, called by the poetic name of 'Dawn', because it suggests the union of those colours in the early morning sky. **1927** *Daily Express* 21 Mar. 2 Colours include cedar, green, silver, new blue, dawn or bois de rose.

c. Phr. ***came the dawn***: a cliché used to announce the break of day; hence *fig.*, used to indicate relief after a time of trouble, the dawning of understanding, etc.

1927 WODEHOUSE *Meet Mr Mulliner* v. 169 A benevolent glow irradiated the other's spectacles. 'Came the Dawn!' he murmured. 'Came the Dawn.' **1929** J. B. PRIESTLEY *Good Companions* III. v. 582 For her sake alone he..renounced wealth and fame. Love was his guiding star. Came the dawn. Yeogh!.. What do you think you are—a little hero from Hollywood? **1948** C. DAY LEWIS *Otterbury Incident* iii. 29 As for Nick, you never saw such a 'Came-the-dawn' expression as he had on his face. **1967** 'A. GARVE' *Very Quiet Place* I. iv. 60 It was fun staying up half the night..but, came the dawn, I was the one who had to..earn the rent. **1967** *Guardian* 18 Oct. 1 'Came the dawn.' In the days of silent films this caption introduced the sequence where the young lovers were united after a night of tropical storm.

2. *fig.* The beginning, commencement, rise, first gleam or appearance (of something compared to light); an incipient gleam (of anything).

1633 P. FLETCHER *Purple Isl.* XII. xlvi, So spring some dawns of joy, so sets the night of sorrow. **1752** JOHNSON *Rambler* No. 196 ¶2 From the dawn of manhood to its decline. **1767** *Babler* II. 100 If he possesses but a dawn of spirit. **1823** LAMB *Elia* Ser. 1 *Old Actors*, You could see the first dawn of an idea stealing slowly over his countenance. **1878** STEWART & TAIT *Unseen Univ.* ii. §50. 69 From the earliest dawn of history to the present day.

3. *attrib.* and *Comb.*, as ***dawn animal, -animalcule*** (see quots.), ***dawn-chill, -cloud, -dew, -flush, -goddess, -light, -mist, -streak, -wind***; ***dawn-illumined, -lit, -tinted*** adjs.; ***dawnward*** adv.; **dawn chorus,** the early-morning bird song; **dawn man,** an extinct primitive man; *spec.* (freq. with capital initials) the (fraudulently postulated) prehistoric type of man, *Eoanthropus dawsoni*: see PILTDOWN; so ***dawn woman***; **dawn raid:** see RAID *sb.* 2 e.

1873 DAWSON *Earth & Man* ii. 23 *Eozoon Canadense*..its name of '*Dawn-animal' having reference to its great antiquity and possible connection with the dawn of life on our planet. **1876** PAGE *Adv. Text-bk. Geol.* x. 189 The organism, *Eozoön Canadense*, or *Dawn-animalcule of Canada. **1899** A. WERNER *Captain of Locusts* 152 Holcroft shivered involuntarily in the *dawn-chill. **1927** E. GREY *Charm of Birds* i. 8 [The robin's song is worth attention.. and, though he may not open the Great Chorus at Dawn in May, he is the last to cease in the evening.] *Ibid.* iv. 70 In May..the great *Dawn Chorus is at its fullest and best. **1966** *Guardian* 23 Mar. 3/2 The dawn chorus project which we carried out last spring produced the interesting result that skylarks apparently don't like singing in the rain. **1969** G. BLACK *Cold Jungle* xi. 160 The birds ought to be busy on their dawn chorus out in the Hebrides, with a new day practically settled in. **1901** KIPLING *Kim* xv. 383 Thence he vanished like a *dawn-cloud on Jakko. **1856** MRS. BROWNING *Aur. Leigh* I. Poems VI. 24 A dash of *dawn-dew from the honeysuckle. **1906** *Daily Chron.* 30 June 4/6 A painter..saw a sunrise and put the *dawn-flush into a picture. **1877** J. E. CARPENTER tr. *Tiele's Hist. Relig.* 107 The Sun-god..and the *dawn-goddess. **1820** SHELLEY *Ode to Liberty* xi, As on a *dawn-illumined mountain. **1850** MRS. BROWNING *Poems* II. 326, I oft had seen the *dawnlight run As red wine, through the hills. **1906** *Westm. Gaz.* 29 Oct. 2/3 Rare and transparent as the *dawn-lit dew. **1912** R. BROOKE *Grantchester* in *Poetry Rev.* Nov. 507 Still in the dawnlit waters cool His ghostly Lordship swims his pool. **1913** *Nature* 2 Oct. 131/2 It is quite certain that they afford the first evidence we have obtained of a hitherto unknown group of the Hominidae so fundamentally distinct from all the early fossil men found in Europe as to be worthy of generic distinction—a '*dawn-man' of a very primitive and generalised type. **1914** W. K. GREGORY in *Amer. Museum Jrnl.* XIV. 189 The Dawn Man of Piltdown. *Ibid.* 191/1 All agree that the Dawn Man dates at the very latest from the Old Stone Age. **1927** H. F. OSBORN in E. Eyre *Europ. Civilization* (1934) I. 1. v. 80 We are descended from 'dawn-men' not from 'ape-men'. **1944** H. G. WELLS *'42 to '44* 190 The breeding season of the Dawn-Men may have been an annual affair. **1904** R. J. FARRER *Garden of Asia* xvi. 151 Across the broad landscape the *dawn-mist lies in heavy, floating wreaths. **1873** LOWELL *Among my Bks.* Ser. II. 221 The *dawn-streaks of a new day. **1822** SHELLEY *Hellas* 963 *Dawn-tinted deluges of fire. **1881** W. WILKINS *Songs of Study* 44 In joyful praises *dawnward rolled. **1887** KIPLING *Departmental Ditties* (1888) 35 The *dawn-wind, softly, slowly, Brought to burning eyelids sleep. **1916** BLUNDEN *Pastorals* 35 And through green sprigs a little dawn-wind plains. **1944** H. G. WELLS *'42 to '44* 190 The hardy steppe-bred *Dawn-Woman of the early Solutrean.

dawn (dɔːn), *v.* Also 6 **daune, dawne.** [Known only from end of 15th c., since which it has displaced the earlier verb DAW. App. deduced from DAWNING, q.v. Cf. also DAYN *v.*]

I. 1. *intr.* To begin to grow daylight: said of the day, morning, light; also simply with *it*.

1499 PYNSON *Promp. Parv.*, Dawnyn or dayen [*c* **1440** dawyn], *auroro.* **1526** TINDALE *Matt.* xxviii. 1 The Sabboth daye at even which dauneth the morowe after the Sabboth [WYCLIF bigynneth to schyne, *Geneva* & **1611** began to dawne]. —— *2 Pet.* i. 19 Vntill the daye dawne. *c* **1532** DEWES *Introd. Fr.* in Palsgr. 938 To dawne, *ajourner.* **1611** BIBLE *Matt.* xxviii. 1 In the ende of the Sabbath, as it began to dawne towards the first day of the weeke. **1711** STEELE *Spect.* No. 142 ¶5 Before the Light this Morning dawned upon the Earth. **1726** *Adv. Capt. R. Boyle* 23 As soon as ever the Morning dawn'd. **1860** TYNDALL *Glac.* I. xxi. 150 Day at length dawned and gradually brightened.

b. *transf.* To begin to shine, as the sun or any luminary.

1702 ROWE *Tamerl.* v. i. 2017 Women, like Summer Storms are Cloudy..But strait the Sun of Beauty dawns abroad. **1811** HEBER *Hymn*, Brightest and best of the sons of the morning, Dawn on our darkness. **1832** TENNYSON *Margaret* v, Look down, and let your blue eyes dawn Upon me thro' the jasmine-leaves.

2. *fig.* To begin to develop, expand, or brighten, like the daylight at dawn.

1717 POPE *Epist. to Jervas* 4 Where Life awakes, and dawns at ev'ry line. **1848** MACAULAY *Hist. Eng.* I. 412 In the year 1685 his fame..was only dawning. **1852** MISS YONGE *Cameos* I. xxviii. 234 When prosperity dawned on the elder brother.

3. To begin to brighten, with or as with the light of dawn.

1647 CRASHAW *Poems* 165 When the dark world dawn'd into Christian day. **1651** *Fuller's Abel Rediv., Zanchius* 390 Zanchius..became such a light..that many parts in Christendome dawned with the luster of his writings. **1832** TENNYSON *Œnone* 46, I waited underneath the dawning hills.

b. *transf.* To begin to appear, become visible.

1744 AKENSIDE *Pleas. Imag.* I. 146, I see them dawn! I see the radiant visions, where they rise. **1812** J. WILSON *Isle of Palms* III. 307 Its porch and roof of roses dawn Through arching trees.

4. *fig.* Of ideas, facts, etc.: To begin to become evident to the mind; to begin to be understood, felt, or perceived. Const. *on, upon.*

1852 MRS. STOWE *Uncle Tom's C.* xv. 129 The idea that they had either feelings or rights had never dawned upon her. **1866** G. MACDONALD *Ann. Q. Neighb.* ix. 137 It dawned on my recollection that I had heard Judy mention her Uncle. **1875** JOWETT *Plato* (ed. 2) V. 66 The distinction between ethics and politics has not yet dawned upon Plato's mind.

II. †5. *transf.* To bring to life; to arouse or awake from a swoon, resuscitate; = DAW *v.* 3.

1530 PALSGR. 507/2, I dawne or get life in one that is fallen in a swoune, *je reuigore*..I can nat dawne him. **1551** T. WILSON *Logike* (1580) 33 If Alexander dawned a weake Soldiour when he was almoste frosen for cold. **1593** MUNDAY *Def. Contraries* 71 After he had dawned him to remembrance by the helpe of vinager and colde water.

dawne, obs. form of DOWN *sb.*

dawned (dɔːnd, *poet.* 'dɔːnɪd), *ppl. a. rare.* [f. DAWN *v.* + -ED[1].] That has begun to brighten.

1818 KEATS *Endym.* I. 94 The dawned light.

dawner, var. of DANDER *v. Sc.*

dawnger(e, etc., obs. forms of DANGER, etc.

dawning ('dɔːnɪŋ), *vbl. sb.* Also 4 **dawynyng,** 4–5 **dawenyng(e,** 4–6 **dawnyng(e,** 5–6 **daunyng(e.** [Known before 1300, when it appears beside the earlier DAWING (from DAW *v.*, OE. *daȝung, daȝ-ian*), which it gradually superseded. The corresponding verb *to dawn*, which has similarly displaced *daw*, is not exemplified till the 15th c., and appears to have been deduced from *dawning*; the sb. *dawn* appeared still later, app. from the vb. As ME. *daw-en* had also an early doublet form *daiȝ-en, day-yn* (see DAY *v.*[1]), so beside *dawen-yng* is found *daiȝen-ing, daien-ing, dain-ing* (see DAYN *v.*). No form corresponding to *dawening, dawning* is recorded in OE., and it was probably from Norse; Sw. and Da. have a form *dagning* (OSw. *daghning c* 1300), either from *daga* to dawn, with suffix *-n-ing*, as in *kvað-n-ing, sað-n-ing, tal-n-ing*, etc. (Vigf. *Introd.* xxxi), or from a deriv. vb. **dagna.*]

1. The beginning of daylight; dawn, daybreak. In reference to time, now *poetic* or *rhetorical.*

1297 R. GLOUC. (1724) 557 To Keningwurþe hii come in þe dawninge. *c* **1385** CHAUCER *L.G.W.* 1188 *Dido*, The dawenyng vp rist out of the se. **1387** TREVISA *Higden* (Rolls) VI. 439 Chasede his enemyes al þat dawenynge [*v.r.* dawyng]. **1470–85** MALORY *Arthur* x. lxxxvi, Vppon a day in the daunynge. **1480** CAXTON *Chron. Eng.* ccvii. 189 Erly in the dawenynge of the day. **1586** COGAN *Haven Health* ccxliii. (1636) 311 Drinke it in the morning at the dawning of the day. **1602** SHAKS. *Ham.* I. i. 160 The Bird of Dawning. **1712** W. ROGERS *Voy.* 104 So we ran North till Dawning. **1810** SCOTT *Lady of L.* I. xxxii, At dawning to assail ye, Here no bugles sound reveillé. **1858** KINGSLEY *Poems, Night Bird* 13 Oh sing, and wake the dawning.

b. *transf.* The east, the 'orient'.

1879 BUTCHER & LANG *Odyssey* 215 Those who dwell toward the dawning.

2. *fig.* The first gleam or appearance, earliest beginning (of something compared to light).

a **1612** DONNE *Βιαθανατος* (1644) 17 A man as..illustrious, in the full glory and Noone of Learning, as others were in the dawning, and Morning. **1697** DRYDEN *Virg. Georg.* I. 68 In this early Dawning of the Year. **1781** GIBBON *Decl. & F.* III. liii. 314 In the ninth century, we trace the first dawnings of the restoration of science. **1843** PRESCOTT *Mexico* (1850) I. 75 The dawnings of a literary culture. **1856** SIR B. BRODIE *Psychol. Inq.* I. v. 198 That principle of intelligence, the dawning of which we observe in the lower animals.

'dawning, *ppl. a.* [f. DAWN *v.* + -ING[2].] That dawns; beginning to grow light. **a.** *lit.*

1588 SHAKS. *Tit. A.* II. ii. 10 Dawning day new comfort hath inspir'd. **1667** MILTON *P.L.* XII. 423 Fresh as the dawning light. **1791** COWPER *Iliad* XI. 60 The dawning skies. **1843** TENNYSON *Two Voices* 405 The light increased With freshness in the dawning east.

b. *fig.* Showing its early beginning, nascent.

1697 DRYDEN *Virg. Æneid* (L.), In dawning youth. **1751** JOHNSON *Rambler* No. 165 ¶5 Those who had paid honours to my dawning merit. **1879** FARRAR *St. Paul* (1883) 765 The distinctive colour of the dawning heresy.

dawnt(e, obs. form of DAUNT.

dawsonite ('dɔːsənaɪt). *Min.* [Named 1874, after Sir J. W. Dawson of Montreal: see -ITE.] A hydrous carbonate of aluminium and sodium, in white transparent or translucent crystals.

1875 *Amer. Jrnl. Sc.* Ser. III. IX. 64 On Dawsonite, a new mineral.

dawt, dawtie (-y): see DAUT, DAUTIE.

daxie: see DACHSIE.

day (deɪ), *sb.* Forms: 1 dæʒ, 2 deʒ, deiʒ, daiʒ, 2–3 dæi, dei, daʒ, 3 (*Orm.*) daȝȝ, 3–5 dai, 3– day, (5–6 daie, daye, 6 *Sc.* da). *Pl.* 3– days (3–5 dawes; *dat.pl.* 2–6 dawen, dawe; daw, dau; see below). [A Com. Teut. sb.: OE. *dæȝ* (*dæȝes*, pl. *daȝas*, *-a*, *-um*) = OFris. *dei, dey, di*, OS *dag* (MDu. *dach* (*gh*), Du. *dag*, MLG., LG. *dag*), OHG., MHG. *tac*(*g*), G. *tag*, ON. *dag-r* (Sw., Da. *dag*), Goth. *dag-s*:—OTeut. **dago-z*. In no way related to L. *dies*; usually referred to an Aryan vb. *dhagh-*, in Skr. *dah* to burn: cf. Lith. *dagas* hot season, OPruss. *dagis* summer. From the WGer. *dag*, OE. had regularly in the sing. *dæȝ*, *dæȝes*, *dæȝe*; in the plural *daȝas*, *daȝa* (later *-ena*), *daȝum*. This phonetic exchange *æ*:*a* survived in early ME., so that while in the sing. the final ʒ was regularly palatal (see forms above; gen. *dæiʒes*, *dæies*, *deies*, *daies*, *dayes*, dat. *dæiʒe*, *daie*, etc.), the pl. was (from *daȝas*), *daʒes*, *dahes*, *daʒhes*, *dawes*, genit. (:—*daȝa*, *-ena*) *daȝa*, *dawene*, *dahene*, *daʒen*, dat. (:—*daȝum*) *daʒon*, *-en*, *daghen*, *dawen*, *dawe*, *daw*, *dau*. The last survived longest in the phrase *of dawe* 'from (life) days' (see 17 and ADAWE), and in *in his dawe*, etc. (see 13 a β). But soon after 1200 plurals phonetically assimilated to the sing. (*dæʒes*, *daiʒes*, *daies*) occur, and at length superseded the earlier forms.]

A. Illustration of early forms.

α. *plural, nom.* and *accus.*

c **1000** *Ags. Gosp.* Matt. xxviii. 20 Ic beo mid eow ealle daȝas. *c* **1160** *Hatton G.* ibid., Ich beo mid eow ealle daʒes. *c* **1200** ORMIN 4356 Seffne daȝhess. *c* **1205** LAY. 8796 Fif dæiʒes [*c* **1275** dawes]. *a* **1225** *Leg. Kath.* 1844 Al þe tweolf dahes. *a* **1225** *Ancr. R.* 70 þreo dawes. **1297** R. GLOUC. (1724) 383 þre dawes & nan mo. **1399** *Pol. Poems* (Rolls) I. 377 As it is said by elderne dawis. *c* **1430** LYDG. *Bochas* VI. i. (1554) 144 a, In thy last dawes.

β. *pl. gen.*

c **1000** *Ags. Ps.* ci. 21 On midle minre daȝena. *c* **1000** *Ags. Gosp.* Matt. iv. 2 He fæste feowurtiȝ daȝa [*Lindisf.* feuortiȝ daȝa, *Hatton G.* feortiʒ dæʒes]. *c* **1175** *Lamb Hom.* 87 Fram þam ester tid fifti daʒa. *c* **1205** LAY. 3615 þe forð wuren agan feuwerti daʒene [*c* **1275** daiʒes]. *Ibid.* 4605 Vnder fif dawene [*c* **1275** daiʒene] ʒeong heo comen to þisse londe. *a* **1225** *Leg. Kath.* 2502 Twenti dahene ʒong.

γ. *pl. dat.*: see also 13 a β.

c **1000** *Ags. Gosp.* Matt. xxvi. 61 Æfter þrym daȝum [xxvii. 63 daȝon]. *c* **1160** *Hatton G.* ibid., Æfter þrem daʒen. *c* **1175** *Lamb. Hom.* 89 On moyses daʒen. *c* **1205** LAY. 5961 Bi heore ældre dæwen [*c* **1275** dawes]. *c* **1300** *K. Alis.* 5631 In twenty dawen. *c* **1300** *St. Margarete* 3 Bi olde dawe Patriarch he was wel heʒ. *c* **1320** *Sir Tristr.* 2480 Etenes bi old dayn Had wrouʒt it. *c* **1430** *Freemasonry* 394 After the lawe That was y-fownded by olde dawe.

δ. In some places *daʒen, dawen*, may be nom. or acc. plural.

c **1175** *Lamb. Hom.* 119 Ic seolf beo mid eow alle daʒen [OE. ealle daȝas].

ε. The genitive sing. OE. *dæȝes*, early ME. *daies*, etc., was formerly used adverbially, by day, on the day (Ger. *des Tags*): see 1 b; it survived in ME. *bi daies, a daies*, A-DAYS, mod. *now-a-days*.

B. Signification.

I. The time of sunlight.

1. a. 'The time between the rising and setting of the sun' (J.); the interval of light between successive periods of darkness or *night*; in ordinary usage including the lighter part of morning and evening twilight, but, when strictly used, limited to the time when the sun is above the horizon, as in 'at the equinox day and night are equal'. ***break of day***: dawn: see BREAK, DAYBREAK.

This is the ***artificial day*** of astronomers: see ARTIFICIAL. It is sometimes called the ***natural day*** (Ger. *natürlicher tag*), which however usually means sense 6.

c **1000** ÆLFRIC *Gen.* i. 5 God..het þæt leoht dæȝ & þa þeostra niht. *c* **1200** *Trin. Coll. Hom.* 258 þu ʒifst þe sunne to þe daiʒ, þe mone to þe nichte. *c* **1290** *S. Eng. Leg.* I. 97/173 In þat prison þat Maide lai twelf dawes and twelf niʒt. *c* **1340** *Cursor M.* 390 (Trin.) To parte þe day fro þe nyʒt. *c* **1400** *Lanfranc's Cirurg.* 41 Ofte tymes in þe dai & in þe nyʒt. **1523** LD. BERNERS *Froiss.* I. cxxviii. 155 It was then nyne of the day. **1580** BARET *Alv.* B 1200 The Breake of the daie. **1592** DAVIES *Immort. Soul* vi. (1742) 15 O Light, which mak'st the Light which makes the Day. **1635** N. CARPENTER *Geog. Del.* I. v. 106 The longest day is equall to the longest night. **1770** GOLDSM. *Des. Vill.* 15 How often have I bless'd the coming day. **1807** ROBINSON *Archæol. Græca* III. xxv. 331 The more ancient Greeks distinguished the natural day—that is, the time from the rising to the setting of the sun—into three parts. **1840** *Penny Cycl.* XVI. 326/1 At North Cape..the longest day lasts from the 15th of May to the 29th of July, which is two months and a fortnight.

b. *Const.* The notion of time *how long* is expressed by the uninflected word (repr. an original accus. or dative), as in ***day and night***, ***all (the) day, this day***, and the like; the notion of time *when* (without respect to duration) was expressed in OE. by *on dæȝ*, early ME. *on, uppon dai, o day, a-day*; also by the genitive *dæȝes*, esp. in the collocation *dæȝes and nihtes*, and in *far days, far forth days*, = 'far on in the day', still used in 17th c. (see FAR *adv.* 3 c); about 1200 we find *bi daʒes*, and soon after *bi daie* by day. See BY *prep.* 19 b.

c **1000** *Ags. Gosp.* Mark v. 5 Symle dæȝes & nihtes he wæs on byrȝenum. *c* **1200** *Trin. Coll. Hom.* 87 Swiche hertes fondeð þe fule gost deies and nihtes. *c* **1200** ORMIN 11332 Heold Crist hiss fasste..Bi daȝhess & bi nahhtess. *a* **1250** *Owl & Night.* 241 Bi daie þu art stare-blind. *c* **1250** *Hymn to Virgin* 257 Min hope is in þe daʒ & nicht. *a* **1300** *Cursor M.* 15159 (Cott.) Ilk night of oliuete To þe mont he yode..And euer on dai þe folk he gaf O godds word þe fode. **1386** *Rolls of Parlt.* III. 225/1 [He] made dyverse enarmynges bi day and eke bi nyght. *c* **1400** *Lanfranc's Cirurg.* 34, I heeld þe wounde open aldai. *a* **1450** *Knt. de la Tour* (1868) 45 She happed to abide so longe on a sonday that it was fer dayes. **1513** MORE in Grafton *Chron.* II. 778 The pageauntes were a making day and night at Westminster. *a* **1563** BALE *Sel. Wks.* (Parker Soc.) 120 It is far days and ye have far to ride to night. **1600** HOLLAND *Livy* XLV. xxxvi. 1225 It was so far forth dayes as being the eighth houre therof. **1697** DRYDEN *Virg. Georg.* III. 318 Untir'd at Night, and chearful all the Day. **1835** THIRLWALL *Greece* I. 219 He might prosecute his voyage as well as by day. **1848** MACAULAY *Hist. Eng.* (1880) I. iii. 184 The bags were carried..day and night at the rate of about five miles an hour.

2. In ***before day, at day*** = daybreak, dawn.

a **1300** *Cursor M.* 6106 (Gött.) þat þai Sould vte of hous cum bi-for day. *c* **1420** *Avow. Arth.* ix, To ride this forest or daye. **1576** FLEMING *Panopl. Epist.* 39 A little before day. **1719** DE FOE *Crusoe* (1840) II. ii. 48 They got up in the morning before day. **1793** NELSON in Nicolas *Disp.* I. 309 This morning at day we fell in with a Spanish..Ship.

3. a. Daylight, the light of day.

c **1340** *Cursor M.* 8676 (Fairf.), I hit knew quen hit was day. **1382** WYCLIF *Rom.* xiii. 13 As in day wandre we honestly. *c* **1489** CAXTON *Sonnes of Aymon* ix. 223 Whan Reynawde sawe the day, he rose vp. **1580** NORTH *Plutarch* (1676) 355 Such as could see day at a little hole. **1662** J. DAVIES tr. *Olearius' Voy. Ambass.* 276 In his Conversion of the darkest Night to bright Day. **1710** STEELE *Tatler* No. 142 ¶1 She had now found out, that it was Day before Nine in the Morning. **1719** DE FOE *Crusoe* (1840) II. x. 218 It was broad day. **1883** STEVENSON *Treasure Isl.* III. xiii. (1886) 107 It was as plain as day.

b. *fig.* A light like that of day; 'daylight' in a difficult question.

1667 MARVELL *Corr.* lxxx. Wks. 1872–5 II. 225, I can not yet see day in the businesse, betwixt the two Houses. **1702** ROWE *Tamerl.* v. i. 2191 They cast a Day around 'em.

†4. One of the perpendicular divisions or 'lights' of a mullioned window. [F. *jour*, med.L. *dies.*]

[**1409** *Will of Ware* (Somerset Ho.), Lego vna fenestra trium dierum.] **1447** *Will Hen. VI* (Hare's MSS. Caius Coll.), In the east ende of the s[d] Quier shalbe sat a great gable window of vij daies. **1484** *Will of Chocke* (Somerset Ho.), A wyndow..of iij dayes. *a* **1490** BOTONER *Itin.* (Nasmith 1778) 296 Et quælibet fenestra..continet tres dayes vitreatas. **1838** J. BRITTON *Dict. Archit.* 40 A part of a window between the mullions is often called a bay, or day. **1859** *Archit. Publ. Soc. Dict., Day*, the mediæval term for each perpendicular division or light (Fr. *jour*) of a mullioned window.

5. *Mining.* The surface of the ground over a mine. Hence ***day-coal, -drift, -hole*** (see also 24).

1665 *Phil. Trans.* I. 80 By letting down Shafts from the *day* (as Miners speak). **1676** HODGSON *ibid.* XI. 762 According as the Day-coal heightens or deepens. **1708** J. C. *Compl. Collier* (1845) 32 Draw your Coals to Bank (or Day) out of the Pit. **1747** HOOSON *Miner's Dict.* N iij b, The Ore that is found on the Tops of Veins, especially near to the Day. **1881** RAYMOND *Mining Gloss., Day*, the surface of the ground over a mine.

II. As a period, natural division, or unit of time.

6. a. The time occupied by the earth in one revolution on its axis, in which the same terrestrial meridian returns to the sun; the space of twenty-four hours, reckoned from a definite or given point. Const. *during, in*, formerly *on, o, a*, retained in twice *a day*, etc.: see A *prep.*[1] 8, 8 b.

The ***solar day*** (and, formerly, the ***astronomical day***) is reckoned from noon to noon; and, as the length of this time varies (within narrow limits) according to the time of the year, its mean or average length is the ***mean solar day***. (The astronomical day is now reckoned from midnight to midnight.) The ***civil day*** in civilized countries generally is the period from midnight to midnight, similarly adjusted to its mean length. Ancient nations variously reckoned their day to begin at sunrise, at noon, or at sunset. The ***sidereal day*** is the time between the successive meridional transits of a star, or specifically of the first point of Aries, and is about four minutes shorter than the solar day. (The term ***natural day*** is sometimes used in this sense, sometimes in sense 1.)

c **950** *Lindisf. Gosp.* Matt. xv. 32 Ðrio dogor ȝe ðerhuunas mec mið. *c* **1000** ÆLFRIC *Gen.* i. 5 þa wæs ȝeworþen æfen and morȝen an dæȝ. *Ibid.* ii. 3 God ȝebletsode þone seofeðan dæȝ and hine ȝehalȝade. *c* **1175** *Lamb. Hom.* 87 Fram þan halie hester dei boð italde fifti daʒa to þisse deie. *c* **1205** LAY. 19216 þreo dæies [*c* **1275** daʒes] wes þe king wuniende þere. **1297** R. GLOUC. (1724) 144 Aftur fyftene dawes..To London he wende. **1382** WYCLIF *Acts* ix. 9 He was thre daies not seynge. **1561** T. NORTON *Calvin's Inst.* I. 10 b, Symonides..desired to haue a daies respite graunted him to study vpon it. *a* **1631** DONNE *Poems* (1650) 6 Hours, daies, months, which are the rags of time. **1822** BYRON *Werner* I. i. 377 Twenty years Of age, if 't is a day. **1831** BREWSTER *Newton* (1855) I. xiii. 365 We may regard the length of the day as one of the most unchangeable elements in the system of the world.

c **1386** CHAUCER *Sqr's. T.* 108 In the space of o day natureel, (This is to seyn, in foure and twenty houres). **1398** TREVISA *Barth. de P.R.* IX, xxi. (1495) 358 Some daye is artyfycyall and some naturell..a naturell daye conteynyth xxiiij houres. **1551** RECORDE *Cast. Knowl.* (1556) 244 The Naturall daye..is commonly accompted from Sonne risinge one daye, to Sonne rising the nexte daye. **1764** MASKELYNE in *Phil. Trans.* LIV. 344 The interval between the transit of the first of Aries across the meridian one day, and its return to it the next day, is called a sidereal day..The interval between the transit of the sun across the meridian one day, and his transit the next day, is called an apparent solar day. **1812** WOODHOUSE *Astron.* xxii. 222 The interval between two successive noons is a natural day. **1834** *Nat. Philos., Astron.* i. 13/2 (Useful Knowl. Soc.) Although..the solar day is of variable length, we can..ascertain its mean or average length; and this quantity is called a *mean solar day*. *Ibid.* 14/2 The length of the sidereal day is found to be uniformly 23 hours, 56 minutes, or more accurately $23^h\ 56^m\ 4^s\cdot092$.

†b. ***all days***: always, for ever. *Obs.*

c **1000** *Ags. Gosp.* Matt. xxviii. 20 Ic beo mid eow ealle daȝas [*Lindisf.* allum daȝum]. *c* **1160** *Hatton G.* ibid., Ich beo mid eow ealle daʒes. **1480** CAXTON *Chron. Eng.* cii, For that time forth losten Britons the royame for al dayes.

†c. A day's travel; a day's journey. *Obs.*

1362 LANGL. *P. Pl.* A. x. 1 Sire Dowel dwelleþ..not a day hennes. **1624** CAPT. SMITH *Virginia* I. 4 A Towne called Pomeiock, and six dayes higher, their City Skicoak.

d. ***of a day***: lit. lasting only a day, ephemeral; transitory, fleeting, fugitive.

1640 B. JONSON *Under-Woods* 234 A Lillie of a Day, Is fairer farre, in May, Although it fall, and die that night. **1746** WESLEY *Serm.* (1769) I. Pref. p. vi, I am a Creature of a Day, passing thro' Life, as an Arrow thro' the Air. **1818** KEATS *Let.* 3 May (1931) I. 153 My song should die away...Rich in the simple worship of a day. **1834** *Rival Sisters* 14 Man—the insect of a day. **1865** M. ARNOLD *Ess. Crit.* 1st Ser. Pref., Apparations of a day.

e. A day noteworthy for its eventfulness, exertion, etc. *colloq.*

1926 HEMINGWAY *Fiesta* (1927) vii. 65, I say. We have had a day... I must have been blind [*sc.* drunk]. **1963** 'W. HAGGARD' *High Wire* xii. 127, I expect you've had a day—I know I have. But there's one small thing still.

7. a. The same space of time, *esp.* the civil day, treated (without reference to its length) as a point or unit of time, on which anything happens, or which fixes a date. Const. *on, upon* (ME. *o, a-*: cf. A *prep.*[1] 8, A *adj.*[2] 4).

c **1000** *Ags. Gosp.* Matt. xx. 19 And þam þryddan dæȝe he arist. **1154** *O.E. Chron.* (Laud. MS.) an. 1135 Ð[at] oþer dei þa he lai an slep in scip. *a* **1400** *Cursor M.* 5108 (Cott.) Forgiue it vs, lauerd, fra þis dau. *Ibid.* 19045 (Cott.) Petre and iohn a dai at none Went to þe kirc. *Ibid.* 19810 (Edin.) Apon a dai at tide of none. *c* **1400** *Lanfranc's Cirurg.* 343 Sumtyme men..weren hool in þe same dai. **1523** LD. BERNERS *Froiss.* I. cxl. 167 Some day ye one part lost, and some day the other. **1533–4** *Act 25 Hen. VIII*, c. 21 §25 Before the saide .xii. daie of Marche. **1600–12** ROWLANDS *Four Knaves* (Percy Soc.) 75 They say, The better the day the better the deede. **1704** NELSON *Fest. & Fasts* i. (1739) 16 The first Day of the Week called the Lord's Day. **1726** tr. *Gregory's Astron.* I. 262 You need only to know what Day of each Month the Sun enters a Sign of the Ecliptic, and compute one Degree for every Day from thence. **1799** F. LEIGHTON *Let. to J. Boucher* 21 Sept. (MS.), Pray treat me with a letter on an early day as parliament folks say. **1865** TROLLOPE *Belton Est.* x. 109 She would return home on the day but one after the funeral.

b. Phrases. ***one day***: on a certain or particular day in the past; on some day in the future. So of future time, ***some day***; and of the present or proximate future, ***one*** or ***some of these days***. ***one of those days***: a day of misfortune.

1535 COVERDALE *1 Sam.* xxvii. 1 One of these dayes shal I fall into the handes of Saul. **1586** A. DAY *Eng. Secretary* II. (1625) 66 His meaning is one of these daies to entreate your paines hitherwards. **1594** SPENSER *Amoretti* lxxv, One day I wrote her name upon the strand. **1613** SHAKS. *Hen. VIII*, II.

ii. 22 The King will know him one day. **1659** B. HARRIS *Parival's Iron Age* 53 Had it not been, to revenge himself one day, upon the Spaniards. **1838** DICKENS *O. Twist* xxxvi, You will tell me a different tale one of these days. **1855** SMEDLEY *H. Coverdale* xxxv, Some of these days I shall be obliged to give him a lesson. **1936** P. FLEMING *News from Tartary* I. ix. 55 As we arrived at the inn, the building next to it.. collapsed... It was one of those days. **1967** 'S. WOODS' *Case is Altered* xiv. 166 Old Mr. Mallory was waiting to pounce on him, and it soon became obvious that it was going to be one of those days.

c. Used without a preposition or article. *U.S.*

1886 S. W. MITCHELL *R. Blake* 292, I saw a man at the Cape wharf day before yesterday, inquirin' about Mrs. Wynne. **1905** *N.Y. Even. Post* 20 May 4 Day before yesterday the President was again in a state of terrific determination. *Ibid.* 26 Sept. 6 Day after election people will want to know [etc.].

III. A specified or appointed day.

8. a. A specific period of twenty-four hours, the whole or part of which is assigned to some particular purpose, observance, or action, or which is the date or anniversary of some event, indicated by an attributive addition or by the context; e.g. ***saints' days, holy days, New Year's day, Lady-day, Christmas-day, St. Swithin's-day, þay-day, rent-day, settling-day, birth-day, wedding-day, coronation-day***, etc. (See the various defining words.)

c **1175** *Lamb. Hom.* 11 Nu beoð icumen..þa halie daȝes uppen us. **1297** R. GLOUC. (1724) 368 A Seyn Nycolas day he com. *c* **1450** *St. Cuthbert* (Surtees) 7007 Ilk ȝere..In þe day of bedis deying. **1577** HOLINSHED *Chron.* IV. 504 To put us in mind how we violate the Sabboth daie. **1595** SHAKS. *John* v. i. 25 Is this Ascension day? **1600** J. PORY tr. *Leo's Africa* A ij, At London this three and fortieth most joifull Coronation-day of her sacred Majestie. 1600. **1615** J. STEPHENS *Satyr. Ess.* (ed. 2) 222 Like a bookesellers shoppe on Bartholomew day. **1825** HONE *Every-day Bk.* I. 100 In each term there is one day whereon the courts do not transact business..These are termed *Grand* days in the inns of court; and *Gaudy* days at the two Universities. **1884** *Christian World* 9 Oct. 764/1 Lord Bramwell..had spoken of Saturday as 'pay-day, drink-day, and crime-day'.

b. ***Last day*** (OE. *ytemesta dæȝ*), ***Day of Judgement*** or ***of Doom, Doomsday, Judgement day, Day of the Lord, of Accounts, Retribution, Wrath, Great Day***, etc.: the day on which the dead shall be raised to be 'judged of the deeds done in the body'. See also the various qualifying words.

971 *Blickl. Hom.* 57 Seo saul..onfehþ hire lichoman on þæm ytmestan dæȝe. *a* **1300** *Cursor M.* 27362 (Cott.) Þe dai of wreth. **1382** WYCLIF *2 Pet.* iii. 10 Forsothe the day of the Lord shal come as a theef. *c* **1386** CHAUCER *Pars. T.* ¶ 305 He schal ȝelde of hem account at þe day of doome. *a* **1400** *Prymer* (1891) 82 Haue mercy of me whan þow comest in þe laste day. *a* **1533** LD. BERNERS *Huon* clviii. 606 Vnto the day of Iugemente. **1583** STUBBES *Anat. Abus.* II. (1882) 86 The generall resurrection at the last day. *Ibid.* II. 96 At yᵉ gret day of the Lord. **1690** LOCKE *Hum. Und.* II. xxvii. (1695) 187 In the great Day, wherein the Secrets of all Hearts shall be laid open. **1746–7** HERVEY *Medit.* (1818) 75 The severer doom, and more public infamy, of the great day. **1860** PUSEY *Min. Proph.* 109 The Day of Judgment or vengeance.

†**c.** Hence in early versions of N.T. = Judgement: a literal rendering of Gr. ἡμέρα in reference to the Judgement Day. *Obs.*

1382 WYCLIF *1 Cor.* iv. 3 To me it is for the leeste thing that I be demyd of ȝou, or of mannis day [TINDALE, *Rhem.* daye, CRANMER, *Geneva*, **1611**, **1881** judgement]. *a* **1628** PRESTON *New Covt.* 19 He would not regard to be judged by mans day, as long as he was not judged by the Lord.

d. That period of the day allotted by usage or law for work; as, *an eight-hour day*. (See EIGHT HOURS, WORKING-DAY.)

1813, **1853** [see WORKING-DAY]. **1850** *Working Man's Friend & Fam. Instr.* 14 Dec. 300/1 Being at the rate of 4s. 2d. per day of ten hours. **1870** *Chambers's Jrnl.* 10 Sept. 586/2 In government workshops,..by special act of Congress, eight hours has been constituted a legal day's work. **1880** C. MARVIN *Our Public Offices* (ed. 2) 121 [They] worked hard the whole of the seven hours of their official day. **1884** J. E. T. ROGERS *Six Cent. Work & Wages* xii. 327 It is plain that the day was one of eight hours. **1889** R. TANGYE *One & All* vii. 116 In 1871 a great agitation sprung [*sic*] up amongst the operative engineers at Newcastle-on-Tyne in favour of a nine hours' day. **1891**, etc. [see EIGHT HOURS].

9. a. A day appointed, a fixed date, *esp.* for payment.

c **1175** *Lamb. Hom.* 35 Ne beo he nefre swa riche forð he scal þenne is dei cumeð. *c* **1290** *S. Eng. Leg.* I. 250/334. **1387** TREVISA *Higden* III. 189 (Mätz.) Þe dettoures myȝte nouȝte pay here money al here day. *c* **1400** *Gamelyn* 792 He wold.. Come afore þe Iustice to kepen his day. *c* **1500** *Merch. & Son* in Halliwell *Nugæ Poet.* 21 In cas he faylyd hys day. **1535** STEWART *Cron. Scot.* I. 556 The king of Scottis..come thair to keip his da. **1596** SHAKS. *Merch. V.* I. iii. 165 If he should breake his daie, what should I gaine By the exaction of the forfeiture? **16..** DRYDEN (J.), Or if my debtors do not keep their day. *a* **1883** in J. G. Butler *Bible Work* II. 343 Christ, in the interval between the resurrection and ascension, keeps day with his disciples.

b. A day in each week (or other period) fixed for receptions, etc.; a day on which a hostess is 'at home'.

1694 CONGREVE *Double Dealer* III. ix, You have been at my lady Whifler's upon her day, madam? **1801** LEMAISTRE *Rough Sk. Mod. Paris* iv. 59 Each of the ministers has a day, to which all foreigners may be taken by their respective ministers. **1888** MRS. H. WARD *R. Elsmere* (1890) 307 We found she was in town, and went on her 'day'.

c. ***The Day*** [tr. G. *Der Tag*]: a day on which an important event is expected to occur; esp. a day of military conflict or victory.

1914 O. SEAMAN in *Punch* 9 Dec. 470/1 [German Crown Prince loq.] Thank Father's God that I can say My constant aim was Peace; I simply lived to see the Day (*Den Tag*) when wars would cease. **1914** G. B. SHAW *What I really Wrote* (1930) ii. 30 When the German fire-eaters drank to The Day (of Armageddon) they were drinking to the day of which our Navy League fire-eaters had first said 'It's bound to come'. **1919** *Ibid.* xii. 321 Just as the lieutenants of the German and British navies..looked forward to 'der Tag' when the preparations would be brought to the test of warfare, the lieutenants of the United States navy are already looking forward..to 'The Day' when the British and American fleets shall fight for that power to blockade [etc.]. **1936** J. BUCHAN *Island of Sheep* xiii. 256 The reconnaissance is complete, gentlemen. Tomorrow is The Day. **1959** J. BRAINE *Vodi* iv. 68 My Dad..says we'll all have to fight for our country when Der Tag comes. That's German for the Day.

10. = *day of battle* or *contest*; day's work on the field of battle: *esp.* in phrases ***to carry, get, win, lose the day***. Cf. FIELD, and CARRY 15 c, etc.

1557 TUSSER 100 *Points Husb.* xci, The battell is fought, thou hast gotten the daye. **1600** E. BLOUNT tr. *Conestaggio* 23 Without his aide the day would be perillous. **1642** ROGERS *Naaman* 492 Shew us how we may get the day of our adversary. **1659** B. HARRIS *Parival's Iron Age* 196 The Imperialists, thinking the Day was theirs. **1721** R. BRADLEY *Wks. Nature* 139 The Silk Worm at present carries the Day before all others of the Papilionaceous Tribe. **1848** MACAULAY *Hist. Eng.* II. 168 The bloody day of Seneff.

IV. A space of time, a period.

†**11.** A space (of time). Its extent is usually defined by the accompanying words. Now *Obs.* or *Sc.*

1451 *Paston Lett.* No. 171 I. 227 They have be fals both to the Clyffordys and to me thys vij yeere day. *c* **1470** HARDING *Chron.* Proem xxii, Who laye afore Paris a moneth daye. **1550** CROWLEY *Epigr.* 1462 You shall..lende but for a monethes day. **1552** T. GRESHAM in Strype *Eccl. Mem.* II. App. C. 148 No man convey out any parcel of lead five years day. **1568** E. TILNEY *Disc. Mariage* C j, I could recite many examples..if the time woulde suffer mee. You have yet day ynough, quoth the Lady Julia. *a* **1670** HOBBES *Dial. Com. Laws* 145 Which Statute alloweth to these Provisors Six weeks Day to appear. **1825–79** JAMIESON, *A month's day*, the space of a month; *A year's day*, the space of a year.

†**12.** Time allowed wherein to be ready, *esp.* for payment; delay, respite; credit. *Obs.*

c **1386** CHAUCER *Frankl. T.* 847 And him bysecheth..To graunte him dayes of the remenaunt. **1428** *E.E. Wills* (1882) 82 To have ther-of resonable daies of paiement. **1523** LD. BERNERS *Froiss.* I. ccxiii. 263 The truce..is nat expired, but hath day to endure vnto the first day of Maye next. *c* **1530** —— *Arth. Lyt. Bryt.* (1814) 477, I giue her daye for a moneth, & truse in the meane season. **1576** GASCOIGNE *Steele Gl.* (Arb.) 80 When drapers draw no gaines by giuing day. **1614** BP. HALL *Recoll. Treat.* 616 Ye Merchants.. make them pay deare for daies. **1644** QUARLES *Barnabas & B.* 18 I'll give no day..I must have present money. **1659** RUSHW. *Hist. Coll.* I. 640 That he might have day until the 25 of October, to consider of the return.

13. The time during which anything exists or takes place; period, time, era.

a. expressed more literally by the *pl.*: e.g. ***in the days of King Arthur, days of old, in those days, in days to come, men of other days***, etc. ***better days***: times when one was better off: so ***evil days***. See also SEE *v.* 10 a.

c **1200** *Trin. Coll. Hom.* 3 Oðre men þe waren bi þo daȝes. *a* **1300** *Cursor M.* 17546 (Cott.) In ald dais. *Ibid.* 21712 (Cott.) Nu in vr daies. **1362** LANGL. *P. Pl.* A. I. 96 Dauid, in his dayes he Dubbede knihtes. **1470–85** MALORY *Arthur* x. lxxxvi, Yet had I neuer reward..of her the dayes of my lyf. **1513** DOUGLAS *Æneis* XIII. ix. 69 Twichyng the stait, quhilum be days gone, Of Latium. **1548** HALL *Chron.* 239 b, Of no small authoritie in those dayes. **1576** FLEMING *Panopl. Epist.* A ij, I know not where we shall finde one in these our dayes. **1614** BP. HALL *Recoll. Treat.* 953 What sonne of Israel can hope for good daies, when hee heares his Fathers were so evill? **1652** CULPEPPER *Eng. Physic.* 183 An Herb of as great Use with us in these dayes. **1732** BERKELEY *Alciphr.* VI. §26 The Jewish state in the days of Josephus. **1806** FORSYTH *Beauties Scotl.* IV. 102 The whole town bears evident marks of having seen better days. **1848** LYTTON *Harold* I. i, In the good old days before the Monk-king reigned. **1880** T. FOWLER *Locke* i. 7 During his undergraduate and bachelor days.

†*β.* In this sense, *esp.*, ME. used *dawen, dawe*, from the OE. dat. pl. *on þæm daȝum*. When *dawe* (*daw*) began to be viewed as sing., *dawes* was often used in the pl.

c **1000** *Ags. Gosp.* Matt. iii. 1 On þam daȝum com Iohannes. *c* **1160** *Hatton G.* ibid., On þam daȝen. *c* **1200** *Trin. Coll. Hom.* 47 Swich þeu wes bi þan daȝen. *c* **1275** LAY. 397 After þan heþene lawe þat stot [= stood] in þan ilke dawe. *a* **1300** *Cursor M.* 4082 (Cott.) Als it bitidd mikel in þaa dauus [*v.r.* be alde dawes]. *c* **1314** *Guy Warw.* (A.) 3852 Non better nar bi þo dawe. *c* **1386** CHAUCER *Frankl. T.* 452 Felawes, The which he had y-knowen in olde dawes. *c* **1430** LYDG. *Bochas* III. xiii. 86 b, Neuer..in their dawes. *c* **1430** *Freemasonry* 509 (Mätz.) Suche mawmetys he hade yn hys dawe. **1501** DOUGLAS *Pal. Hon.* III. xliv, Tullus Seruillius douchtie in his daw.

b. expressed more *fig.* by the *sing.* Now *esp.* in phrases ***at or to this*** or ***that day, at the present day, in our own day, at some future day***, etc.; (***in***) ***this day and age***, (at) the present time; (at) the moment of speaking or writing.

1382 WYCLIF *John* xiv. 20 In that day ȝe schulen knowe, for I am in my fadir, and ȝee in me. **1578** TIMME *Calvin on Gen.* 242 Which Men at this day call Cairum. **1611** BIBLE *Ezek.* xxx. 9 In that day shall messengers goe foorth from me in shippes. **1662** STILLINGFL. *Orig. Sacr.* I. vi. §1 To this day ..the Coptites and antient Egyptians call the end of the year νειοι. **1771** SMOLLETT *Humph. Cl.* I. 23 Apr., The inconveniences which I overlooked in the high day of health. **1805** SCOTT *Last Minstr.* Introd. 4 His wither'd cheek and tresses grey Seem'd to have known a better day. **1848** MACAULAY *Hist. Eng.* I. 403 To this day Palamon and Arcite ..are the delight both of critics and of schoolboys. **1875** JOWETT *Plato* (ed. 2) V. 48 They were..more just than the men of our day. [**1917** A. WOOLLCOTT *Let.* 4 Dec. (1944) 41 You will receive a modest Christmas gift..of no conceivable use in this day and generation.] **1933** *Week-end Rev.* 7 Oct. 348/1 (*title of film*) This day and age. **1941** *Time* 13 Jan. 44/1 She knew that in this day and age a nun could be a scientist, if she were smart as well as conscientious. **1944** H. CROOME *You've gone Astray* xxi. 209 Do you mean to say that in this day and age..you're going to come the conventional? **1958** *Spectator* 18 July 116/2 The needs of this day and age. **1970** *New Yorker* 17 Oct. 39/2 What a comfort it was in this day and age to meet someone obliging.

(*b*) ***the day***: the time under consideration, time (now or then) present; (cf. *the hour, the moment*). ***order of the day***: see ORDER. ***the day***: Sc. for TO-DAY, q.v.

1814 SCOTT *Wav.* xlii,'But we maun a' live the day, and have our dinner. **1839** SIR C. NAPIER in W. N. Bruce *Life* iv. (1885) 127 Funk is the order of the day. **1893** W. P. COURTNEY in *Academy* 13 May 413/1 The gardens were planned by the best landscape gardeners of the day. *a* **1895** *Mod.* Men and women of the day. The book of the day.

14. With personal pronoun: Period of a person's rule, activity, career, or life; lifetime.

a. in *sing.*

1297 R. GLOUC. (1724) 376 Heye men ne dorste by hys day wylde best nyme noȝt. *a* **1300** *Cursor M.* 8315 (Cott.) Salamon..sal be king efter þi dai. *c* **1300** *Beket* 649 Heo that was so freo and heȝ bi myn ancestres daye. *c* **1400** *Gamelyn* 65 Thus dalte the knight his lond by his day. *a* **1500** *Childe of Bristowe* 360 in Hazl. *E.P.P.* I. 124 Yet dwel y stille in peyn..tyl y haue fulfilled my day. **1795** SOUTHEY *Joan of Arc* III. 293 Holy abbots honour'd in their day. **1850** L. HUNT *Autobiog.* (1860) I, I have had vanities enough in my day.

b. in *pl.* Time of one's life, span of existence. ***to end one's days***: to die.

1466 *Paston Lett.* No. 552 II. 282 Like as the said John Paston deceased had in any time of his daies. **1484** CAXTON *Curiall* 1 That thou myghtest vse thy dayes in takyng companye wyth me. **1513** MORE in Grafton *Chron.* II. 756 In his later dayes..somewhat corpulent. **1526** *Pilgr. Perf.* (W. de W. 1531) 289 b, They had neuer feled suche before, in all theyr dayes. *a* **1533** LD. BERNERS *Huon* lxv. 222 There myserably he shall ende his dayes. *c* **1600** SHAKS. *Sonn.* xcv, That tongue that tells the story of thy days. **1600** E. BLOUNT tr. *Conestaggio* 304 The griefe he conceived..hastened his daies. **1697** DRYDEN *Virg. Georg.* IV. 815, I at Naples pass my peaceful Days. **1867** FREEMAN *Norm. Conq.* (1876) I. App. 753 The kingdom of Burgundy was now in its last days.

15. Time of action, period of power or influence. Proverb. ***a*** (***every***) ***dog has his*** (***a***) ***day***.

1550 Q. ELIZ. in Strype *Eccl. Mem.* II. xxviii. 234 Notwithstanding, as a dog hath a day, so may I perchance have time to declare it in deeds. **1562** J. HEYWOOD *Prov. & Epigr.* (1867) 30 But as euery man saith, a dog hath a daie. **1602** SHAKS. *Ham.* v. i. 315 The Cat will Mew, and Dogge will haue his day. **1633** B. JONSON *Tale Tub* II. i, A man has his hour, and a dog his day. **1703** ROWE *Ulyss.* I. i. 71 Suffer the Fools to laugh..This is their Day. **1837** CARLYLE *Fr. Rev.* I. i. 2 Each dog has but his day. **1841** MIALL *Nonconf.* I. i Diplomacy has had its day, and failed. **1850** TENNYSON *In Mem.* Prol. v, Our little systems have their day, They have their day and cease to be.

V. Phrases.

16. A-DAY, A-DAYS, q.v. (see also 1 b); BY DAY, BI-DAY (see 1 and BY *prep.* 19, 20); ***by the day*** (BY *prep.* 24 c); TO-DAY.

†**17. of daw(e** (OE. type **of daȝum*, ME. *of daȝen, of daȝe, of dawe, of dawes, of daw* (*day*), *a daw*; corruptly *on, to daw*(*e*): in ***to bring, do of*** or ***out of dawe, life's dawe***, to deprive of life, to kill; ***to be of dawe***, to be dead. *Obs.* See also ADAWE *adv.*

a **1225** *Juliana* 31 He walde don hire..ut of dahene. *a* **1300** *Cursor M.* 4168 (Gött.) Þan wil na man of vs mak saue, þat we him [Joseph] suld haue done of daue [*v.rr.* on dau, of daghe]. *Ibid.* 7808 (Fairf.) He me be-soȝt..I sulde him bringe on liues dawe [*v.rr.* o dau, o daw, of dawe]. *c* **1300** *Seyn Julian* 193 Þat heo of dawe be. *c* **1325** *E.E. Allit. P.* A. 282, I trawed my perle don out of dawez. ?*a* **1400** *Morte Arth.* 2056 That oure soveraygne sulde be distroyede, And alle done of dawez. *c* **1420** *Chron. Vilod.* 107 Mony a mon was þᵗ day y do to dawe. *c* **1425** WYNTOUN *Cron.* VIII. xxxi. 119 Ðe erle þus wes dwne of day. **1513** DOUGLAS *Æneis* II. iii. 58 He was slane, allace, and brocht of daw.

18. *this* or ***that day week*** (in Sc. ***eight days***), ***twelve months***, etc.: used of measurement of time forward or backward: the same day a week or a year after or before.

1526 TINDALE *Acts* x. 30 This daye nowe .iiij. dayes I fasted. **1651** CROMWELL *Lett.* 3 Sept. (Carlyle), The third of September, (remarkable for a mercy vouchsafed to your forces on this day twelvemonth in Scotland). **1801** ELIZ. HELME *St. Margaret's Cave* III. 244 On the day month that he had made the dreadful avowal. **1815** BYRON *Let. to Moore* 10 Jan., I was married this day week. **1865** KINGSLEY *Herew.* xv. (1877) 189 Let Harold see how many..he holds by this day twelve months. *Mod.* He is expected this day week (or, in *Sc.*, this day eight days).

19. day about, on alternate days in rotation, each on or for a day in his turn: cf. ABOUT, A. 5 b.; **day by day**, on each successive day, daily, every day in its turn (without any notion of cessation); also *attrib.*; **day after day**, each day as a sequel to the preceding, on every day as it comes (but without intending future continuance); **day in (and) day out**, every day for an indefinite number of successive days, continuously; **day off**, a day away from work, school, etc.; **day out**, a day away from home or one's lodgings; *spec.* a servant's free day; also *fig.*; **(from) day to day**, continuously or without interruption from one day to another (said of a continuation of state or conditions); also *attrib.*; hence *day-to-dayness*.

1297 R. Glouc. (1724) 505 Fram daye to daye hii dude the mansinge. **1362** Langl. *P. Pl.* A. viii. 177 What þou dudest day bi day. *c* **1385** Chaucer *L.G.W.* Prol. 175 In whiche me thoughte I myghte, day by day, Dwellen alwey. *c* **1440** *Promp. Parv.* 112 Day be day, or ouery day, *quotidie.* **1483** *Cath. Angl.* 88 From Day to day, *die in diem, in dies, dietim.* **15..** Moffat *Wyf of Auchtirmuchty* (Bannatyne MS.), Content am I To tak the pluche my day about. **1548–9** (Mar.) *Bk. Com. Prayer* 2 b, *Te Deum*, Day by day we magnifie thee. **1556** *Aurelio & Isab.* (1608) I iij, From daye to daye you have beane worse. **1605** Shaks. *Macb.* v. v. 20 To morrow, and to morrow, and to morrow, Creepes in this petty pace from day to day. **1712** Addison *Spect.* No. 445 ¶ 3 Whether I should still persist in laying my Speculations, from Day to Day, before the Publick. **1771** Mrs. Griffith tr. *Viaud's Shipwreck* 178, I cannot give you, day by day, an account of this..journey. **1828** W. Carr *Dial. Craven* (ed. 2) I. 102 'Day in and day out', all the day long. **1830** Tennyson *Poems* 33 A world of peace And confidence, day after day. **1836** Kingsley *Lett.* (1878) I. 38, I am sickened by its day-by-day occurrence. **1848** *Punch* 4 Nov. 182/2 The Servant-Girl's Idea of Life:—one long day out with 'the journeyman'. **1865** Kingsley *Herew.* xv. (1877) 195 Passing each other day by day. **1869** *Punch* 20 Mar. 111/2 Having made this a holiday with a view to having a 'day out', my landlady had not had notice to call me at any particular hour. **1883** *Manch. Exam.* 8 Dec. 4/1 For day-to-day loans the general charge was 2 to $2\frac{1}{4}$ per cent. **1883** B. Harte *Carquinez Woods* ii. 51 It has been already intimated that it was his 'day off'. **1887** M. E. Wilkins *Humble Romance* (1890) 127 Sewing as she did, day in, day out. **1890** *Peel City Guardian* 4 Jan. 5/5 It was Fayle's day out, and he made the most of the chances offered. **1892** Mrs. A. Ireland *Lett. G. E. Jewsbury* p. xiii, Their fulfilment is wholly incompatible with a *migraine* or a 'day off'. **1893** *Eng. Illustr. Mag.* 488/2 The bus-driver spends his 'day off' in driving on a pal's bus, on the box-seat by his pal's side. **1898** A. E. T. Watson *Turf* i. 17 It may not have been the animal's 'day out', it may do better later on. **1904** Kipling in *Windsor Mag.* Dec. 10/1 Whatever 'e's done, let us remember that 'e's given us a day off. **1927** *Public Opinion* Jan. 56/3 The British Broadcasting Company will have to offer, day in and day out, a service. *Ibid.* Feb. 109/2 Work—day in day out—and not much money. **1933** S. Jameson (*title*) A day off. **1933** *Granta* 26 Apr. 370/1 Those interested only in the day to day politics of the fall of the dollar and the Russian embargo. **1942** W. S. Churchill *End of Beginning* (1943) 33 Even in the.. United States the Executive does not stand in the same direct, immediate, day-to-day relation to the Legislative body as we do. **1948** F. R. Leavis *Great Tradition* iv. i. 200 That kind of self-sufficient day-to-dayness of living Conrad can convey. **1960** C. Day Lewis *Buried Day* vi. 116 One boy ..was kicked around, jeered at or ostracised, day in day out for several years. **1963** *Higher Educ.* (*Cmnd. 2154*) xv. 220 The day-to-day conduct of policy must rest with the heads of institutions. **1966** G. N. Leech *Eng. in Advertising* xv. 138 Lifebuoy Toilet Soap With Puralin gives day in-day out protection against B.O. **1971** *Daily Tel.* 1 July 1 (*heading*) Teachers' strike gives 400,000 pupils day off.

20. a. ***all day***: the whole day; †*every day*: see 1 b, and alday. ***all days***: always, for ever: see 6 b. ***better days***: see 13 a. every-day, first day, q.v. ***good day***: see good. ***late in the day***: see late. ***now-a-days***, †*now bi-dawe*: see now and a-days. ***one day, one of these days***: see 7 b. ***the other day***: two (or a few) days ago: see other. ***some day, some of these days***: see 7 b. ***time of day***: hour of the clock, period of the world's history, etc.: see time. ***the day after*** (or ***before***) ***the fair***: too late (or too early); see fair *sb.*[1] ***days in bank, days of grace***, etc.: see bank[2] 2, grace, etc. Also All Fools' Day, Ascension, black-letter, lawful day, etc.: see these words.

b. In various colloq. phrases, as ***to make a day of it***: to devote a day to some pursuit, usu. one of pleasure; to spend the day in enjoyment or revelling (see make *v.*[1] 18 c and cf. night *sb.* 4 e); ***to make (one's) day***: see make *v.*[1]; ***if it's*** (or ***he's***, etc.) ***a day***: of a period of time or a person's age, at least; ***any day (of the week)***: at all times; without exception or doubt; cf. *every time* (every *a.* 1 e and time *sb.* 18 b); ***to call it (half) a day***: to consider that one has done a day's work; *fig.* to rest content, to leave off; ***between two days*** U.S.: overnight; ***that'll*** (or ***that will***) ***be the day*** (app. orig. *N.Z.*): (*a*) that will be a day worth waiting for, experiencing, etc.; (*b*) (*ironically*) that is most unlikely; that will never happen; ***those were the days***: an expression (nostalgic or ironic) of regret for time past.

1660 [see make *v.*[1] 18 c]. **1731–8** Swift *Polite Conv.* (1963) 78 She's on the wrong Side of thirty, if she be a Day. **1763** Boswell *London Jrnl.* 28 July (1950) 327 Come..let us make a day of it. Let us go down to Greenwich and dine. **1777** [see if *conj.* 1 a]. **1828** Lamb *Let.* Dec. (1935) III. 198 From this paradise, making a day of it, you go to see the ruins of an old convent at March Hall. **1829** G. Griffin *Collegians* II. xxiii. 169 It's a long time since you an' I met. .. 'Tis six years if its a day. [**1833** J. Neal *Down-Easters* I. ix. 134 He'll do it any day o' the week..let alone Saturdays —of course the speaker was a Marylander of Irish parentage.] **1838** J. C. Neal *Charcoal Sk.* 140, I've a great mind to knock off and call it half a day. **1839** Thackeray *Catherine* i, in *Fraser's Mag.* May 609/2 She's seventeen if she's a day, though he is the very first sweetheart she has had. **1840** Dickens *Old. C. Shop* xxxix, in *Master Humphrey's Clock* (1841) II. 11 Why *you* are a good deal better-looking than her, Barbara... You are, any day. **1840** R. H. Dana *Bef. Mast* (1854) xxviii. 177 Some rascally deed sent him off 'between two days'. **1843** *Spirit of Times* 4 Mar. 1/2 When a thing isn't 'worth a fig', one 'might as well call it half a day and quit'. **1885** [see night *sb.* 4 e]. **1889** 'Mark Twain' *Yankee* 271 It would have been best for Merlin..to quit and call it half a day. **1902** Conrad *Youth* 4 He was sixty if a day. **1903** A. D. McFaul *Ike Glidden in Maine* ii. 12 Hadn't been't he left town 'tween two days he'd be good way on the road to the pen'tentiary now. **1906** G. K. Chesterton *Dickens* viii. 188 Susan Nipper..is more of a heroine than Florence any day of the week. **1919** Wodehouse *Damsel in Distress* ix. 116 Albert rose, not unwilling to call it a day. **1922** S. Lewis *Babbitt* xv. 193 'Remember how..we pinched the pants-pressing sign and took and hung it on Prof. Morrison's door? Oh, gosh, those were the days!' Those, McKelvey agreed, were the days. **1930** W. S. Maugham *Cakes & Ale* 268 I've had my time and I'm ready to call it a day. **1931** A. L. Rowse *Politics & Younger Gen.* 155 They would prefer a despotism of the civil service to a despotism of the law any day. **1934** J. T. Farrell *Young Manhood* xvi, in *Studs Lonigan* (1936) 347 Jesus, those were the days, weren't they, Studs? **1936** J. B. Priestley *They walk in City* 240 He had to be there at nine ..and then worked on until the Belvedere Trading Company..'called it a day'. **1941** Baker *N.Z. Slang* vi. 50 *That'll be the day!*..a cant phrase expressing mild doubt following some boast or claim by a person. **1943** N. Marsh *Colour Scheme* vi. 101 He's a beaut. Wait till I get him. That'll be the day. **1951** —— *Opening Night* xi. 248 'If I've bungled,' Alleyn muttered, 'I've..bungled in a big way.'.. Bailey astonished everyone by saying..'That'll be the day.' 'Don't talk Australian,' Mr. Fox chided. **1957** G. Bellairs *Death in High Provence* xiii. 149 Madeleine's sister is a great age, too. Eighty, if a day. **1957** J. Braine *Room at Top* xiii. 129 We'll call it a day... Don't think badly of me. **1960** H. Pinter *Room* in *Birthday Party* 107 'Maybe there are two landlords.'.. 'That'll be the day.' **1963** V. Nabokov *Gift* iii. 185 A friend of his..complained that Carlsbad was no longer what it used to be. Those were the days! he said: 'you stand with your mug of water and there next to you is King Edward.' **1965** L. Sands *Something to Hide* v. 83 'Got any free road-maps?' 'That'll be the day. Bob apiece.'

VI. Attributive uses and Combinations.

21. The common use of the possessive genitive *day's* (as in other nouns of time) somewhat restricts the simple attributive use of *day*. The genitive is used in, e.g., ***the day's duties, needs, sales, takings; a day's length, sunshine; a day's fighting, journey, march, rest; a day's allowance, fast, pay, provisions, victuals, wages***, etc. So with the pl. ***two days' journey, three days' pay***, etc. See also daysman, day's work.

a **1250** *Owl & Night.* 1588 That gode wif..Haveth daies kare and niȝtes wake. **1388** Wyclif *Luke* ii. 44 Thei..camen a daies iourney [**1382** the wey of a day]. **1422** *E.E. Wills* (1882) 50 Myn eche daies gowne. **1548** Hall *Chron.* 228 b, Ponderynge together yestardayes promise, and two-dayes doyng. **1784** Cowper *Task* ii. 6 My ear is pained..with every day's report. **1859** Tennyson *Enid* 476 In next day's tourney. *Mod.* 'He has neither night's rest nor day's ease', as the saying is. A distance of three days' journey.

22. Such combinations as ***eight days*** when used attrib. may become ***eight-day***.

1803 M. Wilmot *Jrnl.* 13 Apr. in Londonderry & Hyde *Russ. Jrnls.* (1934) I. 3 My precious Father..saw us safely into the *two day* Coach. **1836** [see eight]. **1847** *Nat. Encycl.* I. 413 Six-day licenses may be granted. *Mod.* An eight-day clock.

23. General combinations: **a.** *simple attrib.* 'of the day, *esp.* as opposed to the night, the day's', as ***day-beam, -blush, -fall, -glory, -god, -going, -hospital, -hours, -season, -spirit***; 'of a day, as a period of time, a day's', as ***day-bill, -journey, -name, -respite, -sum, -ticket, -warning; day-old*** adj. (also *sb.* = day-old chick, etc.).

1811 Shelley *Let.* 6 Jan. (1964) I. 38 The *day-beam returning. **1813** Hogg *Queen's Wake* 265 The day-beam.. O'er Queensberry began to peep. **1825** D. L. Richardson *Sonnets* 60 The day-beams fade Along the crimson west. **1952** C. Day Lewis tr. *Virgil's Aeneid* iv. 76 As Aurora was rising out of her ocean bed And the day-beam lofted. **1824** Byron *Juan* xv. lxii, A single *day-bill Of modern dinners. **1813** —— *Br. Abydos* ii. xxviii, When the *day-blush bursts from high. **1889** F. Thompson in *Merry England* XIII. 300 Who set upon her brow the *day-fall's carcanet? **1960** T. Hughes *Lupercal* 55 Waking, dragged suddenly From a choir-shaken height By the world, Lord, and its dayfall. **1827** *Blackw. Mag.* XXI. 81 Why, *Day-god, why so late? **1638** Jackson *Creed* ix. xxiv. Wks. VIII. 353 Betwixt three of the clock and the *day-going. **1843** *Chambers's Jrnl.* 30 Dec. 398/1 A kind of *day-hospital, to keep the children from wandering idly abroad. **1951** *Brit. Jrnl. Psychol.* Aug. 307 The Day Hospital does not belong to the era of Individual Psychiatry. **1958** *New Statesman* 10 Jan. 34/1 It has long been recognised that given adequate out-patient facilities, day hospitals, occupation centres and hostels, many persons suffering from mental disorder need not enter a mental hospital. **1963** *Guardian* 16 May 4/6 The Marlborough day hospital, in London..had had no beds and has been working as a 'day' hospital where patients after attendance return to their homes and families at night; and as a 'night' hospital where patients can go to work during the day, returning for help in the evenings. **1669** Sturmy *Mariner's Mag.* ii. 77 The upper half of the circle..is the *Day-Hours, and the lower..is the Night-Hours. **1483** *Cath. Angl.* 88 A *Day iornay, *dieta.* **1907** *Daily Chron.* 8 July 4/4 Many poultry-keepers dispose of several thousand *day-old chicks every season. **1911** R. Brooke *Let.* Feb. (1968) 280 Every night I sit in a *café* near here..and read the day-old *Times.* **1928** *Daily Tel.* 11 May 19/4 Day-olds from reliable pedigree strains cost only 21s a dozen. **1930** Masefield *Wanderer of Liverpool* 67 It was fine clear easterly weather with a day-old moon. **1959** *B.S.I. News* Apr. 18/2 Priority is being given to arrangements for the carriage of day-old chicks. **1960** *Farmer & Stockbreeder* 5 Jan. 109/3 Year after year crops of goslings are..in big demand as day-olds or 'growers'. *c* **1489** Caxton *Sonnes of Aymon* xix. 429 A *day respyte is worthe moche. *a* **1568** Coverdale *Bk. Death* i. xxi, Neither need to fear any inconvenience by night, neither swift arrow in the *day-season. **1850** Mrs. Browning *Poems* II. 274 Thy *day-sum of delight. *c* **1530** Ld. Berners *Arth. Lyt. Bryt.* (1814) 443 To be redy at a *day warning.

b. *attrib.* 'Pertaining to or characteristic of the day, existing by day, diurnal'; as ***day-bell, -bird, -breeze, -clothes, -guest, -haul, -moth, -shift, -task, -watch, -watchman, -wind***.

15.. *Tale of Basyn* 172 in Hazl. *E.P.P.* III. 51 Thei daunsyd all the nyȝt, till the son con ryse; The clerke rang the *day-bell, as it was his gise. **1774** White in *Phil. Trans.* LXV. 266 It does not withdraw to rest till a quarter before nine..being the latest of all *day-birds. **1808** J. Barlow *Columb.* ii. 540 The *day-breeze fans the God. **1644** A. Burgesse *Magistrates Commission* 15 It ought to be your *day-care and your night-care, and your morning-care. **1856** Emerson *Eng. Traits, Voy. to Eng.* Wks. (Bohn) II. 12 The master never slept but in his *day-clothes whilst on board. **1654** Whitlock *Zootomia* 33 If griefe lodges with us over night, Joy shall be our *Day Guest. **1888** E. J. Mather *Nor'ard of Dogger* 103 The smacks had their gear down for a *day-haul. **1831** Carlyle *Sart. Res.* (1858) 73 Your very *Daymoth has capabilities in this kind. **1872** *Daily News* 12 Oct., The people of the *day-shift trooping in to relieve the night-workers. **1630** Brathwait *Eng. Gentlem.*, Our Ordinary Gentleman, whose *day-taske is this. **1837** Wheelwright tr. *Aristophanes* I. 263 Eluding our *day-watch. **1722** De Foe *Plague* (1840) 51 Till the morning-man, or *day-watchman, as they called him, came to relieve him. **1846** Keble *Lyra Innoc.* (1873) 50 How soft the *day-wind sighed.

c. With agent-nouns and words expressing action, '(that acts or is done) by day, during the day, as distinguished from night', as ***day-devourer, -drudge, -flier, -lurker, -nurse, -seller, -sleeper, -trip, -tripper; day-drowsiness, -fishing, -journeying, -reflection, -slumber, -somnambulism, -vision***; also adjectives, as ***day-appearing, -flying, -shining***, etc.

1821 Shelley *Fragments, Wandering* i, Like a *day-appearing dream. **1725** Pope *Odyss.* xix. 83 A *day-devourer, and an evening spy! **1852** *Meanderings of Mem.* I. 149 *Day-drowsiness—and night's arousing power. **1837** J. S. Mill in *Westm. Rev.* XXVII. 22 He [*sc.* Carlyle] possesses in no less perfection..the quality of the historical *day-drudge. **1840** Carlyle *Heroes* (1858) 237 Show him the way of doing that, the dullest daydrudge kindles into a hero. **1653** Walton *Angler* 126 There is night as well as *day-fishing for a Trout. **1889** A. R. Wallace *Darwinism* 248 *Day-flying moths. **1876** Geo. Eliot *Dan. Der.* IV. lxiv. 274 In leisurely *day-journeying from Genoa to London. **1657** Tomlinson *Renou's Disp.* 4 Jugglers, *Day-lurkers, and Deceivers. **1844** Dickens *Mart. Chuz.* xxv. 309 The night-nurse..well beknown to Mrs. Prig the *day-nurse. **1855** J. R. Beste *Wabash* I. ii. 48 Our little Isabel amused the youngest children, and constituted herself their day nurse. **1725** Pope *Odyss.* iv. 1062 The *day-reflection, and the midnight-dream! **1889** *Tablet* 3 Aug. 167 Two classes of flower-girl—the *day-sellers and the night-sellers. **1580** Sidney *Arcadia* (1622) 2 The *day-shining starres. **1549** Cheke *Hurt Sedit.* (1641) 41 *Day-sleepers, pursse-pickers. **1836–9** Todd *Cycl. Anat.* II. 767/2 The bat.. awoke from its deep *day-slumber. **1849** H. Mayo *Truths in Pop. Superst.* vi. 86 Let me narrate some instances..one of *day-somnambulism. **1903** A. Bennett *Leonora* viii. 215 He had gone to London by a *day-trip on the previous Thursday. **1967** C. Drummond *Death at Furlong Post* viii. 107 A customer who had taken a day trip to Calais. **1897** *Daily News* 27 Sept. 3/5 The '*day-tripper' class of excursionists. *Ibid.*, Day trippers by the Marguerite from the Thames. **1960** E. W. Hildick *Jim Starling & Colonel* vii. 57 Day-trippers on their way to Blackpool. **1677** Gale *Crt. Gentiles* II. iii. 58 Their night-dreams and *day-visions, whereby they divined things.

d. objective or objective genitive, as ***day-dispensing, -distracting, -loving*** adjs.; ***day-hater, -prolonger***; **e.** instrumental, as ***day-lit, day-wearied*** adjs.; **f.** adverbial, as ***day-born, -hired, -lasting, -lived*** adjs.; **g.** similative and parasynthetic, as ***day-bright, -clear, -eyed*** adjs.

1849 Thoreau *A Week* 59 The Society Islanders had their *day-born gods. **1903** *Westm. Gaz.* 26 Nov. 2/3 The day-born, hopeless longing dies. **1590** T. Watson *Poems* (Arb.) 159 Virgo make fountains of thy *daie-bright eine. *a* **1592** Greene & Lodge *Looking Glasse* (1861) 124 The day-bright eyes that made me see. **1785** Burns *2nd Ep. to J. Lapraik* xvii, Some *day-detesting owl. **1725** Pope *Odyss.* xx. 102 The *day-distracting theme. **1796** T. Townshend *Poems* 49 *Day-eyed Fancy. **1597** Daniel *Civ. Wars* ii. c, The *day-hater, Minerva's bird. **1751** *Female Foundling* II. 159 *Day-hired Servants. *a* **1649** Drumm. of Hawth. *Fam. Epist.* Wks. (1711) 139 *Day-lasting ornaments. **1885** R. L. Stevenson *Dynamiter* 136 The broad, *daylit unencumbered paths of universal scepticism. **1839** Bailey *Festus* v. (1848) 48 Things born of vice or *day-lived fashion. **1824** J. Bowring *Batavian Anthol.* 158 *Day-prolonger—summer's mate. **1595** Shaks. *John* v. iv. 35 Feeble, and *day-wearied Sunne.

24. Special combinations: **day-and-night** *attrib.*, throughout the day and night; †**day-and-night-shot**, the name of some disease; **day-**

before *attrib.*, of the previous day; **day-boarder**, see BOARDER; †**day-body**, a person taken up with the things of the day; **day-boy**, a schoolboy (at a boarding-school) who attends the classes but goes home for the evening, as distinguished from a BOARDER, q.v.; also *transf.* and *attrib.*; **day-bug** *Schoolboy slang*, = *day-boy*; **day-car, -coach** *U.S.*, any railway passenger carriage other than a sleeper; also *transf.*; **day care**, the supervision and care of young children during the day, esp. while their mothers are at work; freq. *attrib.*; **day centre**, a non-residential centre which provides social, recreational, and other facilities, esp. for the elderly or handicapped; **day-clock**, a clock which requires to be wound up daily; **day-coal** (see 5); **day continuation school**, a school for educating young workers released temporarily by their employers; †**day, day!** a childish expression for 'good day', 'goodbye' (cf. *ta-ta sb.*); **day-degree** (see quot.); **day dress**, = *day-gown*; **day-drift, -hole** (see quot. and 5); **day editor**, the editor in charge of a newspaper during the day; **day-eye** (*Coalmining*), a working open to daylight; **day-gang**, †(*a*) a day's march or journey (*obs.*); (*b*) a gang of miners, etc., forming the *day-shift*; **day-gown**, a woman's gown worn by day; **day-holding**, the holding of an appointed day (for arbitration); **day-hours** (*pl.*), those offices for the Canonical Hours which are said in the day-time; **day-house** (*Astrol.*), a house in which a planet is said to be stronger by day than by night (Wilson *Dict. Astrol.*); **day-length**, the length of the day, esp. as it varies at different times of the year; also *attrib.*, *spec.* designating clothes of a suitable length for wear during the day (see also quot. 1949); †**day-liver**, one who lives for a day, or for the day; **dayman**, one employed for the day, or for duty on a special day; **day-nettle**: see DEAD-NETTLE and DEA-NETTLE; **day nursery**, (*a*) a nursery used by children during the day (as distinguished from *night nursery*); (*b*) a nursery where children are cared for while their mothers are at work; **Day of Atonement** [tr. Heb. *Yōm Kippūr*], a Jewish fast day, observed from the ninth to the tenth of Tishri; **day-on** *Naut. slang*, one who does duty as officer of the day; **day release**, a system whereby employers allow employees days off from work for education; also *attrib.*; **day-room**, a room occupied by day only; †**day-set**, sun-set; **day-shine**, day-light; †**day-shutting**, close of day, sunset; **dayside**, (*a*) *U.S.*, the division of a newspaper's staff that works during the day; more generally (*attrib.*), of or pertaining to the day-shift; that works or is performed by day; cf. *night-side* (*c*) s.v. NIGHT *sb.* 14; (*b*) the side of a planet that is facing the sun and is therefore in daylight, esp. in phr. ***on the dayside***; cf. *night-side* (*d*) s.v. NIGHT *sb.* 14; **day-stone**, a naturally detached block of stone found on the surface (see 5); **day-streak**, streak of dawn; **day-student**, a student who comes to a college, etc. during the day for lectures or study, but does not reside there; **day-ticket**, a railway or other ticket covering return on the same day; also, a ticket covering all journeys or entrances made by the purchaser on the day of issue; **day-tide** (*poet.*,) day-time; **day-wages**, wages paid by the day; so **day-wage** *attrib.*; †**day-wait**, a watcher or watchman by day; **day-'ward** *sb.*, ward kept by day; **'dayward** *a.* and *adv.*, towards the day; **day-water**, surface water (see 5).

1899 *Westm. Gaz.* 16 Mar. 10/2 The work will be carried out by *day and night relays of men. **1964** S. DUKE-ELDER *Parsons' Dis. Eye* (ed. 14) xxvii. 436 Unless day-and-night nursing is available it is a wise precaution with many patients to tie their hands loosely to the bed at night. **1527** ANDREW *Brunswyke's Distyll. Waters* K ij b, The same water is good agaynste a sore named the *daye and nyght shotte. **1828** COBBETT *Serm., Drunkenness* 45 Nobody is so dull as the *daybefore drunkard. **1853** E. SEWELL *Exper. Life* iii. 26 A very tolerable school..where they were allowed..to attend as *day boarders. **1567-8** ABP. PARKER *Corr.* 310, I trust, not so great a *day-body..but can consider both reason and godliness. **1848** THACKERAY *Van. Fair* II. xxi, Georgy was, like some dozen other pupils, only a *day-boy. **1888** BURGON *Lives 12 Gd. Men* I. iii. 302 The attempt was made to send [him]..as a day-boy, to Rugby school. **1914** *Spectator* 17 Oct. 516/2 We would train a portion of the men in what we may describe as 'day-boy' battalions... Up till the time of the Boer War..there were two battalions of London Militia who were always trained on the 'day-boy' system. The men lived in their own homes, and came to the depot each day for their recruit training. **1909** WARE *Passing Eng.* 105/1 Don't row with that fellow, he's only a *day-bug. **1913** C. MACKENZIE *Sinister Street* I. i. vii. 103 When an older boarder called him a 'day-bug' Michael was discreetly silent. **1870** W. F. RAE *Westward by Rail* (1871) 50 This company build and run their own elegant sleeping coaches and palace *day cars. **1904** *Westm. Gaz.* 26 Sept. 6/3 [Accident in Tennessee] Day-car and day-car were telescoped, buckled, and thrown over. **1964** *Economist* 4 Jan. 24/2 Adequately staffed day-care centres for children. **1961** *Lancet* 16 Sept. 648/1 A local authority can provide *day-centres or social clubs for them if it wishes to do so. **1976** *Bridgwater Mercury* 21 Dec. 1/3 Grant aid to elderly persons' clubs, luncheon clubs and day centres will be continued. **1984** *Listener* 26 July 21/1 The health team beavers unobtrusively, arranging a home help here, a weekly visit to a day centre there. **1859** GEO. ELIOT *A. Bede* 38 No sound..but the loud ticking of the old *day-clock. **1873** *Winfield* (Kansas) *Courier* 11 Jan. 2/7 Elegant *Day Coaches, [etc.]..are some of the modern improvements used on this Line. **1887** C. B. GEORGE *40 Yrs. on Rail* xi. 226 A passenger on his way to the dining-car came out of the day coach into the ladies' end of my car. **1947** *Shell Aviation News* CXII. 4/1 Atlantic has applied to the Civil Aeronautics Board for permission to operate day coach services in the triangular area, New York, Washington and Pittsburg. **1919** *Times Educ. Suppl.* 25 Sept. 487/1 The *day continuation school must sit between eight in the morning and seven in the evening. **1943** *Ann. Reg. 1942* 68 The Council..advocated..day continuation schools for young persons up to the age of 18. **1952** *Oxf. Jun. Encycl.* X. 142/2 A system of Day Continuation Schools was also included in the 1918 Fisher Act. All young people between the ages of 14 and 18 who had ended full-time schooling were to continue their education at such schools for a period of 320 hours each year. **1712** ARBUTHNOT *John Bull* IV. vii, Bye! bye, Nic!.. Won't you like to shake your *day-day, Nic? **1784** P. OLIVER in *T. Hutchinson's Diary* II. 213 Day, day! Yrs, P. Oliver. **1886** *Daily News* 17 May 3/4 The result is expressed in *day-degrees, a day-degree signifying one degree of excess or deficit of temperature above or below 42 deg. continued for 24 hours, or any other number of degrees for an inversely proportional number of hours. **1922** *Liberty Dresses* Spring 10 *Day Dress, in crèpe-de-chine... Price 12½ guineas. **1891** *Labour Commission* Gloss., **Day drifts* or *day holes*, galleries or inclined planes driven from the surface so that men can walk underground to and from their work without descending and ascending a shaft. **1873** W. MATHEWS *Getting on in World* xiv. 218 Mr. Brooks..acting as leading editor [of the *New York Express*], reporter, *day editor, night editor, and even typesetter. **1877** *Harper's Mag.* Dec. 53/2 The day editor in charge. **1890** H. T. CROFTON in *Trans. Lanc. & Cheshire Antiq. Soc.* VII. 27 Coal would probably be obtained first by 'drifts', '*day-eyes', or 'breast-highs.' *a* **1300** *Cursor M.* 5842 Vte of his land *dai-ganges thre. **1840** T. A. TROLLOPE *Summ. Britt.* II. 163 When the day-gangs come up, and those for the night go down. **1875** L. TROUBRIDGE *Life amongst Troubridges* (1966) x. 116 My old peacock cashmere evening, transformed into a *day gown with long sleeves. **1889** *Pall Mall G.* 14 Nov. 1/3 Another day gown for a well-known society woman. **1565** in *Child Marriages* (E.E.T.S.) 44 Ther was diuerse *daie-holdinges to get them to abide together; which they neuer cold bringe to passe. **1892** *Pall Mall. G.* 11 Feb. 5/1 The coal is won by means of a *day hole. **1855** P. FREEMAN *Princ. Div. Service* I. 220 There is, however, attached to each of these '*day-hours' a 'mid-hour' Office. **1920** GARNER & ALLARD in *Jrnl. Agric. Res.* XVIII. 582 The Stewart Cuban Mammoth tobacco which requires a *day length of 12 hours or less to attain the blossoming stage has been grown commercially to some extent under an artificial shade. **1944** A. G. HATCHER in *Mod. Lang. Notes* Dec. 515 Among the many relationships expressed by noun combinations..the three-member compound is peculiarly modern..day-length dresses..bronze-finish lamp. **1949** *New Biol.* VII. 52 *Day length neutral plants*..flowered whatever the length of day. **1965** *Harper's Bazaar* Jan. 54/1 He will charge you about 20 or 25 gns. for a day-length dress. **1630** DRUMM. OF HAWTH. *Hymn to Fairest Fair*, *Day-livers, we rememberance do lose Of ages worn. **1880** *Times* 8 Oct. 8/5 The Liberal secretaries..mentioned the names of the chairmen, treasurers, executive '*daymen', and captains of the respective wards. **1882** NARES *Seamanship* (ed. 6) 98 Marines, Idlers or Daymen. **1844** MRS. PARKES in Webster & Parkes *Encycl. Domestic Econ.* XXVI. i. 1187 *Day nurseries should be prepared for the children by having the windows open early in the morning. **1850** *Househ. Words* II. 110/1 These institutions were to be Day-Nurseries for the children of the poor. **1884** *Harper's Mag.* Apr. 782/2 A 'Day Nursery and Temporary Home for Children', charging two cents a day to busy mothers. **1896** H. FRIEDERICHS *In the Evening of his Days* 70 (*caption*) The Day Nursery at Hawarden Castle. **1908** H. DE V. STACPOOLE *Patsy* ii, They were in the day nursery, which was also the schoolroom. **1955** *Times* 15 July 5/7 Under the scheme the boroughs would become responsible for maternity and child welfare, day nurseries, [etc.]. [**1611** BIBLE *Lev.* xxiii. 27 On the tenth day of this seuenth moneth there shalbe a day of atonement.] **1819** L. ALEXANDER *Hebrew Ritual* 82 The Conclusion Prayer..concludes the service of the *Day of Atonement. **1893** ZANGWILL *Ghetto Tragedies* 47 The great White Fast, the Day of Atonement. **1932** L. GOLDING *Magnolia Street* I. ii. 33 When she absented herself on the Feast of the New Year and the Day of Atonement, the understanding was she had a cold. **1914** 'BARTIMEUS' *Naval Occasions* (1918) iv. 27 The *Day-on flopped exhaustedly on to a Wardroom settee. **1945** *Youth's Opportunity* (Min. Educ. Pamphlet III) 12 Part-time *day release by industry for the purpose of technical commercial and art courses. **1955** *Times* 23 May 6/2 In part-time day-release courses an effective proportion ..of the students' time should be devoted to non-vocational work. **1965** J. MELVILLE *There lies your Love* i. 24 She was what was called a day-release student: a student who also had a job but was continuing her education. **1823** NICHOLSON *Pract. Builder* 577 A Small County Prison..A spacious *day room on the ground floor. *c* **1386** CHAUCER *Clerk's T.* 718 At *day set he on his way is goon. *c* **1822** BEDDOES *Pygmalion* Poems 154 By moon, or lamp, or sunless *day shine white. **1872** TENNYSON *Gareth & L.* 1065 Naked in open dayshine. **1673** in Picton *L'pool Munic. Rec.* (1883) I. 316 That every publick house hang out lanthornes..till 8 a clock at night, from *day shutting. **1927**, etc. *Day side [see *night side* s.v. NIGHT *sb.* 14]. **1963** *Daily Tel.* 20 May 26/4 He could see the larger stars on the 'dayside' of the Earth if he kept both sunshine and earthshine out of his capsule window. **1979** *Washington Post* 8 Jan. D11/1 Postal clerks who sort mail for Zone 11 on the midnight shift..missed the big dayside collection. **1980** *Washington Post Mag.* 20 Jan. 8/3 At 11:30 he dropped it into the city desk basket and went home, thinking that the dayside would get a kick out of it. **1982** *Nature* 4 Feb. 365/2 When the solar wind magnetic field points south,..magnetic 'reconnection' can occur across the dayside boundary. **1877** A. H. GREEN *Phys. Geol.* x. §3. 441 *Day-stones. **1850** CLOUGH *Dipsychus* 83 The chilly *day-streak signal. **1883** *Durham Univ. Jrnl.* 17 Dec. 141 Sorry indeed to see the *day-student system becoming the rule. **1846** *Railway Reg.* III. 248 *Day tickets—The charge is a fare and a half. **1818** KEATS *Endym.* III. 365 At brim of *day-tide. *a* **1592** GREENE *Orpharion* Wks. (Grosart) XII. 86 A labourer for *day wages. **1625** tr. *Camden's Hist. Eliz.* I. (1688) 49 Souldiers, Servants, and all that took Day-Wages for their Labour. **1963** *Times* 10 May 6/5 The recent provisional agreement on pay increases for day-wage men and craftsmen had been endorsed. **1496** *Dives & Paup.* (W. de W.) v. xi. 210, I haue made the a *dayewayte to the people of Israell. **1597-1602** *W. Riding Sessions Rolls* 49 (*Yorks. Archæol. Assoc.*), Vigilias suas in diebus *anglice* their *daywarde. **1876** LANIER *Poems, Psalm of West* 367 Whilst ever *dayward thou art steadfast drawn. **1698** CAY in *Phil. Trans.* XX. 369 A meer *Day-Water..immediately from the Clouds. **1808** CURWEN *Econ. Feeding Stock* 198 A poor clay..extremely retentive of day-water.

†**day**, *v.*[1] *Obs.* In 3 **dæȝen, daiȝen.** [A form of DAW *v.*, assimilated to *day* sb.] To dawn.

c **1205** LAY. 21726 Lihten hit gon dæȝen [*c* **1275** daȝeie]. —— 21854 Faire hit gon daȝiȝen. —— 26940 Hit agon daiȝen [*c* **1275** daȝeȝe]. *c* **1275** *Ibid.* 1694 A morwe þo hit daȝede [*c* **1205** dawede]. *c* **1440** *Promp. Parv.* 112 Dayyn, or wexyn day..*diesco.* *Ibid.* 114 Dawyn idem est, quod dayyn [PYNSON dayen], *auroro.* *c* **1460** *Towneley Myst., Jacob* 108 Farewell now, the day dayes. **1483** *Cath. Angl.* 88 To Day, *diere, diescere.*

Hence **'daying** *vbl. sb.* = DAWING, DAWNING.

c **1420** *Anturs of Arth.* xxxvii, In þe daying of þe day. *c* **1532** DEWES *Introd. Fr.* in Palsgr. 927 At the dayeng, *a l'ajourner.*

†**day**, *v.*[2] *Obs.* [f. DAY *sb.*; in several disconnected senses.]

1. *trans.* To appoint a day to any one; to cite or summon for an appointed day. [transl. Flem. *daghen.*]

1481 CAXTON *Reynard* (Arb.) 19 That he shold be sente fore and dayed ernestly agayn, for t[o] abyde such Iugement.

2. To submit (a matter) to, or decide by, arbitration. Cf. DAYMENT.

1484 [see DAYING *vbl. sb.*]. **1580** LUPTON *Sivqila* 117 They haue bin enforced when all their money was..spent, to haue their matter dayed, and ended by arbitrement.

3. To give (a person) time for payment; *absol.* to postpone payment. (Cf. DAY *sb.* 12.)

1566 WAGER *Cruell Debter*, The most part of my debtters have honestly payed, And they that were not redy I have gently dayed. **1573** TUSSER *Husb.* lxii. (1878) 139 Ill husbandrie daieth, or letteth it lie: Good husbandrie paieth, the cheaper to bie.

4. To appoint or fix as a date.

1594 CAREW *Tasso* (1881) 114 So when the terme was present come, that dayd The Captaine had.

5. To measure by the day; to furnish with days.

1600 ABP. ABBOT *Exp. Jonah* 545 Is it nothing that their life is dayed and houred, and inched out by a fearful God and terrible? **1616** BUDDEN tr. *Aerodius' Parent's Hon.* 168 Naturall duty, can neither be dayde nor yeard, nor determined by age, or eldership. **1839** BAILEY *Festus* xiii. (1848) 122 When earth was dayed—was morrowed.

6. ***to year and day***: to subject to the statutory period of a year and a day.

1523 FITZHERB. *Surv.* 28 b, And put them in sauegarde to the lordes vse till they be yered and deyd. *a* **1626** W. SCLATER *Serm. Exper.* (1638) 186 Whiles favours are new, we can..say, God be thanked; but, once year'd and day'd, they scarce ever come more into our thought.

day, var. of DEY, dairywoman.

dayabeah, var. DAHABEEYAH.

Daya(c)k, Dayakker, varr. DYAK.

†**'dayage.** *Obs.* [? f. DAY *sb.* + -AGE.] ? Demurrage.

1592 in Picton *L'pool Munic. Rec.* (1883) I. 70 [Various heads under which dues were claimed]..Ferriage; Daiage; Lastage; Wharfage; Keyage; Cranage.

‖**dayal** ('dɑːjəl). *India.* Also **dhyal.** [See DIAL-BIRD.] = DIAL-BIRD.

1855 *Orr's Circle Sci., Org. Nat.* III. 307 The Dayal.. which..is called the Magpie Robin by the English residents in Ceylon. **1893** NEWTON *Dict. Birds* 133 Dayal, or more correctly, it would seem, Dhyal (corrupted into Dial-bird), the Hindostani name commonly adopted by Anglo-Indians.

‖**dayan** (da'jɑːn). Also **dayyan.** Pl. **dayanim, dayans.** [Heb.] A religious judge in a Jewish community.

1880 *Encycl. Brit.* XIII. 687/1 Each congregation requires the services of a dayan or religious chief. **1891** M. FRIEDLÄNDER *Jewish Religion* II. vi. 463 The meat must not be used as food unless the animal has been examined by a competent person (Rabbi or *dayyan*) and declared..*kosher*. **1892** ZANGWILL *Childr. Ghetto* I. 4 The Dayanim, those cadis of the East End, administered justice. **1902** *Daily Chron.* 3 Jan. 5/1 The Rev. B. Spiers, the Dayan of the Beth Hamedrash of London. **1928** *Daily Tel.* 3 Jan. 10/4 Dayan Dr. Feldmann. **1928** *Sunday Dispatch* 30 Dec. 7/2 Problems of divorce and marriage brokerage as well as disputes between synagogues and questions of ritual are settled by the bench of five Dayans—or judges. **1957** L. P. GARTNER *Jewish Immigrant in Eng.* (1960) vii. 204 Rabbi Avigdor Chaikin..sat as a Dayan upon the Beth Din of the Chief Rabbi.

ˈday-bed. A bed to rest on in the daytime; a sofa, couch, lounge; *transf.* (the using of) a bed by day.

1594 SHAKS. *Rich. III*, III. vii. 72 (Qo. 1) He is not lulling on a lewd day bed. *a* **1613** OVERBURY *Charac., Ordinarie Fencer* Wks. (1856) 111 A bench, which in the vacation of the afternoons he uses as his day-bed. —— *Distaster* 127 He is a day-bed for the Devill to slumber on. **1818** SCOTT *Rob Roy* xxxix, An old-fashioned day-bed, or settee. **1831** CAPT. TRELAWNY *Adv. Younger Son* II. 193 Day-beds, fetid air, nightly waltzes and quadrilles, rob her of youth. **1940** *Chambers's Techn. Dict.* 225/2 *Day bed*, a low lounge with sloping head rest. **1969** L. J. CHIARAMONTE in Halpert & Story *Christmas Mumming in Newfoundland* 100 The girls sit down on a day bed (a single cot-type couch found in every kitchen).

ˈdayberry. *local.* (*Cornw.*) Also **deberry** (*Devon*), **dabberry** (*Kent*). A local name of the gooseberry, chiefly in its wild form.

1736 PEGGE *Kenticisms, Dabberries* pl., gooseberries. **1847–78** HALLIWELL, *Deberries*, gooseberries. *Devon.* **1880** *Cornwall Gloss., Day-berry*, the wild gooseberry.

ˈday-blindness. A visual defect in which the eyes see indistinctly, or not at all, by daylight, but tolerably well by artificial light.

1834 GOOD *Study Med.* (ed. 4) III. 145. **1838** *Penny Cycl.* XII. 114/2 Nyctalopia, night-vision, or day-blindness, probably never occurs as a separate disease.

ˈdaybook, day-book. a. A book in which the occurrences or transactions of the day are entered; a diary, journal; †also, a book for daily use or reference; *Naut.* a log-book (*obs.*).

1580 HOLLYBAND *Treas. Fr. Tong, Papier iournal*, a day booke. **1583** J. HIGINS tr. *Junius' Nomenclator* (N.), *Diarium* ..*Registre journel*..A daie booke, conteining such acts, deedes, and matters as are dailie done. **1603** FLORIO *Montaigne* (1634) 111 The daybooke of houshold affaires. **1615** R. BRUCH (*title*) Gerhard's Soule's Watch; or a Day-booke for the devout Soule, consisting of one and fiftie Heavenly Meditations. **1654** TRAPP *Comm. Ps.* v. 4 The young Lord Harrington, and sundry others, kept Journals, or Day-books, and oft read them over, for an help to Humiliation. **1709** STEELE *Tatler* No. 10 ¶3, I see a Sentence of Latin in my Brother's Day-Book of Wit. **1866** MRS. GASKELL *Wives and D.* I. 328, 'I don't like his looks', thought Mr. Gibson to himself at night, as over his daybooks he reviewed the events of the day. **1867** SMYTH *Sailor's Word-bk., Day-book*, an old and better name for the log-book.

b. *Book-keeping.* Originally, a book in which the commercial transactions of the day, as sales, purchases, etc., are entered at once in the order in which they occur; now, very generally restricted to a book containing the daily record of a particular class of transactions, as a ***purchases daybook, sales daybook***, and more especially used of the latter, in which credit sales are recorded.

In Book-keeping by double entry, often a synonym of the *wastebook*, whence transactions are posted in the *journal*; in the methods of single entry commonly used by tradesmen, the book in which goods sold on credit are entered to the debit of the purchaser, and whence they are posted into the ledger, is called variously *daybook* or *journal*.

1660 T. WILLSFORD *Scales of Commerce* 208 The Diary, or Day-book, ought to be in a large folio. **1682** SCARLETT *Exchanges* 222 In some Fairs they use only to note the Resconter in their Day-books, or Memorial, or Pocket-Books that can be blotted out again. **1727–51** CHAMBERS *Cycl.* s.v. *Book*, The waste-book..is in reality a journal or day-book; but that name being applied to another, the name *waste* book is given to this by way of distinction..*Journal-book* or *day book*, is that wherein the affairs of each day are entered orderly down, as they happen, from the waste-book. **1887** *Westm. Rev.* June 276 The ledgers and daybooks of every-day business life are his guides.

ˈdaybreak. [Cf. BREAK *v.* 41 and *sb.*[1] 2.] The first appearance of light in the morning; dawn.

1530 PALSGR. 804/1 At daye breake, *au jour creuer*. **1683** BURNET tr. *More's Utopia* (1684) 81 It is ordinary to have Publick Lectures every Morning before day-break. **1841** LANE *Arab. Nts.* I. 17 Between daybreak and sunrise.

attrib. **1825** WATERTON *Wand. S. Amer.* I. i. 99 The crowing of the hannaquoi will sound in thine ears like the daybreak town-clock.

So †**ˈday-breaking**, the breaking of the day.

1598 GRENEWEY *Tacitus' Ann.* I. xiv. (1622) 26 At day breaking, the legions..abandoned their standings. **1647** (*title*), The Day-breaking if not the Sun-rising of the Gospel with the Indians in New England.

day-daw. *Sc.* = next.

ˈday-dawn. Chiefly *poetic.* The dawn of day, daybreak.

1813 COLERIDGE *Remorse* IV. ii. 53 His tender smiles, love's day-dawn on his lips. **1857** S. OSBORN *Quedah* ix. 109 The daydawn had already chased the stars away. **1887** MORRIS *Odyssey* IV. 192 Now doth the Day-dawn speed, And at hand is the mother of morning.

ˈday-dream. A dream indulged in while awake, *esp.* one of happiness or gratified hope or ambition; a reverie, castle in the air.

1685 DRYDEN *Lucret.* (T.), And when awake, thy soul but nods at best, Day dreams and sickly thoughts revolving in thy breast. **1711** STEELE *Spect.* No. 167 ¶3 The gay Phantoms that dance before my waking Eyes and compose my Day-Dreams. **1815** SCOTT *Guy M.* iv, We shall not pursue a lover's day-dream any farther. **1864** C. KNIGHT *Passages Work. Life* I. i. 122 The realities of life had cured me of many day-dreams.

attrib. **1829** I. TAYLOR *Enthus.* ix. 231 The object of day-dream contemplation.

So **ˈday-dream** *v.*, to indulge in day-dreams; *refl.*, to transport (oneself) imaginatively by means of a day-dream; **ˈday-dreamer**; **ˈday-dreaming** *vbl. sb.* and *ppl. a.*; **ˈday-dreamy** *a.*, pertaining to day-dreams; also, having the quality of a day-dream.

1820 W. IRVING *Sketch-Bk., The Voyage*, One given to day-dreaming, and fond of losing himself in reveries. **1849** THACKERAY *Pendennis* I. xxviii. 272 This young day-dreamer built castles in the air for himself. **1873** SYMONDS *Grk. Poets* xi. 376 All day-dreamers and castle-builders. **1884** *Athenæum* 6 Dec. 738/1 The girl..who sits day-dreaming in a vignette. **1899** *Crampton's Mag.* Jan. 109 Mr. Jones fell into a retrospective mood, day-dreaming himself back into the past. **1906** *Daily Chron.* 3 Aug. 8/5 Day-dreaming children can pass into this fairy world at will. **1921** T. S. ELIOT in *Times Lit. Suppl.* 31 Mar. 202/1 The day-dreamy feeling of Morris is essentially a slight thing. **1949** 'M. INNES' *Journeying Boy* (1961) 170 There is no doubt, however, that Humphrey can day-dream himself into some rather alarming world of romantic adventure, with nervous consequences that are by no means desirable.

‖**daye** (daɪ, ˈdɑːɪ). *India.* Also **dai, dhaye, dhye, dy, dyah.** [f. Hind. *dāī*, Pers. *dāyah*.] In N. India and Persia, a nurse; a wet-nurse; a midwife.

1782 *India Gaz.* 12 Oct. (Y., Suppl.), Dy (Wet-nurse) 10 Rs. **1810** T. WILLIAMSON *East India Vade-Mecum* I. 341 The *Dhye* is more generally an attendant upon native ladies. **1825** M. M. SHERWOOD (*title*) History of little Lucy and her dhaye. **1877** E. S. DALLAS *Kettner's Bk. of Table* 154 The English child born in India has a nurse called a da'i. **1883** C. J. WILLS *In Land of Lion & Sun* xxix. 326 The 'dyah', or wet-nurse, is looked on as a second mother. **1920** *Outward Bound* Oct. 82/1 The doctor and her least dangerous *dai* (nurse) clambered into the waiting barouche. **1927** *Other Lands* Apr. 89/2 The indigenous dais are..absolutely ignorant.

dayerie, -ry, obs. forms of DAIRY.

dayesie, dayesegh, obs. forms of DAISY *sb.*

†**ˈday-fever.** *Obs.* A fever of a day's duration or coming on in the day-time; the sweating-sickness, *ephemera anglica pestilens* of old authors.

1601 HOLLAND *Pliny* II. 155 Those who vpon the Suns heat haue gotten the headach or a day-feuer. **1610** —— *Camden's Brit.* I. 24 That pestilent day-fever in Britaine, which commonly wee call the British or English swet.

ˈday-flower. A flower that opens by day; *spec.* in U.S. the genus *Commelyna* or Spiderwort.

1688 R. HOLME *Armoury* II. 99/2 The Virginian Spiderwort..may be called the Day Flower, for it opens in the day, and closes in the night. **1866** *Treas. Bot., Day-flower*, an American name for Commelyna.

ˈday-fly. An insect of the family *Ephemeridæ*, which in the imago or perfect state lives only a few hours or at most a few days; an ephemerid.

1601 HOLLAND *Pliny* I. 330 A foure footed flie..it liueth not aboue one day, whereupon it is called Hemerobion (*i.* a day-fly. *a* **1711** KEN *Preparatives* Poet. Wks. 1721 IV. 36 This Fly..Never lives longer than a single Day; 'Tis therefore styl'd a Day-Fly. **1860** GOSSE *Rom. Nat. Hist.* 15 The triple-tailed larvæ of dayflies creep in and out.

Day-Glo (ˈdeɪgləʊ). Also **day-glo, dayglo, dayglow**, etc. [f. DAY *sb.* + GLOW *sb.* or *v.*[1]]

1. A proprietary name for a make of fluorescent paint or other colouring matter; also (*transf.*) applied *attrib.* to the vivid colours characteristic of Day-Glo paints, as ***Day-Glo orange***, etc.

1951 *Trade Marks Jrnl.* 3 Oct. 917/1 Day-Glo B 698,104. Pigments and fluorescent coating materials (in the nature of paint). Dane & Co., Limited, 1 and 2, Sugar House Lane, Stratford, London, E.15; Manufacturers. **1952** *Official Gaz.* (U.S. Patent Office) 15 Jan. 662/1 Switzer Brothers Inc., Cleveland, Ohio... *Day-Glo*... For oil paints, water colors, [etc.]. **1963** *Punch* 19 June 884/2 Sailing ladies can wear.. day-glo vermilion jackets. **1968** *Sunday Times* 14 Apr. 15 The George Mitchell Choir, greasepaint and day-glo and soft-shoe, was hamming it up on the jetty. **1968** A. DIMENT *Bang Bang Birds* vii. 132, I walked down the narrow stairs, painted day-glo orange and decorated by crude paintings of Pop cult figures. **1969** *Listener* 24 Apr. 578/2 Sitting at home painting the trees with Dayglo. **1978** J. UPDIKE *Coup* (1979) iv. 169 He..came at last to a stairway. Day-Glo-orange arrows pointed down. **1984** J. ARCHER *First among Equals* (1985) ii. 21 Sitting on his own in the corner of a room decorated with wilting balloons and day-glo orange crêpe paper.

2. *attrib.* **a.** Chiefly of garments: made with a material which incorporates Day-Glo colouring; painted or marked with Day-Glo. Hence *loosely*, fluorescent.

1959 P. B. ABERCROMBIE *Little Difference* vi. 108 The day-glo socks of the innumerable little girls. **1967** *Bahamas Handbk. & Businessmen's Ann.* (ed. 7) 52 There was..an undisclosed number of cloth 'dayglo' markers in geometric shapes. **1976** *Punch* 11 Aug. 210/2 Through the near-impenetrable soup of brine there shone an irridescent dot, pinpointing the blundering shark by the day-glo vest it had snagged on its mighty dorsal fin. **1982** BARR & YORK *Official Sloane Ranger Handbk.* 130/1 You disappear..in a car trailing balloons and shoes, wreathed in squirts of synthetic day-glo spaghetti (the new confetti). **1986** A. CLAMPITT *What Light was Like* IV. 75 The lit night glares like a day-glo strawberry.

b. *fig.*

1968 *Listener* 19 Sept. 380/3 The energetic vulgarity of Jack Cardiff's filming—day-glow flashes for ecstasy and orgasm—has to be seen to be believed. **1974** A. LURIE *War between Tates* (1977) xvi. 347 Erica flops back..laughing with delight at Zed, whose arms and torso shine with a watery day-glo light.

day-house: see DEY-HOUSE.

†**ˈdaying**, *vbl. sb.* *Obs.* [f. DAY *v.*[2]] The action of the verb DAY, esp. arbitration, settlement of a dispute by 'daysmen'.

1484 *Churchw. Acc. St. Dunstan's, Canterb.*, Spent at the dayng betwene Baker and the paryshe. **1556** J. HEYWOOD *Spider & F.* K iv, To bie at a newe pryce Or bringe..To an vncertentie by douwtfull daying. *Ibid.* O iij, That we maie name our daisemen to this daiyng. **1565** JEWEL *Def. Apol.* (1611) 42 Our Doctrine hath bin approued too long, to be put a daying in these daies. **1598** R. BERNARD tr. *Terence, Andria* III. ii, If I doe obtaine her, why should I make any more daying for the matter? **1611** SPEED *Hist. Gt. Brit.* IX. viii. §16 Neither indeed did Philip thus put the matter to daying.

†**ˈdayish**, *a.* *Obs. rare.* [f. DAY *sb.* + -ISH.] Of or pertaining to day; diurnal.

1398 TREVISA *Barth. de P.R.* VIII. ix. (Tollem. MS.), Dayische signis [*diurna*; **1535** daye signes].

dayl, obs. form of DALE *sb.*[2]

day labour, ˈday-ˌlabour. Labour done as a daily task, or for daily wages; labour hired by the day.

c **1449** PECOCK *Repr.*, His dai labour. *c* **1655** MILTON *Sonn. Blindness*, 'Doth God exact day labour, light denied?' I fondly ask. **1659** B. HARRIS *Parival's Iron Age* 245 Such as escaped, fled into Holland, to save their unhappy lives by Day-labour. **1749** BERKELEY *Word to Wise* Wks. III. 446 By pure dint of day-labour, frugality, and foresight. **1793** SMEATON *Edystone L.* §101 An expence..as low, in regard to the value of day labour, as could..be expected. **1839** DE LA BECHE *Rep. Geol. Cornwall*, etc. xv. 569 Though in some mines day-labour is also used under ground. **1850–2** J. M. WILSON *Farmer's Dict.* I. 498/1 The same class of men who perform all kinds of drudgery and day-labour in large towns. **1908** W. ST. CLAIR BADDELEY *Cotteswold Shrine* 76 At the same hour ended his day-labours. **1911** *Rep. Labour & Soc. Cond. Germany* III. VI–VII. 207 Half the labour is piece and the other half is day labour.

ˌday-ˈlabourer. A labourer who is hired to work at a certain rate of wages per day; one who earns his living by day labour.

1548 *Act 2–3 Edw. VI*, c. 13 §7 Other than such as beene common day labourers. **1585** ABP. SANDYS *Serm.* (1841) 104 Should a king then..prefer a mean artificer or a day-labourer before himself? **1632** MILTON *L'Allegro* 109 His shadowy flail hath threshed the corn That ten day-labourers could not end. **1699** *Poor Man's Plea* 16 In the Southern parts of England, where a Day-labourer can gain 9*s.* per Week for his Labour. **1755** SMOLLETT *Quix.* (1803) IV. 43 It makes me sweat like a day-labourer. *a* **1853** ROBERTSON *Lect. Cor.* xxiii. (1878) 171 A nation may exist without an astronomer, or philosopher, but a day-labourer is essential to the existence of man.

So **ˈday-ˈlabouring** *ppl. a.*, that works for daily wages.

1739 CIBBER *Apol.* (1756) I. 313 The day-labouring actors. **1810** *Sporting Mag.* XXXV. 213 Simpson is a day-labouring man.

dayless (ˈdeɪlɪs), *a.* [f. DAY *sb.* + -LESS.]

†**1.** Without redress, resource, or result. *Obs.*

[? Having lost his day, or the day.]

c **1380** WYCLIF *Wks.* (1880) 92 þes vanytes wasten pore mennus goodis & suffren hem goo dailes whanne þei han nedis to pursue. *Ibid.* 129 Pore men schullen stonde with oute & goo dailes but ȝif þei geten knockis. **1387** TREVISA *Higden* (Rolls) V. 159 His enemy was bigiled and passed dayles [*in vanum*]. **1519** HORMAN *Vulg.* 247 b, He came ageyne dayless, or nothynge done [*re infecta rediit*].

2. Devoid of the light of day; dark.

1816 BYRON *Prisoner of Chillon* Sonnet, To fetters and the damp vault's dayless gloom. **1892** LD. LYTTON *King Poppy* Prol. 356 Gleaming thro' a dayless world.

3. Not divided into days.

1839 BAILEY *Festus* xix. (1848) 218 Deep in all dayless time, degreeless space.

daylight (ˈdeɪlaɪt).

1. a. The light of day. (Formerly also *day's light.*) †***to burn daylight***: see BURN *v.* 11 b.

a **1300** *Cursor M.* 6195 (Cott.) Drightin self þam ledd þair wai..Wit cluden piler on dai light. *Ibid.* 17344 þar he o naman suld ha sight, Ne nankins leme o dais light. *c* **1386** CHAUCER *Can. Yeom. Prol. & T.* 328 A bak to walke inne by day-light. **1484** CAXTON *Fables of Alfonse* (1889) 1 He had shame by daye lyȝt to go in to the hows of his Frend. **1592** SHAKS. *Rom. & Jul.* II. ii. 20 The brightnesse of her cheeke would shame those starres As day-light doth a Lampe. **1715** *Lond. Gaz.* No. 5283/2 We..resolved to pursue as long as we had Day-light. **1725** POPE *Odyss.* XVIII. 353 The day-light fades. **1862** DARWIN in *Life & Lett.* (1887) I. 187 His Lectures on Botany were..as clear as daylight.

b. *fig.* The full light of knowledge and observation; openness, publicity.

1690 LOCKE *Hum. Und.* IV. xiv. (1695) 374 God has set some things in broad Day-light; as he has given us some certain Knowledge. **1856** EMERSON *Eng. Traits, Character* (Wks. Bohn) II. 58 They are good at..any desperate service which has daylight and honour in it. **1892** *Law Times* 417/1 A healthy condition of such [jury] lists is not to be relied upon unless they are kept in plenty of daylight.

c. *to let daylight into* or *through*: to open up, make a hole in; to stab or shoot a person. *slang.*

1712 [SWIFT] *Law is a Bottomless-Pit* III, in *John Bull Still in his Senses* vi. 25 I'll warrant ye, you shall see Day-light through them. **1793** A. YOUNG *Example of France* (ed. 3) 172 In the language of the streets, day-light is let into him. **1841** *Punch* I. 101/2 (Farmer) With the..intention of letting day-light into the wittling department. **1890** *Illustr. Lond. News* Christm. No. 2/1 Some..sharpshooter will..let daylight into one of us. **1922** JOYCE *Ulysses* 322 The Molly Maguires looking for him to let daylight through him.

2. a. The time of daylight, the day-time; *spec.* the time when daylight appears, day-break, as in *before* or *at daylight.*

(In early use not clearly separable from 1.)

c **1205** LAY. 27337 þa þas ferde wes al idiht þa wes hit dai-light. *a* **1250** *Owl & Night.* 332 From eve fort hit is dai-liȝt. *c* **1400** *Ywaine & Gaw.* 233 Alsone als it was dayes lyght. *a* **1533** LD. BERNERS *Huon* lxvi. 228 To departe or it be day lyght. **1670** NARBOROUGH *Jrnl.* in *Acc. Sev. Late Voy.* I. (1694) 112 At Daylight the Wind was at South-West. **1836** MARRYAT *Midsh. Easy* xiv. 51 Mesty was up at daylight. **1885** E. ARNOLD *Secret of Death* 5 Ofttimes at daylight I would go To watch the sunlight flood the skies.

b. *Photography.* The period during which film can be 'taken' by natural light; *spec.* (see quot. 1940). Freq. *attrib.*, occurring or performed during daylight (see also 6).

1889 E. J. WALL *Dict. Photogr.* 61 Daylight enlarging. **1940** *Chambers's Techn. Dict.* 225/2 *Daylight*, the average colour of sky and sun at noon, corresponding to a colour temperature of 6500 K. **1940** F. J. MORTIMER *Wall's Dict. Photogr.* (ed. 15) 258 Daylight enlargers.

3. A clear visible space or interval: **a.** between boats, etc. in a race; **b.** between the rim of a wine-glass and the surface of the liquor, which must be filled up when a bumper is drunk; **c.** between a rider and the saddle, etc. *slang.*

1820 SHELLEY *Œdipus Tyr.* II. ii. 35 *All.* A toast! a toast! .. *Dakry.* No heel-taps—darken daylights! **1836** E. HOWARD *R. Reefer* xliv, No heel-taps after, and no day-light before. **1884** *Camb. Rev.* 10 Dec. 132 After about a quarter of a mile, daylight was visible between the two boats.

d. (See quots.)

1930 *Engineering* 3 Jan. 14/1 The 'daylight', i.e. the distance [*sc.* in a hydraulic press] between the faces of the vertical rams in their highest positions and the surface of the work table. **1968** *Gloss. Terms Mechanized & Hand Sheet Metal Work (B.S.I.)* 7 *Daylight.* 1. *On the press.* The distance between the bed of the press and the face of the slide with the press at the top of its stroke and with the adjustment up. 2. *On the die set.* The distance between the inner faces of the die set with the press slide at the bottom of its stroke. 3. *On the press tool.* The distance between the closest points of a press tool with the press fully open and the adjustment up.

4. *pl.* The eyes. Also in extended use of any vital organ. Also *to beat, scare*, etc., ***the (living) daylight(s) out of*** (a person), to beat, scare (a person) severely. *slang.*

1752 FIELDING *Amelia* I. x. (D.), If the lady says such another word to me..I will darken her daylights. **1821** *Blackw. Mag.* X. 586, I saw the storm..through my half-bunged-up daylights. **1848** E. BENNETT *Mike Fink* i. 10/1 We'll catch the fever and ager,..and that'll shake the day-lights out o' us. **1884** E. W. NYE *Baled Hay* 79 The driver bangs the mule, that is ostensibly pulling his daylights out. **1923** R. D. PAINE *Comr. Rolling Ocean* ii. 22 Putting seven of 'em in irons after they shot the daylights out of me left us mighty short-handed. **1944** E. CALDWELL *Tragic Ground* (1947) xiv. 163 If I could find a stick I'd grab it and beat the daylights out of you. **1951** E. TAYLOR *Game of Hide-and-Seek* II. i. 174 Though they scared the daylight out of me, I contempted them. **1955** F. YERBY *Treasure of Pleasant Valley* (1956) iii. 36 Didn't mean to hit him... Meant to throw close to him and scare the living daylights out of him. **1960** N. HILLIARD *Maori Girl* III. viii. 229 I'll go down there and belt the daylights out of him! **1960** R. RAE *Custard Boys* I. viii. 92 We'll get yer an' all the rest of yer gang, an' when we do we'll beat the living daylights out of yer. **1963** *N.Z. Listener* 13 Sept. 10/4, I hated him. He used to beat the daylight out of me. **1964** *Illustr. London News* 18 Jan. 102/3, I might have chuckled throughout 'The Suitor' if its chief actor did not happen to scare the living daylights out of me, as the current saying goes.

5. (See quot.)

1889 *Century Dict.*, *Daylight*, a name of the American spotted turbot, *Lophopsetta maculata*, a fish so thin as to be almost transparent. Also called *window-pane.*

6. *attrib.* and *Comb.*, as *daylight colour*, etc.; **daylight factor** (see quots.); †**daylight-gate**, the going or close of the day; **daylight-loading** *a.*, (of a film-spool, cartridge, etc.) adapted for loading by daylight without the use of a dark-room; **daylight robbery**: see ROBBERY 3; **daylight-saving**, a method of securing a longer period of daylight at the end of the day, viz. by putting the clock forward (e.g. an hour). Cf. SUMMER TIME 2.

1613 T. POTTS *Disc. Witches* (Chetham Soc.) B ij b, The sayd Spirit..appeared at sundry times unto her..about Daylight-gate. **1704** NEWTON *Opticks* (J.), Their own day-light colours. **1753** HOGARTH *Anal. Beauty* xii. 95 A day-light piece. **1842** G. S. FABER *Provinc. Lett.* (1844) II. 301 Through darkling suggestions rather than through day-light assertions. **1850** HT. MARTINEAU *Hist. Peace* II. 705 True to broad daylight English life. **1902** *Photographic Catal.*, Rollable daylight loading Films. **1908** *Hansard* 4th Ser. CLXXXIV. 155 Daylight Saving Bill... Mr. R. Pearce..in moving the Second Reading said that the object of the Bill was to promote the earlier use of daylight in the summer. **1915** *First Rep. Dep. Comm. on Lighting* (Cd. 8000) I. p. vi, The ratio of the actual value of the illumination to this enhanced value, expressed as a percentage, is termed the daylight factor, and is a measure of the lighting efficiency of the building at the point under consideration. **1916** *Hansard* 5th Ser. LXXXII. 321 The advocates of daylight saving are adept in securing the consent of one body of opinion on the ground that some other body has adopted it with enthusiasm. **1924** *Punch* 24 Sept. 338 Two more.. weeks of daylight-saving. **1930** *Engineering* 25 Apr. 550/1 'Daylight Factor', the ratio of the internal illumination to the illumination of a horizontal surface exposed to a hemisphere of sky. **1931** GALSWORTHY *Maid in Waiting* vi. 45 'Too early,' said Sir Lawrence, 'owing to Daylight Saving.' **1953** *Terms Illum. & Photometry (B.S.I.)* 14 *Daylight factor.* At a given point inside a building. The ratio of the illumination..at that point to that simultaneously existing..under an unobstructed sky. **1958** *Newnes Complete Amat. Photogr.* 257 Roll film tanks. There are two types: daylight loading and daylight developing.

Hence **'daylighter**, one of a body of men who sought to enforce the decrees of the Land League in Ireland by violence during the daytime; **'daylighty** *a.* (*nonce-wd.*), full of daylight, as a picture.

1880 W. SEVERN in *Macm. Mag.* No. 245. 379 A truthful simple Müller, or a daylighty Cox. **1886** *St. James's Gaz.* 25 Nov. 11/2 Seeing the 'Day-lighters' she ran into the room where she knew the gun to be and closed the door.

'daylighting, *vbl. sb.* [f. DAYLIGHT.]

1. (See DAYLIGHTER.)

1894 *Daily Tel.* 2 Apr., A case of 'daylighting' instead of moonlighting has been reported to the local police.

2. The process, degree, etc., of the illumination of buildings by daylight. Also *attrib.*

1937 *Archit. Rec.* Sept. 111/2 The problem of daylighting is therefore bound up with the problem of heating and it is ..desirable to orientate the house so as to obtain the best results for both. **1958** *House & Garden* Mar. 53/1 Lectures ..on..Daylighting and Architecture. **1959** *Guardian* 19 Dec. 2/4 A slab..200 feet high..would infringe daylighting rights in Denman Street. **1961** E. A. POWDRILL *Vocab. Land Planning* iii. 29 Daylighting standards have therefore been devised. *Ibid.* 32 It is not thought likely that the attainment of good sunlighting will normally demand a more generous spacing than daylighting.

'day-lily. A lily, the flower of which lasts only for a day; a genus of liliaceous plants, *Hemerocallis*, with large yellow or orange flowers.

1597 GERARDE *Herbal* I. lxxiii. (ed. 1633), *Day-lilie.* This plant bringeth forth in the morning his bud, which at noone is full blowne, or spred abroad, and the same day in the evening it shuts itselfe. **1706** J. GARDINER tr. *Rapin* (1728) I. 48 (Jod.) Thou..Shalt of daylily the fair name receive. **1882** *Garden* 3 June 391/3 Bouquets are of yellow Day Lily.

daylle, obs. north. form of DOLE.

daylong (ˈdeɪlɒŋ), *a.* and *adv.* [f. DAY *sb.* + LONG: cf. *life-long.*] **a.** *adj.* Lasting all day. **b.** *adv.* All through the day.

1855 TENNYSON *The Brook* 53 His weary daylong chirping. **1870** MORRIS *Earthly Par.* I. I. 187 He mounted.. And daylong rode on from the north. *Ibid.* III. IV. 195 As firm as rocks that stand The day-long beating of the sea.

dayly(e, obs. forms of DAILY, DALLY.

'day-mare. [After *night-mare.*] A condition similar to night-mare occurring during wakefulness. Also *attrib.*

1737 M. GREEN *Spleen* 39 The day-mare Spleen, by whose false pleas Men prove mere suicides in ease. **1796** COLERIDGE *Biog. Lit.* (1872) II. 744, I necessarily have day-mare dreams that something will prevent it. **1871** SIR T. WATSON *Princ. Physic* (ed. 5) I. 737 A lady..subject to these attacks of imperfect catalepsy: which have..been called whimsically, but expressively, attacks of day-mare. **1889** LOWELL in *Atlantic Monthly* LXIV. 147 Help me to tame these wild day-mares That sudden on me unawares.

†**day math, day's math.** *Obs.* A day's mowing; the extent of meadow-land mown by a man in one day; cf. DAY-WORK 2.

1669 *Will of R. Mayor* in *Lichfield Merc.* (1889) 23 Aug. 8/1 Alsoe all that parcell of meadow grounds, contayninge one acre or dayes math of ground for her naturall life. And after her deceyse, the above three acres or daye's workes of arrable land, and one day-math of meadow ground to my daughter, Ursula Mayor. **1804** DUNCUMB *Herefordsh.* I. Gloss. (App.), *Day's math*, is..about a statute acre; in other words, it is that quantity of grass usually mown by one man in one day, for the purpose of making hay. **1864** SIR F. PALGRAVE *Norm. & Eng.* IV. 61.

†**'dayment.** *Obs.* Also **daiment.** [f. DAY *v.*² + -MENT.] Arbitration.

1519 HORMAN *Vulg.* 204 b, Wylt thou be tryed by the lawe: or by dayment. **1562** J. HEYWOOD *Prov. & Epigr.* (1867) 207 Many arbitterments without good dayment. **1580** LUPTON *Sivqila* 117 To spende all..that money and put it to dayment at last.

†**dayn**, *v. Obs.* [By-form of DAWN, assimilated to *day.*] To dawn. So **'dayening** (in 3 *daiȝen-, daien-, dain-, daning*), dawning, dawn.

c **1250** *Gen. & Ex.* 77 Ðe daiȝening cam eft agon. *Ibid.* 1808 Til ðe daning. *Ibid.* 1810 Ðe daining. *Ibid.* 3264 Ðo sprong ðe daiening. **1515** *Scot. Field* 204 Sone after dayned the daie. *Ibid.* 422 Then dayned the daie.

dayn, -e, obs. forms of DEIGN.

dayn-: see DAIN-.

†**'day-net.** *Obs.* A net used by day in daring larks or in catching small birds; a clap-net.

1608 MACHIN *Dumb. Knt.* II, Madam, I would not have you with the lark Play yourself into a day net. **1621** BURTON *Anat. Mel.* Democr. to Rdr. (1676) 3/2 As Larks come down to a day net. **1661** BOYLE *Style of Script.* 27 Some he catches with light (as Larks with day-nets). **1766** PENNANT *Zool.* (1768) II. 330 These nets are known in most parts of England by the name of day-nets or clap-nets.

daynous, var. of DEIGNOUS *a. Obs.*

'day-owl. The diurnal or Hawk-owl, which seeks its prey in the day-time.

1840 MACGILLIVRAY *Hist. Brit. Birds* III. 404 *Syrnia Funerea*, the Hawk Day-owl. *Ibid.* 407 *Syrnia Nyctea*, the Snowy Day-owl.

'day-peep. Peep of day; earliest dawn.

[**1530** PALSGR. 804/1 At daye pype, *a la pipe du jour.*] **1606** *Wily Beguiled* in Hazl. *Dodsley* IX. 250 She'll run out o'nights a-dancing, and come no more home till day-peep. **1641** MILTON *Animadv.* xiii. (1851) 231 The honest Gardener, that ever since the day-peepe..had wrought painfully. **1828** SCOTT *F.M. Perth* v, Good night, or rather, good morrow, till day-peep.

†**'day-rawe, -rewe.** *Obs.* [f. DAY + *rawe, rewe*, ROW.] The first streak of day; the dawn.

c **1200** *Trin. Coll. Hom.* 255 Þu ateȝe so þe daiȝ rewe þe deleð from daiȝ þe deorke nicht. *c* **1275** [see DAY-RED] *c* **1325** *E.E. Allit. P.* B. 893 Ruddon of þe day-rawe ros vpon vȝten. *a* **1400-50** *Alexander* 392 Qwen þe day-raw rase he rysis be-lyfe.

†**'day-red.** *Obs.* The red of the break of day; the rosy dawn.

c **1000** *Ags. Gosp.* Luke xxiv. 1 On anum reste-dæȝe swyþe ær on dæȝered hiȝ comun to þære byrȝene. *c* **1275** *Doomsday* 17 in *O.E. Misc.* 162 (Cotton MS.) Þe engles in þe dai-red [*Jesus MS.* daye-rewe] bleweð heore beme.

dayri, -rie, -ry, obs. forms of DAIRY.

†**'day-rim.** *Obs.* In 1 -rima, 2–3 -rime. [f. DAY + RIM.] The 'rim' or border of the (coming) day; the dawn.

c **1000** in Thorpe's *Hom.* I. 442 (Bosw.) Hwæt is ðeos ðe astihþ swilce arisende dæȝrima? *c* **1050** *Voc.* in Wr.-Wülcker 175 *Aurora*, dæȝrima. *c* **1200** *Trin. Coll. Hom.* 167 Hwat is þis þe astihȝð alse dai rieme? *a* **1250** *Owl & Night.* 328 Wone ich i-so arise verre Other dai-rim other dai-sterre.

'day-rule. Formerly, 'A rule or order of court, permitting a prisoner in custody in the King's Bench prison, etc. to go without the bounds of his prison for one day' (Tomlins *Law Dict.*); also called *day-writ.*

c **1750** W. STROUD *Mem.* 37, I effected an Escape from the Tipstaff's Man, who had me out by a Day-rule. **1801** *Sporting Mag.* XVII. 139 An officer confined in the King's Bench for debt, and a gentleman in the same situation in Newgate, having each obtained a day-rule, met, and quarrelled. **1808** SYD. SMITH *Wks.* (1859) I. 127/1 Absenting themselves from their benefices by a kind of day-rule, like prisoners in the King's Bench. **1813** LAMB *Prol.* to Coleridge's *Remorse*, Could Quin come stalking from Elysian glades, Or Garrick get a day-rule from the shades.

'day-ˌscholar. A pupil who attends a boarding-school for daily instruction without boarding there; a day-boy (see DAY *sb.* 24).

1833 HT. MARTINEAU *Berkeley the Banker* I. i. 5 The four elder ones, therefore, between four and nine years old, became day-scholars only. **1851** MAYHEW *Lond. Labour* (ed. 2) I. 284 (Hoppe) He resumed his studies as a day-scholar at the Charterhouse.

'day-school. a. An elementary week-day school, as distinguished from a *Sunday school*; or one carried on in the day-time, as distinguished from an *evening* or *night school.* **b.** A school at which there is no provision for boarding pupils, as distinguished from a *boarding school.*

a **1785** in WALPOLE *Letters to Horace Mann* (F. Hall). **1816** J. HAIGH (*title*), A practical Treatise on Day Schools; exhibiting their defects, and suggesting Hints for their Improvement. **1838** in *Penny Cycl.* XXI. 41 *Headings*: Number of Children of Working Classes attending..Dame Schools and common Day Schools..Number Uneducated in Week-day Schools. *Ibid.* 42 Number Attending Day or evening schools only..Both day or evening and Sunday schools. **1841** *Ibid.* XXI. 42/1 They found many thousands who went to neither day nor Sunday schools. **1840** DICKENS *Old C. Shop* viii, She maintained a very small day-school for young ladies of proportionate dimensions. **1889** R. KIPLING *Willie Winkie* 39 It was decided that he should be sent to a day-school. *Mod.* (*title*) The Girls' Public Day-school Company.

dayse, obs. form of DAZE.

'day-sight. A visual defect in which the eyes see clearly only in the daylight.

1834 GOOD *Study Med.* (ed. 4) III. 147 Day-sight is said to be endemic in some parts of France. **1851-60** in MAYNE *Expos. Lex.*

daysman (ˈdeɪzmən). [f. DAY *sb.* + MAN. For sense 1, cf. DAY *v.*² 2, and DAYMENT.]

1. An umpire or arbitrator; a mediator. *arch.*

1489 *Plumpton Corr.* 82 Sir, the dayesmen cannot agre us. **1535** COVERDALE *Job* ix. 33 Nether is there eny dayes man to reproue both the partes, or to laye his honde betwixte us. **1573** *New Custom* I. ii. in Hazl. *Dodsley* III. 14 If neighbours were at variance, they ran not straight to law: Daysmen took up the matter, and cost them not a straw. **1621** BURTON *Anat. Mel.* Democr. to Rdr. (1657) 50 They had some common arbitrators, or dayesmen, in every towne, that made a friendly composition between man and man. **1681** W. ROBERTSON *Phraseol. Gen.* (1639) 427 A days man or umpire, *arbiter*. **1746-7** HERVEY *Medit.* (1818) 15 Death, like some able daysman, has laid his hand on the contending parties. **1844** MACAULAY *Barère* Misc. Wks. 1860 II. 128 Spurning out of their way the daysman who strives to take his stand between them.

2. A worker by the day; a day-labourer.

a **1639** WARD *Serm.* (1862) 105 (D.) He is a good day's-man, or journeyman, or tasker. **1706** PHILLIPS (ed. Kersey), *Days-man*, a Labourer that works by the Day, as a Thresher, Hedger, etc. **1750** ELLIS *Country Housew.* 16 (E.D.S.) A day's-man, as we call them in Hertfordshire. **1868** BUSHNELL *Serm. Living Subjects* 111 We..pile up what we think good acts on one another, as some day's man might the cents of his wages.

†3. *Obs. nonce-uses.* (See quots.)

1598 BACON *Sacred Medit.* (Arb.) 109 For we ought to be daies-men, and not to-morrowes men, considering the shortnesse of our time. **1658** ROWLAND *Moufet's Theat. Ins.* 951 We are in Pindars account but ἐπώμεροι, Daiesmen, i.e. of a daies continuance.

Hence †**'daysmanship**, the office of a daysman; reconciliation.

1649 LIGHTFOOT *Battle w. Wasp's Nest* Wks. 1825 I. 407 If you be so good a reconciler, I pray begin at home: the Evangelists need none of your day'smanship.

'day-spring. Daybreak, early dawn. Now chiefly *poet.* or *fig.*

c **1300** *K. Alis.* 4290 Day spryng is jolyf tide. **1382** WYCLIF *Job* xxxviii. 12 Whether..thou..hast shewid to the dai spring his place. **1526-34** TINDALE *Luke* i. 78 The daye springe from an hye hath visited vs. **1555** EDEN *Decades* 264 The day sprynge or dawnynge of the daye gyueth a certeyne lyght before the rysinge of the soonne. **1671** MILTON *Samson* 11 The breath of Heav'n fresh-blowing, pure and sweet, With day-spring born. **1791** COWPER *Iliad* I. 588 The day-spring's daughter rosy palm'd. **1837** HT. MARTINEAU *Soc. Amer.* II. 181 The driver declared that he must wait for the day-spring, before he could proceed another step. **1875** SCRIVENER *Lect. Text N. Test.* 4 The thousand years and more which separated the Council of Nice from the dayspring of the Reformation.

'day-star. Also 3 -stern, 5 -sterne, -starne.

1. The morning star.

c **1000** ÆLFRIC *Gen.* xxxii. 26 Nu gæð dæȝ steorra up. *c* **1000** *Sax. Leechd.* III. 270 Seo sunne & se mona & æfen steorra & dæȝ steorra. *a* **1250** [see DAY-RIM]. *a* **1300** *E.E. Psalter* cix. 3 Bifore dai-stern gat I þe. **14..** LYDG. *Temple of Glas* 1355 Fairest of sterres..o Venus..O myȝti goddes, daister after nyȝt. **1483** *Cath. Angl.* 89 A Day-sterne, *lucifer vel phosphoros.* **1576** FLEMING *Panopl. Epist.* 39 Early in the morning, so soone as the day starre appeared. **1845** R. W. HAMILTON *Pop. Educ.* vii. (ed. 2) 157 Such men are as day-stars, breaking the night and hastening the dawn.

2. The sun, as the orb of day. *poet.*

1598 SYLVESTER *Du Bartas* II. ii. *Babylon* 577 His Heav'n-tuned harp, which shall resound While the bright day-star rides his glorious Round. **1637** MILTON *Lycidas* 168 So sinks the day-star in the ocean bed, And yet anon repairs his drooping head, And tricks his beams. **1789** WORDSW. *Evening Walk* 190 Sunk to a curve, the day-star lessens still, Gives one bright glance, and drops behind the hill.

3. *fig.*

1382 WYCLIF *2 Pet.* i. 19 Til the day bigynne for to ȝiue liȝt, and the day sterre springe in ȝoure hertis. *c* **1460** *Towneley Myst.* 118 Haylle lytylle tyne mop [the infant Jesus] Of oure crede thou art crop: I wold drynk on thy cop, Lytylle day starne. **1500-20** DUNBAR *Ballat of our Lady* 26 Haile, bricht, be sicht, in hevyn on hicht! Haile, day sterne orientale! **1738** WESLEY *Hymns*, '*We lift our Hearts*' i, We lift our Hearts to Thee, O Day-Star from on High! **1876** BANCROFT *Hist. U.S.* III. xiii. 466 The day-star of the American Union.

†**day-sun.** *Obs.* The sun. *rhetorical* and *fig.*

1571 GOLDING *Calvin on Ps.* xlix. 15 The chosen..shall behold Christ the daysun. **1587** —— *De Mornay* ix. 115 God ..commaunded the daysunne to be, and it was don. **1577** *Test 12 Patriarchs* (1604) 76 The day-sun of righteousness.

day's-work ('deɪzwɜːk). (Also written as two words.) **a.** The work of a day, work done on or proper to a day. Also = DAYWORK 2 (*obs.*).

1594 SHAKS. *Rich. III*, II. i. 1 Now haue I done a good daies work. **1610** W. FOLKINGHAM *Art of Survey* II. vii. 59 Foure square Pearches make a Daiesworke, 10 Daie-workes a Roode. **1640** G. H. *Witt's Recreations* H ij a, Your dayes work's done, each morning as you rise. *c* **1836** GEN. P. THOMPSON *Exerc.* (1842) IV. 395 Paying him for more day's works. *c* **1850** *Rudim. Navig.* (Weale) 10 The logboard, the contents of which are termed 'the log',—the working it off, 'the day's work'.

b. *all in the day's work*, something unusual but nevertheless taken as part of one's ordinary duty or routine. Freq. ironical.

[**1738** SWIFT *Polite Conv.* i. 39 Will you be so kind to tie this *String* for me..? it will go all in your Day's Work.] **1820** SCOTT *Monastery* I. ix. 248 That will cost me a farther ride, ..but it is all in the day's work. **1857** KINGSLEY *Two Y. Ago* III. iii. 91 All in the day's work, my boy. **1897** [see WORK *sb.* 33]. **1939** *War Illustr.* 220/2 He is not deeply impressed by his experience. 'It is all in the day's work' were his parting words to me. **1953** A. CHRISTIE *Pocket full of Rye* x. 60 This sort of thing seems ordinary enough to you, Inspector. All in the day's work.

day-tale, daytal, datal ('deɪteɪl, 'deɪtəl, 'deɪt(ə)l). [f. DAY + TALE reckoning, etc. In sense 1 parallel to *nighter-tale* in Chaucer, etc., where the sense 'reckoning' appears to pass into that of 'the time counted or reckoned' (to night or to day). There appears to be no direct connexion between this and sense 2.]

†1. Day-time. *a daye tale*: by day. *Obs.*

1530 PALSGR. 699/2 A daye tale he scoulketh in corners and a nyghtes he gothe a thevyng.

2. The reckoning (of work, wages, etc.) by the day. Chiefly *attrib.*, reckoned, paid, or engaged by the day, as in ***day-tale hand, labour, wages, work***, etc.; ***day-tale man***, a day-labourer; ***day-tale pace***, 'a slow pace' (Halliw.).

1560 *Summ. Certain Reasons* in *Harl. Misc.* (Malh.) II. 478 Men that tooke dayetall wages. **1641** BEST *Farm. Bks.* (Surtees) 45 It shall bee accounted but for halfe a day with those that worke with yow by daytaile. **1761** STERNE *Tr. Shandy* (1770) III. 143 (D.) Holla! you chairman, here's sixpence; do step into that bookseller's shop, and call me a day-tall critick. **1770** *Holmesfield Crt. Rolls* in *Sheffield Gloss.* Addenda, Being daytall-man to Mathias Webster. **1788** W. MARSHALL *Yorksh.* Gloss. (E.D.S.), *Daitle* (that) (that is, *day-tale*), *adj.* by the day; as, 'daitle-man', a day-labourer; 'daitle-work', work done by the day. **1855** ROBINSON *Whitby Gloss.*, *Daytal*, tale or reckoning by the day. **1888** *W. Somerset Word-bk.*, *Day-tale fellow*, *Day-tale man*, a labourer hired by the day. Hence a term of reproach, meaning a lazy, slack workman whose only care is to have his wages, and to do as little as he can to earn them. **1892** *Labour Commission* Gloss., *Datal hands*, hands employed in cotton-mills at a fixed rate per week of $56\frac{1}{2}$ hours.

day-taler, dataller ('deɪtələ(r)). *local.* [f. prec. + -ER[1].] A day-labourer, a workman engaged and paid by the day.

1875 *Lanc. Gloss.*, *Dataller* (S. Lanc.), *Daytal-labourer* (Furness), a day labourer. **1881** *Manch. Guardian* 29 Jan. 7/7 Hurst, dataller at Wharton Hall Collieries. **1886** *Engineer* 13 Aug. 138/1 The wages were paid to datallers for packing and putting the roads in repair.

'day-time. The time of daylight.

1535 COVERDALE *Ps.* xxi[i]. 2, I crie in the daye tyme..and in the night season. *a* **1626** BACON *Ess. Fame* (Arb.) 579 In the day time she sittith in a Watch Tower, and flyeth, most, by night. **1782** PRIESTLEY *Corrupt. Chr.* II. VI. 18 Lights in the day-time were usual. **1856** KANE *Arct. Expl.* II. ix. 95 Implying that I never sleep o' daytimes.

daytimes ('deɪtaɪmz), *adv. U.S.* [f. DAYTIME + advb. suff. *-s.*] In the daytime, during the day.

1854 M. S. CUMMINS *Lamplighter* xvii, Willie was very busy daytimes, but was always with them in the evening. **1936** L. C. DOUGLAS *White Banners* viii. 187 Her bed, daytimes, was strewn with illustrated magazines.

day-woman, dairy-woman: see DEY-.

'daywork, day-work. [Cf. also DARG.]

†1. The work of a day; = DAY'S WORK. *Obs.* or *north. dial.*

a **1000** *Cædmon's Exod.* 151 (Gr.) þæt he þæt dæȝweorc dreore ȝebohte. *c* **1425** WYNTOUN *Cron.* VIII. xvi. 224 Na man..evyr herd, or saw befor..A Daywerk to þat Daywerk lyk. **1535** COVERDALE *1 Chron.* xvii. [xvi.] 37 Euery daye his daye worke. **1832** *Specimens Yorkshire Dialect*, Monny a daywark we ha' wrought togither.

†2. The amount of land that could be worked (ploughed, mown, etc.) in a day. *Obs.*

[*c* **1270** *Merton Coll. Rec.* No. 1257 (Essex) Sex Day-wercatas terrae meae.] **1318-19** *MS.* (Sotheby's Sale Catal. 7 Apr. (1892) 22), Grant from Richard de Twysdenne..of a Garden of 13 Dayworks of Land in Gudhurst. **1492** *Will of Reede* (Somerset Ho.), xj day werkes of land. **1534** *Inv. Sir L. Bagot* in *Lichfield Merc.* (1889) 23 Aug. 8/1, xxviij day-warke of pea..xij daye-warke of barley..xxiiij daye-warke of whet. **1641** BEST *Farm Bks.* (Surtees) 38 The South Wandell close, with its bottomes, is 8 dayworkes, or will serve one mower 8 dayes.

3. Work done by the day and paid by daily wages; day labour.

1580 NORTH *Plutarch* (1676) 950 With Masons that had their day-work. **1702** *Lond. Gaz.* No. 3786/4 Committed by one who does Day-work in Deptford and Woolwich Yards. **1751** LABELYE *Westm. Br.* 79 All the workmanship..being suffered to be done by Day-Work. **1851** *Ord. & Regul. R. Engineers* §16. 64 To state the weekly delivery of Materials and performance of Day-work.

†**'day-writ.** *Obs.* = DAY-RULE.

1809 TOMLINS *Law Dict.* s.v., It is against law to grant liberty to prisoners in execution by other writs than day writs (or rules).

daze (deɪz), *v.* Forms: 4-6 dase, (5 dayse, 6-9 daise), 6- daze. [ME. *dase-n*, a. ON. **dasa*, found in Icel. in the refl. *dasa-sk* to become weary and exhausted, *e.g.* from cold, Sw. *dasa* intr. to lie idle; cf. Icel. *dasi* a lazy fellow. Sense 3 was possibly the earliest in Eng. No cognate words appear in the other Teutonic langs.]

I. *trans.* 1. To prostrate the mental faculties of (a person), as by a blow on the head, a violent shock, weariness, intoxicating drink, etc.; to benumb or confuse the senses; to stun, stupefy.

c **1325** [see DAZED 1]. *a* **1400-50** *Alexander* 3997 He was dased of þe dint & half dede him semyd. *c* **1400** *Destr. Troy* 7654 The deire of his dynt dasit hym but litle. *a* **1563** BALE *Sel. Wks.* (Parker Soc.) 443 These things daseth their wits, and amazeth their minds. **1590** SPENSER *F.Q.* III. vii. 7 But shewd by outward signes that dread her sence did daze. **1669** DRYDEN *Tyrannic Love* IV. ii, Poor human kind, all dazed in open day, Err after bliss, and blindly miss their way. **1825** JAMIESON *s.v.*, He daises himself with drink. **1848** MRS. GASKELL *M. Barton* xxiii, Jane Wilton was (to use her own word, so expressive to a Lancashire ear) 'dazed'. **1877** MRS. OLIPHANT *Makers Flor.* i. 26 A man dazed and bewildered by such a calamity.

2. *esp.* To confound or bewilder (the vision) with excess of light or brilliance; to dazzle. *lit.* and *fig.*

a **1529** SKELTON *Ph. Sparowe* 1103 She made me sore amased Vpon her when I gased..My eyne were so dased. **1570** B. GOOGE *Pop. Kingd.* I. (1880) 11 They are but trumprye and deceytes, to daze the foolish eies. **1631** HEYWOOD *Fair Maid of West* II. I. Wks. 1874 II. 352 To daze all eyes that shall behold her state. **1847** TENNYSON *Princ.* V. 11 The sudden light Dazed me half-blind. **1864** SKEAT *Uhland's Poems* 152 Shall earthly splendour that strong eyesight daze?

3. To benumb with cold; to blight or destroy with cold. *north. Eng.* and *Sc.*

1340 HAMPOLE *Pr. Consc.* 6647 For-þi þat þai..Brynned ay here in þe calde of malice, And ay was dased in charité. **1513** DOUGLAS *Æneis* VII. Prol. 88 The callour air..Dasing the blude in euery creature. **1696** *Money masters all Things* lxx. 52 They [birds] stay not too long off, lest th' Eggs be daz'd. **1876** *Mid-Yorkshire Gloss.*, *Dêaze*, to blight, or cause to pine from cold, as when vegetables are frost-nipped, or chickens die in the shell for want of warmth. **1891** ATKINSON *Moorland* 336 He assumed that it [a water rail] was dazed with cold.

II. *intr.* †4. To be or become stupefied or bewildered; to be benumbed with cold; to remain inactive or torpid. *Obs.*

c **1325** *E.E. Allit. P.* C. 383 þer he [the king of Nineveh] dased in þat duste, with droppande teres. *c* **1460** *Towneley Myst.* 28, I dase and I dedir For ferd of that taylle. **14..** *Kyng & Hermit* 418 in Hazl. *E.P.P.* I. 29 Hopys thou, I wold for a mase Stond in the myre there, and dase Nye hand halve a dey? **1483** *Cath. Angl.* 90 To Dayse (A. Dase), *vbi* to be callde. **1529** MORE *Supplic. Soulys* Wks. 331/2 Whan his head first began to dase, of that evill drynke.

†5. Of the eyes or vision: To be or become dazzled. *Obs.*

c **1386** [see DASWEN]. **1529** MORE *Dyaloge* IV. Wks. 252/1 Which law if it were laied in their light..wold make al theyr eyen dase. **1635** QUARLES *Embl.* III. i. (1718) 125 Whose more than Eagle-eyes Can..gaze On glitt'ring beams of honour, and not daze.

†**b.** To gaze stupidly or with bewildered vision (*after, upon*). *Obs.*

1523 SKELTON *Garl. Laurel* 641, I saw dyvers..Dasyng after dottrellis. **1535** COVERDALE *Deut.* xxviii. 32 Thine eyes shal dase vpon them all the daye longe.

6. Of bread or meat: To become DAZED (sense 3). Now *local.*

1769 MRS. RAFFALD *Eng. Housekpr.* (1778) 54 Observe always to have a brisk clear fire, it will prevent your meat from dazing.

7. 'To wither; to become rotten or spoiled, from keeping, dampness, etc.' (Jamieson). *Sc.* and *north. Eng.*

daze (deɪz), *sb.* [f. DAZE *v.*]

1. A dazed condition: **a.** of the mental faculties; **b.** A benumbed, deadened condition; loss of virtue or freshness (*north. dial.*).

1825 JAMIESON, *To get a daise*, to receive such injury as to become rotten or spoiled, applied to clothes, wood, etc. **1855** MRS. GASKELL *North & S.* xix, I'm all in a swounding daze to day. **1870** DICKENS *E. Drood* ii, A little time and a little water brought him out of his daze.

2. *Min.* An old name for mica (from its glitter).

1671 *Phil. Trans.* VI. 2103 *Daze* is a kind of glittering stone..some softer, some harder, of different colours. **1715** THORESBY *Leeds* 467 A brown daze, full of the small sparks of the Mica. **1753** CHAMBERS *Cycl. Supp.*, The word *Daze* takes in, with them [miners] every stone that is hard and glittering. **1788** *Cronstedt's Min.* 106 Glimmer, Daze, or Glist.

dazed (deɪzd), *ppl. a.* [f. DAZE *v.* + -ED. Cf. ON. *dasað* exhausted.]

1. Benumbed in the mental faculties; stupefied, bewildered.

c **1325** *E.E. Allit. P.* A. 1084, I stod as stylle as dased quayle. *c* **1425** WYNTOUN *Cron.* VI. iv. 56 He wes þan In hys Deyd bot a dasyd man. *c* **1440** *Promp. Parv.* 114 Dasyd, or be-dasyd, *vertiginosus.* **1501** DOUGLAS *Pal. Hon.* I. xxvi, My daisit heid fordullit disselie. **1587** TURBERV. *Trag. T., etc.* (1837) 317 It wil delight my dazed sprites. **1789** BURNS *2nd Ep. to Davie* iv, Whyles daez't wi' love, whyles daez't wi' drink. **1866** G. MACDONALD *Ann. Q. Neighb.* xxii. (1878) 408 She looked dazed, perhaps from the effects of her fall.

b. Dazzled with excess of light.

1581 MARBECK *Bk. of Notes* 153 If for a while you fixe your sight thereon, dimnesse & darknesse doe follow your dazed eies. **1590** SPENSER *F.Q.* I. viii. 21 As where th' Almighties lightning brond does light, It dimmes the dazed eyen. **1870** MORRIS *Earthly Par.* I. II. 512 His troubled eyes and dazed He lifted from the glory of that gold.

2. Benumbed or deadened with cold. *north.*

1513 DOUGLAS *Æneis* V. vii. 58 The dasyt bluid..Walxis dolf and dull throw myne unweildy age. **1674** RAY *N.C. Words* 14 *I'ze dazed*, I am very cold. **1811** WILLAN *W. Riding Gloss.*, *Dazed*..benumbed with frost. **1873** *Swaledale Gloss.*, *Dazzed*, chilled.

3. Spoiled in baking or roasting, by using a too strong or too slow heat. *north. dial.*

1674 RAY *N.C. Words*, *Dazed Bread*, dough-baked. *Dazed Meat*, ill roasted by reason of the badness of the fire. **1855** ROBINSON *Whitby Gloss.*, *A deazed loaf*, the dough or paste ill baked, or when the leaven or yeast has failed in its work. **1876** *Mid-Yorkshire Gloss.*, *Dêazed* bread is overbaked outwardly, and not enough baked within.

4. Applied to anything that has lost its freshness and strength, as to wood when it loses its proper colour and texture. *Sc.* and *north. Eng.*

1825 JAMIESON, *Daised wud*, rotten wood. 1892 *Specification* (Durham), No dazed wood to be used.

dazedly ('deɪzɪdlɪ), *adv.* [-LY².] In a dazed way or manner; †inertly, torpidly (as from cold).

13.. [see DAZEDNESS]. 1886 MISS BROUGHTON *Dr. Cupid* III. iv. 90 An idea dazedly flashes across her brain. 1888 *Chamb. Jrnl.* July 462 They looked dazedly at the judge.

'dazedness. [-NESS.] Dazed condition; †the state of being numbed or deadened with cold.

1340 HAMPOLE *Pr. Consc.* 4906 Thurgh fire þat sal swa brinnand be, Agayn þe dasednes [*MS. Lansd.* coldnes] of charite. 13.. *MS. Tib.* E. vii. fol. 24 Dasednes of hert als clerkes pruves Es when a man god dasedly loves, And slawly his luf in god settes. 1817 *Blackw. Mag.* I. 577 What Dan [Chaucer] calls the dasedness of study.

dazel, -ell, -ile, obs. forms of DAZZLE.

dazement ('deɪzmənt). *rare.* [mod. f. DAZE *v.* + -MENT.] The state of being dazed.

1855 ROBINSON *Whitby Gloss.*, *Deeazement*, a sensation of cold all over the body from checked perspiration. 1873 L. WALLACE *Fair God* VII. iv. 457 The king relapsed into his dazement.

dazie, dazied, obs. forms of DAISY *sb.*, -IED.

†**'daziness.** *Obs. rare*⁻¹. [See DAZY *a.* and -NESS.] Dazedness, dizziness.

1554 KNOX *Godly Let.* D iij, Oftentymes theyr posteritie are stryken with blindenes and dasynes of mynde.

dazing ('deɪzɪŋ), *vbl. sb.* [-ING¹.] The action of the verb DAZE; benumbing, stupefaction, as a condition or influence.

a 1535 MORE *De quat. Noviss.* Wks. 101 When the dasyng of death, shall kepe al swete slepe oute of their waterye eyes. 1535 COVERDALE *Deut.* xxviii. 65 The Lorde shal geue the there a fearfull hert and dasynge of eyes. 1577 B. GOOGE *Heresbach's Husb.* IV. (1586) 191 It helpeth against the dasing, or giddinesse of the heade. 1877 *Holderness Gloss.*, *Deeazins*, a severe cold, especially in the head.

†**b.** A disease of sheep; = DAZY *sb. Obs.*

1799 *Ess. Highl. Soc.* III. 404 (Jam.) *Daising* or *Vanquish*. This disease..is..most severe upon young sheep.

'dazing, *ppl. a.* [-ING².] That dazes; †that is dazed.

c 1325 *E.E. Allit. P.* B. 1538 Such a dasande drede dusched to his hert. 1531 FRITH *Judgment upon Tracy* Pref. (1829) 245 Whether of a godly zeal, or of a dasing brain, let other men judge.

dazle, obs. form of DAZZLE.

dazy ('deɪzɪ), *a. rare.* [f. DAZE *v.* or *sb.* + -Y.] **a.** In a dazed condition. **b.** Chill, chilling, benuming with cold (*dial.*).

1825 JAMIESON s.v., *A daisie day*, a cold raw day, without sunshine. 1880 BLACKMORE *Erema* vi. 30 With..a head still weak and dazy.

†**'dazy,** *sb. Obs. rare*⁻¹. [f. DAZE *v.* or from prec. adj.] The 'gid' or 'sturdy', a disease of sheep and young cattle.

1577 B. GOOGE *Heresbach's Husb.* (1586) 134 If your Bullocke turne round, and have the Dasye, you shal..feele upon his forehead; and you shall feele it with your thumbe.

dazzle ('dæz(ə)l), *v.* Forms: 5-7 dasel(l, 6 dasill, -yll, dazile, dassel(l, 6-7 dazel(l, dasle, 6-8 dazle, (7 daisle), 6- dazzle. [In 15-16th c. *dasel, dasle*, freq. and dim. of *dase*, DAZE *v.* (esp. in sense 2).]

†**1.** *intr.* Of the eyes: To lose the faculty of distinct and steady vision, *esp.* from gazing at too bright light. (*lit.* and *fig.*) *Obs.*

1481 CAXTON *Reynard* (Arb.) 96 Parauenture his eyen daselyd as he loked from aboue doun. 1530 PALSGR. 507/1, I dasyll, as ones eyes do for lokyng agaynst the sonne or for eyeng any thyng to moche, etc. 1581 G. PETTIE tr. *Guazzo's Civ. Conv.* III. (1586) 156 b, Her eyes dazell with the least beame thereof [the Sunne]. 1588 SHAKS. *Tit. A.* III. ii. 85. 1621 FLETCHER *Pilgrim* v. vi, *Ped.* Ha? doe I dazell? *Rod.* Tis the faire Alinda. 1672 MARVELL *Reh. Transp.* I. 64 His Eyes dazled at the Precipice of his Stature.

†**2.** To be or become mentally confused or stupefied; to become dizzy. *Obs.*

1571 GOLDING *Calvin on Ps.* xxxiii. 5 How shamefully the most part of the world dazeleth at Gods righteousnesse. 1621 BURTON *Anat. Mel.* I. ii. III. ii. (1651) 95 Many.. tremble at such sights, dazel, and are sick, if they look but down from an high place.

3. *trans.* To overpower, confuse, or dim (the vision), *esp.* with excess of brightness. (Also *fig.*)

1536 STARKEY *Let. to Cromwell* in *England* (1878) p. xliii, Wyth a clere ye [= eye] not dasyllyd wyth the glyteryng of such thyngys as are present. 1563 *Mirr. Mag.*, *Jane Shore* xiii, Doth not the sonne dasill the clearest eyes? 1626 BACON *Sylva* §276 If you come.. out of the Dark into a Glaring Light, the eye is dazeled for a time. *a* 1640 J. BALL *Answ. to Can* i. (1642) 88 You doe only raise a dust to daisle the eye. 1761 HUME *Hist. Eng.* II. xxviii. 135 He tried to dazzle the eyes of the populace by the splendour of his equipage. 1857 MRS. CARLYLE *Lett.* II. 334 The gas-light, which dazzles my eyes.

absol. 1752 JOHNSON *Rambler* No. 207 ¶12 Light after a time ceases to dazzle.

4. *fig.* To overpower or confound (the mental faculties), *esp.* with brilliant or showy qualities; 'to strike or surprise with splendour' (J.).

1561 T. NORTON *Calvin's Inst.* I. xiv. 43 The excellence of the nature of Angels hath so dasellled the mindes of many. 1622 E. ELTON *Compl. Sanct. Sinner* (ed. 2) 94 Their vnruly passions..dazeling and dimming their iudgements. 1643 J. M. *Soveraigne Salve* Pref., Rhetorick may dazle simple men. 1711 ADDISON *Spect.* No. 112 ¶8 The ordinary People; who are so used to be dazzled with Riches. 1880 L. STEPHEN *Pope* iv. 97 Pope seems to have been dazzled by the amazing vivacity of the man.

b. *absol.*

1649 MILTON *Eikon.* xii. (1851) 434 If the whole Irishry of Rebels had feed some advocate to speak..sophistically in their defence, he could have hardly dazl'd better. 1764 GOLDSM. *Trav.* 336 Thine are those charms that dazzle and endear. 1879 M. ARNOLD *Fr. Critic on Milton* Mixed Ess. 238 A style to dazzle, to gain admirers everywhere.

5. To outshine, dim, or eclipse with a brighter light. Const. †*down, out. rare.*

1643 BURROUGHES *Exp. Hosea* v. (1652) 243 They can see ..into the beauty of his wayes, so that it dazeleth all the glory of the world in their eies. 1647 WARD *Simp. Cobler* 60 It hath not ray's enough left, to dazle downe the height of my affections. 1858 HAWTHORNE *Fr. & It. Jrnls.* (1872) I. 47 This church was dazzled out of sight by the Cathedral.

6. *trans.* To camouflage (a ship) by painting large patches of colour on it (cf. DAZZLE *sb.* 3).

1920 *Glasgow Herald* 12 Mar. 7 A number of lantern slides were shown of ships 'dazzled' during the war.

dazzle ('dæz(ə)l), *sb.* [f. prec.]

†**1.** Dazzled state or condition. *Obs.*

1627-77 FELTHAM *Resolves* I. xxvii. 47 We meet with nothing but the puzzle of the soul, and the dazle of the minds dim eyes.

2. a. An act of dazzling; a brightness or glitter that dazzles the vision.

1651 N. BACON *Disc. Govt.* II. xl. (1739) 177 This was but a dazzle, an Eclipse ensues. 1751 PALTOCK *P. Wilkins* (1884) I. xiv. 144, I could see the lake very well by the dazzle of the water. 1821 LOCKHART *Valerius* I. iv. 46 Fatigued with the uniform flash and dazzle of the Mediterranean waves. 1890 *Spectator* 13 Sept., One is taking precautions to avoid a draught or a dazzle.

b. *fig.*

1654 WHITLOCK *Zootomia* 338 Through whose red and white..the Glory of the Maker shineth with more Dazle than through any part of the Creation. 1846 RUSKIN *Mod. Paint.* I. I. I. i. §5 Amidst the tumult and the dazzle of their busy life.

3. The painting of large patches of colour on warships, etc., as camouflage in time of war. Also *Comb.* in ***dazzle-paint, -painted, -painting, -pattern.*** Also *transf.*

1917 *Admiralty Order* 2 July (MS.), The 'Dazzle' painting of a ship with large patches of strong colour in a carefully thought-out pattern and colour scheme. 1919 *Times* 29 May 8/1 'Dazzle', to use the term employed by the camouflage department of the Admiralty. *Ibid.* 5 June 10/2 A 'dazzle' painted ship is on the whole more visible against sky and sea than the usual grey vessel, and this was its chief disadvantage. Furthermore, 'dazzle' painting was designed for short range, at which it is impossible to conceal a vessel against its background. 1919 *Ibid.* 9 June 6/4 Dazzle painting was never intended for use on 'ships of the line', but only for merchantmen..and war vessels working with them. 1919 *Athenæum* 11 July 583/2 The other service [*sc.* the Navy] invented 'dazzle'. 1920 *Blackw. Mag.* Oct. 94/2 A geological 'dazzle-painting' in ochre and red, brown, purple, and buff. 1921 W. STEVENS *Let.* 5 Dec. (1967) 223 From time immemorial the philosophers and other scene painters have daubed the sky with dazzle paint. 1922 *Glasgow Herald* 28 Apr. 9 A 'tramp' steamer, 'dazzle' painted. 1928 C. F. S. GAMBLE *North Sea Air Station* xxii. 400 It was decided that all flying-boats should have their hulls 'dazzle-painted'. 1932 KIPLING *Limits & Renewals* 309 Then, area by area, she [*sc.* a sow] was painted with dazzle-patterns of greenish-yellow and purple-brown. 1948 C. DAY LEWIS *Otterbury Incident* i. 9 The superstructure was made of wood, and we'd dazzle-painted the sides.

4. *attrib.* Designating shoes, etc., in very bright or luminous colours.

1931 *Star* 8 May 7/4 Although the majority of women seem to prefer shoes with just two colours to match their frocks, 'dazzle' footwear are a good second. 1958 *Economist* 11 Jan. 94/1 Girls in tight jeans and dazzle socks. 1958 J. TOWNSEND *Young Devils* i. 11 The boy..his yellow dazzle socks flashing like twin beacons.

dazzled ('dæz(ə)ld), *ppl. a.* [f. DAZZLE *v.*]

1. Overpowered or confounded by too strong light or splendour.

1581 J. BELL. *Haddon's Answ. Osor.* 499 So forcible is the dazeled blindenes of selfe Love. *a* 1628 F. GREVILLE *Sidney* (1652) 89 [He] cleareth the daseled eyes of that army. *a* 1628 —— *Poems, Hum. Learning* xvi, Those dazled notions.. Which our fraile understanding doth retaine. 1811 WORDSW. *Sonn. 'Here pause, etc.'*, An accursed thing it is to gaze On prosperous tyrants with a dazzled eye. 1856 R. A. VAUGHAN *Mystics* (1860) II. IX. ii. 131 This indistinct and dazzled apprehension.

2. Outshone or dimmed by a stronger light.

1576 FLEMING *Panopl. Epist.* 292 As the bright beames of the Sunne passe the dimme and dazeled light of the Moone. 1833 TENNYSON *Fatima* iv, My spirit.. Faints like a dazzled morning moon.

dazzlement ('dæz(ə)lmənt). [-MENT.]

1. The act of dazzling; a cause of dazzling.

1633 J. DONE *Hist. Septuagint* 55 (T.) It beat back the sight with a dazzlement. 1837 CARLYLE *Fr. Rev.* I. II. vi, Confused darkness, broken by bewildering dazzlements. 1881 STEVENSON *Virg. Puerisque* 289 Many holes, drilled in the conical turret-roof of this vagabond Pharos, let up spouts of dazzlement into the bearer's eyes.

2. The fact or condition of being dazzled.

1840 CARLYLE *Heroes* v. (1858) 324 The blinkard dazzlement and staggerings to and fro of a man sent on an errand he is too weak for.

†**'dazzleness.** *Obs. rare*⁻¹. [app. for *dazzledness.*] Dazzled condition.

1581 J. BELL *Haddon's Answ. Osor.* 315 Overwhelmed with a perpetuall dazellnes of sight.

dazzler ('dæzlə(r)). [-ER.]

1. One who dazzles: said *e.g.* of a 'showy' woman. Chiefly *slang* or *colloq.*

a 1800 COWPER tr. *Andreini's Adam* v. ix. Wks. 1837 X. 383 Thou Lord immutable.. Thou dazzler and obscurer of the sun! 1838 DICKENS *Nich. Nick.* xxxvi, Mr. Lumbey shook his head with great solemnity, as though to imply that he supposed she must have been rather a dazzler. 1889 *Columbus (Ohio) Dispatch* 27 Sept., [He] appears to be one of these dazzlers. He succeeded in dazzling two of the jury.

2. A dazzling blow. *slang.*

1883 READE *Many a Slip* in *Harper's Mag.* Dec. 132/1 The carter..received a dazzler with the left, followed by a heavy right-hander.

'dazzling, *vbl. sb.* [-ING¹.] The action of the verb DAZZLE; the condition of being dazzled.

1579 LANGHAM *Gard. Health* (1633) 672 To take away all giddinesse and dasling of the head. 1581 PETTIE *Guazzo's Civ. Conv.* II. (1586) 95 If your eies bee able to beholde it without dazeling.

dazzling ('dæzlɪŋ), *ppl. a.* [-ING².]

†**1.** That is, or becomes, dazzled or dazed. (See DAZZLE *v.* 1, 2.) *Obs.*

1571 GOLDING *Calvin on Ps.* lxviii. 4 His hoarce throt and dazeling eyes. *a* 1592 GREENE *Alphonsus* (1861) 227 Do my dazzling eyes Deceive me? 1641 MILTON *Reform.* II. (1851) 67 Unlesse God have smitten us..with a dazling giddinesse at noon day. 1654 H. L'ESTRANGE *Chas. I* (1655) 3 This unexpected proposall put his Catholique majesty into such a dazling demur.

2. That dazzles the eyes (*esp.* with brightness); bright to a degree that dazzles.

1581 J. BELL *Haddon's Answ. Osor.* 216 b, Drivyng away the dazelyng darkenes of the ugly night. 1667 MILTON *P.L.* I. 564 A horrid Front Of dreadful length and dazling Arms. 1791 COWPER *Odyss.* XXIV. 246 Clad in dazzling brass. 1841 BORROW *Zincali* I. ix. I. 155 In hot countries, where the sun and moon are particularly dazzling.

3. *fig.* That dazzles the mind of the observer; brilliant or splendid to a degree that dazzles.

1749 SMOLLETT *Regicide* I. i, The fair one comes, In all the pride of dazzling charms array'd. 1839 DE QUINCEY *Recoll. Lakes* Wks. 1862 II. 113 A neighbourhood so dazzling in its intellectual pretensions.

4. quasi-*adv.*

1696 TATE & BRADY *Ps.* cxxxix. 6 Too dazling bright for mortal Eye! 1860 TYNDALL *Glac.* I. ii. 13 Its general surface was dazzling white.

dazzlingly ('dæzlɪŋlɪ), *adv.* [-LY².]

†**1.** In a dazzled manner. (See prec. 1.) *Obs.*

1610 *Mirr. Mag.*, *K. Bladud* 56 [They] blinded are, and dazelingly they looke.

2. In a dazzling manner; to a degree that dazzles.

a 1711 KEN *Hymnotheo* Poet. Wks. 1721 III. 322 His Scales the Sun-beams dazzlingly reflect. 1807 SOUTHEY *Espriella's Lett.* III. 99 Nothing was to be seen but what was perfectly and dazzlingly white. 1879 FROUDE *Cæsar* x. 118 Pompey's success had been dazzlingly rapid.

D-Day ('di:deɪ). Also D Day, D-day. [*D* for *day.*] The military code-name for a particular day fixed for the beginning of an operation; *spec.* the day (6 June 1944) of the invasion of the Atlantic coast of German-occupied France by Allied forces. Also *transf.*, of non-military undertakings; later also used for *decimalization day* (e.g. in Britain 15 Feb. 1971, on which day decimal currency came into official use).

1918 *Field Order No. 8, First Army, A.E.F.* 7 Sept., The First Army will attack at H-Hour on D-Day with the object of forcing the evacuation of St. Mihiel salient. 1928 J. M. SAUNDERS *Wings* 210 The word went out that 'D' day was to be Sept. 12. 1942 *Newsweek* 23 Nov. 27 A major Russian offensive long in preparation abiding the eventful D-day. 1944 *Times* 10 June 4/1 The Canadians landed on D Day at Bernières-sur-Mer. 1944 *Hutchinson's Pict. Hist. War* 12 Apr.-26 Sept. 342 By the end of D-Day plus two they had cleared their respective areas of dead and wounded. 1945 W. S. CHURCHILL *Victory* (1946) 102 The total [of Germans] captured by the Allies since D-Day was 2,055,575. 1947 *Economist* 27 Dec. 1047 (*heading*) D-Day for the [Marshall] Plan. 1948 G. MIKES *How to scrape Skies* 21 You know that the pipes *will* burst one day but how exciting it is to spend first of all three pleasant days wrapping them up and then retiring to wait for D-day. 1950 [see *air-drop* s.v. AIR *sb.*¹ B. III. 2].

1963 *Rep. Comm. Inquiry Decimal Curr.* p. xiv, 'D-day'. Short for 'Decimalisation Day'. *Ibid.* xiii. 132 We hope.. that as many organisations as possible will change on 'D-day' [in South Africa]. 1970 *New Scientist* 5 Feb. 245/2 The Anti-Decimal Group will doubtless be busy between now and D-day. 1971 *Oxford Mail* 15 Feb. 1/2 D-day dawned with a minimum of fuss, and shoppers were taking the new coinage in their stride.

D.D.T. (di:di:'ti:). Also DDT. An abbreviation for *d*ichloro*d*iphenyl*t*richloroethane, a white, crystalline, chlorinated hydrocarbon used as an insecticide in the form of a powder, an aqueous emulsion, or a non-aqueous solution. Also *attrib.* and *Comb.*

1943 *Soap & Sanitary Chemicals* Dec. 117/1 An insecticide material of similar type is now being made in the United States by Geigy & Co., New York, under the name 'DDT'. 1944 W. S. CHURCHILL *Memo.* 9 Mar. in *2nd World*

War (1952) V. 612 The demand for the new insecticide, D.D.T., is urgent and increasing. **1944** *Chemical Age* 9 Sept. 246/2 All the DDT produced is at present reserved for the use of the armed forces. *Ibid.*, The DDT powder..was found effective. **1959** *New Statesman* 13 June 820/3 The mustard is to be powdered by helicopter with a DDT-type chemical. **1964** *Ann. Reg. 1963* 399 The accumulation of D.D.T. now going on in many people's fatty tissues might ..be harmful in the long run. **1968** M. PYKE *Food & Society* viii. 118 The chlorinated hydrocarbon pesticides, of which DDT is by far the commonest, are very persistent in soil.

de, obs. Sc. form of DIE *v.*

de, a dialectal (Kentish), foreign, or infantile representation of THE.

Sometimes in early MSS. a scribal error for *ðe* = *the.*

‖**de** (diː). **I.** A Latin preposition, meaning 'down from, from, off, concerning', occurring in some Latin phrases more or less used in English. The chief of these are the following:

1. de bene esse (*Law*), as of 'well-being', as being good, of conditional allowance for the present.

'To take or do any thing *De bene esse*, is to accept or allow it, as well done for present,..but [on fuller examination] to be allowed or disallowed, according to the Merit or Well-being of the thing in its own nature' (Blount, *Law Dict.* 1670).

1603 *Egerton Papers* (Camden) 372 (Stanf.) Wherefore, *de bene esse*, I have provisionally made a warrant redy for his Ma[tyes] signature. **1656** BLOUNT *Glossogr.* s.v., The Court.. often orders that Defendant to be examined De bene esse, i. that his depositions are to be allowed or suppressed at the hearing, as the Judge shall see cause. **1885** *Law Rep.* 29 Ch. Div. 290 (Stanf.) The Court ultimately determined that it should be read *de bene esse*.

2. de congruo, of CONGRUITY.

a **1623** W. PEMBLE *Justif.* (1629) 33 When they tell vs, that faith merits justification *de Congruo* they intrap themselues in grosse contradiction; seeing to deserve *de Congruo* is not to deserve at all. **1841, 1856** [see CONGRUITY 5 a].

3. de facto, in fact, in reality, in actual existence, force, or possession, as a matter of fact. Very frequently opposed to *de jure*. Used also as an *adj.* = 'actual, actually existing', and then sometimes so far anglicized as to be prefixed to its sb.

1602 W. WATSON *Quodlibets* 73 (Stanf.) That the Pope erred *de facto* in the reconciliation of the French King. **1638** CHILLINGW. *Relig. Prot.* I. iii. §30 He may doe it *de facto*, but *de iure* he cannot. **1691** NORRIS *Pract. Disc.* 29 It will appear, that *de facto* it is so. **1696** *Growth Deism* 12 The Shiboleth of the Church now is King William's *de facto* Title. **1765** BLACKSTONE *Comm.* I. 371 That temporary allegiance, which was due to him as king *de facto*. **1870** [see *de jure*, below]. **1891** *Law Rep.* Weekly Notes 70/1 The acts of the *de facto* directors might..bind the company.

Hence †**de'facto-man** (also **defacto** *sb.*), one who recognised William III as king *de facto*. †**de'factoship**, a *de facto* standing, position, or title.

1696 *Growth Deism* 15 For these *de facto*-men, and the Jacobites, were but lately the same sort of People. *Ibid.* 13 And when the King had better Titles..yet he must be made to pay..Dr. S—— Sixteen Hundred Pounds a Year, for a *Defactoship* only. **1710** *Managers' Pro & Con* 39 The one allows the *Defactoship* of the Queen.

4. de fide, of faith, to be held as an article of faith.

1638 CHILLINGW. *Relig. Prot.* I. iii. §5 Some [hold] that the Popes indirect Power over Princes in Temporalities is *de Fide*; Others the contrary. **1865** PUSEY *Eirenicon* 115 The poorer classes are not, for the most part, even acquainted with the distinction between what is to be believed to be *de fide* and what is popularly taught them as truth. **1951** *Essays in Criticism* I. 4 Modern critics..treat this as self-evident or *de fide*.

5. de jure, of right, by right, according to law. Nearly always opposed to *de facto*; like that also (though less usually), treated as an *adj.* = 'legal', and placed before the sb.

1611 *Court & Times Jas. I* (1848) I. 136 (Stanf.) Done *de facto*, and not *de jure*. **1638** [see *de facto* above]. **1694** *Poet Buffoon'd*, etc. 7 (Stanf.) Husband or Gallant, either way, *De facto* or *De jure* sway. **1837** HT. MARTINEAU *Soc. Amer.* II. 81 States that are *de facto* independent, without having anything to do with the question *de jure*. **1870** LOWELL *Study Wind.* (1886) 74 It is a *de jure*, and not a *de facto* property that we have in it.

6. de novo, anew, afresh, over again from the beginning. Rarely as *adj.* = 'new, fresh', and prefixed to sb.

1627 *Court & Times Chas. I* (1848) I. 304 (Stanf.) It is said they have opened *de novo* Calais to our English trade. **1817** PEEL in *Edin. Rev.* XXIX. 121 We cannot make a constitution *de novo*. **1847–9** TODD *Cycl. Anat.* IV. 143/2 A *de novo* development of such texture. **1881** *Med. Temp. Jrnl.* XLIX. 18 In which it is developed by circumstances *de novo*.

7. de profundis, the first words of the Latin version of Psalm cxxx (cxxix) = 'Out of the depths (have I cried)'; hence subst. **a.** the name of this psalm; **b.** a psalm of penitence; **c.** a cry from the depths of sorrow, misery, or degradation.

1463 *Bury Wills* (Camden) 18 Saying *De profundis* for me, for my fader and my moder. **1500–20** KENNEDIE *Flyting w. Dunbar* 447 With *De profundis* fend the, and that failye. **1589** NASHE *Pref. Greene's Menaphon* (Arb.) 17 Let subiects for all their insolence, dedicate a *De profundis* euerie morning to the preseruation of their Cæsar. **1890** *Open Court* 10 Apr. 2204/2 (Stanf.) The Labor cry, the new *De Profundis*, the passionate psalm of the workers appealing out of the depths of misery and degradation for more wages and less hours of daily toil.

II. The French preposition *de, d'* (də, anglicized diː, dɪ, də), meaning 'of, from', occurring in names of places, as *Ashby de la Zouch*, in territorial titles, as *Earl Grey de Wilton*, *Lord Talbot de Malahide*, and in personal surnames, as *De Lisle*, *D'Israeli*, *De Quincey*; also, in French phrases more or less in English use, as *coup d'état*, *coup de main*, etc. (see COUP); ***de haut en bas***, from height to lowness, condescendingly as from a lofty position, with an air of affected superiority; ***de nouveau***, anew, afresh; ***de rigueur***, of strictness, (a matter) strictly or rigorously obligatory, according to strict etiquette; ***de trop***, too much, (one) too many, in the way.

1697 VANBRUGH *Relapse* I. ii, Not if you treat him *de haut en bas*, as you use to do. **1752** CHESTERF. *Lett.* (1792) III. 274, I know no company in which you are likely to be *de trop*. **1775** GIBBON in *Life & Lett.* (1869) 237 (Stanf.) The first chapter has been composed *de nouveau* three times. **1778** H. WALPOLE *Let.* 4 July (1904) X. 271 The Congress has ratified the treaty with France, and intend to treat the Commissioners *de haut en bas*. **1848** THACKERAY *Van. Fair* vi, 'I should only be *de trop*', said the Captain. **1849** —— *Pendennis* xxix, All the young men go to Spratt's after their balls. It is *de rigueur*, my dear. **1868** *Good Words* 1 Aug. 516/1 A de-haut-en-bas-like drawling gait. **1882** W. R. GREG *Misc. Essays* ix. 181 But her *de-haut-en-bas* judgment of Macaulay is perhaps widest of the mark. **1885** A. EDWARDS *Girton Girl* I. ii. 39 Noble French family who.. dropped the 'de' from before their name, and settled here [*sc.* in Guernsey]. **1887** *Illust. Lond. News* 5 Mar. 269/3, I am decidedly *de trop* this morning. **1888** C. M. YONGE *Our New Mistress* v. 43 The names with a De before them are always the grandest. **1915** MRS. H. WARD *Eltham House* vii. 119 Ask an officer to do without his uniforms. My frocks are just as much *de rigueur*. **1944** A. L. ROWSE *English Spirit* 134 It seems to have been *de rigueur* to say that the Queen looked twenty. **1965** R. FERGUSON *Woman with Secret* vi. 42 Her father thought he wasn't good enough for somebody with the 'de' in her name. **1966** *Listener* 17 Nov. 747/2 Hopkins has a distinct tendency to talk *de haut en bas* to his captive audience.

de-, *prefix*. The Latin adverb and preposition, used in combination with verbs, and their derivatives. A large number of verbs so formed lived on in French as popular words, or were taken over into the language in earlier or later times as learned words, and thence came into English, as *dēcrēsc-ĕre, décreis-tre, decrease*; *dēfend-ĕre, défend-re, defend*; *dēsīderāre, désire-r, desire*. In later times English verbs, with their derivative adjectives and substantives, as also participial adjectives and substantives without any verbs, have been adapted directly from Latin, or formed from Latin elements, without the intervention of French. The following are the chief uses in Lat. and Eng.

I. As an etymological element. In the senses:

1. Down, down from, down to: as *dēpendēre* to hang down, DEPEND (DEPENDENT, -ENCE, etc.); *dēpōnĕre* to lay down, DEPONE, DEPOSE; *dēprimĕre* to press down, DEPRESS; *dēscendĕre* to climb down, DESCEND; *dēvorāre* to gulp down, DEVOUR. So of English formation, DEBREAK.

2. Off, away, aside: as *dēclīnāre* to turn aside, DECLINE; *dēdūcĕre* to lead away, DEDUCE; *dēfendĕre* to ward off, DEFEND; *dēportāre* to carry off, DEPORT; *dēsignāre* to mark off, DESIGNATE; *dēsistĕre* to stand off, DESIST.

b. Away from oneself: as *dēlēgāre* to make over, DELEGATE; *dēprecārī* to pray away, DEPRECATE.

3. Down to the bottom, completely; hence thoroughly on and on, away; also methodically, formally: as *dēclāmāre* to shout away, DECLAIM; *dēclārāre* to make quite clear, DECLARE; *dēnūdāre* to strip quite bare, DENUDE; *dēplōrāre* to weep as lost, DEPLORE; *dērelinquĕre* to abandon completely, DERELICT; *dēspoliāre* to spoil utterly, DESPOIL.

b. To exhaustion, to the dregs: as *dēcoquĕre* to boil down or away, DECOCT; *dēliquēscĕre* to melt away, DELIQUESCE.

4. In a bad sense, so as to put down or subject to some indignity: as *dēcipĕre* to take in, DECEIVE; *dēlūdĕre* to make game of, DELUDE; *dērīdēre* to laugh to scorn, DERIDE; *dētestārī* to abominate, DETEST.

5. In late L., *dēcompositus* was used by the grammarians in the sense 'formed or derived from a compound (word)', passing later into that of 'compounded over again, doubly or further compounded'; in this sense the word has in modern times been taken into chemistry, botany, etc. (see DECOMPOSITE, DECOMPOUND), and the prefix has been similarly used in other words, as DECOMPLEX, DEMIXTURE.

6. In Latin, *dē-* had also the function of undoing or reversing the action of a verb, e.g. *armāre* to arm, *dearmāre* to disarm, *decorāre* to grace, *dēdecorāre* to disgrace, *jungĕre* to join, *dējungĕre* to unyoke, *vēlāre* to veil, *dēvēlāre* to unveil, and of forming verbs of similar type from substantives, as *deartuāre* to dismember, from *artus* member, joint, *dēcollāre* to behead, from *collum* neck, *dēcorticāre* to deprive of bark, from *corticem* bark, *dēflōrāre* to rob of its flowers, from *flōrem* flower. A like notion was usually expressed in classical Latin by the prefix *dis-*; e.g. *cingĕre* to gird, *discingĕre* to ungird, *convenīre* to agree, *disconvenīre* to disagree, *jungĕre* to join, *disjungĕre* to disjoin, *diffībulāre* to unclasp, *dīlōrīcāre* to uncorslet, *discalceātus* unshod. In late L., *dis-*, Romanic *des-*, became the favoured form; and although some L. words in *dē-* lived on, or were by scholars adopted into the Romanic langs., all new compounds were formed with *des-*, and many even of the Latin words in *dē-* were refashioned in Romanic with *des-*: thus L. *dearmāre*, *dēcarnāre*, *dēcolōrāre*, *dēcorticāre*, *dēdignārī*, *dēformāre*, **dēcapitāre*, Romanic *desarmare*, *descarnare*, *descorticare*, *desdegnare*, *de-* and *des-formare*, *de-*, *des-capitare*, OF. *desarmer*, *descharner*, *descorchier*, *desdaigner*, *de-* and *desformer*, *de-*, *descapiter*. In later F. *des-* became, first in speech, and finally in writing, *dé-*, in which form it was identical with the *dé-* of learned words from L. *dē-*. In English, early words taken from OF. with *des-* retained this form (now altered back under Latin influence to *dis-*), as in *disarm*, *disband*, *disburse*, *discolour*, *disdain*, *disfrock*, *disjoin*, *disrobe*; but later words have *de-*, which, although coming from F. *dé-*: —OF. *des-*:—L. *dis-*, is usually viewed and treated as identical with Latin *dē-*; e.g. *debauch*, *debord*, *defy*, *defile*, *depeople*, *derange*, *develop*. In some words both forms have passed into English, as *disburse*, †*deburse*, *discard*, †*decard*, *disconcert*, †*deconcert*, *disfrock*, *defrock*. In French the prefix *des-*, *dé-*, has received an ever increasing extension as a privative, freely prefixed to verbs, as in *débarasser*, *débrutaliser*, *décentraliser*, *déconstiper*, etc., or used to form verbs of the same type from nouns, as *débanquer*, *débonder*, *déchaperonner*, *défroquer*, etc. From the free adoption of these into English, *de-* has here also become a living privative element, freely prefixed to verbs (esp. in *-ize*, *-ate*, *-fy*), and forming verbs of a similar type from substantives or adjectives. Hence:

II. As a living prefix, with privative force.

1. Forming compound verbs (with their derivative sbs., adjs., etc.), having the sense of undoing the action of the simple verb, or of depriving (anything) of the thing or character therein expressed, e.g. *de-acidify* to undo or reverse the acidifying process, to take away the acid character, deprive (a thing) of its acid; hence *de-acidified*, *-fying*, *-fication*; *de-anglicize* to undo the anglicizing of, to divest of its English character, render no longer English. Some of these are formed by prefixing *de-* to the original verb, but others are more logically analysed as formed with *de-* + sb. or adj. + verbal suffix, the resulting form being the same in either case. In others, again, no corresponding simple verb is in use: *e.g.* *decephalize*, *decerebrize*, *decolourize*, *defibrinate*. The older and more important of these words are given in their places as main words: *e.g.* DECHRISTIANIZE, DECOMPOSE, DEMAGNETIZE, DEMORALIZE, etc. Of others of less importance, of recent use, and of obvious meaning, examples, nearly all of the 19th c. (but *decanonize* 1624, *decardinalize* 1645), here follow.

(The hyphen is conveniently used when the *de-* comes before a vowel, and sometimes elsewhere to emphasize the occasional nature of the combination, or draw special attention to its composition; otherwise it is not required.)

de-a'cidify (*-fied*, *-fication*), ***de-'alcoholize*** (*-ed*, *-ization*, *-ist*), ***de-'alkalize*** (*-ed*), ***de-a'mericanize***, ***de-a'nathematize***, ***de-'appetize*** (*-ing*), ***de-ar'senicize*** (*-ing*), ***de-'aspirate*** (*-ing*, *-ation*, *-ator*), ***debi'tumenize*** (*-ation*), ***de'brutalize***, ***de'bunnionizer***, ***de'cæsarize***, ***de'calvinize***, ***de'canonize*** (*-ation*), ***de'camphorize***, ***de'cardinalize***, ***deca'thedralize***, ***de'celticize***, ***de'chemicalize*** (*-ation*), ***de'choralize***, ***de'ciceronize***, ***de'citizenize***, ***de'classicize***, ***de'clericalize*** (*-ation*), ***de'climatize***, ***decon'catenate***, ***de'concentrate*** (*-ation*), ***decon'vention-***

alize, de'copperize (-ization), de'cultivate, de'doggerelize, de'dogmatize (-ed), de-'educate, de-e'lectrify, de-e'lectrize (-ation), de'feudalize, de'flexionize (-ed, -ation), de'formalize, de'fortify, de'ganglionate (-ed), de'generalize, de'gentilize (-ing), de'germanize, de'heathenize, de'hellenize, (-ation), dehi'storicize, de-i'dealize (-ed, -ing, etc.), de-indi'vidualize (-ation), de-indi'viduate, de-in'dustrialize (-ation, -ized, -izer), de-'insularize, de-'integrate, de-inte'llectualize (-ed, -ing), de-i'talian-ize, de'jansenize, de'junkerize, de'latinize (-ed, -ation), dele'gitimize (-ation), de'liberalize, de'limitize, de'localize, de'martialize, de'mentholize (-ed), de'metallize, de'metricize, de'narcotize, de'nucleate (-ed), de-'organize (-ation), de-ori'entalize, de-'ossify (-fication), de-'ozonize (-ation), de'paganize, de'pantheonize (to put out of the pantheon), *de'partizanize, dephi'losophize, de'physicalize* (to do away with physical development; *-ation*), *de'piedmontize, depo'liticalize, de'priorize* (deprive of priority), *depro'fessionalize, de'protestantize, depro'vincialize, de'rabbinize (-ation), dere'ligionize (-ing), de'ruralize, de'saxonize, dese'miticize, desenti'mentalize (-ed), de'skeletonize* (to rid of its skeleton), *de'socialize (-ation), desuper'naturalize, deta'rantulize (-ation), de'theorize* (to divest of theories), *devo'latilize*.

1786 *Phil. Trans.* LXXVI. 134 *Deacidified nitrous air. **1866** *Pall Mall G.* 21 Sept. 11 Like blank cartridge or *dealcoholized wine. **1873** M. COLLINS *Sqr. Silchester's* III. xxi. 236 It is a capital dealcoholist. **1877** ROBERTS *Handbk. Med.* (ed. 3) I. 74 The substance consists of *de-alkalized fibrin. **1884** TENNYSON *Becket* v. ii. 176 Can the King *de-anathematise this York? **1888** *Academy* 28 Jan. 56 A *de-appetising feast of dry bones. **1876** F. DOUSE *Grimm's L.* App. F. 210 They both *deaspirated the initial. *Ibid.* §12. 24 Similar deaspirating movements both in Greek and Sanskrit. *Ibid.* §22. 47, I have frequently observed..that when a group of deaspirators are talking together, an *h* is rarely heard at all. **1879** WHITNEY *Sanskrit Gram.* Index 478/2 Deaspiration of aspirate mutes. **1862** DANA *Man. Geol.* II. 410 The *debitumenization of the coal. **1891** *Chicago Advance* 30 Apr., Not merely to '*debrutalize' the police force, but to purify and ennoble it. **1872** DASENT *Three to One* I. 250 An eminent chiropodist and *debunnionizer. **1882** *Pall Mall G.* 20 May 3/2 The Republicans..wish to decentralize, to *decæsarize France. **1832** SOUTHEY in *Q. Rev.* XLVIII. 280 He did not talk of *decalvinizing certain of our provinces, nor of dejansenizing certain corporations. **1891** *Chicago Advance* 4 June, That this committee intended to de-Calvinize the church. **1624** T. JAMES in *Abp. Ussher's Lett.* (1686) 318 He hath..inlarged his Book of Bochel's *Decanonization. *c* **1645** HOWELL *Lett.* (1650) I. II. xix. 32 He [the Cardinal of Guise] is but young, and they speak of a Bull that is to come from Rome to *decardinalize him. **1881** *Academy* 28 May 388/3 Ireland is..more *decelticised now than the Scottish Highlands. **1878** *Scribner's Mag.* XVI. 436/1 An aroma which no chemistry, or *dechemicalization is potent enough to retain. **1864** *Reader* 19 Mar. 374/1 Handel meant his oratorios to be choral works. This *dechoralizes them. **1873** H. A. J. MUNRO *Lucret.* 473 One of the numerous artifices of Tacitus to *deciceronise the style of his annals. **1890** *Columbus* (Ohio) *Dispatch* 27 May, Any..plan of *decitizenizing free Americans. **1848** CLOUGH in *Life & Lett.* (1869) I. 125 The 'jeunes filles'..were *declassicised by their use of parasols. **1870** *Sat. Rev.* 12 Feb. 209/1 Nor ..to allow its Bishops to *declericalize any of its priests and deacons by a penny post letter. *Ibid.*, To accept..a declericalization which was not degradation. **1870** *Lit. Churchman* XVI. 451/2 Englishmen who have lived much abroad seem to become *de-climatised in this particular. **1862** MRS. SPEID *Last Years Ind.* 157 So the whole concatenation *deconcatenated. **1893** *Sat. Rev.* 25 Mar. 333/1 The style of the great Mr. Smith..greatly *deconventionalized. **1784** B. FRANKLIN in *Ann. Reg.* 1817 Chron. 381 The odious mixture of pride and beggary..that have half depopulated and *decultivated Spain. **1890** J. DAVIDSON in *Academy* 15 Mar. 183/1 An example of the failure of high literary ability to *dedoggerelise it thoroughly. **1878** GURNEY *Tertium Quid* (1887) I. 113 The joylessness and dulness of the 'dereligionised' (more truly *dedogmatised) life. **1887** *Parish Problems* 36 Poverty, care, work..had slowly *deëducated the Man! **1881** *Nature* XXIV. 21 Method of *de-electrifying woollen yarn. **1824** *Mech. Mag.* No. 61. 77 Might not steam be further *de-electrized? *Ibid.*, By following up the means which produced it, namely, by de-electrization. **1871** EARLE *Philol. Eng. Tongue* §445 *Deflectionized languages are said to be Analytic. **1880** GRANT WHITE *Every-Day Eng.* 275 This *deformalizing of the English language. **1877** P. THOMSON in *Bible Students' Aids* 146 Antiochus *defortifies the Temple. **1885** ROMANES *Jelly-fish* 180 The *deganglionated tissue. **1864** *Reader* 23 Apr. 511/3 It may be within the compass of critical science to *degeneralize portions of it into the suggesting particulars. **1839** *New Monthly Mag.* LVI. 454 The *degentilizing distinction above mentioned. **1892** *Pall Mall G.* 7 Sept. 6/1 His theory is that Germany is being fast *de-Germanized. **1893** *Chicago Advance* 31 Aug., The vast student-world was being *de-heathenized. **1866** *Pall Mall G.* 8 Oct. 10 The urban population..is either thoroughly *de-Hellenized, or is in the process of de-Hellenization. **1865** W. KAY *Crisis Huffeldiana* 27 Their attempts to *de-historicize..the oldest and most venerable document of human history. **1865** J. GROTE *Treat. Mor. Ideas* vii. (1876) 93 The notion..was very early *de-idealized or positivized. **1890** W. S. LILLY *Right & Wrong* 226 The fine arts, as they exist among us, bear witness..to the deidealising of life. *a* **1866** J. GROTE *Exam. Utilit. Philos.* v. (1870) 94 Reason binds men together, and, if we may so speak, *deindividualizes them. *Ibid.*, The growth of virtue is a gradual deindividualization of men. **1880** FAIRBAIRN *Stud. Life of Christ* xv. (1881) 262 Men *deindividuated are almost dehumanised. **1882** B. LEIGHTON in *Standard* 5 May, To *de-industrialize the population. **1940** *Economist* 23 Nov. 634/1 The 'new European order', in which de-industrialised France is to be reduced to an agricultural hinterland of the Reich. *Ibid.* 634/2 Their [*sc.* the Germans'] plan is to create just one more economic vassal, and in sponsoring the movement for 'de-industrialisation' the Vichy Government have stupidly..given their backing to that plan. **1972** *Nat. Geographic* Sept. 359/2 If man were enlightened..he would deindustrialize many areas of the Connecticut Valley. **1979** *Daily Tel.* 13 Dec. 21 The accelerated rundown of British Steel has disturbing implications about the future health of manufacturing industry and the process of 'de-industrialisation' that is now the vogue Whitehall phrase. **1985** *Inc* Apr. 36/1, I began to realize that there were lots of people out there with axes to grind—the small-business camp, the big-business camp, the deindustrializers and the reindustrializers, [etc.]. **1882** *Daily Tel.* 2 June, In the face of the tunnel that is to *de-insularise us. **1861** BAGEHOT *Biog. Ess.* (1881) 142 Years of acquiescing..usually *de-intellectualise a parliamentary statesman before he comes to half his power. **1891** ABBOTT *Philomythus* 129 The de-intellectualising influence of this resolute faith in miracles. **1889** *Pall Mall G.* 16 Oct. 2/2 The possibility of first *de-Italianising the Sacred College. *Ibid.* 13 Nov. 2/2 The de-Italianizing of the Church. **1832** *Dejansenizing [see *decalvinizing*]. **1866** *Pall Mall G.* 13 Aug. 3 Will a junker be allowed to *dejunkerize himself. **1883** *Spectator* 27 Jan. 126 A certain amount of *delatinisation and some simplification of phraseological structure. **1969** C. DAVIDSON in Cockburn & Blackburn *Student Power* 349 People will not move *against* institutions of power until the legitimizing authority has been stripped away... And we should be forewarned; it is a tricky job and often can backfire, *de-legitimizing us. **1981** *Church Times* 4 Dec. 1/2 The report recommends that the Churches should urgently consider 'the delegitimisation of the production, possession and use of nuclear weapons as a crime against humanity'. **1983** *MacNeil/Lehrer Newshour* 23 Dec., UNESCO..has become..highly discriminatory against Israel, for example — it's where the delegitimization campaign against Israel first got under way. **1984** *Listener* 2 Feb. 9/3 Terrorism is something of a catch-all category in official thinking, used to de-legitimise a variety of enemies. **1835** *Tait's Mag.* II. 461 To *deliberalize the principles of the youthful patriot. **1887** GURNEY *Tertium Quid* II. 194 Further liberalising and *delimitising the conditions of poetic appreciation. **1881** *Ohio State Jrnl.* 29 Jan., Worthless *dementholized oil. **1754** HUXHAM in *Phil. Trans.* XLVIII. 861 Tin and copper..are reduced to ashes, and *demetallized. **1883** *Athenæum* 28 July 104/2 That passage ..should..be forthwith *demetricized and turned into honest prose. **1829** TOGNO, DURAND, etc. *Mat. Med.* The *denarcotized opium. **1892** POULTON & SHIPLEY tr. *Weismann's Heredity* II. 92 Boveri..succeeded in rearing such *denucleated eggs by the introduction of spermatozoa. **1864** *Homeward Mail* 17 Oct. 901 The tendency..is to *de-orientalize the European mind in India. **1881** *Athenæum* 9 July 42/3 Glimpses of Anglo-Indian life before it became de-Orientalized. **1874** W. A. MILLER *Elem. Chem.* (ed. 5) II. §341 Ozonized air is also *deozonized by transmission over cold manganese dioxide. **1873** C. B. FOX *Ozone & Antozone* 95 The deozonisation of air passing over densely populated towns. **1847-8** DE QUINCEY *Protestantism* Wks. VIII. 156 Rome, it was found, could not be *depaganised. **1859** *Lit. Churchman* V. 332/1 Among the slowly depaganized people. **1892** *Harper's Mag.* Sept. 629/2 The bones of Mirabeau.. were carried in great pomp to the Pantheon in 1791; and were *depantheonized..a year or two later. **1885** *American* IX. 198 To *departizanize the public service. **1862** *Sat. Rev.* XIII. 21/2 The work is resumed..in the Italian language.. as a means for *depiedmontizing the author's style. **1872** *Contemp. Rev.* XX. 831 To press philosophy into its service is to *dephilosophize it. **1872** S. BUTLER *Erewhon* xi. 99 A time of universal *dephysicalisation would ensue. **1859** *Sat. Rev.* VIII. 573/2 Dr. Cullen has really..*de-politicalized the Irish priesthood. **1866** DE MORGAN in Graves *Life Sir W. R. Hamilton* (1889) III. 562 You cannot..let him take any licence which can damage or *de-priorise anything you choose to write on your own subject. **1884** *St. James's Gaz.* 22 Mar. 4/1 It helps to some extent..to '*deprofessionalize' the English clergy. **1888** *Mission Herald* (Boston) Oct. 442 To *deprotestantize the nation. **1861** O. W. HOLMES *Pages fr. Old Vol. Life* (1891) 10 The camp is *deprovincializing us very fast. **1865** LOWELL *New Eng. Two Cent. Ago* Prose Wks. 1890 II. 12 Commerce is deprovincializing the minds of those engaged in it. **1891** *Review of Reviews* 15 Sept. 267/1 The Jews must be *derabbinised and denationalised. *Ibid.*, The derabbinisation is far advanced. **1878** *Dereligionized [see *dedogmatized*]. **1879** W. H. MALLOCK *Is Life Worth Living?* 64 To de-religionize life, then, it is not enough to condemn creeds and to abolish prayers. *Ibid.* 136 The gradual de-religionizing of life. **1888** H. F. LESTER *Hartas Maturin* I. i. 7 The gradual process of *deruralizing his townlet. **1890** *Daily News* 19 Nov. 2/5 He hoped the Council would not entirely 'de-ruralise' the park. **1869** LOWELL *Poems, Cathedr.*, A brain *desaxonized. **1892** W. WATSON in *Bookman* Oct. 23/1 Grotesque efforts to get inside the English character and *de-Semiticise his own. **1882** TRAILL *Sterne* vi. 88 That thoroughly *desentimentalized 'domestic interior'. **1886** *Blackw. Mag.* CXL. 747 She ..*deskeletonized the wretched closet with unsparing dexterity. **1889** *Harper's Mag.* June 102/1 The way in which darkness isolates and *desocializes the citizen. **1883** MAUDSLEY *Body & Will* III. iii. 258 Demoralization following desocialization. **1885** *Pall Mall G.* 3 Sept. 5/2 He will steep himself to the lips in falsehood sooner than allow it to be *desupernaturalized. **1836** *Tait's Mag.* III. 168 The singular ceremony of '*de-tarantulization' (since a word must needs be coined). **1883** A. B. EDWARDS in *Academy* 10 Nov. 309/2 A *de-theorised American. **1868** *Birm. Jrnl.* Sept. 12 The oil..has been *devolatilised, so that all danger of explosion is annihilated.

2. Less frequently verbs (and their derivatives) are formed by prefixing *de-* to a noun (cf. L. *dēfāmāre*, F. *défroquer*), with the sense: **a.** To deprive, divest, free from, or rid of the thing in question: as DEBOWEL (1375), ***deflesh, defoliage, deglaze, deglycerin, dehandle, delawn, †demast, demiracle, demonastery, †depark, deprivilege, deprotestant, detenant, †detruth; depetticoated, dereligioned*** ppl. adjs.; ***de-legitimation.*** (Some of these have forms in DIS-, which is the usual prefix for words of this type.) **b.** To turn out of, dislodge or expel from, as ***decart, †deparliament*** (1648); DECOURT, DEHUSK.

1860 RUSSELL *Diary India* (1863) I. 299, I completed my journey, and was safely *decarted at the door of a substantial house. **1837-40** HALIBURTON *Clockm.* I. 76 He was teetotally *defleshed, a mere walking skeleton. **1831** HUISH *Mem. Geo. IV*, 57 The lovely rosebud fell *defoliaged. **1879** *Scribner's Mag.* July 402 They..completely defoliage the trees. **1885** W. L. CARPENTER *Soap & Candles* 151 The French process ..for *deglycerining neutral fats. **1893** in *Chicago Advance* 9 Mar., She had broken the cover of a tureen, and *dehandled a china pitcher. **1726** AMHERST *Terræ Fil.* xxxix. 215 The bishop ought to be *de-lawn'd. **1666** *Lond. Gaz.* No. 89/4 Very little damage, besides the *demasting of one Fireship. **1884** TENNYSON *Becket* III. iii. 137 For as to the fish, they *de-miracled the miraculous draught, and might have sunk a navy. *c* **1808** BYRON *Occas. Pieces* xvi. *note*, Some..monk of the abbey, about the time it was *demonasteried. *a* **1700** B. E. *Dict. Cant. Crew*, *Whetstones-park*, a Lane..fam'd for a Nest of Wenches, now *de-park'd. **1648** J. GOODWIN *Right & Might* 19 The men *deparliamented by the Army. **1892** *Chicago Advance* 14 Jan., She is not a *depetticoated virago, who wants to inaugurate a general swapping of sex. **1979** *Times* 27 Nov. 2/7 Headings of his document included 'Investigate and publicize restrictive labour practices'..'*Deprivilege (sic) the Civil Service'. **1986** *Times* 26 Apr. 8/7 The government believes there is..a connection between legislation to deprivilege unions and macro-economic improvement. **1890** *Guardian* 5 Nov. 1745/2 The result..is, to use the phrase of *The Times*, the '*deprotestanting' of the greater part of Ireland. **1835** *Athenæum* 443 The demoralized, *de-religioned invaders of privilege and property. **1883** C. A. CAMERON in *Pall Mall G.* 4 Dec. 1/2 Many unsanitary houses have been *detenanted. **1647** WARD *Simp. Cobler* 67 He feares there is Truth in them: Could he *de-truth them all, he would defie them all.

3. By an extension of use *de-* is sometimes prefixed to adjectives or substantives, as in DEBARE, DECHEERFUL, DEGALANT, DEDOCTOR. (Cf. *dis-* in *discontent, dissatisfied*, etc.)

dea, deac. U.S. colloq. abbrevs. of DEACON *sb.* 1 c, d.

1821 *Massachusetts Spy* 28 Feb. (Th.), Deac Josiah Bridge. *Ibid.* 4 Apr., Dea. Ebenezer Read. **1907** *Springfield Weekly Republ.* 17 Jan. 11 Dea Wilson was among the foremost of the town's citizens. **1913** *Sat. Even. Post* 1 Feb. 34/3 Look at 'er, deac!

de-accession (diːæk'sɛʃən), *v.* Chiefly *U.S.* [f. DE- II. 1 + ACCESSION *v.*] *trans.* To remove an entry for (an exhibit, book) from the accessions register of a museum, library, etc., usu. in order to sell the item concerned. Also *absol.*

1972 *N.Y. Times* 27 Feb. II. 21/2 The Museum of Art recently de-accessioned (the polite term for 'sold') one of its only four Redons. **1973** *Time* 26 Feb. 43/2 'De-accessioning' pictures—the barbaric museum jargon for preparing to sell. **1974** J. GOLDMAN *Man from Greek & Roman* v. 33 You deaccessioned, you took something off your shelves and sold it. **1981** *Times* 16 Feb. 4/1 The sale of Japanese art included a group of 38 lots of Japanese lacquer 'recently de-accessioned by the Metropolitan Museum in New York'. **1987** *London Rev. Bks.* 19 Mar. 5/4 Curators may soon be tempted to start..'de-accessioning' what their recent predecessors have..acquired.

Hence as *sb.*, the act or process of de-accessioning; **de-ac'cessioned** *ppl. a.*, **de-ac'cessioning** *vbl. sb.*

1973 *Newsweek* 29 Jan. 76 Richard F. Brown, director of Fort Worth's Kimbell Museum of Art, felt that..the 'principle' of de-accession is right although he might 'disagree with the particular object chosen for de-accession'. **1973** *Art in Amer.* Jan.–Feb. 24 In order to illustrate..Mr. Hoving's policy, he should show all the de-accessioned works. **1973** *New Yorker* 31 Mar. 83/1 Money gained through sales—or 'de-accessioning', in museum parlance —is often used for acquisitions. **1976** *Times Lit. Suppl.* 24 Dec. 1604/2 The acquisition by Mellon from the Hermitage of famous paintings... This early twentieth-century instance of sensational 'de-accessioning' as it was to be uneuphoniously called by later adepts of the technique.

de-acidify, etc.: see DE- II. 1.

deacon ('diːkən, -k(ə)n), *sb.*[1] Forms: α. 1 diacon, deacon; β. 2 diacne, diakne, 4 dyakne, *pl.* diaknen; γ. 2 dæcne, 2-4 deakne, 3-5 dekne, (3 *gen. pl.* deknene); 3-6 deken (-in, -on, -un, -yn(e), 4 deeken (*pl.* deeknys), decoun, 4-6 decon, decane, 5-6 deaken, deakon, 6 diacon(e, deacone, 5- deacon. [ad. L. *diāconus*, a. Gr. διάκονος servant, waiting man, messenger, whence *spec.* in Christian use, servant or minister of the church; an order of ministers in the church. The OE. *diacon* (*deacon*) was a learned form immed. from the L.; beside it there appears to have been a popular form **dǽcna* (? from **diǽcna*, **deǽcna*), whence 12th c. *dæcne, deakne*, and later *dêkne*, pl. *deaknen*. From *dêkne, deakne*, came *deken, deaken*, whence under L. influence *deacon*. The early ME. *diacne, dyakne* was perhaps immed. a. OF.

diacne, *dyacne* (12th c.; later *diacre*); it might also represent a semi-popular OE. **diacna*: cf. ON. *djákn*, *djákni*. There were many intermediate forms of the word, from mixture of popular and learned types.]

1. *Eccl.* The name of an order of ministers or officers in the Christian church.

a. In Apostolic times.

Their first appointment is traditionally held to be recorded in Acts vi. 1-6, where however the title διάκονος does not occur, but only the cognate words διακονεῖν ('serve') and διακονία ('ministration').

c **1000** ÆLFRIC *Homilies* (Thorpe) I. 44 Ða apostolas ȝehádodon seofon diaconas.. Ðæra diacona wæs se forma Stephanus. *a* **1300** *Cursor M.* 19482 (Cott.) Steuen..was o þe seuen dekens an. **1382** WYCLIF *Phil.* i. 1 Poul and Tymothe..to alle the hooly men..at Philippis, with bischopis and dekenes. *c* **1450** *Mirour Saluacioun* 4442 Deken Steven be his name. **1597** HOOKER *Eccl. Pol.* v. 419 Deacons were stewards of the Church, vnto whome at the first was committed the distribution of Church-goods. **1611** BIBLE *1 Tim.* ii. 8 Likewise must the deacons bee graue, not double tongued. **1782** PRIESTLEY *Corrupt. Chr.* II. VI. 20 The deacons generally administered the elements. **1875** MANNING *Mission H. Ghost* xv. 417 The Apostles set apart a special order—the Sacred order of deacons—to be ministers of the charity of Jesus Christ to His poor.

b. In Episcopal Churches, a member of the third order of the ministry, ranking below bishops and priests, and having the functions of assisting the priest in divine service, *esp.* in the celebration of the eucharist, and of visiting the sick, etc.

c **900** *Bæda's Eccl. Hist.* III. xiv. [xx.] (1891) 220 Honorius se ærcebiscop..ȝehalȝode Thomam his diacon to biscope. **1122** *O.E. Chron.*, Se dæcne hæfde ongunnan þone godspel. *c* **1175** *Lamb. Hom.* 81 Nu comeð þes diakne. *c* **1290** *S. Eng. Leg.* I. 392/49 Preostes he made and deknene al-so. **1340** *Ayenb.* 190 He acsede at onen of his diaknen. *c* **1386** CHAUCER *Pars. T.* ¶817 Folk that ben entred into ordre, as sub-dekin, or dekin, or prest. *c* **1450** *St. Cuthbert* (Surtees) 6943 A preste sange at ane altere, And his dekyn þat stode him nere. **1513** BRADSHAW *St. Werburge* I. 2221 Whan the Deken redde the holy gospell. **1647** N. BACON *Disc. Govt. Eng.* I. x. (1739) 18 Deacons..attending upon the Presbyters to bring the offerings to the Altar to read the Gospel, to Baptize, and Administer the Lord's Supper. *a* **1771** GRAY *Remarks Lydgate's Poems* Wks. 1843 V. 292 He was ordained a deacon in 1393, which is usually done in the twenty-third year of a man's age. **1844** LINGARD *Anglo-Sax. Ch.* (1858) I. iv. 133 The three orders of bishops, priests, and deacons.

c. In the Presbyterian system, one of an order of officers appointed to attend to the secular affairs of the congregation, as distinguished from the *elders*, whose province is the spiritual. (But they do not always exist, at least under this name, their functions, when they are absent, being performed by the elders.) **d.** In Congregational churches, one of a body of officers elected to advise and assist the pastor, distribute the elements at the communion, administer the charities of the church, and attend to its secular affairs.

1560-1 *Bk. Discipline* viii. (*heading*), The Eyght Heid, tuiching the Electioun off Elderis and Deaconis, etc... The office of the Deaconis..is to receave the rentis, and gadder the almous of the Churche, to keip and distribute the same, as by the ministerie of the Kirk shall be appointed. Thay may also assist in judgement with the Ministeris and Elderis. **1584** J. MELVILL *Diary* (1842) 183 Ther salba twa Deacones: an till attend upon the box..to collect and distribut to the outward pure..ane uther to haiff the cair of our awin inward indigent or diseased. **1644** OWEN *Wks.* XIX. 537-8. *a* **1647** T. HOOKER *Summe Ch. Discipl.* II. i, This Deacon being the steward or Treasurer of the Church, the thing for which he is mainly to be imployed..is for the husbanding of the estate and temporalls of the Church. **1647** *Resolutions, etc. Congreg. Ch. Canterbury* 30 Mar. (MS.), The church..did order that..there bee 3 nominated out of wch on shall bee chose to the office of a Deacon. **1648** J. COTTON *Way Congreg. Ch.* II. 10 It is an Ordinance of Christ to elect Officers (Deacons and Elders), for this is the power and privilege of the Church of Brethren. *a* **1657** W. BRADFORD *New Eng. Mem.* 355 They had..in our time four grave men for ruling elders, and three able and godly men for deacons. **1702** C. MATHER *Magn. Chr.* v. vii, The Office and Work of a Deacon is..to keep the Treasury of the Church, and therewith to serve the Tables, which the Church is to provide for, as the Lord's Table, the Table of the Ministers, and of such as are in Necessity, to whom they are to distribute in simplicity. **1884** R. W. DALE *Congreg. Manual* v. 116 In some Congregational churches there are both 'elders' and 'deacons'.

e. *fig.*

1642 MILTON *Apol. Smect.* xi. (1851) 311 Their office is to pray for others, and not to be the lip-working deacons of other mens appointed words. **1796** C. BURNEY *Mem. Metastasio* III. 170 As an old Deacon of Apollo. **1887** *Mission. Herald* (Boston) Apr. 153 It [the African Lakes Company] acts as deacon to the mission stations themselves, caring for them in secular things.

†**2.** Applied to the Levites, as an order inferior to the priests in the Jewish Church: cf. BISHOP 2.

c **1000** *Ags. Gosp.* John i. 19 þa Iudeas sendon heora sacerdas and heora diaconas fram Ierusalem. *c* **1175** *Lamb. Hom.* 79 þer com a prost be þi weie..and wende forð, þer com an diacne. *a* **1300** *Cursor M.* 7009 (Cott.) For luue of a deken wijf,—Mani man þar tint þair lijf [cf. Judges xx. 4]. **1388** WYCLIF *Num.* ii. 51 The dekenes schulen do doun the tabernacle. *c* **1449** PECOCK *Repr.* III. i. 280 To the dekenis were ȝouun xlviij citees.

3. a. In Scotland, the president of an incorporated 'craft' or trade in any town; formerly *ex officio* a member of the town-council.

1424 *Sc. Acts Jas. I* (1597) §39 Ilke Craft suld haue ane Deakon. **1563** WINȜET *Four Scoir Thre Quest.* xxxix. Wks. 1888 I. 102 As thair is in euery craft almaist ane decane [*MS.* dekin]. *a* **1649** DRUMM. OF HAWTH. *Hist. Jas. V* Wks. (1711) 88 A deacon of the crafts is killed by the faction of the Hamiltons. **1771** SMOLLETT *Humph. Cl.* Wks. 1806 VI. 260 The council [of the Edinburgh magistracy] is composed of deacons, one of whom is returned every year in rotation, as representative of every company of artificers or handicraftsmen. **1787** BURNS *Brigs of Ayr* 154 Ye dainty Deacons, an' ye douce Conveeners. **1828** SCOTT *F.M. Perth* xx, The presidents, or deacons, as they were termed, of the working classes.

b. *fig.* A 'master' of his craft; a thoroughly capable man.

1814 SCOTT *Wav.* xlvi, Yon man is not a deacon o' his craft. **1823** GALT *Entail* III. x. 98, I had got an inkling o' the law frae my father, who was a deacon at a plea.

4. *Freemasonry.* Name of a particular inferior office in a lodge: see quot.

1813 J. ASHE *Masonic Manual* (1825) 227 The Deacons are then named and invested; upon which the new Master addresses them as follows:—'Brothers J. K., and L. M., I appoint you Deacons of this Lodge. It is your province to attend on the Master, and to assist the Wardens in the active duties of the lodge.'

†**5.** A set of eucharistic garments for a deacon.

1534 in Peacock *Engl. Ch. Furniture* 201 A whole vestment for a preist wt deacon and subdeacon of white damaske. **1552** *Trans. Essex Arch. Soc.* N.S. I. 14 Two chesables, othr ways cawlyd deakyn and subdeaken. **1558** *Wills & Inv. N.C.* I. (Surtees 1835) 171 One Cope, a vestment and a deacon all.. of red silk.

6. A very young or aborted calf, or its hide. *U.S. colloq.*

1873 *Chicago Tribune* 2 Jan. 6/2 Hides..deacons, 50 @ 65 ¢. **1898** E. N. WESTCOTT *D. Harum* xvii, I guess you got a 'deakin' in that lot... That calf died, that's what that calf done. **1923** *Dialect Notes* V. 234 *Deacon*, a calf of veal age; the hide or skin of such a calf. 'That hide ain't worth much; it's only a deacon.'

7. *Comb.*, as **deacon-seat** (*U.S.*), a long settee in a log-cabin, cut from a single log.

1851 J. S. SPRINGER *Forest Life* 71 Directly over the foot-pole..and in front of the fire, is the deacon-seat. This seat constitutes our sofa or settee. **1864** LOWELL *Fireside Trav.* 152 We sat down upon the *deacon-seat* before the fire. **1889** FARMER *Americanisms*, *Deacon seat*, a lumberer's camp term ..why so called is difficult to say..unless, indeed, it is an allusion to the seats round a pulpit, facing the congregation, reserved for deacons.

Deacon, *sb.*² The name of Henry *Deacon* (1822-76), English industrial chemist, used attrib. or in the possessive to designate a process for the manufacture of chlorine by the catalytic oxidation of hydrochloric acid.

1876 *Encycl. Brit.* V. 491/1 The production of chlorine by Deacon's process. **1921** *Dict. Occup. Terms* (1927) §143 Deacon plant man, deacon process man. **1965** PHILLIPS & WILLIAMS *Inorg. Chem.* I. xii. 446 Chlorine has been prepared by displacement with oxygen, in such exothermic reactions as..the Deacon process.

'deacon, *v. U.S. colloq.* or *slang*. [f. prec. sb.]

1. *trans.* (usually ***to deacon off***). To read aloud (a hymn) one or two lines at a time, the congregation singing the lines as soon as read, according to the early practice of the Congregational Churches of New England. Hence *fig. U.S. colloq.*

1845 T. W. COIT *Puritanism* 232 The insult..was given by deaconing out, as the phrase goes..the following verses from the 52d Psalm. **1848** LOWELL *Biglow P.* Ser. I. ix, Without you deacon off the toon you want your folks should sing. **1888** —— *Heartsease & Rue* 166 Well he knew to deacon-off a hymn. **1857** GOODRICH *Remin.* I. 77 (Bartlett) The chorister deaconed the first two lines.

2. To pack (fruit, etc.) with the finest specimens on the top. *U.S. slang.*

1866 LOWELL *Biglow P.* Introd., To *deacon* berries is to put the largest atop. **1868** MISS ALCOTT *Lit. Women* xi. (Farmer), The strawberries [were] not as ripe as they looked, having been skilfully deaconed.

b. In various uses connoting unfair or dishonest dealing or the like (cf. *to doctor*): see quots. *U.S. slang.*

1860 BARTLETT *Dict. Amer.*, *To deacon a calf* is to knock it in the head as soon as it is born.—*Connecticut.* **1889** FARMER *Americanisms*, *To deacon land*, to filch land by gradually extending one's fences or boundary lines into the highway or other common property. **1889** *Century Dict.*, *Deacon*, to sophisticate; adulterate; 'doctor': as, to deacon wine or other liquor. *slang.*

3. *Eccl.* To make (someone) a deacon; to ordain to the diaconate, to admit to deacon's orders. Cf. PRIEST *v.* 2. Hence **'deaconing** *vbl. sb.*

1980 *Church Times* 26 Dec. 16/3 Everyone agreed that the cathedral protest had been dignified. But many were puzzled that it should occur now, as ten women had already been deaconed. *Ibid.* 16/4 This is the first public deaconing of a woman in the Diocese of Llandaff. **1985** *Oxf. Diocesan Mag.* Sept. 20/3 To be deaconed by the Bishop of Reading ..on Michaelmas Day: Brian Blackman, [etc.]. **1986** *Church Times* 30 May 5/2 She believes that the proposed deaconing of women..is a mark of the respect earned by deaconesses already serving the churches.

'deaconal *a.*, **'deaconate** *sb.*, forms sometimes used instead of the more correct DIACONAL, -ATE.

1890 *Chicago Advance* 7 Aug., Clerical hospitality.. deaconal hospitality. **1882-3** SCHAFF *Encycl. Relig. Knowl.* III. 2256 The subdeaconate [developed] from the deaconate. **1892** *Daily News* 2 Feb. 5/7 After a meeting of the deaconate.

deaconess ('diːkənɪs). Forms: 6 decon-, diacon-, 6-7 deaconisse, 7 diacon-, deaconness, 8- deaconess. [f. DEACON + -ESS, formed after med.L. *diāconissa*, fem. of *diāconus*: cf. F. *diaconisse* (14-18th c.), now usually *diaconesse*.]

1. *Eccl.* **a.** The name of an order of women in the early church, 'who appear to have undertaken duties in reference to their own sex analogous to those performed by the deacons among men' (*Dict. Chr. Antiq.*). **b.** Also, in some modern churches, of an order of women having functions parallel to those of the deacons in the same, or intermediate between these and those of the women in sense 2.

a **1536** TINDALE *Wks.* 250 (R.) Phebe the deaconisse of the church of Cenchris. **1561** T. NORTON *Calvin's Inst.* IV. 89 There were created deaconisses, not to delite God with singing and wyth mumbling not vnderstanded..but that they should execute publike ministration towarde the poore. **1685** BAXTER *Paraphr. N.T. 1 Tim.* iii. 11 The Deaconnesses that then were appointed to some Care of Women, which Men were less fit for. **1709** J. JOHNSON *Clergym. Vade M.* II. 100 The office of Deaconesses was..especially to attend women in the Baptistery, undressing and dressing them again. **1847** MASKELL *Mon. Rit.* III. p. xcv. *note*, The deaconesses of the primitive ages..their functions being.. limited to the performance of mere secular duties, such as visiting the sick, and catechizing women. **1885** *Catholic Dict.* s.v., [Deaconesses] were employed in assisting at the baptism of women..In the tenth century the office was extinct in the West..At Constantinople the office survived till 1190.

1617 F. JOHNSON *Plea* xx. 317 To the Elders..that rule the Church; and to the Deacons and Deaconesses that serve and minister therein. *a* **1657** W. BRADFORD *New Eng. Mem.* 355 They had..one ancient widow for a deaconess..She usually sat..in the congregation with a little birchen rod in her hand, and kept little children in great awe from disturbing the congregation. She did frequently visit the sick and weak, and especially women. **1892** *Bk. Ch. of Scotl.* 33 Women who being able to make Christian work the chief object of their lives..having passed throught two years' training and service in connection with our Homes in Edinburgh or Glasgow, may apply to be set apart as Deaconesses by their kirk-sessions and presbyteries, and will then..be expected to go to any part of Scotland where they may be required, there to work under the supervision of minister and kirk-session. **1893** *British Weekly* 30 Nov. 88/2 Miss Hargreave was a deaconess of Carr's Lane Church, and has been of great service in many ways.

2. The name taken by certain Protestant orders of women with aims similar to those of Sisters of Mercy.

1867 LADY HERBERT *Cradle L.* iii. 102 The Kaiserswerth Deaconesses..have a school, hospital, and dispensary near the English Protestant Church. **1871** *Daily News* 4 Nov., The Deaconesses' Institute prides itself upon being 'evangelically Protestant'. **1890** *Whitaker's Almanack* 276 General Hospitals—(No. 7) Deaconesses' Institution and Training Hospital, Tottenham.

3. *nonce-use.* A deacon's wife.

1858 O. W. HOLMES *Aut. Breakf.-t.* (1883) 221 Deacon and deaconess dropped away.

4. *Comb.*

1884 *Pall Mall G.* 10 Sept. 2/1 A deaconess-house was opened. **1893** *Ch. Times* 27 Jan. 81/1 The deaconess-widows, and the widows of the higher clergy.

†**'deaconhead.** *Obs.* [-HEAD.] = next.

c **1400** *Apol. Loll.* 32 þe minstri of presthed, & of dekunhed. **1656** *Burgh Rec.* in J. Irving *Hist. Dumbartonshire* (1860) 534 The crafts of the said burgh sould enjoy the lyke fredome priviledge and deaconhead.

deaconhood ('diːkənhʊd). [-HOOD.]

1. The office of a deacon: see DEACON *sb.*¹ 1 b, 3.

1382 WYCLIF *1 Tim.* Prol., The ordynaunce of byschophood, and of the dekenehood. *c* **1449** PECOCK *Repr.* III. ix. 332 Dekenhode was profitable to his clergie.

2. A body of deacons collectively.

In mod. Dicts.

deaconry ('diːkənrɪ). [-RY.]

1. The office of a deacon; deaconship, diaconate.

1483 *Cath. Angl.* 95 A Dekenry, *diaconatus*. **1560-1** *Bk. Discipline* v., *Privilege of Univ.*, Tutorie, Curatorie, Deaconrie, or ony siclike. **1642** SIR E. DERING *Sp. on Relig.* 133 S. Paul calleth his Apostleship but a Deaconry. **1824** G. CHALMERS *Caledonia* III. v. §7. 474 An act annulling that incorporation for having a deaconry.

b. A body of deacons collectively,

a **1679** T. GOODWIN *Wks.* IV. IV. 188 (R.) The deacons of all those churches should make up a common deaconry.

2. *R.C.Ch.* The chapel and charitable institution of a 'region' of Rome, in charge of a cardinal or regionary deacon.

1670 G. H. *Hist. Cardinals* I. III. 67 The Chapels that were ordinarily united to these Religious houses, being called Deaconries. *Ibid.* I. III. 68 Deaconries, where the Cardinals had their Residence, and..were call'd Cardinal Deacons, because of their residence in the Deaconry. **1751** CHAMBERS *Cycl.*, *Deaconry* is also a name still reserved to the chapels and oratories in Rome, under the direction of the several deacons, in their respective regions..To the deaconries were annexed a sort of hospitals..governed by the regionary deacons, called cardinal deacons. **1855** MILMAN *Lat. Chr.* (1864) II. III vii. 117 The churches and monasteries, the hospitals, deaconries or ecclesiastical boards for the poor.

deaconship (ˈdiːkənʃɪp). [-SHIP.] The office or position of a deacon.

1565 HARDING in Jewel *Def. Apol.* (1611) 85 The Priesthood & Deaconship. **1610** J. ROBINSON *Just. Separ. Church* Wks. II. 364 The office of deacon-ship which Christ hath left by his apostles for the collection and distribution of the Church's alms. **1615** WADSWORTH in Bedell *Lett.* 13 Priesthood is giuen by the deliuerie of the Patena..and of the Chalice..Deaconship by the deliuerie of the booke of the Gospels. **1681-6** J. SCOTT *Chr. Life* (1747) III. 400 That none shall be..ordained an Elder, till after he had well acquitted himself in the Deaconship. **1849-53** ROCK *Ch. of Fathers* IV. 51 In due time the Subdeacon was raised to the Deaconship.

†**deˈaction.** *Obs.* [ad. L. *deaction-em*: DE- I. 3.]

1656 BLOUNT *Glossogr.*, *Deaction*, a finishing or perfecting.

deactivate (diːˈæktɪveɪt), *v.* [f. DE- + ACTIVATE *v.*] *trans.* To render inactive or less reactive; *spec.* to deprive of chemical action, to render less chemically reactive. So **deactiˈvation**, the process or result of deactivating; **deˈactivator**, a substance which deactivates.

1904 *Sci. Amer.* Suppl. 20 Feb. 23523/1 He finds that the law of de-activation is still the same throughout this range of temperature. **1938** *Jrnl. Chem. Soc.* June 905 Just as the methyl substituent activates all positions,..so the carbethoxyl group deactivates all positions. **1939** *Nature* 29 Apr. 734/1 The stabilization of petrols by small quantities of organic compounds known as deactivators, which prevent oxidation, is an important advance. **1947** *Science News* V. 160 This drift activates or deactivates the aromatic nucleus. **1956** A. K. OSBORNE *Encycl. Iron & Steel Industry* 105/2 *Deactivation*, the process of prior removal of the active constituents, usually oxygen, from a corrosive liquid. **1958** *Economist* 20 Dec. 1051/1 (Advt.), Gum inhibitors and metal deactivators used in motor and aviation fuels to maintain quality during storage and use. **1970** J. EARL *Tuners & Amplifiers* i. 24 A switch for deactivating the stereo decoder on a weak stereo signal.

dead (dɛd), *a.* (*sb.*[1], *adv.*) Forms: 1-3 **déad**, 2-3 **dæd**, (3 **deæd**), 2-7 **ded**, (4 **deede**, **deid**, **did**, *Ayenb.* **dyad**, **dyead**), 4-6 **deed**, **dede**, 5 **deyde**, **dyde**, 6 **dedde**, 6-7 **deade**, (5- *Sc.* **deid**), 6- **dead**. [A common Teut. adj.; orig. pple.: OE. *déad* = OFris. *dâd* (WFris., NFris. *dead*), OS. *dôd*, MDu. *dôt(d)*, Du. *dood*, MLG. *dôt*, *dôd*, LG. *dôd*, OHG., MHG. *tôt* (Ger. *todt*, *tot*), ON. *dauðr* (Sw., Da. *död*), Goth. *dauþs*:—OTeut. **dau-do-z*, pre-Teut. **dhau-ˈtos*, pa. pple. from vb. stem *dau-* (pre-Teut. *dhau-*), preserved in ON. *deyja* (:—*dau-jan*) and in OS. *dôian*, OHS. *touwen*, to DIE. The suffix is = L. *-tus*, Gr. *-τός*, Skr. *-tas*.

The suffixal *d* in OTeut. **daudo-z*, Eng. *dead* (pre-Teut. **dhauˈtos*), as opposed to the *þ* in *dauþu-z*, *death* (pre-Teut. **ˈdhautus*), shows the influence of the position of the stress accent on the Teutonic representation of original breath mutes, as set forth in Verner's Law.]

A. *adj.* I. Literally, and in senses directly connected.

* *Said of things that have been alive.*

1. That has ceased to live; deprived of life; in that state in which the vital functions and powers have come to an end, and are incapable of being restored: a. of men and animals.

Beowulf 939 Þa wæs Heregar dead min yldra mæȝ. *c* **1000** *Ags. Gosp.* Matt. ix. 24 Nys þys mæden dead. **1154** *O.E. Chron.* (Laud MS.) an. 1135 Þat ilc ȝær warth þe king ded. *c* **1205** LAY. 19229 Hire lauerd wes dæd [*c* **1275** dead]. *a* **1300** *Cursor M.* 6130 (Cott.) Na hus..þat þar ne was ded [*v.rr.* deed, dede] man ligand. *a* **1400** *Poems Vernon MS.* 534 Better is a quik and an hol hounde þen a ded lyon. **1458** in Turner *Dom. Archit.* III. 41 To drawe a deed body out of a lake. **1592** SHAKS. *Rom. & Jul.* v. i. 6, I dreamt my Lady came and found me dead. **1606** —— *Tr. & Cr.* IV. v. 251 Where thou wilt hit me dead. **1660** BOYLE *New Exp. Phys. Mech.* Digress. 360 The Bird..within about a minute more would be stark dead. **1722** DE FOE *Col. Jack* (1840) 233 He was shot dead. **1795** BURKE *Corr.* IV. 239 Dead men, in their written opinions, are heard with patience. **1850** TENNYSON *In Mem.* lxxiv. 1 As sometimes in a dead man's face..A likeness..Comes out—to some one of his race.

b. of plants.

1382 WYCLIF *Jude* 12 Heruest trees withouten fruyt, twies deede, drawun up bi the roote. **1521** FISHER *Wks.* (1876) 326 As a deed stoke, a tree withouten lyfe. **1855** TENNYSON *Maud* I. iii. 14, I..found The shining daffodil dead.

c. of parts or organs of animals or plants. See also DEADHEAD *sb.* 6.

c **1000** ÆLFRIC *Interrog. Sigewulf* (*Anglia* VII. 30), Mid ðam deadum fellum. **1398** TREVISA *Barth. De P.R.* XVI. xciv. (1495) 586 Salte fretyth awaye deed flessh. **1484** CAXTON *Æsop* v. x, He had kytte awey the dede braunches fro the tre. **1561** EDEN *Arte Nauig.* Pref. ¶ij b, Vnsensate by reason of dead fleshe. **1643** J. STEER tr. *Exp. Chyrurg.* vii. 27 If..the skin be burnt dead. **1787** C. B. TRYE in *Med. Commun.* II. 154 The absorbents will remove very little of dead bone. **1821** SHELLEY *Adonais* xvi, The young Spring..threw down Her kindling buds, as if she Autumn were, Or they dead leaves.

d. Specifically used of that which has died of itself, instead of being killed or cut down when alive, as in *dead shell* (of a mollusc), *dead wood*, etc.

1877 *Encycl. Brit.* VI. 539 Dead shells appear in some cases to be thus employed, but..in most..the [Hermit] crab kills the mollusk in order to secure its shell.

¶ *to be dead* was anciently used in the sense 'to die', and later in that of 'to have died'; also = 'To die at the hands of anyone, to be put to death, be killed'.

c **1000** *Ags. Gosp.* Matt. xxii. 24 Gif hwa dead syȝ, & bearn næbbe. *c* **1205** LAY. 196 After þa feourðer ȝere he was dead. *c* **1340** *Cursor M.* 14269 (Trin.) Alle that lyuen & trowen me Deed shul þei neuer be. *c* **1386** CHAUCER *Prol.* 148 Soore wepte she if any of hem were deed. **1388** WYCLIF *2 Cor.* v. 14 If oon died for alle, thanne alle weren deed [*R.V.* then all died]. [**1557** *Tottell's Misc.* (Arb.) 169, I will be dead at once To do my Lady good.]

1382 WYCLIF *Rom.* v. 15 If thorw the gilt of oone many ben deed [ἀπέθανον: *Rhem. & R.V.* 'many died']. **1592** SHAKS. *Rom. & Jul.* v. iii. 210 Alas my liege, my wife is dead to night. **1605** —— *Lear* v. iii. 292 Your eldest Daughters haue fore-done themselues, And desperately are dead. *c* **1676** LADY CHAWORTH in *12th Rep. Hist. MSS. Comm.* App. v. 34 Lord Chesterfields lady is dead in her child-bed month. **1784** JOHNSON *Lett.* (1788) II. 373 Macbean, after three days of illness, is dead of a suppression of urine. **1803** BEDDOES *Hygëia* xi. 75 *note*, I heard..that he was dead of scarlet fever.

a **1300** *Cursor M.* 6688 (Cott.) Qua smites his thain wit a wand, And he be deid vnder his hand. *c* **1375** *Sc. Leg. Saints*, *Andreas* 8 For one þe cors bath ded þai were. **1460** CAPGRAVE *Chron.* 265 Condempned to be ded as a tretoure. *c* **1477** CAXTON *Jason* 10 How many men and..women haue ben slayn and ded by thy poysons.

2. Bereft of sensation or vitality; benumbed, insensible. a. Of parts of the body. (Also *fig.*)

See also DEAD PALSY.

a **1225** *Ancr. R.* 112 A lutel ihurt i þen eie derueð more þen deð a muchel iðe hele: vor þet fleschs is deadure þere. **1398** TREVISA *Barth. De P.R.* IV. i. (1495) 77 Thynges that be deed and dystroyed wyth colde. **1590** SPENSER *F.Q.* I. vii. 21 The messenger of so unhappie newes Would faine have dyde: dead was his hart within. **1607** TOPSELL *Serpents* (1658) 593 They take Serpents in the Winter time, when they grow dead and stiffe through cold. **1806** COLERIDGE in Flagg *Life W. Allston* (1893) 77 My head felt like another man's head; so dead was it [etc.]. **1893** J. HUTCHINSON *Archives Surg.* No. 12 III. 311 The liability to 'dead fingers'. *Ibid.* 312 This pair of fingers on each hand had been liable for at least two years to become 'dead' in the morning after washing.

b. Of persons: deathlike, insensible, in a swoon. *Obs.* Also of *sleep*, a *faint*.

c **1369** CHAUCER *Dethe Blaunche* 127 She..Was wery, and thus the ded slepe Fil on hir. **1598** FLORIO, *Sópore*, a dead swoune, deepe sleepe or drousie sicknes. **1610** SHAKS. *Temp.* v. i. 230 We were dead of sleepe. **1610** BARROUGH *Physick* (1639) I. xx. 30 Coma..may be called in English dead sleep. **1666-7** PEPYS *Diary* 7 Feb. (D.), He was fallen down all along upon the ground dead..he did presently come to himself. **1752** FIELDING *Amelia* III. ix. (D.), We there beheld the most shocking sight in the world, Miss Bath lying dead on the floor..Miss Bath was at length recovered. *Mod.* She fell on the floor in a dead faint.

c. In hyperbolical phrases expressing extreme fatigue or indisposition.

1813 ANNABELLA MILBANKE *Diary* (MS.), At home dead. **1894** *Pall Mall Mag.* Feb. 583 I'm nearly dead from being boxed up in the house all day. **1915** W. S. MAUGHAM *Of Human Bondage* xliii. 208 You know, I'm simply dead. I don't think I can absorb anything more profitably. Let's go and sit down. **1962** J. BRAINE *Life at Top* xiv. 185 'It doesn't matter who started it now,' I yawned. 'Honestly, I'm dead on my feet, Susan.' **1970** P. CARLON *Death by Demonstration* xvi. 175 One job's enough. Come evening and I'm dead on my feet usually.

d. Of pain: dull and continuous, as opposed to sharp and sudden pain.

1863 T. B. CURLING *Dis. Rectum* (ed. 3) 24 He complained of suffering from a dead, aching pain. **1894** MRS. H. H. GARDENER *Unoff. Patriot* 348 She only sat and stared, and was conscious of the dull dead pain.

3. a. As good as dead in respect *to* (something); insensible *to*.

1340 *Ayenb.* 240 He ssel by dyead to þe wordle, and libbe to god. **1601** ? MARSTON *Pasquil & Kath.* I. 307 You are dead to natiue pleasures life. **1647** N. BACON *Disc. Govt. Eng.* I. lix. (1739) 114 He that is in a Monastery is dead to all worldly affairs. **1726** SHELVOCKE *Voy. round World* 224 Obstinate fellows who were dead to reason. **1813** SHELLEY *Q. Mab* v. 33 Sensual, and vile; Dead to all love. **1874** GREEN *Short Hist.* viii. 550 Charles was equally dead to the moderation and to the wisdom of this great Act of Settlement.

b. Hence, As good as dead, in some particular respect or capacity: *spec.* in *Law*, cut off from civil rights and so legally reckoned as dead.

1710 POPE *Let. to Cromwell* 17 May, Dead in a poetical Capacity, as a damn'd Author; and dead in a civil Capacity, as a useless Member of the Common-wealth. **1828** WEBSTER, *Dead*..In *law*, cut off from the rights of a citizen ..as one banished or becoming a monk is civilly dead. *Blackstone*.

c. Colloq. phr. *dead to the world*: unconscious or fast asleep; unaware of the external world.

1899 ADE *Doc' Horne* ii. 19 Our host is dead to the world,' observed the actor... 'Let him rest,' said Doc'. **1906** E. DYSON *Fact'ry 'Ands* iii. 31 Heaven knows what blissful emotions were stirring softly in his bony breast, but he was 'dead to the world'. **1906** *Dialect Notes* III. II. 133 *Dead to the world*, unconscious. 'He fell down and was dead to the world for a while.' **1955** E. HILLARY *High Adventure* 166 He stumbled and fell slowly on to his face and lay there—dead to the world! **1957** G. FRICK tr. *Yourcenar's Coup de Grâce* 56 A muffled sound of snoring rose from the great hall.. where thirty exhausted lads lay dead to the world.

4. Destitute of spiritual life or energy.

1382 WYCLIF *Eph.* ii. 1 Whanne ȝe weren deede in ȝoure giltis and synnes. **1534** TINDALE *1 Tim.* v. 6 She that liveth in pleasure, is deed even yet alive. **1651** HOBBES *Leviath.* I. viii. 35 To have no Desire, is to be Dead. **1668** HOWE *Bless. Righteous* (1825) 206 How often are men the deader for all endeavours to quicken them. **1793** COWPER *Stanzas Yearly Bill of Mortality* i, He lives, who lives to God alone, And all are dead beside. **1884** J. PARKER *Apost. Life* III. 111 There is no deader thing unburied..in many places, than the professing Church of Christ.

5. *fig.* Of things (practices, feelings, etc.): No longer in existence, or in use; extinct, obsolete, perished, past; *esp.* of languages, no longer spoken. (See also DEAD LETTER.)

1591 SHAKS. *Two Gent.* II. vi. 28 My Loue to her is dead. **1641** J. JACKSON *True Evang. T.* I. 71 These..are dead tenets and opinions. **1712** ADDISON *Spect.* No. 285 ¶5 The Works of Ancient Authors, which are written in dead Languages. **1847** TENNYSON *Princ.* VII. 327 My doubts are dead. **1861** BERESF. HOPE *Eng. Cathedr. 19th C.* 167 The lapse from vernacular to dead tongue services. **1884** J. SHARMAN *Hist. Swearing* vi. 102 Seeking to revive this dead past.

** *Said of things naturally without life.*

6. a. Not endowed with life; inanimate.

1430 *E.E. Wills* (1882) 85 Alle necessarijs longynge to housold of dede store. **1534** MORE *On the Passion* Wks. 1274/1 He made it haue a beyng, as hathe the dead stone. **1636** SANDERSON *Serm.* II. 57 Shooting sometimes at a dead mark. **1712** ADDISON *Spect.* No. 519 ¶6 There are some living creatures which are raised but just above dead matter. **1857** H. MILLER *Test. Rocks* iii. 156 The long ascending line from dead matter to man.

b. Applied rhetorically, emphasizing the inert and negative qualities of mere matter.

(In the quot. there are also associations with branch III.)

c **1380** WYCLIF *Wks.* (1880) 23 And þus þese rome renneris beren þe kyngys gold out of oure lond, and bryngen aȝen deed leed, and heresie and symonye and goddis curse.

*** *Transferred applications of the literal senses.*

7. Composed of dead plants, or of dead wood, as *a dead hedge* or *fence* (opposed to *quickset*).

1563 HYLL *Art Garden.* (1593) 7 A..rude inclosure.. made of..bushes hauing no life, which wee name a dead hedge. **1686** PLOT *Staffordsh.* 357 For a dead-fence, none.. better..than those heathy-turf walls. **1728** DOUGLAS in *Phil. Trans.* XXXV. 567 The Fences consist of what they call dead Hedges, or Hurdles to keep out..Cattle. **1805** FORSYTH *Beauties Scotl.* I. 524 A dead hedge is generally placed on the top of the bank.

8. Of, pertaining or relating to a dead person, animal, plant, etc., or to some one's death.

(In some cases not easily separated from the attributive use in B. 6, or from *dead*, northern form of DEATH *sb.*)

1580 SIDNEY *Arcadia* II. (1674) 130 (D.) The tomb.. which they caused to be made for them with..notable workmanship, to preserve their dead lives. **1595** SHAKS. *John* v. vii. 65 You breath these dead newes in as dead an eare. **1662** R. MATHEW *Unl. Alch.* §89. 140 His water [was] shewn to two Doctors, whose judgement was that it was a dead water; and..he would die that night. **1712** J. JAMES tr. *Le Blond's Gardening* 173 It is more difficult to make Plants grow in Gaps and dead Places, than in a new Spot. **1791** W. COOMBE *Devil upon Two Sticks* (1817) IV. 182 It is what the medical people call a dead case..a consultation..to discover the disorder of which their patient died. **1846** J. BAXTER *Libr. Pract. Agric.* (ed. 4) I. 399 (*Hop-growing*) When a dead hill occurs in a garden..the following is the quickest mode of replacing it.

†9. Causing death, deadly, mortal. *Obs.*

c **1400** *Destr. Troy* 1339 In a ded hate. *Ibid.* 11017 Pyrrus ..come..þat doghty to dere with a dede stroke. **1606** *Choice, Chance, &c.* (1881) 72 Beares a dead wound but as a little stripe. **1611** SHAKS. *Wint. T.* IV. iv. 445 Thou Churle, for this time (Though full of our displeasure) yet we free thee From the dead blow of it.

10. Devoid of 'life' or living organisms; hence, barren, infertile, yielding nothing. (Cf. B. 4.)

1577 B. GOOGE *Heresbach's Husb.* (1586) I. 21 b (*marg.*), Though the land be as riche as may be, yet yf you goe any deapth, you shall have it barren [*margin* Dead mould]. **1674** N. FAIRFAX *Bulk & Selv.* 186 You cannot dig many spades in mold or growthsom earth, before you come at a dead soyl. **1747** HOOSON *Miner's Dict.* G ij b, *Dead* [is] where there is no Ore..*Deads* are the Gear or Work got in such dead Places. **1806** FORSYTH *Beauties Scotl.* IV. 57 A rich friable clay on a bottom of dead sand. **1820** SCORESBY *Acc. Arct. Reg.* II. 211 The parallel of 77° to 77½° is considered a 'dead latitude' by the fishers, but occasionally it affords whales. **1874** KNIGHT *Dict. Mech.*, *Dead-ground* (*Mining*), a body of non-metalliferous rock dividing a vein, which passes on each side of it.

II. Deprived of or wanting some 'vital' or characteristic physical quality.

11. Without fire, flame, or glow; extinguished, extinct. (Opposed to *live*, as in *live coal*.)

1340 *Ayenb.* 205 A quic col bernide ope ane hyeape of dyade coles. **1530** PALSGR. 212/2 Deed cole, *charbon*. **1611** SHAKS. *Wint. T.* v. i. 68 Starres, Starres, And all eyes else, dead coales. **1639** HORN & ROB. *Gate Lang. Unl.* v. §46 Wood burning is called a fire-brand; being quenched..a dead brand. **1833** H. COLERIDGE *Sonn.* xviii, The crackling embers on the hearth are dead. **1884** *Illust. Lond. News* 19 Jan. 66/3 Putting his dead cigar in his mouth and puffing as though it had been alight.

12. Having lost its active quality or virtue.

a. Of drink, etc.: That has lost its sharpness, taste, or flavour; flat, vapid, insipid. ? *Obs.*

1552 HULOET, Dead, pale, or vinewed to be, as wyne which hath lost his verdure, *muceo*. **1580** BARET *Alv.* D 132 Dead and vnsauorie salt. **1596** NASHE *Saffron Walden* 115 A cup of dead beere, that had stood pawling by him in a pot three dayes. **1607** TOPSELL *Four-f. Beasts* (1673) 430 If..it [Musk] lose the savour and be dead. **1664** EVELYN *Pomona* Advt., It will not ferment at all, and then the Cider will be dead, flat, and soure. **1747** WESLEY *Prim. Physic* (1765) 68 Dip a soft Rag in dead small Beer.

b. *dead lime*: opposed to *quick-lime*; *dead steam*, exhausted steam.

1831 *Mech. Mag.* XVI. 79 In certain circumstances carbonate of lime is changed by burning into lime which does not heat with water, and which is called dead lime. **1874** KNIGHT *Dict. Mech.*, Dead steam.

c. *Electr.* Of a circuit, conductor, etc.: carrying or transmitting no current; not connected to a source of electricity.

1903 A. H. BEAVAN *Tube, Train*, etc. xi. 134 The studs are 'alive' while the car is over them, and 'dead' as soon as it has passed. **1906** *Westm. Gaz.* 13 July 5/2 There was another stoppage..caused by a 'dead' car. **1929** D. HAMMETT *Dain Curse* (1930) xi. 109 The phone was there, but dead. **1937** DAVID JONES *In Parenthesis* v. 112 Every telephonist with a dead instrument about his ears. **1968** *Globe & Mail* (Toronto) 3 Feb. 5/5, I tried to call the operator but the phone was dead.

13. Without colour or brightness: †**a.** Of the countenance, etc.: Deadly pale, wan. *Obs.*

c **1386** CHAUCER *Doctor's T.* 209 With a face deed as aisshen colde. *c* **1430** LYDG. *Bochas* III. xx. 91 b, With pale and dead visage. **1500–20** DUNBAR *Tua Mariit Wemen* 420, I drup with a ded luke, in my dule habit. **1567** R. EDWARDS *Damon & Pithias* in Hazl. *Dodsley* IV. 98 Why is thy colour so dead? **1604** SHAKS. *Oth.* II. iii. 177 Honest Iago, that lookes dead with greeuing. **1668** DRYDEN *Maiden Queen* II. i, The dead colour of her face.

b. Of colour, etc.: Without brightness, dull, lustreless. (See also DEAD COLOUR.)

1640 PARKINSON *Theat. Bot.* 483 Such like flowers, but of a sadder or deader colour. **1720** DE FOE *Capt. Singleton* viii. (1840) 138 A thick moss..of a blackish dead colour. **1805–17** R. JAMESON *Char. Min.* 59 The principal colours are divided into two series..bright colours, [and] dead colours; red, green, blue, and yellow belong to the first; and white, grey, black, and brown, to the second. **1855** BRIMLEY *Ess.* 58 The deader green of ordinary foliage. **1874** KNIGHT *Dict. Mech.*, *Dead-gold*, the unburnished surface of gold or gold-leaf..Parts of objects are frequently left unburnished as a foil to the..burnished portions. **1883** J. MILLINGTON *Are we to read backwards?* 93 Paper of a brown or yellow tint, with a dead or non-reflecting surface.

14. a. Of sound: without resonance, dull, muffled.

c **1530** LD. BERNERS *Arth. Lyt. Bryt.* (1814) 289 The lady called them again, but..very softely, for it was with a dead voice. **1580** BARET *Alv.* D 131 Ones voice..neither dead in sowne, nor ouer shrill. **1660** BOYLE *New Exp. Phys. Mech.* xxvii. 209 The Bell seem'd to sound more dead. **1675** WOOD *Life* (Oxf. Hist. Soc.) II. 332 They being so cast, severall were found to be ugly dead bells. **1712** F. T. *Shorthand* 5 The sound of D being like a flat dead T. **1783** BLAGDEN in *Phil. Trans.* LXXIII. 332 A solid..metallic mass..yielding a dull dead sound like that metal [lead]. **1847** MRS. SHERWOOD *Fairchild Fam.* III. viii. 110 A dead sound of some heavy, though soft body, in the..act of falling.

b. *Acoustics.* Allowing little or no reverberation.

1907 *Science* XXVI. 879/2 The small room..when closed ..also serves to act as a dead air space between the larger room and the building wall. **1923** GLAZEBROOK *Dict. Appl. Physics* IV. 694/2 A room considered to be right for speech may be just a little too *dead* for music. **1930** *Bell. Syst. Techn. Jrnl.* IX. 596 (*heading*) Reverberation Time in 'Dead' Rooms. *Ibid.*, With the advent of radio broadcasting and sound pictures very 'dead' rooms have been built. **1962** A. NISBETT *Technique Sound Studio* ii. 33 To do away with reverberation entirely and try to create entirely 'dead' studios. *Ibid.* 47 A section of the studio with almost completely dead acoustics, i.e. a 'dead-room'.

15. Not fulfilling the normal and ostensible purpose. (See also *dead door* (in D. 2), DEAD-EYE, DEAD-LIGHT 1, DEAD WELL 2.)

1806 FORSYTH *Beauties Scotl.* IV. 381 A..bridge..over the water of Bervie, the dead arches of which have been fitted up as a town-hall. **1874** KNIGHT *Dict. Mech.*, *Dead*.. 2. False; as of imitation doors and windows, put in as architectural devices to balance parts.

III. Without animation, vigour, or activity; inactive, quiet, dull.

16. a. Without vigour or animation, lifeless.

a **1000** *Seafarer* 65 (Bosw.) Me hatran sind Dryhtnes dreamas ðonne ðis deade lif. *c* **1422** HOCCLEVE *Learn to Die* 714 Where is your help now, where is your chiertee?..al as deed is as a stoon? **1579** TOMSON *Calvin's Serm. Tim.* 691/1 To shewe that wee are Gods true seruants we must not go to work with a dead hand (as the prouerb is). **1646** H. LAWRENCE *Comm. Angells* 167 Patience without hope is the deadest thing in the world. *c* **1665** MRS. HUTCHINSON *Mem. Col. Hutchinson* 24 Or can be gathered from a bare dead description. *a* **1719** ADDISON (J.), How cold and dead does a prayer appear..when it is not heightened by solemnity of phrase from the sacred writings. **1856** EMERSON *Eng. Traits, Race* Wks. (Bohn) II. 22 Active intellect and dead conservatism.

b. *slang.* Of a race-horse: not intended to win; fraudulently run in such a way that it cannot win; chiefly in *dead one, dead 'un*.

1864 *Baily's Mag.* June 121 A horse which has been regarded occasionally as a dead one has proved lively enough to beat the winner of the Two Thousand. **1868** *London Review* 11 July 38/2 The stable and owners might safely lay against what was technically a 'dead 'un' from the first. **1880** H. SMART *Social Sinners* v, Lord, what 'dead 'uns' he did back, to be sure! **1922** *N. & Q.* 12th Ser. XI. 206/2 *Dead meat.* Horses which are not out to win are so described.

c. Lacking resiliency or springiness; esp. of turf.

1870 *N.Y. Herald* 22 July 5/6 A dead ball was used, and again it was clearly demonstrated that this is the proper kind to play with. **1895** H. W. W. WILBERFORCE *Lawn Tennis* ix. 29 This form of game..arose from the very wet and dead state of the courts. **1909** P. A. VAILE *Mod. Golf* viii. 120 You will do well, should you have to choose [a driver] for yourself, to exercise moderation. Avoid too much spring. Don't have a 'dead' one. **1930** *Morning Post* 16 July 16/2 So well did Squires and Peach perform on the dead pitch that the Kent total of 317 was passed without the loss of another wicket.

17. Without active force or practical effect; ineffectual, inoperative. (See also DEAD LETTER 1.)

c **1380** WYCLIF *Wks.* (1880) 22 ȝif it be ded feiþ as fendis han. *c* **1400** *Apol. Loll.* 3 Seynt Jam seiþ, Feiþ wiþ outun werkis is deed. **1548** in *Vicary's Anat.* (1888) App. iii. 133 Good and necessarye ordres..with-out the which, all lawes and ordenaunces..ar butt baryn, ded, and vayne. **1647** N. BACON *Disc. Govt. Eng.* I. xvi, Nor was this a dead word; for the people had formerly a trick of deposing their Kings. **1842** J. H. NEWMAN *Par. Serm.* VI. xii. 179 To have been so earnest for a dead ordinance.

18. a. Characterized by absence of physical activity, motion, or sound; profoundly quiet or still. (Cf. B. 2.)

1548 HALL *Chron.* 107 In the dedde tyme of the night. **1573** G. HARVEY *Letter-bk.* (Camden) 12 It was in the deadist time of winter. **1603** SHAKS. *Meas. for M.* IV. ii. 67 'Tis now dead midnight. *a* **1610** KNOLLES (J.), They came in the dead winter to Aleppo. **1863** KINGLAKE *Crimea* (1876) I. xiv. 294 The dead hours of the night.

b. Of a house: uninhabited. *slang.*

1879 J. W. HORSLEY in *Macm. Mag.* XL. 505/2 Me and the screwsman went to Gravesend, and I found a dead 'un (uninhabited house). **1896** A. MORRISON *Child Jago* 231 On the look out for a dead 'un. **1922** *Daily Mail* 8 Aug. 2/2 We thought it was a 'dead' house, but we walked into a girl's room and she squealed.

c. *Mil.* Denoting an area which cannot be fired on from a particular point because of the nature of the ground, intervening obstacles, etc. (Cf. *dead angle* in D. 2.)

1899 *Westm. Gaz.* 9 Dec. 5/3 Besides the great advantage which we shall reap from the smashing power of these howitzers against field defences, we shall also find them most valuable to search out hollow or hidden ground 'dead' to other fire. **1900** *Daily News* 5 May 3/2 A high and rather steep hill, surrounded by a good deal of 'dead' ground. **1919** *Proc. Soc. Antiq. Scot.* LIII. 38 There is not a single piece of 'dead' ground in the whole fortress.

19. Without alertness or briskness, inert.

1884 *St. James's Gaz.* 4 Apr. 6/1 His recovery [in rowing] is dead, but his work strong.

20. a. Without commercial, social, or intellectual activity; inactive, dull. (Of places, seasons, trade, etc.).

1581 RICHE *Farewell* (Shaks. Soc.) 11 Traffique is so dead by meanes of thes foraine broiles, that [etc.]. **1615** STEPHENS *Satyr. Ess.* (ed. 2) 193 As much leasure..in the most busie Terme, as in the deadest Vacation. **1665** *Surv. Aff. Netherl.* 25 Complaints against dead Trade. **1676** TEMPLE *Let. to Sir W. Godolphin* Wks. 1731 II. 395 This Place is now as dead as I have seen any great Town. **1758** JOHNSON *Idler* No. 55 ¶10 Some [publishers] never had known such a dead time. **1774** FOOTE *Cozeners* II. Wks. 1799 II. 161 The town is thin, and business begins to grow dead. **1883** FROUDE in *Mrs. Carlyle's Lett.* I. 59 It was the dead season; but there were a few persons still in London.

b. Of capital or stock: Lying commercially inactive or unemployed, unproductive.

1570–1 GRESHAM *Let.* 7 Mar. in Burgon *Life* II. 421 There is yet in the Towre xxv or xxx M *li.* in Spannyshe monney; which is great pity should lye there dead and put to no use. **1622** MALYNES *Anc. Law-Merch.* 325 They will not keep it by them as a dead stocke..they must imploy it in trade. **1691** LOCKE *Lower. Interest* 7 That so none of the money.. may lie dead. **1708** *Lond. Gaz.* No. 4419/6 A considerable quantity of Arms and Ammunition, which were the dead Stock of the African Company. **1729** FRANKLIN *Ess.* Wks. (1840) II. 267 The money, which otherwise would have lain dead in their hands, is made to circulate again. **1813** SIR S. ROMILLY in *Examiner* 15 Feb. 101/2 A fund, out of which part of this salary was proposed to be paid, was the *Dead Fund*, amounting to 9000*l.* **1818** JAS. MILL *Brit. India* I. I. iii. 44 The dead stock, as it is technically called.

c. Of goods: Lying unsold, unsaleable, for which there is no market.

1669–70 DRYDEN *Tyrannic Love* v. i, And all your goods lie dead upon your hands. **1681** R. KNOX *Hist. Ceylon* in Arb. *Garner* I. 390 And now caps were become a very dead commodity. **1879** HIBBS in *Cassell's Techn. Educ.* IV. 263/2 A large quantity of finished articles lying as dead stock in the market.

d. *Typogr.* That has been used or is no longer required, as copy after composition, or type ready for distribution or discarded.

a **1877** KNIGHT *Dict. Mech.* I. 679/2 *Dead-letter*, type which has been used for printing, and is ready for distribution. *Dead matter.* **1898** J. SOUTHWARD *Mod. Printing* I. xxiv. 154 The 'dead' letter..would, if of uniform face, constitute in itself a strong fount.

e. Of a cinema set: out of use. Cf. also quot. 1933.

1929 A. C. & C. B. EDINGTON *Studio Murder Myst.* i. 7 The skeletons of 'dead' sets clothed in flowing veils of gray. **1933** P. GODFREY *Back-Stage* i. 20 Every stage accessory which becomes 'dead'—that is to say, which is not used again during the performance—must be cleared to below-stage.

21. a. Of a ball in a game: Inactive (for the time being), out of play. Cf. DEAD WOOD 1.

1658 OSBORN *Adv. Son* (1673) 104 A place that seems equally inclined to different Opinions, I would advise to count it as Bowlers do, for dead to the present understanding. **1828** *Boy's Own Bk. Diversions* (ed. 2) 55 If any player shall stop the ball intentionally..it shall then be considered dead. **1844** *Laws of Cricket* xxxiii, It any fieldsman stop the ball with his hat, the ball shall be considered dead. **1868** W. J. WHITMORE *Croquet Tact.* 9 The term 'dead' ball is borrowed from cricket, and means the ball which, having just been played, has nothing actively to do for one turn. **1875** *Encycl. Brit.* III. 407/1 (Baseball) A ball which hits the bat without being struck at, or the person of the striker or umpire, is a dead ball and out of play. **1876** *Ibid.* IV. 180/2 A 'dead bowl' is one knocked off the green, or against one lying in the ditch, or an illegally played bowl, and must at once be removed from the green. **1900** *Laws of Cricket* 4, 33a. If the ball, whether struck with the bat or not, lodges in a batsman's clothing, the ball shall become 'Dead'. **1902** *Encycl. Brit.* XXVIII. 426/2 So the game [*sc.* Rugby football] proceeds until the ball is once more 'dead'—that is, brought to a standstill. **1966** B. JOHNSTON *Armchair Cricket* 97 A ball does *not* become dead when it strikes an umpire.

b. *Golf.* Of the ball: placed so near the hole that it can be holed with certainty at the next stroke. Also as *adv.*

1857 H. B. FARNIE *Golfer's Manual* (1947) vii. 73 A ball is said to be dead..when it lies so close to the hole that the put is a certainty. **1881** R. FORGAN *Golfer's Handbk.* iii. 30 If you can possibly win a 'half' [i.e. halve a hole] by running your ball 'dead' at the side of the hole,..then the cautious game is to be preferred. **1898** H. G. HUTCHINSON *Golf* (ed. 6) 83 Missing a four-inch put which your partner has left you.. and receiving the cheery consolation, 'Never mind, partner, never mind—another time I'll try to lay you dead.' **1909** P. A. VAILE *Mod. Golf* v. 73 A man may lie 'dead' off a run up, but I am referring now to the well-lofted shot that falls 'plump' within an easy put of the hole and scarcely moves.

IV. Without motion (relatively or absolutely).

22. a. Of water, air, etc.: Without motion or current; still, standing. (See also DEAD WATER.)

a **1000** *Gnomica* (Exon.) 79 (Gr.) Deop deada wæȝ dyrne bið lengest. *a* **1552** LELAND *Collect.* (1774) II. 546 The Water of Forth beyond Banokesburne, a deade depe Water. **1601** HOLLAND *Pliny* (1634) I. 55 The dead and slow riuer Araris. **1653** WALTON *Angler* 91 As he [the Trout] growes stronger, he gets from the dead, still water, into the sharp streames and the gravel. **1861** HUGHES *Tom Brown at Oxf.* xxxvi. (1889) 357 The wind had fallen dead. **1867** BAKER *Nile Trib.* ii. 32 The banks..had evidently been overflowed during floods, but at the present time the river was dead.

b. *Mining.* Having no current of air, unventilated.

1867 W. W. SMITH *Coal & Coal-mining* 27 It would leave the mass of the openings inside of the working 'bords' dead or stagnant.

c. Of molten metal: thick and sluggish, either from insufficient melting or from having stood too long in a ladle. Cf. DEAD-MELT *v.*

1884 W. H. GREENWOOD *Steel & Iron* xviii. 425 Too long exposure to the heat, or extreme 'dead-melting', produces a metal that runs dull and dead, affording ingots also of inferior quality.

d. Of ice: see quots.

1909 *Cent. Dict.* Suppl. I. 619/3 *Dead ice*, ancient ice retained in 'fossil glaciers' or elsewhere under the soil and not moving downward. **1937** WOOLDRIDGE & MORGAN *Physical Basis Geogr.* xxii. 381 In Spitzbergen and elsewhere the ice has sometimes advanced over the low ground, but there has been no correspondingly rapid retreat. It has simply been left as 'dead ice', decaying by melting very slowly and without the production of large quantities of water. **1966** T. ARMSTRONG et al. *Gloss. Snow & Ice* 13 *Dead ice*, any part of a glacier which has ceased to flow. Dead ice is usually covered with moraine.

23. Said of parts of machines or apparatus which do not themselves rotate or move. (Cf. also *dead-rope* (in D. 2), DEAD-CENTRE 2, -LINE 1.)

1807 GREGORY *Mechanics* II. 474 One of these pulleys called the dead pulley is fixed to the axis and turns with it. **1874** KNIGHT *Dict. Mech.*, *Dead*..3. Motionless; as the dead spindle of a lathe, which does not rotate.

24. a. Characterized by complete and abrupt cessation of motion, action, or speech: as *a dead stop*, a sudden complete stop.

1647 WARD *Simp. Cobler* 19 Others..are at a dead stand. **1765** STERNE *Tr. Shandy* VII. xliii, My mule made a dead point. **1775** MAD. D'ARBLAY *Early Diary, Lett. Dr. Burney* Mar., My poor book—at a dead stop now. **1853** LYTTON *My Novel* I. xi, There was a dead pause. **1861** DICKENS *Gt. Expect.* ix, The answer spoilt his joke, and brought him to a dead stop.

b. Characterized by abrupt stoppage of motion without recoil; cf. DEAD BEAT *sb.*[1]

1761 HIRST in *Phil. Trans.* LII. 396 It did not stop in winding up, and scaped dead seconds. **1768** tr. *P. Le Roy's Attempts for finding Longitude* 29 [The escapement] of my watches is a dead one. **1874** KNIGHT *Dict. Mech.*, *Dead-stroke hammer*, a power-hammer which delivers its blow without being affected by the recoil of the shaft.

c. *Cricket.* Of a bat: held in a defensive position with a slightly loose grip so that the ball strikes it and immediately drops to the ground.

1955 *Times* 13 July 8/6 But subsequently Bailey was simply Bailey, calm and unshakable, his whole defence built round the dead bat forward stroke. **1956** R. ALSTON *Test Commentary* 113 These days of dead-bat technique and over-cautious defence.

V. Unrelieved, unbroken; absolute; complete; utmost.

These senses arise out of several of the preceding (cf. 18, 22, 24); and in some cases there is a blending of two or more notions.

25. a. Of a wall, level, etc.: Unbroken, unrelieved by breaks or interruptions; absolutely uniform and continuous.

In *dead level* there is at once the sense 'unrelieved, unvaried, monotonous', and that of 'having no fall or inclination in any direction, absolute'.

1597 BACON *Coulers Good & Evil* (Arb.) 143 It seemeth.. a shorter distance..if it be all dead and continued, then if it haue trees or buildings or any other markes whereby the eye may deuide it. **1670** DRYDEN *Conq. Granada* II. III. i, By the dead wall, you, Abdelmelech, wind. **1742** POPE *Dunc.* IV.

268 We bring to one dead level every mind. **1860** Tyndall *Glac.* I. xxii. 153, I become more weary upon a dead level.. than on a steep mountain side. **1868** Yates *Rock Ahead* II. i, On every hoarding and dead-wall. **1887** Lowell *Democr.* 19 To reduce all mankind to a dead level of mediocrity.

†**b.** Flat. *Obs.*

1782 *Specif. Conway's Patent* No. 1310. 2 The oven..has a dead or flat hearth.

26. Of calm or silence: Profound, deep (passing into the sense of 'complete, absolute': from 18).

1673 Ld. Shaftsbury in *Coll. of Poems* 248 That we may not be tossed with boisterous Winds, nor overtaken by a sudden dead Calm. **1783** Blagden in *Phil. Trans.* LXXIII. 354 A dead silence on the subject seems to have prevailed. **1839** T. Beale *Sperm Whale* 205 There was a 'dead calm'.. not a breath of wind stirring. **1847** Tennyson *Princ.* IV. 371 We heard In the dead hush the papers that she held Rustle.

27. Said of the lowest or stillest state of the tide, as ***dead low water, dead neap***: cf. 31.

1561 [see dead-water 3]. **1589** Greene *Menaphon* (Arb.) 29 The Ocean at his deadest ebbe returns to a full tide. **1626** Capt. Smith *Accid. Yng. Seamen* 17 A lowe water, a dead lowewater. *a* **1641** Spelman *Hist. Sacrilege* (1698) 285 Such a dead Neipe (as they call it) as no Man living was known to have seen the like, the Sea fell so far back from the Land at Hunstanton. **1679** Dryden *Troil. & Cr.* Pref., At high-flood of passion, even in the dead ebb, and lowest water-mark of the scene. **1724** *Lond. Gaz.* No. 6290/3 At dead Low-Water upon a Spring Tide. **1809** Rennell in *Phil. Trans.* XCIX. 403 *note*, The..accident happened at dead neaps. **1857** Livingstone *Trav.* xxxii. 669, I crossed it at dead low-water.

28. In ***dead pull, dead strain***, applied to the absolute or utmost exertion of strength to move an inert or resisting body; sheer; also to such tension exerted without producing motion. See also dead-lift.

1812-6 Playfair *Nat. Phil.* (1819) I. 109 The weight which the animal exerting itself to the utmost, or at a *dead pull*, is just able to overcome. **1855** Bain *Senses & Int.* II. ii. §12 This power taking the form of movement as distinct from dead strain. **1857** Whewell *Hist. Induct. Sc.* I. 73 We may have pressure without motion, or dead pull..as at the critical instant when two nicely-matched wrestlers are balanced by the exertion of the utmost strength of each. **1890** B. L. Gildersleeve *Ess. & Stud.* 64 There are things that must be learned by a dead pull.

29. Pressing with its full or unrelieved weight like an inanimate or inert body: see dead-weight. ***dead load***, a load whose weight is constant and invariable; also *attrib.*

1781 Cowper *Truth* 354 But royalty, nobility, and state, Are such a dead, preponderating weight. **1866** [see factor *sb.* 8]. **1891** *Scribner's Mag.* X. 7 The greater engine-power will add to the dead load, thus still further diminishing the vessel's capability for carrying. **1930** *Engineering* 18 Apr. 503/2 To relieve the main girders of dead-load deflection and live-load stress. **1970** *Fremdsprachen* 43 The stratum.. could be used for safe bearing pressures of 1,200 and 1,800 psf, for dead load and total load respectively.

30. Said of a charge, expense, loss: Unrelieved, absolute, complete, utter; also, of outlay, Unproductive, without returns. ***dead rent***: a fixed rent which remains as a constant and unvarying charge upon a mining concession, etc. ***dead loss***: a complete loss; freq. *colloq.* , a person or thing that is totally worthless, inefficient, or unsuccessful; a complete failure; an utter waste of time. (Cf. quot. 1757.)

a **1715** Burnet *Own Time* (1823) I. 452 The intrinsic wealth of the nation was very high when it could answer such a dead charge. **1757** Jos. Harris *Coins* 79 The deficiency upon the coins is so much dead loss to the public. **1796** Burke *Regic. Peace* i. Wks. VIII. 152 It required a dead expence of three Millions sterling. **1825** Scott *Let.* 25 May in Lockhart, I am a sharer to the extent of £1500 on a railroad which will..double the rent..but is dead outlay in the mean time. **1826** Cobbett *Rur. Rides* (1885) II. 7 Those colonies are a dead expense to us without a possibility of their ever being of any use. **1893** Sir J. W. Chitty in *Law Times Rep.* LXVIII. 428/2 The royalty reserved was fourpence a ton..the dead rent was 30*l.* a year. **1907** *Sears, Roebuck Catal.* 607/2 We seldom have two orders 'just alike' in every particular, consequently if the net was returned it would be a 'dead loss' to us. **1927** T. E. Lawrence *Let.* 27 Dec. in *To his Biographer, R. Graves* (1938) II. 144 This time it was a really good guard, and so I feel that the holiday has not been a dead loss. **1934** *Discovery* Nov. 317/2 Dead weight [on railways] means dead loss. **1951** 'J. Wyndham' *Day of Triffids* v. 82 Certain unmistakable *derniers cris*, some of them undoubtedly destined..to become the rage of tomorrow: others, I would say, a dead loss from their very inception. **1956** D. M. Davin *Sullen Bell* 92 You think a dead loss like myself has no right to say it.

31. a. Absolute, complete, entire, thorough, downright. Also *dead-earnest* in adjectival use.

[Arising out of various earlier senses.]

1660 Sharrock *Vegetables* 20 Till the seed..be come to a full and dead ripenesse. **1766** Goldsm. *Vic. W.* xii, I had them a dead bargain. **1805** Scott *Let. to J. Ballantyne* 12 Apr., This is a dead secret. **1842** S. Kettell *Quozziana* 47, I saw, to a dead certainty, that if I should..be caught with my mouth open, I should be expected to say something. **1860** *Players* I. 154 'Done brown, to a dead certainty' said Buzzen to himself, as he went on eating. **1875** 'Mark Twain' in *Atlantic Monthly* Mar. 288/2 The grimmest and most dead-earnest of reading-matter. **1878** *Print. Trades Jrnl.* No. 25. 15 We know to a dead certainty that [etc.]. **1883** *Century Mag.* XXV. 372/2, I am in dead earnest. **1883** 'Mark Twain' *Life Mississippi* xviii. 223 Ritchie's good-natured badgering was pretty nearly as aggravating as Brown's dead-earnest nagging.

b. Quite certain, sure, unerring. (Cf. *dead certainty* in prec. sense.) ***dead shot***, one whose aim is certain death; so ***dead on the bird***. ***dead-on***: certain, unerring, exactly right (see quot. 1889). See also dead-hand 2.

a **1592** Greene *Jas. IV*, III. i. 203 I, I am dead at a pocket sir..I can..picke a purse as soone as any theefe in my countrie. **1681** Chetham *Angler's Vade-m.* x. §4 (1689) 104 It's a dead Bait for a Trout. **1776** F. Marion in *Harper's Mag.* Sept. (1883) 547/2 It was so dead a shot they none of them said a word. **1826** Miss Mitford *Village* Ser. II. (1863) 330 A silent, stupid, and respectable country gentleman, a dead vote on one side of the House. **1852** Dickens *Bleak Ho.* xxvi, With a gun in his hand, with much the air of a dead shot. **1874** Dasent *Half a Life* II. 227 Those who do so.. are almost always dead plucks. **1889** Barrère & Leland *Dict. Slang* I. 300/2 *Dead-on* (riflemen), straight on. A rifle-shot talks of the aiming being dead-on when the day is so calm that he can aim straight at the bull's eye instead of having to allow to the right or left for wind. He is said to be dead-on himself when he is shooting very well. **1959** *Punch* 17 June 815/1 She sang all night with pure, dead-on tone. **1966** 'K. Nicholson' *Hook, Line & Sinker* ix. 102 Don't you think a gesture like this is simply dead-on, when it comes to showing how with-it the Church is today?

c. Exact.

Mod. Iron bars cut to a dead length are charged a little more.

d. Direct, straight. ***dead wind*** (Naut.): a wind directly opposed to the ship's course. (Cf. C. 3.) ***dead run***: a run at full speed without any let-up. *U.S.*

1881 *Daily Tel.* 28 Jan., It was a dead head-wind. **1888** *Harper's Mag.* July 184 Keeping the sight of my rifle in a dead line for Gobo's ribs. **1889** K. Munroe *Golden Days* xii. 130 He..started on a dead run back over the trail. **1920** C. E. Mulford *J. Nelson* xii. 131 Striking into a dead run as he approached the rocky hump in the trail.

VI. 32. Phrases. **a.** ***dead and gone*** (usually in literal sense); hence ***dead-and-goneness***. Also ***dead and alive*** (see dead-alive *a.*); ***dead and buried***; ***dead and done (for, with)***. All these phrases are also used *attrib.* (with hyphens).

1482 *Monk of Evesham* (Arb.) 62 He fownde me ded and gonne. **1523** Skelton *Garl. Laurel* 1247 Of one Adame all a knave, dede and gone. **1602** Shaks. *Ham.* IV. v. 29 He is dead and gone Lady, he is dead and gone. **1737** Pope *Hor. Epist.* II. i. 34 Advocates for folly dead and gone. **1840** Dickens *Barn. Rudge* xix, When she was dead and gone, perhaps they would be sorry for it. **1863** *All Year Round* IX. 473/1 The grave of Carthage, and other dead and buried cities of the Carthaginians. **1886** Baumann *Londinismen* 39/1 *Dead-and-done for*, rein futsch; *it had such a dead-and-done for look*, es sah so ganz erbärmlich aus. **1891** J. L. Kipling *Beast & Man in India* i. 7 Buddhism has been dead and done with in India proper for centuries. **1891** H. Herman *His Angel* ii. 40 The dead-and-goneness of emotional fervour. **1897** S. Erskine *Lord Dullborough* v, We ..saw some six-months'-old playbills, announcing some dead-and-gone performance. **1909** *Westm. Gaz.* 10 Mar. 11/2 It is urged that the intellect of the Pollman is starved and himself broken on the wheel of a dead-and-done system. **1934** D. L. Sayers *Nine Tailors* II. iv. 158, I won't have you fretting yourself about that old business no more. All that's dead and buried. **1956** *Essays in Criticism* VI. 222 The dead-and-goneness of the past.

b. ***dead as a door-nail, dead as a herring***: completely or certainly dead. Also, ***(as) dead as the*** (or ***a***) ***dodo, (as) dead as mutton***.

c **1350** *Will. Palerne* 628 For but ich haue bote of mi bale I am ded as dorenail. **1362** Langl. *P. Pl.* A. I. 161 Fey withouten fait is febelore þen nou3t, And ded as a dore-nayl. **1593** Shaks. *2 Hen. VI*, IV. x. 42 If I doe not leaue you all as dead as a doore naile. [**1598** Shaks. *Merry W.* II. iii. 12 By gar, de herring is no dead, so as I vill kill him.] **1664** Butler *Hud.* II. iii. 1148 Hudibras, to all appearing, Believ'd him to be dead as Herring. **1680** Otway *Caius Marius* 57 As dead as a Herring, Stock-fish, or Door-nail. **1792** I. Bickerstaffe *Spoil'd Child* II. ii. 32 Thus let me seize my tender bit of lamb—there I think I had her as dead as mutton. **1838** [see mutton 7]. **1856** Reade *Never too late* lx, Ugh! what, is he, is he—Dead as a herring. **1884** *Pall Mall G.* 29 May 5/2 The Congo treaty may now be regarded as being as dead as a doornail. **1904** H. O. Sturgis *Belchamber* iv. 51 The Radicalism of Mill..is as dead as the dodo. **1919** W. S. Maugham *Moon & Sixpence* ii. 10 Mr. Crabbe was as dead as mutton, but Mr. Crabbe continued to write moral stories in rhymed couplets. **1935** *Ann. Reg. 1934* II. 305 References appearing in the London newspapers to the effect that 'war debts are as dead as the Dodo' were cabled to the American press. **1960** *Guardian* 24 Mar. 11/1 Mr. Menzies..refused a request for a boycott..saying he had hoped this 'was as dead as a dodo'.

c. ***dead horse***: see horse.

d. ***to wait for dead men's shoes***: see shoe.

e. ***to be dead on***: cf. death *sb.* 16. *slang.*

1891 'S. C. Scrivener' *Fields & Cities* 22 These boys always were 'dead' on a rat, no matter what its size.

f. ***to be dead nuts on***: see nut *sb.*[1] 6.

g. Colloq. phr. ***(I, etc.) wouldn't be seen*** (or ***found) dead in, with***: (I shall) have nothing to do with (something or someone); (I) hate, detest.

1915 Kipling *Debits & Credits* (1926) 29 'Wouldn't be found dead in *Hilarity*,' was Winchmore's grateful reply. **1931** T. R. G. Lyell *Slang, Phrase & Idiom* 671 No decent person would be seen dead with a specimen like that! **1933** A. G. Macdonell *England, their England* xiii. 222, I have to hang on to one [*sc.* a car] that my daughters say they wouldn't be seen dead in. **1937** M. Sharp *Nutmeg Tree* ix. 103 In the whole of France there wasn't a hat she would be seen dead in. **1966** A. E. Lindop *I start Counting* ix. 110 Do you think I'd be seen dead in gear like that?

h. Colloq. phr. ***dead from the neck up***: brainless, stupid.

1930 J. Dos Passos *42nd Parallel* ii. 161 Most of the inhabitants were dead from the neck up. **1963** Wodehouse *Stiff Upper Lip* vi. 64 The sort of dead-from-the-neck-up dumb brick who wouldn't have thought of it.

¶ The compar. *deader* and superl. *deadest* are in use where the sense permits; chiefly in *transf.* and *fig.* senses (*e.g.* 4, 16, above).

B. *sb.* (or *absol.*)

1. a. *sing.* One who is dead, a dead person. Formerly with *a*, and with possessive *dead's* (*dedes, dedis*). **b.** pl. ***the dead***.

c **1175** *Lamb. Hom.* 51 Al swa me deað bi þe deade. *c* **1340** *Cursor M.* 18043 (Trin.) þat dede [Lazarus] from deþ to lif he di3t. **1340** *Ayenb.* 258 Huanne me yzi3þ bere ane byrie þet is tokne þet þer is wyþine a dyad. **1465** *Paston Lett.* No. 510 II. 202 Tochyng the savacyon of the dedys gode. **1529** S. Fish *Supplic. Beggers* 2 Or elles they will accuse the dedes frendes. **1601** Shaks. *Jul. C.* III. ii. 131, I rather choose To wrong the dead..Then I will wrong such Honourable men. **1691** tr. *Emilianne's Frauds Rom. Monks* 32 The Dead, raising himself the third and last time. **1850** Tennyson *In Mem.* lxxxv, So hold I commerce with the dead; Or so methinks the dead would say.

c **1000** *Ags. Gosp.* Matt. viii. 22 And læt deade bebyri3ean hyra deadan. *c* **1200** *Trin. Coll. Hom.* 23 To demen þe quike and þe deade. **1426** Audelay *Poems* 7 Vysyte the seke..And beré the ded. **1661** Cowley *Disc. Govt. O. Cromwell*, The Monuments of the Dead. **1776** Adam Smith *W.N.* v. ii. (1869) II. 453 The transference of..property from the dead to the living. **1842** Tennyson *Two Voices* lxix, Nor canst thou show the dead are dead.

c. ***from the dead*** [orig. tr. Lat. *a mortuis*, Gr. ἐκ νεκρῶν, ἀπὸ τῶν νεκρῶν in N.T.]: from among those that are dead; hence nearly = from death.

c **950** *Lindisf. Gosp.* John ii. 22 Miððy uutudlice ariseð from deadum. **1340** *Ayenb.* 263 þane þridde day a-ros uram þe dyade. **1557** N. T. (Genev.) *Rom.* xi. 15 What shal the receauing of them be, but lyfe from the dead? **1652** Gataker *Antinom.* 5 His rising from the ded. **1722** De Foe *Col. Jack* (1840) 299 This was a kind of life from the dead to us both. **1862** Trollope *Orley F.* xiii, Her voice sounded..like a voice from the dead.

2. = Dead period, season, or stage. ***dead of night, of winter***: the time of intensest stillness, darkness, cold, etc.; = 'depth' (of winter). †***dead of neap***, the extreme stage of neap tide. (Cf. A. 18, 27.)

1548 Hall *Chron.* 109 b, In the dedde of the night..he brake up his campe and fled. **1583** Stanyhurst *Æneis* IV. (Arb.) 113 Neere toe dead of midnight yt drew. **1601** Shaks. *Twel. N.* I. v. 290 Euen in the dead of night. **1613** Sherley *Trav. Persia* 4 My iourney was under-taken in the dead of winter. **1793** Smeaton *Edystone L.* §266 At dead of neap, when the tides run less rapid. **1807-8** W. Irving *Salmag.* xx. (1860) 452 In the dead of winter, when nature is without charm. **1840** Macaulay *Clive* (1867) 25 At dead of night, Clive marched out of the fort.

†**3.** = dead heat *sb. Obs.*

1635 Quarles *Embl.* x. (D.), Mammon well follow'd, Cupid bravely led; Both touchers; equal fortune makes a dead.

4. *Mining.* ***deads***: earth or rock containing no ore (see A. 10); *esp.* as thrown out or heaped together in the course of working.

1653 Manlove *Rhymed Chron.* 271 Deads, Meers, Groves. **1671** *Phil. Trans.* VI. 2102 By Deads here are meant, that part of the Shelf which contains no metal. **1757** Borlase *ibid.* L. 503 Noise..as if a studdle had broke, and the deads were set a running [*note*, Loose rubbish and broken stones of the mine]. **1851** Kingsley *Yeast* xiii. (D.), A great furze-croft, full of deads (those are the earth-heaps they throw out of the shafts).

†**5.** *U.S. college slang.* A complete failure in 'recitation'. *Obs.*

a **1856** *Harvard Reg.* 378 in B. H. Hall *College Wds. & Customs*, One must stand up in the singleness of his ignorance to understand all the mysterious feelings connected with a dead. **1857** *Harvard Mag.* Oct. 332, I had made a dead that day, and my Tutor's rebuke had touched my pride.

¶ **6.** The absolute sense is also used *attrib.*, as in ***dead money***, money paid for saying masses for the dead; ***dead list***, list of the dead, etc. See various examples under D. 1, 2.

Grammatically, these pass back again into the adjective uses in A, from which, in some cases, they are not easy to separate, as *dead meat*, the flesh of slaughtered animals, or flesh which is itself dead (in sense 1); *dead wool*, the wool of dead or slaughtered sheep.

1476 *Churchw. Acc. Croscombe* (*Somerset Rec. Soc.*) 5 There is left of the ded money..xlvi[s] j[d]. **1692** Luttrell *Brief Rel.* (1857) II. 544 Some..in the dead list were not killed, but made prisoners. *a* **1845** Mrs. Bray *Narleigh* xlii. (1884) 304 Examined into by the 'dead jury', for so was an inquest termed, at the date of our tale. **1851** Mayhew *Lond. Labour* I. 177 'Dead salesmen'.. that is, the market salesmen of the meat sent..ready slaughtered. **1867** Smyth *Sailor's Word-bk.* s.v., Persons dying on board..are cleared from the ship's books by a dead-ticket, which must be filled up in a similar manner to the *sick-ticket*. **1879** A. P. Vivian *Wand. in Western Land* 115 American dead meat can be delivered in perfect condition in English ports. *Ibid.*, The dead-meat trade is only in its infancy. **1880** *Victorian Rev.* Feb. 664 Unlimited supplies of dead beef available for export from the United States. **1897** *Westm. Gaz.* 18 May 2/3 One hideous monster was seen in the Park last week, puffing and rocking along and looking as much out of place as a dead-meat van in a Jubilee procession. **1908** *Ibid.* 22 July 4/3 If we are soon to get cheap beef and mutton it must be by developing the dead-meat trade.

7. ***on the dead***: in dead earnest; honestly. *U.S. slang.*

1896 ADE *Artie* i. 7 On the dead, I don't believe any o' them people out there ever saw a good show. **1902** H. L. WILSON *Spenders* xxix. 340 Say, on the dead, Uncle Peter, I wish you'd come. **1903** A. H. LEWIS *Boss* 184 But, on the dead! I'd like to learn how you..reconcile yourselves to things.

C. *adv.*

1. a. In a manner, or to a degree, characteristic of or suggesting death; with extreme inactivity, stillness, etc.; utterly, profoundly, absolutely (as ***dead asleep, dead calm***); to extremity, 'to death' (as ***dead run, dead tired***). Cf. also *dead sick* (in D. 2), DEAD DRUNK, etc.

Often connected with the qualified word by a hyphen, and thus passing into combinations.

[**1393** GOWER *Conf.* III. 259 Whereof she swouned in his honde, And as who saith lay dede oppressed.] **1596** R. L[INCHE] *Diella* (1877) 61 Leaden-footed griefe, Who neuer goes but with a dead-slowe pace. *a* **1631** LAUD *Serm.* (1847) 125 Elias bid them cry louder; their God was 'asleep'.. Yes, dead asleep. **1637** RUTHERFORD *Lett.* (1862) I. 267 Deferred hopes need not make me dead-sweir (as we used to say). **1727** BRADLEY *Fam. Dict.* s.v. *Hart*, Dead run deer have upon occasion taken very great leaps. **1818** KEATS *Endym.* I. 405 As dead-still as a marble man. **1840** R. H. DANA *Bef. Mast* x. 24 In a few minutes it fell dead calm. **1842** MRS. CARLYLE *Lett.* I. 157 For all so dead-weary as I lay down. *Ibid.* I. 160 Whether I fainted, or suddenly fell dead-asleep. **1861** HUGHES *Tom Brown at Oxford* vi. (1889) 51 To drive into Farringdon.. both horses dead done up. **1881** *Times* 25 July 4/5 Her engines were going dead slow.

b. With absolute or abrupt cessation of motion (or speech). (Cf. A. 24.)

1856 WHYTE MELVILLE *Kate Cov.*, My companion stopped dead short and concealed her blushes in a glass of champagne. **1865** DICKENS *Mut. Fr.* II. iv, He stopped dead.

c. With the full weight of an inert body. (Cf. A. 29.)

1875 J. C. WILCOCKS *Sea Fisherman* 83 What is this on my line which hauls as dead as if I had hooked a weed?

2. a. Hence more generally: Utterly, entirely, absolutely, quite. (Cf. A. 31.) Esp. ***dead broke*** (see BROKE *ppl. a.* 3), ***certain, easy, level, right, sure***. Now *colloq.*

1589 NASHE *Almond for Parrat* 5 b, Oh he is olde dogge at expounding, and deade sure at a Catechisme. **1741** RICHARDSON *Pamela* (1824) I. 62 A dead-spiteful, grey, goggling eye. **1826** DISRAELI *Viv. Grey* I. v, He cut the Doctor quite dead to-day. **1857** R. TOMES *Amer. in Japan* ix. 196 Before the rice is 'dead ripe'. **1860** HOOK *Lives Abps.* (1862) II. ii. 93 Only one horse.. which soon became dead lame. *a* **1861** T. WINTHROP *Canoe & Saddle* (1863) 280 Prairieland lies dead level for leagues. **1871** J. HAY *Pike County Ballads* 10 He'd seen his duty a dead-sure thing. **1883** 'MARK TWAIN' *Life Mississippi* xxxix. 414 We'll cotton-seed his salad for him.. that's a dead-certain thing. **1885** [see GO *v.* 48 e]. **1888** GREENWELL *Gloss. Coal Tr. Terms Northumb. & Durh.* (ed. 3) 2 The small coals..are then passed over a second skreen, [to separate] the nuts.. and the dead small, or duff which falls through the skreen. **1894** in E. R. Lamson *Yale Wit & Humor* 47 (*caption*) A Dead Easy Queen Caught His Eye. **1895** J. L. WILLIAMS *Princeton Stories* 166 You're dead right in saying he's too young. **1903** A. BENNETT *Let.* 24 Aug. (1960) 96 She is dead right all through. **1904** W. H. SMITH *Promoters* v. 92 For a dead easy mark in a business way, commend me to a preacher. **1908** G. H. LORIMER *J. Spurlock* i. 19 It was like having one of those mushy girls dead gone on you. **1922** D. H. LAWRENCE *Aaron's Rod* vii. 71 She liked him because of his dead-level indifference to his surroundings. **1923** 'B. M. BOWER' *Parowan Bonanza* i. 15 'You're dead right, old girl,' Bill agreed. **1930** 'J. J. CONNINGTON' *Two Tickets Puzzle* xiv. 222 There's no great trouble in guessing who's mixed up in the business—that's dead easy. **1930** W. GIBSON *Hazards* 12 He could always plane the deal Dead-level; ay, his work was always true. **1959** J. BRAINE *Vodi* i. 22 You're mardy. You're dead mardy. **1961** SIMPSON & GALTON *Hancock* 43/2 Tony and Sid are dead bored. **1963** D. LESSING *Man & Two Women* 140 'That's right,' said Charlie, 'you're dead right.'

b. Slang phr. ***dead to rights***: (*a*) completely, certainly, (*b*) red-handed; in the act; 'bang to rights' (BANG *v.*[1] 10). (Cf. RIGHT *sb.*[1] 14.) orig. *U.S.*

1859 G. W. MATSELL *Vocabulum* 25 *Dead to rights*, positively guilty, and no way of getting clear. **1872** G. P. BURNHAM *Mem. U.S. Secret Service* p. v, A brief glossary of terms in the vernacular of criminals.. *dead to rights*, caught, with positive proof of guilt. **1881** *City Argus* (San Francisco) 2 July 4/4 Jimmy..was caught 'dead to rights', and now languishes in the city Bastile. **1889** BARRÈRE & LELAND *Dict. Slang* I. 301/1 I've got him dead to rights. **1947** 'A. A. FAIR' *Fools die on Friday* 189 We've got her this time dead-to-rights.

3. Directly, straight. ***dead against***: *lit.* in a direction exactly opposite to one's course (so ***dead on end***); *fig.* (in a way) directly or utterly opposed to. (Cf. A. 31 d.)

1800 C. STURT in *Naval Chron.* IV. 394 Carrying me dead upon the Shambles. **1840** DICKENS *Barn. Rudge* xxxiii, The wind and rain being dead against me. **1840** R. H. DANA *Bef. Mast* iv. 7 We continued running dead before the wind. **1851** DIXON *W. Penn* ix. (1872) 77 The councillors were dead against his prayer. **1875** J. C. WILCOCKS *Sea Fisherman* 109 Observing..that..the wind was dead on end, and the sail 'would not be a ha'porth of good'.

D. Combinations (of the *adj.* or *sb.*).

1. General combs. **a.** With other adjectives or participles (in adjectival or advb. const.) = 'so as to be or seem dead, as if dead, to death, etc.', as in ***dead-blanched, -cold, -drifting, -frozen, -grown, -heavy, -killing, -live*** (cf. DEAD-ALIVE), ***-living, -seeming, -set, -sounding, -speaking, -wounded***; **b.** parasynthetic, as ***dead-coloured, -eyed***, DEAD-HEARTED; **c.** attributive combs. of the sb. = 'of the dead', as † ***dead-burier, dead-land***.

1879 BROWNING *Halbert & Hob* 42 Temples, late black, *dead-blanched. **1535** COVERDALE *Ezek.* xxxix. 14 They shal ordene men also to be *deedburiers. **1611** BEAUM. & FL. *Maid's Trag.* II. ii, Two *dead-cold aspicks. **1611** COTGR., *Blaime*, pale..whitish, *dead coloured. **1818** KEATS *Endym.* III. 411 A swoon Left me *dead-drifting to that fatal power. **1570** *Ane Tragedie* 16 in *Sat. Poems Ref.* (1890) I. 83 Paill of the face..*Deid eyit, dram lyke, disfigurat was he. **1594** KYD *Cornelia* II. in Hazl. *Dodsley* V. 190 My *dead-grown joys. **1819** KEATS *Sonn., Picture of Leander*, See how his body dips *Dead-heavy. **1593** SHAKS. *Lucr.* 540 With a cockatrice *dead-killing eye. **1594** —— *Rich. III*, IV. i. 36 This dead-killing newes. **1871** TYLOR *Prim. Cult.* II. 281 Mictlanteuotli, ruler of the dismal *dead-land in the shades below. **1591** SYLVESTER *Du Bartas* I. iii. 945 Th'admired Adamant, Whose *dead-live power my Reasons power doth dant. **1605** *Ibid.* II. iii. *Lawe* 694 (D.) He smot the sea with his *dead-liuing rod. **1598** *Ibid.* II. i. *Imposture* 260 *Dead-seeming coals but quick. **1820** SCOTT *Monast.* iii, Her quivering lip, and *dead-set eye. **1726** LEONI *Alberti's Archit.* I. 42 a, Of Stones, some..are heavy and sonorous; others are..light, and *dead sounding. **1598** SYLVESTER *Du Bartas* II. ii. IV. *Columnes* 717 The Guide of supplest fingers On (living-dumb, *dead-speaking) sinnew-singers. *c* **1400** *Destr. Troy* 6528 All þat met hym..Auther dyet of his dynttes, or were *ded wondit.

2. Special combs. **dead angle** (*Fortif.*), 'any angle of a fortification, the ground before which is unseen, and therefore undefended from the parapet' (Stocqueler *Milit. Encycl.*); **dead-ball line**, in Rugby Football, a line behind the goal-line, beyond which the ball is considered 'dead' (sense 21 a); **dead-bird** (see quot. 1898); † **dead-birth**: see BIRTH 3 b; **dead-box**, a vehicle used for conveying dead bodies out of a mine; **dead-burned** or **-burnt** *a.*, of substances obtained by calcining refractory minerals such as gypsum or limestone: heated so strongly that vitrification occurred; of lime thus produced: that does not slake readily; **'dead-cart**, a cart in which dead bodies are carried away (*e.g.* during pestilence); **'dead-clothes**, the clothes in which the dead are dressed; **dead dipping**, a process by which a 'dead' or dull surface is given to ornamental brass-work (Ure *Dict. Arts* 1875); also **dead-dipped** *ppl. a.*; **dead doors** (*Naut.*), doors fitted to the outside of the quarter-gallery doors, to keep out water in case the quarter-gallery should be carried away (Weale 1850); **dead-dress** = *dead-clothes*; **dead duck** *slang* (orig. *U.S.*), a person or thing that is useless, unsuccessful, bankrupt, etc.; **dead earth** *Electr.*, a complete or very low-resistance connection with the earth (see quots.); **dead-file** = *dead-smooth* file; **dead fin**, name for the second dorsal fin of a salmon; **dead finish** *Austral. colloq.*, (*a*) the 'limit' or extreme point (with regard to excellence, endurance, etc.); (*b*) any of several Australian trees or shrubs, esp. *Albizzia basaltica* or *Acacia farnesiana*; also, the thicket formed by such trees or shrubs; **'dead-fire**, the luminous appearance called St. Elmo's Fire, superstitiously believed to presage death; **dead-flat** (*Naut.*), that timber or frame in a ship that has the greatest breadth; the midship-bend (Weale 1850); **dead-fold**, a sheep-pen; **dead-freight**, the amount paid for that part of a vessel not occupied by cargo, when the vessel is chartered for a lump sum; **dead furrow** *U.S.*, the last or finishing furrow left between 'lands' in ploughing; **Dead Heart** *Austral. colloq.*, the remote inland area of Australia; **'dead-hole** (see quots. and cf. DEAD-WELL 1); **dead horse** (see HORSE *sb.* 19); **'dead-house**, a building or room in which dead bodies are kept for a time, a mortuary; (see also sense A. 18 b above); **dead-latch** (see quot.); **dead leaf**, (*a*) the colour of a dead leaf; chiefly as *adj.*, = FEUILLEMORTE *a.*; (*b*) *Aeronaut.* (see quot. 1918); **dead load**, (*a*) (see sense A. 29 above); (*b*) *pl.* (*U.S. colloq.*), great quantities; **dead march**, a piece of solemn music played at a funeral procession, *esp.* at a military funeral; a funeral march; **dead marine** (see MARINE *sb.* 4 d); **'dead-office**, the office or service for the burial of the dead; **dead oil**, a name given to those products of the distillation of coal-tar which are heavier than water; also called *heavy oil*; **dead-plate**, an ungrated iron plate at the mouth of a furnace, on which coal is coked before being pushed upon the grate; † **'dead-pledge** = MORTGAGE; **'dead-'rising** (*Naut.*), 'those parts of a ship's floor or bottom, throughout her whole length, where the floor-timber is terminated upon the lower futtock' (Falconer, *Mar. Dict.* 1830); **'dead-room**, a room in which dead bodies are kept; **dead rope**, (*a*) a rope that does not run in a block or pulley (Phillips 1706); cf. A. 23; (*b*) a bell-rope working on a half-wheel, for chiming; **dead-share** (see quot. 1867, and cf. DEAD PAY); **dead sheave**, 'a scored aperture in the heel of a top-mast, through which a second top-tackle pendant can be rove' (Smyth, *Sailor's Word-bk.*); **dead-shore** (see quot.); **dead-sick** *a.*, (*a*) as sick as one can be, prostrate with sickness; † (*b*) sick unto death, death-sick (common in Coverdale); † **'dead-slayer**, one guilty of manslaughter; **dead-smooth** *a.*, said of the finest quality of file; **dead-space**: see quot.; **dead stick** *Aeronaut. colloq.* (orig. *U.S.*), (see quot. 1934); also *attrib.*, as **dead-stick landing**, a landing made with the engine 'dead'; **dead stock, deadstock**, (*a*) (see sense A. 20 b); (*b*) (see STOCK *sb.*[1] 53 a); **dead-stroke** (*Billiards*), see quot.; **'dead-struck**, † **-strooken** *ppl. a.*, struck dead; *fig.* struck with horror, paralyzed, etc.; † **dead-sweat**, the cold sweat of death: = *death-sweat*; **dead time**, (*a*) (see quot. 1909); (*b*) *Physics*, the period immediately after the registering of a pulse, a count, etc., when a detector or counter is not yet ready to register another pulse, etc.; **'dead-tops**, a disease of trees (see quot.); hence **dead-top** *attrib.*; **dead-turn**: see quot.; **dead wagon** *U.S.*, a vehicle for conveying the dead; † **dead wed** (Sc. *wad*) = MORTGAGE; **dead white, dead-white**, (*a*) flat or lustreless white; (*b*) absolute white; pure white; also as *adj.* See also following words, DEAD-ALIVE to DEAD-WORK.

1892 *Football Calendar 1892–93* 63 Not more than 25 yards behind the goal line, and parallel thereto, shall be lines, which shall be called the *Dead-Ball Lines. **1905** *Westm. Gaz.* 30 Nov. 8/3 The necessity of lengthening the playing area to admit of the extensions behind the goals to the 'dead-ball' line. **1892** STEVENSON & OSBOURNE *Wrecker* xxii. 349 Can't you give us 'a *dead bird' for a good trade-room? **1898** MORRIS *Austral Eng.* 115/2 *Dead-bird*, in Australia, a recent slang term, meaning 'a certainty'. The metaphor is from pigeon-shooting, where the bird being let loose in front of a good shot is as good as dead. **1685** COOKE *Marrow Chirurg.* VII. ii. 269 The round [Birthwort] is.. more effectual in moving speedily the Menses, *dead-Birth, and after-Birth. **1897** *Daily News* 12 May 5/7 He arrived at the pit's mouth in the *dead-box, having fainted whilst below. **1939** *Iron & Steel Inst. First Rep. on Refractory Materials* 64 The addition of a small proportion of *dead-burned magnesite to the chrome batch has been a common practice for many years. **1903** *Nature* 19 Nov. 64/2 Under favourable conditions gypsum actually breaks up at 63°·5, and forms insoluble anhydrite found in nature and identical with *dead-burnt gypsum. **1904** GOODCHILD & TWENEY *Technol. & Sci. Dict.* 151/1 *Dead burnt*, a term applied to lime which has become vitrified by fusion of calcium silicate in the limekiln. **1958** A. D. MERRIMAN *Dict. Metall.* 54/1 This causes the lime to slake very slowly, and it is then referred to as 'dead burnt', in contradistinction to the pure lime. **1722** DE FOE *Plague* (1840) 35 Many..were..carried away in the *dead-carts. **1887** *Pall Mall G.* 18 Mar. 2/2 In Monte Video..the dead carts pass through the streets with dead and dying all mixed up. **1861** RAMSAY *Remin.* Ser. II. 5 'Those are fine linens you have got there, Janet.' 'Troth, mem..they're just the gudeman's *deed claes.' **1888** *Contemp. Rev.* Mar. 409 The men set themselves to dig out actual catacombs, while the women made dead-clothes. **1866** TIMMINS *Industr. Hist. Birmingham* 300 Burnishing.. furnishes a contrast to other portions of *dead dipped work. *Ibid.* 299 Dead dipping..has now become the recognized mode of finish where acid is employed. **1879** *Cassell's Techn. Educ.* IV. 299/2 'Dead' dipping produces a beautiful frosted appearance on the work. **1854** H. MILLER *Sch. & Schm.* vii. (1857) 138 Like the pointed tags that roughen a *dead-dress. [**1829** *N.Y. Courier* 15 June 2/1 There is an old saying 'never waste powder on a *dead duck'; but we cannot avoid flashing away a few grains upon an old friend, Henry Clay.] **1844** A. JACKSON *Let.* 7 May in M. James *A. Jackson* (1937) xxiii. 481 Clay [is] a dead political duck. **1867** *New Mexican* 30 Mar. 2/2 The 'powerful' efforts of certain 'dead ducks' to prevent his appointment. **1888** *N.Y. Clipper* (Farmer), Long Branch is said to be a dead duck. **1958** 'A. GILBERT' *Death against Clock* 187 Once a chap's proved innocent..he's a dead duck to the Press. **1863** R. S. CULLEY *Handbk. Pract. Telegr.* vii. 105 *Dead Earth. All the current passing through the fault.. No signal whatever beyond the fault. **1910** *Hawkins' Electr. Dict.* 109/1 *Dead earth*, in telegraphy, a fault in the line involving a complete grounding or connection with the earth; a total earth. **1914** *Work* 26 Sept. 490/2 When cables are earthed intentionally the connection is complete, or a 'dead earth'. There are also 'partial earths' when a cable..leaks. **1865** J. G. BERTRAM *Harvest of Sea* (1873) 88 About 1300 of these [salmon] were marked by cutting off the *dead or second dorsal fin..25 were marked with a silver ring behind the dead fin. *Ibid.* 138 Cutting off the dead fin is not thought a good plan of marking. **1881** A. C. GRANT *Bush Life* xiv, 'He's the *dead finish—go right through a man,' rejoins Sam, rather sulkily. **1885** H. FINCH-HATTON *Advance Australia!* xvii. 272 On the western slopes, rose-wood, myall, dead-finish, plum-tree..all woods with a fine grain suitable for cabinet-making and fancy work. **1889** J. H. MAIDEN *Useful Native Plants* 355 *Acacia farnesiana*... Sometimes called by the absurd name of 'Dead Finish'. This name given to some species of *Acacia* and *Albizzia*, is on account of the trees or shrubs shooting thickly from the bottom, and forming an impenetrable barrier to the traveller, who is thus brought to a 'dead finish' (stop). **1902** J. H. M. ABBOTT *Tommy Cornstalk* 64 There are few colloquialisms more expressive of wearisome disgust, dissatisfaction and discontent than is 'Dead Finish'. It is almost synonymous with 'the Last Straw'. **1907** *Daily Chron.* 18 Mar. 4/4 There is a corporation which grows roses to compete with Nature's 'dead finish' trees. **1934** *Bulletin* (Sydney) 24 Jan. 21/3 They were made from myall, dead finish, ringed gidya and other fancy woods. **1959** C. & E. CHAUVEL *Walkabout* x. 69 If you go out that gate over there past the 'dead finish' tree and take the middle track you'll be right enough. **1854** H. MILLER *Sch. & Schm.* (1858) 15 We looked up, and saw a *dead-fire sticking to the cross-trees. 'It's all over with us now, master,' said I. **1897** L. ROBINSON *Wild Traits* vi. 168 A sudden change of diet from the frugal fare on the hill-turf and in the '*dead-fold' to that of lush cereals [etc.]. **1906** G. A. B. DEWAR *Faery Year* 32 The dead-fold is formed of wattle hurdles bound about with swathes of straw. **1730-6** BAILEY (folio), **Dead Freight*, the Freight a Ship looses for want of being full, or the Freight paid by the Merchant, by agreement, tho' he has not sent his full Compliment of Goods on board. **1880** *Clause in Charter-parties*, Captain or Owners to have an absolute lien on the Cargo for all Freight, Dead-freight, and Demurrage due to the ship under this Charter Party. **1838** H. COLMAN *1st Rep. Agric. Mass.* 68 It [*sc.* the side hill plough]..avoids a *dead furrow in the center. **1873** *Trans. Dep. Agric. Illinois* X. 94 The land between the rows should be plowed toward the trees, so as to have the 'dead furrow' in the center, to allow the water to pass off freely. **1894** *Irrigation Age* Jan. 34/2 With the discs straddling the dead furrow. **1906** J. W. GREGORY (*title*) The *dead heart of Australia. **1935** F. W. JONES in H. H. Finlayson *Red Centre* 8 That strange and undefinable attraction that the Dead Heart always has. **1945** *Salt* 2 July 23/1 Collective effort can radically alter the future of the so-called 'dead-heart' of Australia. **1856** *Jrnl. R. Agric. Soc.* XVII. II. 504 For these *dead-holes we would substitute cesspools..The open cesspools, or dead-holes, which are too frequently used. **1812** J. J. HENRY *Campaign against Quebec* 134 Many carioles..passed our dwelling loaded with the dead..to a place, emphatically, called the '*dead-house'. **1833** *Edin. Rev.* LVII. 348 The keeper of the dead-house. **1850** *Ecclesiologist* X. 339 To the right of the lich-gate we have placed the 'Dead-House'. **1874** KNIGHT *Dict. Mech.*, **Dead-latch*, a kind of latch whose bolt may be so locked by a detent that it cannot be opened from the inside by the handle or from the outside by the latch-key. **1864** M. B. CHESNUT *Diary* 27 May (1905) 311 Brushing scant locks which were fleecy white. Her maid would be doing hers, which were *dead-leaf brown. **1896** *Daily News* 17 Oct. 6/5 A woollen skirt of a dead-leaf shade. **1905** *Westm. Gaz.* 21 Oct. 18/2 That delightful sort of golden browny shade that is really best described as dead leaf. *Ibid.*, This same peculiar dead-leaf colour. *Ibid.*, Some folds of dead-leaf-coloured crêpe de Chine. **1918** E. S. FARROW *Dict. Mil. Terms, Dead leaf*, in aviation, the term applied to an aircraft when its movement resembles that of a falling dead leaf. **1930** R. LEHMANN *Note in Music* 35 The dead-leaf colour of the walls gave back a feeble reflection. **1869** 'MARK TWAIN' *Innoc. Abr.* lvii. 616 The old man's got *dead loads of books. **1603** KNOLLES *Hist. Turks* 827 The ensigns were..let fall..a *dead march sounded, and heavy silence commanded to be kept through all the Campe. **1852** DICKENS *Bleak Ho.* xxi, That's the Dead March in Saul. They bury soldiers to it. **1858** FABER *Life Xavier* 446 Where there was no Christian burial ground, he dug the grave with his own hands, buried them, and then recited the *Dead-Office on the spot. **1849** MANSFIELD in *Jrnl. Chem. Soc.* I. 250 The heavy oil whose extrication forms the second period of the process, is technically called '*dead oil'. **1854** RONALDS & RICHARDSON *Chem. Technol.* (ed. 2) I. 135 More heat [is] applied, until the distillation of the dead oil is complete. **1875** URE *Dict. Arts* III. 395 The dead oils..are found in the very last portions that pass in the distillation of coal-tar. **1855** LARDNER *Museum Sc. & Art* V, The fuel..should be laid on that part of the grate nearest to the fire door, called the *dead plates. **1881** RAYMOND *Mining Gloss.* s.v., The gases evolved on the dead-plate pass over the grate and are burned. **1658** PHILLIPS, **Dead pledge*, land or moveables pawned for money, which is to be the Creditours for ever, if the money be not repaid at the time agreed on; it is also called Mortgage. **1664** E. BUSHNELL *Compl. Shipwright* 10 Then I set off the *Dead Rising. **1691** T. H[ALE] *Acc. New Invent.* 120 The..Stern-post, and Dead-rising up the Tuck. *c* **1850** in *Rudim. Navig.* (Weale) 114. **1835** WILLIS *Pencillings* I. 16 My friend proposed to me to look into the *dead-room. **1751** CHAMBERS *Cycl. Supp.*, **Dead ropes*, in a ship, are such as are not running, i.e. do not run in any block. **1846-54** OLIVER *Monasticon Exon.* 269 Rung with a half wheel, or dead rope. **1872** ELLACOMBE *Bells of Ch.* x. 359 At this time ..the bells were altered from the dead rope pull to the sally. **1517** in *Archæologia* XLVII. 311 For xviij *dedshares..at v.s. a moneth— vj. li. vj. s. **1867** SMYTH *Sailor's Word-bk., Dead-shares*, an allowance formerly made to officers of the fleet, from fictitious numbers borne on the complement (*temp.* Henry VIII.), varying from fifty shares for an admiral, to half a share for the cook's mate. **1857** J. G. WILKINSON *Egyptians t. Pharaohs* 112 A single square sail..raised or lowered by lifts running in *dead-sheeve holes at the top of the mast. **1823** in P. NICHOLSON *Pract. Build.* 584 **Dead-shoar.* **1850** WEALE *Dict. Terms, Dead shore*, a piece of timber worked up in brickwork to support a superincumbent mass until the brickwork which is to carry it has set or become hard. **1535** COVERDALE *2 Kings* xx. 1 At that tyme was Ezechias *deedsicke. [So Isa. xxxviii. 1, John iv. 47, etc.] *c* **1621** S. WARD *Life of Faith* (1627) 88 When thou..(as in a Sea-sicknesse) art dead sicke for the present, remember thou shalt be the better..after. **1535** COVERDALE *Josh.* xx. 2 Fre cities..that a *deed sleyer which sleyeth a soule vnawarres..may flye thither. **1874** KNIGHT *Dict. Mech.* s.v., The grades [of files] are as follows:—Rough. Middle-cut. Bastard. Second-cut. Smooth. *Dead-smooth. **1884** F. J. BRITTEN *Watch & Clockm.* 79 Dead Smooth..the cut of the finest kind of file. **1887** BRUNTON *Pharmacology, etc.* (ed. 3) 1100 *Dead-space: this name has been given by O. Liebreich to the part of a fluid in which no reaction occurs between substances dissolved in it... If the mixture be placed in horizontal capillary tubes the dead-space is at each end of the fluid. **1932** *Word Study* Jan. 3/2 The use of the phrase 'a *dead stick' by some aviators. **1934** WEBSTER, *Dead stick* (*Aviation*), a propeller that has ceased to revolve because the engine has stopped. — *dead-stick* adj. **1943** C. H. WARD-JACKSON *It's a Piece of Cake* 24 *Dead stick*, engine stopped. **1946** B. SUTTON *Jungle Pilot* 40 Poor Jimmy had had his motor stopped and was forced to make a 'dead stick' landing on the aerodrome. **1836** *Dead stock [see STOCK *sb.*[1] 53 a]. **1879** J. SCOTT *Farm Valuer* ix. 97 Interest is charged on the dead stock and the working cattle. **1958** *Times* 1 July p. i/7 His capital invested in livestock, deadstock and equipment. **1873** CAVENDISH & BENNETT *Billiards* 193 A *dead-stroke is played by striking the white gently in the centre, or, if anything, very slightly below it. *a* **1593** MARLOWE *Hero & Leander* I. 121 With fear of death *dead-strooken. **1597-8** BP. HALL *Sat.* I. iii. (T.), [To] appall The *dead-struck audience. **1839** DARLEY *Introd. Beaum. & Fl. Wks.* I. 31 Shakspeare himself scrawls bytimes with a dead-struck hand. **1609** HOLLAND *Amm. Marcell.* 390 Having a *dead sweat comming all over him, he died within a while after. **1909** *Cent. Dict.* Suppl., **Dead time*, time during which the active work of accomplishing a purpose is not going on, although preparations for it may be in progress. Such, in pile-driving, is the time occupied in lifting the hammer. **1949** *Electronic Engin.* XXI. 455 There elapses about 10^{-4} sec., during which time a particle entering cannot initiate a count. This interval is the 'dead-time' for the counter. **1963** B. FOZARD *Instrumentation Nucl. Reactors* v. 44 Geiger-Mueller counters have thus an inherent 'dead time' and are different in this respect from other types of ionisation detector. **1966** *Electronics* 17 Oct. 111 The sampling would be an integral part of the computer's program. It would occur many times during the wait or dead time of the tactical program. **1706** PHILLIPS (ed. Kersey), **Dead-tops*, a Disease in Trees: For large Plants that upon their Removal have had their tops cut off, are apt to die from the Place they were cut off at, to the next Sprig, or Branch. *a* **1711** KEN *Sion* Poet. Wks. 1721 IV. 320 When they saw a dead-top Oak decline. **1888** S. P. THOMPSON *Dynamo-Electr. Mach.* (ed. 3) 405 In every dynamo the current..is proportional to the speed less a certain number of revolutions per second. The latter number is familiarly known as the *dead-turns. **1894** *Outing* (U.S.) XXIV. 7/1 *Dead wagons, hospital ambulances and sanitary corps vehicles were the most prominent objects in the streets. **1340** *Ayenb.* 36 Hy betakeþ hyre londes and hare eritage ine wed and *dead wed. **1609** SKENE *Reg. Maj.* 50 The secund ..ane deidwad..is forbiddin in the Kings court to be made or vsed. Because it is esteemed to be ane kinde of ocker or vsurie. **1794** R. KIRWAN *Elem. Min.* (ed. 2) I. 327 Its colour white, two opposite faces silvery white, two others *dead white, or yellowish. **1825** J. NICHOLSON *Oper. Mech.* 640 If it is to be finished flat, or, as the painters style it, dead white, grey, fawn, &c. **1857** G. LAWRENCE *Guy Liv.* xxx, The straight, beautifully-turned ankle, cased in dead-white silk. **1863** MRS. H. WOOD *Verner's Pride* xiv, The dead white of the roses was not more utterly colourless than Sibylla's face. **1920** R. MACAULAY *Potterism* II. i. 67 Jane in a square-cut, high-waisted, dead white frock. **1922** D. H. LAWRENCE *England, My England* (1924) 110 She turned white—dead white.

dead, *sb.*[2] Also 3-6 **ded, dede**, 4- **deid**. The nothern form of DEATH *sb.*, formerly in regular use with Northern writers (*dede*), and still dialectal in Scotch (*deid*, pronounced (diːd), esp. in certain locutions, e.g. ***tired to dead*** (***deid***), ***to be the dead*** (***deid***) ***of***, ***dead-bell***, ***dead-candle***, ***dead-rattle***, ***dead-spoke***, ***dead-thraw***, etc. For examples of the simple word, see the *β* forms under the various senses of DEATH *sb.*; for the combinations see under the standard English forms DEATH-BELL, DEATH-THROE, etc.

In some instances it is difficult to decide whether *dead-* in combination is the sb. = death, or the ordinary adj. And it is evident that later writers have often used phrases and combinations containing the sb., with the notion that it was the adj. Thus *dead-bell* could easily be understood as the bell of the dead, or rung for the dead, *dead-sweat* as the sweat characteristic of the dead.

† **dead** (dɛd), *v. Obs.* exc. in local or nonce-use; replaced by DEADEN. Forms: 1 **déadian**, 4-5 **dede**, 5-9 **dead**. [OE. *déadian* (also *adéadian*) to become dead (corresp. to a Gothic **dauþôn*), f. *déad*, DEAD *a.* Branch II corresponds in sense to OE. *díedan, dýdan* to kill (Gothic **daudjan*, Ger. *tödten*); but is app. only a transitive use of the original intr. vb.]

I. *intr.* **1.** To become dead. **a.** *lit.* To die.

c **950** *Lindisf. Gosp.* John viii. 21 And in synno iuero deadaȝeð. [*c* **975** *Rushw. Gosp.*, In synnum iowrum ȝe deodiȝað.] [*c* **1050** *Gloss.* in Wr.-Wülcker 408/6 *Fatescit*, adeadaþ.] *c* **1420** *Pallad. on Husb.* I. 752 The seed of thorn in it wol dede and dote. *c* **1425** *Seven Sag.* 623 (P.) The holde tre bygan to dede.

b. *fig.* To lose vitality, force, or vigour; to become numb; to lose heat or glow.

c **1384** CHAUCER *H. Fame* II. 44 Al my felynge gan to dede. **1626** BACON *Sylva* §774 Iron, as soon as it is out of the Fire, deadeth straight-ways. **1654** FULLER *Ephemeris* Pref. 5 Their loyalty flatteth and deadeth by degrees.

2. *U.S. college slang.* 'To be unable to recite; to be ignorant of the lesson; to declare one's self unprepared to recite' (B. H. Hall *College Wds. & Customs*, 1856).

1848 *Oration before H.L. of I.O. of O.F.*, Be ready, in fine, to cut, to drink, to smoke, to dead.

II. *trans.*

3. To make dead (*lit.* and *fig.*); to cause to die; to put to death, kill, slay, destroy.

c **1340** *Cursor M.* 13070 (Fairf.) Herodias couet Iohn to dede. *c* **1374** CHAUCER *Boeth.* IV. iv. 127 Aftir þat þe body is dedid by þe deþe. **1591** SPENSER *Teares of Muses* 210 Our pleasant Willy..is dead..With whom all joy and jolly merriment Is also deaded. **1594** NASHE *Unfort. Trav.* 52 Tree rootes..stubbed downe to the ground, yet were they not vtterly deaded. *c* **1624** LUSHINGTON *Resurr. Serm.* in *Phenix* (1708) II. 480 This would murder His divinity, and dead His immortality. **1677** GALE *Crt. Gentiles* II. IV. 140 By burning to set a marque, or to dead the flesh.

4. *fig.* To deprive of some form of vitality; to deaden: **a.** To deprive of sensation or consciousness; to stupefy, benumb.

1382 WYCLIF *1 Sam.* xxv. 37 And the herte of hym with yn forth is deed [*v.r.* deadyd, deadid, dedid]. **1599** B. JONSON *Ev. Man out of Hum.* I. iii, O my senses, Why lose you not your powers, and become Dull'd, if not deaded, with this spectacle? **1641** FRENCH *Distill.* iv. (1651) 96 It..quickens any deaded member, as in the palsie. **1692** R. L'ESTRANGE *Josephus' Antiq.* VII. x, His hearing was deaded and lost.

b. To deprive of force or vigour.

1586 *Epit. Sidney* Spenser's Wks. (Globe) 572/2 Endlese griefe, which deads my life, yet knowes not how to kill. *a* **1631** LAUD *Serm.* (1847) 13 Let nothing dead your spirits in God's and your country's service. **1653** A. WILSON *Jas. I*, 95 This..deaded the matter so, that it lost the Cause. **1687** SHADWELL *Juvenal* Ded. A iij b, In all Paraphrases upon the Greek and Roman Authors..the Strength and Spirit of them is deaded, and in some quite lost.

c. To render spiritually dead.

1656 R. ROBINSON *Christ all* 108 Carnal security deads the heart. **1676** HALE *Contempl.* I. (1689) 281, I have been very jealous..of wounding..or deading my conscience.

d. To make dead or insensible *to* something.

1612 T. TAYLOR *Comm. Titus.* i. 7 Drunkennes is..an oppressing, and deading of it [the heart] unto dutie. **1655** GURNALL *Chr. in Arm.* (1669) 175/1 The sense of this Gospel-peace will dead the heart to the creature.

5. To deprive of its active or effective physical quality; to deaden, make 'dead', extinguish.

1611 COTGR., *Buffeté*..deaded, as wine that hath taken wind, or hath beene mingled with water. **1626** BACON *Sylva* §158 If a Bell hath Cloth or Silk wrapped about it, it deadeth the Sound more. **1652** J. WRIGHT tr. *Camus' Nature's Paradox* 100 The Ashes of Love, whose coals were deaded on a sodain. **1657** W. COLES *Adam in Eden* i, [Walnut oil] is better for Painters' use to illustrate a white colour than Linseed Oyl, which deadeth it. **1719** D'URFEY *Pills* (1872) V. 163 Common Prey so deads her Dart, It scarce can wound a noble Game. **1748** THOMSON *Cast. Indol.* I. lxvi, When..thy toils..Shall dead thy fire, and damp its heavenly spark.

6. To check, retard (motion or force); to destroy the force or effect of (a missile, etc.).

1602 CAREW *Cornwall* 155 b, Great trusses of hay..to blench the defendants sight, and dead their shot. **1626** BACON *Sylva* §15 Yet it doth not dead the Motion. **1663** PEPYS *Diary* 15 Apr., Which..in dry weather, turns to dust and deads the ball. **1670** *Phil. Trans.* V. 2067 The wind was at South-East; which deads the Tydes there.

7. *U.S. college slang.* 'To cause one to fail in reciting. Said of a teacher who puzzles a scholar with difficult questions, and thereby causes him to fail' (B. H. Hall *College Wds. & Customs*, 1856).

1884 J. HAWTHORNE in *Harper's Mag.* Aug. 386/2 Whose ..enquiry, 'What is ethics?' had deaded so many a promising..student.

dead, obs. form of DEED.

'dead-a'live, *a.* Also **dead-and-alive.** Dead while yet alive; alive, but without animation; dull, inactive, spiritless.

1591 SYLVESTER *Du Bartas* I. v. 953 Leaving a Post-hume (dead-alive) seed behind her. **1617** COLLINS *Def. Bp. Ely* 453 The Monke that liues in pleasure, and delicacie, and idlenesse, is dead aliue. **1794** MISS GUNNING *Packet* II. 103 A dawdling, dead-alive..drowsy subject. **1840** HOOD *Up the Rhine* 2 A..dead-alive, hypochondriacal old bachelor uncle. **1854** THOREAU *Walden* 166 He is dead-and-alive to begin with. *a* **1862** THOREAU *Lett.* (1865) 198, I have performed this journey in a very dead and alive manner. **1868** HOLME LEE *B. Godfrey* xxvi. 138 This..dreary..dead-alive place. **1901** 'M. FRANKLIN' *My Brilliant Career* iii. 16 It's the dead-and-alivest hole I ever seen. **1908** E. J. BANFIELD *Confessions of Beachcomber* I. i. 9 The 'scrub fowl' ..wastes no valuable time in the dead-and-alive duty of sitting. **1909** H. G. WELLS *Tono-Bungay* I. ii. 67 This place ..gives me no Scope... It's dead-and-alive. Nothing happens. **1936** W. HOLTBY *South Riding* II. iii. 112 A bit dead-and-alive, isn't it? Other end of nowhere, eh?

Hence **dead-alivism.**

1887 JESSOPP *Arcady* 170 Dismal, dull, dead-alivism.

dead beat, 'dead-'beat, *sb.*[1] (*a.*) *Watch- and Clock-making*, etc. [DEAD *a.* 24 b.] A beat or stroke which stops 'dead' without recoil. Usually *attrib.* or *adj.*, as in ***dead-beat escapement.***

1768 tr. *P. Le Roy's Attempts finding Longitude* 29 The dead beat is made upon a part that is unconcerned with the regulator. **1874** KNIGHT *Dict. Mech., Dead-beat Escapement.* This..was invented by Graham about 1700. **1881** MAXWELL *Electr. & Magn.* II. 351 Galvanometers, in which the resistance is so great that the motion is of this kind, are called dead-beat galvanometers. **1882** J. MILNE in *Nature* XXVI. 628 Pendulums, so far controlled by friction as to be 'dead-beat'. **1927** *Motor Boat* 9 Sept. 226/3 The..Dead Beat compass..returns after being displaced from its equilibrium position by one direct movement to the north pointing position. **1960** E. L. DELMAR-MORGAN *Cruising Yacht Equipt.* ii. 33 A light, dry card compass... The liquid-filled 'dead-beat' instrument has taken its place.

dead beat, 'dead-'beat, *ppl. a.* (*sb.*[2]) [DEAD *adv.* 1, 2.]

A. *adj.* (or *pa. pple.*) Completely 'beat', utterly exhausted. *colloq.*

1821 P. EGAN *Tom & Jerry* (1890) 34 So dead-beat, as to be compelled to cry for quarter. **1836** HOOK *G. Gurney* I. 218, I never was so dead beat in my life. **1887** SIR R. H. ROBERTS *In the Shires* ii. 30 His horse lay dead beat in a ditch beside him.

B. *sb. slang* (orig. *U.S.*). A worthless idler who sponges on his friends; a sponger, loafer; also (orig. *Austral.*), a man down on his luck. Also *attrib.* Cf. BEAT *sb.*[1] 16.

1863 *Cornhill Mag.* Jan. 94 'Beau' Hickman [was] a professional pensioner, or, in the elegant phraseology of the place 'a deadbeat'. **1875** *Chicago Tribune* 13 Oct. 4/4 To go on a dead-beat spree. **1877** BLACK *Green Past.* xli. (1878) 325 A system of local government controlled by 30,000 bummers, loafers, and dead-beats. **1882** B. HARTE *Flip* ii, Every tramp and dead-beat you've met. **1898** MORRIS *Austral Eng.* 115/2 *Deadbeat.* In Australia, it means a man 'down on his luck', 'stone-broke', beaten by fortune. **1902** W. SATCHELL *Land of Lost* iii. 18 This is the stranding-ground of the dead-beats of the world. **1909** WODEHOUSE *Mike* liv. 304 The Wrykyn team that summer was about the most hopeless gang of dead-beats that had ever made an exhibition of itself on the school grounds. **1912** E. PUGH *Harry the Cockney* xi. 114 He was a full private..attached to London's vast army of dead-beats..these miserable stricken creatures. **1958** *Spectator* 16 May 633/1 A company of British soldiers arrives in trucks, led by a deadbeat Temporary Major. **1959** 'J. WELCOME' *Stop at Nothing* vi. 107 You don't want help from an old dead-beat like me. **1971** *Guardian* 18 Jan. 8/2 He didn't write me off as 'Oh, that dead-beat' when my name was mentioned.

'dead-'beat, *v. rare.* [f. the ppl. adj.] **1.** *trans.* To exhaust, wear out. *colloq.*

1868 M. E. BRADDON *Run to Earth* II. ix. 169 If I ain't dead-beat, it's only because it isn't in circumstances to dead-beat me.

2. *U.S. slang.* **a.** *intr.* To sponge; to loaf. **b.** *trans.* To sponge on; to cheat.

1881 W. O. STODDARD *E. Hardery* 177 He's dead beated on you. **1888** *Boston Jrnl.* (Farmer), No party can dead-beat his way on me these hard times.

So **dead-'beaten** *ppl. a.*, exhausted.

1875 J. G. HOLLAND *Sevenoaks* i. 3 One by one—sick, disabled, discouraged, dead-beaten—they drifted into the poor-house. **1933** MASEFIELD *Bird of Dawning* 220 He felt dead-beaten, yet saw endless things to be done.

dead-beatism. *U.S. slang.* [f. DEAD BEAT *sb.*[2]] Worthlessness.

1869 J. H. BROWNE *Great Metropolis* 192, I have known men of fine talents..fall to the under plane of dead-beatism. **1882** *Congress. Rec.* 25 Jan. 615/1 [Are we] going to put a premium on judicial trumpery and dead-beatism?

dead-beatness. *rare.* [f. DEAD-BEAT *a.* or *ppl. a.* + -NESS.]

1. The quality or property of being aperiodic.

1898 E. J. HOUSTON *Dict. Electr. Words* (ed. 4) App. B. 737/1 *Dead beatness*, possessing the property of aperiodicity. **1918** K. EDGCUMBE *Industr. Electr. Measuring Instr.* (ed. 2) 154 A most important feature of all moving coil instruments lies in their dead-beatness.

2. Utter exhaustion.

1907 M. C. HARRIS *Tents of Wickedness* III. v. 299 The light came streaming in at the window that in the dead-beatness of last night everyone had forgotten to close.

dead-bell: see DEATH-BELL.

'dead-born, *ppl. a.* Now chiefly *dial.*

a. Born dead, still-born.

c **1330** *King of Tars* 914 The child ded-boren was. **1483** *Cath. Angl.* 93 Dedeborne..*abortiuus.* **1613** PURCHAS *Pilgrimage* VIII. xiii. 812 Children which were dead-borne. **1781** BLAND in *Phil. Trans.* LXXI. 357 The number of the children that were dead-born. **1840** R. BREMNER *Excurs. Denmark, etc.* II. 396 The dead-born and those who long wielded the sceptre, are laid side by side.

b. *fig.*

a **1300** *Cursor M.* 26500 (Cott.) þe dedis..þat forwit ded born ware, þai mai be quickend neuer mare. **1725** POPE *Odyss.* xx. 354 A Samian Peer..who teem'd with many a dead-born jest. **1738** —— *Epil. Sat.* II. 226 All, all but Truth, drops dead-born from the Press. **1830** MACAULAY *Southey, Ess.* (1848) I. 222 The History..is already dead: indeed, the second volume was deadborn. **1837** CARLYLE *Fr. Rev.* I. v. viii. 247 Messieurs of the dead-born Brogiie-Ministry.

deadbote: see DEDBOTE.

'dead-,centre. *Mech.* **1.** = DEAD-POINT.

1874 in *Spon's Dict. Engineering* 161.

2. In a lathe, a centre which does not revolve: see CENTRE 5.

1879 HOLTZAPFFEL *Turning* IV. 44 The dead centre with loose pulley. *Ibid.* 45 The dead center lathe.

'dead ,colour. *Painting.* [DEAD *a.* 13 b.] The first or preparatory layer of colour in a painting. So **'dead-,colour** *v. trans.*, to paint in dead colour; **'dead-,colouring** *vbl. sb.*

1658 W. SANDERSON *Graphice* 63 First to speak of dead-colours. **1672** in H. WALPOLE *Vertue's Anecd. Painting* (1786) III. 128, 5 June, Dr. Tillotson sat..to Mr. Lely for him to lay in a dead colour of his picture. **1788** SIR J. REYNOLDS *Disc.* xiv. (1876) 94 That lightness of hand which was in his dead colour, or first painting. *c* **1843** H. GREENOUGH in Flagg *Life W. Allston* (1893) 182 This dead color I paint solidly, with a good body of color.

1658 W. SANDERSON *Graphice* 64 Pictures by a good Master, begun, and dead-coloured only. **1668** *Excellency of Pen & Pencil* 82 In this Dead-colouring you need not be over curious..the colours may be mended at the second Operation. *Ibid.* 101 For a light-red Garment, first dead-colour it with Vermilion. *c* **1790** IMISON *Sch. Art.* II. 58 After the student has covered over, or as artists term it, has dead-coloured the head. **1859** GULLICK & TIMBS *Paint.* 230 The Dead-colouring is the first or preparatory painting, and is so termed because the colours are laid cold and pale to admit of the after-paintings.

dead-day: see DEATH-DAY.

†**'dead-'doing**, *ppl. a. Obs.* 'Doing to death', killing, murderous.

1590 SPENSER *F.Q.* II. iii. 8 Hold your dead-doing hand. **1594** —— *Amoretti* i, Those lilly hands, Which hold my life in their dead-doing might. **1633** B. JONSON *Tale Tub* II. i, Put up..Your frightful blade, and your dead-doing look. **1702** C. MATHER *Magn. Chr.* I. ii. (1852) 53 Such dead-doing things, as powder and shot. **1778** WESLEY *Wks.* (1872) XI. 150 These dead-doing men.

dead drunk, 'dead-'drunk, *a.* [DEAD *adv.* 1: cf. *dead-sick* in DEAD D. 2.] So drunk as to be insensible or unable to move, in a state of prostration through intoxication. Hence **dead-'drunkenness.**

1599 BUTTES *Dyets Dry D.* P vij, They..receive..the smoak through a Cane, till they fall doune Dead-drunke. **1604** SHAKS. *Oth.* II. iii. 85. **1667** DRYDEN *Wild Gallant* v. ii. **1709** STEELE *Tatler* No. 5 ¶1 Cupid is not only Blind at present, but Dead-drunk. **1840** MRS. CARLYLE *Lett.* I. 124 My penitent was lying on the floor, dead-drunk. **1837** HAWTHORNE *Twice Told T., David Swan*, An awful instance of dead drunkenness.

deade, obs. form of DEAD, DEED.

deaded *ppl. a.*: see DEAD *v.* 4.

deaden ('dɛd(ə)n), *v.* [f. DEAD *a.* + -EN[5]: a comparatively recent formation, taking the place of the earlier DEAD *v.*]

I. 1. *intr.* To become dead (*lit.* and *fig.*); to lose vitality, force, vigour, brightness, etc.

1723 *Lond. Gaz.* No. 6171/3 The Wind deadning..we could not make the Way we expected. **1801** SOUTHEY *Thalaba* XII. viii, The dash Of the out-breakers deaden'd. **1835** *New Monthly Mag.* XLIII. 157 The bells, which you hear loudly at first, begin to deaden. **1869** LOWELL *Pictures from Appledore* VI, Yet they momently cool and dampen and deaden.

II. *trans.*

2. a. To deprive of life, kill (*e.g.* the tissues).

1807–26 S. COOPER *First Lines Surg.* (ed. 5) 145 By which ..some of the fibres around the track of the ball are deadened. *Mod.* To deaden the nerve of the tooth.

b. *spec.* (*U.S.*) To kill (trees) by 'girdling', *i.e.* cutting out a section of the bark all round; to clear (ground) by killing the trees in this manner.

1775 ADAIR *Amer. Ind.* 405 They deadened the trees by cutting through the bark. **1855** W. SARGENT *Braddock's Exped.* 84 A good woodsman will soon deaden a number of acres, which by the next seed-time will be ready for cultivation.

3. *fig.* **a.** To deprive of vitality, force, or sensibility; to benumb, to dull.

1684–9 T. BURNET *Th. Earth* (J.), We will..by a soft answer deaden their force by degrees. **1712** ADDISON *Spect.* No. 487 ¶3 That Activity which is natural to the human Soul, and which is not in the power of Sleep to deaden or abate. **1798** T. JEFFERSON *Writ* (1859) IV. 205 It deadens also the demand for wheat. **1863** WHYTE MELVILLE *Gladiators* II. 105 Any anodyne that could deaden or alleviate her pain. **1876** MOZLEY *Univ. Serm.* vi. (1877) 129 To benumb and deaden worship.

b. To render dead or insensible *to.*

a **1690** E. HOPKINS *Serm. Acts* xxvi. 28 (R.) How deadned are they to those sinful ways, which before they much delighted in? **1874** GREEN *Short Hist.* viii. §1. 447 Its [the Bible's] words..fell on ears which custom had not deadened to their force and beauty.

4. To deprive of some effective physical quality: **a.** To deprive of lustre or brilliancy; to make dull in colour or aspect; to give a dull surface to (metal, glass, etc.): see DEAD *a.* 13 b.

1666 PEPYS *Diary* 24 Oct., He..lays the fault of it upon the fire, which deadened..the glory of his services. **1706** POPE *Let. to Walsh* 2 July, In painting, a man may lay colours one upon another, till they stiffen and deaden the piece. **1799** G SMITH *Laboratory* I. 185 How to deaden the glass and fit it to paint upon. **1855** OWEN *Anat. Vertebr. Anim.* ii. (L.), [It] deadens the whiteness of the tissue.

b. To deprive (liquor) of sharpness or flavour, to make vapid. **c.** To make (sound) dull or indistinct. **d.** To reduce (quicksilver) from the liquid to the granular state in the process of amalgamation.

1683 TRYON *Way to Health* 208 Nothing..does more deaden and flat the Spirits, especially in green Herbs, than slack Fires. **1725** [see DEADENED]. **1828** WEBSTER, *Deaden*.. to make vapid or spiritless; as, to deaden wine or beer. **1828** SCOTT *F.M. Perth* xxvii, To shut out, or deaden at least, a sound so piercing. **1872** [see DEADENED]. **1881** RAYMOND *Mining Gloss., Deadened Mercury.*

e. To make impervious to sound; = DEAFEN *v.* 3.

1901 R. STURGIS *Dict. Archit.* I. 751/1 *Deaden*,..to construct so as to be dead, in the sense of..impervious to sound, as a floor which has been made non-conducting. **1926** 'J. J. CONNINGTON' *Death at Swaythling Court* vii. 121 The kitchen is next the workshop and the walls are very badly deadened, so I could hear voices talking next door.

5. To destroy or reduce the energy of (motion).

1665 GLANVILL *Sceps. Sci.* (J.), This motion would be quickly deadened by countermotions. **1828** WEBSTER, *Deaden*..3. To deaden the motion of a ship or of the wind. **1867** SMYTH *Sailor's World-bk., Deaden a ship's way*, to retard a vessel's progress by bracing in the yards.

dead end, 'dead-'end. [DEAD *a.* D. 2.]

1. A closed end of a water-pipe, passage, etc., through which there is no way; also *attrib.*

1886 *Pall Mall G.* 12 Oct. 2/1 There are, of course, fire-cocks and valves on dead-ends, but these are not efficient to thoroughly free water-pipes from incrustations and deposits. **1889** G. FINDLAY *Eng. Railway* 199 This is what is termed a 'dead-end' warehouse..the waggons come in and go out the same way, and cannot be taken through the warehouse. **1960** D. & V. NABOKOV tr. *V. Nabokov's Invit. to Beheading* xv. 147 Several times Cincinnatus found himself in a cul-de-sac, and then M'sieur Pierre would tug at his calves, making him back out of the dead end.

2. *fig.* Esp. a policy, course of action, etc., that leads nowhere; a 'blind alley'.

1922 M. ARLEN *Piracy* III. xiv. 257, I felt..that there was a 'dead-end' at the end of my life. **1928** *Daily Tel.* 24 July 12/1 Young men..who are either working into a dead end or engaged in an industry that has a restricted future. **1934** *Discovery* Mar. 60/2 Once we came to a dead-end when we had no idea which way to turn. **1941** AUDEN *New Year Let.* III. 46 From the dead-ends of greed and sin.

b. *attrib.* or as *adj.* (*a*) That leads nowhere; having no possibilities for advance, promotion, etc.; (*b*) ***dead-end kid***: a tough young person such as lives in back-streets or slums; also *transf.*

1928 *Observer* 15 Jan. 5 He deplores the fate of boys who get into dead-end employments. **1940** J. B. PRIESTLEY *Postscripts* 17 Overgrown, tormenting, cruel schoolboys—middle-aged 'dead end kids'. **1943** J. S. HUXLEY *TVA* xi. 86 No dead-end formula has killed the creative ability of the team. **1946** [see *dead-ending* below]. **1958** *New Statesman* 20 Dec. 869/2 It is not difficult to present France..as Europe's Dead End Kid. **1963** *Economist* 20 Apr. 254/1 Workers shifting out of dead-end jobs and dead-end areas into 'approved' new spots.

3. *Electr.* (See quot. 1940.)

1922 GLAZEBROOK *Dict. Appl. Physics* II. 670/1 A large increase in effective resistance also results from the attachment of a 'dead' end coil having large mutual inductance to the section. **1925** P. J. RISDON *Crystal Receivers & Circuits* 10 The unused portion of the coil, although not directly in the circuit, is joined on to it, and produces an effect known as dead-end loss. **1940** *Chambers's Techn. Dict.* 226/1 *Dead end*, the unused portion of an inductance coil in an oscillatory circuit. *Dead-end effect*, the increase in effective resistance of an inductance coil due to currents circulating in the unused end-turns shunted by their self-capacity.

Hence **dead-'end** *v. trans.*, to bring to a dead end; *intr.*, to come to a dead end; **dead-'endedness**, the quality of leading nowhere or failing to advance; **dead-'ending** *vbl. sb.* (see quot. 1946).

1921 *Blackw. Mag.* Nov. 641/2 Engineers..are not dead-ended so easily. **1946** A. PHELPS *I couldn't care Less* x. 75 There were some..Americans who..made a habit of flying through the most appalling weather. We nicknamed them the 'Deadend Kids'... To this day the term 'Dead-ending' persists to describe flying through unusually bad weather. **1950** H. J. MASSINGHAM *Curious Trav.* iii. 53 The dead-endedness of modern life in which the rational faculty has overborne the poetic perception of reality. **1958** G. USHER *Death in Bag* xi. 105 The car..took an even narrower lane dead-ending in a concreted farmyard.

deadened ('dɛd(ə)nd), *ppl. a.* [f. DEADEN *v.* + -ED[1].] Deprived of life or force; dulled, muffled, etc.

1720 WELTON *Suff. Son of God* I. x. 245 Obedience renews the Life of Deadened Love. **1725** POPE *Odyss.* XXII. 284 With deaden'd sound, one on the threshold falls. **1789** T. WHATELY in *Med. Commun.* II. 393 The exfoliated or deadened part [of a bone]. **1872** BLACK *Adv. Phaeton* ix. 121 The deadened tolling of a bell.

deadener ('dɛd(ə)nə(r)). [-ER[1].] **a.** One who or that which deadens: see the verb.

1846 LANDOR *Imag. Conv.* Wks. II. 60/2 Incumbrances and deadeners of the harmony. **1884** GOLDW. SMITH in *Contemp. Rev.* Sept. 316 Unless they are strong.. Conservative institutions are..deadeners of responsibility.

b. *Logging.* (See quot.) *U.S.*

1905 *Terms Forestry & Logging* 34 *Deadener*, a heavy log or timber, with spikes set in the butt end, so fastened in a log slide that the logs passing under it come in contact with the spikes and have their speed retarded.

deadening ('dɛd(ə)nıŋ), *vbl. sb.* [-ING[1].]

1. The action of the verb DEADEN, q.v.

1866 TIMMINS *Industr. Hist. Birmingham* 300 The [brass] work becomes speckled or irregular in the 'deadening'. **1875** WHITNEY *Life Lang.* vii. 118 The deadening of the native processes of composition and derivation and inflection. **1883** *League Jrnl.* 20 Oct. 657/3 Mental depression and moral deadening.

b. *concr.* That which deadens sound, colour, etc.

1874 KNIGHT *Dict. Mech., Deadening.* 1. (*Carpentry.*) Packing in a floor, ceiling, or wall, to prevent conduction of sound [cf. DEAFEN 3]. 2. (*Gilding.*) A thin coat of glue.. smeared over a surface that is gilded in distemper, and is not to be burnished.

2. *U.S.* The action of killing trees by 'girdling'; *concr.* a clearing in which the trees have been 'girdled'. (See DEADEN 2 b.)

1800 ADDISON *Amer. Law. Rep.* 306 There was a deadening on C's land as early as 1769. **1855** W. SARGENT *Braddock's Exped.* 83 A deadening..signifies the effect produced on the trees by girdling, or cutting a ring about their trunks.

'deadening, *ppl. a.* [-ING[2].] That deadens: see the verb.

1805 SOUTHEY *Madoc in Azt.* xviii, From his shield The deadening force communicated ran Up his stunn'd arm. **1875** HAMERTON *Intell. Life* XI. i. 402 The deadening influences of routine.

deadeningly ('dɛd(ə)nɪŋlɪ), *adv.* [f. DEADENING *ppl. a.* + -LY[2].] In a deadening manner; so as to deaden.

1939 R. MURRAY *Good Pagan's Failure* iii. 150 The amazing material achievements to which we are almost deadeningly accustomed. **1962** I. MURDOCH *Unofficial Rose* vii. 77 That honest simplicity..which made her for him so deadeningly structureless.

† **'deader**[1]. *Obs.* [f. DEAD *v.* + -ER[1].] = DEADENER.

a **1640** W. FENNER *Christ's Alarm* II. (1657) 26 The giving way to sin..which thing is an horrible deader of the heart.

deader[2] ('dɛdə(r)). *slang.* [f. DEAD *a.* + -ER[1] 1.] A dead person, a corpse.

1853 (in *American Newspaper*). **1887** A. C. DOYLE *Study in Scarlet* II. i, Then mother's a deader too. **1887** *Cyclist* 13 Apr. 640/1 The half-dozen..troopers would have been manufactured into deaders in the twinkling of an eye.

dead-eye ('dɛdaɪ). [DEAD *a.* 15.] *Naut.* A round laterally flattened wooden block, pierced with three holes through which a lanyard is reeved, used for extending the shrouds. Also applied to the triangular blocks with one large hole, usually called *hearts*, similarly used for extending the stays. (Cf. DEAD MAN'S EYE.)

1748 *Anson's Voy.* I. viii. 78 The main topsail split, and one of the straps of the main dead-eyes broke. **1835** SIR J. C. ROSS *Narr. 2nd Voy.* xxviii. 398 The dead eyes were preparing for the mainmast. **1891** *Times* 14 Oct. 6/5 The William Bateman has lost her main yard, and several of her chain plates and dead eyes are broken.

b. ***crowfoot dead-eye*** = EUPHROE.

1815 in FALCONER *Marine Dict.* (ed. Burney). **1867** SMYTH *Sailor's Word-bk.* s.v., The *crowfeet dead-eyes* are long cylindrical blocks with a number of small holes in them, to receive the legs or lines composing the crowfoot.

deadfall, dead-fall ('dɛdfɔːl). *Chiefly U.S.*

1. a. A kind of trap used esp. for large game, in which a weighted board or heavy log is arranged to fall upon and kill or disable the prey. Also *attrib.* with *trap.*

1611 MARKHAM *Countr. Content.* I. xvi. (1668) 78 Some do use to take them with hutches, or dead-falls, set in their haunts. **1829** *Massachusetts Spy* 8 July (Th.), In the act of getting in, the log or dead-fall fell upon his back and held him fast. **1843** CARLTON *New Purchase* I. 2 We..were setting dead-falls and snares. **1877** COUES *Fur Anim.* vi. 175 In addition to our steel traps, we built numerous deadfalls. **1902** S. E. WHITE *Blazed Trail* xvii. 128 He had bound together..several of the oddly shaped pine timbers to form a species of dead-fall trap. **1959** J. D. CLARK *Prehist. S. Afr.* vi. 132 The use of dead-fall traps.

b. *fig.* A trap, snare (cf. TRAP *sb.*[1] 1 b).

1860 *Richmond Enquirer* 23 Nov. 1/8 (Th.), A continuance on the part of the Banks to issue specie would..catch us completely under the dead fall of Northern absorptive predominance. **1962** K. ORVIS *Damned & Destroyed* xvi. 113 This rendezvous is a deadfall.

2. a. A tangled mass of fallen trees. Also *attrib.*

1883 *Century Mag.* XXIX. 195/1 Extensive 'dead-falls' of trees thrown pell-mell over, under, and astraddle of each other by gales. **1898** *Westm. Gaz.* 12 Sept. 8/2 Travelling painfully over deadfall timber. **1968** R. M. PATTERSON *Finlay's River* 89 Then through deadfall and around small canyons they made their way down the west slope of the main range.

b. (See quot.)

1874 KNIGHT *Dict. Mech., Dead-fall,* a dumping-platform at the mouth of a mine.

c. 'A low drinking or gaming-place. *Western U.S.*' (*Cent. Dict.*). Also, see quots.

1837 A. WETMORE *Gaz. Missouri* 337 A small pot-house grocery or dead-fall of the village. **1867** *Harper's Mag.* June 131/1 In California, old Judge C—— kept *a little dead fall,* as they call a rum-mill out there. **1903** A. ADAMS *Log Cowboy* xvi. 251 There's a deadfall down here on the river.. that robs a man coming and going. **1937** D. RUNYON *More than Somewhat* v. 100 The Bohemian Club is nothing but a deadfall.

dead-fallow. A complete year's fallow, i.e. rest for the land for both a summer and a winter. Hence **'dead-'fallow** *v.*

1881 *Daily News* 5 Sept. 2/2 Nearly the whole of the arable has been dead-fallowed this summer.

'dead-hand. Also dead hand. **1. a.** = MORTMAIN (of which it is a translation).

[*c* **1380** WYCLIF *Wks.* (1880) 131 þei wolle not cesse til alle be conquerid in-to here dede hondis.] **1612** BP. HALL *Serm.* v. 64 What liberal revenues..were then put into Mortmain, the dead-hand of the Church! **1670** BLOUNT *Law Dict.* s.v. *Ad quod damnum,* The Land so given, is said to fall into a *Dead hand.* For a Body Politick dies not, nor can perform personal service to the King, or their Mesne Lords, as single Persons may do. **1879** MORLEY *Burke* (1880) 162 Forty-thousand serfs in the gorges of the Jura, who were held in dead-hand by the Bishop of Saint-Claude. **1880** A. J. WILSON in *Macm. Mag.* 469 That benevolence of the 'dead hand', which corrupts and blights all its victims.

b. *fig.* An oppressive and retarding influence. Cf. MORTMAIN sense c.

[**1871** *Scribner's Monthly* Nov. 19/1 The dead hand of Wesley has been stronger than the living hand of any pope.] **1935** *Discovery* Oct. 301/2 This cannot fairly be described as the 'dead hand' of the National Trust. **1955** *Times* 29 June 11/2 He would have fought the Government dead hand which fantastically enforces small papers ten years after the war. **1971** *Daily Tel.* (Colour Suppl.) 25 June 13/3 Eisenhower's dead hand on space was an obvious electoral issue for the two incoming presidential candidates to seize on.

2. *colloq.* An expert (*at* doing something).

1848 THACKERAY *Bk. Snobs* vii, He is a dead hand at piquet. **1862** G. O. TREVELYAN *Interludes in Verse & Prose* (1905) 181 A young member of the Secretariat, a dead hand at a minute. **1888** 'R. BOLDREWOOD' *Robbery under Arms* I. xv. 194 First-rate work it was, too; he was always a dead hand at splitting.

Hence **dead-'handed** *a.*, oppressively old-fashioned or out-dated.

1928 D. H. LAWRENCE *Lady Chatterley* xviii. 333 It was stupid, dead-handed higher authority that made the army dead.

'deadhead, dead-head, dead head, *sb.*

†**1.** *Old Chem.* = CAPUT MORTUUM 2. *Obs.*

1576 BAKER *Jewell of Health* 195a, See whether the deadehead be blacke. **1662** R. MATHEW *Unl. Alch.* §109. 177 Take from the Dunghil at the Refiners, his dead head, commonly called, *Caput mortuum.* **1707** *Curios. in Husb. & Gard.* 329, I made a Lixivium with clear Water, and filter'd it to take away the dead head of it.

2. *Techn.* **a.** *Founding.* The extra length or 'head' of metal at the muzzle end of a gun-casting, which contains the dross formed on the molten metal, and which is cut off when cool; see also quot. 1874. **b.** *Mech.* The tail-stock of a lathe, containing the *dead spindle* (see DEAD *a.* 23). **c.** *Naut.* (See quot. 1867.)

1867 SMYTH *Sailor's Word-bk., Dead-head,* a kind of dolphin (a stout post on a quay head to make hawsers fast to); also, a rough block of wood used as an anchor-bouy. **1869** *Eng. Mech.* 17 Dec. 320/1 When castings are required to be particularly solid..they are generally made with what is termed a 'dead head'. **1874** KNIGHT *Dict. Mech., Dead-head..* That piece on a casting which fills the ingate at which the metal entered the mold. A *feeding-head.*

3. *colloq.* **a.** A person admitted without payment to a theatrical performance, a public conveyance, etc. Also *attrib.* and *transf.* orig. *U.S.*

1841 *Spirit of Times* 23 Jan. 564/1 The house on Tuesday was filled as far as $300 could fill, barring 'the dead heads'. **1848** BARTLETT *Dict. Amer.* App. s.v., Persons who drink at a bar, ride in an omnibus, or railroad car, travel in steamboats, or visit the theatre without charge, are called *dead heads.* **1853** LOWELL *Moosehead Jrnl.* Prose Wks. 1890 I. 19 Those 'attentive clerks' whose praises are sung by thankful deadheads. **1863** *Rep. Maine Board Agric.* 15 The milch cow which barely pays the expense of keeping and care is a 'dead head' yielding no profit. **1864** SALA in *Daily Telegraph* 1 Nov., A friend of mine, a very eminent 'dead-head'—that is to say, one who has free admissions everywhere and to everything. **1869** W. H. BREWER *Rocky Mt. Lett.* (1930) 11 We had quite a train—some congressmen who have dead-head tickets over the road. **1887** C. B. GEORGE *40 Yrs. on Rail* ii. 32 Once in a while the conductor found it desirable to eject some would-be dead-head passenger while between stations. **1892** *Daily News* 16 Sept. 5/6 The natural antipathy between peformers and what are known in the theatrical profession as 'deadheads'.. who do not pay for their entertainment. **1892** *Congress. Rec.* 31 May, App. 385/1 The free-delivery service is burdened by the collection and delivery of thousands of dead-head matter under the 'penalty-postage system'.

b. Used predicatively without article. *U.S.*

1874 'MARK TWAIN' & C. D. WARNER *Gilded Age* xxx. 275 Senators and Representatives..always traveled 'dead-head' both ways. **1888** *Portland Transcript* 14 Mar. (Farmer), [Those letters] which had to do with the stage business and went dead-head.

c. A non-combatant accompanying a fighting force. *U.S.*

1864 T. C. REYNOLDS in J. N. Edwards *Shelby & his Men* (1867) xxvii. 470 The real fighting men did little injury, sneaks and dead-heads being the principal plunderers. **1867** J. N. EDWARDS *Shelby & his Men* xxi. 396 Accompanied by at least five hundred 'dead-heads', loafers, and amateur cavalry gentlemen.

d. A train, freight car, truck, etc., carrying no passengers or freight. Also *attrib. U.S.*

1938 L. M. BEEBE *High Iron* 220 *Deadhead,*..empty passenger car. **1945** *Greeley* (Colorado) *Daily Tribune* 15 Dec. 1/7 The headon collision of a deadhead engine and a 37-car freight train. **1950** A. LOMAX *Mr. Jelly Roll* 109 A deadhead, an empty mail car.

4. In full ***dead head log***: a sunken or submerged log. *U.S.*

1902 S. E. WHITE *Blazed Trail* lv. 380 He was enabled to catch the slanting end of a 'dead head' log whose lower end was jammed in the crib. **1905** *Terms Forestry & Logging* 34. **1907** *Black Cat* June 17 Numerous 'dead-heads' bobbed in the current like otters swimming with the stream.

5. A person who contributes nothing to an enterprise, activity, etc.; an unenterprising person.

1942 N. STREATFEILD *I ordered Table* 215 It's an awfully sticky party this... I'm a deadhead to-night, but I can't help it. **1952** *Landfall* VI. 265 You can ignore him [God] too, as these Te Parenga deadheads do. **1964** *Economist* 4 Apr. 40/1 A 'dead head agency', a safe berth for unenterprising civil servants.

6. A faded flower head. See DEAD *a.* A. 1 c.

1960 D. HOLMAN-HUNT *My Grandmothers & I* i. 7 Did you cut off *all* the deadheads? **1962** N. MARSH *Hand in Glove* v. 177 I'll go and snip the deadheads off the roses. **1970** C. LLOYD *Well-Tempered Garden* i. 48 The culling of dead heads is a ploy that figures persistently in the garden in summer.

Hence **'deadheadism,** the practice of admitting persons as 'deadheads'.

1887 *Miss Bayle's Romance* III. 92, I mean to abolish dead-headism.

dead-head, *v.* [see the sb.]

1. *colloq.* (chiefly *U.S.*). **a.** *trans.* To admit as a 'deadhead' (sense 3), without payment. **b.** *intr.* To act the 'deadhead', obtain a privilege without payment.

1854 LOWELL in *Atlantic Monthly* Dec. (1892) 746/2, I will not be deadheaded. **1860** O. W. HOLMES *Elsie V.* ii. (1891) 13 He had been 'dead-headed' into the world some fifty years ago, and had sat with his hands in his pockets staring at the show ever since. **1885** J. BIGELOW in *Harper's Mag.* Mar. 542/1 Mr. Jefferson was not in the habit of deadheading at hotels.

2. *intr.* Of logs: to jam. *U.S. colloq.*

1922 H. TITUS *Timber* viii. 79 Your hardwood will begin dead-heading in a hurry. *Ibid.* x. 89 If the raft goes to pieces and that one log dead-heads.

3. *intr.* To drive an empty train, truck, taxi, etc.; to travel in an empty vehicle. Also *trans. colloq.* (chiefly *U.S.*).

1911 *Daily Colonist* (Victoria, B.C.) 15 Apr. 3/3 Only O'Leary and the conductor..were in the car, which was deadheaded. **1929** *Folk-Say* I. 111 He [*sc.* a taxi-driver] has to deadhead all the way back. **1956** WALLIS & BLAIR *Thunder Above* (1959) xi. 107 Kyle had flown up to Berlin..as a check pilot and now had forty-eight hours before dead-heading back. **1962** K. ORVIS *Damned & Destroyed* xii. 81 He hated to deadhead back an empty boat. **1970** *People* (Austral.) 26 Aug. 27/5 Another fireman was deadheading in the cab with us and he took over for me.

4. *trans.* To remove a dead flower or flowers from (a plant). Cf. DEADHEADING *vbl. sb.* 2.

1952 C. E. L. PHILLIPS *Small Garden* xi. 106 A great many herbaceous plants will go on and on if dead-headed. **1956** E. H. M. & P. A. COX *Mod. Rhododendrons* 17 In a large collection,..it is impossible to dead head every plant. **1966** A. E. LINDOP *I start Counting* vii. 96 The daffs were going off, and I dead-headed them and tied them down. **1970** C. LLOYD *Well-Tempered Garden* i. 48 One can distinguish broadly between those plants that are dead-headed with no further object than to tidy them up and those from which we are hoping to encourage another flowering.

'deadheading, *vbl. sb.* [f. the vb.] **1.** *U.S. colloq.* = DEADHEADISM; also, the act or practice of being a deadhead.

1873 *Newton Kansan* 27 Feb. 3/4 Railroads occasionally complain of the deadheading, but no institution suffers so much from it as the press. **1903** G. C. EGGLESTON *First of Hoosiers* 263 Edward..objected..to all 'dead-heading' of the clergy, and to all 'discounts' made to preachers on the ground of their calling.

2. *Hort.* (See quot. 1954.)

1952 C. E. L. PHILLIPS *Small Garden* vii. 62 The most elementary pruning is the 'dead-heading' of border flowers, by which we remove spent blooms in order to induce new ones. **1954** A. G. L. HELLYER *Encycl. Garden Work* 198/1 Faded flower heads may sometimes be removed... This.. is often known as dead-heading. **1970** C. LLOYD *Well-Tempered Garden* i. 48 The first principle in dead-heading is always to cut back to something definite.

'dead-'hearted, *a.* Dead in feeling, callous, insensible. Hence **dead-'heartedly** *adv.*; **dead-'heartedness.**

1642 J. EATON *Honey-combe* 378 Such dead-hearted, unbeleeving, and wrangling Sophisters. *Ibid.* 378 *margin,* Zealous against dead-heartednesse and unbeliefe. **1670** T. BROOKS *Wks.* (1867) VI. 351 God will deliver you from.. security..formality, dead-heartedness, lukewarmness. **1839** *Standard* 6 July, The callous dead-hearted sensualist.

dead heat, *sb. Racing,* etc. [Cf. DEAD *a.* 28, 31.] A 'heat' or race in which two (or more) competitors reach the goal at the same instant.

1796 *Sporting Mag.* VII. 260/2 The whole race was run *head* and *head,* terminating in a *dead heat.* **1823** 'J. BEE' *Dict. Turf* 94 'Dead heat', is when two winners come in nose to nose. **1840** HOOD *Kilmansegg, Her Accident* viii, She could ride a dead heat With the Dead who ride so fast and fleet. **1878** LEVER *Jack Hinton* viii. 54 What year there was a dead heat for the St. Leger.

Hence **dead-heat** *v. intr.*, to run a dead heat (*with*); *trans.* to run a dead heat with (another competitor). **dead-heater,** one who runs a dead heat.

1887 *Cyclist* 22 June, Ralph Temple..Dead-heated Howell in the Quarter-mile Match. **1892** *Black & White* 19 Mar. 384/1 The two clubs who dead-heated..express themselves as very anxious to decide the matter by a race. **1868** *Daily Tel.* 29 Apr., About four lengths in the rear of the dead-heaters was St. Ronan, third. **1902** *Daily Chron.* 21 May 3/5 Hitherto the London and North-Western have deliberately 'dawdled' over the thirty miles after Crewe, so as to only 'dead-heat' with their competitors. **1922** *Daily Mail* 22 Nov. 7 Chuck-a-Penny distinguished himself..by dead-heating with Eton and dividing the spoils.

† **deading** ('dɛdɪŋ), *vbl. sb. Obs.* [f. DEAD *v.*] The action of the verb DEAD; deadening.

c **1400** *Lanfranc's Cirurg.* 293 Cancrene..comeþ of dedinge of þe skyn. **1607** HIERON *Wks.* I. 219 To the deading of their hearts, like Nabals. **1645** USSHER *Body Div.* (1647) 430 A further deading of the old man.

† **'deading,** *ppl. a. Obs.* [-ING[2].] Deadening.

1647 H. MORE *Song of Soul* III. I. ii, Deading liquor.

deadish ('dɛdɪʃ), *a.* Now *rare.* [f. DEAD *a.* + -ISH.] Somewhat dead (in various senses).

a **1450** *Fysshynge with Angle* (1883) 11 The browne colour seruyth for that water that is blacke dedisshe in ryuers or in other waters. **1562** BULLEYN *Dial. Soarnes & Chir.* 10a, When thei seme to bee colde, pale, deddishe, or partelie not felte. **1611** A. STAFFORD *Niobe* II. 186 (T.) The lips put on a deadish paleness. **1697** R. PEIRCE *Bath Mem.* II. ii. 264 His left Arm and Hand were numb'd and deadish. **1742** *Lond. & Country Brew.* I. (ed. 4) 55 To recover deadish Beer. **1783** *Phil. Trans.* LXXIII. 368 It beat out flat, yielded a deadish sound, and became fluid in less than a minute.

de-adjectival (diːædʒɪk'taɪvəl), *a.* [f. DE- + ADJECTIVAL *a.*] Derived from an adjective.

1934 PRIEBSCH & COLLINSON *German Lang.* iii. 225 De-adjectival verbs like *füllen* from *voll*, *heilen* from *heil*. **1962** B. M. H. STRANG *Mod. Eng. Structure* vi. 97 Words that I shall call de-adjectival class nouns..are homonymous with adjectives.

dead letter.

1. a. *orig.* A writing, etc. taken in a bare literal sense without reference to its 'spirit', and hence useless or ineffective (cf. Rom. vii. 6, 2 Cor. iii. 6).

1579 FULKE *Heskin's Parl.* 6 The scriptures, which this dogge calleth the deade letters. **1652** STERRY *Eng. Deliv. North. Presb.*, 10 This..taken singly by it selfe, is but a breathlesse Carkasse, or a Dead Letter. **1831** CARLYLE *Sart. Res.* II. iii, First must the dead Letter of Religion own itself dead..if the living Spirit of Religion..is to arise on us.

b. A writ, statute, ordinance, etc., which is or has become practically without force or inoperative, though not formally repealed or abolished.

1663 HEATH *Flagellum* (ed. 2) 6 To which all other dictates and Instructions were uselesse, and as a dead letter. **1726** AMHERST *Terræ Fil.* xlii. 220 The best laws, when they become dead letters, are no laws. *a* **1754** FIELDING *Voy. Lisbon* (1755) 145 (Farmer) And to enact laws without doing this, is to fill our statute-books..still fuller with dead letter, of no use but to the printer of the Acts of Parliament. **1848** MACAULAY *Hist. Eng.* II. 132 The few penal laws..which had been made in Ireland against Protestant Noncomformists, were a dead letter. **1869** FREEMAN *Norm. Conq.* (1876) III. xii. 249 Many a treaty of marriage became a dead letter almost as soon as it was signed.

c. *transf.* and *fig.* (See quots.)

1864 HOTTEN *Slang Dict.* 118 *Dead-letter*, an action of no value or weight; an article, owing to some mistake in its production, rendered utterly valueless. **1926** FOWLER *Mod. Eng. Usage* 104/1 *Dead letter*..; the application of it [*sc.* the phrase] to what was never a regulation but has gone or is going out of use, as quill pens, horse-traction, amateur football, &c., or to a regulation that loses its force only by actual abolition (*the one-sex franchise will soon be a d.l.*), is a slipshod extension.

2. A letter which lies unclaimed for a certain time at a post-office, or which cannot be delivered through defect of address or other cause. ***Dead-letter Office***: a department of a general post-office in which dead letters are examined, and returned to the writers, or destroyed after a certain time; *c* 1880 officially styled *Returned Letter Office*.

1703 in *Mass. Hist. Soc. Coll.* (1838) 3rd Ser. VII. 62 The other penny is lost in dead letters (remaining in the several Post Offices). **1737** *London Mag.* Jan. 54/1 John Jesse, Esq; Deputy Secretary of the Post-Office, succeeds the late Mr Williamson as Deputy Cashier; as does Mr John Barber, as Inspector of dead letters at the said Office. **1771** P. PARSONS *Newmarket* II. 126, I sent to the Posthouse, and purchased a pacquet of dead letters. **1812** M. EDGEWORTH *Absentee* in *Tales Fash. Life* VI. xvii. 423 The letter went coursing after you... I took it for granted that it found its way to the dead-letter office. **1845** MCCULLOCH *Taxation* II. vii. (1852) 316 With these exceptions, all packets above the weight of 16 oz. will be immediately forwarded to the Dead Letter Office. **1881** *Standard* 1 Nov. 2/2 The old name, 'Dead Letter Office', has had to be altered to the present appellation, 'Returned Letter Office', partly in consequence of the fatuity of the public, who would insist upon associating the title 'Dead' letter with the 'land of the leal'.

3. *Typogr.* See DEAD *a.* A. 20 d.

Hence **dead-'letterism** (*nonce-wd.*), devotion to the 'dead letter' to the neglect of the 'spirit' (see 1 a).

1879 BARING-GOULD *Germany* II. 186 Pietism..is also a necessary revulsion from the dead-letterism into which German Protestantism had lapsed.

dead lift. [See DEAD *a.* 28, and LIFT *sb.*]

1. The pull of a horse, etc., exerting his utmost strength at a dead weight beyond his power to move.

1551 R. ROBINSON tr. *More's Utop.* II. (Arb.) 76 Oxen.. they graunte to be not so good as horses at a sodeyne brunte, and (as we saye) at a deade lifte. **1888** ELWORTHY *W. Somerset Word-bk.* 186 When horses are attached to a weight beyond their strength to move, they frequently refuse to try a second time; in such a case it is said 'they won't pull at a dead lift'. On the other hand it is common to hear a seller say of a horse, 'I'll warn un to pull twenty times following to a dead-lift'.

2. *fig.* A position or juncture in which one can do no more, an extremity, 'a hopeless exigence' (J.). Usually in phrase ***at a dead lift***. (Very common in the 17th c.: now *arch.* or *dial.*)

1567 HARMAN *Caveat* 34 And to these at a ded lyft, or last refuge, they maye..repayre. **1588** J. UDALL *Diotrephes* (Arb.) 25 You must helpe vs at that dead lift, or else we are vndone. **1625–6** SHIRLEY *Maid's Rev.* III. ii, Medicine he carried always in the pommel of his sword, for a dead lift; a very active poison. **1641** J. SHUTE *Sarah & Hagar* (1649) 7 All-sufficient, he comes in at a dead lift, and he is able to turn things in a moment. **1642** FULLER *Holy & Prof. St.* II. xxi. 137 Then [in a shipwreck] they betook themselves to their prayers, the best lever at such a dead lift indeed. **1754** BERTHELSON *Eng.-Dan. Dict.*, He helped me at a dead lift, *hand satte mig paa fœd igien.* **1783** AINSWORTH *Lat. Dict.* (Morell) IV. s.v. *Nero*, None would do the wretch [Nero] the favour to kill him; and..he had not the heart to help himself at a dead lift. **18..** MAR. EDGEWORTH *Stories of Ireland* v, It's only jockeying—fine sport—and very honourable, to help a friend, at a dead lift. **1814** J. GILCHRIST *Reason* 88, I would not slip off from a dead lift, forgetting to come back to it.

3. An effort in which the whole strength is applied to lift or move something; a sheer lift; a supreme effort. *rare.*

1882 MORRIS *Hopes & Fears for Art* i. 21 It is such a heavy question by what effort, by what dead-lift, you can thrust this difficulty from you.

'dead-light. [In sense 1, f. DEAD *a.* 15; in 3, f. DEAD *sb.*, or Sc. form of *death-light.*]

1. *Naut.* A strong wooden or iron shutter fixed outside a cabin-window or port-hole in a storm, to prevent water from entering.

1726 SHELVOCKE *Voy. round World* 3 A sea struck us..and drove in one of our quarter and one of our stern dead lights. **1836** MARRYAT *Midsh. Easy* xxvi, The water..had burst into the cabin through the windows..for the dead lights.. had not yet been shipped. *a* **1845** BARHAM *Ingol. Leg.*, *Bros. Birchington*, The dead-lights are letting the spray and the rain in.

2. A skylight not made to open.

1882 *Trade Catalogue*, Skylights for which we have no corresponding sizes of Deadlights.

3. A luminous appearance seen over putrescent bodies, in grave-yards, etc.; a 'corpse-light' or ' corpse-candle'. *Sc.*

1813 HOGG *Queen's Wake* Introd., Dead-lights glimmering through the night. **1854** H. MILLER *Sch. & Schm.* ix. (1860) 85/2 The many floating Highland stories of spectral dead-lights and wild supernatural sounds, seen and heard by nights in lonely places of sepulture.

†**'deadlihead.** *Obs. rare.* [f. DEADLY *a.* + -HEAD.] Dead condition; the state of the dead.

1612 AINSWORTH *Annot. Ps.* xvii. 10 By the Hebrew word *Sheol*..we are to understand the place, estate, or depth of death, deadlihed. **1642** G. HUGHES *Embalming Dead Saints* 19 Some kind of losse..which this deadlyhed brings upon the soule. *Ibid.* 20 Deadly-head.

†**'deadlihood.** *Obs. rare*$^{-1}$. = prec.

1659 PEARSON *Creed* 476 In the state or condition of the dead; in deadlyhood, as some have learn't to speak.

deadlily ('dɛdlɪlɪ), *adv. rare.* [f. as prec. + -LY².] In a deadly manner; mortally, fatally; excessively; = DEADLY *adv.*

1621 LADY M. WROTH *Urania* 116 Musing..how hee should so farre and deadlily fall out with himselfe. **1662** J. CHANDLER *Van Helmont's Oriat.* 122 A young man, A Companion in the Duel, to the Earl..being deadlily pricked, thrust Loniguius thorow. **1849** SOUTHEY *Comm.-pl. Bk.* Ser. II. 257 Dull, dull—deadlily dull. **1860** PUSEY *Min. Proph.* 312 They bit, as serpents, treacherously, deadlily. **1863** —— *Lent. Serm.* 4 Deadlily delusive to the soul.

'dead-line.

1. A line that does not move or run. [DEAD *a.* 23.]

1860 *Chamber's Encycl.*, *Barbel*, Angling..with a dead-line, called a ledger. **1892** *Pall Mall G.* 5 Aug. 3/1 The scene is worked with miniature pulleys, 'working lines', and 'dead lines'.

2. a. *Mil.* A line drawn around a military prison, beyond which a prisoner is liable to be shot down. orig. *U.S.*

1864 in *Congress. Rec.* 12 Jan. (1876) 384/1 The 'dead line', beyond which the prisoners are not allowed to pass. **1868** LOSSING *Hist. Civ. War U.S.* III. 600 Seventeen feet from the inner stockade was the 'dead-line', over which no man could pass and live. **1888** *Contemp. Review* Mar. 449 Should he some day escape alive across the dead-line of Winchesters, he will be hunted with bloodhounds.

fig. **1889** BRUCE *Plant. Negro* 45 The instant he sought.. to cross the social dead-line.

b. *Printing.* A guide-line marked on the bed of a printing-press.

1917 F. S. HENRY *Printing for School & Shop* xi. 183 If the chase is one that just fits the bed of the press, make certain that the type does not come outside of the dead-line on the press.

c. = TIME-LIMIT; esp. a time by which material has to be ready for inclusion in a particular issue of a publication. orig. *U.S.*

1920 *Chicago Herald & Examiner* 2 Jan. 10/4 Corinne Griffith..is working on 'Deadline at Eleven', the newspaper play. **1929** *Publishers' Weekly* 27 July 349 Deadline for *Poetry's* $250 prize poem contest is September 1. **1948** *Daily Tel.* 31 May 6/5 The Security Council will not meet again until Wednesday, about 20 hours after the dead-line. **1958** *Woman's Jrnl.* Feb. 96/1 We wait till midnight... That's the deadline.

deadliness ('dɛdlɪnɪs). [f. DEADLY *a.* + -NESS.]

†**1.** The condition of being subject to death (see DEADLY *a.* 1); mortality. *Obs.*

a **1225** *Ancr. R.* 382 We beoren in ure bodie Iesu Cristes deadlicnesse. *a* **1340** HAMPOLE *Psalter* lxxxiii. 2 My hert.. and my fleyss..þof þai be brisel & heuy in dedlynes. **1434** MISYN *Mending of Life* 123 Þe fettyr of dedelynes. *c* **1440** *Promp. Parv.* 115 Dedelynesse, *mortalitas.*

2. a. The quality of being deadly or fatal.

c **1450** *Mirour Saluacioun* 518 Smyten with a sore wounde of eendeles dedelynesse. **1532** MORE *Confut. Tindale* Wks. 598/2 Ye deadlynesse of the sinne. **1612–5** BP. HALL *Contempl.* IV. (T.), The deadliness of Lazarus his sickness. **1863** GEO. ELIOT *Romola* III. xii, That sharp edge might give deadliness to the thrust. **1870** ROGERS *Hist. Gleanings* Ser. II. 13 A new disease of astonishing deadliness.

b. Dead accuracy. Cf. DEADLY *a.* 8 b.

1905 *Daily Chron.* 24 Aug. 6/4 A lack of deadliness in approaching.

dead lock, 'dead-lock, *sb.* [Cf. DEAD *a.* 28, 31.]

1. A condition or situation in which it is impossible to proceed or act; a complete stand-still.

1779 SHERIDAN *Critic* III, I have them all at a dead lock! for every one of them is afraid to let go first. **1858** HAWTHORNE *Fr. & It. Jrnls.* (1872) I. 1 In Newgate Street, there was such a number of market-carts, that we almost came to a dead-lock with some of them. **1888** BRYCE *Amer. Commw.* I. v. 60 It often happens that one party has a majority in the Senate, another party in the House, and then ..a deadlock results.

2. An ordinary lock which opens and shuts only with a key, as opposed to a spring lock; sometimes, locally, a padlock. [DEAD *a.* 24 b.]

1866 TIMMINS *Industr. Hist. Birmingham* 87 Dead locks are those which have only one large bolt, worked by the key.

Hence **'dead-ˌlock** *v. trans.*, to bring to a deadlock or stand-still; *intr.*, to come to a deadlock; **'deadlocked** *ppl. a.*, brought to a deadlock; **'deadˌlocking** *vbl. sb.*

1880 *Daily Tel.* 17 Feb., An entire population is dead-locked through no fault of its own. **1882** *N.Y. Tribune* 3 May, The disgraceful deadlocking which the session of 1882 has witnessed. **1892** *N.Y. Nation* 4 Aug. 81/2 They..have deadlocked the Legislature. **1897** *Rev. Reviews* (N.Y.) Jan. 10/2 Mr. Cleveland makes it perfectly plain that the struggle going on in Cuba is a useless and ruinous one,—a *deadlocked* situation. **1903** *N.Y. Even. Post* 25 Nov. 6 The Legislature would have deadlocked over the vote had not Gov. Odell come to his rescue. **1931** BUCK & ANTHONY *Bring 'em back Alive* 297 For several seconds we remained deadlocked, the animal making a perfect bedlam of the mess-room with his cries of rage. **1968** *Guardian* 24 Oct. 9/5 The deadlocked Vietnam peace talks.

'deadlong, *a.* Humorous nonce-formation after *livelong* (as if f. *live* adj.).

1844 DICKENS *Mart. Chuz.* xxiv, Through half the dead-long night.

deadly ('dɛdlɪ), *a.* Forms: 1 déadlíc, 3 dædlich, diadlich, 3–4 deadlich, 3–5 dedlich, -lych, dedelik(e, 4 dedli, dedeli, deadli, dyadlich, dyeadlich, 4–5 deedli, 4–6 dedly, dedely, 5 deadlike, dedlyke, 5–6 deedly, 6 deadlie, -lye, deedely, dedlie, 6–7 *Sc.* deidly, deidlie, 5– deadly. [OE. *déadlíc*, f. *déad* DEAD: see -LY¹. Cf. OHG. *tôtlich*, MD. *doodlick.*]

†**1. a.** Subject to death, mortal. *Obs.*

c **1000** *Homilies* (Thorpe) II. 186 (Bosw.) Ðæt an deadlic man mihte ealne middaneard oferseon. *c* **1230** *Hali Meid.* 13 Þis deadlich lif. *a* **1300** *Cursor M.* 10919 (Cott.) Godd bicom man dedli. **1340** *Ayenb.* 244 Ne eȝe dyeadlich ne may [þet] naȝt ysy. *c* **1400** MAUNDEV. (Roxb.) vii. 24, I am a creature dedly. **1477** EARL RIVERS (Caxton) *Dictes* 123 Thinke thou art dedely. **1533** GAU *Richt Vay* (1888) 67 This deidlie body sal be cled with immortalite. *a* **1563** BALE *Sel. Wks.* (Parker Soc.) 97 Many holy prophets that were deadly men were martyred. **1839** BAILEY *Festus* xx. (1852) 351 Even man's deadly life Can be there, by God's leave.

†**b.** *absol.* A mortal; usually as *pl.* Mortals, human beings. *Obs.*

c **1450** *St. Cuthbert* (Surtees) 2867 Þare is nane dedely ..þat suffice to serche þe domes of god. **1590** JAS. I *Sp. Gen. Assembly* Aug., I..shall Maintain the same against all deadly. **1685** *Lond. Gaz.* No. 2009/2 Whom we shall humbly Obey..Maintain and Defend with our Lives and Fortunes, against all deadly, as our only Righteous King and Soveraign.

†**2. a.** In danger of death, like to die. *Obs.*

a **1300** *E.E. Psalter* xliii. 22 (Mätz.) For al dai dedelik er we [*morte afficimur*] for þe. *c* **1386** CHAUCER *Frankl. T.* 312 My lady hath my deeth y-sworn..but thy benignytee Vpon my dedly herte haue some pitee. *a* **1616** BEAUM. & FL. *Cust. Country* V. iv, How does the patient? *Clod.* You may inquire Of more than one; for two are sick and deadly..her health's despaired of, And in hers, his.

†**b.** Of or belonging to death. *Obs.*

1470–85 MALORY *Arthur* XIII. xi, Not longe after that Ioseph was layd in his dedely bed. **1483** CAXTON *G. de la Tour* cxxxv. 191 She..became seke, and laye in her dedely bedde.

†**3.** Without life, inanimate; = DEAD *a.* 6. *rare.*

a **1225** *Juliana* 22 To luten dedliche schaften as ȝe schulden to godd. *c* **1440** *Secrees* 132 It is swilk a secre þat vnnethis mannys brest may it vnderstonde, how may it þanne be wrete in dedly skyns?

4. a. Causing death, or fatal injury; mortal, fatal.

c **893** K. ÆLFRED *Oros.* III. viii. §3 Forbræcon Romane heora aþas..and þær deadlicne siȝe ȝeforan. **1297** R. GLOUC. (1724) 223 Ac ouercome vas he noȝt, þey ys wounden dedlych were. *c* **1377** CHAUCER *Anel. & Arc.* 258 The cause..Of my dedely adversitie. *c* **1430** *Pilgr. Lyf Manhode* I. xxvii. (1869) 19 Þer is no wounde so cruelle; for with out remedye it is dedlych. **1562** WINȜET *Certain Tractates* Wks. (1888) I. 3 Lyke..to ane schip in ane dedly storme. **1603** KNOLLES *Hist. Turks* (1621) 48 Every houre expecting the deadly blow of the hangman. **1768** BEATTIE *Minstr.* II. xii, Tho' Fortune aim her deadliest blow. **1874** MORLEY *Compromise* (1886) 34 The narrowing and deadly effect of the daily iteration of short-sighted commonplaces.

b. As a quality of things: Having the property or capacity of causing death or fatal injury; poisonous, venomous, pestilential.

c **1380** WYCLIF *Serm.* Sel. Wks. I. 361 Dedli drynke, ȝif þei taken it..anoieþ hem not. **1567** MAPLET *Gr. Forest* 57 b, The inhabitants..doe set the whole Groue on fire, and by that meanes the deadly Serpents..are driuen away. **1697**

DRYDEN *Virg. Georg.* iii. 447 Dire Stepdames..mix, for deadly Draughts, the pois'nous Juice. **1788** GIBBON *Decl. & F.* l. (1846) V. 3 The winds..from the south-west, diffuse a noxious and even deadly vapour. **1845** DARWIN *Voy. Nat.* x. (1879) 220 Many savages..have seen..small animals killed by the musket, without being..aware how deadly an instrument it is. **1866** *Treas. Bot.* 1140 To camels..it is a deadly poison.

c. *spec.* In names of poisonous plants.

deadly carrot, the genus *Thapsia* of umbelliferous plants, natives of Southern Europe. ***deadly nightshade***, the *Atropa Belladonna* (N.O. *Solanaceæ*), a rare shrub with dark purple flowers and large round black berries; the name is often popularly misapplied to the common Woody Nightshade, *Solanum Dulcamara*, with ovoid scarlet berries.

1578 LYTE *Dodoens* III. xxi 446 Of great Nightshade, or Dwale. This noughtie and deadly plant is taken for a kinde of Solanum..The..fresh leaues of this deadly Nightshade may be applyed outwardly..The fruite of this Solanum is deadly. **1774** T. WEST *Antiq. Furness* 94 There grows the Lethal Bekan, or deadly nightshade. **1842** *Penny Cycl.* XXIV. 282/2 The species [of Thapsia] are mostly natives of the countries of the Mediterranean, and are known under the generic name Deadly Carrot. **1886** *Pall Mall G.* 27 Aug. 4/1 The plant..popularly known as deadly nightshade in England is the woody nightshade or bitter-sweet..The appearance of the deadly nightshade, *atropa belladonna* of botany and medicine, is very different.

5. *Theol.* **a.** Of sin: Entailing spiritual death; mortal (opposed to *venial*); *esp.* applied to the seven chief or 'cardinal' sins: see SIN.

a **1225** *Ancr. R.* 56 He [David] dude þreo vtnummen heaued sunnen & deadliche. **1340** HAMPOLE *Pr. Consc.* 3362 Thir er tha hede syns that er dedely. **1340** *Ayenb.* 9 Lecherie ..is on of þe zeuen dyadliche zennes. *Ibid.* 16 Hi byeþ heaued..of alle zennes, and ginninge of alle kueade, be hy dyadliche, be hy uenial. *c* **1400** MAUNDEV. (Roxb.) iii. 10 Þai say also þat fornicacion es na dedly bot a kyndely thing. **1483** CAXTON *G. de la Tour* H iij, By this synne of glotonye men falle in alle the other sixe dedely synnes. **1548–9** (Mar.) *Bk. Com. Prayer, Litany*, Fornicacion, and all other deadlye synne. **1603** SHAKS. *Meas. for M.* III. i. 111 Sure it is no sinne, Or of the deadly seuen it is the least. *a* **1711** KEN *Hymnotheo* Poet. Wks. 1721 III. 269 The Seven curs'd deadly Sins..Pride, Envy, Sloth, Intemp'rance, Av'rice, Ire, And Lust. **1819** SHELLEY *Cenci* IV. iii. 37 We do but that which 'twere a deadly crime To leave undone.

†**b.** *deadly sinner*: one who commits deadly sin. *Obs.*

1622 DONNE *Serm.* i. 5 He that comes alive out of that field [a duel] comes a dead man, because he comes a deadly sinner, and he that remains dead in the field is gone to an everlasting death.

6. Aiming, or involving an aim, to kill or destroy; implacable, mortal, to the death.

c **1205** LAY. 8550 þine dædliche iuan. *c* **1380** *Sir Ferumb.* 600 A leyde to þe Sarsyn strokes smerte riȝt als til his dedly fo. *c* **1430** *Freemasonry* 309 Throwghe envye, or dedly hate. **1583** STANYHURST *Aeneis* I. (Arb.) 17 Junoes long fostred deadlye reuengement. *a* **1661** FULLER *Worthies* (1840) III. 382 Betwixt whom and Sir Henry Berkeley was so deadly a quarrel. **1703** ROWE *Fair Penit.* I. i. 206 With deadly Imprecations of her Self. **1813** BYRON *Br. Abydos* II. xii, Although thy Sire's my deadliest foe. **1845** M. PATTISON *Ess.* (1889) I. 4 The contest..becomes sharp and deadly.

7. Resembling or suggestive of death, death-like. **a.** Of colour or aspect: pale like that of a corpse.

c **1385** CHAUCER *L.G.W.* 869 *Thisbe*, Who koude wryte which a dedely chere Hath Tesbe now. *c* **1400** *Beryn* 1337 His coloure gan to chaunge in-to a dedely hewe. **1561** EDEN *Arte Nauig.* II. xix. 50 If [the Sunne] shew yealowe or deadly, tempest is like to folow. **1590** SHAKS. *Com. Err.* IV. iv. 96, I know it by their pale and deadly looks. **1795** SOUTHEY *Joan of Arc* 289 By the flush'd cheek..And by the deadly paleness which ensued. **1803** *Med. Jrnl.* x. 152 In consequence of the..deadly look of the child.

b. Death-like in unconsciousness or physical prostration.

1548 HALL *Chron.* 56 The Normans hearyng of the kynges arrival wer sodenly striken with a deadly feare. **1562** WINȜET *Cert. Tractates* i. Wks. 1888 I. 6 Quhat deidly sleip is this that hes oppressit ȝow? **1671** SALMON *Syn. Med.* III. xxii. 413 Narcotick, causing deadly sleep. **1853** LYTTON *My Novel* XI. vii, A deadly faintness seized her.

c. Death-like in darkness, gloom, dullness, silence, etc.

a **1300** *Cursor M.* 17881 (Gött.) Þe folk in dedeli mirknes stadd. **1529** MORE *Conf. agst. Trib.* II. Wks. 1171/1 Continuall fatigacion woulde make it [the mind] dull and deadlye. **1600** E. BLOUNT tr. *Conestaggio* 29 There was such a deadlie silence in the porte. **1605** SHAKS. *Lear* V. iii. 290 All's cheerlesse, darke, and deadly. **1638** ROUSE *Heav. Univ.* (1702) 166 Sitting in darkness and a deadly shadow.

8. a. Excessive, 'terrible', 'awful'. *colloq.*

1660 PEPYS *Diary* 1 Nov., A deadly drinker he is, and grown exceedingly fat. **1660** *Ibid.* 7 Dec., So to the Privy Seale where I signed a deadly number of pardons. **1745** MRS. DELANY *Life & Corr.* (1861) II. 382 It has been a deadly while I have taken to answer your kind letter. **1773** GOLDSM. *Stoops to Conq.* I. ii, You're come a deadly deal wrong! **1843** CARLYLE *Past & Pr.* (1858) 281 Why such deadly haste to make money? **1847** J. WILSON *Chr. North* (1857) I. 146 The quantity of corn that a few sparrows can eat..cannot be very deadly.

b. Characterized by dead accuracy.

1909 P. A. VAILE *Mod. Golf* v. 95 The peculiarity of the stymie stroke, played parallel with the ground, is its deadly direction.

9. *Comb.*, as ***deadly-dinted***, ***-handed***, ***-headed***, ***-like*** adjs.; **deadly-lively** *a.*, combining dullness and liveliness, lively in a gloomy and depressing way (*colloq.*); hence ***deadly-liveliness***.

1593 SHAKS. *2 Hen. VI*, v. ii. 9 The deadly handed Clifford slew my Steed. **1596** FITZ-GEFFREY *Sir F. Drake* (1881) 51 An hundred deadlie-dinted staves. **1630** RUTHERFORD *Lett.* (1862) I. 55 She is in a most dangerous and deadly-like condition. **1838** DICKENS *Nich. Nick.* xli, Even her black dress assumed something of a deadly-lively air from the jaunty style in which it was worn. **1881** MRS. OLIPHANT in *Macm. Mag.* XLIII. 492 He was taken to Mentone..to the deadly-liveliness..and invalid surroundings of that shelter of the suffering. **1891** *Spectator* 12 Dec. 855 The deadly-liveliness of flippant and forced humour.

deadly ('dɛdlɪ), *adv.* Forms: 1 **déadlíce**, 3–4 **deadliche**, 4 **dyadliche**, **dedlyk**, 4–6 **dedely**, 5 **dedly**, 6 **deedly**, *Sc.* **deidly**, 7 **deadlie**, 6– **deadly**. [OE. *déadlíce*, f. *déad* DEAD: see -LY².]

†**1.** In a way that causes death; mortally, fatally; to death. *Obs.*

c **1050** *Gloss.* in Wr.-Wülcker 436/8 *Loetaliter*, deadlice. *a* **1330** R. BRUNNE *Chron.* (1810) 33 He wonded þe Kyng dedely fulle sore. *c* **1440** *Promp. Parv.* 115 Dedely, *mortaliter*, *letaliter*. **1561** T. NORTON *Calvin's Inst.* I. xiv. (1634) 71 They are wounded, but not deadly. **1627** MAY *Lucan* IX. (1431) 21 The snakes bite deadly, fatall are their teeth. *c* **1679** *Roxb. Ball.* VI. 147 Killing Beauty..Be no more so deadly Cruel. **1816** BYRON *Ch. Har.* III. xxix, When shower'd The death-bolts deadliest.

†**b.** *Theol.* In a way that entails spiritual death; mortally; see DEADLY *a.* 5. *Obs.*

a **1225** *Ancr. R.* 58 ȝif he is ivonded so þet he suneȝie, deadliche. **1340** *Ayenb.* 223 Ine oþre cas me may zeneȝi, oþer liȝtliche, oþer dyadliche. *c* **1400** MAUNDEV. (Roxb.) iii. 10 Þai say we synne dedly in þat we schaue oure berdes. **1503** HAWES *Examp. Virt.* xiii. 273 A dongeon longe and wyde Made for theym that do synne dedely. **1579** TOMSON *Calvin's Serm. Tim.* 112/2 To see those men, which were as it were Angels of God, fall: yea, & that deadly.

†**2.** Implacably, mortally; to the death. *Obs.*

c **1330** R. BRUNNE *Chron. Wace* (Rolls) 2644 Sheo louede mykel þe slayn broþer, & dedlyk [*v.r.* dedely] hated sche þat oþer. **1393** GOWER *Conf.* I. 332 Thus hate I dedely thilke vice. **1579** LYLY *Euphues* (Arb.) 95, I haue heard that women either loue entirely or hate deadly. **1650** S. CLARKE *Eccl. Hist.* I. (1654) 44 The spitefull Devil deadly pursuing him.

3. In a manner resembling or suggesting death; as if dead; without animation.

a **1300** *Cursor M.* 18155 (Cott.) Þaa waful wras sa dedli dim, All lighted þe lem þat come wit him. *c* **1430** *Pilgr. Ly. Manhode* I. lxxxix. (1869) 50 Al dedliche [*tout mornement*] he answerde hire. **1594** SHAKS. *Rich. III*, III. vii. 26 They.. Star'd each on other, and look'd deadly pale. **1633** P. FLETCHER *Purple Isl.* VII. (R.), How comes it then, that in so near decay We deadly sleep in deep security? **1865** DICKENS *Mut. Fr.* I. i, Seeming to turn deadly faint.

4. To a fatal or extreme degree; 'mortally', 'to death'; extremely, excessively. *colloq.*

[*a* **1300** *Cursor M.* 17225 (Cott.), I þat es sa dedli dill.] **1589** PUTTENHAM *Eng. Poesie* III. xviii. (Arb.) 205 He..did ..deadly belie the matter by his description. **1591** SPENSER *Virg. Gnat* 446 Judgement seates, whose Iudge is deadlie dred. **1688** MIEGE *Fr. Dict.* s.v. *Slow*, He is deadly slow, *il est furieusement long.* **1703** ROWE *Ulyss.* Epil. 31 These Cups are pretty, but they're deadly dear. **1809** SCOTT *Let. to Southey* 14 Jan. in *Lockhart*, In this deadly cold weather. **1865** TROLLOPE *Belton Est.* ix. 102 It is so deadly dull. **1878** MRS. STOWE *Poganuc P.* xiii, We were deadly tired.

5. In a dead manner; like a dead thing. *rare.*

1581 G. PETTIE tr. *Guazzo's Civ. Conv.* II. (1586) 50 To fall deadlie to the grounde, as a bodie without breath. **1844** MOZLEY *Ess.* (1878) II. 126 There is a belief in the Bible which is mere Bibliolatry, and..rests deadly in a mere book.

'deadman.

†**I. 1.** (*deadman*). = *dead man*: formerly written and pronounced as one word. (Cf. BLINDMAN.) *Obs.* exc. in names, as *Deadman's Walk.*

a **1300** *Cursor M.* 11504 (Cott.) A smerl o selcuth bitturnes, þat dedman cors wit smerld es. *c* **1440** *Gesta Rom.* lxx. 387 (Add. MS.) Atte derige of a dedeman that laye on the bere. **1611** SHAKS. *cymb.* V. iii. 12 The strait passe was damm'd With deadmen.

II. Used in various *fig.* applications and combinations; chiefly in *pl.* (See also following entries.)

2. pl. (*dead men.*) Empty bottles (at a drinking-bout, etc.) *slang* or *colloq.*

a **1700** B. E. *Dict. Cant. Crew*, *Dead-men*, empty Pots or bottles on a Tavern-table. **1738** SWIFT *Polite Convers.* 188 Let him carry off the dead Men, as we say in the army (meaning the empty bottles). **1825** C. M. WESTMACOTT *Eng. Spy.* I. 151 The wine bin surrounded by a regiment of dead men. **1851** THACKERAY *Eng. Hum.* iii. (1876) 244 Fresh bottles were brought; the 'dead men'..removed.

3. *slang.* (See quot. 1873.)

1764 *Low Life* 40 Journeymen Bakers..are casting up what Dead-Men they cheated their Masters of the past Week. **1819** MOORE *Tom Crib's Mem.* 16 (Farmer) Dead men are bakers, so called from the loaves falsely charged to their master's customers. **1873** *Slang Dict.*, *Dead-man*, a baker. Properly speaking, it is an extra loaf smuggled into the basket by the man who carries it out, to the loss of the master. Sometimes the dead-man is charged to a customer, though never delivered.

4. a. *Cards.* A dummy at whist.

1786 MACKENZIE in *The Lounger* No. 79 ¶13 As if one should..sit down with three *dead men* at whist.

b. *dial.* or *slang.* A scarecrow.

1839 in G. C. LEWIS *Gloss. Words in Herefordshire* 31. **1889** BARRÈRE & LELAND *Dict. Slang* I. 299/2 *Dead man*, ..(Popular), a scarecrow; a man made of rags.

5. *Naut.* (*pl.*) 'The reef or gasket-ends carelessly left dangling under the yard when the sail is furled, instead of being tucked in' (Adm. Smyth).

1825 W. N. GLASCOCK *Naval Sketch-Bk.* (1826) I. 11 Why don't they tuck-in those '*dead-men*' out of sight!

6. a. *techn.* Any of various objects buried in or secured to the ground and used as an anchorage or leverage (see quots.).

1840 W. T. SPURDENS *Vocab. E. Anglia* (1858), *Deadman*, a piece of timber buried in the earth, to secure posts, or other timbers by. **1901** *Daily Colonist* (Victoria, B.C.) 15 Oct. 5/4 A deck hand..was killed by being struck on the head by a 'dead man', which is a post imbedded on a [river gravel] bar to haul the steamer over. **1930** *Engineering* 28 Nov. 667/3 The sand..was levelled by the scraper pulled along by tackle attached to a dead man. **1940** *Chambers's Techn. Dict.* 226/2 *Deadman*, the concrete, plate, or other anchorage for land ties. **1950** *N.Z. Jrnl. Agric.* Jan. 61/3 Where it is difficult to obtain ground hold for fence strainer posts, such as in swamps or rocky hill country, fences may be strained with a 'deadman', and the strainer post should be cast [of concrete] with wire holes suitably placed.

b. *Logging.* (See quot.)

1905 *Terms Forestry & Logging* 34 *Deadman*, a fallen tree on the shore, or a timber to which the hawser of a boom is attached.

†**dead man's eye(s.** *Naut. Obs.* Also **dead men's eye(s.** = DEAD-EYE.

1466 *Mann. & Househ. Exp.* 214 A bolt for the stemme, also the closynge of dedemen yen. **1598** FLORIO, *Morto*..a pullie in a ship called the dead man he. **1626** CAPT. SMITH *Accid. Yng. Seamen* 15 Pullies, blockes, shiuers and dead mens eyes. **1706** PHILLIPS (ed. Kersey), *Dead-mens Eyes* (in a Ship), a kind of little Blocks, or Pulleys, having many Holes, but no Shivers; wherein run small Ropes.

dead man's finger(s. Also **dead men's finger(s.**

1. A local name for various species of *Orchis*, properly those with palmate tubers, as *O. maculata* and *latifolia*; in Shaks. prob. the Early Purple Orchis, *O. mascula.* Also applied to *Arum maculatum*, *Lotus corniculatus*, and *Alopecurus pratensis.* (Britten & Holland.)

1602 SHAKS. *Ham.* IV. vii. 173 Long Purples..our cold Maids doe Dead Mens Fingers call them. **1853** G. JOHNSTON *Nat. Hist. E. Bord.* 193 *Orchis latifolia.* The root, from its shape, is sometimes called..Dead-men's-fingers.

2. The zoophyte *Alcyonium digitatum*: = next 1.

1860 DALLAS *Nat. Hist. Anim. Kingd.* 54. **1865** GOSSE *Year at Shore* 73. **1872** DANA *Corals* 83.

3. The finger-like divisions of the *branchiæ* or gills in a lobster or crab.

1806–7 J. BERESFORD *Miseries Hum. Life* (1826) IX. xlv, In eating lobster—getting..half a dozen of the dead man's fingers into your mouth.

dead man's hand.

1. A zoophyte, *Alcyonium digitatum*, forming lobed fleshy masses: see ALCYONIUM.

1755 J. ELLIS *Corallines* 83 Dead Man's Hand or Dead Man's Toes. This extraordinary Sea-production is indebted for the English name to the Fishermen, who often take it up in their Nets, when they are trawling for flat Fish. **1756** SCHLOSSER in *Phil. Trans.* XLIX. 450 The alcyonium.. commonly called dead-man's hand.

2. a. A local name for *Orchis maculata* and *O. mascula* (cf. prec. 1). **b.** Also for '*Nephrodium Filix-mas*, and some other ferns, from the appearance of the young fronds before they begin to open, resembling a closed fist'. **c.** Also for the seaweed Tangle, *Laminaria digitata.* (Britten & Holl.)

1853 G. JOHNSTON *Nat. Hist. E. Bord.* 193 *Orchis maculata*..Dead-man's-hand.

dead man's handle.

In an electric train, a controlling handle which must be held in position for the current to pass, so that the train is automatically brought to a standstill should the driver release his grasp through illness or accident. So ***dead man's device***, ***knob***, ***pedal***, ***treadle***. Also *transf.*

1908 *Internat. Libr. Technol. Electr.-Railway..Multiple-Unit Syst.* 11 Should an accident befall the motorman, causing him to release knob 14, the train will be automatically stopped. On this account knob 14 is sometimes called the dead man's knob, or handle. **1924** *Westm. Gaz.* 2 Dec., The Dead Man's handle..is a safety device for pulling up Underground trains. **1951** *Engineering* 13 Feb. 231/2 The usual dead-man's pedal..can be operated from both sides of the cab. **1958** *Times Rev. Industry* Sept. 48/2 The throttle is arranged as a 'dead-man's handle', and it is impossible to start the bus until the sliding doors have been closed. **1964** *Daily Tel.* 18 Feb. 20 The dead man's treadle..should automatically stop a train if the driver becomes unconscious. *Ibid.*, A deadman's device.

†**dead man's head.** *Obs.* A 'death's head'; a skull or figure of a skull.

1557 *Bury Wills* (Camden) 146 My ringe with the dead manes head. **1562** J. HEYWOOD *Prov. & Epigr.* (1867) 66, I neuer meete the at fleshe nor at fishe, But I haue sure a deade mans head in my dishe.

dead man's thumb.

1. A local name for *Orchis mascula*, from the shape of the tubers. (Cf. DEAD MAN'S FINGER 1.)

1652 *Roxb. Ballads* (Britten & Holland), Each flower.. Such as within the meddowes grew, As dead man's thumbs and harebell blew [*v.r.* an hearb all blew]. **1853** G. JOHNSTON *Nat. Hist. E. Bord.* 193 From the colour and shape of the tuber the plant is called Dead-man's thumb;

and children tell one another, with mysterious awe, that the root was once the thumb of some unburied murderer.

2. = DEAD MAN'S HAND I.

1863 G. ROWE in *Intell. Observ.* Sept. 84 The swelling lobes of the dead man's thumb.

† **dead man's toes.** *Obs.* = prec. 2.

1755 [see DEAD MAN'S HAND I]. **1786** J. ELLIS *Nat. Hist. Zoophytes* 83 Round white eggs, like those described in the *Alcyonium digitatum* or Dead Man's Toes.

dead-melt ('dɛdmɛlt), *v. trans.* To keep (metal) at a melting temperature until it is perfectly fluid and no more gas is evolved. Hence **dead-melted** *ppl. a.*, **dead-melting** *vbl. sb.*

1880 *Encycl. Brit.* XIII. 341/2 If cast immediately it is found that a much larger quantity of gas separates during solidification, rendering the steel porous, than is evolved if the metal is dead-melted, *i.e.*, allowed to remain melted for an extra half hour or more. *Ibid.*, The 'dead melting' effect of the extra time allowed in fusing steel for the molten metal to stand in the furnace after fusion is brought about is due [etc.]. **1884** [see DEAD *a.* A. 22 c]. **1952** C. A. EDWARDS *Struct. & Prop. Mild Steel* i. 15 Towards the end of the operation of making steel by the acid process..the oxygen content of the metal will be extremely low... A charge of this kind is known as 'dead melted' steel, which means that ..solidification proceeds without the liberation of gas.

So **dead melt** *sb.*, the state of a melt when it contains no solid and is evolving no gas.

1929 W. LISTER *Pract. Steelmaking* viii. 48 When the whole charge has come to a dead melt, but not before, commence to feed.

dead men's bells. A local name in Scotland for the Foxglove, *Digitalis purpurea*; also *dead man's bells*.

1818 *Edin. Mag.* Oct. 328/1 But dinnae pu' the dead men's bells. **1848** W. GARDINER *Flora Forfarshire* 139 It is known to the peasantry by the name of 'dead men's bells'. **1853** G. JOHNSTON *Nat. Hist. E. Bord.* 157. **1878** BRITTEN & HOLLAND *Dict. Eng. Plant-Names* 34 Bell, or Bells, Dead Man's, or Men's. **1960** ARY & GREGORY *Oxf. Bk. Wild Flowers* 122/2 Other names for this common plant..are Dead Man's Bells (the plant is poisonous) and Fairy Thimbles.

deadness ('dɛdnɪs). The condition or quality of being dead, in various senses:

1. *lit.*

1607 TOPSELL *Four-f. Beasts* (1673) 481 To Pluto and to the Earth, they sacrificed black Sheep or Lambs, in token of deadnesse. *a* **1716** SOUTH *Serm.* VII. i. (R.), Cursing it [the barren fig-tree] to deadness with a word. **1764** WOOLCOMB in *Phil. Trans.* LX. 97 A numbness and deadness of his little ..finger. **1881** MISS YONGE *Lads & Lasses* ii. 95 The man that..gets the creeping deadness in his bones.

2. *fig.*

1611 BIBLE *Rom.* iv. 19 The deadnesse of Saraes wombe. *c* **1620** Z. BOYD *Zion's Flowers* (1855) 121 They Have bloodlesse cheekes, and deadnesse in their eyes. *a* **1628** PRESTON *Saints Daily Exerc.* (1629) 74 What is a man to doe when hee findes a great indisposition to prayer..a dulnesse, and deadnesse in him. **1642** *Petition* in Clarendon *Hist. Reb.* IV. (1843) 165/2 By the deadness of trade. **1738** WESLEY *Wks.* (1872) I. 162 Hence my deadness and wanderings in public prayer. **1749** BP. G. LAVINGTON *Enthus. Methodists* (1754) II. 55 Spiritual Desertions, inward Deadnesses. **1883** H. DRUMMOND *Nat. Law in Spir. W.* v. (1884) 160 The spiritual deadness of humanity.

b. The state of being dead *to* something.

1745 WESLEY *Answ. Ch.* 7 Your Deadness to the World. **1786** MAD. D'ARBLAY *Diary* 17 Sept., The deadness of the whole Court to talents and genius. **1858** BUSHNELL *Nat. & Supernat.* xiv, Deadness to God and all holy things.

3. Want of some characteristic physical quality; absence of lustre or colour, dullness; want of taste; flatness, insipidity, etc.

1707–16 J. MORTIMER (J.), Deadness or flatness in cyder. **1785** SARAH FIELDING *Ophelia* I. xix, I had perceived.. deadness in the best complexions.

dead-nettle ('dɛd,nɛt(ə)l). See also DEANETTLE. The English name for plants of the genus *Lamium* (N.O. *Labiatæ*), having leaves like those of a nettle, but which do not sting; esp. *L. album* white dead-nettle, and *L. purpureum* red dead-nettle; also applied to *L. Galeobdolon* (*G. luteum*) yellow dead-nettle or archangel, and occasionally to species of *Stachys* or other labiates.

1398 TREVISA *Barth. De P.R.* XVII. cxciii. (1495) 730 Of netles is dowble kynde, one brennyth and bytyth, and another manere hyghte the deed nettyll or the blynde nettyll. **1578** LYTE *Dodoens* I. lxxxviii. 130 There be two kindes of Dead Nettel. The one..smelleth but little, the other..hath a strong and stinking sauour. **1794** MARTYN *Rousseau's Bot.* iv. 43 The white dead-nettle..has no affinity with nettles..except in the shape of the leaves. **1879** LUBBOCK *Sci. Lect.* i. 1 The Common White Deadnettle.

dead-oh ('dɛdəʊ), *a. Naut. colloq.* [f. DEAD *a.* + OH *int.*] **a.** = DEAD DRUNK. **b.** Deeply asleep.

1889 BARRÈRE & LELAND *Dict. Slang* I. 300/1 *Dead-oh!* (naval), is said of a man in the last stage of intoxication. **1924** MASEFIELD *Sard Harker* 160 He slept, as sailors say, 'dead-oh'.

dead oil: see DEAD D. 2.

† **dead palsy, 'dead-,palsy.** *Obs.* [DEAD *a.* 2 a.] Palsy producing complete insensibility or immobility of the part affected.

1592 CONSTABLE *Sonn.* III. vii, Dead-palsey sicke of all my chiefest parts. **1642** FULLER *Holy & Prof. State* v. vi. 382 Now our Atheist hath a dead palsey, is past all sense. **1697** R. PEIRCE *Bath Mem.* I. iv. 59 The 'Ἡμιπληγία, or half stroke (vulgarly call'd the Dead Palsie, or Palsie of one Side). **1702** PEPYS *Corr.* 405 About three weeks since, Sir R. Dutton was struck with the dead-palsy on his left side. He has recovered the motion, though not the use, of his hand and foot. **1712** ARBUTHNOT *John Bull* III. x, Frog was seized with a dead palsy in the tongue. **1761** MRS. F. SHERIDAN *Sidney Bidulph* III. 217.

dead-pan ('dɛdpæn), *a.*, *sb.*, *adv.*, and *v.* orig. *U.S.* Also **dead pan, deadpan.** [f. DEAD *a.* + PAN *sb.*[1] 6 c.]

A. *adj.* Of a face, look, etc.: expressionless, impassive. Of a person: having such a face. Also *transf.*, applied to speech, behaviour, etc.: detached, impersonal.

1928 *N.Y. Times* 11 Mar. VIII. 6/1 *Deadpan*, playing a rôle with expressionless face. **1929** *Variety* 17 Apr. 51/3 They clicked better at the Palace where the intimacy heightened the dead-pan comic's expression. **1939** I. BAIRD *Waste Heritage* i. 5 Matt's eyes lost their cold deadpan look. **1942** *Tablet* 19 Sept. 135/2 Mr. Attlee and Sir Stafford Cripps did their best to assume what in America is called a 'dead-pan' expression. **1947** *People* 22 June 2/6 Perhaps that accounts for Flynn's dead-pan immobility, his flat emotionless voice, and the air of bored indifference. **1949** *Times Lit. Suppl.* 5 Aug. 502/3 An official career far more eventful than most, and one oddly belying his mild demeanour and dead-pan wit. **1950** *Manch. Guardian Weekly* 23 Mar. 3/2 A dispatch from Washington reporting in dead-pan outline Mr. Acheson's Berkeley speech. **1953** L. A. G. STRONG *Personal Remarks* 256 Malcolm Scott was severe, suety, impassive; what nowadays would be called dead-pan. **1957** *Sunday Times* 3 Mar. 3/3 For what is known as 'dead pan' humour no one can challenge Miss Jean Mann, whose facial expression gives no warning of the thrust to come. **1965** *Listener* 20 May 745/3 The superbly dead-pan warning: 'The publication of this book does not directly or indirectly imply that it can be regarded as authorized for use in churches.'

B. *sb.* An expressionless or impassive face, esp. one deliberately assumed; also, a person with such a face; the assumption of such a face.

Freq. treated as two separate words.

1933 'N. WEST' *Miss Lonelyhearts* (1949) 34 He practiced a trick used much by moving-picture comedians— the dead pan. No matter how fantastic or excited his speech, he never changed his expression. **1937** E. LINKLATER *Juan in China* xxi. 282, I told him it wasn't his..and all I got was a dead pan. **1939** N. COWARD *Words & Music* 11, in *Second Play Parade* 159 Now the wife of an Acrobat Is the 'Dead Pan' of the troupe. **1943** P. CHEYNEY *You can always Duck* iii. 53 This bar-tender is an interestin' sorta guy. A dead pan. Nothin' seems to worry him. **1951** E. HYAMS *Sylvester* xx. 96 Eyes..set in round, flabby..faces, the dead-pans of a caste of men who..had given up their humanity. **1957** J. BRAINE *Room at Top* iv. 34 The millhand with the Alan Ladd deadpan.

C. *adv.* With a dead-pan face; in a dead-pan manner.

1933 RUNYON in *Collier's* 28 Oct. 36/3 She does not scowl or anything else, but only looks very dead-pan. **1944** 'P. QUENTIN' *Puzzle for Puppets* xviii. 139 He said that completely dead-pan. For a moment I didn't take it in. Then I grinned. **1962** *New Yorker* 10 Mar. 157/1, 3 claims no authority and merely records, mostly deadpan, what in fact every Tom, Dick, and Harry is now doing..to the language.

D. *v. trans.* and *intr.* To speak, perform, behave, etc., with a dead-pan face or in a dead-pan manner.

1942 BERREY & VAN DEN BARK *Amer. Thes. Slang* §275/2 *Dead-pan*, to maintain an expressionless face. **1959** N. MARSH *False Scent* (1960) ii. 40 'After this,' she said slowly, dead-panning her voice to a tortured monotone, 'there is only one thing for me to do.' **1962** W. KNOX *Little Drops of Blood* iv. 87 Moss dead-panned. 'I don't mind. Of course, I'll need to phone Miss Murdoch and disappoint her, but —' he winked.

† **dead pay.** *Obs.* [Cf. F. *morte-paye.*]

1. Pay continued to a soldier, etc. no longer in active service; a soldier receiving such pay.

1585 T. WASHINGTON tr. *Nicholay's Voy. Turkie* III. iv. 76 b, When these men..can serve no longer in the warres.. they are sent as..keepers of castles and towns, whom we do cal dead payes. **1611** COTGR., *Morte-payes*, Dead-payes; Souldiers in ordinarie pay, for the gard of a fortresse, or frontier Towne, during their liues. **1685** F. SPENCE *House of Medici* 339 The citizens and Dead-payes nabb'd the French at unawares. **1686** *Lond. Gaz.* No. 2196/1 Janisaries..that being Superannuated..receive a dead Pay of so much a day.

2. Pay continued in the name of a soldier or sailor actually dead or discharged, and appropriated by the officer; a person in whose name such pay is drawn. (Cf. *dead-share* in DEAD D. 2.)

1565 CALFHILL *Answ. Treat. Crosse* (1846) 62 Like a covetous Captain will needs indent for a dead pay. **1627** BP. HALL *Gt. Impostor* Wks. 507 Like to some vnfaithfull captaine that hath..filled his purse with dead payes, made vp the number of his companies with borrowed men. **1639** MASSINGER *Unnat. Combat* IV. ii, O you commanders That, like me, have no dead pays, nor can cozen The commissary at a muster. **1663** PEPYS *Diary* 13 Oct., The King.. mustering the Guards the other day himself..found reason to dislike their condition..finding so many absent men, or dead pays. **1867** SMYTH *Sailor's Word-bk.*, *Dead-pay*, that given formerly in shares, or for names borne, but for which no one appears.

'dead-point, dead point. *Mech.* [DEAD *a.* IV.] That position of a crank at which it is in a direct line with the connecting-rod, and at which therefore the force exerted tends to thrust or pull instead of turning the crank.

1830 KATER & LARDN. *Mech.* xviii. 254 The cranks are so placed that when either is at its dead point, the other is in its most favourable position. **1875** R. F. MARTIN tr. *Havrez' Winding Mach.* 72 One piston is on the dead point, and, therefore, the other one alone must turn the engine round.

dead reckoning. *Naut.* and *Aeronaut.* [DEAD *a.* V.] The estimation of a ship's position from the distance run by the log and the courses steered by the compass, with corrections for current, leeway, etc., but without astronomical observations. Hence *dead* LATITUDE (q.v.), that computed by dead reckoning.

1613 M. RIDLEY *Magn. Bodies* 147 Keeping a true, not a dead reckoning of his course. **1760** PEMBERTON in *Phil. Trans.* LI. 911 The latitude exhibited by the dead reckoning of the ship. **1840** R. H. DANA *Bef. Mast* xxxii. 124 We had drifted too much to allow of our dead reckoning being anywhere near the mark. **1891** *Nature* 3 Sept., The log, which for the first time enabled the mariner to carry out his dead-reckoning with confidence, is first described in Bourne's 'Regiment for the Sea', which was published in 1577. **1917** BOSANQUET & CAMPBELL *Navigation for Aerial Navigators* i. 4 In aerial navigation..Dead Reckoning is the position arrived at as calculated from the estimated track and the estimated speed made good over the ground. *Ibid.* 5 These data enable us to find a Dead Reckoning position. **1935** C. G. BURGE *Compl. Bk. Aviation* 477/1 Dead reckoning..is a compromise between pilotage and navigation.

fig. **1868** LOWELL *Witchcraft* Prose Wks. 1890 II. 372 The mind, when it sails by dead reckoning..will sometimes bring up in strange latitudes.

Dead Sea. [transl. L. *mare mortuum*, Gr. ἡ νεκρὰ θάλασσα (Aristotle). By the Greeks and Romans the same name was given also to the Arctic Ocean in the North of Europe: ? as devoid of the presence of life, or of motion, currents, etc.]

a. The lake or inland sea in the south of Palestine, into which the Jordan flows; it has no outlet, and its waters are intensely salt and bitter.

c **1250** *Genesis & Exod.* 1123 Ðe swarte flum, ðe dede se. *c* **1325** *E.E. Allit. P.* B. 1020 Þer faure citees wern set, nov is a see called, þat ay is drouy and dym, and ded in hit kynde, Blo, blubrande, and blak..Forþy þe derk dede see hit is demed. **1387** TREVISA *Higden* (Rolls) I. 105 (Mätz.) Iudea.. haþ in þe souþe side þe dede Se. **1559** W. CUNNINGHAM *Cosmogr. Glasse* 144 It is also called the dead sea, because the water moveth not..nether can..any fishe live there. **1825** J. NEAL *Bro. Jonathan* II. 350 Deader than the dead-sea itself.

b. *attrib.*, as in **Dead Sea apple, Dead Sea fruit** = *Apple of Sodom*: see APPLE *sb.* 3; **Dead Sea Scrolls,** the collective name for a series of fragmentary manuscripts dating from the third century BC to the first century AD, which contain a unique historical and social record of Palestine and early Jewish and Christian traditions, discovered since 1947 in caves to the west of the Dead Sea; occas. in *sing.*; cf. QUMRAN.

1817 MOORE *Lalla Rookh* 222 Like Dead Sea fruits, that tempt the eye, But turn to ashes on the lips! **1868** MISS BRADDON (*title*), Dead Sea Fruit. **1869** *Eng. Mech.* 24 Dec. 354/1 Dead Sea apples, Sodom apples, or mad apples..are occasionally imported from Bussorah. **1882** *The Garden* 1 Apr. 220/1 The Asclepias above alluded to is what has been called the Dead Sea Fruit. **1883** L. WINGFIELD *A. Rowe* III. vi. 119 The baked meats were Dead Sea fruit, and stuck in her throat. **1949** *Palestine Exploration Q.* 112 (*title*) The Dead Sea Scrolls. **1956** J. M. ALLEGRO (*title*) The Dead Sea Scrolls. *Ibid.* i. 31 A small piece of Dead Sea Scroll may look very nice..hung over the mantelpiece. **1965** A. CHRISTIE *At Bertram's Hotel* vii. 76 A pleasant acrimonious discussion on ..the dating of the Dead Sea scrolls. **1986** *N.Y. Times* 1 Jan. 1. 9/5 Among the most important are the Habakkuk Commentary, the first found and the best-preserved of the Dead Sea Scrolls.

dead set: see SET *sb.*

dead-thraw (-throw), Sc. ff. DEATH-THROE.

'dead-tongue. A name for the umbelliferous plant *Œnanthe crocata*, from its paralysing effect on the organs of speech.

1688 T. LAWSON *Let.* in *Ray's Corr.* (1848) 205 *Œnanthe Cicutæ-facie*..about Kendal and Hiltondale, Westmoreland,..where it is commonly called Dead Tongue. **1746** WATSON in *Phil. Trans.* XLIV. 233 This Oenanthe in Cumberland, where the Country-People call it Dead Tongue. **1878** *Cumbrld. Gloss.*, *Deed tongue*, the water hemlock or dropwort plant, *Œnanthe crocata*.

dead water, dead-water. [DEAD *a.* 22.]

1. Water without any current; still water.

1601 HOLLAND *Pliny* I. 240 A standing poole or dead water. **1691** T. H[ALE] *Acc. New Invent.* 122 Its broad side lying to the Wind in dead water. **1874** BURNAND *My Time* xxii. 197 We pulled in..and made for a quiet nook in dead-water.

attrib. **1792** J. PHILLIPS *Hist. Inland Navig.* Add. (1795) 29 The advantages of a dead-water navigation.

2. *Naut.* The eddy water just behind the stern of a ship under way.

1627 CAPT. SMITH *Seaman's Gram.* ix. 42 Dead water is the Eddie water followes the sterne of the ship, not passing away so quickly as that slides by her sides. *c* **1850** *Rudim. Navig.* (Weale) 114 Vessels with a round buttock have but little or no dead-water.

3. The stillest state of the tide, when the rise and fall are at a minimum; the neap tide. (Cf. DEAD *a.* 27.)

1561 EDEN *Arte Nauig.* II. xviii. 50 Whiche the Mariners call nepe tyde.. dead waters, or lowe fluddes.

4. (See quot.)

1904 GOODCHILD & TWENEY *Technol. & Sci. Dict.* 151/2 *Dead water*, water which does not come into contact with the effective heating surface of a boiler.

dead weight, 'dead-weight. [DEAD *a.* 29.]

1. a. The heavy unrelieved weight of an inert body. (*lit.* and *fig.*)

1660 BOYLE *New Exp. Phys. Mech.* xxxiii. 238 When the Sucker came to be moved onely with a dead weight or pressure. **1702** SAVERY *Miner's Friend* 81 The Moving Cause, as Mens Hands, Horses, or Dead Weight. **1711** SHAFTESB. *Charac.* I. iii. (1737) I. 67 Pedantry and Bigotry are Mill-stones able to sink the best Book which carries the least part of their dead weight. **1844** DICKENS *Mart. Chuz.* xlvi, Mrs. Gamp.. forced him backwards down the stairs by the mere oppression of her dead-weight.

b. *techn.* (See quots.)

1858 SIMMONDS *Dict. Trade*, *Dead Weight*, heavy merchandise forming part of a ship's cargo. **1867** SMYTH *Sailor's Word-bk.*, *Dead weight*, a vessel's lading when it consists of heavy goods, but particularly such as pay freight according to their weight and not their stowage. **1874** KNIGHT *Dict. Mech.*, *Dead-weight*, the weight of the vehicle of any kind; that which must be transported in addition to the load. **1881** LUBBOCK in *Nature* No. 618. 412 The saving in dead weight, by this improvement alone, is from 10 to 16 per cent.

2. A heavy inert weight: *fig.* a heavy weight or burden pressing with unrelieved force upon a person, institution, etc.

1721 DE FOE *Mem. Cavalier* (1840) 282 The Scots.. were always the dead weight upon the king's affairs. **1785** C. THOMAS in *Med. Commun.* II. 79 A lump or dead weight, as he termed it, in his inside. **1792** A. YOUNG *Trav. France* 113 His character is a dead weight upon him. **1822** HAZLITT *Table-t.*, *Convers. of Lords* (1852) 242 We not only deter the student from the attempt, but lay a dead-weight upon the imagination. **1876** F. E. TROLLOPE *Charming Fellow* III. xviii. 229 It was extremely exhilarating.. to find himself free .. of the dead weight of debt.

†3. 'A name given to an advance by the Bank of England to Government on account of the half-pay and pensions of the retired officers of the Army and Navy' (Simmonds *Dict. Trade*). *Obs.*

The debt was paid off by an annuity which ceased in 1867.

1823 COBBETT *Rur. Rides* (1885) I. 320 The six hundred millions of Debt and the hundred and fifty millions of dead-weight. **1826** J. HUME in Hansard XVI. 184–5 The year 1822, when Mr. Vansittart brought before parliament the notable expedient to pay for the dead-weight.. The country were induced to believe, that in forty-four years the whole of the dead-weight would be annihilated by the gradual decrement, by death, of the persons to whom the allowances out of it were payable.

4. *attrib.*, as **dead-weight debt**, a debt not covered by assets, such as the greater part of the British National Debt; **dead-weight (safety-)valve**, a safety-valve kept down by a heavy weight.

1827 *Gentl. Mag.* XCVII. II. 13 Placed on the superannuation or dead weight list. **1894** *Westm. Gaz.* 7 May 3/1 Dead-weight expenses have almost reached the irreducible minimum. **1902** *Encycl. Brit.* XXXIII. 373/1 *Deadweight capacity*.. is.. the amount of deadweight which can be carried on the holds at load draught when the vessel is fully charged with coals and stores. **1904** GOODCHILD & TWENEY *Technol. & Sci. Dict.* 151/2 Dead weight safety valve. **1905** *Daily Chron.* 16 May 4/4 There is dead-weight debt, and there is remunerative debt. **1909** *Ibid.* 29 Apr. 4/4 Having brought the dead-weight Debt down to the total at which it stood twenty years ago. **1927** T. WOODHOUSE *Artificial Silk* 16 A dead-weight safety valve. **1930** *Engineering* 10 Oct. 461/2 Should the steam stop valve on the boiler be closed.. the deadweight valve is opened.

dead well, 'dead-'well. [DEAD *a.* 15, 22.]

1. A well dug down into a porous stratum, to carry off surface or refuse water: called also *absorbing well*, *dumb well*. Cf. *dead-hole* (DEAD *a.* D. 2).

1852–61 *Archit. Publ. Soc. Dict.* I. 5 In some parts of England absorbing wells are known under the name of dead wells. **1875** URE *Dict. Arts* II. 10 *Dead wells*, wells which are made to carry off refuse waters.

2. A 'well' or excavation into which the weights of a large clock descend.

1867 MUSGRAVE *Nooks & Corners Old Fr.* I. 261 A 'dead well' of some twenty feet depth, which used to receive the descending weights of a great clock.

dead wood, 'dead-wood.

1. a. Wood dead upon the tree; the dead branches of fruit-trees, or the like; hence *fig.* Also (*U.S.*) in tenpins, a pin that has been knocked down and lies in the alley in front of those remaining.

to get, have, possess the dead-wood (U.S. slang); to have one at a disadvantage, secure the advantage.

1851 L. CLAPPE *Shirley Lett.* (1922) 84 If they ask a man an embarrassing question, or in any way have placed him in an equivocal position, they will triumphantly declare that they have 'got the dead-wood on him'. **1858** *Southern Lit. Messenger* XXVII. 351/1 He.. sent his ball.. straight to the left quarter of the Centre-Pin, and never left any dead wood on the alley. **1867** A. D. RICHARDSON *Beyond Miss.* xi. 134 'The deadwood'—from the game of 'tenpins', in which a fallen pin sometimes lies in front of the standing ones so that the first ball striking it will sweep the alley. 'I have the dead wood on him' was used familiarly, meaning: 'I have him in my power.' **1872** C. KING *Mountain Sierra Nev.* x. 211 He considered himself to possess the 'dead-wood'. **1947** *Time* 17 Mar. p. i, An automatic bowling pin spotter that sets up pins.. removes dead wood.. and even calls fouls! **1951** E S. GARDNER *Case of Borrowed Brunette* xix. 207 Well, they've evidently got the dead-wood on you now, Perry. They know that you took Eva Martell to that rooming-house.

b. ***dead-wood fence***: a fence made of rough logs, fallen branches, etc. Chiefly *Austral.*

1813 J. TAYLOR *Arator* 208 They [*sc.* hogs] are the cause of dead wood fences, which render.. labour unproductive. **1852** MRS. L. A. MEREDITH *My Home in Tasmania* I. x. 157 A 'dead-wood fence', that is, a mass of timber four or five feet thick, and five or six high, the lower part being formed of.. logs.. and the upper portion consisting of the smaller branches skilfully laid over. **1959** in S. J. BAKER *Drum* II. 103.

2. *Naut.* Solid blocks of timber fastened just above the keel at each end of the ship, to strengthen those parts.

1727–52 CHAMBERS *Cycl.* s.v. *Ship* (Plate), The rising or Dead Wood. **1769** FALCONER *Dict. Marine* (1789), It determines the heighth of the dead-wood, afore and abaft. **1879** *Cassell's Techn. Educ.* IV. 187/2 The deadwood, stemson, and other strengthenings.

attrib. **1792** *Trans. Soc. Encourag. Arts* X. 225 To draw the Kelson and dead-wood bolts out. **1867** SMYTH *Sailor's Word-bk.*, *Dead-wood knees*, the upper foremost and aftermost pieces of dead wood.

3. *fig.* A person or thing regarded as useless or unprofitable; a hindrance or impediment. Also *attrib.* orig. *U.S.*

1887 *Sci. Amer.* 1 Oct. 209/1 The commissioner [of patents] has made some effort.. to cut the deadwood out of the examining and clerical forces left him as a legacy by his predecessor. **1903** *McClure's Mag.* July 326 No dead wood is taken into the concern unless it is through the supposed necessities of family or business relations. **1928** *Daily Express* 11 Aug. 9/5 These papers do not receive any advertising support from us unless they make a price which we consider is adequate when you cut out their dead-wood circulation. **1929** *Daily Tel.* 15 Jan. 6/3 Amalgamations of what have hitherto been competing concerns are being formed, the specific objects being to cut out any dead-wood which may be handicapping the smooth working of the machine, to promote efficiency by the pooling of brains and experience.

'dead-work, dead work.

†1. *Naut.* (See quots.) *Obs.*

1653 H. COGAN tr. *Pinto's Trav.* xxi. 75 Together with all the dead works, as the cabins and galleries without. **1769** FALCONER *Dict. Marine* (1789), *Dead-work*, all that part of a ship which is above water when she is laden. *c* **1850** *Rudim. Navig.* (Weale) 154 *Supernatant part of the ship*, that part which, when afloat, is above the water; anciently expressed by the name of *dead-work*.

2. *Mining.* Work not directly productive, but done in preparation for future work.

1839 *Penny Cycl.* XV. 246/1 All the underground work of mines in Cornwall.. is of two distinct kinds: dead work, or that carried on in the rock or metalliferous deposit, for the purpose of trial and discovery; and productive labour. **1869** R. B. SMYTH *Goldfields of Victoria* 609 *Dead-work*, the opening up or preparatory work for mining by sinking shafts and winzes, driving levels and cross-cuts. **1872** RAYMOND *Statist. Mines* 60 They will.. save the expense of timbering, and much 'dead work' in prospecting. **1954** S. PIGGOTT *Neolithic Cultures* ii. 39 The flint seam was at such a depth that a considerable amount of 'dead work' had to be done before the flint was reached.

3. Work in hand, not finished.

1888 *Chicago Inter-Ocean* (Farmer), To-night the joint committee issued a circular commanding the men to quit everything but dead work. [**1891** *Daily News* 23 May 6/5 (*Tailors' Strike*) Another man declared.. that they should refuse to touch any of their 'dead' (i.e., work in hand) until the strike was over.]

deady ('dɛdɪ). *slang.* A name for gin, or for a particular quality of gin.

[So called app. from the name of the distiller. The London Directory for 1812 has D. Deady, Distiller and Brandy-merchant, Sol's Row, Tottenham Court Rd.]

[**1812** *Sporting Mag.* XXXIX. 138 At a public house where Sam had been copiously sipping Deady's max.] **1819** T. MOORE *Tom Crib's Mem. Congress* App., To quaff Our Deady o'er some State Affairs. *a* **1843** SOUTHEY *Doctor* Interchapter xvi. (D.), Some of the whole-hoggery in the House of Commons he would designate by Deady, or Wet and Heavy; some by weak tea, others by Blue-Ruin.

de-'aerate, *v.* [f. DE- + AERATE *v.*] *trans.* To remove air from. So **de-'aerated** *ppl. a.*; **de-'aerating** *vbl. sb.* and *ppl. a.*; **de-aer'ation, de-'aerator.**

1791 *Edin. New Disp.* 65 Calling them aerated and de-aerated. **1830** *Westm. Rev.* XII. 38 The dirt and the stagnation and the de-aeration of the water. **1878** URE *Dict. Arts* (ed. 8) IV. 240 A flask.. filled up with hot de-aerated water. **1919** H. G. WELLS *Outl. Hist.* (1920) I. 17/2 The water has become deaerated and foul. **1940** *Chambers's Techn. Dict.* 227/1 *De-aerator*, a vessel in which boiler feed water is heated under reduced pressure in order to remove dissolved air. **1960** *Times* 12 Feb. 3/1 Condensing, Feed Heating and De-aerating plant.

dea ex machina: see DEUS EX MACHINA.

deaf (dɛf), *a.* Forms: 1–3 deaf, *Orm.* dæf, (2–3 *pl.* deaue), 3–6 def, (3–5 *pl.* deue, 4 *Ayenb.* dyaf, dyaue, dyeaue), 4–5 deef(f, (*pl.* deeue), 4–6 defe, (deff(e, 5 deif, deyf(fe), 6 deefe, deaffe, (*Sc.* deif(f), 6–7 deafe, 7– deaf. [A Common Teutonic adj.: OE. *déaf* = OFris. *dâf* (WFris. *doaf*), OS. *dôf* (MDu., Du., MLG. *doof* (*v*), LG. *dôf*), OHG. *toup* (*b*), (MHG. *toup*, Ger. *taub*), ON. *daufr* (Sw. *döf*, Da. *döv*), Goth. *daufs* (*b*) :—OTeut. **dauƀ-oz*, from an ablaut stem *deuƀ-*, *dauƀ-*, *duƀ*, pre-Teut. *dheubh-*, to be dull or obtuse of perception: cf. Goth. *afdaubnan* to grow dull or obtuse, also Gr. *τυφλός* (:—*θυφ-*) blind. The original diphthong remains in north. dial.; in standard Eng. the vowel was long until the modern period, and so late as 1717–8 it was rimed with *relief* by Prior and Watts; the pronunciation (diːf) is still widely diffused dialectally, and in the United States.

In many Eng. dialects the *ea* is still diphthongal, *deeaf*]

1. a. Lacking, or defective in, the sense of hearing.

c **825** *Vesp. Psalter* xxxvii[i]. 14 Swe swe deaf ic ne ȝe[herde]. *c* **1200** *Trin. Coll. Hom.* 129 Alse to deue men. *c* **1200** ORMIN 15500 Dumbe menn & dæfe. *a* **1225** *St. Marher.* 20 Noðer dumbe ne deaf. *c* **1386** CHAUCER *Prol.* 446 But she was somdel deef [*v.r.* def, defe] and þat was scathe. **1398** TREVISA *Barth. De P.R.* XVII. clxxxviii. (1495) 729 Vynegre helpith deyf eeres. *c* **1440** *Promp. Parv.* 115 Deffe, *surdus.* **1538** STARKEY *England* 212 As you wold tel a tale to a deffe man. **1601** SHAKS. *Jul. C.* I. ii. 213 Come on my right hand, for this eare is deafe. **1717** PRIOR *Alma* II. 366 Till death shall bring the kind relief, We must be patient, or be deaf. **1718** WATTS *Ps.* cxxxv. 7 Blind are their eyes, their ears are deaf [*rime* relief]. **1818** SCOTT *Hrt. Midl.* xxxv, You know our good Lady Suffolk is a little deaf. **1871** B. TAYLOR *Faust* (1875) II. I. i. 5 In the rocks beneath the leaf, If it strikes you, you are deaf.

b. *absol.*, esp. in pl. ***the deaf***, deaf people.

c **1000** *Ags. Gosp.* Matt. xi. 5 Blinde ȝeseoþ.. deafe ȝehyraþ. *c* **1200** *Vices & Virtues* (1888) 75 þe blinde, ðe dumbe, ðe deaue, ðe halte. *a* **1300** *Cursor M.* 13107 (Cott.) þe def has hering, blind has sight. **1611** BIBLE *Isa.* xxxv. 5 Then.. the eares of the deafe shalbe vnstopped. **1855** BROWNING *Master Hugues* xxvi, Who thinks Hugues wrote for the deaf?.. try again; what's the clef?

c. *fig.* said of things.

a **1000** *Juliana* 150 þæt ic.. dumbum and deafum deofolȝieldum.. gaful onhate. **1605** SHAKS. *Macb.* v. i. 81 Infected mindes To their deafe pillowes will discharge their secrets. **1821** SHELLEY *Prometh. Unb.* I. 29 Have its deaf waves not heard my agony?

d. Proverbial phrases. ***as deaf as an adder*** or ***a post*** (formerly and still dialectally ***as deaf as a door, door-post, door-nail***, etc.); ***none so deaf as those who won't hear***. (Deafness is attributed in the Bible, Ps. lviii. 5, to the adder (= *pethen* the asp); cf. the name *deaf-adder* in 7.)

[*a* **1400–50** *Alexander* 4747 Dom as a dore-nayle & defe was he bathe.] **1551** CROWLEY *Pleas. & Pain* 93 Ye deafe dorepostis, coulde ye not heare? **1562** J. HEYWOOD *Prov. & Epigr.* (1867) 143 Who is so deafe, as he that will not heare. **1606** BRETON *Mis. Mavillia* Wks. (Grosart) 49 (D.) He is as deafe as a doore. **1611** COTGR., *Sourd comme vn tapis*, as deafe as a doore-nayle (say we). *a* **1693** URQUHART *Rabelais* III. xxxiv, He was as deaf as a Door-nail. **1824** BENTHAM *Bk. of Fallacies* Wks. 1843 II. 412 None are so completely deaf as those who will not hear. *a* **1845** HOOD *Tale of Trumpet* iv, She was deaf as a post.. And as deaf as twenty similes more, Including the adder, that deafest of snakes.

[*c* **825** *Vesp. Ps.* lvii. 4 (5) Swe nedran deafe. **1535** COVERD. *ibid.*, Like the deaf Adder that stoppeth hir eares.]

e. ***deaf and dumb***: also used *absol.* (= DEAF-MUTE) and thence *attrib.*, as 'a deaf-and-dumb alphabet'.

a **1225** *Ancr. R.* 108 Ich heold me al stille.. ase dumbe & deaf deð þet naueð non onswere. *c* **1400** *Destr. Troy* 4281 þof it defe were & doumbe, dede as a ston. **1625** SIR J. STRADLING *Divine Poems* III. xlvi. 96 The deaf-and-dumbe he made to heare and speake. **1669** HOLDER *Elem. Speech* App. 114 Now as to the most general case of those who are deaf and dumb, I say they are dumb by consequence from their deafness. **1774** JOHNSON *West. Isl.* Wks. X. 520 There is.. in Edinburgh.. a college of the deaf and dumb. **1865** TYLOR *Early Hist. Man.* ii. 17 The real deaf-and-dumb language of signs.

f. In restricted sense: Insensible *to* certain kinds of sounds, musical rhythm, etc.

1784 COWPER *Task* VI. 646 Deaf as the dead to harmony. **1860** TYNDALL *Glac.* I. xxiii. 167 A world of sounds to which I had been before quite deaf. **1870** LOWELL *Study Wind.* (1886) 241 His remarks upon versification are.. instructive to whoever is not rhythm-deaf.

2. *fig.* Not giving ear; unwilling to hear or heed, inattentive. Const. *to* (†*at*). Phrase. ***to turn a deaf ear*** (***to***).

1297 R. GLOUC. (Rolls) 7220 Hii beþ deue & blinde iwys, þat hii noileþ non god þyng yhure ne yse. **1393** LANGL. *P. Pl.* C. XII. 61 For god is def now a dayes and deyneþ nouht ous to huyre. *c* **1440** HYLTON *Scala Perf.* (W. de W. 1494) II. xxii, Make deef ere to hem as though þou herde hem not. **1548** UDALL, ETC. *Erasm. Par. Matt.* iii. 30 Mankinde was in a manner deaffe at the law of nature. **1607** SHAKS. *Timon* I. ii. 257 Oh that mens eares should be To Counsell deafe, but not to Flatterie. **1655** JENNINGS *Elise* 100 The reason that hath caused.. your pitty to be deaf at my prayers. **1700–11** SWIFT *Jrnl. Stella* 7 Feb., I was deaf to all intreaties. *c* **1780** BURNS *Duncan Gray*, Duncan fleech'd and Duncan pray'd; Meg was deaf as Ailsa Craig. **1838** THIRLWALL *Greece* II. xiii. 167 They were deaf to his summons. **1887** R. N. CAREY *Uncle Max* xxvi. 207, I prudently turned a deaf ear to this question.

†3. Dull, stupid; absurd. *Obs.*

c **1440** *Promp. Parv.* 116 Deffe, or dulle (K. defte, H.P. deft), *obtusus, agrestis.* **1482** in *Eng. Gilds* (1870) 315 Tailors', Exeter, Callenge hym knaffe, or horson, or deffe, or any yoder mysname. **1541** R. COPLAND *Galyen's Terapeutyke* 2 B iv b, Otherwyse it shulde be a deafe thynge that yᵉ thynge whiche is no more beynge shulde requyre curacyon.

†4. Numb, without sensation. *Obs. rare.*

15.. L. ANDREW *Noble Lyfe* III. xcii. in *Babees Bk.* 239 Torpido is a fisshe, but who-so handeleth hym shalbe lame & defe of lymmes, that he shall fele no thyng.

†5. Of sounds: So dull as to be hardly or indistinctly heard; muffled. *Obs.* [Cf. F. *bruit sourd.*]

1612 SHELTON *Quix.* I. III. vi. 156 The deaf and confused Trembling of these Trees. **1647** W. BROWNE *Polex.* II. 106 Assoone as Almanzor had made an end, there was a deafe noise among all the assembly. **1700** DRYDEN *Fables, Meleager & Atal.* 221 A deaf murmur through the squadron went. —— *Ovid's Met.* XII. 72 Nor silence is within, nor voice express, But a deaf noise of sounds that never cease.

6. a. Lacking its essential character or quality; hollow, empty, barren, unproductive; insipid. Cf. *deaf nettle* in 7. Now chiefly *dial.*

c **897** K. ÆLFRED *Gregory's Past.* lii. 411 Unʒefynde corn ..ōððe deaf. **14..** *Gloss.* in Wr.-Wülcker 718/36 *Hee sunt partes fructuum.. Hoc nauci..* defe. **1552** HULOET, Deaffe or doted, as that whyche hath no sauoure, *surdus.* **1633** D. ROGERS *Treat. Sacraments* I. 189 Tremble yow for your sitting so long upon the divels deafe egges. **1788** MARSHALL *Yorksh.* Gloss., *Deaf*, blasted, or barren; as a *deaf* ear of corn, or a *deaf* nut. **1878** *Cumbrld. Gloss.*, *Deef, Deeaf..* Applied to corn, it means light grain; and to land, weak and unproductive. **1883** *Standard* 27 Aug. 6/4 The grain is bulky, the ears are large..although a few here and there are 'deaf'. **1888** *W. Somerset Word-bk.*, *Deaf*..applied to any kind of fruit or seed enclosed in a shell or husk, which when opened is barren.

b. ***deaf nut***: one with no kernel; used *fig.* for something hollow, worthless, or unsubstantial.

1613 BP. HALL *Serm. 1 Sam.* xii. 24 He is but a deaf nut therefore, that hath outward service without inward fear. **1637** RUTHERFORD *Lett.* (1862) I. 331, I live upon no deaf nuts, as we use to speak. **1788** [see prec.]. **1808** SCOTT *Let. to C. K. Sharpe* 30 Dec. in Lockhart, The appointments.. are £300 a year—no deaf nuts. **1858** DE QUINCEY *Autobiog. Sk.* Wks. I. 88 A blank day, yielding absolutely nothing—what children call a deaf nut, offering no kernel.

†**c.** ***deaf arch*** = blind arch. *Obs. rare.*

1815 *Ann. Reg.* Chron. 43 In one of the deaf Arches, immediately adjoining the middle arch of the bridge.

7. *Comb.*, etc., as *deaf-eared*, †*-minded* adjs.; **deaf-adder** [cf. 1 d], a local name in England for the slow-worm or blind-worm, in U.S. for certain snakes supposed to be venomous; **deaf-aid**, a hearing aid; **deaf-dumb** = DEAF-MUTE; **deaf-dumbness**, dumbness or aphonia arising from deafness; **deaf-ear**, (*a*) = AURICLE 3; †(*b*) a cotyledon or seed-leaf of some plants; (*c*) the ear-lobe of the domestic fowl; **deaf-nettle** = DEAD-NETTLE.

1806 POLWHELE *Hist. Cornwall* VII. 120 We have a kind of viper which we call the long-cripple: it is the slow-worm or *deaf-adder of authors. **1860** BARTLETT *Dict. Amer.*, *Blauser*, the name given by the Dutch settlers to the hog-nosed snake..Other popular names in New York are Deaf-Adder and Buckwheat-nosed Adder. **1934** *Discovery* Nov. 324/2 The combined radio-gramophone and *deaf-aid. **1939** *Nature* 15 Apr. 633/1 An efficient type of deaf-aid is operated by a pick-up coil, in which are induced currents from an energized cable hung round the auditorium or placed under the carpet. **1834** GOOD *Study Med.* (ed. 4) I. 423 A *deaf-dumb boy. *Ibid.* 421 The extent of Knowledge ..which the deaf-dumb have occasionally exhibited. *Ibid.* 418 *Aphonia Surdorum*, *Deaf-dumbness. **1883** B. W. RICHARDSON *Field of Disease* vi. 262 Deafness, resulting.. from actual disease, or from deaf-dumbness. **1615** CROOKE *Body of Man* 374 At the Basis of the heart on either side hangeth an appendixe..which is called the Eare, not from any profite, action or vse it hath sayeth Galen..and therefore wee in English call it commonly the *deafe-eare, but for the similitude. *Ibid.* 375 The hollow veine..is receiued by the right deafe-eare. **1725** BRADLEY *Fam. Dict.* s.v. *Melon*, The two first leaves, which are call'd the Deaf Ears of the plant, will twirl or coffer. **1796** MRS. GLASSE *Cookery* v. 68 Wash a large beast's heart clean, and cut off the deaf-ears. **1854** *Poultry Chron.* I. 225 The cock..should have large wattles, and a clear white *deaf-ear. **1855** *Ibid.* III. 443 The importance of white deaf-ears seems however to have been overlooked by some of the competitors. **1877** *N. W. Linc. Gloss.*, Dēaf-ears, the auricles of the heart. **1565** GOLDING *Ovid's Met.* IX. (1593) 229 And words of comfort to her *deafeard mind they spake. **1581** MARBECK *Bk. of Notes* 149 These which are dumme and are *deafe minded. *c* **1440** *Promp. Parv.* 116 *Deffe nettylle, *arch-angelus.* **1599** A. M. tr. *Gabelhouer's Bk. Physicke* 201/1 Deafe Nettles. **1877** *N.W. Linc. Gloss.*, *Dēaf-nettle*, the stingless nettle.

deaf (dɛf), *v. arch.* or *dial.* Forms: 5 deffe, 6 *Sc.* deif(f, 6–7 deeff(e, deafe, deaff, 7– deaf. [f. DEAF *a.*; or an assimilation of the earlier DEAVE *v.* to the form of the adj.]

†**1.** *intr.* To become deaf. *Obs. rare.*

1530 PALSGR. 509/2 I deefe, I begyn to wante my hearing.

2. *trans.* To make deaf, to deafen.

c **1460** *Towneley Myst.* 314 Then deffes hym with dyn the bellys of the kyrke When thai clatter. **1530** PALSGR. 509/2 Thou deeffest me with thy kryeng so loude. **1595** SHAKS. *John* II. i. 147 What cracker is this same that deafes our eares With this abundance of superfluous breath? **1697** DRYDEN *Æneid* VII. 130 A swarm of thin aërial shapes appears, And, flutt'ring round his temples, deafs his ears. **1728** VANBR. & CIB. *Prov. Husb.* II. i, Lord! this Boy is enough to deaf People. **1877** *Holderness Gloss.*, *Deeaf*, to deafen with noise.

b. *fig.* and *transf.*

1596 LODGE *Marg. Amer.* 7 Then marched forth ech squadron, deaffing the aire with their cries. **1615** T. ADAMS *Blacke Devill* 13 Yet still [he] deafes himselfe to the cry of his owne conscience. **1637** NABBES *Microcosm.* in *Dodsley* IX. 127 If she urge Those accusations, deaf thy understanding To her suggestions. **1821** BYRON *Heav. & Earth* iii. 283 No more..Than their last cries shall shake the Almighty purpose, Or deaf obedient ocean, which fulfils it.

3. To drown (a sound) *with* a louder sound.

1640 G. ABBOTT *Job Paraphr.* xxxix. 251 Deafing their noise..with his loud and daring neighings. **1821** CLARE *Vill. Minstr.* II. 95 The birds..Were often deaf'd to silence with her song.

Hence **'deafing** *vbl. sb.* and *ppl. a.*

1612 *Two Noble Kinsm.* v. iii. 9 Gainst the which there is No deafing but to hear. **1647** H. MORE *Poems, Oracle* 39 The deafing surges, that with rage do boyl.

deafen ('dɛf(ə)n), *v.* Also 7 **deaffen.** [f. DEAF *a.*: see -EN⁵. A later synonym of prec.]

1. *trans.* To make deaf, to deprive of the power of hearing; to stun with noise. Also *fig.*

1597 [see DEAFENING *ppl. a.* 1]. **1611** COTGR., *Assourdir*, to deafen, or make deafe. **1634** HABINGTON *Castara* (Arb.) 79 We beginne To live in silence, when the noyse oth' Bench Not deafens Westminster. **1717** LADY M. W. MONTAGU *Lett.* 1 Jan., Hunting horns..that almost deafen the Company. **1855** MACAULAY *Hist. Eng.* IV. 269 Racine left the ground..deafened, dazzled, and tired to death.

2. To render (a sound) inaudible; to drown *by* a louder sound.

1823 CHALMERS *Serm.* I. v. 126 With whom the Voice of God is therefore deafened by the voice and testimony of men. **1827** COOPER *Prairie* I. vii. 102, I tarried till the mouths of my hounds were deafened by the blows of the chopper.

3. *Building.* To make (a floor or partition) impervious to sound by means of pugging. Hence **'deafening** *vbl. sb.*, material used for this purpose, pugging: ***deafening-board***, a board fixed between floor-joints to prevent sound from passing through the floor.

c **1814** T. SOMERVILLE *Life* (1861) 337 Few of the floors were deafened or plastered. **1839** M. LAFEVER *Mod. Archit.* 111 Strips nailed on the sides of the beams, to support the deafening board. **1864** *Glasgow Herald* 9 Apr., The heavy load of earth which has been put in for deafening.

†**4.** *intr.* To become deaf. *Obs. rare.*

1680 [see DEAFENING 2].

Hence **'deafened** *ppl. a.*

1608 SHAKS. *Per.* v. i. 47 She..with her sweet harmonie.. would..make a battrie through his deafend parts. **1678** DRYDEN & LEE *Œdipus* II. Wks. (1883) VI. 172 Methinks my deafened ears Are burst.

deafening ('dɛf(ə)nɪŋ), *ppl. a.* [-ING².]

1. That deafens or stuns with noise.

1597 SHAKS. *2 Hen. IV*, III. i. 24 With deaff'ning Clamors. **1667** MILTON *P.L.* II. 520 All the host of Hell With deafning shout return'd them loud acclaim. **1791** COWPER *Iliad* IX. 714 The tumult and the deaf'ning din of war. **1858** FROUDE *Hist. Eng.* III. 498 The deafening storm of denunciation which burst out.

b. ***deafening silence***, a silence heavy with significance; *spec.* a conspicuous failure to respond to or comment on a matter.

1968 *Sci. News* XCIII. 328/3 (*heading*) Deafening silence; deadly words. **1976** *Survey* Spring 195 The so-called mass media made public only these voices of support. There was a deafening silence about protests and about critical voices. **1985** *Times* 28 Aug. 5/1 Conservative and Labour MPs have complained of a 'deafening silence' over the affair.

†**2.** Becoming deaf. *Obs. rare.*

1680 EARL ROSCOM. *Poems* (1780) 81 Music no more delights our deaf'ning ears.

Hence **'deafeningly** *adv.*, in a deafening manner.

1827 HARE *Guesses* (1859) 326 And beat it they do deafeningly, at every corner of a street.

deaffe, obs. form of DEAF.

de-afforest (diːə'fɒrɪst), *v.* [ad. med.L. *deafforest-āre*: see DE- *pref.* II. 1 and AFFOREST *v.*] = DISAFFOREST.

1640 *Act 16 Chas. I*, c. 16 §5 The grounds Territories or places which have been or are Deafforrested. **1670** BLOUNT *Law Dict.*, *De-afforested*, that is discharged from being Forest; or, that is freed and exempted from the Forest-Laws. **1839** BAILEY *Festus* xix. (1848) 208 The paradise Initiate of the soul..that pleasant place, Erst deafforested.

So **de-,affore'station** = DISAFFORESTATION.

1659 *Anc. Land-Mark betw. Prince & People* 15 [They] procured many deafforrestations for the people. **1671** F. PHILLIPS *Reg. Necess.* 498 Their many deafforrestations.

†**'deafhead.** *Obs.* [See HEAD.] Deafness.

c **1350** in *Archaeol.* XXX. 351 For defhed of hed & for dul herynge.

deafish ('dɛfɪʃ), *a.* [f. DEAF *a.* + -ISH.] Somewhat deaf.

1611 COTGR., *Sourdastre*, deafish, thicke of hearing. **1664** COTTON *Scarron.* IV. (1741) 85 For still thou deafish art to 't. **1794–6** E. DARWIN *Zoon.* (1801) II. 443 Ether dropped into the ears of some deafish people. **1899** G. MEREDITH *Let.* 11 July (1970) III. 1332, I am daily more and more a cripple, and am deafish. **1907** ZANGWILL *Jewish Trinity* 5 Unfortunately, the Mayoress of Middleton was deafish.

deafly ('dɛflɪ), *adv.* [f. as prec. + -LY².] In a deaf manner: **a.** Without hearing (*lit.* and *fig.*); **b.** Dully, indistinctly; 'obscurely to the ear' (J.).

c **1330** R. BRUNNE *Chron. Wace* 5236 Bot Iulius Cesar wold hym nought here; fful deflike [*v.r.* defly] herde he his preyere. **1552** HULOET, Deaflye, *surde.* **1626** T. H[AWKINS] *Caussin's Holy Crt.* 36 They might (perhaps) deafly attend deuotion in the silence of a little family. **1827** POLLOK *Course T.* III. 1022 Blindly, deafly, obstinate. *a* **1861** CLOUGH *Misc. Poems, Uranus* 21 Deafly heard Were hauntings dim of old astrologies.

¶ ***deafly deep.*** Of uncertain meaning. With quot. 1400 cf. *devely*, DEVILY *a.*

c **1400** *Sowdone Bab.* 265 The Dikes were so develye depe, Thai helde hem selfe Chek-mate. **1605** SYLVESTER *Du Bartas* II. iii. IV. (1641) 184/2 Rivers the most deafly-deep.

deafly, var. form of DEAVELY *a.*

deaf-mute, *a.*, *sb.* [After F. *sourd-muet.*] **a.** Deaf and dumb. **b.** One who is deaf and dumb.

1837 *Penny Cycl.* VIII. 322/2 s.v. *Deaf and Dumb*, In all these conditions of deafness, the person is consequently *mute*, or *dumb*. Hence the expression *Deaf-Mute*, as used in the continental languages, and *Deaf and Dumb*, as used in England and America. **1865** *New Syd. Soc. Year-Bk. for 1864.* 479 A deaf-mute child. **1881** H. JAMES *Portr. Lady* xxv, He might as well address her in the deaf-mute's alphabet.

Hence **'deaf-'muteness, 'deaf-'mutism**, the condition of a deaf-mute.

1874 H. R. REYNOLDS *John Bapt*, ii. 109 The deaf-muteness of Zacharias. **1865** *New Syd. Soc. Year-Bk. for 1864.* 318 Congenital deaf-mutism. **1874** ROOSA *Dis. Ear* 515 Deaf-muteism is caused by diseases of the middle and internal ears. **1884** A. J. ELLIS in *Athenæum* 12 Jan. 55/2 This art [of lip-reading], the keystone of the modern bridge from deaf-mutism to deaf sociality.

deafness ('dɛfnɪs). For forms see DEAF *a.* [See -NESS.] The state of condition of being deaf.

1398 TREVISA *Barth. de P.R.* v. xii. (1495) 117 Yf colera be wasted in deyf men, deifnes is taken awaye. *c* **1440** *Promp. Parv.* 116 Deffenesse, *surditas.* **1610** SHAKS. *Temp.* I. ii. 106 Your tale, Sir, would cure deafenesse. **1682** J. NORRIS *Hierocles* 138 The blindness and deafness of those Souls which fall into Vice. **1860** TYNDALL *Glac.* I. xxiii. 167 The deafness was probably due to a strain of the tympanum.

deaken, -on, deakne, obs. ff. DEACON.

deal (diːl), *sb.*¹ Forms: 1–3 dǽl, (1 dael), 3–6 del, 4–5 deel, delle, 4–6 dell, 4–7 dele, 5 deyll, 5–6 deele, deill(e, 6 deyle, (daill), 5–7 deale, 6 deall, 6– deal. [A common Teut. sb.: OE. *dǽl*, corresp. to OFris. *dêl*, OS. *dêl* (MDu., Du. *deel*, MLG. *del*, *deil*, LG. *deel*, *dêl*), OHG, MHG., mod.G. *teil*, Goth. *dail-s*:—OTeut. **daili-z*: cf. Lith. *dalis*, OSlav. *dêlŭ* part, *dêlitĭ* to divide. Beside the form *dǽl* (with *ǽ* umlaut of *á* = OTeut. *ai*), OE. had also, without umlaut, *dâl*, whence DOLE and DALE².]

I. A part, portion, amount

†**1.** A part or division of a whole; a portion, fraction, section. *Obs.*

a **800** *Corpus Gloss.* 548 *Competentes portiunculas*, ʒelimplice daele. *c* **888** K. ÆLFRED *Boeth.* xxxiii. §2 Hi.. heora god on swa maniʒe dælas todælaþ. *c* **1000** *Ags. Gosp.* Matt. xxvii. 51 Ðæs temples wah-ryft wearð tosliten on tweʒen dælas. *c* **1205** LAY. 21125 He a fif dæle dælde his ferde. **1340** *Ayenb.* 164 þe filozofes..to-delden þise uirtues ine zix deles. **1398** TREVISA *Barth. de P.R.* XIV. iii. (1495) 469 Monteynes..passe vpwarde aboue the other deale of the londe. *c* **1440** *Promp. Parv.* 117 Dele, or parte, *porcio.* **1594** CAREW *Tasso* (1881) 9 He ceast, and vanisht flew to th' vpper deale, And purest portion of the heauenly seat.

†**b.** With an ordinal number, expressing an aliquot part of the whole. See also HALF-DEAL.

971 *Blickl. Hom.* 35 We sceolan..syllan þone teoþan dæl ure worldspeda. *c* **1205** LAY. 3019 þea þridde del of mine londe. *c* **1350** *Will. Palerne* 1284 þe furþe del of a furlong. **1393** GOWER *Conf.* II. 198 Be so that he the halve dele Hem graunt. *c* **1430** *Two Cookery-bks.* 21 Take þe to del ȝolkys of eyron, þe þridde dele Hony. **1534** *Act 26 Hen. VIII*, c. 3 §23 The moitie and halfe deale of euery suche pension. **1535** COVERDALE *Lev.* xiv. 10 Thre tenth deales of fyne floure. **1601** HOLLAND *Pliny* VII. 1, A good moity and halfe deale thereof. **1611** BIBLE *Num.* xv. 9, A meate offering of three tenth deales of flowre. **1737** WHISTON *Josephus' Antiq.* III. x. §5 They..bring one tenth deal to the altar.

†**c.** With indefinite and distributive numerals, as *a, each, every, never a, no, some*, etc. See also EVERY-DEAL, SOME-DEAL, etc. *Obs.* or *arch.*

c **1200** ORMIN 1720 All wass it filledd iwhillc dæl þurh Crist i Cristess time. *a* **1300** *Cursor M.* 20276 (Cott.) O pine ne sal i thol na dele. *c* **1384** CHAUCER *H. Fame* I. 331 Suche godelyhede In speche and neuer a dele of trouthe. **15..** *Merline* 896 in Furniv. *Percy Folio* 450 That this woman hath told eche deale, certez I beleeue itt weele. **1531** ELYOT *Gov.* I. xx, The straunge kynge..understode euery dele of the mater. [**1870** MAGNUSSON & MORRIS *Volsunga Saga* 67 Then Sigurd ate some deal of Fafnir's heart. **1884** J. PAYNE *1001 Nights* IX. 166 Moreover, they ate not anydele of the food that remained in the tray.]

†**d.** With *other*, and comparative words, as *more, most, less, better*, and the like, distinguishing one of two parts, or a part from the remainder. ***the other deal***: the other part, the rest, the remainder. ***the better deal*** (fig.): the superiority, the better. ***for the most deal***: for the most part, mostly, on most occasions. *Obs.*

1258 *Eng. Proclam. Hen. III* (*Trans. Philol. Soc.* 1868/9, 19), Vre rædesmen alle, oþer þe moare dæl of heom. **1297** R. GLOUC. (Rolls) 7582 þe mestedel of heyemen..Beþ icome of þe Normans. *c* **1380** *Sir Ferumb.* 669 He..ne a-ȝen no man ne tok querel..þat he ne hadde þe betere deel. **1387** TREVISA *Higden* (Rolls) II. 219 Now for þe moste deel he fleeþ mannys siȝt. **1398** —— *Barth de P.R.* v. i. (Tollem. MS.), þey beþ greuous to oþer dele of þe body [*residuo corporis*]. *a* **1400–50** *Alexander* 5568 þe dreȝest deele of þaim died of his dukis handis. **1447** BOKENHAM *Seyntys* (Roxb) 164

Whan she hys feet anoyntyd had weel.. Upon hys heed she porvd the tothir deel. **1481** CAXTON *Reynard* xvi. (Arb.) 35 He made it so that he had the beste dele, I gate not halfe my parte. *c* **1511** *1st Eng. Bk. Amer.* (Arb.) Introd. 30/1 Wherof ye moost deyle is.. kyt of of the holy Romes chyrche. **1572** BOSSEWELL *Armorie* II. 53 b, All the other deale of his body hathe the fourme of a litle hounde.

†**e.** ***by the tenth deal***: ten-fold; ***by a thousand deal***: a thousandfold. Apparently an erroneous use originating in negative expressions where it means 'not by the tenth or thousandth part' (see quot. 1400).

c **1330** R. BRUNNE *Chron.* (1810) 261 If þei now powere had of vs, wite ȝe wele, Streiter we suld be lad bi þe tend dele. *c* **1384** CHAUCER *H. Fame* III. 405 Woxen on high.. Wel more be a thousande dele Than hyt was erst. *c* **1400** *Rom. Rose* 1074 In this world is noone it lyche, Ne by a thousand deelle so riche. **1401** *Pol. Poems* (Rolls) II. 31 Then was it better doe than is nowe.. by a thousand dele.

†**2.** A part allowed or apportioned to any one; a portion, share, dole. *Obs.* exc. *dial.*

c **825** *Vesp. Psalter* cxli. 6 [cxlii. 5] Ðu earð hyht min dæl min in eorðan lifȝendra. *c* **1000** *Ags. Gosp.* Luke xv. 12 Fæder, syle me minne dæl minre æhte. *c* **1325** *Coer de L.* 2220 Their tresour and their meles He toke to his own deles. **1387** TREVISA *Higden* (Rolls) I. 407 He deleþ his mete at þe mel, And ȝeueþ eueriche manis del. **15..** *Kyng & Hermyt* 337 in Hazl. *E.P.P.* I. 25 Every man schall have his dele. **1535** COVERDALE *1 Sam.* i. 5 But vnto Anna he gaue one deale heuely for he loued Anna. **1647** HERRICK *Noble Numbers, Widdowes Teares,* The deale Of gentle paste and yeelding Dow That thou on widdowes didst bestow. **1806** FORSYTH *Beauties Scotl.* IV. 132 The remainder [of the money] is divided into shares, called *deals*, according to the number of persons entitled to a portion of it.

b. A portion or share of land; cf. DALE[2] 1 and DOLE *sb.*[1]

1600 *Sc. Acts Jas. VI* (1814) IV. 241 The cottaris deallis, and aucht akeris of land occupyit be þe fischeris of Ferne. **1633** *Sc. Acts Chas. I* (1814) V. 125 The tua dealles of land lyand betuix the lands of Grainge and Haltounehill. **1851** *Cumbrld. Gloss., Deail,* a narrow plot of ground in a common-field, set out by land-marks.

3. A quantity, an amount; qualified as *good, great, vast,* or the like; formerly, also, as *poor, small, little,* etc. ***a great deal***: a large part, portion, allowance, or amount (*of* anything), very much. ***a good deal***: a considerable amount. Cf. LOT (in *a great lot, good lot,* etc.).

c **1000** *Sax. Leechd.* II. 202 Micel dæl bewylledes wæteres on huniȝes godum dæle. *c* **1230** *Hali Meid.* 29 Ha.. ȝisceð þah after muchele deale mare. *a* **1300** *Cursor M.* 13493 (Cott.) Hai þar was a mikel dele. *a* **1400–50** *Alexander* 3703 Coupis.. þai fande bot a fewe dele forged of siluir. *c* **1430** *Two Cookery-bks.* 15 Safroun, & a gode dele Salt. **1570** LEVINS *Manip.* 207/37 A lyttle deale, *parum.* **1596** SHAKS. *1 Hen. IV*, II. iv. 592 But one halfepenny-worth of Bread to this intollerable deale of Sacke! **1609** BIBLE (Douay) *2 Macc.* iii. 6 The treasurie at Ierusalem was ful of innumerable deale of money. **1621** J. MAYER *Eng. Catech.* 207 Where ignorance preuaileth there can be but a poore deale of loue. **1673** RAY *Journ. Low C.* 57 There being so vast a deal of room, that 40,000 people may shelter themselves in it. **1685** H. MORE *Some Cursory Refl.* A ij b, To make such a Tragical deal ado about it. **1711** HEARNE *Collect.* (Oxf. Hist. Soc.) III. 223 A great Deal of Lead. **1771** FRANKLIN *Autobiog.* Wks. 1840 I. 6 He was also a good deal of a politician. **1790** BEATSON *Nav. & Mil. Mem.* I. 183 A most violent hurricane, which did an incredible deal of damage. **1874** C. GEIKIE *Life in Woods* vi. 102 A good deal of rain having fallen. **1875** JOWETT *Plato* (ed. 2) I. 103 There is a great deal of truth in what you say.

b. *absol.* (the thing referred to being implied or understood).

c **1450** *St. Cuthbert* (Surtees) 2971 Aftirwarde a litel dele, Cuthbert was prayde to karlele, Prestes to ordayne. **1659** *Burton's Diary* (1828) IV. 451, I see no need of it. The danger is a great deal. **1711** STEELE *Spect.* No. 51 ¶2 But there is a great deal to be said in Behalf of an Author. **1720** DE FOE *Capt. Singleton* xvi. (1840) 271 Our beef and hogs.. being not yet all gone by a good deal. **1765** A. DICKSON *Treat. Agric.* (ed. 2) 160 A great deal depends upon the just proportions of its several parts. **1871** B. TAYLOR *Faust* I. Prelude 3 They've read an awful deal. **1891** in *Law Times* XCI. 233/2 Whatever may be thought of the.. propriety of a good deal that was done.

4. ***a deal*** is used pregnantly for ***a good*** or ***great deal***, etc.; an undefined, but considerable or large quantity (*rarely* number); a 'lot'. *colloq.*

15.. *Mylner of Abyngton* 50 in Hazl. *E.P.P.* III. 102 Of each mannes corne wolde he steale More than his toledish by a deale. **1597** GERARDE *Herbal* I. xxxi. §1. 42 Nothing else but a deale of flocks set and thrust togither. **1601** SHAKS. *Twel. N.* III. i. 157 O what a deale of scorne lookes beautifull In the contempt and anger of his lip! **1627–77** FELTHAM *Resolves* I. xxx. 52 What a deal of sweetness do we find in a mild disposition? **1741** RICHARDSON *Pamela* (1824) I. xxii. 34 He and Mrs. Jervis had a deal of talk, as she told me. **1777** JOHNSON *Let.* 16 Oct., I have a deal to look after. **1780** *Phil. Trans.* LXX. 493 A tornado last night, with a deal of rain, thunder, and lightning. **1832** HT. MARTINEAU *Life in Wilds* v. 62 Saving us a deal of trouble. **1875** JOWETT *Plato* I. 351 Talking a deal of nonsense.

II. Adverbial uses.

†**5.** Connected with the notion of 'part, bit, whit': ***any deal***, to any extent, any whit; ***some deal***, to some extent, somewhat; ***each deal, each a deal, every deal, ilk a deal***, every bit, every whit, entirely; ***halfen deal***, half; ***mesten del***, for the most part, mostly. See also EVERYDEAL, HALFENDEAL, SOMEDEAL, etc. *Obs.*

a **700** *Epinal Gloss.* 731 *Partim,* sume daeli [*Erfurt* sumæ dæli]. *a* **1225** *St. Marher.* 17 We lueð bi þe lufte alre mesten del. *a* **1300–1440** [see EACH 1 d]. *a* **1300** *Cursor M.* 17400 (Cott.) Your sagh es lese, euer-ilk del. *c* **1340** *Ibid.* 23532 (Trin) Wiþouten tariynge any dele. **1375–1715** [see EVERYDEAL 2]. *c* **1400** *Sowdone Bab.* 2016 Tille he were rosted to colis ilkadele. **1471** RIPLEY *Comp. Alch.* II. in Ashm. (1652) 138 The whych unknowen thy Warke ys lost ech dele. **1513** DOUGLAS *Æneis* II. iv. 33 As I sall schew the verite ilka deil. **1553** GRIMALDE *Cicero's Offices* 106 a, Was hee any deale the richer? **1590** SPENSER *F.Q.* III. ix. 53 The.. hevenly lampes were halfendeale ybrent. **1710** PHILIPS *Pastorals* iv. 25 Albeit some deal I pipe.

†**b.** In the negative ***never a deal, no deal, not a deal***: never a bit, not a whit, not at all. *Obs.*

c **1250** *Gen. & Ex.* 230 It ne wrocte him neuere a del. *c* **1340** *Cursor M.* 23332 (Trin.) Of hem shul þei rewe no del. *c* **1422** HOCCLEVE *Tale Jonathas* 277 Hir conpaignie he nat a deel forsooke. *c* **1450** *St. Cuthbert* (Surtees) 4678 þe pepill it lyked neuer a dele. **1548** UDALL, etc. *Erasm. Par. John* vii. 57 Neuer a deale moued to cum to better aduisement. **1569** STOCKER *Diod. Sic.* II. xliv. 100 His father was no deale contented with the league. **1579** TOMSON *Calvin's Serm. Tim.* 392/1 They.. are neuer a deale more acceptable to God. *a* **1600** *Captaine Care* xxvi. in Child *Ballads* III. VI. clxxviii. 431/2 His harte was no dele lighte.

6. Connected with the notion of 'amount' or 'extent': ***a great deal***, to a great extent or degree, greatly, very much; ***a good deal***, to a considerable extent or degree, considerably; ***a vast deal***, vastly; †***much deal***, etc. **a.** as verbal adjuncts.

1562 WINȜET *Certain Tract.* i. Wks. 1888 I. 3 To lat down ane grete dele thair hie sailis. **1572** FORREST *Theophilus* 169 (in *Anglia* VII.) The iuste prayer much deale for to prevayle. **1719** DE FOE *Crusoe* (1840) II. viii. 183, I.. bled.. a great deal. *a* **1845** HOOD *Last Man* xxvii, The beggar man grumbled a weary deal. **1887** SALA in *Illust. Lond. News* 19 Mar., I had travelled a good deal in earthquaking lands.

b. as adjuncts of adjectives or adverbs in the comparative or superlative, or their equivalents.

1526 TINDALE *Mark* x. 48 He cryed the moore a greate deale. **1578** LYTE *Dodoens* VI. xiii. 713 Wilde Peares.. do drie and stop a great deale more then the others. **1581** G. PETTIE tr. *Guazzo's Civ. Conv.* (1586) II. 88 b, The kitchin was a greate deale too little. **1692** LOCKE *Educ.* §160 To have them [letters] a pretty deal bigger than he should ordinarily write. **1796** JANE AUSTEN *Pride & Prej.* vi. (1813) 11 You are a great deal too apt.. to like people in general. **1870** DICKENS *E. Drood* viii, You take a great deal too much upon yourself. **1875** JOWETT *Plato* I. 493 At a point a good deal lower than that at which they rose.

7. ***a deal***: to an undefined but considerable amount or extent; much. *colloq.*

1756 TOLDERVY *Hist. Two Orphans* III. 21 She talked a deal. **1811** LAMB *Guy Faux,* The first part of this dilemma is a deal too shocking to think of. **1855** MRS. GASKELL *North & S.* xvii, Beside, I shall be a deal here to make it more lively for thee. **1857** HUGHES *Tom Brown* I. iv, You boys of this generation are a deal tenderer fellows than we used to be.

III. 8. *Comb.* (in OE. and early ME.), as †***del (dal) neominde, -takand***, participator, sharer; †***del-taking***, participation; †***dealsman*** (*Sc.*), a partner, sharer.

c **825** *Vesp. Psalt.* cxviii[i]. 63 Daelniomend ic eam alra ondredendra ðec. *c* **1175** *Lamb. Hom.* 47 Beo heo dal neominde of heofene riches blisse. *a* **1300** *E. E. Psalter* cxviii. 63 Del-takand I am of al þe dredand. *Ibid.* cxxi[i]. 3 Of wham in him self del-taking hisse. **1563** *Aberdeen Reg.* V. 25 (Jam.) The awnaris and delismen of the said schip.

deal (di:l), *sb.*[2] [f. DEAL *v.*] An act or the act of dealing.

1. The act or system of dividing into parts for distribution; sharing.

1873 J. G. BERTRAM *Harvest of Sea* 331 At that time most of the herring boats of Shellbraes were managed on the sharing system, or by 'the deal', as it was called.

†**2.** Dealing; intercourse. *Sc.* See DALE[2] 2.

1588 A. KING tr. *Canisius' Catech.* 6 To haue carnel deale with ane vþer mans vyffe. **1594** WILLOBIE *Avisa* xix, Because you love a secret deale.

3. *Cards.* The distribution to the players of the cards required for a game; a single round or game marked by one distribution of the cards (= HAND *sb.* 23 c).

1607 HEYWOOD *Woman Killed with Kindness* Wks. 1874 II. 123 My minds not on my game; Many a deale I haue lost. **1674** COTTON *Compl. Gamester* xi, At French Ruff you must lift for deal. **1728** SWIFT *Jrnl. of Mod. Lady,* How can the muse.. in harmonious numbers put The deal, the shuffle, and the cut? **1739** GRAY *Let. to Mother* 21 June, You sit down, and play forty deals without intermission. **1778** C. JONES *Hoyle's Games Impr.* 61 You risk the losing of three or four Tricks in that Deal to gain one only. **1860** Bohn's *Handbk. Games* II. 68 If a card is faced in the deal, there must be a new deal, unless it is the last card.

4. a. An act of dealing or buying and selling; a business transaction, bargain. *vulgar* or *slang.*

1837–40 HALIBURTON *Clockm.* (1862) 305 Six dollars apiece for the pictures is about the fair deal for the price. **1861** HUGHES *Tom Brown at Oxf.* vi. (1889) 52 He wanted to have a deal with me for Jessy [mare]. **1879** E. K. BATES *Egypt. Bonds* I. iii. 51 He wants to make a deal for some chickens and vegetables in the morning.

b. *spec.* A transaction of an underhand or questionable nature; a private or secret arrangement in commerce or politics entered into by parties for their mutual benefit; a 'job'. orig. *U.S.*

1863 J. SHERMAN in R. S. Thorndike *Sherman Lett.* (1894) 205 The war is prolonged, and but little chance of its ending until we have a new deal. **1881** *N.Y. Nation* XXXIII. 487 [The party boss] his power of making 'deals'. **1882** *Ibid.* XXXV. 411/1 The shifts and expedients and 'deals' which had illustrated his rise to political prominence. **1888** BRYCE *Amer. Commw.* II. III. lxiii. 461 The chiefs of opposite parties.. will even go the length of making (of course secretly) a joint 'deal', i.e. of arranging for a distribution of offices whereby some of the friends of one shall get places, the residue being left for the friends of the other. **1891** *Boston* (Mass.) *Jrnl.* 27 Nov. 6/4 It is not known who are Deacon White's heirs in this corn deal. **1892** *Ibid.* 5 Nov. 12/7 An alleged Deal between the Republicans and the Democrats. **1928** *Manch. Guardian Weekly* 10 Aug. 102/2 We are.. dependent on Parisian sources for information about our latest deal with the French. *Ibid.* 104/1 [He] tries to explain the attitude of British Liberalism towards the naval deal. **1931** H. F. PRINGLE *T. Roosevelt* I. vi. 66 There had been deals and counterdeals between Tammany and anti-Tammany Democrats.

c. (*a*) ***bad, raw*** or ***rough deal***, harsh or unfair treatment, swindling; (*b*) ***fair*** or ***square deal***, equitable treatment, fair dealing. *colloq.* (orig. *U.S.*).

[**1838** T. C. HALIBURTON *Clockmaker* 2nd Ser. 266 Six dollars apiece for the pictur's is about the fair deal for the price.] **1876** W. G. NASH *New England Life* ii. 30 That was a square deal, Mis Brown. **1912** J. SANDILANDS *Western Canadian Dict.* 37 *Raw deal,* a bare-faced swindle. **1927** LADY ASTOR in *Daily Tel.* 15 Nov. 9/3 Although we have got the vote we women have a long way to go before we get a positive square deal. **1928** *Daily Chron.* 9 Aug. 6/2 The men have had a fair deal. **1931** *Week-end Rev.* 18 Apr. 580/1, I do not believe that in ordinary life Martin would have had such a rough deal. **1938** E. BOWEN *Death of Heart* I. viii. 145 No outside people deserve the bad deal they get from love. **1940** E. C. BENTLEY *Those Days* viii. 237 The Opposition were quite content with this situation. If it was what is known nowadays as a raw deal, they did not mind. **1958** *New Statesman* 22 Feb. 219/1 The government in Djakarta refused to give Sumatra a fair deal.

d. ***new deal, New Deal***, a new arrangement with a view to reform and betterment; *spec.* the programme of social and economic reform in the United States of America planned by the Roosevelt administration of 1932 onwards. Also *transf.* and *attrib.* Hence ***new dealer, New Dealer***, one who advocates or supports a 'new deal'.

1834 in M. James *Andrew Jackson, Portrait of Pres.* (1937) II. xvii. 376 A new bank and a New Deal. **1863** [see sense 4 b above]. **1876** *Chicago Tribune* 7 Aug. 1/6 The 'New-Dealers' appointed a committee to confer with the old State Central Committee. **1909** H. JAMES *Princess Casamassima* (N.Y. ed.) II. xxxiv. 199 I'm one of those who believe that a great new deal is destined to take place. **1932** F. D. ROOSEVELT in *N.Y. Times* 3 July 1. 8/7, I pledge you—I pledge myself—to a new deal for the American people. **1934** *Amer. Mercury* June 246/2 Fifty New Dealers who are helping the President make the country laugh. **1940** H. G. WELLS *New World Order* 61 The New Deal is plainly an attempt to achieve a working socialism and avert a social collapse in America. **1943** J. S. HUXLEY *TVA* 7 The Tennessee Valley Authority Act was one of the earliest New Deal measures, having been passed in May 1933—less than three months after Roosevelt took office. **1955** *Times* 3 Aug. 9/6 He ousts the 'new dealer', Malenkov, and re-directs Russian economy towards heavy industry. **1965** *Listener* 24 June 947/3 As a member of the New Deal team his position was in the highest degree anomalous.

e. ***big deal***, an important business transaction; also *transf.*, something important, exciting, or satisfying; freq. used as an ironical exclamation. orig. *U.S.*

1928 Z. GREY *Nevada* xvi. 279 'Are you open to a big deal?' queried the rustler bluntly. **1949** A. MILLER *Death of Salesman* II. 100 My brother.. pulled off a big deal today. I think we're going into business together. **1951** J. D. SALINGER *Catcher in Rye* i. 6 The game with Saxon Hall was supposed to be a very big deal around Pencey. *Ibid.* xviii. 163 The whole bunch of them—*thousands* of them—singing 'Come All Ye Faithful!' like mad. Big deal. It's supposed to be religious as hell. **1953** POHL & KORNBLUTH *Space Merch.* (1955) vii. 77 My bunk was all mine, twenty-four hours a day. Big deal. **1966** 'S. HARVESTER' *Treacherous Road* ii. 22 So, I can charge an evening's entertainment to business expenses. Oh, big deal. Carry on.

deal (di:l), *sb.*[3] Forms: 5 dele, 6 dell, deil, 6–8 deale, 7 dale, 8 *Sc.* dail, 6– deal. [Introduced from Low German *c* 1400: cf. MLG. *dele* fem. plank, floor (mod.Du. *deel* plank, *dele, delle* floor), corresp. to OHG. *dil, dillo* m., *dilla* f., MHG. *dil* m. f., *dille* f. board, deal, boarding, mod.G. *diele* f. deal-board, fir-plank, in north Germany 'floor' (see Grimm); ON. *þilja* fem. deal, plank, planking; OE. *þille* stake, board, plank, THILL:—OTeut. **þeljôn-* (whence *þiljôn, þilljô, þille*: cf. Finnish *teljo* from Teutonic). Another OE. derivative was *þelu* hewn wood, board, flooring: see THEAL.]

1. A slice sawn from a log of timber (now always of fir or pine), and usually understood to be more than seven inches wide, and not more than three thick; a plank or board of pine or fir-wood.

In the timber trade, in Great Britain, a *deal* is understood to be 9 inches wide, not more than 3 inches thick, and at least 6 feet long. If shorter, it is a *deal-end*; if not more than 7 inches wide, it is a BATTEN. In N. America, the standard deal (to which other sizes are reduced in computation) is 12 feet long, 11 inches wide, and $2\frac{1}{2}$ inches thick. By carpenters, deal of half this thickness ($1\frac{1}{4}$ inches) is called *whole deal*; of half the latter ($\frac{5}{8}$ inch) *slit deal*.

The word was introduced with the importation of sawn boards from some Low German district, and, as these consisted usually of fir or pine, the word was from the first associated with these kinds of wood.

1402 in C. Frost *Early Hist. Hull* (1827) App. 6 Mari Knyght de Dansk..xvj deles, iij^m waynscots. *Ibid.* 18, iij dusen deles. *a* **1450** *Rature* (in Hull Trin. House Records), Item for euerie hundreth of firre deales, xijd. **1558** *Wills & Inv. N.C.* (Surtees) I. 183 Ffyrdells of the biggest sorte.. litle firdells..doble firr sparrs. **1583–4** *Bk. Accts. Hull Charterhouse* in *N. & Q.* 6th Ser. VIII. 217/1, 7 deals to seale the windows. **1595** A. Duncan *Appendix Etymol., Asser*, a deele or planke. **1604** *Vestry Bks.* (Surt.) 283 For fortie firre dales, xxiijs. iiijd. **1641** Best *Farm. Bks.* (Surtees) 111 Robert Bonwicke of Wansworth demanded for everie deale a pennie, for bringing them from Hull to Parsonpooles, alledging that everie deale weighed three stone. **1762** Sterne *Tr. Shandy* VI. xxiii, A little model of a town..to be run up together of slit deals. **1820** Scoresby *Acc. Arctic Reg.* I. 141 These huts, some constructed of logs, others of deals two inches in thickness. **1886** *Law Times* LXXX. 212/1 To there load a cargo of deals.

b. (Without *a* or *plural*.) Wood in the form of deals.

a **1618** Raleigh *Obs.* in *Rem.* (1661) 180 The huge piles of Wainscot, Clapboard, Firdeal, Masts, and Timber..in the Low-countries. **1627** Capt. Smith *Seaman's Gram.* ii. 14 Laying that Decke with spruce Deale of thirty foot long, the sap cut off. **1667** Primatt *City & C. Builder* 85, A handsom Door, lyned with Slit-deal. **1794** *Builder's Price-Bk.* 41 Whole deal dove-tailed dado. **1876** Gwilt *Encycl. Archit.* §2365 The table shows that the value of 1½ inch deal is 8*d.* per foot. *Ibid.* Gloss. 1196 Fir boards..one inch and a quarter thick, are called whole deal, and those a full half inch thick, slit deal.

2. As a kind of timber: The wood of fir or pine, such as deals (in sense 1) are made from.

white deal, the produce of the Norway Spruce (*Abies excelsa*); ***red deal***, the produce of the Scotch Pine (*Pinus sylvestris*); ***yellow deal***, the produce of the Yellow Pine (*P. mitis*), or kindred American species.

1601 Holland *Pliny* I. 476 Some..haue their boughes disposed in good order, as the Pitch-tree, Firre, or Deale. *Ibid.* I. 488 For Mast-poles and crosse saile-yards in ships, the Fir or Deale [*abies*] is commended. **1673–4** Grew *Anat. Trunks* II. vii. §2 Deal, especially the white Deal, if it be cut cross, it tears. **1765** Parsons in *Phil. Trans.* LV. 3 What we call white deal, which is esteemed the lightest and tenderest of all the class of firs. **1833** *Penny Cycl.* I. 31/2 The Norway Spruce Fir..In the market [its wood] is known under the name of white or Christiania deal. **1840** *Ibid.* XVIII. 170/2 The Scotch Pine..Its timber furnishes the red deal of the carpenters. **1877** Japp *De Quincy* I. vii. 143 Preferring mahogany to deal for book-shelves.

3. *attrib.* and *Comb.*, as ('made of or consisting of deal'), ***deal box, door, -shaving, table***, etc.; ('engaged in the trade in deals') ***deal-carrier, -merchant, -porter, -runner***, etc.; **deal-apple** (*dial.*), a fir-cone; **deal-end** (see 1 note); **deal-fish** (see quots.); **deal-frame**, a gang-saw for cutting deals; **deal tree** (*dial.*), a fir-tree; **deal-worker**, a joiner who works up deal; **deal-yard**, a yard where deals are stacked. Also deal-board.

a **1825** Forby *Voc. E. Anglia*, *Deal-apples, the conical fruit of the fir-tree. **1728** Vanbr. & Cib. *Prov Husb.* I. i, Four mail-trunks, besides the great *deal-box. **1893** *Daily News* 26 Apr. 6/1 If the Union *deal-carriers did not return to work their places would be filled by free labourers. **1886** Ruskin *Præterita* I. vii. 232 Neatly brass-latched *deal doors. **1812** J. Smyth *Pract. Customs* (1821) 285 What constitutes the difference between a Deal and a Batten, is the width: the former being above 7 inches wide, and the latter not above 7 inches wide. This distinction..applies also to *Deal Ends and Batten Ends. **1845** in Yarrell *Brit. Fishes* Suppl., *Deal-fish. **1856** J. Richardson in *Encycl. Brit.* XII. 303/2 The Vaagmaer or Deal-fish has also been recorded by Dr. Fleming as a British species. **1862** *Chambers' Encycl., Dealfish*..a genus of fishes of the ribbon-fish family, having the body much compressed, and so named from the resemblance of the form to a piece of deal. **1706** *Lond. Gaz.* No. 4246/7 John Thomas, late of Lambeth ..*Deale-Merchant. **1883** *Gd. Words* Aug. 543/1 Dock-labourers, *deal-porters and coal-heavers. **1889** *Daily News* 24 Oct. 6/6 Dock labourers, wharfingers, *deal runners. **1693** *Phil. Trans.* XVII. 998 *Deal-shavings or brown Paper. *a* **1825** Forby *Voc. E. Anglia*, *Deal-tree, a fir-tree. **1705** *Lond. Gaz.* No. 4126/4 At the Cock in the hoop *Deal-Yard..are to be sold, Deal-Boards, Laths. **1840** *Evid. Hull Docks Comm.* 9 There are no timber-yards..they are deal-yards. *Ibid.* 12 A deal-yard is for sawn timber.

†**deal** *sb.*[4], **deal-wine.** *Obs.* Also dele-wine. Some unidentified kind of wine, supposed to have been of Rhenish origin.

1613 in Rogers *Agric. & Prices* V. 449 [cf. also VI. 416/3]. **1616** T. Adams *Souls Diseases* xvi, He..cals for wine, that he may make knowne his rare vessell of deale at home not forgetting to [tell] you that a Dutch merchant sent it him. **1616** B. Jonson *Masques, Mercury Vind.*, Paracelsus man.. that he promised you out of white bread and Dele-wine. **1635** Shirley *Lady of Pleas.* v. i, To the Dutch magazine of sauce, the Stillyard; Where deal and backrag, and what strange wine else..Shall flow into our room.

deal (diːl), *v.* Pa. t. and pple. dealt (delt). Forms: *Inf.* 1 dǽlan, 2–3 dealen, 3 dælen, deale(n, 3–5 delen, 3–6 dele, (4 del, 4 daile, 4–6 *Sc.* deill, 5 delyn, deele), 6–7 deale, 6– deal. *Pa. t.*, 1–3 dǽlde, 3 delde, 3–4 deld(e, 3–6 delt, 3–5 dalte, 4 dalt, delte, delit, 4–6 deled, -id, -yd, 5 dellyd, 5–6 dealed, -id, -yd, 6 dealte, 6– dealt. *Pa. pple.*, 1 dǽled, 3–4 i-deld, 4 ideled, 3–7 delt, 4–6 dalt, 6 dault, 4– as *pa. t.* [A common Teut. verb: OE. *dǽlan* = OFris. *dêla*, OS. *dêljan*, MDu., Du., MLG. *deelen*, OHG. *teilan*, Ger. *teilen*, ON. *deila* (Sw. *dela*, Da. *dele*), Goth. *dailjan*, derivative of **daili-z*, OE. *dǽl* deal *sb.*[1], part, division.]

I. To divide, distribute, share. Mainly *trans.*

†**1.** *trans.* To divide. *Obs.*

c **950** *Lindisf. Gosp.* xxiv. 51 *Dividet eum* dæles hine [*c* **1000** *Ags. Gosp.* todælþ hyne]. *c* **1205** Lay. 21125 And he a fif dæle dælde his ferde. *c* **1290** *S. Eng. Leg.* I. 239/715 þis watur..delez þis world a-two. *a* **1300** *Cursor M.* 6883 (Cott.) þe folk þat delt [*Trin* dalt] war in kinrede tuelue. **1387** Trevisa *Higden* (Rolls) I. 45 ȝif we deleþ þe somme on þre and þe seuenþe parte of þe þridde. **1480** Caxton *Descr. Brit.* 24 This kyngdome of Northumberland was first deled in two prouynces. **1535** Coverdale *Dan.* v. 28 Thy kyngdome is delt in partes. **1570** *Sat. Poems Reform.* (1890) I. 128 Our Lords are now delt in twa sydis.

†**2. a.** To separate, sever. *Obs.*

a **1000** *Daniel* 21 (Gr.) Swa no man scyle his gastes lufan wið gode dælan. *c* **1200** *Trin. Coll. Hom.* 7 He deleð þe sowle and þe lichame. *a* **1300** *Earth* 13 in *E.E.P.* (1862) 152 He.. deliþ þe dai from niȝt. *c* **1325** *Poem Times Edw. II* 205 in *Pol. Songs* (Camden) 333 I-deled from his riht spous. *a* **1400** *Poems Vernon MS.* 358 He ȝaf him wittes fyue, To delen þat vuel from þe good.

b. *intr.* (for *refl.*) To separate oneself, go away, part (*from*). *Obs. rare.*

c **1000** *Ags. Ps.* liv. 7 [lv. 7] Efne ic feor ȝewite, fleame dæle. *c* **1205** Lay. 7566 Julius þe kaisere mid alle þan Romanisce here dalden from þan fihte. *Ibid.* 18897 þer heo gunnen dælen. Merlin ferde riht suð.

†**3. a.** *trans.* To divide (property, etc.) among a number so that each may have his due share; to distribute in shares; to portion out, apportion. *Obs.*

c **1000** *Ags. Gosp.* Luke xxii. 17 Onfoð and dælað betwux eow. **1002** *Will of Wulfric* in *Cod. Dipl.* VI. 147 Ðæt heo hig dælan him betweonan. *c* **1205** Lay. 4053 Heo wuolden al þis lond dælen heom bi-twenen. *a* **1300** *Cursor M.* 3395 (Cott.) Bituix his childer he delt his aght. *c* **1460** *Emare* 42 He was curtays in all thyng..And well kowth dele and dyght. **1535** Coverdale *Josh.* viii. 2 Ye shal deale amonge you their spoyle & catell.

b. To share (property, etc.) *with* others. *Obs.*

a **1000** *Cædmon's Gen.* 2788 (Gr.) Næfre Ismael wið Isace wið min aȝen bearn yrfe dæleð. *a* **1175** *Cott. Hom.* 219 Hu he mihte delen rice wið god. *a* **1225** *Ancr. R.* 248 Uorto sechen feolawes, & delen mid ham þet god. *a* **1536** Tindale *Exp. Matt.* Wks. II. 83 If thou give us abundance..give us an heart to use it..and to deal with our neighbours.

4. a. To distribute or bestow among a number of recipients; *esp.* to distribute in the form of gifts or alms. Now mostly *fig.*, or with *out*: see b.

(In 3 the main notion is the division into shares; here it is the giving away or bestowing.)

a **1000** *Andreas* 548 (Gr.) Hu þrymlice..[þu] þine ȝife dælest. *c* **1000** *Ags. Gosp.* Mark v. 26 þæt wif ðe..fram maneȝum læcum fela þinga þolode and dælde eall þæt heo ahte. *c* **1175** *Lamb. Hom.* 109 þe ðe deleð elmessan for his drihtnes luuan. *a* **1225** *Ancr. R.* 224 To dealen his feder chetel to neodfule and to poure. *c* **1300** *Beket* 332 A sum of pans I deld on eche side. **1393** Langl. *P. Pl.* C. iv. 76 Let nat þy lyft half..Ywite what þow delest with þy ryht syde. *c* **1400** Maundev. (Roxb.) xxii. 102 He..delez þam þis relefe in faire siluer vessell. *c* **1450** *St. Cuthbert* (Surtees) 4151 Thurgh myght of god þat all gude deelys. **1588** A. King tr. *Canisius' Catech.* 12 He..deillis his sindrie giftis of graces. **1645** Evelyn *Diary* 25 Feb., There are many charities dealt publicly here. **1815** W. H. Ireland *Scribbleomania* 227 In comments they deal to the public dull diet.

b. *to deal out*; †formerly also ***abroad, away, forth***, etc.

1382 Wyclif *Luke* xi. 22 He schal..dele abrood his spuylis. *c* **1430** *Hymns Virg.* (1867) 55, I schal newe tungis in ȝou frame Alle maner of langagis forþ to deele. **1535** Coverdale *2 Sam.* vi. 19 He..dealte out vnto all the people ..vnto euery one a cake of bred. **1795** Southey *Joan of Arc* v. 447 The provident hand deals out its scanty dole. **1866** Rogers *Agric. & Prices* I. xxiv. 609 To deal out a certain number of herrings to their servants.

†**c.** *absol* or *intr.* To make distribution *of*. *Obs.*

Also with the recipients as indirect obj. (dative) or with *to*.

1297 R. Glouc. (Rolls) 7866 Of his fader tresorie..He delde uor his soule. **1362** Langl. *P. Pl.* A. xi. 237 We shuln ȝiue & dele oure enemys And alle men þat arn nedy as pore men & suche. **1456** *How Wise Man taught Son* 154 in Hazl. *E.P.P.* I. 175 And pore men of thy gode thou dele.

5. To deliver or give (*to* a person) as his share; to apportion. Also with *out*.

c **1340** *Gaw. & Gr. Knt.* 2285 Dele to me my destiné, & do hit out of honde. *c* **1400–50** *Alexander* 3475 Driȝtin deyne him to dele a dele of his blis. **1563** B. Googe *Eglogs* ii. (Arb.) 36 For she thy seruyce nought estemes, but deales the griefe for gayne. **1667** Milton *P.L.* iv. 70 To me..it deals eternal woe. **1704** Swift *Mech. Operat. Spirit*, This Grain of Enthusiasm, dealt into every Composition. **1766** Goldsm. *Vic. W.* iv, The hard measure that was dealt me. **1849** M. Arnold *Mod. Sappho*, Hast thou yet dealt him, O life, thy full measure? **1851** Ht. Martineau *Hist. Peace* (1877) III. iv. xiii. 115 The same measure was dealt out to the family of Napoleon.

6. †**a.** To bestow, give forth, render, deliver. *Obs.* exc. as in b, c.

a **1250** *Owl & Night.* 952 He mihte bet speken a sele, þan mid wraþþe wordes dele [*v.r.* deale]. *c* **1325** *E.E. Allit. P.* B. 344 þenne con dryȝttyn hym [Noe] dele dryȝly þyse wordez. *c* **1330** R. Brunne *Chron. Wace* (Rolls) 11890 Ffaire folden, and wel enseled, And to þer maister was hit [a letter] deled. *c* **1400** *Destr. Troy* 5646 And the dom þat he dulte [? dalte] duly was kept. *c* **1400** *Apol. Loll.* xxvii. 100 So may God delen it til an oþer.

b. *esp.* To deliver *blows*.

(The earlier notion was that of distributing them (as in sense 4) among several opponents or in various quarters, in all directions, now more definitely expressed by *deal about*; later, the sense become either 'to give one as his portion' (as in 5), or simply 'to deliver'.)

c **1314** *Guy Warw.* (A.) 2219 Strokes hii togider delden, ywis, On helmes & on briȝt scheldes. **1375** Barbour *Bruce* III. 32 [He] saw thaim swa gret dyntis deill. *c* **1400** *Destr. Troy* 6547 Mony dedly dint delt hom amonge. **1470–85** Malory *Arthur* XI. xi, Syr percyuale delt soo his strokes.. that there durste no man abyde hym. **1640** Rawlins *Rebellion* II. i, He's no true souldier that deales heedlesse blowes. **1700** Dryden *Pal. & Arc.* III. 612 One with a broken truncheon deals his blows. *a* **1732** Gay (J.), The nightly mallet deals resounding blows. **1810** Southey *Kehama* I. v, Rejoiced they see..That Nature in his pride hath dealt the blow. **1878** Bosw. Smith *Carthage* 337 Fortune or fraud soon gave Scipio the chance of dealing a decisive blow.

c. Hence in various expressions, apparently arising out of prec.

1642 Fuller *Holy & Prof. St.* v. vii. 385 He was perfect in the devilish art of dealing an ill turn. **1697** Dryden *Virg. Georg.* I. 447 By fits he deals his fiery bolts about. **1700** —— *Pal. & Arc.* III. 222 When hissing through the skies the feathered deaths were dealt. **1702** Rowe *Tamerl.* I. ii. 671, I Would..deal like Alha My angry Thunder on the frighted World. **1822** Lamb *Elia* Ser. II. *Confess. Drunkard*, We dealt about the wit, or what passes for it after midnight, jovially.

7. *Cards.* **a.** To distribute (the cards to be used in a game) to the various players; to give a player (such or so many cards) in distributing. Also with *out*, and *absol.*

1529 Latimer *Serm. at Camb.* in Foxe *A. & M.* (1583) 2142, I purpose againe to deale vnto you another carde almost of the same sute. **1562** J. Heywood *Prov. & Epigr.* (1867) 174 Were it as parellous to deale cardes at play. *c* **1592** Marlowe *Mass. Paris* I. ii, Take this as surest thing, That, right or wrong, thou deal thyself a king. **1673** Cotton *Compl. Gamester* in Singer *Hist. Cards* 345 He that deals hath the advantage of this game. **1709** *Brit. Apollo* II. 2/2 D. deals T. thirteen Cards. **1878** H. H. Gibbs *Ombre* 18 The Dealer's office is to deal and to see that there is no mistake in the cards dealt. **1891** *Speaker* 2 May 534/2 At baccarat.. the stakes are made before the cards are dealt.

b. To include (someone) *in* those to whom one deals cards for a game; freq. *fig.*, to include (a person) *in* an undertaking; to give (someone) a share or part. *colloq.* (orig. *U.S.*).

1942 Berry & Van den Bark *Amer. Thes. Slang* §369/4 Give a share,..deal one in (on). **1965** J. M. Cain *Magician's Wife* (1966) xiii. 101 You know everything, and yet you dealt yourself in. **1969** D. Bagley *Spoilers* iii. 72 He was on my original list, but he dealt himself in regardless and it would be too risky to leave him out now. **1969** W. Garner *Us or Them War* xvi. 121 If they won't deal us in we may end up having to steal it.

8. †**a.** In *Hurling*, etc.: To deliver or throw (the ball). *Obs.*

1602 Carew *Cornwall* 74 a, Then must hee cast the ball (named Dealing) to some one of his fellowes. **1603** Owen *Pembrokeshire* (1891) 277 The horsemen..will alsoe assault anye..that hath not the Knappan..or cudgell him after he hath delt the same from him. **1827** Hone *Every-day Bk.* II. 1008 (*Cornish hurling*,) The ball [is] thrown up, or *dealt*.

b. Of a horse.

1737 Bracken *Farriery* (1757) II. 34 His Carriage, and way of dealing his Legs. *Ibid.* II. 77 There are Horses that lead, or deal their Legs well.

II. To take part *in*, have to do *with*, occupy oneself, do business, act. Mainly *intr.*

†**9.** *intr.* To take part *in*, share or participate *in* or *with*, be a partaker *of*. *Obs.*

c **1175** *Pater Noster* 225 in *Lamb. Hom.* 67 þu aȝest to hatien wel his sunne, þet ðu ne dele noht þer inne. *a* **1240** *Ureisun* in *Cott. Hom.* 187 Hwa se euer wule habbe lot wiþ þe of þi blisse, he mot deale wiþ þe of þine pine. *c* **1330** R. Brunne *Chron.* (1810) 109 Of o side ne of other no þing deles he. **1481** Caxton *Reynard* (Arb.) 46 Ye shal be partener of my pylgremage, and dele of the pardon that I shal..fecche ouer the see.

†**10. a.** To engage *with* in conflict; to contend.

[Cf. ON. *deila við* to be at feud or quarrel with, to contend.]

993 *Byrhtnoth* 33 Betere..ðonne we swa hearde hilde dælon. *c* **1205** Lay. 30418 þus heo gunnen delen þene dæi longe. *c* **1330** R. Brunne *Chron.* (1810) 113 Steuen stoutly deles. *c* **1400** *Destr. Troy* 11027 Wold haue dongyn hym to dethe, hade þai delt long. **1577** Hammer *Anc. Eccl. Hist.* (1619) 385 How Areobindus slue a mighty Persian after dealing with him hand to hand. **1596** Harington *Metam. Ajax* (1814) 14 To deal with him at his own weapon. **1667** Milton *P.L.* vi. 125 Brutish that contest and foule, When Reason hath to deal with force.

b. *trans.* To contend or fight about. *Obs.*

c **1205** Lay. 26042 Nu wit scullen delen þen dæd of mire maȝen.

11. a. *intr.* To have to do *with* (a person); to have intercourse or dealings *with*; to associate *with. arch.* (and now associated with 13).

a **1300** *Cursor M.* 12249 (Cott.) Sum angels wit him deles To lede his wordes þat he meles. *c* **1380** Wyclif *Sel. Wks.* II. 404 þei delen not wiþ þes newe ordris, but supposen hem heretikes. *c* **1400** *Rom. Rose* 3265 Thou delest with angry folk, ywis. **1514** Barclay *Cyt. & Uplondyshm.* (Percy Soc.) 26 Her name was wanton Besse, Who leest with her delt he thryved not the lesse! **1586** A. Day *Eng. Secretarie* II. (1625) 36 With a resolute vow never to deale with him, I then had cast him [his son] off. **1711** Steele *Spect.* No. 27 ¶6 The Noble Principle..of Benevolence to all I have to deal with. **1869** Freeman *Norm. Conq.* (1876) III. xii. 98 One of the charges against him was that of dealing with a familiar spirit.

†**b.** Of sexual intercourse. *Obs.*

c **1340** *Cursor M.* 1197 (Fairf.) Our lorde..bad he salde wiþ his wyf dele. **1387** Trevisa *Higden* (Rolls) VI. 37 þey eteþ nouȝt, noþer deleþ wiþ hir wifes. *a* **1450** *Knt. de la Tour* 49 An ye loue ani other than youre husbonde, or ani other dele withe you, sauf he only. **1662** J. Davies tr. *Olearius' Voy. Ambass.* 94 They go not to Church the day they have dealt with a woman, till they have wash'd themselves.

12. To have business communications *with*; to carry on negotiations, negotiate, treat *with*; sometimes implying secret or sinister dealings. *arch.* (and now associated with 13).

a **1300** *Cursor M.* 5848 (Gött.) Wid þe eldest folk of israel, wid pharao þai went to dele. **1393** GOWER *Conf.* I. 267 The grete clerken..com..To tret upon this lordes hele, So longe they to-gider dele [etc.]. **1597** BACON *Ess. Negotiating* (Arb.) 86 It is generally better to deale by speech, then by letter, and by the mediation of a thirde then by a mans selfe. **1601** B. JONSON *Poetaster* IV. ii, Now have they dealt with my pothecary to poison me. **1625** *Camden's Hist. Eliz.* I. (1688) 127 The Bishop of Rosse dealt with the Duke, as they were Hawking, about the Marriage. **1625** USSHER in *Lett. Lit. Men* (Camden) 132, I doubt not, but before this time you have dealt with Sir Peter Vanlore for obtaining Erpinus his ..Persian books. *a* **1715** BURNET *Own Time* (1823) II. 285 Wilkinson, a prisoner for debt..was dealt with to accuse him.

13. a. To carry on commercial transactions; to do business, trade, traffic (*with* a person, *in* an article).

[**1523** LD. BERNERS *Froiss.* I. cclxvii. 395 People, suche as I haue dault with all in their marchaundyse. **1599** MINSHEU *Sp. Dict.*, *Negociar*, to deale in businesse, to follow a trade. **1611** COTGR., *Trafiquer*, to trafficke, trade,..commerce, deale in marchandise.] *a* **1627** MIDDLETON *Mayor Quinb.* III. ii, I deal in dog's leather. **1667** *Decay Chr. Piety* (J.), This is to drive a wholesale trade, when all other petty merchants deal but for parcels. **1699** DAMPIER *Voy.* II. I. iii. 65 Merchants care not to deal with him. **1735** POPE *Donne Sat.* iv. 140 Who in the secret, deals in Stocks secure, And cheats th' unknowing Widow and the Poor. **1833** HT. MARTINEAU *Manch. Strike* vii. 82 A traveller who deals..with several firms in this place. **1866** ROGERS *Agric. & Prices* I. xxi. 530 Such persons dealt in finished goods.

†**b.** *trans.* To offer for sale. *Obs. rare.*

1760 FOOTE *Minor* II. Wks. 1799 I. 252 You would not have..the flints?.. Every pebble of 'em..He shall deal them as new pavement.

14. To have to do *with* (a thing) in any way; to busy or occupy oneself, to concern oneself *with*.

a **1300** *Cursor M.* 1517 Jobal..Was first loger, and fee delt [*v.r.* dalt] wit. *c* **1400** MAUNDEV. (Roxb.) xvii. 80 Any man þat deles with sorcery or enchauntementz. **1477** *Paston Lett.* 807 III. 211 Ther is no man wyllyng to del with your swanes. **1535** COVERDALE *Ps.* lvii. 2 Youre handes deale with wickednesse. **1586** A. DAY *Eng. Secretarie* II. (1625) 112 Speaking of Friendship, I onely deale with such, whose actions [etc.]. **1845–60** ABP. THOMSON *Laws of Thought* Introd. 5 The mind deals with truth. **1869** HUXLEY in *Sci. Opinion* 21 Apr. 464 The first question with which I propose to deal. **1893** *Law Times* XCV. 26/2 That part of the Companies Act 1862 which deals with guarantee companies.

15. with *in*: To occupy, employ, or exercise oneself in (a thing); to have to do with, to make use of. (Now often approaching a fig. use of 13.)

1581 MULCASTER *Positions* ix. (1887) 54 Among the best writers that deale in this kinde. **1597** BACON *Ess. Suitors* (Arb.) 44 Plaine dealing, in denying to deale in Sutes at first, is grown..honourable. **1724** WATTS *Logic* Ded., True Logic is not that noisy thing that deals all in dispute and wrangling. **1748** CHESTERF. *Lett.* II. clviii. 65 All malt liquors fatten, or at least bloat; and I hope you do not deal much in them. **1770** *Junius Lett.* xxxix. 200 A poor contracted understanding deals in little schemes. **1885** *Manch. Exam.* 6 July 5/2 Lord E. F——..deals in vague outlines, as if afraid of being too specific.

16. a. *to deal with*: to act in regard to, administer, handle, dispose in any way of (a thing); **b.** to handle effectively; to grapple with; to take successful action in regard to.

1469 *Plumpton Corr.* (Camden) 23 He said that..he wold deele with you & yours, both be the law & besides the law. *a* **1586** SIDNEY (J.), If she hated me, I should know what passion to deal with. **1661** BRAMHALL *Just Vind.* vi. 153 He so abated their power..that a Dean and Chapter were able to deal with them. **1737** BRACKEN *Farriery Impr.* (1757) II. 120 The Lungs are formed accordingly, so that they may the better deal with the Air admitted in Inspiration. **1848** MACAULAY *Hist. Eng.* I. 142 A power more than sufficient to deal with Protector and Parliament together. *a* **1859** *Ibid.* V. 33 The Long Parliament did not..propose to restrain him from dealing according to his pleasure with his parks and his castles, his fisheries and his mines. **1874** GREEN *Short Hist.* iii. §5 (1882) 137 It was with the general anarchy that Hubert had first to deal. **1891** *Law Times* XC. 462/2 Mrs. Headley ..swore that she had never knowingly transferred or dealt with the mortgage. *Ibid.* XCII. 93/2 Restraining the defendants from selling or otherwise dealing with the shares.

17. a. *to deal with*: to act towards (any one), to treat (in some specified way).

a **1300** *Cursor M.* 16461 (Cott.) Iudas..be-hald and se Hu vile þat þai wit him delt. *c* **1340** *Gaw. & Gr. Knt.* 1661 He ..dalt with hir al in daynte. **1494** FABYAN *Chron.* VI. clxvii. 133 In lyke maner as they had dalt with Burdeaux. **1535** COVERDALE *Ps.* cii[i]. 10 He hath not dealt with vs after our synnes. **1568** GRAFTON *Chron.* II. 360 Sore displeased, that they were so hardly delt withall. **1611** BIBLE *2 Sam.* xviii. 5 Deale gently for my sake with..Absalom. **1729** BUTLER *Serm.* ix. Wks. 1874 II. 116 We ourselves shall one time or other be dealt with as we deal with others. **1874** GREEN *Short Hist.* viii. §6. 521 The Commons were dealing roughly with the agents of the Royal system.

b. with *by* (= in regard to) in same sense.

1573 G. HARVEY *Letter-bk.* (Camden) 3 That he wuld not deale so hardly bi me. **1675** tr. *Machiavelli's Prince* (1883) 305 The Venetians..have..dealt..honourably by him. **1754** CHATHAM *Lett. Nephew* vi. 43 If we would deal fairly by ourselves. **1877** MISS BRADDON *Weavers & Weft* 324 It will not be found that I have dealt unjustly by any one.

18. *to deal on, upon*: to set to work upon. *arch.*

1594 SHAKS. *Rich. III*, IV. ii. 76 Two deep enemies, Foes to my Rest..Are they that I would haue thee deale vpon. **1599** B. JONSON *Ev. Man out of Hum.* V. iv, *Mit.* What, will he deal upon such quantities of wine, alone? **1816** BYRON *Ch. Har.* III. lxxxiii, Allured By their new vigour, sternly have they dealt On one another. **1828** SCOTT *F.M. Perth* xv, 'There is a man thou must deal upon, Bonthron,' said the knight.

19. To act towards people generally (in some specified way); to conduct oneself, behave, act.

c **1340** *Gaw. & Gr. Knt.* 1114 þay dronken & daylyeden, & dalten vntyȝtel, þese lordez & ladyez. *Ibid.* 1668 þer þay dronken & dalten. **1535** COVERDALE *Josh.* i. 7 Yt thou mayest deale wysely whither so euer thou goest. **1593** SHAKS. *2 Hen. VI*, IV. ix. 46, I..doubt not so to deale, As all things shall redound vnto your good. **1602** —— *Lear* III. vi. 42 Let us deal justly. **1652** NEEDHAM *Selden's Mare Cl.* 152 Michaël Attaliates truly did ill..Nor indeed hath that eminent man dealt any better, who [etc.]. *c* **1680** BEVERIDGE *Serm.* (1729) I. 446 O Lord I have..dealt falsly before thee. **1711** SWIFT *Jrnl. to Stella* 17 Dec., They had better give up now, if she will not deal openly.

†**20.** To take action, act, proceed (usually *in* some matter or affair). *Obs.*

1470–85 MALORY *Arthur* IV. xiii, Wel said syr Vwayne go on youre waye and lete me dele. **1568** GRAFTON *Chron.* II. 188 To the which the French King aunswered, that without the presence of the .XII. peeres he could not deale in so weightie a matter. **1577** HANMER *Anc. Eccl. Hist.* (1619) 144 To deale in matters of religion both by word and deed. **1586** J. HOOKER *Girald. Irel.* in *Holinshed* II. 44/1 No man would medle or deale to carrie the same awaie. **1599** SHAKS. *Much Ado* V. i. 101 Do not you meddle, let me deale in this.

†**21.** *trans.* To treat. *Obs. rare.*

1586 *Let. Earle Leycester* 1 A late and weightie cause dealt in this Parliament.

dealable ('diːləb(ə)l), *a.* [f. DEAL *v.* + -ABLE.] Capable of being dealt *with*; suitable for dealing.

1667 WATERHOUSE *Fire Lond.* 91 Fled before the Fire, leaving it to its forradge, and not checquing it while dealable with. **1890** *Daily News* 11 Sept. 3/3 [It] did not vary much in the quotations—7 to 1 being a dealable rate.

dealbate (diː'ælbət), *a.* [ad. L. *dealbāt-us*, pa. pple. of *dealbāre* (see next).] Presenting a whitened surface; *esp.* in *Bot.* 'covered with a very opaque white powder' (*Treas. Bot.* 1866).

†**de'albate**, *v. Obs.* [f. ppl. stem of *dealbāre*, to whiten over, whitewash, f. *de-* + *albāre* to whiten, f. *albus* white; cf. DAUB. *v.*] *trans.* To whiten.

1623 COCKERAM, *Dealbate*, to whitelime a thing. **1638** T. WHITAKER *Blood of Grape* 30 Milke is bloud dealbated or thrice concocted. **1657** TOMLINSON *Renou's Disp.*, This dentifrice also will dealbate the teeth.

dealbation (diːæl'beɪʃən). [ad. L. *dealbātiōnem*, n. of action f. *dealbāre* (see prec.); cf. F. *déalbation* (Littré).] The action of whitening; blanching, bleaching.

1607 TOPSELL *Serpents* (1653) 646 The dealbation of the hair. *a* **1634** RANDOLPH *Muses Looking-glasse* IV. i, She.. hath forgot to whiten The naturall rednesse of my nose, she knowes not What 'tis wants dealbation! **1678** R. R[USSELL] *Geber* II. I. II. x. 59 Therefor they cannot whiten [lead] with good Dealbation. **1882** *Syd. Soc. Lex.*, *Dealbation*, the art of making white the skin and teeth; also of whitening bones for the purposes of anatomy.

b. The 'blanching', or reduction to its assay value, of silver coin containing alloy.

1888 W. RYE *Records & Record-searching* 29 The dealbation is always specially mentioned, and the only mention of blanched silver is in the statement of the farm [etc.].

'deal-'board. [f. DEAL *sb.*[3] + BOARD.] = DEAL *sb.*[3] 1; a thin board of fir or pine.

1568–9 in Burgon *Life Gresham* II. 284 One shippe of Brydges [Bruges] in Flanders, in the which is mastes, clappe-borde, deel-bordes. **1583** in *Northern N. & Q.* I. 77 A new cheste of Deal-bourd. **1667** PRIMATT *City & C. Build.* 146 Deal-Boards from ten to twelve inches broad, and about ten foot long. **1722** DE FOE *Plague* (1884) 99 Doors having Deal-Boards nail'd over them. **1883** READE in *Harper's Mag.* July 208/1 He could see through a deal board.

de-alcoholize, -izer, ist, etc.: see DE- II. 1.

†**deale, dele.** *Obs.* Of uncertain meaning.

It seems to be used for the purpose of calling attention, and may be an interjection, or a verb in the imperative, with the force of 'See!' 'mark!' or 'note!'

a **1225** *Ancr. R.* 276 Kumeð þerof smel of aromaz, oðer of swote healewi? Deale [*v.r.* Dele]. Ofte druie sprintles bereð winberien? *Ibid.* 362 Crist [moste] þolien pine & passiun, & so habben ingong into his riche. Lo, deale hwat he seið,—so habben ingong into his riche. *Ibid.* 286. **1330** R. BRUNNE *Chron.* (1810) 167 O dele, said þe kyng, þis is a fole Briton.

dealer ('diːlə(r)). [f. DEAL *v.* + -ER[1].] One who deals (in various senses of the verb).

1. a. One who divides, distributes, delivers.

c **1000** ÆLFRIC *Voc.* in Wr.-Wülcker 129 *Diuisor*, dælere. *c* **1440** *Promp. Parv.* 117 Delare, or he þat delythe, *distributor*, *partitor*. Delare, or grete almysse yevere, *rogatorius*. **1611** COTGR., *Distributeur*, a distributor, dealer, diuider. **1879** FARRAR *St. Paul* (1883) 3 The dealer of the death-wound to the spirit of Pharisaism was a Pharisee.

b. *spec.* The player who distributes the cards.

1600 ROWLANDS *Let. Humours Blood* iii. 58 Make him but dealer..If you do finde good dealing, take his eares. **1673** COTTON *Compl. Gamester* in Singer *Hist. Cards* 345 Then the dealer..shuffling them, after cutting, deals to every one three apiece. **1878** H. H. GIBBS *Ombre* 19 The Dealer then deals nine cards to each player.

2. One who has dealings *with* a person; one who deals *in* (a thing); †an agent, negotiator. *Obs.* in general sense except as *transf.* from next.

c **1000** ÆLFRIC *Deut.* v. 5 Ic wæs dælere betwix Gode and eow. **1586** *St. Trials, Q. Mary* (R.), I was acquainted, I confess, with their practices, but I never did intend to be a dealer in them. *c* **1610** SIR J. MELVIL *Mem.* (1735) 396 He was accused to have been a Dealer with the Earl of Bothwell. **1611** COTGR., *Agent*, an Agent, a dealer, a negotiator. **1727** DE FOE *Syst. Magic* I. iv. (1840) 112 A sorcerer and enchanter, a witch, or dealer with the Devil. *a* **1745** SWIFT (J.), These small dealers in wit and learning.

3. One who deals in merchandise, a trader; *spec.* one who sells articles in the same condition in which he has bought them; often in combination, as ***cattle-***, ***corn-***, ***horse-***, ***money-dealer.***

1611 COTGR., *Trafiqueur*, a trafficker, trader, marchant, occupier, dealer in the world. **1651** DAVENANT *Gondibert* I. iii. (R.), Such small money (though the people's gold With which they trade) great dealers skorne to take. **1745** *De Foe's Eng. Tradesman* Introd. (1841) I. 2 A very great number of considerable dealers, whom we call tradesmen. **1793** CAPT. BENTINCK in *Ld. Auckland's Corr.* (1862) III. 48 He is supplied with horses by some dealer in Town. **1848** MILL *Pol. Econ.* (1876) III. xi. §5. 315 Dealers in money (as lenders by profession are improperly called). **1891** *Pall Mall G.* 29 Oct. 2/1 Costers and hucksters and those not too particular buyers who are euphemistically known as 'general dealers'.

†**4.** One who acts (in some specified manner) in his relation to others. *Obs.*

1547–64 BAULDWIN *Mor. Philos.* (Palfr.) VIII. i, Hypocrites and double dealers. **1561** T. HOBY tr. *Castiglione's Courtyer* I. Hiij, An vntrue dealer, and a despiser of men. **1611** BIBLE *Isa.* xxi. 2 The treacherous dealer. **1677** WYCHERLEY (*title*), The Plain Dealer. **1840** THACKERAY *Catherine* i, What! call Peter Brock a double-dealer?

5. A jobber on the Stock Exchange.

1719 DEFOE *Anat. Exchange-Alley* 4 A young Dealer that has Money to lay out. **1837** *Penny Mag.* VI. 186/2 Dealers in bills purchase them either to get a commission, or in return for goods exported. **1870** *Gentl. Mag.* New Ser. V. 484 The dealers were almost unable to sell stock of any kind. **1890** *Cassell's Sat. Jrnl.* June 724/3 A jobber was engaged in 'banging' the market... Another dealer saw through the trick. **1902** *Encycl. Brit.* XXV. 23/2 Much of the work of the Stock Exchange account is carried out by a department of that institution corresponding to the bankers' clearing house. Its function is to bring into direct communication the ultimate buyer and the ultimate seller as represented by their respective brokers, thus eliminating, for the purposes of the settlement, the middleman known as the 'dealer' or 'jobber'. **1907** *Westm. Gaz.* 25 Mar. 9/3 Those dozens of other dealers are on the look-out for orders from brokers whose clientèle lies amongst the great body of the public. **1970** *Encycl. Brit.* XXI. 259/1 Dealers or jobbers in these securities take up their posts in this space every day, and dealers in other classes of securities similarly occupy the floor space allotted to their particular markets.

dealerdom ('diːlədəm). [f. DEALER + -DOM.] The sphere or influence of a dealer or dealers; dealers collectively.

1921 W. DE MORGAN *Old Man's Youth* xxix. 287 Men have been so often taken at their own valuation, and have been worked up by dealerdom. **1963** *Spectator* 29 Mar. 393 The new Establishment of officialdom and dealerdom.

dealership ('diːləʃɪp). [f. DEALER + -SHIP.] The position, business, or privileges of a dealer; an authorized trading establishment.

1916 W. P. WERHEIM in *Sales Promotion by Mail* viii. 295 Getting more business, establishing more agencies and dealerships. **1964** *Economist* 24 Oct. 384/2 A row of dealerships along the same stretch of main road. **1967** *Boston Sunday Herald* 26 Mar. I. 45/2 (Advt.), Right now our dealership has openings for new and used car men. **1970** *Daily Tel.* (Colour Suppl.) 2 Oct. 9 A certain proportion became interested in real estate, car dealerships, restaurants, and so forth.

deal-fish: see DEAL *sb.*[3] 3.

dealing ('diːlɪŋ), *vbl. sb.* [-ING[1].] The action of the verb DEAL.

1. a. Division; distribution (of gifts, blows, cards, etc.); sharing.

1377 LANGL. *P. Pl.* B. XIX. 374 Þorw bedes-byddynge and ..þorw penyes delynge. **1382** WYCLIF *Num.* xxxvi. 4 The delynge [**1388** departyng] of lottis. **1382** —— *1 Cor.* x. 16 The delynge or part takynge of the body of the Lord. *a* **1400–50** *Alexander* 451 In delingis of dyntis. *a* **1533** FRITH *Disput. Purgatory* §27 All thyne Executours dealyng, and offeryng of masse pence, help thee not a myte. *a* **1602** W. PERKINS *Cases of Consc.* (1619) 347 Others that..iudge the very dealing of the cardes to bee a lotte. **1885** J. MARTINEAU *Types Eth. Th.* I. I. ii. §3. 161 If this dealing out of ideas by exigency is assigned to God.

attrib. **1577–87** HOLINSHED *Chron.* III. 1257/2 His feeding ..all commers thrise a weeke appointed for his dealing daies.

†**b.** *concr.* A part, division. *Obs.*

a **1300** *E.E. Psalter* cxxxv. 13 Þat delt the Rede See in delinges wele.

2. Intercourse, friendly or business communication, connexion. Now usually *pl.*

1538 STARKEY *England* I. ii. 38 To loue euery man iche other, wyth al ryghtwyse and just delyng togyddur. **1586** A. DAY *Eng. Secretarie* I. (1625) 92 About two moneths since, he had dealings with a neighbour of yours, touching a Farme. **1611** BIBLE *John* iv. 9 The Iewes haue no dealings with the Samaritanes. **1674** N. FAIRFAX *Bulk & Selv.* 55 The dealing or business that is between body and body, being as real as that between body and ghost. **1712**

ARBUTHNOT *John Bull* I. viii, Hocus had dealings with John's wife. **1855** MACAULAY *Hist. Eng.* III. 678 It was rumoured..he had dealings with St. Germains.

3. Trading, trafficking; buying and selling.

1664 EVELYN *Kal. Hort.* (1729) 234 Such as would not be impos'd upon, will find the best Ware and Dealing at Brumpton-Park. **1868** ROGERS *Pol. Econ.* iii. (ed. 3) 22 Where dealings are transacted on a large scale, it is not difficult for commodities to be exchanged against commodities.

4. a. Acting (in some specified way) towards others; way of acting, conduct, behaviour.

1483 CAXTON *G. de la Tour* E vij b, For of good delyng and of good guydynge cam neuer but worship and honoure. *c* **1500** *Melusine* 310 His vnkynd & abhomynable deelyng. **1523** LD. BERNERS *Froiss.* I. cxxvii. 154 To ryde out to se the dealyng of thenglysshmen. **1573** G. HARVEY *Lett.-bk.* (Camden) 1 A present redres of so wrongful delings. **1674** in *Essex Papers* (Camden) I. 176 The unworthy dealing of Sir Robt Howard. **1874** MORLEY *Compromise* (1886) 37 Want of faithful dealing in the highest matters.

b. with *with*: Acting towards, treatment of.

a **1679** T. GOODWIN *Wks.* (1861) III. 288 What if God will use his absoluteness..in this his dealing with his children. **1718** HICKES & NELSON *J. Kettlewell* II. lvi. 175 Such a Dealing with their Soveraign as they..would not have allowed in any of their own..Servants. **1885** *Spectator* 8 Aug. 1043/1 The fluctuations of policy which have marked England's dealings with the Soudan.

5. *attrib.*, ***dealing-book*** (Stock Exch.).

1899 *Westm. Gaz.* 19 July 8/2 Dealing-books that have been innocent for weeks of more than two or three bargains a day have been filling rapidly. **1907** *Ibid.* 25 Mar. 9/3 There ..is one man very much absorbed in his dealing-book.

dealkylation (di:,ælkɪ'leɪʃən). *Chem.* [f. DE- + ALKYLATION.] The removal of an alkyl group or groups. So **de'alkylate** *v. trans.*; **de'alkylated** *ppl. a.*

1921 *Chem. Abstr.* XV. 865 Toluene is produced from xylene by the action of H..in the presence of Fe_2O_3 as a catalyst. Other similar dealkylations may be effected by the same method. **1937** *Jrnl. Amer. Chem. Soc.* LIX. 1418 Di-*t*-butylbenzene is dealkylated in the presence of phosphoric acid and benzene. **1946** *Nature* 30 Nov. 800/1 A broad programme on alkylation and dealkylation. **1968** S. PATAI *Chem. Amino Group* vi. 332 The formation of the major products—dealkylated amine and formaldehyde.

†**dealth.** *Obs. nonce-wd.* [f. DEAL *v.*, after *wealth*, *growth*.] Portion dealt.

1637 N. WHITING *Hist. Albino & B.* (N.), Then know, Bellama, since thou aimst at wealth, Where Fortune has bestowed her largest dealth.

†**de'ambulate**, *v. Obs.* [f. L. *deambulāre* to walk abroad: see DE- I. 3.]

1623 COCKERAM, *Deambulate*, to walke abroad.

deambulation (di:,æmbjʊ'leɪʃən). [ad. L. *deambulātiōn-em*, n. of action f. *deambulāre*.] The action of walking abroad or taking a walk.

a **1529** SKELTON *Image Hypocr.* 148 They make deambulations With great ostentations. **1531** ELYOT *Gov.* I. xvi, Suche exercises, as may be used within the house, or in the shadowe..as deambulations or moderate walkynges. **1545** JOYE *Exp. Dan.* iv. H ij b, In this kinges ydle deambulacion. **1648** W. SCLATER Jun. in *W. Sclater's Malachi* (1650) Ep. Ded., At your refections, deambulations, conferences. **1843** NEALE & WEBB *Durandus's Symbol. Ch.* p. lxvii, They had void spaces for deambulation. **1849** LYTTON *Caxtons* I II. ix, Book in hand, he would, on fine days, pace to and fro..In these deambulations, as he called them, he had generally a companion.

†**de'ambu,lator.** *Obs.* [L. *deambulātor*, agent-n. f. *deambulāre* (see above).] One who walks abroad.

1630 J. TAYLOR (Water P.) *Trav.* Wks. III. 76 The Odcombyan Deambulator, Perambulator, Ambler, Trotter, or vntyred Traueller, Sir Tho. Coriat.

de'ambulatory, *a.* and *sb.* [ad. L. *deambulātōri-us* fit for walking in, etc., whence *-ātōrium* sb., place to walk in.]

A. *adj.* Moving about from place to place; movable, shifting.

1607 COWELL *Interpr.* s.v. *Eschequer*, In Scotland the Eschequer was stable, but the other session was deambulatorie. *a* **1633** LENNARD tr. *Charron's Wisd.* II. iii. §3 (1670) 238 In it self unequal, wavering, deambulatory. *a* **1659** BP. MORTON *Episc. Justified* 142 The deambulatory actors used to have their *quietus est*.

B. *sb.* A place to walk in for exercise; *esp.* a covered walk or cloister.

1430 LYDG. *Chron. Troy* II. xi, Fresche alures..That called were deambulatoryes, Men to walke to geder twayne & twayne, To kepe them drye when it dyde rayne. **1447** *Will Hen. VI* in T. J. Carter *King's Coll. Chapel* 13 Of the which [cloistre square] the deambulatorie xiiij fete wide. **1834** *Gentl. Mag.* CIV. I. 55 An inscription in a Roman garden informed the walker, that when he had made five turns of the deambulatory he had completed a mile.

†**deambula'tour.** *Sc. Obs.* [Suffix repr. F. *-atoir*.] = prec. sb.

1513 DOUGLAS *Æneis* VII. iv. 62 Wythin the cheif deambulatour on raw Of forfaderis gret ymagis did stand. *a* **1572** KNOX *Hist. Ref.* Wks. 1846 I. 392 Thair suldiouris in greit cumpaneis..resortit to Sanct Geillis Kirk in Edinburgh, and maid thair commune deambulatour thairin.

deame, obs. form of DEEM, DIME.

de-americanize: see DE- II. 1.

deamination (di:æmɪ'neɪʃən). [f. DE- + AMIN(E + -ATION.] The removal of an amino group or groups. Hence **de'aminate** *v. trans.*; **de'aminating** *ppl. a.*

1912 *Chem. Abstr.* VI. 1912 Deamination. Emulsions of liver..when incubated with asparagine, glycocoll or leucine, liberate NH_3. **1926** *Jrnl. Biol. Chem.* LXX. 140 Tyrosine is also deaminated during the fermentation. *Ibid.* 147 The bacillus is able to deaminate tyrosine. **1927** *Glasgow Herald* 4 June 4/2 The exogenous metabolism by which amino-acids are de-aminated. *Ibid.*, The preliminary process of splitting off the ammonia and forming a fatty acid is called de-amination. **1951** M. ABERCROMBIE et al. *Dict. Biol.* 65 *Deamination*, removal of amino (NH_2) group. In mammals occurs to many amino-acid molecules by action of deaminating enzymes in liver and kidney. **1962** DARDENNE & KIRSTEN in A. Pirie *Lens Metabolism Rel. Cataract* 419 Arginine and glutamic acid were rapidly deaminated. **1970** *Nature* 6 June 969/1 Nitrous acid causes deamination of primary amino groups attached to the ring structure of nucleic acid bases.

†**de-'ample**, *v. Obs. nonce-wd.* [f. DE- II. 2 + AMPLE.] To deprive of amplitude, belittle.

1657 REEVE *God's Plea* 207 It doth grieve me to see how great things are deampled and dismagned amongst you.

dean[1] (di:n). Forms: 4–5 **dene, deen(e, den,** 5 **deyn(e (dyen),** 6 *Sc.* **dane,** 5–7 **deane,** 7– **dean.** [ME. *deen, dēn*, a. OF. *deien, dien.* mod.F. *doyen* = Sp. and It. *decano*, Pg. *deão*, Cat. *degá*:—L. *decān-um* one set over ten (cf. Exod. xviii. 21 Vulg.), also Gr. δεκᾱνός, explained from δέκα, *dec-em* ten.

Whether viewed as Gr. or L., the form of the word offers difficulties. In both languages, it had also an early astrological sense, 'the chief of ten parts, or of ten degrees, of a zodiacal sign': see DECAN. Salmasius, *De annis climactericis et antiqua Astrologia* (Leyden, 1648), considers this the original sense, and holds it to be a term of oriental astrology, which was merely assimilated to δέκα, *decem*, in Gr. and L. As a military term, the Gr. derivative δεκανία occurs = L. *decuria*, in the *Tactica* of Ælian and of Arrian (both c. 120); the L. *decanus* occurs in Vegetius *De Re Militari* c. 386. The word is then used by Jerome *c* 400 in his translation of Exodus xviii. 21, 25, where the Old Latin had *decurio*; and about the same time the monastic use (sense 3 below) appears in *Cod. Theodos.* xvi. 5. 30, and Cassian's *Instit.* iv. 10. In later times of the empire it was applied to various civil functionaries. From these monastic and civil uses come all the modern senses of *dean*.]

†**1.** Representing various uses of late L. *decānus*: A head, chief, or commander of a division of ten.

1388 WYCLIF *Ex.* xviii. 21 Ordeyne thou of hem tribunes, and centuriouns, and quinquagenaries, and deenys [**1382** rewlers vpon ten, Vulg. *decanos*]. *c* **1440** *Secrees* 187 Ffolwe þanne vche comandour ffoure vicaires, & vche vicaire tene lederes, & vche ledere tene denys, & vche deyn ten men. *Ibid.*, With vche a ledere tene dyens, and with vche a dyen ten men. **1483** CAXTON *Gold. Leg.* 59/2 Ordeyne of them trybunes & centuriones & denes that may in all tymes juge the peple.

†**2.** As a translation of med.L. *decānus*, applied in the 'Laws of Edward the Confessor' to the *teoðing-ealdor*, borsholder, headborough, or tithingman, the headman of a *friðborh* or *tenmannetale*. (See Stubbs, *Const. Hist.* I. v. 87.) *Obs.*

[*a* **1200** *Laws of Edw. Conf.* xxviii, Sic imposuerunt justitiarios super quosque x friðborgos, quos decanos possumus dicere, Anglicè autem *tyenþe heued* vocati sunt, hoc est caput x.] **1647** N. BACON *Disc. Govt. Eng.* I. xxvi. (1739) 44 If any controversy arose between the pledges, the chief pledge by them chosen, called also the Dean or Headburrough, might determine the same. **1695** KENNETT *Par. Antiq.* (1818) II. 338 Which justices, or civil deans, were to examine and determine all lesser causes between villages and neighbours.

3. As a translation of Eccl. L. *decānus*, applied to a head or president of ten monks in a monastery.

In the OE. transl. of the Rule of St. Benedict, c. xxi, rendered *teoþingealdor* 'tithing-elder'.

[*a* **430** AUGUSTINE *De Moribus Eccl. Cath.* I. 31 Eis quos decanos vocant eo quod sint denis propositi.] *a* **1641** BP. MOUNTAGU *Acts & Mon.* 437 Only the Deanes, or Tenth men, goe from Cell to Cell to minister consolation. **1695** KENNETT *Par. Antiq.* (1818) II. 339–340 The like office of deans began very early in the greater monasteries, especially in those of the Benedictine order; where the whole convent was divided into decuries, in which the dean or tenth person did preside over the other nine..And in the larger houses, where the numbers amounted to several decuries, the senior dean had a special preeminence, and had sometimes the care of all the other devolved upon him alone. And therefore the institution of cathedral deans was certainly owing to this practice. **1885** *Catholic Dict.* s.v., The senior dean, in the absence of the abbot and provost, governed the monastery.

4. The head of the chapter or body of canons of a collegiate or cathedral church.

Arising out of the monastic use. 'As a cathedral officer, the *decanus* dates from the 8th c., when he is found, after the monastic pattern, as subordinate to the *praepositus*, or provost, who was the bishop's vicegerent as head of the chapter'. But 'the office in its full development dates only from the 10th or 11th c...the Dean of St. Pauls, A.D. 1086, being the first English dean'. *Dict. Chr. Antiq.*

c **1330** R. BRUNNE *Chron.* (1810) 337 Sir Alisander was hie dene of Glasgow. **1377** LANGL. *P. Pl.* B. XIII. 65 Þis freke bifor þe den of poules Preched of penaunces. **1494** FABYAN *Chron.* VII. 327 Ye great deane of Pawlis, Mayster Richarde Wethyrshed. **1577** HARRISON *England* II. j. (1877) I. 14 Cathedrall churches, wherein the deanes (a calling not knowne in England before the Conquest) doo beare the cheefe rule. **1641** *Termes de la Ley* 101 Deane and Chapter is a body Corporate spirituall, consisting of..the Deane (who is chiefe) and his Prebends, and they together make this Corporation. **1689** WOOD *Life* 17 June, Dr. Aldridge, canon of Ch. Ch. [was] installed deane. **1714** SWIFT *Imit. Hor. Sat.* II. vi. 43 Good Mr. Dean, go change your gown. **1846** MCCULLOCH *Acc. Brit. Empire* (1854) II. 263 There may be a chapter without any dean, as the chapter of the collegiate church of Southwell..Every dean must be resident in his cathedral chuch four score and ten days..in every year. **1862** MRS. H. WOOD *Mrs. Hallib.* xxviii, 'Will you pardon my intruding upon you here, Mr. Dean?' he began.

5. A presbyter invested with jurisdiction or precedence (under the bishop or archdeacon) over a division of an archdeaconry; more fully called ***rural dean***; formerly (in some cases) ***dean of Christianity***; see CHRISTIANITY 4. (There were also ***urban deans*** (*decani urbani*): see Kennett *Par. Antiq.* II. 339.)

The rural dean had, in England till the Reformation, and in France till the Revolution, large powers of visitation, administration, and jurisdiction, which are still retained in some Roman Catholic countries. In England the office and title became almost obsolete from the 16th c., but have, since 1835, been generally revived for purposes of diocesan organization. See DANSEY, *Horæ Decanicæ Rurales*, 1835.

(Kennett, Du Cange, etc., have cited *decanus episcopi* in this sense from the 'Laws of Edward the Confessor' xxvii; but *episcopi* is an interpolation not in the original text, the *decanus* spoken of being really in sense 2 above.)

a **1350** *Cursor M.* 29539 (Cotton Galba MS.) And of a prest assoylid be, þat power has to vnbind þe, þat es he þat it first furth sent, Als dene of officiall by iugement. *c* **1380** WYCLIF *Wks.* (1880) 249 Whanne þei ben falsly amendid by officialis & denes. *c* **1450** HOLLAND *Howlat* 215 The Ravyne ..Was dene rurale to reid. **1456** *Pol. Poems* (Rolls) II. 236 With offycyal nor den no favour ther ys, But if sir symony shewe them sylver rounde. **1482** *Monk of Evesham* (Arb.) 80 Of the negligens of denys of archedekons and of other officers. **1514** FITZHERB. *Just. Peas* (1538) 121 It shalbe leful to al Archedecons, Deanes, &c...to weare Sarcenet in theyr lynynges of theyr gownes. **1697** BP. GARDINER *Advice Clergy Lincoln* 6 The Assistance of Rural Deans, which Office is..yet exercised in some Dioceses..but has unhappily been disused in this, (for how long time I know not). **1712** PRIDEAUX *Direct. Ch.-wardens* (ed. 4) 104 Bishop Lloyd went so far..as to name Rural Deans in every Deanry of the Diocese. **1765** BLACKSTONE *Comm.* I. 382 The rural deans are very antient officers of the church, but almost grown out of use; though their deaneries still subsist as an ecclesiastical division of the diocese, or archdeaconry. **1826** POLWHELE *Trad. & Recoll.* II. 610 On visiting the church at L. St. Columb as Dean-rural.

b. In the American Episcopal Church, the president of a CONVOCATION (q.v., 3 b).

6. In other ecclesiastical uses:

Dean of Peculiars: one invested with the charge of a peculiar, i.e. a particular church, parish, or group of parishes which is exempt from the jurisdiction of the bishop of the diocese within which it is situated, e.g. the Dean of Battle in Sussex. Such is also the ***Dean of the Chapels Royal*** in England (St. James's and Whitehall); in Scotland the ***Deans of the Chapel Royal*** are six clergymen of the Ch. of Scotl., who receive a portion of the revenues formerly belonging to the Chapel Royal of Holyrood.

Dean of the Arches: the lay judge of the Court of Arches, who has peculiar jurisdiction over thirteen London parishes called a deanery, and exempt from the authority of the bishop of London.

Dean of the Province of Canterbury: the Bishop of London, who, under a mandate from the archbishop, summons the bishops of the province to meet in Convocation.

[**1496** see DECAN 3.] **1647** CLARENDON *Hist. Reb.* I. (1843) 33/2 The then Bishop of London, Dr. Laud, attended on his majesty, throughout that whole journey [into Scotland] which, as he was dean of the chappel, he was not obliged to do. **1660** R. COKE *Power & Subj.* 203 The King shall present to his free chappels (in default of the Dean). **1726** AYLIFFE *Parergon* 192 The Judge of this Court..is distinguished by the title of Dean or Official of the Court of Arches. *Ibid.* 205 There are also some Deans in England without any Jurisdiction; only for Honour so stiled; as the Dean of the Royal Chapel, the Dean of the Chapel of St. George at Windsor. **1846** MCCULLOCH *Acc. Brit. Empire* (1854) II. 265 The third species of Deans are those of *peculiars*..Deans of peculiars have sometimes jurisdiction and cure of souls, as the Dean of Battle, in Sussex, and sometimes jurisdiction only, as the Dean of the Arches, London. **1893** *Whitaker's Almanack*, Dean of the Chapels Royal, The Bishop of London.

7. In the colleges of Oxford and Cambridge: The title of one or more resident fellows appointed to supervise the conduct and studies of the junior members and to maintain discipline among them, to present them for graduation, etc.

The office came originally from that of the monastic dean, and was disciplinary; one important function of the dean in early times was to preside at the disputations of the scholars, and in the Oxford colleges of the new foundation deans were appointed in the different faculties, e.g. at New College, two in Arts, one in Canon Law, one in Civil Law, and one in Theology, who presided at the disputations of the students in these faculties; from the end of the 16th c., it became customary also in most colleges for the dean to present for degrees. At present the functions pertaining to discipline, attendance at chapel, graduation, etc., are sometimes discharged by a single dean, alone or in conjunction with a sub-warden, vice-president, or other vice-gerent, sometimes distributed among two or three deans; hence the offices of ***senior*** and ***junior dean***, or ***sub-dean***, ***dean of arts***, ***dean of divinity***, ***dean of degrees***, existing in some colleges.

[In the Statutes of Merton Coll., 1267–74, such officers are appointed 'numero cuilibet vicenario vel etiam decenario,' but the title *decanus* is not used. **1382** *Stat. New Coll. Oxon.* xiv, Quinque socii..qui sub dicto custode tanquam ejus coadjutores Scholarium et Sociorum ipsorum curam et regimen habeant, qualiter scilicet in studio scholastico et morum honestate proficiant..Quos omnes sic præfectos Decanos volumus nuncupari. Permittentes quod illi ambo Decani facultatum Juris Canonici et Civilis eligi poterunt, etc.]

1577 HARRISON *England* II. iii. (1877) I. 81 There is moreouer in euerie house a maister or prouost, who hath vnder him a president, and certeine censors or deanes, appointed to looke to the behauour and maners of the students there. **1847** TENNYSON *Princ.* Prol. 161 At college..They lost their weeks: they vext the souls of deans. **1853** C. BEDE *Verdant Green* iv, He had been Proctor and College Dean there. **1891** RASHDALL in Clark *Coll. Oxford* 157 (*New Coll.*) The discipline was mainly in the hands of the Sub-Warden and the five deans—two Artists, a Canonist, a Civilian, and a Theologian—who presided over the disputations of their respective Faculties.

8. The president of a faculty or department of study in a University, as in the ancient continental and Scotch Universities, and in the colleges affiliated to the modern Universities of London, Victoria, etc.

In U.S., the dean is now a registrar or secretary.

[**1271** *Chartul. Univ. Paris.* I. 488 Magistro J. de Racheroles tunc existente decano facultatis medicine. **1282** *Ibid.* I. 595 Canonicus Parisiensis et decanus theologice facultatis. **1413** *Juramentum Bachalariorum, St. Andrews*, Ego juro quod ero obediens facultati arcium et decano eiusdem. **1453** JAS. II. *Letter* in *Munim. Univ. Glasg.* I. 6 Facultatum decanos procuratores nacionum regentes magistros et scholares in prelibata Universitate.] **1524** JAS. V *Letter to St. Andrews* 19 Nov., Maister Mertyne Balfour vicar of Monymeil, den of faculte of art of the said universite. **1535** *Ibid.* 28 Feb., Dean of facultie of Theologie of the said university. **1578** *Contract* in *Munim. Univ. Glasg.* I. 119 Maister Thomas Smeitoun minister of Paslay and dean of facultie of the said Universitie. **1708** J. CHAMBERLAYNE *St. Gt. Brit.* II. III. (1743) 438 The University of Glasgow..had originally considerable Revenues for the Maintenance of a Rector, a Dean of Faculty, a Principal or Warden, etc. **1875** *Edin. Univ. Cal.* 37 The affairs of each Faculty are presided over by a Dean, who is elected from among Professors of the Faculty. **1893** tr. *Compayré's Abelard* 135 The deans..were the real administrators of their respective Faculties. They presided in the assemblies of their company, and were members of the council of the University.

b. ***Dean of Faculty***: the president of the Faculty of Advocates in Scotland.

1664 *Minutes Faculty of Advocates* 4 June (MS. in Adv. Libr.), Motione being made anent the electione of ane deane of faculty. **1826** SCOTT *Diary* 7 June in *Lockhart*, I went to the Dean of Faculty's to a consultation about Constable.

c. Also the usual title of the head of a school of medicine attached to a hospital.

1849 *Minutes of Committee St. Thomas's Hosp.* 23 May, The Committee having been summoned for the purpose of taking into consideration the appointment of a Dean..it was agreed..that some one member of the Medical School shall for each year act in the capacity and with the title of 'Dean of the Medical School'. **1893–4** *Prospectus St. Thomas's Med. Sch.* 16 Dean of the School, G. H. Makins, F.R.C.S.

9. ***dean of guild***: **a.** in the mediæval guilds, an officer who summoned the members to attend meetings, etc.; **b.** in Scotland, the head of the guild or merchant-company of a royal burgh, who is a magistrate charged with the supervision of all buildings within the burgh.

Except in the four cities of Edinburgh, Glasgow, Perth, and Aberdeen, where he is still elected by the guildry, this officer is now chosen by the town-councillors from among their own number.

1389 in *Eng. Gilds* 46 On Dene, for to warnyn alle þe gild breþren and sistren. **1469** *Sc. Acts Jas. III* (1597) §29 Al Officiares perteining to the towne: As Alderman, Baillies, Deane of Gild, and vther officiares. **1754** ERSKINE *Princ. Sc. Law* (1809) 43 The Dean of Guild is that magistrate of a royal borough, who is head of the merchant-company; he has the cognisance of mercantile causes within borough..and the inspection of buildings. **1806** *Gazetteer Scotl.* (ed. 2) 506 Selkirk is a royal borough..It is governed by 2 bailies, a dean of guild, treasurer, and 10 counsellors. **1864** KIRK *Chas. Bold* I. II. i. 451 The deans of the guilds and the principal citizens, who had come out to meet him.

10. The president, chief, or senior member of any body. [= F. *doyen*.]

1687 *Lond. Gaz.* No. 2215/2 At the Boots of the Coach went the Pages..and by them the Dean or chief of the Footmen in black Velvet. **1827** HARDMAN *Battle of Waterloo* 15 Ah! ah! Boney, must you, or our Duke, be the chief dean? **1889** *Times* 25 Nov. 6 The Diplomatic Agents at Cairo..met at the residence of the dean, the Consul-General of Spain, Señor de Ortega.

b. ***Dean of the Sacred College***: see quot. 1885.

1703 *Lond. Gaz.* No. 3921/1 The Cardinal de Bouillon will return hither..to exercise his Function of Dean of the College of Cardinals. **1885** *Catholic Dict.* s.v., The Cardinal Dean is the chief of the sacred college; he is usually the oldest of the Cardinal Bishops..He presides in the consistory in the absence of the Pope.

11. *Comb.*

1862 *Sat. Rev.* XIV. 706/1 If Lord Shaftesbury is to be a Dean-maker. *Ibid.*, The whole system of Dean-making needs reform.

dean², dene (diːn). Forms: 1 denu, 1– dene, 2–4 dane, 5 deyne, 6 *Sc.* dyne, 8–9 dean. [OE. *denu*, acc. *dene*, valley:—OTeut. **dani-*, from the same root as OE. *den(n*, DEN (:—OTeut. *danj-o*ᵐ), q.v.] A vale: **a.** formerly the ordinary word, literal and figurative (as in OE. *déaþ-denu* valley of death, ME. *dene of teres*), and still occurring in the general sense in some local names, as *the Dean*, Edinburgh, *Taunton Dean*, the wide valley of the Tone above Taunton, and perh. *Dean Forest*; **b.** now, usually, the deep, narrow, and wooded vale of a rivulet.

As a common appellative, used in Durham, Northumberland, and adjacent parts of Scotland and England; as part of a proper name, separate or in composition, occurring much more widely, e.g. *Denholm Dean* in Roxburghshire, *Jesmond Dean* or *Dene* near Newcastle, *Castle Eden Dean* or *Dene* and *Hawthorndene* in Durham, *Chellow Dene* near Bradford, *North Dean* near Halifax, *Hepworth Dene* near Huddersfield, *Deepdene* near Dorking, *East Dean*, *West Dean*, *Ovingdean*, *Rottingdean*, in deep wooded vales in the chalk downs near Brighton. The spelling *dene* is that now prevalent in Durham and Northumberland. In composition often shortened to *den*, as *Marden*, *Smarden*, *Biddenden*, etc. in Kent.

c **825** *Vesp. Psalter* lxxxiii. 7 In dene teara [*in convalle lacrimarum*]. *Ibid.* ciii. 10 In deanum. *c* **1000** ÆLFRIC *Gram.* (Z.) 56 *Uallis*, dene. *c* **1000** *Ags. Gosp.* Luke iii 5 Ælc denu [*Lindisf.* dene, *Hatton* dane] bið ȝefylled. *a* **1300** *E.E. Psalter* lxxxiii. 7 (Mätz.) In dene of teres. *c* **1325** *E.E. Allit. P.* A. 295 Þou says þou trawez me in þis dene. **1340** *Ayenb.* 59 Ich wille maki þe helles and þe danes. *a* **1400–50** *Alexander* 5421 Þan dryues he furth..into a deyne entris, A vale full of vermyn. **1594** *Batt. Balrinness* in *Sc. Poems 16th C.* II. 355 Now must I flie, or els be slaine..With that he ran ouer ane dyne Endlongis ane lytill burne. **1612** DRAYTON *Polyolb.* iii. 418 Tauntons fruitfull Deane. **1794** W. HUTCHINSON *Hist. Durham* III. 1 There are some deep and woody vales or deans near this mansion [at Castle Eden]. **1806** *Hull Advertiser* 11 Jan. 2/2 The Estate offers..deans for plantations, sheltered from the sea. **1816** SURTEES *Hist. Durham* I. II. 44 The wild beauties of the Dene [at Castle Eden]. **1873** MURRAY *Handbk. Durham* 13 The deep wooded *denes* which débouche upon the coast.

dean³. As a Cornish mining term: The end of a level.

1874 in KNIGHT *Dict. Mech.* **1881** in RAYMOND *Mining Gloss.*

de-anathematize, *v.*: see DE- II. 1.

deand, obs. north. form of DYING.

deane, obs. form of DIN; var. of DAIN *sb.*

deaner, deener (ˈdiːnə(r)). *slang.* Also dener, diener. [Immediate origin uncertain, but prob. ultimately identical with DENARIUS, DENIER³.] A shilling.

Before the advent of decimal currency esp. freq. in Australia and N.Z.

1839 H. BRANDON *Poverty, Mendicity & Crime*, Deaner, a shilling (country phrase). **1846** R. L. SNOWDEN *Mag. Assistant* 342 Shilling, Deaner, also twelver. **1851** MAYHEW *London Labour* I. 313/1 No, I'll give you a deuce o' deeners (two shillings). **1864** *Times* 12 Oct. 11/6 One woman said, 'Where's the "deaner".' **1901** H. LAWSON *Joe Wilson & his Mates* II. 280 'Stumped?' inquired Jim. 'Not a blanky, lurid deener!' drawled Bill. **1904** *Daily Chron.* 27 Dec. 4/4 I've played it [*sc.* a cornet] six hour for a deaner and a haddock-bone disguised in batter as a bit o' cold, fried fish. **1907** *Ibid.* 26 July 4/7 In Ireland the 'denarius' lingers in the name for a shilling—a dener. **1908** *Ibid.* 5 Feb. 4/7 Here we come to classic reminiscences of the denarius! It is a 'bob', and 'owt deners' is a florin. **1922** *Contemp. Rev.* Sept. 367 A shilling..is frequently a 'deener' [in cockney speech]. **1930** V. PALMER *Men are Human* xxix. 273 I'd like a diener for every quart of whisky the old boy's sunk in his day. **1933** *Bulletin* (Sydney) 13 Dec. 31/1 O' course I waited, after spendin' the bob; 'e looked a bloke 'oo'd be good for more than a deener. **1937** A. UPFIELD *Mr. Jelly's Business* xiv. 146 If I 'ad lorst a deaner I'd have got hell. **1946** F. SARGESON *That Summer* 77 Could you give me the lend of a bob?..I'm on the beach myself, I said, but I can make it a deener.

deanery (ˈdiːnərɪ). Also 5 denerye, deynrye, 6 denry, 6–9 deanry. [f. DEAN¹ + -ERY: the AFr. form *denrie* was prob. from Eng.]

1. The office or position of a dean.

[**1292** BRITTON II. xvii. §6 Dené [*v.rr.* denee, denrie], ou thresorie, ou chaunterie.] *c* **1440** *Promp. Parv.* 118 Denerye, *decanatus.* **1483** *Cath. Angl.* 95 A Deynrye, *decania.* **1534** *Act 26 Hen. VIII*, c. 3 §9 Any..Priorie, Arch-deaconry, Deanry..or any other benefice or promocion spirituall. **1588** J. UDALL *Diotrephes* (Arb.) 26 To beg the Byshoppricks, Deanries, and such great places. **1647** CLARENDON *Hist. Reb.* I. (1843) 37/2 When he could no longer keep the deanery of the chappel royal. **1706** HEARNE *Collect.* 25 Dec., Upon quitting his Deanery in the College [St. John's Oxford]. **1724** SWIFT *Drapier's Lett.* vii, The deanries all..are in the donation of the crown. **1848** MACAULAY *Hist. Eng.* II. vi. 87 The Deanery of Christ-church became vacant.

2. The group of parishes, forming a division of a diocese, over which a rural dean presides; formerly, also, the jurisdiction of a dean.

a **1440** *Found. St. Bartholomew's* xii. 47 A Preiste..that gouerynd the Chirche of seynt Martyn..had receyuyd one hym..the deynrye of nygh chirches for maters ecclesiasticall to discusse. **1587** HARRISON *Engl.* II. i. (1877) I. 15 Vnto these deanerie churches also the cleargie in old time of the same deanrie were appointed to repaire at sundrie seasons, there to receiue wholesome ordinances, and to consult. **1642** SIR E. DERING *Sp. on Relig.* 91 Appeale may be to the rurall Deanery. **1695** KENNETT *Par. Antiq.* (1818) II. 338 The bishops divided each diocese into deaneries or tithings, each of which was the district of ten parishes or churches. **1727–51** CHAMBERS *Cycl.* s.v. *Arches*, The judge of the court of arches, is called the dean of the arches..with which officialty is commonly joined a peculiar jurisdiction over thirteen parishes in London, termed a deanry. **1835** DANSEY *Horæ Dec. Rur.* I. 19 The division of dioceses at that time into decennaries or deanries. **1837** *Penny Cycl.* VIII. 340/1 The report of the Ecclesiastical Commissioners, 1835, recommends that each parish shall be assigned to a deanery, and each deanery to an archdeaconry. **1890** BP. WESTCOTT in *Durham Dioc. Gaz.* IV. 34 Some improvements will, I trust, be made in the assignment of parishes to the several Deaneries.

3. The official residence of a dean.

1598 SHAKS. *Merry W.* IV. vi. 31 And at the Deanry, where a Priest attends, Strait marry her. **1727** EARL OF OXFORD in *Swift's Lett.* 12 Oct., I was in hopes..that you would not have gone to your deanery till the Spring. **1855** MACAULAY *Hist. Eng.* IV. 251 Late at night he was brought to Westminster, and was suffered to sleep at his deanery.

4. *Comb.*, as † ***deanery church*** (the church of a rural dean), ***deanery house***.

1587 HARRISON *England* II. i. (1877) I. 15 But as the number of christians increased, so first monasteries, then finallie parish churches, were builded in euery iurisdiction: from whence I take our deanerie churches to haue their originale, now called mother churches, and their incumbents archpreests. **1720** SWIFT *Poems, Apollo to Dean*, That traitor Delany..seditiously came..To the deanery house.

deaness (ˈdiːnɪs). [f. DEAN¹ + -ESS.]

1. A woman who is head of a female chapter. [L. *decāna*, F. *doyenne*.]

1759 STERNE *Tr. Shandy* II. xxxv, The Abbess of Quedlingberg..with the four great dignitaries of her Chapter, the prioress, the deaness, the sub-chantress, and senior canoness. **1878** SEELEY *Stein* II. 347 Abbess v. Gilsa, Deaness vom Stein, and Canoness v. Metzsch.

2. *humorous.* The wife of a dean.

1848 E. RUSKIN *Let.* 1 July in W. M. James *Order of Release* (1948) v. 115 A large party today at the Master of Pembroke's..and ditto in the evening at the Deaness of Christ Church (Mrs. Gaisford). **1884** G. ALLEN *Philistia* I. 113 Fancy little Miss Butterfly a rural deaness!

ˈdea-nettle. *Obs.* exc. *dial.* Forms: 6– dee-, 8– day-, 9 dea-, deea-, deye-, dae-. [Generally held to be a reduction of *dead-nettle* (in Trevisa *deed-nettyll*); but the phonology is not clear.] A name given to the species of *Lamium* (DEAD-NETTLE) and other Labiates having nettle-like leaves; but in Scotland and the North of England more especially to the Hemp-nettle, *Galeopsis Tetrahit*, the acute calyx-segments of which, when dry and rigid, often wound the hands of reapers.

1523 FITZHERB. *Husb.* §20 There be other wedes not spoken of, as dee-nettylles, dodder, and suche other, that doo moche harme. **1788** MARSHALL *Rur. Econ. E. Yorksh.* Gloss., Dea-nettle, *galeopsis tetrahit*, wild hemp. **1853** G. JOHNSTON *Nat. Hist. E. Bord.* 162 Labourers in harvest are sometimes affected with whitlow, and they ascribe the disease invariably to the sting of the Deye-nettle. **1878** *Cumbrld. Gloss.*, Deäa, Dēea, *Dee nettle*, the dead nettle—*Lamium album.*

de-anglicize (diːˈæŋglɪsaɪz), *v.* [DE- II. 1.] *trans.* To remove English characteristics or influence from. Hence **de-angliciˈzation**; **de-ˈanglicized** *ppl. a.*; **de-ˈanglicizing** *vbl. sb.*

1883 F. HALL in *N.Y. Nation* XXXVII. 435/1 Deanglicized Englishmen. **1890** *Sat. Rev.* 15 Feb. 201/1 He even thinks we must de-anglicize our language. **1894** D. HYDE in C. G. Duffy et al. *Revival of Irish Lit.* 117 (*title*) The necessity for de-anglicising Ireland. **1901** *Daily Chron.* 22 Aug. 6/4 Talking about Celticism and de-Anglicisation. **1905** *Westm. Gaz.* 27 Nov. 5/1 The Gaelic revival meant the de-Anglicising of Ireland. **1961** *20th Cent.* CLXIX. 70 Mencken had launched his de-Anglicization campaign in literature.

de-ˈanimalize, *v.* [DE- II. 1.] *trans.* To deprive of its animal character.

1865 *Intell. Observer* XXXVIII. 96 The negative evidence..does not deanimalise it. **1887** E. P. POWELL *Heredity from God* 155 The tendency is to deanimalize the organs, and to create an intellectual type.

deanship (ˈdiːnʃɪp). [f. DEAN¹ + -SHIP.]

1. The office, position, or rank of a dean; the tenure of this office.

1611 COTGR., *Doyenné*, a Deanerie, or Deaneship. **1761** WARTON *Life Bathurst* 214 (T.) Those [chapter-acts] that were made during his deanship. **1827** COBBETT *Protestant Reform.* II. §47 The Bishopricks, the Parish-livings, the Deanships..are in fact all in their gift. **1881** *New Eng. Jrnl. Educ.* XXIV. 347 Prof. P. J. Williams to the deanship of the Normal department.

2. The personality of a dean: used humorously as a title.

1588 *Marprel. Epist.* (Arb.) 3 May it please you..to ride to Sarum and thanke his Deanship for it. **1729** SWIFT *Poems, Grand Question* xxxiii, I then shall not value his Deanship a straw. **1812** PARR *Let.* Dec. 12 Wks. (1828) VII. 470 His Deanship perhaps has brought from his escrutoire his old Concio for the Doctorate.

de-anthropoˈmorphize, *v.* [DE- II. 1.] *trans.* To deprive of its anthropomorphic character; to divest of its (attributed) human form. So **de-anthropomorph-iˈzation, -ized, -izing, -ism.**

1874 FISKE *Cosmic Philos.* I. 176 A continuous process of deanthropomorphization. **1879** J. JACOBS in *19th Cent.* Sept. 499 The deanthropomorphised Deity of Maimonides. **1884** *Pall Mall G.* 4 Jan. 4/2 The 'de-anthropomorphising' process will continue, says Mr. Spencer. **1886** ROMANES in *Contemp. Rev.* July 52 A continuous growth of 'deanthropomorphism'..passing through polytheism into monotheism..a progressive 'purification' of theism.

de-appetize, -ing: see DE- II. 1.

†**dear,** *sb.*[1] *Obs.* In 3–4 dere. [app. repr. an unrecorded OE. *díeru, *déoru = OHG. *tiurî*, MHG. *tiure*, OLG. *diuri* fem. preciousness, glory, high value, dearness, dearth. Cf. DEAR *a.*[1]] Dearness, dearth.

1297 R. GLOUC. (1724) 416 Gret..dere of þyng þe seuene ȝer me say. *c* **1300** *Havelok* 824 A strong dere Bigan to rise of korn of bred. *Ibid.* 841, I wene that we deye mone For hunger, þis dere is so strong. *c* **1330** R. BRUNNE *Chron. Wace* (Rolls) 16419 In his tyme failled þe corn..Of þat defaute cam gret dere [*et en après fu la cherté*].

dear (dɪə(r)), *a.*[1] and *sb.*[2] Forms: 1 díore, déore, dýre, 2–3 deore, 2 dære, 3–6 dere, (3 dure, diȝere, 4 dir, diere, dyere), 4–5 der, 4–7 deere, (4 duere, 5 deure), 5–6 deyr, 5–7 deir, 6–7 deare, 6– dear; 5–6 *Sc. compar.* darrer, *superlat.* darrest. [OE. *déore*, earlier *díore*; in early WS. *díere*, late WS. *dýre* (but also *déore* as in non-WS.); a Com. Teut. adj., = OFris. *diore*, *diure* (WFris. *djoer*, EFris. *dūr*). MDu. *diere*, *dûre* (Du. *dier* beloved, *diuer* high-priced), OS. *diuri* (MLG. *düre*, LG. *dūr*), OHG. *tiuri* glorious, distinguished, worthy, costly (MHG. *tiure*, *tiur*, MG. *türe*, Ger. *teuer*), ON. *dýrr* worthy, precious, costly (Sw., Da. *dyr*); Goth. not recorded. These forms point to OTeut. type **deur-jo-*, **diur-jo-*.]

A. *adj.* I. Of persons:

†**1. a.** Glorious, noble, honourable, worthy. *Obs.*

a **1000** *Riddles* xxxiv. (Gr.), Is min modor mæȝþa cynnes þæs deorestan. *c* **1000** *Ags. Ps.* cxvii. 10 On Dryhtnes naman deorum. *c* **1340** *Gaw. & Gr. Knt.* 445 To-ward þe derrest on þe dece he dressez þe face. **1375** *Cant. de Creatione* 701 in *Anglia* I, I am Michel, þe angel dere Ordeyned abouen man. ? *a* **1400** *Morte Arth.* 1601 Þe dere kynge hyme selfene Comaundyd syr Cadore with his dere knyghttes..To ryde with þe Romaynes. *a* **1400–50** *Alexander* 4644, I, sir Dyndyn þe derrest at duells in þis Ile, þe best of þe bragmeyns. *c* **1450** HOLLAND *Howlat* 281 With dukis and with digne lordis, darrest in dale. **1595** T. EDWARDES *Cephalus & P., L'Envoy* (1878) 61–2 Oh deere sonnes of stately kings. **1596** SHAKS. *1 Hen. IV*, IV. iv. 31 Corriuals and deare men Of estimation and command. **1606** —— *Tr. & Cr.* V. iii. 27 Life euery man holds deere, but the deere man Holds honor farre more precious, deere, then life.

b. Often used *absol.*

c **1325** *E.E. Allit. P.* B. 1394 Dere droȝen þer-to & vpon des metten. *c* **1420** *Anturs of Arth.* i, Wythe dukys, and with dosiperus, that with the deure dwellus.

2. a. Regarded with personal feelings of high estimation and affection; held in deep and tender esteem; beloved, loved.

† *to have dear, hold dear*: to love [= Ger. *lieb haben*, Du. *liefhebben*].

The earlier sense was that of 'esteemed, valued' rather than 'loved' (= Ger. *teuer*, not *lieb*), but the passage of the one notion into the other is too gradual to admit of their separation.

a **1000** *Juliana* 725 (Gr.) Fæder frofre gæst..and se deora sunu. *c* **1000** *Ags. Gosp.* Luke vii. 2 Sumes hundred-mannes þeowa..se wæs him dyre. *c* **1205** LAY. 4377 Þe king haueð ane dohter þe him is swuðe dure [*c* **1275** þat he loueth swiþe]. *a* **1300** *Cursor M.* 3626 (Cott.) Mi leue sone..þou ert mi derest barn. *Ibid.* 20133 (Cott.) Saint iohn hir keped & had ful dere. *c* **1386** CHAUCER *Knt.'s T.* 590 Ther nas no man that Theseus hath so derre. *c* **1435** *Torr. Portugal* 931, I have a dowghttyr that ys me dere. **1526** *Pilgr. Perf.* (W. de W. 1531) 291 His dere darlynges and well beloved frendes. **1535** STEWART *Cron. Scot.* II. 174 He that wes his darrest sone in law. **1644** MILTON *Educ.* Wks. (1847) 100/1 Dear to God, and famous to all Ages. **1650** W. BROUGH *Sacr. Princ.* (1659) 138 All those Thou hast made near and dear unto me. **1797** MRS. RADCLIFFE *Italian* xiii, Ellena, you have long witnessed how dear you are to me. **1891** E. PEACOCK *N. Brendon* I. 225 He was a very dear friend of mine.

b. Used in addressing a person, in affection or regard.

c **1250** *Gen. & Ex.* 1569 Fader dere, bidde ic ðe, Ðat sum bliscing gif ðu me. *c* **1314** *Guy Warw.* (A.) 3375 Mi dere frende Gij. *c* **1340** *Cursor M.* 10483 (Trin.) Dere god here preyere myne. *c* **1489** CAXTON *Sonnes of Aymon* xxii. 470 'Dere syre', sayd the duke Naymes, 'ye sende vs for noughte.' **1641** *More's Edw. V*, 12 My Lords, my deare kinsmen and allies. **1737** POPE *Hor. Ep.* I. vi. 3 Plain truth, dear Murray, needs no flow'rs of speech. **1820** SHELLEY *Œdipus* I. 102 Why what's the matter, my dear fellow, now? **1875** JOWETT *Plato* (ed. 2) I. 277 Do not all men, my dear sir, desire good?

c. In the introductory address or subscription of a letter. ***Dear John***, as *sb.* (chiefly *N. Amer.*): see quot. 1945; also *transf.* and *attrib.*

Dear Father, Brother, Friend, Dear John, and the like, are still affectionate and intimate, and made more so by prefixing *My*; but *Dear Sir* (or *Dear Mr. A.*) has become since the 17th c. the ordinary polite form of addressing an equal.

1450 Q. MARGT. in *Four C. Eng. Lett.* 7 Right dere and welbeloved. **1503–4** Q. MARGT. (of Scotl.) *to Hen. VII* in Ellis *Orig. Lett.* I. I. 41 My most dere lorde and fader. **1516** —— *to Hen. VIII*, ibid. I. 129 Derest broder, As hartly as I can I recomend me onto you. *a* **1610** MERIEL LITTLETON *to Mrs. Barnaby*, ibid. II. III. 218 Deare Aunt, I ame as willinge [etc.]. **1623** DK. BUCKINGHAM *to Jas. I*, ibid. III. 146 Dere Dad, Gossope, and Steward. **1628** ABP. USHER *Let. to Sir R. Cotton* in *Lett. Emin. Lit. Men* (Camden) 138 Deare Sir, I know not who should beginne first [etc.]. **1656** JER. TAYLOR *Let.* in *Evelyn's Mem.* (1857) III. 72 Believe that I am, in great heartiness and dearness of affection, Dear Sir, your obliged and most affectionate friend and servant J. Taylor. **1665** PEPYS *to Lady Carteret* 4 Sept., Dear Madam, Your Ladyship will not (I hope) imagine [etc.]. **1690** HARRISON *to Strype* in Ellis *Orig. Lett.* II. IV. 209 Dear Sir, after some few days stay at Liverpool for a wind [etc.]. **1757** R. SYMMER *to A. Mitchell* ibid. IV. 392 Dear Mitchell, I write a few lines [etc.]. **1865** G. M. HOPKINS *Let.* 28 Aug. (1935) 1 Dear Bridges,—I left Manchester more than a month ago. **1908** D. H. LAWRENCE *Let.* 4 May (1962) I. 7 Dear Miss Jennings: With hot, boyish, impatience I looked for a letter from you. **1945** *Democrat & Chron.* (Rochester, N.Y.) 17 Aug. 17/2 'Dear John,' the letter began. 'I have found someone else whom I think the world of. I think the only way out is for us to get a divorce,' it said. They usually began like that, those letters that told of infidelity on the part of the wives of servicemen... The men called them 'Dear Johns'. **1947** *Amer. Speech* XXII. 187 It was a 'Dear John'. Quite a lot of the fellows had already had their 'Dear Johns'. **1957** W. CAMP *Prospects of Love* xvi. 103 There was a note from Fenny on the kitchen table. For the moment he enjoyed the irony of thinking it might be what the Americans called a 'dearjohn'. **1964** J. PHILIPS *Laughter Trap* (1965) I. ii. 13 Peter..had gone to war..in love with a girl named Elizabeth Schofield... He had received a 'Dear John' letter from Elizabeth, telling him she was married. **1970** *Post Office Subscriber Trunk Dialling: Dialling Instructions (London)* 1 Dear Customer, In 1966 we changed your old 3 letter and 4 figure numbering to all figures. **1971** *Guardian* 7 Jan. 11/8 The going is getting distinctively gritty for Pan Am, so much so that 1,876 of its staff are now walking round with a new year 'Dear John' from..the airline's president.

d. The adj. is often used *absol.* = 'dear one', especially in 'dear' or 'my dear' addressed to a person; also in the superlative degree, 'dearest', 'my dearest'. Its use otherwise than in address, as in 'his dear', leads to its treatment as a sb., for which see B.

a **1225** *Ancr. R.* 98 Hwo haueð ihurt te, mi deore? **1362** LANGL. *P. Pl.* A. VII. 241 Lere hit me, my deore. **1590** SHAKS. *Mids. N.* V. 286 O dainty Ducke: O Deere! **1611** —— *Wint. T.* I. ii. 88 Hermione (my dearest). *Ibid.* IV. iii. 15 Shall I go mourne for that (my deere)? *a* **1631** DONNE *Poems* (1650) 14 And, Deare, I die As often as from thee I goe. **1712** TICKELL *Spect.* No. 410 ¶6, I therefore came abroad to meet my Dear, And lo, in happy Hour I find thee here. **1813** MAR. EDGEWORTH *Patron.* II. xxiii. 57 'Really, my dear', answered she, 'I can't say.' **1833** HT. MARTINEAU *Berkeley* I. vii. 143 Do not exhaust yourself at once, dearest. **1879** MISS BRADDON *Clov. Foot* xxxviii, 'I am not in the clouds, dear; I am only anxious.'

e. ***dearest friend*** may have suggested ***dearest enemy*** or ***foe***; but see also DEAR *a.*[2] 2.

1596 SHAKS. *1 Hen. IV*, III. ii. 123 Which art my neer'st and dearest Enemie. **1602** —— *Ham.* I. ii. 180 Would I had met my dearest foe in heauen Ere I had [etc.]. **1818** SHELLEY *Rev. Islam* XI. xv, O that I..could set my dearest enemy free From pain and fear!

†**3.** The attribute is sometimes transferred to the subject of the feeling: Affectionate, loving, fond.

1602 SHAKS. *Ham.* I. ii. 111 With no lesse Nobility of Loue, Then that which deerest Father beares his Sonne. **1610** —— *Temp.* I. ii. 179 Bountifull Fortune (Now my deere Lady). **1653** WALTON *Angler* Ep. Ded., Sir Henry Wotton, a dear lover of this Art.

II. Of things.

†**4. a.** Of high estimation, of great worth or value; precious, valuable. *Obs.*

c **888** K. ÆLFRED *Boeth.* xiii, God word and god hlisa ælces monnes biþ betera & deorra þonne æniȝ wela. *c* **893** —— *Oros.* v. ii. (Sw.) 216/5 Corrinthisce fatu..sint fæȝran & dierran þonne æneȝu oþru. *c* **1200** ORMIN 6732 Rihht all swa summ hord off gold Mang menn iss horde deresst. *c* **1325** *E.E. Allit. P.* B. 1792 Now is a dogge also dere þat in a dych lygges. *c* **1400** *Destr. Troy* 1683 Dubbed ouer with dyamondes, þat were dere holdyn. **1470–85** MALORY *Arthur* I. xvii, There may no rychesse be to dere for them. **1500–20** DUNBAR *Thistle & Rose* 101 And crownit him with dyademe full deir. **1596** SHAKS. *Merch. V.* I. i. 62 Your worth is very deere in my regard. *c* **1600** —— *Sonn.* xxx, And with old woes new wail my dear time's waste.

†**b.** Precious in import or significance; important. *Obs.*

1592 SHAKS. *Rom. & Jul.* V. ii. 19 The Letter was not nice, but full of charge, Of deare import, and the neglecting it May do much danger. **1596** —— *1 Hen. IV*, IV. i. 34 So dangerous and deare a trust. **1605** —— *Lear* III. i. 19 Sir, I do know you, And dare..commend a deere thing to you.

†**c.** In weakened sense of 'precious'. *Obs.*

1530 PALSGR. 539 You have erred many a dere daye ..*maynt jour*. **15..** *Tournam. Tottenham* 10 It befel in Totenham on a dere day, Ther was mad a shurtyng be the hy-way. **1596** SHAKS. *Merch. V.* III. v. 70 O deare discretion, how his words are suted.

5. a. The preceding passed gradually into a sense in which personal affection or attachment became the predominant notion as in 2 above: Precious in one's regard, of which one is fond, to which one is greatly attached.

c **1175** *Pater Noster* 34 in *Lamb. Hom.* 57 Þis is þe furste bode here, þet we aȝen to habben deore. *c* **1250** *Gen. & Ex.* 3483 His word ȝu wurðe diȝere al-so lif, Diȝere or eiðer child or wif. *c* **1450** *St. Cuthbert* (Surtees) 3703 Our haly faders statutes dere. **1535** COVERDALE *Ps.* cxv. 3 Right deare in the sight of ye Lorde is the death of his sayntes. **1593** SHAKS. *Rich. II*, II. i. 57 This Land of such deere soules, this deere-deere Land, Deere for her reputation through the world. **1651** HOBBES *Leviath.* II. xxx. 179 Those that are dearest to a man are his own life and limbs. **1742** FIELDING *J. Andrews* II. iv, Bellarmine, in the dear coach and six, came to wait on her. **1746** HERVEY *Medit.* (1818) 209 Liberty, that dearest of names; and property, that best of charters. **1848** MACAULAY *Hist. Eng.* II. 306 Those ties, once so close and dear, which had bound the Church of England to the House of Stuart. **1866** PR. ALICE *Mem.* (1884) 158 How dear of you to have written to me on the 14th. **1891** *Anti-Jacobin* 17 Oct. 903/2 Clad in the black surtout dear to bourgeois taste.

†**b.** Affectionate, fond, loving. *Obs.* or *rare.*

1591 SHAKS. *Two Gent.* IV. iii. 14 Thou art not ignorant what deere good will I beare vnto the banish'd Valentine. *c* **1600** —— *Sonn.* cxxxi, For well thou know'st to my dear doting heart Thou art the fairest and most precious jewel. **1683** *Pennsylv. Archives* I. 70 With dear Love in ye lasting truth I salute thee. *a* **1866** KEBLE *Lett. Spir. Counsel* (1870) 35 My dear love to —— and ——.

c. Often as an attribute of *life, heart, heart's blood*, etc., as things dear to one. ***to ride*** (etc.) ***for dear life***: to ride for one's life, as a thing dear to one; to ride as though life were at stake. Cf. next.

1591 SHAKS. *1 Hen. VI*, III. iv. 40 Or else this Blow should broach thy dearest Bloud. **1602** —— *Ham.* III. ii. 68 Since my deere Soule was Mistris of my choyse. **1604** —— *Oth.* III. iii. 261 Though that her Iesses were my deere heart-strings. **1703** ROWE *Fair Penit.* II. i. 413 My dear Peace of Mind is lost for ever. **1793** BURNS '*Scots wha hae*' v, We will drain our dearest veins But..they shall be free. **1887** FRITH *Autobiog.* I. xxi. 279 Never so happy as when galloping for dear life after a pack of hounds. **1892** *Boy's Own Paper* Nov. 58/2 The men were working for 'dear life' to get her [the cutter] ready for sail.

6. a. Of a high price, high-priced, absolutely or relatively; costly, expensive: the opposite of *cheap*.

1044 *O.E. Chron.*, On ðisum ȝere wæs swyðe mycel hunger ofer eall Englaland and corn swa dyre..swa þæt se sester hwætes eode to LX pen. **1154** *Ibid.* an. 1137 §3 Þa was corn dære. *c* **1320** *Seuyn Sag.* 3724 (W.) Than so bifell that corn was dere. **1375** BARBOUR *Bruce* XVIII. 283 This is the derrest beiff that I Saw euir ȝeit; for sekirly It cost ane thousand pund and mar. **1509** HAWES *Past. Pleas.* IV. xix, Nothynge I wanted, were it chepe or dere. **1595** SHAKS. *John* I. i. 153 Sell your face for fiue pence and 'tis deere. **1668** ROLLE *Abridgment* 40 He swore, that the Wood was worth 40s. where it was dear of 13s. 4d. **1745** *De Foe's Eng. Tradesman* (1841) II. xxxviii. 109 Our manufactures..may be dear, though low-priced, if they are mean in their value. **1857** RUSKIN *Pol. Econ. Art* ii. (1868) 89 Pictures ought not to be too dear, that is to say, not as dear as they are.

b. Said of *prices, rates*: = High. Now less usual.

c **1250** *Gen. & Ex.* 2247 Fruit and spices of dere pris. **1502** ARNOLDE *Chron.* (1811) 128 He bought the said peper at derrar price. **1582–8** *Hist. James VI* (1804) 169 And pat the timber to the mercat to be sauld at the darrest price be the weyght. **1654** tr. *Martini's Conq. China* 37 Considering at how dear a rate he had bought the mastering of that City. **1750** JOHNSON *Rambler* No. 46 ¶3 Privileges, which I have purchased at so dear a rate. **1891** *Law Times* XCI. 33/1 Economy is a good thing, but you may pay for it..at far too dear a price.

c. Said of a time or place in which prices for provisions, etc. are high; ***dear year***, a year of dearth; also of a dealer who charges high prices.

c **1290** *S. Eng. Leg.* 278/25 A deore ȝer þare cam. *c* **1400** MAUNDEV. (1839) v. 44 Therfore is there dere Tyme in that Contree. **1535** COVERDALE *Ps.* xxxii. 19 To fede them in the deare tyme. **1596** SHAKS. *1 Hen. IV*, III. iii. 52 The dearest Chandlers in Europe. **1637** RUTHERFORD *Lett.* (1862) I. 216 The hard fare of the dear inn. *a* **1661** FULLER *Worthies* (1840) II. 501 It is the dearest town in England for fuel. **1765** MRS. HARRIS in *Priv. Lett. Ld. Malmesbury* I. 122, I have myself paid Mademoiselle Peignerelle..In my life I never saw so dear a woman. **1888** BRYCE *Amer. Commw.* III. cxiv. 640 To..send it..by the cheapest routes to the dearest markets.

d. *fig.* Costly in other than a pecuniary sense; difficult to procure; scarce.

a **1330** *Otuel* 1680 Þo alle foure weren ifere, There nere none strokes dere. *a* **1533** LD. BERNERS *Gold. Bk. M. Aurel.* (1546) K vj b, Thou art so dere in vertues, and makeste vyces good chepe. **1535** COVERDALE *1 Sam.* iii. 1 The worde of ye Lorde was deare at the same tyme. **1553** KENNEDY *Compend. Tract.* in *Wodr. Soc. Misc.* (1844) 159 And therefore is deir of the rehersing, because it wes evir misknawin to the Kirk of God. **1576** TURBERV. *Venerie* 248 The experience which hath bene dearer unto me particularly than it is meete to be published generally.

e. Of money: that can be borrowed only at a high rate of interest.

1878 [see MONEY *sb.* 3 c]. **1930** *Economist* 1 Feb. 239/2 A year of dear money, when Bank rate averaged a full one per cent. above the level of 1928.

†**7.** Senses vaguely connected with the prec. *Obs.*

It is possible that a was influenced by DEAR *a.*[2]

a. 'Heartfelt; hearty; hence earnest' (Schmidt).

1588 SHAKS. *L.L.L.* II. i. 1 Now Madam summon vp your dearest spirits. **1596** —— *1 Hen. IV*, V. v. 36 You Sonne John..Towards Yorke shall bend you, with your deerest speed. **1606** —— *Tr. & Cr.* V. iii. 9 Consort with me in loud and deere petition: Pursue we him on knees.

b. ? Rare, unusual, or ? loving, kind.

1592 SHAKS. *Rom. & Jul.* III. iii. 28 This is deare [Qo. 1 meare] mercy, and thou seest it not.

†**8.** ***to think dear***: to seem right or proper; to seem good. *Const.* with dative as in *methinks*.

1340–70 *Alex. & Dind.* 1133 Whan þis makelese man..Hadde..lettrus..Endited to dindimus as him dere þoute. *c* **1400** *Destr. Troy* 2391 To deme as þe dere thinke. *a* **1400–50** *Alexander* 1638 To do with Darius..how so me dere thinke.

B. as *sb.* = Dear one, darling.

This comes from A. 2 d, through intermediate uses like 'I met my dear', 'he found his dear', in which the adj., although capable of being compared ('his dearest'), can also be treated as a sb. with plural *dears*.

c **1400** *Destr. Troy* 9225 On suche couenaund to kepe, yf þat dere wold. *c* **1460** *Towneley Myst.* 281 Waloway! my lefe deres, there I stand in this sted. **1590** SPENSER *F.Q.* I. vi. 16 From that day forth Duessa was his deare. **1611** SHAKS. *Wint. T.* IV. iv. 227 Golden Quoifes, and Stomachers For my Lads, to giue their deers. **1709** PRIOR *Epil. to Phaedra*, The Spouse alone, impatient for her Dear. **1782** COWPER *Gilpin* 19 You are she, my dearest dear, Therefore it shall be done. **1824** BRYON *Juan* xv. lxxvi, Things Are somehow echoed to the pretty dears. **1856** WHYTE MELVILLE *Kate Cov.* xi, Come on, there's a dear! **1880** MISS BRADDON *Just as I am* xlv, You are such a devoted old dear.

C. Used interjectionally. ***Dear!, Oh dear!, Dear, dear!, Dear me!***: exclamations expressing surprise, astonishment, anxiety, distress, regret, sympathy, or other emotion. ***dear bless, help, love, save us*** (*you*): ejaculations of astonishment, usually implying an appeal for higher help (*obs.* or *dial.*). ***dear knows!*** goodness knows, Heaven knows (*I* do not).

These uses with a verb suggest that *dear* represents or implies a fuller *dear Lord!* Thus *dear knows!* is exactly equivalent to *the Lord* or *God knows!*; cf. also the elliptical *Save us! Help us! Keep us!* and the like; but the historical evidence is not conclusive. (A derivation from It. *dio*, God, as conjectured by some, resting upon mod. Eng. pronunciation of *dea(r*, finds no support in the history of the word.)

1694 CONGREVE *Double Dealer* v. xxii, O dear, you make me blush. **1719** A. RAMSAY *Ep. J. Arbuckle* 27 Then did ideas dance (dear safe us!) As they'd been daft. **1769** MAD. D'ARBLAY *Early Diary* (1889) I. 36 O dear! O dear! how melancholy has been to us this last week. *Ibid.*, O dear! I shall die. **1773** GOLDSM. *Stoops to Conq.* IV, Dear me! dear me! I'm sure there is nothing in my behavior to put me on a level with one of that stamp. **1805** E. CAVANAGH *Let.* 4 Oct. in Londonderry & Hyde *Russian Jrnls. of M. & C. Wilmot* (1934) III. 190, I never seen such a good Lady..nor so generous I've reason to say dear knows. *c* **1813** MRS. SHERWOOD *Stories Ch. Catech.* ix. 65 'O, dear!' says Mrs. Hicks, 'do you think I am like your fine folks?' **1818** —— *Fairchild Fam.* xii. (1829) 98 'Dear! how tiresome it must be to be so religious!' **1838** DICKENS *O. Twist* iv, Dear me!.. he's very small. **1844** —— *Mart. Chuz.* xlv, Hers was not a flinty heart. Oh dear no! **1839** CATH. SINCLAIR *Holiday House* iii. 40 'Oh dear! oh dear! what shall I do?' cried Harry. **1849** LYTTON *Caxtons* 17 'Dear, dear', cried my mother ..'my poor flower pot that I prized so much.' **1876** *White Cross* xxxvii. 236 'Dear knows', said Catharine, 'when we shall see them back.' **1880** *Antrim & Down Gloss.*, *Dear bless you!.. Dear help you!.. Dear knows*, a common rejoinder, meaning 'who knows' or 'nobody knows', probably meant originally, 'God only knows'. *Dear love you!* God love you, an exclamation. **1914–15** JOYCE *Portrait of Artist* (1916) v. 203 The dear knows you might try to be in time for your lectures. **1969** *Outlook* Mar. 226 The curate waded out into the sea of dear knows what but mostly rubbish.

†**dear, dere,** *a.*[2] *poetic. Obs.* or *arch.* Forms: 1 dior, déor, 3–5 dere, 6–7 deere, deare, 7– dear. [OE. *déor*; not known in the cognate langs., and of uncertain etymology.

By some held to be intimately related to OE. *déor* animal (see DEER). By others thought to contain the same radical form as DEAR *a.*[1], and to differ only in the stem-suffix (**deur-o-*). In OE., from the levelling of *o-* stems and *jo-* stems, *déor* was formally distinguishable from *déore* only in the nom. sing. (of all genders), the acc. sing. neuter, and nom. acc. pl. neuter, which had *déor*, as against *déore, déoru* (*-o*). Hence, when the final *-e* was lost or mute in ME., the two words became entirely identical in form. But in OE., their senses appear to have been quite distinct; and, in later times, the sense of *dere, dear*, from *déor* was highly incongruous with those developed from *déore* (though intermediate or connecting links of meaning also arose). This difference of sense is a serious objection to the view that the two words are merely different formations from the same base, as in the pairs *strong strenge, weorð wierðe*, etc., where the two forms agree in sense. The ultimate etymology has been discussed by Karsten, *Mod. Lang. Notes*, 1892, 345.

Common in OE. poetry, but found in no prose writing. In ME. poetry, not known in southern writers, but in the East-Midland *Genesis & Exodus*, the West Midland *Allit. Poems, Gawain & Green Knight, Piers Plowman*, and the metrical *Destruction of Troy* (all these except the first being alliterative); it then appears in Spenser (by whom it was perhaps revived), occurs frequently in Shakspere, in 17th c. poets, and archaically in Shelley. By these later writers it was probably conceived of only as a peculiar poetical sense of DEAR *a.*[1], and there are uses in Shakspere evidently associated with both sense-groups.]

†**1.** Brave, bold, strenuous, hardy. *Obs.*

a **1000** *Andreas* 1310 (Gr.) Se halᵹa wæs to hofe læded, deor and domᵹeorn. —— *Cædmon's Satan* 543 Ðæt wæs se deora, Didimus wæs haten. —— *Sal. & Sat.* 387 For hwam nele mon..ᵹeorne ᵹewyrcan deores dryhtscipes. —— *Seaman's Lament* 41 Nis mon in his dædum to ðæs deor. *Ibid.* 76 Deorum dædum. [*c* **1450** *Golagros & Gaw.* I. 9 Dukis and digne lordis, douchty and deir.]

2. Hard, severe, heavy, grievous; fell, dire. *arch.*

Beowulf (Th.) 4186 Dior dædfruma. *a* **1000** *Cædmon's Daniel* (Gr.) 372 Deor scur. *a* **1000** *Sal. & Sat.* 122 Swenga ne wyrnaþ deorra dynta. *Ibid.* 361 Ne mæᵹ man foryldan þone deoran siþ. *c* **1250** *Gen. & Ex.* 3742 He ben smiten in sorwes dere. *c* **1325** *E.E. Allit. P.* B. 214 Dryᵹtyn with his dere dom hym drof to þe abyme. *c* **1340** *Gaw. & Gr. Knt.* 564 Of destinees derf & dere, What may mon do bot fonde. **1377** LANGL. *P. Pl.* B. XIV. 171 May no derth ben hem [riche men] dere, drouth, ne wete. *c* **1400** *Destr. Troy* 920 Withdroghe the deire of his dere attur. **1590** SPENSER *F.Q.* II. v. 38 On him that did Pyrochles deare dismay. *Ibid.* II. xi. 34 To seize upon his foe..Which now him turnd to disadvantage deare. **1593** SHAKS. *Rich. II*, I. iii. 151 The datelesse limit of thy deere exile. *c* **1600** —— *Sonn.* xxxvii, I, made lame by Fortunes dearest spight. **1607** —— *Timon* v. i. 231 What other meanes is left vnto vs In our deere perill. **1607** DELONEY *Strange Hist.* (1841) 14 But this their meriment did turne to deare annoy. *a* **1626** MIDDLETON *Mayor of Q.* IV. ii, Here's no dear villainy. **1637** MILTON *Lycidas* 6 Bitter constraint and sad occasion dear Compels me to disturb your season due. **1819** SHELLEY *Cenci* v. iv. 32 Now I forget them at my dearest need.

†**3.** Hard, difficult. *Obs.*

a **1225** *Leg. Kath.* 948 For nis him no derure for to adweschen feole þen fewe. *c* **1230** *Hali Meid.* 21 Eauer se deore þing se is derure to bewitene. **1340** HAMPOLE *Pr. Consc.* 1469 Now eese us a thyng, now fele we it dere.

dear (dɪə(r)), *adv.* For forms see DEAR *a.*[1] [OE. *díore, déore* = OHG. *tiuro*, MHG. *tiure, tiuwer*, G. *teuer* : in OE., through the reduction of the termination to *e*, not distinct in form from DEAR *a.*[1] in Anglian.]

1. At a high price; at great cost; usually with such verbs as *buy, cost, pay, sell*, etc. (See also ABY *v.*, BUY *v.* 3, COST *v.* 2 b, etc.)

a **1000** *Boeth. Metr.* xxvi. 37 Diore ᵹecepte drihten Creca Troia burh. *c* **1000** ÆLFRIC *Voc.* in Wr.-Wülcker 130 *Care uendidit*, deore he hit bohte vel sealde. *c* **1200** *Trin. Coll. Hom.* 213 þe sullere loueð his þing dere and seið þat it is wel wurð oðer betere. *a* **1225** *Ancr. R.* 392 Ure luue..þet kostnede him so deorre. *c* **1374** CHAUCER *Anel. & Arc.* 2155 Ellas youre love I bie it all to dere. *c* **1400** MAUNDEV. (Roxb.) viii. 29 It es salde wonder dere. *c* **1440** *Bone Flor.* 1479 Be god, he seyde, that boght me dere. **1574** tr. *Littleton's Tenures* 82 b, To have solde the tenementes more deerer to some other. **1600** J. PORY tr. *Leo's Africa* II. 127 Each pretious..thing, though it costeth deere, yet if it be beautifull it..be good cheape. **1677** YARRANTON *Eng. Improv.* 7 The people there [Holland] pay great Taxes, and eat dear. **1774** GOLDSM. *Nat. Hist.* (1776) II. 350 Horses.. are sold extremely dear. **1822** SCOTT *Pirate* xix, That knowledge, which was to cost us both so dear. **1833** HT. MARTINEAU *Cinnamon & P.* vii. 124 It must do without some articles..or pay dear for them.

2. = DEARLY *adv.* 2. (In quots 1601, 1606, perh. associated with DEAR *a.*[2])

c **1314** *Guy Warw.* (A.) 152 þerl him loued swiþe dere, Ouer al oþer þat þer were. *a* **1400** *Destr. Troy* 583 If destyny me demys, hi is dere welcum. *a* **1400–50** *Alexander* 5143 All was done as scho demed & he hire dere thankis. **1485** CAXTON *Chas. Gt.* 30 He was byloued & dere reputed of euery body. **1548–9** (Mar.) *Bk. Com. Prayer* 127 Through thy most dere beloued sonne. **1592** SHAKS. *Rom. & Jul.* II. iii. 66 Is Rosaline that thou didst loue so deare So soone forsaken? **1601** —— *Jul. C.* III. i. 196 Shall it not greeue thee deerer then thy death. **1606** SYLVESTER *Du Bartas* II. iv. II. 248 Let that All-Powerfull dear-drad Prince descend. **1807** BYRON *Ho. Idleness, To E. N. Long* 99 The dear-loved peaceful seat.

dear (dɪə(r)), *v.* [f. DEAR *a.*[1]]

1. *trans.* To make dear or expensive; to raise the price of. *Sc. Obs. rare.*

1424 *Sc. Acts Jas. I* (1814) 7 (Jam.) That na vittalis..be deryt apon our lorde the kyngis men in ony place. **14..** *Chalmerlan Ayr* in *Sc. Stat.* I. 700/2 þai deir þe kingis mercate and þe cuntre of eggis bying. **1462** *Edinb. Rec.* (1870) 7 Oct. (Jam. Supp.), That na neichtbour tak in hand to by the saidis victualis or tymmer to regrait and deir agane upoun the nychtbouris.

†**2.** To endear. *Obs. rare.*

1603 J. DAVIES *Microcosmos* Wks. (1876) 64 (D.) He is his Sire, in nature dear'd.

3. To address (a person) as 'dear'; so to ***dear sir, dear cousin.*** *nonce-use.*

1816 SCOTT *Antiq.* v, I have no leisure to be *Dear Sirring* myself. *Ibid.* xli, He *dears* me too, you see. **1829** MARRYAT *F. Mildmay* xxiv, Don't dear *me*, Sir Hurricane, I am not one of *your dears.* **1875** TENNYSON *Q. Mary* III. iv, Their two graces Do so dear-cousin and royal-cousin him.

dear, obs. form of DEER, DERE.

dearborn (ˈdɪəbɔːn). *U.S.* [From the name of the inventor.] A vehicle, a kind of light four-wheeled wagon used in country districts in parts of the United States.

1841 CATLIN *N. Amer. Ind.* (1844) II. xlv. 81 He had purchased at St. Louis a very comfortable dearborn waggon. **1844** *Blackw. Mag.* LVI. 641, I resolved to leave my gig at New Orleans, procuring in its stead a sort of dearborn or railed cart. **1881** *Harper's Mag.* 181 The country people bring their produce to town in carts, dearborns, and market-wagons.

'dear-'bought, *a.* [DEAR *adv.*] Bought at a high price, obtained at great cost.

c **1384** CHAUCER *H. Fame* III. 662 For that is dere boghte honour. **1562** J. HEYWOOD *Prov. & Epigr.* (1867) 31 Dere bought and far fet Are deinties for Ladies. **1591** SHAKS. *1 Hen. VI*, I. i. 252 Englands deere bought Queen. **1719** DE FOE *Crusoe* (1840) I. xiv. 232 Dear-bought experience. **1813** SCOTT *Rokeby* III. xxii, Our dear-bought victory.

†**dearch, derch,** Sc. var. *duergh*, obs. f. DWARF.

c **1500** KENNEDIE in *Flyting w. Dunbar* 33 Dreid, dirtfast dearch. *Ibid.* 395 Duerch [*v.r.* derch] I sall ding the.

deare, obs. f. DARE *v.*[2], DEAR, DEER, DERE.

dearfe, var. of DERF *Obs.*

†**deargen'tation.** *Obs. rare*[−0]. [f. L. *deargentāre* to plate with silver, f. *de-* (DE- I. 3) + *argentum* silver.] 'A laying over with silver' (Bailey, vol. II. 1727).

†**'dearing.** *Obs. ? nonce-wd.* [f. DEAR *sb.*[2] + -ING (? for the sake of the rime).] Darling.

1601 J. WEEVER *Mirr. Martyrs* B vii b, The seauenth not appearing..Venus white dove, and Mars his onely dearing.

†**dear joy.** *Obs.* A familiar appellation for an Irishman.

1688 *Vox Cleri pro Rege* 47 It seems his Power is absolute, but, not arbitrary, which is, like a Dear-Joy's Witticism, a distinction without a difference. **1698** FARQUHAR *Love & Bottle* v. iii, Oh my dear Roebuck!—And faith is it you, dear joy. **1699** B. E. *Dict. Cant. Crew, Dear Joies*, Irishmen. **1710** *Brit. Apollo* II. *Quarterly No.* 3. 7/2 A Dear Joy, by Shaint Patrick's Shoe-Buckle..With Usquebaugh warm'd.

dearling, obs. form of DARLING.

dearly (ˈdɪəlɪ), *adv.* Forms: see DEAR *a.*[1] [OE. *déorlíce*, = OS. *diurlíco*, OHG. *tiurlíhho*, f. OE. *déorlíc* glorious, precious, OS. *diurlîc*, OHG. *tiurlîh*, f. DEAR *a.*[1]: see -LY[2].]

†**1.** In a precious, worthy, or excellent manner; worthily, choicely, finely, richly. *Obs.*

a **1000** CYNEWULF *Elene* 1159 (Z.) To hwam hio þa næᵹlas [i.e. of the cross] selost and deorlicost ᵹedon meahte. *c* **1325** *E.E. Allit. P.* A. 994 As derely deuysez þis ilk toun, In apocalyppez þe apostel Iohan. **1377** LANGL. *P. Pl.* B. XIX. 2, I..diᵹte me derely & dede me to cherche. *c* **1400** *Destr. Troy* 3463 And double fest þat day derely was holdyn, With all þe reuell & riolte þat Renkes couthe deuise. **1483** CAXTON *G. de la Tour* H j b, The lady..made him [Moses] to be nourysshed in her wardrobe more derely. **1606** SHAKS. *Tr. & Cr.* III. iii. 96 Man, how dearely euer parted..Cannot make boast to haue that which he hath..but by reflection.

2. As one who is held dear; with feelings of tender affection; affectionately, fondly. (Now used only with the vb. *love* or its equivalents.)

c **1205** LAY. 18896 þæ æremite gon to weopen, deorliche he hine custe. *c* **1350** *Will. Palerne* 4374 Ne to hire do no duresse, as þou me derli louest. **1488** CAXTON *Chast. Goddes Chyld.* 14 Loth she is to forgoo her chylde the whiche she derely louyth. **1570** T. NORTON tr. *Nowel's Catech.* (1853) 132 The dearlier that any man is beloved of God. **1611** TOURNEUR *Ath. Trag.* II. iv, So deerely pittifull that ere the poore Could aske his charity with dry eyes he gaue 'em Reliefe wi' teares. **1650** W. BROUGH *Sacr. Princ.* (1659) 42 All whom Thou hast made more nearly and dearly mine. **1789** MRS. PIOZZI *Journ. France* I. 6 Poor Dr. James..loved profligate conversation dearly. **1856** EMERSON *Eng. Traits, Manners* Wks. (Bohn) II. 48 Born in a harsh and wet climate ..he dearly loves his house.

b. with *ppl. adj.*; often hyphened as in 4.

1526–34 TINDALE *Rom.* xii. 19 Derly beloued, avenge not youre selves. **1625** MILTON *Death Fair Infant* iv, His dearly-lovèd mate. **1838** DICKENS *O. Twist* II. xii. 200 Dearly-attached companion. **1878** Q. VICTORIA *Let.* in *Lond. Gaz.* 27 Dec., To call away from this world her dearly-beloved daughter, the Princess Alice.

†**3.** With reference to other feelings than love or affection: **a.** From the heart, heartily, earnestly. *Obs.*

a **1310** in Wright *Lyric P.* xxxix, Drynke to hym deorly of fol god bous. *c* **1340** *Gaw. & Gr. Knt.* 1031 He..derely hym þonkkez. *a* **1400–50** *Alexander* 2352 A doctour, ane Domystyne þai derely beseke To consaile þaim. **1485** CAXTON *Paris & V.* 24 Prayed hir moche derly that she shold not open it. **1606** SHAKS. *Tr. & Cr.* IV. v. 18 Most deerely welcome to the Greekes, sweete Lady.

†**b.** Carefully. *Obs.*

c **1400** MAUNDEV. (1839) x. 112 The Sarrazines kepen that place fulle derely.

†**c.** Deeply, keenly. *Obs.* Cf. DEAR *a.*[2]

1590 SHAKS. *Com. Err.* II. ii. 132 How deerely would it touch thee to the quicke Shouldst thou but heare I were licencious. **1600** —— *A.Y.L.* I. iii. 35 My father hated his father dearly. **1602** —— *Ham.* IV. iii. 43 We deerely greeue For that which thou hast done.

4. At a high price; at great cost; = DEAR *adv.* 1. Now usually *fig.* When modifying an adj. used attributively it is usually hyphened, as 'a *dearly-bought* advantage'.

c **1489** CAXTON *Sonnes of Aymon* xx. 454 For suche dyde folowe..that payd derely for it. *a* **1533** LD. BERNERS *Huon* xciv. 305 He shal derely abye it. **1550** CROWLEY *Epigr.* 1324 Suche maner stones as are most dearlye solde. **1568** GRAFTON *Chron.* II. 264 Such hurtes and dammages.. should be deerely revenged. **1671** MILTON *Samson* 1660 Oh dearly-bought revenge, yet glorious! **1797** G. COLMAN *Br. Grins, Lodgings for Single Gent.* i, Some [lodgings] are good and let dearly. **1848** MACAULAY *Hist. Eng.* I. 611 The Mendip miners stood bravely to their arms, and sold their lives dearly. **1856** KANE *Arct. Expl.* II. xxiv. 237 All the dearly-earned documents of the expedition.

†**'dearly,** *a. Obs.* [OE. had *déorlíc* illustrious, splendid, brave: but the later examples are app. nonce-formations from DEAR *a.*[1] + -LY[1].] Dear.

Beowulf (Th.) 1174 Swa deorlice dæd. *a* **1300** *Cursor M.* 3700 (Cott.) Bot hend and hals es als i tru Mi dereli suns child esau [*F.* my derly sone hit ys esaw, *G. & Tr.* dere son]. **18..** *Ballad, 'Jamie Douglas'* vi. in Child *Ballads* VII. cciv. 98/1 She was a dearly nurse to me.

†**de'arm,** *v. Obs. rare*[−0]. [ad. L. *dearmāre* to disarm: see DE- I. 5.] 'To disarm' (Bailey, vol. II. 1727).

dearn(e, -ful, -ly: see DERN, -FUL, -LY.

dearn, obs. form of DARN *v.*[1]

dearness (ˈdɪənɪs). [f. DEAR *a.*[1] + -NESS.]

1. The quality of being dear: **a.** of being held in esteem and affection; hence **b.** Intimacy, mutual affection; **c.** Affection, fondness.

c **1320** *Seuyn Sag.* (W.) 3144 Dame, said the erl ful sone, For grete derenes es yt done. *a* **1440** *Sir Eglam., MS. Lincoln* A. i. 17 f. 138 (Halliw.) With the erle es he lent In derenes nyghte and daye. **1599** SHAKS. *Much Ado* III. ii. 101, I thinke, he holds you well, and in dearenesse of heart. **1624** BEDELL *Lett.* i. 40 Neither soothing vntruth for the dearnesse of your person, nor breaking charitie. **1656** JER. TAYLOR in *Evelyn's Mem.* (1857) III. 72, I am, in great heartiness and dearness of affection..your..most affectionate friend. *a* **1715** BURNET *Own Time* (1766) II. 185

The dearness that was between them, was now turned..to a most violent enmity. **1842** TENNYSON *Locksley Hall* 91 The child too clothes the father with a dearness not his due. **1871** T. ERSKINE *Spirit. Order* (1876) 20 The nearness and dearness of my relation to Him.

†**d.** *concr.* An expression or token of affection.

1641 MILTON *Ch. Govt.* vi. (1851) 131 All the duties and dearnesses which ye owe to God. **1721** STRYPE *Eccl. Mem.* I. ii. 26 The peace between the two kings, whatever mutual dearnesses there had appeared, was but short.

2. a. The quality of being dear in price; expensiveness, costliness.

1530 PALSGR. 213/1 Derenesse, *chiertè.* **1599** HAKLUYT *Voy.* III. 269 (R.) The want of wood and deerenesse thereof in England. **1631** GOUGE *God's Arrows* ii. §26. 171 Scarcity and dearenesse of corne. **1699** BENTLEY *Phal.* Pref. 63 The dearness of Paper, and the want of good Types. **1796** MORSE *Amer. Geog.* I. 258 The impracticability of success, arising from scarcity of hands, dearness of labour. **1891** *Leeds Mercury* 28 May 4/5 The withdrawal of the Treasury bills.. was due solely to the temporary dearness of money.

b. *attrib.*, as **dearness allowance**, **pay**, an allowance added to a basic salary, esp. in India, to cover an increase in the cost of living.

1955 *Times* 1 July 1/4 (Advt.), Pay. Rs. 1,000 to Rs. 1,600 p.m., according to qualifications and experience, plus dearness allowance. **1969** *National Herald* (New Delhi) 29 July 8/6 A part of dearness allowance was merged with basic pay last year. *Ibid.*, All employees whose basic pay and dearness pay do not total more than Rs. 620 will become eligible for overtime allowance.

†**de-a'rrest**, *v. Obs. rare*⁻¹. [DE- II. 1.] To release from arrest; = DISARREST.

1791 J. BREE *Cursory Sketch* 231 A ship dearrested or released by order of Council.

de-arsenicize: see DE- II. 1.

dearth (dɜːθ), *sb.* Forms: 3-4 **derþe**, (4 **dierþe**), 4-5 **derthe**, 4-6 (7 *Sc.*) **derth**, 6 **darth**, **deerth**, 6- **dearth**. [ME. *derþe*, not recorded in OE. (where the expected form would be *díerðu*, *díerð*, *dýrð*: cf. 14th c. *dierþe* in Ayenb.); but corresp. formally to ON. *dýrð* with sense 'glory', OS. *diurida*, OHG. *tiurida*, MHG. *tiûrde*, MG. *tûrde* glory, honour, value, costliness; abstr. sb. f. WGer. *diuri*, OE. *diere*, *déore*, DEAR *a.*[1]: see -TH[1].

The form *derke* in *Gen. & Exod.* (*bis*) and *Promp. Parv.* seems to be a scribal error for *derþe*, *derðe*; but its repeated occurrence is remarkable.]

†**1.** Glory, splendour. *Obs. rare.* [= ON. *dyrð.*]

c **1325** *E.E. Allit. P.* A. 99 Þe derþe þerof for to deuyse Nis no wyȝ worþe that tonge berez.

†**2.** Dearness, costliness, high price. *Obs.*

(This sense, though etymologically the source of those that follow, is not exemplified very early, and not frequent. In some of the following instances it is doubtful.)

[**1480** CAXTON *Chron. Eng.* cii. 82 Ther felle grete derth and scarsyte of corne and other vytailles in that land. **1596** BP. BARLOW *Three Serm.* i. 5 Dearth is that, when all those things which belong to the life of man..are rated at a high price.] **1632** in Cramond *Ann. Banff* (1891) I. 67 Compleining of..the dearthe of the pryce thairof. **1644** R. BAILLIE *Lett. & Jrnls.* (1841) II. 175, I cannot help the extraordinarie dearth: they say the great soume the author putts on his copie, is the cause of it. **1793** BENTHAM *Emanc. Colonies* Wks. 1843 IV. 413 When an article is dear, it is.. made so by freedom or by force. Dearth which is natural is a misfortune: dearth which is created is a grievance.

fig. **1602** SHAKS. *Ham.* v. ii. 123 His infusion of such dearth and rareness.

3. A condition in which food is scarce and dear; often, in earlier use, a time of scarcity with its accompanying privations, a famine; now mostly restricted to the condition, as ***in time of dearth.***

c **1250** *Gen. & Ex.* 2237 Wex derk [? derþe], ðis coren is gon. *Ibid.* 2345. *a* **1300** *Cursor M.* 4700 (Cott.) Sua bigan þe derth to grete. *c* **1400** MAUNDEV. (Roxb.) vi. 20 If any derth com in þe cuntree [*quant il fait chier temps*]. *c* **1440** *Promp. Parv.* 119 Derthe (P. or derke), *cariscia.* **1526** TINDALE *Luke* xv. 14 There rose a greate derth thorow out all that same londe. **1552** *Bk. Com. Prayer, Litany*, In the tyme of dearth and famine. **1590** SPENSER *F.Q.* I. ii. 27 Dainty they say maketh derth. **1606** SHAKS. *Ant. & Cl.* II. vii 22 They know ..If dearth Or Foizon follow. **1625** BACON *Ess. Seditions* (Arb.) 403 The Causes and Motiues of Seditions are.. Dearths: Disbanded Souldiers. *a* **1687** PETTY *Pol. Arith.* (1690) 80 The same causes which make Dearth in one place do often cause plenty in another. **1781** GIBBON *Decl. & F.* III. li. 217 The fertility of Egypt supplied the dearth of Arabia. **1841** W. SPALDING *Italy & It. Isl.* I. 361 Augustus in a dearth, gave freedom to twenty thousand slaves. **1848** MILL *Pol. Econ.* (1857) II. IV. ii. 270 In modern times, therefore, there is only dearth, where there formerly would have been famine.

b. *of* (†*for*) *corn, victuals*, etc.

c **1400** MAUNDEV. (Roxb.) vi. 23 Þer falles oft sithes grete derth of corne [*chier temps*]. **1538** STARKEY *England* II. i. 174 The darth of al such thyngys as for fode ys necessary. **1556** *Chron. Gr. Friars* (Camden) 33 This yere [1527] was a gret derth in London for brede. *Ibid.* 45 This yere was a gret derth for wode and colles. **1720** GAY *Poems* (1745) I. 139 At the dearth of coals the poor repine. **1721** SWIFT *Let. fr. Lady conc. Bank* Wks. (1841) II. 67 The South-Sea had occasioned such a dearth of money in the kingdom.

4. *fig.* and *transf.* Scarcity *of* anything, material or immaterial; scanty supply; practical deficiency, want or lack *of* a quality, etc.

1340 *Ayenb.* 256 Þe meste dierþe þet is aboute ham is of zoþnesse an of trewþe. *c* **1386** CHAUCER *Pars. T.* ¶340 Precious clothyng is cowpable for the derthe of it. *c* **1477** CAXTON *Jason* 42 b, Ther is no grete derthe ne scarcete of women. **1596** DRAYTON *Legends* iv. 45 A time when never lesse the Dearth Of happie Wits. **1667** DRYDEN *Ess. Dram. Poesie* Wks. 1725 I. 55 That dearth of plot and narrowness of Imagination, which may be observed in all their Plays. **1671** C. HATTON in *Hatton Corr.* (1878) 60 The absence of yᵉ Court occasions a great dirth of news here. **1754** RICHARDSON *Grandison* IV. xvii. 130 We live in an age in which there is a great dearth of good men. **1815** WORDSW. *White Doe* II. 8 Her last companion in a dearth Of love. **1875** J. CURTIS *Hist. Eng.* 151 The great pestilence of 1349 led to such a dearth of labourers.

†**dearth**, *v. Obs.* [f. prec. sb.] *trans.* To make dear in price; to cause or produce a scarcity of or in anything; to beggar.

c **1440** *Promp. Parv.* 119 Derthyn or make dere, *carisco, carioro.* **1594** *Zepheria* ii. in Arb. *Garner* V. 66 Thy Worth hath dearthed his Words, for thy true praise! **1743** in Cramond *Ann. Banff* (1891) I. 153 Thomas Murray having dearthed the flesh Mercat by buying up some pork.

Hence †**'dearthing** *vbl. sb.* and *ppl. a.*

a **1572** KNOX *Hist. Ref.* Wks. 1846 I. 404 To susteane thowsandis of strangeris..to the derthing of all viweris [= vivres]. **1593** NASHE *Christ's T.* (1613) 64 This huge word-dearthing taske.

†**'dearther.** *Obs.* [f. DEARTH *v.* + -ER.] One who causes a dearth or scarcity in commodities.

1622 MALYNES *Anc. Law-Merch.* 445 Against Forestallers, Regraters, and dearthers of corne and victualls. **1708** J. CHAMBERLAYNE *St. Gr. Brit.* II. II. vi. (1743) 389 Punishing forestallers, regraters, and dearthers of corn.

†**'dearthful.** *Obs. nonce-wd.* [f. DEARTH *sb.* + -FUL.] Costly, expensive.

1786 BURNS *Sc. Drink* xvi, It sets you ill, Wi' bitter, dearthfu' wines to mell, Of foreign gill.

†**de-ar'ticulate**, *a. Obs.* [Cf. next, and ARTICULATE *a.*] Divided by joints; freely articulated. Also **de-ar'ticulated** *a.*

1650 BULWER *Anthropomet.* vii. 87 His Ears not too big nor too little, well engraved, de-articulate. **1615** CROOKE *Body of Man* v. (1616) 286 It hath bin observed that the geniture yssuing from a woman..hath bin dearticulated.

ˌde-articu'lation. *Anat.* [ad. med.L. *dearticulātio*, used to translate διάρθρωσις in Aristotle and Galen.] **a.** Division by joints; **b.** 'Articulation admitting of movement in several directions; = DIARTHROSIS' (*Syd. Soc. Lex.*); **c.** Distinct articulation (of the voice).

1615 CROOKE *Body of Man* 333 A dearticulation of the parts. **1634** T. JOHNSON *Parey's Chirurg.* VI. xlii. (1678) 165 De-articulation is a composition of the bones with a manifest and visible motion. **1650** BULWER *Anthropomet.* 144 There would be much of the voice lost in dearticulation. **1651** BIGGS *New Disp.* ¶98 The dearticulation of the operations of nature.

†**de'artuate**, *v. Obs. rare.* [f. L. *deartuāre*, f. *artus* joint, member: see DE- I. 6.] *trans.* To dismember. So †**deartu'ation**, dismemberment.

1623 COCKERAM, *Deartuate.* **1653** GATAKER *Vind. Annot. Jer.* 175 Framing a very maimed and mangled dismembration and deartuation..of it.

†**'dearworth, derworth**, *a. Obs.* Forms: 1 **déorwurþe**, **dyrwurþe**, 2 **derwurðe**, **derwurð**, **dierewurd**, 2-3 **deor-**, **deore-**, **derewurðe**, 3 **durewurðe**, 3-5 **dere-**, **derworþe**, **derworþ**, **-worth**, 4 **derwurþ**, **direwerþe**, 4-5 **darworth**, 5 **derwurthe**, **dirworthe**, **dyrworth**, **derwarde**, 4-6 **dereworth**, 6 **dearworth**. [OE. *déor-*, *dýrwurþe*, app. f. *dieru*, *déoru* DEAR *sb.*[1] + *wyrþe* worthy.]

1. Worthy of high estimation, highly valuable, precious, costly.

c **888** K. ÆLFRED *Boeth.* x. 28 Ðæt is ȝit deorwyrþre ðonne monnes lif. **971** *Blickl. Hom.* 31 ȝe on gold ȝe on deorwyrþum hræȝlum. *c* **1000** *Ags. Gosp.* Matt. xiii. 46 He funde þæt an deorwyrðe [*c* **1160** *Hatton* derwurðe] meregrot. *c* **1175** *Lamb. Hom.* 19 He..alesde us..mid his derewurðe flesse and mid his blode. *c* **1200** *Trin. Coll. Hom.* 145 Hie nam ane box..and hine fulde mid derewurðe smerieles. *a* **1300** *Ten Commandm.* 1 in *E.E.P.* (1862) 15 Þi derworþ blode þat þou schaddist for mankyn. *c* **1374** CHAUCER *Boeth.* II. iv. 41 Þat þei ne ben more derworþe to þe þen þine owen lijf. *c* **1400** *Lanfranc's Cirurg.* 26 Þat þat is wiþynne þe arterye is ful derwarde & nediþ gret kepynge. *c* **1422** HOCCLEVE *Learn to Die* 448 Of satisfaccioun the leeste deede Right dereworthe were it in this neede.

2. Worthy, honourable, noble, glorious.

c **1175** *Lamb. Hom.* 79 Þet he alihte..from derewurð wuninge. *a* **1175** *Cott. Hom.* 231 Se hlaford into þar halle come mid his dierewurd ȝeferede. **1340-70** *Alex. & Dind.* 243 Whan dereworþe dindimus þe enditinge hurde. *a* **1400-50** *Alexander* 2679 Now dose him fra Darius, a dereworth [*v.r.* darworth] prince. *c* **1420** *Avow. Arth.* xxii, Bidus me Sir Gauan, Is derwurthe on dese!

3. Of persons: Dearly esteemed, dear, beloved.

a **1225** *Ancr. R.* 2 Louerd! seið Godes Spuse to hire deorewurðe Spus. **1382** WYCLIF *2 Cor.* vii. 1 Moost dereworthe britheren. *c* **1400** *Sowdone Bab* 1512 My fader so dereworth and der. *c* **1422** HOCCLEVE *Learn to Die* 498 Of alle freendes thow, the derwortheste. **1557** *Tottell's Misc.* (Arb.) 117 A dearworth dame.

†**'dearworthily**, *adv. Obs.* [f. DEARWORTHY + -LY[2].] Worthily, honourably; preciously, richly; affectionately.

a **1300** *Cursor M.* 13669 (Gött.) Ful derworthili his lauerd he gret. ? *a* **1400** *Morte Arth.* 3252 A duches dere-worthily dyghte in dyaperde wedis. *c* **1410** LOVE *Bonavent. Mirr.* iv. (Gibbs MS.), [Sche] roos uppe and clypped hire derworthyly [ed. **1530** worthily] and tenderly. *Ibid.* xiv, Sche..clyppynge hym derworthyly [*v.r.* derworthely; ed. **1530** louyngely] in hyre armes.

†**'dearworthiness.** *Obs.* [f. as prec. + -NESS. OE. had *déorwyrþnes.*] Preciousness, worthiness, valuableness; *pl.* (in OE.), valuables, treasures.

[*c* **888** K. ÆLFRED *Boeth.* vii. §4 Mid golde, ȝe mid seolfre, ȝe mid eallum deorwyrþnessum.] *c* **1325** *Metr. Hom.* 11 Than es the gret derworthines Of precheours that bers witnes. *Ibid.* 73 Wit lovely worde and dereworthynes.

†**'dearworthly**, *adv. Obs.* In 3-4 **-liche**, 4 **-lye**, **-li**, **-ly**, (**derwurly**). [Early ME. f. DEARWORTH *a.* + *-liche*, -LY[2].] = DEARWORTHILY.

c **1205** LAY. 15151 Twa hundred cnihten..þe sculen biwiten þene king, durewurðliche þurh alle þing. *a* **1225** *Ancr. R.* 410 Þeos beon deoruwurðliche i-wust. *a* **1300** *Cursor M.* 5322 (Cott.) He..mensked him derworthli [*v. rr.* dereworthly, -worþely]. *c* **1320** R. BRUNNE *Medit.* 180 How derwurly, afore hys ende, A derwurþ ȝyfte he wulde with þe lete. *c* **1325** *Metr. Hom.* 84 Wel birs us blis the derworthelye. **1413** LYDG. *Pilgr. Sowle* II. lxiii. (1859) 59 Thou..keptest me ful derworthly, that I went nought from the.

†**'dearworthy, derworthy**, *a. Obs.* [A ME. formation from DEARWORTH, with assimilation of the second element to WORTHY.] = DEARWORTH.

a **1300** *Cursor M.* 4731 (Cott.) Mi stiward ioseph al fedes me, For darworthi þar-til es he. *c* **1374** CHAUCER *Boeth.* II. i. 31 Is present fortune derworþi to þe. **1414** BRAMPTON *Penit. Ps.* vii, Helde noȝt thi wrethe on my frealnesse, Thi derworthi childeryn whan thou schalt blesse. *c* **1430** *Hymns Virg.* (1867) 52 Þe derworþiest oile þat euere was. *c* **1485** *Digby Myst.* (1882) III. 1086 O, þou dere worthy emperowere!

deary, -rie ('dɪərɪ), *sb.* and *a.* Also 7-8 **dearee.** [f. DEAR *a.*[1] + -IE, -Y[4].] Diminutive of *dear.*

A. *sb.* A little dear; a darling: a familiar term of amatory and conjugal endearment.

1681 OTWAY *Soldier's Fort.* III. i, Lose thee, poor Love, poor Dearee, poor Baby. **1705** VANBRUGH *Confed.* v. ii. 301 [To their husbands] Bye, dearies! **1739** R. BULL tr. *Dedekindus' Grobianus* 151 You'll be her Love, her Dearee, what you will. **1795** WOLCOTT (P. Pindar) *Pindariana* Wks. 1812 IV. 73 He hugs and kisses his old Deary. **1870** DICKENS *E. Drood* i, Here's another ready for ye, deary. **1890** W. A. WALLACE *Only a Sister!* 88 A Mapleton in love is a Mapleton still, for all your pretty ways, dearie.

B. *adj. dial.* See quots.

1691 RAY *N.C. Words*, *Deary*, little. **1828** *Craven Dial.*, *Deary*, an adjunct to little and equivalent to very; 'This is a deary little bit'. **1877** *N.W. Linc. Gloss.* s.v., 'I never seed such deary little apples in all my life.' **1888** ELWORTHY *W. Somerset Word-bk.* s.v., 'There is a deary little gibby lamb.'

C. *interj.* ***deary me!*** an extension of ***dear me!*** usually more sorrowful in its tone.

1785 HUTTON *Bran New Wark* 343 (E.D.S.) Deary me! deary me! forgive me good Sir. I'll steal naa maar..My mother, my brothers and sisters, and my ald neam, O deary me! **1815** JANE TAYLOR *Display* xi. (ed. 2) 132 'Deary me!' said she. **1833** MARRYAT *P. Simple* i, O deary me! he must have lost a mint of money.

deas(e, deasse, obs. forms of DAIS.

‖**deasil, deiseal** ('djɛʃəl, 'dɛsəl), *adv.*, *sb.* Also **deisal**, **deisul.** [Gaelic *deiseil* (*deiseal*, *deasal*) adj. and adv., righthandwise, turned toward the right, *dextrorsum*, f. *deas* right hand, south, in OIr. *dess*, *des*, Welsh *dehau*, cognate with Lat. *dex-ter*, Gr. δεξ-ιός. (The meaning of the latter part is unknown.)]

Righthandwise, towards the right; motion with continuous turning to the right, as in going round an object with the right hand towards it, or in the same direction as the hands of a clock, or the apparent course of the sun (a practice held auspicious by the Celts).

1771 PENNANT *Tour Scotl. in 1769*, 309 (Jam. s.v. *Widdersinnis*) At marriages and baptisms they make a procession round the church, Deasoil, i.e., sunways. **1774-5** —— *Tour Scotl. in 1772*, II. 15 (Jam.) The unhappy lunatics are brought here by their friends, who first perform the ceremony of the Deasil thrice round a neighbouring cairn. **1794** *Statist. Acc. Perthshire* XI. 521 (Jam.) If a person's meat or drink were to..come against his breath, they instantly cry out, Deisheal! which is an ejaculation praying that it may go the right way. **1814** SCOTT *Wav.* xxiv, The surgeon..perambulated his couch three times, moving from east to west, according to the course of the sun..which was called making the deasil. **1875** LUBBOCK *Orig. Civiliz.* vi. 300 There was a sacred stone in Jura round which the people used to move 'deasil', i.e. sunwise. **1897** *Daily News* 26 July 5/1 'Walking the deisul' round a person or place was lately, perhaps is still, a ceremony in the Highlands. **1945** *Archit. Rev.* XCVII. 49/3 English roundabouts run deisul, clockwise. **1947** AUDEN *Age of Anxiety* (1948) ii. 49 O Primal Age When we danced deisal.

de-aspirate, -ation, -ator: see DE- II. 1.

death (dɛθ), *sb.* Forms: α. 1-4 **déaþ**, 2 **daþ**, **dieþ**, 2-3 **dæþ**, 2-4 **deþ**, 3 **death**, **diaþ**, **diath**, **diþ**, 4 **deeþ**, **dyaþ**, **dyeaþ**, 4-5 **deythe**, 4-6 **deth**, **dethe**, 5 **deeth**, 6 *Sc.* **deith**, 6- **death.** Also β. 3 **dead**, **dæd**, 3-6 **ded**, **dede**, (4 **dedd**, **did**), 4-5 (6-8 *Sc.*) **deed**, 5-6 **deyd**, 6-9 (chiefly *Sc.*) **dead**, 4-9 *Sc.* **deid.** [A Common Teut. sb.: OE. *déaþ*= OFris. *dâth*, *dâd* (WFris. *dead*), OS. *dôð, dôd* (MDu. and MLG. *dôt(d-)*, Du. *dood*), OHG. *tôd*, MHG. *tôt* (Ger. *tod*), ON. orig. *dauðr*, usually *dauði* (Sw., Da. *död*), Goth. *dauþus*, an OTeut. deriv. in *-þu-z* (= L. *-tu-s*) of the verbal stem *dau-* (pre-Teut. type *dhau-*, *'*dhau-tu-s*), whence ON. *deyja* to DIE. (Cf. also DEAD.) Of the ME. form *ded, dede*, usual in the northern dial. (but not confined to it), *Sc.* 4- *deid* (did), also spelt 6- *dead*, the history is not quite clear; the final *d* agrees with Sw. and Da., and suggests Norse influence, but the vowel regularly represents OE. *éa*: cf Sc. *breid, heid, steid* (brid, etc.).]

I. 1. The act or fact of dying; the end of life; the final cessation of the vital functions of an animal or plant. **a.** of an individual.

971 *Blickl. Hom.* 33 He mid his costunge ure costunge oforswiþde, and mid his deaþe urne deaþ. *c* **1250** *Old Kentish Serm.* in *O.E. Misc.* 36 Non ne wot þane dai of his diaþe. *a* **1300** *K. Horn* 58 So fele mi3ten yþe Bringe hem þre to diþe. *c* **1449** PECOCK *Repr.* 376 The wommen..whiche after hir husbondis deethis wolden..lyue chaast. **1590** SHAKS. *Mids. N.* v. i. 293 The death of a deare friend. **1667** MILTON *P.L.* IX. 832 With him all deaths I could endure, without him live no life. **1887** J. A. HAMILTON in *Dict. Nat. Biog.* IX. 370/2 He bore the scar to his death.

β. c **1205** LAY. 8424-6 Herigal..sweor, þat Euelin i ðon dæi Dæd sculde þolien. Euelin wes swiðe of-dred, For me him dead bi-hæhte. *a* **1300** *Cursor M.* 905 (Cott.) þou sal be slan wit duble dedd. *c* **1400** MAUNDEV. (Roxb.) Pref. 1 He wald..suffer hard passioun and dede. *c* **1450** *St. Cuthbert* (Surtees) 2577 Sho saw hir deed semed nere at hande. **1533** GAU *Richt Vay* (1888) 13 Sayand to ane oder god giff the ane ewil deid. **1570** BUCHANAN *Ane Admonitioun* Wks. 23 To revenge his faderis deid. *a* **1605** MONTGOMERIE *Misc. Poems* xxii. 41 Then wer I out of dout of deed.

b. in the abstract.

c **888** K. ÆLFRED *Boeth.* viii. 26 Se deaþ hit huru afirreþ. *a* **1200** *Moral Ode* xcviii. in *E.E.P.* (1862) 28 Dieð com in þis middenerd þurh þe ealde deofles onde. *c* **1340** *Cursor M.* 835 (Trin.) Fro þat tyme furst coom deþ to man. **1398** TREVISA *Barth. De P.R.* VI. ii. (1495) 187 Deth is callyd mors for it is bitter. **1583** HARSNET *Serm. Ezek.* (1658) 128 There are no two things so opposite as Life and Death. **1667** MILTON *P.L.* I. 3 The Fruit Of that Forbidden Tree, whose mortal tast Brought Death into the World. **1769** COWPER *Lett.* 21 Jan., Death is either the most formidable, or the most comfortable thing we have in prospect. **1859** SEELEY *Ecce Homo* iv. (ed. 8) 35 The Greek did not believe death to be annihilation.

β. a **1300** *Cursor M.* 20841 (Gött.) þat lijf, ne dede, ne wele, ne wa, Mai neuer turn mi hert þe fra. **1340** HAMPOLE *Pr. Consc.* 1666 Ded es þe mast dred thing þat es. **1375** BARBOUR *Bruce* I. 269 Thryldome is weill wer than deid. *c* **1420** *Sir Amadas* (Weber) 152 Then com deyd..And partyd my dere husbond and me. **1533** GAU *Richt Vay* (1888) 45 As S. Paul sais..Deid is swolit throw wictore.

c. as a personified agent. (Usually figured as a skeleton; see also DEATH'S-HEAD.)

971 [see 7]. *a* **1300** *Cursor M.* 18116 (Cott.) To ded i said, 'quar es þi stang?' **1504** *Bury Wills* (Camden) 105 A blak clothe steynyd wt an image of deth. **1596** SHAKS. *Merch. V.* II. vii. 63, O hell! what haue we here? A carrion death, within whose emptie eye There is a written scroule. **1667** MILTON *P.L.* XI. 490 Over them triumphant Death his Dart Shook; but delaid to strike. **1839** LONGF. *Reaper & Flowers* i, There is a Reaper, whose name is Death. **1874** J. FOWLER in *Proc. Soc. Antiq.* 19 Feb. 143 A figure of Death, represented as a skeleton with mattock and spade.

2. The state of being dead; the state or condition of being without life, animation, or activity. ***death-in-life***, life that lacks any satisfaction or purpose; living death. (Cf. quot. 1841 *s.v.* DEATHLINESS.)

a **1000** *Andreas* 583 (Gr.) He..men of deaðe worde awehte. *c* **1175** *Lamb. Hom.* 91 Crist aras of deaðe. *c* **1250** *Gen. & Ex.* 265 Quan al man-kinde..Sal ben fro dede to liue bro3t. **1340** *Ayenb.* 7 Oure lhord aros uram dyaþe to lyue. *c* **1450** *St. Cuthbert* (Surtees) 871 Rays þis bryd to lyfe fra deed. **1827** POLLOK *Course T.* III. 1000 This wilderness of intellectual death. **1864** TENNYSON *En. Ard.* 561 One..Lay lingering out a five-years' death-in-life. **1864-6** MRS. GASKELL *Wives & Daughters* (1866) II. xxv. 255 The Squire stood by in dumb dismay, touched in spite of himself by the death-in-life of one so young. *a* **1895** *Mod.* His eyes were closed in death. **1907** *Folk-Lore* June 228 A seven years' death-in-life trance. **1934** 'G. ORWELL' *Burmese Days* xxiv. 358 The sort of horrible death-in-life! The decay, the loneliness. **1955** E. BOWEN *World of Love* vi. 115 They conceived of no death, least of all death-in-life.

¶ In preceding senses ***the death*** was frequent in Old and Middle English, and down to the 16th c. See also 7, 12 c, 13; *to die the death*: see DIE.

c **888** K. ÆLFRED *Boeth.* viii. 26 Se deaþ ne cymð to nanum oðrum þingum. *c* **1175** *Lamb. Hom.* 109 þe alde mei him witan iwis þone deð. *a* **1225** *Ancr. R.* 52 þus eode sihðe biuoren..& com þe deað þer efter. **1340** HAMPOLE *Pr. Consc.* 355 Of þe dede and whi it es to drede. *a* **1400** *Relig. Pieces fr. Thornton MS.* (1867) 3 When þe dede has sundyrde oure bodyes and oure saules. *c* **1430** *Syr Tryam.* 104 Tylle thou be broght to the dedd. **1513** DOUGLAS *Æneis* I. i. 54 Quhilk hed the deid eschapit. *a* **1555** LATIMER *Serm. & Rem.* (1845) 3 He..rose again from the death. **1594** SHAKS. *Rich. III*, I. ii. 179, I lay it [his breast] naked to the deadly stroke, And humbly begge the death. **1599** —— *Hen. V*, IV. i. 181 Where they feared the death, they haue borne life away.

3. *transf.* The loss or cessation of life in a particular part or tissue of a living being.

1800 *Med. Jrnl.* III. 543 So great a torpor, as to produce 'the death or mortification of the parts'. **1869** HUXLEY *Physiol.* i. 23 When death takes place, the body, as a whole, dies first, the death of the tissues not occurring until after a considerable interval.

†**4.** Loss of sensation or vitality, state of unconsciousness, swoon. *Obs. rare.* (Cf. DEAD *a.* 2.)

1596 SIR J. SMYTHE in *Lett. Lit. Men* (Camden) 97 It brought sodeyne death itself upon me for three quarters of an houre.

5. *fig.* **a.** The loss or want of spiritual life; the being or becoming spiritually dead. ***the second death***: the punishment or destruction of lost souls after physical death.

c **1000** *Ags. Gosp.* John v. 24 Ic secge eow þæt se þe min word gehyrð..færð fram deaðe to life. *c* **1175** *Lamb. Hom.* 39 þenne bure3est þu here saule..from þan ufele deaðe. *c* **1200** ORMIN 19052 þiss lif niss nohht rihht nemmnedd lif Acc dæþ itt ma33 ben nemmnedd. *c* **1325** *E.E. Allit. P.* A. 651 [He] delyuered vus of þe deth secounde. **1382** WYCLIF *Rev.* xxi. 8 The pool brennynge with fijr and brunston, that is the secounde deeth. *c* **1400** MAUNDEV. (Roxb.) Pref. 1 To by and delyuer vs fra deed withouten end. **1483** CAXTON *G. de la Tour* D vj, The perille of the deth of helle. **1534** TINDALE *Rom.* viii. 6 To be carnally mynded, is deeth. **1885** S. COX *Expositions* I. xx, The want of this [eternal] life is eternal death.

b. Loss or deprivation of civil life; the fact or state of being cut off from society, or from certain rights and privileges, as by banishment, imprisonment for life, etc. (Usually ***civil death***.)

1622 FLETCHER *Sp. Curate* IV. i, This banishment is a kind of civil death. **1765** BLACKSTONE *Comm.* I. I. ii. 145 A dissolution is the civil death of the parliament. **1767** *Ibid.* II. 121 It may also determine by his civil death; as if he enters into a monastery, whereby he is dead in law. **1772** FLETCHER *Appeal* Wks. 1795 I. 100 Does not the spirit of persecution ..inflict at least academic death upon [them]? **1871** MARKBY *Elem. Law* §120 A sort of conventional death, or, as it is sometimes called, a civil death.

c. Of a thing: Cessation of being, end, extinction, destruction.

1413 LYDG. *Pilgr. Sowle* III. x. (1483) 56 And oure deth is withouten deth for it hath none ende. **1718** WATTS *Hymns* III. xxiii, Our faith beholds the dying Lord, And dooms our sins to death. **1821** SHELLEY *Boat on Serchio* 29 From the lamp's death to the morning ray. **1884** W. C. SMITH *Kildrostan* 48 Suspicion murders love, and from its death Come anguish and remorse.

6. Bloodshed, slaughter, murder.

a **1626** BACON (J.), Not to suffer a man of death to live. **1822** SHELLEY *Hellas* 431 The dew is foul with death. **1883** CHURCH & BRODRIBB tr. *Livy* XXII. li. 118 Some were cut down by the foe as they rose covered with blood from the field of death.

7. Cause or occasion of death, as in ***to be the death of***; something that kills, or renders liable to death; often hyperbolically; *poet.* a deadly weapon, poison, etc.

971 *Blickl. Hom.* 67 He cwæþ, 'Eala deaþ, ic beo þin deaþ'. **1382** WYCLIF *2 Kings* iv. 40 Thei crieden oute, seyinge, Deth in the pott! deth in the pott! **1596** SHAKS. *1 Hen. IV*, II. i. 14 Poore fellow neuer ioy'd since the price of oats rose, it was the death of him. **1599** —— *Much Ado* II. ii. 19 What life is in that, to be the death of this marriage? **16..** DRYDEN (J.), Swiftly flies The feather'd death, and hisses through the skies. **1704** POPE *Windsor For.* 132 The clam'rous lapwings feel the leaden death. **1773** GOLDSM. *Stoops to Conq.* I, A school would be his death. **1816** JANE AUSTEN *Emma* II. iii. 56 Oh! dear, I thought it would have been the death of me! **1842** MIALL *Nonconf.* II. 49 These churchmen magistrates will be the death of us. **1847** TENNYSON *Princ.* VI. 260 You might mix his draught with death. **1863** 'OUIDA' *Held in Bondage* I. iii. 63 A mill-wheel monotony would be the death of me. **1956** S. BECKETT *Waiting for Godot* I. 35 *Estragon* (convulsed with merriment). He'll be the death of me!

β. c **1314** *Guy Warw.* (A.) 365 þou art mi liif, mi ded y-wis ..Y dye for þe loue of þe. *c* **1500** *Melusine* 26 He thenne pulled out of hys brest the piece of the swerd, and knew that it was hys dede. **1725** RAMSAY *Gent. Sheph.* II. ii, Her cheeks, her mouth, her een, Will be my dead. **1792** BURNS *Auld Rob Morris* iii, The wounds I must hide that will soon be my dead. *a* **1894** *Mod. Sc.* You have been the deid o' him.

†**8. a.** A general mortality caused by an epidemic disease; a pestilence. *Obs.* exc. as in b.

[*c* **1358** EDW. III. *Let. to Pope Innocent VI* in *Hist. Lett. N. Registers* (Rolls) 405 Quodam morbo incurabili in tibia, mala mors vulgariter nuncupato, percussus.] *c* **1400** KNIGHTON *Chron.* IV. an. 1348, Scoti..sumpserunt in juramentum.. sub hac forma quando jurare volebant, *Per fœdam mortem Anglorum*, anglice *be the foul dethe of Engelond.* **1480** CAXTON *Descr. Brit.* 35 This was moche vsed to-for ye grete deth [TREVISA þe furste moreyn]. **1480-90** *Chron. Scots* in Pinkerton *Hist. Scot.* I. App. 502 (an. 1482) Thar was ane gret hungyr and deid in Scotland. **1556** *Chron. Gr. Friars* (Camden) 29 Thys yere was a gret deth at the Menerys. **1577-87** HOLINSHED *Chron.* III. 961/1 In this yeare a great death of the pestilence reigned in London.

b. Black Death, the name now commonly given to the Great Pestilence or visitation of the Oriental Plague, which devastated most countries of Europe near the middle of the 14th c., and caused great mortality in England in 1348-9; sometimes also including the recurrences of the epidemic in 1360 and 1379.

The name 'black death' is modern, and was app. introduced into English history by Mrs. Penrose (Mrs. Markham) in 1823, and into medical literature by Babington's transl. of Hecker's *Der Schwarze Tod* in 1833. In earlier writers we find *the pestilence, the plague, great pestilence, great death*, or in distinction from later visitations *the furste moreyn, the first pestilence*; Latin chroniclers have *pestis, pestilentia, epidemia, mortalitas*. The distinctive *magna mortalitas*, 'great mortality' or 'death', and its equivalents, prevailed in many languages: Ger. *das grosse sterben*, LGer. *de grote dot*, Flem. *de groete doet*, Da. *den store död* or *mandööth*, Swed. (1402) *store dödhin*, later *stordöden, digerdöden* (thick or frequent mortality), Norweg. (14th c.) *manndauði hinn mikli*; cf. It. *mortalega grande*, F. *la grande peste*, etc. The epithet 'black' is of uncertain origin, and not known to be contemporary anywhere. It is first found in Swedish and Danish 16th c. chroniclers (*swarta dödhen, den sorte död*). Hence, in German, Schlözer in 1773 used *der schwarze Tod* in reference to Iceland, and Sprengel in 1794 took it as a general appellation. From modern German the name has passed into Dutch (*de zwaarte dood*) and English, and has influenced French (*la peste noire*). The quots. 1758 and 1780 below are translations from Danish and Swedish through German, and refer not to the pestilence of 1348, which did not reach Iceland, but to a later visitation in 1402-3, known at the time as *plagan mikli* (the great plague), but called by modern Icelandic historians, from 17th c., *svarti dauði* (black death).

[*c* **1440** WALSINGHAM *Chron.* Title of chap., De magna mortalitate in anglia, quæ a modernis vocatur prima pestilentia. **1758** tr. *Horrebow's Nat. Hist. Iceland* in *Gentl. Mag.* XXVIII. 79 In the 14th century a disease called the *Sorte död*, or *black death*, destroyed almost all the inhabitants in the place [Iceland]. **1780** tr. *Lett. from Ihre* (1776) in *Von Troil's Lett. Iceland* 305 Schlozer divides the Icelandic literature into three periods..the golden period, from the introduction of christianity to the close of the thirteenth [*sic*—should be fourteenth] century, when the black death or the great plague..checked the progress of poetry. **1800** *Med. Jrnl.* IV. 365 He [Cit. Papon] speaks of the plague..in 1347, otherwise called the black plague.]

1823 MRS. MARKHAM [Eliz. Penrose] *Hist. Eng.* xviii, Edward's successes in France were interrupted during the next six years by a most terrible pestilence—so terrible as to be called the black death. **1833** B. G. BABINGTON (*title*) The Black Death in the Fourteenth Century. From the German of J. F. E. Hecker, M.D. **1874** GREEN *Short Hist.* v. §4. an. 1349, The Black Death fell on the village almost as fiercely as on the town. **1885** *Encycl. Brit.* XIX. 164/2 s.v. *Plague*, The mortality of the black death was..enormous. It is estimated in various parts of Europe at two-thirds or three-fourths of the population in the first pestilence, in England even higher. **1893** F. A. GASQUET (*title*) The Great Pestilence (A.D. 1348-9), now commonly known as the Black Death.

†**9.** *Hunting.* A blast sounded at the death of the game; = MORT. *Obs.*

1741 *Compl. Fam. Piece* II. i. 293 He that first gets in cries *Hoo-up*..and blows a Death.

10. As a vehement exclamation or imprecation. See also 'SDEATH.

1604 SHAKS. *Oth.* III. iii. 396 Death and damnation! Oh! **1668** DRYDEN *Evening's Love* IV. ii, Death, you make me mad, sir! **1766** GOLDSM. *Vic. W.* xi, Death! to be seen by ladies..in such vulgar attitudes!

II. Phrases.

†**11.** In ME. the genitive was occasionally (as in nouns of time) used adverbially = In the condition of death, dead; so *lives* (gen. of *life*) = alive. *Obs.*

a **1250** *Owl & Night.* 1630 Ah thu nevre mon to gode Lives ne deathes, stal ne stode. *c* **1314** *Guy Warw.* (A.) 5459 Ni3t no day swiken y nille Liues or deþes that ich him se.

12. ***to death*** (Sc. *to deid*, occas. in Eng. *to dead*): **a.** *lit.* following verbs as an adverbial extension expressing result, as *to* †*slay, beat, stone*, etc. *to death*; hence *to do to (the) death* (arch.), to kill, slay; ***to put to death***, to kill, *esp.* in the execution of justice, to execute.

c **1000** *Ags. Gosp.* Matt. xx. 18 Hig ge-nyþeriað hyne to deaþe. *a* **1225** *Juliana* 62 He sloh him wið a stan to deaðe. *a* **1300** *Cursor M.* 6711 (Cott.) To ded [*v.r.* deþe] þat beist man sal stan. *c* **1330** R. BRUNNE *Chron* (1810) 127 þe date ..þat Steuen to dede was dight. *c* **1400** *Destr. Troy* 9533 The Troiens..dong hom to dethe. *c* **1489** CAXTON *Blanchardyn* v. (1890) 21 Wounded to deth. **1560-1** *Bk. Discipl. Ch. Scot.* vii. §2 For suche..the Civill swearde aught to punische to death. *c* **1600** SHAKS. *Sonn.* xcix. A vengeful canker eat him up to death. **1611** —— *Cymb.* v. v. 235 The Gods do meane to strike me To death with mortall ioy. **1734** tr. *Rollin's Anc. Hist.* (1827) II. III. 189 Shot to death with darts. **1852** MRS. STOWE *Uncle Tom's C.* xix, The slave-owner can whip his refractory slave to death.

c **1314** *Guy Warw.* (A.) 3581 So mani to ded ther he dede. *c* **1400** *Destr. Troy* 11932 The knightes..The pepull with pyne puttyn to dethe. *a* **1400** *Sir Perc.* 930 Ther he was done to the dede. **1503-4** *Act 19 Hen. VII*, c. 34 Preamb., Dyvers [were] put to deth. **1570-6** LAMBARDE *Peramb. Kent* (1826) 391 Iack Cade..did to death the Lord Say, and others. **1599** SHAKS. *Much Ado* v. iii. 3 Done to death by slanderous tongues. **1631** GOUGE *God's Arrows* III. §60. 295 Ministers of Justice in putting capitall malefactors to death. **1847** GROTE *Greece* (1862) III. xxxiv. 225 They were all put to death. **1858** GEN. P. THOMPSON *Audi Alt.* II. lxxx. 36 Haunted by pictures of some he had done to death.

b. intensifying verbs of feeling, as *hate, resent*, or adjs., as *sick, wearied*: to the last extremity, to the uttermost, to the point of physical or nervous exhaustion, beyond endurance.

a **1300** *Cursor M.* 13070 (Cott.) Herodias him hated to ded. **1583** HOLLYBAND *Campo di Fior* 241 Clodius is inamoured to dead of a certaine yong woman. **1613** SHAKS. *Hen. VIII*, IV. ii. 1 *Grif.* How do's your Grace? *Kath.* O Griffith, sicke to death. **1670** G. H. *Hist. Cardinals* I. II. 58 The Hereticks abhor me to death. **1670** DRYDEN *Conq. Granada* Pt. II. III. iii, I'm sad to death, that I must be your foe. **1773** MRS. CHAPONE *Improv. Mind* (1774) II. 80 A gentleman who would resent to death an imputation of falsehood. **1806** BLOOMFIELD *Wild Flowers* Poems (1845) 220 Some almost laugh'd themselves to dead. **1840** DICKENS *Barn. Rudge* xxii, My stars, Simmun!.. You frighten me to death! **1850** MRS. CARLYLE *Lett.* II. 142, I have also been bothered to death with servants.

c. ***to the death*** formerly interchanged with *to death* in all senses; it is now used only in certain expressions, as ***to pursue, persecute, wage war to the death.***

1382 WYCLIF *Matt.* xxvi. 38 My soule is sorowful til to the deth. *c* **1400** *Three Kings Cologne* iv. 12 Ezechias was syke to þe dethe. *c* **1450** *Merlin* 122 These shull the [= thee] love and serue euer to the deth. **1563** WINȜET *Four Scoir Thre Quest.* Wks. 1888 I. 95 To baneis Christianis..and condemne thame to the dethe. **1568** GRAFTON *Chron.* II. 217 The which Castell the king hated to the death. **1586** T. B. *La Primaud. Fr. Acad.* (1589) 261 With such speeches he fought unto the death. **1599** SHAKS. *Much Ado* I. iii. 73 You are both sure, and will assist mee? *Conr.* To the death my Lord. **1673** DRYDEN *Marr. à la Mode* v. i, And she takes it to the death. **1842** S. LOVER *Handy Andy* ii, When he [an attorney] was obliged..to hunt his man to the death. **1848** MACAULAY *Hist. Eng.* II. 207 Four generations of Stuarts had waged a war to the death with four generations of Puritans.

d. *to do* (a thing) *to death*, to overdo; to repeat too often or *ad nauseam*.

1882 H. D. TRAILL *Recaptured Rhymes* 112, I am also called Played-out and Done-to-death, And It-will-wash-no-more. **1886** H. BAUMANN *Londinismen* 43/2 *Done to death*,..überspannt geschrieben. *a* **1889** in Barrère & Leland *Dict. Slang* (1889) I. 320/2 Caricature of Academy pictures done to death in comic journals with utmost regularity for many past years. **1909** W. S. SPARROW *Hints on House Furnishing* II. iii. 134 Diapered patterns for wall-papers and carpets..were 'done to death'. **1965** *New Statesman* 16 Apr. 605/1 It [*sc.* a tune] was mercilessly done to death by countless performers.

13. a. † *to have* or *take the death*: to meet one's death, to die. *Obs.* So *to catch one's death*: see CATCH *v.* 30. *to be the death of*: see sense 7. *to be* (or *make it*) *death* (*for*): i.e. to be (or make it) a matter of death of capital punishment.

c **1435** *Torr. Portugal* 1229 The kyng had wend he had the dede. *c* **1470** HENRY *Wallace* XI. 837 Throuch cowatice, gud Ector tuk the ded. **1652** H. BELL *Luther's Colloq.* (Cassell's Ed.) 13 It should be death for any person to have..a copy thereof. **1847** TENNYSON *Princ.* Prol. 150, I would make it death For any male thing but to peep at us.

†**b.** *to go one's death* (*on* or *upon*), to do one's utmost (for); to risk one's all (on). *Obs. U.S. slang.*

1833 D. CROCKETT *Sketches* 74 My little boys at home will go their death to support my election. *Ibid.* 173 You think they don't go their death upon a jig, but they do. **1835** A. B. LONGSTREET *Georgia Scenes* (1840) 199 I'll go my death upon you at the shooting match. **1878** *Scribner's Mag.* XV. 400/1 The consulship at Rio Janeiro is vacant, and being worth $6,000, he is moved to 'go his death on Rio'.

14. *death's door*, *the gates* or *jaws of death*: figurative phrases denoting a near approach to, or great danger of, death.

1382 WYCLIF *Ps.* cvi[i]. 18 And they neȝheden to the ȝatis of deth. **1550** COVERDALE *Spir. Perle* xviii, To bring unto deaths door, that he may restore unto life again. **1646** P. BULKELEY *Gospel Covt.* To Rdr. 1 When death comes to our dores, and we are at deaths-dore. **1746** BERKELEY *2nd Let. Tar-water* §12 Many patients might thereby be rescued from the jaws of death. **1855** TENNYSON *Charge Lt. Brigade*, Into the jaws of Death, Into the mouth of Hell, Rode the six hundred. **1860** TROLLOPE *Framley P.* xliii, Poor Mrs. Crawley had been at death's door.

15. *to be in at the death* (in *Fox-hunting*): to be present when the game is killed by the hounds. Also *fig.*

1788 W. COWPER *Let.* 3 Mar. (1904) III. 240, I have been in at the death of a fox. **1800** WINDHAM *Speeches Parl.* (1812) I. 337 For the empty fame of being in at the death. **1841** LYTTON *Nt. & Morn.* v. ix, A skilful huntsman..who generally contrived to be in at the death. **1919** L. STRACHEY in *Athenæum* 13 June 454/1 Creevey..had a trick of being 'in at the death' on every important occasion:..he invariably popped up at the critical moment. **1933** N. COWARD *Design for Living* II. iii. 71 You have a tremendous sense of the 'right moment', Ernest. It's wonderful. You pop up like a genie out of a bottle, just to be in at the death!

16. *to be death on* (slang): to be eminently capable of doing execution on, or a very good hand at dealing with; to be very fond of. orig. *U.S.*

1839 *Spirit of Times* 5 Oct. 368/3 [His] nose is so red that no musquito can stand the blaze of it. It's death upon gallinipers, too. **1855** HALIBURTON *Nat. & Hum. Nat.* 225 (Bartlett) Women..are born with certain natural tastes. Sally was death on lace. **1860** BARTLETT *Dict. Amer.* s.v., To be *death on* a thing, is to be..a capital hand at it, like the quack doctor who could not manage the whooping-cough, but was, as he expressed it, 'death on fits'. Vulgar. **1884** E. FAWCETT *Gentl. of Leisure* i. 9 Fanny hasn't forgotten you.. she was always death on you English chaps. **1892** LENTZNER *Australian Word-bk.* 19 *Death on*, good at..'Death on rabbits', would mean a very good rabbit shot.

17. a. In various other phraseological expressions; as *as pale as death* (see PALE); and *colloq. as sure as death*, to ride, come on, hang on, etc., *like death*, or *like grim death*.

c **1384** CHAUCER *H. Fame* 502 But this as sooth as deeth, certeyn, Hit was of golde. *c* **1440** *Partonope* 6999 And in þis wise cristenyd was he, As siker as dethe, with-outen nay. **1598** B. JONSON *Ev. Man in Hum.* II. i, They would giue out ..That I were iealous! nay, as sure as death, That they would say. **1766** GOLDSM. *Vicar* xix, As sure as death there is our master and mistress come home. **1786** BURNS *Scotch Drink* x, Then Burnewin comes on like death, At every chaup. **1831** S. E. FERRIER *Destiny* xlviii, Oh, as sure as death, then, that's just owning that you are going to be married. **1836** D. CROCKETT *Exploits & Adventures in Texas* x. 151 He hung on like grim death. **1837** T. HOOK *Jack Brag* III. v. 182 Jack..was holding on, like grim Death, by the companion. **1847** [see GRIM *a.* 4 b]. **1893** *Tit Bits* 23 Dec. 211/3 The baby..holds on to that finger like grim death. **1928** D. L. SAYERS *Unpleasantness at Bellona Club* ix. 112 If ever you see him again, Fentiman, freeze on to him like grim death. **1928** R. CULLUM *Myst. Barren Lands* xi. 106 'Think you'll ever get it?'..'Sure,' he said emphatically. 'Just as sure as —— death.'

b. (*a fate*) *worse than death*, a misfortune, situation, etc., regarded as being worse than death; *spec.* loss of virginity; rape (formerly *euphem.*, now usu. jocular).

[**1653** D. OSBORNE *Let.* ? 28 Aug. (1903) 141 The Roman courage, when they killed themselves to avoid misfortunes that were infinitely worse than death. **1781** GIBBON *Decl. & F.* III. xxxi. 238 The matrons and virgins of Rome were exposed to injuries more dreadful, in the apprehension of chastity, than death itself.] **1810** JANE PORTER *Scottish Chiefs* III. iii. 68 But where was he who had delivered herself from a worse fate than death? **1832** F. TROLLOPE *Dom. Manners* (1949) 421 Then would a parliament of love ..doom to worse than death the spitter and tobacco chewer. **1894** RIDER HAGGARD *People of Mist* vi. 40 It is the custom of my mistress to carry a portion of this poison hidden in her hair, since a time might come when she must use it to save herself from worse than death. **1914** E. R. BURROUGHS *Tarzan of Apes* (1917) xix. 168 [The ape] threw her roughly across his broad, hairy shoulders, and leaped back into the trees, bearing Jane Porter away toward a fate a thousand times worse than death. **1926** *Sat. Rev.* 6 Feb. 166/1 The heroine, Countess Olga, is saved from a fate worse than death. **1949** R. HARVEY *Curtain Time* 22 If she hadn't got across, she would've had what they call a Fate Worse than Death. **1952** 'C. BRAND' *London Particular* vii. 95 Madonna Lily was obviously marked up for a double dose of Worse than Death.

c. *like death* (*warmed up*), colloq. phr. indicating a feeling or appearance of extreme illness or exhaustion.

1939 *Soldiers' War Slang Dict.* 7/2 *To feel like death warmed up*, to feel ill. **1942** N. MARSH *Death & Dancing Footman* ii. 42, I look like death warmed up and what I feel is nobody's business. **1964** J. PENDOWER *Sinister Talent* xx. 185 It damned near killed me... I still feel like death warmed up. **1969** *Guardian* 14 Feb. 11/1 Much of the time I feel like death. I am in rather a bad temper.

d. *in the death*, in the end; finally. *slang.*

1958 F. NORMAN *Bang to Rights* 172 In the death this geezer got a repreave. **1962** R. COOK *Crust on its Uppers* iii. 42 In the death, though, it went the way of all the best bent jams. *Ibid.* xvi. 157 After all, you had to marry someone in the death.

III. Combinations.

18. General combinations of obvious meaning.

These may be formed at will, and to any extent: examples are here given. The use of the hyphen is mainly syntactical; it usually implies also a main stress on *death-*, as in *'death-grasp*, *'death-,sickness*, *'death-po,lluted*.

a. *attributive.* [As with other names of things, employed instead of the genitive *death's* (see note below). In this construction already freely used in OE., as in *déaþ-béam*, *-bedd*, *-cwealm*, *-dæȝ*, *-denu*, *-spere*, *-stede*, etc.] Of death; belonging or pertaining to death; as ***death-agony***, ***-angel***, ***-camp***, ***-cart***, ***-chamber***, ***-chime***, ***-cry***, ***-cult***, ***-dew***, ***-dirge***, †***-door***, †***-fall***, ***-fever***, ***-flower***, ***-grapple***, ***-groan***, ***-hour***, ***-knell***, ***-march***, ***-note***, ***-pang***, ***-pill***, ***-sentence***, ***-shot***, ***-shriek***, ***-sleep***, ***-song***, ***-stab***, ***-stiffening***, ***-terror***, ***-token***, ***-train***, ***-vacancy***, ***-wraith***, etc.; also *objective*, as ***death-control*** (after *birth-control*), ***-dealer***, ***-worship***.

c **1440** CAPGRAVE *Life St. Kath.* v. 1751 Soo sodeynly onto deth for to falle. Som men wene that deth-fal were myserye. **1601** CHESTER *Love's Mart.* (1878) 39 Many Death-doore-knocking Soules complaine. **1606** SHAKS. *Tr. & Cr.* II. iii. 187 He is so plaguy proud, that the death tokens of it Cry no recouery. **1635** COWLEY *Davideis* IV. 972 One would have thought..That Nature's self in her Death-pangs had been. *a* **1780** J. CARVER *Trav.* 334 The number of the death-cries they give, declares how many of their own party are lost. *Ibid.* 337 They are then bound to a stake.. and obliged for the last time to sing their death-song. **1792** R. CUMBERLAND *Calvary* Poems 1803 II. 67 Christ's death-hour. **1795** SOUTHEY *Joan of Arc* IV. 262 He knew That this was the Death-Angel Azrael, And that his hour was come. **1798** SOTHEBY tr. *Wieland's Oberon* (1826) II. 25 Pale as the cheek with death-dew icy cold. **1799** NELSON in Nicolas *Disp.* IV. 82 To name Sidney Smith's First Lieutenant to the Death-vacancy of Captain Miller. **1811** W. R. SPENCER *Poems* 96 And our death-sentence ends the book. **1813** BYRON *Giaour* xxiii, The deathshot hissing from afar. **1813** SHELLEY *Q. Mab.* VII. 14 Nature confirms the faith his death-groan sealed. *Ibid.* IX. 104 The melancholy winds a death-dirge sung. **1814** SCOTT *Ld. of Isles* VI. xviii, I must not Moray's death-knell hear! **1816** J. WILSON *City of Plague* II. iv. 103 Now may I ask whose pious care Hath plac'd these death-flowers here! **1829** CARLYLE *Misc.* (1857) II. 55 He gave the death-stab to modern Superstition. **1834** HT. MARTINEAU *Demerara* ix. 128 The animal was not to be restrained..till the long death-grapple was over. **1838** LYTTON *Leila* I. v, The death-shriek of his agonised father. **1841** BORROW *Zincali* II. III. ii. 60 The death-carts..went through the streets..picking up the dead bodies. **1842** PUSEY *Crisis Eng. Ch.* 100 From this deathsleep..Protestant Germany was awakened by another battle-cry. **1851** CARPENTER *Man. Phys.* (ed. 2) 221 The *Rigor Mortis*, or death-stiffening of the muscles. **1882** J. H. BLUNT *Ref. Ch. Eng.* II. 3 The gallery out of which the death-chamber opened. **1883** A. I. MENKEN *Infelicia* 22 The last tremble of the conscious death-agony. **1884** GURNEY & MYERS in *19th Cent.* May 792 Alleged apparitions of living persons, the commonest of which are death-wraiths. **1897** *Daily News* 10 Dec. 7/2 During what was known as the 'death march' from Gundamuk to Peshawur..one battalion was..decimated.. by cholera. **1903** *Daily Chron.* 20 Oct. 5/1 Said he, You death dealers, I'll stop you. **1904** R. J. FARRER *Garden of Asia* vi. 44 The glow of the death-flowers..has faded. **1917** —— *On Eaves of World* I. iv. 71 The inevitable death-terror impels every human soul. **1920** MASEFIELD *Enslaved* 78 That devil's horn Its quavering death-note blew. **1922** JOYCE *Ulysses* 579 The deathflower of the potato blight on her breast. **1925** D. H. LAWRENCE *St. Mawr* 201 They had found their *raison d'être* in self-torture and death-worship. *a* **1930** —— *Etruscan Places* (1932) ii. 60 On the sculptured side of the sarcophagus the two death-dealers wield the hammer of death. **1938** AUDEN & ISHERWOOD *On Frontier* III. ii. 115 Your dreary death-cult is hardly likely to amuse a young lady. **1944** *Ann. Reg. 1943* 204 In the course of a three-day 'liquidation'..the Germans killed more than 1,000 Jews in 'death camps'. **1948** S. GILBERT tr. *Camus's Plague* III. i. 164 This system..was really a great improvement on the death-carts driven by negroes. **1949** KOESTLER *Promise & Fulfilment* vi. 58 At that time the death trains had started rattling through Eastern Europe. **1955** *World Population & Resources* (*P.E.P.*) I. i. 9 Whereas death-control has always been actively fostered by Governments, birth-control has almost always been left to voluntary action. **1962** *Guardian* 16 Feb. 7/2 This is the authentic Jewish experience: herding, the death-march, endless hunger. **1963** I. FLEMING *On H.M. Secret Service* xvi. 175 Had Campbell got a death pill, perhaps one of the buttons on his ski-jacket or trousers? **1970** *Nature* 14 Feb. 595/1 Population growth, death control and the expansion of the labour force are proceeding rapidly.

b. *objective*, with pres. pples. [already in OE., as *déaþ-berende*], as ***death-bearing***, ***-boding***, ***-braving***, ***-bringing***, ***-counterfeiting***, ***-darting***, ***-dealing***, ***-defying***, ***-giving***, ***-subduing***, ***-threatening***, etc., adjs.

1580 SIDNEY *Arcadia* (1622) 269 The..summons of the death-threatning trumpet. **1581** —— *Apol. Poetrie* (Arb.) 27 Death-bringing sinnes. **1590** SHAKS. *Mids. N.* III. ii. 364 Death-counterfeiting sleepe. **1592** —— *Rom. & Jul.* III. ii. 47 The death-darting eye of Cockatrice. **1593** —— *Lucr.* 165 No noise but Owles & wolues death-boding cries. **1633** FORD *Broken H.* I. ii, Death-braving Ithocles. *a* **1711** KEN *Hymns Evang.* Poet. Wks. 1721 I. 171 Their Death-subduing King. **1774** GOLDSM. *Nat. Hist.* (1776) VII. 156 This death-dealing creature. **1821** SHELLEY *Fugitives* iv. 7 As a death-boding spirit. **1860** *Sat. Rev.* X. 574/1 When these death-dealing missiles fell among them. **1878** GEO. ELIOT in *Macm. Mag.* July 168 What is martyrdom But death-defying utterance of belief? **1882** LONGFELLOW *In Harbor* 39 Life-giving, death-giving, which will it be? **1942** S. SPENDER *Life & Poet* 30 Tyrants who wish to freeze institutions into death-giving instead of life-giving forms. **1950** W. DE LA MARE *Inward Companion* 68 This death-defying acrobat.

c. *instrumental*, with pa. pples., and *parasynthetic*, as ***death-begirt***, ***-dewed***, ***-divided***, ***-laden***, ***-marked***, ***-polluted***, ***-shadowed***, ***-sheeted***, ***-slain***, ***-winged***, ***-wounded***, etc., adjs.

1592 SHAKS. *Rom. & Jul.* Prol. 9 The fearful passage of their death-mark'd love. ? *c* **1600** *Distracted Emp.* II. i. in Bullen *O. Pl.* III. 192 Having his deathe-slayne mistres in his armes. **1623** MASSINGER *Dk. Milan* v. ii, Secrets that restore To life death-wounded men! **1647** H. MORE *Song of Soul* I. III. xxi, Through the death-shadowed wood. **1787** MARY WOLLSTONECR. *Wks.* (1798) IV. 139 Those mansions, where death-divided friends should meet. **1809** BYRON *To Florence* viii, The death-wing'd tempest's blast. **1818** SHELLEY *Rev. Islam* X. xiii, The death-polluted land. **1832** MOTHERWELL *Poet. Wks.* (1847) 4 The dark death-laden banner. *a* **1839** MILMAN *Good Friday* Wks. II. 336 By thy drooping death-dew'd brow. **1871** G. MACDONALD *Songs Winter Days* III. iv, Death-sheeted figures, long and white. **1879** BROWNING *Ivan Ivanov.* 30 Each village death-begirt.

d. *adverbial* relations of various kinds, with adjs. and pples., rarely verbs. [With adjs. already in OE., as *déaþ-fǽȝe*, *-scyldiȝ*, *-wériȝ*.] In, to, unto, of, like, as death; as ***death-black***, ***-cold***, ***-dark***, ***-deaf***, ***-deep***, ***-devoted***, ***-doomed***, ***-due***, ***-great***, ***-pale***, ***-still***, ***-weary***, ***-white***, ***-worthy***, etc., adjs.; ***death-doom*** vb. See also DEATH-SICK.

1614 SYLVESTER *Bethulia's Rescue* VI. 210 So, the Saint-Thief, which suffered with our Saviour Was led to Life by his Death-due Behaviour. **1742** FRANCIS *Horace* IV. xiv. (Jod.), The death-devoted breast. **1742** YOUNG *Nt. Th.* v. 75 This Death-deep Silence, and incumbent Shade. **1776** MICKLE tr. *Camoens' Lusiad* 350 Death-doom'd man. **1795** SOUTHEY *Joan of Arc* x. 596 The death-pale face. **1796** T. TOWNSHEND *Poems* 105 What tho' the sigh or wailing voice Can't soothe the death-cold ear. **1829** E. ELLIOTT *Village Patriarch* Pref., With only one star..in the death-black firmament. **1839** BAILEY *Festus* ii. (1848) 11 Like Asshur's death-great monarch. **1863** BARING-GOULD *Iceland* 259, I can death-doom him as I please. **1864** LOWELL *Fireside Trav.* 242 To death-deaf Carthage shout in vain. **1866** HOWELLS *Venet. Life* iii. 34 All the floors..are death-cold in winter. **1906** *Westm. Gaz.* 19 Oct. 2/4 Wild lilies lie on a death-white heart. **1907** *Daily Chron.* 20 Aug. 3/2 Those death-still places which have no houses. **1921** W. DE LA MARE *Veil* 91 Rouse the Old Enemy from his death-still swoon. **1932** E. SITWELL *Bath* 81 They will play with..their death-dark negro slave.

¶ The genitive, now used (as a possessive) only in poetry or when death is personified, was formerly freely used where we should now use *of*, or *death-* in combination, as in ***death's evil***, ***sorrow***, ***sting***; ***death's bed***, ***day***, ***wound*** (see DEATH-BED, etc.). See also DEATH'S-FACE, -HEAD, -HERB, -RING.

a **1000** *Guthlac* 350 (Gr.) Nis me þæs deaþes sorȝ. *c* **1200** ORMIN 1374 Þær Cristess mennisscnesse Drannc dæþess drinnch. *c* **1230** *Hali Meid.* 17 Þat dreori dede..ȝiueð þat deaðes dunt. *c* **1422** HOCCLEVE *Learn to Die* 538 Thogh thow seeke in thy bed now lye, Be nat agast, no dethes euel haast thow. **1847** LYTE *Hymn*, '*Abide with me*' vi, Where is death's sting? Where, grave, thy victory?

19. Special combs.: **death-adder**, a name for the genus *Acanthophis* of venomous serpents, esp. *A. antarctica* of Australia; also erron. f. *deaf-adder*, *deaf adder*: see DEAF *a.* 1 d, 7; **death-baby** (*U.S.*), see quot.; **death-bill** (*Eccl.*), a list of dead for whom prayers were to be said (see quot.); **death-blast**, (*a*) a blast of a horn, etc. announcing or presaging death; (*b*) a storm or wind of destructive or deadly character; **death-bone** *Austral.*, a bone pointed at a person and intended to cause his death (cf. BONE *sb.* 1 e); **death camas(s)** = *death quamash*; **death cap** = *death-cup*; **death-chair**, the electric chair; **death-cord**, the rope used for hanging, the gallows-rope; **death-cup**, the poisonous fungus *Amanita phalloides*; **death-dance**, a dance at or in connexion with death; the Dance of Death; **death-doing** *a.*, doing to death, killing, murderous (see also DEAD-DOING); **death-drake** (*Angling*), a kind of artificial fly (see DRAKE); **death-duty**, a duty levied on the devolution of property in consequence of the owner's death; legacy, and probate and succession duties; †**death-evil** (*dede-*, *deed-*), a mortal disease; also, the name of a specific disease (quot. 1559); **death-feigning**, the feigning of death, esp. by an animal; **death-feud**, a feud prosecuted to the death; **death-flame** = DEATH-FIRE 1; **death-flurry** (*Whale-fishery*), the convulsive struggles of a dying whale after being harpooned (see FLURRY); also *fig.*; **death grant**, a State benefit payable towards the expenses, esp. of a funeral, incurred in connection with a person's death; †**death-head** = DEATH'S-HEAD; **death-house**, (*a*) a place where a person dies; (*b*) *colloq.*, that part of a prison where persons awaiting execution are housed; also, the execution shed; †**death-ill** (Sc. †*dede-ill*), mortal illness; **death-instinct** [tr. G. *todestrieb* (Freud 1920, *Jenseits des Lustprinzips* vi)], a destructive or self-destructive tendency postulated by Freud (cf. DEATH-WISH); **death-mask**, a cast of plaster or the like, taken from a person's face after death; **death-moss** (see quot.); **death-moth**, the Death's-head Moth; **death-or-glory** *attrib. phr.*, (*a*) (with capital initials) a regimental nickname (see quot. 1890); (*b*) *transf.*; **death-penalty**, the penalty of death, capital punishment; **death-penny**, the obolus placed in the mouth of a corpse, with which to pay the ferryman in Hades; **death-pile**, a funeral pile; **death quamash**, a plant of the western U.S., the bulb of which is poisonous to animals; **death-rate**, the proportion of the number of deaths to the population of a country, town, etc., usually reckoned at so much per thousand per annum; **death-rattle**, a rattling sound in the throat of a dying person, caused by the partial stoppage of the air-passage by mucus; **death-ray**, (chiefly in Science Fiction) a ray that causes death; **death-ring**, a finger-ring constructed to convey poison in shaking hands (W. Jones, *Finger-rings* 1877, 435); **death-roll**, a list of the names of those who have been killed in an accident, battle, etc.; **death-rope**, a gallows-rope; **death-ruckle**, **-ruttle** (Sc.) = *death-rattle*; **death-sough** (*Sc.*), 'the last inspiration of a dying person' (Jam.); **death squad**, an armed paramilitary group formed to murder political enemies, suspected subversives, etc.; **death-tick** = DEATH-WATCH 1; **death-trance**, a trance in which the action of the heart, lungs, etc. is so reduced as to produce the semblance of death (*Syd. Soc. Lex.* 1882); **death-trap**, applied to any place or structure which is unhealthy or dangerous without its being suspected, and is thus a trap for the lives of the unwary; **death-wave** (see quots.); **death-weight**, a small weight placed on the eyelids of a corpse to keep them closed.

1860 *Chambers' Encycl.* s.v. *Adder*, A very venomous serpent of New South Wales (*Acanthophis tortor*) is sometimes called the *death-adder. **1615** SIR E. HOBY *Curry-combe* 59 The gracelesse people, who stopped their eares like the death Adder. **1881** *A Chequered Career* 321 The deaf adder, or death adder, as some people miscall it. **1892** *N.Y. Nation* 11 Aug. 107/1 A certain fungus called '*death-baby'..fabled to foretell death in the family. **1849** ROCK *Ch. of Fathers* II. 383 *note*, Abp. Lanfranc..allotted the office of drawing up and sending off these *death-bills to the precentor. **1820** SCOTT *Abbot* xxviii, A bugle sounded loudly..'It is the *death-blast to Queen Mary's royalty', said Ambrosius. **1875** tr. *Comte de Paris' Hist. Civ. War Amer.* I. 456 The storm which in consequence of its periodical return in the beginning of November, sailors call the death-blast. **1933** *Bulletin* (Sydney) 19 Apr. 20/3 Even the semi-civilised Binghi of to-day is not proof against the old belief in the *death-bone. **1889** *Cent. Dict.* s.v. *Camass*, **Death camass*, the poisonous root of *Zygadenus venenosus*. **1937** *Range Plant Handbk.* (*Forest Service, U.S. Dept. Agric.*) W209 The more virulent species of death camas cause the majority of sheep losses. **1820** *St. Kathleen* IV. 23 (Jam.) She had for three nights successively seen a *death-candle flitting..along the cliffs. **1925** R. T. & F. W. ROLFE *Romance of Fungus World* iii. 37 *Amanita phalloides*, sometimes known as the *Death Cap. **1949** *Oxf. Jun. Encycl.* II. 172/1 Many fungi are mildly poisonous, but only one British species, the Death Cap, is deadly poisonous. **1890** *N.Y. Tribune* 7 Aug. 2/1 Kemmler stepped into the *death-chair. **1919** KIPLING *Lett. Travel* (1920) 269 Pinioned men in the death-chair before the current is switched on. *a* **1851** JOANNA BAILLIE (Ogilvie), Have I done well to give this hoary vet'ran..To the *death-cord, unheard? **1904** *Westm. Gaz.* 6 Oct. 10/1 The '*death-cup' is very abundant in woods in this country. **1865–8** F. PARKMAN *France & Eng. in Amer.* (1880) 275 The ghostly *death-dance of the breakers. *a* **1652** BROME *New Acad.* I. Wks. 1873 II. 9 Here's the *death-doing point. **1795** SOUTHEY *Joan of Arc* VII. 362 That death-doing foe. **1799** G. SMITH *Laboratory* II. 298 (*Angling*) *Death-drake..taken chiefly in an evening, when the May-fly is almost gone. **1881** GLADSTONE in *Daily News* 5 Apr. 2/6 My attention has been turned to a much larger subject—the subject of *death duties. *c* **1330** R. BRUNNE *Chron.* (1810) 32 Siþen at Gloucestre *dede euelle him toke. **1559** MORWYNG *Evonym.* 256 Angry byles, such as in some mens legges the late wrytars call the deed evill. **1924** J. A. THOMSON *Science Old & New* vi. 33 The '*death-feigning' or 'playing 'possum' of various animals. **1959** SOUTHWOOD & LESTON *Land & Water Bugs* xii. 355 Pressure on the bug, as by forceps in the laboratory, causes 'death-feigning' immobilization. **1820** SCOTT *Abbot* xi, They have threatened a *death-feud if any one touches us. **1813** HOGG *Queen's Wake* 65 That fays and spectres..spread the *death-flame on the wold. **1860** GEN. P. THOMPSON *Audi Alt.* III. ci. 2 The convulsive effort,—'*death-flurry' as the whalers call it,—which is taking place in America on the subject of slavery. **1946** *National Insurance Act* 9 & 10 *Geo.* 6 c. 67 § 22 A person shall be entitled to a *death grant in respect of the death of any person..if..he has reasonably incurred..expenses..in connection with the funeral of the deceased. **1971** *Reader's Digest Family Guide to Law* 293/1 The Government makes a lump-sum payment, called a death grant, to the next-of-kin of a person who has died, or to the person paying for the funeral. **1771** WESLEY *Wks.* (1872) V. 287 They are mere *death-heads; they kill innocent mirth. **1851** LONGF. *Gold Leg.* IV. *Refectory*, None of your death-heads carved in wood. **1920** MASEFIELD *Enslaved* 8 The place was like a *death-house save for cawings overhead. **1923** E. WALLACE *Missing Million* xxxviii. 293 He has three murders behind him, and the grey doors of the death-house in front of him. **1930** E. RICE *Voyage to Purilia* xiii. 168 The death-house—a huge edifice, crowded..with condemned men awaiting execution. **1958** G. MIKES *East is East* 120 The Death House is a Chinese institution. People are sent there to die because the Chinese regard it as bad luck if people die at home. **1960** *Guardian* 2 May 1/7 There is less than 24 hours to go before Chessman leaves the death house ..and goes to his..Maker. *c* **1425** WYNTOUN *Cron.* VII. x. 230 In-til hys *Dede-ill quhen he lay. **1675** DURHAM *Exp. Commandm.* To Rdr. 1 b (Jam.) The death-ill of a natural unrenewed man. **1822** GALT *Steam-boat* 292 (Jam.) Na, na! There's nae dead-ill about Loui. **1922** C. J. M. HUBBACK tr. *Freud's Beyond Pleasure Principle* vi. 38 The opposition between the ego or *death instincts and the sexual or life instincts would then cease. **1961** J. A. C. BROWN *Freud & Post-Freudians* ii. 27 The Death instinct is a force which is constantly working towards death. **1877** DOWDEN *Shaks. Primer* ii. 29 There exists a *death-mask..which bears the date 1616 and which may be the original cast from the dead poet's face. **1838** MISS PARDOE *River & Desert* I. 247 On many..venerable pines hung wreaths of the greyish-coloured, silken parasite which is called in 'wood-craft' the **death-moss*. *a* **1821** KEATS *Ode to Melancholy* 6 Nor let the beetle, nor the *death-moth be Your mournful Psyche. **1890** FARMER *Slang* I. 199/1 The 17th [Lancers] are still well-known as the *Death or Glory Boys, from their badge, which consists of a death's head, with the words, 'or glory'. **1959** W. K. RICHMOND *Brit. Birds of Prey* ix. 116 He is content to play second fiddle and leaves the death-or-glory stuff to his partner. **1962** *Guardian* 20 Dec. 6/1 Sir Roy Welensky's death-or-glory approach to political problems. **1875** E. WHITE *Life in Christ* II. xiv. (1878) 155 The *death-penalty of the law of Moses. **1863** WHYTE MELVILLE *Gladiators* III. 258 Scatter a handful of dust over my forehead, and lay the *death-penny on my tongue. **1851** MRS. BROWNING *Casa Guidi Windows* II. 76 Had all the *death-piles of the ancient years Flared up in vain before me? **1884** MILLER *Plant-n.* 264/2 *Zygadenus venenosus*. '*Death Quamash', Hog's Potato. **1859** *Ann. Rep. Registrar-General* p. ii, The *death rate was below the average. **1864** *Soc. Sc Rev.* 68 The death rates in the army had been reduced..by sanitary measures. **1873** B. STEWART *Conserv. Force* i. 1 The death rate..varies with the temperature. **1829** LYTTON *Devereux* VI. iv, His lips quivered wildly—I heard the *death-rattle. **1919** B. MUNN *Skeleton Man* xxvii. 90 Had the man once used his *death rays he was watched carefully enough to have been caught..red-handed. **1947** CROWTHER & WHIDDINGTON *Science at War* 4 The situation was grave and the public had already begun to long for death-rays that would dispatch the strongest enemy at will. **1961** J. B. PRIESTLEY *Saturn over Water* vi. 85 You may have some ridiculous ideas..that we are..discovering fantastic gases or death rays out of science fiction. **1963** *Ann. Reg. 1962* 386 Unlikely rumours were also heard that it might be developed as a military death ray or anti-missile weapon. **1864** M. B. CHESNUT *Diary* 1 Aug. (1949) 425 Day after day we read the *death roll. **1873** *Porcupine* XIV. 725/2 Two other actresses also appear on this week's death-roll. **1906** *Westm. Gaz.* 17 Oct. 10/1 The terrible disaster at Seaham in 1880, when the death-roll approximated to nearly 200. **1940** *Manch. Guardian Weekly* 5 Jan. 5 The full extent of the death-roll and damage will not be known for several days. **1815** SCOTT *Guy M.* xxvii, That was the *death-ruckle—he's dead. **1820** *Blackw. Mag.* Sept. 652 (Jam.) Heard nae ye the lang drawn *death-sough? **1969** *Times* 3 Jan. 3/7 In São Paulo..the new year has brought the macabre news from a mysterious *death squad that 1969 will be 'a year full of work'. **1976** *Guardian Weekly* 3 Oct. 8 The victims of the assassination schemes are for the most part political moderates, and there seems to be no geographical limit to the operations of the death squads. **1984** *Daily Mail* 20 Oct. 10/1 A student found dead in a London courtyard is believed to have been the victim of a death squad sent from Africa to kill his father. **1853** H. MELVILLE *Cock-A-Doodle-Doo!* in *Harper's Mag.* Dec. 81/1, I might as well have asked him if he had heard the *death-tick. **1879** JEFFERIES *Wild Life in S.C.* 207 In the huge beams or woodwork, the death-tick is sure to be heard in the silence of the night. **1835** BROWNING *Paracelsus* v. 128 This murky, loathsome *Death-trap, this slaughter-house. **1889** *Spectator* 14 Dec. 830 If..the Board schools are death-traps. **1848** C. A. JOHNS *Week at Lizard* 103 About one in every nine is more boisterous..than the rest: this the fishermen call 'the *death wave'. **1886** J. MILNE *Earthquakes* 171 Phenomena..on the Wexford coast..popularly known as 'death waves', probably in consequence of the lives which have been lost by these sudden inundations. **1850** MRS. BROWNING *Poet's Vow* v. iv–v, They laid the *death-weights on mine eyes.

death *a.*, var. of DEAF *a.* in some MSS., and in mod. dial. See also *death-adder* in DEATH *sb.* 19.

a **1500** *Metr. Life St. Kath.* 436 There is made hole dethe and dombe. **1574** HELLOWES *Gueuara's Fam. Ep.* 116 As he was death, and most dunch, I cried out more in speaking unto him, than I do use in preaching. **1875** *Sussex Gloss.*, *Death*, deaf..'afflicted with deathness'.

So **death** *v.* = DEAF *v.* to deafen.

c **1440** *York Myst.* xxxi. 186 Lo! sirs, he dethis vs with dynne!

death-bed ('dɛθbɛd). Also 5–6 ded-, dead-; 6 death's bed. **a.** The bed on which a person dies; the bed of death. (In OE. the grave.)

Beowulf 5795 Nu is..dryhten Geata, deað-bedde fæst. *c* **1400** *Gamelyn* 24 On his deep bed to a-bide Goddes wille. *a* **1500** *Childe of Bristowe* 100 in Hazl. *E.P.P.* I. 115 On his ded bed he lay. **1550** COVERDALE *Spir. Perle* xii, By him that lieth on his dead-bed. **1567** MAPLET *Gr. Forest* 29 When as he..lay vpon his deathes bed. **1604** SHAKS. *Oth.* v. ii. 51 Sweet Soule, take heed, take heed of Periury, Thou art on thy death-bed. **1732** POPE *Ep. Cobham* 116 He dreads a death-bed like the meanest slave. **1874** STUBBS *Const. Hist.* (1875) I. vii. 201 Canute's division of his dominions on his death-bed.

b. *attrib.* Freq. (with derogatory implication) in ***death-bed confession***, ***repentance***; also *transf.*, of a belated change of conduct or policy.

1691–8 NORRIS *Pract. Disc.* (1707) IV. 185 Such a Death-bed charity is too near akin to a Death-bed repentance, to be much valued. **1771** 'JUNIUS' *Lett.* I. p. vi, A death-bed repentance seldom reaches to restitution. **1816** SCOTT *Tales of Landlord* Introd., To answer funeral and deathbed expenses. **1888** A. C. GUNTER *Mr. Potter of Texas* vi, Curse him and his death-bed confession! **1963** *Times* 2 May 17/3 It was deplorable that it should have needed unemployment of more than 900,000..to extract even this rather meagre deathbed repentance from the Government.

death-bell ('dɛθbɛl). Also **dead-bell** (*Sc.* deid-bell).

1. A bell tolled at the death of a person; a passing-bell.

1781 C. J. FIELDING *Brothers*, The Village death-bell's distant sound. **1784** COWPER *Task* II. 51 A world that seems To toll the death-bell of its own decease. **1889** E. PEACOCK in *Cath. Household* 5 Jan. 13/3 The custom of ringing the death-bell at night.

β. a **1740** *Barbara Allan* viii. in Child *Ballads* (1886) IV. 277/2 She heard the dead-bell ringing. **18..** WHITTIER *Cry of Lost Soul* iv, The guide, as if he heard a dead-bell toll, Starts.

2. A sound in the ears like that of a bell, supposed by the superstitious to portend a death.

1807 HOGG *Mountain Bard* 17 (Jam.) O lady, 'tis dark, an' I heard the death-bell, An' darena gae yonder for gowd nor fee.

'death-bird. A bird that feeds on dead bodies; a carrion-feeding bird; a bird supposed to bode death; a popular name of a small North American owl, *Nyctala Richardsoni*.

1821 SHELLEY *Prometh. Unb.* I. 340. **1822** —— *Hellas* 1025 The death-birds descend to their feast. **1864** T. TAYLOR *Ballads of Brittany* (1865) 93 Sudden I heard the death-bird's cry.

'death-blow. A blow that causes death.

1795 SOUTHEY *Joan of Arc* VII. 135 For the death-blow prepared. *c* **1813** MRS. SHERWOOD *Stories Ch. Catech.* xiv. 118 It was her death-blow—down she dropped, and never spoke after. **1876** BANCROFT *Hist. U.S.* II. xxxii. 302 Never to receive the death-blow but with joy.

fig. **1811** BYRON *Lines written beneath Picture*, The death-blow of my Hope. **1838** THIRLWALL *Greece* V. 103 That event..was generally considered as a death-blow to the Spartan power.

'death-day. Forms: see DEATH *sb.*; also 7 death's-.

1. The day on which a person dies.

735 BÆDA *Death-song*, Huaet his gastae, godaes aeththa yflaes, aefter deothdaege doemid uueorthae. **1362** LANGL. *P. Pl.* A. III. 104 Hennes to þi deþ day do so no more. **1389** in *Eng. Gilds* 121 At þe ded day of a broþer, euery couple to ȝeuyn iij. penys. *c* **1450** *St. Cuthbert* (Surtees) 1540 My deed day comes at hand. *a* **1649** DRUMM. OF HAWTH. *Cypress Grove* Wks. (1711) 124 The death-day of thy body is thy birth-day to eternity. **1882** J. PARKER *Apost. Life* I. 15 Your death-day need not come upon you as a surprise.

2. The anniversary of this day.

1639 HORN & ROB. *Gate Lang. Unl.* xcvii. §964 Keeping a deaths-day as well as a birth-day. **1817** W. TAYLOR in *Monthly Mag.* XLIV. 234 The 7th of November was kept as a solemn anniverse by Lorenzo dei Medici..as the birth-day and death-day of Plato. **1855** THACKERAY *Newcomes* II. 332 The death-day of the founder..is still kept.

'death-fire.

1. A luminous appearance supposed to be seen over a dead body, etc.: = DEAD-LIGHT 3.

1796 COLERIDGE *Ode Departing Year*, Mighty armies of the dead, Dance like death-fires round her tomb. **1818** SHELLEY *Rev. Islam* XI. xii, From the choked well, whence a bright death-fire sprung.

2. A fire for burning a person to death.

1857 T. Flanagan *Hist. R.C. Church Eng.* II. 81 A large wooden statue of the blessed Virgin was brought.. to make the death-fire.

deathful ('dɛθfʊl), *a.* [See -ful.]

1. Full of death; fraught with death; mortal, fatal, destructive, deadly.

a **1240** *Lofsong* in *Cott. Hom.* 207 Bi his deaðfule grure and bi his blodie swote. **1580** Sidney *Arcadia* (1622) 104 Manie deathfull torments. **1617** Collins *Def. Bp. Ely* II. ix. 362 As Homer saies of the champions in their deathfull combat. **1621** G. Sandys *Ovid's Met.* II. (1626) 23 The deathfull Scorpion's far-out-bending clawes. **1742** Collins *Ode to Mercy* 7 Amidst the deathful field. **1850** Blackie *Æschylus* I. 154 The man, that dealt the deathful blow. **1878** Bayne *Purit. Rev.* viii. 340 Man under sinful and deathful conditions.

2. Subject to death, mortal. *arch. rare.*

1616 Chapman *Homer's Hymn to Venus* (N.), That with a deathless goddess lay A deathful man. **1887** Morris *Odyss.* III. 3 Unto deathful men on the corn-kind earth that dwell.

3. Having the appearance of death, deathly.

1656 [see deathfulness]. **1803** Jane Porter *Thaddeus* viii. (1831) 74 The deathful hue of his countenance. **1850** Mrs. Browning *Vision of Poets* xcii, Deathful their faces were. **1881** W. Wilkins *Songs of Study* 97 Her.. white body spotted o'er With deathful green.

Hence '**deathfully** *adv.*, '**deathfulness.**

1809 Campbell *Gertr. Wyom.* I. xvi, Deathfully their thunders seem'd to sweep. **1810** Scott *Lady of L.* IV. xxv, She was bleeding deathfully. **1656** *Artif. Handsom.* 70 To adorn our lookes, so as may be most remote from a deathfulnesse. *a* **1853** Robertson *Lect.* i. (1858) 116 There is nothing to break the deep deathfulness of the scene.

'**death-,hunter.** *slang.* One who furnishes a newspaper with reports of deaths (*obs.*); a vendor of dying speeches or confessions (*obs.*); an undertaker; see also quot. 1816.

1738 (*title* in Farmer), Ramble through London, containing observations on Beggars, Pedlars.. Death Hunters [etc.]. **1776** Foote *Capuchin* II. Wks. 1799 II. 391 When you were the doer of the Scandalous Chronicle, was not I death-hunter to the very same paper? **1816** C. James *Milit. Dict.* (ed. 4) 377/2 *Death Hunters*, followers of an army, who, after the engagement, look for dead bodies, in order to strip them. **1851** Mayhew *Lond. Lab.* I. 228 (Farmer) The 'running patterers', or death-hunters, being men engaged in vending last dying speeches and confessions.

deathify ('dɛθɪfaɪ), *v. nonce-wd.* (See quot.)

a **1834** Coleridge in *Remains* (1836) II. 163 Warburton would scarcely have made so deep a plunge into the bathetic as to have deathified 'sparrow' into 'spare me!'

deathiness ('dɛθɪnɪs). *rare.* [f. deathy *a.* + -ness.] The state or quality of being 'deathy'.

1801 Southey *Thalaba* v. (D.), It burns clear; but with the air around Its dead ingredients mingle deathiness. **1843** Sara Coleridge in *Mem.* (1873) I. 275 The recumbent figure.. looks deathy with too real and actual a deathiness.

deathless ('dɛθlɪs), *a.* [see -less.]

1. Not subject to death; immortal.

1598 Sylvester *Du Bartas* II. i. *Eden* 741 Should (like our death-less Soule) have never dy'd. **1648** Boyle *Seraph. Love* iii. (1700) 19 Though Angels and humane Souls be Deathless. **1790** Cowper *Odyssey* IV. 582 The deathless tenants of the skies. **1871** Tylor *Prim. Cult.* I. 425 The faith that animals have immaterial and deathless souls.

2. *fig.* Of things.

1646 Crashaw *Sospet. d'Her.* iii, The dew of life, whose deathless springs Nor Syrian flame, nor Borean frost deflow'rs. **1667** Milton *P.L.* x. 775 Deathless pain. **1867** Freeman *Norm. Conq.* (1876) I. vi. 408 The deathless name of Godwine.

Hence '**deathlessly** *adv.*, '**deathlessness.**

1682 H. More *Annot. Glanvill's Lux O.* 94 The deathlessness of the Soul. **1865** G. Meredith *Rhoda Fleming* xvi. (1889) 119 Our deathlessness is in what we do, not in what we are. **1850** Mrs. Browning *Vision of Poets* cxi, His brown bees hummed deathlessly.

'**death-light.**

1. = dead-light 3, death-fire 1.

1823 Joanna Baillie *Collect. Poems* 105 A death-light that hovers o'er Liberty's grave.

2. A light burning in a death-chamber.

1871 Carlyle in *Mrs. Carlyle's Lett.* I. 146 The two candles.. reserved.. to be her own death-lights.

deathlike ('dɛθlaɪk), *a.* [f. death *sb.* + -like; formed after the OE. *déaþ-líc* had become *deathly*.]

†**1.** Deadly, fatal, mortal; = deathly 2. *Obs.*

1548 Udall, etc. *Erasm. Par. John* 77 b, The sickenes was not deathlyke. **1608** Shaks. *Per.* I. i. 29 Death-like dragons here affright thee hard. **1621** Lady Mary Wroth *Urania* 418 Most cruell, and the death-lik'st kind of ill.

2. Resembling death.

1605 Sylvester *Du Bartas* II. iii. *Vocation* 616 A deep and death-like Letharge. **1795** Southey *Joan of Arc* IV. 435 A death-like paleness. **1856** Stanley *Sinai & Pal.* i. (1858) 14 The deathlike silence of a region where the fall of waters.. is unknown.

'**deathliness.** [f. deathly *a.* + -ness.] The quality of being deathly; resemblance to death.

1841 Lytton *Nt. & Morn.* (1851) 349 The utter, total Deathliness in Life of Simon. **1862** Mrs. Stowe *Agnes of Sorrento* xviii. 215 The utter deathliness of the scene.

deathling ('dɛθlɪŋ). *rare.* [See -ling.]

1. One subject to death, a mortal. Also *attrib.*

1598 Sylvester *Du Bartas* II. i. *Imposture* 374 Alas fond death-lings! **1839** Bailey *Festus* xiv. (1848) 151 Deathlings! on earth drink, laugh and love! **1886** Way tr. *Iliad* xii, Zeus.. Who over the deathling race and the deathless beareth sway.

2. *pl.* Young Deaths, the offspring of Death personified. (*nonce-use.*)

1730 Swift *Poems, Death & Daphne*, His realm had need That Death should get a num'rous breed; Young deathlings.

†**3.** *Gogs deathlings*: 'by God's death', an oath.

1611 Cotgr., *Mordienne*, Gogs deathlings; a foolish oath in Rab[elais].

deathly ('dɛθlɪ), *a.* Forms: 1–2 **déaþlíc**, 2 **deaðlich, deþlich**, 6 **deathlie, -lye**, 6– **deathly.** [OE. *déaþlíc* = OHG. *todlîh*: f. death *sb.* + -ly[1]; cf. deadly.]

†**1.** Subject to death, mortal. *Obs.*

971 *Blickl. Hom.* 21 Bið þonne undeaþlic, þeah he ær deaþlic wære. *a* **1175** *Cott. Hom.* 221 Þu wurst deaðlic, ȝef þu þes trowes westm ȝeétst. *c* **1200** *Trin. Coll. Hom.* 9 Mid ure deaðliche liue.

2. Causing death, deadly.

c **1175** *Lamb. Hom.* 75 Deþliche atter. **1548** Udall, etc. *Erasm. Par.* 2 Cor. ii. (R.), Vnholsome and deathlye to such as refuse it. **1555** *Cohabitacyon of Faithfull* 19 The byting of deathlie serpentes. **1568** T. Howell *Newe Sonnets* (1879) 119 When deathly seas compels weake hart to quaile. **1862** Trollope *North Amer.* I. 263 That deathly flow of hot air coming up.. from the neighbouring infernal regions. **1885** W. de Gray Birch *Life K. Harold* v. 135 His wounds, many and deathly.

3. Of the nature of or resembling death, deathlike; gloomy, pale, etc. as death.

1568 T. Howell *Arb. Amitie* (1879) 69 The deathly day in dole I passe. **1852** Mrs. Carlyle *Lett.* II. 204 She, poor thing, looking deathly. **1865–8** F. Parkman *France & Eng. in Amer.* (1880) 57 A deathly stillness.

4. Of or pertaining to death. *poetical.*

1850 Mrs. Browning *Soul's Trav.* 176 That deathly odour which the clay Leaves on its deathlessness alway. **1878** Browning *La Saisiaz* 65 As soul is quenchless by the deathly mists.

'**deathly,** *adv.* In 2 **deaðliche.** [See prec. and -ly[2]. Cf. deadly *adv.* 1, 3, 4.]

†**1.** In a way causing or tending to death. *Obs.*

a **1240** *Lofsong* in *Cott. Hom.* 211 Herþurh ich deie þet spec er of swuche þinge and deaðliche sunegi.

2. To a degree resembling death.

1817 Coleridge *Biog. Lit.* (1847) I. 185 Here and thus I lay, my face.. deathly pale. **1884** C. F. Woolson in *Harper's Mag.* Jan. 197/1 It was 'deathly cold' in these 'stony lanes'.

death-place ('dɛθpleɪs). [f. death *sb.* + place *sb.*] The place where a person dies.

1830 Moore *Byron's Life & Lett.* II. 778 His lost friend's melancholy deathplace, Missolonghi. **1901** *Spectator* 28 Sept. 430/1 Why.. is the deathplace of Constantius given as Mopsucrenam? **1906** *Daily Chron.* 19 Dec. 4/5 Brocket Hall, Herts,.. the death-place of two Premiers, Lord Melbourne and Lord Palmerston. **1908** *Westm. Gaz.* 16 Nov. 9/2 Violating the precedents which prescribe the death-place of the rulers of China. **1937** *Tablet* 23 Oct. 553/2 To follow Moses from birth- to death-place (neither of which will ever be ascertainable).

†'**death's-face.** *Obs.*[−1] = death's-head 1.

1623 Shaks. *L.L.L.* v. ii. 616 A deaths face in a ring.

death's-head ('dɛθshɛd). [See death *sb.* 1 c.]

1. The head of Death figured as a skeleton; a human skull; a figure or representation of a skull, *esp.* as an emblem of mortality.

1596 Shaks. *Merch. V.* I. ii. 55, I had rather to be married to a deaths head with a bone in his mouth. **1597** —— *2 Hen. IV*, II. iv. 255 Doe not speake like a Deaths-head: doe not bid me remember mine end. **1684** *Lond. Gaz.* No. 1987/4 Several Jewels and Rings, one of which was Enamelled with a Deaths-head. **1768–74** Tucker *Lt. Nat.* (1852) II. 659 Hermits and holy men are described sighing over death's heads, sobbing and groaning at their being men and not angels. **1822** Scott *Pirate* xl, The old black flag, with the death's head and hour-glass. **1864** Thackeray *D. Duval* ii, His appearance.. was as cheerful as a death's head at a feast. *fig.* **1641** May *Old Couple* III. ii. (1810), As the two old death's-heads to-morrow morning Are to be join'd together.

†**b.** A ring with the figure of a skull. *Obs.*

(About 1600 commonly worn by procuresses.)

1605 Marston *Dutch Courtezan* I. ii, Their wickednesse is always before their eyes, and a deathes-head most commonly on their middle finger. **1607** Dekker *Northward Hoe* IV. Wks. 1873 III. 50 As if I were a bawd, no ring pleases me but a death's head. **1670** *Devout Commun.* (1688) 8 Shall not I wear thy ring, who am so ready to wear a Death's-head to preserve alive the memorial of a dead friend?

2. A name given to a South American species of squirrel-monkey, *Chrysothrix sciureus*, from the appearance of its face and features.

3. *attrib.* **death's-head moth,** a large species of hawk-moth (*Acherontia atropos*), having markings on the back of the thorax resembling the figure of a skull.

1781 Barbut *Genera Insect.* 179 *Deaths-head moth*.. It has a grey irregular spot upon which are two black dots which very plainly represent a death's head, whence this insect takes its name. **1816** Kirby & Sp. *Entomol.* (1843) II. 414 The bees.. protected themselves from the attacks of the death's head moth.. by closing the entrance of the hive. **1879** Lubbock *Sci. Lect.* ii. 50 The Death's head hawk-moth caterpillar feeds on the potato.

†'**death's-herb.** *Obs.* Deadly Nightshade.

1607 Topsell *Four-f. Beasts* (1673) 99 Dwall or Night-shade, which is also called Deaths-herb.

'**death-sick,** *a.* [death *sb.* 18 d.] Sick unto death, mortally sick or ill. So '**death-,sickness,** mortal illness.

1628 Bp. Hall *Quo Vadis?* §19 Apparitions.. wherewith some of our death-sick gentlemen.. haue bin frighted into catholickes. **1661** *Petit. E. Chaloner* in *7th Rep. Hist. MSS. Commission* 147 During his imprisonment.. he took his death sickness. **1846** Manning *Serm.* (1848) II. ii. 33 After the partial cure of a death-sickness.

deathsman ('dɛθsmən). *arch.* A man who puts another to death; an executioner.

1589 Greene *Menaphon* (Arb.) 90 Democles commanded the deathsman to doo his deuoyre. **1605** Shaks. *Lear* IV. vi. 263, I am onely sorry He had no other Deathsman. *a* **1632** T. Taylor *God's Judgem.* II. vii. (1642) 104 Loath to have any other deaths-man but himselfe, he was found slaine by his owne hand. **1813** Scott *Rokeby* VI. xxxii, The very deaths-men paused to hear.

death-song. [death *sb.* 18 a. Cf. G. *todesgesang*, earlier †*todtengesang*.] A song sung immediately before death, or to commemorate the dead. In U.S. *spec.* with reference to Indian customs.

1778 J. Carver *Travels* 337 They are then bound to a stake.. and obliged.. to sing their death-song. **1843** *American Pioneer* II. 225 Four of the missionaries.. were then led into the camp of the Delawares, where the death-song was sung over them. **1873** J. Miller *Life amongst Modocs* ii. 21 They will not revisit their own camp.. until it is first visited by their priest or medicine man, who chaunts the death-song. **1885** H. Sweet *Oldest Eng. Texts* 149 (*title*) Bede's Death-song. **1892** S. A. Brooke *Hist. Early Eng. Lit.* I. 74 Like an Indian chief, he [*sc.* Beowulf] sang his death-song. **1947** B. A. De Voto *Across Wide Missouri* 84 Some of the Gros Ventres began to sing their death songs.

†'**death's-ring.** *Obs.* A death's-head ring.

1649 Bp. Hall *Cases Consc.* IV. vii. (1654) 360 The old posie of the deaths-ring.

'**death-struck,** *a.* Also **death-stricken,** †**-strucken.** Smitten with death, *i.e.* with a mortal wound or disease.

1622 J. Reynolds *God's Revenge* II. vii. 83 They see her death-strooken with that Plannet, and therefore adiudge their skill but vaine. **1653** H. More *Antid. Ath.* III. ii. (*heading*), A strange Example of one Death-strucken as he walked the Streets. **1688** Norris *Love* I. iii. 25 When all his Rational Facultys are as 'twere benumm'd and death-struck. **1812** Byron *Ch. Har.* I. lxxvii, Tho' death-struck, still his feeble frame he rears. **1855** Robinson *Whitby Gloss.*, *Death-strucken*, smitten with death. **1887** A. Jessopp in *Dict. Nat. Biog.* IX. 402/2 It is only when he [Cecil] is death-stricken.. that we find the curtain raised.

death-throe. Forms: α. 4 **deþ þrowe,** 6 *Sc.* **deitht thrau,** 7–9 **death-throe;** β. *Sc.* and *north. dial.* 4 **ded thrau, dede þrawe,** 6 **dede-, deid-thraw,** 7 **dead-throe,** 9 **dead-thraw, -throw.** [f. death *sb.* + throe; most frequent in the northern form *dede-thraw*, mod.Sc. *deid-thraw.*] The agony of death, the death-struggle; also *fig.*

c **1305** *St. Christopher* 192 in *E.E.P.* (1862) 64 Þat hire deþ þrowes were stronge. **1549** *Compl. Scot.* xiv. 121 Darius vas in the agonya and deitht thrau. **1849** Robertson *Serm.* Ser. I. xii. (1866) 210 The death-throes of Rome were long and terrible.

β. *a* **1300** *Cursor M.* 26659 (Cott.) Quen ded thraus smites smert. **1535** Stewart *Cron. Scot.* III. 119 Sum in the deid-thraw la walterand in swoun. **1597** Montgomerie *Cherrie & Slae* 286 Like to an fische fast in the net, In deid-thraw vndeceist. **1645** Rutherford *Tryal & Tri. Faith* (1845) 279 In the dead-throe. **1815** Scott *Guy M.* ix, Ye maun come hame, sir,—for my lady's in the dead-thraw. **1826** E. Irving *Babylon* I. II. 144 While it is the dead-throw, the last gasp and termination of life to the Papal Beast.

b. *fig.* (*Sc.*)

1808 Jamieson *s.v.*, Meat is said to be in the deadthraw, when it is neither cold nor hot. **1822** Hogg *Perils Man* III. 116 (Jam.) One of those.. winter days.. when the weather is what the shepherds call in the dead-thraw, that is, in a struggle between frost and thaw.

deathward ('dɛθwəd), *adv.* and *a.* Forms: see death *sb.*. [See -ward.] **A.** *adv.* In the direction of death, towards death. **a.** orig. *to* (*one's*) *deathward* = towards one's death.

c **1430** Lydg. *Bochas* I. ix. (1544) 18 b, Kind [= Nature] to his deathward.. doth him dispose. *c* **1440** *Gesta Rom.* xlvii. 202 (Harl. MS.), I sawe him go to deþeward. *c* **1530** Ld. Berners *Arth. Lyt. Bryt.* (1814) 129 Ye shall not go to your dethward. **1876** Swinburne *Erechth.* 705 And wash to deathward down one flood of doom.

β. **1340** Hampole *Pr. Consc.* 807 When he drawes to dedward. *c* **1400** Maundev. (Roxb.) xxi. 96 When þaire frendez drawez to þe deed ward.

b. without *to.*

1844 Mrs. Browning *Poems, Lady Geraldine's Courtship* Concl. ix, So.. Would my heart and life flow onward, deathward. **1887** Swinburne *Locrine* IV. i. 77 Our senses sink From dream to dream down deathward.

B. *adj.* Tending towards death.

1854 'G. Greenwood' *Haps & Mishaps* 43 O immortal stones,.. mocking.. the mournful mortality, the deathward throbbing, of the brows ye encircle! **1882** Swinburne *8 Yrs. Old* in *Tristram of L.* 257 Sounds of dying and dawning years, Now quickened on his deathward way. **1899** *Daily News* 17 Oct. 8/3 A pleasant-looking, neatly-dressed woman on the deathward side of fifty. **1937** J. M. Murry *Necessity of Pacifism* v. 86 The individualized, by the very fact of its individualization, belongs to the deathward movement of society.

'deathwards, *adv.* (*a.*). [See -WARDS.] = prec.
1839 BAILEY *Festus* v. (1848) 12/1 All mortal natures fall Deathwards. **1880** R. H. HUTTON in *Fraser's Mag.* May 665 The 'life-wards' or 'death-wards' tendency of our actions.

'death-,warrant. Also 7-8 dead-. A warrant for the execution of the sentence of death.
1692 LUTTRELL *Brief Rel.* (1857) II. 644 The dead warrant is come to the sheriffe of London for the execution of 13 of the late condemned criminally. **1757** SYMMER in Ellis *Orig. Lett.* II. IV. 398 The Lords of the Admiralty..signed the Dead Warrant appointing him to be shot. **1886** C. BULLOCK *Queen's Resolve* 51/1 Before Parliament relieved her of the necessity, she [Queen Victoria] had to sign the death-warrant of all prisoners sentenced to suffer capital punishment.
fig. **1814** SCOTT *Life of Swift* Swift's Wks. (1824) I. 250 It was her death-warrant. She sunk at once under the disappointment. **1874** MORLEY *Compromise* (1886) 232 An institution whose death-warrant you pretend to be signing.

death-watch ('dɛθwɒtʃ). Also 8 dead-.
1. The popular name of various insects which make a noise like the ticking of a watch, supposed by the ignorant and superstitious to portend death; *esp.* the death watch beetle, *Xestobium rufovillosum*, or *Trogium pulsatorium*, a book louse of the order Psocoptera.
1668 WILKINS *Real Char.* II. v. §2. 127 Sheathed Winged Insects..That of a long slender body, frequent about houses, making a noise like the minute of a Watch..Death Watch. **1700** ASTRY tr. *Saavedra-Faxardo* II. 385 The Death-watch Spiders spread their curious Hair. **1762** GOLDSM. *Cit. W.* xc, I listened for death-watches in the wainscot. **1817** KIRBY & SPENCE *Introd. Ent.* II. xxiv. 383 A little wood-louse..—which on that account has been confounded with the death-watch—is said also..to emit a ticking noise. **1828** STARK *Elem. Nat. Hist.* II. 272 Both sexes, in the season of love, have the habit of calling one another by striking rapidly with their mandibles on the wood..This noise, similar to the accelerated beating of a watch, has occasioned..the vulgar name of *Death-watch.* **1877** *Encycl. Brit.* VI. 132/2 Many of the *Malacodermata* are wood-borers; these include the Death-watch Beetles (*Anobium*). **1881** BESANT & RICE *Chapl. of Fleet* I. 294 Last night I heard the death-watch. **1925** E. G. BLAKE *Enemies of Timber* vi. 136 The death-watch beetle..confines its activities exclusively to structural timbers, and is practically identical in its methods and habits with the common furniture beetle. **1955** *Times* 9 May 5/2 The death-watch beetle did not attack sound and permanently dry timber. **1964** N. E. HICKIN *Household Insect Pests* v. 56 One interesting habit shown by the species *Trogium pulsatorium* is the tapping noise which it produces by vibrating its abdomen against a material such as paper. It is probable that the first reference to the 'Death Watch' concerned this Book Louse and not the wood-boring beetle. **1969** R. F. CHAPMAN *Insects* xxviii. 575 The death watch beetle, *Xestobium*, produces tapping sounds by bending its head down and banging it against the floor of its burrow.
comb. **1710** E. WARD *Brit. Hud.* 60 Thy Melancholy Tick, That sounds, alas, so Death-watch like.
2. A watch or vigil by the dead or dying.

'death-wish. [tr. G. *todeswunsch*, f. *tod* death + *wunsch* wish.] A conscious or unconscious wish for the death of oneself or another; also *fig.*
1896 L. HOUSMAN *Green Arras* 68 And I, at the death-wish then, Stood looking upon it all. **1913** A. A. BRILL tr. *Freud's Interpr. of Dreams* v. 218 The death-wish towards parents is to be explained by reference to earliest childhood. **1929** P. MAIRET *Adler's Problems of Neurosis* vi. 84 After having triumphed over him and having had the death-wish granted by fate, he remained still unsatisfied. **1937** 'C. CAUDWELL' *Illusion & Reality* 97 The same secret death-wishes are shown by these aristocrats if they turn revolutionary. **1947** *Partisan Rev.* XIV. 233 Even in America..the death-wish of the business community appears to go beyond the normal limits of political incompetence and geographical security. **1953** X. FIELDING *Stronghold* 153 A death-wish, a longing to be underground, to be in a tomb, buried. **1958** *New Statesman* 11 Jan. 29/1 Whatever handicaps Mr. Macmillan labours under as Prime Minister, they do not include the death-wish; he is still jauntily determined to win the next election.

'death-worm.
†**1.** = DEATH-WATCH 1. *Obs.*
1773 *Gentl. Mag.* XLIII. 195 No ticking death-worm told a fancied doom.
2. *poet.* A 'worm of death'.
1821 SHELLEY *Prometh. Unb.* II. i. 16 How like death-worms the wingless moments crawl! **1850** MRS. BROWNING *Romaunt of Margret* xxiv, Behold, the death-worm to his heart Is a nearer thing than thou.

'death-worthy, *a.* Also 4 ded-. Worthy or deserving of death.
a **1300** *Cursor M.* 11967 (Cott.) Quat has it don þis bodi, ded worþei to be? **1532** MORE *Confut. Barnes* VIII. Wks. 780/2 He was death worthy yᵗ wythdrewe from god the mony which himself had giuen to god. **1593** SHAKS. *Lucr.* 635 This guilt would seem death-worthie in thy brother. **1882** H. ST. CLAIR FEILDEN *Short Const. Hist. Eng.* iv. 157 One [of Alfred's laws] makes treason deathworthy.

'death-wound. Forms: see DEATH *sb.*; formerly also *β.* dedes-, death's-. A wound causing death, a mortal wound.
c **1314** *Guy Warw.* (A.) 3490 Smiteþ wiþ swerdes & speres ..and ȝif hem deþ wounde. *c* **1489** CAXTON *Sonnes of Aymon* xxvi. 562 He made him a grete wounde but no deed wounde. **1793** LD. AUCKLAND *Corr.* (1862) III 122 Jacobinism is.. more likely to receive its death-wound in the South of France than in Flanders. **1867** SMYTH *Sailor's Word-bk.*, *Death-wound*, a law term for the starting of a butt end, or springing a fatal leak. **1879** FARRAR *St. Paul* (1883) 3 The dealer of the death-wound to the spirit of Pharisaism was a Pharisee.
β. **13..** *Cursor M.* 7592 (Gött.) Mani fledd wid dedes wound [*v.r.* deþes wounde]. **1489** CAXTON *Chron. Eng.* ccxliii. 290 There he caught deths wounde. **1536** BELLENDEN *Cron. Scot.* (1821) II. 465 Ane deidis wound in his heid. **1667** MILTON *P.L.* III. 252 Death his deaths wound shall then receive. **1763** SCRAFTON *Indostan* (1770) 43 Mustapha Caun..received his death's wound from an arrow.

deathy ('dɛθɪ), *a.* and *adv.* [f. DEATH *sb.* + -Y.]
A. *adj.* Of the nature or character of death; = DEATHLY *a.* 3, 4.
1801 [cf. DEATHINESS]. **1820** SHELLEY *Witch Atl.* lxx, A mimic day within that deathy nook. **1825** SOUTHEY *Tale of Paraguay* iv. 38 A deathy paleness settled in its stead. **1826** *Blackw. Mag.* XX. 665 The Raven dislikes all animal food that has not a deathy smack.
B. as *adv.* To a degree resembling death; = DEATHLY *adv.* 2.
1796 SOUTHEY *Ballads, Donica* xx, Her cheeks were deathy white and wan. **1811** SHELLEY *Moonbeam* ii. 1 Now all is deathy still.

†**de'aurate,** *a. Obs.* [ad. L. *deaurāt-us*, pa. pple. of *deaurāre* (late L.) to gild over, f. DE- I. 3 + *aurāre* to gild, f. *aurum* gold.] Gilded, golden.
c **1430** LYDG. *Compl. Bl. Knt.* lxxxvi, And whyle the twylyght and the rowes rede Of Phebus lyght were deaurat a lyte. *c* **1510** BARCLAY *Mirr. Gd. Manners* (1570) B iij, The tree of this science with braunches deaurate. **1599** NASHE *Lenten Stuffe* (1871) 57 Of so eye-bewitching a deaurate ruddy dye is the skin-coat of this landgrave. **1616** BULLOKAR, *Deaurate*, guilded, glistering like gold.

deaurate (diː'ɔːreɪt), *v.* ? *Obs.* [f. L. *deaurāt-*, ppl. stem of *deaurāre* to gild: see prec.] *trans.* To gild over. Hence **deaurated** *ppl. a.*
1562 BULLEYN *Bk. Simples* 95 a, Golde is holsome to deaurate or gilde Losinges. **1603** H. CROSSE *Vertues Commw.* (1878) 54 To..deaurate and guild ouer his spottes and sores with the tincture and dye of holynesse. **1656** BLOUNT *Glossogr.*, *Deaurate*, to gild or lay over with gold [also in BAILEY (folio) and JOHNSON]. **1818** J. BROWN *Psyche* 62 She..to illuminate his pen, A deaurated thought inspires, But instantaneously retires.
Hence **deau'ration**, the action of gilding.
1658 PHILLIPS, *Deauration*, a gilding over. **1706** —— (ed. Kersey), *Deauration*, a gilding, or laying over with Gold: Among Apothecaries, the gilding of Pills to prevent ill Tastes. **1721** in BAILEY. **1755** in JOHNSON; and mod. Dicts.

deave (diːv), *v.* Now *Sc.* and *north. dial.* In 4-6 (9) deve, (4-5 dewe), 6 *Sc.* deiv(e, 9 deeve. [OE. *déafian* in *adéafian* (*f* between vowels = *v*) to wax deaf. The trans. type **díefan*, **dýfan* to make deaf, corresp. to Goth. (*ga*)*daubjan*, OHG., MHG. *touben*, *töuben*, Ger. (*be*)*täuben*, does not appear in OE., and the trans. seems to be an extension of the intrans. use in ME.: cf. DEAD *v.*]
†**1.** *intr.* To become deaf. *Obs. rare.*
[*c* **1050** *Gloss.* in Wr.-Wülcker 179/25 *Obsurduit* adeafede.] **13..** in *Pol. Rel. & L. Poems* 224 Hyse eres shullen dewen, And his eyen shullen dymmen.
2. *trans.* To deafen; to stun or stupefy with noise (formerly also with a blow); to bewilder, worry, or confuse, esp. by 'dinning' in one's ears.
c **1340** *Gaw. & Gr. Knt.* 1286 Þe dunte þat schulde hym deue. *a* **1400** *Cov. Myst.* (Shaks. Soc.) 348 Wyttys ben revid, Erys ben devid. *c* **1420** *Anturs of Arth.* xxii, Alle the Duseperis of Fraunse [are] with your dyn deuyt. *c* **1470** HENRY *Wallace* x. 285 Dewyt with speris dynt. **1500-20** KENNEDIE *Flyting w. Dunbar* 360 Thow devis the deuill, thyne eme, wyth dyn. **1597** MONTGOMERIE *Cherrie & Slae* 671 He greuis vs and deues vs With sophistries and schiftis. **1792** BURNS *Willie's Wife* ii, She has..A clapper tongue wad deave a miller. **1818** SCOTT *Hrt. Midl.* v, Dinna deave me wi' you nonsense. **1825** in BROCKETT, *Deave.* **1874** DASENT *Tales fr. Fjeld* 31 It deaved one to hear. **1888** *Sheffield Gloss.*, *Deave*, to deafen; to embarrass, to confuse. Also in Glossaries of *Northumb.*, *Cumbrld.*, *Lanc.*, *Cheshire*, *Cleveland*, *Whitby.*
Hence **'deaving** *ppl. a.*
1832 MOTHERWELL in *Whistle-Binkie* (Sc. Songs) Ser. I. 45 The deavin' dinsome toun. **1883** READE *Tit for Tat* i. in *Harper's Mag.* Jan. 251/2 A new peal of forty church bells, mounting..from a muffin man's up to a deaving dome of bell-metal.

deave, obs. inflex. of DEAF *a.*

'deavely, deafly, *a. dial.* [The form suggests derivation from DEAF (like *goodly*, *sickly*, *weakly*), and the etymological sense may be 'where nothing is heard, silent'.] Lonely, solitary and silent.
1611 COTGR., *Desolé*, desolate, deavelie, desart. *Lieux destournez*..deauelie habitations, solitarie lodgings. **1674-91** RAY *N.C. Words* 14 *Deafely*, lonely, solitary, far from neighbours. **1855** ROBINSON *Whitby Gloss.*, *Deeafly* or *Deafly*, lonely. 'They live in a far off deeafly spot,' retired from all noise, secluded. **1884** *Cheshire Gloss.*, *Dovely*. *Deavely*, *Deafly*, lonely. 'It's a davely road.'
Hence **'deaveliness.**
1611 COTGR., *Solitude*..lonelinesse..want of companie, deauelinesse. *Silence*, a deauelinesse, or solitarinesse.

deavour, var. of DEVER, DEVOIR.

deaw, -y, obs. forms of DEW, DEWY.

†**de-a'warren,** *v. Obs. rare.* [f. WARREN: cf. *de-afforest.*] = DISWARREN.
1727 W. NELSON *Laws conc. Game* (1736) 32 Deawarrened, is when a Warren is diswarrened, or broke up and laid in Common.

deb (dɛb). orig. *U.S.* Also **debby.** Colloq. abbrev. of DÉBUTANTE; hence ***debs'*** (or ***deb's***, ***debbies'***) ***delight***, an eligible or attractive young man in high society. Also *attrib.* or as *adj.*
1920 F. SCOTT FITZGERALD *This Side of Paradise* II. ii. 227 Dancing with mid-Western or New Jersey debbies. **1922** JOYCE *Ulysses* 437 Josie Powell that was, prettiest deb in Dublin. **1926** *Ladies' Home Jrnl.* July 26 One of my deb cousins makes a transcendent cocktail. **1927** *Sunday Express* 10 July 10 It appears that her comments on society have roused the ire of the great army of debutantes... How the angry 'debs' propose to deal with their victim..I cannot imagine. **1928** *Sunday Dispatch* 9 Dec. 11/2 The impossibility of parents doing any of the old kind of chaperonage in the hours kept by the present day (or night) 'debbies' during their present season. **1934** J. O'HARA *Appointment in Samarra* v. 135 Joe Montgomery could be classified under many headings... Well-dressed man. Debbies' delight. Roué. **1940** M. DICKENS *Mariana* vii. 217 She presents her at Court, drags her to all the deb. dances. **1948** N. MARSH *Death in White Tie* iii. 33 Lord Robert half suspected his nephew Donald of being a Debs' Delight. **1958** *Oxf. Mail* 1 July 6/6 His girl is a dim creation and Pauline Arden makes her unnecessarily 'debby'. **1958** *Daily Mail* 4 July 10/4 She danced with —— at a debby night spot clad in little more than a nylon nightie. **1966** J. BETJEMAN *High & Low* 56 The debs may turn disdainful backs On Pearl's uncouth mechanic slacks. **1970** *Daily Tel.* 5 Sept. 16 Somewhat debby (though none was in fact a deb), the girls must also be ready to display their social graces at Council cocktail parties.

†**de'bacchate,** *v. Obs. rare.* [ad. L. *dēbacchāri*, f. *Bacchus*: see DE- I. 3.] To rage or rave as a bacchanal. Hence †**debac'chation.**
1623 COCKERAM, *Debacchate*, to reuile one after the manner of drunkards. **1633** PRYNNE *Histrio-M.* I. VI. xii. (R.), Who defile their holiday with..most wicked debacchations, and sacrilegious execrations. **1727** BAILEY vol. II, *Debacchation*, a raging or madness. *a* **1751** in Bp. Lavington *Enthus. Method. & Papists* (1754) III. 93 Then falling into a Fit of Rage, Quarrelling, and Debacchation.

debace, obs. form of DEBASE.

debacle (dɪ'bɑːk(ə)l). Also **débâcle.** [a. F. *débâcle*, vbl. sb. from *débâcler* to unbar, remove a bar, f. *dé-* = *des-* (see DE- I. 6) + *bâcler* to bar.]
1. A breaking up of ice in a river; in *Geol.* a sudden deluge or violent rush of water, which breaks down opposing barriers, and carries before it blocks of stone and other debris.
1802 PLAYFAIR *Illustr. Hutton. Th.* 402 Valleys are so particularly constructed as to carry with them a still stronger refutation of the existence of a debacle. **1823** W. BUCKLAND *Reliq. Diluv.* 158 They could have been transported by no other force than that of a tremendous deluge or debacle of water. **1893** *Daily Tel.* 1 Feb., The debacle in the United States..Telegrams state that the breaking up of the ice is being attended with great damage.
2. *transf.* and *fig.* A sudden breaking up or downfall; a confused rush or rout, a stampede.
1848 THACKERAY *Van. Fair* xxxii, The Brunswickers were routed and had fled..It was a general *débâcle.* **1887** *Graphic* 15 Jan. 59/2 In the nightly *débâcle* [he] is often content to stand aside.

debadge (diː'bædʒ), *v.* [f. DE- II. 2 a + BADGE *sb.*] *trans.* To deprive of the badge which in the war of 1914-18 exempted a man from military service. Also **de'badged** *ppl. a.*
1916 *Daily Mail* 23 Sept. 5/7 All single men under, say, twenty one, to be immediately debadged. *Ibid.* 1 Nov. 5/5 This practice of capturing debadged men has been brought prominently before the Man-Power Board.

debag (diː'bæg), *v. slang.* [f. DE- II. 2 a. + BAG *sb.* 16.] *trans.* To remove the trousers from (a person) as a punishment or for a joke. Hence **de'bagging** *vbl. sb.*
1914 C. MACKENZIE *Sinister St.* II. III. vi, At Oxford..we should be out of sympathy with him, even up to the point of debagging him. *Ibid.* vii, 'We ought to debag him,' he cried. Appleby was thereupon debagged; but as..he continued to walk about trouserless and dispense hospitality without any apparent loss of dignity, the debagging had to be written down a failure. **1927** *Daily Express* 5 Oct. 3/3 If the Gun Room wishes to pay a tribute to one whom it loves, it debags the adored after dinner; if the Gun Room wishes to hurt the feelings of one it hates, it de-bags the hated one after dinner. **1958** B. NICHOLS *Sweet & Twenties* 118 A number of us chased Sir Robert down the moonlit High Street in an endeavour to debag him.

†**debaid.** *Sc. Obs.* [Arising from mixture of *abaid*, ABODE with *debate.*] Delay.
1375 BARBOUR *Bruce* x. 222 (Edinb. MS.) Than Bonnok.. Went on hys way, but mar debaid [*Camb. MS.* abaid].

debait, obs. Sc. form of DEBATE.

deballast (diː'bæləst), *v.* [DE- II. + BALLAST *sb.* and *v.*] *trans.* To remove ballast from (esp. an oil-rig platform or barge). Also **de'ballasting** *vbl. sb.*
1962 *Oil & Gas Jrnl.* 20 Aug. 78/1 In this control room, one man can ballast and deballast the barge to offset

changing loads. **1965** *Economist* 16 Jan. 221/2 The deballasting system which might have been adequate for a conventional submarine. **1975** *Lamp* (Exxon Corp.) Winter 18/2 From a sheep pasture, the platform is seen deballasted and ready for towing, with Stavanger harbor and town in the background. **1976** *Offshore Platforms & Pipelining* 51/1 Deballast the temporary launching barge until the end of the buoyant tower floats. **1976** *Offshore Engineer* Apr. 9/3 Barge deballasting was scheduled to start so that they rose to make contact just before high tide on Monday, 5 April. **1980** *Jrnl. R. Soc. Arts* July 526/1 De-ballasting lines and ballast treatment plant would be very expensive to instal [sic] and operate. **1982** *Sci. Amer.* Apr. 38/1 After mating, the hull and topside assembly is towed to the installation site, submerged to allow its tethers to be connected to preset foundations and deballasted to tension the tethers.

de-bam'boozle, *v.* [f. DE- II. 1 + BAMBOOZLE *v.*] *trans.* To undeceive, disabuse.

1919 J. M. KEYNES *Econ. Conseq. of Peace* (1920) iii. 50 It was harder to de-bamboozle this old Presbyterian than it had been to bamboozle him. **1921** *Sat. Westm. Gaz.* 12 Feb. 18/2 Even with such an account before them, it is doubtful whether they [*sc.* visitors to Russia] will ever be 'de-bamboozled'. **1958** *Times Lit. Suppl.* 31 Jan. 54/5 Our rationalists and our materialistic demagogues alike, having found it relatively easy to debamboozle the masses of belief in God, love of neighbours, reason, etcetera, now find it extremely difficult to bamboozle them into believing or hoping anything.

debar (dɪ'bɑː(r)), *v.* In 6–7 debarre. [a. F. *débarrer*, in OF. *desbarer*, to unbar, f. *des-* (see DE- I. 6) + *barer*, *barrer*, to BAR.]

1. *trans.* **a.** To exclude or shut out *from* a place or condition; to prevent or prohibit *from* (entrance, or *from* having, attaining, or doing anything).

c **1430** LYDG. *Flour of Curtesie* (R.), Man alone.. Constrained is and by statute bound And debarred from all such pleasaunce. *a* **1557** MRS. M. BASSET tr. *More's Treat. Passion* Wks. 1394/1 Vtterlye to debarre from heauen all mankynde for euer. **1586** W. WEBBE *Eng. Poetrie* (Arb.) 39 Poetry is not debarred from any matter, which may be expressed by penne or speeche. **1624** CAPT. SMITH *Virginia* v. 195 To debarre true men from comming to them for trade. **1633** T. STAFFORD *Pac. Hib.* iii. (1821) 243 His brother John was not debarred by the Law from the title. **1775** JOHNSON *Tax. no Tyr.* 42 The multitudes, who are now debarred from voting. **1867** SMILES *Huguenots Eng.* ix. (1880) 144 The Huguenots were again debarred from holding public offices.

b. const. *of.* (Cf. *deprive of.*) *arch.*

1541 *Act 33 Hen. VIII*, c. 6 Euery other person.. be vtterly excluded and debarred of their said suites. **1599** BP. HALL *Sat.* v. iii. 49 The thred bare clients pouertie Debarres th' atturney of his wonted fee. **1670** EACHARD *Cont. Clergy* 34 Shall we debar youth of such an innocent and harmless recreation? *c* **1750** SHENSTONE *Elegies* xxii. 41 Tho' now debarr'd of each domestic tear. **1822** HAZLITT *Table-t.* Ser. II. iii. (1869) 75 [To] debar themselves of their real strength and advantages.

c. with double object.

c **1600** SHAKS. *Sonn.* xxviii, I.. That am debard the benefit of rest. **1630** WADSWORTH *Pilgr.* viii. 83 My Pension.. was debarred me. **1712** HEARNE *Collect.* (Oxf. Hist. Soc.) III. 413 He was afterwards debarr'd the Library. **1754** J. HILDROP *Miscell. Wks.* II. 209 To debar him the prayers and Sacraments. **1863** H. COX *Instit.* III. iii. 619 Persons who profess the Popish religion or marry Papists are, by the Bill of Rights, debarred the Crown.

†**d.** with *infin.* *Obs.*

1600 HOLLAND *Livy* XLII. xxv. 1129 He was.. debarred to levie warre upon any confederate allies. **1655** FULLER *Ch. Hist.* III. ii. §3 Bishops.. are.. debarred by their Canons to be Judges of Lay-Peers in like cases.

†**e.** with simple object: To shut out, exclude.

1593 T. WATSON *Tears of Fancie* xlix. (Arb.) 203 If shee debarre it whither shall it go. **1601** HOLLAND *Pliny* II. 400 That vitall spirit which giueth life vnto all things is debarred, stopped and choaked. **1647** H. MORE *Song of Soul* II. III. III. xlviii, Venus orb debars Not Mars, nor enters he with knocks and jars.

2. To set a bar or prohibition against (an action, etc.); to prohibit, prevent, forbid, stop.

1526 SKELTON *Magnyf.* 61 Somwhat I could enferre, Your consayte to debarre. **1557** N. T. (Genev.) *Matt.* v. 34 *note*, All superfluous othes are vtterly debarred. **1597** DRAYTON *Mortimeriados* 115 Seldome aduantage is in wrongs de-bard. **1628** T. SPENCER *Logick* 78 Even as the dore when it is shut, debarres all entrance. **1695** WOODWARD *Nat. Hist. Earth* III. i. (1723) 169 Its Egress [would have been] utterly debarr'd. *a* **1848** R. W. HAMILTON *Rew. & Punishm.* viii. (1853) 401 Adherence to such a speculation debars all Christian fellowship. **1872** JENKINSON *Guide Eng. Lakes* (1879) 73 At the head of the glen is a low height which appears to debar the passage.

Hence **de'barred** *ppl. a.*, **de'barring** *vbl. sb.* and *ppl. a.*

1640 O. SEDGWICKE *Christs Counsell* 184 It is of singular good.. to a debarred person. **1604** HIERON *Wks.* I. 503 A law for the debarring of young men from the ministery. **1656** TRAPP *Comm. Matt.* vii. 8 The door of the tabernacle was not of any hard or debarring matter, but a veil. **1709** W. STEUART *Collect. & Observ. Ch. Scotl.* II. IV. §14 (1802) 89 The minister and Session having.. debarred persons from the Lord's Table.. this doctrinal debarring may fear such from partaking.

†**de'barb**, *v.* *Obs.*$^{-0}$ [f. DE- II. 2 + L. *barba* beard.] 'To deprive of his beard' (J.).

1727 BAILEY vol. II, *Debarbed*, having his beard cut or pulled off.

de'barbarize, *v.* [f. DE- II. 1 + BARBARIZE *v.*] *trans.* To divest of its barbarous character, to render not barbarous; = UNBARBARIZE *v.* Hence **debarbari'zation**.

1823 DE QUINCEY *Lett. Education* v. (1860) 103 Wherever law and intellectual order prevail, they *debarbarize* (if I may be allowed such a coinage) what in its elements might be barbarous. **1848** WISEMAN *Ess.* (1853) III. 427 To bring.. the blessing, not of civilization, but of debarbarization. **1857** DE QUINCEY *China* Wks. 1871 XVI. 241 No Asiatic state has ever debarbarised itself. **1885** G. MEREDITH *Diana* II. iii. 72 Before society can be civilized it has to be debarbarized. **1930** W. R. INGE *Christian Ethics* v. 223 The Catholic Church might.. have.. found a congenial task in debarbarising Christianity. **1963** *Guardian* 19 Feb. 4/2 Our chance to de-barbarise our society.

debarcation, var. of DEBARKATION.

†**de'bare**, *v.* *Obs.* [DE- II. 3.] *trans.* To strip down, make quite bare. Hence †**de'bared** *ppl. a.* So †**de'bare** *a.*, intensive of BARE *a.*

1567 DRANT *Horace's Arte of Poetrie* A ij, As wooddes are made debayre of leaues by turnyng of the yeare. *c* **1620** T. ROBINSON *M. Magd.* 223 Next her debared brests bewitch mine eyes.

debarg(e: see next.

debark (dɪ'bɑːk), *v.*[1] Also 7 **debarque, debarg(e**. [a. F. *débarquer*, f. *dé* = *des-* (see DE- *pref.* I. 6) + *barque* BARK *sb.*[2], ship. Cf. DISBARK. For *debarging* (quot. 1692) cf. BARGE.] = DISEMBARK.

a. *trans.*

1654 H. L'ESTRANGE *Chas. I* (1655) 69 Untill he had debarqued all his Horse. **1762** *Gentl. Mag.* 4 The Dutch debarked 700 Europeans. **1880** K. JOHNSTON *Lond. Geog.* 91 A refuge at which the slaves captured.. were debarked.

b. *intr.*

1694 LUTTRELL *Brief Rel.* (1857) III. 349 The forces on board are to debarque. **1883** BURTON & CAMERON *To Gold Coast* I. iii. 76 A strip of beach upon which I should prefer to debark.

Hence **de'barking** *vbl. sb.* and *ppl. a.*

1692 LUTTRELL *Brief Rel.* (1857) II. 463 To row the new debarging vessells to Portsmouth. *Ibid.* 505 Well boates.. for debarging soldiers. **1867** GARFIELD in *Century Mag.* Jan. (1884) 410/1 Three cheers for the ship, answered by our debarking friends with three more.

debark (dɪ'bɑːk), *v.*[2] [f. DE- II. 2 + BARK *sb.*[1]: cf. DISBARK.] *trans.* To strip of its bark, decorticate. Also *fig.* Hence **de'barking** *vbl. sb.*

1742 W. ELLIS *Timber-Tree* II. 197 The Debarking of Oak in the common Season. **1744–50** —— *Mod. Husb.* IV. iii. 58 They de-bark their [hop] poles, that they may dry sooner. **1791** E. DARWIN *Bot. Gard.* I. Notes 114 To debark oak-trees in the spring. **1818** J. BROWN *Psyche* 46 Let us exemplify the matter De-bark'd of scientific chatter. **1963** R. R. A. HIGHAM *Handbk. Papermaking* v. 114 Any logs which have not been properly de-barked are picked out and returned by hand to the inlet side of the barker. **1965** G. McINNES *Road to Gundagai* x. 166 The more enterprising de-barked the saplings. **1970** *Daily Tel.* 4 May 14 Last year two large chestnuts were deliberately killed by poison and debarking.

debark (diː'bɑːk), *v.*[3] [f. DE- II. 2 + BARK *sb.*[3]] *trans.* To perform an operation on (a dog) to prevent it from barking. Hence **de'barking** *vbl. sb.*

1943 *Biol. Abstr.* XVII. 70 Dogs debarked by removal of the true vocal cords soon learned to bark again. **1959** *Times* 30 Sept. 8/4 A 'debarking' operation. *Ibid.*, A new operation for debarking dogs. **1961** *Daily Tel.* 19 Oct. 19/5 (*heading*) No de-barking. *Ibid.*, Two mongrels which annoyed neighbours with their barking are not to be 'debarked'.

debarkation (diːbɑː'keɪʃən). Also **debarcation**. [f. DEBARK *v.*[1] + -ATION.] The action of landing from a ship; disembarkation.

1756 *Gentl. Mag.* XXVI. 324 They kept on their guard, and prevented the intended debarkation. **1850** MERIVALE *Rom. Emp.* (1865) II. xvii. 248 The construction of the Roman galleys gave great facilities for debarkation. **1859** LEWIN *Invas. Brit.* 81 So much controversy has been raised as to the place of [Cæsar's] debarcation.

de'barkment. *rare.* [f. as prec. + -MENT: cf. F. *débarquement.*] = prec.

1742 JARVIS *Quix.* I. IV. xii. (D.), Our troops ought to.. have met the enemy.. at the place of debarkment.

de'barment. *rare.* [f. DEBAR *v.* + -MENT.] The act of debarring or fact of being debarred.

a **1655** VINES *Lord's Supp.* (1677) 231 It may be a cause.. of his debarment. **1709** KENNET *Erasmus on Folly* 95 Add to this.. their debarment from all pleasures. **1869** BLACKMORE *Lorna D.* (1889) 265 Thinking of my sad debarment from the sight of Lorna.

debarrance (dɪ'bɑːrəns). *rare.* [f. as prec. + -ANCE.] The action of debarring; *spec.* the formal debarring of unworthy communicants from the Lord's Table by the 'fencing of the table' in Presbyterian churches: see DEBARRATION.

1861 J. MACFARLANE *Life G. Lawson* II. (1862) 81 It is doubtful if these 'debarrances' (another name for this peculiar service) ever kept away one who had determined to communicate.

debarrass (dɪ'bærəs), *v.* [a. F. *débarrass-er*, f. *dé-* = *des-* (see DE- I. 6) + *-barrasser* in *embarrasser* to EMBARRASS.] *trans.* To disembarrass; to disencumber *from* anything that embarrasses.

1789 T. JEFFERSON *Writ.* (1859) III. 97 So as to debarrass themselves of this. **1792** W. ROBERTS *Looker-on* (1794) I. 390 To debarrass its motions, and to display its attractions. **1796** LD. SHEFFIELD in *Ld. Auckland's Corr.* (1862) III. 348 If the armies of France should be debarrassed from all other enemies. **1848** C. BRONTË *J. Eyre* x, I was debarrassed of interruption. **1853** READE *Chr. Johnstone* 165 Jean Carnie, who debarrassed her of certain wrappers.

deba'rration. *rare.* [f. DEBAR *v.*: see -ATION.] The action of debarring; = DEBARRANCE.

1882 G. W. SPROTT *Worship Ch. Scot.* iii. 109 This address came to be popularly known as the Fencing of the Table.. its most prominent feature came to be a series of debarrations beginning thus: 'I debar from the Table of the Lord' such and such a class.

de'barrent. *rare*$^{-1}$. [f. DEBAR *v.*, after *deterrent*, etc.] Anything that debars.

1884 *Times* 8 Aug. 4/6 The Chinaman generally does not indulge in beer or wine—a great debarrent being the cost when delivered from Europe.

debase (dɪ'beɪs), *v.* Also 6 **debace**. [Formed in 16th c. from DE- I. 1, 3 + BASE *v.*[1]: cf. ABASE.]

†**1.** *trans.* To lower in position, rank, or dignity; to abase. *Obs.*

1568 GRAFTON *Chron.* II. 69 The king hath debased himselfe ynough to the Bishop. *Ibid.* II. 75 Debasyng himselfe with great humilitie and submission before the sayde two Cardinalles. **1593** SHAKS. *Rich. II*, III. iii. 190 Faire Cousin, you debase your Princely Knee, To make the base Earth prowd with kissing it. **1610** HEALEY *St. Aug. Citie of God* III. xvi. (1620) 121 Brutus debased Collatine and banished him the city. **1648** WILKINS *Math. Magick* I. i. 4 The ancient Philosophers.. refusing to debase the principles of that noble profession unto Mechanical experiments. **1671** MILTON *Samson* 999 God sent her to debase me. **1751** JOHNSON *Rambler* No. 187 ¶4 A man [in Greenland] will not debase himself by work, which requires neither skill nor courage. **1827** POLLOK *Course T.* v, Debased in sackcloth, and forlorn in tears.

†**2.** To lower in estimation; to decry, depreciate, vilify. *Obs.*

1565 T. STAPLETON *Fortr. Faith* 62 The Manichee.. would so extol grace, and debace the nature of man. **1600** HOLLAND *Livy* IX. xxxvii. 341 Praising highly.. the Samnites warres, debasing the Tuscanes. **1704** J. BLAIR in W. S. Perry *Hist. Coll. Amer. Col. Ch.* I. 98, I have heard him often debase and vilify the Gentlemen of the Council, using to them the opprob[r]ious names of Rogue, Rascal [etc.]. **1746** HERVEY *Medit.* (1818) 15 Why should we exalt ourselves or debase others?

3. To lower in quality, value, or character; to make base, degrade; to adulterate. **b.** *spec.* To lower the value of (coin) by the mixture of alloy or otherwise; to depreciate.

1591 SPENSER *Tears of Muses, Urania* iii, Ignorance.. That mindes of men borne heavenlie doth debace. **1602** FULBECKE *1st Pt. Parall.* 54 Or els it may be changed in the value, as if a Floren, which was worth 4 li to be debased to 3 li. **1606** *State Trials, Gt. case of Impositions* (R.), That these staple commodities might not be debased. **1751** JOHNSON *Rambler* No. 168 ¶4 Words which convey ideas of dignity.. are in time debased. **1789** *Trans. Soc. Encourag. Arts* I. 16 Much of the Zaffre brought to England is mixed with matters that debase its quality. **1879** FROUDE *Cæsar* xiii. 177 Laws against debasing the coin.

debased (dɪ'beɪst), *ppl. a.* [f. prec. + -ED[1].]

1. Lowered in estimation (*obs.*), in quality, or character: see the verb.

1594 HOOKER *Eccl. Pol.* II. vii. (1611) 76 This so much despiced and debased authoritie of man. *a* **1859** MACAULAY *Hist. Eng.* V. 3 A debased currency. **1863** FR. A. KEMBLE *Resid. in Georgia* 9 One of a debased and degraded race.

2. *Her.* Of a charge: Borne upside down; reversed.

1864 in WEBSTER.

Hence **de'basedness**, debased character.

a **1720** W. DUNLOP in Spurgeon *Treas. Dav.* Ps. cxix. 59 The folly and danger of sin, the debasedness of its pleasures. **1885** L. OLIPHANT *Sympneumata* xii. 189 The fettering debasedness of material cravings.

debasement (dɪ'beɪsmənt). [f. as prec. + -MENT.]

1. The action or process of debasing; the fact or state of being debased; lowering, degradation; *concr.* anything wherein this is involved.

1602 FULBECKE *1st Pt. Parall.* 54 If the debasement were before the day of paiment the debtor may pay the det in the coin embased. **1641** MILTON *Reform.* II. (1851) 37 The Primitive Pastors of the Church.. avoiding all worldly matters as clogs.. and debasements to their high calling. **1776** ADAM SMITH *W.N.* I. xi. (1868) I. 205 The great debasement of the silver coin, by clipping and wearing. **1835** LYTTON *Rienzi* I. viii, I weep for the debasement of my country.

†**2.** Abasement. *Obs.*

1593 NASHE *Christ's T.* (1613) 32 It is debasement and a punishment to me to inuest and enrobe my selfe in the dregs and drosse of mortality. *a* **1711** KEN *Man. Prayers* Wks. (1838) 388 With what debasement and dread ought I to appear before thy awful presence. **1855** MILMAN *Lat. Chr.* (1864) IV. VII. ii. 102 The history of Henry's debasement.

debaser (dɪ'beɪsə(r)). One who debases.

1611 COTGR., *Abbaisseur*, an abaser, debaser.. humbler, bringer downe of. **1621–31** LAUD *Serm.* (1847) 102 To punish the debasers of 'justice'. **1794** SIR W. JONES *Laws of Menu* ix. 258 Debasers of metals. **1805** J. CARTWRIGHT *State* *of Nation* x. 53 A debaser of the character of our nation. **1847** R. E. TYRWHITT *Serm.* II. 378 The debasers of baptism.

†**de'bash**, *v. Obs. nonce-wd.* [f. DE- I. 1, 3 + BASH *v.*[1]] To abash.

1610 NICCOLS *England's Eliza* Induct. (N.), But sillie I.. Fell prostrate down, debash'd with reverent shame.

debash, var. of DUBASH *Anglo-Ind.*, interpreter.

debasing (dɪ'beɪsɪŋ), *vbl. sb.* [-ING[1].] The action of the verb DEBASE.

1891 *Athenæum* 3 Oct. 448/1 In the fatal debasing of the coinage.

de'basing, *ppl. a.* [-ING[2].] That debases.

1775 in ASH. **1837** HT. MARTINEAU *Soc. Amer.* III. 191 The misery of a debasing pauperism. **1876** J. H. NEWMAN *Hist. Sk.* I. I. iv. 198 Mahometanism.. is as debasing.. as it is false.

Hence **de'basingly** *adv.*

1847 in CRAIG. **1892** *Harper's Mag.* Nov. 946/1 It indicated more ignorance of what is debasingly called Life than knowledge of it.

†**de'basure.** *Obs. rare*[−1]. [See -URE.] Debasement.

1683 CAVE *Ecclesiastici* 207 To propound a place that might look like a debasure and degrading of him.

débat: see DEBATE *sb.*[1]

debatable (dɪ'beɪtəb(ə)l), *a.* Also 7-9 debateable. [a. OF. *debatable* (Cotgr.), *debattable*, f. *debat(t)-re* + -ABLE: med. (Anglo-)L. *debatabilis*.]

1. Admitting of debate or controversy; subject to dispute; questionable.

1581 MULCASTER *Positions* iii. (1887) 11 The difference of opinion is no proufe at all, that the matter is debatable. **1685** *Lond. Gaz.* No. 2031/2 A Committee for considering the debateable Elections. **1817** J. SCOTT *Paris Revisit.* (ed. 4) 201 Observations on certain debateable points. **1883** FROUDE *Short Stud.* IV. II. i. 177 Doctrines, which degraded accepted truths into debatable opinions.

2. *esp.* Said of land or territory, *e.g.* on the border of two countries and claimed by both: applied to lands on the borders of England and Scotland, *esp.* a tract between the Esk and Sark, claimed (before the Union) by both countries, and the scene of frequent contests.

[**1453, 1531-2** See BATABLE.] **1492** in Rymer *Fœdera* XII. 467/2 Terras debatabiles ibidem adjacentes. **1536** BELLENDEN *Cron. Scot.* (1821) I. 162 Gret contentioun betwix the Scottis and Pichtis, for certane debaitabill landis, that lay betwix thair realmes. **1549** *Compl. Scot.* viii. 74 Neutral men, lyik to the ridars that dueillis on the debatabil landis. **1604** (*title*), A Booke of the survaie of the debatable and border lands. **1609** SKENE *Reg. Maj.* 11 Quhither the defender hes any other land in the towne, quhere the debaitable land lyes, or nocht. **1777** NICOLSON & BURN *Hist. Westm. & Cumb.* I. p. lxxii, The Debateable Land.. became a further bone of contention between the two snarling parties. *c* **1800** K. WHITE *Lett.* (1837) 338 The debateable ground of the Peloponnesians. **1820** SCOTT *Abbot* ii, The Græmes who then inhabited the Debateable Land. **1838** THIRLWALL *Greece* III. 129 Guarding a debatable frontier.

b. *fig.* Of regions of thought, etc.

1814 CHALMERS *Evid. Chr. Revel.* i. 31 Christianity is now looked upon as debateable ground. **1870** FARRAR *Fam. Speech* iv. (1873) 118 The.. debateable lands of the separate linguistic kingdoms.

†**B.** as *sb.* The Debatable Land (on the border of England and Scotland: see 2 above); also *pl.* the residents on this land (sometimes *debatablers*).

1551 EDW. VI *Lit. Rem.* (Roxb.) II. 389 The lord Maxwell did upon malice to the English debatables overrun them. *Ibid.* 390 Then shal the Scottis wast their debatablers, and we ours. *Ibid* 407 The commissionars for the Debatable. **1568** in H. Campbell *Love-Lett. Mary Q. Scots* App. (1824) 15 The contraversy yerely arising by occasion of certain grounds upon the frontiers in the East Marches, commonly called the 'Threap-land', or 'Debatable'.

debate (dɪ'beɪt), *sb.*[1] Also 4-5 debaat, 4-6 debat, 5-6 *Sc.* debait. [ME. *debat*, a. F. *debat* (13th c. in Littré) = Pr. *debat*, It. *dibatto*, Romanic deriv. of the verb: see DEBATE *v.*[1]].

1. a. Strife, contention, dissension, quarrelling, wrangling; a quarrel. *at debate*: at strife, at variance. *Obs.* or *arch.*

a **1300** *Cursor M.* 9684 (Cott.) Bituix mi sisters es a debat. **1340** HAMPOLE *Pr. Consc.* 3473 To accorde þam þat er at debate. *c* **1386** CHAUCER *Friar's T.* Prol. 24 Ye schold been heende And curteys.. In company we wol haue no debaat. **1481** CAXTON *Godfrey* clxxix. 263 Whan.. alle the debates [had ben] appeased that were emong them. **1535** COVERDALE *Luke* xii. 51 Thynke ye that I am come to brynge peace vpon earth—I tell you nay but rather debate. **1536** BELLENDEN *Cron. Scot.* (1821) I. 61 Thus rais ane schameful debait betwix thir two brethir. **1612** ROWLANDS *Knaue of Harts* 24 To.. set good friends and neighbors at debate. **1715** POPE *Iliad* III. 321 To seal the truce and end the dire debate. **1882** J. PARKER *Apost. Life* I. 138 The spirit of debate is opposed to the spirit of love.

comb. *c* **1440** *Promp. Parv.* 115 Debate maker, or baratour, *incentor*.

†**b.** Physical strife, fight, conflict. *Obs.*

15.. *Felon Sowe Rokeby* in R. Bell *Anc. Poems Peasantry* (1857), Hee wist that there had bin debate. *a* **1533** LD. BERNERS *Gold. Bk. M. Aurel.* (1546) R v b, Their debate was so cruell, that there was slaine v. capitaynes. **1590** SPENSER *F.Q.* II. viii. 54 The whole debate, Which that straunge knight for him sustained had.

†**c.** *to make debate*: to make opposition or resistance. *Obs.*

c **1350** *Will. Palerne* 4380 þe werwolf was ful glad of Williams speche.. And made no more debat in no maner wice. **1500-20** DUNBAR *Freris of Berwik* 535 Se this be done and mak no moir debait. *c* **1565** LINDESAY (Pitscottie) *Chron. Scot.* (1728) 10 Or else, if they made no debate, without consideration and pity would cut their throats.

2. a. Contention in argument; dispute, controversy; discussion; *esp.* the discussion of questions of public interest in Parliament or in any assembly.

1393 GOWER *Conf.* III. 348 Tho was betwene my prest and me Debate and great perplexete. *a* **1450** *Knt. de la Tour* (1868) 21 He is of highe wordes.. wherfor y praie you.. that ye take no debate with hym. **1548** HALL *Chron.* 188b, Wherefore the Commons after long debate, determined to send the speaker of the Parliament to the kinges highness. **1561** T. NORTON *Calvin's Inst.* IV. 56 If there happen debate about any doctrine. **1640** in Rushw. *Hist. Coll.* (1692) III. I. 58 Thursday next is appointed for the Debate of the New Canons. **1727** SWIFT *Gulliver* II. iii. 119 After much debate, they concluded unanimously that [etc.]. **1774** J. BRYANT *Mythol.* II. 431 Sor-Apis had another meaning: and this was the term in debate. **1855** MACAULAY *Hist. Eng.* IV. 155 An account.. which gives a very high notion of his talents for debate. **1883** GILMOUR *Mongols* xvii. 207 Difficulties.. welcomed rather as subjects for debate.

b. (with *a* and *pl.*) A controversy or discussion; *spec.* a formal discussion of some question of public interest in a legislative or other assembly.

c **1500** *Three Kings Sons* 95 Thise debates that were made, of good wille, and by noon hate. **1648** DK. HAMILTON in *H. Papers* (Camden) 245, I shall not trouble your Lo. now with the debats. **1709** STEELE *Tatler* No. 17 ¶1 A full Debate upon Publick Affairs in the Senate. **1880** MCCARTHY *Own Times* IV. lxii. 391 The debate, which lasted four nights, was brilliant and impassioned.

c. (Freq. in French form *débat.*) A type of literary composition, taking the form of a discussion or disputation, commonly found in the vernacular medieval poetry of many European countries, as well as in medieval Latin.

1841 T. WRIGHT *Latin Poems W. Mapes* 346 (*title*) Debate between the Body and the Soul. **1897** G. SAINTSBURY *Flourishing of Romance* v. 203 A form so popular with the French *trouvères* as the *débat*. **1903** E. K. CHAMBERS *Mediæval Stage* I. iv. 79 The *débat* is a kind of poetical controversy put into the mouths of two types or two personified abstractions, each of which pleads the cause of its own superiority, while in the end the decision is not infrequently referred to an umpire in the fashion familiar in the eclogues of Theocritus. *Ibid.* II. xxiii. 153 This *débat*-like theme is of course familiar in every branch of allegorical literature. **1933** R. TUVE *Seasons & Months* i. 12 The conflict between the vital and ascetic principles.. seen in the *Owl and the Nightingale* débat. **1939** R. M. WILSON *Early M.E. Lit.* vii. 168 The *Thrush and the Nightingale*.. is .. a compromise between the debate and the lyric. **1963** M. D. LEGGE *Anglo-Norman Lit.* xiii. 335 The violent language used by both parties to the debate is, like the language of flytings, not to be taken seriously.

†**3.** Fighting for any one, defence, aid, protection. *Sc. Obs. rare.* (Cf. DEBATE *v.* 3.)

1581 *Sat. Poems Reform.* xliii. 61 Quha findis hir [Dame Fortune's] freindship of fauour hes aneuch.. How far may Darius bragge of her debait!

†**de'bate**, *sb.*[2] *Obs.* [f. DEBATE *v.*[2]] Lowering; depreciation; degradation.

c **1460** SIR R. ROS *La Belle Dame* 456 in *Pol. Rel. & L. Poems* 67 Yf a lady doo soo grete outrage to shewe pyte, and cause hir owen debate.

debate (dɪ'beɪt), *v.*[1] Also 4 debat. 6-7 *Sc.* debait. [a. OF. *debat-re*, in Pr. *desbatre*, *debatre*, Sp. *debatir*, Pg. *debater*, It. *dibattere*, f. Romanic *batt-ĕre* to fight (see ABATE, COMBAT), with L. *de-*, occasionally replaced in Rom. by *des-*; the sense is rather from L. *dis-*: cf. *discuss*, *dispute*.]

†**1.** *intr.* To fight, contend, strive, quarrel, wrangle. *Obs.*

c **1340** *Cursor M.* 5913 (Trin.) For he wol þus debate on me I shal him drenche in þe see. *c* **1386** CHAUCER *Sir Thopas* 157 His cote-armour.. In which he wold debate. **1490** CAXTON *How to Die* 9, I wyll not debate ne stryue ayenst the. **1530** PALSGR. 508/1, I debate, I stryve.. I wyll nat debate with you for so small a mater. **1590** SPENSER *F.Q.* II. i. 6 Well could he tourney, and in lists debate. **1665** MANLEY *Grotius' Low C. Warres* 592 The Spanish General.. together with his Officers, debate of the right thereof against all force.

fig. **1393** GOWER *Conf.* II. 300 What shame it is to ben unkinde, Ayein the which reson debateth. *c* **1600** SHAKS. *Sonn.* xv, Wastefull time debateth with decay To change your day of youth to sullied night.

2. *trans.* To contest, dispute; to contend or fight for; to carry on (a fight or quarrel). *Obs.* or *arch.*

c **1489** CAXTON *Blanchardyn* xxiii. 79, I haue debated þe quarelle ayenst the god of loue. **1597** T. BEARD *Theatre Gods Judg.* (1612) 486 As though they would debate a privat quarrell before his presence. **1697** DRYDEN *Æneid* (T.), They see the boys and Latian youth debate The martial prizes on the dusty plain. **1813** SCOTT *Rokeby* I. xvi, In many a well debated field. **1838** PRESCOTT *Ferd. & Is.* (1846) I. Introd. 11 The cause of religion was debated with the same ardour in Spain, as on the plains of Palestine.

†**3.** To fight for, defend, protect; also *absol.* (for *refl.*) to defend oneself. *Sc. Obs.*

1500-20 DUNBAR *Poems* xxi. 32 Is non so armit in-to plait That can fra truble him debait. **1536** BELLENDEN *Cron. Scot.* (1821) I. 46 The residew.. fled to the montanis; and debaitit thair miserabill liffis.. with scars and hard fude. *Ibid.* I. 60 Exercit in swift running and wersling, to make thaim the more abill to debait his realme. *a* **1605** MONTGOMERIE *Devotional Poems* vi. 64 Then prayers, almes-deids, and tearis.. Sall mair availl than jaks and spearis, For to debait thee. *a* **1605** POLWART *Flyting w. Montgomerie* 745 Now debate, if thou dow.

4. To dispute about, argue, discuss; *esp.* to discuss a question of public interest in a legislative or other assembly. (With simple obj. or obj. clause.)

c **1340** [see 5]. *a* **1439** in *Warkworth's Chron.* (Camden) Notes 60 The wyche comyns, after the mater debatet.. grawntyt and assentyt to the forseyd premisses. *c* **1489** CAXTON *Blanchardyn* xxviii. 103 This matere.. they sore debatyd emonge them self by many & dyuerse oppynyons. **1550** CROWLEY *Inform. & Petit.* 2 Most weyghty mattiers.. to be debated.. in this present Parliament. **1590** SHAKS. *Com. Err.* III. i. 67 In debating which was best, wee shall part with neither. **1653** WALTON *Angler* ii. 42 The question has been debated among many great Clerks. **1782** PRIESTLEY *Corrupt. Chr.* I. IV. 392 It was debated in the Greek Church. **1874** GREEN *Short Hist.* viii. §7. 533 The Lords debated nothing but proposals of peace.

b. *intr.* To engage in discussion or argument; *esp.* in a public assembly. Const. *upon*, *on*, †*of*.

1530 PALSGR. 508/1 They have debated upon this mater these fiftene dayes. **1548** [see DEBATING *vbl. sb.*]. **1591** SHAKS. *1 Hen. VI*, v. i. 35 Your seuerall suites Haue bin consider'd and debated on. **1655** FULLER *Ch. Hist.* v. iii. §60 To grant or deny them [Convocations] Commission to debate of Religion. **1828** D'ISRAELI *Chas. I*, I. xi. 307 The Commons .. debated in an open committee on certain parts of these speeches. **1835** W. IRVING *Tour Prairies* 183 Beatte.. came up while we were debating.

5. *trans.* To discuss or consider (*with* oneself or in one's own mind), deliberate upon.

c **1340** *Gaw. & Gr. Knt.* 2179 Debetande with hym-self, quat hit be myȝt. **1530** PALSGR. 508/1, I wyll debate this mater with my selfe, and take counsayle of my pylowe. *c* **1530** H. RHODES *Bk. Nurture* 570 in *Babees Bk.* (1868) 98 Be not hasty, aunswere to giue before thou it debate. **1623** CONWAY in Ellis *Orig. Lett.* I. III. 155 These tender considerations.. his Majestie debated some dayes. **1859** TENNYSON *Enid* 1215 Enid.. Debating his command of silence given.. Held commune with herself.

b. *intr.* To deliberate, consider (with oneself).

1593 [see DEBATING *vbl. sb.*]. **1599** SHAKS. *Hen. V*, IV. i. 31, I and my Bosome must debate awhile. **1651** HOBBES *Leviath.* II. xxix. 168 From this false doctrine, men are disposed to debate with themselves, [etc.]. **1733** SWIFT *Poems, On Poetry*, A founder'd horse will oft debate Before he tries a five-barr'd gate. **1870** MORRIS *Earthly Par.* I. I. 371 She sat, Debating in her mind of this and that.

¶ quasi-*passive* const.: *debating* stands for *a-debating* = in debate, i.e. the vbl. sb. preceded by prep. *a-* = on, in.

1682 D'URFEY *Butler's Ghost* 149 What cursed Case is now debating? **1788** MRS. HUGHES *Henry & Isab.* I. 86 This subject was still earnestly debating.

†**debate**, *v.*[2] *Obs.* [app. f. DE- I. 1, 3 + BATE, aphetic f. ABATE.]

1. *trans.* To abate; to beat down, bring down, lower, reduce, lessen, diminish.

c **1450** *St. Cuthbert* (Surtees) 4727 þai.. prayed for pardoune of þat attaynt, þair mysdede to debate. **1513** DOUGLAS *Æneis* XIII. iii. 35 Thir Rutilianys.. Gan at command debait thar voce and ceis. *c* **1537** *Thersites* in Hazl. *Dodsley* I. 414, I will debate anon.. thy bragging cheer. **1564** J. RASTELL *Confut. Jewell's Serm.* 56 That body, which was.. with fast debated.

b. To depreciate, decry; = DEBASE 2.

1598 GRENEWEY *Tacitus' Ann.* VI. viii. (1622) 134 The Parthian put his souldiers in mind of.. the renowned nobility of the Arsacides: and.. debated Hiberius as ignoble.

c. To subtract, take away. (*absol.* in quot.)

1658 A. FOX *Wurtz' Surg.* II. i. 48 To debate from the one, and to add to the other.

2. *intr.* To abate, fall off, grow less.

a **1400-50** *Alexander* 2506 (Dubl. MS.) þe more I meng our maieste þe more it debates. *c* **1450** *St. Cuthbert* (Surtees) 2548 þe werkenes of hir sekenes with in Began to debate and blyn. **1586** W. WEBBE *Eng. Poetrie* (Arb.) 94 Artes.. when they are at the full perfection, doo debate and decrease againe. **1657** TOMLINSON *Renou's Disp.* 113 The strength of the symptoms being debated.

debateable: see DEBATABLE.

†**de'bateful**, *a. Obs.* [See -FUL.]

1. Of persons: Full of strife, contentious.

1491 CAXTON *Vitas Patr.* (W. de W. 1495) II. 279b/1 Men full of noyse & debatefull. **1557** PAYNEL *Barclay's Jugurth* Biij, Sowers of dyscord and debatful. **1611** COTGR., *Litigieux*.. litigious, debatefull, contentious.

2. Of things: **a.** Pertaining to strife or contention; **b.** Controversial, contentious.

1580 SIDNEY *Arcadia* (1622) 412 Her conscience.. stil nourishing this debateful fire. **1587** FLEMING *Contn. Holinshed* III. 1320/2 In the triall of this debatefull question.

Hence †**de'batefully** *adv.*

1611 COTGR., *Contentieusement*, contentiously.. debatefully, with much wrangling.

†**de'batement**[1]. *Obs.* [a. OF. *debatement* (later *debattement*), f. *debat-re* + -MENT.]

1. The action of debating; debate, controversy, discussion, deliberation.

1536 *Articles about Relig.* Pref. 16 Our bishops.. assembled.. for the full debatement and quiet determination of the same. **1586** A. DAY *Eng. Secretary* I. (1625) 11 The matter requireth long debatement. **1602** SHAKS. *Ham.* V. ii. 45 Without debatement further. **1641**

MILTON *Reform.* I. (1851) 5 A serious question and debatement with my selfe.

2. Contention, strife. *rare*$^{-1}$.

1590 SPENSER *F.Q.* II. vi. 39 He with Pyrochles sharp debatement made.

†**de'batement**[2]. *Obs. rare*$^{-1}$. [f. DEBATE *v.*[2] + -MENT.] = ABATEMENT.

c **1550** BALE *K. Johan* (Camden) 75 Sir, disconfort not, for God hath sent debatementes.. From thys heavye yoke delyveryinge yow.

debater (dɪ'beɪtə(r)). In 5 -our. [a. AF. *debatour* = OF. *debateor, -eur*, agent-n. f. *debat-re* to DEBATE *v.*[1]: see -ER[2] 3.]

†**1.** One who contends or strives; a quarrelsome or contentious person. *Obs.*

1388 WYCLIF *Rom.* i. 30 Detractouris, hateful to God, debateris, proude. **1413** LYDG. *Pilgr. Sowle* IV. xxxv. (1483) 83 Fyghters and debatours. *c* **1440** CAPGRAVE *Life St. Kath.* IV. 1519 A fals traytour.. debater and robbour.

2. One who takes part in debate or public discussion; a disputant, controversialist. Often, one skilled in debate, an able disputant.

1593 SHAKS. *Lucr.* 1019 Debate where leisure serves with dull debaters. *a* **1773** CHESTERFIELD (T.), It is only knowledge and experience that can make a debater. **1823** BYRON *Juan* XIII. xx, The Lord Henry was a great debater, So that few members kept the house up later. **1848** MACAULAY *Hist. Eng.* II. 611 Their debates lasted three days.. Sir Patrick Hume was one of the debaters. **1887** *Westm. Rev.* June 277 Mr. C. is a debater.

debating (dɪ'beɪtɪŋ), *vbl. sb.* [-ING[1].] **a.** The action of DEBATE *v.*[1]; discussion; deliberation.

1548 HALL *Chron.* 110 After long debatyng, the Commons concluded to graunte .ii.s. of the pound. **1593** SHAKS. *Lucr.* 274 Then childish feare auaunt, debating die. **1732** BERKELEY *Alciphr.* IV. §2 The end of debating is to persuade. **1845** S. AUSTIN *Ranke's Hist. Ref.* II. 71 After a great deal of debating a resolution was passed.

b. *attrib.*, as in **debating club** = *debating society*; **debating point**, a point which, though not necessarily essential to the matter in hand, furnishes a useful or interesting subject for debate; a proposition, contention, etc., used mainly to impress or disconcert one's opponent in a debate; **debating society**, a society whose members meet for practice in debating.

1741 *Athen. Lett.* (1792) II. 18, I find myself in such a debating humour, that you must indulge me. **1792** *Gentl. Mag.* LXII. II. 1146 Proceedings.. with respect to a debating-society at the house formerly the King's Arms tavern, in Cornhill. **1808** *Med. Jrnl.* XIX. 445 To answer every base attack on Vaccination, in Newspapers or in Debating Societies. **1830** C. C. BALDWIN *Diary* 6 Feb. (1901) 52 The Debating Club, composed of law students generally, hold a public debate. **1857** BUCKLE *Civiliz.* I. vii. 394 In the middle of the 18th century debating societies sprung up among tradesmen. **1862** BAGEHOT *Coll. Works* (1965) II. 225 The House of Commons.. became.. the debating-club of fashion. **1885** *Leeds Mercury* 24 June 4/4 The new Government will be.. weak in debating power. **1927** G. B. SHAW *Doctors' Delusions* (1932) 135 Shallow petulances and *tu quoques* which have remained part of the vivisector's stock of debating points ever since. **1928** *Daily Tel.* 9 Oct. 6 'I do plead for the liberties of the people of England more than any of you do.' It was not a bad debating point, if such things had then been of any avail. **1965** *Listener* 2 Sept. 348/2 It may be no more than an interesting debating point, but in fact this eastern area was.. little used or even visited by Indians.

de'bating, *ppl. a.* [-ING[2].] That debates: see DEBATE *v.*[1]

1702 ROWE *Tamerl.* I. ii. 665 Debating Senates. **1749** *Deity, A Poem* 30 As just the structure, and as wise the plan, As in the lord of all—debating man!

Hence **de'batingly** *adv. rare*$^{-0}$.

1847 in CRAIG.

†**de'bative**, *a. Obs. rare.* [f. DEBATE *v.*[1] + -IVE. Cf. OF. *debatif* (14th c. in Godef.).] Relating to, or of the nature of, debate or discussion.

1606 G. W[OODCOCKE] tr. *Ivstine* 25 b, They were driuen into a debatiue meditation. **1642** FULLER *Answ. Ferne* 14 If this decisive faculty, after the debative had passed upon the sence of the Law, were not some where resident in the Government.

†**de'batous**, *a. Obs. rare.* [f. *debat*, DEBATE *sb.* + -OUS. (Possibly in AF.)] Quarrelsome, contentious.

1483 *Cath. Angl.* 92 Debatouse, *contensiosus. c* **1520** *Treat. Galaunt* (1860) 14 Aduenture and angre ben aye so debatous.

debauch (dɪ'bɔːtʃ), *v.* Forms: 6- debauch; 6-7 (9 *Sc.*) debosh, 7 debaush, debausch, debosche, 7-8 deboash, 9 *Sc.* debush. [a. (*c* 1600) F. *débauch-er*, in OF. *desbaucher* (13-14th c.) to entice away from the service of one's master, seduce from duty, etc. Of obscure derivation. The original pronunciation after modern F., and its gradual change, are seen in the spellings *debosh, debaush, deboach, debauch* riming in 1682 with *approach*: see the *sb.* See also DEBOISE.

F. *débaucher* is, according to Littré and Hatzfeld, derived from a sb. *bauche*, of which the precise sense and origin are according to the latter unknown; according to the former it = 'a place of work, workshop', so that *desbaucher* would mean orig. 'to draw away from the workshop, from one's work or duty': so Diez. Cotgr. has *bauche*, 'course of stones or bricks in building', *baucher* 'to chip, hew, or square timber, etc.; also to ranke, order, array, lay euenly'; hence *desbaucher* might primarily mean 'to disorder, bring into disarray or disorder'. The sense 'draw away from service or duty' appears however to be the earliest in French, though that of 'corrupt', had also been developed before the word was taken into English.]

†**1.** *trans.* To turn or lead away, entice, seduce, *from* one to whom service or allegiance is due; *e.g.* soldiers or allies from a leader, a wife or children from husband or father, etc. (Usually with the connotation 'lead astray, mislead'.) Rarely with *against*. *Obs.*

a **1595** SIR. R. WILLIAMS *Actions Low C.* (1618) 5 (T.) That Count Egmont would be deboshed from them by the Spanish instruments. **1614** LODGE *Seneca* 49 Not to have such a woman to his wife that was not debauched from her husband. **1677** G. HICKES in Ellis *Orig. Lett.* II. IV. 42 To debauch the military and gentry.. from their duty to his Majesty. **1697** DRYDEN *Virg. Past.* Pref. (1721) I. 80 He who had the Address to debauch away Helen from her Husband. **1702** *Eng. Theophrast.* 72 Money debauches children against their parents. **1712** ARBUTHNOT *John Bull* IV. i, He had hardly put up his sign, when he began to debauch my best customers from me. **1754** HUME *Hist. Eng.* I. xvi. 211 He debauched prince John from his allegiance. **1765** GOLDSM. *Ess. Taste* Wks. (Globe) 315/2 Thus debauched from nature, how can we relish her genuine productions?

†**b.** To entice, seduce, or gain over *to* a party or course of action, or *to do* a thing. *Obs.*

1667 PEPYS *Diary* 3 July, Two young men whom one of them debauched by degrees to steal their fathers' plate and clothes. **1694** *Col. Rec. Pennsylv.* I. 459 The five Indian nations wer now debauched to the french interest. **1765** GOLDSM. *Ess. Taste* Wks. (Globe) 313/2 Hence the youth of both sexes are debauched to diversion. **1797** BURKE *Regic. Peace* iv. Wks. IX. 100 Their amity is to debauch us to their principles.

†**c.** (Without const.) To seduce from allegiance or duty, induce to desert; to render disaffected; to pervert or corrupt in regard of allegiance or duty to others. *Obs.* (exc. as merged in the more general sense of 2.)

1623 FAVINE *Theat. Hon.* I. iv. 25 To debosh and corrupt the subiects. **1651** EVELYN *Mem.* (1857) I. 285 Mr. John Cosin, son of the Dean, debauched by the priests. **1691** LUTTRELL *Brief Rel.* (1857) II. 204 Persons dispersing Tyrconnells declarations to debauch our soldiers. **1712** ARBUTHNOT *John Bull* III. App. i, If a servant ran away, Jack had debauched him. **1741** MIDDLETON *Cicero* I. II. 126 His army.. debauched by his factious officers. **1807** PIKE *Sources Mississ.* II. App. 51 The Spaniards were making such great exertions to debauch the minds of our savages. **1818** JAS. MILL *Brit. India* I. III. iv. 584 To betray their master and debauch his army.

2. To seduce from virtue or morality; to pervert, deprave, or corrupt morally; *esp.* to corrupt or deprave by intemperance, or sensual indulgence.

1603 FLORIO *Montaigne* (1613) 536 (T.) Young men, such as I imagine to be least debaushed and corrupted by ill examples. **1611** COTGR., *Desbaucher*, to debosh.. seduce, mislead; make lewd, bring to disorder, draw from goodnesse. *a* **1665** J. GOODWIN *Filled w. the Spirit* (1867) 40 Though Paul had been a grievous sinner.. yet he had not debauched his conscience. *a* **1694** TILLOTSON (J.), To debauch himself by intemperance and brutish sensuality. **1718** *Col. Rec. Pennsylv.* III. 47 The young men.. had been lately so generally debaucht with Rum. **1745** FIELDING *True Patriot* Wks. 1775 IX. 311 For fear of enervating their minds and debauching their morals. **1816** J. SCOTT *Vis. Paris* (ed. 5) 133 If a father debauches his children, is his family likely to be noted for subordination and respectability? **1829** LYTTON *Devereux* II. ii, Their humour debauches the whole moral system. **1879** FROUDE *Cæsar* xii. 163 The seat of justice has been publicly debauched.

b. To seduce (a woman) from chastity.

(Closely related to 1: see quots. 1614, 1697 there; but eventually also associated with the notion 'corrupt'.)

1711 STEELE *Spect.* No. 151 ¶1 A young lewd Fellow.. who would.. debauch your Sister, or lie with your Wife. **1791** BOSWELL *Johnson* 20 Mar. an. 1776, An abandoned profligate may think that it is not wrong to debauch my wife. **1817** W. SELWYN *Law Nisi Prius* (ed. 4) II. 1039 A compensation in damages for debauching his daughter. **1843** JAMES *Forest Days* II. iii, Debauching a country girl.

3. To deprave, vitiate (the taste, senses, judgement, etc.).

(In first quot. perhaps = mislead, *fig.* of 1 c.)

[**1635** COWLEY *Davideis* III. 700 Her Pride debauch'd her Judgment and her Eyes.] **1664** EVELYN *Sylva* (1679) 28 Acorns were heretofore the food of Men.. till their luxurious palats were debauched. **1686** PLOT *Staffordsh.* 151 Most other animals are nicer in their Senses (having no way debauch't them) than Mankind is. **1710** BERKELEY *Princ. Hum. Knowl.* §123 A mind not yet debauched by learning. **1794** GODWIN *Cal. Williams* 51 Having never been debauched with applause, she set light by her own qualifications. **1805** *Med. Jrnl.* XIV. 379 A person, whose understanding has not been debauched by superannuated prejudice. **1816** SCOTT *Antiq.* xiii, They debauch the spirit of the ignorant and credulous with mystical trash.

†**4.** To vilify, damage in reputation; to depreciate, disparage. *Obs.*

1601 SHAKS. *All's Well* V. iii. 206 He's quoted for a most perfidious slaue, With all the spots a' th' world taxt and debosh'd. **1632** HEYWOOD *2nd Pt. Iron Age* IV. Wks. 1874 III. 396 Whil'st Cethus like a forlorne shadowe walkes Dispis'd, disgrac't, neglected, and deboshit. *a* **1659** OSBORN *Misc.*, Pref. (1673) Qq ij b, It is contrary to my own Aphorism to debosh what I present, by saying it was writ before I was Twenty.

†**b.** To damage or spoil in quality. *Obs.* (Cf. DEBOIST 2.)

1633 *True Trojans* IV. iii. in Hazl. *Dodsley* XII. 512 Last year his barks and galleys were debosh'd; This year they sprout again.

†**5.** To dissipate, spend prodigally, squander.

1632 [see DEBOISE *v.*]. **1637-50** ROW *Hist. Kirk* (1842) 419 To.. give them in rent more thousands (to debosh and mispend) nor honest men hes hundreds. **1649** LD. FOORD in M. P. Brown *Suppl. Decis.* (1826) 399 Since her husband had debausched all, and left nothing to her.

6. *intr.* (formerly *refl.*) To indulge to excess in sensual enjoyment, *esp.* that of eating and drinking; to riot, revel. ? *Obs.*

1644 EVELYN *Mem.* (1857) I. 73 Which causes the English to make no long sojourn here, except such as can drink and debauch. **1687** MONTAGUE & PRIOR *Hind & P. Transv.* A iv, 'Tis hard to conceive how any man could censure the Turks for Gluttony, a People that debauch in Coffee. **1689** *Minutes Kirk Session* in McKay *Hist. Kilmarnock* (1880) 10 Such as they find drinking there, or in any way deboshing. **1703** SAVAGE *Lett. Antients* cvii. 269 More proper for you, than to debauch with Sicilian Wine. **1719** D'URFEY *Pills* (1872) I. 355 We, to grow hot, deboash ourselves in Beef. **1732** LAW *Serious C.* xiii. (1761) 203 That he neither drank, nor debauched; but was sober and regular in his business. **1825** JAMIESON, *To debosh*, to indulge one's self in the use of any thing to excess; as tea, snuff, &c.

fig. **1742** YOUNG *Nt. Th.* viii. 557 Hatred her brothel has, as well as love, Where horrid epicures debauch in blood.

Hence **de'bauching** *vbl. sb.* and *ppl. a.*

1645 MILTON *Tetrachordon* I. (1851) 217 A most negligent and debaushing tutor. **1660** —— *Free Commw.* 428 To the debauching of our prime Gentry both Male and Female. **1662** PETTY *Taxes & Contrib.* 48 If we should think it hard to giue good necessary cloth for debauching wines.

debauch (dɪ'bɔːtʃ), *sb.* (Also 7 deboach.) [a. F. *débauche*, f. *débaucher* to DEBAUCH. For the phonology, etc., see the verb.]

I. 1. A bout of excessive indulgence in sensual pleasures, *esp.* those of eating and drinking.

1603 FLORIO *Montaigne* 488 My debauches or excesses transport me not much. **1661** PEPYS *Diary* 3 Apr., My head akeing all day from last night's debauch. **1682** N. O. *Boileau's Lutrin* III. 203 Snoring after late Debauches, Nor dream'st what mischief now thy Head approaches. **1737** L. CLARKE *Hist. Bible* (1740) II. XII. 714 Extravagant and beastly debauches. **1839-40** W. IRVING *Wolfert's R.* (1855) 125 The dissolute companions of his debauches. **1874** GREEN *Short Hist.* iii. §3. 126 The fever.. was inflamed by a gluttonous debauch.

2. The practice or habit of such indulgence; debauchery.

1673 DRYDEN *Marr. à la Mode* IV. i, Masquerade is Vizor-mask in debauch. **1699** —— *Ep. to J. Dryden* 73 The first physicians by debauch were made. **1784** COWPER *Task* IV. 470 A whiff Of stale debauch, forth-issuing from the styes That law has licensed. **1874** BLACKIE *Self-Cult.* 74 All debauch is incipient suicide.

3. *transf.* and *fig.*

1672 MARVELL *Reh. Transp.* I. 41 He flyes out into a furious Debauch, and breaks the Windows. **1710** SHAFTESB. *Advice to Author* II. §2 (R.) Thro' petulancy, or debauch of humour. **1752** HUME *Ess. & Treat.* (1777) I. 148 The gentle Damon.. inspires us with the same happy debauch of fancy by which he is himself transported. **1873** LOWELL *Among my Bks.* Ser. II. 195 Such a debauch of initial assonances.

†**II. 4.** = DEBAUCHEE. *Obs.* [perh. for F. *débauché*, through the pl. in *-és*.]

1681 GLANVILL *Saddücismus* II. (1726) 452 A greater charge against these quibbling Debauches. **1689** JAS. CARLISLE *Fortune-Hunters* 6 He grew the Debauch of the Town. **1719** D'URFEY *Pills* (1872) IV. 319 When Debauches of both Sexes, From Hospitals crept.

†**de'bauch, debaush**, *a. Obs.* [perh. ad. F. *débauché*, with *-e* mute, or ? corruption of *debaucht*.] = DEBAUCHED. (Cf. DEBAUCHNESS.)

1616 R. C. *Times' Whistle* v. 1758 Mock them as despisde And debaush creatures.

debauchable (dɪ'bɔːtʃəb(ə)l), *a.* [-ABLE.] That can be debauched.

1865 MILL in *Morn. Star* 6 July, To spend 10,000*l.* in corrupting and debauching the constituents who are debauchable and corruptible.

debauched (dɪ'bɔːtʃt), *ppl. a.* [f. DEBAUCH *v.*, or immed. after F. *débauché*, with native ending -ED.] Seduced or corrupted from duty or virtue; depraved or corrupt in morals; given up to sensual pleasures or loose living; dissolute, licentious.

1598 FLORIO *Suiato*.. Also an vnthriftie, careles, debaucht or mislead man. **1624** CAPT. SMITH *Virginia* IV. 167 To rectifie a common-wealth with debaushed people is impossible. **1647** R. STAPYLTON *Juvenal* 18 Whose debauchter face and miene disclose His mind's diseases. **1653** HOLCROFT *Procopius* I. 4 He.. made love to other mens wives, and was extreamly debaucht. **1790** PENNANT *London* (1813) 259 Bartholomew-fair.. becoming the resort of the debauched of all denominations. **1796** H. HUNTER tr. *St.-Pierre's Stud. Nat.* (1799) II. 495 The money of strangers disappears, but their debauched morals remain. **1864** KINGSLEY *Rom. & Teut.* ii. (1875) 46 Decrepit and debauched slave-nations.

de'bauchedly, *adv.* [-LY[2].] In a debauched manner.

1644 BP. HALL *Rem. Wks.* (1660) 133 If I see a man live debauchedly in drunkennesse [etc.]. **1663** COWLEY *Of Liberty*, To live.. desperately with the bold, and debauchedly with the luxurious.

de'bauchedness. [-NESS.] The state or quality of being debauched.

1618 MYNSHUL *Ess. Prison* 29 By being giuen to drunkennes or whoring..or by any other debauchednes. **1660** H. MORE *Myst. Godl.* III. xi. 79 *Cybele, mater Deorum*, the celebration of whose Rites had so much villany and debauchedness in it. **1837** *New Monthly Mag.* XLIX. 168 Strange pranks of humorous debauchedness.

debauchee (dɛbɒ'ʃiː). Also 7 deboichee, 8 deboshee; also **debauché(e.** [a. F. *débauché* debauched (person), sb. use of pa. pple. of *débaucher* to DEBAUCH. In 17th and 18th c. also *deboichee, deboshee*: cf. DEBOISE, DEBOSHED.]

One who is addicted to vicious indulgence in sensual pleasures.

a **1661** HOLYDAY *Juvenal* 81 Cicero, describing the debauchées [*printed* -oes] of his time, says they were *vino languidi*. **1665** PEPYS *Diary* 23 July, If he knew his son to be a debauchee (as many and most are now-a-dayes about the Court). **1677** B. RIVELEY *Fun. Serm. Bp. of Norwich* 14 A great Deboichee. **1741** tr. *D'Argens' Chinese Lett.* xxxiii, Perhaps if the People could be Deboshees and Gluttons with Impunity, they would not be more sober there than in Europe. **1751** JOHNSON *Rambler* No. 174 ¶9, I never betrayed an heir to gamesters, or a girl to debauchees. **1882** FARRAR *Early Chr.* I. 67 No man is more systematically heartless than a corrupted debauchee.

b. *attrib.*

1768–74 TUCKER *Lt. Nat.* (1852) I. 262 A debauchee physician. **1862** *Sat. Rev.* 15 Mar. 305 A debauchee peer.

debaucher (dɪ'bɔːtʃə(r)). [f. DEBAUCH *v.* + -ER[1].] One who debauches; a corrupter or seducer.

1614 B. JONSON *Barth. Fair* V. vi, Thou strong debaucher and seducer of youth. **1670** G. H. *Hist. Cardinals* I. II. 47 A continual Swearer and Debaucher. **1727** BLACKWALL *Sacred Classics* I. 399 (T.) Insidious underminers of chastity, and debauchers of sound principles. **1828** SCOTT *F.M. Perth* xx, Destroyers of men, and debauchers of women.

debauchery (dɪ'bɔːtʃərɪ). Also 7 debaushery, deboshery, deboichery. [f. as prec. + -ERY.]

1. Vicious indulgence in sensual pleasures.

1642 MILTON *Apol. Smect.* (1851) 309 What with truanting and debaushery. **1647** R. STAPYLTON *Juvenal* 146 Those that excuse youth's deboichery. *c* **1665** MRS. HUTCHINSON *Mem. Col. Hutchinson* (R.), The nobility and courtiers, who did not quite abandon their deboscheries. **1727** DE FOE *Syst. Magic* I. i. (1840) 13 Noah himself..fell into the debaucheries of wine. **1838** THIRLWALL *Greece* IV. 109 Unworthy favourites, the companions of his debaucheries. **1841** ELPHINSTONE *Hist. Ind.* II. 155 He was ..fond of coarse debauchery and low society.

†**2.** Seduction from duty, integrity, or virtue; corruption. *Obs.*

1713 STEELE *Guardian* No. 17 ¶8 To contrive the debauchery of your child. **1752** JOHNSON *Rambler* No. 189 ¶6 There are men that boast of debaucheries of which they never had address to be guilty. **1790** BURKE *Fr. Rev.* 78 The republick of Paris will endeavour to compleat the debauchery of the army. **1863** H. COX *Instit.* I. viii 99 In no case was an election questioned on account of *treating*, or, as it was then called, debauchery at elections.

debauchment (dɪ'bɔːtʃmənt). ? *Obs.* Also 7 -baush-, -bosh-. [a. F. *débauchement* (in Cotgr. *des-*), f. *débaucher* to DEBAUCH: see -MENT.]

1. The action or fact of debauching or corrupting; seduction from duty or virtue.

1606 DANIEL *Queen's Arcadia* I. iv, These strange debaushments of our nymphes. **1611** COTGR., *Desbauchement*, a deboshement. **1625** W. B. *True School War* 64 He first outraged them by the debauchment of their Councellors and subiects. **1685** SOUTH *Serm.* (1843) II. xvii. 282 A corruption and debauchment of men's manners.

2. Debauched condition; debauchery; a debauch.

1628 BP. HALL *Quo Vadis?* §10 They are growne to that height of debauchment as to hold learning a shame to nobility. **1629** EARLE *Microcosm., Honest Fellow* (Arb.) 102 A good dull vicious fellow, that complyes well with the deboshments of the time. **1658** CLEVELAND *Rustic Rampant* Wks. (1687) 506 There is a Proneness in unruly Man to run into Debauchments.

†**de'bauchness.** *Obs. rare.* [f. DEBAUCH *a.* + -NESS, or corruption of *debauchedness.*]

Debauchedness.

1640 QUARLES *Enchirid.* IV. xcix, Let him avoyd Debauchnesse. **1650** ARNWAY *Alarm* 115 (T.) Their throats to drunkenness, gluttony, and debauchness. **1659** GAUDEN *Tears of Church* 390 Occasioned, yea necessitated, by their own debauchnesse and distempers.

†**debaurd.** *Obs.* [properly *debord*, a. F. *débord.* Cf. DEBORD *v.*] Departure from the right way; excess.

1671 ANNAND *Myst. Pietatis* 118 (Jam.) Which verily is the ground of all our sinful debaurds.

debayre, debefe: see DEBARE *a.*, LANG DE BŒUF.

debby: see DEB.

de-beak (diː'biːk), *v.* [f. DE- II. 2 + BEAK *sb.*[1]] *trans.* To remove the beak from. Hence **de'beaking** *vbl. sb.*

1937 *Ohio Agric. Experiment Station Bimonthly Bull.* Jan.–Feb. 37 There is only one way to debeak [chickens] properly and effectively. Only the upper beak is removed. The beak is not cut off; it is torn off. **1955** *Sci. News Let.* 16 July 46/3 Debeaking turkeys reduces losses from cannibalism. **1959** *Observer* 8 Mar. 3/4 The ill-fated chicks ..have to be..debeaked to prevent them tearing one another to pieces. **1960** *Farmer & Stockbreeder* 15 Mar. 133/1 Once feather pecking and cannibalism become established as a vice in intensively kept layers the only cure is debeaking.

†**de'bel, -ell,** *v. Obs.* [a. F. *débell-er* (Oresme, 14th c.), ad. L. *dēbellāre* to subdue in fight, f. *dē-* down + *bellāre* to war.] *trans.* To put down in fight, subdue, vanquish; to expel by force of arms. Hence †**debelling** *vbl. sb.*

1555 ABP. PARKER *Ps.* cviii. 320 He our foes shall sone debell. *a* **1564** BECON *Pleas. New Nosegay* Early Wks. (1843) 201 Humility..debelleth and valiantly overcometh the enemy of all grace. **1586** WARNER *Alb. Eng.* II. viii, Spanish Cacus..Whom Hercules from out his Realme debelled at the length. **1651** HOWELL *Venice* 42 This..made him more illustrious than by debelling of Afric. **1671** MILTON *P.R.* IV. 604 Him long of old Thou didst debel, and down from Heav'n cast. **1825** HOGG *Queene Hynde* 202. **1897** H. N. HOWARD *Footsteps Proserpine* 12 Many mourned by man, by fate debelled.

†**de'bellate,** *v. Obs.* [f. L. *dēbellāt-*, ppl. stem of *dēbellāre*: see DEBEL and -ATE.] = DEBEL. Hence †**debellating** *vbl. sb.*

1611 SPEED *Hist. Gt. Brit.* IX. xii. 138 Though in two or three battles inferior, yet not to haue beene clearely debellated. *a* **1626** BACON *Holy War* (J.), The extirpating and debellating of giants, monsters, and foreign tyrants.

†**debe'llation.** *Obs.* [n. of action f. L. *dēbellāre*: see prec. and -ATION.] The action of vanquishing or reducing by force of arms; conquest, subjugation.

1526 *St. Papers Hen. VIII*, I. 180 The debellacion of the Thurkes, enemyes of Christes feith. **1533** MORE (*title*), The Debellacyon of Salem and Bizance. **1627–77** FELTHAM *Resolves* I. lxxvii. 118 We often let Vice spring, for wanting the audacity and courage of a Debellation. **1653** T. ADAMS *Serm. Ps.* xciv. 19 Wks. (1861) III. 281 An insurrection and a debellation; a tumult and its appeasement. **1830** *Fraser's Mag.* I. 748 The internecine and flagrant debellation which I have had with..Sir James Scarlett.

†**de'bellative,** *a. Obs. rare*[−1]. [f. as prec. + -IVE.] Tending to overthrow or reduce by war. (In quot. '(mutually) destructive'.)

1651 BIGGS *New Disp.* ¶199 Warres of debellative contraries.

†**debe'llator.** *Obs. rare*[−1]. [a. L. *dēbellātor*, agent-n. f. *dēbellāre.*] A subduer, vanquisher.

1713 SWIFT *Char. of Steele* Wks. 1814 VI. 216 (Stanf.) Behold..the terror of politicians! and the debellator of news-writers!

†**de'bellish,** *v. Obs. rare.* [f. DE- I. 6 + *-bellish* in EMBELLISH: cf. BELLISH *v.*] *trans.* To rob of beauty, disfigure.

1610 G. FLETCHER *Christ's Vict.* (1632) 59 What blast hath thus his flowers debellished?

de bene esse: see DE I.

debenture (dɪ'bɛntjʊə(r)). Also 5–7 debentur, 6–7 debenter. [In early use *debentur*, stated by BLOUNT in 17th c. to be the L. word *debentur* 'there are due or owing', supposed to have been the initial word of formal certificates of indebtedness. This is, from the early use of the term, probable; though no actual examples of documents containing the Latin formula have been found.]

1. A certificate or voucher certifying that a sum of money is owing to the person designated in it; a certificate of indebtedness.

a. A voucher given in the Royal household, the Exchequer or other Government office, certifying to the recipient the sum due to him for goods supplied, services rendered, salary, etc., and serving as his authority in claiming payment. A principal application of the word during the 17th and 18th centuries was to the vouchers given by the Ordnance Office in payment of stores.

c **1455** in *Paston Lett.* No. 264 I. 364 Owyng to the seyd Fastolf for costys and chargys that he bare when he was Lieutenant of the towne of Harflew in Normandie [1415], as yt shewith by a debentur made to the seyd Fastolf, with hym remaynyng..Cxxxiijli. vjs. viijd. *Ibid.* 366 Certeyn debentur conteynyng the seyd sommes. **1469** *Mann. & Househ. Exp.* 537 Item, my master hath delyvered ij. debentures in the name of Norres, one of viij. marces fore fyshe, and nodere of vij. marces. *a* **1483** *Liber Niger* in *Househ. Ord.* 66 That none other person make suche debentures or bylles but the Clerkes of the self offyce, so that theyre wryting and hand may be certaynly knowne to them that pay in the countyng house. **1526** *Ibid.* 236 The clerke of the office [Accatrie] shall make out debentures to the parties of whom such provision is made..which he shall present into the Compting-house within two dayes after. **1567** R. EDWARDS *Damon & P.* in Hazl. *Dodsley* IV. 78 Let us rifle him so..And steal away his debenters [for coal delivered to the king's kitchen] too. **1666** W. FIELDING *Petit.* in *10th Rep. Hist. MSS. Comm.* App. v. 6 Before he gives debentures unto your petitioner for what creation-mony fell due unto your petitioner's said father. **1682** *Lond. Gaz.* No. 1689/4 Two Debenters were lost..One for Nine Months..for the Sum of 37*l.* 10*s.* The other for Six Months..for 25*l.* **1697** *Act* 8–9 *Will. III*, c. 27 (For better observation of ancient course of the Exchequer) No Teller..shall Trust or Depart With such Money..without an Order or Debenture for the same. **1701** *Lond. Gaz.* No. 3698/4 Lost..an Irish Transport Debenture, No. 191, made out the 20th of August, 1695, to Richard Haynes, for the Service of the Ann Ketch. **1708** J. CHAMBERLAYNE *St. Gt. Brit.* I. II. xii. (1743) 101 The chief Clerk [of the Kitchen] keeps all the Records, Ledger books, and Debentures for Salaries, and Provisions and Necessaries issuing from the Offices of the Pantry, Buttery, and Cellar. **1730–6** BAILEY (folio), *Debenture* [in the *Exchequer* and *King's House*], a Writing given to the Servants for the Payment of their Wages, etc. **1837** *Penny Cycl.* VIII. 340/2 Debentures..are in use now in the receipt of Exchequer and Board of Ordnance, and it is believed in the king's household.

†**b.** *spec.* A voucher certifying to a soldier or sailor the audited amount of his arrears for pay: see quot. 1674. *Obs.*

This was a regular feature of 17th c. army organization; such certificates, issued 'upon the public faith of the kingdom', were given to the Parliamentary Army during the Civil War, app. from November 1641 onwards, and similar bonds were also given in subsequent reigns; in some cases these certificates were secured upon and redeemed in forfeited land, esp. in Ireland.

1645 in Rushw. *Hist. Coll.* IV. I. 17 That particular Committee which are appointed to..take in your Accompts, and pay you part of your Arrears at present, and for the rest you are to have a Debentur upon the Public Faith of the Kingdom. **1647** *Thomasson Tracts* (Br. Mus) CCCXIV. No. 26. 2 Very sensible..how tedious..it is for soldiers after disbanding to get their particular accompts audited, and debenters for arrears. **1672** PETTY *Pol. Anat.* (1691) 6 The Debentures of Commission Officers, who serv'd eight years till about December 1649, comes to 1,800,000*l.* **1674** BLOUNT *Glossogr.* (ed. 4), *Debentur* (the third person plural of *debeor* to be due or owing) was by a Rump-act of 1649 cap. 43. ordained to be in the nature of a Bond or Bill to charge the Common-wealth to pay the Souldier-creditor or his Assigns, the sum due upon account for his Arrears. **1698** FARQUHAR *Love & Bottle* I. i. 8 The merciful bullet, more kind than thy ungrateful country, has given thee a Debenture in thy broken leg, from which thou canst draw a more plentiful maintenance than I with all my limbs in perfection. **1756** *Gentl. Mag.* XXVI. 391 In Limerick, a county, of which the greater part was..in the possession of families whose ancestors were adventurers in the reign of Q. Elizabeth, or had got debentures under Oliver Cromwell.

c. At the Custom-house: A certificate given to an exporter of imported goods on which a drawback is allowed, or of home produce on which a bounty was granted, certifying that the holder is entitled to the amount therein stated.

See M. POSTLETHWAITE, *Dict. Trade & Commerce* 1751–66, s.v., for full account, and 'forms of several kinds of debentures'.

1662 *Act 14 Chas. II*, c. 11 §14 The Moneys due upon Debentures for such forein Goods exported by Certificate. **1704** *Dict. Rust.*, *Debenture*..as most commonly used among Merchants is the allowance of Custom paid inward, which a Merchant draws back upon exportation of that Commodity, which was formerly imported. **1711** *Act 9 Anne*, c. 23 Any Certificate or Debenture for Drawing back any Customs or Duties. **1763** *Gentl. Mag.* Apr. 185 Without any suspicion of fraud, a debenture was granted, and a clearance made to Rotterdam, where a certificate was obtained for landing so many casks of rice. **1889** *Whitaker's Almanac* s.v. *Excise, Stamps, & Taxes*, Debenture or Certificate for drawback, or goods exported, etc., not exceeding £10..1*s.*

†**d.** *transf.* An acknowledgement of indebtedness by a corporation, private person, etc. *Obs.* exc. as in 3.

1583 in Picton *L'pool Munic. Rec.* (1883) I. 98 The said stipend paid at Halton is iiij[li] xvij[s] v[d] Deducted viz. ffirst for a Debenter xij[d] Postage iiij[s] x[d] [etc.]. **1615** SIR R. BOYLE *Diary* (1886) I. 85, I cleered all accompts with Iustice Gosnold and took in his debenter. **1654** GAYTON *Pleas. Notes* III. iv. 94 An Accessary..in all the pilferings, Hedge-robberies, Debenturs at Inns, and Farrier scores.

†**e.** *fig.* Acknowledgement of indebtedness; obligation; debt. *Obs.*

1609 HEYWOOD *Brit. Troy* XVI. ix, His Throne he fils Twenty foure yeares, then pays his last Debenter [*rime* aduenter] To Nature. **1658** OSBORN *Adv. Son* (1673) 38 If you consider beauty alone, quite discharged from such Debentur's, as she owes to the Arts of Tire-women, Taylers, Shoomakers and perhaps Painters. **1694** STEELE *Poet. Misc.* (1714) 40 You modern Wits..Have desperate Debentures on your Fame; And little would be left you, I'm afraid, If all your debts to Greece and Rome were paid.

†**2.** A certificate of a loan made to the government for public purposes, a government bond bearing annual interest. *Obs.*

The first quot. connects this with sense 1; it refers to government debentures given to the inhabitants of Nevis and St. Christopher's to recoup them for losses sustained from the invasions of the French.

1710 *Act 9 Anne* c. 23 Which Debentures shall be signed by the said Commissioners of Trade and Plantations..and shall bear interest for the Principal Sums to be contained, after the Rate of Six Pounds per Centum per Annum. **1756** NUGENT *Gr. Tour, France* IV. 7 Vast sums are levied by raising and lowering the coin at pleasure, by compounding debentures and government-bills, and by other oppressive methods. **1810** 'PHOCION' *Opinions on Public Funds* 8 If legal paper such as state debentures or bills had, in 1790, been of ten or fifty times their then magnitude. *Ibid.* 9 Give me a state debenture or an exchequer bill. **1811** *Wetenhall's Course of Exchange* 22 Oct., Irish Funds, Government Debentures, 3½ per cent. **1813** *Act 53 Geo. III*, c. 41 An Act for granting Annuities to satisfy certain Exchequer Bills, and for raising a Sum of Money by Debentures for the Service of Great Britain.

3. A bond issued by a corporation or company (under seal), in which acknowledgement is made that the corporation or company is indebted to a particular person or to the holder in a specified sum of money on which interest is to be paid until repayment of the principal.

Not occurring in the Companies Clauses Consolidation Act of 1845, but used shortly after in connexion with the loans raised by Railway Companies and the like, the name being evidently taken from sense 2. The term is in general use, especially for those bonds by which public companies raise money at a fixed rate of interest, with a prior charge on the assets of the company or corporation issuing them.

mortgage debenture: a debenture the principal of which is secured by the pledging of the whole or a part of the property of the issuing company.

1847 *East Ind. Railway, Deed of Settlement* 9 Apr., Debenture, bond, Bill of Exchange, Promissory note, or other Security. **1858** SIMMONDS *Dict. Trade, Debenture*.. The term has now got to be applied to railway companies', municipal, and other bonds or securities for money loaned. **1861** *Larceny, &c. Act 24-25 Vict.* c. 96 §1 The term.. valuable Security shall include..any Debenture, Deed, Bond, Bill, &c. **1863** FAWCETT *Pol. Econ.* III. xv. **1865** *Mortgage Debenture Act 28-29 Vict.* c. 78 An Act to enable certain Companies to issue Mortgage Debentures founded on Securities upon or affecting Land. *Ibid.* §26 Every Mortgage Debenture..issued by the Company shall be a Deed under the Common Seal of the Company duly stamped. **1887** CHITTY in *Law Rep.* 36 *Chanc. Div.* 215 The term *debenture* has not, so far as I am aware, ever received any precise legal definition. *Ibid.* 215 In my opinion a debenture means a document which either creates a debt or acknowledges it, and any document which fulfils either of these conditions is a 'debenture'..It is not either in law or commerce a strictly technical term, or what is called a term 'of art'.

4. *attrib.* and *Comb.*, as †***debenture goods***, †***lands***, ***debenture-holders***; **debenture-bond**, a bond of the nature of a debenture; = DEBENTURE 3; **debenture-stock**, debentures consolidated into, or created in the form of, a stock, the nominal capital of which represents a debt of which only the interest is secured by a perpetual annuity.

1736 BP. WILSON in Keble *Life* xxvii. (1863) 903 Shipping tobacco and other debenture goods into the running wherries. **1742** FRANCIS *Horace* II vii. (R.), Yet, prithee, where are Cæsar's bands Allotted their debenture-lands? **1863** *Act 26-7 Vict.* c. 118 §24 The Interest on Debenture Stock shall have Priority of Payment over all Dividends or Interest on any Shares or Stock of the Company, whether Ordinary or Preference or guaranteed, and shall rank next to the Interest payable on the Mortgages or Bonds for the Time being of the Company. **1866** *Spectator* 1 Dec. 1331 That faith stands already pledged to the existing debenture-holders, who lent their money on the security of a legislative Act. **1870** *Daily News* 22 Nov., Vice-Chancellor Malins..in the claim of the holders of debenture bonds issued by the Imperial Land Company of Marseilles..decided that..the bonds in question were virtually promissory notes, and that the holders were consequently entitled to recover in full. **1887** *Pall Mall G.* 8 June 12/1 It is proposed to create £285,000 Six per cent. Debenture stock, or rather more than the existing debentures of the company. **1893** *Midl. Rail. Circular* Dec. 30 They all benefited..by consolidation into one uniform 3 per cent. Debenture Stock.

debentured (dɪˈbɛntjʊəd), *a.* [f. prec. + -ED.] Furnished with or secured by a debenture. ***debentured goods***: goods on which a custom house debenture for a drawback, etc., is given.

1805 J. STEPHEN *War in Disguise* 60 (L.) Official clearances were given, in which no mention was made that the cargo consisted of bonded or debentured goods.

deberry, dial. var. of DAYBERRY, gooseberry.

debet(e, obs. f. DEBIT; var. DEBITE *Obs.*

†**ˈdebeth**, *v.* *3rd pers. sing.* *Obs.* App. an adaptation of Latin *dēbet* owes, oweth.

1481-90 *Howard Househ. Bks.* (Roxb.) 423 And so debeth to hym stylle xx.li. **1532** *Croscombe Churchw. Acc.* (Somerset Record Soc.) 40 Iohn Bolle for pewter vessells debeth ix[d]. *Ibid.* 41 Thos. Downe debeth unto the chyrch for the rentte for the lamp viii[s].

debile (ˈdɛbɪl), *a.* *Obs.* or *arch.* [a. F. *débile* (14-15th c.), ad.L. *dēbil-is* weak, *orig.* wanting in ability or aptitude, f. *dē-* (DE- I. 6) + *habilis*, ABLE, apt, nimble, expert, etc.] Weak, feeble, suffering from debility.

1536 LATIMER *Serm. & Rem.* (1845) 372 He being so debile, so weak, and of so great age. **1599** A. M. tr. *Gabelhouer's Bk. Physicke* 110/1 So debile, and feble of stomacke. **1607** SHAKS. *Cor.* I. ix. 48 For that I haue not.. foyl'd some debile Wretch. **1659** BAXTER *Key Cath.* xliii. 308 Where the fact or Proposition from the Light of Nature is more debile. **1788** MAY in Pettigrew *Life of Lettsom* (1817) III. 278 She..was still very restless, and extremely debile. **1802** *Med. Jrnl.* VIII. 111 Causes, which induce a debile frame. **1890** E. JOHNSON *Rise of Christendom* 158 In the form of a very debile old man of 202 years.

b. *Bot.* 'Applied to a stem which is too weak to support the weight of leaves and flowers in an upright position' (*Syd. Soc. Lex.*).

deˈbilitant, *a.* and *sb.* [a. F. *débilitant* or ad. L. *dēbilitānt-em*, pr. pple. of *dēbilitāre*: see DEBILITATE *v.*]

A. *adj.* Debilitating. **B.** *sb. Med.* (See quot.)

1857 DUNGLISON *Dict. Med.* s.v. *Debilitant*, Antiphlogistics are, hence, debilitants. **1882** *Syd. Soc. Lex.*, *Debilitants*, remedies or means employed to depress the powers of the body, such as antimony and low diet.

†**deˈbilitate**, *a.* *Obs.* [ad. L. *dēbilitāt-us*, pa. pple. of *dēbilitāre*.] Enfeebled; feeble.

1552 HULOET, Debilitate, or feble, or wythout synnowes, *eneruis*. **1737** H. BRACKEN *Farriery Impr.* (1757) II. 41 Help and strengthen the Part that is debilitate.

debilitate (dɪˈbɪlɪteɪt), *v.* [f. L. *dēbilitāt-*, ppl. stem of *dēbilitāre* to weaken, f. *dēbilis* weak.] *trans.* To render weak; to weaken, enfeeble.

1533 ELYOT *Cast. Helthe* (1541) 46 a, Immoderate watch ..doth debilitate the powers animall. **1541** PAYNEL *Catiline* xlv. 71 To debylitate and cutte asunder theyr endeuoir and hope. *a* **1625** BEAUM. & FL. *Faithful Friends* v. ii, If you think His youth or judgment..Debilitate his person..call him home. **1717** BULLOCK *Woman a Riddle* I. i. 8, I am totally debilitated of all power of elocution. **1715** LEONI *Palladio's Archit.* (1742) I. 57 The Sun shining..would be apt to heat, debilitate, and spoil the Wine or other Liquors. **1829** I. TAYLOR *Enthus.* ix. 233 Whose moral sense had been debilitated. **1871** NAPHEYS *Prev. & Cure Dis.* I. i. 45 A feeble constitution, which he further debilitated by a dissipated life.

†**b.** *Astrol.* Cf. DEBILITY 4 b. *Obs.*

a **1625** BEAUM. & FL. *Bloody Bro.* IV. ii, Venus..is..clear debilitated five degrees Beneath her ordinary power.

deˈbilitated, *ppl. a.* [f. prec. + -ED[1].] Enfeebled; reduced to debility.

1611 COTGR., *Debilité*, debilitated, weakened, enfeebled. **1646** SIR T. BROWNE *Pseud. Ep.* I. i. 3 Their debilitated posterity. **1803** T. BEDDOES *Hygëia* ix. 175 Those who exact efforts from the debilitated. **1841** BREWSTER *Mart. Sc.* vi. (1856) 91 His debilitated frame was exhausted with mental labour.

deˈbilitating, *vbl. sb.* [-ING[1].] Enfeeblement, debilitation.

1539 ELYOT in Ellis *Orig. Lett.* I. II. 117, I no thing gate but the Colike and the Stone, debilitating of Nature. **1765** *Univ. Mag.* XXXVII. 237/2 The debilitating of the affected part.

deˈbilitating, *ppl. a.* [-ING[2].] That debilitates; weakening, enfeebling.

1674 R. GODFREY *Inj. & Ab. Physic* Pref., Their poisonous and debilitating Methods. **1805** W. SAUNDERS *Min. Waters* 500 A long and debilitating sickness. **1865** LIVINGSTONE *Zambesi* vi. 143 The..debilitating effects of the climate.

debilitation (dɪbɪlɪˈteɪʃən). [a. F. *débilitation*, *-acion* (13th c.), ad. L. *dēbilitātiōn-em*, n. of action f. *dēbilitāre* to DEBILITATE.] The action of debilitating; debilitated condition; weakening.

1491 CAXTON *Vitas Patr.* (W. de W. 1495) II. 247 a/2 Some sykenes or debylytacyon of his bodye. **1524** *St. Papers Hen. VIII*, IV. 93 For the debilitacion and discomfort of thenemye. **1645** BP. HALL *Rem. Discont.* 25 How often doth sicknesse prevent the debilitations of age. **1875** LYELL *Princ. Geol.* I. I. ix. 168 The debilitation of the subterranean forces. **1876** DOUSE *Grimm's L.* §10. 19 An accelerated phonetic debilitation.

debilitative (dɪˈbɪlɪteɪtɪv), *a.* [f. L. *dēbilitāt-*, ppl. stem + -IVE.] Tending to debilitate; causing debilitation.

1682 H. MORE *Annot. Glanvill's Lux O.* 37 The deteriorating change in the Body..is understood of a debilitative..deterioration. **1810** BENTHAM *Packing* (1821) 153 The morbid and debilitative influence. **1886** *Lond. Med. Record* 15 Mar. 131/1 The debilitative effect of these preparations.

†**debilite**, *v.* *Obs.* [a. F. *débilite-r*, ad. L. *dēbilitāre*.] = DEBILITATE.

1483 CAXTON *Cato* B viij, [Drinking] debyliteth and maketh feble the vertues of the man. **1489** —— *Faytes of A.* IV. xvii. 279 A man debylyted and nyghe dede. **1545** RAYNOLD *Byrth Mankynde* 52 Ouer much heate debylitith, weakenith, and fayntith both the woman and the chyld.

†**deˈbilitude**. *Obs. rare.* [f. L. *dēbili-s* weak + -TUDE.] Debility, weakness; also in *Astrol.*

1669 W. SIMPSON *Hydrol. Chym.* 125 From a debilitude of the womb. **1686** GOAD *Celest. Bodies* II. v. 221 Weaker Signs must be debilitudes.

debility (dɪˈbɪlɪtɪ). Also 5-6 **debyli-**, **debilyte**, **-tee**, **-tye**, 6-7 **-tie**. [a. F. *débilité* (Oresme, 14th c.), ad. L. *dēbilitās*, f. *dēbili-s* weak.]

1. The condition of being weak or feeble; weakness, infirmity; want of strength; *esp.* that condition of the body in which the vital functions generally are feebly discharged.

1484 CAXTON *Æsop* v. xii, The grete feblenesse and debylyte of thy lene body. **1494** FABYAN *Chron.* VII. 556 For his feblenesse or debylyte of age. **1545** RAYNOLD *Byrth Mankynde* H h vij, To help the debilite of nature with cupping glassis. **1563** *Homilies* II. *Idleness* (1859) 517 By reason of age, debility of body, or want of health. **1650** BULWER *Anthropomet.* 105 By reason of the debility of his stomack. **1748** *Anson's Voy.* III. iv. 331 After full three hours ineffectual labour..the men being quite jaded, we were obliged, by mere debility, to desist. **1867** KINGSLEY *Lett.* (1878) II. 260 With the cure of stammering, nervous debility decreases. **1879** HARLAN *Eyesight* vi. 89 After long illness, the muscle of accommodation shares the debility of the whole system.

†**b.** Weakness of a material structure. *Obs.*

1563-87 FOXE *A. & M.* (1596) 247/1 Either by the debilitie of the bridge, or subtiltie of the soldiors..3000 of them with bridge and all fell armed into the violent stream.

2. Weakness in a mental or moral quality.

1474 CAXTON *Chesse* 65 For the debylite and feblenes of corage. **1502** *Ord. Crysten Men* (W. de W. 1506) IV. xi. 197 After the debylyte of fragylyte humayne. **1758** H. WALPOLE *Catal. Roy. Authors* (1759) II. 219 This Lord had much debility of mind, and a kind of superstitious scruples. **1805** FOSTER *Ess.* II. iv. 176 This debility of purpose. **1829** I. TAYLOR *Enthus.* ii. (1867) 33 A wretched debility and dejection of the heart.

3. Political, social, or pecuniary weakness.

1525 LD. BERNERS *Froiss.* II. ccxxxviij [ccxxxiv] 738 The debylyte of the realme of Englande. **1540** *Act 32 Hen. VIII*, c. 1 §1 Wylling to releue and helpe his saide subiectes in their said necessities and debilitye. **1818** CRUISE *Digest* (ed. 2) I. 139 Which B. could not have for the debility of his estate. **1871** MORLEY *Voltaire* (1886) 182 The debility of the courts of Austria and France.

†**4.** (with *pl.*) An instance of weakness. *Obs.*

a **1533** LD. BERNERS *Gold. Bk. M. Aurel.* (1546) E viij, The open honestee supplyeth many fautes and debilytees. **1654** tr. *Scudery's Curia Pol.* 61 They to guarde us from humane passions, and the debilities of Nature. **1825** T. JEFFERSON *Autobiog.* Wks. 1859 I. 82 Among the debilities of the government of the Confederation.

b. *Astrol.* Of a planet: A weakness or diminution of influence due to unfavourable position, etc.

1647 LILLY *Chr. Astrol.* To Rdr. 2, I would have him.. well to understand the Debilities and Fortitudes of every Planet. **1706** PHILLIPS (ed. Kersey) *s.v.*, Debilities are either Essential, when a Planet is in its Detriment, Fall, or Peregrine; or Accidental, when it is in the 12th, 8th, or 6th Houses; or Combust, etc. So that by each of those Circumstances, a Planet is more or less afflicted, and said to have so many or so few Debilities.

†**deˈbind**, *v.* *nonce-wd.* [DE- I. 1.] To bind down. (Put by Scott into the mouth of Baron Bradwardine.)

1814 SCOTT *Wav.* xli, A prisoner of war is on no account to be coerced with fetters, or debinded in *ergastulo*.

debit (ˈdɛbɪt), *sb.* Forms: (5 dubete), 6 **debitte**, **debette**, 6-7 **debet**, 8- **debit**. [ad. L. *dēbit-um* owed, due, *sb.* a debt. Cf. F. *débit* (1723 in Hatzfeld). In early use app. a further latinization of *debte*, from earlier *dette*, *det*: see DEBT.]

†**1.** *gen.* Something that is owed, a debt. *Obs.*

c **1450** *Paston Lett.* xlix. I. 61 Of certein dubete that I owe unto you. **1515** *Plumpton Corr.* p. cxxi, Be yearly worth over all charges or debittes. **1547** *Ludlow Churchw. Acc.* (Camden) 32 Parcelle of the debet that the churche restede in his dett. **1598** R. QUINEY *Let. to Shaks.* in *Leopold Shaks.* Introd. 105 In helpeing me out of all the debettes I owe in London. **1614** T. ADAMS *Devil's Banquet* 108 The Deuill tyes his Customers in the bond of Debets.

2. *Book-keeping.* **a.** An entry in an account of a sum of money owing; an item so entered. **b.** The whole of these items collectively; that side of an account (the left-hand side) on which debits are entered. (Opposed to CREDIT *sb.* 12.)

1776 *Trial of Nundocomar* 15/2 There are debits and credits between them in Bolankee Doss's books to a great amount. **1868**, **1889** [see CREDIT *sb.* 12]. **1872** BAGEHOT *Physics & Pol.* (1876) 189 There is a most heavy debit of evil. *a* **1895** *Mod.* This has been placed to your debit.

c. *attrib.*, as ***debit-entry***, ***-side*** (of an account).

1776 *Trial of Nundocomar* 83/2 The debit side of my master's account. **1887** *Pall Mall G.* 8 June 12/1 The year's operations show a debit balance of £42,000.

3. Special Comb. **debit card** orig. *U.S.*, a card issued by an organization, giving the holder access to an account, via an appropriate computer terminal, esp. in order to authorize the transfer of funds to the account of another party when making a purchase, etc., without incurring revolving finance charges for credit; = *asset card* s.v. ASSETS 5.

1975 M. G. BENDER *EFTS: Electronic Funds Transfer Syst.* iii. 53 Customer cards which have the primary function of effecting third party payments or of otherwise allowing the card holder remote access to his asset accounts, including a savings account or checking account, are becoming commonly known as '*debit' cards or 'asset' cards. **1977** *McGraw-Hill Yearbk. Sci. & Technol.* 143/2 Unlike bank credit cards.., debit cards..are presently used mainly in a local or regional environment. **1982** *Sci. Amer.* Sept. 119/1 By inserting a plastic card known as a debit card the customer can directly debit his checking account by the amount of a purchase rather than paying for that purchase in cash or with a check.

debit (ˈdɛbɪt), *v.* [f. DEBIT *sb.* Cf. F. *débiter* (1723 in Hatzfeld).]

1. *trans.* To charge with a debt; to enter something to the debit of (a person).

1682 SCARLETT *Exchanges* 203 He must and may debit the Principal for the said Value. **1768-74** TUCKER *Lt. Nat.* (1852) I. 621 Accounts are regularly kept, and every man debited or credited for the least farthing he takes out or brings in. **1809** R. LANGFORD *Introd. Trade* 26, I have debited your account with Lire 5000 Austriache. **1892** *Law Times* XCIV. 105/1 The bank were not entitled to debit the plaintiffs with the amount paid on the said cheques.

2. To charge as a debt; to enter on the debit side of an account.

1865 MISS BRADDON *H. Dunbar* i. 10 Pay the money, but don't debit it against his lordship. *Mod.* To whom is it to be debited?

3. (*Gallicism.*) To put into circulation; to spread (news, etc.).

1879 T. F. SIMMONS *Lay Folks Mass Book* 366 In respect of those who debited these fables. **1916** G. B. SHAW *Pen Portraits & Reviews* (1932) 43 Mr Bennett talks shop and debits harmless tosh about technique for the entertainment of literary amateurs in a very agreeable and suggestive manner.

debitable ('dɛbɪtəb(ə)l), *a.* [f. DEBIT *v.* + -ABLE.] That can be debited.

1895 *19th Cent.* Oct. 650 Salaries and establishments out of, but debitable to, India. **1899** *Westm. Gaz.* 12 Oct. 5/3 The monthly maintenance is estimated at £11,000 sterling, all of which is debitable to England.

† **debite**, *sb. Obs.* Also 5 debet, -ete, 5–6 debyte. [A corruption of DEPUTE: cf. DEBITY.] A deputy, lieutenant.

1482 in *Eng. Gilds* (1870) 312 The Master .. every þursday to be at the common halle, or els a debet ffor hym. **1526** TINDALE *Acts* xxiii. 24 Felix the hye debite. **1535** COVERDALE *Dan.* ii. 15 Arioch being then the Kynges debyte. **1549** ALLEN *Jude's Par. Rev.* 26 The vycar and debyte of Christ.

† **debite**, *a. Obs. rare.* [ad. L. *dēbit-us* owed, due: cf. DEBT.] That is owed or due.

1678 GALE *Crt. Gentiles* III. 5 Sin, as to its formal cause, is .. a privation of debite perfection.

debiteuse (dɛbɪ'tɜːz, -'tjuːz). *Glass-making.* [a. F. *débiteuse*, fem. of *débiteur* one who spreads (gossip), f. *débiter* to cut up, yield, MF. *débiter* to cut wood, sell retail, f. *de-* DE- I + *bitte* post on ship for fastening cables, f. ON. *biti* (see BITT).]

An open, oblong, trough-like object made of refractory material and having a slit along the bottom, which in the Fourcault method of making sheet glass floats on the surface of the molten glass.

1922 *Encycl. Brit.* XXXI. 290/1 In drawing a sheet of glass a bait consisting of a narrow flat woven iron sheet of a length equal to the slit in the *débiteuse* is lowered within the lips forming the slit. **1948** W. C. SCOVILLE *Revolution in Glassmaking* 330 His 'debiteuse' .. rested in a shallow tub of glass connecting with the melting furnace. **1969** R. PERSSON *Flat Glass Technol.* ii. 9 The glass sheet is drawn vertically from a slot in a refractory floater or debiteuse, which floats on the glass in the drawing chamber.

† **'debitor.** *Obs.* Also 5 debytour. [a. OF. *débitor* (14th c.), *débiteur*, ad. L. *dēbitor*, agent-n. f. *dēbēre* to owe. *Débitor, -eur*, was in French a learned term, the popular and proper F. form being *dettor, -ur, -eur*: see DEBTOR. In English, *debitor* no doubt owed its 16–17th c. use to its identity with the L.] A by-form of DEBTOR, current from 15th to 17th c., *esp.* in Book-keeping.

1484 CAXTON *Curiall* 4 Thenne art thou debytour of thy self. **1543** (*title*), A profitable Treatyce .. to learne .. the kepyng of the famouse reconynge, called in Latyn, Dare and Habere, and in Englyshe, Debitor and Creditor. **1588, 1660** [see CREDITOR 2]. **1611** SHAKS. *Cymb.* v. iv. 171 Oh the charity of a penny Cord, it summes vp thousands in a trice: you haue no true Debitor, and Creditor but it. **1660** WILLSFORD *Scales Comm.* 209 By Debitor or Debitors in a Merchants books, is understood the account that oweth or stands charged, and .. so all things received, or the Receiver is alwayes made Debitor. **1689** G. HARVEY *Curing Dis. by Expect.* i. 2 The Physician .. doth commonly .. insinuate, that the Patient is Debitor for his Life. **1795** WYTHE *Decis. Virginia* 15 A debitor who oweth money on several accounts. *attrib.* **1588** J. MELLIS *Briefe Instr.* C v, This Debitor side of your Leager.

† **'debitory.** *Obs. rare.* [f. L. *dēbit-us* owed, *dēbitor* debtor: see -ORY.] A statement or item of debt.

1575 *Richmond. Wills* (Surtees) 259 Inventorie of all the goodes and cattells of Sir Edmond Smissons .. Summa, vj^{li}. The debitorie. William Wormley for tithes xv^{d}–x^{d} Dame Wormley, xx^{d}. **1580** *Wills & Inv. N.C.* (Surtees) I. 432 The Resydewe of all my goodes .. as well as all debitoryes to me Owinge, I doe geue and Bequeithe vnto my Sonne.

† **'debitrice.** *Obs. rare*$^{-1}$. [a. F. *débitrice* (16th c.), fem. of *débiteur*, ad. L. *dēbitrix, -īcem*, fem. of *dēbitor*.] A female debtor.

1588 J. MELLIS *Briefe Instr.* F v b, And if [you buy] for ready money, make Creditrice the stocke, and Debitrice the shoppe.

debitumenize, -ation: see DE- II. 1.

† **debity.** *Obs.* In 5 -te, 5–6 -tee, 6 -tie, -tey, -bytie, -ty. Corruption of DEPUTY: cf. DEBITE.

1467 *Mann. & Househ. Exp.* 170, I was my lordes debyte at is dessyre. **1475** *Bk. Noblesse* (1860) 72 Hir debitees or commissioneris. **1535** COVERDALE *Esther* i. 3 The Debities and rulers of his countrees. **1548** UDALL, etc. *Erasm. Par. Acts* ix. 38 The Lieftenaunt of the citie, who was the debytie of King Aretas. **1559** *Mirr. Mag., Jack Cade* xxiii, Lieutenauntes or debities in realmes.

‖ **déblai** (deblɛ). *Fortif.* [Fr., vbl. sb. f. *déblayer* for *déblaer*, in OF. *desblaer*, f. *des-*:—L. *dis-* + *blé* (:—*blad, blat*) wheat: orig. to clear from corn, hence to clear of any mass of material.] (See quot.)

1853 STOCQUELER *Milit. Encycl.*, *Deblai*, the hollow space or excavation formed by removing earth for the construction of parapets in fortification. Thus, the ditch or fosse whence the earth has been taken represents the *déblai*.

deblat, var. of DABLET *Obs.*, little devil.

1473 *Ld. Treas. Acc. Scotl.* I. 68 Item to thare ij deblatis .. xx s. **1494** *Ibid.* 239.

de'blaterate, *v. rare.* [f. L. *dēblaterāre* trans., to prate of, blab out, f. DE- I. 3 + *blaterāre* to prate.] *intr.* To prate. (*affected.*)

1623 COCKERAM, *Deblaterate*, to babble much. **1893** R. L. STEVENSON in *Brit. Weekly* 27 Apr. 6 Those who deblaterate against missions have only one thing to do, to come and see them on the spot.

Hence **de'blateration**.

1817 *Blackw. Mag.* I. 470 (Caricaturing Sir T. Urquhart), Quisquiliary deblaterations.

† **de'blaze**, *v. Obs. rare*$^{-1}$. [f. DE- + BLAZE *v.*] = next.

1640 *Yorke's Union Hon.* Commend. Verses, Who weare gay Coats, but can no Coat deblaze.

† **de'blazon**, *v. Obs.* [f. DE- + BLAZON: cf. *depict, describe*.] = BLAZON *v.* (in various senses).

1621 BRATHWAIT *Nat. Embass.* (1877) 34 Now more amply meane I to deblazon the forlorne condition of these vnnatural maisters. **1630** —— *Eng. Gentlem.* (1641) 33 They no sooner became great, than they deblazoned their own thoughts. **1631** —— *Whimzies, Traveller* 92 Cities hee deblazons as if he were their herald.

Hence † **de'blazoning** *ppl. a.*

1640 *Yorke's Union Hon.* Commend. Verses, Those Coat-deblaz'ning Windowes.

† **'deblerie.** *Obs.*$^{-1}$ [a. OF. *deablerie*, now *diablerie*, f. *diable* devil.] *prop.* Demoniacal possession: but in quot. transl. a L. word meaning 'demon'.

a **1325** *Prose Psalter* cv[i]. 34 Hij sacrifiden her sones and her douters to debleries [*dæmoniis*].

deblet: see DABLET.

ˌ**deblo'ckade.** *rare.* [DE- II. 2.] The removal of a blockade.

1871 *Daily News* 5 Jan., General Trochu .. having formed in his own mind a plan for the deblockade of Paris.

deboach, -boash, obs. forms of DEBAUCH.

deboichee, -ery, deboicht, -ness: see DEBAUCHEE, -ERY, DEBOIST, -NESS.

† **de'boise**, *v. Obs.* Also 7 deboyst, -boish, -boysh. [A by-form of *debosh* DEBAUCH, with which it is connected by various intermediate forms: see DEBOIST *ppl. a.* The phonetic history is not clear.]

1. *refl.* To leave one's employment; to take recreation. [= F. *se débaucher*, Littré.]

1633 J. DONE *Hist. Septuagint* 44 Worke-men .. whom hee helde so close to their businesse that hee would not give them any leasure to deboyst themselves nor to idle sport by no meanes.

2. *trans.* To corrupt morally; to deprave by sensuality; = DEBAUCH *v.* 2. Also *fig.*

1654 GAYTON *Pleas. Notes* II. i. 35 Wicked wretch as I am, to be at such a late houre deboysing my selfe. **1654** Z. COKE *Logick* (1657) A iij b, Corruption of manners .. doth deboish a people. **1656** in Burn *Poor Laws* (1764) 47 They do make it their trade .. to cheat, deboyst [? deboyse], cozen, and deceive the young gentry. **1662** J. DAVIES *Olearius' Voy. Ambass.* 333 To make a temperate use of the Philosophy of Aristotle .. not deboysting himself.

3. To spend prodigally; to squander; = DEBAUCH *v.* 5.

1632 QUARLES *Div. Fancies* III. lxxv. (1664), One part to cloath our pride, Another share we lavishly deboise To vain, or sinful joyes.

† **de'boise**, *a. Obs.* [Corruption of DEBOIST: cf. DEBAUCH *a.*] = next.

1632 RANDOLPH *Jealous Lovers* III. ii, The deboisest Roarers in the citie. **1644** BULWER *Chiron.* 34 One Polemon a deboyse young man. **1667–9** BUTLER *Rem.* (1759) II. 205 (*A clown*) All the worst Names that are given to Men .. as *Villain, Deboyse, Peasant*, &c.

† **de'boist**, *ppl. a.* (*sb.*) *Obs.* Forms: 7 deboist, -oyst; -oysed; -ost(e; -oished, -oisht, -oyshed, -oysht, -oicht. [By-form of DEBAUCHED: cf. DEBOISE vb.]

1. = DEBAUCHED.

1604 [see DEBOISTLY]. **1612** WOODALL *Surg. Mate* Pref. Wks. (1653) 18 A general deboist and base kind of habit. **1622** F. MARKHAM *Bk. War* I. viii. 31 Froathy, base and deboysed Creatures. **1626** L. OWEN *Spec. Jesuit.* (1629) 63 A very wicked, deboysht, and prophane man. **1639** R. JUNIUS *Sin Stigmatized* 359 (T.) Our debauched drunkards, and deboyshed swearers. *a* **1657** W. BRADFORD *Plymouth Plant.* II. (1856) 240 This wicked and deboste crue. **1694** CROWNE *Married Beau* III. 27 Stand off, you base, unworthy, false, deboist man. **1722** SEWEL *Hist. Quakers* (1795) III. 217 Knowing him to be a deboist fellow.

2. Damaged. (Cf. DEBAUCH *v.* 4.)

1641 HEYWOOD *Priest Judge & Patentee*, The price of French and Spanish wines are raisd How ever in their worth deboyst and craisd.

3. Used as a *sb.* = DEBAUCHEE.

1657 R. LIGON *Barbadoes* (1673) 21 For one woman that dyed, there were ten men; and the men were the greater deboystes.

Hence **de'boistly** *adv.*, **de'boistness**.

1604 T. WRIGHT *Passions* II. iii. §3. 74 A multitude of Passions .. breake out debostly. **1628** PRYNNE *Love-lockes* 34 Licentiousnesse, Deboistnesse, and the like. **1647** R. STAPYLTON *Juvenal* 148 Nero's cruelty and deboich'tnesse. **1671** *Westm. Drollery* 78 Tell me no more that long hair can Argue deboistness in a man.

† **de'bolish**, *v. Obs.* [DE- II. 1; cf. ABOLISH *v.*.] *trans.* To demolish, sweep away.

1615 G. SANDYS *Trav.* 214 The passage was soon after debolished by assaulting seas.

debonair, -bonnaire (ˌdɛbə'nɛə(r)), *a.* (*sb.*) Forms: 3–4 debonere, 4 -eir(e, -ure, 4–5 -ar, 4–6 -er, -ayr(e, 6 *Sc.* -are, 4– debonaire, 5– debonair, (7–9 debonnaire, 8–9 debonnair). [a. OF. *debonaire*, prop. a phrase *de bonne aire* (11th c.) of good disposition. Very common in ME., but obsolescent from the 16th c., and now a literary archaism, often assimilated in spelling to mod.F. *débonnaire*.]

A. *adj.* † **a.** Of gentle disposition, mild, meek; gracious, kindly; courteous, affable (*obs.*); **b.** Pleasant and affable in outward manner or address; often in mod. quots. connoting gaiety of heart.

a **1225** *Ancr. R.* 186 Auh þet debonere child hwon hit is ibeaten, ȝif þe ueder hat hit, cusseð þe ȝerd. **1297** R. GLOUC. (1724) 167 So large he was & so hende, & al so de bonere. *Ibid.* 374 To hem, þat wolde hys wylle do, debonere he was & mylde. *c* **1374** CHAUCER *Boeth.* I. v. 22 Zepherus þe deboneire wynde. *c* **1385** —— *L.G.W.* 276 So good, so faire, so debonayre. **1375** BARBOUR *Bruce* I. 362 Wyss, curtaiss, and deboner. **1382** WYCLIF *Ecclus.* v. 13 Be thou debonere to here the wrd of God. *c* **1430** LYDG. *Chichev. & Bycorne*, Pacient wyfes debonayre, Whiche to her husbondes be nat contrayre. **1545** RAYNOLD *Byrth Mankynde* Prol. (1634) 6 By honest, sober, debonnaire and gentle manners. **1590** SPENSER *F.Q.* I. ii. 23 Was neuer Prince so meeke and debonaire. **1685** EVELYN *Mem.* (1857) II. 216 He was a prince of many virtues, and many great imperfections: debonaire, easy of access. **1707** COLLIER *Refl. Ridic.* 379 He has too debonair and free a Deportment with the Women. **1782** COWPER *Table T.* 236 The Frenchman, easy, debonair, and brisk. **1812** MAR. EDGEWORTH *Vivian* ii, In spite of his gay and debonair manner, he looked old. **1843** LYTTON *Last of Barons* I. vi, She became so vivacious, so debonnair, so charming. **1847** DISRAELI *Tancred* II. xvi, A carriage a degree too debonair for his years.

B. *sb.* † **1.** [the adj. used *absol.*] Gracious being or person. *Obs.*

c **1366** CHAUCER *A.B.C.* 6 Help and releeue thou mihti debonayre. **1393** GOWER *Conf.* III. 192 Trajan the worthy debonaire, By whom that Rome stood governed.

† **2.** Graciousness of manner; = DEBONAIRTY.

1697 EVELYN *Numism.* ix 305 A serious Majesty attemper'd with such strokes of Debonaire, as won Love and Reverence. **1748** RICHARDSON *Clarissa* Wks. 1883 IV. 185 Shall my vanity extend only to personals, such as the gracefulness of dress, my debonnaire, and my assurance.

debo'nairly, *adv.* [f. prec. + -LY^{2}.] In a debonair manner; meekly, gently, graciously, affably, etc.; see the adj.

c **1300** *Cursor M.* 23872 (Edin.) He þat can mar þan anoþer, debonerlik [*v.rr.* de-bonerli, debonerly] .. teche his broþer. *c* **1350** *Will. Palerne* 730 Mi hauteyn hert bi-houes me to chast, And bere me debonureli. *c* **1386** CHAUCER *Melib.* ¶ 98 Whan dame Prudence, ful debonerly and with gret pacience, hadde herd al that hir housbonde liked for to seye. *c* **1430** *Pilgr. Lyf Manhode* I. lxi. (1869) 37, I am .. thilke that debonairliche suffreth al pacientlich. **1483** CAXTON *Cato* G viij b, Thou oughtest to bere and suffre debonayrlye the wordes of thy wyf. **1597** TOFTE *Alba* Introd. (1880) p. xxvii, Hoping your Honour will .. debonairly accept of these trifles. **1633** FORD *Love's Sacr.* II. i, Your apparel sits about you most debonairly. **1785** H. WALPOLE *Lett. C'tess Ossory* II. 214 My hand, you see, Madam, has obeyed you very debonairly. **1849** C. BRONTE *Shirley* viii, 'Good morning, Mr. Barraclough,' said Moore, debonairly.

debo'nairness. [f. as prec. + -NESS.] The quality of being debonair: see the adj.

1382 WYCLIF *Ps.* xliv. [xlv.] 5 For treuthe, and debonernesse, and riȝtwisnesse. **1664** H. MORE *Myst. Iniq.* 548 That there should be all Kindness, Condescending, Benignity and Debonairness in them. **1753** RICHARDSON *Grandison* (1810) VI. xxxi. 213 From whom can spirits, can cheerfulness, can debonnairness be expected, if not from a good man? **1768** STERNE *Sent. Journ.* (1778) II. 42 With all the gaiety and debonairness in the world. **1929** W. DEEPING *Roper's Row* x. 99 A notable claim to decency and debonairness. **1964** *Listener* 13 Aug. 248/1 His breezy debonairness depends on the convention of public-school illiteracy.

† **debo'nairship.** *Obs. rare*$^{-1}$. [f. as prec. + -SHIP.] = next.

a **1240** *Wohunge* in *Cott. Hom.* 275 Þenne þi deboneirschipe mai make þe eihwer luued.

† **debo'nairty, debo'narity.** *Obs.* Forms: 3–5 debonerte, -airte, 4 -eirete, 4–5 -airete, 5 -ertee, -ayrte(e, -airty, -arte, -arete, 6 debonnairetie, 6–7 debonaritie, 7 -airitie, -ty, -arety, -erity, -arity. [ME. a. OF. *debonaireté, -eretié* (13th c.), f. *debonaire*: see -TY. *Debonarity* is a later assimilation to the type of *similarity*, etc.]

Debonair character or disposition; mildness, gentleness, meekness; graciousness, kindness; courtesy, affability.

a **1225** *Ancr. R.* 390 Þuruh his debonerté, luue hefde ouerkumen hine. *a* **1240** *Wohunge* in *Cott. Hom.* 269 Debonairte of herte. *c* **1386** CHAUCER *Pars. T.* ¶ 466 This Ire is with debonerete and it is wroþ withoute bitternes. *c* **1430** *Pilgr. Lyf Manhode* III. liii. (1869) 163 This cometh .. of youre debonayrtee. **1491** CAXTON *Vitas Patr.* (W. de W.

1495) II. 209a/2 Pacyence, humylyte, debonarete, & wyllefull obedyence. **1600** HOLLAND *Livy* XL. xlvi. 1089 The goodnature and debonairitie [*facilitas*] of the two Censors. **1637** BASTWICK *Litany* II. 3 A Prince of surpassing deboneritу. *a* **1677** BARROW *Serm.* (1687) I. viii. 95 The chearfull debonairity expressed therein. **1688** BP. S. PARKER *Enq. Reasons Abrogating Test* 2 He quickly repents him of that Debonarity.

†**debo'narious,** *a. Obs. rare*⁻¹. [f. DEBONAIR after words in *-arious*, f. L. *-ārius*, F. *-aire.*] = DEBONAIR; cf. next.

c **1485** *Digby Myst.* (1882) III. 447 Your debonarius obedyauns ravyssyt me to trankquelyte!

†**'debonary,** *a. Obs.* [f. DEBONAIR after words in -ARY, an alteration of F. *-aire*, e.g. *ordinaire, ordinary*.] = DEBONAIR.

1402 HOCCLEVE *Letter of Cupid* 347 They [women] ben.. ful of humylite, Shamefaste, debonarie and amyable. *c* **1430** LYDG. *Bochas* (1558) II. v. 8 To her declaring with reasons debonary [*rime* tary]. **1630** *Tinker of Turvey* 46 Of a comely visage, courteous, gentle and debonary.

de'bord, *v.* ? *Obs.* Also 7 deboard, *Sc* deboird. [a. F. *débord-er*, in 15–16th c. *desborder*, f. *des-*:—L. *dis-* (DE- I. 6) + *bord* border.]

1. *intr.* Of a body of water: To pass beyond its borders or banks, to overflow.

1632 LITHGOW *Trav.* VII. 316 As the Water groweth in the River, and so from it debording. *Ibid.* 317 Violent streames do ever deface, transplant, and destroy all that they debord upon. **1635** PERSON *Varieties* I. 24 Such as aske, why the Sea doth never debord. **1859** R. F. BURTON in *Jrnl. Geog. Soc.* XXIX. 194 A wide expanse.. over which the stream when in flood debords to a distance of two miles.

†**2.** *fig.* To go out of bounds, deviate; to go beyond bounds, go to excess. *Obs.*

c **1620** Z. BOYD *Zion's Flowers* (1855) 77 That hence I from my duety not debord. *a* **1658** DURHAM *Ten Commandm.* (1675) 362 (Jam.) It is a wonder that men should take pleasure to deboard in their cloathing. **1671** *True Nonconf.* 401 Debording from common methods. *a* **1678** WOODHEAD *Holy Living* (1688) 113 Least.. your passions sometimes debord where you would not have them.

Hence **de'bording** *vbl. sb.* = next.

1635 PERSON *Varieties* II. 66 Great debording of waters. **1652** URQUHART *Jewel* Wks. (1834) 225 Too great proness to such like debordings and youthful emancipations.

†**de'bordment.** *Obs.* [a. F. *débordement*, f. *déborder*: see prec. and -MENT.] Going beyond bounds, excess.

1603 FLORIO *Montaigne* III. ix. (1632) 540 Against the ignorance and debordement of Magistrates. **1646** H. LAWRENCE *Comm. Angells* 88 The debordments and excesses of no beasts are so great as those of mankind. **1659** GAUDEN *Tears of Church* 214 To cleanse it of all those debordments and debasements faln upon Christian Religion.

debosh, -bosche, obs. or arch. f. DEBAUCH.

de'boshed, *ppl. a.* Also 7 debosht. An early variant of DEBAUCHED, representing the pronunciation of F. *débauché*; connected with the main form by *debaushed, debausht*. *Obs.* in Eng. before the middle of 17th c.; retained longer in Scotch; revived by Scott, and now frequent in literary English, with somewhat vaguer sense than *debauched*.

1599 JAMES I *Βασιλ. Δωρον* (1603) 110 Ouer superfluous like a deboshed waister. **1605** SHAKS. *Lear* I. iv. 263 Men so disorder'd, so debosh'd, and bold. **1624** HEYWOOD *Gunaik.* II. 16 One Herostratus, a wicked and debosht fellow. **1637–50** Row *Hist. Kirk* (1842) 358 Ignorant and debosht ministers are tolerated. **1826** SCOTT *Woodst.* iii, Swash-bucklers, deboshed revellers, bloody brawlers. **1859** KINGSLEY *Plays & Purit.* Misc. II. 109 An utterly deboshed, insincere, decrepit, and decaying age. **1867** LOWELL *Biglow P.* Ser. II. 55 Many deboshed younger brothers of.. good families may have sought refuge in Virginia.

deboshee, -ery, -ment, obs. ff. DEBAUCHEE, etc.

debost(e: see DEBOIST.

debouch (dɪ'buːʃ, ‖debuʃ), *v.* Also debouche. [mod. a. F. *débouche-r*, in 17th c. *desboucher*, OF. *desbouchier* (13th c.), f. *dé-*:—*des-*, L. *dis-* (see DE- I. 6) + *bouche* mouth. Cf. It. *sboccare* 'to mouth or fall into the sea as a river' (Florio).]

1. *Milit.* (*intr.*) To issue from a narrow or confined place, as a defile or a wood, into open country; hence *gen.* to issue or emerge from a narrower into a wider place or space.

[**1665** EVELYN *Mem.* (1857) III. 161 We have hardly any words that do so fully express the French.. *ennui, bizarre, débouche*.. Let us therefore.. make as many of these do homage as are like to prove good citizens.] **1760** *Lond. Mag.* XXIX. 177 We saw the column of infantry debouching into Minden plain. **1812** *Examiner* 24 Aug. 531/2 These two companies gave the.. cavalry time to *debouche*. **1813** *Ibid.* 7 June 355/2 General Bertrand.. appearing to intend debouching from Jaselitz upon the enemy's right. **1840** BARHAM *Ingol. Leg.: Leech of Folkestone* (1877) 370 The travellers debouched on the open plain on Aldington Frith.

fig. **1839** *Times* 4 Oct., Mr. Labouchere debouches upon the cabinet.

2. *transf.* Of a ravine, river, etc.: To issue as at a mouth or outlet into a wider place or space.

1834 MEDWIN *Angler in Wales* I. 168 This little stream that debouches from the lake. **1850** B. TAYLOR *Eldorado* xxii. (1862) 236 The ravine finally debouched upon the river at the Middle Bar. **1878** H. M. STANLEY *Dark Cont.* I. viii. 167 Nakidino Creek, into which an important stream debouches.

3. *trans.* (*causal*). To lead forth into open ground; to provide an outlet for.

1745 DUNCAN FORBES in Ellis *Orig. Lett.* II. IV. 355 No more than a hundred and fifty or a hundred and sixty of the Mackenzies have been debouched. **1844** W. H. MAXWELL *Sports & Adv. Scotl.* xxiii. (1855) 190 Huge outlets which *débouche* the waters.

de'bouch, *sb. rare.* Also debouche. [f. prec. vb.] = next (sense 1).

1813 *Examiner* 7 June 354/2 Fortified rising points, which defended the debouches from the Spree. *Ibid.* 3 May 274/2 The debouch from the Hartz. **1823** SOUTHEY *Hist. Penins. War* I. 696 The debouches of Villarcayo, Orduña, and Munguia.

‖**débouché** (debuʃe). [Fr.: f. *déboucher* (see above).]

1. *Milit.* An opening where troops debouch or may debouch; *gen.* a place of exit, outlet, opening.

1760 *Lond. Mag.* XXIX. 171 The generals will take particular notice of the nine *Debouché's*, by which the army may advance to form in the plain of Minden. **1813** WELLINGTON in Gurw. *Desp.* (1838) X. 545 Desirable to obtain possession of the *débouchés* of the mountains towards Vera. **1857** J. W. CROKER *Ess. Fr. Rev.* iv. 202 (Stanf.) One gate, as an additional *débouché* for the crowd.

2. *fig.* An opening, outlet, or market for goods.

1846 WORCESTER cites RAWSON.

de'bouchment. Also debouchement. [a. F. *débouchement*, f. *déboucher* (see DEBOUCH *v.*) + -MENT.]

1. *Milit.* The action or fact of debouching.

1827 J. F. COOPER *Prairie* II. iii. 44 To unravel the mystery of so sudden a debouchement from the cover. **1871** *Daily News* 19 Sept., The debouchment of Stephenson's brigade through the railway arch.

2. The mouth or outlet of a river, a pass, etc.

1859 BURTON *Centr. Afr.* in *Jrnl. Geog. Soc.* XXIX. 42 The coast.. presents but three debouchments that deserve the name of rivers.

debouchure (debuʃyr). [In form, French, f. *déboucher* to DEBOUCH + -URE; but this sense is not Fr.] = DEBOUCHMENT 2, EMBOUCHURE I.

1844 KINGLAKE *Eothen* xii. (1878) 168 Towards the debouchure of the river. **1890** *Spectator* 11 Jan. 41 Thence two railways would connect her with Zanzibar and the debouchure of the Zambesi.

debourse, var. of DEBURSE.

†**de'bout,** *v. Obs.* [a. F. *débouter*, in OF. *deboter* (10th c.), f. *de-* (DE- I. 2) + *bouter*, OF. *boter* to push.] *trans.* To thrust out, expel, oust.

1619 *Time's Storehouse* 208 (L.) Not able enough to debout them out of their possessions. **1644** HUME *Hist. Ho. Douglas* 264 (Jam.) His fraud was detected.. and he debouted, and put from that authority.

†**de'boutement.** *Obs.* [a. OF. *debotement, déboutement*, f. *débouter*: see prec. and -MENT.] A thrusting forth, expulsion.

1481 CAXTON *Myrr.* II. xxviii. 121 Deboutemens and brekyng out of wyndes that mete aboue the clowdes.

†**de'bowel,** *v. Obs.* [DE- II. 2.] = DISBOWEL, disembowel.

1375 BARBOUR *Bruce* XX. 285 He debowalit wes clenly, And bawlmyt syne full rychly. **1513** DOUGLAS *Æneis* IV. ii. 25 The beistis costis, as thai debowalit wer. *a* **1547** SURREY *Æneid* IV. 80 With giftes that day, and beastes debowled.

deboyse, deboyst, var. DEBOISE *Obs.*

†**de'braid,** *v. Obs. rare.* In 4–5 debreyd. [f. DE- I. 1 + BRAID *v.*¹ 3 to snatch.] To snatch down (rendering L. *decerpere*).

1388 [see DEBREAK].

†**de'branch,** *v. Obs. rare.* [ad. F. *desbranchir* (Palsgr. & Cotgr.), or *desbranche-r* (15–16th c. Godef.), f. *dé-, des-* (DE- I. 6) + *branche* branch.] *trans.* To deprive of branches, to lop. Hence **de'branching** *vbl. sb.*

1601 HOLLAND *Pliny* I. 538 After such pruning and debranching.

†**de'break,** *v. Obs. rare.* [f. DE- I. 1 + BREAK *v.*] *trans.* To break down (transl. L. *decerpere*).

1382 WYCLIF *Mark* i. 26 The onclene goost debrekynge [*v.r.* to-braydynge, **1388** debreidynge, to-breidinge] hym, and cryinge with grete vois.

Debrett (dɪ'brɛt), *sb.* A colloquial designation of 'Debrett's Peerage of England, Scotland and Ireland', the first edition of which, issued in 1803, was compiled by John *Debrett* (*c* 1750–1822). Also *transf.*

1848, etc. [see BURKE *sb.*]. **1849** THACKERAY *Pendennis* I. ix. 85 You cannot begin your genealogical studies too early; I wish.. you would read in Debrett every day. **1873** [see WET-NURSE *v.* b]. **1910** BARONESS ORCZY *Lady Molly of Scotland Yard* iv. 82 If you have studied Debrett at all, you know.. that the peerage is one of those old English ones which date back some six hundred years. **1970** *Guardian* 18 Aug. 1/5 The 1970 Debrett was published yesterday.

débridement (debridmɑ̃). *Surg.* [Fr., lit. 'unbridling'.] The removal from a wound, etc., of damaged tissue or foreign matter (see also quot. 1842). Hence **de'bride** *v. trans.*, to perform débridement on.

1842 DUNGLISON *Med. Lex.* (ed. 3) 217/2 *Débridement*, the removal of filaments, &c., in a wound or abscess, which prevent the discharge of pus. In a more general acceptation, it means the cutting of a soft, membranous or aponeurotic part, which interferes with the exercise of any organ whatever. **1929** F. A. POTTLE *Stretchers* (1930) 149 Débridement about half the extensor muscles of thigh. Wounds of entrance and exit in knee joint debrided. **1967** S. TAYLOR et al. *Short Textbk. Surg.* xxxii. 473 Where there is .. contamination of the wound by dirt and foreign bodies, full débridement must be carried out.

debrief (diː'briːf), *v. colloq.* [f. DE- II. 1 + BRIEF *v.*²] *trans.* To obtain information from (a person) on the completion of a mission or after a journey. Usu. *pass.* So **de'briefing** *vbl. sb.*

1945 *Picture Post* 31 Mar. 9/1 Crump and his men go through a medical test,.. de-briefing and customs. **1945** *John o' London's* 16 Nov. 70/2 The R.A.F. use of the atrocity debrief. When airmen receive their orders for an operation they are said to be briefed for it—a quite legitimate extension of the legal term. But when they return to give their report, they do not just report, as one would think. They are debriefed. **1951** *Life* 17 Dec. 31/2 He went to the debriefing shed and made a routine report on the railroad bombing mission. **1964** *Observer* 13 Sept. 2/2 He [*sc.* a defecting Russian scientist] is now in the U.S., presumably being debriefed by American intelligence. **1964** J. PORTER *Dover One* xi. 138, I want everybody back at the station.. for a de-briefing session. **1965** *Guardian* 22 Mar. 9/6 Leonov and Belyaev.. will stay at the space station for several days to be debriefed and medically examined.

‖**debris, débris** (debri, 'deɪbriː, 'dɛbriː). [F. *débris*. vbl. sb. from obs. *débriser* (Cotgr.), OF. *debrisier*: see DEBRUISE *v.*] **1.** The remains of anything broken down or destroyed; ruins, wreck: **a.** orig. (in Eng.) *fig.*; **b.** in *Geol.* applied to any accumulation of loose material arising from the waste of rocks; also to drifted accumulation of vegetable or animal matter (Page); thence, **c.** any similar rubbish formed by destructive operations.

1708 COLLIER *Eccl. Hist.* I. A.D. 685 To retire with the *debris* of the army. **1735** SWIFT *Lett. to Dk. of Dorset*, Your Grace is now disposing of the *debris* of two bishoprics. **1778** H. WALPOLE *Let. to W. Mason* 18 July, The best they can hope for, is to sit down with the *débris* of an empire. **1802** PLAYFAIR *Illustr. Hutton. Th.* 363 A temporary receptacle for the *debris* of the Alps. **1849** MURCHISON *Siluria* xiv. 356 The *débris* of the ancient rocks. **1851** D. WILSON *Preh. Ann.* (1863) II. III. iii. 105 Accumulated rubbish and debris. **1858** GEIKIE *Hist. Boulder* ix. 176 The sandstone cliffs.. are battered down and their debris carried out to sea. **1885** *Act 48–9 Vict.* c. 39 §5 The sanitary authority shall remove the same and all foundations, débris, and other materials.

d. = SLIME *sb.* 4, TAILING *vbl. sb.*¹ 2 b.

1871 *Cape Monthly Mag.* June 358 In the paucity of materials in the *débris* of pans worked for diamonds, I would have less difficulty in finding traces of these rocks. **1882** H. G. HANKS *Sec. Rep. State Min. Calif.* 283 *Debris*,.. the silt, sand and gravel that flow from the hydraulic mines; called in miner's parlance, tailings, slums, and sometimes by the outlandish name of 'slickens'. **1902** D. WARD *Digest Criminal Cases Superior Courts Colony C.G.H.* 5/2 The accused, an employé, *not of De Beers*, but of a *débris* washer. **1967** *Gloss. Mining Terms* (*B.S.I.*) VIII. 12 *Dirt*, (*debris*),.. any material, such as rock or clay, etc., associated with the mineral and extracted during mining operations.

2. *attrib.*, as **debris-cone**, a cone formed by the accumulation of volcanic ejecta, debris, etc.

1890 J. D. DANA *Char. Volcanoes* 113 The cone was found to be literally a debris-cone, not a lava-cone or cinder-cone in any part. *Ibid.* 171 Between 1880 and 1882 another debris cone began in the basin of Halema'uma'u. **1895** —— *Man. Geol.* (ed. 4) III. v. 285 The basin contained a debris-cone made of the fallen blocks, and not at all of ejected material.

de Broglie (də 'brəʊljiː). The name of L. V. *de Broglie* (born 1892), French physicist, used *attrib.*, esp. in *de Broglie wave*, the wave which in wave mechanics is taken as accounting for or representing the wave-like properties of a material particle, esp. an elementary particle.

1922 *Nature* 17 June 781/1 An improved De Broglie photographic spectrometer was used. **1927** *Proc. R. Soc.* A. CXV. 208 (*heading*) The de Broglie Phase Wave in Generalised Space-Time. **1928** G. BIRTWISTLE *New Quantum Mechanics* xxiii. 189 The de Broglie wave length associated with the particle. **1952** R. E. MARSHAK *Meson Physics* iii. 97 The de Broglie wave length of the meson is much larger and comparable with the nuclear radius. **1966** D. G. BRANDON *Mod. Techniques Metallogr.* 38 The energy, E, of a single photon of light of wavelength λ is given by the de Broglie relation, $E = hc/\lambda = h\upsilon$, where υ is the frequency, c the velocity of light and h Planck's constant.

debruise (dɪ'bruːz), *v.* Forms: 3–8 **debruse,** 4 debrise, 7– debruise. [a. ONF. *debruisier*, *debrusier* = OF. *debrisier*, to break down or in pieces, crush, f. *de-* (DE- I. 1) + *brisier* to BREAK.]

†**1.** *trans.* To break down, break in pieces, crush, smash. *Obs.*

1297 R. GLOUC. (1724) 298 Hii.. stenede hym wyþ stones As me stenede Seynt Steuene, and debrusede ys bones. *a* **1300** *Fragm. Pop. Sc.* (Wright) 178 Tho oure Louerd.. debrusede helle ȝates. **1382** WYCLIF *Ezek.* xxxiv. 27 Whan I shal debrise the chaynes of her ȝoc. **1618** M. DALTON

Countrey Justice 195 Though it were lawfull to make the trenches, and to debruse the Nusans [a Weare on the Trent].

†**b.** *intr.* To be dashed to pieces. *Obs.*

1297 R. GLOUC. (1724) 288 þe flor to brac vnder hem.. And hii velle and debrusede somme anon to deþe. *Ibid.* 537 He hupte & debrusede, & deide in an stounde.

2. *Her.* (*trans.*) To cross (a charge, *esp.* an animal) with an ordinary so as partially to hide it, and as it were press it down; usually in *pa. pple.* **debruised**; also said of a serpent so bent or 'folded' that its head or tail is partly covered by its body. ***counter-debruised***: see quot. 1830.

1572 BOSSEWELL *Armorie* II. 114 His fielde is de Argent, a Lyon salient Gules, debrused with a Barre de Azure. **1661** MORGAN *Sph. Gentry* II. i. 10 Composed of the two bodies of trees laid crosse each other: but then one must Debruse and bear down the other. **1830** ROBSON *Brit. Herald* III. Gloss., *Counter-debruised*, when either the head or tail of a serpent in the bowing or embowing, is turned under, in a contrary direction the one to the other. **1848** MACAULAY *Hist. Engl.* I. 252 He..exhibited on his escutcheon the lions of England and the lilies of France without the baton sinister under which, according to the law of heraldry, they were debruised in token of his illegitimate birth.

de-brutalize: see DE- II. 1.

debt (dɛt), *sb.* Forms: 3-4 dete, 3-6 dette, 4-6 dett, det, deytt(e, 5-7 debte, 7- debt. [ME. *det*, *dette*, a. OF. *dete*, *dette*:—pop. L. **debita* for L. *dēbitum* (pa. pple. of *dēbēre* to owe), lit. (that which is) owed or due, money owed, debt. Often made masc. in OF. after *debitum*, and from 13th to 16th c. sometimes artificially spelt *debte*, after which *debt* has become the English spelling since the 16th c.]

1. That which is owed or due; anything (as money, goods, or service) which one person is under obligation to pay or render to another: **a.** a sum of money or a material thing.

a **1300** *Cursor M.* 7642 Dauid..wightli wan o þam his dete [*v.rr.* dette, dett]. *c* **1380** WYCLIF *Sel. Wks.* III. 293 ȝif a trewe man teche þis pore man to paie his dettis. **14..** *Merchant & Son* in Halliw. *Nugæ Poet.* 28 Then Wyllyam payde hys fadur dettys. **1548-9** (Mar.) *Bk. Com. Prayer* Offices 20 To declare his debtes, what he oweth. **1559** *Mirr. Mag., Dk. Glocester* xxiii, To paye large vsury besides the due det. **1596** SHAKS. *Tam. Shr.* IV. iv. 24 Hauing com to Padua To gather in some debts. **1707** HEARNE *Collect.* 23 Aug., To pay his small debts. **1767** BLACKSTONE *Comm.* II. 464 A debt of record is a sum of money, which appears to be due by the evidence of a court of record. **1845** STEPHEN *Laws Eng.* II. 144 Whenever a man is subject to a legal liability to pay a sum of money to another, he is said to owe him a debt to that amount.

b. a thing immaterial.

c **13..** *Cursor M.* 27808 (Cotton Galba) Rightwis es he, to gif ilk man his det. *c* **1386** CHAUCER *Wife's Prol.* 130 Why sholde men elles in hir bookes sette That a man shal yelde to his wyf hire dette. *c* **1400** *Destr. Troy* 534 This curtysy he claymes as for clere det. **1754** RICHARDSON *Grandison* II. xxxv. 343 Look upon what is done for you..as your debt to ..Providence. **1832** TENNYSON *Miller's Dau.* 217 Love the gift is love the debt.

†**c.** That which one is bound or ought to do; (one's) duty. *Sc. Obs.*

c **1450** HOLLAND *Howlat* 135 The trewe Turtour has.. Done dewlie his det. *c* **1470** HENRY *Wallace* VIII. 546 It is my dett to do all that I can To fend our kynrik out off dangeryng. **1513** DOUGLAS *Æneis* IX. iii. 184 So douchtely we schaype to do our det. **1573** *Sat. Poems Reform.* xxxix. 319, I haue lang forȝet, Quhairfor indeid I haue not done my det.

2. a. A liability or obligation to pay or render something; the condition of being under such obligation.

c **1290** *S. Eng. Leg.* I. 250/345 He with-sok þe giwes [= Jew's] dette and was i-don to ane oþe. *c* **1325** *Metr. Hom.* 18 And he..forgaf thaim thair dette bathe. **1388** WYCLIF *Rom.* iv. 4 And to hym that worchith mede is not arettid bi grace, but bi dette. **1513** MORE in Grafton *Chron.* II. 771 Neither king nor Pope can geve any place suche a privilege that it shall discharge a man of his debtes beyng able to pay. *c* **1532** DEWES *Introd. Fr.* in *Palsgr.* 1064, I have herd say that promysse is dette. **1611** BIBLE *Transl. Pref.* 5 He hath for euer bound the Church vnto him, in a debt of speciall remembrance and thankefulnesse. *a* **1699** LADY HALKETT *Autobiog.* (1875) 65, I was free of that Dept. **1844** H. H. WILSON *Brit. India* III. 513 Debts contracted..as far back as 1796. **1883** S. C. HALL *Retrospect* II. 502 He considered he thus contracted a debt to the country.

b. *in debt*: under obligation to pay something; owing something, *esp.* money (see also c); ***in any one's debt***: under obligation to pay or render something to him; indebted to him. So ***out of debt, out of any one's debt; to fall*** or ***run into*** (or ***in***) ***debt; out of debt out of danger***: see DANGER, and cf. quot. 1551.

c **1314** *Guy Warw.* (A.) 462 'Þat dint', he seyd, 'was iuel sett. Wele schal y com out of þi dette.' *c* **1386** CHAUCER *Prol.* 280 Ther wiste no man that he [the Marchaunt] was in dette. **1393** LANGL. *P. Pl.* C. XXIII. 10 Ne neuere shal falle in dette. **1478** *Paston Lett.* No. 824 III. 237 For he seythe ye be xx^ti^ in hys dette. **1513** MORE in Grafton *Chron.* II. 770 Now unthriftes riott and runne in debt. **1551** ROBINSON tr. *More's Utop.* II. (Arb.) 104 Men, in whose debte and daunger they be not. **1568** GRAFTON *Chron.* II. 434 Out of the debt of other men, and well able to pay. **1615** SIR E. HOBY *Curry-combe* 215, I see you meane not to die in Iabals debt for an Epigram. *a* **1624** BP. M. SMITH *Serm.* (1632) 5 Being ouer head and eares in debt. **1745** *De Foe's Eng. Tradesman* vi. (1841) I. 39 They are under no necessity of running deep into debt. **1763** *Gentl. Mag.* July 331 The black traders are often in debt to the chiefs. **1812** MAR. EDGEWORTH *Absentee* xiv, Lord Clonbrony, for the first time since he left Ireland, found himself out of debt, and out of danger. **1845** DISRAELI *Sybil* (1863) 155 To run in debt to the shopkeepers.

†**c.** Obligation to do something; duty. ***in debt***: under obligation, in duty bound. ***of*** or ***with debt***: as a matter of debt, as is due or right; as in duty bound. *Obs.* (Cf. 1 c.)

c **1300** *Cursor M.* 23888 (Edin.) A besand he me taht to sette þat ik him ah to yeld wit dette. *c* **1330** R. BRUNNE *Chron.* (1810) 261 We ere in dette, at nede to help þe kyng. **1393** GOWER *Conf.* III. 52 And as it were of pure dette They yive her goodes to the king. *c* **1425** WYNTOUN *Chron.* III. Prol. 23 Oure Eldrys we sulde folowe of det. *a* **1400** *Relig. Pieces fr. Thornton MS.* (1867) 2 Prelates and persons..þat ere haldene by dett for to lere þame. **1488** CAXTON *Chast. Goddes Chyld.* 10, I..cannot thanke the as I ought of dette. **1535** STEWART *Cron. Scot.* (1858) I. 35 This fatall stone.. Quhair it wes brocht in ony land or erd..Of verrie det the Scottis thair suld ring.

3. *fig.* Used in Biblical language as the type of an offence requiring expiation, a sin.

a **1225** *Ancr. R.* 126 We siggeð forȝif us ure dettes, al so ase we vorȝiueð to ure detturs. *a* **1400** *Prymer* (1891) 20 Forȝiue us oure dettes: as we forȝeue to oure detoures. **1508** FISHER *Wks.* (1876) 242 Whiche be our dettes? Truly our synnes. **1557** N. T. (Genev.) *Matt.* vi. 12 And forgeue vs our debtes [WYCLIF dettis, CRANM., *Rhemish* dettes, **1611** debts] euen as we forgiue our debters. **1858** TRENCH *Parables* xvi, God is the creditor, men the debtors, and sins the debt.

4. *Phrases.* **a.** ***debt of honour***: a debt that cannot be legally enforced, but depends for its validity on the honour of the debtor; usually applied to debts incurred by gambling.

1646 EVANCE *Noble Ord.* 37 He is become a voluntary debitor..in a debt of honour. **1732** BERKELEY *Alciphr.* I. 98 He..is obliged to pay debts of Honour, that is, all such as are contracted by Play. **1839** CATH. SINCLAIR *Holiday House* xiii. 265 Pay your debt of honour, Master Harry!

b. ***debt of*** (or ***to***) ***nature***: the necessity of dying, death; ***to pay the debt of*** (or ***one's debt to***) ***nature***: to die. [Lat. *debitum naturæ*.]

[*c* **1315** SHOREHAM 2 And his deythes dette ȝelde. **1375** BARBOUR *Bruce* XIX. 209 Hym worthit neyd to pay the det That no man for till pay may let.] **1494** FABYAN *Chron.* II. xli. 28 Fynally he payde the dette of nature. **1590** MARLOWE *Edw. II*, Wks. (ed. Rtldg.) 212/1 Pay nature's debt with cheerful countenance. **1635** QUARLES *Embl.* II. xiii, The slender debt to nature's quickly paid. **1727** A. HAMILTON *New Acc. E. Ind.* II. lii. 265 He had paid his great Debt to Nature, without taking Notice of the small one due to me. **1812** *Examiner* 23 Nov. 747/1 One of them has..paid the debt of nature.

c. ***action of debt***: an action at law for recovering a debt.

1552 in *Vicary's Anat.* (1888) App. iii. 152 The gouernours..to haue an accion of dett[e] for the same. **1603** OWEN *Pembrokeshire* (1891) 192 A plaintiffe in an action of debte. **1800** ADDISON *Amer. Law. Rep.* 111 The ground of an action of debt is the consideration or equivalent given by the debtee to the debtor.

†**d.** ***bill of debt***: a promissory note, I.O.U., or other acknowledgement of indebtedness, in some countries used, like a bill of exchange, as a negotiable document. *Obs.*

1530 PALSGR. 198/1 Byll of dette, *cedule.* **1622** MALYNES *Anc. Law-Merch.* 96 The most vsuall buying and selling of commodities beyond the Seas, in the course of Trafficke, is for Bills of Debt, or Obligations, called Billes Obligatorie, which one Merchant giueth vnto another, for commodities bought or sold, which is altogether vsed by the Merchants Adventurors at Amsterdam, Middleborough, Hamborough, and other places. **1690** CHILD *Disc. Trade* (ed. 4) 16 If..a law for transferring bills of debt should pass, we should not miss the Dutch money. *Ibid.* 139 In other Kingdoms and Countries abroad..transference of Bills of Debt is in use.

e. ***National Debt***: a debt owing by a sovereign state to private individuals who have advanced money to it for the public needs; *esp.* that main part of the ***public debt***, which has been converted into a fund or stock of which the government no longer seeks to pay off the principal, but to provide the annual interest; hence called ***funded debt***, as opposed to the ***floating debt***, which includes the ever-varying amounts due by the government and repayable on demand or by a certain time.

1653 CHIDLEY (*title*), Remonstrance concerning the Public Faith, Soldier's Arrears, and other Public Debts. **1721** A. HUTCHESON (*title*), Collection of Treatises, relating to the National Debts and Funds. **1752** HUME *Ess. Public Credit* (1875) I. 364 National debts cause a mighty confluence of people and riches to the capital. **1812** G. CHALMERS *Dom. Econ. Gt. Brit.* (New ed.) 210 The most efficient measure..was to fund..the floating debts, of the victualling, and of the ordnance departments. **1840** *Penny Cycl.* XVI. 100 The contracting of the National Debt cannot be said to have been begun before the Revolution of 1688. **1860** KNIGHT *Pop. Hist. Eng.* VI. iii. 40 There was a floating debt of about ten millions. **1878** EDITH THOMPSON *Hist. Eng.* xxxix. 275 The South Sea Company..for the purpose of reducing the National Debt, engaged..to buy up certain annuities. **1889** *Whitaker's Alman.* 493 The French National Debt is the largest in the world..Public debt, funded £957,000,000; Public debt, floating, annuities, etc., capitalized £728,372,372.

f. ***small debt***: a debt of limited amount, for which summary jurisdiction is provided, in England in the *County Court*, in Scotland in the *Small Debt Court* held by the sheriff. Also *attrib.*

(In Scotland the limit of these debts was in 1788 £5, in 1837 £8 6*s.* 8*d.*, and in 1853 £12.)

1603-4 *Act 1 Jas. I*, c. 14 (*title*), An Acte for Recouerie of Small Debtes. **1795** *Act 35 Geo. III*, c. 23 (*title*) An Act for the more easy and expeditious Recovery of Small Debts. **1861** W. BELL *Dict. Law Scot.* 762 The Statute 39 and 40 Geo. III, c. 46, commonly called the *Small-Debt Act. Ibid.* 764 The sheriff's exclusive jurisdiction in small debts was introduced by 6 Geo. IV, c. 24. *Ibid.* 766 The sheriffs must, in addition to their ordinary small-debt courts, hold circuit courts for the purposes of this act. *Ibid.* 767 By the act 16 and 17 Vict. c. 80, 1853, the small-debt jurisdiction of sheriffs is extended to causes not exceeding £12.

5. *attrib.* and *Comb.* ***debt-collecting, -collector, -dealer, -exchange, -fraud, -reduction***; **debt-raiser**, one who undertakes to raise money to pay off a debt; **debt-slave**, one who is in slavery for the redemption of debt; so ***debt-slavery***.

1897 *Westm. Gaz.* 13 Apr. 2/1 But not by any means must it be supposed that the work of the County Courts is confined to debt-collecting. *Ibid.*, The small debt-collecting work which now largely occupies them. *a* **1852** in G. B. Hill *Talks about Autographs* (1896) 3 F.-M. the Duke of Wellington begs to inform Mr. Snip that he is neither the Marquis of Douro's steward nor Mr. Snip's debt collector. **1826** COBBETT *Rur. Rides* (1885) II. 255 Large part of the rents must go to the Debt-Dealers, or Loan-makers. **1682** SCARLETT *Exchanges* 236 In mixed or Debt Exchanges the Drawer receives no Monyes, but is Debtor, and gives Bills to his Creditor..for payment of his Debt. **1883** *19th Cent.* May 884 Punishment of debt-frauds as crimes. **1881** *Instr. Census Clerks* (1885) 121. **1899** *Westm. Gaz.* 19 May 3/1 Lord Salisbury may be an admirable political 'debt raiser'. **1905** *Daily Chron.* 1 Feb. 6/1 We have handed over £93,376 more towards debt reduction. **1895** MRS. GRINDROD *Siam* 40 People still sell themselves and their families to a wealthy chief, who will pay off their debts contracted through thriftlessness or gambling. These debt slaves give service for a specified term. **1962** *Daily Tel.* 23 Apr. 6 Mortgaging him as a debt-slave to a Pakistani employer already in Britain. **1895** F. A. SWETTENHAM *Malay Sketches* 229 The revolting practice of debt-slavery.

†**debt**, *ppl. a. Obs.* Forms: 4-5 dett(e, 6- debt. [ad. L. *dēbit-us* owed (cf. DEBITE *a.*), conformed to *debt* sb.] Owed, due, owing.

a **1340** HAMPOLE *Psalter* lxxviii. 5 ȝeldand til þe[e] dett [*v.r.* duwe] honur. *c* **1440** HYLTON *Scala Perf.* (W. de W. 1494) I. xl, That it is nedeful to the & dette for to traueyle soo. *a* **1555** RIDLEY *Wks.* (1843) 305 Promises so openly made, and so duly debt. **1576** J. KNEWSTUB *Confut.* (1579) Q vj a, That which is det and due on their behalfe. **1602** SHAKS. *Ham.* III. ii. 203 To pay our selues, what to ourselues is debt.

†**'debtable**, *a. Obs. rare*⁻¹. [f. DEBT + -ABLE.] Under pecuniary obligation, chargeable.

1516 *Plumpton Corr.* 217 That your mastership shold be debtable to the King for the lordship of Plompton.

†**debt-bind**, *v. Obs. nonce-wd. trans.* To bind by obligation, render indebted.

a **1608** SACKVILLE *Dk. Buckingham* xliii. (D.), Banish'd by them whom he did thus debt-bind.

'debt-book. An account-book in which debts are recorded. Often *fig.*

a **1600** HOOKER *Serm.* Wks. 1845 II. 609 We dare not call God to a reckoning, as if we had him in our debt-books. **1617** HIERON *Wks.* II. 90 Forgiuenesse of sins is (as it were) the wiping out of a score, or the crossing of a debt-booke. **1745** *De Foe's Eng. Tradesman* xxxii. (1841) II. 34 The proper method for a debt-book for a small tradesman.

†**'debt-bound**, *ppl. a. Obs.* Also -bounden.

1. Under obligation, bound by duty, obliged.

1513 DOUGLAS *Æneis* XI. iv. 62 This mysfortoun is myne of ald thirlage, As tharto detbund in my wrachit age. **1553** BALE *Gardiner's Devera Obed.* Pref. A iv, All true subiectes were dettebounden to defende..and upholde, the supreme autoritie of the crowne. **1597** MORLEY *Introd. Mus.* 28, I will ..acknowledge myself debt bound to him. **1603** in Ellis *Orig. Lett.* I. III. 73 *note*, I shall acknowledge myself exceedingly debt-bound to your Excellency.

2. Of things: Obligatory, due, bounden.

1588 A. KING tr. *Canisius' Catech.* 32 And daylie giwe det-bound thankes to the for sua greate benefites.

†**'debted**, *ppl. a. Obs.* [? after OF. *deté* (DETTY): see -ED; or aphetic form of *an-, en-, indebted* (13th c.).]

1. Of things: Owed, due.

c **1375** *Sc. Leg. Saints, Agnes* 171, & gyf he ȝald dettyt honoure Til god þat al thinge has in cure. **1388** WYCLIF *Deut.* xv. 2 To whom ony thing is dettid, *ethir owid. c* **1440** HYLTON *Scala Perf.* (W. de W. 1494) II. vii, The payne detted for the synne. **1552** ABP. HAMILTON *Catech.* (1884) 9 Obediens dettit til our natural fatheris. **1599-16..** MASSINGER, etc. *Old Law* I. i, In my debted duty.

2. Of persons: Under obligation; indebted.

c **1425** WYNTOUN *Cron.* IX. xxvii. 267 In sic affynite Ilkane dettit wes til uthire. **1536** BELLENDEN *Cron. Scot.* (1821) I. 16 We ar dettit to you as faderis to thair childrin. **1590** SHAKS. *Com. Err.* IV. i. 31 Three odde Duckets more Then I stand debted to this Gentleman.

debtee (ˌdɛ'tiː). [f. DEBT-OR + -EE.] One to whom a debt is due: a creditor.

1531 *Dial. on Laws Eng.* I. xxix. (1638) 51 To appoint the libertie and the judgement of Conscience..to the debtee then to the debtor. *a* **1626** BACON *Max. & Uses Com. Law* ix. (1636) 39 Where the debtor makes the debtee his executor. **1800** ADDISON *Amer. Law Rep.* 111 The consideration or equivalent given by the debtee to the debtor.

†**'debtful**, *a. Obs.* Chiefly *Sc.* Also 5 dettefull, 5-7 detful(l. [f. DEBT *sb.* + -FUL.]

1. Owed, bounden, due; dutiful.

c **1425** WYNTOUN *Cron.* VII. viii. 13 The Kyng of Frawns Hys Lord be detful Alegeawns. *a* **1440** *Found. St. Bartholomew's* (E.E.T.S.) 54 Sum penyes, the whiche of a vowe were dettefull to the Chirche of seynt Barthylmewe. **1556** LAUDER *Tractate* 176 And do ȝow homage and reuerence, With all detfull Obedience. **1621** *Bk. Discipl. Ch. Scot.* Pref., The obligation, whereby they are bound for debtfull obedience.

2. Indebted.

1649 LD. FOORD in M. P. Brown *Suppl. Dec.* I. 434 That..Patrick Keir..was debtful to him in greater sums.

Hence † **'debtfully** *adv. Sc.*, duly, dutifully.

c **1425** WYNTOUN *Cron.* VII. viii. 704 Thare charge thai dyd nocht detfully. **1478** *Sc. Acts Jas. III* (1814) 123 (Jam.) That oure souuerain lord..sal..execut detfully the panys of proscripcioun & tresoun aganis the saidis personis.

debtless ('dɛtlɪs), *a.* [See -LESS.] Free from, or clear of, debt.

c **1386** CHAUCER *Prol.* 582 To make him lyve by his propre good, In honour detteles, but if he were wood. **1570** E. ROBSON in *Durham Depositions* (Surtees) 228 He is worth £30, debtless, of his own goods. **1590** SWINBURNE *Testaments* 103 Legacies to be paid out of the cleere debtlesse goods. **1766** G. CANNING *Anti-Lucretius* III. 184 Debtless to power, but Fortune's and it's own. **1848** *Tait's Mag.* 276 America, free and debtless, was there before their eyes.

debtor ('dɛtə(r)). Forms: α. 3 **dettor**, 3–5 **det(t)ur**, 4–6 **det(t)our**, **-or**, 5 **dettere**, 6–7 **detter**; β. 6–7 **debtor**, 7 **-our**, 6– **-or**. See also DEBITOR. [ME. *det(t)ur*, *-our*, a. OF. *det(t)or*, *-ur*, *-our* (later *detteur*, *debteur*):—L. *dēbitōr-em*, acc. of *dēbitor* (whence OF. *det(t)re*). In later OF. often artificially spelt with *b*, after L.; in Eng. the *b* was inserted between 1560 and 1668, being first prevalent in legal documents, where it was probably assisted by the parallel form DEBITOR. (The Bible of 1611 has *detter*, *debter*, each thrice: *debtor* twice, *debtour* once.)]

1. One who owes or is indebted to another: **a.** One who owes money to one or more persons: correlative to *creditor*.

c **1290** *S. Eng. Leg.* I. 465/117 An vsurer..þat hadde dettores tweyne. **1387** TREVISA *Higden* III. 189 (Mätz), þe dettoures myȝte nouȝt pay here money at here day. **1464** *Mann. & Househ. Exp.* 102 Thomas Hoo is become detor to my sayd mastyre. **1535** COVERDALE *2 Kings* iv. 1 Now commeth the man that he was detter vnto. **1568** GRAFTON *Chron.* II. 360 The Admyrall became debter to them all.. Suche summes of money as he was become debtor for. **1611** BIBLE *Luke* xvi. 5 So he called euery one of his lords detters vnto him [so all 16th c. *vv.*; WYCLIF dettours]. **1644** MILTON *Areop.* (Arb.) 59 Dettors and delinquents may walk abroad without a keeper. **1745** *De Foe's Eng. Tradesman* v. (1841) I. 34 Acts of grace for the relief of insolvent debtors. **1865** DICKENS *Mut. Fr.* III. i, Pubsey & Co., are so strict with their debtors. **1875** MAINE *Hist. Inst.* ix. 257 Execution against the person of a judgment debtor.

b. One who owes an obligation or duty.

a **1225** *Ancr. R.* 126 Louerd, we siggeð forȝif us ure dettes, al so ase we uorȝiueð to ure detturs. **1382** WYCLIF *Matt.* vi. 12 Forȝeue to vs oure dettes as we forȝeue to oure dettours [**1388** -ouris, COVERD., CRANMER, *Rhem.*, detters, *Geneva*, **1611**, debters]. —— *Rom.* i. 14 To Grekis and barbaryns.. to wyse men and vnwyse men, I am dettour. *a* **1535** MORE *De quat. Nouiss.* Wks. 91 To whom we be al dettours of death. **1593** SHAKS. *Lucr.* 1155 When life is sham'd, and death Reproches detter. *c* **1645** HOWELL *Lett.* (1726) 10 Of joy ungrudg'd may each Day be a Debter. **1653** WALTON *Angler* i. 38, I must be your Debtor..for the rest of my promised discourse. *a* **1677** BARROW *Wks.* (1716) II. 140 He being..master of all things and debtor to none. **1847** TENNYSON *Princ.* II. 334 Debtors for our lives to you.

c. ***poor debtor*** (U.S.): One who, being imprisoned in a civil action for debt, is, under the laws of several States, entitled to be discharged after a short period, on proof of poverty, etc.

1831 W. L. GARRISON in *Liberator* I. 28 The Poor Debtor.

2. *Book-keeping.* *Debtor* (or *Dr.*) being written at the top of the left-hand or debit side of an account is hence applied to this side of an account, or to what is entered there.

[**1543–1660**: see DEBITOR.] **1714** (*title*), The Gentleman Accomptant or an Essay to Unfold the Mystery of Accompts, by Way of Debtor and Creditor. **1745** [see CREDITOR 2]. **1836** *Penny Cycl.* V. 164/1 Exacting.. equilibrium between debtor and creditor in each entry.

attrib. [**1588**: see DEBITOR.] **1712** ADDISON *Spect.* No. 549 ¶1 When I look upon the Debtor-side, I find such innumerable Articles, that I want Arithmetick to cast them up. **1836** *Penny Cycl.* V. 164/1 All the debtor accounts on one side, compared with..the creditor accounts on the other. **1866** C. W. HOSKYNS *Occas. Ess.* 133 Every human right, however absolute and accredited, has its corresponding debtor-page of duty and obligation.

3. *attrib.* and *Comb.*, as ***debtor law***, ***country***; ***debtor side***, etc. (see 2); ***debtor-like*** adj.

1669 DRYDEN *Tyran. Love* v. i, Debtor-like, I dare not meet your eyes. **1810** MINCHIN (*title*), A Treatise on the Defects of the Debtor and Creditor Laws. **1881** H. H. GIBBS *Double Stand.* 68 The debtor country..will pay its debts in Silver.

Hence **'debtorship.**

1798 H. T. COLEBROOKE tr. *Digest Hindu Law* (1801) I. 7 The debtorship of others than women, or the like. **1859** G. MEREDITH *R. Feverel* I. ix. 173 Without incurring further debtorship.

† **de'buccinate**, *v. Obs.*⁻⁰ [f. L. *dēbuccināre* to trumpet forth (Tertull.), prop. *debūcināre*, f. *de-* (DE- I. 3) + *būcināre* to trumpet.] 'To report abroad' (Cockeram 1623).

debug (diː'bʌg), *v.* [f. DE- II. 2 + BUG *sb.*²]

1. *trans.* = DELOUSE *v.*

1960 J. STROUD *Shorn Lamb* vi. 70 We'll..take them round to the Clinic, and..get them debugged there.

2. *slang.* To remove faults from (a machine, system, etc.).

1945 *Jrnl. R. Aeronaut. Soc.* XLIX. 183/2 It ranged from the pre-design development of essential components, through the stage of type test and flight test and 'debugging' right through to later development of the engine. **1959** *New Scientist* 26 Mar. 674/1 The 'debugging' time spent in perfecting a non-automatic programme. **1964** *Discovery* Oct. 51/3 This failure report plays a vital role in the process by which the scientist corrects or de-bugs his programme. **1964** T. W. MCRAE *Impact of Computers on Accounting* iv. 99 Once we have ' debugged' our information system. **1970** A. CAMERON et al. *Computers & O.E. Concordances* 49 Program translation, debugging, and trial runs of the concordance were performed at the University of Michigan Computer Center. *Ibid.*, By Christmas the program was debugged.

3. To remove a concealed microphone or microphones from (a room, etc.); to free of such listening devices by electronically rendering them inoperative. Cf. BUG *sb.*² 3f. orig. *U.S.*

1964 *Business Week* 31 Oct. 154 (*heading*) When walls have ears, call a debugging man. *Ibid.* 158/2 He quotes high fees for his work, saying that debugging equipment is expensive. **1966** in Random House Dict. **1969** *New Scientist* 16 Jan. 128/3 'Debugging' the boardroom and the boss's telephone may become as common in industry as in the unreal world of the super-spy. **1976** M. MACHLIN *Pipeline* xxxi. 353 The room..had steel walls and had been rigorously de-bugged. **1978** *Sunday Mail Mag.* (Brisbane) 9 Apr. 3/6 Jamil, America's leading 'debugging' expert, discovered the secret of an exported 'bug' which should not have worked. **1987** *Daily Tel.* 3 Apr. 1/8 American officials are scrambling to 'de-bug' their embassy in Moscow before the arrival of Mr Shultz, Secretary of State, on Monday week.

Also **de'bugging** *vbl. sb.* (see senses 2, 3 above).

† **de'bulliate**, *v. Obs.*⁻⁰ [Improperly f. *de-* (DE- I. 1) + L. *bullīre* to boil. Cf. F. *débouillir*.] 'To bubble or seeth over' (BLOUNT 1656).

† **debu'llition.** *Obs.* [n. of action f. L. **dēbullīre*: see prec.] A bubbling or boiling over.

1727 in BAILEY vol. II. **1730–6**—(folio). Whence in JOHNSON, ASH and mod. Dicts.

debunk (dɪ'bʌŋk), *v.* orig. *U.S.* [f. DE- II. 2 + BUNK *sb.*⁴] *trans.* To remove the 'nonsense' or false sentiment from; to expose (false claims or pretensions); hence, to remove (a person) from his 'pedestal' or 'pinnacle'. Also *absol.* Hence **de'bunker**, one who debunks; **de'bunking** *vbl. sb.* and *ppl. a.*

1923 W. E. WOODWARD *Bunk* i. 2 De-bunking means simply taking the bunk out of things. *Ibid.*, I'm a professional de-bunker. *Ibid.* 4 To keep the United States thoroughly de-bunked would require the continual services of..half a million persons. *Ibid.*, Just how do you go about your de-bunking operations? *Ibid.* 6 Recently we de-bunked the head of a large financial institution. **1927** *Daily Express* 21 Nov. 2/3 The Thucydidean school of what are known as 'debunking' historians. **1927** *Brit. Weekly* 29 Dec. 327/2 The somewhat ruthless process which in America is called 'debunking'—that is, pricking pretentious bubbles [etc.]. **1930** *Times Lit. Suppl.* 6 Mar. 174 The present fashion for 'debunking' great men. *Ibid.* 13 Mar. 217 He is not indeed a 'debunker', but he is as far from being a blind hero-worshipper. *Ibid.* 8 May 378 The aim of 'debunking' a reputation that has been swollen by the uncritical eulogies of contemporaries. **1934** *Municipal Engineering* 12 July 31/1 The London C.C. has decided to 'debunk' Waterloo Bridge, or, in other words, to take away the bunkum that has been attached to it. **1940** *Illustr. Lond. News* CXCVI. 758/2 In fact, he is a reverent man, who enjoys 'debunking' the 'debunkers', if that word may be taken now as acceptable and established English. **1948** *Sat. Rev.* 26 June 13/1 In dealing with military reputations, the author neither glorifies nor debunks. **1958** *Spectator* 13 June 777/1 It is his duty..to debunk the claims of the Fabians. **1960** *Guardian* 10 Dec. 5/3 No cynic, but a debunker.

† **de'burse**, *v. Obs. Sc.* Also 6 **deburs**, **-burce**, 7 **debourse.** [a. F. *débourse-r*, in OF. *desbourser*, f. *des-*:—L. *dis-* (see DE- I. 6) + *bourse*:—late pop. L. *bursa* purse.] To pay out, DISBURSE.

1529 W. FRANKELEYN in Fiddes *Wolsey* II. (1726) 167 Your grace shuld not deburse owt of your coffers very myche monye. **1561** in W. H. Turner *Select. Rec. Oxford* 286 Suche..somes as they shall deburse. *c* **1610** SIR J. MELVIL *Mem.* 318. **1705** *Kirk-Session Rec.* in *Sc. Leader* 22 June 1888 Debursed upon thatching the schoolhouse £11 3s. 4d.

Hence **de'bursing** *vbl. sb.* = next.

1598 *Sc. Acts Jas. VI* (1814) 179 (Jam.) Necessar debursingis in thair hienes..maist honorabill effairis.

† **de'bursement.** *Obs. Sc.* [a. F. *déboursement*, f. *débourser*: see prec.] = DISBURSEMENT.

1637–50 Row *Hist. Kirk* (1842) 153 Provyding alwayes his debursements exceed not 400 merks. **1689** R. SINCLAIR in *Leisure Hour* (1883) 205/1 Accompt of debursements for my son Jhon.

debus (diː'bʌs), *v.* orig. *Army slang.* Also **debuss.** [f. DE- II. 1 + BUS *sb.*²] *intr.* To alight from motor transport. Hence **de'bus(s)ing** *vbl. sb.*

1915 G. ADAM *Behind Scenes at the Front* iv. 126 The battalion has 'embussed', as the orders now phrase it, 'at X, and will debuss at Y'. **1915** *Times* 12 Mar. 10/1 The words 'embuss' and 'debuss' have been consecrated in Staff orders. Many is the battalion which has received orders to 'embuss' at dusk at X, and 'debuss' at Z. **1917** *Ibid.* 28 Sept. 9/5 This Division had already had a very hard time... From the moment of 'de-busing' its life was made very difficult for it. **1958** P. SCOTT *Mark of Warrior* I. 20 The cadets arrived in trucks... They debussed in a tarmac-laid square. **1962** *Times* 26 Oct. (Suppl.) p. v/7 All are close to a car park and debussing station.

debusscope ('dɛbəskəʊp). [f. the name of the inventor M. Debus + -SCOPE, after *kaleidoscope*.] An optical contrivance consisting of two mirrors placed at an angle of 72°, so as to give four reflections of an object or figure placed between them and form composite figures for purposes of decorative design, etc.

1862 TIMBS *Year-Bk. of Facts* 144 M. Debus has invented this new form of kaleidoscope. The debusscope may be made of any size. *c* **1865** J. WYLDE in *Circ. Sc.* I. 43/1 In the Debusscope, any object placed between the mirrors is multiplied, so as to present a fourfold appearance.

Debussyan (də'byːsɪən), *a.* and *sb.* [-IAN.]

A. *adj.* Of or pertaining to the French composer Claude *Debussy* (1862–1918), his music or his style of musical composition. **B.** *sb.* An admirer or follower of Debussy.

1923 P. ROSENFELD *Mus. Chron. 1917–23* 147 There is no Debussyan fluidity, dreamfulness, satin. **1938** *Scrutiny* VII. 170 Any other composer of the time using the same more or less Debussyan idiom. **1959** *Radio Times* 16 Jan. 25/3 An individual mixture of Hungarian folk-song, Debussyan orchestration, and modal inflexions. **1959** R. RUSSELL in M. T. Williams *Art of Jazz* (1960) xviii. 209 The light polychrome orchestral palette of the Debussyians [*sic*].

So **Debussy'esque** *a.*, resembling the style of Debussy.

1946 R. BLESH *Shining Trumpets* (1949) x. 229 A rambling piece in unresolved Debussyesque harmonies. **1963** *Economist* 8 June 1008/1 This is not a Debussyesque hallucination.

‖ **début** (deby, 'deɪbuː, -juː), *sb.* [F. vbl. sb., f. *débuter* to make the first stroke in billiards, etc., lead off: see Littré and Hatzfeld.] Entry into society; first appearance in public of an actor, actress, or other performer. Also *transf.*

1751 CHESTERF. *Lett.* ccxxxviii. (1792) III. 88, I find that your *début* at Paris has been a good one. **1806** BYRON *Occas. Prol.* 15 To-night you throng to witness the *début* Of embryo actors, to the Drama new. **1837** LD. BEACONSFIELD in *Corr. w. Sister* (1886) 78, I state at once that my *début* [in House of Comm.] was a failure. **1955** *Times* 6 May 14/3 Its considerable acuteness of observation make it a most promising *début* for its director. *Ibid.* 9 May 3/7 All [paintings] making their public London *début* in the Gardens. *Ibid.* 12 May 16/4 Lady Megan Lloyd George made her *début* on the Labour platform tonight. **1971** *Daily Tel.* 27 Apr. 20 The day's newcomer to the equity sections, Hilton's Footwear, made a rather disappointing debut.

So **début(e** *v.* [cf. F. *débuter*], to make one's début; to 'come out'.

1830 *Fraser's Mag.* II. 52 He debuted at Naples, about five years ago, and has since performed..in the principal theatres of Italy. **1885** F. ARTHUR *Coparceners* v. 69 The moment..is..a proud one for the debuting youth. **1889** *Pall Mall G.* 21 Sept. 6/1 When a popular actor's son 'débuts' with a flourish of trumpets.

débutant (debytɑ̃). [F. pr. pple. of *débuter*: see prec.] A male performer or speaker making his first appearance before the public. So **débutante** (-tɑ̃t) [F. fem. of the same], a female appearing for the first time before the public or in society; also, a young woman who has recently 'come out' (see COME *v.* 67 o); also *transf.* and *attrib.*; see also DEB.

1801 *Monthly Mirror* Aug. 134 The amiable *debûtante* was called for after the play, and crowns were thrown upon the stage. **1817** U. FOSCOLO *Let.* 20 July in H. C. B. Campbell *Journey to Florence* (1951) 14 The..Adonises, who from February until today, the end of the London season, have discussed the ten thousand *débutantes* of London Society. **1824** W. IRVING *T. Trav.* I. 282 The character was favourable to a debutant. **1826** DISRAELI *Viv. Grey* IV. i, Under different circumstances from those which usually attend most political debutants. **1837** *Blackw. Mag.* XLII. 343/1 Gentlemen are apt to dismiss all serious thoughts in addressing a very young débutante. **1900** E. GLYN *Visits of Eliz.* 20 It was by far the prettiest débutante frock she had ever seen. **1903** *Daily Chron.* 20 June 8/4 The gauging of the skirt proclaims it a débutante among dresses. **1904** *Ibid.* 14 June 4/4 Lord Northampton's postponed ball for his débutante daughter. **1927** [see DEB]. **1971** *Guardian* 3 Feb. 11/3 Her recollections as a debutante—the coming out balls and the charity balls and the hunt balls.

Debye (də'baɪ). The name of P. J. W. *Debye* (1884–1966), Dutch physicist, used *attrib.* to designate certain phenomena observed and principles enunciated by him, as ***Debye effect*** (see quots.); ***Debye-Hückel theory***, a theory concerned with the inter-ionic forces in electrolytes; ***Debye-Scherrer method***, a method for the identification of crystals by photographing the diffraction pattern formed by a beam of X-rays directed on to a powdered sample of the crystal under investigation; ***Debye temperature***, a temperature characteristic of an idealized crystal lattice in Debye's theory of specific heats; also, a temperature calculated for a crystalline solid on the assumption that Debye's theory is a correct description of it; ***Debye unit***, a unit of electrical dipole moment equal to 10^{-18} e.s.u. (approximately 3·336 × 10^{-30} coulomb metre).

1914 *Chem. Abstr.* VIII. 2845 A theoretical and mathematical discussion of the Debye effect, *i.e.*, the influence of rizing temp. on Röntgen ray interference phenomena. **1918** *Ibid.* XII. 2488 A mathematical paper dealing with the Bragg and Debye-Scherrer methods of X-ray spectrometry. **1930** *Chem. Soc. Ann. Rep.* XXVII. 327 The basis of the Debye-Hückel theory of the properties of electrolytic solutions is the idea of an ionic atmosphere. **1934** *Nature* 22 Sept. 459/1 The slopes of these lines yield the following moments in Debye units ($D = 1 \times 10^{-18}$ E.S.U.)... The average is 4·25 D. **1944** *Jrnl. Chem. Physics* XII. 289 A theory in which the Debye characteristic temperature θ was related to the curvature of the interatomic potential energy curve. **1947** *Thorpe's Dict. Appl. Chem.* (ed. 4) VIII. 228/2 Electric dipole moments are expressed in Debye units (represented D.); 1 D. is equivalent to 10^{-18} C.G.S. unit. **1955** H. B. G. CASIMIR in W. Pauli *Niels Bohr* 119 At temperatures well below the so-called Debye temperature θ only lattice waves with a wave-length of many atomic distances are excited. **1957** *Encycl. Brit.* XXI. 35/1 When ultrasonic radiation passes through an electrolyte, the ions of one sign are affected differently by rapid changes in density from those of the other sign (Debye effect).

debylite, -yte: see DEBILITE.

debylle, obs. form of DIBBLE.

debyte, -tie, -ty, -tour: see DEBITE, etc.

Dec. Abbrev. of DECEMBER; in *Music* of DECRESCENDO; in *Med.* of L. *decoctum* (= decoction).

deca-, dec-, Gr. δεκα- ten, an initial element in numerous technical words: see below. Also

1. deca'canthous *a.* [Gr. ἄκανθα thorn], having ten spines (*Syd. Soc. Lex.* 1882). **deca-'carbon** *a. Chem.* in ***decacarbon series***, the series of hydrocarbon compounds containing C_{10}, as *decane, decene, decine, decyl*, q.v. ‖**De'cacera** *sb. pl. Zool.* [Gr. κέρας, κερατ- horn], a name proposed by some naturalists for the ten-armed cephalopods, otherwise called *Decapoda*. **de'cacerate** (*Syd. Soc. Lex.* 1882), **de'cacerous** *a.*, ten-horned, pertaining to the *Decacera*. **deca'dactylous** *a. Zool.*, having ten rays or fingers (*Syd. Soc. Lex.*). **deca'dianome** *Math.* [Gr. διανομή distribution, DIANOME], a quartic surface (dianome) having ten conical points. **'decafid** *a.* [L. *-fidus* -cleft] = DECEMFID (*Syd. Soc. Lex.*). **'decalet** *nonce-wd.* [after *triplet*], a stanza of ten lines. **de'calobate** *a.* [Gr. λοβός lobe], ten-lobed. **de'camerous** *a.* [Gr. μέρος part], consisting of ten parts or divisions, decempartite (*Syd. Soc. Lex.*). **de'cameter** *nonce-wd.* [Gr. μέτρον measure], a verse consisting of ten metrical feet. **de'cangular** *a.* [L. *angulus*, corner], having ten angles = DECAGONAL. **de'cantherous** *a. Bot.* [ANTHER], having ten anthers. **deca'partite** *a.* = *decempartite*: see DECEM-. **deca'petalous** *a. Bot.* [PETAL], having ten petals (*Syd. Soc. Lex.*). **deca'phyllous** *a. Bot.* [Gr. φύλλον leaf], ten-leaved. **decapte'rygious** *a. Ichth.* [πτερύγιον fin], having ten fins; so **decapte'rygian** *a.* and *sb.* **deca'semic** (-'siːmɪk) *a.* [cf. the Gr. comp. τεσσαρεσκαιδεκάσημος, f. σῆμα mark, sign], consisting of ten units of metrical measurement as a 'decasemic colon'. **deca'sepalous** *a. Bot.* [SEPAL], having ten sepals. **deca'spermal, -'spermous** *a. Bot.* [Gr. σπέρμα seed], having ten seeds.

1874 SALMON *Analyt. Geom. Three Dim.* (ed. 3) 507 Decadianome. **1861** BENTLEY *Man. Bot.* iv. §4. 274 A flower with Ten carpels or Ten styles is Decagynous. **1882** VINES *Sachs's Bot.* 654 Whorls dimerous to octamerous..or pentamerous and decamerous. **1821** *Blackw. Mag.* X. 387 They might have appeared as decameters, had that structure of verse pleased the eyes of the compositor. **18..** LEE (cited by Webster 1828), *Decangular*. **1879** SIR G. SCOTT *Lect. Archit.* II. 197 The vaulting, having its sides divided.. making in all a decapartite vault. **1793** MARTYN *Lang. Bot.* s.v., *Decaphyllus calyx*, a decaphyllous or ten-leaved calyx; as in *Hibiscus*. **1847** CRAIG, *Decapterygians*, a name given by Schneider to an artificial division of fishes, including such as have ten fins. *Ibid.*, *Decaspermal, Decaspermous*, containing ten seeds, as the berry of *Psidium decaspermum*.

2. *esp.* in the nomenclature of the French metric system, the initial element in names of measures and weights, composed of ten times the standard unit of the series in question. (Cf. DECI-.) Hence, **'decagramme, -gram** (F. *décagramme*), the weight of 10 grammes (= 154·32349 troy grains, or ·353 oz. avoird.). **decalitre** ('dɛkəliːtə(r)), [F. *déca-*], a measure of capacity, containing 10 litres (= 610.28 cubic inches, or a little over $2\frac{1}{5}$ gallons). **decametre** ('dɛkəmiːtə(r)), [F. *déca-*], a lineal measure of 10 metres (= 32 ft. 9.7079 inches Eng.). **decastere** ('dɛkəstiːə(r)), [F. *décastère*], a solid measure = 10 steres or cubic metres. Also †**decare** (*obs.*), a measure of 10 ares = 1000 square metres.

1810 *Naval Chron.* XXIV. 301-2. [Has *decagram, decalittre, decameter, decar*.] **1828** J. M. SPEARMAN *Brit. Gunner* (ed. 2) 417 Decametre signifies ten metres. *Ibid.* 419 Kiliare..Hectare..Decare. **1860** *All Year Round* No. 69. 448 A decalitre..would contain a hundred thousand grains [of wheat]. **1890** *Daily News* 10 Dec. 3/3 He then brought up the dose of lymph to two decagrammes, a potent one.

†**de'cachinnate**, *v. Obs.*—⁰ [f. L. *dēcachinnāre* (Tertull.) to deride (DE- I. 4).] 'To scorn' (Cockeram, 1623).

decachord ('dɛkəkɔːd), *a.* and *sb.* Also 6 -corde. [ad. L. *decachord-us, -um*, a. Gr. δεκάχορδ-ος, -ον, ten-stringed, f. δέκα + -χορδή string.]

A. *adj.* Ten-stringed (cf. *Ps.* xxxii. 2 ἐν ψαλτηρίῳ δεκαχόρδῳ). **B.** *sb.* A musical instrument with ten strings.

c **1525** SKELTON *Replyc.* 340 Dauid, our poete, harped.. melodiously..in his decacorde psautry. **1555** ABP. PARKER *Ps.* (1556) A ij, In Lute and Harpe rejoyce to sing, Syng Psalmes in decachorde. **1609** DOULAND *Ornith. Microl.* 23 It is called a Monochord, because it hath but one string, as ..a Decachord which hath tenne. **1659** HAMMOND *On Ps.* Wks. 1684 IV. I. 91 Dechacord or instrument of ten strings. *Ibid.*, On a dechachord Psaltery. **1858** NEALE *Bernard de M.* 33 Whose everlasting music Is the glorious decachord.

†**deca'chordon**. *Obs.* (In 7 -cordon.) [a. Gr. δεκαχορδον: see prec.] = prec. B. Also *fig.*

1602 W. WATSON (*title*), Decacordon of Ten Quodlibeticall Questions concerning Religion and State. **1613** R. C. *Table Alph.*, *Decacordon*, an instrument with tenne strings.

†**deca'cuminate**, *v. Obs.*—⁰ [f. L. *dēcacūmināre* to deprive of the top (DE- I. 6).]

1656 BLOUNT *Glossogr.*, *Decacuminate*, to take off the top of any thing. **1727** BAILEY vol. II, *Decacuminated*, having the Tops lopped off. (So in J. and mod. Dicts.)

decad ('dɛkəd). [ad. Gr. δεκάς, δεκαδ-, collective sb. from δέκα ten.]

1. The number ten (the perfect number of the Pythagoreans).

1616 in BULLOKAR. **1655-60** STANLEY *Hist. Philos.* (1701) 379/2 The Decad comprehends every Reason of Number, and every Proportion. **1865** GROTE *Plato* I. i. 11 The Dekad, the full and perfect number. **1881** tr. *Zeller's Presocratic Phil.* I. 427 All numbers and all powers of numbers appeared to them [the Pythagoreans] to be comprehended in the decad.

2. *Music.* A group of ten notes out of which may be formed the consonant triads, and all the discords possible without a modulation.

1875 A. J. ELLIS tr. *Helmholtz* 663 Decad.

3. An earlier spelling of DECADE, q.v.

decadactylous: see DECA- *prefix* 1.

decadal ('dɛkədəl), *a.* [f. L. *decas, decad-em*, a. Gr. δεκάς, δεκάδ-α DECADE + -AL¹.] Of or relating to the number ten; belonging to a decade or period of ten years.

1753 CHAMBERS *Cycl. Supp.* s.v. *Arithmetic, Decadal Arithmetic*, that performed by the nine figures and a Cypher. **1881** M. L. KNAPP *Disasters* 45 The decadal character of epidemics has been noticed.

'decadarch. *Gr. Hist.* [ad. Gr. δεκάδαρχ-ος, f. δεκάδ-α DECADE + ἀρχός chief.] A commander of ten, a decurion.

1794 T. TAYLOR tr. *Pausanias* III. 16 The Decadarchs, or governors of companies consisting each of ten men.

'decadarchy, deka-. *Gr. Hist.* [ad. Gr. δεκαδαρχία: see prec.] A ruling body of ten. Cf. DECARCHY.

1849 GROTE *Greece* II. lxv. V. 547 He constituted an oligarchy of ten native citizens, chosen from among his—partisans, and called a Dekarchy, or Dekadarchy. **1852** *Ibid.* II. lxxvii. X. 137 The oppressions exercised by the Spartan harmosts and the dekadarchies.

decadary ('dɛkədərɪ), *a.* [f. L. *decad-em* DECADE + -ARY, after F. *décadaire*.] Relating to a decade or period of ten days (in the French Republican calendar of 1793).

1801 DUPRÉ *Neolog. Fr. Dict.* 71 *Décadaire*..A decadary festival dedicated to the Eternal. **1823** SOUTHEY in *Q. Rev.* XXVIII. 508 For the purpose of giving a religious character to the Decadary fêtes. **1876** G. F. CHAMBERS *Astron.* 454 The whole of the decadary days were kept, or ordered to be kept, as secular festivals.

deca'dation. *Music.* [f. DECAD 2 + -ATION.] The process of converting one decad into another in order to obtain a new series of consonant triads, etc.

1875 A. J. ELLIS tr. *Helmholtz* 665 This change of one decad into another is called *decadation*.

decade ('dɛkeɪd, -əd). Also 7-9 decad. [a. F. *decade* (14th c. in Littré), ad. L. *decas, decad-em*, a. Gr. δεκας, δεκάδα, a group of ten, f. δέκα ten. Cf. DECAD.]

1. a. An assemblage, group, set, or series of ten.

1594 PLAT *Jewell-ho.* III. 81 Your subiectes must consist of Decades, whereof the first is a man, and the fifth a woman. **1612** R. SHELDON *Serm. St. Martin's* 41 Of which some bring into this Kingdome Decades of thousands. **1679** T. PIERCE (*title*), A decad of Caveats to the people of England. **1725** POPE *Odyss.* XVI. 265 Can we engage, not decads, but an host? **1830** GODWIN *Cloudesley* III. xv. 298 His prisoners were divided into two decads. **1830** D'ISRAELI *Chas. I*, III. xiv. 301 In two hours, our fervid innovator drew up that decade of propositions. **1872** O. SHIPLEY *Gloss. Eccl. Terms* s.v. *Beads* 61 The practice of saying fifteen decades of the Ave Maria, with one Our Father after each decade, was invented by St. Dominic.

b. (i) A set of resistors (or capacitors or inductors) connected so as to provide a resistance of any integral value between one and ten times the lowest at a single setting of a switch, etc.; a decade is usu. one of several in a box which cover successive multiples of ten in value (so ***decade box***, etc.).

1911 W. H. TIMBIE *Elem. Electr.* v. 121 (*caption*) Wheatstone bridge, 'decade' form. *Ibid.*, The coils composing the variable resistance are arranged in such an ingenious way that 10 variations in value in each 'decade' or row are made by the use of only 4 coils. *Ibid.* 122 One decade represents 1000-ohm steps, the next 100-ohm steps, etc. This gives a total range in the four decades of 9999 ohms, by one-ohm steps. **1952** TERMAN & PETTIT *Electronic Measurem.* (ed. 2) xiv. 615 In grouping condensers together to form decade units, it is desirable to employ the smallest possible number of condensers. **1952** F. K. HARRIS *Electr. Measurem.* vii. 229 There may be ten 1-ohm coils for the unit decade, ten 10-ohm coils for the ten decade, etc. *Ibid.* 231 The switching arrangement most common in decade resistance boxes..is the rotary switch having brushes which bear on contact studs.

(ii) A set of ten electronic devices each used to represent a digit in the counting of pulses. So ***decade counter, system***, etc.

1948 *Sci. News* VII. 118 Each accumulator contains 10 decade counters and each decade counter 10 gadgets with the..name 'flip-flop'. *Ibid.* 119 The ten flip-flops within a decade counter represent from left to right the digits 0 to 9, while the whole decade represents one place of a ten-digit number. **1952** *Electronic Engin.* XXIV. 376 With a suitably larger power supply there is no limit to the number of decade units which can be used. **1958** *Engineering* 28 Mar. 389/3 The pulses are counted by a three decade system using multi-cathode discharge tubes which display in a digital form the measured voltage. **1963** B. FOZARD *Instrumentation Nucl. Reactors* viii. 88 The display for each decade consists of ten neon lamps arranged in a vertical column corresponding to the numbers 0 to 9.

2. *spec.* **a.** Short for 'decade of years'; a period of ten years.

1605 T. HUTTON *Reasons for Refusal* 121 So many tens or decads of yeares. **1709** J. PALMER *Latter Day Glory* 112 That Decad of Years in which the Empire ceased. **1869** RAWLINSON *Anc. Hist.* 296 The war..might still have continued for another decade of years. *c* **1655** T. DUGARD in S. Ashe *Fun. Serm.* (1655) 71 His smoother brow..made me hope that He might raise eight Decads to a Century. **1837** HALLAM *Hist. Lit.* I. i. §19 In the second decad of the 12th Cent. **1864** TENNYSON *Aylmer's F.* 82 Since Averill was a decad and a half His elder. **1878** DOWDEN *Stud. Lit.* 1 The last decade of that century.

b. A period of ten days, substituted for the week in the French Republican calendar of 1793.

1798 *Anti-Jacobin* in *Spirit Public Jrnls.* (1799) II. 43 In the course of the next decade I shall sail to the canal which is now cutting across the Isthmus of Suez. **1801** DUPRÉ *Neolog. Fr. Dict.* 71 Three decades make a month of thirty days.

3. A division of a literary work, containing ten books or parts; as the decades of Livy.

1475 *Bk. Noblesse* 53 I rede in the Romayns stories of Titus Livius, in the booke of the first decade. **1555** EDEN (*title*), The Decades of the newe worlde or West India. **1594** (*title*), Diana: or the excellent conceitful Sonnets of H. C[onstable]..Deuided into viij Decads. **1651** WALTON *Reliq Wotton.* (1672) 46 'Tis the first Epistle in his Printed Decads. **1789** MRS. PIOZZI *Journ. France* I. 394 He was a blockhead, and burned Livy's decads. **1840** MACAULAY *Ranke* Ess. 1851 II. 139 It is now as hopelessly lost as the second decade of Livy. **1882** *Encycl. Brit.* XIV. 726/1 (*Livy*), The division into decades is certainly not due to the author himself, and is first heard of at the end of the 5th century.

4. *Comb.* †**decade-day** = DÉCADI; **decade-ring**, a finger-ring having ten projections or knobs for counting the repetition of so many Aves.

1798 *Anti-Jacobin* in *Spir. Public Jrnls.* (1799) II. 134 When father had been keeping his Decade-day, as he calls it (for we had no Sundays now, though we did no work). **1861** C. W. KING *Ant. Gems* (1866) 296 The decade rings of medieval times..are readily known by their having ten projections like short cogs on their circumference, representing so many *Aves*, whilst the round head, engraved with I.H.S., stands for the Pater Noster.

†**de'cade, decaid**, *v. Sc. Obs.* [ad. L. *dēcad-ĕre* DECAY.] To fall down, fail.

15.. *Aberdeen Reg.* (Jamieson).

decadence ('dɛkədəns, dɪ'keɪdəns). In 6-7 *Sc.* decadens. [a. F. *décadence* (1413 in Hatzf.), ad. med.L. *decadentia*, Sp., Pg. *decadéncia*, It. *decadenza* 'a declyning, a decaying' (Florio), f.

decadĕre to decay, f. *de-* down + *cadĕre* to fall (the Comm. Romanic repr. of L. *cadĕre* to fall; cf. Sp. *caer*, F. *choir*). The prevalent accentuation was formerly *de'cadence*, perh. after *decay* (see the dictionaries); *'decadence* was 'considered more scholarly' *c* 1895 (*N.E.D.*); it is now standard.]

The process of falling away or declining (from a prior state of excellence, vitality, prosperity, etc.); decay; impaired or deteriorated condition.
1549 *Compl. Scot.* vii. 71 My triumphant stait is succumbit in decadens. **1623** FAVINE *Theat. Hon.* II. xii. 177 Forewarning of the entire decadence of the Kingdom. *a* **1649** DRUMM. OF HAWTH. *Poems* 185 Doth in Decadens fall and slack remaine. *a* **1734** NORTH *Exam.* II. v. §144 (1740) 406 The Decadence of all the Good he had hoped, or could hope for, in the World. **1762** GOLDSM. *Cit. W.* xl, Every day produces some pathetic exclamation upon the decadence of taste and genius. **1815** SCOTT *Guy M.* ii, The old castle, where the family lived in their decadence. **1847** LD. LINDSAY *Chr Art* I. 114 The eleventh century, commonly considered as marking the lowest decadence of Byzantine art. **1871** J. B. MAYOR in *Jrnl. Philol.* III. 348 'Decadence' seems to have made little way in England until the last quarter of a century, when.. it came into fashion, apparently to *denote* decline, and *connote* a scientific and enlightened view of that decline on the part of the user.

b. *spec.* Applied to a particular period of decline in art, literature, etc.
e.g. the Silver Age of Latin literature (chiefly a French use); in *Art*, the period subsequent to Raphael and Michael Angelo.
1852 MRS. JAMESON *Leg. Madonna* Introd. (1857) 73 The style of art belongs to the decadence. **1874** STUBBS *Const. Hist.* III. xxi. 615 The men of the decadence, not less than the men of the renaissance, were giants of learning.

c. *lit.* Falling down, falling off. *nonce-use.*
1812 SIR R. WILSON *Diary* I. 136, I fell to the ground in the dirtiest soil that could be selected by a man in a state of decadence. **1884** *Birm. Weekly Post* 15 Nov. 1/4 This process is said to prevent the decadence of the hair.

decadency ('dɛkədənsɪ, dɪ'keɪdənsɪ). Also 7 decaydency. [f. as prec. with suffix -ENCY.] Decaying condition: also = prec.
1632 J. HAYWARD tr. *Biondi's Eromena* 132 The infirmitie and decadency of the King. **1685** F. SPENCE *House of Medici* 239 During the decaydency and restauration of the Roman empire. **1777** *Misc.* in *Ann. Reg.* 189/2 The causes of the decadency of an empire. **1779** SWINBURNE *Trav. Spain* XLIV. (T.), Burgos.. long since abandoned by its princes to obscurity and decadency. **1812** W. TAYLOR in *Monthly Mag.* XXXIV. 14 Of a cadaverous man the decay, of a paralytic man the decadency, is sensible. **1844** *Fraser's Mag.* XXIX. 313 He enumerated all the causes of the Spanish decadency.

decadent ('dɛkədənt, dɪ'keɪdənt), *a.* [f. DECADENCE: see -ENT. So mod.F. *décadent* (Hatzf.).]

1. That is in a state of decay or decline; falling off or deteriorating from a prior condition of excellence, vitality, prosperity, etc.
1837 CARLYLE *Fr. Rev.* I. I. ii, Those decadent ages in which no Ideal either grows or blossoms? **1872** BLACKIE *Lays Highl.* Introd. 50 A grey, old town with an air of decadent respectability about it. **1885** MME. DARMESTETER in *Mag. of Art* Sept. 477/1 To establish in his kingdom the already decadent and modern art of Italy.

‖**2. a.** Said of a French school which affects to belong to an age of decadence in literature and art. Hence *sb.*, a member of this fraternity.
[**1885** *Figaro* 22 Sept., Le décadent n'a pas d'idées. Il n'en veut pas. Il aime mieux les mots.. C'est au lecteur à comprendre et à mettre des idées sous les mots. Le lecteur s'y refuse généralement. De là, mépris du décadent pour le lecteur.] **1888** *Sat. Rev.* 6 Oct. 417/2 M. Darmesteter has written in a style occasionally a little decadent and over-elaborate. **1890** *Ibid.* 22 Nov. 602/2 The very noisy and motley crew of younger writers in France.. naturalists, decadents, scientific critics, and what not. **1889** *Daily News* 8 Nov. 5/2 A wonderful piece of 'decadent' French, in a queer new style, as if Rabelais's Limousin had been reborn, with a fresh manner of being unintelligible.

b. Said of other schools of literature and art characterized by decadence; *spec.* = ÆSTHETIC *a.* 4. So as *sb.*
1894 M. BEERBOHM in *Yellow Bk.* II. 284 English literature.. must fall at length into the hands of the decadents. **1906** R. BROOKE *Let.* Jan. (1968) 37, I contrive to keep the *mens insana in corpore sano* which is all the English decadent may hope for. **1942** WYNDHAM LEWIS *Let.* (1963) 324 The artist is labelled 'decadent' who departs from the Salon norm, or that of the Royal Academy, by the Hitlerite pundit of 'sanity'. **1958** *Times* 20 May 3/7 The last public appearance of Dadaism was that of an aesthetic outlaw under the Nazi ban and during the campaign of 1937 against 'Decadent Art'. **1961** M. LEVY *Studio Dict. Art Terms* 39 *Decadent movement*, a critical and disparaging term sometimes used loosely as a synonym for the Aesthetic Movement.

Hence **'decadently** *adv.*
1892 *Sat. Rev.* 23 Apr. 492/2 It is very prettily and decadently written.

decadentism ('dɛkədəntɪz(ə)m). [f. DECADENT *a.* + -ISM.] The distinctive qualities or spirit of the decadent school in art, literature, and music; decadent behaviour or characteristics.
[**1886** *Athenæum* 24 July 117/1, I shall speak to you some other time about the *décadents* and the *décadentisme*, a malady of the hour.] **1895** *Westm. Gaz.* 27 May 2/1 The ego-mania of decadentism, its love of the artificial.. and its exaggeration of the importance of art, have found their English representative among the Æsthetes. **1949** *Mind* LVIII. 114 Existentialism is the philosophy of decadentism.

decadescent (dɛkə'dɛsənt), *a.* *nonce-wd.* [f. assumed L. type *decadescere*, inceptive from med.L. or Romanic *decadĕre*: see DECADENCE and -ESCENT.] Beginning or tending to decay.
1858 *National Rev.* Oct. 351 Those perils of matrimony over which decadescent virgins sigh so affectingly.

‖**décadi.** [Fr.: f. Gr. δέκα ten + *-di* day in *Lundi*, etc] The tenth day of the 'decade' in the French Republican calendar, superseding Sunday as a day of rest.
1795 BURKE *Let. to W. Elliot* Wks. VII. 358 Annulling the Calvinistic sabbath, and establishing the decadi of atheism in all his states. **1801** H. M. WILLIAMS *Sk. Fr. Rep.* I. xxii. 323 The fossé, formed into a walk, furnishes a ball-room to the villagers on the decadi.

decadianome: see DECA- *prefix.*

decadic (dɪ'kædɪk), *a.* [a. Gr. δεκαδικός, f. Gr. δεκαδ- (see DECADE) + -IC.] Belonging to the system of counting by tens; denary.
1838 SIR W. HAMILTON *Logic* xxvi. (1866) II. 42 We select the decadic scheme of numeration. **1877** E. CAIRD *Philos. Kant* II. vi. 293 The decadic system of numbers. **1883** *Times* 5 July 7/3 The reduction of a Decadic Binary Quantic.

decadist ('dɛkədɪst). *rare.*—0 [f. Gr. δεκαδ- DECADE + -IST.] One who writes in decades.
1674 BLOUNT *Glossogr.* (ed. 4), *Decadist*, a Writer of Decads, such was Titus Livius.

decadrachm, deka- ('dɛkədræm). *Numism.* [f. Gr. δεκάδραχμος of the value of ten drachmæ, f. δέκα ten + δραχμή DRACHMA.] An ancient Greek silver coin of the value of 10 drachmas.
1856 *Sat. Rev.* II. 735/1 Pre-eminent amongst them was a decadrachm of Syracuse.

decæsarize, etc.: see DE- II. 1.

decaffeinate (dɪ'kæfɪneɪt), *v.* [f. DE- II. 1 + CAFFEINE + -ATE[3].] *trans.* To remove the caffeine from, or to reduce the quantity of, caffeine in (coffee). So **de'caffeinated** *ppl. a.*, **de,caffeini'zation.**
1927 *Times* 24 May (Advt.), Even experts cannot detect that decaffeinisation makes a shade of difference in taste or aroma. **1934** WEBSTER, Decaffeinate, *v.t.* **1955** *Sci. News Let.* 8 Oct. 238/2 Makers of decaffeinated coffee who claim 97% or more of the caffeine has been removed from their products are correct. **1966** P. V. PRICE *France* 77 Decaffeinated coffee.. may always be asked for by people who find that strong black coffee.. interferes with their sleep.

decafid: see DECA- *prefix* 1.

decagon ('dɛkəgən). *Geom.* [ad. med.L. *decagōnum* sb., *-us* adj., a. Gr. δεκάγωνον, -ος, f. Gr. δέκα ten, and γωνία corner or angle, -γωνος angled. Used at first in Latin form. Cf. F. *décagone*, 1652 in Hatzfeld.] A plane figure having ten sides and ten angles. Also *attrib.*
[**1571** DIGGES *Pantom.* IV. xxv. H h iij b, The superficies of an equiangle Decagonum.] **1613-39** I. JONES in Leoni *Palladio's Archit.* (1742) II. 46 A Circle without and Decagon within. **1704** J. HARRIS *Lex. Techn.* s.v., If they are all equal to one another 'tis then called a Regular Decagon, and it may be inscribed in a Circle. **1838** *Murray's Handbk. N. Germ.* 226 The circular portion, or rather the decagon, was not finished till 1227. **1881** *Trans. Victoria Inst.* XIV. 195, I discovered a perfect decagon terra cotta cylinder.

decagonal (dɪ'kægənəl), *a.* [f. med.L. *decagōn-um* + -AL[1].] Of or pertaining to a decagon; of the form of a decagon; ten-sided.
1571 DIGGES *Pantom.* IV. ix. Y j b, The decagonall corde of that circle wheron Icosaedron is framed. **1717** BERKELEY *Tour in Italy* Wks. 1871 IV. 526 What remains is a decagonal building. **1879** SIR G. SCOTT *Lect. Archit.* II. 235 Its surrounding wall is not circular, but decagonal.

decagram: see DECA- *prefix* 2.

decagynous (dɪ'kædʒɪnəs), *a.* *Bot.* [f. mod.Bot. L. *decagyn-us*, f. Gr. δέκα ten + γυνή woman, female, taken by Linnæus in sense of 'female organ, pistil'.] Having ten pistils.

So **deca'gynia**, a name for an order of plants having ten pistils, in a class of the Linnæan Sexual System, as class *Decandria*, order *Decagynia*, genus *Phytolacca*: see Linnæus *Spec. Plant.* ed. 1, 1753, Colin Milne *Bot. Dict.* 1770.

decahedral (dɛkə'hi:drəl), *a.* [f. next + -AL[1].] Having the form of a decahedron; ten-sided.
1811 PINKERTON *Petral.* I. 494 Prismatic decahedral selenite, produced by the elongated octahedron.

decahedron (dɛkə'hi:drən). *Geom.* [Representing a Gr. *δεκάεδρον, neuter of *δεκάεδρος, on the model of ἑξάεδρος, f. δέκα ten + ἕδρα seat, base. Cf. F. *decaèdre*, Hauy 1801.] A solid figure having ten faces.
1828 in WEBSTER.

decahydrate (dɛkə'haɪdrət). *Chem.* [f. DECA- + HYDRATE *sb.*] A compound containing ten molecules of water of crystallization. So **deca'hydrated** *a.*
1880 G. LUNGE *Sulphuric Acid* II. 6 The solubility of the decahydrated salt in water rises from 0° to 34° C. with the temperature. **1902** *Science* 24 Jan. 146/1 The equilibrium conditions were determined by the solid salt being in the form of the decahydrate.

decahydro'naphthalene. *Chem.* Also **deka-**. [f. DECA- + HYDRO- + NAPHTHALENE.] A colourless liquid, $C_{10}H_{18}$, much used in the paint industry as a solvent, with a molecular structure consisting of two fused saturated rings; cf. DECALIN.
1877 *Jrnl. Chem. Soc.* II. 899 Tetrahydroisoxylene absorbs oxygen, while hexhydroisoxylene, like decahydronaphthalene, may be kept without alteration in the air or in oxygen. **1904** *Ibid.* LXXXVI. I. 987 Decahydronaphthalene, $C_{10}H_{18}$, obtained by hydrogenating tetrahydronaphthalene at 175°, is a colourless liquid with an odour of menthol. **1920** *Chem. Abstr.* XIV. 1751 The hydrogenation of naphthalene, converting this ring compd. into dekahydronaphthalene, $C_{10}H_{18}$. **1964** [see DECALIN].

decaid: see DECADE *v.* (*Sc.*).

decairt, var. of DECART *Sc. Obs.*, to discard.

decal ('di:kəl). [Abbrev. of DECALCOMANIA.] A transfer (TRANSFER *sb.* 3) produced by decalcomania.
1952 *Electronic Engin.* XXIV. 512 This firm is producing a book of decals or transfers. **1955** *Ibid.* XXVII. 513 These P.V.C. decals are intended for the identification marking of P.V.C. cables and are supplied in the form of ordinary (reverse) transfers. **1959** *New Yorker* 14 Nov. 53/1 The captain himself stopped the fellow's car at the gate as he was leaving, scraped the decal off with a razor blade. **1970** *Win* 15 Feb. 35/2 (Advt.), Put this decal in your car window and let the American flag freaks know where you stand.

decalage ('di:kəlɑ:ʒ), ‖**décalage** (dekalɑʒ). *Aeronaut.* [Fr. *décalage* displacement, f. *décaler* to displace.] (See quots.)
1917 R. B. MATTHEWS *Aviation Pocket-Bk.* (ed. 5) XII. 267 *Decalage*, the difference in the angle of incidence between any two distinct aerofoils on an aeroplane; *e.g.*, the main plane and the tail; or more usually between the chords of the upper and lower planes of a biplane. **1933** *Flight* (Suppl. Aircraft Engin.) 27 Apr. 396d/1 The term aerodynamic decalage.. defined as the angle that the no lift angle of the upper plane makes with the no lift angle of the lower plane, positive when the upper plane is at greater incidence than the lower.

decalcation (di:kæl'keɪʃən). [f. L. *dē-* down (DE- I. 1) + *calcāre* to tread, to trample: see -ATION.] A treading or trampling down or hard.
1827 STEUART *Planter's G.* (1828) 294 When it will bear the workmen's feet, it is ultimately finished, by a complete decalcation of the surface.

decalcify (dɪ'kælsɪfaɪ), *v.* [f. DE- II. 1 + CALCIFY.] *trans.* To deprive (*e.g.* bone) of its lime or calcareous matter. Hence **de'calcified** *ppl. a.*; **de'calcifying** *vbl. sb.*; **decalcifi'cation**, the action of decalcifying.
1847-9 TODD *Cycl Anat.* IV. 564/1 No vestige of them can be traced in the decalcified shell. **1859** *Ibid.* V. 487/2 Decalcification brings to light no endoplasts in the 'cells'. **1859** J. TOMES *Dental Surg.* (1873) 297 Decalcifying a tooth by the aid of a dilute mineral acid. **1875** DARWIN *Insectiv. Pl.* vi. 105 The normal appearance of decalcified bone.

decalco'mania. Often in Fr. form. [ad. mod.F. *décalcomanie*, f. *décalquer* to transfer a tracing + *manie* mania, craze.] A process or art of transferring pictures from a specially prepared paper to surfaces of glass, porcelain, etc., much in vogue about 1862-4. Also *attrib.*
1864 *The Queen* 27 Feb. 164 There are few employments for leisure hours which for the past eighteen months have proved either so fashionable or fascinating as decalcomanie. **1865** *Morn. Star* 25 Aug., The potichomania.. assumed a still more virulent craze when decalcomania was ushered into the world. **1869** *Eng. Mech.* 12 Nov. 215/1 Gilded scroll-work can be made to show through plain glass by the Decalcomanie process.

decalco'maniac, one who practises this process.
1866 MISS BRADDON *Lady's Mile* 116 The most timid of the décalcomaniacs.

decalescence (di:kə'lɛsəns). *Metallurgy.* [f. DE- II. 1 + CALESCENCE.] (See quot. 1954.) So **deca'lescent** *a.*
1893 *Funk's Stand. Dict.*, Decalescence. **1910** E. F. LAKE *Composition & Heat Treatment of Steel* vi. 68 The temperature again falls uniformly until it reaches.. 1350° F., at which point the second change takes place.. designed Ar 2. After the change has been completed at this point, it again lowers in temperature uniformly to the next point, or Ar 1. .. After this change takes place, it then gradually lowers to atmospheric temperature. These have been named the decalescent points. **1912** A. SAUVEUR *Metallogr. Iron & Steel* vii. 2 The notation Ar_1 and Ac_1 are used for the recalescence point and its reversal... The point Ac_1 has been called point of 'decalescence' by some writers. **1916** D. K. BULLENS *Steel* 417 For the majority of heat-treatment work, it is more important to know the location of the decalescent points than that of the recalescent points. *Ibid.* 425/2 Decalescence. **1954** *Gloss. Terms Iron & Steel* (*B.S.I.*) 1. 11 *Decalescence*, absorption of heat without

increase of temperature when the metal is heated through the critical points.

decalet, -litre, -lobate: see DECA- 1, 2.

Decalin ('dɛkəlɪn). Also Dekalin. [Trade mark in the U.S.] = DECAHYDRONAPHTHALENE.

1920 *Chem. Abstr.* XIV. 1227 New turpentine substitutes .. Dekalin, $C_{10}H_{18}$... In the trade dekalin is not found pure, but always contains tetralin and is handled under the name tetralin extra. **1943** *Thorpe's Dict. Appl. Chem.* (ed. 4) VI. 352/2 The decalin so obtained was the pure *cis*-compound, whereas nickel at 160° yields chiefly *trans*-decalin. **1946** *Nature* 14 Sept. 365/2 The fuel used [in the torpedo] is a by-product of the coal distillation industry known as 'Dekalin'. **1964** N. G. CLARK *Mod. Org. Chem.* xix. 391 At 200° catalytic hydrogenation over nickel yields tetrahydronaphthalene ('tetralin'), while at 250°, decahydronaphthalene ('decalin') results.

Decalogist (dɪ'kælədʒɪst). *rare.* [f. L. *decalogus* DECALOGUE + -IST.] One who expounds the Decalogue or Ten Commandments.

1650 *Gregory's Posthuma* Life 3 Mr Dod the Decalogist. **1738** NEAL *Hist. Purit.* IV. 452. **1889** A. H. DRYSDALE *Hist. Presbyt. Eng.* II. v. 241 John Dod (surnamed the Decalogist, from his book on the Ten Commandments).

Decalogue ('dɛkəlɒg). [a. F. *décalogue* (15th c. in Hatzf.), ad. L. *decalog-us* (Tertullian), a. Gr. δεκάλογος (orig. adj. ἡ δεκάλογος, sc. βίβλος), in Clemens Alexand., etc., from the phrase οἱ δέκα λόγοι the ten commandments, in LXX, Philo, etc. In Wyclif, prob. directly from Latin: cf. quot. 1563.

The word occurs repeatedly in the Latin version of Irenæus *adv. Hæres.*; and was probably in the Greek original.]

The Ten Commandments collectively as a body of law.

1382 WYCLIF *Rom.* Prol. 299 The noumbre of the firste maundementus of the decaloge. **1563** MAN *Musculus' Commonpl.* 34 a, The preceptes of the Decalogus bee called, the tenne wordes. **1642** HOWELL *For. Trav.* (Arb.) 84 They beleeve the Decalog of Moses. **1670** J. GOODWIN *Filled with the Spirit* To Rdr. A iij a, The Second Table of the Decalogue or Ten Commandments. **1755** YOUNG *Centaur* i. Wks. 1757 IV. 111 Both the tables of the decalogue are broken. **1847** H. MILLER *First Impr.* iv. (1857) 55 The great geologic register, graven, like the decalogue of old, on tables of stone.

transf. **a1649** DRUMM. OF HAWTH. *Skiamachia* Wks. (1711) 199 O new and ever till now concealed decalogue! **a1861** CLOUGH *Poems* (*title*), The Latest Decalogue.

†**decal'vation.** *Obs.* [n. of action f. L. *dēcalvāre* to make bald, f. *dē-* (DE- I. 3) + *calvus* bald.] A making bald by removal of hair.

1650 BULWER *Anthropomet.* 48 All those wayes of Decalvation practised by the Ancients. **1737** L. CLARKE *Hist. Bible* (1740) I. vi, For Decalvation, or leaving any part where hair grew, bald, was one great offence.

decalvinize: see DE- II. 1.

decamalee = DIKAMALI, an Indian gum.

Decameron (dɪ'kæmərən). [a. It. *Decamerone*, f. Gr. δέκα ten + ἡμέρα day, after *Hexāmeron*, mediæval corruption of *Hexahemeron* or *Hexaëmeron*, Gr. ἑξαήμερον. The Greek form would be δεχήμερον or δεκαήμερον.] The title of a work by Boccaccio containing a hundred tales which are supposed to be related in ten days; used allusively by Ben Jonson. Hence **Decame'ronic** *a.*, characteristic of or resembling Boccaccio's work.

1609 B. JONSON *Sil. Wom.* I. iii, *Cler.* When were you there? *Daup.* Last night: and such a Decameron of sport fallen out! Boccace never thought of the like.

decamerous, decametre: see DECA- 1, 2.

decamethonium (ˌdɛkəmɪ'θəʊnɪəm). *Pharm.* [f. DECA- + METHONIUM.] A quaternary ammonium cation, $[(CH_3)_3N(CH_2)_{10}N(CH_3)_3]^{++}$; also, the bromide or iodide salt of this, used as a muscle relaxant.

1949 G. ORGANE in *Lancet* 7 May 774/2 Decamethonium iodide (C 10) is a stable, neutral, non-irritant muscle relaxant, roughly five times as potent as *d*-tubocurarine chloride. **1963** *Lancet* 19 Jan. 130/1 With decamethonium muscle fasciculation was only slight, whereas with suxamethonium it was severe and long lasting.

decamp (dɪ'kæmp), *v.* [a. F. *décamper*, earlier *descamper* (Cotgr. 1611); f. *des-*, *dé-* (see DE- I. 6) + *camp*. Cf. It. *scampare* = *discampare*, DISCAMP.]

1. *intr.* (*Mil.*) To break up a camp; to remove from a place of encampment. Hence, said of other bodies or parties leaving a camping-place.

1676 [see b]. **1678** PHILLIPS, *To Decamp*, a term now grown much into use in Military Affairs, and signifies to rise from the present place of Incampment, in order to a removing and incamping in another place. **1692** *Siege Lymerick* 2 Here we incamp'd, and lay till the 14th, on which day we decamp'd. **1725** DE FOE *Voy. round World* (1840) 312 The Spaniards' gentleman caused them to decamp, and march two days further into the mountains, and then they encamped again. **1803** WELLINGTON in Owen *Desp.* 408 We found on our arrival that the armies of both chiefs had decamped. **1868** FREEMAN *Norm. Conq.* (1876) II. viii. 290 The Count and his host had decamped.

b. Const. *from*, etc.

1676 ROW *Suppl. Blair's Autobiog.* x. (1848) 161 That powder had been laid there the year before, when the army decamped from Dunse-law. **1695** BLACKMORE *Pr. Arth.* VI. 429 Decamping thence, his arm'd Battalions gain .. the fertile Plain. **1836** W. IRVING *Astoria* III. 97 They were fain to decamp from their inhospitable bivouac before the dawn.

2. To go away promptly or suddenly; to make off at once, take oneself off: often said of criminals and persons eluding the officers of the law.

1751 SMOLLETT *Per. Pic.* civ, He ordered them [servants] to decamp without further preparation. **1764** STERNE in Traill *Life* 87 Christmas, at which time I decamp from hence and fix my head-quarters at London. **1792** *Gentl. Mag.* 17/2 Probably the rascal is decamped; and where is your remedy? **1828** D'ISRAELI *Chas. I*, I. iv. 76 An idle report that Prince Charles designed to decamp secretly from Spain. **1885** *Manch. Exam.* 29 June 5/2 The murderer had decamped, and taken with him 2,000 francs.

fig. **1806-7** J. BERESFORD *Miseries Hum. Life* (1826) IX. iii, Finding, as you sit down to an excellent dinner, that your appetite has secretly decamped. **1871** ROSSETTI *Poems*, *Jenny* 310 So on the wings of day decamps My last night's frolic.

†**3.** *trans.* To cause to break up a camp. *rare.*

1684 *Scanderbeg Rediv.* v. 120 The next day decampt his whole Army and followed them. **1733** MILLNER *Compend. Jrnl.* 202 The Duke decamp'd our Army from Nivelle.

¶**4.** *catachr.* To camp. *Obs.*

1698 FRYER *Acc. E. India* 42 They .. being beaten from their Works near the City, had decamped Seven Miles off St. Thomas. **1745** POCOCKE *Descr. East* II. II. 120 It leads to a plain spot on the side of the hill where the Urukes were decamping.

Hence **de'camped** *ppl. a.*, **de'camping** *vbl. sb.*

1689 LUTTRELL *Brief Rel.* (1857) I 567 We have the confirmation of the decamping of the Irish from before Derry. **1770** LANGHORNE *Plutarch* (1879) II. 780/1 Cæsar hoped, by his frequent decampings, to provide better for his troops. **1887** *Pall Mall G.* 14 Nov. 12/1 To inquire into the doings of the decamped bankrupt .. and his associates.

de'campment, *sb.* [a. F. *décampement* (16th c.), f. *décamper*: see prec. and -MENT.] The action of decamping; the raising of a camp; a prompt departure.

1706 PHILLIPS (ed. Kersey), *Decampment*, a Decamping, or Marching off. **1733** MILLNER *Compend. Jrnl.* 300 Both Armies march'd from their several Decampments Rightward. **1736** ELIZA STANLEY tr. *Hist. Pr. Titi* 122 Having by some few Decampments .. drawn Ginguet's Army into a spacious Plain. **1751** SMOLLETT *Per. Pic.* (1779) IV. xc. 86 In consequence of this decampment, the borrower had withdrawn himself. **1809** W. IRVING *Knickerb.* (1861) 259 The vigilant Peter, perceiving that a moment's delay were fatal, made a secret and precipitate decampment.

decan ('dɛkən). Also 5-6 decane. [ad. L. *decānus*, Gr. δεκανός; cf. DEAN.]

†**1.** A chief or ruler of ten. *Obs.*

1569 J. SANFORD tr. *Agrippa's Van. Artes* 130 a, Moses did then appoint them .. Centurians, Quinquagenarians and Decans.

2. *Astrol.* The chief or ruler of ten parts, or ten degrees, of a zodiacal sign; also this division itself. Cf. DECANATE[1].

1588 J. HARVEY *Discours. Probl.* 103 The great Coniunction of Saturne and Iupiter in the last Decane of Pisces. **1651** J. F[REAKE] *Agrippa's Occ. Philos.* 391 Angels who might rule the signs, triplicities, decans, quinaries, degrees and stars. **1678** CUDWORTH *Intell. Syst.* I. iv. 317 (transl. Porphyrius) Such of the Egyptians as talk of no other Gods but the planets .. their decans, and horoscopes, and robust princes, as they call them. **1812** BUCHAN in Singer *Hist. Cards* 361 Each of these signs is divided into three decans or thirty degrees.

†**3.** = DEAN[1]. *Obs.*

1432-50 tr. *Higden* (Rolls) VII. 477 Symon .. decan [**1387** TREVISA deen] in the same churche. **1496** *Will of Hawarden* (Somerset Ho.), Decane of the Arches. **1538** LELAND *Itin.* II. 40 Walingford .. There is also a Collegiate Chapel .. There is a Decane, 4 Prestes, 6 Clerkes, and 4 Choristers.

decanal (dɪ'keɪnəl), *a.* [f. L. *decān-us* DEAN + -AL[1].]

1. Of or pertaining to a dean or deanery.

1707 *Lond. Gaz.* No. 4386/3 Libraries of 3 degrees, viz. General, Decanal or Lending, and Parochial. **1862** *Sat. Rev.* XIV. 705/2 The specially Decanal virtues. **1868** MILMAN *St. Paul's* xi. 271 The decanal and prebendal estates.

2. Applied to the south side of the choir of a cathedral or other church, being that on which the dean usually sits.

1792 *Chron.* in *Ann. Reg.* 67/1 The Pall-bearers and executors in the seats on the Decanal side, the other noblemen and gentlemen on the Cantorial side. **1877** J. D. CHAMBERS *Div. Worship* 4 On the Decanal or Southern side.

Hence **de'canally**, also **de'canically**, *advbs.* (*nonce-wds.*), as a dean.

1882 PLUMPTRE in *Spectator* 8 Apr. 465/1 The twin-brother Deans, born decanally on the same day. **1892** A. K. H. BOYD *25 Years of St. Andrew's* I. 286 A great Welsh preacher, though as Stanley said, a babe decanically, a very young dean.

'**decanate**[1]. *Astrol.* [f. DECAN + -ATE.] = FACE *sb.* 11 c: see quot. 1696.

1647 LILLY *Chr. Astrol.* viii. 58 He [Saturn] hath also these [degrees] for his Face or Decanate. **1653** GATAKER *Vind. Annot. Jer.* 23 It is in the last degree of the Decanate of Aries. **1696** PHILLIPS, *Decanate*, by some called *Decurie*, and in Astrology the Face, is one third part, or ten Degrees of each Sign, attributed to some particular Planet, which being therein, shall be said to have one Dignity, and consequently cannot be Peregrine. **a1963** L. MACNEICE *Astrol.* (1964) iv. 126 Certain stones are in 'sympathy' with certain decanates.

'**decanate**[2]. [ad. med.L. *decānātus*, f. *decānus* DEAN.] = DEANERY 2.

1835 DANSEY *Horæ Dec. Rur.* I. xxxiv. (*Contents*), Deans rural, general supervisors and censors of the inhabitants of their decanates.

†**de'cander.** *Bot. Obs.* [See next.] A plant having ten stamens; a member of the decandria.

1828 in WEBSTER.

‖**De'candria.** *Bot.* [mod. Bot. L. (Linnæus) f. Gr. δέκα ten + ἀνδρ- man, male, taken as 'male organ, stamen'.] In the Sexual System of Linnæus, the class of plants having ten stamens.

1775 in ASH. **1794** MARTYN *Rousseau's Bot.* ix. 89 Decandria, which has ten stamens.

Hence **de'candrian** *a.* = next.

1828 in WEBSTER.

decandrous (dɪ'kændrəs), *a. Bot.* [f. as prec. + -OUS.] Characterized by ten stamens.

1808 J. E. SMITH in *Trans. Linn. Soc.* IX. 244 (*title*) Specific Characters of the Decandrous Papilionaceous Plants of New Holland. **1872** OLIVER *Elem. Bot.* II. 148 In some exotic allies the stamens are decandrous.

decane ('dɛkeɪn). *Chem.* [f. Gr. δέκα ten + -ANE 2 b.] The saturated hydrocarbon $C_{10}H_{22}$; one of the paraffins found in coal-tar.

1875 in WATTS *Dict. Chem.* VII. 422.

decane, obs. form of DECAN, DEACON.

†**de'canery, -ary.** *Obs.* [f. L. *decān-us* DEAN + -ERY.] = DEANERY.

1538 LELAND *Itin.* II. 29 The Church .. is impropriate onto the Decanerie of Saresbyri. **1647** N. BACON *Disc. Govt.* I. xii. (1739) 23 Dioceses have also been sub-divided into inferiour Precincts, called Deanaries or Decanaries, the chief of which was wont to be a Presbyter of the highest note, called Decanus.

decangular: see DECA- *prefix* 1.

‖**decani** (dɪ'keɪnaɪ). [L., genitive of *decānus* DEAN.] Of a dean, dean's; in phrases ***decani side, stall*** (of a choir): = DECANAL 2. In *Music* used to indicate the decanal side of the choir in antiphonal singing.

1760 BOYCE *Cathedral Music* I. 8. **1866** *Direct. Angl.* 353 *Decani Stall*, the first return stall on the right upon entering the choir. **1894** J. T. FOWLER (in letter), At Durham the Decani and Cantoris sides are reversed.

decanonize, -ation: see DE- II. 1.

decant (dɪ'kænt), *v.*[1] [a. F. *décanter*, ad. med.L. *dēcanthāre* (a word of the alchemists), f. *dē-* down + *canthus* the angular beak or 'lip' of a cup or jug, a transferred use of Gr. κάνθος corner of the eye (Darmesteter).]

a. *trans.* To pour off (the clear liquid of a solution) by gently inclining the vessel so as not to disturb the lees or sediment; *esp.* in *Chem.* as a means of separating a liquid from a precipitate.

1633 WOTTON *Let.* in *Rem.* 454 (T.) Decant from it [the vessel] the clear juice. **1666** BOYLE *Orig. Formes & Qual.*, Having carefully decanted the Solution into a conveniently siz'd Retort. **1779** FORDYCE in *Phil. Trans.* LXX. 32 Decant the fluid from the copper and iron with great care into another bason, so that .. none of the copper be carried along with it. **1863-72** WATTS *Dict. Chem.* s.v. *Decantation*, It is only .. from very heavy precipitates that a liquid can be thus decanted. (*fig.*) **1872** O. W. HOLMES *Poet Breakf.-t.* iv. 121 If you are not decanted off from yourself every few days or weeks.

b. To pour (wine, etc.) from the ordinary bottle in which it is kept in the cellar into a decanter for use at table; also, *loosely*, to pour out (wine, ale, etc.) into a drinking vessel.

1730 SWIFT *Poems, Market-hill* 23 Attend him daily as their chief, Decant his wine, and carve his beef. **1789** MRS. PIOZZI *Journ. France* II. 35 Some of their wine already decanted for use. **1815** SCOTT *Guy M.* xxii, A sign, where a tankard of ale voluntarily decanted itself into a tumbler. **1873** MRS. ALEXANDER *The Wooing o't* ix, Claret .. ah, you decant it, that is a good sign.

c. *transf.* To pour or empty out (as from or into a decanter).

1742 YOUNG *Nt. Th.* iii. 339 O'er our palates to decant Another vintage? **1823** *Blackw. Mag.* XIV. 586 He .. used to have eighty pails of water decanted over him daily. **1871** M. COLLINS *Mrq. & Merch.* II. vi. 162 All the vegetables in the world are decanted into Covent Garden. **1915** J. BUCHAN *39 Steps* vii. 171, I was decanted at Crewe .. and had to wait till six to get a train for Birmingham. **1925** WODEHOUSE *Carry On, Jeeves!* ii. 46 The nurse .. got up with the baby and decanted it into a perambulator. **1959** T. S. ELIOT *Elder Statesman* II. 47 Let's hope this [conversation] was merely the concoction Which she decants for every newcomer.

Hence **de'canted** *ppl. a.*

1788 CAVENDISH in *Phil. Trans.* LXXVIII. 169 The decanted and undecanted parts. **1793** BEDDOES *Sea Scurvy* 91 The decanted water is to be boiled down.

†**de'cant,** *v.*[2] *Obs.* [ad. L. *dēcantā-re*: see next.] = DECANTATE *v.* Hence **de'canted** *ppl. a.*

[**1546** O. JOHNSON in Ellis *Orig. Lett.* II. II. 176 Dr. Crome's canting, recanting, decanting, or rather double canting.] **1674** BLOUNT *Glossogr.* (ed. 4), *Decant*, to report or speak often, to sing, to enchant. **1711** FORBES in M. P. Brown *Suppl. Dec.* (1824) V. 79 Therefore this decanted notion, of a popular action, can never found a title in this country.

† **de'cantate**, *pa. pple. Obs.* [ad. L. *dēcantāt-us*, pa. pple. of *dēcantāre*: see next.] Decantated.
1620 E. BLOUNT *Horae Subs.* 195 Not to reiterate the so many and so much decantate vtilities and praises of History. **1675** BAXTER *Cath. Theol.* II. I. 10 Augustines saying so much decantate by Dr. Twisse and others.

† **de'cantate**, *v. Obs.* [f. ppl. stem of L. *dēcantāre* to sing off, repeat in singing, sing or chant over and over again, f. DE- I. 3 + *cantāre* to sing.]
1. *trans.* To sing or say over and over again; to repeat often.
1542 BECON *Pathw. Prayer* Early Wks. (1843) 182 Not able sufficiently to decantate, sing, and set forth his praises. **1611** CORYAT *Crudities* 99 The very Elysian fieldes, so much decantated and celebrated by the Verses of Poets. **1650** R. HOLLINGWORTH *Usurped Powers* 14 That late so much decantated Aphorisme, All Power.. is from the People.
2. *intr.* To sing or speak often.
1659 GAUDEN *Tears of Church* 99 These men.. impertinently decantate against the Ceremonies of the Church.

decantation (diːkæn'teɪʃən). [ad. med.L. *dēcanthātio*, in Fr. *décantation*, n. of action f. DECANT *v.*[1]] The action of decanting; *esp.* of pouring off a liquid clear from a precipitate or deposit.
1641 FRENCH *Distill.* i. (1651) 9 *Decantation*, is the pouring off of any liquor which hath a setling, by inclination. **1657** G. STARKEY *Helmont's Vind.* 196 This [sedimen] to be severed from the other juyce by decantation, and dried. **1758** *Elaboratory* 377 The earth.. will.. form a sediment, that makes a decantation necessary. **1837** HOWITT *Rur. Life* VI. ii. (1862) 217 Inviting sounds of scraping plate and decantation. **1883** *Hardwich's Photogr. Chem.* 23 Decantation, is allowing the precipitate to fall by its own weight to the bottom of the liquid, and then pouring the latter off.

decanter (dɪ'kæntə(r)). [f. DECANT *v.*[1] + -ER.]
1. One who decants.
1758 DYCHE, *Decanter*, one that pours or racks off liquor from the lees into other vessels. **1828** in WEBSTER; and in mod. Dicts.
2. A vessel used for decanting or receiving decanted liquors: *spec.* a bottle of clear flint or cut glass, with a stopper, in which wine is brought to the table, and from which the glasses are filled.
[The Dictionaries have variously explained the word from the etymological point of view:
1715 KERSEY, *Decanter*, a Bottle made of clear Flint-Glass for the holding of Wine, etc. to be pour'd off into a Drinking-Glass. **1755** JOHNSON, *Decanter*, a glass vessel made for pouring off liquor clear from the lees. **1775** ASH, *Decanter*, the vessel that contains the liquor after it has been decanted. **1818** TODD, *Decanter*, a glass vessel made for receiving liquor clear from the lees.]
1712 *Lond. Gaz.* No. 5041/3 A pair of Silver Decanters of 20 Guineas value. **1713** ADDISON *Guardian* No. 162 ¶5 The Barmecide.. then filled both their glasses out of an empty decanter. **1725** DE FOE *Voy. round World* (1840) 237 We had .. water in large silver decanters, that held, at least, five quarts apiece; these stood in our chamber. **1823** J. BADCOCK *Dom. Amusem.* 44 Keep this liquor in a glass decanter well stopped. **1849** LYTTON *Caxtons* 46 In virtue of my growing years, and my promise to abstain from the decanters. **1862** G. MACDONALD *D. Elginbrod* I. 40 Away she went with a jug, commonly called a decanter, in her hand. **1870** DICKENS *E. Drood* ii, A dish of walnuts and a decanter of rich-coloured sherry are placed upon the table.
Hence **de'canter** *v. nonce-wd.*, to put wine in a decanter.
1825 C. M. WESTMACOTT *Eng. Spy* II. 117 While the wine was decantering. **1885** *Punch* 16 May 230/2 They're catering and de-cantering.

decantherous, decapartite, -petalous, -phyllous: see DECA- I.

decapacitation (diːkəpæsɪ'teɪʃən). *Physiol.* [f. DE- II. 1 + CAPACITATION b.] The process of removing the effects of capacitation; the action of decapacitating a spermatozoon.
1961 *Federation Proc.* XX. I. i. 418/2 (*heading*) A study of the decapacitation factor present in rabbit seminal plasma. **1969** *New Scientist* 31 July 234/1 Such sperm were said to have suffered decapacitation. **1970** *Nature* 11 July 182/2 To determine whether these compounds would behave like 'decapacitation factor' from seminal plasma, that is whether they would be absorbed by sperm and reverse the capacitated state, the following experiment was carried out.
So **deca'pacitate** *v. trans.*, to deprive (a spermatozoon) of its ability to penetrate the *zona pellucida* of the ovum which it gains by capacitation; **deca'pacitated** *ppl. a.*
1964 T. MANN *Biochem. Semen* (ed. 2) ii. 32 There is some evidence.. that capacitated rabbit spermatozoa brought in contact with seminal plasma can be de-capacitated. **1970** *Nature* 11 July 182/2 We cannot say whether recapacitation represents the recovery of activity by decapacitated spermatozoa, or the activation of sperm not capacitated in the first place.

deca'pillated, *ppl. a. rare.*—[0] [f. pa. pple. of late or med.L. *dēcapillāre* to cut off the hair, f. DE- I. 6 + *capill-us* hair of the head.]
1727 BAILEY vol. II, *Decapillated*, having the Hair pulled or fallen off.

deca'pillatory, *a. nonce-wd.* [f. as prec.: see -ORY.] Pertaining to the removal of hair from the head or face.
1839 *New Monthly Mag.* LVI. 30 A primitive array of decapillatory conveniences or rather necessaries.

de'capitable, *a. rare.* [f. late or med.L. *dēcapitāre* to DECAPITATE + -ABLE.] That can be decapitated.
1843 CARLYLE *Past & Pr.* (1858) 198 Thou,—not even 'natural'; decapitable.

decapitalize (dɪ'kæpɪtəlaɪz), *v.* [f. DE- II. 1 + CAPITAL + -IZE.] *trans.* To reduce from the rank or position of a capital city. Hence **decapitali'zation**.
1871 *Daily News* 13 Apr. 5 Disarm Paris—bind her hand and foot—decapitalise her. **1889** *The Voice* (N.Y.) 26 Dec., Nor is it probable that decapitalization can be enforced by either sentiment or patriotism.

decapitate (dɪ'kæpɪteɪt), *v.* [f. F. *décapiter* (1320 in Hatzf.), also *desc-* (14th c.), = Pr. *de-*, *descapitar*, It. *decapitare*, late or med.L. *dēcapitāre*, f. DE- I. 6 + *caput*, *capit-* head. See -ATE[3].]
1. *trans.* To cut off the head of (a man or animal); to behead, kill by beheading. Also, to poll a tree, etc.
1611 COTGR., *Decapiter, Descapiter*, to decapitate, or behead. **1661** *Arnway's Tablet* Advt. (T.), Charles the First ..murdered, and decapitated before his own door at Whitehall. **1776** *Evelyn's Sylva* I. vii. §2. 154 Hedgerow ashes may the oftener be decapitated, and will show their heads again sooner than other trees so used. **1867** SMILES *Huguenots Eng.* iii. (1880) 50 They decapitated beautiful statues of stone, it is true; but the Guises had decapitated the living men. **1871** MORLEY *Voltaire* (1886) 340 In a time when you are not imprisoned or hung or decapitated for holding unpopular opinions.
b. *Math.* In the symbolical method of calculating seminvariants: To remove the highest number of the symbol.
1884 CAYLEY in *Amer. Jrnl. Math.* VII. I. 9 In every case we decapitate the symbol by striking out the highest number.
2. *U.S. politics.* To dismiss summarily from office.
1872 *Daily Tel.* 5 Jan., At the commencement of any fresh Presidency, hundreds of Democratic *employés* have their heads cut off to make room for Republicans who, in their turn, will be decapitated when the Democrats get the upper hand again. **1889** in FARMER *Americanisms* s.v.
Hence **de'capitated** *ppl. a.*, **de'capitating** *vbl. sb.* and *ppl. a.*
1796 *Ess. by Soc. of Gentlem. Exeter* 228 A very antient decapitated pillar. **1874** CARPENTER *Ment. Phys.* I. ii. §67 A decapitated Frog.. remains at rest until it is touched. **1827** STEUART *Planter's G.* (1828) 76 The decapitating of them [trees] is utterly destructive of their health and growth. **1890** *Athenæum* 8 Mar. 310/1 The suppression of piracy and decapitating expeditions.

decapitation (dɪkæpɪ'teɪʃən). [a. F. *décapitation* = med.L. *dēcapitātion-em*, n. of action f. *dēcapitāre*: see prec.]
1. The action of decapitating; the fact of being decapitated.
1650 ARNWAY *Alarum, etc.* (1661) 76 (T.) His decapitation for the clear truth of God. *a* **1794** SIR W. JONES *Suhridbheda* (R.), It is better to lose life by decapitation, than to desert a prince. **1839** JAMES *Louis XIV*, IV. 355 The punishment for high treason committed by a person of noble family.. was decapitation.
b. *Obstetr. Med.* of the fœtus.
1876 LEISHMAN *Midwifery* xxx. (ed. 2) 565.
c. *Math.* (See DECAPITATE *v.* 1 b.)
1884 CAYLEY in *Amer. Jrnl. Math.* VII. I. 10 By decapitation we always diminish the weight, but we do not diminish the degree.
2. *Zool.* The spontaneous division and detachment of the hydranths of tubularian Hydrozoa when mature. (*Syd. Soc. Lex.* 1882.)
3. *U.S. politics.* Summary dismissal from office.
1869 *N.Y. Herald* 5 Aug. (Farmer), The clerks in the Treasury Department begin to feel anxious, as the work of decapitation will soon make an end of them also. **1885** H. DAVIS *Amer. Const.* 35, I have already referred to Jackson's wholesale decapitation of the Federal officials upon his accession to the Presidency.

decapitator (dɪ'kæpɪteɪtə(r)). [f. DECAPITATE + -OR, after L. type.]
1. One who decapitates.
1820 *Examiner* No. 630. 290/1 Disgust at the decapitators and pity for the beheaded. **1892** *Columbus* (Ohio) *Dispatch* 2 Feb., Mr. S. will be remembered as the official decapitator of fourth-class postmasters under President Cleveland.
2. *Med.* An obstetric instrument for decapitation of the fœtus.
1841 F. H. RAMSBOTHAM *Obstetr. Med.* (1851) 371. **1882** in *Syd. Soc. Lex.*

‖**decapité** (dɪ'kæpɪte), *a. Her.* [F. *décapité*, decapitated.] (See quot.)
1727 BAILEY vol. II, *Decapité* (in Heraldry) signifies that the Beast has the Head cut off smooth, and is different from *erazed*.

decaploid ('dɛkəplɔɪd), *a. Biol.* [f. DECA- + -PLOID.] (See quot. 1940.)
1932 SANSOME & PHILP *Recent Advances in Plant Genetics* v. 165 In the first case the species with the highest chromosome number has ten sets as the basic number of the genus (decaploid). **1940** *Chambers's Techn. Dict.* 227/2 *Decaploid*, having ten times the haploid number of chromosomes. **1946** *Ann. Reg. 1945* 351 In the U.S.S.R. Zhebrak has worked on the properties of.. decaploid wheats with seventy chromosomes. **1946** *Nature* 17 Aug. 239/2 Since the basic haploid number of *Artemia salina* is known to be 21, the present race must be considered as decaploid with a slight augmentation of the number of 105 tetrads.

decapod ('dɛkəpɒd). *Zool.* [a. F. *décapode* (Latreille 1806), ad. mod.L. *Decapoda*: see next.]
A. *sb.* **1.** A member of the *Decapoda*; a ten-footed crustacean; also, a ten-armed cephalopod; in *pl.* = DECAPODA.
1835-6 TODD *Cycl. Anat.* I. 520/2 The Decapods are.. characterized by having a pair of fins attached to the mantle. **1885** C. F. HOLDER *Marvels Anim. Life* 169 I have never succeeded in capturing one of these beautiful decapods [*Spirula*] alive.
2. A heavy-freight locomotive with ten driving wheels originating in the United States. Also *attrib.*
1888 *Scribner's Mag.* Aug. 183 Consolidation and decapod types of engines, which have four and five pairs of driving-wheels. **1903** *Westm. Gaz.* 25 Feb. 5/2 'Decapod'! New Hustling Locomotive for G.E.R. **1906** *Daily Mail* 17 Dec. 5/7 Messrs. Robert Stephenson and Co. of Darlington have just completed three.. huge 'decapod' locomotives. **1947** L. M. BEEBE *Mixed Train Daily* 276 Decapods and other classifications with 250-pound engine pressure.
B. *adj.* Belonging to the *Decapoda*.
1835 KIRBY *Hab. & Inst. Anim.* II. xv. 37 In most of the Decapod Crustaceans the anterior legs are become strictly arms. **1847** CARPENTER *Zool.* §892 The Decapod family [of Cephalopods].

‖**Decapoda** (dɪ'kæpədə), *sb. pl. Zool.* [mod.L. (Latreille 1806), prop. adj. pl. neuter sc. *animalia*, a. Gr. δεκάποδα, neut. pl. of δεκάπους ten-footed.]
1. The highest order of *Crustacea*, having ten feet or legs; it includes the lobster, crab, crayfish, shrimp, etc.
[**1806** LATREILLE *Gen. Crust. et Ins.* I. 9 Crustaceorum Distributio generalis.. Legio Secunda Malacostraca.. Ordo I. Decapoda, *Décapodes*.] **1878** BELL *Gegenbauer's Comp. Anat.* 242 In most of the Decapoda, the number of gills is greatly increased.
2. The ten-armed *Cephalopoda* (order *Dibranchiata*), distinguished from the *Octopoda*. Called also *Decacera*.
1851 RICHARDSON *Geol.* viii. 254 The 10-armed cephalopods, called *decapoda*.
Hence **de'capodal** *a.*; **de'capodan** *a.* and *sb.*; **de'capodous** *a.*; **deca'podiform** *a.*, having the form or shape of a decapod crustacean.
1852 DANA *Crust.* II. 1528 The two types, the Decapodan and Tetradecapodan. **1835-6** TODD *Cycl. Anat.* I. 525/2 The locomotive appendages of the mantle in the Decapodous Cephalopods. **1870** ROLLESTON *Anim. Life* 101 The Decapodous Crustaceans.

decapsulate (diː'kæpsjuːleɪt), *v. Surg.* [f. DE- II. 1 + CAPSULE *sb.* + -ATE[3].] *trans.* To remove the capsule of. So **decapsu'lation**, the removal of a capsule.
1907 *Practitioner* Oct. 471 The decapsulation of the normal healthy kidney. *Ibid.* Dec. 778 The renal artery of a cat, whose corresponding kidney had been decapsulated and fixed two months previously. **1962** H. L. KERN et al. in A. Pirie *Lens Metabolism Rel. Cataract* 386 The lenses were either decapsulated or mashed in the culture tubes. **1963** J. P. MERRILL in Strauss & Welt *Dis. Kidney* xiii. 457/1 Decapsulation of the kidney is of little value after acute renal failure has been present for several days.

decapterygious: see DECA- *prefix* I.

† **de'capulate,** *v. Obs.*—[0] [f. L. **dēcapulāre*, f. *dē-* away + *capulāre* to pour off (f. *capula* small vessel).]
1623 COCKERAM, *Decapulate*, to poure out from one thing to another. **1727** in BAILEY vol. II.
Hence † **decapu'lation.**
1681 tr. *Willis' Rem. Med. Wks.* Vocab., *Decapulation*, a pouring off.

de'carbonate, *v. rare.* [Cf. F. *décarbonater* and CARBONATE.] = DECARBONIZE.
1831 J. HOLLAND *Manuf. Metal* I. 270 They [forks, common snuffers, etc.] are annealed, or, in other words, decarbonated in the requisite degree. **1882** *Syd. Soc. Lex.*, *Decarbonated*, an old term applied to an oxide, such as quicklime, which has been formed by expelling the carbonic acid from a carbonate of the metal.

decarboni'zation. [f. next: see -ATION.] **a.** The action or process of decarbonizing.
1831 J. HOLLAND *Manuf. Metal* I. 276 To subject the cast steel.. to the process of decarbonisation. **1835-6** TODD *Cycl.*

Anat. I. 428/2 Blood rendered black by defective decarbonization.

b. Removal of carbon deposit from inside an internal combustion engine.

1912 *Motor Manual* (ed. 14) vi. 232 Certain preparations in liquid form are sold for which it is claimed that, when injected in the cylinders, decarbonisation and thorough cleansing is effected.

decarbonize (dɪ'kɑːbənaɪz), *v.* [f. DE- II. 1 + CARBONIZE.] **a.** *trans.* To deprive of its carbon or carbonic acid.

1825 E. TURRELL in *Philos. Mag.* LXV. 421 Engravings upon decarbonized steel plates. **1836–9** TODD *Cycl. Anat.* II. 493/2 The liver is..the true decarbonising organ in the animal kingdom. **1876** HARLEY *Mat. Med.* 197 In Bessemer's process, liquid crude iron is decarbonised by forcing air through it by machinery.

b. To remove carbon deposit from (an internal combustion engine). Also *absol.*

1915 R. D. PRICE *U.S. Patent 1,148,403*, Decarbonizing compound... My invention relates to a compound for use in removing the carbon deposits from the cylinders of gasolene engines and like internal combustion motors... I provide a decarbonizing composition consisting of the following ingredients. **1916** R. T. NICHOLSON *Book of Ford* vii. 93 Decarbonizing tools are sold, which can be inserted through the sparking-plug holes, and used to scrape the carbon out thus. *Ibid.*, Have nothing to do with chemical decarbonizing processes. **1925** *Morris Owner's Manual* x. 70 Materials required—for decarbonizing only—are the standard tool kit and a bottle of gold size. *Ibid.*, The head has to be lifted to decarbonize. *Ibid.* 71 When decarbonizing the Morris engine. **1930** *Engineering* 10 Jan. 44/1 This engine can be decarbonised and the valves ground in in less than an hour. **1967** E. RUDINGER *Consumer's Car Gloss.* (ed. 2) 30 Decarbonising, that is, scraping off the carbon..from the cylinder head and pistons.

Hence **de'carbonized** *ppl. a.*, **de'carbonizing** *vbl. sb.* and *ppl. a.* (see above).

decarbonizer (diː'kɑːbənaɪzə(r)). [f. DECARBONIZE *v.* + -ER[1].] One who or that which decarbonizes; *spec.* see quot. 1921.

1890 in WEBSTER. **1921** *Dict. Occup. Terms* (1927) §449 *Decarboniser* (sugar refining); attends a number of steam-heated cylinders..in which animal charcoal is decarbonised after revivification in char kiln.

decarboxylase (diːkɑː'bɒksɪleɪz, -eɪs). *Biochem.* [f. DE- + CARBOXYL + -ASE.] Any enzyme which effects decarboxylation.

1940 E. F. GALE in *Biochem. Jrnl.* XXXIV. 399 When the organism is grown on the surface of broth agar, it has negligible decarboxylase activity. *Ibid.* 411 The production of decarboxylases may be the method by which the organism extends its range of existence, utilizing amino-acid decarboxylation when other substrates and methods of attack are no longer available. **1947** *Sci. News* IV. 64 The particular enzyme, containing B1, was called pyruvic oxidase, sometimes decarboxylase.

decarboxylate (diːkɑː'bɒksɪleɪt), *v.* *Chem.* [Back-formation from next.] **a.** *trans.* To remove a carboxyl group from. **b.** *intr.* To lose a carboxyl group, to undergo decarboxylation. Hence **decar'boxylated**, **decar'boxylating** *ppl. adjs.*

1922 *Jrnl. Biol. Chem.* L. 132 Are all strains of colon bacilli capable of decarboxylating histidine in our standard medium? **1930** *Biochem. Jrnl.* XXIV. 262 It is necessary to employ a decarboxylating reagent. **1946** *Nature* 27 July 132/1 The carboxyl group..is very unstable and in the presence of alkali readily loses carbon dioxide, forming a decarboxylated compound. **1959** A. ALBERT *Heterocyclic Chem.* vii. 269 Dehydracetic acid undergoes ring-opening to aceto-acetylacetone-3-carboxylic acid: this decarboxylates to acetoacetylacetone which cyclizes to 2:6-dimethyl-γ-pyrone. **1962** S. G. WALEY in A. Pirie *Lens Metabolism Rel. Cataract* 354 Only certain carboxylic acids ..decarboxylate readily non-enzymatically. **1964** W. G. SMITH *Allergy & Tissue Metabolism* iii. 36 Mast cells can decarboxylate histidine at an appreciable rate.

decarboxylation (ˌdiːkɑːbɒksɪ'leɪʃən). *Chem.* [f. DE- II. 1 + CARBOXYL + -ATION.] The removal of a carboxyl group.

1922 *Jrnl. Biol. Chem.* L. 189 The decarboxylation of histidine is influenced by the presence of other amino-acids. **1940** [see DECARBOXYLASE]. **1956** *Nature* 18 Feb. 333/2 The very high initial values for production of carbon dioxide in nitrogen..may be due to rapid decarboxylation.

de'carburize, *v.* [Cf. F. *décarburer* and CARBURIZE.] = DECARBONIZE *v.* So **de'carburized** *ppl. a.*; **decarburi'zation**; **decarbu'ration**.

1856 W. FAIRBAIRN in *Encycl. Brit.* XII. 553/2 The crude iron is..decarburised by the action of a blast of air. *Ibid.* 553/1 Difficulties have attended the decarburisation of iron containing so much carbon. *Ibid.*, Converted into malleable iron..by decarburation in the refinery. **1881** J. REESE in *Metal World* No. 22. 344, I first decarburize and desiliconize the cast iron. **1880** W. C. ROBERTS *Introd. Metallurgy* 33 For determining the point at which decarburization has ceased in the Bessemer converter.

decarch, dek- ('dɛkɑːk), *sb.* *Gr. Hist.* [ad. Gr. δεκάρχ-ης or *δέκαρχος, f. δέκα ten + -αρχης, -αρχος ruler.] One of a ruling body of ten.

1656 BLOUNT *Glossogr.*, *Decarck*, the same with *Dearck* ['a Captain or Governor of ten']. **1849** GROTE *Greece* II. lxxii. (1862) VI. 350 As at Athens..the Dekarchs would begin by putting to death notorious political opponents.

decarch, dek- ('dɛkɑːk), *a.* *Bot.* [f. Gr. δέκα ten + ἀρχή beginning, origin.] Proceeding from ten distinct points of origin: said of the primary xylem (or wood) of the root.

1884 BOWER & SCOTT *De Bary's Phaner.* 350 In the two species mentioned [*Lycopodium clavatum, Alpinum*] the xylem is hexarch to dekarch, very often heptarch.

decarchy, dek- ('dɛkəkɪ). *Gr. Hist.* [ad. Gr. δεκαρχία: see prec. sb.] = DECADARCHY.

a **1638** MEDE *Ep. Dr. Meddus* Wks. IV. 781 The Beast's Horns, that is, the 'eyed' and 'mouthed' Horn with that Decarchy of Horns subject to him. **1838** THIRLWALL *Greece* IV. 155 A council of ten (a decarchy, as it was commonly called) nominated by himself, was the ordinary substitute for all the ancient forms of polity. **1849** GROTE *Greece* II. lxv, The enormities perpetrated by the Thirty at Athens and by the Lysandrian dekarchies in the other cities.

†**de'card**, *v.* *Obs.* [f. DE- II. 2 + CARD; cf. OF. *descarter* and DE- I. 6.] = DISCARD.

1. *trans.* To throw away or reject (a card) from the hand; also *absol.* Hence **de'carded** *ppl. a.*

c **1550** *Manif. Detect. Diceplay* C viij a, Stealing the stocke of the decarded cardes. **1608** MACHIN *Dumb Knt.* in Hazl. *Dodsley* X. 187 Can you decard, madam?

2. *gen.* To reject, set aside, get rid of, dismiss.

1605 BACON *Adv. Learn.* II. viii. §5. 34 That..they bee from thenceforth omitted, decarded, and not continued. **1621** FLETCHER *Pilgrim* IV. ii. (ed. 1647) You cannot sir; you have cast those by; decarded 'em.

decardinalize, decasualize: see DE- II. 1.

decare: see DECA- *prefix* 2.

decarnate (dɪ'kɑːnət), *a.* [ad. L. *dēcarnātus* divested or stripped of flesh, f. DE- prep. I. 6 + *carn-em* flesh.] Divested of incarnation, no longer incarnate. So **decarnated** *ppl. a.*

1865 *Reader* 16 Dec., Logic Comte never liked, but it became to him at last a sort of devil decarnated. **1886** *Ch. Times* 42/1 The idea..that the Incarnate Word will ever become decarnate.

†**decar'nation.** *Obs.* [f. as prec. with reference to *incarnation.*] Deliverance from the flesh or from carnality.

1648 W. MOUNTAGUE *Devout Ep.* II. i. 13 Gods incarnation inableth man for his own decarnation, as I may say, and devesture of carnality.

†**decart**, *v.* *Sc.* *Obs.* Also decairt. [a. OF. *descarter*, f. *des-*, *de-* (DE- I. 6) + *carte* CARD.] = DECARD, DISCARD.

a **1572** KNOX *Hist. Ref.* Wks. 1846 I. 262 The articles of his beleve war; 'I Referr: Decarte yow' [etc.]. *a* **1605** MONTGOMERIE *Misc. Poems* xxxii. 87 3our vter ansueir courteously I crave, Quhom 3e will keep, or vhom 3e will decairt. **1641** R. BAILLIE *Lett. & Jrnls.* (1841) I. 303 He hes such a hand among the ministris and others that it was not thought meet to decairt him.

decart *v.*, to turn out of a cart: see DE- II. 2.

decartel(l)ization (diːˌkɑːtəlaɪ'zeɪʃən). [f. DE- + CARTEL(L)IZATION.] The abolition of the system of trade cartels. Hence **de'cartellizer**, one who favours decartellization.

1947 *Times* 20 Oct. 5/6 At least three senior American officials have resigned from the decartellization branch. *Ibid.* 5/7 The socializers and decartellizers may expect to be displaced by experts in management and production. **1948** *Hansard* CCCCXLV. 338 The functions of the Division are supervisory and cover disarmament, decartelisation and the revival of peaceful industry. **1955** *Times* 4 July 9/7 Whereas only lately..decartelization in Germany was the order of the day, it is now again cartelization.

†**de'cas.** *Obs.* *rare*[−1]. [a. OF. **decas*, ad. med.L. *dēcāsus* falling down, decay.] Decay, ruin.

1393 GOWER *Conf.* I. 32 The walle and al the citee withinne Stant in ruine and in decas [*rime* was].

decasemic, -sepalous, -spermal, -spermous: see DECA- 1.

†**de'cass**, *v.* *Obs.* *rare.* [a. OF. *decasser*, *desquasser* to break or beat down, f. *de-*, *des-* (DE- I. 1,3) + *casser* to break: see CASS *v.*] *trans.* To discharge, dismiss, cashier.

1579 FENTON *Guicciard.* 1170 They decassed hym from his charge.

decastellate (dɪ'kæstəleɪt), *v.* *rare.* [f. med.L. *dēcastellāre*, f. DE- I. 6 + *castellāre* to CASTELLATE.] *trans.* To deprive of its castellation, take away the battlements of.

1880 A. TH. DRANE *Hist. St. Cath. Siena* 356 To sanction the dismantling, or rather decastellating of one of the fortresses.

decastere: see DECA- *prefix* 2.

decastich ('dɛkəstɪk). *rare.* [f. Gr. δέκα ten + στίχος verse.] A poem of ten lines.

[**1601** HOLLAND *Pliny* II. 402 This Decasticon.] *c* **1645** HOWELL *Lett.* 6 Oct. 1632 According to your friendly request, I send you this decastic. **1891** S. R. DRIVER *Introd. Lit. O.T.* viii. 376 A short poem (on the value of industry to the farmer), consisting of a decastich.

decastyle ('dɛkəstaɪl), *a.* *Arch.* [mod. ad. L. *decastȳlus*, a. Gr. δεκάστυλος having ten columns, f. δέκα ten + -στυλος column. Cf. F. *décastyle* (1694 in Hatzf.), *décastile* (1762 in Acad. Dict.).]

Consisting of ten columns; (of a building) having ten columns in front. Also *sb.* A portico or colonnade of ten columns.

1727–51 CHAMBERS *Cycl. Decastyle*, in the antient architecture, a building with an ordonnance of ten columns in front.—The temple of Jupiter Olympius was decastyle. *Ibid.* s.v. *Hypæthros*, Of *hypæthrons*, some were decastyle, others pycnostyle. **1727** BAILEY vol. II, *Decastyle*, that has 10 Pillers. **1832** W. WILKINS in *Philol. Museum* I. 543 We should have an octostyle and a hexastyle temple as illustrations of the hypæthral decastyle species.

decasualize (diː'kæzjuːəlaɪz), *v.* [f. DE- + CASUAL *a.* + -IZE.] *trans.* To remove the casual element from (labour). So **deˌcasuali'zation**, the abolition of casual labour.

1892 T. H. NUNN in *Toynbee Record* 30 There is being effected..a permanent decasualization of labour at the Docks..The casual docker [must] lose his work. **1907** *Ann. Rep. Universities' Settlement in E. London* 34 In its demand for nationalisation before means are taken to decasualise labour. **1910** *Fabian News* XXI. 16/2 Taxi-driver desires to decasualize his profession by acquiring regular clientèle. **1928** *Daily Tel.* 15 May 12/4 Bermondsey contains a large number of casual riverside labourers, whose decasualisation has been the steady aim of the Port authorities. **1961** *New Statesman* 5 May 698/2 The process of de-casualisation begun by Ernest Bevin. **1962** *Economist* 10 Feb. 497/1 Mr Cousins..spoke of the need to 'decasualise' labour relations in the docks.

decasyllabic (dɛkəsɪ'læbɪk), *a.* (*sb.*) [f. Gr. δέκα ten + SYLLABIC. Cf. F. *décasyllabique* (1752 in Hatzf.).] **A.** *adj.* Consisting of ten syllables. **B.** *sb.* A line of ten syllables.

a **1771** GRAY *Observ. Eng. Metre* Wks. 1843 V. 242 Spenser has also given an instance of the decasyllabic measure. **1837–9** HALLAM *Hist. Lit.* I. viii. §28 Every line is regularly and harmoniously decasyllabic. **1854** EMERSON *Lett. & Soc. Aims, Poet. & Imag.* Wks. (Bohn) III. 159 The decasyllabic quatrain. **1880** S. LANE-POOLE in *Macm. Mag.* No. 246. 498 Over four thousand lines of decasyllabics have not stifled his fervour.

decasyllable (dɛkə'sɪləb(ə)l), *sb.* and *a.* [f. Gr. δέκα ten + SYLLABLE. Cf. F. *décasyllabe* adj. and sb.] **A.** *sb.* A line of ten syllables. **B.** *adj.* Of ten syllables.

1837–9 HALLAM *Hist Lit.* I. viii. §28 The normal type, or decasyllable line. **1859** THACKERAY *Virgin.* lxxix, I had rather hear Mrs. Warrington's artless prattle than your declamation of Mr. Warrington's decasyllables. **1892** *Academy* 17 Sept. 230/2 The decasyllable couplet.

‖**deca'syllabon.** *Obs.* [a. assumed Gr. δεκασύλλαβον, neuter of -ος adj.: cf. prec. and Gr. δισύλλαβος, -ον, etc.] A ten-syllable verse.

1589 NASHE *Introd. Greene's Menaphon* (Arb.) 6 The spacious volubilitie of a drumming decasillabon.

†**deca'tessarad.** *Obs.* *nonce-wd.* [f. late Gr. δεκατέσσαρες = τέσσαρες καὶ δέκα fourteen + -AD.] A poem of 14 lines.

1600 J. MELVILL *Diary* (1842) 437 In memoriall wharoff this Decatessarad was maid.

decathlon (dɛ'kæθlən). [f. Gr. δέκα ten + ἆθλον contest.] In the modern Olympic games, a composite contest consisting of ten specific events. Also *attrib.* Hence **de'cathlete** *sb.*

1912 *Times* 16 July 13/1 The Decathlon was brought to a close to-day, the events to be decided being the pole jump, throwing the javelin..and 1,500 metres flat race. **1920** *Glasgow Herald* 23 Aug. 10 In the stadium proper most of the morning was given up to a succession of Decathlon events, including hurdles, throwing the discus, and pole jump. **1928** *Daily Tel.* 6 Nov. 19/4 The Springboks' Decathlon champion..broke down. **1968** *Evening Standard* 9 Aug. 30/5 Britain's leading decathlete. **1970** *Encycl. Brit.* VII. 154/2 Similar to the decathlon is the all-around championship of the U.S. Amateur Athletic Union.

deca'tholicize, *v.* [DE- II. 6 + CATHOLICIZE.] *trans.* To deprive of catholicity or Catholicism; to divest of its catholic character.

1794 *Barruel's Hist. Clergy Fr. Rev.* (1795) 63 But then France would not have been decatholicised. **1867** *Ch. Times* 18 May 175/2 Means by which the Book of Common Prayer may be decatholicised. **1889** *Catholic Union Gaz.* 27 *note*, If you wish to regenerate France, first decatholicise her.

decatise ('dɛkətaɪz), *v.* [f. Fr. *décatir* to sponge or steam (cloth).] *trans.* To subject (cloth) to the action of steam in order to give it a permanent lustre or finish. Hence **'decatising** *vbl. sb.*

1907 *Textile Mercury* 16 Feb. 124/2 Fabrics of good quality should be decatised before dyeing. **1921** *Dict. Occup. Terms* (1927) §384 Decatising machine minder. **1963** A. J. HALL *Textile Sci.* v. 224 A machine for decatising wool fabrics.

decatyl ('dɛkətɪl). *Chem.* [f. Gr. δέκατ-ος tenth + -YL.] A synonym of DECYL, the univalent hydrocarbon radical $C_{10}H_{21}$.

1869 ROSCOE *Elem. Chem.* 333 We..consider this body as decatyl hydride, and as not belonging to the amyl group.

decaudate (dɪˈkɔːdeɪt), *v.* [f. DE- II. 1 + L. *cauda* tail + -ATE[3].] *trans.* To deprive of the tail.

1864 *N. & Q.* V. 165 The P. was originally an R. which has had the misfortune to be dacaudated.

So **deˈcaudalize** *v. nonce-wd.*

1840 *New Monthly Mag.* LVIII. 273 Puss..was decaudalized.

decaudation (diːkɔːˈdeɪʃən). [f. DECAUDATE *v.* + -ATION.] Removal of the tail or 'tails'.

1897 *19th Cent.* May 805 Decaudation with mutilation is seen in *bike* for *bicycle*. **1927** *Daily Tel.* 9 Aug. 8/5 The decaudation and blanching and unstiffening of the waiter are another phase of the transformation which has abolished the frock-coat and the silk hat and women's hair.

Decauville (dəˈkəʊvɪl). The surname of P. *Decauville* (1846–1922), French engineer, used *attrib.* or alone to designate a type of narrow-gauge railway invented by him.

1899 W. H. COLE *Light Railways* xiv. 245 The 2ft. rolling-stock on a French 'Decauville' line. *a* **1935** T. E. LAWRENCE *Mint* (1955) I. xxix. 98 We ran eight lorry loads of the Decauville rails. **1958** F. STARK *Alexander's Path* ix. 125 The little decauville running down from the sheds.

decay (dɪˈkeɪ), *sb.* For forms see the verb. [f. DECAY *v.* Cf. med.L. *decheium* in Du Cange.]

1. a. The process of falling off from a prosperous or thriving condition; progressive decline; the condition of one who has thus fallen off or declined.

c **1460** FORTESCUE *Abs. & Lim. Mon.* xvi, The estate off þe Romans..hath ffallen alwey sythyn, into suche decay, þat nowe [etc.]. **1558** BP. WATSON *Sev. Sacram.* i. 3 He repayreth all our decaies in grace. **1587** *Mirr. Mag., Albanact* lxvi, Discord brings all kingdomes to decay. **1611** BIBLE *Lev.* xxv. 35 If thy brother bee waxen poore, and fallen in decay with thee. **1718** HICKES & NELSON *J. Kettlewell* III. §103. 439 Perceiving..a very Sensible Decay of his Spirits. **1856** FROUDE *Hist. Eng.* (1858) I. i. 9 At present, the decay of a town implies the decay of the trade of the town. **1874** GREEN *Short Hist.* v. §3. 228 The decay of the University of Paris..had transferred her intellectual supremacy to Oxford.

†**b.** Formerly sometimes = Downfall, destruction, ruin; *poet.* fall, death. *Obs.*

1535 COVERDALE *Ps.* cv[i]. 36 They worshipped their ymages, which turned to their owne decaye. **1590** SPENSER *F.Q.* I. vi. 48 In hope to bring her to her last decay. *Ibid.* II. ix. 12 Fly fast, and save yourselves from neare decay. **1593** SHAKS. *Lucr.* 516 To kill thine honour with thy lives decaie. **1595** —— *John* IV. iii. 154. *a* **1724** *Battle of Harlaw* xxv. in Ramsay *Evergreen*, Grit Dolour was for his Decay, That sae unhappylie was slain.

2. †**a.** Falling off (in quantity, volume, intensity, etc.); dwindling, decrease. *Obs.*

1636 BLUNT *Voy. Levant* (1637) 46 The opinion of our decay in stature from our forefathers. **1662** STILLINGFL. *Orig. Sacr.* III. iv. §6 The decay of many of them [springs] in hot and dry weather. **1669** A. BROWNE *Ars Pict.* (1675) 39 The shadows..being caused by the decay of the light. **1691** T. H[ALE] *Acc. New Invent.* p. lxxxiv, Complaints were brought to the Council-Board, of the great Decay of that River. **1816** J. SMITH *Panorama Sc. & Art* II. 62 The decay of sound has been supposed by some to be nearly in the direct ratio of the distances.

b. *Physics.* The gradual decrease in the radioactivity of a substance; hence, the spontaneous transformation of a single atomic nucleus or elementary particle into one or more different nuclei or particles. Also *attrib.*

1897 RUTHERFORD in *Phil. Mag.* XLIV. 425 The intensity of the radiation varied widely, but in all cases the rate of decay was found to be in close agreement with theory. **1902** RUTHERFORD & ALLEN in *Phil. Mag.* IV. 708 The decay-curve for a copper wire exposed 210 minutes inside the laboratory. **1905** *Nature* 13 Apr. 574/1 Different samples gave for the half-period of decay from 52 to 55 seconds. **1931** G. GAMOW *Constitution of Atomic Nuclei* ii. 31 One of the most important characteristics of a decaying nucleus is its decay constant.., giving the probability of disintegration per unit time. **1938** R. W. LAWSON tr. *Hevesy & Paneth's Man. Radioactivity* (ed. 2) xxiii. 223 Uranium Z..may be a decay product of a uranium isotope other than ^{238}U. **1958** J. L. PERKIN in O. R. Frisch *Nucl. Handbk.* iii. 7 The decay of a nucleus via various excited levels of the final nucleus is shown diagrammatically. **1962** H. D. BUSH *Atomic & Nuclear Physics* iv. 81 The half-life of uranium I..is obviously too long to determine by measuring the decay of its activity. **1968** M. S. LIVINGSTON *Particle Physics* xi. 196 The most fundamental weak interaction is the decay of the neutron into a proton, an electron, and an antineutrino. **1969** *Times* 12 Mar. 4/7 The radioactive decay of uranium..has long been recognized as a means of fixing the ages of remote cosmological events.

c. A progressive diminution in the amplitude of an oscillation or vibration.

1906 J. A. FLEMING *Princ. Electr. Wave Telegr.* i. 15 Frictional resistance causes decay in the amplitude of the oscillations by dissipating their energy as heat. **1922** GLAZEBROOK *Dict. Appl. Physics* II. 111/1 The damping of the oscillations is determined by *b*..which is called the damping coefficient or the coefficient of decay. **1950** STEPHENS & BATE *Wave Motion & Sound* 357 This decay of amplitude is known as damping and the motion is referred to as damped harmonic motion. **1962** A. NISBETT *Technique Sound Studio* iii. 56 Some percussive instruments, such as tympani, continue to sound for some time, and have decay characteristics which are somewhat similar to that of reverberation.

3. a. Of material things: Wasting or wearing away, disintegration; dilapidation, ruinous condition.

1523 FITZHERB. *Surv.* 1 Those castelles..that be fallen in dekay and nat inhabyted. *c* **1600** SHAKS. *Sonn.* xiii. 9 Who lets so fair a house fall to decay? **1756–7** tr. *Keysler's Trav.* (1760) II. 248 That edifice, by length of time, fell to decay, and lay in ruins. **1839** KEIGHTLEY *Hist. Eng.* II. 41 The decay of these sacred edifices.

†**b.** *pl.* Dilapidations; *concr.* ruined remains, ruins, debris, detritus. (Rarely in *sing.*) *Obs.*

1582 in W. H. Turner *Select. Rec. Oxford* 427 The Bayliffs ..shall..make relation unto this howsse what the decayes are. **1615** G. SANDYS *Trav.* 176 Beyond are the decayes of a Church. **1632** LITHGOW *Trav.* v. 200 The decayes whereof being much semblable to..the stony heapes of Jericho. **1655** FULLER *Ch. Hist.* III. vi. §26. 82 Jehoida was careful to amend the decayes of the Temple. **1777** G. FORSTER *Voy. round World* I. 313 A vegetable mould, mixed with volcanic decays.

fig. **1605** SHAKS. *Lear* v. iii. 297 What comfort to this great decay may come Shall be appli'd. **1662** SOUTH *Serm.* I. ii. *Gen.* i. 27 And certainly that must needs have been very glorious the decayes of which are so admirable.

c. *fig.* The gradual 'wearing down' of words or phonetic elements in language.

1874 SAYCE *Compar. Philol.* i. 18 Contraction and decay may be carried so far as to become an idiosyncracy of a particular language. **1877** PAPILLON *Man. Comp. Philology* iv. 56 The principle of 'Phonetic Decay', which plays so large a part in the history of language.

4. a. Decline of the vital energy or faculties (through disease or old age); breaking up of the health and constitution; formerly also (with *pl.*), effect, mark, or sign of physical decay.

c **1600** SHAKS. *Sonn.* xi, Age and could decay. **1611** B. JONSON *Catiline* II. i, She has been a fine lady..and paints, and hides Her decays very well. **1720** WODROW *Corr.* (1843) II. 498 Notwithstanding my great age and decays, I am able to preach..in the largest meeting-house in Boston. **1752** JOHNSON *Rambler* No. 203 ¶12 In the pains of disease, and the languor of decay. **1860** HOOK *Lives Abps.* (1869) I. vii. 421 The archbishop..had begun to show symptoms of decay.

†**b.** *spec.* Consumption, phthisis; 'a decline'.

1725 N. ROBINSON *Th. Physick* 150 A perfect Hectic, which inseparably accompanies Wastes, Decays, and Consumptions. **1746** BERKELEY *Let. Tar-Water* §23 Dropsies, decays, and other maladies. **1818** SCOTT *Hrt. Midl.* xviii, Her son that she had left at hame weak of a decay.

5. The destructive decomposition or wasting of organic tissue; rotting.

1594 PLAT *Jewell-ho.* II. 42 One day, or two, before you feare the decay of your decoction, set the same on the fire. **1748** F. SMITH *Voy.* I. 138 Such Wood as is upon the Decay, but not yet become rotten. **1771** J. HUNTER *Hist. Teeth* 122 Fill the hole with lead, which prevents the pain and retards the decay. **1775** HARRIS *Philos. Arrangem.*, The body ceases to live, and the members soon pass into putrefaction and decay. **1860** RUSKIN *Mod. Paint.* V. VIII. i. 159 The decay of leaves. **1878** L. P. MEREDITH *Teeth* 115 The teeth will come together, and further decay will almost infallibly result.

†**6.** A cause of decay; the 'destruction' or 'ruin *of*' anything. *Obs.*

1563 *Homilies* II. x. Pt. i, Som worldly witted men think it a great decaye to the quiete and prudent gouernynge of their commonwelthes to geue eare to the simple and playne rules ..of our Sauiour. **1584** POWEL *Lloyd's Cambria* 21 This partition is the very decaie of great families. *c* **1600** SHAKS. *Sonn.* lxxx, My loue was my decay. **1674** WOOD *Life* (O.H.S) II. 300 The decay of study, and consequently of learning, are coffy houses. **1690** CHILD *Disc. Trade* (ed. 4) 235 Trade, to which the high rate of Usury is a great prejudice and decay.

†**7.** Failure of payment or rent; arrears. *Obs.* [med.L. *decasus redditus, decatum.*]

1546 in *Eng. Gilds* (1870) 199 The possessiones of the Guyld, wyth the decayes, ben yerly valued at [etc.]. *Ibid.*, Decayes and defautes of Rentes. **1546** *Mem. Ripon* (Surtees) III. 31 One Annuall Rent..in decay and not payde.

decay (dɪˈkeɪ), *v.* Forms: 5– decay; also 5–6 **dekay(e, dekey, 6–7 decaye, -aie.** [a. OF. *decair, dekair* (subj. pres. *decaie*), var. of *decaoir, dechaoir, decheoir*, now *déchoir* = Sp. *decaer*, Pg. *decahir*, It. *decadēre*, a Com. Rom. compound of *de-* down + *cadēre* = L. *cadĕre* to fall. The F. forms in *-eir, -oir* correspond to the *-ēre* type, those in *-ir* in OF. and Pg. have passed over to the *-īre* conjugation.]

I. *intr.*

1. a. To fall off (in quality or condition); to deteriorate or become impaired; to lose its characteristic quality, strength, or excellence; to be in a failing condition.

1494 FABYAN *Chron.* v. xcv. 69 The seruyce of God..by mean of yͤ Saxons was greatly decayde through all Brytayne. **1511–2** *Act 3 Hen. VIII*, c. 3 Preamb., Archerie..is right litell used, but dayly mynessheth, decayth and abateth. **1583** STUBBES *Anat. Abus.* II. (1882) 73 Whereby learning greatlie decaieth. **1602** ROWLANDS *Kind Gossips* (1609) 18 His loue to me now daily doth decay. **1677** YARRANTON *Eng. Improv.* 49 Common Honesty is necessary for Trade, and without it Trade will decay. **1728** POPE *Dunc.* I. 277 How Prologues into Prefaces decay. **1812** J. WILSON *Isle of Palms* III. 273 Entranced there the Lovers gaze Till every human fear decays.

b. To decline from prosperity or fortune.

1483 *Act 1 Rich. III*, c. 12 §1 The Artificers of this seid Realme..ben greatly empoveresshed and dailly dekeyn. **1483** CAXTON *Cato* H ij, It is seen selde the juste to dekaye ne to haue nede. **1535** COVERDALE *Prov.* xi. 11 When the iust are in wealth, the cite prospereth: but whan the vngodly haue the rule, it decayeth. **1663** PEPYS *Diary* 15 May, The Dutch decay there [in the East Indies] exceedingly. **1816** SCOTT *Old Mort.* i, Ancient..families..decayed into the humble vale of life.

2. †**a.** To fall off or decrease (in number, volume, amount, intensity, etc.); to dwindle away. *Obs.*

1489 *Act 4 Hen. VII*, c. 16 The which Isle is lately decayed of people. **1568** BIBLE (Bishops') *Job* xiv. 11 The fludde decayeth and dryeth vp. **1634** SIR T. HERBERT *Trav.* 168 It became a hard question, whether my spirits or Gold decayed faster. **1691** T. H[ALE] *Acc. New Invent.* p. xc, The Shipping and Number of our Seamen were decay'd about a third part. **1698** FRYER *Acc. E. Ind.* 67 The Water drank is usually Rain-water preserved in Tanks, which decaying, they are forced to dig Wells. **1725** POPE *Odyss.* XII. 237 Till, dying off, the distant sounds decay. *c* **1790** IMISON *Sch. Art.* I. 126 The candle will burn a minute; and then, having gradually decayed from the first instant, will go out.

b. Of an oscillation or vibration: gradually to decrease in amplitude, so that each swing is smaller than the one before. Also said of the amplitude of the oscillation.

1879 *Encycl. Brit.* VIII. 11/2 Sir W. Thomson investigated mathematically the discharge of a Leyden jar.. and predicted that under certain circumstances the discharge would consist of a series of decaying oscillations. **1906** J. A. FLEMING *Princ. Electr. Wave Telegr.* 573 A very important matter in connection with practical electric wave telegraphy is the rate at which the wave amplitude decays during the emission of a wave train from the antenna. **1927** I. B. CRANDALL *Theory of Vibr. Syst.* i. 8 The natural oscillations may be made to decay very rapidly, or to disappear altogether, if the damping factor is made very large. **1944** A. WOOD *Physics of Music* ii. 23 Sound-waves are carrying energy more rapidly away from the fork, and the vibrations therefore decay more rapidly. **1959** *Chambers's Encycl.* I. 375/1 The amplitude of the swing about the final true position decays exponentially with time.

c. *Physics.* Of radioactivity: gradually to diminish in intensity; of a substance: to suffer a gradual decrease in its radioactive power, to undergo nuclear disintegration. Hence, of a radioactive substance, an atomic nucleus, or an elementary particle: to change or disintegrate *into* one or more different substances, etc.

1900 RUTHERFORD in *Phil. Mag.* XLIX. 177 The intensity of the 'excited' radiation falls to half its value in about eleven hours, or one decays 660 times faster than the other. **1913** —— *Radioactive Substances* viii. 339 The active deposit.. decays *in situ* and this results in an apparent decrease of the activity. **1942** J. D. STRANATHAN '*Particles*' *Mod. Physics* viii. 326 The half life period *T* of a radioactive substance is defined as the time required for one half of the active material present at any time to decay. **1958** W. K. MANSFIELD *Elem. Nuclear Physics* iii. 21 It is found experimentally that the probability of an unstable nucleus, known as a radioactive nucleus, decaying within a given time is constant. **1962** H. D. BUSH *Atomic & Nuclear Physics* iv. 80 Uranium X does not decay into a stable product but is the parent of a chain of radioactive daughter products. **1968** M. S. LIVINGSTON *Particle Physics* iv. 72 In matter, when π^+ pions are slowed down by ionizing impacts, they decay into positive muons and muon neutrinos.

3. a. To fall into physical ruin; to waste away, wear out, become ruined.

1494 FABYAN *Chron.* III. lvi. 36 Aruiragus..with great dilygence Repayred Cyties and Townes before decayed. **1570–6** LAMBARDE *Peramb. Kent* (1826) 283 This house, by that time..was decaied, either by age, or flame, or bothe. **1635** MILTON *On Hobson* ii, Made of sphear metal, never to decay Until his revolution was at stay. **1694** *Coll. Sev. Late Voy.* (1711) I. 45 There was Water over the Salt, which began to decay with the Rain and Weather being on it. **1748** F. SMITH *Voy.* I. 51 The Ise being inseparable, as it was very little decayed.

b. To suffer decomposition; to rot.

1580 BARET *Alv.* D 178 That soone is ripe, doth soone decaie. **1737** POPE *Hor. Epist.* II. ii. 319 As winter fruits grow mild ere they decay. **1771** J. HUNTER *Hist. Teeth* 122 When an opening is made into the cavity of the Tooth, the inside begins to decay. **1851** CARPENTER *Man. Phys.* (ed. 2) 22 The parent-cell having arrived at its full development..dies and decays.

4. To fall off in vital energy; to lose health and strength (of body or faculties); also, to lose the bloom of youth and health.

1538 STARKEY *England* I. ii. 48 Wythout the wych hys helth long can not be maynteynyd; but, schortly, of necesstye hyt must dekay. **1655** CULPEPPER *Riverius* I. xi. 38 His Imagination began to decay. **1712–14** POPE *Rape Lock* v. 25 But since, alas! frail beauty must decay. **1795** SOUTHEY *Joan of Arc* VII. 337 Feel life itself with that false hope decay. **1875** JOWETT *Plato* (ed. 2) V. 20 An author whose original powers are beginning to decay.

II. *trans.*

†**5.** To cause to fall off or deteriorate. *Obs.*

1529 MORE *Comf. agst. Trib.* II. Wks. 1200/2 For feare of decaying the common wele, men are driuen to put malefactors to pain. **1565** JEWEL *Def. Apol.* (1611) 362 We haue decaied no mans Power or right. **1665** MANLEY *Grotius' Low C. Warres* 299 His last five years had much decayed his Reputation. **1691** LOCKE *Lower. Interest* Wks. 1727 II. 38 A High Interest decays Trade.

†**6.** To cause to fall off (in number, amount, etc.); to reduce, cause to dwindle. *Obs.*

1550 CROWLEY *Epigr.* 734 Yet can there nothynge My flocke more decaye, Then when hyrelynges suffer My shepe go astraye. **1600** HOLLAND *Livy* I. xlix. 35 a, When he had decaied the number of the nobles. *a* **1626** BACON *Max. & Uses Com. Law* iv. (1636) 23 If I do decay the game whereby there is no Deere.

†**7. a.** To waste or ruin physically; to disintegrate, dilapidate; to bring to decay or ruin. *Obs.*

1536 *Exhort. North* in Furniv. *Ballads from MSS.* I. 306 Downe stregth to the grownde Many are besy them [abbeys] to dekay. **1605** BACON *Adv. Learn.* I. viii. §6 (1873) 72 Palaces, temples, castles, cities, have been decayed and demolished. **1636** SIR H. BLOUNT *Voy. Levant* (1637) 46 Where there were any raine, it would settle..and decay the building. **1703** MOXON *Mech. Exerc.* 239 No time will impair or decay those Grey Kentish Bricks.

b. To destroy by decomposition; to rot.

1616 B. JONSON *Divell an Asse* IV. iii, [It] decayes the fore-teeth. **1626** BACON *Sylva* §995 To lay that which you cut off to putrefie, to see whether it will decay the rest of the stock. **1703** T. N. *City & C. Purchaser* 210 Lime and Wood are insociable, the former very much corroding and decaying the latter. **1893** MRS. A. ARNOLD in *Westm. Gaz.* 27 Feb. 9/2 Is it probable that a blooming girl would defile her breath, decay her teeth, and damage her complexion [by smoking]?

8. To cause (the body or faculties) to fail in vital energy, health, or beauty.

1540-54 CROKE *Ps.* (Percy Soc.) 24 Ther is no tyme can the decaye. **1568** E. TILNEY *Disc. Mariage* C j b, Wine..if it be abused..decaying womens bewtie. *a* **1668** DENHAM *Of Old Age* 217 'But Age', 'tis said, 'will memory decay'. **1713** ADDISON *Guardian* No. 120 ¶7 Almost every thing which corrupts the soul decays the body. **1718** LADY M. W. MONTAGU *Let. to C'tess of Mar* 10 Mar., She had the remains of a fine face..more decayed by sorrow than time.

decayable (dɪˈkeɪəb(ə)l), *a.* [f. DECAY *v.* + -ABLE. Cf. OF. *decheable.*] Capable of, or liable to, decay; perishable.

1617 MORYSON *Itin.* II. III. i. 243 Such victuals as are decaiable. **16..** T. ADAMS *Wks.* (1861-2) III. 111 (D.) Were His strength decayable with time there might be some hope in reluctation. **1640** BP. HALL *Episc.* III. vii. 252 His truths are..not changeable by time, not decayable by age. **1889** *Voice* (N.Y.) 14 Mar., 13 dead cats, besides other decayable matter, were found.

decayed (dɪˈkeɪd), *ppl. a.* [f. as prec. + -ED.]

1. Fallen off, impaired, or reduced in quality, condition, health, freshness, prosperity, fortune, etc.; *spec.* in phr. ***decayed gentlewoman***.

1513 DOUGLAS *Æneis* XI. Prol. 148 To haue bene in welth and hartis blys, And now to be dekeit and in wo. **1563** *Homilies* II. *Idleness*, To reliefe such decayed men in syckenes. **1577** B. GOOGE *Heresbach's Husb.* IV. (1586) 190b, For the comforting..of a decayed memorie. **1605** VERSTEGAN *Dec. Intell.* Pref. Ep., A restitution of decaied intelligence. **1677** YARRANTON *Eng. Improv.* 16 The neglected, and I may say decayed Trade of Fishing. **1711** ADDISON *Spect.* No. 164 ¶1 Theodosius was the younger Son of a decayed Family. **1766** FORDYCE *Serm. Yng. Wom.* (1767) II. viii. 29 A decayed beauty. **1851** HAWTHORNE *Ho. Sev. Gables* (1852) ii. 27 We might point to several little shops of a similar description..where a decayed gentlewoman stands behind the counter. **1863** H. COX *Instit.* I. viii. 97 It was contended that decayed boroughs ought to be disfranchised. **1893** *Bookman* June 83/1 A decayed civilization with many repulsive features. **1921** G. B. SHAW *Lett.* (1952) 218 The celebrated decayed gentlewoman who had to cry laces in the street for a living but hoped that nobody heard her. **1961** J. GLOAG *Victorian Comfort* viii. 212 Impoverished widows and spinsters of the middle classes, who were officially described as 'decayed gentlewomen'.

2. Physically wasted or impaired; that has begun to crumble or fall in pieces or to rot; ruined.

1528 GARDNIER in Pocock *Rec. Ref.* I. xlvi. 89 The pope lieth in an old palace..ruinous and decayed. **1599** BUTTES *Dyets Dry Dinner* D v b, Walnuts..repaire decaied teeth. **1632** LITHGOW *Trav.* VI. 247 Thence wee came to the decayed lodging of Caiphas. *a* **1716** BLACKALL *Wks.* (1723) I. 147 Wine, tho' it be decayed..is nevertheless useful as Vinegar. **1794** S. WILLIAMS *Vermont* 80 Formed of decayed or rotten leaves. **1883** *Daily News* 17 May 6/1 Decayed gooseberry—a sickly, bluish lilac.

de'cayedness. [-NESS.] Decayed condition.

1647 CLARENDON *Hist. Reb.* V. (1702) I. 544 Their lowness, and decaiedness of their Fortunes. **1719** LONDON & WISE *Compl. Gard.* p. xx, The decayedness of the Trees.

decayer (dɪˈkeɪə(r)). [-ER.] One who, or that which, causes decay; a waster.

a **1541** WYATT in *Tottell's Misc.* (Arb.) 63 The enmy of life, decayer of all kinde. **1602** SHAKS. *Ham.* V. i. 188 Your water is a sore Decayer of your horson dead body. **1691** T. H[ALE] *Acc. New Invent.* 81 This Sheathing is an extraordinary decayer of the Iron-work. **1711** ADDISON *Spect.* No. 73 Old Age is likewise a great Decayer of your Idol.

decaying (dɪˈkeɪɪŋ), *vbl. sb.* [-ING[1].] The action of the verb DECAY.

1530 PALSGR. 212/1 Decayeng of a thyng, *ruine, decadence, decline.* **1632** MASSINGER *City Madam* I. i, These [a leg and foot], indeed, wench, are not so subject to decayings as the face. **1796** MORSE *Amer. Geog.* I. 396 This..has been in a state of thriving and decaying many times.

de'caying, *ppl. a.* [-ING[2].] That decays; falling off, declining; falling into ruin; decomposing.

1530 PALSGR. 309/2 Dekayeng..*ruyneux.* **1591** SHAKS. *1 Hen. VI*, II. v. 1 Kind Keepers of my weake decaying Age. **1651** HOBBES *Leviath.* I. ii. 5 Imagination..is nothing but decaying sense. **1774** PENNANT *Tour Scotl. in* 1772. 4 The castle is a decaying pile. **1855** MACAULAY *Hist. Eng.* IV. 629 Her decaying industry and commerce. **1884** *Law Reports* 16 Q. Bench Div. 65 A house..situate in a decaying borough. *Mod.* An odour of decaying leaves.

de'cayless, *a. rare.* [f. DECAY *sb.* + -LESS.] Not subject to decay, undecaying.

1828 MOIR *Castle of Time* Wks. 1852 II. 399 For shadows ..Left not a trace on that decayless sky. **1864** NEALE *Seaton. Poems* 155 Untended, decayless, Sleeping the infinite sleep, the monarch reposed.

decayue, obs. form of DECEIVE.

Decca (ˈdɛkə). The name of a British company, used *attrib.* to designate air and sea radio-navigational systems developed by them.

1946 *Int. Meeting Radio Aids to Marine Navigation* II. III. xiii. 48 The Decca System of Radio Navigation consists of a number of transmitting beacon stations at fixed positions on shore, and special receiving equipment to be carried in the ship or aircraft by means of which the navigator can determine his position relative to these beacons. **1950** *Jrnl. Inst. Navigation* III. 330 The useful range of the Decca Navigator system is about 500 miles by day,..to about 300 miles by night. **1959** *Observer* 8 Feb. 4/5 A..flying aid invented in America and developed here—the 'Decca Navigator'; its technical description is a 'high accuracy hyperbolic navigation system'. This replaces the traditional string of radio beacons by a fine grid of radio signals sent out from four transmitters linked to make a Decca 'chain'.

dece, obs. form of DAIS.

deceaph, -ue, deceat, obs. ff. DECEIVE, DECEIT.

decease (dɪˈsiːs), *sb.* Forms: α. 4 deces, deses, dises, 4-7 decess(e, 5 decez, dicese, 6 dicesse, *Sc.* deceis, 7 deceyse, 5- decease. β. 4 desces, *Sc.* desceiss, 4-5 dessece, 5 desseyse, discese, -cees, -sese, -sees, dysces, -sees, -seys, -sease, 5-6 disease, dyssese, 6 *Sc.* diseis. [ME. *deces*, etc., a. F. *décès*, ad. L. *dēcess-us* departure, death, vbl. sb. f. ppl. stem of *dēcēdĕre* to depart, go away. In OF. often also *desces* (see DE- *pref.* I. 6), hence also in ME. with *des-, dis-, dys-*, spellings which often confused it in form with DISEASE. See the vb.] Departure from life; death.

In its origin a euphemism (L. *dēcessus* for *mors*), and still slightly euphemistic or at least less harsh and realistic than *death*; it is the common term in legal and technical language where the legal or civil incidence of death is in question, without reference to the act of dying.

α. *c* **1330** R. BRUNNE *Chron.* (1810) 15 After his fader decesse. *Ibid.* 126 If þat Henry die, or Steuen mak his deses. *c* **1440** *Gesta Rom.* lv. 237 (Harl. MS.) Aftir hir dicese, þe Emperoure weddid anoþer woman. **1513** MORE in Grafton *Chron.* II. 761 At the time of his fathers decease. **1654** GATAKER *Disc. Apol.* 79 The decesse of one Pope..and entrance of another. **1751** SMOLLETT *Per. Pic.* lxxiii, A groan which announced his decease. **1818** CRUISE *Digest* (ed. 2) II. 289 In case his said daughter should die without issue of her body living at her decease. **1849** LINGARD *Hist. Eng.* (1855) I. vi. 182/2 The surname of 'the Confessor' was given to him [Edward] from the bull of his canonization, issued by Alexander III, about a century after his decease.

β. *c* **1330** R. BRUNNE *Chron.* (1810) 254 After Blanche desces. *c* **1350** *Will. Palerne* 4101 After mi deseece. *c* **1440** *Gesta Rom.* xv. 49 Aftere his dissese. **1494** FABYAN *Chron.* V. cxxxi. 113 Worde came to hym of his faders disease. **1580** LYLY *Euphues* (Arb.) 293 A Lady..who after the disease of hir Father hadde three sutors.

γ. **1417** *E.E. Wills* (1882) 29 After þe sesse [corruption of *decease*] of her.

†**b.** Said of the death of many; mortality, slaughter. *Obs.*

1513 DOUGLAS *Æneis* XII. ix. 5 Sa feill and diuers slauchteris as war thair, And gret deces of dukis.

decease (dɪˈsiːs), *v.* Forms: α. 5 decess, -sesse, 5-6 -cesse, 5-7 -cease, 6 -cese, -sece, dicesse, *Sc.* deceiss, 6- decease. β. 5 disceas, -ceyse, -sese, -sease, 5-6 -cess(e, -cease, 6 descece, -cess, -sece, disceasse, dyscess, -cece, -scesse, -sese, -sesse, disease. [f. DECEASE *sb.* Taken as the Eng. repr. of L. *dēcēdere* and F. *décéder*. In L. *dēcēdĕre* and *discēdĕre* were nearly synonymous in the sense 'depart, go away', and in med.L. *discēdĕre, discessus*, were also used for *dēcēdĕre, dēcessus* in senses 'die, death'; hence OF. *descès* = *decès*, and the ME. and 16th c. forms in *des-, dis-, dys-*, some of which were identical with variant spellings of *disease*. Cf. the sb.]

intr. To depart from life; to die.

α. **1439** *E.E. Wills* (1882) 123 Yf the saide Iohn decesse withoute heires. **1513** MORE *Rich. III* Wks. 36/2 So deceased..this noble Kynge. **1623** FAVINE *Theat. Hon.* IX. i. 356 Deceassing without children. **1639** FULLER *Holy War* III. x. (1840) 132 Queen Sibyll who deceased of the plague. **1777** *Life Abp. Abbot* 41 He deceased at his palace of Croydon. **1868** BROWNING *Ring & Bk.* IV. 103 If the good fat easy man..decease..being childless.

β. **1439** *E.E. Wills* (1882) 123 If he discesse without heires. **1463** *Bury Wills* (1850) 28 As God disposith for me to dissese. **1530** PALSGR. 517/2, I disceasse, I dye or departe out of this worlde. **1556** *Chron. Gr. Friars* (Camden) 41 Thys yere the good qwene Jane dessecid the xxiij. day of October.

†**b.** *to decease this world* (cf. *to depart this life*). *Obs. rare.*

1515 *Epitaph* in Wood *Ath. Oxon.*, James Stanley..who decessed thys transytory wourld the xxi of March.

c. *fig.* To come to an end, perish; CEASE.

1538 *Lichfield Gild Ord.* 8 Bring the parties together that ther may be made a good end, and discord clene desecedd. **1591** SYLVESTER *Du Bartas* I. vii. (1641) 60/2 How often had this world deceast, except Gods mighty arms had it upheld and kept. **1635** SWAN *Spec. M.* (1670) 93 This circle never corrupteth nor deceaseth.

Hence †**de'ceasing** *vbl. sb.*, death, decease.

1591 PERCIVALL *Sp. Dict.*, *Finamiento*, the dieng, the deceasing, death. **1691** E. TAYLOR *Behmen's Threefold Life* xviii. 313 At deceasing of the Body.

deceased (dɪˈsiːst, *poet.* dɪˈsiːsɪd), *ppl. a.* Forms: see DECEASE *v.*; also 7 deceast. [f. DECEASE *v.* + -ED[1]. From the intermixture of the prefixes *de-* and *dis-*, and of the letters *c* and *s*, it was frequently written *diseased.*]

1. a. That has departed this life, dead, 'departed'; *esp.* lately dead, 'late'.

c **1489** CAXTON *Sonnes of Aymon* ix. 227 After that a man is ones decessed. **1523** LD. BERNERS *Froiss.* I. ccxliv. 364 The bysshop of Wynchestre discessed..was chancellour of England. **1564** GRINDAL *Fun. Serm. Pr. Ferd.* Wks. (1843) 10 [He] highly commended the parties discessed. **1586** A. DAY *Eng. Secretary* I. (1625) 63 The deceased ghost of him that loved you. **1651** HOBBES *Leviath.* III. xxxviii. 242 Those deceased Giants. **1762** GOLDSM. *Cit. W.* xii, There..I shall see justice done to deceased merit. **1810** WORDSW. *Ess. Epitaphs* Wks. (1888) 814/1 The character of a deceased friend. **1893** *Law Times* XCV. 82/1 The heir of a deceased licence-holder.

fig. **1597** SHAKS. *2 Hen. IV*, III. i. 81 Figuring the nature of the Times deceas'd.

b. ***deceased wife's sister question***: the question of a widower's marrying the sister of his deceased wife, such a marriage being legal in some countries and illegal in others.

c. *transf.* Of a deceased person.

1906 *Times* 29 Aug. 11/2 London and North-Western stock was noticeably plentiful for delivery, and was said to have been sold heavily during the account on behalf of a deceased estate.

2. *absol.* †**a.** *pl.* ***the deceased***: those who are dead, the dead (*obs.*). **b.** The person (lately) dead, or whose death is in question.

1625 MASSINGER *New Way* V. i, It might have argued me of little love To the deceased. **1648** MILTON *Ps.* lxxxviii. 42 Shall the deceas'd arise? **1751** SMOLLETT *Per. Pic.* civ, He.. sealed up all the papers of the deceased. **1840** C. PELHAM *Chron. Crime* (1886) II. 349 An inquest was held upon the remains of deceased at the Dog and Gun. **1841** LYTTON *Nt. & Morn.* I. i, Mr. Jones..promised to read the burial-service over the deceased.

†**de'ceasure.** *Obs. rare.* [f. DECEASE *v.* + -URE; corresp. to a L. type **dēcessūra.*] Decease.

1580 LODGE *Forb. & Prisc.* (Shaks. Soc.) 97 To lament my deceasure and her froward destinie.

deceave, etc., obs. form of DECEIVE *v.*

†**de'cede,** *v. Obs.* [ad. L. *dēcēd-ĕre* to go away, depart, remove, f. DE- I. 2 + *cēdĕre* to go. (French has had *décéder* in sense 'to die' since 15th c.).] *intr.* To depart; to secede; to give place, yield.

1655 FULLER *Ch. Hist.* V. iii. §25 To justifie the English Reformation, from the scandal of Schisme, to shew, that they had 1. Just cause for which, 2. True authority by which they deceded from Rome. **1658** J. WEBB tr. *Cleopatra* VIII. II. 63 That violent passion..deceding to the pitty she conceived. **1697** J. SERGEANT *Solid Philos.* 262 With their Quantity and Figure acceding and deceding to the Individuum.

decedent (dɪˈsiːdənt), *sb.* (*a.*) [ad. L. *dēcēdent-em*, pr. pple. of *dēcēdĕre* to depart, die.]

A. *sb.* One who retires from an office (*obs.*), deceases, or dies; a deceased person. *U.S.*, chiefly in *Law.*

1599 CRAUFURD *Hist. Univ. Edinb.* (1880) 52 Mr. Andrew Young..was appointed to succeed to the next decedent. **1730** BP. WILSON in Keble *Life* xxi. (1863) 724 Taking care of orphan's and decedent's goods. **1828** WEBSTER, *Decedent*, a deceased person. *Laws of Pennsylv.* **1884** *Boston* (Mass.) *Jrnl.* Jan., In North Andover last year there were 65 deaths. Twenty-two of the decedents were more than 70.

†**B.** *adj.* (See quot.) *Obs.*[-0]

1727 BAILEY vol. II, *Decedent*, adj. departing, going away.

deceife, deceipt, deceis(s, obs. ff. DECEIVE, DECEIT, DECEASE.

deceit (dɪˈsiːt). Forms: α. 4 deseyt(e, 4-5 -sait(e, 4-6 -ceyt(e, 4-7 -ceite, 5 -sayte, -sate, 6 -ceat, -seite, -seytte, -saitte, -sette, 4- deceit. β. 5 deceipte, 5-7 -ceipt, 5-6 -cept(e. γ. 4-6 desceit, -sayte, 5 desseit, -seyt(e, -sait, -sate, 6 desceyt. δ. 4 disseyte, -saite, -sayte, *Sc.* dissat, 4-5 disseit, -ceite, 5 dissayet, dysseyte, -sayt, 5-6 dissait, -sate, dis-, dysceyt(e, 5-7 disceit, 6 -ceat(e, -sayt(e. ε. 6 dis-, dyscept, -ceipte. [ME. *deceite, deseyte, desaite*, etc., a. OF. *deceite, -eyte* (later *deçoite*): sb. fem. from pa. pple. of *deceveir, décevoir*, with assimilation of vowel, as in *deceive*. (Cf. CONCEIT.)

In ME. and early mod.Eng. with many varieties of spelling, partly inherited from Fr., partly due to Eng. change of OF. *ei* to *ai, ay*, and consequent interchange of *c* and *s*, whence arose such forms as *desait*, Sc. *desate*. In OF. the spelling was sometimes assimilated to Latin *decepta*, as *decepte*, whence in Eng. *deceipte*. But in both langs. the *p* was mute; the oldest Gower MSS. have *deceipte, deceite*, but the word rimes with *streite* (*strait*); the ordinary 17th c. pronunciation rimed it with *-ait*, as in Wither *a* 1667 *bait: deceit*; cf. the common 16th c. spellings in *-sait, -sate, -ceat*. The narrowing of *ē* to *ī* came later. In OF. the prefix *de-* was sometimes changed to *des-* (see DE- I. 6), which became very common in ME., and was here, moreover, in the general alteration of the French form *des-* back to the Latin *dis-*, subjected to the same change, so as to give, in 15-16th c., such odd spellings as *dis-ceat, dis-sait, dis-sate* (all meaning (dɪˈseːt)): cf. DECEIVE.]

1. The action or practice of deceiving; concealment of the truth in order to mislead; deception, fraud, cheating, false dealing.

c **1300** *K. Alis.* 6157 By queyntise to don, other deseyte. c **1386** CHAUCER *Pars. T.* ¶703 Deceipt bitwixe marchaunt and marchaunt. **1393** GOWER *Conf.* II. 318 And that he dide for deceipt, For she began to axe him streit. **1426** AUDELAY *Poems* 6 Dysseyte ne theft loke thou do non. **1483** *Cath. Angl.* 101 Dissate, *vbi* dessate. **1535** COVERDALE *Mal.* iii. 8 Shulde a man vse falsede and disceate with God? **1552** LYNDESAY *Monarche* 5780 Leif ȝour dissait and crafty wylis. **1667** MILTON *P.L.* v. 243 By violence? no..But by deceit and lies. **1794** S. WILLIAMS *Vermont* 170 The deceit, knavery, and fraud of the European traders. **1849** RUSKIN *Sev. Lamps* ii. §6. 32 Gilding, which in architecture is no deceit, because it is therein not understood for gold.

b. in *Law*.

[**1275** *Act 3 Edw. I*, c. 29 Nul manere deceyte ou collusion.] **1495** *Nottingham Rec.* III. 285 Accion of desseyte ffor brekynge off promyse. **1531** *Dial. on Laws Eng.* II. xlii. (1638) 135 A false returne whereupon an action of disceit lyeth. **1672** COWELL, *Deceit*..is a subtle, wily shift or device, having no other name. **1818** CRUISE *Digest* (ed. 2) IV. 294 All manner of deceit is hereby avoided in deeds.

†**c.** Phr. ***in deceit of***: so as to deceive; so ***to the deceit of, upon d., under d. with no deceit, without deceit***: without mistake, assuredly, certainly. *Obs.*

[**1275** *Act 3 Edw. I*, c. 29 De fere la en deceyte de la Court.] **1303** R. BRUNNE *Handl. Synne* 3814 He durst come oute on no party Of all þe twelve monþe wyþ no deseyt. c **1350** *Will. Palerne* 2041 Wiþoute disseyte, I wold alle hire werk do ȝou wite sone. **1393** LANGL. *P. Pl.* C. I. 77 Hus sele sholde noȝt be sent in deceit of þe puple. c **1425** *Hampole's Psalter* Metr. Pref. 32 Betwene dancastir and Poumefreyt this is þe way.. euen streygth wiþ out deseyt. **1534** *Indictm. Eliz. Bocking* in Hall *Chron.* (1550) 221 To the great deceit of the prince and people of this realme. **1535** COVERDALE *1 Chron.* xiii. 17 Yf ye come vpon disceate, and to be mine aduersaries. **1535** —— *1 Macc.* vii. 10 Speakinge vnto them with peaceable wordes: but vnder disceate. a **1626** BACON *Max. & Uses Com. Law* (1636) 8 Selling..things unwholsome, or ill made in deceipt of the people.

2. (with *a* and *pl.*) An instance of deception; an act or device intended to deceive; a trick, stratagem, wile.

c **1340** *Cursor M.* 897 (Fairf.) For þi dissayte at þou dede. c **1380** WYCLIF *Wks.* (1880) 104 þe deuelis disceitis. **14..** *Piers of Fulham* 95 in Hazl. *E.P.P.* II. 5 The fowler with hys deseyttes bryngeth The gentyll fowles in to hys false crafte. **1548–9** (Mar.) *Bk. Com. Prayer, Litany*, Al the deceytes of the worlde, the fleshe, and the deuill. **1559** CECIL in Robertson *Hist. Scotl.* II. App. i, To avoid the decepts and tromperies of the French. a **1667** WITHER *Stedfast Shepherd* i, Thy painted baits, And poor deceits, Are all bestowed on me in vain. **1713** SWIFT *Cadenus & V.*, Venus thought on a deceit. c **1793** COLERIDGE *Autumnal Evening* ii, O dear deceit! I see the maiden rise.

3. The quality of deceiving; deceitfulness.

1303 R. BRUNNE *Handl. Synne* 12494 What doust þou byfore þe prest and hast deseyt yn þy brest? c **1400** *Destr. Troy* 3788 Ulexes..was..full of disseit. **1526** TINDALE *Rom.* i. 29 Full of envie, morther, debate, disseyte. **1577** tr. *Bullinger's Decades* (1592) 20 The care of this world and the deceipt of riches. **1845** MANNING *Serm.* I. ix. *On Jas.* i. 22 It is a vain and hurtful thing, full of deceit and danger, to hear and not to do.

†**de'ceit**, *v. Obs. rare.* Hence 5 **desetyng** *vbl. sb.* [f. DECEIT *sb.*] To construct deceitfully, to forge (a document).

1484 in *Surtees Misc.* (1890) 43 Declaracion concernyng the disetyng of a fals testimoniall [*called* p. 42 the forsaid forged, false testymonyall].

†**de'ceiteous**, *a. Obs. rare.* [f. DECEIT, with suffix fashioned after *righteous*, *courteous*: see -EOUS 3.] Deceitful. Hence **de'ceiteously** *adv.*

1481 in *Eng. Gilds* (1870) 332 And all other ware..whiche is desceyteously wrought.

deceitful (dɪ'siːtfʊl), *a.* Forms: see DECEIT. [f. DECEIT + -FUL.] Full of deceit; given to deceiving or cheating; misleading, false, fallacious. (As said of things often = DECEPTIVE.)

1483 *Cath. Angl.* 97 Desatefulle, *vbi* false. **1500–20** DUNBAR *Flyting* 75 Dissaitfull tyrand, with serpentis tung, vnstable. **1513** DOUGLAS *Æneis* IX. vii. 52 Throw the dern wod dyssaitfull and onplane. **1584** POWEL *Lloyd's Cambria* 104 A Deceiptfull and Subtile man. **1641** WILKINS *Math. Magick* I. iii. (1648) 19 Such deceitfull ballances may be discovered..by changing the weights. **1842** LYTTON *Zanoni* 29 Appearances are deceitful. **1862** LD. BROUGHAM *Brit. Const.* ix. §1. 113 They may be the most false and deceitful of human kind.

de'ceitfully, *adv.* [f. prec. + -LY².] In a deceitful manner; with intent to deceive. (In first quot.: By deceit or treachery.)

c **1470** HENRY *Wallace* VII. 34 Desaitfully I may nocht se thaim hang. **1523** *Act 14–15 Hen. VIII*, c. 2 Workemanship ..falsely and disceitfully made. **1611** BIBLE *2 Cor.* iv. 2 Not walking in craftines, nor handling the word of God deceitfully. **1667** *Decay Chr. Piety* viii. ¶1 If this foundation be deceitfully laid, the superstructure must necessarily sink and perish. **1873** SYMONDS *Grk. Poets* viii 265 His allegory ..must always show them [the clouds] deceitfully beautiful, spreading illusion over earth and sky.

de'ceitfulness. [f. as prec. + -NESS.] The quality of being deceitful; disposition or tendency to deceive or mislead; deceptiveness.

1509 BARCLAY *Shyp of Folys* (1874) II. 223 Beware disceytfulnes, All fraude and gyle take hede that thou despyce. **1526** TINDALE *Matt.* xiii. 22 The dissaytfulnes off ryches. **1671** GLANVILL *Disc. M. Stubbe* 21 The deceitfulness of Telescopes. **1741** RICHARDSON *Pamela* (1824) I. 64 O, the deceitfulness of the heart of man! **1870** ANDERSON *Missions Amer. Bd.* III. xv. 238 The deceitfulness of the people.

de'ceitless, *a. rare.* [f. DECEIT + -LESS.] Free from deceit.

1630 BP. HALL *Old Relig.* §2 (L.) So he that should call Satan an unclean devil, should imply that some devil is not unclean; or deceivable lusts, some lusts deceitless!

de,ceiva'bility. *rare.* [f. next + -ITY. OF. had *decevablete*.] Capacity of being deceived.

1861 GEN. P. THOMPSON *Audi Alt.* III. cxlix. 142 The deceivability of the masses.

deceivable (dɪ'siːvəb(ə)l), *a.* Forms (about 40 variants): *α.* with **de-** 4–, *β.* with **des-** 4–5, *γ.* with **dis-** 4–6; variations of the stem as in DECEIVE. [a. OF. *decevable*, f. stem of *décevoir* to DECEIVE + -ABLE.]

†**1.** *actively.* Having the quality or habit of deceiving; deceitful, deceptive. *Obs.* (or *arch.*)

(*Obs.* since c 1688; exc. as used after the biblical *deceivableness*.)

1303 R. BRUNNE *Handl. Synne* 471 So ben dremys deseyuable. **1382** WYCLIF *Prov.* xiv. 17 The desseyuable man is hateful. c **1400** MAUNDEV. (Roxb.) xxx. 135 A fantom and a dessayuable thing to þe sight. **1428** *Surtees Misc.* (1890) 4 John Lyllyng had salde mykell swylk deceyvable tyn to bellemakers. **1503–4** *Act 19 Hen. VII*, c. 6 Deceivable and untrewe Beames and scales. c **1510** DUNBAR *Poems* lxviii, I seik abowte this warld onstable, To find..it is dissavable. **1535** COVERDALE *2 Pet.* i. 16 We folowed not deceaueable fables. **1558** KNOX *First Blast* App. (Arb.) 59 Yf I should flatter your grace I were no freind, but a deceavabill trater. **1682** BUNYAN *Holy War* 55 Deceivable speech. **1688** R. HOLME *Armoury* II. 305 A wicked deceivable person, who indeavouring to chate others, chats himself. **1860** TRENCH *Serm. Westm. Abb.* xxxiii. 376 We may have proved them false and deceivable a thousand times, and yet they are still able to attract and to allure.

2. *passively.* Capable of being, or liable to be, deceived; fallible. Now *rare.*

1646 SIR T. BROWNE *Pseud. Ep.* I. i, Man was not only deceiveable in his integrity, but the Angels of light in all their clarity. **1658** *Whole Duty Man* iv. §4. 38 As deceivable, and easie to be deluded. **1705** STANHOPE *Paraphr.* III. 559 To deal with him, as if he were such a deceivable Creature as our selves. **1841–4** EMERSON *Ess., Politics* Wks. (Bohn) I. 239 With such an ignorant and deceivable majority.

de'ceivableness. Now *rare.* [-NESS.]

†**1.** The capacity of deceiving; deceitfulness, deceit; deceptiveness. *Obs.* (or *arch.* after N.T.)

1526 TINDALE *2 Thess.* ii. 10 In all deceavablenes of unrighteswenes [**1611** with all deceivableness; **1881** R. V. with all deceit]. **1530** PALSGR. 213/1 Desceyvablenesse, *deceuableté.* a **1653** GOUGE *Comm. Heb.* iii. 14 Sin prevails the more by the deceiveablenesse thereof. **1671** GLANVILL *Disc. M. Stubbe* 26 The Discourse about the deceivableness of Opticks. **1826** E. IRVING *Babylon* II. 439 They are deceived into false security by that mystery of deceivableness. **1853** I. WILLIAMS *Serm. Epist.* (1875) I. xvii. 193 With all deceivableness and power of seduction.

2. Liability to be deceived, fallibility.

1674 *Govt. Tongue* viii. ¶11 His negligence and deceivableness.

†**de'ceivably**, *adv. Obs.* or *arch.* [-LY².] Deceitfully, fraudulently, falsely.

1387 TREVISA *Higden* (Rolls) VII. 109 Aftirward he [Edwyne] was reconsiled desceyvably and i-slayn. **1428** *Surtees Misc.* (1890) 4 Castyng of fals tyn menged with lede and pewtre, and sellyng of yt deceyvably for gude tyn. **1532–3** *Act 24 Hen. VIII*, c. 1 Hydes..vntruly, insufficiently and deceiuably tanned. **1637** *Declar. Pfaltzgraves' Faith* 3 When the one shall..deceiveably lay imputations of errour on the other. **1865** NICHOLS *Britton* v. ii. §3 If dower be deceivably [*deceivablement*] established.

†**decei'vance.** *Obs.* Forms: see DECEIVE. [a. OF. *decevance*, f. *decev-ant*: see next and -ANCE.] Deceit, deception.

c **1330** R. BRUNNE *Chron.* (1810) 133 þe Kyng sister of France Henry allied him to, Here of a desceyuance þei conseild him to do. c **1430** LYDG. *Bochas* I. i. (1554) 4 a, Beware the serpent, with his disceivance. **1483** CAXTON *Gold. Leg.* 129/1 Ayenst the deceyuaunces of the feend. **1486** *Surtees Misc.* (1890) 57 Set[h] yat it is your citie not filid with dissavaunce.

†**decei'vant**, *a.* and *sb. Obs. rare.* (In 4 -aunt.) [a. F. *decevant*, pr. pple. of *deceveir*, -*oir*:—L. *dēcipient-em*.] **A.** *adj.* Deceiving, deceitful, deceptive. **B.** *sb.* A deceiver.

1393 GOWER *Conf.* I. 82 That þou ne be noght deceiuant. *Ibid.* I. 222 The fourthe deceivaunt, The whiche is cleped fals semblaunt. *Ibid.* II. 72 This Achelous was a Geaunt, A subtil man, a deceivaunt.

deceive (dɪ'siːv), *v.* Forms: *α.* 4 deseue, -sayue, -saife, -ceife, -cayue, dicayue, 4–5 deseyue, 4–6 deceyue, 4–7 deceyue, 5–6 desave, (*Sc.* -sawe), 6 deceaph, 6–7 deceaue, 5– deceive. *β.* 4 desceiue, 4–5 -ceyue, -sayue, 5 -saue, -sayfe, 5–6 -seyue. *γ.* 4 (*Sc.*) dissaf, 4–5 disceyue, -seyue, dysceue, -saue, 4–5 (6 *Sc.*) dissaue, 4–6 dyssayue, 5 disceue, -saiue, -sayue, (*Sc.* -sayf, -sawe), dysseyue, 5–6 dysceyue, -seue, 6 disceiue, -ceaue, *Sc.* -saif. [a. OF. *decev-eir* (stressed stem *deceiv-*), mod.F. *décevoir*:—L. *dēcipĕre*, f. DE- I. 1 or 4 + *capĕre* to take. Cf. CONCEIVE.

The stem was subject in ME. and 16th c. to the same variations as those mentioned under DECEIT, and the prefix varied in like manner as *de-*, *des-*, *dis-*, whence came such curious spellings as *disceave*, *dissave*, *dissaif*; the stem vowel has passed through the stages (ɛɪ, ɛː, eː, iː). Quarles in 1635 (*Emblems* III. ii.) rimed *deceiv'd thee*: *sav'd thee*.

(The literal sense of L. *dēcipĕre* was app. to catch in a trap, to entrap, ensnare; hence, to catch by guile; to get the better of by fraud; to cheat, mislead.)]

†**1.** *trans.* To ensnare; to take unawares by craft or guile; to overcome, overreach, or get the better of by trickery; to beguile or betray into mischief or sin; to mislead. *Obs.* (or *arch.*)

a **1300** *Cursor M.* 3172 (Gött) þat þe child were noght percayued, ar þe suord him had dicayued. c **1340** *Ibid.* 27214 (Fairf.), & queþer he was þus dessayuid, sone ofter his creature he resceyuid. **1398** TREVISA *Barth. De P.R.* XII. vii. (1495) 418 Somtyme a tame culuoure is..taughte to begyle and to dysceyue wylde colouures and ledyth theym in to the foulers nette. c **1450** *Merlin* 4 The deuell..devised how he myght best disceyve the thre doughtres of this rich man. **1594** WILLOBIE *Avisa* Ljb, Apply her still with dyvers thinges (For giftes the wysest will deceave). **1611** CORYAT *Crudities* 2 A certaine English man..was deceiued by those sands: for..he was suddenly ouertaken and ouerwhelmed with the waters. **1667** MILTON *P.L.* I. 35 He it was whose guile..deceived The mother of mankind. **1741** RICHARDSON *Pamela* I. 170 As we deceived and hooked the poor carp, so was I betrayed by false baits. **1794** SULLIVAN *View Nat.* II, The mother of mankind, who was deceived by the serpent.

2. To cause to believe what is false; to mislead as to a matter of fact, lead into error, impose upon, delude, 'take in'.

c **1320** *Seuyn Sag.* (W.) 109, I wald noght he decayued ware. **1375** BARBOUR *Bruce* IV. 237 Thai mak ay thair answering In-till dowbill vndirstanding, Till dissaf thame that will thame trow. **1382** WYCLIF *Matt.* xxiv. 11 Many false prophetis schulen ryse, and disceyue many. c **1460** *Towneley Myst.* (Surtees) 124 Or els the rewlys of astronomy Dyssavys me. c **1489** CAXTON *Sonnes of Aymon* xxi. 462 Soo dysguysed for to dysceve us. a **1533** LD. BERNERS *Huon* xxiv. 69 By hys fayr langage he may dyssayue vs. c **1600** SHAKS. *Sonn.* civ, Mine eye may be deceaued. **1667** MILTON *P.L.* II. 189 Who [can] deceive his mind, whose eye Views all things at one view? **1781** GIBBON *Decl. & F.* xxx. III. 179 Two statesmen, who laboured to deceive each other and the world. **1856** FROUDE *Hist. Eng.* (1858) I. ii. 98 Wolsey..was too wise to be deceived with outward prosperity. **1862** MRS. H. WOOD *Mrs. Hallib.* II. xix, He denied it..and I believed he was attempting to deceive me.

b. *absol.* To use deceit, act deceitfully.

c **1340** HAMPOLE *Prose Tr.* (1866) 3 If þou will nowthire be dyssayuede ne dyssayue. **1500–20** DUNBAR *Poems* (1893) xxi. 102 Quhair fortoun..dissavis With freyndly smylingis of ane hure. **1594** HOOKER *Eccl. Pol.* I. xv. §4 He can neither erre nor deceiue. **1769** *Junius Lett.* xxxv. 163 A moment of difficulty and danger, at which flattery and falsehood can no longer deceive. **1808** SCOTT *Marm.* VI. xvii, Ah, what a tangled web we weave, When first we practise to deceive! **1875** JOWETT *Plato* (ed. 2) V. 160 The makers of household implements..should be ashamed to deceive in the practice of their craft.

c. *refl.* To allow oneself to be misled; to delude oneself. [F. *se tromper.*]

1382 WYCLIF *Jas.* i. 22 Be ȝe doers of the word and not herers onely, deceyuynge you silf. **1535** COVERDALE *Bel & Dr.* 7 Daniel smyled, and sayde: O kynge, disceaue not thyselfe. **1791** MRS. RADCLIFFE *Rom. Forest* ii, I can no longer deceive myself. **1884** GLADSTONE in *Standard* 29 Feb. 2/7 Do not let us deceive ourselves on that point.

d. In *pass.* sometimes merely: To be mistaken, be in error.

c **1315** SHOREHAM 93 Ac many man desceyved hys..And weyneth that he be out of peryl. c **1325** *Poem temp. Edw. II* (Percy) lv, Forsoth he is deseyved, He wenyth he doth ful wel. a **1450** *Knt. de la Tour* 33 We are foule deceiued in you the tyme passed. **1553** EDEN *Treat. Newe Ind.* (Arb.) 41 He was not deceaued in his opinion. **1596** SHAKS. *Merch. V.* v. i. 111 That is the voice, Or I am much deceiu'd, of Portia. **1603** —— *Meas. for M.* III. i. 197 How much is the good Duke deceiu'd in Angelo. **1749** FIELDING *Tom Jones* XIV. vi, I am very much deceived in Mr. Nightingale, if..he hath not much goodness of heart at the bottom.

†**3.** To be or prove false to, play false, deal treacherously with; to betray. *Obs.*

a **1300** *Cursor M.* 1894 (Cott.) Quen noe sagh..þat þis rauen had him deceueid, Lete vt a doue. c **1470** HENRY *Wallace* VI. 480 Thai swor that he had dissawit thair lord. **1526** *Pilgr. Perf.* (W. de W. 1531) 6 The corruptyble rychesse of this worlde..forsaketh and deceyueth hym whan he weneth best. **1596** SHAKS. *1 Hen. IV*, v. i. 11 You have deceiu'd our trust. **1605** CAMDEN *Rem., Epitaphs* 53 Fame deceaues the dead mans trust. **1658** *Whole Duty Man* xv. §26. 125 He that does not carefully look to his masters profit, deceives his trust.

b. *fig.* To prove false to; †to frustrate (a purpose, etc.) *obs.*; to disappoint (hope, expectation, etc.).

1571 *Act 13 Eliz.* in Bolton *Stat. Irel.* (1621) 360 Which good meaning of that good lawe..is daylie..deceyved by diverse evill disposed persons. **1666** DRYDEN *Ann. Mirab.* lxviii, Till..doubtful moonlight did our rage deceive. **1697** —— *Virg. Georg.* III. 190 The weak old Stallion will deceive thy Care. a **1700** —— (J.), Nor are my hopes deceiv'd. **1818** JAS. MILL *Brit. India* II. IV. ii. 89 Never was expectation more completely deceived.

†**4.** To cheat, overreach; defraud. *Obs.*

c **1330** R. BRUNNE *Chron.* (1810) 319 þat mad þe Tresorere þou has desceyued him. **1382** WYCLIF *1 Thess.* iv. 6 That no man ouer go nether disceyue his brother in chaffaringe. **1481** in *Eng. Gilds* (1870) 332 Desceteously wrought as in tannyng, where-thurgh the kynges lege peopell scholde be disceuyd. **1533** GAU *Richt Vay* (1888) 16 Thay that sellis ald and ewil guidis for new and thair throw dissauis oders falslie. **1625** BACON *Ess. Gardens* (Arb.) 563 That the Borders..be

..Set with Fine Flowers, but thin and sparingly, lest they Deceiue the Trees. **1626** —— *Sylva* §479 Where two Plants draw (much) the same Juyce, there the Neighbourhood hurteth; for the one deceiveth the other.

†**b.** with *of*: To cheat out of. *Obs.*

a **1300** *Cursor M.* 8626 (Cott.) Sco parceuid, þat sco was of hir child deceuid. *c* **1380** WYCLIF *Wks.* (1880) 73 Whanne þei be raueine & ypocrisie disceyuen hem of here goodis. **1525** *Wido Edyth*, The sixt merye Jest: how this wydowe Edyth deceiued a Draper..of a new Gowne and a new Kyrtell. **1620** J. WILKINSON *Coroners & Sherifes* 62 To deceive them of it and to gain it for themselves. **1667** MILTON *P.L.* x. 990 Childless thou art, Childless remain; so Death Shall be deceav'd his glut. *a* **1761** OLDYS in D'Israeli *Cur. Lit.* (1866) 563[He] deceived me of a good sum of money which he owed me.

†**5.** To beguile, wile away (time, tediousness, etc.). *Obs.* (Cf. CHEAT *v.* 5.)

1591 FLORIO *Sec. Fruites* 65 Let us do something to deceaue the time, and that we may not thinke it long. **1663** BP. PATRICK *Parab. Pilgr.* ii. (1668) 5 To deceive the tediousness of the pilgrimage. **1697** DRYDEN *Virg. Past.* x. (R.), This while I sung, my sorrows I deceiv'd. **1784** COWPER *Task* III. 362 Happy to deceive the time, Not waste it. **1841** CATLIN *N. Amer. Ind.* (1844) II. xxxvii. 36 Amusements to deceive away the time.

deceived (dɪ'siːvd, *poet.* dɪ'siːvɪd), *ppl. a.* [f. prec. + -ED[1].] Deluded, imposed upon, misled, mistaken, etc.: see the verb.

1569 T. NORTON (*title*) To the Quenes Maiesties poore deceyued Subjects of the North Countrey, drawen into rebellion. **1611** BIBLE *Job* xii. 16 The deceiued and the deceiuer are his. **1651** HOBBES *Leviath.* I. iii. 11 Speeches taken..from deceived Philosophers, and deceived, or deceiving Schoolemen. **1820** KEATS *St. Agnes* xxxvii, I curse not..Though thou forsakest a deceived thing.

b. *absol.*

1652 J. WRIGHT tr. *Camus' Nature's Paradox* 158 The Deceived, as well as the Deceivers. **1847** SIR W. HAMILTON *Let. to De Morgan* 5, I was wrong..in presuming you to be a deceiver, and not rather a deceived.

deceiver (dɪ'siːvə(r)). Forms: α. 4 deceiuour, 4–5 deceyuour(e, -or, 5–6 -ar, 6 deceyuer, deceauer, 7– deceiver. β. 4–6 dis-: see DECEIVE. [a. AF. *decevour* = OF. *deceveur*, earlier *deceveor*, f. stem of *decev-oir*; subsequently taking the form of an Eng. derivative of DECEIVE *v.*: see -ER[1] 2.]

1. One who (or that which) deceives; a cheat, impostor.

1382 WYCLIF *2 John* 7 Many deceyuours [**1388** disseyueris] wenten out in to the world. *c* **1450** tr. *De Imitatione* III. i, What are all temporale þinges but deceyuours. **1483** *Cath. Angl.* 101 A Dissauer, *deceptor*. **1535** COVERDALE *Job* xii. 16 Both the deceaver, and him that is deceaved. **1555** EDEN *Decades* 313 An Italian deceauer who had before deluded the kynges of Englande and Portugale. **1634** MILTON *Comus* 596 Hence with thy brew'd enchantments, foul deceiver! **1832** LYTTON *Eugene A.* I. v, The passions are at once our masters and our deceivers.

2. *Comb.*

1624 W. HALL *Man's Gt. Enemy* in Farr *S.P. Jas. I* (1848) 199 Deceiuer-like, hee said, Yee shall not dye.

deceiving (dɪ'siːvɪŋ), *vbl. sb.* [-ING[1].] The action of the verb DECEIVE; deception.

c **1400** *Rom. Rose* 1590 Withouten any deceiving. **1523** LD. BERNERS *Froiss.* I. xviii. 25 Than the Englisshe lordes.. for doubte of deceyuyng..kept styll the two trompettis pryuely. **1568** BIBLE (Bishops') *2 Pet.* ii. 13 Delighting them selues in their deceiuings. **1833** MRS. BROWNING *Prometh. Bound* Poems 1850 I. 171 For in my mind Deceiving works more shame than torturing.

de'ceiving, *ppl. a.* [-ING[2].] That deceives; deceitful, misleading, fallacious.

1500–20 DUNBAR *Poems* xlvii. 87 This fals dissavand warldis bliss. **1603** SHAKS. *Meas. for M.* III. ii. 260 Manie deceyuing promises of life. *a* **1653** GOUGE *Comm. Heb.* xiii. 5 Covetousnesse is a deceiving sin. *c* **1793** *Telegraph* in *Spir. Publ. Jrnls.* (1799) I. 26 The most deceiving tongue.

Hence **de'ceivingly** *adv.*

14.. *Prose Legends* in *Anglia* VIII. 143 Hydynge deceyuaundly wikke wiþ medelynge of good. *c* **1440** *York Myst.* xiii. 140 At carpe to me dissayuandly. **1888** *Harper's Mag.* Oct. 806 To listen appreciatingly even if deceivingly.

decelerate (diː'sɛləreɪt), *v.* [f. DE- + AC)CELERATE *v.*] *trans.* To diminish the speed of; to cause to go slower. Also *intr.* or *absol.*

1899 *Times* 30 Sept. 3/5 The 7.45 a.m. ex Exeter..is decelerated nine minutes. **1902** *Westm. Gaz.* 22 Oct. 2/1 Two years ago this timing was decelerated by 5 min. **1924** *Public Opinion* 26 Apr. 399/3 Pushing the third button decelerates the whole system. **1928** *Evening Standard* 18 Mar., There would be a catastrophe if you decelerated too suddenly. **1957** *Times* 3 Sept. 4/2 Their thrust reversal unit, designed to assist in decelerating aircraft after landing.

deceleration (diːsɛlə'reɪʃən). [f. as prec. + -ATION.] The action or process of decelerating.

1897 *Daily News* 20 July 5/2 As far as the Great Northern and Caledonian Companies are concerned, 'deceleration' has been the order of the day in making the summer arrangements. **1900** *Ibid.* 24 Mar. 5/6 These alterations and 'decelerations' affect only Chatham trains. **1922** *Field* 18 Feb., Our travel was one of smooth acceleration and deceleration. **1926** *Bulletin* 1 Dec. 5/6 Drive cautiously and avoid sudden acceleration or deceleration. **1930** A. BENNETT *Imperial Palace* iv. 17 Her accelerations and decelerations, her brakings, could hardly be perceived. **1955** *Roadcraft* (H.M.S.O.) VII. 70 There are two normal methods by which the speed of a motor vehicle may be reduced—(a) by the deceleration of the engine as the pressure on the accelerator is relaxed, and (b) by the application of the brakes. **1971** *Daily Tel.* 1 July 30/5 The cosmonauts could have died of a lack of blood supply to the brain caused by the strong deceleration during re-entry from space.

decelerator (diː'sɛləreɪtə(r)). [f. DECELERATE *v.* + -OR.] An apparatus for reducing the speed of an engine.

1907 *Westm. Gaz.* 18 Nov. 6/3 The decelerator which automatically throttles the engine whenever the clutch is disengaged.

decelerometer (ˌdiːsɛlə'rɒmɪtə(r)). [f. DECELERATE *v.* + -METER, after ACCELEROMETER.] An instrument for ascertaining the deceleration of a moving body.

1924 *Sci. Amer.* Mar. 171/3 A decelerometer..is being used for making tests of the effectiveness of brakes. **1958** *Engineering* 21 Mar. 371/3 Recording decelerometers were found capable of giving a complete record of braking behaviour.

decelticize, etc.: see DE- II. 1.

decem-, L. *decem* ten, used in combination, as *decemjugis* ten-yoked, *decempedālis* ten feet long, *decemplicātus* ten-fold, etc.; hence in various technical words: **decem'costate** *a.* [COSTA], having ten ribs. **decem'dentate** *a.* [L. *dens* tooth], having ten teeth or points (Smart 1836). **de'cemfid** *a.* [L. *-fidus* cleft], divided into ten parts, segments, or lobes (*ibid.*). **decem'florous** *a.* [L. *-flōr-us*, -flowered], 'having ten flowers' (*Syd. Soc. Lex.* 1882). **decem'foliate, -'foliolate** [L. *folium* leaf, *foliolus* leaflet], having ten leaves or leaflets. **de'cemjugate** *a.* [L. *jugāt-us* yoked], 'having ten pairs of leaflets or of other organs' (*Syd. Soc. Lex.* 1882). **decem'locular** *a.* [L. *loculus* little bag], ten-celled, having ten little cells for seeds (Smart 1836). †**decemnovenal** *a.* [L. *decemnovem* nineteen], of nineteen years = DECENNOVENNAL. **ˌdecemnove'narian**, a man of the Nineteenth Century; hence **decemnove'narianism**, the characteristics distinctive of a man of the Nineteenth Century; **decemnove'narianize** *v.*, to act the decemnovenarian. **de'cempedal** *a.* [L. *decempedālis*, f. *pes, ped-* feet], (*a*) ten feet in length (*obs.*); (*b*) having ten feet. **de'cempedate** *a.* = prec. b (*Syd. Soc. Lex.* 1882). **decem'pennate** *a.* [L. *penna* wing], having ten flight-feathers on the pinion-bone. **'decemplex** *a.* [L. *-plex* -fold], tenfold (*S.S. Lex.*). **'decemplicate** *a.* [L. *plicātus* plaited, folded], 'having ten plaits or folds' (*ibid.*). **decem'punctate** *a.* [L. *punctum* a point], 'having ten points or spots' (*ibid.*). **decem'striate** *a.* [L. *striātus* grooved], 'having ten striæ' (*ibid.*).

1858 BENTHAM *Handbk. Brit. Flora* 7 *Decemdentate ..Decemfid..Decemfoliate..Decemfoliolate.* **1588** J. HARVEY *Disc. Probl.* 95 The Golden, decemnouenall, or Lunarie circle. **1698** WALLIS in *Phil. Trans.* XX. 187 That is, this is the Eighth Year of such Decem-novenal Cycle, or Circle of Nineteen Years. **1863** [DE MORGAN] *From Matter to Spirit* Pref. 6 We, respectable decemnovenarians as we are, have been so nourished on theories..that most of us cannot live with an unexplained fact in our heads. **1890** F. HALL in *N.Y. Nation* L. 316/1 Though a decemnovenarian, as some would call him, he is not to be allowed to decemnovenarianize in language. **1864** MISS COBBE *Studies New & Old* (1865) 359 We have all heard much concerning this 'Decemnovenarianism' for a long time before he received his formidable cognomen. *Ibid.* 379 Is it Steam which has made 'Decemnovenarianism', or 'Decemnovenarianism' which has created Steam? **1827** G. S. FABER *Sacr. Cal. Proph.* (1844) I. 48 A yet future decempartite division of that Empire. **1656** BLOUNT *Glossogr.*, *Decempedal*, of ten foot, or ten foot long. **1708** MOTTEUX *Rabelais* IV. lxiv. (1737) 262 The shadow is decempedal.

December (dɪ'sɛmbə(r)). Also 4–6 -bre, 4 -bir, descembre, 5 decembyr, 6 desember. Abbreviated Dec. [a. OF. *décembre*, *dezembre*, ad. L. *December*, f. *decem* ten, this being originally the tenth month of the Roman year. The meaning of *-ber* in this and the names of the three preceding months is uncertain.]

1. The twelfth and last month of the year according to the modern reckoning; that in which the winter solstice occurs in the northern hemisphere.

[*a* **1000** *Menologium* 220 (Gr.) þænne folcum bringð morȝen, to mannum monað to tune Decembris..ærra Jula.] **1297** R. GLOUC. (1724) 408þe endlefþe day of December þe toun hii wonne so. *a* **1300** *Cursor M.* 24916 (Cott.) þat moneth þat man clepes..Decembre [*v.r.* -ber, -bir, descembre]. **1460** *Plumpton Corr.* (Camden) 20 Written at London 9 of December. **1573** TUSSER *Husb.*, *December's husbandrie*, O dirtie December For Christmas remember. **1593** T. MORLEY *Madrigals*, '*Aprill is my mistris face*', Within her bosom is September, But in her heart a cold December. *a* **1643** CARTWRIGHT *Ordinary* I. ii, Don't you see December in her face? **1775** N. WRAXALL *Tour N. Europe* 88 The weather, which..was become in a few hours as cold and piercing as our Decembers. **1805** SCOTT *Last Minstr.* I. xxi, Alike to him was time or tide, December's snow or July's pride. **1841** T. H. KEY in Smith *Dict. Antiq.* s.v. *Calendar, Roman*, The winter solstice at Rome, in the year 46 B.C., occurred on the 24th of December of the Julian Calendar. **1886** MISS BRADDON *Under Red Flag* vi, The Man of December and Sedan—it was thus Blanquists and Internationals spoke of the late Emperor [Napoleon III]—was dethroned.

2. *attrib.* and *Comb.* **December moth** (see quots.).

1593 SHAKS. *Rich. II*, I. iii. 298 Or wallow naked in December snow. *a* **1679** EARL ORRERY *Guzman* III, Were our Hearts as much mortified as those December-Lovers Looks! **1832** J. RENNIE *Consp. Butterfl. & M.* 38 The December Moth (*Pœcilocampa Populi*, Stephens) appears in December. **1863** KINGSLEY *Water Bab.* iv. (ed. 2) 160 Pleasant December days. **1907** R. SOUTH *Moths Brit. Isles* I. 113 (*heading*) The December Moth (*Pœcilocampa populi*). **1945** V. TEMPLE *Butterflies & Moths in Brit.* Pl. 80 (*caption*) Caterpillar of the December Moth.

Hence **De'cember** *v. nonce-wd.*, (*a*) *trans.* to give the character of December to; (*b*) *intr.* to celebrate December (as the time of Christmas festivities). **De'cemberish** *a.*, †**De'cemberly** *a.*, resembling December in dreariness and darkness. **De'cembrist**, one connected in some specific way with this month; see quot. 1882.

1876 J. ELLIS *Cæsar in Egypt* 332 Now balls are deserted, and plays unremember'd, And all the May joys prematurely December'd. **1888** *Times* (Weekly Ed.) 7 Dec. 7/1 The Cabinet was seeking a pretext for 'Decembering'. **1795** BURNS *Let. to Mrs. Dunlop* 15 Dec., As I am in a complete Decemberish humour, gloomy, sullen, stupid. **1765** STERNE *Tr. Shandy* VIII. ix, In the many bleak and Decemberly nights of a seven years widowhood. **1882** H. LANSDELL *Through Siberia* II. 2 Certain of them called 'Decembrists', who in December 1825 tried to raise a revolt among the soldiers of Nicolas, and deprive him of his throne.

‖**decemvir** (dɪ'sɛmvə(r)). [L., sing. of *decemvirī*, originally *decem virī* 'the ten men'.]

Rom. Antiq. (*pl.*) A body of ten men acting as a commission, council, college, or ruling authority; *esp.* the two bodies of magistrates appointed in 451 and 450 B.C. to draw up a code of laws (the laws of the Twelve Tables) who were, during the time, entrusted with the supreme government of Rome.

[**1579** NORTH *Plutarch* (1612) 864 Cicero..did one day sharply reproue and inueigh against this law of the Decemuiri.] **1600** HOLLAND *Livy* III. xxxii. 109 Agreed it was that there should be created Decemvirs above all appeale. **1781** GIBBON *Decl. & F.* xliv, The Decemvirs, who sullied by their actions the honour of inscribing, on brass, or wood, or ivory, the Twelve Tables of the Roman Laws. **1838** ARNOLD *Hist. Rome* I. 253 A commission invested with such extraordinary powers as those committed to the decemvirs. **1868** SMITH *Sm. Dict. Rom. Antiq.* 127/2 *Decemviri Litibus Judicandis*..Augustus transferred to these decemvirs the presidency in the courts of the centumviri.

b. *transf.* A council or ruling body of ten, as the Council of Ten of the Venetian Republic.

1615 R. COCKS *Diary* 2 Aug., I had much adowe with Zanzabars desemvery. **1821** BYRON *Two Foscari* I. 188. I look Forward to be one day of the decemvirs. **1832** tr. *Sismondi's Ital. Rep.* ix. 202 The decemvirs dared unblushingly propose to their colleagues, etc.

c. *sing.* A member of such a body.

1703 ROWE *Fair Penit.* IV. i. (Jod.), He slew his only daughter To save her from the fierce Decemvir's lust. **1744** tr. *Livy* I. 272 (Jod.) C. Julius, a decemvir, appointed him a day for taking his trial. **1849** GROTE *Greece* II. lxxii. (1862) VI. 351 Like the Decemvir Appius Claudius at Rome.

Hence **de'cemvirship**, the office of decemvir.

1600 HOLLAND *Livy* 115 (R.) The decemvirship, and the conditions of his colleagues together, had so greatly changed.

decemviral (dɪ'sɛmvɪrəl), *a.* [ad. L. *decemvirālis*, f. *decemvir*: see -AL[1].] Of or pertaining to the decemvirs.

1600 HOLLAND *Livy* 127 (R.) The decemvirall lawes (which now are knowne by the name of the twelve Tables). **1651** HOWELL *Venice* 13 Three Senators..have power to summon the Decemvirall Colledg. **1833** THIRLWALL in *Philol. Museum* II. 477 The advantages of the consular over the decemviral form of government. **1852** GROTE *Greece* II. lxxiv. IX. 416 His decemviral governments or Dekarchies.

decemvirate (dɪ'sɛmvɪreɪt). [ad. L. *decemvirātus*, f. *decemvir*: see -ATE[1].] The office or government of decemvirs; a body of decemvirs.

1620 E. BLOUNT *Horæ Subsec.* 233 After the Decemvirate, they returned againe to Consuls. **1704** HEARNE *Duct. Hist.* (1714) I. 369 The Decemvirate regarded neither Senate nor people, but cut off the most considerable Citizens of both sorts. **1838** ARNOLD *Hist. Rome* I. xv. 302 The decemvirate seems indeed to have exhibited the perfect model of an aristocratical royalty, vested not in one person but in several.

b. *transf.* A body of ten rulers, councillors, etc., as the Venetian Council of Ten. Also *attrib.*

1651 HOWELL *Venice* 13 They read the letters addressd to the Decemvirat Colledg. **1653** SIR E. NICHOLAS in *N. Papers* (Camden) II. 12 The room..is now possessed by the Decemvirate or ten Worthies that now reign far more absolutely than ever any King did in England. *c* **1776** SIR W. JONES *Let. Ld. Althorpe*, If such a decemvirate should ever attempt to restore our constitutional liberty by constitutional means.

de'cenary, *improp.* **de'cennary**, *a.* and *sb.* [ad. med.L. *decēnārius* (*decennārius*), f. med.L. *decēna* (*decenna*) a tithing: see DECENER.]

A. *adj.* Of or pertaining to a *decēna* or tithing.

1752 FIELDING *Causes Incr. Robbers* §5 (R.) To prevent idle persons wandering from place to place..was one great point of the decennary constitution.

B. *sb.* = med.L. *decēna*, a tithing: see quot. 1881.

Apparently taken by the 17th c. antiquaries as formed on *decenner* DECENER + -Y, and so accepted by later writers.

[*c* **1250** BRACTON III. II. x, Diligenter erit inquirendum si [latro] fuerit in franco plegio et decenna, et tunc erit decenna in misericordia coram justitiarios nostros.] **1647** N. BACON *Disc. Govt. Eng.* I. xlviii. (1739) 84 View of free Pledges must be, to see that the Decennaries be full. *c* **1670** HOBBES *Dial. Com. Laws* 201 The whole Land was divided into Hundreds, and those again into Decennaries. **1765** BLACKSTONE *Comm.* I. 114 No man was suffered to abide in England above forty days, unless he were enrolled in some tithing or decennary. **1881** T. S. FRAMPTON *Hundred of Wrotham* 36 All males..should..be enrolled in a tithing, or decennary, which originally consisted of ten free families. [Cf. **1866** ROGERS *Agric. & Prices* I. 66 He was registered in the decenna before he reached adolescence.]

†**'decence.** *Obs.* [a. F. *décence* (13–14th c. in Hatzf.), ad. L. *decēntia*: see next.] = next.

1678 SPRAT *Serm. Gal.* vi. 10 In good works..there may be goodness in the general; but decence and gracefulness can be only in the particulars in doing the good. **1683** W. CLAGETT *Answ. Dissenter's Object.* 7 When the Decence and Convenience of a thing is considered, we should attribute much to the Wisdom of Authority. **1697** DRYDEN *Virg. Æneid* x. 96 And must I own.. my secret smart—What with more decence were in silence kept.

¶ *As confessedly Fr.*:

1836 GREVILLE *Diary* 94 (Stanford) To the opera to see Taglioni dance..Her grace and *décence* are something that no one can imagine who has not seen her.

decency ('diːsənsɪ). [ad. L. *decēntia*, f. *decēnt-em* becoming, fitting, DECENT.] The quality or fact of being decent.

†**1.** Appropriateness or fitness to the circumstances or requirements of the case; fitness, seemliness, propriety: **a.** of speech, action, or behaviour.

1567 DRANT *Horace, Arte of Poetrie* (R.), Of sortes and ages thou must note the manner and the guyse, A decensie for stirring youth, for elder folke likewise. **1589** PUTTENHAM *Eng. Poesie* III. xxiii. (Arb.) 269 To πρεπον.. we in our vulgar call it by a scholasticall terme [*decencie*] our owne Saxon English terme is [*seemelynesse*]. *Ibid.* 271 Your decencies are of sundrie sorts, according to the many circumstances accompanying our writing, speech or behauiour. **1636** HEALEY *Epictetus' Manuall* lix. 79 Thou neglectest another [function] which thou mightest execute with full decency. **1647** CLARENDON *Hist. Reb.* I. (1843) 33/1 The king was always the most punctual observer of all decency in his devotion. **1719** WATERLAND *Vind. Christ's Divinity* 107 Why so concern'd about the fitness, and decency of his Interpretation? **1725** WATTS *Logic* II. v. §4 The great Design of Prudence..is to determine and manage every Affair with Decency, and to the best Advantage. **1762** HUME *Hist. Eng.* III. liv. 173 His discourse on the scaffold was full of decency and courage.

†**b.** What is appropriate to a person's rank or dignity. *Obs.*

1584 POWEL *Lloyd's Cambria* 364 Reseruing two things, that is to say his conscience, and also the decencie of his state. **1649** MILTON *Eikon.* 17 With Scholastic flourishes, beneath the decencie of a king. **1661** MORGAN *Sphere Gentry* IV. v. 78 According to the Decency of the said Name of the Duke of Somerset and the nobility of his..estate.

†**c.** Fitness of form or proportion: Comeliness.

1610 GUILLIM *Heraldry* III. xiv. (1660) 170 Neither cán Art forme a fashion of more stately decencie, than she hath done on the Stage. **1667** PRIMATT *City & C. Builder* 80 For decency it will be requisite not to have the girders altogether so deep as ten inches in the second, third, and fourth Story.

†**2.** Decent or orderly condition of civil or social life. *Obs.*

1651 HOBBES *Govt. & Soc.* x. §1. 148 In [the state of civill Government there is] the Dominion of reason, peace, security, riches, decency, society, elegancy [etc.]. **1660** R. COKE *Power & Subj.* 89 Decencie and order must presuppose laws and directions. **1705** STANHOPE *Paraphr.* II. 121 God, as he is a God of Decency and Order, and not of Anarchy and Confusion [etc.].

3. Propriety of behaviour or demeanour; due regard to what is becoming; conformity (in behaviour, speech, or action) to the standard of propriety or good taste.

1647 CLARENDON *Hist. Reb.* I. (1843) 23/2 He [Wm. Earl of Pembroke]..lived towards the favourites with that decency, as would not suffer them to censure or reproach his master's judgment. **1682** NORRIS *Hierocles* 39 To bear..the loss of our goods with mildness and decency. **1702** *Eng. Theophrastus* 342 We do sometimes out of vanity or decency what we could do out of inclination and duty. **1732–3** SWIFT *Let. Mrs. Pilkington* 1 Jan., I cannot with decency shew them, except to a very few. **1749** FIELDING *Tom Jones* x. viii, If I had not the patience of fifty Jobs, you would make me forget all decency and decorum. **1798** WORDSW. *Old Cumbrld. Beggar*, Many, I believe, there are Who live a life of virtuous decency. **1855** LD. HOUGHTON in *Life* (1891) I. xi. 516 As I have got two letters from you to-day, I must write in decency before I go to sleep. **1883** GLADSTONE in *Times* 9 June, Less than that I cannot say in justice and in decency.

b. *esp.* Compliance with recognized notions of modesty or delicacy; freedom from impropriety.

1639 tr. *Du. Bosq's Compl. Woman* F iv, Peradventure they would..accuse him for not writing, as decency obliged him therein..Is there one sole word in all this worke..to make one blush in reading it? **1684** EARL ROSCOM. *Ess. Transl. Verse*, Immodest words admit of no defence; For want of decency is want of sense. *a* **1715** BURNET *Own Time* (1724) I. 137 Sir Elisha Leightoun..maintained an outward decency..yet he was a very vicious man. **1886** H. H. JOHNSTON *Kilimanjaro Exp.* ii. 28 The black glistening forms of the burly negroes on whom nakedness sits with decency. *Ibid.* xix. 433 Both sexes have little notion or conception of decency, the men especially seeming to be unconscious of any impropriety in nakedness.

c. Conformity to the standard of living becoming one's position; respectability.

1751 JOHNSON *Rambler* No. 166 ¶2 Those whom a very little assistance would enable to support themselves with decency. **1785** PALEY *Mor. Philos.* III. ix, There is a certain appearance, attendance, establishment, and mode of living, which custom has annexed to the several ranks and orders of civil life (and which compose what is called decency).

4. *pl.* Decent or becoming acts or observances; the established observances of decent life or decorum; proprieties. (Rarely *sing.*)

1667 MILTON *P.L.* VIII. 601 Those graceful acts, Those thousand decencies that daily flow From all her words and actions mixed with love And sweet compliance. **1673** DRYDEN *Marr. à la Mode* Ep. Ded., They have copied..the delicacies of expression, and the decencies of behaviour from your lordship. **1700** —— *Sigismonda & G.* 701 O ever faithful heart, I have perform'd the ceremonial part, The decencies of grief. **1723** DE FOE *Col. Jack* (1840) 204, I told her I thought it was a decency to the ladies. **1735** POPE *Ep. Lady* 164 Virtue she finds too painful an endeavour, Content to dwell in decencies for ever. **1827** MACAULAY *Machiavelli* Ess. (1854) 49/2 He became careless of the decencies which were expected from a man so highly distinguished in the literary and political world.

b. *pl.* The outward conditions or requirements of a decent life.

1798 MALTHUS *Popul.* (1878) 375 He may be..better able to command the decencies..of life. **1832** LEWIS *Use & Ab. Pol. Terms* xiii. 111 In this sense the poor are those who.. severally enjoy a less quantity of decencies and necessaries. **1842** S. LOVER *Handy Andy* xxiv. 213 The little man was buttoning on a pair of black gaiters, the only serviceable decency he had at his command. **1894** H. SIDGWICK in *Times* 13 Jan. 11/4 It was not easy to distinguish decencies and comforts on the one hand and luxuries on the other.

decend, etc.: see DESCEND, etc.

decene ('diːsiːn). *Chem.* [f. Gr. δέκα ten + -ENE.] The olefine of the decacarbon or DECYL series, $C_{10}H_{20}$. Also called *decylene*.

1877 WATTS *Fownes' Chem.* 52.

†**'decener.** *Obs.* Forms: 6 decenier, disener, 7 deciner, -or, 7–8 decenner. [a. AngloFr. *decener* = OF. *decenier*, mod.F. *dixenier*, *dizenier*, *dizainier*, in med.L. *decēnārius* (improp. *decennārius*), f. *decēna*, in OF. *dizeine*, *-aine*, Pr. *desena*, Sp. *decena*, a group of ten, a tithing.]

1. One in command of ten soldiers.

1555 WATREMAN *Fardle Facions* II. x. 211 Their capitaines ouer ten, whiche, by a terme borowed of the Frenche, we calle Diseners. **1589** IVE tr. *Du Bellay's Instr.* 80 The Souldiers [should exercise] by themselues euerie holie day, with their Deceniers [*chefs de chambre*] Chiefs of squadrons, and Corporals. **1627** S. WARD *Serm., Jethro's Justice*, From the Gouernour of the thousand to the Centurion, from him to the Tithing-man or Decinor.

2. a. The head of a *decena* or tithing; a tithing-man or borsholder; **b.** A member of a tithing.

1607 COWELL *Interpr., Deciners*..signifieth..such as were wont to have the oversight and checke of ten friburgs for the maintenance of the king's peace. **1624** *Termes de la Ley* s.v., Deciner is not now used for the chiefe man of a Dozein, but for him that is sworne to the Kings peace. **1647** N. BACON *Disc. Govt. Eng.* I. xxvi. (1739) 43 All Free-men were Decenners, that is, ranked into several tens. **1752** FIELDING *Causes Incr. Robbers* §5 (R.) In case of the default of appearance in a decenner, his nine pledges had one and thirty days to bring the delinquent forth to justice. [**1869** W. MOLYNEUX *Burton on Trent* 105 There was a staff of men six in number called 'Deciners', whose duty it was in modern times to assist the constables in preserving the peace of the manor and borough..The name commonly given to these officers was *dozener*, and under it at the present day they are associated in many instances with municipal boroughs.]

decennal (dɪ'sɛnəl), *a.* ? *Obs.* [ad. L. *decennāl-is* of ten years, f. *decem* + *ann-us*. Cf. F. *décennal* (16th c. in Hatzf.).] = DECENNIAL.

1648 'MERCURIUS PRAGMATICUS' *Plea for King* 26 They.. appointed Archons, or Decennall Governors, that is, one Prince for ten years. **1708** MOTTEUX *Rabelais* (1737) V. 235 A Decennal Prescription.

†**dece'nnalian**, *a. Obs.* = prec.

1794 T. TAYLOR *Pausanias* I. 376 The Medontidæ still held the decennalian government.

decennary (dɪ'sɛnərɪ), *a.* and *sb.* [f. L. *decenn-is* of ten years + -ARY: cf. DECENNIAL.]

A. *adj.* Of or pertaining to a period of ten years; DECENNIAL.

1855 *Jrnl. R. Agric. Soc.* XVI. II. 577 The average home-produce of wheat..during each of these decennary periods.

B. *sb.* A period of ten years; a decennium.

1822 W. R. HAMILTON in *Parr's Wks.* (1828) VIII. 34 The awful predictions of the Whigs during the last decennary. **1826** H. C. ROBINSON *Diary* (1869) II. 322 The fifth decennary of the nineteenth century. **1873** C. ROBINSON *N.S. Wales* 72 Dividing the decennary into two equal parts, it will be found that..during the earlier five years [etc.].

decennary: see DECENARY.

de'cenniad. [irreg. f. L. DECENNIUM + -AD, after *triad*, *chiliad*, etc.] = DECENNIUM.

1864 *Soc. Science Rev.* 239 The increase..was found in the ten years ending in 1851 to be less than it had been in any previous decenniad. **1882** *Athenæum* 3 June 692/1 During three decenniads of the latter half of the present century.

decennial (dɪ'sɛnɪəl), *a.* (*sb.*) [f. L. *decenni-um* (see next) + -AL[1]: cf. *centennial*. The L. adj. was *decennāl-is*, whence DECENNAL.]

A. *adj.* Of or pertaining to a period of ten years.

1656 BLOUNT *Glossogr.*, *Decennial*, belonging to or conteining ten years. **1685** H. MORE *Paralip. Prophet.* 91 At a complete decennial interval. **1798** W. TAYLOR in *Monthly Mag.* IV. 111 The interest of a majority of the house.. illegally to perpetuate its authority and vote itself decennial. **1866** ROGERS *Agric. & Prices* I. xxv. 625 A table in which decennial averages may be stated. **1868** M. PATTISON *Academ. Org.* iii. 52 The decennial return of income to be made by each college.

b. Of persons: Holding office for ten years.

1728 NEWTON *Chronol. Amended* 37 Charops, the first decennial Archon of the Athenians. **1866** FELTON *Anc. & Mod. Gr.* II. v. 74 Seven decennial archons carried on the government till B.C. 683.

B. *sb.* A decennial anniversary or its celebration. *U.S.*

1889 in *Century Dict.*

Hence **de'cennially** *adv.*, every ten years.

1874 *Daily News* 16 Feb. 5/5 Opportunity of decennially reviewing the progress throughout the world of fine arts.

‖**decennium** (dɪ'sɛnɪəm). Pl. **-ia.** [L., f. *decenn-is* of ten years, f. *decem* ten + *annus* year: cf. *biennis*, *biennium*, and CENTENNIUM.] A space of ten years, a decade (of years).

1685 H. MORE *Paralip. Prophet.* 91 Reckoning on still by complete Decenniums. **1801** W. TAYLOR in *Monthly Mag.* XII. 590 To unteach all their lessons of the last decennium. **1864** PUSEY *Lect. Daniel* i. 8 In the last decennia of the last century. **1881** *Census Eng. & Wales* Prelim. Report p. xii, The decrease of the population of Ireland..in each succeeding decennium.

†**decennoval** (dɪ'sɛnəvəl), *a. Obs.* [ad. L. *decennovāl-is*, f. *decem-novem* nineteen: see -AL[1].] Of or pertaining to nineteen (years).

1681 HOOKE *Phil. Collect.* XII. 28 Dionysius Exiguus introduced the Decennoval Cycle (called the Golden Number) for the Celebration of Easter. **1694** HOLDER *Disc. Time* 75 Meton..constituted a Decennoval Circle, or of 19 years.

So †**de'cennovary**, †**decenno'vennal**, = prec.

1694 HOLDER *Disc. Time* 77 In this whole Decennovary Progress of the Epacts. **1677** CARY *Chronol.* I. II. I. ii. 57 An Interval of 1257 Years, which make 66 Decenovenal Cycles, and somewhat more. **1686** PLOT *Staffordsh.* 425 Through the whole Decennovennal Cycle.

decension, -sor, obs. DESCENSION, -SOR.

decent ('diːsənt), *a.* [a. F. *décent* (15th c. in Hatzf.), or ad. L. *decēnt-em*, pr. pple. of *decēre* to become, to be fitting. It is used etymologically by Wynkyn de Worde (perh. as French) in

1495 *Trevisa's Barth. De P.R.* v. xxix., The fyngres highte digiti..of this worde decent [*Bodl. MS.* decere], to saye in Englysshe semely, for they ben semely sette.]

1. a. Becoming, suitable, appropriate, or proper to the circumstances or special requirements of the case; seemly, fitting. *Obs.* or *arch.*

1539 [see b]. **1547** LATIMER *1st Serm. bef. Edw. VI* (Arb.) 33 It was not decent that the kings horsses shuld be kept in them [abbeys]. **1589** PUTTENHAM *Eng. Poesie* III. xxiii. (Arb.) 279 Tell thine errand in such termes as are decent betwixt enemies. **1661** EVELYN *Diary* 20 Dec., The funeral of the Bishop of Hereford..was a decent solemnity. *a* **1677** BARROW *Serm. Matt.* i. 20 (Wks. 1716) II. 257 Decent it was that as man did approve so man also should condemn sin in the flesh. **1695** DRYDEN *Parall. Poetry & Paint.*, Since there must be ornaments both in painting and poetry, if they are not necessary, they must at least be decent, that is in their due place, and but moderately used. **1710** STEELE *Tatler* No. 231 ¶2 After a decent Time spent in the Father's House, the Bridegroom went to prepare his Seat for her Reception. **1749** FIELDING *Tom Jones* v. iii, So total a change..that we think it decent to communicate it in a fresh chapter. **1827** POLLOK *Course T.* III. Showing, too, in plain and decent phrase. **1848** MACAULAY *Hist. Eng.* I. 75 The founders of the Anglican Church had retained episcopacy as an ancient, a decent, and a convenient ecclesiastical polity, but had not declared that form of church government to be of divine institution.

†**b.** Appropriate with regard to rank or dignity.

1539 *Act 31 Hen. VIII*, c. 5 A goodly..manour, decent and convenient for a king. **1547** LATIMER *1st Serm. bef. Edw. VI* (Arb.) 33 God teacheth what honoure is decente for the kynge. **1640** YORKE *Union Hon.* 77 The Tombe..is not so decent, nor convenient as his honour and acts deserved. **1657** J. SMITH *Myst. Rhet.* 67 He useth a decent and due epithet, thus, Honourable Judge. **1716** LADY M. W. MONTAGUE *Basset Table* 77 When kings, queens, knaves are set in decent rank. *a* **1794** GIBBON *Autobiog.* 84 The court was regulated with decent and splendid economy.

†**2.** Of such appearance and proportions as suit the requirements of good taste; comely, handsome.

1600 J. PORY tr. *Leo's Africa* II. 237 Most of their houses are but of one storie high, yet are they very decent, and have each one a garden. **1616** BULLOKAR, *Decent*, comely, handsome. **1625** BACON *Ess. Buildings* (Arb.) 552 An Inward Court..Which is to be..Cloistered on all Sides, vpon Decent and Beautifull Arches, as High as the first Story. **1669** A. BROWNE *Ars Pict.* (1675) 4 It is impossible to make any decent or well proportioned thing, without this Symetrical measure of the parts orderly united. **1725** POPE *Odyss.* XIII. 273 Her decent hand a shining jav'lin bore. **1725** DE FOE *Voy. round World* (1840) 268 He had five or six apartments in his house..two of them were very large and decent.

3. a. In accordance with or satisfying the general standard of propriety or good taste, in conduct, speech, or action; *esp.* conformable to or satisfying the recognized standard of modesty or delicacy; free from obscenity.

1545 JOYE *Exp. Dan.* vii. 124 A fayer decent semely shewe of vtwarde deuocion. **1613** SHAKS. *Hen VIII*, IV. ii. 145 For vertue, and true beautie of the soule, For honestie, and decent carriage. **1625** BACON *Ess. Praise* (Arb.) 357 To Praise a Mans selfe, cannot be Decent, except it be in rare Cases. **1712** HEARNE *Collect.* 29 Oct., 'Twill not be decent for me to inquire into y[t] Affair. **1732** BERKELEY *Alciphr.* II. §10 The regular decent life of a virtuous man. **1754** CHATHAM *Lett. Nephew* iv. 20 Be sure to associate..with men of decent and honourable lives. **1770** GIBBON *On Æneid* VI. Misc. Wks. 1796 II. 507 The laws of honour are different in different ages; and a behaviour which in Augustus was decent, would have covered Æneas with infamy. **1830-2** CARLETON *Traits Irish Peasant.* (Tegg's ed.) 375 Are you ladin' a decenter or more becominer life? **1855** MACAULAY *Hist. Eng.* IV. 265 Much more than they had any decent pretence for asking. **1865** MILL in *Morn. Star* 6 July, Would it have been decent in me to have gone among you and said, 'I am the fittest man?'

b. of persons. *spec.* in mod. colloq. use (see quot. 1949).

1731 SWIFT *Poems, Strephon & Chloe*, Women must be decent, And from the spouse each blemish hide. **1886** H. H. JOHNSTON *Kilimanjaro Exp.* xix. 437 The Wa-Caga cannot be accused of indecency, for they make no effort to be decent, but walk about as Nature made them. **1949** R. HARVEY *Curtain Time* 63 Sometimes, if she knew one of the actors or actresses, she would knock at a door and call 'Are you decent?' (That old theatrical phrase startled people who didn't belong to the theatre, but it simply meant 'Are you dressed?')

4. a. Satisfying (in character, mode of living, behaviour, manners, etc.) the standard of one's position or circumstances; respectable.

1712 STEELE *Spect.* No. 443 ¶7 Honestus..makes modest Profit by modest Means, to the decent Support of his Family. **1738** POPE *Epil. Sat.* II. 71 Even in a bishop I can spy desert: Secker is decent. **1771** MRS. HARRIS in *Priv. Lett. Ld. Malmesbury* I. 239 Lord Herbert is at Wilton with his tutor..a decent well-behaved man. **1807** CRABBE *Par. Reg.* I. 403 Next, with their boy, a decent couple came. **1831** T. L. PEACOCK *Crotchet Castle* iii, *Captain F.*—Many decent families are maintained on smaller means. *Lady C.*—Decent families: ay, decent is the distinction from respectable. Respectable means rich, and decent means poor. I should die if I heard my family called decent. **1879** GEO. ELIOT *Theo. Such* ii. 27 Most of us who have had decent parents. **1882** SERJT. BALLANTINE *Exper. Barrister's Life* I. xxiii. 290, I remember a pantaloon..He was a very sober decent fellow.

b. of appearance, dress, etc.

1696 tr. *Du Mont's Voy. Levant* 45 Others go about in a pretty decent Garb. **1745** *De Foe's Eng. Tradesman* (1841) I. xxii. 210 A well-furnished shop with a decent outside. **1773** JOHNSON *Let. Mrs. Thrale* 6 Sept., In the afternoon tea was made by a very decent girl in a printed linen. **1843** MRS. CARLYLE *Lett.* I. 227, I am getting together one decent suit of clothes for her. **1884** F. M. CRAWFORD *Rom. Singer* I. 5 We made him look very decent.

5. a. Satisfying a fair standard; fair, tolerable, passable, 'respectable'; good enough in its way.

Distinct examples of this sense are late; within brackets are given some earlier quots. which may belong to it.

[*c* **1642** TWYNE in Wood *Life* (Oxf. Hist. Soc.) I. 55 They were put into battell arraye, and skirmished together in a very decent manner. **1697** DRYDEN *Virg. Georg.* Ded. (1721) I. 180 If his Constitution be healthful, his Mind may still retain a decent Vigour.]

1711 ADDISON *Spect.* No. 34 ¶10 At length, making a Sacrifice of all their Acquaintance and Relations, [they] furnished out a very decent Execution. **1773** J. BERRIDGE *Chr. World Unmasked* (1812) 29 Some debts I shall pay myself, a decent part of the shot. **1826** COBBETT *Rur. Rides* (1885) II. 27 The locusts..appeared..to be doing pretty well, and had made decent shoots. **1863** FR. A. KEMBLE *Resid. in Georgia* 132 There was not another decent kitchen, or flower garden in the State. **1880** MISS BRADDON *Just as I am* xi, She had just learnt enough English to write a decent letter. *Mod.* (*Oxford Tutor*) He ought to be able to write decent Latin prose.

b. Of a person: kind, accommodating, pleasant. *colloq.*

1902 E. NESBIT *Five Children & It* iii. 101 'Well,' said Cyril, 'if you ask me I think it was rather decent of her'——'Decent?' said Anthea; 'it was very nice indeed of her...' **1909** GALSWORTHY *Joy* I 11, Couldn't you just go up and give her a message..it would be most awfully decent of you. **1910** L. A. HARKER *Master & Maid* xvii. 255 Fellows had told him how cut up old Nick was when that chap died in his house, and Bruiser was a jolly sight decenter than old Nick. *Ibid.* xx. 308 He was a very decent chap, quite a man of the world. **1928** W. DEEPING *Old Pybus* ix. §3 The pater has been rather decent. **1932** 'N. SHUTE' *Lonely Road* vi. 125 That's really very decent of you. **1944** R. LEHMANN *Ballad & Source* 36 This is a ripping place, and they're being jolly decent to us.

6. quasi-*adv.* Decently.

1715-20 POPE *Iliad* VII. 513 Nor less the Greeks their pious sorrows shed, And decent on the pile dispose the dead. **1761** ELIZ. BONHOTE *Rambles of Frankly* (1797) II. 176 The woman was dressed neat and decent.

7. *Comb.*, as *decent-lived*, *-looking*.

1800 MRS. HERVEY *Mourtray Fam.* II. 152 A small but tolerably decent-looking house. **1892** *Pall Mall G.* 5 Apr. 6/1, I never stole any spoons, and am a decent-lived man as a whole.

decentish ('di:səntɪʃ), *a. colloq.* [f. prec. + -ISH.] Somewhat decent, pretty decent.

a **1814** DIBDIN '*Tom Tough*' in *Univ. Songster* (1825) 83 Laid up at last in a decentish condition. **1820** *Blackw. Mag.* VII. 298 The Jenkinsops had maintained a decentish sort of character. **1854** MOTLEY *Corr.* 8 May, I have a decentish kind of room here, and I think I shall stop.

decently ('di:səntlɪ), *adv.* [-LY[2].]

1. In a decent manner; with decency; †suitably; †fittingly; becomingly; respectably.

1552 HULOET, Decentlye, *decenter.* **1556** LAUDER *Tractate* 39 To rewle his ryng In Godlie maner, decentlie. **1611** BIBLE *1 Cor.* xiv. 40 Let all things be done decently [Vulg. *honeste*; WYCLIF, *and all 16th c. vv.* honestly] and in order. **1639** FULLER *Holy War* IV. viii. (1840) 192 He also caused the corpses of the Christians..decently to be interred. **1662** *Bk. Com. Prayer, Churching of Women*, The woman..shall come into the Church decently appareled. **1723** DE FOE *Col. Jack* (1840) 221 My wife..treated me more decently than she had been wont to do. **1751** JOHNSON *Rambler* No. 170 ¶2 My father was burthened with more children than he could decently support. **1814** SOUTHEY *Roderick* III, There upon the ground Four bodies, decently composed, were laid. **1871** MORLEY *Voltaire* (1886) 74 In England, Voltaire noticed, the peasant is decently clad.

2. In a fairly satisfactory way or measure; tolerably, passably.

1846 MRS. CARLYLE *Lett.* I. 368, I cannot even steady my hand to write decently. **1859** DARWIN in *Life & Lett.* (1887) I. 151 If I keep decently well.

†**'decentness.** *Obs.* [-NESS.] The quality of being decent; decency, propriety.

1561 VERON *Hunting of Purg.* 37 Shall they [our dead] be caried forth, wythout any decentnesse, as we be wont to cary forth dead horses? **1581** MULCASTER *Positions* xxxviii. (1887) 178 There is a comlynesse in eche kinde, and a decentnesse in degree. **1670** EVELYN *Diary* 6 Feb., The lawfulnesse, decentnesse, and necessitie of subordinate degrees and ranks of men.

decentralist (di:'sɛntrəlɪst), *sb.* (and *a.*) [f. DECENTRALIZE *v.*: see -IST.] One who believes in a policy of decentralization. Also *attrib.* or as *adj.*

1920 *Glasgow Herald* 18 Mar. 9 The struggle between the Centralists and the Decentralists or Regionalists in the matter of administration. **1921** *Q. Rev.* Apr. 398 The Centralists and Decentralists are about equal in numbers. **1941** *Commonweal* 20 June 204 For several years, we have had an evident decentralist movement. People have fled from the big cities, and landed outside. **1964** M. MCLUHAN *Understanding Media* I. i. 8 Automation technology..is integral and decentralist in depth.

decentralization (di:,sɛntrəlaɪ'zeɪʃən). [n. of action from next. So mod.F. *décentralisation* (1878 in *Acad. Dict.*).]

The action or fact of decentralizing; decentralized condition; *esp.* in *Politics*, the weakening of the central authority and distribution of its functions among the branches or local administrative bodies. Also *attrib.*

1846 BASTIAT & PORTER *Gen. Interest* 40 An irresistible power of decentralization. **1872** M. D. CONWAY *Republ. Superst.* I. i. 10 The illustration of the dangers of extreme decentralisation in a republic furnished by the history of the United States. **1898** *Daily News* 8 Sept. 5/1 The recommendations of Lord Lansdowne's decentralisation Committee. **1906** *Daily Chron.* 23 Jan. 5/2 The decentralisation schemes introduced by the late Government. **1908** *Ibid.* 12 May 6/4 With these larger and wider reforms the Decentralisation Commission has nothing to do. **1961** *Ann. Reg. 1960* 219 The decentralization reform..had to be modified.

decentralize (di:'sɛntrəlaɪz), *v.* [f. DE- II. 1 + CENTRALIZE. Cf. mod.F. *décentraliser* (1878 in *Acad. Dict.*).]

trans. To undo the centralization of; to distribute administrative powers, etc., which have been concentrated in a single head or centre. Hence **de'centralized, de'centralizing** *ppl. adjs.*

1851 NICHOL *Archit. Heav.* 91 These unconcentrated, or rather de-centralized masses of stars. **1859** BRIGHT *Sp. India* 1 Aug., What you want is to decentralize your Government. **1860** *Sat. Rev.* IX. 803/2 Decentralizing influences wax faint and few. **1875** MERIVALE *Gen. Hist. Rome* lxx. (1877) 575 During the last century the government of the empire had become completely decentralized.

decentralizer (di:'sɛntrəlaɪzə(r)). [f. DECENTRALIZE *v.*] = DECENTRALIST.

1898 J. E. C. BODLEY *France* i. 36 The venerable savant, himself a decentralizer. **1963** *Economist* 19 Oct. 240/1 The 'decentralisers', who were ready to let Angola..and the rest move some way towards autonomy.

decentre (di:'sɛntə(r)), *v.* Also decenter. [f. DE- + CENTRE *sb.* or *v.*] **1.** *trans.* To remove the centre from (in quot., CENTRE *sb.* 13).

1870 *Engineering* X. 485/1 In 1847, M. Beaudemoulin..made use of sand in decentering arches.

2. To place out of centre; to render eccentric; *spec.* in *Optics* (see quot. 1889). So **de'centrated** *ppl. a.*; **decen'tration**; **de'cent(e)red** *ppl. a.*; **de'cent(e)ring** *vbl. sb.* and *ppl. a.*

1889 E. E. MADDOX *Clinical Use of Prisms* II. 45 A lens is said to be normally centred when the optical and geometrical centres coincide..but to be decentred when, as in *Fig.* 21, the optical centre O, and the geometrical centre G, are apart. *Ibid.* 47 The word 'decentering' is generally applied to the removal of the optical centre away from the geometrical centre of the lens. *Ibid.* 49 The dislocation of the optical centre..to be obtained by decentration proper, that is by decentering the lens *in* its rim. **1909** *Cent. Dict.* Suppl., Decentrated. **1946** A. HUXLEY *Let.* 26 Oct. (1969) 551 Too much concentration defeats its own end, and..effective concentration has to work by a process of decentration. **1962** L. S. SASIENI *Optical Dispensing* v. 126 The right lens may be decentred out and the left lens decentred inwards. *Ibid.*, The amount of decentration produced by the asymmetry..is..likely to have appreciable prismatic effect. **1964** *Yearbook Astr. 1965* 96 The stresses ..tend to de-centre the secondary, making it move off the optical axis.

†**deceper**, *v. Obs.* [Illiterate spelling of *desepare* or *dessepare*, a. OF. *desseparer*, *deseparer*, ad. late L. *dis-sēparāre*, f. *dis-* asunder + *sēparāre* to SEPARATE, SEVER.] *trans.* To dissever. Hence †**de'ceperation** [OF. *deceperacion* (Godef.)], separation, severance.

1547 BOORDE *Brev. Health* 13 b, The one decepered from the other. *a* **1450** *Knt. de la Tour* (1868) 98 Deceperacion of the loue be twene hem.

decephalize (di:'sɛfəlaɪz), *v. Biol.* [DE- II. 1: cf. CEPHALIZATION (Gr. κεφαλή head).] To reverse the cephalization of; to reduce, degrade, or simplify the parts of the head of (an animal). Hence **decephali'zation**, the simplification or reduction of cephalic parts; reduction of the complexity or specialization of the head, as compared with the rest of the body; decephalized condition. (Introduced by Dana, in article cited.)

1863 DANA in *Amer. Jrnl. Science & Arts* 2nd Ser. XXXVI. 3 Examples of *cephalization*..by a transfer of members from the locomotive to the cephalic series (or of *decephalization* by the reverse) occur in the two highest sub-kingdoms, those of *Vertebrates* and *Articulates*. *Ibid.* 5 The Entomostracans exemplify decephalization by degeneration.

deceptation, obs. f. DISCEPTATION, discussion.

†**de'ceptible**, *a. Obs.* [? a. obs. F. *déceptible* or directly f. L. type **dēceptibilis*: see -BLE.] Apt to be deceived.

1646 SIR T. BROWNE *Pseud. Ep.* I Humane nature; of whose deceptible condition..perhaps there should not need any other eviction. *Ibid.* I. iii. 8 An erroneous inclination of the people; as being the most deceptible part of mankind.

Hence **decepti'bility**.

1665 GLANVILL *Sceps. Sci.* i. 6 Considering the shortness of our intellectual sight, the deceptibility and impositions of our senses. **1837** CARLYLE *Diam. Necklace* Misc. Ess. (1888) V. 162 A fixed idea..has produced a deceptibility..that will clutch at straws.

deception (dɪ'sɛpʃən). Also 6 dis-. [a. F. *déception* (13th c. in Hatzf.), ad. L. *dēceptiōn-em*, n. of action from *dēcipĕre* to DECEIVE.]

1. The action of deceiving or cheating.

c **1430** LYDG. *Min. Poems* (1840) 76 Hope dispeyred, a gwerdonles gwerdone; Trusty disceyte, feythful decepcioune. **1477** EARL RIVERS (Caxton) *Dictes* F ij, þ[t] ben harme-doers & loveth falshode and desepcion. **1490** CAXTON *Eneydos* xxvi. 95 What grete decepcions and iniuries she ymagyneth ayenst the. *c* **1500** *Doctr. Gd. Servauntes* in *Anc. Poet. Tracts* (Percy Soc.) 4 Fle dysceyte, gyle, and decepcyon. **1535** STEWART *Cron. Scot.* II. 126 For greit disceptioun all this thing he did. *a* **1716** SOUTH (J.), All deception is a misapplying of those signs which..were made the means of mens signifying or conveying their thoughts. **1794** S. WILLIAMS *Vermont* 170 He was accustomed to no falsehood or deception. **1862** DARWIN *Fertil. Orchids* i. 45 These plants exist by an organized system of deception.

b. The fact or condition of being deceived.

1646 SIR T. BROWNE *Pseud. Ep.* III. iv. 113 Hee is surely greedy of delusion, and will hardly avoide deception. **1769** *Junius Lett.* xxxi. 144 The public has fallen into the deception. **1836** HOR. SMITH *Tin Trump.* (1876) 118 Deception—a principal ingredient in happiness.

2. That which deceives; a piece of trickery; a cheat, sham.

1794 MRS. RADCLIFFE *Myst. Udolpho* xx, There is some deception, some trick. **1833** RITCHIE *Wand. Loire* 176 Launching the anathemas of what we call taste against so paltry a deception. **1841** MISS MITFORD in L'Estrange *Life* III. viii. 130 There was no background to form a phantasmagoria deception.

Hence **de'ceptionist**, one who performs feats of illusion; a juggler.

1883 *Society* 20 Jan. 22/1 'The American Deceptionist'..with his marvellous juggling tricks.

de'ceptional, *a. rare.* [f. prec. + -AL[1].] Of or pertaining to deception; deceptive.

1830 GALT *Lawrie T.* v. vii. (1849) 224, I played a deceptional part.

deceptious (dɪ'sɛpʃəs), *a.* Now *rare.* [a. obs. F. *deceptieux*, *-cieux*, in med.L. *dēceptiōs-us* (Du Cange), f. *dēceptiōn-em*: see -OUS.] Of the nature of or characterized by deception; that tends to deceive, cheat, or mislead.

1606 SHAKS. *Tr. & Cr.* v. ii. 123 An esperance..That doth inuert th'attest of eyes and eares; As if those organs had deceptious functions. **1789** *Bath Jrnl.* 20 July Advt., To puff off an old stock in a deceptious manner. **1824** BENTHAM *Bk. Fallacies* Wks. 1843 II. 437 Deceptious terms. 1. In the war department,—*honour* and *glory*. 2. In international affairs, *honour*, *glory*, and *dignity*. **1829** *Examiner* 706/2 False attacks, feints, and deceptious demonstrations. **1843** *Tait's Mag.* x. 622 Stripped of its deceptious summer verdure.

† **de'ceptiously**, *adv. Obs.* [f. prec. + -LY².] In a way characterized by deception; in such a way as to deceive.

1797 W. TAYLOR in *Monthly Rev.* XXIII. 582 She then appoints him deceptiously in the bath house. **1817** BENTHAM *Plan Parl. Reform* cxv, Circumstantially but deceptiously evidentiary.

deceptitious (diːsɛp'tɪʃəs), *a. rare.* [f. L. stem *dēcept-* (see next) + *-itious* (from L. *-īcius*).] Of a deceptive kind or character.

1827 BENTHAM *Ration. Evid.* Wks. 1843 VII. 15 Any deceptitious representation of psychological facts.

deceptive (dɪ'sɛptɪv), *a.* [a. F. *déceptif, -ive* (1378 in Hatzf.), in med. or mod.L. *dēceptīvus*, f. *dēcept-* ppl. stem of *dēcipĕre* to deceive; see -IVE. In English a recent word (not in Shaksp.), which has taken the place of DECEPTIOUS.] Apt or tending to deceive, having the character of deceiving.

deceptive cadence (Music): false or interrupted cadence: see FALSE *a.* 2 b.

1611 COTGR., *Deceptif*, deceptiue, deceitfull, deceiuing. **1656** in BLOUNT *Glossogr.* *c* **1780** V. KNOX *Remarks Gram. Schools* (R.), It is to be feared..that this mode of education ..is ultimately deceptive. **1787** HARGRAVE *Tracts, Case of Impositions* (R.), The deceptive verbal criticism from words no longer understood. **1840** CARLYLE *Heroes* (1858) 295 A mere shadow and deceptive nonentity. **1874** MORLEY *Compromise* (1886) 171 We see the same men..kneeling, rising, bowing, with deceptive solemnity.

† **b.** as *sb.* Deceiving faculty. *Obs.*

1652 GAULE *Magastrom.* 268 By learning the deceptive, and proving the experience, of the magical Art.

deceptively (dɪ'sɛptɪvlɪ), *adv.* [-LY².] In a deceptive manner, so as to deceive.

1825 COLERIDGE *Aids Refl.* (1848) I. 104 If he use the words, *right* and *obligation*, he does it deceptively. **1863** BATES *Nat. Amazon* II. 58 Two smaller kinds, which are deceptively like the little Nemeobius Lucina.

de'ceptiveness. [-NESS.] The quality of being deceptive.

1837 CARLYLE *Fr. Rev.* II. v. vi, An Executive 'pretending', really with less and less deceptiveness now, 'to be dead'. **1873** BURTON *Hist. Scot.* VI. lxx. 201 A characteristic deceptiveness that must have comprehended self-deceit.

deceptivity (diːsɛp'tɪvɪtɪ). [f. as DECEPTIVE + -ITY.] = DECEPTIVENESS; also *concr.* a thing of deceptive character.

1843 CARLYLE *Past & Pr.* (1858) 230 A Deceptivity, a Sham-thing.

† **de'ceptor.** *Obs.* In 5 -our. [ad. (through Fr.) L. *dēceptōr-em* deceiver, agent-n. from *dēcipĕre* to deceive. Cf. later F. *décepteur* (Littré).] A deceiver.

1484 CAXTON *Æsop* IV. xi. (1889) 116 Ypocrytes and deceptours of god and of the world.

† **de'ceptory**, *a. Obs.* [ad. L. *dēceptōri-us* deceitful, f. *dēceptōr-em* deceiver: see -ORY. In obs. F. *déceptoire.*] Apt to deceive.

c **1430** LYDG. *Bochas* I. xi. (1554) 25 a, See how deceptorye Been all these worldly revolucions. **1727-30** in BAILEY vol. II. and folio; whence **1755** in JOHNSON.

de'ceptress. *rare.* [fem. of DECEPTOR, answering in sense to L. *dēceptrix*: see -ESS.] A female deceiver.

1880 M. CROMMELIN *Black Abbey* II. viii. 139 The pretty deceptress woke refreshed.

† **de'cepture.** *Obs.* [f. L. *dēcept-* ppl. stem of *dēcipĕre* + -URE.] 'Fraud, deceit' (Halliwell).

decerebrate (diː'sɛrɪbrət), *a.* [f. DE- + CEREBRUM: see -ATE².] Deprived of the cerebrum; having the cerebrum removed or the brain-stem cut; also, resulting from this, as ***decerebrate rigidity***, a state in which the limbs are extended and certain skeletal muscles rigidly contracted. So **decere'bration**, removal of the cerebrum, cutting of the brain-stem.

1897 C. S. SHERRINGTON in *Proc. R. Soc.* LXI. 244, I have found the 'long intra-spinal reflexes', like sub-cerebral rigidity ('decerebrate tonus',) locally abolished..by total severance of the sensory spinal roots belonging to their own region of terminal discharge. **1898** —— in *Jrnl. Physiol.* XXII. 319 In a communication to the Royal Society in 1896 I described under the name decerebrate rigidity a condition of long-maintained muscular contraction supervening on removal of the cerebral hemispheres. **1900** DORLAND *Med. Dict.* 192/2 *Decerebration*, the removal of the brain in performing craniotomy. **1902** *Encycl. Brit.* XXXI. 744/1 The decerebrate monkey exhibits 'cataleptoid' reflexes. Father Kircher's *experimentum mirabile* with the fowl and the chalk line succeeds best with the decerebrate hen. **1915** W. OSLER *Let.* 29 July in H. Cushing *Life* (1925) II. 484 It is a sort of psychical decerebration... I suppose it is the shock & strain. **1927** HALDANE & HUXLEY *Anim. Biol.* vi. 139 A 'decerebrate' animal, i.e. one in which the cerebral hemispheres have been removed, though unconscious, can to some extent adjust its standing posture. **1950** *Sci. News* XV. 19 An anaesthetised, or decerebrate animal. **1969** 'M. INNES' *Family Affair* xvii. 187 Oswyn's virtually decerebrate, of course. **1970** J. CROSSLAND *Lewis's Pharmacol.* (ed. 4) ix. 181 Decerebration (which involves destruction of the brain above the level of the midbrain) releases this restraint and causes decerebrate rigidity.

de'cerebrize, *v.* [f. DE- II. 1 + CEREBR-UM + -IZE.] To deprive of the cerebrum; to pith.

decern (dɪ'sɜːn), *v.* [a. F. *décerne-r* (1318 in Godef.), ad. L. *dēcernĕre* to decide, pronounce a decision, f. DE- I. 2 + *cernĕre* to separate, distinguish, decide: see CERN *v.* In OF. *décerner* was confused in form with *descerner, discerner*; the clear distinction between the two dates only from the 16th c.; hence, in English also, *decern* is found with the sense DISCERN.]

I. To decide, determine, decree.

† **1.** *trans.* To decide, determine (a matter disputed or doubtful). *Obs.* **a.** with simple obj.

c **1425** WYNTOUN *Cron.* VIII. ii. 110 Be þe Text þai decerne all Tha casis. **1555** EDEN *Decades* 80 The controuersie shulde bee decerned by the bysshope of Rome.

b. with *inf.* or *object clause.*

1491 CAXTON *Vitas Patr.* (W. de W. 1495) II. 220 a/1 Holy faders..decerned & concluded that it sholde be buryed with theyr myster. **1502** ARNOLDE *Chron.* (1811) 162 Whan my noble prince..had decerned to send me his oratour to France. **1535** STEWART *Cron. Scot.* I. 531 This ilk Donald.. Decernit hes thairfoir richt suddantlie To gif battell. **1547** *Homilies* I. *Charity* I. (1859) 69 He shall not be deceived, but truly decern and judge. *a* **1619** FOTHERBY *Athcom.* I. v. §2 (1622) 31 To make them decerne, there should be no God.

c. *intr.*

1553 KENNEDY *Compend. Tract.* in *Wodr. Soc. Misc.* (1844) 105 The Apostolis and Eldaris convenit to dispute and decerne upoun the questioun.

2. *trans.* To decree by judicial sentence. Now a technical term of Scottish judicature; the use of the word 'decerns' being necessary to constitute a DECREE: see quot. 1774 in d.

a. with simple obj.

c **1555** HARPSFIELD *Divorce Hen. VIII* (1878) 182 She.. was denounced..contumax, and a citation decerned for her appearance. **1637** GILLESPIE *Eng. Pop. Cerem.* III. viii. 181 But onely pronounce the sentence according to that which he who sitteth judge in the Court, hath decreed and decerned. *a* **1850** ROSSETTI *Dante & Circ.* I. (1874) 118 Since thou, Death, and thou only, canst decern Wealth to my life, or want, at thy free choice.

b. *that* something be done.

1460 CAPGRAVE *Chron.* 274 The lordis of this present Parlement [1399] decerne and deme, That the dukes..schal lese..her dignite. **1515** R. SAMPSON in Strype *Eccl. Mem.* I. i. 17 A commission to some men..to decern [that] the same one exception and process..were of no strength. **1582-8** *Hist. James VI* (1804) 21 It was decernit that..shoe sould be transportit to the fortalice of Lochlevin, and thair decernit to remain in captivity.

c. a person, etc. *to be* or *to do* something. † *to decern in*: to mulct in by decree of court.

1526 *Sc. Acts Jas. V* (1814) 306 (Jam.) Decernit to haif incurrit the panis contenit in said actis. **1559** *Diurn. Occurr.* (1833) 52 The forthe of Aymouth decernit to be cassin down. **1568** GRAFTON *Chron.* Rich. II an. 23 II. 405 We.. by the power, name, and authoritie to us..committed, pronounce, decerne[**1494** FABYAN dyscerne] and declare, the same king Richard..to be..unworthy to the rule and governaunce. **1640-1** *Kirkcudbr. War-Comm. Min. Bk.* (1855) 41 Roger Gordoun..for his contumacie in not coming to the Committie..is decernit in xx merks monie of fyne. *Ibid.* 43 Decerns Alexander Gordoun..to content and pey to George Glendonyng..the soume of xxij lib. xiijs. iiijd. **1682** *Lond. Gaz.* No. 1682/1 The Lords Commissioners of Iusticiary, therefore Decerne and Adjudge the said Archibald Earl of Argile to be Execute to the Death. **1753** *Stewart's Trial* 283 They..decern and adjudge the said James Stewart to be carried back to the prison. **1754** ERSKINE *Princ. Sc. Law* (1809) 438 If a bastard might be decerned executor as next of kin to his mother.

d. *intr.*

1541 PAYNEL *Catiline* xvii. 29 b, Whan they suffre, they decerne: whan they hold theyr peace, they crye aloude. **1588** A. KING tr. *Canisius' Catech.* 52 Authoritie, in gouerning, iudging, and decerning. **1774** *Interlocutor* in A. McKay *Hist. Kilmarnock* (ed. 4) 363 Therefore [the Lord Ordinary] suspends the letters *simpliciter*, and decerns. **1817** *Blackw. Mag.* I. 437/1 The court below..decerned in terms of the prayer of the complaint. **1880** *Chambers' Encycl.* s.v. *Debts*, If the sum decerned for..do not exceed, etc.

e. *transf.*

1850 *Tait's Mag.* XVII. 106/1 One has said, 'It is not this': another avers, 'It is not that': one decerns it [a book] too elaborate.

II. To discern.

† **3.** *trans.* To distinguish or separate by their differences (things that differ, one thing *from* another). *Obs.*

a **1535** [see DECERNING]. **1546** BP. GARDINER *Declar. Art. Joye* 16 b, That belefe was a condicion which decerned them that shall enioye the fruite of Christes passion, and them that shall not. *a* **1572** KNOX *Hist. Ref.* Wks. 1846 I. 188 We must decerne the immaculat spous of Jesus Christ, frome the Mother of confusioun. **1586** T. B. *La Primaud. Fr. Acad.* I. 99 That rule..whereby..he decerneth and chooseth good from bad. *a* **1649** DRUMM. OF HAWTH. *Disc. Impresa's Wks.* (1711) 228 Things which cannot be decerned from others; as fowls like to others.

b. *intr.* To distinguish, discriminate *between.*

a **1535** SIR T. MORE *Wks.* 528 (R.) To deserne betwene the true doctrine and the false. **1892** A. R. WATSON *Geo. Gilfillan* iii. 38 With little skill to decern between the good and the evil in literature.

4. To see distinctly (with the eyes or the mind); to distinguish (an object or fact); to discern.

1559 W. CUNNINGHAM *Cosmogr. Glasse* 9 Then all that we ether by sight may decerne, or by arte conceive. **1595** *Blanchardine* Pt. II. Ded., You may well decerne, that my willing minde dooth bewraie my good meaning. *c* **1610** SIR J. MELVIL *Mem.* (1735) 94 A Princess who could decern and reward good Service. *a* **1638** MEDE *Apostasie* Wks. (1672) 54 The starres and lights therein should not easily be decerned. **1891** H. S. CONSTABLE *Horses, Sport, & War* 37 Differences ..that cannot be decerned by the eye.

Hence **de'cerning** *vbl. sb.*, † **de'cernment.**

a **1535** SIR T. MORE *Wks.* 528 (R.) The decerning of the true woord of God..from the countrefet woorde of man. **1551** ROBINSON tr. *More's Utop.* II. (Arb.) 125 *marg.*, The decerning of punishment putte to the discretion of the magistrates. **1586** A. DAY *Eng. Secretary* I. (1625) 142 Judge by your owne decernement, how much. *a* **1679** T. GOODWIN *Wks.* III. I. 488 (R.) A yet more refined elective discretion or decernment.

decernable, var. of DISCERNABLE.

† **de'cernent**, *a. Obs.* [ad. L. *dēcernent-em*, pr. pple. of *dēcernĕre* to DECERN.] Decerning; = DECRETORY I.

1677 GALE *Crt. Gentiles* II. IV. 341 The reasons of good and evil extrinsic to the Divine Essence are al dependent on the Divine Wil either decernent or legislative.

decerniture (dɪ'sɜːnɪtjʊə(r)). *Sc. Law.* [f. DECERN *v.* (or its source); the formation is irregular, imitative of such pairs as *invest, investiture.* Cf. CERNITURE.] The action of decerning; a DECREE of a (Scotch) court of justice.

1632 LITHGOW *Trav.* IX. 380 Being urged to it by Captaine Wairds decernitour, I freely performed his Direction. **1666** in Brown *Supplt. Morrison's Decisions* (1826) I. 517 Sufficient to maintain his right of the stipend, and to infer decerniture against the heritors. **1885** D. BEVERIDGE *Culross & Tulliallan* I. iv. 130 We find two decernitures in favour of Bessie Bur. **1885** LD. SELBORNE in *Law Rep.* 10 *Appeal* 500 The first question..is, whether the decerniture in terms of the declaratory conclusions of the summons is..correct.

† **de'cerp**, *v. Obs.* Pa. pple. decerped, decerpt. [ad. L. *dēcerp-ĕre* to pluck off, crop, cull, f. DE- I. 2 + *carpĕre* to pluck, etc. With the pa. pple. *decerpt*, cf. L. *dēcerpt-us.* (Cf. DISCERP: the two were often confused.)]

trans. To pluck off or out; to extract, excerpt.

1531 ELYOT *Gov.* III. xxiv, Tulli saieth..Mannes soule, beinge decerpt or taken of the portion of diuinitie called Mens, may be compared with none other thinge..but with god hym selfe. **1566** PAINTER *Pal. Pleas.* Ded. I. 2 Out of whom I decerped and chose (*raptim*) sondry proper and commendable Histories. **1657** TOMLINSON *Renou's Disp.* 255 Plums, decerped from..different trees. **1678** CUDWORTH *Intell. Syst.* 373 That God was a Mind passing through the whole Nature of things, from whom our Souls were, as it were, decerped or cut out.

¶ for DISCERP, to pull to pieces, divide.

1531 ELYOT *Gov.* I. ii, Howe this most noble Isle of the worlde was decerpt and rent in pieces.

† **de'cerpt**, *v. Obs.* [f. L. *dēcerpt-*, ppl. stem of *dēcerpĕre*: see prec. Cf. EXCERPT.] = prec.

a **1612** DONNE Βιαθανατος (1644) 83 The rags of Fathers decerpted and decocted by Gratian, and the glosses of these. **1651** *Raleigh's Ghost* 355 The soule of the world, from which ..they..taught..that..the Soules of men, were decerpted.

† **de'cerptible**, *a. Obs. rare.*⁻⁰ [f. L. ppl. stem *dēcerpt-* (see prec.) + -IBLE: cf. *contemptible.*] 'That may be cropped off' (Bailey, vol. II, 1727).

† **de'cerption.** *Obs. rare.* [n. of action f. L. *dēcerpĕre, dēcerpt-*: see DECERPT and -ION¹.] 'A cropping off, or pulling away' (Phillips 1657); that which is plucked off.

1662 GLANVILL *Lux Orient.* iii. (1682) 25 If our souls are but particles and decerptions of our parents.

† **decer'tation.** *Obs.* [ad. L. *dēcertātiōn-em*, n. of action f. *dēcertāre* to fight it out, contend, f. DE- I. 3 + *certāre* to contend.] Contention, strife, contest; dispute.

1635 HEYWOOD *Hierarch.* VI. 334 Great hath the Decertation Bin mongst the Learned men, 'bout the Creation of blessed angels. **1646** SIR T. BROWNE *Pseud. Ep.* IV. xii. 213 A decertation betweene the disease and nature. **1661** ARNWAY *Tablet* 213 (L.) The day of decertation, 'pro aris et focis'.

decertify (diː'sɜːtɪfaɪ), *v.* [f. DE- + CERTIFY *v.*] *trans.* To remove a certificate or certification from; *spec.* to remove certification of insanity from. Hence **,decertifi'cation.**

1918 *Oxf. Times* 11 May 7/3 The duty was cast on him of decertifying certain men if he thought they came within the terms of the order. *Ibid.*, I have decertified certain men. **1947** B. F. TUCKER *Guide to Nat. Labor Relations Act* 138 Decertification. The Board has power to revoke a certification already issued. **1959** *Times* 16 Mar. 10/2 The Newfoundland action in decertifying this union, which is affiliated to the powerful Canadian Labour Congress. **1960** *Sunday Times* 3 Jan. 11/4 The 1960s are likely to see the decertification of the majority of the remaining certified mental defectives. **1964** G. L. COHEN *What's Wrong with Hospitals?* viii. 177 They did all the pleasant jobs. I didn't dare open my mouth; I wanted to be de-certified.

deces, decese, decess(e, obs. ff. DECEASE.

decess (dɪˈsɛs). *rare.* [ad. L. *dēcēssus* going down, decrease, f. *dēcēdĕre* to go down, depart, etc.: cf. DECEASE.] Decrease, diminution.

1854 SYD. DOBELL *Balder* iii. 17 Whatever..from below Receives nor of accession or decess. *Ibid.* xxiv. 167.

decession (dɪˈsɛʃən). Now *rare.* [ad. L. *dēcēssiōn-em*, n. of action from *dēcēdĕre* (see prec.). (Cf. OF. *décession* 15th c.)] Departure, withdrawal; secession; deviation from a given standard, 'coming down'; decrease, diminution (opp. to *accession*).

1606 WARNER *Alb. Eng.* xv. xcvii. (1612) 387 The Brittish Church in primatiue Profession Proceeded, till did Slaughter make therein a forst Decession. **1611** SPEED *Hist. Gt. Brit.* IX. xvi. §36 By rebellious decessions, and absentments of himselfe. **1623** T. SCOT *Highw. God* 39 Succession of Persons without succession of Doctrine is a decession, a defection. **1635** W. SCOTT *Ess. Drapery* 7 (T.) By the accession and decession of the matter. **1655** FULLER *Ch. Hist.* III. vi. §48 By this..decesion of the Jews. **1822** SOUTHEY *Lett.* (1856) III. 336 In the event of Gifford's decession, or decease, a new 'Quarterly Review' has been talked of.

Hence **de'cessionist**, an advocate of secession.

1866 *Morn. Star* 20 Aug. 6/3 The Democrats, and..the decessionists.

† **de'cessor.** *Obs.* [a. L. *dēcēssor* one who retires, a retiring officer, in late L. (Augustine, etc.) 'predecessor', agent-n. from *dēcēdĕre* to depart, retire.] = PREDECESSOR.

1647 JER. TAYLOR *Lib. Proph.* vii. 128 The Popes may deny Christ as well as their Cheife and Decessor Peter. **1651–3** —— *Serm. for year* I. iv. 42 David..humbled himself for the sins of his Ancestors and Decessors.

deceue, -eyue, deceyt(e, obs. ff. DECEIVE, DECEIT.

deceuer, decez, obs. ff. DISSEVER, DECEASE.

† **de'charm,** *v. Obs.* [a. F. *décharmer*, in Cotgr. *descharmer* 'to vncharme, vnspell', f. *dé-, des-*, L. *dis-* (see DE- I. 6) + *charmer* to charm.] *trans.* To undo the effect of (a charm or spell); to disenchant.

16.. HARVEY (J.), He was..cured by decharming the witchcraft.

† **de'chay,** *v. Obs.* [ad. OF. *decha-eir, decha-ir*: see DECAY.] By-form of DECAY *v.*

1549 *Compl. Scot* i. (1873) 21 Al dominions altris, dechaeis, ande cummis to subuersione.

† **deche,** *v. Obs.* [OE. *décan*: app. not known in the other Teut. langs.] To daub; to smear, to lute.

a **1000** ÆLFRIC *Hom.* (Thorpe) II. 260 Hi bewundon his lic mid linenre scytan ʒedéced mid wyrtum. *c* **1000** *Sax. Leechd.* I. 150 Déc þonne anne clað þær of, leʒe to ðam sare. *Ibid.* I. 182 lxxviii, Cnuca mid rysle, and ʒedec anne clað þærmid [cf. lxxix, Smyre þonne anne clað þærmid, leʒe to þære miltan]. *c* **1420** *Pallad. on Husb.* I. 1124 Al thees comixt wol deche Every defaute, and all the woundes leche. *Ibid.* IX. 185 Oil-tempred lyme this joyntes shal scyment, Thenne ysels myxt with litel water renne Thorough, deching alle this holsom instrument.

† **de'cheerful,** *a. Obs. nonce-wd.* [See DE- II. 3.] Void of cheerfulness, melancholy.

1607 MIDDLETON *Five Gallants* IV. vii, O decheerful 'prentice, uncomfortable servant.

dechemicalize, -ation, dechoralize, deciceronize: see DE- II. 1.

dechenite (ˈdɛxənaɪt, ˈdɛk-). *Min.* [Named after the geologist von Dechen: see -ITE.] A vanadate of lead and zinc, occurring in red or reddish-yellow masses.

1851 *Amer. Jrnl. Sc.* Ser. II. XII. 208 Dechenite comes from..Bavaria. **1884** in DANA *Min.* 604.

de-'christianize, *v.* [DE- II. 1 (OF. had *deskrestianer*).] *trans.* To deprive or divest of its Christian character; to make no longer Christian.

1834 *Fraser's Mag.* X. 17 The Jew-bill has de-Christianised one branch of our legislature already. **1884** DEAN BURGON in *Pall Mall G.* 11 Dec. 1/2 To de-Christianize the place—to disestablish Religion in Oxford—was the great object of those individuals.

Hence **de-'christianized** *ppl. a.*, **-izing** *vbl. sb.*, **de-christiani'zation.**

1869 D. P. CHASE in *Standard* 27 Oct., The De-Christianising of the Colleges of Oxford. **1882** *Church Q. Rev.* July 434 A dechristianized nation. **1882** W. S. LILLY in *Spectator* 25 Mar. 391 The dechristianisation and the demoralisation of that country [France] are proceeding *pari passu.*

deci- (dɛsɪ), shortened from L. *decimus* tenth.

1. In the French metric system, the initial element in names of measures and weights which are one tenth of the standard unit. (Cf. DECA-.) Thus ***deciare, decigramme, -gram, decilitre, decimetre, decineper, decistere***, the tenth part of the *are, gramme, litre, metre, neper,* and *stere* respectively.

1801 DUPRÉ, *Neol. Fr. Dict.* s.v., In dry measure, the..décilitre is equal to one eighth of the litron. **1809** *Naval Chron.* XXII. 363 It was about three decimetres in length. **1810** *Ibid.* XXIV. 301 Deciar = 2·63 square toises. *Ibid.*, Decimeter..decilittre..decistere..decigram. **1871** C. DAVIES *Metr. Syst.* I. 14, 1 decilitre = 6·102338 cubic inches. **1883** *Daily News* 12 July 3/7 Cartridges of one decimetre in length each. **1890** *Ibid.* 14 Nov. 6/2 A decigram of liquid is used for each injection. **1931** *Telegr. & Teleph. Jrnl.* Mar. 119/2 The unit [of attenuation] adopted in France and Germany is the neper or decineper.

2. Rarely in technical terms, as † **deci-duodecimal** *a.*, (a crystal) having the form of a ten-sided prism with twelve additional planes at the ends (six at each end).

1805–17 R. JAMESON *Char. Min.* (ed. 3) 206 *Sex-decimal*, when the planes that belong to the prism..and those which belong to the two summits, are the one six, and the other ten in number or *vice versa*..In the same manner, we say, *octo-decimal..octo-duodecimal*, and *deci-duodecimal.*

Decian (ˈdiːʃ(ɪ)ən), *a.* [f. *Decius* + -AN.] Of or pertaining to the Roman emperor Decius or his reign (A.D. 249–251), and esp. the persecution of Christians which took place under him.

1695 J. SAGE *Cyprianic Age* 92 He tells Cornelius Bishop of Rome, Ep. 59. That he was Proscribed in the Days of the Decian Persecution. **1717** N. MARSHALL *Wks. St. Cyprian* II. 13 The Decian persecution..began in Africa with a popular tumult. **1846** C. MAITLAND *Ch. in Catacombs* iv. 118 The Decian persecution at Carthage. **1869** T. W. ALLIES *Formation Christendom* II. xii. 323 At the eve of the great Decian persecution in 249. **1939** A. J. TOYNBEE *Study Hist.* VI. 203 The Decian persecution of the Christian Church.

decibar (ˈdɛsɪbɑː(r)). *Meteorol.* [f. DECI- + BAR *sb.*[6] 2.] A unit of barometric pressure equal to one-tenth of a bar.

1910, 1914 [see BAR *sb.*[6] 2]. **1967** *Oceanogr. & Marine Biol.* V. 90 The difference between the geostrophic circulation at 1750 decibars and that at 1000 decibars is negligible.

decibel (ˈdɛsɪbɛl). [f. DECI- + BEL.] The usual unit (equal to one-tenth of a bel) used in comparing the power levels in two electrical communication circuits (or two parts of the same circuit) or the intensities of two sounds; freq. used to express a single power level or sound intensity relative to some reference level (stated or understood). Also used loosely in non-technical contexts. Abbrev. db.

1928 *Electrical Communication* VII. I. 33/2 If common logarithms are used, the reproduction is obtained in Decibels. **1929** W. H. MARTIN in *Bell System Techn. Jrnl.* VIII. 2 The Bell System has adopted the name 'decibel' for the 'transmission unit', based on a power ratio of $10^{\cdot 1}$... For convenience, the symbol 'db' will be employed to indicate the name 'decibel'. **1930** *Discovery* Dec. 398/2 The band-pass filter, which follows the low frequency modulator, allows the lower side-band to pass with an attenuation of six decibels. **1930** J. R. FIRTH *Speech* iv. 34 In order to measure differences of powers in units of sensation telephone engineers have adopted a logarithmic unit called the decibel (db.). **1937** *Nature* 28 Aug. 370 The First International Acoustical Conference... The 'phon'..was adopted as the unit in the subjective scale of equivalent loudness, while the use of the 'decibel'..was restricted to the scale of the associated energy or pressure level. **1948** *Punch Miscellany* 54/1 No one misses a single decibel of your conversation. **1953** L. F. BROSNAHAN *Some O.E. Sound Changes* iii. 28 The differences are measured in decibels, a decibel corresponding roughly to the change in loudness of a sound which is perceived as such. **1955** S. GIBBONS *Shadow of Sorcerer* iv. 37 A deep, fierce droning, louder by many decibels than the noise of wasps. **1958** *Engineering* 31 Jan. 133/3 Measurement at 800 c/s of the attenuation of a physical circuit with loss up to 10 db. **1959** K. HENNEY *Radio Engin. Handbk.* (ed. 5) xxviii. 23 Noise measurements are commonly expressed in decibels above a base, which is approximately at 85 db below 1 mw. **1970** *Daily Tel.* 4 Nov. 12/4 Patrons are in for a fairly high rate of decibel battering from these two muscular and very loud players.

decidability (dɪsaɪdəˈbɪlɪtɪ). [f. DECIDABLE *a.* + -ITY, tr. G. *entscheidbarkeit.*] The quality of being decidable (see next).

1940 in W. V. QUINE *Math. Logic* 344. **1959** K. R. POPPER *Logic of Sci. Disc.* viii. 191 The questions I have raised..constitute the problem of decidability.

decidable (dɪˈsaɪdəb(ə)l), *a.* [See -ABLE.]

1. a. Capable of being decided.

1594 CAREW *Huarte's Exam. Wits* v. (1596) 52 What the vse..of them may be..is not easily decideable. **1638** CHILLINGW. *Relig. Prot.* I. ii. §156. 115 Controversies..about Faith, are either not at all decidable..or they may be determined by Scripture. **1708** J. CHAMBERLAYNE *St. Gt. Brit.* II. II. vi. (1743) 396 All cases of trade..are there decidable. **1851** CARLYLE *Sterling* III. i. (1871) 169 The thing not being decidable by that kind of weapon.

b. *Logic* and *Math.* Of a statement or formula: capable, within the system to which it belongs, of being proved or disproved, or of being shown to be true or false, or to have some other property or not to have it; of theories, systems, etc.: having a solvable decision problem or computability problem.

1942 R. CARNAP *Introd. Semantics* xxvi. 163 *Ti* is decidable. **1950** W. V. QUINE *Methods Logic* (1952) 247 Elementary algebra is completable and mechanically decidable while elementary number theory is not. **1958** [see *decision method* s.v. DECISION 5]. **1963** G. T. KNEEBONE *Math. Logic* x. 279 In other cases..a system is to be reckoned decidable as long as both the derivable and the underivable formulae are recursively enumerable. **1964** E. BACH *Introd. Transformational Gram.* vii. 161 A decidable set of strings is a set such that after a finite number of steps it is possible to determine whether or not a given string is in the set.

† **2.** To be decided, open to decision. *Obs.*

1611 SPEED *Hist. Gt. Brit.* IX. xv. (1632) 788 It was a question decideable, whether of the kingdoms was first to be dealt with.

decide (dɪˈsaɪd), *v.*[1] Forms: 4–7 **descide**, 5 **deside**, 5–6 **decyde**, 6 **dissyde**, **discede**, 7 **discide**, 6– **decide**. [a. F. *décider* (1403 in Hatzf.), ad. L. *dēcīdĕre* to cut off, cut the knot, decide, determine, f. DE- I. 2 + *-cædĕre* to cut. In OF. also *des-cider*, in Eng. *des-, dis-*: cf. DE- I. 6.]

1. *trans.* To determine (a question, controversy, or cause) by giving the victory to one side or the other; to bring to a settlement, settle, resolve (a matter in dispute, doubt, or suspense).

c **1380** WYCLIF *Sel. Wks.* III. 429 Bifore þis cause were descided bytwene wyse men. **1484** CAXTON *Fables of Alfonce* (1889) 4 The cause came before the kyng to be decyded and pletyd. **1559** W. CUNNINGHAM *Cosmogr. Glasse* 43 There is great controversie touching the Earthes fourme: which must be descided..or we can safely procede further. **1594** HOOKER *Eccl. Pol.* IV. x. (1611) 146 Till it be..decided who have stood for truth. **1597** SHAKS. *2 Hen. IV*, IV. i. 182 Either end in peace..Or to the place of difference call the Swords Which must decide it. **1667** MILTON *P.L.* VI. 303 Fit to decide the Empire of great Heav'n. *a* **1677** BARROW *Wks.* (1830) I. 363 Advocates plead causes, and judges decide them. **1860** TYNDALL *Glac.* I. xxiv. 170 The proper persons to decide the question. *Mod.* This day will decide his fate.

2. To bring to a decision or resolve.

1710 STEELE *Tatler* No. 141 ¶2 Have agreed to be decided by your Judgment. **1836** SOUTHEY *Lett.* (1856) IV. 463 This 'Tasso' came in good time to decide me in a matter upon which I was hesitating.

3. *absol.* or *intr.* To settle a question in dispute; to pronounce a final judgement. Const. *between, in favour of, against*; also with *clause* (or its equivalent).

1732 POPE *Ep. Bathurst* 1 Who shall decide, when Doctors disagree? **1749** SMOLLETT *Regicide* II. ii, Let heaven decide Between me and my foes. **1794** SULLIVAN *View Nat.* II. 265 To judge and to decide on the authority of historical monuments. **1844** MARRYAT *Privateersman* xvii. 124 You shall be the arbitress of her fate, and what you decide shall be irrevocable. **1852** T. D. HARDY *Mem. Ld. Langdale* 10 His father..had decided that he should be brought up to the medical profession. **1863** GEO. ELIOT *Romola* II. xxii, Moments when our passions speak and decide for us.

4. *intr.* To come to a conclusion, make up one's mind; determine, resolve. Const. *inf.*, *on, upon, against.*

1830 D'ISRAELI *Chas. I.* III. i. 8 An English monarch now decided to reign without a Parliament. **1887** C. J. ABBEY *Eng. Ch. & its Bps.* II. 54 Butler soon after this decided against Nonconformity. *Mod.* Have you decided on going? I have fully decided upon this course.

† **5.** *trans.* To cut off, separate. *Obs. rare.*

1579 in Fuller *Holy & Prof. St.* II. xix. 122 Again, our seat denies us traffick here, The sea too near decides us from the rest.

† **de'cide,** *v.*[2] *Obs. rare.* [ad. L. *dēcid-ĕre* to fall down or off, f. DE- I. 1 + *cadĕre* to fall.] *intr.* To fall off.

1657 TOMLINSON *Renou's Disp.* 265 [The flowers of Hellebore] in whose middle when they are ready to decide, grow short husks.

decided (dɪˈsaɪdɪd), *ppl. a.* [f. DECIDE *v.*[1]]

1. Settled, certain; definite; unquestionable.

1790 *Impartial Hist. War in Amer.* 319 Such various accounts have been given..that it is difficult to form any decided opinion. **1858** DICKENS *Lett.* (1880) II. 61 It was a most decided and complete success. **1879** ROOD *Chromatics* xviii. 315 Decided greens are not admitted except in small touches.

2. Resolute, determined, unhesitating.

1790 PALEY *Horæ Paul., Rom.* ii. 17 They had taken a decided part in the great controversy. **1828** SCOTT *F.M. Perth* vii, Henry Smith spoke out boldly, and in a decided voice. **1840** ALISON *Hist. Europe* VIII. xlix. §13. 14 He found them vacillating, he left them decided.

decidedly (dɪˈsaɪdɪdlɪ), *adv.* [-LY[2].]

1. Definitely, in such a manner as to preclude question or doubt.

1790 HAN. MORE *Relig. Fash. World* (ed. 3) 46 The balance perhaps will not turn out so decidedly in favour of the times. **1841** W. SPALDING *Italy & It. Isl.* I. 33 All the rustic dresses are not graceful, and..some are decidedly ugly. **1860** TYNDALL *Glac.* II. xxvii. 382 The lateral portions [of a glacier] are very decidedly laminated.

2. In a determined manner, with decision, unhesitatingly.

1802 MAR. EDGEWORTH *Moral T.* (1816) I. xiv. 117 He decidedly answered, No. **1884** SIR J. STEPHEN in *Law Reports 12 Q. Bench Div.* 281 If the House had resolved ever so decidedly that [etc.].

de'cidedness. [-NESS.] The quality of being decided; see the adj.

1804 W. TAYLOR in *Ann. Rev.* II. 359 That decidedness of practical counsel which always accompanies clearness of intellect. **1827** J. AIKMAN *Hist. Scot.* IV. VII. 21 Decidedness of principle.

† **de'cidement.** *Obs. rare.* [f. DECIDE *v.*[1] + -MENT: cf. *judgement.*] = DECISION.

a **1625** FLETCHER *Love's Pilgr.* II. i, Descidements able To speak ye noble gentlemen.

† **decidence** ('dɛsɪdəns). *Obs.* [f. as DECIDENT: see -ENCE. Cf. DECADENCE.] **1.** Falling off.

1646 SIR T. BROWNE *Pseud. Ep.* III. ix. 127 The decidence of their [deer's] hornes.

2. Falling off in strength, vigour, etc.; decline.

1684 tr. *Bonet's Merc. Compit.* VI. 165 If the bloud, constituted in this state of decidence, decay so far as [etc.]. *Ibid.* XVIII. 611 When Children are in a neutral state of decidence.

† **'decidency.** *Obs. rare.* [f. as prec.: see -ENCY.] Falling, failing, subsidence.

1651 BIGGS *New Disp.* ¶238 Flowes not, till the ebb or decidency.

† **'decident,** *a. Obs.* [ad. L. *dēcident-em*, pr. pple. of *dēcidĕre* to fall down or off, f. DE- I. 1, 2 + *cadĕre* to fall: cf. DECADENT.] Falling.

1674 DURANT in *Phil. Trans.* XLIV. 223 Decident lapidescent Waters.

decider (dɪ'saɪdə(r)). [f. DECIDE *v.* + -ER[1].] One who or that which decides (a controversy, question, etc.).

1592 WYRLEY *Armorie* 23 The Scriptures of God, the decider of all controuersies. **1764** FOOTE *Patron* I. Wks. 1799 I. 329 The paragon of poets, decider on merit, chief justice of taste. **1862** WILBERFORCE *Let.* in *Life* III. 106 The.. danger of having..the Irish Bishops made the actual deciders of our doctrine.

b. *spec.* in *Racing.* A final race or heat which decides the contest; *esp.* an extra one run for that purpose, *e.g.* after a dead heat.

1883 *Standard* 18 June 2/4 He..disposed of Egerie in the decider. **1887** *Daily News* 8 June 6/5 This pair ran a dead heat last year..and in the decider Button Park proved..the better.

deciding (dɪ'saɪdɪŋ), *vbl. sb.* [-ING[1].] The action of the verb DECIDE; decision.

1576 in W. H. Turner *Select. Rec. Oxford* 382 For the decyding of the same matter. **1690** LOCKE *Hum. Und.* II. xiii. §20 In deciding of Questions in Philosophy.

de'ciding, *ppl. a.* [-ING[2].] That decides; decisive.

1658–9 *Burton's Diary* (1828) IV. 68 This is a very great question, and a deciding question. **1856** R. A. VAUGHAN *Mystics* (1860) II. VIII. vii. 74 The deciding epoch of his [Behmen's] life.

Hence **de'cidingly** *adv.*, decisively, by way of decision.

1646 SIR T. BROWNE *Pseud. Ep.* VII. xiii. 366 Herodotus.. hath cleared this point..and so decidingly concludeth.

‖**decidua** (dɪ'sɪdju:ə). [mod. or med.L. for *membrāna dēcidua* deciduous membrane: see DECIDUOUS.]

1. *Phys.* A name given by Dr. W. Hunter to the membrane formed, in the impregnated uterus of certain orders of Mammalia, by alteration of the upper layer of its lining mucous membrane; it forms the external envelope of the ovum, and is cast off at parturition (whence the name).

1785 *Anat. Dialogues* (ed. 2) 356 There is the false or spongy chorion, which Dr. [W.] Hunter has found to consist of two distinct layers; that which lines the uterus he styles membrana caduca or decidua, because it is cast off after delivery... The decidua and decidua reflexa, differ in appearance from the true chorion. **1794** J. HUNTER *Wks.* 1837 IV. 57 The enlargement of the uterus, the newly formed vascular membrane, or decidua, lining the cavity.. sufficiently prove conception to have taken place. **1841** E. RIGBY *Syst. Midwifery* I. iii. 27 To Dr. W. Hunter are we indebted for the first correct description of the decidua.

attrib. **1875** tr. *Ziemssen's Cycl. Med.* X. 335 The so called decidua cells.

2. *Path.* The lining membrane of the unimpregnated uterus discharged in some cases of dysmenorrhæa.

1864 F. CHURCHILL *Dis. Women* II. iv. (ed. 5) 211 Ovarian congestion, calling forth a sympathetic growth of the uterine glands, forming a false decidua. **1869** *New Syd. Soc. Biennial Retrospect* 378 The idea that it is a simple menstrual decidua.

decidual (dɪ'sɪdju:əl), *a. Phys.* [f. DECIDU-A + -AL[1].] Of or pertaining to the decidua.

1837 OWEN *Note* in J. Hunter's Wks. IV. 69 The continuation of the uterine veins into decidual canals. **1859** TODD *Cycl. Anat.* V. 653 These two decidual coats. **1889** W. S. PLAYFAIR *Treat. Midwifery* I. II. ix. 264 The decidual cells are greatly increased in size.

de'ciduary, *a. rare.* [f. as DECIDU-OUS + -ARY: not on L. analogies.] Deciduous.

1871 DARWIN *Desc. Man* II. xiii. 80 The shedding of the deciduary margins may be compared with the shedding by very young birds of their down.

‖**Deciduata** (dɪˌsɪdju:'eɪtə), *sb. pl. Zool.* [mod.L. adj. pl. neut. (sc. *animālia*) of *deciduāt-us*: see next.] A term comprising all placental Mammalia which possess a decidua or deciduate placenta: with some systematists the *Deciduata* and *Non-deciduata* are major divisions of monadelphous mammals.

1879 tr. *Haeckel's Evol. Man* II. xix. 161 All Placental Animals which possess this deciduous membrane are classed together as Deciduata.

deciduate (dɪ'sɪdju:ət), *a. Zool.* [ad. med.L. *dēciduāt-us*, f. DECIDUA: see -ATE[2] 2.] **a.** Possessing a decidua; belonging to the *Deciduata.* **b.** Of the nature of a decidua: said of a placenta which is cast off at parturition.

1868 OWEN *Anat. Vert.* III. xxxviii. 724 The deciduate type of lining substance. **1875** tr. *Schmidt's Desc. & Darw.* 273 As non-deciduate mammals, the Cetacea are held to be more closely allied to the Ungulata than to the Carnivora which are deciduate. **1881** MIVART *Cat* 474 The placenta is deciduate.

deciduity (dɛsɪ'dju:ɪtɪ). *rare.* [f. L. type **dēciduitās*, f. *dēcidu-us*: see -ITY.] Deciduousness.

1846 WORCESTER cites KEITH.

deciduoma (dɪsɪdju:'əʊmə). *Path.* [mod.L., f. DECIDUA + -OMA.] An intra-uterine tumour probably caused by portions of the decidua remaining after abortion; ***deciduoma malignum***, a malignant and cancerous deciduoma.

1890 in BILLINGS *Med. Dict.* **1902** [see *chorio-epithelioma*]. **1907** F. J. MCCANN *Cancer of Womb* xi. 119 The deciduoma malignum consists as a rule of a small primary growth. *Ibid.* 122 Deciduoma may occur at any age during the child-bearing period. **1932** S. ZUCKERMAN *Soc. Life Monkeys* v. 79 The development of large masses of hypertrophied endometrium—deciduomata. **1967** R. A. WILLIS *Path. Tumours* (ed. 4) lxii. 1004 There is now universal recognition of its origin [*sc.* that of a chorion-epithelioma] from the chorionic epithelium, and of the erroneousness of the old name 'deciduoma malignum'.

deciduous (dɪ'sɪdju:əs), *a.* [f. L. *dēcidu-us* falling down, falling off (f. *dēcid-ĕre*: see DECIDENT) + -OUS. Cf. mod.F. *décidu.*]

†**1.** Falling down or off. *Obs.*

1656 H. MORE *Enthus. Tri.* (1712) 32 The Lightnings without Thunder are as it were the deciduous flowers of the Æstival Stars.

†**b.** Sinking, declining, *Obs. rare.*

1791 E. DARWIN *Bot. Gard.* I. 16 Yon round deciduous day, Tressed with soft beams.

2. *Bot.* and *Zool.* Of parts of plants or animals (as leaves, petals, teeth, horns, etc.): Falling off or shed at a particular time, season, or stage of growth. Opposed to *persistent* or *permanent.*

1688 R. HOLME *Armoury* II. 115/1 Deciduous leaf. **1690** BOYLE *Chr. Virtuoso* II. II. §i, Which some anatomists therefore call deciduous parts, such as the placenta uterina, and the different membranes that involve the fœtus. **1704** J. HARRIS *Lex. Techn., Deciduous*, is that which is apt or ready to fall..Thus the Botanists say, in some Plants the Perianthium or Calyx is *deciduous* with the Flower, i.e. falls from off the Plant with it. **1766** PENNANT *Zool.* I. p. xxii, Upright branched horns, annually deciduous. **1784** COWPER *Task* III. 468 Ere the beech and elm have cast their leaf Deciduous. **1872** HUXLEY *Phys.* xii. 290 The first set of teeth, called deciduous or milk teeth. **1875** DARWIN *Insectiv. Pl.* xv. 353 The deciduous..scales of the leaf buds.

b. *Bot.* Of a tree or shrub: That sheds its leaves every year; opposed to *evergreen.*

1778 BP. LOWTH *Transl. Isaiah* Notes (ed. 12) 144 The oak [and] the terebinth..being deciduous; where the Prophet's design seems to me to require an ever-green. **1816** KIRBY & SP. *Entomol.* (1843) I. 176 The insects injurious to deciduous trees mostly leave the fir and pine tribes untouched. **1875** LYELL *Princ. Geol.* I. II. xix. 459 The deciduous cypress.

c. *Zool.* Of insects: That shed their wings after copulation, as the females of ants and termites.

d. *Phys.* = DECIDUAL.

1829 BELL *Anat. Hum. Body* (ed. 7) III. 445 That the ovum..upon its descent gets entangled behind the deciduous membrane. **1868** OWEN *Anat. Vert.* III. xxxviii. 725 note, The normal canal of the uterus is obliterated by the accumulated deciduous substance.

3. *fig.* Fleeting, transitory; perishing or disappearing after having served its purpose.

1811 W. R. SPENCER *Poems* Ded., E'en Fancy's rose deciduous dies. **1841–4** EMERSON *Ess., Love* Wks. (Bohn) I. 79 They discover that all which at first drew them together ..was deciduous. **1870** LOWELL *Among my Bks.* Ser. I. (1873) 177 There is much that is deciduous in books.

Hence **de'ciduously, de'ciduousness.**

1868 OWEN *Anat. Vert.* III. xxxviii. 725 The deciduously developed lining substance of the womb. **1727** BAILEY vol. II, *Deciduousness*, aptness to fall. **1871** EARLE *Philol.* viii. 395 This early deciduousness of our reflex pronoun.

decigram, -gramme: see DECI-.

'decil, decile. [Corresponds to F. *décile* (also *dextil*, Littré), prob. med.L. **decīlis*, app. f. *decem* ten, after *quintīlis, sextīlis.*] **1.** *Astrol.* The aspect of two planets when distant from each other a tenth part of the zodiac, or 36 degrees.

1674 S. JEAKE *Arith. Surv.* I. (1696) 11 Aspects..Semi-quintil or Decil. **1686** GOAD *Celest. Bodies* I. xi. 39 The Quintile..the Biquintile..the Vigintile, and Quindecile, and Decile, etc.,..We hope..we shall never be forced to own such Driblets of Aspects.

2. (Spelt decile.) *Statistics.* Any of the nine values of a variate which divide a frequency distribution into ten groups, each containing one tenth of the total population; also, any of the ten groups so produced.

1882 GALTON in *Rep. Brit. Assoc. 1881* 245 The Upper Decile is that which is exceeded by one-tenth of an infinitely large group, and which the remaining nine-tenths fall short of. The Lower Decile is the converse of this. **1907** G. P. WATKINS *Growth of Large Fortunes* ii. 18 Convenient relative numbers are the ratio of the upper decile, or the upper centile, to the median. **1934** *Brit. Jrnl. Psychol.* XXIV. 277 The group [of subjects] was formed by combining the highest and lowest deciles of a larger group, and there was thus too large a scatter. **1939** *Nature* 11 Mar. 439/1 Mr. Yule has selected the mean, median, upper and lower quartiles, interquartile range, and ninth decile. **1971** *Ibid.* 22 Jan. 224/3 The range of salaries indicated by the survey extends from $24,500 or more in the highest decile to $9,500 or less in the lowest decile.

decilitre: see DECI-.

decillion (dɪ'sɪljən). [f. DECI-, L. *decem* ten, on the analogy of *million*: cf. *billion.*] The tenth power of a million; a number which would be denoted by 1 followed by 60 ciphers. Hence **de'cillionth** *a.* and *sb.*; **de'cillionist** (*nonce-wd.*), one who deals in infinitesimal doses (of homœopathic drugs), such as the decillionth of a grain.

a **1845** HOOD *To Hahnemann* xii, Leave no decillionth fragment of your works. **1880** BEALE *Slight Ailm.* 21 Popular prescribers of decillionths of grains. **1865** *Athenæum* 11 Mar. 345 If the homœopathists should finally carry the day, would a generation of decillionists have a right to call Jenner and Holland quacks?

† **'decim.** *Obs.* [ad. L. *decima*: see next.] A tenth part, tithe.

1638 SIR R. COTTON *Abstr. Rec. Tower* 19 It was so..in the best govern'd State [Rome] which let out their portions and Decims to the Publicans.

‖**decima** ('dɛsɪmə). [L., for *decima pars*, tenth part, tithe, as a tax, offering, or largess.]

1. A tenth part; a tax of one-tenth, a tithe.

c **1630** in Rushw. *Hist. Coll.* (1659) I. App. 14 Subsidies, Fifteens, and such like..are fit to be released..in recompence of the said Decima, which will yield your Maiesty more. **1811** WELLINGTON in Gurw. *Desp.* VIII. 299 Giving up the new decima in order to obtain means of transport.

2. *Mus.* **a.** The interval of a tenth. (Common in med.L. but rare in Eng.) **b.** An organ-stop sounding a tenth above the normal or 8-feet pitch; called also a double-tierce. *rare.*

1819 in REES *Cycl.* XI.

decimal ('dɛsɪməl), *a.* and *sb.* [ad. med.L. *decimāl-is* of or pertaining to tenths or tithes, f. L. *decima* tenth, tithe; whence sense 2, and F. *décimal* in sense 'relating to tithes' (13th c. in Godef.); in mod. use, treated as derivative of L. *decimus* tenth, or *decem* ten, in which sense the F. word was admitted by the Academy only in 1762.]

A. *adj.* **1. a.** Relating to tenth parts, or to the number ten; proceeding by tens.

decimal arithmetic: the common arithmetic in which the Arabic or *decimal notation* is used; in a restricted sense the arithmetic of decimals or decimal fractions (see b). ***decimal classification*** (or ***system***), a system of classifying library or archival material with a numerical notation subdivided as a decimal fraction allowing expansion after any figure; *spec.* the DEWEY system. ***decimal numeration***, the numerical system generally prevalent in all ages, of which 10 forms the basis; i.e. in which the units have distinct names up to 10, and the higher numbers are expressed by multiples or powers of 10 with the units added as required. ***decimal coinage*** or ***currency***, a monetary system in which each successive division or denomination is ten times the value of that next below it; so ***decimal system*** of adoption of weights and measures, one in which the successive denominations rise by tens, as in the French *metric* system.

1608 R. NORTON tr. *Stevin* (title) *Disme*: The Art of Tenths, or *Decimall Arithmetike*, teaching how to performe all computations whatsoeuer, by whole numbers without fractions, by the foure principles of common Arithmeticke .. Invented [1585] by the excellent Mathematician Simon Stevin. **1619** H. LYTE *Art of Tens or Decimall Arithmeticke* 24 Here followeth two Tables of Decimall accounts for money. **1659** T. PECKE *Parnassi Puerp.* 154 Some Magistrates, void Cyphers we may call: Uselesse, but to make others Decimal. **1684** *Lond. Gaz.* No. 1985/4 Cocker's Decimal Arithmetick: Shewing the nature and use of Decimal Fractions. **1782** GOUV. MORRIS in Sparks *Life & Writ.* (1832) I. 273 It is very desirable that money should be increased in decimal ratio. **1841** ELPHINSTONE *Hist. Ind.* I. 245 The Hindūs are distinguished in arithmetic by the acknowledged invention of the decimal notation. **1842** *Times* 23 Apr. 6/2 The standard measures are to be restored under the superintendence of three scientific gentlemen, who are inclined to introduce the decimal system. **1854** WILLIAM BROWN (*title*) Decimal coinage. A letter..to Francis Shand, Esq. chairman of the Liverpool Chamber of Commerce. **1858** TROLLOPE *Three Clerks* I. xi. 243 The much-vexed question of penny *versus* pound, as touching the new standard for the decimal coinage. **1864** COLENSO *Arithmetic* (1874) 145 'Decimal Coinage', A Decimal Coinage..has been recommended for adoption by a Committee of the House of Commons. **1876** M. DEWEY in *Public Libraries in U.S.A.* I. xxviii. 623 (*sub-heading*) A decimal classification and subject-index. **1885** [see DEWEY]. **1930** *Library Jrnl.* 13 Dec. 1000 Why the Science Library adopted the Universal Decimal Classification. **1948** S. C. BRADFORD *Documentation* iii. 26 In 1883, a decimal classification was introduced in the Bodleian Library..and ..is still in use. **1963** *Rep. Comm. Inquiry Decimal Currency* ii. 8 By far the most common decimal currency systems are two-place systems in which the major unit is divided into one hundred minor units or 'cents'. **1971** *Guardian* 22 Feb. 5/2 Bus services in many towns and cities went decimal yesterday.

b. ***decimal fraction*** († ***number***): a fraction whose denominator is some power of ten (10, 100, 1000, etc.); *spec.* a fraction expressed (by an extension of the ordinary Arabic notation) by figures written to the right of the units figure after a dot or point (the ***decimal point***), and denoting respectively so many tenths, hundredths, thousandths, etc. The number of ***decimal places*** († ***parts***) is the number of figures after the decimal point.

† *decimal thirds*: the parts expressed by a decimal fraction to 3 places, i.e. thousandths; so *d. fourths*, etc. (For a historical sketch of the notation of decimal fractions, the introduction of the decimal point, etc., see W. W. R. Ball, *Short Hist. Mathem.* (1888) 176.)

1616 E. WRIGHT tr. *Napier's Logarithms* 19 Logarithms.. to fall upon decimal numbers..which are easie to be added or abated to or from any other number. **1660** WILLSFORD *Scales Comm.* 60, $\frac{094}{1000}$*l*, which decimal fraction is 1*s.* 10½*d.* *Ibid.* 69, 1.060000..is a mixt decimal fraction. *Ibid.* 70 To finde Decimal Numbers for any parts of a year, as moneths, weeks. **1674** JEAKE *Arith.* (1696) 222 So 0,003125 divided by 0,125, shall make the Quotient Decimal Thirds. **1704** J. HARRIS *Lex. Techn.* s.v. *Decimal*, There must be just as many Decimal Parts cut off by the Separating Point, from the Product, as there are Decimals in both Factors. **1706** W. JONES *Introd. Math.* 103 A Figure in the 1st, 2d, 3d, etc. Decimal Place, is 10, 100, 1000, etc. times less than if it were an Integer. **1840** LARDNER *Geom.* 61 The number expressing the circumference of the circle has been determined to 140 decimal places. **1873** J. HAMBLIN SMITH *Arith.* (ed. 6) 79 Placing a decimal point at the end of the Dividend, and affixing as many zeros as we please. *Ibid.* 83 A Vulgar Fraction may be converted into a Decimal Fraction.

c. Of or relating to a decimal coinage, a decimal system of weights and measures, etc.

1859 *Sat. Rev.* VIII. 13/2 The decimal project. *Ibid.*, During the progress of the decimal agitation.

†**2.** Relating to tithes. *Obs.*

1641 'SMECTYMNUUS' *Vind. Answ.* §10. 106 Can one Bishop..discharge all businesses belonging to testamentary and decimall causes and suites? **1653** MILTON *Hirelings* Wks. (1851) 377, I see them still so loth to unlearn their decimal Arithmetic, and still grasp thir Tithes. *a* **1662** HEYLIN *Hist. Presbyterians* (1670) 469 (D.) The jurisdiction of Ecclesiastical Courts in causes testamentary, decimal, and matrimonial.

B. *sb.* †**1.** A tenth part. *Obs.*

1641 WILKINS *Math. Magick* I. xiii. (1648) 89 As a decimall, or one tenth. **1665** HOOKE *Microgr.* C j b, And the inches..I subdivide into Decimals. **1669** STURMY *Mariner's Mag.* IV. iij. 156 If you keep your Account by Arithmetick, by Decimals or 10 Parts.

2. a. A decimal fraction (see 1 b); in *pl.* often = the arithmetic of decimal fractions, 'decimal arithmetic' (see 1): cf. CONICS.

recurring decimal: one in which the exact equivalent to a common fraction can be expressed only by the continual repetition of one or more decimal figures; called *repeating d.* when one figure recurs as ·111 etc., written ·i̇ (= ⅑), and *circulating d.* when two or more recur as ·142857 (= ⅐).

1651 R. JAGER (*title*), Artificial Arithmetick in Decimals. **1660** WILLSFORD *Scales Comm.* 83, I find the decimal ..·971286. *Ibid.* 87 According to the rules of Multiplication in Decimals. **1706** W. JONES *Introd. Math.* 107 When a Decimal..is to be multiplied by an Unit with Cyphers. **1805** SYD. SMITH *Elem. Mor. Philos.* (1850) 180 The decimal of a farthing. **1816** J. SMITH *Panorama Sc. & Art* II. 41 The force of the wind on a square foot, would have been 29 pounds and a decimal. **1858** LARDNER *Handbk. Nat. Phil.* 23 A portion..expressed by the decimal 0·036065.

b. *fig.* A 'fraction'; a (small) portion or part.

1869 BLACKMORE *Lorna D.* (1889) 265 Beholding.. faintest decimal of promise. **1892** W. W. PEYTON *Memorab. Jesus* I. 1 Fractions of doubts and decimals of guesses.

Hence **'decimalism**, a decimal system or theory. **'decimalist**, an advocate of a decimal system (of coinage, or weights and measures). **'decimalization**, the process of decimalizing. **'decimalize** *v.*, to render decimal, reduce to a decimal system, divide into tenths (*trans.* and *absol.*).

1864 WEBSTER, *Decimalism.* **1859** *Sat. Rev.* VIII. 13/2 The ranks of the decimalists. **1887** *Ibid.* 11 June 831/1 The decimalists..pester the general community with mils..and dimes and half dimes. **1855** R. SLATER (*title*), Inquiry into the Principles involved in the Decimalisation of the Weights, Measures, etc., of the U.K. **1887** *Longm. Mag.* Sept. 517 The subject of our coinage and its decimalisation. **1856** *Leisure Hour* V. 231/2 If we begin with the sovereign, and decimalize downwards, we come first to the florin. **1859** *Sat. Rev.* VIII. 13/2 The decimalizing opinions of the 'Standard' Commissioners. **1867** *Contemp. Rev.* IV. 19 There would be no advantage in decimalizing the penny; the halfpenny and farthing are all we want.

decimally ('dɛsɪməlɪ), *adv.* [-LY².] In a decimal manner; by tens or tenths; into tenths.

1704 J. HARRIS *Lex. Techn.* s.v. *Decimal*, As Cyphers set on the right Hand of Integers do increase the Value of them Decimally, as 2, 20, 200, etc. So when set on the left Hand of Fractions, they decrease their Value Decimally, as ·5, ·05, ·005, etc. **1828** HUTTON *Course Math.* II. 82 The edge of the rule is commonly divided decimally, or into tenths. **1859** *Sat. Rev.* VIII. 13/1 To have weights and measures decimally divided.

b. In the form of a decimal fraction.

1692 in *Capt. Smith's Seaman's Gram.* II. xvi. 125 The Weight..is 7 Pound 5 Ounces, (or Decimally) 7.31.

†**'decimate**, *sb. Obs.* [ad. med.L. *decimāt-us* tithing, area whence tithe is collected, f. L. *decimāre* to tithe.] Tithing, tithe.

1641 HEYWOOD *Reader here, etc.* 1 That not with their due Decimates content Both Tythe and Totall must encrease their rent?

decimate ('dɛsɪmeɪt), *v.* [f. L. *decimā-re* to take the tenth, f. *decim-us* tenth: see -ATE³. Cf. F. *décimer* (16th c.).]

†**1.** To exact a tenth or a tithe from; to tax to the amount of one-tenth. *Obs.* In *Eng. Hist.*, see DECIMATION 1.

1656 in BLOUNT *Glossogr.* **1657** MAJOR-GEN. DESBROWE *Sp. in Parlt.* 7 Jan., Not one man was decimated but who had acted or spoken against the present government. **1667** DRYDEN *Wild Gallant* II. i, I have heard you are as poor as a decimated Cavalier. **1670** PENN *Lib. Consc. Debated* Wks. 1726 I. 447 The insatiable Appetites of a decimating Clergy. **1738** NEAL *Hist. Purit.* IV. 96 That all who had been in arms for the king..should be decimated; that is pay a tenth part of their estates. *a* **1845** [see DECIMATED].

†**2.** To divide into tenths, divide decimally. *Obs.*

1749 SMETHURST in *Phil. Trans.* XLVI. 22 The Chinese.. are so happy as to have their Parts of an Integer in their Coins, &c. decimated.

3. *Milit.* To select by lot and put to death one in every ten of (a body of soldiers guilty of mutiny or other crime): a practice in the ancient Roman army, sometimes followed in later times.

1600 DYMMOK *Treat. Ireland* (1843) 42 All..were by a martiall courte condemned to dye, which sentence was yet mittigated by the Lord Lieutenants mercy, by which they were onely decimated by lott. **1651** *Reliq. Wotton.* 30 In Ireland..he [Earl of Essex] decimated certain troops that ran away, renewing a peece of the Roman Discipline. **1720** OZELL *Vertot's Rom. Rep.* I. III. 185 Appius decimated, that is, put every Tenth Man to death among the Soldiers. **1840** NAPIER *Penins. War* VI. XXII. v. 293 The soldiers could not be decimated until captured. **1855** MACAULAY *Hist. Eng.* IV. 577 Who is to determine whether it be or be not necessary ..to decimate a large body of mutineers?

4. *transf.* **a.** To kill, destroy, or remove one in every ten of. **b.** *rhetorically* or *loosely.* To destroy or remove a large proportion of; to subject to severe loss, slaughter, or mortality.

1663 J. SPENCER *Prodigies* (1665) 385 The..Lord.. sometimes decimates a multitude of offenders, and discovers in the personal sufferings of a few what all deserve. **1812** W. TAYLOR in *Monthly Rev.* LXXIX. 181 An expurgatory index, pointing out the papers which it would be fatiguing to peruse, and thus decimating the contents into legibility. **1848** C. BRONTE *Let.* in Mrs. Gaskell *Life* 276 Typhus fever decimated the school periodically. **1875** LYELL *Princ. Geol.* II. III. xlii. 466 The whole animal Creation has been decimated again and again. **1877** FIELD *Killarney to Golden Horn* 340 This conscription weighs very heavily on the Mussulmen..who are thus decimated from year to year. **1883** L. OLIPHANT *Haifa* (1887) 76 Cholera.. was then decimating the country.

Hence **'decimated, 'decimating** *ppl. adjs.*

1661 MIDDLETON *Mayor of Q.* Pref., Now whether this magistrate fear'd the decimating times. **1667, 1670** [see 1]. *a* **1845** SYD. SMITH *Wks.* (1850) 688 The decimated person.

decimater: see DECIMATOR.

decimation (dɛsɪ'meɪʃən). [ad. L. *decimātiōn-em* the taking of a tenth, tithing, n. of action from *decimāre* to DECIMATE.]

1. The exaction of tithes, or of a tax of one-tenth; the tithe or tax itself.

Popularly applied to the tax levied by Cromwell on the Royalists in 1655: see *Calendar Domestic St. Pap.* 1655, 347. Cf. DECIMATE *v.* 1.

1549 LATIMER *6th Serm. bef. Edw. VI* (Arb.) 165 Their doctrine was..but of Lotions [*mispr.* Lolions], of decimations of anets seade, and Cummyn. *c* **1630** in Rushw. *Hist. Coll.* (1659) I. App. 14 The first means..to increase your Majesty's revenues..I call it a Decimation, being so tearmed in Italy..importing the tenth of all Subjects Estates to be paid as a yearly Rent to their Prince. **1655** EVELYN *Mem.* (1857) I. 327 This day came forth the Protector's Edict, or Proclamation..with the decimation of all the royal party's revenues throughout England. **1657** MAJOR-GEN. DESBROWE *Sp. in Parlt.* 7 Jan., I think it is too light a tax, a decimation; I would have it higher. **1669** WORLIDGE *Syst. Agric.* vii. §1 (1681) 111 One that would not improve a very good piece of ground..with Fruit-trees, because the Parson would have the decimation of it. **1738** NEAL *Hist. Purit.* IV. 123 To sequester such as did not pay their Decimation. **1827** POLLOK *Course T.* II. 669 The priest collected tithes, and pleaded rights Of decimation, to the very last. **1869** W. MOLYNEUX *Burton on Trent* 40 This decimation was under a punishment of excommunication by Pope Alexander IV.

2. *Milit.* The selection by lot of every tenth man to be put to death, as a punishment in cases of mutiny or other offence by a body of soldiers, etc.

1580 NORTH *Plutarch* (1676) 768 Antonius..executed the Decimation. For he divided his men by ten Legions, and then of them he put the tenth Legion to death. **1617** COLLINS *Def. Bp. Ely* I. ii. 99. **1717** DE FOE *Mem. Ch. Scot.* III. 75 After the Decimations and Drafts made out of them for the Gibbet and Scaffold were over, these were sentenc'd to Transportation. **1827** MACAULAY *Machiavelli* Ess. (1854) 39/2 Whether decimation be a convenient mode of military execution.

b. The execution of nine out of every ten. *rare.*

1867 FREEMAN *Norm. Conq.* (1876) I. App. 674 A systematic decimation of the surviving male adults. By decimation is here meant the slaying, not of one out of ten, but of nine out of ten.

†**c.** The selection of every tenth member for any purpose. *Obs. rare.*

1632 J. LEE *Short Surv.* 36 The foot forces are culled and pickt out from among the choicest youth..by decimation, or taking every tenth man. **1742** WARBURTON *Wks.* (1811) XI. 155 Of a hundred arguments from reason and authority..he has not ventured so much as at a decimation.

3. *transf.* **a.** The killing or destruction of one in every ten. **b.** *loosely.* Destruction of a large proportion; subjection to severe loss, slaughter, or mortality.

1682 SIR T. BROWNE *Chr. Mor.* 65 The mercy of God hath singled out but few to be the signals of His justice..But the inadvertency of our natures not well apprehending this merciful decimation, etc. **1856** J. H. NEWMAN *Callista* 267 The population is prostrated by..pestilence, and by the decimation which their riot brought upon them. **1871** *Daily News* 21 Sept., In situations where their decimation by smart rifle practice would be almost a foregone conclusion.

decimator, -er ('dɛsɪmeɪtə(r)). [a. med.L. *decimātor* tithe-taker, n. of action from *decimāre* to DECIMATE; or f. DECIMATE + -ER¹. In F. *décimateur.*]

†**1.** An exactor or receiver of tithes, or of taxes to the amount of one-tenth. *Obs.*

1673 RUDYARD & GIBSON *Tythes ended* 13 Why then do not the Decimators take their Tenth themselves? *a* **1716** SOUTH *Serm.* 30 Jan. (T.), We have complained of.. sequestrators, triers, and decimators.

2. One who decimates: see DECIMATE *v.* 3, 4.

1862 MERIVALE *Rom. Emp.* (1865) V. xlv. 355 The decimater of the Senate.

†**'decime¹.** *Obs.* [ad. med.L. *decima* tenth, tithe, tithing. Cf. next.] A tithing as a division of the *hundred* in the English counties.

1611 SPEED *Theat. Gt. Brit.* II. 3/2 Elfred ordained Centuries, which they terme Hundreds, and Decimes, which they call Tithings. *c* **1630** RISDON *Surv. Devon* Title in orig. MS., The Decimes or a Corographicall description of the County of Devon.

‖**décime²** (desim). [F., ad. L. *decima* tenth.] A French coin of the value of one-tenth of a franc.

1810 *Naval Chron.* XXIV. 302 Decime = 2 Sols. 0,3 Deniers.

decimestrial (dɛsɪ'mɛstrɪəl), *a. rare.* [f. L. *decimēstri-s*, var. reading of *decemmēstris* (f. *decem* ten + *-mēstris*, deriv. of *mensis* month; cf. *menstruus* monthly) + -AL¹.] Consisting of ten months.

1842 SMITH *Dict. Gr. & Rom. Antiq.* s.v. *Calendar*, The decimestrial year still survived long after the legal government had ceased. **1862** G. C. LEWIS *Astron. Ancients* i. 9 Varro is also stated to have accepted the decimestrial year of Romulus.

decimeter, -metre: see DECI-.

'decimo-'sexto. ? *Obs.* [for L. *sexto decimo*, ablative case (due to original occurrence with *in*) of *sextus decimus* sixteenth.] A term denoting the size of a book, or of the page of a book, in which each leaf is one-sixteenth of a full sheet; properly SEXTO-DECIMO (usually abbreviated 16mo.). Also applied *fig.* to a diminutive person or thing.

1599 B. JONSON *Cynthia's Rev.* I. i, How now! my dancing braggart in decimo sexto! charm your skipping tongue. **1608** MIDDLETON *Five Gallants* I. i, Neither in folio nor in decimo sexto, but in octavo. **1656** *Artif. Handsom.* 75 Our stature.. if shrunk to a dwarfishnesse and epitomized to a Decimo-sexto. **1659** D. PELL *Impr. of Sea* 286 The little decimo sextos that be both in the Sea and Land..the small fish..as well as..the great folios of the Whale, and Elephant. **1706** HEARNE *Collect.* 4 Feb., As in Octavo's and Decimo-Sexto's.

†**'decinary¹**, *a. Obs.* Properly **decenary.** [f. med.L. *decēnāri-us*, f. *decēna* body of ten; cf. *deciner*, var. of DECENER.] Divisible by ten.

1650 ASHMOLE *Chym. Collect.* 88 That so in a Decinary number, which is a perfect number, the whole Work may be consummate. *Ibid.* 92.

decinary², -ner: see DECENARY, -NER.

decine, *Chem.*: see DECYL.

decinormal (dɛsɪ'nɔːməl), *a. Chem.* [f. DECI- + NORMAL *a.*] Of a solution: having a concentration one-tenth of that of a normal solution; containing one-tenth of a gramme-molecule or gramme-equivalent of the dissolved substance per litre of solution.

1863 F. SUTTON *Syst. Handbk. Volumetric Anal.* 19 The decinormal solutions may be made either by weighing $\frac{1}{10}$ atom of test direct and diluting to 1000, or by diluting 100 parts of normal solution to 1000. **1898** *Rev. Brit. Pharm.* 32 Deci-normal silver nitrate. **1964** *Oceanogr. & Marine Biol.* II. 291 Water..acidified with decinormal hydrochloric or nitric acids.

decipher (dɪ'saɪfə(r)), *v.* Forms: 6–7 des-, discipher, -cypher, (6 discifer, -sipher, 7 decyfer), 6– decipher, -cypher. [f. CIPHER *sb.*, after F.

déchiffrer, in 15th c. *deschiffrer*, f. *des-*, *de-* (DE- I. 6) + *chiffre* cipher. Cf. It. *deciferare* (Florio).]

1. *trans.* To convert into ordinary writing (what is written in cipher); to make out or interpret (a communication in cipher) by means of the key.

1545 EARL HERTFORD *Let. Hen. VIII* in Tytler *Hist. Scotl.* (1864) II. 404 A letter in cipher..which we have deciphered. **1552** ASCHAM in *Lett. Lit. Men* (Camden) 12 Seeing our lettres fittly dissiphered. **1605** BACON *Adv. Learn.* II. xvi. §6 The virtues of them [ciphers]..are..that they be impossible to decipher. *a* **1674** CLARENDON *Hist. Reb.* x. (1843) 595/2 The following letter was sent him by the Lord Jermyn, in whose Cipher it was writ, and deciphered by his lordship. **1709** HEARNE *Collect.* 24 Nov., Mr. Blincoe, being her Majesty's Officer in decyphering Letters, when there is occasion. **1839** JAMES *Louis XIV*, I. 9 The Queen was too closely watched to put the correspondence in cypher herself, or to decypher the answers she received. [See also CIPHER *sb.* 5 and *v.* 2.]

2. *transf.* To make out the meaning of (characters as difficult as those of a cipher): **a.** of obscure or badly-formed writing.

1710 STEELE *Tatler* No. 104 ¶5 With much ado I deciphered another Letter. **1799** C. DURNFORD *Willes' Rep.* Pref. 4 The necessity of decyphering and transcribing myself the manuscripts of the learned Chief Justice which are in a character peculiar to himself. **1855** BAIN *Senses & Int.* III. ii. §21 In deciphering bad hand-writing there is scope for identifying sameness in diversity.

b. of hieroglyphics, or writing in a foregin alphabet. Also *fig.*

1681-6 J. SCOTT *Chr. Life* (1747) III. 264 When our Saviour came into the World he unveiled the Jewish Religion, and deciphered all those mystical Characters wherein its spiritual Sense was expressed. **1750** JOHNSON *Rambler* No. 19 ¶11, I have found him..decyphering the Chinese language. **1794** SULLIVAN *View Nat.* II. 361 Coins ..with legends in a character not to be decyphered by the antiquaries of Europe. **1843** PRESCOTT *Mexico* (1850) I. 175 He deciphered the hieroglyphics. **1858** F. HALL in *Jrnl. Asiatic Soc. Bengal* 217 The Khaira inscription..has been partially deciphered.

3. To make out the meaning of (anything obscure or difficult to understand or trace): **a.** of things *fig.* treated as writings; **b.** of other things.

a. 1605 DANIEL *Philotas*, These secret figures Nature's message beare Of comming woes, were they deciphered right. **1862** C. P. HODGSON in *Guardian* 30 Apr. 424 The history of the 'Ainos' also is a singular book to decipher. **1865** LIVINGSTONE *Zambesi* xxv. 535 Attempting to decipher the testimony of the rocks.

b. 1669 GALE *Crt. Gentiles* I. I. vi. 33 Learned Bochart.. does thus decipher this riddle. **1788** REID *Aristotle's Log.* vi. §2. 141 We may at last decypher the law of nature. **1874** SPURGEON *Treas. Dav.* Ps. lxxxiv. 6 Probably there is here a local allusion, which will never now be deciphered. **1884** BOWER & SCOTT *De Bary's Phaner.* 367 A structure which at the first glance is difficult to decipher.

†**4.** To find out, discover, detect. *Obs.*

1528 GARDINER in Pocock *Rec. Ref.* I. l. 104 To the intent we might the better discipher the very lett and sticking. **1574** DEE in *Lett. Lit. Men* (Camden) 37 Yf by such a secret ..Threasor hid may be deciphered in precise place. **1588** SHAKS. *Tit. A.* IV. ii. 8 That you are both decipherd, thats the newes, For villaines markt with rape. **1599** SIR R. WROTHE in Ellis *Orig. Lett.* II. III. 181, I have appoynted sum especiall spyall of them to bewray them and to know them..and I hope in time to have them discifared.

†**5.** Of actions, outward signs, etc.: To reveal, make known, indicate; to give the key to (a person's character, etc.). *Obs.*

1529 MORE *Suppl. Soulys* Wks. 329/1 If he would nowe.. believe those .iij. or .iiij. noughty persones, against those .iij. or .iiij. C. good and honest men: he then should well decypher himselfe, and well declare therby, etc. **1598** SHAKS. *Merry W.* v. ii. 10 What needes either your Mum or her Budget? The white will decipher her well enough. *a* **1649** DRUMM. OF HAWTH. *Fam. Epist.* Wks. (1711) 143 Crosses serve for many uses, and more than magistracies decipher the man. **1793** HOLCROFT *Lavater's Physiog.* xxxviii. 197 Each man has his favorite gesture which might decypher his whole character.

†**b.** Of persons: To reveal. *Obs.*

1594 J. DICKENSON *Arisbas* (1878) 37 I haue a secret to disclose, a sorrowe to disciphre.

†**6.** To represent verbally or pictorially; to describe, delineate, portray, depict; = CIPHER *v.* 3.

a **1572** KNOX *Hist. Ref.* Wks. (1846) I. 191 Thane begane he to dissipher the lyves of diverse Papes, and the lyves of all the scheavelynges for the most parte. **1579** GOSSON *Sch. of Abuse* (Arb.) 19 Whether he were better with his art to discifer the life of ye Nimphe Melia, or Cadmus encounter with the Dragon, or [etc.]. **1601** HOLLAND *Pliny* II. 145 First I will discipher the medicinable vertues of trees. **1607** TOPSELL *Four-f. Beasts* (1658) 112 Those Painters which could most artificially decipher a Dog..were greatly reverenced among the Egyptians. **1626** MASSINGER *Rom. Actor* I. i, On the stage Decipher to the life what honours wait On good and glorious actions. **1714** ADDISON *Spect.* No. 613 ¶8 Decyphering them on a carpet humbly begging admittance. **1753** L. M. tr. *Du Boscq's Accompl. Woman* I The fancied Loves which these romantic Tales decipher.

†**7.** To represent or express by some kind of character, cipher, or figure; = CIPHER *v.* 2. *Obs.*

1586 A. DAY *Eng. Secretary* I. (1625) 144 One tearmed by the name of Friendship, and this other challenging onely to be deciphered by Love. **1644** BULWER *Chiron.* 15 The ancient Masters of the Hieroglyphiques..used to decypher a distinct and articulate voyce by a Tongue. **1720** WATERLAND *8 Serm.*, The Son being decipher'd and figur'd under those names or Characters. **1727** SWIFT *Gulliver, Brobdingnag* vi, Of these hairs I likewise made a neat little purse,..with her majesty's name decyphered in gold letters.

Hence **de'ciphered** *ppl. a.*

1845 GRAVES *Rom. Law* in *Encycl. Metrop.* 776/1 A copy of the decyphered text.

de'cipher, *sb.* [f. prec. vb.] The decipherment or translation of a cipher.

1545 EARL HERTFORD *Let. to Hen. VIII* in Tytler *Hist. Scotl.* (1864) II. 404 A letter in cipher..which we have deciphered, and send both the cipher and the decipher to your majesty herewith. **1571** *State Trials, Dk. of Norfolk* (R.), Baker brought me a decypher, telling me, That forty was for me, and thirty for the Queen of Scots. *a* **1670** HACKET *Abp. Williams* I. (1692) 22 His Majesty had pointed at no person, nor disclosed his meaning by any decipher or intimation. **1812** WELLINGTON in Gurw. IX. 280, I wish that the Marques had sent the ciphered letter here, or at least an accurate copy of the decipher. **1878** N. POCOCK *Harpsfield's Divorce Hen. VIII* Notes 324 The passage is in cypher, and runs as follows in the decypher given by Mr. Brewer.

†**b.** Description, delineation. *Obs.*

a **1670** HACKET *Abp. Williams* II. 220 (D.) A Lord Chancellour of France, whose decipher agrees exactly with this great prelate, sometimes Lord Keeper of the Great Seal.

decipherable (dɪˈsaɪfərəb(ə)l), *a.* [f. DECIPHER *v.* + -ABLE. Cf. F. *déchiffrable* (17th c.).] Capable of being deciphered, made out, or interpreted.

1607 DEKKER *Knt.'s Conjur.* (1842) 67 In his countenance there was a kinde of indignation fighting with a kind of exalted ioy, which by his very gesture were apparently decipherable. **1787** T. JEFFERSON *Writ.* (1859) II. 334 The form which affairs in Europe may assume, is not yet decipherable by those out of the cabinet. **1854** H. MILLER *Sch. & Schm.* (1858) 135 Half-effaced but still decipherable characters.

Hence **de'cipherably** *adv.* *nonce-wd.*, in a decipherable manner.

1890 *Temple Bar Mag.* Aug. 480 [They] still tell their curious faint tale decipherably.

de'cipherage. *nonce-wd.* Decipherment.

1851 H. TORRENS *Jrnl. Asiat. Soc. Bengal* 42 This is due to the decypherage of the Behistun and other inscriptions.

deciphe'ration. *nonce-wd.* = prec.

1838 *Fraser's Mag.* XVIII. 235 Our strongest microscope and concentrated powers of decipheration.

decipherer (dɪˈsaɪfərə(r)). [f. DECIPHER *v.* + -ER: cf. F. *déchiffreur* (16th c. in Hatzf.).] One who deciphers; one who makes out the meaning of what is written in cipher, or in indistinct or unknown characters.

Formerly the title of a government official.

1587 GOLDING *De Mornay* Pref. 9 Anatomists or Decipherers of nature; such as Pythagoras, Plato, Aristotle. **1605** BACON *Adv. Learn.* II. xv. §6 Suppose that cyphars were well managed, there bee multitudes of them which exclude the discypherer. **1715** *Hist. Register, Chron. Diary* 63 John Keil, Esq.; appointed his Majesty's Decypherer. **1863** KINGLAKE *Crimea* II. xvi. 100 The message came in an imperfect state. Part of it was..beyond all the power of the decipherer.

de'cipheress. *rare*$^{-1}$. [See -ESS.] A female decipherer.

a **1763** BYROM *Astrologer* 6 And thou, O Astrology, Goddess divine, Celestial decypheress.

deciphering (dɪˈsaɪfərɪŋ), *vbl. sb.* [-ING[1].] The action of the verb DECIPHER in various senses.

1552 ASCHAM in *Lett. Lit. Men* (Camden) 13 And bicause I perceyve this in siphering, I think other may perhaps light upon the same in dissiphring. **1712** HEARNE *Collect.* (Oxf. Hist. Soc.) III. 439 He..understood the Art of Decyphering tolerably well. **1883** *Athenæum* 17 Nov. 629/3 Much of it is actually due to his own deciphering.

decipherment (dɪˈsaɪfəmənt). [DECIPHER *v.* + -MENT: a modern word, not in Craig 1847. Cf. F. *déchiffrement* (16th c. in Hatzf.).] The action of deciphering; *esp.* interpretation of hieroglyphics or of obscure inscriptions.

1846 in WORCESTER [who cites *For. Q. Rev.* and notes it as *rare*]. **1851** D. WILSON *Preh. Ann.* (1863) II. IV. iv. 287 Inscriptions more elaborate and difficult of decipherment. **1862** MAX MÜLLER *Chips* (1880) I. v. 122 His later decipherments of the Cuneiform inscriptions. **1874** SAYCE *Compar. Philol.* App. 392 The decipherment of the records of Assyria and Babylonia.

decipium (dɪˈsɪpɪəm). *Chem.* [mod. irreg. f. L. *decĭp-ĕre* to deceive, with ending of *sodium*, *potassium*, *cerium*, etc.] A supposed rare metallic element of the cerium earth group.

Its oxide, **decipia**, was discovered by Delafontaine in 1878 in the samarskite of North Carolina, and the iodate, sulphate, and other salts have been prepared. On the supposition that decipia, of which the molecular weight is 390, is Dp_2O_3, it is inferred that decipium is a triad element of atomic weight 171. (See *Comptes Rendus* LXXXVII. 632 and XCIII. 63, and Watts *Dict. Chem.* (1881) VIII. 2156.)

deciple, -pel, obs. forms of DISCIPLE.

†**de'circinate**, *v.* *Obs.* [f. L. *dēcircinā-re* to round off, f. DE- I. 2, 3 + *circin-us* circle.] To round off, form into a circle.

1656 in BLOUNT *Glossogr.* [but wrongly explained]. **1686** GOAD *Celest. Bodies* I. v. 14 He [the Sun] imprinteth his Face on the Roscid Cloud, and decircinates the Iris with his Pencil. *Ibid.* II. xiii. 337 If the ☽ decircinates the Circle. **1721** BAILEY, *Decircinate*, to bring into a compass or roundness: to draw a Circle with a pair of Compasses.

Hence †**decirci'nation.**

1731 in BAILEY vol. II.

†**de'cise**, *v.* *Obs.* [f. L. *dēcīs-*, ppl. stem of *dēcīdĕre* to DECIDE: cf. *excise*, *incise*.] = DECIDE *v.*[1] Hence **de'cised, de'cising** *ppl. adjs.*

1538 BALE *Brefe Comedy* in *Harl. Misc.* (Malh.) I. 210 Soch vertuouse men to despyse As the lawes of God to hys people doth decyse. **1551** RECORDE *Pathw. Knowl.* II. Pref., In decising some controuersy of religion. **1570** LEVINS *Manip.* 148/11 To decise, *decidere, discutere.* **1641** R. BAILLIE *Lett. & Jrnls.* (1841) I. 360 To make that short, decised and nervous answer. **1662** J. DAVIES tr. *Olearius' Voy. Ambass.* 325 A Judge finds not so much difficulty in decising the differences of a Province, as [etc.].

deciser: see DECISOR.

decision (dɪˈsɪʒən). Also 5 **decysion**, 6 **-syon, decisioun, desision.** [a. F. *décision* (14th c. in Hatzf.), ad. L. *dēcīsiōn-em* cutting down, decision, n. of action from *dēcīd-ĕre* to DECIDE.]

1. a. The action of deciding (a contest, controversy, question, etc.); settlement, determination.

1490 CAXTON *Eneydos* vi. 23 He hath not rendred the reason or made ony decysion. **1538** STARKEY *England* II. ii. 192 Thys causyth sutys to be long in decysyon. **1651** HOBBES *Leviath.* II. xviii. 91 The decision of Controversies. **1769** *Junius Lett.* i. 9 In the decision of private causes. **1833** HT. MARTINEAU *Manch. Strike* vii. 73 For the decision of questions daily arising.

b. (with *a* and *pl.*) The final and definite result of examining a question; a conclusion, judgement: *esp.* one formally pronounced in a court of law.

1552 ABP. HAMILTON *Catech.* (1884) 5 The decisiouns and determinatiouns of general counsallis. **1611** BIBLE *Transl. Pref.* 11 Then his word were an Oracle, his opinion a decision. **1651** HOBBES *Leviath.* III. xlii. 311 To compell men to obey his Decisions. **1827** JARMAN *Powell's Devises* (ed. 3) II. 95, I have not been able to discover more than one dictum and one decision in favour of the distinction. **1883** FROUDE *Short Stud.* IV. I. iii. 35 The decisions of the clergy were more satisfactory to themselves than to the laity.

2. The making up of one's mind on any point or on a course of action; a resolution, determination.

1886 ST. GEORGE STOCK tr. *Aristotle's Ethics* III. i. 43 It is hard at times to decide what sort of thing one should choose ..and still harder to abide by one's decisions. *Mod.* Let me know your decision. Decision for Christ.

3. As a quality: Determination, firmness, decidedness of character.

1781 BURKE *Corr.* (1844) II. 438 We want courage and decision of mind. **1805** FOSTER *Ess.* ii. (*title*), Decision of Character. **1856** EMERSON *Eng. Traits* Wks. (Bohn) II. 30 On the English face are combined decision and nerve.

†**4.** Cutting off, separation. *Obs.*

1584 R. SCOT *Discov. Witchcr.* IV. ii. 59 Without decision of seed. **1602** WARNER *Alb. Eng.* x. lvi. (1612) 246 By.. decision of the Lymme whence all the bayne did floe. **1603** HOLLAND *Plutarch's Mor.* 827 (R.) From rocks and stones along the sea..there be decisions pass of some parcels and smal fragments. **1659** PEARSON *Creed* I. 221 Human generation..is performed by derivation or decision of part of the substance of the Parent.

5. *attrib.* and *Comb.*, as ***decision-maker, -making, -taker, -taking, theory***; **decision method** = *decision procedure*; **decision problem** [tr. G. *entscheidungsproblem*] *Math.* and *Logic*, the problem of finding a decision procedure for a class of formulas; the ENTSCHEIDUNGSPROBLEM; **decision procedure** *Math.* and *Logic*, an effective formal routine or mechanical method for deciding whether any selected formula of a given system, or a given class of formulas, is true or derivable within the system to which it belongs.

1938 S. CHASE *Tyranny of Words* xviii. 233 Mr. Baldwin was long the chief *decision-maker for the British Empire. **1955** D. CHAPMAN *Home & Social Status* 2 Collaboration between researchers and 'decision-makers'. **1953** *Amer. Political Sci. Rev.* Mar. 7 The right of every voter to participate equally in the community's *decision-making process. **1956** J. KLEIN *Study of Groups* xi. 148 The group moves into the decision-making phase. *Ibid.*, Progress in decision-making. **1960** *Times* 24 Mar. 2/2 An electronic laboratory (specialising in decision-making machines). **1965** M. FRAYN *Tin Men* v. 27 The decision-making faculties of a professional decision-maker like himself had to be nursed. **1948** A. TARSKI (*title*) A *decision method for elementary algebra and geometry. **1958** FRAENKEL & BAR-HILLEL *Found. Set Theory* v. 297 A formalized theory *T* is decidable if there exists an effective, uniform method—a so-called decision method—of determining whether a given sentence, formulated in the vocabulary of *T*, is valid in *T*. **1939** *Jrnl. Symbolic Logic* IV. 1 (*heading*) On the reduction of the *decision problem. **1954** I. M. COPI *Symbolic Logic* vii. 235 The decision problem for any deductive system is the problem of stating an effective criterion for deciding whether or not any statement or well-formed formula is a theorem of the system. **1945** W. V. QUINE in *Jrnl. Symbolic Logic* X. 3 No *decision procedure is possible for the validity of polyadic schemata. **1950** —— *Methods of Logic* (1952) §15. 82 A 'decision procedure'—i.e., a mechanical routine for deciding validity, implication, consistency, etc. **1957** *Technology* July 182/2 Any game of a finite kind which can be completed in a finite number of moves—and this includes simple games like noughts and crosses as well as draughts and chess—must have a decision procedure, even though we may not know for any particular game what this procedure is. **1962** *Times Lit. Suppl.* 24 Aug. 634/1 Wider ranges of privilege for economic *decision-takers (and their wives and children). **1964** T. W. MCRAE *Impact of Computers on*

Accounting iii. 98 Raw statistics, the backbone of the *decision-taking process. **1964** J. Z. YOUNG *Model of Brain* iii. 28 'Signals' are the physical events in the communication channels that operate the decision-taking mechanism. **1961** *Jrnl. Acous. Soc. Amer.* XXXIII. 358/1 An algorithm based on statistical *decision theory. **1964** T. W. MCRAE *Impact of Computers on Accounting* v. 120 Decision theory is probing the psychology of decision making, and attempts to provide an algorism for taking decisions.

de'cisional, *a. rare.* [f. prec. + -AL[1].] Of, or of the nature of, a decision.

1883 *Encycl. Brit.* XVI. 503/2 These opinions of the minority can have no decisional effect.

decisive (dɪ'saɪsɪv), *a.* (*sb.*) [ad. med.L. *dēcīsīv-us*, f. *dēcīs-*, ppl. stem of *dēcīdĕre*: see -IVE. Cf. F. *décisif, -ive* (1413 in Godef. *Suppl.*).]

1. Having the quality of deciding or determining (a question, contest, etc.); conclusive, determinative.

1611 COTGR., *Decisif*, decisiue, deciding, determining, fit or able to end a controuersie. **1647** CRASHAW *Poems* 147 That sure decisive dart. **1794** SULLIVAN *View Nat.* I. 255 Notions..unsupported by decisive experiments. **1835** THIRLWALL *Greece* I. vii. 260 Tisamenus was slain in the decisive battle. **1892** L. W. CAVE in *Law Times Rep.* LXVII. 199/2 The case..is really decisive of the point raised.

2. Characterized by decision; unhesitating, resolute, determined; = DECIDED 2.

1736 BUTLER *Anal.* II. vii. 355 To determine at once with a decisive air. **1858** MAX MÜLLER *Chips* (1880) III. iii. 68 The age..was not an age of decisive thought or decisive action. **1861** DICKENS *Gt. Expect.* v. 20 The serjeant, a decisive man, ordered that the sound should not be answered.

3. That is beyond question or doubt, that cannot be mistaken; hence often = DECIDED 1.

1794 S. WILLIAMS *Vermont* 160 Operate with a decisive influence to give them new force. **1835** I. TAYLOR *Spir. Despot.* ii. 38 A decisive leaning toward what is most simple and intelligible. **1880** L. STEPHEN *Pope* iii. 71 The sustained vivacity and emphasis of the style give it [Pope's Iliad] a decisive superiority over its rivals.

¶ *ellipt.* as *sb.*

a **1734** NORTH *Exam.* I. ii. §64 (1740) 63 The Roman Catholic Peers were so many, as nearly if not wholly made a Decisive, for they went altogether as one Man.

decisively (dɪ'saɪsɪvlɪ), *adv.* [-LY[2].] In a decisive manner.

1. Conclusively; so as to decide the question.

1651 BAXTER *Inf. Bapt.* 121 The Authority of Synods in matters of Faith is..declarative, and not decisively judiciall. **1756** WATSON in *Phil. Trans.* XLIX. 491, I..cannot determine decisively about it, till the whole be cleared by digging. **1854** MAURICE *Mor. & Met. Philos.* (ed. 2) 5 Seneca disposed rapidly and decisively of the objection.

2. With decision; unhesitatingly, resolutely.

1809–10 COLERIDGE *Friend* (1865) 129 Major Cartwright has expressed himself as decisively, and with as much warmth, against [etc.]. **1870** ANDERSON *Missions Amer. Bd.* II. xii. 95 It was now time..to act decisively.

3. In a manner beyond question or doubt; unmistakeably, decidedly.

1792 YOUNG *Trav. France* 257 It is fine sun-shine weather, decisively warmer than ever felt in England at this season. **1800** FOSTER in *Life & Corr.* (1846) I. 126 Decisively Calvinistic. **1893** *British Weekly* 8 June 105/5 Poe is decisively the first of American poets.

decisiveness (dɪ'saɪsɪvnɪs). [-NESS.] The quality of being decisive; conclusiveness; resoluteness, decision.

1727 in BAILEY vol. II. **1797** *Hist.* in *Ann. Reg.* 45/2 They knew the decisiveness of his temper. **1837** CARLYLE *Fr. Rev.* II. II. vi, The Mutineers pronounce themselves with a decisiveness, which to Bouillé seems insolence. **1856** FROUDE *Hist. Eng.* (1858) II. vi. 23 The King, with swift decisiveness, annihilated the incipient treason.

† **de'cisor, -er.** *Obs.* [a. med.L. *dēcīsor*, agent-n. from *dēcīdĕre* to decide.] One who decides causes or controversies: a decider, arbiter.

1563 FOXE *A. & M.* 68 b, Thys King [Hen. II], to whom other Princes dyd so resort, as to their arbitrer and deciser. **1564** HAWARD *Eutropius* I. 9 Two whome they called Tribuni plebis..to be peculier decisers and determiners of their causes. **1888** B. PICK in *Libr. Mag.* Mar. 245 They were called *Saboraim*, 'Decisors', 'Opinionists'.

† **de'cisory,** *a. Obs. rare*$^{-0}$. [ad. med.L. *dēcīsōri-us*, f. *dēcīsor*: see prec. and -ORY. In F. *décisoire* (14th c. in Godef. *Suppl.*).] Decisive.

1611 COTGR., *Decisoire*, decisorie, deciding; fit, vsed, or able, to decide controuersies. **1755** in JOHNSON.

decistere: see DECI-.

decitizenize: see DE- II. 1.

decivilize (dɪ'sɪvɪlaɪz), *v.* [DE- II. 1.: in mod.F. *déciviliser* (Littré).] To divest of civilization, to degrade from a civilized condition. Hence **de'civilized** *ppl. a.*, **de'civilizing** *vbl. sb.* and *ppl. a.*; **decivili'zation**, the process or condition of losing civilization.

1831 MRS. M. HOLLEY *Texas* (1833) 43 It sometimes happens that a white man from the States, who has become somewhat *decivilized* (to coin a word), is substituted. *a* **1859** DE QUINCEY has *decivilized* (F. Hall). **1876** H. SPENCER *Princ. Sociol.* §71 We have but to imagine ourselves de-civilized. **1892** *Sat. Rev.* 27 Aug. 246/1 He was barbarized, de-civilized, and enslaved. **1889** *Ch. Times* 15 Feb. 159/1 The decivilising effect of the wars. **1878** *N. Amer. Rev.* CXXVII. 447 General harm, and decivilization, of the people. **1885** E. W. BENSON in *Law Times* LXXVIII. 338/1 If it might stem by even its own ruin the process of decivilisation.

deck (dɛk), *sb.*[1] Also 5 dekke, 6–7 decke. [In sense 1, app. of Flemish or LG. origin.

In sense 1, prob. a MDu. *dec* (neuter) roof, covering, cloak, pretext (app. from *decke*:—OTeut. *þakjo*^{m}, from same root as DECK *v.*): cf. Kilian '*decke* operimentum, lodix = *decksel* operimentum, opertorium, tegumen, tegumentum, tegmen, stragulum'; also mod.Du. *dek* bed-covering, horse-cloth'. But in the nautical sense, 2, the word is not known in Du. before 1675–81, when *dek* (neuter) appears as a synonym of *verdek*, quoted in the nautical sense in 1640, but recorded by Kilian, 1599, only in the general sense 'tegumen, velamen'. Thus, *deck* in the nautical sense, appears to be known in Eng. 160 years earlier than in Dutch. It may be simply a specific application of the general sense 'covering', or it may come more immediately from the MDu. sense 'roof.']

I. † **1.** A covering. *Obs.*

In quot. 1466 app. some material used for covering; with 1712 cf. Du. *dek* 'horse-cloth'.

1466 *Mann. & Househ. Exp.* 348 My mastyr paid to John Felawe, for xij. yerdes of dekke for the spynas, iijs. **1509** BARCLAY *Shyp of Folys* (1874) I. 38 Do on your Decke, Slut, ..I mean your Copyntanke. **1712** *Lond. Gaz.* No. 4997/4 A red Saddle with 2 Ovals in the Skirt, and the under Decks edg'd with blue.

2. a. *Naut.* A platform extending from side to side of a ship or part of a ship, covering in the space below, and also itself serving as a floor; formed of planks, or (in iron ships) of iron plating usually covered with planks.

The primary notion was 'covering' or 'roof' rather than 'floor': see quots. 1550 and 1624, and cf. 1466 in sense 1, where the 'dekke for the spynas' or pinnace, may have been a covering of canvas, tarpaulin, or the like. In early craft there was a deck only at the stern, so that 16th c. writers sometimes use *deck* as equivalent to *poop*. In Elyot (1538), whence in Cooper, Huloet, and Baret, *deck* is erroneously made the equivalent of *prora*, instead of *puppis*.

1513 ECHYNGHAM *to Wolsey* 5 May (MS. Cott. Calig. D. vi. lf. 110), And bycause I hade no Rayles upon my dek I coyled a cable rounde a [boute the] dek brest hye and likwise in the waste. **1531** C. MORRES *Inv. Great Bark* (Cott. MS. App. xxviii), In primis, the shype with oon over-lop. Item, a somer castell & a cloos tymber deck made from the mast forward whyche was made of laet. Item aboue the somer castel A deck from the mayne mast aftward. **1550** NICOLLS *Thucyd.* (tr. Seyssel's Fr. version of Valla's Lat.) 191 They couered the former parte, and the mooste parte of their deckes [Fr. la plus part du couvert de leurs navires] w[t] copper [F *cuir*, leather]. *c* **1585** ? J. POLMON *Famous Battles* 192 (Seafight at Cape of Orso, 1528) Philippino..levelling the first shotte of his Basilisco, with piercing the *Emperiall Admirall*, passed from the stemme to the decke, slaying thirtie men. *Ibid.* 193 The *Moore* hitting the decke, strake off the rudder. *Ibid.* 320 (Battle of Lepanto) The decke of this galley..chequered and wroughte marvellous fayre with diuers colours and hystories..ingraued and wrought in golde. **1587** W. BOURNE *Arte of Shooting* 59 It is very evil for to have the Orlop or Deck too low under the port. **1610** SHAKS. *Temp.* I. ii. 197 Now on the Beake, Now in the Waste, the Decke, in euery Cabyn. **1624** CAPT. SMITH *Virginia* III. 63 In a broad Bay, out of danger of their shot.. we vntyed our Targets that couered vs as a Deck. **1692** DELAVAL in *Lond. Gaz.* No. 2769/3, 15 Capital Ships, 10 whereof are of 3 Decks. **1720** DE FOE *Capt. Singleton* ii. (1840) 36 A boat with a deck and a sail. **1840** R. DANA *Bef. the Mast* xxxiii. 125 The captain walked the deck at a rapid stride.

b. With qualifying words.

The largest ships of the line had ***main-deck, middle*** and ***lower*** deck; also the ***upper*** or ***spar-deck***, extending from stem to stern over the main-deck, and the ***orlop deck*** (which carried no guns) below the lower deck; they had also a ***poop-deck***, or short deck in the after part of the ship above the spar-deck, and sometimes a ***forecastle deck***, or similar short deck in the fore-part of the ship, sometimes retained in merchant ships and called the ***top-gallant forecastle***. See also HALF-DECK, HURRICANE-DECK, QUARTER-DECK, etc.

1598 FLORIO *Dict.* To Reader 9, I was but one to sit at sterne, to pricke my carde, to watch vpon the vpper decke. *c* **1620** Z. BOYD *Zion's Flowers* (1855) 12, I see a man that's in the lower deck. **1627** CAPT. SMITH *Seaman's Gram.* ii. 6 A Flush Decke is when from stem to sterne, it lies upon a right line fore and aft. **1637** HEYWOOD *Royal Ship* 45 She hath three flush Deckes, and a Fore-Castle, an halfe Decke, a quarter Decke, and a round-house. *a* **1642** SIR W. MONSON *Naval Tracts* III. 346/1 They make close the Forecastle and Half-Deck. **1836** MARRYAT *Midsh. Easy* xii, Easthupp would constantly accost him familiarly on the forecastle and lower deck. *Ibid.* xiii, He then proceeded to the quarter-deck. *Ibid.* xxvi, To comply with the captain's orders on the main deck.

c. In phrases, as ***above deck*** (also *fig.*), BETWEEN-DECKS, ***on deck, under deck(s; to clear, sweep the decks*** (see CLEAR *v.*, SWEEP *v.*).

on deck fig. (orig. U.S.): at hand; ready for action; alive; in *Baseball*, next at the bat, with the right or privilege of batting next.

1598 SHAKS. *Merry W.* II. i. 94 *F.* Ile be sure to keepe him aboue decke. *P.* So will I: if hee come vnder my hatches, Ile neuer to Sea againe. **1647** CLARENDON *Hist. Reb.* VI. (1843) 297/2 Committed to prison on board the ships..where they were kept under decks. **1659** D. PELL *Impr. of Sea* 419 Now hang the lighted Lanthorns betwixt decks and in the Hold. *a* **1679** GURNALL in Spurgeon *Treas. Dav.* Ps. lxv. 3 Poor Christian, who thinkest that thou shalt never get above deck. **1720** DE FOE *Capt. Singleton* xi. (1840) 194 The rest ran.. down between decks. **1857** R. TOMES *Amer. in Japan* iv. 110 [He] left the banquet to be discussed by his officers and men, who..soon cleared the decks. **1867** *Ball Players' Chron.* 26 Sept. 5/4 Well, I went on deck and took up a bat. **1889** 'MARK TWAIN' *Yankee* xxii. 274 Angels..are always on deck when there is a miracle to the fore. **1889** *Lisbon* (Dakota) *Star* 26 Apr. 4/2 A. H. Moore..was kicked by a horse, a cow and a colt.., but is still on deck. **1946** K. TENNANT *Lost Haven* (1968) xix. 346, I couldn't bring it [*sc.* oakum] up here if Jame was on deck. She'd be down on me like a ton of lead. **1950** *Here & Now* (N.Z.) Dec. 12/1 If I am on deck when that time comes you will have a strong advocate for reinstatement in the service. **1966** *Times* 28 Feb. (Canada Suppl.) p. x/4 Dice games and three-card monte are not, so to speak, on deck but bingo flourishes.

3. a. *Mining.* (See quot.)

1888 GREENWELL *Coal-trade Terms Northumb. & Durh.* (ed. 3) 31 *Deck*, the platform of a cage upon which the tubs stand when being drawn up or lowered down the pit.

b. By extension, any kind of floor or platform, as the floor of a pier or landing-stage, or the platform or roadway of a deck-bridge (see also quot. 1938).

1872 *Porcupine* XIV. 314/2 The decks of the three stages being swept pretty clear, by the devastating fire of the enemy. **1876** *Ibid.* XVIII. 330/1 Its deck is fairly rotting away. **1883** *Specif. Alnwick & Cornhill Rlwy.* 45 The girders are connected by a wrought-iron deck. **1910** A. WILLIAMS *Engin. Wonders of World* III. 282 The old suspension truss, which could then be removed piece by piece to make room for the upper deck. **1938** L. M. HARROD *Librarians' Gloss.* 56 *Deck*, one floor of a stack room containing the bookshelves, lifts, and workrooms. (American.) **1955** *Times* 9 May 18/2 Multi-deck car parks with direct access to the stores. **1961** *Daily Tel.* 19 Jan. 13/2 Other upper level walkways.. include those on a 'deck' on the London Pavilion site. **1970** *Times* 9 Feb. 13/3 A service area and parking deck for 650 vehicles on the second floor.

c. *Aeronaut.* A main aeroplane surface, esp. of a biplane or multiplane; a wing.

1843 G. CAYLEY in *Mech. Mag.* XXXVIII. 275/1 Would it not be more likely to answer the purpose to compact it into the form of a *three decker*, each deck being 8 to 10 ft. from the other, to give free room for the passage of air between them? **1910** A. WILLIAMS *Engin. Wonders of World* III. 7/2 The biplane, with two 'decks' set one above the other. **1929** *Papers Mich. Acad. Sci. & Arts* X. 287 *Decks*, the wings of an airplane.

d. The floor of an omnibus or tramcar; ***top*** or ***upper deck***, the upper floor or compartment of a double-decked vehicle.

1869 [implied in DOUBLE-DECKED *a.*]. **1906** *Daily Chron.* 11 Sept. 7/1 The cars..have no upper deck, and carry only thirty-six passengers, as compared with accommodation for sixty-six in and on the double-deck pattern. **1966** P. MOLONEY *Plea for Mersey* 33 The best place to hear examples of all these quaint circumlocutions is the top deck of Liverpool's buses. **1968** *Listener* 26 Dec. 855/2 Two American soldiers sat on the lower deck of a bus smoking cigars.

e. *Aeronaut. slang.* The ground; *spec.* the landing-ground of an aerodrome.

1925 *Punch* 11 Nov. 521 *R.A.F. Officer* (unhorsed). Oh, he just stalled on top of the loop, did a roll and left me hangin' on the straps; then spun into the deck. **1941** *War Illustr.* 29 Aug. 93/1, I didn't see the bombs drop, but Mac, the rear-gunner, yelled over the inter-comm in a broad Scots accent —'There's one on the deck.' **1958** 'N. SHUTE' *Rainbow & Rose* vii. 276 She spun her Moth into the deck.

f. The surface of a tape recorder above which the tape moves, together with its attachments such as the motor(s) and other mechanisms, the magnetic heads, and the circuits immediately associated with them, the whole being built as a single unit; any device for moving tape from one spool to another past magnetic heads; more fully as ***tape deck***. Also, the corresponding part of a system for playing gramophone records.

1949 *Electronic Engin.* XXI. 149/3 At present the 'Tapedeck' recorder is available to manufacturers only who will fit the recorder into their own amplifying equipment. **1962** A. NISBETT *Technique Sound Studio* 249 Professional tape decks and some domestic decks have two further motors for the feed and take up spools. **1964** F. L. WESTWATER *Electronic Computers* iv. 67 Tape does not run continuously, but as required by the computer. It is mounted on what is called a Tape Deck. *a* **1965** *Manual of 'Ferrograph' Series 6* (*Model 631*) 4 The instrument resolves itself into three main units:—A. The mechanical deck carrying the motors, heads, reels, etc. B. The power unit and oscillator. C. The amplifier chassis containing the amplifier, monitor meter, etc. *Ibid.* 27 The mechanical unit is situated entirely on the hinged deck of the instrument. **1971** *Observer* (Colour Suppl.) 28 Feb. 33/2 (Advt.), The Garrard range..means you can tailor a deck to suit your needs... Perfect sound and record care for years.

4. In U.S. 'A passenger-car roof, particularly the clear-story roof' (*Standard Dict.*).

II. 5. a. 'A pack of cards piled regularly on each other' (J.); also the portion of the pack left, in some games, after the hands have been dealt. Since 17th c. *dial.* and in *U.S.*

1593 SHAKS. *3 Hen. VI*, v. i. 44 But whiles he thought to steale the single Ten, The King was slyly finger'd from the Deck. **1594** ? GREENE *Selimus* Wks. 1881–3 XIV. 251 If I chance but once to get the decke, To deale about and shuffle as I would. **1594** BARNFIELD *Sheph. Cont.* viii, Pride deales the Deck whilst Chance doth choose the Card. **1609** ARMIN *Two Maids Moreclacke* (N.), I'll deal the cards, and cut you from the deck. **16..** GREW (J.), The Selenites, of parallel plates, as in a deck of cards. **1777** BRAND *Pop. Antiq.* (1849) II. 449 In some parts of the North of England a pack of cards is called to this day..a deck of cards. **1860** in BARTLETT *Dict. Amer.* **1882** BRET HARTE *Gentl. La Porte* in *Flip*, etc. 135, I reckon the other fifty-one of the deck ez as pooty. **1884** *Chesh. Gloss.*, *Deck o' cards*, a pack of cards. **1885** *Century Mag.* XXIX. 548/1 An old ratty deck of cards.

b. A packet of narcotics; a small portion of some drug wrapped in paper. *U.S. slang.*

1922 E. F. MURPHY *Black Candle* (1926) I. v. 52 Small paper packages [of cocaine]..are called 'decks', and contain about a couple of sniffs. **1927** *Flynn's* 9 July 462/2 At night it was 'snow' that went over the counter..to poor devils who left behind them three dollars..for a deck. **1949** 'J. Evans' *Halo in Brass* (1951) iv. 29 A deck of nose candy for sale to the right guy. **1966** C. Himes *Heat's On* iii. 27 When it's analysed, they'll find five or six half-chewed decks of heroin.

† **6. a.** A pile of things laid flat upon each other.

1625 F. Markham *Bk. Hon.* II. vi. §5 Any whose Pedigree lyes so deepe in the decke, that few or none will labour to find it. **1631** *Celestina* xix. 185 Subtill words, whereof such as shee are never to seeke, but have them still ready in the deck. **1634** Sanderson *Serm.* II. 287 So long as these things should hang upon the file, or lie in the deck, he might perhaps be safe. **1673** Marvell *Reh. Transp.* II. 394 A certain Declaration..which you have kept in deck until this season.

b. Part of a newspaper, periodical, etc., headline containing more than one line of type, esp. the part printed beneath the main headline. Also *attrib.*

1935 H. Straumann *Newspaper Headlines* i. 28 These are first decks (and streamers) only. *Ibid.* iii. 87 The first three lines or 'decks' as they would be called in present-day journalism. **1965** L. H. Whitten *Progeny of Adder* (1966) 127 The eight-column headline told him of Pantelein's body being found. But it was the 'deck' headline that held him: *county coroner cites 'vampirism'.*

† **7.** Of a cannon: see quot. *Obs.*

1672 W. T. *Compleat Gunner* I. iv. 5 The Pumel or Button at her Coyl or Britch-end is called the Casacabel or Deck.

III. *attrib.* and *Comb.* (from sense 2), as ***deck-cabin, -cleat, -cricket, -flat, -framing, -game, -officer, -passage, -passenger, -plank, -pump, -scrubber, -seat, -stool, -stringer, -swabber, -transom, -trumpet, -watch***; also, **deck-beam**, one of the strong transverse beams supporting the deck of a ship; **deck-boy**, a boy employed on the deck of a vessel; **deck-bridge**, (*a*) a narrow platform above and across the deck of a steamer amidships; = bridge *sb.*[1] 5; (*b*) a bridge in which the roadway is laid on the top of the truss (opp. to a *through bridge*); **deck-cargo** = *deck-load*; **deck class**, a grade of accommodation entitling a person to deck-space only on board a ship; **deck-collar** (U.S.), the iron collar or ring through which the stove-pipe passes in the roof of a railway carriage; cf. *deck-plate*; **deck-feather** (see quot.); **deck-flats** (see flat *sb.*); **deck-hand**, a 'hand' or workman employed on the deck of a vessel; **deck-head**, a name for the slipper limpet (*Crepidula*); **deck-hook**, 'the compass timber bolted horizontally athwart a ship's bow, connecting the stem, timber, and deck-planks of the fore-part; it is part and parcel of the *breast-hooks*' (Smyth *Sailor's Word-bk.*); **deck-house**, a 'house' or room erected on the deck of a ship; **deck-lander**, an aeroplane designed to be able to land on a ship's deck; **deck-light**, a thick glass let into a deck to light a cabin below; **deck-load** *sb.*, hence **deck-load** *v.*, to load with a cargo upon the deck; also *fig.*; **deck-nail**, 'a kind of spike with a snug head, commonly made in a diamond form' (Smyth); **deck-pipe**, 'an iron pipe through which the chain cable is paid into the chain-locker' (Smyth); **deck-plate** (see quot.); **deck-pot**, a pot used on whaling vessels to receive the scraps; **deck quoits**, a game played, chiefly on board ships, by throwing a rope quoit over a peg; **deck-sheet**, 'that sheet of a studding-sail which leads directly to the deck, by which it is steadied until set' (Smyth); **deck-stopper**, 'a strong stopper used for securing the cable forward of the capstan or windlass while it is overhauled; also abaft the windlass or bitts to prevent more cable from running out' (Smyth); **deck-tackle**, a tackle led along the deck, for hauling in cable, etc.; **deck tennis**, a game played esp. on the deck of a ship by tossing a ring or quoit of rubber, rope, etc., back and forth over a net.

1858 Simmonds *Dict. Trade*, *Deck-beams. **1876** Davis *Pol. Exp.* i. 29 New deck-beams of increased size were put in. **1900** *Westm. Gaz.* 22 Mar. 5/2 Prisoner said he was *deck-boy on board the *Carisbrook Castle.* **1908** *Ibid.* 28 Aug. 12/1 The owner..sent his son, the deck-boy, down to the engineer. **1902** *Ibid.* 28 July 2/1 He..writes pictured post-cards at the *deck-cabin table. **1861** *Chambers' Encycl.* s.v. *Cargo*, The term *deck-cargo is given to the commodities on the deck of a ship, which are not usually included in the policy of insurance. **1953** A. Smith *Blind White Fish* ii. 32 The second and third classes were more cosmopolitan;..all three could look down with equal disdain upon the *deck class. *Ibid.*, The deck class passengers began to look around for sheltered niches in which to spend the night. **1969** J. H. Vance *Deadly Isles* (1970) iii. 23 If he was lucky he might still find a berth available. If not, he'd go deck class, like the Polynesians. **1867** Smyth *Sailor's Word-bk.*, *Deck-cleats, pieces of wood temporarily nailed to the deck to secure objects in bad weather. **1891** *Scribner's Mag.* X. 278 *Deck cricket, quoits, and cock-fighting enliven the forenoons. **1879** *Encycl. Brit.* IX. 7/1 *Deck feathers, the two centre tail-feathers. **1879** *Cassell's Techn. Educ.* IV. 60/1 Wood ships with wood beams have their *deck-flats formed by planking laid upon and fastened to the beams. **1894** *Outing* (U.S.) XXIV. 396/1 Everything else, including the *deck-framing and deck is of the same kind of material as those used in a regular battleship. **1896** S. A. Barnett *Let.* Sept. in H. Barnett *Canon Barnett* (1918) II. xxxvii. 118 Of course there are the *deck games. **1971** 'A. Garve' *Late Bill Smith* ii. 45 There was..little provision for deck games. **1844** *Knickerbocker* XXIII. 88 On board of one of the steam-boats on the Mississippi, I encountered a *deck-hand, who went by the name of Barney. **1885** Gen. Grant *Pers. Mem.* xxi. I. 288 From captain down to deck-hand. **1881** *Scribner's Mag.* XXII. 656/1 Beds of jingles or amber-shells..*deck heads ..limpets, and other rock-loving mollusks. *c* **1850** *Rudim. Navig.* (Weale) 101 The breast-hooks that receive the ends of the deck-planks are also called *Deck-Hooks. **1856** Kane *Arct. Expl.* I. x. 106 Ohlsen and Petersen building our *deck-house. **1882** *Daily News* 24 May 1/1 Good accommodation is..provided for second-class passengers in a commodious deck-house. **1928** *Daily Tel.* 18 Sept. 11/4 It [*sc.* the autogiro] should be able to act as a *deck-lander on almost any ship. **1961** E. Brown *Wings on my Sleeve* viii. 83 The Sea Hornet, a twin-engined deck-lander developed from the Mosquito, followed on the heels of the single-seater Hawker Sea Fury. **1849** N. Kingsley *Diary* 7 Mar. (1914) 7 Mate arrived today, Mr. Webb, put in *deck lights & scuttle to house on deck. **1757** in *Essex Inst. Hist. Coll.* (1910) XLVI. 273 They hove overboard the *Deck Load of Lumber. **1840** Longfellow in *Life* (1891) I. 357 Horrible negligence,—a deck-load of cotton! **1867** Smyth *Sailor's Word-bk.*, *Deck-load*, timber, casks, or other cargo not liable to damage from wet, stowed on the deck of merchant vessels. **1884** Gladstone in *Standard* 29 Feb. 2/7 We are determined..not to *deck-load our Franchise Bill. **1703** T. N. *City & C. Purchaser* 126, 211 *Deck-nails..are proper for fastning of Decks in Ships. **1828** 'C. Sealsfield' *Americans* ix. 105 The great difference of fare between a cabin and a *deck passage..contributes to establish a distinction in this assemblage of people. **1883** 'Mark Twain' *Life Mississippi* vi. 79 He only traveled deck passage because it was cooler! **1824** W. Owen *Diary* 6 Dec. in *Indiana Hist. Publ.* (1906) IV. 57 Here the steerage, or as they are called *deck passengers, sit, eat and sleep. **1859** *Autobiog. Beggar Boy* 114 Among the deck passengers there was a man and his wife with seven children. **1872** E. Eggleston *End of World* xxviii. 187 He passed through to the place where the steerage or deck passengers are. *c* **1860** H. Stuart *Seaman's Catech.* 55 The hawse boxes, or *deck pipe. **1884** Sir E. J. Reed in *Contemp. Rev.* Nov. 620 The steel decks..being..covered with *deck-plank of teak or of pine. **1874** Knight *Dict. Mech.*, **Deck-plate*, a plate around the chimney of a marine-engine furnace to keep the same from contact with the wood of the deck. **1904** *Sci. Amer. Suppl.* 5 Mar. 23551 The oil flows freely..into the pots, while the refuse..is thrown into another receptacle, called the *deck-pot. **1907** *Yesterday's Shopping* (1969) 1022/2 *Deck quoits. As used on all steamships, and can be played in any sized room or lawn. **1971** 'A. Garve' *Late Bill Smith* ii. 64 The last time I was on a cruise a man died through over-exertion in a deck quoits competition. **1920** *Blackw. Mag.* Apr. 509/2 He..belaboured them methodically with a *deck-scrubber. *c* **1860** H. Stuart *Seaman's Catech.* 56 A 'double wall' or *deck stopper-knot. **1874** *Deck stringer [see stringer 5 b]. **1874** Thearle *Naval Archit.* 102 The deck-stringer plate. **1883** F. M. Crawford *Dr. Claudius* ix, In ten minutes, the parade of *deck-swabbers had passed. **1927** *Delineator* Mar. 9 They played *deck-tennis and shuffleboard. **1932** L. Golding *Magnolia St.* III. vi. 530 The deck-tennis court was empty when Bella and Mick wanted to play. **1965** E. Brown *Big Man* ix. 77 The other passengers..had declined..preferring the Sports Deck and their deck tennis. **1874** Knight *Dict. Mech.*, **Deck-transom*, a horizontal timber under a ship's counter. **1838** J. F. Cooper *Eve Effingham* I. ii. 52 A capital watch..and a *deck-trumpet, in solid silver. **1856** Kane *Arct. Expl.* I. xvii. 201 One of our *deck-watch, who had been cutting ice for the melter.

deck (dɛk), *sb.*[2] *colloq.* (orig. *Anglo-Indian*). Also **dekh.** [ad. Hind. *dekha* sight, *dekhnā* to see, look at.] A look, peep. Cf. dekko.

1853 'Punjabee' *Oakfield* iv. 85 Some officer, stopping, as he passed by..'just to have a dekh at the steamer'. **1886** Yule & Burnell *Hobson-Jobson*, Deck. **1951** E. Milne in J. Marriott *Best One-Act Plays of 1950–51* (1952) 99 Crickey, have a deck at Ronald Colman!

deck (dɛk), *v.* Also 5–7 decke, 6 dek, dekke. [Not known before 16th c.: app. then of recent adoption from Flem. or Low Ger.; cf. Du. *dekken*, MDu. *deken*, *decken* to cover. The latter is = MLG., MHG. *decken*, OHG. *dachjan*, *decchan*:—OTeut. *þakjan* (whence ON. *þekja*, OFris. *thekka*, OE. *þeccan* to cover, roof over) a derivative verb from an ablaut-stem *þek-*, *þak-*, Indog. *teg-* to cover, whence ON. *þak*, OHG. *dah*, Ger. *dach* covering, roof, OE. *þæc*, thatch. In branch II a derivative of deck *sb.*[1]: cf. to *roof*, *floor*, etc.]

I. † **1.** *trans.* To cover; *esp.* to cover with garments, clothe. *Obs.*

1513 Douglas *Æneis* x. xiii. 106 Ene, That..hys sovir targe erekkit, And thar vndre hym haldis closly dekkyt. *Ibid.* xi. v. 92 Queyn Amatha..Dekkis and defendis hym with wordis sle. **1515** Barclay *Egloges* iv. (1570) Ciij/1 This lusty Codrus was cloked for the rayne And doble decked with huddes one or twayne. **1526** Skelton *Magnyf.* 759 Decke your hofte. **1535** Coverdale *Haggai* i. 6 Ye decke [**1611** clothe] youre selues, but ye are not warme. **1594** Carew *Tasso* (1881) 91 No place is vnder sky so closely deckt, Which gold not opes. **1600** Surflet *Countrie Farme* III. xviii. 461 Take away the barke..and after inuest and decke vp therewith some shoote that is of the like thickenes with the graft.

2. a. To clothe in rich or ornamental garments; to cover with what beautifies; to array, attire, adorn.

1514 Barclay *Cyt. & Uplondyshm.* (Percy Soc.) lxvii, Then is he decked as poet laureate. **1535** Coverdale *2 Kings* ix. 30 She coloured hir face, and decked hir heade. —— *Ps.* ciii. 2 Thou deckest thyself with light as it were with a garment. **1602** Shaks. *Ham.* v. i. 268, I thought thy Bride-bed to haue deckt (sweet Maid), And not t' haue strew'd thy Graue. **1628** Prynne *Love-lockes* 35 Much lesse, may we Curle, Die, or ouer-curiously decke our Haire. **1633** G. Herbert *Temple, Jordan* i, Curling with metaphors a plain intention, Decking the sense. **1808** Scott *Marm.* I. xxvii, The scallop shell his cap did deck. **1821** Clare *Vill. Minstr.* II. 63 Daisies deck the green. **1885** *Manch. Exam.* 9 July 4/7 The shipping..was profusely decked with flags.

b. with *out*, †*up*.

1587 Harrison *England* II. vii. (1877) I. 169 In decking up of the body. **1640** Sir R. Baker in Spurgeon *Treas. Dav.* Ps. cxvi. 11–15 To serve for a jewel in the decking up of God's cabinet. **1745** *De Foe's Eng. Tradesman* v. (1841) I. 34 Decked out with long wigs and swords. **1882** B. D. W. Ramsay *Recoll. Mil. Serv.* II. xv. 64 Every vessel being gaily decked out with flags.

† **3.** To array, fit out, equip. *Obs.*

? **15..** *Agincourt* 90 in Hazl. *E.P.P.* II. 97 The wastes decked with serpentynes stronge, Saynt Georges stremers sprede ouer hede. **1548** Hall *Chron.* an. 25 Hen. VIII (1809) 798 The kyng..decked and vitailed dyuers shippes of warre and sent them to the North seas to defende his subiectes.

II. 4. *Naut.* To cover as with a deck; to furnish with a deck; ***to deck in, over***, to cover in with the deck, in ship-building.

1624 Capt. Smith *Virginia* v. 175 At last it was concluded, to decke their long boat with their ship hatches. **1700** S. L. tr. *Fryke's Voy.* 6 Flat Boats..tho' small, yet so close Deck't, that in a rough Sea they will go quite under the waves and retain no water. **1774** Goldsm. *Nat. Hist.* (1776) VI. 256 The five-men-boat is decked at each end, but open in the middle. **1874** J. Deady in *Law Times Rep.* XXXI. 231/2 The vessel..was..decked over, fore and aft. **1893** R. Kipling *Many Invent.* 121 Your ship has been built and designed, closed and decked in.

5. *Mining.* To load or unload (the tubs upon the cage). (See deck *sb.*[1] 3.) Chiefly *U.S.*

1883 Gresley *Gloss. Coal-mining* 76 *Decking*, the operation of changing the tubs on a cage at top and bottom of a shaft.

6. In *Lumbering*: to pile *up* (logs) on a skidway. *U.S.*

1901 *Munsey's Mag.* XXV. 392/1 Other men pile—technically, 'deck'—them [*sc.* logs] exactly as in the woods. **1905** *Terms Forestry & Logging* 35 Deck up.

† **'deckage.** *Obs. rare.* [f. deck *v.* + -age.] Adornment, embellishment.

1642 Lightfoot *Observ. Genesis* i. Wks. 1822 II. 333 The Earth..had not received as yet its perfection, beauty and deckage.

deck-chair. [deck *sb.*[1]] A folding chair, often with an adjustable leg-rest, used esp. on the deck of a ship as seating accommodation for passengers; a hammock chair. Also *attrib.*

1884 E. Nesbit *Let.* in D. L. Moore *E. Nesbit* (1933) v. 69, I sit here in my 'deck' chair. **1886** J. H. McCarthy *Doom* 9 The group comfortably arranged on deck-chairs. **1888** W. S. Caine *Trip round World* i. 3 Ladies are grouped about in pleasant corners in easy deck-chairs. **1904** *Daily Chron.* 6 Oct. 8/1 At eleven o'clock soup and crackers..are served and little deck-chair groups are formed. **1926** *Spectator* 11 Sept. 372/2 To spend one's leisure lying on a deck-chair. **1937** J. Betjeman *Coll. Poems* (1958) 33 A tennis court, a summerhouse, deckchairs by the walnut tree. **1958** *Times* 23 Aug. 8/6 It is the weather and not the client that rules the days of the deck-chair attendant.

decked (dɛkt), *ppl. a.* [f. deck + -ed.]

1. Adorned, embellished, set out: see the verb.

? *a* **1500** *Chester Pl.* (Shaks. Soc.) I. 4 See that you fourth bringe In well decked order, that worthie storie Of Balaam and his asse. **1593** Q. Eliz. *Boeth.* 16 The decked wode seak not whan thou violetz gather. **1865** J. G. Bertram *Harvest of Sea* (1873) 307 The well-decked and well-plenished dwellings.

b. *Her.* Applied to an eagle or other bird when the edges of the feathers are of a different tincture.

In mod. Dicts.

2. Having a deck, or decks (as in ***two-decked***).

1792 A. Young *Trav. France* 78 By the passage-packet, a decked vessel, to Honfleur. **1837** Marryat *Dog-fiend* iii, On board of a two-decked ship. **1879** Butcher & Lang *Odyssey* 28 Such tackling as decked ships carry.

decker[1] ('dɛkə(r)). [f. deck *v.* + -er[1].] One who decks or adorns.

1555 Watreman *Fardle Facions* II. viii. 167 The Yndians are..greate deckers and trimmers of them selues. **1591** Percivall *Sp. Dict.*, *Afeytador*, a barber, a trimmer, a decker. **1803** *Pic Nic* No. 2 (1806) I. 53, I am but a sort of table-decker.

decker[2] ('dɛkə(r)). [f. deck *sb.*[1] + -er[1] 1.]

1. a. A vessel having (a specified number of) decks, as in ***two-decker, three-decker***, etc., q.v. **b.** *transf.* Applied to a kind of oven: see quot. 1884. See also double-decker, *single-decker* (s.v. single *a.* 17 b), three-decker, two-decker.

1795 *Hull Advertiser* 25 July 2/4 Admiral Hotham's large ships, that is, the three deckers. **1805** in *Naval Chron.* XV. 204 The *Santissima Trinidada*, the Spanish four-decker. **1884** *Health Exhib. Catal.* 120/2 Mason's Patent Hot-Air Continuous Baking Two Decker Oven. **1884** *Pall Mall Gaz.* '*Extra*' 24 July 3/2 Patent continuous-baking 'decker' ovens —i.e., ovens piled upon each other, which are heated by one furnace.

2. A gun belonging to a particular deck of a ship of war; as in *lower-decker*, a gun belonging to the lower deck.

1781 ARCHER in *Naval Chron.* XI. 287 Double breech'd the lower deckers. **1809** *Ibid.* XXII. 344 Having only fourteen of her main-deckers mounted.

3. a. A workman employed on the deck of a ship. **b.** A deck-passenger. *colloq.*

1800 COLQUHOUN *Com. Thames* iv. 180 The Deckers, or persons who hoist up the Cargo upon deck. **1866** *The Colonist* (Belize) 5 May 2/1 Passengers arrived. In the Packet—Mr. and Mrs. D... and 79 deckers.

deckie (ˈdɛkɪ). *Naut. colloq.* Also **decky.** [f. DECK *sb.*[1] + -IE.] A deck-hand; = DECKER[2] 3a. So **deckie-learner**, an apprentice deck-hand on a fishing-boat.

1913 *Q. Rev.* Apr. 435 This 'deckie'.. has usually no more knowledge of seamanship than a ploughboy. **1934** 'TAFFRAIL' *Seventy North* v. 113 He had passed through every grade—'deckie-learner', deck-hand.. and finally skipper. **1935** 'L. LUARD' *Conquering Seas* ii. 30 Alf making his first voyage as decky-learner. **1971** *Daily Tel.* 21 May (Colour Suppl.) 24/3 A young deckie sorts the arrivals [*sc.* fish] and throws them on to the ice.

decking (ˈdɛkɪŋ), *vbl. sb.* [f. DECK *v.* and *sb.*[1] + -ING[1].]

1. The action of the verb DECK; †*concr.* that with which something is decked (*obs.*); adornment, embellishment, ornament.

1531 ELYOT *Gov.* II. iii, Semblable deckynge oughte to be in the house of a nobleman or man of honour. **1562** J. SHUTE *Cambine's Turk. Wars* 38 Somtuouse and magnifique ornamentes and deckings. *c* **1620** Z. BOYD *Zion's Flowers* (1855) 157 Spending on decking many precious houres. **1673** *Lady's Call.* I. §1 ¶26. 10 Their most exquisit deckings are but like the garlands on a beast design'd for sacrifice.

2. a. The work or material of the deck of a ship; planking or flooring forming a deck.

1580 HOLLYBAND *Treas. Fr. Tong.*, *Le tillac d'vne navire*, the decking of a ship. **1879** BUTCHER & LANG *Odyssey* 81 Fashion a wide raft.. and lay deckings high thereupon. **1887** *Daily News* 26 June 6/2 The building is considered to be absolutely fireproof, the floors being all of steel 'decking' and solid breeze concrete.

b. In extended uses (see DECK *sb.*[1] 3 b).

1883 *Specif. Alnwick & Cornhill Rlwy.* 45 The superstructure consists of two wrought-iron plate girders.. connected together by cross-bracing and by a decking of curved strips. **1897** *Daily News* 3 May 2/1 Piles, beams, and decking. **1898** *Ibid.* 4 Oct. 3/2 A huge decking.. is being constructed in the river. *Ibid.* 12 Dec. 3/3 It was some time before the decking of the pier collapsed. **1900** *Westm. Gaz.* 29 Dec. 5/2 Some of the decking of St. Leonards pier was wrenched away by the waves. **1924** *Times Trade & Engin. Suppl.* 29 Nov. 252/3 The general design of decking is that of a reinforced concrete slab. **1954** *Archit. Rev.* CXVI. 129 Roof deckings are now well established in the vocabulary of present-day building materials. **1963** *Gloss. Build. Terms* (*B.S.I.*) 18 *Decking*, prefabricated units for the construction of a floor or roof. **1970** *Financial Times* 13 Apr. 13/7 Coated steel.. has found particular outlets in cladding, as well as roofing and decking.

3. In *Lumbering*: the action of piling logs on a skidway. Also *attrib. U.S.*

1901 *Munsey's Mag.* XXV. 392/1 A decking chain more than three hundred feet long is required to roll the logs to their places. **1902** S. E. WHITE *Blazed Trail* xi. 83 A shout of surprise or horror would have stopped the horse pulling on the decking chain.

deckle (ˈdɛk(ə)l). Also **deckel.** [a. Ger. *deckel* in same sense, prop. 'little cover, lid, tympan', and in other technical applications, dim. of *decke* cover.]

1. A contrivance in a paper-making machine to confine the pulp within the desired limits, and determine the size or width of the sheet: **a.** in hand paper-making, a thin rectangular frame of wood fitting close upon the mould on which the pulp is placed; **b.** in a paper-machine, a continuous band or strap on either side of the apron. Hence used as a measure of the width of paper, as '50-inch deckle paper,' and short for *deckle-edge.*

1810 [see *deckle-strap* in 2]. **1816** *Specif. Cameron's Patent* No. 4002. 2 The deckle being attached to the carriage, falls on the bottom of the mould. **1858** SIMMONDS *Dict. Trade*, *Deckle*.. also the rough or raw edge of paper. **1888** *N. & Q.* 7th Ser. V. 227 It seems as if the deckle, fitting on the mould, should produce a sheet of paper with a smooth and even edge.

2. *Comb.* **deckle edge**, the rough uncut edge of a sheet of paper, formed by the deckle; also *attrib.* = next; **deckle-edged** *a.*, having a rough uncut edge, as hand-made paper; **deckle-strap**, see 1 b.

1874 KNIGHT *Dict. Mech.* s.v., The uncut edge of paper is known as the *deckel edge. **1884** *Bookseller* 6 Nov. 1176/2 The deckle edges are left at the side and bottom, the top edge alone being cut. **1887** *Nimmo's Catal.* Oct., One Hundred Copies on fine deckle-edge royal 8vo paper. **1888** *N. & Q.* 7th Ser. V. 227/2 **Deckle-edged.* This term has lately been adopted in the advertisements of books to indicate that the edges of the paper have not been cut or trimmed, so that it is equivalent to.. 'rough edged'. **1899** T. VEBLEN *Theory of Leisure Class* vi. 163 A somewhat cruder type, printed on hand-laid deckel-edged paper. **1955** S. C. GILMOUR *Paper* vii. 65 Small sizes of deckle-edged notepaper are made in this way. **1810** *Trans. Soc. Encourag. Arts* XXVIII. 193 The *deckle-straps.. are made perfectly smooth and true. **1875** URE *Dict. Arts* III. 490 We have to notice the deckle or boundary straps.. which regulate the width of the paper.

deckled (ˈdɛk(ə)ld), *a.* [f. DECKLE + -ED[2].] Formed by a deckle; deckle-edged. Also *transf.*

1906 C. G. MCCRIE *Contemp. Portraits of Reformers* (dust-jacket), Vellum gilt, gilt top, deckled edges. **1947** D. M. DAVIN *Gorse blooms Pale* 150 The ash-tray was deckled and each time as my eye came to its degenerate line it winced with dissatisfaction.

deckless (ˈdɛklɪs), *a. rare.* [-LESS.] Without a deck.

1823 BENTHAM *Not Paul but Jesus* 328 In a deckless vessel. **1890** *Harper's Mag.* Mar. 558/1 Deckless and cabinless.

decky, var. DECKIE.

declaim (dɪˈkleɪm), *v.* Also 5-7 **-clame**, 7 **-claime**, **-clayme.** [Formerly *declame*, ad. L. *dēclāmāre*, f. DE- I. 3 + *clāmāre* to cry: subseq. assimilated to *claim*. Cf. F. *déclamer* (1549 in Hatzf.).]

I. *intr.*

1. To speak aloud with studied rhetorical force and expression; to make a speech on a set subject or theme as an exercise in public oratory or disputation. **b.** To recite with elocutionary or rhetorical effect (chiefly U.S.).

1552 HULOET, Declame or exercise fayned argument in pleadynge, vsed among lawers called mooting. **1553** T. WILSON *Rhet.* 83 When you and I declamed together last. **1641** EVELYN *Mem.* (1857) I. 11, I offered at my first exercise in the Hall, and answered my opponent: and upon the 11th following, declaimed in the Chapel before the Master, Fellows and Scholars, according to the custom. **1748** J. MASON *Elocut.* 11 A Weakness of Voice; which he cured by frequently declaiming on the Sea-Shore, amidst the Noise of the Waves. **1856** EMERSON *Eng. Traits, First Visit* Wks. (Bohn) II. 10 Wordsworth, standing apart, and reciting to me.. like a schoolboy declaiming.

2. *to declaim against*: to speak in an impassioned oratorical manner in reprobation or condemnation of; to inveigh against.

1611 B. JONSON *Catiline* IV. ii, What are his mischiefs, consul? You declaim Against his manners, and corrupt your own. **1646** SIR T. BROWNE *Pseud. Ep.* I. vi. 21 Thus is it the humour of many heads to extoll the dayes of their forefathers, and declaime against the wickednesse of times present. **1855** PRESCOTT *Philip II*, I. II. ix. 239 They loudly declaimed against the King's insincerity. **1880** L. STEPHEN *Pope* viii. 196 A generous patriot declaiming against the growth of luxury.

3. To speak aloud in an impassioned oratorical manner, with appeals to the emotions rather than the reason of the audience; to harangue.

1735 BERKELEY *Def. Free-thinking Math.* §33 Instead of giving a reason you declaim. **1759** STERNE *Tr. Shandy* I. xl, Let him declaim as pompously as he chooses upon the subject. **1833** HT. MARTINEAU *Brooke Farm* ii. 27 Tom Webster bustled and declaimed, while Sergeant Rayne quietly argued. **1884** R. GLOVER in *Christian World* 9 Oct. 766/3 To declaim is more easy than to convince.

b. quasi-*trans.* with extension.

1755 *Monitor* 16 Aug. ¶2 Some late patriots.. declaimed themselves into power.

II. *trans.*

†**4.** To discuss aloud; to debate. *Obs. rare*[-1].

(The early date of the quotation, so long before the verb is otherwise known in Eng. or French, as well as the sense, is notable.)

CHAUCER *Troylus* II. 1198 As þey declamede [4 *MSS.* 1410-25; *Harl.* 3943 declarid] þis matere, Lo Troylus.. Come rydende.

5. To speak or utter aloud with studied rhetorical expression; to repeat or recite rhetorically.

1577 B. GOOGE *Heresbach's Husb.* II. (1586) 49 Weriyng you with the declaimyng of my poore skill in the tilling of the feelde. *a* **1716** SOUTH *Serm.* VIII. 82 (T.) Whoever strives to beget, or foment in his heart, such [malignant] persuasions concerning God, makes himself the devil's orator, and declaims his cause. **1818** SCOTT *Hrt. Midl.* i, He then declaimed the following passage rather with too much than too little emphasis. **1885** R. L. STEVENSON in *Contemp. Rev.* 555 In declaiming a so-called iambic verse, it may so happen that we never utter one iambic foot.

†**6.** = *declaim against*; to decry, denounce. *Obs.*

1614 T. ADAMS *Devil's Banquet* 42 This Banket then.. is at once declared and declaimed, spoken of and forbidden. **1623** COCKERAM, *Declaime*, to speake ill of.

Hence **deˈclaiming** *vbl. sb.* and *ppl. a.*

1577 [see 5]. **1603** HOLLAND *Plutarch's Mor.* 931 He used otherwhiles to goe downe to the water side.. for to exercise himselfe in declaiming. **1656** *Artif. Handsom.* 95 Humane fallacies and declaymings. **1701** ROWE *Amb. Step-Moth.* IV. i. 1684 Yield much matter to declaiming flatterers. **1735** BERKELEY *Def. Free-thinking Math.* §11 In the same manner as any declaiming bigot would defend transubstantiation.

deˈclaim, *sb.* *rare*[-1]. [f. the vb.] = DECLAMATION.

1922 T. HARDY *Late Lyrics* 165, I went where my friend had lectioned The prophets in high declaim.

deˈclaimant. *rare*[-1]. [f. DECLAIM *v.* + -ANT, after *claimant*, etc.] = DECLAIMER.

a **1763** SHENSTONE *Ess.* 28 The company was a little surprised at the sophistry of our declaimant.

declaimer (dɪˈkleɪmə(r)). [f. DECLAIM + -ER[1].] One who declaims; one who speaks with rhetorical expression, or as an exercise in elocution; one who harangues, or speaks with impassioned force.

1432-50 tr. *Higden* (Rolls) IV. 401 Iulius Gallo, a noble declamer. **1580** HOLLYBAND *Treas. Fr. Tong*, *Declamateur*, a Declaimer, a mooter. **1640** G. WATTS tr. *Bacon's Adv. Learn.* IV. ii. (R.), A certaine declaimor against sciences. **1712** STEELE *Spect.* No. 521 ¶4 The Declaimers in Coffee-houses. **1752** JOHNSON *Rambler* No. 202 ¶2 The pompous periods of declaimers, whose purpose is only to amuse with fallacies. **1848** MILL *Pol. Econ.* I. iii. §2 Such.. is the labour of the musical performer, the actor, the public declaimer or reciter.

declamation (dɛkləˈmeɪʃən). [ad. L. *dēclāmātiōn-em*, n. of action from *dēclāmāre* to DECLAIM, or ad. F. *déclamation* (15th c. in Hatzf.).]

1. The action or art of declaiming; the repeating or uttering of a speech, etc. with studied intonation and gesture.

1552 HULOET, Declamation often heard, and tedious to the hearers, *crambe repetita.* **1597** MORLEY *Introd. Mus.* 86 Your plainsong is as it were your theme, and your descant as it were your declamation. **1776** GIBBON *Decl. & F.* I. xxiv. 680 He publicly professed the arts of rhetoric and declamation. **1834** MACAULAY *Pitt* Ess. (1854) I. 294 That which gave most effect to his declamation was the air of sincerity, of vehement feeling, or moral elevation, which belonged to all that he said.

attrib. **1806** BYRON *Thoughts College Exam.* 25 The declamation prize.

b. *Music.* The proper rhetorical rendering of words set to music.

1876 in STAINER & BARRETT.

2. A public speech or address of rhetorical character; a set speech in rhetorical elocution.

1523 SKELTON *Garl. Laurel* (R.), Olde Quintillian with his declamations; Theocritus with his Bucolicall relacions. **1573** G. HARVEY *Letter-bk.* (Camden) 11 Theams more fit for schollars declamations. **1603** HOLLAND *Plutarch's Mor.* 55 The Orations and declamations.. of these Sophisters, who make shew of their eloquence. **1782** J. WARTON *Ess. Pope* II. xiii. 381 Able to compose Essays, Declamations, and Verses, in Greek, in Latin, and in English. **1830** DRURY in Moore *Life Byron* (1866) 20/1 He suddenly diverged from the written composition.. I questioned him, why he had altered his declamation?

3. Declaiming or speaking in an impassioned oratorical manner; fervid denunciation with appeals to the audience.

1614 T. ADAMS *Devil's Banquet* 42 The more accurately the Scriptures describe sinnes, the more absolutely they forbid them: where wickednesse is the subject, all speech is declamation. **1750** JOHNSON *Rambler* No. 172 ¶3 [Not so universal] as some have asserted in the.. heat of declamation. **1789** BENTHAM *Princ. Legisl.* i. §1 But enough of metaphor and declamation. *a* **1794** GIBBON *Autobiog.* 90, I was conscious myself that my style, above prose and below poetry, degenerated into a verbose and turgid declamation. **1874** MORLEY *Compromise* (1886) 53 Exacerbated declamation in favor of ancient dogma against modern science.

4. A speech of a rhetorical kind expressing strong feeling and addressed to the passions of the hearers; a declamatory speech, a harangue.

1594 HOOKER *Eccl. Pol.* III. viii. (1611) 98 The cause why such declamations preuaill so greatly, is, for that men suffer themselues to be deluded. **1631** WEEVER *Anc. Fun. Mon.* 23 But this was but one of Cæsars rodamantadoes, or thundring declamations. **1688** PENTON *Guardians Instr.* 47 The constant Declamations against us of those intruding members. *a* **1715** BURNET *Own Time* (1766) II. 216 It was only an insolent declamation.. full of fury and indecent invectives. **1856** EMERSON *Eng. Traits, First Visit* Wks. (Bohn) II. 4 On this, he [Coleridge] burst into a declamation on the folly and ignorance of Unitarianism.

†**ˈdeclamator.** *Obs.* [a. L. *dēclāmātor*, n. of action from *dēclāmāre* to DECLAIM.] One who practises declamation; a declaimer.

1387 TREVISA *Higden* (Rolls) IV. 401 Iulius Gallio.. was [the] best declamator of alle. **1530** ELYOT *Gov.* I. xiii, They whiche do onely teache rhetorike.. ought to be named rhetoriciens, declamatours, artificiall spekers.. or any other name than oratours. **1624** F. WHITE *Repl. Fisher* 590 Sir Declamator, you vsurpe Radamanthus his office. **1699** BENTLEY *Phal.* Introd. 7 Was ever any Declamator's Case so extravagantly put? **1710** STEELE *Tatler* No. 56 ¶1 Who could, I say, hear this generous Declamator without being fired by his noble Zeal?

declamatory (dɪˈklæmətərɪ), *a.* (*sb.*) [ad. L. *dēclāmātōri-us*, f. *dēclāmātōr-em*: see prec. and -ORY.] Of or pertaining to rhetorical declaiming; of the nature of, or characterized by, declamation.

1581 MULCASTER *Positions* x. (1887) 57 To pronounce.. orations and other declamatory argumentes. **1621** BURTON *Anat. Mel.* II. ii. VI. iii, To leaue all declamatory speeches in praise of divine Musick. *a* **1639** WOTTON (J.), This.. became a declamatory theme amongst the religious men of that age. **1795** MASON *Ch. Mus.* i. 5 That peculiar species of Music, which may be called declamatory. **1807** G. CHALMERS *Caledonia* I. III. vii. 393 *note*, This pretended charter is very suspicious; its style is too declamatory. **1880** L. STEPHEN *Pope* iii. 75 It is in the true declamatory passages that Pope is at his best.

†**b.** Characterized by declamation against something; denunciatory. *Obs.*

1589 NASHE *Greene's Menaphon* Ded. 10 Least in this declamatorie vaine, I should condemne all and commend none.

†**B.** *sb.* A declamatory speech. *Obs.*

1688 L'ESTRANGE *Brief Hist. Times* III. 12 Then's the Time for Declamatoryes, and Exaggerations.

Hence **de'clamatoriness**, the quality of being declamatory.

1844 *Foreign Q. Rev.* XXXIII. 351 The general characteristics of Linguet's oratory are declamatoriness and paradox.

† **de'clarable**, *a. Obs.* [f. L. *dēclārā-re* + -BLE; viewed also as f. DECLARE + -ABLE.] Capable of being declared, shown, or made known.

1646 SIR T. BROWNE *Pseud. Ep.* III. iv. 112 This is declareable from the best and most professed Writers. *Ibid.* IV. xiii. **1678** CUDWORTH *Intell. Syst.* 23 Right Reason is of two sorts.. Of which the Divine is inexpressible, but the Humane declarable.

declarant (dɪ'klɛərənt). [f. F. *déclarant* or L. *dēclārānt-em*, pr. pple. of *dēclārāre* to DECLARE: see -ANT.] One who makes a declaration: *esp.* in *Law*.

1681 GLANVILL *Sadducismus* II. 296 Declares, that [etc.].. and that this was after the Declarant's renouncing of her Baptism. **1752** J. STEWART in *Scots Mag.* June (1753) 285/2 The declarant was at Edinburgh. **1818** SCOTT *Rob Roy* viii, The declaration farther set forth that..he, the said declarant, was informed that they were of the worst description. **1888** *Times* 29 Oct. 5/3 The object of requiring the signature of the declarant is to fix liability for false declarations.

declaration (dɛklə'reɪʃən). Also 4-5 **-acioun**, 4-6 **-acion**. [a. F. *déclaration* or ad. L. *dēclārātiōn-em*, n. of action f. *dēclārāre* to DECLARE.]

†**1.** The action of making clear or clearing up (anything obscure or not understood); elucidation, explanation, interpretation. *Obs.*

c **1374** CHAUCER *Boeth.* III. x. (Camb. MS.) 71-2 Thyse geometryens whan they han shewyd hyr proposiciouns ben wont to bryngen in thinges þat they clepyn porysmes or declaraciouns of forseyde thinges. *c* **1391** —— *Astrol.* I. §4 And for the more declaracioun, lo here the figure. **1527** R. THORNE in Hakluyt *Voy.* (1589) 253 For more declaration of the said Card [= map]. **1532-3** *Act 24 Hen. VIII*, c. 5 For the declaracion of the whiche ambyguitee and doubte. **1656** H. PHILLIPS *Purch. Patt.* (1676) 57 This Table is so plain, that it needs no declaration.

†**2.** The setting forth or expounding of a topic; exposition, description, relation. *Obs.*

1382 WYCLIF *Deut.* xvii. 18 He shal discriue..a declaracioun of this lawe [*deuteronomium legis hujus*] in a volym. **1460** CAPGRAVE *Chron.* 17 The childirn of Noe..of whos issew here schal be a declaration. **1553** T. WILSON *Rhet.* 95 A description or an evident declaration of a thyng as though we sawe it even now doen. **1619** *Mirr. Mag.* Title-p., With a Declaration of all the Warres, Battels and Sea-fights, during her Reigne. **1642** PERKINS *Prof. Bk.* v. §437. 189 Of Dower 'ad ostium ecclesiæ' a good declaration hath beene made by Master Littleton in his first book.

3. a. The action of stating, telling, setting forth, or announcing openly, explicitly or formally; positive statement or assertion; an assertion, announcement or proclamation in emphatic, solemn, or legal terms.

1340 HAMPOLE *Pr. Consc.* 2606 Þan sal he deme ilka nacyon, And mak a fynal declaracyon Of alle þe domes byfor shewed. **1426** in *Surtees Misc.* (1890) 9 Apon þis declaracion made. **1547** in *Vicary's Anat.* (1888) App. iii. 161 Crosses to be sett vpon mens dores for the declaracion of the plage. **1594** HOOKER *Eccl. Pol.* I. ii. (1611) 5 His promises are nothing else but declarations what God will do for the good of men. **1651** HOBBES *Leviath.* II. xxi. 114 If he dye.. without declaration of his Heyre. **1751** JOHNSON *Rambler* No. 152 ⁋3 Declarations of fidelity. **1796** JANE AUSTEN *Sense & Sens.* (1849) 33 In spite of Marianne's declaration that the day would be lastingly fair. **1856** FROUDE *Hist. Eng.* (1858) I. iii. 262 The pope made a public declaration with respect to the dispute. **1881** BAGEHOT *Biog. Studies* 290 The first declaration of love was made by the lady.

b. *spec.* A declaration of love; a proposal of marriage.

1739-40 RICHARDSON *Pamela* (1740) I. 192, I am glad at my Heart, Madam, that I was *before-hand* in my Declarations to you. *Ibid.* 193 What Necessity was there for you to talk of your *former* Declaration? **1766** GOLDSMITH *Vicar* xvi. 144 My wife undertook to sound him..in the choice of an husband for her eldest daughter. If this was not found sufficient to induce him to a declaration, it was then fixed upon to terrify him with a rival. **1850** DICKENS *Dav. Copp.* xxxiii. 344, I went to Miss Mills's, fraught with a declaration. **1937** 'E. M. DELAFIELD' *Ladies & Gentlemen in Victorian Fiction* iii. 89 The Victorian papa..was by no means invariably consulted before a 'declaration' took place.

4. a. ***declaration of war***: formal announcement or proclamation by a Power of the commencement of hostilities against another Power. Also ***declaration of peace***.

1387 TREVISA *Higden* (Rolls) I. 243 When þe Romaynes wolde werry in eny lond, schulde oon goo..and clereliche declare..þe matire and cause of the werre, and þat declaracioun was i-cleped clarigatio. **1548** HALL *Chron.* 207 She was sent..with a plain overture and declaracion of peace. **1762** *Univ. Mag.* Feb. 99 The following is a Declaration of War by Spain against Great Britain dated the 16th of January. **1803** *Edin. Rev.* Jan. 389 Declarations of war and peace, when presented by the executive to the legislative body, are to be adopted [etc.]. **1828** NAPIER *Hist. Penins. War* I. 137 The invasion of Napoleon produced a friendly alliance between those countries without a declaration of peace. **1845** POLSON in *Encycl. Metrop.* 728/1 The custom of making a declaration of war to the enemy, previous to the commencement of hostilities, is of great antiquity, and was practised even by the Romans..Since, however, the peace of Versailles, in 1763, such declarations have been discontinued, and the present usage is, for the state with whom the war commences to publish a manifesto within its own territories.

b. ***declaration of the poll***: the public official announcement of the numbers polled for each candidate at an election. Hence *attrib.* in ***declaration day***.

1835 DICKENS *Let.* 18 Dec. (1965) I. 109 It will be unnecessary for me to remain here for the Declaration of the Poll on Monday. **1863** H. COX *Instit.* I. viii. 114 Upon the closing of the poll, the poll-books are sealed, and kept under seal until the declaration of the poll. **1892** *Daily News* 14 Oct. 6/1 On the morning of declaration day, there arrived reports about some districts in which the polling had been large. **1906** [see POLL *sb.*[1] 7c].

5. The action of declaring *for* or *against* (see DECLARE *v.* 8).

1736 BUTLER *Anal.* I. iii. Wks. 1874 I. 53 The natural fear ..which restrains from such crimes, is a declaration of nature against them.

6. A proclamation or public statement as embodied in a document, instrument, or public act.

Declaration of Indulgence: see INDULGENCE.

Declaration of Rights: the Parliamentary declaration of 1689: see RIGHT.

Declaration of Independence: the public act by which the American Continental Congress, on July 4th, 1776, declared the North American colonies to be free and independent of Great Britain; the document in which this is embodied.

Declaration of Paris: a diplomatic instrument signed by the representatives of the powers at the Congress of Paris in 1856, settling and defining important points of maritime law affecting belligerents and neutrals in time of war.

1659 B. HARRIS *Parival's Iron Age* 208 A petition from some Lords in England, conformable in the main points to a Declaration of the Scots, which they called the intention of their Army. **1660** MARVELL *Corr.* vi. Wks. 1872-5 II. 25 To-morrow the Bill for enacting his Majestye's Declaration in religious matters is to haue its first reading. **1776** *Ann. Reg.* 261 A Declaration by the Representatives of the United States of America, in General Congress assembled, July 4. **1780** *Impartial Hist. War Amer.* 335 These Articles, as well as the Declaration of Independence, were published in all the Colonies. **1816** SCOTT *Old Mort.* xxxvii, The declaration of Indulgence issued by Charles II. **1846** MᶜCULLOCH *Acc. Brit. Empire* (1854) II. 209 The principal abuses that had characterized the government of the two preceding reigns, were also enumerated and digested into an instrument, called a Declaration and Claim of Rights, presented and assented to, by the new sovereigns.

7. *Law.* **a.** The plaintiff's statement of claim in an action; the writing or instrument in which this is made.

1483 *Act 1 Rich. III*, c. 6 §1 The Plaintiff..[shall] make Oath..that the Contract..comprised in the same Declaration [etc.]. **1579** W. RASTELL *Termes of Law*, *Declaratyon* is a shewinge forth in writing of the griefe and complaynt of the demaundant or pleintife, against the tenant or defendant. **1642** PERKINS *Prof. Bk.* ii. §151. 67 The declaration shall abate. **1672** WYCHERLEY *Love in Wood* Ded., No man with papers in 's hand is more dreadful than a poet; no, not a lawyer with his declarations. **1768** BLACKSTONE *Comm.* III. 203 As soon as this action is brought, and the complaint fully stated in the declaration. **1817** W. SELWYN *Law Nisi Prius* II. 783 The first count in the declaration.

b. A simple affirmation allowed to be taken, in certain cases, instead of an oath or solemn affirmation.

1834 *Act 5-6 Will. IV*, c. 62. **1848** WHARTON *Law Lex.* 164 By 5 & 6 Wm. IV, c. 62, for the abolition of unnecessary oaths, any justice..is empowered to take voluntary declarations in the form specified in the act. And any person wilfully making such declaration false, in any material particular, shall be guilty of a misdemeanour.

c. In the Custom-house; see DECLARE *v.* 10c.

1853 *Act 16 & 17 Vict.* c. 107 §186 The master of the ship in which such goods shall be laden shall before clearance make and subscribe a declaration before the proper officer of customs. **1876** *Act 39 & 40 Vict.* c. 36 §58.

d. The creation or acknowledgement of a *trust* or *use* in some form of writing; any writing whereby a trust or use is constituted or proved to exist.

a **1626** BACON *Max. & Uses Comm. Law* xiv. (1636) 56 Declarations evermore are countermandable in their natures. **1818** CRUISE *Digest* (ed. 2) I. 449 The only point for which they contended was, that the articles..under which they claimed, amounted to a good declaration of the uses of recovery. *Ibid.* 463 A declaration of trust requires no particular form, provided it be proved or manifested in writing. **1827** JARMAN *Powell's Devises* (ed. 3) II. 75 There being no declaration of the trust of the money beyond the life of the wife, it resulted to the heir.

e. *Scots Law.* 'In criminal proceedings the account which a prisoner, who has been apprehended on suspicion of having committed a crime, gives of himself on his examination, which is taken down in writing' (Bell *Dict.* s.v.).

dying declaration: a declaration made by a person on his deathbed, which is admitted as evidence in a prosecution for homicide.

judicial declaration: the statement, taken down in writing, of a party when judicially examined as to the particular facts in a civil action.

1818 SCOTT *Hrt. Midl.* xxiii, It..usually happens that these declarations become the means of condemning the accused, as it were, out of their own mouths. **1861** W. BELL *Dict. Law Scot.* 256 The magistrate's proper duty is distinctly to inform the prisoner not only that it is optional for him to make a declaration or not as he pleases, but also that what he says may afterwards be used against him on his trial.

8. a. In the game of bezique: see quot.

1870 *Mod. Hoyle* 153 Declaration is the act of declaring a score by the process of placing certain cards upon the table. *Ibid.* 148 The last declaration must be made before the last two cards are drawn.

b. In the game of Bridge, the naming of the trump suit or the declaring of 'no trumps' by any of the players.

1895 'BOAZ' *Laws of Bridge* 10 His partner must thereupon make the necessary declaration. **1905** in W. Dalton *'Saturday' Bridge* (1910) 12 If the dealer's partner make the trump declaration without receiving permission from the dealer, the eldest hand may demand: I. That the declaration so made shall stand. II. That there shall be a new deal. **1910** *Ibid.* 38 The declaration at Bridge affords an opportunity for the exercise of certain qualities which were never called into use in the game of Whist. *Ibid.* 39 The most expensive declaration..being No Trumps, when the value of each trick is twelve points.

c. *Cricket.* The closing, by the team batting, of an innings. (Cf. DECLARE *v.* 11b.)

1908 W. E. W. COLLINS *Country Cricketer's Diary* ix. 158 The Malvern boys had proved equal to the emergency.. after an apparently safe 'declaration' [by their opponents]. **1963** A. ROSS *Australia 63* i. 40 Benaud delayed his declaration.

decla'rationist. *nonce-wd.* One who joins in or signs a declaration.

1892 *Times* 7 Jan. 10/5 We are indebted to the declarationists for bringing this controversy again before the public.

declarative (dɪ'klærətɪv), *a.* (*sb.*) [a. F. *déclaratif, -ive*, or ad. L. *dēclārātīv-us*, f. ppl. stem of *dēclārāre* to DECLARE: see -IVE.] Characterized by declaring (in the various senses of the vb.).

†**1.** Making clear, manifest, or evident. *Obs.*

a **1536** TINDALE *Wks.* 67 (R.) Notwithstanding ye sonne is the cause declaratiue wherby we know that the other is a father. **1644** BULWER *Chirol.* 1 All the declarative conceits of Gesture. **1646** P. BULKELEY *Gospel Covt.* IV. 337 These kind of promises..are declarative, making manifest who be those true beleivers to whom the life promised..doth belong. *a* **1665** J. GOODWIN, *Filled w. the Spirit* (1867) 329 Holy and zealous impressions upon the hearts..of men may be declarative of their being filled with the Spirit of God. **1772** FLETCHER *Logica Genev.* 43 The declarative evidences.. whether or no he was among the trees of righteousness.

†**b.** That manifests itself or is capable of manifestation. *Obs.*

1642 T. HODGES *Glimpse* 36 Every thing whereby the declarative highnesse of this great God is advanced. *a* **1679** GURNALL in Spurgeon *Treas. Dav.* Ps. cii. 16 His declarative glory then appears, when the glory of his mercy, truth and faithfulness break forth in his people's salvation.

2. Characterized by making declaration; of the nature of a declaration or formal assertion. ***declarative act, statute***, etc. = DECLARATORY *act*, etc.

1628 T. SPENCER *Logick* 153 A declaratiue, or pronouncing sentence. **1646** S. BOLTON *Arraignm. Err.* 136 Ministeriall, declaratiue, subordinate Judges. **1661** BRAMHALL *Just Vind.* iii. 31 Whether the Act or Statute.. were operative or declarative, creating new right, or manifesting, or restoring old right. **1692** BP. PATRICK *Answ. Touchstone* 97 The only Question is, Whether their Absolution be only declarative, or also operative? **1755** CARTE *Hist. Eng.* IV. 335 It was a declarative law. **1824** L. MURRAY *Eng. Gram.* (ed. 5) I. 270 The best method of discovering the proper case of the pronoun, in such phrases ..is, to turn them into declarative expressions.

b. Const. *of*.

1642 CHAS. I *Answ. Declar. Both Houses* 1 July, According to the Common Law (of which the Statute is but declarative). **1774** PENNANT *Tour Scotl.* in *1772*, 16 An inscription, declarative of his munificence towards the church. **1866** GROSART in *Lismore Papers* Introd. 12 Much of the record..is declarative of a wish on the part of the Founder of the History to win the ear of posterity.

†**3.** Of a person: Declaring oneself, declaring or uttering one's opinion; communicative. *Obs.*

1647 N. BACON *Disc. Govt. Eng.* I. vi. (1739) 14 The times were too tender to endure them to be declarative on either part. **1748** RICHARDSON *Clarissa* (1811) III. xli. 240 He was still more declarative afterwards.

B. *sb.* A declaratory statement or act.

1651 N. BACON *Disc. Govt. Eng.* II. x. (1739) 57 Not as an Introduction of a new Law, but as a Declarative of the old. **1865** BUSHNELL *Vicar. Sacr.* III. i. 201 As declaratives of natural consequence.

de'claratively, *adv.* [f. prec. + -LY[2].] In a declarative manner, by way of declaration or distinct assertion; † by way of manifestation.

1625 USSHER *Answ. Jesuit* 132 [They] doe discharge that part of their function which concerneth forgivenesse of sinnes, partly operatively, partly declaratively. **1652** *Englands Commonw.* 20 A man whom..this State had declaratively disclaimed. **1671** FLAVEL *Fount. of Life* xii. 55 Not only declaratively or by way of manifestation. *a* **1848** R. W. HAMILTON *Rew. & Punishm.* iv. (1853) 175 Still more declaratively is the connexion told.

† **'declarator**, *sb.*[1] *Obs.* [a. L. *dēclārātor*, agent-n. from *dēclārāre* to DECLARE.] One who declares or makes manifest; an informer.

a **1577** SIR T. SMITH *Commw. Eng.* (1633) 100 The other part to the Declarator, Detector or Informer.

declarator (dɪ'klærətə(r)), *sb.*[2] *Sc.* [representing F. *déclaratoire* (*acte, sentence déclaratoire*), med.L. *dēclārātōrius, -a, -um*: see DECLARATORY.] A declaratory statement, 'a legal or authentic declaration' (Jam.). (*action of*) ***declarator*** (Sc.Law): a form of action in the Court of Session, in which something is prayed to be declared judicially, the legal consequences being left to follow as a matter of course.

1567 *Sc. Acts Jas. VI* (1814) 28 (Jam.) Desyring our souerane lord, etc., to gif declaratour to the said William Dowglas..that he has done his detfull diligence. **1599** JAS. I *Βασιλ. Δωρον* (1603) 17 Your pronouncing of sentences, or declaratour of your will in judgement. **1746–7** *Act 20 Geo. II*, c. 50 §3 The citation in the general declarator of non-entry. **1864** *Daily Tel.* 13 June, The Scotch courts have a kind of action called a declarator of marriage, in which they affirm or negative the abstract proposition that two persons are married persons. **1876** GRANT *Burgh Sch. Scotl.* II. i. 92 They raised a summons of declarator against the Council concluding that Elgin Academy was a public School. **1884** *Law Reports* 9 App. Cases 305 The present action was brought..for declarator of his right to one-half of the heritable estate.

declaratorily (dɪˈklærətərɪlɪ), *adv.* [f. DECLARATORY + -LY[2].] In a declaratory manner; in the form of a declaration.

1588 J. HARVEY *Disc. Probl.* 103 The resolution of Cyprianus Leouitius..is declaratorily deliuered in the end of this Prognosticon. **1616** JAS. I *Sp. in Starre-Chamber* 20 June 10, I tooke this occasion..here in this Seate of Iudgement, not judicially, but declaratorily and openly to giue those directions. **1646** SIR T. BROWNE *Pseud. Ep.* VII. xvii. 376 [They] have both declaratorily confirmed the same.

declaratory (dɪˈklærətərɪ), *a.* and *sb.* [ad. L. type *dēclārātōri-us, -a, -um*, f. *dēclārātōr-em* a declarer: see -ORY. Cf. F. *déclaratoire* (16th c.).] Having the function of declaring, setting forth, or explaining; having the nature or form of a declaration; affirmatory.

declaratory act or ***statute***: one which declares or explains what the existing law is. ***declaratory action*** (Sc. Law) = action of DECLARATOR. ***declaratory judgement*** or ***decree***: one which simply declares the rights of the parties or the opinion of the court as to what the law is.

1587 FLEMING *Contn. Holinshed* III. 1362/2 The explication or meaning of the bull declaratorie made by Pius the fift against Elisabeth. *a* **1631** DONNE in *Select.* (1840) 67 Neither would this profit without the declaratory justification. **1648** in Clarendon *Hist. Reb.* XI. (1843) 679/2 A recital in a new law, which was not a declaratory law of what the law was formerly in being. **1699** BURNET *39 Art.* xxv. (1700) 276 The power of pardoning is only declaratory. **1787** J. BARLOW *Oration 4 July* 7 That declaratory Act of Independence, which gave being to an empire. **1845** POLSON in *Encycl. Metrop.* 852/1 Actions known to Scottish law ..*Declaratory* actions, wherein the right of the pursuer is craved to be declared, but nothing is claimed to be done by the defender. **1857** GLADSTONE *Glean.* VI. xliii. 74 The case is not one of divorce at all, but of a declaratory process where the marriage had been originally null. **1884** A. R. PENNINGTON *Wiclif* viii. 257 With regard to Penance and Absolution, he holds the view of the Church of England, that the office of the priest is declaratory.

b. Const. *of.*

1660 R. COKE *Power & Subj.* 227 That the Statute.. should be but declaratory of the ancient and common Law of this Land. **1791** MACKINTOSH *Vind. Gallicæ* Wks. 1846 III. 26 Resolutions declaratory of adherence to their former decrees. **1876** BANCROFT *Hist. U.S.* III. x. 431 The decision was declaratory of the boundary. **1884** *Law Reports* 9 App. Cases 95 The Bills of Exchange Act, 1882..is declaratory of the prior law.

†**B.** *sb.* A declaratory order; a declaration. *Obs.*

1571 *State Trials, Dk. of Norfolk* (R.), A summary cognition in the cases of controversy, with a small declaratory to have followed. **1691** *Agreement w. Denmark* (MS. Treaties 96), His Majesty..has thought fit to issue out a Declaratory or Ordonnance..concerning the Shipping and the carrying on of their Commerce with France.

†**deˈclarature.** *Obs. rare.* [f. ppl. stem of L. *dēclārāre* to DECLARE + -URE.] = DECLARATION.

1729 *Wodrow Corr.* (1843) III. 440 That deposition was not the fit state of the vote, but acquiesce and harmony if possible in the declarature.

declare (dɪˈklɛə(r)), *v.* Also 4–5 declar, 6 declair, -ayre. [a. F. *déclare-r*, ad. L. *dēclārā-re* to clear up, make clear or evident, f. DE- I. 3 + *clār-us* clear, *clārāre* to make clear. OF. had *desclairier*, f. *des-*, *de-* (DE- I. 6) + *clair* clear, which was gradually brought, through *declairir*, *declairer*, into conformity with the L. type.]

†**1.** *trans.* To make clear or plain (anything that is obscure or imperfectly understood); to clear up, explain, expound, interpret, elucidate.

c **1325** *E.E. Allit. P.* B. 1618 And þaȝ þe mater be merk.. He shal de-clar hit also, as hit on clay stande. *c* **1400** *Lanfranc's Cirurg.* 72 Declarynge & openynge doutis. **1526** *Pilgr. Perf.* (W. de W. 1531) 56 Yf I sholde reherse them.. excepte I sholde also declare them, they sholde not moche profyte. **1530** PALSGR. 508/2 It is no nede to declare it, the mater is playne ynoughe. **1638** CHILLINGW. *Relig. Prot.* I. ii. §12. 58 That those [things] which are obscure should remain obscure, untill he please to declare them. *a* **1691** BOYLE (J.), To declare this a little, we must assume that the surfaces of such bodies are exactly smooth.

†**2.** To manifest, show forth, make known; to unfold, set forth (facts, circumstances, etc.); to describe, state in detail; to recount, relate. *Obs.*

c **1340** HAMPOLE *Prose Tr.* 23, I schalle telle and declare to the a litille of this more opynly. *c* **1400** MAUNDEV. (1839) v. 53 For to declare ȝou the othere weyes, that drawen toward Babiloyne. **1526** *Pilgr. Perf.* (W. de W. 1531), The cause.. shall be more playnly declared in the seconde boke. *a* **1533** LD. BERNERS *Huon* xlii. 140 He declared to them the dethe of his brother. **1582** N. T. (Rhem.) *Acts* xx. 27 For I haue not spared to declare vnto you al the counsel of God. **1606** HOLLAND *Sueton.* 76 He wrote..somewhat of his owne life: which hee declared [L. *exposuit*] in thirty books. **1703** MOXON *Mech. Exerc.* 237, I will declare their Method of Working.

†**3.** *intr.* To make exposition or relation *of.*

1393 GOWER *Conf.* III. 128 Of other sterres how they fare, I thinke hereafter to declare. *c* **1400** MAUNDEV. (Roxb.) xvi. 72 Here hafe I talde ȝow and declared of þe Haly Land and of cuntreez þer aboute. *c* **1470** HENRY *Wallace* v. 528 He.. To thaim declarde off all this paynfull cas. **1526** TINDALE *Acts* xvii. 2 And thre saboth dayes declared of the scriptures unto them. *a* **1533** LD. BERNERS *Huon* cxxv. 452 The whiche he shewyd to syr Barnarde, and declaryd of the fountayne and gardayne.

4. *trans.* Of things: To manifest, show, demonstrate, prove.

In later quots. there is association with 5.

c **1386** CHAUCER *Knt.'s T.* 1498 The fires which that on myn auter brenne Shulle thee declaren..Thyn auenture of loue. *c* **1391** —— *Astrol.* II. §6 ȝif any degree in thi zodiak be dirk, his nadire shal declare him. **1533** ELYOT *Cast. Helthe* (1539) 57 b, Suche maner of vomite declareth corruption. **1535** COVERDALE *Ps.* xviii. [xix.] 1 The very heauens declare the glory off God. **1568** E. TILNEY *Disc. Marriage* C iij, Much babling declareth a foolishe head. **1667** MILTON *P.L.* IV. 300 His fair large Front and Eye sublime declar'd Absolute rule. **1668** CULPEPPER & COLE *Barthol. Anat.* IV. ii. 338 Many Sceletons..declare that the *Cartilago scutiformis* ..is changed into the hard substance of a Bone. **1810** SCOTT *Lady of L.* I. xxv, Nor track nor pathway might declare That human foot frequented there.

5. a. To make known or state publicly, formally, or in explicit terms; to assert, proclaim, announce or pronounce by formal statement or in solemn terms.

c **1330** R. BRUNNE *Chron.* (1810) 314 Þer foure at Rome ware, to areson þe pape, þe right for to declare. **1397** *Rolls of Parlt.* III. 378/2 As it is more pleynleche declared in the same Commission. *c* **1400** *Destr. Troy* 2147 Qwen the kyng had his counsell declaret to the ende. **15..** ? DUNBAR *Wks.* (1893) 264/3 His name of confort I will declair, Welcom, my awin Lord Thesaurair! **1648** DK. HAMILTON in *H. Papers* (Camden) 234 You shall declare in name of this kingdome that they nor their forces will not admitt..the excepted persons. **1827** JARMAN *Powell's Devises* (ed. 3) II. 165 A testator, after declaring his intention to dispose of all his worldly estate. **1856** FROUDE *Hist. Eng.* (1858) I. ii. 111 The parliament itself declared in formal language that they would resist any attempt.

b. with ***compl.***: ***a person***, etc. (to be) ***something***.

1538 STARKEY *England* I. iv. 124 To declayre penytent heartys..to be absoluyd from the faute therof. **1640** *State Trials, Earl Strafford* (R.), No man hath ever been declared a traitor, either by king or parliament, except [etc.]. **1659** B. HARRIS *Parival's Iron Age* 269 The Chanceller declared him Major, as being entred into the fourteenth yeare of his age. **1667** MILTON *P.L.* VI. 728 That thou in me well pleas'd declarst thy will Fulfill'd. **1765–9** BLACKSTONE *Comm.* I. xvi. (1793) I. 578 When a woman..declares herself with child. **1848** MACAULAY *Hist. Eng.* II. 115 [He] declared himself a member of the Church of Rome. **1874** GREEN *Short Hist.* vi. §4. 312 The end of all punishment he declares to be reformation.

c. ***to declare war***: to make formal and public proclamation of hostilities *against* (†*to*) another power.

1552 HULOET, Declare warres, *arma canere, bellum indicere.* **1681** SALGADO *Symbiosis* 6 Of Angels..some declared war against God. **1761** CHESTERF. *Lett.* IV. ccclx. 178, I have now good reason to believe that Spain will declare war to us. **1763** *Gentl. Mag.* Mar. 108 Before the war just now concluded was declared. **1827** *Examiner* 422/1 France..has formally declared war against Algiers. **1831** *Ibid.* 321/1 The Duke..had declared war.

d. ***to declare a dividend***: to announce officially a (specified) dividend as payable.

6. a. To state emphatically; to affirm, aver, assert.

1709 STEELE *Tatler* No. 135 ¶1 He declares, he would rather be in the Wrong with Plato, than in the Right with such Company. **1752** JOHNSON *Rambler* No. 199 ¶15 One young lady..declared that she scorned to separate her wishes from her acts. **1841** D'ISRAELI *Amen. Lit.* (1867) 136 Spenser..declared that the language of Chaucer was the purest English. **1860** TYNDALL *Glac.* I. x. 67 Who at first declared four guides to be necessary.

b. Used as a mere asseveration.

1811 L. M. HAWKINS *C'tess & Gertr.* i. 8, I declare to goodness. **1839** CATH. SINCLAIR *Holiday House* xv. 300, I declare poor Frisk is going to be sick! **1849** LONGF. *Kavanagh* Prose Wks. 1886 II. xxix. 408 Well, I declare! If it is not Mr. Kavanagh! **1889** EARL OF DESART *Lit. Chatelaine* II. xxiii. 107, I declare, I long to see your niece.

7. ***to declare oneself***: **a.** to avow or proclaim one's opinions, leanings, or intentions; **b.** to make known or reveal one's true character, identity, or existence; also *fig.* of things.

c **1529** WOLSEY in Ellis *Orig. Lett.* I. II. 5 So declaryng your sylf therin that the world may perceive [etc.]. *a* **1626** BACON (J.), In Cæsar's army somewhat the soldiers would have had, yet they would not declare themselves in it, but only demanded a discharge. *a* **1680** BUTLER *Rem.* (1759) I. 237 As Thistles wear the softest Down, To hide their Prickles till they're grown; And then declare themselves and tear Whatever ventures to come near. *a* **1719** ADDISON (J.), We are a considerable body, who, upon a proper occasion, would not fail to declare ourselves. **1883** *Standard* 7 Sept. 4/6 A politician who could hardly declare himself with frankness without..alienating one or other of the sections of which his Party was composed. **1884** *Weekly Times* 7 Nov. 2/4 Wherever a spark fell..a little fire promptly declared itself.

c. with *for* or *against*, etc. Cf. 8.

1631 BEAULIEU *Let.* in *Crt. & Times Chas. I* (1848) II. 155 The circle of the Lower Saxony have now declared themselves for him. **1697** DAMPIER *Voy.* I. Introd. p. vi, I.. now declared myself on the side of those that were Out-voted. **1840** THIRLWALL *Greece* VII. 303 Alexander.. declared himself for Cassander. **1867** SMILES *Huguenots Eng.* ix. 144 Protestant children were invited to declare themselves against the religion of their parents.

d. *refl.* To declare one's love for another person; to propose marriage. Cf. DECLARATION 3 b.

1840 DICKENS *Old C. Shop* viii, A concerted plot..having for its object the inducing Mr. Swiveller to declare himself in time. **1879** TROLLOPE *Eye for Eye* II. ii. 29 You should have thought of that before you declared yourself to her, Mr. Neville. **1907** M. E. BRADDON *Dead Love has Chains* ii. 40 People were beginning to say ill-natured things about us; and he must either declare himself, or must go away. **1965** C. D. BROAD in G. Cummins *Swan on Black Sea* p. xviii, This was his love for Catherine Mary Lyttelton; her tragic death..before he had declared himself.

8. a. *intr.* (for *refl.*) ***to declare for*** (***in favour of***), or ***against***: to make known or avow one's sympathy, opinion, or resolution to act, for or against.

16.. JER. TAYLOR (J.), The internal faculties of will and understanding, decreeing and declaring against them. **1659** B. HARRIS *Parival's Iron Age* 216 Poyer, and Powell, formerly for the Parliament..declared against them. **1706** HEARNE *Collect.* 3 Apr., A Man..for siding with both Parties..and not declaring..for either. **1754** CHATHAM *Lett. Nephew* iv. 23 The adhering..to false and dangerous notions, only because one has declared for them. **1823** LAMB *Elia* Ser. II. *Poor Rel.*, He declareth against fish. **1855** MACAULAY *Hist. Eng.* III. 642 Wexford had declared for King William. **1881** HENTY *Cornet of Horse* xvii. 175 Rupert naturally declared at once for the journey to Paris.

†**b.** ***to declare for***: to declare oneself a candidate for; to make a bid for. *Obs.*

1666 PEPYS *Diary* (1879) VI. 44 To discourse of the further quantity of victuals fit to be declared for. **1701** W. WOTTON *Hist. Rome* 385 These Fancy's led one Severus.. to declare for the Empire. **1769** GOLDSM. *Hist. Rome* (1786) II. 456 Those who at first instigated him to declare for the throne.

9. ***to declare off***: to state formally that one is 'off' with a bargain or undertaking; to break off an engagement, practice, etc.; to withdraw, back out. *colloq.* (Rarely *trans.*)

1749 FIELDING *Tom Jones* XV. ix, Propose marriage..and she will declare off in a moment. **1766** GOLDSM. *Vic. W.* xiii, No, I declare off; I'll fight no more. **1791** GOUV. MORRIS in Sparks *Life & Writ.* (1832) III. 19, I contrived to get clear by declaring off from being a candidate. **1812** *Sporting Mag.* XXXIX. 188 Many declared off their bets. **1876** G. ELIOT *Dan. Der.* VIII. lxiv. 573 When it came to the point, Mr. Haynes declared off, and there has been no one to take it since.

10. *Law.* **a.** *intr.* To make a declaration or statement of claim as plaintiff in an action. Also with *that.*

1512 *Act 4 Hen. VIII*, c. 20 §2 If..eny of theym be non-suite in any of the said Appelis after they have appered and declared in the same. *a* **1626** BACON *Max. & Uses Com. Law* iii. (1636) 20 Her demand is of a moity, and shee declares upon the custome of the Realme. **1642** PERKINS *Prof. Bk.* ii. §151 If an action of debt be brought by administrators and they declare that [etc.]. **1768** BLACKSTONE *Comm.* III. 113 The party applying for the prohibition is directed by the court to declare in prohibition.

b. *trans.* To make a formal statement constituting or acknowledging (a trust or use).

1677 *Act 29 Chas. II*, c. 3 §7 That all declarations or creations of trusts or confidences..shall be..proved by some writing, signed by the party who is by law enabled to declare such trust. **1767** BLACKSTONE *Comm.* II. 363 If these deeds are made previous to the fine or recovery, they are called deeds to lead the uses; if subsequent, deeds to declare them. **1818** CRUISE *Digest* (ed. 2) VI. 392 Where the trusts and limitations were expressly declared.

c. To make a full and proper statement of or as to (goods liable to duty); to name (such and such dutiable goods) as being in one's posession. *trans.* and *intr.*

1714 *Fr. Bk. of Rates* 158 Without declaring and reporting thereof, and paying the Duties and Customs which they are so subject to. **1762** *Univ. Mag.* Feb. 99 All merchants who shall have in their possession any cod, or other fish..shall.. declare the same and deliver an account thereof. **1872** HOWELLS *Wedd. Journ.* 279 'Perhaps we'd better declare some of these things'..'I won't declare a thread!' *Mod.* (*Revenue Officer*) 'Have you anything to declare?'

11. a. In the game of bezique: To announce (a particular score) by laying down the cards which yield the score; to lay the cards face up on the table for this purpose. *trans.* or *absol.*

1870 *Mod. Hoyle* 147 (*Besique*) The winner of the trick now declares, if he has anything to declare.

b. *trans.* and *intr.* *Cricket.* To close an innings before the usual ten wickets have fallen; orig. 'to *declare* the innings at an end'.

1889 *Cricketer's Guide* 7 On the last day of a double-innings match, or in a one-day match, the batting side may, at any time, declare their innings at an end. **1897** *Encycl. Sport* I. 245/2 *Declare*, to close an innings. **1901** *Daily News* 5 June 4/4 Warwickshire made 532 for four wickets, and then declared. **1955** *Times* 15 July 3/3 Barnett showed that he is still worth a few runs before Insole declared.

c. *trans.* and *intr.* In the game of Bridge, to name the trump suit, or to announce the intention to play 'no trumps'; in auction or contract bridge, to announce the number of tricks that one intends to make.

1895 'BOAZ' *Laws of Bridge* 10 The dealer, having examined his hand, has the option of declaring what suit shall be trumps, or whether the hand shall be played without trumps. **1899** 'J. DOE' *Bridge Conventions* iii. 21 Before declaring ask yourself the question, Have we a better chance of making 30 than of losing 18? **1899** A. DUNN *Bridge* 27 The dealer should declare trumps 'on the top' of his cards. **1910** [see BID *v.* 3 c].

†**12.** *trans.* To clear (a person) of a charge or imputation. *Obs.*

1460 *Paston Lett.* No. 347 I. 508 [We were] mistrusted to our grete vilanye and rebuke, wheche muste be answerd the causes why, and we declared. **1463-4** *Plumpton Corr.* p. lxx, Our welbeloved William Plompton Kt. hath truly, sufficiently, & clearly declared himself of all manner matters that have been said or surmised against him, & so we hold him thereof for fully excused & declared.

13. *Racing.* To announce the withdrawal of (a horse) from a race for which it has been entered; said also *intr.* of the horse.

1847 *Weekly Times* 9 Oct., Stakes of 10 sovs each, 5 f[orfei]t, and only 3 if declared. **1897** *Westm. Gaz.* 5 Feb. 9/2 Two Grand National winners have just declared.

declared (dɪˈklɛəd), *ppl. a.* [f. prec. + -ED.] Openly or formally made known by words or something equivalent; openly avowed, professed.

1651 HOBBES *Leviath.* II. xxviii. 163 Harme inflicted upon one that is a declared enemy. **1722** *Wodrow Corr.* (1843) II. 661, I was glad to observe a declared inclination to write the lives of our remarkably learned men. **1781** GIBBON *Decl. & F.* III. 92 Declared and devout Pagans. **1828** SCOTT *F.M. Perth* xxv, A declared lover. **1884** *Pall Mall G.* 2 Sept. 8/1 The present condition of affairs is most trying, and a declared state of war would be preferable.

declaredly (dɪˈklɛərɪdlɪ), *adv.* [f. prec. + -LY².] In a declared manner; with formal declaration; professedly, avowedly, etc.

1644 J. GOODWIN *Innoc. Triumph.* (1645) 44 Many by being declaredly ingag'd for such or such an opinion. **1664** MORE *Myst. Iniq.* xiii. 42 They apertly and declaredly profess that there is only one true God. **1748** RICHARDSON *Clarissa* (1811) I. 10 Had not her uncle brought him declaredly as a suitor to her? **1844** H. H. WILSON *Brit. India* III. 130 The states..were not declaredly at war.

deˈclaredness. *rare.* [f. as prec. + -NESS.] The state of being declared.

1846 WORCESTER cites MORE.

†**deˈclarement.** *Obs.* [f. DECLARE *v.* + -MENT. Cf. OF. *declarement* (*desclairiement, declairement*) 14-15th c.; but this was app. obs. when the Eng. word was formed.]

1. The act of showing or setting forth; exposition, explanation, manifestation, declaring.

1646 SIR T. BROWNE *Pseud. Ep.* I. i, The frequent errors, we shall our selves commit, even in the expresse declarement hereof. **1665** GLANVILL *Sceps. Sci.* xiv. 78 For the Declarement of this, we are to observe [etc.].

2. Declaration, express or formal statement; the act of declaring *against* anything.

1633 T. ADAMS *Exp. 2 Peter* ii. 3 When by our comfortable declarements, we have testified our assurance of blessedness. **1679** 'TOM TICKLEFOOT' *Trial Wakeman* 7 A declarement against shedding innocent blood.

declarer (dɪˈklɛərə(r)). [f. DECLARE *v.* + -ER.]

1. One who declares: †**a.** One who expounds, explains, or interprets. Obs.

1527 R. THORNE in Hakluyt *Voy.* (1589) 258 That I be the declarer or gloser of mine owne worke. **1530** PALSGR. 212/1 Declarer, expounder, *declarevr, exposevr.* *a* **1714** J. SHARP *Serm.* VII. iv. (R.), To be the infallible declarers and interpreters of the sense of Scripture to all the Christian world.

b. One who (or that which) exhibits, sets forth, or makes known; one who proclaims or publishes.

1548 UDALL, etc. *Erasm. Par. Luke* xviii. (R.), He became ..an open declarer of Gods goodness. **1632** *State Trials, W. Prynne* (R.), He is not the declarer of his intentions. **1670** EACHARD *Cont. Clergy* 96 Such as are His peculiar servants, and declarers of His mind and doctrine. **1870** RUSKIN *Lect. Art* iii. (1887) 89 The declarer of some true facts or sincere passions.

2. One who makes or signs a declaration.

1649 C. WALKER *Hist. Independ.* II. 144 The Declarers play the Orators in behalfe of the felicity of Government. **1817** COBBETT *Pol. Reg.* 8 Feb. 173 This is declaration for declaration..But, my worthy Declarers, I am not going to stop here.

3. a. One who declares at bezique.

1870 *Mod. Hoyle* 153 (*Besique*) The declarer cannot declare Sequence and Royal Marriage at a blow.

b. In the game of Bridge, one who declares (see DECLARE *v.* 11 c).

1905 in W. Dalton '*Saturday' Bridge* (1910) 13 The declarer of the trump shall have the right to say whether or not the double shall stand. **1927** M. C. WORK *Contract Bridge* iii. 55 A double which is not 'free' may produce for the Declarer a game otherwise unobtainable. **1965** *Listener* 17 June 915/3 When Mrs Markus was declarer South led the two of diamonds.

declaring (dɪˈklɛərɪŋ), *vbl. sb.* [-ING¹.] The action of the verb DECLARE in its various senses; declaration.

c **1374** CHAUCER *Boeth.* III. x. (Camb. MS.) 72 Clepe it as thow wolt, be it porisme..or declarynges. *c* **1386** —— *Monk's T.* 94 Lo, this declaryng ought y-nough suffise. **1530** PALSGR. 212/2 Declaryng of armes, *blason.* **1611** BIBLE *2 Macc.* vi. 17 And nowe will wee come to the declaring of the matter in few words. **1612** BREREWOOD *Lang. & Relig.* xii. 108 For the better declaring of which point. **1667** J. CORBET *Disc. Relig. Eng.* 40 Their hazardous declaring against the designed Death of our late Soveraign.

deˈclaringly, *adv. rare.* In a manner that declares, manifests, or demonstrates.

1581 NOWELL & DAY in *Confer.* I. (1584) E iv, *Fides justificat apprehensiuè*, faith doth iustifie apprehendingly, *opera iustificant declaratiuè*, workes doe iustifie declaringly.

declass (dɪˈklɑːs, -klæs), *v.* [a. mod.F. *déclasser*, f. *dé-, des-* (see DE- I. 6) + *classe* class, *classer* to class.] *trans.* To remove or degrade from one's class. Hence **deˈclassed** *ppl. a.* (= F. *déclassé*).

1888 *Pall Mall Budget* 5 July 30/2 Mrs. E, who declasses herself once for all by painting her face. **1891** *New Review* June 563 The declassed Judith Marsett.

‖**déclassé** (deklase), *a.* and *sb.* Fem. **-ée.** [Fr., pa. pple. of *déclasser* DECLASS *v.*] **A.** *adj.* Reduced or degraded from one's social class; having come down in the world. **B.** *sb.* One who has been so reduced or degraded.

1887 *Fortn. Rev.* Aug. 227 It is only the *déclassé*, the ne'er-do-well, or the really unfortunate, who has nothing to call his own. **1905** *Spectator* 28 Jan. 144/2 Pamela..quits the company of artists and actresses, *declassés* and *divorcées*. **1921** *Glasgow Herald* 3 Aug., The attempt by a body of declassés to form the policy of the entire working-class of this country. **1921** *Times Lit. Suppl.* 29 Sept. 626/2 A girl of any family may, by force of circumstances, become *déclassée*. **1961** A. WILSON *Old Men at Zoo* ii. 97 Déclassé nations are very touchy.

declassicize see DE- II. 1.

declassify (diːˈklæsɪfaɪ), *v.* [f. DE- II. 1 + CLASSIFY *v.*] *trans.* To undo the action of classification; *spec.* to remove (information, etc.) from the category of being 'classified' (see CLASSIFIED *ppl. a.* c). So **declassiˈfiable** *a.*, **deˌclassifiˈcation, deˈclassified** *ppl. a.*

1865 GROTE *Plato* II. xxiv. 246 Logical exposition proceeding by way of classifying and declassifying. **1946** *Nature* 14 Sept. 355/2 Much of the nuclear research material ..is now declassifiable and provision has been made for revision of the rules for declassification of the secret documents. **1946** *Rep. Internat. Control Atomic Energy* IV. 53 This Committee was directed to report on a policy of declassification—that is disclosure—of scientific and technical material now classified as Secret. **1948** *Birmingham* (Ala.) *News* 21 Dec. 14/6 Forrestal asked Adm. Souers and Gen. Gruenther to 'declassify' it (make it non-secret) immediately. **1951** *Economist* 13 Oct. 864/1 No effective machinery is created for 'declassifying' secret information. **1953** *Encounter* Oct. 58/2 In the United States, the entire declassification procedure, by which work of potential military value is sifted and eventually tossed into the open, was devised by the scientists themselves. **1955** *Bull. Atomic Sci.* Apr. 145/3 Even the handling of declassified documents can cause trouble.

declension (dɪˈklɛnʃən). [Represents L. *dēclīnātiōn-em* (n. of action f. *dēclīnāre* to DECLINE), F. *déclinaison* (13th c.). The form is irregular, and its history obscure: possibly it came from the F. word, by shifting of the stress as in *comparison, orison, benison*, and loss of *ĭ*, as in *venison, ven'son*, giving *declin'son* (cf. 1565 in 4), with subsequent assimilative changes; the grammatical sense was the earliest, and the word had no doubt a long colloquial existence in the grammar schools before the English form appears in print. Cf. CONSTER.]

I. 1. The action or state of declining, or deviating from a vertical or horizontal position; slope, inclination; a declining or sinking into a lower position, as of the sun towards setting; the dip of the magnetic needle (= DECLINATION 8 a). ? *Obs.*

1640-4 LD. FINCH in Rushw. *Hist. Coll.* III. (1692) I. 13 To make us steer between the Tropicks of Moderation, that there be no declension from the Pole of Security. *a* **1659** OSBORN *Q. Eliz.* Epist. D d iv b, The ignorant Traveller may see by the Dial, the Time is in a declension. **1684-90** T. BURNET *Th. Earth* (J.), Allow as much for the declension of the land from that place to the sea. **1764** GRAINGER *Sugar Cane* I. iii. *note*, The declension of the needle was discovered A.D. 1492 by Columbus. **1799** W. TOOKE *View Russ. Emp.* I. 67 The northern part..has a sensible declension towards the White Sea. **1802-3** tr. *Pallas' Trav.* (1812) II. 201 This elevated ridge extends, with gradual declensions..towards the sea.

2. *fig.* Deviation or declining from a standard; falling away (from one's allegiance), apostasy.

1594 SHAKS. *Rich. III*, III. vii. 189 A Beautie-waining.. Widow..Seduc'd the pitch, and height of his degree, To base declension, and loath'd Bigamie. **1647** CLARENDON *Hist. Reb.* VII. (1843) 432/1 A declension from his own rules of life. *c* **1665** MRS. HUTCHINSON *Mem. Col. Hutchinson* (1846) 336 All their prudent declensions saved not the lives of some nor the estates of others. **1814** CARY *Dante, Parad.* IV. 69 That..is argument for faith, and not For heretic declension. **1881** W. R. SMITH *Old Test. in Jew. Ch.* xii. 344 The declensions of Israel had not checked the outward zeal with which Jehovah was worshipped.

3. The process or state of declining, or sinking into a lower or inferior condition; gradual diminution, deterioration, or decay; falling off, decline.

1602 SHAKS. *Ham.* II. ii. 149 He..Fell into a Sadnesse.. thence into a Weaknesse, Thence to a Lightnesse, and by this declension Into the Madnesse whereon now he raues. **1660** JER. TAYLOR *Worthy Commun.* ii. §1. 115 In the greatest declension of Religion. **1677** *Govt. Venice* Ep. Ded. 1 The State of Venice is at this day in its declension. **1734** tr. *Rollin's Anc. Hist.* (1827) I. Pref. 1 The causes of their declension and fall. **1874** MAURICE *Friendship Bks.* ii. 55 Symptoms of declension or decay.

b. Sunken or fallen condition.

1642 JER. TAYLOR *Episc.* (1647) 214 It hath..come to so low a declension, as it can scarce stand alone. **1734** tr. *Rollin's Anc. Hist.* (1827) VII. XVII. 345 Till Sparta sunk to her last declension. **1776** ADAM SMITH *W.N.* I. xi. I. 213 The declension of Spain is not, perhaps, so great as is commonly imagined.

II. 4. *Gram.* **a.** The variation of the form of a noun, adjective, or pronoun, constituting its different cases (see CASE *sb.*¹ 9); case-inflexion. **b.** Each of the classes into which the nouns of any language are grouped according to their inflexions. **c.** The action of declining, *i.e.* setting forth in order the different cases of, a noun, adjective, or pronoun.

1565-78 COOPER *Thesaurus* Introd., Substantives may be perceyved by their gender and declenson. **1569** J. SANFORD tr. *Agrippa's Van. Artes* 10 Rules of Declensions. **1598** SHAKS. *Merry W.* IV. i. 76 Show me now (William) some declensions of your Pronounes. **1612** BRINSLEY *Lud. Lit.* 58 The seueral terminations of euery case in euery Declension. **1640** G. WATTS tr. *Bacon's Adv. Learn.* VI. i. (R.), Ancient languages were more full of declensions, cases, conjugations, tenses, and the like. **1845** STODDART in *Encycl. Metrop.* 187/1 Those inflections, which grammarians call declensions and conjugations. **1871** ROBY *Lat. Gram.* I. 113 §334 The ordinary division of nouns substantive was into five declensions. *Ibid.* 116 §344 Ordinary declension of *-o* stems.

†**d.** Formerly, in a wider sense: Change of the form or of the ending of a word, as in derivation. (Cf. note under CASE *sb.*¹ 9.) *Obs. rare.* [So L. *declinatio* in early use.]

1678 CUDWORTH *Intell. Syst.* 524 The God..was called not *Bellum* but *Bellona*..not *Cuna* but *Cunina*..At other times, this was done without any Declension of the Word at all.

III. 5. The action of declining; courteous refusal, declinature. *rare.*

1817 BYRON *Let. to Murray* 21 Aug., You want a 'civil.. declension' for the..tragedy? **1886** *Echo* 13 Nov. 3/1 Prince Waldemar's declension.

declensional (dɪˈklɛnʃənəl), *a.* [f. prec. + -AL¹.] Of or belonging to grammatical declension.

1856 *Sat. Rev.* II. 461/2 The Albanian declensional inflections. **1875** WHITNEY *Life Lang.* x. 200 Conjugational and declensional inflections.

Hence **deˈclensionally** *adv.*

1888 RHYS *Hibbert Lectures* 69 This *taran* does not correspond declensionally to Taranis.

declericalize, declimatize: see DE- II. 1.

declinable (dɪˈklaɪnəb(ə)l), *a. Gram.* [a. F. *déclinable* (14th c.), ad. L. *dēclīnābilis* (Priscian), f. *dēclīnā-re* to DECLINE: see -BLE.] Capable of being declined; having case-inflexions.

1530 PALSGR. 135 Any word declynable in this tong. **1659** PEARSON *Creed* (1839) 242 The latter with a Greek termination, declinable. **1871** ROBY *Lat. Gram.* I. §795 Declinable adjectives of number.

declinal (dɪˈklaɪnəl), *sb. rare*⁻¹. [f. DECLINE *v.* (sense 13): cf. *denial* and -AL¹.] The action of declining; courteous refusal, declinature.

1837 SIR F. PALGRAVE *Merch. & Friar* (1844) 2 The declinals were grounded upon reasons neither unkind nor uncomplimentary.

†**deˈclinal,** *a. Obs. rare*⁻¹. [irreg. f. DECLINE.] = DECLINABLE.

1509 HAWES *Past. Pleas.* v. xxvii, A nowne substantyve.. wyth a gender is declynall [*rime* substancyall].

declinant (ˈdɛklɪnənt), *a.* and *sb.* [a. F. *déclinant*, pr. pple. of *décliner* to DECLINE.]

A. *adj.* **1.** *Her.* 'Applied to a serpent borne with the tail straight downwards' (Robson, *Brit. Herald*, 1830).

2. Declining. *nonce-use.*

1893 *National Observer* 20 May 17/2 Auriga..drooped declinant, perilously near the horizon.

†**B.** *sb.* One who is declining (in fortunes, etc.).

a **1734** NORTH *Lives* II. 64 The aspirant dealt with all imaginable kindness and candour to the declinant.

declinate (ˈdɛklɪnət), *a. Bot.* [ad. L. *dēclīnāt-us*, pa. pple. of *dēclīnāre* to bend away or down.] Inclined downwards or leaning to one side.

1810 W. ROXBURGH in *Asiatic Res.* XI. 346 Zinziber Zerumbet..Stems declinate. **1870** HOOKER *Stud. Flora* 235 Stamens..erect or declinate.

† **'declinated**, *a.* [f. as prec. + -ED.] = prec.
1757 PULTNEY in *Phil. Trans.* L. 66 The Atropa comes in among those, that have declinated stamina.

declination (dɛklɪ'neɪʃən). [a. OF. *déclinacion*, ad. L. *dēclīnātiōn-em*, n. of action f. *dēclīnāre* to DECLINE. In some senses perh. a direct adaptation of the L. word.] The action of declining.

†**1.** A turning aside, swerving, deviation from a standard; turning aside (from rectitude, etc.); falling away; = DECLENSION 2. *Obs.*
1533 MORE *Answ. Poysoned Bk.* Wks. 1035/2 Declinacion into foule and filthy talking. **1605** BACON *Adv. Learn.* II. 128 The declinations from Religion. **1659** HAMMOND *On Ps.* ci. 3. 496 The least declination from the rules of justice. **1673** *Lady's Call.* I. §3. 24 The declinations to any vice are gradual. **1814** SOUTHEY *Roderick* x. *Poems* IX. 94 The slight bias of untoward chance Makes his best virtue from the even line, With fatal declination, swerve aside.

†**2.** An inclination or leaning (away *from* or *towards* anything); a mental bias. *Obs.*
a **1605** STOW *Q. Eliz.* an. 1581 (R.), Letters..signefying the queen's declination from marriage, and the people's unwillingnesse to match that way. **1622** DONNE *Serm.* (1624) 15 Saint Augustine himself had, at first, some declination towards that opinion.

3. A leaning, bending, or sloping downwards; slope, inclination from the vertical or horizontal position.
1594 PLAT *Jewell-ho.* II. 16 Let it settle..then by declination poure away the cleerest. **1616** BULLOKAR, *Declination*, a bending downeward. **1662** STILLINGFL. *Orig. Sacr.* III. ii. §16 For this purpose he invented a motion of declination..he supposed..the descent not to be in a perpendicular right line, but to decline a little. *a* **1742** BENTLEY (J.), This declination of atoms in their descent, was itself either necessary or voluntary. **1816** SCOTT *Antiq.* xiii, A declination of the Antiquary's stiff backbone acknowledged the preference. **1846** JOYCE *Sci. Dial.* x. 23 A small declination..would throw the line of direction out of the base.

†**4.** A sinking into a lower position; descent towards setting; = DECLINING *vbl. sb.* 4. *Obs.*
1503 HAWES *Examp. Virt.* i. 5 In Septembre in fallynge of the lefe Whan phebus made his declynacyon. **1630** J. TAYLOR (Water P.) *Trav.* Wks. III. 84/2 Beeing a man famous through Europe, Asia, Affricke, and America, from the Orientall exhaltation of Titan, to his Occidental declination.

†**5.** The gradual falling off from a condition of prosperity or vigour; decline; decay. *Obs.*
1533 MORE *Apol.* xviii. Wks. 878/2 In this declinacion of the worlde. **1589** PUTTENHAM *Eng. Poesie* I. vi. (Arb.) 27 Then aboutes began the declination of the Romain Empire. *a* **1638** MEDE *View Apoc.* Wks. (1672) v. 923 His Declination and Ruine we see is already begun. **1673** H. STUBBE *Vind. Dutch War* 82 The declination of antient Learning. **1799** WASHINGTON *Let.* Writ. (1893) XIV. 191 Although I have abundant cause to be thankful for..good health..yet I am not insensible to my declination in other respects.

†**6.** The withholding of acceptance; non acceptance, modest or courteous refusal; declinature. ? *Obs.*
1612-5 BP. HALL *Contempl. O.T.* XII. v, A modest declination of that honour, which he saw must come. —— *Contempl. N.T.* IV. x, A voluntary declination of their familiar conversation. **1884** *Pall Mall G.* 21 Aug. 5/1 [The author] must excuse our declination to accept as possible characters in any possible social system, people so unnatural.

7. *Astron.* The angular distance of a heavenly body (north or south) from the celestial equator, measured on a meridian passing through the body: corresponding to terrestrial *latitude*. Formerly also the angular distance from the ecliptic.
(The earliest and now most usual sense.)
circle or *parallel of declination*: see CIRCLE 2 a, PARALLEL.
c **1386** CHAUCER *Frankl. T.* 518 Phebus..That in his hoote declynacion Shoon as the burned gold with stremes brighte. *c* **1391** —— *Astrol.* I. §17 In this heued of Cancer is the grettest declinacioun northward of the Sonne. *Ibid.* II. §17 Al be it so þat fro the Equinoxial may the declinacion or the latitude of any body celestial be rikned..riht so may the latitude or the declinacion of any body celestial, saue only of the sonne..be rekned fro the Ecliptik lyne. **1549** *Compl. Scot.* vi. 47 The mouyng, eleuatione, and declinatione of the sone, mune, and of the sternis. **1594** BLUNDEVIL *Exerc.* II. (ed. 7) 113 The greatest declination which is 23 degrees, 28'. **1794** SULLIVAN *View Nat.* I. 390 In consequence of the different declinations of the sun and moon at different times. **1816** PLAYFAIR *Nat. Phil.* II. 7 The arch of that circle intercepted between the star and the Equator is called the Declination of the star. **1872** PROCTOR *Ess. Astron.* i. 2 To Herschel astronomy was not a matter of right ascension and declination.

8. Of the magnetic needle: †**a.** Formerly, the DIP or deviation from the horizontal (*obs.*); **b.** the deviation from the true north and south line, *esp.* the angular measure of this deviation; also called VARIATION.
1635 N. CARPENTER *Geog. Del.* I. iii. 66 The Declination is a magneticall motion, whereby the magneticall needle conuerts it selfe vnder the Horizontall plaine, towards the Axis of the Earth. **1646** SIR T. BROWNE *Pseud. Ep.* II. ii. 61 The Inclination or Declination of the Loadstone; that is, the descent of the needle below the plaine of the Horizon. **1865** LIVINGSTONE *Zambesi* vi. 133 Magnetical observations, for ascertaining the dip and declination of the needle. **1878** HUXLEY *Physiog.* i. 10 The divergence of the position of the magnetic needle from the true north-and-south line is called its declination, or by nautical men, its variation.

9. *Dialling.* Of a vertical plane (*e.g.* that of a wall): The angular measure of its deviation from the prime vertical (the vertical plane through the east and west points of the horizon), or from the meridian (that through the north and south points).
1593 [see DECLINE *v.* 2 b]. **1669** STURMY *Mariner's Mag.* VII. vi. 11 The Declination of a Plane is the Azimuthal Distance of his Poles from the meridian. **1703** MOXON *Mech. Exerc.* 314 If it do not point directly either East, West, North, or South, then so many degrees is the Declination of the Plane. **1737-51** CHAMBERS *Cycl.*, *Declination* of a plane, or wall, in dialling.

†**10.** *Gram.* = DECLENSION 4. *Obs.*
c **1440** CAPGRAVE *Life St. Kath.* I. i. 259 To teche hir of retoryk and gramer the scole..The declynacions, þe personys, the modys, þe tens. **1530** PALSGR. Introd. 29 Pronownes of the fyrst declynation. **1603** FLORIO *Montaigne* I. xxv. (1632) 85 We did tosse our declinations, and conjugations to and fro. **1751** SMOLLETT *Per. Pic.* (1779) I. xii. 105 A perfect *ignoramus*, who scarce knows the declination of *musa*.

11. *attrib.* and *Comb.*, as ***declination-needle***; **declination axis**, that axis of an equatorial telescope which is at right angles to the polar axis, and to which is attached at one end the telescope and at the other the declination circle, so called because when the position of the telescope is changed by turning the declination axis there is an alteration in the declination of the object viewed; **declination circle**, (*a*) (see quot. 1854); (*b*) the graduated circle on an equatorial telescope which marks the declinations of the heavenly bodies; **declination compass** (see quot.); **declination magnet**, a magnet used in determining the magnetic declination and the magnetic axis.
1835 *Mech. Mag.* XXIV. 210/2 On these rollers turns the *declination axis. **1888** *Encycl. Brit.* XXIII. 146/2 The equatorial in its simplest form consists of an axis parallel to the earth's axis, called the 'polar axis'; a second axis, at right angles to this, called the 'declination axis'; and a telescope fixed at right angles to the latter. **1905** *Westm. Gaz.* 17 Apr. 1/3 A large equatorial with a 26-in. photographic refractor at one end of the declination axis and a 30-in. reflector at the other. **1964** R. H. BAKER *Astron.* (ed. 8) iv. 108 The circle on the declination axis is graduated in degrees of declination. **1835** *Mech. Mag.* XXIV. 211, Y is the *declination circle, fixed on the declination axis. **1854** MOSELEY *Astron.* ix. (ed. 4) 41 Declination-circles are those great circles which pass round the heavens from one pole to the other. **1888** *Encycl. Brit.* XXIII. 149/1 The declination circle is attached to the farther end of the declination axis. **1862** *Chambers's Encycl.* III. 461/1 The ordinary compass which must be used by making allowance for declination, is a *declination compass. **1883** *Encycl. Brit.* XV. 238/1 The first step is to remove the torsion as far as possible from the suspension fibre by hanging to it a brass plummet E of the same weight as the *declination magnet. After this weight has come to rest, it is replaced by the declination magnet. **1899** *Daily News* 3 Mar. 5/2 They have placed out here a declination magnet, a dip instrument for the inclination of the needle, and a deflexion instrument. **1870** R. M. FERGUSON *Electr.* 19 Instruments for determining magnetic declinations are called *declination needles or declinometers.

decli'national, *a.* [f. prec. + -AL[1].] Relating to declination.
1881 J. G. BARNARD in *Smithsonian Contrib. Knowl.* No. 310. 15 Absence of right ascension and declinational motions of the attracting body.

declinator[1] ('dɛklɪneɪtə(r)). [agent-n. on L. type f. L. *dēclīnāre* to DECLINE. F. *déclinateur*.]
†**1.** One who declines or refuses; a dissentient; also = DECLINER 2. *Obs.*
1606 BP. W. BARLOW *Serm.* (1607) A iv a, Declinators from their lawful Princes tribunall. *a* **1670** HACKET *Abp. Williams* II. (1692) 65 The votes of the declinators could not be heard for the noise.
2. *Dialling.* An instrument for determining the declination of planes.
1727-51 CHAMBERS *Cycl.*, *Declinator* or *Declinatory*, an instrument in dialling, whereby the declination, inclination, and reclination, of planes is determined.

† **declinator**[2] (dɪ'klaɪnətə(r)), *a.* and *sb.* *Sc. Law.* *Obs.* Also 7 -our. [Sc. repr. of F. *déclinatoire*: see DECLINATORY.]
A. *adj.* In ***exception declinatour*** = B. **B.** *sb.* A written instrument declining the jurisdiction of a judge or court.
1609 SKENE *Reg. Maj.* 113 Exceptions declinatours against the Judge. **1639** (*title*), Declinator and Protestation of the Archbishops and Bishops of the Church of Scotland. **1681** *Lond. Gaz.* No. 1651/4 The same day were likewise past, An Act gainst Protections, An Act against Declinators. **1733** NEAL *Hist. Purit.* II. 324 The Bishops Declinator being read, was unanimously rejected.

declinatory (dɪ'klaɪnətərɪ), *a.* and *sb.* [ad. med.L. *dēclīnātōri-us* (f. ppl. stem *dēclīnāt-* of *dēclīnāre*: see -ORY), in the legal expression *exceptio dēclīnātōria*, in F. *exception déclinatoire*. French has also the sb. use (1381 in Hatzf.).]
A. *adj.* That declines (sense 13); expressing refusal. ***declinatory plea*** (Law): a plea intended to show that the party was exempt from the jurisdiction of the court, or from the penalty of the law; abolished in 1826.
1673 MARVELL *Corr.* ccxi. Wks. 1872-5 II. 412 Return an answer..in a civill but declinatory way. **1769** BLACKSTONE *Comm.* IV. 327 Formerly..the benefit of clergy used to be pleaded before trial or conviction, and was called a declinatory plea. **1848** WHARTON *Law Lex.*, *Declinatory plea*, a plea of sanctuary, also pleading benefit of clergy before trial or conviction.
B. *sb.* **1.** *Law.* A declinatory plea.
a **1693** URQUHART *Rabelais* III. xxxix. 326 Declinatories [Fr. *declinatoires*], Anticipatories. *a* **1734** NORTH *Lives* (1826) I. 342 They had a declinatory of course: viz..'That matters of Parliament were too high for them'.
†**2.** *Dialling.* = DECLINATOR[1] 2. *Obs.*
1703 MOXON *Mech. Exerc.* 311 If the Situation of the Plane be not given, you must seek it..the readiest and easiest [way] is by an Instrument called a Declinatory. **1727-51** [see DECLINATOR[1] 2].

declinature (dɪ'klaɪnətjʊə(r)). [f. L. type *dēclīnātūra*, f. ppl. stem *dēclīnāt-*: see -URE. In sense 1 perhaps a 'rectification' of DECLINATOR[2].]
1. *Sc. Law.* A formal plea declining to admit the jurisdiction of a court or tribunal; *spec.* 'the privilege which a party has in certain circumstances to decline judicially the jurisdiction of the judge before whom he is cited' (Bell): = DECLINATOR[2], DECLINATORY *sb.* 1.
1637-50 ROW *Hist. Kirk* (1842) 321 He had given in a declinature, containing reasons why he could not acknowledge that judicatorie to be lawfull. **1639** BAILLIE *Let. to W. Spang* 28 Sept., To passe from his declinature of the Generall Assemblie. **1754** ERSKINE *Princ. Sc. Law* (1809) 19 The defender pleads a declinature, which is repelled. **1861** W. BELL *Dict. Law Scot.* 258/2 The relationship of the judge to one or both of the parties is a ground of declinature. **1883** GARDINER *Hist. Eng.* I. 60 Black ..having once more declined its jurisdiction, a formal resolution was passed to the effect that..the Court refused to admit the declinature.
2. *gen.* The action of declining or refusing; courteous refusal.
1842 ALISON *Hist. Europe* (1853) XIV. xcv. §29. 104 This second declinature irritated the government in the highest degree. **1882** A. B. BRUCE *Parab. Teaching* (1889) 504 It was nothing more than a declinature to be burdened with their neighbours' affairs. **1885** *Manch. Exam.* 15 June 5/5 The reported declinature of office by the Marquis of Salisbury.

decline (dɪ'klaɪn), *sb.* Also 4 **declyn**, 5 **declyne**. [a. F. *déclin*, f. *décliner* to DECLINE.]
1. The process of declining or sinking to a weaker or inferior condition; gradual loss of force, vigour, vitality, or excellence of quality; falling off, decay, diminution, deterioration. ***on the decline***: in a declining state; declining, falling off.
a **1327** in *Pol. Songs* (Camden) 154 Al hit cometh in declyn this gigelotes geren. *c* **1430** LYDG. *Thebes* III. (R.), The high noblesse shall draw to decline Of Greekes blood. **1638** C. ALEYN *Hist. Hen. VII*, 138 When Bodies cease to grow, 'tis the presage Of a decline to their decrepit Age. **1711** STEELE *Spect.* No. 78 ¶4 The Lady had actually lost one Eye, and the other was very much upon the Decline. **1766** GOLDSM. *Vic. W.* xxviii, The decline of my daughter's health. **1776** GIBBON (*title*), History of the Decline and Fall of the Roman Empire. **1844** H. H. WILSON *Brit. India* III. 436 The ascendancy, decline, and final overthrow of the Mahrattas. **1892** *Law Times* XCII. 138/1 It is said that reading in barristers' chambers is on the decline.
b. Fallen or sunken condition. *rare.*
1705 STANHOPE *Paraphr.* I. 108 In the lowest Decline of Oppression and Disgrace, he was in no degree less worthy of Veneration than when in his highest Glory.
c. A gradual failure of the physical powers, as in the later years of life.
1770 LANGHORNE *Plutarch* (1879) I. 85/1 Numa..wasted away insensibly with old age and a gentle decline. **1801** *Med. Jrnl.* V. 545 A gradual decline had apparently begun.
d. Any disease in which the bodily strength gradually fails; *esp.* tubercular phthisis, consumption.
1783 *Gentl. Mag.* LIII. II. 1066 [Died] at his brother's at Enfield, of a deep decline, by bursting a blood-vessel in coughing. **1790** MAD. D'ARBLAY *Diary* Dec., A general opinion that I was falling into a decline. **1845** S. AUSTIN *Ranke's Hist. Ref.* I. 285 He fell into a rapid decline, and died prematurely. **1857** HUGHES *Tom Brown* II. i, She said one of his sisters was like to die of decline. **1882** *Syd. Soc. Lex.*, *Decline*..applied to the later stages of phthisis pulmonalis. Also, a term for the condition formerly called *Tabes*.
e. *Comm.* A downward movement or gradual fall in price or value.
1885 *Manch. Guardian* 20 July 5/5 The decline in the value of labour has not hitherto kept pace with that of commodities and property. **1887** *Daily News* 23 Feb. 2/6, 560 bags Demerara syrups at 6d decline. **1893** *Ibid.* 25 Dec. 7/3 The market was weak, but declines were unimportant.
2. Of the sun or day: The action of sinking towards its setting or close.
14.. *Epiph.* in *Tundale's Vis.* 103 Westryng or drawyng to declyne. **1590** GREENE *Orl. Fur.* (1861) 111 Where Phœbus ..kisses Thetis in the days decline. **1667** MILTON *P.L.* IV. 792 This Evening from the Sun's decline arriv'd. **1827** POLLOK *Course T.* x, At dawn, at mid-day, and decline.
b. In ***the decline of life*** there is a mixture of senses 1 and 2.
1711 STEELE *Spect.* No. 2 ¶5 A Gentleman who according to his Years should be in the Decline of his Life. **1848** MACAULAY *Hist. Eng.* I. 269 The king and his heir were nearly of the same age. Both were approaching the decline of life.

3. A downward incline, a slope. *rare.*
1538 LELAND *Itin.* II. 46 Farington, standing in a stony Ground in the Decline of an Hille. **1844** *Mech. Mag.* XL. 397 The frightful precipitation of a railway train down a decline. **1859** R. F. BURTON *Centr. Afr.* in *Jrnl. Geog. Soc.* XXIX. 237 §1 On the declines, more precipitous than Swiss terraces, manioc and cereals grow luxuriantly.

decline (dɪˈklaɪn), *v.* Also 4–6 declyne. [a. F. *décline-r* (Chans. Roland 11th c.), ad. L. *dēclīnāre* to turn or bend away or aside from the straight course, etc., f. DE- I. 2 + *-clīnāre* (in comb.) to bend, cognate with Gr. *κλίν-ειν* to bend, and Teut. **hlinôjan*, OSax. *hlinôn* to lean. In the sense-development the prefix *de-* has also been taken in the sense 'down', of which there is little trace in L. *dēclīnāre.*]

I. Intransitive senses.

* *To turn aside, deviate.*

†**1. a.** To turn or bend aside; to deviate (from the straight course); to turn away. *Obs.*
c **1325** *E.E. Allit. P.* A. 333 Now rech I neuer for to declyne, Ne how fer of folde þat man me fleme. **14..** *Epiph.* in *Tundale's Vis.* 122 No thyng may be hyd from thy presence Ne from thyne eye declyne ne astart. **1483** CAXTON *Gold. Leg.* 65/4 Dauid said what haue I doo..and declyned fro hys brother to other of the peple. **1555** EDEN *Decades* 1 Colonus directynge his visage towarde the weste..declining somwhat towarde the left hande, sayled on forwarde xxxiii. dayes. **1632** LITHGOW *Trav.* VI. 291 Againe night we declined towards Gaza. **1691** RAY *Creation* I. (1704) 62 A line..much declining from the Object. **1703** MAUNDRELL *Journ. Jerus.* (1732) 57 Here we began to decline from the Sea-Coast. **1778** BP. LOWTH *Transl. Isaiah* (ed. 12) 55 Turn aside from the way; decline from the straight path. **1839** LINGARD *Hist. Eng.* (ed. 4) XI. 286 The few individuals who ventured abroad..when they met, declined on opposite sides, to avoid the contact of each other.

†**b.** To turn aside *from* (anything) so as to avoid it: cf. the trans. sense in 12. *Obs.*
1526 *Pilgr. Perf.* (W. de W. 1531) 93 b, We can not beare yᵉ presence of our neyghbour..but declyne from his company. **1563** FOXE *A. & M.* 723 b, Naturally euery creature declineth gladly from that thyng which goth about to hurt it.

†**2. a.** *Astron.* and *Geog.* To deviate, diverge, or fall away from the equator (formerly also, from the ecliptic); to have DECLINATION (sense 7). *Obs.*
c **1391** CHAUCER *Astrol.* I. §21 þat on half [of the Zodiac] declinith sowthward, & þat other northward. *Ibid.* II. §17 The Ecliptic lyne: fro which lyne alle Planetes som tyme declinen north or south. **1634** SIR T. HERBERT *Trav.* 200 Java is an Ile..declining seven degrees from the Æquator towards the Antarctique Pole. **1726** tr. *Gregory's Astron.* I. 331 At London the least Twilight is when the Sun declines from the Equator towards the South 6ᵈ 7′.

†**b.** *Dialling.* Of a vertical plane: To have an aspect oblique to the prime vertical or to the meridian; to have DECLINATION (sense 9). *Obs.*
1593 FALE *Dialling* 4 The East and West are not said to decline, because the declination is accounted from the south and North to the direct East and West points. **1669** STURMY *Mariner's Mag.* VII. x. 15 AB is a Wall or Plane declining East..so much as the Wall bendeth from the East Azimuth, so much doth his Pole at P decline or bend from the Meridian. **1703** MOXON *Mech. Exerc.* 311 The South Erect Plane, declining more or less towards the East or West.

†**c.** Of the magnetic needle: To deviate from the true north and south line; cf. DECLINATION 8.
1662 J. DAVIES tr. *Olearius' Voy. Ambass.* 180 In that place the needle declin'd 22 degrees from the North, towards the West. **1674** BOYLE *Excell. Theol.* II. v. 215 The magnetick needle not onely declining in many places from the true points of N. and S. but..varying in tract of time its declination in the self-same place.

†**3.** *fig.* **a.** To turn aside in conduct; *esp.* to swerve or fall away (from rectitude, duty, allegiance, instructions, etc.). *Obs.*
c **1374** CHAUCER *Boeth.* IV. vii. 145 Of hem þat eschewen and declinen fro vices and taken þe weye of vertue. *c* **1450** tr. *De Imitatione* I. xx. 24 Ner lete hem not liȝtly decline to outwarde consolacions. **1495** *Act 11 Hen. VII*, c. 1 §2 Persones..which shall hereafter declyne from..their seid alliegeaunce. ?**1507** *Communyc.* Biij, Alas why..so unkyndly from hym declyne That is our god so gracyous. **1558** KNOX *First Blast* (Arb.) 31 Frome the highest to the lowest, all were declined frome the. *a* **1580** *Farrant's Anthem, 'Lord, for thy tender mercies' sake'*, Give us grace to amend our sinful lives, to decline from sin and incline to virtue. **1611** BIBLE *Ps.* cxix. 157 Yet doe I not decline from thy testimonies. **1728** NEWTON *Chronol. Amended* vi. 352 They declined from the worship of this Eternal Invisible God. **1749** F. SMITH *Voy.* II. 201 He had formed a Design ..of declining from his Instructions.

†**b.** To turn aside from the subject, in speaking or writing; to digress. *Obs.*
1544 PHAER *Regim. Lyfe* (1560) Nvb, Here I have declined by occasion, but now to our intent. **1600** HOLLAND *Livy* IX. xvii. 325 a, I have nothing lesse sought..than to digresse and decline [*declinarem*] more than was needfull, from the order and course of mine historie.

†**c.** Of things: To diverge, deviate (in character, excellence, etc.) *from. Obs.*
1615 G. SANDYS *Trav.* 12 There is a Bannia, which little declines from the state of a Temple. **1632** J. HAYWARD tr. *Biondi's Eromena* 174 Nor doth thy last alleaged excuse.. decline any whit from thy other reasons.

†**4.** *fig.* To incline or lean *to. Obs.*
1541 R. COPLAND *Guydon's Quest. Chirurg.*, It is set in the myddes of the brest, nat declynynge to one parte more than to another. **1580** FRAMPTON *Monardes' Med. agst. Venome* 127 The Bezaar stone is..full of spottes, declining to the colour of a sad blewe. —— *Dial. Yron* 151 b, Yron..doth more decline to be hot than colde. **1590** SHAKS. *Com. Err.* III. ii. 44 Your weeping sister is no wife of mine..Farre more, farre more, to you doe I decline. *a* **1636** HOLLAND (Webster), That purple luster..declineth in the end to the color of wine. **1671** tr. *Palafox's Conq. China* xi. 230 It was quickly perceived to which side the victory declined.

¶ Not to consent or agree (*to do something*); to refuse. See sense 13.

** *To slope, incline, or bend downward.*

5. To deviate from the horizontal or vertical position; to have a downward inclination, to slant or slope downward.
c **1420** *Pallad. on Husb.* I. 298 On south and este se that it [the land] faire enclyne..But from the colde Septemptrion declyne. **1607** TOPSELL *Four-f. Beasts* (1658) 159 Some plain place..declining by the space of some four or five furlongs. **1665** SIR T. HERBERT *Trav.* (1677) 152 The ground on each side declining gently. **1725** DE FOE *Voy. round World* (1840) 258 The way..having first mounted gently a pleasant slope declined again. **1843** PRESCOTT *Mexico* (1850) I. 5 Table land which..gradually declines in the higher latitudes of the north.

6. To bend down, bow down, droop.
a **1400–50** *Alexander* 2289 (Dubl. MS.) 'My louely Lord', quod þe lede, and law he declynes. **1598** ROWLANDS *Betraying of Christ* 4 As a fruitfull tree the more it is fruitladen, the more it declineth. *a* **1612** DONNE *Biathan.* (1644) 190 Our heads decline after our death by the slackness of the sinews and muscles. **1632** LITHGOW *Trav.* II. 49 The wearisome creatures of the world declining to their rest. **1749** FIELDING *Tom Jones* VI. viii, His eyes were eagerly fixed on Sophia, and hers declining towards the ground. **1891** T. HARDY *Tess* I. 10 Declining from his sitting position..[he] stretched himself..among the daisies.

†**7. a.** To come down, fall, descend, sink. *Obs.*
a **1400–50** *Alexander* 2714 (Ashm. MS.) He þat enhansis him to heȝe, þe heldire he declynes. **1602** SHAKS. *Ham.* II. ii. 500 His Sword Which was declining on the Milkie head Of Reuerend Priam, seem'd i' the air to stick.

†**b.** To descend in lineage. *Obs. rare.*
1598 YONG *Diana* 98 On th' one side Dukes most excellent decline, And from the other scepter, throne, and crowne.

8. a. Of the sun or other heavenly body: To descend in the sky after culmination; to sink towards setting.
c **1430** LYDG. *Compl. Bl. Knt.* xcii, Er that thy bemes go up to declyne, And er that thou now go fro us adoune. **1513** DOUGLAS *Æneis* X. xiv. 194 Be this the son declynyt was almost. **1607** ROWLANDS *Fam. Hist.* 22 The Sun declines, day ancient grows. **1812** WOODHOUSE *Astron.* xxx. 299 As the Moon, having passed the meridian, declines. **1837** DISRAELI *Venetia* I. ii, The sun was beginning to decline.

b. *transf.* Said of the day (evening, etc.), also *fig.* of one's life: To draw towards its close. (Often with mixture of sense 10.)
1697 [see DECLINING *ppl. a.* 3]. **1704** F. FULLER *Med. Gymn.* (1711) 108 When People decline in Years, there are some extraordinary Means requisite. **1724** DE FOE *Mem. Cavalier* (1840) 146 The day declined. **1770** LANGHORNE *Plutarch* (1879) I. 152/1 The summer was now declining. **1871** R. ELLIS *Catullus* lxi. 94 The day declines. Forth, fair bride.

9. *fig.* To fall morally or in dignity, to sink (to evil courses, etc., or to an unworthy object). (Now only *literary*, and after Shaks.)
[*c* **1440** *Gesta Rom.* lxiv. 279 (Add. MS.) But that in no wise from hens forward he declyn to synne agayn. **1579** FULKE *Heskins' Parl.* 485 Many of the elect do decline to vices.] **1602** SHAKS. *Ham.* I. v. 50 Oh Hamlet, what a falling off was there, From me, whose loue was of that dignity..and to decline Vpon a wretch, whose Naturall gifts were poore To those of mine. **1667** MILTON *P.L.* XII. 97 Yet somtimes Nations will decline so low From vertue. **1691** E. TAYLOR *Behmen's Theos. Philos.* xx. 30 The direful shameful state Adam declined into. **1708** SWIFT *Sent. Church of Eng. Man*, He declines..from his office of presiding over the whole, to be the head of a party. **1842** TENNYSON *Locksley Hall* 43 Having known me—to decline On a range of lower feelings and a narrower heart than mine!

10. *fig.* To fall off or fail in force, vigour, or vitality; to decay, wane, diminish, decrease; to fall from prosperity or excellence, to deteriorate.
1530 PALSGR. 508/2 Whan thynges be at the hyghest, than they begyn to declyne. **1577** tr. *Bullinger's Decades* (1592) 515 After the subuersion of Hierusalem the Romane Empire began to decline. **1597** MORLEY *Introd. Mus.* 182 Your health, which I feare is already declining. **1607** SHAKS. *Cor.* I. i. 197 Who's like to rise, Who thriues, and who declines. **1687** WALLER (J.), That empire must decline, Whose chief support and sinews are of coin. **1697** DRYDEN *Virg. Georg.* II. 435 When Autumnal Warmth declines. **1728** YOUNG *Love Fame* v. 517 She grants, indeed, a lady may decline (All ladies but herself) at ninety-nine. **1818** JAS. MILL *Brit. India* II. v. viii. 675 The net territorial revenues..instead of increasing, had actually declined. **1852** MRS. STOWE *Uncle Tom's C.* xxvi, Eva after this declined rapidly: there was no more any doubt of the event. **1888** M. ROBERTSON *Lombard St. Myst.* iv, Mr. Alldis had declined considerably in his estimation.

II. Transitive senses.

* *To cause to turn aside, to avert; to turn aside from, avoid, refuse.*

†**11.** To turn aside (*lit.* and *fig.*): **a.** To avert.
c **1430** LYDG. *Bochas* VI. iv. (1554) 151 a, For remedies.. Was prouided theyr malice to declyne. **1606** HOLLAND *Sueton.* Annot. 25 Counterfeiting a woman, thereby to decline suspicion. **1638** COWLEY *Love's Riddle* v, Thanks to the juster Deities for declining From both the Danger, and from me the Sin. *a* **1661** FULLER *Worthies* (1840) III. 422 Here Johnson lies: could physic fence Death's dart, Sure death had been declined by his art. **1750** JOHNSON *Rambler* No. 31 ¶5 Subterfuges and evasions are sought to decline the pressure of resistless arguments.

†**b.** To turn (a person) aside *from* or *to* a course of conduct, from duty, etc.; to divert. *Obs.*
a **1555** LATIMER *Serm. & Rem.* (1845) 230 Of them which decline their ear from hearing the law of God. **1610** DONNE *Pseudo Martyr* 185 The immensnesse..auerts me from beleeuing it to bee just, so doeth this also decline me that they will not bee brought to tell vs, etc. **1617** BEAUM. & FL. *Valent.* III. i, Nor any way decline you to discredit. **1633** BP. HALL *Hard Texts* 175 When I wᵈ doe good I am in the meane while declined to evill. *c* **1634** STRAFFORD in Browning *Life* (1890) 129 This alliance shall not decline me from those more sovereign duties I owe my master. **1658** SLINGSBY *Diary* (1836) 207 Sundry disputes with sinewy Arguments to decline my opinion.

†**c.** In physical sense: To cause to deviate, deflect (from a straight course, etc.). *Obs.*
1646 SIR T. BROWNE *Pseud. Ep.* II. ii. 59 Contrary poles or faces attract each other, as the North the South, and the like decline each other, as the North the North. **1692** BENTLEY *Boyle Lect.* ii. 71 A Byas, that may decline it a little from a straight Line. *Ibid.* 137 How can he conceive, that any parcel of dead matter can spontaneously divert and decline it self from the line of its motion.

†**d.** *refl.* To withdraw oneself, turn away. *Obs.*
a **1635** NAUNTON *Fragm. Reg.* (Arb.) 49 Rawleigh.. undertook a new peregrination, to leave..the Court..and, by declining himself, and by absence, to expell his, and the passion of his enemies.

†**12.** To turn aside from; to get or keep out of the way of; to avoid, shun. *Obs.* (or merged in 13.)
a **1400–50** *Alexander* 4263 All þat ouire mesure is to mekill emell we declyne. **1526** *Pilgr. Perf.* (W. de W. 1531) 9 What company to vse, & whome to declyne and eschewe. **1607** TOPSELL *Four-f. Beasts* (1658) 452 Except they meet them in some path way where the man cannot decline the Beast, nor the Beast the Man. **1656** TRAPP *Comm. Matt.* vii. 13 Certain dangerous rocks..carefully to be declined. **1705** PURSHALL *Mech. Macrocosm* 145 In Autumn, when the Sun declines us, and its Tendency is towards the Southern Hemisphere. *a* **1711** KEN *Preparatives* Poet. Wks. 1721 IV. 49 Guilty sinners, self-condemn'd, Despairing to decline their Fate. **1761** *New Companion Fest. & Fasts* xx. §2. 177 When the fire of persecution breaks out among us, we have our Lord's permission by all prudent and honourable methods to decline it.

13. a. To turn away from (anything suggested or presenting itself) as from a thing which one is unwilling to take up, undertake, or engage in; to withhold oneself from; not to consent to engage in, practise, or do. Now only with nouns of action: to decline a *discussion*, *contest*, *challenge*, etc.: cf. c.
1631 *Star Chamb. Cases* (Camden) 58 That Sʳ Arthur Savage should humbly acknowledge that he had committed a great offence..Sʳ Arthur declyned this acknowledgement. **1643** SIR T. BROWNE *Relig. Med.* I. §6, I have no Genius to disputes in Religion, and have often thought it wisedome to decline them. **1672** PETTY *Pol. Anat.* (1691) 320 Declining all military means of settling and securing Ireland in peace and plenty. *c* **1750** JOHNSON, Melissa..gained the victory by declining the contest. **1754** RICHARDSON *Grandison* I. xxviii. 206 What must the man have been that had declined his aid in a distress so alarming. **1786** BURKE *W. Hastings* Wks. 1842 II. 187 Bristow, declining the violent attempt on the life of Almas Ali, deceitfully ordered by the said Warren Hastings. **1793** —— *Conduct of Minority* ibid. I. 617 To throw an odium upon those who were obliged to decline the cause of justice from their impossibility of supporting a cause which they approve. **1806** SURR *Winter in Lond.* (ed. 3) I. 11 The fisherman..at one moment was on the point of setting out for Brighton immediately, and the next declined it till the morning. **1824** T. JEFFERSON *Writ.* (1830) IV. 407, I decline all newspaper controversy. **1848** MACAULAY *Hist. Eng.* xiv, They far more readily forgive a commander who loses a battle than a commander who declines one.

b. Not to consent or agree to *doing*, or *to do* (something suggested, asked, etc.); hence, practically = REFUSE: but without the notion of active repulse or rejection conveyed by the latter word, and therefore a milder and more courteous expression. (Constr. *vbl. sb.*, *inf.*; also *absol.* or *intr.*)
a **1691** BOYLE (J.), That would not be to render a reason of the thing proposed, but, in effect, to decline rendering any. **1696** tr. *Du Mont's Voy. Levant* 288, I cannot reasonably decline giving Credit to a Thing..so often confirm'd. **1751** JOHNSON *Rambler* No. 143 ¶14 Provided he declines to tread in their footsteps. **1865** CARLYLE *Fredk. Gt.* VI. XVI. xv. 314, I declined satisfying his curiosity. **1891** *Pall Mall G.* 12 Jan. 3/2 The Archbishop..declined to accept their apology. *Mod.* He was invited, but declined. Shall we accept or decline?

c. Not to accept (something offered); implying polite or courteous refusal.
c **1712** ADDISON (J.), She generously declined them [the glories of this world], because she saw the acceptance of them was inconsistent with religion. **1771** SMOLLETT *Humph. Cl.* (L.), The squire said they could not decently decline his visit. **1833** HT. MARTINEAU *Manch. Strike* vii. 84 Being aware of this, Allen would have declined the gift. **1838** THIRLWALL *Greece* IV. xxxiii. 312 Ariæus declined the offer of the Greeks. **1884** G. ALLEN *Philistia* III. 18 Writing magazine articles..which were invariably declined with thanks.

d. *Chess.* To refuse to take a piece or pawn offered in (a gambit).
[**1833** W. LEWIS *Progr. Less. Chess* (ed. 2) 138 King's Gambit... The best move for the Black is to take your K.B.P.; but he may decline doing so.] **1847** H. STAUNTON *Chess-Player's Handbk.* IV. x. 347 (*heading*) The gambit declined. **1875** G. H. D. GOSSIP *Chess-Player's Man.* 705 The Queen's Gambit accepted and declined. **1899** E. E. CUNNINGTON *How to play Chess* 48 P-QKt4, offering the sacrifice of a P. to get an attack. Black need not take it (he

may retreat the B to Kt3), in which case the Opening is called the Evans declined.

†**14.** *Sc. Law.* To refuse, disown, or formally object to the jurisdiction of (a judge or court). Cf. DECLINATOR², DECLINATURE 1. ? *Obs.*

c **1450** HENRYSON *Tale of Dog* 49 Thairfoir as juge suspect, I yow declyne. **1638** *Short Relat. State Kirk Scotl.* 11 The Supplicants declined the Bishops from being their Iudges, as beeing now their parties. *a* **1715** BURNET *Own Time* (1823) I. 193 He would not appear, but declined the King and his council, who, he said, were not proper judges of matters of doctrine. **1754** ERSKINE *Princ. Sc. Law* (1809) 18 A judge may be declined, i.e. his jurisdiction disowned judicially, 1. *ratione causæ*, from his incompetency to the special cause brought before him. **1861** W. BELL *Dict. Law Scot.* s.v. *Declinature*, A judge who is a partner in a trading company may be declined in a question where the interest of that company is concerned.

†**15.** To abandon, forsake, give up (a practice).

1672 PETTY *Pol. Anat.* 368 As for the interest of these poorer Irish, it is manifestly to be transmuted into English ..so as to decline their language. **1679** PENN *Addr. Prot.* II. 74 The Christians had declin'd the Simplicity of their own Religion and grew Curious and Wanton. **1699** BENTLEY *Phal.* 317 Herodotus, Dionysius Halic. etc. had great reason to decline the use of their vernacular Tongue, as improper for History. **1749** FIELDING *Tom Jones* XIV. viii, Having acquired a very good fortune, he had lately declined his business.

** *To cause to bend down, descend, or slope.*

16. a. To bend down, bow down, lean.

a **1400-50** *Alexander* 5322 And hitterly on ilk side his heued he declines. *a* **1547** SURREY *Aeneid* IV. 239 Ne doth decline to the swete sleepe her eyes. **1583** STUBBES *Anat. Abus.* I. (1879) 55 As they can verie hardly eyther stoupe downe, or decline them selues to the grounde. **1697** POTTER *Antiq. Greece* IV. v. (1715) 202 Another Token of Dejection was, to decline their Heads upon their Hands. **1814** SOUTHEY *Roderick* xvii, He sate with folded arms and head declined Upon his breast. **1856** BRYANT *Poems, Summer Wind* 11 The clover droops..and declines its blooms.

†**b.** To move or direct obliquely downwards.

15.. SPENSER (J.), And now fair Phœbus 'gan decline in haste, His weary waggon to the western vale. **1725** POPE *Odyss.* IV. 145 His good old Sire with sorrow to the tomb Declines his trembling steps.

†**17.** To lower, bring down, depress, bring low, degrade, debase. *lit.* and *fig. Obs.*

a **1400-50** *Alexander* 2334, I þar pompe and þaire pride to poudire declined. **1599** DANIEL *Let. Octavia* Wks. 1717 I. 72 For I could never think the aspiring Mind Of worthy and victorious Anthony, Could be by such a Syren so declin'd. **1621** FLETCHER *Isl. Princess* I. i, A dull labour that declines a gentleman. *a* **1649** DRUMM. OF HAWTH. *Hist. Jas. I*, Wks. (1711) 15 To decline the rank growth of these usurpers. **1659** D. PELL *Impr. Sea* 131 The more they run Northward, the more they..raise the Septentrional Pole, and decline the Austral. *c* **1790** IMISON *Sch. Art* I. 236 To elevate or decline the glass according to the sun's altitude.

18. To cause to slant or slope, incline downwards.

1578 BANISTER *Hist. Man* I. 30 Those partes beyng also flat..but somewhat inward declined with all. **1812** J. J. HENRY *Camp. agst. Quebec* 149 Built on a plain pretty much declined towards the street. **1849** RUSKIN *Sev. Lamps* iv. §23. 113 The uprightness of the form declined against the marble ledge.

†**19.** To undervalue, disparage, depreciate. *Obs.*

1509 HAWES *Past. Pleas.* XI. ix, She can not declyne The noble science, whiche, after poverte, Maye bryng a man agayne to dignitie. **1626** SHIRLEY *Brothers* I. i, Unless you disaffect His person, or decline his education. **1649** SIR E. NICHOLAS in *N. Papers* (Camden) I. 143 What is here said is not with intencion to undervallue or decline yᵉ Presbiterians.

*** *To inflect grammatically.*

20. a. *Gram.* To inflect (a noun, adjective, or pronoun) through its different cases; to go through or recite in order the cases of. (Cf. DECLENSION 4.)

Also used more widely, or loosely, of verbs (for which the proper word is CONJUGATE).

1387 TREVISA *Higden* (Rolls) I. 327 (Mätz.) ȝif þou canst declyne þilke tweye names and speke Latyn. **1398** —— *Barth. De P.R.* XVIII. xc. (1495) 839 Rinoceron is declined, hic Rinoceron, huius Rinocerontis. **1530** PALSGR. 65 Of whiche [IX partes of speche] v be declined, that is to say varie their last letters: article, nowne, pronowne, verbe and participle. **1612** BRINSLEY *Lud. Lit.* vi. (1627) 56 Of these eight parts, the foure first onely are such as may be declined. **1654** TRAPP *Comm. Ps.* xvi. 4 It was the Serpents grammar that first taught man to decline God in the plurall number. *a* **1843** SOUTHEY *Doctor* (1862) 40 That verb is eternally being declined. **1871** ROBY *Lat. Gram.* I. §339 The substantive stems in *-a* (chiefly feminine), and the feminine form of those adjectives which have stems in *-o*, are declined alike.

†**b.** *transf.* To say or recite formally or in definite order. *Obs.*

1594 SHAKS. *Rich. III*, IV. iv. 97 Decline all this, and see what now thou art. **1606** —— *Tr. & Cr.* II. iii. 55 Ile declin the whole question. **1627** DRAYTON *Agincourt* 201 That you no harsh, nor shallow rimes decline, Vpon that day wherein you shall read mine.

declined (dɪˈklaɪnd, *poet.* dɪˈklaɪnɪd), *ppl. a.* [f. DECLINE *v.* + -ED¹.] Turned aside, deflected; sloped, oblique; brought low, debased, decayed; advanced towards its close: see the verb.

1591 *Declar. Gt. Troubles* in *Harl. Misc.* (Malh.) II. 210 Now in his declined yeeres. **1593** SHAKS. *Lucr.* 1705 My low declined Honor to aduance. **1667** HALE *Prim. Orig. Man.* I. i. 10 Their declined Motions. **1792** MRS. C. SMITH *Desmond* I. 129 Ecclesiastics..whose declined authority..you regret. **1798** WASHINGTON *Let.* Writ. (1893) XIV. 38 My earnest wish, that the choice had fallen on a man less declined in years.

Hence **deˈclinedness.**

1648 BP. HALL *Select Thoughts* §68 The common fault of age, loquacity, is a plain evidence of the world's declinedness.

†**deˈclinement.** *Obs. rare.* [f. DECLINE *v.* + -MENT.] = DECLINATURE.

1680 *Privy Council Proc. Edin.* in *Cloud of Witnesses* (1810) 30 The causes of his declinement are, because they have usurped the supremacy over the church..and have established idolatry, perjury, and other iniquities.

decliner (dɪˈklaɪnə(r)). [-ER¹.] One who or that which declines.

†**1.** One who turns aside, deviates, or falls away (from his duty or allegiance, or from an approved standard of conduct or belief). *Obs.*

1601 DENT *Pathw. Heaven* 259 Backsliders, Decliners, and cold Christians. **1651** BAXTER *Inf. Bapt.* 193 Censured as decliners or erroneous. **1684** RENWICK *Serm.* iv. (1776) 44 All that join with decliners in an ill time.

2. One who refuses or waives; in *Sc. Law*, one who declines the jurisdiction of a judge or court.

1639 R. BAILLIE *Lett.* I. 161, A chief declyner of the Assemblie. **1641** EVELYN *Diary* (1871) 20 My Father..(who was one of the greatest decliners of it). **1748** RICHARDSON *Clarissa* (1811) III. liv. 301 Do not..be so very melancholy a decliner as to prefer a shroud, when the matter you wish for is in your power.

3. *Dialling.* A plane which (or a dial whose plane) 'declines' or deviates from the meridian or prime vertical, and therefore does not pass through any of the four cardinal points.

[**1669** STURMY *Mariner's Mag.* VII. xvi. 25 For these East Recliners be in very deed South Decliners to those that live 90 deg. from us Northward or Southward.] **1684** *Ibid.* (ed. 3) VII. vi. 118 Direct Dials have their Poles in the Meridian or prime Vertical, Decliners have their Poles in some other Azimuth. **1703** MOXON *Mech. Exerc.* 311 Of Decliners there are infinite; and yet may be reduced into..1. The South Erect Plane, declining more or less towards the East or West. 2. The North Erect Plane, declining more or less towards the East or West.

declining (dɪˈklaɪnɪŋ), *vbl. sb.* [-ING¹.] The action of the verb DECLINE, q.v. (Formerly frequent as a sb.; now usually gerundial.)

1. Turning aside, falling away; = DECLENSION 2.

1526 *Pilgr. Perf.* (W. de W. 1531) 34 b, Our general labour must stande in.. declynynge from euyll, and in dylygent workynge of good. **1574** W. TRAVERS (*title*), Full and plaine Declaration of Ecclesiasticall Discipline and off the Declininge off the Churche off Englande. **1646** P. BULKELEY *Gospel Covt.* IV. 347 In times of general declining. **1650** R. HOLLINGWORTH *Exerc. Usurped Powers* 39 Partiall and temporary declinings in men from their said integritie.

2. Avoidance (*obs.*); non-acceptance; refusal.

1607 TOPSELL *Four-f. Beasts* (1673) 111 If any fall or sit down on the ground and cast away his weapon, they bite him not; taking that declining for submissive pacification. **1636** MASSINGER *Bashf. Lover* V. i, There is now No contradiction or declining left: I must and will go on. **1786** MAD. D'ARBLAY *Diary* 7 Aug., To save myself from more open and awkward declinings.

3. Gradual sinking or descent; downward slope or declivity.

1601 CORNWALLYES *Disc. Seneca* (1631) 7 Being once brought to that declining, they never leave rolling untill they come to the bottome of unhappinesse. **1602** CAREW *Cornwall* 145 b, Upon the declyning of a hill the house is seated. **1612** BREREWOOD *Lang. & Relig.* xiii. 139 Pliny, in the derivation of water, requireth one cubit of declining in 240 foot of proceeding. *a* **1703** POMFRET *Poet. Wks.* (1833) 9 A short and dubious bliss On the declining of a precipice.

4. Of the sun, etc.: Descent towards setting; hence of the day, one's life, etc.: Drawing to its close; = DECLINE *sb.* 2.

1588 A. KING tr. *Canisius' Catech.* I viij, Ye hicht and declyning of ye sone. *a* **1610** HEALEY *Theophrastus* xxvii. (1636) 92 The going downe of our strength, and the declining of our age. *a* **1662** HEYLIN *Laud.* I. 64 In the declining of the year 1616.

5. Falling off, decay, decreasing, waning, etc.; = DECLINE *sb.* 1.

1481 CAXTON *Myrr.* III. i. 131 Yf the sonne and therthe were of one lyke gretenesse, this shadowe shold haue none ende, but shold be all egal without declynyng. **1581** MULCASTER *Positions* xxxvii. (1887) 159 All that..write of the declining and ruine of the Romain Empire. **1622** DRAYTON *Poly-olb.* xix. (1748) 333 Rest content, nor our declining rue. **1645** MILTON *Tetrach.* (1851) 201 The next declining is, when law becomes now too straight for the secular manners, and those too loose for the cincture of law.

6. *Gram.* = DECLENSION 4; formerly in wider sense: Inflexion, including conjugation.

1565-78 COOPER *Thesaurus* Introd., Nownes and verbes maye be knowne by their declining. **1599** MINSHEU *Span. Gram.* 35 The verbes Irregular (in which is found hardnes and difficultie to the learner for their declining). **1612** BRINSLEY *Pos. Parts* (1669) 108 There are certain Adjectives which have two manner of endings and declinings..both in *us* and *is*. **1740** J. CLARKE *Educ. Youth* (ed. 3) 82 The Article is of no Manner of Use for the Declining of Nouns.

deˈclining, *ppl. a.* [-ING².] That declines: see the verb.

1. Having a downward inclination, sloping downwards; oblique.

1553 EDEN *Treat. Newe Ind.* (Arb.) 14 It standeth in a place somewhat declyning. **1571** DIGGES *Pantom.* III. Q b, This perpendicular..in directe solides falleth within the body, and vppon the base, but in declyning solides, it falleth without the bodies and bases. **1655-60** STANLEY *Hist. Philos.* (1701) 9/2 The height of the great Pyramid..is by its perpendicular..499 Feet, by its declining ascent, 693 Feet. **1792** *Copper-plate Mag.* No. 1 The mansion..is approached by a circular sweep through a declining lawn. **1802-3** tr. *Pallas' Trav.* (1812) I. 61 The Volga, which flows..through a gradually-declining valley.

b. *Dialling.* Deviating from the prime vertical or meridian: see DECLINATION 9.

1593 FALE *Dialling* 4 All such plats as behold not some principall part of the world directly, are called Declining. The quantity of their declination is found out thus. **1640** WILKINS *New Planet* ii. (1707) 165 In all declining Dials, the Elevation of whose Pole is less than the Sun's greatest Declination. **1669** STURMY *Mariner's Mag.* VII. xvi. 25 All Declining Planes lie in some Azimuth, and cross one another in the Zenith and Nadir. **1703** MOXON *Mech. Exerc.* 311.

2. Bending or bowing down; drooping.

1596 SHAKS. *Tam. Shr.* I. i. 119 With..tempting kisses, And with declining head. **1776** WITHERING *Brit. Plants* (1796) III. 605 Pedicles declining, Flower-scales cloven. **1816** BYRON *Siege Cor.* xix, Declining was his attitude.

3. Of the sun: Sinking towards setting; *transf.* of the day: Drawing to its close.

c **1620** T. ROBINSON *M. Magd.* 375 The Sun peep'd in with his declininge raye. **1697** DRYDEN *Virg. Georg.* IV. 273 Nor end their Work, but with declining Day. **1833** HT. MARTINEAU *Vanderput & S.* ix. 133 The beams of the declining sun glistering on the heaving surface. **1834** S. ROGERS *Poems* 126 Till declining day, Thro' the green trellis shoots a crimson ray.

4. Falling off from vigour, excellence, or prosperity; becoming weaker or worse; failing, waning, decaying (in health, fortunes, etc.); in a decline.

1593 SHAKS. *Rich. II*, II. i. 240 In this declining Land. **1603** KNOLLES *Hist. Turks* Introd., The long and still declining state of the Christian Commonweale. **1745** *De Foe's English Tradesman* (1841) I. vii. 53, I speak it to every declining tradesman. **1776** GIBBON *Decl. & F.* I. 401 The declining health of the emperor Constantius. **1876** J. H. NEWMAN *Hist. Sk.* I. I. iii. 121 This desolation is no accident of a declining empire.

b. Of a person's age, life, years, etc. (Mixture of senses 3 and 4.)

1615 LATHAM *Falconry* (1633) 31 Towards their declining age. **1697** DRYDEN *Æneid* IX. 638 Thus looks the prop of my declining years! **1780** JOHNSON *Lett. to Mrs. Thrale* 18 Apr., Declining life is a very awful scene. **1875** JOWETT *Plato* (ed. 2) V. 7 Such a sadness was the natural effect of declining years and failing powers.

5. That declines (jurisdiction); that refuses to accept, etc.

1639 BAILLIE *Lett. & Jrnls.* I. 155 A present excommunicating of all the declyning Bishops.

deˈclinist. *nonce-wd.* [f. DECLINE *sb.* + -IST.] (See quot.)

1831 WHEWELL in Todhunter *Acc. Whewell's Writ.* (1876) II. 122 [Dr. Brewster] has now chosen to fancy that we are all banded together to oppose his favourite doctrine of the decline of science; though the only professor who has written at all on the subject is Babbage, the leader of the Declinists.

declinograph (dɪˈklaɪnəʊgrɑːf, -æ). [irreg. f. L. *dēclīnāre* (as etymon of *declination*) + -GRAPH, Gr. -γραφος writing.] An astronomical instrument or arrangement for automatically recording the declination of stars with a filar micrometer.

1883 D. GILL in *Encycl. Brit.* XVI. 256 It is found with this declinograph on the Berlin equatorial, that the observed declinations have only a probable error of ±0·9″.

declinometer (dɛklɪˈnɒmɪtə(r)). *Magn.* [irreg. f. as prec. + -METER, Gr. μέτρον measure.]

1. *Magn.* An instrument for measuring the variation of the magnetic needle.

1858 in SIMMONDS *Dict. Trade.* **1870** R. M. FERGUSON *Electr.* 19 Instruments for determining magnetic declination are called declination needles or declinometers. **1881** MAXWELL *Electr. & Magn.* II. 112 The declinometer gives the declination at every instant.

2. *Astr.* An instrument for observing and registering declination.

1883 D. GILL in *Encycl. Brit.* XVI. 255 Bond's mica declinometer.

[**declinous**, *a.* Error for DECLIVOUS.

1864 in WEBSTER; hence in some later Dicts.]

[**declivant**, *a.* Error for DECLINANT.

1830 ROBSON *Brit. Herald*, Declinant or Declivant. Hence **1881** OGILVIE (Annandale), Declinant, Declivant. **1890** in *Century Dict.*]

deˈclivate, *a.* [irreg. f. L. *dēclīv-is*: see DECLIVE.] 'Descending; declining; inclining downward' (*Syd. Soc. Lex.* 1881).

†**declive** (dɪˈklaɪv), *a. Obs.* [a. F. *déclive* (Paré 16th c. in Surg. sense), ad. L. *dēclīvis* sloping downward, f. DE- I. 1 + *clīv-us* slope, hill.]

Sloping downwards.

1635 SWAN *Spec. M.* vi. §2 (1643) 188 The waters coming down from the Caspian hills settling themselves in those declive and bottomie places where the said Sea is. **1644** DIGBY *Nat. Bodies* xx. (1658) 228 An easier and more declive bed. **1669** W. SIMPSON *Hydrol. Chym.* 284 Declive currents out of brooks.

†**declived**, *a. Obs.* [f. L. *dēclīvis* (see prec.) or ? error for *declined*.]

1575 BANISTER *Chyrurg.* II. (1585) 373 Open the skull in the most bending or declived place.

declivitous (dɪˈklɪvɪtəs), *a.* [f. L. type **dēclīvitōs-us*, f. *dēclīvitās*: see DECLIVITY and -OUS: cf. ACCLIVITOUS.] Having a (considerable) declivity or slope; steep.

1799 R. WARNER *Walk* (1800) 94 The approach to Culbone church is by a small foot-path, narrow, rugged and ..declivitous. 1802 BRAY *Jrnl.* in Mrs. Bray *Descr. Devon* (1835) I. 237 The declivitous sides of this tor. 1882 *Proc. Berw. Nat. Club* IX. 454 In descending the next declivitous hill.

de'clivitously, *adv.* [f. DECLIVITOUS *a.* + -LY².] In a declivitous manner; on or down a steep slope.

1878 I. L. BIRD in *Leisure Hour* 5 Oct. 637/2 A good hotel declivitously situated. 1930 W. J. LOCKE *Town of Tombarel* vii. 215 The path lands you declivitously into the Place Georges Clemenceau.

declivity (dɪˈklɪvɪtɪ). [ad. L. *dēclīvitāt-em*, f. *dēclīv-is*: see DECLIVE and -ITY. Cf. F. *déclivité* (Dict. Acad. 1762).]

1. Downward slope or inclination (of a hill, etc.).

1612 BREREWOOD *Lang. & Relig.* xiv. 147 It is the property of water ever to fall that way, where it findeth declivity. 1666 *Phil. Trans.* I. 361 With what declivity the Water runs out of the Euxine Sea into the Propontis. 1818 BYRON *Ch. Har.* IV. lxvii, Upon a mild declivity of hill. 1860 HAWTHORNE *Fr. & It. Jrnls.* II. 301 The declivity of most of the streets keeps them remarkably clean.

2. *concr.* A downward slope.

1695 WOODWARD *Nat. Hist. Earth* VI. (1723) 280 They will not flow unless upon a Declivity. 1794 MRS. RADCLIFFE *Myst. Udolpho* i, A grove which stood on the brow of a gentle declivity. 1860 TYNDALL *Glac.* I. viii. 58, I could see the stones..jumping down the declivities.

declivous (dɪˈklaɪvəs), *a.* [f. L. *dēclīv-us*, rare var. of *dēclīv-is* (see DECLIVE) + -OUS: cf. ACCLIVOUS.] Having a downward inclination; sloping, slanting. (Now *rare* exc. as in b.)

1684 tr. *Bonet's Merc. Compit.* v. 141 Pus..may this way better run out, because of the more declivous site of the opening. *a*1722 LISLE *Husb.* (1752) 173 On a ground declivous from the sun. 1786 GILPIN *Pict. Beauty Cumbrld.* (1808) I. xiv. 211 We left the Derwent in its declivous course between two mountains. 1853 G. JOHNSTON *Nat. Hist. E. Bord.* I. 251 This hurries along as the gap deepens, and becomes, at every step, more declivous.

b. *spec.* in *Zool.* Sloping downwards.

1847 JOHNSTON in *Proc. Berw. Nat. Club* II. 228 Rostrum long, tapered, porrect, declivous. 1877 COUES *Fur Anim.* iv. 99 Frontal profile..strongly declivous.

†**de'clivy**, *a. Obs. rare.* [f. L. *dēclīvi-s*: cf. CLIVY.] Sloping downwards.

1609 HEYWOOD *Brit. Troy* VII. xii. 143 There is a steepe declivy way lookes downe.

†**de'close**, *v. Obs. rare.* [See DE- I. 6.] = DISCLOSE.

14.. *Prose Legends* in *Anglia* VIII. 115 It maye not be perceyued þat she holdith þe sacramente in hir mouþe..or swolowes or decloseþ hit in her mouþe.

declutch (diːˈklʌtʃ), *v.* [f. DE- II. 1 + CLUTCH *sb.*¹ 6 a.] *intr.* To disengage the clutch of a motor vehicle; so **double-declutch** *v. intr.*, to release and re-engage the clutch twice when changing gear. Hence **de'clutching** *vbl. sb.*

1905 *Daily Chron.* 21 Mar. 7/4 Without once using a brake, changing his gear, declutching or slipping the clutch. 1906 *Westm. Gaz.* 16 July 5/1 The driver of the 'bus declutched at the top of the hill. 1925 *Morris Owner's Man.* 10 The expert driver will have recourse to double declutching. 1934 *Neuphilologische Mitteilungen* XXXV. 130 To *double-declutch*, to let the clutch in twice (instead of the more usual once) when changing gear. 1937 *Autocar Handbk.* (ed. 13) vi. 108 Syncromesh..rendered double declutching a refinement but no longer a necessity. 1963 *Which?* (Car Suppl.) Jan. 30 To make proper downward gear changes you had to double-declutch. 1966 'D. RUTHERFORD' *Black Leather Murders* i. 7 He double-declutched and rammed the gear-lever into bottom.

'Deco. Also deco. Short for *art deco* s.v. ART *sb.* VI c. Usu. *attrib.*

1969 *Harper's Bazaar* Oct. 36/3 'Fish', that most Decadent of Deco designers. 1974 K. MILLETT *Flying* (1975) II. 130 We inspect the great Deco mansion now decaying. 1981 *Times* 13 Apr. 14/5 A London dealer paid a surprisingly high price in the deco section. 1984 *Washington Post* 13 May D6/2 We loved the Deco feel of the place, the tile floor, the banquettes of red velvet.

†**de'coct**, *sb. Obs. rare*⁻¹. [ad. L. *dēcoct-um* sb., prop. neuter of pa. pple. *dēcoct-us*: see next.] A decoction.

1551 TURNER *Herbal* I. (1568) O ij a, To gyue the decoct or broth of it wyth wyne vnto nurses, when they want mylke.

†**de'coct**, *ppl. a. Obs.* [ad. L. *dēcoct-us*, pa. pple. of *dēcoqu-ĕre* to boil down or away. In earlier use, both as pple. and adj., than DECOCT *v.*, after the introduction of which this continued for some time as its pa. pple., till gradually superseded by the regular *decocted*.]

1. Decocted; subjected to heat; digested, etc.: see the verb.

*c*1420 *Pallad. on Husb.* I. 650 Puls decoct and colde. 1505 FISHER *Penit. Ps.* Wks. (1876) 177 The hete of thy charyte whereby we may be decocte and made harde as stones. 1533 ELYOT *Cast. Helth* (1541) 9 a, Matter decocte or boyled in the stomacke. 1545 RAYNOLD *Byrth Mankynde* II. vi. (1634) 122 Wine in which is decoct Motherwort. 1671 SALMON *Syn. Med.* III. xxii. 434 The root decoct in water purgeth Flegm and Choller.

2. Bankrupt. [L. *dēcoquĕre* to run through one's estate, become bankrupt.]

1529 WOLSEY *To Ambassadors at Rome* (*MS. Cott. Vit. B.* xi. f. 83), The banker of Venice, to whom ye wer assigned by Anthony Viualde for viij^m ducates is decoct.

decoct (dɪˈkɒkt), *v.* [f. DECOCT *ppl. a.* or L. *dēcoct-*, ppl. stem of *dēcoqu-ĕre* to boil down or away, f. DE- I. 3 b + *coquĕre* to boil, cook.]

†1. To boil down or away; to concentrate by boiling. *Obs.*

1538 LELAND *Itin.* IV. 111 The Wychmen use the Commodity of their Sault Springes in drawinge and decocting the Water of them onely by 6 Monthes in the Yeare. 1548 VICARY *Englishm. Treas.* (1626) 177 Let all these be decocted to the forme of a Syrope. 1620 VENNER *Via Recta* (1650) 141 This being the third time diluted and decocted.

fig. *a*1661 FULLER *Worthies* (1840) I. ii. 7 A Proverb is much matter decocted into few words.

†2. *fig.* To diminish, consume, waste. *Obs.* [So L. *dēcoquĕre*.]

1629 N. CARPENTER *Achitophel* III. 54 To haue decocted his fortunes and an ancient family. 1654 H. L'ESTRANGE *Chas. I* (1655) 130 Had he wasted and decocted his Treasure in luxury and riot. *a*1677 BARROW *Serm.* Wks. 1716 I. 123 When the predominant vanities of the age are somewhat decocted.

†3. To prepare as food by the agency of fire; to boil, cook. *Obs.*

*c*1420 [see DECOCT *ppl. a.*]. 1547 BOORDE *Brev. Health* cccxxxv. 108 b, As the fyre doth decocte the meates and the broth in the pot, so doth the liuer vnder the stomake decoct the meat in mannes body. 1657 TOMLINSON *Renou's Disp.* 66 Flesh is decocted at the fire on a spit.

†b. *transf.* To warm up, as in cooking. *Obs.*

1599 SHAKS. *Hen V*, III. v. 20 Can sodden Water..Decoct their cold blood to such valiant heat?

†4. To digest in the stomach. (Regarded as a kind of cooking; cf. CONCOCT *v.* 4.) Also *fig.*

1533 [see DECOCT *ppl. a.*]. 1542 BOORDE *Dyetary* ix. (1870) 250 A surfyt is whan..the lyuer, whiche is the fyre vnder the potte..can not naturally nor truely decocte, defye, ne dygest, the superabundaunce of meate & drynke the whiche is in the potte or stomacke. 1547 [see prec.]. 1592 DAVIES *Immort. Soul* XII. ii. (1714) 64 There she decocts, and doth the Food prepare. 1608 S. HIERON *2nd Pt. Def. Ministers' Reas. Refus. Subscription* 121 More gredily disposed to devoure and swallowe..then to decocte and reteine.

†5. To prepare or mature (metals or mineral ores) by heat. (Pertaining to old notions of natural science: cf. CONCOCT *v.* 2.) *Obs.*

1505 [see DECOCT *ppl. a.*]. 1610 GUILLIM *Heraldry* III. vi. (1660) 126 Metals are bodies imperfectly living, and are decocted in the veins of the Earth. 1653 H. COGAN *Diod. Sic.* 231 The iron which is made of these stones decocted in furnaces, they divide into pieces.

†6. *fig.* To prepare, devise, CONCOCT. *Obs. rare.*

1602 MARSTON *Antonio's Rev.* IV. iii, What villanie are they decocting now? 1613 T. MILLES *Treas. Aunc. & Mod. Times* 718/1 A word to win Laughter must be quickly decocted, woorking upon some sudden and unexpected thing.

7. To boil so as to extract the soluble parts or principles; to prepare a decoction of.

1545 [see DECOCT *ppl. a.*]. 1599 A. M. tr. *Gabelhouer's Bk. Physicke* 79/1 Decocte a vivificente Eele, in a pot of water, skimme therof the axungietye of the Eele, reserve the same, & let it stand a certayn time. 1664 EVELYN *Sylva* (1679) 29 Young red Oaken leaves decocted in wine, make an excellent gargle for a sore mouth. 1743 *Lond. & Country Brew.* II. (ed. 2) 101 The common Way of infusing and decocting Herbs a long Time, is injurious to Health.

Hence **de'cocted** *ppl. a.*

*a*1593 MARLOWE *Ignoto*, To do thee good, I'll freely spend my thrice-decocted blood [cf. CONCOCTION 1 b]. 1616 R. C. *Times' Whistle* vi. 2770 Fine gellies of decocted sparrowes bones. 1725 BRADLEY *Fam. Dict.* s.v. *Sallet*, Some few tops of the decocted Leaves may be admitted.

de'coctible, *a. rare*⁻⁰. [f. L. *dēcoct-* ppl. stem: see DECOCT and -BLE.] Capable of being decocted.

1656 BLOUNT *Glossogr.*, *Decoctible*, easie to be sodden or boyled. 1730–6 in BAILEY (folio). Hence in JOHNSON, etc.

decoction (dɪˈkɒkʃən). Also 4–5 -cyon, 5–6 -cioun, 6 decokcien. [a. OF. *decoction*, *-cocciun* (13th c.), ad. L. *dēcoctiōn-em*, n. of action f. *dēcoquĕre* to DECOCT.]

1. The action of decocting; *esp.* boiling in water or other liquid so as to extract the soluble parts or principles of the substance.

*c*1430 LYDG. *Min. Poems* (1840) 82 (Mätz.) The coke by mesour sesonyth his potages..By decoccioune to take theyr avauntages. 1502 ARNOLDE *Chron.* 165 Moysted wᵗ water of the decokcien of benes. 1605 TIMME *Quersit.* I. vi. 24 The airey..parts..are separated by decoction. 1718 QUINCY *Compl. Disp.* 112 This Plant affords a very soft mucilaginous Substance in Decoction. 1807 T. THOMSON *Chem.* (ed. 3) II. 357 Catechu..is a substance obtained by decoction and evaporation from a species of mimosa which abounds in India.

†b. Digestion. *Obs.*

1533 ELYOT *Cast. Helth* (1541) 8 b, By insufficient decoction in the second digestion. 1658 A. FOX *Wurtz' Surg.* I. ix. 36 The stomack hath a decoction to digest the meats he feedeth on.

†2. Maturing or perfecting by heat; *esp.* of metals or mineral ores. *Obs.*

(Pertaining to old notions as to the composition and formation of metals: cf. CONCOCTION 2.)

1430 LYDG. *Chron. Troy* IV. xxxiii, To white he tourneth with his beames shene Both sede and graine by decoction. 1555 EDEN *Decades* 334 By the helpe of fermentacion and decoction of the minerall heate. 1577–87 HARRISON *England* III. xi. 237 The substance of sulphur and quicksiluer being mixed in due proportion, after long and temperate decoction in the bowels of the earth..becommeth gold. 1671 J. WEBSTER *Metallogr.* iv. 73 According to the variety of the degrees of decoction and alteration, into divers metallick forms.

†3. Reduction by evaporation in boiling, boiling down; *fig.* reduction. *Obs.*

1650 FULLER *Pisgah* I. II. viii. 174 The body of his men remaining was still too big, and must pass another decoction. 1655 —— *Ch. Hist.* III. v. §34 Four and twenty prime persons were chosen..which soon after (to make them the more cordiall) passed a decoction, and were reduced to three.

4. A liquor in which a substance, usually animal or vegetable, has been boiled, and in which the principles thus extracted are dissolved; *spec.* as a medicinal agent.

1398 TREVISA *Barth. De P.R.* XVI. ciii. (Tollem. MS.), þis ston [lapis lazuli] schal not be ȝeue with decoccyon. *c*1400 *Lanfranc's Cirurg.* 216 Waische þe place wiþ a decoccioun of camomille. 1563 T. GALE *Antidot.* II. 8 Decoctions..be liquors and other thynges boyled together and then strayned. 1607 TOPSELL *Four-f. Beasts* (1673) 332 A 'decoction' is..the broath of certain hearbs or simples boyled together in water till the third part be consumed. 1741 BERKELEY *Let.* Wks. 1871 IV. 266 The receipt of a decoction of briar-roots for the bloody flux. 1833 J. RENNIE *Alph. Angling*, Lines..tinted by a decoction of oak bark.

de'coctive, *a. rare*⁻⁰. [f. L. *dēcoct-* ppl. stem + -IVE.] Pertaining to decoction; having the quality of decocting.

1727 BAILEY vol. II, *Decoctive*, easily sodden. 1775 in ASH. 1828 in WEBSTER. Hence in mod. Dicts.

†**de'coctor.** *Obs. rare.* [a. L. *dēcoctor*, agent-n. f. *dēcoquĕre* to DECOCT.] One who wastes or squanders; a ruined spendthrift.

1615 CROOKE *Body of Man* 37 Wee..may worthily be accounted decoctors and prodigals, if we keepe not our Patrimony together. 1622 MALYNES *Anc. Law-Merch.* 224 The Ciuilians..haue attributed vnto this kind of people, the name of Decoctor..otherwise called disturbers or consumers of other mens goods in the course of trafficke.

†**de'cocture.** *Obs.*⁻⁰ [ad. L. *dēcoctūra*, f. *dēcoct-*: see DECOCT, and -URE.] = DECOCTION 4.

1727 BAILEY vol. II, *Decocture*, a Decoction, a Broth or Liquor wherein things have been boiled. Hence in JOHNSON, and mod. Dicts.

decode (diːˈkəʊd), *v.* [f. DE- II + CODE *sb.*¹ 3 b or CODE *v.* 1 b.] *trans.* To decipher or translate (a coded message). Also *absol.* and *transf.* Hence **de'coded** *ppl. a.*; **de'coder**, one who or that which decodes (see also quots. 1962 and 1964); **de'coding** *vbl. sb.*

1896 *N. Brit. Daily Mail* 28 Aug. 5 The message was decoded. 1897 *Westm. Gaz.* 26 Jan. 2/1 If it seems desirable, I shall decode and publish at my own time. *Ibid.* 18 May 7/1 The decoded cables. 1897 *Daily News* 15 May 4/6 Formal evidence as to the de-coding of the Harris-Rhodes telegrams was given. 1897 *Times* 30 June 9 The cipher telegrams in which they and Mr. Rhodes are concerned, and which have now been decoded. 1920 *Glasgow Herald* 20 Aug. 8 The alleged decoded messages..contain ludicrous statements. As to whether it is due to incompetence in decoding,..we are not competent to judge. *Ibid.*, The decoder on his own showing was doubtful as to his interpretation. 1937 KOESTLER *Spanish Testament* II. iii. 263 Finally we landed up somewhere in the decoding department. 1956 *Spaceflight* I. 27/2 Received at the ground station, this signal is decoded automatically and interpreted as a series of line graphs. 1957 *Electronic Engin.* XXIX. 574 The decoders were produced in the laboratory at a cost of about £50 each. 1962 *Gloss. Autom. Data Processing* (*B.S.I.*) 83 *Decoder.* 1. A device capable of decoding a group of signals and generating other signals which may initiate an operation. 2. In data-processing equipment. A device with a number of input and output lines in which a specified combination of input signals causes a particular output line to give a signal. 1964 F. L. WESTWATER *Electronic Computers* (ed. 2) i. 2 Before it can operate, the computer must have numbers presented in the form which it can understand. This requires some kind of decoder or mechanism which will translate a number into a suitably recognisable electrical impulse. *Ibid.* vi. 99 Information on a card is normally decimal in character and has to be decoded into whatever binary code a computer employs. The decoding circuitry is..part of the computer design.

†'**decognize**, *v. nonce-wd.* [f. DE- I. 6 + COGNIZE.] *trans.* To cease or fail to recognize.

1658–9 *Burton's Diary* (1828) III. 275 There was no recognition to King Charles, and no need of it..I can decognize Charles Stuart and that family, but recognize I cannot.

decohere (diːkəʊˈhɪə(r)), *v.* [f. DE- II. 1 + COHERE *v.*] *trans.* To restore (a coherer) to its normal condition of sensitiveness. Also *absol.*, and *intr.* for *pass.* (Disused.)

1902 *How to make Useful Things* 5/1 The purpose of the tapper is to decohere the filings after they are affected by the etheric waves. *Ibid.* 6/1 The tapper keeps busily at work decohering in response to the continuously closing circuit caused by the waves. **1923** E. W. MARCHANT *Radio Telegr.* iv. 38 By using mercury, Lodge and others made coherers which decohered without tapping. **1924** S. R. ROGET *Dict. Electr. Terms* 58/2 A coherer is said to 'decohere' when it resumes its normal feebly conducting state on tapping or disturbance, after it has been made conducting by electrical oscillations, etc.

Hence **decoˈherence, decoˈhesion; decoˈherer,** a device for bringing a coherer back to its normal condition.

1899 MARCONI in *Jrnl. Inst. Electr. Engin.* XXVIII. 275 This coherer forms part of a circuit.. which circuit works a trembler or decoherer and a recording instrument. **1902** *Science* 21 Mar. 466 A short description of the single contact coherer used by him and an explanation of the so-called decohesion. **1902** *Young Engineer* I. 371/2 As the coherer is continuously rotating, decoherence follows immediately on coherence. **1903** *Sci. Abstr.* B. VI. 128 The self-induction of the telephone may have been sufficient to cause the decoherence. **1913** *Work* 4 Oct. 7/2 The decoherer circuit.

decoir, -ment, variants of DECORE, -MENT.

decoit, decoity: see DACOIT, -Y.

decoke (diːˈkəʊk), *v. colloq.* [f. DE- II. 2 + COKE *sb.*] **a.** *trans.* = DECARBONIZE *v.* **b.** Also *transf.* Hence **deˈcoking** *vbl. sb.*

1928 *Daily Express* 19 May 13/2 My advice to all motorists who are puzzled about.. the 'knocking' which invariably accompanies carbonisation, is that they should lose not an hour in getting the engine 'decoked'. *Ibid.* 31 May 3/7 Good car, but wants decoking. **1931** *Boys' Mag.* XLV. 169/1 The presence of the carbon will cause overheating, bad hill-climbing and loss of power, so when any of these things persist, it is time for the engine to be 'decoked'. **1958** M. PUGH *Wilderness of Monkeys* iii. 32 He found his pipe, decoked it with a spike intended to hold papers and was about to light it. *Ibid.* viii. 98 A meat skewer, which he normally used in decoking his pipe.

decoke (diːˈkəʊk), *sb. colloq.* [f. the vb.] = DECARBONIZATION b.

1962 'A. GARVE' *Prisoner's Friend* i. 35 Mr. Winter's car.. it's in for a de-coke. **1967** *Observer* (Colour Suppl.) 28 May 35/1 Do your own de-coke for.. half the normal garage charge.

†**deˈcoll,** *v. Obs.* [a. F. *décolle-r*, or ad. L. *dēcollā-re.*] *trans.* To behead; = DECOLLATE *v.*[1] Hence **deˈcolling** *vbl. sb.* and *ppl. a.*

1648 *Parliamentary Hist.* (R.), By a speedy public dethroning and decolling of the King. **1649** PRYNNE *Vind. Liberty Eng.* 19 In the King's own case, whom they decolled. **1653** E. CHISENHALE *Cath. Hist.* 462 The only decolling instrument of Principality and Temporal Power.

†**decollate,** *ppl. a. Obs.* or *arch.* [ad. L. *dēcollāt-us*, pa. pple. of *dēcollāre*: see next.] Beheaded: in early use as *pa. pple.*

c **1470** HARDING *Chron.* LXX. iii, He was heded with swerd and decollate. **1868** BROWNING *Ring & Bk.* XII. 268 All five, to-day, have suffered death.. he, Decollate by mere due of privilege, The rest hanged decently and in order.

decollate (dɪˈkɒleɪt, ˈdɛkəleɪt), *v.*[1] [f. L. *dēcollāt-*, ppl. stem of *dēcollā-re* to behead, f. DE- I. 6 + *collum* neck. As adaptation of L. *dēcollāt-us*, *decollate* as pa. pple. was in use before any other part of the verb: see prec.]

1. *trans.* To sever at the neck; to behead.

1599 A. M. tr. *Gabelhouer's Bk. Physicke* 30/2 With on blow beheaded, or decollated. **1635** HEYWOOD *Hierarch.* VII. 474 A statue with three heads.. two of them were quite beat off and the Third was much bruised but not decollated. **1656** H. PHILLIPS *Purch. Patt.* (1676) 257 Sir Walter Rawleigh decollated. **1782** W. F. MARTYN *Geog. Mag.* I. 720 The murderer.. is instantly decollated. **1814** SOUTHEY in *Q. Rev.* XII. 223 Upon taking off the cloth he beheld a human head just decollated.

2. *Conch.* To break off the apex of (a shell).

1854 WOODWARD *Mollusca* (1856) 96 The inner courses of this shell probably break away or are 'decollated' in the progress of its growth.

decollate (diːkəˈleɪt, ˈdɛkəleɪt), *v.*[2] [f. DE- II. 1 + COLLATE *v.*] *intr.* To separate sheets of paper, etc., esp. multi-part continuous stationery, mechanically into different piles. Hence **decoˈllating** *vbl. sb.* Cf. DECOLLATOR[2].

1967 D. WILSON in Wills & Yearsley *Handbk. Managem. Technol.* 46 A wide range of document-handling equipment is marketed, which will decollate (separate carbons from printed sheets). **1979** *Fortune* 12 Mar. 27 There's no need for.. printing and storing preprinted forms. Going through the trouble of changing them. Or bursting, decollating, reloading or retyping. **1982** *Computerworld* 29 Nov. SR/19 One-part computer paper costs $33 per thousand pages... To that must be added the costs for the actual printing, collating, decollating and distribution. **1984** *Mag. Bank Admin.* Jan. 84/3 [The] T7070 burster bursts and slits one to four-ply forms at a rate of up to 300 feet per minute and can also decollate as it bursts.

decollated, *ppl. a.* [f. DECOLLATE *v.*[1] + -ED.]

1. Severed at the neck; beheaded, decapitated.

1662 OGILBY *King's Coronation* 3 A Trophy with decollated Heads. **1756** BURKE *Subl. & B.* Introd. 23 A fine piece of a decollated head of St. John the Baptist was shewn to a Turkish emperor. *a* **1845** BARHAM *Ingol. Leg.*, *Jerry Jarvis's Wig*, Speaking of the decollated Martyr St. Dennis's walk with his head under his arm.

2. *Conch.* Of a spiral shell: Truncated at the apex.

This occurs normally in some univalve molluscs; in the course of growth, the animal ceases to occupy the apex, and throws a partition across, when the dead part breaks off.

1847 CARPENTER *Zool.* §909 A shell thus deprived of its apex is said to be *decollated.* **1854** WOODWARD *Mollusca* iv. (1856) 45 The deserted apex is sometimes very thin, and becoming dead and brittle, it breaks away, leaving the shell truncated, or decollated.

decollation (diːkɒˈleɪʃən). [a. F. *décollation* (13th c. in Hatzfeld), ad. L. *dēcollātiōn-em*, n. of action f. *dēcollāre*: see prec.]

1. The action of decollating or beheading; the fact of being beheaded; *spec.* in *Obstetric Surg.*, severance of the head from the body of a fœtus.

Feast of the Decollation of St. John the Baptist: a festival in the Roman, Greek, and other Christian churches in commemoration of the beheading of St. John the Baptist, observed on the 29th of August.

1387 TREVISA *Higden* (Rolls) IV. 345 Oþer men telleþ þat it is nouȝt þe feste of þe decollacioun. *Ibid.* V. 49 (Mätz.) Of the decollacioun of Seint John. **1485** CAXTON *St. Wenefr.* 13 The lyf whiche she after hyr decollacion lyued by the space of 15 yere. **1494** FABYAN *Chron.* III. 462 In this xxv. yere, aboute the feast of the Decollacion of Seynt Iohn Baptyst. **1647** WHARTON *Ireland's War* Wks. (1683) 262 The Decollation of Mary Queen of Scots. **1654** VILVAIN *Epit. Ess.* vii. 31 A fourth is added of King Charls decollation. **1793** W. HODGES *Trav. India* 91 The grand sacrifice was preceded by the decolation of a kid and a cock, the heads of which were thrown upon the altar. **1848** MRS. JAMESON *Sacr. & Leg. Art* (1850) 131 The decollation of St. Paul. **1884** SALA *Journey due South* I. i. (1887) 18 [He] strenuously denied the painlessness of decollation by the guillotine.

fig. **1646** SIR T. BROWNE *Pseud. Ep.* I. ii. 7 He by a decollation of all hope annihilated his mercy.

2. *Conch.* The truncating or truncated condition of a spiral shell: see DECOLLATED 2.

1866 TATE *Brit. Mollusks* iv. 185 The decollation of the upper whorls of the shells.

decollator[1] (ˈdiːkɒleɪtə(r)). [agent-n. in L. form from *dēcollāre* to DECOLLATE *v.*[1]]

1. One who decollates; a decapitator.

1843 *Blackw. Mag.* LIII. 522 The Sans-culottes.. would have raised you by acclamation to the dignity of Decollator of the royal family.

2. *Surg.* An obstetric instrument for performing decollation of the fœtus; a decapitator.

1871 BARNES *Lect. Obst. Oper.* 217–8 If Braun's decollator be used the movement employed is rotatory from right to left.

decollator[2] (diːkəˈleɪtə(r), ˈdɛkəleɪtə(r)) [f. DECOLLATE *v.*[2] + -OR.] A piece of office machinery which separates sheets of paper, esp. multi-part continuous stationery, into different piles.

1978 *Computer Users' Handbk.* 490/1 (*heading*) Continuous stationery, decollators. **1980** *Daily Tel.* 23 Apr. 3 (Advt.), Filing cabinets.. bursters, decollators and forms handling equipment. **1983** *Dict. Computing* 101/1 *Decollator*, a machine that can process multicopy printed output into separate stacks of copy and used carbon paper.

‖**décollement** (dekɔlmɑ̃). [Fr., f. *décoller* to unstick, disengage.] **1.** *Med.* The process of separating organs or tissues from surrounding parts; also, the state of being thus separated.

1842 DUNGLISON *Med. Lex.* (ed. 3), *Décollement*, the state of an organ that is separated from the surrounding parts, owing to destruction of the cellular membrane which united them; the skin is *décollée*; i.e., separated from the subjacent parts. **1908** *Practitioner* Sept. 455 The third danger zone is behind in the neighbourhood of the portal vein and vena cava. Injury to these vessels may be avoided by practising 'decollement' of the duodenum. *Ibid.*, The stage of decollement being completed, ablation may be proceeded with.

2. *Geol.* A process in which some strata are supposed to become partly detached from those underneath and slide over them, becoming folded.

1927 L. W. COLLET *Structure of Alps* II. viii. 129 The folds of the Jura must be considered.. to be due to a phenomenon of '*décollement*'. *Ibid.* 139 Owing to the push exerted by the Alps in formation, the sedimentary rocks of the Jura have been detached on the Middle Muschelkalk, of which the salt beds played the rôle of a lubricant, and folded. This kind of folding is a '*décollement*'. **1935** E. B. BAILEY *Tectonic Ess.* xi. 176 Complications have developed along a plane of *décollement* (ungluing) in the Trias. **1969** M. G. RUTTEN *Geol. W. Europe* x. 204 The French literature has become permeated almost completely by the idea of 'décollement' in the sense of gravity sliding since about 1950.

‖**décolletage** (dekɔltɑʒ). Also **decolletage, decoltage.** [Fr.: see DÉCOLLETÉ *ppl. a.*]

1. The low-cut neck of a bodice.

1894 *Season* X. 34/2 Into the breast pleats are placed fan-shaped gores.. loosely smocked into the decoltage. **1896** *Westm. Gaz.* 14 Mar. 3/2 The sleeves and upper bodice are in creamy white chiffon, and the dark line round the décolletage of black jet. **1902** *Queen* 10 May 816/2 A soft fold of pink silk at the decolletage. **1933** MRS. C. S. PEEL *Life's Enchanted Cup* iv. 47 The decolletage was, in the case of young girls, decorously cut.

2. Exposure of the neck and shoulders by the low cut of the bodice. Also *fig.*

1894 *Sat. Rev.* LXXVIII. 596 Such art as that of John Oliver Hobbes, so typically feminine in its discreet décolletage, is not truth but effect. **1921** *Public Opinion* 8 July 37/3 A bold *decolletage* of shoulders still young and white. **1924** *Blackw. Mag.* Nov. 678/1 *Skeletta's* ever-increasing décolletage had a sort of embarrassed fascination for us. **1937** J. LAVER *Taste & Fashion* xiii. 192 A considerable proportion of young women will be *décolleté*, for *décolletage* is a powerful weapon of attractiveness.

‖**décolleté** (dekɔlte), *ppl. a.*; fem. **-ée.** [Fr., pa. pple. of *décolleter* to expose the neck, etc., f. *de-*, *des-* (DE- I. 6) + *collet* collar of a dress.] **a.** Of a dress, etc.: Cut low round the neck; low-necked. **b.** Wearing a low-necked dress.

1831 GREVILLE *Mem. Geo. IV* (1875) II. xiii. 106 The Queen is a prude, and will not let the ladies come *décolletées* to her parties. **1848** THACKERAY *Van. Fair* xlviii, A stout countess of sixty, décolletée. **1884** *West. Daily Press* 16 Dec. 7/4 Englishwomen will imitate their French sisters in.. the excessively decolleté bodices.. they patronise.

c. *fig.*

1890 *Forum* IX. 682 Of an American writer whose questionable book ran like wildfire into every reading home.., a publisher said: 'You cannot blame her; she was born *décolleté*.' **1952** S. KAUFFMANN *Philanderer* (1953) iii. 49 Before the wildness of the twenties, there was Victorianism; and before that there was the eighteenth century, very *décolleté*. **1966** *Listener* 20 Jan. 99/3 The glittering Mrs Cheveley, with her décolleté dresses and décolleté past.

‖**décolletée** (dekɔlte). [fem. pa. pple. of *décolleter*: see DÉCOLLETÉ *ppl. a.*] The low-cut neck of a bodice.

1907 *Daily Chron.* 2 July 10/5 Mohair braid round the décolletée and armpits in bretelles and as bands on the skirt. **1908** *Ibid.* 24 Aug. 7/5 Décolletée and sleeves are in Malines.

ˌdecoloniˈzation. [f. DE- II. 2 + COLONIZATION *sb.*] The withdrawal from its former colonies of a colonial power; the acquisition of political or economic independence by such colonies. Also *transf.*

1938 M. J. BONN *Crumbling of Empire* II. 101 A decolonization movement is sweeping over the continents. An age of empire-breaking is following an age of empire-making. **1957** *Economist* 19 Oct. 213/2 Nor did the postwar return of the colonial powers reverse or halt the process of 'decolonisation'. **1960** *Guardian* 6 Oct. 10/4 Britain, as a liberal state, engaged in working out the logic of decolonisation. **1967** *Times* 30 Nov. 11/1 If the full glory of decolonization is to throw the alien power out neck and crop, this satisfaction can hardly be denied the National Liberation Front.

decolorant (dɪˈkʌlərənt), *a.* and *sb.* [a. F. *décolorant*, pr. pple. of *décolorer*, repr. L. *dēcolōrānt-em*: see DECOLOUR.]

A. *adj.* Decolorizing.

1886–8 in *Encycl. Dict.*

B. *sb.* A decolorizing agent.

1864 in WEBSTER.

decolorate (dɪˈkʌlərət), *a.* [ad. L. *dēcolōrātus*, pa. pple. of *dēcolōrāre.*] 'Having lost its colour' (*Syd. Soc. Lex.* 1882).

decolorate (dɪˈkʌləreɪt), *v.* [f. ppl. stem of L. *dēcolōrāre* to DECOLOUR.] †**a.** = DISCOLOUR (*obs.*). **b.** To deprive of colour, decolour.

1623 COCKERAM, *Decolorate*, to staine. *a* **1846** *Phil. Mag.* (cited in WORCESTER). In mod. Dicts.

decoloration (dɪkʌləˈreɪʃən). Also **-colour-.** [a. F. *décoloration*, ad. L. *dēcolōrātiōn-em*, n. of action from *dēcolōrāre* to DECOLOUR.] Deprivation or loss of colour; †discoloration.

1623 COCKERAM, *Decoloration*, a staining. **1640** E. CHILMEAD tr. *Ferrand's Love Melancholy* 121 (T.), We must not understand by this word *pale* a simple decoloration or whiteness of the skin. **1727** BAILEY vol. II, *Decoloration*, a staining or marring the Colour. **1876** tr. *Schützenberger's Ferment.* 113 If we now add a fresh quantity of the reducing fluid until the second decolouration.

decolorimeter (dɪˌkʌləˈrɪmɪtə(r)). [f. L. *dēcolōr-em* deprived of colour + Gr. μέτρον measure: see -METER.] An instrument for measuring the power or effect of a decolorizing agent.

1863–72 in WATTS *Dict. Chem.* II. 308.

decolorize, -ourize (dɪˈkʌləraɪz), *v.* [f. DE- II. 1. + COLORIZE.] **1.** *trans.* To deprive of colour.

1836–9 TODD *Cycl. Anat.* II. 503/2 Chlorine passed through a solution of hæmatosine decolorizes it. **1870** P. M. DUNCAN *Transform. Insects* (1882) 170 The leaves, and even the variegated flowers, are in this way often completely decolourised.

fig. **1887** F. ROBINSON *New Relig. Med.* 78 Temperament plays a part, colouring or decolourizing present and future.

2. *intr.* To lose colour; to become colourless.

1908 *Practitioner* Feb. 205 Characteristics of the gonococcus... Its characteristic half-moon shape, and the fact that it decolourises with Gram's method.

Hence **decoloriˈzation, -izing,** the action of depriving of its colour; **deˈcolorizer,** an agent that decolorizes; **deˈcolo(u)rized, deˈcolorizing** *ppl. a.*

1871 *Athenæum* 19 Aug. 251 The decolourization of flowers and leaves by electrical discharges. **1879** *St. George's Hosp. Rep.* IX. 509 Decolorised blood-clot. **1890** W. J. Gordon *Foundry* 177 Decolourized indigo. **1965** R. Cruikshank *Med. Microbiol.* (ed. 11) xlv. 646 In order to render the decolourised organisms visible..a contrast or counterstain is then applied. *c* **1865** Letheby in *Circ. Sc.* I. 125/2 The charcoal is very valuable as a decoloriser and disinfectant. **1861** Hulme tr. *Moquin-Tandon* II. III. 160 Its decolorizing properties.

decolour, -or (dɪˈkʌlə(r)), *v.* [a. F. *décolore-r*, or ad. L. *dēcolōrāre*, to deprive of its colour, discolour, f. de- I. 6 + *colōrāre* to colour. Cf. discolour.] †**1.** *trans.* To discolour; *fig.* to stain.

c **1618** E. Bolton *Hypercritica* (1722) 210 That Herb, with which the Britanns are reported to have painted and decolour'd their Bodies. **1630** Brathwait *Eng. Gentlem.* (1641) 198, I remember with what character that proud Cardinall was decoloured.

2. To deprive of colour, decolorize. Hence **deˈcolouring** *ppl. a.*

1832 G. R. Porter *Porcelain & Gl.* 196 To which are added manganese and oxide of cobalt as decolouring substances. **1861** Hulme tr. *Moquin-Tandon* II. III. 160 Animal charcoal is used for the purpose of decolouring various liquids.

†**deˈcoloured,** *ppl. a. Obs. rare*⁻¹. [For *decollared*.] Cut low in the neck; low-necked.

c **1430** *Pilgr. Lyf Manhode* II. civ. (1869) 113 To nekke and breste white a coote wel decoloured [*escolletees*] to be wel biholde.

decommission (diːkəˈmɪʃɒn), *v.* [f. de- II. 1 + commission *v.*] *trans.* To take (a ship, aeroplane, etc.) out of service; to close down (esp. a nuclear reactor).

1922 *Ann. Rep. Sec. Navy* (U.S.) 8 A large number of vessels were decommissioned with a view to retaining them in good condition for future service. **1971** *Flying* Apr. s2/3 Some [flight service stations] were closed when they doused the bonfires, and some more were decommissioned after World War II. **1980** *Daily Tel.* 4 Nov. 11/3 This is not because we cannot totally decommission power station reactors or that it is too dangerous to do so. **1983** *Sci. Amer.* Dec. S5/3 Municipal heating systems will also make use of the heat produced in 'back-pressure' power plants, which we will have to build when all the nuclear reactors have been decommissioned. **1987** *Aviation News* 6–19 Mar. 1034/4 On 16 March 1959, VF-871 was decommissioned and amalgamated with VF-870.

Hence **decoˈmmissioned** *ppl. a.*, **decoˈmmissioning** *vbl. sb.*

1922 *Ann. Rep. Sec. Navy* (U.S.) 8 (*heading*) Decommissioning of ships. **1929** *Ann. Rep. U.S. Navy Dept.* (1930) 12 The *Rigel*, tending the decommissioned destroyers at San Diego, requires a great deal of work. **1947** *New Yorker* 12 July 18/2 The Navy used to count on taking seven months to activate a decommissioned destroyer. **1967** 'J. Winton' *HMS Leviathan* (1969) ii. 25 The ship's present decommissioned state. **1978** R. M. Nixon *Memoirs* 536 We ordered the decommissioning of the two large Navy yachts that had been maintained exclusively for the President's use. **1979** *Nature* 22 Mar. 297/3 The second [chapter] discusses routine emission of radiation and radiological protection,..and the eighth decommissioning.

ˌdecompenˈsation. *Med.* [f. de- II. 2 + compensation 1 c.] A state or condition of having lost compensation (sense 1 c), *spec.*, as in ***cardiac decompensation, circulatory decompensation***, a failure of the heart to maintain adequate circulation, after a period of compensation. Hence **deˈcompensated** *ppl. a.*

1905 Gould *Dict. New Med. Terms* 208/1. **1938** H. A. Christian *Osler's Princ. & Pract. Med.* (ed. 13) 1037 Treatment of the Permanently Decompensated Cardiac. *Ibid.*, Sooner or later irremediable decompensation will come. **1953** *Faber Med. Dict.* 114/1 Cardiac or circulatory decompensation. **1961** *Lancet* 5 Aug. 314/2 We considered they had died from decompensated hypertensive cardiac failure. **1961** *Ibid.* 19 Aug. 429/1 Patients with enlarged hearts, cardiac decompensation, and diabetes.

decomplex (ˈdiːkɒmˌplɛks), *a.* [f. de- I. 5 + complex, after *decomposite, decompound.*] Repeatedly complex; compounded of parts which are themselves complex.

1748 Hartley *Observ. Man* I. i. 77 The Varieties of the Associations hinder particular ones from being so close and permanent, between the complex Parts of decomplex Ideas, as between the simple Parts of complex ones. **1840** De Quincey *Style* i. Wks. 1890 X. 150 This monster model of sentence, bloated with decomplex intercalations..is the prevailing model in newspaper eloquence.

†**decomˈpone,** *v. Sc. Obs.*⁻¹ [ad. med.L. *dēcompōnĕre*, back-formation from *dēcompositus*: see decomposite.] = decompound *v.* 1. Hence †**decomˈponit** *ppl. a.* = decompound *a.*

1522 Vaus *Rudiment.* Dd iiij b (Jam.), How mony figures is there in ane pronowne? Thre. Quhilk thre? Ane simple, & ane componit, and ane decomponit. The simple as *is*, the componit as *idem*, the decomponit as *identidem*.

decomponent (diːkəmˈpəʊnənt). ? *Obs.* [Formed on a L. type *dē-compōnent-em*, f. *dē-compōnĕre*, not in ancient L., but inferred from *decompose, decomposition*: see de- I. 6.] A decomposing agent.

1797 Henry in *Phil. Trans.* LXXXVII. 409 That the decomponent of the water..is not a metallic body, will appear highly probable. **1800** *Ibid.* XC. 189 The action of the electric fluid itself, as a decomponent.

decomˈponible, *a. rare.* [f. assumed L. *dēcompōnĕre* (see prec.) + -ble.] Capable of being decomposed or resolved into its elements.

1859 H. Coleridge in *Philol. Soc. Trans.* 19 The word is decomponible in that language into simpler elements.

decomposability (diːkəmpəʊzəˈbɪlɪtɪ). Also **-ibility.** [f. next + -ity.] The quality or property of being decomposable.

1862 Ansted *Channel Isl.* I. iv. (ed. 2) 64 A proof of the decomposability of the granite rock. **1881** Lockyer in *Nature* No. 617. 397 This decomposibility of the terrestrial elements.

decomposable (diːkəmˈpəʊzəb(ə)l), *a.* Also **-ible.** [f. next + -able; so F. *décomposable* (1790 in Hatzf.).] Capable of being decomposed, or separated into its constituent elements. (Usually in reference to chemical decomposition.)

1784 Kirwan in *Phil. Trans.* LXXIV. 180 Plumbago cannot be supposed decomposable by red precipitate. **1800** Henry *Epit. Chem.* (1808) 419 Decomposible substances. **1831** Brewster *Optics* vii. 73 This white light will possess the remarkable property of..being decomposable only by absorption. **1872** Huxley *Phys.* iv. 83 Animal matter of a highly decomposable character.

decompose (diːkəmˈpəʊz), *v.* [a. F. *décompose-r* (16th c. in Littré), f. *dé-, des-* (de- I. 6) + *composer* to compose.]

1. *trans.* To separate or resolve into its constituent parts or elements. (Of the separation of substances into their chemical elements, of light into its constituent colours; also of force or motion. Cf. decomposition 2.)

a **1751** Bolingbroke *Ess.* i. *Hum. Knowl.* (R.), The chemist who has..decomposed a thousand natural, and composed as many artificial bodies. **1805** *Med. Jrnl.* XIV. 272 Attempts to decompose water by the Galvanic pile. **1831** Brewster *Optics* vii. §66. 72 We have therefore by absorption decomposed green light into yellow and blue. *c* **1860** Faraday *Forces Nat.* i. 28, I can decompose this marble and change it.

b. To disintegrate; to rot.

1841 W. Spalding *Italy & It. Isl.* I. 19 The seasons decompose its cliffs.

c. *fig.* of immaterial things.

1796 Burke *Lett. Noble Ld.* Wks. VIII. 61 Analytical legislators, and constitution-venders, are quite as busy in their trade of decomposing organization. **1816** Scott *Antiq.* i, Were I compelled to decompose the motives of my worthy friend. **1846** Mill *Logic* Introd. §7, I do not attempt to decompose the mental operations in question into their ultimate elements.

†**d.** *Printing.* To distribute (type that has been set up or *composed*). *Obs.*

1816 Singer *Hist. Cards* 153 Go and take out the pieces from the press, and decompose them.

2. *intr.* (for *refl.*) To suffer decomposition or disintegration; to break up; to decay, rot.

1793 Beddoes *Calculus, etc.* 215 The mucus, contained in great quantities in the lungs, and which is continually decomposing. **1865** *Sat. Rev.* 11 Mar. 269/1 These broken armies decompose into bands of roving marauders. **1872** Huxley *Phys.* vii. 156 Such compounds as abound in the mineral world, or immediately decompose into them. *Mod.* Soon after death the softer parts of organized bodies begin to decompose.

decomposed (diːkəmˈpəʊzd), *ppl. a.* [f. prec. + -ed¹.] Subjected to organic decay, rotten.

1846 *Nonconf.* VI. 28 Why should decomposed potatoes be more objectionable than decomposed partridges?

decomˈposer. [-er¹.] Something that decomposes; a decomposing agent.

1821 *Examiner* 10/1 The turn for parody seems..to be, in its very essence, a decomposer of greatness. **1850** *Jrnl. R. Agric. Soc.* 135 The soil is a slow decomposer of manure.

decomposible, -ibility: see decomposable, -ability.

decomˈposing, *ppl. a.* [-ing².] That decomposes; usually *intr.* undergoing decomposition, in process of organic decay.

1833 Thirlwall in *Philol. Museum* II. 546 The decomposing hand has grown tired of its work. **1862** Ansted *Channel Isl.* II. x. (ed. 2) 263 Veins of soft clay and some of decomposing greenstone. **1870** H. Macmillan *Bible Teach.* viii. 153 These plants die, and form by their decomposing remains a rich and fertile mould.

decomposite (diːˈkɒmpəzɪt), *a.* and *sb.* [ad. late L. *dēcompositus*, a Latin rendering of Gr. παρασύνθετος used by Priscian in the sense 'formed or derived from a compound word', by mediæval and modern L. writers as 'further or more deeply compounded'. Cf. decompone. Hence a series of senses, found also in *decompound, decomposition*, in which *de-* is used differently from the more ordinary sense in *decompose* and derivatives. See de- I. 5.]

A. *adj.* Further compounded; formed by adding another element or constituent to something already composite.

1655 Gouge *Comm. Heb.* Epist., Simple, compound, or decomposite notions. **1869** Latham s.v., The decomposite character of such words is often concealed or disguised.

B. *sb.* A decomposite substance, word, etc.; a compound formed from something already composite.

1622 T. Jackson *Judah* 48 That elegant metaphoricall decomposite of the Apostle unto Timothie [2 Tim. i. 6, ἀναζωπυρεῖν 'rekindle']. *a* **1626** Bacon *Minerals* Wks. 1857 III. 807 The decomposites of three metals or more, are too long to enquire of. **1678** Phillips, *Decomposite*, a term in Grammar, signifying a word equally compounded, that is by the addition of two other words, as *In-dis-positio*. **1706** —— (ed. Kersey), *Decomposite* (in Grammar), a Word doubly compounded; as *In-dis-position*; also, a Term us'd by Apothecaries, when a Physical Composition is encreas'd. **1848** Latham *Eng. Lang.* §299 Compounds wherein one element is Compound are called Decomposites. **1863** W. Smith tr. *Curtius' Gr. Gram.*, Eng. Index, Decomposites, Augm[ent] in, §239 [Some verbs, which are not merely compounded with prepositions, but derived from already compound nouns (Decomposita), have the Augment at the beginning].

decomposition (diːkɒmpəˈzɪʃən). [n. of action f. decompound and decompose, with the respective senses of the prefix in these words: cf. *decomposite*. Mod.F. has *décomposition* in sense 2, of date 1694 in Acad. Dict., whence perhaps the English uses.

For the adventitious association of *compose* and *composition*, see these words.]

I. Allied to decomposite: with de- I. 5.

†**1.** Further composition or compounding; compounding of things already composite. (Cf. decomplex, decompound.) *Obs.*

1659 O. Walker *Instruct. Oratory* 52 The English..hath an elegant way of expressing them [Epithets]..in a dexterous decomposition of two, or three words together. As: Tast-pleasing-fruits. **1674** Boyle *Corpusc. Philos.* 11 The almost innumerable diversifications, that compositions and decompositions may make of a small number, not perhaps exceeding twenty, of distinct things. **1690** Locke *Hum. Und.* IV. iv. §9 The many Decompositions that go to the making up the complex Ideas of those modes.

II. Allied to decompose: with de- I. 6.

2. The action or process of decomposing, separation or resolution (of anything) into its constituent elements. **a.** Used of the separation of substances into their chemical elements, of light into the prismatic colours. ***decomposition of forces***, in Dynamics = resolution of forces.

1762 *Univ. Mag.* Jan. 12 If then the vinegar be used for precipitating it, there will be scarce any further decomposition of this magistery. **1794** G. Adams *Nat. & Exp. Philos.* IV. xli. 119 The decomposition of forces into parallelograms. **1800** tr. *Lagrange's Chem.* I. 53 Hydrogen gas..is always produced in the greatest purity by the decomposition of water. **1828** Hutton *Course Math.* II. 142 Called the decomposition, or the resolution of forces. **1831** Brewster *Optics* vii. 66 In the decomposition and recomposition of white light. **1860** Thomson in Bowen *Logic* x. 348 Chemistry..the science of the decomposition and combinations of the various substances that compose and surround the earth.

b. The natural dissolution of compound bodies; disintegration; the process or condition of organic decay; putrescence.

1777 Priestley *Mat. & Spir.* (1782) I. xvii. 200 Death, with its..dispersion of parts, is only a decomposition. **1794** Sullivan *View Nat.* I. 77 This ancient rocky substance, and the sand produced by its decomposition. **1845** Darwin *Voy. Nat.* (1852) 164, I am inclined to consider that the phosphorescence is the result of the decomposition of the organic particles. **1865** Lubbock *Preh. Times* iv. (1869) 91 The bones were in such a state of decomposition, that the ribs and vertebræ crumbled into dust.

c. *fig.* of immaterial things.

1762–71 H. Walpole *Vertue's Anecd. Paint.* (1786) I. 81 Allegoric personages are a poor decomposition of human nature. **1793** Burke *Policy of Allies* Wks. 1842 I. 599 In France..in the decomposition of society. **1874** Sayce *Compar. Philol.* vi. 240 It is very possible that the Aryan roots are capable of still further decomposition.

Hence **decompoˈsitionist**, an advocate or supporter of decomposition, *e.g.* that of an empire, confederation, etc.

1849 *Tait's Mag.* XVI. 756 'But,' say the decompositionists, 'we seek not the destruction of this empire—we agitate not for its abolition.'

†**decomˈposure.** *Obs. rare.* [f. decompose; see -ure.] Decomposition, resolution (of forces).

1740 Stack in *Phil. Trans.* XLI. 420 There will be no Decomposure, and the Force IC will not change into a Force that has the Radius OC for its Direction.

decompound (ˈdiːkəmˌpaʊnd), *a.* and *sb.* [f. de- I. 5 + compound *a.*: after late and med.L. *dēcompositus* decomposite in same sense.]

A. *adj.* Repeatedly compound; compounded of parts which are themselves compound; *spec.* in *Bot.* of compound leaves or inflorescences whose divisions are further divided (L. *decompositus*, Linnæus).

a **1691** Boyle (J.), The pretended salts and sulphur are so far from being elementary parts extracted out of the body of mercury, that they are rather, to borrow a term of the grammarians, decompound bodies, made up of the whole metal and the menstruum, or other additaments employed to disguise it. **1793** Martyn *Lang. Bot.* s.v., Decompound leaf, *Folium decompositum*, when the primary petiole is so divided that each part forms a compound leaf. **1835**

LINDLEY *Introd. Bot.* (1848) II. 360 *Decompound*, having various compound divisions or ramifications. **1837–8** SIR W. HAMILTON *Logic* xv. (1866) I. 275 Erroneous to maintain ..that a reasoning or syllogism is a mere decompound whole, made up of concepts. **1870** H. MACMILLAN *Bible Teach.* vii. 145 The lobed leaf passes by various stages into the compound, decompound, and supra-decompound.

B. *sb.* A decompound thing, word, etc.; a compound further compounded, or of which one or more elements are themselves compound.

1614 BP. ANDREWES *96 Serm.* (1641) 472 *Super-exaltavit* is a de-compound. There is, *Ex* and *Super* (both) in it. **1622** HEYLIN *Cosmogr.* (1627) 469 That the English language is a decompound of Dutch, French, and Latine, I hold. **17..** ARBUTHNOT, etc. (J.), No body should use any compound or decompound of the substantial verbs. **1836–7** SIR W. HAMILTON *Metaph.* xxi. (1859) II. 19 To use the word *to cognise* in connection with its noun *cognition*, as we use the decompound *to recognise* in connection with its noun *recognition*. **1881** CHANDLER *Gr. Accent.* §429 Decompounds, or words consisting of more than two factors.

decompound (ˌdiːkəm'paʊnd), *v.* [f. DE- I. 5, II. 1 + COMPOUND *v.*: cf. prec., and DECOMPOSE.]

I. Connected with DECOMPOUND *a.* and DECOMPOSITE.

†**1.** *trans.* To compound further; to form by combining compound constituents, or by adding another constituent to something already compound. *Obs.*

1673 NEWTON in *Phil. Trans.* VIII. 6110 The resulting White..was compounded of them all, and only de-compounded of those two. **16..** —— (J.), If the intercepted colours be let pass, they will fall upon this compounded orange, and, together with it, decompound a white. **1690** LOCKE *Hum. Und.* III. ix. §6 A very complex Idea that is compounded and decompounded. **1747** WESLEY *Prim. Physic* (1762) p. xv, The common Method of compounding and decompounding Medicines can never be reconciled to common sense.

II. Connected with DECOMPOSE.

2. To separate the constituent parts or elements of; to DECOMPOSE.

Johnson 1755 says—'This is a sense that has of late crept irregularly into chymical books.'

a **1751** BOLINGBROKE *Ess.* i. *Hum. Knowl.* (R.), If we consider that in learning..the signification of these names, we learn to decompound them. **1766** CAVENDISH in *Phil. Trans.* LVII. 102 To decompound as much of the solution of chalk as contains 16½ grains of earth. **1793** J. BOWLES *Real Ground War w. France* (ed. 5) 25 Other States are to be broken up and decompounded. **1830** HERSCHEL *Stud. Nat. Phil.* II. ii. (1851) 92 The chemist in his analysis, who accounts every ingredient an element till it can be decompounded and resolved into others.

Hence **decom'poundable** *a.*, capable of being decomposed.

1797 *Brit. Crit.* Jan. IX. 58 Discoveries..which shew the universal dominion of air of different kinds, and that all nature seems to be decompoundable into fluidity.

decom'pounded, *ppl. a.* [f. prec. + -ED[1].]

I. 1. Further compounded; made up of compound constituents: *spec.* in *Bot.* and *Zool.* = DECOMPOUND.

1674 BOYLE *Corpusc. Philos.* 26 Amel is manifestly not only a compounded, but a decompounded body, consisting of salt and powder of pebbles or sand, and calcined tin. **1794** MARTYN *Rousseau's Bot.* xix. 268 The leaves being decompounded. **1852** DANA *Crust.* I. 205 The areolation is very deep and the areolets not decompounded.

II. 2. Separated into its constituent parts, decomposed.

1797 PEARSON in *Phil. Trans.* LXXXVII. 152 The oxygen and hydrogen gaz of the decompounded water. **1807** VANCOUVER *Agric. Devon* (1813) 22 Composed of the decompounded shale. **1841** HOR. SMITH *Moneyed Man* II. ix. 309 The very dust..may consist of decompounded human hearts.

decompress (diːkəm'prɛs), *v.* [f. DE- II. 1 + COMPRESS *v.*; cf. next.] *trans.* To relieve or reduce pressure. **a.** To subject (a diver, etc.) to decompression; to reduce the pressure of the air or other gas in. Also *absol.*

1905 *Jrnl. Physiol.* XXXIII. p. vi, We placed rats in 10–15 or 20 atmospheres of air.., and then decompressed them in about three seconds. **1909** G. W. M. BOYCOTT *Compressed Air Work* i. 2 When decompressing from great depths or high pressures after short exposures, the saturation..is obviated by the first rapid drop in pressure. *Ibid.* 12 When a worker is suddenly decompressed by some such accident ..he should immediately be placed in the air-lock. **1911** *Engineer* 10 Mar. 243/1 To decompress slowly but continuously. **1925** *Literary Digest* 27 June 24/1 When they have finished their labors, it is necessary that they be 'decomprest', that is, slowly restored to normal air conditions. *Ibid.*, The two air-locks..are used in putting the compress-air workers gradually under pressure and for decompressing them after they have finished work. **1962** [see DECOMPRESSION 1 a].

b. *Surg.* To relieve excessive internal pressure in (a part of the body) by surgical means.

1914 A. P. C. ASHHURST *Surgery* xvii. 574 The most imperative indication is to 'decompress' the brain by removing some of the overlying cranium. **1954** E. L. FARQUHARSON *Textbk. Oper. Surg.* xxv. 708 When the bladder has been chronically distended over a period of several days..it should be decompressed gradually. **1967** T. J. MCNAIR *Bailey's Emergency Surg.* (ed. 8) lxxxviii. 970 Grossly distended intestine is decompressed by the method of Savage.

decompression (diːkəm'prɛʃən). [f. DE- II. 2 + COMPRESSION.] **1.** The process of relieving or reducing pressure. **a.** A reduction of the pressure of the air or other gas in an enclosed space; *esp.* (*a*) the process of subjecting a diver, etc., who has been in air under pressure to a gradual reduction in pressure in a special chamber until atmospheric pressure is reached; (*b*) in an aircraft, etc., a reduction of the air-pressure from that of the atmosphere to a lower value, *e.g.* as a result of a rupture of the cabin during high-altitude flight.

1905 *Jrnl. Physiol.* XXXIII. p. vi (*heading*) Estimation of the gas set free in the body after rapid decompression from high atmospheric pressures. **1906** *Westm. Gaz.* 27 Jan. 10/1 The men who controlled the airlocks, and were subjected to compression and decompression every few minutes, were in no case affected. **1939** H. G. ARMSTRONG *Aviation Med.* xx. 335 The effects of sudden decompressions at less than one atmosphere. **1951** A. GROLLMAN *Pharmacol. & Therapeutics* xxix. 688 The incidence of 'divers' bends' may also be reduced appreciably by using a mixture of helium and oxygen to replace the air in the pressure chamber used in decompression. **1962** J. GLENN in *Into Orbit* 41 You have one large handle for repressurizing the cabin with oxygen in case of a bad leak, plus another handle to decompress it..in case of fire. (Decompression—or getting rid of the oxygen —is the quickest way to put out a fire.)

b. *Surg.* The surgical relief of excessive internal pressure in a part of the body.

1906 *Trans. College Phys.* (Philadelphia) 3rd Ser. XXVIII. 73 (*heading*) Cerebral decompression; palliative operations in the treatment of tumors of the brain. **1949** I. AIRD *Compan. Surg. Studies* xliii. 956 A distended bladder is prone to infection. If catheterization succeeds, gradual decompression is continued for five or seven days. **1966** E. L. FARQUHARSON *Textbk. Oper. Surg.* (ed. 3) ix. 328 Subtemporal decompression was formerly employed as a method of relieving intra-cranial pressure.

2. *attrib.*, as ***decompression symptom***; **decompression chamber**, (*a*) a chamber in which pressure is reduced gradually to that of the outside air; (*b*) a chamber in which a person or animal can be subjected to a reduction in the pressure of the air (or oxygen) below that of the atmosphere; **decompression sickness**, sickness resulting from the effects of too rapid decompression.

1932 *Daily Express* 28 Jan. 1/2 The minesweeper Tedworth..is equipped with special decompression chambers and the latest appliances for deep-sea diving. **1958** *Times Lit. Suppl.* 30 Oct. 564/2 He walks..into a decompression chamber to test his cameras for high altitude work on Mount Everest. **1961** *Lancet* 26 Aug. 484/1 Concern with..anoxia..led Haldane to expose himself to low oxygen-pressures in decompression chambers. **1941** *Observations on Decompression Sickness in Man* (*Flying Personnel Res. Comm.*, Farnborough) 2 The term decompression sickness is retained because it covers the whole range of phenomena that occur, while 'bends' refers only to one of many symptoms..while aeroembolism.. refers to only one aspect. **1962** Decompression sickness [see BEND *sb.*[4] 2 b]. **1971** *Sunday Times* 7 Mar. 45/7 Prolonged investigations by the Medical Research Council's experts on decompression sickness. **1906** *Jrnl. Physiol.* XXXV. p. vi, It would seem probable that any animal whose respired gases are conveyed to the cells without the intervention of a circulating liquid should be immune from decompression symptoms.

decompressive (diːkəm'prɛsɪv), *a.* [f. DECOMPRESS *v.* + -IVE.] Of or pertaining to decompression (sense 1 b).

1910 H. CUSHING in Osler & McCrae *Mod. Med.* VII. 457 Tumor-palliation (decompressive operations). **1931** H. BAILEY *Emergency Surg.* II. xxv. 86 With the slight decompressive action of the injection the veil may be lifted sufficiently to enable us to decide on which side to trephine.

decompressor (diːkəm'prɛsə(r)). [f. DECOMPRESS *v.* + -OR.] An apparatus for reducing compression in a motor engine.

1919 *Chambers's Jrnl.* Dec. 830/2 The only levers needed to control this motor are one connected to a decompressor and clutch. **1923** *Daily Mail* 7 June 12 An ingenious decompressor to lower the engine compression..for easy starting.

†**de'compt.** *Sc. Obs.*[−1] [Cf. F. '*descompt*, an account giuen for things receaued; a backe-reckoning' (Cotgr.).] Account, reckoning.

1584 *Sc. Acts Jas. VI* (1814) 325 (Jam.) Thair obligationis and decompt respectiue, meid be thair commissaris deput be thame to that effect, particularly thairvpon will testifie.

decon, obs. form of DEACON.

deconcatenate, deconcentrate, -ation, etc.: see DE- II. 1.

de'concentrate, *v.* [See DE- II. 1.] *trans.* To reverse or diminish the concentration of; *spec.* to dissolve (cartels or other large industrial groupings), to decentralize. Also *intr.*

1889 in *Cent. Dict.* **1958** *Times* 1 May 9/2 Why, it is asked, should Krupp be obliged to deconcentrate?

deconcen'tration. [See DE- II. 2.] The reversal or diminution of concentration; *spec.* the dissolution of cartels or other large industrial groupings; decentralization. Also *attrib.*

1889 in *Cent. Dict.* **1925** E. B. WILSON *Cell* (ed. 3) 545 The chromosomes are..in a state of deconcentration. **1955** *Times* 6 July 7/5 Some families..weathered the storm of deconcentration, and still control large business organizations. **1959** *Economist* 17 Jan. 204/1 Under the allied deconcentration laws Herr Alfried Krupp was obliged to sell his holdings in coal and steel.

†**decon'cert,** *v. Obs. rare.* [a. F. *déconcerter* (16th c.), f. *dé-*, *des-* (DE- I. 6) + *concerter.*] *trans.* To put out of concert or agreement, disarrange; = DISCONCERT 1.

1715 M. DAVIES *Athen. Brit.* I. 322 A more heterogene Metamorphosis, capable of deconcerting the closest Union and Interest.

†**decon'coct,** *v. Obs. rare.* [f. DE- I. 3 or 5 + CONCOCT *v.*] According to earlier physiological notions: To reduce (imperfectly concocted humours or ill digested food) by further digestion: cf. CRUDITY 2. (In quot. *fig.*)

1655 FULLER *Ch. Hist.* VI. i. 267, I doubt not but since these Benedictines have had their crudities deconcocted, and have been drawn out into more slender threds of sub-divisions.

decondition (diːkən'dɪʃən), *v.* [f. DE- II. 1 + CONDITION *v.* 9.] *trans.* To reverse or remove the conditioned reflexes of (someone); to undo the results of conditioning in (a person); (in quot. 1940, to lower the charged condition of). So **decon'ditioned** *ppl. a.*, **decon'ditioning** *vbl. sb.* and *ppl. a.*

1940 *Physical Rev.* 1 Dec. 993 The reapplication of potential showed that the tube had become partially deconditioned. *Ibid.*, The deconditioning of the tube was not due to any leak. **1941** *Spectator* 5 Sept. 232/1 Experiments in what is described as 'de-conditioning'. The idea is to reproduce warlike sounds and disturbing noises until the patients regain their normal reactions. **1959** *Times Lit. Suppl.* 27 Mar. 181/3 Man is a transient being, subject to time, from which all his other 'conditionings' ensue. The need to 'decondition' man is..acknowledged in the Christian rite of baptism in which 'the world, the flesh and the devil' are abjured. **1960** KOESTLER *Lotus & Robot* II. xi. 264 Zen started as a de-conditioning cure and ended up as a different type of conditioning.

decongestant (diːkən'dʒɛstənt), *a.* and *sb.* [f. DE- II. 1 + CONGEST *v.* + -ANT[1].] **A.** *adj.* = DECONGESTIVE *a.* **B.** *sb.* A decongestive agent.

1950 *Therapeutic Notes* Dec. 259 Benylin Expectorant is antispasmodic, decongestant, expectorant, [etc.]. **1952** *Official Gaz.* (U.S. Pat. Off.) 1 July 23/1 Decongestants, Digestants. **1958** FALCONER & NORMAN *Drug, Nurse, Patient* xviii. 294 While nasal decongestants do have value, as a general rule there is a great tendency to overuse this type of medication. **1962** *Which?* Apr. 123/1 Decongestants constrict blood vessels and relieve the burning feeling and heaviness in the eyes. **1965** C. ANDREWES *Common Cold* IV. 173 People then tend to take more of the decongestant spray. **1966** in G. N. LEECH *Eng. in Advertising* xviii. 159 Never go to bed with a cold without decongestant Vick Vapour Rub.

decongestion (diːkən'dʒɛstjən). [f. DE- II. 2 + CONGESTION.] The relief of congestion. So **decon'gest** *v. trans.*, to relieve congestion in; **decon'gestive** *a.*, that relieves congestion.

1903 *Med. Record* 1 Aug. 167 Treatment..by electricity ..has a decongestive local action. **1908** *Practitioner* Oct. 569 Heat relieves the pain, not by the old-fashioned theory of 'de-congestion', but by causing hyperæmia. **1945** *Ann. Reg. 1944* 49 The 'decongestion' of congested areas and the encouragement of reasonable balance between different regions. **1958** *Times* 8 Aug. 9/6 Suppose, for example, Devonshire County Council wishes to 'decongest' its main towns, while preserving green belts, beauty spots, and the best farmland.

deconsecrate (diː'kɒnsɪkreɪt), *v.* [f. DE- II. 1 + CONSECRATE *v.*] *trans.* To undo the consecration of; to deprive of sacredness, secularize. Hence **de'consecrated** *ppl. a.*; **deconse'cration**, the action or ceremony of deconsecrating.

1867 *Ch. & St. Rev.* 16 Feb. 150 The last new..word 'deconsecration'..intended to convey to the public mind the fact, without the unpleasant associations, of what has hitherto been known under the..title of 'desecration'. **1876** *City Press* 21 Oct. 4/6 This Church was deconsecrated on Thursday. **1882** *Q. Rev.* Oct. 438 The bare deconsecrated Nature which our author offers us as the substitute for God.

decon'sider, *v. rare.* [a. mod.F. *déconsidérer*: see DE- II. 1 and CONSIDER.] *trans.* To treat with too little consideration. Hence **decon-side'ration.**

1881 *Med. Review* Apr., *Med. Profession & Morality*, In the Army and Navy, the surgeons, long unfairly deconsidered, now haughtily claim equally unreasonable precedence. **1882** MISS COBBE *Peak in Darien* 219 Women are..actually much deconsidered by men. *Ibid.*, Would not their deconsideration be reflected on Religion itself were they to become its authorized ministers?

decon'struct, *v.* [Back-formation f. DECONSTRUCTION b.] *trans.* **a.** To undo the construction of, to take to pieces. **b.** *Philos.* and *Lit. Theory.* To subject to deconstruction; to analyse and reinterpret in accordance with the 'strategy' associated with Jacques Derrida.

1973 D. B. ALLISON tr. *Derrida's Speech & Phenomena* vi. 77 One cannot attempt to deconstruct this transcendence. **1976** G. C. SPIVAK in J. Derrida *Of Grammatology* 322, Ricoeur delivers hermeneutic interpretations of several texts that Derrida deconstructs. **1977** *Dædalus* II. 108 This second perspective deconstructs the first; it seems to bring about a reversal, explaining meaning not by prior conventions but by acts of imposition. **1979** *PN Rev.* X. 38/1 Derrida sets out to uncover (or 'deconstruct') the manifold traps and illusions which philosophy has created for itself. **1980** *Times Lit. Suppl.* 26 Dec. 1466/4 One 'deconstructs' the confused, erroneous picture of knowledge as representation, philosophy as foundational, the mind as a separate locus. **1984** A. BROOKNER *Hotel du Lac* v. 76 If I were younger and more trendy I should probably say that I could deconstruct the signifiers of your discourse.

deconstruction. [f. DE- + CONSTRUCTION.]

a. The action of undoing the construction of a thing.

1882 McCARTHY in *19th Cent.* 859 A reform the beginnings of which must be a work of deconstruction.

b. *Philos.* and *Lit. Theory.* A strategy of critical analysis associated with the French philosopher Jacques Derrida (b. 1930), directed towards exposing unquestioned metaphysical assumptions and internal contradictions in philosophical and literary language. Also *transf.*

1973 D. B. ALLISON tr. *Derrida's Speech & Phenomena* vi. 74 The prerogative of being cannot withstand the deconstruction of the word. **1973** MATIAS & WILLEMEN tr. M. Cegarra in *Screen* Spring/Summer 130 A radical reading of the texts/films, a turning back upon theories and types of criticism, effecting deconstructions, ruptures, deletions and renewals. **1976** G. C. SPIVAK in J. Derrida *Of Grammatology* p. lxxvii, To locate the promising marginal text, to disclose the undecidable moment, to pry it loose with the positive lever of the signifier; to reverse the resident hierarchy, only to displace it; to dismantle in order to reconstitute what is always already inscribed. Deconstruction in a nutshell. **1979** *London Rev. Bks.* 25 Oct. 2/4 We are not in favour of the current fashion for the 'deconstruction' of literary texts, for the elimination of the author from his work. **1982** *Encounter* May 87/1 The strength of these critiques is that they offer alternative constructions as well as critical deconstructions of language. **1983** *N. & Q.* Dec. 549/2 Boucher, Lemoyne, Natoire, discard space as it was created by Masaccio and their work is a 'deconstruction' of quattrocento achievement.

Hence **decon'structionism**, the theory or practice of deconstruction (sense b); **decon'structionist** *a.* and *sb.*, (characteristic of) an adherent or practitioner of deconstructionism.

1980 R. M. ADAMS in Michaels & Ricks *State of Lang.* 584 The coincidence of vulgar with erudite deconstructionism is a circumstance worth remarking. **1982** *N. & Q.* June 193/2 To see in this poem a 'structureless habit of proceeding' is too determinedly deconstructionist. **1983** *N. & Q.* June 286/2 In 1979 he rather recommended J. Hillis Miller's Yale deconstructionism. **1983** D. LODGE in *Times Lit. Suppl.* 11 Nov. 1237/2 'Bartleby' is indeed the sort of story that makes deconstructionists' mouths water, an astonishingly early assault on the conventions and assumptions of the 'classic realist text'. **1984** *Listener* 15 Mar. 16/2 This follows, as the deconstructionists never tire of telling us, 'from the systematic and collective nature of language and literary convention'.

deconstructive (diːkən'strʌktɪv), *a.* *Philos.* and *Lit. Theory.* [f. DECONSTRUCT(ION + -IVE, after *constructive.*] Characterized by deconstruction (sense b).

1977 *Dædalus* Fall 108 The semiotics of literature thus gives rise to a 'deconstructive movement' in which each pole of an opposition can be used to show that the other is in error. **1981** M. WHITFORD in J. Wintle *Makers of Mod. Culture* 130/1 The deconstructive strategy is controversial, partly because it is not entirely clear whether.. Derrida has altogether avoided implicit *a priori* arguments. **1983** *N. & Q.* Dec. 568/1 Bloom vaunts an 'American tradition of criticism'.. to be distinguished from the deconstructive dialectics of Europe.

deconstructor (diːkən'strʌktə(r)). *Philos.* and *Lit. Theory.* [f. DECONSTRUCT *v.* + -OR.] One who deconstructs, a deconstructionist.

1978 *Times Lit. Suppl.* 16 June 668/1 Jacques Derrida, the great Deconstructor. **1983** *N. & Q.* Apr. 192/1 The deconstructors are not the first American intellectuals to seek in France the means to such an end. **1986** *Paragraph* Oct. 2 Would-be deconstructors of sexual difference necessarily speak from a position inside that difference.

decontaminate (diːkən'tæmɪneɪt), *v.* [f. DE- II. 1 + CONTAMINATE *v.*] *trans.* To remove contamination or the risk of contamination from (a person, area, etc.) affected by poison gas, radioactivity, etc.

1936 *Daily Tel.* 17 Oct. 13/5 Cars sped through the streets carrying men wearing gas-masks, whose task it was to decontaminate 'mustard gas' areas. **1938** *Protection of Your Home against Air Raids* 25 Mustard gas.. 'contaminates' clothing, or other objects exposed to it, making them dangerous to have near you or to touch until they have been 'decontaminated'. **1948** *Times* 5 Mar. 3/2 The vessels.. were still so radio-active that the cost of decontaminating them.. would have been greater than their value as scrap. **1958** *Observer* 12 Oct. 1/3 The package was elaborately decontaminated both by chemicals and radiation to prevent the placing of any live organisms on the moon's surface. **1971** *Nature* 5 Feb. 363/2 Breeders pay too little attention to the arduous task of decontaminating buildings where infected birds have been housed, before moving in fresh, healthy stock.

So **decontami'nation**, the action or result of the verb; also *attrib.*

1935 *Discovery* July 186/2 The scheme of gas defence requires.. that there should be an organisation for the decontamination of the areas affected. **1937** *Evening News* 15 Mar. 7/1 Decontamination squads, who would clear areas sprayed by mustard gas. **1955** *Times* 30 May 7/7 The techniques of decontamination..: a householder, on emerging from his cellar, should immediately take a broom and sweep down his roof. **1957** *Ibid.* 12 Oct. 6/1 Traces of radioactivity lingered on his hands and he was given a pair of surgical gloves to wear until to-morrow when the decontamination process can be completed. **1966** D. F. GALOUYE *Lost Perception* ii. 18 The original airport had been swallowed by a gaping crater where, even after two years, decontamination crews were still scouring the inner slope.

decontextualize (diːkən'tɛkstjuːəlaɪz), *v.* *Sociol.* [f. DE- II. 1 + CONTEXTUALIZE *v.*] *trans.* To study or treat (something) in isolation from its context, to take out of context. So **decon,textuali'zation**, the activity or result of decontextualizing; the condition of existing out of context; **decon'textualized** *ppl. a.*, **decon'textualizing** *vbl. sb.*

1971 *Sociol. Rev.* XIX. 305 The imposition of analysts' decontextualised models. **1976** *Brit. Jrnl. Sociol.* XXVII. 359 'The second [danger to avoid].. is to emphasize the bond between language and existence so much that the proper character of speech is denied.' That proper character resides in the peculiar capacity of speech to acquire a limited phenomenological decontextualization. **1977** D. L. ALTHEIDE in Douglas & Johnson *Existential Sociol.* iv. 148 Their methods and research decontextualize these features to focus on *invariant* procedures for processing information. **1979** *Archivum Linguisticum 1978* IX. 107 This stage, 'decontextualisation', is where various linguistic elements are added which have the effect of reducing as far as possible any necessity to rely on the surrounding context in order to interpret the given utterance. **1980** *N.Y. Times* 9 Sept. E11/3 The 'decontextualizing' of experience on page and screen. **1984** *Guardian* 25 July 11/2 Individual stories linked to their social context can reveal much more about distress than decontextualised biochemical experiments.

†**decon'tract**, *v.* *Obs. rare.* [f. DE- I. 3 or 5 + CONTRACT *v.*] *trans.* To contract further.

1647 FULLER *Good Th. in Worse T.* (1841) 93 This also seems too long: I decontract and abridge the abridgment of my prayers, yea.. too often I shrink my prayers to a minute.

decontrol (diːkən'trəʊl), *sb.* [DE- II.] The removal of control; *spec.* the removal of government control, esp. of a control imposed in wartime or in an emergency. Also *attrib.* So **decon'trol** *v. trans.*, to free from control; **decon'trolled** *ppl. a.*, **decon'trolling** *vbl. sb.*

1919 G. H. ROBERTS in *Times* 14 Feb. 3/1, I am told that every one wants to get rid of Government control... The moment I can see those conditions safeguarded in respect of any commodity, decontrol will come. *Ibid.* 3/2, I do not propose to risk decontrolling any commodity while there is the slightest possibility of decontrol resulting in higher prices. **1919** *Observer* 23 Mar. 12/6 (*headline*) De-controlled. Tea after to-morrow: bacon next week. **1923** *Daily Mail* 27 Jan. 8 Rent decontrol. **1923** RAMSAY MACDONALD in *Hansard Commons* 5th Ser. CLX. 21 To decontrol a certain block of middle-class tenants.. will do more harm than good. Look at what happens the moment decontrol comes. Either the rent goes up, or.. the house will be sold. **1946** *New Statesman* 14 Sept. 182/2 The decision of the Price Decontrol Board to lift the controls on grains and dairy products. **1955** *Times* 27 Aug. 10/1 At least two million tons more domestic house-coal, it is considered, is needed before decontrol can be envisaged. **1957** *Ibid.* 23 Dec. 11/4 Of the tenants of our newly decontrolled flats some 85 per cent. have accepted and signed new agreements on the basis we offered. **1971** *Daily Tel.* 1 May 19/4 The decontrol of gold coins on April 1 has coincided with a slight increase in demand for gold in London and Zurich. **1971** *Ibid.* 23 June 19/4 The decontrolling of bank competition.. suggests that the Government should also withdraw from supporting local authorities.

deconventionalize, decopperize, -ation: see DE- II. 1.

†**de'coped**, *ppl. a.* *Obs. rare*$^{-1}$. [f. OF. *décopé*, mod.F. *découpé*, cut down, minutely cut, slashed.] Cut in figures; slashed; cf. COUP *v.*[2] 1.

*c*1400 *Rom. Rose* 843 And shode he was with grete maistrie, With shoon decoped.

‖**decor** ('dɛkə(r)). *Obs.* [a. L. *decor* (*decōr-*), seemliness, comeliness, grace, beauty. Earlier Eng. had *de'cur*, *de'cour*, *de'core* app. through French: see DECORE *sb.*] Comeliness, beauty, ornament.

1656 BLOUNT *Glossogr.*, *Decor*, comeliness or beauty. **1664** EVELYN tr. *Freart's Archit.* 117 For the apt Distribution, Decor and fitness. **1681** H. MORE *Exp. Dan.* vi. 179 Riches are the Political glory and decor of any Kingdom.

‖**décor** ('deɪkɔː(r)). Also **decor.** [Fr., ad. L. *decor* (see DECOR).] The scenery and furnishings of a theatre stage. Also *transf.* and *fig.*, setting, surroundings.

1897 G. SAINTSBURY *Sir W. Scott* iii. 64 Scott had obtained part of the scenery.. in his yachting voyage.., which also gave the *décor* for *The Pirate.* **1900** H. HARLAND *Cardinal's Snuff-Box* ii. 12 Not too much like a *décor de théâtre.* **1902** C. H. E. BROOKFIELD *Random Reminiscences* x. 182 He was afraid some heavy piece of the *décor* had fallen upon me. **1931** *Times Lit. Suppl.* 29 Jan. 76/2 This author.. seems to lavish all his art.. on fitting to them [*sc.* his characters].. a telling *décor.* **1953** 'M. INNES' *Christmas at Candleshoe* xii. 135 Then he sees that this is another ghost —the ghost of some departed modest revelry, a tattered remnant of stage *décor.*

b. The decoration or furnishings of a room, building, etc.; the layout or method of display of an exhibition, etc.

1926 R. MACAULAY *Crewe Train* II. vi. 131 What with.. the Russian ballet *decor* of Evelyn Gresham, and the.. gunroom notions of Denham, the flat was a queer hotchpotch. **1927** *Observer* 24 July 18/3 Olympia last week marked a revolution in exhibition *décor.* **1953** E. TAYLOR *Sleeping Beauty* ix. 161 Those little silver cups which his mother seemed to think part of the décor of a schoolboy's bedroom. **1955** *Times* 11 July 12/5 A *décor* including washable walls of the useful material now commonly used for kitchen table tops.

decorable ('dɛkərəb(ə)l), *a.* *rare.* [f. L. *decorā-re* to DECORATE + -BLE. So in mod.F. (Littré).] Capable of decoration.

1889 *Pall Mall G.* 9 Jan. 6/1 The 'decorable' parts of the church were still adorned with.. evergreens.

decorament ('dɛkərəmənt). *rare.* [ad. L. *decorāment-um* (Tertull.), f. *decorāre* to DECORATE: see -MENT.] Decoration, ornament.

1727 BAILEY vol. II, *Decorament*, an Ornament, an adorning. **1730–6** —— (folio). **1755–73** in JOHNSON. **1826** SCOTT *Jrnl.* 24 Mar., It is foolish to encourage people to expect mottoes and such-like decoraments. [**1888** ELWORTHY *W. Somerset Gloss.* 189 'Thick there thing idn no decriment.']

decorate ('dɛkərət), *ppl. a.* *Obs.* or *arch.* [ad. L. *decorāt-us* adorned, beautiful, pa. pple. of *decorāre*: see next. For some time after the adoption of the vb., *decorat, -ate* continued to serve as the pa. pple., until superseded by *decorated*, which has also taken its place in ordinary use as adjective.] Adorned, decorated; ornate.

1460 in *Pol. Rel. & L. Poems* (1866) 81 Heyle flece of gedion, with vertu decorate! **1491** CAXTON *Vitas Patr.* (W. de W. 1495) I. xlviii. 92 b/2 They sawe a chirche decorate and ornate aboue alle puyssaunce humayne. **1513** BRADSHAW *St. Werburge* I. 3248 The place was decorat with myracles many. **1550** J. COKE *Eng. & Fr. Heralds* (1877) §203 Considre the magnifique and decorate churches [of London]. **1876** J. ELLIS *Cæsar in Egypt* 56 Rigg'd in gay colours, decorate with flowers. **1886** BURTON *Arab. Nts.* (abr. ed.) I. 102 A fair hall and richly decorate.

decorate ('dɛkəreɪt), *v.* [f. L. *decorāt-*, ppl. stem of *decorāre* to adorn, beautify, f. *decus, decor-* grace, honour, embellishment. As in other verbs of similar formation, the L. pa. pple. was first adapted as a ppl. adj. (see prec.), and subsequently the same type was taken as the stem of a vb.]

1. *trans.* To adorn, beautify, embellish; to grace, honour. *Obs.* or *arch.*

1530 PALSGR. 509/1, I decorate, I make fayre or gay, *je decore.* You have decorate our assemblye with your presence. **1541** *Act 33 Hen. VIII*, c. 37 The same.. with goodli and parkely parks.. to beautifie adorne and decorite. **1577–87** HOLINSHED *Scot. Chron.*, *Malcolm* (R.), His familie .. is decorated with the office of the marshalship of Scotland. **1642** W. BALL *Caveat for Subjects* 15 The name of the House of Austria decorates their dominions. **1781** GIBBON *Decl. & F.* lxviii. VI. 282 His mother has been decorated with the titles of Christian and princess. **1856** FROUDE *Hist. Eng.* (1858) II. viii. 245 War and plunder were decorated by poetry as the honourable occupation of heroic natures.

2. To furnish or deck with ornamental accessories: **a.** said of the personal agent.

1782 MAD. D'ARBLAY *Diary* 26 Oct., I.. was then decorated a little, and came forth to tea. **1820** W. IRVING *Sketch Bk.* I. 81 The head was decorated with a cocked hat. **1874** PARKER *Goth. Archit.* I. vi. 207 The custom of decorating churches with flowers at certain seasons is very ancient.

b. said of the things serving as ornaments.

1870 E. PEACOCK *Ralf Skirl.* III. 193 The old armour which decorated its walls. **1887** *Times* 7 Mar. 9/3 In ages.. more robustly conscious of the difference between evil and good their heads would have decorated the City gates.

3. To invest (a person) with a military or other decoration, as the badge of an order, medal of honour, or the like.

1816 [see DECORATED]. **1878** *Print. Trades Jrnl.* XXIII. 7 Prince Charles of Roumania has decorated two printers in his dominions.

Hence **'decorating** *vbl. sb.* and *ppl. a.*

1877 *Athenæum* 3 Nov. 571/3 An apprenticeship to a decorating carver. *Mod.* In the decorating of the church.

decorated ('dɛkəreɪtɪd), *ppl. a.* [f. DECORATE *v.* + -ED.] Adorned, embellished; furnished with anything ornamental; invested with a decoration.

1727 BAILEY vol. II, *Decorated*, beautified, adorned. **1816** J. SCOTT *Vis. Paris* (ed. 5) p. xlvii, Disturbances.. caused by decorated officers attempting to make the passers-by cry *Vive l'Empereur.* **1874** BOUTELL *Arms & Arm.* v. 76 The least decorated pieces of ancient Greek armour.

b. *Archit.* Applied to the second or Middle style of English Pointed architecture (which prevailed throughout the greater part of the

14th c.), wherein decoration was increasingly employed and became part of the construction.

'The most prominent characteristic of this style is to be found in the windows, the tracery of which is always either of geometrical figures, circles, quatrefoils, etc., as in the earlier instances [hence called *geometrical decorated*], or flowing in wavy lines, as in the later examples' (Parker *Gloss. Archit.*).

1812 RICKMAN *Styles Goth. Archit.* (1817) 44 Decorated English, reaching to the end of the reign of Edward III in 1377. *Ibid.* 71 Of the Third, or Decorated English Style. **1847** *Hand-Bk. Eng. Ecclesiology* 3 Second, or Middle Pointed (which has been known by the name of *Decorated*). **1848** POOLE *Eccl. Archit.* 245 Geometrical or very early Decorated. **1849** FREEMAN *Archit.* II. II. iii. 347 The exquisite Decorated church of Wymmington in Bedfordshire. **1874** PARKER *Goth. Archit.* I. v. 161 The change from the Early English to the Decorated style was.. very gradual.

decoration (dɛkə'reɪʃən). [ad. late L. *decorātiōn-em*, n. of action from *decorāre* to DECORATE: perh. a. F. *décoration* (1393 in Hatzf.).]

1. a. The action of decorating; embellishment, adornment, ornamentation. (See also quot. 1957.)

Decoration Day (U.S.): the day (now May 30th) kept in memory of those who fell in the civil war of 1861–65, on which their graves are decorated with flowers.

1585 JAS. I *Ess. Poesie* (Arb.) 65 It is also meit, for the better decoratioun of the verse to vse sumtyme the figure of Repetitioun. **1589** —— in Ellis *Orig. Lett.* I. III. 29 Ornamentes requisit for decoration of our mariage. **1611** COTGR., *Decoration*, a decoration, beautifying, bedecking, adorning, garnishing, trimming, gracing. **1752** JOHNSON *Rambler* 189 ⁋12 She.. applied all her care to the decoration of her person. **1844** EMERSON *Lect. Yng. Amer.* Wks. (Bohn) II. 295 To facilitate the decoration of land and dwellings. **1871** *Michigan Gen. Statutes* (1882) I. 455 The thirtieth day of May, commonly called decoration day. **1877** *Independent* 24 May 25/1 Decoration Day dawned bright and beautiful. **1886** *Century Mag.* XXXII. 475/1 On Decoration day he met them on their way to a neighbouring cemetery. **1957** *Encycl. Brit.* VII. 126/1 *Decoration day*, a holiday.. observed in the northern states.. on May 30, originally in honour of soldiers killed in the U.S. Civil War, but subsequently also in honour of those who fell in later wars.

b. The fact or condition of being decorated. **c.** †The quality of being decorated; ornateness.

1633 J. DONE *Hist. Septuagint* 68 Amazement.. for the manner and decoration of one thing and another. *Ibid.* 43 The beauty and Decoration of the things we found in Hierusalem. **1838** LYTTON *Leila* I. iv, The fashion of its ornament and decoration was foreign to that adopted by the Moors of Granada.

2. That which decorates or adorns; an ornament, embellishment; *esp.* an ornament temporarily put up on some special occasion; formerly used (after the French) of scenery on the stage.

a **1678** MARVELL *Wks.* II. 208 (R.) Our church did even then exceed the Romish in ceremonies and decorations. **1706** PHILLIPS (ed. Kersey), *Decoration*, an Ornament, Imbellishment, or Set-off; as The Decorations of the Stage. **1716** LADY M. W. MONTAGU *Let. to Pope* 14 Sept., No [opera] house could hold such large decorations. **1760** tr. *Juan & Ulloa's Voy.* (1772) I. 63 Mariposas or butterflies.. differing visibly in figure, colours, and decorations. **1769** MRS. RAFFALD *Eng. Housekpr.* (1778) 199 A pretty decoration for a grand table. **1845** M. PATTISON *Ess.* (1889) I. 17 Basilicas.. more remarkable for the richness of their decorations than for beauty of architectural proportions. **1864** BURTON *Scot. Abr.* I. i. 2 When its history is stripped of the remote antiquity and other fabulous decorations.

3. A star, cross, medal, or other badge conferred and worn as a mark of honour.

1816 J. SCOTT *Vis. Paris* (ed. 5) p. xiii, To sport the decoration of the Legion of Honour. *Ibid.* 294 All the young men who had not military decorations. **1882** CUSSANS *Her.* 252 The Royal Order of Victoria and Albert.. The Decoration of the Order consists of an onyx cameo, bearing a profile likeness of the late Prince Consort.

4. The composition placed in the head of a rocket firework which makes the display when the case explodes.

1873–4 W. H. BROWNE *Art of Pyrotechny* (1874) 23 The rocket is now ready for its cap or pot which is to contain the stars or other decorations that are to be used. *Ibid.* 30 We have another exceedingly beautiful decoration for our rocket heads, which is called golden rain.

deco'rationist. [f. prec. + -IST.] A professional decorator.

1828 CARLYLE *Misc.* (1857) I. 192 Which the more cunning Decorationist.. may have selected. **1829** *Ibid.* I. 276 If the tailor and decorationist do their duty.

decorative ('dɛk(ə)rətɪv), *a.* [f. L. ppl. stem *decorāt-* (see DECORATE *v.*) + -IVE. Cf. F. *décoratif, -ive* in Academy's Dict. of 1878, but also occurring in OF. in 15th c.] Having the function of decorating; tending to, pertaining to, or of the nature of decoration.

1791 SIR W. CHAMBERS *Civil Archit.* (ed. 3) 17 The orders ..may be considered as the basis of the whole decorative part of architecture. **1815** W. H. IRELAND *Scribbleomania* 130 *note*, To have the piece elegantly printed in quarto with decorative engravings. **1849** FREEMAN *Archit.* 237 A decorative arch is formed on the west wall. **1855** BAIN *Senses & Int.* III. iv. §27 In the fancies of decorative art, nature has very little place.

Hence **'decoratively** *adv.*, in a decorative manner, in reference to decoration; **'decorativeness**, the quality of being decorative.

1882 SALA *America Revis.* (1885) 55 A New York hack coupé is superior structurally, decoratively, and locomotively to one of our four-wheelers. **1847** CRAIG *Decorativeness.* **1890** *Times* 5 Feb. 9 Nowhere, in shape, decorativeness, and certainty of effects for eye, ear, and touch is there the least superfluity or deficiency.

decorator ('dɛkəreɪtə(r)). [agent-n. in L. form from *decorāre* to DECORATE: see -OR. In F. *décorateur* (*c* 1600 in Hatzf.).] One who decorates; *spec.* one who professionally decorates houses, public buildings, etc., with ornamental painting, plaster-work, gilding, and the like.

1755 in JOHNSON. **1787** SIR J. HAWKINS *Life Johnson* Wks. I. 373 *note*, James and Kent were mere decorators. **1836–9** DICKENS *Sk. Boz* (1850) 154/1 The ornamental painter and decorator's journeyman. **1885** *Law Reports 14 Q. Bench Div.* 600 They carried on.. the business of upholsterers, house painters, and decorators.

decoratory ('dɛkərətərɪ), *a. rare.* [f. L. *decorāt-* ppl. stem (see DECORATE) + -ORY.] Pertaining to decoration; decorative.

1889 J. HIRST in *Archæol. Inst.* No. 181. 34 Creations of the decoratory and representative Arts.

†**de'core**, *sb. Obs.* Also 6 decur, decoure. [app. a. AngloFr. *decour, ad. L. *decor, decōrem*: see DECOR. Littré has mod.F. *décor*, in 16th c. *décore* masc., as a deriv. of *décorer* to DECORATE.] Grace, honour, glory, beauty, adornment.

1513 BRADSHAW *St. Werburge* II. 337 With great worship, decoure and dignite.. She was receyued. *Ibid.* II. 1925 In worship, praisyng, beaute and decur. **1596** DALRYMPLE tr. *Leslie's Hist. Scot.* (1885) 49 Quhais decore cheiflie does consiste in Nobilitie of gentle men, etc. **1616** LANE *Sqr.'s T.* 43 He fraught theare minde with faire decore Of truith, iustice (twins), groundes of virtues lore.

†**de'core**, *a. Sc. Obs.* Also 6 decoir. [ad. L. *decōr-us* becoming, comely, f. *decor, -ōrem* becomingness, f. *decēre* to become.] Comely, beautiful.

1500–20 DUNBAR *Ballat of our Lady* 49 Hail, more decore, than of before, And swetar be sic sevyne. **1501** DOUGLAS *Pal. Hon.* II. 300 Ane sweit nimphe maist faithfull and decoir.

†**de'core**, *v. Obs.* or *arch.* Also 6–7 *Sc.* decoir. [a. F. *décore-r* (14th c.), ad. L. *decorā-re* to DECORATE.] To decorate, adorn, embellish.

1490 CAXTON *Eneydos* vi. (1890) 24 The name thenne and Royalme of Fenyce hath be moche hiely decored by merueyllous artes and myryfyke. **1548** HALL *Chron.* (1809) 59 To decore and beautifye the House of God. **1583** STUBBES *Anat. Abus.* I. (1879) 64 The Women of Ailgna vse to colour their faces.. whereby they think their beautie is greatly decored. **1603** *Philotus* xlvii, Deck vp and do thyself decoir. **1634** RUTHERFORD *Lett.* (1862) I. 129 Decored and trimmed as a bride. *a* **1661** FULLER *Worthies* II. 6 Which Church he decored with many Ornaments and Edifices. **1818** SCOTT *Br. Lamm.* ix, 'Without the saddle being decored wi' the broidered sumpter-cloth!'

Hence †**de'coring** *vbl. sb.*

1618 JAS. I *Decl. Lawful Sports* in Arb. *Garner* IV. 515 Leave to carry rushes to the church for the decoring of it.

†**de'corement.** *Obs.* Also 6–7 *Sc.* decoir-, decor-. [a. OF. *decorement* (15th c.), f. *décorer* to DECORATE: repr. L. *decorāmentum.*]

a. Decoration, ornamentation. *rare.* **b.** *concr.* An ornament, an embellishment.

1587 *Sc. Acts Jas. VI* (1814) III. 506 Very commodious and convenient for the.. decoirment of þis realme. **1632** LITHGOW *Trav.* I. 41 The decorements of their beautifull Palaces. **1635** HEYWOOD *Lond. Sinus Salutis* Wks. 1874 IV. 288 The Decorements that adorne the Structure, I omit. **1681** JAS. STEWART in *Cloud of Witnesses* (1810) 156 What brethren did cast upon him as a shame was his glory and decorement. *c* **1720** W. GIBSON *Farrier's Guide* I. i. (1738) 4 The Main, Tail, and Foretop.. of a Horse.. are a suitable Decorement to a Creature of so much Fire and Mettle.

de'corist. *nonce-wd.* [f. DECOR-UM + -IST.] One attached to artistic proprieties.

1839 POE *Assignation* Wks. (1864) I. 381 Proprieties of place and especially of time are the bugbears which terrify mankind from the contemplation of the magnificent. Once I was myself a decorist.

decorous (də'kɔərəs, 'dɛkərəs), *a.* [In form ad. late L. *decorōs-us* elegant, beautiful (It. *decoroso* decorous, decent), f. *decus, decor-*: see DECORATE; but in sense corresp. to L. *decōr-us* becoming, seemly, fitting, proper, f. *decor, decōr-em* becomingness, f. *decēre* to become, befit. In harmony with this Johnson, Walker, and Smart 1849 pronounce *de'cōrous.* Bailey 1730 and Perry 1805 have '*decŏrous*; Craig 1847 and later dictionaries record both. The word is not very frequent colloquially.]

†**1.** Seemly, suitable, appropriate. *Obs.*

1664 H. MORE *Myst. Iniq.* 225 That decorous embellishment in the external Cortex of the Prophecy [is] punctually observed. **1680** —— *Apocal. Apoc.* 75 So decorous is the representation. **1691** RAY *Creation* I. (1704) 57 It is not so decorous with respect to God, that he should immediately do all the meanest and triflingest things himself, without any inferiour or subordinate minister.

2. Characterized by decorum or outward conformity to the recognized standard of propriety and good taste in manners, behaviour, etc.

[**1673** *Rules of Civility* 144 It is not decorous to look in the Glass, to comb, brush, or do any thing of that nature to ourselves, whilst the said person be in the Room.] **1792** V. KNOX *Serm.* ix. (R.), Individuals, who support a decorous character. **1795** BURKE *Corr.* (1844) IV. 291 Their language ..is cool, decorous, and conciliatory. **1821** BYRON *Vis. Judg.* xcv, Some grumbling voice, Which now and then will make a slight inroad Upon decorous silence. **1858** HAWTHORNE *Fr. & It. Jrnls.* I. 293 Washington, the most decorous and respectable personage that ever went ceremoniously through the realities of life. **1874** HELPS *Soc. Press.* iii. 40 In a great city everything has to be made outwardly decorous.

b. Of language: Exemplifying propriety of diction.

1873 LOWELL *Among my Bks.* Ser. II. 224 A treatise of permanent value for philosophic statement and decorous English.

¶ Explained in the sense of L. *decorōsus.*

1727 BAILEY vol. II, *De'corous, Decoro'se*, fair and lovely, beautiful, graceful, comely.

decorously (see prec.), *adv.* [-LY².] In a decorous manner; with decorum.

1809 HAN. MORE *Cœlebs* I. 189 (Jod.) Oh! if women in general knew.. with what a charm even the appearance of modesty invests its possessor, they would dress decorously. **1855** MACAULAY *Hist. Eng.* IV. 566 He endured decorously the hardships of his present situation.

decorousness (see prec.). [-NESS.] The quality of being decorous; †seemliness, fitness (*obs.*); propriety of behaviour.

1678 CUDWORTH *Intell. Syst.* I. v. 874 The will of God is Goodness, Justice, and Wisdom; or Decorousness, Fitness. **1834** CAMPBELL *Life Mrs. Siddons* II. iii. 72 The decorousness of the national character.

†**de'corporate**, *v. Obs.* [DE- II. 1 + L. *corpus, corpor-* body.] (See quot.) Hence **de-corpo'ration.**

1660 HEXHAM, *Ontlijven*, to Decorporate, Kill or make Bodylesse.. *een Ontlijvinge*, a Decorporation, or a making Bodylesse.

†**decorre**, *v. Obs.* Also decourre. [? a. OF. *decourre, decorre* 'to runne downe, to haste or hy apace' (Cotgr.):—L. *dēcurrĕre* to run down.] *intr.* To run or flow away, pass or haste away.

(But the sense of the passage quoted is uncertain.)

1377 LANGL. *P. Pl.* B. XIV. 193 Of pompe and of pruyde þe parchemyn [of þis patent] decorreth [*v.r.* decourreþ] And principalliche of alle peple, but þei be pore of herte.

de'corrugative, *a.* [f. DE- II. 1 + CORRUGATIVE.] Tending to remove wrinkles.

a **1876** M. COLLINS *Pen Sketches* (1879) II. 175 Seeing that wrinkles are not unknown in these days, it might be worth inquiry whether bean-flower has any decorrugative effect.

de'corticate, *a.* [ad. L. *dēcorticāt-us*, pa. pple. of *dēcorticāre*: see next.] Destitute of a cortex or cortical layer: *spec.* applied to those Lichens which have no cortical layer.

1872 LEIGHTON *Lichen-Flora Gt. Brit.* p. xxiii.

decorticate (dɪ'kɔːtɪkeɪt), *v.* [f. ppl. stem of L. *dēcorticāre* to deprive of its bark, f. DE- I. 6 + *cortex, cortic-em* bark.] *trans.* To remove the bark, rind, or husk from; to strip of its bark.

1611 CORYAT *Crudities* 472 Decorticating it [hemp] or as we call it in Somersetshire, scaling it with their fingers. **1620** VENNER *Via Recta* v. 90 Wheate decorticated, and boyled in milke, commonly called Frumentie. **1693** *Phil. Trans.* XVII. 763 Black and white Pepper.. are the same, only the latter is decorticated. **1727** BRADLEY *Fam. Dict.* s.v. *Cork*, The Manner of decorticating, or taking off the Bark of the Cork-tree. **1860** BERKELEY *Brit. Fungol.* 8 An oak-trunk.. felled and decorticated.

b. *fig.* To divest of what conceals, to expose. **c.** To 'flay'.

1660 WATERHOUSE *Arms & Arm.* 18 Arms ought to have analogie and proportion to the bearer, and in a great Measure to decorticate his nature, station, and course of life. **1862** *London Rev.* 16 Aug. 148 It is impossible to 'decorticate' people, as the writer now and then does, without inflicting pain.

d. *intr.* To peel or come *off* as a skin.

1805 *Med. Jrnl.* XIV. 496 The scabs will decorticate and peel off from the scalp.

Hence **de'corticated** *ppl. a.*; *spec.* having had the cortex (CORTEX 3 a) removed.

1798 W. BLAIR *Soldier's Friend* 12 Decorticated oats, cut groats, dried peas. **1859** DARWIN *Orig. Spec.* viii. (1872) 208 A cement.. with which he had covered decorticated trees. **1875** H. C. WOOD *Therap.* (1879) 581 The decorticated seeds of the common barley, the pearl barley of commerce. **1927** G. V. ANREP tr. *Pavlov's Conditioned Reflexes* i. 14 This difference in the dynamic balance of life between the normal and the decorticated animal. **1933** *Brit. Jrnl. Psychol.* Oct. 145 A similar difference in the behaviour of normal and partially decorticated animals.

decortication (dɪkɔːtɪ'keɪʃən). [ad. L. *decorticātiōn-em*, n. of action from *decorticāre* (see DECORTICATE *v.*).] The action of decorticating; *spec.* in *Surg.* (see quots.).

1623 COCKERAM, *Decortication*, peeling. **1657** TOMLINSON *Renou's Disp.* 119 They do ill that extract oil out of almonds before decortication. **1816** KEITH *Phys. Bot.* II. 482 The decortication of a tree, or the stripping it of its bark. **1900** DORLAND *Med. Dict.* 193/1 *Decortication*,..removal of portions of the cortical substance of the brain. **1909** *Practitioner* Nov. 661 Where the surgeon finds during the course of a nephrectomy that the decortication of the sac is very difficult. **1936** PUNCH & KNOTT *Mod. Treatm. Dis. Respiratory Syst.* vi. 97 *Decortication.* The justification for this operation is based on the assumption that the lung cannot..obliterate the empyema cavity because it is bound down by..thickened and fibrous visceral pleura. The operation of decortication consists in freeing the lung of this inelastic coat. **1962** *Lancet* 5 May 946/1 This procedure was followed by a tension pneumothorax which eventually necessitated thoracotomy and decortication to produce good re-expansion of the lung.

decorticator (dɪˈkɔːtɪkeɪtə(r)). [agent-n. in L. form from *dēcorticāre* to DECORTICATE: see -OR.] He who or that which decorticates; a machine, tool, or instrument for decortication.

1874 KNIGHT in *Dict. Mech.* **1879** *Encycl. Brit.* IX. 344/2 Child's decorticator, an implement..for simply rubbing and scouring the grain, or for removing the thin bran and germ previous to the operation of grinding. **1954** D. UNWIN *Governor's Wife* iii. 58 The decorticator was a mile from the bungalow... The huge jaws devoured an endless belt of sisal leaves, chewing them up and spewing out flaccid heaps of blond fibre.

decorum (dɪˈkɔərəm). [a. L. *decōrum* that which is seemly, propriety; subst. use of neuter sing. of *decōr-us* adj. seemly, fitting, proper. So mod.F. *décorum* (since 16th c.).]

1. That which is proper, suitable, seemly, befitting, becoming; fitness, propriety, congruity.

†**a.** *esp.* in dramatic, literary, or artistic composition: That which is proper to a personage, place, time, or subject in question, or to the nature, unity, or harmony of the composition; fitness, congruity, keeping. *Obs.*

a **1568** ASCHAM *Scholem.* (Arb.) 139 Who soeuer hath bene diligent to read aduisedlie ouer, Terence, Seneca, Virgil, Horace..he shall easelie perceiue, what is fitte and *decorum* in euerie one. **1576** FOXE *A. & M.* 990/1, I..lay all the wyte in maister More, the authour and contriuer of this Poeticall booke, for not kepyng *Decorum personæ*, as a perfect Poet should haue done. *Ibid.*, Some wyll thinke..maister More to haue missed some part of his *Decorum* in makyng the euill spirite..to be messenger betwene middle earth and Purgatory. **1621** BURTON *Anat. Mel.* II. ii. VI. iv, If that Decorum of time and place..be observed. **1644** MILTON *Educ.* Wks. 1738 I. 140 What the Laws are of a true Epic Poem, what of a Dramatic, what of a Lyric, what Decorum is, which is the grand master-piece to observe. **1686** AGLIONBY *Painting Illust.* ii. 67 Simon Sanese began to understand the Decorum of Composition. *Ibid.* iii. 119 The second part of Invention is Decorum; that is, that there be nothing Absurd nor Discordant in the Piece. **1704** HEARNE *Duct. Hist.* (1714) I. 132 Neither is a just Decorum always observ'd, for he sometimes makes Blockheads and Barbarians talk like Philosophers. **1756** J. WARTON *Ess. Pope* I. i. 5 Complaints..[which] when uttered by the inhabitants of Greece, have a decorum and consistency, which they totally lose in the character of a British shepherd.

b. That which is proper to the character, position, rank, or dignity of a real person. *arch.*

1589 PUTTENHAM *Eng. Poesie* III. xxiv. (Arb.) 303 Our soueraign Lady (keeping alwaies the decorum of a Princely person) at her first comming to the crowne, etc. **1594** J. DICKENSON *Arisbas* (1878) 87 The minde of man degenerating from the decorum of humanitie becomes monstrous. **1606** SHAKS. *Ant. & Cl.* v. ii. 17 Maiesty to keepe *decorum*, must No lesse begge then a Kingdome. **1683** CAVE *Ecclesiastici, Athanasius* 171 He was a Prince of a lofty Mind, careful to preserve the Decorum of State and Empire. *a* **1715** BURNET *Own Time* (1766) I. 130 He..did not always observe the decorum of his post. **1848** MACAULAY *Hist. Eng.* I. 180 It was necessary to the decorum of her character that she should admonish her erring children.

c. That which is proper to the circumstances or requirements of the case: seemliness, propriety, fitness; = DECENCY 1. *arch.*

1586 T. B. *La Primaud. Fr. Acad.* I. 171 A waie how to frame all things according to that which is decent or seemely, which the Latines call *decorum.* **1598** J. DICKENSON *Greene in Conc.* (1878) 147 She deemd it no decorum to blemish her yet-during pleasures with not auailing sorrow. **1677** GALE *Crt. Gentiles* II. IV. 19 Temperance formally consistes in giving al persons and things their just decorum and measure. **1809** MATHIAS in *Gray's Corr.* (1843) 16 There was a peculiar propriety and decorum in his manner of reading. **1858** TRENCH *Parables* (1860) 126 They argue that it is against the decorum of the Divine teaching, that, etc.

2. Qualities which result from sense 1: †**a.** Beauty arising from fitness, or from absence of the incongruous; comeliness; grace; gracefulness.

1613 R. C. *Table Alph.* (ed. 3), *Decorum*, comelinesse. **1618** DEKKER *Owles Almanacke*, A coloured cloute will set the stampe of *decorum* on a rotten partition. **1635** SWAN *Spec. M.* vii. §3 (1643) 320 To shew the due decorum and comely beauty of the worlds brave structure. **1729** SHELVOCKE *Artillery* v. 334 The Decorum and Gracefulness of any Pile, the making the whole Aspect of a Fabric so correct.

†**b.** Orderly condition, orderliness. *Obs.*

1610 HEALEY *St. Aug. Citie of God* XII. xxv. 442 Whose wisedome reacheth from end to end, ordering all in a delicate *decorum. Ibid.* XXII. xxiv. 847 And brings the potentiall formes into such actuall *decorum.* **1684** T. BURNET *Th. Earth* I. 132 The first orders of things are more perfect and regular, and this decorum seems to be observ'd afterwards.

†**c.** Orderly and grave array. *Obs.*

1634 SIR T. HERBERT *Trav.* (1638) 238 In this Decorum they march slowly, and with great silence [at a funeral].

3. Propriety of behaviour; what is fitting or proper in behaviour or demeanour, what is in accordance with the standard of good breeding; the avoidance of anything unseemly or offensive in manner.

1572 tr. *Buchanan's Detect. Mary* M iij a, To obserue decorum and comely conuenience in hir pairt..sche counterfeiteth a mourning. *a* **1628** F. GREVILLE *Sidney* (1652) 93 She resolved to keep within the Decorum of her sex. **1668** DRYDEN *Evening's Love* Epil. 19 Where nothing must decorum shock. **1704** F. FULLER *Med. Gymn.* (1711) 143, I can't see any breach of Decorum, if a Lady..should ride on Horse-back. **1791** MRS. RADCLIFFE *Rom. Forest* iii, The lady-abbess was a woman of rigid decorum and severe devotion. **1803** *Med. Jrnl.* IX. 442 A spirit of levity and wrangling, wholly inconsistent with the grave decorum due to the investigation and decision of a philosophical subject. **1814** JANE AUSTEN *Mansf. Park* (1851) 81 My father.. would never wish his grown-up daughters to be acting plays. His sense of decorum is strict. **1866** G. MACDONALD *Ann. Q. Neighb.* xxvii. (1878) 475 If the mothers..are shocked at the want of decorum in my friend Judy.

4. (with *a* and *pl.*) †**a.** A fitting or appropriate act. *Obs.*

1601 A. C. *Answ. to Let. Jesuited Gent.* 114 (Stanf.) It had bin a decorum in them, to have shewd themselves thankful unto such kind office. **1692** DRYDEN *St. Evremont's Ess.* 372 The Laugh, the Speech, the Action, accompanied with Agreements and Decorums. **1717** BERKELEY *Tour Italy* 21 Jan. Wks. 1871 IV. 532 The tragedy of Caligula, where, amongst other decorums, Harlequin..was very familiar with the Emperor himself.

b. An act or requirement of polite behaviour; a decorous observance; chiefly in *pl.*, proprieties.

1601 R. JOHNSON *Kingd. & Commw.* (1603) 245 The Spanish nation..using a certaine decorum (which they call an obeysance or..a compliment or cerimonious curtesie). **1676** WYCHERLEY *Pl. Dealer* I. i, Tell not me..of your Decorums, supercilious Forms, and slavish Ceremonies. **1706** ESTCOURT *Fair Examp.* I. i, My Lady Stately longs to see you, had paid you a Visit but for the Decorums: She expects the first from you. **1766** GOLDSM. *Vic. W.* xxx, No decorums could restrain the impatience of his blushing mistress to be forgiven. **1865** MERIVALE *Rom. Emp.* VIII. lxvi. 202 The dignity of his military character was hedged round by formalities and decorums.

Decoudun (dɪˈkuːdʌn). [Named after Jules *Decoudun.*] A calender ironing machine of French invention, first made in England in 1876.

1889 *Laundry Management* p. xxi, The Decoudun Ironer. .. The decoudun varies in size and construction with each maker. A simple form consists of a polished metal bed (concave) and a heavy roller, fitted in a strong cast-iron frame. **1905** *Daily Chron.* 23 Feb. 9/2 Wanted to purchase, Decoudon Ironer, a Cudlipp Perfect preferred. *Ibid.* 31 Oct. 9/5 Laundry.—Wanted really good calender hands, for calender and Decoudun. **1911** in *Encycl. Brit.* XVI. 282/1. **1921** *Dict. Occup. Terms* (1927) §918 Decoudun hand.

decoun, obs. form of DEACON.

†**deˈcount**, *v. Obs. rare.* [f. DE- + COUNT *v.*: cf. *depict, describe.*] *trans.* To set down in a reckoning or account; to reckon.

1762 tr. *Busching's Syst. Geog.* V. 23 He was afterwards decounted a denizen, and the correspondent duties were required of him.

‖**découpage** (dekupɑʒ). [Fr., lit. 'the action of cutting up or out', f. *découper* to cut up or out.]

1. The decoration of a surface with an applied paper cut-out; an object produced by this technique.

1960 H. HAYWARD *Antique Coll.* 94/1 *Découpage.* Until the mid-1670's the mounts of folding fans were cut with open-work lace-like patterns copying the intricate designs of French and Flemish lace. **1961** *Times* 30 Aug. 11/1 The programme cover..is decorated with a *découpage.*

2. *Cinemat.* = CUTTING *vbl. sb.* 1 d.

1963 *Times* 7 Mar. 8/6 Such is..the precision of the *découpage* that the mysterious tale unfolds in a completely fascinating way. **1963** *Times Lit. Suppl.* 15 Mar. 180/1 A post-production script following closely the final *découpage* of the film.

deˈcouple, *v.* [a. F. *découple-r* to uncouple: see DE- I. 6.]

†**1.** To uncouple. *Obs. rare*$^{-1}$.

1602 *2nd Pt. Return fr. Parnass.* II. v. (Arb.) 32 Another company of houndes..had their couples cast off and we might heare the Huntsmen cry, horse, decouple, Auant.

2. a. To make the coupling between (two oscillatory systems, or two modes of oscillation of a single system) very loose, so that there is little transfer of oscillations from one to the other; chiefly *Electr.* So **deˈcoupling** *vbl. sb.*

1931 *Wireless World* 19 Aug. 175/2 A large-capacity paper type condenser may have a higher internal impedance..and so give less effective de-coupling. **1938** *Wireless Engineer.* Sept. 480 The time constants of the series and parallel type of filter, used for decoupling the A.V.C. bias from the grid circuit of the R.F. controlled valves, are examined. **1940** *Amateur Radio Handbk.* (ed. 2) 86/2 In some cases it is necessary to use decouplings which are effective for R.F. but which allow currents of speech frequency to pass. **1961** HARRIS & CREDE *Shock & Vibration Handbk.* II. xxx. 27 The natural modes of vibration of a body supported by isolators may be decoupled one from another by proper orientation of the isolators. Each mode of vibration then exists independently of the others. **1962** SIMPSON & RICHARDS *Junction Transistors* xv. 370 A collector decoupling filter, in which a resistor of value *R* is placed between the collector bias resistor and the power supply. **1964** R. F. FICCHI *Electrical Interference* x. 187 Another technique that is useful for decoupling power supply leads is the decoupling capacitor.

b. To muffle the sound or shock of (a nuclear explosion) by causing it to take place in an underground cavity.

1960 *Guardian* 15 June 1/2 He wanted to know whether 'de-coupling' (the way of muffling underground tests) was to be tested. **1960** *New Scientist* 24 Nov. 1369/1 There have been claims in the United States that an explosion conducted in a large spherical cavity is greatly muffled, or 'decoupled'. **1966** *Ibid.* 28 July 191/3 The decoupling effects of a nuclear explosion in a large sphere..are a mystery.

‖**découplé.** *Her.* [F.: see prec.] (See quots.)

1727-51 CHAMBERS *Cycl.*, *Decouplé*, in heraldry, the same as uncoupled, i.e. parted, or severed. Thus, a chevron decouplé is a chevron wanting so much towards the point, that the two ends stand at a distance from each other. **1830** in ROBSON *Brit. Herald.*

decoure, decourre, var. DECORE, DECORRE.

‖**decours.** *Her.* [F.: see next] = DECREMENT 1 c.

1727-51 in CHAMBERS *Cycl.*, A *moon-decressant* or *en decours.*

†**deˈcourse.** *Obs.* [a. F. *décours* (12th c.):—L. *dēcurs-um* a running down, f. *dēcurrĕre* to run down: cf. DECURSE and COURSE.] Downward course, descent. Also *fig.*

1585 T. WASHINGTON tr. *Nicholay's Voy. Turkie* IV. xx. 134 b, The Euphrates..in the channell and decourse whereof are founde many pretious stones. **1597** J. KING *On Jonas* (1618) 213 In the decourse of many generations.

†**deˈcourt**, *v. Obs.* [f. DE- II. 2 + COURT *sb.*] *trans.* To expel or banish from court.

c **1610** SIR J. MELVIL *Mem.* (1683) 198 He was accused.. and..for a time decourted. **1633** T. ADAMS *Exp. 2 Peter* ii. 4 If the king's favourite be forever decourted and banished. **1676** W. ROW *Contn. Blair's Autobiog.* xii. (1848) 462 Middleton is thus decourted and all his places taken from him.

†**deˈcovered**, *ppl. a. Obs.* [f. DE- II. 1 + COVERED: cf. F. *découvert.*] Uncovered.

1658 J. WEBB tr. *Cleopatra* VIII. ii. 19 His face remained almost quite decovered.

†**deˈcoy**, *sb.*[1] *Obs.* [Derivation and history unknown.] A game of cards played in the sixteenth and beginning of the seventeenth century.

c **1550** *Diceplay* C viij a, Primero now as it hath most use in courts, so is there most deceit in it... At trump, saint, & such other like, cutting at yͤ neck is a good uantage so is cutting by a bum card (finely) vnder & ouer..At decoy, they drawe easily xx handes together, and play all vpon assurance when to win or lose. **1591** GREENE *Disc. Coosnage* (1592) 4 Ile play at mumchance, or decoy, he shal shuffle the cards, and ile cut. **1608-9** DECKER *Belman Lond.* F iij (N.), Cardes are fetcht, and mumchance or decoy is the game.

decoy (dɪˈkɔɪ, ˈdiːkɔɪ), *sb.*[2] Also 7 decoye, dequoy, de quoi, duckquoy, 7-8 duckoy, duck-coy, duccoy. [*Decoy*, in all its senses (exc. 4 a) and combinations, was preceded by a simple form COY *sb.*[1] (known in 1621), a. Du. *kooi* of the same meaning. Thus senses 1 and 3 are identical with 1 and 3 of COY; sense 2 is a fig. use of 1; 4 b. and 5 are closely related to 3. The combinations *decoy-bird, -dog, -duck, -man*, etc., were preceded generally by the forms *coy-bird, -dog, -duck, -man*, etc. It is thus evident that *de-coy* is a derivative, compound, or extension, of COY *sb.*; but the origin of the *de-* is undetermined.

It has been variously conjectured to be the prefix DE-, the Dutch article in *de kooi* 'the coy' or 'decoy', the second half of Du. *eende* in *eende-kooi* 'duck-coy', and an obscuration of *duck* itself in *duck-coy*, which is indeed found in the 17th c., and (what is notable) not merely as the sb., but as the vb. (see below). Yet we do not find it as the earlier form, which suggests that it is really a later spelling of popular etymology. The likelihood that *decoy* is the Du. *de kooi* has been forcibly urged by C. Stoffel in *Englische Studien* X. (1887) 180. But direct evidence is wanting. And, since DECOY *sb.*[1] appears to be an entirely distinct word, being much older in the language than either this word or *coy* itself, and was probably still in use when *coy* was introduced from Dutch, it is possible that the latter was made into *de-coy* under the influence of that earlier word. It is to be noted also that the sense 'sharper', 4 a below, actually appears earlier than any other, literal or figurative, and may possibly not be a sense of this word at all, but an independent and earlier cant or slang term; if so, it may also have influenced the change of *coy* to *decoy.*]

1. A pond or pool out of which run narrow arms or 'pipes' covered with network or other contrivances into which wild ducks or other fowl may be allured and there caught.

1625 [see DECOY-DUCK 2]. [**1626-41** SPELMAN in Payne-Gallwey *Bk. Duck Decoys* (1886) 2 Sir W. Wodehouse (who lived in the reign of James I., 1603-25) made among us the first device for catching Ducks, known by the foreign name of a *koye*.] **1641** EVELYN *Diary* 19 Sept., We arrived at Dort, passing by the Decoys, where they catch innumerable quantities of fowle. **1665** —— 29 Mar., His Majestie was now finishing the Decoy in the Parke. **1676** WORLIDGE *Bees* (1678) 23 Allured..as Ducks by Dequoys. **1678** RAY *Willughby's Ornith.* (1680) 286 Piscinas hasce cum allectatricibus et reliquo suo apparatu Decoys sei Duck-coys vocant, allectatrices coy-ducks. **1679–88** *Secr. Serv. Money Chas. II & Jas. II* (Camden) 82 A kennell for the dogs, and a new ducquoy in the park. **1714** *Flying-Post* 4–7 Dec., Keeper of New Forest in Hampshire, and of the Duckoy there. **1750** R. POCOCKE *Trav.* (1888) 94 The duckoy close to the Fleet, where the swans..breed, as well as wildfowl. **1839** STONEHOUSE *Axholme* 68 The decoy has superseded all those ancient methods of taking water fowl. **1846** MCCULLOCH *Acc. Brit. Empire* (1854) I. 179 Decoys for the taking of wild ducks, teal, widgeons, etc. were..at one time, very common in the fens; but a few only exist at present. **1886** PAYNE-GALLWEY *Bk. Duck Decoys* 17 A Decoy is a cunning and clever combination of water, nets, and screens, by means of which wildfowl, such as Wigeon, Mallard, and Teal, are caught alive.

2. *fig.* A place into which persons are enticed to the profit of the keeper.

1678 OTWAY *Friendship in F.* IV. i. (R.), You who keep a general decoy here for fools and coxcombs [a brothel]. *a* **1839** PRAED *Poems* (1864) I. 197 The place was cursed with an evil name, And that name was 'The Devil's Decoy!'

3. A bird (or other animal) trained to lure or entice others (usually of its species) into a trap.

1661 *Humane Industry* 170 Wilde Ducks, that are tamed and made Decoyes, to intice and betray their fellows. **1663** COWLEY *Verses & Ess.* (1669) 132 Man is to man..a treacherous Decoy, and a rapacious Vulture. **1774** GOLDSM. *Nat. Hist.* (1862) II. VII. xii. 235 A number of wild ducks made tame, which are called decoys. **1859** TENNENT *Ceylon* II. VIII. v. 366 A display of dry humour in the manner in which the decoys thus played with the fears of the wild herd [of elephants].

4. Applied to a person:

†**a.** A swindler, sharper; an impostor or 'shark' who lives by his wits at the expense of his dupes. *Obs.*

(It is, from the early date and sense, very doubtful if this belongs to this word. In the 'character' by Brathwait (quot. 1631), there is no reference explicit or implicit to the action of a decoy-duck. It rather looks as if this were a slang term already in use when *coys* and *coy-ducks* were introduced into England, and as if *coy-duck* were changed into *decoy-duck* with allusion to this.)

1618 MYNSHUL *Ess. Prison* 30 Iaylors..are..indeed for the most part the very off-scum of the rascall multitude, as Cabbage-carriers, Decoyes, Bum-bayliffes, disgraced Purseuants, Botchers..and a rabble of such stinkardly companions. **1630** J. TAYLOR (Water P.) *Wks.* I. 71/1 To Sharkes, Stales, Nims, Lifts, Foysts, Cheats, Stands, Decoyes. **1631** BRATHWAIT *Whimzies, Char. Decoy* 25 A Decoy Is a brave metall'd Blade, as apt to take as give. *Ibid.* 31 Which simplicitie of his our Decoy observes and workes upon it.

b. One who entices, allures, or inveigles another into some trap, deception, or evil situation; = DECOY-DUCK 2.

1638 FORD *Lady's Trial* V. i, I foster a decoy here [his niece, a strumpet]; And she trowls on her ragged customer, To cut my throat for pillage. **1656** EARL MONM. *Advt. fr. Parnass.* 186 These were the true de quois, or call-ducks, which ticed in the scum of the city. **1667** *Decay Chr. Piety* xviii. ¶5 To lead captive silly women, and make them the duck-coys to their whole family. **1744** BERKELEY *Siris* §108 Some tough dram-drinker, set up as the devil's decoy, to draw in proselytes. **1843** DICKENS *Mart. Chuz.* xli, I want you, besides, to act as a decoy in a case I have already told you of. **1849** JAMES *Woodman* xxxii, I have the pretty decoy [a girl] in my own hand, I can whistle either bird back to the lure.

5. Anything employed to allure and entice, especially into a trap; an enticement, bait, trap.

1655 FULLER *Ch. Hist.* III. iii. §24 Intending onely a short Essay, and to be (let me call it) an honest Decoy, by entering on this subject, to draw others into the compleating thereof. **1679** PENN *Addr. Prot.* II. 178 She that makes her Pretences to Religion a Decoy to catch the World. **1698** FRYER *Acc. E. India & P.* 45 Antilopes, not to be taken but by a Decoy made of Green Boughs, wherein a Man hides himself. **1705** HICKERINGILL *Priest-cr.* (1721) I. 27 [By] the Duckoy of a Wedding..trepan'd to Death and Murther'd. **1865** LUBBOCK *Preh. Times* xiv. (1869) 500 A decoy roughly representing the head and antlers of a reindeer has been put up. **1883** A. K. GREEN *Hand & Ring* xx, The note had been sent as a decoy by the detective.

6. *attrib.* and *Comb.*, as ***decoy-bird***, ***-dog***, ***-goose***, ***-place***; **decoy-man**, **decoyman**, one whose business it is to attend to a decoy for wildfowl; **decoy ship**, one used to decoy enemy vessels.

1643 *Soveraigne Salve* 39 Some dequoy indulgence may be used towards them to draw others, till all be in [their] power. **1711** KING tr. *Naude's Refined Pol.* v. 195 The Bird-catchers, to succeed in their sport, make use of decoy birds. **1775** *Epit.* in *Birm. Weekly Post* 17 Jan. (1891) 11/1 Andrew Williams..lived under the Aston family as Decoy-man 60 years. **1778** *Sportsman's Dict., Decoy-duck*..by her allurement draws [wild ones] into the decoy-place. **1799** W. TOOKE *View Russ. Emp.* III. 83 The Ostiaks..placed at some distance several decoy-geese. **1839** STONEHOUSE *Axholme* 68 Screens, formed of reeds, are set up..to prevent the possibility of the fowl seeing the decoy man. *Ibid.*, The decoy birds resort to..the mouth of the pipes, followed by the young wild fowl. **1883** G. C. DAVIES *Norfolk Broads* xxii. (1884) 164 The decoy-dog..was a retriever of reddish colour. **1887** *Daily News* 21 Nov. 2/8 The prisoner had used his shop as a decoy place for poor little girls. **1915** *War Illustrated* III. 262/2 Decoy ships flying a neutral flag. **1923** W. S. CHURCHILL *World Crisis 1915* 290 Our two principal devices for destroying the German submarines were the Bircham Indicator Nets and the Decoy Ships, afterwards called the Q-boats. **1925** FRASER & GIBBONS *Soldier & Sailor Words* 73 *Decoy ships*, a name for certain vessels (also known as 'Mystery Ships' and 'Q-Ships'), introduced in 1915.

decoy (dɪˈkɔɪ), *v.* [See prec.

The vb. is considerably later than the sb., and its earliest examples are spelt *duckoy*; it was evidently formed directly from the sb., of which it reflects the contemporary varieties of spelling.]

1. *trans.* To alure or entice (wildfowl or other animals) into a snare or place of capture: said usually when this is done by, or with the aid of, another animal trained to the work.

1671 *Phil. Trans.* VI. 3093 The Wild Elephants are by the tame Females of the same kind as 'twere duckoy'd into a lodge with trap-doors. **1697** DAMPIER *Voy.* I. 168 Their Hogs..at night come in..and are put up in their Crauls or Pens, and yet some turn wild, which nevertheless are often decoyed in by the other. **1735** *Sportsman's Dict.*, Decoy-birds..are usually kept in a cage and from thence decoy birds into the nets. **1788** REID *Act. Powers* III. II. iv. 565 The arts they use..to decoy hawks and other enemies. **1835** W. IRVING *Tour Prairies* 170 A black horse on the Brasis..being decoyed under a tree by a tame mare. **1845** YARRELL *Hist. Birds* (ed. 2) III. 266 The outer side..is the one on which the person walks who is decoying the fowl.

2. To entice or allure (persons) by the use of cunning and deceitful attractions, *into* a place or situation, *away*, *out*, *from* a situation, *to do* something.

1660 HICKERINGILL *Jamaica* Pref. (1661) A ij b, To allure and Duckoy the unwary world. *a* **1674** CLARENDON *Hist. Reb.* XI. (1888) §195 Rolph answered, that the King might be decoyed from thence..and then he might easily be despatched. **1709** STEELE *Tatler* No. 59 ¶1 That they may not be decoyed in by the soft Allurement of a Fine Lady. **1774** GOLDSM. *Nat. Hist.* (1776) II. 261 Two of whom the mariners decoyed on ship-board. **1776** ADAM SMITH *W.N.* II. v. I. 365 [They] may sometimes decoy a weak customer to buy what he has no occasion for. **1833** HT. MARTINEAU *Fr. Wines* iv. 63 They would not be decoyed away by a false alarm. **1865** BARING-GOULD *Werewolves* vi. 81 This wretched man had decoyed children into his shop.

Hence **de'coyer**, **de'coying** *vbl. sb.*

1883 G. C. DAVIES *Norfolk Broads* xxii. (1884) 162 Decoying was the only item of the wild life still existing in the Broad district with which we had not made ourselves acquainted.

decoy-duck (dɪˈkɔɪˌdʌk, ˈdiːkɔɪ-). [f. DECOY *sb.* + DUCK. Cf. Du. *kooieend* in same sense.]

1. A duck trained to decoy its fellows.

1651 C. WALKER *Hist. Independ.* III. 34 These..are rewarded like Decoy Duckes for their paines. **1883** G. C. DAVIES *Norfolk Broads* xxii. (1884) 167 These decoy ducks are kept in the decoy, and trained to come in for food whenever they..hear a low whistle from the decoy-man.

2. *fig.* A person who entices another into danger or mischief.

1625 FLETCHER *Fair Maid* IV. ii, You are worse than simple widgeons, and will be drawn into the net by this decoy-duck, this tame cheater. **1688** SHADWELL *Sqr. Alsatia* Dram. Personæ, Shamwell..being ruined by Cheatly, is made a decoy-duck for others. **1887** *Daily News* 11 July 3/1 At Monte Carlo..he was employed as a decoy duck.

de'crassify, *v. rare.* [f. DE- II. 1 + L. *crass-us* thick, gross + -FY.] *trans.* To divest of what is crass, gross, or material.

1855 BROWNING *Bp. Blougram's Apol.* Wks. IV. 267, I hear you recommend, I might at least Eliminate, decrassify my faith. **1885** COUPLAND *Spirit Goethe's Faust* vi. 202 Our attempt to decrassify this symbol, to see in it the wonderful power of the creative human brain.

decrease (dɪˈkriːs, ˈdiːkriːs), *sb.* Forms: 4 decrees, 4–7 discrease, 5 decresse, 6– decrease. [a. OF. *decreis*, *descreis* (later *des-*, *de-crois*, now *décroît*), verbal sb. f. stem of *de-*, *descreis-tre* (*de(s)creiss-ant*) to DECREASE.]

The process of growing less; lessening, diminution, falling off, abatement; the condition which results from this. (Opposed to INCREASE *sb.*)

1383 GOWER *Conf.* III. 154 That none honour fall in decrees [*v.r.* discrease]. **1488–9** *Act 4 Hen. VII*, c. 1 To decresse and destruccion of your lyvelode. **1555** EDEN *Decades* 119 They see the seas by increase and decrease to flowe and reflowe. **1665** PEPYS *Diary* 28 Nov., Soon as we know how the plague goes this week, which we hope will be a good decrease. **1674** PLAYFORD *Skill Mus.* I. viii. 24 Notes of Diminution or Decrease. **1742** YOUNG *Nt. Th.* v. 717 While man is growing, life is in decrease. **1874** GREEN *Short Hist.* iv. §2. 168 The steady decrease in the number of the greater nobles.

†**b.** *spec.* The wane of the moon. *Obs.*

1626 BACON *Sylva* §626 Such Fruits..you must gather..when the Moon is under the Earth, and in decrease. **1661** LOVELL *Hist. Anim. & Min.* 29 The same taken in the decrease of the moon..helpeth the fits of quartans. **1746** HERVEY *Medit.* (1818) 266 The moon in her decrease prevents the dawn.

decrease (dɪˈkriːs), *v.* Forms: α. 4–5 discrese, 5 discrease, -creace, dyscres, -crece, 6 discresse, dyscrease; β. 4–5 decreesse, 4–6 decrese, 5 -crece, -creace, 5–6 -cresse, 6 *Sc.* dicres, 6– decrease. [f. OF. *de-*, *descreiss-*, ppl. stem of *descreistre* (later *descroistre* (Cotgr. 1611), now *décroître*) = Pr. *descreisser*, Cat. *descrexer*, Sp. *descrecer*, It. *di'screscere*, which took in Romanic the place of L. *dēcrēscĕre*, f. *dē-* down + *crēscĕre* to grow: see DE- I. 6. Under the influence of the L., *decreistre* was an occasional variant in OF., and under the same influence, *de-crese*, found beside *descrese* in ME., eventually superseded it. An AngloFr. *decresser*, influenced by Eng. *decrese* or L. *decrescere*, is found in the Statutes of Hen. VI.]

1. *intr.* To grow less (in amount, importance, influence, etc.); to lessen, diminish, fall off, shrink, abate. (Opposed to INCREASE *v.*)

α. **1393** GOWER *Conf.* II. 189 Knowend how that the feith discreseth. *a* **1400** *Cov. Myst.* (1841) 224 Oure joy wylle sone dyscres. **1490** CAXTON *Eneydos* Prol. 2 The mone..euer wauerynge, wexynge one season and waneth & dyscreaseth another season. **1526** SKELTON *Magnyf.* 2545 Now ebbe, now flowe, nowe increase, nowe dyscrease. **1530** PALSGR. 518/2, I discresse, I growe lasse or dymynysshe.

β. **1382** WYCLIF *Gen.* viii. 5 The watres ȝeden and decreesseden [**1388** decresiden] vnto the tenthe moneth. *c* **1400** MAUNDEV. (Roxb.) vi. 23 Þan begynnes Nilus to decreesse. **1483** *Cath. Angl.* 92 To Decrese (A. Decresse), *decrescere*. **1530** PALSGR. 509/1, I decrease, I waxe lesse, or vanysshe awaye. **1534** TINDALE *John* iii. 30 He must increace: and I must decreace. **1608** SHAKS. *Per.* I. ii. 85 Tyrants' fears Decrease not, but grow faster than the years. **1776** GIBBON *Decl. & F.* ii. (1838) I. 36 The number of citizens gradually decreased. **1854** BREWSTER *More Worlds* iv. 68 The temperature..decreases as we rise in the atmosphere.

2. *trans.* To cause to grow less; to lessen, diminish.

c **1470** HARDING *Chron.* XVI. vii, For couetyse his brother to discreace. **1587** *Mirr. Mag.*, *Cordila* xlv, He first decreast my wealth. **1596** SHAKS. *Tam. Shrew* II. 119 His Lands and goods, Which I haue bettered rather then decreast. **1651** *Life Father Sarpi* (1676) 80 Yet the Father knew very well that age decreaseth strength. *c* **1718** PRIOR *An Epitaph* 42 Nor cherish'd they relations poor, That might decrease their present store. **1865** MILL in *Even. Star* 10 July, That did not decrease in the least the hundreds of miles which London was distant from Edinburgh.

Hence **de'creasing** *vbl. sb.* and *ppl. a.*, **de'creasingly** *adv.*

1398 TREVISA *Barth. De P.R.* VIII. ii. (1495) 298 In the whyche waters..it makyth encreasynge and decresynge. **1591** PERCIVALL *Sp. Dict.*, *Descrecimiento*, decreasing. **1633** FLETCHER *Purple Isl.* IX. l. 134 Which yet increases more with the decreasing day. **1796** MORSE *Amer. Geog.* I. 277 [Quakers] hold that..baptism with water belonged to an inferior and decreasing dispensation. **1822** *Examiner* 219/1 Glaring on its contiguous objects, and decreasingly gleaming to the foreground. *Mod.* Food was decreasingly scarce.

decreation (diːkriːˈeɪʃən). [f. DE- I. 6 + CREATION. (In sense of 'diminution' *décréation* is found in 14th c. F.)] The undoing of creation; depriving of existence; annihilation.

1647 WARD *Simp. Cobler* 47 As he is a creature, hee feares decreation. **1678** CUDWORTH *Intell. Syst.* I. i. §37. 45 More Reasonable..then the continual Decreation and Annihilation of the souls of Brutes. **1918** P. T. FORSYTH *This Life & Next* x. 97 It is creation not out of a chaos but a wreck. It is the recreation of a decreation. *a* **1930** D. H. LAWRENCE *Pornography & so On* (1936) 26 The excrementory flow is towards dissolution, de-creation, if we may use such a word.

†**decre'ator**. *Obs.* [f. DE- I. 6 + CREATOR, implying a vb. *decreate*: see prec.] One who uncreates or annihilates.

1678 CUDWORTH *Intell. Syst.* I. iv. §25. 426 Not only the Creator of all the other gods, but also..the Decreator of them.

decrece, obs. form of DECREASE.

decree (dɪˈkriː), *sb.* Also 4–6 decre. [a. OF. *decré*, var. of *decret* (in pl. *decrez*, *decres*) = Pr. *decret*, Sp., It. *decreto*, ad. L. *dēcrētum*, subst. use of neuter of *dēcrētus*, pa. pple. of *dēcernĕre* to decree: see DECERN.]

1. An ordinance or edict set forth by the civil or other authority; an authoritative decision having the force of law.

c **1325** *E.E. Allit. P.* B. 1745 Þen watz demed a de-cre bi þe duk seluen. *c* **1330** R. BRUNNE *Chron.* (1810) 122 At London þei wer atteynt, decre was mad for þate. **1483** *Cath. Angl.* 92 A Decree, *decretum*. **1596** SHAKS. *Merch. V.* IV. i. 102 There is no force in the decrees of Venice. **1637** (*title*), A Decree of the Starre-Chamber concerning Printing. **1697** DRYDEN *Virg. Georg.* III. 7 The dire Decrees Of hard Euristheus. **1796** H. HUNTER tr. *St.-Pierre's Stud. Nat.* (1799) III. 639 The Constituent Assembly..abolished, by it's decree of September 1791, the justice which it had done to persons of colour in the Antilles. **1821** J. Q. ADAMS in C. Davies *Metr. Syst.* III. (1871) 140 This report was sanctioned by a decree of the assembly. **1851** TENNYSON *To the Queen* ix, To take Occasion by the hand, and make The bounds of freedom wider yet By shaping some august decree.

fig. **1596** SHAKS. *Merch. V.* I. ii. 20 The braine may deuise lawes for the blood, but a hot temper leapes ore a colde decree. **1697** DRYDEN *Virg. Georg.* I. 289 Whether by Nature's Curse, Or Fate's Decree.

2. *Eccl.* An edict or law of an ecclesiastical council, usually one settling some disputed or doubtful point of doctrine or discipline; in *pl.* the collection of such laws and decisions, forming part of the canon law. (Cf. DECRETAL.)

1303 R. BRUNNE *Handl. Synne* 4640 Hyt ys forbode hym, yn þe decre, Myracles for to make or se. **1377** LANGL. *P. Pl.* B. xv. 373 Doctoures of decres and of diuinite Maistres.

1393 GOWER *Conf.* I. 257 The pope..hath made and yove the decre. **1531** in W. H. Turner *Select. Rec. Oxford* 95 Master Morgan Johns, bachelor of decrees. **1564** *(title)*, A godly and necessarie Admonition of the Decrees and Canons of the Counsel of Trent. **1691** WOOD *Ath. Oxon.* I. 20 He was..admitted to the extraordinary reading of any Book of the Decretals, that is to the degree of Bach. of Decrees, which some call the Canon Law. **1726** AYLIFFE *Parergon* p. xxxvii, A Decree is an Ordinance which is enacted by the Pope himself, by and with the advice of his Cardinals in Council assembled, without being consulted by any one thereon. **1843** *Penny Cycl.* XXV. 189/1 The king and the queen-mother promised..that they would accept the decrees of the Council [of Trent]. **1893** P. T. FORSYTH in *Faith & Criticism* 106 If that infallibility be carried beyond Himself..there is no logical halting-place till we

3. *Theol.* One of the eternal purposes of God whereby events are foreordained.

1570 B. GOOGE *Pop. Kingd.* I. (1880) 1 All the Deuils deepe in hell, at his decrees doe quake. **1648** *Assembly's Larger Catech.* Q. 12 God's Decrees are the wise, free, and holy acts of the counsel of his will, whereby from all eternity, he hath, for his own glory, unchangeably fore-ordained whatsoever comes to passe in time. *a* **1711** KEN *Hymnarium* Poet. Wks. 1721 II. 108 Her Conscience tells her God's Decree Full option gave, and made her free. **1860** MOTLEY *Netherl.* (1868) I. i. 4 Philip stood enfeoffed, by divine decree, of..possessions far and near.

4. *Law.* A judicial decision. In various specific uses: **a.** *Rom. Law.* A decision given by the emperor on a question brought before him judicially.

1776–81 GIBBON *Decl. & F.* xliv, The rescripts of the emperor, his grants and decrees, his edicts and pragmatic sanctions, were subscribed in purple ink. **1880** MUIRHEAD *Gaius* I. §5 An imperial constitution is what the emperor has established by decree, edict, or letter. It has never been disputed that such a constitution has the full force of a *lex*.

b. *Eng. Law.* The judgement of a court of equity, or of the Court of Admiralty, Probate, and Divorce. But since the Judicature Act of 1873–5, the term 'judgement' is applied to the decisions of courts having both common law and equity powers.

Decree is still used in *Admiralty* cases. In *Divorce* cases, a *decree* is an order of the Court declaring the nullity of dissolution of marriage, or the judicial separation of the parties. *decree nisi*: the order made by the court for divorce, which remains conditional for at least six months, after which, *unless* cause to the contrary is shown, it is made absolute. In *Ecclesiastical* cases, *decree* is a special form of citation of the party to the suit.

1622 CALLIS *Stat. Sewers* (1647) 231 A Decree is..only a Sentence of Judgement in a Court of Justice, delivered or declared by the Judges there. **1735** *Col. Rec. Pennsylv.* IV. 39 But two Causes, and both by Consent, have been brought to a Decree. **1768** BLACKSTONE *Comm.* III. 451 When all are heard, the court pronounces the *decree*, adjusting every point in debate according to equity and good conscience. **1848** WHARTON *Law Lex.* s.v., Courts of equity may adjust their decrees so as to meet different exigencies..whereas courts of common law are bound down to a fixed and invariable form of judgment. **1860**, **1872** [see NISI]. **1873** *Act 36 & 37 Vict.* c. 66 §100 In the construction of this Act..the several words herein-after mentioned shall have, or include, the meanings following; (that is to say)..'Judgment' shall include Decree. **1873** PHILLIMORE *Eccles. Law* 1254 These decrees or citations are signed by the Registrar of the Court. **1892** GEARY *Law of Marriage* 354 A decree of judicial separation may be subsequently turned into a decree for dissolution. **1893** BARNES in *Law Rep.* Probate Div. 154 The decree I make will be: that the crew other than the captain shall receive salvage according to their ratings. *a* **1894** *Mod. Newspr.*, A decree *nisi* was pronounced. The decree was made absolute. **1922** [see ABSOLUTE *a.* 5c]. **1934** A. P. HERBERT *Holy Deadlock* 163 She was a lonely decree-nisi mongrel of a woman.

c. *Sc. Law.* The final judgement or sentence of a civil court, whereby the question at issue between the parties is decided; strictly, a judgement which can be put in force by containing the executive words 'and decerns': cf. DECERNITURE.

Decrees are said to be *condemnator* or *absolvitor* according as the decision is in favour of the pursuer or the defender. A *decree in absence* is a decree pronounced against a defender who has not appeared and pleaded on the merits of the cause = 'Judgement by Default' in English Common Law. *decree of registration* is a decree *fictione juris* of a court, interposed without the actual intervention of a judge, in virtue of the party's consent to a decree going out against him. *decree arbitral*: an award by one or more arbiters: see ARBITRAL. *decree dative*: see DATIVE. *decree of locality, modification,* and *valuation of teinds*: various decisions of the Teind Court. (Bell, *Dict. Law Scotl.* 1861.) Cf. earlier DECREET 1 b.

1754 ERSKINE *Princ. Sc. Law* (1809) 484 Before horning could pass on the decree of an inferior judge, the decree was, by our former practice, to have been judicially produced before the Session, and their authority interposed to it by a new decree. **1861** W. BELL *Dict. Law Scot.* s.v., The decree issued by the Court of Session in aid of the inferior court decree, was called a *decree conform*. **1877** MACKAY *Practice Crt. Session* I. 581 The term *decree* is now sometimes used interchangeably with *interlocutor*, though it might be convenient to apply the former to a final determination by which the whole or a substantive part of the cause is decided, and the latter to an order pronounced in its course.

decree (dɪkriː), *v.* Also 6 decre, decrey. [f. DECREE *sb.*: cf. F. *décréter*, f. *décret*.]

1. *trans.* To command (something) by decree; to order, appoint, or assign authoritatively, ordain.

1399 *Rolls of Parlt.* III. 424/1 [Their] Commissaries..declared and decreed, and adjugged yowe fore to be deposed and pryved..of the Astate of Kyng. **1538** STARKEY *England* I. i. 20 No partycular mean by cyuyle ordynance decred. **1590** MARLOWE *Edw. II*, Wks. (Rtldg.) 194/2 The stately triumph we decreed. *a* **1627** MIDDLETON *Mayor of Q.* IV. ii, Upon the plain of Salisbury A peaceful meeting they decreen. **1637** *Decree Star Chamber* §11 It is further Ordered and Decreed, that no Merchant, Bookseller..shall imprint..any English bookes [etc.]. *a* **1718** ROWE (J.), Their father..has decreed His sceptre to the younger. **1858** FROUDE *Hist. Eng.* III. xii. 13 The English parliaments were ..decreeing the dissolution of the smaller monasteries. **1876** J. H. NEWMAN *Hist. Sk.* I. III. i. 309 The cities sent embassies to him, decreeing him public honours.

b. *fig.* To ordain as by Divine appointment, or by fate.

c **1580** C'TESS PEMBROKE *Ps.* (1823) CXIX. B. iii, What thou dost decree. **1594** HOOKER *Eccl. Pol.* I. ii. (1611) 4 Wherewith God hath eternally decreed when and how they should be. **1601** SHAKS. *Twel. N.* I. v. 330 What is decreed, must be: and be this so. **1795** SOUTHEY *Joan of Arc* VI. 68 For Heaven all-just Hath seen our sufferings and decreed their end. **1841** LANE *Arab. Nts.* I. 111 Give me patience, O Allah, to bear what Thou decreest.

2. *Law.* †To pronounce judgement on (a cause), decide judicially (*obs.*); to order or determine by a judicial decision; to adjudge; *absol.* to give judgement in a cause.

1530 PALSGR. 509/1, I shall decree it or it be to morowe noone. **1570** LEVINS 46/39 To Decree, *decernere*. **1621** ELSING *Debates Ho. Lords* (Camden) 112 He decreed the cause not hearing any one wytnesse. **1818** CRUISE *Digest* (ed. 2) I. 469 It was decreed to be a resulting trust for the grantor. *Ibid.* VI. 489 Lord Bathurst decreed accordingly. **1891** *Law Reports* Weekly Notes 43/1 The Court would not decree specific performance of a contract of service.

3. To decide or determine authoritatively; to pronounce by decree.

a **1571** JEWEL *Serm. Haggai* i. 4 Our fathers in the Councill holden at Constance..have decreed..that, to minister the Communion to a lay man under both kinds, is an open heresie. **1651** HOBBES *Leviath.* II. xxii. 116 Whatsoever that Assembly shall Decree. **1837** CARLYLE *Fr. Rev.* I. v. ii, The Third Estate is decreeing that it is, was, and will be nothing but a National Assembly.

†**b.** *to decree (a person) for*: to put him down as, pronounce him to be. *Obs. rare.*

1616 BEAUM. & FL. *Scornful Lady* IV. i, Such a Coxcomb, such a whining Ass, as you decreed me for when I was last here.

†**4.** To determine, resolve, decide (*to do* something). *Obs.* or *arch.*

1526 *Pilgr. Perf.* (W. de W. 1531) 86 b, Decreyinge with them selfe..to beare and suffre all thynges. **1599** SHAKS. *Much Ado* I. iii. 35, I haue decreed not to sing in my cage. **1697** DRYDEN *Virg. Georg.* IV. 333 When thou hast decreed to seize their Stores. **1754** FIELDING *Jon. Wild* IV. viii, Here we decreed to rest and dine. **1871** R. ELLIS *Catullus* viii. 17 Who decrees to live thine own?

5. *absol.* or *intr.* To decide, determine, ordain.

1591 SPENSER *Ruines of Rome* vi. 11 So did the Gods by heavenly doome decree. **1600** SHAKS. *A. Y. L.* I. ii. 111 As the destinies decrees. **1647–8** COTTERELL *Davila's Hist. Fr.* (1678) 3 Laws, decreed of in the fields [of battle]. **1667** MILTON *P.L.* III. 172 As my Eternal purpose hath decreed.

Hence **de'creed** *ppl. a*, **de'creeing** *vbl. sb.* and *ppl. a.*

1548 UDALL, etc. *Erasm. Par. Phil.* ii. (R.), Suche was the decreed wyll of the father. **1591** SPENSER *Ruins of Time* 35 Bereft of both by Fates vniust decreeing. **1618** BOLTON *Florus* III. xxi. 242 Hee laboured by the law of Sulpitius to take from Sulla his decreed employment. **1878** SEELEY *Stein* II. 133 The decreeing and executing Power not being combined.

decreeable (dɪ'kriːab(ə)l), *a. rare.* [-ABLE.] Capable of being decreed.

1846 WORCESTER cites VERNON.

†**de'creement.** *Obs.* [-MENT.] A decreeing, a decree.

1563–87 FOXE *A. & M.* (1596) 5/1 These..expresse decreements of general councels. **1601** BP. W. BARLOW *Defense* 197 The sole..iudge of all writings and decreementes.

decreement, obs. (erron.) f. DECREMENT.

decreer (dɪ'kriːə(r)). [-ER[1].] One who decrees.

1660 H. MORE *Myst. Godl.* VII. ii. 283 The word naturally signifies a Commander or Decreer. **1664** —— *Myst. Iniq.* 285 A Decreer of Idolatrous practices. *a* **1679** T. GOODWIN *Wks.* I. III. 103 (R.), The first decreer of it.

decrees, decreesse, obs. forms of DECREASE.

decreet (dɪ'kriːt), *sb. Obs.* or *arch.* Forms: 4–5 decret, 5–7 decreit, decrete, 6– decreet. [a. F. *décret*, or ad. L. *dēcrēt-um*: see DECREE *sb.*]

†**1.** An earlier form of the word DECREE, entirely *Obs.* in English, and in Sc. retained only as in b.

c **1374** CHAUCER *Boeth.* I. iv. 17 þoruȝ her decretz and hire iugementys. *c* **1425** WYNTOUN *Cron.* VIII. v. 172 He gert þame þare decrete retrete, And all tyl wndo þaire sentens. **1483** CAXTON *Gold. Leg.* 108 b/1 Lyke as it is had in the decrete. **1552** ABP. HAMILTON *Catech.* (1884) 5 The decreet maid in our provincial counsale. **1571** *Sat. Poems Reform.* xxviii. 78 Aganis thair Cannoun Law thay gaif decreit. *a* **1605** MONTGOMERIE *Misc. Poems* xxxii. 10 Nane dou reduce the Destinies decreit.

b. *Sc. Law.* = DECREE 4 c. (The vernacular form in Sc.; now *arch.*)

1491 *Sc. Acts Jas. IV* (1597) §30 Within twentie daies after the decreet of the deliuerance be given there vpon. **1584** *Sc. Acts Jas. VI* (1597) §139 All decreetes giuen be quhatsumeuer Judges. **1609** SKENE *Reg. Maj.* 21 The effect of ane decreit given be Arbiters is, that it sall be obeyed, quhither it be just or nocht. **1752** in *Scots Mag.* June (1753) 287/2 He had procured a sist..against the decreet. **1812** CHALMERS *Let.* in *Life* (1851) I. 272 The only effect of this decreet of the Court of Teinds. **1824** SCOTT *Redgauntlet* ch. ii, It went..just like a decreet in absence. **1833** *Act* 3–4 *Will. IV*, c. 46 §70 Such summary decreets and warrants.

†**2.** A decision, determination. *Obs. rare.*

c **1400** *Apol. Loll.* 101 Chaunge þi decret, & do not þis þat þu hast vowid unwarly. *c* **1470** HENRY *Wallace* VIII. 630 This decret thar wit amang thaim fand; Gyff Wallace wald apon him tak the croun, To gyff battaill thai suld be redy boun.

†**decreet** (dɪ'kriːt), *v. Obs.* Forms: see prec. [a. F. *décréte-r*, f. *décret* DECREE. Only *Sc.* after 15th c.]

1. *trans.* To decree, order, ordain.

c **1425** WYNTOUN *Cron.* VI. iv. 72 He Decretyd hym þar Kyng to be. **1457** *Sc. Acts Jas. II* (1814) II. 48/1 It is decretyt & ordainyt þ[t] wapinschawings be haldin be þe lords. **1491** CAXTON *Vitas Patr.* (W. de W. 1495) I. xlix. 97 a/1 It is decreted by sentence dyuyne. *c* **1565** LINDESAY (Pitscottie) *Chron. Scot.* (1728) 62 It is also..decreeted that all faithful men shall lay to their shoulders for expelling of thir common enemies. **1633** *Sc. Acts Chas. I* (1817) V. 42/2 Quhat they sall decreit and determine.

2. To decide, determine, resolve (*to do* something).

1582–8 *Hist. James VI* (1804) 138 He decrettit to pas hame, and to leaue the Regent's company.

3. *intr.* To pronounce a decision or judgement.

1563 WINȜET *Wks.* (1890) II. 30 Paraduentuir he..hes brestit out erar of a manlie passioun, than decretit be heuinlie ressoun. **1597** MONTGOMERIE *Cherrie & Slae* 1324 Since ȝe ȝoursells submit To do as I decreit. **1609** SKENE *Reg. Maj.* 21 Be consent of the parties, the Arbiters may decreit as they please. *Ibid.* 65 Arbiters..may not decreit vpon ane halie day.

Hence **de'creeted** *ppl. a.*, decreed.

172. *Wodrow Corr.* (1843) II. 558 A Decreeted Non-juror. **1761** HUME *Hist. Eng.* II. xxx. 168 The more to pacify the king he showed to him..the decreted bull.

decrement ('dɛkrɪmənt). [ad. L. *dēcrēment-um*, f. *dēcrē-* stem of inceptive *dēcrē-sc-ĕre* to DECREASE: see -MENT.]

1. a. The process or fact of decreasing or growing gradually less, or (with *pl.*) an instance of this; decrease, diminution, lessening, waste, loss. (Opposed to *increment*.)

1621 MOUNTAGU *Diatribæ* 310 The decrements of the First-fruits. **1631** BRATHWAIT *Whimzies* 93 Hee would finde his decrements great, his increments small: his receits come farre short of his disbursements. **1660** BOYLE *New Exp. Phys. Mech.* xxi. 151 The greater decrement of the pressure of the Air. **1695** WOODWARD *Nat. Hist. Earth* v. (1723) 253 Rocks..suffer a continual Decrement, and grow lower and lower. **1774** J. BRYANT *Mythology* I. 339 A society..where there is a continual decrement. **1840** J. H. GREEN *Vital Dynamics* 81 Signs of the decrement of vital energy.

†**b.** *spec.* Bodily decay, wasting away. *Obs.*

1646 SIR T. BROWNE *Pseud. Ep.* VI. iv. 289 Our decrement accelerates, we set apace, and in our last dayes precipitate into our graves. **1692** RAY *Dissol. World* III. v. (1732) 340 There is a Decrement or Decay both of Things and Men.

c. The wane (of the moon): *spec.* in *Heraldry*.

1610 GUILLIM *Heraldry* III. iii. (1611) 91 Her divers denominations in Heraldrie, as her increment in her increase..her decrement in her waning and her detriment in her change and eclipse. **1822** T. TAYLOR *Apuleius* 292 The Moon..defining the month through her increments, and afterwards by her equal decrements.

d. *decrement of life*: in the doctrine of annuities and tables of mortality: The (annual) decrease of a given number of persons by death.

1752 *Phil. Trans.* XLVII. liii. 335 The decrements of life may be esteemed nearly equal, after a certain age. **1755** BRAKENRIDGE *ibid.* XLIX. 180 It will be easy to form a table of the decrements of life. **1851** HERSCHEL *Stud. Nat. Phil.* II. vi. 178 The decrement of life, or the law of mortality.

e. *Crystallography.* 'A successive diminution of the layers of molecules, applied to the faces of the primitive form, by which the secondary forms are supposed to be produced' (Webster).

1805–17 R. JAMESON *Char. Min.* (ed. 3) 146 The decrements on the edges concur with those in the angles to produce the same crystalline form. **1823** H. J. BROOKE *Introd. Crystallogr.* 18 When the additions do not cover the whole surface of a primary form, but there are rows of molecules omitted on the edges, or angles or the superimposed plates, such omission is called a *decrement*. **1858** BUCKLE *Civiliz.* II. vii. 402 The secondary forms of all crystals are derived from their primary forms by a regular process of decrement.

2. a. The amount lost by diminution or waste; *spec.* in *Math.* a small quantity by which a variable diminishes (*e.g.* in a given small time).

1666 BOYLE *Orig. Formes & Qual.*, [What] the obtained powder amounts to over and above the decrement of weight. **1758** I. LYONS *Fluxions* 90 Let *Y* be the decrement of *y*. **1812–6** PLAYFAIR *Nat. Phil.* (1819) I. 227 The decrements of heat in each second. **1846** H. ROGERS *Ess.* (1860) I. 202 Admitting increase or diminution by infinitely small increments or decrements. **1883** *Economist* 15 Sept., If the unearned increment is to be appropriated by the State.. The undeserved decrement, as perhaps it may be called, would surely claim compensation.

b. The ratio of the amplitudes of two successive cycles of a damped oscillation; also (more fully ***logarithmic decrement***), the natural logarithm of this.

1879 *Encycl. Brit.* X. 50/1 Such needles have great advantages—where, for instance, the time of oscillation, the logarithmic decrement, or the extent of swing of the needle has to be observed. **1908** E. H. BARTON *Text-bk. Sound* x. 577 Hartmann-Kempf found that the relation between logarithmic decrement and amplitude for three makes of tuning-fork is almost linear. **1913** [see DECREMETER]. **1927** E. G. RICHARDSON *Sound* iv. 121 To estimate the rate of decay, the ratio of the amplitudes in two successive periods is obtained, a quantity which is known as the decrement. It is the logarithm of this quantity..which usually figures in calculations. **1929** J. A. RATCLIFFE *Physical Principles of Wireless* i. 14 The reciprocal of this quantity, $R\sqrt{\frac{C}{L}}$, is of great importance in the theory of oscillatory circuits; it is known as the decrement of the circuit, and corresponds to the logarithmic decrement of a mechanical oscillatory system. **1936** L. S. PALMER *Wireless Engin.* iii. 47 Circuits with small decrements have good selectivity. **1966** W. T. THOMSON *Vibration Theory* ii. 48 A body vibrating in a viscous medium has a period of 0·20 sec. and an initial amplitude of 1·0 in. Determine the logarithmic decrement if the amplitude after 10 cycles is 0·02 in.

†**3.** Applied to certain college expenses at Oxford: see quot. 1726. *Obs.*

[**1483** in Arnolde *Chron.* (1811) 271 Item in decrementis, iij. li, vij. s'. i. d'.] **1726** R. NEWTON in *Reminiscences* (Oxf. Hist. Soc.) 64 Decrements, each Scholar's proportion for Fuel, Candles, Salt, and other common necessaries: originally so call'd as so much did, on these accounts, *decrescere*, or was discounted from a Scholar's Endowment.

decremeter ('dɛkrɪmiːtə(r), dɛ'krɛmɪtə(r)). *Electr.* [f. DECRE(MENT + -METER.] An instrument which measures the logarithmic decrement of an oscillatory circuit.

1913 *Year-Bk. Wireless Telegr. & Teleph.* 294 The Marconi Company has brought out an instrument called a decremeter, which enables an approximate measurement of the decrement of a circuit to be made. **1931** MOYER & WOSTREL *Radio Handbk.* III. 112 The decremeter..may be considered as a wave meter in which the movable plates of the variable condenser carry a dial graduated in values of decrements... This device gives a direct reading of the decrement on a dial.

de'creolize, *v.* [f. DE- II. 1 + CREOLIZE *v.* 2 b.] *trans.* To modify from a creolized towards a standard language; to cause (a language) to lose its creolization. Chiefly as *pa. pple.* and *ppl. a.* Also **de'creolizing** *vbl. sb.*; **de,creoli'zation**.

1933 BLOOMFIELD *Language* xxvi. 474 It is a question whether during this process the dialect that is being decreolized may not influence the speech of the community. **1968** *Word* XXIV. 260 The Negro speech has influenced the dialect of the entire region but has itself often become quite thoroughly 'decreolized'. **1971** I. F. HANCOCK in J. Spencer *Eng. Lang. W. Afr.* 116 Krio,..as with Gullah, Jamaican Creole, Guyana Creole and Cameroon Pidgin, is spoken side by side with English, which constantly exerts a 'standardizing' pressure on the language, resulting in its gradual decreolisation, especially with regard to pronunciation. **1974** *Florida FL Reporter* XII. 78/3 Grammatical differences (accountable for by perhaps some late-ordered, over-generalised rules or by perhaps decreolizing rules). **1977** *Language* LIII. 334 The strongest motive for variation in decreolization is the pressure to avoid the basilect. **1982** *English World-Wide* II. 245 A pidgin English which eventually became a plantation Creole language and ultimately a decreolized language. **1983** *Word* XXXIV. 207 According to Valdman.., decreolization plays a considerable role in Haiti, not only among the bilinguals.

†**decre'pidity**. *rare*⁻¹. [f. *decrepid*, variant of DECREPIT, after *timidity*, etc.] = DECREPITUDE.

1760 *Misc.* in *Ann. Reg.* 190/2 Age pictured in the mind is decrepidity in winter, retiring in the evening to the comfortable shelter of a fire-side.

decrepit (dɪ'krɛpɪt), *a.* (*sb.*) Also 6 decrepute, decreaped, 6–7 decrepite, -et, 7 -ate, 7–9 decrepid, 8 decripid, -ed, decripped. [a. F. *décrépit* (16th c.), in 15th c. *descrepy*, ad. L. *dēcrepitus* very old, decrepit, f. *dē-* down + *crepit-*, ppl. stem of *crepāre* to crack, creak, rattle. The final *-it* has had many forms assimilated to pa. pples., adjs. in *-id*, etc.]

1. Of living beings (and their attributes): Wasted or worn out with old age, decayed and enfeebled with infirmities; old and feeble.

c **1450** HENRYSON *Praise of Age* 2 Ane auld man, and decrepit, hard I sing. **1511–2** *Act 3 Hen. VIII*, c. 3 §1 Every man..not lame decrepute or maymed. **1550** CROWLEY *Inform. & Petit.* 463 To sustayne theyr parents decrepet age. **1606** WARNER *Alb. Eng.* XIV. lxxxix. 361 A fourth farre older decrepate with age. **1689–90** TEMPLE *Ess. Health & Long Life* Wks. 1731 I. 273 With common Diseases Strength grows decrepit. **1752** FIELDING *Amelia* (1775) X. 4 Poor old decrepit people, who are incapable of getting a livelihood by work. **1872** BLACK *Adv. Phaeton* xx. 283 Some poor old pensioner, decrepit and feeble-eyed.

β. decrepid, etc.

a **1616** BEAUM. & FL. *Lit. Fr. Lawyer* I. i, Thou shalt not find I am decrepid. **1696** DRYDEN *Let. Mrs. Stewart* 1 Oct. Wks. 1800 I. II. 66 How can you be so good to an old decrepid man? **1719** D'URFEY *Pills* (1872) IV. 317 Decripped old Sinners. **1820** W. IRVING *Sketch Bk.* I. 216 A poor decrepid old woman. **1845** G. E. DAY tr. *Simon's Anim. Chem.* I. 204 An old, decrepid..animal.

2. *fig.* of things.

1594 NASHE *Unfort. Trav.* 23 The decrepite Churches in contention beyond sea. **1646** SIR T. BROWNE *Pseud. Ep.* v. xxi. 264 Decrepite superstitions. **1780** BURKE *Sp. Econ. Reform* Wks. III. 261 The poor wasted decrepid revenue of the principality. **1863** D. G. MITCHELL *My Farm of Edgewood* 124 The decrepid apple trees are rooted up. **1878** LECKY *Eng. in 18th C.* I. i. 116 The military administrations of surrounding nations were singularly decrepit and corrupt.

B. *sb.* One who is decrepit. *Obs.* or *local.*

1578 BANISTER *Hist. Man* I. 25 In men full of dayes, and such decrepittes as old age hath long arrested. **1887** *S. Cheshire Gloss.*, *Decrippit*, a cripple, lame person.

†**de'crepit**, *v.* *Obs.*⁻¹ [f. prec.] To make decrepit (see quot.).

1688 R. HOLME *Armoury* III. 310/2 The Tying Neck and Heels, is a Punishment of decrepiting, that is benumming the Body, by drawing it all together, as it were into a round Ball.

†**decrepitage, decrepitancy.** *Obs.* Irregular formations = DECREPITUDE.

1670 G. H. *Hist. Cardinals* II. III. 176 Of his goodness and decrepitage [*bontà e decrepità*]. *Ibid.* III. II. 302 His age..his infirmities, and decrepitancy.

decrepitate (dɪ'krɛpɪteɪt), *v.* [f. med. or mod.L. *dēcrepitāre*, f. *dē-* down, away + *-crepitāre* to crackle, freq. of *crepāre* to crack. Cf. F. *décrépiter* (1690 in Hatzf.).]

1. *trans.* To calcine or roast (a salt or mineral) until it no longer crackles in the fire.

1646 SIR T. BROWNE *Pseud. Ep.* II. v. 87 And so will it come to passe in a pot of salt, although decrepitated. **1684** BOYLE *Porousn. Anim. & Solid Bod.* viii. 125 A pound of Dantzick Vitriol and a pound of Sea Salt, after the former had been very lightly calcined, and the latter decrepitated. **1799** G. SMITH *Laboratory* I. 379 Decrepitate them, *i.e.* dry them till they crack, in a pan, crucible, or clean fire shovel. **1832** G. R. PORTER *Porcelain & Gl.* 82 The salt purified and decrepitated,—that is, subjected to the action of heat until all crackling noise has ceased.

2. *intr.* Of salts and minerals: To make a crackling noise when suddenly heated, accompanied by a violent disintegration of their particles.

This is owing to the sudden conversion into steam of the water enclosed within the substance, or, as in some natural minerals, to the unequal expansion of the laminæ which compose them. Watts *Dict. Chem.*

1677 PLOT *Oxfordsh.* 54 Put in the fire, it presently decrepitates with no less noise than salt itself. **1800** tr. *Lagrange's Chem.* I. 331 If transparent calcareous spar be exposed to a sudden heat, it decrepitates and loses its transparency. **1849** DANA *Geol.* v. (1850) 324 *note*, It decrepitates..but does not fuse.

Hence **de'crepitated** *ppl. a.*, **de'crepitating** *vbl. sb.* and *ppl. a.*

1662 R. MATHEW *Unl. Alch.* §101. 165 Let thy salt stand meanly red til it wil crack no more, and that is called decrepitating. **1765** *Univ. Mag.* XXXVII. 84/2, I..take equal parts of decrepitated salt and nitre. **1819** H. BUSK *Vestriad* v. 53 Decrepitating salts with fury crack. **1874** GROVE *Contrib. Sc.* in *Corr. Phys. Forces* 304 A brilliant combustion, attended with a decrepitating noise.

decrepitation (dɪkrɛpɪ'teɪʃən). [n. of action f. DECREPITATE: see -ATION. Also mod.F. (1742 in Hatzf.), and prob. in 16–17th c. Latin.] The action of the verb DECREPITATE: **a.** The calcining of a salt or mineral until it ceases to crackle with the heat. **b.** The crackling and disintegration of a salt or mineral when exposed to sudden heat.

1669 W. SIMPSON *Hydrol. Chym.* 142 Unless the hydropick moisture..be exhausted by flagration or decrepitation. **1685** *Phil. Trans.* XV. 1061 In the decrepitation of common Salt. **1827** FARADAY *Chem. Manip.* v. 169 Decrepitation is generally occasioned by the expansion of the outer portions before the interior has had time to heat. **1830** LINDLEY *Nat. Syst. Bot.* 242 Said to contain nitre, a proof of which is shewn by their frequent decrepitation when thrown on the fire.

decrepitly (dɪ'krɛpɪtlɪ), *adv.* [-LY².] In a decrepit manner.

1848 LOWELL *Sir Launfal* II. i, And she rose up decrepitly For a last dim look at earth and sea.

†**de'crepitness**. *Obs.* Also 7–8 decrepid-. [-NESS.] = DECREPITUDE.

1601 CORNWALLYES *Ep.* x, Before decrepitness and death catch me. **1677** WYCHERLEY *Pl. Dealer* II. i, Wou'dst thou make me the Staff of thy Age, the Crutch of thy Decrepidness? **1703** J. SAVAGE *Lett. Antients* viii. 49 The Decrepidness of extream Old Age.

decrepitude (dɪ'krɛpɪtjuːd). [a. F. *décrépitude* (14th c.), prob. repr. a med.L. **dēcrepitūdo*, f. *dēcrepitus*, or on the model of similar formations: see -TUDE.] The state or condition of being decrepit; a state of feebleness and decay, *esp.* that due to old age. *lit.* and *fig.*

1603 FLORIO *Montaigne* I. xix. (1632) 37 She..dies in her decrepitude. **1751** JOHNSON *Rambler* No. 151 ¶1 The several stages by which animal life makes its progress from infancy to decrepitude. **1784** COWPER *Task* II. 489 Praise from the rivel'd lips of toothless, bald Decrepitude. **1871** R. ELLIS *Catullus* lxi. 161 Still when hoary decrepitude..Nods a tremulous Yes to all. **1875** MERIVALE *Gen. Hist. Rome* lxxv. (1877) 627 Paganism thus stricken down in her decrepitude never rose again.

†**de'crepity**. *Obs.* [a. OF. *décrépité* (15th–17th c. in Godef.), ad. med.L. *dēcrepit-ās, -tātem* (Du Cange), f. L. *dēcrepitus*.] = DECREPITUDE.

1576 NEWTON tr. *Lemnie's Complex.* 30a, The firste enteraunce and steppe into Olde Age, which is the nexte neighboure to decrepitie and dotage. **1598** FLORIO, *Decrepità*..olde age, decrepitie. **1603** —— *Montaigne* II. xxix. (1632) 394 Being demanded what his studies would stead him in his decrepity. **1605** CHAPMAN *All Fooles* Plays 1873 I. 160 A true Loadstone to draw on Decrepity.

decrescence (dɪ'krɛsəns). *rare.* [ad. L. *dēcrēscentia* decreasing, waning, f. *dēcrēscĕre* to DECREASE: see -ENCE.] Waning state or condition.

1872 *Contemp. Rev.* XX. 899 They have attained their maximum of development, and, by inevitable sequence, have begun their decrescence.

‖**decrescendo** (dekreʃ'ʃɛndo, deɪkrə'ʃɛndəʊ). *Mus.* [It. = decreasing.] A musical direction indicating that the tone is to be gradually lessened in force or loudness; = DIMINUENDO. As *sb.*: A gradual diminution of loudness of tone. Also *attrib.* and as *v. intr.*

1806 in T. BUSBY *Dict. Mus.* (ed. 2). **1880** GROVE *Dict. Mus.* s.v., A decrescendo of 48 bars from *fff*. **1890** G. B. SHAW *London Music* (1937) 365 The Wagnerian interpretation of the *decrescendo* mark over the chord. **1903** R. LANGBRIDGE *Flame & Flood* xvi. 165 Her voice.. crescendoed..and decrescendoed. **1968** *Language* XLIV. 87 A long decrescendo and downglide typically follow the peak of stress.

decrescent (dɪ'krɛsənt), *a.* and *sb.* Also 7–8 **decressant**. [ad. L. *dēcrēscent-em*, pr. pple. of *dēcrēscĕre* to DECREASE: see -ENT. For the earlier spelling, cf. CRESCENT.]

A. *adj.* Decreasing, growing gradually less. Chiefly of the moon: Waning, in her decrement; in *Her.* represented with the horns towards the sinister side. In *Bot.* applied to organs which decrease gradually from the base upwards.

1610 GUILLIM *Heraldry* III. iii. (1660) 111 He beareth Azure, a Moon decressant Proper. **1674** JEAKE *Arith.* I. (1696) 30 Then draw the Decrescent Lunular, or Separatrix. **1727–51** CHAMBERS *Cycl.* s.v. *Decrement*, The moon looking to the left side of the escutcheon is always supposed to be decressant. **1811** PINKERTON *Petrol.* II. 167 A dozen specimens, which presented a decrescent progression, with regard to the size of the grain. **1872** TENNYSON *Gareth & Lyn.* 518 Between the increscent and decrescent moon.

B. *sb.* The moon in her decrement or wane: used in *Her.* as a bearing. (Opposed to *increscent.*)

1616 BULLOKAR, *Decressant*, the Moone in the last quarter. ? **1620** FELTHAM *Resolves* xxviii. (1st ed.) 88 Thus while he sinnes, he is a Decressant; when he repents, a Cressant. **1691** *Lond. Gaz.* No. 2674/4 A Cross Moline between 2 Increscents and 2 Decrescents. **1851** J. B. HUME *Poems, Glenfinlas* 162 The wan decrescent's slanting beams.

decrese, decresse, obs. forms of DECREASE.

decresion, var. of DECRETION *Obs.*, decrease.

decretal (dɪ'kriːtəl), *a.*, *sb.* Also 4–7 -ale, -all(e, (7 decreetall). [a. F. *décrétal, -ale* (13th c.), ad. L. *dēcrētālis* of or containing a decree, whence med.L. *dēcrētāles* (sc. *epistolæ*) papal letters containing decrees, *dēcrētāle* a decree, statute, constitution.]

A. *adj.*

1. Pertaining to, of the nature of, or containing, a decree or decrees. **a.** Pertaining to the papal decrees: see B. 1. †*decretal right*: canon law.

1489 CAXTON *Faytes of A.* III. v. 175 After the decretall and cyuyll ryght. **1561** T. NORTON *Calvin's Inst.* IV. vii. 43 The decretall epistles heaped together by Gregorie the .ix. **1563–87** FOXE *A. & M.* (1596) 5/1 Decided by certeine new decretal or rather extradecretal and extravagant constitutions. *a* **1631** DONNE in *Select.* (1840) 18 The word inspired by the Holy Ghost; not apocryphal, not decretal, not traditional. **1682** BURNET *Rights Princes* v. 165 That impudent Forgery of the Decretal Epistles. **1765** BLACKSTONE *Comm.* I. 59 The canon laws, or decretal epistles of the popes, are..rescripts in the strictest sense. **1823** LINGARD *Hist. Eng.* VI. 193 Campeggio had read the decretal bull to him and his minister.

b. Pertaining to, or of the nature of, a decree of Chancery or other civil court.

1689 *Col. Rec. Pennsylv.* I. 253 Persuant to a Decretall order of yᵉ Provinll. Judges. **1714** *Lond. Gaz.* No. 5253/4 A Decretal Order made in the High Court of Chancery. **1819** SWANSTON *Reports* (Chancery) III. 238 The bill could not be dismissed by motion of course. That order was decretal, and necessarily retained the cause. **1884** *Weekly Notes* 20 Dec. 242/2 Such an order is decretal only and not a final foreclosure judgment.

†**2.** Having the force of a decree or absolute command, imperative. **b.** *transf.* of the person who commands. *Obs.*

a **1610** HEALEY *Epictetus' Man.* lxxiv. (1636) 95 To observe all these as decretall lawes, never to bee violated. **1610** —— *St. Aug. Citie of God* XXI. viii. (1620) 793 What more decretall law hath God laid vpon nature. **1679** J. GOODMAN *Penit. Pardoned* II. ii. (1713) 192 When he [the Almighty]..seems to have been most peremptory and decretal in his threatenings.

†**3.** Decisive, definitive. *Obs. rare.*

1608 CHAPMAN *Byron's Trag.* Plays 1873 II. 319 So heer's a most decreetall end of me. **1697** EVELYN *Numism.* vii. 252 The decretal Battel at Pharsalia.

B. *sb.*

1. *Eccl.* A papal decree or decretal epistle; a document issued by a Pope, containing a decree or authoritative decision on some point of doctrine or ecclesiastical law. **b.** *pl.* The collection of such decrees, forming part of the canon law.

c1330 R. BRUNNE *Chron.* (1810) 337, & if þe decretal ne were ordeynd for þis, þe clerkes ouer alle ne rouht to do amys. **1377** LANGL. *P. Pl.* B. v. 428 Ac in canoun ne in þe decretales I can nouȝte rede a lyne. **1481** CAXTON *Myrr.* I. v. 26 They..goo lerne anon the lawes or decretals. *c* **1555** HARPSFIELD *Divorce Hen. VIII* (1878) 191 That..the Pope would sign a Decretall drawn out for his purpose. **1645** MILTON *Colast.* Wks. (1851) 358 To uphold his opinion, by Canons, and Gregorian decretals. **1725** tr. *Dupin's Eccl. Hist. 17th C.* I. v. 69 The Name of Decretals is particularly given to Letters of the Popes which contain Constitutions and Regulations. **1818** HALLAM *Mid. Ages* (1841) I. vii. 524 Upon these spurious decretals was built the great fabric of papal supremacy over the different national churches. **1856** FROUDE *Hist. Eng.* II. ix. 312 The first decretal, which was withheld by Campeggio, in which he had pronounced the marriage with Catherine invalid. **1860** *Lit. Churchman* VI. 304/2 The false decretals of Isidore.

¶ The *sing.* was occasionally used instead of the *pl.* in sense b above. *Obs.*

1531 *Dial. Laws Eng.* II. xxvi. (1638) 110 They that be learned in the law..hold the decretall bindeth not in this Realme. **1563-87** FOXE *A. & M.* (1684) III. 307 They brought forth a Decretal, a Book of the Bishop of Romes Law, to bind me to answer.

2. *transf.* A decree, ordinance.

1588 GREENE *Perimedes* 3 To phlebotomie, to fomentacions, and such medicinall decretals. *a* **1652** J. SMITH *Sel. Disc.* v. 171 Which are not the eternal dictates and decretals of the devine nature. **1858** J. MARTINEAU *Stud. Chr.* 86 A repeal of the decretals of Eternity.

†decretaliarch. *Obs.* [F. *décrétaliarche.*] A word of Rabelais: the lord of decretals, the Pope.

1656 in BLOUNT *Glossogr.* [from Cotgrave]. **1708** MOTTEUX *Rabelais* IV. liv, The blessed Kingdom of Heaven, whose Keys are given to our good God and Decretaliarch.

†de'cretaline, *a. Obs.* [f. DECRETAL + -INE.] Of or belonging to the Decretals.

1600 O. E. *Repl. Libel* II. iii. 59 They haue..receiued a new decretaline law, wherein they walke more curiously, then in the law of God. *Ibid.* II. iv. 90 Their decretaline doctrine is neither sound, nor holy. **1708** MOTTEUX *Rabelais* IV. xlix. (1737) 199 Our old Decretaline Scholiasts.

decretalist (dɪˈkriːtəlɪst). [mod.f. DECRETAL (B. 1) + -IST: cf. F. *décrétaliste* (14th c.), and DECRETIST.] One versed in the Decretals. **†b.** One who holds the Calvinistic doctrine as the decrees of God (cf. DECRETAL *a.* 2).

1710 D. WHITBY *Disc. Five Points* vi. i. (1817) 400 If these Decretalists may take sanctuary in the fore-knowledge God hath of things future, the Hobbists and the Fatalists may do the same. **1872** R. JENKINS in *Archæol. Cant.* VIII. 66 *note*, Apostacy according to the decretalists is a threefold crime.

de'cretally, *adv.* [-LY².] In a decretal way, by way of decree.

1621 W. SCLATER *Tythes* (1623) 215 Doctrinally, or rather decretally, its deliuered by Vrban. **1626** —— *Expos. 2 Thess.* (1629) 104 When were these dogmatized and decretally stablished for catholique doctrine? **1716** M. DAVIES *Athen. Brit.* II. To Rdr. 43 The Supream Divinity of Jesus Christ, as decretally Pre-existing in the Hypostatick Union.

†de'cretary. *Obs.* [f. L. *dēcrēt-um* DECREE + -ARY.] One versed in the Decretals.

1581 J. BELL *Haddon's Answ. Osor.* 358b, For Evangelistes, cruell Canonistes, Copistes, Decretaries.

de'crete. 1. = DECREE 4 a. [A special adaptation of L. *decrētum.*]

1832 AUSTIN *Jurispr.* (1879) II. xxviii. 534 The most important..of these special constitutions were those decretes and rescripts which were made by the Emperors..a decrete being an order made on a regular appeal from the judgment of a lower tribunal.

2. Obs. var. of DECREET.

†de'cretion. *Obs.* Also 7 decresion. [n. of action from L. *dēcrēt-*, ppl. stem of *dēcrēscĕre* to DECREASE: cf. *accretion, concretion.* (Not used in L., which had a different *dēcrētio* from *dēcernĕre* to decree.)] Decrease, diminution.

1635 SWAN *Spec. M.* iv. §2 (1643) 68 The clouds..by descending make no greater augmentation then the decresion was in their ascending. **1659** PEARSON *Creed* (1839) 73 By which decretion we might guess at a former increase.

decretist (dɪˈkriːtɪst). [ad. med.L. *dēcrētista*, f. *dēcrētum* DECREE: see -IST. So OF. *décrétiste* (1499 in Godef.), earlier *décrétistre* (see next).] One versed in the Decretals; a decretalist.

c **1400** *Apol. Loll.* 75 þe decretistis, þat are Israelitis..as to þe part of sciens þat þey han tane of Godis lawe, & Egipcians, as to þe part þat þey haue of worldly wysdam. **1656** BLOUNT *Glossogr.*, *Decretist*, a Student, or one that studies the Decretals. **1726** AYLIFFE *Parergon* xx, The Decretists had their Rise and Beginning, even under the Reign of the Emperor Frederick Barbarossa. **1871** VAUGHAN *Life St. Thomas* 352 To attend the lectures of the decretists.

†decre'tistre. *Obs.* [a. OF. *décrétistre* (13th c. in Littré), ad. med.L. *dēcrētista*: see -ISTRE: later *décrétiste* (see prec.).] = prec.

1393 LANGL. *P. Pl.* C. xvi. 85 This doctor and diuinour, and decretistre of canon, Hath no pite on vs poure.

decretive (dɪˈkriːtɪv), *a.* [f. L. *dēcrēt-*, ppl. stem of *dēcernĕre* to DECREE + -IVE.] Having the attribute of decreeing; = DECRETORY 1.

1609 BP. W. BARLOW *Answ. Nameless Cath.* 170 Either discretiue..or directiue..and thirdly decretiue, which is in the Prince, either affirmatiuely to binde those within his compasse [etc.]. **1651** BAXTER *Inf. Bapt.* 269 To distinguish between event and duty; the Decretive and Legislative will of God. **1770** WESLEY *Wks.* (1872) XIV. 195 Both the choice of the former, and the decretive omission of the latter were owing..to the sovereign will..of God. **1874** H. R. REYNOLDS *John Bapt.* iii. §3. 206 They are..too specific and too decretive in their essence.

Hence **de'cretively** *adv.*

1610 HEALEY *St. Aug. Citie of God* 808 The thousand years are decretively meant of the devills bondage onely.

decre'torial, *a.* [f. L. *dēcrētōri-us* DECRETORY + -AL¹.]

†1. = DECRETORY 3. *Obs. rare.*

1588 J. HARVEY *Disc. Probl.* 25 The great Climactericall, Hebdomaticall, Scalary, Decretoriall yeere. *Ibid.* 93 Is it therefore impossible..that any of these should see as far into Decretoriall numbers? **1646** SIR T. BROWNE *Pseud. Ep.* IV. xii. 212 The medicall or Decretoriall month.

2. = DECRETORY 1.

1778 FARMER *Lett. to Worthington* i. (R.), That I..overrule the Scripture itself, in a decretorial manner. **1909** G. TYRRELL *Christianity at Cross Roads* 179 He understood this destination as more than moral or decretorial, as an inherent potentiality of His spirit. **1921** *Glasgow Herald* 18 Apr. 7 The argument..which that gentleman plainly considers decretorial.

†decre'torian, *a. Obs.* [f. as prec. + -AN.] Decisive, critical; = DECRETORY 2, 3.

1679 J. GOODMAN *Penit. Pardoned* III. ii. (1713) 289 There is no decretorian battle, nor is the business decided upon a push. **1716** M. DAVIES *Athen. Brit.* III. *Diss. Physick* 54 The ancient Greek Physicians made..Astrology or Astronomy, with their Critical and Decretorian Days, a considerable Part of their Medicinal Studies.

de'cretorily, *adv.* ? *Obs.* [f. next + -LY².] In a decretory manner; positively, decisively.

1660 JER. TAYLOR *Duct. Dubit.* II. ii. rule vi. §33 All which speak..decretorily and dogmatically and zealously. **1684** J. GOODMAN *Wint. Ev. Conf.* III. (T.), Deal concisely and decretorily, that I may be brought..to the point you drive at.

decretory (dɪˈkriːtərɪ), *a.* Now *rare* or *Obs.* [ad. L. *dēcrētōri-us*, f. *dēcrēt-* ppl. stem of L. *dēcernĕre* to determine, DECREE: see -ORY.]

1. Of the nature of, involving, or relating to, a decree, authoritative decision, or final judgement.

a **1631** DONNE in *Select.* (1840) 83 We banish..all imaginary fatality, and all decretory impossibility of concurrence and co-operation to our own salvation. **1649** JER. TAYLOR *Gt. Exemp.* II. vii. 37 Those decretory and finall words of S. Paul: He that defiles a Temple, him will God destroy. **1673** BAXTER *Let.* in *Answ. Dodwell* 82 You appropriate the Decretory Power to your Monarch; and communicate only the executive. **1737** J. CLARKE *Hist. Bible* (1740) II. v. 128 Jesus, knowing they had passed a decretory sentence against Him. **1807** ROBINSON *Archæol. Græca* I. xvi. 77 The decretory sentence was passed.

†b. Of persons: Characterized by pronouncing a definite decision or judgement; positive, decided.

1651 JER. TAYLOR *Serm. for Year* I. xi. 136 They that with..a loose tongue are too decretory, and enunciative of speedy judgement. **1655** —— *Unum Necess.* vii. §1, I will not be decretory in it, because the Scripture hath said nothing of it. **1680** H. DODWELL *Two Lett. Advice* (1691) 105 If I may seem decretory in resolving positively some things controverted among learned men.

†2. Such as to decide the question; decisive, determinative. *Obs.*

1674 EVELYN *Navig. & Comm.* Misc. Writ. (1805) 644 That decretory battle at Actium. **1692** M. MORGAN *Poem on Victory over Fr. Fleet* 7 In which was struck this decretory Blow. **1718** BP. HUTCHINSON *Witchcraft* (1720) 172 They tried..their Claims to Land, by Combat, or the Decretory Morsel. **1737** WHISTON *Josephus* Diss. 105 There is one particular Observation..that seems to me to be decretory.

†3. *Old Med.* and *Astrol.* Pertaining to or decisive of the final issue of a disease, etc.; also *fig.* of a course of life; = CRITICAL 4. *Obs.* or *arch.*

1577 B. GOOGE *Heresbach's Husb.* (1586) 78b, The third of Maie (which is the late decretorie daie of the Vine). **1601** HOLLAND *Pliny* I. 500 The foure decretorie or criticall daies, that giue the doome of Oliue trees, either to good or bad. **1646** SIR T. BROWNE *Pseud. Ep.* IV. xii. 213 The medicall month; introduced by Galen..for the better compute of Decretory or Criticall dayes. **1702** C. MATHER *Magn. Chr.* III. IV. vii. (1852) 610 When the decretory hour of death overtakes you. **1890** E. JOHNSON *Rise Christendom* 104, I look intrepidly forward to yonder decretory hour [of death].

‖decretum (dɪˈkriːtəm). [L.] A decree; sometimes short for *Decretum Gratiani.*

1602 W. WATSON *Decacordon* 163 The *decretum* of the order obserued in all elections. **1888** *Encycl. Brit.* XXIV. 639/1 The *Decretum* specially inculcated subjection of the wife to the husband.

†de'crew, *v. Obs. rare.* [f. OF. *décreu*, now *décru*, pa. pple. of *décreistre*, *décroître* to DECREASE: cf. ACCRUE.] To decrease, wane.

1596 SPENSER *F.Q.* IV. vi. 18 Sir Arthegall renewed His strength still more, but she still more decrewed.

decrial (dɪˈkraɪəl). *rare.* [f. DECRY *v.* + -AL¹ 5.] The act of decrying; open disparagement.

1711 SHAFTESB. *Charac.* Misc. v. i. (1737) III. 266 The Decrial of an Art, on which the Cause and Interest of Wit and Letters absolutely depend. *Ibid.* v. ii. (R.), A decrial or disparagement of those raw works.

decried (dɪˈkraɪd), *ppl. a.* [f. DECRY *v.* + -ED.] Cried down, disparaged openly, etc.: see the verb.

1655 H. VAUGHAN *Silex Scint.* I. (1858) 36 Prayer was such A decryed course, sure it prevailed not much. **1783** BURKE *Report Affairs India* Wks. 1842 II. 6 A suspected and decried government. **1818** J. C. HOBHOUSE *Italy* (1859) II. 372 A decried effort since the edict of Dr. Johnson.

decrier (dɪˈkraɪə(r)). One who decries.

1698 FRYER *Acc. E. India* A iiij b, It is a Justice only intended my Country against its Decriers. *a* **1716** SOUTH *Serm.* VII. ii. (R.), The late fanatic decryers of the necessity of human learning. **1881** SAINTSBURY *Dryden* v. 103 Dryden's principal decrier.

ˌdecriminaliˈzation. [f. DE- II. 2 + CRIMINAL *a.* + -IZATION.] The action or process of decriminalizing, esp. the legalization of (the possession and use of) certain narcotic drugs.

1945 S. & E. T. GLUECK *After-Conduct Discharged Offenders* viii. 99 This legislation is of great significance as probably constituting an entering wedge to the later *decriminalisation* of other behaviour categories of psychopaths. **1948** M. GRÜNHUT *Penal Reform* xvii. 451 Decriminalization has a twofold meaning. First, it implies that although the new sanction can be legally applied only if a criminal offence has been committed, the treatment is selected and administered not in relation to the gravity of the offence, but to the prospects and needs of the individual... Decriminalization means, secondly, the substitution for punishment of another type of sanction, either reformative or protective. **1968** *N.Y. Times* 23 Aug. 67/3 Dr. Fort..called present drug laws 'extreme, barbaric and inefficient', and said that 'immediate de-criminalization of the whole thing' was needed. **1973** *Daily Tel.* 21 June 18 From time to time it is held against stores and firms that they adopt their own policy of 'decriminalisation' and do not take action against offenders where sums below a certain amount are involved. **1975** *High Times* Dec. 113/2 The National Organization for the Reform of Marijuana Laws (NORML) is laying plans for an autumn attack on the recently passed California decriminalization legislation. **1984** *Listener* 3 May 3/1 The emerging policy theory was..summed up as the three Ds: decriminalisation, diversion (from court) and de-institutionalisation.

decriminalize, *v.* [Back-formation f. DECRIMINALIZATION.] **1.** *trans.* To reform (an offender or one with criminal tendencies) through psychiatric treatment. (In quot. as *vbl. sb.*) *rare.*

1963 *Punch* 26 June 915/3 The *Mentor* carries news of..'decriminalizing' through psychiatry.

2. To reclassify (an activity) so that it is no longer considered criminal in law; *spec.* to legalize (a narcotic drug, its possession, or use). (*Rarely*, with person as obj.)

1972 *Sat. Rev. Sci.* (U.S.) 15 Apr. 21/3 The recommended removal of all penalties for the private possession of marihuana would do much to decriminalize a large number of those involved with this drug. **1972** *N.Y. Times Mag.* 2 July 8 Glasser would decriminalize heroin and make it available in pharmacies for addicts. **1973** *Nature* 30 Mar. 292/1 Restating his opposition to decriminalizing the use of marihuana. **1975** *Listener* 18 Dec. 822/3 Homosexuality was decriminalised, and homosexuals came to be treated with unprecedented tolerance. **1977** *Rolling Stone* 5 May 30/3 The likely trend of decriminalized prostitution is already suggested by massage parlors. **1983** *Daily Tel.* 20 June 2/1 A programme of reform was urged which would 'decriminalise' certain offences.

†de'criminate, *v. Obs. rare.* [f. med.L. *dēcrīmināre* (Du Cange), f. DE- I. 3 + *crīmināre* to accuse of crime.] To denounce as a criminal, to accuse. Hence **de'criminating** *ppl. a.*

1670 *Tryal Rudyard, etc.* in *Phenix* (1721) I. 398 A whole sea of their Decriminating and Obnoxious Terms.

†de'crott, *v. Obs. nonce-wd.* [a. F. *décrotter*, in 12th c. *descroter*, f. *de-*, *des-* (DE- I. 6) + *crotte* dirt.] *trans.* To clean from dirt, remove dirt from.

1653 URQUHART *Rabelais* I. xx, To decrott themselves in rubbing of the dirt of either their shoes or clothes.

decrown (dɪˈkraʊn), *v.* ? *Obs.* [f. DE- II. 2 + CROWN *sb.* Cf. F. *découronner* 'to vncrowne' (Cotgr.), OF. *descoroner* (12th c.); also *dethrone.*] *trans.* To deprive of the crown, to discrown.

1609 BP. W. BARLOW *Answ. Nameless Cath.* 153 Authoritie to de-Throan and de-Crowne Princes. **1624** F. WHITE *Repl. Fisher* 56 Throning and dethroning, crowning and decrowning them. **1778** *Phil. Surv. S. Irel.* 322 If the Pope had not arrogated a right to dethrone and decrown Kings. **1835** LYTTON *Rienzi* I. iii, How art thou decrowned and spoiled by thy recreant and apostate children.

Hence **de'crowning** *vbl. sb.*

a **1613** OVERBURY *A Wife* (1638) 212 The decrowning of Kings.

decrustation (diːkrʌˈsteɪʃən). *rare*⁻⁰. [n. of action f. L. *dēcrust-āre* to peel off (an outer layer or crust), f. DE- I. 6 + *crusta* CRUST, *crustāre* to

CRUST: see -ATION.] The removal of a crust or incrustation.

1611 COTGR., *Decrustation*, a decrustation, or vncrusting; a paring away of the vppermost part, or outmost rind. **1656** in BLOUNT *Glossogr.* **1658** in PHILLIPS. **1721** in BAILEY; and in mod. Dicts. **1882** in *Syd. Soc. Lex.*

decry (dɪ'kraɪ), *v.* Also 6-7 decrie. Pa. t. and pple. decried. [a. F. *décrier*, in 14th c. *descrier*, f. *des-*, *de-* (see DE- I. 6) + *crier* to cry. In Eng. the prefix appears always to have been taken in sense 'down': see DE- I. 4.]

1. *trans.* To denounce, condemn, suppress, or depreciate by proclamation; = *cry down* (CRY *v.* 17 a); chiefly said of foreign or obsolete coins; also to bring down the value (of any article) by the utterance or circulation of statements.

1617 MORYSON *Itin.* I. III. vi. 289 Having a singular Art to draw all forraine coynes when they want them, by raising the value, and in like sort to put them away, when they haue got abundance thereof, by decrying the value. **1633** T. STAFFORD *Pac. Hib.* iv. (1821) 267 The calling downe, and decrying of all other Moneys whatsoever. **1697** EVELYN *Numism.* vi. 204 Many others [medals of Elagabalus] decried and called in for his infamous life. **1710** WHITWORTH *Acc. Russia* (1758) 80 Next year..the..gold..was left without refining, which utterly decried those Ducats. **1765** BLACKSTONE *Comm.* I. 278 The king may..decry, or cry down, any coin of the kingdom, and make it no longer current. **1844** *Act 7-8* Vict. c. 24 §4 Spreading..any false rumour, with intent to enhance or decry the price of any goods.

2. To cry out against; to disparage or condemn openly; to attack the credit or reputation of; = *cry down* (CRY 17 b).

1641 J. JACKSON *True Evang. T.* I. 75 We goe..to law one with another (which S. Paul so decryed). **1660** R. COKE *Justice Vind.* Pref. 1 All men..have with one voice commended Virtue, and decried Vice. **1665** PEPYS *Diary* 27 Nov., The goldsmiths do decry the new Act. **1756** C. LUCAS *Ess. Waters* I. Pref., 'Who is this', says one, 'that is come to decry our waters?' **1867** LEWES *Hist. Philos.* II. 105 He does not so much decry Aristotle, as the idolatry of Aristotle. **1872** YEATS *Growth Comm.* 371 The zeal with which the Church decried the taking of interest or usury.

Hence **de'crying** *vbl. sb.*

1633 [see 1 above]. **1637** *State Trials, John Hampden* (R.), There hath been a decrying by the people and they have petitioned in parliament against it. **1863** KINGLAKE *Crimea* (1876) I. vi. 84 A general decrying of arms.

†**de'cry,** *sb. Obs. rare*⁻¹. [f. prec. vb.] The decrying (of money); decrial.

1686 tr. *Chardin's Trav.* i. 9 The English were the Procurers of this Decry. For had that Money continu'd Currant, their Trade had been ruin'd.

decrypt (dɪ'krɪpt), *v.* [f. DE- II. 1 + *crypt* as in CRYPTOGRAM, CRYPTOGRAPH; cf. It. *decriptare.*] **a.** *trans.* To solve (a cryptogram) without knowledge of the key. **b.** To convert (a cryptogram) into plaintext by proper application of the key. So **de'crypted** *ppl. a.*, **de'crypting** *vbl. sb.*, **de'cryption**, the deciphering of a cryptogram.

1936 *Cryptogram* June 4 Those who succeeded in decrypting Message No. 1 of the last issue. **1938** R. CANDELA *Milit. Cipher of Commandant Bazeries* 111 Decrypting or Cryptanalysis is that discipline which teaches us how to attempt the restoration of ciphered texts to their intended meaning without the knowledge or use of the cipher or key involved. **1946** *Rep. Joint. Comm. Investigation Pearl Harbor Attack. 79th Congress 2nd Sess.* IV. 230 The message was decrypted and translated in rough form on December 6. *Ibid.*, The December 3 dispatch..was turned over on December 5, 1941, to the Radio Intelligence Unit for decryption and translation. *Ibid.* 231 No basis exists for criticizing the system which was set up for decrypting and translating the intercepted Japanese messages. **1957** R. WATSON-WATT *Three Steps to Victory* liii. 318 Burn all codes save that needed to decrypt the final note. **1962** G. JENKINS *Grue of Ice* v. 72, I can get a bearing if a ship sends eleven letters. I proved it to the German Decryption Service. **1967** *Punch* 30 Aug. 327/1 The lower case was used for decrypted messages.

decrystallization (diː,krɪstəlaɪ'zeɪʃən). [f. DE- II. 1.] Deprivation of crystalline structure.

1860 *Sat. Rev.* X. 83/1 The decrystallization of ice by the solar rays. **1878** HUXLEY *Physiogr.* 56 Developed by the breaking-down or decrystallisation of the ice.

†**decu'bation.** *Obs. rare.* [n. of action f. L. *dēcubāre* to lie away (from one's own bed), taken in sense of L. *dēcumbĕre* to lie down.] The action of lying down.

1664 EVELYN *Sylva* (1776) 613 At this Decubation upon boughs the Satyrist seems to hint, when he introduces the gypsies (Juv. Sat. vi. 543-5).

decubital (dɪ'kjuːbɪtəl), *a.* [f. next + -AL¹.] Pertaining to or resulting from decubitus.

1876 BRAITHWAITE *Retrospect Med.* LXXIII. 4 Dr. Handfield Jones on decubital inflammation.

‖**decubitus** (dɪ'kjuːbɪtəs). *Med.* [mod.L. f. *dēcumbĕre* to lie down, after *accubitus* and other parallel forms. Used also in French from 1747.]

1. The manner or posture of lying in bed.

1866 A. FLINT *Princ. Med.* (1880) 190 The dorsal decubitus should not be constantly maintained; changes of position are important. **1879** J. M. DUNCAN *Lect. Dis. Women* xxx. (1889) 245 The decubitus is rarely on the healthy side.

2. 'Also, a synonym of *Bedsore*' (*Syd. Soc. Lex.*); see BED *sb.* 19.

†**de'culcate,** *v. Obs.*⁻⁰ [f. late L. *dēculcāre* + -ATE³: cf. *inculcate.*] (See quots.)

1623 COCKERAM, *Deculcate*, to tread somthing vnder foot. **1656** BLOUNT *Glossogr.*, *Deculcate*..to tread or trample upon.

†**de'cult,** *v. Obs.*⁻⁰ [ad. L. *dēcultāre* (rare and doubtful) = *valde occultare.*] (See quot.)

1623 COCKERAM, *Decult*, to hide priuily.

decultivate: see DE- II. 1.

decuman ('dɛkjuːmən), *a.* Also 7-8 **-ane**. [ad. L. *decumān-us*, var. of *decimānus* of or belonging to the tenth part, or the tenth cohort, f. *decim-us* tenth: see -AN; also, by metonymy, considerable, large, immense.]

1. Very large, immense: usually of waves.

(As to the vulgar notion that the tenth or decuman wave, *fluctus decumanus*, is greater and more dangerous than any other: see SIR THOS. BROWNE *Pseud. Ep.* VII. xvii. 2, DE QUINCEY *Pagan Oracles* Wks. 1862 VII. 183.)

1659 GAUDEN *Tears of Church* 30 To be overwhelmed and quite sunk by such decumane billowes as those small vessels have no proportion to resist. **1708** MOTTEUX *Rabelais* IV. xxiii. (1737) 97 That decumane Wave that took us fore and aft. **1838** *Fraser's Mag.* XVII. 122 The tenth, or decuman, is the last of the series of waves, and the most sweeping in its operation. **1870** FARRAR *Witn. Hist.* i. (1871) 5 Confidence, that even amid the decuman billows of modern scepticism it [the Church] shall remain immovable.

absol. **1870** LOWELL *Poems, Cathedr.*, Shocks of surf that clomb and fell, Spume-sliding down the baffled decuman.

2. *Rom. Antiq.* Belonging to the tenth cohort: applied to the chief entrance to a camp, or that farthest from the enemy (*porta decumana*).

1852 WRIGHT *Celt, Roman, & Saxon* (1861) 148 The decuman gate.

†**decumanal,** *a. Obs. rare.* [f. as prec. + -AL¹.] = prec. 1.

1652 URQUHART *Jewel* Wks. (1834) 229 The decumanal wave of the oddest whimzy of all.

decumbence (dɪ'kʌmbəns). [f. DECUMBENT: see -ENCE.] Lying down; = next.

1646 SIR T. BROWNE *Pseud. Ep.* III. i. 105 If..they lye not downe and enjoy no decumbence at all. **1882** *Syd. Soc. Lex.*, *Decumbence*, the state or attitude of lying down.

decumbency (dɪ'kʌmbənsɪ). [f. as prec.: see -ENCY.]

1. Lying down, reclining; decumbent condition or posture.

1646 SIR T. BROWNE *Pseud. Ep.* v. vi. 244 Theophylact.. not considering the ancient manner of decumbency, imputed this gesture of the beloved Disciple unto Rusticity. **1877** ROBERTS *Handbk. Med.* (ed. 3) II. 32 The mode of decumbency is generally on the back, with the head high.

2. Taking to one's bed; = DECUMBITURE 2. In quot. 1820 *humorously* for 'going to bed'.

1651 C. WALKER *Hist. Independ.* III. 52 One peece of cure ..must be Phlebotomy, but then you must begin before Decumbency. **1652** GAULE *Magastrom.* 240 The hour of decumbency. **1820** L. HUNT *Indicator* No. 15 (1822) I. 117 Candid enquirers into one's decumbency.

decumbent (dɪ'kʌmbənt), *a.* (*sb.*) [ad. L. *dēcumbent-em*, pr. pple. of *dēcumb-ĕre* to lie down, f. DE- I. 1 + *-cumbĕre* to lie.]

1. Lying down, reclining. Now *rare* or *Obs.*

1656 BLOUNT *Glossogr.*, *Decumbent*, that lyes or sits down; or dyes. *a* **1692** ASHMOLE *Antiq. Berksh.* I. 2 (R.) The decumbent portraiture of a woman, resting on a death's head. **1748** HARTLEY *Observ. Man* I. i. 46 The decumbent Posture which is common to Animals in Sleep. **1798** W. YONGE in Beddoes *Contrib. Phys. Knowledge* (1799) 303 The advantage of a decumbent posture.

†**b.** Lying in bed through illness. *Obs.*

1689 G. HARVEY *Curing Dis. by Expect.* xv. 114 An elder Brother decumbent of a Continual Fever. *a* **1732** ATTERBURY (T.), To deal with..decumbent dying sinners.

2. *spec.* **a.** *Bot.* Lying or trailing upon the ground, but with the extremity ascending: applied to stems, branches, etc.

1791 E. DARWIN *Bot. Gard.* II. 24 *note*, This species of Fern..with a decumbent root. **1830** LINDLEY *Nat. Syst. Bot.* 83 Herbaceous plants, native of sandy plains..and usually decumbent. **1874** M. C. COOKE *Fungi* 249 The fertile flocci were decumbent, probably from the weight of the spores.

b. *Nat. Hist.* Of hairs or bristles: Lying flat on the surface, instead of growing out at right angles.

1826 KIRBY & SP. *Entomol.* III. xxxiv. 398 The covering of hairs is silky and decumbent. *Ibid.* III. 645 Short decumbent hairs or bristles.

†**B.** as *sb.* One lying ill in bed: cf. 1 b. *Obs.*

1641 J. JACKSON *True Evang. T.* II. 138 When the Christian decumbent growes near to the grave. **1699** 'MISAURUS' *Honour of Gout* (1720) 10 He tells the Decumbent a long story of the..Misery of Life.

Hence **de'cumbently** *adv.*, in a decumbent manner.

In mod. Dicts.

decumbiture (dɪ'kʌmbɪtjʊə(r)). ? *Obs.* [An irregular formation from L. *dēcumbĕre*; the etymological form being *decubiture*: see DECUBITUS.]

1. Lying down; *spec.* as an invalid in bed.

1670 MAYNWARING *Vita Sana* viii. 94 As for the manner of decumbiture, the body must lie easie. **1681** WHARTON *Crises Dis.* Wks. (1683) 115 The time when the Sick-party takes his Bed, is the beginning of his Decumbiture. **1741** ETTRICK in *Phil. Trans.* XLI. 565 The Band..is to be kept on, the whole Time of Decumbiture.

2. The act or time of taking to one's bed in an illness. **b.** *Astrol.* A figure erected for the time at which this happens, and affording prognostics of recovery or death.

1647 LILLY *Chr. Astrol.* xliv. 255 At the hour of Birth, at time of Decumbiture of the sick. **1671** BLAGRAVE *Astrol. Physic* 23 The Moon being returned unto the place she was in at the decumbiture. *a* **1700** DRYDEN (J.), The planetary hour must first be known, And lucky moment: if her eye but akes, Or itches, its decumbiture she takes. **1707** J. FRAZER *Disc. Second Sight* 4 The boy died..the eleventh night from his decumbiture. **1819** J. WILSON *Dict. Astrol.*, *Decumbiture*, a horary question or figure, erected for a sick person. It should be made to the time when the patient first perceives his disease.

†**decupe'lation.** *Obs.*⁻⁰ [cf. CUPEL, CUPELLATION.] 'The same as Decantation.'

1706 in PHILLIPS (ed. Kersey); hence **1721** in BAILEY, etc.

†'**decuplate,** *a. Obs.* [ad. L. *decuplāt-us*, pa. pple.: see DECUPLE *v.*] Multiplied by ten.

1690 LEYBOURN *Cursus Math.* 339 There remains..Root Decuplate, b = 20.

decuplate ('dɛkjuːpleɪt), *v.* [f. L. *dēcuplāre*: see DECUPLE *v.* and -ATE³.] = DECUPLE *v.*

1690 LEYBOURN *Cursus Math.* 340 The first Root decuplated, b = 30. **1887** *19th Cent.* Aug. 152 All this decuplating our production.

Hence †**decu'plation**, multiplication by ten, increase tenfold.

1690 LEYBOURN *Cursus Math.* 340 The Decuplation of the Roots.

decuple ('dɛkjuːp(ə)l), *a.* and *sb.* [a. F. *décuple* (1484 in Hatzf.), ad. L. *decuplus* tenfold, f. *decem* ten + *-plus*, as in *du-plus*, *tri-plus*, etc.]

A. *adj.* Ten times as much; tenfold.

[**1501** DOUGLAS *Pal. Hon.* I. xli, Duplat, triplat, diatesseriall, Sesqui altera, and decupla resortis.] **1613** M. RIDLEY *Magn. Bodies* 87 Sometimes decuple or ten times as much againe. **1646** SIR T. BROWNE *Pseud. Ep.* 192 Man, whose length..is sextuple unto his breadth..and decuple unto his profundity. **1771** RAPER in *Phil. Trans.* LXI. 534 Reckoning..the value of gold decuple that of silver. **1817** COLEBROOKE *Algebra, etc.* 4 Increasing regularly in decuple proportion. **1843** *Fraser's Mag.* XXVII. 461 Double, treble, and more than decuple the amount.

B. *sb.* A number or quantity ten times another; a tenfold amount.

c **1425** *Craft Nombrynge* (E.E.T.S.) 20, 20 is þe decuple of 2, 10 is þe decuple of 1. **1691** RAY *Creation* I. (R.), If the same proportion holds..(that is, as I guess, near a decuple). **1864** PUSEY *Lect. Daniel* 623 During a period of years, which was to be a decuple of their own number. **1885** *Times* 12 Dec. 9/5 To abolish one or two of the doubles, trebles, and decuples which afflict postmen and cabmen [in street nomenclature].

decuple ('dɛkjuːp(ə)l), *v.* [ad. L. *decuplāre* (only in pa. pple. *decuplātus*), f. *decuplus* tenfold: see prec.: cf. F. *décupler* (18th c. in Hatzf.).]

trans. To increase or multiply tenfold.

1674 JEAKE *Arith.* (1696) 201 The Square of 1 decupled is 10. *a* **1687** PETTY *Pol. Arith.* i. (1691) 9 If France hath scarce doubled its Wealth and Power, and that the other have decupled theirs. **1837** GEN. P. THOMPSON *Exerc.* (1842) IV. 253 If the demand for muscle were decupled at every commercial and manufacturing station.

Hence '**decupled** *ppl. a.*

1854 H. H. WILSON tr. *Rig-veda* II. 5 To partake of the decupled (libation).

decuplet ('dɛkjuːplɪt). *Mus.* [f. L. *decuplus* DECUPLE + -ET¹ in *triplet*, etc.] 'A group of ten notes played in the time of eight or four' (Stainer & Barrett *Dict. Mus. Terms*).

decur, var. of DECORE *Obs.*

decure, obs. form of DECURY.

†**de'curiate,** *v. Obs.*⁻⁰ [f. ppl. stem of L. *decuriāre* to divide into *decuriæ*: see DECURY.] (See quot.) So †**decuri'ation** [L. *decuriātio*].

1623 COCKERAM, *Decuriate*, to diuide into bands, to separate. **1721** in BAILEY. **1623** COCKERAM, *Decuriation*, a making of Knights or Captaines.

decurion (dɪ'kjʊərɪən). In 4-5 -ioun. [ad. L. *decurio*, *-ōnem*, f. *dec-em* ten, after *centurio* CENTURION: see DECURY.]

1. *Rom. Antiq.* A cavalry officer in command of a *decuria* or company of ten horse. Also *gen.* A commander or captain of ten men.

1382 WYCLIF *1 Macc.* iii. 55 Decuriouns, leders of ten. **1533** BELLENDEN *Livy* IV. (1822) 361 Sixtus Tempanius, decurion of horsmen. **1581** STYWARD *Mart. Discipl.* I. 61 He shall charge euerie decurion or Captaine of ten men vpon their othes. **1701** W. WOTTON *Hist. Rome* v. 83 He had got away, if a Decurion had not fallen upon him. **1838** ARNOLD *Hist. Rome* I. 75 The poorest citizens..followed the army.. acting as orderlies to the centurions and decurions.

b. *transf.* An overseer of ten households, a tithing-man.

1591 G. FLETCHER *Russe Commw.* (Hakluyt Soc.) 43 The constable hath certaine..decurions under him, which haue the ouersight of ten households a peece. **1689–90** TEMPLE *Ess. Heroic Virtue* §3 Wks. 1731 I. 207 He [Mango Capac] instituted Decurions thro' both these Colonies, that is, one over every Ten Families.

2. *Roman Hist.* A member of the senate of a colony or municipal town; a town councillor.

In later times the capacity for the office became hereditary, and the decurions formed an order charged with heavy financial and other responsibilities to the imperial government.

1382 WYCLIF *Mark* xv. 43 Ioseph of Armathie, the noble decurioun [Vulg. *decurio*, Gr. βουλευτής]. **1606** HOLLAND *Sueton.* 60 A new kind of Suffrages which the decurions or elders of Colonies gave every one in their owne Towneshippe. **1635** PAGITT *Christianogr.* III. (1636) 2 Ioseph of Arimathea, that noble Decurion. **1781** GIBBON *Decl. & F.* II. 63 The laborious offices, which could be productive only of envy and reproach, of expence and danger, were imposed on the Decurions, who formed the corporations of the cities, and whom the severity of the Imperial laws had condemned to sustain the burthens of civil society. **1872** E. W. ROBERTSON *Hist. Ess.* 37 *note*, The Decurio, and filius Decurionis, the Plebeius, and the Servus of the law of Constantine, answer exactly to the Noble, Free, and Servile orders of the Germanic codes.

3. A member of the Great Council in modern Italian cities and towns.

1666 *Lond. Gaz.* No 97/1 The Colledge of the Jurists, the sixty Decurions [at Milan]. **1708** *Ibid.* No. 4448/1 After these came eight Trumpeters..preceding the 60 Decurions, the great Chancellor, the Privy-Council, and Senate. **1841** W. SPALDING *Italy & It. Isl.* III. 343 In Genoa, whose municipality was constituted by laws of 1814 and 1815, there is a Great Council of forty decurions (half nobles, half merchants and other citizens), who were named in the first instance by the crown, but have since filled up their own vacancies. **1865** MAFFEI *Brigand Life* II. 47 At one time a syndic, a decurion, profited by his post to persecute his private enemies.

4. *Astrol.* = DECAN 2.

1652 GAULE *Magastrom.* 87 Their houses..thrones, decurions, faces, joys.

¶ Erron. for DECURY, a company of ten.

1555 EDEN *Decades* 23 A coompanye of armed men diuided into .xxv. decurions, that is, tenne in a company with theyr capitaynes.

de'curionate. [ad. L. *decuriōnāt-us*, f. *decuriōn-em*: see -ATE[1].] The office of a decurion.

1840 MILMAN *Hist. Chr.* II. 382. **1863** DRAPER *Intell. Devel. Europe* ix. (1865) 209 Exempting the priesthood from burdensome offices such as the decurionate. **1880** MUIRHEAD *Gaius* I. §95 *note*, Not only the magistracy but also the decurionate was a stepping-stone to citizenship.

de'curionship. [See -SHIP.] = prec.

1873 WAGNER tr. *Teuffel's Hist. Rom. Lit.* II. 340 Exemption..from the decurionship and military service.

decurrence ('dɪˈkʌrəns). [f. DECURRENT: see -ENCE.]

†**1.** The act or state of running down; downward flow or course; lapse (of time). *Obs.*

1659 GAUDEN *Tears of Church* 536 The errata's which, by long decurrence of time, through many mens hands have befaln it, are easily corrected. **1677** P. A. *Pref. Poem* in *Cary's Chronol.*, The Course of Humane Beeing even from the Source Of it's Decurrence.

2. *Bot.* The condition of being DECURRENT (q.v.).

1835 LINDLEY *Introd. Bot.* (1848) I. 228 The decurrence of the fibres. **1883** G. ALLEN in *Nature* 29 Mar. 511 There will be a strong tendency towards the long pointed ribbon-like form, and also a marked inclination towards decurrence.

de'currency. [f. as prec. + -ENCY.] = prec.

1651 J. GOODWIN *Redemption Red.* ii. §17 The flowing of Rivers from their Fountaines together with the decurrency of their Waters into the Sea. **1882** *Syd. Soc. Lex.*, *Decurrency*, the condition or appearance of a decurrent leaf.

decurrent (dɪˈkʌrənt), *a.* [ad. L. *dĕcurrent-em*, pr. pple. of *dĕcurrĕre* to run down, f. DE- I. 1 + *currĕre* to run.]

†**1.** Running or flowing down. *Obs.*

1432–50 tr. *Higden* (Rolls) I. 225 An ymage of Venus.. whiche was made so subtily that a man myȝhte see in that ymage as bloode decurrente.

2. *Bot.* Of leaves, etc.: Extending down the stem or axis below the point of insertion or attachment.

1753 CHAMBERS *Cycl. Suppl.*, Decurrent leaf. *a* **1794** SIR W. JONES *Bot. Obs.* in *Asiat. Res.* (1795) IV. 259 [Leaves] downy on both sides, mostly decurrent on the long hoary petiols. **1870** HOOKER *Stud. Flora* 260 Verbascum Thapsus ..leaves very decurrent..anthers of long stamens slightly decurrent.

Hence **de'currently** *adv.*

1807 J. E. SMITH *Phys. Bot.* 178 [Pinnate] *decursivè*, decurrently, when the leaflets are decurrent.

de'curring, *ppl. a.* = DECURRENT (in *Bot.*).

1889 in *Cent. Dict.*

†**de'curse.** *Obs.* [ad. L. *dĕcurs-us*, f. ppl. stem of *dĕcurr-ĕre*: cf. DECOURSE.] Downward course, lapse.

1593 BILSON *Govt. Christ's Ch.* 237 By degrees, in decurse of time. **1657** TOMLINSON *Renou's Disp.* 225 Nor that the decurse of years would work some change in it.

†**decursion** (dɪˈkɜːʃən). *Obs.* [ad. L. *dĕcursiōn-em*, n. of action f. *dĕcurr-ĕre* (ppl. stem *dĕcurs-*) to run down.]

1. The action of running, flowing, or passing downwards; also *fig.* of time, etc.

c **1630** JACKSON *Creed* VI. x. Wks. V. 277 The perpetual ascent of springing waters into the hills, their continual decursion from them into the sea. **1664** H. MORE *Myst. Iniq.* 206 In the decursion of..twelve or thirteen hundred years. **1680** —— *Apocal. Apoc.* 24 The whole decursion and succession of the church to the end of the world.

2. *Antiq.* A military manœuvre, exercise or evolution, performed under arms; a solemn procession round a funeral pile.

[**1623** COCKERAM, *Decursion*, a running of souldiers on their enemies.] **1658** W. BURTON *Itin. Anton.* 68 His body.. was laid on the *Rogus*, or Pile..and honored with the περίδρομή, decursion, or running round it by his Sons and Souldiers. **1697** POTTER *Antiq. Greece* IV. vi. (1715) 211 In this Decursion the Motion was towards the Left hand. **1702** ADDISON *Dial. Medals* i. 19 Charged..with many Ancient Customs, as sacrifices..allocutions, decursions, lectisterniums.

de'cursive, *a. Bot.* [ad. mod. Bot. L. *dĕcursīvus*, f. L. *dĕcurs-*, ppl. stem of *dĕcurr-ĕre* to run down: see -IVE.] = DECURRENT.

1828 in WEBSTER.

Hence **de'cursively** *adv.*, as ***decursively-pinnate*** [mod.L. *decursivè pinnatus*: cf. DECURRENTLY].

1823 CRABB *Technol. Dict.*, *Decursively-pinnate*, an epithet for a leaf having its leaflets decurrent, or running along the petiole. **1866** in *Treas. Bot.*

†**de'curt,** *a. Obs.*$^{-0}$ [Cf. CURT and DE- II. 3.]

1623 COCKERAM, *Decurt*, short.

†**de'curt,** *v. Obs.* [ad. L. *dĕcurt-āre* to cut off, curtail, f. DE- I. 2 + *curtāre* to shorten: see CURT *v.*] *trans.* To cut down, shorten, dock, curtail, abridge. Hence **de'curted** *ppl. a.*

1550 BALE *Apol.* 147 Your decurted or headlesse clause, *Angelorum enim, et cet.* **1631** J. DONE *Polydoron* 88 [It is] plain Roguerie to Decurte or mispoint their Writings. **1648** HERRICK *Hesper.*, *Julia's Churching* (1869) 307 To him bring Thy free, and not decurted offering.

de'curtate, *a. rare.* [ad. L. *dĕcurtāt-us*, pa. pple. of *dĕcurtāre*: see prec.] Cut down, shortened, abridged, curtailed.

a **1638** MEDE *Ep. to Hayn* Wks. (1672) IV. 755 The preposition [*b*] being decurtate of [*bên*] *inter.* **1859** F. HALL *Vâsavadattâ* Preface 8 Bâna..lopped off his own hands and feet..In this decurtate condition he dictated a poem of a hundred couplets.

†**de'curtate,** *v. Obs.* [f. ppl. stem of L. *dĕcurtāre*: see prec. and -ATE[3].] *trans.* = DECURT *v.*

1599 NASHE *Lenten Stuffe* Ep. Ded. A ij b, Hee sendes for his barber to depure, decurtate, and spunge him. **1623** COCKERAM, *Decurtate*, to shorten. **1676** COLE in *Phil. Trans.* XI. 607 Those, which had been decurtated by the unequal cutting of the knife.

†**decur'tation.** *Obs.* [ad. L. *dĕcurtātiōn-em*, n. of action f. *dĕcurtāre*: see DECURT *v.* So in mod.F.] Shortening, abridging, or cutting down.

1652 GAULE *Magastrom.* To Rdr., Ambiguous equivocations, affected decurtations, sophisticated expressions. **1652–62** HEYLIN *Cosmogr.* III. (1682) 38 By the like decurtation we have turned Hispania unto Spain. **1700** *Phil. Trans.* XXII. 568 The Contraction..is performed by the decurtation or shortening of the Fleshy Fibres.

decurvation (diːkɜːˈveɪʃən). [n. of action f. L. *dē-* down + ppl. stem of *curvāre* to bend, CURVE: see -ATION.] The action or process of decurving; the condition of being bent downwards.

1881 A. NEWTON in *Encycl. Brit.* XII. 358/2 There are *Trochilidæ* which possess almost every gradation of decurvation of the bill.

decurvature (dɪˈkɜːvətjʊə(r)). [f. as prec. + -URE: cf. *curvature.*] = prec.

1887 E. D. COPE *Orig. Fittest* 376 Constant jarring.. would tend to a decurvature of both inferior and superior adjacent end walls.

decurve (dɪˈkɜːv), *v. rare.* [f. L. *dē-* down + *curvāre* to CURVE.] To curve or bend down. Hence **de'curved** *ppl. a.*, curved downwards.

1835 KIRBY *Hab. & Inst. Anim.* I. ix. 274 An incipient decurved spire. **1892** *Athenæum* 18 June 795/2 The upper mandible [of a parakeet] was so abnormally decurved.

decury ('dɛkjʊərɪ). Also 6 decure. [a. OF. *decurie* or ad. L. *decuria* a division or company of ten, f. *dec-em* ten, after *centuria* CENTURY.]

Rom. Hist. and *Antiq.* A division consisting of ten men, a company or body of ten; applied also to larger classes or divisions (*e.g.* of the *judices*, *scribæ*, etc.).

1533 BELLENDEN *Livy* I. (1822) 30 The faderis, quhilk war ane hundreth in nowmer, devidit thaimself in ten decuris, ilk decure contening ten men in nowmer. **1563–7** BUCHANAN *Reform. St. Andros* Wks. (1892) 8 The regent sal..assigne thayme place in hys classe diuidit in decuriis. **1586** T. B. *La Primaud. Fr. Acad.* I. 643 The Pretors..tooke a certain number of Iudges..who..were distributed by decuries or tens. **1695** KENNETT *Par. Antiq.* (1818) II. 340 In the larger houses, where the numbers amounted to several decuries, the senior dean had a special preeminence. **1847** GROTE *Greece* II. xxxi. IV. 189, 5000 of these citizens were arranged in ten pannels or decuries of 500 each.

decus ('diːkəs). *slang.* [From the Latin motto *decus et tutamen* on the rim.] A crown-piece.

1688 SHADWELL *Sqr. Alsatia* II. Wks. (1720) IV. 48 To equip you with some Meggs, Smelts, Decus's and Georges. **1822** SCOTT *Nigel* xxiii, 'You see', he said, pointing to the casket, 'that noble Master Grahame..has got the *decuses* and the *smelts.*'

decuss (dɪˈkʌs), *v. rare.* [ad. L. *decuss-āre* to divide crosswise, or in the form of an X, f. *decussis* the number ten (X), also a ten-as piece, and so supposed to be f. *dec(-em)assis.*] = DECUSSATE *v.*

1782 A. MONRO *Compar. Anat.* (ed. 3) 25 A double row of ..fibres decussing one another.

†**de'cussant,** *a. Obs. rare.* [ad. L. *decussant-em*, pr. pple. of *decussāre*: see prec.] Decussating, intersecting.

1685 H. MORE *Para. Prophet.* 462 Placed on those produced decussant Lines.

decussate (dɪˈkʌsət), *a.* [ad. L. *decussāt-us*, pa. pple. of *decussāre*: see DECUSS.]

1. Having the form of an X.

1825 HONE *Every-day Bk.* I. 1538 The letter X, styled a cross decussate. **1882** FARRAR *Early Chr.* I. 85 The decussate cross now known as the cross of St. Andrew.

2. *Bot.* Of leaves, etc.: Arranged on the stem in successive pairs, the directions of which cross each other at right angles, so that the alternate pairs are parallel.

1835 LINDLEY *Introd. Bot.* (1848) II. 382 *Decussate*, arranged in pairs that alternately cross each other. **1884** BOWER & SCOTT *De Bary's Phaner.* 259 The stem has four angles, and bears decussate pairs of opposite leaves.

Hence **de'cussately** *adv.*, in a decussate manner.

1846 DANA *Zooph.* (1848) 329 Folia..transversely coalescent or intersecting one another (decussately aggregated).

decussate ('dɛkəseɪt, dɪˈkʌseɪt), *v.* [f. L. *decussāt-*, ppl. stem of *decuss-āre*: see DECUSS.]

1. *trans.* To cross, intersect, lie across, so as to form a figure like the letter X.

1658 SIR T. BROWNE *Gard. Cyrus* iii. 53 The right and transverse fibres are decussated by the oblick fibres. **1665–6** *Phil. Trans.* I. 221 These Rainbows did not..decussate one another at right angles. **1737** BRACKEN *Farriery Impr.* (1756) I. 58 The inner [fibres] always decussate or cross the outer. **1835–6** TODD *Cycl. Anat.* I. 583/1 Their medullary fibres.. converge and decussate each other.

2. *intr.* To cross or intersect each other; to form a figure like the letter X.

1713 DERHAM *Phys. Theol.* IV. vii. 153 The Fibres of the external and internal Intercostals decussate. **1835–6** TODD *Cycl. Anat.* I. 251/1 Sometimes they [ligaments] cross or decussate with each other. **1875** BLAKE *Zool.* 198 Optic nerves, commissurally united, not decussating.

decussated (see prec.), *ppl. a.* [f. prec. + -ED[1].] Formed with crossing lines like an X; crossed, intersected; having decussations or intersections.

1658 SIR T. BROWNE *Gard. Cyrus* i. 37 The decussated characters in many consulary coynes. **1686** PLOT *Staffordsh.* 430 A decussated cross. **1755** JOHNSON, *Network*, any thing reticulated or decussated, at equal distances, with interstices between the intersections. **1841** JOHNSTON in *Proc. Berw. Nat. Club* I. 267 Shell..spirally ridged with fine decussated striæ in the interstices.

b. *Rhet.* Consisting of or characterized by two pairs of clauses or words, those in each pair corresponding to those in the other, but in reverse order; chiastic.

1828 WEBSTER s.v., In rhetoric, a decussated period is one that consists of two rising and two falling clauses, placed in alternate opposition to each other.

decussating, *ppl. a.* [-ING[2].] Crossing, intersecting.

1839–47 TODD *Cycl. Anat.* III. 680/1 These decussating fibres. **1855** HOLDEN *Hum. Osteol.* (1878) 9 Arranged in decussating curves like the arches in Gothic architecture.

decussation (dɛkʌˈseɪʃən). [ad. L. *decussātiōn-em*, n. of action f. *decussāre*: see DECUSS and -ATION.] Crossing (of lines, rays, fibres, etc.) so as to form a figure like the letter X; intersection.

1656 in BLOUNT *Glossogr.* **1658** SIR T. BROWNE *Gard. Cyrus* i. 37 The letter χ, that is the Emphatical decussation, or fundamental figure. **1662** EVELYN *Chalcogr.* (1769) 90 Performed in single and masterly strokes, without decussations, and cross hatchings. **1672** NEWTON in Rigaud *Corr. Sci. Men* (1841) II. 344 By the iterated decussations of the rays, objects will be rendered less distinct. **1713** DERHAM *Phys. Theol.* IV. ii. 95 A Coalition or Decussation of the Optick Nerves. **1839–47** TODD *Cycl. Anat.* III. 480/1 The point at which the decussation [of nerve-fibres in the brain] takes place is about ten lines below the margin of the pons Varolii.

b. *Rhet.* An arrangement of clauses, etc. in which corresponding terms occur in reverse order; chiasmus.

1841 *Tait's Mag.* VIII. 561 They have.. become weary of these pretty grammatico-metrical cuttings and decussations.

¶ Erroneous use, app. for DECUSSION, striking off.

1654 H. L'ESTRANGE *Chas. I* (1655) 117 He yeilded his head to de-cussation, to the striking off.

† **de'cussative**, *a. Obs. rare.* [f. L. *decussāt-*, ppl. stem of *decuss-āre* + -IVE.] Characterized by decussation; crossing. Hence **de'cussatively** *adv.*

1658 SIR T. BROWNE *Gard. Cyrus* iii. 56 By decussative diametrals, Quincunciall Lines and angles. *Ibid.* i. 38 The High-Priest was anointed decussatively or in the form of a X.

† **de'cussion.** *Obs. rare.* [ad. L. *dēcussiōn-em*, n. of action f. *dēcutĕre* to shake down, beat down, etc., f. DE- I. 1 + *quatĕre* to shake.] A shaking down or off.

1664 EVELYN *Pomona* (1729) 94 Making a Quantity of Cider with Windfalls, which he let ripen in the Hoard, near a month interceding between the time of their Decussion, and that which Nature intended for their Maturity. **1674** BLOUNT *Glossogr.*, *Decussion*, a striking or shaking off; a beating down.

‖ **decu'ssorium.** *Surg.* [mod.L. f. *dēcuss-*, ppl. stem of *dēcutĕre*: see prec. and -ORIUM. In mod.F. *décussoire.*] 'An instrument for keeping down, or separating to a sufficient extent, the dura mater in the operation of trepanning, to protect it from injury, and to facilitate the discharge of matters from its surface' (*Syd. Soc. Lex.* 1882).

† **de'cute**, *v. Obs.*$^{-0}$ [ad. L. *dēcutĕre* (see above).]

1623 COCKERAM, *Decute*, to cut off.

† **de'cutient**, *a. Obs.*$^{-0}$ [ad. L. *dēcutient-em*, pr. pple. of *dēcutĕre* (see above).]

1656 BLOUNT *Glossogr.*, *Decutient*, that shakes or beats down.

decyl ('dɛsɪl). *Chem.* [f. Gr. δέκα ten + -YL.] The tenth member of the series of hydrocarbon radicals having the formula C_nH_{2n+1}; the monatomic alcohol radical $C_{10}H_{21}$; also called *decatyl*. Used *attrib.* in ***decyl series, compounds, chloride***, etc.

Hence derivatives as **'decylene**, the olefine of the decyl series $C_{10}H_{20}$; **de'cylic**, of or pertaining to decyl, as in ***decylic alcohol, hydride***, etc. So **'decine**, the liquid hydrocarbon $C_{10}H_{18}$, the ethine or acetylene member of the decyl series. Cf. DECANE, DECENE.

1868 WATTS *Dict. Chem.* V. 1090 Decyl, Rutyl, Capryl,.. $C_{10}H_{21}$.. Hydride of Decyl.. Chloride of Decyl. **1872** *Ibid.* VI. 542 *Decylic compounds*.. derived from the fundamental hydrocarbon $C_{10}H_{22}$, decyl hydride.. *Decylene*, $C_{10}H_{20}$. **1875** *Ibid.* VII. 423 *Decene* and *Decine.*

decypher, obs. form of DECIPHER.

ded, obs. form of DEAD, DEATH *sb.*, DEED, DID (see DO *v.*).

dedain, early form of DISDAIN.

Dedal, Dedalian, etc.: see DÆDAL, etc.

‖ **dédale** (dedal). *rare.* [Fr.] = DÆDAL *sb.* 2.

1916 H. G. WELLS *Mr. Britling* II. ii. 260 The roads, he said, were not a means of getting from place to place, they were a *dédale.*

Dedalic, var. DÆDALIC *a.*

dedane, var. of DEDEIGN *v.*[2]

‖ **dedans** (də'dɑ̃). *Tennis.* [F. *dedans* gallery of a tennis court, special application of *dedans* inside, interior, subst. use of *dedans* adv. inside, f. *de* of, from, by, with, etc. + *dans* within:—OF. *denz*, itself f. *de* + *enz*:—L. *intus* inside, within.] The open gallery at the end of the service-side of a tennis-court.

1706 in PHILLIPS (ed. Kersey). **1878** J. MARSHALL *Ann. Tennis* 36 At Lord's.. the net, instead of being equidistant from each end of the Court, is nearer to the dedans than to the other end by 1 ft. **1885** *Pall Mall G.* 12 May 11/1 The forcing for the dedans and the stopping were magnificent. **1890** *Athenæum* 21 June 794/3 Let any young man.. go into the 'dedans' of a tennis court while a good match is going on.

dedayn, -e, early forms of DISDAIN.

dedbote, var. of DEEDBOTE *Obs.*

dedd(e, dede, obs. ff. DEAD, DEATH *sb.*, DEED.

dede, obs. pa. t. of DO.

† **de'decorate**, *a. Obs.* [ad. L. *dēdecorāt-us*, pa. pple. of *dēdecorāre* to disgrace; see next.] Disgraced, disgraceful.

15.. *Phylogamus* in *Skelton's Wks.* (1843) I. p. cxvi, O poet.. Dedecorate and indecent, Insolent and insensate.

dedecorate (dɪ'dɛkəreɪt), *v.* [f. L. *dēdecorāt-*, ppl. stem of *dēdecorāre* to disgrace, f. *dēdecus*, *dēdecor-* disgrace, f. DE- I. 6 + *decus*, *decor-*, grace, etc. In sense 2, f. DE- II. 1 + DECORATE.]

† **1.** *trans.* To disgrace, dishonour. *Obs.*

1609 J. DAVIES *Holy Roode* 13 (D.) Why lett'st weake Wormes Thy head dedecorate With worthlesse briers, and flesh-transpiercing thornes? **1623** COCKERAM, *Dedecorate*, to dishonor, or shame one.

2. To disfigure; to do the opposite of decorating.

1804 SYD. SMITH *Mor. Philos.* xi. (1850) 137 If a tradesman.. were to slide down gently into the mud, and de-decorate a pea green coat. **1887** *Spectator* 25 June 867/1 The vulgar and misleading caricatures which de-decorate these admirable chapters.

dedeco'ration. *rare*$^{-0}$. [ad. L. *dēdecorātiōn-em*, n. of action f. *dēdecorāre*: see prec.] 'A disgracing or dishonouring' (Phillips 1658); hence in Bailey, Johnson, and mod. Dicts.

de'decorous, *a. rare.* [ad. L. *dēdecorōs-us*, later synonym of *dēdecōrus* disgraceful, f. DE- I. 6 + *decōrus*: see DECOROUS.] Disgraceful, unbecoming. So † **de'decorose** *a.*

1727 BAILEY vol. II, *Dedecorose*, full of shame and dishonesty. *Dedecorous*, uncomely, unseemly, dishonest. **1755** JOHNSON, *Dedecorous*, disgraceful, reproachful, shameful. *a* **1913** F. ROLFE *Desire & Pursuit of Whole* (1934) 59 He avoided them, because of the dedecorous way in which some of them had treated him.

† **dedeign, -dein, -deyne**, *sb.* and *v.*[1] Early form of DISDAIN.

† **de'deign**, *v.*[2] *Sc. Obs.* Forms: 4-6 dedeynȝe, dedeinȝe, 5 dedyne, 6 dedeyne, dedenye, deden(e, dedane, deding. [A derivative of DEIGN *v.*, in which the prefix *de-* appears to be taken in the sense 'down' (DE- I. 1), so as to strengthen the notion of condescension; or which may have arisen by confusion of *dedeign* (= *disdain*) with *deign*. It seems to be confined to Scotch, and to have no analogies in French or Latin.]

1. = DEIGN *v.* 1. (In first quot. *impers.*)

1375 BARBOUR *Bruce* I. 376 He wes in all his dedis lele; For him dedeynȝeit nocht to dele With trechery. **1423** JAS. I *Kingis Q.* clxviii, Madame.. bot that ȝour grace dedyne, Off ȝour grete myght, my wittis to enspire. **14..** HOCCLEVE *Mother of God* 51 For Christ of the dedeynyt [*Ph. MS.* hath deyned] for to take Bothe flesche and blood. *c* **1500** *Lancelot* 240 And in his body.. The tronsione of o brokine sper that was, Quhich no man out dedenyt to aras. **1535** STEWART *Cron. Scot.* I. 618 That wald deding with his auctoritie Ws to support in oure necessitie. **1513-53** DOUGLAS *Æneis* I. vi. 53 (ed. 1553), I dedeinȝe [*v.r.* denȝe] not to ressaue Sic honour.

2. To lower.

1536 BELLENDEN *Cron. Scot.* (1821) I. 123 The Romains wald nocht dedenye thair majeste, to satefy the desire of barbar pepill.

dedely, obs. form of DEADLY.

deden(e, var. of DEDEIGN *v.*[2]; obs. pa. t. pl. of DO.

dedendum (di:'dɛndəm). *Mech.* [L., neut. gerundive of *dēdere* to give up, surrender.]

a. 'That part of the tooth of a cog-wheel or gear which is inside the pitch-circle and is intercepted between the pitch-line and the circle which limits all the roots of the teeth and the spaces between them' (*Cent. Dict.* Suppl., 1909). Also *attrib.* **b.** (See quot. 1958.)

1901 *Internat. Libr. Technol.* II. (*Gear-Cutting*) §17. 7 A tooth is composed of two parts, the addendum, or part outside the pitch circle, and the part inside, which is called either the root or the dedendum. **1909** N. HAWKINS *Mech. Dict.* 185/2 The dedendum circle is the circle within the pitch circle, to which the bottom of each tooth extends. **1925** BERARD & WATERS *Elem. Machine Design* x. 180 The bottoms of the grooves are limited by a root or dedendum circle, distant from the pitch circle by an amount called the dedendum. **1949** E. BUCKINGHAM *Analytical Mech. Gears* xii. 256 We shall use a constant axial pitch of 1 in... This would give us the following thread proportions:.. Dedendum 0·3247 [in.]. **1958** *Chambers's Techn. Dict.* Add. 971/1 *Dedendum*, radial distance between the pitch and minor cylinders of an external screw thread; radial distance between the major and pitch cylinders of an internal thread. **1961** P. S. HOUGHTON *Gears* (ed. 2) i. 6 The dedendum of spur, helical and worm gearing is the radial distance of the tooth measuring from the pitch circle to the bottom of the tooth space. For a bevel gear it is the depth of the tooth space below the pitch circle measuring along the back cone generator or edge angle.

dedentition (di:dɛn'tɪʃən). *Phys.* [f. DE- II. 1 + DENTITION.] The shedding of the teeth; *esp.* of the first set.

1646 SIR T. BROWNE *Pseud. Ep.* IV. xii. 216 In the first [Septenary] is Dedentition or falling of teeth. **1857** DUNGLISON *Dict. Med.* s.v. *Dentition*, Dedentition begins about the age of 6 or 7. **1882** in *Syd. Soc. Lex.*

dedenye, dedeyn(e, etc., var. DEDEIGN *v.*[2], and early ff. DISDAIN.

dedes ('di:dɛs). [Javanese.] Musk obtained from the rasse.

1817 [see RASSE[1]]. **1843** *Penny Cycl.* XXVI. 406/2 This is the *Rasse* of the Javanese, who term the odoriferous secretion *dedes* or *jibet.*

de-de'velopment. [f. DE- II. 2 + DEVELOPMENT.] The reversal of economic or industrial development, esp. in (over-) developed countries, for the benefit of the country concerned; return to a less advanced economy.

1974 *Ecologist* IV. VIII. 309/3 It has been the theme of the Ecologist for the last four years that development is an unmitigated catastrophe. What is needed is de-development even in Africa. **1976** *Church Times* 10 Dec. 10 The snag about.. 'de-development' (Professor Birch at the WCC) as the aim is that in the past mankind has found satisfaction largely through trying to do better materially. **1978** *Nature* 18 May 176/2 Where some developed countries (such as Italy) are experiencing an enforced de-development, and others are hovering from crisis to crisis, a little isolation from western science and technology may not be a bad thing for the developing countries.

dedicant ('dɛdɪkənt). [ad. L. *dēdicānt-em*, pr. pple. of *dēdicāre* to DEDICATE.] One who dedicates.

1881 HÜBNER in *Encycl. Brit.* XIII. 127 (*Rom. Inscriptions*), The proper form of the dedication.. also the name of the dedicants.. and the formulæ of the offering.

† **'dedicate**, *pa. pple.* and *ppl. a. Obs.* or *arch.* Also 4-6 dedicat. [ad. L. *dēdicāt-us* consecrated, formally devoted, pa. pple. of *dēdicāre* (see next). Used both as pa. pple. and adj., but now only as an archaic synonym of *dedicated.*] Dedicated.

c **1386** CHAUCER *Pars. T.* ¶890 In chirche, or in chirche-hawe, in chirche dedicate, or in noon. **1494** FABYAN *Chron.* I. ii. 9 An old Temple dedycat in the honoure of.. Diana. **1535** COVERDALE *Ezek.* xliv. 29 Euery dedicate thinge in Israel shall be theirs. **1565** CALFHILL *Answ. Treat. Crosse* (1846) 5 You have dedicate your book to the Queen's highness. **1643** MILTON *Divorce* vii. (1851) 35 Every true Christian.. is a person dedicate to joy and peace. **1646** P. BULKELEY *Gospel Covt.* III. 275 The dedicate things which should have been to the honouring of God. **1798** COLERIDGE *Nightingale*, Like a Lady vow'd and dedicate To something more than Nature in the grove. **1814** SOUTHEY *Roderick* x, I vow'd, A virgin dedicate, to pass my life Immured.

dedicate ('dɛdɪkeɪt), *v.* [f. L. *dēdicāt-*, ppl. stem of *dēdicāre* to declare, proclaim, devote (to a deity) in a set form of words, to consecrate, f. DE- + *dicāre* to say, proclaim, make over formally by words, a weak vb. from stem *dic-* of *dīcĕre* to say, tell; cf. the adj. formative *-dicus* -saying, -telling; also *abdicate*. For the pa. pple., *dedicate* (see prec.) has been used, and in 16th c. the same form was used for the pa. t., as if short for *dedicated.*]

1. a. *trans.* To devote (*to* the Deity or to a sacred person or purpose) with solemn rites; to surrender, set apart, and consecrate to sacred uses.

(The leading sense, which more or less colours the others.)

1530 PALSGR. 509/1, I dedycate a churche. **1548-9** (Mar.) *Bk. Com. Prayer, Publ. Baptism*, Whosoeuer is here dedicated to thee by our office and ministerie. **1555** EDEN *Decades* 73 To whom he buylded and dedicate a chapell and an altare. **1651** HOBBES *Leviath.* III. xxxix. 247* Any Edifice dedicated by Christians to the worship of Christ. **1659** PEARSON *Creed* (1839) 223 Many are the enemies of those persons who dedicate themselves unto his service. **1822** K. DIGBY *Broadst. Hon.* (1846) II. 337 (*Tancredus*), The 29th of September has been dedicated to St. Michael and all Angels ever since the fifth century. **1885** *Pall Mall G.* 2 Jan. 10/2 The precedent set by the Bishop of St. Albans in dedicating a cemetery, in lieu of consecrating it in a strictly legal way.

b. *fig.*

1599 SHAKS. *Hen. V*, IV. Chor. 37 Nor doth he dedicate one iot of colour Vnto the wearie and all-watched Night. **1606** —— *Tr. & Cr.* III. ii. 110 Well Vnckle, what folly I commit, I dedicate to you. **1678** SALMON *Lond. Disp.* 578/1 A Pectoral Decoction.. is Dedicated to the Lungs.

2. *transf.* To give up earnestly, seriously, or wholly, *to* a particular person or specific purpose; to assign or appropriate; to devote.

1553 T. WILSON *Rhet.* 3 We must dedicate our myndes wholly to folowe the moste wise and learned menne. **1595** SPENSER *Col. Clout* 472 To her my thoughts I daily dedicate. **1653** WALTON *Angler* Ep. Ded. 3 When you.. devest your self of your more serious business, and.. dedicate a day or two to this Recreation. **1718** PRIOR *Solomon* II. 818 It bid her .. dedicate her remnant life To the just duties of an humble wife. **1771** *Junius Lett.* xlix. 257 The remainder of the summer shall be dedicated to your amusement. **1818** HALLAM *Mid. Ages* (1872) I. 504 The dukes of Savoy were .. completely dedicated to the French interests. **1841** W. SPALDING *Italy & It. Isl.* I. 236 It assumed the title of the Via Triumphalis, from the processions to which it was dedicated.

3. a. To inscribe or address (a book, engraving, piece of music, etc.) *to* a patron or friend, as a compliment, mark of honour, regard, or affection.

1542 BOORDE *Dyetary* Pref. (1870) 227 And where I haue dedycted this boke to your grace [etc.]. **1605** BACON *Adv. Learn* I. iii. §9 The ancient custom was to dedicate them only to private and equal friends, or to entitle the books with their names. **1737** FIELDING *Hist. Reg.* Ded., Asking leave to dedicate, therefore, is asking whether you will pay for your dedication, and in that sense I believe it is understood by both authors and patrons. **1832** W. L. GARRISON *Thoughts African Colon.* p. iii, I dedicate this work to my countrymen. **1848** THACKERAY *Van. Fair*, To B. W. Procter this story is affectionately dedicated.

†**b.** To address (a letter or other communication) *to*. *Obs. rare.*

1688 *Col. Rec. Pennsylv.* I. 236 That some things of that Nature had been proposed and Dedicated to ye proprietor, by himself..to which he believed he should receive his Answer by ye ffirst Shipping hether. **1776** BLACK *Lett. to Adam Smith* 26 Aug., I heard that he had dedicated a letter to you, desiring you not to come.

4. a. *Law.* To devote or throw open to the use of the public (a highway or other open space).

1843 *Penny Cycl.* XXVII. 153/2 It is necessary that the party dedicating should have a sufficient interest in the land to warrant such dedication.

b. To open formally to the public; to inaugurate, make public.

1892 *Times* (Weekly ed.) 21 Oct. 5/4 President Harrison cannot visit Chicago to dedicate the World's Fair.

c. *Forestry.* (See quots.)

1943 *Post-War Forest Policy* 50 in *Parl. Papers 1942–3* (Cmd. 6447) IV. 419 Woodland which is required for timber production should be *dedicated* to that specific purpose, and ..woodland owners who so dedicate their land and also provide adequate assurances for subsequent good management should receive State assistance. **1953** H. L. EDLIN *Forester's Handbk.* xxi. 348 In order to obtain financial assistance from the Forestry Commission, for any substantial area of privately owned woodland, it is necessary to Dedicate it. This implies that the owner undertakes to manage it on an approved plan, more or less in perpetuity.

dedicated (ˈdɛdɪkeɪtɪd), *ppl. a.* [f. prec. + -ED.] **1. a.** Sacredly, solemnly, or formally devoted; wholly given up, etc.; inscribed (as a book).

c **1600** SHAKS. *Sonn.* lxxxii. 3 The dedicated words which writers use Of their fair subject, blessing every book. **1611** BIBLE *2 Kings* xii. 4 All the money of the dedicated things. **1661** BOYLE *Style of Script.* Ep. Ded. (1675) 2 In the dedicated book. **1805** WORDSW. *Prelude* IV. Wks. (1888) 261/2 That I should be..A dedicated Spirit.

b. Of a person: devoted to his aims or his vocation; single-minded in loyalty to his beliefs, or in his artistic or professional integrity.

1944 AUDEN *For Time Being* (1945) I. iii. 55 Having learnt his language, I begin to feel something of the serio-comic embarrassment of the dedicated dramatist. **1955** N. KING *Shadow of Doubt* II, in J. Trewin *Plays of Year 1954–55* XII. 527 *Laura*... Have you ever met a really...dedicated person? *Frank.* Yes. Yes, I think so. Particularly one during the War. He was a doctor. **1971** M. RUSSELL *Deadline* xi. 130 I'm dedicated, Smutty... Let me show my true worth.

2. Of equipment, a facility, etc.: designed, manufactured, or installed so as to be available only for a particular purpose or a particular category of user.

1969 *Times* 27 Oct. 19/4 The bulk of M.I.T.'s computers are the so-called 'dedicated' computers, like the stolen one. They are dedicated, that is, to a particular function—usually some on-line process control function. **1970** *Globe & Mail* (Toronto) 28 Sept. 9/4 Line costs are negligible. A dedicated line open 24 hours a day costs $4 a mile a month. **1972** *Sci. Amer.* Sept. 112/3 If one user wants to correspond with another user frequently and on an exclusive basis, it makes sense to set up a 'dedicated' channel between the two. **1978** *Industr. Photogr.* Nov. 27/1 'Dedicated' electronic flash units matched to the sophisticated exposure controls and capabilities of specified 35 mm single lens reflex cameras. **1983** *What's New in Computing* Jan. 25/1 It is a dedicated word processor which is small..and has the advantage of a proven user-friendly operating system. **1985** *Personal Computer World* Feb. 30/2 (Advt.), All but the smallest documents tie up the computer while being printed... This is more so in a network which does not have a dedicated computer for printer operation. **1986** *Which?* May 215/1 Some cameras set the aperture automatically.. when the dedicated flash is turned on.

dedicatee (ˌdɛdɪkəˈtiː). [A modern formation from DEDICATE *v.* + -EE, correlative to *dedicator*.] One to whom anything is dedicated.

1760–72 H. BROOKE *Fool of Qual.* I. Introd. iv, The writer and his patron, the dedicator and the dedicatee. **1802** SYD. SMITH in *Edin. Rev.* I. 22 The worthy dedicatees, the Lord Mayor and Aldermen. **1881** SAINTSBURY *Dryden* 108 Assiduous visits to patrons and dedicatees.

dedicating (ˈdɛdɪkeɪtɪŋ), *vbl. sb.* [-ING¹.] The action of the verb DEDICATE; dedication.

1535 COVERDALE *Dan.* iii. 3 The dedicatynge of ye ymage. **1611** BIBLE *Num.* vii. 11 The dedicating of the Altar.

ˈdedicating, *ppl. a.* [-ING².] That dedicates.

1666 J. SERGEANT *Let. Thanks* 32 He is Mr. Stillingfleets dedicated and dedicating friend.

dedication (dɛdɪˈkeɪʃən). [a. OF. *dédication*, *-cion* (14th c. in Godef.), ad. L. *dēdicātiōn-em*, n. of action from *dēdicāre* to DEDICATE.]

1. a. The action of dedicating, the fact of being dedicated; a setting apart and devoting to the Deity or to a sacred purpose with solemn rites.

1382 WYCLIF *Num.* vii. 88 Thes thinges ben offrid in the dedicacioun of the auter, whanne it is anoynt. **1387** TREVISA *Higden* VII. 351 Kyng William..commaundede nyh alle þe bisshoppes of Engelond þat þey schulde come to þat dedicacioun þe fiftenþe day of May. **1460** CAPGRAVE *Chron.* 165 William..aftir tyme that he had biggid the Cherch ageyn, desired that the Kyng schuld com to the dedicacion. **1643** BURROUGHES *Exp. Hosea* viii. (1652) 292 Dedication is when I give a thing out of my own power, for a pious use, that I cannot make use of for anything again. **1665** SIR T. HERBERT *Trav.* (1677) 296 The Monks..shave the upper part of their head by way of distinction from the Laity and for dedication. **1776** GIBBON *Decl. & F.* I. xvii. 444 The founder prepared to celebrate the dedication of his city.

b. The form of words in which this act is expressed.

1520 *Caxton's Chron. Eng.* IV. 38/1 He ordeyned the dedycacyon of the chirche every yere sholde be sayd. **1607** TOPSELL *Four-f. Beasts* (1673) 264 Metellus the Macedonian raised two porches..without inscription or dedication.

c. The commemoration of such an act; the day or feast of dedication (of a church).

Feast of the Dedication: the annual commemoration of the purification of the Second Temple by Judas Maccabæus. *c* **1400** MAUNDEV. (Roxb.) xix. 87 When grete festez commez..as þe dedicacioun of þe kirk. **1483** *Cath. Angl.* 93 Dedicacion, *dedicacio, encennia.* **1530** PALSGR. 212/2 Dedication a feestfull day, *dedicace.* **1695** KENNETT *Par. Antiq.* (1818) II. 305 The dedication of churches should in all places be celebrated on the first Sunday of the month October.

2. *fig.* The giving up or devoting (of oneself, one's time, labour, etc.) to the service of a person or to the pursuit of a purpose.

1601 SHAKS. *Twel. N.* v. i. 85 His life I gaue him, and did thereto adde My loue without retention or restraint, All his in dedication. **1611** —— *Wint. T.* IV. iv. 577 A Course more promising, Then a wild dedication of your selues To vnpath'd Waters. **1841–44** EMERSON *Ess., Experience* Wks. (Bohn) I. 177 We need change of objects. Dedication to one thought is quickly odious. **1875** JOWETT *Plato* (ed. 2) I. 345 The dedication of himself to the improvement of his fellow-citizens.

3. The dedicating of a book, etc.; the form of words in which a writing, engraving, etc., is dedicated to some person.

1598 FLORIO *Dict.* Ep. Ded. 1 This dedication..may haply make your Honors muse. **1605** BACON *Adv. Learn.* I. iii. §9 Neither is the modern dedication of books and writings, as to patrons, to be commended. **1751** JOHNSON *Rambler* No. 136 ¶6 Nothing has so much degraded literature from its natural rank, as the practice of indecent and promiscuous dedication. **1887** BOWEN *Virgil, Eclogue* vi. Argt., The Eclogue opens with a dedication to the Roman general Varus.

†**4.** Special appropriation. *Obs.*

1570–6 LAMBARDE *Peramb. Kent* (1826) 225 It should seeme by the dedication of the name [Sheppey], that this Ilande was long since greatly esteemed either for the number of the sheepe, or for the finenesse of the fleese.

5. a. *Law.* The action of dedicating (a highway, etc.) to the public use.

1809 TOMLINS *Law Dict.* s.v. *Highway*, A street built upon a person's own ground is a dedication of the Highway so far only as the publick has occasion for it, viz. for a right of passage. **1843** *Penny Cycl.* XXVII. 153 The dedication of a way to the public may be by writing or by words. **1883** E. P. WOLSTENHOLME *Settled Land Act* 28 Dedication to the public is a term generally applied to the act of throwing roads open to the use of the public.

b. *Forestry.* The assignment of land under certain conditions for the production of timber. Cf. DEDICATE *v.* 4 c.

1943 *Post-War Forest Policy* 50 in *Parl. Papers 1942–3* (Cmd. 6447) IV. 419 The act of dedication on the part of the owner would include the following undertakings:—(1) To use the land in such a way that timber production is the main object. (2) To work to a plan..approved by the Forest Authority. **1946** *Q. Jrnl. Forestry* XL. 69 Dedication is a covenant under which both the owner of the land and the Government undertake certain obligations. **1950** *Ibid.* XLIV. 53 It is just two years since the proposed Covenant of Dedication was published, and although the Society had always been strongly in favour of dedication, the covenant, as drafted, was received with considerable misgiving and distrust.

6. *attrib.* and *Comb.*, as ***dedication feast, festival***; **dedication cross**, a cross painted or carved on a church or altar at its dedication; **dedication day**, the anniversary of the dedication of a church, observed as a festival.

1581 J. BELL *Haddon's Answ. Osor.* 323 b, The feastes..of the patrone of the church, dedication day, and Relick-sonday. **1695** KENNETT *Par. Antiq.* (1818) II. 306 The primitive fair in Oxford was on the day of St. Frideswide, because it was the dedication day of the chief conventual church. *Ibid.* 308 The dedication feasts fell on those days. **1848** B. WEBB *Continent. Ecclesiol.* 57 Remains of..a dedication-cross. **1882** BLOXAM *Gothic Arch.* II. 155 We sometimes meet with dedication or consecration crosses imbedded in the external walls of churches.

dediˈcational, *a.* [f. prec. + -AL¹.] Of or pertaining to dedication.

1884 *Springfield Wheelmen's Gaz.* Nov. 103/2 The members..met at the new rooms..to witness the dedicational exercises.

dedicative (ˈdɛdɪkeɪtɪv), *a.* [ad. L. *dēdicātīv-us*, f. *dēdicāt-*, ppl. stem of *dēdicāre* to DEDICATE: see -IVE.] Having the attribute of dedicating.

1655 tr. *Francion* xi. 14 Which is..not dedicative, but it is rather a negative Epistle. **1816** KEATINGE *Trav.* (1817) II. 79 Here is a temple of Mars with a dedicative inscription. **1825** COLERIDGE *Aids Refl.* (1848) I. 28 The religious nature and dedicative force of the marriage vow.

dedicator (ˈdɛdɪkeɪtə(r)). [a. L. *dēdicātor*, agent-n. f. *dēdicāre* to DEDICATE.] One who dedicates; *esp.* one who inscribes a book to a friend or patron.

1596 W. BARLEY *New Bk. Tabliture* A ij b (Stanf.), The first of these causes doth shew a greedie minde in the Dedicator. **1663** DAVENANT *Siege of Rhodes* Ded., The ill manners and indiscretion of ordinary Dedicators. **1709** POPE *Ess. Crit.* 593 Leave dang'rous truths to unsuccessful Satyrs, And flattery to fulsome Dedicators. **1763** H. WALPOLE *Lett. Montagu* clxxxi, It is usual to give dedicators something. **1855** LEWIS *Cred. Early Rom. Hist.* I. ix. 312 Here they dedicate some brazen bowls..with the names of the dedicators.

dedicaˈtorial (ˌdɛdɪkəˈtɔərɪəl), *a.* [f. as DEDICATORY + -AL¹.] = DEDICATORY.

1844 J. W. DONALDSON *Varronianus* 131 Tuscan inscriptions..of a sepulchral or dedicatorial character.

dedicatorily (ˈdɛdɪkeɪtərɪlɪ, -kət-), *adv.* [f. DEDICATORY *a.* + -LY².] In a dedicatory manner.

1821 *Blackw. Mag.* X. 200 The Thomas Hope, who writes so dedicatorily to Louisa from Duchess Street.

dedicatory (ˈdɛdɪkeɪtərɪ, -kətərɪ), *a.* and *sb.* [f. L. type **dēdicātōri-us*, f. *dēdicātōr-em* DEDICATOR: see -ORY. Cf. mod.F. *dédicatoire.*]

A. *adj.* Relating to, or of the nature of, dedication; that has the attribute of dedicating, serving to dedicate. Used chiefly of literary dedication, as in ***epistle dedicatory***.

1565 *Randolphes Phantasey* (in *Satir. Poems Reform.* (1890) i.), The Epistle dedicatorie..to Mr. Thomas Randolphe. **1604** DEKKER *Honest Wh.* Wks. 1873 II. 121 Whose face is as ciuill as the outside of a Dedicatory Booke. **1611** BIBLE, The Epistle Dedicatorie. To the Most High and Mightie Prince, Iames, etc. **1717** BERKELEY *Tour in Italy* Wks. 1871 IV. 514 The epistle dedicatory is full of respect to the pope. **1846** ELLIS *Elgin Marb.* II. 108 We read of similar dedicatory offerings in the Bible.

†**B.** *sb.* A dedicatory inscription or address.

1598 YONG *Diana*, As Collin in his French dedicatorie to the Illustrous Prince Lewis of Lorraine at large setteth downe. **1642** MILTON *Apol. Smect.* (1851) 259 Neere a kin to him who set forth a Passion Sermon with a formall Dedicatory in great letters to our Saviour. **1674** HICKMAN *Quinquart. Hist.* (ed. 2) Ep. A v, Commended in the Dedicatory as being [etc.].

dedicature (ˈdɛdɪkeɪtjʊə(r)). *rare.* [f. L. *dēdicāt-*, ppl. stem + -URE.] The act of dedication.

c **1850** MRS. BROWNING *Sabbath Morning at Sea* viii, I would not praise the pageant high Yet miss the dedicature.

†**dedie,** *v. Obs.* [a. F. *dédie-r* (12th c. in Hatzf.), ad. L. *dēdicāre* to DEDICATE.] To dedicate.

c **1430** *Pilgr. Lyf Manhode* I. xv. (1869) 12 Whan thou dediedest and halwedest and blissedest the place. **1485** CAXTON *Chas. Gt.* 16 Yf thou haddest dedyed hym to my goddes he were now alyue. **1549** *Compl. Scot.* Ep. 7 The quhilk tracteit i hef dediet ande direckyt to ȝour nobil grace.

dedifferentiation (ˌdiːdɪfərɛnʃɪˈeɪʃən). *Biol.* [ad. F. *dédifférentiation* (C. Champy): see DE- II. 2.] The loss or reversal of differentiation (see DIFFERENTIATION 1). Hence **ˌdediffeˈrentiate** *v. intr.*, to undergo such a process; **ˌdediffeˈrentiated** *ppl. a.*

1917 *Amer. Jrnl. Anat.* XXII. 188 Dedifferentiation or return to a more embryonic condition probably underlies all types of regeneration. *Ibid.* 189 Champy..has maintained that most of the cells in the body dedifferentiate in tissue culture. **1926** *Glasgow Herald* 18 Sept. 4 A good example of the dedifferentiated inert state of suspended animation is the 'brown body' of some of the moss-animals. **1926** J. S. HUXLEY *Ess. Pop. Sci.* 80 The sea squirt..can in unfavourable surroundings de-differentiate, or revert to an embryonic state. **1960** *New Biol.* XXXI. 90 Tissue cells undergo an apparent de-differentiation to form the young regenerate or the bud.

†**ˈdedify, dedefy,** *v. Obs.* [app. a confused form from F. *dédier*, or L. *dēdicāre*, to DEDICATE, and *edify* (†*edefy*), F. *édifier*, L. *ædificāre*.] To dedicate (a building). Hence **ˈdedifying** *vbl. sb.*

1482 *Monk of Evesham* (Arb.) 30 The awter that is dedifyed and halowd in the worschipe of seynte laurence. **1483** CAXTON *Gold. Leg.* 194/2 Saynt remyge dyd halowe and dedefye hit. **1483** *Cath. Angl.* 93 Dedyfye, *dicare, dedicare, sanctificare.* **1494** FABYAN *Chron.* v. cxxxii. 115 Any forther busynesse touchyng the dedyfying of ye sayd Churche.

†**dedigˈnation.** *Obs.* [a. OF. *dédignation* (Godef.), ad. L. *dēdignātiōn-em*, n. of action from *dēdignāre*, *-ārī* to reject as unworthy, DISDAIN, f. DE- I. 6 + *dignārī* to think worthy, f. *dignus* worthy.]

1. Disdain, scorn, contempt.

c **1400** *Lanfranc's Cirurg.* 298 Manie men have dedignacioun for to worche wiþ her hondis. *c* **1450** tr. *De Imitatione* III. lxiii, Wo to hem þat haue dedignacion to meke hem self wilfully wiþ smale children. **1633** T. ADAMS *Exp. 2 Peter* ii. 3 Not only with a dedignation of good works, but also with an indignation against good workers. **1716** M. DAVIES *Ath. Brit.* II. 270 The Socinians reject the Imputation..with the utmost Horror and Dedignation.

2. Displeasure, anger (= DISDAIN *sb.* 2); *pass.*, state of being under a person's displeasure, disfavour.

1538 LELAND *Itin.* IV. 33 Wainflete was very great with Henry the vi, wherby he was in great Dedignation with Edward the iv.

†**'dedigne**, *v. Obs.*$^{-0}$ [ad. L. *dēdignāre* (see prec.)]
1623 COCKERAM, *Dedigne*, to disdaine.

†**de'dignify**, *v. Obs.* [f. DE- II. 1 + DIGNIFY *v.*] *trans.* To deprive of dignity or worthiness; to disparage, flout.
1654 GAYTON *Pleas. Notes* III. xi. 151 What greater affront could he put upon himselfe, then to dedignifie his countenance, as not worthy to be look'd on by a Lady.

‖**dedimus** ('dɛdɪməs). *Law.* [From the words of the writ, *dedimus potestatem*, Lat. 'we have given the power'.] A writ empowering one who is not a judge to do some act in place of a judge.
1489–90 *Plumpton Corr.* 92 Afore Easter, send upp your pardons, wrytes of *dedimus.* **1712** ARBUTHNOT *John Bull* I. vii, He talks of nothing but..Writs of Error, Actions of Trover and Conversion, Trespasses, *Precipes et Dedimus.* **1771** SMOLLETT *Humph. Cl.* II. 26 June, He..found means to obtain a *Dedimus* as an acting justice of peace. **1800** BENTHAM *Method of Census* Wks. (1843) X. 353/1 Acting justices..who have taken out their respective *dedimuses.*

deding, var. of DEDEIGN *v.*² *Sc.*

dedir, obs. form of DIDDER *v.*, to tremble.

dedist, obs. form of *didst*: see DO *v.*

deditician (dɛdɪ'tɪʃən), *sb.* and *a. Rom. Law.* Also **-itian.** [f. L. *dēditīci-us*, orig. an alien enemy who had surrendered unconditionally, then a freedman of the class described below; f. *dēdit-*, ppl. stem of *dēdĕre* to surrender: see -ICIOUS and -AN.]
A freedman who, on account of some grave offence committed during his state of slavery, was not allowed the full rights of citizenship. Also *attrib.* or as *adj.*
1880 MUIRHEAD *Ulpian* i. §11 Those freedmen are ranked as dediticians who have been put in chains by their owners as a punishment, or branded, or put to the torture because of some offence and thereof found guilty, or given up to fight either with the sword or with wild beasts, or cast into a gladiatorial training-school or into prison, and have afterwards been manumitted, no matter how. *Ibid.* vii. §4 A woman of deditician condition.
Hence **dedi'ticiancy**, the condition or state of a deditician.

dedition (dɪ'dɪʃən). Now *rare* or *Obs.* [ad. L. *dēditiōn-em*, n. of action from *dēdĕre* to lay down, give up, f. DE- I. 3 + *dăre* to give, to put.] Giving up, yielding, surrender.
1523 *St. Papers Hen. VIII*, VI. 135 For dedicion of their places townes and strengthes to the Kinges subjection. **1659** HAMMOND *On Ps.* cx. 7. 566 Eastern Princes..in token of dedition exacted from subjugated provinces Earth and Water. **1667** *Decay of Chr. Piety* xiii. §1. 334 [They] make an entire dedition of themselves, and submit to the severest and ignoblest vassalage. **1705** STANHOPE *Paraphr.* IV. 598 He disputes not the..Dedition made by his Faction. **1851** GALLENGA *Italy* 367 He insisted upon distinct and positive terms of dedition.

†**dedi'titious**, *a. rare*$^{-0}$. [f. L. *dēditīci-us*, *-ītius* (see above) + -OUS.] (See quot.)
1727 BAILEY vol. II, *Dedititious*, yielding, or delivering himself up into the power of another.

dedly, obs. form of DEADLY.

†**dedoctor.** *Obs. nonce-wd.* [cf. DE- II. 3; agent-n. f. L. *dēdocēre* to cause to unlearn, to teach the contrary of, f. DE- I. 6 + *docēre* to teach: cf. DOCTOR.]
1656 HOBBES *Six Lessons* vi. *ad fin.*, Dedoctors of morality.

dedoggerelize, dedogmatize: see DE- II. 1.

dedolation (diːdəʊ'leɪʃən). *Med.* [n. of action from L. *dēdolāre* to hew away, f. DE- I. 2 + *dolāre* to chip, hew.] 'The shaving off of a portion of the skin or other part of small importance by an oblique cut' (*Syd. Soc. Lex.*).
1857 DUNGLISON *Med. Dict.* s.v., It is commonly on the head that wounds by dedolation are observed.

†**de'doleate**, *v. Obs.*$^{-0}$ [irreg. f. L. *dēdolēre*: see DEDOLENT.]
1623 COCKERAM, *Dedoleate*, to end ones sorrow or griefe.

†**'dedolence.** *Obs.* [ad. L. *dēdolēntia* abandonment of grief, ceasing to grieve, f. *dēdolēre*: see DEDOLENT.] Absence of grief or sorrow; insensibility, callousness.
1606 BIRNIE *Kirk-Buriall* (1833) 10 Our Heroik burials.. wherein the touting of trumpets, trampling of steades, and trouping of men, may sufficiently testifie the dedolence of men. **1633** ROGERS *Treat. Sacraments* II. 127 This chases away the cloudes of dedolence and impenitency. **1633** T. ADAMS *Exp. 2 Peter* iii. 15 There is a dedolence, to be in pain and not to feel it.

†**'dedolency.** *Obs.* [f. L. *dēdolēntia*: see next and -ENCY.] = prec.
a **1617** BAYNE *On Coloss.* (1634) 100 That is a blockish head which can..goe on in a Stoicall dedolency. **1655** GURNALL *Chr. in Arm.* v. (1669) 33/2 Riches & treasures in their Coffers, numness and dedolency in their Consciences.

'dedolent, *a. rare.* Also **dedolant.** [ad. L. *dēdolēnt-em*, pr. pple. of *dēdolēre* to give over grieving, f. DE- I. 6 + *dolēre* to grieve.] That feels sorrow no more; feeling no compunction; insensible, callous.
1633 ROGERS *Treat. Sacraments* II. 23 With an insensible, dedolent heart, with a dead benummed spirit. **1647** WARD *Simp. Cobler* 20 Men..accursed with indelible infamy and dedolent impenitency. **1698** R. FERGUSSON *View Eccles.* 46 His Forehead is Brass double gilt and his Understanding.. Callous and Dedolent. **1893** 'S. GRAND' *Heavenly Twins* I. v. i. 3 She was sleeping soundly, not because she was dedolent but because she was exhausted. **1951** AUDEN *Nones* (1952) 34 A tanker sinks into a dedolant sea.

dedolomitization (ˌdiːdɒləmɪtaɪ'zeɪʃən). *Petrol.* [f. DE- + DOLOMITIZE *v.* + -ATION.] The changing of dolomite into rock of another kind. So **de'dolomitize** *v. trans.*, **de'dolomitized** *ppl. a.*
1903 J. J. H. TEALL in *Geol. Mag.* 4th Ser. X. 514 The cherty dolomites have been dedolomitised by the formation of magnesian silicates... But dedolomitisation has also been produced in another way... The carbonic acid freed itself more readily from the magnesia..converting the original dolomite into an aggregate calcite and periclase. **1930** PEACH & HORNE *Geol. Scotl.* 113 Another method of dedolomitization should be added to those enumerated by Teall. **1969** *Nature* 9 Aug. 607/2 The partially dedolomitized rocks have three components—calcite of the original limestone, unreplaced dolomite and calcite after dolomite.

deducate ('dɛdjuːkeɪt), *v.* (See quot.) So **'deducated, deduc'cation, 'deducator.**
1867 FURNIVALL *Pref.* to *Hymns to Virgin* p. viii, Many educated (or deducated) persons. *Note*, We sadly want some word like this *deducate*, *deducation*, &c., to denote the wilful down-leading into prejudice and unreason..Let any one think of the amount of deducation attempted about the Repeal of the Corn Laws..&c., and then see how hard the deducators still are at their work!

deduce (dɪ'djuːs), *v.* Also 6–7 *erron.* **diduce.** [ad. L. *dēdūc-ĕre* to lead down, derive, in med.L. to infer logically, f. DE- I. 1, 2 + *dūcĕre* to lead. Cf. DEDUCT. In 16–17th c. there was frequent confusion of the forms of *deduce* and DIDUCE, q.v.
(The sense-development had already taken place in Latin, and does not agree with the chronological data in English.)]
1. *lit. trans.* **a.** To bring, convey; *spec.* (after Lat.), to lead forth or conduct (a colony). *arch.*
1578 BANISTER *Hist. Man* v. 71 If any of the wayes deducyng choler, come vnto the bottome of the ventricle. **1612** SELDEN *Illustr. of Drayton* §17 (R.) Advising him he should hither deduce a colony. **1685** STILLINGFL. *Orig. Brit.* i. 5 The Romans began to deduce Colonies, to settle Magistrates and Jurisdictions here. **1822** T. TAYLOR *Apuleius* 340 Sagacious nature may from thence deduce it [the blood] through all the members. **1866** J. B. ROSE *Virgil's Georg.* 88 Still Ausonian colonists rehearse, Deduced from Troy, the incoherent verse.
†**b.** To bring or draw (water, etc.) *from. Obs.*
1602 FULBECKE *2nd Pt. Parall.* 54 By that meane he deduced water out of the earth. *c* **1630** RISDON *Surv. Devon* §107 (1810) 104 Conduits..nourished with waters deduced from out of the fields.
†**c.** To bring or draw down. *Obs.*
1621 G. SANDYS *Ovid's Met.* XII. (1626) 244 Orions mother Mycale, eft-soone Could with her charmes deduce the strugling Moone.
†**2.** *fig.* **a.** To lead, bring. *Obs.*
1545 JOYE *Exp. Dan.* Ded. A. iv, Christ himself doth.. deduce us unto the readinge of thys boke. **1585** J. HILTON in Fuller *Ch. Hist.* IX. vi. §27 That..we be..made partakers of his Testament, and so deduced to the knowledge of his godly will. **1706** COLLIER *Refl. Ridic.* 25 He continually deduces the conversation to this topick.
†**b.** *Law.* To bring before a tribunal.
1612 BACON *Ess. Judicature* (Arb.) 458 Many times, the thing deduced to Iudgement, may bee *meum et tuum* [etc.].
†**c.** To lead away, turn aside, divert.
1541 *Act 33 Hen. VIII*, c. 32 The vicar..wolde deduce them from their said most accustomable parishe church of Whitegate, vnto his said church of Ouer. **1647** LILLY *Chr. Astrol.* clxvii. 720 The force of a Direction may continue many yeers, untill the Significator is deduced to another Promittor.
†**d.** To bring down, convey by inheritance.
1633 BP. HALL *Hard Texts* 483 If Abraham..had this land given to him for his inheritance, how much more may wee, his seed, (to whom it is deduced)..challenge a due interest in it. **1641** 'SMECTYMNUUS' *Answ.* §6 (1653) 32 How this should have beene deduced to us in an uninterrupted Line, wee know not.
3. To draw or obtain *from* some source; to derive. Now somewhat *rare.*
1565–78 COOPER *Thesaurus* Introd., Whether the word be a Primative or derivative deduced of some other. **1596** H. CLAPHAM *Briefe Bible* I. 15 He, of Nothing, created Something..whereout, Al other Creatures were to be diduced. **1634** SIR T. HERBERT *Trav.* (1638) 232 A ceremony diduced from the Romans. **1665** *Ibid.* (1677) 181 Rivers that deduce their Springs near each other. **1790** COWPER *My Mother's Picture* 108 My boast is not, that I deduce my birth From loins enthron'd, and rulers of the earth. **1869** FARRAR *Fam. Speech* i. (1873) 20 The attempt to prove that all languages were deduced from the Hebrew.
b. *intr.* To be derived. *rare.* (Cf. *to derive.*)
1866 J. B. ROSE tr. *Ovid's Fasti* Notes 240 The former notion of a bird..may deduce from the eastern word Gaph. **1889** COURTNEY *Mill* 20 The very first principles from which it deduces, are so little axiomatic that, etc.

4. *trans.* To trace the course of, trace out, go through in order (as in narrative or description); to bring down (a record) *from* or *to* a particular period. †Formerly, also, To conduct (a process), handle, treat, deal with (a matter).
1528 GARDINER in Pocock *Rec. Ref.* I. l. 115 Considering how the process might be after the best sort deduced and handled. *c* **1645** HOWELL *Lett.* VI. 61, I will deduce the business from the beginning. **1659** BP. WALTON *Consid. Considered* 259 These things are largely deduced and handled in the same Prolegomena. **1685** STILLINGFL. *Orig. Brit.* iii. 88 Having deduced the Succession of the British Churches down to..the first Councel of Arles. **1728–46** THOMSON *Spring* 577 Lend me your song, ye nightingales.. while I deduce, From the first note the hollow cuckoo sings, The symphony of Spring. **1776** GIBBON *Decl. & Fall* I. 296 The general design of this work will not permit us..to deduce the various fortunes of his private life. **1818** JAS. MILL *Brit. India* I. (1840) I. 2 To deduce to the present times a history of..the British transactions, which have had an immediate relation to India. **1866** J. MARTINEAU *Ess.* I. 149 All the optical history..is elaborately deduced.
5. To trace the derivation or descent of, to show or hold (a thing) to be derived *from.*
a **1536** TINDALE *Wks.* 21 (R.) Deducyng the loue to God out of fayth, and the loue of a man's neighbour out of the loue of God. **1579** W. FULKE *Ref. Rastel* 715 They could not deduce the beginning from yᵉ Apostles. **1658** USSHER *Annals* 593 They deduced themselves from the Athenians. **1676** HODGSON in *Phil. Trans.* XI. 766 Those..who deduce the Scurvy from the use of Sugar. **1767** BLACKSTONE *Comm.* II. 114 He cannot deduce his descent wholly by heirs male.
6. To derive or draw as a conclusion *from* something already known or assumed; to derive by a process of reasoning or inference; to infer. (The chief current sense.)
1529 MORE *Dyaloge* III. Wks. 215/2 Yᵉ case once graunted, ye deduce your conclusion very surelye. **1651** BAXTER *Inf. Bapt.* 87 It must be [known] rationally by deducing it from some premises. **1696** WHISTON *Th. Earth* II. (1722) 184 The knowledge of Causes is deduc'd from their Effects. **1788** REID *Aristotle's Log.* iv. §4. 83 Rules..deduced from the particular cases before determined. **1812** SIR H. DAVY *Chem. Philos.* p. viii, It was deduced from an indirect experiment. **1849** MURCHISON *Siluria* i. (1867) 2 This inference has been deduced from positive observation. **1885** LEUDESDORF *Cremona's Proj. Geom.* 277 From this we deduce a method for the construction.
b. Less commonly with *obj. clause.*
1532 MORE *Confut. Tindale* Wks. 461/2 We deduce therupon that he wil not suffer his church fal into yᵉ erronious belief of anie damnable vntrouthe. **1646** SIR T. BROWNE *Pseud. Ep.* v. vi. 243 That the custome of feasting upon beds was in use among the Hebrewes, many diduce from the 23. of Ezekiel.
†**7.** To deduct, subtract. *Obs.*
1563–7 BUCHANAN *Reform. St. Andros* Wks. (1892) 14 The principal sal deduce sa mekle of hys gagis. **1614** BP. HALL *Recoll. Treat.* 514 The more we deduce, the fewer we leave. **1632** B. JONSON *Magn. Lady* II. i, A matter of four hundred To be deduced upon the payment. **1662** STILLINGFL. *Orig. Sacr.* I. v. §3, 1117. which being deduced from 3940. the remainder is 2823.
†**8.** To reduce (to a different form). *Obs.*
1586 J. HOOKER *Girald. Irel.* in *Holinshed* II. 10/1 By these meanes the whole land, which is now diuided into fiue prouinces or portions, maie be deduced and brought into one. **1654** GATAKER *Disc. Apol.* 36 After that my Morning Lecture was reduced, or deduced rather, to the ordinarie hour in most places. **1749** J. MILLAN (*title*), Coins, Weights, and Measures, Ancient and Modern, of all Nations, deduced into English on above 100 Tables.
Hence **de'ducing** *vbl. sb.*, deduction.
1530 PALSGR. 212/2 Deducyng, *discours.* **1532** MORE *Confut. Tindale* Wks. 461/2 Termes..of drawyng oute & deducinges and depending vpon scrypture. **1651** HOBBES *Leviath.* II. xxv. 133 Consisting in a deducing of the benefit, or hurt that may arise, etc. **1827** WHATELY *Logic* (1837) 258 The deducing of an inference from those facts.

deduceable, obs. var. of DEDUCIBLE.

†**de'ducement.** *Obs.* Also 7 (*erron.*) **diducement.** [f. DEDUCE + -MENT.]
1. A deduction, inference, conclusion.
1605 BACON *Adv. Learn.* II. xxiii. §7. 104 If I woulde haue broken them and illustrated them by diducements and examples. *a* **1631** DONNE *Serm.* xii. 114 All the Deducements and Inferences of the Schooles. **1682** DRYDEN *Relig. Laici* Pref. (Globe ed.) 186 Those deducements, which I am confident are the remote effects of Revelation.
2. A tracing out (see DEDUCE 4). *rare.*
1820 *Blackw. Mag.* VII. 362 A regular deducement of the Batavian line through all the varieties of place and fortune.

deducible (dɪ'djuːsɪb(ə)l), *a.* Also 7 (*erron.*) **diducible**, 7–8 **deduceable.** [f. L. *dēdūcĕre* to DEDUCE + -BLE.]
1. That may be deduced or inferred.
1617 COLLINS *Def. Bp. Ely* I. iii. 126 Nothing is deducible out of his doctrine, which fauours the Popedome. **1678** R. BARCLAY *Apol. Quakers* XII. §x. 451 There [is] not any difference or ground for it visible in the Text, or deduceable from it. **1752** J. GILL *Trinity* i. 14 These are consequences justly deducible from our principles. **1867** J. MARTINEAU *Ess.* II. 62 Precept is not deducible from precept.
b. as *sb.* That which is deducible; an inference that may be drawn.
1654 WHITLOCK *Zootomia* 511 Yet since it is from Truth, and her Secretaries (the Casuists), heare their deducibles. **1861** J. MARTINEAU *Ess. etc.* (1891) II. 435 As if they were deducibles from the primary spiritual truth. **1881** CASEY *Sequel to Euclid* 16 A large number of deducibles may be given in connexion with..Prop. xlvii.

†**2.** That may be or is to be deducted. *Obs. rare.*

1613 F. ROBARTS *Revenue of Gospel* 94 Before I come to define the charge diducible.

Hence **deduci'bility, de'ducibleness,** the quality of being deducible.

1846 WORCESTER cites COLERIDGE for *deducibility*. **1881** WESTCOTT & HORT *Grk. N.T.* Introd. §67 The easy deducibility, direct or indirect, of all their readings from a single text. **1727** BAILEY vol. II, *Deducibleness*, capableness of being deduced.

de'ducive, *a. rare*⁻⁰. [f. DEDUCE + -IVE: cf. *conducive*.] (See quot.)

1755 JOHNSON, *Deducive*, performing the act of deduction. *Dict.*

†**de'duct,** *ppl. a. Obs.* [ad. L. *dēduct-us*, pa. pple. of *dēdūcĕre*: see next. After the formation of *deduct* vb., used as its pa. pple. till superseded by *deducted*.] Deducted.

1439 *Rolls of Parl.* 5 Aftur the summes in the seid Commissions to be deducte. **1495** *Act 11 Hen VII*, c. 61 §1 Aftir all ordinary charges deducte. **1532** FRITH *Mirror or Glass* (1829) 273 The poor, which..are the owners, under God, of all together, the minister's living deduct.

deduct (dɪ'dʌkt), *v.* [f. L. *dēduct-*, ppl. stem of L. *dēdūc-ĕre* to lead or bring down or away, lead off, withdraw, f. DE- I. 1, 2 + *dūcĕre* to lead, draw. Cf. DEDUCE: the two verbs were formerly to a great extent synonymous, but are now differentiated in use, by the restriction of this to sense 1.]

1. *trans.* To take away or subtract from a sum or amount. (The current sense.)

Now said usually of amounts, portions, etc., while *subtract* is properly said only of numbers; but *deduct* was formerly used also of the arithmetical operation.

1524 *Ch. Accts. Kingston-on-Thames* in Lysons *Environs of London* I. 226 Recᵈ at the Church Ale and Robyn-hode, all things deducted, 3*l.* 10*s.* 6*d.* **1530** PALSGR. 509/1, I deducte, I abate partyculer sommes out of a great somme, *Je rabats*. **1542** RECORDE *Gr. Artes* (1575) 107 Deducte the digit from the figure that is ouer him, and write the remayner. **1631** GOUGE *God's Arrowes* v. §18. 430 His Master might buy him bow, and arrowes, and deduct the price out of his wages. **1646** SIR T. BROWNE *Pseud. Ep.* IV. ii. 182 Deducting the waight of that five pound. **1751** JOHNSON *Rambler* No. 108 ¶2 When we have deducted all that is absorbed in sleep. **1850** PRESCOTT *Peru* II. 115 The royal fifth was first deducted, including the remittance already sent to Spain. **1874** MASSON *Milton* (Gold. Treas. ed.) I. p. xi, If we deduct the two Psalm Paraphrases..Milton's literary life may be said to begin exactly with the reign of Charles I.

absol. **1824** *Examiner* 641/1 Every shilling squandered by Ministers..deducts from the value of their property.

†**2.** To lead forth, conduct (a colony); = DEDUCE 1 a. *Obs.*

1549 COVERDALE *Erasm. Par. Phil.* Argt., A people deducted oute of the citie of Philippos. **1582** [see DEDUCTING]. **1600** HOLLAND *Livy* Pref. 3 Venice was a Colonie deducted and drawne from thence. **1627** [see DEDUCTED].

†**3.** To draw or convey (a streamlet) aside (*from* the main stream). *Obs. rare.*

1621 BURTON *Anat. Mel.* Democr. to Rdr. 10 Which as a rillet is deducted from that maine channell of my other studies. *c* **1626** *Dick of Devon.* II. ii. in Bullen *O. Pl.* II. 31 A rivolet but deducted From the mayne Channell.

†**4.** To derive; to trace the derivation or descent of; = DEDUCE 3, 5. *Obs.*

1530 PALSGR. 17 All suche wordes as be deducted out of Latin wordes. **1565** T. STAPLETON *Fortr. Faith* 94* For more safety to deduct that succession from the See of Rome. **1577–87** HOLINSHED *Chron.* II. 9/1 Touching the name Ibernia, historiographers are not yet agreed from whence it is deducted. *a* **1641** BP. MOUNTAGU *Acts & Mon.* (1642) 108 In deducting the Maccabees from Iudah. **1648** GAGE *West Ind.* xx. (1655) 174 From whence commonly in the Church of Rome the Texts and subjects of Sermons are deducted. **1660** R. SHERINGHAM *King's Suprem. Asserted* ii. (1682) 10 All authority..is derived and deducted from the King's Majesty.

†**5.** To trace out in order: to bring down *from* or *to* a particular period; = DEDUCE 4. *Obs. rare.*

1545 LELAND *New-year's Gift* in Strype *Eccl. Mem.* I. App. cxviii. 330 The first boke, begynnyng at the Druides, is deducted vnto the tyme of the comyng of S. Augustyne. **1586** MARY Q. SCOTS *Let. to Babington* 12 July in Howell *St. Trials* (1809) I. 1177 For divers great and importunate considerations which were here too long to be deducted.

†**6.** To derive by reasoning, infer, deduce. *Obs.*

1563 FOXE *A. & M.* 850b, This parte he deducted and proued by sundry ensamples, and similitudes. **1609** SIR E. HOBY *Lett. to T. Higgins* 37 Which by Logicall consequence is not Necessarily deducted out of the Premisses. **1660** tr. *Amyraldus' Treat. conc. Relig.* I. iii. 32 A conception.. deducted from sober influence of reason. **1889** *Cape Law Jrnl.* 203 To take all the circumstances into consideration and to deduct therefrom..the act of desertion.

†**7.** To reduce. *Obs.* (Cf. DEDUCE 8.)

1599–16.. MASSINGER, etc. *Old Law* III. i. *Clerk.* 'Tis but so many months, so many weeks, so many—. *Gnotho.* Do not deduct it to days, 'twill be the more tedious.

Hence **de'ducted** *ppl. a.*, **de'ducting** *vbl. sb.*

1582 *Divers Voy.* (Hakluyt Soc. 1850) 9 The deducting of some Colonies of our superfluous people into those temperate and fertile partes of America. **1596** SPENSER *Hymn Love* 106 Man..hauing yet in his deducted spright, Some sparks remaining of that heauenly fyre. **1598** YONG *Diana* Ded., It befell to my lot..to performe the part of a French Oratour by a deducted speech in the same toong. **1627** MAY *Lucan* IV. 434 Though no deducted colony.

deductible (dɪ'dʌktɪb(ə)l), *a.* and *sb.* Also deductable. [f. L. *deduct-* (see prec.) + -BLE.]

A. *adj.* Capable of being deducted; *spec.* that can be deducted from one's tax or from one's taxable income.

1856 MRS. BROWNING *Aur. Leigh* II. (1888) 71 Not one found honestly deductible From any use that pleased him. **1894** *Westm. Gaz.* 14 Aug. 2/1 Now tax is deductable either at the rate actually in force at the date of payment. **1913** *Standard* 3 Apr. 11/4 A dividend entrusted to an agent for payment on a date before April 6 is chargeable with the duty in force for the year 1912–13, and the duty is deductible notwithstanding that payment in individual cases may not happen to be claimed until after that date. **1925** *Glasgow Herald* 30 Jan. 9 The time within which..discount was deductable under the contract. **1954** I. LEVIN *Kiss before Dying* II. ii. 89 We are..beginning the contruction of a new gymnasium... Perhaps your father would be interested in making a contribution... Such contributions are tax-deductible. **1965** *Listener* 17 June 899/3 The all-in price for a London plane tree, including maintenance, is £40—not exactly cheap, but it is tax-deductible.

B. *sb.* The amount of a loss which must be borne by the policy-holder in the event of a claim upon an insurance policy. Chiefly *N. Amer.*

1927 *Annals Amer. Acad. Pol. & Soc. Sci.* CXXX. 158/1 The popular deductibles are in the amounts of $50, $100 and $250. The cost of deductible collision insurance, especially on the larger deductibles, is small. **1956** *U.S. News & World Rep.* 30 Mar. 144/2 They set up a $25 deductible to eliminate these 'nuisance' payments. **1971** *Wall St. Jrnl.* 11 Aug. 28/2 Many companies say they would buy the coverage ..if the 'deductible' (the amount of loss which the insured company must absorb before benefits begin) were lower. **1984** *Times* 8 Sept. 21/7 The policy is reported to provide cover up to about $200m for Brazil, Argentina, Venezuela.. and to have a deductible of about one-quarter of the coverage for each country.

de'ductile, *a. rare*⁻⁰. [ad. L. type *dēductil-is*, f. *dēduct-* DEDUCT.]

1727 BAILEY vol. II, *Deductile*, easy to be deducted.

deduction (dɪ'dʌkʃən). Also 5 deduxion, 5–6 deduccion, 6 deduccoun. [In some senses a. F. *déduction* (Oresme 14th c.), but in most ad. L. *dēductiōn-em*, n. of action from L. *dēdūcĕre*: see DEDUCT, DEDUCE.] The action of deducting.

1. a. The action of deducting or taking away from a sum or amount; subtraction, abatement.

1483 in Arnolde *Chron.* (1811) 110 The sayde Ri. shall be chargeable for the hoole somme..wythot ony deduxion. **1496–7** *Act 12 Hen. VII*, c. 12 §4 Any deduccion or abatement befortyme allowed. **1646** SIR T. BROWNE *Pseud. Ep.* IV. xii. 217 He dyed in the day of his nativity, and without deduction justly accomplished the year of eighty one. **1776** SMITH *W.N.* I. viii. (1869) I. 68 His rent..makes the first deduction from the produce of the labour which is employed upon land. **1827** JARMAN *Powell's Devises* II. 55 The interest given to them was exclusive of, and with a deduction of, that sum. **1868** FREEMAN *Norm. Conq.* (1876) II. vii. 33 Charges of this kind must always be taken with certain deductions.

b. That which is deducted or subtracted.

1546 in *Eng. Gilds* (1870) 197 Wyth the yerely Resolutes and deduccions goyng out of the same. **1557** RECORDE *Whetst.* Xj, For subtraction your nombers are sette downe after the common maner, firste the totall, and then the deduction. **1703** T. N. *City & C. Purchaser* 55 In taking out the Deductions for the Doors and Windows.

2. a. A leading forth or away (*spec.* of a colony); conduct. Now *rare* or *Obs.*

1615 CHAPMAN *Odyss.* VI. 455 Take such way, That you yourself may compass..Your quick deduction by my father's grace. **1677** HALE *Prim. Orig. Man.* II. x. 228 Deductions of Colonies, and new Plantations. **1832** *Blackw. Mag.* XXXI. 574 The solemn *deduction* (to use the technical term) of a legitimate Roman colony.

†**b.** *fig.* A leading up *to* something, introduction. *Obs. rare.*

1513 MORE *Rich. III*, Wks. 61 (R.) He sodainly lefte the matter, with which he was in hand, and without any deduction thereunto..began to repete those wordes again.

†**3.** The action or result of tracing out or setting forth in order; a detailed narration or account. *Obs.* (Cf. DEDUCE 4, DEDUCT *v.* 5.)

a **1532** *Remedie of Love* (R.), Ordinately behoveth thee first to procede In deduction thereof [this werke]. **1603** FLORIO *Montaigne* I. ix. (1632) 17 A long counterfet deduction of this storie. **1670** EVELYN *Mem.* (1857) III. 222 A solemn deduction and true state of all affairs and particulars. **1748** CHESTERF. *Lett.* II. clix. 71 It..gives a clear deduction of the affairs of Europe from the treaty of Munster to this time. **1826** C. BUTLER *Life Grotius* 34 We have thus brought down our historical deduction of the German Empire to the accession of the Emperor Charles.

†**4.** *Mus.* The succession of notes forming a HEXACHORD: the singing of these in order. *Obs.*

1597 MORLEY *Introd. Mus.* 7 Now for the last tryall of your singing in continuall deduction sing this perfectly. **1609** DOULAND *Ornith. Microl.* 26 There are..three Deductions of this kinde. **1876** STAINER & BARRETT *Dict. Mus. Terms.*

†**5. a.** The process of deducing or deriving from some source; derivation. *Obs.*

1612 DRAYTON *Poly-olb.* ix. Notes 145 Affirming that our Britons from them..had deduction of this nationall title. **1669** GALE *Crt. Gentiles* I. I. ii. 12 The deduction of the Greek Leters from the Hebrew. **1755** JOHNSON *Dict.*, *Grammar Eng. Tongue*, Etymology teaches the deduction of one word from another.

b. *concr.* That which is derived. *rare.*

a **1835** RICKMAN *Archit.* 30 There may be some doubt, whether the modern Ionic capital is not rather a deduction from the Composite than the contrary.

6. a. The process of deducing or drawing a conclusion from a principle already known or assumed; *spec.* in *Logic*, inference by reasoning from generals to particulars; opposed to INDUCTION.

1594 HOOKER *Eccl. Pol.* I. xiv. (1611) 42 And show the deduction thereof out of Scripture to be necessarie. **1651** HOBBES *Govt. & Soc.* iii. §26 The deduction of these Lawes is so hard, that [etc.]. **1736** BUTLER *Anal.* II. vi. 308 A matter of deduction and inference. **1789** BELSHAM *Ess.* I. i. 4 It follows by easy and irrefragable deduction. **1860** ABP. THOMSON *Laws Th.* §113 Deduction the process of deriving facts from laws, and effects from their causes. *a* **1862** BUCKLE *Civiliz.* (1869) III. v. 291 By deduction we descend from the abstract to the concrete.

b. *transf.* That which is deduced; an inference, conclusion.

1532 MORE *Confut. Tindale* Wks. 461/2 Yet if he would.. neither vse false deduccions of hys owne, nor refuse our deduccions yf we deduce them wel. **1671** J. WEBSTER *Metallogr.* i. 9 From all this we shall only draw these Deductions. **1736** BUTLER *Anal.* I. ii. 35 It is not so much a Deduction of Reason, as a Matter of Experience. **1876** FREEMAN *Norm. Conq.* V. xxii. 21 The whole evidence.. bears out the general deductions which I have made.

†**7.** Reduction. *Obs. rare.* (Cf. DEDUCT 7.)

1650 BULWER *Anthropomet.* 172 The Deduction and Moderation of their Excrescencie.

8. *attrib.*, **deduction theorem** *Logic*, the rule or metatheorem that if within a system a formula B is derivable from a formula A, then 'If A then B' is a theorem of the system; the principle of conditionalization.

1941 O. HELMER tr. *Tarski's Introd. Logic* vi. 127 A general law..which..is known as the law of deduction (or the deduction theorem). **1951** *Mind* LX. 382 The Deduction Theorem holds for the calculus of causal propositions. **1962** W. & M. KNEALE *Devel. Logic* v. 320 The principle of conditionalization (or 'deduction theorem').. was taken for granted by Aristotle.

de'ductional, *a. rare.* [f. prec. + -AL¹.] Of, pertaining to, or of the nature of deduction.

1683 E. HOOKER *Pref. Ep. Pordage's Mystic Div.* 44 As for Doctrines Traditional, Superstitional, and Deductional, these are (world !) without end.

deductive (dɪ'dʌktɪv), *a.* and *sb.* [ad. L. *dēductīv-us*, f. *dēduct-*, ppl. stem of *dēdūcĕre* to DEDUCE: see -IVE. Cf. mod.F. *déductif, -ive*.]

A. *adj.* **1. a.** Of the nature of, or characterized by the use of, deduction; *spec.* in *Logic*, reasoning from generals to particulars; opposed to *inductive*.

1665 GLANVILL *Scepsis Sci.* xxiii. §1 All knowledge of causes is deductive. **1665** HOOKE *Microgr.* D, The rational or deductive Faculty. **1846** MILL *Logic* II. iv. §4 Geometry is a Deductive Science. *a* **1862** BUCKLE *Misc. Wks.* (1872) I. 7 Women naturally prefer the deductive method to the inductive.

b. Of persons: Employing the method of deduction; reasoning deductively.

1861 TULLOCH *Eng. Purit.* iii. 378 Of all the divines of his time, none was more bold, or deductive. **1867** LEWES *Hist. Philos.* II. 153 The mathematical cultivators of Physics and the deductive cultivators of Philosophy.

c. ***deductive system*** (Logic): a set of propositions or formulas, in which some are derived from others according to rules of proof, all such possible derivations being held to be included.

1910 WHITEHEAD & RUSSELL *Principia Math.* I. p. vi, A deductive system such as that contained in the present work. **1936** A. J. AYER *Lang., Truth & Logic* ii. 40 Among the superstitions..is the view that it is the business of the philosopher to construct a deductive system. **1940** W. V. QUINE *Math. Logic* 88 The highly explicit way of presenting formal deductive systems which is customary nowadays dates back only to Hilbert (1922) or Post (1921). **1951** *Mind* LX. 266 The calculus, or deductive system, of truth-functions.

†**2.** Derivative.

1646 SIR T. BROWNE *Pseud. Ep.* I. x. 38 He labours to introduce a secondary and deductive Atheisme, that although they concede there is a God, yet should they deny his providence.

†**B.** *sb.* Deductive reasoning; a deduction.

1677 HALE *Prim. Orig. Man.* To Rdr., If there be any Errours..in my Deductives, Inferences, or Applications.

deductively (dɪ'dʌktɪvlɪ), *adv.* [f. prec. + -LY².] In a deductive manner, by deduction, inferentially; †by derivation or descent.

a **1641** BP. MOUNTAGU *Acts & Mon.* (1642) 132 Holinesse ..deductively passed from himselfe to others, members and parts of his body mysticall. **1646** SIR T. BROWNE *Pseud. Ep.* I. x. 39 Yet doth it diductively and upon inference include the same. **1857** WHEWELL *Hist. Induct. Sc.* I. 114 Which trace deductively the results. **1862** H. SPENCER *First Princ.* II. viii. §73 The truth as arrived at deductively, cannot be inductively confirmed.

deductivism (dɪ'dʌktɪvɪz(ə)m). *Philos.* [f. DEDUCTIVE *a.* + -ISM.] The preference for, use of, or belief in the superiority of, deductive as opposed to inductive methods; *esp.* either the doctrine that induction has no place in scientific method, or that induction in some manner requires justification by deduction. So **de'ductivist**, one who advocates deductivism; also *attrib.* or as *adj.*

1908 *Fabian News* June 56/2 The parallel sociological advance from metaphysics to deductivism. **1936** A. L. Rowse *Mr. Keynes* ii. 7 That excessive and unenlightening deductivism in economics. *Ibid.* 9 It is simply to recommend a more modest habit of mind to the deductivists. **1959** K. R. Popper *Logic of Sci. Disc.* i. 30 The theory of the deductive method of testing, or..the view that a hypothesis can only be empirically *tested*..might be called 'deductivism'. *Ibid.*, Duhem..held pronounced deductivist views. **1962** in E. Nagel et al. *Logic, Methodol., etc.* 265 (*title*) The Controversy: Deductivism Versus Inductivism.

deductory (dɪ'dʌktərɪ), *a. rare.* [ad. L. *dēductōri-us*, f. *dēductor*, agent-n. from *dēdūcĕre* to DEDUCE: see -ORY.]

†**1.** *Law.* Having the effect of bringing a matter before a court (see DEDUCE 2 b). *Obs.*

1613 Sir H. Finch *Law* (1636) 490 Being not diductory to bring any matter into plea or solemne action, but onely Commandatorie or Prohibitorie.

2. = DEDUCTIVE *a.*

1655 Fuller *Ch. Hist.* IX. viii. §3 A consequential and deductory felonie. **1889** J. D. Hunting in *National Rev.* XIV. 219 Ascertained by fair deductory evidence.

†**deduit**, *sb. Obs.* Forms: 3-4 dedut, 4 dedute, dedwt, 4-5 deduit(e, 5 deduyt(e. See also DUTE. [a. F. *déduit* (12th c. in Littré):—L. *dēduct-um*, subst. use of pa. pple. of *dēdūcĕre* in sense of 'divert'. In Prov. *desduch*, *desdui*, from *desduire*, *desdure* = F. *déduire*, L. *dēdūcĕre*.] Diversion, enjoyment, pleasure.

1297 R. Glouc. (1724) 564 [Hy] were in hor dedut, iwend an hontinge. *c* **1350** *Will. Palerne* 4998 þan driue þei forþ þe day in dedut and in murþe. **1393** Gower *Conf.* III. 371 In which the yere hath his deduit Of grass, of lefe, of floure, of fruit. *c* **1450** *Merlin* 307 This Dionas loved moche the deduyt of the wode and the river. **1480** Caxton *Ovid's Met.* XI. xiii, I [Venus] am lady of all courtoisye and of al deduyt. **1483** —— *Gold. Leg.* 119 b/1 All the delytes and deduytes of the world.

†**deduit, -e**, *ppl. a. Obs. rare.* [a. F. *déduit, -ite*, pa. pple. of *déduire*:—L. *dēdūcĕre*: see DEDUCE.] Drawn out.

1485 Caxton *Chas. Gt.* 26 He had the face deduyte in lengthe.

deduplication (di:,dju:plɪ'keɪʃən). *Bot.* [a. F. *déduplication*, latinized deriv. of F. *dédoubler* (*desdoubler*, 1429 in Hatzf.) to separate what is double, divide into two halves, f. *des-*, *dé-* (DE- I. 6) + *doubler* to double.] Congenital division of one organ into two (or more); = CHORISIS.

1835 Lindley *Introd. Bot.* (1848) I. 332, I thought I might extend the primitive meaning of the word *deduplication*, and consider it synonymous with separation, disjunction. *Ibid.* 333 The theory of deduplication has its supporters among French Botanists of eminence. **1850** Gray *Lett.* I. 365. **1880** —— *Struct. Bot.* vi. §3. 202 Chorisis or Deduplication..the division of that which is morphologically one organ into two or more (a division which is of course congenital), so that two or more organs occupy the position of one.

dedur, obs. form of DIDDER *v.*

dedut(e, deduyt(e, var. DEDUIT *Obs.*

dedye, dedyne, var. DEDIE *v.* and DEDEIGN *v.*[2]

dedyn, obs. pl. of *did*, from DO *v.*

dee (di:), *sb.* **1. a.** Name of the letter D; applied to a D-shaped iron or steel loop used for connecting parts of harness, or for fastening articles to the saddle: cf. D I. 2.

1794 W. Felton *Carriages* (1801) II. 145 The Collar-Dee, an iron ring in the form of a D, sewed in the front of the collar, for the pole-piece to loop through; there are various other dees used about some harness, but of a small size, and mostly plated. **1880** *Blackw. Mag.* Feb. 164 (*Bush Life Queensland*) The pommel was also furnished with strong iron dees driven firmly into the woodwork. **1884** W. Westall in *Contemp. Rev.* July 69 The cheeks are furnished with 'dees' for holding bridle and curb chain. **1888** Elworthy *W. Somerset Gloss.*, *Dee*, an iron shaped like letter D. Such an iron is used in cart-harness to connect the leather of the breeching with the chains.

b. *Comb.* **dee-lock** (see quot.)

1888 Elworthy *W. Somerset Gloss.*, *Dee-lock*, a very common, cheap kind of padlock, used for gates, etc. It is a simple piece of iron in the shape of letter D, having a joint at one angle and a screw working in a short pipe at the other.

2. Either of the two hollow, D-shaped electrodes used to accelerate particles in a cyclotron.

1936 Lawrence & Cooksey in *Physical Rev.* L. 1131/2 The accelerating electrodes..are called duants, or dees. **1966** *New Scientist* 24 Nov. 464/1 In the traditional type of cyclotron, the particles are accelerated by being driven electrostatically from one to another of a pair of matched semicircular devices called dees.

3. Slang abbrev. of DETECTIVE *sb.* Cf. D III. 3.

1882 *Sydney Slang Dict.* 3/2 Dee (D.), a detective policeman. **1895** *Brewer's Dict. Phr. & Fable* 339/2 Look sharp! the dees are about. **1943** *Penguin New Writing* XVIII. 72 Occasionally I'd see people we passed who'd pick them for dees. **1949** E. de Mauny *Huntsman in Career* 127 You've got to look out, if the dees come.

dee (di:), *v.* **a.** Pronunciation of d ——, euphemistic for *damn* (see D I. 3); usually in pa. pple. *deed* (also *deedeed*) = d —— d, damned.

a **1845** Barham *Ingol. Leg.*, *The Poplar*, We'll be *Deed* if it isn't an O! **1859** Reade *Love me little* III. 25 Your three graces are three deed fools. **1864** Lowell *Fireside Trav.* 61 A satirist..whose works were long ago dead and (I fear) deedeed to boot.

b. as *adj.* = DAMNED *ppl. a.* 4 a.

1889 Kipling *From Sea to Sea* (1899) 212 Dee fool. It's different in Upper Burma, where you get command and travelling allowances.

dee, d'ee, earlier way of writing *d'ye* = do ye? do you?

1611 Chapman *May Day* Plays 1873 II. 344 And how dee Sir? **1625** Fletcher *Fair Maid* III. i, De'e forsooth? **1632** Brome *Northern Lasse* I. ii, Dee hear?

dee, var. of DEY; obs. or dial. f. DIE.

deea-nettle: see DEA-NETTLE.

deed (di:d). Forms: 1 *W. Sax.* dǽd, *Anglian* déd; 2-3 dæd, 2-5 ded, 2-6 dede, (3 dead, dade, 4-5 dide, 4-6 deid(e, 5 deyd(e), 5-7 deede, (6 deade), 5- deed. [OE. *dǽd*, *déd* = OFris. *dēde*, OSax. *dâd* (MDu. *daet* (*dâde*), Du. *daad*), OHG., MHG. *tât* (Ger. *that, tat*), ON. *dáð* (Sw. *dåd*, Da. *daad*), Goth. *dêds*:—OTeut. **dǣdi-z* :—**dhē̆tis*, f. verb root ˌ*dhēdhō*, OTeut. ˌ*dǣdô*: see DO *v.* The second *d* from original *t*, is in accordance with Verner's Law: cf. DEAD.

The early ME. was *dede*, from the OE. acc. *dǽde*, *dēde*. The OE. pl. *dǽda*, *déda*, regularly became *dede* in 12-13th c. But this was identical with the sing., whence, for distinction, new plurals came into use after other OE. types, viz. *deden* in the south, *dedes* in the midl. and north; the former was still used *c* 1320 (*Castel of Loue*), but, as in other words, the *-s* form (found *c* 1200 in *Ormulum* and *Trin. Coll. Hom.*) eventually prevailed.]

1. That which is done, acted, or performed by an intelligent or responsible agent; an act.

c **825** *Vesp. Psalter* lxiii. 10 [lxiv. 9] And ondreord oȝhwelc mon, & seȝdun werc godes, & dede his onȝetun. **971** *Blickl. Hom.* 23 We sceolon..þæt ondȝit mid gédum dædum ȝefyllan. **1154** *O.E. Chron.* (Laud MS.) an. 1137 §5 þe land was al fordon mid suilce dædes. *c* **1200** *Trin. Coll. Hom.* 9 Hit is riht þat we forleten and forsaken nihtliche deden. *Ibid.* 15 To done þe six dede. *Ibid.* 131 Godes paðes ben ure gode dedes. *c* **1205** Lay. 7024 His deden [*c* **1275** deades] weoren for-cuðe. *c* **1250** *Gen. & Ex.* 2983 And quane ðe king wurð war ðis dead. *a* **1300** *Cursor M.* 1085 (Cott.) Quen caym had don þat dreri d[e]ide [*v.r.* dede], Til his fader hamward he ȝeide. *c* **1320** *Cast. Love* 938 Bi-hold now..his deden hou heo beoþ diht. **1340** Hampole *Pr. Consc.* 2498 Our gud dedis pur gud er noght. **1375** Barbour *Bruce* v. 278 He had done mony thankfull deid. *c* **1440** *Promp. Parv.* 115 Dede, or werke, *factum*. **1491** *Act 7 Hen. VII*, c. 2 §4 The seid Warrant is not the dede of hym that is named to be the maker of the seid Warrant. **1570** *Sc. Satir. Poems Reform.* xviii. 5 O cursit hour! O deid of fellonie! **1601** Shaks. *Jul. C.* III. ii. 216 They that haue done this Deede, are honourable. **1667** Milton *P.L.* XI. 256 And one bad act with many deeds well done Mayst cover. **1809-10** Coleridge *Friend* ix. (1887) 37 What are noble deeds but noble truths realized? **1875** Jowett *Plato* (ed. 2) V. 52 Their deeds did not agree with their words.

b. An act of bravery, skill, etc.; a feat; *esp.* in *deed of arms*, and the like.

Beowulf 5668 (Th.) þeah ðe he dæda ȝehwæs dyrstiȝ wære. **1340** *Ayenb.* 163 By playtinge me ne proueþ naȝt þet he by guod knyȝt ac be moche dede of armes. **1375** Barbour *Bruce* I. 18 The dedys Of stalwart folk that lywyt ar. **1568** Grafton *Chron.* II. 262 Desiryng nothing so much as to have deedes of Armes. **1570** *Sc. Satir. Poems Reform.* x. 60 ȝit we his hart with Martiall deidis dotit. **1666** Dryden *Ann. Mirab.* clxxvi, Thousands..Whose deeds some nobler poem shall adorn. **1869** Tennyson *Coming of Arthur* 46 And Arthur yet had done no deed of arms. **1871** R. Ellis *Catullus* lxiv. 357 Deeds of such high glory Scamander's river avoucheth. **1875** Jowett *Plato* (ed. 2) III. 609 Many great and wonderful deeds are recorded of your State.

†**c.** *Deeds of the Apostles*: the Acts of the Apostles. *Obs.*

c **1380** Wyclif *Wks.* (1880) 195 Peter saiþ in dedis of apostlis..þat to him neiþer was gold ne siluer. **1382** —— *Acts* (*title*), Heere begynnen the Apostles Dedes. **1533** Gau *Richt Vay* (1888) 37 In ye xx c. of the dedis of the Apostlis.

2. (without *a* or *pl.*) Action generally; doing, performance. (Often contrasted with *word*.)

c **1000** Ælfric *Gram.* xix. (Z.) 122 *Deponentia verba significant actvm* þa alecgendlican word ȝetacnjað dæde. *c* **1200** *Trin. Coll. Hom.* 187 þe man þe nis stedefast ne on dade ne on speche ne on þonke. **1297** R. Glouc. (1724) 501 Ower dede ne may be no wors, than ower word is. *a* **1300** *Cursor M.* 3402 (Cott.) His suns dughti ware o dede. *c* **1386** Chaucer *Pars. T.* ¶282 þanne wol I sle him with my hond in dede of synne. *c* **1460** *Towneley Myst.* 1 At the begynnyng of oure dede Make we heuen & erth. *c* **1500** *Melusine* 371 In som cas the good wylle of a man is accepted for the dede. **1667** Milton *P.L.* v. 549 To be both will and deed created free. **1871** Ruskin *Fors Clav.* I. ii. 5 The strength of Hercules is for deed not misdeed.

b. *collect.* Doings; ado, to-do. *dial.*

1788 W. Marshall *E. Yorks.* Gloss., *Deed*, doings; *whent deed*, great to-do. **1828** *Craven Dial.*, *Deed*, doings. 'There's sad deed, I'll uphodto.' **1855** Robinson *Whitby Gloss.*, 'Here's bonny deed!' great to do..'Great deed about nought', large stir about trifles. **1867** Waugh *Home Life Factory Folk* xvi. 145 (*Lanc. Dial.*) 'Aw consider we'n had as hard deed as anybody livin.'

†**3.** Thing to be done, work (in contemplation); the task or duty of any time or person. *Obs.*

c **1325** *E.E. Allit. P.* C. 354 On to þrenge þer-þurȝe [a city] watz þre dayes dede. *c* **1400** *Destr. Troy* 274 Sone he dressit to his dede & no dyn made, And made vp a mekyll ship. *c* **1460** *Towneley Myst.* 57 To dyke and delf, bere and draw, and to do all vnhonest deyde. **1580** North *Plutarch* (1676) 812 You shall..set the poor distressed City of Syracusa again on foot, which is your deed.

4. *Law.* An instrument in writing (which for this purpose includes printing or other legible representation of words on parchment or paper), purporting to effect some legal disposition, and sealed and delivered by the disposing party or parties.

Signature to a deed is not generally required by English law, but is practically universal; and in most jurisdictions outside England where English law or legal forms prevail, signature has been substituted for or made equivalent to sealing. *Delivery* (q.v.) is now a moribund formality. Contracts of most kinds, as well as dispositions of property *inter vivos*, may be made by deed, and in common practice are often so made.

c **1300** R. Brunne *Chron.* (1810) 69 Edward..suore..to me..his heyre suld I be. þerof he mad me skrite..& for to sikere his dede, set þer to his seale. *Ibid.* 259 Bituex him & þe was mad a priue dede..Forto feffe him ageyn in þat tenement. **1362** Langl. *P. Pl.* A. II. 81 In þe Date of þe deuel þe Deede was a-selet, Be siht of sir Symoni and Notaries signes. **1435** *Nottingham Rec.* II. 358 For ye exchaunge of Heyberd Stener be a ded undder ye seel of his armes. *c* **1590** Marlowe *Faust.* v. 35 And write a deed of gift with thine own blood. **1596** Shaks. *Merch. V.* IV. ii. 1 Enquire the Iewes house out, giue him this deed, And let him signe it. **1613** *Bury Wills* (Camd. Soc.) 162 As I and the said Edmond longe agoe did give vnto her by a jointe deede of guift. **1642** Perkins *Prof. Bk.* ii. §130. 58 A writing cannot be a deed if it be not sealed. **1767** Blackstone *Comm.* II. 295 A deed is a writing sealed and delivered by the parties..it is called a deed..because it is the most solemn and authentic act that a man can possibly perform, with relation to the disposal of his property. **1844** Williams *Real Prop.* (1877) 148 The sealing and delivery of a deed are termed the execution of it. **1893** Sir J. W. Chitty in *Law Times' Rep.* LXVIII. 430/1 The statute..requires a deed in cases where formerly a mere writing would have sufficed.

5. Phrases. †**a.** *with the deed*: in the act. *Obs.*

c **1450** *Erle Tolous* 522 Of myrthe schalt thou not mys; Thou schalt take us wyth the dede. **1470-85** Malory *Arthur* XX. ii, And it be sothe as ye saye I wold he were taken with the dede. **1585** T. Washington tr. *Nicholay's Voy. Turkie* IV. xxxiii. 156 The Adulterer being found with the deed.

b. *in deed*: in action, in actual practice.

c **1340** *Cursor M.* 13830 (Trin.) þe lif þat he ledeþ in dede Hit is aȝeyn oure lede. *c* **1385** Chaucer *L.G.W.* 2138 *Ariadne*, And every poynt was performed in dede. *c* **1440** *Gesta Rom.* i. 2 (Harl. MS.), I am redy to fulfille alle in dede þat þou wolt sey vnto me. **1553** T. Wilson *Rhet.* (1580) 29, I trust that not onely all men will commende justice in worde, but also will live justly in deede. **1613** Sir H. Finch *Law* (1636) 202 Offering to beat one, though he doe not beat one in deed. **1862** Stanley *Jew. Ch.* (1877) I. vii. 130 Graven images..set up in deed or in word.

c. *in deed*, *in very deed*, † *of very deed* (Sc.): in fact, in effect, in reality, in truth: hence INDEED.

c **1386** Chaucer *Prol.* 659 But wel I woot he lyed right in dede. **1535** Coverdale *2 Chron.* vi. 18 For thinkest thou that God in very dede dwelleth amonge men vpon earth? **1549** *Compl. Scot.* xv. 123 Thai ar my mortal enemes of verray deid. **1581** W. Fulke in *Confer.* III. (1584) S iij, They eate not the body of Christ in deede. **1615** Bedwell *Moham. Imp.* III. §97 They are in very deed holy bookes. **1862** Ld. Brougham *Brit. Const.* App. iii. 458 Making all principles be treated in very deed as the counters wherewith the game of faction was to be played. **1862** Stanley *Jew. Ch.* (1877) I. xiv. 273 The chiefs became the chiefs in deed as well as in name.

6. *Comb.*, as †*deed-doer*, †*-doing*; *deed-achieving*, *-worthy* adjs.; **deed-box**, a box, usually of tin-plate, for keeping deeds or other documents in; **deed-offering**, Coverdale's word in some instances for the 'peace-offering' of the 1611 version. Also DEED-BOTE, DEED POLL.

1607 Shaks. *Cor.* II. i. 190 By *deed-atchieuing Honor newly nam'd. **1835** Marryat *Jac. Faithf.* xxxi, Taking with him the tin-box (it was what they called a *deed-box). **1858** Ld. St. Leonards *Handy Bk. Prop. Law* xiv. 85 It is advisable to keep your own securities in your own deed-box at home. **1548** Hall *Chron.* 20 b, Thei would be lokers on and no *deede doers. **1663** Spalding *Troub. Chas. I* (1792) I. 272 (Jam.) But the deed doer was fled. *c* **1380** Wyclif *Wks.* (1880) 70 þe *dede doynge is proff of loue, as gregory seiþ. **1586** T. B. *La Primaud. Fr. Acad.* 430 One of his horse-keepers..taking him at the deed doing..bestowed so many blowes on him..that he left him half dead. **1535** Coverdale *2 Sam.* vi. 17 And Dauid offred burnt offerynges and *deed offerynges before ye Lorde. **1865** J. Grote *Treat. Moral Ideas* viii. (1876) 103 *Deedworthy conduct, or the faciendum.

deed (di:d), *v. U.S.* [f. DEED *sb.*] *trans.* To convey or transfer by deed. Also *fig.*

1816 J. Pickering *Vocabulary* 76 To *deed*..We sometimes hear this word used colloquially; but rarely, except by illiterate people... None of our writers would employ it. **1828** Webster *Deed*, to convey or transfer by deed; a popular use of the word in America; as, he deeded all his estate to his eldest son. **1865** *Morn. Star* Sept., A..complete farm..in Connecticut has been deeded over to his wife. **1890** *Century Mag.* Jan. 475/1 The act of 1864, deeding to that state the Yosemite Valley and the Mariposa Big Tree Grove.

deed, *adv.* In 6 dede. Aphetic form of *i'deed*, INDEED; now chiefly Sc.

1547 Coverdale *Old Faith* Prol. A vij a, Let vs be true scolers of the same; and dede, let vs euen entre in to the nature and kynde therof. **1816** Scott *Antiq.* xxxvi, "Deed, sir, they hae various opinions.' **1848** Thackeray *Van. Fair*

235 "Deed and she will', said O'Dowd. **1868** RAMSAY *Remin.* 183 'Deed', said the laird..'I wad ha' wondered if ye had.'

deed, -e, obs. forms of DEAD.

†ˈdeedbote. *Obs.* Also **dædbote, dead-, dedbote.** [OE. *dǽd* deed + *bót*, BOOT *sb.*[1] 10, amends, expiation.] Amends-deed, penance, repentance.

c **1000** *Ags. Gosp.* Matt. iii. 2 Doð dæd bote. *c* **1160** *Hatton G.* ibid., Doð deadbote. *c* **1175** *Lamb. Hom.* 21 Mid sodðe dedbote his sunne bi reowsumnesse. *c* **1200** ORMIN 9191 Sannt Johan..bigann to spellenn þa Wiþþ fulluht off dædbote. *a* **1225** *Ancr. R.* 372 Bireousunge and dedbote uor sunne. **1340** *Ayenb.* 33 Amendinge and dedbote. **13..** *Verses Palm-Sunday* in *Rel. Antiq.* II. 243 Wyth sorwthe of herte and schryft of mouthe, Doth deedbote this tyme nouth.

†ˈdeeded, *a. Obs.* [f. DEED *sb.* + -ED[2].] Characterized by deeds (of such a kind).

1606 WARNER *Alb. Eng.* 377 Well educated of the king, and proving nobly deeded.

deedeed: see DEE *v.*

deedful (ˈdiːdfʊl), *a.* [f. DEED *sb.* + -FUL.] Full of deeds, active, effective.

1834 *Blackw. Mag.* XXXV. 150 He is a trusty and deedful friend to that bold..insurgent. **1842** TENNYSON *To* ——, A deedful life. **1879** J. TODHUNTER *Alcestis* 3 That fair past, Bright with our deedful days, is all our own.

Hence **ˈdeedfully** *adv.*, actively, effectively.

1615 T. ADAMS *Lycanthropy* 9 It is not yet enough to go speedfully and heedfully except also deedfully.

deedily (ˈdiːdɪlɪ), *adv. dial.* [f. DEEDY + -LY[2].] Actively, busily.

1813 JANE AUSTEN *Lett.* II. 173 They are each [busy] about a rabbit net, and sit as deedily to it, side by side, as any two Uncle Franks could do. **1815** —— *Emma* (1870) II. x. 204 Frank Churchill..most deedily occupied about her spectacles. **1859** BURTON in *Jrnl. Geog. Soc.* XXIX. 241 They row in 'spirts', applying deedily to their paddling.

†ˈdeeding, *vbl. sb. Obs. rare*[−1]. [f. DEED *sb.* + -ING[1].] Actual doing, carrying out in deed.

1606 WARNER *Alb. Eng.* XVI. ciii. 407 And in the Deeding none more tough.

†ˈdeedle. *Obs.* or *dial.* An alteration of *devil*.

1653 URQUHART *Rabelais* I. xii, What a deedle [*que diantre*], you are it seems but bad horsemen.

ˈdeedless, *a.* Without action or deeds.

1598 ROWLANDS *Betray. Christ* 28 Thy deedlesse words, words vnconfirmed by truth. *a* **1625** FLETCHER *Bloody Bro.* IV. iii, Th' undaunted power of Princes should never be Confin'd in deedless cold calamity. **1890** BLACKIE *To Mr. Gladstone* in *Pall Mall G.* Mar., And to dull length of deedless days retire.

b. Of persons: Performing no deeds, doing nothing, inactive; also *dial.* incapable, helpless.

1606 SHAKS. *Tr. & Cr.* IV. v. 98 Firme of word, Speaking in deedes, and deedelesse in his tongue. **1621** G. SANDYS *Ovid's Met.* VII. (1626) 140 The generous Horse..Grones at his manger, and there deedlesse dyes. **1718** POPE *Iliad* v. 796 What art thou, who, deedless, look'st around? **1855** ROBINSON *Whitby Gloss., Deedless*, helpless, indolent. 'A deedless sort of a body.' **1870** MORRIS *Earthly Par.* I. II. 503 As deedless men they there must sit.

ˈdeed poll, deed-poll. Also 6 **poll deed.** [See POLL.] *Law.* A deed made and executed by one party only; so called because the paper or parchment is 'polled' or cut even, not indented.

[**1523** FITZHERB. *Surv.* 20 Estates made of free lande by polle dede or dede indented.] **1588** FRAUNCE *Lawiers Log.* II. iii. 89 b, The nature of a deede indented and a deede polle. **1628** COKE *On Litt.* 229 A Deed poll is that which is plaine without any indenting, so called, because it is cut euen, or polled. **1767** BLACKSTONE *Comm.* II. 296. **1818** CRUISE *Digest* (ed. 2) IV. 357 George Everinden by deed-poll..did give, grant, and confirm, to his two daughters, all the rents and profits of two tenements. **1847** C. G. ADDISON *Law of Contracts* I. i. §1 (1883) 22 Deed poll.

deeds, dial. form of *deads* (see DEAD *a.* B. 4), waste material from an excavation.

1802 C. FINLATER *Agric. Surv. Peebles* 131 (Jam.) What is taken out of the ditch (vernacularly the *deeds*) [to be] thrown behind this facing to support it. **1825** BROCKETT *N.C. Words, Deeds*, rubbish of quarries or drains.

deed-sicke, -sleyer: see DEAD *a.* D. 2.

de-educate: see DE- II. 1.

deedy (ˈdiːdɪ), *a.* Chiefly *dial.* [f. DEED *sb.* + -Y[1]: found first in the combination ILL-DEEDY.]

1. Full of deeds or activity; active. Also, earnest, serious.

[*c* **1460** *Towneley Myst.* 320 Riche and ille-dedy, Gederand and gredy. **1535** LYNDESAY *Satyre* 4028 Luke quhat it is to be evil-deidie.] **1615** T. ADAMS *Lycanthropy* 7 In a messenger..is required..that he be speedy, that he be heedy, and that he be deedy. **1623** BINGHAM *Xenophon* 72 The horse of that Country are..more deedy, and full of metall. **1721** CIBBER *Double Gallant* III. i, If she is not a Deedy Tit at the Bottom, I'm no Jockey. **1787** GROSE *Provinc. Gloss., Deedy*, industrious, notable. *Berksh.* **1876** J. ELLIS *Cæsar in Egypt* 135 A deedy conclave were we. **1883** G. MACDONALD *Castle Warlock* I. xvii. 263 Grizzie was live as the new day, bustling and deedy. **1895** HARDY *Jude* I. ii. 14 There! don't ye look so deedy! Farmer Troutham is not so much better than myself. **1938** F. D. SHARPE *Sharpe of Flying Squad* xxiii. 241 He said that he had seen four men in a pub in Bethnal Green in 'deedy' conversation. **1951** M. KENNEDY *Lucy Carmichael* VI. v. 310 He was feeling genial and deedy, and..his imagination toyed with new campaigns. *Ibid.* vii. 326 The train came puffing in half empty, so he did not have to be so deedy on her behalf as he would have liked. **1959** *Listener* 19 Nov. 900/2 The opening scenes..were just a shade too fruity and deedy.

†2. Actual, real. *Obs. rare.*

1781 COWPER *Let. to Newton* 18 Mar., There are soldiers quartered at Newport and at Olney. These..performed all the manœuvres of a deedy battle, and the result was that this town was taken. **1788** —— *Let. to Lady Hesketh* 27 June, Retirement indeed, or..what we call *deedy* retirement.

deef(f, deefe, obs. forms of DEAF.

†deeful, defull, var. of, or error for *delful*, DOLEFUL.

c **1380** *Sir Ferumb.* 4208 'Alas!' said he..'þis is a deeful þyng!' *c* **1460** *Emare* 606 Sertes this ys a fowle case, And a defull dede.

dee-jay, deejay (diːˈdʒeɪ). *slang* (orig. *U.S.*). [Pronunciation of *D.J.* (see D III. 3).] A disc-jockey.

1955 in L. FEATHER *Encycl. Jazz* (1956) 346/1. **1956** *Life* (U.S.) 19 Nov. 143/1 Some 1,200 radio disk jockeys.. journeyed..to Nashville..to attend..'Dee Jay' (for disk jockey) convention. **1958** [see *A. and R.* s.v. A III]. **1964** *Melody Maker* 28 Nov. 3 Deejays and promoters must stop being idiots.

deeken, obs. form of DEACON.

deel(e, obs. ff. DEAL, DEIL (DEVIL), DOLE.

de-electrify, de-electricize: see DE- II. 1.

Deely-bobber (ˈdiːlɪ ˈbɒbə(r)). Chiefly *U.S.* Also **Deelie-bobber. 1.** A proprietary name for a make of construction toy comprising a number of inter-linking building blocks. (Manufactured 1969–73.) *U.S. temporary.*

1969 *Official Gaz.* (U.S. Patent Office) 1 July TM15/2 Products of the Behavioral Sciences, Inc., San Jose, Calif. Filed Aug. 5, 1968. Deelie-bobbers for building toys. **1969** *Telegraph* (Brisbane) 2 July 46/5 *Deelie Bobbers*... They lobbed on my desk in a flower-patterned drawstring bag which, upended, sent 100 plastic daisy cutouts spilled every whichway. **1973** *Toys Directory Issue* LXXII. VI A. 206/2 Deelie Bobbers—Parker Brothers.

2. A proprietary name (in the U.S.) for a variety of children's novelty headgear consisting of a pair of ornaments (e.g. balls) attached antenna-like by springs or wires to a head-band.

1982 *People* 26 July 67/1 Those little plastic headbands with the springs, topped with glittery balls, pinwheels, stars or hearts, are called Deely Bobbers. **1982** *New Statesman* 24 Sept. 17 Deely-bobbers—the glittering, bouncing baubles on wire which are the latest craze in headgear—caused a row in a hospital's X-ray department when all the staff there decided to wear them at once. **1982** *Official Gaz.* (U.S. Patent Office) 29 Nov. TM578 Ace Novelty Co., Inc., Bellevue, Wash...Deely bobbers. For Novelty Item—Namely, a Head Band with Springs Carrying Ornaments... First use Dec. 4, 1981.

deem (diːm), *v.* Forms: 1 **dœ́man,** 1–2 **déman,** 2–4 **demen,** 2–7 **deme,** (3–6 **deame,** 4–5 **dem, deyme,** 5 **dyme,** 6 *Sc.* **deim,** 7 **dim),** 4–7 **deeme,** 5– **deem.** *Pa. t.* and *pa. pple.* **deemed:** 1 **dœ́mde, démed,** 3–7 **dempt.** [A Common Teut. derivative vb.; OE *dœ́man, déman* + OFris. *déma*, OS. *a-dômian* (Du. *doemen*), OHG. *tuomian, tuomen* (MHG. *tüemen*), ON. *dœma* (*dæma*), (Sw. *döma*, Da. *dömme*), Goth. *dômjan*:—OTeut. **dômjan*. f. *dômo-z*, Goth. *dôm-s*, judgement, DOOM. Cf. DEME *sb.*, DOOM *v.*]

†1. *intr.* To give or pronounce judgement; to act as judge, sit in judgement; to give one's decision, sentence, or opinion; to arbitrate. *Obs.*

In OE. construed with a dative of the person, 'to pronounce judgement to, to act as judge to', equivalent to the trans. sense in 2.

c **825** *Vesp. Psalter* ii. 10 Alle ða ðe doemað eorðan. **971** *Blickl. Hom.* 11 He cymeþ to demenne cwicum & deadum. *c* **1000** *Ags. Gosp.* Matt. vii. 2 Witodlice ðam ylcan dome þe ȝe demað, eow byð ȝedemed. —— John viii. 15 Ge demað æfter flæsce, ic ne deme nanum men [*c* **1160** *Hatton G.*, Ich ne deme nane men]. *a* **1300** *Cursor M.* 17415 (Cott.), If yee þan rightwisli wil deme, Yeild vs ioseph þat yee suld yeme. **1393** GOWER *Conf.* I. 304 They..toke a juge therupon.. And bede him demen in this cas. *c* **1440** CAPGRAVE *St. Kath.* III. 1464 She..Spak and commaunded, bothe dempte and wrot. **1556** in W. H. Turner *Select. Rec. Oxford* 262 To arbytrate, deme, and judge betwixt the said Citie and..John Wayte. **1579** SPENSER *Sheph. Cal.* Aug. 137 Neuer dempt more right of beautye I weene The shepheard of Ida that iudged beauties Queene.

†2. *trans.* To judge, sit in judgement on (a person or cause). *Obs.*

The construction with a personal object takes, in Northumbrian and ME., the place of the OE. const. with dative in 1.

c **950** *Lindisf. Gosp.* Matt. vii. 2 In ðæm dome ȝie doemes ȝe biðon ȝedoemed [*Rushw. Gl.* ȝe beoþ doemde]. —— John viii. 15 Ic ne doemo æniȝne monno. *c* **1200** *Trin. Coll. Hom.* 171 Ure drihten cumeð al middeneard to demen. *Ibid.* 225 þat sal deme þe quica and þe deade. *a* **1300** *Cursor M.* 21965 (Cott.), In þe first he com dempt to be. **1382** WYCLIF *John* xvi. 11 The prince of this world is now demyd. **1483** CAXTON *Gold. Leg.* 59/2 Moyses satte & juged & demed the peple fro moryng vnto euenyng. **1596** SPENSER *F.Q.* IV. iii. 4 At th' one side sixe iudges were dispos'd, To view and deeme the deedes of armes that day. **1605** HEYWOOD *1st Pt. If you know not me* Wks. 1874 I. 203 Deeme her offences, if she haue offended, With all the lenity a sister can. **1609** SKENE *Reg. Maj.* 111 Thou Judge be ware, for as ye deme, ȝe sall be demed.

†b. To rule (a people) as a judge. *Obs.*

a **1300** *Cursor M.* 7283 (Cott.), Fourti yeir dempt he israel. *c* **1330** R. BRUNNE *Chron.* (1810) 280 Edward now he wille, þat Scotlond be wele ȝemed, And streitly in skille þorgh wise men demed.

c. To administer (law). *arch.*

1393 LANGL. *P. Pl.* C. v. 175 By leel men and lyf-holy my lawe shal be demyd. **1718** BP. WILSON in Keble *Life* xii. (1863) 397 That..the 24 Keys may be called, according to the statute and constant practice to deem the law truly. **1887** HALL CAINE *Deemster* viii. 54 The Deemster was a hard judge, and deemed the laws in rigour.

†d. To decide (a quarrel). *Obs.*

1494 FABYAN *Chron.* v. cxxv. 105 To suffre his quarell to be demyd by dynt of swerde atwene them two.

†3. To sentence, doom, condemn (*to* some penalty, *to do* or *suffer* something). *Obs.*

a **1000** *Elene* 500 (Gr.) Swa he..to cwale moniȝe Cristes folces demde, to deaþe. *c* **1175** *Lamb. Hom.* 73 He wurð idemed to þolien wawe mid dovelen in helle. *c* **1200** *Trin. Coll. Hom.* 223 þe sulle ben to deaðe idemd. *a* **1300** *Cursor M.* 15343 To-morn dai sal i be dempt On rode tre to hang. *c* **1386** CHAUCER *Sompn. T.* 316 For which I deme the to deth certayn. **1426** AUDELAY *Poems* 12 Leve he is a lyere, his dedis thai done hym deme. **1529** RASTELL *Pastyme* (1811) 243 For whiche rebellyon they were there demyd to dethe. **1602** in J. Mill *Diary* (1889) 180 John Sinclair..is dempt to quyt his guddis.

†b. *fig.* To pass (adverse) judgement upon; to condemn, censure. *Obs.*

a **1300** *Cursor M.* 28148 (Cott.) Oþer men dedis oft i demyd. **1488** CAXTON *Chast. Goddes Chyld.* 21 Many thynges they deme and blame. **1500–20** DUNBAR *Poems* xviii. 36 Wist thir folkis that vthir demis, How that thair sawis to vthir semis. **1555–86** *Satir. Poems Reform.* xxxvii. 33 Do quhat ȝe dow, detractouris ay will deme ȝou. **1598** D. FERGUSSON *Scot. Prov.*, Dame, deem warily; ye watna wha wytes yersell.

†4. To decree, ordain, appoint; to decide, determine; to adjudicate or award (a thing *to* a person).

c **900** tr. *Bæda's Hist.* IV. xxix [xxviii.] (1891) 368 Ne wæs ða hweðre sona his halȝunge ȝedemed. *a* **1000** *Exeter Bk.* vii. 16 Næfre God demeð þæt æniȝ eft þæs earm ȝeweorðe. *c* **1175** *Lamb. Hom.* 95 He demað stiðne dom þam forsuneȝede. *c* **1205** LAY. 460 He habbeð idemed þat ich am duc ofer heom. *Ibid.* 22116 He hæhte alle cnihtes demen rihte domes. *a* **1300** *Cursor M.* 21445 (Cott.) þe quen has biden us to deme To þe al þat to right es queme. *c* **1386** CHAUCER *Doctor's T.* 199, I deme anoon this clerk his seruaunt haue. **1399** *Rolls of Parlt.* III. 452/1 The Lordes..deme and ajuggen and decreen, that [etc.]. *c* **1400** *Destr. Troy* 606 Whateuer ye deme me to do. **1464** *Paston Lett.* No. 493 II. 166 Fynes therefore dempt or to be dempt. **1483** CAXTON *Gold. Leg.* 72/2 In demyng of rightful domes. **1503–4** *Act 19 Hen. VII*, c. 38 Preamb., It was enacted stablisshed ordeyned demed & declared..that [etc.]. **1568** GRAFTON *Chron.* II. 13 The Epistle, in the which Gregory..demed that the Church of Yorke and of London should be even Peres. *a* **1605** MONTGOMERIE *Flyting* 373 Syne duelie they deemde, what death it sould die.

†b. To decide (*to do* something). *Obs.*

c **1340** *Gaw. & Gr. Knt.* 1089 ȝe han demed to do þe dede þat I bidde.

†5. To form or express a judgement or estimate on; to judge, judge of, estimate. *Obs.*

a **1225** *Ancr. R.* 290 Euer bihold hire wurð þet he paide uor hire, and dem þerefter pris. *c* **1325** *E.E. Allit. P.* (A.) 312 To leue no tale be true to tryȝe, Bot þat hys one skyl may dem. **1388** WYCLIF *Matt.* xvi. 4 Thanne ȝe kunne deme the face of heuene, but ȝe moun not wite the tokenes of tymes. *c* **1400** *Rom. Rose* 2200 A cherle is demed by his dede. **1533** ELYOT *Cast. Helthe* Proem (1541) A iv b, I desyre men to deme well myne intente. **1596** SPENSER *Hymne Love* 168 Things hard gotten men more dearely deeme.

†b. To judge between (things), to distinguish, discern. *Obs.*

1530 PALSGR. 511/1 A blynde man can nat deme no coulours. **1581** RICH *Farewell* (1846) 67 He is not able to deeme white from blacke, good from badde, vertue from vice. **1596** SPENSER *F.Q.* V. i. 8 Thus she him taught In all the skill of deeming wrong and right.

†c. *intr.* To judge *of*, to distinguish *between*.

1340 *Ayenb.* 82 þet hi ne conne yknawe þane day uram þe nyȝt, ne deme betuene grat and smal. *a* **1542** WYAT *Of Courtiers Life* 94 Nor Flaunders chere lettes not my syght to deme Of blacke and white. **1586** A. DAY *Eng. Secretary* I. (1625) 27 Here, by judging of our estate, thou maist accordingly deeme of our pleasures. *Ibid.* II. 111 Conversing among such as have discretion to deeme of a Gentleman.

6. To form the opinion, to be of opinion; to judge, conclude, think, consider, hold. (The ordinary current sense.)

a. *intr.* or *absol.* (Now chiefly parenthetical.)

a **800** *Corpus Gloss.* 440 *Censeo*, doema. *c* **900** tr. *Bæda's Hist.* I. xvi. [xxvii.] (1890) 86 þæs þe ic demo [*ut arbitror*]. *c* **1000** ÆLFRIC *Gram.* xxvi. (Z.) 155 *Censeo* ic deme oððe ic asmeaȝe. *c* **1385** CHAUCER *L.G.W.* 1244 (*Dido*) And demede as hem liste. *c* **1386** —— *Clerk's T.* 932 For sche is fairer, as thay demen alle, Than is Grisild. *a* **1400** *Relig. Pieces fr. Thornton MS.* (1867) 20 To fele and with resone to deme. **1586** A. DAY *Eng. Secretary* II. (1625) 15 He is not..here in the countrey, but as I deeme and you have enformed, about London. **1725** POPE *Odyss.* III. 61 He too, I deem, implores the power divine.

b. with *obj.* and *complement* (*sb.*, *adj.* or *pple.*, or *infin. phrase*; †formerly often with *for*, *as*).

c **1205** LAY. 22140 þene þe king demde for-lore. *a* **1225** *Ancr. R.* 120 þet tu schalt demen þi suluen wod. *a* **1300** *Cursor M.* 26814 (Cott.) It mai nan him for buxum deme. **1340–70** *Alex. & Dind.* 218 Oure doctourus dere, demed for wise. *c* **1400** *Lanfranc's Cirurg.* 102, I demede him for deed.

c **1450** *St. Cuthbert* (Surtees) 5163 Þai demed it better all' to dye. **1548** HALL *Chron.* 191 b, What so ever jeoperdy or perill might bee construed or demed, to have insued. **1581** PETTIE *Guazzo's Civ. Conv.* I. (1586) 35 A vertue which you deeme yourselfe to have. **1628** DIGBY *Voy. Medit.* 51, I deemed it much my best and shortest way. **1681** P. RYCAUT *Critick* 201 He went to the House of the World, which was always deemed for a Deceiver. **1697** DRYDEN *Virg. Past.* I. 9 For never can I deem him less than God. **1754** SHEBBEARE *Matrimony* (1766) I. 45 Deemed as very unjust in Gaming. **1827** JARMAN *Powell's Devises* II. 293 A general permission ..appears to have been deemed sufficient. **1852** MISS YONGE *Cameos* I. xxxii. 277 Harold..deemed it time to repress these inroads. **1875** JOWETT *Plato* (ed. 2) V. 398 Works..which have been deemed to fulfil their design fairly.

c. with *that* and *clause*.

c **1205** LAY. 24250 Men gunnen demen þat nes i nane londe burh nan swa hende. *c* **1386** CHAUCER *Man of Law's T.* 940, I ought to deme..That in the salte see my wyf is deed. *c* **1430** LYDG. *Bochas* I. ii. (1544) 5 a, Nembroth..Dempt.. He transcended al other of noblesse. *c* **1450** *Merlin* 10 She demed that it was the enmy that so hadde hir begiled. **1597** HOOKER *Eccl. Pol.* v. i. (1611) 184 Wee may boldly deeme there is neither, where both are not. **1739** MELMOTH *Fitzosb. Lett.* (1763) 291 Nor dempt he, simple wight, no mortal may The blinded god..when he list, foresay. **1887** BOWEN *Virgil Æneid* II. 371 (1889) 126 Deeming we come with forces allied.

7. *intr.* To judge or think (in a specified way) *of* a person or thing.

c **1384** CHAUCER *H. Fame* II. 88 Thow demest of thy selfe amys. *c* **1400** *Rom. Rose* 2198 Of hem noon other deme I can. *c* **1440** *Generydes* 4710 Wele I wote in hym ye demyd amys. **1581** SIDNEY *Apol. Poetrie* (Arb.) 24 Let vs see how the Greekes named it [Poetry], and howe they deemed of it. **1586** A. DAY *Eng. Secretary* I. (1625) 146, I shall..give you so good occasion to deeme well of me. **1667** MILTON *P.L.* VIII. 599 Though higher of the genial Bed by far, And with mysterious reverence I deem. **1762** BLACKSTONE in Gutch *Coll. Cur.* II. 362 These capital mistakes..occasion'd the Editor..to deem with less reverence of this Roll. **1814** SCOTT *Wav.* lxi, Where the ties of affection were highly deemed of. **1860** J. P. KENNEDY *Horse Shoe R.* ix. 105, I cannot deem otherwise of them.

†**8.** To think *to do* something, to expect, hope.

c **1400** *Apol. Loll.* 51 Symon Magus..was reprouid of Petre, for he demid to possede þe ȝeft of God bi money. **1819** BYRON *Juan* II. clxxii, A creature meant To be her happiness, and whom she deem'd To render happy.

†**9.** *trans.* To think of (something) as existent; to guess, suspect, surmise, imagine. *Obs.*

c **1400** *Destr. Troy* 528 Ne deme no dishonesty in your derfe hert, þof I put me þus pertly my purpos to shewe. **1470–85** MALORY *Arthur* x. xxvi, As Kynge mark redde these letters, he demed treson by syr Tristram. **1586** A. DAY *Eng. Secretary* I. (1625) 114 Your imaginations doe already deeme the matter I must utter. **1598–9** *Parismus* I. (1661) 15 All the companie began to deeme that which afterward proued true.

b. *intr.* To think *of*, have a thought or idea *of*.

1814 CARY *Dante* (Chandos) 302 The shining of a flambeau at his back Lit sudden ere he deem of its approach. **1818** BYRON *Ch. Har.* IV. cxxxvii, Something unearthly which they deem not of.

†**10.** *trans.* To pronounce, proclaim, celebrate, announce, declare; to tell, say, utter. Also *intr.* with *of*. [An exclusively poetic sense, found already in OE., probably derived from sense 4. Cf. also ON. *dœma* in poetry, to talk.]

a **1000** *Fat. Apost.* (Gr.) 10 þær hie dryhtnes æ deman sceoldon, reccan fore rincum. *a* **1000** *Guthlac* (Gr.) 498 þæt we æfæstra dæde demen, secȝen dryhtne lof ealra þara bisena. *c* **1205** LAY. 23059 Ælles ne cunne we demen [*c* **1275** telle] of Arðures deden. *c* **1325** *E.E. Allit. P.* C. 119 Dyngne Dauid..þat demed þis speche, In a psalme. *c* **1330** R. BRUNNE *Chron. Wace* (Rolls) 154 Alle þer lymmes, how þai besemed, In his buke has Dares demed, Both of Troie & of Grece. *c* **1350** *Will. Palerne* 151 Hire deth was neiȝ diȝt, to deme þe sope. *a* **1400–50** *Alexander* 1231 þan he dryfes to þe duke, as demys [*Dubl. MS.* tellys] þe textis. *a* **1547** SURREY *Aeneid* II. 156 Then some gan deme to me The cruell wrek of him that framde the craft [*crudele canebant artificis scelus*].

†**b.** with *double obj.* To celebrate as, style, call, name. *poetic. Obs.*

c **1325** *E.E. Allit. P.* B. 1020 Forþy þe derk dede see hit is demed euer more. *Ibid.* 1611 Baltazar..þat now is demed Danyel of derne coninges.

†**deem** (diːm), *sb. Obs.* [f. DEEM *v.*] Judgement, opinion, thought, surmise.

1606 SHAKS. *Troylus & Cressida* IV. iv. 61 *Troy.* Here me my loue: be thou but true of heart. *Cres.* I true? how now? what wicked deeme is this? **1629** GAULE *Holy Madn.* 163 Honour what is it; but an imposed..Hight, and Deeme? **1648** SYMMONS *Vind. Chas. I*, 292 Much wrong should they have in the world's deem.

de-emanate (diːˈɛməneɪt), *v.* [f. DE- II. 1 + EMANATE *v.*] *trans.* To deprive (a radioactive substance) of the power of emitting its characteristic radioactive gas or 'emanation'. Hence **de-'emanated** *ppl. a.*; **de-ema'nation**.

1902 RUTHERFORD & SODDY in *Phil. Mag.* IV. 371 If thorium oxide be exposed to a white heat its power of giving an emanation is to a large extent destroyed. Thoria that has been so treated is referred to throughout as 'de-emanated'. *Ibid.* 575 Water-vapour exerts no influence..in de-emanating thoria. **1902** —— in *Jrnl. Chem. Soc.* LXXXI. 333 (*heading*) The de-emanation of thoria. **1904** RUTHERFORD *Radio-activity* 216 Thus de-emanation does not permanently destroy the power of thorium of giving out an emanation. *Ibid.*, The de-emanated thoria was dissolved.

deeme, obs. form of DIME.

deemed (diːmd), *ppl. a.* [f. DEEM *v.* + -ED.] Judged, thought, supposed.

1667 H. MORE *Divine Dial.* II. xxviii. 346 Then with pure Eyes thou shalt behold..That deemed mischiefs are no harms. **1671** MILTON *P.R.* I. 21 And with them came From Nazareth the son of Joseph deemed.

deemer (ˈdiːmə(r)). Forms: 1 **dœ́mere**, 1–5 **démere**, 3 **demare**, 3–5 **demer**, 5– 6 **demar**, 5– **deemer**. [OE. *dœ́mere*, f. *dœ́man* to DEEM: see -ER[1].] One who deems.

†**1.** A judge. *Obs.*

c **950** *Lindisf. Gosp.* Matt. xii. 27 Ða dœmeras [*iudices*] biðon iuera. *a* **1225** *Ancr. R.* 306 Let skile sitten ase demare upon þe dom stol. **1382** WYCLIF *Ps.* vii. 12 God riȝtwis demere [**1388** iust iuge]. *c* **1440** *York Myst.* xxiii. 142 So schall bothe heuen & helle Be demers of þis dede. *c* **1440** *Promp. Parv.* 118 Demar (P. or domes man), *judicator.* *c* **1580** C'TESS PEMBROKE *Ps.* cxix. V ii, Then be my causes deemer.

2. One who deems, judges, or opines; †one who censures or (unfavourably) criticizes others.

c **1410** LOVE *Bonavent. Mirr.* xv. 37 (Gibbs MS.) þat þowe be not a presumptuouse and temerarye deemer of oþer men. **1500–20** DUNBAR *Poems* xviii. 42 To wirk vengeance on ane demar. **1557** SIR J. CHEKE in T. Hoby tr. *Castiglione's Courtyer* (1561) ad fin., Counted ouerstraight a deemer of thinges. **1610** BARROUGH *Meth. Physick* Ep. Ded. (1639) 2 Plato that most grave and wise deemer of the state tyrannical. **1854** TRENCH *Synon. N.T.* xi. 44 Our profound English proverb, 'Ill doers are ill deemers'.

†**b.** One that distinguishes or discriminates. *Obs.*

c **1400** *Lanfranc's Cirurg.* 29 Ne þe skyn of þe fyngris endis ..ne schulde nouȝt be a good demere in knowynge hoot, cold [etc.]. **1548–77** VICARY *Anat.* ii. (1888) 23 The Skinne ..is made temperate, because he should be a good deemer of heate from colde.

deeming (ˈdiːmɪŋ), *vbl. sb.* [-ING[1].]

†**1.** Judging, judgement. *Obs.*

1303 R. BRUNNE *Handl. Synne* 1495 Ȝyf he demeþ pytyfully At hys demyng getyþ he mercy. *c* **1440** *Promp. Parv.* 118/1 Demynge or dome, *judicium.* *c* **1450** *Mirour Saluacioun* 4197 This wise shalle crist..the day of his demyng.

2. The forming or expressing of a judgement or opinion; thinking, opining; †censure; †a surmise or suspicion.

1340 *Ayenb.* 27 þe venimouse herte of þe enuiouse zene-ȝeþ..ine ualse demynges. **1476** SIR J. PASTON in *Lett.* No. 771 III. 152 Iff I had hadde any demyng off my lordys dethe iiij howrs or he dyed. **1500–20** DUNBAR *Poems* xviii. 25 God send thame a widdy wicht, That can not lat sic demyng be. **1513** DOUGLAS *Æneis* x. ix. 1 Nane incertane rumor nor demyng, Bot sovyr bodword cam thar. **1580** HOLLYBAND *Treas. Fr. Tong, Souspeçon*, suspition, deeming. **1697** J. SERGEANT *Solid Philos.* 418 Doubts, Deemings, and Uncertainties. **1821** BYRON *Sardan.* II. i. 379 You may do your own deeming.

de-emotionalize (diːɪˈməʊʃənəlaɪz), *v.* [f. DE- II. 1 + EMOTIONALIZE *v.*] *trans.* To render emotionless. So **de-e'motionalized** *ppl. a.*

1942 *Mind* LI. 84 The defence of the obsessional neurotic, namely de-emotionalised talk. **1957** J. S. HUXLEY *Religion without Revel.* (ed. 2) iii. 55 Hypostasised 'forces' and 'principles' are de-emotionalised refinements of personalised thinking.

de-emphasis (diːˈɛmfəsɪs). [f. DE- II. 2 + EMPHASIS.] A lessening or removal of emphasis; *spec.* in radio communications, a reduction in the relative strength of higher audio frequencies made in order to restore the original form of the signal.

1940 *RCA Review* Jan. 359 A de-emphasis circuit at the receiver. **1942** A. HUND *Frequency Modulation* ii. 221 Networks for a-f accentuation and deaccentuation are also known as circuits for a-f preemphasis and deemphasis respectively. **1957** K. W. WITTFOGEL *Oriental Despotism* 7 These methods, which use distortion and de-emphasis rather than open discussion. **1962** A. NISBETT *Technique Sound Studio* 254 Pre-emphasis of top (i.e. prior to transmission), with a corresponding de-emphasis at the receiver, helps to reduce the noise level still further. **1965** *Economist* 2 Jan. 27/3 The new policy aims were marked by major de-emphasis on air defence.

de-emphasize (diːˈɛmfəsaɪz), *v.* [f. DE- II. 1 + EMPHASIZE *v.*] *trans.* To remove emphasis from, or reduce emphasis on.

1938 *Time* 28 Nov. 22 One way to de-emphasize football is to hold the games in the morning. **1949** M. MEAD *Male & Female* vii. 152 The dual character of the eliminative tract also provides a background for re-emphasizing and de-emphasizing sex differences. **1952** *Essays in Criticism* II. II. 212 Without de-emphasizing feeling, he..emphasizes that poetic sensitivity is a correlative of a poet's knowledge. **1956** A. H. COMPTON *Atomic Quest* ii. 107 Ernest Lawrence.. urged that this process be de-emphasized so that greater effort could be applied to the methods that gave greater promise of immediate production. **1961** A. WEST *Trend is Up* vii. 306 We're trying to make it a good college. We've de-emphasized football. **1970** *Economics* VIII. 145 The examination de-emphasizes technical detail.

deemster (ˈdiːmstə(r)). [One of the modern representatives of ME. *dēmestre*, in form fem. of *dēmere* DEEMER, judge; the other (and, phonetically, more regular form) is DEMPSTER. q.v. The form *deemster* is that proper to the Manx judges, and has been used in the general sense as a historical archaism by some modern writers.]

1. A judge. *Obs.* or *arch.* in general sense.

[*a* **1300** *Cursor M.* 5585 (Fairf.) Prest & demestre [*v. rr.* demister, demmepster, domes man] forsothe say I.—For other examples see DEMPSTER.] **1748** RICHARDSON *Clarissa* (1811) VI. xlix. 206 The deemster, or judge, delivers to the woman a rope, a sword, and a ring. **1820** *Edin. Rev.* XXXIV. 192 King Sigurd..craved that the deemsters should pronounce sentence of outlawry. **1857** SIR F. PALGRAVE *Norm. & Eng.* II. 258 The decree was the Deemster's 'Breastlaw'.

2. The title of each of the two justices of the Isle of Man, one of whom has jurisdiction over the southern, the other over the northern division of the island.

1611 SPEED *Theat. Gt. Brit.* xlvi. (1614) 91/1 All controversies are there [Man Iland] determined by certaine judges..and them they call Deemsters and chuse forth among themselves. **1656** J. CHALONER *Descr. I. of Man* in Dr. King *Vale Royall* IV. 30 There are four Merchants.. chosen..and sworn by the Deemsters. **1863** KEBLE *Life Bp. Wilson* v. 163 The steward was assisted in these trials by one or both of the Deemsters. **1883** *Birm. Weekly Post* 15 Dec. 3/5 His honour Richard Sherwood, her Majesty's Northern Deemster, or second judge of the island..Deemster Sherwood was appointed one of the judges of the island in March last.

deemstership (ˈdiːmstəʃɪp). [f. DEEMSTER + -SHIP.] The office of deemster in the Isle of Man.

1894 HALL CAINE *Manxman* III. iii, Let the Deemstership go to perdition. **1902** *Daily Chron.* 28 Mar. 5/2 When he retired from his deemstership of the Isle of Man in 1897.

deen(e, obs. forms of DEAN[1], DIN.

deener: see DEANER.

dee-nettle: see DEA-NETTLE.

deep (diːp), *a.* Forms: 1 **díop**, **déop**, 2–3 **deop**, 2–5 **dep**, (3 **dop**, **deap**, **dup**, 4 **dipe**, **dupe**, **duppe**, (*Ayenb.*) **dyep**), 4–6 **depe**, (5 **deype**, 5–6 *Sc.* **deip**, 6 **deape**, **diep(e)**, 5–7 **deepe**, 4– **deep**. *Compar.* **deeper**; in 1 **déopre**, 4 **deppere**, 4–6 **depper**. *Superl.* **deepest**; in 1 **déopost**, 4 **depperste**, 4–5 **deppest(e**, 5 **deppist**, **dyppest**. [A Com. Teut. adj.; OE. *díop*, *déop* = OFris. *diop*, *diap*, *diep*, OS. *diop*. *diap* (MDu., Du., LG. *diep*), OHG. *tiof* (MHG., mod.Ger. *tief*), ON. *djupr* (Sw. *djúp*, Da. *dyb*), Goth. *diups*:—OTeut. **deupo-z*, *-â*, *-om*, belonging to an ablaut series *deup-*, *daup-*, *dup-*, whence OE. *dyppan* (:—*dupjan*) to DIP; pre-Teut. root *dhub*: *dhup*. The regular early ME. form was *dēp*; the forms *dipe*, *düp*, *düpe*, *dyep*, correspond to an OE. by-form *diepe*, *dýpe*, with ablaut; perh. taken from *díepe*, *dýpe*, DEEP *sb.*]

I. Literal senses.

1. a. Having great or considerable extension downward.

854 *Chart.* in *Cod. Dipl.* V. 111 Of lusan þorne to deopan delle. *c* **1000** *Ags. Gosp.* John iv. 11 þes pytt is deop. *c* **1205** LAY. 647 He lette makien enne dic þe wes wnderliche deop [*c* **1275** swiþe deap]. **1297** R. GLOUC. (1724) 6 Grante-brugge and Hontyndone [have] mest plente of dup fen. *c* **1300** *St. Brandan* 574 Ich caste him in a dupe dich. **13..** *Poems fr. Vernon MS.* 578 Schip is more siker in luitel water þen in þe deope see. **1340** *Ayenb.* 264 Helle is..dyep wyþ-oute botme. *c* **1420** *Avow. Arth.* xvii, In a dale depe. *c* **1450** *St. Cuthbert* (Surtees) 1679 Twa bestes come fra þe depe se. **1559** W. CUNNINGHAM *Cosmogr. Glasse* 44 The greate deepe valleis. **1594** SHAKS. *Rich. III*, I. i. 4 In the deepe bosome of the Ocean buried. **1632** LITHGOW *Trav.* v. 232 Wee buried the slayne people in deep graves. **1774** GOLDSM. *Nat. Hist.* (1776) I. 380 Holes..so deep as not to be fathomed. **1819** SHELLEY *Fragm. Serpent* 4 Through the deep grass of the meadow. **1860** TYNDALL *Glaciers* I. vii. 55 [The stream] had cut a deep gorge in the clean ice.

b. Having great or considerable extension inward from the surface or exterior, or backward from the front.

a **1000** *Riddles* lvii. 4 (Gr.) Heaðoglemma feng, deopra dolȝa. *c* **1250** *Pol. Rel. & L. Poems* (1866) 214 His wund dop ant wide. *a* **1300** *Cursor M.* 12923 (Cott.) He..yode in-to depe desert. *c* **1400** *Destr. Troy* 1876 Depe woundes to the dethe. **1513** DOUGLAS *Æneis* VII. viii. 2 Mony wild beistis den and deip caverne. **1662** J. DAVIES tr. *Olearius' Voy. Ambass.* 88 She presented me a Handkercher..with a deep fringde. **1665** HOOKE *Microgr.* 181 A deep Convex-glass. **1703** MOXON *Mech. Exerc.* 127 Make the Rooms next the Front deeper, or shallower. **1775** WRAXALL *Tour North. Europe* 303 Very deep and gloomy woods, of twenty English miles in length. **1820** SHELLEY *Summer & Winter* 12 When birds die In the deep forests. **1842** TENNYSON *Morte D' Arthur* 5 His wound was deep.

c. *deep water(s)*: see WATER *sb.* 6 c.

d. *deep end*: the end of a swimming-pool at which the water is deepest; so in colloq. fig. phr. *to go (in) off the deep end*, etc.: to give way to emotion or anger; to 'let oneself go'.

1921 *Times Lit. Suppl.* 22 Dec. 853/3 Saint-Saëns rarely, if ever, takes any risks; he never, to use the slang of the moment, 'went in off the deep end'. **1922** JOAD *Highbrows* vi. 186 She passed her life metaphorically at the end of a diving-board, ready at the slightest provocation to go in at the deep end. **1923** *Weekly Dispatch* 21 Jan. 5 Mr. Nicholas Hannen

..plays the second fiddling husband admirably, except when, once or twice, he goes off the deep end a trifle too explosively. **1924** GALSWORTHY *White Monkey* II. iv, Would it not be more in the mode, really dramatic—if one 'went over the deep end', as they said, just once? **1927** W. E. COLLINSON *Contemp. Eng.* 115 A very common phrase since the war is to go (in) off the deep end, an expression evidently taken from the deep end of a swimming-bath where the diving board is. **1934** F. W. CROFTS *12.30 from Croydon* vii. 84 Yes, I've been. And found the old boy brimming over with wrath against you. And when he heard I was coming on the same job he fairly went off the deep end. **1963** T. PARKER *Unknown Citizen* iii. 88 I'm not going to do what I've done before, go off the deep end, nothing like that. **1966** G. GREENE *Comedians* I. iv. 113 Mr Smith trundled to the deep-end before he emerged. **1970** V. GIELGUD *Candle-Holders* vii. 62 Simon Astley was too much like the instructor in a swimming-bath, who throws you in at the deep end.

2. a. Having a (specified) dimension downward.

The depth is sometimes indicated by prefixing a word giving the equivalent of a measure, as ***ankle-***, ***knee-deep***.

a **1000** *Cædmon's Gen.* 1398 (Gr.) Fiftena stod deop ofer dunum flod elna. *c* **1420** *Pallad. on Husb.* I. 207 Two foote depe is good for corne tillage. **1576** in W. H. Turner *Select. Rec. Oxford* 386 He penned the water but one foote deepe. **1608** MIDDLETON *Mad World* III, This puts me in mind of a hole seven foot deep; my grave. **1696** WHISTON *Th. Earth* II. (1722) 221 The Waters might cover the Earth in general about 50 Miles deep. **1826** SCOTT *Woodst.* xxviii, Long grass ..almost ancle-deep in dew. **1832** *Examiner* 44/2 The ditch ..was eight feet deep. **1875** F. HALL in *Lippincott's Mag.* XVI. 750/2 The mud was everywhere ankle-deep.

b. Having a (specified) dimension inward from the surface, outer part, or front; *spec.* (with simple numeral prefixed) of persons, chiefly soldiers, having (so many) ranks standing one behind another. Also, with numeral prefixed, having so many engagements or obligations.

1646 H. LAWRENCE *Comm. Angells* 63 The pleasure is but skin deepe. **1698** FRYER *Acc. E. India* 107 The first File.. was as deep as the Street would admit. **1703** MOXON *Mech. Exerc.* 127 The Front-Room is 25 Foot, and the Back-Room 15 Foot deep. **1780** LANGTON in Boswell *Johnson* (1848) 646/2 The company began to collect round him..four, if not five deep. **1835** BURNES *Trav. Bokhara* (ed. 2) I. 133 Five regiments..drawn up in line, three deep. **1838** THIRLWALL *Greece* III. xxiii. 280 The Thebans..stood five-and-twenty deep. **1921** *Discovery* Sept. 242/2 He proposed to her, and she accepted him—if he would wait his turn; she was four deep already! **1935** LADY FORTESCUE *Perfume from Provence* 109 The lawyer was always engaged six deep whenever I called to see him.

c. *Cricket.* Of a fielder or fielding position: farther than normal from the batsman. (See also *deep field* below.)

1867 G. H. SELKIRK *Guide to Cricket Ground* ii. 25 Deep Cover, etc. When twenty-two are in the field the men that stand far out are designated by the names of the positions of the men they support, with the word 'deep' prefixed. **1897** K. S. RANJITSINHJI *Jubilee Bk. Cricket* ii. 54 When a man is put on the boundary behind extra-cover or cover, he is usually called deep-extra-cover or deep-cover.

3. a. Placed or situated far (or a specified distance) down or beneath the surface; of a ship, low in the water. **b.** Far in from the margin, far back.

c **1000** *Ags. Ps.* cxiv. 8 Þu mine sawle..ofer deopum deaþe ʒelæddest. *a* **1340** HAMPOLE *Psalter* ix. 8 Þai þat has synned mare sall be deppest in hell. *c* **1400** MAUNDEV. (1839) xxiv. 255 This Lond of Cathay is in Asye the depe. **1641** BP. OF LINCOLN in Cobbett *Parl. Hist.* 1807 II. 798 Yet shall you find St. Paul..intermeddle, knuckle deep, with Secular Affairs. **1669** STURMY *Mariner's Mag.* I. ii. 19 It is a hot Ship, but deep and foul..a Prize worth fighting for. **1697** DRYDEN *Virg. Georg.* III. 548 The frozen Earth lyes buried there..seven Cubits deep in Snow. **1720** DE FOE *Capt. Singleton* xiv. (1840) 246 We were now a very deep ship, having near two hundred tons of goods on board. **1842** E. WILSON *Anat. Vade M.* 334 The deep veins are situated among the deeper structures of the body. **1885** GEN. GRANT *Personal Mem.* I. xxi. 297 A portion of the ground..was two feet deep in water.

c. *spec.* Of mining operations: far below the surface of the ground; so **deep-mined** *a.* (contrasted with *opencast*); ***deep lead***: see LEAD *sb.*[2] 6 b.

1839 *Penny Cycl.* XV. 239/2 Even in very deep shafts, when complete, daylight may be seen from the bottom. **1860** *Mining Gloss.* (ed. 2) 37 *Deep level*, the watercourse leading to the engine-shaft, being always the deepest adit in the mine. **1862** *Otago: Its Goldfields & Resources* 18 The deep sinking has not, so far, realised the sanguine expectations once entertained regarding it. **1899** *Daily News* 3 May 3/5 Deep-level mines and deep-level mining. **1921** *Dict. Occup. Terms* (1927) §581 *Deep sinking labourer*; navvy or miner engaged in sinking deep holes or shafts. **1948** *Ann. Reg. 1947* 493, 4 million tons of deep-mined coal a week.

4. Of physical actions: Extending to or coming from a depth; also *transf.* of agents.

1483 CAXTON *Gold. Leg.* 437b/1 He maketh a depe enclynacion. **1589** R. HARVEY *Pl. Perc.* 15 To be compted high fliers and deepe swimmers. **1632** J. HAYWARD tr. *Biondi's Eromena* 106 Fetching a deepe sigh. **1711** ADDISON *Spect.* No. 159 ¶8, I here fetched a deep sigh. **1784** COWPER *Task* v. 64 Fearful of too deep a plunge. **1866** HUXLEY *Physiol.* iv. (1869) 102 In taking a deep inspiration.

†**5.** Of ground or roads: Covered with a depth of mud, sand, or loose soil. *Obs.*

c **1386** CHAUCER *Friar's T.* 243 Deep was the way, for which the carte stood. *c* **1470** HENRY *Wallace* v. 285 His hors stuffyt, for the way was depe and lang. **1523** *Act 14–15 Hen. VIII*, c. 6 Many other common waies..be so depe and noyous, by wearyng and course of water. **1632** LITHGOW *Trav.* VI. 253 We incountred with such deep sandy ground. **1748** SMOLLETT *Rod. Rand.* viii, To walk upwards of three hundred miles through deep roads. **1828** C. CROKER *Fairy Leg.* 167 The roads were excessively deep, from the heavy rains. [We now say 'deep in mud, dust, etc.']

II. Figurative senses.

* *Of things, states, actions, etc.*

6. a. Hard to fathom or 'get to the bottom of'; penetrating far into a subject, profound.

c **1000** *Ags. Ps.* xci[i]. 4 Wæran ðine ʒeþancas þearle deope. *c* **1200** ORMIN 5501 Off all þe boc i Godess hus þe deope diȝhellnesse. *Ibid.* 7205 Bisshopess off dep lare. *c* **1325** *E.E. Allit. P.* B. 1609 For his depe diuinité & his dere sawes. *c* **1450** *St. Cuthbert* (Surtees) 1553 Þai left all depe questyouns. **1535** COVERDALE *Ps.* xci[i]. 5 Thy thoughtes are very depe. **1600** J. PORY tr. *Leo's Africa* II. 315 A man of deepe learning. **1611** BIBLE *1 Cor.* ii. 10. **1798** FERRIAR *Illustr. of Sterne* i. 5 They suppose a work to be deep, in proportion to its darkness. **1860** RUSKIN *Mod. Painters* V. VII. iv. 150 A deep book..for deep people. **1875** HELPS *Anim. & Mast.* iv. 86 In this work..hopeful that I should find something very deep, and very significant.

b. Lying below the surface; not superficial; profound.

1856 EMERSON *Eng. Traits, Char.* Wks. (Bohn) II. 60 It is in the deep traits of race that the fortunes of nations are written. **1871** MORLEY *Voltaire* (1886) 6 In all that belongs to its deeper significance. **1874** —— *Compromise* (1886) 28 Of these deeper causes, the most important..is the growth of the Historic Method.

†**7.** Solemn; grave: **a.** of oaths, protestations, etc. *Obs.* (In OE. also of divine messages, etc.: Awful, dread, stern.)

a **1000** *Cædmon's Exod.* 518 (Gr.) Moyses sæʒde haliʒe spræce, deop ærende. *a* **1000** *Guthlac* 641 (Gr.) þurh deopne dom. *c* **1000** *Ags. Ps.* cxxxi. 11 Þæs deopne áþ Drihten aswor. **1297** R. GLOUC. (1724) 233 Grettore oþ non nys, þan by þe olde chyrche of Glastynbury [h]wo so dep oþ nome. **1587** TURBERV. *Trag. T.* (1837) 117 To sweare by deepe And very solemne othes. **1646** SIR T. BROWNE *Pseud. Ep.* I. vii. 25 Nor are the deepest sacraments..of any force to perswade. **1649** BP. HALL *Cases Consc.* 59 Beleeving the sellers deepe protestation.

†**b.** Of grave consequence or effect; grave, serious, weighty, important. *Obs.*

1596 SHAKS. *1 Hen. IV*, I. iii. 190 Ile reade you Matter, deepe and dangerous. **1605** —— *Macb.* I. iii. 126 The Instruments of Darknesse..Winne vs with honest Trifles, to betray's In deepest consequences. **1643** MILTON *Divorce* I. vi, This is a deep and serious verity. **1711** ADDISON *Spect.* No. 26 ¶6 A View of Nature in her deep and solemn Scenes.

8. As an attribute of moral qualities or of actions in which sinking or abasement is present.

a. Of sin, crime, guilt (into which one may fall or sink): Grave, heinous.

a **1000** *Guthlac* 830 (Gr.) Onguldon deopra firena. *a* **1000** *Juliana* 301 (Gr.) þurh deopne ʒedwolan. *c* **1200** *Trin. Coll. Hom.* 73 Þanne þe sinfulle man beoð bifallen on depe sinne. *a* **1400–50** *Alexander* 1866 A depe dishonoure ȝe do to ȝoure name. **1594** SHAKS. *Rich. III*, II. ii. 28 And with a vertuous Vizor hide deepe vice. **1605** —— *Macb.* I. vii. 20 The deepe damnation of his taking off. *Mod.* He is in deep disgrace.

b. Of humility, or of things humble or lowly.

a **1225** *Ancr. R.* 246 Auh habbe ȝe dope dich of deope edmodnesse. **1340** *Ayenb.* 211 He ssel to god grede mid dyepe herte. [**1843** CARLYLE *Past & Pr.* (1858) 159 Letters ..answered with new deep humilities.]

9. Deep-rooted in the breast; that comes from or enters into one's inmost nature or feelings; that affects one profoundly.

a **1400–50** *Alexander* 265 With depe desire of delite. **1594** SHAKS. *Rich. III*, I, iv. 69 If my deepe prayres cannot appease thee. **1697** DRYDEN *Virg. Georg.* I. 451 Deep Horrour seizes ev'ry Humane Breast. **1698** FRYER *Acc. E. India* 389 A deep sense of Honour. **1709** STEELE *Tatler* No. 107 ¶1, I saw in his Countenance a deep Sorrow. **1795** SOUTHEY *Joan of Arc* IX. 13 Through every fibre a deep fear Crept shivering. **1832** HT. MARTINEAU *Demerara* i. 7 Alfred ..yet entertained a deep dislike of the system. **1855** MACAULAY *Hist. Eng.* III. 107 The manner, they said, is one ..in which every Englishman..has a deep interest. **1891** E. PEACOCK *N. Brendon* II. 72 John's feelings were too deep for words.

10. Said of actions, processes, etc. in which the mind is profoundly absorbed or occupied.

1586 A. DAY *Eng. Secretary* I. (1625) 127 From the deep consideration and hard suppose of my present evils. **1658** SIR T. BROWNE *Hydriot.* Introd., In the deep Discovery of the Subterranean World. **1791** MRS. RADCLIFFE *Rom. Forest* v, Gazing on her with that deep attention which marks an enamoured mind. **1841** LANE *Arab. Nts.* I. 85 He passed the next night in deep study.

†**11. a.** Said of things involving heavy expenditure or liability; expensive; heavy. *Obs.*

1614 BP. HALL *Recoll. Treat.* 616 Ye Merchants lode them with deepe and unreasonable prices. **1649** —— *Cases Consc.* 43 The deep expence he hath beene at. **1655** FULLER *Ch. Hist.* II. vi. §5 The people paid deep Taxes. **1710** SWIFT *Jrnl. to Stella* 29 Sept., I have the first floor, a dining-room and bed-chamber, at eight shillings a week; plaguy deep. **1728** VANBR. & CIB. *Prov. Husb.* II. i, Overjoy'd for winning a deep Stake. **1781** COWPER *Expostulation* 608 Chargeable with deep arrears.

b. Of drinking, gaming, or other practices.

1577 tr. *Bullinger's Decades* (1592) 131 Deep swearings, not only needlesse, but also hurtfull. **1709** SWIFT *Adv. Relig.*, That ruinous practice of deep gaming. **1732** BERKELEY *Alciphr.* ii. §4 She took a turn towards expensive Diversions, particularly deep Play. **1827** SCOTT *Jrnl.* 8 Jan., He could not resist the temptation of deep play. **1838** THIRLWALL *Greece* V. xlii. 220 Deep drinking was customary among the Thracians. [Here there is a mixture of senses.]

12. a. Of conditions, states, or qualities: Intense, profound, very great in measure or degree. Of actions: Powerfully affecting, mighty, influential.

1605 BP. HALL *Medit. & Vows* II. §50 Without a deepe check to my selfe for my backwardnes. **1616** tr. *De Dominis' Motives* 13 This consideration..hath in deepe measure seized upon mee. **1642** ROGERS *Naaman* 11 If the Lord having man at a deepe, yea infinite advantage. **1873** MORLEY *Rousseau* I. 188 That influence..[gave] a deep and remarkable bias, first to the American Revolution, and a dozen years afterwards to the French Revolution. **1889** J. M. DUNCAN *Dis. Women* xx. (ed. 4) 162 And in order to their examination, the deep influence of an anæsthetic is necessary.

b. Said esp. of sleep, silence, and similar conditions, in which one may be deeply plunged or immersed.

1547 BOORDE *Brev. Health* (1587) 34a, The 83. Chapter doth shew of a terrible and depe slepe. *c* **1585** ? J. POLMON *Famous Battles* 262 They maye be wrapped in deepe silence. **1601** HOLLAND *Pliny* I. 84 Drowned in deepe and thick darkenes. **1611** BIBLE *2 Cor.* viii. 2 Their deepe pouertie abounded vnto the riches of their liberalitie. **1734** tr. *Rollin's Anc. Hist.* (1827) VII. XVII. 345 Which at last ended in deep consumption. **1805** WORDSW. *Waggoner* I. 6 In silence deeper far than that of deepest noon. **1853** KANE *Grinnell Exp.* xxxii. (1856) 279 Now comes the deep stillness after it.

c. Used of the intense or extreme stage of winter, night, etc., when nature is 'plunged' in darkness or death.

a **1555** LATIMER *Serm. & Rem.* (1845) 323, I would be very loth, now this deep winter. to take such a journey. **1593** SHAKS. *2 Hen. VI*, I. iv. 19 Deepe Night, darke Night, the silent of the Night. **1607** TOPSELL *Four-f. Beasts* (1658) 459 In the deepest cold weather he cometh into the Mountains of Norway. **1633** T. STAFFORD *Pac. Hib.* To Rdr. 3 In her deepe and declining age. **1797** MRS. RADCLIFFE *Italian* vii, It was deep night before he left Naples. **1806–7** J. BERESFORD *Miseries Hum. Life* (1826) v. iii, During the deepest part of the tragedy. **1821** JOANNA BAILLIE *Met. Leg., Columbus* xlix, But when the deep eclipse came on. **1851** HAWTHORNE *Wonder Bk., Gorgon's Head* (1879) 87 It was now deep night.

13. a. Of colour (or coloured objects): Intense from the quantity of colour through or on which one looks; highly chromatic. The opposite of *faint, thin.*

1555 EDEN *Decades* 236 Iacinthes..are best that are of diepeste colour. *c* **1600** SHAKS. *Sonn.* liv. 5 The canker-blooms have full as deep a dye As the perfumed tincture of the roses. **1665** HOOKE *Microgr.* 74 All manner of Blues, from the faintest to the deepest. *Ibid.*, As the liquor grew thicker and thicker, this tincture appear'd deeper and deeper. **1668** *Excell. Pen & Pencil* 81 In putting the deep and dark shadows in the Face. **1799** G. SMITH *Laboratory* I. 394 According as you would have it deeper or lighter. *a* **1839** PRAED *Poems* (1864) I. 6 Like the glow of a deep carnation. **1873** BLACK *Pr. of Thule* x. 164 Deeper and deeper grew the colour of the sun.

b. Qualifying names of colours.

Orig. with sbs. of colour, as 'a deep blue' (F. *un bleu foncé*); when the colour word is used as an adj., *deep* becomes functionally an adv., and is sometimes hyphened: cf. DEEP *adv.* 2, 3 b.

1597 SHAKS. *Lover's Compl.* 213 The deepe greene Emrald. **1665** HOOKE *Microgr.* 73 Of a deep Scarlet colour. **1776** WITHERING *Brit. Plants* (1796) II. 485 Petals..deep orange. **1831** BREWSTER *Optics* xi. 99 Deep crimson red. **1883** *L'pool Courier* 25 Sept. 4/6 Glittering on the deep blue dome.

c. ***deep mourning***: complete or full mourning: that which symbolizes deep grief.

1722 *Lond. Gaz.* No. 6084/6 The Coachman in deep Mourning. **1762** GOLDSM. *Cit. W.* xviii. ¶6 A lady dressed in the deepest mourning. **1863** MRS. CARLYLE *Lett.* III. 167 [She] was very tall, dressed in deep black.

14. a. Of sound (or a source of sound): Low in pitch, grave; full-toned, resonant.

1591 SHAKS. *1 Hen. VI*, II. iv. 12 Between two Dogs, which hath the deeper mouth. **1610** —— *Temp.* III. iii. 98 That deepe and dreadfull Organ-Pipe. **1629** MILTON *Ode Nativity* xiii, And let the bass of heaven's deep organ blow. **1704** POPE *Autumn* 20 And with deep murmurs fills the sounding shores. **1828** SCOTT *F.M. Perth* ii, 'Why, so I can' ..said one of the deepest voices that ever answered question. **1886** *Pall Mall G.* 28 Sept. 14/1 He possesses a very fine deep bass voice.

b. with mixture of senses. Cf. 7, 9.

1605 SHAKS. *Macb.* v. iii. 27 Curses, not lowd, but deepe. **1818** SHELLEY *Rev. Islam* VII. vii, They began to breathe Deep curses.

†**15.** Far advanced (in time), late. *Obs. rare.*

1599 B. JONSON *Cynthia's Rev.* IV. i, I marle how forward the day is..'slight, 'tis deeper than I took it, past five.

** *Of persons, and their faculties.*

16. 'Having the power to enter far into a subject' (J.), penetrating, profound; having profound knowledge, learning, or insight.

c **1200** ORMIN 7084 Þatt haffdenn dep innsihht and witt. *c* **1400** *Destr. Troy* 9237 Of wit noble, Depe of discrecioun. **1577–87** HOLINSHED *Chron.* II. 43/2 A deepe clerke, and one that read much. **1594** SHAKS. *Rich. III*, III. vii. 75 Meditating with two deepe Diuines. *c* **1610** MIDDLETON, etc. *Widow* I. ii, I shall be glad to learn too, Of one so deep as you are. **1640** BP. HALL *Episc.* I. v. 20 Wise Fregivillæus (a deep head, and one that was able to cut even betwixt the league, the Church, and the State). *a* **1661** FULLER *Worthies* (1840) III. 212 He was no deep seaman. **1749** FIELDING *Tom Jones* XV. vi, The deepest politicians, who see to the bottom. **1781** COWPER *Conversation* 741 The World grown old her deep discernment shows, Claps spectacles on her sagacious nose. **1856** EMERSON *Eng. Traits* I. Wks. (Bohn) II. 9 He [Carlyle] was clever and deep, but he defied the sympathies of everybody. **1875** JOWETT *Plato* (ed. 2) V. 19 There is none of Plato's writings which shows so deep an insight into the sources of human evil.

17. Profound in craft or subtlety; in *mod. slang*, profoundly cunning, artful, or sly.

1513 MORE in Grafton *Chron.* (1568) II. 758 He was close and secret and a depe dissimuler. **1568** GRAFTON *Chron.* II. 776 Oh depe and wretched dissimulation. **1594** SHAKS. *Rich. III*, II. i. 38 Deepe, hollow, treacherous, and full of guile. **1663** BUTLER *Hud.* I. i. 743 There is a Machiavelian plot.. And deep design in 't. **1688** SHADWELL *Sqr. Alsatia* III. (1720) 63 Fools! nay there I am sure you are out: they are all deep, they are very deep and sharp. **1712** STEELE *Spect.* No. 485 ⁋8 Which is the deeper man of the two. **1861** DICKENS *Gt. Expect.* xxxii, You're a deep one, Mr. Pip. **1877** *N.W. Linc. Gloss.* s.v., 'He's as deep as a well', and 'He's as deep as Wilkes', are common expressions to indicate subtilty and craft.

18. Of an agent: Who does (what is expressed) deeply, profoundly, gravely, excessively.

1526 *Pilgr. Perf.* (W. de W. 1531) 242 b, Amonge the most depe synners. **1594** SHAKS. *Rich. III*, IV. ii. 73 Two deepe enemies, Foes to my Rest. **1615** STEPHENS *Satyr. Ess.* (ed. 2) 378 Yet she is a deepe Idolater. **1722** DE FOE *Col. Jack* (1840) 279 She had been the deepest sufferer by far. **1865** M. ARNOLD *Ess. Crit.* i. (1875) 9 Shakspeare was no deep reader. **1884** A. R. PENNINGTON *Wiclif* ii. 28 A great favourite with deep thinkers.

19. a. Much immersed, involved, or implicated (*in* debt, guilt, ruin, drink, etc.); far advanced, far on.

Often passing into the adverb.

1567 *Damon & P.* in Hazl. *Dodsley* IV. 76 For all their high looks, I know some sticks full deep in merchants' books. **1587** R. HOVENDEN in *Collectanea* (Oxford Hist. Soc.) I. 215 Being.. deepe in your Lordships debt. **1594** SHAKS. *Rich. III*, I. iv. 220 For in that sinne, he is as deepe as I. **1600** —— *A.Y.L.* IV. i. 220 How deepe I am in loue. **1638** JUNIUS *Painting of Anc.* 58 Comming from a drink-feast.. deepe in drinke. **1662** HOBBES *Consid.* (1680) 6 To his dammage some thousands of pounds deep. **1771** T. HULL *Sir W. Harrington* (1797) I. 53, I shall be at as great a loss, being the sum deep with my banker already. **1782** COWPER *Boadicea* 16 Rome shall perish.. Deep in ruin as in guilt. **1784** —— *Task* v. 494 The age of virtuous politics is past, And we are deep in that of cold pretence. **1856** MACLEOD in Crump *Banking* i. 9 The Plebeians.. got deeper and deeper into debt.

b. Greatly immersed, engrossed, absorbed (*in* some occupation).

1735 POPE *Ep. Lady* 63 Now deep in Taylor and the Book of Martyrs. ?**1746** GRAY *Lett. to J. Chute* Wks. 1884 II. 131, I was in the Coffee-House very deep in advertisements. **1820** BYRON *Mar. Fal.* I. i. 3 Still the Signory is deep in council. **1855** BROWNING *By the Fireside* iii, There he is at it, deep in Greek.

III. a. Examples of the comparative and superlative. Cf. Also DEEPMOST.

a **1000** *Cædmon's Exod.* 364 (Gr.) Đone deopestan drencfloda. *c* **1330** R. BRUNNE *Chron. Wace* (Rolls) 6567 In deppest flod. *c* **1380** WYCLIF *Sel. Wks.* III. 344 þe depperste place of helle. **1398** TREVISA *Barth. De P.R.* XIV. lv. (Tollem. MS.), þe depper [**1495** deper] þe diche is withinne. *c* **1400** *Lanfranc's Cirurg.* 21 To þe deppest place. **1503** HAWES *Examp. Virt.* xiii. 278 Then went we downe to a depper vale. **1613** PURCHAS *Pilgrimage* VIII. v. 760 Still waters are deepest. **1651** HOBBES *Leviath.* III. xxxviii. 242 As well the Grave, as any other deeper place.

b. The superl. is used *absol.* = deepest part.

a **1400-50** *Alexander* 712 Into þe dyppest of þe dyke bothum. *c* **1489** CAXTON *Sonnes of Aymon* iv. 115 They wente and dwelled in the deppeste of the foreste of Ardeyne. **1556** *Aurelio & Isab.* (1608) c, From the depest of the earth unto the greatest height of the heaven. *a* **1861** CLOUGH *Song of Lamech* 92 And in his slumber's deepest he beheld.. our father Cain.

IV. *Comb.* **a.** Attributive uses of phrases, as ***deep-mouth*** (= DEEP-MOUTHED), ***deep-water***, ***deep-well***, DEEP-SEA.

1795 J. PHILLIPS *Hist. Inland Navig.* 324 A deep-water canal at this place would be essentially useful. **1806** *Sporting Mag.* XXVIII. 192 A deep-mouth Norman hound. *a* **1877** KNIGHT *Dict. Mech.* I. 682/2 *Deep-well pump*, a pump specifically adapted for oil and brine wells which are bored of small diameters and to great depths. **1890** *Nature* 10 Apr. 541 There will be no deep-water channel into the river. **1906** *Daily Chron.* 5 Sept. 3/3 To allow these deep-well waters.. to run heedlessly to waste, is a policy of which a later generation of Australians may have bitter cause for complaint. **1963** *Gloss. Mining Terms (B.S.I.)* IV. 6 *Deep well pump*, any kind of pump delivering from a well, shaft or borehole.

b. Parasynthetic derivatives, forming adjectives, as ***deep-bellied*** [*deep belly* + *-ed*], having a deep belly, ***-bosomed*** [Gr. βαθύκολπος], ***-brained***, ***-breasted***, ***-browed***, ***-chested***, ***-coloured***, ***-ditched***, ***-eyed***, ***-faced***, ***-flewed***, ***-grassed***, ***-nosed***, ***-piled***, ***-rutted***, ***-sighted***, ***-thoughted***, ***-throated***, ***-toned***, ***-vaulted***, ***-voiced***, ***-waisted***, etc.

1682 *Lond. Gaz.* No. 1744/4 A dark brown Mare.. fat, and *deep-bellied. **1851** BUCKLEY *Iliad* 346 Trojan (dames) and *deep-bosomed Dardanians. **1876** PATER *Greek Studies* (1895) 81 The deep-bosomed daughters of the Ocean. **1905** R. GARNETT *Shakespeare* 56 Not all deep-bosomed earth's wide fruitfulness. **1909** *Westm. Gaz.* 14 Aug. 2/3 The brown-faced, deep-bosomed peasant women. **1597** SHAKS. *Lover's Compl.* 209 *Deep-brained sonnets. **1935** W. G. HARDY *Father Abraham* 101 A tall, *deep-breasted woman was standing in the door of the tent. *a* **1821** KEATS *Sonn. Chapman's Homer*, *Deep-browed Homer. **1838** JAMES *Robber* i, He was both broad and *deep-chested. **1770** HAMILTON in *Phil. Trans.* LXI. 22 *Deep-coloured flames burst forth. **1548** HALL *Chron.* 56 No stronger walled then *depe ditched. **1818** SHELLEY *Rev. Islam* I. li, Sculptures like life and thought; immovable, *deep-eyed. **1908** *Westm. Gaz.* 23 Dec. 4/1 A number of golfers playing with *deep-faced, round-headed drivers. **1735** SOMERVILLE *Chase* I. 286 The *deep-flew'd Hound Breed up with Care. **1846** J. BAXTER *Libr. Pract. Agric.* (ed. 4) I. 219 All light sharp-nosed dogs will always be much more inclined to riot than deep-flewed dogs. **1906** *Westm. Gaz.* 21 May 1/3 The hedge on either side is just high enough to hide the *deep-grassed meadows. **1859** YARRELL *Brit. Fishes* (ed. 3) II. 406 The *Deep-nosed Pipe-fish is immediately recognised by the compressed form of the face. **1876** ROCK *Text. Fabr.* 67 A dark blue *deep-piled velvet. **1836** T. HOOK *G. Gurney* I. iii. 217 At the corner of the *deep-rutted lane. **1899** *Daily News* 19 Oct. 6/1 Transports stopped in the deep-rutted roads. **1622** MASSINGER *Virg. Mart.* II. i, Pimpled, *deep-scarleted, rubified, and carbuncled faces. **1577** B. GOOGE *Heresbach's Husb.* III. (1586) 128 A long, a large, and *deepe sided body. *a* **1797** H. WALPOLE *Mem. Geo. III* (1845) I. viii. 117 Wholesome and *deep-sighted advice. **1668** *Lond. Gaz.* No. 272/4 A *deep skirted Saddle of red Cloth. **1882** *Times* 27 June, English wools.. of the *deep-stapled class. **1839** J. R. DARLEY *Introd. Beaum. & Fl. Wks.* (1839) I. 17 Jonson ..repaid both with the following *deep-thoughted lines. **1844** MRS. BROWNING *The Dead Pan* xxii, The hoarse *deep-throated ages Laugh your god-ships unto scorn. **1780** COWPER *Progr. Err.* 605 Strike on the *deep-toned chord the sum of all. **1876** GEO. ELIOT *Dan. Der.* III. xxxvi. 86 With deep-toned decision. **1842** TENNYSON *Gardener's Dau.* 45 Fields.. browsed by *deep-udder'd kine. **1671** MILTON *P.R.* I. 113 Hell's *deep-vaulted den. **1847** LONGF. *Ev.* II. v. 247 The *deep-voiced.. ocean. **1769** FALCONER *Dict. Marine* (1789), *Encastillé*, *deep-waisted, or frigate-built; as opposed to galley-built.

c. deep-breathing *vbl. sb.*, the act of breathing deeply as a form of physical exercise; hence ***deep-breathe*** v. intr.; **deep-cover** *attrib.*, applied to an intelligence agent whose real identity and allegiance are thoroughly protected; **deep-dish pie** *U.S.*, 'a pie, usually a fruit pie, baked in a deep dish and having no bottom crust' (Webster 1934); **deep-draft** or **-draught** *a. Naut.*, that displaces deep water; **deep drawing**, a kind of cold-working in which a sheet or strip of metal is subjected to considerable plastic deformation by being forced through a die, so producing hollow parts such as cylinders; **deep-etch, -etching**, a photo-engraving process in which the lithographic plate is slightly etched; hence **deep-etch** *v. trans.* and *intr.*; **deep field** *Cricket*, that part of the field which is near the boundary, esp. behind the bowler; also, a fieldsman or his position there; hence ***deep-fielder***; **deep-(fat-)frying**, the frying of food in sufficient oil or fat to cover it completely; so ***deep-(fat-)fry*** v. trans. and intr., ***deep-(fat-)frier***, ***-fryer***; **deep kiss** (see quot. 1951); so ***deep kissing*** vbl. sb.; **deep litter**, a deep layer of litter (LITTER *sb.* 3 b) used in poultry-houses, etc.; a method of keeping poultry in such conditions; also *attrib.*; **deep-milking**, the production of a good yield of milk; so ***deep-milker***; **deep-rooter**, something which takes deep root; **deep-sinker** *Austral. slang*, (*a*) a drinking-glass of the largest size, so called from a fanciful resemblance to a deep mineshaft; (*b*) the drink served in such a glass; **Deep South**, the southernmost parts of the United States, usually taken to include the states of Alabama, Georgia, Louisiana, Mississippi, and sometimes South Carolina; also *attrib.*; **deep space**, a term for the regions of space that are either (*a*) beyond the solar system or (*b*) well outside the earth's atmosphere; also *attrib.*; **deep structure** *Linguistics* (see quot. 1965); **deep tank**, a tank for water ballast or fuel oil, formed by cutting off a part of a ship's hold; **deep therapy**, the treatment of disease by short-wave X-rays (see quots.); **deep throat**, a person working within an organization who supplies anonymously information concerning misconduct by other members of the organization; orig. applied (with capital initials) to the principal informant in the WATERGATE scandal [after a pornographic film (1972) so titled]; **deep trance**, a deep hypnotic state; also *attrib.*; hence ***deep-tranced*** used as *pa. pple.*

1964 *Punch* 26 Feb. 315/1 In the morning he *deep-breathed. **1904** B. A. MACFADDEN *Building of Vital Power* 115 Through *deep breathing conducted as an exercise, the lungs become larger. **1936** W. FAULKNER *Absalom, Absalom!* vii. 217 He will raise the window and do deep-breathing. **1965** F. SARGESON *Memoirs of Peon* vi. 161 The rules were, nothing to drink except water; deep-breathing exercises and no tobacco. **1963** *N.Y. Times* 7 Apr. 9/1 He was born Abraham Hackelman and was a '*deep cover' agent in the eighteen nineties. **1979** *Courier-Mail* (Brisbane) 26 Jan. 5/2 This corroborated information supplied to the FBI by a deep-cover Soviet double agent in New York. **1936** WODEHOUSE *Laughing Gas* ii. 29, I polished off the steak and put in a bid for *deep-dish apple pie with a bit of cheese on the side. **1943** *Gen* 2 Jan. 33/2 Their [American] diet.. consists of little but.. deep-dish apple tart. **1908** *Westm. Gaz.* 30 Oct. 6/4 None of our inward water-borne traffic enters the Port in *deep-draft vessels. **1925** *Forging, Stamping, Heat Treating* XI. 428/1 Several annealing and pickling operations.. are necessary on extremely *deep drawing. **1929** *Jrnl. Iron & Steel Inst.* CXX. 460 The force required and the stresses set up at various stages in the deep drawing of sheet metal. **1932** *Ibid.* CXXV. 559 The deep-drawing qualities of steel sheets. **1948** H. MISSINGHAM *Stud. Guide Comm. Art* II. 141 **Deep-etch*, used on half-tone blocks where the white parts of the drawing would have a very small screen dot over them unless this instruction were given for their removal. **1960** G. A. GLAISTER *Gloss. of Book* 99/2 *Deep-etch process*, a method of making a lithographic plate by photo-mechanical means. It involves the printing on to metal of a photographic positive, and the very slight.. etching of the plate. **1967** E. CHAMBERS *Photolitho-Offset* 270 *Deep-etch*, lithographic platemaking process in which the work areas are slightly etched (about 0·003 in.) into the surface of the plate. Positives are used for printing to metal using special solutions, with the etches supplying space for the lacquer base of the ink-receptive printing image. **1897** *Process Photogram* Sept. 143 For a *deep etching the solution would have to be renewed several times. **1955** in *Amer. Speech* (1956) XXXI. 84 They *deep-fat-fry them. **1947** M. GIVEN *Modern Encycl. Cooking* II. 1609 **Deep fat fryer*. Buy as a unit. **1926** S. E. NASH *Cooking Craft* vi. 35 French or *Deep Fat Frying. **1870** *Times* 20 July 10/3 Mr. Francis was caught at *deep field. **1900** *Westm. Gaz.* 22 June 3/1 There is scarcely a bowler nowadays who does not station at least one man in the deep-field. *Ibid.* 3/2 Our first two batsmen.. succeeded in getting the ball between his deep fields. **1933** A. G. MACDONELL *England, their England* vii. 114 Mr. Southcott.. went away into the deep field, about a hundred and twenty yards from the wicket. **1870** *Times* 9 Aug. 3/4 *Deep-fielders have now a better chance of compassing with effect the space allotted them. **1951** E. DAVID *French Country Cooking* 18 A *deep frier with a basket is necessary for chips. **1933** *Mod. Pract. Cookery* 195/2 Be very careful when *deep-frying not to fill the pan too full. **1970** *New Yorker* 24 Oct. 43/2 It's cornmeal and onions, deep fried. **1932** E. CRAIG *Cooking with E. Craig* 113 Use 1 or 1½ lb... fat, lard or olive oil, for *deep frying. **1951** FORD & BEACH *Patterns Sex. Behav.* iii. 49 The '*deep kiss' ..involves thrusting the tongue of one partner into the mouth of the other. **1948** A. C. KINSEY et al. *Sexual Behavior in Human Male* x. 369 *Deep kissing is utilized as a prime source of erotic arousal... A deep kiss may involve considerable tongue contacts. **1946** LIPPINCOTT & CARD *Poultry Production* (ed. 7) xii. 292 The usual procedure with *deep litter is to start in the fall with two to four inches of dry litter, and add to this gradually until the floor is covered eight to ten inches deep. **1947** R. SEIDEN *Poultry Handbk.* 106 Deep-litter nests keep eggs clean. **1958** *Times* 19 Sept. 3/5 There had been a drop in egg production since they changed from batteries to deep litter. **1969** *Guardian* 25 Aug. 13/5 The sheep were all in deep litter. **1879** J. P. SHELDON *Dairy Farming* 5/2 It is important that she should be a '*deep milker'. **1833** *Ridgemont Farm Rep.* in *British Husbandry* (1840) III. I. 148 The large, heavy, slow-fattening but *deep-milking cows of this country. **1879** J. P. SHELDON *Dairy Farming* 36/2 Deep milking.. is a question of breeding and training. **1923** *Discovery* Sept. 244/2 The deep-milking propensity of some cows may be transmitted through the bull to the next generation of female calves. **1960** *Farmer & Stockbreeder* 8 Mar. 31/1 An opportunity to purchase well-framed, deep-milking Ayrshire cattle. **1898** *Westm. Gaz.* 19 Mar. 2/1 Her first cousin.. is a *deep-rooter, and must be looked after betimes. **1927** *Smallholder* 26 Mar. 105/2 The main-crop, deep-rooters should be sown at the end of May. **1886** F. COWAN *Australia: a Charcoal Sketch* 32 *Long-sleever, Bishop Barker*, and **Deep-sinker*, synonyms of Yankee Schooner. **1897** *Argus* 15 Jan. 6/5 (Morris), A tumbler—whether medium, small, or deep-sinker. **1936** 'R. WEST' *Thinking Reed* i. 23 He had thought himself right out of the illusions common to the *Deep South. **1938** C. H. MATSCHAT *Suwannee River* 285 A trip to the Deep South. **1940** C. MCCULLERS *Heart is Lonely Hunter* (1943) I. i. 3 The town was in the middle of the deep South. **1941** W. S. MAUGHAM *Writer's Notebook* (1949) 327 The vicissitudes of the war have brought her down to the deep South, but till then she had always lived in Portland, Oregon. **1952** *Spectator* 21 Nov. 710/2 A 'Deep South' American novel. **1967** *Times* 8 July 11/1 In the two years since the voting rights Act was passed the registration of Negro voters in the deep South has increased by 78 per cent. **1952** M. ST. CLAIR in 'E. Crispin' *Best SF* (1955) 184, I am aware of an intense loneliness. It's a normal response to the *deep space situation. **1954** *Jrnl. Brit. Interplanetary Soc.* XIII. 16 These specialized 'deep-space' rocket vehicles would, of course, be refuelled and serviced from satellite ships. **1960** F. GAYNOR *Dict. Aerospace* 69 *Deep space*, a colloquial term for space beyond the outermost boundaries of our solar system. **1962** *New Scientist* 22 Mar. 676/2 Deep-space missiles.. being fired far out into space and then falling back to approach the target at a steep angle and a high velocity. **1969** *Daily Tel.* 11 Jan. 1/4 They will also send back to Earth information about deep space during the 155 million-mile journey [to Venus]. **1965** N. CHOMSKY *Aspects Theory Syntax* i. 16 The syntactic component of a grammar must specify, for each sentence, a **deep structure* that determines its semantic interpretation and a *surface structure* that determines its phonetic interpretation. **1966** L. J. COHEN *Diversity of Meaning* (ed. 2) ii. 37 The basic rules generate so-called 'deep structures' which receive an interpretation from the semantic rules. **1909** *Cent. Dict. Suppl.*, *Deep tank. **1935** *Jane's Fighting Ships* 113 No. 1 stokehold now converted into four oil-fuel deep-tanks. **1944** R. PHILLIPS *Super-voltage X-ray Therapy* ii. 4 These descriptive terms—'superficial' therapy for voltages up to 130 kv., '*deep' therapy for the 200–400 kv. range, and 'supervoltage' therapy for 500 kv. upwards—have little to recommend them except brevity. **1967** *New Scientist* 29 June 760/1 Whereas the term 'deep therapy' formerly implied X-ray generators of several hundred kilovolts, it now implies accelerators of, effectively, several million volts. [**1973** *National Rev.* (U.S.) 22 June 697/2 So you want to write a best-seller... Well, for starters, how about the hijacking bit?.. Characters? Mafia and *Deep Throat* types are winners this season.] **1974** *Time* 22 Apr. 55/1 Foremost among their key sources was a man whom the authors still tantalizingly refuse to name. They called him '*Deep Throat', and report only that he was a pre-Watergate friend of Woodward's, with 'extremely sensitive' antennae. **1974** BERNSTEIN & WOODWARD in *Playboy* May 218/2 In newspaper terminology, this meant the discussions were on 'deep background'. Woodward explained the arrangements to managing editor Howard Simons one day. He had taken to calling the source 'my friend', but Simons dubbed him 'Deep Throat'. The name stuck. **1982** *Times* 3 Nov. 1 A fresh threat of industrial action emerged last night after the publication of documents leaked by a 'deep throat' in the National Coal Board. **1892** *Deep trance [see HYPNOSIS 2].

1959 *Listener* 31 Dec. 1165/3 Deep-trance subjects. **1927** W. DE LA MARE *Stuff & Nonsense* 48 A panther spies them there, *Deep-tranced in speechless rapture.

deep (diːp), *sb.* Forms: 1 déop, dýpe, 4 deope, 4–6 depe, 4–7 deepe, 5–6 *Sc.* deip(e, (8 dip (sense 8)), 6– deep. [OE. *déop*, neuter of *déop* a., used subst.; also *díepe*, *dýpe*, in non-WSax. *déope* depth, deepness = OS. *diupî*, *diopî*, OHG. *tiufî* (Ger. *tiefe*), ON. *dýpi*, Goth. *diupei*:—OTeut. *deupîn-*, *diupîn-*, f. *deupo-z* DEEP.]

†**1.** Depth, deepness. *Obs. rare.*

c **1000** *Ags. Gosp.* Matt. xiii. 5 Hiȝ næfdon þære eorþan dypan [*c* **1160** *Hatton G.* deopan]. **1624** BACON *New Atlantis* Wks. (1676) 259 Caves of several deeps. **1635** L. FOXE *N.-W. Voy.* 128 Hee lessed his deepe 3 fathom.

2. The deep part of the sea, or of a lake or river (opposed to *shallow*); deep water; a deep place.

a **1000** *Cædmon's Exod.* 281 (Gr.) Ic sloh garsecges deop. *c* **1000** *Ags. Ps.* lxviii. 14–15 Ado me of deope deorces wæteres..Ne me huru forswelȝe sæ-grundes deop. **1483** CAXTON *Gold. Leg.* 58/2 And sancke doun in to the depe of the see. *c* **1500** *Melusine* 273 They had take the deep of the porte. **1568** GRAFTON *Chron.* II. 325 The Frenchmen.. passed by and tooke the deepe of the Sea. **1681** CHETHAM *Angler's Vade-m.* xxxiii. §1 Dib in the still deeps. **1700** S. L. tr. *Fryke's Voy.* 265 Till we were quite out of the deep, and in full sight of the Land. **1831** CARLYLE *Sart. Res.* I. iv, Some silent, high-encircled mountain-pool, into whose black deeps you fear to gaze. **1855** KINGSLEY *Heroes* v. ii. (1868) 155 They sailed on through the deeps of Sardinia. **1865** J. G. BERTRAM *Harvest of Sea* (1873) 108 The best places for this kind of fishing are the deeps at Kingston Bridge, Sunbury Lock. *Mod.* A ship crossing Boston deeps.

3. ***the deep***: **a.** The deep sea, the ocean, the main. *poetic* and *rhetorical* (without pl.)

c **1000** *Ags. Gosp.* Luke v. 4 Teoh hit [scip] on dypan [*c* **1160** *Hatton G.* deopan]. *c* **1315** SHOREHAM 146 Fisches ine the depe. *c* **1386** CHAUCER *Man of Law's T.* 357, I schal drenchen in þe deepe. *a* **1400–50** *Alexander* 64 Dromonds dryfes ouer þe depe. **1590** SHAKS. *Mids. N.* III. i. 161 They shall fetch thee Iewels from the deepe. **1614** BP. HALL *Recoll. Treat.* 442 The swelling waves of the Deepe. **1662** *Bk. Com. Prayer, Burial at Sea*, We therefore commit his body to the Deep. **1713** STEELE *Englishman* No. 26. 171 Monsters of the Deep. **1801** CAMPBELL *Mariners of Eng.* iv, Britannia needs no bulwark, No towers along the steep; Her march is o'er the mountain waves, Her home is on the deep. **1870** BRYANT *Iliad* I. II. 65 Barks To cross the dark blue deep.

†**b.** Formerly also in *pl.* in same sense. *Obs.*

1598 CHAPMAN *Iliad* I. 310 They..cast the offal of all to the deeps. **1659** D. PELL *Improv. Sea* Ep. Ded. A iij b, Among the Lords wonders in the Deeps. **1725** POPE *Odyss.* II. 372 The dangers of the deeps he tries. *Ibid.* III. 410 The monstrous wonders of the deeps.

c. The abyss or depth of space. (Sometimes a fig. use of a.)

1596 SHAKS. *1 Hen. IV*, III. i. 52 *Glend.* I can call Spirits from the vastie Deepe. **1667** MILTON *P.L.* VII. 168 Boundless the Deep, because I am who fill Infinitude, nor vacuous the space. **1794** BLAKE *Songs Exper., Tiger* 5 In what distant deeps or skies Burnt the fire of thine eyes? **1820** SHELLEY *Skylark* 9 The blue deep thou wingest. **1830** TENNYSON *Poems* 114 And thunder through the sapphire deeps. **1877** E. R. CONDER *Bas. Faith* iv. 192 That boundless deep of space.

d. *Cricket.* Ellipt. for *deep field* (see DEEP *a.* IV. c).

1906 BELDAM & FRY *Gt. Bowlers & Fielders* 438 A fine example of the throw in from 'the deep'. **1924** H. DE SELINCOURT *Cricket Match* (1928) iv. 89 One catch in the deep which he had held in a school cricket match..was still vividly remembered. **1954** J. H. FINGLETON *Ashes crown the Year* 112 Lindwall having nobody in the deep. **1963** A. ROSS *Australia 63* iii. 85 Graveney, chasing one in the deep, pulled a muscle and left the field.

4. a. A deep place in the earth, etc.; a deep pit, cavity, valley; an abyss; a depression in a surface.

1393 GOWER *Conf.* II. 200 They go by night unto the mine ..A wilde fire into the depe Thei caste among the tymberwerke. *c* **1470** HENRY *Wallace* VI. 719 A thousand in the myre, Off hors with men, was plungyt in the deipe. **1576** LAMBARDE *Peramb. Kent* (1826) 189 Newendene is such, as it may likely enough take the name..of the deepe and bottome. **1667** MILTON *P.L.* IV. 76 And in the lowest deep a lower deep Still threatning to devour me opens wide. **1855** SINGLETON *Virgil* I. 331 The madding prophetess..Who in a deep of cliff the fates doth chant. **1891** COTES *2 Girls on Barge* 161 Noting the deeps and curves of the curious pensive face.

b. *Cornish Mining.* 'The lower portion of a vein; used in the phrase ***to the deep***, i.e. downward upon the vein' (Raymond *Mining Gloss.* 1881).

5. The remote central part, the 'depths'. *rare.*

c **1400** MAUNDEV. (1839) vii. 79 He wan..all the othere kyngdoms unto the depe of Ethiope. **1879** BROWNING *Ivan Ivanovitch* 17 In the deep of our land 'tis said, a village from out the woods Emerged.

†**6.** The middle (of winter, of night) when the cold, stillness, or darkness is most intense; the 'depth'. *Obs.*

1530 PALSGR. 543/1 In the depe of wynter, all flowers be faded quyte awaye. **1598** SHAKS. *Merry W.* IV. iv. 40 Many that do feare In deepe of night to walke by this Hernes Oake. *a* **1661** HOLYDAY *Juvenal* 13 An hour at the deep of winter, being but a twelfth part of their shortest day. **1682** BUNYAN *Holy War* 80 The Captains also, in the deep of this Winter, did send..a summons to Mansoul.

7. *fig.* A deep (*i.e.* secret, mysterious, unfathomable, or vast) region of thought, feeling, or being; a 'depth', ' abyss'. *poet.* and *rhet.*

1614 BP. HALL *Recoll. Treat.* 631 Hee is happily waded out of those deepes of sorrowes, whereof our conceites can finde no bottome. **1632** LITHGOW *Trav.* x. 485 Low plunge my hopes, in dark deepes of despaire. **1781** COWPER *Retirement* 135 To dive into the secret deeps within. **1820** SHELLEY *Ode Liberty* ix, From the human spirit's deepest deep. **1832** TENNYSON *Palace of Art* lvi, God, before whom ever lie bare The abysmal deeps of Personality.

8. *Naut.* A term used in estimating the fathoms intermediate to those indicated by marks on the 20-fathom sounding-line. Formerly also *dip.*

The marks are at 2, 3, 5, 7, 10, 13, 15, 17, 20 fathoms; the 'deeps' or 'dips' are therefore 1, 4, 6, 8, 9, 11, 12, 14, 16, 18, 19.

1769 FALCONER *Dict. Marine* (1789) M m iv, As there is no mark at 4, 6, 8, &c., he estimates those numbers, and calls, 'By the dip four, &c.' *c* **1860** H. STUART *Seaman's Catech.* 42 How many marks and deeps are there in a 20-fathom lead line? Nine marks and eleven deeps. **1867** SMYTH *Sailor's Word-bk., Hand-line*, a line bent to the hand-lead, measured at certain intervals with what are called *marks* and *deeps* from 2 and 3 fathoms to 20. **1882** NARES *Seamanship* (ed. 6) 17 If he judges that the depth corresponds with a deep, [the leadsman calls] 'by the deep 8 or 9, etc.'

9. *Comb.*, as ***deep-commanding***.

c **1590** GREENE *Fr. Bacon* xi. 112 Hell trembled at my deep-commanding spells.

deep (diːp), *adv.* Forms: 1 díope, déope, 3 diep, 3–6 depe, 4 dep, dipe, 5–7 deepe, 6– deep. *Comp.* deeper, *superl.* deepest; also 2 deoppre, 4 deppere, 4–5 depper, 5 deppir; 4 deppest, depperst. [OE. *díope*, *déope* = OS. *diopo*, *diapo*, OHG. *tiufo* (MHG. *tiefe*, Ger. *tief*).]

1. a. *lit.* Deeply; to, at, or with, a great, or specified depth; far down, in, etc.

a **1000** *Riddles* liv. 6 (Gr.) Deope ȝedolȝod, dumb in bendum. *c* **1175** *Lamb. Hom.* 49 Heo delueð deihwamliche heore put deoppre and deoppre. *a* **1300** *Cursor M.* 494 (Cott.) Þan fell þai depe. *c* **1380** WYCLIF *Sel. Wks.* III. 344 Þes ben depperst dampned in helle. *c* **1489** CAXTON *Aymon* iv. 116 They..wente in to the forest of Ardeyn, sore deepe in it. **1601** R. JOHNSON *Kingd. & Commw.* (1603) 190 Waters do ebbe as deepe as they flow. **1667** MILTON *P.L.* III. 201 That they may stumble on, and deeper fall. **1727** SWIFT *Gulliver* III. i. 178 My sloop was so deep laden that she sailed very slow. **1870** E. PEACOCK *Ralf Skirl.* I. 33 His hands were stuck deep into the waistband of his breeches.

b. *transf.* in reference to time: Far on.

1822 SCOTT *Nigel* xviii, The Abbess..died before her munificent patroness, who lived deep in Queen Elizabeth's time. **1871** DIXON *Tower* III. xx. 211 The three men sat up deep into the night. **1890** W. C. RUSSELL *Ocean Trag.* III. xxx. 137 The work ran us deep into the afternoon.

c. In *to lie deep* and the like, the adv. approaches the adj.

a **1704** LOCKE (J.), If the matter be knotty, and the sense lies deep, the mind must stop and buckle to it. **1803** WORDSW. *Ode Intim. Immort.* xi, Thoughts that do often lie too deep for tears. **1812** MRS. HEMANS *Graves of Househ.* iv, The sea, the blue lone sea hath one, He lies where pearls lie deep. *Prov.* Still waters run deep.

d. *Cricket.* In the deep field (see DEEP *a.* IV. c).

1849 W. LILLYWHITE *Young Cricketer's Guide* 21 This fieldsman must stand deeper. **1857** HUGHES *Tom Brown* II. viii, The batter..cuts it beautifully to where cover-point is standing very deep, in fact almost off the ground. **1891** W. G. GRACE *Cricket* x. 265 Mid-on..is placed close in or deep according to the wish of the bowler.

2. *fig.* Deeply (in various figurative senses); profoundly, intensely, earnestly, heavily, etc.

As qualifying an adj. (cf. quots. 1600, 1602) *deep* is obs. (exc. with words of colour, as '*deep-red* stain', where *deep* is historically an *adj.*: see DEEP *a.* 13 b); qualifying a verb, it is generally superseded in prose use by *deeply*, although still used in particular cases; cf. quots. 1810–75.

a **1000** *Desc. Hell* 108 (Gr.) Nu ic þe hatsie deope. *c* **1000** *Ags. Ps.* cvi. 26 Gedrefede ða deope syndan. *a* **1300** *Cursor M.* 8269 (Cott.) Ferr and depe he vmbi-thoght, Hu þat hus it suld be wroght. *c* **1385** CHAUCER *L.G.W.* 1234 *Dido*, And swore so depe to hire to be trewe. **1526** *Pilgr. Perf.* (W. de W. 1531) 15 b, Anone they ouerthrowe hym as depe in aduersite. **1600** SHAKS. *A.Y.L.* II. vii. 31 That Fooles should be so deepe contemplatiue. **1602** MARSTON *Antonio's Rev.* IV. iii. Wks. 1856 I. 127, I am deepe sad. **1621** ELSING *Debates Ho. Lords* (Camden) 90 That for honour's sake Yelverton be fyned deepe. **1709** POPE *Ess. Crit.* 216 A little learning is a dangerous thing; Drink deep, or taste not the Pierian spring. *a* **1715** BURNET *Own Time* (1823) I. 436 The King was so afraid to engage himself too deep. **1762** GOLDSM. *Nash* 53 To tie him up..from playing deep. **1810** SCOTT *Lady of L.* I. iii, A hundred dogs bayed deep and strong. **1823** LAMB *Elia* Ser. II. *Old Margate Hoy*, The reason..scarcely goes deep enough into the question. **1833** THIRLWALL in *Philol. Mus.* II. 538 Moral inquiries..were those in which he engaged the deepest. **1866** KINGSLEY *Hereward* iii. 77 They drank deep of the French wine. **1875** JOWETT *Plato* (ed. 2) IV. 417 The thoughts of Socrates.. have certainly sunk deep into the mind of the world.

3. *Comb.* **a.** Frequent in combination with pres. and pa. pples. (in which *deeply*, not hyphened, may usually be substituted); as ***deep-going***, ***-lying***, ***-questioning***, ***-reaching***, ***-sinking***, ***-thinking***, ***-trenching***; ***deep-cut***, ***-felt***, ***-grown***, ***-sunk***; DEEP-DRAWN, -LAID, -SET, etc. In poetical language, especially, these combinations are formed at will, and their number is unlimited, e.g. ***deep-affected***, ***-affrighted***, ***-biting***, ***-brooding***, ***-buried***, ***-crimsoned***, ***-damasked***, ***-discerning***, ***-drawing***, ***-drunk***, ***-dyed***, ***-engraven***, ***-laden***, ***-persuading***, ***-searching***, ***-sunken***, ***-sworn***, ***-throbbing***, ***-worn***, ***-wounded***; DEEP-ROOTED, DEEP-SEATED, etc. It is sometimes difficult to separate these from parasynthetic combinations of the adj. such as ***deep-vaulted***: see DEEP *a.* IV. b.

1598 SYLVESTER *Du Bartas* II. i. *Imposture* 305 Sweet, courting, *deep-affected words. *Ibid.* II. i. *Furies* 581 *Deep-affrighted Sadnesse. **1647** H. MORE *Song of Soul* App. III. ix, By Nemesis *deep-biting whips well urged. **1776** MICKLE tr. *Camoens' Lusiad* 339 *Deep-brooding silence reign'd. **1855** SINGLETON *Virgil* I. 142 Wealth.. broodeth over his *deep-buried gold. *a* **1826** LONGF. *Autumn* 19 The..woods of ash *deep-crimsoned. **1860** TYNDALL *Glac.* I. viii. 59 Streams..rushing through *deep-cut channels. **1820** KEATS *St. Agnes* xxiv, The tiger-moth's *deep-damask'd wings. **1844** MARG. FULLER *Wom. in 19th C.* (1862) 51 Deep-eyed *deep-discerning Greece. **1606** SHAKS. *Tr. & Cr.* Prol. 12 The *deep-drawing barks do there disgorge. **1593** —— *Lucr.* 1100 She, *deep-drenched in a sea of care. **1703** ROWE *Ulyss.* II. i. 954 Mounting Spirits of the *deep-drunk Bowl. **1818** BYRON *Ch. Har.* IV. xxviii, Gently flows The *deep-dyed Brenta. **1614** T. ADAMS *Devil's Banquet* 47 *Deepe-ingrauen and indelible characters. **1808** J. BARLOW *Columb.* I. 52 *Deep felt sorrows. **1859** I. TAYLOR *Logic in Theol.* 178 A *deep-going error. **1883** *Daily News* 17 Sept. 2/3 *Deep-grown English wools are still out of fashion. **1845** LONGF. *Belfry Bruges* xii, With *deep-laden argosies. **1864** MARSH *Man & Nature* 439 The *deep-lying veins. **1876** GEO. ELIOT *Dan. Der.* II. xxviii. 215 The deep-lying though not obtrusive difference. **1594** BARNFIELD *Compl. Chastitie* vii, Gold is a *deepe-perswading Orator. **1871** MORLEY *Voltaire* (1886) 213 Moods of egotistic introspection and *deep-questioning contemplation. **1599** MARSTON *Sco. Villanie* II. v. 196 For Flavus was a knaue, A damn'd *deep-reaching villain. **1873** M. ARNOLD *Lit. & Dogma* 362 The truth is really..more wide and deep-reaching than the Aberglaube. **1776** MICKLE tr. *Camoens' Lusiad* 125 *Deep-settled grief. **1858** LYTTON *What will he do* I. vi, Under the *deep-sunk window. *c* **1600** SHAKS. *Sonn.* ii, Within thine owne *deep-sunken eyes. **1845** LONGF. *To a Child* ii, Far-down in the deep-sunken wells Of darksome mines. **1862** E. ARNOLD in *Fraser's Mag.* July 113 Unto us, thy *deep-sworn votaries. **1768–74** TUCKER *Lt. Nat.* (1852) I. 613 To deal with the sagacious and *deep-thinking, one must go to the bottom of things. **1845** G. MURRAY *Islaford* 126 When this *deep-throbbing heart shall be wed. **1862** ANSTED *Channel Isl.* IV. xx. (ed. 2) 475 The *deep-trenching plough..turning up a thickness of a foot of subsoil. **1827** KEBLE *Chr. Y., Holy Innocents*, The *deep-worn trace of penitential tears. **1590** SPENSER *F.Q.* I. ii. 24 A virgin widow; whose *deepe-wounded mind With love long time did languish.

b. *deep* was also formerly used with adjectives (see 2), and these were (or are by editors) sometimes hyphened (to make the grammatical construction clear), as ***deep-naked***, ***deep-sore***, ***deep-sweet***: cf. *deep contemplative* in 2. So still sometimes with adjs. of colour, as '***deep-blue*** sea', '***deep-green*** grass': see DEEP *a.* 13 b.

1592 SHAKS. *Ven. & Adon.* 432 Ear's deep-sweet music, and heart's deep-sore wounding. *a* **1618** SYLVESTER *Tobacco Battered* 377 Chaprones..with broad deep-naked Brests.

c. with another *adv.*, as **deep-down** *adv.* and *adj.*

1832 TENNYSON *Lotos-eaters* 35 His voice was thin..And deep-asleep he seem'd. **1861** L. L. NOBLE *Icebergs* 108 If he [iceberg] move, he dashes a foot against the deep down stones. **1876** TENNYSON *Harold* II. ii. (1877) 55 And deeper still the deep-down oubliette, Down thirty feet below the smiling day. **1890** *Daily News* 3 Feb. 5/3 These deep-down curtseys are reported to be now coming into common use abroad. **1915** E. B. HOLT *Freudian Wish* i. 5 The person does, in his dream, what he deep-down wishes to do. **1962** E. BOWEN *Afterthought* 81 A slowly acquired deep-down knowledge.

d. with verbs (*rare*), as **deep-fish** [f. *deep fishing*, *fisheries*], to fish in the DEEP SEA (q.v.).

1844 W. H. MAXWELL *Sports & Adv. Scotl.* xvi. (1855) 148 A fleet of boats had gone out to deep-fish.

deep (diːp), *v. rare.* [OE. *díepan*, *dýpan* trans., OFris. *diupa* (Du. *diepen*), MHG. *tiefen*, Goth. *ga-diupjan*. The intr. would correspond to an OE. **déopian*, Goth. **diupôn* to be deep, but is app. an analogical form of later age.]

†**1.** *trans.* To make deep, deepen. *Obs.*

c **930** *Laws of Æthelstan* iv. §6 We cwædon be ðam blaserum, ðæt man dypte ðone aþ be þryfealdum. *c* **1205** LAY. 15473 Þa þe dic wes idoluen & allunge ideoped. **1616** *MS. Acc. St. John's Hosp., Canterb.*, For the deping of it, iiijd.

2. *intr.* To become deep, deepen. *rare.*

1598 HAKLUYT *Voy.* I. 436 Vse your leade oftener.. noting diligently the order of your depth, and the deeping and sholding. **1849** KINGSLEY *Misc., N. Devon* II. 254 Nature's own glazings, deeping every instant there behind us.

†**3.** To go deep, penetrate. *Obs.*

a **1225** *Ancr. R.* 288 Þer waxeð wunde & deopeð into þe soule.

†**4.** *trans.* To plunge or immerse deeply (*lit.* and *fig.*); to drown. *Obs.*

c **1380** WYCLIF *Serm.* Sel. Wks. I. 13 It is noo nede to depe us in þis story more þan þe gospel tellith. *a* **1541** WYATT *Poet. Wks.* (1861) 173 And deep thyself in travail more and more. **1578** *Chr. Prayers* in *Priv. Prayers* (1851) 444 A droopy night ever deepeth the minds of them.

deep-drawn (ˈdiːpˌdrɔːn), *ppl. a.* [DEEP *adv.* 3.] **1.** Drawn deeply or from the depths (esp. of the breast).

1813 T. JEFFERSON *Writ.* (1830) IV. 224 They can never suppress the deep-drawn sigh. **1860** TYNDALL *Glac.* I. xvi.

107 The hollow cave resounded to the deep-drawn snore. **1870** BRYANT *Iliad* II. XVI. 114 With a sigh Deep-drawn.

2. Of metals: produced or worked by deep drawing; suitable for deep drawing (cf. DEEP *a.* IV. c).

1925 *Forging, Stamping, Heat Treating* XI. 427 The importance of selecting the proper stock for deep drawn shells. **1926** *Jrnl. Iron & Steel Inst.* CXIII. 589 The manufacture of deep-drawn cylinders. **1959** *Motor Manual* (ed. 36) i. 7 The sheet is not pushed into the die by the punch, but is stretched into it, which is why the type of sheet steel known as deep drawn must be used.

deepen ('di:p(ə)n), *v.* [Like most verbs in *-en*, a comparatively modern formation from DEEP *a.*, taking the place of the earlier DEEP *v.* See -EN[5].]

1. *trans.* To make deep or deeper (in various senses); to increase the depth of.

a **1605** STOW *Q. Eliz.* an. 1601 (R.) He..heightened the ditches, deepened the trenches. **1612** PEACHAM *Gentl. Exerc.* xxiii. 80 You must deepen your colours so that the Orpiment may be the highest. **1665** HOOKE *Microgr.* 75 Nor will the Blues be diluted or deepened after the manner I speak of. **1785** J. PHILLIPS *Treat. Inland Navig.* 45 To widen and deepen the River Stort. **1858** *Merc. Marine Mag.* V. 226 The ship will have passed the shoal and deepened her water to 9 fathoms. **1870** RUSKIN *Lect. Art* ii. (1875) 43 Means of deepening and confirming your convictions.

2. *intr.* To become deep or deeper.

1699 DAMPIER *Voy. New Holland* (R.), The water deepned and sholdned so very gently. **1774** GOLDSM. *Nat. Hist.* (1776) II. 234 We shall find..the shades gradually to deepen. **1801** CAMPBELL *Hohenlinden*, The combat deepens. **1838** T. THOMSON *Chem. Org. Bodies* 851 The colour gradually deepens by exposure to the air. **1863** GEO. ELIOT *Romola* I. xx, The evening had deepened into struggling starlight.

deepened ('di:p(ə)nd), *ppl. a.* [f. prec. + -ED[1].] Made deep or deeper: see DEEPEN 1.

1598 CHAPMAN *Iliad* I. 418 In the ocean's deepen'd breast. **1873** TRISTRAM *Moab* Pref. 4 Read with deepened interest.

deepener ('di:p(ə)nə(r)). [f. as prec. + -ER[1].] One who or that which deepens.

1823 *Blackw. Mag.* XIV. 487 A deepener of her sorrows. **1845–6** TRENCH *Huls. Lect.* Ser. II. ii. 168 The deepener of the curse.

deepening ('di:p(ə)nɪŋ), *vbl. sb.* [-ING[1].]

1. The action of the verb DEEPEN, q.v.

1785 J. PHILLIPS *Treat. Inland Navig.* 45 The cleansing and deepening would be exactly the same..expence. **1802** PLAYFAIR *Illustr. Hutton. Th.* 360 The draining off of the water, by the deepening of the outlet. **1884** *Athenæum* 1 Nov. 558/1 The gradual deepening of the mystery.

attrib. **1767** *Specif. Downes' Patent* No. 872 A certain instrument or tool called a deepening tool.

†**2.** *Painting.* The process of intensifying colour or shadow; a shaded part of a picture. *Obs.*

1622 PEACHAM *Compl. Gent.* 114 White Lead for the heightning, and Smalt for your deepning, or darkest shadow. **1638** JUNIUS *Painting of Anc.* 275 To adde unto their workes some shadowes and deepnings. **1669** A. BROWNE *Ars Pict.* (1675) 84 The strong touches and deepnings.

3. A depression in a surface.

1859 R. F. BURTON *Centr. Afr.* in *Jrnl. Geog. Soc.* XXIX. 314 The bridge of the nose is..not without a deepening in the interorbital portion. **1880** J. CAIRD *Philos. Relig.* vii. 192 Dints, marks, spatial deepenings and elevations.

'deepening, *ppl. a.* [-ING[2].] That deepens; becoming deep or deeper: see DEEPEN 2.

1762 FALCONER *Shipwr.* I. (R.), Ere yet the deepening incidents prevail. **1791** MRS. RADCLIFFE *Rom. Forest* ii, The deepening gloom. **1867** MISS BRADDON *Aur. Floyd* i. 5 Against the deepening crimson of the sky.

Hence **'deepeningly** *adv.*

1878 GROSART in *H. More's Poems*, Introd. 19/2 The same impression is inevitable in reading More..and deepeningly as you ponder his Poetry.

deep-fetched, †**-fet** ('di:p,fɛtʃt, -,fɛt), *ppl. a.* [DEEP *adv.* 3.] Fetched from deep in the bosom, or from far below the surface of things; far-fetched.

1562 COOPER *Answ. Priv. Masse* (1850) 130 O profound and deep-fetched reason. **1593** SHAKS. *2 Hen. VI*, II. iv. 33 To see my teares, and heare my deepe-fet groanes. **1604** *Meeting of Gallants* 20 Vomiting out some two or three deepe-fetch Oaths. *a* **1618** SYLVESTER *Panaretus* 465 And sending forth a deep-fet sigh. **1647** H. MORE *Poems, Resolution* 109 By deep-fetchd sighs and pure devotion. **1708** OZELL tr. *Boileau's Lutrin* 10 With deep fetch'd Bellowings the noble Beast Exhales his Spirits.

deep-freeze, deep freeze. orig. *U.S.* [f. DEEP *a.* + FREEZE *sb.*[1]] **1.** (Written *Deep-freeze.*) The registered American trade-name of a type of refrigerator capable of rapid freezing. Hence, a refrigerator or process in which food can be quickly frozen and stored almost indefinitely at a very low temperature. Also *attrib.*

1941 *Official Gaz. U.S. Pat. Off.* 8 July 260/2 *Deepfreeze.* For Refrigerating Apparatus and Parts Thereof. **1942** *Science Illustr.* Mar. 3/1 The Deepfreeze home locker looks like an up-ended white enameled barrel with an encased compressor housing at its side. **1951** *Good Housek. Home Encycl.* 218/1 'Polythene'..is particularly suitable for deep-freeze and quick-frozen foods. *Ibid.* 473/2 A refrigerator with a special deep-freeze compartment. **1957** W. H. WHYTE *Organization Man* 250 The chickens are stacked high in the deep freeze. **1958** *Sunday Times* 27 Apr. 22/6 The housewife with a deep freeze can keep them for six months. **1969** *News of World* 23 Nov. 9/5 They paid a deposit on a deep-freeze but then heard nothing more.

2. *transf.* and *fig.* 'Cold storage'; suspension of activity; suspended animation. Also *attrib.*

1949 L. C. WROTH in C. F. Bühler et al. *Standards of Bibliogr. Description* 114 Most historians won't bother. They are not interested in bibliography. For all that they may do about it, the meat will lie in the deep-freeze compartment until the end of time. **1950** *N.Y. Times Bk. Rev.* 8 Oct. 3/1 This can never be reprinted too often; it is a classic of deep-freeze. **1951** I. SHAW *Troubled Air* iv. 84 You must have led your life in deep freeze for the last twenty years. **1952** *Birmingham* (Ala.) *News* 6 May 26/3 A Swedish doctor has predicted that 'deep freeze' operations on human beings may not be far off. He said this is a technique in which heart action is purposely stopped by lowering the body temperature. **1957** *Daily Mail* 26 Sept. 9/5 The 'deep-freeze' girl who lay in a coma for 14 weeks. **1958** *Spectator* 6 June 722/1 It [*sc.* a suburb] is not alive either, of course; perhaps suspended animation is the best description, a kind of socio-economic deep freeze.

deep-freeze, *v.* orig. *U.S.* [f. prec.] *trans.* To subject to a deep-freeze process; to refrigerate; also *transf.* and *fig.* So **deep-freezer**, a deep-freeze; **deep-freezing** *vbl. sb.*; **deep-frozen** *ppl. a.*

1949 *Time* 18 July 34/1 Helen Hayes stuck a hand into her deep freezer. **1951** *Good Housek. Home Encycl.* 63/1 Deep freezer. *Ibid.* 438/1 Most fruits are suitable for deep freezing. **1953** A. HUXLEY *Let.* 8 Dec. (1969) 689 The product is deep-frozen the moment it leaves the pod. **1956** *Sci. News Let.* 3 Nov. 279/2 Deep-frozen shrimps from India may soon be making an appearance on dining tables in the United States. **1957** 'B. BUCKINGHAM' *Boiled Alive* xxxiii. 249 If the cook deep-froze the body, he knew about the murder. **1959** *Listener* 5 Feb. 263/2 We all know the deep-frozen expert from the one who is humanly concerned to put something across. **1959** *Observer* 15 Mar. 16/3 Why should Gilbert and Sullivan be specially exempt?.. Perpetuity would deep-freeze them as well. **1959** *Woman* 2 May 33/1 With deep freezing and modern refrigerated transport, fish doesn't depend on the season nearly as much as it used to. **1970** *Daily Tel.* 28 Apr. 17 Leading manufacturers of refrigerators and deep-freezers..are producing space-saving models which are ideal for our small British kitchens. **1971** *Ibid.* 25 Jan. 10 No doubt these arguments are today accepted by all but a few deep-frozen ideologues on Labour's Left wing.

deepie ('di:pɪ). *colloq.* [f. DEEP *a.* + *-ie*, as in TALKIE.] A three-dimensional cinematographic or television film.

1953 DILYS POWELL in *Sunday Times* 8 Feb. 9/7 Twentieth-Century Fox..has announced that all its important films are now to be what I will venture to call deepies. **1954** *Britannica Bk. of Year* 637/2 The normal kind of film was called a flat or flattie, the three-dimensional a deepie. **1966** *T.V. Times* (Australia) 7 Dec. 10/2 Three-D television is now the subject of experiment... This week, I discussed the future of 'deepies' with Mr B. Brownless.

deeping ('di:pɪŋ). [f. DEEP *v.* + -ING[1].] Each of the sections (a fathom deep) of which a fishing-net is composed.

1615 E. S. *Britain's Buss* in Arb. *Garner* III. 629 Each net must be in depth seven deepings. Each deeping must be a fathom, that is two yards, deep. **1879** E. ROBERTSON in *Encycl. Brit.* IX. 251/2 They [twine drift-nets] are..netted by hand, and are made in narrower pieces called deepings, which are laced together one below the other to make up the required depth.

deepish ('di:pɪʃ), *a.* [f. DEEP *a.* + -ISH[1].] Somewhat or rather deep.

1878 I. L. BIRD *Lady's Life Rocky Mountains* (1879) 197 We crossed a deepish stream on the ice. **1920** *Blackw. Mag.* July 86/2 It's only a deepish scratch. **1925** A. S. M. HUTCHINSON *One Increasing Purpose* I. xx. 128 Rather, rather deepish things. **1926** *Spectator* 6 Mar. 408/2 The Government was now in deepish water. **1959** *Times* 27 May 5/2 Dixon was caught at deepish mid-off.

deep-laid ('di:p,leɪd), *ppl. a.* [DEEP *adv.* 3.] Deeply laid; planned with profound cunning.

1768–74 TUCKER *Lt. Nat.* (1852) II. 104 Any deep-laid scheme or fine spun artifice. **1783** *Miss Baltimores* I. 74 He is a deep-laid villain after women. **1846** GROTE *Greece* I. xv. (1862) I. 241 The deep-laid designs of Zeus. **1869** TROLLOPE *He Knew* xxiii. (1878) 130 He himself had had no very deep-laid scheme in his addresses to Colonel Osborne.

deeply (di:plɪ), *adv.* Also dep-, depe-, diepe-, -lie. [OE. *díoplíce*, *déoplíce*, adv. f. *déoplíc* adj., deriv. of *déop*, DEEP: see -LY[2].]

1. To a great or considerable depth; far downwards, inwards, etc. (See 7.)

a **1400–50** *Alexander* 1396 (Dubl. MS.) Þai..Dryves dartez at owr dukez deply þaim wounden. **1573** TUSSER *Husb.* xlviii. (1878) 104 Three poles to a hillock..set deeplie and strong. **1594** HOOKER *Eccl. Pol.* I. i. (1611) 2 Preiudices deepely rooted in the hearts of men. **1597** GERARDE *Herbal* I. xliv. (1633), They..who have deepliest waded in this sea of simples. **1627** MAY *Lucan* VII. 725 All people there Are deeplyer wounded than our age can beare. **1707** SLOANE *Jamaica* I. 96 The leaves were thinner, deeplier, and more regularly cut. *a* **1717** PARNELL *Gift of Poetry* (R.), I..sink in deep affliction, deeply down. **1845** M. PATTISON *Ess.* (1889) I. 3 It is a tendency deeply seated in the mind of our age. **1860** TYNDALL *Glac.* I. xvi. 118 The glacier was deeply fissured.

b. In reference to drinking; also to sighing. (Here other notions than the literal enter in.)

1557 N. T. (Genev.) *Mark* viii. 12 Then he syghed diepely in his spirite. **1695** LD. PRESTON *Boeth.* IV. 176 They deeply tasted of th' infected Bowl. **1697** DRYDEN *Virg. Georg.* III. 610 When the Kids their Dams too deeply drain. **1813** SCOTT *Rokeby* I. vi, Deeply he drank, and fiercely fed.

2. *fig.* With deep thought, insight, knowledge, etc.; profoundly, thoroughly.

c **888** K. ÆLFRED *Boeth.* xxxv. §1 Swa hwa swa wille dioplice spiriȝan æfter ryhte. *c* **1000** ÆLFRIC *Colloquy* (Wright's *Vocab.* 12), þearle deoplice [þu] spricst. *a* **1225** *Ancr. R.* 154 Isaac..uorto þenchen deoplic[h]e souhte onlich stude. *c* **1400** MAUNDEV. (1839) xiii. 144 He preched & spak so depely of Dyvynyty. **1523** *Act 14–15 Hen. VIII* c. 5 Persons..lerned, and depely studied in Phisicke. **1561** T. NORTON *Calvin's Inst.* III. 329 To search depelier of vnknowen things. **1605** SHAKS. *Macb.* II. ii. 30 Consider it not so deeply. **1798** FERRIAR *Illustr. Sterne* ii. 35 He was deeply read in Beroalde. **1875** JOWETT *Plato* (ed. 2) IV. 22, I should like to consider the matter a little more deeply.

b. With profound craft, subtlety, or cunning.

1596 SHAKS. *Tam. Shr.* IV. iv. 42 Both dissemble deepely their affections. **1617** FLETCHER *Valentinian* v. vi, Either you love too dearly, Or deeply you dissemble. *Mod.* The plot was deeply laid, but it has been discovered.

†**3.** With deep seriousness, solemnly. *Obs.*

c **1300** *Havelok* 1417 Deplike dede he him swere. *a* **1400–50** *Alexander* 1186 þat me was done many day depely to swere. ? **1503** *Plumpton Corr.* p. lxiv, And, yf nede be, depely depose afore the Kynge & hys counsell, that yt is matter of trawth. **1513** BRADSHAW *St. Werburge* I. 2881 Charged full depely Theyr offyce to execute. **1600** J. PORY tr. *Leo's Africa* II. 22 And this I dare most deeply take mine oath on. **1602** SHAKS. *Ham.* III. ii. 234 'Tis deepely sworne. **1671** H. M. *Erasm. Colloq.* 401 Even when he had deeply sworn to it.

4. Gravely, seriously, heavily; *esp.* in reference to being involved in guilt, liability, obligation, or the like.

1382 WYCLIF *Hos.* ix. 9 Thei synneden depely. **1576** FLEMING *Panopl. Epist.* 343 F. G. who is so deepely in your bookes of accountes. **1586** *Let. Earl Leycester* 13 For which I count my selfe the deeplyest bounde to give him my humblest thankes. **1601** R. JOHNSON *Kingd. & Commw.* (1603) 17 Henry..left the kingdome deeply indebted. **1621** SANDERSON *12 Serm.* (1632) 51 And stoutly maintaine Gods truth, when it is deepeliest slandered. **1700** S. L. tr. *C. Fryke's Voy.* 76 Now the other Buffel was deeply engaged too. **1848** MACAULAY *Hist. Eng.* I. 658 Of all the enemies of the government he was..the most deeply criminal. **1883** FROUDE *Short Stud.* IV. I. ix. 103 The archbishop had committed himself so deeply that he could not afford to wait.

†**b.** In reference to fines: Heavily. *Obs.*

1631 *Star Chamb. Cases* (Camden) 36 If it had not been that this man hath suffered as he hath I should have sentenced him deepely. **1655** FULLER *Ch. Hist.* IX. vii. §20 The Starr-Chamber deeply fined S[r]. Richard Knightly..for entertaining and receiving the Press Gentelmen.

5. With deep feeling, emotion, etc.; in a high degree, profoundly, intensely, extremely.

a **1400–50** *Alexander* 1673 Sire, þis I depely disire, durst I it neuyn. *Ibid.* 1698 Summe..depely þam playnt Quat.. euill þai suffird. **1568** GRAFTON *Chron.* II. 111 With them the sayd Pope had bene so depely offended. **1611** SHAKS. *Wint. T.* II. iii. 14 He straight declin'd, droop'd, tooke it deeply. **1634** SIR T. HERBERT *Trav.* 120 They curst him deeply. **1781** COWPER *Hope* 333 His soul abhors a mercenary thought, And him as deeply who abhors it not. **1851** DIXON *W. Penn* xv. (1872) 131 All this was deeply interesting to Penn. **1857** BUCKLE *Civiliz.* I. xiv. 850 Of these shortcomings I am deeply sensible.

6. Of physical states or qualities: **a.** Profoundly, soundly, with complete absorption of the faculties. **b.** With deep colour, intensely. **c.** With a deep, grave, or sonorous voice.

1632 J. HAYWARD tr. *Biondi's Eromena* 122 Deeply plunged in a profound sleepe. **1695** BLACKMORE *Pr. Arth.* III. 706 Some deeply Red, and others faintly Blue. **1820** SHELLEY *Vision of Sea* 77 Smile not, my child, But sleep deeply and sweetly. *a* **1845** HOOD *Ruth* ii, On her cheek an autumn flush Deeply ripened. **1883** *Harper's Mag.* Nov. 948/2 A pack of hounds came..baying deeply.

7. *Comb. Deeply* (mostly in sense 1) qualifying a pple. is now usually hyphened when the pple. is used attributively, preceding its sb., but not when it follows; as 'the leaf is deeply serrated', 'a deeply-serrated leaf'.

1816 J. SCOTT *Visit Paris* Pref. 35 Deeply-bottomed bravery. **1854** J. S. C. ABBOTT *Napoleon* (1855) I. xxvii. 424 Deeply-rooted popular prejudices. **1865** HOWELLS *Venet. Life* xix. 295 That deeply-serrated block of steel. **1879** SIR G. SCOTT *Lect. Archit.* I. 166 Lofty and deeply-receding jambs.

'deepmost, *a.* (*superl.*) *rare.* [f. DEEP *a.* + -MOST. Cf. *topmost*, *inmost*, etc.] Deepest.

1810 SCOTT *Lady of L.* II. xx, From her deepmost glen. **1841** LADY F. HASTINGS *Poems* 233 Shout, echo! from thy deepmost cell.

deep-mouthed ('di:pmaʊðd, -maʊθt), *a.* [f. *deep mouth* + -ED[2].]

1. Having a deep or sonorous voice: *esp.* of dogs.

1595 SHAKS. *John* v. ii. 173 And mocke the deepe mouth'd Thunder. **1599** —— *Hen. V*, v. Prol. 11 Out-voyce the deep-mouth'd Sea. **1662** DRYDEN *Wild Gallant* III. i, A Serenade of deep-mouth'd Currs. **1696** *Lond. Gaz.* No. 3204/4 A Pack of deep mouth'd Hounds to be sold. **1725** POPE *Odyss* XIX. 504 Parnassus..With deep-mouthed hounds the hunter-troop invades. **1818** BYRON *Juan* I. cxxiii, 'Tis sweet to hear the watch-dog's honest bark Bay deep-mouth'd welcome. **1842** S. LOVER *Handy Andy* ii, The sound..awoke the deep-mouthed dogs around the house.

2. *lit.* Having a deep or capacious mouth. *rare.*

1844 MRS. BROWNING *Wine of Cyprus* ii, Some deep-mouthed Greek exemplar Would become your Cyprus wine.

deepness (diːpnɪs). Now *rare*; displaced by DEPTH. Forms: see DEEP *a.*, and -NESS; in ME. 4-5 depnes(se. [OE. *díopnes, déopnes*, f. *déop* DEEP: see -NESS.]

1. The quality of being deep, or of considerable extension or distance downwards, or inwards; depth.

1382 WYCLIF *Matt.* xiii. 5 For thei hadde nat depnesse of erthe. *c* **1400** *Lanfranc's Cirurg.* 89 þouȝ þat þei acorden togidere in depnes & in streitnesse of þe mouþ. **1530** PALSGR. 213/1 Depnesse of any thyng, *profundité*. **1653** H. COGAN tr. *Pinto's Trav.* XLII. 169 A river..which for the bredth and deepness of it is frequented with much shipping. **1765** A. DICKSON *Treat. Agric.* (ed. 2) 121 Seeds, many of which, from their deepness in the earth, will not vegetate. **1823** SCOTT *Peveril* iv, The deepness of his obeisance.

†**b.** Of ground or roads: cf. DEEP *a.* 5. *Obs.*

1603 KNOLLES (J.), By reason of the deepness of the way and heaviness of the great ordnance. **1632** LITHGOW *Trav.* vi. 292 The deepnesse of the Way. **1780** *Impart. Hist. War Amer.* 240 [The troops] had suffered excessively from the severity of the climate, the deepness of the roads.

2. Measurement or dimension downwards, inwards, or through; depth.

c **1330** R. BRUNNE *Chron. Wace* (Rolls) 10, 312 Fyue fot hit haþ of depnes. **1413** LYDG. *Pilgr. Sowle* v. xiv. (1483) 107 Ther is no body parfit withouten thre dymensions that is breede lengthe and depnesse. **1551** RECORDE *Pathw. Knowl.* I. Defin., As I take it here, the depenesse of his bodie is his thicknesse in the sides. **1665** SIR T. HERBERT *Trav.* (1677) 252 The deepness of the Sea usually answers to the height of Mountains. **1703** MAUNDRELL *Journ. Jerus.* (1732) 138 In deepness they were four yards each.

3. *fig.* Of thought, knowledge, etc.: Depth; penetration; profundity.

a **1000** *Hymns* iii. 33 (Gr.) Swa þæt ænig ne wat eorðbuendra ða deopnesse Drihtnes mihta. *a* **1225** *Leg. Kath.* 980 þis is nu þe derfschipe of þi dusi onsware, and te deopnesse. **1340** *Ayenb.* 105 þe dyepnesse of his zoþhede. *c* **1440** *Secrees* 127 þe clernesse of ȝoure wyt & þe depnesse of ȝoure conynge passys all men. **1548-77** VICARY *Anat.* Ep. Ded. (1888) 7 We who..practise in Surgerie, according to the deepnes of the Arte. **1653** MANTON *Exp. James* i. 25 Deepness of Meditation. *a* **1720** SHEFFIELD (Dk. Buckhm.) *Wks.* (1753) I. 271 Deepness of thought.

†**b.** In bad sense: Deep cunning or subtlety.

1526 TINDALE *Rev.* ii. 24 Vnto you..which have not knowen the depnes of Satan. **1646** J. GREGORY *Notes & Obs.* xxvi. (T.), The greatest deepness of Satan.

4. Of moral qualities, feelings, etc.: Depth, intensity; gravity.

c **1175** *Lamb. Hom.* 49 þes put bitacneð deopnesse of sunne. *a* **1533** LD. BERNERS *Gold. Bk. M. Aurel.* (1546) H vi, The depenesse of good wylles ought to be wonne with the depnes of the hearte. **1632** LITHGOW *Trav.* III. 114 In the deepnesse of sorrow.

5. Of physical qualities, etc.: **a.** Of sound: Sonorousness, or lowness of pitch. **b.** Of colour, etc.: Intensity.

1626 BACON *Sylva* §852 Heat also dilateth the Pipes, and Organs, which causeth the Deepnesse of the Voice. **1684** R. H. *School Recreat.* 11 For Deepness of Cry, the largest Dogs having the greatest mouths. **1711** BUDGELL *Spect.* No. 116 ¶3 These [hounds]..by the Deepness of their Mouths and the Variety of their Notes. **1822** SCOTT *Pirate* xx, Her glowing cheek..in the deepness of its crimson.

†**6.** *concr.* A deep place or cavity, an abyss; a deep part of the sea, etc. *Obs.*

a **1000** *Lamb. Ps.* lxviii. 3 (Bosw.) Ic com on deopnysse sæ. *c* **1000** *Gosp. Nicod.* 24 (Bosw.) On ðære hellican deopnysse. *a* **1300** *E.E. Psalter* lxviii. 16 Ne ouerswelyhe me depenes. **1382** WYCLIF *Ps.* cxlviii. 7 Dragonnes, and alle depnessis. *c* **1440** *Promp. Parv.* 118 Depenesse of watur, *gurges*. **1450-1530** *Myrr. our Ladye* 203 In heuen & in erthe & in see and in all depnesses. **1502** *Ord. Crysten Men* (W. de W. 1506) I. ii. 10 The destruccyon and the fallynge into depnes of al the townes, castelles and cytees of yᵉ world.

†**b.** *fig.* A depth of thought, feeling, or being.

1340 *Ayenb.* 211 þe bene þet comþ of þe dyepnesse of þe herte. **1535** COVERDALE *1 Cor.* ii. 10 All thinges yee euen the depenesses of the Godhead. **1549** *Compl. Scot.* i. 21 The iugement of gode..is ane profound onknauen deipnes.

deep-read (ˈdiːpˈrɛd), *ppl. a.* [DEEP *adv.* 3.] Deeply read; skilled by profound reading.

1639 MASSINGER *Unnat. Combat* IV. i, A deep-read man. **1790** BURNS *The Whistle* vi, Gallant Sir Robert, deep-read in old wines. **1822** T. MITCHELL *Aristoph.* II. 286 Great scholars, Deep-read—full to a plethora with knowledge.

deep-rooted (diːp,ruːtɪd), *a.* [DEEP *adv.* 3.] Deeply rooted or implanted; chiefly *fig.*, of feelings, opinions, prejudices, etc.

1669 WOODHEAD *St. Teresa* II. xxxiv. 228 Where Vertue is deep-rooted, occasions work little upon them. **1672** OTWAY *Titus & B.* I. ii, So long establish'd and deep-rooted Love. **1834** PRINGLE *African Sk.* x. 314 The Governor's jealousy..was too deep-rooted. **1871** MORLEY *Voltaire* (1886) 70 A deep-rooted reverence for truth.

Hence **deep-ˈrootedness.**

1860 PUSEY *Min. Proph.* 90 The strength and deeprootedness of the soul in grace.

deep sea, deep-sea. Also 7 dipsie, dipsy. The deeper part of the sea or ocean at a distance from the shore. Used *attrib.* or as *adj.*: Of or belonging to the deep sea.

deep-sea lead, line, a head and line used for soundings in deep water. *deep-sea fisheries*, fisheries prosecuted at a distance from land, in which the fishermen are absent from home for a lengthened period.

1626 CAPT. SMITH *Accid. Yng. Seamen* 29 Heaue the lead, try the dipsie line. **1627** —— *Seaman's Gram.* ix. 43 The Dipsie line..is a small line some hundred and fifty fadome long, with a long plummet at the end..which is first marked at twenty fadome, and after increased by tens to the end. **1698** FRYER *Acc. E. India* 13 Heaving our Dipsy-lead we were in soundings eighty Fathom depth. **1769** FALCONER *Dict. Marine* (1789), *Sonder*, to sound: to heave the hand-lead, or deep-sea-lead. **1835** SIR J. ROSS *Narr. 2nd Voy.* iv. 55 We now sounded with the deepsea lead every two hours. **1853** HERSCHEL *Pop. Lect. Sc.* ii. §2 (1873) 48 Among deep-sea fishes. **1875** J. H. BENNET *Winter Medit.* I. v. 128 The pioneer of deep-sea dredging, the late Edward Forbes. **1880** WYVILLE THOMSON in *Rep. Challenger Exp. Zool.* I. 50 Faunæ which have successively occupied the same deep-sea. **1887** E. J. MATHER (*title*), Nor'ard of the Dogger: the story of..the Mission to Deep Sea Fishermen.

deep-searching (ˈdiːpˈsɜːtʃɪŋ), *ppl. a.* [DEEP *adv.* 3.] That searches or penetrates deeply.

1599 MARSTON *Sco. Villanie* I. i. 174 O for some deep-searching Corycean. *a* **1643** W. CARTWRIGHT *Ordinary* II. iii, He's nois'd about for a deep-searching head. **1844** MARG. FULLER *Wom. 19th C.* (1862) 19 The only sermons of a persuasive and deep-searching influence.

deep-seated (ˈdiːp,siːtɪd), *a.* [DEEP *adv.* 3.] Having its seat far beneath the surface.

1741 MONRO *Anat.* (ed. 3) 5 The deep-seated kind of *Paronychia*. **1813** J. THOMSON *Lect. Inflam.* 375 A deep-seated abscess. **1878** HUXLEY *Physiogr.* 190 The conversion into steam of water which..obtains access to the deep-seated molten rocks.

fig. **1847** GROTE *Greece* II. xliv. (1862) IV. 13 Causes, deep-seated as well as various. **1887** JESSOPP *Arcady* ii. 35 The deep-seated faith in charms and occult lore.

†**ˈdeep-seen,** *a. Obs.* [DEEP *adv.* 3.] That sees or has seen deeply into things.

1597-8 BP. HALL *Sat.* IV. i. 170 Some nose-wise pedant..whose deepe-sene skil Hath three times construed either Flaccus ore.

deep-set (ˈdiːp,sɛt), *ppl. a.* [DEEP *adv.* 3.] Deeply set.

1832 TENNYSON *Palace of Art* xiii, The deep-set windows, stain'd and traced. **1877** BLACK *Green Past.* iv. (1878) 28 Deep-set keen grey eyes.

†**ˈdeepship.** *Obs. rare*$^{-1}$. In 3 deopschipe. [f. DEEP *a.* + -SHIP.] Depth, profound mystery.

a **1225** *Leg. Kath.* 1341 Ha [= she] Crist cleopede..and schawde seoððen suteliche þe deopschipe and te derne run of his deað on rode.

deepsome (ˈdiːpsəm), *a. poetic. rare.* [f. DEEP *a.* or *sb.* + -SOME. Cf. *darksome, gladsome.*] Having deepness or depths; more or less deep.

1615 CHAPMAN *Odyss.* IV. 769 He dived the deepsome watery heaps. **1855** SINGLETON *Virgil* I. 133 The hollow vales are filled And deepsome glades. *Ibid.* I. 218 He plunged him with a bound Into the deepsome sea.

deep-waterman (,diːpˈwɔːtəmən). [f. *deep water* + MAN *sb.*[1]] A sea-going vessel as opposed to a coaster.

1906 *Daily Chron.* 21 Mar. 6/4 Owners, not of 'deep-watermen' only, but of coasting craft as well. **1909** *Ibid.* 13 Aug. 3/1 What of the hundreds of fine deep-water men that still fly the Red Ensign? **1924** R. CLEMENTS *Gipsy of Horn* 57 This..constitutes the time-honoured decoration of a deep-waterman.

deer (dɪə(r)). Forms: 1 díor, déor, 2-3 deor, (2 dær), 2-4 der, (2-3 dor, 3 dier, 3-4 duer, 4 dur, 5 dure, deure), 4-6 dere, (4-7 deere, 5, 7 diere, 5- (*Sc.*) deir, 6-7 deare), 4- deer, (5 theer). *Pl.* 1-9 normally same as sing.; also 2 deore, deoran, 2-3 -en; 3-4 deores, dueres, 7-9 *occas.* deers. [A Comm. Teut. sb.: OE. *dior, déor* = OS. *dier*, OFris. *diar, dier* (MDu. and Du. and LG. *dier*), OHG. *tior* (MHG. *tier*, Ger. *tier, thier*):—WG. *dior*, ON. **djúr* (Icel. *dýr*, Sw. *djur*, Da. *dyr*); Goth. *dius, diuz-*:— OTeut. *deuzo*^{m}:—pre-Teut. *dheu'som.*

Generally referred to a root *dhus* to breathe (cf. *animal* from *anima*), and thought by some etymologists to be the neuter of an adj. used subst. Cf. DEAR *a.*[2]. (Not connected with Gr. θήρ wild beast.)]

†**1.** A beast: usually a quadruped, as distinguished from birds and fishes; but sometimes, like *beast*, applied to animals of lower orders. *Obs.*

c **950** *Lindisf. Gosp.* Luke xviii. 25 Se camal þæt micla dear. *a* **1000** *Boeth. Metr.* xxvii. 24 Swa swa fugl oððe dior. *c* **1000** ÆLFRIC *Voc.* in Wr.-Wülcker 118/31 *Fera*, wild deor. *Bellua*, reðe deor..*Unicornis*, anhyrne deor. **1154** *O.E. Chron.* (Laud MS.) an. 1135 Pais he makede men & dær. *c* **1200** ORMIN 1176 Shep iss..stille der. *Ibid.* 1312 Lamb iss sofFte & stille deor. *a* **1250** *Owl & Night.* 1321 Al swo deth mani dor and man. *c* **1250** *Gen. & Ex.* 4025 Also leun is miȝtful der. **1481** CAXTON *Reynard* (Arb.) 18 The rybaud and the felle diere here I se hym comen.

β. plural.

c **1000** ÆLFRIC *Gen.* i. 25 And he siȝ ofer þa deor. *c* **1175** *Lamb. Hom.* 43 Innan þan ilke sea weren un-aneomned deor, summe feðerfotetd, summe al bute fet. *Ibid.* 115 þene bið his erd ihened..on wilde deoran. *c* **1200** *Trin. Coll. Hom.* 177 Oref, and deor, and fishshes, and fugeles. *Ibid.* 209 Hie habbeð geres after wilde deore. *Ibid.* 224 Of wilde diere. *c* **1250** *Gen. & Ex.* 4020 On ilc brend eft twin der. *Ibid.* 4032 Efte he sacrede deres mor. *a* **1310** in Wright *Lyric P.* xiii. 44 Deores with huere derne rounes. *Ibid.* xiv. 45 In dounes with this dueres plawes. *c* **1340** *Gaw. & Gr. Kt.* 1151 Der drof in þe dale..bot heterly þay were Restayed with þe stablye.

2. a. The general name of a family (*Cervidæ*) of ruminant quadrupeds, distinguished by the possession of deciduous branching horns or antlers, and by the presence of spots on the young: the various genera and species being distinguished as ***rein-deer, moose-deer, red deer, fallow deer***; the MUSK DEER belong to a different family, *Moschidæ*.

A specific application of the word, which occurs in OE. only contextually, but became distinct in the ME. period, and by its close remained as the usual sense.

[*c* **893** K. ÆLFRED *Oros.* I. i. (Sw.) 18 He [Ohthere] hæfde þa ȝyt ða he þone cyningc sohte, tamra deora unbebohtra syx hund. þa deor hi hatað hranas.] *a* **1131** [see *der fald* in 4]. *c* **1205** LAY. 2586 To huntien after deoren [*c* **1275** after deores]. **1297** R. GLOUC. (Rolls) 9047 He let [make] þe parc of Wodestoke, & der þer inne do. *c* **1325** *Song on Passion* 59 (*O.E. Misc.*) He was todrawe so dur islawe in chace. **1375** BARBOUR *Bruce* VII. 497 [He] went..to purchase venysoun, For than the deir war in sesoun. *c* **1420** *Anturs of Arth.* (Camden) iv, Thay felle to the female dure, feyful thyk fold. **1464** *Mann. & Househ. Exp.* 195 A payr bregandery cueryd wyth whyte deris leder. **1470-85** MALORY *Arthur* x. lxi, He chaced at the reed dere. **1538** STARKEY *England* I. iii. 98 A dere louyth a lene barren..ground. **1601** SHAKS. *Jul. C.* III. i. 209 Like a Deere, strocken by many Princes. **1611** CORYAT *Crudities* 10 A goodly Parke..wherein there is Deere. **1774** GOLDSM. *Nat. Hist.* (1776) III. 80 An hog, an ox, a goat, or a deer. **1855** LONGF. *Hiaw.* III. 169 Where the red deer herd together.

b. occasional plural *deers.*

c **1275** [see **1205** in prec.]. **1674** N. COX *Gentl. Recreat.* II. (1677) 58 The reasons why Harts and Deers do lose their Horns yearly. **1769** HOME *Fatal Discov.* III, Stretch'd on the skins of deers. *c* **1817** HOGG *Tales & Sk.* II. 89 The place of rendezvous, to which the deers were to be driven.

†**c.** *deer of ten*: a stag of ten, i.e. one having ten points or tines on his horns; an adult stag of five years at least, and therefore 'warrantable' or fit to be hunted. *Obs.*

1631 MASSINGER *Emp. of East* IV. ii, He will make you royal sport, He is a deer Of ten, at the least.

3. ***small deer***: a phrase originally, and perhaps still by Shakspere, used in sense 1; but now humorously associated with sense 2.

14.. *Sir Beues* (1885) p. 74/2 (MS.C.) Ratons & myse and soche smale dere, That was hys mete that vii yere. **1605** SHAKS. *Lear* III. iv. 144 But Mice, and Rats, and such small Deare, Haue bin Toms food, for seuen long yeare. **1883** G. ALLEN in *Colin Clout's Calender* 14 Live mainly upon worms, slugs, and other hardy small deer.

transf. **1857** H. REED *Lect. Eng. Poets* x. II. 17 The small deer that were herded together by Johnson as the most eminent of English poets.

4. a. *attrib.* and *Comb.*, as ***deer bed, herd, -hide, -keeper, kind, life, -sinew, -snaring***, etc.; ***deer-like, deer-loved*** adjs. [Several already in OE., as *déor-fald* an enclosure or cage for wild beasts in the amphitheatre, or for beasts of the chase, a deer-park, *déor-edisc* deer-park, *déor-net* net for wild animals, etc.]

1835 W. IRVING *Tour Prairies* xi, The tall grass was pressed down into numerous *'deer beds', where those animals had couched. *a* **1000** *Ags. Gloss.* in Wr.-Wülcker 201 *Cauea, domus in theatro*, *deorfald. *a* **1131** *O.E. Chron.* an. 1123 Se king rad in his der fald [æt Wudestoke]. **1860** G. H. K. *Vac. Tour.* 123 Peaks..where the scattered remnants of the great *deer herds can repose in security. **1814** SCOTT *Ld. of Isles* III. xix, Goat-skins or *deer-hides o'er them cast. **1849** JAMES *Woodman* vii, I have got my *deer-keepers watching. **1875** LYELL *Princ. Geol.* II. III. xxxix. 359 Animals of the *deer kind. **1860** G. H. K. *Vac. Tour.* 122 The shepherds..see a good deal of *deer life. **1840** MRS. NORTON *Dream* 127 The dark, *deer-like eyes. **1876** GEO. ELIOT *Dan. Der.* IV. liv. 114 Deer-like shyness. **1831** LYTTON *Godolph.* 23 The *deer-loved fern. *c* **1000** ÆLFRIC *Voc.* in Wr.-Wülcker 167 *Cassis*, *deornet. **1856** KANE *Arct. Expl.* II. vii. 79 To walk up Mary River Ravine until we reach the *deer-plains. **1866** KINGSLEY *Herew.* I. vi. 178 Sea-bows of horn and *deer-sinew. **1862** S. ST. JOHN *Forests Far East* II. 34, I have been out *deer-snaring in this neighbourhood.

b. Special comb.: **deer-ball**, an underground fruit body of a fungus of the genus *Elaphomyces*; **deer-bleat** *U.S.*, an instrument serving to imitate the bleating of a deer; **deer-brush**, an American shrub in Arizona; **deer-cart**, the covered cart in which a tame stag to be hunted is carried to the meet; **deer-culler** *N.Z.* (see quot. 1947); so *deer-culling*; **deer-dog** = DEER-HOUND; **deer-drive**, a shooting expedition in which the deer are driven past the sportsman; so *deer-driving*; **deer-eyed** *a*, having eyes like deer, having soft or languid eyes; **deer-fence**, a high railing such as deer cannot leap over; **deer-flesh**, venison; **deer-fly**, any one of various flies which infest deer; also *attrib.*; **deer-forest**, a 'forest' or extensive track of unenclosed wild land reserved for deer; †**deer-goat**, an old name for the capriform or caprine antelopes; **deer-grass**, species of Rhexia (N.O. *Melastomaceæ*); **deer-horn**, (*a*) the material of a deer's horn; (*b*) *U.S.*, a large rough mussel of the Mississippi, *Trigonia* or *Unio verrucosa*, the shell of which is used for making buttons; **deer-leap**, a lower place in a hedge or fence where deer may leap; **deer-meat** = *deer-flesh*; **deer-neck**, a thin neck (of a horse) resembling a deer's; **deer-park**, a park in which deer are kept; †**deer-reeve**, a township officer in New England in the colonial days, whose duty it was to execute the laws as to deer; **deer-plain**, a plain inhabited by deer; **deer-saddle**, a saddle on which a slain deer is carried away; **deer's eye** = BUCK-EYE (the tree); **deer's foot** (*grass*), the fine grass *Agrostis setacea*; **deer's hair** = DEER-HAIR; **deer's milk**, a local name of the wood spurge, *Euphorbia amygdaloides*; **deer-stand** *U.S.*, a station for the shooters at a deer-drive; **deer's tongue, deer-tongue**, a N. American Cichoraceous plant, *Liatris odoratissima*; **deer-tiger**, the puma or cougar; **deer-track**, (*a*) the marks of a deer's passage; (*b*) a route habitually taken by deer; **deer-yard** *U.S.*, an open spot where deer herd, and where the ground is trodden by them.

[**1640** PARKINSON *Theat. Bot.* 1320 *Tubera cervina.* The Deares underground balles or Mushromes are another sort of these Tuberaes.] **1854** MAYNE *Expos. Lex.*, *Deer-Ball. **1866** LINDLEY & MOORE *Treas. Bot.*, *Deer balls*, a synonym of Hart's Truffles, Lycoperdon Nuts, and *Elaphomyces*. **1950** AINSWORTH & BISBY *Dict. Fungi* (ed. 3) 95 *Deer balls*, (Lycoperdon nuts or harts' truffles), *Elaphomyces* fruit bodies. **1852** MARCY & MCCLELLAN *Explor. Red River* 27 June (1853) vi. 50 The idea occurred to me of attempting to call them with a *deer-bleat, which one of the Delawares had made for me. **1883** W. H. BISHOP in *Harper's Mag.* Mar. 502/2 The '*deer brush' resembles horns. **1840** HOOD *Up the Rhine* 186 The hearse, very like a *deer-cart. **1947** P. NEWTON *Wayleggo* (1949) 153 **Deer cullers*, men who shoot deer professionally for the Government or an acclimatization society. **1965** M. SHADBOLT *Among Cinders* xxvi. 260 He was a deer-culler when he wasn't writing. **1959** —— *New Zealanders* 113 He went *deer-culling for a year. **1814** SCOTT *Ld. of Isles* v. xxiii, Many a *deer-dog howl'd around. **1834** W. A. CARRUTHERS *Kentuckian* II. 108 Would you put this clamjamfry against a *deer drive? **1882** *Society* 21 Oct. 19/1 Setting out for a deer-drive. **1860** G. H. K. *Vac. Tour.* 143 Mr. Scrope..was a great hand at *deer-driving. **1884** Q. VICTORIA *More Leaves* 14 The gate of the *deer-fence. *a* **1300** *Cursor M.* 3603 (Cott.) If þou me *dere flesse [*v.r.* venisun] ani gete. **1853** J. BENWELL *Travels* 127 Dusky-looking *deer-flies constantly alighted on our faces and hands. **1937** E. FRANCIS in *Public Health Reports* (U.S.) 22 Jan. 1 This name [*sc.* tularaemia] was given to the disease by the writer in 1920 after establishing the identity of ..'deer-fly fever' in man. **1950** A. P. HERBERT *Independent Member* 276 The discomforts and dangers we should have to face ashore in Labrador—including black-fly, mosquitoes, deer-fly and dogs. **1854** *Act 17-8 Vict.* c. 91 §42 Where such shootings or *deer forests are actually let. **1892** E. WESTON BELL *Scot. Deerhound* 80 Probably not more than twenty deer forests, recognized as such, were in existence prior to the beginning of the present century. **1607** TOPSELL *Four-f. Beasts* (1658) 93 Of the first kinde of Tragelaphvs which may be called a *Deer-goat. **1693** SIR T. P. BLOUNT *Nat. Hist.* 30 The Deer-Goat..being partly like a deer partly like a Goat. **1866** *Treas. Bot.* 972/2 Low perennial often bristly herbs, commonly called *Deer-grass, or Meadow-beauty, [with] large showy cymose flowers. **1843** 'R. CARLTON' *New Purchase* I. xvii. 122 A powder horn, and its loader of *deer-horn. **1880** *Encycl. Brit.* XII. 167/2 Deer-horn is almost exclusively used for handles by cutlers and walking-stick and umbrella makers. **1897** *Daily News* 1 Feb. 6/2 A saddle, probably Burgundian workmanship of 1400, composed of polished deer-horn plates. **1540-2** *Act 31 Hen. VIII*, c. 5 To make *dere leapes and breakes in the sayde hedges and fences. **1838** JAMES *Robber* i, In front appeared a *deer-park. **1860** G. H. K. *Vac. Tour.* 172 It is no light business to get our big stag..on the *deer saddle. **1762** J. CLAYTON *Flora Virginica* 57 *Æsculus floribus octandris* Linn... *Dear's Eye, and Bucks Eyes. **1835** J. H. INGRAHAM *South-West* II. 137 After a farther ride of a mile..we arrived at the '*deer-stand'. **1883** *Century Mag.* XXVI. 383 Among the lily-pads, *deer-tongue, and other aquatic plants. **1787** W. ATTMORE *Jrnl. Tour N. Carolina* (1922) 24 One part of the Company go into the Wood..to trail for the *Deer Tracks, and put the Dogs on the Scent. **1829** J. F. COOPER *Wish-ton-Wish* ix, Several times did I fall upon a maze of well-beaten deer-tracks, that as often led to nothing. **1859** J. CONWAY *Lett. from Highlands* 17 A pass, or deer-track, winding up through places apparently inaccessible. **1849** C. LANMAN *Lett. Alleghany Mts.* viii. 58, I discovered a large spot of bare earth, which I took to be a *deer-yard. **1880** *7th Rep. Surv. Adirondack Reg. N.Y.* 159 We reached an open forest plateau on the mountain, where we were surprised to find a 'deer-yard'. Here the deep snow was tramped down by deer into a broad central level area.

deer(e, obs. f. DEAR, and DERE *v.*, to injure.

deerberry ('dɪəˌbɛrɪ). A name given to the berry or succulent fruit of several North American procumbent shrubs or herbs, esp. of *Gaultheria procumbens* (N.O. *Ericaceæ*), commonly called Winter-green in U.S. Also of *Vaccinium stamineum*, also called Squaw Huckleberry, and *Mitchella repens* (N.O. *Cinchonaceæ*), a creeping herb, widely distributed in America. The name is also sometimes applied to the plants themselves.

1862 *Chambers' Encycl.* 649. **1866** *Treas. Bot.* 522 The berries [of *Gaultheria*] are known by various names, as Partridge-berry, Chequer-berry, Deer-berry, Tea-berry, Box-berry, and afford winter food to partridges, deer, and other animals.

'deer-ˌcoloured, *a.* Of the colour of a deer; tawny-red.

1611 COTGR., *Blond*..bright tawnie, or deer-coloured. **1688** *Lond. Gaz.* No. 2408/4 A brown Gelding [with].. Deer-coloured Haunches. **1746-7** MRS DELANY *Autobiog.* (1861) II. 447 A flowered silk..on a pale deer-coloured figured ground.

'deer-hair, deer's hair.

1. The hair of deer.

1494 *Act 11 Hen. VII*, c. 19 Cushions, stuffed with Horse hair..Deers-hair, and Goats-hair.

2. The common name in Scotland and north of England of a small moorland species of club-rush, *Scirpus cæspitosus.*

1772-8 LIGHTFOOT *Flora Scot.* (1789) II. 1080 (App.) *Scirpus cæspitosus* Deer's Hair *Scotis australibus.* *a* **1802** LEYDEN *Ld. Soulis* lxvi, And on the spot, where they boil'd the pot, The spreat and the deer-hair ne'er shall grow. **1816** SCOTT *Old Mort.* i, Moss, lichen, and deer-hair are fast covering those stones. **1853** G. JOHNSTON *Nat. Hist. E. Borders* 203 *Deer's Hair.* Abundantly on all our moors.

†**'deer-hay.** *Obs.* [f. DEER + HAY, a net set round an animal's haunt.] A net set for the capture of deer.

1503 *Act 19 Hen. VII*, c. 11 The greatest Destruction of Red Deer and Fallow..is with Nets called Deer-hays and Buck-stalls. **1598** MANWOOD *Lawes Forest* xviii. §9 (1615) 135. **1796** *Sporting Mag.* VIII. 177 Taking a buck in a deer-hayes, or net, is not unfrequent in parks.

'deer-hound A dog of a breed used for hunting red-deer, a stag-hound; particularly, one of a Scottish breed, a large variety of the rough greyhound, standing 28 inches or more.

[**1814** SCOTT *Wav.* lxiii, Two grim and half-starved deer greyhounds.] **1818** W. H. SCOTT *Brit. Field Sports* 384 Few Packs of Deer Hounds are now kept. **1838** W. SCROPE *Deerstalking* xii. 260 The deerhound is known under the names of Irish wolfhound, Irish greyhound, Highland deerhound, and Scotch greyhound. **1858** JESSE *Anecd. Dogs* (Bohn) 121 The Highland greyhounds, or deerhounds as they are called in the Highlands, have a great antipathy to the sheep-dogs. **1892** E. WESTON BELL (*title*), The Ancient Scottish Deerhound.

'deericide. *nonce-wd.* [f. DEER + -CIDE.] The killing or killer of a deer.

1832 J. R. HOPE-SCOTT in R. Ornsby *Mem.* (1884) I. 41 The second [day] crowned with the above-mentioned deericide.

†**'deer-kin.** *Obs.* In 2-3 -cyn, -cen. [See KIN.] Beast-kind as distinct from man.

a **1175** *Cott. Hom.* 221 Niatenu and deor-cen and fuȝel-cyn. *Ibid.* 225 Of diercynne and of fugel cynne. *c* **1250** *Gen. & Ex.* 556 And ouer-flowȝed men & deres-kin.

deerlet ('dɪəlɪt). [See -LET.] A little or tiny deer; *spec.* the chevrotain.

1878 *Cassell's Nat. Hist.* II. 336 In the Water Deerlet of West Africa the external toes are smaller, whilst..each metacarpal..is independent of its neighbour, the Javan Deerlet differing in having the third and fourth fused into a 'cannon' bone. **1924** *Glasgow Herald* 8 Nov. 4 While camels chew the cud they resemble the old-fashioned chevrotains or deerlets in having only three chambers in their 'stomach' instead of the usual four.

'deer-lick. *U.S.* A small spring or spot of damp ground, impregnated with salt, potash, alum, or the like, where deer come to lick.

1778 *Maryland Jrnl.* 2 June (Th.), I never saw a Deer-lick. Hunters have told me that Deer frequent those places for the mud. **1823** W. FAUX *Memorable Days Amer.* 234, I saw a deer-lick, at which I dismounted and took a lick. **1876** R. L. PRICE *Two Americas* (1877) 217 A deer-lick is a small spring of saline or sulphur-impregnated water, to which..all the deer in the country for miles and miles will come to 'liquor up'. **1890** HALLETT *1000 miles* 362 The place is a deer-lick, and the caravans of cattle which passed..so enjoyed licking the puddles, that they could hardly be driven from the place.

'deer-mouse. The popular name of certain American mice; esp. the widely-distributed white-footed mouse (*Hesperomys leucopus*) brown above and white beneath; also the common jumping-mouse (*Zapus hudsonius*), so called from its agility.

1840 E. EMMONS *Rep. Quadrupeds of Mass.* 62 *Arvicola Emmonsii*... This beautiful animal..is known by the name of Deer Mouse. **1841** CATLIN *N. Amer. Indians* I. xxiv. 194 A small 'deer mouse', of which little and very destructive animals their lodges contained many. **1884-90** *Cassell's Nat. Hist.* III. 111 The white-footed, or Deer Mouse..is perhaps the best known of all the species, and its varieties, or rather local permanent races, are distributed all over the continent of North America. **1970** *Sci. Amer.* Feb. 58 The deer mouse (*Peromyscus maniculatus*), a small, white-footed species that is noted for its ubiquitous presence throughout North America.

†**de-'err**, *v.* *Obs. rare*$^{-1}$. [ad. L. *deerrāre* to wander off, f. DE- I. 2 + *errāre* to wander, stray.] *intr.* To go astray, diverge.

1657 TOMLINSON *Renou's Disp.* 108 That it may deerre into the breast.

'deerskin. The skin of a deer, especially as a material for clothing. Also *attrib.*

1396 *Will of Wodehous* (Commissary Crt.), Meam togam blod' cum furrure & vn deriskyn. **1751** JOHNSON *Rambler* No. 187 ⁋3 [She] laid aside from that hour her white deer skins. **1820** SCOTT *Monast.* xiv, In his home-spun doublet, blue cap, and deerskin trousers. **1876** BANCROFT *Hist. U.S.* II. xxxiv. 362 Dressed..each in a large deerskin.

'deer-ˌstalker. [See STALK *v.*]

1. One who stalks deer; a sportsman who furtively approaches the deer, so as to get within shooting-distance without being discovered.

1830-35 D. BOOTH *Analyt. Dict. Eng. Lang.* 257 In the woodcraft of former times, many devices for catching deer were employed by the deer stalkers. **1833** *Chamber's Jrnl.* 19 Oct. 298/1 One who really knew the mountains well, having been an incorrigible deer-stalker. **1875** J. H. BENNET *Winter Medit.* I. vii. 189 Reached by Scottish deer-stalkers and hardy mountaineers. **1885** BLACK *White Heather* ii, The smartest deer-stalker and the best trainer of dogs in Sutherlandshire.

2. Name given to a low-crowned close-fitting hat fit to be worn by deer-stalkers.

1881 *Cheq. Career* 135 In the winter a 'billycock' or 'deer-stalker' is considered quite dressy enough.

So **'deer-ˌstalking** *vbl. sb.*

1816 SCOTT *Bl. Dwarf* ii, On his return from deer-stalking. **1885** *New Bk. Sports* 20 There is no sport in the world about which more nonsense is talked than deer-stalking. **1885** BLACK *White Heather* i, Clad in a smart deer-stalking costume.

'deer-ˌstealer. A poacher who kills and steals deer. So **'deer-ˌstealing** *vbl. sb.*

c **1640** J. SMITH *Lives Berkeleys* (1883) II. 296 Old notorious deerestealers. **1679-88** *Secr. Serv. Money Chas. II & Jas. II* (Camden) 75 To discover dear-stealers and trespassers within the said forest. **1714** MANDEVILLE *Fab. Bees* (1725) I. 172 He promises never to be a deer-stealer, upon condition that he shall have venison of his own. **1710** *Lond. Gaz.* No. 4702/2 Leave..to bring in a Bill to prevent Dear-stealing. **1818** SCOTT *Hrt. Midl.* xxxiii, Among smugglers and deer-stealers.

deerth, obs. form of DEARTH.

dees(se, obs. forms of DAIS, DICE.

de-escalation (diːɛskə'leɪʃən). orig. *U.S.* [f. DE- II. 2 + ESCALATION.] The reversal of escalation. So **de-'escalate** *v. trans.* and *intr.*

1964 *Christian Sci. Monitor* 28 Jan. 14/5 Just as the military must be able to escalate operations if the situation demands, they must be able to de-escalate also. **1965** H. KAHN *On Escalation* v. 91 Subsequent popular reaction, if the crisis de-escalates, may be an all-important influence. *Ibid.* xii. 230 In de-escalation, concessions and conciliation play something of the same role that demands and coercion play in escalation. **1965** *Observer* 29 Aug. 2/7 The Americans..are making the suggestion that a process of de-escalation should be tried. **1967** *Spectator* 15 Sept. 293/3 A good case can be made for the thesis that the administration is seriously preparing to de-escalate the war. **1970** *Nature* 26 Sept. 1371/2 It is full of sound advice to administrators on how to de-escalate situations deliberately contrived to lead to confrontation. **1971** *Daily Tel.* 27 Jan. 7 It is perfectly possible to have de-escalation of the level of wage settlements and at the same time an increase in the real earnings of people.

deese, *sb. dial.* A place where herrings are dried.

1682 J. COLLINS *Salt & Fishery* 67 That they be suddenly put into the Deese, and well or sufficiently Deesed. **1847-78** HALLIWELL, *Dees*, a place where herrings are dried, *East Sussex.* **1875** PARISH *Sussex Gloss.*, *Deese*, a place where herrings are dried, now more generally called a herring-hang, from the fish being on sticks to dry.

deese, *v. dial.* [f. prec.] *trans.* To dry (herrings). Hence **'deesing-room.**

1682 J. COLLINS *Salt & Fishery* 66 The worser sort..are deesed over a Wood-fire, and are thereby dried and rendered..Red-Herrings. *Ibid.* 124 Dried..on Racks in a Fire or Deesing-roome.

deeshy ('diːʃɪ), *a. Anglo-Irish.* [Orig. unknown.] Tiny; insignificant.

1825 T. C. CROKER *Fairy Leg. S. Ireland* I. 200 A deeshy daushy leather apron hanging before him. *Ibid.* 209 The three original diminutives are *tiny*, *dony*, and the Scottish *wee*... From the first and third they [*sc.* the Irish] form *weeny*, and by the use of the termination *shy*, they make *deeshy*, *doshy*, and *weeshy*. **1907** G. B. SHAW *John Bull's Other Island* II. 31 For shame, Patsy!..to be afraid of a little deeshy grasshopper.

†**'deess, deesse.** *Obs.* [a. F. *déesse* (12th c.), variant, influenced by L. *dea*, of *dieuesse*, fem. of *dieu* god. Cf. Pr. *deuessa*, *diuessa*, Sp. *diosa*, Pg. *deosa.* See -ESS.] A goddess.

1549 *Compl. Scot.* Prol. 11 Ane fayr ymage of the deesse iuno. **1685** BP. H. CROFT on *Burnet's Th. Earth* Pref. A vij (T.), He does so much magnifie Nature..that he hath made her a kind of joint deess with God. **1698** VANBRUGH *Æsop* I. 285 Wks. (1893) I. 169 The Déesse who from Atropos's breast preserves The names of heroes and their actions.

deet, Sc. f. *died*: see DIE *v.*

deeth, obs. form of DEATH *sb.*

de-'ethicize, *v.* [DE- II. 1.] *trans.* To deprive of its ethical character; to separate from ethics. Hence **de-'ethicized** *ppl. a.*, **de-'ethicizing** *vbl. sb.*, **de-ethici'zation.**

1887 BOYD CARPENTER *Perm. Elem. Relig.* v. §2 (1891) 188 Religionism is the shadow of religion..its effect is to *de-ethicize* religion. **1890** W. S. LILLY *Right & Wrong*, The newspaper press..has done more than any thing else to de-ethicise public life. **1890** *Guardian* 30 Apr. 711/3 Suspicion of that demoralising (or de-ethicising) tendency. **1893** FAIRBAIRN *Christ in Mod. Theol.* 405 The invariable tendency in Metaphysics is to the de-ethicization of deity.

deeve, obs. form of DEAF, DEAVE *v.*

deevil, dial. var. of DEVIL.

deevy ('di:vɪ), *a. colloq.* Also deevey, deevie, devey, devy. [Affected alteration of DIVVY *a.*] 'Divine'; delightful, sweet, charming.

1900 E. GLYN *Visits Eliz.* 11 Miss La Touche..said my hat was 'too devey for words'. **1904** E. F. BENSON *Challoners* xi, 'Martin,' she cried, 'you are too deevey!' **1905** *Punch* 8 Mar. 178/1 Do look at this sweet little monkey on the organ! Isn't he deevie! **1906** *Ibid.* 13 June 422/2, I had the most *devy* doll you can imagine. **1909** H. A. VACHELL *Paladin* i, The affair..was so appropriate, so obviously fashioned in heaven, so 'deevy'—a word coined in those days, and now regrettably become obsolete. **1930** V. M. SACKVILLE-WEST *Edwardians* i. 17 Tommy, you're going, aren't you? How too deevy! **1942** *English Studies* XXIV. 186 'Too deevy (divine) for words' is the flapper's reaction to what she moderately approves of.

Hence **'deevily** *adv.*

1905 E. F. BENSON *Image in Sand* vii, How too deliciously eerie! How deevily mysterious!

deewan: see DEWAN.

de-exci'tation. *Physics.* [DE- II. 1.] The induced transition of an atom or other quantized system from an excited state to the ground state (or a lower excited state); the action of producing such a transition.

1964 *Proc. Physical Soc.* LXXXIII. 769 The theory of vibrational de-excitation in collisions should be most accurate for these simple molecular systems. **1968** M. S. LIVINGSTON *Particle Physics* xii. 217 Neutrinos are also not constituents of matter, but are radiated..in a variety of deexcitation transitions of nucleonic or particle states. **1970** *Nature* 17 Oct. 277/2 The de-excitation of a molecule and the appearance of a quantum of luminescent light is a discrete process.

So **de-ex'cite** *v. trans.*, to cause the de-excitation of.

1960 *McGraw-Hill Encycl. Sci. & Technol.* IX. 85/2 Spontaneous neutron emission takes place and serves very rapidly to de-excite the nucleus. **1964** *Proc. Physical Soc.* LXXXIII. 769 The theory..predicts that light molecules will be effective in de-exciting vibrationally excited oxygen molecules.

def, obs. f. DEAF.

deface (dɪ'feɪs), *v.* Also 4 defaas, 5 defface, defase, diface, 6 dyface. [a. obs. F. *deface-r*, earlier *deffacer*, orig. *desfacier*, f. *des-*, *dé-* (DE- 6) + *face* FACE *sb.* Cf. It. *sfacciare*.]

1. *trans.* To mar the face, features, or appearance of; to spoil or ruin the figure, form, or beauty of; to disfigure.

to deface coin includes the stamping on a legally current coin of any name or words other than those impressed on it; made illegal by Act 16 & 17 Vict. c. 102.

c **1374** CHAUCER *Troylus* v. 915 And clepe A-yen þe beute of your face, That ye with salte Teeris so deface. **1430** LYDG. *Chron. Troy* III. xxvii, But in her rage to the kinge she ran.. So diffaced and rewefull of her sight That by her hewe knoweth her no wyht. **1555** EDEN *Decades* 48 The hole woorke..defaced with blottes and interlynynge. **1579** LYLY *Euphues* (Arb.) 39 One yron Mole, defaceth the whole peece of Lawne. ? **1661** in *12th Rep. Hist. MSS. Comm.* App. v. 7 Lucas..cut downe all the trees about the Castle, which utterly defaced the seat. **1716** LADY M. W. MONTAGU *Let.* 10 Oct. (1887) I. 130 There are some few heads of ancient statues; but several of them are defaced by modern additions. **1818** CRUISE *Digest* (ed. 2) IV. 497 A deed..is.. cancelled, by tearing off the seals, or otherwise defacing it. **1848** MACAULAY *Hist. Eng.* I. 160 Fine works of art and curious remains of antiquity, were brutally defaced.

b. *fig.* (of things immaterial).

c **1325** *Deo Gratias* 70 in *E.E.P.* (1862) 126 þi vertues let no fulþe defaas. *c* **1450** *Crt. of Love* iii, Minerva, guide me with thy grace, That language rude my matter not deface. **1509** FISHER *Fun. Serm. C'tess Richmond* Wks. (1876) 290 A noblenes of maners, withouten whiche the noblenes of bloode is moche defaced. **1656** HOBBES *Liberty, Necess. & Chance* (1841) 286 Those readers whose judgments are not defaced with the abuse of words. **1706** ADDISON *Poems, Rosamond* I. iv, How does my constant grief deface The pleasures of this happy place! **1878** P. BAYNE *Purit. Rev.* i. 5 Every religion..will be more or less defaced by error.

†**2.** To destroy, demolish, lay waste. *Obs.*

1494 FABYAN *Chron.* VI. clxxx. 178 The cytie of Maynchester, that sore was defaced with warre of the Danys. **1568** GRAFTON *Chron.* II. 751 They woulde..race, and clerely deface the walles, toures, and portes of the Castell. **1575** CHURCHYARD *Chippes* (1817) 148 Now cleane defaste the goodly buildings fayre. **1600** J. PORY tr. *Leo's Africa* I. 29 The Portugals erected a fortresse, which their king afterward commanded them to deface. **1632** LITHGOW *Trav.* II. 47 Croatia..then by lawlesse, and turbulent souldiers, was miserably defaced. **1871** R. ELLIS *Catullus* lxvi. 12 Hotly the King to deface outer Assyria sped.

3. To blot out, obliterate, efface (writing, marks).

1340 *Ayenb.* 191 Hi lokede..ine hare testament and hi yzeȝ þe þousend pond defaced of hire write. *c* **1400** MAUNDEV. (Roxb.) xxv. 117 When þis monee es waxen alde, and þe prynte þeroff defaced by cause of vsyng. **1438** CAXTON *Gold. Leg.* 333/2 The lyon..defaceth his traces and stappes with his taille whan he fleeth. **1587** FLEMING *Contn. Holinshed* III. 1372/1 To deface a letter, which he was then in writing..in cipher. **1646** SIR T. BROWNE *Pseud. Ep.* I. iv, To deface the print of a cauldron in the ashes. **1692** BENTLEY *Boyle Lect.* i. 4 In Characters that can never be defaced. **1839** MISS MITFORD in L'Estrange *Life* III. vii. 100 The beginning of this letter is irreparably defaced.

b. *fig.* To blot out of existence, memory, thought, etc.; to extinguish.

c **1386** CHAUCER *Clerk's T.* 454 This wyl is in myn herte and ay shal be No lengthe of tyme or deeth may this deface. *c* **1430** LYDG. *Min. Poems* (1840) 198 (Mätz.) Than comyth a storm and doth his lihte diffface. **1570** T. NORTON tr. *Nowel's Catech.* (1853) 160 Defacing with everlasting forgetfulness the memory of our sins. **1621** BURTON *Anat. Mel.* II. iii. II, For want of issue they [families] are defaced in an instant. **1709** POPE *Ess. Crit.* 25 By false learning is good sense defac'd. **1796** [see DEFACED].

†**4.** To destroy the reputation or credit of; to discredit, defame. *Obs.*

1529 MORE *Dyaloge* I. Wks. 109/1 To deface that holy worke, to the ende, that they might seme to haue some iust cause to burne it. **1548** UDALL *Erasm. Par.* Pref. 11 To bryng hym out of credite, to deface hym. **1570** LEVINS 7/16 To Deface, *dehonestare*. **1600** E. BLOUNT tr. *Conestaggio* 223 Reasons to deface the Dukes merits. **1641** PRYNNE *Antip.* p. x, Iohn White..would have defaced Queene Elizabeth gladly, if hee durst, in his Funerall Sermon of Queene Mary, whom he immoderately extolled.

†**5.** To put out of countenance; to outface, abash. *Obs.*

1537 in W. H. Turner *Select. Rec. Oxford* 143 There stode ..Parret..and his face flatt ageynst for to deface me. *c* **1570** LADY HUNGERFORD *to W. Darrell* in H. Hall *Eliz. Soc.* (1887) 253 Seeke oute what possabell may be to deface and disprove those varlettes that soo vily hathe youwsed us.

†**6.** To outshine by contrast, cast in the shade.

c **1590** GREENE *Fr. Bacon* xvi. 48 So rich and fair a bud, whose brightness shall deface proud Phœbus flower. **1639** tr. *Du Bosq's Compl. Woman* C ij, Women who..put on many diamonds..make them contemplate their jewels.. The luster of the flash they give, defaceth that of their own hue. **1796** MORSE *Amer. Geog.* I. 142 The Aurora Borealis ..not to be defaced even by the splendour of the full moon.

†**de'face**, *sb. Obs.* [f. prec.] Defacement.

1556 J. HEYWOOD *Spider & F.* lxi. 5 That trewth trewlie might appere without deface. **1563** SACKVILLE *Compl. Dk. Buckhm.* xix. Wks. (1859) 130 Yet God..At last descries them to your sad deface, You see the examples set before your face. **1601** CHESTER *Love's Mart.* (1878) 61 His fathers Coate, his Mothers Countries grace, His honors Badge, his cruell foes deface. *c* **1611** CHAPMAN *Iliad* VI. 298 He hath been born, and bred to the deface, By great Olympius, of Troy.

defaceable (dɪ'feɪsəb(ə)l), *a.* [-ABLE.] Liable to or capable of defacement.

1889 *Bookseller* Feb. 146/2 A nickel coin..[is] not so easily defaceable as ordinary bullion.

defaced (dɪ'feɪst), *ppl. a.* [-ED[1].] Disfigured, marred, destroyed, blotted out, etc.: see DEFACE.

1776 ADAM SMITH *W.N.* I. v. (1869) I. 43 One-and-twenty worn and defaced shillings. **1796** BURKE *Regic. Peace* i. Wks. VIII. 83 With defaced manufactures, with a ruined commerce. **1845–6** TRENCH *Huls. Lect.* Ser. I. iv. 57 The idea of a..defaced and yet not wholly effaced image of God in man. **1860** TYNDALL *Glac.* I. ix. 61 Defaced statuary.

Hence **de'facedness.**

1668 HOWE *Bless. Righteous* (1825) 109 To recover the defacedness of God: to be again made like him, as once I was.

de'facement. [f. DEFACE *v.* + -MENT.] The action or process of defacing; the fact or state of being defaced; *concr.* a disfigurement.

1561 T. NORTON *Calvin's Inst.* I. xi. (1634) 38 It cannot be done without some defacement of his glory. **1622** BACON *Hen. VII*, 55 In defacement of his former benefits. **1630** NAUNTON *Fragm. Reg.* (Arb.) 64 Modesty in me forbids the defacements of Men departed. **1664** H. MORE *Myst. Iniq.* 566 Such disorderly breaches are a great defacement of the lustre of the Protestant Reformation..which..was the special work of God. **1796** BURKE *Regic. Peace* iii. Wks. VIII. 310 Amidst the recent ruins and the new defacements of his plundered capital. **1878** P. BAYNE *Pur. Rev.* i. 8 The removal of their excrescences and defacements. **1885** *Manch. Exam.* 23 May 5/1 The defacement of French copper coins..by having an advertisement stamped upon them.

defacer (dɪ'feɪsə(r)). [f. as prec. + -ER[1].] One who or that which defaces.

1534 in Froude *Hist. Eng.* ix. II. 320 The most cruellest capital heretic, defacer and treader under foot of Christ and his church. **1611** SPEED *Hist. Gt. Brit.* IX. ix. (1632) 625 Clippers and defacers of his Coyne. **1613** SHAKS. *Hen. VIII*, v. iii. 41 Nor is there liuing..A man that more detests.. Defacers of a publique peace then I doe. **1876** M. ARNOLD *Lit. & Dogma* 120 A defacer and disfigurer of moral treasures which were once in better keeping.

defacing (dɪ'feɪsɪŋ), *vbl. sb.* [-ING[1].] The action of the verb DEFACE; defacement.

c **1400** *Test. Love* I. (1560) 273/1 The defacing to you is verily imaginable. **1543–4** *Act 35 Hen. VIII*, c. 10 For satisfaction of any suche breakyng and defacyng of the grounde. **1631** WEEVER *Anc. Fun. Mon.* 50 Proclamation.. against defacing of Monuments. *a* **1718** PENN *Tracts* Wks. 1726 I. 686 To preserve them from the Defacings of Time. **1871** R. ELLIS *Catullus* lxviii. 171 So your household names no rust nor seamy defacing Soil this day.

de'facing, *ppl. a.* [-ING[2].] That defaces; disfiguring; †destroying, etc.

1583 M. ROYDON *Commend. Verses* in Watson *Poems* (Arb.) 35 Reproofe with his defacing crewe Treades vnderfoote that rightly should aspyre. **1886** RUSKIN *Præterita* I. vi. 176 The defacing mound [at Waterloo] was not then built. **1887** *Times* 27 Aug. 10/2 He asks for a removal of the defacing advertisements.

Hence **de'facingly** *adv.*, in a defacing manner.

1847 in CRAIG.

de facto: see DE I. 3.

†**de'fade**, *v. Obs.* Also 4 diff-, 5 dyff-. Pa. t. and pple. in *Sc.* defaid, -fayd. [prob. representing an OF. or AF. **defader*, f. *des-*, *de-* (DE- I. 3, 6) + OF. *fader*: see FADE *v.*]

1. *intr.* To lose freshness or fairness; to fade away.

c **1325** *Song of Yesterday* 8 in *E.E.P.* (1862) 133 þei wene heore honoure and heore hele Schal euer last and neuer diffade. ? *a* **1400** *Morte Arth.* 3304 Now es my face defadide, and foule is me hapnede. **1470–85** MALORY *Arthur* X. lxxxvi, A Palomydes..why arte thow dyffaded thou that was wonte to be called one of the fayrest knyȝtes of the world. **1513** DOUGLAS *Æneis* XI. ii. 34 His schene cullour, and figur glaid Is nocht all went, nor his bewte defayd. **1570** LEVINS 9/1 To Defade, *deficere*.

2. *trans.* To cause to fade; to deprive of lustre, freshness, or vigour; cf. FADE *v.* 3.

1423 JAS. I *Kingis Q.* clxx, All thing..That may thy ȝouth oppressen or defade. *c* **1440** HYLTON *Scala Perf.* (W. de W. 1494) II. xii, Beholde me not that I am swart for the sonne hath defaded me. **1461** *Liber Pluscard.* XI. viii. (Hist. Scot. VII. 383).

defæcate, -cation: see DEFECATE, -CATION.

defaict, obs. form of DEFEAT, DEFECT.

defaik, obs. Sc. form of DEFALK.

†**de'fail**, *v. Obs.* [a. F. *défaill-ir* (Ch. de Roland, 11th c.) = Pr. *defalhir*, OCat. *defallir*: f. DE- 3 + *fallire*, Rom. repr. of L. *fallĕre*: see FAIL.]

1. *intr.* Used in various senses of FAIL *v.* (the prefix adding little to the force of the word): **a.** To be or become absent or wanting (*to* a person, or with *dative*); **b.** To lose vigour, become weak, decay; **c.** *to defail of*: to lack, want.

13.. SHOREHAM *Ps.* xxii[i]. 1 in *Wyclif's Bible* I. Pref. 4 Nothyng shal defailen to me. **1340** *Ayenb.* 33 Efterward comþ werihede þet makeþ þane man weri and worsi uram daye to daye al huet he is al recreyd and defayled. **1382** WYCLIF *Deut.* xxviii. 32 Thin eyen..defaylynge at the siȝt of hem al day. *a* **1420** HOCCLEVE *De Reg. Princ.* 3525 Whether supposest thow bette that noblesse Begynne in me, or noblesse and honour Defaile in the? *c* **1440** *York Myst.* xxviii. 146 If all othir for-sake þe I schall neuere fayntely defayle þe. **1481** CAXTON *Myrr.* III. vi. 140 Whan the mone ..cometh right bytwene vs and the sonne, thenne..the mone taketh and reteygneth the lyght of the sonne on hye, so that it semeth to vs that is defaylled. **1490** —— *Eneydos* xiii. 48 Her speche deffaylleth alle sodeynly and can not kepe purpos ne countenaunce. **1556** *Aurelio & Isab.* N iv, I forcede of love, defailinge of goode jugemente, discover myne illes to her.

2. *trans.* To cause to fail; to defeat.

1608 MACHIN *Dumb Knight* I. (1633) B iv, Which to withstand I boldly enter thus, And will defaile, or else prove recreant.

Hence †**de'failing** *vbl. sb.*

1502 *Ord. Crysten Men* (W. de W. 1506) IV. xxix. 331 The fourth lettynge is dyffaylynge of wytte humayne. **1580** HOLLYBAND *Treas., Defaillance & langueur*, defayling, languor.

de'failance, -faillance. Also 7–8 -fail(l)iance. [a. F. *défaillance*, f. *défaill-ir*: see -ANCE.] Failing, failure.

1603 FLORIO *Montaigne* II. vi. (1632) 207 So great a.. deffailance of senses [as in fits]. **1613–18** DANIEL *Coll. Hist. Eng.* (1626) 55 He had a fayre Title, by the defaillance of issue. *a* **1668** SIR W. WALLER *Div. Medit.* (1839) 42 In the defailliance of all these transitory comforts. *a* **1677** BARROW *Serm.* Wks. 1716 II. 57 By transgression of his laws and defailance in duty. **1727** A. HAMILTON *New Acc. E. Ind.* II. xxxviii. 206 Those Eastern Desperadoes are very faithful where..Covenants are duly observed when made with them, but in Defailiance, they are revengeful and cruel. **1892** E. DOWSON *Let.* ?23 Nov. (1967) 254 Forgive my *défaillance*. I hope you didn't wait long; most contrite. **1902** BELLOC *Path to Rome* 194 This defaillance and breakdown which comes from time to time over the mind. **1938** HEMINGWAY *Fifth Column* (1939) III. i. 86 If you have a little *defaillance* I understand.

†**de'faillancy.** *Obs. rare.* [f. as prec. with suffix -ANCY.] Failure.

1649 JER. TAYLOR *Gt. Exemp.* II. viii. 71 Our life is full of defaillancies. **1689** *Def. Liberty agst. Tyrants* 144 Neither can the others defaillancy [*printed* defalliancy] be excused, in the bad managing of the tutorship.

†**de'failment.** *Obs.* [a. obs. F. *défaillement* (Cotgr.), f. *défaillir*: see -MENT.] Failure.

1612 *Proc. Virginia* in *Capt. Smith's Wks.* (Arb.) 89 All the world doe see a defailement. **1624** CAPT. SMITH *Virginia* III. xi. 88 We..sent him for England, with a true relation of the causes of our defailments. **1652–62** HEYLIN *Cosmogr.* To Rdr. (1674) A iij, After the defailment of his Projects.

†**de'failure.** *Obs. rare.* [f. DEFAIL *v.* after *failure*: see -URE.] Failure.

a **1677** BARROW *Pope's Suprem.* (1687) 272 Why may not the Successour of Peter, no less than the Heir of Adam, suffer a defaileur of Jurisdiction? **1753** L. M. tr. *Du Bosq's Accompl. Woman* II. 69 Who is there that thinks he shall die by defailure of strength?

defaisance, obs. form of DEFEASANCE.

defait(e, obs. forms of DEFEAT.

defaite, defate, *ppl. a. Sc.* [Sc. form of *defeat* for *defeated*: cf. DEFEIT.] Defeated, vanquished.

1597 MONTGOMERIE *Cherrie & Slae* 1255 For he esteemt his faes defate, Quhen anes he fand them fald. **1814** *Saxon & Gael* I. 96 (Jam.) A' defaite thegither.

†**de'falcable**, *a. Obs. rare*$^{-1}$. [f. med.L. *dēfalcāre* (see below) + -BLE.] Liable to be deducted.

1622 SIR R. BOYLE *Diary* (1886) II. 43 He had paid and disbursed for me defalcable on his accompt 714^{li} 17^{s} 6^{d}.

†**de'falcate**, *ppl. a. Obs.* [ad. med.L. *dēfalcāt-us*, pa. pple. of *dēfalcāre*: see next.] Curtailed, diminished.

1531 ELYOT *Gov.* II. x, All thoughe philosophers in the description of vertues haue deuised to set them as it were in degrees..yet be nat these in any parte defalcate of their condigne praises.

defalcate (dɪ'fælkeɪt), *v.* Also 6–7 **-at**. [f. *dēfalcāt-*, ppl. stem of med.L. *dēfalcāre* (see Du Cange), f. DE- I. 1, 2 + L. *falx, falc-em* sickle, reaping-hook, scythe. Cf. F. *défalquer* (14th c. in Littré), Sp. *defalcar*, It. *diffalcare*.]

†**1.** *trans.* To cut or lop off (a portion from a whole); to retrench, deduct, subtract, abate.

1540–1 ELYOT *Image Gov.* (1549) 25 He shall defalcate that thyng that semeth superfluouse. **1611** SPEED *Hist. Gt. Brit.* IX. viii. §54 Rather..then to defalcate any jot of their couetous demaunds. **1624** F. WHITE *Repl. Fisher* 496 To defalcate a substantiall part. **1653** MANTON *Exp. James* ii. 10 Man is not..to defalcate and cut off such a considerable part of duty at his own pleasure. **1721** STRYPE *Eccl. Mem.* II. xxiv. 450 Those that had accounts to make to the king..used to defalcate a part and put it into their own pockets. **1755** MAGENS *Insurances* I. 439 Defalcating from the Money due to the English, the Sum which his Subjects demanded for their Indemnification. **1810** BENTHAM *Packing* (1821) 195 The least desire to see defalcated any the least particle of abuse from a system composed wholly of abuse. **1817** —— *Plan of Parl. Reform* cccxvi.

†**2.** To take or deduct a part from; to curtail, reduce. *Obs.*

a **1690** E. HOPKINS *Exp. Ten Commandm.* (R.), To..defalcate, and as it were to decimate the laws of the great God. **1712** PRIDEAUX *Direct. Ch.-wardens* (ed. 4) 90 Such an one shall..be defalcated all those Particulars in his Account, where the Fraud appears. **1793** W. ROBERTS *Looker-on* No. 66 ¶2 If it [the mind] were defalcated and reduced. **1817** BENTHAM *Ch.-of-Englandism* (1818) 386 Let all pay..be defalcated, and applied to the real exigencies of the State.

b. To diminish or lessen in luminosity, heat, etc.

1808 HERSCHEL in *Phil. Trans.* XCVIII. 156 Both phases appear to me sufficiently defalcated, to prove that the comet did not shine by light reflected from the sun only.

3. *intr.* To commit defalcations; to misappropriate property in one's charge.

1864 in WEBSTER. **1888** *Daily News* 23 July 5/1 Head clerks have defalcated. **1891** *Law Times* XCII. 19/1 The secretary of the society having defalcated, and being threatened..with criminal proceedings.

defalcation (diːfæl'keɪʃən). [ad. med.L. *dēfalcātiōn-em*, n. of action from *dēfalcāre*: see prec. So mod.F. *défalcation* (18th c. in Hatzf.).]

†**1.** Diminution or reduction by taking away a part; cutting down, abatement, curtailment. *Obs.*

1476 *Will of Sir J. Crosby*, An equall defalcacion or diminucion pounde poundelike penny pennylike and rate ratelike of all the legates aforesaide. **1526** *Househ. Ord.* 139 To be corrected..by the checking and defalcation of their wages. **1611** SPEED *Hist. Gt. Brit.* IX. xii. (1632) 685 This treasonable defalcation and weakening of the royall meanes. **1650** FULLER *Pisgah* 412 In such defalcation of measures by Cyrus allotted, he shewed little courtship to his master the Emperour. **1712** ADDISON *Spect.* No. 488 ¶2 The Tea Table shall be set forth every Morning with its Customary Bill of Fare, and without any manner of defalcation.

b. *spec.* Reduction of an account, claim, etc., by the amount of a counter-account or claim, allowed as a set-off.

1622 MALYNES *Anc. Law-Merch.* 117 The Factor is to haue the benefit of the Salt in defalcation of the said fraight. **1830** C. HUSTON in *Houk v. Foley* 2 Pen. & W. (Pa.) 250 (Cent.) Defalcation is setting off another account or another contract—perhaps total want of consideration founded on fraud, imposition, or falsehood, is not defalcation: though, being relieved in the same way, they are blended.

2. The action or fact of cutting or lopping off or taking away; deduction. *arch.*

1624 F. WHITE *Repl. Fisher* 471 The defalcation of one kind is against the integritie of the substance of the Eucharist. **1652** BP. HALL *Rem. Wks.* (1660) 145 If we be still our old selves..without defalcation of our corruptions, without addition of Grace. **1673** *Essex Papers* (Camden) I. 147 To allow twelve thousand Pds to ye Farmers, by way of defalcation, out of ther Rents for ye Customs. **1684** T. BURNET *Th. Earth* I. 285 If these deductions and defalcations be made. **1755** MAGENS *Insurances* I. 440 His Majesty..will order the Defalcation of the Sum adjudged to his Subjects. *a* **1832** BENTHAM *Mem. & Corr.* Wks. 1843 X. 69 The stock of knowledge..from which, after a certain period [of life], large defalcations are every minute making by the scythe of Time.

b. A deduction; a diminution or abatement to which an amount (income, etc.) is liable, on account of debts or expenses. *arch.*

1621 BURTON *Anat. Mel.* Democr. to Rdr. 63 To defray this charge of wars, as also all other public defalcations, expenses, fees, pensions. **1622** F. MARKHAM *Bk. War* II. iv. 55 After his debts and defaulcations are paid. **1690** BOYLE *Chr. Virtuoso* II. 20 This inward Recompense is received, not only without any Defalcations, but with great improvements. **1701** J. LAW *Counc. Trade* (1751) 9 Repairs, risques, damages by fire and other defalcations. **1823** BENTHAM *Not Paul* p. iii, A reprint..but with some defalcations, additions, and alterations.

3. Diminution suffered or sustained; falling off. *arch.*

1649 JER. TAYLOR *Gt. Exemp.* XI. i. §9 Nothing but a very great defalcation or ruin of a man's estate will..justify such a controversy. **1792** HERSCHEL in *Phil. Trans.* LXXXII. 27 The brightness of the moon, notwithstanding the great defalcation of light occasioned by the eclipse. **1793** *Ld. Auckland's Corr.* II. 514 The duty, which last year produced 160,000*l*, is betted this year at under 50,000*l*; a terrible defalcation..especially after the falling off of the last quarter. **1801** WELLESLEY in Owen *Desp.* 202 The causes of this increasing defalcation of revenue are manifest, and daily acquire new strength. **1831** BREWSTER *Optics* xiv. 122 Its tint varied with the angle of incidence, and had some relation to the defalcation of colour in the prismatic images. **1844** H. H. WILSON *Brit. India* III. 452 A serious defalcation of the public revenue was incurred.

4. Falling away, defection; shortcoming, failure, delinquency.

1750 CARTE *Hist. Eng.* II. 304 Its power would have been so much lessened by the defalcation of the vassal provinces. **1782** MISS BURNEY *Cecilia* (1820) III. 38 Defalcation of principle. **1820** LAMB *Elia* Ser. I. *Oxford in Vacation*, I..could almost have wept the defalcation of Iscariot. **1822** ELIZA NATHAN *Langreath* I. 192 Tears of..regret streamed down her cheeks at the defalcation of her vows to Dalton. **1839** JAMES *Louis XIV* IV. 158 The defalcation of one or two members from the league. **1868** MISS BRADDON *Run to Earth* III. i. 16 Pointing out Reginald's neglect, all his defalcations, the cruelty of his conduct to her.

5. A monetary deficiency through breach of trust by one who has the management or charge of funds; a fraudulent deficiency in money matters; also *concr.* (in *pl.*), the amount so misappropriated.

1846 WORCESTER, *Defalcation*, a breach of trust by one who has charge or management of money. [Not in CRAIG, 1847.] **1856** E. A. BOND *Russia at Close 16th C.* (Hakluyt Soc.) Introd. 130 Although they had clamoured loudly of his defalcations..at the termination of his connection with them, the balance..was in his favour. **1866** *Morn. Star* 20 Aug. 6/4 The ground of the action taken being an alleged defalcation to the extent of 11,000*l.* **1885** *Manch. Exam.* 6 July 4/7 The prosecutors estimate the defalcations at about £1,800.

defalcator ('diːfælkeɪtə(r)). [agent-n. on L. type from med.L. *dēfalcāre*: see DEFALCATE.] One guilty of defalcation; one who has misappropriated money or other property committed to his care.

1813 *Chron.* in *Ann. Reg.* 14/1 A..collector of the income tax in the parish of Christchurch Surry, has lately become a defalcator to the amount of £3,700. **1858** CARLYLE *Fredk. Gt.* (1865) I. IV. iii. 290 Prevaricators, defalcators, imaginary workers, and slippery unjust persons. **1890** *Harper's Mag.* Apr. 760/1 A defalcator convicted and sentenced.

†**de'falce**, *v. Obs. rare.* [ad. med.L. *dēfalcāre*: see next.] = DEFALK.

1651 FULLER *Abel Rediv.*, *Berengarius* 5 When we read Baronius calling him *hominem mendacissimum*—we know how to defalce our credit accordingly.

defalk (dɪ'fɔːlk), *v. Obs.* or *arch.* Also 5–7 **-falke**, 6 **-falck**, **-faik** (*Sc.*), 6–7 **-faulk(e**. [a. F. *défalque-r* (14th c. in Littré), ad. med.L. *dēfalcāre*: see DEFALCATE.]

†**1.** *trans.* To diminish by cutting off a part, to reduce by deductions. *Obs.*

1475 *Bk. Noblesse* 72 None of youre officers roialle..shalle darre doo the contrarie to take no bribe, rewarde, or defalke the kingis wagis. **1526** *Househ. Ord.* 230 The Clerkes Comptrolers..to defaulk [*printed* default] & check the wages of all [those]..absent without lycense. **1552** HULOET, Defalke or mynyshe, *defalcare.* **1587** FLEMING *Contn. Holinshed* III. 1543/1 Vpon euerie default their wages was totted and defalked. **1613–8** DANIEL *Coll. Hist. Eng.* (1626) 158 In the second Statute..hee defalked the Jurisdiction of Ecclesiasticall Judges. **1630** *R. Johnson's Kingd. & Commw.* 323 The monethly expence of the Court (being thirtie thousand Crownes) is in these times defalked unto five thousand. **1747** CARTE *Hist. Eng.* I. 164 Not thinking it lawful to defalk any of their dues.

2. To cut or lop off; to deduct, subtract, abate.

†**a.** *gen. Obs.*

1536 BELLENDEN *Cron. Scot.* (1821) I. 118 Thir novellis maid Cesius to defaik sum part of his curage *remiserit ardorem*]. **1577** STANYHURST *Descr. Irel.* in Holinshed VI. 2 Ireland is divided into foure regions..and into a fift plot, defalked from everie fourth part. **1647** JER. TAYLOR *Lib. Proph.* iii. 61 That the Jewes had defalk'd many sayings from the Books of the old Prophets. **1659** *Gentl. Calling* VIII. §1. 441 These days have taught the vulgar to defalk much of that respect which former ages paid to superiors of all sorts. **1701** BEVERLEY *Glory of Grace* 51 The..Noble Part of the Redemption of Christ were then Defaulked, If He did not save From the Filth of Sin.

b. a part or sum from an account, payment, etc. (Still locally in U.S. legal use.)

1524–5 *Burgh Rec. Edin.* 20 Feb., Quilk sowme the said president..grantis to be allowit and defalkit to the said fermoraris in thair latter quarter. **1530** PALSGR. 509/2, I wyll nat defalke you a peny of your hole somme..This shall be defalked from your somme. **15..** *Aberdeen Reg.* (Jam.), The skiper aucht to defaik sa mekle of his fraucht as wald fuyr the merchandis gudis to..Sanctandrois. **1562** *Act 5 Eliz.* c. 4 To..forfeit 1^d for euery houres absence, to be deducted and defaulked out of his wages. *a* **1610** HEALEY *Theophrastus* (1636) 41 If any of his seruants breake but a pitcher..he defalketh it out of their wages. **1666** PEPYS *Diary* (1879) III. 486 He bids me defalk 25*l* for myself. **1736** CARTE *Ormonde* II. 401 Money..payable out of the treasury of Ireland, and afterwards defalked out of the Duke's salary and entertainment. **1886** JUSTICE STERRETT in *Gunnis v. Cluff* (Cent.), The question is whether the damages sustained can be defalked against the demand in this action.

†**c.** *absol.* or *intr. Obs.*

1604 *Househ. Ord.* 305 Our Officers..to whom it appertaineth to defaulk from their entertainement. *a* **1631** DONNE *Serm.* lxxv. 765 Why should I defalke from his generall propositions and..call his omnes (his all) a Few. **1649** BP. HALL *Cases Consc.* (1650) 194 He lyes to the holy Ghost, that defalkes from that which he engaged himselfe to bestow. **1757** WARBURTON in *Garrick's Corr.* I. 77 You see at last if I defalk from their human science, I repay them largely in divine.

†**3. a.** To allow (any one) a deduction. **b.** To deprive or mulct *of* (anything due). *Obs.*

1541 *Act 33 Hen. VIII* in *Stat. Irel.* (1621) 230 The Kings said lessees..shall be defalked, abated, and allowed..of and for such and so much yearely rent and ferme. **1565** CALFHILL *Answ. Treat. Crosse* (1846) 206 That, for default of solemnity, she shall be defaulked of fruit of Sacraments.

Hence **de'falking** *vbl. sb.*

1475 *Bk. Noblesse* 31 Bethout any defalking [or] abregging of here wagis. **1581** ANDRESON *Serm. Paules Crosse* 22 Without addition or defalking too or fro the worde of God. **1659** GAUDEN *Tears of Ch.* 235 Few do pay them without delayings, defalkings, and defraudings.

†**defa'llation.** *Obs.* [irreg. f. F. *défaillir*, OF. also *defallir*: see -ATION.] Failure, failing.

1490 CAXTON *How to Die* ad fin., That God hath promysed trust it well without defallacyon.

defalt, -ive, obs. forms of DEFAULT, -IVE.

de'famable, *a. rare*$^{-0}$. Also **diff-**. [See below and -ABLE.] Liable to be defamed.

1570 LEVINS 3/12 Defamable, *defamabilis.* **1721** BAILEY, *Diffamable*, that may be slandered.

'defamate, *v. rare*$^{-0}$. [f. ppl. stem of L. *diffāmāre* after following words.] To defame, slander.

In mod. Dicts.

defamation (diːfə'meɪʃən, dɛf-). Forms: 4–6 **diff-**, **dyffamacion**, **-oun**, etc., 6–8 **diffamation**, 5– **defamation**. [ad. OF. *diffamation*, L. *diffāmātiōn-em*, n. of action from *diffāmāre*, with same change of prefix as in DEFAME.]

†**1.** The bringing of ill fame or dishonour upon any one; disgrace, shame. *Obs.*

1303 R. BRUNNE *Handl. Synne* 7427 Þe dede ys confusyun, And more ys þe dyffamacyun. **1387** TREVISA *Higden* (Rolls) II. 313 Som tyme it were a greet diffamacioun for a man to vse more rynges þan oon. **1533** BELLENDEN *Livy* II. (1822) 164 The Romanis has maid thair playis allanerlie this day to youre diffamacioun and schame. **1633** PRYNNE *Histrio-Mastix* I. III. vi. (R.), Their ayme is onely men's defamation, not their reformation. **1711** STEELE *Spect.* No. 262 ¶2 Any thing that may tend to the Defamation of particular Persons, Families, or Societies.

2. The action of defaming, or attacking any one's good fame; the fact of being defamed or slandered; also (with *pl.*), an act or instance of defaming.

c **1386** CHAUCER *Friar's T.* 6 In punysshynge..Of diffamacioun and auowtrye. *c* **1425** WYNTOUN *Cron.* V. xii. 1322 Wylful Defamatyownys. **1529** MORE *Dyaloge* I. Wks. 127/1 The priest sued him before ye bishoppes offyciall for Dyffamatyon. **1630** *R. Johnson's Kingd. & Commw.* 113 Defamations breathed from the poyson of malice. **1633** AMES *Agst. Cerem.* II. 530 It was necessarie to speak againe for a good cause, lest diffamation should prævayl against it. **1709** STEELE *Tatler* No. 105 ¶4 The Father of Boniface brought his Action of Defamation..and recovered Dammages. **1726** AYLIFFE *Parergon* 212 Diffamation, or Defamation..is the uttering of reproachful Speeches, or contumelious Language of any one, with an Intent of raising an ill Fame of the Party thus reproached; and this extends to Writing..and to Deeds. **1883** *Law Rep. 11 Q. Bench Div.* 595 An advocate is protected from an action for defamation only when the words he utters are spoken bonâ fide, and are relevant to the matters before the Court.

†**de'famative**, *a. Obs.* In 6 **dyff-**. [f. L. *diffāmāt-*, ppl. stem of *diffāmāre*, with change of prefix as in DEFAME: see -IVE.] Defamatory.

1502 *Ord. Crysten Men* (W. de W. 1506) IV. xxii. 295 Yf he hath caused wrytynges dyffamatyues for to be founde in place openly. **1634** A. WARWICK *Spare Min.* (1637) 91 Defamative reports.

†**'defamator.** *Obs. rare*$^{-1}$. [f. as prec.: see -OR.] One who defames, a slanderer.

1704 *Gentl. Instructed* (1732) 66 (D.) We should keep in pay a brigade of hunters to ferret our defamators, and to clear the nation of this noxious vermin.

defamatory (dɪ'fæmətərɪ), *a.* Also 6–7 **diff-**. [ad. med.L. *diffāmātōrius*, F. *diffamatoire* (14th c.), f. as prec.: see -ORY.]

1. Of the nature of, or characterized by, defamation; having the property of defaming.

1592 SUTCLIFFE (*title*), Answere to a certaine libel, supplicatory, or rather Diffamatory. **1656** EARL MONM. *Advt. fr. Parnass.* 144 Though the poets let fly diffamatory verses. **1669** CLARENDON *Ess.* Tracts (1727) 157 Defamatory writings. **1749** FIELDING *Tom Jones* (1775) II. 177 Who..condemn the whole in general defamatory terms. **1848** MACAULAY *Hist. Eng.* I. 482 James..had instituted a civil suit against Oates for defamatory words.

b. Const. *of*, *to*.

1655 Fuller *Ch. Hist.* IX. iii. §23 For dispersing of scandalous Pamphlets defamatory to the Queen and State. *Ibid.* X. i. §26 Such papers defamatory of the present Government. **1868** Stanley *Westm. Abb.* vi. 523 A passage defamatory of ten Bishops. **1891** *Times* 14 Jan. 5/5 The Portuguese Government has protested..against the posting ..of bills and circulars defamatory to its credit.

2. Of persons: Employing or addicted to defamation.

1769 *Junius Lett.* ii. 13 All such defamatory writers. **1836** Hor. Smith *Tin Trump.* (1876) 333 They have a good excuse for being defamatory.

defame (dɪˈfeɪm), *v.* Forms: 4–7 **diff-**, 4–5 **deff-**, 4–6 **dyff-**, 6 **diffame**, 4– **defame.** [ME. *diffame-n* and *defame-n*, a. OF. *diffame-r*, rarely *desfamer*, *deffamer*, *defamer* (mod.F. *diffamer*) = Pr. *diffamar*, It. *diffamare*, ad. L. *diffāmāre* to spread abroad by an ill report, f. *dif-* = dis- + *fāma* rumour, report, fame. In this word and its derivatives, while French retains the prefix as *dis-*, *des-*, *dé-*, Eng. has the form *de-*, prob. after med.L. *dēfāmāre* (Du Cange); cf. post-cl. L. *dēfāmātus* dishonoured, infamous, *dēfāmis* shameful.

(Etymologically, perhaps, sense 1 belongs to *dēfāmāre*, senses 2–4 to *diffāmāre*.)]

1. *trans.* To bring ill fame, infamy, or dishonour upon, to dishonour or disgrace in fact; to render infamous. *Obs.* or *arch.*

1303 R. Brunne *Handl. Synne* 6571 For to make hym be ashamede þat he shulde be so defamede. *c* **1374** Chaucer *Troylus* IV. 537 Me were leuere ded than hire defame. *c* **1489** Caxton *Sonnes of Aymon* xxviii. 580 We ben dyffamed bi thys grete knave, that doth somoche labour. **1526** Tindale *Matt.* i. 19 Ioseph, loth to defame her. **1615** G. Sandys *Trav.* 92 The hauen of Alexandria, newly defamed with a number of wracks. **1684** *Contempl. State of Man* I. ix. (1699) 103 Crimes so Infamous, as they not only defame the Person who commits them, but [etc.]. **1725** Pope *Odyss.* XIX. 16 Lest..Dishonest wounds, or violence of soul, Defame the bridal feast. **1850** Tennyson *In Mem.* cxi. 23 The grand old name of gentleman, Defamed by every charlatan.

2. To attack the good fame or reputation of (a person); to dishonour by rumour or report.

1303 R. Brunne *Handl. Synne* 11636, Y dar weyl seye þou hym dyffamest. *c* **1330** —— *Chron.* (1810) 321 Þe kyng did grete trespas, diffamed þe pape's se. *c* **1386** Chaucer *Miller's Prol.* 39 It is a synne..To apeyren eny man or him defame [*v.r.* diffame]. **1470–85** Malory *Arthur* XVIII. v, I am now in certayne she is vntruly defamed. **1547** *Homilies* I. *Love & Charity* (1859) 67 Speak well of them that diffame you. **1602** Marston *Antonio's Rev.* IV. iii. Wks. 1856 I. 122, I have defam'd this ladie wrongfully. **1701** De Foe *True-born Eng.* 34 He never fails his Neighbour to defame. **1837** Lytton *E. Maltrav.* 240 You would darkly slander him whom you cannot openly defame. **1883** *Law Rep.* 11 *Q. Bench Div.* 597 The plaintiff has been defamed, and has primâ facie a cause of action.

†**3.** To raise an imputation *of* (some specific offence) against (any one); to accuse. Const. also with *with*, *by*, or clause. *Obs.*

1303 R. Brunne *Handl. Synne* 8304 Ioye he haþ hym self to dyffame Of alle hys synnes. **1398** Trevisa *Barth. De P.R.* XV. clix. (1495) 546 One Tenes..was deffamyd that he had lyen by his stepdame. *c* **1460** Fortescue *Abs. & Lim. Mon.* v. (1885) 118 His creauncers shul..defame his highnes off mysgouernance. **1482** Caxton *Trevisa's Higden* VII. iii, One bisshop that was sharply defamed by symonye. **1564** Grindal *Fun. Serm.* Wks. (1843) 20 As diffaming him, that for ambition' sake he would do a thing contrary to his conscience. **1672** Cave *Prim. Chr.* III. iv. (1673) 347 You defame us with Treason against the Emperour. **1736** Chandler *Hist. Persec.* 213 Others are defamed for heresy; such who are spoken against by common report. **1820** Scott *Ivanhoe* xxxviii, Rebecca..is, by many frequent and suspicious circumstances, defamed of sorcery.

†**4.** To publish, spread abroad, proclaim. [Rendering *diffāmāre* in the Vulgate]. *Obs.*

1382 Wyclif *Wisd.* ii. 12 He..defameth aȝen vs [Vulg. *diffamat in nos*] the synnes of oure disciplyne. —— *Matt.* ix. 31 Thei goynge out defameden [**1388** diffameden] hym thorwȝ al that lond. —— *1 Thess.* i. 8 Forsoth of ȝou the word of the Lord is defamyd, [or *moche told*.

†**defame** (dɪˈfeɪm), *sb. Obs.* Forms: see the verb. [ME. *diffame* and *defame*, a. OF. *deffame* (usually *disfame*, *diffame*), f. *def-*, *diffamer*, to defame. Cf. L. *diffāmia* (Augustine, 4th c.), f. **diffāmis* (cf. *dēfāmis*, and *infāmis*, *infāmia*), f. *dis-* privative + *fāma* fame.]

1. Ill fame, evil repute; dishonour, disgrace, infamy.

1375 Barbour *Bruce* XIX. 12 Schyr Wilyame Off that purches had maist defame, For principale tharoff wes he. **1474** Caxton *Chesse* III. vi. Hiv, His vertue is torned to diffame. **1533** Bellenden *Livy* III. (1822) 301 To the grete diffame and reproche of Romanis. **1596** Spenser *F.Q.* V. iii. 38 So ought all faytours..From all brave knights be banisht with defame. **1603** Knolles *Hist. Turks* (1638) 146 Now he lieth obscurely buried, shrouded in the sheet of defame. **1630** Lord *Persees* 50 Such as are..of publique defame in the world for some evill. **1659** *Crown Garland of Roses* (1845) 60 Yet lives his famous name Without spot or defame.

2. Defamation, slander, calumny.

a **1450** *Knt. de la Tour* 2 Gret defames and sclaundres withoute cause. **1502** *Ord. Crysten Men* (W. de W. 1506) IV. xxi. 270 Those to whome he hath spoken the dyffame of his neyghbour. **1599** Porter *Angry Wom. Abingd.* in Hazl. *Dodsley* VII. 376 *Mrs. Gour.* She slandered my good name. *Fran.* But if she now deny it, 'tis no defame. **1609** Rowlands *Knaue of Clubs* 36 Fond men vniustly do abuse your names, With slaundrous speeches and most false defames. **1654** Whitlock *Zootomia* 447 Nibles at the Fame Of's absent Friend; and seems t' assent By silence to 's Defames.

defamed (dɪˈfeɪmd), *ppl. a.* [f. prec. vb. + -ed.]

1. †**a.** Brought to disgrace, dishonoured, of ill fame (*obs.*). **b.** Attacked in reputation, slandered.

1474 Caxton *Chesse* 4 The euyl lyf and diffamed of a kyng is the lyf of a cruel beste. **1536** Bellenden *Cron. Scot.* (1821) I. 176 Maist vile and diffamit creaturis. **1548** Udall, etc. *Erasm. Par. Matt.* iii. 30 Souldyoures, a violent and a diffamed kynde of people. **1631** Weever *Anc. Fun. Mon.* 146 None were to be admitted if of a defamed life. **1691** Wood *Ath. Oxon.* I. 74 The defamed dead recovereth never. **1891** Scrivener *Fields & Cities* 159 The defamed character of a fellow-workman.

2. *Her.* Said of a lion or other beast which is figured without a tail. [F. *diffamé*.]

1863 *Chambers' Encycl.* s.v. *Infamed* 570 *Defamed* is an epithet applied to a lion or other animal which has lost its tail, the loss being supposed to disgrace or defame it. **1882** Cussans *Heraldry* vi (ed. 3) 86.

Hence **deˈfamedly** *adv.*

1567 in Tytler *Hist. Scotl.* (1864) III. 265 Let her [Queen Mary] know that the Earl of Moray never spoke defamedly of her for the death of her husband.

deˈfameless, *a. rare.* [f. defame *sb.* or *v.* + -less.] Free from discredit or reproach.

1888 Ramsay *Scotl. & Scotsmen 18th C.* II. ix. 151 Nothing could be more defameless than their manners.

defamer (dɪˈfeɪmə(r)). Also 5 **deff-**, 5–6 **diff-**, **dyff-**. [f. defame *v.* + -er. Cf. OF. *diffameur*, *deffameur*.] One who defames.

a **1340** Hampole *Psalter* v. 10 Bakbiters and defamers. **1481** Caxton *Reynard* (Arb.) 96 A deffamer of wymmen. **1550** Nicolls *Thucyd.* Pref. 3 (R.) Pryuye dyffamours of dylygent and vertuous laboure. **1654** Whitlock *Zootomia* 460 Blushes for the Defamer, as well as Defamed. **1797** Mrs. Radcliffe *Italian* ii, Impatient to avenge the insult upon the original defamer.

ˌdefamiliariˈzation. *Lit. Theory.* [de- II. 1; tr. Russ. *ostranenie* (V. Shklovskiĭ, in *Poétika* (1919), II. 105), lit. 'making strange'.] In structuralist (esp. Russian Formalist) theory: the process or result of rendering unfamiliar; *spec.* of literature, in which formal devices are held to revitalize the perception of words and their sounds by differentiation from ordinary language or (subsequently) from other habituated formal techniques.

1971 E. M. Thompson *Russ. Formalism* II. ii. 94 Šklovskij ..did not look at defacilitation and defamiliarization only in terms of their being noticeable in one epoch and unnoticeable in another. **1972** F. Jameson *Prison-House of Lang.* II. 60 The techniques for plot defamiliarization and those of lyric are analogous. **1976** T. Eagleton *Crit. & Ideology* iii. 79 Defamiliarisation may revitalise an ideology for reactionary ends. **1982** *N. & Q.* June 278/2 Terms like 'authenticity', 'phenomenology', 'alienation' and 'defamiliarization' float free of any historically determining pain.

Also **defaˈmiliarize** *v. trans.*, to render unfamiliar; to subject to defamiliarization.

1971 E. M. Thompson *Russ. Formalism* III. 129 As far as Romantic imagery is concerned, Nekrasov 'defamiliarized' it by twisting its conventional meaning. **1976** T. Eagleton *Crit. & Ideology* iii. 79 A text may so 'foreground' its signifiers as to radically deform, distantiate, and defamiliarise its signified. **1984** *Review Eng. Stud.* XXXV. 352 He attempts to defamiliarize and deconstruct the text and thus account for its persuasive power.

defaming (dɪˈfeɪmɪŋ), *vbl. sb.* [-ing[1].] The action of the verb defame.

a **1340** Hampole *Psalter* lxiv. 5 Þis is wickidnes and defamynge of God. **1556** *Aurelio & Isab.* (1608) H, Fearinge the diffaminge of youre poisenede tonges. **1611** Bible *Jer.* xx. 10, I heard the defaming of many. **1611** Beaum. & Fl. *Philaster* III. ii, They draw a nourishment Out of defamings, grow upon disgraces.

deˈfaming, *ppl. a.* [-ing[2].] That defames. Hence **deˈfamingly** *adv.*

1641 Milton *Animadv.* (1851) 189 What defaming invectives have lately flown abroad against the Subjects of Scotland.

†**defamous**, *a. Obs.* [a. AF. *deffamous*, OF. type **deffameux*, f. *diffame* sb., defame: cf. *famous*, *infamous*. (The stress varies in the metrical examples.)] **a.** Infamous, disgraceful. **b.** Defamatory.

c **1430** *Pilgr. Lyf Manhode* I. lii. (1869) 32 No sinne so fowl, so defamowse. *c* **1430** Lydg. *Bochas* III. x. (1554) 84 a, A word defamous, most foule in al languages. **1500–20** Dunbar *Poems* (1893) lix. 10 With rycht defamowss speiche off lordis. **1557** North *Gueuara's Diall Pr.* 61 b/2 To haue set on his graue so defamous a title. **1577–87** Holinshed *Chron.* II. Kkj (N.), There was a knighte that spake defamous words of him.

Hence **defamously** (*diff-*) *adv.*, defamatorily.

1557 R. Allerton in S. R. Maitland *Ess. Reform.* 556 (D.) Whereupon should your lordship gather or say of me so diffamously?

†**ˈdefamy.** *Obs.* Also **diff-**. [a. OF. *diffamie*, ad. L. *diffāmia*: see defame *sb.* Cf. *infamy*: for prefix see defame.] = defamation 1, 2.

1490 Caxton *Eneydos* xxviii. 109 Wherof they of cartage shalle haue a blame that shalle torne vnto them to a grete diffamye. **1494** Fabyan *Chron.* v. cxiv. 87 By whose defamy and report, Sygebert was more kyndelyd to set vpon his brother. **1523** Ld. Berners *Froiss.* I. ccxlii. 359 Yt we be reputed for false and forsworne, and to ryn into suche blame and diffamy, as [etc.].

defar, defarre, obs. forms of defer *v.*[1]

†**deˈfarm**, *v. Obs. rare*[−1]. [ad. OF. *desfermer*, *défermer* to unshut, disclose, turn out from an enclosure, f. *des-*, *dé-*, de- I. 6 + *fermer* to shut, close.] *trans.* To shut out from, dispossess.

1648 Symmons *Vind. Chas. I.* 237 Should they part with it [the Militia] they should not only..defarme themselves of safety but of their wealth and riches too.

defase, obs. Sc. form of defease.

defaste, obs. pa. t. and pa. pple. of deface.

de-fat, defat (diːˈfæt), *v.* [f. de- II. 2 + fat *sb.*[2]] *trans.* To remove fat or fats from. So **deˈfatted** *ppl. a.*; **deˈfatting** *vbl. sb.*

1923 Dreyer in *Times* 15 June 11/6 If the bacillus is 'defatted'..it no longer retains the acid stain. *Ibid.*, Dr. A. C. Inman..began..to treat cases of human tuberculosis with the 'defatted' antigen. **1924** *Glasgow Herald* 15 Feb. 6 These 'defatted' vaccines. **1960** *Farmer & Stockbreeder* 29 Mar. 117 (Advt.), Quickly mixed powder; no waste. De-fats rubbers; prolongs their life. **1962** *New Scientist* 24 May 409/3 Methods involving simultaneous defatting and dehydration.

defate, obs. f. defeat; var. of defaite.

deˈfatigable, *a.* [ad. L. type *dēfatīgābil-is* (found in negative *indēfatīgābilis*), f. *fatīgāre* to fatigue: see -ble.]

1. Apt to be wearied; capable of being wearied.

1656 Blount *Glossogr.*, *Defatigable*, easily to be wearyed. **1659** D. Pell *Impr. Sea* 244 That when this bird is defatigable, and wearied with flying, that hee will betake himself to any ship. **1662** Glanvill *Lux Orient.* (1682) 116 We were made on set purpose defatigable, that so all degrees of life might have their exercise. **1948** E. Waugh *Loved One* (1949) 2 Then they lost interest. I did too. I was always the most defatigable of hacks. **1958** *Times Lit. Suppl.* 25 July 418/3 Mr Toynbee, by his own admission the most defatigable of marchers, has reverted to the written word.

†**2.** Apt to weary or fatigue. *Obs.*

1657 Tomlinson *Renou's Disp.* Pref., My Imployments.. and defatigable diuturnal Labours.

Hence **deˈfatigableness.**

1727 Bailey vol. II, *Defatigableness*, aptness to be tired.

†**deˈfatigate**, *v. Obs.* [f. L. *dēfatīgāt-*, ppl. stem of *dēfatīgāre* to weary out, exhaust with fatigue, f. de- I. 3 + *fatīgāre* to weary, fatigue.] *trans.* To weary out, to exhaust with labour. Hence **deˈfatigated, deˈfatigating** *ppl. adjs.*

1552 Huloet, Defatigate, *defatigo.* **1566** Painter *Pal. Pleas.* (1575) I. To Rdr., Mindes defatigated either with paineful trauaile or with continuall care. **1634** Sir T. Herbert *Trav.* (1638) 190 Up which defatigating hill we crambled. *a* **1666** C. Hoole *School Colloq.* (1688) Ep. Ded., This defatigating task of a Schoolmaster.

†**defatiˈgation.** *Obs.* [ad. L. *dēfatīgātiōn-em*, n. of action from *dēfatīgāre* (see prec.).] The action of wearying out, or condition of being wearied out; fatigue.

1508 Fisher Wks. (1876) 196 Whereby we shall come into everlastynge defatygacyons and werynesse in hell. **1610** Barrough *Meth. Physick* IV. ii. (1639) 218 Sometime it is caused through wearinesse and vehement defatigation. **1654** tr. *Scudery's Curia Pol.* 175 A defatigation and dispiritedness will accompany that oppression.

defaulcation, -faulk, obs. ff. defalcation, -falk.

default (dɪˈfɔːlt), *sb.* Forms: 3–6 **defaut, -e**, (4 **defauȝte**), 4–5 **def-, diffaute**, 5 **defawt(e, (deffawte, defauute)**, 5–7 **defalt**, 5–6 **defalte, -faulte**, (5 **deffault(e**, 6 **difalt, deafaulte**), 6– **default.** [ME. a. OF. *defaute*, deriv. of *defaillir*, after *faute* and *faillir*: see fault. Nearly superseded in Fr. by a masc. variant *defaut* (in Froissart 14th c.), mod.F. *défaut*; in Eng., forms without final *-e* appear also in 14th c., but those with *-e* came down as late as the 16th.

The spellings *defalte*, *defaulte*, appear in Anglo-Fr. of 13–14th c.; and *defalt*, *default*, in English of 15th c., but the *l* was not generally pronounced until the 17th or 18th c.: cf. fault.]

I. Failure of something, want, defect.

†**1. a.** Absence (*of* something wanted); want, lack, scarcity *of*; = fault *sb.* 1. *Obs.* or *arch.*

a **1300** *Cursor M.* 1718 (Cott.) [That] þou haue defaut [*v.rr.* defaute, deffaute] of mete and drink. *Ibid.* 4601 (Gött.) Suilk diffaute sal be of bred, þe folk sal be for hunger dede. **1375** Barbour *Bruce* II. 569 Gret defaut off mete had thai. *Ibid.* XIV. 368 Defalt of mete. *c* **1380** Wyclif *Serm* Sel. Wks. I. 70 Certis defaute of bileve is cause of oure sleuthe. *c* **1400** *Lanfranc's Cirurg.* 199 Bi necligence & defaute of help manie men ben perischid. *a* **1470** Tiptoft *Cæsar* iv. (1530) 6 They had defawte of all things as be convenyent. **1548** Udall *Erasm. Par.* Pref. 14 Ignoraunce and defaulte of litterature.

1594 CAREW *Huarte's Exam. Wits* (1616) 90 Through default of a well made penne he is forced to write with a sticke. **1654** H. L'ESTRANGE *Chas. I* (1655) 19 And a great default there was..of sufficient pay, of holesome meat, and unanimity. **1823** J. BADCOCK *Dom. Amusem.* 94 Two kinds of deafness are those arising from an excess of wax in the ear, or its total default.

†**b.** *absol.* Lack of food or other necessaries; want, poverty. *Obs.*

c **1290** *S. Eng. Leg.* I. 261/16 For non ne scholde for defaute bi-leue þe foule sunne. *a* **1300** *Cursor M.* (Cott.) 4760 þan iacob and his suns warn For defaut wel ner for-farn. **1393** LANGL. *P. Pl.* C. XVIII. 67 He..fedde þat a-fyngred were and in defaute lyueden. **1483** CAXTON *Gold. Leg.* 166 b/1 They of the towne within had so grete defaulte that they ete theyr shoys and lachettis. **1494** FABYAN *Chron.* VI. clxxxvi. 186 Many dyed for defaute.

c. ***for default of*** (obs.), ***in default of***: through the failure or want of, in the absence of; †***in default***: failing these (this, etc.).

1297 R. GLOUC. (1724) 457 Vor defaute of wyt. *c* **1369** CHAUCER *Dethe Blaunche* 5, I haue so many an idel þou3t Purli for defaute of slepe. **1393** GOWER *Conf.* III. 93 The fissh, if it be drie, Mote in defalte of water deie. **1464** *Bury Wills* (Camden) 24 For the defawte of eyr male. **1568** TURNER *Herbal* III. 29 In defaut of it he teacheth to take halfe as much of Asarabacca. **1586** A. DAY *Eng. Secretary* II. (1625) 47 And for default of other matter forsooth, how they laught at me. **1650** in W. S. Perry *Hist. Coll. Amer. Col. Ch.* (1860) I. 2 It shall be lawful..to make Probates of Wills, and default of a will to grant Letters of Administration in the Colony. **1689** HICKERINGILL *Ceremony-Monger*, *Wks.* (1716) II. 468 The Presbyters or (in default) any Church Member. **1729** BUTLER *Serm.* Wks. 1874 II. 104 In default of that perfection of wisdom and virtue. **1818** CRUISE *Digest* (ed. 2) IV. 340 And for default of issue of the body of the said Thomas, to [etc.]. **1865** J. C. WILCOCKS *Sea Fisherman* (1875) 27 Pilchards for bait may frequently be procured..in default of which Mussels can be obtained.

2. A failure in being perfect; an imperfection, defect, blemish, flaw; = FAULT 3: **a.** in character or things immaterial. *Obs.* or *arch.*

1389 in *Eng. Gilds* (1870) 4 He shal be put out..in-to tyme þ^t he haue hym amended of þe defautes to-fore said. *a* **1450** *Knt. de la Tour* (1868) 160 She is with oute defauute. *a* **1533** LD. BERNERS *Gold. Bk. M. Aurel.* (1546) N ij b, Al defautes in a gouernour may be borne saue ignoraunce. **1680–90** TEMPLE *Ess. Learn.* Wks. 1731 I. 151 New [books]..have many of them their Beauties as well as their Defaults. **1704** SWIFT *T. Tub* v. 80 Forcing into light my own excellencies and other men's defaults. **1880** KINGLAKE *Crimea* VI. vi. 143 Grave defaults all the while lay hidden under the surface.

†**b.** in appearance, structure, etc.: Physical defect or blemish. *Obs.*

1340 HAMPOLE *Pr. Consc.* 5016 And if any lym wanted..or any war over smalle..God þan wille Alle þe defautes of þe lyms fulfille. *c* **1400** MAUNDEV. (Roxb.) iii. 9 þai..fand þe same letters..als fresch as þai ware on þe first day withouten any defaute. **1487** *Churchw. Acc. Wigtoft, Linc.* (Nichols 1797) 82 For mending and stoppyng of the botrasses, and other defauts in the chirche walles. **1562** TURNER *Herbal* II. 39 Lynt sede..when it is raw it taketh away the defautes of the face and frekles. **1634** T. JOHNSON tr. *Parey's Chirurg.* XXVI. xvi. (1678) 639 All such defaults must be taken away, and then..an epulotick applied.

II. Failure in performance.

3. a. Failure to act; neglect; *spec.* in *Law*, failure to perform some legal requirement or obligation, *esp.* failure to attend in a court on the day assigned; often in the phrase ***to make default. judgement by default***: a judgement given for the plaintiff on the defendant's failing to plead or put in his answer within the proper time. ***to go by default***: of a legal judgement, to be given for the plaintiff by default of the defendant; hence in *gen.* use, to fail or be overlooked by reason of negligence, lack of exposition, etc.

[**1292** BRITTON I. ii §8 Et si le pleyntif face defaute a nuli Counté.] *c* **1330** R. BRUNNE *Chron.* (1810) 58 Defaute he mad þat day. þerfor was þe dome gyuen..To exile þe erle Godwyn. **1411** *E.E. Wills* (1882) 20 Takynge a distresse in defawte of payment. **1495** *Act 11 Hen. VII*, c. 7 If any..make defaute at the day and place. **1588** FRAUNCE *Lawiers Log.* 53 b, If hee bee nonsuite in an action, or doe commit any such like default. **1666** PEPYS *Diary* (1879) IV. 208 The calling over the defaults of Members appearing in the House. **1736** NEAL *Hist. Purit.* III. 540 His Majesty persisting in his refusal to plead, the clerk was ordered to record the default. **1764** CROKER, etc. *Dict. Arts & Sc.* s.v., Where a defendant makes default, judgment shall be had against him by default. **1827** JARMAN *Powell's Devises* (ed. 3) II. 155 The period of foreclosure is the date of the final order of the Court, following default of payment on the day appointed. **1851** HT. MARTINEAU *Hist. Peace* (1877) III. IV. ix. 21 He had allowed judgment to go by default. **1955** *Bull. Atomic Sci.* June 216/3 The problem must not be allowed to go by default. **1985** *Guardian* 18 Nov. 6/7 Part of the new Soviet policy of using the media more professionally has meant that the US side of the case went by default.

attrib. **1892** *Boston* (Mass.) *Jrnl.* 15 Jan. 8/3 John F. Delaney was arrested..this morning on a default warrant issued by the Superior Court. **1894** *Daily News* 7 Feb. 7/8 A default summons in which the company sought to recover payment of an account.

b. *Computing.* A preselected option adopted by a computer when no alternative is specified by the user or programmer. Usu. *attrib.*

1966 G. M. WEINBERG *PL/1 Programming Primer* iv. 74 The use of default attributes can contribute to the ease of writing and modifying a program. **1969** —— *PL/1 Programming* ii. 106/1 The entire secret of successful defaults lies in the ability of the language designer to make a good guess at what the programmer is going to want to do in most cases. **1971** A. RALSTON *Introd. Programming & Computer Sci.* vi. 239 The best compilers now being written have default conditions for all syntactic errors which attempt to correct the error in the most likely fashion. **1971** *Computers & Humanities* V. 155 FORTRAN..has more default options (thus requiring far fewer declarations of variables). **1974** R. HANNULA *Computers & Programming* v. 91 There are four subfields in the operand field of which only *type* is required. The duplication factor, if used, may be any nonnegative integer from 1 to 65,535. The default for this subfield is one. **1985** *Personal Computer World* Feb. 211/4 This area is unaffected by any screen operations using the default screen sizes.

†**4. a.** Failure in duty, care, etc.; as the cause of some untoward event; culpable neglect of some duty or obligation; = FAULT 7. *Obs.*

to be in default: to fail in one's duty.

a **1300** *Cursor M.* 26241 (Cott.) If þi barne for þi defaut be for-farne. *c* **1400** *Lay Folk's Mass Bk.* App. iii. 126 He is continuelly in defaute a3en þat my3tteful lord. *c* **1400** MAUNDEV. (Roxb.) Pref. 2 Thurgh whilk ilk man es saued, bot if it be his awen defaute. *c* **1460** *Towneley Myst.* 60 Greatt defawte with hym youre fader fand. **1523** LD. BERNERS *Froiss.* I. ccclxxix. 634 The rebellion..hath coste ..many a mans lyfe in Gaunt, and parauenture many a one that were in no defaulte. **1549** LATIMER *5th Serm.* (Arb.) 149 They shall aunswere for all the soules that peryshe throughe theyr defaute. **1614** RALEIGH *Hist. World* II. 473 Those calamities which happen by their owne default. **1671** MILTON *Samson* 45 What if all foretold Had been fulfilled but through mine own default, Whom have I to complain of but myself? **1742** POPE *Dunciad* IV. 486 A God without a Thought, Regardless of our merit or default.

†**b.** *transf.* of things: Failure to act or perform its normal or required functions. ***default of the sun*** (L. *defectus solis*): eclipse. *Obs.*

1340 HAMPOLE *Pr. Consc.* 5015 If any lym wanted..Thurgh þe defaut here of kynd. **1520** *Caxton's Chron. Eng.* III. 19/1 Talus founde fyrste the defaute of the sonne and the moone. **1586** A. DAY *Eng. Secretary* I. (1625) 131 It is your Oxe that by default of your owne fence hath entred my ground. **1621** BURTON *Anat. Mel.* I. i. III. §2 Faith, opinion ..Ratiocination, are all accidentally depraved by the default of the imagination. **1736** GRAY *Let. to West* in Mason *Life* (ed. 2) 14 If the default of your spirits and nerves be nothing but the effect of the hyp, I have no more to say.

†**5. a.** (with *a* and *pl.*) A failure in duty; a wrong act or deed; a fault, misdeed, offence; = FAULT 5.

a **1225** *Ancr. R.* 136 Beon icnowen ofte to God of..hire defautes touward him. *a* **1340** HAMPOLE *Psalter* cxl. 4 It is þe manere of vnqueynt men when þai ere takyn with a defaute to excuse þaim wiþ falshede. *c* **1386** CHAUCER *Sompn. T.* 102 Ye god amende defautes sire quod she. **1539** *Manual of Prayers, Lauds*, Grant us pardon of our defaults. **1548** GEST *Pr. Masse* 74 To murder a gyltlesse personne is a defaulte full grevouse. **1635** QUARLES *Embl.* III. iv. 139 Thine owne defaults did urge This twofold punishment. **1703** MOXON *Mech. Exerc.* 264 That no Timber be laid within the Tunnel of any Chimny, upon penalty to the Workman for every Default ten Shillings. **1719** BP. OF LONDON in W. S. Perry *Hist. Coll. Amer. Col. Ch.* I. 201 It is..a grief to hear of any defaults and irregularities among you.

†**b.** A failure in what is attempted; an error, mistake; = FAULT 5 b. *Obs.*

c **1386** CHAUCER *Clerk's T.* 962 With so glad chier his gestes sche receyveth, And so connyngly everich in his degre, That no defaute no man aparceyveth. **1426** *Paston Lett.* No. 7 I. 25 Hem semyth..by the defautes ye espied in the same..that the processe..is false and untrewe. **1590** HUTCHINSON in Greenwood *Collect. Sclaund. Art.* C b, Your vnsufficient Argument hath 2. defaults in it. **1737** L. CLARKE *Hist. Bible* IV. (1740) 192 One great Default..was, that they did not make a right use of their victories. **1822** SOUTHEY *Vis. Judgement* 111 There he..accuses For his own defaults the men who too faithfully served him.

†**6.** Failure in any course; *spec.* in *Hunting*, failure to follow the scent; loss of the scent or track by the hounds; = FAULT *sb.* 8. *Obs.*

a **1300** *Leg. Rood* (1871) 22 Our stapes worþ isene þer-by þou my3t wiþþoute defaute to paradys euene gon. *c* **1369** CHAUCER *Dethe Blaunche* 384 The houndis hade ouershet hem al, And were on a defaute [*v.r.* defaulte] ifal. **1486** *Bk. St. Albans* E vj b, And iff yowre houndis chase at hert or at haare and thay renne at defaute. **1602** *2nd Pt. Return fr. Parnass.* II. v. (Arb.) 31 Thrise our hounds were at default. **1741** *Compl. Fam. Piece* II. i. 291 The Huntsman..assisting them at every Default, when they have either lost the Slot, or follow not the right.

7. Failure to meet financial engagements; the action of defaulting in money matters.

1858 SIMMONDS *Dict. Trade*, *Default*, a failure of payment of instalments, etc., agreed upon, or in the due execution of a contract. **1875** JEVONS *Money* (1878) 209 Convicted of fraud or default. **1890** *Daily News* 8 Nov. 5/4 Some defaults are expected at the Stock Exchange settlement next week.

8. *attrib.* Dealing with or connected with a default, as ***default authority, interest, price.***

1897 *Westm. Gaz.* 29 July 5/3 If a client borrowed £100, say, and paid off £90, 'default interest' at the rate of one halfpenny per shilling per week..was at once charged on the £10 in arrear. **1908** *Daily Chron.* 13 May 7/7 While the county council is the default authority in case of the failure of the district council in sanitation, the Local Government Board is the default authority in case of the district council's failure to do what is needed in housing. **1909** *Westm. Gaz.* 9 Nov. 8/2 The Army authorities saying that if plaintiffs would not take the cattle the beasts would subsequently be issued at default prices.

default (dɪˈfɔːlt), *v.* Forms: 4–5 **defaut(e**, 5 **defawte**, 6–7 **defalt**, 6 **difalt**, 6– **default**. [ME. ad. OF. *defaillir* (in 3rd sing. pres. *defalt*, *defaut*, *default*) to fail, be wanting, make default, = Pr. *defalhir*, *defaylhir*, OCat. *defallir*, Romanic type *defallīre*, f. DE- + *fallīre*, *fallĕre*, L. *fallĕre*: see FAIL. Cf. It. *sfallire* (*disfallire*), Sp. *defallecer*, to fail. In English associated with DEFAULT *sb.*]

1. *intr.* To be wanting; to fail. *Obs.* (exc. as in quot. 1860, transf. from sense 3.)

c **1340** *Cursor M.* 8572 (Fairf.) Riches sal þe defaute nane. **1382** WYCLIF *Num.* xi. 33 3it flesh was in the teethe of hem, ne defautide siche a maner mete. **1860** *Merc. Marine Mag.* VII. 121 The Court advised the Captain to account to his Owners for the money which was defaulting.

†**b.** To have want *of*, be deprived *of*. *rare*⁻¹.

c **1440** *Gesta Rom.* xxxvi. 140 (Add. MS.), I leue to the my doughtir..and I comaunde the, that she defaute of none thyng..as longeth to a maiden for to haue.

†**2.** To fail in strength or vigour, faint; to suffer failure. *Obs.*

1382 WYCLIF *Judg.* viii. 5 And he seide..3yueth looues to the puple, that is with me, for greetlich thei defauten [**1388** for thei failiden greetli]. *Ibid.* 15 That we 3euen to the men, that ben wery and han defautid, looues. *a* **1440** [see DEFAULTING *vbl. sb.*]. *a* **1592** GREENE *James IV*, II. ii, And can your..king Default, ye lords, except yourselves do fail? *a* **1617** BAYNE *On Eph.* (1658) 34 No inferiour cause can default beside his intention.

3. To make default; to be guilty of default; to fail to fulfil an obligation, *esp.* one legally required, as to appear in court at the proper time.

1596 SPENSER *F.Q.* VI. iii. 21 He..pardon crav'd for his so rash default That he gainst courtesie so fowly did default. **1621** BP. MOUNTAGU *Diatribæ* 479 This was..punishable if defaulted in. **1730–6** in BAILEY (folio). **1828** [see DEFAULTING *ppl. a.*]. **1845** R. W. HAMILTON *Pop. Educ.* viii. (ed. 2) 199 The Dissenters..in the Weekly Schools..are grievously defaulting. **1857** [see DEFAULTING *ppl. a.*]. **1858** CARLYLE *Fredk. Gt.* II. VIII. iv. 318 There is one Rath..who has been found actually defaulting; peculating from that pious hoard. **1892** *Boston* (Mass.) *Jrnl.* 15 Jan. 8/3 Delaney was arrested by officers..this morning..He was arrested July 21..and defaulted.

b. To fail to meet financial engagements.

1868 ROGERS *Pol. Econ.* xix. (1876) 256 The colony..will cease to get fresh creditors, as assuredly as any defaulting foreign Government does. **1885** *Truth* 11 June 925/2 To insist upon Egypt paying her creditors, and to let Turkey default to hers is a palpable contradiction. **1886** *Manch. Exam.* 9 Jan. 5/1 Last year..44 companies, with 8,386 miles of main line, defaulted and passed into receiverships.

4. *trans.* To put in default; to make or adjudge a defaulter; in *Law*, to declare (a party) in default and enter judgement against him (see quot. 1828).

1375 BARBOUR *Bruce* I. 182 Ihone the balleoll, that swa sone Was all defawtyt & wndone. **1574** tr. *Littleton's Tenures* 87 a, No man of full age shalbe received in any ple by the law to difalt or disable his owne person. **1597** SKENE *De Verb. Sign.* s.v. *Sok*, The court beand fensed, the Serjand thereof sall call the Soytes, and defalt the absentes. **1828** WEBSTER, *Default*, to call a defendant officially, to appear and answer in court, and on his failing to answer, to declare him in default, and enter judgment against him; as, let the defendant be defaulted..[also] the cause was defaulted.

†**5.** To fail to perform; to omit, neglect. *Obs.*

1648 MILTON *Tenure Kings* (1649) 32 Wee shall not need dispute..what they have defaulted towards him as no king. **1656** SANDERSON *Serm.* (1689) 388 He that defalteth anything of that just honour.

6. To fail to pay.

1889 *Pall Mall G.* 27 Apr. 6/3 Mexico..defaulted her interest after promising to pay 5 per cent.

de'faultant, *a.* [f. DEFAULT *v.* + -ANT. Not repr. any Fr. form.] Defaulting, guilty of default.

1884 A. A. PUTNAM *10 Yrs. Police Judge* v. 30 It did not transpire that the offending officials had been delinquent, defaultant, or otherwise derelict.

defaulted (dɪːˈfɔːltɪd), *ppl. a.* [f. DEFAULT *sb.* or *v.* + -ED.]

†**1.** Having defaults or defects; defective. *Obs.*

1580 E. KNIGHT *Trial Truth* 63 (T.) The old defaulted building being rid out of the way.

2. Not paid by reason of default.

1897 *Westm. Gaz.* 26 May 5/1 Nearly all the bonds issued of late by the Greek Government in respect of defaulted interest having found their way to London.

defaulter (dɪˈfɔːltə(r)). [f. DEFAULT *v.* + -ER.]

a. One who is guilty of default; *esp.* one who fails to perform some duty or obligation legally required of him; one who fails to appear when required.

1666–7 MARVELL *Corr.* lxv. Wks. 1872–5 II. 206 On Friday the defaulters upon the call of the House are to be called over. **1686** PLOT *Staffordsh.* 436 The defaulters being many, and the amercements by the Officers perhaps not sometimes over reasonable. **1727–51** CHAMBERS *Cycl.* s.v. *Default*, Judgment may be given against the defaulter. **1848** THACKERAY *Van. Fair* lvi, Master Osborne, you came a little late this morning, and have been a defaulter in this respect more than once. **1877** BLACK *Green Past.* xi. (1878) 85 There was no chance of a defaulter sneaking off in the night without paying his fourpence.

b. *Mil.* A soldier guilty of a military crime or offence. Also *attrib.*

1823 in CRABB *Techn. Dict.* **1844** *Regul. & Ord. Army* 119 Confinement to the Defaulters' Room for any period not exceeding seven days..being drilled with the Defaulters during that time. **1853** STOCQUELER *Milit. Encycl.*, *Defaulters' Book*, a regimental record of the crimes of the men. **1892** *Daily News* 25 Mar. 3/2, I attach a copy of Private O'Grady's defaulter-sheet.

c. One who fails properly to account for money or other property entrusted to his care, *esp.*

through having misappropriated it to his own use.

1806 WEBSTER, *Defaulter*, one who fails in payment, a debtor. **1823** CRABB *Techn. Dict.*, *Defaulter* (Com.), one who is deficient in his accounts, or fails in making his accounts correct. **1856** E. A. BOND *Russia at Close 16th C.* (Hakluyt Soc.) Introd. 81 He was soon..denounced..as a defaulter in his accounts. **1887** *Westm. Rev.* June 298 The Receiver-General for Lower Canada became a defaulter to the extent of £96,000 of public money.

d. One who fails to meet his money engagements; one who becomes bankrupt.

1858 SIMMONDS *Dict. Trade*, *Defaulter*..a trader who fails in his payments, or is unable to meet his engagements. **1887** *Pall Mall G.* 28 June 9/2 Mr. H——. has been officially declared a defaulter upon the Stock Exchange.

†de'faultiness. *Obs.*⁻⁰ In 6 defalt-. [f. DEFAULTY *a.* + -NESS.]

1530 PALSGR. 212/2 Defaltynesse, *favte*.

defaulting (dɪ'fɔːltɪŋ), *vbl. sb.* [f. DEFAULT *v.* + -ING¹.] Failing, failure (*obs.*); failing in an obligation.

1382 WYCLIF *Wisd.* xi. 5 The enemys..suffreden peynes, fro the defauting of ther drinc. *a* **1440** *Found. St. Barthol.* 45 For defawtynge of his hert, the vtteryng of his voice beganne to breke. **1870** EMERSON *Soc. & Solit.*, *Work & Days* Wks. (Bohn) III. 67 Shameful defaulting, bubble, and bankruptcy.

de'faulting, *ppl. a.* [-ING².] That defaults: see the vb. (*esp.* in sense 3).

1828 WEBSTER, *Defaulting, ppr.* 1. Failing to fulfill a contract; delinquent. 2. Failing to perform a duty or legal requirement; as, a defaulting creditor. *Walsh.* **1857** G. WILSON *Let.* in *Mem.* x. (1860) 444, I took a defaulting lecturer's place at the Philosophical Institution. **1889** *Law Times* LXXXVIII. 115/2 A writ of sequestration..against a defaulting trustee.

†de'faultive, *a. Obs.* [f. DEFAULT *sb.* + -IVE, after F. *fautif, -ive*: cf. FAULTIVE.] Deficient, faulty, remiss.

a **1400** WYCLIF *Exod.* vi. 12 (MS. B, etc.) Hou schal Farao here, moost sithen Y am vncircumcidid [*v.r.* that is, defautiyf] in lippis. *c* **1400** *Lanfranc's Cirurg.* 149 þilke ryngis whanne þei ben joyned wiþ merie þei ben defautif aȝens þe merie. *a* **1641** BP. MOUNTAGU *Acts & Mon.* (1642) 274, I never was behinde, nor defaltive in any thing which might conduce unto, or advance your benefit.

†de'faultless, *a. Obs. rare*⁻¹. [-LESS.] Faultless.

1340 HAMPOLE *Pr. Consc.* 8699 Alle fayrnes of þis lyfe here ..þat any man myght ordayne defautles War noght a poynt to þat fairnes.

de'faultress. *rare.* [f. DEFAULTER + -ESS.] A female defaulter.

1736 SWIFT *New Prop. Quadrille*, The defaultress to be amerced as foresaid at the next meeting.

†de'faulture. *Obs. rare.* [f. DEFAULT *v.* + -URE: cf. *failure*.] The action of defaulting; failure to fulfil an engagement.

1632 *Indenture* in Arb. *Garner* I. 317 If any one of the aforesaid parties..should fail in the payment of such money ..then it should be lawful to and for the rest of the said parties..to supply the same, or to admit some other person or persons to have the share of such defaulture, paying the sum imposed on the said share.

†de'faulty, *a. Obs.* Also 5 defawty, 5-6 -fauti, -fautie, -fauty. [f. DEFAULT *sb.* + -Y: cf. DEFAULTIVE, FAULTY.] Faulty, defective, in fault.

c **1440** *Promp. Parv.* 115 Defawty, *defectivus*. *c* **1449** PECOCK *Repr.* I. xiii. 72 Excusing what ellis in hem schulde be untrewe and defauti. **1462** MARG. PASTON in *Lett.* No. 436 II. 84 He..swore sore he was nevyr defawty in that ye have thowte hym defawty in. **1526** *Pilgr. Perf.* (W. de W. 1531) 214 In the whiche werkes who so be founde defauty, it shall be layde to his charge. **1530** PALSGR. 309/2 Defaulty, in blame for a matter, *fauteux, fauteuse*.

defayte, obs. form of DEFEAT.

defe, obs. form of DEAF.

defeasance (diː'fiːzəns). Forms: 5 defesance, *Sc.* defasance, 6 depheazance, *Sc.* defaisance, 6-7 defeasans, defeysance, 7 defeisance, 6-9 defeazance, 6- defeasance. [ME. a. AF. *defesaunce*, OF. *defesance* undoing, destruction, f. OF. *defesant, des-*, pr. pple. of *desfaire* (now *défaire*) to undo, destroy, f. *des-, dé-*, DE- I. 6 + *faire* to do. See -ANCE.]

1. Undoing, bringing to nought; ruin, defeat, overthrow. (Now always coloured by 2.)

1590 SPENSER *F.Q.* I. xii. 12 Where that champion stout After his foes defeasaunce did remaine. **1616** R. CARPENTER *Christ's Larum-bell* 61 Notwithstanding the discouery and defeysance of their manifold mischieuous designments. *a* **1617** BAYNE *On Eph.* (1658) 35 He may suffer defeasance in the intentions hee purposeth. **1847** GROTE *Greece* II. ix. III. 21 It was always an oligarchy which arose on the defeasance of the heroic kingdom. **1874** STUBBS *Const. Hist.* I. viii. 235 The extinction or other defeasance of the old royal houses.

2. *Law.* The rendering null and void (of a former act, an existing condition, right, etc.).

1592 GREENE *Def. Conny Catch.* (1859) 15 The gentleman ..promised to acknowledge a statute staple to him, with letters of defeysance. **1602** FULBECKE *2nd Pt. Parall.* 68 As to conditions impossible in facte, such conditions if they go to the defeasans of an estate, the estate notwithstanding remaineth good. **1628** COKE *On Litt.* 236 b, Indentures of Defeasance. **1765** BLACKSTONE *Comm.* I. 211 It was not a defeazance of the right of succession. **1827** JARMAN *Powell's Devises* (ed. 3) II. 242 An executory devise, limited in defeazance of a preceding estate.

3. *Law.* A condition upon the performance of which a deed or other instrument is defeated or made void; a collateral deed or writing expressing such condition.

1428 *Surtees Misc.* (1890) 9 An obligacyon..and a defesance made yer apon yat ye sayd John Lyllyng fra yan furth suld be of gude governaunce. **1580** SIDNEY *Arcadia* III. 293 A sufficient defeazance for the firmest bond of good nature. **1634** FORD *P. Warbeck* II. iii, No indenture but has its counterpawn; no noverint but his condition or defeysance. **1641** *Termes de la Ley* 103 A defeasance is usually a deed by it selfe concluded and agreed on betweene the parties, and having relation to another deed or grant. **1767** BLACKSTONE *Comm.* II. 327 A defeazance is a collateral deed, made at the same time with a feoffment or other conveyance, containing certain conditions, upon the performance of which the estate then created may be defeated or totally undone. **1875** POSTE *Gaius* III. Comm. (ed. 2) 414 The warrant being accompanied by a defeazance declaring it to be merely a security for payment.

†4. *Sc.* Acquittance or discharge from an obligation or claim. *Obs.*

1478 [see DEFEASE *v.* 2]. **1489** *Sc. Acts Jas. IV* (1597) §9 The saidis letters of discharge to be na defaisance to them. **1551** *Sc. Acts Mary* (1597) §10 It sal be leasum to the annuelleres, notwithstanding the defaisance maid presently, gif they please to bye in againe..Defaisance of payment.

Hence **de'feasanced** *pa. pple.* or *a.*

1846 WORCESTER, *Defeasanced* (*Law*), liable to be forfeited. *Burrows.*

defease, *v.* Also 5 *Sc.* defese, 6 *Sc.* defase, 7 defeise. [f. *defeas-ance, defeas-ible*, etc., and thus representing OF. *de(s)fes-*, stem of *desfaire* to undo: see DEFEASANCE.]

1. *trans.* To undo, bring to nought, destroy. *rare.*

1621 G. SANDYS *Ovid's Met.* IV. (1626) 76 What? could that Strumpets brat the form defeise Of poore Mæonian Saylers, drencht in Seas? **1866** J. B. ROSE *Ovid's Fasti* VI. 836 Now on the Ides all order is defeased.

†2. *Sc.* To discharge from an obligation, acquit. **b.** To discharge (a part), deduct. *Obs.*

1478 *Act. Dom. Conc.* 22 (Jam.) Becauss the thane of Caldor allegis that he has charteris to defese him tharof [payment], the lordis assignis him..to schew tha charteris, and sufficiand defesance. **1551** *Sc. Acts Mary* (1597) §10 The awner..sall not bee halden to paye mair..then cummis to the residue thereof, the saidis sext, fifth and fourth partes, *respectiuè*, being defaised. **1664** NEWBYTH in M. P. Brown *Suppl. Decis.* (1826) I. 499 Notwithstanding of the twenty shillings Scots to be defeased to the defender upon the boll.

†defease, *sb. Sc. Obs.* [f. prec. vb.] Discharge, acquittance; = DEFEASANCE 4.

1491 *Ld. Treas. Acc. Scotl.* I. 166 Chauncellare, we charge ȝow that..ȝe here the Thesauraris compt and defeis, and allow as ȝe think accordis to resone.

defeasible (dɪ'fiːzɪb(ə)l), *a.* Also 6 defeazable, 9 -ible, 7 defesible, -eable, 7-9 defeasable. [a. AF. *defeasible* (Lyttelton):—OF. type **de(s)faisible*, **de(s)fesible*, f. *de(s)faire*, *de(s)fes-*, to undo + -BLE. Cf. FEASIBLE.] Capable of being, or liable to be, undone, 'defeated' or made void; subject to forfeiture.

1586 FERNE *Blaz. Gentrie* 301 There be two or three rules to be obserued, otherwise the adoption is defeasible. **1612** DAVIES *Why Ireland, etc.* (1747) 81 He came to the Crowne of England by a defeasible title. **1767** BLACKSTONE *Comm.* II. 393 In all these creatures, reclaimed from the wildness of their nature, the property is not absolute, but defeasible. **1818** CRUISE *Digest* (ed. 2) IV. 105 A confirmation may make a voidable or defeazible estate good. **1876** BANCROFT *Hist. U.S.* I. xv. 456 The unlettered savage..might deem the English tenure defeasible.

Hence **de'feasibleness, defeasi'bility**.

1610 DONNE *Pseudo Martyr* 158 Much lesse..were our Lawes subject to that frailty and Defeseablenesse. **1885** SIR F. NORTH in *Law Rep.* 29 Ch. Div. 542 The defeasibility of the gift in favour of Mrs. White.

defeat (dɪ'fiːt), *sb.* [Appears at end of 16th c.: f. DEFEAT *v.*, prob. after F. *défaite* sb. (1475 in Hatzf.): the latter was the ordinary fem. sb. from *défait, -e*, pa. pple. of *défaire* vb., = It. *disfatta* 'an vndoing, an vnmaking' (Florio), a defeat, a rout; Romanic type **disfacta*: see DEFEAT *v.*]

†1. Undoing; ruin; act of destruction. ***to make defeat upon*** (***of***): to bring about the ruin or destruction of. *Obs.*

1599 SHAKS. *Much Ado* IV. i. 48 If you..Haue vanquisht the resistance of her youth, And made defeat of her virginitie. **1602** —— *Ham.* II. ii. 598 A king, Vpon whose property, and most deere life, A damn'd defeate was made. **1621** BEAUM. & FL. *Thierry & Theo.* v. ii, After the damned defeat on you. *a* **1634** CHAPMAN *Rev. Honour*, That he might meantime make a sure defeat On our good aged father's life. **1636** DAVENANT *Wits* v. v, I cannot for my heart proceed to more Defeat upon thy liberty.

2. The action of bringing to nought (schemes, plans, hopes, expectations); frustration. (Now usually *fig.* of 3.)

1599 SHAKS. *Hen. V*, I. ii. 213 So may a thousand actions once a foote..be all well borne Without defeat. **1645** EVELYN *Mem.* (1857) I. 191 After I had sufficiently complained of my defeat of correspondence at Rome. **1667** LD. G. DIGBY *Elvira* I. ii, Th' ingenious defeats..You are prepar'd to give to her suspicions. **1675** *Art Contentm.* ix. §3. 224 With him..whose perpetual toil makes him insensible what the defeat of sport signifies. **1738** WARBURTON *Div. Legat.* II. Notes (R.), The defeat of Julian's impious purpose to rebuild the temple of Jerusalem. **1859** TENNYSON *Guinevere* 621, I must not dwell on that defeat of fame.

3. The act of overthrowing in a contest, the fact of being so overthrown or overcome; overthrow.

With objective genitive, or its equivalent, as 'after their defeat by the Romans', 'the defeat of Bonaparte at Waterloo'; phrases, ***to inflict a defeat upon***, ***†give a defeat to***, to defeat; ***to suffer, sustain***, ***†receive a defeat***, to be defeated.

a. in a military contest or fight. (The usual term from *c* 1650.)

1600 E. BLOUNT tr. *Conestaggio* 298 They had newes in Fraunce of the defeat of the armie. **1657** *North's Plutarch, Addit. Lives* 57 To revenge the Defeat which they received at Derbent. **1659** B. HARRIS *Parival's Iron Age* 213 Prince Rupert..notwithstanding his late defeat at Marston Moore. *Ibid.* 298 They gave a totall defeat to the Turkish Fleet. **1667** MILTON *P. L.* I. 135 The dire event, That with sad overthrow and foul defeat Hath lost us Heav'n. **1710** STEELE *Tatler* No. 74 ¶ 12 He received the News of the Defeat of his Troops. **1841** ELPHINSTONE *Hist. Ind.* II. 103 He at last suffered a total defeat, and lost all his acquisitions. **1874** GREEN *Short Hist.* vii. §8. 430 The defeat of the Armada.

b. in other contests or struggles, *e.g.* in parliament, the defeat of a ministry, of the supporters of a measure, of a measure itself.

1697 JER. COLLIER *Ess. Mor. Subj.*, *Confidence* (1698) 103 A Man of Confidence..is ready to rally after a Defeat; and grows more troublesome upon Denial. **1848** MACAULAY *Hist. Eng.* II. 26 In that House of Commons..the Court had sustained a defeat on a vital question. **1884** GLADSTONE in *Standard* 29 Feb. 2/7 The vote upon redistribution of power brought about the defeat of the first Reform Bill.

4. *Law.* The action of rendering null and void.

defeat (dɪ'fiːt), *v.* Forms: 4-5 deffete, 4-7 defete, 5 deffayt, dyffeat, 5-7 defait, 6 defayte, -fette, -feict, -faict, disfeat, 6-7 defeate, 7 defeit, 6- defeat. [f. OF. *defeit, -fait*, orig. *desfait*, pa. pple. of *desfaire* = It. *disfare*, late L. *diffacĕre*, *disfacĕre*, to undo, unmake, mar, destroy (in *Salic Law* and *Capitula Car. Magn.*), f. L. *dis-* (see DE- I. 6) + *facĕre* to do, make. Apparently the OF. pa. pple. *defait*, *defeit* was first taken into Eng. as a pa. pple. (see DEFEIT, *defet*); this was soon extended to *defeted*, and *defete* taken as the stem of an Eng. verb: cf. the dates of these.

(The pa. pple., and even the pa. t., were sometimes *defeat* in 16-17th c.)]

†1. *trans.* To unmake, undo, do away with; to ruin, destroy. *Obs.*

1435 *Rolls Parl.* 490 Ye saide pouere Toune of Caleys, yat by ye continuance of ye saide Staple hath hiderto been gretly maintened..[is] like to bee defaited and lost. **1481** CAXTON *Myrr.* I. i. 7 God may make alle thyng & alle deffete or vnmake. **1481** —— *Godfrey* 21 Whan Titus..deffeted and destroyed al the cyte. **1509** HAWES *Past. Pleas.* XXXVIII. xii, Her lusty rethoryke My courage reformed..My sorowe defeted, and my mynde dyde modefy. **1548** HALL *Chron.* 184 To subverte and defaict all conclusions and agrementes, enacted and assented to, in the last Parliament. **1604** SHAKS. *Oth.* IV. ii. 160 Vnkindnesse may do much; And his vnkindnesse may defeat my life. **1605** BACON *Adv. Learn.* II. xxii. §5 (1873) 207 Great and sudden fortune for the most part defeateth men. **1611** COTGR., *Desfaire*, to vndoe;.. defeat, discomfit, ouercome; ruine, destroy, ouerthrow. **1632** LITHGOW *Trav.* VIII. 343 Thy wals defeat, were rear'd with fatall bones.

†2. To destroy the vigour or vitality of; to cause to waste or languish; *pa. pple.* wasted, withered.

c **1374** CHAUCER *Boeth.* II. i. 30 þou languissed and art deffeted for talent and desijr of þi raþer fortune. **1483** CAXTON *Gold. Leg.* 136/1 My body is deffeted by the tormentis, that the woundes suffre nothyng to entre in to my thought.

†3. To destroy the beauty, form, or figure of; to disfigure, deface, spoil. *Obs.*

1491 CAXTON *Vitas Patr.* (W. de W. 1495) I. xli. 65 a/2 She was soo deffayted and dysfygured by the grete abstynences that she made. *Ibid.* I. l. 101 b/2 His vysage..was also pale and dyffeated as of a deed man. **1495** *Trevisa's Barth. De P.R.* IV. iii. (ed. W. de W.) 83 Dryenesse..makyth the body euyll colouryd, and defacyth and defetyth [*corpus discolorat et deformat*; Harl. MS. 4787 (*c* **1410**) euel y-hewed & defaceþ & defete; Addit. MS. 27944 (*c* **1425**) euel I-hewed & defactif & defete; *orig. probably* euel yhewed & defaced & defet]. **1604** SHAKS. *Oth.* I. iii. 346 Defeate thy fauour, with an vsurp'd Beard.

†4. *Hunting.* To cut up (an animal). *Obs.*

14.. *Le Venery de Twety* in *Rel. Ant.* I. 153 And whan the hert is take..and shal be defeted. *Ibid.* 154 And whan the boor is i-take, he be deffetyd al velue.

5. To bring to nought, cause to fail, frustrate, nullify (a plan, purpose, scheme, etc.).

1474 CAXTON *Chesse* 65 Thynges and honoures shal ben defetid by sodeyn deth. **1526** *Pilgr. Perf.* (W. de W. 1531) 34 b, Whiche illusyon..as soone as it was detected..anone it auoyded & was defeted. **1538** STARKEY *England* iv. 118 Yf hyt were wel ordryd justyce schold not be so defettyd. **1602** SHAKS. *Ham.* III. iii. 40 My stronger guilt, defeats my strong intent. **1660** HICKERINGILL *Jamaica* (1661) 73 The most promising designs..are many times easily defeated. **1708** J. CHAMBERLAYNE *St. Gt. Brit.* I. III. x. (1743) 204 Almost sufficient to defeat the old adage, 'Rome was not built in a day'. **1781** COWPER *Charity* 38 To thwart its influence, and its end defeat. **1818** CRUISE *Digest* (ed. 2) IV. 414 To.. defeat the ulterior objects of the articles. **1855** EMERSON *Misc.* 223 A man who commits a crime defeats the end of his existence.

6. *Law.* To render null and void, to annul.

1525 TUNSTAL, etc. *To Wolsey* (MS. Cott. Vesp. C III. 189b), In case ye wold have these points at this tyme be expresse convention defeatyd. **1583** *Wills & Inv. N.C.* (Surtees) II. 62 Herbye defeating all former will and willes, by me att anye tyme made. **1642** PERKINS *Prof. Bk.* iv. §279 This exchange is good until it be defeated by the wife or her heire. **1767** BLACKSTONE *Comm.* II. 142 The lessee's estate might also, by the antient law, be at any time defeated, by a common recovery suffered by the tenant of the freehold. **1818** CRUISE *Digest* (ed. 2) II. 49 A condition that defeats an estate. **1848** WHARTON *Law Lex.* s.v. *Defeasance*, A Defeasance on a bond.. defeats that in the same manner.

7. To do (a person) out *of* (something expected, or naturally coming to him); to disappoint, defraud, cheat.

1538 STARKEY *England* I. iv. 121 The credytorys holly are defayted of theyr dette. **1542-3** *Act 34-5 Hen. VIII*, c. 20 §1 Feined recoueries..to binde and defete their heires inheritable by the limitacion of suche giftes. **1569** NEWTON *Cicero's Olde Age* 14a, That they might defeate him from the use and possession of his goods. **1633** BP. HALL *Hard Texts* 382 That thou maist not be defeated of that glory which awaits for thee. **1667** MILTON *P. L.* XI. 254 Death.. Defeated of his seisure. **1767** BLACKSTONE *Comm.* II. 475 A means of defeating their landlords of the security which the law has given them. **1777** JOHNSON *Let. to Mrs. Thrale* 6 Oct., Having been defeated of my first design. **1846** MILL *Logic* III. xxvi. §3 The assertion that a cause has been defeated of an effect that is connected with it by a completely ascertained law of causation.

†**b.** To deprive *of* (something one already possesses); to dispossess. *Obs.*

1591 HARINGTON *Orl. Fur.* XXXVI. xlvii. (1634) 301 Rogero sunders them..Then of their daggers he them both defeateth. **1606** DAY *Ile of Guls* I. ii. (1881) 12 That whosoeuer..can defeate him of his daughters shall with theyr loues inioy his dukedome. **1677** *Govt. Venice* 29 They are never defeated of those marks of Honour, unless they have done something dishonourable.

8. To discomfit or overthrow in a contest; to vanquish, beat, gain the victory over: **a.** in battle.

The sense gradually passes from 'undo, annihilate, ruin, cut to pieces, destroy, rout', in the early quots., to that merely of 'beat, gain the victory over, put to the worse', in the modern ones. (Not in Shaks.)

1562 J. SHUTE *Cambine's Turk. Wars* 6 The armie of Baiazith was defeicted, and he taken by Tamerlano. **1579** E. K. *Gloss. Spenser's Sheph. Cal.* June, Great armies were defaicted and put to flyght at the onely hearing of hys name. **1606** HOLLAND *Sueton.* 15 After this, he defeited Scipio and Ivba. *Ibid.* 47 When Lollius and Varrus were defaited. **1653** H. COGAN tr. *Pinto's Trav.* 47 Then..he made an end of defeating them, the most of them being constrained to leap into the Sea. **1667** LD. ORRERY *State Lett.* (1743) II. 213 Three English ships..fell on the Irish, killed some, and defeat the rest. **1776** *Trial of Nundocomar* 64/2 Their army was defeated before the walls of Patna. **1838** THIRLWALL *Greece* IV. 437 An engagement followed, in which Therimachus was defeated and slain. **1861** *Westm. Rev.* Oct. 497 But though defeated the Cotton States were not vanquished.

b. *transf.* and *fig.*

1781 COWPER *Retirement* 781 'Tis love like his that can alone defeat The foes of man. **1818** SHELLEY *Rev. Islam* VI. lii, But that she Who loved me did with absent looks defeat Despair. **1870** E. PEACOCK *Ralf Skirl.* III. 139 Isabell was not to be so easily defeated.

†**de'featance.** *Obs. rare.* [f. DEFEAT *v.* + -ANCE. (Not in Fr.)] Defeat.

a **1612** BROUGHTON *Wks.* (1662) III. 693 By 3000 well giuen to a courtier and a lady, procured grief to Q. Elizabeth and defeatance.

defeated (dɪ'fi:tɪd), *ppl. a.* [-ED[1].] Undone, frustrated, vanquished, etc.; see the verb.

1602 SHAKS. *Ham.* I. ii. 10 As 'twere, with a defeated ioy. **1660** HICKERINGILL *Jamaica* (1661) 86 Daring to rally defeated courage. *a* **1859** MACAULAY *Hist. Eng.* V. 239 The malevolence of the defeated party soon revived in all its energy.

defeater (dɪ'fi:tə(r)). [-ER[1].] One who or that which defeats.

1844 TUPPER *Crock of G.* xiii, That inevitable defeator of all printed secrets—impatience. **1864** SALA in *Daily Tel.* 11 Oct., The loss inflicted by the defeated on the defeater.

de'feating, *vbl. sb.* [-ING[1].] The action of the verb DEFEAT, q.v.

1592 *Good Newes fr. Fraunce* Title-p., Together with the defeating, drowning, and taking of much victuaille, corne and money, sent by the enemy. **1593** WATSON *Tears of Fancie* xxvi. Poems (Arb.) 191 So liue I now and looke for ioyes defeating. **1659** B. HARRIS *Parival's Iron Age* 94 The defeating of some companies of Dragoons.

de'feating, *ppl. a.* [-ING[2].] That defeats; see the verb.

1674 BOYLE *Excell. Theol.* I. iii. 106 The defeating dispositions of his providence.

defeatism (dɪ'fi:tɪz(ə)m). [ad. F. *défaitisme*, f. *défaite* DEFEAT *sb.*: see -ISM.] Conduct tending to bring about acceptance of (the certainty of) defeat; a disposition to accept defeat.

1918 *Observer* 9 June 6/4 Irish Nationalists will henceforth support Pacifism, and that means defeatism. **1922** *Daily Mail* 13 Nov. 10 At an order from the leaders, the Labour Press has broken into a campaign of defeatism, lamenting that organised capital is still too strong to admit of any possible chance of the levy becoming law this time. **1926** C. L. GRAVES *Hubert Parry* II. 79 He was as far removed from foolish optimism as from 'defeatism'. **1928** GALSWORTHY *Swan Song* 124 To acknowledge the limitations of human nature was a sort of defeatism. **1942** F. G. HACKFORTH-JONES *One-One-One* vi. 65 Defeatism.. must be guarded against; it was as dangerous an attitude of mind as the twin-headed monsters of Complacency and Wishful Thinking.

defeatist (dɪ'fi:tɪst). [ad. F. *défaitiste*: cf. prec.] One who advocates defeatism or accepts defeat. Also *attrib.* or as *adj.*

1918 *Observer* 9 June 8/6 The political creed of the party, ..is to support the Government in winning the war and in defeating the intrigues of Pacifists and Defeatists. **1918** *Times* 19 June 6/4 The Independent Nationalist Press..has applied the label 'defeatist' to those Nationalists who voted for a moderate policy at the Irish Convention. **1920** *19th Cent.* Mar. 556 The shop-stewards, too, in the great factories in Berlin and other towns were disloyal and 'defeatist'. **1921** N. ANGELL *Fruits of Victory* vii. 207 The repression of pacifist and defeatist propaganda during the War. **1921** *19th Cent.* Jan. 151 Throughout the Great War, as in the Japanese War, he was a defeatist. **1927** C. E. MONTAGUE *Right off Map* xxii, Lovel sat down to his separate table and map, but could not take his eyes from the abhorred defeatist. **1929** *Daily Tel.* 8 Jan. 10/3 The defeatist tactics of those who belittle his leadership.

†**de'featment.** *Obs.* [f. DEFEAT *v.* + -MENT.] The action of defeating, defeat.

1. In battle or war; = DEFEAT *sb.* 3.

1598 BARRET *Theor. Warres* IV. i. 98 The cause of many defeatments. *a* **1635** NAUNTON *Fragm. Reg.* (Arb.) 19 Considering the defeatments of Blackwater. **1733** MILLNER *Compend. Jrnl.* 167 The Seat of the War was wholly in Flanders, removed thither by the French Defeatment.

2. Undoing, frustration, disappointment (of a purpose, design, etc.); = DEFEAT *sb.* 2.

1647 SPRIGGE *Anglia Rediv.* I. vi. (1854) 53 Had these letters been delivered to the King (as they might have been but for this defeatment). **1674** OWEN *Wks.* (1851) VIII. 491 The defeatment of these advantages. **1681** H. MORE *Exp. Dan.* 261 In defeatment of his Power and Laws in the Church.

defeature (dɪ'fi:tjʊə(r)), *sb. Obs.* or *arch.* Also 7 **defaiture, defeiture, diffeature.** [a. OF. *deffaiture, desfaiture*, f. *desfaire* to undo, etc., after *faiture*:—L. *factūra* making, doing. In Eng. conformed in spelling to *defeat*, and in sense 2 associated with *feature*.]

†**1.** Undoing, ruin; = DEFEAT *sb.* 1. *Obs.*

1592 DANIEL *Compl. Rosamond*, The Day before the Night of my Defeature. **1596** SPENSER *F.Q.* IV. vi. 17 For their first loves defeature. **1615** *Life Lady Jane Grey* B iij b, After her most vnfortunate marriage and the utter defaiture almost of her name and honours. **1616** R. C. *Times' Whistle* iii. 900 To make defeature Of his estate in blisse he doth intend.

2. Disfigurement, defacement; marring of features. *arch.* Cf. DEFEAT *v.* 3.

Now chiefly an echo of the Shaksperian use.

1590 SHAKS. *Com. Err.* v. i. 299 Carefull houres with times deformed hand, Haue written strange defeatures in my face. *Ibid.* II. i. 98. **1592** — *Ven. & Ad.* 736 To mingle beauty with infirmities, And pure perfection with impure defeature. **1797** MRS. A. M. BENNETT *Beggar Girl* (1813) V. 312 All the defeatures of guilt..stood on the brow of the former. **1829** SOUTHEY *Colloq. Society* Ded. I. iv, Ere heart-hardening bigotry..With sour defeature marr'd his countenance. **1842** *Tait's Mag.* IX. 354 To see the veil uplifted from the deformities and defeatures of my fellow-creatures.

†**3.** Frustration; = DEFEAT *sb.* 2. *Obs.*

1609 BP. W. BARLOW *Answ. Nameless Cath.* 14 The defeature and discouerie of those horrible Traitors. **1668** E. KEMP *Reasons for Use of Ch. Prayers* 10 Have they had no disappointments, no defeatures? **1681** GLANVILL *Sadducismus* I. (1726) 31 The Defeature of its Purposes.

†**4.** Defeat in battle or contest. *Obs.*

1598 FLORIO, *Soffratto*, a defeature or ouerthrow. **1601** HOLLAND *Pliny* II. 481 After the defeiture of K. Perseus. **1623** MASSINGER *Bondman* IV. i, Have you acquainted her with the defeature Of the Carthaginians. **1810** SOUTHEY *Kehama* XI. ii, Complaining of defeature twice sustain'd. **1834** *Fraser's Mag.* X. 417 This comfort we to our defeature lend.

de'feature, *v.* [f. prec. sb., sense 2. Cf. OF. *deffaiturer* (13th c. in Godef.), with which however the Eng. word is not historically connected.] *trans.* To disfigure, deface, mar the features of. Hence **de'featured** *ppl. a.*

1792 J. FENNELL *Proc. at Paris* (L.), Events defeatured by exaggeration. **1818** *Blackw. Mag.* II. 493 A..face, defeatured horribly. **1863** LD. LYTTON *Ring Amasis* II. 137 Ruined defeatured shapes of Beauty.

defeazable, -ance, var. DEFEASIBLE, -ANCE.

†**'defecate,** *ppl. a. obs.* Also 5 **deficate,** 7 **defæcate.** [ad. L. *dēfæcāt-us* pa. pple. of *dēfæcāre* (see next). In early times used as pa. pple. of DEFECATE *v.*]

1. Purified from dregs, clarified, clear and pure. **a.** as *pple.*

1533 ELYOT *Cast. Helthe* (1541) 34b, Ale or biere welle and perfytely brewed and clensed, and.. settled and defecate. **1650** W. BROUGH *Sacr. Princ.* (1659) 257 Joys.. defecate from your dregs of guilt.

b. as *adj.*

1576 NEWTON *Lemnie's Complex.* (1633) 143 This pure, cleare, defecate, lovely, and amiable juyce. **1621-51** *Anat. Mel.* II. ii. I. i. 233 Many rivers..defecate and clear. **1671** R. BOHUN *Wind* 235 The Air is generally defecate and serene. **1684** tr. *Bonet's Merc. Compit.* v. 146 It renders the mass of bloud defæcate.

2. Mentally, morally, or spiritually purified.

c **1450** HENRYSON *Test. Cres.* (R.), Sith ye are all seven deficate Participant of diuine sapience. **1621** BURTON *Anat. Mel.* III. iv. I. i, Calvinists, more defecate than the rest, yet ..not free from superstition. **1653** H. MORE *Conject. Cabbal.* (1713) 23 A pure and defecate Æthereal Spirit. **1742** YOUNG *Nt. Th.* ix. 1209 Minds elevate, and panting for unseen, And defecate from sense.

defecate ('dɛfɪkeɪt), *v.* Also 6 **deficate,** 7-9 **defæcate.** [f. ppl. stem of L. *dēfæcāre* to cleanse from dregs, purify, f. DE- I. 6 + *fæx*, pl. *fæc-es* dregs. Cf. F. *déféquer* (16th c. in Littré).]

1. *trans.* To clear from dregs or impurities; to purify, clarify, refine.

1575 LANEHAM *Let.* (1871) 58 When..it iz defecated by al nights standing, the drink iz the better. **1621** BURTON *Anat. Mel.* I. ii. II. i, Some are of opinion that such fat standing waters make the best Beere, and that seething doth defecate it. **1707** SLOANE *Jamaica* I. 20 The gum, which they defecate in water by boiling and purging. **1753** HERVEY *Theron & Asp.* (1757) I. xii. 457 Some like the Distillers Alembick sublimate; others like the Common sewers defæcate. **1881** H. NICHOLSON *From Sword to Share* xxxii. 255 The juice should be.. defecated and concentrated on the most approved methods.

2. *fig.* To purify from pollution or extraneous admixture (of things immaterial).

1621 BURTON *Anat. Mel.* III. iv. I. iii, Till Luther's time.. who began upon a sudden to defecate, and as another sun to drive away those foggy mists of superstition. **1648** BOYLE *Seraph. Love* (1700) 58 To Defecate and Exalt our Conceptions. **1665** GLANVILL *Scepsis Sci.* i. 17 If we defæcate the notion from materiality. **1751** JOHNSON *Rambler* No. 177 ¶4 To defecate and clear my mind by brisker motions. **1866** LOWELL *Biglow P.* Introd. Poems 1890 II. 162 A growing tendency to curtail language into a mere convenience, and to defecate it of all emotion. **1870** W. M. ROSSETTI *Life of Shelley* p. xx, To defecate life of its misery.

3. To remove (dregs or fæces) by a purifying process; to purge away; to void as excrement. Also *fig.*

1774 GOLDSM. *Nat. Hist.* (1862) I. iv. 13 It [the air] soon began to defecate and to depose these particles upon the oily surface. **1862** GOULBURN *Pers. Relig.* IV. vii. (1873) 311 To defecate the dregs of the mind. **1872** H. MACMILLAN *True Vine* iii. 91 By the death of the body, sin is defecated.

b. *absol.* To void the fæces.

1864 in WEBSTER. **1878** A. HAMILTON *Nerv. Dis.* 108 The patient should not be allowed to get up to defecate. **1889** J. M. DUNCAN *Clin. Lect. Dis. Women* xiv. (ed. 4) 96.

Hence **'defecating** *vbl. sb.* and *ppl. a.*

1855 MAURICE *Let.* in *Life* (1884) II. vii. 277 Get it clear by any defæcating processes. **1885** *Manch. Even. News* 29 May 2/2 The use of defecating powders.

defecated ('dɛfɪkeɪtɪd), *ppl. a.* [f. prec. + -ED.]

1. Cleared of dregs or impurities; clarified, clear.

1641 WILKINS *Math. Magick* II. v. (1648) 185 Have the air ..so pure and defecated as is required. **1677** GREW *Anat. Fruits* iii. §6 A more defecated or better fined Juyce. **1733** CHEYNE *Eng. Malady* Pref. (1734) 5 Generous, defecated, spirituous Liquors. **1865** *Sat. Rev.* 17 June 721/1 We have a right to ask..that our rivers should flow with water, and not with defecated sewage.

2. *fig.* Mentally, morally, or spiritually purified.

1611 SPEED *Hist. Gt. Brit.* IX. xx. §4 A great deale of cleare elocution, and defæcated conceit. **1793** T. TAYLOR *Orat. Julian* 39 Consider the defecated nature of that pure and divine body. **1862** F. HALL *Hindu Philos. Syst.* 279 His judgment daily becomes more and more defecated.

3. *transf.* Of evil: Unmixed, unmitigated.

1796 BURKE *Let. Noble Ld.* Wks. VIII. 57 The principle of evil himself, incorporeal, pure, unmixed, dephlegmated, defecated, evil. **1827** HARE *Guesses* Ser. I. (1873) 92 The Penal Colonies..have been the seats of simple, defecated crime.

defecation (dɛfɪ'keɪʃən). Also **defæcation.** [ad. L. *dēfæcātiōn-em*, n. of action from *dēfæcāre* to DEFECATE. Also in mod.F.] The action or process of defecating.

1. The action of purifying from dregs or lees; cleansing from impurities; clarification.

1656 BLOUNT *Glossogr.*, *Defecation*, a purging from dregs, a refining. **1666** J. SMITH *Old Age* (ed. 2) 218 Depuration and defæcation..of the blood and vital spirits. **1865** *Standard* 26 Jan., Unless some means are taken for the defecation of the sewage before it is discharged into the river.

2. Purification of the mind or soul from what is gross or low.

1649 JER. TAYLOR *Gt. Exemp.* I. Ad §ix. 142 A defecation of his faculties and an opportunity of Prayer.

3. The discharging of the fæces.

1830 R. KNOX *Béclard's Anat.* 310 In coughing, sneezing, vomiting, defecation..a greater or less number of the muscles..act in unison. **1847-9** TODD *Cycl. Anat.* IV. 142/2 Cases of defecation of hair..are..to be received with distrust. **1872** HUXLEY *Phys.* vi. 153 When defæcation takes place.

defecator ('dɛfɪkeɪtə(r)). [agent-n. f. DEFECATE *v.*: see -OR.] One who or that which defecates or purifies; *spec.* in *Sugar-manufacture*: see quot. 1874.

1864 WEBSTER, *Defecator*, that which cleanses or purifies. **1874** KNIGHT *Mech. Dict.*, *Defecator*, an apparatus for the removal from a saccharine liquid of the immature and feculent matters which would impair the concentrated result... Defecators for sorghum partake of the character of filters. **1875** URE *Dict. Arts* III. 944 (*Sugar*), This dissolving pan is sometimes..called a 'defecator'.

defect (dɪˈfɛkt, ˈdiː-), *sb.* Also 5 **defaicte**, 5–6 **defecte**. [ad. L. *dēfect-us* defect, want, f. ppl. stem of *dēficĕre* to leave, desert, fail, etc.: see DEFECT *v.* In early use repr. OF. *defaicte* privation, or *defaict* evil, misfortune: see DEFEAT *v.*]

1. The fact of being wanting or falling short; lack or absence of something essential to completeness (opposed to *excess*); deficiency.

1589 NASHE *Introd. Green's Menaphon* (Arb.) 11 To supplie all other inferiour foundations defects. **1592** DAVIES *Immort. Soul* Introd. v. 2 Which Ill being nought but a Defect of Good. **1632** J. HAYWARD tr. *Biondi's Eromena* 112 Holding on a meane path betweene excesse and defect. **1719** DE FOE *Crusoe* (1840) II. ii. 43, I must supply a defect in my former relation. **1798** MALTHUS *Popul.* (1817) I. 360 The excess of one check is balanced by the defect of some other. **1848** MACAULAY *Hist. Eng.* I. 495 Having little money to give, the Estates supplied the defect by loyal protestations and barbarous statues. **1878** MORLEY *Crit. Misc.*, *Condorcet* 66 The excess of scepticism and the defect of enthusiasm.

b. *in defect*: wanting, deficient, defective. *in* (†*for*) *defect of*: in default of, for want of.

1612 T. TAYLOR *Comm. Titus* i. 1 The latter being in defect. *Ibid.* i. 5 Our bodies are..prone to pine away for defect of daily food. **1641** FRENCH *Distill.* i. (1651) 3 In defect of a Furnace..we may use a Kettle. **1643** SIR T. BROWNE *Relig. Med.* (1659) 174 That [quality]..in whose defect the Devils are unhappy. **1767** BLACKSTONE *Comm.* II. 76 Besides the scutages they were liable to in defect of personal attendance. **1865** GROTE *Plato* I. i. 47 In other [animals] water was in excess and fire in defect.

2. A shortcoming or failing; a fault, blemish, flaw, imperfection (in a person or thing).

c **1420** *Pallad. on Husb.* I. 44 An hidde defaicte is sumtyme in nature Under covert. **1592** SHAKS. *Ven. & Ad.* 138 But having no defects, why dost abhor me? **1594** HOOKER *Eccl. Pol.* I. i. (1611) 2 The manifold defects whereunto every kind of regiment is subiect. **1647** CLARENDON *Hist. Reb.* I. (1843) 25/1 The very good general reputation he had, notwithstanding his defects, acquired. **1752** FIELDING *Covent Gard. Jrnl.* No. 56 Ill breeding..is not a single defect, it is the result of many. **1857** H. REED *Lect. Eng. Poets* II. x. 18 Its incurable defect is an utter absence of imagination. **1878** MORLEY *Crit. Misc.*, *Vauvenargues* 14 Vauvenargues has the defects of his qualities.

b. *Naut.* (See quots.)

1829 MARRYAT *F. Mildmay* v, Having delivered..an account of our defects, they were sent up to the Admiralty. **1867** SMYTH *Sailor's Word-bk.*, *Defects*, an official return of the state of a ship as to what is required for her hull and equipment, and what repairs she stands in need of. Upon this return a ship is ordered to sea, into harbour, into dock, or paid out of commission.

†**3.** The quality of being imperfect; defectiveness, faultiness. *Obs.*

1538 STARKEY *England* II. i. 178 The defecte of nature ys with vs such. *c* **1600** SHAKS. *Sonn.* cxlix. 11 When all my best doth worship thy defect. **1776** SIR J. REYNOLDS *Disc.* vii. (1876) 414 The merit or defect of performances.

4. The quantity or amount by which anything falls short; in *Math.* a part by which a figure or quantity is wanting or deficient.

1660 BARROW *Euclid* VI. xxvii, The greatest is that AD which is applied to the half being like to the defect KI. **1674** JEAKE *Arith.* (1696) 223 Supplying the defect of the Dividend with Cyphers. **1823** H. J. BROOKE *Introd. Crystallogr.* 290 When a decrement by 1 row of molecules takes place on the edge of any parallelopiped, the ratio of the edges of the defect [etc.]. **1858** HERSCHEL *Astron.* §545 An allowance..proportional to the excess or defect of Jupiter's distance from the earth above or below its average amount.

†**5.** Failure (of the heavenly bodies) to shine; eclipse; wane of the moon. *Obs.* [L. *dēfectus.*]

1603 HOLLAND *Plutarch's Mor.* 1307 The defect of the Moone and her occultation. **1607** TOPSELL *Four-f. Beasts* (1658) 4 When the moon is in the wane, they [Apes] are heavie and sorrowful..for, as other beasts, so do these fear the defect of the stars and planets. **1692** RAY *Dissol. World* 259 Prodigious and lasting Defects of the Sun, such as happened when Cæsar the Dictator was slain.

†**6.** A falling away (*from*), defection. *Obs.*

1540 in Strype *Eccl. Mem.* I. xlix. 367 The king..made a defect from his purpose of reformation with great precipitancy. *c* **1790** WILLOCK *Voy.* 308 When a priest apostatizes..they seldom place his defect to the account of conscience.

†**deˈfect**, *a.* *Obs.* [ad. L. *dēfectus*, pa. pple. of *dēficĕre*: see next.] Defective, deficient, wanting.

1600 TOURNEUR *Transf. Metamorph.* Prol. i, This huge concauitie, defect of light. **1630** J. TAYLOR (Water P.) *Wks.* (N.), Their service was defect and lame. **1664** *Flodden F.* vi. 56 And sage advice was clean defect.

deˈfect, *v.* [f. L. *dēfect-*, ppl. stem of *dēficĕre* to leave, desert, depart, cease, fail, f. DE- + *facĕre* to make, do.] **I.** *intr.*

†**1.** To fail, fall short, become deficient or wanting; to fall off *from* (a standard, etc.). *Obs.*

1586 J. HOOKER *Girald. Irel.* in *Holinshed* II. 143/2 After he perceiued that nature began to faile and defect, he yeelded himselfe to die. **1598** BARCKLEY *Felic. Man* IV. (1603) 315 The vertue and goodnesse of men seemeth to defect from that of former ages. **1646** SIR T. BROWNE *Pseud. Ep.* I. v. 18 Yet have the inquiries of most defected by the way. **1652** GAULE *Magastrom.* 295 The Moon suddenly defected in an ecclipse. *a* **1677** BARROW *Serm.* Wks. 1716 III. 16 Not..to defect from the right..course thereto.

2. To fall away *from* (a person, party, or cause); to become a rebel or deserter; *spec.* to desert *to* a Communist country from a non-Communist country, or vice versa.

1596 DALRYMPLE tr. *Leslie's Hist. Scot.* IV. liii. 241 Thay had defected frome the Christiane Religioune. **1646** BUCK *Rich. III*, I. 15 The Duke was now secretly in his heart defected from the King, and become male-content. **1652** GAULE *Magastrom.* 340 He defected, and fled to the contrary part. **1860** RUSSELL *Diary India* I. xviii. 280 The native troops and gunners defected. **1955** *Times* 10 May 11/2 There must be many soldiers in the satellite armies who commit ideological sin in thought, but it is difficult to see how they could defect in action. *Ibid.* 27 Aug. 6/1 Dr. John ..defected to east Berlin last year. **1959** *Ibid.* 28 May 15/5 A plot by a member of Parliament and a lobby correspondent to persuade a top Russian scientist to 'defect'. **1960** *Guardian* 16 Sept. 13/2 One of the two code clerks who defected to Russia.

II. *trans.*

†**3.** To cause to desert or fall away. *Obs.*

1636 PRYNNE *Unbish. Tim.* Ded. (1661) 7 Defect me from (the Episcopal) throne, expell me the City. **1685** F. SPENCE *House of Medici* 373 The means of defecting his garrison.

†**4.** To hurt, damage, make defective; to dishonour. *Obs.*

1579 *Remedie agst. Loue* C ij, To brydell all affectes, As.. Drunkennesse, Whordome, which our God defectes. **1639** *Troubles Q. Eliz.* (N.), Men may much suspect; But yet, my lord, none can my life defect.

Hence †**deˈfected** *ppl. a.*, †**deˈfecting** *vbl. sb.*

1589 WARNER *Alb. Eng.* V. xxviii. (R.), Defected honour neuer more is to be got againe. **1596** DALRYMPLE tr. *Leslie's Hist. Scot.* (1885) 62 A certane gret schip, bot throuch aldnes defected. **1602** CAREW *Cornwall* (1723) 140 a, There dwelt another, so affected, or rather defected [being deaf and dumb]. **1635** HEYWOOD *Hierarch.* II. Comm. 104, I finde myselfe much defected and disabled in my knowledge and understanding. **1686** EVELYN *Mem.* (1857) II. 262 The Archbishop of York now died..I look on this as a great stroke to the poor Church of England, now in this defecting period.

defectant (dɪˈfɛktənt). *rare.* [f. DEFECT *v.* + -ANT. (No corresp. L. or F.)] = DEFECTOR.

1883 *Field* 1 Dec. 759 Defectant after defectant causing.. the honorary secretary an immense amount of trouble.

defectibility (dɪˌfɛktɪbɪ ˈlɪtɪ). [f. next + -ITY.] Liability to fail or become defective.

a **1617** BAYNE *On Eph.* (1658) 108 This is..to detect..the defectibility..in his creature. **1678** GALE *Crt. Gentiles* III. 4 Sin came first into the world from the Defectibilitie of our first Parents their Free-wil. **1705** PURSHALL *Mech. Macrocosm* 13 A Defectibilty in these is Inconsistent with Infinite Wisdom. **1845** R. W. HAMILTON *Pop. Educ.* viii. (ed. 2) 192 The certain defectibility of all institutions, which depend not upon the principle of self-government.

deˈfectible, *a.* Also 7 **-able**. [f. L. *dēfect-*, ppl. stem of *dēficĕre* (see DEFECT *v.*) + -BLE: cf. *perfectible*.] Liable to fail or fall short.

a **1617** BAYNE *On Eph.* (1658) 104 The sin of a creature defectable maybe ordained. **1674** HICKMAN *Quinquart. Hist.* (ed. 2) 12 The defectible nature of the will. **1736** BUTLER *Anal.* I. v. Wks. (1874) I. 101 Such creatures..would for ever remain defectible.

defection (dɪˈfɛkʃən). In 6 **defeccion**. [ad. L. *dēfectiōn-em* desertion, revolt, failure, eclipse, deficiency, fainting, etc., n. of action from L. *dēficĕre*: see DEFECT *v.* Cf. F. *défection* (in OF. 13–15th c., and in mod.F. 18–19th c., but obs. in 16th c., when the Eng. word was adopted from L.).]

1. The action or fact of failing, falling short or becoming defective; failure (*of* anything).

1544 PHAER *Regim. Lyfe* (1553) G vj b, Mani times foloweth defeccion of the strength. **1576** FLEMING *Panopl. Epist.* 36 You..suffer no defection of your renoune, nor eclipse of dignitie. **1650** FULLER *Pisgah* II. 62 The stopping of the waters [of Jordan] above must necessarily command their defection beneath. **1655–60** STANLEY *Hist. Philos.* (1701) 29/2 As soon as he remembred these words, he fell into a great defection of Spirit. **1853** C. BRONTË *Villette* xxiv, I underwent..miserable defections of hope, intolerable encroachments of despair. **1874** H. R. REYNOLDS *John Bapt.* iii. §1. 129 All the cumbrous ceremonial might be strictly attended to without flaw or defection.

†**b.** *spec.* Failure of vitality; a fainting away or swooning. *Obs.*

1615 CROOKE *Body of Man* 417 The vrine that hee auoyded in his defections or swounds. **1684** tr. *Bonet's Merc. Compit.* XIX. 680 It may be sometimes good in sudden Defections of the Soul to sprinkle cold water on the Face.

†**c.** Imperfection, defectiveness; an instance of this, a defect. *Obs.*

1576 FLEMING *Panopl. Epist.* 273 In whom, if there be any defection..it is to be referred to Nature. **1651** *Life Father Sarpi* (1676) 93 He himself in his anatomy of his affections and defections..acknowledges himself to be severe. **1656** BLOUNT *Glossogr.*, *Defection*..an infirmity. **1677** HALE *Contempl.* II. 38 The Light of Nature shews us, that there is a great defection and disorder in our Natures.

2. The action of falling away from allegiance or adherence to a leader, party, or cause; desertion.

1552 HULOET, *Defection*, properly wheras an armye doth forsake their owne captayne. **1583** STUBBES *Anat. Abus.* II. (1882) 92 After the defection of Iudas the traitour. **1653** H. COGAN tr. *Pinto's Trav.* lxx. 284 Fearing lest the defection of his souldiers should daily more and more increase. **1670** R. COKE *Disc. Trade* Pref., When the United Netherlands made their defection from the Crown of Spain. **1777** ROBERTSON *Hist. Amer.* (1778) II. VI. 251 A spirit of defection had already begun to spread among those whom he trusted most. **1884** *Nonconf. & Indep.* 21 Feb. 186/3 The Liberal defection on Wednesday morning was..small.

3. A falling away from faith, religion, duty, or virtue; backsliding; apostasy.

1546 BALE *Eng. Votaries* II. (R.), Suche a defection from Christ as Saint Paul speketh of. **1549** LATIMER *5th Serm. bef. Edw. VI* (Arb.) 132 Also the defection is come and swaruinge from the fayth. **1612** T. TAYLOR *Comm. Titus* ii. 1 The Lord for this end permitteth many generall defections and corruptions. **1677** HALE *Prim. Orig. Man.* IV. vii. 355 The defection and disobedience of the first Man, which brought Death into the World. **1738** WARBURTON *Div. Legat.* I. 287 Their frequent Defections into Idolatry. **1772** PRIESTLEY *Inst. Relig.* (1782) I. 300 The times of defection and idolatry. **1882** FARRAR *Early Chr.* II. 436 For each such defection we must find forgiveness.

Hence **deˈfectionist**, one who advocates defection.

1846 WORCESTER cites *Morn. Chron.*

†**deˈfectious**, *a.* *Obs.* [f. DEFECTION: see -OUS. Cf. *infectious*.]

1. Having defects, defective.

1581 PETTIE *Guazzo's Civ. Conv.* I. (1586) 11 b, Without Conversation our life would bee defectious. **1581** SIDNEY *Apol. Poetrie* (Arb.) 43 Perchance in some one defectious peece, we may find a blemish.

2. Of the nature of defection or desertion.

1630 LORD *Relig. Persees* Ep. Ded., Relapse and defectious apostasie.

defectivation (dɪˌfɛktɪˈveɪʃən). *Linguistics.* [f. DEFECTIVE *a.* + -ATION.] The process or result of making, or becoming, defective.

1957 HJELMSLEV & ULDALL *Outl. Glossematics* 83 It involves syncretism, defectivation, and manifestation. **1963** *Language* XXXIX. 328 The intensive term of an opposition is also the one on which 'defectivations' and 'syncretisms' depend.

defective (dɪˈfɛktɪv), *a.* and *sb.* Also 5 **defectif**, **-yf**, **def(f)ectyff(e**, 5–6 **def(f)ectyve**. [a. F. *défectif*, *-ive* (14th c. in Littré), ad. L. *dēfectīv-us* (Tertull.), f. *dēfect-*, ppl. stem of *dēficĕre*: see DEFECT *v.*]

A. *adj.* **1. a.** Having a defect or defects; wanting some essential part or proper quality; faulty, imperfect, incomplete.

1472 in *Surtees Misc.* (1890) 25 The crosse in the markythe his defectyff & lyke to fall. **1480** CAXTON *Chron. Eng.* clxiv. 148 And tho lete kyng edward amende the lawes of walys that were defectif. **1495** *Act 11 Hen. VII*, c. 4 Weightes and mesures so found defectif to be forfeit and brent. **1528** PAYNEL *Salerne's Regim.* X iv b, Saffron comfortethe defectiue membres, and principallye the harte. **1599** SANDYS *Europæ Spec.* (1632) 153 For a Prince hee hath beene thought somwhat defective. **1663** GERBIER *Counsel* 8 Why modern and daily Buildings are so exceedingly Defective? **1781** COWPER *Poems, Ep. to Lady Austen* 62 In aid of our defective sight. **1860** TYNDALL *Glac.* I. xxiv. 171 My defective French pronunciation. **1893** *Law Times' Rep.* LXVIII. 309/1 The defective condition of the drains.

b. *defective fifth* (in *Music*): an interval containing a semitone less than the perfect fifth. *defective hyperbola* (in *Math.*): = DEFICIENT hyperbola.

1706 PHILLIPS (ed. Kersey), *Semi-Diapason*, a Term in Musick, signifying a defective or imperfect Octave. **1727–51** CHAMBERS *Cycl.* s.v. *Curve*, [Newton's] Enumeration of the Curves of the second kind..Six are defective parabolas, having no diameters..Seven are defective hyperbolas, having diameters. **1730–6** BAILEY (folio), *Semidiapente*, a defective fifth, called a false fifth.

c. *spec.* Mentally defective.

1898 *Amer. Jrnl. Sociology* Nov. 334 Numerous are the cases of idiotic women, the mothers of defective illegitimate children. **1899** *Act 62 & 63 Vict.* c. 32 § 1 A school authority ..may..make such arrangements..for ascertaining—(*a*) what children in their district, not being imbecile, and not being merely dull or backward, are defective, that is to say, what children by reason of mental or physical defect are incapable of receiving proper benefit from..instruction in the ordinary..schools. **1908** A. F. TREDGOLD *Mental Deficiency* viii. 123 A group of children existed who were so far defective that they could not be satisfactorily taught in the ordinary public schools, but who were not sufficiently defective to be certified as imbeciles or idiots. *Ibid.* 124 These defective children would suffer by association with imbeciles. **1933** L. P. CLARK *Amentia* p. xi, Though our compassion be great for the defective child, the need of understanding [etc.].

2. *defective in* (†*of*): wanting or deficient in.

1599 SANDYS *Europæ Spec.* (1632) 112 A soveraigne preservative, and defective of no vertue save Iustice and Mercy. **1604** SHAKS. *Oth.* II. i. 233 All which the Moore is defectiue in. *a* **1639** W. WHATELEY *Prototypes* I. xi. (1640) 107 Why are we so defective in this duty? **1689** EVELYN *Mem.* (1857) III. 305 Hence it is that we are in England so defective of good libraries. **1713** ADDISON *Guard.* No. 110 ¶ 2 Our tragedy writers have been notoriously defective in giving proper sentiments to the persons they introduce. **1875** JOWELL *Plato* (ed. 2) IV. 121 The first portion of the dialogue is in no way defective in ease and grace.

†**3.** At fault; that has committed a fault or offence; guilty of error or wrongdoing. *Obs.*

1401 *Pol. Poems* (Rolls) II. 106 Thou puttist defaut to prestes, as erst thou didist to curates. I wot thai ben defectif, bot ȝit stondith Cristis religion. **1467** in *Eng. Gilds* (1870) 389 Yf suche a persone may be founde defectyf by xij. men lawfully sworen. **1504** ATKYNSON tr. *De Imitatione* III. xv, If thou founde thy aungels defectyue & impure. **1518** *Act 10 Hen. VIII* in *Stat. Irel.* (1621) 56 Persons..so founden defective or trespassing in any of the said statutes. **1677** *Govt. Venice* 189 When any of them is defective, he is responsible to that terrible Court.

4. Wanting or lacking (to the completeness of anything).

1603 HOLLAND *Plutarch's Mor.* 55 To supply that which was defective in some, or to correct what was amisse in others. **1711** STRYPE *Parker* IV. iii. (R.), To have written thereon what was defective. **1714** tr. *Rivella* 68 He..did not then dream there was any thing in her Person defective to his Happiness. **1864** CARLYLE *Fredk. Gt.* (1865) IV. XII. v. 162, I wish you had a Fortunatus hat; it is the only thing defective in your outfit.

5. *Gram.* Wanting one or more of the usual forms of declension, conjugation, etc.

1530 PALSGR. Introd. 30 Verbes parsonall be of thre sortes, parfyte, anomales, and defectyves. *Ibid.* 36 Some be yet more deffectyves. **1824** L. MURRAY *Eng. Gram.* (ed. 5) I. 168 Defective Verbs are those which are used only in some of their moods and tenses, (*e.g.*) Can, could..Ought..quoth.

†**6.** *defective cause*: see DEFICIENT *a.* 3. *Obs.*

1624 N. DE LAWNE tr. *Du Moulin's Logick* 60 Under the Efficient cause we comprehend the cause which is called Defective. As the want of sight is the cause of going astray. **1678** GALE *Crt. Gentiles* III. 195 Albeit Gods wil be the effective and predeterminative cause of the substrate mater of sin, yet it is no way a defective or moral cause of sin.

B. *sb.* †**1.** A thing defective or wanting. *Obs.*

1497 BP. ALCOCK *Mons Perfect.* A iij/2 No defectyue to their comforte.

†**2. a.** *gen.* One who is defective. *Obs.*

a **1592** H. SMITH *Wks.* (1866–7) I. 444, I cannot tell what to make of these defectives..they neither weep nor dance..they weep almost, and dance almost.

b. *spec.* A person who is deficient in one or more of the physical senses or powers. *U.S.*

1881 G. S. HALL *German Culture* 267 She [Laura Bridgman] is not apt, like many defectives, to fall asleep if left alone or unemployed. **1892** J. B. WEBER in *N. Amer. Rev.* Apr. 425 Their paupers, criminals, or other defectives.

c. A mental defective (see MENTAL *a.*).

1899 *Pop. Sci. Monthly* Apr. 747 Laws preventing the marriage of defectives and of their immediate descendents would go far to stem the tide of harmful heredity. **1908** A. F. TREDGOLD *Mental Deficiency* viii. 127 A proportion of the urban defectives attending special schools are returned as cured to the ordinary schools. **1913** *Act 3 & 4 Geo. V* c. 38 §1 The following classes of persons who are mentally defective shall be deemed to be defectives within the meaning of this Act:—(*a*) Idiots...(*b*) Imbeciles [etc.]. **1922** [see MENTAL *a.*]. **1937** H. G. WELLS *Star Begotten* vi. 90 Institutions for defectives, lunatic asylums. **1964** M. CRITCHLEY *Developmental Dyslexia* xiii. 74 Any total series will probably include some children who are dullards, if not indeed defectives.

3. *Gram.* A defective part of speech. (Also *fig.*)

1612 BRINSLEY *Pos. Parts* (1669) 100 Rehearse the several sorts of Defectives..Aptots, Monoptots, Diptots, [etc.]. **1627–77** FELTHAM *Resolves* II. iv. 166 Certainly a Lyer, though never so plausible, is but a defective of the present tense. **1863** W. SMITH tr. *Curtius' Gr. Gram.* §200 Observe further the Defectives: ὕστερος later, ὕστατος *ultimus*, [etc.].

defectively (dɪˈfɛktɪvlɪ), *adv.* [-LY².] In a defective manner; imperfectly, faultily.

1611 SPEED *Hist. Gt. Brit.* Proem, Fabius Maximus is reprehended by Polybius for defectiuely writing the Punicke warres. **1653** BAXTER *Chr. Concord* Pref. C ii, Because..the Duties..[are] so Defectively performed. **1818** CRUISE *Digest* (ed. 2) IV. 274 To carry it into execution, though defectively made. *a* **1850** ROSSETTI *Dante & Circ.* I. (1874) 84 It seemed to me that I had spoken defectively.

defectiveness (dɪˈfɛktɪvnɪs). [-NESS.] Defective quality or condition; the fact or state of being defective; faultiness.

1622 MALYNES *Anc. Law-Merch.* 402 Let there be made a Notariall Instrument or Act concerning the defectiuenesse of the commodities. **1643** MILTON *Divorce* i. (1851) 22 The unfitnes and defectivenes of an unconjugall mind. **1727** SWIFT *Gulliver* II. iii. 118 The queen giving great allowance for my defectiveness in speaking. **1884** W. J. COURTHOPE *Addison* iii. 47 Owing to the defectiveness of his memory. **1884** *Law Times* 16 Feb. 275/2 The radical defectiveness of leasehold tenure as now applied to urban holdings.

defectless (dɪˈfɛktlɛs), *a.* [-LESS.] Without defect; flawless.

1883 S. L. CLEMENS [MARK TWAIN] *Life on Mississippi* 485 An absolutely defectless memory.

defector (dɪˈfɛktə(r)). [a. L. *dēfector* revolter, agent-n. f. *dēficĕre*: see DEFECT *v.*] One who falls away; a seceder or deserter.

1662 PETTY *Taxes* 62 If the minister should lose part of the tythes of those whom he suffers to defect from the church, (the defector not saving, but the state wholly gaining them). **1879** SIR G. CAMPBELL *White & Black* 372 Independents and all other defectors from the party.

†**deˈfectual,** *a. Obs. rare.* [f. L. *dēfectu-s* DEFECT + -AL¹: cf. *effectual.*] Defective.

1582 N. T. (Rhem.) *Acts* xv. 2 *note*, Without which order ..the Church had been more defectuall and insufficient, then any Common wealth..in the world.

†**deˈfectuose,** *a. Obs. rare.* [ad. med.L. *dēfectuōs-us*: see -OSE.] = DEFECTUOUS.

1678 GALE *Crt. Gentiles* III. 195 The same act which is defectuose and sinful in regard of the wil of man is most perfect and regular in regard to the wil of God.

†**defectuˈosity.** *Obs.* [ad. med.L. *dēfectuōsitās*, f. *dēfectuōs-us*: see next and -ITY. Cf. F. *défectuosité*, in 15th c. *deffectueusité* (Hatzf.).] Defectiveness, faultiness.

1597 LOWE *Chirurg.* (1634) 185 The Hare-shaw is a defectuositie of nature..in the Lip, Eare, or Nose. **1648** W. MOUNTAGUE *Devout Ess.* I. xiv. §2 (R), This mercifull indulgence given to our defectuosities.

†**deˈfectuous,** *a. Obs.* [ad. med.L. *dēfectuōs-us*, f. *dēfectu-s* DEFECT: see -OUS. Cf. F. *défectueux* (1336 in Littré), Pr. *defectuos*, Sp. *defectuoso*, It. *difettuoso.*] Having defects; defective, faulty; imperfect.

1553 CDL. POLE in Strype *Cranmer* II. (1694) 177 The former Act of the ratifying of the matrimony seemed unto me much defectuous. **1681** H. MORE *Exp. Dan.* App. ii. 272 The correspondence betwixt this Vial and this Trumpet is visibly lame and defectuous. **1726** *Nat. Hist. Ireland* 92 The Irish air is greatly defectuous in this part.

Hence †**deˈfectuously** *adv.*, †**deˈfectuousness.**

1604 PARSONS *3rd Pt. Three Convers. Eng.* 43 Relating their stories corruptly or defectuously of purpose. **1684** H. MORE *Answer* 307 Which are more obscurely and defectuously here intimated. **1662** —— *Enthus. Tri.* (1712) 48 Touching the Defectuousness in my Enumeration of the Causes of Enthusiasm. **1680** —— *Apocal. Apoc.* 39 This insinuates the defectuousness of the Sardian Church.

†**defedate,** *v. Obs.* [f. ppl. stem of late L. *dēfœdāre* to defile, f. DE- I. 3 + *fœdāre* to make foul, defile, f. *fœdus* foul.] *trans.* To defile, pollute.

1669 W. SIMPSON *Hydrol. Chym.* 26 The same spurious acidity..defedates the blood.

†**defedation** (ˌdiːfiːˈdeɪʃən). *Obs.* Also defœd-. [ad. med.L. *dēfœdātiōn-em*, in F. *défédation* (15–16th c.), n. of action from late L. *dēfœdāre*: see prec.] The action of making impure; befoulment, pollution (*esp.* of the blood or skin; also *fig.*).

1634 T. JOHNSON *Parey's Chirurg.* XX. vii. (1678) 461 A Morphew or defedation of all the skin. **1669** W. SIMPSON *Hydrol. Chym.* 73 An extraordinary defedation of the blood. **1684** tr. *Bonet's Merc. Compit.* v. 153 A purge must not be given in any defœdation of the skin. *a* **1742** BENTLEY (J.), The defœdation of so many parts by a bad printer, and a worse editor. **1764** GRAINGER *Sugar Cane* IV. 282 Successive crops Of defœdations oft will spot the skin. **1793** D'ISRAELI *Cur. Lit.* (1843) 134 All these changes are so many defœdations of the poem.

defeict, obs. form of DEFEAT.

defeisance, obs. form of DEFEASANCE.

†**deˈfeit, deˈfet,** *a. Obs.* Also 5 defect, deffait. [a. OF. *defeit*, *desfeit*, *-fait*, pa. pple. of *desfaire*, *défaire* to undo: see DEFEAT *v.*] Marred, disfigured.

c **1374** CHAUCER *Troylus* v. 618 To ben defet [*v.r.* defect] and pale, and woxen lesse. *Ibid.* v. 1219 He so defet [*v.r.* disfigured] was, þat no maner man Vnneþe myght hym knowe þer he wente. **1483** CAXTON *G. de la Tour* xcii. 121 Hadde her uisage deffait in such wise that she was unknowe to eueri creatoure. *a* **1605** MONTGOMERIE *The Elegie* 56 It weeping said:—'O deidly corps, defet!'

defeit, defeiture, obs. ff. DEFEAT, -URE.

†**deˈfeke,** *v. Obs.* [a. F. *déféquer*, ad. L. *dēfæcāre* to DEFECATE.] = DEFECATE *v.* 3.

1605 TIMME *Quersit.* I. i. 3 By the meanes whereof all impure and corrupt matter is defeked and separated.

defeminize (diːˈfɛmɪnaɪz), *v.* [f. DE- II. 1 + L. *femina* woman + -IZE.] *trans.* To deprive of femininity. So **defeminiˈzation**; **deˈfeminized** *ppl. a.*

1900 *Amer. Jrnl. Psychol.* July 546 The most defeminized of these specimens, who are so prone to diminutives suggesting endearment. **1905** *Daily Chron.* 25 May 3/6 He thought this was 'monstrous and de-feminised'. **1907** *Ibid.* 9 Mar. 4/6 The so-called Feminism tends in reality to the 'defeminisation' of women. **1907** *Standard* 23 Mar., There was no need for women's suffrage, which would defeminise women.

defence, defense (dɪˈfɛns), *sb.* Forms: 3–6 defens, 3– defence, defense; (5 diffens, -ense, -ence, difence, 5–6 deffence, 6 deffens). [Two forms: ME. *defens*, a. OF. *defens* (*deffans*, *deffenz*, *desfens*, *-fans*, etc.), Ph. de Thaun 1119, ad. L. *dēfensum* thing forbidden, defended, etc., sb. use of pa. pple. of *dēfendĕre* (see DEFEND); also ME. *defense*, a. OF. *defense* defence, prohibition, ad. L. *dēfensa* (Tertullian = *defensio*), f. pa. pple. *dēfensus*, analogous to sbs. in *-āta*, *-ade*, *-ée*. In Eng. where *e* became early mute, and grammatical gender was lost, the two forms naturally ran together; app. the spelling *defence* comes from the *defens* form; cf. *hennes*, *hens*, *hence*; *penis*, *pens*, *pence*; *ones*, *ons*, *once*; *sithens*, *since*; *Duns*, *dunce*. The spelling *defense* is that now usual in the United States.

(The pop. Romanic forms were *de-*, *diffēso*, *-fēsa*, cf. It. *difesa*, OF. *des-*, *def-*, *defeis*, *defois*, Norman *défais*, and *defeise*, *defoise*.)]

The action of defending, in the various senses of the verb, q.v.

The order here followed is as in the verb, though this does not quite agree with the chronological data in hand.

I. The action of warding off, and of prohibiting. (*Obs.* or *arch.*)

†**1. a.** The action of keeping off, or resisting the attack *of* (an enemy). *Obs.*

c **1400** *Destr. Troy* 4715 In defense of hor fos, þat on flete lay. **1494** FABYAN *Chron.* VI. cxcix. 206 For yᵉ defence of his enemyes. **1543–4** *Act 35 Hen. VIII*, c. 12 For the maintenaunce of his warres, inuasion and defence of his enemies. **1588** LD. BURGHLEY *Let. to Sir F. Walsyngham* 19 July, 5000 footmen and 1000 horsemen for defence of the enemy landing in Essex.

†**b.** ? Offence. *Obs.*

c **1400** *Destr. Troy* 2692 What defense has þou done to our dere goddes?

†**2. a.** The action of forbidding; prohibition. *Obs.* (exc. as in b, c.)

a **1300** *Ten Commandm.* 15 in *E.E.P.* (1862) 16 Hou he ssold þe folke tech, and to ssow ham godis defens boþe to ȝung and to olde of þe .x. commandemens. **1303** R. BRUNNE *Handl. Synne* 11098 Þe sekesteyn, for alle þat defense, Ȝyt he ȝaue þe body ensense. **1377** LANGL. *P. Pl.* B. XVIII. 193 Adam afterward aȝeines his defence, Frette of þat fruit. *a* **1450** *Knt. de la Tour* (1868) 56 Eve..bethought her not aright of the defence that God had made to her husbonde and her. **1526** J. HACKET *Let.* in MS. Cott. Galba IX. 35 The Gowernour wyll macke a partyculer deffens and comandment..for the anychyllment and destruccion of thys nywe bokes. **1600** E. BLOUNT tr. *Conestaggio* 94 The pope..wrote unto him by an other briefe, with defence not to proceede in the cause. *a* **1698** TEMPLE (J.), Severe defences may be made against wearing any linen under a certain breadth.

b. *in defence*: (of fish, or waters) prohibited from being taken, or fished in. ***defence-month*** = *fence-month.* (Cf. FENCE *sb.* 7, 11.)

1607 COWELL *Interpr.* s.v. *Fencemoneth*, All waters where salmons be taken, shall be in defence..from the nativitie. **1736** W. NELSON *Laws conc. Game* 77 The Fence-Month, by the antient Foresters was called the Defence-Month, and is the Fawning Time. **1758** *Descr. Thames* 174 Salmon shall be in Defence, or not taken, from 8th September to St. Martin's Day. **1818** HASSELL *Rides & Walks* II. 63 During the defence months, which are March, April, and May, at which time the fish..are spawning. **1887** *Pall Mall G.* 6 May 10/1 Streams which were 'put in defence in the reign of his late Majesty King Henry II., and have been so maintained thereafter'.

c. In the game of *Ombre*: see quot.

1878 H. H. GIBBS *Ombre* 32 If there be Defence, that is to say, if either of his adversaries undertake to forbid the Surrender.

II. The action of guarding or protecting from attack.

3. a. Guarding or protecting from attack; resistance against attack; warding off of injury; protection. (The chief current sense.)

1297 R. GLOUC. (1724) 197 Wanne hii forsoke ys, and for slewþed, and to non defence ne come. *c* **1300** *K. Alis.* 2615 Alle that hadde power To beore weopene to defence. *c* **1325** *Coer de L.* 6840 Withe egyr knyghtes of defens. *c* **1386** CHAUCER *Clerk's T.* 1139 Ye archewyves, stondith at defens. **1393** GOWER *Conf.* III. 214 With thritty thousand of defence. *c* **1400** *Destr. Troy* 9518 In deffence of þe folke. **1418** *E.E. Wills* (1882) 31 A Doubeled of defence couered with red Leþer. *a* **1533** LD. BERNERS *Huon* lxvii. 230 His defence coude not auayle hym. **1548** HALL *Chron.* 57 He would rather dye in the defence than frely yeld the castle. *a* **1699** LADY HALKETT *Autobiog.* (1875) 53 [He] drew his sword in the deffence of the inocentt. **1709** *Tatler* No. 63 ⁋2 His Sword, not to be drawn but in his own Defence. **1797** MRS. RADCLIFFE *Italian* i, What are your weapons of defence? **1875** JOWETT *Plato* (ed. 2) V. 123 They are to take measures for the defence of the country.

†**b.** Faculty or capacity of defending. *Obs.*

[*c* **1470** HENRY *Wallace* VIII. 803 The defendouris was off so fell defens.] **1568** GRAFTON *Chron.* II. 1078 The walles were of that defence that ordinaunce did litle harme. **1593** SHAKS. *3 Hen. VI*, v. i. 64 The Citie being but of small defence. **1596** SPENSER *F.Q.* v. ii. 5 A man of great defence. **1634** SIR T. HERBERT *Trav.* 20 Pikes and Targets of great length and defence. **1654** WHITELOCKE *Swed. Ambassy* (1772) I. 203 A castle..neither large nor beautifull, or of much defence.

c. In games: *e.g.* in *Cricket*, the guarding of the wicket by the batsman. Opposed to *attack*. Also, the batting strength or batsmen collectively.

1828 G. T. KNIGHT in *Sporting Mag.* Mar. 338/2 The object is not to bring the batting down to the bowling..not to diminish the means of defence, but to add to the powers of attack. **1830** M. R. MITFORD *Our Village* IV. 29 His hits were weak, his defence insecure. **1851** J. PYCROFT *Cricket Field* x. 203 Many a man..whose talent lies in defence, tries hitting. **1863** *Baily's Mag. Sports & Past.* Sept. 44 The bowling..the wicket-keeping,..and the fine defence shown ..was all cricket in perfection. **1875** J. D. HEATH *Croquet Player* 43 Upon the introduction of the heavy mallet..it was found that the ' attack' was a great deal too strong for the 'defence'. **1883** *Daily Tel.* 15 May 2/7 Peate [bowler] got past his defence. **1901** R. H. LYTTELTON *Out-door Games* iv. 81 Any reform of cricket law has for its object a levelling up of attack and defence—in other words, of batting and bowling.

d. ***line of defence*** (*Mil.*): (*a*) a line or series of fortified points at which an enemy is resisted; (*b*) *Fortif.* a line drawn from the curtain to the salient angle of the bastion, representing the course of a ball fired from the curtain to defend the face of the bastion.

1645 N. Stone *Enchirid. Fortif.* 18 And that shall cut off the flanke at F, and bring the line of defence in towards the middle of the Curtain. **1802–3** tr. *Pallas' Trav.* (1812) II. 7 The reader will find a distinct view..of the gate and line of defence drawn from the side opposite to the Crimea. **1821** *Examiner* 216/1 Compelled to fall back to Capua, a strong point in the second line of defence. **1853** Stocqueler *Milit. Encycl., Line of Defence*..is either *fichant* or *razant*. The first is, when it is drawn from the angle; the last, when it is drawn from a point in the curtain, ranging the face of the bastion in fortification.

e. *Psychol.* Behaviour which seeks to protect an organism from a real or apparent danger, esp. behaviour which seeks to resist the exposure of a neurosis. Also *attrib.*, as **defence mechanism**, a type of mental process, usually unconscious, that allows the ego or conscious mind to avoid conflict or anxiety, *e.g.*, by compensation, projection, or repression; also *transf.*

1909 A. A. Brill tr. *Freud's Sel. Papers on Hysteria* (1912) iii. 51 The ideas of the 'defense' (abwehr) against an unbearable presentation, the origin of hysterical symptoms through conversion of psychic into physical excitement, the formation of a separate psychic group by an arbitrary act, leading to the defense—all these were..presented before my eyes. *Ibid.* 61 The assumption of a defense hysteria (abwehr hysterie) includes the requisite that at least one such moment has already occurred. **1913** *Amer. Jrnl. Insanity* 569 The psychosexual anaesthesia is nothing but a defense mechanism. **1917** D. Hecht in C. E. Long tr. *Jung's Analytical Psychology* (ed. 2) xiv. 424 By these means she remains at an infantile homosexual stage, which serves her as a defence. **1920** C. S. Myers *Mind & Work* vi. 167 The true causes of one's emotional conduct are replaced by reasons which are invented subconsciously..Such 'defence mechanisms', as they have been called, may come into play in any insoluble emotional situation. **1935** *Essays & Studies* XX. 131 Teachers, afraid of literature...put up a defence-mechanism of literariness. **1941** *Times Lit. Suppl.* 2 Aug. 372/2 The faith of modern Germany is, in psychological language, a 'defence' against reasoning. **1942** A. Christie *Body in Library* xiii. 115 The breaking of a piece of bad news nearly always sets up a defence reaction. It numbs the recipient. **1946** H. Nicolson *Eng. Sense of Humour* 49 Freud was not alone in defining the sense of humour as a defence mechanism having as its main function the protection of the self against discomfort.

f. ***defence in depth***, a system of defence comprising successive areas of resistance or mutually supporting fortifications.

1941 *Ann. Reg. 1940* 55 An elaborate system of 'defence in depth' was also formed all round the east and south coasts. **1949** Koestler *Promise & Fulfilment* II. ii. 205 Finally, the tiny area of Israel..gave them no opportunity for defence in depth.

4. The practice, art, or 'science' of defending oneself (with weapons or the fists); self-defence; fencing or boxing.

1602 Shaks. *Ham.* iv. vii. 98 Hee..gaue you such a Masterly report, For Art and exercise in your defence; And for your Rapier most especially. **1639** tr. *Camus' Moral Relat.* 148 An excellent Master of defence, with whom no man will fight..for feare of his dexterity. **1684** R. H. *School Recreat.* 56 The Noble Science of Defence. **1711** *Lond. Gaz.* No. 4886/4 Has fought several Prizes, setting up for Master of Defence. **1828** Scott *Tales of Grandf.* Ser. ii. I. ii. 63 Fencing with a man called Turner, a teacher of the science of defence.

5. a. Something that defends; a means of resisting or warding off attack; *spec.* (*pl.*) fortifications, fortified works. Also, a defending force.

c **1400** *Lanfranc's Cirurg.* 55 (MS. B), Leye a defens [*MS. A* defensif] aboute þe wounde. **1526** *Pilgr. Perf.* (W. de W. 1531) 5 b, Whiche..is our sauegarde and defence. **1548** Hall *Chron.* 123 The duke strake the kyng on the browe right under the defence of yᵉ hedpece. **1600** E. Blount tr. *Conestaggio* 316 The galleies..often discharged all their artillerie against the defences. **1611** Bible *Ps.* xciv. 22 The Lord is my defence. **1688** R. Holme *Armoury* iii. 457/2 Baskets filled with earth, are good defence in tymes of warr and hostility. **1796** Morse *Amer. Geog.* I. 62 Mountains are necessary..as a defence against the violence of heat, in the warm latitudes. **1853** Sir H. Douglas *Milit. Bridges* (ed. 3) 208 The defences of the Austrians on the right bank were strengthened by numerous batteries. **1916** 'Boyd Cable' *Action Front* 27 The defence, demoralised by that tornado of explosion, was pushed a good fifty yards further back.

b. *Her.* (See quot.)

1727–51 Chambers *Cycl.*, *Defences*, are the weapons of any beast; as, the horns of a stag, the tusks of a wild boar, etc.

c. The military resources of a country. Freq. *attrib.*

1935 C. R. Attlee in *Hansard Commons* 5th Ser. CCCII. 378 We talk about the co-ordination of defence; the co-ordination of the peace forces of the world is quite as important..as the co-ordination of the different services of this country. *Ibid.* 382, I am glad to hear that the Government are thinking of the question of having a Defence Minister. **1937** *Ann. Reg. 1936* i. 16 The Prime Minister still desired to keep the chief authority in defence matters in his own hands. *Ibid.* 17 The official title of the new Minister would be 'Minister for the Co-ordination of Defence'. **1937** F. P. Crozier *Men I Killed* i. 20 These are the men who are planning 'Defence' at the risk of peace. *Ibid.* 21 To be *accused* of being anxious to avoid the wholesale slaughter of countless thousands..despite our £1,500,000,000 Defence Bill! **1966** *Listener* 6 Jan. 13/2 The diversion of money and productive resources to defence. *Ibid.*, Certain parts of industry have turned from civilian to defence production.

6. a. The defending, supporting, or maintaining by argument; justification, vindication.

1382 Wyclif *Phil.* i. 16 Witinge for I am putt in the defence of the gospel. **1563** Winȝet *Four Scoir Thre Quest.* Wks. 1888 I. 69 Corroboring our iugement with sufficient defensis. **1573** G. Harvey *Letter-bk.* (Camden) 10, I never yit tooke vppon me the defenc of ani quæstion. **1653** Gauden (*title*), Defence of the Ministry and Ministers of the Church of England. **1732** Law *Serious C.* xviii. (ed. 2) 333 In defense of this method of education. **1848** Macaulay *Hist. Eng.* II. 212 Nor is it possible to urge in defence of this act of James those pleas by which many arbitrary acts of the Stuarts have been vindicated or excused.

b. A speech or argument in self-vindication.

1557 N. T. (Genev.) *Acts* xxii. 1 Ye men, brethren and fathers, heare my defence which I now make vnto you. **1611** Bible *Acts* xix. 33 And Alexander beckened with the hand, and would haue made his defence vnto the people. **1672** Marvell *Reh. Transp.* i. 82 Mr. Bayes his Defence was but the blew-John of his Ecclesiastical Policy. **1875** Jowett *Plato* (ed. 2) IV. 241 Socrates prefaces his defence by resuming the attack.

†**7.** ***without defence***: without remedy or help; unavoidably, inevitably. *Obs.*

c **1385** Chaucer *L.G.W.* 279 (Fairf. MS.), I hadde ben dede withouten any defence For drede of loves wordes. *c* **1430** *Hymns Virg.* (1867) 66 Glotenie coostiþ wiþouten diffence Boþe in diuerse drinkis and meete.

III. *Law.* [Originally allied to sense 1, but now influenced by senses 3, 6: see defend *v.* 6.]

8. The opposing or denial by the accused party of the truth or validity of the complaint made against him; the defendant's (written) pleading in answer to the plaintiff's statement of claim; the proceedings taken by an accused party or his legal agents, for defending himself.

1595 *Termes of Lawes* 57 b, Defence is that which the defendant ought to make immediately after the count or declaration made, that is to say, that he defendeth all the wrong, force, and dammage, where and when he ought, and then to proceede farther to his plee, or to imparle. **1632** *High Commission Cases* (Camden) 314 The defence is that the same was printed before he was borne, and he hath but renewed it, and is very sorry for it. **1768** Blackstone *Comm.* iii. xx. III. 296–7 Defence, in it's true legal sense, signifies not a justification, protection, or guard, which is now it's popular signification; but merely an opposing or denial (from the French verb *defender*) of the truth or validity of the complaint. **1769** Goldsm. *Roman Hist.* (1786) I. 63 Brutus ..demanded..if they could make any defence to the crimes with which they had been charged. **1817** W. Selwyn *Law Nisi Prius* (ed. 4) II. 1001 *Malicious Prosecution.* The usual defence to this action is, that the defendant had reasonable or probable grounds of suspicion against the plaintiff. *Mod. Newspr.* The examination of the witnesses for the defence. The prisoner refused counsel, and conducted his own defence.

IV. 9. *attrib.*, as ***defence area***; **defence bond**, a bond (bond *sb.*[1] 10) issued by a government borrowing money for military defence (cf. sense 5 c above); also ***defence loan bond***; **defenceman, defenseman** *N. Amer.*, in ice-hockey and lacrosse, a player in a defence position.

1940 *Economist* 6 July 10/2 The declaration of certain parts of the country to be *defence areas in which movements of all persons are controlled—to be distinguished from protected areas where the restrictions apply to aliens only. **1941** *Ann. Reg. 1940* 46 The sale of ..*Defence Bonds..was going on apace. **1947** *News of World* 26 Jan. 1/2 A conversion offer is shortly to be made of holders of three per cent. Defence Bonds purchased between May 1 and Oct. 31 1940, which mature this year. **1940** *Ann. Reg. 1939* 118 The Government..issued ..*defence loan bonds..bearing interest at 3½ per cent. **1895** *Athletic Life* Feb. 78/1 You will generally find it easiest to skate past a *defence man if such tactics are necessary, by tiling straight at him and at the critical moment severing [*sic*] to his right hand side. **1940** T. Stanwick *Lacrosse* v. 41 Defense men who must play near the center stripe..should place themselves several yards behind their respective attack men. **1963** J. N. Harris *Weird World Wes Beattie* (1964) iii. 25 Rick Phelan was a hockey player... He was, in fact, the greatest prospective defenseman to come down the pike since the late Bill Barilko. **1966** Evans & Anderson *Lacrosse Fundamentals* iv. 142 The defense man must not reach so far forward that he is off balance. **1970** *Toronto Daily Star* 24 Sept. 16/7 Brad Selwood, rookie Leaf defenceman, was sidelined after stopping a shot with his right hand in the second period.

†**defence, defense,** *v. Obs.* [f. defence *sb.*; perh. in part a. OF. *defenser, deffencer*, ad. L. *dēfensāre*, freq. of *dēfendĕre* to defend.] *trans.* To provide with a defence or defences; to defend, protect, guard. (*lit.* and *fig.*)

c **1400** *Lanfranc's Cirurg.* 82 Þis defensiþ [*v.r.* defendiþ] a membre fro corrupcioun. *c* **1440** *Promp. Parv.* 115 Defensyn, *defenso, munio.* **1460** Capgrave *Chron.* 184 [How] this lond schulde be defensed ageyn the cruelte of Scottis. **1559** Morwyng *Evonym.* 307 A bely of glasse diligently defenced with clay. **1570–6** Lambarde *Peramb. Kent* (1826) 155 For the defensing of this Realme against forreine invasion. **1587** Turberv. *Trag. T.* (1837) 260 Out he gate, defenst with darke of night. **1629** Shirley *Wedding* ii. ii, Wert thou defenced with circular fire..yet I should Neglect the danger. **1637** Heywood *Lond. Mirrour* Wks. 1874 IV. 313 This Fort..is stil'd Imperiall, defenc'd with men and officers. **1791** [see defenced].

defenceable, obs. form of defensible.

†**de'fenced,** *ppl. a. Obs.* [f. defence *sb.* and *v.* + -ed.] Provided with defences; fenced, protected, fortified.

1535 Coverdale *Jer.* xxxiv. 6 Stronge defensed cities of Iuda. **1551** Robinson tr. *More's Utop.* (Arb.) 161 The well fortified and stronglie defenced wealthe..of many Cities. **1616** Surfl. & Markh. *Country Farme* 2 Wee must dresse some well-defenced piece of ground or greene plot for fruits. **1633** Shirley *Bird in Cage* v. i, Where She could be more defenc'd from all men's eyes. **1791** J. Townsend *Journ. Spain* III. 309 Perello was formerly a defenced city.

de'fenceful, *a. nonce-wd.* [f. defence *sb.* + -ful: after *defenceless.*] Full of defences; well protected or fortified.

1864 Carlyle *Fredk. Gt.* IV. 478 A commanding and defenceful way.

defenceless, defenseless (dɪˈfɛnslɪs), *a.*

1. Without defence; unguarded, unprotected.

c **1530** *Remedie of Love* (R.), O ther disceit vnware and defencelesse. **1589** Warner *Alb. Eng.* v. xxvi. (R.), King Dermote..Was left defencelesse..And fled to England. **1667** Milton *P.L.* x. 815 That fear Comes thundring back with dreadful revolution On my defensless head. **1713** *Lond. Gaz.* No. 5149/3 It is a Place entirely Defenceless. **1740** Wesley *Hymn, 'Jesus, Lover of my soul'* ii, Cover my defenceless head With the shadow of Thy wing. **1755** *Monitor* No. 12 ¶10 In the murder of the innocent and defenceless. **1841** Borrow *Zincali* I. xi. 50 To attack or even murder the unarmed and defenceless traveller.

†**2.** Affording no defence or protection. *rare.*

1697 Dryden *Virg. Georg.* iii. 811 Defenceless was the Shelter of the Ground.

Hence **de'fencelessly** *adv.*, **de'fencelessness.**

a **1723** Bp. Fleetwood [according to Todd uses] Defencelessness. **1802** Paley *Nat. Theol.* xxvi. (R.), Defencelessness and devastation are repaired by fecundity. **1813** Shelley *Q. Mab* iv. 136 All liberty and love And peace is torn from its [the soul's] defencelessness. **1818** Todd, Defencelessly. **1824** Miss Mitford *Village* Ser. i. (1863) 9 His unprotectedness, his utter defencelessness.

defencer: see defensor.

defencible, -ive, obs. ff. defensible, -ive.

defend (dɪˈfɛnd), *v.* Also 3–6 defende, 4–6 diffend(e, deffend(e, 5–6 dyffende; 5 *pa. t.* and *pple.* defend(e, deffende. [ME. a. OF. *defend-re* (11th c.) = Pr. *defendre*, Sp. *defender*, It. *difendere*:—L. *dēfend-ĕre* to ward off, defend, protect, etc., f. de- I. 2 + *fendĕre* (obs. exc. in compounds).

The primary sense in Latin was (I.) to ward off (attack, danger, evil) from a person or thing. Hence, by exchange of objects, came (II.) To guard (the person or thing) from the attack or evil. (Cf. to keep harm off a person, and to keep a person from harm.) By a Romanic extension of I, the sense *ward off* passed into *prohibit, forbid* (I. 3). Branch I is obsolete in Eng. exc. as retained in legal phraseology (III.); but the latter has also uses from II.]

I. To ward off, avert, repel, restrain, prevent; with its extension, To prohibit. (*Obs.* exc. as in III.)

†**1.** To ward off, keep off (an assailant, attack, etc.); to repel, avert (*lit.* and *fig.*). *Obs.* or *dial.*

c **1314** *Guy Warw.* (A.) 3046 Ich the defende sikerly. *c* **1400** *Lanfranc's Cirurg.* 101 If þat þou myȝtist nouȝt defende þe crampe. **1480** Caxton *Chron. Eng.* lxi. 45, I ne had myght ne power hym to defende fro me. *a* **1533** Ld. Berners *Gold. Bk. M. Aurel.* (1546) U iij b, Venim is defended by the horne of an vnicorne, by triacle. **1568** Grafton *Chron.* II. 17 To withstand and defend his enimyes. **1580** J. Frampton *Monardes' Dial. Yron* 142 b, The houses are made of boordes, to defende the great colde. **1609** Blundevil *Dieting of Horses* 11 Horses..would be housed in Summer season with canuas to defend the flies. **1636** Denham *Destr. Troy* 431 And, with their shields on their left arms, defend Arrows and darts. **1793** Smeaton *Edystone L.* §300 Men..with staves in their hands, who could..have defended it from the wall. **1808** Jamieson, *Defend*, to ward off. [In north of Scotl.] they commonly speak of 'defending a stroke'.

†**2.** To keep (*from* doing something), to prevent, hinder. *Obs.*

c **1320** *Seuyn Sag.* 667 (W.) Themperour saide, 'God the defende Fram god dai and fram god ende!' *c* **1400** *Test. Love* iii. (1560) 295/1 No love to be defended from the will of loving. *c* **1450** *Merlin* 29 Let vs diffende the kynge, that he se hym not quyk. **1577–87** Holinshed *Chron.* III. 1262/2 Which walles greatlie defended the fire from spreading further. **1660** R. Coke *Power & Subj.* 196 Trees..planted to defend the force of the wind from hurting of the Church.

†**b.** with *negative clause.*

c **1400** *Lanfranc's Cirurg.* 95 Þis oynement is myche worþ for to defende þat þe malise of þe cancre schal not wexen. **1586** Cogan *Haven Health* Ep. Ded., It keepeth the body from corruption and defendeth that natural moisture be not lightly dissolved and consumed.

†**c.** To restrain; *refl.* to keep oneself, refrain.

a **1325** *Prose Psalter* xxxix. [xl.] 12 Lord, y ne shal nouȝt defenden myn lippes. *a* **1340** Hampole *Psalter* cxviii. 101 Ffra all ill way .i. defendid my fete. *c* **1400** *Rom. Rose* 5800 If they hem yeve to goodnesse, Defendyng hem from ydelnesse.

†**3.** To prohibit, forbid. *Obs.* exc. *dial.*

a. with simple obj. (with or without personal indirect (dative) obj.).

a **1300** *Cursor M.* 21764 (Cott.) Þe tre þat was defend. *c* **1340** *Ibid.* 27314 (Fairf.), I defende þe hit. **1377** Langl. *P. Pl.* B. xv. 19 Is noyther peter þe porter, ne poule with his fauchoune, þat wil defende me þe dore. *c* **1386** Chaucer *Pars. T.* ¶532 Al þis þing is defended by god and holy chirche. **1474** Caxton *Chesse* 17 Hit was defended vpon payn of deth. **1549** *Compl. Scot.* 140 The ciuil lauis defendis and forbiddis al monopoles and conuentions of the comont pepil. **1616** B. Jonson *Devil an Ass* i. iv, I doe defend 'hem any thing like action. **1671** Milton *P.R.* ii. 368 No interdict Defends the touching of these viands pure. *a* **1698** Temple *Ess. Cure Gout* Wks. 1731 I. 146 The Use of it pure being so little practised, and in some Places defended by Customs or Laws.

†**b.** with infin. (usually preceded by personal obj.).

c **1330** R. BRUNNE *Chron.* (1810) 303 Þe pape me defendes .. To renne on þo landes. *c* **1400** MAUNDEV. (Roxb.) xxv. 120 He defendeth no man to holde no law other þan him lyketh. **1483** CAXTON *Gold. Leg.* 14/2 He defended to paye the trewage. **1536** BELLENDEN *Cron. Scot.* (1821) I. xliii, It is defendit be our lawis, to sla ony salmond fra the viii day of September to the xv day of Novembre. **1604** E. G. *D'Acosta's Hist. Indies* v. xxvii. 409 It was defended vpon paine of death, not to marry againe together.

†**c.** with obj. clause (with or without personal obj.); usually with pleonastic negative.

c **1330** R. BRUNNE *Chron. Wace* (Rolls) 12614 He comaundes þe, & defendes, þat þou of ffraunce nought entremet. *a* **1450** *Knt. de la Tour* (1868) 81 He defended her in payne of her lyff she shulde no more come there. *c* **1530** LD. BERNERS *Arth. Lyt. Bryt.* 164 The other knightes wolde have fought with Arthur; but theyr mayster defended them the contrary. *Ibid.* 281. **1577** FENTON *Gold. Epist.* 220 It was defended that none shoulde doe sacrifice in the temple of Minerua. **1660** STILLINGFL. *Iren.* II. viii. §2 Whether .. it be defended by Gods Law, that he and they should preche.

†**d.** *ellipt.* with personal obj. only; also *absol.*

c **1325** *Coer de L.* 1477 Thus deffendes Modard the kyng. **1382** WYCLIF *Num.* xi. 28 My Lord, Moyses, defend hem. **1382** —— *Judg.* xv. 1 And whanne he wold goo .. as he was wont, the fadir of hir defendide hym.

†**e.** a person *from* doing something.

a **1533** LD. BERNERS *Huon* l. 167 Eue was dyffendyd fro y[e] etinge of fruyte. **1672** WYCHERLEY *Love in Wood* III. ii, To .. put you to bed to Lucy and defend you from touching her. **1864** *N. & Q.* 3rd Ser. V. 296/1 A few years ago I heard a governess [in Nottinghamshire] say to a round-backed pupil, 'I defend you from sitting in easy chairs'.

¶ In *God defend* = 'God forbid', the senses 'prohibit' (3) and 'avert' (1) seem to unite.

1389 *Eng. Gilds* 4 ȝif it be so þ[t] eny debat chaunselich falle among eny of hem, þ[t] god defende. **1425** *Paston Lett.* No. 5 I. 19 God defende that any of my saide kyn shuld be of swyche governaunce. **1552** T. BARNABE in Ellis *Orig. Lett.* Ser. II. II. 202 Yf so be yt that we shoulde warre with them, (as God defende). **1599** SHAKS. *Much Ado* II. i. 98 God defend the Lute should be like the case. **1663** PEPYS *Diary* 31 Oct., The plague is much in Amsterdam, and we in fears of it here, which God defend. **1695** CONGREVE *Love for L.* II. i, Marry, Heaven defend!—I at midnight practices!

II. To guard from attack, etc.; to protect, vindicate.

4. *trans.* To ward off attack from; to fight for the safety of; to keep safe from assault or injury; to protect, guard.

c **1250** *Old Kentish Serm.* in *O.E. Misc.* 28 Mirre .. is biter, and be þo biternesse defendet þet Cors þet is mide i-smered þet no werm nel comme i-hende. **1297** R. GLOUC. (1724) 173 Fyȝteþ vor ȝure kunde, and defendeþ ȝoure ryȝte. **1393** GOWER *Conf.* III. 208 She, which wolde her lond defende. **1398** TREVISA *Barth. De P.R.* XVIII. i. (1495) 739 Smalle beestys that lacke sharpe teeth and clawes and hornes ben deffendyd wyth ablynesse of membres. *c* **1400** MAUNDEV. (Roxb.) ix. 33 Armour hafe þai nane to defend þam with. *a* **1450** *Le Morte Arth.* 2034 That he had ofte here landis deffende. **1549–62** STERNHOLD & H. *Ps., Prayer* 395 From Turke and Pope defend vs Lord. **1601** HOLLAND *Pliny* I. 515 Trees .. defended and clad with thick leaued branches. **1700** S. L. tr. *Fryke's Voy. E. India* 108 One of the Buffels defended himself very well of the first Dog that came at him. *c* **1750** in 'Bat' *Crick. Man.* (1850) 30 It [cricket] is performed by a person, who, with a clumsy wooden bat, defends a wicket. **1874** GREEN *Short Hist.* ii. §7. 98 The citizens swore to defend the King with money and blood.

b. *absol.* (for *refl.*) To make defence.

a **1533** LD. BERNERS *Huon* xlix. 164 Yf he come and assayle me I shall defende as well as I can. **1548** HALL *Chron.* 50 Some strake, some defended. **1667** MILTON *P.L.* XI. 657 Others from the Wall defend.

†**c.** To 'fence' a court: see FENCE *v.* 8. *Obs.*

1609 SKENE *Reg. Maj.* 115 Item, after the Court be affirmed, and defended, na man aught to speik .. bot they ilke parties, and their forespeakers, and their counsell.

5. To support or uphold by speech or argument, maintain, vindicate; to speak or write in favour of (a person or thing attacked).

1340 HAMPOLE *Pr. Consc.* 5359 In nathyng may þai be excused þan; .. þai may defende þam be na ways. **1395** W. DYNET *Oath of Recantn.* in *Academy* 17 Nov. (1883) 331/1 þat I .. ne defende [no] conclusions ne techynges of the lollardes. *c* **1450** *St. Cuthbert* (Surtees) 856 Þe bischop þe clerkes malyce kende, Bot nouthir party he defende. **1512** *Act 4 Hen. VIII*, c. 19 Preamble, Erronyously defendyng & maynteynyng his seid obstynate opynyons. **1581** J. BELL *Haddon's Answ. Osor.* 29 b, Whose lyfe and doctrine I did not undertake to defende. **1708** J. CHAMBERLAYNE *St. Gt. Brit.* III. xi. (1743) 280 That he defend three questions in Natural Philosophy. **1782** PRIESTLEY *Corrupt. Chr.* I. II. 235, I am far from pretending .. to defend this passage of Irenæus. **1874** MORLEY *Compromise* (1886) 2 Are we only to be permitted to defend general principles?

†**b.** with obj. clause: To maintain (a statement impugned); to contend. *Obs.*

c **1489** CAXTON *Sonnes of Aymon* xxvi. 546 Here ben our gages, how that we will defende that our fader slew never foulques of moryllon by treyson. **1541** BARNES *Wks.* (1573) 357/2 Their Masse .. whiche our Papistes so wickedly defende to bee a sacrifice. **1580** NORTH *Plutarch* (1676) 9 Others to the contrary defended it was not so. **1607** TOPSELL *Four-f. Beasts* (1658) 25 But that these [animals] can be properly called Asses, no man can defend. *c* **1620** A. HUME *Brit. Tongue* 21 This [vowel] sum defend not to be idle.

III. *Law.* (Originally belonging to I, but also with uses from II.)

6. a. Of the defendant: To deny, repel, oppose (the plaintiff's plea, the action raised against him); *absol.* To enter or make defence. **b.** To vindicate (himself or his cause). **c.** Of a legal agent: To take legal measures to vindicate; to appear, address the court, etc. in defence of (the accused).

[*c* **1200** *Select Pleas of Crown* (1888), Petrus venit et totum defendit de verbo in verbum. *c* **1222** *Bracton's Note-bk.* I. 250 Et Alicia venit et defendit ius eorum.] **1428** *Surtees Misc.* (1890) 5 Seand þat he myght .. deny nor defend this mater na langer, he knawleged and graunted his trespas. **1484** CAXTON *Fables of Alfonce* (1889) 3 After that the cause had be wel deffended and pleted by bothe partyes. **1561** T. NORTON *Calvin's Inst.* IV. xx. (1634) 742 The right use [of law is] both for the plaintife to sue, and for the defendant to defend. **1768** BLACKSTONE *Comm.* III. 296/7. **1883** J. HAWTHORNE *Dust* xxxvii. 306 A letter announcing that the defendants in the case of Desmoines v. Lancaster declined to defend. **1891** *Law Rep.* Weekly Notes 201/2 A solicitor to a trust has authority to defend legal proceedings, though not to initiate them. *Mod.* The prisoners were defended by Mr. L. On his trial he defended himself (or conducted his own defence) with great ability.

†**de'fend**, *sb.* *Sc. Obs. rare.* [f. DEFEND *v.*] Defence.

c **1450** HENRYSON *Mor. Fab.* 69 Sir .. made I not fair defend? *c* **1470** HENRY *Wallace* x. 1154 Sum men tharfor agaynys makis defend.

defendable (dɪˈfɛndəb(ə)l), *a. rare.* Also 8 -ible. [f. DEFEND *v.* + -ABLE. Cf. F. *défendable* (from 13th c.).]

1. Capable of being defended or protected from assault or injury.

1611 COTGR., *Defensable*, defendable .. which may be defended, guarded, or preserued. **1713** DERHAM *Phys. Theol.* v. vi. (R.), [The skin] being easily defendible by the power of man's reason and art. **1870** *Daily News* 25 Nov., That they should establish a defendable frontier.

2. Capable of being maintained or vindicated; defensible.

1683 CAVE *Ecclesiastici* 90 The death of Arsenius, which they knew was not defendable at a fair Audit.

†**de'fendance.** *Obs.* Also 5 -ens. [a. OF. *defendance, deff-* (13th c. in Godefroy), defence, resistance, f. *defendre* to DEFEND.] Defence.

a **1500** *Orol. Sap.* in *Anglia* X. 389 Heelful defendens in alle dyuerse periles. **1600** ABP. ABBOT *Exp. Jonah* 550 Our chalenges, and defendances for combats in the field.

defendant (dɪˈfɛndənt), *a.* and *sb.* Also 4–6 -aunt, 6 -ante, 7 -ent. [a. F. *défendant* (OF. *deffendant*), pr. pple. of *défendre* to DEFEND; also used absol.] **A.** *adj.*

†**1.** Used as *pres. pple.* Defending; *him self defendaunt* = in his own defence. *Obs.*

c **1314** *Guy Warw.* (A.) 6890 ȝif ich þi sone owhar a-slouȝ, It was me defendant anouȝ. *c* **1320** *Sir Beues* 660 Men ne slouȝ he nouȝt, Boute hit were him self defendaunt!

2. Defending oneself, or an opinion, cause, etc., against attack; making one's defence; being defendant in a suit (see B. 3).

1596 *Foxe's A. & M.* 658/2 The defendant part was driven for a while to keepe silence. **1598** HAKLUYT *Voy.* I. 240 (R.) Then commeth an officer and arresteth the party defendant. **1682** DRYDEN *King & Queen* Epil. 16 'Tis just like puss defendant in a gutter. **1896** *Daily News* 24 Nov. 5/7 Detailing my instructions to the defendant surgeon. **1907** *Westm. Gaz.* 6 Dec. 9/1 The defendant directors. **1924** *Pocket Oxf. Dict.* s.v., The defendant company.

†**3.** Affording defence; defensive. *Obs.*

1599 SHAKS. *Hen. V*, II. iv. 8 With men of courage, and with meanes defendant.

B. *sb.* †**1. a.** A defender against hostile attack; opposed to *assailant*. *Obs.*

a **1533** LD. BERNERS *Huon* cxiii. 398 The citye was so sore assayld on all partyes that the defendauntys wyste not where to make resystence. **1548** HALL *Chron.* 54 Neither the assailauntes nor defendantes loke for any refuge. **1614** RALEIGH *Hist. World* II. v. iii. §15. 442 To beat the defendants from the Wall. **1731** J. GRAY *Gunnery* Pref. 21 The defendants .. of the city .. were sorely gauled with all sorts of missive weapons. *a* **1787** BP. LOWTH *Serm & Rem.* 289 Had a potent enemy invaded Sodom .. nothing could have inspired the defendants with truer courage, than virtue and the fear of God.

†**b.** One who defends (an opinion, etc.). *Obs.*

1665 HOOKE *Microgr.* 100 Nor will it be enough for a Defendant of that Hypothesis to say, etc.

†**2.** The party who denies the charge and accepts the challenge of the *appellant* in wager of battle.

1520 *Caxton's Chron. Eng.* VII. 143/2 Gloucestre .. was the appellaunt and Arthur was the defendaunt. **1593** SHAKS. *2 Hen. VI*, II. iii. 49 Ready are the Appellant and Defendant. *a* **1645** HEYWOOD *Fortune by Land* II. Wks. 1874 VI. 385 Neither challenger nor defendant are yet in field. **1828** SCOTT *F.M. Perth* xxiii, The Knight of Kinfauns, the challenger, and .. the young Earl of Crawford, as representing the defendant.

3. *Law.* A person sued in a court of law; the party in a suit who defends; opposed to *plaintiff*.

'A "defendant" is originally a *denier*, but the notion of his *protecting himself* comes in early and prevails.' Prof. F. W. Maitland.

a **1400** in *Eng. Gilds* (1870) 361 And þat commune law hym be y-entred, þe axere and þe defendaunt. **1550** CROWLEY *Last Trump.* 923 Retained of playntyfe, or of defendaunt. **1553** T. WILSON *Rhet.* 47 The complainaunt commenseth his action, and the defendaunt thereupon answereth. **1596** SHAKS. *Merch. V.* IV. i. 361. **1809** J. MARSHALL *Const. Opin.* (1839) 123 The state cannot be made a defendant in a suit brought by an individual. **1859** DICKENS *T. Two Cities* II. xii, The counsel for the defendant threw up his brief.

†**4.** Phrase. *in my, his* (etc.) *defendant*: in one's defence. *Obs.*

[App. a corruption of *me, him, defendant* in A. 1.]

c **1386** CHAUCER *Pars. T.* ¶498 Whan o man sleeth another in his defendaunt. **1470–85** MALORY *Arthur* II. vii, Balyn that slewe this knyght in my defendaunt.

defended (dɪˈfɛndɪd), *ppl. a.* [f. DEFEND *v.*]

†**1.** Forbidden. *Obs.*

c **1386** CHAUCER *Pars. T.* ¶258 Þe beaute of þe fruyt defendid. **1633** MASSINGER *Guardian* IV. ii, How justly am I punish'd .. For my defended wantonness! **1667** MILTON *P.L.* XI. 86 To know both Good and Evil, since his taste Of that defended Fruit.

2. Guarded, protected, maintained against attack, etc.: see DEFEND *v.*

1615 STEPHENS *Satyr. Ess.* (ed. 2) 426 A Fidler .. is a defended night-walker: and under privilege of Musicke takes occasion to disquiet men. **1694** *Amadis of Greece* Title p., His conquering of the defended mountain. **1891** *Daily News* 7 Dec. 6/1 The defended action of Duplany v. Duplany .. was set down .. for hearing on the following day.

defen'dee. *rare*⁻⁰. [f. as prec. + -EE.] One who is defended.

1864 in WEBSTER. (Described as rare.)

defendens, -ent: see DEFENDANCE, -ANT.

defender (dɪˈfɛndə(r)). Forms: 3, 6 defendor, 4–7 -our, (4 -owr, 5 deffendour), 5– defender. [ME. and AFr. *defendour* = OF. *defendeor* (nom. *defendere*), mod.F. *défendeur*, f. *defend-re* to DEFEND. See -ER² 3.

The OF. oblique case *defendeor, -edor*, comes from a Romanic type *dēfenditōr-em*: cf. Pr., Sp., Pg. *defendedor*, It. *difenditore*; the nom. *defendere, -ierre*, Pr. *defendaire*, was formed on the analogy of sbs. with *-eor, -edor*, in the oblique case from L. *-ātōr-em*.]

1. a. One who defends, or wards off an attack; *esp.* one who fights in defence of a fortress, city, etc.

1297 R. GLOUC. (1724) 198 He may ys owe lese, ȝyf þe defendor aþ þe myȝte. *a* **1325** *Prose Psalter* xxxix. [xl.] 24 Þou art myn helper and my defendour. **1483** *Cath. Angl.* 93 A defender, *defensor*. **1526** *Pilgr. Perf.* (W. de W. 1531) 13 Our kynge and defender. **1594** HOOKER *Eccl. Pol.* I. (1611) 26 Men always knew that when force and iniury was offered, they might be defendours of themselues. **1607** SHAKS. *Cor.* III. iii. 128 The power .. To banish your Defenders. *c* **1750** in 'Bat' *Crick. Man.* (1850) 30 The oftener is the defender able to run between the wicket and the stand. **1844** H. H. WILSON *Brit. India* II. 474 After a severe struggle the defenders were driven out. **1878** SEELEY *Stein* II. 128 All the inhabitants of the State are born defenders of it.

†**b.** The person who accepts the challenge to combat in wager of battle: = DEFENDANT *sb.* 2.

1586 FERNE *Blaz. Gentrie*, If it be on the defendors side, he may refuse the combat offered.

†**c.** A dog kept for purposes of defence; a watch-dog. *Obs.*

1607 TOPSELL *Four-f. Beasts* (1658) 124 *margin*, The greater sociable Dogs or defenders. **1688** R. HOLME *Armoury* II. 184/1 The Defenders are Dogs that forsake not their Master in Life nor Death.

d. *Irish Hist.* (with capital.) Originally, one who defended his home against marauders; later, towards the end of the 18th c., the name assumed by a society of Roman Catholics formed to resist the Orangemen. (See Lecky, *Eng. in Eighteenth Cent.* VII.)

1796 *Hull Advertiser* 13 Feb. 3/1 Defenders!! .. a party of these miscreants attacked a small public-house .. on the Trim road. **1798** *Ann. Reg.* 155 Irritated by this usage, the Catholics also associated for their defence, whence they were called Defenders. **1842** S. C. HALL *Ireland* II. 121 The Peep-of-day-boys originated in the north, about the year 1785 .. they were met by a counter association, 'the Defenders'. **1890** LECKY *Eng. in 18th C.* VII. 12 For six or eight months Defender outrages continued in this county almost uncontrolled.

e. *Sport.* The holder of a championship, cup, etc., who defends the title (opp. to *challenger*).

2. a. One who defends, upholds, or maintains by argument; one who speaks or writes in defence of a person, cause, or opinion.

1544 (*title*), A Supplycacion to our most soveraigne Lorde Kynge Henry the Eyght, Kynge of England, .. and moste ernest defender of Christes gospell. **1594** HOOKER *Eccl. Pol.* IV. iv. (1611) 134 Defenders of that which is Popish. **1685** STILLINGFL. *Orig. Brit.* i. 3 The Defenders of this Tradition. **1856** EMERSON *Eng. Traits, Char.* Wks. (Bohn) II. 58 They are headstrong believers and defenders of their opinion. **1875** JOWETT *Plato* (ed. 2) IV. 377 The Sophists have found an enthusiastic defender in the distinguished historian of Greece.

b. *defender of the faith*: a title borne by the sovereigns of England since Henry VIII, on whom it (i.e. *Fidei defensor*) was conferred by Pope Leo X in 1521 as a reward for writing against Luther. Cf. DEFENSOR.

[**1530** *Act 21 Hen. VIII* (*title*), Anno regni inuictissimi principis Henrici octaui, Angliæ et Franciæ regis, fidei defensoris .. vicesimi primi.] **1528** TINDALE *Obed. Chr. Man* Wks. I. 186 One is called Most Christian King; another, Defender of the faith. **1540** *Act 31 Hen. VIII*, Henry the eight by the grace of God, King of England and of France, Defendor of faith. **1558** in Strype *Ann. Ref.* I. App. i. 2 Elizabeth, by the grace of God .. defendour of the faith. **1623** LD. HERBERT *to Jas. I* in Ellis *Orig. Lett.* Ser. I. III. 165 Your sacred Majestie .. beeinge Defender of our Faithe.

3. The party sued in an action at law; = DEFENDANT *sb.* 3. (Now the term in *Sc. Law*; opposed to *pursuer*; also used in Roman Law treatises.)

c **1450** in *Surtees Misc.* (1890) 59 Als well þe playntyffe as þe defender in all maner of playnttes. **1752** J. LOUTHIAN *Form of Process* (ed. 2) 146 All Prosecutors may compear with four, and the Defenders with six of their Friends. **1861** W. BELL *Dict. Law Scot.*, *Defender* is the party against whom the conclusions of a process or action are directed. **1880** MUIRHEAD *Gaius* IV. §102 In certain cases..the defender in an action *in personam* must give security even when conducting his own defence.

4. In the game of *Ombre*: see DEFENCE *sb.* 2 c. **1878** H. H. GIBBS *Ombre* 33 The Defender has to fight out the game against the other two players.

Hence **De'fenderism** (*Irish Hist.*), the principles or policy of the Defenders. (Sense 1 d above.)

1795 *Hull Advertiser* 19 Sept. 1/4 He..avowed the principles of Defenderism. **1796** BURKE *Corr.* (1844) IV. 330 It is now plain that Catholic *defenderism* is the only restraint upon Protestant ascendency. **1837** *Fraser's Mag.* XV. 54 Defenderism finds fuel in Connaught, Leinster, and Munster. **1890** LECKY *Eng. in 18th C.* VII. 13.

defenderesse, obs. form of DEFENDRESS.

defendible: see DEFENDABLE.

defending (dɪ'fɛndɪŋ), *vbl. sb.* [-ING[1].] The action of the verb DEFEND: **a.** The warding off of attack, etc.

c **1300** *K. Alis.* 676 Now con Alisaundre..of sweordis turnyng, Apon stede, apon justyng, And 'sailyng, of defendyng. **1382** WYCLIF *Phil.* i. 7 In defendyng and confermyng of the gospel. **1483** *Cath. Angl.* 93 A Defendynge, *brachium, custodia, defensio.* **1583** STUBBES *Anat. Abus.* II. (1882) 97 Power of defending of life. **1675** tr. *Machiavelli's Prince* (Rtldg. 1883) 273 The storming or defending of towns.

†**b.** Forbidding, prohibition. *Obs.*

c **1400** *Test. Love* III. (1560) 295/1 Prohibicion, that is, defendyng.

de'fending, *ppl. a.* [-ING[2].] That defends: see the verb.

1881 *Daily News* 5 Nov. 5/8 Some of those discrepancies which defending counsel delight in discovering.

†**de'fendless**, *a. Obs. rare.* [See -LESS.] Defenceless.

1737 *Common Sense* (1738) I. 42 Pointing a Musket to a defendless Man's Breast.

defendor, -our, -owr, obs. ff. DEFENDER.

defendress (dɪ'fɛndrɪs). Now *rare.* In 6-7 -eresse, -resse. [a. F. *défenderesse*, fem. of *défendeur*: see -ESS.]

1. A female defender, protector, or maintainer.

1509 FISHER *Wks.* (1876) 301 Good preestes and clerkes to whome she was a true defenderesse [ed. **1708** defendresse]. **1581** MULCASTER *Positions* Ded., Elizabeth by the Grace of God Queene of England, Fraunce, and Ireland, defendresse of the faith, &c. **1627-47** FELTHAM *Resolves* I. lxxv. (1677) 115 Virtue is a Defendress, and valiants the heart of man. **1749** H. WALPOLE *Lett. H. Mann* (1834) II. cxcix. 265 Gracious Anne..would make an admirable defendress of the new faith.

†**2.** A female defendant in a suit. *Obs.*

1611 E. GRIMSTONE *Hist. France* 1042 That which afflicts the Defendresse much more, is that the Complainants obiect against her, that she loued not her child.

†**de'fendrix.** *Obs. rare.* [f. DEFENDER, after L. feminines in -(*t*)*rix*: the L. word was *defenstrix.*] = prec. 1.

1597 J. PAYNE *Royal Exch.* 35 You fight..for your Soveraigne Lady, defendrix vnder God of the same [gospell].

†**defene'ration.** *Obs. rare.*—[0] [n. of action from L. *dēfēnerāre* to involve in debt, exhaust by usury, f. *fænus*, *fēnus* interest, usury.]

1656 BLOUNT *Glossogr.*, *Defeneration*, a taking mony upon usury.

defenestration (di:fɛnɪ'streɪʃən). [mod. f. L. DE- I. 1, 2 + *fenestra* a window: so in mod.F.] The action of throwing out of a window.

Defenestration of Prague, the action of the Bohemian insurgents who, on the 21st of May 1618, broke up a meeting of Imperial commissioners and deputies of the States, held in the castle of the Hradshin, and threw two of the commissioners and their secretary out of the window; this formed the prelude to the Thirty Years' War.

1620 *Reliq. Wotton.* (1672) 507 A man saued at the time of the defenestration. **1837** SOUTHEY *Lett.* (1856) IV. 521, I much admire the manner in which the defenestration is shown [in a picture]. **1863** NEALE *Ess. Liturgiol.* 238 Which commencing at the defenestration of Prague..terminated in the peace of Westphalia.

Hence (as a back-formation) **de'fenestrate** *v. trans.* (usu. joc.), to throw out of a window; **de'fenestrated** *ppl. a.* (in quot. 1927 punningly = 'windowless'?).

1620 H. WOTTON *Lett.* (1907) II. 199 Two of the defenestrated men. **1915** *Lit. Digest* 20 Mar. 668/3 The word *defenestrate* means 'to throw out of the window'..but there is no good authority for its use. **1927** C. CONNOLLY *Let.* 27 Apr. in *Romantic Friendship* (1975) 298 Prague..seemed a good place, gloomy and defenestrated. **1958** J. C. HEROLD *Mistress to Age* (1959) xii. 246 'I am like the Irishman who kept coming back until he was thrown out of a fourth-floor window.' So confident was she of not being defenestrated that she rented a house at 540 rue de Lille. **1974** *Publishers Weekly* 30 Sept. 52/2 Anne Ramsdell, a brilliant math professor at Oxford,..escapes death by stabbing but is thrown out of her third-story window...Anne meets and falls in love with the man who had defenestrated her at Oxford.

defens, obs. form of DEFENCE.

defensable, ME. form of DEFENSIBLE, q.v.

†**defensal**, *a. Obs. rare.* [f. med.L. *dēfensāl-is*, f. *defens-um* DEFENCE: see -AL[1]. (OF. had *deffensal* sb. defence.)] Pertaining to defence.

1560 ROLLAND *Crt. Venus* I. 800 Charge him compeir befoir my Maiestie..To heir him self accusit of crueltie..With exceptionis, and causis defensall.

†**de'fensative**, *a.* and *sb. Obs.* Also -itive. [f. L. type **dēfensātīv-us* (prob. used in 15-16th c. Latin), f. *dēfensāt-*, ppl. stem of *dēfensāre* to ward off, defend, freq. of *dēfendĕre* to DEFEND: see -IVE.]

A. *adj.* **1.** Having the property of defending; defensive, protective.

1603 HOLLAND *Plutarch's Mor.* 19 As with a defensative band about it. **1615** MARKHAM *Eng. Housew.* II. i. (1668) 41 Lay it within the defensitive plaister before rehearsed. **1668** HOWE *Bless. Righteous* (1825) 240 The efficacy and defensative power of moral goodness.

b. = DEFENSIBLE 1 b.

1591 F. SPARRY *Geomancie* 85 The Citie..is not defensatiue and [is] ill maintayned by men of force.

2. Made in defence or vindication of something.

a **1703** BURKITT *On N.T.* Mark ii. 22 Observe the defensative plea which our blessed Saviour makes.

B. *sb.* = DEFENSIVE *sb.* 1. (Very common in 17th c.)

1576 BAKER *Jewell of Health* 7b, Defensatives..for expelling the Plague. **1583** H. HOWARDE (*title*), A Defensatiue against the Poyson of supposed Prophecies. **1612** WOODALL *Surg. Mate* Wks. (1653) 28 A good defensative against all venemous humours. **1658** SIR T. BROWNE *Gard. Cyrus* iii. 126 Houseleek, which old superstition set on the tops of houses, as a defensative against lightening. *a* **1711** KEN *Serm.* Wks. (1838) 160 Abstinence, the best defensitive a Christian can have. **1758** J. S. *Le Dran's Observ. Surg.* (1771) 94 A Defensitive composed of Bole Armenia[c], The White of an Egg, and Vinegar. **1783** AINSWORTH *Lat. Dict.* (Morell) 1, A defensative against poison.

†**de'fensatrice.** *Obs. rare.* [ad. late L. *dēfensātrix, -trīcem*, fem. of *dēfensātor*, agent-n. from *dēfensāre*: see prec.] Defendress.

c **1450** *Mirour Saluacioun* 3984 Virgine Marie..is oure blissed deffensatrice.

defense, -fenser, var. of DEFENCE, DEFENSOR.

defensibility (dɪfɛnsɪ'bɪlɪtɪ). [f. next + -ITY.] The quality of being defensible; capacity of being defended.

1846 GROTE *Greece* II. ii. II. 344 The extreme defensibility of its frontier. **1859** J. WHITE *Hist. France* (1860) 5 The perfect defencibility of the French territory.

defensible (dɪ'fɛnsɪb(ə)l), *a.* Forms: α. 3-6 defensable, (5 -abill, -abylle, deffensable, 6 *Sc.* defensabil, 6-7 defenceable); β. 5- defensible, (5 diffensyble, 5-6 defensyble, 7 defencible). [Etymologically there are here two distinct words: α. *defensable*, a. F. *défensable* (12th c. in Hatzf.):—L. *dēfensābil-em* (St. Ambrose, *c* 375), f. *dēfensāre* to ward off, freq. of *dēfendĕre* to defend. In the latter part of the 15th c. this began to be displaced by β. *defensible*, ad. L. *dēfensibil-em* (Cassiodorus, *c* 550), f. L. *dēfens-*, ppl. stem of *dēfendere*. This expelled the former before 1700. In French also *défensible* appears in 17-18th c., but both forms are there archaic, the ordinary word being *défendable.*]

†**1.** Affording, or capable of affording, defence; defensive. (Cf. FENCIBLE A. 1-3.) **a.** Of men-at-arms: Fit or able to defend a fortress, etc. *Obs.*

1297 R. GLOUC. (1724) 549 Hii hulde hom there defensables, to libbe other to deie. **1481** CAXTON *Godfrey* 306 Ther were therin turkes many, hardy and defensable. **1502** ARNOLDE *Chron.* (1811) 289 Wyth certayn nombre off defensible parsones. **1549** *Compl. Scot.* xix. 163 Sa mony of you that ar defensabil men. **1599** SHAKS. *Hen. V*, III. iii. 50 We no longer are defensible. **1636** PRYNNE *Humb. Remonstr.* 4 Great Navies of Ships and people defensible. **1828** SCOTT *F.M. Perth* xix, Every defensible man of you..keep his weapons in readiness.

†**b.** Of fortresses, fortified places, etc. *Obs.* (but often not distinguishable from sense 3).

1382 WYCLIF *Judg.* vi. 2 Thei maden to hem..moost defensable placis to withstonden. *c* **1400** *Rom. Rose* 4168 A portecolys defensable. *c* **1489** CAXTON *Sonnes of Aymon* vi. 149 Barbacanes well defensable. **1585** T. WASHINGTON tr. *Nicholay's Voy. Turkie* I. xvi. 17 This Bourg is not defensible agaynst any great siege. **1627** SPEED *England, Garnsey* §2 A Pale of Rockes..uery defensible vnto the Iland. **1699** DAMPIER *Voy.* II. I. viii. 161 What charges have been bestowed on it since to make it defenceable. **1781** GIBBON *Decl. & F.* III. lxiv. 609 He maintained the most useful and defensible posts. **1818** HALLAM *Mid. Ages* (1872) II. 129 Notwithstanding the vast population and defensible strength of Constantinople.

†**c.** Of weapons, armour, or habiliments. *Obs.*

1418 HEN. V in Riley *Lond. Mem.* (1868) 664 In here best and most defensable harneys. **1480** *Plumpton Corr.* 40 In there most defensible arrey. **1513** *Act 5 Hen. VIII*, c. 6 Any Armour or defenceable Geer of War. **1548** HALL *Chron.* 56 The citezens..had provided for al thinges necessary and defensible.

†**d.** *gen.* Defensive, protective. *Obs.*

1545 *Primer Hen. VIII* (1546) 156 Be thou unto me..a defensible God. **1574** HYLL *Planting* 77 Covered with clay, or some other defensable playster.

†**2.** In a state of defence against attack or injury; safe. *Obs.*

1581 J. BELL *Haddon's Answ. Osor.* 276 b, That such as are buryed in the cowle and weede of a Franciscane Fryer, are forthwith defensible enough agaynst all the Devilles and furies of hell. *Ibid.* 487 b, Y[t] her life might have eskaped safe, and defensible from those raging stormes. **1793** SMEATON *Edystone L.* §253 We could not leave the work in a more defensible state.

3. Capable of being defended against attack or injury.

1600 E. BLOUNT tr. *Conestaggio* 207 The rocke with such unexpert soldiers was not defensible. **1704** ADDISON *Italy* (1733) 304 Defensible by a very little Army against a numerous Enemy. **1816** KEATINGE *Trav.* (1817) I. 259 His fortress was defensible against all the power of man. **1873** BURTON *Hist. Scotl.* VI. lxxii. 256 Dumbarton was supposed to be more defensible.

4. *fig.* Capable of being defended (in argument), maintained, or vindicated; justifiable. (The chief current sense.)

1413 LYDG. *Pilgr. Sowle* I. xvii. (1859) 18 My cause..was nought defensable by ought that I couthe se. *c* **1555** HARPSFIELD *Divorce Hen. VIII* (1878) 48 The marriage is defenceable enough. **1674** OWEN *Holy Spirit* (1693) 153 This is scarce defensible. **1769** *Junius Lett.* xvi. 71 The..resolution..is defensible on general principles of reason. **1863** FAWCETT *Pol. Econ.* III. vii. 387 A more defensible, or a juster claim. **1875** WHITNEY *Life Lang.* ix. 154 In a true and defensible sense.

Hence **de'fensibleness.**

a **1689** PETTY *Pol. Arith.* (1690) 14 The defensibleness of the Country by reason of its Situation on the Sea. **1830** GEN. P. THOMPSON *Exerc.* (1842) I. 229 The defensibleness of particular branches of a system.

defensibly (dɪ'fɛnsɪblɪ), *adv.* Also 5-6 -sably, 6 -cibly. [f. prec. + -LY[2].]

†**1.** In a 'defensible' manner; so as to afford defence or protection: see prec. 1. *Obs.*

1464 in Rymer *Fœdera* (1710) XI. 524 Every Man..be Well and Defensibly arrayed. *a* **1533** LD. BERNERS *Huon* cxliii. 530 Aboue .iii. M. horses defensably aparaylyd. **1599** R. CROMPTON *Mansion of Magnan.* N iv b, The houses were all of stone, very strongly and defencibly builded.

2. In a manner defensible by argument; justifiably.

1880 *Variorum Teachers' Bible* Isa. vii. 14 The Hebrew prefixes the article, which A.V. defensibly regards as that of species.

defension (dɪ'fɛnʃən). Also 6 -syon, -cion. [ad. L. *dēfensiōn-em*, n. of action from *dēfendĕre* to DEFEND. Cf. OF. *defension, -siun* (11-16th c. in Godef.).]

†**1.** = DEFENCE; protection, vindication, etc.

1382 WYCLIF *Ecclus.* xlviii. 7 Domes of defensioun [**1388** defence]. **14..** *Balade, IX Ladies Worthie* (Chaucer's Wks. 1561), Against the proud Grekes made defencion With her victorious hand. **1514** R. PACE in Fiddes *Wolsey* II. (1726) 203 In the defension of your gracis causis. *a* **1555** PHILPOT *Exam. & Writ.* (Parker Soc.) 325 The just defension against his unjust accusation.

2. In R.C. Colleges: The formal defence of a thesis or proposition as an academic exercise.

1563 FOXE *A. & M.* 862 a, He withstandeth the Popes Supremacie..in his disputations and defensions. **16..** W. BLUNDELL in *Crossby Records* 175 My said brother did make his public defension of Philosophy in the Roman college. **1862** F. C. HUSENBETH *Life J. Milner* 8 He never taught in the Schools, nor made any public defensions. **1886** J. GILLOW *Lit. Hist. Eng. Catholics* II. 458 This defension took place in the palace of Cardinal Guise.

Hence †**de'fensional** *a.*, pertaining to defence.

1762 tr. *Busching's Syst. Geog.* III. 682 The arsenal, the defensional office [at Freiburg, Switzerland].

defensist (dɪ'fɛnsɪst). *Russian Hist.* [f. DEFENCE, DEFENSE *sb.* + -IST.] One who, towards the end of the war of 1914-18, advocated the continuation of the war by Russia against Germany rather than the conclusion of a separate peace. Also *attrib.* or as *adj.* Hence **de'fensism.**

1920 E. ANTONELLI *Bolshevist Russia* I. ii. 57 The sophistry of the self-styled 'liberal defensists'. *Ibid.*, *Defensist* in contradistinction to *defeatist*, meaning one who advocated continuing the war against Germany for the defence of Russia. **1932** M. EASTMAN tr. *Trotsky's Hist. Russian Rev.* I. xv. 303 'Our slogan..is pressure upon the Provisional Government..to induce all the warring countries to open immediate negotiations..and until then every man remains at his fighting post!' Both the idea and its formulation are those of the defensists. **1949** I. DEUTSCHER *Stalin* v. 131 The patriotic attitude or the 'defensism' of the Mensheviks. *Ibid.* 133 Stalin welcomed the semi-pacifist and semi-defensist Manifesto..The argument...implied that the defensists, Menshevik or even Liberal, acted in good faith.

defensitive: see DEFENSATIVE.

defensive (dɪˈfɛnsɪv), *a.* and *sb.* Also 4–5 **-sif**, 5 **-syue**, 6 **-sife**, **deffensive**, 7 **defencive**. [a. F. *défensif*, *-ive* (14th c. in Hatzf.), ad. med.L. *dēfensīv-us*, f. *dēfens-*, ppl. stem of L. *dēfendĕre*: see -IVE.] **A.** *adj.*

1. a. Having the quality of defending against attack or injury; serving for defence; protective.

c **1400** *Lanfranc's Cirurg.* 13 Aboute þe wounde leie a medicyn defensif. **1495** *Act 11 Hen. VII*, c. 64 Preamb., Armours Defensives, as Jakkes, Salettis, Brigandynes. **1548** HALL *Chron.* 169 b, Any weapon, either invasive or defensive. **1593** SHAKS. *Rich. II*, II. i. 48 As a Moate defensiue to a house. **1636** SIR H. BLOUNT *Voy. Levant* (1637) 100 A boorded Arche..defensive against sunne and raine. **1634** SIR T. HERBERT *Trav.* (1638) 330 The Nut is cloathed with a defensive husk. **1655** FULLER *Ch. Hist.* IX. II. §21 IV. 357 A Castle (then much decayed, never much defensive for this City). **1774** GOLDSM. *Nat. Hist.* (1776) VI. 361 An hard, firm shell, which furnishes..both offensive and defensive armour. **1874** BOUTELL *Arms & Arm.* ii. 9 When they invaded Gaul, the Romans..wore defensive armour formed of iron.

†**b.** Of fortified places: = DEFENSIBLE 1 b. *Obs.*

1601 R. JOHNSON *Kingd. & Commw.* (1603) 259 To immure themselves in such defensive places. **1634** SIR T. HERBERT *Trav.* (1638) 81 The Citie is..made defensive by many helps of nature and industry.

†**c.** Of persons: Capable of making defence. *Obs. rare.*

1667 MILTON *P.L.* VI. 393 The faint Satanic Host Defensive scarse, or, with pale fear surpris'd.

†**d.** With *of*: Serving to ward off, or to protect against. *Obs. rare.*

1725 POPE *Odyss.* XXIII. 196, I rais'd a nuptial bow'r And roof'd defensive of the storm and show'r.

e. *Cricket.* Of batting: characterized by cautiousness; having the protection of the wicket as the chief consideration.

1872 *Baily's Monthly Mag.* Aug. 167 Mr. Ottaway played a perfect defensive innings, while Mr. Grace was hitting. **1904** P. F. WARNER *How we recovered Ashes* i. 13 He can play a forcing or defensive game as circumstances demand. **1965** P. SHARPE *Cricket for Schoolboys* vii. 82 *Defensive stroke*,..stroke intended to protect wicket rather than score. **1967** C. J. GOODWIN *Coming in to Bat* i. 9 (*heading*) The defensive back stroke.

f. Of a person, attitude, expression, etc.: self-protective, defiant, ready to reject criticism. Cf. SELF-DEFENSIVE *a.*

1919 J. CONRAD *Arrow of Gold* V. v. 275 The perfect stillness and silence made her raise her eyes at last, reluctantly, with a hard, defensive expression which I had never seen in them before. *a* **1930** D. H. LAWRENCE *Mod. Lover* (1934) 42 He recognized the woman defensive, playing the coward against her own inclination. **1938** *Psychoanalytic Q.* VII. 254 It is an important function of the analyst to distinguish these defensive attitudes from the underlying emotions. **1945** E. WAUGH *Brideshead Revisited* I. v. 120 We were instructed by a man of about my age, who treated us with defensive hostility. **1956** *Jrnl. Gen. Psychol.* LIV. 191 Rogers..and Snygg and Combs..imply..that the more an individual tends to deny threatening experiences to awareness (i.e., the more *defensive* he is), the greater will be the degree of threat he experiences. **1971** *Black Scholar* Jan. 48/1, There is..what I have called the Defensive Posture of black writers: that is, a certain fear of strongly criticizing black people and attacking them for their weaknesses. **1986** *Monthly Rev.* Apr. 20 P. W. Botha appeared to fumble the ball with his ill-starred 'Rubicon' speech,..—a speech..characterized by an all too familiar defensive truculence.

2. Made, formed, or carried on for the purpose of defence: opposed to *offensive* (= aggressive).

1580 NORTH *Plutarch* (1676) 455 The Athenians made League offensive and deffensive with them. **1631** GOUGE *God's Arrows* III. §60. 293 The bloud which in defensive warre is shed. **1678** LADY CHAWORTH in *12th Rep. Hist. MSS. Comm.* App. v. 44 A league offencive and defencive with Holland. **1777** WATSON *Philip II* (1839) 353 Able to wage only a tedious defensive war. **1787** MAD. D'ARBLAY *Diary* Mar., I was obliged to resolve upon a defensive conduct in future. **1869** RAWLINSON *Anc. Hist.* 180 Alliance, offensive and defensive, between Sparta and Bœotia.

3. Of or belonging to defence.

1643 SLINGSBY *Diary* (1836) 102 They..lay at a defensive guarde. **1684** R. H. *School Recreation* 67 Having shewn you the Defensive part, I shall now proceed to the Offensive. **1739** J. TRAPP *Right. over-much* (1758) 16 Going to law is absolutely unlawful, even on the defensive side. **1845** S. AUSTIN *Ranke's Hist. Ref.* III. 175 Their position was entirely a defensive one.

4. Spoken or written in defence *of* something; of the nature of a defence or vindication.

1604 BROUGHTON (*title*), Two little Workes defensive of our Redemption. **1768** BLACKSTONE *Comm.* III. 100 His defensive allegation, to which he is entitled in his turn to the plaintiff's answer upon oath. **1893** *Bookman* June 85/2 An appreciative essay, partly defensive of his memory.

B. *sb.*

†**1.** Something that serves to defend or protect; *esp.* in *Med.* and *Surg.* a bandage, plaster, ointment, or medicine, serving to guard against injury, inflammation, corruption, infection, etc. *Obs.*

c **1400** *Lanfranc's Cirurg.* 214 Þou schalt algate aboute þe sijknes leie a defensif of bole & terra sigillata. **1544** PHAER *Pestilence* (1553) P iv b, Lay a defensiue about the sore. **1562** TURNER *Herbal* II. 41 b, If it be layd vnto woundes, it is a good defensiue for them. **1610** MARKHAM *Masterpiece* II. clxxiii. 485 It is also an excellent defensiue against fluxes of blood. *a* **1626** BACON (J.), Wars preventive upon just fears, are defensives, as well as on actual invasions. **1665** EVELYN *Mem.* (1857) III. 150 Wear this defensive for my sake. **1725** BRADLEY *Fam. Dict.* s.v. *Wounds*, If a Nerve happens to be cut, you must close it, and use a Defensive, to prevent a concourse of Humours.

2. a. A position or attitude of defence: usually in phr. *to stand* (*act*, etc.) *on the defensive*. [Absolute use of A. 3.]

1601 R. JOHNSON *Kingd. & Commw.* (1603) 178 Onely to stand upon the defensive. **1708** SWIFT *Predictions*, The French army acts now wholly on the defensive. **1797** BURKE *Corr.* IV. 431 In debate, as in war, we confine ourselves to a poor, disgraceful, and ruinous defensive. **1828** SCOTT *F.M. Perth* xxxiv, The two brethren..striking both at once, compelled him to keep the defensive. **1869** FREEMAN *Norm. Conq.* (1876) III. xii. 152 The plan of the Duke was to stand wholly on the defensive.

b. *Cricket.* Defensive batting (see A. 1 e, above); blocking.

1851 J. PYCROFT *Cricket Field* iv. 58 The defensive was comparatively unknown: both the bat and the wicket, and the style of bowling too, were all adapted to a short life and a merry one. **1906** A. E. KNIGHT *Complete Cricketer* 344 To act on the defensive is to play with care, mindful of not getting out rather than of adding to the score.

†**3.** One who defends himself against attack: opposed to *assailant* or *aggressor*. *Obs. rare.*

1634 SIR T. HERBERT *Trav.* 79 They..retired home, leaving the Georgians Victors, though defensives.

defensively (dɪˈfɛnsɪvlɪ), *adv.* [-LY².] In a defensive manner; by way of defence.

1670 MILTON *Hist. Eng.* II. Wks. (1851) 59 Camalodunum, where the Romans had seated themselves to dwell pleasantly, rather than defensively, was not fortifi'd. **1692** LUTTRELL *Brief Rel.* (1857) II. 370 We shall, it's beleived, act only defensively. **1884** MRS. OLIPHANT in *Blackw. Mag.* Jan. 5/2 Lady Mary put up her hand defensively.

deˈfensiveness. [-NESS.] The quality of being defensive.

1600 F. WALKER *Sp. Mandeville* 131 a, They want no defensiuenes against the cold. **1828** *Examiner* 643/1 The position of defensiveness. **1885** G. MEREDITH *Diana* I. xv. 323 Arousing her instincts of defensiveness.

defensor (dɪˈfɛnsə(r), -ɔː(r)). Forms: 4–5 **defensour**, (4–6 **-oure**, 5 **-owre**), 6 **defencer**, 6– **defensor**. [ME. and AFr. *defensour* = OF. **defenseor*, in 13th c. *deffenceour*, mod.F. *défenseur*:—L. *dēfensātōr-em* (Jerome), agent-n. from *dēfensāre*, freq. of *dēfendĕre* to DEFEND. By later changes in Eng. the word is completely assimilated to L. *dēfensor*, agent-n. from *dēfendĕre*.]

†**1.** A defender. *Obs.*

Chief Defensor of the Christian Church, a title formerly bestowed by the Pope upon individual kings, as upon Henry VII of England.

1375 BARBOUR *Bruce* XVII. 745 Sum of the defensouris war All dede, and othir woundit sare. *c* **1430** LYDG. *Bochas* I. xvi. (1554) 33 a, To holy churche he was chief defensour. **1509** FABYAN VII. (1533) 690. **1530** PALSGR. Introd. 10 Henry by the grace of God, kynge of Englande and of France, defensor of the faythe. **1596** *Foxe's A. & M.* 591/1 Any of their fautors, comforters, counsellers, or defensers. **1611** SPEED *Hist. Gt. Brit.* IX. xx. 72 Chiefe Defensor of Christs Church. **1670** *Famous Conclave Clement VIII* 29 The only defensor and supportor of the Catholick Religion.

2. *Rom. Hist.* 'In the later period of the empire (after 365 A.D.), title of a magistrate in the provincial cities, whose chief duty was to afford protection against oppression on the part of the governor' (Lewis & Short).

c **1370** WYCLIF *Eng. Wks.* (1880) 395 And saynte gregori wrote to þe defensoure of rome in þis maner. [**1818** HALLAM *Mid. Ages* (1872) I. 341 But the *Defensores* were also magistrates and preservers of order.] **1841** W. SPALDING *Italy & It. Isl.* I. 112 The defensors differed in both respects. **1855** MILMAN *Lat. Chr.* (1864) II. III. v. 45 What the defensor had been in the old municipal system.

3. *Roman Law.* One who took up the defence and assumed the liability of a defendant in an action.

1875 POSTE *Gaius* IV. Comm. (ed. 2) 569 A defensor may prevent a forfeiture of the stipulation. *Ibid.*, A defensor (unauthorized representative) of the defendant gave security judicatum solvi.

4. *Eccl.* An officer in charge of the temporal affairs of a church.

[**1875** SMITH & CHEETHAM *Dict. Chr. Antiq.* I. 33/2 In Rome..the *Defensores* became by the time of Gregory the Great a regular order of officers.] **1905** F. H. DUDDEN *Greg. Gt.* I. 327 A certain defensor of the Milanese Church, named Valentinus.

Hence **deˈfensorship**, the office of defensor.

1855 MILMAN *Latin Chr.* III. 292 The golden diadem, the insignia of the Patriciate and Defensorship of the city of Rome.

defensory (dɪˈfɛnsərɪ), *a.* and *sb.* Now *rare* or *Obs.* [ad. L. *dēfensōri-us*, f. *dēfensōr-em*: see DEFENSOR and -ORY.]

A. *adj.* That is intended, or serves, to defend; defensive.

1552 HULOET, Defensorye, *praesidiarius.* **1586** A. DAY *Eng. Secretary* II. (1625) 14 A Letter defensory answering by confutation all the objections. **1647** *Royall & Royallist's Plea* 13 The warre on the Kings side is vindicatory and defensorie. **1849** *Fraser's Mag.* XXXIX. 669 One of the defensory provisions which the Creator has assigned to some of His creatures.

†**B.** *sb.* Something defensive; a defence. *Obs.*

1588 GREENE *Perimedes* 6 As a defensorie against ensuing griefes. **1592** (*title*), Martin Mar-Sixtus. A second Replie against the Defensory and Apology of Sixtus the fifth. **1677** GALE *Crt. Gentiles* II. III. 154 A Defensorie of the Scripture and Church.

defenst, obs. f. *defenced*: see DEFENCE *v.*

†**deˈfensure.** *Obs.* [f. L. *dēfens-* ppl. stem of *dēfendĕre* + -URE.] Something that defends; = DEFENSIVE *sb.* 1.

1586 W. BAILEY *Briefe Treat.* (1633) 21 Wee must defend the eye with some defensure to avoid the offence of a fluxe.

defer (dɪˈfɜː(r)), *v.*¹ Forms: 4–7 **differre**, 5–7 **deferre**, (4 **defere**, 5–6 **defar**, **-arre**, 4 **dyfferre**, 7 **deferr**), 5–7 **differ**, 5–6 **differr**, 6 **differe**, **dyferre**, **dyffer**, **dyffer(r-)**, **diffar(r-)**, 6–7 **differ(r-)**, 5– **defer(r-)**. Inflexions **deferred**, **deferring**. [ME. *differre-n*, a. OF. *differer* (*il diffère*), 14th c. in Littré, ad. L. *differ-re* to carry apart, put off, postpone, delay, protract; also, *intr.*, to bear in different directions, have diverse bearings, differ. Orig. the same word as DIFFER *v.* (q.v. for the history of their differentiation), and often spelt *differ* in 16–17th c.; but forms in *de-*, *def-*, are found from the 15th, and have prevailed, against the etymology, mainly from the stress being on the final syllable; but partly, perhaps, by association with *delay*.]

†**1.** *trans.* To put on one side; to set aside. *Obs.*

1393 GOWER *Conf.* I. 262 At mannes sighte Envie for to be preferred Hath conscience so differred, That no man loketh to the vice Whiche is the moder of malice. *c* **1430** LYDG. *Hors, Shepe & G.* 96 The Syrcumstaunce me lyst nat to defer. —— *Min. Poems* (Percy Soc.) 14 Grace withe her lycour cristallyne and pure Defferrithe vengeaunce off ffuriose woodnes.

†**b.** To set or put 'beside oneself'; to bereave of one's wits. *Obs. rare*⁻¹.

c **1375** *Sc. Leg. Saints, Matthæus* 84 Quhame þat þai [two sorcerers] had euir marryte Ine þare wittis or differryte.

†**c.** *refl.* To withdraw or remove oneself. *Obs.*

c **1375** *Sc. Leg. Saints, Martha* 171 Hely, defere þe nocht fra me, Bot in myn helpe nov haste þu þe!

2. *trans.* To put off (action, procedure) to some later time; to delay, postpone.

1382 WYCLIF *Num.* xxx. 15 If the man..into another day deferre the sentence. **14..** *Prose Legends* in *Anglia* VIII. 132 [She] differred þe questyone. **1483** *Cath. Angl.* 99 To Differ, *differre, prolongare.* **1489** CAXTON *Faytes of A.* II. vii. 104 The Lacedemonyens with drewe them self and differde the bataylle. **1526** TINDALE *Matt.* xxiv. 48 My master wyll differ his commynge. **1593** SHAKS. *2 Hen. VI*, IV. vii. 141 Soldiers, Deferre the spoile of the Citie vntill night. **1651** HOBBES *Leviath.* II. xxx. 183 Sometimes a Civill warre, may be differred, by such wayes. **1711** ADDISON *Spect.* No. 92 ¶2, I have deferred furnishing my Closet with Authors, 'till I receive your Advice. **1795** SOUTHEY *Joan of Arc* IV. 499 O chosen by Heaven! defer one day thy march. **1863** GEO. ELIOT *Romola* II. iv, She deferred writing the irrevocable words of parting from all her little world.

b. Const. with *inf.* ? *Obs.*

1426 H. BEAUFORT in Ellis *Orig. Lett.* Ser. II. I. 102 He hath long differred to parfourme them. *c* **1450** *St. Cuthbert* (Surtees) 7118 To wende hame þai noȝt deferde. **1535** COVERDALE *Josh.* x. 13 The Sonne..dyfferred to go downe for the space of a whole daye after. **1609** BIBLE (Douay) *Ps.* lxxix. Comm., How long wilt thou differre to heare our prayer? *a* **1656** USSHER *Ann.* (1658) 880 Neither did he long defer to put those Jews to death. *a* **1732** ATTERBURY (J.), The longer thou deferrest to be acquainted with them, the less every day thou wilt find thyself disposed to them.

c. *absol.* or *intr.* To delay, procrastinate: rarely with *off*.

1382 WYCLIF *Deut.* vii. 10 So that he scater hem, and ferther differre not [**1388** differr [*v.r.* tarie] no lengere]. *c* **1450** *St. Cuthbert* (Surtees) 7523 He defard, and walde noȝt trus. **1577** NORTHBROOKE *Dicing* (1843) 180 Whyles he desired, they deferred. *a* **1592** GREENE & LODGE *Looking Glass* Wks. (Rtldg.) 129/1 Defer not off, to-morrow is too late. **1614** BP. HALL *Recoll. Treat.* 935 God differ's on purpose that our trials may be perfect. **1635** R. BOLTON *Comf. Affl. Consc.* ix. 252 The longer thou putst off and defferest the more unfit shalt thou be to repent. **1742** YOUNG *Nt. Th.* i. 390 Be wise to-day; 'tis madness to defer. **1771** P. PARSONS *Newmarket* I. 21, I have waited (demurred, my gentle reader, if you be a lawyer, deferred, if you be a divine)..a full year.

3. *trans.* To put off (a person or matter) to a future occasion: †**a.** a person. *Obs.*

1382 WYCLIF *Acts* xxiv. 22 Sothli Felix deferride hem [**1388** delayede, *MS. K.* ether differride; TINDALE differde, **1539** *Great B.* deferede, **1557** *Genev.* differed, **1582** *Rhem.* differred, **1611** and **1881** deferred]. **1545** BRINKLOW *Compl.* 20 b, Men be differyd from tyme to tyme, yea from yere to yere. **1642** ROGERS *Naaman* 137 If it seem good to thy wisdome to deferre me. **1709** STRYPE *Ann. Ref.* I. xxxviii. 440 He was deferred until Monday.

b. a time, matter, question.

1509 BARCLAY *Shyp of Folys* (1570) 49 Where they two borowed, they promise to pay three, Their day of payment longer to deferre. **1536** *Exhort. fr. North* 135 in Furniv. *Ballads* I. 309 Differ not your matteres tyll a new ȝere. **1559** MORWYNG *Evonym.* 95 Which conserveth the good health of man's body, prolongeth a man's youth, differeth age. **1559** WILLOCK *Lett. to Crosraguell* in Keith *Hist. Church Sc.* App. 198 (Jam.), I wold aske quhilk of us differreth the Caus. **1611** BIBLE *Prov.* xiii. 12 Hope deferred maketh the heart sicke.

c. To relegate to a later part of a treatise.

1538 STARKEY *England* I. iv. 123 Let us not entur into thys dysputatyon now, but..dyffer hyt to hys place. **1558** KNOX *First Blast* (Arb.) 37 The admonition I differe to the end.

1611 CORYAT *Crudities* 480, I had differred it till the end of the sermon. **1695** WOODWARD *Nat. Hist. Earth* I. (1723) 41 Which I choose, rather than trouble the Reader with a Detail..here, to deferr to their proper Place. **1877** J. D. CHAMBERS *Divine Worship* 284 It has been found necessary to defer them to the Appendix.

†**4.** To put off (time), waste in delay. *Obs.*

1382 WYCLIF *Ezek.* xii. 22 Dais shulen be differrid, or drawen, in to loong [**1388** differrid in to long tyme]. **1548** HALL *Chron.* 184 Not mynding to differre the time any farther. **1579** LYLY *Euphues* (Arb.) 123 Idle to deferre yᵉ time lyke Saint George, who is euer on horsebacke yet neuer rydeth. **1591** SHAKS. *1 Hen. VI*, III. ii. 33 Deferre no tyme, delayes haue dangerous ends. **1633** G. HERBERT *Temple, Deniall* vi, O cheer and tune my heartlesse breast, Deferre no time.

†**b.** To protract; also *intr.* to linger. *Obs.*

1546 LANGLEY *Pol. Verg. De Invent.* I. xii. 24a, The Warres were longe differred. **1561** NORTON & SACKV. *Gorboduc* IV. ii, Why to this houre Have kind and fortune thus deferred my breath? **1561** HOLLYBUSH *Hom. Apoth.* 42b, If the disease woulde differre, and the jaundis woulde not voyde.

defer (dɪˈfɜː(r)), *v.*² Also 5–6 differ, 6–7 deferre, (8 defere). Inflexions deferred, deferring. [a. F. *déférer* (*il défère*), 16th c. in Littré (*defferer* 14th c. in Godef. *Suppl.*), in same sense as Eng., ad. L. *dēfer-re* to bring or carry away, convey down, to bring or carry with reference to destination, to confer, deliver, transfer, grant, give, to report, to refer (a matter) to any one; f. DE- I. 1, 2 + *ferre* to bear, carry.]

†**1.** *trans.* To carry down or away; to convey (*to* some place); to bring away. *Obs. rare.*

1626 BACON *Sylva* §254, I do not think that if a Sound should pass through divers mediums..it would deliver the Sound in a differing place, from that unto which it is deferred. **1654** R. CODRINGTON tr. *Hist. Ivstine* 552 He was so much amazed at it, that he could not forbear to vomit or defer the forced burthen of his belly.

†**2.** To offer, proffer, tender; in *Law*, to offer for acceptance. Const. *to*, rarely *on*. ***to defer an oath*** = F. *déférer un serment*, L. *deferre jusjurandum. Obs.*

1563 FOXE *A. & M.* 782b, Vpon a corporall othe to them deferred by the iudges. **1565** JEWEL *Repl. Harding* (1611) 379 That Godly worship which..of the Diuines is called Latria, is deferred only to the Blessed Trinity. **1651** HOBBES *Leviath.* II. xxx. 177 To deferre to them any obedience, or honour. **1677** GALE *Crt. Gentiles* III. 172 Apuleius..does in vain defer or bestow this honor on those Demons. **1764–7** LD. G. LYTTELTON *Hist. Hen. II*, II. 95 (Seager) How very wonderful is it that all the princes..when a king renowned for his valour..was actually at their head, should defer the command to a monk. **1832** AUSTIN *Jurispr.* (1879) II. liii. 894 Until he accept the inheritance, he has a right deferred or proffered by the law (*jus delatum*) but he has not a right fully acquired (*jus acquisitum*).

†**3.** To submit (a matter *to* a person, etc.) for determination or judgement; to refer. *Obs.*

1490 *Acta Dom. Conc.* 204 (Jam.) The lordis will differ the hale mater to the said Robert spoussis aitht. **1541** BARNES *Wks.* (1573) 345/1 This matter was deferred of both partes to the sentence of the kyng. **1660** R. COKE *Power & Subj.* 160 We teach, that among Priests there be no strifes and wrangling, nor let them be deferred to the Secular power. **1691** BLAIR in W. S. Perry *Hist. Coll. Amer. Col. Ch.* (1860) I. 4 The council, he said, would defer it to the committee for plantations.

†**4.** *absol.* To refer for information *to*. *Obs.*

1563 FOXE *A. & M.* 797b, Concernynge the depositions of this Lorde Paget, here producted, we differ to the xx. act, where you shal fynde hym examined.

†**5.** *intr.* (for *refl.*) To submit oneself *to*. *Sc. Obs.*

1479 *Acta Dom. Audit.* 90 (Jam.) Decretis..that Johne Stewart..sall..pay to Archibald Forester of Corstorfin xx L yerly of viii yeris bigain..becauss the said Archibald differit to his aith, and he refusit to suere in presens of the lordis. **1490** *Acta Dom. Conc.* 194 (Jam.) The lordis aboue writtin wald nocht defer to the said excepcioun.

6. *intr.* To submit in opinion or judgement *to*; to pay deference *to*.

It is probably with reference to this that Evelyn, 1667 (*Mem.* III. 161 ed. 1857), says, We have hardly any words that do..fully express the French *emotion, defer, effort*.

1686 F. SPENCE *House of Medici* 306 (L.) They not only deferred to his counsels in publick assemblies, but he was moreover the umpire of domestic matters. **1730** A. GORDON *Maffei's Amphith.* 8 How far we must defere to his Authority? **1792** BURKE *Let. to Sir H. Langrishe* Wks. 1842 I. 543 If you had not deferred to the judgment of others. **1855** PRESCOTT *Philip II*, I. ix. (1857) 165 Philip..had the good sense to defer to the long experience and the wisdom of his father. **1870** BRYANT *Iliad* I. I. 31 And let me warn my mother, Wise as she is, that she defer to Jove.

deference (ˈdɛfərəns). [a. F. *déférence* (16th c.), f. *déférer* to DEFER *v.*²: see -ENCE.]

†**1.** The action of offering or proffering; tendering, bestowing, yielding. *Obs. rare*⁻¹.

1660 tr. *Amyraldus' Treat. conc. Relig.* I. iii. 35 Our deference of all honor and glory to that which we venerate.

2. Submission to the acknowledged superior claims, skill, judgement, or other qualitites, of another. Often in phr. ***to pay, show, yield deference.***

1647 CLARENDON *Hist. Reb.* I. (1843) 9/2 He was.. negligent..to correspond with him with that deference he had used to do, but had the courage to dispute his commands. **1706** ESTCOURT *Fair Examp.* III. i, Now, Sir, you shall stay and see what a Deference they pay to my Skill and Authority. **1711** ADDISON *Spect.* No. 62 ¶7 With all the Deference that is due to the Judgment of so great a Man. **1798** FERRIAR *Illustr. Sterne, Varieties of Man* 196 Much of this evil has certainly proceeded from undue deference to authorities. **1830** D'ISRAELI *Chas. I*, III. vii. 148 Charles often yielded a strange deference to minds inferior to his own. **1836** H. COLERIDGE *North. Worthies* (1852) I. 6 That voice of authority to which he would have paid most willing deference.

3. Courteous regard such as is rendered to a superior, or to one to whom respect is due; the manifestation of a disposition to yield to the claims or wishes of another. Const. *to*, †*for*.

a **1660** HAMMOND *Wks.* II. I. 137 (R.) Why was not John who was a virgin chosen, or preferred before the rest?..his answer is, because Peter was the Elder, the deference being given to his age. **1662** J. DAVIES tr. *Olearius' Voy. Ambass.* 80 Nor have they any more complyance one for another, than they have deference for strangers: for instead of being civil one to another [etc.]. **1678** *Lively Orac.* v. §15. 296, I shall consider to which God himself appears in Scripture to give the deference. **1712** STEELE *Spect.* No. 497 ¶2 He was conducted from room to room, with great deference, to the minister. **1754** CHATHAM *Lett. Nephew* iv. 20 Their age and learning..entitle them to all deference. **1855** H. REED *Lect. Eng. Hist.* iii. 411 That indescribable and instinctive deference to the feelings of others, which constitutes the gentlemanly spirit.

4. ***in deference to***: in respectful acknowledgement of the authority of, out of practical respect or regard to.

1863 H. COX *Instit.* I. x. 249 The resignation of a Prime Minister in deference to the will of the House of Commons. **1867** SMILES *Huguenots Eng.* xi. (1880) 195 In deference to public opinion, he granted some relief to the exiles from his privy purse. **1879** M. ARNOLD *Irish Cathol.* Mixed Ess. 101 It is in deference to the opinion..of such a class that we shape our policy.

deference, obs. form of DIFFERENCE.

†**'deferency.** *Obs. rare*⁻¹. [f. as DEFERENCE with ending -ENCY, q.v.] = DEFERENCE.

1678 OWEN *Mind of God* v. 132 A due reverence and deferency unto the Wisdom..of God.

deferent (ˈdɛfərənt), *a.*¹ and *sb.* Also 5–7 different, 6 defferent. [a. F. *déférent* (Paré 16th c.), or immed. ad. L. *dēferent-em*, pr. pple. of *dēfer-re* to carry down or away.]

A. *adj.* Carrying or conveying down or to a particular destination.

1626 BACON *Sylva* Argt. to §221, etc., The Figures of Pipes, or Concaues, thorow which Sounds passe; or the other Bodies different; conduce to the Variety and Alteration of the Sounds. **1686** SNAPE *Anat. Horse* I. xxiii. 47 These deferent Vessels are two, one on each side. **1877** HUXLEY *Anat. Inv. Anim.* vii. 378 The..testes end in a pair of deferent ducts.

B. *sb.*

1. A carrying or conducting agent; *spec.* in *Phys.*, a canal or duct for conveying fluids.

1626 BACON *Sylva* §133 Though Aire be the most favourable Deferent of Sounds. *Ibid.* §217 All of them are dull and unapt Deferents except the Air. **1730–6** BAILEY (folio), *Deferents*, those vessels of the body appointed for the conveyance of humours from one part to another.

2. In the Ptolemaic astronomical system: The circular orbit of the centre of the epicycle in which a planet was conceived to move: corresponding (roughly) to the actual orbit of the planet. Cf. EPICYCLE 1.

1413 LYDG. *Pilgr. Sowle* v. i. 70 Within eueryche of these seuen speres, there was a Cercle embelyfyng som what.. whiche Cercle clepeth the different. **1594** BLUNDEVIL *Exerc.* III. I. xv. (ed. 7) 306 The Circle that carrieth the Moon, called her Defferent. **1690** LEYBOURN *Cursus Math.* 757 The Semidiametre of the Deferent..is equal to 56½ Semidiametres of the Earth. **1704** J. HARRIS *Lex. Techn.* s.v., The two points where the Epicicle intersects the Deferent are called the Points of the greatest Elongation. **1834** *Nat. Philos., Hist. Astron.* vi. 31/2 (Useful Knowl. Soc.), He [Ptolemy] himself considered his system of deferents and epicycles merely as a means of determining mathematically the positions of the heavenly bodies for any given time.

3. One who reports a matter; the communicator of a notice.

1670 EVELYN in *Phil. Trans.* V. 1056, I communicate to them, through your hands, not only the Instrument..but the Description of the Use and Benefit of it from such a Deferent, as I am sure they will very highly value. **1671** —— *Mem.* (1857) III. 238 Unless you approve of what I write, and assist the deferrent, for I am no more.

deferent (ˈdɛfərənt), *a.*² [f. DEFER *v.*², and DEFERENCE: see -ENT.] Showing deference, deferential.

1822 *Blackw. Mag.* XI. 167 His opposition..was always modest, deferent. **1856** MISS MULOCK *J. Halifax* (ed. 17) 413 Never in all his life had Guy been so deferent, so loving, to his father. **1886** MALLOCK *Old Order Changes* II. vii, Easiness and want of deferent distance in his manner.

deferential (dɛfəˈrɛnʃəl), *a.*¹ [f. DEFERENCE (or its L. type **dēferentia*) + -AL¹: cf. *essence, essential, prudence, prudential*, etc.] Characterized by deference; showing deference; respectful.

1822 SCOTT *Nigel* xxii, If you seek deferential observance and attendance, I tell you at once you will not find them here. **1838** DICKENS *Nich. Nick.* xvii, She was marvellously deferential to Madame Mantalini. **1870** DISRAELI *Lothair* xxviii, The Duke..could be soft and deferential to women.

Hence **deferentiˈality** *sb.*, deference; **defeˈrentially** *adv.*, in a deferential manner.

1880 *Cornh. Mag.* Feb. 183 His master he recognises as such with respectful deferentiality. *a* **1846** *Gentlem. Mag.* cited in WORCESTER for *deferentially*. **1848** C. BRONTË *J. Eyre* vii. (1873) 61 These ladies were deferentially received..and conducted to seats of honour. **1865** DICKENS *Mut. Fr.* III. i, Deferentially observant of his master's face.

defeˈrential, *a.*² *Phys.* [a. F. *déférentiel* (e.g. *artère déférentielle*), f. *déférent*, DEFERENT *a.*¹: see -AL¹.] Serving to convey or conduct; pertaining to the deferent duct.

1877 HUXLEY *Anat. Inv. Anim.* xi. 640 The deferential end of the testicular tube opens into a sac close to the anus. **1883** *Syd. Soc. Lex.*, *Deferential artery*, a small branch supplied to the vas deferens by one of the branches of the superior vesical artery.

deferment (dɪˈfɜːmənt). [f. DEFER *v.*¹ + -MENT. Possibly from F.: Godefroy *Suppl.* cites an example of *déferrement* of 14th c.] A putting off; postponement, delay.

1612 W. PARKES *Curtaine Dr.* (1876) 31 Mercers and Taylors may their customes hire, With long deferment of their tedious bils. **1832** SOUTHEY *Hist. Penins. War* III. 191 The cases which could bear no deferment of relief. **1884** M. ARNOLD in *Pall Mall G.* 1 Dec. 6/2 The delays and the deferments which they are certain to lead to.

deferral (dɪˈfɜːrəl). [f. DEFER *v.*¹ + -AL.] = DEFERMENT.

1895 W. J. LINTON *Love-Lore* 17 To-morrow will amend To-day's deferral. **1957** W. H. WHYTE *Organization Man* 130 The effect has been a large-scale deferral of dead-ends and pigeonholes for thousands of organization men. **1963** *Economist* 16 Mar. 1001/2 The new law ends this right of 'deferral' for so-called 'tax-haven' income.

deferred (dɪˈfɜːd), *ppl. a.* [f. DEFER *v.*¹ + -ED.] Postponed, put off for a time, delayed.

deferred annuity, an annuity that does not begin till after a certain period or number of years, or till the occurrence of a future event, as the decease of some person. ***deferred bonds***: see quot. 1882. ***deferred pay***, a part of the pay of a soldier, etc., which is held over to be paid at his discharge, or at death; in the British Army the amount of deferred pay for soldiers and non-commissioned officers is twopence a day; to men in the reserve force the amount is paid annually. ***deferred payment***, payment that is postponed; *spec.* payment in instalments (see quot. 1951); also *fig.* ***deferred rate***, a cheaper rate charged for a telegram, cable, etc., which may be delayed in transit. ***deferred shares, stock***: see quot. 1882. ***deferred shoot***: see quot. 1883. ***deferred telegram***, one not for immediate delivery (see quot. 1908).

1651 HOBBES *Leviath.* III. xxxii. 198 An immediate, or a not long deferr'd event. **1674** *Essex Papers* (Camden) I. 215 That no surprise might be put upon yʳ Excellency by the defered hearing. **1796** *Deb. Congress U.S.* (1849) 792 A sum ..will then become due and payable on the deferred stock. **1804** J. POOLE *Narr. Foreign Corps* 63 My first knowledge of the deferred list. **1819** SHELLEY *Cenci* V. ii. 23 'Tis my hate, and the deferred desire To wreak it, which extinguishes their [the cheeks'] blood. **1855** MACAULAY *Hist. Eng.* IV. 381 The effect..of bitter regrets and of deferred hopes. **1863** *Sydney Morning Herald* 25 Dec., Information regarding free selection, conditional purchase, deferred payment, or grazing rights. *Ibid.*, In the year previous to free selection and deferred payment, that is, during the year 1861. **1882** BITHELL *Counting-house Dict.* s.v., *Deferred Bonds* are bonds issued by a Government or by a company, entitling the holder to a gradually increasing rate of interest, till the interest amount to a certain specified rate, when they are classed as, or are converted into *Active Bonds*. *Deferred Shares* are shares issued by a Trading Company, but not entitling the holder to a full share of the profits of the company, and sometimes to none at all, until the expiration of a specified time, or the occurrence of some event. **1883** *Syd. Soc. Lex.*, *Deferred shoots*, the shoots produced from dormant buds in the axils of bud-scales. **1883** *Chambers's Jrnl.* 1 Sept. 545/2 The training undergone for the sake of the future recompense which forms the deferred payment. **1883** F. A. WALKER *Pol. Econ.* III. iii. 115 The Standard of Deferred Payments, usually called the Standard of Value. **1889** *Whitaker's Alm.* 645 Deferred pay is an additional payment of £3 per annum made to all non-commissioned officers and soldiers on discharge who have fulfilled certain conditions. **1896** *Chambers's Jrnl.* 26 Sept. 610/1 It is this system of 'deferred payment', as it may be called, that enables the speculator to deal in shares although he may not possess any appreciable capital. **1898** MORRIS *Austral Eng.*, *Deferred payment*, a legal phrase. 'Land on deferred payment'; 'Deferred payment settler'; 'Pastoral deferred payment'. These expressions in New Zealand have reference to the mode of statutory alienation of Crown lands. **1907** *Westm. Gaz.* 18 June 4/2 The introduction of the deferred-payment system in connexion with the automobile business. **1908** *Ibid.* 3 Apr. 10/1 All deferred rate telegrams are posted instead of being wired. **1929** *Times* 2 Feb. 8/3 The cost of 'Urgent' telegram to be 1s., and 'Deferred' 6d., for 15 words. **1951** *Oxf. Jun. Encycl.* VII. 148/2 The other system of instalment selling is called 'deferred payments'. A written agreement is drawn up, as for a hire-purchase transaction, but the goods become the property of the buyer after payment of the first deposit.

deferrer (dɪˈfɜːrə(r)). [f. DEFER *v.*¹ + -ER¹.] One who defers; a delayer, postponer.

1552 HULOET, Deferrer, *cunctator*. **1559** WILLOCK *Let. to Crossraguel* in Keith *Hist. Ch. Scotl.* App. 198 Quhilk of both is the Differrer of the Caus? *a* **1637** B. JONSON tr. *Horace's Art Poetry* 245 A great deferrer, long in hope, grown numb With sloth, yet greedy still of what's to come. **1880** G. MEREDITH *Trag. Com.* xiv. (1892) 200 One of those delicious girls in the New Comedy..called The Postponer, The Deferrer, or, as we might say, The To-Morrower.

deferring (dɪˈfɜːrɪŋ), *vbl. sb.* [f. DEFER *v.*^{1} + -ING^1.] The action of the verb DEFER^1; delaying, postponement.

14.. LYDG. *Temple of Glas* 1206 Abide awhile..Let no sorow in þin herte bite For no differring. **1583** STUBBES *Anat. Abus.* II. (1882) 9 This deferring of iustice is as damnable before God. **1621** BP. HALL *Heaven upon Earth* §6 After all these friuolous deferrings, it [sinne] will returne vpon thee. **1633** EARL MANCH. *Al Mondo* (1636) 112 By deferring wee presume upon that we haue not, and neglect that we haue.

deferring (dɪˈfɜːrɪŋ), *ppl. a.*^{1} [f. DEFER *v.*^{1} + -ING^2.] That defers; putting off, delaying.

c **1565** LINDESAY (Pitsc.) *Chron. Scot.* (1728) 105 Gave them a differring answer which was little to effect.

deˈferring, *ppl. a.*^{2} [f. DEFER *v.*^{2} + -ING^2.] Manifesting deference; deferential.

1829 S. TURNER *Hist. Eng.* IV. II. xxvii. 198 The language of very deferring but of rather strong affection.

†**deˈferve**, *v. Obs. rare.* [ad. L. *dēfervēre* to boil down, boil thoroughly, f. DE- I. 3 b + *fervēre* to boil.] To boil down.

c **1420** *Pallad. on Husb.* XI. 485 Defrut, carene..Of must is made: Defrut of defervyng Til thicke.

defervesce (diːfəˈvɛs), *v.* [ad. L. *dēfervēscĕre* to cease to boil, cool down, f. DE- I. 6 + *fervēscĕre*, inceptive of *fervēre* to be hot.] *intr.* To cool down.

1859 *Sat. Rev.* VIII. 735/2 The pamphlet..has experienced the fate incidental to effervescent things—it has defervesced.

defervescence (diːfəˈvɛsəns). [f. L. *dēfervēscent-em* DEFERVESCENT: see -ENCE.]

1. Cooling down; abatement of heat.

1721 BAILEY, *Defervescence*, a growing cool, an abating. **1775** in ASH. Hence in mod. Dicts.

2. *Path.* The decrease of bodily temperature which accompanies the abatement of fever or feverish symptoms; the period of this decrease.

(Introduced in German (*defervescenz*) by Wunderlich.)

1866 BRAITHWAITE *Retrospect of Med.* LIII. 14 The height of the fever was reached on December 31st..after this defervescence went on gradually. **1875** H. C. WOOD *Therap.* (1879) 145 It is evident that..in some of these cases of Wunderlich's the drug was given about the time natural defervescence would be expected to occur. **1877** ROBERTS *Handbk. Med.* (ed. 3) I. 78 Occasionally defervescence is quite irregular in its progress.

†**deferˈvescency**. *Obs.* [f. as prec. + -ENCY.] = prec.; also *fig.*

1649 JER. TAYLOR *Great Exemp.* v. §20. 155 After a long time..they are abated by a defervescency in holy actions. **1684** tr. *Bonet's Merc. Compit.* VI. 160 A Loosness, which follows in the defervescency of a Fever.

defervescent (diːfəˈvɛsənt), *a.* and *sb.* [f. L. *dēfervēscent-em*, pr. pple. of *dēfervēscĕre* to DEFERVESCE.] 'That which can reduce fever and high temperature, as cold and bloodletting' (*Syd. Soc. Lex.*).

defesance, defese, etc., obs. ff. DEFEASANCE, DEFEASE, etc.

defet, var. of DEFEIT *a. Obs.*, wasted.

defete, -fette, obs. forms of DEFEAT *sb.* and *v.*

†**deˈfeud**. *nonce-wd.* [f. DE- + FEUD: on some mistaken analogy, such as *spite, despite.*] = Feud.

1648 EVELYN *Mem.* (1857) III. 22 If the commanders were all at defeud one amongst the other.

defeudalize: see DE- II. 1.

defeysance, obs. form of DEFEASANCE.

deff(e, obs. forms of DEAF.

‖**deffait**, *a. Her. Obs.*$^{-0}$ [F. *défait*, in OF. *desfait, deffait*, undone, deprived, etc.]

1727 BAILEY vol. II, *Deffait*, is used to signify the Head of a Beast cut off smooth, the same as *Decapité*. **1727–51** CHAMBERS *Cycl.*, *Deffait* or *Decapité*, a term used by the French heralds.

deffame, deffawte, obs. ff. DEFAME, DEFAULT.

deffayt, deffete, obs. forms of DEFEAT.

deffe, var. of DAFF *sb.*, fool, stupid fellow.

1482 in *Eng. Gilds* (1870) 315 Yf any brother dysspysse anoder callenge hym knaffe or horson, or deffe.

deffence, defform, etc.: see DEFENCE, etc.

deffer, var. of DEVER *Obs.*, duty.

defference, obs. form of DIFFERENCE.

deffly, erron. form of DEFTLY.

defhed: see DEAFHEAD.

defi: see DEFY *sb.*

defiable (dɪˈfaɪəb(ə)l), *a.*^{1} *rare.* [f. DEFY *v.*^{1} + -ABLE.] Capable of being defied; †defiant.

1874 M. & F. COLLINS *Frances* I. 14 Oh! I think he's rather a defiable young gentleman.

†**deˈfiable**, *a.*^{2} *Obs. rare*$^{-1}$. [f. DEFY *v.*^{2} + -ABLE.] Capable of being digested; digestible.

a **1450** *Fysshynge wyth an Angle* (1883) 2 And ete norysching metes & defyabul.

defial (dɪˈfaɪəl). *rare.* [In ME., a. OF. *defiaille* (13–14th c. in Godef.), f. *defier* to DEFY: see -AL^1 5. In modern use perh. directly from the Eng. verb: cf. *denial.*] = DEFIANCE.

c **1470** HARDING *Chron.* CLIV. iv, He helde the felde and kyng Philyp warred, And letters sent hym, defyals and vmbrayde, Of hys sueraunce and othe. **1793** W. TAYLOR tr. *Goethe's Iph. in Tauris* Note 119 This defial is not a Gothic and misplac'd idea. **1824** W. TAYLOR in *Monthly Mag.* LVII. 509 King Meliad, And Danayn..took part In the defial. **1848** W. H. KELLY tr. *L. Blanc's Hist. Ten Y.* II. 267 Abuse, which he met with lofty defial or silent contempt.

defiance (dɪˈfaɪəns). Forms: 4 defye-, 5 defy-, diffi-, diffye-, dyffy-, 5–6 defi-, deffyaunce, 6 diffyans, diffi-, defyance, 5- defiance. [a. OF. *defiance, deff-, desf-*, the action of defying = Pr. *desfiansa*, OSp. *desfianza*, It. *disfidanza* :—Romanic **disfidāntia*, f. *disfidāre*, med.L. *diffidāre*: see DEFY *v.*^{1} and -ANCE. Mod.F. *défiance* in sense of 'distrust' appears to be influenced by L. *diffidentia* distrust: see DIFFIDENCE.]

†1. Renunciation of faith, allegiance, or amity; declaration of hostilities. *Obs.*

c **1300** *K. Alis.* 5545 Alisaunder the wryt behelde, And saugh therinne thretyng belde, And defyeaunce, the thrid day. *c* **1430** LYDG. *Min. Poems* 92 (Mätz.) Arbachus..sent to hym, for his mysgovernaunce, Of highe disdayne a ful playne defyaunce. *c* **1500** *Melusine* 350 They lete make a lettre of deffyaunce of whiche the tenour foloweth. **1523** LD. BERNERS *Froiss.* I. xxxiv. 48 That who soeuer wolde any hurte to other, shuld make his defyance thre dayes before his dede. **1622** R. HAWKINS *Voy. S. Sea* (1847) 231 Spaine broke the peace with England..and that by ymbargo, which of all kindes of defiances is most reproved, and of least reputation..the most honourable is with trumpet and herald to proclaime and denounce the warre by publicke defiance. **1649** MILTON *Tenure of Kings* Wks. 238/2 The whole protestant league raised open war against Charles the Fifth..sent him a defiance, renounced all faith and allegiance toward him.

†**b.** *at defiance*: at enmity or hostility. *Obs.*

1563–87 FOXE *A. & M.* (1684) III. 574 Cleave unto God, and be at defiance with his enemies the Papists. **1598** GRENEWEY *Tacitus' Ann.* III. vii. (1622) 74 The Prouinces at defiance with vs. **1634** SIR T. HERBERT *Trav.* (1638) 28 The two kings..live at defiance, and oft times the poore Savages pay deerely for eithers ambition. **1705** J. LOGAN in *Pa. Hist. Soc. Mem.* X. 58, I have been ever since the sending of that letter..at defiance with him.

2. The act of defying or challenging to fight; a challenge or summons to a combat or contest; a challenge to make good or maintain a cause, assertion, etc. *cartel of defiance*: see CARTEL and quots.

c **1430** LYDG. *Bochas* II. Prol. (1554) 40 a, Vertue on fortune maketh a defiaunce. **1587** *Mirr. Mag.*, *Brennus* xxv, To sound defiaunce, fyre, and sword and fight. **1593** SHAKS. *Rich. II*, III. iii. 130 Shall we..send Defiance to the Traytor? **1639** tr. *Camus' Moral Relat.* 303 Saluted by a letter of defiance, which marked out the houre and the place where he should come with a second. **1755** JOHNSON, *Defiance*..a challenge to make any impeachment good. **1831** BREWSTER *Newton* (1855) II. xv. 64 He could not dispense with answering..Sir Isaac Newton..who had given him a defiance in express terms. **1856** FROUDE *Hist. Eng.* (1858) II. ix. 372 To the king, the pope's conduct appeared a defiance; and as a defiance he accepted it.

3. The act of setting at nought; open or daring resistance offered to authority or any opposing force.

1710 STEELE *Tatler* No. 98 ¶3 Remarkable for that Piece of good Breeding peculiar to natural Britons, to wit Defiance. *a* **1714** SHARP *Wks.* VI. Dis. VIII. (R.), This open and scandalous violation and defiance of his most sacred fundamental laws. **1883** FROUDE *Short Stud.* IV. I. ix. 105 The open disobedience of the order..could be construed only as defiance.

4. *Phr.* **a.** *to bid defiance to*: to defy, declare hostility to; to brave, set at nought; so *to set at defiance.*

1621 BURTON *Anat. Mel.* II. iii. III. (1676) 210 He set her [Fortune] at defiance ever after. **1667** *Decay Chr. Piety* (J.), The Novatian heresy..bade such express defiance to apostacy. **1757** *Centinel* No. 34 The fire of youth..when agitated by any violent passion..sets everything at defiance. **1794** SULLIVAN *View Nat.* II, The Alps. See how scornfully they look down upon you, and bid defiance to the elements. **1842** MISS MITFORD in L'Estrange *Life* III. ix. 144 They might have set the Tories at defiance.

b. *in defiance of*: with daring disregard of; setting at nought.

1750 JOHNSON *Rambler* No. 75 ¶15 He carries me the first dish, in defiance of the frowns and whispers of the table. **1816** KEATINGE *Trav.* (1817) I. 15 Clung to..in defiance of reason and sensation. **1874** GREEN *Short Hist.* iv. §5. 202 Gaveston..was beheaded in defiance of the terms of his capitulation.

†5. Declaration of aversion or contempt; rejection. *Obs. rare*$^{-1}$.

1603 SHAKS. *Meas. for M.* III. i. 143 Such a warped slip of wildernesse Nere issu'd from his blood. Take my defiance, Die, perish.

†6. Distrust. *Obs. rare*$^{-1}$. [= mod.F. *défiance.*]

1662 PEPYS *Diary* 6 Jan., Major Holmes..I perceive, would fain get to be free and friends with my wife; but I shall prevent it, and she herself hath a defyance against him.

defiant (dɪˈfaɪənt), *a.* [a. F. *défiant*, OF. *des-, deff-, defiant*, pr. pple. of *desfier, défier*: see DEFY and -ANT. App. quite of modern use.]

1. Showing a disposition to defy; manifesting a spirit of defiance.

a **1837** BRYDGES cited in WORCESTER. **1840** CARLYLE *Heroes* (1858) 289 The man's heart that dare rise defiant..against Hell itself. **1856** FROUDE *Hist. Eng.* II. xi. 510 The defiant attitude which she had assumed. **1863** GEO. ELIOT *Romola* II. viii, She had started up with defiant words ready to burst from her lips.

‖2. Feeling distrust. [= mod.F. *défiant.*]

1872 LEVER *Ld. Kilgobbin* xv. (1875) 98 He was less defiant, or mistrustful.

defiantly (dɪˈfaɪəntlɪ), *adv.* [f. prec. + -LY^2.] In a defiant manner; with defiance; daringly.

1859 HALLIWELL *Evid. Chr.* 150 The early Christians..defiantly neglected the polytheistic worship. **1874** GREEN *Short Hist.* viii. §3. 487 Buckingham..stood defiantly at his master's side as he was denounced.

deˈfiantness. *rare.* [-NESS.] The quality of being defiant.

1872 GEO. ELIOT *Middlem.* lxi, He answered..speaking with quick defiantness.

†**deˈfiatory**, *a. Obs. rare*$^{-1}$. [f. DEFY *v.*^{1}, after words like *commend-atory.*] Bearing or conveying defiance.

1635 SHELFORD *Learned Disc.* 276 (T.) The letters defiatory of Achmet to Sigismund the Third.

defibrillation (ˌdiːfaɪbrɪˈleɪʃən). *Med.* [f. DE- II. 1 + FIBRILLATION.] **1.** The separation of the fibres of tissues, *e.g.* cerebral tissues.

1935 H. J. WILKINSON tr. *Hultkrantz's Brain Preparations* i. 6 In the defibrillation method, spatulae and awl-shaped instruments are those most frequently used.

2. The stopping of fibrillation of the heart. Hence **deˈfibrillating** *ppl. a.*; **deˈfibrillator**, an apparatus used to control fibrillation of the heart.

1940 C. J. WIGGERS in *Amer. Heart Jrnl.* XX. 419 Defibrillation can be accomplished in the dog by the..application of several comparatively weak shocks. **1956** *Blakiston's New Gould Med. Dict.* (ed. 2) 321/1 Defibrillator. **1958** *Electronic Engin.* XXX. 24 The complete circuit of the defibrillator is shown. **1961** *Lancet* 5 Aug. 293/2 Heart action is restored within a few minutes of releasing the aortic clamp. This results in perfusion of the coronaries with comparatively warm blood, and although ventricular fibrillation seems to be invariable at this stage it reverts easily with a defibrillating shock. **1967** *Spectator* 11 Aug. 159/3 Ventricular fibrillation may be controlled by a piece of electrical apparatus known as a defibrillator.

defibrinate (dɪˈfaɪbrɪneɪt), *v.* [f. DE- II. 1 + FIBRIN + -ATE^3.] *trans.* To deprive of fibrin. Hence **deˈfibrinated** *ppl. a.*; **defibriˈnation**, the process of depriving of fibrin. So **deˈfibrinize** *v.* [see -IZE] = DEFIBRINATE.

1845 G. E. DAY tr. *Simon's Anim. Chem.* I. 249 Density of defibrinated blood. **1880** *Nature* XXI. 453 On diluting the fresh blood..and exposing it after rapid defibrination. **1881** G. F. DOWDESWELL in *Jrnl. Microsc. Sc.* Jan. 160, I have not found it necessary to defibrinate the blood. **1883** *Syd. Soc. Lex.*, *Defibrinize*. **1885** OGILVIE, *Defibrinize*.

†**deficience** (dɪˈfɪʃəns). *Obs.* [ad. late L. *dēficientia*, f. *dēficient-em* DEFICIENT: see -ENCE.] The fact of being deficient; failure, want, deficiency.

1605 BACON *Adv. Learn.* II. ii. §4. 11 In these kindes of vnperfect Histories I doe assign no deficience. **1641** LD. J. DIGBY *Sp. in Ho. Com.* 19 Jan. 20 The deficience of Parliament hath bin the *Causa Causarum* of all the Mischiefs. **1667** MILTON *P.L.* VIII. 416 Thou in thy self art perfect, and in thee Is no deficience found. **1762–71** H. WALPOLE *Vertue's Anecd. Paint.* (1782) V. 2 Want of colouring is the capital deficience of prints. **1784** JOHNSON *Lett. to Mrs. Thrale* 10 Mar., Imputing every deficience to criminal negligence.

deficiency (dɪˈfɪʃənsɪ). [f. as prec.: see -ENCY.]

1. a. The quality or state of being deficient or wanting; failure; want, lack, absence; insufficiency.

1634 E. KNOTT *Charity maintained* v. §9 The Doctrine of the total deficiency of the visible Church, which..is maintained by divers chief Protestants. **1646** SIR T. BROWNE *Pseud. Ep.* IV. v. 188 Scaliger finding a defect in the reason of Aristotle, introduceth one of no lesse deficiency himselfe. **1767** BLACKSTONE *Comm.* II. 246 Escheats..arising merely upon the deficiency of the blood, whereby the descent is impeded. **1793** BEDDOES *Math. Evid.* 62 We may make up, by continued attention, for their deficiency of original acuteness. **1797** M. BAILLIE *Morb. Anat.* Pref., Patients often explain very imperfectly their feelings, partly from the natural deficiency of language. **1865** GROTE *Plato* I. i. 83 These particles might be in excess as well as in deficiency.

b. with *a* and *pl.*: An instance of this condition; something wanting; a defect, an imperfection.

1664 H. MORE *Myst. Iniq.* 116 That there is a deficiency in the Merits of Christ. **1664** POWER *Exp. Philos.* I. 53 They discover the flaws and deficiencies of the latter. **1736** BUTLER *Anal.* I. v. Wks. 1874 I. 92 Nature has endued us with a power of supplying those deficiencies, by acquired knowledge. **1817** J. SCOTT *Paris Revisit.* (ed. 4) 184 The battle..proved the existence of a deficiency in the latter quarter. **1828** D'ISRAELI *Chas. I*, II. vii. 168 This consciousness of his own deficiencies is an interesting trait in his character. **1853** J. H. NEWMAN *Hist. Sk.* (1876) I. I. iii. 127 Where art has to supply the deficiencies of nature.

c. *Math.* ***deficiency of a curve***: the number by which its double points fall short of the highest number possible in a curve of the same order.

1865 CAYLEY *Proc. Lond. Math. Soc.* I. No. iii, It will be convenient to introduce the term 'Deficiency', viz. a curve of the order *n* with $\frac{1}{2}(n-1)(n-2) - D$ double points, is said to have a deficiency $= D$. **1893** FORSYTH *Theory of Functions* 356 The deficiency of a curve is the same as the class of the Riemann surface associated with its equation.

d. The amount by which the revenue of a state, company, etc. falls short of the expenditure; a deficit; hence ***deficiency act, bill, law*** (i.e. one to meet such a deficiency); the amount by which the assets of a debtor fall short of his liabilities; hence ***deficiency account, statement.*** (For quots., see 2 below.)

e. *Genetics.* = DELETION 3.

1916 C. B. BRIDGES in *Genetics* I. 150 *Deficiency*... Tests showed..that a small section of the X in the bar region had become genetically non-existent! **1917** *Ibid.* II. 445 The general term 'deficiency' is used to designate the loss or inactivation of an entire, definite, and measurable section of genes and framework of a chromosome. **1956** *New Biol.* XX. 41 A deficiency arises when a chromosome is broken in two spots and the two end pieces join up to form a new chromosome from which the middle piece is missing... Large deficiencies, by which many genes have been removed from the cell, act as dominant lethals. Smaller deficiencies act as recessive lethals. **1969** G. W. BURNS *Sci. Genetics* xii. 220 Probably the best known disorder to be associated definitely with a chromosomal deficiency in man is the 'cri du chat' or cat-cry syndrome described by Le Jeune (1963).

2. *attrib.* and *Comb.*, as **deficiency disease**, a disease caused by the lack of an essential or important substance in the diet; usu. = AVITAMINOSIS; **deficiency payment**, a subsidy paid by the government to farmers to cover differences between market prices of agricultural produce and minimum prices guaranteed by the government. See also 1 d above.

1887 *Daily News* 26 Oct. 6/8 None of the debtors have as yet filed deficiency accounts. **1912** C. FUNK in *Jrnl. State Med.* XX. 341 (*title*) The etiology of deficiency diseases. **1914** *Lancet* 15 Aug. 460/1 If pellagra is a deficiency disease its relation to maize is similar to that of beri-beri to rice. **1933** *Discovery* July 234/1 The relief of deficiency diseases by the ever-increasing number of vitamins. **1968** M. PYKE *Food & Society* ii. 17 Expensive multivitamin tablets protect the well-fed people who can afford them against deficiency diseases they will never experience. **1719** W. WOOD *Surv. Trade* 168 A considerable Sum of Money arising by the Deficiency Law. **1932** *Act 22 & 23 Geo. V* c. 24 §1 If, in any cereal year, the..average price of..wheat is less than the standard price, every registered grower shall.. be entitled to receive..a payment (hereinafter referred to as a 'deficiency payment') representing..the difference.. between the said average price and the standard price. **1963** *Ann. Reg. 1962* 462 Britain's system of support for home agriculture (by means of deficiency payments). **1969** *Times* 13 Jan. 11/2 Although the primary intention at Oxford was to look at alternatives to the present deficiency payment system as a means of farm support, other problems kept intruding. **1887** *Pall Mall G.* 30 Nov. 9/1 The bankrupt was then questioned upon his deficiency statement.

deficient (dɪˈfɪʃənt), *a.* and *sb.* [ad. L. *dēficient-em*, pr. pple. of *dēficĕre* to fail, orig. to undo, do away, take oneself away, leave, forsake; f. DE- I. 6 + *facĕre* to make, do. Cf. mod.F. *déficient* (1754 in Hatzf.).] **A.** *adj.*

1. a. Wanting some part, element, constituent, or characteristic which is necessary to completeness, or having less than the proper amount of it; wanting or falling short *in* something; defective.

1604 SHAKS. *Oth.* I. iii. 63 Being not deficient, blind, or lame of sense. **1632** LITHGOW *Trav.* A iv, Howsoever the Gift, and the Giver be deficient. **1651** T. RUDD *Euclide* A iv, The [Manuscript] Copie, in many places, was deficient. **1659** O. WALKER *Oratory* 32 Latine words (where our language is deficient) Englished. **1663** COWLEY *Disc. Govt. O. Cromwell* (1669) 74 In the point of murder..we have little reason to think that our late Tyranny has been deficient to the examples..set it in other Countreys. **1713** STEELE *Englishman* No. 19. 121 We find our selves deficient in any thing else sooner than in our Understanding. **1758** JOHNSON *Idler* No. 72 ¶1 Men complain..of deficient memory. **1861** FLO. NIGHTINGALE *Nursing* 5 The best women are wofully deficient in knowledge about health. **1891** *Law Times* XCII. 94/1 Milk which on analysis proved to be deficient in fatty matter to the extent of about 33 per cent.

†**b.** *Gram.* = DEFECTIVE *a.* 5. *Obs.* **c.** *Arith.* ***deficient number***: a number the sum of whose factors is less than the number itself. **d.** *Geom.* ***deficient hyperbola***: a cubic curve having only one asymptote. †**e.** *Mus.* Applied to any interval diminished by a comma. *Obs.*

1727–51 CHAMBERS *Cycl.*, *Defective*, or *Deficient Nouns*, in grammar. *Ibid.*, *Deficient Hyperbola*. *Ibid.*, *Deficient numbers* ..Such, *e.gr.* is 8; whose quota parts are, 1, 2, and 4; which, together, only make 7. **1753** *Ibid.*, *Supp.* s.v. *Interval*, Limma of the Greek Scale, or deficient Semi-tone Major.

2. Present in less than the proper quantity; not of sufficient force; wholly or partly wanting or lacking; insufficient, inadequate.

1632 J. HAYWARD tr. *Biondi's Eromena* 14 Meere conjectures were deficient because the meanes (whereby to conjecture) were wanting. **1663** COWLEY *Disc. Govt. O. Cromwell* (1669) 70 If I should say, that personal kind of courage had been deficient in the man. **1748** *Anson's Voy.* III. iv. 333 Apprehensions that our stock of water might prove deficient. **1856** EMERSON *Eng. Traits, Lit.* Wks. (Bohn) II. 109 Hallam is uniformly polite, but with deficient sympathy. **1881** MAXWELL *Electr. & Magn.* I. 40 The quantity of fluid which would be required to saturate it is sometimes called the Deficient fluid.

†**3.** ***deficient cause***: that 'deficience', failure to act, or absence of anything, which becomes the cause or negative condition of some result. *Obs.*

The conception and the phrase (*causa deficiens*) appear first in St. Augustine, in his discussion of the origin of evil and of God's relation to it, and are connected with his doctrine that evil being nothing positive, but merely a *defect*, could have no *efficient*, but only a *deficient* cause. It was also used by Thomas Aquinas (who distinguished the physical sense of the phrase from the moral); in English it came into vogue during the Calvinistic-Arminian controversy in 16–17th c., in reference both to the origin of evil and to the reprobation of the wicked. Cf. DEFECTIVE *a.* 6.

[ST. AUGUST. *De Civ. Dei* XII. vii, Nemo igitur quærat efficientem caussam malæ voluntatis, non enim est efficiens, sed deficiens; quia nec illa effectio est, sed defectio; deficere namque ab eo quod summum est, ad id quod minus est, hoc est incipere habere voluntatem malam.] **1581** J. BELL *Haddon's Answ. Osor.* 204 And hereof commeth the destruction of the reprobates..yͤ efficient cause wherof consisteth truely in every of their own corruption, but the cause deficient in the will of God. **1598** BARCKLEY *Felic. Man* (1631) 666 It [the cause of evil and sin] is no efficient but a deficient cause. **1658** WOMOCK *Exam. Tilenus* 40 There are sins of omission..and if the deficient cause in things necessary be the efficient, you know to whom such sins are to be imputed. **1677** GALE *Crt. Gentiles* IV. II. vi. §3. 380 As for moral evil he [God] is not the author or cause thereof as it is evil: because moral evils as such have no efficient cause but only deficient. **1678** *Ibid.* IV. III. vi. 195 Gods concurse is neither the efficient nor deficient cause of sin.

†**4.** Failing, fainting; of or pertaining to swooning. *Obs.*

1605 SHAKS. *Lear* IV. vi. 23 Ile looke no more, Least my braine turne, and the deficient sight Topple downe headlong. **1632** LITHGOW *Trav.* x. 438 A..giddy headed Foole, (full of deficient Vapours).

B. *sb.*

†**1. a.** Something that is wanting, or absent where it should be present. **b.** The want or absence of something; a deficiency. *Obs.*

1640 G. WATTS tr. *Bacon's Adv. Learn.* Pref. 23 To set down more than the naked Titles, or brief Arguments of Deficients. **1660** SHARROCK *Vegetables* 1 Lord Bacon.. reckons it among the Deficients of Natural History. **1686** WILDING in *Collect.* (Oxf. Hist. Soc.) I. 263 To yͤ mercer for deficients to my new suit.

†**2.** *Gram.* A defective noun. *Obs.*

1647 WARD *Simp. Cobler* 25 Like the *Quæ Genus* in the Grammer, being Deficients, or Redundants, not to be brought under any Rule.

†**3.** A person who fails to do what is required; a defaulter. *Obs.*

1697 *Col. Rec. Pennsylv.* I. 521 Yͤ Collectors had neither brought in the Monies they had Received, nor yͤ names of the deficients. **1719** *Ayr Presbyt. Rec.* in *Ch. Life Scotl.* (1885) I. i. 22 *note*, The deficients have all engadged to do it.

4. = DEFECTIVE *sb.* 2 c.

1906 F. THORESBY in *Westm. Rev.* Jan. 39 There are the deficients, *i.e.*, those who from, or before birth, or by reason of their rearing, or both, never have..a fair start. **1927** CARR-SAUNDERS & JONES *Soc. Struct. Eng. & Wales* 213 [Authorities] vary notoriously... Some are active, while others close their eyes to the existence of deficients within their areas.

deˈficiently, *adv.* [f. prec. + -LY².] In a deficient manner; defectively, insufficiently.

1702 ECHARD *Eccl. Hist.* (1710) 279 After she had sacrificed many of her gallants who were too deficiently serviceable to her. **1818** TODD, *Deficiently*, in a defective manner.

deficile, obs. var of DIFFICILE *a.*

†**deˈficious**, *a. Obs. rare.* [irreg. f. L. *dēficĕre* to fail; cf. DEFICIENT.] Deficient, lacking.

1540–1 ELYOT *Image Gov.* 6 Because they have been so deficiouse of knowlage.

deficit (ˈdɛfɪsɪt, ˈdiːfɪsɪt). [a. F. *déficit* (1690 in Hatzf.), a. L. *dēficit* 'it is wanting, there is wanting' (from *dēficĕre*: see DEFICIENT), formerly used in inventories, etc., to designate things wanting.]

A falling short, a deficiency; the amount by which a sum of money, or the like, falls short of what is due or required; the excess of expenditure or liabilities over income or assets.

1782 *Gentl. Mag.* LII. 122/1 The deficit in the accounts of men entrusted with public employment. **1787** T. JEFFERSON *Writ.* (1859) II. 209 They see a great deficit in their revenues. **1817** BENTHAM *Parl. Ref. Catech.* (1818) 75 In congress, where, in the very last year, there was a *surplus*.. instead of a *deficit*, as here. **1861** MUSGRAVE *By-roads* 215 The hardier sex was compelled to make good the deficit arising from the withdrawal of female exertion. **1879** H. FAWCETT in *19th Cent.* Feb. 194 (Government of India) Deficits have been repeatedly recurring, and debt has been steadily and surely accumulated.

de fide: see DE I. 4.

defie, obs. form of DEFY *v.* and *sb.*

defied (dɪˈfaɪd), *ppl. a.* [f. DEFY *v.*¹ + -ED.] Treated with defiance, challenged, braved.

1816 BYRON *Stanzas to Augusta* (I.) vi, There's more in one soft word of thine Than in the world's defied rebuke.

defier (dɪˈfaɪə(r)). [f. DEFY *v.*¹ + -ER¹.] One who defies, challenges, or braves.

1585 T. WASHINGTON tr. *Nicholay's Voy. Turkie* IV. xiii. 126 Zatasnicis, which signifieth..defyers of men, for that every one of them are bounde to fight agaynst tenne. **1612** *Two Noble K.* V. i. 120, I am..To those that boast, and have not, a defyer. **1703** ROWE *Ulyss.* V. i, This Defier of the Gods. **1826** MISS MITFORD *Village* Ser. II. (1863) 372 The girls..more sturdy defiers of heat, and cold, and wet, than boys themselves.

†**defiguration** (diːfɪgjʊˈreɪʃən). *Obs.* [n. of action from med.L. *dēfigūrāre* to disfigure, f. DE- I. 6 + *figūrāre* to figure, *figūra* figure; cf. F. *défigurer.*] The action of disfiguring; marring the figure or appearance (of a thing); disfigurement.

1585 T. WASHINGTON tr. *Nicholay's Voy. Turkie* II. iii. 73 b, By such defiguration they do shew very horrible. **1628** BP. HALL *Rem. Wks.* (1660) 30 These traditions are defigurations and deformations of Christ exhibited. **1830** LAMB *Lett.* (1837) II. 263 A certain personal defiguration in the man-part of this extraordinary centaur.

†**deˈfigure**, *v.*¹ *Obs.* [a. OF. *defigurer* (12th c.), var. of *des-*, *deffigurer*, mod.F. *défigurer*:—late L. and Rom. *disfigūrāre* to DISFIGURE.] An early synonym of DISFIGURE.

1340 HAMPOLE *Pr. Consc.* 2340 Horribely defygurd thurgh syn. **14..** *Eng. Misc.* (Warton Club) 24 Thow art defygurt, thi eyne beth depe hollowed.

†**defigure** (dɪˈfɪgjʊə(r)), *v.*² *Obs.* [f. DE- I. 3 + FIGURE *v.* (cf. *depict*, *delineate*).]

1. *trans.* To represent by a figure or image; to figure, delineate.

1599 A. M. tr. *Gabelhouer's Bk. Physicke* 114/2 To be.. defigured or portraitede in woode. **1631** WEEVER *Anc. Fun. Mon.* 844 Two stones as they are here defigured.

2. *fig.* To represent symbolically, symbolize.

1615 G. SANDYS *Trav.* II. 113 By this defigured they the perplexed life of man.

†**defil**, *v. Obs. rare.* To be or become stupid; = dialectal *daffle*: see DAFF *v.*

1570 LEVINS 126/37 To défil, neutre, *stupére.*

defilade (dɛfɪˈleɪd), *sb. Fortif.* [f. DEFILE *v.*³ + -ADE. *Défilade* in F. appears not to have this sense, but only to be related to DEFILE *v.*²] = DEFILEMENT².

1851 J. S. MACAULAY *Field Fortif.* 105 The object of defilade is so to regulate the relief of the parapets or covering masses, that the defenders may be perfectly screened by them from the view of the enemy. *Ibid.* 111 It often happens ..that a single plane of defilade would give too great a relief. **1855** PORTLOCK in *Encycl. Brit.* IX. 801/2 It is preferable to excavate behind the parapet, whenever the defilade requires so great an increase of height. **1879** *Cassell's Techn. Educ.* II. 106 The various practical operations that are gone through to ascertain how much the parapets should be raised to obtain cover, are called *defilade.*

defilade (dɛfɪˈleɪd), *v. Fortif.* [f. DEFILADE *sb.*: answering to mod.F. *défiler*, DEFILE *v.*³] To arrange the plan and profile of fortifications, so that their lines shall be protected from enfilading fire, and the interior of the works from plunging or reverse fire (Stocqueler *Mil. Encycl.*). Hence **defiˈlading** *vbl. sb.*

1828 J. M. SPEARMAN *Brit. Gunner* (ed. 2) 217 When a work is commanded by a height in front, the interior must be defiladed by elevating the parapet to such a height, that a line of fire from..the hill..may be every where at least eight feet above the terre-plein of the work. *Ibid.* 218 When a work is commanded in reverse, the parapet or traverse must be high enough to defilade the defenders of the banquette opposite the height. **1830** E. S. N. CAMPBELL *Dict. Mil. Sc.* s.v. *Defilement*, The operation..called Defilement, or Defilading, is of two kinds, in altitude and in direction. **1851** J. S. MACAULAY *Field Fortif.* 297 Proof that the defilading operations have been incorrectly executed.

defile (ˈdiːfaɪl, dɪˈfaɪl), *sb.*¹ Formerly 7–9 **defilé**, 8 **defilee**. [a. F. *défilé* (17th c.), ppl. sb. from *défiler* to DEFILE *v.*²: the final *-é* was formerly often made *-ee* in Eng., but being generally written *-e* without accent, has come to be treated as *e* mute, the word being identified in form with DEFILE *v.*]

1. *Mil.* A narrow way or passage along which troops can march only by files or with a narrow front; *esp.* (and in ordinary use) a narrow pass or gorge between mountains.

α. *defilé, defilee.*

1685 *Lond. Gaz.* No. 2064/2 They repassed the Defilés on the side of the Moras. **1698** T. FROGER *Voy.* 62 They are surrounded with high Mountains; so that one cannot enter, or go out, but thro' a *Defilé* or narrow Passage. **1701** *Lond. Gaz.* No. 3723/2 In a Defilee between a great Moras and the River Adige. **1720** OZELL *Vertot's Rom. Rep.* II. XIV. 340 He was seized in the Defilees of those Mountains. **1796–7** *Instr. & Reg. Cavalry* (1813) 259 The Regiment passes a defilé, and forms in line of divisions. **1830** E. S. N. CAMPBELL *Dict. Mil. Sc., Defilé.*

β. defile.

1686 *Lond. Gaz.* No. 2161/1 A Valley, to which there was no passage but by a very narrow Defile. **1719** DE FOE *Crusoe* I. xx. 353 A long narrow Defile or Lane, which we were to pass to get through the Wood. **1776** GIBBON *Decl. & F.* I. xiv. 437 Constantine had taken post in a defile about half a mile in breadth, between a steep hill and a deep morass. **1818** BYRON *Ch. Har.* IV. lxii, By Thrasimene's lake, in the defiles Fatal to Roman rashness. **1860** TYNDALL *Glac.* I. xx. 139 [The glacier] squeezes itself through the narrow defile at the base of the Riffelhorn.

2. The act of defiling, a march by files. (Also as Fr., *défilé*.)

1835 in H. Greville *Diary* 65 (Stanf.) In the Place Vendôme, where the King placed himself for the *défilé* of the troops. **1880** C. E. NORTON *Church-build. Mid. Ages* III. 100 She watched the defile through her narrow and embattled streets of band after band of the envoys.

de'file, *sb.*² *Fortif. rare.* [f. DEFILE *v.*³] The act of defilading a fortress.

1864 in WEBSTER.

defile (dɪ'faɪl), *v.*¹ Also 5–6 **defyle**. [An altered form of *defoul*, *defoil*, by association with FILE *v.* DEFOUL, orig. a. OF. *defouler* 'to trample down, oppress, outrage, violate', had, by the 14th c., come to be associated with the Eng. adj. *foul*, and, in accordance with this, to be used in the sense 'pollute'; in this sense Eng. had already the native verbs *befoul* and *befile*, also *foul* and *file* (the latter:—OE. *fýlan* umlaut deriv. of OE. *fúl*, foul); and the example of these synonymous pairs appears to have led to the similar use of *defile* beside *defoul*. What share, if any, the variant *defoil* had in the process does not appear.]

†**1.** *trans.* To bruise, maul: cf. DEFOUL *v. Obs.*

c **1400** *Rom. Rose* (C) 7317 Men ne may..Tearen the wolfe out of his hide, Till he be slaine backe and side, Though men him beat and all defile [Fr. *Ja tant n' iert batus ne torchies. Rime* 'beguile'].

2. To render (materially) foul, filthy, or dirty; to pollute, dirty; to destroy the purity, cleanness, or clearness of.

[**1432–50** tr. *Higden* (Rolls) I. 185 Letters wryten were founde vndefilede at the end of the yere.] **1530** PALSGR. 509/2, I defyle, I araye or soyle a thing. *Je salis*..This garment is sore defyled. **1535** COVERDALE *Job* ix. 31 Yet shuldest thou dyppe me in yᵉ myre, & myne owne clothes shulde defyle me. **1594** LATIMER *6th Serm. bef. Edw. VI* (Arb.) 165 An evyll birde that defiles hys own nest. **1626** J. PYER in Ellis *Orig. Lett.* Ser. I. III. 247 The French had so defiled that House, as a weeks worke would not make it cleane. **1846** TRENCH *Mirac.* xix. (1682) 325 It is not the agitation of the waters, but the sediment at the bottom, which troubles and defiles them. **1887** STEVENSON *Underwoods* I. xxx. 63 While I defile the dinner plate.

fig. **1885** PRESCOTT *Philip II*, I. II. iii. 182 The stain of heresy no longer defiled the hem of her garment.

3. To render morally foul or polluted; to destroy the ideal purity of; to corrupt, taint, sully.

c **1325** [see DEFILED]. *c* **1450** *Pol. Rel. & L. Poems* (1866) 104 I am..defyled with syne. **1460** CAPGRAVE *Chron.* 63 Domician..was..in his last ȝeres al defiled wiṫ vices. **1526–34** TINDALE *Mark* vii. 15 Thoo thinges which procede out of him are those which defyle the man. **1555** *Tract* in Strype *Eccl. Mem.* III. App. xliv. 126 Oh! miserable England, defiled with bloud by the Pope's sword! **16..** STILLINGFLEET (J.), God requires rather that we should die than defile ourselves with impieties. **1747** BUTLER *Serm.* Wks. 1874 II. 302 Christianity, free from the superstitions with which it is defiled in other countries. **1875** JOWETT *Plato* (ed. 2) V. 167 The best things in human life are liable to be defiled and perverted.

†**4.** To violate the chastity of, to deflower; to debauch. *Obs.* Cf. DEFOUL 4.

a **1400** *Cov. Myst.* (Shaks. Soc.) 5 She wold not be defylyde With spot or wem of man. **1530** PALSGR. 509/2, I defyle, I ravysshe a mayden of her maydenheed, *Je viole*.. God defende that I sholde defyle her, and she a mayden. **1556** *Aurelio & Isab.* (1608) Hj, She that..hathe lever to dey than to be defilede. **1611** BIBLE *Gen.* xxxiv. 2 Shechem the son of Hamor..tooke her, and lay with her, and defiled her. **1718** PRIOR *Solomon* III. 453 The husband murder'd, and the wife defil'd. **1769** BLACKSTONE *Comm.* IV. 208 It must..appear, that she was afterwards married, or defiled.

5. To violate the sacredness or sanctity of; to desecrate, profane.

[Cf. *c* **1450** *St. Cuthbert* (Surtees) 335 And þat þis haly place be fyled.] ? *a* **1500** *Wyclif's Wycket* (1828) 2 The armes of hyme shall stonde, and shall defyle the sanctuarye. **1535** COVERDALE *2 Chron.* xxxvi. 14 [They] dyfyled the house of the Lorde. **1611** BIBLE *Neh.* xiii. 29 They have defiled the priesthood. **1683** BURNET tr. *More's Utopia* (1684) 144 Those that defile the Marriage-Bed.

b. To render ceremonially unclean.

1535 COVERDALE *Lev.* xi. 44 Ye shal not defyle youre selues on eny maner of crepynge beest. **1611** BIBLE *Lev.* xxii. 8 That which dieth of it selfe..hee shall not eate to defile himselfe therewith. —— *John* xviii. 28 They themselves went not into the Iudgement hall, lest they should be defiled. **1882** F. M. CRAWFORD *Mr. Isaacs* i, It is a criminal offence..for a non-Hindu person to defile the food of even the lowest caste man.

†**6.** To sully the honour of, to dishonour. *Obs.*

1581 J. BELL *Haddon's Answ. Osor.* 29 b, This foule mouthed Gentleman depraveth and defileth the death of that godly man. **1590** SHAKS. *Mids. N.* III. ii. 410 Come, recreant..Ile whip thee with a rod. He is defil'd That drawes a sword on thee. **1708** SWIFT *Let. Sacram. Test*, However his character may be defiled by such mean and dirty hands.

†**7.** *absol.* To cause defilement or filth; to drop excrement. *Obs.*

1547 BOORDE *Brev. Health* 4 Asses and moyles dyd defyle within the precynct of the churche. **1596** SHAKS. *1 Hen. IV*, II. iv. 456 This Pitch (as ancient Writers doe report) doth defile; so doth the companie thou keepest.

†**8.** *intr.* To become foul or unclean. *Obs.*

1673 J. CARYL *Nat. & Princ. Love* 79 If you do not daily sweep your houses they will defile.

defile (dɪ'faɪl), *v.*² *Mil.* [a. F. *défiler* (1648 in Hatzf.), f. DE- I. 6 + *file* sb., FILE.]

1. *intr.* To march in a line or by files; to file off. Also *transf.*

1705 A. R. *Accompl. Officer* vii. 90 Lest the Army being too long Defiling should be defeated by degrees, before it can form its Lines. **1732** LEDIARD *Sethos* II. x. 393 He began by making the troops defile. **1812** *Examiner* 24 Aug. 531/2 The division..defiled on the right. **1857** H. MILLER *Test. Rocks* ii. 111 That long procession of being which..is still defiling across the stage.

2. *trans.* To traverse by files. ? *Obs.*

1761–2 HUME *Hist. Eng.* (1806) IV. lvi. 293 He briskly attacked them, as they were defiling a lane.

de'file, *v.*³ *Fortif. rare.* [a. F. *défiler* (14th c. *desfilher* to unthread, in Hatzf.), f. *dé-*, DE- I. 6 + radical part of *enfiler* (= *désenfiler*): see ENFILE, ENFILADE.] = DEFILADE *v.*

1864 in WEBSTER, and in later Dicts.

defiled (dɪ'faɪld), *ppl. a.* [f. DEFILE *v.*¹ + -ED.] Polluted, sullied.

[*c* **1325** *E.E. Allit. P.* A. 724 Bot he com þyder ryȝt as a chylde..Harmlez, trwe and vndefylde.] **1530** PALSGR. 309/2 Defyled as a thynge that is soyled, *polu.* **1660** JER. TAYLOR *Worthy Commun.* Introd. 6 Nor eat of this sacrifice with a defiled head. **1746–7** HERVEY *Medit.* (1818) p. iii, Men of defiled habits and unclean lips. **1858** J. MARTINEAU *Stud. Chr.* 154 To tear out the defiled page of the past.

Hence †**de'filedness**.

1607 HIERON *Wks.* I. 328 The corruption and defilednesse of nature, which man brings with him into the world. **1642** ROGERS *Naaman* 541, I speake of a defilednesse of heart.

defilee, obs. form of DEFILE *sb.*¹

defilement¹ (dɪ'faɪlmənt). [f. DEFILE *v.*¹ + -MENT.] The act of defiling, the fact or state of being defiled.

1634 MILTON *Comus* 466 When lust..Lets in defilement to the inward parts. **1712** STEELE *Spect.* No. 286 ¶1 The Chaste cannot rake into such Filth without Danger of Defilement. **1814** SOUTHEY *Roderick* ii, Where..It might abide..From all defilement safe. **1861** GEN. P. THOMPSON *Audi Alt.* III. cxxxii. 97 Those sources of ceremonial defilement.

b. An instance of this; *concr.* anything that defiles.

1571 GOLDING *Calvin on Ps.* x. 16 Yᵉ holy land was at length purged from yᵉ defylements and filthines, wherewith it was berayed. **1643** MILTON *Divorce* Pref. (1851) 16 Mariage lay in disgrace..as a work of the flesh, almost a defilement. **1699** W. SALMON *Ars Chirurgica* Title-p., Removal of Defilements. **1834** HT. MARTINEAU *Farrers* ii. 33 Purifying himself from the defilements of the counter. **1871** *Echo* 31 Jan., The defilements in water which are most fatal to man.

de'filement². *Fortif.* [a. mod.F. *défilement* (1785 in Hatzf.), f. *défiler*: see DEFILE *v.*³] The act or operation of defilading.

1816 in JAMES *Milit. Dict.* **1828** J. M. SPEARMAN *Brit. Gunner* (ed. 2) 218 The banquettes and terre-pleins of ramparts that are commanded, should be formed in planes parallel to the plane of defilement of the crest of the parapet. **1830** E. S. N. CAMPBELL *Dict. Mil. Sc.* 51 The operation.. called Defilement, or Defilading, is of two kinds, in altitude and in direction..Defilement in Altitude is performed by raising the parapet, sinking the terrepleine, or constructing Traverses.

defiler (dɪ'faɪlə(r)). [f. DEFILE *v.*¹ + -ER.] One who defiles; also *fig.* of things.

1546 BALE *Eng. Votaries* II. (R.), As a defyler of relygion and polluter of their holye ceremonyes. **1580** HOLLYBAND *Treas. Fr. Tong, Corrompeur de femmes ou de filles*, a defiler of women, a deflourer of maydes. **1607** SHAKS. *Timon* IV. iii. 383 Thou bright defiler Of Himens purest bed. *a* **1719** ADDISON (J.), I shall hold forth in my arms my much wronged child, and call aloud for vengeance on her defiler. **1882** SPURGEON *Treas. Dav.* Ps. cxix. 9 The world, the flesh, and the devil, that trinity of defilers.

defili'ation. *nonce-wd.* [f. DE- II. 1 + L. *fīli-us* son, *fīli-a* daughter + -ATION, after *affiliation*.] Deprivation of a son.

1822 LAMB *Elia* Ser. I. *Praise Chimney-Sw.*, The recovery of the young Montagu [may] be but a solitary instance of good fortune out of many irreparable and hopeless defiliations.

defiling (dɪ'faɪlɪŋ), *vbl. sb.* [f. DEFILE *v.*¹ + -ING¹.] The action of DEFILE *v.*¹; defilement.

1585 ABP. SANDYS *Serm.* (1841) 67 We need not their after-cleansings, which in truth are defilings. **1586** J. HOOKER *Girald. Irel.* in *Holinshed* II. 140/2 Indignation for this defiling of his holie sanctuarie. **1846** KEBLE *Lyra Innoc.* (1873) 38 Washed from the world and sin's defiling.

de'filing, *ppl. a.* [-ING².] That defiles. Hence **de'filingly** *adv.*

1889 MONA CAIRD *Wing of Azrael* I. ix. 149 It clung to her defilingly, as some slimy sea-weed clings.

definability (dɪˌfaɪnə'bɪlɪtɪ). [f. next + -ITY.] The quality of being definable.

1865 PUSEY *Eiren.* 390 Many..profound theologians.. have impugned its definability. *a* **1866** J. GROTE *Exam. Utilit. Philos.* vii. (1870) 131 The legal definability of it.

definable (dɪ'faɪnəb(ə)l), *a.* [f. DEFINE *v.* + -ABLE.] Capable of being defined.

a **1660** HAMMOND *Wks.* I. 291 (R.) Great variety..of.. opportunities, not defineable particularly. **1682** DRYDEN *Relig. Laici* Pref. (Globe) 186 As if infinite were defenable, or infinity a subject for our narrow understanding. **1840** CARLYLE *Heroes* (1858) 227 Islam is definable as a confused form of Christianity. **1863** GEO. ELIOT *Romola* II. xxvii, Something apart from all the definable interests of her life. **1893** F. HALL in *Nation* LVII. 45/2 The ordinary *predicate*, that briefly definable by 'affirm'.

Hence **de'finably** *adv.*

1805 FOSTER *Ess.* I. iii. 31 A state most definably corresponding to the subject of your attention.

define (dɪ'faɪn), *v.* Forms: 4 **deffine**, 4–6 **diff-**, **defyne**, 5 **deffyne**, 5–6 **diffine**, **dyffyne**, 5– **define**. [ME., a. Anglo-F. and OF. *define-r* to end, terminate, determine = Pr. *definar*; a Romanic parallel form to L. *dēfīnīre* to end, terminate, bound (f. DE- I. 3 + *fīnīre* to end, FINISH), whence It. *definire*, Sp. *definir*, Pr. and OF. *defenir*, *definir*. *Definer*, the common form in OF., is the only form given by Cotgr. 1611, and survives in Picard, but has been superseded in F. by *définir*, with adoption of the transferred senses of L. *dēfīnīre*. In mod. English also *define* is in sense the representative of L. *dēfīnīre*. A parallel form *diffīnīre*, with *dis-* (see DE- I. 6) is also found in Latin texts, and the forms *diffiner*, *desfinir*, *diffinir* (14–17th c.) in F.; thence the Eng. variants in *deff-*, *diff-*, *dyff-*.]

†**1. a.** *trans.* To bring to an end. Also *intr.* To come to an end. *Obs. rare.*

c **1384** CHAUCER *H. Fame* 344 For though your loue laste a seson Wayte vpon the conclusyon, And eke how that ye determynen And for the more part diffynen. **1466** *Mann. & Househ. Exp.* 370 My mastyr gaff to Gorney the excheatour, to deffyne an offyse afftyr Water Gorges dethe, xx. s. **1494** FABYAN *Chron.* 5 The fourth [part] endyth than at Constantyne: The fyft at Cadwaladyr I haue also diffyned. **1562** *Pyramus & Th.*, (Alas my loue) and liue ye yet, did not your life define By Lyones rage?

†**b.** To bring to an end (a controversy, etc.); to determine, decide, settle. *Obs.*

1538 STARKEY *England* II. iii. 199 And as for al othir controversys, I wold they schuld be defynyd at home. **1596** SPENSER *F.Q.* IV. iii. 3 These warlike Champions.. Assembled were in field the chalenge to define. **1611** SPEED *Theat. Gt. Brit.* ii. (1614) 4/1 What could not there be defined, was referred to the whole Shire. *a* **1677** BARROW *Pope's Suprem.* (1687) 148 A more ready way to define Controversies.

2. a. To determine the boundary or spatial extent of; to settle the limits of. Also *fig.*

c **1400** MAUNDEV. (1839) xxxi. 315 Gowtes, Artetykes, that me distreynen, tho diffynen the end of my labour aȝenst my wille. **1843** PRESCOTT *Mexico* I. 16 The limits already noticed as defining its permanent territory. **1861** M. PATTISON *Ess.* (1889) I. 47 The duties of the guild towards the country and city..were strictly defined. **1874** GREEN *Short Hist.* iv. §2. 164 His first step was to define the provinces of the civil and ecclesiastical jurisdictions.

b. To make definite in outline or form. Also *refl.* (See also DEFINED.)

1815 WORDSW. *Essay* Wks. (1888) 873/1 In nature everything is distinct, yet nothing defined into absolute independent singleness. **1859** GEO. ELIOT *Lifted Veil* ii, I.. saw the light floating vanities of the girl defining themselves into the systematic coquetry, the scheming selfishness, of the woman. **1869** TYNDALL *Notes Lect. Light* §174 For perfectly distinct vision it is necessary that the image on the retina should be perfectly defined. **1888** MRS. H. WARD *R. Elsmere* xv, The slender figure suddenly defined itself against the road. *Ibid.* xxxii, The difficulties began to define themselves more sharply. *Ibid.* xliii, The half-coherent enigmatical sentences..began gradually to define themselves.

†**3.** To set bounds to, to limit, restrict, confine.

1513 DOUGLAS *Æneis* IV. ii. 30 Quhilkis na way diffynis The force nor strenth of luif with his hard bandis! **1624** DE LAWNE tr. *Du Moulin's Logick* 27 God is..so present in all places, as he is neither limited, nor defined by any place. **1643** SIR T. BROWNE *Relig. Med.* I. §27 Wee doe too narrowly define the power of God, restraining it to our capacities.

4. a. To determine, lay down definitely; to fix, decide; †to decide upon, fix upon.

1535 STEWART *Cron. Scot.* II. 120 All the lordis for that samin thing, And commoun pepill..did defyne The kingis bruther, callit Constantyne. **1647** CLARENDON *Hist. Reb.* II. (1843) 43/1 The first canon defined and determined such an unlimited power and prerogative to be in the king. **1790** GIBBON *Misc. Wks.* (1814) III. 510 The situation, the measure and the value of the estate cannot now be exactly defined. *a* **1794** *Ibid.* I. 158 Two or three years were loosely defined for the term of my absence. **1867** E. QUINCY *Life J. Quincy* 280 He 'defined his position', to use a later political formula, very clearly.

†**b.** *intr.* To determine, decide. *Obs.*

c **1374** CHAUCER *Troylus* IV. 362 Forthi I thus defyne:—Ne truste no wight to fynden in Fortune Aye proprete; her yiftes ben commune. **1402** HOCCLEVE *Letter of Cupid* 463 Than wol we thus concluden and dyffyne: we yow comaunde..that, of thise false men our reble foon, ye do punyshment. **1568** GRAFTON *Chron.* II. 351 Authoritie to enquire, intreate, defyne and determine of all maner of causes, querels, debtes. **1582** MUNDAY *Disc. E. Campion* C b, Neither was that barre appointed to define on causes of conscience. **1612** BACON *Ess. Judicature* (Arb.) 450 The vniust Iudge..when hee defineth amisse of lands and property.

†**5. a.** To state precisely or determinately; to specify. (Const. with *obj. clause* or *simple obj.*) *Obs.*

c **1374** CHAUCER *Troylus* III. 834 Wherfore I wol deffyne.. That trewely for ought I kan espie Ther is no verray wele is þis world here. **1561** DAUS tr. *Bullinger on Apoc.* (1573) 166 b, The day of iudgement can no man diffine. **1563** W. FULKE *Meteors* (1640) 46 Cardan plainly defineth, that Amber is a mineral. **1669** BOYLE *Cont. New Exper.* I. (1682) 80 Even clouds..may reach much higher than Carden, Kepler, and others have defin'd.

†**b.** *intr.* or *absol.* To make precise statement.

c **1380** WYCLIF *Serm.* xciii. Sel. Wks. I. 330 Men shulden not here diffyne, but ʒif God tolde it hem. *c* **1430** LYDG. *Bochas* I. ix. (1544) 17 a, Of her byrth fyrst he doth defyne. **1570** *Act 13 Eliz.* c. 7 §2 Persons being Bankrupt as is before defined. **1600** HAKLUYT *Voy.* III. 54 (R.) How then can such men define upon other regions..whether they were inhabited or not.

6. a. To state exactly what (a thing) is; to set forth or explain the essential nature of. (In early use: To state the nature or properties of, to describe.)

c **1374** CHAUCER *Troylus* V. 271 Swych a wo my wit kan not defyne. **1413** LYDG. *Pilgr. Sowle* V. i. (1859) 72 The beaute of this mansion ne maye no man telle, ne diffyne the ioye, and the grete arraye. **1484** CAXTON *Curiall* 5 That thou mayst the better knowe now the courte I wyl descryue and dyffyne it to the. **1526** *Pilgr. Perf.* (W. de W. 1531) 67 b, What it is, Saynt Bernarde declareth..diffynynge or discribynge it in this wyse. **1555** EDEN *Decades* Pref. (Arb.) 49 Cicero defineth trewe glory to bee a fame of many and greate desertes. **1677** GALE *Crt. of Gentiles* IV. 292 He that perfectly comprehends and defines a thing gives limits and bounds to that thing in his intellect. **1710** ADDISON *Whig Exam.* No. 4 ¶1 Hudibras has defined nonsense (as Cowley does wit) by negatives. **1777** PRIESTLEY *Matt. & Spir.* (1782) I. xx. 257 Descartes defined the essence of the soul to consist in thinking. **1846** MILL *Logic* Introd. §1 To define, is to select from among all the properties of a thing, those which shall be understood to be designated and declared by its name. **1875** JOWETT *Plato* (ed. 2) III. 184 Genius has been defined as 'the power of taking pains'.

b. To set forth or explain what (a word or expression) means; to declare the signification of (a word). [Not recognized by J.]

1532 MORE *Confut. Tindale* Wks. 608/2 All hys other sygnificacions I lette passe..except onely that which he hath also diffyned false. **1551** T. WILSON *Logike* (1580) 14 Therefore ye muste needes have these Predicamentes ready, when soever ye will define any worde, or give a naturall name unto it. **1724** WATTS *Logic* I. vi. §2 In defining the name there is no need that we should be acquainted with the intimate nature or essence of the thing. **1791** BOSWELL *Johnson* an. 1755 (1887) I. 293 A lady once asked him how he came to define *Pastern* 'the *knee* of a horse'. **1885** DAVIDSON *Logic of Definition* 86 *Horse* cannot be otherwise defined in a dictionary than as a well-known quadruped, used as a beast of burden and in war.

c. *intr.* or *absol.* To frame or give a precise description or definition.

1587 TURBERV. *Trag. T.* (1837) 200 For that of love so derely he definde. **1645** MILTON *Tetrach.* (1851) 168 Then only we know certainly, when we can define. **1756** BURKE *Subl. & B.* Introd. Wks. I. 97 When we define we seem in danger of circumscribing nature within the bounds of our own notions. **1863** OUIDA *Held in Bondage* (1870) 81 Hang it, Arthur, why do you set me defining?

7. *transf.* Of properties: To make (a thing) what it is; to give a character to, characterize; to constitute the definition of.

1633 G. HERBERT *Temple, Invitation* ii, Come ye hither all, whom wine Doth define, Naming you not to your good. **1648** MILTON *Tenure Kings* (1650) 55 Being lawfully depriv'd of all things that define a magistrate. **1875** BENNETT & DYER *Sachs's Bot.* I. iii. 180 The *tout ensemble* of properties which define the character of the natural group, class, or order.

8. To separate by definition, to distinguish by special marks or characteristics (*from*). *rare.*

1807–8 W. IRVING *Salmag.* xii. (1860) 280 By this is defin'd The fop from the man of refinement and mind. **1839** MURCHISON *Silur. Syst.* I. xxxiv. 456 It is difficult to define the subsoil of Silurian rock from that of the Old Red Sandstone.

defined (dɪˈfaɪnd), *ppl. a.* [f. prec. + -ED.] Having a definite outline or form; clearly marked. Also *fig.*

a **1727** NEWTON (J.), When the rings appeared only black and white, they were very distinct and well defined. **1849** MRS. SOMERVILLE *Connect. Phys. Sc.* xxxvii. 436 The central matter is so vivid and so sharply defined that the nebula might be taken for a bright star. **1852** H. ROGERS *Ecl. Faith* (1853) 125 His [man's] animal nature is more defined than his intellectual.

Hence **de'finedly** *adv.*

1821 SCOTT *Kenilw.* xxiii, Definedly visible against the pure azure blue of the summer sky.

definement (dɪˈfaɪnmənt). *rare.* [a. obs. F. *définement* (1611 in Cotgr.), in OF. *de-*, *def-*, *diffinement* (see Godef.) termination, end, f. OF. *definer*: see DEFINE *v.*]

1. Definition, description.

1602 SHAKS. *Ham.* V. ii. 117 Sir, his definement suffers no perdition in you. **1867** *Eng. Leader* 15 June 326 Definement is always by the contrary. Everything is defined by its contrary: night by day, dark by light.

†**2.** Limitation, restriction. *Obs.*

1643 HUNTON *Treat. Monarchy* I. ii. 16 This Legall Allay and definement of Power. **1644** —— *Vind. Treat. Monarchy* iv. 27 A Civill and Legall definement of Authority.

definer (dɪˈfaɪnə(r)). [f. DEFINE *v.* + -ER[1].] One who or that which defines.

1589 PUTTENHAM *Eng. Poesie* III. xix. (Arb.) 239 *margin*, Orismus, or the Definer of difference. **1645** MILTON *Colast.* (1851) 347 Yee see already what a faithfull definer wee have him. **1779–81** JOHNSON *L.P., Pope* Wks. IV. 137 To circumscribe poetry by a definition will only shew the narrowness of the definer. **1847** EMERSON *Repr. Men, Uses Gt. Men* Wks. (Bohn) I. 278 A definer and map-maker of the latitudes and longitudes of our condition.

definiendum (dɪˌfɪnɪˈɛndəm). *Logic.* [a. L. *dēfiniendum* 'thing to be defined', neut. of gerundive of *dēfinīre* DEFINE *v.*] That which is, or is to be, defined; the phrase of which a definition states or purports to state the meaning; in *Mathematical Logic*, the word or symbol (or the formula devised to contain the symbol) that is being introduced by definition into a system. (Cf. next.)

1871 [see DEFINIENS]. *a* **1897** W. WALLACE *Lect.* (1898) 81 If definition that may be called which practically negatives the existence of the *definiendum*. **1910** WHITEHEAD & RUSSELL *Principia Math.* I. i. 11 We will give the names of *definiendum* and *definiens* respectively to what is defined and to that which it is defined as meaning. **1941** O. HELMER tr. *Tarski's Introd. Logic* vi. 150 The definiens is an arbitrary sentential function containing exactly the same variables as the definiendum, and containing no constants except primitive terms and terms previously defined. **1964** N. RESCHER *Introd. Logic* iii. 30 The expression whose meaning the definition attempts to explain..is called the *definiendum*.

definiens (dɪˈfɪnɪɛnz). *Logic.* [a. med.L. *dēfiniens* (not in Du Cange), pres. pple. of L. *dēfinīre* DEFINE *v.*] The defining part of a definition; the phrase that states the meaning; in *Mathematical Logic*, the verbal or symbolic expression to which a word or symbol being introduced by definition into a system is declared to be equivalent. (Cf. prec.)

[*a* **1277** PETRUS HISPANUS *Summulae Logicales* (1947) 3.03 Unumquodque definiens in sua definitione sive definito.] **1871** T. M. LINDSAY tr. *Ueberweg's Syst. Logic* 173 The definiens has here a wider extent than the definiendum. **1910, 1941** [see DEFINIENDUM].

defining (dɪˈfaɪnɪŋ), *vbl. sb.* [-ING[1].] The action of the verb DEFINE; definition.

1382 WYCLIF *Ezek.* xliii. 13 The diffynyng, *or certeyntee*, therof [*definitio ejus*] vn to the lippe..therof in cumpas, o palme. **1530** PALSGR. 213/2 Diffyning, *diffinissement*, *diffinition*. **1581** MULCASTER *Positions* xxxvi. (1887) 138 Plato in his..defining of naturall dignities. **1668** WILKINS *Real Char.* Ded. A ij, The business of Defining, being amongst all others the most nice and difficult. **1847** EMERSON *Repr. Men, Plato* Wks. (Bohn) I. 292 This defining is philosophy.

de'fining, *ppl. a.* [-ING[2].] That defines.

1773 J. ROSS *Fratricide* I. 17 (MS.) Defining ears, which idolize The dignifying climax of thy verse. **1885** *Athenæum* 4 Apr. 441/2 The various defining spheres.

†**de'finish,** *v. Obs. rare.* In 4 **diffinisse, -issh.** [ad. OF. *definiss-*, *diffiniss-*, lengthened stem of *definir*: see DEFINE.] *trans.* To define.

c **1374** CHAUCER *Boeth.* III. x. 88 þilke goode þat þou hast diffinissed a lytel her byforne.

definite (ˈdɛfɪnɪt), *a.* (*sb.*) Also 6 **diffynite,** 7 **definit.** [ad. L. *dēfīnīt-us* defined, bounded, limited, distinct, precise, pa. pple. of *dēfīnīre*: see DEFINE. Cf. obs. F. *définit, -ite* (1504 in Godef.).]

1. Having fixed or exact limits; clearly defined, determinate, fixed, certain; exact, precise. (Of material, or, more commonly, immaterial things.)

1553 T. WILSON *Rhet.* 1 Either it is an infinite question and without ende, or els it is definite and comprehended within some ende..Those questions are called definite, which set forthe a matter, with the..namyng of place, tyme, and persone. *a* **1586** SIDNEY (J.), The goddess, who in a definite compass can set forth infinite beauty. **1644** MILTON *Educ.* Wks. (1847) 98/1 Either by the definite will of God so ruling, or the peculiar sway of nature, which also is God's working. **1691** T. H[ALE] *Acc. New Invent.* 122 The clear and definite understanding of the several parts of the Ship. **1726** AYLIFFE *Parergon* 50 In a charge of Adultery, the Accuser ought to set forth..some certain and definite time. **1823** LAMB *Elia* Ser. II. *Confess. Drunkard*, Those uneasy sensations..worse to bear than any definite pains or aches. **1859** DICKENS *Lett.* (1880) II. 85, I must give some decided and definite answer. **1860** TYNDALL *Glac.* I. xxiv. 174 A definite structure was in many places to be traced. **1874** GREEN *Short Hist.* v. §4. 238 Even this class [serfs] had now acquired definite rights.

b. *transf.* Said of persons, in reference to their actions (opinions, statements, etc.).

1611 SHAKS. *Cymb.* I. vi. 43 Idiots in this case of fauour, would Be wisely definit. *a* **1619** FOTHERBY *Atheom.* II. vii. §7 (1622) 277 As definite as hee was in appointing the set time of the dissolution of Babilon. *Mod.* Be more definite in your statements.

c. ***definite description*** (Philos.): in the theory of descriptions proposed by Bertrand Russell, a denoting phrase that is introduced by the definite article or its equivalent.

1911 B. RUSSELL in *Proc. Aristotelian Soc. 1910–11* XI. v. 112 A phrase of the form 'a so-and-so' I shall call an 'ambiguous' description; a phrase of the form 'the so-and-so' (in the singular) I shall call a 'definite' description. **1944** [see CONTEXTUAL *a.* 1 b]. **1974** *Encycl. Brit. Macropædia* XI. 49/2 The correct analysis of propositions containing definite descriptions has been the subject of considerable philosophical controversy. **1977** *Canad. Jrnl. Linguistics 1976* XXI. 143 We are..obliged to accept that in some sense 'Smith's murderer' is not even a definite description, if used referentially.

2. *Gram.* **a.** Applied, in German and Early English grammar, to those inflexions of the adjective which are used when preceded by the definite article or some equivalent. **b.** Of verbs: = Finite. *rare.* **c.** ***definite article***: a name for the demonstrative adjective *the*, and its equivalents in other languages, as indicating a defined or particularized individual of the species denoted by the noun. **d.** ***past*** or ***preterite definite***: the name in French Grammar of the tense which coincides historically with the Latin preterite or perfect, and corresponds in sense to the Greek aorist and English simple past: e.g. *il vint*, he came.

1727–51 in CHAMBERS *Cycl.* **1765** W. WARD *Grammar* I. xxii. 103 'The' is called the definite article. *Ibid.* IV. ii. 158 The verb in this character [i.e. infinitive] may be..used as a nominative case, on which a definite verb depends. **1824** L. MURRAY *Eng. Gram.* (ed. 5) I. 68 *The* is called the definite article; because it ascertains what particular thing or things are meant: as, 'Give me *the* book'. **1855** FORBES *Hindūstānī Gram.* (1868) 18 Arabic nouns have frequently the definite article..of the language prefixed to them. **1874** R. MORRIS *Chaucer's Prol.*, etc. (Clar. Press Ser.) Introd. 33 Adjectives, like the modern German, have two forms—Definite and Indefinite. The definite form preceded by the definite article, a demonstrative adjective, or a possessive pronoun, terminates in *-ë* in all cases of the singular.

3. *Bot.* **a.** Said of inflorescence having the central axis terminated in a flower-bud which opens first, those on the lateral branches following in succession: also called *centrifugal* or *determinate*. **b.** Of stamens or other parts of the flower: Of a constant number not exceeding twenty.

1845 LINDLEY *Sch. Bot.* iv. (1858) 25 Stamens definite; that is to say, obviously corresponding in number with the sepals and petals. **1876** J. D. HOOKER *Bot. Primer* 45 Definite, because the axis is terminated by a flower and does not elongate. **1880** GRAY *Struct. Bot.* v. 144 The kinds of Inflorescence..are all reducible to two types..Indefinite and Definite, or..Indeterminate and Determinate.

B. *sb.* **1.** Something that is definite; *spec.* in *Gram.*: †**a.** A definite tense; **b.** A noun denoting a definite thing or object.

1530 PALSGR. Introd. 31 The fyrst [conjugation] is chefly ruled by E, saufe that in his diffynites he torneth into A. **1817** COLERIDGE *Biog. Lit.* 144 Fancy..has no other counters to play with, but fixities and definites. **1845** STODDART *Gram.* in *Encycl. Metrop.* I. 55 The Latin nouns in *io* [as *actio*] seem properly to have been definites; that is to say, that they originally signified only a certain number of acts, and not action in general.

†**2.** 'Thing explained or defined' (J.). *Obs.*

1726 AYLIFFE *Parergon* 110 *Special* Bastardy is nothing else but the Definition of the *general*, and the *general* again, is nothing else but a *Definite* of the *Special*.

definitely (ˈdɛfɪnɪtlɪ), *adv.* [f. prec. + -LY[2].]

a. In a definite manner; determinately, precisely.

1581 MULCASTER *Positions* xxxvi. (1887) 140 For the choice of wittes definitely. **1651** HOBBES *Govt. & Soc.* xvi. §4. 265 He must definitely acknowledge him. *a* **1800** H. BLAIR *Serm.* III. iv. (R.), [Middle age] cannot have its peculiar character so definitely marked and ascertained. **1867** FREEMAN *Norm. Conq.* (1876) I. iv. 187 The relations between Normandy and Brittany were now definitely settled.

b. *colloq.* Used as an emphatic affirmative: certainly; yes.

1931 A. A. MILNE *Two People* xvii. 329 'It would be disconcerting, wouldn't it?' 'Definitely,' said Reginald. **1933** WODEHOUSE *Heavy Weather* vii. 132 'So you wish to return to Tilbury House?' 'Definitely.' 'You shall.' **1959** *Sunday Times* 12 Apr. 32/4 Did they get more work done than at home? 'Definitely.' Would they recommend that the experiment is repeated another year? 'Oh, definitely.' **1967** L. J. BRAUN *Cat who ate Danish Modern* x. 88 'Do you design interiors around this theme?' 'Definitely!'

definiteness (ˈdɛfɪnɪtnɪs). [-NESS.] The quality of being definite.

1727 BAILEY vol. II, *Definiteness*, certainty, limitedness. **1837–9** HALLAM *Hist. Lit.* I. ix. §5 The definiteness of solution, which numerical problems admit and require. **1875** JOWETT *Plato* (ed. 2) V. 487 From this want of definiteness in their language they do a great deal of harm.

definition (dɛfɪˈnɪʃən). Forms: α. 4–6 **diffinicioun,** etc. (with usual interchange of *i* and *y*), 5–6 **-tion,** etc., 6 *Sc.* **-tioun;** β. 5–6 **defi-,** 6 **defynicion(e,** 6– **definition.** [a. OF. *de-*, *def-*, *diffinicion* (also *definison*), ad. L. *dēfīnītiōn-em* (also in MSS. *diff-*), n. of action from *dēfīnīre*: see DEFINE. Cf. Pr. *diff-*, *deffinicio*, Sp. *definicion*, It. *difinizione*.]

†**1.** The setting of bounds or limits; limitation, restriction. *Obs. rare.*

c **1386** CHAUCER *Wife's Prol.* 25 Yit herd I never tellen.. Uppon this noumbre diffinicioun. **1483** CAXTON *Gold. Leg.* 403 b/2 Thenne said he ben they knowen which men shal suffre thyse passyons without dyffynycion.

2. The action of determining a controversy or question at issue; determination, decision; *spec.* a formal decision or pronouncement of an ecclesiastical authority. *Obs.* exc. in specific use.

1382 WYCLIF *Dan.* xi. 36 Diffinicioun, *or dome* [**1388** determynynge] is fully don. **1532-3** *Act 24 Hen. VIII*, c. 12 §9 A finall decree, sentence, judgement, diffinicion, and determinacion. **1552** ABP. HAMILTON *Catech.* (1884) 41 The determinatiouns and diffinitiouns of general counsellis. **1634** R. H. *Salernes Regiment* 13 This question.. whether a man should eate more at Dinner, or at Supper. For definition hereof, it is to be noted [etc.]. **1661** BRAMHALL *Just Vind.* viii. 241 This challenge of infallibility diminisheth their [councils'] authority, discrediteth their definitions. **1864** J. H. NEWMAN *Apol.* 392 Infallibility cannot act outside of a definite circle of thought, and it must in all its decisions, or definitions, as they are called, profess to be keeping within it.

3. *Logic*, etc. The action of defining, or stating exactly what a thing is, or what a word means.

1645 MILTON *Tetrach.* (1851) 168 Definition is that which refines the pure essence of things from the circumstance. **1690** LOCKE *Hum. Und.* III. iii. §10 Definition being nothing but making another understand by Words, what Idea the Term defin'd stands for. **1730** BAILEY (folio), *Definition* (with *Logicians*), an unfolding the essence or being of a thing by its kind and difference. **1858** J. MARTINEAU *Stud. Chr.* 226 Definition is always an enclosure of the true by exclusion of the false. **1860** ABP. THOMSON *Laws Th.* §54. 82 Definition expounds all the marks implied in the notion, and so represents to us the nature or specific character of it. —— §69. 111. **1885** W. L. DAVIDSON *Logic of Definition* 32 It is the object of Definition to determine the nature or meaning or signification of a thing; in other words, definition is the formal attempt to answer the question, 'What is it?'

4. a. A precise statement of the essential nature of a thing; a statement or form of words by which anything is defined.

1398 TREVISA *Barth. De P.R.* XIX. cxvi. (1495) 920 Some thynges haue but one dyffynycyon. *c* **1450** tr. *De Imitatione* I. i. 2, I desire more to knowe compunccion þen his diffinycion. **1551** T. WILSON *Logike* 14 A definition of the substaunce is a speach which sheweth the very nature of the thing. **1571** DIGGES *Pantom.* II. v. M ij b, Of quadrangles.. there are fiue sortes, as appeereth in the Diffinitions. **1633** MASSINGER *Guardian* v. iv, His victories but royal robberies, And his true definition—A Thief. **1710** STEELE *Tatler* No. 62 ¶14 Propriety of Words and Thoughts, which is Mr. Dryden's Definition of Wit. **1758** JOHNSON *Idler* No. 1 ¶4 It has been found hard to describe man by an adequate definition. **1842** GROVE *Corr. Phys. Forces* 75 The old definition of force was, that which caused change in motion. **1864** BOWEN *Logic* 94 A Definition consists primarily of two parts, the Proximate Genus and the Specific Difference of the Concept defined.

b. A declaration or formal explanation of the signification of a word or phrase. [Not recognized by Johnson.]

?*a* **1500** *Wyclif's Wycket* Sub-Title, A verye brefe diffinition of these wordes, *Hoc est corpus meum.* **1551** T. WILSON *Logike* 14 A definition of a word is any maner of declaration of a word. **1724** WATTS *Logic* I. vi. §2 A definition of the name being only a declaration in what sense the word is used, or what idea or object we mean by it. **1755** JOHNSON *Pref. to Dict.*, As nothing can be proved but by supposing something intuitively known, and evident without proof, so nothing can be defined but by the use of words too plain to admit a definition. **1791** BOSWELL *Johnson* an. 1755 (1887) I. 293 The definitions have always appeared to me such.. as indicate a genius of the highest rank... A few of his definitions must be admitted to be erroneous. **1885** W. L. DAVIDSON *Logic of Definition* 87 No [dictionary] definition of 'Gold' will be sufficient that does not contain a reference to its colour, which supplies us with the distinct meaning 'golden'.

c. ***definition in use***: a definition which does not provide an equivalent for the expression to be defined, but instead replaces the whole context in which that expression occurs by an equivalent not containing that expression; a contextual definition (cf. CONTEXTUAL *a.* b).

1910 WHITEHEAD & RUSSELL *Principia Math.* I. iii. 69 Incomplete.. symbols have what may be called a 'definition in use'... We define the *use* of ∇^2, but ∇^2 by itself remains without meaning. **1936** A. J. AYER *Lang., Truth & Logic* iii. 66 In a dictionary we look mainly for what may be called *explicit* definitions; in philosophy, for definitions *in use*. **1963** A. PAP *Introd. Philos. Sci.* ii. 30 Contextual definition (also called 'definition in use').

5. a. The action of making definite; the condition of being made, or of being definite, in visual form or outline; distinctness; *spec.* the defining power of a lens or optical instrument, i.e. its capacity to render an object or image distinct to the eye.

1859 REEVE *Brittany* 137 We were content.. to sacrifice the artistic definition of the trees. **1860** TYNDALL *Glac.* I. xviii. 125 The stratification.. was shown with great beauty and definition. **1878** NEWCOMB *Pop. Astron.* II. i. 138 The definition of this telescope is very fine.

b. *gen.* Definiteness, precision, exactitude. *rare.*

1866 ARGYLL *Reign Law* i. (ed. 4) 8 A fallacy is getting hold upon us from a want of definition in the use of terms.

c. The degree of distinctness of the details in a photograph, film, television picture, etc.; so ***high-***, ***low-definition***, used to designate television systems using different numbers of scanning lines.

1889 E. J. WALL *Dict. Photogr.* 38 *Detail*, the definition of each minute part or parts of the material of a picture, whether in the negative or print therefrom. **1928** *Television* I. II. 7/3 It is claimed that much better definition and detail are obtained. *Ibid.* 10/1 A difference of phase of only one per cent. between the transmitter and the receiver is sufficient to spoil the definition of the received image. **1933** *Ibid.* VI. LXIX. 373/1 Other companies, too, may.. be given similar opportunities of providing high-definition television apparatus for transmission experiments. **1935** *Discovery* Sept. 277/2 The pioneer work of Baird.. with low and high definition scanning. *Ibid.* 278/1 The iconoscope camera, which is said to be capable of definition up to 500 lines. **1937** *Amateur Photography* (Newnes) 50 This explains the superb definition of the tiny cine-film pictures, in spite of their enormous enlargement when projected. **1943** *Gloss. Terms Telecomm.* (*B.S.I.*) 77 ***High-definition television***, a system of television in which the number of scanning-lines exceeds 200 for each picture. **1946** *Nature* 20 July 88/2 In 1929.. the B.B.C. decided to give Messrs. Baird Television, Ltd., facilities for experimental transmissions through the medium-wave London station. These transmissions, which were afterwards referred to as 'low-definition', employed 30 scanning lines and 12½ pictures per second. **1955** J. LIPINSKI *Miniature & Precision Cameras* ii. 34 It is not generally realized how serious a contribution camera shake makes in degrading the definition of a photograph taken with a miniature. **1969** M. J. LANGFORD *Adv. Photogr.* iii. 58 A high resolution lens may well form separate images of closely spaced lines, but unless the blacks and whites are also clearly definable by their contrast the impression of 'definition' will be poor.

6. *Comb.*

1856 R. A. VAUGHAN *Mystics* (1860) I. 209 Alas, for our poor definition-cutter, with his logical scissors!

defi'nitional, *a.* [f. prec. + -AL¹.] Of, pertaining to, or of the nature of a definition.

1869 *Athenæum* 11 Sept. 329 The definitional rule judiciously laid down by Mr. Hazlitt, that a proverb should have a figurative sense, an inner sense or an approximate sense. **1883** *Encycl. Brit.* XX. 49/2 Two distinct presentations are necessary to the comparison.. but we cannot begin with such definitional differentiation. **1948** L. SPITZER *Linguistics* iii. 113 There is in the phrase *objet pour les yeux* something definitional and intellectual. **1963** J. LYONS *Structural Semantics* ii. 23 These are definitional statements, which will be amplified in what follows. **1970** *Economics* VIII. 126 We now have Y = C + I + X − M; or alternatively, Y + M = C + I + X which signifies a definitional equality between total supply and total demand.

Hence **defi'nitionally** *adv.*, by means of a definition; as a definition.

1940 W. V. QUINE *Math. Logic* 100 Only a single occurrence of ϕ appears in our definitionally abbreviated notations. **1947** *Mind* LVI. 74, *f* might be a definitionally constructed, property determining a subclass of a class determined by a more abstract or less complex property.

definitive (dɪ'fɪnɪtɪv), *a.* and *sb.* Forms: 4-6 **diffinityf, -inytif, -ynytif(e,** 5 **defynytyfe, defenytyffe,** 6 **dyffinatyue, definytiue,** 6-7 **diffinitive,** 7 **definative,** 6- **definitive.** [a. OF. *definitif, diffinitif, -ive* (12th c.), ad. L. *dē-, diffīnītīv-us*, f. ppl. stem of *dēfīnīre*: see DEFINITE.]

A. *adj.* Having the function of defining, or of being definite.

1. a. Having the function of finally deciding or settling; decisive, determinative, conclusive, final: esp. in ***definitive sentence***, and the like.

c **1386** CHAUCER *Doctor's T.* 172 The Iuge answerd of þis in his absence I may not ȝiue diffinityf sentence. **1474** CAXTON *Chesse* III. vi. H v b, The theef was.. taken.. and by sentence diffynytif was hanged. **1523** LD. BERNERS *Froiss.* I. xxiv. 35 It was the moneth of May folowyng, or [= ere] they had aunswere dyffinatyue. **1583** STUBBES *Anat. Abus.* II. (1882) 106 Maye they as Capytall Iudges, geue definytiue sentence of lyfe and death vpon malefactors. **1601** R. JOHNSON *Kingd. & Commw.* (1603) 57 Upon hearing of both parties, judgment definative is given, and may not be repealed. **1688** *Answ. Talon's Plea* 3 Barely to say with a definitive Gravity, Here's a great abuse. **1748** RICHARDSON *Clarissa* (1811) I. 11 Expecting a definitive answer. **1763** WILKES *Corr.* (1805) I. 84 The definitive treaty is now signed. **1855** MACAULAY *Hist. Eng.* IV. 527 A jury had pronounced: the verdict was definitive.

†**b.** *transf.* of persons. *Obs.*

1603 SHAKS. *Meas. for M.* v. i. 432 Neuer craue him, we are definitiue.. Away with him to death. **1639** FULLER *Holy War* IV. v. (1647) 176 Desiring rather to be scepticall then definitive in the causes of Gods judgements. **1741** RICHARDSON *Pamela* (1824) I. 104, I will make you.. my adviser in this matter, though not, perhaps, my definitive judge.

c. That settles or determines bounds or limits.

1860 J. P. KENNEDY *W. Wirt* I. xiii. 164 [This] point of view should lead to a just and definitive limitation of the boundaries.

2. Having the character of finality as a product; determinate, definite, fixed and final. Of an edition of a literary work, a textbook, etc.: authoritative; the most complete and authoritative to date. In *Biol.* opposed to *formative* or *primitive*, as ***definitive organs***, ***definitive aorta***.

a **1639** WOTTON (J.), [It] being the very definitive sum of this art, to distribute usefully and gracefully a well chosen plot. **1646** SIR T. BROWNE *Pseud. Ep.* I. vi, Other Authors write often dubiously, even in matters wherein is expected a strict and definitive truth. **1821** J. Q. ADAMS in C. Davies *Metr. Syst.* III. (1871) 174 The temporary system established by the law of 1st August, 1793. The definitive system established by the law of 10th December, 1799. **1865** *Daily Tel.* 30 Oct. 4/4 Some days will probably elapse before we shall be able to announce a definitive result. **1878** NEWCOMB *Pop. Astron.* III. v. 399 A definitive orbit of the comet. **1882** SWINBURNE *Let.* 27 Sept. in *N. & Q.* (1965) CCX. 304/2 Dr. Grosart.. is about to publish what the French would call a 'definitive edition' of Daniel. **1887** *Amer. Jrnl. Philol.* VIII. 484 With the four volumes first mentioned the Goethe Society in Weimar begins the publication of the definitive edition of Goethe's works. **1888** ROLLESTON & JACKSON *Forms of Animal Life* 803 The primitive ovum divides; one of the cells thus produced grows into the definitive ovum. **1928** T. S. ELIOT in E. Pound *Sel. Poems* p. vii, This book is, in my eyes, rather a convenient Introduction to Pound's work than a definitive edition. **1949** 'G. ORWELL' *Nineteen Eighty-Four* I. iv. 44 Ampleforth.. was engaged in producing garbled versions—definitive texts, they were called—of poems which had become ideologically offensive. **1959** *Spectator* 21 Aug. 235/1 That vague uneasiness one has come to feel in the presence of American 'definitive' biographies.

†**3.** *Metaph.* Having a definite position, but not occupying space: opposed to *circumscriptive*. *Obs.*

[**1529, 1624** see DEFINITIVELY 2.] **1657** HOBBES *Absurd Geom.* Wks. VII. 385 Definitive or circumscriptive, and some other of your distinctions.. are but snares. **1665** GLANVILL *Sceps. Sci.* xiii. 73 Who is it that retains not a great part of the imposture, by allowing them a definitive *Ubi*, which is still but Imagination?

4. That makes or deals with definite statements.

a **1619** FOTHERBY *Atheom.* II. ix. §2 (1622) 296 Plutarch is more definitiue, and punctuall, in this point. **1862** *Lit. Churchman* VIII. 6/1 We should be glad to see more definitive teaching on the nature of Church Communion.

5. That serves to define or state exactly what a thing is; that specifies the individual referred to; *esp.* in *Gram.* (Formerly used of the DEFINITE article, and of the FINITE verb.)

1731 BAILEY vol. II, s.v. *Article, Definitive Article*, the article (*the*) so called, as fixing the sense of the word it is put before to one individual thing. **1765** W. WARD *Gram.* IV. iv. 164 Of the verb definitive. **1800** W. TAYLOR in *Monthly Mag.* VIII. 797 To preserve a name of sect, which ought to be simply definitive, from sliding into a term of reproach. **1824** L. MURRAY *Eng. Gram.* (ed. 5) I. 231 When a noun of multitude is preceded by a definitive word, which clearly limits the sense to an aggregate with an idea of unity, it requires a verb.. in the singular number: as, '*A* company of troops *was* detached'. **1854** ELLICOTT *Galat.* 87 The.. definitive force of the article.

6. Concerned with the definition of form or outline. *rare.*

1815 W. TAYLOR in *Monthly Rev.* LXXVI. 115 The lineless delicate contours of youth and bloom embarrass the definitive skill even of a Correggio.

B. *sb.* (the *adj.* used *ellipt.*)

†**1.** A definitive sentence, judgement, or pronouncement. *Obs.*

1595 HUBBOCKE *Apol. Infants Unbapt.* 11 Is there no pardon from this general damnatorie sentence and cruell definitiue? **1660** R. COKE *Power & Subj.* 134 Judgment is the definitive of him who by right commands, permits, or forbids a thing. **1804** *Europ. Mag.* in *Spirit Pub. Jrnls.* (1805) VIII. 135 In spite of the Definitive, we shall have another battle of the books.

2. *Gram.* A definitive word.

1751 HARRIS *Hermes* (1841) 179 Definitives.. are commonly called by grammarians, 'articles,' *articuli*, ἄρθρα. They are of two kinds, either those properly.. so called, or else the pronominal articles, such as *this, that, any*, &c. **1786-98** H. TOOKE *Purley* I. 20 About the time of Aristotle, when a fourth part of the speech was added,—the definitive, or article. **1824** L. MURRAY *Eng. Gram.* (ed. 5) I. 71 As articles are by their nature definitives.. they cannot be united with such words as are.. as definite as they may be; (the personal pronouns for instance).

definitively (dɪ'fɪnɪtɪvlɪ), *adv.* [f. prec. + -LY².] In a definitive manner.

1. So as to decide or settle the matter; decisively, conclusively, finally, definitely.

1532-3 *Act 24 Hen. VIII*, c. 12 §2 All causes testamentarie.. shall be.. finallye and diffinitiuely adiudged and determined within the Kynges iurisdiction. **1639** GENTILIS *Servita's Inquis.* xxxvi. (1676) 833 Contumacious Persons shall be banished, either definitively, or for a time. **1659** MILTON *Civil Power in Eccl. Causes* Wks. (1847) 415/1 No man, no synod, no session.. can judge definitively the sense of Scripture to another man's conscience. **1753** HANWAY *Trav.* (1762) I. III. xlii. 198, I desired he would tell me definitively what number of men he would give me for a guard. **1856** FROUDE *Hist. Eng.* (1858) I. ii. 132 Henry.. definitively breaking the Spanish alliance, formed a league with Francis I. **1871** BLACKIE *Four Phases* i. 55 To settle definitively that much-vexed question.

†**2.** *Metaph.* So as to have a definite position, but not take up space: see prec. 3. *Obs.*

1529 MORE *Dyaloge* II. Wks. 188/1 Though thei be not cyrcumscribed in place.. yet are thei and angels also diffinitiuely so placed where thei be for the time. **1624** DE LAWNE tr. *Du Moulin's Logick* 27 The Philosophers.. say that Bodies are in a place circumscriptiuely, and Soules definitiuely; because Soules are not limited or circumscribed by place, and yet a man may say.. that they are here, or there, and not els-where. **1711** tr. *Werenfels' Disc. Logom.* 96.

de'finitiveness. [-NESS.] The quality of being definitive; determinativeness, decisiveness.

1727 BAILEY vol. II, *Definitiveness*, decisiveness, etc. **1841** *Blackw. Mag.* L. 160 Southey is.. thoroughly English, however, in the historical definitiveness and decision of his religious convictions. **1875** POSTE *Gaius* III. Comm. (ed. 2) 361 The earnestness and definitiveness of the resolution.

ˈdefinitize, *v. rare.* [f. DEFINITE *a.* + -IZE.] *trans.* To make definite.

1876 A. M. FAIRBAIRN in *Contemp. Rev.* June 135 The Church..definitized and generalized opinions. **1882** *Blackw. Mag.* Nov. 632 The 'his' then outstanding had to be definitised.

definitor (dɛfɪˈnaɪtə(r)). Also 7 **diffinitor** [a. L. *dēfīnītor*, agent-n. from *dēfīnīre* to DEFINE.]

1. An officer of the chapter in certain monastic orders, charged with the 'definition' or decision of points of discipline.

1648 GAGE *West Ind.* iii. (1655) 7 When the Provinciall Chapter is kept, then..is there one named by name of Procurator or Diffinitor, who is to goe in the name of the whole Province to the next election of the Generall. **1704** *Collect. Voy.* (Church.) III. 51/1 [St. Francis] having been Definitor of his Order. **1745** A. BUTLER *Lives Saints, Bonaventure* VII. 194 The saint held a general chapter at Narbonne, and in concert with the definitors gave a new form to the old Constitutions. **1867** R. PALMER *Life P. Howard* 15 *note*, The order [Dominicans] is governed by a master-general with his council of definitors.

†**2.** A kind of surveying instrument: see quots.

1664 EVELYN tr. *Freart's Archit.* 153 This whole Instrument..consisting of Horizon, Ruler, and Plummet we shall call our Definitor. **1793** SMEATON *Edystone L.* §97 The instrument will shew the situation, distance from the center, and depression of any given point..below the plane of the dial..which instrument he calls a Definitor.

Deˈfinitory, *sb.* [f. as DEFINITOR + -ORY[1].] Definitors (see DEFINITOR 1) collectively, or a council of these.

1898 FR. THADDEUS *Franciscans in England* 334 He lost no time in calling his Definitory together, and laying the matter before them. **1904** *Month* Mar. 245 At the Definitory itself he was chosen to be the first President of the renovated and perpetuated English Benedictine Congregation. **1960** J. B. DOCKERY *C. Davenport* i. 30 Provincial, Custos, and four Definitors constitute the governing body of a Province. These six are known as the Definitorium or Definitory.

definitory (dɪˈfɪnɪtərɪ), *a.* [f. L. *dēfīnīre* to DEFINE, on type of adjs. such as AUDITORY: see -ORY[2].] Relating or belonging to definition.

a **1914** C. S. PEIRCE *Coll. Papers* (1932) II. §271 Such propositions might be termed Definiform, or Definitory. **1928** W. A. PICKARD-CAMBRIDGE tr. *Aristotle's Topica* I. v. 102[a] In a word we may call 'definitory' everything that falls under the same branch of inquiry as definitions. **1935** *Mind* XLIV. 291 In ordinary discourse we are very seldom indeed conscious of the full definitory meaning of the complex terms that we use.

definitude (dɪˈfɪnɪtjuːd). [f. L. *dēfīnīt-us*, DEFINITE, after *infinitude, multitude*: see -TUDE.] The quality of being definite; definiteness, precision.

1836 SIR W. HAMILTON *Study Math.* Discuss. (1852) 275 Destitute of the light and definitude of mathematical representations. **1862** LATHAM *Channel Isl.* III. xiv. (ed. 2) 332 Results of remarkable precision and definitude. **1875** VEITCH *Lucretius* 66 There would be no definitude of leaf or flower.

definitum (dɛfɪˈnaɪtəm). *Logic.* [a. L. *dēfīnītum* 'thing defined', neut. of pa. pple. of *dēfīnīre* DEFINE *v.*] The thing or expression which a definition defines. Cf. DEFINIENDUM.

[*a* **1277** PETRUS HISPANUS *Summulae Logicales* (1947) 5.10 Locus a definitione est habitudo definitionis ad definitum.] **1629** A. RICHARDSON *Logician's School-Master* 215 If the *definitum* bee larger than the *definitio*, then it outreacheth the limits of the thing. **1855** [see RESOLUTION 7b]. **1944** G. E. MOORE in P. A. Schilpp *Philos. B. Russell* II. v. 197 It is only where..the sentence used to express the *definiens*..forms a part of the sentence which is the *definitum*, that one can be said to be giving a definition in spite of the fact that (1) is not fulfilled.

†**defix** (dɪˈfɪks), *v. Obs.* [f. L. *dēfix-*, ppl. stem of *dēfīgĕre* to fasten down, f. DE- I. 1 + *fīgĕre* to FIX, fasten. The early example of the pa. pple. appears to have been formed immed. after L. *defix-us*, with Eng. ppl. suffix.]

trans. To fasten down; to fix firmly, definitely, or earnestly (*lit.* and *fig.*).

1432-50 tr. *Higden* (Rolls) I. 243 The spere of the messengere defixede in to the erthe schewede a prenosticacion and as a begynnenge of fiȝhte. **1598** HAKLUYT *Voy.* I. II. 89 (R.) They were constrained to defixe their princely seate and habitation in that extreme prouince of the north. **1605** J. DOVE *Confut. Atheism* 16 The eyes of the people will be defixed vpon them. **1664** H. MORE *Myst. Iniq.* 264 Those Ten Horns answerable to the Beast with ten Horns in Daniel..seem to defix and determinate the Prophecy to that sense. **1679** J. GOODMAN *Penit. Pard.* II. i. (1713) 146 When a man..defixes his thoughts, and suspends his determination till he see plain reason to incline him this way or that.

Hence †**deˈfixed, defixt** *ppl. a.*

1652 GAULE *Magastrom.* 280 With defixed eyes and distracted countenance. **1681** GLANVILL *Sadducismus* 116 In intent and defixed thoughts upon some..object.

†**defixion** (dɪˈfɪkʃən). *Obs.* [ad. late L. *dēfixiōn-em*, n. of action f. *dēfīgĕre* to fasten down, etc. (see prec.).] Fixing, fastening.

1660 H. MORE *Myst. Godl.* I. ix. 29 By the defixion of our Phansy upon what is most gross and sensible.

deflagraˈbility. *rare.* [f. next: see -ITY.] Deflagrable quality, readiness to deflagrate.

a **1691** BOYLE *Wks.* I. 362 (R.) The opinion of the ready deflagrability (if I may so speak) of salt-petre.

deflagrable (ˈdɛfləgrəb(ə)l), *a. rare.* [f. L. *dēflagrā-re* to DEFLAGRATE + -BLE.]

a **1691** BOYLE *Wks.* I. 538 (R.) More inflammable and deflagrable.

deflagrate (ˈdɛfləgreɪt), *v. Physics.* [f. L. *dēflagrāt-*, ppl. stem of *dēflagrāre* to burn away, burn up, consume, f. DE- I. 3 + *flagrāre* to burn.]

1. *trans.* To cause to burn away with sudden evolution of flame and rapid, sharp combustion (*e.g.* a mixture of charcoal and nitre thrown into a red-hot crucible).

1727 BAILEY vol. II, *Deflagrate*, to inkindle and burn off in a Crucible a Mixture of Salt or some mineral Body with a Sulphureous one. **1794** J. HUTTON *Philos. Light, etc.* 208 When coal is deflagrated with nitre. **1876** *S. Kens. Mus. Catal.* No. 1369 The spark from this battery deflagrates a platinum wire a foot long.

2. *intr.* To burst into flame and burn away rapidly.

1750 *Phil. Trans.* XLVI. 449 Neither these, nor those of Cheltenham, will deflagrate or flash in Touch-Paper, nor on burning Charcoal, as true Nitre will do. **1794** G. ADAMS *Nat. & Exp. Philos.* II. xx. 376 Such a degree of heat as would cause the nitre to deflagrate. **1803** *Edin. Rev.* III. 25 Let a drop of water be projected upon this liquor..it instantly deflagrates with a slight explosion. **1876** HARLEY *Mat. Med.* 161 When thrown on the fire it deflagrates.

Hence **ˈdeflagrated, ˈdeflagrating** *ppl. adjs.*

1766 AMORY *Buncle* (1770) IV. 93 The deflagrating nitre consumes the sulphur of the antimony. **1788** KEIR in *Phil. Trans.* LXXVIII. 327 Giving a deflagrating quality to paper soaked in this liquor. **1822** FARADAY *Exp. Res.* xvi. 78 A black residuum is left..which..when heated..is found to be deflagrating. **1831** T. P. JONES *Convers. Chem.* xxii. 229 The deflagrated charcoal.

ˈdeflagrating, *vbl. sb.* The action of the verb *to deflagrate*; used *attrib.* in **deflagrating spoon,** a metal spoon with a long handle, used for holding small quantities of materials that deflagrate.

1827 [see SPOON *sb.* 4b]. **1867** BLOXAM *Chem.* 7 The experiment is most conveniently performed by heating the sulphur in a deflagrating spoon. **1936** G. H. J. ADLAM *Sci. Masters' Bk.* (2nd Ser.) 98 (*heading*) Deflagrating spoon.

deflagration (dɛfləˈgreɪʃən). [ad. L. *dēflagrātiōn-em*, n. of action from *dēflagrāre* to DEFLAGRATE. Cf. mod.F. *déflagration.*]

†**1.** The rapid burning away of anything in a destructive fire; consumption by a blazing fire. *Obs.*

1607 J. KING *Serm.* 30 A type of the deflagration of Sodome and Gomorre. *a* **1633** LENNARD tr. *Charron's Wisd.* III. iv. VIII. §1 (1670) 390 Witness that great deflagration..in Constantinople. **1659** PEARSON *Creed* (1839) 88 By supposing innumerable deluges and deflagrations. **1788** POTTER *Sophocles* Pref. to Œdipus (R.), Till the mountain..discharges its torrent fires, which..carry with them deflagration, ruin, and horror. **1811** PINKERTON *Petrol.* II. 547 In Fifeshire..a coal-mine has continued in a state of deflagration, at least since the time of Buchanan, 1560. **1836-7** SIR W. HAMILTON *Lect. Metaph.* (1877) II. xxxix. 381 We see..the fall of a spark on gunpowder, for example, followed by the deflagration of the gunpowder.

†**b.** Of a volcano: A blazing out into flame.

1691 RAY *Creation* II. v. (1732) 259 The great Deflagrations or Eruptions of Vulcanos.

2. *Physics.* The action of deflagrating; rapid, sharp combustion with sudden evolution of flame; *esp.* the sudden combustion of a substance for the purpose of producing some change in its composition by the joint action of heat and oxygen (cf. quot. 1831); also, the sudden combustion and oxidation of a metal by the electric spark.

1666 BOYLE *Orig. Formes & Qual.*, Nor were all its inflammable parts consum'd at one deflagration. **1674** *Phil. Trans.* IX. 102 The deflagration of Niter. **1706** PHILLIPS (ed. Kersey), *Deflagration*..In Chymistry, the inkindling and burning off in a Crucible a Mixture of a Salt or of some Mineral Body with a Sulphureous one, in order to purify the Salt, or to make a *Regulus* of the Mineral; as in the preparing of *Sal Prunellæ* and *Regulus of Antimony*. **1754** *Phil. Trans.* XLVIII. 679 A violent deflagration arose, and the platina was almost instantly dissolved. **1816** J. SMITH *Panorama Sc. & Art* II. 282 Galvanic batteries..the larger the plates, the greater is their power of deflagration. **1831** T. P. JONES *Convers. Chem.* xxii. 228 The metals are sometimes oxidized by what is called deflagration. That is, by mixing them with nitre, and projecting the mixture into a red hot crucible.

deflagrator (ˈdɛfləgreɪtə(r)). [agent-n. in L. form, from *dēflagrāre* to DEFLAGRATE.] An instrument or apparatus for producing deflagration, *esp.* a voltaic arrangement for the production of intense heat.

1824 LONGF. in *Life* (1891) I. v. 51 The galvanick heat produced by Professor Hare's deflagrator. **1827** WEEKES in *Mech. Mag.* VII. 425 The Safety gas deflagrator, an oxyhydrogen blowpipe on an entirely new principle. **1876** *S. Kens. Mus. Catal.* No. 1256 Hare's Calorimotor, or Deflagrator.

deflate (dɪˈfleɪt), *v.* [f. L. *dēflāt-*, ppl. stem of *dēflāre*, to blow away, f. DE- I. 2 + *flāre* to blow; but in mod. use the prefix is taken as DE- I. 1, down, or DE- II. 1.]

1. a. *trans.* To release the air from (anything inflated).

1891 *Strand Mag.* II. 498/1 Spencer proceeds to deflate the balloon. **1892** *Cycl. Tour. Club Gaz.* Aug. 229 In case of repairs the tyre is deflated.

b. *intr.* for *pass.* Of an inflated object: to become emptied of the inflating gas; to 'go down'.

1902 *Daily Chron.* 2 Sept. 4/5 Mr. Spencer turning aside from the deflating balloon. **1925** *Glasgow Herald* 18 Apr. 9 When the bag deflated it formed a new bulkhead. **1971** *Country Life* 14 Jan. 59/3 The turkey cock deflated and rushed away, squawking for dear life.

2. a. *intr.* To 'climb down'; to lose spirit, confidence, etc.

1912 D. H. LAWRENCE *Let.* 5 Apr. (1962) I. 107 I'll write to Harrison. He seems inclined to deflate. On Tuesday he wrote me a cocky letter, yesterday, a sweet and friendly one. **1933** T. E. LAWRENCE *Lett.* (1938) 772 'Mr. Garnett' said the village postman importantly 'is gone to Spain.' 'Mr. Garnett is unfortunate' I replied..and the postman deflated. **1960** L. WRIGHT *Clean & Decent* 264 We may or may not deflate when a statistician tells us that of our neighbours on a London bus today, one in five *never* takes a bath.

b. *trans.* To reduce the size or importance of (a thing). Of a person's reputation, character, etc.: to depreciate, to 'debunk'.

1920 *Glasgow Herald* 17 Mar. 11, I rather wish not to inflate the currency of optimism, but I want to deflate the note of pessimism which is sometimes present. **1933** H. G. WELLS *Bulpington* iii. 113 Comfort, bathrooms, punctuality, duty, were all jumbled and deflated together under the blight of that word [*bourgeois*]. **1934** —— *Exper. in Autobiogr.* I. v. 247 Strong as is my disposition to deflate the reputation of Marx I have to admit [etc.]. *Ibid.* II. ix. 763 The belief in the possible world leadership of England had been deflated. **1940** J. BUCHAN *Memory Hold-the-Door* viii. 185 They were sansculottes who sought to deflate majestic reputations. **1940** *Manch. Guardian Weekly* 5 Jan. 2 The war's lack of intensity has deflated what military fervour there ever was. **1958** *Essays & Studies* XI. iv. 53 Lytton Strachey uses the tone of Gibbon in order to deflate the Victorians.

3. a. *trans.* To reduce the inflation of (a currency). Also *absol.*, to pursue a policy of deflation. **b.** *intr.* for *pass.* To be reduced by deflation.

1919 R. G. HAWTREY *Currency & Credit* 352 Every country will seek to keep pace with its neighbours. If one does not deflate its currency as quickly as the others the exchanges will turn against it. **1922** *Glasgow Herald* 7 Aug. 8 All of these costs..would require to deflate to pre-war standard to enable the sixpenny loaf to reappear. **1923** R. MCKENNA in *Daily Mail* 27 Jan. 3 If at this stage we made no further effort to deflate, trade would soon recover. **1926** *Westm. Gaz.* 30 July, To 'deflate' the franc from 240 or 200 ..to a level of only 25 to the £ is beyond the realms of practicability. **1963** *Ann. Reg. 1962* 15 Treasury belief that Britain could afford to deflate its way out of its balance of payments difficulties.

Hence **deˈflated, deˈflating** *ppl. adjs.*

1894 *Sat. Rev.* 8 Dec. 618/1 There are narrow edges to the rims on which a deflated tyre would rest. **1908** H. G. WELLS *War in Air* iv. 133 He left him in an extremely deflated condition, with all his little story told. **1931** —— *Work, Wealth & Happiness* (1932) xii. 616 Operations with the deflated armament firms, metallurgical industries and petroleum. **1933** *Mind* XLII. 266 The effect is to put Taine in his place (in the 'deflating' sense of these words). **1960** N. COWARD *Pomp & Circumstance* iv. 28 There's nothing more deflating than telling someone some exciting news and discovering that they already know it.

deflater: see DEFLATOR.

deflation (diːˈfleɪʃən). [f. DEFLATE *v.* + -ION.]

1. The release of air from something inflated.

1891 *Pall Mall G.* 6 Aug. 1/3 A new patent valve, possessing the long-desired means for deflation as well as inflation. **1968** PASSMORE & ROBSON *Compan. Med. Studies* I. xxix. 22/2 An imposed, maintained deflation of the lungs increases the frequency, or force, or both, of spontaneous inspiratory efforts.

2. *Physical Geogr.* [a. G. *deflation* (J. Walther 1891, in *Abhandl. d. math.-phys. Classe d. k. sächsischen Ges. d. Wissenschaften* XVI. 38).] The removal of particles of rock, sand, etc., by the wind.

1893 J. WALTHER in *Nat. Geogr. Mag.* IV. 176 We say of the wind that it 'sweeps' over the ground; for this word means nothing else than that the wind cleans the ground of all loose particles that cover it. Translated into technical geologic language, it is called 'deflation', but that means nothing else than the every-day word 'sweep'. **1898** J. GEIKIE *Earth Sculpture* 20 The transporting action of the wind, or 'deflation' as it is termed, goes on without ceasing. **1910** LAKE & RASTALL *Text-bk. Geol.* 73 Erosion by wind divides itself naturally into two parts—removal by material or *deflation*, which of course comes under the heading of transport, and actual corrasion or wearing away of the rocks by the dynamical effect of moving sand. **1954** W. D. THORNBURY *Princ. Geomorphol.* xii. 302 Some geologists..believe that deflation is a relatively insignificant process..in the reduction of desert landscapes. **1970** R. J. SMALL *Study of Landforms* ix. 300 Deflation could gradually deepen the hollow until the water-table was exposed.

3. The action or process of deflating currency; an economic situation characterized by a rise in the value of money and a fall in prices, wages, and credit, usually accompanied by a rise in unemployment. Cf. INFLATION, DISINFLATION.

1920 R. G. HAWTREY in *Rep. Brit. Assoc. 1919* 252 To restore a depreciated unit to its normal gold value requires a measure of deflation. Deflation, which is a reversal of the process of inflation, must mean a decrease in the aggregate of money incomes. **1920** *Glasgow Herald* 11 May 10 The process of deflation likely to result from the new rights of the Federal Reserve system to discount on a graded scale. **1923** *Guernsey Star* 25 Jan., The primary ground on which a policy of gradual deflation is recommended is that it raises the exchange value of the pound sterling in relation to the dollar and hastens our return to the gold standard. **1956** *Ann. Reg. 1955* 227 Influential bankers and industrialists complained that the 'credit squeeze' had been overdone and warned against the danger of deflation.

4. *fig.* (Cf. DEFLATE *v.* 2 a and b.)

1933 H. G. WELLS *Shape of Things to Come* II. §12. 243 The mindless exaltation and the subsequent mindless deflation of American spiritual life. **1944** —— *'42 to '44* 157 Maybe his mental trouble is not hopeless. He may be cured by his deflation. **1958** G. J. WARNOCK *Eng. Philos. since 1900* xiii. 173 The contemporary philosopher's eye is characteristically cold and his pen, perhaps, apt to be employed as an instrument of deflation.

deflationary (dɪˈfleɪʃənərɪ), *a.* [f. DEFLATION + -ARY[1].] Of, pertaining to, or tending to deflation.

1920 *Glasgow Herald* 21 Aug. 7 The transition from an inflationary to a deflationary period in prices. **1923** J. M. KEYNES *Tract on Monetary Reform* iv. 152 Aurelian's deflationary zeal to restore the integrity of the coin excited an insurrection which caused the death of 7000 soldiers. **1929** *New Statesman* 1 June 231 The falling price level of recent years has been in large part the result of a world-wide deflationary movement which has inevitably reacted on credit and unemployment. **1957** G. E. HUTCHINSON *Treat. Limnol.* I. i. 125 There are a number of basins, the origin of which appears to involve wind action, either through its effect on the distribution of sand or through the deflationary or erosive action of wind acting on broken rock. **1959** *Ann. Reg. 1958* 478 The deflationary policies adopted by the Government in September 1957. **1962** *Listener* 5 Apr. 611/2 This makes him apply a deflationary technique to just those matters which have most strikingly affected British party life in the last century and a half. **1963** *Ibid.* 24 Jan. 179/1 Beneath the deflationary mockery of Beatrice and Benedick there is much human affection and goodwill.

deflationist (diːˈfleɪʃənɪst). [f. DEFLATION 3 + -IST.] One who advocates a policy of deflation. Also *attrib.* or as *adj.*

1921 *Glasgow Herald* 10 Feb. 4 If the deflationists have their way, the pound will be raised again to the value of 20s. **1922** *Edin. Rev.* July 194 The decision to get back to gold would divide the country into inflationists and deflationists. **1928** *Observer* 19 Feb. 18/2 The policy of the Suiyukai is positive and inflationist, while that of the Minseito is negative and deflationist.

deflator (diːˈfleɪtə(r)). Also -er. [f. DEFLATE *v.* + -OR.] One who or that which deflates.

1896 *Westm. Gaz.* 2 Nov. 9/1 Some person..had strewn the road with a number of 'boot protectors', perhaps the most deadly deflator that could be constructed. **1964** *Economist* 12 Dec. 1205/2 The European common market deflaters.

deflect (dɪˈflɛkt), *v.* [ad. L. *dēflect-ĕre* to bend aside, or downwards; f. DE- I. 1, 2 + *flectĕre* to bend.] **I.** *trans.*

1. To bend down. Cf. DEFLECTED 2.

1630 LORD *Banians* 72 They pray with demissive eyelids ..and with their knees deflected under them.

2. To bend or turn to one side or from a straight line; to change the direction of; to cause to deviate from its course.

c **1630** JACKSON *Creed* IV. v. Wks. III. 57 It would argue no error sometimes to deflect our course. **1845** DARWIN *Voy. Nat.* xxi. (1852) 491 The current seemed to be deflected upward from the face of the cliff. **1860** TRISTRAM *Gt. Sahara* xvii. 287 The French..will do all in their power to deflect the stream of commerce to a more northerly channel. **1879** G. PRESCOTT *Sp. Telephone* 1 In 1820, Oersted discovered that an electric current would deflect a magnetic needle.

b. *Optics.* To bend (a ray of light) from the straight line; *esp.* to bend away from a body.

1796 BROUGHAM in *Phil. Trans.* LXXXVI. 264 The first knife deflected the images formed by the second, in precisely the same degree that it inflected those images which itself formed. **1811** A. T. THOMSON *Lond. Disp.* (1818) p. xxxvii, When a ray of light moving in a straight line passes within a certain distance of a body parallel to its direction, it bends towards the body, or is *inflected*; but when the body parallel to its course is at a greater distance, the ray is bent from it, or *deflected*. **1879** HARLAN *Eyesight* iii. 36 If we look at an object through a prism, the rays of light coming from it are deflected.

3. *fig.* (in reference to a course of action, conduct, and the like.)

c **1555** HARPSFIELD *Divorce Hen. VIII* (1878) 66 To averte and deflect him from this enterprise. **1620** SHELTON *Quix.* IV. ix. II. 118 Let me cleave to the Supporter from whom neither thy Importunity nor Threats..could once deflect me. **1863** KINGLAKE *Crimea* I. i. 7 The personal and family motives which deflect the state policy of a prince who is his own minister. **1878** LECKY *Eng. in 18th C.* II. ix. 540 The evil of all attempts to deflect the judgment by hope or fear.

4. To turn or convert (a thing) *to* something different from its natural quality or use.

1613 PURCHAS *Pilgrimage* VII. iii. (1614) 670 That Title of *Prestegian* (easily deflected and altered to *Priest Iohn*). *a* **1711** KEN *Hymns Evang.* Poet. Wks. 1721 I. 109 How God's All-wise Superintending Will To greatest Good deflected greatest ill.

II. *intr.*

5. To turn to one side or from a straight line; to change its direction; to deviate from its course.

1646 SIR T. BROWNE *Pseud. Ep.* II. ii, At some parts of the Azores it [the needle] deflecteth not, but lyeth in the true meridian. **1696** WHISTON *Th. Earth* I. (1722) 53 They seem to deflect from that great Circle in which they before were seen to move. **1726** tr. *Gregory's Astron.* I. 155 The same part of the Moon is turned towards the Earth, or at least does not deflect much from it. **1879** R. H. ELLIOT *Written on Foreheads* II. 6 Then deflecting a little to their right, they got on a long ridge of grassy hill.

6. *fig.*

1612 T. JAMES *Jesuits Downfall* 59 Kings do deflect from the Catholike Religion. **1646** SIR T. BROWNE *Pseud. Ep.* VI. x, Many creatures exposed to the ayre, deflect in extremity from their naturall colours. **1753-4** WARBURTON *Nat. & Rev. Relig.* ii, The Mind..can, every moment, deflect from the line of truth and reason. **1879** M. ARNOLD *Equality* Mixed Ess. 81 The points where this type deflects from the truly humane ideal.

deflect (dɪˈflɛkt), *ppl. a.* [f. as prec. after ppl. forms in *-ct*, as *erect.*] Deflected, bent aside.

1851 MRS. BROWNING *Casa Guidi Windows* 105 So swept ..The marshalled thousands,—not an eye deflect To left or right.

deflectable (dɪˈflɛktəb(ə)l), *a.* [f. DEFLECT *v.* + -ABLE.] Capable of being deflected.

1893 in *Funk's Standard Dict.* **1925** *Contemp. Rev.* July 89 Woman..being less deflectable and in her nature more impressionable [than man].

deflected (dɪˈflɛktɪd), *ppl. a.* [f. DEFLECT *v.* + -ED.]

1. Turned aside; bent to one side.

1860 MAURY *Phys. Geog. Sea* xvi. 881 Monsoons are, for the most part, trade-winds deflected. **1874** S. COX *Pilgr. Ps.* vi. 121 Walking in subtle and deflected paths.

2. *Zool.* and *Bot.* Bent or curved downwards; = DEFLEXED.

1828 WEBSTER, *Deflected.* In botany, bending downward archwise. **1854** WOODWARD *Mollusca* II. 165 Glandina.. eye-tentacles deflected at the tips, beyond the eyes. **1867** F. FRANCIS *Angling* vi. (1880) 195 The wings..come up to an angle..as it is termed, they are deflected.

3. *Philol.* Used to translate F. *fléchi*, a term proposed for the 'strong' grade in ablaut series.

1890 R. T. ELLIOTT tr. *V. Henry's Compar. Gram.* §41. 47 We may distinguish three chief grades, the normal grade, the weak or reduced grade, and the deflected grade (*fléchi*). *Ibid.* 48 I.-E. types, **bhĕydh* (to trust), weak **bhidh*, deflected **bhoydh*.

de'flecting, *vbl. sb.* [-ING[1].] The action of the verb DEFLECT.

1623 COCKERAM, *Deflectings*, turnings from good to bad.

de'flecting, *ppl. a.* [-ING[2].] That deflects.

deflecting magnet: a magnet used for deflecting a magnetic needle, as in a galvanometer.

1796 BROUGHAM in *Phil. Trans.* LXXXVI. 229 The ray moves in an ellipse by the inflecting, and an hyperbola by the deflecting force. **1851-9** SABINE *Man. Sci. Enq.* 91 When the weather does not permit the manipulation of the weights, deflecting magnets are substituted. **1857** WHEWELL *Hist. Induct. Sc.* II. 23 Gravity must act as a deflecting force.

deflection: see DEFLEXION.

deflective (dɪˈflɛktɪv), *a.* [f. DEFLECT *v.* + -IVE. (L. analogies would give *deflexive*.)] Having the quality of deflecting.

1813 P. BARLOW *Math. Dict.*, *Deflective forces.* **1881** LUBBOCK in *Nature* No. 618. 411 In 1819..Oersted had discovered the deflective action of the current on the magnetic needle.

deflectometer (diːflɛkˈtɒmɪtə(r)). [See -METER.] An instrument for measuring the deflection or deformation of a body, esp. a metal bar, under stress.

1836 *Mech. Mag.* 6 Feb. 367/1 The effects produced [on the rails] by the passing engines and trains were minutely observed with this deflectometer. **1874** KNIGHT *Dict. Mech.*, *Deflectometer*, an instrument for measuring the deflection of a rail by a weight in rapid motion. **1962** *Engineering* 23 Feb. 268/3 A series of deflectometers at the column positions was used to give an indication of the movement. A central deflectometer recorded the deflections in the new steel girder.

deflector (dɪˈflɛktə(r)). [f. DEFLECT *v.* + *-or* for -ER: the corresponding form on L. analogies is *deflexor.*] **1.** An instrument or contrivance for deflecting; e.g. (*a*) a deflecting magnet; (*b*) a plate or diaphragm for deflecting a current of air, gas, etc.

1837 BREWSTER *Magnet.* 344 Dipping needle Deflector, for measuring the Variation and Dip of the Needle. **1879** THOMSON & TAIT *Nat. Phil.* I. I. §198 The 'Deflector', an adjustible magnet laid on the glass of the compass bowl and used..to discover the 'semicircular' error produced by the ship's iron. **1887** *Pall Mall G.* 4 June 12/1 These sprinklers consist of a plate and a deflector..The deflector is for the purpose of breaking the column of water into spray, which falls in a dense shower over the flames.

2. *attrib.*

1940 *Chambers's Techn. Dict.* 230/1 *Deflector coil*, a coil so arranged that a current passing through it produces a magnetic field which deflects the beam in a cathode ray tube employing magnetic deflection. *Deflector plates*, electrodes so arranged in a cathode ray tube that the electrostatic field produced by a difference of potential between them deflects the beam. **1961** *Lancet* 30 Sept. 755/1 For protection of the area in front of the face, there was no significant difference between the performances of fabric 'filter masks' and paper or paper-insert 'deflector masks'. **1962** *Which?* Dec. 359/1 Eight of the typewriters had an erasure table which also acted as a deflector plate to stop the paper wrapping round the platen.

†**de'fletion.** *Obs.*[—0] [ad. L. *dēflētiōn-em*, n. of action from *dēflēre* to weep over, bewail, f. DE- I. 3 + *flēre* to weep.]

1656 BLOUNT *Glossogr.*, *Defletion*, a bewayling or bemoaning.

deflex (ˈdiːflɛks), *a.* [ad. L. *dēflex-us*, pa. pple. of *dēflectĕre* to DEFLECT.] = DEFLEXED.

1794 MARTYN *Rousseau's Bot.* xxvii. 420 In the common Bee Orchis it [the lip of the nectary] consists of five lobes, which are deflex or bent downwards.

deflexed (dɪˈflɛkst), *ppl. a. Zool.* and *Bot.* [f. prec. + -ED.] Bent downwards; deflected.

1826 KIRBY & SP. *Entomol.* xlvii. (1828) IV. 386 The organs of flight are deflexed and do not lap over each other. **1845** LINDLEY *Sch. Bot.* iv. (1858) 41 Stem rough with deflexed bristles. **1871** STAVELEY *Brit. Insects* 127 Such insects as have the wings, when at rest, deflexed—lying over the body like a shelving roof. **1877-84** F. E. HULME *Wild Fl.* p. vi, Pedicels bearing fruit deflexed.

deflexi'bility. [f. next + -ITY.] Capability of being deflected.

1796 BROUGHAM in *Phil. Trans.* LXXXVI. 263 The inflexibilities of the rays are directly as their deflexibilities. **1805** *Edin. Rev.* VI. 25 He attempts to demonstrate some connexion between the greater deflexibility and the less reflexibility of the red rays.

deflexible (dɪˈflɛksɪb(ə)l), *a.* [f. L. *dēflex-us* (see DEFLEX) + -BLE.] Capable of being deflected.

1796 BROUGHAM in *Phil. Trans.* LXXXVI. 234 It is evident that the most inflexible rays are also most deflexible.

deflexion, deflection (dɪˈflɛkʃən). [ad. L. *dēflexiōn-em*, n. of action f. *dēflectĕre* (ppl. stem *dēflex-*) to DEFLECT. Cf. mod.F. *déflexion* (Dict. Acad. 1762, occurring also in 16th c. as *déflection*). The non-etymological spelling *deflection*, now very common, is taken from the present-stem *deflect-*, associated with nouns of action from L. ppl. stem in *-ect-*, as *collection*, *dissection*, etc.]

1. The action of bending down; the condition of being bent or curved; also, a bend or curve (as a result).

In *Mech.* The bending of any body under a transverse strain; the amount of this. In *Entom.* The state of being bent downward, as the deflexion of the wings when folded; also, a deflected part or margin.

1665 SIR T. HERBERT *Trav.* (1677) 296 The Mahometans signifie the same onely by a moderate deflexion of the head. **1821** TREDGOLD *Ess. Cast Iron* (1824) 73 When the weights were removed, the piece retained a permanent deflexion. **1879** *Cassell's Techn. Educ.* IV. 276/2 The deflection of a beam supporting a lateral weight.

2. The action of turning, or state of being turned, away from a straight line or regular path; the amount of such deviation; also, a turn or deviation (as an effect or result).

1665 *Phil. Trans.* I. 105 Of which deflection he ventures to assign the cause. **1831** BREWSTER *Newton* (1855) I. xii. 292 In 1684..Newton discovered that the moon's deflexion in a minute was sixteen feet, the same as that of bodies at the earth's surface. **1833** HERSCHEL *Astron.* viii. 267 Deflection from a straight line is only another word for *curvature* of path. **1862** MERIVALE *Rom. Emp.* (1865) VII. lxi. 329 They ..possibly noted the great deflection of the coast southward from Cape Wrath.

b. Of things immaterial.

1605 BACON *Adv. Learn.* II. i. §3 Of the works of nature which have a digression and deflexion from the ordinary course of generations, productions, and motions. **1648** W. MOUNTAGUE *Devout Ess.* I. 112 (T.) King David found this deflection and indirectness in our minds. **1649** JER. TAYLOR *Gt. Exemp.* II. ix. 123 Deflexions in manners. **1840** DE QUINCEY *Style* iii. Wks. X. 190 We shall point out the deflexion, the bias, which was impressed upon the Greek speculations in this particular. **1851** CARLYLE *Sterling* I. xiv. (1872) 86 At this extreme point of spiritual deflexion and depression. **1876** MOZLEY *Univ. Serm.* iv. (1877) 84 The type of religion it has produced is a deflection from simplicity.

3. The turning of a word or phrase aside from its actual form, application, or grammatical use. *arch.*

1603 HOLLAND *Plutarch's Mor.* 1311 By a little deflexion of the name..that Canicular or Dogge starre is called *Κυων*. *a* **1619** FOTHERBY *Atheom.* II. i. §8 (1622) 191 That censure of Catullus (with a little deflexion) might very fitly bee applied vnto him. **1659** O. WALKER *Oratory* 34 By a gentle deflexion of the same word, in changing the substantive with the adjective. **1807** G. CHALMERS *Caledonia* I. I. iv. 119 *Grym* signifies strength; and hence, by a little deflexion, *Grym* came to signify any strength. **1830** DE QUINCEY *Bentley* Wks. 1890 IV. 131 *note*, A practice arose of giving to Greek names in *as* their real Greek termination, without any Roman deflexion.

4. *Electr.* and *Magn.* The turning of a magnetic needle away from its zero; the measured amount by which it is deflected.

1646 SIR T. BROWNE *Pseud. Ep.* II. ii. 62 The variation of the compass is..a deflexion and siding East and West from the true meridian. **1863** TYNDALL *Heat* i. 4 A moment's contact suffices to produce a prompt and energetic deflection of the needle. **1865** *Pall Mall G.* 3 Aug. 1/2 The curious electrical phenomenon known to electricians as 'deflection', has to-day been observed through the United Kingdom.

5. *Optics.* The bending of rays of light from the straight line. By Hooke applied specifically to the apparent bending or turning aside of the rays passing near the edge of an opaque body, called by Newton *inflexion*, and now explained as a phenomenon of DIFFRACTION.

(Brougham tried to differentiate *inflexion* and *deflexion*: see quot.)

1674-5 HOOKE *Lect. Light* Wks. (1705) 188 The Light from the Edge [of a card or razor] did strike downwards into the Shadow very near to a Quadrant, though still I found, that the greater the Deflection of this new Light was from the direct Radiations of the Cone, the more faint they were. **1727-51** CHAMBERS *Cycl., Deflection of the Rays of Light*, is a property which Dr. Hook observed 167⅘..He says, he found it different both from reflexion, and refraction..This is the same property which Sir Isaac Newton calls *Inflection*. **1796** BROUGHAM in *Phil. Trans.* LXXXVI. 228 *Def.* 1. If a ray passes within a certain distance of any body, it is bent inwards; this we shall call Inflection. 2. If it passes at a still greater distance it is turned away; this may be termed Deflection. **1808** J. WEBSTER *Nat. Phil.* 174 This deflection is supposed to proceed from the attraction of the denser medium. **1831** BREWSTER *Newton* viii. (1839) 99 In his paper of 1674..he [Hooke]..described the leading phenomena of the inflexion, or the deflexion of light, as he calls it.

6. *Naut.* The deviation of a ship from her true course in sailing.

1706 PHILLIPS (ed. Kersey), *Deflection*..In Navigation, the Tendency of a Ship from her true Course, by means of Currents, &c. which divert or turn her out of her right Way.

deflexionize, -ed, -ation: see DE- II. 1.

†**de'flexity.** *Obs.* [f. L. *dēflex-us* DEFLEX + -ITY.] The quality of being deflected (said of rays of light: see DEFLECT 2 b, DEFLEXION 5).

1797 BROUGHAM in *Phil. Trans.* LXXXVII. 360 We may ..say that the rays of light differ in degree of refrangity, reflexity, and flexity, comprehending inflexity and deflexity ..these terms..allude to the degree of distance to which the rays are subject to the action of bodies.

deflexure (dɪ'flɛksjʊə(r), -'flɛkʃə(r)). *rare.* [f. L. *dēflex-*, ppl. stem of *dēflectĕre* to DEFLECT + -URE: cf. *flexure*.] Deflexion, deviation; the condition of being bent (down or away).

1656 BLOUNT *Glossogr., Deflexure*, a bowing or bending. **1675** OGILBY *Brit.* Pref. 4 Deductions for the..smaller Deflexures of the Way. **1845** *Florist's Jrnl.* 17 The lip.. instead of being saddle-shaped by the usual deflexure of the sides, is perfectly flat.

†**de'floccate,** *v. Obs. rare*⁻⁰. [f. L. *dēfloccāre, dēfloccāt-* to pluck off, pluck, f. DE- I. 6 + *flocc-us* lock, flock.] (See quot.)

1623 COCKERAM, *Defloccate*, to weare out a thing.

deflocculant (diː'flɒkjʊlənt). [f. as next + -ANT¹.] A deflocculating agent.

1930 *Engineering* 26 Dec. 814/1 Using alkaline deflocculants only, it would be possible to produce goods.. superior to those obtained from the same mixes, hand-moulded. **1956** *Science News* XL. 66 Deflocculants are added in ceramic practice to give fluid suspensions containing high concentrations of solid matter.

deflocculate (diː'flɒkjʊleɪt), *v.* [f. DE- II. 1 + FLOCCULATE *v.*] *trans.* and *intr.* To undergo, or to cause to undergo, deflocculation. So **de'flocculated** *ppl. a.*; **de'flocculating** *vbl. sb.* and *ppl. adj.*

1907 *Sci. Amer.* 11 May 387 In the deflocculated condition..graphite has a condition of fineness far beyond [etc.]. **1909** WEBSTER, Deflocculate *v.i.* **1940** *Geogr. Jrnl.* XCV. 67 The distinct turbidity of the White Nile was no doubt related to the deflocculating effect of its slightly alkaline water in contrast with that of the Blue Nile. **1956** *Sci. News* XL. 66 Dispersions of clays in water..brought about by deflocculating agents..are very sensitive to the addition of electrolytes. **1957** *Encycl. Brit.* X. 645/2 A soft, unctuous form results on treating carbon with ash or silica in special furnaces, and this gives the so-called 'deflocculated' variety [of graphite] when treated with gallotannic acid. **1963** D. W. & E. E. HUMPHRIES tr. *Termier's Erosion & Sedimentation* xi. 225 The marl is deflocculated and hydrolysis of the alumino-silicates occurs.

deflocculation (ˌdiːflɒkjʊ'leɪʃən). [f. DE- + FLOCCULATION.] The process by which floccules present in a liquid break up into fine particles, producing a dispersion; the action of deflocculating.

1904 *Nature* 7 July 238/2 The removal of the finest particles from the surface soil is attributed to deflocculation induced by the use of sodium nitrate. **1930** *Engineering* 18 July 61/1 The process of passing from sol to gel is termed coagulation, the reverse process is deflocculation. **1957** *New Biol.* XXIV. 37 The displacement of calcium by sodium from the clay particles in the flooded land caused them to contract and show the phenomena of 'deflocculation'.

deflorate (dɪ'flɔərət, 'dɛflɒrət), *a.* [ad. L. *dēflōrāt-us*, pa. pple. of *dēflōrāre*: see next. Cf. L. *dēflōrēre* to shed its bloom.]

1. *Bot.* Past the flowering state: applied to anthers that have shed their pollen, or to plants when their flowers have fallen.

1828 WEBSTER, *Deflorate*, in *botany*, having cast its farin, pollen, or fecundating dust. *Martyn.* **1858** GRAY *Struct. Bot.* Gloss., *Deflórate*, past the flowering age.

2. = DEFLOWERED; having lost virginity.

1883 in *Syd. Soc. Lex.*

deflorate ('dɛflɒreɪt), *v. rare.* In 5 defflorate. [f. ppl. stem of late L. *dēflōrāre* to deprive of its flowers, ravish, f. DE- I. 6 + *flōs, flōr-em* flower.]

†1. *trans.* To deflower (a woman). *Obs.*

c **1470** HARDING *Chron.* CVII. vii, The women euer they diuiciate In euery place, and fouly defflorate.

2. To strip (a plant) of its flowers.

1829 E. JESSE *Jrnl. Nat.* 165 They [the chaffinches] will deflorate too the spikes or whorls of the little red archangel.

defloration (dɛflɒ'reɪʃən). In 4-5 -acioun, 5-6 -acion, -acyon, 6 -atioun, deflouration. [a. OF. *defloracion* (14th c. in Hatzf.), ad. L. *dēflōrātiōn-em* plucking of flowers, of virginity, n. of action from *dēflōrāre* to DEFLOWER.] The action of the verb DEFLOWER.

1. The action of deflowering a virgin.

c **1400** MAUNDEV. (Roxb.) xxxi. 141 Þe defloracioun of maydens. **1483** CAXTON *Gold. Leg.* 196 b/2 Tellyng to hir the place & tyme of hir defloracion. **1536** BELLENDEN *Cron. Scot.* (1821) I. 199 He..complanit hevily the defloration of his dochteris. **1763** CHESTERF. *Lett.* IV. ccclxxvi. 198. **1803** *Med. Jrnl.* IX. 71 Opinions generally entertained on the subject of Defloration. **1883** *Syd. Soc. Lex., Defloration*, a term for sexual connexion for the first time without violence, in distinction from rape.

2. The culling or excerpting of the flowers or finest parts of a book; a selection of choice passages.

1387 TREVISA *Higden* (Rolls) VII. 271 Þe whiche book þis Robert defloured solempneliche, and took out þe beste, so þat it semed þat þat defloracioun is now more worþy þan al þe grete volume. **1612** SELDEN in *Drayton's Poly-olb.* To Rdr. A iij, The common printed Chronicle, which is..but an Epitome or Defloration made by Robert of Lorraine. **1696** RAY in *Lett. Lit. Men* (Camden) 203 Your History, were it reasonable for me to beg the defloration of it, would afford the greatest ornaments to it. **1747** CARTE *Hist. Eng.* I. Pref. 8 The Historia Britonum out of which he says, he made those deflorations. **1890** R. ELLIS in *Hermathena* XVI. 184 The *deflorations* or MSS. containing excerpts.

'**deflorator.** *rare.* [agent-n. f. L. *dēflōrāre*: see prec.] One who excerpts the finest parts of a book or author.

1647-8 G. LANGBAINE in *Abp. Ussher's Lett.* (1686) 524 This is the same Robert, the deflorator of Marianus mentioned by Malmesbury.

deflore, deflour, obs. forms of DEFLOWER.

†**de'flourish,** *v. Obs.* In 5 de-, diffloryssh, 6 deflorisch. [ad. OF. *de(s)flouriss-*, lengthened stem of *de(s)flourir*, now *défleurir*, to DEFLOWER, f. DE- I. 6 + *florir, fleurir* to FLOURISH.]

1. *trans.* To deflower; also *fig.* to spoil, ravage.

1494 FABYAN *Chron.* VII. 304 Yᵗ he shuld..also defloryssh yᵉ emperours doughter. *Ibid.* VII. 410 The sayd bysshop.. had difflorysshed a mayden and doughter of the sayde sir Gautier. **1538** LELAND *Itin.* V. 4 Montgomerike deflorisched by Owen Glindour.

2. *intr.* To lose its flowers, to cease to flourish.

1656 TRAPP *Comm. Philip.* iv. 10 It had deflourished then for a season, and withered, as an oak in winter.

†**de'flourished** *ppl. a.*, having lost its flowers.

1616 DRUMM. OF HAWTH. *Sonn.* xlix, Deflourisht mead, where is your heavenly hue?

†**de'flow,** *v. Obs. rare*⁻¹. [f. DE- I. 1 + FLOW, after L. *dēfluĕre* to flow down or away: see DEFLUENCE, etc.] *intr.* To flow down.

1646 SIR T. BROWNE *Pseud. Ep.* III. iv. 114 A collection of some superfluous matter deflowing from the body.

deflower (dɪ'flaʊə(r)), *v.* Forms: 4-7 deflore, defloure, 5-7 deflowre, 4-9 deflour, 6- deflower. [a. OF. *desflorer, desflourer* (13th c. in Hatzf.), later *defflorer, défleurer* (Cotgr.), mod.F. *déflorer* = Pr. *deflorar*, Sp. *desflorar*, It. *deflorare*, repr. L. *dēflōrāre* to deprive of its flowers, to ravish, f. DE- I. 6 + *flōs, flōr-em* flower. With this prob. is blended OF. *desflorir, -flourir* (14th c.), in 16th c. *defflorir*, mod.F. *défleurir* in same sense, and *intrans.* The form is now assimilated to *flower.*]

1. *trans.* To deprive (a woman) of her virginity; to violate, ravish.

1382 WYCLIF *Ecclus.* xx. 2 The lust of the gelding deflourede the ȝunge womman. **1393** GOWER *Conf.* II. 322 Which sigh her suster pale and fade..Of that she hadde be defloured. **1494** FABYAN *Chron.* VII. ccxxxviii. 278 The whiche..he deflowred of hyr vyrgynytie. **1559** W. CUNNINGHAM *Cosmogr. Glasse* 196 They have thys use that when any manne marieth, he must commit his wife to the priest to be defloured. **1611** BIBLE *Ecclus.* xx. 4 As is the lust of an Eunuch to defloure a virgine. **1775** ADAIR *Amer. Ind.* 164 The French Indians are said not to have deflowered any of our young women they captivated.

2. *fig.* To violate, ravage, desecrate; to rob of its bloom, chief beauty, or excellence; to spoil.

1486 in *Surtees Misc.* (1890) 56 This citie..Was never deflorid be force ne violence. **1500-20** DUNBAR *Poems* lxxii. 53 With blude and sweit was all deflorde His face. **1596** SPENSER *Hymne Hon. Beautie* 39 That wondrous paterne.. layd up in secret store..that no man may it see with sinfull eyes, for feare it to deflore. **1654** tr. *Martini's Conq. China* A iv, I will not..deflower that worth of its greatest beauty. **1660** GAUDEN *Antisacrilegus* 7 It would never recover its beauty..of late so much deflored. *a* **1716** SOUTH *Serm.* I. i. (R.), Actual discovery (as it were) rifles and deflowers the newness and freshness of the object. **1889** LOWELL *Walton* Lit. Ess. (1891) 60 [To] find a sanctuary which telegraph or telephone had not deflowered.

†3. To cull or excerpt from (a book, etc.) its choice or most valuable parts. *Obs.*

1387 TREVISA *Higden* (Rolls) I. 39 Þe whiche book Robert Bishop of Herforde deflorede. *Ibid.* VII. 271 [see DEFLORATION 2]. **1781** J. T. DILLON *Trav. Spain* 229 After they had in a manner deflowered the mine, and got as much ore as they could easily extract.

4. To deprive or strip of flowers.

c **1630** DRUMM. OF HAWTH. *Poems* 173 The freezing winds our gardens do defloure. **1648** W. MOUNTAGUE *Devout Ess.* I. xix. §6 (R.), An earthquake..rending the cedars, deflowering the gardens. **1800** CAMPBELL *Ode to Winter* 27 Deflow'ring nature's grassy robe. **1820** KEATS *Lamia* II. 216 Garlands..From vales deflower'd, or forest trees branch-rent.

deflowered (dɪ'flaʊəd), *ppl. a.* [-ED.] Deprived of virginity, violated; robbed of beauty or bloom; marred, disfigured.

1509 HAWES *Past. Pleas.* XI. xvi, Of Cerebus the deflowred pycture..Lyke an horrible gyaunt fyrce and wonderly. **1603** SHAKS. *Meas. for M.* IV. iv. 24 A deflowred maid. **1647** COWLEY *Mistress, Agst. Hope* ii, The Joys which we entire should wed, Come deflowr'd Virgins to our bed. **1887** T. HARDY *Woodlanders* iii, She would not turn again to the little looking-glass..knowing what a deflowered visage would look back at her.

deflowerer (dɪ'flaʊərə(r)). [-ER.] One who deflowers.

1536 BELLENDEN *Cron. Scot.* (1821) II. 53 Hir freindis.. commandit hir to schaw the deflorar of hir chastite. **1645** MILTON *Tetrach.* (1851) 189 The punishment of a deflowrer, and a defamer. *a* **1677** BARROW *Wks.* (1687) I. xviii. 256 A deflowrer and defiler of his reputation. **1713** *Guardian* No. 123 These deflourers of innocence. **1824-9** LANDOR *Imag. Conv.* Wks. (1846) II. 7 Our Italy would rise up in arms against the despoiler and deflowerer.

deflowering (dɪ'flaʊərɪŋ), *vbl. sb.* [-ING¹.] The action of the verb DEFLOWER: violation.

c **1400** MAUNDEV. (1839) xxviii. 286 Of old tyme, men hadden bede for deflourynge of Maydenes. **1561** T. NORTON *Calvin's Inst.* IV. 138 b, Yᵉ rauishment and deflouring of his daughter. **1609** ROWLANDS *Knaue of Clubbes* 8 Villain..Before the Lord you die, For this deflowring of my wife. **1673** *Lady's Call.* II. §1 ¶7. 59 Every indecent curiosity..is a deflowring of the mind.

de'flowering, *ppl. a.* That deflowers.

1642 MILTON *Apol. Smect.* (1851) 273 If unchastity in a woman..be such a scandall and dishonour, then certainly in a man..it must, though commonly not so thought, be much more deflouring and dishonourable.

defluction, bad form of DEFLUXION.

defluence ('dɛfluːəns). *rare.* [f. L. type **dēfluentia*, f. *dēfluent-em*, pr. pple. of *dēfluĕre*, f. DE- I. 1 + *fluĕre* to flow.] A flowing down or away.

1681-6 J. SCOTT *Chr. Life* (1747) III. 281 They suffer a continual Defluence of old, and Access of new Parts. **1803** *Methodist Mag.* XXVI. 36 There is a continual defluence and access of parts.

†**de'fluency.** *Obs. rare.* [f. as prec. + -ENCY.] The quality of flowing; fluidity.

1665 BOYLE *Hist. Cold* xxi. 630 The cold having taken away the defluency of the oyl.

defluent ('dɛfluːənt) *a.* and *sb. rare.* [ad. L. *dēfluent-em*, pr. pple. of *dēflu- ĕre* to flow down.]

A. *adj.* Flowing down, decurrent. B. *sb.* That which flows down (from a main body).

1652 GAULE *Magastrom.* 87 Planets, in respect of motion, positure, aspect; sc. combust, peregrine..applicate, defluent. **1890** *Athenæum* 20 Dec. 845/3 This ice..breaking off into icebergs when its defluents reach the sea in the fjords which intersect Greenland. *Ibid.* 846/1 The defluents of the inland ice.

†**defluous** ('dɛfluːəs), *a. Obs. rare.* [f. L. *dēflu-us* (f. stem of *dēflu-ĕre* to flow down) + -OUS.] Flowing down; also, falling off, shedding.

1727 BAILEY vol. II, *Defluous*, flowing down, falling, shedding. **1822** T. TAYLOR *Apuleius* XI. 261 Her most copious and long hairs..were softly defluous.

defluvium (dɪ'fluːvɪəm). *Path.* [L.] A complete shedding of some part (as the hair or the finger-nails) as a result of disease (see quots.).

1817 J. M. GOOD *Physiol. Syst. Nosol.* (1820) 501 Baldness. *a* Simplex. Hairs of the scalp of a natural hue: gradually dying at the bulbs, or loosened by relaxation of the integument. Defluvium capillorum. Sennert. Alopecia simplex. Sauv. **1899** G. T. JACKSON *Dis. Skin* (ed. 3) 93 The variety [of alopecia] called Defluvium Capillorum is that sudden and general fall and manifest thinning of the hair which comes on during or after some severe illness. **1906** *Practitioner* Nov. 692 All loss of hair is abnormal, and the popular belief in a physiological defluvium is false. **1910** J. N. HYDE *Pract. Treat. Dis. Skin* (ed. 8) 992 Onychomadesis (..Alopecia Unguialis; Defluvium Unguium; Onychoptosis).—Total and so-called intermittent shedding of the nails occurs, as in the partial form, in connection with systemic affections of a severe grade. **1930** W. J. O'DONOVAN *Hair* xii. 123 The defluvium of hair that coincides or follows severe general illness is a matter of common knowledge. **1940** L. MCCARTHY *Diagn. & Treatm. Dis. Hair* vi. 553 In cases of sudden loss of hair following a shock, in which the eyebrows and eyelashes are also involved, it may be impossible to say whether we are dealing with defluvium capillorum or with an alopecia totalis.

†**deflux** ('diːflʌks), *sb. Obs.* [ad. L. *dēflux-us* a flowing down, a running off, f. ppl. stem of *dēfluĕre*: see above.]

1. A flowing or running down; defluxion.

1599 H. BUTTES *Dyet's Dry Din.* Aa iij b, Head o'reflowne with brinie deluge of defluxes hot. **1626** BACON *Sylva* (1677) §677 The Deflux of Humors. **1636** FEATLY *Clavis Myst.* xxviii. 365 A great defluxe of penitent teares. **1710** T. FULLER *Pharm. Extemp.* 172 A Frontal with Mastic.. hinders the deflux of Humours.

2. *transf.* A falling off or shedding. *rare.*

1682 NORRIS *Hierocles* 130 Having suffered a deflux of her wings.

3. *concr.* An effluence, emanation; = DEFLUXION 3 b. *rare.*

1603 HOLLAND *Plutarch's Mor.* 1336 But say there should happly be some deflux or effluence that passeth from one world to another. **1682** CREECH *Lucretius* (1683) Notes 3 The constant deflux of divine Images which strike the Mind.

†**de'flux**, *v. Obs. rare.* [f. L. *dēflux-*, ppl. stem of *dēfluĕre.*] *intr.* **a.** To flow down. **b.** To fall off in influence. Hence **de'fluxed** *ppl. a.*

1647 NEEDHAM *Levellers Levelled* 9 If wee observe the middle time of this Eclipse or full Moone..shee defluxeth from the opposition of the Sunne, to the Conjunction of Saturne. **1657** TOMLINSON *Renou's Disp.* 520 It cohibits all fluxions, and cocts the defluxed humours.

defluxion (dɪ'flʌkʃən). Also 7-9 **defluction**. [a. F. *défluxion* (16th c., Calvin, Paré), or ad. L. *dēfluxiōn-em*, n. of action from L. *dēfluĕre* to flow down, also, to fall off (as hair).]

†**1.** A flowing or running down. *Obs.*

1549 *Compl. Scot.* Prol. 14 The defluxione of blude hed payntit ande cullourt all the feildis. **1616** HAYWARD *Sanct. Troub. Soul* I. ii. (1620) 38 The emptying of an Houre-glasse consisteth, not onely in the falling of the last graine of sand, but in the whole defluxion thereof from the beginning. **1677** HALE *Prim. Orig. Man.* IV. viii. 370 By the defluxion of Waters. **1832** *Blackw. Mag.* XXXII. 644 It would be a needless defluxion of time to relate what took place.

†**b.** A falling off (of hair). *Obs. rare.*

1658 ROWLAND *Moufet's Theat. Ins.* 945 They cure.. defluxion of hair, and the thinnesse thereof however contracted.

2. *Path.* **a.** A supposed flow of 'humours' to a particular part of the body, in certain diseases. **b.** The flow or discharge accompanying a cold or inflammation; a running at the nose or eyes; catarrh. Now *rare*, *Obs.*, or *dial.*

1576 LYTE *Dodoens* V. xx. 576 [It] stoppeth all defluxions and falling downe of humours. **1586** SIR A. PAULET in Ellis *Orig. Lett.* I. III. No. 220. 7 Whome we found in her bed troubled..with a defluxion which was fallen into the syde of her neck. **1626** BACON *Sylva* (1651) 11 So doth Cold likewise cause Rheumes, and Defluxions from the Head. **1666** *Lond. Gaz.* No. 65/2 Monsieur Colbert is fallen very ill of a defluction upon his throat. **1744** FRANKLIN *Pennsylv. Fire-Places* Wks. (1887) I. 496 Women..get colds..and defluctions, which fall into their jaws and gums. **1781** GIBBON *Decl. & F.* II. xli. 517 A defluxion had fallen on his eyes. **1842** ABDY *Water Cure* (1843) 221 A scorbutic ulcer in the leg..attended with a great defluction on the part. **1860** MOTLEY *Netherl.* (1868) I. vii. 455 Owing to a bad cold with a defluxion in the eyes, she was unable at once to read.

†**3.** *concr.* Something that flows or runs down.

1615 CROOKE *Body of Man* 277 The Nature of Seede no man that I know hath yet essentially defined..Plato [calleth it] The defluxion of the spinall marrow. **1633** T. ADAMS *Exp. 2 Pet.* iii. 18 (1865) 884 We know..that he can..pour down putrid defluxions from above.

†**b.** *fig.* An effluence, emanation. [tr. Gr. ἀπορροή.] *Obs.*

1603 HOLLAND *Plutarch's Mor.* 1307 The defluxion of Osiris, and the very apparent image of him. **1678** CUDWORTH *Intell. Syst.* 15 According to Empedocles, Vision and other Sensations were made by ἀποῤῥοαὶ σχημάτων, the Defluxions of Figures, or Effluvia of Atoms.

†**de'fluxive**, *a. Obs.* [f. L. *deflux-*, ppl. stem (DEFLUX *v.*) + -IVE.] That is characterized by flowing down. Hence **de'fluxively** *adv.*

1655-60 STANLEY *Hist. Philos.* III. II. 133 Aliment, distributed by the veines through the whole frame defluxively.

defocus (diː'fəʊkəs), *v.* [f. DE- II. 1 + FOCUS *v.*] *trans.* To put out of focus; also *intr.*, to go out of focus. So **de'focus(s)ed** *ppl. a.*

1935 *Proc. Inst. Radio Engineers* XXIII. 1338 A defocused beam will cause..spot or pattern distortion. **1950** H. PENDER *Electr. Engineers' Handbk.* (ed. 4) II. 66 The apparent resolution is not appreciably impaired when the blue image is severely defocused. **1955** *Gloss. Terms Automatic Digital Computers (B.S.I.)* 9 The 'writing' beam is initially defocused so as to excite a small circular area of the screen. **1958** *Engineering* 21 Feb. 233/2 A more pleasing effect was obtained with the circular soft edged arrangement than with a de-focused primary beam. **1961** G. MILLERSON *Television Production* iii. 49 The director's only solution is.. to have cameras defocus when their shots are not being taken.

defœdation: see DEFEDATION.

de'fogger (diː'fɒgə(r)). [f. DE- II. 2 + FOG *sb.*[2] + -ER[1].] = DEMISTER, esp. one which clears condensed water vapour from the rear window of a motor vehicle.

1966 *Economist* 24 Dec. 1329/1 Some concessions are made to the industry's objections—rear window defoggers are not insisted on, for example. **1968** *Globe & Mail* (Toronto) 15 Jan. 19/7 (Advt.), 1968 Meteor; S33 Tudor hardtop... Power disc brakes, rear window de fogger. **1978** *Detroit Free Press* 16 Apr. F14/1 (Advt.), '76 Datsun B210 hatchback..tinted glass, rear defogger $2150.

†**de'foil**, *v.*[1] *Obs.* Also 7 deffoile, diff-. [ad. F. *défeuille-r*, in 13th c. *des-*, *deffueiller*, f. *des-*, *dé-* (DE- I. 6) + *feuille* leaf. Cf. med.L. *dēfoliāre.*] *trans.* To strip of leaves; = DEFOLIATE *v.*

1601 HOLLAND *Pliny* XVII. xxii, In disburgening and defoiling a vine. *Ibid.*, How much thereof must be diffoiled. *Ibid.*, It is not the manner to disburgen or deffoile altogether such trees.

defoil, *v.*[2] To trample down, crush, oppress, violate, defile: see DEFOUL *v.*

defoil *sb.*, var. form of DEFOUL *sb.*

defoliant (dɪ'fəʊlɪənt). [f. DEFOLI(ATE *v.* + -ANT[1].] A chemical used to cause defoliation.

1943 *N.Y. Herald Tribune* 7 Nov. 6 A cotton crop sprinkled with a specially prepared defoliant to make machine picking easier was harvested recently. **1956** *Nature* 3 Mar. 417/2 Research on the use of herbicides, arboricides and defoliants in East Africa. **1963** *Guardian* 1 May 8/5 The defoliants..are widely used by farmers. **1967** *Punch* 1 Mar. 302/2 The most powerful technological nation in the world has deployed its invention in massive weight; from 70,000-ton attack carriers, through flying headquarters equipped with computers, to defoliants for stripping the jungle of concealing vegetation.

defoliate (dɪ'fəʊlɪət), *a. rare.*[−0] [ad. med.L. *dēfoliāt-us*: see next.] 'Having cast, or being deprived of, its leaves' (*Syd. Soc. Lex.* 1883).

defoliate (dɪ'fəʊlɪeɪt), *v.* [f. med.L. *dēfoliāre*, f. DE- I. 6 + *folium* leaf. Cf. DEFOIL.] *trans.* To strip of leaves; also *fig.*

1793 W. ROBERTS *Looker-on* (1794) II. No. 48. 213 To contemplate the decay of a great and ornamented mind..to see it defoliated and withered. **1816** KIRBY & SP. *Entomol.* (1843) I. 173 One of these caterpillars..is often so numerous as to defoliate the apple trees by the road sides for miles. **1882** *Proc. Berw. Nat. Club* IX. 435 *Arbutus Unedo* was not only defoliated, but the stems..have been split.

Hence **de'foliator**, that which defoliates; an insect that strips trees of their leaves.

1887 *Amer. Naturalist* XXI. 580 Dr. Riley has published Bulletin No. 10 of the Division of Entomology, U.S. Dept. Agr., entitled 'Our Shade-Trees and their Insect Defoliators'. **1897** *Pop. Sci. Monthly* IV. 428 The leaf defoliators, as the rose chafer and flea beetle. **1936** *Forestry* X. 47 Repeated attacks by such forest insects as defoliators.

defoliation (diːfəʊlɪ'eɪʃən). [ad. L. type **dēfoliātiōn-em*, n. of action f. *dēfoliāre*: see prec. So in mod.Fr.] **a.** Loss or shedding of leaves.

1659 H. L'ESTRANGE *Alliance Div. Off.* 222 At the time of the defoliation, or fall of the leaf. **1791** E. DARWIN *Bot. Gard.* II. 18 *note*, The defoliation of deciduous trees is announced by the flowering of the Colchicum. **1866** *Treas. Bot.*, *Defoliation*, the casting off of leaves. **1884** *Nature* 9 Oct. 558/2 The observation of the first flowering and fruiting of plants, the foliation and defoliation of trees.

b. The deliberate destruction of foliage (for military purposes).

1964 *Economist* 25 July 345/2 'Defoliation' of the jungle by tactical atomic bombs. **1965** *Times* 25 Mar. 10/1 Mr. Goldwater was demanding the nuclear defoliation of the Vietnamese jungles.

deforce (dɪ'fɔəs), *v.* Also 5-6 deforse. [a. AF. *deforcer* (11th c.) = OF. *deforcier* (*des-*, *def-*), f. *des-*, *de-* (DE- I. 6) + *forcier*, *forcer* to FORCE (or from the Romanic forms of these): in med.L. *dif-*, *dēforciare* (Du Cange). Cf. EFFORCE, ENFORCE.]

1. *Law.* (*trans.*) To keep (something) by force or violence (*from* the person who has a right to it); to withhold wrongfully.

[**1292** BRITTON I. xix. §8 Nos eschetes defforcez (*transl.* Escheats deforced from us). *Ibid.* III. xxi. §1 Tiel qi la.. rente deforce tient (*tr.* who holds the rent deforced).] *c* **1470** HARDING *Chron.* lxxx. i, Arthure.. emperour of Rome by title of right, [Whiche deforced] by Lucius Romain, Pretendyng hym for emperour of might. **1609** SKENE *Reg. Maj.* 28 Command B. that..he..restore to M...her reasonabill dowrie..And inquire him, for quhat cause he deforces and deteins the samine fra her. **1765** *Lond. Chron.* 23 Nov. 500 The cutter is said to have deforced Capt. Duncan's boat..off the island of May. **1865** NICHOLS *Britton* II. 6 It sometimes happens..that he who has no right deforces the wardship from him who has a better right [*deforce la garde a celi qi major dreit ad*].

†**b.** *gen.* To take or keep away by force. *Obs.*

1430 LYDG. *Chron. Troy* II. xiv, For you my wyfe, for you myne owne Heleine, That be deforced fro me, welaway. **1494** FABYAN *Chron.* I. 215 (R.) This Lowys..maryed the doughter of Guy..the which after, for nerynesse of kynne, was deforced from the sayd Lowys.

2. To eject (a person) by force *from* his property; to keep (him) forcibly out·of the possession *of*; to deprive wrongfully.

1531 *Dial. on Laws Eng.* II. xxv. (1638) 109 Where a Parson of a Church is wrongfully deforced of his Dismes. **1540** *Act 32 Hen. VIII*, c. 7 §7 Personnes..dysseased, deforsed, wronged, or otherwyse..put from their lawfull inheritance. **1586** FERNE *Lacies Nobilitie* 35 Stephen was a wrongfull possessour of the Crowne, for he deforced Mawd ..of her right. **1602** FULBECKE *2nd Pt. Parall.* 57 A *Nuper obijt* ought to be brought by that Coparcener, who is deforced from the tenements, against all the other Coparceners which do deforce her. **1741** T. ROBINSON *Gavelkind* vi. 105 [He] enters on the whole Land on the Death of the Ancestor and deforces the other. **1865** NICHOLS *Britton* II. 257 Peter wrongfully deforces her of the third part of so much land.

3. *Sc. Law.* To prevent by force (an officer of the law) from executing his official duty.

1461 *Liber Pluscardensis* XI. xi. (1877) I. 399 Deforsand serrefis, masaris or sergeand. **1579** *Sc. Acts Jas. VI* (1597) §75 In case the officiar..beis violently deforced and stopped in execution of his office. **1609** SKENE *Reg. Maj.* Table 75 He quha deforces the kings officiars, and stops the taking of poynds. **1816** SCOTT *Antiq.* xlii, If you interrupt me in my duty, I will..declare myself deforced. **1885** *Manch. Exam.* 18 Mar. 4/7 Crofters charged with deforcing a sheriff's officer while attempting to serve summonses for arrears of rent.

†**4.** To commit rape upon, to force. *Sc. Obs.*

1528 LYNDESAY *Dreme* 1098 Tak tent, how prydful Tarquyne tynt his croun, For the deforsyng of Lucres. **1536** BELLENDEN *Cron. Scot.* (1821) I. 173 Mogallus..deforsit virginis and matronis.

†**de'force**, *sb. Sc. Obs.* [f. the vb.] = DEFORCEMENT.

1479 *Act. Dom. Conc.* 33 (Jam.) That Johne Lindissay.. sall restore to James lord Hammiltoune..a kow of a deforce, a salt mert, a mask fat. *Ibid.* 38 That he has made na deforss.

deforcement (dɪ'fɔəsmənt). *Law.* [a. AF. and OF. *deforcement* (12th c.), f. *deforcer*; in med.L. (Scotch Stat.) *deforciamentum*: see prec. and -MENT.]

1. 'The holding of any lands or tenements to which another person has a right' (Wharton, *Law Lex.*); the action of forcibly keeping a person out of possession of anything.

1609 SKENE *Reg. Maj.* cxxxv. 137 Gif any man complaines ..that he is vnjustlie deforced be sic ane man, of sic lands, or sic ane tenement..the maker of the deforcement sall be summoned incontinent. **1768** BLACKSTONE *Comm.* III. 172 The fifth and last species of injuries by ouster or privation of the freehold..is that by deforcement. *Ibid.* 174 Another species of deforcement is, where two persons have the same title to land, and one of them enters and keeps possession against the other.

2. *Sc. Law.* The forcible preventing of an officer of the law from execution of his office; such obstruction or resistance as is construed to amount to this.

1581 *Sc. Acts Jas. VI* (1597) §117 In all actiones of deforcementes, and breaking of arreistmentes. **1609** SKENE *Reg. Maj.* 2 Ane deforcement done to the kings officiar. **1708** J. CHAMBERLAYNE *St. Gt. Brit.* II. III. x. (1743) 434 The resisting him [the messenger at arms] is a crime in the law of Scotland, called deforcement. *a* **1805** A. CARLYLE *Autobiog.* 22 *note*, The thieves were collecting..in order to come to Dumfries on the day of the execution, and make a deforcement as they were conducting Jock to the gallows. **1884** *N. Brit. Daily Mail* 5 Aug. 4/3 Two aged women, tried at Stornoway for deforcement of a sheriff officer.

deforcer (dɪ'fɔəsə(r)). Also 6-9 deforceor, 6 *Sc.* -forsare, 7 -forsour. [a. AF. *deforceour*, *-eor*, f. *deforcer* to DEFORCE.]

1. *Law.* One who wrongfully ejects or keeps another out of possession; = DEFORCIANT.

1628 COKE *On Litt.* 331 b, The Deforceor holdeth it so fast, as the right owner is driuen to his reall Præcipe. **1641** *Termes de la Ley*, *Deforceor* is hee that overcommeth and casteth out with force, and he differeth from a disseisor, first in this, that a man may disseise another without force..then because a man may deforce another that never was in possession. **1656** BLOUNT *Glossogr.*, Deforsour. **1700** TYRRELL *Hist. Eng.* II. 1106 The Deforceors withal to be amerced. **1865** NICHOLS *Britton* II. 25 Let the deforceor be punished according to the tenor of our statutes.

2. *Sc. Law.* One who deforces an officer of the law: see DEFORCE 3.

1587 *Sc. Acts Jas. VI* (1597) §84 All deforcers of Officiares, in execution of their Office. **1609** SKENE *Reg. Maj.* 2 Gif the deforcer is convict..of the said deforcement.

†**3.** One who commits a rape: see DEFORCE 4.

1533 BELLENDEN *Livy* I. (1822) 101 Gif me youre handis and faith that the adulterare and deforsare of me [Lucretia] sall nocht leif unpunist.

deforciant (dɪ'fɔəsɪənt). *Law.* Also 7 deforceant. [a. AF. *deforceant*, pr. pple. of *deforcer*. Cf. med. (Anglo) L. *dēforcians.*] A person who deforces another or keeps him wrongfully out of possession of an estate.

[**1292** BRITTON III. xv. §3 Si le deforceaunt ne puse averrer la soute [unless the deforciant can aver payment].] **1585** in H. Hall *Soc. Eliz. Age* (1886) 239 Edward Essex levyed a fyne of the premyses to Hughe Stukeley deforciant. **1613** SIR H. FINCH *Law* (1636) 279 A fine is the acknowledging of an hereditament..to be his right that doth complaine. He that complaineth is called plaintife, and the other deforceant. **1767** BLACKSTONE *Comm.* II. 350 An acknowlegement from the deforciants (or those who keep the other out of possession). **1768** *Ibid.* III. 174 In levying a fine of lands, the person, against whom the fictitious action is brought upon a supposed breach of covenant, is called the *deforciant*. **1885** L. O. PIKE *Year-bks.* 12-13 *Edw. III* Introd. 60 Actions..in which the deforciant could not know the nature of the claim *per verba brevis*.

†**deforci'ation.** *Obs.* [ad. med.L. *dēforciātiōn-em* (*Leg. Quat. Burg.*), *disforciation-em* (*Leg.*

Normann.), n. of action f. *dē-*, *disforciāre* to DEFORCE.] = DEFORCEMENT.

[1695 KENNETT *Paroch. Antiq.* II. *Gloss.*, *Deforciatio*, a distraint or seizure of goods for satisfaction of a lawful debt.—Hence in Law Dictionaries, and under the anglicized form in BAILEY 1721 and modern Dicts. But the explanation is incorrect, the meaning in Kennett's Latin quot. being 'what is taken or held by force'.]

1864 WEBSTER, *Deforciation* (*Law*), a withholding by force or fraud from rightful possession; deforcement.

†**deforci'ator.** *Obs.* [a. med.L. *dēforciātor* (Du Cange), agent-n. from *dēforciāre* to DEFORCE.] = DEFORCER 1.

1549 *Act 3-4 Edw. VI*, c. 3 §1 Their Ingress and Egress were..letted by the same Deforciators.

deforest (dɪ'fɒrɪst), *v.* [f. DE- II. 2 + FOREST: cf. the synonyms DEAFFOREST, DISAFFOREST, DISFOREST, OF. *desforester*, *deforester*, med.L. *deafforestare*, *disafforestare*: see DE- I. 6.]

1. *Law.* To reduce from the legal position of forest to that of ordinary land; to make no longer a forest; = DISAFFOREST 1, DISFOREST 1.

1538 LELAND *Itin.* IV. 115 John Harman.. B. of Excester ..obteyned License to deforest the Chase there. **1759** B. MARTIN *Nat. Hist. Eng.* II. 105 One entire Forest, till deforested by the Kings.

2. *gen.* To clear or strip of forests or trees.

1880 [see DEFORESTING]. **1887** *Scribner's Mag.* II. 450 The region should be forest-clad; or even if now deforested, [etc.]. **1891** BRET HARTE *First Fam. Tasajara* x, [He] deforested the cañon.

Hence **de'forested** *ppl. a.*; **de'foresting** *vbl. sb.* and *ppl. a.*; also **defore'station**; **de'forester**.

1538 LELAND *Itin.* VII. 101 At the Deforestinge of the old Foreste of Kyngeswood. **1880** *Scribner's Mag.* Feb. 502 Most speculating deforesters go to the bad pecuniarily. **1880** *Standard* 10 Dec., By the deforesting of plains he has turned once fertile fields into arid deserts. **1884** *Chicago Advance* 25 Dec. 853 The native newspapers fear the deforestation of Japan. **1887** *Scribner's Mag.* I. 568 The deforested surface.

de'form, *sb. nonce-wd.* [f. DEFORM *v.*] The action of deforming, deformation: opp. to *reform.*

1831 *Fraser's Mag.* IV. 2 He..permitted the actual deform of his windows sooner than testify any sort of sympathy with the sham reform of parliament.

deform (dɪ'fɔːm), *a. arch.* Forms: 4–6 defourme, 6–7 deforme, 7– deform. [a. obs. F. *deforme* (1604 in Godef.) = mod.F. *difforme*, or ad. L. *dēform-is* (in med.L. also *difformis*) deformed, misshapen, ugly, disgraceful, f. DE- I. 6 + *forma* shape. Cf. also DIFFORM.] Deformed, misshapen, shapeless, distorted; ugly, hideous.

1382 WYCLIF *Gen.* xli. 19 Other seven oxen..defourme and leene. **1508** FISHER *Wks.* (1876) 98 With many..spottes of synne we haue..made it defourme in the syght of god. **1591** SYLVESTER *Du Bartas* I. i. (1641) 3/2 A confus'd heap, a Chaos most deform. **1667** MILTON *P.L.* XI. 494 Sight so deform what heart of rock could long Drie-ey'd behold? *a*1734 NORTH *Examen* I. iii. ¶16. 133 The monstrous and deform Tales of Oates. **1872** BROWNING *Fifine* xliii, Every face, no matter how deform.

deform (dɪ'fɔːm), *v.*[1] Also 5–7 dif-, 5 dyf-. [a. OF. *deformer*, also *desformer*, *defformer*, and (15th c.) *difformer*, mod.F. *déformer*. The first is ad. L. *dēformāre*, f. DE- I. 6 + *forma* shape; the second represents the Rom. var. *disformare*, and the last its med.L. repr. *difformāre*. Thence the Eng. variants in *de-*, *dif-*. Cf. also Pr. *deformar*, It. *deformare*, Sp. *desformar*.]

1. *trans.* To mar the appearance, beauty, or excellence of; to make ugly or unsightly; to disfigure, deface. **a.** *lit.*

*c*1450 [see DEFORMED 1]. **1509** BARCLAY *Shyp of Folys* (1570) 8 Thus by this deuising such counterfaited things, They diffourme that figure that God himselfe hath made. **1530** RASTELL *Bk. Purgat.* Prol., Some spot..wherby he is somwhat deformed. *a*1627 HAYWARD *Edw. VI* (1630) 16 He ..wasted Tinedale and the marches, and deformed the country with ruine and spoile. **1634** SIR T. HERBERT *Trav.* (1638) 80 Never did poore wretch shed more teares.. deforming her sweet face. **1702** ROWE *Tamerlane* v. i. 2012 To deform thy gentle Brow with Frowns. **1858** HAWTHORNE *Fr. & It. Jrnls.* (1872) I. 37 The square..had mean little huts, deforming its ample space. **1861** GEN. P. THOMPSON *Audi Alt.* III. clxxv. 208 The blackest pirate that ever deformed his face with beard.

b. *fig.*

1533 BELLENDEN *Livy* III. (1822) 308 This honest victorie ..wes deformit be ane schamefull jugement gevin be Romane pepil. **1756** C. LUCAS *Ess. Waters* I. Ded., It is a vice that deforms human nature. **1855** MACAULAY *Hist. Eng.* IV. 535 The earlier part of his discourse was deformed by pedantic divisions and subdivisions.

†**c.** To put out of proper form, disarrange. *Obs.*

1725 POPE *Odyss.* XIV. 252 The fair ranks of battle to deform. **1783** *Hist. Europe* in *Ann. Reg.* 66/2 Breaking the British line, and totally deforming their order of battle.

†**d.** *intr.* To become deformed or disfigured; to lose its beauty. *Obs. rare.*

1760 BEATTIE *Ode to Hope* II. iii, To-morrow the gay scene deforms!

2. *trans.* To mar the form or shape of; to misshape. See also DEFORMED.

*c*1400, **1483** [see DEFORMED 2]. **1500–20** DUNBAR *Poems* lxxxiv. 19 A crippill, or a creatour Deformit as ane oule be dame Natour. **1590** SHAKS. *Com. Err.* I. ii. 100 Darke working Sorcerers that change the mind: Soule-killing Witches, that deforme the bodie. **1594** —— *Rich. III*, I. i. 20 Cheated of Feature by dissembling Nature, Deform'd, vnfinish'd. **1703** MOXON *Mech. Exerc.* 94 Keep the Bitt straight to the hole you pierce, lest you deform the hole.

3. To alter the form of; in *Physics*, to change the normal shape of, put out of shape: cf. DEFORMATION 3.

1702 *Eng. Theophrast.* 116 Nothing so deforms certain Courtiers, as the Presence of the Prince; it so alters their Air and debases their Looks that a Man can scarce know them. **1876** GLADSTONE *Homeric Synchr.* 222 This completely alters and deforms the idea of the earth as a plane surface. **1883** *Nature* XXVII. 405 The hard steel..breaks up or deforms the projectiles.

¶**4.** Obs. var. of DIFFORM *v.*

†**deform,** *v.*[2] *Obs. rare.* In 4 defourme, defforme. [ad. L. *dēformāre* to form, fashion, describe, f. DE- I. 1, 3 + *formāre* to FORM.] *trans.* To form, fashion, delineate.

1382 WYCLIF *2 Cor.* iii. 7 The mynistracioun of deeth defformyd [*v.r.* defourmyde, Vulg. *deformata*] by lettris [**1388** write bi lettris] in stoones.

deformable (dɪ'fɔːməb(ə)l), *a.* [f. DEFORM *v.* or *a.* (or their L. originals) + -ABLE. Cf. CONFORMABLE.]

†**1.** Affected with, or of the nature of, a deformity; deformed; ugly. *Obs.*

*c*1450 *Mirour Saluacioun* 4296 Thaire bodyes than shalle be more defourmable. **1576** BAKER *Jewell of Health* 99 The hyghe rednesse of the face being deformable. **1677** GALE *Crt. Gentiles* IV. 17 Splendor and Brightnesse is essential to Beautie..Shadows and Darknesses are deformed, and render althings deformable.

2. Capable of being deformed or put out of shape. Hence **deforma'bility**.

deformalize: see DE- II. 1.

†**deformate,** *a. Obs. rare.* [ad. L. *dēformāt-us*, pa. pple. of *dēformāre*.] Deformed, disfigured.

*c*1450 HENRYSON *Compl. Creseide* (R.), Whan she sawe her visage so deformate.

deformation (diːfɔː'meɪʃən). Also 5 diff-, 6 dyff-. [ad. L. *dēformātiōn-em* (in med.L. also *dif-*), n. of action from L. *dēformāre* to DEFORM. Cf. F. *déformation* (14th c. in Hatzf., and in Cotgr.); admitted into *Dict. Acad.* 1835.]

1. The action (or result) of deforming or marring the form or beauty of; disfigurement, defacement.

*c*1440 LYDG. *Secrees* 500 Difformacyons of Circes and meede. **1623** COCKERAM, *Deformation*, a spoiling. **1633** BP. HALL *Hard Texts* 86 If by these means of deformation thy heart shall be set off from her. **1650** BULWER *Anthropomet.* 96 Which deformation is so pleasing to their Eyes, that men ..are commonly seen with their Eares so arrayed. **1734** WATTS *Relig. Juv.* (1789) 85 Could you..recover them from the deformations and disgraces of time. **1877** J. D. CHAMBERS *Div. Worship* 13 The deformations perpetrated by Wyatt [in a building].

2. a. Alteration of form for the worse; *esp.*, in controversial use, the opposite of *reformation.*

1546 BALE *Eng. Votaries* II. (1550) 48 b, Johan Capgraue writeth y[t] a great reformacyon (a dyfformacyon he shulde haue seyd) was than in the Scottish churche. **1581** PETTIE *Guazzo's Civ. Conv.* II. (1586) 81 To seeme young..[they] convert their silver haires into golden ones..this their transformation or rather deformation [etc.]. *a*1638 MEDE *Disc.* xlii. Wks. (1677) 236 These are the Serpents first-born .. begotten..by spiritual deformation, as they are Devils. **1651** N. BACON *Disc. Govt. Eng.* II. xxxv. (1739) 159 The great work of Reformation, or rather Deformation in the Worship of God. **1774** A. GIB *Present Truth* II. 246 The grievous deformation which has been taking place in the Church state. **1832** WHATELY in *Life* (1866) I. 153 A most extensive ecclesiastical reformation (or deformation, as it may turn out). **1891** W. LOCKHART *Chasuble* 7 Before the Protestant Deformation of religion in the sixteenth century.

b. An altered form of a word in which its proper form is for some purpose perverted:

e.g. the various deformations of the word *God*, as *'od, cod, dod, cot, cock, cop*, etc., formerly so common in asseverations, etc., to avoid overt profanity of language, and the breach of the Third Commandment, or of statutes such as that of 3 James I, c. 21 'For the preventing and avoiding of the great abuse of the holy name of God in stage-plays, interludes' [etc.].

3. a. Alteration of form or shape; relative displacement of the parts of a body or surface without breach of continuity; an altered form *of.*

1846 CAYLEY *Wks.* I. 234 Two skew surfaces are said to be deformations of each other, when for corresponding generating lines the torsion is always the same. **1857** WHEWELL *Hist. Induct. Sc.* III. 54 The isogonal curves may be looked upon as deformations of the curve. **1869** PHIPSON tr. *Guillemin's The Sun* (1870) 81 The deformation of the solar disc by refraction. **1893** FORSYTH *Functions of a Complex Variable* 333 In the continuous Deformation of a surface there may be stretching and there may be bending; but there must be no joining. **1900** *Proc. R. Soc.* LXV. 90 'Flow' or non-elastic deformation in metals. **1916** C. A. EDWARDS *Physico-Chem. Properties of Steel* xi. 125 One of the most useful properties possessed by metals is the facility with which they undergo plastic deformation when pressed, hammered, or rolled. **1953** AITCHISON & PUMPHREY *Engin. Steels* ix. 364 The deformation or warping is also partly attributable to the thermal stresses which are set up in the metal. **1967** H. J. STERN *Rubber* (ed. 2) xi. 490 Rapidly alternating stresses or deformations..give rise to the development of heat in the rubber. **1968** COULSON & RICHARDSON *Chem. Engin.* (ed. 2) II. iv. 152 Deformation of the drop is opposed by the surface tension forces so that very small drops retain their spherical shape.

b. *Geol.* The process by which a stratum, mass of rock, etc., undergoes change of form or structure by being compressed, faulted, folded, etc.; also, the result of this process. Also *attrib.*

1882 A. GEIKIE *Text-bk. Geol.* 312 Evidences of actual deformation within the mass of rock. **1904** CHAMBERLIN & SALISBURY *Geol.* (1905) I. 547 It is theoretically possible that deformation of the sub-crust may result from the internal transfer of heat without regard to external loss. **1937** *Q. Jrnl. Geol. Soc.* XCIII. 602 Such [sedimentation] fabrics in rocks of this type are never so well marked as deformation fabrics. **1955** *Sci. Amer.* July 40/1 There is little doubt that these four huge fracture zones resulted from some massive deformation of the earth's crust. **1963** E. S. HILLS *Elem. Struct. Geol.* iv. 77 It is therefore admissible to draw analogies between the mechanics of deformation of such rocks with the deformation of metals, both as to the effects in individual crystals and for the crystal aggregate as a whole.

deformational (diːfɔː'meɪʃənəl), *a.* [f. DEFORMATION + -AL.] Of or pertaining to deformation.

1903 *Nature* 12 Feb. 359/1 Several deformational movements had affected this district. **1965** G. J. WILLIAMS *Econ. Geol. N.Z.* vi. 66/2 Retrogressive metamorphism accompanying a deformational phase. **1970** *Physics Bull.* Apr. 174/2 Physical properties such as deformational behaviour, strength characteristics,..and thermal properties.

deformative (dɪ'fɔːmətɪv), *a. nonce-wd.* [f. L. *dēformāt-*, ppl. stem + -IVE.] Having the property of deforming or altering for the worse.

1641 *Prelat. Episc.* 10 Whither their courts be reformative or deformative.

deformed (dɪ'fɔːmd), *ppl. a.* Also 5 dyffourmed, difformed. [f. DEFORM *v.* + -ED[1].]

†**1.** Marred in appearance; disfigured, defaced.

*c*1450 *St. Cuthbert* (Surtees) 4115 His face was deformed and bolnyd. **1535** COVERDALE *Isa.* lii. 13 Y[e] multitude shal wondre vpon him, because his face shalbe so deformed & not as a mans face. **1553** EDEN *Treat. Newe Ind.* (Arb.) 23 Theyr women are deformed by reason of theyr greate eyes, greate mouthes and greate nosethrilles. **1631** WEEVER *Anc. Fun. Mon.* 791 Beholding the deformed ruines, he could hardly refraine from teares. **1632** LITHGOW *Trav.* VI. 253 In all this deformed Countrey, wee saw neyther house, nor Village.

2. Marred in shape, misshapen, distorted; unshapely, of an ill form. Now chiefly of persons: Misshapen in body or limbs.

*c*1400 MAUNDEV. (1839) v. 47 A monster is a þing difformed aȝen kynde. **1483** CAXTON *Gold. Leg.* 427/2 The most dysfourmed and most myserable he sat nyghe hym. **1574** tr. *Littleton's Tenures* 24 a, One that hath but one foote, or one hande, or is deformed. *c*1600 SHAKS. *Sonn.* cxiii, The most sweet fauor, or deformedst creature. **1665** SIR T. HERBERT *Trav.* (1677) 338 Many deformed Pagotha's are here worshipped. **1675** TRAHERNE *Chr. Ethics* vi. 69 Lions have an inclination to their grim mistresses, and deformed bears a natural affection to their whelps. **1752** JOHNSON *Rambler* No. 196 ¶7 Of his children, some may be deformed, and others vicious. **1869** W. P. MACKAY *Grace & Truth* (1875) 247 A poor deformed fellow.

†**3.** Of irregular form; shapeless, formless. *Obs.*

1555 EDEN *Decades* 200 Branches full of large and deformed leaves. **1567** *Satir. Poems Reform.* iii. 7 Ane King at euin..At morne bot ane deformit lumpe of clay. **1655–60** STANLEY *Hist. Philos.* (1701) 186/1 Which..he from a deformed confusion reduced to beautiful order. **1677** HALE *Prim. Orig. Man.* IV. ii. 297 The great Moles Chaotica..in its first deformed exhibition of its appearance..had the shape of Water.

4. *fig.* Perverted, distorted; morally ugly, offensive, or hateful.

1555 EDEN *Decades* To Rdr. (Arb.) 53 The monstrous and deformed myndes of the people mysshapened with phantastical opinions. **1604** MARSTON *Malcontent* IV. iii, Sure thou would'st make an excellent elder in a deformed Church. **1628** PRYNNE *Love-lockes* 49 What a deformed thing is it for a man to doe any womanish thing! **1667** MILTON *P.L.* VI. 387 Deformed rout Enter'd, and foul disorder. **1860** PUSEY *Min. Proph.* 182 Deformed as is all oppression, yet to oppress the poor, has an unnatural hideousness of its own.

deformedly (dɪ'fɔːmɪdlɪ, dɪ'fɔːmdlɪ), *adv.* Now *rare.* [f. prec. + -LY[2].] In a deformed or disfigured manner; misshapenly, ill-favouredly.

1593 NASHE *Christ's T.* (1613) 21 You..cast them to the Foules of the ayre, to bee deformedly torne in peeces. **1611** SPEED *Hist. Gt. Brit.* IX. viii. (1632) 588 His fingers deformedly growing together. **1634** SIR T. HERBERT *Trav.* (1638) 349 A speckled Toad-fish..not unlike a Tench, but ..more..deformedly painted. **1667** H. MORE *Div. Dial.* v. v. (1713) 411 He that keeps not to the right cloathing will be found most deformedly naked. **1685** —— *Paralip. Prophet.* 412.

†**b.** *fig.* With moral deformity. *Obs.*

1610 HEALEY *St. Aug. Citie of God* 858 Erring more deformedly..against the expresse word of God.

†**de'formedness.** *Obs. rare.* [-NESS.] The quality of being deformed; deformity, ugliness.

1588 W. AVERELL *Comb. Contrarieties* B ij b, Howe doth your gluttonie chaunge Natures comlines into foule deformednes?

deformer (dɪˈfɔːmə(r)). [f. DEFORM *v.*[1] + -ER[1].] One who or that which deforms; in controversial use, the opposite of *reformer*.

1562 WINȜET *Cert. Tractates* iii. Wks. 1888 I. 26 The principall deformare of his allegeit reformatioun. **1592** NASHE *P. Penilesse* F, A mightie deformer of men's manners and features is this vnnecessarie vice [drunkenness]. **1639** T. GOODWIN *On Revelation* Wks. II. II. 129 (R.) To reduce our worship, etc. now into the pattern of the first four or five hundred years (which is the plausible pretence of our new deformers) is to bring Popery again in. **1689** T. PLUNKET *Char. Gd. Commander* 54 Deformers, not Reformers, still excite Informers, Non-conformers, to indite. **1882** *Atlantic Monthly* XLIX. 336 These literary deformers.

deformeter (dɪˈfɔːmɪtə(r)). [f. DEFORM *v.*[1] + -METER.] An instrument for measuring deformation. Also *attrib.*

1927 G. E. BEGGS in *Jrnl. Franklin Inst.* CCIII. 380 The deformeter apparatus..consists of very precise means for producing known, but very small, displacements at sections where stress is sought, and optical means for measuring the deflections of the model at..load points. *Ibid.*, An indeterminate frame connected to the deformeter gauges and in position for deformation readings. **1946** *Nature* 20 July 91/2 Research work into structural analysis by the deformeter.

†**deˈformidable**, *a. Obs. rare*[−1]. [? A mixture of *deformable* and *formidable*.] Tending to deformation.

1631 WEEVER *Anc. Fun. Mon.* Ep. to Rdr. 1 Their brasen Inscriptions erazed, torne away, and pilfered, by which inhumane, deformidable act, the honourable memory of many..persons deceased, is extinguished.

deforming (dɪˈfɔːmɪŋ), *vbl. sb.* [-ING[1].] The action of the verb DEFORM, q.v.

1552 HULOET, Deformynge, *vitiatio.*

deˈforming, *ppl. a.* [-ING[2].] That deforms: see the verb.

1870 *Daily News* 19 Dec., Incongruity is a deforming feature. **1892** LD. KELVIN in *Pall Mall G.* 1 Dec. 6/3 He had now..a..demonstration of elastic yielding in the earth as a whole, under the influence of a deforming force.

deformity (dɪˈfɔːmɪtɪ). Also 5 dif-, 5–6 dyff-. [a. OF. *deformité* (*deffformeteit*, *defformité*, *desformité*), ad. L. *dēformitās*, f. *dēformis*: see DEFORM *a.* and -ITY. In mod.F. *difformité*.]

1. The quality or condition of being marred or disfigured in appearance; disfigurement; unsightliness, ugliness.

c **1450** *Crt. of Love* clxvii, For other have their ful shape and beaute, And we..ben in deformite. **1483** CAXTON *Gold. Leg.* 431/1 Wythout abhomynacion of dyfformyte ne of ordure or fylthe. **1514** BARCLAY *Cyt. & Uplondyshm.* (Percy Soc.) 25 No fautes with Moryans is blacke dyfformyte, Because all the sorte lyke of theyr favour be. **1530** RASTELL *Bk. Purgat.* III. viii. 2 [The linen cloths] had no such spottes or tokens of deformyte to the eye. **1658** SIR T. BROWNE *Hydriot.* iii. (1736) 31 Christians have handsomely glossed the Deformity of Death by careful Consideration of the Body, and civil Rites. **1634** SIR T. HERBERT *Trav.* (1638) 261 Lastly, they cleanse themselves with purer water, supposing contaminated deformitie washt off. **1762–71** H. WALPOLE *Vertue's Anecd. Paint.* (1786) I. 181 Beautifull Gothic architecture was engrafted on Saxon deformity. **1805** *Med. Jrnl.* XIV. 107 To prevent the propagation of disease [small-pox], and its consequent effects, deformity.

2. The quality or condition of being deformed or misshapen; *esp.* bodily misshapenness or malformation; abnormal formation of the body or of some bodily member.

c **1440** *Gesta Rom.* lxxviii. 396 (Add. MS.), A dwerfe of a litill stature, hauyng..a bose in his back, ande crokide fete ..ande full of alle diformyte. **1494** FABYAN *Chron.* VII. 330 Edmunde..surnamed Crowke backe, was the..eldest; albe it he was put by, by y[e] meane of his fadre, for his deformytye. **1587** GOLDING *De Mornay* x. 138 But how can mater be without forme, seeing that euen deformitie it selfe is a kinde of forme? **1594** SHAKS. *Rich. III*, I. i. 27 To see my Shadow in the Sunne, And descant on mine owne Deformity. *Ibid.* I. ii. 57 Blush, blush, thou lumpe of fowle Deformitie. **1643** SIR T. BROWNE *Relig. Med.* I. §16 The Chaos: wherin..to speak strictly, there was no deformity, because no forme. **1717** LADY M. W. MONTAGU *Let. to C'tess of Mar* 16 Jan., Their fondness for these pieces of deformity [dwarfs]. **1801** *Med. Jrnl.* V. 41 In cases of deformity of the pelvis. **1856** KANE *Arct. Expl.* II. i. 22 Rightly clad, he is a lump of deformity waddling over the ice.

3. (with *a* and *pl.*) An instance of deformity; a disfigurement or malformation; now usually *spec.* a malformation of the body or of some bodily member or organ.

1413 LYDG. *Pilgr. Sowle* II. xlv. (1859) 52 The fowle spottys, and wonderful defourmytees, whiche he shold apperceyuen in his owne persone. **1578** LYTE *Dodoens* IV. lvii. 518 Sonne burning, and other suche deformities of the face. *a* **1662** HEYLYN *Laud* I. (1671) 204 Those deformities in it [St. Paul's] which by long time had been contracted. **1794** SULLIVAN *View Nat.* V. 382 Others..carry..maladies and deformities about them, from the cradle to the grave. **1807–26** S. COOPER *First Lines Surg.* (ed. 5) 411 The tumour sometimes creates no particular inconvenience; and is merely a deformity.

b. *transf.* A deformed being or thing.

1698 FRYER *Acc. E. India* 44 Their Gods..were cut in horrid Shapes.. to represent the Divinity..yet I cannot imagine such Deformities could ever be invented for that end. **1817** BYRON *Manfred* I. i, A bright deformity on high, The monster of the upper sky! **1838** DICKENS *Nich. Nick.* viii, Children with the countenances of old men, deformities with irons upon their limbs.

4. *fig.* Moral disfigurement, ugliness, or crookedness.

c **1400** MAUNDEV. (Roxb.) xxi. 141 Purged and clene of all vice and alkyn deformitee. **1561** T. NORTON *Calvin's Inst.* I. xv. (1634) 74 The corruption and deformitie of our nature. **1696** STANHOPE *Chr. Pattern* (1711) 71 If the deformity of his neighbour's actions happen to represent that of his own. **1741** MIDDLETON *Cicero* II. vii. 109 The deformity of Pompey's conduct. **1860** EMERSON *Cond. of Life, Behaviour* Wks. (Bohn) II. 382 It held bad manners up, so that churls could see the deformity.

b. (with *a* and *pl.*) A moral disfigurement.

1571 CAMPION *Hist. Irel.* II. v. (1633) 80 They declined now to such intollerable deformities of life and other superstitious errors. **1576** FLEMING *Panopl. Epist.* 248, I supposed it a great deformitie, and disorder. **1705** STANHOPE *Paraphr.* I. 22 Those Vicious Habits which are a Deformity to Christians. **1855** MACAULAY *Hist. Eng.* IV. 333 Cromwell had tried to correct the deformities of the representative system.

¶**5.** Misused for DIFFORMITY, difference or diversity of form; want of uniformity or conformity.

1531–2 LATIMER in Foxe *A. & M.* (1563) 1331/1 Better it were to haue a deformitie in preaching..then to haue suche a vniformitie that the sely people shoulde..continue still in ..ignoraunce. *a* **1623** PEMBLE *Grace & Faith* (1635) 49 The greatest deformity and disagreement..betweene his knowledge..and his application thereof to practice. **1658** SIR T. BROWNE *Garden of Cyrus* ii. 45 The Funeral bed of King Cheops..which holds seven in length and four foot in bredth, had no great deformity from this measure. *a* **1708** BEVERIDGE *Priv. Th.* I. (1730) 12 This Deformity to the Will and Nature of God, is that which we call Sin. **1788** KAMES *Elem. Crit.* (ed. 7) II. 490 A remarkable uniformity among creatures of the same kind, and a deformity [*other edd.* diff-] no less remarkable among creatures of different kinds.

†**deˈformly**, *adv. Obs.* [f. DEFORM *a.* + -LY[2].] In a 'deform' manner, with distortion, deformedly.

a **1684** LEIGHTON *Serm. Habak.* iii. 17, 18 (R.) A limb out of joint, which..moves both deformely and painfully. *a* **1734** NORTH *Lives* (1890) II. 335 [He] often laughed, but (as his visage was then distorted) most deformly.

deforse, etc., obs. forms of DEFORCE, etc.

defortify: see DE- II. 1.

defossion (dɪˈfɒʃən). [mod.L. *dēfossiōn-em*, n. of action from L. *dēfodĕre* to bury (in the earth).] (See quot.: but the etymological meaning of the word is simply 'burying, interment'.)

1753 CHAMBERS *Cycl. Supp.*, *Defossion*, *Defossio*, the punishment of burying alive, inflicted among the Romans, on vestal virgins guilty of incontinency. [Hence in mod. Dicts.]

†**deˈfoul, deˈfoil**, *v. Obs.* Forms: α. 3–5 defoule-n, 4–6 defoul(e, defowl(e, (5 defoulle, devoul, def(f)ule, diffowl, dyffowl, 5–6 diffoule). β. 4–6 defoyle, (5 defuyl(e, diffoyle, defoylle), 5–6 defoil. See also DEFILE. [ME. a. OF. *defoule-r* (*defoler*, *-fuler*, *-fuller*) to trample down, oppress, outrage, violate, deflower, f. DE- I. 1 + *fouler* (*foler, fuler*) 'to tread, stampe, or trample on, to bruise or crush by stamping' Cotgr. (= Pr. *folar*, Sp. *hollar*, It. *follare*):—late L. **fullāre* to stamp with the feet, to full (cloth), connected with L. *fullo, -ōnem* fuller, med.L. *fullātōrium* a fulling-mill, etc. Senses 1–5 existed already in OF.; the senses 'trample in the mud', and 'violate chastity', thus coming with the word into English, naturally suggested that it contained the native adjective FOUL, OE. *fúl*, and gave rise to senses 6–8, which derive from 'foul', as well as (apparently) to the collateral form DEFILE (q.v.), on the analogy of the equivalence of *befoul*, *befile*. The phonology of the variant *defuyle*, *defoyle* (found nearly as early as *defoule*), has not been satisfactorily made out: see FOIL *v.* It occurs in the earlier senses, and does not appear to have been specially connected with *defile*.]

1. *trans.* To trample under foot; tread down.

α. *c* **1290** *S. Eng. Leg.* I. 375/297 Defoulede huy [þe bones] weren so. **1297** R. GLOUC. (1724) 536 Hii..orne on him mid hor hors, & defoulede him vaste. *a* **1340** HAMPOLE *Psalter* xc. 13 Þou sall defoul þe lyon & þe dragon. **1340** *Ayenb.* 167 Mochel is defouled mid þe uet of uolleres þe robe of scarlet, erþan þet þe kuen his do an. **1382** WYCLIF *Matt.* vii. 6 Nethir sende ȝe ȝoure margaritis..bifore swyne, lest perauenture thei defoulen hem with theire feet [Vulg. *conculcent*]. *c* **1400** *Three Kings Cologne* 50 On þe morwe þei siȝen þe weye gretlich defowled with hors fete and oþir beestys. **1483** CAXTON *Gold. Leg.* 181 b/1 Thenne the knyghtes..bete & defowleden nazaryen under theyr feet. **1574** tr. *Littleton's Tenures* 66 b, Wasting and defouling of their grasse.

β. *c* **1330** *Arth. & Merl.* 9297 Ther was defoiled King Rion Vnder stedes fet mani on. **1470–85** MALORY *Arthur* I. xiv, That were fowle defoyled vnder horsfeet. **1525** LD. BERNERS *Froiss.* II. xv. 30 As they rode abrode, thay beate downe and defoyled their cornes..and wolde nat kepe the highe wayes.

b. *absol.* or *intr.*

β. *a* **1300** *K. Alis.* 2463 Me myghte y-seo ther knyghtis defoille, Heorten blede, braynes boyle, Hedes tomblen.

2. To bruise, break, crush (materially).

c **1300** *Beket* 1100 The bond is undo And al defouled, and we beoth delyvred so [cf. Psalm cxxiv. 7]. *a* **1325** *Prose Psalter* xlv[i]. 9 He shal de-foule bowe and breke armes. *c* **1386** CHAUCER *Pars. T.* ¶207 He was woundid for oure mysdede, and defouled by oure felonyes. **14..** *Voc.* in Wr.-Wülcker 575/12 *Contero*, to breke or defoule. *a* **1533** LD. BERNERS *Huon* cxxi. 433 The Gryffon so sore defowlyd and bet hym that he could not ryse vp.

3. To trample down or crush (figuratively); to oppress; to outrage, maltreat, abuse.

α. *c* **1300** *St. Brandan* 508 The develen..nome thane wrecche faste, And defoulede him stronge y-nouȝ and amidde the fur him caste. *c* **1325** *E.E. Allit. P.* B. 1129 If folk be defowled by vnfre chaunce. **1393** LANGL. *P. Pl.* C. XVIII. 195 How ryght holy men lyueden, How thei defouleden here fleessh. *a* **1400** *Relig. Pieces fr. Thornton MS.* (1867) 46 To refuse it [ilke a bodily ymagynacyone] and to defule it, þat it may see the selfe swylke as it es. **1485** CAXTON *Chas. Gt.* 108 Thou hast gretely defouled me by oultrage. **1508** DUNBAR *Flyting* 236 Oule, rere and ȝowle, I sall defowll thy pryde.

β. *c* **1350** *Will. Palerne* 4614 Alle ȝour fon þat with fors defoyled ȝou long. **1494** FABYAN *Chron.* 4 Of Danes, whiche both landes defoyled By their outrage. **1548** HALL *Chron.* (1809) 486 Perkyn..so many times had been defoyled and vanquished.

4. To violate the chastity of, deflower, debauch. Often, esp. in later use, with the sense of *defile.*

α. *c* **1290** *S. Eng. Leg.* I. 181/24 Woldest þov defouli mi bodi? *c* **1330** R. BRUNNE *Chron.* (1810) 317 Philip..Defoules þer wyues, þer douhtres lay bi, þer lordes slouh with knyues. *c* **1400** MAUNDEV. (Roxb.) xxxi. 141 After þe first nyght þat þase wymmen er so defouled. *c* **1450** LONELICH *Grail* xliii. 163 And for Child beryng neuere defowlid was, but Evere Clene virgine be Goddis gras. **1483** CAXTON *G. de la Tour* C vj, Their suster that so had be depuceled or defowled. **1523** LD. BERNERS *Froiss.* I. xxxvii. 51 The Spanyerdes.. pilled the towne, and slewe dyuers, and defowled maydens. **1596** DALRYMPLE *Leslie's Hist. Scot.* I. 122 Gif quha defoulis a nothir manis wyfe.

β. **1430–40** *Chaucer's Frankl. T.* 668 (Camb. MS.) Now sythe that maydenys haddyn swich dispit To been defoyled [*other MSS.* defouled] with manys foule delyt. **1486** *Act 3 Hen. VII*, c. 2 Women..been..married to such Mis-doers ..or defoiled, to the great Displeasure of God.

5. To violate (laws, holy places, etc.); to break the sanctity of, profane, pollute.

α. **13..** *Version of Ps.* lxxviii. 1 (in *Wyclif's Bible* Pref. 4 *note*), Thei defouledyn thin hooli temple. **1382** WYCLIF *Matt.* xii. 5 In sabothis prestis in the temple defoulen the sabothis. *c* **1400** MAUNDEV. (1839) xii. 137 The Jewes..han defouled the Lawe. **1485** CAXTON *Chas. Gt.* 42 He hath.. deffuled chyrches. **1491** —— *Vitas Patr.* (W. de W. 1495) I. xxxv. 29 a/1 The name of our blessyd sauyour..[was] horrybly dispysed & defouled. **1513** DOUGLAS *Æneis* X. vii. 69 The quhilk..Defowlit his fadderis bed incestuusly. **1614** T. WHITE *Martyrd. St. George* B ij b, It moued not the Tyrant to behold The Martirs goodly body so defowld.

β. **13..** *Prose Psalter* lxxviii. 1 Hij filden [*Dublin MS.* defoilyd] þyn holy temple. *c* **1450** *St. Cuthbert* (Surtees) 7373 My kirke þou hase defuyled. **1481** CAXTON *Tulle on Friendsh.* C iij, That frendship were hurte or defoylled. **1549–62** STERNHOLD & H. *Ps.* lxxix, Thy temple they defoile.

6. To render (materially) foul, filthy, or dirty; to pollute, defile, dirty.

α. *c* **1320** R. BRUNNE *Medit.* 506 With wete and eke dung þey hym defoule. **1402** HOCCLEVE *Letter of Cupid* 186 That bird..ys dyshonest..that vseth to defoule his ovne neste. **1530** RASTELL *Bk. Purgat.* III. viii, Yf ony of those table clothes or napkyns be defouled with dust fylth or other foule mater. **1576** TURBERV. *Venerie* 100 An Hart defowlant the water.

β. **1483** CAXTON *Gold. Leg.* 15 b/1 Thy desyrous vysage.. the Jewes with their spyttynges have defoylled. **1528** ROY *Rede me* (Arb.) 113 Henns and capons Defoylynge theym with their durt. **1548** UDALL, etc. *Erasm. Par. Luke* xxiv. 191 Not stained or defoiled. **1600** FAIRFAX *Tasso* VIII. lx, With dust and gore defoiled.

7. *fig.* **a.** To defile or pollute morally; to corrupt.

α. *a* **1340** HAMPOLE *Psalter* 518 Defouland his elde in syn. *c* **1380** WYCLIF *Wks.* (1880) 129 To kepe hym self unblekkid or defoulid fro þis world. *c* **1440** HYLTON *Scala Perf.* (W. de W. 1494) I. lxiii, Wyth thy pryde thou defowlest all thy good dedes. **1484** CAXTON *Chivalry* 45 Chyualrye..is defouled by coward men and faynt of herte. **1540** TAVERNER *Postils, Exhort. bef. Commun.*, Man, which is so much defouled & corrupt in all kynde of unryghtuousnes. *a* **1555** PHILPOT *Exam. & Writ.* (Parker Soc.) 373 He defouleth the whole faith of his testimony, by the falsifying of one part.

β. **1398** TREVISA *Barth. De P.R.* II. ii. (1495) 29 Angels.. ben not defoyled wyth none affeccyon. *c* **1440** HYLTON *Scala Perf.* (W. de W. 1494) I. xliii, Yf thou be defoyled wyth vaynglory. **1450–1530** *Myrr. our Ladye* 98 Yt was defoyled and darkyd and mysshape by synne.

b. To render ceremonially or sentimentally unclean; to defile, sully.

c **1449** PECOCK *Repr.* 465 To ete with hondis not wayschen defoulith not a man. **1483** CAXTON *Gold. Leg.* 141 b/1 The mouth whyche god had kyssed ought not to be defouled in touchyng. **1611** SPEED *Hist. Gt. Brit.* VII. xlii. §14. 352 Must I needs defoule my self, to be his only faire foule.

c. To sully (fame, reputation, or the like); to defame.

α. *c* **1400** *Destr. Troy* 2475 Your suster..þat our fame so defoules, & is in filth holdyn. *c* **1450** *Golagros & Gaw.* 1038 Wes I neuer yit defoullit, nor fylit in fame.

β. **1470–85** MALORY *Arthur* IX. xxxii, I..am defoiled with falshede and treason.

8. To make unsightly or ugly [cf. FOUL *a.*], to disfigure.

α. **1387** TREVISA *Higden* (Rolls) I. 389 And þey be faire of schap, þey beeþ defouled and i-made vnsemelich i-now wiþ here owne cloþinge. **1430** LYDG. *Chron. Troy* II. xi, The soyle defouled with ruyne Of walles olde.

β. **1398** TREVISA *Barth. De P.R.* VII. lx. (1495) 276 Blaynes defoylle the skynne and maketh it vnsemely.

† **de'foul, de'foil,** *sb. Obs.* Also defoule, -fowle; defoile. [f. DEFOUL *v.*]

1. Trampling down; oppression, outrage.

c **1330** *Arth. & Merl.* 7999 (Mätzn.) Ther was fighting, ther was toile, And vnder hors knightes defoile. *Ibid.* 9191 Ther was swiche cark and swiche defoil. **1400** EARL OF DUNBAR *Let.* in C. Innes *Scot. Mid. Ages* ix. (1860) 263 The wrongs & the defowle that ys done me. *c* **1425** WYNTOUN *Cron.* VIII. xxvi. 54 (Jam.) Lychtlynes and succwdry Drawys in defowle comownaly. **1563–87** FOXE *A. & M.* (1684) I. 460/1 If we take this defoule and this disease in patience.

2. Defilement, pollution.

c **1325** *E.E. Allit. P.* C. 290 þer no de-foule of no fylþe watz fest hym abute. **1387** TREVISA *Higden* (Rolls) I. 109 þat þe water..takeþ no defoul, but is clene i-now. **1398** —— *Barth. De P.R.* XVII. cxxiii. (Tollem. MS.), Picche defouleþ ..and suche defoule [**1535** defoylynge] is unneþe taken awey from cloþe.

† **de'fouled,** *ppl. a. Obs.* [f. DEFOUL *v.* + -ED.] Defiled, polluted, corrupt.

c **1440** *Promp. Parv.* 116 Defowlyd, *deturpatus..feculentus,* (P. *dehonestatus*). **1460** W. THORPE *Test.* in Arb. *Garner* VI. 114 Covetous simoners and defouled adulterers. **1483** *Cath. Angl.* 94 Defowled, *maculatus, pollutus,* etc.

† **de'fouler.** *Obs.* [f. as prec. + -ER^{1}.] One who defouls.

14.. *Voc.* in Wr.-Wülcker 617/34, *Tritor,* a defoulere. *c* **1440** *Jacob's Well* 62 þise dyffoulerys & depryueres of holy cherche.

† **de'fouling, de'foiling,** *vbl. sb. Obs.* [f. DEFOUL *v.* + -ING^{1}.]

The action of the verb DEFOUL: **a.** Trampling down; **b.** Violation, deflowering; **c.** Defiling, pollution, defilement; **d.** Disfigurement.

c **1380** WYCLIF *Sel. Wks.* III. 200 No defoulynge þerof may askape unpeyned. **1382** —— *2 Sam.* xxii. 5 There han envyround me the defoulyngis of deeth. **1398** TREVISA *Barth. De P.R.* XVII. cxxiii. (1495) 685 Defoyllyng of pytche is vneth taken awaye from clothe. **14..** *Prose Legends* in *Anglia* VIII. 158 Made dule for defoylinge of chirches. **1440** J. SHIRLEY *Dethe K. James* (1818) 5 Yn dispusellyng and defowlyng of yong madyns. *a* **1450** *Knt. de la Tour* 23 That defoulyng of her uisage. **1483** *Cath. Angl.* 94 A Defowlynge, *conculcacio, pollucio,* etc. **1535** STEWART *Cron. Scot.* II. 124 For the defoulling of his dochter deir. **1548** HALL *Chron.* 247 b, The bytyng of her tethe..defoulynge of her tayle.

defound, var. of DEFUND *v. Obs.*

defourme, obs. form of DEFORM.

deframe (diː'freɪm), *v.* [f. DE- II. 1 + FRAME *v.* 9.] *trans.* To remove (a picture) from its frame. So **de'framed** *ppl. a.*

1908 T. HARDY *Dynasts* III. II. iii. 78 A deframed old master. **1950** E. HEMINGWAY *Across the River* xv. 141 The portrait had been de-framed.

† **de'fraud,** *sb. Obs.* [f. DEFRAUD *v.*, after FRAUD *sb.*] = DEFRAUDATION.

c **1440** *Jacob's Well* iii. (E.E.T.S.) 21 þo arn acursyd, þat ..ȝyuen awey here good..in defraude of here wyves & chylderyn. **1493** *Sc. Acts Jas. IV* (1597) §85 For the defraud done to our Soveraine Lorde in his customes be strangers. **1495** *Act 11 Hen. VII*, c. 22 Preamb., Their subtill ymagynacion in defraude of the seid estatutes. **1581** *Sc. Acts Jas. VI* (1597) §117 Anent..Alienationes maid in defraud of Creditoures. **1800** *Trans. Soc. Encourag. Arts* XVIII. 216 Without..being liable to the..defrauds of the miller.

defraud (dɪ'frɔːd), *v.* [a. OF. *defrauder* (*des-, def-, dif-*), 14th c. in Godef., ad. L. *dēfraudāre*, f. DE- I. 3 + *fraudāre* to cheat, f. *fraus, fraud-em*, deceit, FRAUD.]

1. To deprive (a person) by fraud of what is his by right, either by fraudulently taking or by dishonestly withholding it from him; to cheat, cozen, beguile. Const. *of* (†*from*).

1362 LANGL. *P. Pl.* A. VIII. 71 He þat beggeþ..bote he habbe neode..defraudeþ þe neodi. **14..** *Epiph.* in *Tundale's Vis.* (1843) 104 They..thanked God with all her hartis furst Whech hathe not defrawded hem of her lust. **1474** CAXTON *Chesse* 98 To defraude the begiler is no fraude. **1555** EDEN *Decades* 39 He had..defrauded the kynge of his portion. **1634** SIR T. HERBERT *Trav.* 46 This poore Citie, was defrauded of her hopes. *Ibid.* 217, I will a little defraude the Reader from concluding with a few lines touching the first Discoverer. **1752** JOHNSON *Rambler* No. 199 ¶7 To defraud any man of his due praise is unworthy of a philosopher. **1838** EMERSON *Addr. Camb., Mass.* Wks. (Bohn) II. 198 Whenever the pulpit is usurped by a formalist, then is the worshipper defrauded. **1880** E. KIRKE *Garfield* 39 We who defraud four million citizens of their rights.

†**b.** with direct and indirect object. *Obs.*

1382 WYCLIF *Luke* xix. 8 If I haue ony thing defraudid ony man I ȝelde the fourefold. **1600** HOLLAND *Livy* IV. xii. 148 Defrauding servants a portion of their daily food. **1670** MILTON *Hist. Brit.* VI. *Harold*, Harold..defrauded his soldiers their due..share of the spoils.

c. *absol.* To act with or employ fraud.

1382 WYCLIF *1 Cor.* vi. 8 Ȝe don wrong and defrauden [**1388** doen fraude] or bigilen and that to britheren. **1611** BIBLE *Mark* x. 19 Doe not beare false witnesse, Defraud not. **1875** JOWETT *Plato* (ed. 2) III. 102 If he is the trustee of an orphan, and has the power to defraud.

2. *fig.* To deprive or cheat (a thing) of what is due to it; to withhold fraudulently. *arch.* or *Obs.*

1497 BP. ALCOCK *Mons Perfect.* Dj/3 They selle Cryst & defraudeth theyr relygyon. **1559** BP. COX in Strype *Ann. Ref.* I. vi. 98 They defrauded the payment of tithes and firstfruits. **1660** BOYLE *Seraph. Love* 26 Where a direct and immediate expression of love to God defrauds not any other Duty. **1764** GOLDSM. *Trav.* 277 Here beggar pride defrauds her daily cheer, To boast one splendid banquet once a year. *a* **1805** PALEY (in Webster 1828), By the duties deserted..by the claims defrauded.

Hence **de'frauding** *vbl. sb.*

1548 UDALL, etc. *Erasm. Par. 1 Cor.* vii. (R.), To denye this right yf eyther of bothe aske it, is a defraudyng. **1651** HOBBES *Leviath.* II. xxvii. 160 The robbing, or defrauding of a Private man. **1659** GAUDEN *Tears of Ch.* 235 Few do pay them without delayings, defalkings, and defraudings.

defrau'dation. [a. OF. *defraudation, -acion* (13–14th c. in Godef.), ad. L. *dēfraudātiōn-em*, n. of action from *dēfraudāre* to DEFRAUD.] The action (or an act) of defrauding; fraudulent deprivation of property or rights; cheating.

1502 ARNOLDE *Chron.* (1811) 286 The sayd cardynal.. porchased hymself in gret deffraudacion of your Hyghnes, a charter of pardon. **1601–2** FULBECKE *2nd Pt. Parall.* 23 b, Here is no defraudation of the Law. **1646** SIR T. BROWNE *Pseud. Ep.* I. iii. 11 Deluding not onely unto pecuniary defraudations, but the irreparable deceit of death. *a* **1716** BLACKALL *Wks.* (1723) I. 190 By such Defraudation we become Accessaries, etc. **1886** H. D. TRAILL *Shaftesbury* 19 This defraudation of personal and constitutional rights.

de'frauder. [f. DEFRAUD *v.* + -ER^{1}: perh. a. OF. *defraudeor, -eur*, ad. L. *dēfraudātōr-em.*] One who defrauds, one who fraudulently withholds or takes what belongs to another.

1552 ABP. HAMILTON *Catech.* (1884) 10 Defraudaris of waigis fra servandis or labouraris. **1651** *Reliq. Wotton.* 257 (R.) Decrees against defrauders of the publick chests. **1754** RICHARDSON *Grandison* (1766) V. 67 Who would not rather be the sufferer than the defrauder? **1878** *N. Amer. Rev.* CXXVII. 287 A defrauder of the revenue.

† **de'fraudful,** *a. Obs. rare*$^{-1}$. [f. DEFRAUD + -FUL; cf. *assistful*, etc.] Full of fraud; cheating, cozening.

c **1585** *Faire Em* II. 402 That with thy cunning and defraudful tongue Seeks to delude the honest-meaning mind!

de'fraudment. ? *Obs.* [f. DEFRAUD *v.* + -MENT: perh. a. OF. *defraudement*, 'a defrauding, deceiuing, beguiling' (Cotgr.).] The action of defrauding; deprivation by fraud.

1645 MILTON *Colast.* Wks. (1851) 352 Perpetual defraudments of truest conjugal society. **1791** BENTHAM *Draught of Code* Wks. 1843 IV. 402 *note*, Offences.. comprised under the name of *felonies*: theft, defraudment, robbery, homicide.

† **de'fray,** *sb. Obs. rare*$^{-1}$. [f. DEFRAY *v.*^{1}: cf. OF. *desfroi, deffray, defrai*, f. *desfrayer*: see next.] Defrayal.

1615 CHAPMAN *Odyss.* XIV. 730 Thou..shalt not need, Or coat, or other thing..for defray Of this night's need.

defray (dɪ'freɪ), *v.*^{1} Also 6 defraie, deffray, 7 defraye. [a. F. *défraye-r*, in 14th c. *deffroier*, 15th c. *deffroyer*, 16th c. *desfrayer*, f. *des-, de-* (DE- I. 3, 6 + OF. *fraier, freier, froyer* to spend, incur expense, f. *frai*, in 14th c. *frait*, pl. *frais*, 13th c. *fres*, expenses, charges, cost.]

†**1.** To pay out, expend, spend, disburse (money).

1543–4 *Act 35 Hen. VIII*, c. 12 Inestimable summes of treasure, to be employed and defrayed about the same. *c* **1555** HARPSFIELD *Divorce Hen. VIII* (1878) 241 There is emption and vendition contracted as soon as the parties be condescended upon the price, though there be no money presently defrayed. **1600** HOLLAND *Livy* XXXIX. v. 1026 The Senate permitted Fulvius to deffray (*inpenderet*) what he would himselfe, so as hee exceeded not the summe of 80000 [Asses]. *a* **1610** HEALEY tr. *Epictetus' Man.* xxxii. (1636) 43 Nor hast thou defrayed the price that the banquet is sold for: namely praise, and flatterie. **1613** R. C. *Table Alph.* (ed. 3), *Defraye*, lay out, pay, discharge.

2. To discharge (the expense or cost of anything) by payment; to pay, meet, settle.

1570–6 LAMBARDE *Peramb. Kent* (1826) 110 The King shall defray the wages. **1587** in Ellis *Orig. Lett.* Ser. II. III. 130 The College cannot possibly defray its ordinary expenses without some other help, over and beyond the ordinary revenues. **1639** FULLER *Holy War* IV. xiii. (1840) 202 Meladin..offered the Christians..a great sum of money to defray their charges. **1745** in *Col. Rec. Penn.* V. 6 To draw Bills for defraying the Expence. **1838** THIRLWALL *Greece* II. 208 The cost of the expedition to Naxos he pledged himself to defray. **1868** FREEMAN *Norm. Conq.* (1876) II. ix. 404 The payment was defrayed out of the spoils.

b. *fig.*

1580 SIDNEY *Arcadia* (1674) 328 With the death of some one striving to defray every drop of his blood. **1590** SPENSER *F.Q.* I. v. 42 Can Night defray The wrath of thundring Ioue. **1596** *Ibid.* IV. v. 31 Nought but dire revenge his anger mote defray.

3. To meet the expense of; to bear the charge of; pay for. Now *rare* or *arch.*

1581 LAMBARDE *Eiren.* IV. xxi. (1588) 623 To bestowe the whole allowance upon the defraying of their common diet. **1587** FLEMING *Contn. Holinshed* III. 1371/2 The enterprise ..to be defraied by the pope and king of Spaine. *c* **1645** HOWELL *Lett.* I. I. xi, It serv'd to defray the expenceful Progress he made to Scotland the Summer following. **1830** DE QUINCEY *Bentley* Wks. VII. 64 A poor exchequer for defraying a war upon Bentley. **1859** C. BARKER *Assoc. Princ.* ii. 51 The estate of the defunct member was not sufficient to defray his funeral.

†**4.** To pay the charges or expenses of (a person); to reimburse; to entertain free of charge.

1580 SIDNEY *Arcadia* I. (1590) 5 Defraying the mariners with a ring bestowed upon them. **1607** SIR E. HOBY in Ellis *Orig. Lett.* Ser. I. III. 87 He..would not land at Dover till he had indented with Sir Thomas Waller that he should be defrayed during his aboad. *a* **1626** BACON *New Atl.* (1650) 7 The State will defray you all the time you stay. **1686** F. SPENCE tr. *Varillas' Ho. Medici* 44 The Pitti's were defray'd at Venice at the public cost. **1724** DE FOE *Mem. Cavalier* (1860) 80 A warrant to defray me, my horses and servants at the King's charge. **1858** CARLYLE *Fredk. Gt.* I. IV. iv. 424 Such a man [Czar Peter] is to be royally defrayed while with us; yet one would wish it done cheap.

Hence **de'fraying** *vbl. sb.*

1587 R. HOVENDEN in Hearne *Collect.* (Oxf. Hist. Soc.) I. 195 The defraieinge of our..expences. **1632** LITHGOW *Trav.* IX. 387 Disbursed..for..high-wayes, Lords pensions, and other defrayings. **1651** HOBBES *Leviath.* IV. xliv. 336 The defraying of all publique charges. **1783** AINSWORTH *Lat. Dict.* (Morell) I, A defraying, *pecuniæ erogatio.*

† **de'fray,** *v.*^{2} *Obs.* [app. a. OF. **des-, defraier*, f. *des-, de-* (DE- II. 3, 6) + *freier, froier, fraier* to rub, rub off, FRAY:—L. *fricāre* to rub.] *trans.* ? To rub off or away.

1532 R. BOWYER in Strype *Eccl. Mem.* I. xvii. 135 He intendeth not to infringe, annul, derogate, defray or minish anything of the popes authority.

[**defray,** error for *desray*, DERAY.]

defrayable (dɪ'freɪəb(ə)l), *a.* [f. DEFRAY *v.*^{1} + -ABLE.] Liable to be defrayed, payable.

1886 *Manch. Exam.* 25 Mar. 5/2 Defrayable out of local contributions.

defrayal (dɪ'freɪəl). [f. DEFRAY *v.*^{1} + -AL^{1}.] The action of defraying; defrayment.

1820 *Examiner* No. 648. 577/2 [He] expects nothing but the defrayal of his expenses. **1883** W. E. NORRIS *No New Thing* II. xiii. 3 Her share..was confined to the defrayal of its cost.

de'frayer. [f. DEFRAY *v.* + -ER^{1}: cf. obs. F. *defrayeur* in Cotgr. 1611.] One who defrays or discharges a monetary obligation; a payer of expenses.

1580 NORTH *Plutarch* (1676) 273 The Registers and Records kept of the defrayers of the charges of common Plays. **1755** JOHNSON, *Defrayer*, one that discharges expences.

defrayment (dɪ'freɪmənt). [a. OF. *deffrayement* (*desfroiement*), f. *deffrayer* to DEFRAY: see -MENT.]

The action or fact of defraying: †**a.** Expenditure. *Obs.* **b.** Payment of expenses or charges, discharge of pecuniary obligations.

1547 *Privy Council Acts* (1890) II. 135 Mmmli... towardes defrayment of the charges of his Majeste. **1579** FENTON *Guicciard.* IX. (1599) 388 To pay within a certaine time for all defrayments, twentie thousand duckets. **1611** SPEED *Hist. Great Brit.* IX. xiii. §85 [To pay..] toward the defraiment of the Dukes huge charges. **1620** SHELTON *Quix.* IV. 7 (T.) Let the traitor pay, with his life's defrayment, that which he attempted with so lascivious a desire. **1656** EARL MONM. *Advt. fr. Parnass.* 354 If we were not fed by the free defrayment of our Cornucopia. **1762** tr. *Busching's Syst. Geog.* V. 541 Applied for the defrayment of the electoral council colleges. **1884** SIR C. S. C. BOWEN in *Law Reports* 13 Q. Bench Div. 91 Part of the disbursements consisted in the defrayment of these expenses.

defreeze (diː'friːz), *v.* [f. DE- II. 1 + FREEZE *v.*] *trans.* = DEFROST *v.* So **de'freezing** *vbl. sb.*

1901 *Westm. Gaz.* 22 July 10/2 A new process of 'defreezing' is now being tried. **1922** *Evening News* 20 Dec. 4/3 When these birds, only lightly frozen for the voyage, are 'defrozen'—the trade term. **1963** *Guardian* 4 Feb. 16/1 (*heading*) Electric charge to defreeze pipes. **1970** *Ibid.* 8 May 9/4 We recently defroze a rock hard salmon which left the sea..on August 16, 1969. It was superb.

de'freeze, *sb.* [f. the vb.] The act or process of unfreezing.

1962 *Daily Tel.* 3 Jan. 1/6 Describing yesterday as 'defreeze day', the Association gave warning of..a covering of water on roads already ice-bound. **1963** *Guardian* 30 Jan. 16/5 The 'de-freeze' of the main roads of Britain was almost complete.

† **de'freight,** *v. Obs. rare*$^{-1}$. [f. DE- II. 1 or 2 + FREIGHT: cf. *disload, disburden.*] *trans.* To relieve of freight or cargo; to unload.

1555 EDEN *Decades* 212 The port or hauen is so commodious to defraight or vnlade shyppes.

† **de'frenate, defrænate,** *v. Obs. Surg.* [f. ppl. stem of L. *dēfrēnāre* to unbridle; f. DE- I. 6 + *frēnum, frænum* bridle, curb, ligament.] To remove a frænum or restraining ligament.

1758 J. S. *Le Dran's Observ. Surg.* (1771) 92 To defrænate the Aponeurosis. *Ibid.* 278, I had..defrænated the Sinus's and scarified the Sides of the Fistula.

defri'cation. *rare.* [ad. L. *dēfricātiōn-em*, n. of action f. L. *dēfricāre* to rub off, rub down.] Rubbing, rubbing off.

1727 in BAILEY vol. II; and in some mod. Dicts.

defrock (dɪ'frɒk), *v.* [a. F. *défroquer*, in 15th c. *deffr-*, f. *des-, dé-* (DE- I. 6) + *froque* FROCK. Cf.

DISFROCK.] *trans.* To deprive of the priestly garb; to unfrock. Hence **defrocked** (dɪˈfrɒkt) *ppl. a.*

1581 J. HAMILTON *Facile Traict.* (1600) 440 This defrokit frere..mariet a zoung las of xv zearis auld. **1891** *Tablet* 21 Feb. 294 The eloquent defrocked have denounced..the vows which they failed to keep.

defrost (diːˈfrɒst), *v.* [f. DE- II. 2 + FROST *sb.*] *trans.* To unfreeze, remove the frost from; *spec.* (*a*) to unfreeze (frozen meat or other provisions); (*b*) to clear the frost from (e.g. the interior of a refrigerator, the windscreen of a motor vehicle or aircraft). Also *absol.* and *refl.*; occas. *intr.*, to become unfrozen. So **deˈfrosted** *ppl. a.*; **deˈfrosting** *vbl. sb.*

1895 *Daily News* 29 May 8/4 It was believed that Queensland defrosted beef could be brought into formidable competition with American chilled. **1895** *Australasian Pastoralists' Rev.* 15 Aug. p. viii, The difficulties hitherto attaching to the defrosting of Beef and Mutton. **1897** *Yearbk. U.S. Dept. Agric. 1896* 26 Each year there is visible improvement in the methods of defrosting meats in European markets. **1924** *Glasgow Herald* 19 Aug. 7 The electrical defrosting process experiments which were recently undertaken in Melbourne. **1937** 'N. BLAKE' *There's Trouble Brewing* ix. 166 Nigel was standing near the door, his back to one of the refrigerators. 'Doesn't seem so cold as when I was here last.' 'No, sir,' said Carruthers. 'We're defrosting now.' **1951** *Good Housek. Home Encycl.* 232/2 An automatic de-frosting mechanism is incorporated in some machines. **1953** C. M. KORNBLUTH *Syndic* (1964) xix. 201 He defrosted some hamburger, fried it and ate it. **1957** *Daily Mail* 5 Sept. 11/5 The vegetables..now defrost in the car on the way from the home to the picnic-ground. **1957** *Economist* 9 Nov. 499/2 The heater provides a generous flow of warm air... The result is extremely efficient demisting and defrosting. **1958** *Listener* 17 July 81/1 The refrigerator that defrosts itself. **1960** *Housewife* Apr. 114/1 Simply defrost a packet of frozen chicken joints. **1965** J. CHRISTOPHER *Wrinkle in Skin* iv. 46 They had a mess of defrosted strawberries afterwards. **1970** *Daily Tel.* 28 Apr. 17 Both refrigerator and deep-freezer de-frost themselves continuously and automatically. **1970** *Which?* Sept. 283/2 Most manufacturers recommend defrosting once a year.

defroster (diːˈfrɒstə(r)). [f. prec. + -ER¹.] A device for defrosting; *spec.* (see quot. 1930).

1927 *Refrigerating Engin.* Jan. 238 Defroster for packing houses and cold storage plants. **1930** *Popular Sci.* Dec. 74/3 This electrical 'defroster' warms the glass and prevents ice and snow from getting a hold on it. The device may be attached to the windshield of any car. **1937** *Sunday Express* 14 Mar. 13/4 The defrosters, unusual in England, created an impression. **1960** *News Chron.* 22 Sept. 13/4 The larger models [of refrigerator] feature an automatic or semi-automatic de-froster.

†**deˈfroysse**, *v. Obs.* [a. OF. *defroissier* (*des-*, *def-*), f. *des-*, *dé-*, (DE- I. 6) + *froissier*, *froisser* to rub violently, bruise, crush:—L. type **frictiare*, deriv. of *frict-us* rubbed, pa. pple. of *fricāre*.] *trans.* To crush to pieces.

1480 CAXTON *Ovid's Met.* XI. xix, The wawes defroyssed and al [to] brake the sterne and other garnysshyng.

†**defrut.** *Obs. rare*⁻¹. [ad. L. *defrutum* must boiled down.] Must boiled down.

c **1420** *Pallad. on Husb.* XI. 484 Defrut, carene, & sape in oon manere Of must is made.

deft (dɛft), *a.* Also 3-5 **defte.** [app. a doublet of DAFT, repr. OE. *ȝedæfte*, for *ȝedefte*, mild, gentle, meek, from stem *dab-* in Gothic *gadaban* to become, befit: cf. OE. *ȝedæfen* becoming, fit, suitable.]

†**1.** Gentle, meek, humble; = DAFT 1. *Obs. rare.*

c **1220** *Bestiary* 36 Ðat defte meiden, Marie bi name Ðe him bar to manne frame.

2. Apt, skilful, dexterous, clever or neat in action.

c **1440** *York Myst.* i. 92, I sall be lyke vnto hym þat es hyeste on heyhte; Owe! what I am derworth and defte. **1592** G. HARVEY *Four Lett.* 57 Whether the Deft writer be as sure a workeman as the neat Taylor. **1598** CHAPMAN *Iliad* I. 580 A laughter never left Shook all the blessed deities, to see the lame so deft At that cup service. **1601** B. JONSON *Poetaster* v. iii, Well said, my divine, deft Horace. **1607** *Lingua* III. v. in Hazl. *Dodsley* IX. 394 Their knowledge is only of things present, quickly sublimed with the deft file of time. **1855** ROBINSON *Whitby Gloss.*, *Deft*, neat, clever. 'She is a deft hand with a needle.' **1863** GEO. ELIOT *Romola* I. ix, Smitten and buffeted because he was not deft and active. **1864** CARLYLE *Fredk. Gt.* IV. XII. xi. 254 A cunning little wretch, they say, and of deft tongue.

b. Of actions: Showing skill or dexterity in execution.

1647 H. MORE *Philos. Poems, Oracle* 90 Break off this musick, and deft seemly Round. **1714** GAY *Sheph. Week* i. 56 The wanton Calf may skip with many a Bound, And my Cur Tray play deftest Feats around. **1853** C. BRONTE *Villette* i, The creature..made a deft attempt to fold the shawl. **1878** H. S. WILSON *Alp. Ascents* iii. 97 With deft blows of the untiring axe.

†**c.** *transf.* Of a metal: Apt for working, easily wrought. *Obs.*

1683 *Phil. Trans.* XIII. 193 How to make brittle gold deft and fit to be wrought.

3. Neat, tidy, trim, spruce; handsome, pretty. Still *dial.*

[The sense 'neat in action' (see 2) appears to have passed into 'neat in person'. Cf. similar developments, under *buxom*, *canny*, *clever*, *handsome*, *tidy*, and other adjectives expressing personal praise.]

1579, **1589** [see DEFTLY 2]. **1600** HEYWOOD *1 Edw. IV* Wks. 1874 I. 83 By the messe, a deft lass! Christs benison light on her. **1600** HOLLAND *Livy* IV. xliv. 168 In her raiment ..not so deft [*scite*] as devout..her garments rather saintcly than sightly. **1611** COTGR., *Greslet*..little, prettie, deft, smallish. **1622** ROWLANDS *Good Newes* 20 Shee came to London very neat and deft, To seeke preferment. **1674-91** RAY *N.C. Words* 20 *Deft*, little and pretty, or neat. A Deft man or thing. It is a word of general use all England over. **1781** J. HUTTON *Tour Caves* Gloss., *Deft*, pretty, agreeable. **1788** W. MARSHALL *E. Yorksh.* Gloss., *Deft*, neat, pretty, handsome. **1873** *Swaledale Gloss.*, *Deft*, neat, pretty.

4. Quiet. Cf. DEFTLY 3. Still *dial.*

a **1763** BYROM *Careless Content* (R.), Or if ye ween, for worldly stirs, That man does right to mar his rest, Let me be deft, and debonair, I am content, I do not care. **1878** *Cumbrld. Gloss.* (Central), *Deft*, quiet, silent.

†**5.** Stupid; = DAFT 2. *Obs.*⁻⁰

c **1440** *Promp. Parv.* 116 Defte [*v.r.* deft] or dulle, *obtusus*, *agrestis*.

6. quasi *adv.* Deftly.

1805 SCOTT *Last Minstr.* I. xv, Merry elves their morrice pacing..Trip it deft and merrily.

7. *Comb.*, as *deft-fingered*, *-handed*.

1860 W. J. C. MUIR *Pagan or Christian?* 36 Being deft-fingered..they grew in good time to be tolerable adepts in their Art. **1889** *Boys' Own Paper* 3 Aug. 698/3 She did not show herself so deft-handed.

defterdar (dɛftəˈdɑːr). Also 6-7 **teftadar**, **teftader**, 7-8 **tefterdar**, 9 **defturdar**. [Turk. f. *defter* (see DUFTER) + Pers. *-dar* holding.] A Turkish officer of finance, *esp.* the accountant general of a province; also formerly, the Turkish minister of finance.

1589 HAKLUYT *Voy.* 205 Vnder him be three Subtreasurers called *Teftaders*. **1601** W. BIDDULPH *Trav. Four Englishmen* (1609) 88 *Defterdare*, that is Treasurer of Aleppo. **1615** G. SANDYS *Trav.* III. 211 Tendring to the *Teftadar* or Treasurer the reuenew of that *Sanziackry*. **1796** J. MORSE *Amer. Univ. Geogr.* II. 463 The first minister of finances is called Defterdar. **1836** E. W. LANE *Mod. Egypt.* I. 154 The Defturdár, having caused the Názir to be brought before him, asked him [etc.]. **1902** *Encycl. Brit.* XXXIII. 508/1 A complete budget of receipts and expenditure is drawn up by its *defterdar*.

deftly (ˈdɛftlɪ), *adv.* Also 6-8 **deffly**, 7 **defly**, **deaftly**. [f. DEFT + -LY².] In a deft manner.

1. Aptly, skilfully, cleverly, dexterously, nimbly.

The sense of the first quot. is doubtful.

c **1460** *Towneley Myst.* (Surtees) 100 God looke over the raw, full defly ye stand. **1579** SPENSER *Sheph. Cal.* Apr. 111 They dauncen deffly, and singen soote. **1605** SHAKS. *Macb.* IV. i. 68 Come high or low: Thy Selfe and Office, deaftly show. **1607** DEKKER *Knt.'s Conjur.* (1842) 71 You shall see swaynes defly piping, and virgins chastly dancing. **1616** SURFL. & MARKH. *Countrey Farme* 655 The mattocke would pull vp the seed, and therefore they must be vnderdigd very deftly. **1710** PHILIPS *Pastorals* i. 29 How deffly to mine Oaten Reed so sweet Wont they upon the Green, to shift their Feet? **1808** SCOTT *Marm.* III. viii, The harp full deftly can he strike. **1856** R. A. VAUGHAN *Mystics* (1860) II. 97 The deftly-woven threadwork of the tissues.

2. Neatly, tidily, trimly; prettily, handsomely. Still *dial.*

1579 G. GILPIN tr. *Marnix's Beehive Rom. Ch.* Z 5 (N.) Deftly deck'd with all costly jewels, like puppets. **1589** *Pasquil's Ret.* Biijb, Verie defflie set out, with Pompes, Pagents, Motions..Impreases. **1847** J. WILSON *Chr. North* (1857) II. 4 Deftly arrayed in home-spun drapery. **1859** HELPS *Friends in C.* Ser. II. II. i. 6 The grass which deftly covers without hiding.

3. Softly, gently, quietly. *dial.*

1787 GROSE *Prov. Gloss.*, *Deftly*, softly, leisurely. **1802** WORDSW. *Stanzas*, 'Within our happy Castle' 58 A pipe on which the wind would deftly play. **1869** *Lonsdale Gloss.*, *Deftly*, quietly, softly. **1873** *Swaledale Gloss.*, *Deftly*, neatly, gently, softly, orderly: see Cannily.

deftness (ˈdɛftnɪs). [-NESS.]

†**1.** Neatness, trimness. *Obs.* or *dial.*

1612 DRAYTON *Poly-olb.* ii. 33 By her, two little Iles, her handmaids (which compar'd With those within the Poole for deftness not out-dar'd).

2. The quality of being deft, cleverness, dexterity, neatness of action.

1853 MISS E. S. SHEPPARD *C. Auchester* I. 316 He assisted me..with that assiduous deftness which pre-eminently distinguishes the instrumental artist. **1868** *Sat. Rev.* 13 June 777/1 They can neither tie a string nor fasten a button with ordinary deftness.

†**defude**, *v. Obs. rare.* [perh. misprint for *defūde* = *defunde*, f. L. *dēfundĕre*.] To pour off.

1599 A. M. tr. *Gabelhouer's Bk. Physicke* 29/2 Then defude the wyne from the Spices, and distille the same.

defule, obs. var. of DEFOUL *v.*

defull: see DEEFUL.

†**defulmiˈnation.** *Obs. rare*⁻¹. [f. DE- I. 1 + FULMINATION.] The sending down of thunderbolts.

1615 T. ADAMS *Spir. Navig.* 21 He is not only as manacles to the hands of God to hold them from the defulmination of judgement.

defunct (dɪˈfʌŋkt), *a.* and *sb.* [ad. L. *dēfunct-us* discharged, deceased, dead, pa. pple. of *dēfungī* to discharge, have done with, f. DE- I. 6 + *fungī* to perform, discharge (duty). Perh. immed. a. F. *defunct* (Cotgr. 1611), now *défunt*.]

A. *adj.* Having ceased to live; deceased, dead.

[**1398** TREVISA *Barth. De P.R.* VI. ii. (1495) 187 A deed body is callyd *Defunctus*, for he hath lefte the offyce of lyfe.] **1599** SHAKS. *Hen. V*, IV. i. 21 The Organs, though defunct and dead before, Breake vp their drowsie Graue. **1603** JAS. I in Ellis *Orig. Lett.* Ser. I. III. 65 To do that and all other honnor that we may unto the Queene defunct. **1605** BACON *Adv. Learn.* II. x. § 5. 42 The anatomy is of a defunct patient. **1694** *Lond. Gaz.* No. 2981/3 Two defunct Knights of the Order. **1828** SCOTT *F.M. Perth* xx, Now, Simon..what was the purport of the defunct Oliver Proudfute's discourse with you? **1872** BAKER *Nile Tribut.* xx. 341 The stock in trade of a defunct doctor.

b. *fig.* No longer in existence; having ceased its functions; dead, extinct.

1741 *Love of Fame* (ed. 4) 74 Defunct by Phœbus' laws, beyond redress. **1809-10** COLERIDGE *Friend* (ed. 3) II. 20 This ghost of a defunct absurdity. **1834** MEDWIN *Angler in Wales* I. 24 It appeared, some months ago, in a defunct periodical. **1878** STEWART & TAIT *Unseen Univ.* iii. §115 Due to the crashing together of defunct suns.

B. *sb. the defunct*: the deceased; hence, with *pl.* (*rare*), one who is dead, a dead person.

1548 HALL *Chron. Hen. VIII*, an. 1 (R.) The corps of the said defunct [the late kyng] was brought..into the great chamber. **1611** SHAKS. *Cymb.* IV. ii. 358 Nature doth abhorre to make his bed With the defunct, or sleepe upon the dead. **1663** WOOD *Life* (Oxf. Hist. Soc.) I. 479 The.. hors-litter..where was the defunct, drawne by six horses. **1715** M. DAVIES *Ath. Brit.* I. 143 Those two great Episcopal Defuncts. **1771** SMOLLETT *Humph. Cl.* (1815) 217 Knavish priests, who pretended that the devil could have no power over the defunct, if he was interred in holy ground. **1828** LANDOR *Imag. Convers.* III. 392 Indifferent whether the pace with which the defunct are carried to the grave be quick or slow. **1839-40** W. IRVING *Wolfert's R.* (1855) 251 Accosting a servant..he demanded the name of the defunct. **1888** H. C. LEA *Hist. Inquisition* I. 391 A sentence condemning five defuncts.

defunction (dɪˈfʌŋkʃən). *rare.* [ad. L. *dēfunctiōn-em* execution, discharge, death, n. of action from *dēfungī* (see prec.).] Dying, decease, death.

1599 SHAKS. *Hen. V*, I. ii. 58 Foure hundred one and twentie yeeres After defunction of King Pharamond. **1617** COLLINS *Def. Bp. Ely* II. ix. 380 Applying it to the daily defunctions of our penitence. **1813** T. BUSBY *Lucretius* III. *Comment.* iii, The soul..in cases of sudden defunction.. will be entirely..dissipated before the body visibly decays. **1859** *Punch* 2 July 8/2 That obnoxious potentate's defunction.

deˈfunctionalize, *v.* [DE- II. 1.] *trans.* To deprive of function or office.

1877 COUES *Fur Anim.* i. 12 Back upper premolar defunctionalized as a 'sectorial' tooth. *Ibid.* xi. 325 The sectorial teeth are defunctionalized as such.

deˈfunctive, *a.* [f. L. *dēfunct-* ppl. stem (see DEFUNCT) + -IVE.] Of or pertaining to defunction or dying. Also, becoming defunct; dying.

1601 SHAKS. *Phœnix & Turtle* 14 Let the priest in surplice white, That defunctive music can, Be the death-divining swan. **1920** T. S. ELIOT *Ara Vos Prec* 14 Defunctive music under sea Passed seaward with the passing bell. **1929** W. FAULKNER *Sound & Fury* 165 The lane..became defunctive in grass, a mere path scarred quietly into new grass. **1939** T. WOLFE *Web & Rock* I. 18 The day was drowsed with quietness and defunctive turnip greens. **1961** *Listener* 26 Oct. 681/1 The theatre has a whole barrel full of conventions for the purpose—slow curtains, quick curtains..defunctive music preparing a slow ending.

deˈfunctness. [-NESS.] The state of being defunct; extinctness.

1883 WRIGHT *Dogmatic Scept.* 7 This gave scepticism its crowning emancipation, finally hurling the miraculous into everlasting defunctness.

†**deˈfund**, *v. Obs. rare.* Also 6 defound. [ad. L. *dēfundĕre* (or its OF. repr. *defondre*, *des-*, *def-*), f. DE- I. 1 + *fundĕre* to pour. See also DIFFUND.] *trans.* To pour down.

1513 DOUGLAS *Æneis* IX. viii. 4 The son scheyn Begouth defund [*v.r.* defound] hys bemys on the greyn. *Ibid.* XII. Prol. 41 Fvrth..ischyt Phebus Defundand [*v.r.* defoundand] from hys sege etheriall Glaid influent aspectis celicall.

defuse (diːˈfjuːz), *v.* [f. DE- II. 2 + FUSE *sb.*] *trans.* To remove the fuse from (an explosive device). Also *fig.*

1943 *Word Study* Oct. 7 A group of fliers defused a 1,000-pound bomb that had jammed in the racks when their plane was flying..over an Italian target. **1958** *Economist* 2 Aug. 352 Thought has to be given now, without delay, to the means of reducing the risks involved in this inevitable act of disengagement—of defusing it, in effect. **1960** *Times* 20 Jan. 6/1 Jack decides to save Barry by defusing the discovered bomb. **1967** *Listener* 1 June 708/2 Mr George Brown..says the Russians are anxious to 'defuse' the middle east. **1968** *Economist* 3 Feb. 11/2 The early release of the crew alone would defuse this crisis, as things now stand. **1970** *Guardian* 9 May 1/3 President Nixon['s]..news conference..which he evidently hopes will defuse much of the students' anger.

defuse, -ed, -edly, defusion, -ive, obs. ff. DIFFUSE, etc.

defusion (diːˈfjuːʒən). *Psychiatry.* [tr. G. *entmischung* (Freud *Das Ich und das Es* (1923) iv. 50), f. DE- II. 1 + FUSION.] A reversal of the normal fusion of the instincts; *spec.* a regression from the normal fusion of the life and death instincts.

1927 J. RIVIERE tr. *Freud's Ego & Id* iv. 57 Once we have admitted the conception of a fusion of the two classes of instincts with each other, the possibility of a 'defusion' of them forces itself upon us. The sadistic component of the sexual instinct would be a classical example of instinctual fusion..and the perversion in which sadism has made itself independent would be typical of defusion. **1945** J. C. FLÜGEL *Man, Morals & Society* viii. 101 The process of defusion, which allows the death instinct to carry on its dread work without the saving grace of love. **1946** *Mind* LV. 83 Such processes as..the 'fusion' and subsequent 'defusion' of the various attitudes of the self. **1955** J. RIVIERE in M. Klein *New Directions in Psycho-Analysis* xiv. 360 They are both situations in which a measure of defusion of instincts has taken place; for the time being either Eros or Thanatos has gained some victory. **1959** G. KENNEDY in S. Hook *Psychoanalysis* 278 A partial defusion of these two normally fused sets of original instincts.

†**de'fust**, *v. Obs. rare*$^{-0}$. [ad. med.L. *dēfustāre* (Du Cange), f. DE- + *fustis* cudgel.]

1623 COCKERAM, *Defust*, to cudgle, or beat one. [**1644** *Vindex Anglicus* 5 How ridiculous..is the merchandise they seeke to sell for currant. Let me afford you a few examples ..Read and censure. *Adpugne, Algate, Daffe..Defust, Depex..Contrast, Catillate*, etc.]

de'fy, *sb.* Now chiefly *U.S.* Also defi. [a. F. *défi*, earlier *deffy* (15th c. in Littré), f. *deffi-er, defi-er* to DEFY.] Declaration of defiance; challenge to fight.

1580 SIDNEY *Arcadia* (1622) 272 Hee..because he found Amphialus was inflexible, wrote his defie vnto him in this maner. **1600** FAIRFAX *Tasso* VI. xx, Arme you, my Lord, he said, your bold defies By your braue foes accepted boldly beene. **1612** BACON *Charge touching Duels*, When he had himself given the lie and defy to the Emperor. **1645** EVELYN *Diary* (1827) I. 279 There had been in the morning a tournament of severall young gentlemen on a formal defy. **1700** DRYDEN *Pal. & Arc.* 1856 At this the challenger with fierce defie His trumpet sounds: the challeng'd makes reply. *a* **1734** NORTH *Exam.* I. ii. §75 (1740) 69 What becomes of his Grace's improper Defy to them? **1888** B. P. BLOOD *Lion of Nile* in *Scribner's Mag.* Dec. 707 And all night long, roaring my fierce defy. **1897** *Harper's Mag.* Jan. 231 He sent out the last defy to the enemy in 1800. **1911** *Boxing* 9 Sept. 454/3 Marcel Denis launches forth with a defi to Young Brooks. **1945** *Sat. Rev. Lit.* 29 Dec. 10 Leonard..still hurls his defy into the teeth of his enemy.

defy (dɪ'faɪ), *v.*^{1} Forms: 4-6 defye, 4-7 -fie, 5- defy, (also 4 defyghe, 4-5 deffie, -fye, dify, diffie, -fy(e, dyffy(e). [ME. a. OF. *des-, def-, defier* (mod.F. *défier*) = Pr. *desfiar, desfizar*, It. *disfidare, diffidare*, med.L. *diffidāre* (Du Cange):—Rom. **disfidāre*, f. DIS- privative + **fīdāre* to trust, give faith to (f. L. *fīdus* faithful). The sense-development appears to have been 'to renounce faith, alliance, or amity with, declare hostility against, challenge to fight'; the later sense 'distrust' found in modern F., and occasionally in Eng., is, according to Darmesteter, perh. taken over from L. *diffīdĕre* to distrust, of which the OF. repr. was *difier*: see sense 7.]

†**1.** *trans.* To renounce faith, allegiance, or affiance to (any one); to declare hostilities or war against; to send a declaration of defiance to. *Obs.*

c **1300** *K. Alis.* 7201 Pors..saide..Yeldith him my feute I no kepe with him have no lewte. Syggith him Y him defyghe, With sweord and with chyvalrye! Of him more holde Y nulle. *c* **1330** R. BRUNNE *Chron.* (1810) 46 Edmunde bi messengers þe erle he diffies. *c* **1450** *Merlin* 70 He hym diffied at the ende of xl dayes, he seide he sholde hym diffende yef he myght. **1568** GRAFTON *Chron.* II. 228 The King sent other Ambassadors..to sommon him: and that if he would not be otherwise advised, then the king gave them full authoritie to defye him. **1885** C. PLUMMER *Fortescue's Abs. & Lim. Mon.* 258 James Douglas..defied the king [of Scotland], and offered his homage to the King of England.

†**b.** To repudiate, disavow. *Obs.*

c **1386** CHAUCER *Knt's. T.* 746, I defye the seurete and the bond Which that thou seist þat I haue maad to thee.

2. To challenge to combat or battle. *arch.*

c **1380** *Sir Ferumb.* 655 If þou art to fiȝte bold com on y þe diffye! **1470-85** MALORY *Arthur* XIII. xv, Tho knyghtes in the Castel defyen yow. **1595** SHAKS. *John* II. i. 406 Defie each other, and pell-mell Make worke vpon our selues, for heauen or hell. **1667** MILTON *P.L.* I. 49 Th' infernal Serpent ..Who durst defie th' Omnipotent to Arms. **1754** RICHARDSON *Grandison* I. xxxix. 291 A man who defies his fellow-creature into the field, in a private quarrel, must first defy his God. **1870** BRYANT *Iliad* I. III. 102 Go now, Defy him to the combat once again.

†**b.** *intr.* To utter defiance. *Obs.*

c **1400** *Rowland & O.* 449 Appon sir Rowlande he gan defy With a full hawtayne steven.

3. *trans.* To challenge to a contest or trial of skill; *esp.* to challenge to do (what the challenger is prepared to maintain cannot be done). Const. *to* and *inf.*

1674 BREVINT *Saul at Endor* 366, I defie all the Roman Preachers to say anything to justifie what they do upon this account. **1697** DRYDEN *Virg. Georg.* II. 773 The Groom his Fellow-Groom at Buts defies. **1770** *Junius Lett.* xxxvii. 181, I defy the most subtile lawyer in this country to point out a single instance in which they have exceeded the truth. **1845** DARWIN *Voy. Nat.* ix. (1890) 211, I defy any one at first sight to be sure that it is not a fish leaping for sport. **1887** BOWEN *Virg. Æneid* VI. 171 In wild folly defying the Ocean Gods to compete.

4. To challenge the power of; to set at defiance; to resist boldly or openly; to set at nought.

1377 LANGL. *P. Pl.* B. xx. 65 Mylde men and holy.. Defyed [C. XXIII. 66 Defieden] al falsenesse and folke þat hit vsed. *c* **1386** CHAUCER *Sompn. T.* 220 For hir lewednesse I hem diffye. **1393** GOWER *Conf.* III. 311 Ha, thou fortune, I the defie, Now hast thou do to me thy werst. **1530** PALSGR. 515/2, I diffye, I set at naught. **1670** DRYDEN *Conq. Granada* I. i, From my walls I defie the Powr's of Spain. **1717** T. TUDWAY in Ellis *Orig. Lett.* Ser. II. IV. 313 With a thousand other insolent speeches defying the Vice-Chancellor and Heads. **1857** MAURICE *Ep. St. John* xiv. 224 The Apostles could not defy the witness of the conscience.

b. Said of things: To resist completely, be beyond the power of.

1715 tr. *Pancirollus' Rerum Mem.* I. II. xix. 116 It [Naphtha]..defies to be quench'd by any Moisture whatever. **1794** MRS. RADCLIFFE *Myst. Udolpho* xv, Others seemed to defy all description. **1838** THIRLWALL *Greece* III. xx. 125 The fortress defied their attacks. **1871** MORLEY *Voltaire* (1886) 242 Holiness, deepest of all the words that defy definition.

†**5.** To set at nought; to reject, renounce, despise, disdain, revolt at. *Obs.*

c **1320** R. BRUNNE *Med.* 743 Y haue be skurged, scorned dyffyed, Wounded, angred, and crucyfyed. *c* **1440** *Promp. Parv.* 115 Dyffyyn, or vtterly dyspysyn, *vilipendo.* **1484** CAXTON *Curiall* 9 Certes, brother, thou demandest that whyche thou oughtest to deffye. **1537** TURNER *Olde Learnyng* To Rdr., Some ther be that do defye All that is newe, and ever do crye The old is better, away with the newe. **1549** OLDE *Erasm. Par. Thess.* 4, I defie all thinges in comparison of the gospel of Christ. **1600** SHAKS. *A.Y.L.* Epil. 21 If I were a Woman, I would kisse as many of you as had..breaths that I defi'de not. **1601** *Downf. Earl Huntington* v. in Hazl. *Dodsley* VIII. 199 No, Iohn, I defy To stain my old hands in thy youthful blood. **1727-38** GAY *Fables* I. xxvi. 17 He next the mastiff's honour try'd, Whose honest jaws the bribe defy'd.

6. ? To reprobate; to curse. *Obs.*

c **1430** *Hymns Virg.* (1867) 95 Hise deedli synnis he gan to defie. **1548** HALL *Chron.* 52 b, The faire damoselles defied that daie [at Agincourt] in the whiche thei had lost their paramors.

†**7.** *intr.* To have or manifest want of faith; to have distrust *of*. *Obs.* [OF. *difier de*, 12th c. in Hatzf.]

c **1380** WYCLIF *Wks.* (1880) 479 He were a fool out of bileue þat diffiede heere of Cristis help. **1502** *Ord. Crysten Men* (W. de W. 1506) II. xviii. 136 We sholde defye aboue all of our strength & our merytes. **1613** R. C. *Table Alph.* (ed. 3), *Defie*, distrust.

†**de'fy**, *v.*^{2} *Obs.* Forms: 4-6 defye, 4-5 defie, deffye, 5 dyffye, difye, defy, defyyn. [The word has all the appearance of being of F. origin, but no equivalent OF. *defier* has yet been recorded, nor is it clear what the etymology of such a form would be. Phonologically, it might answer to L. *dēfæcāre, dēfēcāre* (see DEFECATE); but the sense offers difficulties. It has been suggested, however, that if 1 b were the starting-point, it might conceivably answer to a late L. *dēfæcāre stomachum* (cf. *dissolvere stomachum* Pliny). But the sense-development remains uncertain, and the order here followed is provisional. It may be that 'dissolve' was the primary sense.]

1. *trans.* To digest (food). Said of a person, of the stomach or other organ, of nature, a solvent, etc.

1362 LANGL. *P. Pl.* A. Prol. 108 Good wyn of Gaskoyne And wyn of Oseye, Of Ruyn and of Rochel þe Rost to defye. **1377** *Ibid.* B. XIII. 404 More mete ete and dronke þen kende miȝt defie. *Ibid.* B. xv. 63 Hony is yuel to defye. **1382** WYCLIF *1 Sam.* xxv. 37 Whanne Naabal hadde defied the wyn [Vulg. *digessisset*]. **1393** GOWER *Conf.* III. 25 My stomack may it nought defie. *c* **1400** *Lanfranc's Cirurg.* 240 If..þe patient mai not wel defie his mete. *c* **1440** *Promp. Parv.* 115 Defyyn mete or drynke, *digero.* **1542** BOORDE *Dyetary* ix. (1870) 250 The lyuer..can not truely decocte, defye ne dygest the superabundaunce of meate & drynke the whiche is in the stomacke.

b. *to defy the stomach, a person*; to *digest* the stomach: see DIGEST *v.*

1393 GOWER *Conf.* III. 41 Nero than..slough hem, for he wolde se The whose stomack was best defied. And whan he hath the sothe tried, He found that he, which goth the pas, Defied best of alle was. ? *c* **1475** *Sqr. lowe Degre* 761 Ye shall have rumney and malmesyne..Rochell. The reed your stomake to defye.

2. *intr.* Of food: To undergo digestion, to digest.

c **1315** SHOREHAM 28 Ac [hyt]..defith nauȝt ase thy mete ..Nabyd hyȝt nauȝt ase other mete Hys tyme of defyynge. **1362** LANGL. *P. Pl.* A. v. 219 For hungur oþer for Furst I make myne A-vou, Schal neuer fysch on Fridai defyen in my mawe.

3. *trans.* To make ready by a process likened to digestion, to 'concoct'.

c **1380** WYCLIF *Serm.* xxxiii. Sel. Wks. I. 88 Water..is drawen in to þe vine tree and siþ in to þe grapis, and by tyme defyed til þat it be wyn. **1398** TREVISA *Barth. De P.R.* IV. vii. (Tollem. MS.), It is seyde þat yf blood is wel sode and defied, þerof men makeþ wel talow. *c* **1400** *Lanfranc's Cirurg.* 222 If þou drawist out þe matere þat is neische þe matere þat is hard is yvel to defie.

b. To dissolve, waste by dissolution.

1393 GOWER *Conf.* I. 76 Þilke ymage Thei drowen out and als so faste Fer into Tibre þei it caste, Wher þe riuere it haþ defied. *c* **1430** LYDG. *Bochas* VI. xv. (1554) 162 b, The honde, the head..Were..Upon a stake set vp..There to abyde where it did shyne or reyne With wynde and wether til they wer defyed.

c. *intr.*

c **1420** *Pallad. on Husb.* III. 1160 (Fitz. MS.) The mirtes baies rype..hit is to take And honge hem in thy wyn wessell ywrie All cloos & long in hit let hem defie.

4. *to defy out*: to eject as excrement; to void.

1382 WYCLIF *Deut.* xxiii. 13 Whanne thow sittist, thow shalt delue bi enuyrown, and the defied out thow shalt couer with erthe, in the whych thow art releued.

defyer, obs. form of DEFIER.

de'fying, *vbl. sb.*^{1} [f. DEFY *v.*^{1} + -ING^1.] The action of DEFY *v.*^{1}; a defiance, a challenge.

c **1300** *K. Alis.* 7289 Alisaunder..hath afonge thy deffying. *c* **1440** *Promp. Parv.* 116 Defyynge, or dyspysynge, *vilipencio, floccipencio.* **1483** *Cath. Angl.* 94 Defiynge, *despeccio, etc.*; *vbi* a disspysynge.

†**de'fying**, *vbl. sb.*^{2} [f. DEFY *v.*^{2} + -ING^1.] The action of digesting; digestion.

c **1315** [see DEFY *v.*^{2} 2]. *c* **1400** *Lanfranc's Cirurg.* 162 Þese arterys goiþ to..þe lyvere & geveþ him vertu ful myche & makiþ defiynge. *c* **1440** *Promp. Parv.* 116 Defyynge of mete or drynke, *digestio.* **1483** *Cath. Angl.* 94 A Defiynge, *digestio.*

de'fying, *ppl. a.* [f. DEFY *v.*^{1} + -ING^1.] That defies; defiant.

1834 MACAULAY *Pitt* Ess. (1854) 309/1 His impetuous, adventurous and defying character.

Hence **de'fyingly** *adv.*, defiantly, with defiance.

1831 L. E. L. in *Examiner* 821/1 The petticoat is defyingly dragged through the mud. **1856** MRS. BROWNING *Aur. Leigh* I. 504, I looked into his face defyingly.

defyne, defynicion, etc., obs. ff. DEFINE, DEFINITION, etc.

deg, *v.*^{1} *dial.* [var. of DAG *v.*^{4}] **a.** *trans.* To sprinkle with water; to damp. **b.** *intr.* To drizzle. Hence **degging** *vbl. sb.*; in comb. *degging-can, -cart, -machine* (see quots.).

1674 in RAY *N.C. Words* 14. **1854** W. GASKELL *Lect. Lanc. Dial.* 28 (*Lanc. Gloss.*) The word which a Lancashire man employs for sprinkling with water is 'to deg', and when he degs his garden he uses a deggin-can. **1865** MISS LAHEE *Carter's Struggles* vii. 53 (*ibid.*), Si' tho' what a deggin' hoo's gin me. **1874** KNIGHT *Dict. Mech.*, *Degging-machine* (Cotton), One for damping the fabric in the process of calendering. **1885** *Manch. Exam.* 14 Aug. 2/6 It was usual for the degging cart to go three times over the ground..as twice going over would not deg across the road. **1892** *Northumb. Wds.*, *Deg*, to drizzle = *Dag.*

‖**dégagé** (degaʒe), *a.*; fem. -ée. [F. pa. pple. of *dégager* to disengage, put at ease.] Easy, unconstrained (in manner or address).

1697 VANBRUGH *Relapse* IV. vi. 218, I do use to appear a little more dégagé. **1712** BUDGELL *Spect.* No. 277 ¶8 An Air altogether galant and dégagé. **1762** GOLDSM. *Cit. W.* xxxix, Mamma pretended to be as *dégagée* as I. **1855** DICKENS *Dorrit* (Househ. ed.) 203/2 You ought to make yourself fit for it [Society] by being more dégagé and less preoccupied.

†**degalant**, *a. Obs. rare.* [f. DE- II. 3 + *galant*, GALLANT *a.*] Ungallant, wanting in gallantry.

1778 *Hist. Eliza Warwick* II. 6 The most insensible of lovers, the most degalant bridegroom.

†**de'gamboy.** *Obs.* Short for *viol-de-gamboy* (Shaks.) = *viola-da-gamba*, a musical instrument: see GAMBA and VIOLA.

1618 FLETCHER *Chances* IV. ii, Presuming To medle with my degamboys.

deganglionate, degeneralize: see DE- II. 1.

degarnish (dɪ'gɑːnɪʃ), *v. rare.* By-form of DISGARNISH: see DE- I. 6.

degas (diː'gæs), *v.* [f. DE- II. 2 + GAS *sb.*] *trans.* To remove unwanted gas from. Also **de,gasifi'cation**; **de'gasify** *v.*; **de'gasifying** *ppl. a.*; **de'gasser**; **de'gassing** *vbl. sb.* and *ppl. a.*

1901 D. VON WAGNER *Man. Chem. Technol.* 12 If wood is heated above 150°, it is de-gasified. **1920** *Lit. Digest* 8 May 117 The first 'degassing chamber' was constructed in a cellar ..in the shell-torn village of Cagnicourt, France. **1925** *Chem. Abstr.* 1938 (*heading*) Degasification and reactivity of carbonized fuels. **1928** *Brewer & Maltster & Beverageur* 15 Jan. 50 It is very difficult, once a water is de-gassed, to prevent it absorbing oxygen anew. **1934** WEBSTER, Degasser. **1936** *Nature* 26 Dec. 1091/2 The electrical vehicle used for transporting the degasser is operated by an 80-volt battery. According to recent experiments, an area contained by a circumference of about 300 meters and covering sewers ..can be degassed in 10-15 minutes. **1946** *Nature* 27 July 133/2 We believe that..(3) the type of source, as well as the degassing procedure followed in conditioning the fluoride before coating, affects the hardness [of magnesium fluoride films]. **1949** *Electronic Engin.* XXI. 423 Liquids and melted substances can be de-gassed by ultrasonic waves. **1953** *Jrnl. Iron & Steel Inst.* CLXXIII. 440/1 The author describes a method of desulphurizing and degassing steel in the ladle. **1958** *New Scientist* 7 Aug. 575/3 More information on the Dutch degasifying device..would..be valuable. **1965** *Times* 12 Mar. 24/1 (*caption*) This degasification station [at an oil-drilling rig] makes a strangely unreal picture.

†**de'gast.** *Obs.* [a. OF. *degast* (14th c.), mod.F. *dégât*, f. OF. *degaster* to devastate, f. DE- I. 3 + *gaster* to waste.] Devastation, ruin, waste.

1592 WYRLEY *Armorie* 116 Ech thing almost we turne vnto degaste. **1653** H. COGAN tr. *Pinto's Trav.* liv. 214 He lost in all these degasts eight Thousand of his men.

de Gaullist, *a.* and *sb.* = GAULLIST *a.* and *sb.* So **de Gaullism** = GAULLISM.

1944 H. G. WELLS *'42 to '44* 63 It [*sc.* a novel] is, among other insanities, strongly de Gaullist. *Ibid.* 152 To build up a de Gaullist mentality in the infantile French mind. *Ibid.* 153 The de Gaullists in North Africa. **1946** W. S. CHURCHILL *Secret Session Speeches* 82 Any admixture of De Gaullist troops at the outset would destroy all hope of a peaceful landing. **1955** KOESTLER *Trail of Dinosaur* 199 English Labourites and Conservatives, French Socialists and de Gaullists, spoke from the same platform. **1963** *Daily Tel.* 4 Feb. 20/6 The political implications of 'de Gaullism' as they may affect Italy.

degauss (diː'gaʊs), *v.* [f. DE- II. 2 + the name of K. F. *Gauss*, German scientist (1777–1855). Cf. GAUSS.] *trans.* To protect (a ship) against magnetic mines by encircling it with an electrically charged cable (called the ***degaussing belt*** or ***girdle***), so as to demagnetize it. Also in extended use, to remove unwanted magnetism from, to demagnetize. So **de'gaussed** *ppl. a.*, **de'gaussing** *vbl. sb.*

1940 *Times* 9 Mar. 6/5 Since the object of the device was to render ships non-magnetic, the verb to 'de-gauss'..was coined to indicate its function. *Ibid.*, The 'de-gauss-ing girdle'..consists of ordinary insulated electric cable, energized in a special way by an electric current. *Ibid.*, One of the officers responsible for its development expressed himself perfectly ready himself to take any properly de-gaussed ship over any number of magnetic mines. **1940** *Daily Tel.* 9 Mar. 1/4 A new word (de-gaussing) has been added to the wartime vocabulary of the Royal Navy as the result of the arrival of the German magnetic mine. It implies de-magnetising, or de-polarising a ship. **1940** *Manch. Guardian Weekly* 15 Mar. 201 A device which makes a ship incapable of affecting the magnetic needle in the mine. The apparatus is known as a degaussing girdle. It takes the form of an electric cable following the line of the hull round the ship's upper deck or bulwark. **1946** W. S. CHURCHILL *Secret Session Speeches* 25 The protective measures of the Admiralty—convoy, diversion, degaussing. **1954** C. P. SNOW *New Men* 13 He was working at Rosyth in one of the first degaussing parties. **1960** O. SKILBECK *ABC of Film & TV* 39 *Degaussing*, the process of removing residual magnetism from metallic objects. It is necessary frequently to degauss cutting room equipment. **1960** J. L. BERNSTEIN *Video Tape Recording* xii. 259 It is wise to degauss the heads prior to each recording session. **1968** W. H. BUCHSBAUM *Color TV Servicing* (ed. 2) v. 50 Degaussing a picture tube, just like demagnetizing the tape recorder head, is accomplished by generating a strong AC field around the degaussed object and then gradually reducing this field. **1969** *Daily Tel.* 21 July 10/8 Any colour receiver is sensitive to magnetic influences..and an elaborate degaussing process had to be applied to the first receivers that I used.

degelation (ˌdiːdʒɪ'leɪʃən). *rare.* [f. F. *dégeler* to thaw, f. *des-*, *dé-* (DE- I. 6) + *geler* to freeze.] Melting from the frozen state; thawing.

In mod. Dict.

†**degen** ('deɪgən). *Old Cant.* Also **degan, dagen.** [Ger.; = sword.]

a **1700** B. E. *Dict. Cant. Crew*, *Degen*, a Sword. **1785** in GROSE *Dict. Vulg. T.* **1827** LYTTON *Pelham* (1864) 325 (Farmer) Tip him the degen.

†**de'gender,** *v. Obs.* [ad. L. *dēgenerāre*, F. *dégénérer* (15th c.), after GENDER *v.*] *intr.* To degenerate.

1539 TAVERNER *Gard. Wysed.* II. 18b, He forgatte all goodnes and degendred quyte & cleane from the renowmed & excellent vertues of hys father. **1596** SPENSER *Hymne Heav. Love* 94 So that next off-spring of the Makers love.. Degendering to hate, fell from above Through pride. **1597** LOWE *Chirurg.* (1634) 83 If it [Furuncle]..much inflameth, oftentimes it degendereth into Anthrax.

Hence †**de'gendered** *ppl. a.*, degenerate.

1561 T. NORTON *Calvin's Inst.* II. ii. (1634) 117 The perverted and degendred nature of man.

†**de'gener,** *v. Obs.* [a. F. *dégénér-er*, ad. L. *dēgenerāre*: see DEGENERATE.] *intr.* = prec. Hence **de'genered** *ppl. a.*

1545 JOYE *Exp. Dan.* iv. G ij b, Yᵉ churche..degenered much from her first beutye. **1611** ed. *Spenser's F.Q.* v. Prol. ii, They into that ere long will be degenered [**1596** degendered]. **1614** EARL STIRLING *Doomes-day, Fifth Hour* (R.), Of religion a degener'd seed.

degeneracy (dɪ'dʒɛnərəsɪ). [f. DEGENERATE *a.*: see -ACY.] **1. a.** The condition or quality of being degenerate.

1664 H. MORE *Myst. Iniq.* 206 This grand Degeneracy of the Church. **1711** ADDISON *Spect.* No. 65 ¶9 It is Nature in its utmost Corruption and Degeneracy. **1862** GOULBURN *Pers. Relig.* 117 A degeneracy from the scriptural theory of Public Worship. **1883** FROUDE *Short Stud.* IV. v. 336 The fall of a nobility may be a cause of degeneracy, or it may only be a symptom.

b. An instance of degeneracy; something that is degenerate. *rare.*

1678 CUDWORTH *Intell. Syst.* 133 (R.) We incline..to account this form of atheism..to be but a certain degeneracy from the right Heraclitick and Zenonian cabala. **1862** ALFORD in *Life* (1873) 345 The cathedral of Sens is a sad degeneracy from ours.

2. *Physics.* **a.** A property of a quantized or an oscillatory system (see DEGENERATE *a.* 3 a).

1928 SHEARER & DEANS tr. *Schrödinger's Coll. Papers Wave Mech.* 70 Multiplicity of the proper values corresponds to degeneracy in the theory of conditioned periodic systems and is therefore especially interesting for quantum theory. **1935** J. DOUGALL tr. *Born's Atomic Physics* v. 108 When the relativistic variability of mass is taken into consideration, the degeneracy of the hydrogen atom is certainly removed in part, but the motion is still simply degenerate. **1971** *Nature* 23 Apr. 495/3 Interaction between the free oscillations [of the Earth] and the Earth's rotation removes degeneracy in the spherical harmonics of the same degree.

b. A property of a system of particles or 'gas' (see DEGENERATE *a.* 3 b).

1928 *Proc. Physical Soc.* XL. 327 An example of degeneracy is provided by the free electrons in a metal even at normal temperature. **1958** J. B. SYKES tr. *Ambartsumyan's Theoret. Astrophysics* xxxii. 544 Owing to the high ionisation inside the stars [*sc.* white dwarfs], the gas retains the properties of an ideal gas..up to densities of about 10^2 or 10^3 g/cm³; at higher densities a degeneracy sets in, at first of the electron gas, and later (for densities greater than 10^5 or 10^6 g/cm³) of the heavy particles.

degenerate (dɪ'dʒɛnərət), *a.* Also 5–6 -at, 6 *Sc.* -it. [ad. L. *dēgenerāt-us*, pa. pple. of *dēgenerāre*: see next.]

A. as *pa. pple.* = Degenerated. *Obs.* or *arch.*

1494 [see B. 1]. **1500–20** DUNBAR *Poems* xiv. 42 Sic brallaris and bosteris, degenerat fra thair naturis. **1552** ABP. HAMILTON *Catech.* (1884) 19 How matrimonye was degenerat fra the first perfectioun. **1559** in Strype *Ann. Ref.* I. viii. 23 To what abuses the state of that lyff was degenerate. **1607–12** BACON *Ess. Great Place* (Arb.) 284 Observe wherein and how they have degenerate. **1733** SWIFT *On Poetry* 381 Degen'rate from their ancient brood.

B. as *adj.*

1. Having lost the qualities proper to the race or kind; having declined from a higher to a lower type; hence, declined in character or qualities; debased, degraded. **a.** of persons.

1494 FABYAN *Chron.* VII. ccxxxv. 272 Thou art degenerat, & growen out of kynde. **1605** SHAKS. *Lear* I. iv. 276 *Lear.* Degenerate Bastard, Ile not trouble thee; Yet haue I left a daughter. **1794** S. WILLIAMS *Vermont* 196 The Laplanders are only degenerate Tartars. **1848** MACAULAY *Hist. Eng.* II. 139 Tyrconnel sprang..from one of those degenerate families of the pale which were popularly classed with the aboriginal population of Ireland. **1856** FROUDE *Hist. Eng.* (1858) I. iii. 242 The degenerate representatives of a once noble institution.

b. of animals and plants: *spec.* in *Biol.* (cf. DEGENERATION 1 b).

1611 BIBLE *Jer.* ii. 21 How then art thou turned into the degenerate plant of a strange vine? **1651** N. BACON *Disc. Govt.* II. i. (1739) 4 (As a Plant transplanted into a savage soil) in degree and disposition wholly degenerate. **1665** T. HERBERT *Trav.* (1677) 12 Penguins..the wings or fins hanging down like sleeves, covered with down instead of Feathers..a degenerate Duck. **1879** RAY LANKESTER *Degeneration* 52 The Ascidian Phallusia shows itself to be a degenerate Vertebrate by beginning life as a tadpole. **1890** M. MARSHALL in *Nature* 11 Sept., Animals..which have lost organs or systems which their progenitors possessed, are commonly called degenerate.

c. *fig.* of things. (In *Geom.* applied to a locus of any order when reduced to the condition of an aggregate of loci of a lower order.)

1552 [see A]. **1669** GALE *Crt. of Gentiles* I. I. vii. 36 The several names..were al but corrupt degenerate derivations from Iewish Traditions. **1763** J. BROWN *Poetry & Mus.* xi. 193 The degenerate Arts sunk with the degenerate City. **1878** MORLEY *Carlyle* Crit. Misc. Ser. I. 201 The cant and formalism of any other degenerate form of active faith.

2. *transf.* Characterized by degeneracy.

1651 tr. *Bacon's Life & Death* 8 In Tame Creatures, their Degenerate Life corrupteth them. **1715–20** POPE *Iliad* XII. 540 Such men as live in these degenerate days. **1870** SWINBURNE *Ess. & Stud.* (1875) 101 There has never been an age that was not degenerate in the eyes of its own fools.

3. *Physics.* **a.** Of a quantized system: having two or more linearly independent eigen-functions with the same eigenvalue; *spec.* having two or more states with the same energy; also applied to the eigenfunctions or the states. Also more widely, applied to any oscillatory system having two or more modes of oscillation with the same frequency, and to the modes themselves.

1923 H. L. BROSE tr. *Sommerfeld's Atomic Struct. & Spectral Lines* 564 We follow Schwarzschild and call the exceptional case considered degenerate. A degenerate case thus occurs..when the quantum conditions are not uniquely determined. **1929** CONDON & MORSE *Quantum Mech.* iv. 136 It is better to speak of a particular level as degenerate or non-degenerate, for there are mechanical systems in which some states are degenerate and others are not. **1940** F. SEITZ *Mod. Theory Solids* xii. 411 The six functions do not have the proper symmetry to have the same energy in a cubic crystal. Thus, the degenerate levels would split if interatomic interactions were taken into account. **1961** POWELL & CRASEMANN *Quantum Mech.* vi. 173 The eigenvalue a may be degenerate... Suppose, for example, that a is doubly degenerate, having linearly independent eigenfunctions ψ_1 and ψ_2 which may..be assumed to be orthonormal. **1968** R. C. STANLEY *Light & Sound* xvi. 315 If two or more normal modes [of vibration] formed by different reflection paths have the same resonant frequency ..they are termed degenerate modes... In an irregularly shaped room fewer degenerate or near degenerate modes form.

b. Of a system of particles or 'gas' (such as the electrons in a metal or the interior of a white dwarf star): having properties which depart markedly from those of an ordinary gas as described by classical statistical mechanics, being described either by Fermi-Dirac or by Bose-Einstein statistics.

1928 *Proc. Physical Soc.* XL. 330 Thomas supposes the electrons in an atom to be degenerate in the sense of Fermi and Dirac. **1939** S. CHANDRASEKHAR *Introd. Study Stellar Struct.* x. 358 A completely degenerate electron gas is one in which all the lowest quantum states are occupied. **1951** J. DOUGALL tr. *Born's Atomic Physics* (ed. 5) viii. 265 Pauli and Sommerfeld (1927)..pointed out that the laws of classical statistics ought not to be applied to the electron gas within a metal, since it is bound to behave as a degenerate gas. **1954** D. TER HAAR *Elem. Statist. Mech.* iv. 95 In the interior of some stars such high densities will occur that notwithstanding the very high stellar temperatures the gas is degenerate. **1966** *New Statesman* 15 Apr. 534/1 These x-ray sources..might be made of 'degenerate matter'—matter so compacted that the atoms have collapsed down to the size of their nuclei. Such a star would be fantastically dense.

degenerate (dɪ'dʒɛnərət), *sb.* [subst. use of the adj.] One who has lost, or has become deficient in, the qualities considered proper to the race or kind; a degenerate specimen; a person of debased physical or mental constitution.

1555 J. PROCTOR *Historie of Wyates Rebellion* f. 80 It is to be wished..that prouoked with so greate clemencie these degenerates reforme themselues. **1895** tr. *Nordau's Degeneration* I. iii. 18 In the mental development of degenerates, we meet with the same irregularity that we have observed in their physical growth... That which nearly all degenerates lack is the sense of morality and of right and wrong. **1901** H. ELLIS *Criminal* (ed. 3) iii. 51 Näcke..found the skulls of women..abnormal, and among degenerates generally..the stigmata of degeneracy are more common in women. **1919** M. K. BRADBY *Psycho-analysis* 17 The fact..is compatible with his being a genius or a degenerate, a scoundrel or a valuable citizen. **1952** W. J. H. SPROTT *Soc. Psychol.* viii. 142 The deplorable Jukes family, their dismal record of defectives and degenerates.

degenerate (dɪ'dʒɛnəreɪt), *v.* [f. *dēgenerāt-*, ppl. stem of L. *dēgenerāre* to depart from its race or kind, to fall from its ancestral quality, f. *dēgener* adj. that departs from its race, ignoble, f. DE- I. 1 + *gener-* (*genus*) race, kind. So F. *dégénérer* (15th c. in Hatzf.).]

1. *intr.* To lose, or become deficient in, the qualities proper to the race or kind; to fall away from ancestral virtue or excellence; hence (more generally), to decline in character or qualities, become of a lower type. **a.** of persons.

1553 EDEN *Treat. Newe Ind.* (Arb.) 31 Degeneratinge from al kind of honestie and faithfulnes. **1612** T. TAYLOR *Comm. Titus* i. 12 When men degenerate, and by sinne put off the nature of man. **1651** HOBBES *Leviath.* I. xiii. 63 The manner of life, which men..degenerate into in a civill Warre. **1718** LADY M. W. MONTAGU *Let. to C'tess of Mar* 10 Mar., It is well if I do not degenerate into a downright story-teller. **1863** GEO. ELIOT *Romola* I. v, In this respect Florentines have not degenerated from their ancestral customs.

b. of animals and plants.

1577 BULL *Luther's Comm. Ps. Grad.* (1615) 193 They degenerate, and grow out of kind, and become evil plants. **1626** BACON *Sylva* §518 Plants for want of Culture, degenerate to be baser in the same kind; and sometimes so far, as to change into another kind. **1751** CHAMBERS *Cycl.* s.v. *Degeneration*, It is a great dispute among the naturalists, whether or no animals, plants, etc. be capable of degenerating into other species? **1845** FORD *Handbk. Spain* I. 53 They have from neglect degenerated into ponies.

c. *transf.* and *fig.* of things.

1545 RAYNOLD *Byrth of Mankynde* 40 When they be entered into the nauell, the ii. vaynes degenerat in one. **1605** BACON *Adv. Learn.* I. iii. §2. 12 After that the state of Rome was not it selfe, but did degenerate. **1741** BUTLER *Serm.* Wks. 1874 II. 263 Liberty..is..liable..to degenerate insensibly into licentiousness. **1841** D'ISRAELI *Amen. Lit.* (1867) 125 The Latin of the bar had degenerated into the most ludicrous barbarism.

d. *Geom.* Of a curve or other locus: To become reduced to a lower order, or altered into a locus of a different or less complex form.

1763 W. EMERSON *Meth. Increments* vii, If the parts of the abscissa be taken infinitely small, then these parallelograms degenerate into the curve.

†**2.** To show a falling-off or degeneration *from* an anterior type; to be degenerate. *Obs.*

1548 HALL *Chron.* 176b, Jhon Talbot erle of Shrewesbury, a valeant person, and not degenerating from his noble parent. **1623** BINGHAM *Xenophon* 48 Of such Ancestors are you descended. I speak not this, as though you degenerated from them. **1715–20** POPE *Iliad* IV. 451 Such Tydeus was..Gods! how the son degenerates from the sire. **1739** —— in *Swift's Lett.* (1766) II. 255 Dr. Arbuthnot's daughter does not degenerate from the humour and goodness of her father.

†**3.** To become or be altered in nature or character (without implying debasement); to change in kind; to show an alteration *from* a normal type.

1548 HALL *Chron.* 176b, The Scottes also not degeneratyng from their olde mutabilitie. **1576** FLEMING *Panopl. Epist.* 149 It is now highe time for you to degenerate, and to be unlike your selfe [i.e. less martial]. **1597** GERARDE *Herbal* I. xlii. 62 It is altered..into Wheate it selfe, as degenerating from bad to better. **1600** HAKLUYT *Voy.* (1810) III. 186 Some..followed Courses degenerating from the Voyage before pretended.

†**4.** To fall away, revolt. *Obs. rare.*

1602 CAREW *Cornwall* 98 a, The Cornish men..marched to..Welles, where James Touchet, Lord Audely, degenerated to their party. **1622** MALYNES *Anc. Law-Merch.* 431 His friends forsake him, his wife and children suffer with him, or leaue him, or rebell, or degenerate against him.

5. *trans.* To cause to degenerate; to reduce to a lower or worse condition; to debase, degrade.

1645 MILTON *Tetrach.* 192 It degenerates and disorders the best spirits. **1653** *Cloria & Narcissus* I. 172 The least dejection of spirit..would degenerate you from your birth and education. **1710** *Brit. Apollo* III. 2/1 They..Degenerate themselves to Brutes. **1790–1811** COMBE *Devil upon Two Sticks in Eng.* (1817) IV. 16 Her theatric excellencies..are impaired by physical defects, or degenerated by the adoption of bad habits. **1893** J. PULSFORD *Loyalty to Christ* II. 131 The one seeking to regenerate, and the other to degenerate yet more and more the soul's nature. **1921** E. MACNEILL *Celtic Irel.* 17 Acquired habits..can degenerate and recreate a nation.

†**6.** To generate (something of an inferior or lower type). *Obs. rare.*

1649 G. DANIEL *Trinarch., Hen. V* xciv, A bastard flye, Corrupting where it breaths..Degenerating Putrefaction. **1668** CULPEPPER & COLE *Barthol. Anat.* I. xxxii. 75 It is backwards more deep and broad, that the lower and after-end might degenerate as it were the Ditch or Trench.

Hence **de'generating** *vbl. sb.* and *ppl. a.*

1611 SPEED *Hist. Gt. Brit.* VI. xx. §1. 105 Young Commodus, his soone degenerating Son. **1693** BRANCARD *Phys. Dict.* 140/1 *Metaptosis*, the degenerating of one Disease into another, as of a Quartane Ague into a Tertian. **1746** W. HORSLEY *The Fool* No. 5 ¶6 A Degenerating from this Character is the Progress towards the Formation of a Beau.

de'generated, *ppl. a.* [-ED[1].] Fallen from ancestral or original excellence; degenerate.

1581 PETTIE *Guazzo's Civ. Conv.* II. (1586) 84 Unknowen and degenerated posteritie. **1727** DE FOE *Hist. Appar.* iv. (1840) 31 The Devil is..a degenerated, fallen, and evil spirit. **1808** WILFORD *Sacr. Isles* in *Asiat. Res.* VIII. 302 In the present wicked age and degenerated times.

degenerately (dɪˈdʒɛnərətlɪ), *adv.* [f. DEGENERATE *a.* + -LY[2].] In a degenerate manner.

1645 MILTON *Tetrach.* (1851) 145 Nothing now adayes is more degenerately forgott'n, than the true dignity of man. *a* **1671** J. WORTHINGTON *Misc.* 29 (T.) A short view of Rome, Christian, though apostatized and degenerately Christian.

de'generateness. *rare.* [f. as prec. + -NESS.] Degenerate quality or condition; degeneracy.

1640 WILKINS *New Planet* x. (1707) 272 A Degenerateness and Poverty of Spirit. **1684** tr. *Bonet's Merc. Compit.* VI. 156 This degenerateness, which frequently happens to the bloud in Autumnal Fevers.

degeneration (dɪdʒɛnəˈreɪʃən). [a. F. *dégénération* (15th c. in Hatzf.), n. of action from L. *dēgenerāre* to DEGENERATE: see -ATION.]

1. The process of degenerating or becoming degenerate; the falling off from ancestral or earlier excellence; declining to a lower or worse stage of being; degradation of nature.

1607 TOPSELL *Four-f. Beasts* (1658) 460 That so he might learn the difference betwixt his generation, and his degeneration, and consider how great a loss unto him was his fall in Paradise. **1658** SIR T. BROWNE *Hydriot.* i. 3 Others conceived it most natural to end in fire..whereby they also declined a visible degeneration into worms. **1661** COWLEY *Prop. Adv. Exp. Philos.* Concl., Capable (as many good Institutions)..of Degeneration into any thing harmful. **1845** MAURICE *Mor. Philos.* in *Encycl. Metrop.* II. 598/1 It is possible in each case to trace the process of degeneration.

b. *Biol.* A change of structure by which an organism, or some particular organ, becomes less elaborately developed and assumes the form of a lower type.

[**1751** CHAMBERS *Cycl.* s.v., Others hold, that degeneration only obtains in vegetables; and define it the change of a plant of one kind, into that of another viler kind. Thus, say they, wheat degenerates into darnel..But our..best naturalists maintain the opinion of such a degeneration, or transmutation, to be erroneous.] **1848** CARPENTER *Anim. Phys.* 33 Such a degeneration may take place simply from want of use. **1879** RAY LANKESTER *Degeneration* (1880) 32 Degeneration may be defined as a gradual change of the structure in which the organism becomes adapted to less varied and less complex conditions of life. *Ibid.* 32 Elaboration of some one organ may be a necessary accompaniment of Degeneration in all the others. **1883** *Syd. Soc. Lex.* s.v., In many flowers..the formation of a nectary results from the degeneration of the stamens.

c. *Path.* 'A morbid change in the structure of parts, consisting in a disintegration of tissue, or in a substitution of a lower for a higher form of structure' (*Syd. Soc. Lex.*).

1851–60 in MAYNE *Expos. Lex.* **1866** A. FLINT *Princ. Med.* (1880) 54. **1869** E. A. PARKES *Pract. Hygiene* (ed. 3) 193 The gangrenous degeneration rapidly extended. **1883** *Syd. Soc. Lex.* s.v., Fatty degeneration..consists in the substitution of oil globules for the healthy protoplasm of cells, or other structures, by transformation..of the protoplasmic compound.

2. The condition of being degenerate; degeneracy.

?**1481** CAXTON *Orat. G. Flamineus* F j, Rather..with degeneracion than nobleness. *a* **1652** J. SMITH *Sel. Disc.* ix. 446 It speaks the degeneration of any soul..that it should desire to incorporate itself with any..sensual delights. **1865** MERIVALE *Rom. Emp.* VIII. lxviii. 368 When the popular notion of its degeneration was actually realized.

†**3.** Something that has degenerated; a degenerate form or product. *Obs.*

c **1645** HOWELL *Lett.* (1892) II. 475 What Languages..are Dialects, Derivations, or Degenerations from their Originals. **1646** SIR T. BROWNE *Pseud. Ep.* III. xvii. 147 Cockle, Aracus, Ægilops, and other degenerations which come up in unexpected shapes. **1748** HARTLEY *Observ. Man* I. iv. 453 The Degenerations and Counterfeits of Benevolence.

Hence **degene'rationist** *nonce-wd.*, one who holds a theory of degeneration.

1871 TYLOR *Prim. Cult.* I. 48 The opinions of older writers..whether progressionists or degenerationists.

degenerative (dɪˈdʒɛnərətɪv), *a.* [f. L. *dēgenerāt-*, ppl. stem of *dēgenerāre* to DEGENERATE + -IVE.] Of the nature of, or tending to, degeneration.

1846 WORCESTER cites *Month. Rev.* **1879** RAY LANKESTER *Adv. Science* (1890) 46 Degenerative evolution. **1890** HUMPHRY *Old Age* 149 Other degenerative changes, such as calcification of the costal cartilages.

degeneratory (dɪˈdʒɛnərətərɪ), *a. rare.* [f. as prec. + -ORY.] Tending to degeneration.

1876 R. F. BURTON *Gorilla L.* I. 28 Perhaps six years had exercised a degeneratory effect upon Roi Denis.

degenered: see DEGENER.

degenerescence (-ˈɛsəns). *Biol.* [a. F. *dégénérescence* (1799 in Hatzf.), f. *dégénérescent*, deriv. of *dégénérer* to degenerate, after L. inchoative vbs.: see -ESCENT.] Tendency to degenerate; the process of degeneration.

1882 G. ALLEN in *St. James's Gaz.* 30 May 3 They have all..acquired the same parasitic habits, and..exhibit different stages in the same process of degenerescence. **1884** H. MACMILLAN in *Brit. & For. Evang. Rev.* Apr. 315 The *degenerescence* of Decandolle brings all the parts of the flower back to the leaf.

†**de'generize**, *v. Obs. rare*[−1]. [f. L. *dēgener* (see next) + -IZE.] *intr.* To become degenerate, to degenerate.

1605 SYLVESTER *Du Bartas* II. iii. *Vocation* 104 Degeneriz'd, decaid, and withered quight.

†**de'generous**, *a. Obs.* [f. L. *dēgener* degenerate, bastard, spurious (see DEGENERATE *v.*) + -OUS, after GENEROUS *a.*, of which it is, in some senses, treated as a derivative: cf. *ungenerous*, *degallant*.]

1. Fallen from ancestral virtue or excellence, unworthy of one's ancestry or kindred, degenerate. **a.** of persons.

1600 DEKKER *Gentle Craft* Wks. 1873 I. 74 Your Grace to do me honour Heapt on the head of this degenerous boy Desertless favours. **1643** PRYNNE *Sov. Power Parl.* IV. 35 Disclaiming them as degenerous Brats, and not their sonnes. *a* **1734** NORTH *Lives* I. 199 An upstart and degenerous race.

b. of personal qualities, feelings, actions, etc.

1597 DANIEL *Civ. Wars* I. lii, The least felt touch of a degenerous feare. *a* **1734** NORTH *Exam.* II. v. §41 (1740) 338 That this Passive-Obedience or Non-Resistance of theirs is a slavish and degenerous Principle.

c. *transf.* Characterized by degeneration.

1611 SPEED *Hist. Gt. Brit.* IX. x. (1632) 647 In our effeminate and degenerous age. **1690** BOYLE *Chr. Virtuoso* II. 39 Especially in such a Degenerous age.

d. Const. *from.* (*rare.*)

1657 BP. H. KING *Poems* III. ix. (1843) 91 He n'er had shew'd Himself..So much degen'rous from renowned Vere. **1695** DODWELL *Def. Vind. Deprived Bps.* 36 The Ages he deals in were very degenerous from the Piety and Skill of their Primitive Ancestors.

2. *transf.* and *fig.* of things (*esp.* organisms or organic products).

1635 F. WHITE *Sabbath* Ep. Ded. 4 A good tree hath some degenerous branches. **1748** *Univ. Mag.* Aug. 65 That..a new born child should..be corrupted by the degenerous and adventitious milk of another.

Hence †**de'generously** *adv.*, †**de'generousness.**

1627 H. BURTON *Baiting of Pope's Bull* 94 No true Englishman will be..so vnnaturally and degenerously impious. *a* **1734** NORTH *Lives* I. 371 Naming him so degenerously as he did. **1678** WALTON *Life Sanderson* (1681) 2 All the Rubbish of their Degenerousness ought to fall heavy on such dishonourable heads.

degentilize, degermanize: see DE- II. 1.

de,geomorphi'zation. *nonce-wd.* [f. DE- II. 1, Gr. γῆ (comb. γεω-) earth + μορφή form.] The process of making unlike, or less like, the earth.

1894 *Jrnl. Educ.* 1 Jan. 61/2 [They insist] that religious progress tends towards the de-anthropomorphization of God. Does it not equally tend towards the de-geomorphization of heaven?

de'germ, *v.* [DE- II. 2.] *trans.* To remove the germ from (e.g. wheat).

de'germinator. [DE- II. 1 + L. *germen* germ.] A machine with iron discs for splitting the grains of wheat and removing the germ.

In mod. Dicts.

degeroite (dɛgəˈrəʊaɪt). *Min.* [Named 1850 f. *Degerö* in Finland.] A variety of Hisingerite.

1868 in DANA *Min.* 489.

degest, obs. form of DIGEST.

degging: see DEG *v.*[1]

degh, obs. pres. t. of DOW *v.* to be of use.

degise, obs. form of DISGUISE.

†**de'glabrate**, *v. Obs.* [f. L. *dēglabrāt-*, ppl. stem of *dēglabrāre* to smooth down, make smooth, f. DE- I. 3 + *glabr-* smooth, *glabrāre* to make smooth.] *trans.* To make quite smooth. Hence **de'glabrated** *ppl. a.*

1623 COCKERAM, *Deglabrate*, to pull off skin, hayre, or the like. **1684** tr. *Bonet's Merc. Compit.* XIV. 466 An Eye-lid inverted..was amended by cutting the Circle of the Deglabrated Eye-lid.

deglaciation (diːgleɪʃɪˈeɪʃən). *Geol.* [f. DE- II. 1 + GLACIATION 2.] The disappearance of ice from a previously glaciated region.

1895 J. D. DANA *Man. Geol.* (ed. 4) IV. iv. 969 Partial deglaciation, and the formation of a sheet of drift perhaps 20′ in thickness, with occasional layers of soil embedded in the drift. **1947** R. F. FLINT *Glacial Geol. & Pleistocene Epoch* v. 64 By deglaciation is meant the uncovering of any area as a result of glacier shrinkage. **1961** *New Scientist* 25 May 444/3 It would be interesting to speculate upon the results of sudden deglaciation of the [Antarctic] continent.

degladiation, obs. form of DIGLADIATION.

deglamorize, deglamourize (diːˈglæməraɪz), *v.* Also -ise. [f. DE- II. 1 + GLAMORIZE *v.*] To deprive of glamour. So **de'glamorization**; **de'glamorized** *ppl. a.*

1938 *Covina* (Calif.) *Independent* 22 Mar., The problem..seems to be how the 'deglamorizing' of the 'whataman' idea among the dupes of the dictators is to be accomplished. **1941** *Sunday Jrnl. & Star* (Lincoln, Neb.) 2 Nov., Paulette Goddard recently became the first Hollywood glamor girl to de-glamorize herself in the interest of national defense. **1942** *Time* 27 Apr. 24/1 Deglamorization of the week was performed by an alert news photographer..who caught the handsome face of..Norma Shearer registering desolation. **1942** *Gen* 15 July 31/2 From the minute they join the depot, they find themselves undergoing a de-glamorisation course. **1962** *Times Lit. Suppl.* 26 Oct. 821/4 The deglamorized toughies of the 1960s. **1964** *Punch* 28 Oct. 657/3 It seems rather late to deglamorise war.

deglaze *v.*: see DE- II. 2.

†**de'glory**, *v. Obs. rare.* [f. DE- II. 2 + GLORY *sb.*] *trans.* To deprive of its glory.

1610 G. FLETCHER *Christ's Vict.* I. xvii, To crowne his head, That was before with thornes degloried. **1653** R. MASON in *Bulwer's Anthropomet.* Let. to Author, Neither his soule nor body (both being so degloried).

†**de'glubate**, *v. Obs. rare.* [irreg. f. L. *dēglūbĕre* to peel, flay (f. DE- I. 3 + *glūbĕre* to peel, flay) + -ATE.] *trans.* To flay, excoriate.

1623 COCKERAM, *Deglubate*, to fley a thing. **1698** FRYER *Acc. E. Ind. & P.* 297 To prevent the sharp Winds deglubating us, we housed our selves Cap-a-pee under Felts.

†**de'glubing**, *ppl. a. Obs. rare*[−1]. [f. *deglube vb., ad. L. *dēglūbĕre*: see prec.] Flaying.

a **1658** CLEVELAND *Cl. Vind.* (1677) 96 Now enter his Taxing and deglubing Face, a squeezing Look like that of Vespasianus.

de'glutate, *v. rare*[−1]. [irreg. f. L. *dēglūtīre*: see next.] = DEGLUTE.

1867 *Jrnl. R. Agric. Soc.* Ser. II. III. II. 639 The chance of choking does not depend upon hair which is deglutated.

deglute (dɪˈgluːt), *v. Obs.* exc. as *nonce-wd.* In 6 di-. [f. L. *dēglūtīre*, f. DE- I. 1 down + *glūtīre*, *gluttīre* to swallow.] *trans.* To swallow, swallow down. Also *absol.*

1599 A. M. tr. *Gabelhouer's Bk. Physicke* 101/2 Make little Pilles, contayne them in thy mouth, and by little and little diglute or swallowe them. **1820** L. HUNT *Indicator* No. 64 (1822) II. 95 They champ, they grind, they deglute.

†**de'glutible**, *a. Obs. rare.* [f. L. *dēglūtī-re* (see prec.) + -BLE.] Capable of being swallowed.

1661 LOVELL *Hist. Anim. & Min.* 515 Some are prescribed in a potable forme..Others deglutible, as pills and powders.

de'glutinate, *v.* [f. L. *dēglūtināt-*, ppl. stem of *dēglūtināre* to unglue (Pliny), f. DE- I. 6 + *glūtināre* to glue.]

†**1.** *trans.* To unglue; to loosen or separate (things glued together). *Obs.*

1609 J. DAVIES *Holy Roode* (1876) 16 (D.) The Hand of Outrage that deglutinates His Vesture, glu'd with gore-blood to His backe. **1727** BAILEY vol. II, *Deglutinated.*

2. To deprive of gluten, extract the gluten from.

1889 in *Cent. Dict.*

Hence **degluti'nation.**

1623 in COCKERAM II. s.v. *Vngluing.* **1721** in BAILEY.

†**de'glution.** *Obs.* [a. obs. F. *deglution* (Cotgr.).] = next.

1657 TOMLINSON *Renou's Disp.* 115 Compressed with the tongue or teeth before deglution.

deglutition (ˌdiːgluːˈtɪʃən). *Phys.* [a. F. *déglutition* (Paré 16th c.), n. of action f. L. *dēglūtīre*: see DEGLUTE.] The action of swallowing.

1650 BULWER *Anthropomet.* 118 The action of the Gullet, that is Deglutition. **1748** HARTLEY *Observ. Man* I. ii. 135 The Nerves of the Fauces, and Muscles of Deglutition. **1802** PALEY *Nat. Theol.* (1804) 195 In a city feast..what deglutition, what anhelation! **1804** ABERNETHY *Surg. Obs.* 199 The difficulty of deglutition arose from the unnatural state in which the muscles of the pharynx were placed. **1861** LOWELL *Biglow P.* Poems 1890 II. 216 Persons who venture their lives in the deglutition of patent medicines.

b. In *fig.* senses of *swallow*.

1764 REID *Inquiry* vi. §19 As the stomach receives its food, so the soul receives her images by a kind of nervous deglutition. **1848** C. BRONTE *J. Eyre* (1857) 241 Judgment untempered by feeling is too bitter and husky a morsel for human deglutition. **1858** FROUDE *Hist. Eng.* IV. 187 Even such good Catholics as the Irish chiefs had commenced a similar process of deglutition, much to their comfort.

deglutitious (diːgluːˈtɪʃəs), *a. rare.* [f. prec.: see -OUS.] Pertaining or tending to deglutition.

1822 HEBER in *Jer. Taylor's Wks.* (1828) I. Introd. p. xci, With the poor book which is beslavered with such deglutitious phrases I have no acquaintance.

deglutitive (dɪˈgluːtɪtɪv), *a. rare.* [f. as next + -IVE.] = next.

In some mod. Dicts.

deglutitory (dɪˈgluːtɪtərɪ), *a. rare.* [f. L. *dēglūtīt-*, ppl. stem of *dēglūtīre* to DEGLUTE + -ORY.] Pertaining to deglutition; having the function of swallowing.

1864 in WEBSTER. **1887** *Cornh. Mag.* Jan. 59 The little invalid, whose masticatory and deglutitory powers were now feebler.

deglycerin(e *v.*: see DE- II. 2.

ˌdeˈgorder. *Math.* [Made up of DEGREE + ORDER.] The pair of numbers signifying the degree and order of any mathematical form.

1880 SYLVESTER in *Amer. Jrnl. Mathem.* III. When $n = 2$ we know that the degorder is (4; 4).

†**degorge** (dɪˈgɔːdʒ), *v. Obs.* [a. F. *dégorger*, OF. *desgorger*: see DE- I. 6.] = DISGORGE.

1493 *Festivall* (W. de W. 1515) 142 These people..made dragons for to spytte & degorge flambes of fyre out of theyr mouthes. **1586** B. YOUNG *Guazzo's Civ. Conv.* IV. 181 b, It beehoveth..to chew it [a hastie sentence] well in our mindes before, least it be thought to be degorged..raw and undigested. **1622** BOYS *Wks.* 2 We must degorge our malice before we pray. **1635** PERSON *Varieties* I. 24 All other waters doe degorge themselves into her [the sea's] bosome. **1737** BRACKEN *Farriery Impr.* (1757) II. 69 The Farrier's Dictionary..1726..says, that it proceeds from the *degorging*, tho' I suppose he means the *disgorging*, of the great Vein.

degote: see DAGGETT.

†**deˈgoust, degout.** *Obs. rare.* [a. OF. *des-, degoust*, in mod.F. *dégoût*.] = DISGUST.

1716 M. DAVIES *Athen. Brit.* II. 150 Brinish..and of an Unsavoury Degout. **1720** WELTON *Suffer. Son of God* I. viii. 154 From hence comes all that degoust and surfeit in Matters of Religion.

†**deˈgout**, *v. Obs.* [a. F. *dégoutter*, OF. *deguter* (12th c.), = Pr. *degotar*:—Rom. type **dēguttāre*, f. L. DE- I. 1, down + *gutta* drop; cf. *guttātus* splashed, spotted.]

1. *trans.* To spot, besprinkle with drops or spots.

1423 JAS. I *Kingis Q.* clxi, A mantill..That furrit was with ermyn full quhite, Degoutit with the self in spottis blake. **1486** *Bk. St. Albans* A vij b, Ye shall say she is Degouted to the vttermost brayle.

2. To shed in drops, distil.

1503 HAWES *Examp. Virt.* iv. 42 The chambre where she held her consystory The dewe aromatyke dyde oft degoute Of fragrant floures. **1509** —— *Past. Pleas.* 198 Her redolente wordes..Degouted vapoure moost aromatyke.

degradable (dɪˈgreɪdəb(ə)l), *a.* [f. DEGRADE *v.* + -ABLE.] Capable of being degraded. *spec.* Susceptible to chemical or biological degradation (cf. *biodegradable* adj. s.v. BIO-).

[**1867** H. KINGSLEY *Silcote of S.* xxxvii. (1876) 255 The labourer..is undegradable, being in a chronic state of bankruptcy.] **1963** *Economist* 22 June 1257/1 The detergent industry is..spending $5 million a year to find a more soluble, or 'degradable', 'surface active ingredient'. **1971** *Sci. News* 7 Aug. 92 Public indignation over litter and garbage has caused industry to ask chemists whether self-destroying, or quickly degradable, plastics might be devised to replace indestructible, unburnable and incompressible glass, aluminum and plastics.

Hence **degradaˈbility**.

1969 *Rep. Secretary's Comm. Pesticides* (U.S. Dept. Health) ii. 141 The problem to the consumer..depends upon the degradability of the pesticide. **1971** *Nature* 2 Apr. 326/1 Concern about the persistence of some insecticides in mammals and in the environment has stimulated a consideration of the degradability of widely used compounds. **1974** *Daily Tel.* 11 Oct. 2/6 Assuming that five per cent of the refuse were to be composted it would cost 10 times as much to introduce degradability..as would be saved on the compost.

ˈdegradand. *rare.* [ad. L. *dēgradand-us* to be degraded, gerundive of *dēgradāre* to DEGRADE.] One who is to be degraded from his rank or order.

1891 R. W. DIXON *Hist. Ch. Eng.* IV. 494 The degradand is to be brought in his daily or ordinary dress.

degradation[1] (dɛgrəˈdeɪʃən). [a. F. *dégradation* (14th c. in Hatzf.), ad. med.L. *dēgradātiōn-em*, n. of action f. *dēgradāre*, to DEGRADE: see -ATION.] The action of degrading.

1. Deposition from some rank, office, or position of honour as an act of punishment; *esp.* the depriving of an ecclesiastic of his orders, benefices, and privileges, of a knight, military officer, etc., of his rank, of a graduate of his academical degree.

In *Eccl. Law*, two kinds of degradation are recognized: see quot. 1885.

a **1535** MORE *Wks.* 624 (R.) Vpon..hys degradacion, he kneled downe before the byshoppes chauncellour..& humbli besought him of absolucion fro the sentence of excommunicacion. **1586** *Exam. H. Barrowe* in *Harl. Misc.* (Malh.) II. 35 Since his excommunication and degradation by the Romish church. **1647** CLARENDON *Hist. Reb.* I. (1843) 22/2 He saw many removes and degradations in all the other offices of which he had been possessed. **1726** AYLIFFE *Parergon* 206 *Degradation* is commonly used to denote a Deprivation or Removing of a Man from his Office and Benefice. **1779–81** JOHNSON *L.P.*, *Halifax*, An..active statesman..exposed to the vicissitudes of advancement and degradation. **1885** *Catholic Dict.* 253/2 Degradation is of two kinds, verbal and real. By the first a criminous cleric is declared to be perpetually deposed from clerical orders, or from the execution thereof, so as to be deprived of all order and function..and of any benefice which he might have previously enjoyed..Real or actual degradation is that which, besides deposing a cleric from the exercise of his ministry, actually strips him of his orders, according to a prescribed ceremonial, and delivers him to the secular arm to be punished. **1898** *Westm. Gaz.* 15 Jan. 5/1 Madame Dreyfus..sends to the Press a letter from her husband..written the day after the degradation.

2. Lowering in honour, estimation, social position, etc.; the state or condition of being so lowered.

c **1752** JOHNSON in *Boswell* (1887) IV. 382 *note*, A Table of the Spectators, Tatlers, and Guardians, distinguished by figures into six degrees of value, with notes, giving the reasons of preference or degradation. **1794** S. WILLIAMS *Vermont* 152 This degradation of the female was carried to its greatest extreme. **1833** HT. MARTINEAU *Brooke Farm* v. 70 They would complain of the degradation of obtaining their food by rendering service. **1878** JEVONS *Prim. Pol. Econ.* 85 Enough ought to have been saved to avoid the need of charity or the degradation of the poor-house.

3. Lowering in character or quality; the state or condition of being degraded morally or intellectually; moral debasement.

1697 LOCKE *2nd Vind. Christ.* (R.), The lowest degradation that human nature could sink to. *a* **1716** SOUTH (J.), So deplorable is the degradation of our nature. **1856** SIR B. BRODIE *Psychol. Inq.* I. iii. 77 Nothing can tend more to every kind of..degradation than the vice of gin-drinking. **1866** G. MACDONALD *Ann. Q. Neighb.* xxvii. (1878) 473 She would not submit to the degradation of marrying a man she did not love.

4. a. Reduction to an inferior type or stage of development. Also *attrib.*

1850 H. ROGERS *Ess.* II. iv. 169 The vocabulary would be for the most part retained, and the grammatical forms undergo degradation. **1871** TYLOR *Prim. Cult.* I. 34 The progression-theory recognizes degradation, and the degradation-theory recognizes progression, as powerful influences in the course of culture.

b. *spec. Biol.* Reduction of an organ or structure to a less perfect or more rudimentary condition; degeneration.

1849 BALFOUR *Manual of Bot.* §649 There is thus traced a *degradation*, as it is called, from a flower with three stamens and three divisions of the calyx, to one with a single bract and a single stamen or carpel. **1872** MIVART *Elem. Anat.* 39 'Degradation' is a constant character of the last vertebræ in all classes of Vertebrates. *Ibid.* ii. 59 The maximum of degradation and abortion of the coccyx is in the Bats.

c. *Structural Bot.* A change in the substance of the organized structures of plants, resulting in the formation of products (***degradation-products***) which have no further use in the building up of new cell-walls or protoplasmic structures. In wider use in *Biochem.* and *Chem.*: a simplification of the structure of a molecule, brought about either naturally or artificially, in which it loses some constituent atoms or is broken up into a number of simpler molecules.

1875 BENNETT & DYER *Sachs' Bot.* 628 The substances which cause lignification, suberisation, or cuticularisation are also probably the result of a partial degradation of the cellulose of the cell-walls. **1883** *Syd. Soc. Lex.*, *Degradation products*, a term applied to such compounds as gum in plants. **1884** BOWER & SCOTT *De Bary's Phaner.* 511 The transformation or degradation of the alburnum into duramen takes place in some [trees] gradually, in others suddenly. **1900** *Jrnl. Chem. Soc.* LXXVIII. I. 650 (*heading*) Synthesis and degradation in the coumarone series. **1937** *Jrnl. Biol. Chem.* CXVIII. 781 The general conception has been that the enzymatic degradation of proteins proceeds in two distinct stages; i.e., the proteinases cleave the true protein into polypeptides and..the polypeptidases and dipeptidase complete the degradation to amino acids. **1938** L. SMALL in H. Gilman *Org. Chem.* II. xii. 1027 The cyanogen bromide degradation..often succeeds with compounds that resist the Hofmann degradation... Other vigorous degradations are often employed to determine the fundamental structures present. **1949** *Nature* 15 Jan. 94/2 The identification of this degradation product affords support for the view that one point of attachment of the disulphide grouping in gliotoxin is *via* a carbon atom directly linked to the indole nitrogen. **1954** *Biochem. Jrnl.* LVIII. 392/1 The terminal monoribonucleotide..was obtained by stepwise degradation of the polynucleotides listed in Table 1. **1958** [see DEGRADE *v.* 5 d]. **1966** MORRISON & BOYD *Org. Chem.* (ed. 2) iv. 139 We may carry out a degradation: break the molecule apart, identify the fragments, and deduce what the structure must have been. **1968** *Times* 24 Oct. 7/8 Organic materials that accumulate in deep waters in the sea are relatively resistant to degradation by micro-organisms. **1970** [see DEGRADE *v.* 5 d].

d. *Physics.* The conversion of (energy) into a lower form, *i.e.* one which has a decreased capability of being transformed.

1871 B. STEWART *Heat* §384 When mechanical energy is transmuted into heat by friction or otherwise there is always a degradation in the form of energy. **1876** TAIT *Rec. Adv. Phys. Sc.* vi. 146 A certain amount of degradation (degraded energy meaning energy less capable of being transformed than before).

e. *Soil Science.* (See quot. 1958.)

1927 C. F. MARBUT tr. *Glinka's Great Soil Groups* 95 Holes made by burrowing animals were found filled with a brownish mass on which one could see the evidences of the later degradation which took place under the influence of the acid forest humus. **1958** *Yearbk. Agric. 1957* (U.S. Dept. Agric.) 756/1 *Degradation* (*of soils*), the change of one kind of soil to a more highly leached kind, such as the change of a Chernozem to a Podzol. **1965** B. T. BUNTING *Geogr. Soils* xiii. 157 Invasions of populus on to chernozemic soils in Canada have caused degradation to gray wooded soils.

5. A lowering or reducing in strength, amount, etc.

1769 STRANGE in *Phil. Trans.* LIX. 55 This plant was in the first stage of putrefaction..hence its degradation of colour. **1776** ADAM SMITH *W.N.* I. v. (1869) I. 36 The degradation in the value of silver. *Ibid.* I. xi. I. 243 This degradation, both in the real and nominal value of wool. **1883** *Syd. Soc. Lex.*, *Senile degradation*, the gradual failure of the mental and bodily powers due to age. **1889** J. M. DUNCAN *Lect. Dis. Women* xvi. (ed. 4) 127 Producing as its only great indication, degradation of the general health, and a hydroperitoneal collection. **1958** *Engineering* 21 Mar. 358/1 The picture degradation normally experienced between successive generations of facsimile pictures is largely eliminated with the..machine. **1958** *Times Rev. Industry* June 26/1 Chemical reagents employed may easily lead to the degradation of the silicon. **1959** W. S. SHARPS *Dict. Cinemat.* 89/1 *Degradation*, the degree to which the quality of the film image at any stage is inferior to the original scene, or to the image at some previous stage. **1966** *Electronics* 17 Oct. 103 Indication to the aircrew of the amount of degradation of functions to allow assessment of mission capability.

6. a. *Geol.* The disintegration and wearing down of the surface of rocks, cliffs, strata, etc., by atmospheric and aqueous action.

1799 KIRWAN *Geol. Ess.* 327 Those of siliceous shistus are most subject to this degradation and decomposition. **1802** PLAYFAIR *Illustr. Hutton. Th.* 156 The great degradation of mountains, involved in this hypothesis. **1853** PHILLIPS *Rivers Yorksh.* i. 11 The chalk..yields rather easily to degradation. **1875** CROLL *Climate & T.* xvii. 268 Old sea-bottoms formed out of the accumulated material derived from the degradation of primeval land-surfaces. **1898** [see AGGRADE *v.*]. **1909** W. M. DAVIS *Geogr. Ess.* xviii. 408 'Degradation'..is more properly associated with those leisurely processes..in which a graded slope is reduced to fainter and fainter declivity, although maintaining its graded condition all the while. **1922** C. A. COTTON *Geomorphol. N. Zealand* vi. 61 When..a stream cuts downward to establish or maintain grade, it is said to degrade; and the process is termed degradation.

b. *transf.* Wearing down of any surface.

1849 RUSKIN *Sev. Lamps* vi. §17. 179 The materials to be employed are liable to degradation, as brick, sandstone, or soft limestone. **1861** FLO. NIGHTINGALE *Nursing* 62 There is a constant degradation, as it is called, taking place from everything except polished or glazed articles.

degradation[2] (ˌdiːgrəˈdeɪʃən). [In sense 1, a. F. *dégradation* (Molière, 17th c.), ad. It. *digradazione*, f. *digradare* to come down by degrees. Sense 2 may also be from It.; but cf. GRADATION.]

1. *Painting.* The gradual lowering of colour or light in a painting; *esp.* that which gives the effect of distance; gradation of tint; gradual toning down or shading off. ? *Obs.*

1706 *Art of Painting* (1744) 33 Perspective..regulates..the degradation of colours in all places of the Picture. **1762–71** H. WALPOLE *Vertue's Anecd. Paint.* (1786) II. 231 There is great truth and nature in his heads; but the carnations are too bricky, and want a degradation and variety of tints. **1817** COLERIDGE *Biog. Lit.* 212 Colours..used as the means of that gentle degradation requisite in order to produce the effect of a whole. **1881** C. A. YOUNG *Sun* 250 Vogel's observations show a much more rapid degradation of the light.

†**2.** Diminution (in size or thickness) by degrees or successive steps; the part so reduced. *Obs.*

1730 A. GORDON *Maffei's Amphith.* 285 The internal Degradation of the Wall. *Ibid.* 406 The Retiring of the Wall ..proceeds by a Degradation above that Stone..and more largely in the Degradation of the second Story; so that the third is reduced to a small Thickness. *Ibid.* 407 There being no Marks of Vaults on the Degradation of the Wall.

degradational (dɛgrəˈdeɪʃənəl), *a.* [f. DEGRADATION[1] + -AL[1].] Of or pertaining to (biological) degradation; manifesting structural degradation.

1863 DANA in *Amer. Jrnl. Sc. & Arts* 2nd Ser. XXXVI. 4 They [Entomostracans] are *degradational* forms as well as the Myriapods. *Ibid.* 5 The distinction of the Entomostracans..consists rather in their degradational characters than in any peculiarities of the mouth.

degradative (dɪˈgreɪdətɪv), *a.* [f. *dēgradāt-*, ppl. stem of late L. *dēgradāre* + -IVE.] Causing degradation.

1940 *Jrnl. Research Nat. Bureau of Standards* Oct. 452 They involve the use of treatments which are known to have a degradative effect on the protein. **1950** *New Biol.* VIII. 101 Enzymes are capable of accelerating synthetic as well as degradative reactions. **1958** *New Scientist* 12 June 174/3 The degradative diseases, the pathetic conditions in which it is plain..that some part of the human frame has been worn out by too much use.

ˈdegraˌdator. *rare.* [Agent-n. in L. form, from late L. *dēgradāre* to DEGRADE.] One who degrades or deprives of rank.

1891 R. W. DIXON *Hist. Ch. Eng.* IV. 494 From a degradand of archiepiscopal degree the degradator shall first remove the pall.

† **degradatory,** *a. Obs.* [f. *dēgradāt-*, ppl. stem of late L. *dēgradāre* + -ORY.] Having the quality of degrading; tending to degrade.

1783 W. F. MARTYN *Geog. Mag.* I. 407 Other degradatory circumstances. **1786** *Francis the Philan.* III. 166 A species of imposition so degradatory to the republic of letters.

degrade (dɪˈgreɪd), *v.* Also 5 **degrate, -grayd,** 6 **-graid,** 7 **di-.** [ME. a. OF. *degrader* (12th c.), occasionally *desg-*, = Pr. *de-*, *desgrader*, Sp. *degradar*, It. *degradare*:—late eccl. L. *dēgradāre*, f. DE- I. 1, down, from + *gradus* degree.]

1. *trans.* To reduce from a higher to a lower rank, to depose *from* (†*of*) a position of honour or estimation.

c **1325** *Song of Yesterday* 11 in *E.E.P.* (1862) 133 Hou sone þat god hem may degrade. **1375** BARBOUR *Bruce* I. 175 Schir Ihon the balleoll..was king bot a litill quhile..degradyt syne wes he Off honour and off dignite. *a* **1400–50** *Alexander* 2670 Darye..semblis his knyȝtis..And gessis him wele..to degrayd þe grekis maistir. **1624** MASSINGER *Parl. Love* v. i, Thou dost degrade thyself of all the honours Thy ancestors left thee. **1641** SIR. E. DERING in Rushw. *Hist. Coll.* (1692) III. I. 295 Neither you here, nor Mr. Speaker in the House can degrade any one of us from these Seats. **1662** STILLINGFL. *Orig. Sacr.* III. iii. §2 They degraded him from the very title of a Philosopher. **1788** REID *Aristotle's Log.* iv. §3. 80 An affirmative may be degraded into a negative. **1874** HOLLAND *Mistr. Manse* xii. 56 Change That would degrade her to a thing Of homely use and household care. **1876** J. H. NEWMAN *Hist. Sk.* II. III. vii. 342 The man who made this boast was himself degraded from his high estate.

2. a. *spec.* To depose (a person) formally from his degree, rank, or position of honour as an act of punishment, as to degrade a knight, a military officer, a graduate of a university.

Cf. DISGRADE, which in 15–16th c. was the more usual word to express legal and formal degradation.

c **1400** *Destr. Troy* 12576 The grekes..Ordant hym Emperour by opon assent, And Agamynon degrated of his degre þan. **1508** KENNEDY *Flyting w. Dunbar* 397, I sall degraid the, graceles, of thy greis. **1591** SHAKS. *1 Hen. VI*, IV. i. 43 He then..Doth but vsurpe the Sacred name of Knight..And should..Be quite degraded, like a Hedge-borne Swaine. **1621** ELSING *Debates Ho. Lords* (Camden) 65 Whether Sr Fra. Michell shalbe degraded of his knighthood for parte of his punishment or noe? **1628** MEADE in Ellis *Orig. Lett.* Ser. I. III. 277 His censure was to be degraded both from her ministry and degrees taken in the University. **1709** HEARNE *Collect.* (Oxf. Hist. Soc.) II. 206 The University of Dublin having expell'd and degraded Mr. Forbes. **1875** JOWETT *Plato* (ed. 2) III. 351 The soldier who ..is guilty of any other act of cowardice, should be degraded into the rank of a husbandman or artisan.

b. To inflict ecclesiastical degradation upon; to deprive of his orders.

1395 PURVEY *Remonstr.* (1851) 37 He that..blasfemith God in othere manere be deposid or degratid if he is a clerk. **1480** CAXTON *Chron. Eng.* ccxlvii. 313 The first day of march after was sir william taillour preest degrated of his preesthode. **1555** WATREMAN *Fardle Facions* II. xii. 268 To the Bisshoppe was giuen authoritie..to put Priestes from the Priesthode: and to degrade theim, when thei deserue it. **1681** BAXTER *Apol. Nonconf. Min.* 39 Magistrates might degrade ministers. **1782** PRIESTLEY *Corrupt. Chr.* II. x. 268 A priest could not be degraded but by eight bishops. **1882** J. H. BLUNT *Ref. Ch. Eng.* II. 284 He was formally degraded from the priesthood.

3. To lower in estimation; to bring into dishonour or contempt.

c **1500** *Lancelot* 749 Hyme thoght that it his worschip wold degrade. **1560** ROLLAND *Crt. Venus* IV. 470 Ladie Venus ȝe sall neuer degraid In word, nor deid, nor neuer do hir deir. **1771** *Junius Lett.* liv. 285, I will not insult his misfortunes by a comparison that would degrade him. **1844** EMERSON *Lect. Yng. Amer.* Wks. (Bohn) II. 306 The aristocracy incorporated by law and education, degrades life for the unprivileged classes.

4. a. To lower in character or quality; to debase.

1650 FROYSELL *Gale of Opport.* (1652) Ep. Ded., At this news the Ruffler is sodainly dismounted, and his courage degraded. **1755** JOHNSON, *Degrade*..to reduce from a higher to a lower state, with respect to qualities. **1762** GOLDSM. *Cit. W.* cxviii, How low avarice can degrade human nature. **1776** ADAM SMITH *W.N.* IV. viii. (1869) II. 235 English wool cannot be even so mixed with Spanish wool as to enter into the composition..without spoiling and degrading in some degree the fabric of the cloth. **1857** KINGSLEY *Two Y. Ago* (1877) 432 So will an unhealthy craving degrade a man. **1875** JOWETT *Plato* (ed. 2) V. 41 This custom has been the ruin of the poets, and has degraded the theatre.

b. To lower or reduce in price, strength, purity, etc.; to reduce or tone down in colour (cf. DEGRADATION²).

1844 COBDEN *Speeches* (1878) 73 He proposed to degrade prices instead of aiming to sustain them. **1855** tr. *Labarte's Arts Mid. Ages* ii. 72 How to degrade the tones with this single enamel colour. **1873** E. SPON *Workshop Receipts* I. 320/1 To prevent its greenish tint degrading the brilliancy of dyed stuffs, or the purity of whites.

5. a. *Biol.* To reduce to a lower and less complex organic type. **b.** *Physics.* To reduce (energy) to a form less capable of transformation. **c.** *Optics.* To lower in position in the spectrum; to diminish the refrangibility of (a ray of light) as by the action of a fluorescent substance.

1862, 1876 [see DEGRADED *ppl. a.* 2]. **1870** ROLLESTON *Anim. Life* 139 Annelids degraded by the special habit of parasitism.

d. *Chem.* and *Biochem.* To make (a molecule) simpler in structure; to split into a number of simpler molecules.

1935 TIPSON & STILLER in Harrow & Sherwin *Textbk. Biochem.* ii. 85 Zemplén has used a fundamentally different method to decide the point of union of the two hexose units in a reducing disaccharide. By degrading the reducing component till it no longer forms an osazone, he has determined the constitution of lactose..and other sugars. **1958** BALLENTYNE & WALKER *Dict. Named Effects & Laws* 192 *Weerman degradation.* An α hydroxy or α methoxy amide may be degraded to an aldehyde containing one less carbon atom by the action of a cold aqueous solution of sodium hypochlorite. **1963** *Union Carbide Stockholder News* Sept. 1/1 The detergents..can be quickly destroyed or degraded in sewage systems to non-detergent-like products. **1970** *Nature* 26 Dec. 1313/1 Most body proteins are continually degraded and resynthesized. The protein content of various organs must represent the net balance between synthesis and degradation over some period of time.

6. *Geol.* To wear down (rocks, strata, cliffs, etc.) by surface abrasion or disintegration.

1812 SIR H. DAVY *Chem. Philos.* 101 These agents [water and air] gradually..decompose and degrade the exterior of strata. **1863** A. C. RAMSAY *Phys. Geog.* i. (1878) 6 The quantity of material degraded and spread in the sea by these united means is immense.

7. *intr.* To descend to a lower grade or type; to exhibit a degradation of type or structure; to degenerate.

1850 TENNYSON *In Mem.* cxxvii, No doubt vast eddies in the flood Of onward time shall yet be made, And throned races may degrade. **1863** KINGSLEY *Water Bab.* 77 If he says that things cannot degrade, that is change downwards into lower forms. *a* **1864** WEBSTER (citing DANA) s.v., A family of plants or animals degrades through this or that genus or group of genera.

8. a. *Cambridge Univ.* To postpone entering the examination in honours for the degree of B.A. for one year beyond the statutory time; also occas. at Oxford University. (Now disused.) Now at Cambridge, to take a specified examination when one is above the standing prescribed for it.

1829 *Camb. Univ. Cal.* (1857) 24 That no person who has degraded be permitted, etc. **1869** *Daily News* 13 Nov., To grant permission to students who have degraded or who wish to degrade to become candidates for University scholarships or for any other academical honours during their undergraduateship. **1880** *Eagle Mag.* (St. John's Coll., Camb.) XI. 189 G. S., Scholar, has obtained permission to 'degrade' to the Tripos of 1881. **1906** *Oxf. Univ. Gaz.* 29 May 654/2 John O. Aglionby..was granted permission to degrade till Trinity Term, 1907, and to offer Modern History.

b. See quot. 1883; at Oxford University, to supplicate for a lower degree than that for which one originally entered.

1883 *Encycl. Dic., Degrade,*..to take a lower degree than one is entitled to;..to descend from a higher to a lower class. **1921** *Oxford Univ. Registry Acc. Bks.* 4 Nov. (MS.), Wing, J. L... Degrading to B.Litt. £1.

degrade (dɪˈgreɪd), *sb.* [f. the vb.] A piece of timber containing defects; also, the production of defects resulting in a lowering of the 'grade' or quality of the timber.

1922 R. C. BRYANT *Lumber* 242 This practice..has the disadvantage of producing a higher per cent of 'degrades', because the lumber as it leaves the kiln is bone-dry. **1953** *Oxf. Univ. Gaz.* 7 Aug. 1202/1 A thesis entitled 'A study of degrade in oak logs due to "ambrosia" beetles'. **1970** *Timber Trades Jrnl.* 21 Mar. 61/1 Strips 4½ in. wide by 1 in. thick have been dried without excessive degrade at starting temperatures up to 66°C..coupled with an initial humidity of 75%.

degraded (dɪˈgreɪdɪd), *ppl. a.* [f. DEGRADE *v.*¹ + -ED¹.]

1. Lowered in rank, position, reputation, character, etc.; debased.

1483 *Cath. Angl.* 94 Degradid, *degradatus.* **1614** SYLVESTER *Bethulia's Rescue* v. 499 By long Swathes of their degraded Grasse, Well show the way their sweeping Scithes did pass. **1643** MILTON *Divorce* II. xv. (1851) 101 The restoring of this degraded law. **1781** GIBBON *Decl. & F.* III. 235 The degraded emperor of the Romans. **1858** MAX MÜLLER *Chips* (1880) I. ii. 60 There is, perhaps, no race of men so low and degraded. **1885** *Catholic Dict.* 253/2 The consecration of the Eucharist by a degraded priest is..valid.

2. a. *Biol.* Showing structural or functional degradation.

1862 DARWIN *Fertil. Orchids* vi. 271 The pollen grains.. in all other genera, excepting the degraded Cephalanthera. **1883** H. DRUMMOND *Nat. Law in Spir. W.* iii. (1884) 101 Degeneration..by which the organism..becomes more and more adapted to a degraded form of life.

b. *Physics.* Of energy: Changed into a form less capable of transformation.

1876 TAIT *Rec. Adv. Phys. Sc.* vi. 146 Degraded energy meaning energy less capable of being transformed than before.

c. *Soil Science.* Of soil; (cf. DEGRADATION¹ 4e).

1927 C. F. MARBUT tr. *Glinka's Great Soil Groups* 95 The well known degraded Tschernosem found in many parts of European and Asiatic Russia. **1965** B. T. BUNTING *Geogr. Soil* xv. 173 The westernmost area of modal chernozem is south of Wroclaw, but degraded chernozem occur as far west as Braunschweig.

3. *Geol.* Having suffered degradation, worn down.

1869 PHILLIPS *Vesuv.* viii. 229 Old broken and degraded crateriform ridges.

4. Of colour: Reduced in brilliancy, toned down.

1877 A. B. EDWARDS *Up Nile* i. 9 The outer robe, or gibbeh, is generally of some beautiful degraded colour, such as maize, mulberry, olive, peach.

Hence **deˈgradedly** *adv.*; **deˈgradedness.**

1791 PAINE *Rights of Man* I. (ed. 2) 38 A vast mass of mankind are degradedly thrown into the back-ground. **1824** LANDOR *Imag. Conv.* Wks. (1846) I. 185/2 A government more systematically and more degradedly tyrannical. **1883** *Pall Mall G.* 19 Dec. 2/2 He sees..the misery and degradedness of the poor, the callousness of many rich.

deˈgraded, *a. Her.* [f. DE- I + L. *grad-us* step + -ED.] Of a cross: Set on steps, or having step-like extensions at the ends connecting it with the sides of the shield.

1562 LEIGH *Armorie* (1597) 35 Hee beareth Geules, a Crosse nowye degraded fitche Argent. **1727–51** CHAMBERS *Cycl.* s.v., A *Cross degraded* is a cross marked, or divided into steps at each end, diminishing as they ascend towards the middle, or centre; by the French called perronnée. **1882** CUSSANS *Handbk. Her.* 64 A Cross set on Steps (usually three) is *Degraded*, or *On Degrees.*

† **deˈgradement.** *Obs.* [a. obs. F. *dégradement* (1611 in Cotgr.) = *degradation*: see -MENT.] Degradation, abasement.

1641 MILTON *Reform.* II. (1851) 61 So the words of Ridley at his degradment..expressly shew. **1648** —— *Tenure Kings* 34 By their holding him in prison..which brought him to the lowest degradement.

degrader (dɪˈgreɪdə(r)). [f. DEGRADE *v.* + -ER¹.]

1. One who or that which degrades or debases.

1746 W. HORSLEY *Fool* (1748) No. 51 ¶3 The Degraders were left to laugh at each other in due Order. **1754** RICHARDSON *Grandison* lxiii, What a degrader even of high spirits is vice. **1804–6** SYD. SMITH *Sk. Mor. Phil.* xviii. (1850) 255 As the degraders of human nature have said.

2. *Cambridge Univ.* See DEGRADE *v.* 8.

1860 G. FERGUSON in *Encycl. Brit.* (ed. 8) XXI. 465 A statute was enacted in 1829, by which degraders are not allowed to present themselves for university scholarships, or any other academical honours, without special permission.

degrading (dɪˈgreɪdɪŋ), *vbl. sb.* [f. DEGRADE *v.*¹ + -ING¹.] The action of the verb DEGRADE.

1646 EVANCE *Noble Ord.* 2 Elyes degrading, or Gods revoking of his promise. **1853** KINGSLEY *Hypatia* xxvii. (1879) 341 It was a carnal degrading of the Supreme One.

deˈgrading, *ppl. a.* [-ING².]

1. That degrades or debases.

1684 EARL ROSCOM. *Ess. Transl. Verse* (1709) 43 Degrading Prose explains his meaning ill. **1773** MRS. CHAPONE *Improv. Mind* (1774) II. 15 A..generous kind of anger..has nothing in it sinful or degrading. **1814** SCOTT *Wav.* ix, Engaged in this laborious and..degrading office. **1855** MACAULAY *Hist. Eng.* III. 448 A superstition as stupid and degrading as the Egyptian worship of cats and onions. *Mod. Boarding School Prospectus.* There are no degrading punishments.

2. *Geol.* Wearing down a surface.

1842 H. MILLER *O.R. Sandst.* x. (ed. 2) 228 The degrading process is the same as that to which sandstones.. are exposed during severe frosts. **1880** HAUGHTON *Phys. Geog.* ii. 45 The absence of degrading forces at the sea bottom.

Hence **deˈgradingly** *adv.*; **deˈgradingness.**

1707 NORRIS *Treat. Humility* vi. 289 He that disparages, or speaks degradingly of himself, may possibly be much the prouder man of the two. **1803** *Ann. Reg.* 253 Two men.. were insulted, imprisoned, degradingly used. **1865** DICKENS *Mut. Fr.* I. iv, We are degradingly poor. **1818** BENTHAM *Ch. Eng.* 274 Degradingness: of..its inherency in the very essence of a Sinecure, mention has been already made.

† **deˈgraduate,** *v. Obs.* [f. DE- II. 1 + GRADUATE *v.*] *trans.* To depose from rank or dignity; to degrade from an office or position.

1649 EVELYN *Mem.* (1857) III. 47 Since (after degraduating the Lord Mayor) they have voted five more of the principal aldermen out of the city government. **1814** G. DYER *Hist. Univ. Cambridge* II. 414 By mistaking the character, and degraduating him, we lose sight of the dignity of the *poeta laureatus.*

† **degradu'ation**[1]. *Obs. rare*[−1]. [n. of action f. prec.: see -ATION.] Degradation, abasement from rank or dignity.

1581 RICH *Farewell* (1846) 85 Besides the degraduation of her honour, she thrusteth her self into the pitte of perpetualle infamie.

† **de-gradu'ation**[2]. *Paint. Obs.* [f. DE- I. 1 + *graduation*.] Gradual diminution to give the effect of distance: cf. DEGRADATION[2].

1784 J. BARRY *Lect. Art* v. (1848) 194 Perspective imitations of the aerial as well as lineal de-graduations of the object. *Ibid.* 197 In the ancient bas-reliefs there certainly is not much attention paid to any de-graduation of objects and their effects.

degrain (diː'greɪn). [f. DE- II. 2 + GRAIN *sb.*[1]] Used *attrib.* designating leather from which the grain has been removed. Hence **de'grained** *a.*

1925 *Civil Service Supply Assoc. Ltd. Catal.* 133 Men's Glove Department... Degrain Mocha finish. **1928** *Daily Express* 1 Nov. 8/1 Degrained Glove... Made from supple Degrain skins.

† **degrandinate**, *v. Obs. rare*[−0]. [f. L. *dēgrandināre*, f. DE- I. 1 or 3 + *grandināre* to hail, f. *grando, grandin-em*, hail.] (See quots.)

1623 COCKERAM, *Degrandinate*, to haile downe right. **1656** BLOUNT *Glossogr.*, *Degrandinate*, to hail much.

degras, dégras ('dɛgrəs, ‖de'gra). [F. *dégras*, f. *dégraisser* to remove grease from, with assimilation to *gras* fat.] **a.** The dark wax or grease obtained when fish-oils are rubbed into hides and recovered by expression and by washing the hides with alkali, as in the manufacture of chamois leather; the commercial product usu. contains added quantities of fish-oils and solid fats (cf. MOELLON[2]), and is used in currying and fat-liquoring leather; also, a product made from fish-oils in imitation of this.

1882 *Encycl. Brit.* XIV. 390/2 This uncombined oil is washed out with a warm potash solution, and the fat so recovered, known as *degras*, forms a valuable material for the dressing of common leather by curriers. **1904** J. LEWKOWITSCH *Oils, Fats, & Waxes* (ed. 3) II. xvi. 1129 A large number of artificial dégras are now being prepared by blowing fish, liver, and blubber oils with air.., thus imitating the natural process of oxidation the oils appear to undergo when skins are converted into chamois leather. **1922** H. R. PROCTER *Princ. Leather Manuf.* (ed. 2) xxv. 448 The residual oil..constitutes *moellon*... This is never sold for currying in its original purity; but, mixed with further quantities of fish oils, tallows, and sometimes wool-fat, it constitutes the ordinary dégras of commerce. **1931** WILSON & MERRILL *Anal. Leather* xi. 382 The excess oil is pressed out after saturating the skins with water and constitutes the purest and best grade of moellon *dégras*. **1937** BURTON & ROBERTSHAW in Atkin & Thompson *Procter's Leather Chemists' Pocket-Bk.* (ed. 3) xix. 326 Genuine dégras (moellon) and sod oil were originally obtained as by-products of chamoising.., but are now frequently prepared from scrap skins or by direct oxidation of oils. **1958** A. KUNTZEL in F. O'Flaherty et al. *Chem. & Technol. Leather* II. xxviii. 431 It is a very valuable leather-greasing agent because of its high water compatibility and is known as degras or moellon.

b. *U.S.* The crude mixture of wax and fatty acids obtained by scouring wool or treating it with organic solvents, used industrially (*e.g.* as a source of lanolin and in the manufacture of lubricating greases) and as a substitute for degras (sense a) in leather manufacture; wool-grease, wool-fat.

1894 *Jrnl. Amer. Chem. Soc.* XVI. 535 In this country, the term 'degras' is generally applied to the grease or fatty matter recovered from the water in which wool has been scoured. **1915** F. S. HYDE *Solvents, Oils, Gums, Waxes* 124 Wool grease, the English 'Yorkshire grease', 'Suint', or American 'degras'—but not the true degras—is a dirty grease with a foul odor, obtained by scouring wool of sheep, and contains, besides fatty acids from soap employed in scouring,..esters of palmitic and myristic acids, other waxy substances,..as well as mineral oil used in lubricating the wool. **1954** C. J. BONER *Lubricating Greases* iv. 149 Wool wax is ordinarily sold under the name of degras or wool grease.

† **'degravate**, *v. Obs.* [f. L. *dēgravāre* to weigh down, f. DE- I. 1 + *gravāre* to load, burden: see -ATE[3].] *trans.* To weigh down, burden, load.

1574 NEWTON *Health Mag.* 54 They degravate the tongue and hinder the speech. **1727** BAILEY vol. II, *Degravate*, to make heavy, to burden.

† **degra'vation**. *Obs.* [n. of action f. L. *dēgravāre*: see prec.] The action of making heavy.

1755 in JOHNSON.

degrease (diː'griːs), *v.* [f. DE- II. 2 + GREASE *sb.*] *trans.* To remove grease or fat from. Hence **de'greaser**; **de'greasing** *vbl. sb.* and *ppl. a.*

1889 *Cent. Dict.*, Degrease. **1900** S. P. SADTLER *Handbk. Industr. Org. Chem.* (ed. 3) ix. 310 The only treatment of this kind, known technically as a degreasing process, is that with petroleum-naphtha. **1904** GOODCHILD & TWENEY *Technol. & Sci. Dict.* 153/1 *Degreasing*, the process of extracting fat or grease from wool and bones by means of benzene or other solvent. **1921** *Dict. Occup. Terms* (1927) §158 s.v. Extractor, *Benzine degreaser, bone degreaser (benzine process), degreaser*, extracts grease (or tallow) from kitchen stuff, or butchers' scraps, by dissolving fat in petrol or benzine. *Ibid.* §334 *Degreaser*, in fellmongery puts pelts in tanks..containing benzine..to remove grease. **1930** FIELD & WEILL *Electro-Plating* iv. 80 This principle is achieved by..'de-greasers'. **1939** *Jrnl. Iron & Steel Inst.* CXXXIX. 168 The author compares the results of degreasing tests on a number of steel specimens covered with oil and fat..using petrol and three other unnamed degreasing agents. **1958** *New Scientist* 3 July 305/1 The zinc layer is removed by three minutes' 'pickling' (the steel being degreased at the same time). **1963** A. J. HALL *Textile Sci.* iv. 167 Wool fabric can also be degreased in a continuous manner by use of the I.C.I. trichloroethylene process. **1969** *Jane's Freight Containers 1968–69* 531/1 The complete container is degreased inside and out.

degree (dɪ'griː), *sb.* Forms: 3–6 degre, (3 degrece, 4–5 þegre, 5 decre, dygre), 6 degrie, 4– degree; also *pl.* 5 degrece, degreces. See also GREE. [ME. *degre*, pl. *-ez*, a. OF. *degre*, earlier nom. *degrez*, obl. *degret* (*St. Alexis*, 11th c.) = Pr. *degrat, degra*:—late pop. L. **dēgrad-us, -um*, f. DE- I. 1 down + *grad-us* step.]

I. 1. a. A step in an ascent or descent; one of a flight of steps; a step or rung of a ladder. *Obs.* (exc. in *Heraldry*).

c **1290** *S. Eng. Leg.* I. 482/44 Huy brouȝhten him up-on an he de-grece þat muche folk him i-seiȝh. *c* **1325** *E.E. Allit. P.* A. 1021 Þise twelue degres wern brode and stayre, þe cyte stod abof. *c* **1400** MAUNDEV. (1839) xxvii. 276 The Degrees to gon up to his Throne. *a* **1400–50** *Alexander* 5636 And xij degreces all of gold for gate vp of lordis. **1483** CAXTON *Cato* A v, He sawe a ladder whyche had ten degrees or stappes. **1598** HAKLUYT *Voy.* I. 69 There were certain degrees or staires to ascend vnto it. **1601** SHAKS. *Jul. C.* II. i. 26 He then vnto the Ladder turnes his Backe..scorning the base degrees By which he did ascend. **1682** WHELER *Journ. Greece* v. 385 Raised upon half a dozen steps or degrees. **1738** NEAL *Hist. Purit.* IV. 171 At the upper end there was an ascent of two degrees covered with carpets. **1864** BOUTELL *Heraldry Hist. & Pop.* vi. 28 When placed upon steps..a Cross is said to be on Degrees.

b. *transf.* Something resembling a step; each of a series of things placed one above another like steps; row, tier, shelf, etc.

1611 CORYAT *Crudities* 201 Goodly windowes, with three degrees of glasse in them, each containing sixe rowes. **1611** HEYWOOD *Gold. Age* II. Wks. 1874 III. 28 In chace we clime the high degrees Of euerie steepie mountaine. **1704** HEARNE *Duct. Hist.* (1714) I. 427 The Ship of excessive Magnitude with 20 Degrees of Oars built for King Hiero. **1726** LEONI *Alberti's Archit.* II. 37b, If the Cupola have a cover on the outside made with degrees like steps. **1857** G. J. WIGLEY *Borromeo's Instr. Eccl. Building* xv. 46 On the wooden degree on the after part of the altar.

c. *degree-cut* in gem-cutting: = TRAP-CUT.

1909 in WEBSTER.

2. *fig.* **a.** A step or stage in a process, etc., *esp.* one in an ascending or descending scale.

c **1230** *Hali Meid.* 23 Þu maht bi þe degrez of hare blisse icnawen hwuch and bi hu muchel þe an passed þe oðre. **1550** PAGET in Froude *Hist. Eng.* (1881) IV. 502 Which recognizance is the first degree to amendment. **1600** SHAKS. *A.Y.L.* v. iv. 92 Can you nominate in order now the degrees of the lye? **1600** E. BLOUNT tr. *Conestaggio* 246 The greatest in Spain aspire..to be Viceroy of Naples, where-unto they labour to come by many degrees. **1673** DRYDEN *Marr. à la Mode* IV. ii, To go unknown is the next degree to going invisible. **1713** STEELE *Spect.* No. 422 ¶1 To say a thing which..brings blushes into his Face, is a degree of Murder.

b. *esp.* in phr. *by degrees*: by successive steps or stages, by little and little, gradually.

1563–7 BUCHANAN *Reform. St. Andros* Wks. (1892) 12 Thyr regentis sal pas be degreis the hail cours of dialectic, logic, etc. **1604** SHAKS. *Oth.* II. iii. 377 What wound did euer heale but by degrees? **1684** R. H. *School Recreat.* 31 Fill it by Degrees. **1700** S. L. tr. *Fryke's Voy.* 109 Several of our Company..dropt in by degrees. **1711** ADDISON *Spect.* No. 123 ¶5 His Acquaintance with her by degrees grew into Love. *a* **1721** PRIOR *Henry & Emma* 430 Fine by degrees and beautifully less. **1814** SCOTT *Wav.* lii, The character of Colonel Talbot dawned upon Edward by degrees. **1853** LYTTON *My Novel* IV. iii, By degrees he began to resign her more and more to Jemima's care and tuition.

3. a. A 'step' in direct line of descent; in *pl.* the number of such steps, upward or downward, or both upward to a common ancestor and downward from him, determining the proximity of blood of collateral descendants.

prohibited or ***forbidden degrees***: the number of such steps within which marriage is prohibited; degrees of consanguinity and affinity within which marriage is not allowed. In the Civil Law the degree of relationship between collaterals is counted by the number of steps up from one of them to the common ancestor and thence down to the other; according to the Canon Law by the number of steps from the common ancestor to the party more remote from him; uncle and niece are according to the former related in the third, according to the latter in the second degree.

a **1300** *Cursor M.* 5603 (Gött.) A man was of his genealogy Fra him bot þo toþer degre. *c* **1340** *Ibid.* 9260 (Fairf.) Quasim wil se fra adam þe alde How many degrees to criste is talde. *c* **1450** *Golagros & Gaw.* 1044 Na nane of the nynt degre haue noy of my name. **1512** *Act 4 Hen. VIII*, c. 20 Preamb., Beyng of kyn and alied unto the said John..within the second and third degree. **1540** *Act 32 Hen. VIII*, c. 38 *title*, Concerning precontracts and degrees of Consanguinuite. *c* **1550** CHEKE *Matt.* i. 17 Therfoor from David unto Abraham theer weer feorteen degrees. **1604** *Canons Ecclesiastical* (1852) 48 No person shall marry within the degrees prohibited by the laws of God. **1660** JER. TAYLOR *Duct. Dubit.* 237 The reasons why the Projectors of the Canon law did forbid to the fourth or to the seventh degree. **1762** *Univ. Mag.* Mar. 119 She was the daughter of Margaret, the eldest sister of Henry VIII..and..was one degree nearer the royal blood of England than Mary. **1824** SCOTT *St. Ronan's* xxxi, I thought..there should be no fighting, as there is no marriage, within the forbidden degrees. **1848** WHARTON *Law Lex.* 406 Marriages between collaterals to the third degree inclusive, according to the mode of computation in the civil law, are prohibited. Cousins german or first cousins, being in the fourth degree of collaterals, may marry.

b. Used, by extension, of ethnological relationship through more or less remote common ancestry.

1799 W. TOOKE *Russian Emp.* II. 104 The nations that.. stand in various degrees of affinity with the Samoyedes.

4. a. A stage or position in the scale of dignity or rank; relative social or official rank, grade, order, estate, or station.

c **1230** *Hali Meid.* 15 Se þu herre stondest, beo sarre offearet to fallen for se herre degre. *c* **1325** *E.E. Allit. P.* B. 92 Ful manerly with marchal mad for to sitte, As he watz dere of de-gre, dressed his seete. *c* **1386** CHAUCER *Prol.* 744 Al haue I folk nat set in here degree. —— *Clerk's T.* 369 He saugh that vnder low degree Was ofte vertu y-hid. *c* **1420** *Sir Amadace* (Camden) l, Knyȝte, squiere, ȝoman and knaue, Iche mon in thayre degre. ?*c* **1475** *Sqr. lowe Degre* 1 It was a squyer of lowe degrè That loved the Kings doughter of Hungrè. *c* **1510** MORE *Picus* Wks. 11/2 Holding myself content with my bokes and rest, of a childe haue lerned to liue within my degree. **1548** HALL *Chron.* 186 Men of al ages & of al degrees to him dayly repaired. *a* **1645** HEYWOOD *Fortune by Land* I. ii, Do you think I..would marry under the degree of a Gentlewoman? **1746** W. HARRIS in *Priv. Lett. Ld. Malmesbury* I. 44 They marched out..with great formality..every Lord walking according to his degree. **1851** LONGF. *Gold. Leg.* 140 None of your damsels of high degree! **1864** BURTON *Scot Aboard* I. iii. 125 Regulations.. for settling questions between persons of unequal degrees.

b. A rank or class of persons. ? *Obs.*

c **1325** *Cursor M.* 27715 (Cotton Galba) None.. may fle enuy, Bot pouer caitefs..None has enuy till þat degre. **1470–85** MALORY *Arthur* IX. xxxv, Thenne alle the estates and degrees hyhe and lowe sayd of syr launcelot grete worship. **1577** NORTHBROOKE *Dicing* (1843) 105 So much practised now a dayes amongst all sorts and degrees. **1585** T. WASHINGTON tr. *Nicholay's Voy.* II. xiii. 48b, Without sparyng anye age or degree. **1622** SPARROW *Bk. Com. Prayer* (1661) 249 The Bishop..begins,..all the degrees of Ecclesiasticks singing with him. *a* **1754** FIELDING *Voy. Lisbon* Wks. 1882 VII. 27 This barbarous custom is peculiar to the English, and of them only to the lowest degree.

†**c.** of animals, things without life, etc. *Obs.*

c **1500** *For to serve a Lord* in *Babees Bk.* 370 Thenne the kerver or sewer most asserve every disshe in his degre, after order and course of servise as folowith. **1684** R. H. *School Recreat.* 8 The Coney is first a Rabbet, and then an Old Coney. Thus much for their Names, Degrees, and Ages.. To speak briefly of the proper Names, Degrees, Ages, and Seasons of the several Chases which we Hunt.

5. Relative condition or state of being; manner, way, wise; relation, respect.

c **1330** R. BRUNNE *Chron.* (1810) 55 He stombled at a chance, & felle on his kne, þorgh þe toþer schank he ros, & serued in his degre. *c* **1385** CHAUCER *L.G.W.* 1031 *Dido*, We ..Be now disclaundred, and in swiche degre, No lenger for to lyven I ne kepe. *c* **1420** *Chron. Vilod.* 963 Bot sone afterward he felle into suche dygre, þat gret sekenesse come his body to. *c* **1430** *Two Cookery-bks.* 36 Coloure þat on with Saunderys, and þat oþer wyth Safroune, and þe þrydde on a-nother degre, so þat þey ben dyuerse. *c* **1500** *Merchant & Son* in Halliwell *Nugæ Poet.* 28 To see yow come in thys degre, nere-hande y lese my wytt. **1586** A. DAY *Eng. Secretary* II. (1625) 106, I say of our Secretorie, that as hee is in one degree in place of a Servant, so is he in another degree in place of a friend. **1697** DRYDEN *Virg. Georg.* IV. 258 Studious of Honey, each in his Degree, The youthful Swain, the grave experienc'd Bee. **1867** O. W. HOLMES *Guardian Angel* II. ii. 35 A simple evening party in the smallest village is just as admirable in its degree.

6. a. A step or stage in intensity or amount; the relative intensity, extent, measure, or amount of a quality, attribute, or action.

(Often closely related to sense 2.)

c **1380** WYCLIF *Sel. Wks.* III. 510 Cristene men..shulde have discerved most þank of God in degre possible to hem. **1414** BRAMPTON *Penit. Ps.* i. 1 How I had synned, and what degre. **1538** STARKEY *England* I. ii. 45 By the reson wherof felycyte admyttyth..degres; and some haue more wele, and som les. **1586** B. YOUNG *Guazzo's Civ. Conv.* IV. 192 Judge to what degree or stint he ought to delaie it [wine] with water. **1601** SHAKS. *Twel. N.* I. v. 61 Misprision in the highest degree. **1652** J. WRIGHT tr. *Camus' Nat. Parad.*, Who knew themselves greater and more beautifull many degrees. **1667** MILTON *P.L.* v. 490 The latter most is ours, Differing but in degree, of kind the same. **1739** HUME *Hum. Nat.* (1874) I. I. v. 323 When any two objects possess the same quality in common, the degrees, in which they possess it, form a fifth species of relation. **1824** LONGF. in *Life* (1891) I. v. 55, I have the faculty of abstraction to a wonderful degree.

b. *a degree*: a considerable measure or amount *of*. ***to a degree*** (colloq.): to an undefined, but considerable or serious, extent; extremely, seriously. ***to the last degree***: to the utmost measure.

1639 T. BRUGIS tr. *Camus' Moral Relat.* 165 Whose fire was come to the last degree of it's violence. **1665** DRYDEN *Indian Emp.* II. iv, Thou mak'st me jealous to the last degree. **1721** D'URFEY *New Opera's*, etc. 251 The Cadiz, raging to degree. **1737** BRACKEN *Farriery Impr.* (1757) II. 249 Let any one walk in a cold Air, so that his Feet be cold to a Degree. **1775** SHERIDAN *Rivals* II. i, Assuredly, sir, your father is wrath to a degree. **1865** CARLYLE *Fredk. Gt.* VII. XVII. ii. 18 A Czarina obstinate to a degree; would not consent. **1875** JOWETT *Plato* (ed. 2) IV. 13 Few philosophers will deny that a degree of pleasure attends eating and drinking. **1888** *Spectator* 30 June 878 His argument..is far-fetched to the last degree.

†**c.** Applied in the natural philosophy of the Middle Ages to the successive stages of intensity

of the elementary qualities of bodies (heat and cold, moisture and dryness): see quots. *Obs.*

c **1400** *Lanfranc's Cirurg.* 11 þilke þing þat we seie is hoot in þe firste degree þat is I-heet of kyndely heete þat is in oure bodies. **1578** LYTE *Dodoens* II. lxxxiii. 261 Rue is hoate and dry in the thirde degree. **1727–51** CHAMBERS *Cycl.* s.v., The degrees usually allowed are four, answering to the number of the peripatetic elements. In the school philosophy, the same qualities are divided into eight.. Fire was held hot in the eighth degree, and dry in the fourth degree.

d. *Crim. Law.* Relative measure of criminality, as in ***principal in the first,*** or ***second, degree***: see quots. In *U.S. Law*, A distinctive grade of crime (with different maximum punishments), as 'murder in the first degree', or 'second degree'.

a **1676** HALE *Pleas of Crown* (1736) I. 613 Those, who did actually commit the very fact of treason, should be first tried before those, that are principals in the second degree. *Ibid.* 615 By what hath been formerly deliverd, principals are in two kinds, principals in the first degree, which actually commit the offense, principals in the second degree, which are present, aiding, and abetting of the fact to be done. **1797** *Jacob's Law Dict.* s.v. *Accessary*, A man may be a principal in an offence in two degrees.. he must be certainly guilty, either as principal or accessary.. and if principal, then in the first degree, for there is no.. superior in the guilt, whom he could aid, abet, or assist. **1821** JEFFERSON *Autob.* Writings 1892 I. 65 They introduced [1796] the new terms of murder in the 1st and 2d degree. **1877** J. F. STEPHEN *Digest Crim. Law* art. 35 Whoever actually commits or takes part in the actual commission of a crime is a principal in the first degree, whether he is on the spot when the crime is committed or not.

e. ***third degree***: see THIRD DEGREE.

II. Specific and technical senses.

7. A stage of proficiency in an art, craft, or course of study: **a.** *esp.* An academical rank or distinction conferred by a university or college as a mark of proficiency in scholarship; also (***honorary degree***) as a recognition of distinction, or a tribute of honour. Also in legal use.

Originally used of the preliminary steps to the Mastership or Doctorate, i.e. the Bachelorship and License; afterwards of the Mastership also. (As to the origin, see quot. 1794.)

[**1284** *Chart. Univ. Paris.* I. I. No. 515 Determinatio [i.e. the Disputation for B.A.] est unus honorabilis gradus attingendi magisterium.] *c* **1380** WYCLIF *Wks.* (1880) 427 Degre takun in scole makiþ goddis word more acceptable, and þe puple trowiþ betere þerto whanne it is seyd of a maistir. **1481** CAXTON *Myrr.* I. v. 26 Without hauyng the degree and name of maistre. **1573** G. HARVEY *Letter-bk.* (Camden) 42 That I shuld.. go well enough forward in lerninge but never take any high degree in schooles. **1606** Shaks. *Tr. & Cr.* I. iii. 104. **1614** BP. HALL *Recoll. Treat.* 772 You have twice kneeled to our Vice-Chauncellour, when you were admitted to your degree. **1708** HEARNE *Collect.* 17 June, This day Mr. Carter.. accumulated yᵉ Degrees of Bach. and Doct. of Divinity. *a* **1794** GIBBON *Autobiog.* 29 The use of academical degrees, as old as the thirteenth century, is visibly borrowed from the mechanic corporations: in which an apprentice, after serving his time, obtains a testimonial of his skill, and a licence to practice his trade and mystery. **1828** SCOTT *F.M. Perth* xi, A medal.. which intimated, in the name of some court or guild of minstrels, the degree she had taken in the Gay or Joyous Science. **1868** M. PATTISON *Academ. Org.* v. 128 To pass through the whole of this course.. whose successive steps were called degrees (*gradus*), required at least twenty years. **1880** *Encycl. Brit.* XIII. 87/2 Each inn confers this status or degree [*sc.* of barrister] on its own members only. **1885** *Law Jrnl.* 13 June 364/1 That his Royal Highness.. be called to the degree of the Utter Bar. **1959** JOWITT *Dict. Eng. Law* 601/2 *Degree*,.. the state of a person, as to be a barrister-at-law, or a Master of Arts of a University.

b. *Freemasonry.* Each of the steps of proficiency in the order, conferring successively higher rank on the initiated, as the first or 'entered apprentice degree', the second or 'fellow craft degree', the third or 'degree of master mason'.

There are 33 degrees recognized by the Ancient and Accepted Scottish Rite, besides many others considered more or less irregular. Some bodies recognize only three degrees.

c **1430** *Freemasonry* 727 To the nexte degre loke wysly, To do hem reverans by and by. **1875** FORT *Early Hist. Freemasonry*, A society comprising three degrees of laborers,—masters, fellows, and apprentices. **1881** *Text-bk. Freemasonry* 27 There are several degrees in Freemasonry with peculiar secrets restricted to each.

8. *Gram.* Each of the three stages (POSITIVE, COMPARATIVE, SUPERLATIVE) in the comparison of an adjective or adverb.

[A technical application of sense 6.]

1460–70 *Bk. Quintessence* 22 Þe feuere agu is þe posityue degree, and in þe superlatyue degree. **1530** PALSGR. Introd. 28 Adjectyves have thre degrees of comparation. **1621** BURTON *Anat. Mel.* III. ii. vi. §3 If.. any were *mala, pejor, pessima*, bad in the superlative degree, 'tis a whore. **1707** J. STEVENS tr. *Quevedo's Com. Wks.* (1709) 145 He was the Superlative Degree of Avarice. **1855** FORBES *Hindústání Gram.* (1868) 34 The adjectives in Hindústání have no regular degrees of comparison. **1888** *Pall Mall G.* 31 Oct. 4/1 There are three degrees of comparison in Empire, as in grammar. The positive is the chartered company; the comparative is a protectorate; the superlative, annexation.

9. a. *Geom.* (*Astron.*, *Geog.*, etc.) A unit of measurement of angles or circular arcs, being an angle equal to the 90th part of a right angle, or an arc equal to the 360th part of the circumference of a circle (which subtends this angle at the centre).

The sign for *degrees* is °, thus 45° = forty-five degrees. This division of the circle is very ancient, and appears to have been originally applied to the circle of the Zodiac, a *degree* being the stage or distance travelled by the sun each day according to ancient Babylonian and Egyptian computation, just as a *sign* represented the space passed through in a month.

c **1386** CHAUCER *Sqr.'s T.* 378 The yonge sonne That in the Ram is foure degrees vp ronne. *c* **1391** —— *Astrol.* I. §6 The entring of the first degree in which the sonne arisith. *Ibid.* II. §22 I proue it thus by the latitude of Oxenford.. the heyhte of owre pool Artik fro owre north Orisonte is 51 degrees and 50 Minutes. **1413** LYDG. *Pilgr. Sowle* v. i. (1859) 70 In the hole compas of the spyere ben of such degrees thre honderd and syxty. **1527** in Arber *1st 3 Eng. Bks. Amer.* Pref. p. xiv, We ranne in our course to the Northward, till we came into 53 degrees.. and then we cast about to the Southward, and.. came into 52 degrees. **1559** W. CUNNINGHAM *Cosmogr. Glasse* 58 Cosmographers do place the first degre of Longitude in the West fortunate Ilandes. **1590** WEBBE *Trav.* (1868) 25 Being thus in the land of prester Iohn, I trauelled within Eighteene degrees of yᵉ Sun, euery degree being in distance three score miles. **1665** MANLEY *Grotius' Low C. Warres* 471 A Land full of grass.. pleasantly green, where the Pole is elevated eighty degrees. **1719** DE FOE *Crusoe* (1840) II. ii. 26 In the latitude of 27 degrees 5 minutes N. **1823** H. J. BROOKE *Introd. Crystallogr.* 2 The angle at which they meet is said to measure 90°, and is termed a right angle. **1867** J. HOGG *Microsc.* I. i. 11 Transmitting a pencil of eighteen degrees.

b. *transf.* A position on the earth's surface or the celestial sphere, as measured by degrees (chiefly of latitude).

1647 COWLEY *Mistress, Parting* iii, The men of Learning comfort me; And say I'm in a warm Degree. **1663** BUTLER *Hud.* I. i. 174 He knew the Seat of Paradise, Could tell in what Degree it lies. **1726** *Adv. Capt. R. Boyle* 175 The next Day we discover'd the Magellan Clouds.. These Clouds are always seen in the same Degree, and the same orbicular Form.

10. *Thermometry.* **a.** A unit of temperature, varying according to the scale employed. **b.** Each of the marks denoting degrees of temperature on the scale of a thermometer, or the interval between two successive marks.

The interval between the freezing and boiling points of water is divided in Fahrenheit's scale into 180 degrees, in the Centigrade into 100, in Réaumur's into 80. The symbol ° is used in this sense as in prec.; thus 32° Fahr. means 'thirty-two degrees of Fahrenheit's scale'.

1727–51 CHAMBERS *Cycl.* s.v. *Thermometer*, Various methods have been proposed.. for finding a fixed point, or degree of heat and cold, from which to account the other degrees, and adjust the scale. **1796** HUTTON *Math. Dict.* s.v. *Thermometer*, The distance between these two points he divided into 600 equal parts or degrees; and by trials he found at the freezing point.. that the mercury stood at 32 of these divisions. **1812** SIR H. DAVY *Chem. Philos.* 70 Raised from the degree of freezing to that of boiling water. **1877** WATTS *Dict. Chem.* V. 762 s.v. *Thermometer*, Thermometers intended to show the $\frac{1}{10}$ of a degree (Fahr.), should have degrees not less than $\frac{1}{16}$ inch in length. *Ibid.* 763 For meteorological use, the degrees should still be etched on the glass, but may be repeated on the metal scale.

c. **degree day**, a unit used to determine the heating requirements of buildings (see quots.). Also *attrib.*

1930 *Engineering* 11 July 34/1 The term 'degree-day' is used in the United States to denote the difference in external temperature between the daily mean and 65° F; we have no similar recognized term here. **1958** *Ibid.* 14 Mar. 322/3 The conception of Degree Days as a means of exercising control over heating installations and of forecasting fuel requirements is by no means a new one in this country. The London and Home Counties Coke Association started the first Degree Day Service in 1938. **1964** J. S. SCOTT *Dict. Build.* 94 *Degree-day value*, a figure which describes the relative coldness of a site. It is based on the number of days yearly by which the average temperature falls below 60° F. in Britain... In USA.. the temperature chosen for degree-day charts is 65° F.

11. *Mus.* **a.** The interval between any note of a scale (*esp.* the diatonic scale) and the next note. **b.** Each of the successive notes forming the scale. **c.** Each of the successive lines and spaces on the stave, which denote the position of the notes; the interval between two of these.

[**1597** MORLEY *Introd. Mus.* 12 Those which we now call Moodes, they tearmid degree of Musicke.] **1674** PLAYFORD *Skill Mus.* III. 40 The parts part asunder, the one by degree, the other by leap. **1684** R. H. *School Recreat.* 115 The Five Lines and Spaces.. are useful, as Steps or Gradations whereon the Degrees of Sound are to be expressed. **1727–51** CHAMBERS *Cycl.* s.v., The musical degrees are three; the greater tone, the lesser tone, and the semi-tone. *Ibid.*, *Conjoint degrees*, two notes which immediately follow each other in the order of the scale. **1880** STAINER *Composition* iii, All the degrees of a scale can be harmonized by chords formed by combining sounds of that scale. **1880** C. H. H. PARRY in Grove *Dict. Mus.* s.v., The interval of a second is one degree, the interval of a third two degrees, and so on.

†**12.** *Arith.* A group of three figures taken together in numeration. *Obs.*

1674 JEAKE *Arith.* (1696) 15 These places are distinguished into Degrees and Periods. Degrees are three; Once, Ten times, a Hundred times. *a* **1677** *Cocker's Arith.* (1688) i. §9 A degree consists of three figures, viz. of three places comprehending Units, Tens, and Hundreds, so 365 is a degree. [Hence in JOHNSON, etc.]

13. *Alg.* The rank of an equation or expression as determined by the highest power of the unknown or variable quantity, or the highest dimensions of the terms, which it contains.

Thus $x^3 + x^2$, $x^2y + xy$, are both expressions of the third degree; the terms x^3 and x^2y being each of 3 dimensions. In algebraic geometry, the *degree* of a curve or surface is that of the equation expressing it. † ***parodic degree***: see quot. 1730.

1730–6 BAILEY (folio), *Parodic Degree* (in Algebra) is the index or exponent of any power; so in numbers, 1. is the parodick degree, or exponent of the root or side; 2. of the square, 3. of the cube, etc. **1796** HUTTON *Math. Dict.* s.v., Equations.. are said to be of such a degree according to the highest power of the unknown quantity. **1870** TODHUNTER *Algebra* ix. §166 An equation of the first degree cannot have more than one root. **1872** B. WILLIAMSON *Diff. Calc.* xiv. §204 When the lowest terms in the equation of a curve are of the second degree, the origin is a double point. *Ibid.* §207 The curves considered in this Article are called parabolas of the third degree.

14. ***degree of freedom***: see FREEDOM 10

15. *Comb.* (in sense 7 a), as ***degree-day*** (see also 10 c), ***factory***, ***-fee***, ***-level***; ***degree-conferring***, ***-granting*** adjs.; ***degree-giving*** vbl. sb. and adj.

1903 *Westm. Gaz.* 11 July 2/2 The *degree-conferring Universities of the United Kingdom. **1906** *Daily Chron.* 27 July 6/7 To make the Nottingham University College a degree-conferring University. **1832** J. ROMILLY *Diary* 9 May (1967) 12 A *Degree day: 2 hon. M.A., 6 M.A. & 17 B.A. **1867** G. M. HOPKINS *Let. to Bridges* 5 Dec. (1935) 20 Would it be possible for you to see me on yr. way home? Certainly it would if the degree day does not fall too late. **1900** G. SWIFT *Somerley* 164 When the dance and degree-day were over. **1886** W. HOOPER *Sketches fr. Academic Life* 51 It [an M.A. degree] had been obtained from one of these **degree factories. **1897** *Daily News* 23 Apr. 7/4 Many of the **Degree-Fees have.. been raised. **1888** BRYCE *Amer. Commonw.* III. VI. cii. 462 They complain of the multiplication of *degree-giving bodies. **1905** W. JAMES *Mem. & Stud.* (1911) v. 102 'Civilization', with its herding and branding, licensing and degree-giving. **1946** *Nature* 19 Oct. 531/1 The difficulties.. have led Lord Cherwell to propose the transfer of engineering training from the universities to degree-giving institutes of technology. **1895** *Westm. Gaz.* 27 July 5/3 It.. had never been adequately encouraged by *degree-granting Universities. **1896** *Daily News* 20 Feb. 5/4 The larger degree-granting institutions. **1967** *Times* 28 Feb. (Canada Suppl.) 36 Some 60 degree-granting universities and colleges in Canada. **1956** *Nature* 18 Feb. 296/2 A national council to control the award of ..*degree-level qualification.

degree (dɪ'griː), *v.* [f. DEGREE *sb.*]

†**1.** *trans.* To advance by degrees; to lead or bring on step by step. *Obs.*

1614 T. ADAMS *Devil's Banquet* 168 Thus is the soules death degreed up. Sin gathers strength by custom, and creeps like some contagious disease.. from joint to joint. **1627–77** FELTHAM *Resolves* I. iii. 4, I like that Love, which by a soft ascension, does degree itself in the soul. **1636** HEYWOOD *Challenge* II. Wks. 1874 V. 27 Degree thy tortures, like an angry tempest, Rise calmely first, and keepe thy worst rage last. *a* **1670** HACKET *Abp. Williams* II. 189 (D.), I will degree this noxious neutrality one peg higher.

†**b.** *absol. Obs. rare.*

1638 HEYWOOD *London's Gate* Wks. 1874 V. 273 There's not a stone that's laid in such foundation But is a step degreeing to salvation.

2. To confer a degree upon. *nonce-use.*

[**1560**: see DEGREED.] **1865** MRS. WHITNEY *Gayworthys* ii. (1879) 23 A divine.. degreed in due course as Doctor Divinitatis. **1891** *Sat. Rev.* 22 Aug. 208 The Demographers ....had the good fortune to be welcomed and degreed at Cambridge.

degreed (dɪ'griːd), *a.* [f. DEGREE *sb.* (and *v.*).]

1. Having an academical degree. Also *absol.*

1560 in Strype *Ann. Ref.* I. xvii. 215 Such as be degreed in the Universities. **1905** *Daily Chron.* 11 July 3/2 The unfairness to the rate-payer,.. to the class-teacher, to the non-collegiate, to the academical degreed. **1962** *Guardian* 17 Jan. 6/6 Degreed women are.. very much the exception. **1967** *Ibid.* 28 June 6/5 Abstracts of papers by much-degreed ladies from the University of Saskatchewan.

†**2.** Made or done by gradations, graduated.

1581 MULCASTER *Positions* xi. (1887) 50 Musick.. standeth vpon an ordinate, and degreed motion of the voice.

†**3.** Having a (specified) degree or rank. *Obs.*

1608 HEYWOOD *Rape of Lucrece* II. iii, We, that are degreed above our people. **1656** S. H. *Gold. Law* 43 Are they not both (though differently degree'd), servants to one and the same Lord?

†**4.** Marked out in successive divisions. *Obs.*

1664 POWER *Exp. Philos.* 23 Her two horns are all joynted and degreed like the stops in the germination of some Plants.

5. *Her.* Of a cross: Placed upon 'degrees' or steps; = DEGRADED.

In mod. Dicts.

†**de'greeingly**, *adv. Obs. rare.* [f. *degreeing*, pres. pple. of DEGREE *v.* + -LY².] By degrees, gradually, step by step.

1627–77 FELTHAM *Resolves* I. xcvii. 151 Degreeingly to grow to greatness, is the course that he hath left for Man.

de'greeless, *a. rare.* [-LESS.]

1. Without degree or measurement; measureless.

1839 BAILEY *Festus* xix. (1848) 218 Deep in all dayless time degreeless space.

2. Without an academical degree or degrees.

1825 *New Monthly Mag.* XIII. 414 Parliament could not well refuse a degreeless university to.. Londoners. **1892** *Times* (weekly ed.) 1 Jan. 21/4 The case of those who are.. left degreeless.. is the hardest of all.

†**de'gress**, *v. Obs. rare*$^{-0}$. [f. L. *dēgress-*, ppl. stem of *dēgredī* to descend, dismount; f. DE- I. 1 + *gradī* to step, go.]

1623 COCKERAM, *Degresse*, to vnlight from a Horse.

degression (dɪ'grɛʃən). [ad. L. *dēgressiōn-em* going down, n. of action from *dēgredī* (see prec.).] †**1.** Stepping down, descent. Also a textual variant of DIGRESSION. *Obs.*

1486 *Hen. VII at York* in *Surtees Misc.* (1890) 55 For your blode this citie made never degression. **1618** LITHGOW *Pilgrim's Farewell*, Thy stiffeneckt crew..misregarding God, fall in degression.

2. The decrease in the rate of taxation in a degressive scale.

1896 PALGRAVE *Dict. Pol. Econ.* II. 244/1 Graduated taxation therefore technically includes progression, degression, and regression. **1906** *Westm. Gaz.* 9 June 2/1 The income-tax so long planned in France..is English both in its taxation by schedules and in its exemptions of the less wealthy payers, though it effects the last-named result by a more complete scheme of 'degression' than is in operation here. *Ibid.* 31 July 5/3 If any change was made in the direction of degression by which everybody would first be taxed at the higher rate and then have to apply for abatements.

3. *Bibliogr.* See next, sense 2.

degressive (dɪ'grɛsɪv), *a.* [f. L. *degress-*, ppl. stem of *dēgredī* to descend.] **1.** In taxation, of or pertaining to schemes in which the rate decreases successively on sums below a certain limit. Hence **de'gressively** (Webster 1909).

1886 H. SIDGWICK *Let.* 7 May in *Memoir* (1906) vi. 447 Giffen inclined to back out of his advocacy of 'degressive' taxation. **1911** S. J. CHAPMAN *Outl. Pol. Econ.* xxxii. 379 *Degressive taxation* means that large incomes are taxed at a higher rate than smaller incomes, but not in a degree which involves as great a proportional sacrifice for the former as for the latter. **1962** *Economist* 1 Dec. 939/2 This tax..might be made 'degressive' (i.e. declining in rate each year).

2. *Bibliogr.* (See quot. 1908.)

1908 F. MADAN in *Trans. Bibliogr. Soc.* IX. 53 (*title*) Degressive bibliography. *Ibid.*, The principle of degression ..that is to say, the principle of varying a description [of a book] according to the difference of the period treated or of the importance of the work to be described. It may therefore be worth while to suggest four forms for the description of a book, showing by degressive changes what details may fairly be omitted in short descriptions. **1953** *Library* VIII. 20 Generalizations about degressive bibliography, a phrase increasing in popular esteem at the moment. **1963** *Times Lit. Suppl.* 10 May 348/3 It is flying in the face of the degressive principle to repeat..title-page wording in multi-volumed books.

degrez, obs. pl. of DEGREE *sb.*

‖**dégringolade** (degrɛ̃gɔlad). [Fr., f. *dégringoler* to descend rapidly.] A rapid descent; deterioration, decadence; change from bad to worse. Also as vb.

1883 *Sat. Rev.* 24 Nov. 648/1 The *dégringolade* of Tokka and the catastrophe of Obeid. **1895** G. B. SHAW in *Sat. Rev.* 27 July 109/1 Miss Lottie Collins..will soon find her popularity degringolading from the summit on which the Tarara craze exalted it. **1906** W. DE MORGAN *Joseph Vance* xxxv. 346 This last is a short chapter, but is a record of a steady *dégringolade.* **1909** *Westm. Gaz.* 29 May 5/3 We.. share her distress in the ensuing dégringolade. **1926** *Spectator* 29 May 900/1 This *dégringolade*, this falling back into an undrained, unfenced, unploughed, unweeded prairie. **1926** *Nation* 24 July 460/1 The franc has this week looked the penny in the face, and has acquired a momentum in decline which suggests that a *dégringolade* is close at hand, unless prompt and effective measures are really taken. **1959** *Encounter* Sept. 69/1 The hero..underwent a convincing but totally unsensational *dégringolade*, taking, not to drugs or drink, but to an increasing sluggishness.

‖**Degu** ('dɛguː). *Zool.* [Native name in South America.] A South American genus *Octodon* of hystricomorphous or porcupine-like rodents; *esp.* the species *O. Cumingii*, abundant in Chile.

1843 *List Mammalia Brit. Mus.* 122 The cucurrito or the Degus, *Octodon Degus.* **1883** *Cassell's Nat. Hist.* III. 129 The Degu is a rat-like animal, rather smaller than the Water Vole, the head and body measuring from seven and a half to eight inches in length.

deguise: see DISGUISE.

†**'degulate**, *v. Obs. rare*$^{-0}$. [f. L. *dēgulāre* to consume, devour, f. DE- I. 1 + *gula* gullet.]

1623 COCKERAM, *Degulate*, to consume in belly cheere.

degum (diː'gʌm), *v.* [DE- II. 2 + GUM *sb.*^{2}] To deprive of gum; *spec.* (in the preparation of silk) to deglutinate. So **de'gummed** *ppl. a.*; **de'gumming** *vbl. sb.* Also *fig.*

a **1884** KNIGHT *Dict. Mech.* Suppl. 249/2 *Degumming machine*, a machine used in treating silk before dyeing. **1887** *Encycl. Brit.* XXII. 62/2 The fibres..being now degummed, are separated from each other. **1938** *Thorpe's Dict. Appl. Chem.* (ed. 4) II. 17/2 Generally silk is degummed as hanks of yarn. Degumming as cloth has.. advantages. **1956** *Nature* 3 Mar. 429/2, 4·86 gm. of the radioactive cocoon fibres was cut into small pieces and degummed. **1959** N. MARSH *Singing in Shrouds* vii. 148 He treated his restive audience to a comprehensive degumming of *Hamlet* and *Macbeth.* **1960** A. E. BENDER *Dict. of Nutrition* 38/2 *Degumming agents*, used in refining of fats to remove mucilaginous matter consisting of gum, resin, proteins and phosphatides. **1963** A. J. HALL *Textile Sci.* ii. 42 There is about 20 to 30% of silk-gum associated with the silk fibres so that a weight loss of this order results from degumming—it makes the de-gummed silk so much the more expensive.

degust (dɪ'gʌst), *v. rare.* [ad. L. *dēgustāre*, f. DE- I. 3 + *gustāre* to taste. Cf. mod.F. *déguster.*] *trans.* To taste; *esp.* to taste attentively, so as to appreciate the savour. Also *absol.*

1623 COCKERAM, *Degust*, to taste. **1860** READE *Cloister & H.* ii. (D.), A *soupe au vin*, madam, I will degust, and gratefully. **1883** STEVENSON *Silverado Sq.* 17 Wine..a deity to be invoked by two or three, all fervent, hushing their talk, degusting tenderly.

degustate (dɪ'gʌsteɪt), *v. rare.* [f. L. *dēgustāt-*, ppl. stem of *dēgustāre*: see prec.] = prec.

1599 A. M. tr. *Gabelhouer's Bk. Physicke* 85/2 When as we can not digustate either Meate, or Drincke. **1831** T. L. PEACOCK *Crotchet Castle* iv. (1887) 56 Which gave the divine an opportunity to degustate one or two side dishes.

degustation (diːgʌ'steɪʃən). [ad. L. *dēgustātiōn-em* tasting, making trial of, n. of action from *dēgustāre*: see DEGUST. Cf. F. *dégustation.*] The action of degusting or tasting.

a **1656** BP. HALL *Souls Farew.* Wks. 1837 VIII. 314 Carnal delights; the degustation whereof is wont to draw on the heart to a more eager appetite. **1880** *Daily Tel.* 11 Oct., The 'tasting bars' devoted to the 'degustation' of all kinds of alcoholic compounds.

degustator (dɪ'gʌstətə(r)). *rare.* [agent-n. in L. form from L. *dēgustāre*: see prec. Cf. mod.F. *dégustateur.*] One who degusts, or tastes as a connoisseur.

1833 *New Monthly Mag.* XXXVIII. 223 The numerous degustators of oysters with which our capital abounds.

degustatory (dɪ'gʌstətərɪ), *a.* [f. L. *dēgustāt-*, ppl. stem of *dēgustāre*: see -ORY.] Pertaining to degustation; tasty.

1824 *New Monthly Mag.* XI. 394 A constant ingurgitation of degustatory morsels.

degut (diː'gʌt), *v.* [DE- II. 2 + GUT *sb.*] *trans.* To remove the guts, contents, or essential elements of (in the senses of *gut* vb.).

1933 DYLAN THOMAS *Let.* Sept. (1966) 24 Open him [*sc.* Wordsworth] at any page: and there lies the English language... Degutted and desouled. **1948** WYNDHAM LEWIS *Let.* 25 Oct. (1963) 466 The publisher *who dulls these letters down* and deguts them will not only be doing a great disservice to Ezra but to the public of today and also tomorrow. **1960** *Sunday Times* 6 Mar. 6/8 We are certainly not going to de-gut the centre of London..to provide motorways and parking space. **1962** *Daily Tel.* 17 Dec. 8/8 The latest edition of 'That Was The Week That Was' [B.B.C. Television] was degutted as efficiently as any fish at Yarmouth! *Ibid.*, It was pleasant to watch the farmers degutting the unhappy Mr. Levin.

deguyse, degyse: see DISGUISE *v.*

deh, obs. 3rd sing. pres. of DOW *v.*

‖**déhaché** (deɪ'hæʃeɪ), *a. Her.* [obs. F. *déhaché* 'hacked, hewed, cut into small pieces' (Cotgr. 1611), f. DE- I. 1, 2 + *hacher* to cut.] (See quots.)

1766 PORNY *Heraldry* v. (1777) 158 If a Lion, or any other Beast is represented with its limbs and body separated..it is then termed *Déhaché* or *Couped in all its parts. Ibid.* Gloss., *Déhaché*, this is an obsolete French word..the term *Couped* is now used in stead of it. **1880** G. T. CLARK in *Encycl. Brit.* XI. 698/2 (*Heraldry*) In one or two well-known instances on the Continent he [the lion] is 'déhaché', that is, his head and paws and the tuft of his tail are cut off.

dehair (diː'hɛə(r)), *v.* [f. DE- II. 2 + HAIR *sb.*] *trans.* To remove the hair from (a skin), to unhair. Hence **de'hairer**; **de'hairing** *vbl. sb.*

1902 *Mod. Amer. Tanning* I. 37 When [sulphide of sodium is] used in conjunction with lime a very satisfactory process is obtained which results in the skins being dehaired..in much less time. **1921** *Dict. Occup. Terms* (1927) §338 *Unhairer* (tannery); *dehairer*; (i) a beam man who spreads hides or skins on wooden beam; scrapes hair, by hand, with two-handled knife; (ii) passes hides or skins from lime pits, between unhairing machine, removing hairs. **1959** *Chambers's Encycl.* XIII. 456/2 The hide or skin..after de-hairing is immersed in liquors made from chromium salts.

†**de'haust.** *Obs. rare.* [f. L. *dēhaust-um*, pa. pple. of *dēhaurīre* to draw or drain off, f. DE- I. 2 + *haurīre* to draw, drain.] Drain, exhaustion.

1654 CODRINGTON tr. *Hist. Iustine* 536 He being the cause of the great Dehaust of moneys in the Exchequer.

de haut en bas: see DE II.

deheathenize, dehellenize, dehistoricize: see DE- II. 1.

de'hire, *v. N. Amer. euphem.* [f. DE- II. 1 + HIRE *v.*] *trans.* To discharge (an employee, esp. an executive) from a position; to 'sack' or 'fire'. Also **de'hiring** *vbl. sb.*

1970 *Guardian Weekly* 5 Sept. 22 The pinched corporation..fires the chairman of the board. Fires is a rude word, but the bouncing of the boss is happening now on such a scale that Wall Street is mushrooming with firms bearing the weird names of 'Dehiring Consultants, Inc.' and 'Executive Adjustment Advisers'... In a depression, the boss is sacked and jumps from a window. In the 'recedence', he is 'dehired'. **1977** *Time* May 328/1 These half dozen or so organizations, known in the doublespeak world of consulting as 'out-placement' or 'de-hiring' firms, steel the courage of the executives who have to do the firing. **1980** *Amer. Speech* LV. 272 It is presumably more fashionable to be dehired than to be fired. **1982** *Forbes* (N.Y.) 10 May 200/2 'Outplacement specialists'... That's a fancy name for the folks whose business it is to 'dehire' (*i.e.*, to help fire) executives.

dehisce (dɪ'hɪs), *v.* [ad. L. *dēhisc-ĕre* to open in chinks, gape, yawn, f. DE- I. 2 + *hiscĕre*, inceptive of *hiāre* to stand open, gape.] *intr.* To gape; in *Bot.* to burst open, as the seed-vessels of plants.

1657 TOMLINSON *Renou's Disp.* 259 Dehiscing with frequent chinks. **1830** LINDLEY *Nat. Syst. Bot.* 35 *Ovarium* consisting of 5 carpella..dehiscing in various ways. **1859** TODD *Cycl. Anat.* V. 246/1 The organ..subsequently dehisces in four valves. **1882** O'DONOVAN *Merv* II. xliv. 241 The green carpels..dehisce, separating and bending backwards.

Hence **de'hiscing** *ppl. a.*

1845 LINDLEY *Sch. Bot.* iv. (1858) 33 Valves ventricose.. scarcely dehiscing.

dehiscence (dɪ'hɪsəns). [ad. mod.L. *dehiscentia* 'quum fructus maturus semina dispergat' (Linnæus), f. L. *dēhiscent-em*, pr. pple. of *dēhiscĕre*: see -ENCE. So in mod.F.] Gaping, opening by divergence of parts, *esp.* as a natural process: **a.** *Bot.* The bursting open of capsules, fruits, anthers, etc. in order to discharge their mature contents.

1828 WEBSTER cites MARTYN. **1830** LINDLEY *Nat. Syst. Bot.* Introd. 29 In Hamamelideæ dehiscence is effected by the falling off of the face of the anthers. **1870** BENTLEY *Bot.* 243 The anthers..open and discharge the contained pollen; this act is called the dehiscence of the anther.

b. *Anim. Phys.* Applied to the bursting open of mucous follicles, and of the Graafian follicles, for the expulsion of their contents.

1859 TODD *Cycl. Anat.* V. 56/1 The ova..drop by internal dehiscence into the cavity of the ovary. **1870** ROLLESTON *Anim. Life* Introd. 38 The ova are set free by dehiscence into the perivisceral cavity.

c. *fig.* and *gen.*

1853 KANE *Grinnell Exp.* xxxiii. (1856) 285 The dehiscence..of such tensely-compressed floes, must be the cause of the loud explosions we have heard lately. **1860** O. W. HOLMES *Elsie V.* 139 A house is a large pod with a human germ or two in each of its cells or chambers; it opens by dehiscence of the front door..and projects one of its germs to Kansas, another to San Francisco.

dehiscent (dɪ'hɪsənt), *a.* [ad. L. *dēhiscent-em*, pr. pple. of *dēhiscĕre* to DEHISCE. So in mod.F.] Gaping open; *spec.*, in *Bot.* opening as seed-vessels.

1649 BULWER *Pathomyot.* II. ii. 107 The Mouth..is Dehiscent, yet scarce Dehiscent into a Casme. **1845** LINDLEY *Sch. Bot.* i. (1858) 17 If..[the fruit] splits into pieces when ripe it is called *dehiscent.* **1853** KANE *Grinnell Exp.* xix. (1856) 145 The period when the dehiscent edges and mountain ravines..have been worn down into rounded hill and gentle valley. **1872** H. MACMILLAN *True Vine* iv. 162 The fruits of many plants are dehiscent..they open to scatter the seed.

b. Said of the elytra of insects when they do not meet at the apices; also of antennæ divergent at the tips.

1889 in *Cent. Dict.*

†**dehomi'nation.** *nonce-wd. Obs.* [n. of action from med.L. *dēhomināre* to deprive of the status of a man (Du Cange), f. DE- I. 6 + *homo, homin-em* man.] Deprival of the character or attributes of humanity.

1647 WARD *Simp. Cobler* (1843) 51 He fears..as an Angell dehominations; as a Prince, dis-common-wealthings.

de'honestate, *v. rare.* [f. ppl. stem of L. *dēhonestāre* to dishonour, disgrace (f. DE- I. 6 + *honestus* HONEST): see -ATE^3.] *trans.* To dishonour, disgrace, disparage.

1663 JER. TAYLOR *Fun. Serm. Abp. Bramhall* III. 224 (L.) The excellent..pains he took in this particular, no man can dehonestate or reproach. **1825** LAMB *Vision of Horns*, Knaves who dehonestate the intellects of married women.

Hence **dehone'station** [ad. L. *dēhonestātiōn-em*], dishonouring, dishonour.

c **1555** HARPSFIELD *Divorce Hen. VIII* (1878) 96 The dehonestation and dishonouring of the brother. **1653** GAUDEN *Hierasp.* 482 The infinite shame, dehonestation, and infamy which they bring. **1661** —— *Anti-Baal-B.* 464 (L.) Sacrilege..is the unjust violation, alienation or dehonestation of things truly sacred.

de'horn, *v.* [DE- II. 2.]

1. *trans.* To deprive (an animal) of horns. Also *absol.* and *fig.* Hence **de'horner**, one who, or an instrument which, dehorns animals.

1888 *Voice* (N.Y.) 12 Jan. 2 The champion of dehorning cattle. *Ibid.* 23 Feb. 7 That enthusiastic champion of dehorning, 'Farmer Haaf,' will soon issue a book: 'Every Man His own Dehorner'. **1888** *Missouri Republ.* 15 Feb. (Farmer), Dehorning is performed when the calf is young, and the tips of the horns movable. **1889** FARMER *Americanisms* 197/1 The preferred age at which to dehorn is in the second year of the animal's life. **1895** *Montgomery Ward Catal.* 394/3 Cattle Dehorners... Newton's lately improved dehorning knife, revolving and sliding shear, each one making a draw cut. **1897** *Sears, Roebuck Catal.* (facing p. 33), The Adsit dehorning shears..makes a drawing cut completely encircling the horn, which it removes almost instantly. **1904** WILCOX & SMITH *Farmer's Cycl. Agric.*

339/1 The practice of dehorning cattle is generally recommended by the experiment station. **1907** *Sears, Roebuck Catal.*, This style Dehorner in the large size will clip any size horn from cattle of any age. **1914** *Boston Even. Transcript* 6 June 2/1 Four years ago they dehorned the speaker. **1920** F. B. Hadley *Princ. Vet. Sci.* xiii. 260 When cattle are allowed to run together they should be dehorned. **1935** J. Steinbeck *To a God Unknown* 91 To borrow a dehorner for that long-horned bull. **1959** *Times* 27 Oct. 6/4 The high proportion of dehorned cows in the main cattle section. **1960** *Farmer & Stockbreeder* 26 Jan. 112/3 (Advt.), 6-volt calf dehorner. **1971** *Guardian* 20 Feb. 18/4 A cattle de-horning device.

2. *Forestry.* (See quots.)

1905 *Terms Forestry & Logging* 35 *Dehorn*, to saw off the ends of logs bearing the owner's mark and put on a new mark (Kentucky). **1957** *Brit. Commonw. Forest Terminol.* II. 59 *Dehorn*, to re-mark logs for change of ownership.

3. *Horticulture.* (See quot. 1954.)

1934 in Webster. **1954** A. G. L. Hellyer *Encycl. Garden Work & Terms* 195/1 If..fairly large branches have to be removed..this should be done either right back to the main trunk, or to a suitably placed side branch. This latter process is known as dehorning.

‖**dehors** (dəˈhɔːr), *prep.* and *sb.* [a. OF. *dehors*, prep., mod.F. *dehors* adv. and sb.; OF. also *defors*, Pr. *defors*, Cat. *defora*, Sp. *defuera*, a late L. or Romanic comb. of *de* prep. + L. *forās* out of doors, forth, also in sense of L. *forīs* out of doors, outside, without. Cf. It. *fuor*, *fuora*, *fuori.*]

A. *prep.* (*Law.*) Outside of; not within the scope of.

1701 *Law French Dict.*, *Dehors*, out, without. **1818** Cruise *Digest* (ed. 2) VI. 196 The Judge..was of opinion that nothing *dehors* the will could be received to show the intention of the devisor. **1885** Ld. Esher in *Law Times* LXXIX. 445/1 The trustees were named in the deed, but who they were was a fact *dehors* the deed.

†**B.** *sb.* (*Fortif.*) See quot. *Obs.*

1706 Phillips (ed. Kersey), *Dehors*..in *Fortification*, all sorts of separate Out-works, as Crown-works, Horn-works, Half-moons, Ravelins, etc., made for the better security of the main place. **1721** in Bailey; and in mod. Dicts.

de Horsey (dəˈhɔːsɪ). *Naut.* The name of Admiral Sir A. F. R. *de Horsey* (1827–1922), used to designate a rig for a cutter or launch consisting of a triangular or jib-headed foresail and a gaff mainsail. Hence **de Horsey-rigged** *a.*

1905 *Man. Seamanship* iii. 47 *Launches and Pinnaces.* The de Horsey rig, *i.e.*, one mast, a foresail set on the forestay, and a mainsail bent to a gaff. **1923** 'Bartimeus' *Seaways* xii. 211 She's de Horsey-rigged and is propelled by oars in the absence of a suitable wind. **1953** J. Masefield *Conway* (rev. ed.) IV. 249 The De Horsey-rigged cutters and sloop-rigged dinghies.

dehort (dɪˈhɔːt), *v.* Now *rare.* [ad. L. *dēhortā-rī* to dissuade, f. DE- I. 2 + *hortārī* to exhort.]

1. *trans.* To use exhortation to dissuade (a person) from a course or purpose; to advise or counsel against (an action, etc.). †**a.** with simple (or double) obj. Now *Obs.*

1545 Joye *Exp. Dan.* i. (R.), Jermye wel dehorted and disswaded the peple sayinge [etc.]. **1553** T. Wilson *Rhet.* (1580) 29 Wherby we doe persuade..disswade..exhorte, or dehorte..any man. **1611** Bible *1 Macc.* ix. 9 But they dehorted him, saying, Wee shall neuer be able. *a* **1631** Donne *Lett.* xcvii. Wks. VI. 416, I am far from dehorting those fixed Devotions. *a* **1656** Ussher *Ann.* iv. (1658) 24 Exhorting them to observe the law of God..and dehorting them the breach of that law. **1682** Burthogge *Argument* (1684) 121 He doth Dehort the Baptizing of Infants. **1696** Aubrey *Misc.* (1721) 218, I dehort him who adviseth with me, and suffer him not to proceed with what he is about.

b. Const. *from.*

a **1533** Frith *Another Bk. agst. Rastell* Prol. Wks. (1829) 207 To dehort thee from the vain and childish fear which our forefathers have had. **1603** Sir C. Heydon *Jud. Astrol.* xiii. 333 They dehorted him from going to Babylon. **1758** Jortin *Erasm.* I. 343 No person had taken so much pains as he to dehort all men from cruelty. **1825** Southey *Lett.* (1856) III. 462 Croker dehorts me from visiting Ireland. **1882** Cheyne *Isaiah* xx. Introd., Isaiah had good reason..to dehort the Jews from an Egyptian alliance.

†**c.** *fig.* Said of circumstances, etc. *Obs.*

1579 Lyly *Euphues* (Arb.) 106 If the wasting of our money might not dehort vs, yet the wounding of our mindes should deterre vs. **1697** Potter *Antiq. Greece* II. xvii. (1715) 339 It was unlucky, and dehorted them from proceeding in what they had designed.

2. *absol.*

1574 Whitgift *Def. Aunsw.* i. Wks. (1851) I. 156 Christ doth not here dehort from bearing rule..but from seeking rule. **1660** Jer. Taylor *Duct. Dubit.* III. iv. rule xx. §19 S. Paul does..dehort from marriage not as from an evil but as from a burden. *a* **1703** Burkitt *On N.T.* Heb. xiii. 6 The words are a strong reason to dehort from covetousness, and to exhort to contentedness. **1801** F. Barrett *The Magus* 19 The Creator..dehorting from the eating of the apple.

Hence **deˈhorting** *vbl. sb.* and *ppl. a.*

1553 T. Wilson *Rhet.* 34 b, The places of exhortyng and dehortyng are the same whiche wee use in perswadyng and dissuadyng. **1586** A. Day *Eng. Secretary* I. (1625) 82 After these Epistles Dehorting and Disswading. **1652** Gaule *Magastrom.* 29 Whan God desists from his gracious and serious dehorting.

dehortation (diːhɔːˈteɪʃən). [ad. L. *dēhortātiōn-em*, n. of action from *dēhortārī* to DEHORT.]

1. The action of dehorting *from* a course; earnest dissuasion.

1529 More *Dyaloge* IV. Wks. 273/2 Al the dehortacions and commynacions & threts in scripture. **1633** T. Stafford *Pac. Hib.* xiv. (1821) 164 His Country people vsed loud and rude dehortations to keepe him from Church. **1737** Whiston *Josephus' Hist.* II. viii. §11 Exhortations to virtue, and dehortations from wickedness. **1860** Pusey *Min. Proph.* 240 It is the voice of earnest, emphatic dehortation, not to do what would displease God.

†**2.** Power or faculty of dehorting. *Obs. rare*$^{-1}$.

1655 R. Younge *Agst. Drunkards* 16 Oh that I had dehortation answerable to my detestation of it!

dehortative (dɪˈhɔːtətɪv), *a.* and *sb.* [ad. L. *dēhortātīv-us*, f. ppl. stem of *dēhortārī*: see -IVE.]

A. *adj.* Having the quality or purpose of dehorting; dehortatory.

1620 Woodward in Gutch *Coll. Cur.* I. 181 Wryting..a dehortative letter against the match with Spayn. *c* **1810** Coleridge in *Lit. Rem.* III. 301 The words of the Apostle are exhortative and dehortative.

B. *sb.* A dehortative address or argument.

1671 *True Nonconf.* 431 His words after the usual manner of dehortatives, do seem some what tending to the contrary extreme. **1824** Miss L. M. Hawkins *Memoirs* II. 12 My father suggested that the horse-pond might be the best dehortative. **1850** L. Hunt *Autobiog.* v. (1860) 102 The doctor..warned me against the perils of authorship; adding, as a final dehortative, that 'the shelves were full'.

dehortatory (dɪˈhɔːtətərɪ), *a.* and *sb.* [ad. L. *dēhortātōri-us*, f. *dēhortārī*: see -ORY.]

A. *adj.* Characterized by dehortation; dissuasory.

1576 Fleming *Panopl. Epist.* Epit. B, Those places which are used..in an epistle Exhortatorie and Dehortatorie. **1644** Bp. Hall *Rem. Wks.* (1660) 103 A dehortatory charge to avoid the offence of God. **1804** Southey *Lett.* (1856) I. 251, I wrote to him in rather a dehortatory strain.

†**B.** *sb.* A dehortatory address. *Obs.*

1648 Milton *Observ. Art. Peace* (1851) 581 That fair dehortatory from joyning with Malignants.

dehorter (dɪˈhɔːtə(r)). [f. DEHORT *v.* + -ER.] One who dehorts or advises against an action, etc.

1611 Cotgr., *Desenhorteur*, a dehorter, dissuader. **1755** Johnson, *Dehorter*, a dissuader; an adviser to the contrary. **1866** Lowell *Carlyle* Prose Wks. 1890 II. 91 So long as he was merely an exhorter or dehorter, we were thankful for such eloquence..as only he could give.

†**deˈhortment.** *Obs. rare*$^{-1}$. [f. DEHORT *v.* + -MENT.] Dehortation.

1656 S. Holland *Zara* (1719) 118 Pantalone was too proud to hearken to dehortments.

deˈhuman, *a. nonce-wd.* [DE- II. 3.] Wanting the attributes of humanity.

1889 L. Abbott in *Chr. Union* (N.Y.) 31 Jan., The demoniacs..were distinctively, if I may coin the word, dehuman.

dehumanize (diːˈhjuːmənaɪz), *v.* [DE- II. 1 + HUMAN, HUMANIZE.] *trans.* To deprive of human character or attributes.

1818 Moore *Diary* 4 Dec., Turner's face was a good deal de-humanised. **1889** *Pall Mall G.* 26 Nov. 1/2 Our great towns de-humanize our children.

Hence **deˈhumanized** *ppl. a.*; **deˈhumanizing** *vbl. sb.* and *ppl. a.*; also **dehumaniˈzation**.

1844 *N. Brit. Rev.* II. 109 These almost de-humanized creatures. **1856** R. A. Vaughan *Mystics* IV. ii. *note*, The mystics..representing regeneration almost as a process of dehumanization. **1857** J. Pulsford *Quiet Hours* 156 It would seem as though the world's method of Education were dehumanizing. **1860** O. W. Holmes *Elsie V.* xxii. (1891) 325 Centuries of de-humanizing celibacy. **1882** F. Harrison *Choice Bks.* (1886) 446 To rehumanise the dehumanised members of society. **1889** G. Gissing *Nether World* III. i. 19 The last step in that process of dehumanisation which threatens idealists of his type.

ˌdehuˈmidify, *v.* [f. DE- II. + HUMIDIFY *v.*] *trans.* To reduce the degree of humidity of; to remove moisture from; to dry. So **ˌdehumidifiˈcation**, the removal of moisture; **ˌdehuˈmidified** *ppl. a.*; **ˌdehuˈmidifier**, a device or substance for dehumidification; **ˌdehuˈmidifying** *vbl. sb.* and *ppl. a.*

1921 *Sci. Amer.* 5 Mar. 188/2 Dehumidifier with dew-point control, showing the main parts of the controlling mechanism. **1932** *Engineering* 14 Oct. 458/1 The supply air has to be..dehumidified or dried. *Ibid.*, In this method of drying or dehumidification..the air..is passed through sprays of chilled water. *Ibid.*, The cooled dried air leaving the dehumidifier is warmed. **1933** *BBC Yearbk.* 102 This drying (or 'de-humidifying') of the air supply. **1933** *Archit. Rev.* LXXX. p. lxvi, The air conditioner comprises a slow speed fan and motor, heating coils, cooling and dehumidifying coils, air filter and humidifying spray for winter use. **1940** *Chambers's Techn. Dict.* 230/2 Dehumidified air. **1941** *Chem. Abstr.* 1674 Apparatus for humidifying, dehumidifying and cleaning air. **1947** *Jrnl. R. Aeronaut. Soc.* LI. 93/1 For tropical use, dehumidification is achieved by utilising the refrigerating system to cool the air below the dew point. **1958** *Engineering* 28 Feb. 274/2 Nevertheless, filtered and de-humidified air is supplied which is also heated or cooled as required. *Ibid.* 14 Mar. 352/2 Dehumidification..was very often omitted and 'conditioning' came to mean 'cooling'. **1969** *J.C. Penney Co. Catal.* Fall & Winter 870 (Advt.), 14-pint dehumidifier. Designed for the smaller home—prevents sweating pipes.

†**deˈhusk**, *v. Obs. rare.* [f. DE- II. 2 + HUSK.] *trans.* To deprive of the husk.

1566 Drant *Horace* A iij, An hundreth thousande mets of corne dehuskde. **1567** —— *Epist.* vi. D j, That thy neighbour should haue more Wheate..dehuskd vpon the flore.

dehydracetic (diːhaɪdrəˈsiːtɪk), *a. Chem.* Also **deˌhydroaˈcetic.** [tr. G. *dehydracetsäure* dehydracetic acid (A. Geuther 1866, in *Jenaische Zeitschr. f. Med. u. Naturwissen.* II. 410), f. DEHYDR(O- + ACETIC *a.*] ***dehydracetic acid***: a colourless, crystalline, cyclic compound, $C_8H_8O_4$, usu. obtained by heating ethyl acetoacetate.

1872 Watts *Dict. Chem.* Suppl. 543 *Dehydracetic acid*... An acid said to be produced by the action of hydrochloric or carbonic acid on the sodium salt of ethyl-diacetic acid. **1911** *Jrnl. Amer. Chem. Soc.* XXXIII. 1119 The construction of a satisfactory structural formula for dehydroacetic acid has occupied the attention of chemists ever since its discovery. **1937** *Thorpe's Dict. Appl. Chem.* (ed. 4) I. 63/2 Ethyl acetoacetate loses alcohol on refluxing and forms dehydracetic acid. **1969** R. J. W. Byrde in D.C. Torgeson *Fungicides* II. xii. 549 Dehydroacetic acid has proved of value as a postharvest treatment for fruit.

dehydrase (diːˈhaɪdreɪz, -s). *Biochem.* [a. G. *dehydrase* (H. Wieland 1913, in *Ber. d. Deutsch. Chem. Ges.* XLVI. 3333), f. DE- II. 3 + HYDR- + -ASE.] **a.** = DEHYDROGENASE.

1914 *Chem. Abstr.* VIII. 3051 It is shown by means of a typical dehydrase, Schardinger's milk enzyme, that oxidase, reductase and mutase are 1 and the same enzyme. **1939** *Thorpe's Dict. Appl. Chem.* (ed. 4) III. 553/2 Citric acid dehydrase is present in the liver and in vegetable material acting on citric acid. **1959** N. Campbell in E. H. Rodd *Chem. Carbon Compounds* IVB. viii. 942 Freudenberg also postulates a second process whereby catechins in the presence of dehydrases undergo condensation by dehydrogenation. **1961** [see DEHYDRATASE].

b. = DEHYDRATASE.

1953 *Adv. Enzymol.* XIV. 243 The usual English term 'dehydrase' for an enzyme dehydrating a substrate was changed to dehydratase, because *Dehydrase* in German.. means a dehydrogenating enzyme rather than an enzyme splitting off water. **1957** *Jrnl. Gen. Microbiol.* XVI. 480 The enzymic dehydration of tartaric acid to oxaloacetic acid, first established..for the *d*-isomer, occurs also with the *meso*- and *l*-isomers, and the attack on all three tartaric acids by bacteria of the genus *Pseudomonas* appears to occur principally by means of stereospecific dehydrases. **1961** [see DEHYDRATASE].

dehydratase (diːˈhaɪdreɪteɪz, -s). *Biochem.* [f. DEHYDRAT(E *v.* + -ASE.] Any enzyme that catalyses the removal of a molecule of water from a substrate.

1953 [see DEHYDRASE b]. **1961** *Rep. Comm. Enzymes Internat. Union Biochem.* vi. 34 The name 'dehydrase', which has been used for both dehydrogenating and dehydrating enzymes, will not be used. 'Dehydrogenase' will be used for the former and 'dehydratase' for the latter. **1966** *Proc. Nat. Acad. Sci.* LV. 869 Deamination of homoserine to *a*-ketobutyrate by homoserine dehydratase is the primary reaction in the catabolism of homoserine.

dehydrate (diːˈhaɪdreɪt), *v. Chem.* [f. DE- II. 2 + Gr. ὕδωρ, in comb. ὑδρ- water + -ATE³.]

1. a. *trans.* To deprive of water, or of the elements which compose water in a chemical combination.

1876 Foster *Phys.* II. v. (1879) 388 The sugar becoming ..dehydrated into starch. **1880** Clemenshaw *Wurtz's Atom. Th.* 279 When phosphoric acid is dehydrated. **1886** *Jrnl. Microsc. Soc.* Ser. II. VI. 350 These are then dehydrated in 90–96 per cent. alcohol.

b. *spec.* To remove the water from (foods), so as to preserve them and reduce their bulk.

1921 C. V. Ekroth in A. Rogers *Industr. Chem.* (ed. 3) li. 1158 One of the most important features of the food conservation movement since the outbreak of the war has been the practice of dehydrating fruits and vegetables. **1943** *Daily Tel.* 23 Oct. 4 As early as 1938 British food scientists began to study methods of dehydrating vegetables, meat and eggs and of storing them in that form.

c. *fig.* To render 'dry', lifeless, uninteresting, etc.

1957 *London Mag.* Nov. 73 They dehydrate Joyce, destroying both the devil and the child in him.

2. *intr.* To lose water as a constituent.

1886 *Jrnl. Microsc. Soc.* Ser. II. VI. 350 The celloidin layers are slow in dehydrating.

Hence **deˈhydrated** *ppl. a.*; **deˈhydrater**, an agent that dehydrates; **deˈhydrating** *ppl. a.* and *vbl. sb.*; **dehyˈdration**, the removal of water, or of its constituents, in a chemical combination.

1854 J. Scoffern in *Orr's Circ. Sc.* Chem. 453 The result of difference between hydration and dehydration. **1876** Harley *Mat. Med.* 159 The same complete dehydration is effected more slowly by mere exposure to the air. **1884** Muir & Wilson *Thermal Chem.* iv. §175. 149 Those dehydrated salts which dissolve in water with evolution of heat. **1884** *Pharm. Soc. Prospectus* 6 Action of..dehydrating agents upon them. **1921** C. V. Ekroth in A. Rogers *Industr. Chem.* (ed. 3) li. 1156 Dehydrated or dried food has had practically all of its moisture removed. *Ibid.* 1170 The dehydration of cow's milk, partial or complete, produces, in the former case, the condensed and evaporated milk so familiar to us. **1943** *Harper's* July 166 *Life* shares with its elder brother, *Time*,..a language which..revels in coining nifty, dehydrated words. **1944** *Evening Standard* 5 Dec. 6/4 It seems strange that words like flak..should escape censure by the austere..while such bitter eloquence is directed against dehydrated, deprescribed, hospitalisation [etc.].

1954 KOESTLER *Invis. Writing* ii. 26 Language, and with it thought, underwent a process of dehydration. **1955** *N.Y. Times* 6 Mar. I. 49/4 The Army is putting greater emphasis on dehydrated foods to meet the needs of swiftly moving, widely dispersed fighting units. **1958** *Times* 6 Feb. 11/2 A series of rather dehydrated arguments between a number of intellectual types.

dehydro- (diːˈhaɪdrəʊ), before a vowel also **dehydr-**. *Chem.* A prefix used in forming the names of some organic compounds, denoting (*a*) the loss of one atom of hydrogen (or freq. two), (*b*) the loss of a molecule of water (= ANHYDRO-); as **dehydrotriacetonamine**; **de,hydroaˈscorbic acid**, an oxidation product, $C_6H_6O_6$, of ascorbic acid; **de,hydrochoˈlesterol** [ad. G. *dehydro-cholesteryl* (A. Windaus et al. 1935, in *Ann. Chem.* DXX. 106)], the provitamin, $C_{27}H_{44}O$, of vitamin D_3, naturally formed in human and animal skin under the influence of sunlight.

1877 H. WATTS *Fownes' Man. Chem.* (ed. 12) II. 264 Triacetonamine, $C_9H_{17}NO$... Dehydrotriacetonamine, $C_9H_{15}N$. **1933** *Nature* 3 June 800/2 We found that by the action of a copper acetate solution upon ascorbic acid, a dehydroascorbic acid is formed. **1935** *Chem. Abstr.* XXIX. 7995 (*title*) 7-Dehydrocholesterol. *Ibid.*, 7-Hydrocholesterol..with BzCl in C_5H_5N gives a dibenzoate... Heating..gives 58% of the benzoate..of 7-dehydrocholesterol. **1946** *Nature* 3 Aug. 169/1 The preparation from cholesterol (I) of 7-dehydrocholesterol (III), which on irradiation gave a highly antirachitic product (vitamin D_3). **1959** *New Biol.* XXIX. 35 Dehydroascorbic acid, the oxidized form of vitamin C, is reported as having been obtained..from seawater. **1962** H. HEATH in A. Pirie *Lens Metabolism Rel. Cataract* 365 Present evidence would seem to indicate that it [*sc.* ascorbic acid] is actively secreted [by the ciliary body] in the nonionized, oxidized form, dehydroascorbic acid. **1965** *Nomencl. Org. Chem.* (I.U.P.A.C.) C. 42 Loss of two hydrogen atoms from a compound designated by a trivial name is denoted by a prefix 'didehydro-'... In common usage 'dehydro-' is often used in place of 'didehydro-'. For example the above compound [*sc.* 7, 8-didehydrocholesterol] is often termed dehydrocholesterol. **1968** R. S. CAHN *Introd. Chem. Nomencl.* (ed. 3) iii. 44 Removal of atoms is indicated in a few cases, e.g., dehydro (loss of 2H), anhydro (loss of H_2O).

dehyˈdrogenase. *Biochem.* [f. DE- + HYDROGEN + -ASE.] Any enzyme that transfers hydrogen from a substrate to an acceptor or performs an equivalent oxidation.

1923 *Chem. Abstr.* XVII. 1274 By the agency of dehydrogenases occurring in muscle, H. is abstracted. **1931** *Times Lit. Suppl.* 2 July 530/3 The temperature coefficients and energy exchanges of the citric acid dehydrogenase of cucumber seeds. **1946** *Nature* 17 Aug. 238/2 Different hydrogenase systems..have been studied by the methylene blue technique. **1958** FRUTON & SIMMONDS *Gen. Biochem.* (ed. 2) xii. 319 An important property of alcohol dehydrogenase (from yeast and from liver), and of other dehydrogenases, is that they catalyze not only electron transfer but also direct hydrogen transfer. **1961** [see DEHYDRATASE].

dehydrogenate (diːˈhaɪdrədʒəneɪt, -haɪˈdrɒ-), *v. Chem.* [DE- II. 1.] = DEHYDROGENIZE *v.* Hence **-ating** *ppl. a.*

1850 DAUBENY *Atom. Th.* viii. (ed. 2) 482 *note*, Through the dehydrogenating influence of chlorine or oxygen.

dehydrogenated (diːhaɪˈdrɒdʒəneɪtɪd), *ppl. a. Chem.* [f. DEHYDROGENATE *v.* + -ED¹.] Of a compound: deprived of some or all of its hydrogen.

1909 *Chambers's Jrnl.* Oct. 686/2 A direct conversion of the gas into alcohols and dehydrogenated alcohols.

dehydrogenation (diːhaɪ,drɒdʒɪˈneɪʃən). *Chem.* [f. DEHYDROGENATE *v.*: see -ATION.] The removal or loss of one or more atoms of hydrogen from a compound; = DEHYDROGENIZATION.

1866 ODLING *Anim. Chem.* 129 The oxidation or dehydrogenation of uric acid. **1950** *Sci. News* XV. 69 Such dehydrogenation reactions frequently occur at catalytic surfaces. **1956** *Nature* 17 Mar. 512/2 The structure of methyl linoleate dimer investigated by a dehydrogenation-oxidation procedure. **1964** N. G. CLARK *Mod. Org. Chem.* vi. 92 At high temperatures and in the presence of suitable catalysts, paraffins lose two atoms of hydrogen from adjacent carbons, with the production of a double bond and a molecule of gaseous hydrogen; such a process is known as 'dehydrogenation'.

dehydrogenize (diːˈhaɪdrədʒənaɪz, -haɪˈdrɒ-), *v. Chem.* [f. DE- II. 1 + HYDROGEN + -IZE.] *trans.* To deprive of its hydrogen; to remove hydrogen from (a compound). Hence **deˈhydrogenized** *ppl. a.*; **-izing** *vbl. sb.* and *ppl. a.*; also **deˈhydrogeniˈzation**; **deˈhydroge,nizer**, a dehydrogenizing agent.

1878 URE *Dict. Arts* IV. 77 The oxidations and the dehydrogenisations play the most important part in the production of colour. *Ibid.* IV. 932 The action of dehydrogenisers upon naphthylamine.

dehypnotize (diːˈhɪpnətaɪz), *v.* [DE- II. 1.] To awaken out of the hypnotic state.

dei, obs. form of DAY, DIE *v.*

deiamba (diːˈæmbə). Also **diamba**. [Native name.] Congo tobacco; = HEMP *sb.* 4.

1851 R. O. CLARKE in *Hooker's Jrnl. of Botany* III. 9 (*title*) Short notice of the African Plant Diamba, commonly called Congo Tobacco. **1861** R. BENTLEY *Man. Bot.* 637 Indian hemp is also used for smoking. The plant is also known under the name of *Diamba* in Western Africa. **1864** WATTS *Dict. Chem.* II. 309 Deiamba.

†**ˈdeical**, *a. Obs. rare.* [ad. med.L. *deic-us* (f. L. *de-us* God) + -AL¹.] Pertaining to God, divine.

1662 J. SPARROW tr. *Behme's Rem. Wks.*, *Apol. Perfection* 52 The Triune Totally perfect Divine or Deicall substance.

de-ice (diːˈaɪs), *v.* [f. DE- II. 2 + ICE *sb.*] *trans.* To remove or prevent the formation of ice on (parts of an aeroplane, machine, ship, etc.); to clear of ice. More usually as **de-icing** *ppl. a.* and *vbl. sb.*, removing or preventing ice-formation.

1935 *Jrnl. R. Aeronaut. Soc.* XXXIX. 794 An automatic de-icing device. **1937** *Ibid.* XLI. 731 The high pressure is mainly used for engine starting..and low pressure for de-icing. **1942** *Hutchinson's Pict. Hist. War* 18 Mar.–9 June 11 'De-icing' a Corvette... All hands set to work to strip away the icy covering. **1958** *Engineering* 28 Mar. 404/2 De-icing and de-misting of aircraft control cabin windows. **1961** W. VAUGHAN-THOMAS *Anzio* iv. 53 Parties were standing by to de-ice the mountain passes.

de-icer (diːˈaɪsə(r)). [f. prec. + -ER¹.] A mechanical or other device to remove or prevent ice-formation, esp. on aircraft and on motor-car windscreens.

1932 *Product Engineering* Sept. 357/2 The installation is similar to that of the 'de-icer' without inflation tubes or compressed air equipment. **1934** *Shell Aviation News* No. 37. 20/2 Instal rubber de-icers on the propeller and pneumatic de-icers on the wings. **1941** [see ANTICER]. **1958** *Times Rev. Industry* Aug. 30/1 Electroforms of..nickel are ..fitted on..aircraft propeller blades to guard the delicate de-icer elements against rupture.

deicidal (ˈdiːɪsaɪdəl), *a.* [f. DEICIDE + -AL¹.] Of or pertaining to deicide; god-slaying.

1839 BAILEY *Festus* xix. (1848) 210 And thus the deicidal tribes made quit. **1880** SWINBURNE in *Fortn. Rev.* June 762 A deicidal and theophagous Christianity.

deicide¹ (ˈdiːɪsaɪd). [ad. mod. or med.L. *deicīda* slayer of a god, f. *de-us* god + *-cīda*: see -CIDE 1. Cf. F. *déicide* (1681).] The killer of a god.

1653 GAUDEN *Hierasp.* 139 Uncharitable destroyers of Christians, are rather Deicides, than Homicides. **1657** PIERCE *Div. Philanthr.* 72 Our Saviour..did very heartily pray, even for those very homicides, and parricides, and Deicides that kill'd him. **1731** *Hist. Litteraria* II. 109 The Deicide was immediately conveyed for Refuge to the French Factory, and the dead God privately buried. **1882** *Century Mag.* XXIV. 179 In the Middle Ages, 'the Jews were believed to be an accursed race of deicides.

deicide² (ˈdiːɪsaɪd). [ad. mod. or med.L. type **deicīdium*: see prec. and -CIDE 2.] The killing of a god.

1611 SPEED *Hist. Gt. Brit.* IX. ix. §59 In..killing a Prince, the Traytor is guiltie of Homicide, of Parricide, of Christicide, nay of Deicide. **1688** PRIOR *Exod.* iii. 14 viii, And Earth prophan'd yet bless'd with Deicide. **1818** W. TAYLOR in *Monthly Rev.* LXXXVI. 4 To slaughter a cow for food being in their eyes, an act of deicide. **1860** PUSEY *Min. Proph.* 317 Their first destruction was the punishment of their Deicide, the crucifixion of Jesus, the Christ.

deictic (ˈdaɪktɪk), *a.* and *sb.* Also **deiktic**. [ad. Gr. δεικτικ-ός able to show, showing directly, f. δεικτός vbl. adj. of δείκ-νυ-ναι to show.

The Greek word occurs in Latin medical and rhetorical writers as *dicticos*, which would give *dictic*; but the term is purely academic, and the form *deictic* or *deiktic* is preferred as more distinctly preserving both in spelling and pronunciation the Greek form. Cf. *apodictic*, *-deictic*.]

Directly pointing out, demonstrative; in *Logic*, applied, after Aristotle, to reasoning which proves directly, as opposed to the *elenctic*, which proves indirectly. Also in *Grammar* and as sb.

1828 WHATELY *Rhet.* I. ii. §1 Thirdly into 'Direct' and 'Indirect' (or *reductio ad absurdum*)—the Deictic and Elenctic of Aristotle. **1876** DOUSE *Grimm's L.* §31. 66 In meaning, the word originally covered all deictic action irrespective of direction. **1922** O. JESPERSEN *Language* xix. 383 The relation between a demonstrative pronoun or a deictic particle and genitival function. **1964** [see ANAPHORA 1 b]. **1970** *Archivum Linguisticum* I. 6 The only exceptions to this restriction are the gen. dat. sg. fem. and the gen. pl. of the deictic *theser*.

†**ˈdeictical**, *a. Obs.* Also dict-. [f. Gr. δεικτικ-ός (see prec.) + -AL¹.] = prec.

1638 FEATLY *Strict. Lyndom.* I. 89 Those Arguments which the Logicians tearme Dicticall.

Hence †**ˈdeictically** *adv.*, with direct indication or pointing out.

1659 HAMMOND *On Ps.* lxviii. 8 Annot. 333 It may also be set by it selfe, this is Sinai, to denote deictically, when that shaking of the earth..was heard. *a* **1660** —— *Wks.* I. 703 (R.) And he that dippeth, at that time when Christ spake it deictically, i.e. Judas, is that person.

deid, Sc. and north. f. DEAD, DEATH *sb.*, DEED.

†**deid-doar.** *Sc. Obs.* [= *death-doer*, or *dead-doer*.] Slayer, murderer.

1535 STEWART *Cron. Scot.* II. 502 Thir deid-doaris..War tane ilkone and hangit.

de-idealize, etc.: see DE- II. 1.

deie, deiect, obs. ff. DIE *v.*, DEJECT.

deierie, obs. form of DAIRY.

deif(f, obs. Sc. form of DEAF.

deific (diːˈɪfɪk), *a.* [a. F. *déifique* (1372 in Hatzf.), ad. L. *deific-us* god-making, consecrated, sacred, in med.L. 'divine', f. *de-us* god + *-ficus* making: see -FIC.] Deifying, making divine; also (less properly), divine, godlike.

1490 CAXTON *Eneydos* xvi. 64 The grete vysion deyfyque that he had seen. **1627–77** FELTHAM *Resolves* II. xxxii. 225 Our Saviour..putting all the world in the scale, doth find it far too light for mans Deific soul. **1653** URQUHART *Rabelais* II. i, That nectarian, delicious..and deific liquor. **1706** MOTTEUX *Rabelais* IV. liii. (1737) 219 O Deific Books! **1816** T. TAYLOR *Ess.* VIII. 54 According to a deific energy. **1858** FABER *Foot of Cross* (1872) 145 What the hard style of mystical theology calls deific transformation. **1878** J. COOK *Lect. Orthodoxy* ii. 42 Our Lord displayed a degree of being that was deific.

†**deifical** (diːˈɪfɪkəl), *a. Obs.* [f. L. *deific-us* (see prec.) + -AL¹.] = prec.

1563 *Homilies* II. *Sacrament* I. (1859) 443 The ancient catholic fathers..were not afraid to call this Supper, some of them, 'the salve of immortality'..other, 'a deifical communion'. **1582** *N.T.* (Rhem.) Acts viii. *Annot.*, That he might signe them..with the diuine and deifical ointment. **1627–77** FELTHAM *Resolves* II. xxvii. 215 Those abilities.. beget a kind of Deifical Reverence in their future Readers.

†**deˈificate**, *ppl. a. Obs.* [ad. L. *deificāt-us*, pa. pple. of late L. *deificāre* to DEIFY.] Deified.

1513 DOUGLAS *Æneis* X. v. 48 In this figour has ws all translait, For euirmair to be deificat. **1560** ROLLAND *Crt. Venus* IV. 53 Scho is deificait. **1628** GAULE *Pract. Th.* (1629) 52 Of Man deificate, of God incarnate.

†**deˈificate**, *v. Obs.* [f. ppl. stem of L. *deificāre* to DEIFY.] To deify, to make divine.

1536 BELLENDEN *Cron. Scot.* (1821) I. 119 Claudius.. quhilk was laitly deceissit, and deificat be the Romanis. **1565** JEWEL *Repl. Harding* (1611) 341 It is the Body it selfe of our Lord Deificated.

deification (diːɪfɪˈkeɪʃən). [n. of action from L. *deificāre* to DEIFY: so in F. (1556 in Hatzf.).] The action of deifying; the condition of being deified or made a deity; a deified embodiment.

1393 GOWER *Conf.* II. 158 Lo now, through what creacion He [Apollo] hath deificacion, And cleped is the god of wit. **1606** HOLLAND *Sueton.* 82 His deification after death. **1700** DRYDEN *Fables Pythag. Philos.* Argt. 1 The death and deification of Romulus. **1878** BOSW. SMITH *Carthage* 29 The Phoenician religion has been defined to be a deification of the powers of Nature.

b. The treating or regarding of anything as a god or as divine.

1651 *Nicholas Papers* (Camden) 227 The other part of that book..is the deification of K. Charles. **1709** STEELE *Tatler* No. 33 ⁋7 He had the Audaciousness to throw himself at my Feet..and then ran into Deifications of my Person. **1848** MRS. JAMESON *Sacr. & Leg. Art* (1850) 11 The deification of suffering. **1875** MANNING *Mission H. Ghost* iii. 88 The deification of the human reason as the sole rule of life.

c. The rendering of any one a partaker of the divine nature; absorption in the divine nature.

1856 R. A. VAUGHAN *Mystics* (1860) I. IV. ii. 93 All things have emanated from God, and the end of all is return to God. Such return—deification, he calls it—is the consummation of the creature. **1857** KEBLE *Euchar. Ador.* 19 An union of condescension and power for the deification (so termed by the fathers) of each one of us.

deificatory (diːɪfɪˈkeɪtərɪ), *a.* [f. *deificāt-*, ppl. stem of L. *deificāre* to DEIFY + -ORY.] Of or pertaining to deification; having the function of deifying.

1624 BOLTON *Nero* 249 Expressed by a deificatorie herse, or throne. **1629** J. MAXWELL tr. *Herodian* (1635) 227 *margin*, The Funerall Pile, or Deificatory Throne. **1902** A. M. FAIRBAIRN *Philos. Chr. Relig.* II. II. ii. 474 He is not conceived as the subject of a deificatory process.

deified (ˈdiːɪfaɪd), *ppl. a.* [f. DEIFY *v.* + -ED.] Made into a deity, raised to the rank of a god; considered or treated as divine.

1603 FLORIO *Montaigne* (1634) 296 That Eagle is represented carrying..up towards heaven, those Deified soules. **1686** HORNECK *Crucif. Jesus* ix. 157 Deified vices had their votaries. **1776** GIBBON *Decl. & F.* I. 373 The statues of the deified kings. **1862** STANLEY *Jew. Ch.* (1877) I. iv. 76 Thrice a day before the deified beast the incense was offered.

deifier (ˈdiːɪfaɪə(r)). [f. DEIFY *v.* + -ER.] One who or that which deifies.

1736 H. COVENTRY *Phil. to Hyd.* Conv. iii. (R.), The first deifiers of men. **1874** PUSEY *Lent. Serm.* 325 His Human Nature, the Deifier of our nature.

deiform (ˈdiːɪfɔːm), *a.* [ad. med.L. *deiform-is* (Du Cange), f. *de-us* god: see -FORM.]

1. Having the form of a god; godlike in form.

1642 H. MORE *Song of Soul* II. I. II. xlvii, Onely souls Deiform intellective, Unto that height of happinesse can get. *a* **1667** JER. TAYLOR *Serm. for Year* Suppl. (1678) 245 We can no otherwayes see God..but by becoming Deiform. **1825** *New Monthly Mag.* XIV. 280 Attempting to arrive at the deiform nature. **1856** FABER *Creator & Creature* III. iv. (1886) 383 By these [gifts of glory] we..become..deiform, shining like the Divinity.

2. Conformable to the character or nature of God; godlike, divine, holy.

1654 GATAKER *Disc. Apol.* 68 Admirable and most ravishing Devotions, Deiform Intentions, Heroical acts of Vertu. *a* **1715** BURNET *Own Time* (1766) I. 261 To consider religion as a seed of a deiform nature. **1794** T. TAYLOR *Pausanias* III. 330 Hence these souls..exhibit a deiform power. **1874** PUSEY *Lenten Serm.* 20 Free-will..enfreed and Deiform through grace, or enslaved and imbruted by sin.

† **'deiformed**, *ppl. a. Obs.* [f. as prec. + -ED.] Formed in the image of God.

1652 BENLOWES *Theoph.* II. Argt. 23 The deiform'd Soul deform'd by Sin, repents.

deiformity (diːɪˈfɔːmɪtɪ). [f. DEIFORM + -ITY.] The quality of being deiform; likeness to God; conformity to the divine nature or character.

1642 H. MORE *Song of Soul* IV. xxvii, The souls numerous plurality I've prov'd, and shew'd she is not very God; But yet a decent Deiformity Have given her. *a* **1726** W. REEVES *Serm.* (1729) 370 This immediate influx of the Deity, which the Schoolmen call the Deiformity of the Soul. **1835** SIR A. DE VERE in Graves *Life Sir W. R. Hamilton* II. 163 Deiformity is the Ideal of regenerate Humanity.

deify (ˈdiːɪfaɪ), *v.* [a. F. *déifier* (13th c. in Hatzf.), ad. L. *deificāre* (Augustine and Cassiodorus), f. *de-us* god + *-ficāre*: see -FY.] *trans.* To make a god of; to exalt to the position of a deity; to enroll among the gods of the nation or tribe.

1393 GOWER *Conf.* II. 165 Juno, Neptunus, Pluto, The which of nice fantasy The people wolde deify. **1430** LYDG. *Chron. Troy* I. iii, [They] were both ystellyfyed In the heauen and there defyed. **1530** PALSGR. 510/1, I deifye, I make an erthly man a God, as the gentylles dyd. **1634** HABINGTON *Castara* (Arb.) 123 The Superstition of those Times Which deified Kings to warrant their owne crimes. **1728** NEWTON *Chronol. Amended* i. 134 The first instances that I meet with in Greece of Deifying the dead. **1868** GLADSTONE *Juv. Mundi* v. (1870) 123 Leukotheê, once a mortal, now deified in the Sea-region.

b. To render godlike or divine in nature, character, or spirit.

a **1340** HAMPOLE *Psalter* lxxxi. 1 þe gaderynge of halymen deifide thorgh grace. **1613** R. C. *Table Alph.* (ed. 3), *Deifie*, make like God. **1634** SIR T. HERBERT *Trav.* 77 No vertue more deified a Prince then Clemencie. **1838** [see DEIFYING]. **1874** [see DEIFIER].

c. To treat as a god, in word or action; to regard or adore as a deity.

1590 SPENSER *Teares of Muses* 368 Now change the tenor of your joyous layes, With which ye use your loves to deifie. **1600** SHAKS. *A.Y.L.* III. ii. 381 Oades..and Elegies..all (forsooth) deifying the name of Rosalinde. **1622** BACON *Hen. VII* 38 He did againe so extoll and deifie the Pope. **1649** BP. REYNOLDS *Hosea* iv. 49 Men of power are apt to deifie their own strength..men of wisdome, to deifie their owne reason. **1759** JOHNSON *Rasselas* xxvi, The old man deifies prudence. **1859** SMILES *Self-Help* iii. (1860) 46 It is possible to over-estimate success to the extent of almost deifying it.

Hence **'deifying** *vbl. sb.* and *ppl. a.*

1553 BRENDE *Q. Curtius* 223 (R.) The deifying of Hercules. **1637** NABBES *Hanniball & Sc.* Hij (R.), A man that..merited A deifying by your gratitude. **1649** MILTON *Eikon.* 12 Bequeath'd among his deifying friends that stood about him. **1701** COLLIER *M. Aurel.* Life 21 The Deifying of his Father. **1838** EMERSON *Addr. Cambr. Mass.* Wks. (Bohn) II. 192 This sentiment [religious] is divine and deifying.

deign (deɪn), *v.* Forms: 3–7 **deine**, 4–5 **deyne**, **dayne**, 5–7 **daigne**, 6 **digne**, 6–7 **dain(e**, **deigne**, 7–8 **daign**, 6– **deign**. [a. OF. *degn-ier* (3 sing. *deigne*), later *deignier*, *deigner*, from 14th c. *daigner*, = Pr. *denhar*, *deinar*, It. *degnare*:—L. *dignāre*, by-form of *dignārī* to deem worthy, think fit, f. *dignus* worthy.]

1. *intr.* To think it worthy of oneself (*to do* something); to think fit, vouchsafe, condescend.

c **1314** *Guy Warw.* (A.) 3464 Helman That deined fle for no man. **1340** *Ayenb.* 196 Uolk..þet onworþeþ þe poure, and ne dayneþ naȝt to speke to ham. *c* **1450** *Mirour Saluacioun* 3518 Oure lorde goddе..to become man deynyd. *c* **1477** CAXTON *Jason* 114 He daigneth not to come. *c* **1590** GREENE *Fr. Bacon* vi, Would he daine to wed a Countrie Lasse? **1593** SHAKS. *3 Hen. VI*, IV. vii. 39 And all those friends, that deine to follow mee. **1667** MILTON *P.L.* v. 221 Raphael, the sociable Spirit, that deign'd To travel with Tobias. **1701** ROWE *Amb. Step-Moth.* I. i. 349 Hardly daigning To be controll'd by his Imperious Mother. **1879** M. ARNOLD *Geo. Sand* Mixed Ess. 328 [The] very dog will hardly deign to bark at you.

†**b.** *impers. Obs.*

1297 R. GLOUC. (1724) 557 Him ne deinede noȝt to ligge in þe castel by niȝte. **1340** *Ayenb.* 76 Ham ne daynede naȝt to do zenne. *c* **1374** CHAUCER *Anel. & Arc.* 181 That on her wo ne deyneth him not to thinke. *a* **1400–50** *Alexander* 830 Ne here to dwell with þi douce deynes me na langer.

†**c.** *refl. Obs.*

1500–20 DUNBAR *Poems* lxxxvi. 36 Quhilk deinȝeit him for our trespass to de. **1563** WINȜET *Wks.* (1890) II. 42 He deinȝeit Him aluterlie to do this in deid.

2. *trans.* with *simple obj.* **a.** To condescend to bestow or grant, to vouchsafe. (Now chiefly with *reply*, *answer*, in negative sentences.)

1589 GREENE *Menaphon* (Abr.) 36 Rather..than haue deigned her eyes on the face..of so lowe a peasant. **1605** SHAKS. *Macb.* I. ii. 60 Nor would we deigne him buriall of his men. **1622** F. MARKHAM *Bk. Warre* IV. ix. §6, I will not here daigne a recapitulation of the same. **1634** W. WOOD *New Eng. Prosp.*, *Ded. Note*, I am confident you will daigne it your protection. **1825** SOUTHEY *Tale of Paraguay* III. xviii, A willing ear she well might deign. **1863** MRS. C. CLARKE *Shaks. Char.* iii. 71 The spirit stalks away, deigning no reply.

†**b.** To condescend or vouchsafe to accept; to take or accept graciously. (The opposite of *to disdain.*) *Obs.*

1576 FLEMING *Panopl. Epist.* 50 Those..who did not receive and intertaine my father..nor yet digned other Gentlemen of much worthinesse. **1579** SPENSER *Sheph. Cal.* Jan. 63 Shee deignes not my good will, but doth reproue. **1606** SHAKS. *Ant. & Cl.* I. iv. 63 Thy pallat then did daine The roughest Berry, on the rudest Hedge. **1637–50** ROW *Hist. Kirk* (1842) 255 The Lord dained him. **1661** in Hickeringill *Jamaica* A iij, This Welcome-home..Thou wilt accept from me, And deign it to attend thy smoother Line.

†**c.** In same sense with *of*. (Cf. *to accept of.*) *Obs. rare.*

1589 GREENE *Menaphon* (Arb.) 51 Which if you shall vouch to deigne of, I shall be..glad of such accepted seruice.

†**3.** To treat (a person) as worthy *of*, to dignify (him) *with*. [= L. *dignārī*.] *Obs.*

1579 TWYNE *Phisicke agst. Fort.* II. cxxxii. 341 a, [They] had lyen vnburied, had not their most deadly enimie dained them of a graue. **1591** in De Foe *Hist. Ch. Scot.* Add. D (1844) 57/2 Will ye not daigne his Majesty with an Answer? **1648** E. BOUGHEN *Geree's Case of Consc.* 76 He daines them with this honour.

¶**4.** Short for *dedain*, DISDAIN: see DAIN *v.*

deignfull, var. of DAINFUL, disdainful.

†**'deignous**, *a. Obs.* Forms: 4 **deignouse**, 4–5 **deynous**, 5 **deinous**, 5–6 **daynous**, 6 **daynnous**, 5–7 **deignous**. [app. a shortened form of *dedeignous*, DISDAINOUS, F. *dédaigneux*, OF. *desdeignous* (12th c. in Hatzf.): cf. DAIN *v.*

(Earlier examples of *dedeignous*, *dedainous*, than of *deignous* are not yet known; but the history of DISDAIN shows that they may well have existed.)]

Disdainful, proud, haughty.

c **1330** R. BRUNNE *Chron.* (1810) 289 Deignouse pride & ille avisement. *c* **1374** CHAUCER *Troylus* I. 290 Her chere, Which sumdel deynous was. *c* **1430** LYDG. *Bochas* v. xxiv. (1554) 138 a, Nothing..more deynous, nor more vntreatable Than whan a begger hath dominacion. *c* **1440** *Ipomydon* 1122 A proude knyght and a daynous. *a* **1643** W. CARTWRIGHT *Ordinary* III. i, One Harlotha, Concubine To deignous Wilhelme, hight the Conqueror.

Hence †**'deignoushede** (deyn-), disdainfulness, haughtiness; †**'deignously** (deyn-, dayn-) *adv.*, disdainfully.

c **1330** R. BRUNNE *Chron.* (1810) 129 For deynoushede & pride. *c* **1440** *Partonope* 3434 Many one That loked vpon hym full deynously. *a* **1529** SKELTON *Bouge of Court* Prol. 82 And gan on me to stare Ful daynously.

‖**Dei gratia.** [L.] By the grace of God: see GRACE.

deih, obs. sing. pres. of DOW *v.*

deiktic, var. of DEICTIC.

deil (dil). [Scotch vernacular form of the word DEVIL, corresponding to the ME. monosyllabic types *del*, *dele*, *dewle*, *dule*, etc.]

1. The Devil: *esp.* according to the popular conception of his appearance and attributes.

(For the Biblical Satan, the usual form is *deevil*.)

1500–20 DUNBAR *Turnament* 54 Off all his dennar..His breist held deill a bitt. **1570** *Sempill Ballates* (1872) 117 The mekle Deill. **1725** RAMSAY *Gent. Sheph.* III. ii, Awa! awa! the deil's [*v.r.* deel's] ower grit wi' you. **1785** BURNS *Address to the Deil* ii, I'm sure sma' pleasure it can gie, Ev'n to a deil. **1790** —— *Tam o' Shanter* 78 That night a child might understand, The Deil had business on his hand. **1816** SCOTT *Old Mort.* xxxiii, Being atween the deil and the deep sea.

2. A mischievously wicked or troublesome fellow; one who embodies the spirit of wickedness or mischief.

1786 BURNS *Twa Dogs* 222 They're a' run deils or jads thegither. **1802** SCOTT *Bonnie Dundee* ii, The Guid Toun is well quit of that deil of Dundee. *Mod. Sc.* He's an awfu' laddie, a perfit deil.

3. For *deil a bit*, and other phrases, see DEVIL.

deill, deim, obs. forms of DEAL, DEEM.

dein, obs. form of DEIGN.

dein, deen, Sc. dial. forms of DONE.

†**de-in'cline**, *v. Obs.* [f. DE- I. 2 + INCLINE *v.*] (See quot.) Hence **dein'clined**, **dein'clining**, *ppl. adjs.*; **dein'cliner**.

1727–51 CHAMBERS *Cycl.* s.v. *Dial*, *Secondary Dials*, are all those drawn on the planes of other circles beside the horizon, prime vertical, equinoctial, and polar circles: or those, which either decline, incline, recline, or deincline ..*Deinclined Dials*, are such as both decline and incline, or recline. *Ibid.*, *Deincliners* or *Deinclining Dials*..Suppose..a plane to cut the prime vertical circle at an angle of 30 degrees, and the horizontal plane under an angle of 24 degrees..a dial, drawn on this plane, is called a *deincliner*.

de-index (diːˈɪndɛks), *v.* [f. DE- II. 1 + INDEX *v.*; cf. INDEXATION.] *trans.* To remove indexation to inflation or cost-of-living rates from (pensions or other benefits); to cease to index. Hence **de-inde'xation**.

1979 *Daily Tel.* 17 Dec. 16 Political opposition to making short term benefits liable for tax will be much smaller than to de-indexing pensions. **1980** *Times* 12 Jan. 12/2 Will it [an interview] be remembered for all that dogged detail over possible changes in union immunities and de-indexation of social benefits. **1983** *Listener* 28 July 5/1 If the Cabinet decides to de-index benefits or to cut deeply into the Health Service.., the reaction of its refurbished back benches is not predictable.

de-individualize, de-industrialize, etc.: see DE- II. 1.

deine, obs. form of DENE, sand-hill.

deing, obs. form of DYING, DYEING.

†**'dein,grate**, *v. Obs. rare.* [f. DE- I. 3 + L. *ingrātus* disagreeable: see INGRATE.] *trans.* To render unpopular, bring into disfavour.

1624 *Brief Inform. Affairs Palatinate* 34 To deingrate the Prince Palatine, and to make him more odious.

deinosaur, deinothere, etc.: see DINO-.

deinseyn, obs. form of DENIZEN.

de,insti,tutionali'zation. Chiefly *N. Amer.* [f. DE- II. 2 + INSTITUTIONALIZATION.] The process or action of removing (a person) from an institution, such as a mental hospital, or from the effects of institutional life. Also **de,insti'tutionalized** *ppl. a.* (in quot. 1967, deprived of the qualities of an institution).

[**1955** *Lancet* 31 Dec. 1393/2 The process of disinstitutionalisation is taking place in his own region.] **1967** *Listener* 20 Apr. 518/3 Russell has never been academic; he has not been confined in a university, except for very short periods; and this gives him..a de-institutionalized setting, which enables him to speak as a human being to great numbers of persons. **1974** *Science* 2 Aug. 423/2 A major current trend is toward deinstitutionalization. People who are down on jails believe that the institutional setting is too dehumanizing for any meaningful rehabilitation to take place. **1978** *Sci. Amer.* Feb. 46/3 It is not too soon to review the issues raised by this aspect of the community mental health movement and to consider how such a well-intentioned reform as deinstitutionalization could have created so many problems. **1979** *Time* 2 Apr. 45/2 Under the Community Mental Health Center Act of 1963, 647 local centers have been set up to treat such 'deinstitutionalized' patients. **1980** *Spokane* (Washington) *Daily Chron.* 30 Apr. 4 The 'human rights' faction..decided that criminals and mental patients released to roam the streets should be recognized as persons who are the beneficiaries of deinstitutionalization. **1984** *Listener* 3 May 3/3 They attended a conference on de-institutionalization.

de-insularize, -integrate, etc.: see DE- II. 1.

deinte, -ee, -ie, -y, obs. forms of DAINTY.

deintrelle, var. of DAINTREL *Obs.*, a dainty.

de,ioni'zation. [f. next + -ATION.] The process of deionizing a substance or a space, or of becoming deionized; the removal or loss of ions.

1919 E. W. STONE *Elem. Radiotelegr.* (1920) viii. 157 To enhance both the extinction and ignition voltages..it is necessary to provide adequate means for the deionization of the arc. **1959** *Engineering* 20 Feb. 247/2 Silica is not removed by many demineralisation or deionisation treatments. **1962** M. G. DENAVARRE *Chem. & Manuf. Cosmetics* (ed. 2) II. 351 Deionization has become the most widely used method of purifying water in the cosmetic industry. **1967** H. COTTON *Adv. Electr. Technol.* xv. 641 There is a short interval of time required for the deionization of the discharge path.

deionize (diːˈaɪənaɪz), *v.* [f. DE- II. 1 + ION + -IZE.] *trans.* To deprive of ions or of ionic character; *esp.* (*a*) to cause the positive and negative ions in (a gas or a space) to recombine to form neutral atoms or molecules; (*b*) to take out of (a liquid, esp. water) the ionic constituents. Hence **de'ionized** *ppl. a.*

1906 G. MANN *Chem. Proteids* vi. 216 These compounds are therefore formed by the amphoteric amino-acids, simply adding CO_2, which thereby becomes de-ionised. **1919** E. W. STONE *Elem. Radiotelegr.* (1920) viii. 151 Let us assume that ..the space between the electrodes is very quickly deionized. **1930** *Trans. Amer. Inst. Electr. Engin.* XLIX. 58/2 The layer of gas immediately adjacent to the surface becomes very quickly denuded of ions, and then ions which further reach the surface must diffuse through this layer of deionized gas. **1941** J. D. COBINE *Gaseous Conductors* iv. 102 The presence of the confining walls aids diffusion processes to deionize the entire volume of an ionized gas, for as the ions reach the walls they lose their charge. **1950** KUNIN & MYERS *Ion Exchange Resins* viii. 88 There are three methods for deionizing electrolyte solutions with ion exchange resins. **1956** *Nature* 28 Jan. 187/2 The resin was washed with deionized water. **1970** *Rep. Visitors Ashmolean Mus.* (Oxford) *1969* 20 Mrs. K. Kimber..cleaned this by applying 'packs' of Sepolite..and deionized water to the unpolished surface of the marble.

deionizer (diːˈaɪənaɪzə(r)). [f. prec. + -ER¹.] An apparatus for removing the ions from water or other liquids.

1956 *Nature* 17 Mar. 509/2 The portable deionizer..is supplied with exchangeable cartridges of the mixed resins. **1958** I. W. CORNWALL *Soils for Archaeologist* ix. 165 The best [water] is provided by percolation through a bed of the new ion-exchange resins in a de-ionizer made entirely of polythene. **1962** M. G. DENAVARRE *Chem. & Manuf. Cosmetics* (ed. 2) II. 351 The same water processed in a mixed bed deionizer shows less than 2 p.p.m. total solids.

deip(e, obs. Sc. form of DEEP.

‖**Deipara** (diːˈɪpərə). [late L. (*Cod. Just.* i. 1, 6) = mother of God, f. *de-us* God + *-parus, -a*, bearing, *parĕre* to bear; a L. repr. of Gr. θεοτόκος.] A title of the Virgin Mary, 'Mother of God'.

1664 H. MORE *Myst. Iniq., Synopsis Proph.* 521 He.. would not allow the most holy Virgin, the Mother of Christ as to the flesh..to be called Deipara or the Mother of God. **1860** SOPHOCLES *Gloss. Later Greek* 334/1 Θεοτόκιον..a modulus addressed or relating to the Deipara.

deiparous (diːˈɪpərəs), *a.* [f. as prec. + -OUS.] Bearing or bringing forth a god.

1664 H. MORE *Myst. Iniq., Synopsis Proph.* 520 Nor confess that the holy..Mary is properly and according to truth Deiparous, that is to say, the mother of God. **1827** SIR H. TAYLOR *Isaac Comnenus* III. iv, Deiparous Virgin! Holy Mary mother!

deipno- (ˈdaɪpnəʊ-), repr. Gr. δειπνο-, combining form of δεῖπνον dinner, used in nonce-words and combinations, as **deipno-diplomatic** of or pertaining to dining and diplomacy, **deipnophobia** dread of dinner-parties.

1827 *Brit. Critic* I. 475 An interchange of deipno-diplomatic correspondence. **1891** *Daily News* 23 June 4/8 People who heartily sympathise with the 'deipnophobia' of Gordon.

deipnosophist (daɪpˈnɒsəfɪst). [ad. Gr. δειπνοσοφιστ-ής 'one learned in the mysteries of the kitchen', f. δεῖπνον the chief meal, dinner + σοφιστής a master of his craft, clever or wise man, SOPHIST. The pl. δειπνοσοφισταί was the title of a celebrated work of the Greek Athenæus, written after A.D. 228.]

A master of the art of dining: taken from the title of the Greek work of Athenæus, in which a number of learned men are represented as dining together and discussing subjects which range from the dishes before them to literary criticism and miscellaneous topics of every description.

1656 BLOUNT *Glossogr., Deipnosophists*, Athenæus his great learned books carry that title. **1774** BURNEY *Hist. Mus.* I. 229 (Jod.) To render credible the following assertion of a deipnosophist in Athenæus. **1845** FORD *Handbk. Spain* I. 1. 70 Spanish Cookery, a..subject which is well worth the inquiry of any antiquarian deipnosophist. **1866** LOWELL *Swinburne's Trag.* Prose Wks. 1890 II. 135 With about as much nature in it as a dialogue of the Deipnosophists.

Hence **deipnoso'phistic** *a.*, **deip'nosophism**.

1661 LOVELL *Hist. Anim. & Min.* 23 Diverse other things ..belonging to cookery, are here omitted, as belonging to the dypnosophistick art. **1824** *Blackw. Mag.* XVI. 1 Let me ..luxuriate in the..paradisaical department of deipnosophism. **1836** *Fraser's Mag.* XIII. 336 An elegy.. appended to that deipnosophistic dissertation.

deir, obs. form of DEAR, DEER, DERE.

deirie, obs. form of DAIRY.

deis(e, deische, deiss, obs. forms of DAIS.

deisal, deisul, varr. DEASIL

deishal, -eal, deisul, var. of DEASIL.

deism (ˈdiːɪz(ə)m). [mod. f. L. *de-us* god + -ISM. Cf. F. *déisme* (in Pascal *a* 1660).] The distinctive doctrine or belief of a deist; usually, belief in the existence of a Supreme Being as the source of finite existence, with rejection of revelation and the supernatural doctrines of Christianity; 'natural religion'.

1682 DRYDEN *Religio Laici* Pref. (Globe) 186 That Deism, or the principles of natural worship, are only the faint remnants or dying flames of revealed religion in the posterity of Noah. **1692** BENTLEY *Boyle Lect.* ix. 306 Modern Deism being the very same with old Philosophical Paganism. **1759** DILWORTH *Pope* 63 There breathes in this inscription [*ens entium miserere mei*] the genuine spirit of deism. **1774** FLETCHER *Doctr. Grace* Wks. 1795 IV. 203 Deism is the error of those who..think that man..needs no Redeemer at all. **1861** BERESF. HOPE *Eng. Cathedr. 19th c.* 260 That decorous and philanthropic deism which is a growing peril of the age. **1877** E. R. CONDER *Bas. Faith* i. 25 Deism should etymologically have the same sense with *Theism*, but it is commonly taken to carry with it the denial of what is called revealed religion. Theism conveys no such implication.

†**2.** The condition of being a god or as God. *Obs.*

1726 DE FOE *Hist. Devil* viii, He [the Devil] set her [Eve's] head a madding after deism, and to be made a goddess.

deist (ˈdiːɪst). [a. F. *déiste*, f. L. *de-us* god: see -IST.] One who acknowledges the existence of a God upon the testimony of reason, but rejects revealed religion.

(The term was originally opposed to *atheist*, and was interchangeable with *theist* even in the end of the 17th c. (Locke, *Second Vindication*, 1695, W. Nichols *Conference with a Theist*, 1696); but the negative aspect of deism, as opposed to Christianity, became the accepted one, and *deist* and *theist* were differentiated as in quots. 1878–80.)

[**1563** VIRET *Instruct. Chr.* II. Ep. Ded., J'ai entendu qu'il y en a de ceste bande, qui s'appellent Deistes, d'un mot tout nouveau, lequel ils veulent oposer a Atheiste.] **1621** BURTON *Anat. Mel.* III. iv. II. i, Cosen-germans to these men are many of our great Philosophers and Deists. **1670** R. TRAILL *Serm.* vi. Sel. Writ. (1845) 107 We have a generation among us..called Deists, which is nothing else but a new court word for Atheist. **1692** BENTLEY *Boyle Lect.* 6 Some infidels ..to avoid the odious name of atheists, would shelter and screen themselves under a new one of deists, which is not quite so obnoxious. **1711–37** SHAFTESBURY *Charac.* II. 209 Averse as I am to the cause of *theism*, or name of *deist*, when taken in a sense exclusive of revelation. **1748** HARTLEY *Observ. Man* II. iii. 347 Unless he be a sincere Deist at least, i.e. unless he believe in the Existence and Attributes of God. **1788** WESLEY *Wks.* (1872) VII. 196 A Deist—I mean one who believes there is a God distinct from matter; but does not believe the Bible. **1878** D. PATRICK in *Encycl. Brit.* VII. 33 The later distinction between theist and deist, which stamped the latter word as excluding the belief in providence or the immanence of God, was apparently formulated in the end of the 18th century by those rationalists who were aggrieved at being identified with the naturalists. **1880** *Sat. Rev.* 26 June 820 In speaking of a deist they fix their attention on the negative, in speaking of a theist on the positive aspect of his belief.

deistic (diːˈɪstɪk), *a.* [f. DEIST + -IC.] Of the nature of or pertaining to deists or deism.

1795 G. WAKEFIELD *Reply Paine's Age of Reason* II. 57 From the mouth of Thomas Paine, the most tremendous of all possible deistic dunces! **1880** L. STEPHEN *Pope* vii. 163 Brought up as a Catholic, he had gradually swung into vague deistic belief. **1882–3** SCHAFF *Encycl. Relig. Knowl.* I. 728 The deistic controversy..beginning with Lord Herbert of Cherbury (1581–1648).

deistical (diːˈɪstɪkəl), *a.* [f. as prec. + -AL¹.] = prec.; also, inclined or tending to deism.

1741 WATTS *Improv. Mind* I. v. §3 To support the deistical or antichristian scheme of our days. **1796** MORSE *Amer. Geog.* II. 314 The ingenious and eloquent, but deistical J. J. Rousseau. **1809–10** COLERIDGE *Friend* (1865) 54 Concerning the right of punishing by law the authors of heretical or deistical writings. **1871** TYNDALL *Fragm. Sc.* (1879) II. ix. 168 My object was to show my deistical friends ..that they were in no better condition than we were.

Hence **de'istically** *adv.*, in a deistical way.

1882–3 SCHAFF *Encycl. Relig. Knowl.* II. 1608 Nature.. may be conceived of deistically, as an accomplished fact.. utterly external to God.

deit, Sc. f. *died*, pa. t. of DIE *v.*

de-italianize: see DE- II. 1.

†**'deitate**, *ppl. a. Obs.* [repr. an assumed L. **deitāt-us* (tr. Gr. θεωθείς), f. *deitās, deitāt-em* DEITY.] Made a deity, deified.

1551 CRANMER *Answ. Bp. Gardiner* II. Rem. (1833) III. 450 One person and one Christ, who is God incarnate and man Deitate, as Gregory Nazianzene saith.

Deiters (ˈdaɪtəz). The name of Otto Friedrich Carl *Deiters* (1834–63), German anatomist, used to designate various anatomical structures, as *cells of Deiters*, (*a*) the outer hair cells in the organ of Corti; (*b*) the astrocytes of the neuroglia; ***nucleus of Deiters***, the lateral vestibular nucleus (NUCLEUS *sb.* 6 b) in the brain.

1867 *Quain's Anat.* (ed. 7) III. 767 Alternating with the outer ciliated cells [in the organ of Corti] are the cells of Deiters, which are fusiform and prolonged into a thread at each extremity. **1886** W. R. GOWERS *Man. Dis. Nerv. Syst.* I. III. 107 Fine fibres..form a network. At their intersections are peculiar cells consisting of a nucleus and small cell body ('glia-cells', 'cells of Deiters'). **1890** A. HILL tr. *Obersteiner's Anat. Cent. Nerv. Organs* 225 This region is ..known as the large-celled nucleus of the auditory nerve (Deiters' nucleus). **1964** J. Z. YOUNG *Model of Brain* Gloss. 335/2 *Deiter's* [sic] *nucleus*, nerve-cell region receiving signals from the organ of balance via the vestibular nerve. **1966** R. O. GREEP *Histol.* (ed. 2) xxxvi. 866/1 The supporting cells of the outer hair cells are the outer phalangeal cells, or Deiters' cells.

deith, obs. Sc. form of DEATH *sb.*

deity (ˈdiːɪtɪ, ˈdeɪtɪ). Also 4–6 **deite, deyte**, 4 **deitee**, 6–7 **deitie**, (5 **deyite, -yte, dietie**, 5–7 **diety**, 7 **dyety**). [a. F. *déité*, in 12th c. *deitet, deite* (= Pr. *deitat*, Sp. *deidad*, It. *deità*), ad. L. *deitās, deitāt-em*, f. *de-us* god (formed by Augustine, *De Civ. Dei* VII. i., after L. *dīvīnitās*): see -ITY.]

1. a. The estate or rank of a god; godhood; the personality of a god; godship; *esp.* with *poss. pron.*

c **1374** CHAUCER *Troylus* III. 968 But o þow Ioue..Is þis an honour to þi deite. *c* **1386** —— *Frankl. T.* 319 Though Neptunus haue deitee in the See. *c* **1440** CAPGRAVE *Life St. Kath.* IV. 764 Whi shulde appollo bere ony deyte? **1594** MARLOWE & NASHE *Dido* III. ii, That ugly imp that shall.. wrong my deity with high disgrace. **1594** SHAKS. *Rich. III*, I. i. 76 Lord Hastings..Humbly complaining to her Deitie, Got my Lord Chamberlaine his libertie. **1611** —— *Wint. T.* IV. iv. 26 The Goddes themselues (Humbling their Deities to loue). *a* **1618** RALEIGH (J.), By what reason could the same deity be denied unto Laurentia and Flora, which was given to Venus? **1619** DRAYTON *Man in Moon* (R.), Yet no disguise her deity could smother, So far in beauty she excelled other. **1844** MRS. BROWNING *Dead Pan* xxviii, All the false gods with a cry Rendered up their deity.

b. The divine quality, character, or nature of God; Godhood, divinity; the divine nature and attributes, the Godhead.

1362 LANGL. *P. Pl.* A. XI. 43 Þus þei drauelen on heore deys þe Deite to knowe. *c* **1394** *P. Pl. Crede* 825 Freres wyln for her pride Disputen of þis deyte as dotardes schulden. **1398** TREVISA *Barth. De P.R.* I. (1495) 3 The lyghte of the heuenly dyuyne clarete, couerte, & closid in the deyte or in the godhede. *c* **1489** CAXTON *Blanchardyn* liv. 213 Whose eternall dietie raigneth within the highest heauens. **1502** *Ord. Crysten Men* (W. de W. 1506) Prol. 2 The fader the sone & the holy ghost, one essence of deite. **1514** BARCLAY *Cyt. & Uplondyshm.* (Percy Soc.) 17 To honour our Lorde, & pease his deyte. **1594** T. B. *La Primaud. Fr. Acad.* II. *Seneca*, The creator..hath set such markes of his diety in his workes. **1633** BP. HALL *Hard Texts, N.T.* 57 In my.. infinite Deity I will be ever present with you. **1667** MILTON *P.L.* x. 65. **1736** CHANDLER *Hist. Persec.* 47 The same man opposed the Deity of the Son of God. **1835** *Gentl. Mag.* Oct. 397/1 Mr. Gurney's work..is chiefly confined to the Deity of Christ. There is something open and decided in saying *Deity*, rather than *Divinity*.

†**c.** The condition or state in which the Divine Being exists. *Obs.*

c **1400** *Rom. Rose* 5656 And leven alle humanite, And purely lyve in deite. *c* **1485** *Digby Myst.* (1882) III. 1075, I ded natt asend to my father In deyyte.

2. a. *concr.* A divinity, a divine being, a god; one of the gods worshipped by a people or tribe.

c **1374** CHAUCER *Troylus* IV. 1515, I swere it yow, and ek on ech goddesse, On every nymphe, and deyte infernal. **1589** GREENE *Menaphon* (Arb.) 42 That I helde a supersticious opinion of loue, in honouring him for a Deitie. **1607** SHAKS. *Cor.* IV. vi. 91 A thing Made by some other Deity then Nature, That shapes man Better. **1641** WILKINS *Math. Magick* I. xi. (1648) 69 Temples or Tombes..dedicated to some of their Deities. **1794** SULLIVAN *View Nat.* II. 448 The chief deity, the sun. **1814** CARY *Dante, Paradiso* VIII. 3 The fair Cyprian deity [Venus]. **1851** D. WILSON *Preh. Ann.* (1863) II. III. ii. 71 The Altar appears to be dedicated to one of these obscure local deities.

b. *fig.* An object of worship; a thing or person deified.

1588 SHAKS. *L.L.L.* IV. iii. 74 This is the liuer veine, which makes flesh a deity. **1630** J. TAYLOR (Water P.) *Wks.* II. 113/1 Tobacco (England's bainefull Diety).

3. (*with capital*) A supreme being as creator of the universe; ***the Deity***, the Supreme Being, God. (Especially as a term of Natural Theology, and without explicit predication of personality.)

1647 N. BACON *Disc. Laws Eng.* I. iv. (1739) 10 They worship an invisible and an infinite Deity. **1690** LOCKE *Hum. Und.* I. iv. (1695) 30 A rational Creature, who will but seriously reflect on them, cannot miss the discovery of a Deity. **1774** GOLDSM. *Nat. Hist.* (1776) I. 6 We see the greatness and wisdom of the Deity in all the seeming worlds that surround us. **1786** HAN. MORE *Let.* in *Mem. Ld. Gambier* (1861) I. x. 157 Polite ears are disgusted to hear their Maker called 'the Lord' in common talk, while serious ones think the fashionable appellation of 'the Deity' sounds extremely Pagan. **1812–6** J. SMITH *Panorama Sc. & Art* I. 527 Newton..had recourse, for one of the forces, to the immediate action of the Deity. **1860** PUSEY *Min. Proph.* 193 Men spoke of 'the Deity', as a sort of first cause of all things, and..had lost sight of the Personal God.

'deityship. [f. prec. (sense 2) + -SHIP.] The status or personality of a deity; godship (= DEITY 1).

1694 ECHARD *Plautus* 46 Why shou'dnt my deityship gi' me the same priviledge? **1748** RICHARDSON *Clarissa* Wks. 1883 VI. 503 With due regard to your deityship. **1834** LYTTON *Pompeii* IV. xii, If his deityship were never better served, he would do well to give up the godly profession.

deive, obs. form of DEAVE, to deafen.

†**deivirile**, *a. Obs. rare.* [ad. med.L. *deīvirīl-is* (f. *de-us* god + *virīlis* manly), transl. Gr. θεανδρικός (f. θε-ός god + ἀνδρικός of a man, manly).] 'A term in the school theology signifying something divine and human at the same time' (Chambers, *Cycl.*).

1727–51 CHAMBERS *Cycl.* s.v. *Theandric*, Θεανδρικὴ ἐνεργεια, *theandric* or *dei-virile* operations, in the sense of Dionysius (Bp. of Athens) and Damascenus is thus exemplified by Athanasius..In raising Lazarus, he called as man, but awaked him from the dead as God.

deixis (ˈdaɪksɪs). *Grammar.* [Gr. δεῖξις reference.] Indication, pointing out. Cf. DEICTIC *a.*

1949 *Archivum Linguisticum* I. II. 181 His analysis of the basic personal pronouns in terms of deixis. **1964** R. A. HALL *Introd. Ling.* xxvi. 164 The function of pointing out is often called deixis. **1966** G. N. LEECH *Eng. in Advertising* xviii. 157 The definite article is characteristically employed in advertising in this sense of *absolute* deixis.

‖**déjà entendu** (deʒa ɑ̃tɑ̃dy). [f. F. *déjà* already + *entendu* heard, after DÉJÀ VU.] A feeling that one has already heard a passage of music, etc., before.

1965 *Listener* 22 July 141/2 There is no gainsaying that this kind of large orchestral statement—the Cheltenham Symphony as the genre has been called—has a feeling of *déjà entendu* about its formal structure. **1969** *Daily Tel.* 13 Sept. 13/3 We hear words and phrases snatched from the texts used in the following movements..and set here in an almost, if not quite identical manner so as to give rise to a sense of *déja entendu* [sic] when they are heard again later. **1976** *Listener* 26 Feb. 246/2 Around *To the Shores of the Polar Sea* (Radio 4)..there hung an air of *déjà entendu*.

‖**déjà lu** (deʒa ly). [f. F. *déjà* already + *lu* read, after DÉJÀ VU.] A feeling that one may have read the present passage before, or in a similar form elsewhere.

1960 *Guardian* 29 Apr. 11/5 Rather a barren patch, full of the déja-lu [*sic*] and books that disturb the memory. **1973** *Observer* 19 Aug. 32/5 It is not only Mr Holroyd's own readers who may have a sense..of *déjà lu*. **1979** C. JAMES *Pillars of Hercules* I. iii. 52 The first poem in the book.. induces a fairly heavy effect of déjà lu. Aren't we long used to that massive four-stanza form, that conjectural opening?

dejansenize: see DE- II. 1.

‖**déjà vu** (deʒa vy, deɪʒɑːˈvuː). *Psychol.* [Fr., = already seen.] **a.** An illusory feeling of having previously experienced a present situation; a form of paramnesia. Also *attrib.*

1903 [see PROMNESIA]. **1906** *Jrnl. Abnormal Psychol.* Apr. 9 A feeling that the present is a part of past experience (*déjà vu*). **1914** tr. *Freud's Psychopathol. Everday Life* xii. 323 My own experience of *Déjà vu* I can trace in a similar manner to the emotional constellation of the moment. **1937** KOESTLER *Spanish Test.* i. 21 He is unable to shake off a dream-like feeling that he has had this nightmare before, a feeling that the psychologists term *déjà vu*. **1949** M. DICKENS *Flowers on Grass* v. 107 The queer dreamlike warning came upon him again, that illusion of having experienced everything before. The *déjà vu phenomenon*, he knew it was called. **1953** H. H. PRICE *Thinking & Experience* iii. 80 We have all heard of the *déjà vu* illusion, and most of us have experienced it at some time or other. **1958** I. MURDOCH *Bell* xxv. 297 He had again the strange sensation of *déjà vu*.

b. *occas.* The correct impression that something has been previously experienced; tedious familiarity.

1960 *Times* 18 Feb. 15/2 Although better than her last novel, *Aimez-vous Brahms*..has a depressing air of *déjà vu*. **1962** *Listener* 11 Jan. 82/3 Even when..some of them [*sc.* photogravures] are of well-known sites or monuments, the *déjà vu* is avoided by lighting or angle or texture.

deˈject, *ppl. a. Obs.* or *arch.* Also 6 -gecte. [ad. L. *dēject-us*, pa. pple. of *dējicĕre* (*dēicĕre*) to throw down, f. DE- I. 1 + *jacĕre* to throw. (In OF. *des-*, *degiet*, *-get*, *-git*.)]

1. As *pa. pple.* Thrown down, cast down; †cast away, rejected: see DEJECT *v.*

1430 LYDG. *Chron. Troy* II. xvii, Thorowen and deiect in a pyt horryble. **1483** CAXTON *Gold. Leg.* 37 b/1 Lucifer whiche was dejecte and caste out of heven. **1560** ROLLAND *Crt. Venus* III. 510 He..was deiect with schame fra all honour. **1819** H. BUSK *Vestriad* v. 513 Here on Patroclus' corse deject he lies.

2. As *ppl. a.* Downcast, dispirited, DEJECTED.

1528 ROY *Rede me* (Arb.) 43 They were so abasshed and deiecte That once to hisse they were nott able. **1555** J. PHILPOT in Coverdale *Lett. Mart.* (1564) 228 Dearling..Be not of a deiect mind for these temptations. **1602** SHAKS. *Ham.* III. i. 163 And I, of Ladies most deiect and wretched. **1639** G. DANIEL *Ecclus.* xi. 59 Be not deiect in Miserie. **1863** W. LANCASTER *Præterita* 87 Deject and doubtful thus I forge quaint fears.

b. Cast down from one's position, lowered in fortunes; lowered in character, abject, abased.

1510–20 *Everyman* in Hazl. *Dodsley* I. 101 Like traitors deject. **1605** *Play Stucley* in Simpson *Sch. Shaks.* (1878) I. 234 Is't possible that Stukly, so deject In England, lives in Spain in such respect. *a* **1625** FLETCHER *Love's Cure* II. i, What can be a more deject spirit in man, than to lay his hands under every one's horse's feet? **1820** T. L. PEACOCK *Wks.* (1875) III. 324 The beggar being, for the most part, a king deject.

†**c.** *Astrol.* (See quot.) *Obs.*

1594 BLUNDEVIL *Exerc.* IV. xxxvi. (ed. 7) 494 Such houses as have no familiarity with the Horoscope or Ascendent.. are said to be slow and deject.

deject (dɪˈdʒɛkt), *v.* (In *Sc.*, 6 deiekk, 6– dejeck.) [f. L. *dēject-*, ppl. stem of *dējicĕre* to throw or cast down: see prec.]

1. *trans.* To throw or cast down; to cause to fall down, overthrow. *arch.* or *Obs.*

c **1420** *Pallad. on Husb.* II. 423 Take of the laures bayes.. in sething water hem dejecte. **1536** BELLENDEN *Cron. Scot.* (1821) I. 110 Scho hes dejeckit me at thy feit. **1550** NICOLLS *Thucyd.* 125 Their people..whiche were deiected and dryuen downe from the sayd rocke. **1627** SPEED *England* xli. §7 This Citie..by the furious outrages of the Scots and Picts was deiected. *a* **1638** MEDE *Paraphr. 2 Pet.* iii. Wks. (1672) III. 615 To be exiled and dejected from those high mansions. **1881** [see DEJECTED 1].

b. To bend down.

1601 HOLLAND *Pliny* XVII. xxii. I. 531 What part soeuer of it [the vine] is dejected and driuen downward, or els bound and tied fast, the same ordinarily beareth fruit. **1605** HEYWOOD *If you know not me* Wks. 1874 I. 206 It becomes not You being a Princess, to deiect your knee. **1625** *Modell of Wit* 62 b, Deiecting her head into her bosome. **1809** [see DEJECTED 1 b].

c. To cast down (the eyes).

1612 DRAYTON *Poly-olb.* xii. (T.), One, having climb'd some roof..From thence upon the earth dejects his humble eye. **1727–46** THOMSON *Summer* 1066 Princely wisdom then Dejects his watchful eye. **1768** *Woman of Honor* III. 264 Fixing his eyes on Clara, who modestly dejected her's.

†**2.** To cast away, dismiss, reject. *Obs.*

1530 PALSGR. 510/1, I dejecte, I caste a waye, *je dejecte*. **1549** *Compl. Scot.* Prol. 17 Gyf sic vordis suld be disusit or deiekkit. **1579** FENTON *Guicciard.* III. (1599) 118 These perswasions..he vtterly deiected. **1633** BP. HALL *Hard Texts* 544 Whether your humiliation may not yet..cause him to deject and take off his judgements?

†**3.** *fig.* To cast down from high estate or dignity, depose; to lower in condition or character, to abase, humble. *Obs.*

1515 BARCLAY *Egloges* iv. (1570) C v/2 The coyne auaunceth, neede doth the name deject. **1549** COVERDALE *Erasm. Par. 1 Pet.* II. 14 His delyght is in..suche as deiecte them selues. **1601** F. GODWIN *Bps. of Eng.* 503 Being loath to deiect them whom he had once aduanced. **1660** BOND *Scut. Reg.* 165 Where the superior makes an Inferior officer, he may deject him at his pleasure. **1691** E. TAYLOR *Behmen's Theos. Philos.* 185 Faln Mans dejecting himself may be called Humiliation.

†**4.** To reduce the force or strength of, to weaken, lessen. *Obs.*

1580 SIDNEY *Arcadia* iii, Though in strength exceedingly dejected. **1599** SANDYS *Europæ Spec.* (1632) 190 One disadvantage..impeacheth and dejecteth all other their forces. **1620** VENNER *Via Recta* ii. 22 It doth very greatly deiect their appetite. **1684** tr. *Bonet's Merc. Compit.* I. 15 The Appetite..is often dejected in Consumptive Persons.

5. To depress in spirits; to cast down, dispirit, dishearten. (The ordinary current sense.)

1581 [see DEJECTED 3]. **1603** FLORIO *Montaigne* (1634) 491 Good Authours deject me too-too much, and quaile my courage. **1625** MEADE in Ellis *Orig. Lett.* Ser. I. III. 204 The king was much dejected by a Lettre received from Denmark. **1761** STERNE *Tr. Shandy* III. xx, To deject and contrist myself with so bad and melancholy an account. **1775** JOHNSON *Tax. no Tyr.* 8 Nothing dejects a trader like the interruption of his profits. **1862** LYTTON *Str. Story* I. 68 The things which do not disturb her temper, may, perhaps, deject her spirits.

†**b.** *intr.* (for *refl.*) To be dejected. *Obs. rare.*

1644 QUARLES *Barnabas & B.* 226 Deject not, O my soul, nor let thy thoughts despair.

6. *intr.* To bend downwards. *nonce-use.*

1825 HONE *Every-day Bk.* I. 323 It stands, or rather dejects, over..a pair of wooden gates.

Hence **deˈjecting** *ppl. a.*

1818 MRS. ILIFF *Poems* (ed. 2) 20 The mien assuming of dejecting care.

‖**dejecta** (dɪˈdʒɛktə), *sb. pl.* [L., neut. pl. of *dēject-us*: see DEJECT.] Castings, excrements.

1887 GARNSEY & BALFOUR tr. *De Bary's Fungi* vii. 357 Fungi which grow on the *dejecta* of warm-blooded animals, dung, feathers, etc.

dejectant (dɪˈdʒɛktənt), *a. Her.* [f. DEJECT + -ANT[1].] Cast down, bending down.

1889 [see DEJECTED 1 d].

dejected (dɪˈdʒɛktɪd), *ppl. a.* [f. DEJECT *v.*]

1. *lit.* Thrown or cast down, overthrown. *arch.*

1682 WHELER *Journ. Greece* VI. 427 Buried in the Rubbish of its dejected Roof and Walls. **1881** H. JAMES *Portr. Lady* xxvi, Looking at her dejected pillar.

b. Allowed to hang down.

1809 HEBER *Passage of Red Sea* 12 The mute swain..With arms enfolded, and dejected head.

c. Of the eyes: Downcast.

1600 [see 3 b]. **1663** COWLEY *Pindar. Odes*, *Brutus* ii, If with dejected Eye In standing Pools we seek the Sky. **1715–20** POPE *Iliad* IX. 626 With humble mien and with dejected eyes Constant they follow where Injustice flies.

d. *Her.* Cast down, bent downwards; as *dejected embowed*, embowed with the head downwards.

1889 ELVIN *Dict. Her.*, *Dejected*, cast down, as a garb dejected or dejectant.

†**2.** Lowered in estate, condition, or character; abased, humbled, lowly. *Obs.*

1605 SHAKS. *Lear* IV. i. 3 The lowest and most deiected thing of Fortune. **1641** MILTON *Reform.* II. (1851) 71 The basest, the lowermost, the most dejected..downe-trodden Vassals of Perdition. *a* **1680** BUTLER *Rem.* (1759) II. 14 Able to reach from the highest Arrogance to the meanest, and most dejected Submissions. **1721** [see DEJECTEDNESS].

3. Depressed in spirits, downcast, disheartened, low-spirited.

1581 MARBECK *Bk. of Notes* 115 So that he was deiected and compelled to weepe for very many, which had fallen. **1608–11** BP. HALL *Medit. & Vows* I. §39, I marvell not that a wicked man is..so dejected, when hee feeles sickness. **1667** PEPYS *Diary* (1879) IV. 369 Never were people so dejected as they are in the City. **1793** COWPER *Lett.* 8 Sept., I am cheerful on paper sometimes, when I am absolutely the most dejected of all creatures. **1835** LYTTON *Rienzi* X. viii, Thus are we fools of Fortune;—to-day glad—to-morrow dejected!

b. *transf.* (Of the visage, behaviour, etc.) (Often combining 1 c and 3.)

1600 *Disc. Gowrie Conspir.*, With a very dejected countenaunce, his eies ever fixed upon the earth. **1602** SHAKS. *Ham.* I. ii. 81 The deiected hauiour of the Visage. **1710** STEELE *Tatler* No. 85 ¶2 The Goddess..is to sit in a dejected Posture. **1769** ROBERTSON *Chas. V*, III. XI. 273 In a timid dejected silence. **1822** SCOTT *Pirate* xl, I could not but move with a drooping head, and dejected pace.

dejectedly (dɪˈdʒɛktɪdlɪ), *adv.* [-LY[2].] In a dejected manner.

1611 COTGR., *Bassement*, basely, lowly, deiectedly. **1675** BROOKS *Gold. Key* Wks. 1867 V. 189 As he stood bound before the palace, leaning dejectedly upon a tree. **1805** SCOTT *Last Ministr.* I. Concl., Dejectedly and low he bowed. **1881** MISS BRADDON *Asph.* II. 256 Those early comers who roam about empty halls dejectedly.

dejectedness (dɪˈdʒɛktɪdnɪs). [-NESS.]

†**1.** The state of being cast down or humbled (in fortunes, condition, etc.); abasement. *Obs.*

1608 BP. HALL *Char. Virtues & V.* I. 27 No Man sets so low a value of his worth as himselfe, not out of ignorance.. but of a voluntary and meeke deiectednesse. **1646** JENKYN *Remora* 15 Lownes and dejectednes of estate. **1721** R. KEITH tr. *T. à Kempis's Solil. Soul* iv. 139 Behold, O Lord, the Dejectedness of my State.

2. The state of being downcast or depressed in spirits.

1633 BP. HALL *Hard Texts* 88 An heart full of dejectedness and dismay. *c* **1740** MRS. DELANY *Autobiog.* (1861) I. 13 The dejectedness of my mother's spirits. **1884** *Manch. Exam.* 29 Nov. 5/3 The same spirit of.. dejectedness which marks the long-suffering Cockney.

dejecter (dɪˈdʒɛktə(r)). [f. DEJECT *v.* + -ER. Cf. DEJECTOR.] One who dejects.

1611 COTGR., *Abbaisseur*, an abaser, debaser, deiecter.

dejectile (dɪˈdʒɛktɪl). [f. L. type **dējectil-is*, f. ppl. stem of L. *dējicĕre* to DEJECT; cf. *projectile*, and L. *miss-ilis*, *plect-ilis*: see -ILE.] A body thrown or impelled down upon an enemy.

1886 MRS. RANDOLPH *Mostly Fools* III. x. 297 Harassing the foe by casting dejectiles into their works.

dejection (dɪˈdʒɛkʃən). Also 5 deieccion. [a. OF. *dejection* (14th c. in Godef.), ad. L. *dējectiōn-em*, n. of action from *dējicĕre* (*dēicĕre*) to cast down: see DEJECT *ppl. a.*]

1. *lit.* The action of casting down; the fact of being cast down.

1681 HALLYWELL *Melampr.* 13 (T.) Their [the angels'] dejection and detrusion into the caliginous regions. **1851** RUSKIN *Stones Ven.* I. xiv. §10 A hole between each bracket for the convenient dejection of hot sand and lead.

†**b.** The throwing down or precipitation of a sediment. *Obs.*

1594 PLAT *Jewell-ho.* II. 40 A means how to make deiection of the Lee or fæces of yᵉ best sallet oyle.

†**2.** *fig.* A casting down, deposing or lowering (in fortunes, condition, quality, etc.); humiliation, abasement. *Obs.*

c **1450** tr. *De Imitatione* III. xxii, Se þerfore, lorde, my deieccion and my frailte. **1545** JOYE *Exp. Dan.* iv. (R.), This deiection and humiliacion might not the kynge knowe. **1601** B. JONSON *Poetaster* Prol., Such full-blown vanity he more doth loth Than base dejection. **1641** PRYNNE *Antip.* 35 The Pope writ Letters to all Nobles..to assist Philip for the dejection of Iohn. **1659** PEARSON *Creed* i. (1845) 38 Adoration implies submission and dejection; so that, while we worship, we cast down ourselves.

†**b.** *Astrol.* (See quot. 1727.) *Obs.*

1430 LYDG. *Chron. Troy* IV. xxxiv, But in the Bull is thy kingdom lorne, For therein is thy deiection. **1727–51** CHAMBERS *Cycl.*, *Dejection*, in astrology, is applied to the planets, when in their detriment, *i.e.* when they have lost their force, or influence..by reason of their being in opposition to some others..Or, it is used when a planet is in a sign opposite to that wherein it has its greatest effect, or influence, which is called its exaltation. Thus, the sign *Aries* being the exaltation of the sun..*Libra* is its dejection.

3. Depression of spirits; downcast or dejected condition.

c **1450** tr. *De Imitatione* II. xi, If ihesu hide him ande a litel forsake hem, þei falle into a compleynyng or into ouer gret deieccion. *a* **1631** DONNE in *Select.* (1840) 120 To sink into a sordid melancholy, or irreligious dejection of spirit. **1667** MILTON *P.L.* XI. 301 What besides Of sorrow and dejection and despair Our frailtie can sustain. **1791** BOSWELL *Johnson* an. 1755 (1831) I. 283 That miserable dejection of spirits to which he was constitutionally subject. **1865** PARKMAN *Huguenots* vi. (1875) 72 A deep dejection fell upon them.

†**4.** Lowering of force or strength; diminution or weakening (of the bodily strength or appetite).

1652 FRENCH *Yorksh. Spa* viii. 78 A manifest dejection of the appetite. **1659** HAMMOND *On Ps.* cvi. 15 Annot. 537 A suddain and almost incredible dejection of strength. **1732** ARBUTHNOT *Rules of Diet* 294 Dejection of Appetite. **1883** *Syd. Soc. Lex.*, *Dejection*..applied also to depression, exhaustion, or prostration.

5. *Med.* Evacuation of the bowels, fæcal discharge.

1605 TIMME *Quersit.* I. xvi. 82 Purgations which work.. by deiections, by vomit, by sweates, and by urines. **1691** RAY *Creation* (J.), Where there is good use for it [the choler] ..to provoke dejection. **1805** *Med. Jrnl.* XIV. 430 She..had frequent vomitings and dejections.

6. *concr.* That which is dejected: **a.** Fæcal discharge, excrement.

1727–51 CHAMBERS *Cycl.* s.v., *Dejection* is also, and that more ordinarily, applied to the excrements themselves, thus evacuated. **1849** *Jrnl. R. Agric. Soc.* X. II. 522 Fæcal dejections. **1861** HULME tr. *Moquin-Tandon* II. VII. 409 Dr. Hassall also found the Vibrios in the dejections of cholera.

b. *Geol.* Matter thrown out from a volcano.

1839 MURCHISON *Silur. Syst.* I. xxiii. 291 A greenish grey sandstone, evidently formed of volcanic submarine dejections. **1849** —— *Siluria* iv. 77 By the action of submarine volcanoes, such igneous dejections are supposed to have accumulated.

†**deˈjective**, *a. Obs.* [f. L. *dēject-* ppl. stem (see DEJECT *ppl. a.*) + -IVE.]

1. Characterized by, or betokening, dejection, submission, or abasement.

1591 HORSEY *Trav.* (Hakluyt Soc.) 160 They yeld [the city] with a dejective flag of truce. **1611** SPEED *Hist. Gt. Brit.* IX. iv. §18 Humbling himselfe in a more deiectiue manner, then either his birth, or owne nature could well brooke.

2. *Med.* Causing evacuation, purgative.

1605 TIMME *Quersit.* I. vi. 23 It will be made both deiective and vomitive. **1657** TOMLINSON *Renou's Disp.* 45

Two purging medicaments, one a vomiting or ejective, the other dejective.

† **de'jectly**, *adv. Obs.* [f. DEJECT *ppl. a.* + -LY².] In a 'deject' manner, dejectedly.
1611 Cotgr., *Peneusement*, deiectly, heartlesly. **1653** *Cloria & Narcissus* I. 50 It doth not become a Prince of your birth..to entertaine dejectly these passages. **1767** H. Brooke *Fool of Qual.* (1859) II. 237 (D.), I rose dejectly, curtsied, and withdrew without reply.

† **de'jectment.** *Obs.* [a. obs. F. *dejectement* 'a deiecting, bringing low, also contumelious repulse' (Cotgr.), in earlier F. *degiete-, deget(t)ement, dejet(t)ement*, f. *degieter, déjeter*, f. DE- I. 1 + *jeter*:—L. *jactāre* freq. of *jacĕre* to throw. Cf. med. or mod.L. *dējectāmentum*.] A bringing low, abasement, dejection.
1656 S. Holland *Zara* (1719) 53 To Soto's extream dejectment..the Inchantress..demanded of him [etc.]. **1660** H. More *Myst. Godl.* vi. vi. 229 He..who in his dejectment could raise to life not only a faithless but senseless corps.

dejector (dɪ'dʒɛktə(r)). *Med. rare.* [agent-n. in L. form from L. *dējicĕre* to DEJECT.] A dejectory agent or medicine; an aperient.
1831 Trelawny *Adv. Younger Son* I. 239 An emetocatharticus, an enema, or simple dejectors.

dejectory (dɪ'dʒɛktərɪ), *a.* [f. as prec.: see -ORY.] Capable of promoting evacuation of the bowels; aperient.
1640 E. Chilmead *Ferrand's Love Mel.* 346 (T.) Easily wrought upon and evacuated by the dejectory medicines.

dejecture (dɪ'dʒɛktjʊə(r)). [f. L. type **dējectūra* (cf. *jactūra* a throwing away), f. *dējicĕre* to throw down: see -URE.] Matter discharged from the bowels; excrement.
1731 Arbuthnot *Aliments* vi. (R.), Excess of animal secretions, as of perspiration, sweat, liquid dejectures, &c.

† **'dejerate**, *v. Obs.* [f. L. *dējerāre* to take an oath, f. DE- I. 3 + *jūrāre* to swear.] *intr.* and *trans.* To swear solemnly. Hence † **'dejerated** *ppl. a.* So † **deje'ration**, † **'dejerator**.
1607 J. King *Serm.* Nov. 32 Their vowed and deierated secresie. *a* **1641** Bp. Mountagu *Acts & Mon.* (1642) 302 Antipater..dejerated deeply, and called God to witnesse of his innocency. **1612-15** Bp. Hall *Contempl.*, *O.T.* xxi. viii, Doubtlesse with many vowes and teares, and dejerations, he labours to clear his intentions. **1656** Blount *Glossogr.*, *Deieration*, a solemn swearing. **1623** Cockeram, *Deierator*, a great swearer.

dejeune, dejune. *Obs.* or *arch.* [For earlier *desjeune*, DISJUNE, a. OF. *desjeun* (Froissart), mod.F. dial. *déjun*, f. *desjeuner*, mod.F. *déjeuner* to break fast, to breakfast, f. *des-, dé-* (DE- I. 6) + *jeun*:—L. *jejūn-us* fasting. Superseded in mod.F. (hence also in Eng.) by *déjeuné, déjeuner*.] = next.
[**1589** Greene *Menaphon* (Arb.) 35 He had ended his desiune.] **1630** B. Jonson *New Inn* iii. i, Take a dejeune of muskadel and eggs. **1788** *Disinterested Love* I. 39 He arrived yesterday about twelve, and, shameful to relate, the dejeune was not removed. **1810** *Sporting Mag.* XXXV. 201 To treat them with an elegant dejune. **1837** Dickens *Pickw.* xviii, For two days after the dejeune at Mrs. Hunter's, the Pickwickians remained at Eatanswill.

‖ **déjeuner**, † **déjeuné** (deʒœne). [mod.F. *déjeuner*, formerly often *déjeuné* (cf. COUCHEE), pres. inf. = to breakfast, used subst. = breaking fast, breakfast.] **a.** The morning meal; breakfast.
In France, it often corresponds in time more to the English luncheon, for which *déjeuner* is consequently used as a synonym. ***déjeuner à la fourchette*** [lit. breakfast with the fork], a late *déjeuner* of a substantial character, with meat, wine, etc.; a luncheon.
1787 Maty tr. *Riesbeck's Trav. Germ.* xxxi. II. 47 Every body now gives *dinès, soupès*, and *dejunès*. **1818** Moore *Fudge Fam. Paris* i. 8 This exceeding long letter You owe to a *déjeuner à la fourchette*. **1826** J. R. Best *Four Years in France* 289 We took our déjuné at which we had delicious grapes and execrable wine. **1849** Thackeray *Pendennis* vii, At her *déjeuner-dansant* after the Bohemian Ball. **1864** *Daily Tel.* 31 May, At the tables on which that description of banquet usually called a déjeûner is spread.

b. A breakfast service (see quot. 1875).
1774 *Descr. of Villa of H. Walpole* 105 A dejuné [ed. 1784, p. 74: dejeuné] of Seve china. **1869** Lady C. Schreiber *Jrnl.* (1911) I. 31 A very fine Chelsea Déjeuner which he sold for £90. **1875** E. Meteyard *Wedgwood Handbk.* 395 A déjeuner consists of a tray, one or more cups and saucers, occasionally a teapot, a cream jug, and a slop basin.

c. *attrib.*
1851 *Illustr. Catal. Gt. Exhib.* iii. 726/1 Communion and déjeûne services. *Ibid.* 748/2 Papier maché 'standish', 'déjeûner tray', and bottle-stand. **1865** 'Ouida' *Strathmore* xii, In the breakfast-room every déjeûner delicacy was waiting. **1870** Lady C. Schreiber *Jrnl.* (1911) I. 65 A Sèvres déjeuner service. **1875** J. Grant *One of Six Hundr.* x, A *déjeûner* service of splendid Wedgwood ware. **1899** *Westm. Gaz.* 5 July 1/3 Messrs. Christie sold yesterday the déjeuner-service of Napoleon I.

dejudicate, variant of DIJUDICATE.
1623 Cockeram ii, To *Censure*..Determine, Deiudicate.

dejunkerize: see DE- II. 1.

de jure: see DE- I. 5.

† **dejury.** *Obs. rare*⁻¹. [ad. L. *dējūri-um* an oath, f. *dējūrāre* (earlier *dējerāre*) to take an oath, make oath, f. DE- I. 3 + *jūrāre* to swear.] A solemn oath.
1683 E. Hooker *Pref. Ep. Pordage's Mystic Div.* 15 Common Oaths, cursed Dejuries, monstrous Perjuries.

Dekabrist ('dɛkəbrɪst). Also **Deca-**. [a. Russ. *dekabríst*, f. *dekábr'* December.] One who took part in an uprising which occurred in St. Petersburg on 26 December 1825, on the accession of the Emperor Nicholas I.
1882 in Ogilvie (Annandale). **1885** *Encycl. Brit.* XIX. 649/1 The unfortunate conspiracy of the Dekabrists. **1903** *Daily Chron.* 22 Oct. 3/2 A reactionary policy led to a series of conspiracies—notably that of the Decabrists—which closed the door to enlightened government for many years to come. **1920** *19th Cent.* Sept. 420 *Russian Women* gives a description of the wives of the Dekabrists, aristocrats but our first revolutionists. **1925** *Glasgow Herald* 5 Mar. 4 Prince Wolkonsky, as became a descendant of a Dekabrist, was a liberal.

dekadarchy, -drachm, dekarch, etc.: see DECA-.

Dekatron ('dɛkətrɒn). [f. Gr. δεκα- DECA- + -TRON.] The proprietary name of any of several gas-filled multi-electrode counting tubes, each containing a central anode and a set of ten interconnected cathodes. Also *attrib.*
1950 Bacon & Pollard in *Electronic Engin.* XXII. 173 (*title*) The Dekatron. A new cold cathode counting tube. *Ibid.*, A range of 'Dekatron' tubes has been designed which comprises..three types of multi-electrode cold-cathode tubes. **1951** *Electronic Engin.* XXIII. 85 These valves (Dekatrons) are gas filled tubes which have ten stable glow positions. **1958** *Engineering* 14 Feb. 201/3 The count is therefore shown on dekatron tubes in which the glow rotates through ten positions on each of three tubes which count the hundreds, tens and units respectively. **1963** B. Fozard *Instrumentation Nucl. Reactors* viii. 77 These are multi-electrode gas-filled scaling tubes commonly arranged to give, for nuclear particle counting applications, a scaling factor per tube of ten (hence the name Dekatron).

dekay, dekey, obs. forms of DECAY.

deke (diːk), *sb. N. Amer.* (chiefly *Canad.*). Also **deek**. [Shortened f. DECOY *sb.*²] In Ice Hockey, a deceptive movement or feint that induces an opponent to move out of position.
1960 *Time* (Canad. ed.) 21 Nov. 79/1 On the ice, Moore is one of the league's best players in the split-second art of faking a goalie out of position. 'I've developed a little play of my own,' he says. 'It's a kind of fake shot—we call them 'deeks' for decoys.' **1966** *Globe & Mail* (Toronto) 8 Nov. 34/6 On the fourth deke he moved and I fired her into the corner. **1973** *Weekend Mag.* (Montreal) 27 Jan. 10/2 What proved to be the 'insurance goal'..left the Canadiens' Jimmy Roberts gasping after a fantastic deke, then beat goalie Ken Dryden on the short side.

deke (diːk), *v. N. Amer.* (chiefly *Canad.*). [f. prec.] *trans.* and *intr.* In Ice Hockey: to pass (an opponent) by feinting or making a 'deke'. Also *transf.*
1961 *Kingston* (Ont.) *Whig-Standard* 23 Oct. 8/6 He deked around a Soo defenceman but was spun off balance from behind before he could get his shot away. **1962** *Ibid.* 12 Feb. 8/6 The big Irishman..deked (the defenceman)..almost out of his uniform, and ripped a deadly backhand shot past the helpless Hull netminder. **1974** *Saturday Night* (Toronto) Feb. 43/2 So you decide to deke them out by taking two tiny quick rightward steps and they take one giant step—in the same direction. **1977** *Time Out* 17 June 63/5 Glynne Thomas..has fattened his average at the expense of inexperienced forwards unable or unwilling to go in on goal or 'deke'.

deken, -in, -on, -un, -yn(e, obs. ff. DEACON.

dekh, var. DECK *sb.*²

† **de'king**, *v. Obs.* [f. DE- II. 2 + KING.] *trans.* To depose (a king); to dethrone.
1611 Speed *Hist. Gt. Brit.* ix. xi. §75 Edward being thus de-kinged, the Embassie rode joyfully backe to London.

dekink (diː'kɪŋk), *v.* [f. DE- II. 2 + KINK *sb.*¹] *trans.* To remove kinks from. So **de'kinking** *vbl. sb.*
1936 J. Grierson *High Failure* viii. 189 He would come down to help with the dekinking and rewinding of the aerial. **1957** *Observer* 7 July 2/5 A process for dekinking the hair [of Negro women].

dekko ('dɛkəʊ). *slang* (orig. *Army slang*). Also **decko, † dekho.** [f. Hind. *dekho*, imperative of *dekhnā* to look: cf. DECK *sb.*²] A look. Also as *vb.*, to look, look at.
1894 *Daily News* 8 Sept. 6/3, I had a 'dekho' round every 'house' in the place, but couldn't see you. **1917** A. G. Empey *From the Fire Step* 232 '*Dekko*', to look; a look at something. **1920** M. A. Mügge *War Diary of Square Peg* 219 *Dekko*.—Look! **1927** F. B. Young *Portrait of Clare* vi. x. 744 He's promised to look in this evening, just to have a 'dekko' as he calls it, and see that you're all right. **1927** E. Thompson *These Men thy Friends* 63 'You haven't had a proper *dekko*, padre' he protested. **1933** *Punch* 16 Aug. 181/1 While they were hard-and-fast aground, James took a dekko, or look around. **1936** *Ibid.* 10 June 656/3 'Im and me was 'aving a last decko at the markwee when the housemaid comes out. **1958** *Observer* 11 May 15/1 Once I'd grabbed hold of the script and taken a good dekko at it, my worst fears were confirmed. **1961** J. Stroud *Touch & Go* xvi. 176 Phew! Dekko this, sir!

dekle, variant of DECKLE.

del (dɛl). *Math.* [Short for DELTA, from its being represented by an inverted delta (sense 1).] A name of the symbolic operator ∇, defined as $\mathrm{i}\frac{\partial}{\partial x} + \mathrm{j}\frac{\partial}{\partial y} + \mathrm{k}\frac{\partial}{\partial z}$.
1901 Gibbs & Wilson *Vector Analysis* iii. 138, $\mathrm{i}\frac{\partial}{\partial x} + \mathrm{j}\frac{\partial}{\partial y} + \mathrm{k}\frac{\partial}{\partial z}$. This symbolic operator ∇ was introduced by Sir W. R. Hamilton and is now in universal employment. There seems, however, to be no universally recognized name for it, although owing to the frequent occurrence of the symbol some name is a practical necessity. It has been found by experience that the monosyllable *del* is so short and easy to pronounce that even in complicated formulæ in which ∇ occurs a number of times no inconvenience to the speaker or hearer arises from the repetition. ∇*V* is read simply as 'del *V*'. **1924** C. E. Weatherburn *Adv. Vector Analysis* i. 4 ∇*V* (pronounced *del V*). **1962** Corson & Lorrain *Introd. Electromagn. Fields* i. 6 Gradient is commonly abbreviated as grad, and the operation on the scalar *f* defined by the term gradient is indicated by the symbol ∇, called del. **1964** S. Simons *Vector Anal.* v. 69 If we define a vector differential operator ∇ (called 'del' or 'nabla') by $\nabla = \mathrm{i}(\partial/\partial x) + \mathrm{j}(\partial/\partial y) + \mathrm{k}(\partial/\partial z)$, then it follows..that grad $V = \nabla V$.

del, obs. f. DEAL *sb.*¹, and of DOLE, mourning.

† **de'labe**, *v. Obs. rare.* [ad. L. *dēlābī* to slip down, f. DE- I. 1 + *lābī* to slide, fall.] *intr.* To glide down.
1657 Tomlinson *Renou's Disp.* Pref., There is no Jurgia Mentis to pertarr your Cogitations from delabing through the Golden Chanels of Experience.

delabiali'zation. *Phonetics.* [f. DELABIALIZE *v.* + -ATION.] The action of delabializing.
1907 H. M. Chadwick *Origin Eng. Nation* iv. 66 The delabialisation in E 4..is confined to unaccented words. **1939** *Year's Wk. in Eng. Stud. 1937* 30 The actual phonetic processes involved in the 'delabialization'. **1959** *Brno Studies Eng.* I. 34 The delabialisation of *u*.

de'labialize, *v.* [f. DE- II. 1 + LABIAL *a.* + -IZE.] *trans.* To deprive of its labial character.
1875-6 Sweet in *Trans. Philol. Soc.* 568 When the *o* of *hano* became delabialized into *a* in Frisian.

† **de'labiate**, *v. Obs. rare.* [Incorrectly f. L. *dēlābī* (see DELABE) + -ATE³.] = DELABE.
1632 W. Lithgow *Trav.* vii. 318 The abundant Snow..dissolving in streames, to the Lake Zembria, it ingorgeth Nylus so long as the matter delabiates.

† **de'labrate**, *v. rare.* [f. F. *délabrer* to shatter, dilapidate, *délabré* dilapidated, tattered; of unknown origin: see Littré and Hatzfeld.] To dilapidate, ruin. Hence **de'labrated** *ppl. a.*
1813 Forsyth *Remarks Excurs. Italy* 292 You can distinguish at once the three delabrated craters upon which the city forms a loose amphitheatre.

† **de'lace**, *v. Obs. rare*⁻¹. [a. F. *délacer*, in OF. *des-* (DE- I. 6) + *lacer* to LACE.] *trans.* To untie, undo.
1581 T. Howell *Deuises* (1879) 259 My onely ioy regarde you this my wofull case, Sith none but your disdaine, my sorrow can delace.

delacerate, -ation, obs. ff. DILACERATE, etc.

† **delacrimate**, *v. Obs.*⁻⁰ In 7 delachry-. [f. L. *dēlacrimāre* to shed tears, weep, f. DE- I. 1, 3 + *lacrimāre* to weep, *lacrima* tear.] 'To weepe' (Cockeram 1623).

delacri'mation. Also 7 delachry-, 7-9 delacry-. [ad. L. *dēlacrimātion-em*, n. of action from *dēlacrimāre* (see prec.).] Weeping or shedding of tears (*obs.*); a superabundant flow of an aqueous or serous humour from the eyes; epiphora.
1623 Cockeram, *Delachrymation*, a weeping. **1640** Parkinson *Theat. Bot.* 223 It procureth frequent and strong neesing, often times even unto delacrymation. **1727** Bailey vol. II, *Delacrymation*, the falling down of Humours, the Waterishness of the Eyes, or a weeping much. **1883** *Syd. Soc. Lex.*, *Delacrymation*, a synonym of *Epiphora*.

de'lacrimative, *a.* Also delacry-. [f. ppl. stem of L. *dēlacrimāre* (see prec.) + -IVE.] **a.** 'Having power to stop the flow of tears; also, **b.** applied to substances which produce a great flow of tears' (*Syd Soc. Lex.*).
[**1811** Hooper *Med. Dict.*, *Delachrymativa*, medicines which dry the eyes, first purging them of tears.]

delac'tation. [f. DE- I. 6 + LACTATION.] **a.** The act of weaning; **b.** 'artificial arrest of the secretion of milk' (*Syd. Soc. Lex.*).
1727 Bailey vol. II, *Delactation*, a weaning from the Breast. **1730-6** —— (folio). Hence in Johnson and mod. Dicts.

delafossite (dɛlə'fɒsaɪt). *Min.* [a. F. *delafossite* (C. Friedel 1873, in *Comptes Rendus* LXXVII.

213), f. the name of G. *Delafosse*, French mineralogist (1796–1878): see -ITE[1].] A black oxide of iron and copper, $CuFeO_2$, found chiefly in crystalline form or as botryoidal crusts.

1873 *Jrnl. Chem. Soc.* XXVI. 1107 Finer specimens were subsequently found in the collection of the museum of natural history. The name delafossite is proposed for it. **1968** M. H. HEY in *Mineral. Mag.* XXXVI. 651 Two new microanalyses of delafossite from Nizhniĭ Tagil (the type locality) and Kimberly, Nevada, confirm the accepted formula $CuFeO_2$.

delai, -ance, -ment, etc.: see DELAY, etc.

delaine (dɪ'leɪn). [Short for *muslin delaine*, F. *mousseline de laine* lit. 'woollen muslin', so called as being a woollen tissue of great thinness or fineness.] Originally called in full ***mousseline-*** or ***muslin-de-laine***: A kind of light textile fabric, chiefly used for women's dresses; originally made of wool, now more commonly of wool and cotton, and generally printed.

α. **1840** THACKERAY *Shabby Genteel Story* iii. Dressed in a sweet yellow *mousseline de laine*. **1862** *Lond. Rev.* 26 July 87 These were muslin-de-laines.. made with a cotton weft and a woollen warp.

β. **1849** *Glasgow Exam.* 23 June 3/1 A lot of beautiful De Laine dresses. **1860** O. W. HOLMES *Elsie V.* (1887) 78 The poor old green de-laine. **1891** *Leeds Mercury* 25 May 5/2 Pretty gowns of black delaine figured with coloured flower sprays.

delait(e, obs. ff. DELATE, DILATE; obs. Sc. pa. pple. of DELETE.

delaminate (dɪ'læmɪneɪt), *v. Biol.* [f. DE- I. 1, 2 + L. *lāmina* thin plate, leaf, layer: see -ATE[3]. (Cf. L. *dēlāmināre*, to split in two.)] *trans.* and *intr.* To split into separate layers.

1877 HUXLEY *Anat. Inv. Anim.* iii. 157 *note*, In other species of Actinia and in Alcyonium, the planula seems to delaminate.

delamination (dɪlæmɪ'neɪʃən). *Biol.* [n. of action from prec.] The process of splitting into separate layers: *spec.* applied to the formation of the layers of the BLASTODERM (q.v.).

1877 HUXLEY *Anat. Inv. Anim.* iii. 115 *note*, The formation of the gastrula by delamination, or splitting of the walls of an oval shut planula-sac into two layers. **1886** H. SPENCER in *19th Cent.* May 764 The next stage of development.. is reached in two ways—by invagination and by delamination.

delanovite (dɛlə'nəʊvaɪt). *Min.* Also **delanouite** (dɛ'lænuːaɪt). [ad. G. *delanovit*, f. the name of *Delanoue*, French mineralogist: see -ITE[1].] A manganiferous clay of a rose-red colour.

1854 DANA *Syst. Min.* (ed. 4) II. App. 500 Delanovite, *Kenngott*, (Jahrb. k.k. Geol. Reichs., iv, 633).—A reddish amorphous earthy mineral... Kenngott places it near Montmorillonite. **1934** *Mineral. Mag.* XXII. 469 Substances named montmorillonite, as well as others named confolensite, delanouite, stolpenite, erite, severite, &c., show a great variety of composition.

delapidate, etc., obs. form of DILAPIDATE, etc.

[**delapsation**: a spurious word in Webster, copied in subsequent Dicts.: see DELASSATION.]

†**de'lapse**, *sb. Obs. rare.* [ad. L. *dēlaps-us* downfall, descent, f. *dēlābī* (see next).] Falling down, downfall, descent.

c **1630** JACKSON *Creed.* v. xi. Wks. IV. 85 By their delapse into these bodily sinks of corruption. **1657** TOMLINSON *Renou's Disp.* 548 They [comfrey roots].. cohibit the delapse of humours.

delapse (dɪ'læps), *v. Obs.* or *arch.* [f. L. *dēlaps-*, ppl. stem of *dēlābī* to slip or fall down, f. DE- I. 1 + *lābī* to slip, fall.] *intr.* To fall or slip down, descend, sink. *lit.* and *fig.*

1526 *Pilgr. Perf.* (W. de W. 1531) 203 The diuyne fatherly voyce delapsed & commynge downe from his magnifycent glory. **1651** BIGGS *New Disp.* ⁋243 Nature is delapsed into that dotage and folly. **1848** WORNUM in *Lect. Painting by R.A.'s* 79 *note*, Greece.. delapsed into a Roman province.

Hence **de'lapsed** *ppl. a.*

1622 DRAYTON *Poly-olb.* xxviii. (1748) 379 Which Anne deriv'd alone, the right, before all other, Of the delapsed crown, from Philip her fair mother. **1631** J. DONE *Polydoron* 183 Those Delapsed Angells. **1730–6** BAILEY (folio), *Delapsed* [with Physicians], a bearing or falling down of the womb, of the fundament, etc. [An error for DELAPSION of ed. 1721; reproduced in Johnson and some mod. Dicts.] **1819** H. BUSK *Vestriad* III. 423 Am I debas'd, delaps'd, defunct, forsooth, My orb eclips'd, or day-star set, in truth?

†**de'lapsion**. *Obs.* [f. L. type *dēlapsiōn-em*, n. of action f. *dēlābī*, *dēlaps-*: see prec.] A falling down; in *Path.* = prolapsus.

1603 HOLLAND *Plutarch's Mor.* 954 (R.) That the same rays being carried so great a way, should have their frictions, fluxions, and delapsions. **1706** PHILLIPS (ed. Kersey), *Delapsion*, a slipping, sliding or falling down: In the Art of Physick, a falling or bearing down of the Womb, Fundament, Guts, etc. **1721** in BAILEY (cf. prec.).

†**de'lash**, *v. Sc. Obs.* [a. OF. *delacher* 'to discharge' (Cotgr.), in OF. *deslachier*, f. *des-*, *dé-* (DE- I. 2, 6) + *lacher*:—L. *laxāre* to loosen.] *trans.* To discharge, let fly.

1582–8 *Hist. James VI* (1804) 247 A number of English bowmen delashet some arrowes againes the Scotish company. **1590** R. BRUCE *Serm. Sacrament* G iij b (Jam.), Against this ground they delash their artillerie siclike. **1606** BIRNIE *Kirk-Buriall* (1838) 11 To stand out against the thunder-bolts of death delashed by God.

†**de'lassable**, *a. Obs.*[—0] *erron.* **-ible**. [ad. L. *dēlassābilis*.] Capable of being wearied out.

1727 BAILEY vol. II, *Delassible*, that may be tired. **1730–6** —— (folio). Hence **1775** in ASH.

†**dela'ssation**. *Obs. rare*[—1]. [n. of action f. L. *dēlassāre* to weary or tire out, f. *de-*, DE- I. 3 + *lassāre* to weary.] Fatigue, weariness.

1692 RAY *Dissol. World* II. ii. (1732) 102 [The birds] are able to continue longer on the Wing without Delassation. **1727** BAILEY vol. II, *Delassation*, a tiring or wearying.

‖**délassement** (delɑsmɑ̃). [Fr., f. *délasser*, f. *dé-* DE- + *las* weary.] Relaxation.

1804 M. WILMOT *Let.* 8 Aug. (1934) I. 122 The serpantine Mazes of two Polonaizes, which walk (for 'tis no more) is the only *dilassement* one has. **1854** THACKERAY *Newcomes* xxii, Clive (who had taken a trip to Paris with his father, as a *délassement* after the fatigues incident on his great work).. declared the thing was rubbish. **1860** W. H. RUSSELL *Diary India* I. 56 We had the *délassemens* of many meals, and music, and whist, and songs at night. **1906** W. DE MORGAN *Joseph Vance* xxiv. 232 Illusion—hallucination—*délassement* of the senses—that sort of thing.

de'lassitude, *v. nonce-wd.* [DE- II. 2.] *trans.* To deliver or recover from lassitude.

1807 W. IRVING in *Life & Lett.* (1862) I. 163 The.. method by which you delassitude yourself after the fatigues of an evening's campaign.

delate (dɪ'leɪt), *v.* Also 6 *Sc.* delait, 6–7 dilate, 7 *Sc.* deleat. [f. L. *dēlāt-*, ppl. stem of *dēfer-re* to bear or bring away or down, convey, deliver, report, indict, accuse, etc.; with 4, cf. med.L. *dēlātāre* to bring before a judge, indict, accuse, freq. of *dēferre*: see DEFER *v.*[2].

(The stem *lāt-* (**tlāt-*) belongs to a different root (**tlā-*, Gr. τλά-ειν to bear), used to supply defective parts of *ferre*.)]

†**1.** *trans.* To carry down or away, convey to a particular point; = DEFER *v.*[2] 1. *Obs.*

1578 BANISTER *Hist. Man* I. 15 The bone of the cheeke.. hath a round hole.. through which is transmitted a portion of the thyrd coniugation of Sinewes, delated to the Muscles of the nose. **1626** BACON *Sylva* §209 To try exactly the time wherein Sound is Delated.

†**2.** To tender or offer for acceptance or adoption; = DEFER *v.*[2] 2. *Obs.*

c **1555** HARPSFIELD *Divorce Hen. VIII* (1878) 119 This good Bishop did.. refuse the oath delated to him for the confirmation of the said divorce. **1875** POSTE *Gaius* II. Comm. (ed. 2) 224 On the incapacitation of the first heres institutus the inheritance would be instantaneously delated (offered for acceptance) to the heres substitutus or to the successor ab intestato.

†**3.** To hand down or over, transfer; to refer (a matter to any one). *Obs.*

1651 HOWELL *Venice* 201 Which charge and singular trust was delated unto them for their extraordinary prudence. *a* **1659** OSBORN *Characters*, &c. Wks. (1673) 617 The Abstract of all Delated Dignities. *a* **1734** NORTH *Exam.* II. v. §24 (1740) 330 In a Nation that hath Established Laws, all Questions of Right and Wrong are delated to executive Power. **1858** MASSON *Milton* I. 342 The King delates them [Instructions] to the two Archbishops; each Archbishop is to see to their execution by the bishops of his own province.

4. To accuse, bring a charge against, impeach; to inform against; to denounce to a judicial tribunal, *esp.* that of the Scotch ecclesiastical courts.

1515 in *Douglas's Wks.* (1874) I. p. lxi, Comperit Master Gavin Douglas.. and schew how.. he was delatit to be ane evile man in diuers poyntis. **1536** BELLENDEN *Cron. Scot.* (1821) II. 414 Ane wikit limmare.. quhilk was oftimes dilatit of adultry. **1609** SKENE *Reg. Maj.*, *Treat.* 132 Gif he quha is suspect, or delated to haue committed treason, is fugitiue. **1637–50** Row *Hist. Kirk* (1842) 53 He wes delated to the Presbyterie. **1776** JOHNSON in *Boswell*, *Case Jas. Thomson*, If a minister be thus left at liberty to delate sinners from the pulpit.. he may often blast the innocent. **1834** H. MILLER *Scenes & Leg.* xix. (1857) 280 They deliberated together.. on delating her as a witch before the presbytery of Tain. **1863** SALA *Capt. Dangerous* II. iii. 119 He will delate me to the English Resident at Brussels for a Jacobite spy.

b. To report, inform of (an offence, crime, fault).

1582–8 *Hist. James VI* (1804) 107 He imediatlie come to Edinburgh, and thair delaitit his turpitude to the judge criminall. **1605** G. POWEL *Refut. Epist. Puritan-Papist* 28 To punish the crimes delated vnto him. **1605** B. JONSON *Volpone* II. vi, They may delate My slacknesse to my patron. **1848** J. H. NEWMAN *Loss & Gain* II. ix. 208 Facts like these were, in most cases, delated to the Head of the house to which a young man belonged.

5. To relate, report.

a **1639** SPOTTISWOOD *Hist. Ch. Scot.* IV. (1677) 185 He.. delated the matter to the Queen. **1798** T. JEFFERSON *Writ.* (1859) IV. 246 This party division is necessary to induce each to watch and delate to the people the proceedings of the other. **1862** SIR H. TAYLOR *St. Clement's Eve* I. iii, Still of the art itself I spare to speak, Delating but, in quality of witness, The art's practitioners as I have known them.

Hence **de'lated** *ppl. a.*, **de'lating** *vbl. sb.*

1599 JAS. I Βασιλ. Δωρον (1603) 100 The nature and by-past life of the dilated person. **1708** J. CHAMBERLAYNE *St. Gt. Brit.* II. II. iii. (1743) 366 When the delated father, i.e. the man whom the woman chargeth, appears, he is examined. **1820** *Ess. Witchcraft* 9 Their delating of one another, as it is called.

delate, obs. form of DILATE, DELETE.

delatinize, -ed, -ation: see DE- II. 1.

delation (dɪ'leɪʃən). Also 6–7 **dilation**. [ad. L. *dēlātiōn-em* information, accusation, denunciation, n. of action from *dēlāt-*, ppl. stem of *dēferre*: see DELATE *v.*]

†**1.** Conveyance (to a place), transmission. *Obs.*

1578 BANISTER *Hist. Man* I. 33 Holes in these bones for the delation of nourishment. **1626** BACON *Sylva* §129 In Delation of Sounds, the Enclosure of them preserveth them, and causeth them to be heard further. *Ibid.* §149 A plain Dilation of the Sound, from the Teeth to the Instrument of hearing. *Ibid.* §209 It is certain that the Delation of Light is in an Instant.

2. Handing down (to a new possessor), handing over, transference. *Obs.* (exc. in *Rom. Law*).

1681 WHARTON *Epochæ & Æræ* Wks. (1683) 47 The sole delation of the Empire, on Augustus Cæsar, became of happy consequence to the Spaniards. **1875** POSTE *Gaius* II. Comm. (ed. 2) 190 The only title required.. was the overture or delation of the inheritance and vacancy of possession.

3. An accusing or bringing a charge against, *esp.* on the part of an informer; informing against; accusation, denouncement, criminal information.

1578 *Sc. Poems 16th C.* II. 183 Priests, burne na ma, Of wrang delation ye may hyre.. And let abjuring go. **1604** SHAKS. *Oth.* III. iii. 123 Such things.. in a man that's iust, They're close dilations [so F. 1, Q. 2, 3; Q. 1 denotements] working from the heart, That Passion cannot rule. **1621** *Reliq. Wotton.* (1672) 307 Three Gentlemen.. who receive all secret Delations on matter of practice against the Republick. *a* **1639** SPOTTISWOOD *Hist. Ch. Scot.* II. (1677) 103 Upon some envious delations the King became jealous of him. **1790** BURKE *Fr. Rev.* Wks. V. 372 That court is to try criminals sent to it by the national assembly, or brought before it by other courses of delation. **1862** MERIVALE *Rom. Emp.* (1865) VII. lxii. 386 In criminal cases.. the interference of a mere stranger was unauthorized delation. **1893** *Dublin Rev.* July 649 His [Abbé Dupin's] delation to the Archbishop of Paris by Bossuet.

delation, obs. var. of DILATION, delay.

delative, obs. form of DILATIVE.

delator (dɪ'leɪtə(r)). Also 6 **delatour**, 7 **-later**, **-laiter**; 6–7 **di-**. [a. L. *dēlātor* informer, accuser, denouncer, agent-n. of *dēferre* (ppl. stem *dēlāt-*): see DELATE *v.*] An informer, a secret or professional accuser.

a **1572** KNOX *Hist. Ref.* Wks. (1846) I. 81 Whosoevir wald delaite any of heresye, he was heard: no respect nor consideratioun had what mynd the delatour bayre to the persone delated. **1598** STOW *Surv.* xliii. (1603) 472 In this Court he heard those that are delators or informers in popular and penal actions. **1649** BP. HALL *Cases Consc.* II. vii. 134 Hence it is that Delators, and Informers, have in all happy and well-governed States, been ever held an infamous and odious kind of Cattell. **1776** GIBBON *Decl. & F.* I. xiv. 311 A formidable army of sycophants and delators. **1874** FARRAR *Christ* II. lx. 387 There might be secret delators in that very mob.

delator, -our, obs. forms of DILATOR, a delay.

dela'torian, *a. nonce-wd.* [f. DELATOR after *prætorian*.] Of informers or spies.

1818 MOORE *Fudge Fam. Paris* Pref., That Delatorian Cohort which Lord S—dm—th.. has organized.

†**de'latory**, *a. Obs.* [ad. L. *dēlātōri-us*, f. *dēlātor*: see prec. and -ORY.] Of the nature of criminative information or accusation.

1608 BP. HALL *Char. Virtues & V.* II. 83 (*Busie-Bodie*) There can no Act passe without his Comment, which is ever far-fetch't, rash, suspicious, delatorie. **1609** BP. W. BARLOW *Answ. Nameless Cath.* 107 Which delight in such Calumniations, and vse those Delatory accusations.

delatory, obs. form of DILATORY.

delature, obs. var. of DILATURE, delay.

†**de'lavy, des-, di-, dis-**, *a. Obs.* Also **-lavee**, **lavé**. [a. OF. *deslavé* washed away, overflowed, like a flood or inundation, f. *des-*:—L. *dis-* + *lavé* washed.

The OF. word had also the sense '*un*washed (DE- I. 6), befouled, dirty', retained in Swiss Romance; and perhaps this was present in some of the English examples under sense 2.]

1. Of floods: Overflowing, abundant.

a **1400–50** *Alexander* 1351 (MS. D.) þar flowe owt of fresh wynne flodez enowe, So largly & so delavy [MS. A. delauyly].

2. Of speech or behaviour: Going beyond bounds, immoderate, unbridled, dissolute.

c **1380** WYCLIF *Wks.* (1880) 306 þise freris ben doumbe.. when þei shulde speke.. but þei ben dilauy in heere tungis, in gabbyngis & other iapis. —— *Sel. Wks.* III. 388 [Freris] ben moste dislavy of hor veyn speche and worldly. *c* **1386** CHAUCER *Pars. T.* 555 As seith Salamon, The amyable tonge is the tree of lyf.. and soothly a deslauee [*v.r.* deslaue, dislave, disselaue; Vulg. *Prov.* xv. 4, *immoderata*] tonge sleeth the spirites of hym that repreueth and eek of hym that is repreued. *Ibid.* 760 Mesure also, that restreyneth by reson the deslauee [*v.r.* dislave, delaue, delavy] appetit of etynge. *c* **1422** HOCCLEVE *Jereslaus' Wife* 901 A shipman which was a foul lecchour.. to his contree Him shoop lede hire this man delauee.

Hence †**de'lavily** *adv.* [see above, sense 1]; †**de'laviness.**

c **1380** WYCLIF *Serm.* Sel. Wks. II. 298 Dilavynesse of tunge in spekinge wordis oþer þan Goddis is passynge fro good religioun. **1447** BOKENHAM *Seyntys* (Roxb.) 156 Mary Mawdelyn.. hir youthe in dislavynesse Of hir body so unshamefastly She dispendyd. *a* **1500** *Prose Legends* in *Anglia* VIII. 168, I shent myselfe wiþ so grete delauynesse, turnynge to my-selfe after þe sermon.

Delaware ('dɛləwɛə(r)). [f. the name of an American river (see quot. 1832).] **a.** A member of an Algonquian Indian people, formerly inhabiting the basin of the Delaware river. **b.** The language of this people. Also *attrib.*

1709 *Penn. Col. Rec.* (1852) II. 469 Chiefs of the Delaware Indians, settled at Peshtang above Conestogoe. **1721** *Doc. Col. Hist. N.Y.* (1855) V. 623 All the English.. have.. in Jersey & Pennsylvania, their own or home nations, called Delawares, [who] are exceedingly decreased. *a* **1762** S. NILES *Wars* in *Mass. Hist. Soc. Coll.* (1861) 4th Ser. V. II. 430 A large party of Delaware Indians. *a* **1772** J. WOOLMAN *Jrnl.* (1778) 201 None of them were quite perfect in the English and Delaware tongues. **1826** J. F. COOPER *Last of Mohicans* I. iv. 69 Look to a Delaware, or a Mohican, for a warrior! *Ibid.* 75 They spoke together earnestly in the Delaware language. *Ibid.* viii. 169 He spoke in Delaware. **1832** S. A. FERRALL *Ramble thro' U.S.* 46 The Lenni Lenape, or Delawares, as they were called by the English, from the circumstance of their holding their great 'Council-fire' on the banks of the Delaware river. **1877** L. H. MORGAN *Ancient Society* II. ii. 73 The number of gentes.. varied in the different tribes, from three among the Delawares.. to upwards of twenty among the Ojibwas. **1933** BLOOMFIELD *Lang.* iv. 72 The Algonquian family.. includes the languages.. of New England (.. Mohican, and so on, with Delaware to the south). **1965** *Canad. Jrnl. Linguistics* Spring 135 Some Algonquians.. now speak.. Delaware in Oklahoma.

delay (dɪ'leɪ), *sb.* Forms: 3–6 delaie, 3–7 delaye, 4 delai, (4–6 dilaye, 5 deley, delee), 3– delay. [ME. a. F. *délai* (12th c. in Littré), also in OF. *delei, deloi,* Cotgr. (1611) *delay,* f. OF. *delaier,* in mod.F. *dilayer*: see DELAY *v.* (Not immediately cognate with It. *dilata.*)]

1. a. The action of delaying; the putting off or deferring of action, etc.; procrastination, loitering; waiting, lingering.

1297 R. GLOUC. (1724) 421 Somme feynede a delay, & somme al out wyþ seyde. *c* **1380** WYCLIF *Wks.* (1880) 305 þei seken.. fals dilayes to lette knowyng of treuþe. **1413** LYDG. *Pilgr. Sowle* I. xviii. (1859) 18 Thou shalt nought with such delayes and excepcyons escape. **1548** HALL *Chron.* 241 b, Sent Ambassadors.. with faire woordes, and frivolous delaies. **1583** HOLLYBAND *Campo di Fior* 47 To do so great an enterprise, I make no delay. **1600** SHAKS. *A.Y.L.* III. ii. 207 One inch of delay more, is a South-sea of discouerie; I pre'thee tell me, who is it quickely. **1602** —— *Ham.* III. i. 72 For who would beare.. the Lawes delay, The insolence of Office. *a* **1628** PRESTON *New Covt.* (1634) 435 Delay in all things is dangerous, but procrastination in takeing the offer of Grace, is the most dangerous thing in the World. **1678** OTWAY *Friendship in F.* 39 Come, come, delayes are dangerous. **1887** BOWEN *Virg. Æneid* VI. 846 Fabius thou, whose timely delays gave strength to the state.

b. The fact of being delayed or kept waiting for a time; hindrance to progress.

1748 F. SMITH *Voy. Disc. N.-W. Pass.* I. 79 These Delays from the Wind.. were a great Check to [our] Hopes. **1875** JOWETT *Plato* (ed. 2) I. 384 There will be a delay of a day.

c. *spec. Electr.* (See quot. 1940.)

1930 *Bell Syst. Techn. Jrnl.* IX. 571 The transmission delay suffered by different portions of the frequency band must also be considered. This is necessary because.. this delay tends to be different for different parts of the frequency band and the distortion produced is a function of the frequency-delay characteristics. **1937** W. L. EVERITT *Communication Engin.* (ed. 2) i. 23 *Delay Distortion*.. occurs when the phase angle of the transfer impedance with respect to two chosen pairs of terminals is not linear with frequency .. thus making the time of transmission or delay vary with frequency. **1940** *Chambers's Techn. Dict.* 231/1 *Delay*, the time taken for a signal to travel from one end of an electrical communication system to the other, or along a part of such system. **1956** AMOS & BIRKINSHAW *T.V. Engin.* II. i. 20 The signal takes a finite time, usually termed delay, to pass through the amplifier. **1967** *Electronics* 6 Mar. 165/2 Circuit delay, meaning propagation delay due to the IC alone, is usually expressed on IC data sheets as t_p, but we reserve t_p for the propagation delay... We call this 'system logic delay'.

2. *Phrases.* **a.** *without delay*: without waiting, immediately, at once.

c **1275** LAY. 17480 þat hii come to Ambres-buri wiþ houte delaie. **1375** BARBOUR *Bruce* III. 388 He thocht, but mar delay, In-to þe manland till arywe. **1382** WYCLIF *Acts* xxv. 17 Withoute ony delay.. I.. comaundide the man for to be ladd to. *c* **1420** *Avow. Arth.* (Camden) xxii, He wold pay my rawnnsone With-owtyn delees. **1548** HALL *Chron.* 214 Without delay they armed them selfe, and came to defende the gates. **1747** WESLEY *Prim. Physic* (1762) p. xxvi, Without Delay to apply to a Physician that fears God. *Mod.* I must return without delay.

†**b.** *to put* or *set in delay*: to delay, defer, put off. *Obs.*

1393 GOWER *Conf.* I. 274 The sentence of that ilke day May none appele sette in delay. *c* **1470** HENRY *Wallace* VIII. 704 And thus thai put the battaill on delay. **1490** CAXTON *Eneydos* xxi. 77, I requyre only that he putte this thyng in delaye for a certayn space of tyme.

3. *attrib.*, as **delay-shop**; **delay action** = *delayed action*; **delay cable, line,** a device producing a desired delay in the transmission of an electrical or other signal, used esp. in computers.

1879 *Man. Siege & Garr. Artill. Exerc.* II. 51 Delay Action for base of Battering Shell. **1900** *Daily News* 11 Apr. 5/6 Delay-action projectiles. **1928** in C. F. S. Gamble *N. Sea Air Station* xv. 280, 100-lb. bombs with 2½ seconds delay fuses. **1940** *Chambers's Techn. Dict.* 231/1 The surge .. travels along the delay cable. **1941** S. R. ROGET *Dict. Electr. Terms* (ed. 4) 87/2 *Delay cable*, a cable of special characteristics by which a transmission line is connected to a surge measuring instrument to cause a time lag. **1947** *Electronics* Nov. 136/1 The system of storage used with delay lines depends upon timed distribution of the electrical impulses that represent the information. **1947** EMSLIE & MCCONNELL in L. N. Ridenour *Radar System Engin.* xvi. 667 The simplest delay line is a straight tube with parallel transducers at the end. **1958** *New Biol.* XXVI. 106 A typical storage system for a digital computer is what is called a 'delay line storage'. This is made up of tubes filled with mercury that carry pulses... These pulses travel up and down the mercury tube in a special order where the presence of a pulse stands for 1 and its absence for 0; then a whole collection of those 0s and 1s, say 001 101 10, may represent an instruction word in coded form, or a number on which the instruction will operate. **1962** N. H. CODLING in G. A. T. Burdett *Autom. Control Handbk.* viii. 41 A specialised cable type which finds applications in pulse-forming circuits for computers is the helically wound delay line. Delay cables have a very high inductance. **1964** C. DENT *Quantity Surveying by Computer* iii. 19 Delay line storage comprises units which store binary digits in the form of pulses, which are kept circulating in specially designed circuits called delay lines. **1965** *Economist* 13 Feb. 592/2 At the [colour TV] receiver the first two-colour signal is stored in a delay-line to await the arrival of the second, and the two are then combined. **1970** *Physics Bull.* July 306/2 The acoustic delay lines used in some of the earliest computers. **1810** BENTHAM *Packing* (1821) 264 Observing the House of Lords to have.. become, in respect of its appellate jurisdiction, converted into a sort of delay-shop.

delay (dɪ'leɪ), *v.*[1] Forms: 3 delaiȝen, 3–6 delaie(n, (4 deley, dylaye), 4–6 delaye, 3– delay. [ME. a. OF. *delaier, delayer* (also *deleer, deleier, deloier, desl-, dell-, dil-, dal-, dol-*, to put off (an event, or person), to retard, to defer; in mod.F. *dilayer* (16th c. in Littré and Hatzf.), but *delayer* in Cotgr. 1611.

The derivation of the F. word is difficult. The sense is that of late L. *dīlātāre* (Du Cange), freq. of *differre* to defer, delay, put off; but this does not account for the actual form, since it could only give an OF. *dileer* or (with Rom. prefix) *desleer.*]

1. *trans.* To put off to a later time; to defer, postpone. †*to delay time*: to put off time.

c **1290** *S. Eng. Leg.* I. 87/30 And bide þat he it delaiȝe Ane þreo ȝer. **1297** R. GLOUC. (1724) 513 Me nolde nouȝt, that is crouninge leng delaied were. **1393** GOWER *Conf.* III. 290 For to make him afered, The kinge his time hath so delaied. **1489** CAXTON *Faytes of A.* I. xxii. 68 To delaye the bataylle vnto another day. **1586** B. YOUNG *Guazzo's Civ. Conv.* IV. 181 b, Delaie the sentence no longer. **1594** WEST *2nd Pt. Symbol.* Chancerie § 140 Who.. with faire promises delaied time, and kept the said C. D. in hope from yeare to yeare. **1611** BIBLE *Matt.* xxiv. 48 My Lord delayeth his comming. **1737** POPE *Hor. Epist.* I. i. 41 Th' unprofitable moments.. That.. still delay Life's instant business to a future day. **1821** SHELLEY *Prometh. Unb.* III. iii. 6 Freedom long desired And long delayed. **1847** GROTE *Greece* I. xl. (1862) III. 433 He delayed the attack for four days.

b. with *infin.* To defer, put off.

a **1340** HAMPOLE *Psalter* vi. 3 How lange dylayes þou to gif grace. **1611** BIBLE *Ex.* xxxii. 1 When the people saw that Moses delayed to come downe. **1799** COWPER *Castaway* v, Some succour.. [they] Delayed not to bestow. **1847** TENNYSON *Princ.* iv. 88 Delaying as the tender ash delays To clothe herself, when all the woods are green.

†**c.** With personal object: To put (any one) off, to keep him waiting. *Obs.*

1388 WYCLIF *Acts* xxiv. 22 Felix delayede hem. **1512** *Act 4 Hen. VIII*, c. 6 § 2 If.. the same Collectours.. unreasonably delay or tary the said Marchauntes. **1530** PALSGR. 510/1, I delaye one, or deferre hym, or put hym backe of his purpose. **1639** DU VERGER tr. *Camus' Admir. Events* 88 It was not fit shee should delay him with faire wordes. **1768** BLACKSTONE *Comm.* III. 109 Where judges of any court do delay the parties.

2. To impede the progress of, cause to linger or stand still; to retard, hinder.

1393 GOWER *Conf.* III. 261 Her wo to telle thanne assaieth, But tendre shame her word delaieth. **1634** MILTON *Comus* 494 Thyrsis! whose artful strains have oft delayed The huddling brook to hear his madrigal. **1709** STEELE *Tatler* No. 39 ¶ 4 Joy and Grief can hasten and delay Time. **1813** SHELLEY *Q. Mab* II. 197 The unwilling sojourner, whose steps Chance in that desert has delayed. **1856** KANE *Arct. Expl.* II. xv. 161 To delay the animal until the hunters come up.

3. *intr.* To put off action; to linger, loiter, tarry.

1509 HAWES *Past. Pleas.* XVI. lxix, A womans guyse is evermore to delaye. **1596** SHAKS. *1 Hen. IV*, III. ii. 180 Aduantage feedes him fat, while men delay. **1667** MILTON *P.L.* v. 247 So spake th' Eternal Father.. nor delaid the winged Saint After his charge receivd. **1850** TENNYSON *In Mem.* lxxxiii, O sweet new-year delaying long.. Delaying long, delay no more.

b. To tarry in a place. (Now only *poetic.*)

1654 H. L'ESTRANGE *Chas. I* (1655) 3 Paris being.. in his way to Spain, he delaid there one day. *a* **1878** BRYANT *Poems, October*, Wind of the sunny south! oh still delay, In the gay woods and in the golden air.

c. To be tardy in one's progress, to loiter.

1690 LOCKE *Hum. Und.* II. xiv. § 9 There seem to be certain bounds to the quickness and slowness of the succession of those ideas.. beyond which they can neither delay nor hasten.

†**de'lay**, *v.*[2] *Obs.* Forms: (6 delaye, deley), 6–7 delaie, delay, (dilay). [a. F. *délayer* (13th c. in Hatzf.), in Cotgr. *deslayer* 'to supple, soften, allay, soake, steepe', *delayer* 'to macerate, allay or soften by steeping, &c.; also to make thin', in OF. *desleier, desloier*, app. = Pr. *deslegar*, It. *dileguare*, Sp. *desleir*:—Rom. **dis-ligare*, to unbind, disunite, f. L. DIS- with separative force + *ligāre* to bind. Cf. ALLAY *v.*[1] III, and ALLAY *v.*[2]]

1. *trans.* To weaken by admixture (as wine with water); to dilute, temper, qualify; = ALLAY *v.*[1] 14, 15.

1543 TRAHERON *Vigo's Chirurg.* 35 b/1 His wyne must be claret delaied. **1562** BULLEYN *Bk. Simples* 24 b, The same water is wholsome to delaie wine. **1616** SURFL. & MARKH. *Country Farme* 419 Dilay it with sufficient quantitie of Fountaine water. **1624** R. DAVENPORT *City Nightcap* I. in Hazl. *Dodsley* XIII. 114 She can drink a cup of wine not delayed with water.

fig. **1565** JEWEL *Def. Apol.* (1611) 248 Allowing the words, he thought it best.. to delay, and qualify the same with some Construction.

b. To debase (coin) by admixture of alloy; = ALLAY *v.*[2] 1.

1586 SIR E. HOBY *Pol. Disc. Truth* xlix. 239 They.. which clippe, waste and delaye coyne.

2. To mitigate, assuage, quench; = ALLAY *v.*[1] 8, 11.

1530 PALSGR. 510/2 This is a soverayne medycine for it hath delayed my payne in lesse than halfe an hour. **1578** LYTE *Dodoens* IV. lvii. 518 It delayeth the swelling of them that have the Dropsie. **1590** SPENSER *F.Q.* III. xii. 42 Those dreadfull flames she also found delayd And quenched. **1603** HOLLAND *Plutarch's Mor.* 19 The mingling of water with wine, delaieth and taketh away the hurtfull force thereof.

3. To soak, steep, macerate. *rare.*

1578 LYTE *Dodoens* VI. xxx. 697 Of the same beries [of Buckthorn].. soked or delayed in Allom water, they make a fayre yellowe colour. **1580** HOLLYBAND *Treas. Fr. Tong, Desléer*, and *destremper*, to soake, to deley.

de'layable, *a.* *rare.* [f. DELAY *v.*[1] or *sb.* + -ABLE.] That may be delayed; subject to delay.

1760–72 H. BROOKE *Fool of Qual.* (1792) II. 118 Law thus divisible, debateable, and delayable.

de'layal. *rare.* [f. DELAY *v.*[1] + -AL[1]: cf. *betrayal.*] The action of delaying; retardation.

1890 J. HUTCHINSON *Archives Surg.* 228 The delayal of venous circulation.

†**de'layance.** *Obs.* Also 4 delaiance. [a. OF. *delaiance, delayance* (Godef.), f. *delayer* to DELAY: see -ANCE.] Delaying, delay.

a **1300** *Cursor M.* 26135 (Cott.) Him reu his sinnes sare, and for-think his lang delaiance. **1625** tr. *Boccaccio's Decameron* II. 134 How little delayance.. ought to be in such as would not have an enchantment to be hindered.

delayed (dɪ'leɪd), *ppl. a.*[1] [f. DELAY *v.*[1] + -ED[1].]

a. Deferred, retarded, etc.: see the verb.

1552 HULOET, Delayed, *comperendinatus, procrastinatus, tardatus.* **1879** B. TAYLOR *Stud. Germ. Lit.* 170 It was only a delayed, not a prevented growth. **1880** JEFFERIES *Gt. Estate* 195 Nothing was said about the delayed visit.

b. In specific collocations, as *delayed action*: an action that is delayed, esp. for a particular purpose; an arrangement or device that delays an action; freq. *attrib.*, as *delayed-action bomb*, a bomb that explodes some time after it has struck the target; *delayed-action fuse*, a fuse that delays the detonation of a charge until some time after the projectile has struck the target; *delayed drop, jump*: a parachute jump in which the parachutist delays longer than usual before pulling the rip-cord; *delayed neutron*: a neutron emitted by a nucleus which has been left in an excited state following the decay or fission of its parent nucleus; *delayed shock*: shock (see SHOCK *sb.*[3] 5) that appears a considerable time after the event(s) that produced it; also *transf.*

1892 *Chambers's Jrnl.* 560/1 A *delayed-action fuse. **1909** *Westm. Gaz.* 2 Jan. 13/3 The thickest armour-plate can now be pierced by projectiles fitted with a delayed-action fuse. **1936** F. J. MORTIMER *Wall's Dict. Photogr.* (ed. 14) 175 *Delayed action.* Many shutters on modern cameras.. are now made with a 'delayed action' adjustment. **1940** *Manch. Guardian Weekly* 10 May 362 The debate will prepare an explosion that will go off like a delayed-action bomb in about three weeks' time. **1942** *Aeronautics* June 62/1 Reaching their objective, dropped delayed-action bombs on their targets. **1958** *Listener* 20 Nov. 812/1 The electoral delayed action of those events as it works itself out will be even more difficult to detect and disentangle. **1962** G. LAWTON *John Wesley's English* 162 We find effective delayed-action mechanism such as: 'Indeed if thou canst save the soul of another, do; but at least save one,—thy own.' **1967** *Gloss. Sanitation Terms (B.S.I.)* 59 *Delayed action ballvalve*... The opening of the ballvalve is delayed until the water level in the cistern has fallen through a fixed distance. **1942** A. M. LOW *Parachutes* iv. 60 A *delayed drop of 200 feet. **1946** W. F. BURBIDGE *From Balloon to Bomber* 43 The belief that a person lost consciousness during a parachute descent was widely held until delayed drops proved the contrary. **1942** A. M. LOW *Parachutes* iv. 60 The only really effective method of testing the matter was by a series of *delayed jumps. **1941** M. GOWING *Britain & Atomic Energy 1939–1945* (1964) App. ii. 406 There are a few '*delayed' neutrons arising from products of the fission process. **1950** *Effects of Atomic Weapons* 240 More than 99 percent of the total number of neutrons accompanying the fission of uranium 235 or plutonium 239 are released almost immediately, probably within 10^{-8} second of the explosion. These are referred to as the *prompt neutrons*. In addition, somewhat less than 1 percent, called the *delayed neutrons*, are emitted subsequently. **1963** W. E. BURCHAM *Nuclear Physics* 703 A β-process may leave a product nucleus so highly excited that neutron emission is a predominant alternative to β^--decay. An emission of delayed neutrons, with a half-life corresponding to that of the preceding β-emitter, then ensues. **1938** DORLAND & MILLER *Med. Dict.* (ed. 18) 1272/2 **Delayed shock*, severe physical or mental disturbance, of which the symptoms occur a considerable time after the injury or mental impression is received. **1961** *Guardian* 29 May 12/6 The 'delayed shock' of the state's worst drought on record in 1959–60.

† **de'layed**, *ppl. a.*² *Obs.* [f. DELAY *v.*² + -ED¹.] Diluted, weakened by admixture; also *transf.* of colours.

1543 TRAHERON *Vigo's Chirurg.* II. xix. 29 Ye may gyve hym also delayed wine of small strength. **1597** GERARDE *Herbal* I. xcvii. §2. 155 A fine delaied purple colour. **1610** HOLLAND *Camden's Brit.* (1637) 476 Somewhat yellowish like delayed gold. **1688** R. HOLME *Armoury* II. 295 Of a delayed chestnut-colour.

delayer (dɪˈleɪə(r)). Now *rare*. [f. DELAY *v.*¹ + -ER¹. Cf. OF. *delayeur, dilayeur*.] One who (or that which) delays.

1. One who lingers or tarries; one who puts off doing something, a procrastinator.

1531 ELYOT *Gov.* I. xxiv, Called..*Fabius Cunctator*, that is to saye the tariar or delayer. **1653** HOLCROFT *Procopius* III. 81 Being no Souldier, a coward, and an extreame delayer. **1748** RICHARDSON *Clarissa* (1811) IV. 92 To quicken the delayer in his resolutions. **1890** *Blackw. Mag.* CXLVII. 267 The dear delayers Whose part is over, but they do not go.

† **b.** with *inf.* One who delays *to do* something. *Obs. rare.*

1640–1 *Kirkcudbr. War-Comm. Min. Bk.* (1855) 93 Refuisers or delayers to mak peyment. **1653** BAXTER *Chr. Concord* xix. B ij b, Delayers or deniers to consent to the matter.

2. (With obj. genitive.) One who (or that which) retards or hinders; one who puts off or defers.

1514 BARCLAY *Cyt. & Uplondyshm.* (Percy Soc.) 32 Cratchers of coyne, delayers of processe. **1642** ROGERS *Naaman* 26 The furtherer or delayer of his owne grace. *a* **1745** SWIFT *Char. Hen. II*, Wks. 1824 X. 391 A delayer of justice. **1888** *Pall Mall G.* 16 Jan. 6/1 He was a Yankee inventor. He had patented early-rising machines, burglar delayers..and..other curious appliances.

† **de'layful**, *a. Obs. rare.* [f. DELAY *sb.* + -FUL.] Full of or characterized by delay; dilatory.

1600 HOLLAND *Livy* XXVII. xxi. 644 By whose cold and delayfull proceedings..Anniball now these ten yeares had remained in Italie. **1615** CHAPMAN *Odyss.* IV. 1041 Now the ..queen Will surely satiate her delayful spleen.

delaying (dɪˈleɪɪŋ), *vbl. sb.*¹ The action of DELAY *v.*¹, q.v.; putting off, tarrying, etc.; delay.

a **1340** HAMPOLE *Psalter* xii. 1 Haly men..plenand þaim of delaiynge. *c* **1440** HYLTON *Scala Perf.* (W. de W. 1494) II. vii, And thenne..wythoute ony delayenge he forgeuyth the synne. *c* **1500** *Melusine* 144 Goo we thenne..without dylayeng. **1583** STUBBES *Anat. Abus.* II. (1882) 9 This deferring and delaieng of poore mens causes. **1659** GAUDEN *Tears of Ch.* 235 Few do pay them without delayings, defalkings, and defraudings. *Mod.* By delaying he has lost his chance.

† **de'laying**, *vbl. sb.*² *Obs.* Allaying, tempering; alloying: see DELAY *v.*²

1473 WARKW. *Chron.* 4 The same ryolle was put viij. d. of aley, and so weyed viij. d. more by delaynge. **1549** *Latimer's 3rd Serm. bef. Edw. VI* (Arb.) 86 *margin*, Scrupulous..in delayinge of hys wyne wyth water.

de'laying, *ppl. a.* That delays: see DELAY *v.*¹

1649 BP. GUTHRIE *Mem.* (1702) 74 Yet did his Majesty give it a fair and delaying answer, until the meeting of the Peers.

Hence **de'layingly** *adv.*

1864 TENNYSON *En. Ard.* 465 And yet she held him on delayingly With many a scarce-believable excuse.

† **de'layment.** *Obs.* Also 4 delaiement. [ME. a. OF. *delaie-, delayement* (also *delee-, delie-, deloie-*), f. *delayer* to DELAY *v.*¹ + -MENT.] The action of delaying; delay.

1393 GOWER *Conf.* II. 9 He made non delaiement, But goth him home. **1483** CAXTON *Gold. Leg.* 237/2 He..blamed hym greuously of his delayment and necligence.

† **de'layous**, *a. Obs. rare.* [a. OF. *delaieus*, f. *delai* sb., DELAY: see -OUS.] Given to, or characterized by, delay; dilatory.

1469 SIR J. PASTON in *Lett.* II. No. 619. 368 Ye delt wythe ryght delayous peple. **1494** FABYAN *Chron.* VI. cliii. 140 The parlyament of Fraunce..is lyke vnto the Court of requestys ..in Englonde. How be it that is of moche gretter resorte of people, and therwith veray delayous.

‖ **del credere** (del ˈkrɛdere), *attrib.* and *adv. phr. Comm.* [It. = 'of belief, of trust,' f. *del* of the, *credere* to believe, believing, belief, trust.] A phrase expressing the obligation undertaken by a factor, broker, or commission merchant, when he guarantees and becomes responsible for the solvency of the persons to whom he sells. Hence ***del credere agent, account***, etc.

on del credere terms is a very common heading to invoices of goods sent to agents in foreign or colonial places. ***del credere commission***: see quot. 1849.

1797 *Jacob's Law Dict.*, *Del Credere*, a commission *del credere* is an undertaking by an insurance-broker, for an additional premium, to insure his principal against the contingency of the failure of the under-writer. **1849** FREESE *Comm. Class-bk.* 48 Under the item Charges, must be included a charge for guaranteeing the debt, called *Delcredere* or guarantee commission, when the consignee makes himself responsible for the prompt payment of the debt. **1891** *Law Times* XCI. 224/1 Nor is there any general presumption of law which fixes the broker with liability as a *del credere* agent.

‖ **dele** (ˈdiːliː). [L. *dēlē*, 2nd sing. pres. imper. act. of *dēlēre* to DELETE; but perh. sometimes an abbreviation of *deleatur*.] = DELEATUR, or imperatively, 'Delete (the letter, etc. marked)'. Also as *sb.*, an instance of the use of the sign so called.

Commonly indicated by a *d* with a twisted and crossed head (₰).

1727–51 CHAMBERS *Cycl.* s.v. *Correction*, There are different characters used to express different corrections, *v.gr.* D or δ *dele* for anything to be effaced, or left out. **1821** DIBDIN *Bibliogr., etc. Tour* I. 129, I could discover..that.. he wished me to..leave him to his *deles* and *stets*! **1841** in SAVAGE *Dict. Printing.* **1963** V. NABOKOV *Gift* iv. 258 To take but the word 'I', *ya* (formed in Russian script somewhat like a proof-reader's dele).

Hence **dele**, *v.* = DELETE *v.* 2.

1705 S. SEWALL *Diary* 24 Dec. (1879) II. 150, I deled the Title, *In Obitum Crucis.* **1765** *N. Carolina Col. Rec.* (1890) VII. 81 To the *deleing* the Clause..we..agree. **1869** R. MORRIS *Spenser's Wks.* App. i. 689/2 The comma after ape should be deled.

dele, obs. form of DEAL.

† **de'league, de'legue**, *v. Obs.* [a. F. *déléguer* (3rd sing. pres. *délègue*), 15th c. in Hatzf., ad. L. *dēlēgāre* to DELEGATE.] = DELEGATE *v.*

1567 THROGMORTON *Let.* in Robertson *Hist. Scotl.* (1759) II. App. 43 A number of persons deleagued, and authorized by her. **1623** FAVINE *Theat. Hon.* I. iv. 26 They delegued Great Pompey, to goe and make Warre. *Ibid.* III. vii. 394 The Gentlemen deleagued by the said Commissaries.

deleat(e, obs. form of DELATE *v.*, DELETE *v.*

‖ **deleatur** (diːliːˈeɪtə(r)). [L. = 'let it be deleted'; 3rd sing. pres. subj. passive of *dēlēre* to blot out, delete.] A written direction or mark on a printed proof-sheet directing something to be struck out or omitted; hence *fig.*

1602 PARSONS *Warn-Word, &c.* II. ix. 70 b (Stanf.), We pervert..the ancient Fathers with the censure of *deleatur* when any sentence lyketh us not. **1640** SIR E. DERING *Sp. on Relig.* 23 Nov. iii. 7 The most learned labours of our.. Divines, must bee..defaced with a *Deleatur.* **1696** EVELYN *Let. to W. Wotton* 28 Oct., *Deleatur*, therefore, wherever you meet it.

† **de'leave**, *v. Obs. nonce-wd.* [f. DE- II. 2 + LEAF, pl. *leaves*.] *trans.* To strip off (leaves); to defoliate.

1591 HARINGTON *Orl. Fur.* XXXVII. xxxi, Thrise haue the leaues with winter been deleaued.

deleble, var. of DELIBLE.

† **de'lect**, *v. Obs.* [ad. L. *dēlectāre* to DELIGHT.] = DELIGHT *v.* (*trans.* and *intr.*)

1530 R. WHYTFORD *Werke for Householders* H ij, Yf you.. begyn somwhat to delecte in theyr maters, I advyse you dissymule. **1588** A. KING tr. *Canisius' Catech.* 211 The thing in this lyf that delects indures bot a moment.

delectability (dɪlɛktəˈbɪlɪtɪ). [ad. OF. *delectableté*, f. *delectable*: see next and -ITY. The earlier OF. was *delitableté*, whence DELITABILITY.] The quality of being delectable; delectableness; *concr.* (in *pl.*) delectable things; delights.

c **1440** *Gesta Rom.* lii. 232 (Harl. MS.) þe worlde, that bihotithe to thé swetnesse & dilectabilites. **1834** BECKFORD *Italy* II. 336, I have heard of this court and its delectabilities. **1856** *Lamps of Temple* (ed. 3) 119 We will look..at the delectabilities of these three volumes. **1886** HOLMAN HUNT in *Contemp. Rev.* June 827 Looking at the picture as a picture should always be regarded—for its delectability to the eye.

delectable (dɪˈlɛktəb(ə)l), *a.* [ME. a. OF. *delectable*, ad. L. *dēlectābilis*, f. *dēlectāre* to DELIGHT: see -ABLE. The earlier popular form in OF. was *delitable*, DELITABLE.

In Shaks. and P. Fletcher still stressed '*delectable*.]

Affording delight; delightful, pleasant.

Now little used in ordinary speech, except ironically or humorously; used seriously in poetry and elevated prose.

c **1400** MAUNDEV. (1839) xiv. 155 A gret contree and a fulle delectable. **14..** *Tundale's Vis.* 1782 Musyk clere That full delectabull was to here. **1529** MORE *Comf. agst. Trib.* III. Wks. 1216/2 Delectable allectiues to moue a manne to synne. **1555** EDEN *Decades* 75 Suche newes and presentes as they brought were delectable to the kinge. **1578** LYTE *Dodoens* IV. lxxvi. 540 Woodrowe flowreth in May, and then is the smell most delectable. **1646** SIR T. BROWNE *Pseud. Ep.* I. viii, Athenæus, a delectable Author. **1667** MILTON *P.L.* VII. 539 Trees of God, Delectable both to behold and taste. **1684** BUNYAN *Pilgr.* II. 165 The Shepherds there, who welcomed them..unto the delectable Mountains. **1759** STERNE *Trist. Shandy* I. xi, Of which original journey..a most delectable narrative will be given in the progress of this work. **1838–9** HALLAM *Hist. Lit.* II. v. II. 230 *note*, For the beautiful lines in the second eclogue of Virgil we have this delectable hexametric version. **1871** R. ELLIS *Catullus* lxiv. 31 When the delectable hour those days did fully determine. **1880** H. JAMES *Benvolio* III. 372 The old man had told him that he had a delectable voice. *Mod. Advt.* Delectable Lozenges, for clearing the throat.

de'lectableness. [f. prec. + -NESS.] The quality of being delectable; delightfulness.

1526 *Pilgr. Perf.* (W. de W. 1531) 280 b, The swetnes & delectablenes of this gyfte aboue all yᵉ moost swete thynges. **1555** EDEN *Decades* 132 Pleasauntnesse of hylles, and delectablenes of playnes. **1652–62** HEYLIN *Cosmogr.* III. (1673) 151/2 The delectableness of the Gardens adjoyning. **1852** HAWTHORNE *Blithedale Rom.* I. xiii. 252 A terrible drawback on the delectableness of a kiss. **1879** J. BURROUGHS *Locusts & W. Honey* 16 Half the delectableness is in breaking down these frail walls yourself.

delectably (dɪˈlɛktəblɪ), *adv.* [f. as prec. + -LY².] In a delectable manner, delightfully.

c **1400** MAUNDEV. (1839) xxvii. 278 Bryddes þat songen full delectably. **1550** BALE *Sel. Wks.* (1849) 388 Of myrrh, balm, and aloes, they delectably smell. **1652–62** HEYLIN *Cosmogr.* II. (1682) 51 A neat Town, and very delectably seated. **1754** SHEBBEARE *Matrimony* (1766) II. 157 No life could pass more delectably than his.

† **'delectary**, *a. Obs.* [f. L. type **dēlectāri-us*, whence also OF. *delitaire* delectable, f. *dēlectā-re* to delight: see -ARY¹.] Delectable, pleasant.

c **1485** *Digby Myst.* (1882) III. 751 He hathe made me clene and delectary, the wyche was to synne a subiectary.

delectate (dɪˈlɛkteɪt, ˈdiːlɛkteɪt), *v. rare.* [f. ppl. stem of L. *dēlectāre* to DELIGHT: see -ATE³, 5.] *trans.* To delight. (Affected or humorous.)

1802 LAMB *Curious Fragm. fr. Burton*, The silly man.. thinketh only how best to delectate and refresh his mind. **1841** *Fraser's Mag.* XXIII. 220, I also delectated myself greatly in the library. **1871** B. TAYLOR *Faust* (1875) II. II. iii. 136 His art and favour delectate you [*rime* create you].

delectation (diːlɛkˈteɪʃən). Also 4 -aciun, 4–5 -acioun, 5–6 -acion, -acyon(e, etc.; also dilect-. [a. OF. *delectation* (12th c. in Hatzf.), also *delitacion* (Godef.), ad. L. *dēlectātiōn-em*, n. of action from *dēlectāre* to DELIGHT.] The action of delighting; delight, enjoyment, great pleasure.

Formerly in general use, and denoting all kinds of pleasure from sensual to spiritual; now (since *c* 1700) rarer, more or less affected or humorous, and restricted to the lighter kinds of pleasure.

13.. *S. Augustin* 730 in Horstmann *Altengl. Leg.* 74 þat luttel delectaciun þat he feled in his etyng. **1382** WYCLIF *2 Macc.* ii. 26 Sothely we curiden..that it were delectacioun, or lykyng, of ynwitt to men willynge for to reede. **1435** MISYN *Fire of Love* v. 9 Wyckyd treuly þis warld lufe, settand þere-in þe lust of þere delectacyone. **1526** TINDALE *2 Cor.* xii. 10 Therefore have I delectacion in infirmities. **1570** DEE *Math. Pref.* 32 To the glory of God, and to our honest delectation in earth. **1620** VENNER *Via Recta* iv. 75 It is pleasant to the pallat, and induceth..a smoothing delectation to the gullet. *a* **1711** KEN *Edmund* Poet. Wks. 1721 II. 96 Liking shoots up unheeded to Delight, And Delectations soon Consent excite. **1779–81** JOHNSON *L.P.*, *Garth*, 'The Dispensary'..appears..to want something of poetical ardour and something of general delectation. **1846** DICKENS *Cricket on Hearth* i, Reproducing scraps of conversation for the delectation of the baby. **1892** *Times* 27 Dec. 7/1 A great many other entertainments were provided for the public delectation.

b. *transf.* Something that delights; a delight.

1432–50 tr. *Higden* (Rolls) I. 249 That the citesynnes scholde dispute of the commune profette yn tylle none: and not attende to eny other delectacion. **1536** *Primer Hen. VIII*, 149 Of mind Thou art the delectation, Of pure love the insuation. **1576** FLEMING *Panopl. Epist.* 63 If solitarinesse and living alone be your delectation.

delectible, delection, obs. var. DELECTABLE, DILECTION.

‖ **delectus** (dɪˈlɛktəs). [a. L. *dēlectus* selection, choice, f. *dēligĕre* to choose out, select; f. DE- I. 2 + *legĕre* to gather, cull, choose.] A selection of passages from various authors, *esp.* Latin or Greek, for translation.

[**1814** R. VALPY (*title*), Delectus Sententiarum Græcarum.] **1828** F. E. J. VALPY (*title*), Second Greek Delectus, or New Analecta Minora. **1836** —— Second Latin Delectus, with English notes. **1865** SMILES *Life of Watt* 512 His first school-exercises, down to his college themes, his delectuses. **1888** BERNARD *World to Cloister* v. 114 Such a caning as a small boy gets at school for not knowing his *Delectus*.

‖ **delectus personæ.** *Law.* [Lat. = 'choice of a person'.] The choice or right of selection of a person to occupy any specific position or relation; e.g. of one to be admitted as partner in any firm, or as tenant in a lease; the right which each existing partner or party to a contract has of being satisfied with the person whom it is proposed subsequently to admit into the firm or lease.

1848 WHARTON *Law Dict.* s.v., The *delectus personæ*, which is essential to the constitution of partnership. **1861** W. BELL *Dict. Law Scotl.*, Although the *delectus personæ* does not now exclude the tenant's heirs, yet without the landlord's consent, either express or implied..a lease cannot be voluntarily assigned or sublet.

delee, obs. form of DELAY.

de'leerit, *ppl. a. Sc.* [pa. pple. of *deleer* = DELIRE *v.*, F. *délirer*.] Crazed, out of one's wits.
1785 BURNS *Halloween* xiv, For monie a ane has gotten fright, An' liv'd an' di'd deleerit, On sic a night.

deleet, obs. form of DELETE.

delegable ('dɛlɪgəb(ə)l), *a.* [f. L. *dēlēgā-re* to DELEGATE + -BLE.] Capable of being delegated.
1660 R. SHERINGHAM *King's Suprem.* viii. (1682) 85 The Legislative power is delegable.

delegacy ('dɛlɪgəsɪ). [f. DELEGATE *sb.*: see -ACY.]
1. The action or system of delegating; appointment of a person as a delegate; commission or authority given to act as a delegate.
1533-4 *Act 25 Hen. VIII*, c. 21 §1 Great summes of money..haue ben..taken by the Pope..for delegacies, & rescriptis in causes of contencions and appeles. **1614** RALEIGH *Hist. World* v. ii. §8 Understanding the majesty of Rome to be indeed wholly in the people and no otherwise in the senate than by way of delegacy or grand commission. **1626** *State Trials, Dk. Buckhm.* (R.), They are great judges, a court of the last resort..and this not by delegacy and commission, but by birth and inheritance. **1882** FFOULKES in *Macm. Mag.* XLV. 204 So much for delegacies and appeals in the abstract. **1888** BRYCE *Amer. Commw.* II. III. lxiii. 459 He is..forbidden to hope for a delegacy to a convention.
2. A body or committee of delegates; †formerly also, a meeting of such a body.
In the University of Oxford, a permanent committee, or board of delegates, entrusted with special business; as, the Delegacy of the Non-Collegiate Students: see DELEGATE 2 b.
1621 BURTON *Anat. Mel.* Democr. to Rdr. (1657) 64 The plaintiff shall have his complaint approved by a set delegacy to that purpose. **1631** LAUD *Wks.* (1853) V. 49 Their professed aim was to dissolve the delegacy appointed for the ordering and settling of the statutes [of Oxford]. **1669** WOOD *Life* (Oxf. Hist. Soc.) II. 172 The Delegacy for printing of books met between 8 and 9 in the morn. **1671** *Ibid.* II. 216 A conference or delegacy held in the lodgings of Dr. Jo. Lamphire, principal of Hart hall. **1852** [see DELEGATE 2 b]. **1867** *Times* 13 Dec. 8/6 Youths residing entirely..out of College would require special attention, and therefore it was proposed to create a delegacy—that is, an Academic Board—for that purpose. **1875** M. PATTISON *Casaubon* 90 The town-council of Montpellier proceeded to appoint a delegacy of eight persons to prepare a scheme for the college of Arts.

delegant ('dɛlɪgənt). [ad. L. *dēlēgānt-em*, pr. pple. of *dēlēgāre* to DELEGATE: so mod.F. *délégant*.] One who delegates; in *Civil Law*, one who, to discharge his debt to a creditor, assigns his own debtor to the latter, in his place.
1627 W. SCLATER *Exp. 2 Thess.* (1629) 128 The Iurisdiction of the delegant and delegate is one. **1644** BP. MAXWELL *Prerog. Chr. Kings* iv. 44 Samuel was onely the delegate, God was the principall and delegant. **1818** COLEBROOKE *Oblig. & Contracts* I. 214 The most frequent case of delegation is that of a debtor of the delegant, who, for his own discharge of a debt due by him, delegates that debtor to his own creditor.

delegate ('dɛlɪgət), *sb.* Also 5 *Sc.* diligat(e, 7 delegat. [a. OF. *delegat* (= mod.F. *délégué*, Sp. *delegado*, It. *delegato*), ad. L. *dēlēgāt-us*, pa. pple. of *dēlēgāre* to DELEGATE, used as sb. in Romanic, like L. *lēgātus*.]
1. A person sent or deputed to act for or represent another or others; one entrusted with authority or power to be exercised on behalf of those by whom he is appointed; a deputy, commissioner.
c **1380** *Antecrist* in Todd *3 Treat. Wyclif* 124 Take we heede to þe popes & cardinals..delegates & commyssaries. **1461** *Liber Pluscardensis* XI. viii. (1877) I. 385 His [God's] diligatis dois na thyng heire in vayn. **1614** SELDEN *Titles Hon.* 252 The delegats of Bishops in temporall iurisdiction ..were stil'd *Vicedomini*. *a* **1631** DONNE in *Select.* (1840) 47 Taught..by the Holy Ghost speaking in his delegates, in his ministers. **1725** POPE *Odyss.* I. 501 Elect by Jove his delegate of sway. **1876** E. MELLOR *Priesth.* vii. 324 He [the priest] claims simply to stand as delegate of heaven.
b. Now chiefly applied to one or more persons elected and sent by an association or body of men to act in their name, and in accordance with their instructions, at some conference or meeting at which the whole body cannot be present.
1600 HOLLAND *Livy* XXXIII. xxiv. 838 There were appointed ten Committees or Delegates [*legati*]. **1775** JOHNSON *Tax. no Tyr.* 71 The delegates of the several towns and parishes in Cornwal. **1863** H. COX *Instit.* I. viii. 107 Where there was a district of burghs, each Town Council elected a delegate, and the four or five delegates elected the member. **1878** JEVONS *Prim. Pol. Econ.* 78 Sometimes three or more delegates of the workmen meet an equal number of delegates from the masters.
c. A layman appointed to attend an ecclesiastical council (of which the clergy or ministers are *ex officio* members).
1828 in WEBSTER; and in later Dicts.
2. *spec.* **a.** A commissioner appointed by the crown under the great seal to hear and determine appeals from the ecclesiastical courts. These commissioners constituted the ***Court of Delegates***, or great court of appeal in ecclesiastical and Admiralty causes.
1554 *Act 1–2 Phil. & M.* c. 8 §29 All judicial Process made before any Ordinaries..or before any Delegates upon any Appeals. **1591** HARINGTON *Orl. Fur.* XIV. lxxiii, In courts of Delegates and of Requests. **1726** AYLIFFE *Parergon* 191 The Court of Delegates..wherein all Causes of Appeal by way of Devolution from either of the Archbishops are decided. **1768** BLACKSTONE *Comm.* III. 66 The great court of appeal in all ecclesiastical causes, *viz.* the court of *delegates, judices delegati*, appointed by the king's commission under his great seal, and issuing out of chancery, to represent his royal person.
b. In the University of Oxford: A member of a permanent committee entrusted with some special branch of University business; as, the Delegates of Appeals in Congregation and in Convocation, of the University Press, of University Police, etc.
c **1604** SIR T. BODLEY in *Reliq. Bodl.* (1703) 196 As the Delegates have resolved, there shall be a Porter for the Library. **1660** WOOD *Life* (Oxf. Hist. Soc.) I. 316 In the same convocation, the Delegates' decree was confirmed by the regents and non-regents, scil. that the overplus of the money..should be employed in printing Gregorius Abulpharagus. **1668** *Clarendon Press MSS.*, At a Meeting of the Delegats for Printing. **1671** *Ibid.*, At a Meeting of ye Delegats for the Physick Garden. **1700** *Ibid.*, At a Meeting of ye Delegates for Accts of ye University of Oxford. **1723** *Ibid.*, At a Meeting of the Heads of Houses in ye Delegates Room of the Printing House. **1852** *Rep. Oxford Univ. Commission* 15 The Standing Delegacies or Committees, which are appointed for the purpose of managing various branches of University business..There are Delegates of Accounts, of Estates, of Privileges, of the Press, and of Appeals.
3. *U.S.* **a.** The representative of a Territory in Congress, having a seat and the right of speech in the House of Representatives, but no vote. Before 1789 it was the title of the representatives of the various States in the Congress of the Confederation.
1825 T. JEFFERSON *Autobiog.* Wks. 1859 I. 52, I was appointed by the legislature a delegate to Congress.
b. ***House of Delegates***: (*a*) the lower house of the General Assembly in Virginia, West Virginia, and Maryland; (*b*) the lower house of the General Convention of the Protestant Episcopal Church.
1843 *Penny Cycl.* XXVI. 368/2 The legislature consists of a Senate and a House of Delegates, which are together called the General Assembly of Virginia. *Ibid.*, All laws must originate in the House of Delegates.

delegate ('dɛlɪgət), *ppl. a.* Also 6–7 *Sc.* delegat. [ad. L. *dēlēgāt-us*, pa. pple. of *dēlēgāre* to DELEGATE.]
†**1.** As *pa. pple.* Delegated, deputed, commissioned.
1530 PALSGR. 510/2 The bysshop hath delegate the deane in this mater. **1549** *Compl. Scot.* xiv. 115, I vald god that fuluius flaccus var diligat iuge to puneis them. **1660** R. COKE *Power & Subj.* 54 Supreme power is delegate from God to every Prince.
2. As *adj.* Delegated.
1613 MILLES *Treas. Aunc. & Mod. Times* 713/2 The King and the Queen with all their Servants and delegate Apostles. *a* **1667** JER. TAYLOR (J.), Princes in judgement, and their delegate judges. **1828** GUNNING *Cerem. Cambr.* 420 The Party Appellant..doth desire the Judges Delegate [*Judices Delegati*] that they would decree [etc.].

delegate ('dɛlɪgeɪt), *v.* [f. ppl. stem of L. *dēlēgāre* to send, dispatch, assign, commit, f. DE- I. 2 b + *lēgāre* to send with a commission, depute, commit, etc.]
1. *trans.* To send or commission (a person) as a deputy or representative, with power to transact business for another; to depute or appoint to act.
1623 COCKERAM, *Delegate*, to assigne, to send in commission. **1641** R. BROOKE *Eng. Episc.* II. ii. 71 Will any man..think it reasonable my Lord Keeper should, *ad placitum*, delegate whom hee will to keep the Seale? **1646** H. LAWRENCE *Comm. Angells* 20 Every one from his nativity hath an Angell delegated for his keeper. **1876** GRANT *Burgh Sch. Scotl.* I. i. 10 Commissioners of the Abbot of Dunfermline who had been delegated judge by the pope.
2. To entrust, commit or deliver (authority, a function, etc.) to another as an agent or deputy.
1530 PALSGR. 510/2, I delegate myne auctorite, *je delegue*. **1641** R. BROOKE *Eng. Episc.* II. ii. 72 Can any man think it fit, to *Delegate* the Tuition or Education of a tender Prince, committed to his Charge? **1774** T. JEFFERSON *Autobiog.* App. Wks. 1859 I. 138 Those bodies..to whom the people have delegated the powers of legislation. **1873** HELPS *Anim. & Mast.* v. (1875) 117, I wish we could delegate to women some of this work. **1883** A. L. SMITH in *Law Reports 12 Q. Bench Div.* 95 The defendant delegated to another to utter the slanderous words.
†**3.** In a looser sense: To assign, deliver. *Obs.*
1633 J. DONE *Hist. Septuagint* 74 For this was Published ..a Law, and the reason thereof delegated to the Judges.. that the Peasants should not sojourne [etc.]. **1774** J. BRYANT *Mythol.* I. 310 A number of strange attributes, which by some of the poets were delegated to different personages.
4. *Civil Law.* To assign (one who is debtor to oneself) to a creditor as debtor in one's place.
1818 [see DELEGANT]. **1880** MUIRHEAD *Gaius* III. §130 When, for example, I enter to your debit what is due me by Titius, provided always he has delegated you to me in his stead. **1887** JUTA *Burge's Comm. Law of Holland* 246 It is necessary that there should be the concurrence of the person delegating, that is, the original debtor, and of the person delegated, or the person whom he appoints.

delegated ('dɛlɪgeɪtɪd), *ppl. a.* [f. prec. vb.]
1. Appointed to act as a deputy or representative for another; deputed.
1647 CRASHAW *Poems* 164 The delegated eye of day. **1791** E. DARWIN *Bot. Gard.* I. 109 The delegated throng O'er the wide plains delighted rush along. **1818** COLEBROOKE *Oblig. & Contracts* I. 214 If nothing were due by the delegant, the delegated party need not perform that engagement. **1859** TENNYSON *Enid* 1741 By having..wrought too long with delegated hands, Not used mine own.
2. Entrusted or committed (to a deputy).
1654 H. L'ESTRANGE *Chas. I* (1655) 150 Neither..his Own, nor his delegated Authority to his Council. **1735–8** BOLINGBROKE *On Parties* 209 The Peers have an inherent, the Commons a delegated Right. **1861** W. BELL *Dict. Law Scot.*, *Delegated jurisdiction*, as contradistinguished from *proper* jurisdiction, is that which is communicated by a judge to another, who acts in his name, called a depute or deputy. **1867** FREEMAN *Norm. Conq.* (1876) I. iv. 247 An English Ealdorman ruled only with a delegated authority.

delega'tee. [f. DELEGATE *v.* + -EE.] *Civil Law.* The party to whom a debtor is delegated by the delegant.
1875 POSTE *Gaius* (ed. 2) 670 When the Delegator is indebted to the Delegatee.

'delegateship. [See -SHIP.] The office or position of a delegate.
1892 *Columbus* (Ohio) *Dispatch* 23 Mar., That federal office holders in the South are put forward for delegateships.

delegation (dɛlɪ'geɪʃən). [ad. L. *dēlēgātiōn-em*, n. of action from *dēlēgāre* to DELEGATE. So F. *délégation* (13th c. in Hatzf.).]
1. The action of delegating or fact of being delegated; appointment or commission of a person as a delegate or representative; the entrusting of authority to a delegate.
1612 SELDEN *Drayton's Poly-olb.* xi. Notes 193 Government upon delegation from the King. **1641** R. BROOKE *Eng. Episc.* II. ii. 72 To countenance such Delegation of an entrusted Office, to Deputies. **1775** JOHNSON *Tax. no Tyr.* 33 The business of the Publick must be done by delegation. **1867** FREEMAN *Norm. Conq.* (1876) I. iii. 77 He is a sovereign, inasmuch as he does not rule by delegation from any personal superior.
b. The action of sending on a commission.
1641 SMECTYMNUUS *Vind. Answ.* §13. 130 If the greatest part of Titus his travels had beene before his delegation to Creet.
†**c.** The action of delivering or assigning a thing to a person or to a purpose. *Obs.*
1681 E. SCLATER *Serm. Putney* 7 There are two parts of Moses his power intimated fairly enough in the delegation of these siluer trumpets.
2. A charge or commission given to a delegate.
1611 SPEED *Hist. Gt. Brit.* IX. xii. §66 Lewis..re-called his Vicar-ship or delegation, which hee had made to Edward. **1690** LOCKE *Civ. Gov.* II. xix. (R.), When..others usurp the place, who have no such authority or delegation.
3. A delegated body; a number of persons sent or commissioned to act as representatives.
1818 JAS. MILL *Brit. India* II. IV. vii. 261 The government of India..by a delegation of servants. **1841** CATLIN *N. Amer. Ind.* (1844) I. i. 2 A delegation of some ten or fifteen noble and dignified-looking Indians..suddenly arrived.
b. *U.S.* The body of delegates appointed to represent a State or district in a representative assembly.
1828 WEBSTER s.v., Thus, the representatives of Massachusetts in Congress are called the *delegation*, or *whole delegation*. **1865** H. PHILLIPS *Amer. Paper Curr.* II. 43 The Jersey delegation..presented to congress a number of the counterfeits.
4. *Civil Law.* The assignment of a debtor by his creditor to a creditor of the delegant, to act as debtor in his place and discharge his debt.
1721 BAILEY, *Delegation* [in Civil Law] is when a Debtor appoints one who is Debtor to him, to answer a Creditor, in his Place. **1818** COLEBROOKE *Oblig. & Contracts* I. 208. **1860** J. PATERSON *Compend. Eng. & Sc. Law* 514. **1880** MUIRHEAD *Gaius* Digest 552 A transaction..called delegation of his debtor by the creditor to the third party.
5. A letter or other instrument, unstamped and not negotiable, used by bankers and merchants in the place of a cheque, bill of exchange or other instrument, for the transfer of a debt or credit.
1882 BITHELL *Counting-ho. Dict.* 92 Letters of Credit are mostly simple Delegations.
‖**b.** A share-certificate: used *esp.* in reference to Suez Canal shares. [F. *délégation*.]
1882 *Daily Tel.* 10 Oct. (Cassell), The English government intended purchasing 200,000 Suez Canal delegations.

†**'delegative**, *a. Obs.* [f. ppl. stem of L. *dēlēgāre* to DELEGATE + -IVE.] Having the attribute of delegating; of delegated nature.
1641 R. BROOKE *Eng. Episc.* I. i. 3 Hither also wee may referre his power Juridicall or Legislative in Parliament.. And..his power Delegative. **1690** LOCKE *Govt.* II. xi. §141 It [the Power of making Laws] being but a delegative Power from the People.

delegator (ˈdɛlɪgeɪtə(r)). [ad. L. *dēlēgātor*, agent-n. f. *dēlēgāre* to DELEGATE.] One who delegates, a delegant.
1875 [see DELEGATEE].

delegatory (ˈdɛlɪgətərɪ), *a.* [ad. L. *dēlēgātōri-us*, f. *dēlēgātor*: see prec. and -ORY.] Of or relating to delegation; of the nature of delegation or delegated power; †of a person, holding delegated authority.
1599 NASHE *Lenten Stuffe* in *Harl. Misc.* (1808–13) VI. 170 (D.) Some politique delegatory Scipio..whom they might depose when they list. **1615** CROOKE *Body of Man* 42 No where doth he attribute any delegatory power of Sensation vnto it. **1762** tr. *Busching's Syst. Geog.* III. 547 This jurisdiction was conferred on him by the see of Utrecht, which the Emperor..had invested with a delegatory authority. **1787** ANN HILDITCH *Rosa de Mont.* I. 62 The decrees of an immutable providence, and its delegatory laws on earth.

delegue, var. DELEAGUE *v. Obs.*, to delegate.

deleit, obs. Sc. form of DELETE.

‖**delenda** (dɪˈlɛndə), *sb. pl.* [L., pl. of *dēlēndum* (a thing) to be blotted out, gerundive of *dēlēre* to DELETE.] Things to be deleted.
(In early quot. with additional plural *-s*.)
1645 MRQ. WORCESTER in *Bibl. Regia* (1659) 71, I beseech your Majesty to consider the streiks that are drawn over the Divine writ as so many delendies [quoted in C. Cartwright *Cert. Relig.* I. 6 (1651) as *delenda's*] by such bold hands as these.

delendung, var. of DELUNDUNG.

†**deˈleniate**, *v. Obs. rare.* Also erron. **delineate**. [irreg. f. L. *dēlēnīre* to soften or soothe down.] To soothe, mitigate.
1623 COCKERAM, II, To Pacifie, *Deleniate.* **1657** TOMLINSON *Renou's Disp.* 29 That is called Anodynum which delineates and mitigates any paine.

†**deleˈnifical**, *a. Obs. rare*—⁰. [f. L. *dēlēnific-us* soothing, f. *dēlēnīre* to soothe down + *-ficus* making.] Soothing, pacifying.
1656 BLOUNT *Glossogr.*, *Delenifical*, that mitigates or makes gentle. **1721** in BAILEY. **1755** in JOHNSON ('having virtue to assuage or ease pain').

delerious, erron. form of DELIRIOUS.

delessite (dɪˈlɛsaɪt). *Min.* [Named 1850 after the French mineralogist Delesse: see -ITE.] A dark-green mineral, allied to CHLORITE, but containing much more iron.
1854 in DANA *Min.* 296. **1879** RUTLEY *Stud. Rocks* xii. 219 Augite, which is often altered into pseudomorphs of chlorite or delessite.

delete (dɪˈliːt), *v.* Also 5–6 **delyte**, 6–7 *Sc.* **deleit**, **dilate**, 7 **deleet(e**, **deleate**, 7 *Sc. pa. t.* and *pa. pple.* **deletted**, **delait**: see next. [f. L. *dēlēt-*, ppl. stem of *dēlēre* to blot out, efface.]
†**1.** *trans.* To destroy, annihilate, abolish, eradicate, do away with. *Obs.*
(The first quot. is on various grounds uncertain.)
1495 *Barth. De P.R.* (W. de W.) IV. iii. 82 Drinesse dystroyeth bodyes that haue soules, so he dyssoluyth and delyteth the kynde naturall spyrytes that ben of mayst smoke. **1534** *St. Papers Hen. VIII*, II. 218 Stryke thaym..till they be consumed, and ther generation clene radycat and delytit of this worlde. **1545** *Act 37 Hen. VIII*, c. 17 §1 The Bishop of Rome..minding..to abolish, obscure and delete such Power. **1565** *Satir. Poems Reform.* i. 344 Where no redresse in tyme cold dilate The extreme wrong that Rigor had tought. **1656** PRYNNE *Demurrer to Jews* 69 Confederating..to murder and delete them. **1657** TOMLINSON *Renou's Disp.* 215 It doth perfectly deleate the ulcers which infest the throat. **1851** SIR F. PALGRAVE *Norm. & Eng.* I. 43 Though Carthage was deleted.
2. a. To strike or blot out, obliterate, erase, expunge (written or printed characters).
a **1605** MONTGOMERIE *Misc. Poems* I. 6 Sic tytillis in ȝour sanges deleit. **1637–50** ROW *Hist. Kirk* (1842) 522 His Majestie deletted that clause. *a* **1657** BALFOUR *Ann. Scot.* (1824–5) II. 76 Her proces [was] ordained to be delait out of the recordes. **1667** COLLINS in Rigaud *Corr. Sci. Men* (1841) I. 127 Here the corrector took out more than I deleted. **1862** BEVERIDGE *Hist. India* II. VI. iii. 641 The peerage would be granted if the censure were deleted. **1875** F. HALL in *Nation* XXI. 360/2 Here, to make either sense or metre, the *and* must be deleted.
b. *fig.* To erase, expunge, 'wipe out'.
1650 FULLER *Pisgah* III. x. 340 Studiously deleting the character of that Sacrament out of their bodies. **1785** REID *Int. Powers* III. vii, So imprinted as not to be deleted by time. **1864** *Morn. Star* 12 Jan., Kagosima has been deleted from the list of cities, and there is an end of it.
c. To remove (a gramophone record) from the catalogue and thus no longer offer it for sale.
1937 *Gramophone* Oct. 190/1 H.M.V. are wisely persevering with their policy of announcing in advance which records they intend to delete from the Connoisseur's catalogue. **1949** *Ibid.* Oct. 90/1 The first two Bartók quartets, long deleted, are now eagerly sought after by collectors. **1966** *Melody Maker* 7 May 12/1 These justly famous tracks make a surprise reappearance because it was only in April that EMI deleted them.
3. *pass. Cytology.* Of a segment of a chromosome: to be lost from the chromosome. So **deˈleted** *ppl. a.* Cf. DELETION 3.
1929 PAINTER & MULLER in *Jrnl. Heredity* XX. 296/1 Drawings of the chromosomes have been presented..the deleted *X* being indicated as '*X*—'. **1936** *Discovery* Sept. 269/1 It is usually a section in the middle which disappears, or is 'deleted', the two ends joining up to make a shortened chromosome. **1957** C. P. SWANSON *Cytol. & Cytogenetics* x. 368 At anaphase, the deleted portion is usually freed and does not undergo movement to one or the other of the poles.
Hence **deˈleting** *vbl. sb.*, deletion.
1711 *Countrey-Man's Lett. to Curat* 6 They had the popish missal and breviary with some few Deletings.

†**deˈlete**, *pa. pple. Obs.* Also 7 **deleete**, **delate**. [ad. L. *dēlēt-us* blotted out, effaced, pa. pple. of *dēlēre* to DELETE.] Deleted, abolished, destroyed.
c **1555** HARPSFIELD *Divorce Hen. VIII* (1878) 87 His brother's memory was delete and abolished among the Jews. **1642** *Declar. Lords & Com. to Gen. Ass. Ch. Scot.* 13 An Obligation that cannot be delete. **1682** *Lond. Gaz.* No. 1682/1 His Arms to be..delate out of the Books of Arms.

†**deleˈterial**, *a. Obs.* [f. as next + -AL¹.] = next.
1621 VENNER *Via Recta, Treat. Tobacco* (1650) 397 It hath a deleteriall or venemous quality. **1684** tr. *Bonet's Merc. Compit.* XIX. 701 In his Epistle concerning Paracelsus's Medicines and their deleterial vertues.

deleterious (dɛlɪˈtɪərɪəs), *a.* [f. mod.L. *dēlētēri-us*, a. Gr. δηλητήρι-ος noxious, hurtful, f. δηλήτηρ destroyer, f. δηλέ-εσθαι to hurt: see -OUS.] Hurtful or injurious to life or health; noxious.
1643 SIR T. BROWNE *Relig. Med.* II. §10 They were not deleterious to others onely, but to themselves also. **1646** —— *Pseud. Ep.* III. vii. 119 Deleterious it may bee at some distance and destructive without a corporall contaction. **1762** GOLDSM. *Cit. W.* xci, In some places, those plants which are entirely poisonous at home lose their deleterious quality by being carried abroad. **1821** BYRON *Juan* IV. lii, 'Tis pity wine should be so deleterious, For tea and coffee leave us much more serious. **1869** PHILLIPS *Vesuv.* viii. 213 This gas was well known to be deleterious.
b. Mentally or morally injurious or harmful.
1823 BYRON *Juan* XIII. i, A jest at vice by virtue's called a crime, And critically held as deleterious. **1860** EMERSON *Cond. Life, Power* Wks. (Bohn) II. 335 Politics is a deleterious profession, like some poisonous handicrafts.
Hence **deleˈteriously** *adv.*, **deleˈteriousness**.
1812 SHELLEY *Let.* 29 July (1964) I. 316, I have *no* doubts on the deleteriousness of classical education. **1879** *Cassell's Techn. Educ.* IV. 359/1 The solution should not be deleteriously affected. **1892** W. B. SCOTT *Autobiog.* I. i. 15 David was..deleteriously influenced by studying these able but imperfect artists.

†**deletery** (ˈdɛlɪtərɪ), *a. Obs.* Also *erron.* **-ory**, **-ary**. [a. med.L. *dēlētēri-us* (Du Cange), a. Gr. δηλητήριος DELETERIOUS. In F. *délétère* (*médicament délétère*, Joubert, 16th c.). In the 17th c. often erroneously viewed as a derivative of L. *dēlēre*, *dēlētum*, to blot out, efface, destroy, and consequently both spelt *-ory*, and used in the sense 'effacing, blotting out': cf. DELETORY.
By Butler stressed *ˈdeletery*; but generally perhaps *deˈletery*.]
A. *adj.* Deleterious, noxious, poisonous.
1576 NEWTON *Lemnie's Complex.* (1633) 101 [Venemous hearbes] which by reason of their deletory coldnesse bring destruction unto Creatures, as Henbane, Mandrake, *Napellus*. **1638** A. READ *Chirurg.* xii. 89 The subjects wherein this deletery propertie is lodged. **1657** TOMLINSON *Renou's Disp.* 10 A certain deletary and poysonous quality. **1663** BUTLER *Hud.* I. II. 317 Though stor'd with Deletery Med'cines (Which whosoever took is Dead since). **1684** tr. *Bonet's Merc. Compit.* VI. 196 A Patient..died frantick, as if he had taken a deletery Medicine.
B. 1. A deleterious or noxious drug; a poison. Also *fig.*
1638 A. READ *Chirurg.* xii. 88 You may aske by what meanes these poisons and deleteries doe kill. **1649** JER. TAYLOR *Gt. Exemp.* (1703) 407 Health and pleasure, deletery and cordial. **1651–3** —— *Serm. for Year* I. xvii. 223 [To] destroy Charity..with the same general venom and deletery as apostacy destroyes faith.
2. A drug that destroys or counteracts the effect of anything noxious, as a poison; an antidote. **b.** *fig.* Anything that destroys, or counteracts the poison *of*, sin or evil; an antidote *to* or *for* evil.
¶In this sense evidently associated with L. *dēlēre*, *dēlētum*, and so used as = 'destroyer, effacer, wiper out' (of evil): cf. DELETORY *sb.*
1642 JER. TAYLOR *Episc.* (1647) 5 Episcopacy is the best deletery in the world for Schisme. **1649** —— *Apol. Liturgy* Pref. §34 Inserted as Antidotes, and deleteries to the worst of Heresies. **1649** —— *Gt. Exemp.* II. xii. xi. I. §9 A proper deletery of his disgrace, and purgative of the calumny. **1660** —— *Duct. Dubit.* I. i. rule ii. §23 Intended to be deleteries of the sin and instruments of repentance. —— *Ibid.* I. iii, My thinking that mercury is not poison, nor hellebore purgative, cannot make an antidote or deletery against them.

deletion (dɪˈliːʃən). [ad. L. *dēlētiōn-em*, n. of action from *dēlēre* to blot out, efface.]
1. The action of effacing or destroying; destruction, annihilation, abolition, extinction. Now *arch.*
1606 COKE in *True & Perf. Rel.* D iij b, Tending not onely to the hurt..but euen the deletion of our whole name and Nation. **1651–3** JER. TAYLOR *Serm. for Year* I. v. 58 Unlesse this proceed so far as to a total deletion of the sin. **1677** HALE *Pomp. Atticus* 36 The taking of Alexandria by Augustus, which was the fatal and funeral deletion of Antony. **1845** DAVISON *Disc. Prophecy* v. (1861) 162 Rome remains, though Carthage is gone: the similar fate of deletion has not come. **1881** STEVENSON *Virg. Puerisque, Ordered South* 162 The more will he be tempted to regret the extinction of his powers and the deletion of his personality.
2. a. The action of striking out, erasing or obliterating written or printed matter; the fact of being deleted; a deleted passage, an erasure.
1590 SWINBURNE *Testaments* 271 Although the deletion were in the chiefe part of the testament. **1852** SIR W. HAMILTON *Discuss.* 38 *note*, Some deletions, found necessary in consequence of the unexpected length to which the Article extended..have been restored. **1880** MUIRHEAD *Gaius* I. §31 *note*, With a dot—equivalent to deletion—over some if not all of the letters. **1884** KAY in *Law Times Rep.* LI. 315/1 The deletion was initialed in the margin with the initials of the persons who signed the agreement.
b. The action of deleting a gramophone record from the catalogue; a deleted record.
1937 *Gramophone* Oct. 190/1 The characteristic of last year's deletion list was the preponderance of French works. **1944** *Ibid.* Sept. 52/3 (*heading*) Decca deletions. **1954** *Gramophone Record Rev.* Oct. 574/2 From the many *Schwarzkopf* deletions I would single out the best complete version of the aria 'L'amero, saro costante'. **1969** *Gramophone* June 103/2 (Advt.), Classical, Shows and jazz LPs at reduced prices, mono and stereo deletions.
3. *Cytology.* The loss of a segment from a chromosome; also, the segment lost. Cf. DEFICIENCY I e.
1929 PAINTER & MULLER in *Jrnl. Heredity* XX. 295/1 Deletions of *X* Chromosomes. *Ibid.*, We have obtained..hyperdiploids of a different origin, based upon deletions of the *X*. **1938** E. B. FORD *Study of Heredity* iv. 92 In the instances so far mentioned, the fragment of chromosome which has broken away has succeeded in reattaching itself elsewhere. Sometimes, however, it fails to do so and is lost. This leads to 'deletion', in which some of the genes..find themselves unopposed by their allelomorphs. **1952** C. P. BLACKER *Eugenics* 245 A piece of a chromosome may break off, causing a deficiency or deletion. **1969** BROWN & BERTKE *Textbk. Cytol.* xxi. 480/2 The location where an interstitial deletion was 'extracted' is not represented by a gap in the chromosome.

deleˈtitious, *a. rare*—⁰. [f. L. *dēlētīci-us*, *-ītius* characterized by blotting out or erasure + -OUS.] Characterized by erasure; said of paper from which writing has been, or may be, erased.
1823 CRABB, *Deletitious* (*Ant.*), an epithet for paper on which one may write things and blot them out again, to make room for new matter. Hence **1846** in WORCESTER; and in later Dicts.

deletive (dɪˈliːtɪv), *a. rare.* [f. L. *dēlēt-*, ppl. stem of *dēlēre* to efface + -IVE.] Having the property of deleting, adapted for erasing.
1662 EVELYN *Chalcogr.* 9 Save where the obtuser end [of the *stilus*] was made more deletive, apt to put out, and obliterate.

†**deleˈtorious**, *a. Obs. rare*—⁰. = DELETORY.
1656 BLOUNT *Glossogr.*, *Deletorious* (*deletorius*), that blotteth or raceth out.

deletory (dɪˈliːtərɪ), *a. sb.* [f. L. *dēlēt-* (see above) + -ORY.]
A. *adj.* That is used to delete or efface, effacing.
Also used in 17th c. in sense of DELETERY *a.*: see that word and cf. quot. 1679 here.
1612 T. JAMES *Corrupt. Script.* II. 41 That also must be thrust away with a deletorie sponge. **1679** PULLER *Moder. Ch. Eng.* (1843) 202 The Penances in the Church of Rome, which..are counted deletory of sin.
B. *sb.* That which destroys or effaces.
(Cf. DELETERY *sb.* 2 b, with which this ran together.)
1647 JER. TAYLOR *Dissuas. Popery* ii. (1686) 112 The severity of Confession, which..was most certainly intended as a deletory of sin. **1649** —— *Gt. Exemp.* VI. I. §23 The Spirit of Sanctification..the deletory of Concupiscence. **1699** 'MISAURUS' *Honour of Gout* (1720) 35 It is a perfect Deletory of Folly.

dele-wine: see DEAL *sb.*⁴

deley, obs. form of DELAY.

delf¹ (dɛlf). Now only *local.* Forms: 5–7 **delfe**, 6 **delff**, 7–9 **delft**, 5– **delf**, 6– **delph**; *pl.* 4– **delves**, 6–7 **delfes**, 7– **delfs**, 8– **delphs**. [ME. *delf*, late OE. *dælf* for *delf*, trench, ditch, quarry, occurring in a 12th c. copy of a charter, inserted in the Peterborough OE. Chron. (Laud MS.) anno 963; app. aphetic f. OE. *ȝedelf* digging, a digging, ditch, trench, quarry, mine (*stánȝedelf*, *léadȝedelf*), f. *delfan* to DELVE, dig.]
1. That which is delved or dug: **a.** A hole or cavity dug in the earth, e.g. for irrigation or drainage; a pit; a trench, ditch; *spec.* applied to the drainage canals in the fen districts of the eastern counties.
c **1420** *Pallad. on Husb.* IV. 40 In forowe, in delf, in pastyne. **1502** ARNOLDE *Chron.* 168 Make a delf ther aboute ..til thou com to the gret rote. **1557** *Tottell's Misc.* (Arb.) 179 Daungerous delph, depe dungeon of disdaine. **1633** P. FLETCHER *Purple Isl.* III. xiii, Some lesser delfs [*later ed.* delfts] the fountains bottome sounding. **1661** MORGAN *Sph. Gentry* II. vii. 78 Extracting him out of that Delf or Pit which Reuben put him in. **1675** EVELYN *Terra* (1776) 3 In marshes and fenny Delves. **1713** *Lond. Gaz.* No. 5143/4, 44 Acres of Pasture Ground in the Delphs in..Haddenham in the County of Cambridge. **1851** *Jrnl. R. Agric. Soc.* XII. II. 304 The fens are divided by embanked upland rivulets or

'delphs'. **1877** *N.W. Linc. Gloss.*, *Delf, Delft*, a drain that has been delved..a pond, a clay-pit. a railway cutting, or any other large hole that has been delved out.

b. An excavation in or under the earth, where stone, coal, or other mineral is dug; a quarry; a mine. The ordinary name for a quarry in the northern counties.

1388 WYCLIF *2 Chron.* xxxiv. 11 To bie stoonys hewid out of the delues, *ether quarreris*. **14..** *Vocab. Harl. MS.* 1002 in *Promp. Parv.* 118 *note*², *Aurifedella*, a gold delfe. **1588–9** *Act 31 Eliz.* c. 7 §4 Quarries or Delfes of Stone or Slate. **1598** MANWOOD *Lawes Forest* xxiv. §5 (1615) 242/1 Any Mine, Delph of Coale, Stone, Clay, Marle, Turfe, Iron, or any other Mine. **1692** RAY *Dissol. World* 78 In Coal Delfs and other Mines..the Miners are many times drowned out. **1732** in *L'pool Munic. Rec.* (1886) II. 156 The quarry or delf att Brownlow Hill sho'd be cut thorow. **1878** F. S. WILLIAMS *Midl. Railw.* 390 Limestone..is dug from a quarry, or 'delph', some 30 to 50 ft. beneath the surface. **1888** *Sheffield Gloss.*, *Delf*, a stone quarry. **1891** *Labour Commission Gloss.*, *Delphs*, terms used to denote the working places in Yorkshire ironstone quarries.

†**c.** A grave. *Obs.*

c **1425** WYNTOUN *Cron.* VI. iv. 39 The Grafe, quhare þis dede Pypyne lay, Ðai rypyd..Ðat Delf þai stoppyd hastyly And away sped þame rycht spedyly. *c* **1460** *Towneley Myst.* (Surtees) 230 He rasyd Lazare out of his delfe. *a* **1548** *Thrie Priests Peblis* 37 (Jam.), The first freind, quhil he was laid in delf, He lufit ay far better than himself.

†**2.** A bed or stratum of any earth or mineral that is or may be dug into.

1601 HOLLAND *Pliny* II. 409 Obserue the change of euery coat..of the earth as they dig, to wit from the black delfe, vntil they meet..the veins aforesaid. *Ibid.* II. 415 Under the delfe of sand they met with salt. **1706** PHILLIPS (ed. Kersey), *Delf of Coal*, Coal lying in Veins under ground, before it is digged up.

3. *Sc.* A sod or cut turf.

1812 SOUTER *Agric. Surv. Banffs.* App. 42 If a delph be cast up in a field that hath lien for the space of five or six years, wild oats will spring up of their own accord. **1825–80** JAMIESON, *Delf*, a sod. In this sense the term *delf* is used, Lanarks. and Banffs.

†**b.** *Her.* A square bearing supposed to represent a square-cut sod of turf, used as an abatement. *Obs.*

c **1500** *Sc. Poem Heraldry* 165 in *Q. Eliz. Acad.* (1869) 100 Ȝit in armes, pictes and delphes espy. **1562** LEIGH *Armorie* (1597) 73 He beareth Argent, a delff Geules. To him that revoketh his own challeng, as commonly we cal it eating his worde, this is giuen in token thereof. **1610** GUILLIM *Heraldry* I. viii. (1660) 43 A Delfe for revocation of Challenge. **1688** R. HOLME *Armoury* III. 343/2 Some term..a Tile a Delfe because of its squareness, but in a Delfe there is nothing of a thickness.

†**4.** An act of delving; a thrust of the spade.

1616 SURFL. & MARKH. *Country Farme* 501 You must cut the vpper face and crust of the earth in Aprill, with a shallow delfe. **1688** R. HOLME *Armoury* II. 115/1 Delfe, or Spade-graft..a digging into the earth as deep as a spade can go at once.

5. *attrib.* and *Comb.*

1792 *Trans. Soc. Encourag. Arts* X. 105 Making a delf-ditch, twelve feet wide. **1885** *Law Times Rep.* LI. 589/1 Certain land called delph land, beyond which were sand-hills, protecting the property from the sea.

delf², **delft** (dɛlf, dɛlft). Also **delph**. [a. Du. *Delf*, now *Delft*, a town of Holland, named from the *delf*, *delve* 'ditch', by which name the chief canal of the town is still known: see prec. Since the paragogic *t* was added to the name of the town in mod.Du., it has been extended also to the English word, probably with the notion that *delf* was a corruption.]

1. A kind of glazed earthenware made at Delf or Delft in Holland; originally called ***Delf ware***.

1714 *Fr. Bk. of Rates* 121 Certain Goods, called Delph-Ware, and counterfeit China, coming from Holland and other Parts. **1743** *Lond. & Country Brew.* II. Advt., Potters-Work or Delft-Ware. **1859** SMILES *Self-Help* 40 Large quantities of the commoner sort of ware were imported..from Delft in Holland, whence it was usually known by the name of Delft ware.

1723 SWIFT *Poems, Stella at Woodpark*, A supper worthy of herself, Five nothings in five plates of delf. **1840** DICKENS *Old C. Shop* xv, A corner cupboard with their little stock of crockery and delf. **1880** HOWELLS *Undisc. Country* xvi. 261 From tall standing clocks to the coarsest cracked blue delft.

2. *attrib.* and *Comb.*

1756 *Connoisseur* 103 ¶6, I am never allowed to eat from any thing better than a Delft plate. **1796** MORSE *Amer. Geog.* II. 166 Glass works..delf-houses and paper mills. **1809** W. IRVING *Knickerb.* III. iii. (1849) 161 A majestic delft tea-pot. **1884** MAY CROMMELIN *Brown-Eyes* iv. 33 Rows of blue china and coarser but valuable old delf pottery.

delf, obs. form of DELVE *v.*, to dig.

delfin, -fyn, var. of DELPHIN *Obs.*

delful, -fully, obs. var. of DOLEFUL, -FULLY.

Delhi ('dɛlɪ). The name of the capital of India, used *attrib.* in **Delhi belly** *slang*, an upset stomach accompanied by diarrhœa such as may be suffered by visitors to India; cf. *gippy tummy* s.v. GIPPY 1 c.

1944 *Newsweek* 28 Feb. 76/1 Joe was off again—this time to be the first to hit the heat and filth of India and the desolation of China. He got 'Delhi belly' (a form of dysentery) and greeted Tommy Harmon when the flyer walked out of Jap-controlled China. **1962** E. SNOW *Other Side of River* (1963) xlii. 314, I experienced the usual agonizing symptoms of indiscretion in the East—what the G.I.'s called Delhi-belly. **1980** *Daily Tel.* 25 June 18 In Bombay, shortly after the First World War, our mess was periodically afflicted by a particularly virulent form of 'Delhi belly'.

deli ('dɛlɪ). *colloq.* (orig. *U.S.*). Also **delly**. Abbrev. of DELICATESSEN, usu. in sense b.

1954 J. A. WEINGARTEN *Amer. Dict. Slang* 99/1 *Deli*... I have not yet seen this word in print, but it is used quite frequently. 'I'm having deli tonight.'; 'Mom, let's have deli.' Perhaps to be spelled *dely* or *delly*. **1967** L. DEIGHTON *London Dossier* 40 The next best thing to home cooking might be cooked food from tempting delicatessens. Very few London delis have a place to sit. **1970** 'E. FERRERS' *Seven Sleepers* xi. 128 Stopping at the shop near his flat which his landlady called 'the delly', he bought half a cold chicken. **1973** *Times* 29 Nov. 17/6 In..Adelaide..Jim and Mary Phillips run a *deli*—a cross between a delicatessen and a corner shop. **1978** J. WAMBAUGH *Black Marble* ix. 182 How about a deli on Fairfax? I could go for a nice onion bagel. **1980** A. J. JONES *Game Theory* iii. 173 The manager of a downtown 24-hour Deli has divided an average weekday into four-hour periods and figured out how many assistants he needs serving in each four-hour period. **1982** *Observer* 13 June 39/5 As yet the area is a little light on dellies, wine bars and restaurants as compared with the more established Islington areas. **1983** *Times* 19 July 17/4 Last April in the Haymarket, came London's first Chinese deli, Cohen & Wong, reflecting the mix of Jewish-style delicatessen food and Chinese dishes.

Delian ('diːlɪən), *a.*¹ [f. L. *Dēli-us* (Gr. Δήλι-ος) of or pertaining to Delos, Δῆλος) + -AN.] Of or belonging to Delos, an island in the Grecian archipelago, the reputed birthplace of Apollo and Artemis (Diana). **Delian problem**, the problem of finding the side of a cube having double the volume of a given cube (i.e. of finding the cube root of 2); so called from the answer of the oracle of Delos, that a plague raging at Athens should cease when Apollo's altar, which was cubical, should be doubled. Also †**Deliacal** *a.*

1623 COCKERAM, *Delian twins*, the Sunne and Moone. **1727–51** CHAMBERS *Cycl.* s.v. *Duplication*, They applied themselves..to seek the Duplicature of the cube, which henceforward was called the *Delian Problem*. *Ibid.*, *Deliacal Problem*, a famous problem among the antients concerning the duplication of the cube. **1879** GEO. ELIOT *Coll. Breakf. P.* 679 'Tis our lot To pass more swiftly than the Delian God.

Delian ('diːlɪən), *a.*² and *sb.* **A.** *adj.* Of, relating to, or characteristic of Frederick *Delius* (1862–1934), English composer, or his works. **B.** *sb.* A follower or admirer of Delius.

1958 B. JAMES in P. Gammond *Duke Ellington* II. 149 Delian harmony has become the stock-in-trade of modern popular music by an odd accident which, I am convinced, provokes a smile of..amusement from the ghost of Delius. .. Some of Ellington's reflective pieces have a distinctly Delian flavour of nostalgia and bitter-sweetness. **1962** *Observer* 8 Apr. 28/3 Our Delians are in full bloom this spring. At Bradford on Tuesday they were out in force for Sadler's Wells' new production of 'A Village Romeo and Juliet' and gave it a rapturous reception. **1976** *Daily Tel.* 21 Aug. 7/4 Mr. Palmer's description of the characteristic 'Delian experience' as a 'soaring ecstasy of yearning wistfulness' suggests an art of escape from the ideal. **1977** *Gramophone* June 48/1, I only put these comparisons in for the dedicated Delians who will already have the earlier versions. **1984** *N.Y. Times* 4 Nov. II. 31/3 The cello line in the sonata soars in the Delian manner.

†**de'libate**, *v.* *Obs.* [f. ppl. stem of L. *dēlībā-re* to take a little of, taste, f. DE- I. 2 + *lībāre* to take a little of, taste, etc.]

1. *trans.* To take a little of, taste, sip; also *fig.*

1623 COCKERAM, *Delibate*, to sippe, or kisse the cup. *a* **1639** MARMION *Antiq.* III. ii, When he has travell'd, and delibated the French and the Spanish.

2. To take away as a small part, to pluck, cull.

1655–60 STANLEY *Hist. Philos.* III. II. 104 The mind is induced into the soul from without by divine participation, delibated of the universall Divine mind.

Hence **delibated** *ppl. a.*

1655 FULLER *Serm.*, *Gift for God* 13 A soule..unacquainted with virgin, delibated, and clarified joy.

†**deli'bation.** *Obs.* [ad. L. *dēlībātiōn-em*, n. of action f. *dēlībāre*: see prec.]

1. A 'taste' or slight knowledge *of* something.

a **1638** MEDE *Disc. Acts* xvii. 4 Wks. (1672) I. 19 Nor can it be understood without some delibation of Jewish Antiquity.

2. A portion taken away, culled, or extracted.

1678 CUDWORTH *Intell. Syst.* 216 Either..the substance of God Himself together with that of the Evil Demon, or else certain delibations from both..blended and confounded together. **1794** G. ADAMS *Nat. & Exp. Philos.* II. xxi. 420 They considered the principle of motion and vegetation as delibations from the invisible fire of the universe.

†**de'liber**, *v.* *Obs.* Forms: 4–6 **deliber**, 5 **delibere**, 5–6 **delyber**, 6 **delybre**: see also DELIVER *v.*² [ME. a. F. *délibérer* (15th c. in Littré), or ad. L. *dēlīberāre* to weigh well, consider maturely, take counsel, etc., f. DE- I. 3 + *lībrāre* to balance, weigh, f. *lībra* a balance, pair of scales. In 15–16th c. it varied with *deliver*: cf. the ordinary Romanic *v* from Latin *b*.]

1. a. *intr.* To deliberate, take counsel, consider.

c **1374** CHAUCER *Troylus* IV. 169 He gan deliberyn for the best. *c* **1386** — *Melib.* ¶760 She..delibered and took auys in hir self. **1481** CAXTON *Myrr.* I. v. 21 They deliberid emong them and concluded.

b. *trans.* To deliberate upon, consider.

1545 JOYE *Exp. Dan.* viii. (R.), In delibering, in decerning things delybred.

2. *trans.* To determine, resolve.

a. with *simple obj.* or *infin.*

1482 CAXTON *Polycron.* Prohemye A iij, I haue delybered too wryte twoo bookes notable. **1489** —— *Faytes of A.* I. vi. 13 It is not to be delibered ne lightly to be concluded. *c* **1534** tr. *Pol. Verg. Eng. Hist.* (Camd.) I. 204 But hee..delibered to withstande the adventure. **1580** STOW *Hen. V* an. 1417 (R.) He delibered to goe vnto them in his owne person.

b. *refl.* (with *inf.*)

c **1489** CAXTON *Sonnes of Aymon* xvi. 378, I pray you that ye wyll delibere your self for to gyve vs a good answere. **15..** *Helyas* in Thoms *Prose Rom.* (1858) III. 25 On a day he delibered him for to go to hunt.

c. *pass.* To be determined or resolved.

1470–85 MALORY *Arthur* V. ii, I am delybered and fully concluded to goo. *a* **1529** SKELTON *Bk. Three Fooles* I. 203 Joseph..had vii brethren..the which were delybered of a longe time to haue destroyed him.

deliberalize: see DE- II. 1.

deliberant (dɪ'lɪbərənt). *rare.* [a. F. *délibérant*, or ad. L. *dēlīberānt-em*, pr. pple. of F. *délibérer*, L. *dēlīberāre* to DELIBERATE.] One who deliberates.

1673 O. WALKER *Educ.* 202 Experience, which the Deliberant is supposed not to have. **1824** T. JEFFERSON *Writ.* (1830) IV. 395 Experience has proved the benefit of subjecting questions to two separate bodies of deliberants.

deliberate (dɪ'lɪbərət), *a.* [ad. L. *dēlīberāt-us*, pa. pple. of *dēlīberāre*: see DELIBER.]

1. Well weighed or considered; carefully thought out; formed, carried out, etc. with careful consideration and full intention; done of set purpose; studied; not hasty or rash.

1548 HALL *Chron.* 182 After..deliberate consultacion had among the peeres, prelates, and commons. **1602** SHAKS. *Ham.* IV. iii. 9 This sodaine sending him away, must seeme Deliberate pause. **1667** MILTON *P.L.* I. 554 Such as..in stead of rage Deliberate valour breath'd. **1761** HUME *Hist. Eng.* III. lxi. 322 He seems not to have had any deliberate plan in all these alterations. **1848** RUSKIN *Mod. Paint.* II. III. I. ii. §4. 13 The act is deliberate, and determined on beforehand, in direct defiance of reason. **1856** FROUDE *Hist. Eng.* (1858) II. viii. 244 An impatience of control, a deliberate preference for disorder.

b. Of persons: Characterized by deliberation; considering carefully; careful and slow in deciding; not hasty or rash.

1596 SHAKS. *Merch. V.* II. ix. 80 O these deliberate fooles when they doe choose, They haue the wisdome by their wit to loose. **1802** MAR. EDGEWORTH *Moral T.* (1816) I. xix. 165 'I will tell you, sir', replied the deliberate, unfeeling magistrate; 'you are suspected of having', etc. **1874** GREEN *Short Hist.* viii. §1. 450 Striving to be deliberate in speech.

2. Leisurely, slow, not hurried: of movement or moving agents.

a **1600** HOOKER (J.), It is for virtuous considerations, that wisdom so far prevaileth with men as to make them desirous of slow and deliberate death. **1608–11** BP. HALL *Medit. & Vows* I. §18 There are three messengers of death: Casualty, Sickness, Age..The two first are suddaine, the last leasurely and deliberate. **1626** BACON *Sylva* §252 Eccho's are some more sudden..Others are more deliberate, that is, giue more Space betweene the Voice and the Eccho. **1790** J. BRUCE *Source of Nile* II. III. 232 Sertza Denghel..drew up his army in the same deliberate manner in which he had crossed the Mareb. *Mod.* He is very deliberate in his movements.

deliberate (dɪ'lɪbəreɪt), *v.* [f. L. *dēlīberāt-*, ppl. stem of *dēlīberāre*: see DELIBER and -ATE. The pa. pple. was in early times *deliberat*, *-ate*, from L.: cf. prec.]

†**1.** *trans.* To weigh in the mind; to consider carefully with a view to decision; to think over. *Obs.* (Now usually ***to deliberate upon***: see 2.)

a **1610** HEALEY *Theophrastus*, *Unseasonableness* (1636) 49 An unseasonable fellow..obtrudes his owne affaires to be deliberated and debated. **1611** TOURNEUR *Ath. Trag.* III. i. Wks. 1878 I. 83 Leaue a little roome..For understanding to deliberate The cause or author of this accident. **1681** J. SALGADO *Symbiosis* 14 A thing not to be deliberated.

b. with *obj. clause.*

1555 EDEN *Decades* 83 Deliberatinge therefore with my selfe, from whense these mountaynes..haue such great holowe caues or dennes. **1659** PEARSON *Creed* (1839) 28 The stone doth not deliberate whether it shall descend. **1759** ROBERTSON *Hist. Scotl.* I. v. 371 She deliberated..how she might overcome the regent's scruples. **1829** W. IRVING *Conq. Granada* I. x. 81 A council of war..where it was deliberated what was to be done with Alhama.

2. *intr.* To use consideration with a view to decision; to think carefully; to pause or take time for consideration. Const. †*of* (obs.), *on*, *upon*, etc.

1561 T. NORTON *Calvin's Inst.* Table Scripture Quot., The heart of man doth deliberate of his way. **1591** SHAKS. *Two Gent.* I. iii. 73 Please you deliberate a day or two. **1624** CAPT. SMITH *Virginia* IV. 153 Two daies the King deliberated vpon an answer. **1697** STILLINGFL. *Serm.* II. xi. (R.), If he had time to deliberate about it. **1713** ADDISON *Cato* IV. i, In spight of all the virtue we can boast The woman that deliberates is lost. **1797** MRS. RADCLIFFE *Italian* i, Vivaldi shut himself up in his apartment to deliberate.

1894 *Daily News* 4 May 4/7 They [women] deliberate a great deal, now-a-days; we draw no unfriendly conclusion.

b. Of a body of persons: To take counsel together, considering and examining the reasons for and against a proposal or course of action.

1552 HULOET, Deliberate or take aduice or counsayle, *consulto*. **1665** MANLEY *Grotius' Low C. Warres* 191 When therefore the Common-Council of any Town hath deliberated at home, concerning matters there proposed. **1745** *Col. Rec. Pennsylv.* V. 11 To carry it home to their Council to deliberate upon. **1843** PRESCOTT *Mexico* (1850) I. 145 The three crowned heads of the empire..deliberated with the other members on the respective merits of the pieces. **1858** FROUDE *Hist. Eng.* IV. xviii. 28 The future relations of the two countries could now be deliberated on with a hope of settlement.

†**3.** To resolve, determine, conclude; *pass.* to be resolved or determined. *Obs.*

1550 NICOLLS *Thucyd.* 187 (R.) They deliberated to constrayne theym to fighte by sea ymmediatly. **1582–8** *Hist. James VI* (1804) 260 He was deliberat to resigne his office. **1585** T. WASHINGTON tr. *Nicholay's Voy.* IV. vi. 117, I am deliberated..to follow the most auncient, famous, and moderne Geographers. **1633** J. DONE *Hist. Septuagint* 12, I have deliberated to frame unto you by Writing, a thing.. well deserving to be knowne.

Hence **de'liberating** *vbl. sb.* and *ppl. a.*

1643 MILTON *Divorce* II. ix, The all-wise purpose of a deliberating God. **1885** *Athenæum* 2 May 572/3 The deliberating expression of the student's countenance.

de'liberated, *ppl. a.* [f. prec. + -ED[1].] Carefully weighed in the mind: see the verb.

1597 J. KING *Jonas* (1618) 311 A wise & deliberated speech. *a* **1644** LAUD *Serm.* 226 (T.) If you shall not be firm to deliberated counsels. **1704** *Col. Rec. Pennsylv.* II. 191 After Deliberated and mature Debate thereon.

deliberately (dɪˈlɪbərətlɪ), *adv.* [f. DELIBERATE *a.* + -LY[2].] In a deliberate manner.

1. With careful consideration; not hastily or rashly; of set purpose.

1532 MORE *Confut. Tindale* Wks. 575/2 He..dooeth deliberatelye with long deuice and studye bestowed about it, doe this geare willingly. **1651** BAXTER *Inf. Bapt.* 243, I.. deliberately compared one with the other. **1748** HARTLEY *Observ. Man* II. ii. §43. 188 To deceive the world knowingly and deliberately. **1892** *Law Times' Rep.* LXVII. 232/1 Omitted..through inadvertence and not deliberately and on purpose.

2. Without haste, leisurely, slowly.

1711 STEELE *Spect.* No. 147 ¶2 Those that Read so fast.. may learn to speak deliberately. **1774** PENNANT *Tour Scotl. in 1772*, 169 They swim very deliberately with their two dorsal fins above water. **1871** B. TAYLOR *Faust* (1875) II. IV. i. 228, I tread deliberately this summit's lonely edge.

de'liberateness. [f. as prec. + -NESS.] The quality of being deliberate, or of showing careful consideration; absence of haste in decision.

1602 CAREW *Cornwall* 100 Deliberatenes of vndertaking, & sufficiency of effecting. **1649** *Eikon Bas.* (1824) 21 The order, gravity, and deliberatenesse befitting a Parliament. **1881** W. C. RUSSELL *Ocean Free-Lance* II. 142 The.. chilling deliberateness of Shelvocke's manner and voice.

deliberater, var. of DELIBERATOR.

deliberation[1] (dɪˌlɪbəˈreɪʃən). Also 4–6 delyberacioun, -acion, etc. [a. F. *délibération*, in 13th c. *deliberacion*, ad. L. *dēlīberātiōn-em*, n. of action from *dēlīberāre* to DELIBERATE.]

1. The action of deliberating, or weighing a thing in the mind; careful consideration with a view to decision.

c **1374** CHAUCER *Troylus* III. 470 For he, with grete deliberacion Had every thing..Forcast, and put in execucion. **1477** EARL RIVERS (Caxton) *Dictes* 133 A man ought to do his Werkis by deliberacion..and not sodaynly. **1548** HALL *Chron.* 194 b, Without any farther deliberacion, he determined with himselfe. **1618** BOLTON *Florus* III. x. 198 Asking time for deliberation. **1651** HOBBES *Govt. & Soc.* xiii. §16. 207 Deliberation is nothing else but a weighing, as it were in scales, the conveniencies, and inconveniencies of the fact we are attempting. **1751** JOHNSON *Rambler* No. 184 ¶4 To close tedious deliberations with hasty resolves. **1875** JOWETT *Plato* (ed. 2) I. 386 Make up your mind then..for the time of deliberation is over.

2. The consideration and discussion of the reasons for and against a measure by a number of councillors (*e.g.* in a legislative assembly).

1489 CAXTON *Faytes of A.* IV. x. 256 Grete bataylles are entreprysed by delyberacyon of a grete counseyl. **1555** EDEN *Decades* 57 After deliberation they iudged that *Nicuesa* could no more lacke [etc.]. **1688** in Somers *Tracts* II. 290 Their Lordships assembled together..and prepared, upon the most mature Deliberation, such Matters as they judged necessary. **1771** *Junius Lett.* xlviii. 252 The resolutions.. were made..after long deliberation upon a constitutional question. **1855** MACAULAY *Hist. Eng.* III. xiii. 280 To protect the deliberations of the Royalist Convention. **1861** GEO. ELIOT *Silas M.* 9 On their return to the vestry there was further deliberation. **1871** J. LEWES *Digest of Census* 204 The legislative body [of Guernsey], called the 'States of Deliberation'.

†**b.** A consultation, conference. *Obs.*

1632 LITHGOW *Trav.* III. 80 A long deliberation being ended, they restored backe againe my Pilgrimes clothes, and Letters. **1648** NETHERSOLE *Problems* II. *title*, Advice..very applyable to the present Deliberation.

†**3.** A resolution or determination. *Obs.*

1579 FENTON *Guicciard.* I. (1599) 18 The timerous man carried by despaire into deliberations headlong and hurtfull. **1632** J. HAYWARD tr. *Biondi's Eromena* 10 If the doubt of shewing himselfe too credulous..had not confirm'd him in his former deliberation. **1653** URQUHART *Rabelais* I. xxix. My deliberation is not to provoke, but to appease: not to assault but to defend.

†**b.** The written record of a resolution (of a deliberating body). *Obs.*

1715 LEONI *Palladio's Archit.* (1742) I. 98 Places..where were reposited the deliberations and resolutions of the Senate.

4. As a quality: Deliberateness of action.

c **1386** CHAUCER *Melib.* ¶376 Yow oghte purueyen and apparaillen yow..with greet diligence and greet deliberacioun. **1413** LYDG. *Pylgr. Sowle* IV. xxix. (1859) 62 Al that they sayde or dyde shold be of suche delyberacion, that it myght be taken for autoryte of lawe. **1526** *Pilgr. Perf.* (W. de W. 1531) 92 b, And this enuy is mortall synne, whan it is with delyberacyon of reason and wyll. **1541** R. COPLAND *Guydon's Quest.* 2 C iij b/2 Nowe we wyll dyspose vs with delyberacyon to speake of the curacyon of inueterate vlcers. **1628** EARLE *Microcosm.*, *Alderman* (Arb.) 27 Hee is one that will not hastily runne into error, for hee treds with great deliberation. **1732** LAW *Serious C.* xxiii. (ed. 2) 47 You must enter upon it with deliberation. **1794** S. WILLIAMS *Hist. Vermont* 166 The chiefs consulted with great deliberation. **1856** EMERSON *Eng. Traits, Wealth* Wks. (Bohn) II. 73 Every whim..is put into stone and iron, into silver and gold, with costly deliberation and detail.

b. Absence of hurry; slowness in action or movement; leisureliness.

1855 H. SPENCER *Princ. Psychol.* (1872) I. ix. 495 Psychical changes which..take place with some deliberation. **1860** TYNDALL *Glac.* I. xvii. 119 We saw it [an ice-berg] roll over with the utmost deliberation.

†**delibe'ration**[2]. *Obs. rare.* [ad. med.L. *dēlīberātiōn-em*, n. of action from *dēlīberāre* to DELIVER.] Liberation, setting free.

1502 ARNOLDE *Chron.* 160 That we shulde treat with thy holynesse for his delyberacion.

deliberative (dɪˈlɪbərətɪv), *a.* and *sb.* [ad. L. *dēlīberātīv-us*, f. ppl. stem of *dēlīberāre*: see -IVE. Cf. F. *délibératif, -ive* (14th c. in Hatzf.).]

A. *adj.* **1.** Pertaining to deliberation; having the function of deliberating.

1553 T. WILSON *Rhet.* (1580) 29 An Oracion deliberative. **1586** A. DAY *Eng. Secretary* II. (1625) 88 In a deliberative sort we propound divers things, and refute them all one after another. **1641** SIR E. DERING in Rushw. *Hist. Coll.* (1692) III. I. 393 We neither had a Decisive Voice to determine with them, nor a Deliberative Voice to Consult with them. **1678** *Trans. Crt. Spain* 143 All the Towns which have a deliberative Vote in the State. **1790** BURKE *Fr. Rev.* Wks. V. 377 Erecting itself into a deliberative body. **1874** MORLEY *Compromise* (1886) 105 The growth of self-government, or government by deliberative bodies, representing opposed principles and conflicting interests.

2. a. Characterized by deliberation, or careful consideration in order to decision.

1659 D. PELL *Impr. Sea* 361 A serious meditation, and deliberative ponderating upon the Power and terrible Majesty of God. **1762** KAMES *Elem. Crit.* I. ii. 100 The slower operations of deliberative reason. **1836** *Random Recoll. Ho. Lords* xiv. 326 Things to which, in his cooler and more deliberative moments, he would not on any account give expression.

†**b.** Habitually deliberate; not hasty. *Obs.*

a **1734** NORTH *Lives* I. 431 He was naturally very quick of apprehension but withal very deliberative.

3. *Gram.* Expressing deliberation or doubt.

1842 W. E. JELF *Gram. Gr. Lang.* II. iv. 501 The conjunct. after principal, opt. after historic tenses, has a deliberative force. **1858** J. CONINGTON *Wks. Virgil* I. 38/1 The deliberative conjunctive in Greek. **1893** HAYES & MASON *Tutorial Lat. Gram.* xlii. 238 The interrogative form of the jussive subjunctive is called the deliberative or dubitative subjunctive. **1930** J. F. MOUNTFORD *Kennedy's Rev. Lat. Primer* 160 The Subjunctive of Will (Volitive) expresses.. what ought to be done as a matter of propriety or duty... When used in a question, this Subjunctive is called Deliberative.

†**B.** *sb.* A discussion of some question with a view to settlement; a deliberative discourse; a matter for deliberation. *Obs.*

1597 BACON *Coulers Good & Evill* (Arb.) 138 In deliberatiues the point is what is good and what is euill. **1620** E. BLOUNT *Horæ Subsec.* 77 A man so conceited of himselfe can bee no companion in deliberatiues. **1650** R. HOLLINGWORTH *Exerc. Usurped Powers* 52 A person.. should begin this section of his with a generall deliberative.

de'liberatively, *adv.* [f. prec. + -LY[2].] In a deliberative manner; with deliberation, deliberately (*obs.*); in the way of deliberation or discussion, as a deliberative body.

1654 H. L'ESTRANGE *Chas. I* (1655) 208 An omission studiously and deliberatively resolved upon. **1757** BURKE *Abridgm. Eng. Hist.* Wks. X. 347 Constituent parts of this assembly..whilst it acted deliberatively. **1864** CARLYLE *Fredk. Gt.* IV. 548 Consulted of and deliberatively touched upon.

de'liberativeness. [f. as prec. + -NESS.] The quality of being deliberative.

1653–4 WHITELOCKE *Jrnl. Swed. Emb.* (1772) I. 376 Through the slowness, or rather deliberativeness, of the old chancellor. **1880** *Scribner's Mag.* May 94 The prayerful deliberativeness with which New England made war.

deliberator (dɪˈlɪbəreɪtə(r)). [ad. L. *dēlīberātor*, agent-n. from *dēlīberāre*: see -OR.] One who deliberates; one who takes part in a deliberation.

1782 V. KNOX *Ess.* 133 (R.) The dull and unfeeling deliberators of questions on which a good heart and understanding can intuitively decide. **1813** SIR R. WILSON *Diary* II. 265 They pretend that this multiplicity of supervisors and conflicting deliberators is fatal to the common interest.

delible (ˈdɛlɪb(ə)l), *a.* Also 7–8 deleble. [ad. L. *dēlēbil-is* that may be blotted out, f. *dēlēre* (see DELETE and -BLE): cf. *indelible*.] Capable of being deleted or effaced (*lit.* and *fig.*).

1610 W. FOLKINGHAM *Art of Survey* II. v. 55 Base lines.. for Boundaries or deleble Plant-lines. *a* **1661** FULLER *Worthies* I. 215 An impression easily deleble. **1683** tr. *Erasmus' Moriæ Enc.* 95 Distinguishing between a Delible and an Indelible character. **1715** BENTLEY *Serm.* x. 357 The deleble stains of departed souls. **1793** SMEATON *Edystone L.* §235 To render the marks not easily delible.

†**'delibrate,** *v. Obs. rare*[—0]. [f. L. *dēlibrāre* to take off the bark, f. DE- I. 6 + *liber, libr-*, bark.]

1623 COCKERAM, *Delibrate*, to pull off the rinde of a Tree.

delicacy (ˈdɛlɪkəsɪ). Also 5 -asie, -asye, 5–6 -acie. [f. DELICATE *a.*: see -ACY, and cf. *obstinacy, secrecy*.] I. The quality of being DELICATE (in various senses of the adj.). II. A thing in which this quality is displayed or embodied.

I. †**1.** The quality of being addicted to pleasure or sensuous delights; voluptuousness, luxuriousness, daintiness. *Obs.*

c **1374** CHAUCER *Former Age* 58 Yit was nat Iuppiter the lykerous þat fyrst was fadyr of delicasie. **1393** GOWER *Conf.* III. 21 Of the seconde glotony, Which cleped is delicacy. *Ibid.* III. 115 He shall be..lusty to delicacy In every thing which he shall do. *c* **1550** *Disc. Common Weal Eng.* (1893) 5 Our dylycasye in requyrynge strangers wares. **1593** NASHE *Christ's T.* 140 Thus much of delicacy in general; now more particularly of his first branch, gluttony. **1680** C. BLOUNT tr. *Philostratus* 229 (Trench) Cephisodorus, the disciple of Isocrates, charged him with delicacy, intemperance, and gluttony. **1741** MIDDLETON *Cicero* II. XII. 503 In his [Cicero's] cloaths and dress..avoiding the extremes of a rustic negligence and foppish delicacy.

†**2.** Luxury; pampering indulgence. *Obs.*

1393 GOWER *Conf.* I. 14 Delicacie his swete toþ Haþ fostred so þat it fordoþ Of abstinence al þat þer is. *c* **1450** LONELICH *Grail* xlii. 554 The Cristene men..weren Alle ful Richely..Ifed with alle delicasy. **1577** B. GOOGE *Heresbach's Husb.* I. (1586) 7 The common sort preferreth shamefull and beastly delicasie, before honest and vertuous labour. **1629** MAXWELL tr. *Herodian* (1635) 127 The glory of a Souldier consists in labour, not in lazinesse or delicacie. **1665** G. HAVERS *Sir T. Roe's Voy. E. Ind.* 477 A life that was full of pomp, and pleasure, and delicacy. **1725** POPE *Odyss.* XX. 82 Venus in tender delicacy rears With honey, milk, and wine, their infant years.

†**b.** Gratification, pleasure, delectation. *Obs.*

c **1386** CHAUCER *Monk's T.* 401 He Rome brende for his delicasie. **1667** MILTON *P.L.* V. 333 She turns, on hospitable thoughts intent What choice to chuse for delicacie best.

†**3.** The quality of being delightful to the palate; delicateness or daintiness (of food). *Obs.*

1393 GOWER *Conf.* II. 83 Berconius of cokerie First made the delicacie. **1650** JER. TAYLOR *Holy Living* ii. §1 Be not troublesome to thyself or others in the choice of thy meats or the delicacy of thy sauces.

†**4.** The quality of being delightful, *esp.* to the intellectual senses; beauty, daintiness, pleasantness. *Obs.*

1509 HAWES *Past. Pleas.* XI. xxii, O redolent well of famous poetry..Refleryngе out the dulcet delicacy Of iiii. ryvers in mervaylous wydenesse. **1589** GREENE *Menaphon* (Arb.) 48 Feeding on the delicacie of their features. **1612** DRAYTON *Poly-olb.* i. 5 Euen in the agedst face, where beautie once did dwell..something wil appeare To showe some little tract of delicacie there. *Ibid.* vii. 106 The aire with such delights and delicacie fils, As makes it loth to stirre, or thence those smels to beare. **1634** SIR T. HERBERT *Trav.* 61 Some peculiar Houses..may be competitors for delicacie with most in Europe.

5. Exquisite fineness of texture, substance, finish, etc.; graceful slightness, slenderness, or softness; soft or tender beauty.

a **1586** SIDNEY (J.), A man..in whom strong making took not away delicacy, nor beauty fierceness. **1615** CROOKE *Body of Man* (1616) 730 Anaxagoras..marking diligently.. the postures of the fingers..and the soft delicacy thereof. **1744** HARRIS *Three Treat.* III. II. (1765) 217 No Woman ever equalled the Delicacy of the Medicean Venus. **1756** BURKE *Subl. & B.* IV. xvi, An air of robustness and strength is very prejudicial to beauty. An appearance of delicacy and even of fragility, is almost essential to it. **1874** GREEN *Short Hist.* vii. §3. 363 She [Elizabeth] would play with her rings that her courtiers might note the delicacy of her hands.

6. Tenderness or weakliness of constitution or health; want of strength or robustness; susceptibility to injury or disease.

1632 J. HAYWARD tr. *Biondi's Eromena* 93 Cause to conjecture, that the delicacie of her sex kept disproportioned companie with..her courage. **1711** ADDISON *Spect.* No. 3 ¶3 Whether it was from the Delicacy of her Constitution, or that she was troubled with the Vapours. **1759** DILWORTH *Pope* 136 From the delicacy of his body, his life had been a continual scene of suffering to him. **1816** KEATINGE *Trav.* (1817) II. 181 The silk-cultivation has been on the decline in this part of the world, from the extreme delicacy of the insect. **1872** B. CLAYTON *Dogs* 20 The great drawback [to the Italian Greyhound] is its delicacy; it requires the utmost care.

7. The quality or condition of requiring nice and skilful handling.

1785 BURKE *Sp. Nabob Arcot* Wks. 1842 I. 318 That our concerns in India were matters of delicacy. **1796** MORSE *Amer. Geog.* II. 679 The extreme difficulty and delicacy of drawing the line of limitation [in a list of eminent men]. **1857** WHEWELL *Hist. Induct. Sc.* I. Pref. 7, I was aware.. of the difficulty and delicacy of the office which I had undertaken. **1885** *L'pool Daily Post* 1 June 5/3 Absorbed in negotiations of the utmost delicacy.

8. Exquisite fineness of feeling, observation, etc.; nicety of perception; sensitiveness of appreciation.

1702 ROWE *Tamerl.* Ded., Poetry..will still be the Entertainment of all wise Men, that have any Delicacy in their Knowledge. *a* **1704** T. BROWN *Sat. Antients* Wks. 1730 I. 23 To make the delicacy of his sentiments perceived. **1855** MACAULAY *Hist. Eng.* III. 60 His principles would be relaxed, and the delicacy of his sense of right and wrong impaired. **1869** E. A. PARKES *Pract. Hygiene* (ed. 3) 29 Warming the water is said to increase the delicacy of taste. **1884** CHURCH *Bacon* ix. 216 Their truth and piercingness and delicacy of observation.

b. *transf.* Of instruments, etc.: Responsiveness to the slightest influence or change; sensitiveness.

1871 B. STEWART *Heat* §29 Such an instrument will therefore indicate any difference of temperature with great delicacy.

9. Exquisite fineness or nicety of skill, expression, touch, etc.

1675 tr. *Machiavelli's Prince* (Rtldg. 1883) 198 This double intelligence was managed with..slyness and delicacy. **1683** D. A. *Art Converse* 103 With modest Apologies and delicacy of expression. *a* **1700** DRYDEN (J.), Van Dyck has even excelled him in the delicacy of his colouring. **1759** ROBERTSON *Hist. Scotl.* I. I. 69 Henry VIII of England held the balance with less delicacy, but with a stronger hand. **1848** MACAULAY *Hist. Eng.* I. 66 Scotsmen ..wrote Latin verse with more than the delicacy of Vida. **1885** *Truth* 28 May 848/2 The spray is rendered with much lightness and delicacy.

10. A refined sense of what is becoming, modest or proper; sensitiveness to the feelings of modesty, shame, etc.; delicate regard for the feelings of others.

1712 STEELE *Spect.* No. 286 ¶1 A false Delicacy is Affectation, not Politeness. **1732** MALLET in *Swift's Lett.* (1766) II. 269, I am sure you will do it with all the delicacy natural to your own disposition. **1749** FIELDING *Tom Jones* XVIII. xiii, This..somewhat reconciled the delicacy of Sophia to the public entertainment, which..she was obliged to go to. **1832** LYTTON *Eugene A.* I. x, It would be a false delicacy in me to deny that I have observed it. **1843** MISS MITFORD in L'Estrange *Life* III. x. 171 Nothing can exceed their cordiality and delicacy, so that their benefactions are given as a compliment.

†**11.** Fastidiousness; squeamishness. *Obs.*

1725 POPE *Odyss.* XIX. 397 The delicacy of your courtly train To wash a wretched wand'rer wou'd disdain. **1771** MRS. GRIFFITH tr. *Viaud's Shipwreck* 104 It was almost come to a state of putrefaction, but hunger has no delicacy; so having broiled it [etc.]. **1793** BEDDOES *Math. Evid.* 118 The common old thin 4to. is not adapted to modern delicacy in books.

II. 12. A thing which gives delight; something delightful. *arch.*

1586 A. DAY *Eng. Secretary* I. (1625) 24 [To] beleeve that ..our very senses are partakers of every delicacie in them contained. **1594** T. B. *La Primaud. Fr. Acad.* II. 197 These delicacies and spirituall delights. **1609** BIBLE (Douay) *Isa.* li. 3 He wil make her desert as delicacies [WYCLIF delices]. **1650** JER. TAYLOR *Holy Living* (1727) 242 God..encourages our duty with..sensible pleasure and delicacies in prayer. **1667** MILTON *P.L.* VIII. 526 These delicacies of Taste, Sight, Smell, Herbs, Fruits, & Flours, Walks, and the melodie of Birds. **1882** STEVENSON *New Arab. Nts.* (1884) 22 The President's company is a delicacy in itself.

b. *esp.* Something that gratifies the palate, a choice or dainty item of food; a dainty.

c **1450** LONELICH *Grail* lv. 270 The peple..weren Repleynsched..with alle Maner Metes and delecasyes. **1596** DRAYTON *Legends* iii. 118 Me with Ambrosiall Delicacies fed. **1751** JOHNSON *Rambler* No. 172 ¶10 Untasted delicacies solicit his appetite. **1879** FARRAR *St. Paul* (1883) 194 A pig..was..the chief delicacy at Gentile banquets. **1884** G. ALLEN *Philistia* III. 156 Oysters, sweetbreads, red mullet, any little delicacy of that sort.

†**c.** A luxury; a sensual pleasure. *Obs.*

1581 PETTIE *Guazzo's Civ. Conv.* I. (1586) 19 These lurke loyteringlie plunged in delicacies..as Swine in the mire. **1605** VERSTEGAN *Dec. Intell.* vi. (1628) 165 A people very strong and hardy, and the rather for not beeing weakned with delicacies.

13. A delicate trait, observance, or attention.

1712 STEELE *Spect.* No. 491 ¶2 The Decencies, Honours and Delicacies that attend the Passion towards them [women] in elegant Minds. **1751** JOHNSON *Rambler* No. 98 ¶5 Those little civilities and ceremonious delicacies. **1779** J. MOORE *View Soc. Fr.* II. xciv. 418 A woman, and acquainted with all the weakness and delicacies of the sex.

14. A nicety, a refinement.

1789 STOKES *Let.* in Pettigrew *Mem. Lettsom* (1817) III. 402 In these delicacies we wish to be confirmed or corrected by those who are real masters in the profession. **1876** FREEMAN *Norm. Conq.* V. xxiv. 524 To disregard the grammatical delicacies of the written language.

delicate ('dɛlɪkət), *a.* and *sb.* Forms: 4–6 delicat, 5 -caat, 5–6 de-, dylycate, 6 *Sc.* diligat, 4– delicate. [ad. L. *dēlicāt-us, -a, -um* alluring, charming, voluptuous, soft, tender, dainty, effeminate, etc.; reinforced by later F. *délicat* (15th c. in Hatzfeld), 'daintie, pleasing, prettie, delicious, tender, nice, effeminate, of a weake complexion' (Cotgr.); in mod.F. 'of exquisite fineness' (Hatzf.): cf. Pr. and Cat. *delicat*, Sp. *delicado*, It. *delicato*. The native repr. of L. *dēlicātus* in OF. was *delié* 'fine, slender, delicate': see DELIE.

(The etymology of L. *dēlicātus* appears to be quite uncertain: several distinct suggestions are current. Even the primary sense is doubtful; but, if not originally connected with *dēliciæ* (DELICE), it seems to have been subsequently associated therewith. The word had undergone considerable development of meaning already in ancient Latin; in Romanic it received further extension in the line of meaning 'dainty, tenderly fine, slender, slight, easily affected or hurt'; these Latin and Romanic senses have at various times been adopted in English, often as literal adaptations of the Latin word in the Vulgate, etc.; and the history of the word here is involved and difficult to trace. The following arrangement is more or less provisional.)]

A. *adj.* **I.** Senses more or less = various uses of DAINTY *a.*

1. Delightful, charming, pleasant, nice. †**a.** *gen. Obs.*

1382 WYCLIF *Isa.* lviii. 13 If thou..clepist a delicat sabot [**1388** clepist the sabat delicat, Vulg. *vocaveris sabbatum delicatum*, **1611** call the sabbath a delight]. *c* **1400** MAUNDEV. (1839) v. 39 Anoynted with delicat thinges of swete smelle. **1513** BRADSHAW *St. Werburge* I. 2560 The Worde of god was moost delycate seruyse. **1553** EDEN *Treat. Newe Ind.* (Arb.) 15 Delicate thinges..that may encrease the pleasures of this lyfe. **1665** SIR T. HERBERT *Trav.* (1677) 175 A spacious Garden, which was curious to the eye and delicate to the smell. **1683** THORESBY *Diary* 4 Apr., To Biggleswerth where is nothing observable but a delicate new Inn. **1697** DAMPIER *Voy.* I. xvi. 458 Which our Carpenters afterwards altered, and made a delicate Boat fit for any service. **1712** tr. *Pomet's Hist. Drugs* I. 152 A ravishing Smell..as strong as that of the Quince, but much more delicate. **1791** COWPER *Retired Cat* 60 Cried Puss '..Oh what a delicate retreat! I will resign myself to rest'.

b. Of food, etc.: Pleasing to the palate, dainty.

c **1380** WYCLIF *Wks.* (1880) 13 Delicat metis and drynkis. **1514** BARCLAY *Cyt. & Uplondyshm.* (Percy Soc.) p. xlvi, Then cometh dishes moste swete & delicate. **1535** COVERDALE *Ecclus.* xxix. 22 Better is it to haue a poore lyuynge in a mans owne house, then delicate fayre amonge the straunge. **1624** BP. HALL *Rem. Wks.* (1660) 18 Let the drink be never so delicate and well-spiced. **1700** S. L. tr. *Fryke's Voy. E. Ind.* 21 A very good Dinner of Meat..and Cheese, and delicate Beer. **1760–72** tr. *Juan & Ulloa's Voy.* (ed. 3) I. 79 Some of them [dishes] are so delicate, that foreigners are no less pleased with them, than the gentlemen of the country. **1845** M. PATTISON *Ess.* (1889) I. 22 Not to take delight in delicate meats. **1853** J. H. NEWMAN *Hist. Sk.* (1876) II. I. i. 40 Horseflesh was the most delicate of all the Tartar viands in the times we are now considering.

†**c.** Said of the air, climate, or natural features.

1553 BRENDE *Q. Curtius* L iv, The river Hydaspis which is counted to be a verye delicate water. **1586** A. DAY *Eng. Secretary* I. (1625) 26 A soile delicate..for the aire, and pleasant for the situation. **1605** SHAKS. *Macb.* I. vi. 10 Where they much breed, and haunt: I have obseru'd The ayre is delicate. **1622** DRAYTON *Poly-olb.* xxi. (1748) 339 A purer stream, a delicater brook, Bright Phœbus in his course doth scarcely overlook. **1697** DAMPIER *Voy.* (1729) I. 485 Tabago ..still lies wast (though a delicate fruitful Island). **1700** CONGREVE in *Lett. Lit. Men* (Camden) 299 We had a long passage, but delicate weather. **1756** NUGENT *Gr. Tour* II. 141 There is a small arm of the sea, and another delicate country joining to it. **1789** G. WHITE *Selborne* xxiii. (1853) 94 The sun broke out into a warm delicate day.

†**d.** Delightful from its beauty; dainty to behold; lovely, graceful, elegant. *Obs.*

1583 SEMPILL *Leg. Bp. St. Andrews* 1023 Ane diligat [*v.r.* deligat] gowne..he send him. **1604** SHAKS. *Oth.* II. iii. 20 She's a most exquisite Lady..Indeed she's a most fresh and delicate creature. **1632** LITHGOW *Trav.* VI. 282 Rare Alabaster Tombe..inclosed within a delicate Chappell under the ground. **1641** EVELYN *Mem.* (1857) I. 28 Haerlem is a very delicate town, and hath one of the fairest churches of the Gothic design I had ever seen. **1759** B. MARTIN *Nat. Hist. Eng.* I. 367 Oxford..is a most delicate and beautiful City.

†**2. a.** Characterized by pleasure or sensuous delight; luxurious, voluptuous, effeminate. *Obs.*

c **1386** CHAUCER *Merch. T.* 402, I shal lede now so myrie a lyf So delicat with-outen wo and stryf That I shal haue myn heuene in erthe heere. **1393** LANGL. *P. Pl.* C. IX. 279 Dues for hus delicat lyf to þe deuel wente. **1542–3** *Act 34–5 Hen. VIII*, c. 4 Sundrie persons..consume the substance obteined by credite..for their own pleasure and delicate liuinge. **1576** FLEMING *Panopl. Epist.* 410 You have your sweete and delicate sleepes in your comfortable chambers. **1599** SHAKS. *Much Ado* I. i. 305 Come thronging soft and delicate desires, All prompting mee how faire yonge Hero is. **1737** WHISTON *Josephus' Antiq.* XVII. xii. §2 Softness of body ..derived from his delicate and generous education.

†**b.** Of persons: Given to pleasure or luxury; luxurious; sumptuous. *Obs.*

c **1386** CHAUCER *Monk's T.* 393 Moore delicaat, moore pompous of array, Moore proud was neuere Emperour than he. **1393** GOWER *Conf.* III. 34 He was eke so delicate Of his clothing, that every day Of purpure and bisse he made him gay. *c* **1440** *Promp. Parv.* 117 Delycate or lycorowse, *delicatus* (P. *lautus*). *c* **1450** *Mirour Saluacioun* 1538 Now glutterie is yᵗ vice yᵗ the feend first temptis man inne, ffor rathere a man delicat than abstynent fallis in synne. **1535** COVERDALE *Amos* vi. (*heading*), He reproueth the welthy, ydyll and delicate people. **1613** R. C. *Table Alph.* (ed. 3), *Delicate*, daintie, giuen to pleasure. **1640** HABINGTON *Hist. Edw. IV* 196 (Trench) The most delicate and voluptuous princes have ever been the heaviest oppressors of the people.

†**3.** Self-indulgent, loving ease, indolent. *Obs.*

c **1374** CHAUCER *Boeth.* IV. vii. 149 O ȝe slowe and delicat men, whi fley ȝe aduersites and ne fyȝten nat aȝeins hem by vertue. **1413** LYDG. *Pilgr. Sowle* III. ix. (1483) 56 Suche folke haue ben soo delycate and lothe to good werkes. **1533** MORE *Debell. Salem* Pref. Wks. 931/1 Many men are now a dayes so delicate in reading, and so lothe to laboure. **1579** TOMSON *Calvin's Serm. Tim.* 102/2 They which will be delicate, & persuade themselues yᵗ they shal not suffer much trouble in doing their dutie faithfully. **1601** CORNWALLYES *Ess.* xii, He made choyse rather of a slow delicate people, then of spirits of more excellency.

†**4.** Tenderly or softly reared, not robust; dainty; effeminate. *Obs.* or *arch.*

1382 WYCLIF *Deut.* xxviii. 56 A tendre womman and a delicate, the which vpon the erthe myȝte not go, ne fitch the stap of the foot, for softnes and moost tendrenes. **1526** *Pilgr. Perf.* (W. de W. 1531) 204 b, The delycate persone that can suffre no payne in body. **1556** *Aurelio & Isab.* (1608) E viij, And well that [= *bien que*] the grete colde penetrethe youre delicat fleshes. [Of women]. **1602** SHAKS. *Ham.* IV. iv. 48 Witness this army..Led by a delicate and tender prince. **1611** BIBLE *Jer.* vi. 2, I haue likened the daughter of Zion to a comely and delicate [COVERD. fayre and tendre] woman. **1688** S. PENTON *Guardian's Instr.* 56 This was the unhappiness of a delicate Youth, whose great misfortune it was to be worth Two Thousand A Year before he was One and Twenty.

†**5.** Fastidious, particular, nice, dainty. *Obs.*

1568 GRAFTON *Chron.* II. 88 He was more delicate and deyntie than became a person being so homely appareled. **1649** BP. REYNOLDS *Serm. Hosea* Epist. 1, I speake with such plainess, as might commend the matter delivered rather to the Conscience of a Penitent, then to the fancy of a delicate hearer. **1673** *Rules of Civility* 109 Some people being so delicate, they will not eat after a man has eat with his Spoon and not wiped it. **1712** STEELE *Spect.* No. 493 ¶7 You, who are delicate in the choice of your friends and domestics. **1773** JOHNSON *Lett. Mrs. Thrale* 21 Sept., The only things of which we, or travellers yet more delicate, could find any pretensions to complain. **1796** MORSE *Amer. Geog.* II. 561 They are delicate in no part of their dress but in their hair.

II. Fine: not coarse, not robust, not rough, not gross.

6. a. Exquisitely or beautifully fine in texture, make, or finish; exquisitely soft, slender, or slight.

1577 B. GOOGE *Heresbach's Husb.* III. (1586) 140 Champion Feeldes and Downes, are best for the delicatest and finest woolled Sheepe. **1600** J. PORY tr. *Leo's Africa* II. 237 Their women are white, having blacke haires and a most delicate skin. **1634** SIR. T. HERBERT *Trav.* 190 The people ..weare little clothing, save what is thin and delicate. **1756** BURKE *Subl. & B.* IV. xvi, It is the delicate myrtle..it is the vine, which we look on as vegetable beauties. **1800** tr. *Lagrange's Chem.* II. 188 A salt..under the form of exceedingly delicate needles. **1825** J. NEAL *Bro. Jonathan* III. 175 The delicate gauze over her bosom shook. **1870** LOWELL *Study Wind.* (1886) 38 Delicatest sea-ferns.

b. Fine or exquisite in quality or nature.

a **1533** LD. BERNERS *Gold. Bk. M. Aurel.* (1546) M vij b, Such as are of a delicate bloudde, haue not soo much sollicitude as the rustical people. **1610** SHAKS. *Temp.* I. ii. 272 Thou wast a Spirit too delicate To act her earthy, and abhord commands. *a* **1631** DONNE *Paradoxes* (1652) 47 Nor is it because the delicatest blood hath the best spirits. **1794** S. WILLIAMS *Vermont* 119 Like most of our delicate pleasures it is not to be enjoyed but in the cultivated state. **1858** HAWTHORNE *Fr. & It. Jrnls.* (1872) I. 9 All the dishes were very delicate. **1863** GEO. ELIOT *Romola* II. vi, The meats were likely to be delicate, the wines choice. **1886** RUSKIN *Præterita* I. vi. 186 My father liked delicate cookery, just because he was one of the smallest and rarest eaters.

c. Fine in workmanship; finely or exquisitely constructed.

1756 J. WARTON *Ess. Pope* (1782) I. vi. 301 My chief reason for quoting these delicate lines. **1870** EMERSON *Soc. & Solit.*, *Clubs* Wks. (Bohn) III. 91 We are delicate machines, and require nice treatment to get from us the maximum of power and pleasure.

d. Of colour: Of a shade which is not strong or glaring; soft, tender, or subdued.

1822 PRAED *Poems, Lillian* I. 12 And wings of a warm and delicate hue, Like the glow of a deep carnation. **1860** TYNDALL *Glac.* I. xi. 83 The hole..[in] the snow was filled with a delicate blue light.

7. So fine or slight as to be little noticeable or difficult to appreciate; subtle in its fineness.

1692 DRYDEN *St. Evremont's Ess.* 120 He leaves to be discerned a delicate inclination for the Conspirators. **1700** —— *Fables* Pref. (Globe) 498 The French have a high value for them [turns of words]..they are often what they call delicate, when they are introduc'd with judgment. **1848** MACAULAY *Hist. Eng.* II. 71 Catharine often told the king plainly what the Protestant lords of the council only dared to hint in the most delicate phrases. **1855** BAIN *Senses & Int.* II. i. §23 Discrimination of the most delicate differences is an indispensable qualification.

8. a. So fine or tender as to be easily damaged; tender, fragile; easily injured or spoiled.

1568 TILNEY *Disc. Mariage* E ij b, A good name..is so delicate a thing in a woman, that she must not onely be good, but likewise must apeere so. **1604** SHAKS. *Oth.* I. ii. 74 Thou hast..Abus'd her delicate Youth, with Drugs or Minerals. **1664** EVELYN *Kal. Hort.* (1729) 192 The Nectarine and like delicate mural-Fruit. **1834** MEDWIN *Angler in Wales* I. 75 But they [trout] are so delicate that they will not keep, and must be eaten the day they are killed. **1893** H. DALZIEL *Dis. Dogs* (ed. 3) 104 It [cropping] is cruel..in exposing one of the most delicate organs to the effects of cold, wet, sand, and dirt.

b. Tender or feeble in constitution; very susceptible to injury; liable to sickness or disease; weakly, not strong or robust. Also colloq. phr. ***in a delicate condition*** or ***state of health***: pregnant.

c **1400** *Lanfranc's Cirurg.* 291 If he be a delicat man or a feble drie hem with fumygaciouns maad of pulpa coloquintada. **1574** HELLOWES *Gueuara's Fam. Ep.* (1577) 184 The old man is delicate and of small strength. **1665** SIR T. HERBERT *Trav.* (1677) 164 The excess [in bathing] doubtless weakens the Body, by making it soft and delicate, and subject to colds. **1789** W. BUCHAN *Dom. Med.* (1790) 93 Robust persons are able to endure either cold or heat better than the delicate. **1850** DICKENS *Dav. Copp.* xxvii. 287 Mrs. Micawber, being in a delicate state of health, was overcome by it. **1855** MACAULAY *Hist. Eng.* IV. 532 The Princess.. was then in very delicate health. **1893** H. DALZIEL *Dis. Dogs* (ed. 3) 73 Dogs of a delicate constitution and unused to rough it. **1908** G. SANGER *70 Yrs. a Showman* xxx. 85, I was the more concerned as Mrs. Sanger was in a delicate condition.

9. *fig.* Presenting points which require nice and skilful handling; critical; ticklish.

1742 HUME *Ess. Parties Gt. Brit.* init., The just balance between the republican and monarchical part of our constitution is really, in itself, so extremely delicate and uncertain, that [etc.]. **1777** BURKE *Let. Sheriffs Bristol* Wks. 1842 I. 215 These delicate points ought to be wholly left to the crown. **1779** FORREST *Voy. N. Guinea* 215, I informed him it was a delicate affair, advising him to say nothing about it. **1803** WELLINGTON in Gurw. *Desp.* II. 8, I saw clearly that Amrut Rao's situation was delicate. **1860** MOTLEY *Netherl.* (1868) I. vii. 443 His mission was a delicate one.

III. Endowed with fineness of appreciation or execution.

10. a. Exquisitely fine in power of perception, feeling, appreciation, etc.; finely sensitive.

a **1533** LD. BERNERS *Gold. Bk. M. Aurel.* (1546) E iij, He was but of tender age, and not of great delycate vnderstandynge. **1581** PETTIE *Guazzo's Civ. Conv.* II. (1586) 94 b, To their delicate eares to heare what men saie, they lacke [etc.]. *c* **1680** BEVERIDGE *Serm.* (1729) I. 338 Then our minds.. would be always kept in so fine, so delicate a temper. **1711** STEELE *Spect.* No. 2 ¶2 A very delicate Observer of what occurs to him in the present World. **1856** RUSKIN *Mod. Paint.* IV. v. v. §5 A delicate ear rejoices in the slighter and more modulated passages of sound. **1875** MANNING *Mission H. Ghost* i. 26 Let us learn then to have a delicate conscience.

b. Of instruments: So finely made or adjusted as to be responsive to very slight influences; finely sensitive.

1822 IMISON *Sc. & Art* I. 34 Very delicate balances are not only useful in nice experiments [etc.]. **1849** MRS. SOMERVILLE *Connect. Phys. Sc.* xxxvi. 386 A structure so delicate that it would have made the hundredth part of a degree evident. **1871** B. STEWART *Heat* §193 Our instruments are doubtless very delicate, but.. the most refined apparatus is far less sensitive for dark heat than the eye is for light.

11. a. Endowed with exquisitely fine powers of expression or execution; finely skilful.

1589 PUTTENHAM *Eng. Poesie* I. viii. (Arb.) 33 Horace the most delicate of all the Romain Lyrickes. **1604** SHAKS. *Oth.* IV. i. 199, I do but say what she is: so delicate with her needle: an admirable Musitian. **1611** TOURNEUR *Ath. Trag.* II. i. Wks. 1878 I. 42 O thou'rt a most delicate, sweete, eloquent villaine. **1780** COWPER *Table T.* 653 Pope..(So nice his ear, so delicate his touch) Made poetry a mere mechanic art. **1884** *Public Opinion* 11 July 52/1 The artist is at his best, at his delicatest and subtlest, in his water-colours.

†**b.** Characterized by skilful action; finely ingenious. *Obs.*

1577 B. GOOGE *Heresbach's Husb.* II. (1586) 76 An other more delicater way he speaketh of, which is..laying the braunches in baskettes of earth..obtaining Rootes betwixte the very fruite and the toppes. **1605** SHAKS. *Lear* IV. vi. 188 It were a delicate stratagem to shoo A Troope of Horse with Felt. **1673** R. HEAD *Canting Acad.* 11 The Budge it is a delicate trade.

12. a. Finely sensitive to what is becoming, proper, or modest, or to the feelings of others.

1634 SIR T. HERBERT *Trav.* 103 Her..admirable beautie, a delicate spirit, sweet behaviour and charitable acts surpassing child-hood. **1721** TICKELL *Life of Addison* in *Wks.*, Mr. Addison..was..too delicate to take any part of that [praise] which belonged to others. **1768** STERNE *Sent. Journ.* (1778) II. 201 (*Case of Delicacy*) We were both too delicate to communicate what we felt to each other upon the occasion. **1836** J. GILBERT *Chr. Atonem.* ix. (1852) 260 Appearances of a just ground for the imputation are so unambiguous that it were treason to truth to be delicate.

b. Of actions, etc.: Showing or characterized by feelings of delicacy or modesty.

1818 JAS. MILL *Brit. India* II. IV. vii. 242 All parties recommended a delicate and liberal treatment. **1832** HT. MARTINEAU *Ella of Gar.* viii. 102 It would not have been delicate, I warrant, Mr. Angus. **1887** F. M. CRAWFORD *P. Patoff* II. 83 It was evident from her few words and from the blush which accompanied them that this was a delicate subject.

IV. *Comb.*, as ***delicate-footed***, ***-handed***, ***-looking***, ***-minded*** adjs.

1870 BRYANT *Iliad* I. IX. 293 A *delicate-footed dame. **1855** TENNYSON *Maud* I. viii. 11 The snowy banded, dilettante *Delicate-handed priest. **1853** MRS. GASKELL *Cranford* vi. 82 My mother was very pretty and *delicate-looking. **1906** J. JOYCE *Let.* 12 Sept. (1966) II. 159 He wears spectacles, is delicate-looking. **1806** M. WILMOT *Jrnl.* 14 June (1934) III. 268 She opens into a very cleaver, well judging, *delicate minded, spirited Woman. **1891** M. BEERBOHM *Let.* 20 Aug. (1964) 21 Awkward for delicate-minded English people.

B. *sb.*

†**1. a.** One addicted to a life of luxury. **b.** One who is dainty or fastidious in his tastes. *Obs.*

1382 WYCLIF *Isa.* xlvii. 8 Now here thou these thingus, thou delicat, and dwellende trosteli. **1382** —— *Baruch* iv. 26 My delicatis [Vulg. *delicati mei*] *or nurshid in delicis,* walkiden sharp weies. **1603** HOLLAND *Plutarch's Mor.* 361 (R.) If Lucullus were not a waster and a delicate given to belly-cheare. **1709** ADDISON *Tatler* No. 148 ¶4 The Rules among these false Delicates are to be as Contradictory as they can be to Nature.

2. A thing that gives pleasure (usually in *pl.*): †**a.** *gen.* A luxury, delight. *Obs.*

c **1450** tr. *De Imitatione* I. xxiv, Than shal þe fleshe þat haþ ben in affliccion, ioy much more þan he þat haþ be norisshed in delicats. **1489** CAXTON *Faytes of A.* III. xix. 211 For to knowe and acquyre connyng scolers haue lefte and layde asyde ryhesses, delicates and al eases of body. **1539** CRANMER in Strype *Life* II. (1694) 247 Such as..repute for their chief delicates the disputation of high questions. **1593** SHAKS. *3 Hen. VI*, II. v. 51. **1598** BARCKLEY *Felic. Man* IV. (1603) 345 The pompe and delicates used by the great estates of other ages. **1637** RUTHERFORD *Lett.* (1862) I. 247 There is no reason that His comforts be too cheap, seeing they are delicates. **1742** YOUNG *Nt. Th.* viii. 819 Her nectareous cup, Mixt up of delicates for ev'ry sense.

b. A choice viand; a dainty, delicacy.

c **1450** *Merlin* 6 Yef we hadde but a mossell brede, we haue more ioye and delyte than ye haue with alle the delicatys of the worlde. **1526** *Pilgr. Perf.* (W. de W. 1531) 70 b, To be admytted to the kynges owne table, and to taste of his deyntyue delycates. **1650** W. BROUGH *Sacr. Princ.* (1659) 226 Hunger cooks all meats to delicates. **1676** SHADWELL *Virtuoso* III, Cheshire-cheese..seems to be a great delicate to the palate of this animal. **1710** STEELE *Tatler* No. 251 ¶4 Reflections..which add Delicates to the Feast of a good Conscience. **1820** KEATS *Eve St. Agnes* xxxi, These delicates he heap'd with glowing hand On golden dishes. **1870** MORRIS *Earthly Par.* I. I. 204 And many such a delicate As goddesses in old time ate.

†**c.** Of a person: The delight, joy, darling. *Obs. rare*$^{-1}$.

1531 ELYOT *Gov.* III. xxiv, The Emperour Titus..for his lernynge and vertue, was named the delicate of the worlde [*amor et deliciæ humani generis*].

†**'delicate**, *v. rare. Obs.* [f. DELICATE *a.*] To render delicate.

1614 W. B. *Philosopher's Banquet* (ed. 2) 69 They doe dillicate and mollifie the flesh.

Hence **'delicated** *ppl. a.*

1851 MRS. BROWNING *Casa Guidi Windows* 125 These delicated muslins rather seem Than be, you think?

delicately ('dɛlɪkətlɪ), *adv.* [f. DELICATE *a.* + -LY².] In a delicate manner.

†**1.** In a way that gratifies the senses, *esp.* the palate; sumptuously, luxuriously; daintily, fastidiously. *Obs.*

1377 LANGL. *P. Pl.* B. v. 184 Drynke nouȝte ouer delicatly ne to depe noyther. *Ibid.* B. XIV. 250 He..doth hym nouȝte dyne delycatly ne drynke wyn oft. **1435** MISYN *Fire of Love* 26 þat I wald not abyde bot wher I myght be delicately fed. **1555** EDEN *Decades* 117 Bores fleshe wherwith they fedde them selues dilycately. **1576** FLEMING *Panopl. Epist.* 292 You have received mee honorably, sumptuously and delicatly. **1611** BIBLE *1 Tim.* v. 6 She that liueth in pleasure [*margin*, delicately] is dead while she liueth. **1650** JER. TAYLOR *Holy Living* ii. §1. 57 Eat not delicately or nicely.

b. With enervating or weakening luxury or indulgence; effeminately, tenderly.

1382 WYCLIF *Prov.* xxix. 21 Who delicatli [*delicate*] fro childhed nurshith his seruaunt, afterward shal feelen hym vnobeisaunt. **1552** HULOET, Delicately, *laute, molliter, muliebriter.* **1856** EMERSON *Eng. Traits, Char.* Wks. (Bohn) II. 58 The young coxcombs of the Life Guards delicately brought up. **1893** H. DALZIEL *Dis. Dogs* (ed. 3) 28 Not so liable to attacks of cold as the more delicately reared.

2. †**a.** In a way that gives pleasure or delight; delightfully, beautifully (*obs.*). **b.** 'With soft elegance' (J.); with exquisite or graceful fineness, softness, etc. Opposed to *coarsely*.

1577–87 HOLINSHED *Ireland* an. 1535 (R.) He was.. delicatelie in each limb featured. **1698** FRYER *Acc. E. India & P.* 199 The Moors build with Stone and Mortar..making small shew without, but delicately contrived within. **1735** POPE *Ep. Lady* 43 Ladies..'Tis to their Changes half their charms we owe; Fine by defect, and delicately weak. **1760–72** tr. *Juan & Ulloa's Voy.* (ed. 3) I. 54 The fox here is not much bigger than a large cat; but delicately shaped. **1821** CLARE *Vill. Minstr.* II. 61 Ye cowslips, delicately pale. **1848** MACAULAY *Hist. Eng.* II. 407 The more delicately organised mind of Halifax. **1876** GEO. ELIOT *Dan. Der.* III. xxxv. 39 The delicately-wrought foliage of the capitals.

3. Softly, lightly; with light or delicate touch, gently; with delicacy of feeling. Opposed to *roughly*.

1611 BIBLE *1 Sam.* xv. 32 And Agag came vnto him delicately [COVERD. tenderly, *Genev.* pleasantly]. **1677** S. LEE *Triumph of Mercy* in Spurgeon *Treas. Dav.* Ps. cv. 19–21 Joseph's feet were hurt in irons, to fit him to tread more delicately in the King's Palace. **1825** J. NEAL *Bro. Jonathan* III. 318 Death in his great mercy..had breathed upon it very delicately. **1845** M. PATTISON *Ess.* (1889) I. 19 The thorny subject which they were delicately shunning in their conversation. **1855** MACAULAY *Hist. Eng.* IV. 411 Blame which, though delicately expressed, was perfectly intelligible.

4. In a way that is sensitive or responsive to the slightest influences; sensitively; with nice exactness.

1791 MRS. RADCLIFFE *Rom. Forest* i, Whose mind was delicately sensible to the beauties of nature. **1793** BEDDOES *Calculus* 195 The least degree of heat then produces the most violent effects upon the fibres thus delicately irritable. **1842** S. LOVER *Handy Andy* xx. 179 A very delicately-balanced scale of etiquette. **1879** *Cassell's Techn. Educ.* I. 187 How delicately the adjustment of the pressure can be made with this apparatus.

delicateness ('dɛlɪkətnɪs). [f. as prec. + -NESS.] The quality of being delicate, delicacy. The opposite of *roughness*, *coarseness*, *grossness*.

1530 PALSGR. 212/2 Delycatenesse, *friandise.* **1552** HULOET, Delicatenes, *mollicia, mollicies, muliebritas.* **1555** EDEN *Decades* 49 They fynde the lyke softenes or delicatenes to bee in herbes. **1598** STOW *Surv.* x. (1603) 80 They which delight in delicatenesse may be satisfied with as delicate dishes there as may be found elsewhere. **1611** BIBLE *Deut.* xxviii. 56 The tender and delicate woman..which would not aduenture to set the sole of her foote vpon the ground, for delicatenesse and tendernesse. **1670–98** LASSELS *Voy. Italy* Pref. 19 Any young traveller should leave behind him ..all delicateness and effeminateness. **1678** *Trans. Crt. Spain* 21 The delicateness of our Young Prince suffered him not to bear the Fatigue. **1727** BRADLEY *Fam. Dict.* s.v. *Epilepsy*, Young Children are more subject to the Falling-Sickness..by Reason of the Delicateness of the Nerves. **1873** *Daily News* 21 Aug., To borrow the delicateness of [this] French idiom.

‖**delicatesse** (dɛlɪkə'tɛs). [mod.F. *délicatesse* (1564 in Hatzf.), f. *délicat* DELICATE: cf. It. *delicatezza*, and older pop. F. words like *justesse*, *vilesse*, etc.] Delicacy.

1698 VANBRUGH *Prov. Wife* I. ii. 150 But I have too much *délicatesse* to make a practice on 't. **1704** SWIFT *T. Tub* ii. 40 All which required abundance of *finesse* and *delicatesse* to manage with advantage. **1706** FARQUHAR *Recruit. Off.* Epil., The French found it a little too rough for their *delicatesse.* **1854** SYD. DOBELL *Balder* xxv. 186 Let delicatesse Weave his thin cuticle, and mesh him in.

delicatessen (ˌdɛlɪkə'tɛsən). orig. *U.S.* [G. *delikatessen*, Du. *delicatessen*, ad. F. *délicatesse* (see DELICATESSE).] Delicacies or relishes for the table; esp. *attrib.*, in ***delicatessen shop***, ***store***. **b.** *ellipt.* A delicatessen shop.

[**1877** E. S. DALLAS *Kettner's Bk. of Table* 399 A house which abounds in foreign dainties of all sorts—Lingner's Delicatessen Handlung, 46, Old Compton Street, Soho.] **1889** *Kansas Times & Star* 7 Nov., Burglars broke into Blake's delicatessen store..and..made an awful mess of the juicy stuff, canned and bottled. **1893** *Harper's Mag.* Apr. 660 They [*sc.* Germans in New York] maintain..their delicatessen shops and pork butchers. **1893** W. D. HOWELLS *Coast of Bohemia* 261 The shop of an old German..who dealt in delicatessen. **1904** 'A. DALE' *Wanted: A Cook* 28 Tonight, Anna has provided us what she calls a delicatessen dinner. **1904** *N.Y. Even. Post* 30 June 14 (Advt.), Our Modern Delicatessen Department on the fifth floor is prepared to furnish estimates for picnic luncheons. **1905** *Ibid.* 13 Nov. 7 Next week's opening of Mr. Conried's operatic delicatessen store on Broadway. **1908** *Daily Chron.* 8 Jan. 8/3 The German delicatessen shops which are now becoming such a feature in London life. **1916** *Daily Colonist* (Victoria, B.C.) 7 July 5/1 Home Cooked Meats and Delicatessen Goods in Great Variety. **1930** *Daily Tel.* 8 Apr. 9/6 The New York women,..in their skyscraper niches, where everything can be done by electricity, with the delicatessen and..prepared food as a stand-by. **1969** *P.O. Directory: London Yellow Pages Classified (North)* 62/3 Delicatessens and Cooked Meats.

†**'delicative**, *a. Obs.* In 5 delycatyf. [a. OF. *delicatif, -ive*, dainty, exquisite.] Of the nature of delicacies; dainty.

1491 CAXTON *Vitas Patr.* (W. de W. 1495) v. iii. 337 b/2 Seche no metes ouer delycyous ne delycatyf.

†**'delicatude.** *Obs. rare.* = DELICATENESS.

1727 BAILEY II, *Delicatude*, deliciousness. **1775** in ASH.

†**de'lice.** *Obs.* Forms: 3–7 delice, 3–6 -yce, 4 -ijss, 5 -is, -ys, -yse; *pl.* 3–7 delices, 4–5 -icis, 4 -icys, 5 -ycys, 5–6 -yces. [a. OF. *delice* masc.:—L. *dēlicium*, and OF. *delices* fem. pl.:—L. *dēliciæ, -as*, delight, pleasure, charm; f. *dēlicĕre* to allure, entice, delight. (The L. words have the form of the neuter sing. and fem. pl. of an adj. **dēlicius* charming, alluring. L. had also the fem. sing. *dēlicia*, whence It. *delizia*, Sp., Pg. *delicia* delight.]

1. Delight, pleasure, joy, enjoyment.

a **1225** *Ancr. R.* 340 Vor his delices, he seið, beoð forto wunien þer. 'Et delicie mee cum filiis hominum.' **1382** WYCLIF *Gen.* ii. 8 The Lord God had plawntid paradise of delice fro bigynnyng. **1430** LYDG. *Chron. Troy* III. xxviii, Causinge the ayre enuyron be delyse To resemble a very paradyse. **1435** MISYN *Fire of Love* 96 þe delis of endles lufe. **1450–1530** *Myrr. our Ladye* 174 In thy delyces holy mother of God. **1614** T. ADAMS *Devil's Banquet* 3 If she discouers the greene and gay flowers of delice. **1656** JER. TAYLOR in *Four C. Eng. Lett.* 104 My delices were really in seeing you severe and unconcerned. **1685** EVELYN *Mrs. Godolphin* 47 The love of God and delices of Religion.

b. *spec.* Sensual or worldly pleasure; voluptuousness.

a **1225** *Ancr. R.* 368 þet heo gleowede & gomede..& liuede in delices? **1340** *Ayenb.* 24 þe guodes of hap byeþ heȝnesses, richesses, delices, and prosperites. *c* **1386** CHAUCER *Pars. T.* ¶133 For certis delices ben þe appetites of þy fyue wittes. **1401** *Pol. Poems* (Rolls) II. 50 Take ȝe Cristes crosse, he saith; and counte we delices claye. **1532** MORE *Confut. Tindale* Wks. 535/2 Paule sayde of wanton wiedowes, that the wiedow which liueth in delyces, is dead euen whyle she liueth. **1669** GALE *Crt. Gentiles* I. III. x. 106 No smooth and effeminate delices for itching ears.

2. Something that affords pleasure; a delight.

14.. *Pol. Rel. & L. Poems* (1866) 248 To don hym sorwe was here delys [*rime* prys]. **1564** HAWARD *Eutropius* VII. 73 Hee was called the love and delices of mankynde. **1664** EVELYN tr. *Freart's Archit.* Ep. Ded. 15 S. Germain's and Versailles, which were then the ordinary residence and delices of the King. **1779** SWINBURNE *Trav. Spain* xxxiv. (T.), Zehra, with all its delices, is erased from the face of the earth.

b. A dainty, delicacy.

1483 CAXTON *Gold. Leg.* 195 b/1 She had no thynge but barly brede and sometyme benes, the whiche..she ete for alle delyces. **1599** BUTTES *Dyets drie Dinner* A a viij, There with Cates, Delices, Tabacco, Mell. **1652** C. B. STAPYLTON *Herodian* 91 Whence..many Fragrant Spices Are brought to us, as rare and choise Delices.

¶ Spenser stresses *'delices*, perhaps by confusion with DELICIES.

1590–6 SPENSER *F.Q.* II. v. 28 And now he has pourd out his ydle mynd In daintie delices, and lavish joyes. *Ibid.* IV.

x. 6 An island strong, Abounding all with delices most rare. *Ibid.* v. iii. 40.

†**de'liciate**, *v. Obs. rare.* [Formed after OF. *délicier* (12–16th c.), *trans.* to rejoice, *refl.* to enjoy oneself, feast, med.L. *dēliciārī* to feast, f. L. *dēlicia*, *-æ*: see DELICE, and -ATE³.]

1. *intr.* To take one's pleasure, enjoy oneself, revel, luxuriate.

1633 A. H. *Partheneia Sacra* 18 (R.) When Flora is disposed to deliciate with her minions. **1678** CUDWORTH *Intell. Syst.* 811 These Evil Demons therefore did as it were Deliciate and Epicurize in them.

2. *trans.* To fill with delight, render delightful, delight.

1658 R. FRANCK *North. Mem.* (1821) 77, I perceive you disordered, but not much deliciated. *Ibid.* 122 Whilst the birds harmoniously deliciat the air.

†'**delicies**, *sb. pl. Obs. rare.* [ad. L. *dēliciæ*, *-as*: cf. DELICE.] = DELICES, delights; joys; dainties.

1597 *1st Pt. Return fr. Parnass.* II. III. iv. 1355 Inspire me streight with some rare delicies, Or Ile dismount thee from thy radiant coach. **1607** WALKINGTON *Opt. Glass* 9 Charon and Atropos are com'd to call me away from my delicies.

†**delici'osity.** *Obs. rare.* In 5 -iosite, -iousite, diliciousite. [f. DELICIOUS or its L. or Fr. equivalent. A med.L. **dēliciōsitās* and OF. **deliciouseté* were prob. used, though not yet registered.] The quality of being delicious, or of affording delight; *concr.* something in which this quality is embodied; a delicacy, a luxury.

c **1440** *Gesta Rom.* lxiii. 274 (Harl. MS.) To abide still with þe deliciousites. *Ibid.*, As ofte as the flessh is ouercome with diliciousites. *c* **1449** PECOCK *Repr.* 255 To speke and write tho wordis in sum gaynes and bewte or in sum deliciosite.

delicious (dɪ'lɪʃəs), *a.* Also 4–6 -yci-, -icy-, -ycy-, -ous, -owse, dilicious(e, 5 dylycy-, 6 delicius, di-, 6–7 delitious, 7 delishous. [a. OF. and Anglo-Fr. *delicious* (later F. *delicieus*, *-eux*) = Pr. *delicios*, Sp. *delicioso*, It. *delizioso*, ad. late L. *dēliciōs-us* delicious, delicate (Augustine), f. L. *dēlicia*, *-æ*: see DELICE and -OUS.]

1. a. Highly pleasing or delightful; affording great pleasure or enjoyment.

In mod. use, usually less dignified than 'delightful', and expressing an intenser degree and lower quality of pleasure. *c* **1300** *K. Alis.* 38 Theo wondres, of worm and best, Deliciouse hit is to lest. *c* **1374** CHAUCER *Boeth.* II. iii. 36 þise ben faire þinges..and only while þei ben herd..þei ben deliciouse. *c* **1534** tr. *Pol. Verg. Eng. Hist.* (Camden) I. 20 Plenti of delicius rivers, pleasauntlie wateringe there feldes. **1632** LITHGOW *Trav.* v. 222 A Delicious incircling Harbour, inclos'd within the middle of the Towne. *a* **1661** FULLER *Worthies* (1840) III. 283 [Guy's Cliff] a most delicious place, so that a man in many miles riding cannot meet so much variety, as there one furlong doth afford. **1742** COLLINS *Eclog.* i. 24 Each gentler ray, delicious to your eyes. **1824** DIBDIN *Libr. Comp.* 611 A delicious array of Miltonic treasures. **1861** O'CURRY *MS. Materials Anc. Irish Hist.* 263 The delicious strains of the harp. **1879** FARRAR *St. Paul* (1883) 349 A green delicious plain.

b. Intensely amusing or entertaining.

1642 MILTON *Apol. Smect.* viii. Wks. (1847) 92/1 Delicious! he had that whole Bevie at command whether in Morrice or at May-pole; whilst I..left so impoverish'd of what to say, as to turn my Liturgy into my Lady's Psalter. **1851** RUSKIN *Stones Ven.* (1874) I. App. 362 The strut of the foremost cock, lifting one leg at right angles to the other, is delicious. **1853** KINGSLEY *Hypatia* vi. (1879) 71 A delicious joke it would have been.

2. a. Highly pleasing or enjoyable to the bodily senses, *esp.* to the taste or smell; affording exquisite sensuous or bodily pleasure.

1340 HAMPOLE *Pr. Consc.* 9287 þat savour sal be ful plenteuouse, And swa swete and swa delicious. *c* **1400** MAUNDEV. (Roxb.) xv. 71 Ane oþer maner of drinke gude and delicious. *c* **1440** *York Myst.* xxix. 76 Itt is licoure full delicious. *c* **1532** DEWES *Introd. Fr.* in *Palsgr.* 921 A quyete slepe is right necessary and delycious. **1548** HALL *Chron.* 230 b, In the same delicious climate. **1634** SIR T. HERBERT *Trav.* 183 Bananas or Plantanes..the fruite..gives a most delicious taste and rellish. **1667** MILTON *P.L.* II. 400 The soft delicious Air. **1732** BERKELEY *Alciphr.* I. § 1 We walked under the delicious shade of these trees. **1847** EMERSON *Repr. Men, Uses Gt. Men* Wks. (Bohn) I. 274 In Valencia the climate is delicious. **1850** L. HUNT *Autobiog.* II. x. 31 There is something in the word *delicious* which may be said to comprize a reference to every species of pleasant taste.

b. With capital initial: designating a variety of eating apple of North American origin. Also as *sb.*

1903 BUDD & HANSEN *Amer. Hort. Man.* II. 70 *The Apple ..Delicious.* Originated by Jesse Hiatt..Iowa; tree a regular and heavy bearer. Fruit large, roundish conic, ribbed; skin medium thick..color yellow, washed with mixed red. **1932** *Discovery* July 220/1 Canada is proud of the Mackintosh Red, Delicious, Jonathan, [etc.]. **1959** A. H. MCLINTOCK *Descr. Atlas N.Z.* 42 The most popular export varieties are Sturmer, Delicious, Jonathan, Granny Smith, and Cox's Orange.

†**3. a.** Characterized by or tending to sensuous indulgence; voluptuous, luxurious. *Obs.*

a **1340** HAMPOLE *Psalter* ix. 6 Deliciouse affeccIouns of flescly lust. *a* **1450** *Knt. de la Tour* (1868) 54 The flesshe is tempted by delicious metes and drinkes, the whiche bene leteres and kindelers of the brondes of lecherye. **1563** *Homilies* II. *Fasting* I. (1859) 280 An abstinence..from all delicious pleasures and delectations worldly. **1632** LITHGOW *Trav.* I. 22 Forsaking the delicious lives of the effeminate Affricans. **1651–3** JER. TAYLOR *Serm. for Year* (1678) 339 The habitual Intemperance which is too commonly annexed to festival and delicious Tables.

†**b.** Of persons: Addicted to sensuous indulgence; voluptuous, luxurious, dainty. *Obs.*

1393 GOWER *Conf.* III. 33 If that thou understode, What is to ben delicious, Thou woldest nought ben curious. *c* **1450** *Mirour Saluacioun* 914 Of mete nor drinke was sho neure yhit diliciouse. **1483** CAXTON *Gold. Leg.* 116/2 Thyse monckes ben ouer delycious. **1530** PALSGR. 309/2 Delycyouse, daynty mouthed or delycate. **1598** SYLVESTER *Du Bartas* II. I. *Eden* (1641) 84/1 Idleness..Defiles our body, Yea sobrest men it makes dilicious. **1680** MORDEN *Geog. Rect.* (1685) 71 The Gentry are..Costly in their Apparel, Delicious in their Diet. **1681** W. ROBERTSON *Phraseol. Gen.* (1693) 448 A delicious mouth or palate.

deliciously (dɪ'lɪʃəslɪ), *adv.* [f. prec. + -LY².] In a delicious manner.

1. So as to afford intense pleasure; delightfully.

c **1386** CHAUCER *Sqr.'s T.* 71 Herknynge hise Mynstrals hir thynges pleye Beforn hym at the bord deliciously. **1485** CAXTON *Chas. Gt.* 19 He..repayred the places ryght delycyously. **1747** CARTE *Hist. Eng.* I. 577 No cost being spared either to purchase the greatest rarities, or to dress them deliciously. **1792** A. YOUNG *Trav. France* 259 There was something so deliciously amiable in her character. **1863** E. C. CLAYTON *Queens of Song* II. 322 Her voice was invariably pure, true, and deliciously sweet. **1865** LIVINGSTONE *Zambesi* v. 106 The air was deliciously cool. **1883** *Manch. Exam.* 19 Dec. 5/3 The explanation is deliciously grotesque.

b. With intense delight or enjoyment.

1696 STANHOPE *Chr. Pattern* (1711) 290 Yet does He.. importune us to sit and eat deliciously with him. **1706** *Reflex. upon Ridicule* 239 He deliciously imbibes the Elogies that are given him. **1799** SOUTHEY *Love Elegies* iv, O'er the page of Love's despair, My Delia bent deliciously to grieve. **1864** SKEAT *Uhland's Poems* 294 Beneath its shade he oft would sit And dream deliciously.

†**2.** Luxuriously, voluptuously, sumptuously.

1303 R. BRUNNE *Handl. Synne* 207 I. 6617 Anoþer spyce ys yn glotonye, To ete ouer delycyusly. *c* **1340** HAMPOLE *Prose Tr.* iii. 6 A ȝonge man..vn-chastely and delycyouesly lyfande and full of many synnys. *c* **1400** *Rom. Rose* 6729 If he have peraventure..Lyved over deliciously. **1557** N. T. (Genev.) *Luke* xvi. 19 A certayne ryche man, which..fared deliciously euery day. **1634** SIR T. HERBERT *Trav.* 102 The King..deliciously tooke his pleasure. **1690** J. PALMER in *Andros Tracts* I. 54 Did his Excellency lye upon Beds of Down, and fare Delishously every day? *a* **1800** COWPER *Iliad* (ed. 2) xxiv. 56 The lion..Makes inroad on the flocks, that he may fare Deliciously at cost of mortal man.

†**3.** With fondness, fondly. *Obs.*

c **1400** *Test. Love* I. (1560) 275 b/2 She [Love] gan deliciously me comfort with sugred words. *a* **1440** *Found. St. Barthol.* 61 His hors, that so deliciously he louyd, and so negligently hadde lost. **1483** CAXTON *Gold. Leg.* 143 b/1 An heremyte..reteyned nothyng but a catte wyth whyche he playde ofte and helde it in his lappe deliciously.

deliciousness (dɪ'lɪʃəsnɪs). [f. as prec. + -NESS.]

1. The quality of being delicious, or highly pleasing (now *esp.* to the senses): see the adj.

1398 TREVISA *Barth. De P.R.* VI. xxiii. (1495) 213 Delycyousnes of all that is sette on the borde. *c* **1400** *Test. Love* Prol. (1560) 271 b/2 Many men there been, that with eeres openly sprad, so moch swalowen the deliciousnesse of jestes and of ryme. **1592** SHAKS. *Rom. & Jul.* II. vi. 12 The sweetest honey Is loathsome in its owne deliciousnesse. *a* **1652** J. SMITH *Sel. Disc.* i. 12 There is an inward sweetness and deliciousness in divine truth, which no sensual mind can taste or relish. **1751** JOHNSON *Rambler* No. 127 ¶4 The deliciousness of ease commonly makes us unwilling to return to labour. **1860** HAWTHORNE *Marble Faun* xxiv, There was a deliciousness in it that eluded analysis.

†**b.** (with *pl.*) A delight. *Obs.*

1749 BP. LAVINGTON *Enthus. Meth. & Papists* (1754) I. 57 A Woman quite deserted, and the Vein of her Spiritual Deliciousnesses dried up in her Aridities.

†**2.** Voluptuousness, luxuriousness, luxury. *Obs.*

c **1440** *Gesta Rom.* I. xxvi. 101 (Harl. MS.) He folowithe deliciousnes of the fleshe. **1579** LYLY *Euphues* (Arb.) 179 Philautus, hath giuen ouer himselfe to all deliciousnesse, desiring..to be dandled in the laps of Ladyes. **1580** NORTH *Plutarch* (1676) 37 He thought..to banish out of the City all insolency, envy, covetousness, and deliciousness. **1650** JER. TAYLOR *Holy Living* (1727) 242 Do not seek for deliciousness and sensible consolations in the actions of religion.

†**3.** Fondness for what gives pleasure. *Obs.*

1548 UDALL, etc. *Erasm. Par. Luke* xvi. 25 So great was the deliciousnes of thy mouth.

†**de'licity.** *Obs. rare.* In 5 -ycyte. [A non-etymological formation from DELICE: see -ITY.] Deliciousness, delightfulness.

c **1485** *Digby Myst.* (1882) III. 72 Martha, ful [of] bewte and of delycyte. *Ibid.* III. 2039 And have fed me with fode of most delycyte.

delict (dɪ'lɪkt). [ad. L. *dēlict-um* fault, offence, crime, prop. subst. use of neuter sing. of pa. pple. of *dēlinquĕre* to fail, commit a fault: see DELINQUENT.] A violation of law or right; an offence, a delinquency.

1523 in W. H. Turner *Select. Rec. Oxford* 43 Their delicts and offenses. **1594** PARSONS *Confer. Success.* II. ix. 209 In al criminal affayres and punishing of delictes. **1613** R. C. *Table Alph.* (ed. 3), Delicte, fault, small offence. **1649** JER. TAYLOR *Gt. Exemp.* II. ix. 117 When the Supreme Power either hath not power to punish the delinquent, or may misse to have notice of the delict. *a* **1734** NORTH *Exam.* II. v. § 43 (1740) 340 Whereby the proper Officer may be brought to answer for the Delict. **1832** AUSTIN *Jurispr.* (1879) I. 44 Acts, forbearances and omissions which are violations of rights or duties are styled delicts, injuries or offences. **1871** MARKBY *Elem. Law* § 157 The French code..is no more explicit on the subject of delicts than Blackstone on the subject of civil injuries to which they correspond.

b. *in flagrant delict*: transl. Lat. *in flagrante delicto*, Fr. *en flagrant délit*, in the very act of committing the offence.

[**1772** *Junius Lett.* lxviii. (1875) 327/1 A person..taken *in flagrante delicto*, with the stolen goods upon him, is not bailable.] **1820** SCOTT *Ivanhoe* xxxvi, Taken in the flagrant delict by the avowal of a crime contrary to thine oath. **1837** SIR F. PALGRAVE *Merch. & Friar* (1844) 121 Cases of flagrant delict..required no other trial than the publicity.. of the fact. **1892** G. S. LAYARD *Life C. Keene* i. 4 [She] resorted to all the time-honoured means of catching scholars in flagrant delict.

delictal (dɪ'lɪktəl), *a.* [f. DELICT + -AL.] Of, pertaining to, or of the nature of a delict.

1913 H. GOUDY in P. Vinogradoff *Ess. Legal Hist.* 208 Where..a delictal action was not strictly penal..it transmitted both actively and passively.

delictual (dɪ'lɪktju:əl), *a. rare.* [f. DELICT or L. *dēlictum*, after *effectual*, etc.] Of or belonging to a delict.

1875 POSTE *Gaius* II. Comm. (ed. 3) 303 Both Mora..and Mala fide possessio have a delictual character.

†**delie, delye**, *a. Obs. rare.* [a. F. *délié* (13th c. in Hatzf.), early ad. L. *dēlicāt-us*, on the analogy of popular formations like *plicātus*, *plié*. (As a living word *dēlicātus* passed through to *del'cato*, Sp. *delgado*, Cat. and Pr. *delgat*, OF. *delgiét*, *delgié*, *deljé*, mod.F. dial. *deugé*, *dougé*. A third and still later adaptation is *délicat*: see DELICATE.)] Delicate, fine.

c **1374** CHAUCER *Boeth.* I. i. 5 Her cloþes weren maked of ryȝt delye þredes. *c* **1425** *Govt. Lordschipes* 88 Ffor delye þinge ys more worth þan greet, and þynne more worth þan þycke. [**1692** COLES, *Dely*, little. *Old word.*—Hence in Kersey, Bailey, Ash, etc.]

deligated ('dɛlɪgeɪtɪd), *ppl. a. Surg.* [f. L. *dēligāt-us* bound fast (see next) + -ED.] Tied with a ligature, as an artery.

1840 R. LISTON *Elem. Surg.* (ed. 2) 204 The immediate effect of a tightly-drawn ligature is to divide the internal and middle coats at the deligated point. **1859** TODD *Cycl. Anat.* V. 330/1 With deligated salivary ducts.

deligation (dɛlɪ'geɪʃən). [ad. L. **dēligātiōn-em*, n. of action from *dēligāre* to bind fast, bind up, f. DE- I. 3 + *ligāre* to bind. Cf. mod.F. *déligation* in Surgery. In sense 2, taken in sense of med.L. *disligare*, OF. *deslier*, mod.F. *délier* to untie: see DE- I. 6.]

I. 1. *Surg.* †**a.** Bandaging; a bandage. *Obs.*

1661 LOVELL *Hist. Anim. & Min.* 340 By reason of tumours or delligation. **1676** WISEMAN *Surg.* (J.), The third intention is deligation, or retaining the parts so joined together. **1798** W. BLAIR *Soldier's Friend* 33 Useful for the temporary delegation of wounds. **1857** DUNGLISON *Dict. Med.* 282 s.v. *Deligation*, The delegation of wounds formerly embraced the application of dressings, &c... Deligation is hardly ever used now as an English word.

b. The tying of an artery, etc. with a ligature.

1840 R. LISTON *Elem. Surg.* II. (ed. 2) 477 For aneurism at the angle of the jaw, the point of deligation must in a great measure depend on the size of the tumour. **1884** BRAITHWAITE *Retrospect Med.* LXXXVIII. 22 Delegation of large Arteries by application of two ligatures, and division of the Vessel between them.

II. †**2.** An unbinding, loosening. *Obs.*

1650 ASHMOLE *Chym. Collect.* 73 In such a Dissolution and naturall Sublimation, there is made a deligation of the Elements.

†**de'ligature.** *Obs.* [f. L. *dēligāre* (see prec.), after *ligature*: see -URE.] A bandage.

1610 BARROUGH *Meth. Physick* III. lii. (1639) 183 He must use apt and convenient deligatures and trusses.

deligent, obs. form of DILIGENT.

delight (dɪ'laɪt), *sb.* Forms: 3–6 delit, (3 delijt), 4–6 delyt(e, -lite, (5 delytte, 6 dellyte), 6– delight. [ME. *delit*, a. OF. *delit* (-*eit*), (= Pr. *deliet*, Sp. *deleite*, It. *diletto*), f. stem of *deliter* vb. The etymological *delite* is found as late as 1590, but earlier in 16th c. it had generally been supplanted by *delight*, an erroneous spelling after *light*, *flight*, etc.]

1. a. The fact or condition of being delighted; pleasure, joy, or gratification felt in a high degree.

a **1225** *Ancr. R.* 272 So sone so me..let þene lust gon inward & delit waxen. *a* **1240** *Ureisun* in *Cott. Hom.* 201 þe muchele delit of þine swetnesse. *c* **1340** *Cursor M.* 8164 (Fairf.) þai hailsed him wiþ grete delite. *c* **1386** CHAUCER *Prol.* 335 To lyuen in delit was euere his wone, For he was Epicurus owene sone. **1559** *Mirr. Mag.*, *Dk. Clarence* xxxix, In study set his hole delite. **1610** SHAKS. *Temp.* III. ii. 145 Sounds, and sweet aires, that giue delight and hurt not. **1736** BUTLER *Anal.* I. iii. 72 The gratification itself of every natural passion must be attended with delight. **1793** COLERIDGE *Poems*, *The Rose*, He gazed! he thrilled with deep delight! **1860** TYNDALL *Glac.* I. v. 38, I had read with delight Coleridge's poem.

b. Phr. *to take* or *have delight* (*in* a thing, *in doing*, *to do*).

†*to have delight* was formerly used as = to desire, Fr. *avoir envie* (see quots. 1470, 1477).

c **1230** *Hali Meid.* 7 And habbeð mare delit þerin þen anie oðre habbeð i likinge of þe worlde. *a* **1300** *Cursor M.* 23339 (Cott.) Bot suld þai haf a gret delite, To se þam setlid in þair site. *c* **1470** HENRY *Wallace* VIII. 1626 The nobill king.. Had gret delyte this Wallace for to se. **1477** EARL RIVERS (Caxton) *Dictes* 1, I had delyte & axed to rede some good historye. **1483** CAXTON *G. de la Tour* D vj, The delite that men take in the savour and etyng of them. *a* **1569** KINGESMYLL *Confl. Satan* (1578) 49 When he hath a delite in that that he doeth. *c* **1600** SHAKS. *Sonn.* xxxvii. 1 As a decrepit father takes delight To see his active child do deeds of youth. **1652** J. WRIGHT tr. *Camus' Nature's Paradox* 12 [He] took more delight in Arms than at his Book. **1726** *Adv. Capt. R. Boyle* 28 Gardening was what I always took delight in. **1875** JOWETT *Plato* (ed. 2) III. 184 The branch of knowledge.. in which he takes the greatest delight.

2. Anything in which one takes delight, or which affords delight; an object of delight; a source of great pleasure or joy.

a **1225** *Ancr. R.* 102 þes cos.. is a swetnesse & a delit of heorte. **1340** HAMPOLE *Pr. Consc.* 269 Bot in his delytis settes his hert fast. *c* **1400** MAUNDEV. (Roxb.) xv. 66 It es a place of delytez. **1598** SHAKS. *Merry W.* v. v. 158 Why, Sir Iohn, do you thinke.. that euer the deuill could haue made you our delight? **1697** DRYDEN *Virg. Past.* v. 65 Daphnis, the Fields Delight. **1709** POPE *Ess. Crit.* 124 Be Homer's works your study and delight. **1848** MACAULAY *Hist. Eng.* I. 396 The poetry and eloquence of Greece had been the delight of Raleigh and Falkland.

3. The quality (in objects) which causes delight; quality or faculty of delighting; charm, delightfulness. Now only *poet.*

c **1385** CHAUCER *L.G.W.* 1199 *Dido*, With sadyl red enbroudit with delyt. **1500–20** DUNBAR *Thistle & Rose* 145 No flour is so perfyt, So full of vertew, plesans and delyt. *c* **1600** SHAKS. *Sonn.* cii. 12 Sweets growne common lose their dear delight. **1662** GERBIER *Princ.* 38 The Louver at Paris.. with the delight of the annexed Tuilleries. **1804** WORDSW. *Poem*, She was a Phantom of delight When first she gleamed upon my sight.

4. *lumps of delight*: a former name for *Turkish delight* (see TURKISH *a.* 2 b).

1870 [see TURKISH *a.* 1]. **1875** L. M. ALCOTT *Eight Cousins* v, Phebe.. crunched the 'Lump of Delight' tucked into her mouth. **1894** *Daily News* 4 June 7/7 The Turkish, or rather Greek, sweetmeat known as Rahat Loukoums, or 'Lumps of Delight'.

†Hence *delight-taking*.

1619 W. SCLATER *Expos. 1 Thess.* (1630) 468 Pleasure or delight-taking in the partie loued.

delight (dɪˈlaɪt), *v.* Forms: 3–7 **delite**, 4–6 **delyte**, (4 **delytte**, 4–5 **dilyte**, 6 **delyt**), 6 **delyght**, 6– **delight**. [ME. *delite-n*, a. OF. *delitier* (*-leitier*, *-leter*, *-liter*) = Pr., Sp. *delectar*, Sp., Pg. *deleitar*, It. *delettare*, *dilettare*:—L. *dēlectāre* to allure, attract, delight, charm, please, freq. of *dēlicĕre* to entice away, allure: cf. DELICIOUS. The current erroneous spelling after *light*, etc. arose in the 16th c., and prevailed about 1575: the Bible of 1611 occasionally retained *delite*.]

1. a. *trans.* To give great pleasure or enjoyment to; to please highly. Frequently in *pass.* (const. *with*, *at*, †*in*, or with infin.). Also *absol.*

c **1300** *K. Alis.* 5802 So hy ben delited in that art That wery ne ben hy neuere cert. *c* **1374** CHAUCER *Anel. & Arc.* 266 But for I.. was so besy you to delyte. **1535** FISHER *Wks.* (1876) 366 The loue of this game deliteth him so muche. **1576** FLEMING *Panopl. Epist.* 151, I am merveilously delighted with merrie conceites. **1594** HOOKER *Eccl. Pol.* I. (1676) 70 The stateliness of Houses.. delighteth the eye. **1673** RAY *Journ. Low C.* 395 The Italians are greatly delighted in Pictures. **1704** POPE *Spring* 67 If Windsor-shades delight the matchless maid. **1855** MACAULAY *Hist. Eng.* III. 496 Charles.. was delighted with an adviser who had a hundred pleasant.. things to say. **1873** BLACK *Pr. Thule* xxii. 371 If the money belonged to me, I should be delighted to keep it. **1875** JOWETT *Plato* (ed. 2) I. 476, I was quite delighted at this notion. **1904** E. T. MEADE *Love Triumphant* v, I mean to go to London.. to meet my equals. I shall dazzle, I shall delight. **1908** G. F. ATHERTON *Gorgeous Isle* iii, There had been much to delight and awe.

b. *refl.* = 2.

1303 R. BRUNNE *Handl. Synne* 3086 3yf þou delyte þe oftyn stoundes, Yn horses, haukys, or yn houndes. *c* **1340** *Cursor M.* 1560 (Fairf.) A-mong caymys kyn, þat delitet ham al to syn. **1362** LANGL. *P. Pl.* A. I. 29 Lot.. Dilytede him in drinke. **1477** EARL RIVERS (Caxton) *Dictes* 1 A gentylman.. whiche gretly delited hym in alle vertuouse.. thynges. **1611** BIBLE *Ps.* cxix. 16, I will delight my selfe in thy statutes. **1634** SIR T. HERBERT *Trav.* 199 He has many Elephants with whose Majestie he greatly delights himselfe. **1742** COLLINS *Eclog.* iii. 36 Fair happy maid!.. With love delight thee. **1828** D'ISRAELI *Chas. I*, I. v. 95 A life of pleasure—to delight himself and to be the delight of others.

2. *intr.* (for *refl.*) To be highly pleased, take great pleasure, rejoice: **a.** *in* or *to do* (anything).

a **1225** *Ancr. R.* 52 Eue.. iseih hine euir, & ueng to deliten i þe biholdunge. *a* **1325** *Prose Psalter* l[i]. 17 þou ne shalt nou3t deliten in sacrifices. *c* **1385** CHAUCER *L.G.W.* 415 Yet hath he made lewde folke delyte To serue yow. *a* **1450** *Le Morte Arth.* 3717 Suche we haue delyted in. **1535** JOHN AP RICE in *Four C. Eng. Lett.* 33 He delited moche in playing at dice and cardes. **1548** HALL *Chron.* 201 b, An Inne, wherein he delighted muche to be. **1605** SHAKS. *Macb.* II. iii. 55 The labour we delight in physicks paine. **1611** BIBLE *Ps.* lxviii. 30 Scatter thou the people that delite in warre. **1634** SIR T. HERBERT *Trav.* 16 They delight to dawbe and make their skin glister with grease. **1710** STEELE & ADDISON *Tatler* No. 254 ¶1 There are no Books which I more delight in than Travels. **1869** FREEMAN *Norm. Conq.* (1876) III. xii. 145 The obsolete titles delighted in by the Latin writers. **1874** MORLEY *Compromise* (1886) 39 We know the kind of man whom this system delights to honour.

b. *absol.* (without *const.*).

1393 GOWER *Conf.* III. 243 And she.. So ferforth made him to delite Through lust. **1509** HAWES *Past. Pleas.* x. ii, Divers persons in sundry wyse delyght.

c. *transf.* of things.

1577 B. GOOGE *Heresbach's Husb.* I. (1586) 33 b, The Beane delighteth in riche and wel dounged ground. **1697** DAMPIER *Voy.* I. iii. 34 The Manatee delights to live in brackish Water. **1849** JOHNSTON *Exp. Agric.* 116 The hop delights in woollen rags.

†**3.** *trans.* To enjoy greatly: = *to delight in.*

a **1450** *Knt. de la Tour* (1868) 63 The whiche makithe hym to desire and delite foule plesaunce of the synne of lechery. **1591** SYLVESTER *Du Bartas* I. iv. (1641) 34/2 Brave-minded Mars.. Delighting nought but Battails, blood, and murder. **1602** BASSE *Eleg.* i. 3 Who lou'd no riot, tho delighted sport. **1618** J. SMYTH *Lives Berkeleys* (1883) II. 285 Shee often went with her husband part of those hunting journeys, delighting her crosbowe.

delightable (dɪˈlaɪtəb(ə)l), *a. rare.* [f. DELIGHT *v.* or *sb.* + -ABLE: containing the same elements as the ME. DELITABLE.] Affording delight.

1871 R. ELLIS *Catullus* xxxiv. 10 Queen of mountainous heights, of all Forests leafy, delightable.

delighted (dɪˈlaɪtɪd), *ppl. a.* [f. DELIGHT *v.* and *sb.* + -ED.]

1. Filled with delight, highly pleased or gratified.

a **1687** WALLER *On His Majesty's Escape* (R.), About the keel delighted dolphins play. **1857** LOWELL *Above & Below* I, What health there is In the frank Dawn's delighted eyes.

†**2.** Endowed or attended with delight; affording delight, delightful. *Obs.*

With the first quot. cf. DELIGHTFUL 2, quot. 1600.

1603 SHAKS. *Meas. for M.* III. i. 121 This sensible warme motion to become A kneaded clod; and the delighted spirit To bath in fierie floods, or to recide In thrilling region of thicke-ribbed ice. **1604** —— *Oth.* I. iii. 290 If Vertue no delighted Beautie lacke. **1634** SIR T. HERBERT *Trav.* 104 By supping a delighted cup of extreame poyson. **1667** PRIMATT *City & C. Build.* Ded., Your quick and delighted equitable dispatch of such Differences as have come before you. **1747** COLLINS *Passions* 30 But thou, O Hope.. What was thy delighted measure?

deˈlightedly, *adv.* [-LY².] In a delighted manner.

1800 COLERIDGE *Piccolom.* II. iv, Delightedly dwells he 'mong fays and talismans. **1879** GEO. ELIOT *Theo. Such* ix. 161 A man delightedly conscious of his wealth.

delighter (dɪˈlaɪtə(r)). [-ER.] One who delights; one who takes delight *in* (anything).

a **1677** BARROW *Serm.* Wks. 1687 I. xvii. 250 A delighter in telling bad stories. **1715** *Lond. Gaz.* No. 5360/9 All Persons that are delighters in Plants and Flowers. **1705** STANHOPE *Paraphr.* II. 366 To draw a greater Guilt, upon the Delighter in, than upon the Commiter of, them.

delightful (dɪˈlaɪtfʊl), *a.* Also 6 **delyte-**, **delite-**. [f. DELIGHT (*delite*) *sb.* + -FUL.]

1. Affording delight; delighting; highly pleasing, charming.

1530 PALSGR. 309/2 Delytefull, that moche delyteth, *deliteux*. **1553** T. WILSON *Rhet.* (1580) 3 *marg.*, Oratours muste use delitefull wordes and saiges. **1590** SPENSER *F.Q.* I. iv. 4 Goodly galleries.. Full of faire windowes and delightful bowres. **1659** D. PELL *Impr. Sea* To Rdr. A vij, What delightfuller thing canst thou read than a Theam or Subject of the Sea. **1667** MILTON *P.L.* I. 467 Rimmon, whose delightful Seat Was fair Damascus. **1779** COWPER *Lett.* 31 Oct., Was there ever anything so delightful as the music of the Paradise Lost? **1848** DICKENS *Dombey* xxxv, That delightfullest of cities, Paris. **1870** LOWELL *Study Wind.* (1871) 1 One of the most delightful books in my father's library.

†**2.** Full of or experiencing delight; delighting *in*, delighted *with*. *Obs.*

a **1569** [see DELIGHTFULLY 2]. **1576** FLEMING *Panopl. Epist.* 392 Shake off that delightfull desire whiche you have to be conversaunt in the Citie. **1600** C. SUTTON *Learn to Die* (1634) 16 Too chilling a doctrine for our delightful dispositions. **1602** DANIEL *Hymen's Tri.* v. i, We are glad to see you thus Delightful. **1687** A. LOVELL *Bergerac's Com. Hist.* 24 The Nymph Eccho is so delightful with their Airs.

delightfully (dɪˈlaɪtfʊlɪ), *adv.* [f. prec. + -LY².]

1. In a delightful manner; in a way that affords delight; charmingly.

1580 SIDNEY *Arcadia* I. (R.), The flock of unspeakable virtues, held up delightfully in that best builded fold. **1625** BACON *Ess. Gardens* (Arb.) 558 Those which Perfume the Aire most delightfully. **1788** MAD. D'ARBLAY *Diary* 2 Jan., My dear father was delightfully well and gay. **1848** C. BRONTË *J. Eyre* xvi. (1873) 160 She sang delightfully: it was a treat to listen to her. **1865** MRS. CARLYLE *Lett.* III. 281 The air to-day is delightfully fresh.

†**2.** With experience of delight, delightedly.

a **1569** KINGESMYLL *Confl. Satan* (1578) 7 It must shutte up thine eyes from delightfully seeing sin. **1678** WANLEY *Wond. Lit. World* Ded. A ij, These things I have many times delightfully considered of. **1749** C. WESLEY *Hymn, 'Forth in Thy Name'*, For Thee delightfully [to] employ Whate'er Thy bounteous grace hath given.

delightfulness (dɪˈlaɪtfʊlnɪs). [f. as prec. + -NESS.]

1. The state or quality of being delightful.

1579 LYLY *Euphues* (Arb.) 49, I hope the delightfulnesse of the one wil attenuate the tediousnesse of the other. **1674** PLAYFORD *Skill Mus.* I. 59 Which Musick, by its Variety and Delightfulness, allayeth the Passions. **1777** SIR W. JONES *Ess.* i. 163 The delightfulness of their climate. **1831** GREVILLE *Mem. Geo. IV* (1875) II. xv. 182, Admiration of the beauty and delightfulness of the place.

†**2.** Of persons: The state of being delighted or of feeling delight. *Obs.*

1580 SIDNEY *Arcadia* (1613) 148–9 But our desires' tyrannicall extortion Doth force vs there to set our chiefe delight fulnesse Where but a baiting-place is all our portion. **1608** MACHIN *Dumb Knt.* IV. i, The Queen is all for revels; her high heart.. Bestows itself upon delightfulness.

delighting (dɪˈlaɪtɪŋ), *vbl. sb.* [-ING¹.] The action of the verb DELIGHT; delectation.

a **1325** *Prose Psalter* xv. 11 Delitynges ben in þy ri3t honde vnto þe ende. **1500–20** DUNBAR *Poems* (1893) 311/34 Bettir war leif my paper quhyte, And tak me to vthir delyting. **1581** SIDNEY *Apol. Poetrie* (Arb.) 37 Beautifying it both for further teaching, and more delighting. **1640** SIR R. BAKER in Spurgeon *Treas. Dav.* Ps. lxxxiv. 2 His Tabernacles.. must needs work in me an infinite delighting.

deˈlighting, *ppl. a.* [-ING².] That delights (in the different senses of the verb).

1563 *Form of Medit.* in *Liturg. Serv. Q. Eliz.* (1847) 504 With wines, spices, silks, and other vain costly delighting things. **1599** T. M[OUFET] *Silkwormes* 20 Full of delighting change, and learning greate. **1814** *Forgery* LV. ii. Let me.. praise Heaven for the delighting pledge.

Hence **deˈlightingly** *adv.*

1602 CAREW *Cornwall* 132 b, A walk which.. my selfe haue oftentimes delightingly seene. **1660** JER. TAYLOR *Duct. Dubit.* IV. i. (R.), Though he did not consent clearly and delightingly to Seguiri's death. **1836** *New Monthly Mag.* XLVI. 425 Readers who delightingly believe, that [etc.].

delightless (dɪˈlaɪtlɪs), *a.* [-LESS.] Void of delight; affording no delight. (The opposite of *delightful*.)

1580 SIDNEY *Arcadia* III. (1622) 287 Turning away her feeble sight, as from a delightlesse obiect. *c* **1750** SHENSTONE *Elegies* xi. 8 And we, delightless, left to wander home! **1850** BLACKIE *Æschylus* II. 16 For this thou shalt keep watch On this delightless rock.

delightsome (dɪˈlaɪtsəm), *a.* Also 6 **delyt-**, **delite-**. [f. DELIGHT *sb.* + -SOME.]

= DELIGHTFUL. (In 17th c. in frequent use: now only literary.)

1500–20 DUNBAR *Poems* lxiv. 2 Delytsum lyllie of everie lustynes. **1576** FLEMING *Panopl. Epist.* 409 Up and about the pleasaunt and delightsome hilles. **1601** WEEVER *Mirr. Mart.* E j b, Daie is delightsome in respect of night. **1611** BIBLE *Mal.* iii. 12 Ye shall be a delightsome land. **1697** DAMPIER *Voy.* I. xvi. 454 The whole Town was very clean and delightsome. **1760** STERNE *Serm.* x. (1773) 64 When he reflected upon this gay delightsome structure. **1844** MRS. BROWNING *Vision of Poets*, A mild delightsome melancholy. **1878** SHAIRP in *Contemp. Rev.* 685 All who care to visit.. that delightsome land [the Scottish Border]. **1892** *Field* 19 Nov. 770/1 This delightsome, if quick-fleeting, season.

deˈlightsomely, *adv.* [f. prec. + -LY².] In a delightsome manner; delightfully, joyously.

1576 FLEMING *Panopl. Epist.* 227 The grassehopper.. was delightsomly disposed. **1600** SURFLET *Countrie Farme* VII. lxi. 892 The misken.. singeth sweetly and delightsomely. *a* **1603** T. CARTWRIGHT *Confut. Rhem. N.T.* (1618) 84 A man is willingly, desirously, and delightsomly holden vnder sinne. **1885** TENNYSON *Balin & Balan*, I have not lived my life delightsomely.

deˈlightsomeness. [f. as prec. + -NESS.] = DELIGHTFULNESS.

1576 FLEMING *Panopl. Epist.* 439 The delightsomnesse of his behaviours. **1679** T. SIDEN *Hist. Sevarites* II. i, A little Town called by the Inhabitants *Cola*, from the delightsomness of the place. **1866** RUSKIN *Crown Wild Olive* i. 72 To repent into delight and delightsomeness. **1883** J. PARKER *Tyne Ch.* 334 Tell a stone-deaf man what music is; dwell on its delightsomeness.

†ˈ**deligible**, *a. Obs.* [f. L. *dēlig-ĕre* to choose + -BLE.] Worthy to be chosen, desirable.

1680 HOLLINGWORTH *Penit. J. Marketman* 11 Those joys and pleasures which render humane life any ways deligible.

†**deˈlignate**, *v. nonce-wd.* [f. DE- II. 1 + L. *lign-um* wood.] *trans.* To deprive of wood.

1655 FULLER *Ch. Hist.* IX. iii. §34 Dilapidating (or rather delignating his Bishoprick, cutting down the woods thereof).

delignification (dɪˌlɪgnɪfɪˈkeɪʃən). [f. DE- + LIGN(IN + -IFICATION.] The removal of lignin from woody tissue. So **deˈlignified** *ppl. a.*

1919 *Experiment Station Record* Feb. 160 Its action on the wood is described as one of delignification followed by digestion. **1943** *Chem. Abstr.* 10 Apr. 1877 Decomposition of delignified bast fiber. **1946** *Nature* 20 July 100/2 Jute fibres that have been subjected to intensive delignification. *Ibid.*, Completely delignified and partially mercerized jute fibres.

Delilah (dɪˈlaɪlə). Also 6–8 **Dalilah**. The name of the woman who betrayed Samson to the Philistines (see Judges xvi), used allusively to mean a temptress or treacherous paramour.

1594 J. KING *On Jonas* (1597) xlvi. 630 You who esteeme.. to be the dearlings of the pleasure of Egypt, and be set vpon the knees of the Delilah of this world. **1614** T. ADAMS *Divells Banket* i. 6 If Dalilah inuite Sampson, ware his lockes; she will spoile the Nazarite of his hayres; there are many Dalilahs in these dayes. **1678** BUTLER *Hud.* III. ii. 1115 [Ye] Transform'd all Wives to Dalilahs, Whose Husbands were not for the Cause. **1768** H. BROOKE *Fool of Qual.* III. xiii. 30, I have no foreign Dalilahs, no secret amours. **1879** J. C. SHAIRP *Robert Burns* vi. 141 Other Delilahs on a smaller scale Burns met with during his Dumfries sojourn. **1893** F. ADAMS *New Egypt* 63 This is about as far as the French Delilah dare at present go in the public incitements of her young Egyptian Samson. **1931** W. DE LA MARE *Seven Short Stories* 89 The gloved fingers, Delilah-like, had tapped again.

† **de'limate**, *v. Obs.*—[0] [f. stem of L. *dēlīmāt-us* filed off, f. DE- I. 2 + *līmāre* to file.]

1623 COCKERAM, *Delimate*, to file or shaue from off a thing. **1656** in BLOUNT *Glossogr.*

delimit (dɪˈlɪmɪt), *v.* [a. F. *délimit-er* (1773 in Hatzf.), ad. L. *dēlīmitāre* to mark out as a boundary, f. DE- I. 3 + *līmitāre* to bound, *līmes, līmit-em* boundary, limit.] *trans.* To mark or determine the limits of; to define, as a limit or boundary.

1852 GLADSTONE *Glean.* IV. v. 144 Other nations are to delimit for themselves the possessions and status of the clergy. **1885** *Times* 10 Apr. 9 The question of delimiting the Russo-Afghan frontier.

delimitate (dɪˈlɪmɪteɪt), *v.* [f. ppl. stem of L. *dēlīmitāre*: see prec.] = prec.

1884 *Manch. Exam.* 3 Dec. 5/5 The territory of the Association as delimitated on an appended map. **1891** *Times* 18 May, The Commission to delimitate the frontier between Burmah and Siam.

delimitation (dɪlɪmɪˈteɪʃən). [a. F. *délimitation* (1773 in Hatzf.), n. of action from *délimiter* to DELIMIT.] The action of delimiting; the fact of being delimited; determination of a limit or boundary; *esp.* of the frontier of a territory.

1836 SIR H. TAYLOR *Statesman* xvi. 116 The delimitation of those bounds within which a statesman's dispensation should be confined. **1868** GLADSTONE *Juv. Mundi* iv. (1869) 110 They [territorial names] came to signify districts of fixed and known delimitation. **1884** *Leeds Mercury* 13 Mar., The delimitation of the frontier of Turkestan and Kashgar.

delimitative (dɪˈlɪmɪteɪtɪv), *a.* [f. *dēlīmitāt-*, ppl. stem of *dēlīmitāre* to DELIMIT + -IVE.] Having the function of delimitation.

1887 *Spectator* 3 Sept. 1171 A Delimitative Commission is to mark out the frontier.

delimiter (dɪˈlɪmɪtə(r)). *Computing.* [f. DELIMIT *v.* + -ER[1].] A character, etc., used to indicate the beginning or end of a group of characters or a field.

1960 *Communications Assoc. Computing Machinery* III. 217/1 Break characters may serve merely as separators (e.g., commas to indicate parallel structure), as signs denoting a treatment to be performed on the separated blocks.., or as delimiters (paired parentheses) to impose tree structure on otherwise linear text. **1967** G. H. MEALY in S. Rosen *Programming Syst. & Lang.* 558 The translation phase has two main functions. The first is to scan source statements, breaking them up into symbols, delimiters, literals, etc. **1979** J. E. ROWLEY *Mechanised In-House Information Syst.* II. 191 The variable length records are parsed and analysed for appropriate delimiters of textual fields, and then the data elements are extracted. **1983** *Austral. Personal Computer* Sept. 30, 20H—ASCII space used as a delimiter.

delimitize: see DE- II. 1.

† **de'line**, *v. Obs.* Also 6 delyne. [ad. L. *dēlīneā-re*: see DELINEATE. Cf. ALIGN *v.*, and mod.F. *délinéer* (Littré).] *trans.* To mark out by lines; to outline, sketch; = DELINEATE *v.* 1, 2.

1589 IVE *Fortif.* 36 Proceede as in the delyning of a bulwarke. *a* **1734** NORTH *Exam.* (1740) 523 A certain Plan had been delined out for a farther Proceeding.

delineable (dɪˈlɪniːəb(ə)l), *a. rare.* [f. L. *dēlīneā-re* to DELINEATE: see -BLE.] Capable of being delineated.

1661 FELTHAM *Resolves, Lusoria, etc.* Lett. xvii. 85 In either Vision there is something not delineable.

† **delineament** (dɪˈlɪniːəmənt). *Obs.* [f. L. *dēlīneā-re*: see -MENT; cf. *lineament*.] The action of delineating, or an instance of this; delineation.

1593 NASHE *Christ's T.* (1613) 57 The delineament of wretchednesse. **1612** SELDEN *Drayton's Poly-olb.* xi. Notes 181 For similitude of delineaments and composture. **1653** H. MORE *Antid. Ath.* II. v. (1712) 52 The more rude and careless strokes and delineaments of Divine Providence.

de'lineate, *ppl. a. arch.* or *poetic.* [ad. L. *dēlīneāt-us*, pa. pple. of *dēlīneāre*: see next.] Delineated; traced out, portrayed, described, etc. (Also used as a participle.)

1596 *Edw. III*, II. ii. 27 Still do I see in him delineate His mother's visage. **1607** TOPSELL *Four-f. Beasts* (1658) 247 Such an even and delineate proportion. **1619** BAINBRIDGE *Descr. late Comet* 11 That forme which..is delineate in the planispheare. **1773** J. ROSS *Fratricide* v. 508 (MS.) But where's the Muse can give delineate life To heavenly Thyrsa. **1848** BAILEY *Festus* Proem (ed. 3) 7/1 And for the soul of man delineate here.

delineate (dɪˈlɪniːeɪt), *v.* Also 6 delineat, 6–7 deliniat(e. [f. ppl. stem of L. *dēlīneāre* to outline, sketch out, f. DE- I. 3 + *līneāre* to draw lines, *līnea* line: cf. *depict, describe.*]

1. *trans.* To trace out by lines, trace the outline of, as on a chart or map.

1559 W. CUNNINGHAM *Cosmogr. Glasse* 6 Geographie does deliniat, and set out the universal earth. **1612** DRAYTON *Poly-olb.* A b, The Map, lively delineating to thee every mountaine, forrest, river and valley. **1710** BERKELEY *Princ. Hum. Knowl.* §127 When therefore I delineate a triangle on paper. **1860** MAURY *Phys. Geog. Sea* viii. §409 Other currents..delineated on [the] Plates. **1870** F. R. WILSON *Ch. Lindisf.* 61 The exact position is delineated on the plan.

2. To trace in outline, sketch out (something to be constructed); to outline; 'to make the first draught of' (J.).

1613 R. C. *Table Alph.* (ed. 3), *Delineate*, to draw the proportion of any thing. **1641** MILTON *Ch. Govt.* ii. (1851) 103 God..never intended to leave the government thereof delineated here in such curious architecture to be patch't afterwards. **1670** MARVELL *Corr.* cliv. Wks. 1872–5 II. 338 Not willing nor prepared to deliniate his whole proposall. **1764** REID *Inquiry* vi. §15. 172, I have endeavoured to delineate such a process. **1875** JOWETT *Plato* (ed. 2) V. 394 Our laws and the whole constitution of our state having been thus delineated.

3. To represent by a drawing; to draw, portray.

1610 GUILLIM *Heraldry* III. vii. (1660) 130 Plants.. delineated with lims, sprigs, or branches. **1646** SIR T. BROWNE *Pseud. Ep.* v. xi. 251 With the same reason they may delineate old Nestor like Adonis. **1794** SULLIVAN *View Nat.* II, They were accused of being Anthropomorphites; delineating the Almighty as they did with hands, with eyes, and with feet. **1865** GROTE *Plato* I. i. 17 If horses or lions could paint, they would delineate their gods in form like themselves.

4. *fig.* To portray in words; to describe.

a **1618** RALEIGH (J.), It followeth, to delineate the region in which God first planted his delightful garden. **1680** J. CHAMBERLAYNE (*title*), Sacred Poem, Wherein the Birth, Miracles, &c. of the Most Holy Jesus are Delineated. **1791** BOSWELL *Johnson* Introd., When I delineate him without reserve. **1868** NETTLESHIP *Browning* Introd. 3 Great as is his power in delineating all human passion.

Hence **de'lineating** *vbl. sb.*; also *attrib.*

1603 DRAYTON *Bar. Wars* VI. lx, The Land-skip, Mixture, and Delineatings. **1823** J. BADCOCK *Dom. Amusem.* 142 The Delineating Ink..for delineating upon stone.

delineation (dɪˌlɪniːˈeɪʃən). Also 6–7 deliniation. [ad. L. *dēlīneātiōn-em*, n. of action f. *dēlīneāre*, to DELINEATE. So in F. (Paré, 16th c.).] The action or product of delineating.

1. The action of tracing out something by lines; the drawing of a diagram, geometrical figure, etc.; *concr.* a drawing, diagram, or figure.

1570 BILLINGSLEY *Euclid* I. ii. 11 Whereupon follow diuers delineations and constructions. **1589** PUTTENHAM *Eng. Poesie* III. iv. (Arb.) 159 *Declination, delineation, dimention*, are scholasticall termes in deede, and yet very proper. **1646** SIR T. BROWNE *Pseud. Ep.* VI. viii. 314 In the deliniations of many Maps of Africa, the River Niger exceedeth it about ten degrees in length. **1774** J. BRYANT *Mythol.* II. 234 The delineations of the sphere have by the Greeks..been greatly abused. **1811** PINKERTON *Petral.* I. 335 There are generally several colours together, and these are arranged in striped, dotted, and clouded delineations.

2. The action of tracing in outline something to be constructed; a sketch, outline, plan, rough draft. Usually *fig.*

1581 MARBECK *Bk. of Notes* 939 Painters..when they intend to paint a King, first draw out the proportion upon a table..a man may by that deliniation..easely perceiue that the Image of a King is there painted. **1678** CUDWORTH *Intell. Syst.* 132 In the Seed is conteined the Whole Delineation of the Future man. **1722** WOLLASTON *Relig. Nat.* 6, I call it only a Delineation, or rude draught. **1853** MARSDEN *Early Purit.* 92 Cartwright's bold assertion, that the New Testament contains the exact delineation of a Christian church.

3. The action or manner of representing an object by a drawing or design; pictorial representation, portraiture; *concr.* a portrait, likeness, picture.

1594 CAREW *Huarte's Exam. Wits* (1616) 90 If with a bad pensill he draw ill fauoured shapes, and of bad delineation. **1615** CROOKE *Body of Man* 17 If Galen would not haue Plants and Hearbes painted..how would hee haue endured the delineation of the parts of our body? **1801** STRUTT *Sports & Past.* I. i. 12 This delineation..taken from a manuscript and illuminated early in the fourteenth century. **1831** BREWSTER *Nat. Magic* iv. (1833) 86 We shall have phantasms of the most perfect delineation.

4. The action of portraying in words.

1603 DANIEL *Def. Rhime* (1717) 19 In these Delineations of Men. **1664** H. MORE *Myst. Iniq.* v. 11 Let us begin then with the delineation of the first member of this hideous Mystery. **1781** COWPER *Lett.* 10 Oct., My delineations of the heart are from my own experience. **1870** EMERSON *Soc. & Solit., Bks.* Wks. (Bohn) III. 82 Xenophon's delineation of Athenian manners.

† **5.** Lineal descent or derivation. *Obs. rare.*

1606 G. W[OODCOCKE] tr. *Hist. Ivstine* 69 b From him, by order of delineation and rightfull succession, the kingdom discended to Arimba.

delineative (dɪˈlɪniːətɪv), *a.* [f. ppl. stem of L. *dēlīneāre* to DELINEATE + -IVE.] Pertaining to delineation; tending to delineate.

1841 H. S. FOOTE *Texas & Texans* I. 40 Others were perspicuously delineative of current events. **1854** BAGEHOT *Coll. Works* (1965) I. 260 In the absence of the delineative faculty..minds of this deep..class are apt to put up with reasons which lie on the surface. **1892** CLERKE *Fam. Studies Homer* x. 276 The delineative inlaying of the Shield of Achilles.

delineator (dɪˈlɪniːeɪtə(r)). [agent-n. in L. form from *dēlīneāre* to DELINEATE.]

1. One who delineates, sketches, or depicts.

1782 V. KNOX *Ess.* 52 (R.) We are tempted to exclaim, with a modern delineator of characters, 'Alas, poor human nature'. **1815** W. H. IRELAND *Scribbleomania* 202 An unbiassed delineator of facts. **1865** WRIGHT *Hist. Caricature* vi. (1875) 100 The mediæval artists in general were not very good delineators of form.

2. An instrument for tracing outlines.

1774 *Specif. W. Storer's Patent* No. 1183 An optical Instrument or accurate delineator. **1844** *Civ. Eng. & Archit. Jrnl.* VII. 237 A profile delineator..Improvements in apparatus for obtaining the profile of various forms or figures.

3. (See quots.)

a **1877** KNIGHT *Dict. Mech.* 683/2 *Delineator* 1. (*Tailoring.*) A pattern formed by rule; being expansible in the directions where the sizes vary, as indicated by the varying lengths obtained by measurement. 2. (*Surveying.*) A perambulator, or geodetical instrument on wheels, with registering devices for recording distances between points [etc.]. **1964** *Punch* 23 Sept. 442/3 The delineators are the small reflectors mounted on posts 132 feet apart [on U.S. roads].

delineatory (dɪˈlɪniːətərɪ), *a.* [f. as prec.: see -ORY.] Belonging to delineation; descriptive.

1834 H. O'BRIEN *Round Towers Ireland* 129, I have traced from the Irish..its delineatory name.

delineatress (dɪˌlɪnɪˈeɪtrɪs). *rare.* [f. DELINEATOR: see -ESS.] A female delineator.

1876 *Daily News* 22 Aug. 3 Madame Materna, the delineatress of Brünnhilda.

† **de'lineature.** *Obs.* [f. ppl. stem of L. *dēlīneāre* + -URE.] Delineation; description.

1611 COTGR., *Delineature*, the same [as *Delineation*]; or, a delineature. **1635** BRATHWAIT *Arcad. Pr.* II. 93 In the delineature of those features. **1659** A. LOVEDAY in *R. Loveday's Lett.* (1663) A vj a, Without any other additional delineature.

† **de'liniment.** *Obs.* [ad. L. *dēlīnīment-um*, f. *dēlīn-*, *dēlēnīre*.]

1727 BAILEY vol. II, *Deliniment*, a mitigating or asswaging.

† **deli'nition.** *Obs. rare*—[1]. [irreg. f. L. *dēlinĕre* to besmear (ppl. stem *dēlit-*): see -TION.] The action of smearing.

1664 H. MORE *Myst. Iniq.* xviii. 68 The Delinition also of the Infant's Ears and Nostrils with the Spittle of the Priest.

† **de'linque**, *v. Obs. rare*—[0]. [ad. L. *dēlinqu-ĕre* to fail, be lacking, be at fault, offend, f. DE- I. 3 + *linquĕre* to leave: so F. *délinque-r* (15th c. in Littré).] (See quot.)

1623 COCKERAM II, To Leaue, *delinque.*

† **de'linquence.** *Obs.* [ad. L. *dēlinquentia* (Tertullian), f. *dēlinquent-em*, DELINQUENT *a.*: see -ENCE.] The fact of being a delinquent; culpable failure in duty.

1682 *Address fr. Hereford* in *Lond. Gaz.* No. 1695/1 Prayers..and..Vows of Allegiance..are the best Offerings we have to attone Heaven for our Delinquence. **1779–81** JOHNSON *L.P., Pope* Wks. IV. 103 All his delinquences observed and aggravated. **1832** *Blackw. Mag.* XXXI. 390 Rights..are to be sacrificed without either proved delinquence or tendered compensation.

delinquency (dɪˈlɪŋkwənsɪ). [f. as prec.: see -ENCY.]

1. The condition or quality of being a delinquent; failure in or neglect of duty; more generally, violation of duty or right; the condition of being guilty, guilt.

1648 *Articles of Peace* xxvii. in *Milton's Wks.* (1851) II., In case of Refractories or Delinquency, [they] may distrain and imprison, and cause such Delinquents to be distrained and imprisoned. *a* **1661** FULLER *Worthies* (1840) III. 80 Such as compounded for their reputed delinquency in our late civil wars. **1751** SMOLLETT *Per. Pic.* (1779) II. l. 112 They were old offenders in the same degree of delinquency. **1754** RICHARDSON *Grandison* (1781) II. xxviii. 256, I know not any act of delinquency she has committed. **1892** SIR H. H. LOPES in *Law Times Rep.* LXVII. 142/1 There must be moral delinquency on the part of the person proceeded against.

b. (with *pl.*) An act of delinquency; a fault, sin of omission; an offence, misdeed.

1636 G. SANDYS *Paraphr. Job* (J.), Can Thy years determine like the age of man That thou should'st my delinquencies exquire? **1651** G. W. tr. *Cowel's Inst.* 209 From these Delinquencies proceed greater crimes. **1854** EMERSON *Lett. & Soc. Aims, Comic* Wks. (Bohn) III. 205 The yawning delinquencies of practice. **1876** GRANT *Burgh Sch. Scotl.* II. v. 175 If delinquencies be committed in the playground, they may be reported to the masters.

delinquent (dɪˈlɪŋkwənt), *a.* and *sb.* [ad. L. *dēlinquent-em*, pr. pple. of *dēlinquĕre*: see DELINQUE and -ENT. Caxton used a form in *-aunt*, a. F. *délinquant*, pr. pple. of *délinquer*.]

A. *adj.* Failing in, or neglectful of, a duty or obligation; defaulting; faulty; more generally, guilty of a misdeed or offence.

1603 HOLLAND *Plutarch's Mor.* 93 Having offended or being delinquent in any duetie. **1611** SPEED *Hist. Gt. Brit.* IX. viii. (1632) 562 Whensoeuer one Prince is delinquent against another. *a* **1640** J. BALL *Answ. to Can* I. (1642) 26 The Ministerie may be lawfull, though in many particulars delinquent and deficient. **1709** SACHEVERELL *Serm.* 15 Aug.

4 He stands delinquent. **1824** W. IRVING *T. Trav.* I. 276 A delinquent school-boy. **1891** *Daily News* 5 Feb. 5/4 What are 'delinquent parishes'?.. parishes that have a provoking habit of neglecting to hand over the sums that are due from them on account of the relief of the poor.

b. *transf.* Of or pertaining to a delinquent.

1657 *Burton's Diary* (1828) II. 129 A purchaser of this or any other delinquent lands. **1889** BRUCE *Plant. Negro* 218 Sold out by the public auctioneer for delinquent taxes.

B. *sb.* **1.** One who fails in duty or obligation, a defaulter; more generally, one guilty of an offence against the law, an offender.

1484 CAXTON *Chivalry* 34 To punysshe the trespacers and delynquaunts. **1605** SHAKS. *Macb.* III. vi. 12 Did he not straight In pious rage, the two delinquents teare? **1638** BAKER tr. *Balzac's Lett.* (1654) II. II. 61 When the Delinquent concurs in opinion with the judge. **1709** STEELE & SWIFT *Tatler* No. 74 ¶ 10 Where Crimes are enormous, the Delinquent deserves little Pity. **1836** H. COLERIDGE *North. Worthies* (1852) I. 50 Severe prosecution of delinquents. **1865** LIVINGSTONE *Zambesi* xx. 410 This deliberation however gave the delinquents a chance of escape.

2. *Eng. Hist.* A name applied by the Parliamentary party to those who assisted Charles I or Charles II, by arms, money, or personal service, in levying war, 1642–1660.

The term was exhaustively defined by an Order of 27 March, 1643. As it practically included all Royalists, it became in common parlance almost synonymous with *Cavalier*.

1643 *Ordinance of Parlt.* April 1 Preamb., That the estates of such notorious Delinquents, as have been the causes or Instruments of the publick calamities.. should be converted and applyed towards the supportation of the great charges of the Commonwealth. *c* **1643** *Ballad 'A Mad World'* in *The Rump* I. (1662) 48 A Monster now Delinquent term'd He is declared to be, And that his lands, as well as goods, Sequestered ought to be. **1647** CLARENDON *Hist. Reb.* III. (1702) I. 212 Hereupon, they [the Commons] call'd whom they pleased, Delinquents. **1648** D. JENKINS *Wks.* 7 A Delinquent is he who adhears to the Kings Enemies; *Com. Sur. Litil.* 261. This shewes who are delinquents. **1670** *Moral State Eng.* 21 The bleeding estates of unhappy delinquents. **1761–2** HUME *Hist. Eng.* (1806) IV. liv. 169.

de'linquently, *adv. rare*⁻⁰. [f. prec. + -LY².] In a delinquent manner; so as to fail in duty.

1864 in WEBSTER.

† **de'linquish**, *v. Obs.* [f. L. *dēlinquĕre* (see DELINQUE), after *relinquish*. (OF. had a rare *délinquir* = *délinquer*: so Pr. and Sp. *delinquir*.)] *intr.* To fail in duty or obligation; to be guilty of a delinquency.

1606 J. KING *4th Serm. Hampton Crt.* 13 Must all be remoued.. because some had delinquished?

† **de'linquishment.** *Obs.* [f. prec. + -MENT.] **1.** Failure in duty; a fault, offence, delinquency.

1593 NASHE *Christ's T.* 23 a, Thou shalt be my vninnocence, and whole summe of delinquishment. **1633** T. ADAMS *Exp. 2 Peter* ii. 1 Suffering for our delinquishments.

2. = RELINQUISHMENT. (*bombastic nonce-use.*)

1603 DEKKER *Grissil* (Shaks. Soc.) 21 Though to my disconsolation, I will oblivionize my love to the Welsh widow, and do here proclaim my delinquishment.

delint (diː'lɪnt), *v.* [f. DE- + LINT¹.] *trans.* To remove the fibre from (cotton or similar seeds). Hence **de'linter.** So **de'lint** *sb.* (see quot. 1904).

1902 *Westm. Gaz.* 2 Jan. 7/2 A new process for delinting and hulling the cotton seed. **1904** L. L. LAMBORN *Cottonseed Products* iv. 50 The products of delinting are the linters, which pass to the condenser attached to the delinter. *Ibid.* 51 Linters, or delint, as the short fiber is also called, find extensive application in the arts. **1921** *Dict. Occup. Terms* (1927) §159 *Delinter*;.. attends and feeds machine which removes short fibres adhering to cotton seeds, after long fibres have been detached in ginning process. **1922** *Encycl. Brit.* XXX. 591/1 The United States supplied large quantities of nitro-cellulose propellant for the Allies and for its own army, and used as raw material a considerable proportion of the shorter fibre 'waste' from the delinted cotton seed.

† **'deliquate**, *v. Chem. Obs.* [f. ppl. stem of L. *dēliquā-re* trans. to clear off, clarify (a liquid), f. DE- I. 3 + *liquāre* to liquefy, melt, dissolve.]

1. *trans.* To dissolve (in a liquid), melt down.

1673 RAY *Journ. Low C.* 273 It seemed.. to have a mixture of Sulphur and fixt salt deliquated in it.

2. *intr.* To deliquesce.

1669 BOYLE *Contn. New Exp.* I. (1682) 37, I caused an unusual Brine to be made, by suffering Sea-salt to deliquate in the moist air. **1680** —— *Exp. Chem. Princ.* I. 5 Salt of Tartar left in moist Cellars to deliquate. **1800** *Med. Jrnl.* IV. 373 A salt crystallized in small needles, easily deliquating.

Hence **'deliquated** *ppl. a.*

1675 EVELYN *Terra* (1729) 9 Precipitated by deliquated Oil of Tartar. **1691** RAY *Creation* I. (1704) 50 Oil of Vitriol and deliquated Salt of Tartar.

† **deli'quation.** *Obs.* [n. of action f. prec.: see -ATION.] The process of deliquating; deliquescence.

1612 WOODALL *Surg. Mate* Wks. (1653) 264 Sometimes digestion needful is, and deliquation too. *Ibid.* 270 Deliquation is the liquation of a concrete (as salt, powder calcined, &c.) set in an humid and frigid place.. that it flow, having a watery form. **1657** in *Phys. Dict.*

† **de'lique.** *Obs. rare.* [ad. L. *dēliquium*: see below; cf. *relique.*] = DELIQUIUM¹ 1; failure.

1645 RUTHERFORD *Tryal & Tri. Faith* (1845) 71 It cometh from a delique in the affections.. that there is a swooning and delique of words.

deliquesce (dɛlɪ'kwɛs), *v.* [ad. L. *dēliquēscĕre* to melt away, dissolve, disappear, f. DE- I. 3 + *liquēscĕre* to become liquid, melt, inceptive of *liquēre* to be liquid, clear, etc.] *intr.*

1. *Chem.* To melt or become liquid by absorbing moisture from the air, as certain salts.

1756 C. LUCAS *Ess. Waters* I. 14 They attract the humidity of the air, and deliquesce, or run liquid. **1780** *Phil. Trans.* LXX. 349 This pot-ash.. deliquesces a little in moist air. **1876** PAGE *Advd. Text-bk. Geol.* xvi. 299 Pure chloride of sodium is not liable to deliquesce.

b. *Biol.* To liquefy or melt away, as some parts of fungi or other plants of low organization, in the process of growth or of decay.

1836–9 TODD *Cycl. Anat.* II. 953 [The brain's] disposition to deliquesce when exposed.. to the air. **1872** OLIVER *Elem. Bot.* II. 292 [Fungi] often deliquesce when mature. **1882** VINES *Sachs' Bot.* 272 Zoogonidia which are set free by the wall of the mother-cell becoming gelatinous and deliquescing.

2. *gen.* To melt away (*lit.* and *fig.*). (Mostly *humorous* or *affected.*)

1858 O. W. HOLMES *Aut. Breakf.-t.* xi. (1891) 256, I have known several very genteel idiots whose whole vocabulary had deliquesced into some half dozen expressions. **1860** —— *Elsie V.* 107 Undue apprehensions.. of its tendency to deliquesce and resolve itself.. into puddles of creamy fluid. **1871** JOWETT *Plato* I. 436 If while the man is alive the body deliquesces and decays.

Hence **deli'quescing** *vbl. sb.* and *ppl. a.*

1791 *Phil. Trans.* LXXXI. 330 Some of the deliquescing part of the mass.

deliquescence (dɛlɪ'kwɛsəns). [f. DELIQUESCENT: see -ENCE. (So mod.F. 1792 in Hatzf.)] The process of deliquescing or melting away; *esp.* the melting or liquefying of a salt by absorption of moisture from the air.

1800 HENRY *Epit. Chem.* (1808) 118 This change is termed deliquescence. **1839–47** TODD *Cycl. Anat.* III. 503/2 The nucleated cells.. gradually disappear by a kind of solution or deliquescence. **1863** HAWTHORNE *Our Old Home* (1883) I. 259 The English.. hurry to the seaside with red, perspiring faces, in a state of combustion and deliquescence. *fig.* **1881** *Spectator* 19 Mar. 373 The deliquescence.. of beliefs.

b. *concr.* The liquid or solution resulting from this process.

1756 C. LUCAS *Ess. Waters* I. 148 This deliquescence or solution always has an acrid taste. **1860** O. W. HOLMES *Poems, De Sauty*, Drops of deliquescence glistened on his forehead.

deliquescency (dɛlɪ'kwɛsənsɪ). *rare.* [f. as prec. + -ENCY.] The quality of being deliquescent; tendency to deliquesce.

1756 C. LUCAS *Ess. Waters* II. 42 Some attribute this deliquescency of salt to the redundance of an alcali. **1860** RUSKIN *Mod. Paint.* V. VI. vii. §3. 53.

deliquescent (dɛlɪ'kwɛsənt), *a.* [mod. ad. L. *dēliquēscent-em*, pr. pple. of *dēliquēscĕre* to DELIQUESCE. So in mod.F. (1783 in Hatzf.).]

1. *Chem.* That deliquesces; having the property of melting or becoming liquid by absorption of moisture from the air.

1791 *Edin. New Disp.* 381 Mild fixed alkali is.. considerably deliquescent. **1812–6** J. SMITH *Panorama Sc. & Art* II. 482 A salt is deliquescent, when it has a greater attraction for water than the air, as it will in that case take water from the air. **1845** DARWIN *Voy. Nat.* iv. (1873) 66 Those salts answer best for preserving cheese which contain most of the deliquescent chlorides.

2. a. *Biol.* Melting away in the process of growth or of decay: see DELIQUESCE 1 b.

1874 COOKE *Fungi* 28 It is very difficult to observe the structure of the hymenium, on account of its deliquescent nature.

b. *Bot.* Branching in such a way that the main stem or axis is, as it were, dissolved in ramifications.

1866 *Treas. Bot., Deliquescent*.. as the head of an oak tree. **1880** GRAY *Struct. Bot.* iii. §3. 49 Thus the trunk is dissolved into branches, or is deliquescent, as in the White Elm.

3. *humorously.* Dissolving (in perspiration).

1837 SYD. SMITH *Let. Singleton* Wks. 1859 II. 294/1 Striding over the stiles to Church, with a second-rate wife —dusty and deliquescent—and four parochial children, full of catechism and bread and butter. *a* **1876** M. COLLINS *Pen Sketches* I. 180 The dusty and deliquescent pedestrian. **1937** V. D. SCUDDER *On Journey* I. iv. 83 'Laissez Faire' was in its hey-day then; it is deliquescent now, though it lingers in the liking for 'Rugged Individualism'. **1947** T. H. WHITE *Elephant & Kangaroo* (1948) xvii. 144 A ghostly figure of the Virgin Mary... It was ghostly because Mrs. O'Callaghan had taken it into her head to give it a vigorous scrubbing.. and this had taken off the paint. It had also taken off most of the left cheek, so that the Virgin now hoved in her shadowy corner, chalk-white, leperous and deliquescent.

† **de'liquiate**, *v. Chem. Obs.* [irreg. f. L. *dēliquāre* (DELIQUATE), or f. DELIQUIUM².] *intr.* = DELIQUATE 2, DELIQUESCE.

1782 WEDGWOOD in *Phil. Trans.* LXX. 323 No crystalization was formed: the dry salt.. deliquiated in the air. **1810** HENRY *Elem. Chem.* (1840) II. 397 Urea.. deliquiates, when exposed to the air, into a thick brown liquid. **1854** J. SCOFFERN in *Orr's Circ. Sc. Chem.* 14 Other salts.. become liquid, or *deliquiate*.

† **deliquiation.** *Obs.* [n. of action from prec.] = DELIQUESCENCE.

1782 WEDGWOOD in *Phil. Trans.* LXX. 324 A salt.. which.. would have crystallized long before the alkali became dry, or remained after its deliquiation.

† **de'liquity.** *Obs.* [f. L. *dēliqu-us* lacking, wanting + -ITY: cf. *obliquity.*] Delinquency, guilt.

1692 *Christ Exalted* §158 Christ.. hath infinitely more Holiness than our sins have of Deliquity or Malignity in them.

deliquium¹ (dɪ'lɪkwɪəm). *arch.* [L. *dēliquium* failure, want, f. *dēlinquĕre* (*dēliqu-*): see DELINQUE, DELICT, and cf. DELIQUE.]

1. Failure of the vital powers; a swoon, fainting fit. Also *fig.*

[**1597** J. KING *On Jonas* (1864) 180 (Stanf.) His soul forsook him, as it were, and there was *deliquium animæ*.] **1621** BURTON *Anat. Mel.* I. iii. I. ii, He.. carries Bisket, Aquavitæ, or some strong waters about him, for fear of deliquiums. **1681** GLANVILL *Sadducismus* 14 Strange things men report to have seen during those Deliquiums. **1746** *Brit. Mag.* 102 He.. was seiz'd with a sudden Deliquium. **1867** CARLYLE *Remin.* (1881) II. 10 Jeffrey.. bewildered the poor jury into temporary deliquium or loss of wits.

† **2.** A failure of light, as in an eclipse. *Obs.*

1647 CRASHAW *Poems* 160 Forcing his sometimes eclipsed face to be A long deliquium to the light of thee. **1663** J. SPENCER *Prodigies* (1665) 5 The strange deliquium of Light in the Sun about the death of Cæsar. **1671** SHADWELL *Humorists* III. 33, I have suffer'd a *Deliquium*, viz. an Eclipse.

3. Confused with DELIQUIUM², as if = melting away, or state of having melted away: usually *fig.*

a **1711** KEN *Psyche* Poet. Wks. 1721 IV. 281 Her Pow'rs in Liquefaction soft exhal'd, She into amorous Deliquium falls. **1837** CARLYLE *Fr. Rev.* (1857) I. I. VII. viii. 212 The Assembly melts, under such pressure, into deliquium; or, as it is officially called, adjourns. **1858** —— *Fredk. Gt.* (1865) I. IV. v. 312 Stalwart sentries were found melted into actual deliquium of swooning.

† **de'liquium**². *Obs.* [L. *dēliquium* flowing down, dropping down, f. *dēliquāre*: see DELIQUATE.] = DELIQUESCENCE.

1641 FRENCH *Distill.* i. (1651) 9 *Deliquium*, is the dissolving of a hard body into a liquor, as salt.. in a moist, cold place. **1654** WHITLOCK *Zootomia* 407 Death is a preparing Deliquium, or melting us down into a Menstruum, fit for the Chymistry of the Resurrection to work on. **1727–51** CHAMBERS *Cycl.* s.v., Salt of tartar, or any fixed alcali, set in a cellar.. runs, into a kind of liquor, called by the chymists, oil of tartar *per deliquium*. **1823** J. BADCOCK *Dom. Amusem.* 46 As much hot oil of tartar, per deliquium, as will saturate the acid.

deliracy (dɪ'lɪrəsɪ). *rare.* [f. DELIRATE: cf. *accuracy, piracy*, and see -ACY.] Subjection to delirium: cf. DELIRANCY.

1824 SOUTHEY *Bk. of Ch.* (1841) 543 By lunacy, deliracy, or apathy.

delirament (dɪ'lɪrəmənt). Now *rare.* [ad. L. *dēlīrāment-um*, f. *dēlīrāre*: see DELIRE *v.*, and -MENT.] Raving, frenzy, insanity; a craze.

c **1440** CAPGRAVE *Life St. Kath.* IV. 1421 That thei calle feith, we calle delirament. **1560** ROLLAND *Crt. Venus* III. 593 He was deiect be daft delyrament. **1605** BELL *Motives conc. Romish Faith* Pref. 12 These and like popish deliraments. **1856** FERRIER *Inst. Metaph.* VIII. v. 229 Some of the fashionable deliraments of the day, such as clairvoyance and .. spirit-rapping.

† **de'lirancy.** *Obs.* [f. DELIRANT or L. *dēlīrānt-em*, corresponding to L. type **dēlīrāntia*: see -ANCY.] Raving, frenzy, madness.

1659 GAUDEN *Tears* 208 A Manichean dotage and delirancy seiseth upon them. **1678** CUDWORTH *Intell. Syst.* I. v. 691 This attempt of his was no other than a plain Delirancy, or Atheistick Phrenzy in him. *a* **1734** NORTH *Lives* (1890) III. 144 This was a sort of delirancy.

delirant (dɪ'laɪərənt), *a.* and *sb.* [ad. L. *dēlīrānt-em*, pr. pple. of *dēlīrāre* (see DELIRE *v.*), or a corresponding F. *délirant* (18th c. in Hatzf.), pr. pple. of *délirer*.]

† **A.** *adj.* Raving, mad, insane. *Obs.*

1600 LODGE in *Englands Helicon* D b, Age makes silly swaines delirant. **1681** GLANVILL *Sadducismus* I. (1726) 66 What can be imagined more delirant and more remote from common sense? *Ibid.* 71 This Man.. is either delirant and crazed, or else plays Tricks.

B. *sb. Med.* = DELIRIFACIENT.

1872 *Tanner's Mem. Poison* Pref. (ed. 3) 8 Neurotics: subdivided into Narcotics, Anæsthetics, Inebriants, Delirants [etc.].

† **de'lirate**, *v. Obs. rare*⁻¹. [f. ppl. stem of L. *dēlīrāre*: see DELIRE *v.* and -ATE³.] **a.** *trans.* = DELIRIATE. **b.** *intr.* = DELIRE 2. Hence **de'lirating** *ppl. a.*

1603 HOLLAND *Plutarch's Mor.* II. 393 (L.) They say it [ivy] hath an infatuating and delirating spirit in it. **1623** COCKERAM, *Delirate*, to dote.

deliration (dɛlɪ'reɪʃən). [ad. L. *dēlīrātiōn-em*, n. of action from *dēlīrāre*: see DELIRE *v.*]

1. Delirium, aberration of mind; frenzy, madness.

1600 *Hosp. Inc. Fooles* 9 Deliration is oftentimes a Symptome..of an feuer. *Ibid.* 10 Frensie being a far more violent infirmitie than deliration or dotage. **1668** H. MORE *Div. Dial.* II. xiv. (1713) 132 As idely as those that pill Straws or tie knots on Rushes in a fit of Deliration or Lunacy. **1840** CARLYLE *Heroes* v. (1858) 323 An earnestness..which..drove him into the strangest incoherences, almost delirations. **1855** MISS A. MANNING *O. Chelsea Bun-house* iii. 45 Her Deliration incessantly finding Vent in an incoherent Babble.

†**b.** A rendering delirious or temporarily insane.

1656 H. MORE *Enthus. Tri.* (1712) 19 The Effect is the deliration of the party after he awakes, for he takes his Dreams for..real Transactions.

2. *fig.* Wildly absurd behaviour or speech, as if arising from aberration of mind.

1603 HARSNET *Pop. Impost.* 27 What a Deliration is this in our graue, learned and famous College of..Physicians! **1678** CUDWORTH *Intell. Syst.* 848 The many atheistick hallucinations or delirations concerning it [cogitation]. **1821** *New Monthly Mag.* II. 123 The bombastic deliration of Lee's tragedy. **1860** EMERSON *Cond. Life, Worship* 122 In creeds never was such levity: witness..the periodic 'revivals'..the deliration of rappings.

†**de'lire,** *v.* *Obs.* [ad. L. *dēlīrāre* to be deranged, crazy, out of one's wits, orig. to go out of the furrow, to deviate from the straight, go off; f. DE- I. 2 + *līra* ridge, furrow, in ploughing; with sense 2 cf. F. *délirer* (in Rabelais, 16th c.) 'to doat, rave, do things against reason' (Cotgr.).]

1. *intr.* To go astray, go wrong, err.

a **1400** *Cov. Myst.* (1841) 204 God wyl be vengyd on man ..That wyl nevyr be schrevyn, but evyrmore doth delyre. **1560** ROLLAND *Crt. Venus* II. 339 Sa peirt for to delyre Fra Venus Court, or thairfra for to gyre? **1633** T. ADAMS *Exp. 2 Peter* ii. 5 He repents not as man does, for he cannot delire and err as man does.

2. To go astray from reason; to wander in mind, be delirious or mad, to rave.

Hence **de'liring** *ppl. a.*

1600 *Hosp. Inc. Fooles* 10 Franticke and deliring Fooles.. who..swarue from all sense. **1632** QUARLES *Div. Fancies* IV. xv, How fresh bloud dotes! O how green Youth delires! **1675** R. BURTHOGGE *Causa Dei* 196 He delires, and is out of his Wits, that would preferr it [moonlight] before the Sun by Day.

†**de'lirement.** *Obs.* [a. obs. F. *délirement*, 'a raving or doating' (Cotgr.), ad. L. *dēlīrāmentum.*] = DELIRAMENT.

1613 HEYWOOD *Silver Age* II. i, Thus—thou art here, and there,—With me, at home, and at one instant both! In vain are these delirements, and to me Most deeply incredible. **1637** —— *Dial.* iv. Wks. 1874 VI. 179 With fond delirements let him others charme. **1633** T. ADAMS *Exp. 2 Peter* i. 4 This delirement never came into the holy apostles' minds.

deliria, occas. pl. of DELIRIUM.

deliriant (dɪ'lɪrɪənt), *a.* and *sb.* *Med.* [f. DELIRIUM: cf. next, and *anæsthesiant*, etc.]

1883 *Syd. Soc. Lex.*, *Deliriant*, having power to produce delirium. Applied to such drugs as henbane, Indian hemp, and such like.

†**de'liriate,** *v.* *Obs.* [f. L. *dēlīri-um* DELIRIUM + -ATE[3].] *trans.* To make delirious.

1658 R. FRANCK *North. Mem.* (1821) p. iii, Now so generally and epidemically the kingdom was diseased, that deliriated and distracted, they let one another blood. *a* **1711** KEN *Christophil* Poet. Wks. 1721 I. 478 Their Love misplac'd deliriates their Wit.

delirifacient (dɪlɪrɪ'feɪʃənt). *a.* and *sb.* *Med.* [f. L. *dēlīrium*, DELIRIUM, *dēlīrāre* to be crazy + *facient-em* making.]

A. *adj.* Causing or producing delirium.

B. *sb.* An agent or substance that produces delirium.

1875 H. C. WOOD *Therap.* (1879) 219 In some..morphia acts as a delirifacient.

delirious (dɪ'lɪrɪəs), *a.* [f. L. *dēlīri-um* + -OUS.]

1. Affected with delirium, *esp.* as a result or symptom of disease; wandering in mind, light-headed, temporarily insane.

1706 SWIFT *Death of Partridge*, The people..said, he had been for some time delirious; but when I saw him, he had his understanding as well as ever I knew. **1751** JOHNSON *Rambler* No. 153 ¶11 He caught a fever..of which he died delirious on the third day. **1804** ABERNETHY *Surg. Obs.* 175 He had gradually become delirious, and..could scarcely be kept in bed. **1871** SIR T. WATSON *Princ. Physic* (ed. 5) I. xviii. 350 The patient, complaining probably of his head, becomes all at once and furiously delirious.

b. Belonging to or characteristic of delirium.

1703 J. LOGAN in *Pa. Hist. Soc. Mem.* IX. 188 In what he has wrote to-day one paragraph may appear almost delirious. **1809** *Med. Jrnl.* XXI. 435 March 25th..The whole of this day he has talked quite incoherently..March 26th. The same delirious manner has continued all this day. **1874** CARPENTER *Ment. Phys.* I. i. §7 (1879) 8 The delirious ravings of Intoxication or of Fever.

2. *transf.* and *fig.* **a.** Characterized by wild excitement or symptoms resembling those of delirium; frantic, crazed, 'mad'.

1791 COWPER *Iliad* XV. 156 Frantic, delirious! thou art lost for ever! **1829** I. TAYLOR *Enthus.* iv. (1867) 77 The delirious bigot who burns with ambition to render himself the enemy ..of the Church. **1855** BRIMLEY *Ess.*, *Tennyson* 76 Snatches of song that make the world delirious with delight.

b. Of things, actions, etc.

1599 *Broughton's Lett.* iii. 13 You..charge the High commission of Atheisme, for calling you to account for your delirious doctrine. **1818** BYRON *Ch. Har.* IV. lxx, How the giant element From rock to rock leaps with delirious bound. **1858** CARLYLE *Fredk. Gt.* (1865) I. II. vi. 87 The delirious screech..of a railway train.

de'liriously, *adv.* [f. prec. + -LY[2].] In a delirious manner; madly, frantically.

1820 BYRON *Mar. Fal.* IV. i. 240 The plague Which sweeps the soul deliriously from life! **1863** E. C. CLAYTON *Queens of Song* II. 380 They were deliriously dancing, shouting, singing..with the most hilarious gaiety.

de'liriousness. [f. as prec. + -NESS.] The state of being delirious; delirium.

1779-81 JOHNSON *L.P.*, *Pope* Wks. IV. 86 Pope, at the intermission of his deliriousness, was always saying something kind..of his..friends. **1782** HEBERDEN *Comment.* xii, Giddiness, forgetfulness, slight deliriousness. **1855** SINGLETON *Virgil* I. 268 What such intense deliriousness?

delirium (dɪ'lɪrɪəm). Pl. **deliriums, -ia.** [a. L. *dēlīrium* (Celsus), madness, derangement, deriv. of *dēlīrāre* to be deranged: see DELIRE *v.*]

1. A disordered state of the mental faculties resulting from disturbance of the functions of the brain, and characterized by incoherent speech, hallucinations, restlessness, and frenzied or maniacal excitement.

1599 *Broughton's Lett.* xii. 42 It is but the franticke *delirium* of one, whose pride hath made him φρεναπατᾶν. **1656** RIDGLEY *Pract. Physick* 143 The signs are a weak Pulse ..*delirium.* **1670** COTTON *Espernon* III. XII. 648 His Deliriums had far longer intervals than before. **1707** FLOYER *Physic. Pulse-Watch* 357 The Deliria and Melancholic Fevers are indicated by this Pulse. **1756** BURKE *Subl. & B.* Introd. Wks. I. 103 Opium is pleasing to Turks, on account of the agreeable delirium it produces. **1840** DICKENS *Old C. Shop* xi, In a raging fever accompanied with delirium. **1871** SIR T. WATSON *Princ. Physic* (ed. 5) I. xviii. 360 The delirium you will generally find to be not a fierce or mischievous delirium, but a busy delirium.

2. *fig.* Uncontrollable excitement or emotion, as of a delirious person; frenzied rapture; wildly absurd thought or speech.

1650 HOWELL *Masaniello* I. 126 He had broken out into a thousand delirium's and fooleries. **1709** STEELE *Tatler* No. 125 ¶10 Any Free-thinker whom they shall find publishing his Deliriums. **1791-1823** D'ISRAELI *Cur. Lit.* (1866) 2/1 Testimonies of men of letters of the pleasurable delirium of their researches. **1836** W. IRVING *Astoria* II. 225 He jumped up, shouted, clapped his hands, and danced in a delirium of joy, until he upset the canoe. **1879** GEO. ELIOT *Theo. Such* xiv. 254 The gorgeous delirium of gladiatorial shows.

delirium tremens (dɪ'lɪrɪəm 'triːmɛnz). [mod. Medical Lat. = trembling or quaking delirium.] A species of delirium induced by excessive indulgence in alcoholic liquors, and characterized by tremblings and various delusions of the senses.

'The term was introduced by Dr. Sutton, in 1813, for that form of delirium which is rendered worse by bleeding, but improved by opium. By Rayer and subsequent writers it has been almost exclusively applied to delirium resulting from the abuse of alcohol.' (*Syd. Soc. Lex.*)

1813 T. SUTTON (*title*), Tracts on Delirium Tremens, etc., etc. **1865** TYLOR *Early Hist. Man.* i. 6 The fiends which torment the victim of delirium tremens.

fig. **1832** *Blackw. Mag.* Jan. 123/2 The delirium tremens of radicalism, in which the unhappy patient..imagines himself haunted by a thousand devils, who are not only men but Tories.

†**de'lirous,** *a.* *Obs.* [f. L. *dēlīr-us* doting, crazy (f. DE- I. 2 + *līra* ridge, furrow: cf. DELIRE) + -OUS.] = DELIRIOUS; crazy, raving.

1656 H. MORE *Enthus. Tri.* (1712) 33 The rampant and delirous Fancies of..Paracelsus. *a* **1687** *Ibid.* 54 They that deny this true Enthusiasm, do confirm those wild delirous Fanaticks in their false Enthusiasm. **1673** RAY *Journ. Low C.* 144 We observed in these Countries more Idiots and delirous persons than anywhere else. **1722** *Phil. Trans.* XXXII. 25 He became delirous with Convulsions.

Hence †**de'lirousness.**

a **1687** H. MORE *Antid. Ath.* III. ix. Schol. (1712) 174 Many other circumstances have been told me by them.. without the least species or shadow of delirousness.

†**de'liry.** *Obs.* Pl. **-ies.** [ad. L. *dēlīri-um* DELIRIUM: cf. *ministry*.] = DELIRIUM.

1669 GALE *Crt. Gentiles* I. II. ii. 18 The deliries, or dreams of the Mythologists, touching their Gods. **1677** *Ibid.* III. 137 The Deliries or sick Dreams of Origen.

delish (dɪ'lɪʃ), *a.* Colloq. abbrev. of DELICIOUS *a.*

1920 *Punch* 14 Jan. 38/1 Their music, I gather, is wholly delish. **1953** 'N. BLAKE' *Dreadful Hollow* 51 Have a glass of port, won't you? It's rather delish. **1962** *Woman* 12 May 40/1 Making delish dishes for a picnic.

delisk, var. of DULSE, a sea-weed.

delit, earlier form of DELIGHT.

†**delita'bility.** *Obs.* In 4 **delitabilite, dilat-, diletabilte.** [ME. a. OF. *delitableté*, f. *delitable*: see next.] Delightfulness, delight.

a **1340** HAMPOLE *Psalter* Prol., þe dilatabilte of þis gyft. *Ibid.* lxvii. 36 In diletabilte of luf. *c* **1340** —— *Prose Tr.* 43 Gastely joye and delitabilite.

†**delitable,** *a.* *Obs.* Also 4 delitabill, -byl(l, dilitable, diletabile, 4-6 delyt-, 5 delet-, delite-, deleitable, dylitabile. [ME. a. OF. *delitable* (*deleit-*, *delet-*, *deliet-*), f. *delitier* to DELIGHT: cf. DELECTABLE, DELIGHTABLE.] Affording delight; delightful, pleasant, delectable.

c **1290** *S. Eng. Leg.* I. 220/26 An yle..þat delitable was inou. *a* **1340** HAMPOLE *Psalter* Cant. 523 þe notis of luf er delitabylest in the melody þat sho shewys. **1362** LANGL. *P. Pl.* A. I. 32 Dreede dilitable drinke. *c* **1386** CHAUCER *Clerk's T.* 6 Wher many a tour and toun thou maist byholde..And many anothir delitable [*v. rr.* de-, dilectable] sight. *c* **1400** MAUNDEV. (Roxb.) xii. 51 Appels faire of coloure and delitable to behald. *c* **1450** *Mirour Saluacioun* 660 A delitable floure. *c* **1500** *Lancelot* 1738 Thar giftis mot be fair and delitable. **1500-20** DUNBAR *Goldyn Targe* 120 Ianus, god of entree delytable.

†**delitably,** *adv.* *Obs.* [f. prec. + -LY[2].] In a 'delitable' manner; delightfully, pleasantly.

c **1340** HAMPOLE *Prose Tr.* 18 þe name sowunes in his herte delitably as it were a saunge. *c* **1374** CHAUCER *Boeth.* IV. i. 108 Whanne philosophie hadde songen softly and delitably þe forseide þinges. *c* **1425** WYNTOUN *Cron.* VI. v. 56 He wes..festyd oft delytably. **1450-1530** *Myrr. our Ladye* 210 He abydeth..delytablely with desyre.

†**de'lite,** *sb.* *Obs.* [A derivative, or expansion, of LITE *sb.*, in same sense.] Delay.

a **1300** *Cursor M.* 5790 (Gött.) þar-to sal be na lang dilite [*Cott.* lite, *Trin.* delay]. *c* **1340** *Ibid.* 6679 (Fairf.) Dey þai salle wiþ-out delite [*Cott.* lite, *rime* quite, quitte].

†**de'lite,** *a.* *Obs. rare.* In 5 **delyte.** [a. OF. *delit* delicious.] Delightful.

c **1430** LYDG. *Hors, Shepe & G.* 3 This pascalle Lambe with-owte spott..þis lambe moste delyte.

delite, the earlier form of DELIGHT.

delitescence (dɛlɪ'tɛsəns). [f. DELITESCENT: see -ENCE. (In the medical sense used in F. by Paré in 16th c.)]

1. The condition of lying hid; latent state, concealment, seclusion.

1776 JOHNSON *Lett. to Mrs. Thrale* 22 May, To sooth him into inactivity or delitescence. **1836-7** SIR W. HAMILTON *Metaph.* xxx. (1870) II. 213 The obscuration, the delitescence of mental activities.

2. *Med.* **a.** 'Term applied to the sudden disappearance of inflammation, or of its events, by resolution, no other part of the body being affected.' **b.** 'The period during which poisons, as those of rabies and smallpox, remain in the system before they produce visible symptoms' (= INCUBATION). *Syd. Soc. Lex.*

1835-6 TODD *Cycl. Anat.* I. 513/2 This speedy termination of the disease has been called by the French writers *delitescence.* **1877** ROBERTS *Handbk. Med.* (ed. 3) I. 46 Resolution may take place very quickly, this being termed delitescence.

deli'tescency. [f. as prec.: see -ENCY.] **a.** The quality of being delitescent. **b.** = prec. 1.

1696 AUBREY *Misc.* Introd. (1857) p. xiii, From 1670 to this very day..I have enjoyed a happy delitescency. **1805** *Pref.* to *Brathwait's Drunken Barnaby* (ed. 5), Republishing this facetious little book after a delitescency of near a hundred years. **1821** J. L. ADOLPHUS *Let. to Heber* 8 An extraordinary development of the passion for delitescency.

delitescent (dɛlɪ'tɛsənt, 'diː-), *a.* [ad. L. *dēlitēscent-em*, pr. pple. of *dēlitēscĕre* to hide away, f. DE- I. 2 + *latēscĕre*, inceptive of *latēre* to lie hid.] Lying hid, latent, concealed.

1684 T. HOCKIN *God's Decrees* 212 The vertue of those means..may be long delitescent, and lye hid. **1836-7** SIR W. HAMILTON *Metaph.* xxx. (1870) II. 213 The immense proportion of our intellectual possessions consists of our delitescent cognitions.

†**de'litigate,** *v.* *Obs. rare*[−0]. [f. L. *dēlītigāre*: see -ATE[3].]

1623 COCKERAM, *Delitigate*, to skold or chide vehemently.

Hence **deliti'gation.**

1727 BAILEY vol. II, *Delitigation*, a striving, a chiding, a contending.

†**delitous,** *a.* *Obs.* Also 5 delytous. [a. OF. *delitous* (Bozon), *-eus*, f. *delit* DELIGHT: see -OUS.] Delightful.

c **1400** *Rom. Rose* 90 In this sesoun delytous, Whan love affraieth al thing. *Ibid.* 489 Swich solace, swich ioie, and play..As was in that place delytous.

de'liver, *a.* *Obs.* or *arch.* Also 4-7 delyuer(e, (4 delyure, 5 deliuuer, -liuere, -lyvyr, 6 -liure). [a. OF. *delivre*, *deslivre* (cf. It. *dilibero*), vbl. adj. from *delivrer* to DELIVER.]

†**1.** Free, at liberty. *Obs.*

c **1305** *Edmund Conf.* 290 in *E.E.P.* (1862) 78 He ne miȝte him wawe fot ne hond: his poer him was binome; Ac delyure he hadde al his þoȝt.

2. Free from all encumbrance or impediments; active, nimble, agile, quick in action.

c **1350** *Will. Palerne* 3596 Douȝthi man and deliuer in dedes of armes. **1375** BARBOUR *Bruce* III. 737 Bot the Kingis folk, that war Deliuer off fute. **1387** TREVISA *Higden* (Rolls) VI. 289 Delyvere men strong and swyþer. *c* **1430** LYDG. *Bochas* III. i. (1554) 70 b, Light and deliuer, voyde of al fatness. **1472** *Paston Lett.* No. 696 III. 47 He is one the lyghtest, delyverst, best spokyn, fayrest archer. **1530** PALSGR. 309/2 Delyver of ones lymmes as they that prove mastryes, *souple*. Delyver, redy, quicke to do any thyng, *agile, deliuré*. *a* **1562** G. Cavendish *Wolsey* (1827) 141 A number of the most deliverest soldiers. **1580** Sidney *Arcadia* (1622) 326 Pyrocles, of a more fine and deliuer strength. **1600** Holland *Livy* xxviii. xx. 683 b, Being men light and deliver of bodie.

[*arch.* **1814** Scott *Wav.* xlii, Mr. Waverley looks clean-made and deliver. **1887** *Eng. Illust. Mag.* Nov. 72 He is the most deliver at that exercise I have ever set eyes on.]

†**3.** Delivered (of a child). *Obs.*

c **1325** *E.E. Allit. P.* B. 1084 Alle hende þat honestly moȝt an hert glade, Aboutte my lady watz lent, quen ho delyuer were. *c* **1325** *Metr. Hom.* 168 That this abbas suld paynes dreght, And be delyuer of hir chylde. *c* **1400** Maundev. (Roxb.) xv. 67 Mary was delyuer of hir childe vnder a palme tree. *c* **1460** *Towneley Myst., Purif. Mary* 117 Ffourty dayes syn that thou was Delyuer of thy son.

deliver (dɪˈlɪvə(r)), *v.*[1] Also 3–5 deliure, 3–6 delyuer(e, 4 deliuyr, delyuyr, dilyuer(e, 4–5 delyuir(e, 4–6 delyure, diliuer(e, 6 *Sc.* delywer. [a. F. *délivrer*, in OF. also *deslivrer*, = Pr. *de-, deslivrar*, Cat. *desliurar*, OSp. *delibrar*, It. *diliberare*:—late pop. L. *dēlīberāre*, in Romanic partly refashioned as **deslībrāre* (de- I. 6), used in sense of L. *līberāre* to set free, liberate (see Du Cange). (In cl.Lat. *dēlīberāre* had a different sense: see deliberate.)]

I. 1. *trans.* To set free, liberate, release, rescue, save. Const. *from, out of*, †*of*. †**a.** To release *from* a place. *Obs.* (exc. as merged in b, and as a traditional phrase in reference to gaol-delivery).

c **1325** *Coer de L.* 1140 Whenne I am servyd off that fee, Thenne schal Richard delyveryd bee. *c* **1400** Maundev. (Roxb.) xi. 45 Scho delyuerd þe lordes oute of þe toure. **1513** More in Grafton *Chron.* II. 798 The Lorde Stanley was delivered out of ward. **1725** De Foe *Voy. round World* (1840) 277 The way turned short east..and delivered us entirely from the mountains. **1768** Blackstone *Comm.* III. 134 That they could not upon an *habeas corpus* either bail or deliver a prisoner. **1863** H. Cox *Instit.* ii. x. 534 A commission of general gaol delivery.

b. Now *esp.* To set free *from* restraint, imminent danger, annoyance, trouble, or evil generally.

a **1225** *Ancr. R.* 234 Nolde heo neuer enes bisechen ure Louerd þet he allunge deliurede hire þerof. *c* **1250** *Old Kent. Serm.* in *O.E. Misc.* 33 þet he us deliuri of alle eueles. **1382** Wyclif *Matt.* vi. 13 And leede vs nat in to temptacioun, but delyuere vs fro yuel. *c* **1386** Chaucer *Moder of God* 34 Fro temptacioun deliure me. **1549** *Bk. Com. Prayer, Litany,* From al euill and mischiefe, from synne, from the craftes and assaultes of the deuyll; from thy wrathe, and from euerlastyng damnacion: Good lorde deliuer us. **1611** Bible *1 Sam.* xvii. 37 The Lord that delivered me out of the paw of the lion..he will deliver me out of the hand of this Philistine. **1651** *Reliq. Wotton.* 199, I fell into these thoughts, of which there were two wayes to be delivered. **1719** De Foe *Crusoe* (1840) I. xii. 205 God..had..delivered me from blood-guiltness. **1845** M. Pattison *Ess.* (1889) I. 26 Chilperic was delivered from the necessity of inventing any new expedient. **1871** R. Ellis *Catullus* lxiv. 396 Stood in body before them, a fainting host to deliver.

†**c.** *spec.* To release or free (any one) from his vow, by putting him in a position to discharge it; to accept combat offered by. [So in OF.] *Obs.*

? *a* **1400** *Morte Arth.* 1688 ȝif thow hufe alle the daye, thou bees noghte delyuerede. **1470–85** Malory *Arthur* vii. xiv, I care not..what knyghte soo euer he be, for I shal soone delyuer hym. **1475** *Bk. Noblesse* 77 For to take entreprises, to answere or deliver a gentilman that desire in worship to doo armes in liestis to the utteraunce, or to certein pointis. **1523** Ld. Berners *Froiss.* I. ccclxxiii. 617 Then it was sayd to all the knightes there about, Sirs, is there any of you that will delyuer this knyght?.. Sir Wylliam of Fermyton..sayd ..if it pleases him a lytell to rest hym, he shall anone be delyuered, for I shall arme me agaynst hym.

†**2. a.** To free, rid, divest, clear (*a*) *of*, (*b*) *from*.

c **1314** *Guy Warw.* (A.) 3248 Deliuer þi lond..Of alle þine dedeliche fon. *c* **1374** Chaucer *Boeth.* iii. i. 64 Who so wil sowe a felde plentiuous lat hym first delyuer it of thornes. **1540–1** Elyot *Image Gov.* (1549) 32 At last god hath deliuered the..of him. **1562** *Homilies* ii. *Good Friday* (1859) 411 It pleased him [Christ] to deliver himself of all His godly honour. **1868** Bushnell *Serm. on living Subj.* 21 The salutation will be quite delivered of its harshness by just observing that [etc.].

c **1400** *Lanfranc's Cirurg.* 193 Anoynte þe pacient & þis wole delyvere him fro icching. **1627** Donne *Serm.* v. 50 Yet we doe not deliver Moses from all infirmity herein. **1632** Lithgow *Trav.* vii. 323 A stone..which hath the vertue to deliuer a woman from her paine in child-birth. **1677** Hale *Prim. Orig. Man.* To Rdr., If the Expressions..be..delivered from Amphibologies.

†**b.** *refl.* To free oneself, get clear or rid *of*. *Obs.*

c **1300** *K. Alis.* 1319 Anon they deliverid heom of Macedoyne. *c* **1489** Caxton *Sonnes of Aymon* ix. 208, I counseyll you that ye..delyuer yourselfe of Reynawde assone as ye maye. **1530** Palsgr. 511/1, I can nat delyver me of hym by no meanes. [**1709** Berkeley *Ess. Vision* §51 [He] may be able to deliver himself from that prejudice.]

c. *to deliver a gaol*: to clear it of prisoners in order to bring them to trial at the assizes.

1523 in W. H. Turner *Select. Rec. Oxford* 34 To deliver any gayole wthin the towne. **1535** *Act 27 Hen. VIII*, c. 24 §16 All suche iustices..shal haue auctoritee..to deliuer the same gaoles from time to time. **1890** *Spectator* 26 Apr. 584/2 The gaol must be delivered before the Judge leaves the assize town.

†**d.** *transf.* To make riddance of, get rid of, dispel (pain, disease, etc.); to relieve. *Obs.*

1483 Caxton *Gold. Leg.* 405 b/1 A lytel medecyne ofte delyuereth a grete languor and payne. **1576** Baker *Jewell of Health* 53 b, This water..delyvereth the griefe of the stone. **1610** Guillim *Heraldry* iv. v. (1660) 282 That so his momentany passion..might by some like intermission of time be delivered, and so vanish away.

3. a. To disburden (a woman) *of* the fœtus, to bring to childbirth; in *passive*, to give birth to a child or offspring. Rarely said of beasts. (The active is late and chiefly in obstetrical use.)

c **1325** *Metr. Hom.* 63 For than com tim Mari mild Suld be deliuerd of hir child. *c* **1340** *Cursor M.* 5562 (Fairf.) þer wimmen..ar deliuered be þaire awen sliȝt. **1480** Caxton *Chron. Eng.* lxxi. 53 Tyme come that she shold be delyuered and bere a child. **1484** —— *Fables of Æsop* i. ix, A bytche which wold lyttre and be delyured of her lytyl dogges. **1568** Tilney *Disc. Mariage* C viij, To have thy wyfe with childe safely delyvered. **1611** Shaks. *Wint. T.* ii. ii. 25 She is, something before her time, deliuer'd. **1685** Cooke *Marrow of Chirurg.* iii. i. (ed. 4) 168 The third time they sent and begged I would deliver her. **1754–64** Smellie *Midwif.* I. Introd. 70 A better method of delivering in laborious and preternatural cases. **1805** *Med. Jrnl.* XIV. 521 By making an incision in the urethra..the patient might be delivered. *c* **1850** *Arab. Nts.* (Rtldg.) 448 The queen..was in due time safely delivered of a prince.

fig. **1634** Heywood *Mayden-head well Lost* i. Wks. 1874 IV. 108 My brain's in labour, and must be deliuered Of some new mischeife. *a* **1640** Peacham (J.), Tully was long ere he could be delivered of a few verses. **1875** Jowett *Plato* (ed. 2) I. 281, I have been delivered of an infinite variety of speeches about virtue before now, and to many persons.

†**b.** *pass.* Of the offspring: To be brought forth (*lit.* and *fig.*). *Obs.*

1581 Pettie *Guazzo's Civ. Conv.* i. (1586) 12 All beastes so soone as they are delivered from their dam get upon their feete. *c* **1600** Shaks. *Sonn.* lxxvii. 11 Those children nursed, deliver'd from thy brain. **1604** —— *Oth.* i. iii. 378 There are many Euents in the Wombe of Time, which wilbe deliuered.

4. To disburden, unload. ? *Obs.*

1793 Smeaton *Edystone L.* §289 The Weston was delivered of her cargo. **1805** in A. Duncan *Nelson* 231, 26th. Delivered the Spaniard, and sunk her. **1851** Mayne Reid *Scalp Hunt.* xxxiv. 267 The brace of revellers went staggering over the azotea, delivering their stomachs.

5. *refl.* To disburden *oneself of* what is in one's mind; to express one's opinion or thought; to utter words or sounds; to speak, discourse. (Cf. 10.)

c **1340** *Cursor M.* 20391 (Trin.), I delyuered me of my sermoun. **1654** tr. *Martini's Conq. China* 217 He delivered himself thus unto them, 'I hope by your valour to obtain the Empire of the world'. **1660** *Trial Regic.* 42, I now desire to know, whether it be proper now to deliver my self, before you proceed to the calling of Witnesses. **1713** Steele *Englishman* No. 3. 19 Some Merchants..delivered themselves against the Bill before our Houses of Lords and Commons. **1752** Fielding *Amelia* vi. vii, Amelia delivered herself on the subject of second marriages with much eloquence. **1869** Goulburn *Purs. Holiness* x. 91 Delivering Himself..in sentiments the very tones of which are unearthly.

II. †**6. a.** *trans.* To get rid of or dispose of quickly, to dispatch; *refl.* to make haste, be quick.

c **1340** *Gaw. & Gr. Knt.* 1414 þe mete & þe masse watz metely delyuered. *c* **1475** *Rauf Coilȝear* 302 Deliuer the..and mak na delay. **1523** Ld. Berners *Froiss.* I. cccxxvi. 510 The Romayns..sayd, Harke, ye sir cardynalles, delyuer you atones, and make a pope; Ye tary to longe. **1530** Palsgr. 510/2, I delyver, I rydde or dispatche thynges shortly out of handes, *Je despeche*.

†**b.** ? To dispatch, make away with. *Obs. rare.*

a **1400–50** *Alexander* 3930 þis breme best..Aȝt and tuenti men of armes onone scho delyuird. *c* **1450** *Guy Warw.* (C.) 10140 And wyth the grace of god almyght To delyuyr ther enmyes wyth ryght.

III. 7. a. To give up entirely, give over, surrender, yield; formerly often *spec.* to give up to an evil fate, devote to destruction, ruin, or the like. Also with *over* (obs. or arch.), *up*.

a **1300** *Cursor M.* 5012 (Cott.) Him sal deliuer your yongest child. *c* **1340** *Ibid.* 15879 (Fairf.) He deliuered his maister vp. *c* **1300** *Beket* 724 The Kynges baillyf delivri him to anhonge other to drawe. **1483** Caxton *G. de la Tour* E vij b, The moders of them shall be delyuered to the dolorous deth of helle. **1513** More in Grafton *Chron.* II. 771 That the goods of a sanctuary man, shoulde be deliuered in payment of his debtes. **1593** Shaks. *Rich. II*, iii. i. 29 See them deliuered ouer To execution, and the hand of death. **1600** E. Blount tr. *Conestaggio* 321 The French came from the mountaine, and..delivered up their armes. **1638** Sir T. Herbert *Trav.* 90 Hee also assaults Tzinner, which tho a while well kept..is in the end delivered. **1771** Mrs. Griffith tr. *Viaud's Shipwreck* 97 To take our chance, and deliver ourselves over into the hands of Providence. **1777** Watson *Philip II* (1839) 133 'Count Egmont,' said Alva, 'deliver your sword; it is the will of the King that you give it up, and go to prison.' **1845** M. Pattison *Ess.* (1889) I. 2 When premiers deliver up their portfolios.

†**b.** *refl.* To give oneself up, surrender, devote oneself. *Obs.*

a **1533** Ld. Berners *Gold. Bk. M. Aurel.* (1546) B vj, I delyuered myselfe with greatte desyre to knowe thynges.

8. a. To hand over, transfer, commit to another's possession or keeping; *spec.* to give or distribute to the proper person or quarter (letters or goods brought by post, carrier, or messenger); to present (an account, etc.). Const. *to*, or with simple dative.

1297 R. Glouc. (1724) 430 Alle þe byssopryches, þat delyuered were Of Normandye & Engelond, he ȝef al clene þere. *c* **1300** *K. Alis.* 1011 In a castel heo was y-set, And was deliverid liversoon, Skarschliche and nought foisoun. *c* **1400** Maundev. (Roxb.) xxv. 119 He delyuers þis currour þe lettres. *c* **1440** *Ipomydon* 1282 Delyuere my mayde to me this day. **1530** Palsgr. 510/2, I delyver, I gyve a thyng in to ones handes to kepe. *Je liure*. **1535** Wriothesley *Chron.* (1875) I. 28 Who had his pardon delyvered him on the Tower Hill. **1651** Hobbes *Leviath.* ii. xxii. 122 To joyn in a Petition to be delivered to a Iudge, etc. **1745** *Col. Rec. Pennsylv.* V. 9 He delivered back the String of Wampum sent him. **1843** Prescott *Mexico* (1850) I. 255 A message which he must deliver in person. **1881** Goldw. Smith *Lect. & Ess.* 260 The postmaster had written the letter as well as delivered it. **1892** *Law Times' Rep.* LXVII. 52/2 No bill of costs was ever delivered. *Mod.* Get the address from the postman who delivers in that part of the town. How often are letters delivered here?

fig. **1526–34** Tindale *1 Cor.* xi. 2 That ye..kepe the ordinaunces even as I delyvered them to you. **1598** Shaks. *Merry W.* iv. iv. 37 The superstitious idle-headed-Eld Receiu'd and did deliuer to our age This tale of Herne the Hunter. **1794** Sullivan *View Nat.* II, Seven persons only were necessary to deliver the history of the creation and fall from Adam to Moses.

b. *Law.* To give or hand over formally (*esp.* a deed to the grantee, or to a third party): see delivery 4 b (*b*). So 'to deliver' seisin of hereditaments, or a corporeal chattel.

1574 tr. *Littleton's Tenures* 15 a, If a man make a deede of feoffemente unto another..and delyvereth to him the deed but no livery of seisin. *c* **1590** Marlowe *Faust.* v. 110 Speak, Faustus, do you deliver this as your deed? **1623** in *New Shaks. Soc. Trans.* (1885) 505 Wch said Indentr was sealled and deliuered by all the parties thervnto. **1767** Blackstone *Comm.* II. 306 A seventh requisite to a good deed is that it be delivered, by the party himself or his certain attorney. **1844** Williams *Real Prop.* vii. (1877) 148 The words 'I deliver this as my act and deed', which are spoken at the same time, are held to be equivalent to delivery, even if the party keep the deed himself.

†**c.** *poetic*, with weakened sense of 'To hand over, present'. *Obs.*

1601 Shaks. *Twel. N.* i. ii. 43 O that I..might not be deliuered to the world Till I had made mine owne occasion mellow. **1607** —— *Cor.* v. iii. 39 The sorrow that deliuers vs thus chang'd Makes you think so.

d. Colloq. phr. *to deliver the goods*: see good *a.* C. 8. Now also *absol.* (chiefly *U.S.*); also const. *on*.

1942 in Berrey & Van den Bark *Amer. Thes. Slang* §243/3. **1959** F. Astaire *Steps in Time* (1960) xxi. 244, I have a horror of not delivering—making good, so to speak; and I can't stand the thought of letting everybody down—studio and public as well as myself. **1970** *N.Y. Times* 28 Oct. 46 This autumn the President has a major opportunity to deliver on his pledge. **1976** *Sci. Amer.* Sept. 160/3 Mrs. Gandhi could not deliver on her promises. **1978** *Jrnl. R. Soc. Arts* CXXVI. 351/2 If Toscanini's players didn't deliver at a rehearsal, Toscanini would explode. **1985** *Company* Dec. 82/1 Whether you go there for the art at the Louvre,..or just plain old sightseeing, Paris certainly delivers in full.

IV. 9. To give forth, send forth, emit; to discharge, launch; to cast, throw, project: **a.** things material.

1597 T. J. *Serm. Paules C.* 37 The bow, being ready bent to deliuer the arrowe. **1613** Shaks. *Hen. VIII*, v. iv. 59 A File of Boyes..deliuer'd such a showre of Pibbles. **1633** T. James *Voy.* 71 [The pump] did deliuer water very sufficiently. **1702** Luttrell *Brief Rel.* (1857) V. 207 The earl of Kent, as he was delivering his bowl upon the green at Tunbridge Wells last Wensday, fell down and immediately died. **1834** Medwin *Angler in Wales* I. 291 In delivering his harpoon he lost his balance. **1850** 'Bat' *Crick. Man.* 39 Before a ball is delivered, the umpires station themselves at their respective wickets. **1885** *Manch. Exam.* 15 May 5/2 The enemy..waited till Middleton's volunteers had approached very close before they delivered their fire.

b. a blow, assault, attack, etc. *to deliver battle*: to give battle, make or begin an attack.

1842 Alison *Hist. Europe* XI. lxxv. §36. 349 The Emperor was..obliged to deliver a defensive battle. **1864** *Daily Tel.* 19 Nov., The assaults were badly delivered. **1874** Green *Short Hist.* vii. §6. 405 When Philip at last was forced to deliver his blow.

†**c.** To put forth freely (bodily action, etc.): cf. delivery 6. *Obs.*

a **1586** Sidney (J.), Musidorus could not perform any action..more strongly, or deliver that strength more nimbly. **1845** *Jrnl. R. Agric. Soc.* V. ii. 530 He [a horse] must..be taught to raise his knee and deliver his leg with freedom.

†**d.** *fig.* To give out as produce, to produce, yield. *Obs.*

1605 Verstegan *Dec. Intell.* ii. (1628) 51 The mynes..do deliuer gold, siluer, copper.

10. a. To give forth in words, utter, enunciate, pronounce openly or formally. (Cf. 5.)

Here the object is usually either something in the speaker's mind, as a judgement or opinion, or (now very commonly) the speech or utterance itself, with reference to its mode of delivery.

1576 Fleming *Panopl. Epist.* 56 To a question by him propounded, this answere was delivered. **1589** Puttenham *Eng. Poesie* ii. xiii. [xiv.] (Arb.) 134 The vowell is alwayes more easily deliuered then the consonant. **1615** Crooke *Body of Man* v. xxxi. (1616) 341 Galen deliuering the precepts of health. **1667** Pepys *Diary* (1879) IV. 435 He is..bold to deliver what he thinks on every occasion. **1771** *Junius Lett.* liv. 286, I am called upon to deliver my opinion. **1804** *Med. Jrnl.* XII. 384 Dr. John Reid..intends to deliver ..a Course of Lectures on the Theory and Practice of Medicine. **1873** Hamerton *Intell. Life* 150 Like an orator who knows that he can deliver a passage, and compose at the same time the one which is to follow. **1882** *Times* 25 Nov. 4 The Master of the Rolls, in delivering judgment, said [etc.].

b. *absol.* or *intr.* To 'deliver oneself', discourse; to pronounce an opinion or verdict; to 'make deliverance'.

1807 Robinson *Archæol. Græca* v. xxi. 525 They first delivered on civil affairs: afterwards the discourse turned on war. **1859** Sala *Tw. round Clock* (1861) 97 Poor jurymen..

understanding a great deal more about the case on which they have to deliver at its commencement than at its termination.

†**c.** *absol.* or *intr.* To utter notes in singing.

1530 PALSGR. 510/2, I delyver quickly, as one dothe in syngynge..I never herde boye in my lyfe delyver more quyckely.

†**11. a.** *trans.* To declare, communicate, report, relate, narrate, tell, make known; to state, affirm, assert; to express in words, set forth, describe. *Obs.*

1557 *Order of Hospitalls* H vj, Goe to the Lord Maior, and deliuer unto him the disobedience of the said Constable. **1600** E. BLOUNT tr. *Conestaggio* 219 The Duke..himselfe unto the king, delivered what hee had seene. **1611** SHAKS. *Wint. T.* v. ii. 4, I..heard the old Shepheard deliuer the manner how he found it. **1655–60** STANLEY *Hist. Philos.* (1701) 114/1 The time of his birth is no where expresly delivered. **1664** POWER *Exp. Philos.* I. 80, I will here deliver one or two Optical Experiments. **1768** STERNE *Sent. Journ.* (1778) II. 1 (*Fille de Chambre*) What the old French officer had delivered upon travelling. **1790** PALEY *Horæ Paul.* i. 5 Particulars so plainly delivered..in the Acts of the Apostles. **1800** VINCE *Hydrostat.* (1806) 5 Like his general principles of motion before delivered.

†**b.** with obj. clause. *Obs.*

1586 A. DAY *Eng. Secretary* I. (1625) 44 It was delivered hee hung himselfe for griefe. **1658** BROWNE *Hydriot.* i, That they held that Practice in Gallia, Cæsar expressly delivereth. **1698** FRYER *Acc. E. India & P.* 161 Who founded these, their Annals nor their Sanscript deliver not.

†**c.** with obj. and complement. *Obs.*

1636 MASSINGER *Gt. Dk. Florence* I. ii, She is deliver'd.. For a masterpiece in nature. **1649** MILTON *Eikon.* 11 History delivers him a deep dissembler. *a* **1687** PETTY *Pol. Arith.* iv. (1691) 64 The Author..delivers the Proportion..to be as Thirty to Eighty two.

V. 12. *Pottery* and *Founding*. To set free from the mould; *refl.* and *intr.* To free itself from the mould; to leave the mould easily.

1782 WEDGWOOD in *Phil. Trans.* LXXII. 310 To make the clay deliver easily, it will be necessary to oil the mould. **1832** PORTER *Porcelain & Gl.* 50 The ware..dries in a sufficient degree to deliver itself (according to the workman's phrase) easily from the mould. **1880** C. T. NEWTON *Ess. Art & Archæol.* vi. 272 That oil or grease had been applied..to make the mould deliver.

†**de'liver**, *v.*[2] *Obs.* [A variant of DELIBER *v.*, with Romanic change of L. *b* to *v*, as in prec.] = DELIBER, to deliberate, determine.

1382 WYCLIF *2 Sam.* xxiv. 13 Now thanne delyver, and see, what word I shal answere to hym. *c* **1440** CAPGRAVE *Life St. Kath.* I. 966 Deliuer þis mater, so god ȝour soulys saue. **1535** STEWART *Cron. Scot.* II. 520 Oft in his mynd revoluand to and fro, Syne at the last deliuerit hes rycht sone, To tak his tyme sen it wes oportune.

Hence †**de'livered** *ppl. a.*, determined, resolved.

1536 BELLENDEN *Cron. Scot.* (1821) I. 259 With deliverit mind to assailye thame in the brek of the day. **1552** ABP. HAMILTON *Catech.* (1884) 12 We consent nocht with ane deliverit mynd.

deliverable (dɪˈlɪvərəb(ə)l), *a.* [f. DELIVER *v.*[1] + -ABLE: cf. OF. *deliverable, delivrable* (15–17th c. in Godef.).] That can or may be delivered; to be delivered (according to agreement): cf. *payable*.

1755 MAGENS *Insurances* I. 401 Ten thousand Pounds of good and deliverable Dutch made Starch. **1877** *Act 40–1 Vict.* c. 39 §5 Where the document..makes the goods deliverable to the bearer. **1889** *Macm. Mag.* Mar. 270/2 So wild and shrill a cry of human anguish, that the like of it I could never imagine deliverable by human lips.

deliverance (dɪˈlɪvərəns). [a. OF. *delivrance, desl-* (12th c. in Littré) = Pr. *delivransa, desl-*, f. *délivrer, delivrar* to DELIVER: see -ANCE.]

1. The action of delivering or setting free, or fact of being set free (†*of*, *from* confinement, danger, evil, etc.); liberation, release, rescue.

c **1290** *S. Eng. Leg.* I. 197/118 A-serued heo hath to alle þe contreie deliueraunce of langour. *c* **1330** R. BRUNNE *Chron.* (1810) 121 William Marschalle..gaf for his delyueraunce þe castelle of Schirburne. **1340** HAMPOLE *Pr. Consc.* 3585 For þair deliverance fra payn. **13..** *Poems fr. Vernon MS.* 226/200 Of alle þeos Merueylous chaunces Vr lord haþ sent vs diliueraunces. *c* **1400** MAUNDEV. (1839) xxiii. 247 It hath a round wyndowe abouen that..seruethe for deliverance of smoke. *c* **1450** *Mirour Saluacioun* 4074 Sho..lete hym out at a wyndowe so making his delyvrance. **1483** CAXTON *Gold. Leg.* 275/2 That he shold praye to god for the delyueraunce of his sekenesse. **1568** GRAFTON *Chron.* II. 408 On the behalfe of king Richard for his delyveraunce out of prison. **1651** HOBBES *Leviath.* III. xxxv. 221 Our deliverance from the bondage of sin. **1719** DE FOE *Crusoe* (1858) 139 The greatest deliverances I enjoyed, such as my escape from Sallee. **1871** FREEMAN *Norm. Conq.* (1876) IV. xviii. 144 At no moment..had hopes of deliverance been higher.

†**b.** 'Delivery' of a gaol: see DELIVER *v.*[1] 2 c.

c **1400** *Gamelyn* 745 Þat þou graunte him me Til þe nexte sittyng of delyueraunce. **1464** *Nottingham Rec.* II. 377 Paied to the Justices of Deliuerance for the Gaole Delyuere. **1487** *Act 3 Hen. VII*, c. 3 The next generall gaoles deliveraunce of eny suche gaole.

c. In the ritual observed at a criminal trial.

1565 SIR T. SMITH *Commonw. Eng.* xxv. 99 No man that is once indicted can be deliuered without arraignment. *Ibid.* [Form of proclamation in court when no indictment is produced], A. B. prisoner standeth here at the barre, if any man can say any thing against him, let him now speake, for the prisoner standeth at his deliuerance: If no man do then come, he is deliuered without anie further processe or trouble. [In Budden's Latin transl. 1601: *nam vinctus liberationem expectat: si nemo eum tum incusaverit, in libertatem pristinam asseritur.*] *Ibid.* 102 [Form of procl. on trial by Jury] If any man can giue evidence, or can say any thing against the prisoner, let him come now, for he standeth vpon his deliuerance [Budden: *nam de captivi liberatione agitur*]. **1660** *Trial Regic. 21. Col. Harrison.* 'I do offer myself to be tried in your own way, by God and my Countrey.' *Clerk.* 'God send you a good deliverance.' *Ibid.* 35 For now the Prisoner [Col. Harrison] stands at the Bar upon his Deliverance. **1781** *Trial Ld. Geo. Gordon 7 Clerk.* 'How will you be tried?' *Gordon.* 'By God and my country.' *Clerk.* 'God send you a good deliverance.'

(It is possible that this has been in later times associated with the 'true deliverance' of the Jury: see 8 b.)

†**2.** The being delivered of offspring, the bringing forth of offspring; delivery. *Obs.*

c **1325** *Metr. Hom.* 72 This womane yode wit chylde full lange..myght scho haue na delyueraunce. *c* **1350** *Will. Palerne* 4080 Mi wif..Deied at þe deliueraunce of mi dere sone. *c* **1450** *Merlin* 13 Two women ffor to helpe hir at hir delyueraunce when tyme is. **1548–9** (Mar.) *Bk. Com. Prayer, Churching of Women*, To geue you safe deliuerance. **1611** SHAKS. *Cymb.* v. v. 370 Nere Mother Reioyc'd deliuerance more. **1625** *Gonsalvio's Sp. Inquis.* 122 Within foure dayes after her deliuerance, they tooke the childe away from her.

fig. **1660** WILLSFORD *Scales Comm.* 190 Sulphurious Meteors fir'd in the wombs of clouds, break forth in their deliverance with amazement to mortals.

†**3.** The action of giving up or yielding; surrender. *Obs.*

c **1330** R. BRUNNE *Chron.* (1810) 158, I am not bonden to mak deliuerance. **1404** in Ellis *Orig. Lett.* Ser. II. I. 38 Awyn ..is accordit with all the men that arne therinne save vij, for to have dilyverance of the Castell at a certayn day. **1548** HALL *Chron.* 19 b, The kyng openly saied that if they wolde not deliver them, he woulde take them without deliverance. **1568** GRAFTON *Chron.* II. 227 To make deliverance of the towne of Barwike.

†**4.** The action of handing over, transferring, or delivering a thing to another; delivery. *Obs.*

c **1340** *Cursor M.* 5045 (Fairf.) He made del[i]uerance þer of corne. *c* **1449** PECOCK *Repr.* 404 Eer than the receyuer make Execucioun or Delyuerance of the thing or deede bi him ȝouun. **1528** TYBALL in Strype *Eccl. Mem.* I. App. xvii. 38 After the delyverance of the sayd New Testament to them. **1631** *Star Chamb. Cases* (Camden) 35 The Sheriffe did not make deliverance of 400 sheepe.

b. Law. *writ of second deliverance*: a writ for re-delivery to the owner of goods distrained or unlawfully taken, after they have been returned to the distrainer in consequence of a judgement being given against the owner in an action of replevin.

a **1565** RASTELL tr. *Fitzherbert's Nat. Brevium* (1652) 174 The plaintiff may sue a Writ of second Deliverance. **1618** PULTON *Stat.* (1632) 47 *marg.*, A Writ of Second deliuerance. **1708** *Termes de la Ley* 508 b, Second Deliverance is a Writ made by the Filacer, to deliver Cattel distreined, after the Plaintiff is Non-suit in Replevin. **1845** STEPHEN *Laws Eng.* (1874) III. v. xi. 616 The Statute of Westminster 2 (13 Edw. I c. 2)..allowed him a judicial writ issuing out of the original record (called a writ of second deliverance).

†**5.** Sending forth, emission, issue, discharge.

1626 BACON *Sylva* §9 This Motion worketh..by way of Proofe and Search, which way to deliuer itself; And then worketh in progresse, where it findeth the Deliuerance easiest.

†**6.** The action or manner of uttering words in speaking; utterance, enunciation, delivery. *Obs.*

1553 T. WILSON *Rhet.* (1580) 222 Singyng plaine song, and counterfeictyng those that doe speake distinctly, helpe muche to have a good deliueraunce. **1593** SHAKS. *3 Hen. VI*, II. i. 97 At each words deliuerance. **1609** HOLLAND *Amm. Marcell.* xxx. ix. 397 For his speech, readie he was ynough in quicke deliverance.

†**7.** The action of reporting or stating something; that which is stated; statement, narration, declaration; = DELIVERY 8. *Obs.*

1431 in *Eng. Gilds* (1870) 276 To make a trewe delyueraunce of swiche goodys as thei receyue. **1509** HAWES *Past. Pleas.* xxix. (Percy Soc.) 143 And to Venus he made deliveraunce Of his complaint. **1586** A. DAY *Eng. Secretary* I. (1625) 7 What confused deliverance is this? *Ibid.* II. 44 Doth not the very deliverance of your own fact condemne you? **1621** T. ADAMS *White Devill* (1635) 111, If there wanted nothing in the deliverance.

b. An utterance; *esp.* of a formal character.

1859 MILL *Liberty* ii. (1865) 29 Things which are not provided for..in the recorded deliverances of the Founder of Christianity. **1879** M. ARNOLD *Fr. Critic on Milton* Mixed Ess. 241 Macaulay's writing..often..is really obscure, if one takes his deliverances seriously. **1883** *Manch. Guardian* 29 Sept. 7/3 We can complain of no ambiguity in his present deliverance.

8. *Sc. Law.* Judgement delivered; a judicial or administrative order in an action or other proceeding.

In its most general sense applicable to any order pronounced by any body exercising quasi-judicial functions. In the *Bankruptcy Act* of 1856 (19 & 20 Vict. c. 79 §4) 'deliverance' is defined as including 'any order, warrant, judgement, decision, interlocutor, or decree'. Hence the word has acquired a quasi-technical application to orders in bankruptcy proceedings.

c **1425** WYNTOUN *Cron.* VII. vi. 90 Of þat [he] Stablysyd, and mad ordynance..and full delyverance. **1500–20** DUNBAR *Poems* ix. 133 Of fals solisting ffor wrang deliuerance At Counsale, Sessioun, and at Parliament. **1535** STEWART *Cron. Scot.* II. 562 In this mater..Rycht sone I wald heir ȝour deliuerance. *c* **1565** LINDESAY (Pitscottie) *Chron. Scot.* (1728) 14 (Jam.) Both parties were compromit by their oaths to stand at the deliverance of the arbitrators chosen by them both. *a* **1649** DRUMM. OF HAWTH. *Skiamachia* Wks. (1711) 194 We hope your lordships will give us leave..to remember your lordships of your deliverance, June the first, 1642. **1752** J. LOUTHIAN *Form of Process* (ed. 2) 35 The Deliverance on the Bill is, *Fiat ut petitur, to the — Day of — next to come.* **1833** *Act 3–4 Will. IV*, c. 46 §25 The said sheriff shall..affix a deliverance thereon finding and declaring..that this Act has not been adopted. **1868** *Act 31–2 Vict.* c. 101 §75 The judgment or deliverance so pronounced shall form a valid and sufficient warrant for the preparation in Chancery of the writ.

b. In the (English) Jurors' oath, in a trial for treason or felony, used app. in the sense: Determination of the question at issue, verdict.

1660 *Trial Regic.* 11 Oct. 32 His Oath was then read to him [Sir T. Allen, juror]: You shall well and truly try and true deliverance make between our Sovereign Lord the King, and the prisoners at the Bar, whom you shall have in Charge, according to your Evidence. So help you God! **1892** S. F. HARRIS *Princ. Crim. Law* (ed. 6) xiv. 412. [The current formula: the same words with the last clause expanded to 'and a true verdict give, according to the evidence'.]

(The meaning here has been matter of discussion: cf. 1 c above, and TOMLINS *Law Dict.* s.v. *Jury*.)

c. Formal judgement pronounced, expression of opinion, verdict.

[**1847** DE QUINCEY *Wks.* XII. 184 *Milton* v. *Southey & Landor*, Wordsworth never said the thing ascribed to him here as any formal judgment, or what the Scottish law would call *deliverance*.] **1856** DOVE *Logic Chr. Faith* v. i. §2. 298 We cannot but attach great value to the deliberate deliverance of so impartial..a man. **1871** SARAH TYTLER *Sisters & Wives* 154 Dr. Harris's deliverance was..that Mr. Duke was not looking very well.

†**d.** Used (in *Sc.*) to render L. *senatus consultum*.

1533 BELLENDEN *Livy* (1822) 212 (Jam.) Thir novellis maid the Faderis sa astonist, that thay usit the samen deliverance that thay usit in extreme necessite.

†**9.** = DELIVERNESS; DELIVERY 6. *Obs.*

14.. CHAUCER *Pars. T.* ¶378 (Harl. 7334) Þe goodes of body ben hele of body, strengþe, deliuerance [*six texts* deliuernesse], beaute [etc.]. **1500–20** DUNBAR *Thistle & Rose* 95 Lusty of schaip, lycht of deliuerance.

de'liverancy. *rare*[−1]. [See prec. and -ANCY.] = DELIVERANCE 7 b.

1853 *Tait's Mag.* XX. 365 Being the accredited organ of the Government on Scotch topics, his deliverancy necessarily carries more weight than those of any ordinary member.

†**delive'ration.** *Obs. rare*[−1]. [a. OF. *delivration* (in earlier and more popular form *delivraison, -oison, -ison*), ad. late pop. L. *dēlīberātiōn-em* (Du Cange), n. of action from *dēlīberāre* to liberate.] Deliverance, liberation, release.

1509 HAWES *Past. Pleas.* 148 Who is fettered in chaynes He thinketh long after delyveracion Of his great wo.

delivered (dɪˈlɪvəd), *ppl. a.*[1] [f. DELIVER *v.*[1] + -ED[1].] Set free; disburdened of offspring; handed over; surrendered; formally uttered or stated, etc.: see the verb.

c **1440** *Promp. Parv.* 117 Delyueryd, *liberatus, erutus.* **1588** SHAKS. *Tit. A.* IV. ii. 142 Cornelia, the midwife, and my selfe, And none else but the deliuered Empresse. **1665** MANLEY *Grotius' Low C. Warres* 123 Prince of the delivered City. **1893** *Pall Mall G.* 13 Jan. 2/1 The additional cost..for delivered bread.

†**delivered**, *ppl. a.*[2]: see DELIVER *v.*[2]

deliveree (dɪˌlɪvəˈriː). [f. DELIVER *v.*[1] + -EE.] The person to whom something is delivered.

1887 V. SAMPSON in *Cape Law Jrnl.* 37 The putting of a deliveree in possession. *Ibid.* 43 The deliveror should point out the subject of delivery to the deliveree.

deliveree, obs. form of DELIVERY.

deliverer (dɪˈlɪvərə(r)). Also 4–6 dely-, 4 -ere, 6 -our; see also DELIVEROR. [a. OF. *delivrere* (12th c. in Hatzf.), in obl. case *delivreor, -our, -eur*:—late pop. L. *dēlīberātor, -ōrem*, agent-n. from *dēlīberāre*, F. *délivrer* to DELIVER: see -ER[1].] One who delivers.

1. One who sets free or releases; a liberator, rescuer, saviour.

a **1340** HAMPOLE *Psalter* lxix. 7 My helpere & my delyuerere ert þou. **1382** WYCLIF *Ps.* xvii[i]. 2 My refut, and my delyuerere. *c* **1440** *Promp. Parv.* 117 Delyuerer, *liberator.* **1555** EDEN *Decades* Pref. to Rdr. (Arb.) 53 Thou oughteste to..bee thankefull to thy delyuerer. **1667** MILTON *P.L.* XII. 149 Thy great deliverer, who shall bruise The Serpents head. **1781** GIBBON *Decl. & F.* III. lxv. 622 He stood forth as the deliverer of his country. **1855** MACAULAY *Hist. Eng.* III. 404 Though he had been a deliverer by accident, he was a despot by nature.

2. One who hands over, commits, surrenders, etc.; *esp.* one who delivers letters or goods.

1531–2 *Act 23 Hen. VIII*, c. 16 The seller, exchaunger or deliuerer. **1534** *Act 26 Hen. VIII*, c. 6 §8 By indenture to be made betwene the deliuerour..and the receiuour. **1622** MISSELDEN *Free Trade* 104 The Stranger..would be a deliuerer heere of money at a high rate. **1766** ENTICK *London* IV. 295 There is..a deliverer of letters to the House of Commons, at 6*s.* 8*d.* per day. **1888** *Daily News* 25 Aug. 5/3 Each deliverer of milk will possess a share.

3. One who utters, enunciates, sets forth, etc. (*rare.*)

1597 HOOKER *Eccl. Pol.* VIII. vi. §12 Thereof God himself was..the deviser, the discusser, the deliverer. **1651** *Reliq. Wotton.* 202 Among the Deliverers of this Art. **1822** *New Monthly Mag.* IV. 195 The public deliverers of song at the Grecian festivals.

deliveress (dɪˈlɪvərɪs). *rare.* [Short for *delivreress*, f. DELIVERER + -ESS, in F. *délivreresse*: see -ESS.] A female deliverer.

1644 EVELYN *Mem.* (1857) I. 72 At one side of the cross, kneels Charles VII armed, and at the other Joan d'Arc.. as the deliveress of the town. **1839** *Q. Rev.* June 98 Nancy comes like the deliveress of the pious Æneas.

†**deˈliverhede.** *Obs.* [f. DELIVER *a.* + *-hede*, -HEAD.] Nimbleness, agility.

1496 *Dives & Paup.* (W. de W.) III. xiii. 148/2 They shal haue delyuerhede of body and lightnesse.

delivering (dɪˈlɪvərɪŋ), *vbl. sb.* [f. DELIVER *v.*[1] + -ING[2].] The action of the verb DELIVER, q.v.; deliverance, delivery (in various senses).

c **1320** *Seuyn Sag.* 1536 (W.) The maister.. hadde mani a blessing, For his disciple deliuering. *c* **1450** *St. Cuthbert* (Surtees) 5800 Of his delyueryng gled and blithe. **1571** GOLDING *Calvin on Ps.* lxv. 6 By thy wonderfull deliveringes, thy power may be shewed abrode. **1642** JER. TAYLOR *Episc.* §36 (R.) Excommunications.. were deliverings over to Satan. **1889** J. M. DUNCAN *Dis. Women* vi. (ed. 4) 26 Judgement of the method to be pursued in delivering.

attrib. **1881** *Daily News* 19 Jan. 5/5 A few heavy railway collecting or delivering vans.

deˈlivering, *ppl. a.* [f. as prec. + -ING[2].] That delivers: see the verb.

1887 *Pall Mall G.* 29 Nov. 11/1 There was no evidence that the delivering company.. were not willing to supply the coal at 8*s.* a ton.

†**deˈliverly,** *adv. Obs.* or *arch.* For forms see DELIVER *a.* [f. DELIVER *a.* + -LY[2].]

1. Lightly, actively, nimbly, quickly.

c **1340** *Gaw. & Gr. Knt.* 2009 Deliuerly he dressed vp, er þe day sprenged. *c* **1374** CHAUCER *Troylus* II. 1088 He.. sette [his signet] Upon the wex deliverliche and rathe. *c* **1440** *Partonope* 7051 His Swerd he pulleth oute delyuerly. **1549** CHALONER *Erasmus on Folly* R ij a, The nemblier and more deliverly to goe about theyr charge. **1657** S. PURCHAS *Pol. Flying-Ins.* x. 50 The claw-tailed Humble Bee.. flyes as deliverly when great with young as when she is barren.

2. Deftly, cleverly.

1530 PALSGR. 550, I fynger, I handell an instrument of musyke delyverly. **1612** *Two Noble K.* III. v, Carry it sweetly and deliverly. **1870** EMERSON *Soc. & Solit., Clubs* Wks. (Bohn) III. 93 We get a mechanical advantage in detaching it well and deliverly.

¶ As *adj.* (erroneous archaism).

1820 SCOTT *Monast.* xvii, A deliverly fellow was Hughie—could read and write like a priest, and could wield brand and buckler with the best of the riders.

deˈliverment. *rare.* [f. DELIVER *v.*[1] + -MENT. (Cf. OF. *delivrement* in Godef.)] = DELIVERANCE 7 b; open statement, pronouncement.

1893 *Nat. Observer* 13 May 640/1 Because the Emperor has heretofore spoken unadvisedly, it by no means follows that.. Tuesday's deliverment makes for complete ineptitude.

†**deˈliverness.** *Obs.* [f. DELIVER *a.* + -NESS.] Lightness, activity, nimbleness, agility, quickness.

1340 HAMPOLE *Pr. Consc.* 5900 Delyvernes and bewte of body. *c* **1386** CHAUCER *Melib.* ¶ 199 Grete thinges ben not ay accompliced by strengthe, ne by delyvernes of body. **1489** CAXTON *Faytes of A.* I. xi. 30 To voyde the strokis by delyuernes of body. **1540** ELYOT *Image Gov.* (1556) 69 b, Fewe men surmounted hym in strength and delivernesse. *a* **1607** BRIGHTMAN *Revelation* (1615) 700 Certainly this.. deserueth to be called properly by the Latin name, *Expedition*, for the deliuernes thereof.

deliveror (dɪˌlɪvəˈrɔː(r)). [f. DELIVER *v.*[1]: see -OR.] A technical variant of DELIVERER, used as correlative to *deliveree*: one who makes a legal delivery of goods, etc.

1887 [see DELIVEREE].

delivery (dɪˈlɪvərɪ). Forms: 5 **deliveree**, 5–6 **delyuery(e**, 6 **-ere**, 6–7 **deliverie**, 6– **-ery**. [a. Anglo-Fr. *delivrée*, fem. sb. f. pa. pple. of *délivrer* to DELIVER: cf. *livery*, and see -Y.]

†**1. a.** The action of setting free; release, rescue, deliverance. *Obs.*

1494 FABYAN *Chron.* VII. ccxxxiii. 266 The quene made assyduat laboure for the delyuerye of the kynge her husbonde. **1555** EDEN *Decades* 103 Thankes geuynge to almyghty god for his delyuery and preseruation from so many imminent perels. **1638** SIR T. HERBERT *Trav.* 90 A servant of his.. by force attempting his Lords delivery. **1671** MILTON *Samson* 1505 Thy hopes are not ill founded, nor seem vain, Of his delivery. **1766** GOLDSM. *Vic. W.* xxx, Here is the brave man to whom I owe my delivery. **1784** R. BAGE *Barham Downs* II. 58 Some that called upon the Lord for delivery before there was need.

b. The action of delivering a gaol: see DELIVER *v.*[1] 2 c, and JAIL-DELIVERY.

2. a. The fact of being delivered of, or act of bringing forth, offspring; childbirth.

Usually of the mother; formerly sometimes of the child; cf. DELIVER *v.* 3.

1577 B. GOOGE *Heresbach's Husb.* III. (1586) 139 For this poore creature.. is as much tormented in her deliverie, as a shrew. **1611** BIBLE *Isa.* xxvi. 17 Like as a woman.. that draweth neere the time of her deliuerie. **1648** W. MOUNTAGUE *Devoute Ess.* I. xii. §1 (R.) As they are twins.. their delivery is commonly after such a manner, as that of Pharez and Zara. **1676** LADY CHAWORTH in *12th Rep. Hist. MSS. Comm.* App. v. 29 My prayers shall attend your ladies good delivery of a brave boy. **1868** *Chambers' Encycl.* VI. 446/1 Midwife.. a woman who assists in parturition or delivery.

attrib. **1876** tr. *Ziemssen's Cycl. Med.* XI. 562 That form of paralysis.. in newly-born children.. which we should call delivery-paralysis.

b. As the action of the accoucheur or midwife.

[**1660** SHIRLEY *Andromana* III. i. 8, I am with child to hear the news: Pr'ythee Be quick in the delivery.] **1767** GOOCH *Treat. Wounds* I. 323 Injury in a laborious, hasty or injudicious delivery. **1800** *Med. Jrnl.* III. 483, I therefore did not conceive myself justified.. in proceeding to immediate delivery. **1889** W. S. PLAYFAIR *Treat. Midwifery* II. IV. ii. 163 No other means of effecting artificial delivery was known.

c. *fig.*

a **1639** MARMION *Antiquary* III. ii, My head labours with the pangs of delivery. **1823** SCOTT *Peveril* xlvi, Out started the dwarf.. and the poor German, on seeing the portentous delivery of his fiddlecase, tumbled on the floor.

3. The act of giving up possession of; surrender.

1513 MORE in Grafton *Chron.* II. 772 The whole counsaile had sente him to require of her the deliverie of him [her child]. **1548** HALL *Chron.* 245 b, The delivery of the Castell of Barwyke. **1600** E. BLOUNT tr. *Conestaggio* 181 The deliverie of the rocke of Saint Julian and of the fort. **1780** *Impartial Hist. War Amer.* 147 Marching directly to Boston, there to demand a delivery of the powder and stores, and in case of refusal to attack the troops. **1844** H. H. WILSON *Brit. India* II. 158 The arrest of Trimbak, and his delivery to the British Government.

4. a. The action of handing over, or conveying into the hands of another; *esp.* the action of a carrier in delivering letters or goods entrusted to him for conveyance to a person at a distance.

1480 *Wardr. Acc. Edw. IV* (1830) 140 For the deliveree of the said stuff and bedding. **1556** in Hakluyt *Voy.* (1886) III. 113 Hauing receiued any priuie letters.. you shal.. let the deliuerie of them at your arriuing in Russia. **1634** SIR T. HERBERT *Trav.* 124 He might forge other Letters.. else why kept he them two dayes without delivery. **1679** BURNET *Hist. Ref.* I. I. (R.), The investitures of bishops and abbots.. had been originally given by the delivery of the pastoral ring and staff. **1799** W. TOOKE *View Russian Emp.* III. 652 Extraordinary charges for the delivery of goods. **1838** DICKENS *Nich. Nick.* ii, It [a letter] will be here by the two o'clock delivery. **1851** HT. MARTINEAU *Hist. Peace* (1877) III. IV. xiv. 139 The convenience of two or three deliveries of letters per day. **1879** R. M. BALLANTYNE *Post Haste* vii. (1880) 74 The delivery of a telegram.

fig. **1605** BACON *Adv. Learn.* I. v. §9 Another error is in the manner of the tradition and delivery of knowledge.

attrib. **1720** DE FOE *Capt. Singleton* xviii. (1840) 316 Our proper delivery port.. was at Madagascar. **1889** *Daily News* 11 Dec. 3/2 Carmen's wages:—Delivery men: Driving, 1s. per day and 7d. per ton.

b. *Law.* (*a*) The formal or legal handing over of anything to another; *esp.* the putting of property into the legal possession of another person.

1577 tr. *Bullinger's Decades* (1592) 264 Goods are gotten.. by deliuerie. **1625** GILL *Sacr. Philos.* I. 87 Whereof we have already assurance, yea deliverie, and seisure. **1818** CRUISE *Digest* (ed. 2) IV. 47 Acts which have been held to be a part performance of an agreement.. such as delivery of possession; and payment of the whole, or a considerable part of the consideration. **1887** V. SAMPSON in *Cape Law Jrnl.* 38 We now come to the several species of constructive delivery, of which delivery *brevis manus*, or short-hand is the first. **1891** *Law Times* XC. 473/1 After delivery of defence the plaintiff discontinued his action.

(*b*) The formal transfer of a deed by the grantor or his attorney to the grantee or to a third party, either by act or by word: formerly essential to the validity of the deed.

1660 R. COKE *Power & Subj.* 25 Absolute estates of inheritance which.. do not pass by livery and seisin, but by delivery of the deed or feoffment. **1809** TOMLINS *Law Dict.* s.v. *Deed*, If I have sealed my deed, and after I deliver it to him to whom it is made, or to some other by his appointment, and say nothing, this is a good delivery. **1853** WHARTON *Pennsylv. Digest* 261 Delivery is necessary to give effect to a bond.

5. a. The act of sending forth or delivering (a missile, a blow, etc.); emission, discharge; throwing or bowling of a ball (at cricket, baseball, etc.). Also, = BALL *sb.*[1] 4 c.

1702 SAVERY *Miner's Friend* 46 The delivery of your Water into a convenient Trough. **1787** *Specif. Bryant's Patent* No. 1631 Useful.. by its much greater delivery of water. **1816** W. LAMBERT *Instr. & Rules of Cricket* 22 Very few Bowlers run alike before the delivery of the Ball. **1834** MEDWIN *Angler in Wales* I. 109 The peril.. from the delivery of the spear. **1837** W. MARTIN *Bk. of Sports* 96 If the hand be above the shoulder in the delivery, the umpire must call 'no ball'. **1868** J. LILLYWHITE *Cricketers' Compan.* 54 Mr. Jupp.. played Southerton's 'curly' deliveries with consummate skill. **1882** *Daily Tel.* 19 May (*Cricket*), Crossland at 68 came on with his fast deliveries. **1960** J. FINGLETON *Four Chukkas* 59 He thus played 'doggo' to 388 deliveries.

b. *Founding.* See quot. (Cf. DELIVER *v.*[1] 12.)

1874 KNIGHT *Dict. Mech.*, *Delivery* (*Founding*), the draft or allowance by which a pattern is made to free itself from close lateral contact with the sand of the mold as it is lifted. Also called *draw-taper*.

†**6.** Free putting forth of bodily action, 'use of the limbs, activity' (J.); action, bearing, deportment. *Obs.*

a **1586** SIDNEY (J.), Musidorus could not.. deliver that strength more nimbly, or become the delivery more gracefully. **1586** A. DAY *Eng. Secretary* II. (1625) 127 Men ..for their severall callings questionlesse of very good delivery. **1634** SIR T. HERBERT *Trav.* 223 Observing simplicitie in the Messingers delivery and lookes. *a* **1639** WOTTON (J.), The duke had the neater limbs, and freer delivery. **1741** RICHARDSON *Pamela* (1824) I. xxxii. 319 There is a great deal in a *delivery*, as it is called, in a way, a manner, a deportment, to engage people's attention and liking. **1818** TODD, *Deliverness*, agility.. What we now term *delivery*.

fig. **1762–71** H. WALPOLE *Vertue's Anecd. Paint.* (1786) II. 177 It has the greatest freedom of pencil, the happiest delivery of nature.

7. a. The utterance or enunciation (of words), the delivering (of a speech, etc.).

1581 PETTIE *Guazzo's Civ. Conv.* II. (1586) 58 All their force and vertue lyeth in the sweete deliverie of their wordes. **1586** A. DAY *Eng. Secretary* I. (1625) 37 His skill and delivery of forraigne languages [was] so wonderfull. **1665** LLOYD *State Worthies* (1670) 22 One thing he advised young men to take care of in their publick deliveries. **1818** JAS. MILL *Brit. India* III. ii. 68 Four days were occupied in the delivery of the speech. **1879** MCCARTHY *Own Times* II. xix. 57 The speech occupied some five hours in delivery.

b. Manner of utterance or enunciation in public speaking or singing.

1667 PEPYS *Diary* 19 May, Meriton.. hath a strange knack of a grave, serious delivery. **1769** JOHNSON in Boswell *Life* an. 1781 (1848) 679/2 His delivery, though unconstrained, was not negligent. **1853** HOLYOAKE *Rudim. Public Speaking* 13 The power of distinct and forcible pronunciation is the basis of delivery. **1892** *Sat. Rev.* 15 Oct. 443/1 Few men of his generation had a greater fund of talk or a more telling delivery.

†**8.** The action of setting forth in words, or that which is set forth; communication, narration, statement; = DELIVERANCE 7. *Obs.*

1586 A. DAY *Eng. Secretary* I. (1625) 22 The order hereafter to be observed in delivery of examples. **1611** SHAKS. *Wint. T.* V. ii. 10, I make a broken deliuerie of the Businesse. **1646** SIR T. BROWNE *Pseud. Ep.* I. iv, Which enigmatical deliveries comprehended usefull verities. **1653** H. COGAN tr. *Pinto's Trav.* xxxvii. 145, I will forbear the delivery of many matters, that possibly might bring much contentment.

9. *attrib.* and *Comb.*: ***delivery cart, company, date, port, system, tube, van, wagon***; **delivery box, order** (see quots.); **delivery pipe**, a pipe through which liquids are ejected, *spec.* from a pump; also, a service-pipe; **delivery room**, a room in a hospital in which a mother is delivered (of a child).

1888 *Lockwood's Dict. Mech. Engin.*, **Delivery box*, the upper or delivery chamber of a series of two or three throw pumps, into which the liquid is lifted by the pistons and from which it is delivered. **1859** G. MEASOM *Illustr. Guide Lanc. & Carlisle Railw.* 115 (Advt.), Tradesmen's *Delivery Carts and Vans. **1856** MRS. GASKELL *Let.* ?29 Apr. (1966) 388, I have just sent you off a parcel by the *Delivery Company. **1962** J. BRAINE *Life at Top* iv. 68, I started to worry about the Tiffield order again; Mottram was bound to talk about *delivery dates tomorrow. **1967** O. WYND *Walk Softly* i. 8 It's run like a precision machine. Delivery dates are met. **1882** R. BITHELL *Counting-house Dict.* 93 **Delivery order*, a.. document, entitling.. the legal holder thereof, to the delivery of any goods.. of the value of forty shillings, or upwards, lying in any dock, port, wharf, or warehouse. **1924** *Times Trade & Engin. Suppl.* 29 Nov. 245/1 Ownership in goods can be transferred by mere endorsement of a bill of lading or a delivery order... A delivery order, or formal request, signed by the owner of goods, that they be delivered to the firm or person named, or to 'bearer', must be lodged with the bill of lading or freight release. **1965** PERRY & RYDER *Thomson's Dict. Banking* (ed. 11) 209/1 When delivery orders are taken as security, the banker's letter of lien.. should be signed by the customer. **1870** *Technol. Dict.* (ed. 2) II. 176/1 *Delivery-pipe of a feed-pump (Locom.), Das Druckrohr, Tuyau de refoulement. **1888** *Lockwood's Dict. Mech. Engin.*, *Delivery pipes*, the series of pipes through which the liquids drawn up by pumping machinery are ejected. **1889** P. N. HASLUCK *Model Engin. Handybk.* 111 To connect the delivery-pipe union. **1895** *Daily News* 14 Sept. 5/1 It was noticed that this water had the power to dissolve the lead of the delivery pipes. **1720** *Delivery port [see sense 4]. **1949** M. MEAD *Male & Female* iii. 62 In our own society, our images of the ..rituals of the *delivery-room.. overlay any realization of what a shock birth is. **1967** *Nursing Times* 8 Sept. 1199/2 Once labour is established, the mother should be in a delivery room where in a normal confinement she will have her baby without any further move. **1961** *Listener* 28 Dec. 1098/2 This means developing nuclear weapons and *delivery systems so strong and so varied that no surprise attack could knock out the power to retaliate. **1967** *Guardian* 16 May 16/8 France.. might.. be interested.. in the development of a European delivery system. **1968** *Listener* 19 Dec. 813/1 After the war, the Soviet Union had two defence priorities: the construction of nuclear weapons and delivery systems. **1879** NOAD & PREECE *Electricity* 221 The *delivery tube conducts the gases into a graduated receiver. **1868** *Third Member for Birmingham* 22 Oct. (Advt.), William Keel's, *delivery van. **1906** *Westm. Gaz.* 22 Feb. 11/1 For the purpose of manufacturing in England motor-cars, motor-omnibuses, and delivery-vans. **1907** *Ibid.* 21 Nov. 4/3 Delivered free by express motor delivery-van. **1960** *Library Assoc. Rec.* Aug. 262/2 *Delivery van*, a vehicle intended and adapted primarily for the transport of books in boxes or trays, and providing no facilities for the selection of books. **1882** G. W. PECK *Peck's Fun* 88 Smith took them [*sc.* the goods] out to put them in the *delivery wagon. **1889** *Kansas Times & Star* 14 Dec., The sign painted on one side of the delivery wagon going to the various schools with supplies.

dell[1] (dɛl). [ME. *delle*, corresp. to MDu. and MLG. *delle*, mod.Du. *del*, MHG. and mod.G. *telle*:—WGer. **daljâ-* or **deljôn-* fem., deriv. of **dalo-*, OLG. *dal*, DALE; root meaning 'deep or low place.' Cf. also Goth. *ibdalja*, and OE. *æfdæl*, descent. (*Dell* bears nearly the same etymological relation to *dale*, that *den* does to *dean*.)]

†**1.** A deep hole, a pit. *Obs.*

1531 ELYOT *Gov.* II. ix, Curtius..enforsed his horse to lepe in to the dell or pitte. **1579** SPENSER *Sheph. Cal.* Mar. 51 Thilke same..Ewe..Fell headlong into a dell [*gloss*, a hole in the ground]. **1770** LANGHORNE *Plutarch* (1879) II. 889/1 He met with dells or other deep holes. **1783** AINSWORTH *Lat. Dict.* (Morell) 1, A dell, *fossa.*

2. A deep natural hollow or vale of no great extent, the sides usually clothed with trees or foliage.

c **1220** *Bestiary* 5 Bi wilc weie so he [ðe leun] wile To dele niðer wenden. *c* **1420** *Anturs of Arth.* i, On a day thay hom dyȝt into the depe dellus. *c* **1475** *Rauf Coilȝear* 17 The deip durandlie draif in mony deip dell. **1610** FLETCHER *Faithf. Shepherdess* II. ii, Yon same dell, O'ertopp'd with mourning cypress and sad yew Shall be my cabin. **1634** MILTON *Comus* 312 Every alley green, Dingle, or bushy dell. **1794** MRS. RADCLIFFE *Myst. Udolpho* xxviii, Disputing..on the situation of a dell where they meant to form an ambuscade. **1798** COLERIDGE *Fear in Solitude*, A green and silent spot, amid the hills, A small and silent dell! **1845** B'NESS BUNSEN in Hare *Life* II. iii. 86 Miss Gurney's cottage is in a sheltered dell, with woods on each side.

transf. **1812** SOUTHEY in *Omniana* I. 54 Young ladies would do well to remember, that if laughter displays dimples, it creates dells.

dell² (dɛl). *Rogues' Cant. arch.* A young girl (of the vagrant class); a wench.

1567 HARMAN *Caveat* 75 A Dell is a yonge wenche, able for generation, and not yet knowen..by the vpright man. **1621** B. JONSON *Gipsies Metamorph.* Wks. (Rtldg.) 624/1 Sweet doxies and dells, My Roses and Nells, Scarce out of your shells. **1630** TAYLOR (Water P.) *Wks.* II. 112/1 She's a Priests Lemman, and a Tinkers Pad, Or Dell, or Doxy, (though the names be bad). **1688** R. HOLMES *Armoury* II. iii. §68 *Dells*, trulls, dirty Drabs. **1834** H. AINSWORTH *Rookwood* III. v, 'Sharp as needles', said a dark-eyed dell.

dell(e, obs. form of DEAL.

‖**Della Crusca** (ˌdella ˈkruska). [It. *Accademia della Crusca*, lit. Academy of the bran or chaff.] The name of an Academy established at Florence in 1582, mainly with the object of sifting and purifying the Italian language; whence its name, and its emblem, a sieve.

The first edition of its Dictionary, the *Vocabolario degli Accademici della Crusca*, appeared in 1612, and the fourth, 1729–38, has long been considered as the standard authority for the Italian language. A new edition on more historical lines was begun in 1881.

Hence **Della-ˈCruscan** *a.*, of, pertaining to, or after the style of the Academy della Crusca, or its methods; also, applied to a school of English poetry, affecting an artifical style, started towards the end of the 18th c.; *sb.* a member of this Academy, or English school of poetry. Hence **Della-ˈCruscanism.**

One of the noted writers of this school was Mr. Robert Merry, who (having been elected a member of the Florentine Academy) adopted the signature of *Della Crusca*, whence the name was extended to the school as a whole.

[**1796** GIFFORD *Mæviad* Introd. 8-9 While the epidemic malady was spreading from fool to fool, Della Crusca [i.e. Merry] came over [from Italy], and immediately announced himself by a sonnet to Love..and from one end of the kingdom to the other, all was nonsense and Della Crusca.] **1815** W. H. IRELAND *Scribbleomania* 48 Mr. Pratt has certainly indulged too much in the flimsy Della Cruscan style. **1821** SHELLEY *Boat on Serchio* 67 In such transalpine Tuscan As would have killed a Della-Cruscan. **1857** TRENCH *Defic. Eng. Dicts.* 7 It is for those who use a language to sift the bran from the flour, to reject that and retain this. They are to be the true *Della Cruscans*. **1881** *Athenæum* 20 Aug. 230/1 The detestable Della Cruscanism which makes many new volumes of verse a positive offence.

Della Robbia (ˌdɛlə ˈrɒbɪə). [Name of a family of Italian painters and sculptors of the fifteenth century.] **a.** Used *attrib.* to designate the enamelled terra-cotta ware made by Luca Della Robbia and his successors. **b.** Any similar ware.

1787 P. BECKFORD *Lett. fr. Italy* (1805) I. 307 Some curious specimens in Terra della Robbia. **1850** *Art Jrnl.* 1 Oct. 313/2 Many fine specimens of the Della Robbia ware are yet to be found in the Florentine churches. **1878** *Lloyd's Weekly* 19 May 5/4 (Stanford), A mural tablet in Della Robbia ware. **1886** *Encycl. Brit.* XX. 589/2 Though Luca was not the inventor of the process [*sc.* the production of terra-cotta reliefs covered with enamel], yet his genius so improved and extended its application that it is not unnaturally known now as Della Robbia ware. **1961** M. BEADLE *These Ruins are Inhabited* (1963) i. 11 Della Robbia plaques.

delly (ˈdɛlɪ), *a. rare.* [f. DELL *sb.*¹ + -Y.] Abounding in dells.

1861 G. CALVERT *Univ. Restoration*, Delly woods remote.

delocalize (diːˈləʊkəlaɪz), *v.* [f. DE- II. 1 + LOCALIZE *v.*] *trans.* To detach or remove from its place or locality, or from local limitations.

1855 DE MORGAN in Graves *Life Sir W. R. Hamilton* (1889) III. 505 The *Morning Register* I could not use; you had better not delocalize it. **1867** LOWELL *Study Wind., Gt. Public Character*, We can have no St. Simons or Pepyses till we have a Paris or London to delocalize our gossip and give it historic breadth. **1870** R. B. D. MORIER *Rep. Land Tenure* (Parl. Papers) 208 It was necessary to find some means of effecting the transfers..without delocalizing the Land Register.

Hence **deˈlocalized** *ppl. a.*, **delocaliˈzation.**

1887 *Daily News* 13 Jan. 5/2 A reform in the direction of what may be called dockyard de-localisation.

delomorphic (diːləʊˈmɔːfɪk), *a. Anat.* [ad. G. *delomorph* (A. Rollett 1870, in *Centralbl. f. d. med. Wissenschaften* VIII. 338), f. Gr. δῆλος visible + μορφή form + -IC.] Having a definite form, *spec.* denoting certain cells of the gastric glands of the stomach. Also **deloˈmorphous** *a.*

1882 J. N. LANGLEY in *Jrnl. Physiology* III. 272 He [*sc.* Rollett] found that in winter the gastric glands of the bat contained no delomorphous or border-cells, but contained many in summer. **1890** BILLINGS *Med. Dict., Delomorphous cells*, large parietal cells of secretory portion of peptic glands. **1891** W. D. HALLIBURTON *Chem. Physiol. & Path.* 633 Cells of a different nature called parietal cells (Heidenhain), delomorphic cells (Rollett), or oxyntic cells (Langley).

‖**deloo** (dɪˈluː). [Native name in Dor language (in Sudan) for the gazelle.] A species of antelope, *Cephalolophus grimmia*, found in northern Africa, akin to the duykerbok of South Africa.

1861 J. PETHERICK *Egypt, etc.* 482 (Vocab. Dor language) Gazelle = diloo. **1874** G. SCHWEINFURTH *Heart of Africa* I. 244 The Deloo has only one pair of these glands.

delope (dɪˈləʊp), *v. Hist.* [Of uncertain orgin; cf. LOPE *v.* and Du. *loop* barrel of a gun: revived by Georgette Heyer (1902–74), English historical novelist.] *intr.* Of a duellist: to fire into the air, deliberately missing one's opponent.

1836 *Art of Duelling* 47 Sometimes a man is placed in a situation when he considers it his duty to delope, (or fire in the air). **1868** A. STEINMETZ *Romance of Duelling* I. vi. 113 (as 1836). **1935** G. HEYER *Regency Buck* x. 131 However much Mr. Farnaby might know himself to have been in the wrong, no dependence could be placed on his tacitly acknowledging it on the ground by *deloping*, or firing into the air. **1958** —— *Venetia* vi. 84 He added superb marksmanship to his other accomplishments, and might have put a bullet through me at double the range... In fact, he deloped—fired in the air! **1977** *Observer* 20 Nov. 29/3 Both he and his opponent, Martynov, seemed about to delope, to fire into the air, when he remarked loudly: 'I'm not going to fire at that fool.' Enraged, Martynov..fired. Lermontov fell. **1980** G. WHEELER *Cato's War* xi. 156 Twice I held my fire until they'd missed, then deloped—fired in the air—because the fools weren't worth the bullet.

deloul (dɛˈluːl). Also **delool**, **delul**, **dolool.** [colloq. Arab. *ḏelūl*, Arab. *ḏalūl*, lit. obedient.] A dromedary.

1830 J. L. BURCKHARDT *Notes on Bedouins* 260 What is called in Egypt and Africa *hedjein*, and in Arabia *deloul*, (both terms signifying the camels trained for riding). **1855** R. F. BURTON *El-Medinah* II. xx. 225 Bedouins bestriding naked-backed 'Deluls'. **1865** [see HYGEEN]. **1875** *Encycl. Brit.* II. 242/1 The 'hejeen', or dromedary, sometimes also called 'delool', or 'facile'.

delouse (diːˈlaʊs), *vb.* [f. DE- II. 2 + LOUSE *sb.*; cf. G. *entlausen.*] *trans.* To clear of lice. So **deˈlousing** *vbl. sb.* and *ppl. a.*

1919 *Library Assoc. Rec.* Sept. 6 The inhabitants of each barrack went in turn to the delousing station on the other side of the island, where the delousing process took three days. **1921** *Glasgow Herald* 9 July 7 The fact that there were no adequate means of delousing these men. **1929** A. FORBES *Hist. Army Ordn. Serv.* III. ii. 46 Disinfectors for de-lousing clothing. **1937** AUDEN in B. Dobrée *From Anne to Victoria* 92 The wearing of wigs helped to delouse the upper classes. **1946** G. MILLAR *Horned Pigeon* v. 65 We were going to the delousing-pen. **1964** R. CHURCH *Voyage Home* i. 7 The stench polluted..the holy air of the garden surrounding the temple. They sat delousing each other.

b. *transf.* and *fig.* To free from something unpleasant. *slang.*

1942 BERREY & VAN DEN BARK *Amer. Thes. Slang* §355/2 *Delouse*, to get rid of displeasing companions. **1943** *Times Weekly* 18 Aug. 2 The road itself had been 'deloused' of mines. **1946** BRICKHILL & NORTON *Escape to Danger* xx. 179 His squadron was 'delousing' Fortresses as they came back home out of Holland.

†**deˈloyalty.** *Obs. rare*⁻¹. [ad. F. *déloyauté* formerly *desloyaulté*: see DE- I. 6.] = DISLOYALTY.

1571 *Admon. Regent* 112 in *Sempill Ballads* (1872) 132 Sum hes..Lyfes losit for thair deloyaltie.

delph, var. of DELF.

Delphi (ˈdɛlfɪ). [The name of a town of ancient Greece (see DELPHIAN), the site of a sanctuary and oracle of Apollo.] Applied *attrib.* to a method of forecasting technological and other events by analysing the results of a questionnaire sent to a panel of experts, who are therefore not subject to the inhibiting factors of a round-table discussion.

1963 DALKEY & HELMER in *Managem. Sci.* Apr. 458 'Project Delphi' is the name for a study of the use of expert opinion that has been intermittently conducted at the RAND Corporation. The technique employed is called the Delphi method. **1966** O. HELMER *Social Technol.* I. 16 The Delphi technique has been used recently in a large-scale experiment in which several international panels of respondents were enlisted in an effort to arrive at long-range contingency forecasts of the state of the world twenty-five to fifty years hence. **1969** *Futures* Sept. 417 The Delphi forecasts were..more accurate in 13 cases. **1972** *Times* 9 Mar. 19 He intends to apply the so-called Delphi method in backing future productions—a kind of consensus forecasting technique in which panels of different experts are called in. **1983** *Leisure, Recreation & Tourism Abstr.* IV. no. 1872, An overview and guide to the major forecasting methods currently in use. Trend extrapolation, Delphi forecasting, structural forecasting and dynamic forecasting are reviewed.

Delphian (ˈdɛlfɪən). [f. *Delphi* place name + -AN.] Of or relating to Delphi, a town of ancient Greece on the slope of Mount Parnassus, and to the sanctuary and oracle of Apollo there; hence, of or relating to the Delphic Apollo; and *transf.* oracular, of the obscure and ambiguous nature of the responses of the Delphic oracle.

1625 HART *Anat. Ur.* I. ii. 25 [They] are nothing at all ashamed, by the vrine alone to deliuer their Delphian oracles concerning all diseases. **1631** WEEVER *Anc. Fun. Mon.* 48 This treasure..was a part of the Delphian riches. **1873** LOWELL *Among my Bks.* Ser. II. 322 His eyes had an inward Delphian look. **1887** BOWEN *Virg. Æneid* II. 113 We send, perplexed, to the Delphian fane, Counsel to ask of the god.

So **ˈDelphic**, †**ˈDelphical** *a.*

1599 MARSTON *Sco. Villanie* 169 Some of his new-minted Epithets (as Reall, Intrinsecate, Delphicke). *a* **1661** HOLYDAY *Juvenal* 174 The mathematical table was by the ancients called the Delphick table. **1742** YOUNG *Nt. Th.* vii. 595 Pride, like the Delphic priestess, with a swell, Rav'd nonsense, destin'd to be future sense. **1830** *Fraser's Mag.* I. 60 This delphic fury—this preternatural possession. **1879** *Daily News* 22 Nov. 5/5 This reads rather like a Delphic response. *a* **1603** T. CARTWRIGHT *Confut. Rhem. N.T.* (1618) 174 No riddles or Delphicall answers.

ˈdelphically, *adv.* [f. DELPHIC *a.*: see -ICALLY.] In a manner characteristic of the Delphic oracle; enigmatically, obscurely, prophetically.

1927 *Observer* 15 May 17/2 More Delphically it [*sc.* a report] adds that for industrial purposes the general strike can be serviceable only 'in the hands of men who know how and when to use it'. **1930** BLUNDEN *Leigh Hunt* viii. 106 Hunt had dipped into the future so delphically as to publish the hurried article announcing three 'Young Poets' who would do great things. **1960** *Guardian* 27 July 9/1 M. Nkayi merely read out a vague, almost oracular statement... He then fell delphically silent.

delphin (ˈdɛlfɪn), *sb.* and *a.* Forms: 4 **delfyn**, 5 **-fyne**, 5–6 **delphyn**, 6–7 **-phine**, 6– **delphin.** [a. L. *delphīn*, *delphīn-us*, a. Gr. δελφίν: cf. also It. *delfino*, Sp. *delfin*, Pg. *delfim*, Pr. *dalfin*, *dalphin*, OF. *dalphin*, *daulphin*, mod.F. *dauphin*, whence DOLPHIN, DAUPHIN.]

†**A.** *sb.* **1.** = DOLPHIN. *Obs.*

c **1300** *K. Alis.* 6576 A water..Tiger..Heo noriceth delfyns, and cokadrill. **1387** TREVISA *Higden* (Rolls) I. 41 Thar buth oft ytake delphyns, & se-calues. *c* **1440** *Promp. Parv.* 54 Brunswyne or delfyne..*delphinus.* **1555** EDEN *Decades* 131 Of a maruelous sence or memorie as are the elephant and the delphyn. **1633** P. FLETCHER *Pisc. Ecl.* VII. xiii. 47 The lively Delphins dance, and brisly Seales give eare.

†**b.** A drinking vessel of the shape of a dolphin. *Obs. rare*⁻¹.

1638 JUNIUS *Painting of Ancients* 162 Some artificiall drinking vessels made after the manner of a dolphin, were called delphines.

2. *Chem.* Short for *delphinin* (see -IN): A neutral fat found in the oil of several species of dolphin; called also *dolphin-fat* and *phocenin.*

1863–72 WATTS *Dict. Chem.* II. 309 Delphin is an oil very mobile at 17° C.

B. *adj.*

1. [attrib. use of L. *delphīnī* in phrase *ad usum Delphini* 'for the use of the Dauphin'.] Of or pertaining to the Dauphin of France, and to the edition of Latin classics, prepared 'for the use of the dauphin', son of Louis XIV.

[**1712** STEELE *Spect.* No. 330. ¶4 All the Boys in the School, but I, have the Classick Authors *in usum Delphini*, gilt and letter'd on the Back.] **1775** E. HARWOOD *Gr. & Rom. Classics* (1778) 222 Delphin Classics, quarto. **1802** DIBDIN *Introd. Classics* 10 *note*, One of the rarest of the Delphin editions. **1818** *Advt.* in *Valpy's Grk. Gram.* (ed. 6) 215 The best text will be used, and not the Delphin. **1877** *Globe Encycl.* II. 361 Valpy's Variorum Latin Classics..contain the Delphin notes and *Interpretatio.*

2. *Chem.* A bad form of DELPHINE, DELPHININE.

delphina, delphinate, *Chem.*: see DELPHININE, DELPHINIC.

†**ˈdelphinate**, obs. variant of DAUPHINATE.

1619 BRENT tr. *Sarpi's Counc. Trent* (1676) 474 Some new stirs, raised by the Hugonots in the Delphinate.

ˈdelphine, *a.* and *sb.*¹ [See DELPHIN.]

1. A variant of DELPHIN *a.* (Webster, 1828).
2. *Zool.* = DELPHININE *a.* (Webster, 1828).
3. *Chem.* = DELPHININE, *sb.*

delphine (ˈdɛlfɪn), *sb.*² Also **-in.** [ad. DELPHINIUM.] = DELPHINIUM b.

1909 *Cent. Dict.* Suppl. s.v. *Blue, Delphin blue*, a mordant coal-tar color of the oxazin type. **1923** *Daily Mail* 28 May 1 Shades: Lemon,..Champagne, Delphine.

delphiˈnestrian. *nonce-wd.* [f. L. *delphīn-us* dolphin, after *equestrian.*] A rider on a dolphin.

1820 L. HUNT *Indicator* No. 17 (1822) I. 134 To the great terror of the young delphinestrian.

delphinic (dɛl'fɪnɪk), *a.* [f. L. *delphīn-us* dolphin: see DELPHIN 2.] In ***delphinic acid***, an acid discovered by Chevreuil in dolphin-oil, and afterwards in the ripe berries of the Guelder-rose; it is identical with inactive valeric acid. A salt of it is a '**delphinate**.

delphinidin (dɛl'fɪnɪdɪn). *Chem.* [a. G. *delphinidin* (R. Willstätter 1914, in *Sitzungsber. preuss. Akad. d. Wissenschaften* 405), f. DELPHIN(IUM + -IDIN.] An anthocyanidin which is usu. isolated as the chloride, $C_{15}H_{11}O_7Cl$, and which combined as glycosides forms many plant pigments.

1914 *Chem. Abstr.* VIII. 3421 The anthocyan of larkspur (delphinin) on hydrolysis gave 2 mols. dextrose, 2 mols. *p*-$HOC_6H_4CO_2H$ and 1 mol. delphinidin, $C_{15}H_{11}O_7Cl$. **1937** *Thorpe's Dict. Appl. Chem.* (ed. 4) I. 381/2 The anthocyanins..fall into three groups represented by the pelargonidin, cyanidin, and delphinidin types. **1946** *Nature* 17 Aug. 240/1 A delphinidin flower pigment..in an acid cell sap is normally pink but is blue in the presence of excess aluminium. **1963** F. M. DEAN *Naturally Occurring Oxygen Ring Compounds* xiii. 399 It is now known that violanin is a delphinidin-3-rhamnoglucoside combined in some way with *p*-coumaric acid.

delphinine ('dɛlfɪnaɪn), *sb. Chem.* [f. Bot. L. *Delphīnium* the genus Larkspur.] A highly poisonous alkaloid obtained from the seeds of *Delphinium Staphesagria* or *Stavesacre*. Called also **del'phinia**, and formerly **'delphia**, **del,phina**, **'delphine**.

1830 LINDLEY *Nat. Syst. Bot.* 7 The chemical principle called Delphine. **1838** T. THOMSON *Chem. Org. Bodies* 246 Delphina was discovered, in 1819, by MM. Lassaigne and Feneulle in the seeds of the..*stavesacre*. **1840** HENRY *Elem. Chem.* II. 304 Of Delphia. **1863–72** WATTS *Dict. Chem.* II. 310 Delphinine produces nausea when taken internally. It is said to act on the nervous system, and is used as a remedy in chronic swellings of the glands. **1876** HARLEY *Mat. Med.* 769 The active properties are due to delphinia or delphinine.

'delphinine, *a.* Of the nature of a dolphin: in *Zool.*, of or pertaining to the *Delphininæ* or sub-family of Cetacea, containing the Dolphins and Porpoises.

†**'delphinite.** *Obs. Min.* [f. L. *Delphīnātus*, Dauphiné (f. *delphīnus*, Dauphin), where found.] An obsolete name of yellowish green Epidote.

1804 *Fourcroy's Chem.* II. 426 This is the..delphinite of Saussure.

del'phinity. A humorous nonce-wd. after *humanity*: Dolphin-kind, the nature of dolphins.

1860 LEVER *Day's Ride* x, History has never told that the dolphins..charmed by Orpheus were peculiar dolphins.. they were..fish..taken 'ex medio acervo' of delphinity.

‖**delphinium** (dɛl'fɪnɪəm). *Bot.* [Bot. Lat. *Delphīnium*, a. Gr. δελφίνιον larkspur (Dioscorides), dim. of δελφίν dolphin (so named from the form of the nectary).] **a.** A genus of plants, N.O. *Ranunculaceæ*, with handsome flowers of irregular form, comprising the common larkspur and many other species. The name is in ordinary horticultural use for the cultivated species and varieties.

1664 EVELYN *Kal. Hort.* (1729) 200 Sow divers Annuals.. as double marigold, Digitalis, Delphinium. **1882** *The Garden* 3 June 384/1 Another fine group is formed by a row of tall-growing Delphiniums..in front of Clematises and Roses.

b. A deep blue like that of the indigo-blue delphinium.

1923 *Daily Mail* 23 Apr. 6 Exclusive colourings, including ..Delphinium, Saxe. **1927** *Observer* 9 Oct. 21 Nut Brown, Cocoa, Delphinium. **1970** *Guardian* 5 May 7/1 Mini dress.. coffee, apple, rose or delphinium print on green. **1971** M. LEE *Dying for Fun* xlvii. 220 Pretty girls dressed in pastiche rags and delphinium-blue wellington boots.

'delphinoid, *a.* and *sb. Zool.* [ad. Gr. δελφινοειδής like a dolphin, f. δελφίν dolphin.]

A. *adj.* Like or related to a dolphin; belonging to the *Delphinoidea*, a division of the Cetacea, which includes the dolphins and seals.

In mod. Dicts.

B. *sb.* A member of the *Delphinoidea*.

delphinoidine (dɛlfɪ'nɔɪdaɪn). *Chem.* [f. as DELPHININE + -OID.] An amorphous alkaloid obtained from the same source as delphinine.

1883 in *Syd. Soc. Lex.*

‖**Delphinus** (dɛl'faɪnəs). The Latin word for 'dolphin': in *Zool.*, the name of the cetacean genus containing the Dolphin and its co-species; in *Astron.*, one of the ancient constellations of the northern hemisphere, figured as a dolphin.

a **1672** WILLUGHBY *Ichthyogr.* (1686) Tab. A j, Delphinus. **1835–6** TODD *Cycl. Anat.* I. 566/2 The Delphini..have also a narrow rostrum.

'delphisine. *Chem.* [f. *delphine*, DELPHININE, by insertion of *-is-* repr. Gr. ἴσ-ος equal.] An alkaloid akin to delphinoidine, obtained from the same source, in warty crystals. Also called *Delphisia*.

1883 in *Syd. Soc. Lex.*

delta ('dɛltə). [Gr. δέλτα (ad. Phœnician *daleth*), name of the fourth letter of the Greek alphabet; also the land at the mouth of the Nile (Herod.), the Indus (Strabo), etc.]

1. The name of the fourth letter of the Greek alphabet, having the form of a triangle (Δ), and the power of D.

c **1400** MAUNDEV. (1839) iii. 20 ȝif ȝee wil wite of here A, B, C..thei clepen hem..α Alpha..δ Deltha..ω Omega. **1601** HOLLAND *Pliny* I. 96 Many haue called Ægypt by the name of the Greeke letter Delta. **1860** T. A. G. BALFOUR *Typ. Char. Nature* 118 In Botany the symbol of a perennial plant is a Delta.

b. An examiner's fourth-class mark (often the lowest grading category). Also *transf.*, applied to a person.

1911 T. H. WARREN *Oxford & Poetry in 1911* 19 Swinburne estimated in superlatives or the opposite. His marks were all α+ or δ−. **1932** A. HUXLEY *Brave New World* ii. 24 Why go to the trouble of making it psychologically impossible for Deltas to like flowers? **1958** [see BETA 3].

2. a. *Hist.* (***The Delta.***) The tract of alluvial land enclosed and traversed by the diverging mouths of the Nile; so called from the triangular figure of the tract enclosed between the two main branches and the coast-line.

1555 EDEN *Decades* 250 The goulfe of Arabie..from whense they determyned to brynge a nauigable trench vnto the ryuer of Nilus, where as is the fyrst Delta. **1601** HOLLAND *Pliny* I. 67 As in Ægypt Nilus maketh that which they call Delta. **1636** SIR H. BLOUNT *Voy. Levant* (1637) 57, I enquired of the Delta, and the Niles seven streames. **1732** LEDIARD *Sethos* II. IX. 354 The most convenient port of the Delta. **1875** JOWETT *Plato* (ed. 2) III. 529 At the head of the Egyptian Delta, where the river Nile divides.

b. *Geog.* The more or less triangular tract of alluvial land formed at the mouth of a river, and enclosed or traversed by its diverging branches.

1790 GIBBON *Misc. Wks.* (1814) III. 453 The triangular island or delta of Mesola, at the mouth of the Po. **1794** SULLIVAN *View Nat.* I. 94 The earthy matter, borne down by the floods, is..thrown back upon the shores, into bays and creeks, and into the mouths of rivers, where it forms deltas. **1830** LYELL *Princ. Geol.* I. 13 Islands have become connected with the main land by the growth of deltas and new deposits. **1836** MARRYAT *Olla Podr.* xxvi, The two rivers..enclose a large delta of land. **1893** *Nation* 16 Feb. 125/1 The villages are situated on small deltas, built by torrential streams that descend from the neighboring hills.

3. a. Any triangular space or figure; †the constellation of the Triangle.

1638 C. ALEYN *Hist. Hen. VII*, 134 But if the nobler souls, as they maintein'd, Were fixed in the body of some starre, Then Edwards murder'd sonnes and Warwickes are In those call'd Delta, of Triangle fashion.

b. *Electr.* In three-phase electrical equipment, the arrangement of the three windings in series in a manner represented by a triangle, each of the three wires of the circuit being connected to a junction of two windings; chiefly used *attrib.*, as **delta connection**.

1902 *Encycl. Brit.* XXVII. 582/2 Any three-phase winding may be changed over from the star to the delta connection. *Ibid.* 592/1 If the three coils are closed upon themselves in a mesh or *delta* fashion. **1943** *Gloss. Terms Electr. Engin.* (*B.S.I.*) 19 *Delta connection*, a method of connection, in three-phase A.C. working, in which three conductors or windings are so connected that they may be represented diagrammatically by a triangle.

4. *attrib.* and *Comb.*, as ***delta-formation***, ***-land***; **delta connection** (see above); hence ***delta-connected*** adj.; **delta frequency**, **rhythm**, **wave**, the most slowly varying of the 'brain waves' recorded by an electroencephalograph, having a frequency of less than about three per second and normally present only during deep sleep; **delta-metal**, an alloy of copper, zinc, and iron introduced about 1883, and named in allusion to its *three* constituents; **delta plain**, the flat area of a delta; **delta plateau**, a raised delta plain; **delta-rays** or ***δ-rays***, rays of low penetrating power consisting of slow electrons released by the passage of ionizing particles such as alpha-rays through matter; **delta wing**, a type of triangular swept-back aeroplane wing; so **delta-winged** *a.*, descriptive of aircraft with this type of wing.

1964 R. F. FICCHI *Electrical Interference* x. 201 If it is necessary to establish a neutral with a *delta-connected secondary, grounding transformers are used to form a neutral solidly connected to ground. **1862** DANA *Man. Geol.* II. 647 Stratification of *delta deposits. **1858** GEIKIE *Hist. Boulder* ix. 172 The process of *delta-formation remains essentially the same, both in lakes and at the sea. **1961** *Lancet* 16 Sept. 631/1 Low-amplitude slow activity much of it of *delta frequency, compatible with a delirium. **1806** FORSYTH *Beauties Scotl.* IV. 225 The Carse..considered as the finest sort of alluvial or *delta land. **1883** *Engineer* 23 Feb. 140 Mr. Alexander Dick [has] succeeded in producing an alloy which he calls '*Delta metal'. **1884** *Times* 14 June 8 'Delta metal'..is an alloy of copper, zinc, and iron..A steam launch..has..been built entirely of this metal [by Mr. A. Dick]. **1890** W. M. DAVIS in *Bull. Geol. Soc. America* I. 200 Glacial Sand Plains... A corollary of the rapid growth of the *delta plains compared to the retreat of the ice is, that the growth of the delta plains was a local..spasmodic operation. **1892** —— in *Proc. Boston Soc. Nat. Hist.* XXV. 489 Sand plateaus as deltas, marginal to the decaying ice sheet... The size of the delta would depend on the activity of the feeding stream from the ice, and on..the gravel ridges or eskers so often extending backward from the head of the *delta plateau. **1908** RUTHERFORD & GEIGER in *Proc. R. Soc.* A. LXXXI. 163 It is well known that the α-particles, in their passage through matter, liberate a large number of slow-velocity electrons, or *δ-rays, as they have been termed by J. J. Thomson. **1966** *McGraw-Hill Encycl. Sci. & Technol.* I. 267/2 An appreciable fraction, roughly one-half, of the energy lost by α-rays appears as δ-rays. **1938** *Jrnl. Neurol. & Psychiatry* I. 383 A similar *delta rhythm appears locally when only a part of the cortex is affected. **1943** *Electronic Engin.* XV. 520 A waveform of much lower frequency which is characteristic of a cerebral tumour. The name delta rhythm has been given to this wave which usually has a frequency of 3 c/s or lower. **1936** W. GREY WALTER in *Lancet* 8 Aug. 308/1 It is suggested that..these slow waves from the neighbourhood of tumours be called '*δ waves' until their true nature be discovered. **1957** DORLAND *Med. Dict.* (ed. 23) 1540/2 *Delta waves*, waves in the electroencephalogram which have a frequency of ½ to 3 per second. **1968** *Brit. Med. Bull.* XXIV. 202/1 The background consists of random slow activity which is symmetrical and there are some delta waves mixed with the alpha rhythm. **1946** *Jrnl. Brit. Interplan. Soc.* VI. 94 The first effect..can..be reduced but not eliminated by the use of a very low aspect-ratio triangular wing platform (the so-called '*Delta' wing). **1951** *Engineering* 20 Apr. 474/3 Type of..swept-back 'delta'-wing experimental aircraft. **1970** *Flight* (*Life Science Libr.*) 181 The delta wing of the F-106 Delta Dart..combines the advantages of sweepback with those of a thin wing, and is structurally stronger and easier to build than either. **1950** *Nat. Geogr. Mag.* Sept. 282/2 Among the latest to be tested against Father Time and the laws of aerodynamics is the new Air Force *delta-winged plane. **1954** *Economist* 11 Sept. Suppl. 2/1 This year.. Gloster Aircraft were able to put five delta-winged Javelins in the air at once.

deltafi'cation. [f. DELTA + -FICATION.] The formation of a delta at the mouth of a river.

1864 in WEBSTER.

deltaic (dɛl'teɪɪk), *a.* [mod. f. Gr. δέλτα + -IC: cf. *algebraic*.] Of, pertaining to, or forming a delta; of the nature of a delta.

1846 WORCESTER cites *Edin. Rev.* **1878** C. J. ANDERSON in *Macm. Mag.* Jan. 251/2 A deltaic tract of country traversed by a number of arms of the Cauvery. **1882** SIR R. TEMPLE in *Standard* 26 Aug. 3/3 The deltaic population of the Lower Ganges.

†**Deltan**, *a. Obs. rare*⁻¹. [f. DELTA + -AN: cf. *Roman*.] Of the Delta of Egypt.

1600 TOURNEUR *Trans. Metamorph.* lxv. Wks. 1878 II. 211 Throughout the Deltan soile.

deltation (dɛl'teɪʃən). [mod. f. DELTA.] Formation of a delta at the mouth of a river.

1886 tr. *Pelleschi's Argentine Rep.* 185 Effects produced by the deltation or deposition..of sediment from the rivers of the Gran Chaco.

deltic ('dɛltɪk), *a. rare.* [f. DELTA + -IC: cf. *Indic*.] = DELTAIC.

1865 PAGE *Geol. Terms* 171 *Deltic*, of or belonging to a delta. **1876** —— *Adv. Text-bk. Geol.* xiv. 240 Their plants seem to have grown in marshes and deltic jungles.

‖**deltidium** (dɛl'tɪdɪəm). *Conch.* [mod.L. dim. of Gr. δέλτα DELTA, in reference to its shape. (Cf. Gr. κυνίδιον little dog, from κυν-.)] The triangular space, usually covered in by a horny shell or operculum, between the beak and the hinge of brachiopod shells.

1851 RICHARDSON *Geol.* viii. (1855) 232 The form and structure of the area and deltidium afford good generic characters. **1888** ROLLESTON & JACKSON *Anim. Life* 693 The groove is usually converted into a foramen by a 'deltidium' which consists of two calcareous pieces.

deltiology (dɛltɪ'ɒlədʒɪ). [f. Gr. δελτίο-ν, dim. of δέλτος writing tablet + -OLOGY.] The hobby of collecting postcards. Hence **delti'ologist**, one who collects postcards.

1947 *N.Y. Times* 22 June VI. 20/2 (*heading*) The article on postcards..omits..the current passion for collecting postcards (now called by serious followers of the hobby 'deltiology'). **1959** BUTLAND & WESTWOOD *Picture Post Cards*, In recent years very few attempts have been made to cater for the Deltiologists. **1964** *Dalesman* Dec. 710/2 How many readers know the meaning of 'deltiology'? Certainly I was in the dark about it until a subscriber..wrote to tell me all about her hobby, which is postcard collecting. **1970** *N.Y. Times Encycl. Alm.* 477/2 *Deltiologist*, a person whose hobby is collecting picture postcards.

deltohedron (dɛltəʊ'hi:drən). *Crystall.* [f. δελτο-, taken as combining form of next + -HEDRON.]

1879 ROSSITER *Dict. Sci. Terms*, *Deltohedron*, a solid figure the surface of which is formed by twenty-four deltoids.

deltoid ('dɛltɔɪd), *a.* (*sb.*) [mod. a. Gr. δελτοειδής delta-shaped, triangular: see -OID. So F. *deltoide* (in Paré, 16th c.); mod.L. *deltoides* (Linnæus), and *deltoideus*.]

1. Resembling the Greek letter Δ in shape; triangular; *esp.* in *Bot.*, of a leaf; also triangular in section, as the leaf of *Mesembryanthemum deltoideum*; also in comb., as ***deltoid-ovate***, of an ovate outline but somewhat deltoid; so ***deltoid-hastate***, etc.

1753 CHAMBERS *Cycl. Supp.* s.v. *Leaf*, Deltoide Leaf. 1793 MARTYN *Lang. Bot.* s.v., A leaf of the common Black Poplar.. is given as an instance of a deltoid leaf in Linnæus's specific characters. 1845 LINDLEY *Sch. Bot.* vii. (1858) 122 Leaves ovate, acute, somewhat deltoid. 1870 HOOKER *Stud. Flora* 240 *Cicendia*.. calyx campanulate, teeth deltoid.

b. ***deltoid muscle*** (Anat.): the large muscle of triangular shape which forms the prominence of the shoulder; it serves to raise the arm and draw it from the body. ***deltoid ligament***: see quot. 1835.

1741 MONRO *Anat.* (ed. 3) 237 Some Part of the deltoid Muscle. 1835-6 TODD *Cycl. Anat.* I. 152 The *internal tibio-tarsal ligament*, is also called the *internal lateral*, and by Weithecht, the *deltoid* ligament. 1877 ROSENTHAL *Muscles & Nerves* 92 The elevator of the upper arm, which on account of its triangular shape is called the deltoid muscle.

c. *Entom.* ***deltoid moth***: a moth which in repose spreads its wings over the back in a triangular form; also *absol.*

1859 H. T. STAINTON *Manual Brit. Butterflies & Moths* II. 125 *Deltoides*, these insects form a sort of connecting group between the Noctuæ and the true Pyralidæ.. Any one who has seen that insect in repose will recognize the resemblance in the form of the wings to the Greek Delta, Δ, whence the name. 1869 E. NEWMAN *Brit. Moths* Pref. 3 It was intended to include the Deltoids, Pyrales, Veneers, and Plumes.

2. Of the nature of the delta of a river.

1837 *Penny Cycl.* VIII. 376/1 The whole of Holland is a formation of deltoid islands, created by the anastomosing branches of the Rhine, the Meuse, and the Scheldt. The deltoid form of the mouths of the Petchora is no longer recognizable in the group of islands at its embouchure. 1861 DARWIN in *Life & Lett.* (1887) II. 364 The French superficial deposits are deltoid and semi-marine.

B. *sb.* **1.** The deltoid muscle. Also in L. form *deltoides, deltoīdeus.*

[1681 tr. *Willis' Rem. Med. Wks.* Vocab., Deltoides, a muscle in the top of the arm, having the figure of a Delta, the Greek D.] 1758 J. S. *Le Dran's Observ. Surg.* (1771) 149 The Deltoid was elevated by it and much tumified. 1860 O. W. HOLMES *Elsie V.* iii. (1891) 32 The deltoid, which caps the shoulder like an epaulette.

attrib. 1881 MIVART *Cat* 91 External to this is a slightly roughened and elevated tract called the deltoid ridge.

2. (See quot.)

1879 ROSSITER *Dict. Sci. Terms, Deltoid*, a four-sided figure formed of two unequal isosceles triangles on opposite sides of a common base.

3. A deltoid moth: see A. 1 c.

deltoidal (dɛlˈtɔɪdəl), *a.* [f. prec. + -AL[1].]

a. Pertaining to the delta of a river. **b.** = DELTOID *a.* 1. **c.** Of the shape of a DELTOID (*sb.* 2).

1837 *Penny Cycl.* VIII. 375/2 The alluvial tract is frequently intersected by a great many deltoidal branches. 1873 W. K. SULLIVAN *O'Curry's Anc. Irish* I. Introd. 505 Square, rectangular or deltoidal instruments of the harp kind.

deltoideo-, combining form of mod.L. *deltoīdeus* adj., used to express 'with deltoid tendency', 'deltoid and ——', as ***deltoideo-lunate***.

1850 DANA *Geol.* App. i. 707 Aperture deltoideo-lunate, a little dilated either side.

‖**delubrum** (dɪˈl(j)uːbrəm). [L., f. *dēlu-ĕre* to wash off, cleanse, with instrumental suffix -BRUM.]

1. A temple, shrine, or sanctuary.

2. *Eccl. Arch.* **a.** A church furnished with a font. **b.** A font.

1665 SIR T. HERBERT *Trav.* (1677) 164 The Ethnique Romans.. at the entrance into their Temples had tanks or like places to wash in: *Delubra* they called them. 1698 FRYER *Acc. E. India & P.* 265 Attributing Divine Honour to the Fire, maintaining it always alive in the Delubriums, or Places set apart for their Worship.

†**deˈluce, deˈlys.** *Obs.* A shortening of *flower deluce*, a former anglicized form of F. *fleur de lis* (OF. *lys*), i.e. lily-flower, the ensign of the Bourbons. Also ***deluce flower***.

c 1450 LONELICH *Grail* xliii. 253 Owt of the delys, A rose Owt sprang Of Riht gret pris. 1586 W. WEBBE *Eng. Poetrie* (Arb.) 84 Kyngcuppe and Lillies.. and the deluce flowre. 1594 PLAT *Jewell-ho.* III. 44 The purple part of the leafe of the flower deluce.

delucidate, -itate, obs. ff. DILUCIDATE.

deludable (dɪˈl(j)uːdəb(ə)l), *a.* [f. DELUDE *v.* + -ABLE.] Capable of being deluded.

1646 SIR T. BROWNE *Pseud. Ep.* I. ii, He is not so ready to deceive himself, as to falsifie unto him whose Cognition is no way deludable.

delude (dɪˈl(j)uːd), *v.* [ad. L. *dēlūd-ĕre* to play false, mock, deceive, f. DE- I. 4 + *lūdere* to play. (Cf. rare obs. F. *deluder*, 1402 in Godef.)]

†**1.** *trans.* To play with (any one) to his injury or frustration, under pretence of acting seriously; to mock, *esp.* in hopes, expectations, or purposes; to cheat or disappoint the hopes of. *Obs.*

1494 FABYAN *Chron.* VII. ccxxxiv. 270 The Cristen prynces seinge that they were thus deluded. 1543 in W. H. Turner *Select. Rec. Oxford* 170 A man that.. hadde deluded wyth delayes the.. commissioners. 1596 NASHE *Saffron Walden* 35 There is no Husbandman but tills and sowes in hope of a good crop, though manie times he is deluded with a bad Haruest. 1630 DEKKER *2nd Pt. Honest Wh.* Wks. 1873 II. 138 Yet sure i'th end he'll delude all my hopes. 1671 MILTON *Samson* 396 Thrice I deluded her, and turned to sport Her importunity. 1697 DRYDEN *Virg. Past.* VI. 30 For by the fraudful God deluded long, They now resolve to have their promis'd Song.

b. To disappoint or deprive *of* by fraud or deceit; to defraud *of*.

1493 *Petronilla* 99 Of his purpos Flaccus was deludyd. *c* 1585 *Faire Em* III. 904 Whose ransom.. I am deluded of by this escape. 1586 A. DAY *Eng. Secretary* II. (1625) 88 Yong men.. cauteleously.. deluded of that, whereunto both their parents and birth do commend them. 1594 MARLOWE & NASHE *Dido* v. Wks. (Rtldg.) 272/2 Thou for some petty gift hast let him go, And I am thus deluded of my boy.

†**2.** To deride, mock, laugh at. *Obs. rare.*

1526 *Pilgr. Perf.* (W. de W. 153) 300 b, Thus beaten and deluded Annas sent the bounde to Cayphas. 1586 [cf. DELUDER].

3. To befool the mind or judgement of, so as to cause what is false to be accepted as true; to bring by deceit into a false opinion or belief; to cheat, deceive, beguile; to impose upon with false impressions or notions.

c 1450 HENRYSON *Compl. Creseide* (R.), The idol of a thing in case may be So depe emprinted in the fantasie That it deludeth the wittes outwardly. 1526 TINDALE *Acts* viii. 11 With Sorcery he had deluded their wittes. 1532 FRITH *Mirror* (1829) 272 God.. cannot be deluded, although the world may be blinded. 1687 T. BROWN *Saints in Uproar* Wks. 1730 I. 81 They are seven as arrant imposters as ever deluded the credulous world. 1745 *De Foe's Eng. Tradesman* I. xxii. 211 The world are taken in, deluded, and imposed upon by outside and tinsel. 1853 BRIGHT *Sp. India* 3 June, A system which obscured responsibility and deluded public opinion.

b. with extension (*on, to, into*).

a 1643 W. CARTWRIGHT *Lady-Errant* IV. i, Go, and delude them on. 1719 DE FOE *Crusoe* (1840) I. xv. 259 The many stratagems he made use of, to delude mankind to their ruin. 1875 JOWETT *Plato* (ed. 2) V. 512 Let no one be deluded by poets.. into a mistaken belief of such things.

†**4.** To frustrate the aim or purpose of; to elude, evade. *Obs.*

1536 *Act 28 Hen. VIII*, c. 5 Diuers.. haue.. practised to defraude and delude the sayd.. statutes. 1600 *Hosp. Inc. Fooles* 58 Thus did he delude the last blow of this despitefull Foole. 1601 HOLLAND *Pliny* x. 1, There was a starting hole found to delude and escape the meaning thereof. 1638 SIR T. HERBERT *Trav.* (ed. 2) 11 The 7. of June she againe deluded us, after two houres chase. 1647 N. BACON *Disc. Govt. Eng.* I. xli. (1739) 66 The entailing of Estates.. was very ancient, although by corrupt custom it was deluded. 1680 DRYDEN *Ovid's Ep.* vii. (R.), Tyber now thou seek'st.. Yet it deludes thy search.

†**5.** To beguile (time). *Obs.*

1615 *Val. Welshm.* (1663) B ij b, I need not here delude The precious time. 1660 R. COKE *Power & Subj.* Pref. 1 In entertaining worldly pleasures, thereby to delude, and spend their time.

deluded (dɪˈl(j)uːdɪd), *ppl. a.* [f. prec. + -ED.] Deceived by mocking prospects, beguiled, misled: see the verb.

a 1628 SIR J. BEAUMONT *Transfig. Our Lord* in Farr *S.P. James I* (1848) 145 To weane, deluded mindes From fond delight. 1710 NORRIS *Chr. Prud.* iv. 153 With disappointment and a deluded expectation. 1781 GIBBON *Decl. & F.* III. 237 Their deluded votaries.

Hence **deˈludedly** *adv.*

1830 *Blackw. Mag.* XXVIII. 364 So deludedly stupid as to believe himself Apollo.

deluder (dɪˈl(j)uːdə(r)). [f. DELUDE *v.* + -ER.] One who deludes.

(In quot. 1586, one who mocks or derides.)

1586 A. DAY *Eng. Secretary* II. (1625) 122 That he be no ordinary scoffer, or frivolous deluder of other mens speeches, gestures, reasons, or conditions. 1629 PRYNNE (*title*), God no Impostor nor Deluder. 1713 ROWE *Jane Shore* v, Thou soft deluder, Thou beauteous witch. 1725 POPE *Odyss.* XII. 221 Thus the sweet deluders tune the song. 1840 BARHAM *Ingol. Leg.*, *Look at Clock*, Gin's but a snare of Old Nick the deluder.

deluding (dɪˈl(j)uːdɪŋ), *vbl. sb.* [-ING[1].] The action of the verb DELUDE: cheating.

1645 MILTON *Tetrach.* (1851) 184 No Covnant.. intended to the good of both parties, can hold to the deluding or making miserable of them both. *a* 1650 BR. PRIDEAUX *Euch.* 228 (T.) Annanias and Sapphira's dainty deludings with a smooth lie.

deˈluding, *ppl. a.* [-ING[2].] That deludes.

1596 SHAKS. *Tam. Shr.* IV. iii. 31 Thou false deluding slaue, That feed'st me with the uerie name of meate. 1649 MILTON *Eikon.* xxviii, Not as a deluding ceremony, but as a real condition. 1727 DYER *Grongar Hill* 120 Ey'd thro' hope's deluding glass.

Hence **deˈludingly** *adv.*

1641 'SMECTYMNUUS' *Vind. Answ.* § 5. 63 To performe the contrary to what hee hath deludingly promised.

deluge (ˈdɛljuːdʒ), *sb.* Also 4-5 (7) diluge, 6 diludge, (7 dyluge). [a. F. *déluge* (12th c. in Hatzf.), early ad. L. *dīluvium* (see DILUVIUM), modified after the example of words of popular formation (Hatzf.). OF. forms nearer to the L. were *deluve, delouve, diluve*: cf. Pr. *diluvi*, Sp. and It. *diluvio*. An earlier ME. form was DILUVY. In the 15th c. it rimed with *huge*.]

1. A great flood or overflowing of water, a destructive inundation. (Often used hyperbolically, e.g. of a heavy fall of rain.)

c 1374 CHAUCER *Boeth.* II. vi. 51 Ne no deluge ne doþ so cruel harmes. *c* 1393 —— *Scogan* 14 Thow cawsest this diluge [*v.r.* deluuye] of pestilence. 1601 HOLLAND *Pliny* I. 39 There happen, together with earthquakes, deluges also, and inundations of the sea. 1634 SIR T. HERBERT *Trav.* 54 A violent storme of raine.. caused such a sudden Deluge.. that a Carravan of two thousand camels perisht. 1720 GAY *Poems* (1745) I. 139 When the bursting clouds a deluge pour. 1748 F. SMITH *Voy. Disc. N.-W. Pass.* I. 121 A Harbour.. where they might go free from the Ice and the Spring Deluge, which sometimes happens.. by the Suddenness of the Thaw. 1855 MOTLEY *Dutch Rep.* (1861) II. 270 The memorable deluge of the thirteenth century out of which the Zuyder Zee was born. 1878 HUXLEY *Physiogr.* 131 Where the rain comes down as a deluge.

2. *spec.* The great Flood in the time of Noah (also called ***the general*** or ***universal deluge***).

c 1386 CHAUCER *Pars. T.* ¶765 God dreynte al the world at the diluge [*v.r.* diluve]. 1483 CAXTON *G. de la Tour* D viij, The deluge or gaderyng of waters in the dayes of Noe. 1559 W. CUNNINGHAM *Cosmogr. Glasse* 194 Jaffa, a port whiche was builded before the diludge. 1635 N. CARPENTER *Geog. Del.* II. i. 8 In the generall deluge all mankinde suffered for their sinnes a plague of waters. 1725 DE FOE *Voy. round World* (1840) 289 From the days of the general deluge. 1880 OUIDA *Moths* I. 46 It must have been worn at the deluge.

3. *fig.* and *transf.*

c 1430 LYDG. *Min. Poems* 251 (Mätz.) That worldly wawes with there mortal deluge Ne drowne me nat. 1555 EDEN *Decades* Pref. to Rdr. (Arb.) 51 Drowned in the deluge of erroure. 1632 LITHGOW *Trav.* x. 446 The general deluge of the Gothes, Hunnes and Vandales. 1667 MILTON *P.L.* I. 68 A fiery Deluge, fed With ever-burning Sulphur unconsum'd. 1760-72 tr. *Juan & Ulloa's Voy.* (ed. 3) I. 252 The whole city and.. country were often, as it were, buried under a deluge of ashes. 1872 BLACK *Adv. Phaeton* xxvi. 359 When the waters of this deluge of rhetoric had abated.

†**4.** The inundation (*of*). Also *fig. Obs.*

1601 HOLLAND *Pliny* I. 65 In the generall deluge of the countrey by raine they only remained aliue. 1631 WEEVER *Anc. Fun. Mon.* 768 Demolished long before the violent deluge of such buildings, which happened in the raigne of King Henry the eight.

deluge (ˈdɛljuːdʒ), *v.* [f. the sb.: cf. *to flood.*]

1. *trans.* To flow or pour over (a surface) in a deluge; to flood, inundate; also *absol.* (Often used hyperbolically.)

1649 MONTROSE *Epit. Chas. I* in *Bp. Guthrie's Mem.* (1702) 255, I 'de weep the World in such a Strain, As it should deluge once again. 1715-20 POPE *Iliad* XXI. 383 At every step, before Achilles stood The crimson surge, and delug'd him with blood. 1727 DE FOE *Syst. Magic* I. iv. (1840) 104 Sufficient to deluge the World, and drown Mankind. 1787 *Generous Attachment* III. 82 The heavens now deluged in good earnest. 1790 MAD. D'ARBLAY *Diary* Aug., He left me neither more nor less than deluged in tears. 1869 PHILLIPS *Vesuv.* iii. 48 Hot water from the mountain deluged the neighbourhood.

2. *fig.* and *transf.*

1654 E. COKE *Logick* (1657) A vij b, Truths that before deluged you, will take you now but up to the Ancles. 1732 POPE *Ep. Bathurst* 137 At length Corruption, like a gen'ral flood.. Shall deluge all. 1833 HT. MARTINEAU *Loom & Lugger* I. i. 2 The market was deluged with smuggled silks. 1850 W. IRVING *Goldsmith* xxi. 227 The kingdom was deluged with pamphlets.

Hence **ˈdeluged** *ppl. a.*; **ˈdeluger**, one who deluges (*nonce-wd.*); **ˈdeluging** *vbl. sb.* and *ppl. a.*

1712 BLACKMORE (J.), The delug'd earth. 1824 MISS MITFORD *Village* Ser. I. (1863) 177 The sky promised a series of deluging showers. 1834 *Georgian Era* IV. 463/2 He vented his reproaches upon the deluger. 1887 BOWEN *Virg. Æneid* III. 625 The deluged threshold in gore Ran. 1890 W. C. RUSSELL *Ocean Trag.* II. xxi. 183 These darkening, glimmering, green delugings.

deluginous (dɛˈljuːdʒɪnəs), *a.* [Fantastically f. DELUGE after *ferruginous, salsuginous.*] Like a deluge.

1835 G. DARLEY *Nepenthe* II. 60 He.. enthralls Earth in deluginous ocean. 1923 *Glasgow Herald* 15 Nov. 8 The deluginous flooding of its markets. 1924 *Ibid.* 15 Apr. 8 When the Great War broke deluginous over the world.

†**deˈlumbate**, *v. Obs. rare.* [f. ppl. stem of L. *dēlumbāre* to lame in the loin, f. DE- I. 6 + *lumbus* loin, flank.] *trans.* To lame, maim, emasculate.

1609 BP. W. BARLOW *Answ. Nameless Cath.* 316 His cutting of Fathers when hee cites them for his aduantage; delumbating the positions of Protestants to make their doctrine odious. 1623 COCKERAM, *Delumbate*, to beate, weaken, to breake. 1624 BP. MOUNTAGU *Gagg* Pref. 18 Tertullian, Basil, Chrysostome.. we neither geld nor delumbate for speaking too plaine nor use them like you.

‖**delundung** (ˈdɛləndʌŋ). Also **delendung.** [Native Javanese name.] The weasel-cat of Java and Malacca, belonging to the civet family.

1840 tr. *Cuvier's Anim. Kingd.* 92 Delundung. A rare Javanese animal, of slender form, very handsomely streaked and spotted. Allied to the Genets.

†**deˈlusible**, *a. Obs. rare.* [f. L. *dēlūs-*, ppl. stem of *dēlūdĕre* to DELUDE: see -BLE.] Capable of being deluded; deludable.

1665 BOYLE *Occas. Refl.* I. viii. (1845) 93 After they have been admitted by the more delusible faculty we call Fancy, I make them pass the severer scrutiny of Reason.

delusion (dɪˈl(j)uːʒən). Also 5 delucion. [ad. L. *dēlūsion-em*, n. of action from *dēlūdĕre* to DELUDE: see -ION[1]. (Cf. rare obs. F. *delusion*, 16th c. in Godef.)] The action of deluding; the condition of being deluded.

†**1.** The action of befooling, mocking, or cheating a person in his expectations; the fact of being so cheated or mocked. *Obs.*

1494 FABYAN *Chron.* VII. 438 Whan kyng Charlys was assertaynyd of this delusyon, he was greuouslye dyscontentyd agayne the Gascoynes. **1542** HEN. VIII *Declar. Scots* 197 We haue paciently suffred many delusions, and notably the laste yere, when we made preparation at Yorke for his repaire to vs. **1624** CAPT. SMITH *Virginia* IV. 158 They saw all those promises were but delusions. **1656** BLOUNT *Glossogr.*, *Delusion*, a mocking, abusing or deceiving.

2. The action of befooling with false impressions or beliefs; the fact or condition of being cheated and led to believe what is false.

c **1420** LYDG. *Story of Thebes* I. (R.), But he her put in delusion As he had done it for the nones. **1526–34** TINDALE *2 Thess.* ii. 11 God shall sende them stronge delusion, that they shuld beleve lyes. **1529** MORE *Dyaloge* I. Wks. 177/2 Thinges..done by the deuill for our delusion. **1671** MILTON *P.R.* I. 443 God hath justly giv'n the nations up To thy delusions. **1762** FOOTE *Liar* III. Wks. 1799 I. 319, *Y.W.* By all that's sacred, Sir——. *O. W.* I am now deaf to your delusions. **1853** BRIGHT *Sp. India* 3 June, This concealment ..this delusion practised upon public opinion. **1876** FREEMAN *Norm. Conq.* V. xxiii. 331 In all this there was something of the willing delusion of a people that takes its memories for hopes.

3. a. Anything that deceives the mind with a false impression; a deception; a fixed false opinion or belief with regard to objective things, *esp.* as a form of mental derangement.

1552 HULOET, Delusion wroughte by enchauntmente, *præstigium.* **1588** FRAUNCE *Lawiers Log.* I. ii. 5 For that thereby men..fell headlong into divers delusions and erronious conceiptes. **1638** JUNIUS *Painting of Anc.* 117 It shall resemble a juglers delusion. **1720** GAY *Poems* (1745) II. 163 Some dark delusion swims before thy sight. **1874** C. GEIKIE *Life in Woods* xvi. 275 The poor fellow was only labouring under a delusion.

b. *delusions of grandeur*: a false belief concerning one's personality or status, which is thought to be more important than it is. Also *fig.*

1909 in *Cent. Dict.* Suppl. **1937** E. ST. V. MILLAY *Conversation at Midnight* I. 16 Take the electric refrigerator. .. Take mine... Delusions of grandeur, that's what it's got, all right; Thinks it's the *Queen Mary.* **1956** 'M. INNES' *Old Hall, New Hall* II. i. 101 The University..had given them their impressive title while experiencing delusions of grandeur. **1967** P. MCGERR *Murder is Absurd* iii. 37 Man, you really have delusions of grandeur! You think you're going to audition Mark Kendall?

†**4.** Elusion, evasion. (Cf. DELUDE *v.* 4.) *Obs.*

1606 HOLLAND *Sueton.* 10 That none ever after should by such delusion of the law seeke evasion.

delusional (dɪˈl(j)uːʒənəl), *a.* [-AL[1].] Of the nature of, or characterized by, delusion.

1871 J. R. REYNOLDS *Syst. Med.* (1878) II. 29 Delusional Insanity. **1884** *American* IX. 88 They regarded Taylor as a 'delusional monomaniac'. **1891** *Daily News* 7 July 7/1 She suffers from delusional insanity; that is, her actions depend upon false judgments of existing facts.

delusionist (dɪˈl(j)uːʒənɪst). [-IST.] **a.** One who is addicted to deluding. **b.** One given up to delusions.

1841 A. W. FONBLANQUE in *Life & Labours* (1874) 151 The great delusionist is to make believe that he is pledged to the one [etc.]. **1845** CARLYLE *Cromwell* (1871) IV. 25 Day-dreaming Delusionists.

delusive (dɪˈl(j)uːsɪv), *a.* [f. *dēlūs-*, ppl. stem of L. *dēlūdĕre* to DELUDE: see -IVE.]

1. Having the attribute of deluding, characterized by delusion, tending to delude, deceptive.

1605 B. JONSON *Volpone* I. i, A fox Stretch'd on the earth, with fine delusive sleights, Mocking a gaping crow. **1638** SIR T. HERBERT *Trav.* (ed. 2) 110 In it [Arabia] was hatcht the delusive Alcaron. **1736** BUTLER *Anal. Relig.* I. i. 16 Imagination..that forward delusive Faculty. **1759** JOHNSON *Rasselas* xx, Appearances are delusive. **1855** PRESCOTT *Philip II*, I. IV. iv. 440 Holding out delusive promises of succour. **1869** PHILLIPS *Vesuv.* iii. 88 The lava had a delusive aspect of yielding to any impression.

2. Of the nature of a delusion.

1645 MILTON *Tetrach.* (1851) 156 The breed of Centaures ..the fruits of a delusive mariage. **1833** LONGF. *Coplas de Manrique* xiii, Behold of what delusive worth The bubbles we pursue on earth.

delusively (dɪˈl(j)uːsɪvlɪ), *adv.* [-LY[2].] In a delusive manner.

1646 GAULE *Cases Consc.* 46 God utterly deserting, the Devill delusively invading. **1648** A. BURRELL *Cord. Calenture* 5 The Officers of the Navie did delusively cause Seaven great Frigots to be built. **1818** MAD. D'ARBLAY *Diary* 17 Nov., How sweet to me were those words, which I thought—alas, how delusively!—would soothe and invigorate recovery. **1885** *Manch. Exam.* 6 June 5/3 The senses act delusively and uncertainly.

delusiveness (dɪˈl(j)uːsɪvnɪs). [-NESS] Delusive or deceptive quality.

a **1652** J. SMITH *Sel. Disc.* vi. 208 The wiser sort of the heathen have happily found out the lameness and delusiveness of it. **1811** LAMB *Trag. Shaks.*, This exposure of supernatural agents upon the stage is truly bringing in a candle to expose their own delusiveness. **1873** M. ARNOLD *Lit. & Dogma* (1876) 183 It is needful to show the line of growth of this Aberglaube, and its delusiveness.

†**deluˈsorious,** *a. Obs. rare.* [f. med. or mod.L. *dēlūsōri-us* DELUSORY + -OUS.] = next.

1625 JACKSON *Creed* V. xliii, Delusorious imaginations of brotherly love's inherence in hearts wherein [etc.].

delusory (dɪˈl(j)uːsərɪ), *a.* [ad. med. or mod.L. *dēlūsōri-us*, f. ppl. stem *dēlūs-* (see DELUSIVE): cf. obs. F. *delusoire* (15th c.).] Having the character of deluding; of deluding quality; delusive.

1588 J. HARVEY *Discours. Probl.* 41 Practises deuised onely ..as delusorie experiments, and wilie sleights to make fooles. **1611** SPEED *Hist. Gt. Brit.* IX. ix. §85 His errand was in shew glorious, but in truth both delusory and unprofitable. **1686** GOAD *Celest. Bodies* I. iii. 10 Are all Pretences to a Prescience..delusory and impossible? **1753** HERVEY *Theron & Aspasio* Ded. (1786) 4 Beguiled by delusory pleasures. **1814** MAD. D'ARBLAY *Wanderer* III. 430, I had some hope..but I had already given it up as delusory.

delustre (diːˈlʌstə(r)), *v.* Also (*U.S.*) -luster. [f. DE- II. 2 + LUSTRE *sb.*[1]] *trans.* Of textiles: to deprive of lustre or sheen. So **deˈlustring** *vbl. sb.*, **deˈlustred** *ppl. a.*

1927 *Rayon Jrnl.* Apr. 13 (*title*) Delustering Rayon. *Ibid.* 13/1 The methods of delustering Rayon may be classified into three groups: the delustering of Celanese; the mechanical delustering of other varieties of Rayon (by abrasion); and the loading of Rayon to accomplish delustering. *Ibid.* 13/2 Celanese yarn..has been delustered without otherwise altering its composition of peculiar properties. **1929** *Daily Tel.* 22 Jan. 7/6 To get rid of that cold effect a special delustering process has to be gone through during the dyeing. **1934** B. L. HATHORNE *Rayon Dyeing & Finishing* ii. 49 The procedures used to produce delustered acetate fabrics vary with the type of fabric processed. **1950** '*Mercury*' *Dict. Textile Terms* 171/2 *Delustring*, chemical treatments for dulling the lustre of rayon yarns and fabrics in order to make them more nearly resemble silk. **1960** *Harper's Bazaar* Apr. 84 Dress of delustred oyster satin. **1963** A. J. HALL *Textile Sci.* ii. 61 Delustred acetate fibres. *Ibid.* 62 Delustring is hindered by lowering the temperature of the soap-liquor.

†**deˈlute,** *v. Obs. rare*—0. [ad. L. *dēlutāre*, f. DE- I. 3 + *lutāre* to daub with *lutum* moist clay.]

1623 COCKERAM, *Delute*, to cover with clay.

deluvian, -ate, deluvy: see DI-.

‖**de luxe** (də lyks, lʌks), *adj. phr.* [Fr., lit. 'of luxury'.] Luxurious, sumptuous; of a superior kind.

1819 Edition de luxe [see LUXE 2]. **1865** 'OUIDA' *Strathmore* viii, I wonder governments don't tax good talk; it's quite a luxury, and they might add *de luxe.* **1885** Edition de luxe [see LUXE 2]. **1890** Trains de luxe [see LUXE 2]. **1908** *Westm. Gaz.* 6 June 5/1 We are conscious of something De luxe, but not oppressed by the sense of it. **1934** *Punch* 20 June 679/3 They will disclose Britannia, enthroned on the top of a *de luxe* model of one of those erections from which they mend tram-wires. **1949** E. POUND *Pisan Cantos* lxxvii. 52 Before the deluxe car carried him over the precipice. **1955** T. H. PEAR *Eng. Social Differences* viii. 182 Members of the upper economic strata..who patronise *hotels de luxe.* **1970** K. CHESNEY *Victorian Underworld* 336 These places were often little businesses engaged in a de luxe trade, glovers, bonnet makers, perfumers and so on.

†**delvage** (ˈdɛlvɪdʒ). *Obs.* [f. DELVE *v.* + -AGE.] Delving; the digging, ploughing, or turning up of the soil in process of tillage.

1610 W. FOLKINGHAM *Art of Survey* I. vii. 14 Deluage is applyed about preparing, and putrifying of the Earth by stirring, tossing and turning of the same. **1688** R. HOLME *Armoury* III. 333/2 Delvage..is..Vertillage.

delvauxene (dɛlˈvəʊksiːn). *Min.* Also delvauxine. [ad. F. *delvauxine* (A. H. Dumont 1838, in *Bull. de l'Acad. R. des Sci. et Belles-Lettres de Bruxelles* V. 298), f. the name of J. C. P. J. *Delvaux* de Fenffe (1782–1863), Belgian chemist: see -INE[5].] = next.

1844 DANA *Syst. Min.* (ed. 2) Suppl. 524 Delvauxene. Massive and earthy, with a yellowish-brown color. **1854** [see next]. **1965** *Mineral. Abstr.* XVII. 231/1 Delvauxine, destinezite, torbenite, richellite, and akaganéite at Richelle.

delvauxite (dɛlˈvəʊksaɪt). *Min.* [ad. G. *delvauxit* (W. Haidinger *Handbuch d. Mineral.* (1845) iv. 512), f. DELVAUX(ENE + -ITE[1].] A hydrated ferric phosphate.

1854 DANA *Syst. Min.* (ed. 4) II. v. 427 (*heading*) Delvauxene, *Dumont.* Delvauxit. **1864** *Chem. News* 24 Sept. 145/1 The formula $2Fe_2O_3.PO_5+24HO$ is assigned to delvauxite. **1963** *Mineral. Abstr.* XVI. 220/1 Amorphous coatings of delvauxite.

delve (dɛlv), *sb.* [Partly a variant of DELF *sb.* (cf. *staff, stave*), partly n. of action from DELVE *v.*]

1. A cavity in or under the ground; excavation, pit, den; = DELF *sb.* 1. (The pl. *delves* is found with either sing.)

1590–6 SPENSER *F.Q.* II. vii. Argt, Guyon findes Mammon in a delve Sunning his threasure hore. *Ibid.* IV. i. 20 It is a darksome delue farre vnder ground. **1729** SAVAGE *Wanderer* III. 303 The delve obscene, where no suspicion pries. **1748** THOMSON *Cast. Indol.* II. 682 There left thro' delves and deserts dire to yell. **1815** MOORE *Lalla R.* IV. (1850) 226 The very tigers from their delves Look out. **1820** SHELLEY *Hymn to Mercury* xix, And fine dry logs and roots innumerous He gathered in a delve upon the ground.

2. A hollow or depression in a surface; a wrinkle.

1811 in *Pall Mall G.* 4 Oct. 1892, 3/1 If it be the same bottle I found under his bed, there is a 'delve' in it into which I can put my thumb. **1869** *Daily News* 8 July, The pursed up mouths, the artificial lines and delves, the half-closed eyes of those [marksman] to be seen sighting, and 'cocking', and aiming for the Queen's to-day.

3. An act of delving; the plunging (of a spade) into the ground.

1869 *Daily News* 1 Mar., He quickly learns that every delve of his spade in the earth means money.

†**4.** (See quot.) *Obs.*—0

1706 PHILLIPS (ed. Kersey), *Delve*, as a *Delve of Coals*, i.e. a certain quantity of Coals digged in the Mine or Pit. **1721** in BAILEY; hence in Johnson, etc.

delve (dɛlv), *v.* Forms: 1 delf-an, 2- deluen, (3 dælfen, *Orm.* dellfenn), 3–7 delue, 4 deluyn, 5 delvyn, 4- delve, (5–6 *Sc.* delf, delfe). *Pa. t.* and *pa. pple.* 4- delved: earlier forms see below. [A Common WGer. vb. originally strong: OE. *delfan*; *dealf, dulfon*; *dolfen*; corresp. to OFris. *delva*, OS. (*bi-*)*delƀan*, MDu. and Du. *delven*, LG. *dölben*, OHG. (*bi-*)*telban*, MHG. *telben* :—OTeut. ablaut series *delƀ-*, *dalƀ-*, *dulƀ-*: not known in Norse, nor in Gothic; but having cognates in Slavonic. The original strong inflexions were retained more or less throughout the ME. period, though with various levellings of the singular and plural forms, *dalf, dulven*, in the pa. t., and replacement of the plural form by that of the pa. pple. *dolven*; they are rare in the 16th c.; the weak inflexions are found already in the 14th c., and are now alone in use. The verb has itself been largely displaced by DIG, but is still in common use dialectally.]

A. Forms of past tense and pa. pple.

1. *Past tense. Strong.*

a. *sing.* 1 dealf, 2–5 dalf, 4–5 dalfe, dalue; 4 delf, delue; 6 (9 *arch.*) dolve.

c **1000** ÆLFRIC *Gen.* xxi. 30 Ic dealf þisne pytt. *c* **1250** *Gen. & Ex.* 2718 Stille he dalf him [in] ðe sond. *a* **1300** *Cursor M.* 21530 (Cott.) Lang he delf [*v. rr.* delue, dalue] but noght he fand. **1483** CAXTON *Gold. Leg.* 48/3 He dalfe a pit behynde the cyte. **1489** —— *Faytes of A.* I. xvii. 50 He..dalue the erth. **1598** BARCKLEY *Felic. Man* II. (1603) 66 Wo worth the wight that first dolve the mould.

b. *pl.* α. 1 dulfon; 2–3 dulfen, 3 duluen; 3–4 dolfen, 3–5 dolue(n, dolve(n.

a **1000** *Martyrol.* 138 þa dulfon hi in þære ylcan stowe. *c* **1205** LAY. 21998 Alfene hine dulfen [*c* **1275** dolue]. *a* **1225** *Ancr. R.* 292 Heo duluen mine vet. *c* **1250** *Gen. & Ex.* 3189 Ðor he doluen..and hauen up-broȝt ðe bones. *c* **1290** *S. Eng. Leg.* I. 427/239 Huy doluen and beoten faste. *a* **1400** *Prymer* (1891) 107 They dolfen myn handes and my feet. **1483** CAXTON *Gold. Leg.* 57/1 Thegypciens wente and doluen pittes for water. **1865** S. EVANS *Bro. Fabian* 59 They dolve a grave beneath the arrow.

β. 4 dalfe, dalue, dalf, 5 dalff; 4 delf.

a **1300** *Cursor M.* 7786 (Gött.) þai dalf [*v.r.* dalue] it in a wodis side. *Ibid.* 21146 (Cott.) þe cristen men þar delf [*v.r.* dalue, *Gött.* delued, *Trin.* buryed] him þan. **1489** CAXTON *Faytes of A.* II. xxxv. 153 They dalff the erthe.

Weak sing. and *pl.* 4–5 delued (*pl.* -eden), 4 -id, delfd, 5 deluyde, 4- delved.

a **1300** *Cursor M.* 16877 (Cott.) þai delued him..in a yerd be þe tun. *Ibid.* 18562 (Gött.) þai him hanged..And deluid him. *Ibid.* 19256 (Cott.) þai..þat right nu delfd þi ded husband. **1382** WYCLIF *Gen.* xxi. 30, I deluyde this pit. **1388** —— *Ps.* lvi. 7 Thei delueden [**1382** doluen] a diche bifore my face. **1605** ROWLANDS *Hell's Broke Loose* 15 For when old Adam delu'd, and Euah span, Where was my silken veluet Gentleman?

2. *Pa. pple. Strong.* 1–4 dolfen, 2–6 doluen, 3–4 duluen, dolfe, 3–6 dolue, 4 dollin, -yn, delluin, 4–6 dolven, (-yn), dolve, (5 doluyn, -wyn); 6 delfe. *Weak.* 6–7 delued, (6 *Sc.* deluet), 6- delved.

c **1000** *Ags. Ps.* xciii. 12 Deop adolfen, deorc and ðystre. *c* **1250** *Gen. & Ex.* 1895 Starf ysaac..was doluen on ðat stede. *a* **1300** *Cursor M.* 5428 (Cott.), I be noght duluen in þis land. *Ibid.* 5494 (Gött.) Dede and doluie [*C.* duluen, *F.* dolue, *T.* doluen] þar war þai. *c* **1340** *Ibid.* 3214 (Fairf.) In ebron dalue hir sir abraham, þer formast was dollyn alde adam. *c* **1325** *Leg. Rood* (1871) 113 Quen he riȝt depe had delluí[n] sare. *a* **1400** *Prymer* (1891) 77 He hat[h] opened the lake and dolfe hym. *c* **1430** LYDG. *Bochas* IV. ii. (1554) 102 a, She was ydolue lowe. *a* **1450** *Le Morte Arth.* 3664 Dolwyn dede. **1587** GOLDING *De Mornay* xi. 159 To seeke Death where it seemeth to be doluen most deepe. ? *a* **1600** *Merline* 733 in *Percy Folio* I. 445 Her one sister quick was delfe. **1582** [see B. 1, quot. 1398]. **1596** DALRYMPLE tr. *Leslie's Hist. Scot.* (1885) 7 In sum places of Ingland..is deluet upe na small quantitie of Leid. **1756** [see B. 7].

B. Signification.

1. a. *trans.* To dig; to turn up with the spade; *esp.* to dig (ground) in preparation for a crop. Now chiefly *north.* and *Sc.*, where it is the regular word for 'digging' a garden. In Shropshire, according to Miss Jackson, *to delve* is *spec.* to dig two spades deep.

c **888** K. ÆLFRED *Boeth.* xl. §6 Swelce hwa nu delfe eorþan & finde þær ðonne goldhord. **1398** TREVISA *Barth. De P.R.* XIV. i. (Tollem. MS.) þe more londe is doluen [**1582** delved] and erid and ouerturnid, þe virtu þat is þerin is þe more medlid with all þe parties þerof. *c* **1420** *Pallad. on Husb.* II. 74 Thi lande unclene alle doluen uppe mot be. *c* **1440** HYLTON *Scala Perf.* (W. de W. 1494) I. xlii, Vntyll this grounde be well ransaken & depe doluyn. **1576** GASCOIGNE *Steele Gl.* (Arb.) 58 To delue the ground for mines of glistering gold. **1577–95** *Descr. Isles Scotl.* in Skene *Celtic Scotl.* III. App. 431 Thay use na pleuchis, but delvis thair corn land with spaiddis. *a* **1610** BABINGTON *Wks.* (1622) 269 We ouer and ouer.. plow our land, and delue our gardens. **1799** J. ROBERTSON *Agric. Perth* 247 He directs the moss to be *delved* or dug up with spades, and the manure to be chiefly lime. **1845** R. W. HAMILTON *Pop. Educ.* iii. (ed. 2) 37 Time was when our countrymen united every employment; they delved the soil, they wove the fleece.

fig. **1611** SHAKS. *Cymb.* I. i. 28 What's his name, and Birth?.. I cannot delve him to the roote: His Father Was call'd Sicillius.

b. *transf.* of burrowing animals.

1484 CAXTON *Fables of Æsop* II. v, Of a hylle whiche beganne to tremble and shake by cause of the molle whiche delued hit. **1592** SHAKS. *Ven. & Ad.* 687 Sometime he runs.. where earth-delving conies keep. **1861** LYTTON & FANE *Tannhäuser* 49 The blind mole that delves the earth.

2. a. To make (a hole, pit, ditch, etc.) by digging; to excavate. *arch.*

c **825** *Vesp. Psalter* vii. 16 Seað ontynde & dalf. *c* **1000** ÆLFRIC *Deut.* vi. 11 Wæterpyttas þa þe ʒe ne dulfon. *c* **1205** LAY. 16733 Þe king lette deluen ænne dich [*c* **1275** dealue one dich]. *a* **1300** *Cursor M.* 21063 (Cott.) First he did his graf to deluen. **1393** LANGL. *P. Pl.* C. XXII. 365 To delue and dike a deop diche. **1513** DOUGLAS *Æneis* XI. ix. 68 Sum.. Befor the portis delvis trynschis deip. **1549–62** STERNH. & H. *Ps.* vii. 13 He digs a ditch and delues it deepe. **1659** D. PELL *Impr. of Sea* 338 Sextons to delve the graves of the greatest part of his Army. **1795** SOUTHEY *Joan of Arc* VII. 477 Underneath the tree.. They delved the narrow house. **1821** CLARE *Vill. Minstr.* I. 65 Delving the ditch a livelihood to earn. **1872** AUSTIN DOBSON *Bookworm, Vignettes* (1873) 209 To delve, in folios' rust and must The tomb he lived in, dry as dust.

b. *transf.* and *fig.*

c **1600** SHAKS. *Sonn.* lx, Time.. delues the paralels in beauties brow. **1855** SINGLETON *Virgil* I. 81 The moles have delved Their chambers. **1872** GEO. ELIOT *Middlem.* xi. 169 Mrs. Vincy's face, in which forty-five years had delved neither angles nor parallels.

†**3.** To put or hide in the ground by digging; *esp.* to bury (a corpse). *Obs.*

c **1200** ORMIN 6484 Þatt lic þatt smeredd iss þærwiþþ Biforr þatt mann itt dellfeþþ. **1387** TREVISA *Higden* (Rolls) VII. 77 Ioseph dalf wiþ his fader moche tresour in þe erþe. *c* **1450** *Mirour Saluacioun* 4888 Bespitted, scourgid, and corovned, dede, dolven, and ascendid. **1481** CAXTON *Reynard* (Arb.) 36 My fader had founden kyng ermeryks tresour doluen in a pytte. **1587** GOLDING *De Mornay* xi. 159 Consider how often men go to seeke Death where it seemeth to be doluen most deepe, and yet finde it not.

transf. **1735** SOMERVILLE *Chase* II. 38 In the dry crumbling Bank Their Forms they delve, and cautiously avoid The dripping Covert.

4. To obtain by digging; to dig *up* or *out of* (the ground); to exhume. *arch.* or *dial.*

c **1000** *Ags. Gosp.* Matt. vi. 19 þær ðeofas hit delfað & forstelaþ. *c* **1374** CHAUCER *Boeth.* II. v. 51 He þat first dalf vp þe gobets or þe weyȝtys of gold, couered vndir erþe. *c* **1386** —— *Sqr.'s T.* 630 Now can nought Canace bot herbes delve Out of the grounde. *c* **1440** *Promp. Parv.* 118 Delvyn' vp owte of the erthe, *effodio.* **1587** TURBERV. *Trag. T.* (1837) 255 Do delve it up, and burne it here. **1596** DALRYMPLE tr. *Leslie's Hist. Scot.* IV. (1887) 207 Delfeing vpe his fatheris reliques. **1777** *Barmby Inclos. Act* 26 To cut, dig, delve, gather and carry away any turves or sods. **1866** NEALE *Sequences & Hymns* 35 In the valleys where they delve it, how the gold is good indeed. **1870** HAWTHORNE *Eng. Note-Bks.* (1879) I. 226 Minerals, delved, doubtless, out of the hearts of the mountains.

†**5.** To pierce or penetrate as by digging. *Obs.*

a **1225** *Ancr. R.* 292 Heo duluen mine vet & mine honden. He ne seide nout þet heo þurleden mine vet & mine honden, auh duluen. Vor efter þisse lettre.. þe neiles weren so dulte þet heo duluen his flesch. *c* **1340** *Ayenb.* 263 Yef þe uader of þe house wyste huyche time þe þyef were comynde, uorzoþe he wolde waky and nolde naȝt þolye þet me dolue his hous. **1382** WYCLIF *Ps.* xxi[i]. 17 Thei dolue [*v.r.* delueden] myn hondis and my feet. *c* **1450** *Bk. Curtasye* 327 in *Babees Bk.* 308 Ne delf thou never nose thyrle With thombe ne fyngur.

6. To dint or indent. *dial.*

1788 W. MARSHALL *East Yorks.* Gloss., *Delve*, to dint or bruise, as a pewter or a tin vessel. **1876** *Whitby Gloss., Delve*.. to indent, as by a blow upon pewter; which is then said to be delved. **1877** *Holderness Gloss., Delve*, to indent or bruise a table, or metal surface, by a blow.

7. a. *absol.* or *intr.* To labour with a spade in husbandry, excavating, etc.: to dig. *arch.* or *poet.*, and *dial.* (In most dialect glossaries from Lincolnsh. and Shropsh. northward.)

c **1000** *Ags. Gosp.* Luke xvi. 3 Ne mæʒ ic delfan, me sceamað þæt ic wædliʒe. *a* **1225** *Ancr. R.* 384 ʒif eax ne kurue, ne þe spade ne dulue.. hwo kepte ham uorte holden? *c* **1340** HAMPOLE in *Relig. Pieces fr. Thornton MS.* 79 When Adam dalfe and Eue spane.. Whare was þan þe pride of man? *c* **1430** *Pilgr. Lyf Manhode* III. viii. (1869) 140 Folk howweden and doluen aboute þe cherche. **1512** *Act 4 Hen. VIII*, c. 1 §4 To digge and to delve.. for erth, stones and turfes. **1535** STEWART *Cron. Scot.* III. 41 [He] saw ane ald man.. Delfand full fast with ane spaid in his hand. **1602** SHAKS. *Ham.* III. iv. 208, I will delve one yard below their mines. **1756** C. LUCAS *Ess. Waters* III. 113 Men have.. delved into the bowels of the earth. **1858** LONGF. *M. Standish* viii, When he delved in the soil of his garden.

b. *transf.* of animals.

1727–38 GAY *Fables* I. xlviii. 31 With delving snout he turns the soil. **1855** LONGF. *Hiaw.* xiii. 130 Crows and blackbirds.. jays and ravens.. Delving deep with beak and talon For the body of Mondamin.

c. *to delve about*: to excavate round. (With *indirect passive.*)

1515 *Scot. Field* 19 in *Chetham Misc.* (1856) II., Yt was so deepe dolven with ditches aboute.

8. *fig.* To make laborious search for facts, information, etc., as one who digs deep for treasure.

1649 G. DANIEL *Trinarch., Rich. II* ccxliv, Gloucester.. Delves for himselfe, pretending publick right. **1650** FEATLEY *Pref.* in *S. Newman's Concord.* 1 Why delve they continually in humane arts and secular sciences, full of dregs and drosse? **1836** O. W. HOLMES *Poems, Poetry* IV. iv, Not in the cells where frigid learning delves In Aldine folios mouldering on their shelves. **1864** SIR F. PALGRAVE *Norm. & Eng.* III. 32 The Norman Antiquary delves for the records of his country anterior to the reign of Philip Augustus.

9. To work hard, slave, drudge. *dial.* or *slang.*

1838 C. GILMAN *Recoll. Southern Matron* xxix. 204 The poor mother.. delving at her needle. **1869** MISS L. M. ALCOTT *Lit. Women* I. ii. 171 Delve like slaves. **1876** *Whitby Gloss.* s.v., 'They're delving at it', going ahead with the work. **1879** MISS JACKSON *Shropsh. Word-bk., Delve*.. to slave, to drudge. **1891** FARMER *Slang, Delve it* (tailors'), to hurry with one's work, head down and sewing fast.

†**10.** To dip with violence, plunge down into water. *Obs. rare*$^{-1}$.

1697 DAMPIER *Voy.* I. xiii. 367 He was bound.. on a Bambon.. which was so near the Water, that by the Vessels motion, it frequently delved under water, and the man along with it.

11. Of the slope of a hill, road, etc.: To make a sudden dip or deep descent.

1848 LYTTON *Arthur* VI. lxxxi, The bird beckoned down a delving lane. **1855** *Chamb. Jrnl.* III. 329 The combs delve down precipitously. **1862** LYTTON *Str. Story* II. 115 The path was rugged.. sometimes skirting the very brink of perilous cliffs; sometimes delving down to the sea-shore.

Hence **delved** *ppl. a.*, **delving** *vbl. sb.* and *ppl. a.*

1377 LANGL. *P. Pl.* B. VI. 250 In dykynge or in deluynge. **1576** FLEMING *Panopl. Epist.* 356 Let us.. fall to delving. *c* **1625** MILTON *Death Fair Inf.* v, Hid from the world in a low-delvèd tomb. *a* **1659** CLEVELAND *Count. Com. Man Poems* (1677) 98 One that hates the King because he is a Gentleman, transgressing the *Magna Charta* of Delving Adam. **1883** J. SHIELDS in *Trans. Highland Soc. Agric.* Ser. IV. XV. 38 The delved and ploughed portion, about 2¼ acres. **1888** *Athenæum* 25 Aug. 249/1 Weary delvings among a heterogeneous mass of documents.

delver ('dɛlvə(r)). [f. prec. + -ER.] One who delves, as a tiller of the ground, or excavator.

c **888** K. ÆLFRED *Boeth.* xl. §6 ʒif se delfere ða eorþan no ne dulfe. **1362** LANGL. *P. Pl.* A. Prol. 102 Dykers, and Deluers þat don heore dedes ille. **1413** LYDG. *Pilgr. Sowle* IV. xxxvii. (1483) 84 More necessary to the land is a diker and a deluer than a goldsmyth. **1602** SHAKS. *Ham.* V. i. 15 Nay but heare you Goodman deluer. *a* **1619** FOTHERBY *Atheom.* II. xii. §2 (1622) 338 The Delver bound and clogd in clowted buskin. **1787** BURNS *Twa Dogs* 90. **1859** TENNYSON *Enid* 774 As careful robins eye the delver's toil.

fig. **1859** HOLLAND *Gold. F.* v. 75 The delver in the stratified history of the race.

dely-, obs. form of words in DELI-.

delyte, obs. f. DELETE, DELIGHT; var. DELITE *a.*

dem, *v.*^{1} *Obs.* exc. *dial.* [OE. *-dęmman* in *fordęmman*: see DAM *sb.*^{1}] *trans.* or *absol.* To dam, obstruct the course of water, etc.

[*c* **1000** *Ags. Ps.* (Spelm., Trin. MS.) lvii. 4 (Bosw.) Swa swa nædran deafe, and fordemmende earan heora.] *c* **1325** *E.E. Allit. P.* B. 384 Vche a dale so depe þat demmed at þe brynkez. **1513** DOUGLAS *Æneis* XI. vii. 9 Riuerys.. Brystand on skelleis our thir demmyt lynnis. *Mod.Sc.* (*Roxburghshire*) Trying to dem the stream.

Hence **'demming** *vbl. sb.* and *ppl. a.*

a **1300** *Cursor M.* 1908 (Cott.) [Noe] baid seuen dais in rest, for doute if ani demmyng brest. *c* **1340** *Ibid.* 11934 (Fairf.) Ihesu and othir childryn.. went hem by the rever to gamyn.. And demmynges [*Cott.* lakes] vij made of clay.

dem, *v.*^{2}; formerly **demn.** Minced form of DAMN; so **demd** for *damned.*

†**1.** To damn, condemn. *Obs.*

1377 LANGL. *P. Pl.* B. V. 144 (MS. C.) Þise possessioneres preche and dempne freres. **1650** BAXTER *Saints' R.* I. viii. (1662) 132 He is dead and demned in point of Law.

2. In profane use. (So **dem-me, demmy** = DAMME, damn me!; **dem,** for *demd* adv. = DAMNED 4 b.)

1695 CONGREVE *Love for L.* II. ii, Oh, demn you, toad! **1720** *Humourist* 50 A Beau cries Dem me. **1753** *Scots Mag.* Oct. 491/1, I now advanced to *By Jove*, *'fore Ged*, *Geds curse it*, and *Demme.* **1755** *Gentl. Mag.* XXV. 374 Give me your person, dem your gold! **1801** *Sporting Mag.* XVII. 23 Swear in a commanding military *dem-me.* **1838** DICKENS *Nich. Nick.* xvii, Two demd fine women: real Countesses. **1849** THACKERAY *Pendennis* iii, What a dem fine woman Mrs. Jones was. *Ibid.* liii, Miss Bell's a *little* countrified. But the smell of the hawthorn is pleasant, demmy.

dem (dɛm), Caribbean and Black English var. of THEM *pers. pron.* 1, 3, 5.

1868 T. RUSSELL *Etymol. Jamaica Gram.* 13 The personal pronouns are.. Plur. 3rd person *Dem*, all cases Mas. Fem. Neuter. **1895** BANKS & SMILEY in A. Dundes *Mother Wit* (1973) 256/2 Dem vines is love. **1907** W. JEKYLL *Jamaican Song & Story* 32 Me see enough yam, me feel dem put dem a fire. **1928** J. PETERKIN *Scarlet Sister Mary* xxxi. 336 Pray widout ceastin until dem stripes come clean and you soul gets white as snow. **1953** S. A. BROWN in A. Dundes *Mother Wit* (1973) 41/2 Dem wuz good ole times, marster. **1973** *Sunday Express* (Trinidad & Tobago) 1 Apr. 12/4 At that point, I give the wife a high sign and I take off. Not me and the tourists and dem. **1981** *Westindian World* 28 Aug. 4/1 De lads of Arkville have finally realised that dem have to be practical.

dem, colloq. abbrev. of DEMONSTRATION (sense 5); also, a demonstration of (the operation of) a commercial product, esp. a piece of apparatus.

1968 M. BUTTERWORTH *Walk softly, in Fear* iii. 37 A pencilled scrawl in my old diary: *Dem 2 lb fan Willocks*, which means that a sweet-and-tobacconist named Willocks had half agreed to be shown a two-pound scale that day. *Ibid.*, 'Give us the toffee dem, Hes', pleaded Demauney. **1970** J. EARL *Tuners & Amplifiers* iv. 89 This setting is influenced by the nature of the music, whether we.. want the music purely as a background or whether we wish to impress guests with a fully-fledged hi-fi 'dem'. **1981** *Pop. Hi-Fi* Mar. 75/2, I.. would quibble with one or two turntable/arm/cartridge combinations.. judging by the dem I received of JBE/Dynavector arm/Dynavector Karat Ruby cartridge.

dem, obs. form of DEEM *v.*

demagnetize (diː'mægnɪtaɪz), *v.* [DE- II. 1.]

1. *trans.* To deprive of magnetic quality.

1839 *Brit. Pat. 8255* 2 My said invented improvements consists [*sic*] in employing, as my prime movers, a series of electro-magnets, which are alternately.. magnetized and demagnetized. **1842–3** GROVE *Corr. Phys. Forces* (1887) 56 We must magnetise and demagnetise in order to produce a continuous mechanical effect. **1887** *Times* 9 Sept. 14/5 Hot air traversing the discs and rolls demagnetizes the discs.

fig. **1875** SEARS *Serm. Chr. Life* 43 People whose wills have been demagnetized.

†**2.** To free from 'magnetic' or mesmeric influence; to demesmerize. *Obs.*

1850 W. GREGORY *Lett. Anim. Magnetism* 106 This she ascribed to her not having been demagnetised, and it continued next morning.

Hence **de'magnetizing** *vbl. sb.*; **de,magneti'zation,** the action or process of demagnetizing.

1843 *Rep. Brit. Assoc.* 27 The de-magnetizings produced by operations which serve also to magnetize. **1864** WEBSTER, *Demagnetization.* **1872** F. L. POPE *Electr. Tel.* ii. (1872) 23 The act of demagnetization requires time, but is effected more rapidly than magnetization.

demagnetized (diː'mægnɪtaɪzd), *ppl. a.* [f. DEMAGNETIZE + -ED^1.] Deprived of magnetic quality.

1876 PREECE & SIVEWRIGHT *Telegr.* 246 A demagnetised needle. **1945** [see DOMAIN *sb.* 4 h].

de'magnify, *v.* [f. DE- II. 1 + MAGNIFY *v.*] *trans.* Of a lens, etc.: to make smaller. Also *absol.*

1960 *Sat. Rev. Lit.* (U.S.) 2 Apr. 45/2 We can reverse the lenses of the electron microscope in order to demagnify rather [than] to magnify. **1963** L. S. BIRKS *Electron Probe Microanalysis* iii. 26 The second lens further demagnifies the image and focuses the electron beam on the specimen surface. **1984** *Electronics* 23 Feb. 74/2 The ions shooting through the holes in the mask go through an ion optical-projection lens system that demagnifies the mask's ion image.

Hence **de'magnified, de'magnifying** *ppl. adjs.*; also **demagnifi'cation.**

1959 *Jrnl. Sci. Instruments* XXXVI. 350/1 The limit is set chiefly by the spherical aberration of the final demagnifying lens and the current density per unit solid angle.. of the electron gun. *Ibid.* 352/1 The demagnification of the source takes place in two stages. **1963** L. S. BIRKS *Electron Probe Microanalysis* iii. 25 The first lens forms a demagnified real image of the hot filament. *Ibid.* 26 The working distance is related to the focal length of the second lens and the demagnification required. **1976** *Physics Bull.* Sept. 397/3 A demagnifying image intensifier with an ultraviolet photocathode. **1984** *Electronics* 23 Feb. 73/3 Such 10X demagnification relaxes the accuracy needed in mask fabrication, so that masks can be made by common lithographic methods.

demagogic (,dɛmə'gɒgɪk, -'gɒdʒɪk), *a.* Also **-goguic.** [mod. ad. Gr. δημαγωγικός, f. δημαγωγός, DEMAGOGUE. So mod.F. *démagogique* (in Dict. Acad. 1835).] Of, pertaining to, or of the nature of a demagogue; characteristic of a demagogue.

1831 *Fraser's Mag.* IV. 374 That Spirit which is as far superior to the democratic or demagoguic, as the heavens are to the earth. *a* **1834** COLERIDGE *Shaks. Notes* (1875) 126 Thersites.. is the Caliban of demagogic life. **1866** FELTON *Anc. & Mod. Gr.* II. v. 78 He [Solon] gained, without the need of demagogic arts, the affections of the people.

dema'gogical, *a.* [f. as prec. + -AL^1.] = prec.

a **1734** NORTH *Lives* I. 118 The principles of the former, being demagogical, could not allow much favour to one who rose a monarchist declared. **1853** LYTTON *My Novel* XI. ii. (D.), A set of demagogical fellows who keep calling out, 'Farmer this is an oppressor, and Squire that is a vampyre'. **1867** J. GARFIELD in *Century Mag.* Jan. (1884) 411/1 There seems to be as much of the demagogical spirit here as in our Congress.

demagogism, -goguism ('dɛməgɒgɪz(ə)m). [f. DEMAGOGUE + -ISM.] The practice and principles of a demagogue.

1824 *Blackw. Mag.* XVI. 480 In a government depending on popular support, the vices of demagogism (let us take a Trans-Atlantic privilege of coining a word) will be found. **1831** *Fraser's Mag.* III. 478 His dissolute and detestable demagoguism. **1870** LOWELL *Study Wind.* (1886) 181 The demagogism which Aristophanes derided.

demagogue ('dɛməgɒg), *sb.* [mod. ad. Gr. δημαγωγ-ός a popular leader, a leader of the mob,

f. δῆμος people, populace, the commons + ἀγωγός leading, leader.

In French, *demagoge* was used by Oresme in 14th c.; but in the 17th Bossuet wished that it were permissible to employ the word. *Démagogue* was not admitted by the Academy till 1762.]

1. In ancient times, a leader of the people; a popular leader or orator who espoused the cause of the people against any other party in the state.

1651 HOBBES *Govt. & Soc.* x. §6. 153 In a Democraty, look how many Demagoges (that is) how many powerfull Oratours there are with the people. **1683** DRYDEN *Life Plutarch* 99 Their warriours, and senators, and demagogues. **1719** SWIFT *To Yng. Clergyman*, Demosthenes and Cicero, though each of them a leader (or as the Greeks called it, a demagogue) in a popular state, yet seem to differ. **1832** tr. *Sismondi's Ital. Rep.* x. 224 He was descended from one of the demagogues who, in 1378, had undertaken the defence of the minor arts against the aristocracy. **1874** GREEN *Short Hist.* viii. §6. 520 He [Pym] proved himself..the grandest of demagogues.

2. In bad sense: A leader of a popular faction, or of the mob; a political agitator who appeals to the passions and prejudices of the mob in order to obtain power or further his own interests; an unprincipled or factious popular orator.

1648 *Eikon Bas.* iv, Who were the chief demagogues and patrons of tumults, to send for them, to flatter and embolden them. **1649** MILTON *Eikon.* iv. (1851) 365 Setting aside the affrightment of this Goblin word [*demagogue*]; for the King by his leave cannot coine English as he could mony, to be current..those Demagogues..saving his Greek, were good patriots. *a* **1716** SOUTH *Serm.* II. 333 (T.) A plausible, insignificant word, in the mouth of an expert demagogue, is a dangerous and a dreadful weapon. **1835** LYTTON *Rienzi* I. viii, I do not play the part of a mere demagogue. **1848** MACAULAY *Hist. Eng.* I. 243 He despised the mean arts and unreasonable clamours of demagogues.

3. *attrib.* and *Comb.*

1812 SOUTHEY in *Q. Rev.* VIII. 349 The venom and virulence of the demagogue journalists. **1878** LECKY *Eng. in 18th C.* (1883) III. 61 He stooped to no demagogue art. **1887** *Brit. Mercantile Gaz.* 15 June 29/1 The overheated demagogue-fired imagination of the masses.

'demagogue, *v.* Chiefly *U.S.* [f. prec.]

1. *intr.* To play the demagogue.

1656 HARRINGTON *Oceana* 143 When that same ranting fellow Alcibiades fell a demagoging for the Sicilian War. **1850** *Congress. Globe* 24 July App. 940 In Ohio, the master-spirits of the party, while demagoging upon the stump, have promised the people [etc.]. **1867** *Ibid.* 16 Mar. 146/1 There was a great temptation presented to members of the Republican party now to demagogue. **1876** *Congress. Rec.* 1 July 4338/1, I have not been one of those..trying to cut down a few dollars for the purpose of demagoguing before the county.

2. *trans.* To deal with (a matter) after the fashion of a demagogue.

1890 *Cincinnati Commercial Gaz.* 31 July, The President never thought of demagoging the matter by..spurning the goodly gift. **1897** *Congress. Rec.* 20 Feb. 2041/2 Here is a plain, common-sense question, not to be demogogued in any way.

demagoguery ('dɛməgɒgrɪ, -ˌgɒgərɪ). [f. DEMAGOGUE *sb.* + -RY, -ERY.] Demagogic practices and arts; demagogism.

1866 *N.Y. Nation* 4 Oct. 271/2 At this period the House wholly abandoned itself to 'demagoguery'. **1888** BELLAMY *Looking Backward* 84 The demagoguery and corruption of our public men. **1959** *Times Lit. Suppl.*, The now familiar recipe of aggressive demagoguery and muck-raking. **1966** *Listener* 10 Mar. 338/2 Wherever politicians rely overmuch on demagoguery or on cultivating the mystique of their own personalities, [etc.].

'demagoguish, -gish, *a. rare.* [f. as prec. + -ISH.] Like or of the nature of a demagogue. Hence **'demaˌgoguishness**.

1860 *Chamb. Jrnl.* XIV. 218 Its most prevalent feature is its unblushing demagoguishness.

'demagoguize, *v. nonce-wd.* [f. DEMAGOGUE + -IZE.] *intr.* To play the demagogue.

1889 *Sat. Rev.* Dec. 696/1.

demagogy ('dɛməgɒgɪ, -gɒdʒɪ). [mod. ad. Gr. δημαγωγία leadership of the people, abstr. sb. f. δημαγωγός DEMAGOGUE.]

1. The action or quality of a demagogue.

1655 M. CASAUBON *Enthus.* (1656) 197 A consideration of the efficacy of ancient Rhetorick, I will not insist upon Demagogie, so called anciently, though it be the chiefest. **1835** *Blackw. Mag.* XXXVIII. 382 This insane demagogy. **1849** GROTE *Greece* II. xlvi. V. 488 The arts of demagogy were in fact much more cultivated by the oligarchical Kimon. **1880** *Daily Tel.* 4 Oct., The men least suspected of demagogy, the least revolutionary.

2. The rule of demagogues.

1860 HUXLEY in *Darwin's Life & Lett.* (1887) II. 284 Despotism and demagogy are not the necessary alternatives of government.

3. A body of demagogues.

1878 *N. Amer. Rev.* CXXVI. 156 The defeat..of the greenback demagogy. **1883** *Century Mag.* 570 The economy of an ignorant demagogy.

†demaim, *v. Obs.* [f. DE- I. 1, 3 + MAIM *v.*] *trans.* To maim, mutilate.

a **1670** SPALDING *Troub. Chas. I* (1829) 20 His head to be stricken frae his shoulders, and his body demaimed and quartered, and set up on exemplary places of the town.

demain, obs. form of DEMEAN *v.*[1]

demain(e, an early form of DOMAIN, DEMESNE.

demand (dɪ'mɑːnd, -æ-), *sb.*[1] Also 3-6 demaunde, 4-5 demande. [a. F. *demande* (12th c. in Littré), f. *demander* to DEMAND.]

1. a. An act of demanding or asking by virtue of right or authority; an authoritative or peremptory request or claim; also *transf.*, the substance or matter of the claim, that which is demanded.

c **1290** *S. Eng. Leg.* I. 130/823 Alle þat heorden þeos demaunde In grete wonder stoden þere. **1390-1** in *Coldingham Corr.* (Surtees 1841) 67 The quylk bischop mad hym richt resonable demaundes as we thoucht. **1393** GOWER *Conf.* I. 259 But he..Withstood the wrong of that demaunde. **1484** CAXTON *Fables of Æsop* v. xiii, A fayrer demaunde or request than thyn is I shalle now make. *a* **1533** LD. BERNERS *Huon* lxvi. 229 Graunt to Gerard your brother his demaunde. **1593** SHAKS. *Rich. II*, III. iii. 123 All the number of his faire demands Shall be accomplish'd without contradiction. **1654** WHITELOCKE *Jrnl. Swed. Emb.* (1772) I. 41 A desire, that Whitelocke would putt down his demands in writing. **1769** ROBERTSON *Chas. V.*, V. IV. 377 Henry's extravagant demands had been received at Madrid with that neglect which they deserved. **1883** FROUDE *Short Stud.* IV. I. vii. 81 The king's demand seemed just and moderate to all present.

b. *fig.*

1729 BUTLER *Serm.* Wks. 1874 II. 71 Compassion is a call, a demand of nature, to relieve the unhappy. **1816** L. HUNT *Rimini* III. 83 He made..A sort of fierce demand on your respect. **1885** F. TEMPLE *Relat. Relig. & Sc.* viii. 228 The sense of responsibility is a rock which no demand for completeness in Science can crush.

2. a. The action of demanding; claiming; peremptory asking.

1602 SHAKS. *Ham.* III. i. 178 He shall with speed to England For the demand of our neglected Tribute. **1606** —— *Tr. & Cr.* III. iii. 17 What would'st thou of vs Troian? make demand? **1642-3** EARL OF NEWCASTLE *Declar.* in Rushw. *Hist. Coll.* (1751) V. 134 So a Thief may term a true Man a Malignant, because he doth refuse to deliver his Purse upon demand. **1781** COWPER *Truth* 93 High in demand, though lowly in pretence. **1874** GREEN *Short Hist.* iv. §1. 161 The accession of a new sovereign..was at once followed by the demand of his homage.

b. *on* (†*at*) *demand*: (payable) on being requested, claimed, or presented: said of promissory notes, drafts, etc.

1691 *Lond. Gaz.* No. 2636/4 A Note, signed Samuel Lock to Isaac Stackhouse on Demand, for 158*l.* 7*s.* 3*d.* **1715** *Ibid.* No. 5299/4 They may have their Mony..at Demand. **1880** J. W. SMITH *Manual Com. Law* III. vi. (ed. 9) 287 If a bill or note is payable on demand, the Statute of Limitations runs from the date of the instrument, without waiting for a demand. **1892** J. ADAM *Commercial Corr.* 24 A Bank Note is a Promissory Note payable to Bearer on Demand.

3. *Law.* The action or fact of demanding or claiming in legal form; a legal claim; *esp.* a claim made by legal process to real property.

[*a* **1481** LITTLETON *Tenures* 39 Si homme relessa a un auter toutz maners demandes.] **1485** *Act 1 Hen. VII*, c. 1 As if his ancestor had dyed seised of the said lands and tenements so in demand. **1568** GRAFTON *Chron.* II. 351 Auctoritie to enquire, intreate, defyne and determine of all maner of causes, querels, debtes and demaundes. **1628** COKE *On Litt.* 291 b, There bee two kinde of demands or claimes, viz. a demand or claime in Deed, and a Demand or claime in Law. **1875** POSTE *Gaius* IV. Comm. (ed. 2) 564 In a demand of a heritage, security must be given.

4. a. 'The calling for a thing in order to purchase it' (J.); a call for a commodity on the part of consumers.

1711 STEELE *Spect.* No. 262 ¶3 The Demand for my Papers has increased every Month. **1780** *Impartial Hist. War Amer.* 35 The English, finding a great demand for tobacco in Europe. **1882** *Times* 27 Nov. 11 The demand for tonnage at the Rice Ports has decidedly increased.

b. *Pol. Econ.* The manifestation of a desire on the part of consumers to purchase some commodity or service, combined with the power to purchase; called also ***effectual demand*** (cf. EFFECTUAL 1 c). Correlative to ***supply***.

1776 ADAM SMITH *W.N.* I. xi. (1868) I. 197 The average produce of every sort of industry is always suited, more or less exactly, to the average consumption; the average supply to the average demand. **1776-1868** [see EFFECTUAL 1 c]. **1848** MILL *Pol. Econ.* III. iii. §2 Demand and supply govern the value of all things which cannot be indefinitely increased. **1878** JEVONS *Prim. Pol. Econ.* 99 The Laws of Supply and Demand may be thus stated: a rise of price tends to produce a greater supply and a less demand; a fall of price tends to produce a less supply and a greater demand.

c. *in demand*: sought after, in request.

1825 MCCULLOCH *Pol. Econ.* II. iv. 178 Labourers would be in as great demand as before. **1828** WEBSTER s.v., We say, the company of a gentleman is in great demand; the lady is in great demand or request. **1868** ROGERS *Pol. Econ.* iii. (1876) 2 It is necessary in order to give value to any object, that it should be, as is technically said, in demand.

5. An urgent or pressing claim or requirement; need actively expressing itself.

c **1790** WILLOCK *Voy.* 259 We found the garrison had very urgent demands for provisions. **1856** SIR B. BRODIE *Psychol. Inq.* I. I. 3 He had sufficient fortune to meet the reasonable demands of himself and his family. **1875** JOWETT *Plato* (ed. 2) III. 184 The demands of a profession destroy the elasticity of the mind.

6. A request; a question. *arch.*

c **1386** CHAUCER *Man of Law's T.* 374 Men myghten asken why she was nat slayn..I answere to that demande agayn Who saued danyel in the horrible Caue. *c* **1477** CAXTON *Jason* 61 b, I wolde fayn axe yow a demande if it were your playsir. **1553** T. WILSON *Rhet.* 1 Every question or demaunde in thynges is of two sortes. **1634** CANNE *Necess. Separ.* (1849) 15 There follows an exhortation again, with other demands and answers. **1766** GOLDSM. *Vic. W.* xxv, 'I ask pardon, sir..is not your name Ephraim Jenkinson?' At this demand he only sighed. *Ibid.* xxxi, 'Pray your honour..can the Squire have this lady's fortune if he be married to another?' 'How can you make such a simple demand?' replied the Baronet: 'undoubtedly he cannot.' **1821** SHELLEY *Prometh. Unb.* II. iv. 124 One more demand; and do thou answer me As my own soul would answer, did it know That which I ask.

7. *attrib.* and *Comb.* **demand curve**, a graph showing how the demand for a commodity or service varies with or depends on some other quantity; *spec.* one that shows how the demand, at any particular time, varies according to the price charged; **demand deposit** *U.S.*, a banking account from which the customer can withdraw funds without prior notification; **demand-driven** *a. Econ.*, motivated or propelled by demand, esp. the (usu. increasing) requirements of the user, consumer, etc.; **demand feeding**, the feeding of a baby when it cries, and not according to a timetable; **demand note**, a note payable on demand (2 b); also, a formal request for payment; **demand-pull** *attrib.* (Econ.), designating inflation caused by demand (DEMAND *sb.*[1] 4 b) in excess of available supply; contrasted with *cost-push* s.v. COST *sb.*[2] 6; **demand-side** *attrib.* (Econ.), pertaining to the demand side, esp. of the economy; hence, designating changes in price or output caused by variations in the pressure of demand; also *non-attrib.*; contrasted with *supply-side* adj. s.v. SUPPLY *sb.* 12 a.

1936 *Economist* 11 Apr. 85/2 And how far is the [building society] movement prepared to cope with any future change, such as a downward turn in the '*demand curve' for owner-occupied houses? **1949** *Mind* LVIII. 199 The basis of the theory of demand is the demand-curve, which states a functional relationship between the price and the quantity of a commodity demanded by the aggregate of consumers. **1930** J. M. KEYNES *Treat. Money* II. xxiii. 7 Current Accounts in England and *Demand Deposits in the United States roughly correspond to the Cash-deposits. **1947** L. TARSHIS *Elem. Econ.* III. xxiii. 284 When someone writes a check, he instructs his bank to transfer a part of his demand deposit, or checking account, to another person. **1966** R. G. LIPSEY *Introd. Positive Econ.* (ed. 2) VIII. xlviii. 675 A demand deposit means that the customer can withdraw his money on demand. **1980** *Newsweek* 27 Oct. 89/3 If too many Americans begin to feel the same way, the nation could return to the old *demand-driven inflationary treadmill. **1984** *N.Y. Times* 19 Feb. XXIII. 28/3 Health care is..a demand-driven industry, that is,..a large part of its costs are the result of increased demand for more and better services and technology. **1953** R. LIGHTWOOD in Gaisford & Lightwood *Paediatrics for Practitioner* I. xiii. 118 Some people find that '*demand feeding' obviates this [*sc.* early morning crying of a baby]. **1955** I. ASIMOV *Martian Way* (1964) 123 She followed the demand-feeding system or the 'if-you-want-it-holler-and-you'll-get-it' routine. **1970** *Radio Times* 16 Apr. 57/2 At about the same time that his [Dr. Spock's] book was published, a report came out attempting to prove that a baby could set his own feeding schedule ('demand feeding' as it has come to be known). **1892** *Daily News* 19 Dec. 6/3 *Demand money was valued at 10 to 25 per cent. **1866** CRUMP *Banking* v. 129 On a '*demand' note the statute [of Limitation] would run from the date of the instrument. **1892** J. ADAM *Commerc. Corr.* 22 The most common form is the *Demand Promissory Note. **1958** *Economist* 29 Nov. 784/3 The proper approach to the wage element in inflation is to reduce the spread (itself largely a product of '*demand-pull' inflation) between basic wage rates and earnings. **1980** *Newsweek* 13 Oct. 99/2 Reagan's is basically a demand-pull tax cut, relying on consumer spending and saving to expand the economy. **1975** *Forbes* (N.Y.) 1 Jan. 215 The supply side looks bad, but the *demand side looks worse. **1980** *N.Y. Times* 9 Mar. III. 1/5 This is in contrast to the demand-side, or Keynesian, theory that to cure a lagging economy, one creates demand through government spending or tax cuts; and to cure inflation, one depresses demand by cutting spending or raising taxes.

†de'mand, *sb.*[2] *Sc. Obs.* [a. OF. **desmande* (not in Godef.), f. OF. *desmander*, mod.F. dial. *démander* to countermand, f *des-*, *dé-* (DIS-) + *mander*:—L. *mandāre* to order.] Countermand; opposition to a command, desire, or wish; demur.

c **1500** *Lancelot* 191, I that dar makine no demande To quhat I wot It lykith loue commande. *Ibid.* 3052, I fal at hir command Do at I may, withouten more demand. **1535** STEWART *Cron. Scot.* II. 598 In the passage with drawin sword in hand, Still thair he stude, and maid thame sic demand, Neuir ane of thame he wald lat furth by.

demand (dɪ'mɑːnd, -æ-), *v.* Also 5-7 demaund(e. [a. F. *demander* (= Pr., Sp., Pg. *demandar*, It. *dimandare*):—L. *dēmandāre* to give in charge, entrust, commit (f. DE- I. 3 + *mandāre* to commission, order), in med.L. = *poscere* to demand, request (Du Cange).

The transition from the Latin sense 'give in charge, entrust, commit, commend' to the Romanic sense 'request, ask', was probably made through the notion of *entrusting* or *committing* to any one a duty to be performed, of *charging* a servant, or officer, with the performance of something, whence of *requiring* its performance of him, or *authoritatively requesting* him to do it. Hence the notion of *asking* in a way that commands obedience or compliance, which the word retains in English, and of simple asking, as in French. An indirect personal object (repr. the L. dative) would thus be a necessary part of the original construction, but it had ceased to be so before the word was adopted in England, where the earliest use, both in Anglo-Fr. and English, is to *demand a thing* simply. The verb probably passed into the vernacular from its legal use in Anglo-French.]

I. To ask (authoritatively or peremptorily) for: * *a thing*.

1. *trans.* To ask for (a thing) with legal right or authority; to claim as something one is legally or rightfully entitled to.

[**1292** BRITTON VI. iv. §16 Si..le pleintif se profre et demaunde jugement de la defaute, le pleintif recovera seisine de sa demaunde, et le tenaunt remeindra en la merci.] **1489** CAXTON *Faytes of A.* III. xiv. 199 Hys heyre myght haue an actyon for to demande the hole payement of hys wages. **1568** GRAFTON *Chron.* II. 114 He was compelled to demaund an ayde and taske of all England for the quieting of Irelande. **1594** R. CROMPTON *L'Authoritie des Courts* 8 The Serjeant of the Parliament should..demaund deliuery of the prisoner. **1628** COKE *On Litt.* 127 a, He shall defend but the wrong and the force, & demand the iudgement if he shall be answered. **1634** SIR T. HERBERT *Trav.* 182 And for every tun of fresh water, they demanded and was payed.. foure shillings and foure pence. **1670** *Tryal of Penn & Mead* in *Phenix* (1721) 321, I demand my Liberty, being freed by the Jury. **1763** *Gentl. Mag.* Sept. 463 The peace officer.. demanding entrance, the door was opened a little way. **1894** MIVART in *Eclectic Mag.* Jan. 10 To all men a doctrine was preached, and assent to its teaching was categorically demanded.

b. with *inf. phrase* or *subord. clause*.

1588 SHAKS. *L.L.L.* II. i. 143 He doth demand to haue repaid A hundred thousand Crownes. **1751** JOHNSON *Rambler* No. 161 ¶9 The constable..demanded to search the garrets. **1834** L. RITCHIE *Wand. by Seine* 40 The diocese of Paris..had the cruelty and injustice to demand that the bones..should be returned to their care.

2. *spec.* in *Law.* To make formal claim to (real property) as the rightful owner. Cf. DEMAND *sb.* 3 and DEMANDANT 1.

1485 *Act 1 Hen. VII*, c. 1 That the demandant in euery such case haue his action against the Pernour or Pernours of the profits of the lands or tenements demanded. **1531** *Dial. Laws Eng.* ix. 18 b, If the demandaunt or plaintyffe hangyng his writ wyll entre in to the thyng demaunded his wryt shal abate. **1628** COKE *On Litt.* 127 b, Demandant, *peteur*, is hee which is actor in a reall action because he demandeth lands, etc. **1783** BLACKSTONE *Comm.* (ed. 9) II. App. xviii, Francis Golding Clerk in his proper person demandeth against David Edwards, Esq., two messuages.

3. To ask for (a thing) peremptorily, imperiously, urgently, or in such a way as to command attention. †But formerly often weakened into a simple equivalent of 'to ask' (*esp.* in transl. from French, etc.). Const. *of* or *from* a person.

1484 CAXTON *Curiall* I b, But what demaundest thou? Thou sechest the way to lese thy self by thexample of me. **1548** HALL *Chron.* 236 When Piers Cleret had paied the pencion to the lorde Hastynges, he gently demaunded of hym an acquitaunce, for his discharge. **1600** E. BLOUNT tr. *Conestaggio* 273 By his letter, hee had demaunded pardon of the Catholique King. **1632** J. HAYWARD tr. *Biondi's Eromena* 108 He was to intreate his father to demand for him a wife. **1651** HOBBES *Leviath.* III. xl. 255 They demanded a King, after the manner of the nations. **1812** MAR. EDGEWORTH *Vivian* xi, The physician qualified the assent which his lordship's peremptory tone seemed to demand. **1887** BOWEN *Virg. Æneid* II. 71 Trojans eye me in wrath, and demand my life as a foe!

b. with object expressed by *inf. phrase* or *subord. clause*.

1534 LD. BERNERS tr. *Golden Bk. M. Aurel.* (1546) 56, I demaunded then to haue a compte of the people. **1600** E. BLOUNT tr. *Conestaggio* 242 They demaunded secretly..to borrow beds of silke, silver vessels, and other things fit for a kings service. **1754** HUME *Hist. Eng.* I. v. 304 Anselm.. demanded positively, that all the revenues of his see should be restored to him. **1769** GOLDSM. *Hist. Rome* (1786) I. 39 Two ruffians..demanded to speak with the king. **1798** *Invasion* II. 232 He..demanded to speak with Sherland.

c. *absol.*

1509 HAWES *Past. Pleas.* XXXIII. xxii, Whan I had so obteyned the victory, Unto me than my verlet well sayd: You have demaunded well and worthely. **1597** SHAKS. *Lover's Compl.* 149 Yet did I not, as some my equals did, Demand of him, nor being desired, yielded. **1601** —— *All's Well* II. i. 21 Those girles of Italy, take heed of them, They say our French lacke language to deny If they demand.

†**4.** To make a demand for (a thing) *to* (a person). [= Fr. *demander à*.] *Obs.*

1483 CAXTON *G. de la Tour* D vj, Of whiche god shalle aske and demaunde to them acompte the day of his grete Jugement. *c* **1500** *Melusine* 134 The kinge receyued hym moche benyngly and demanded to hym som tydynges.

5. To ask for (a person) to come or be produced; to ask to see; to require to appear; to summon.

1650 FULLER *Pisgah* II. xii. 257 And first in a fair way the offenders are demanded to justice. **1848** C. BRONTË *J. Eyre* xxxiv, While the driver and Hannah brought in the boxes, they demanded St. John.

6. *fig.* Said of things: **a.** To call for of right or justice; to require.

[**1292** BRITTON I. ix. §1 Et poet estre treysoun graunt et petit; dunt acun demaund jugement de mort, et acun amissioun de membre [etc.].] **1703** POPE *Thebais* 3 Th' alternate reign destroy'd by impious arms Demands our song. **1779** COWPER *Lett.* 2 Oct., Two pair of soles, with shrimps which arrived last night demand my acknowledgments. **1836** J. GILBERT *Chr. Atonem.* vi. (1852) 168 Holiness may demand, but not desire the punishment of transgressors. **1871** FREEMAN *Norm. Conq.* (1876) IV. xvii. 93 The piety of the Duke demanded that the ceremony should be no longer delayed.

b. To call for or require as necessary; to have need of.

1748 F. SMITH *Voy. Disc. N.-W. Pass.* I. 145 Keep the Water..from going down faster, than the [Beaver] Dams which are below the House demand it. **1855** BAIN *Senses & Int.* II. ii. §6 Sensibility everywhere demands a distribution of nerve fibres. **1878** MORLEY *Carlyle* Crit. Misc. Ser. I. 199 Government..more than anything else in this world demands skill, patience, energy, long and tenacious grip.

** *a person* for *or* to do *a thing*.

†**7.** To ask (a person) authoritatively, peremptorily, urgently, etc. *for* (a thing); to require (a person) *to do* a thing. *Obs.*

1632 LITHGOW *Trav.* x. 482, I intreated Sir Richard Halkins to goe a shoare to the Governour, and demand him for my Gold. **1652** J. WADSWORTH tr. *Sandoval's Civ. Wars Spain* 22 Hee demanded the Catalanes to receiv, and acknowledg him their King. **1726–7** SWIFT *Gulliver* I. iii. 49 After they were read, I was demanded to swear to the performance of them. **1795** *Cicely* I. 37 He demanded the traitor to give up his lovely prize.

*** *intrans.*

†**8.** To make a demand; to ask *for* or *after*; to call urgently *for*. *Obs.*

a **1533** LD. BERNERS *Huon* lx. 208 Huon approchyd to the shyppe and demaundyd for the patrone and for the mayster of them that were in the shyppe. **1605** SHAKS. *Lear* III. ii. 65 Which euen but now, demanding after you, Deny'd me to come in. **1654** R. CODRINGTON tr. *Justine* 200 To free himself of it, he demanded for a sword.

II. To ask (authoritatively) to know or be told: * *a thing*.

9. To ask to know, authoritatively or formally; to request to be told.

[**1292** BRITTON I. v. §9 Qe il verite dirrount de ceo qe hom les demaundera de par nous.] **1548–9** (Mar.) *Bk. Com. Prayer, Baptism*, Then the prieste shall demaunde the name of the childe. **1593** SHAKS. *Lucr.* Argt., They..finding Lucrece attired in mourning habit, demanded the cause of her sorrow. **1600** E. BLOUNT tr. *Conestaggio* 262 The Portugals demaunded the state of the realme. **1634** SIR T. HERBERT *Trav.* 77 In bravery and shew of insolence, demanding her businesse. **1818** SHELLEY *Rev. Islam* III. vii, Ere with rapid lips and gathered brow I could demand the cause. **1859** TENNYSON *Enid* 193 And Guinevere..desired his name and sent Her maiden to demand it of the dwarf.

b. with the object expressed by a clause.

1494 FABYAN *Chron.* I. xiv. 14 Y^e^ fader..demaunded of Ragan, the seconde doughter, how wel she loued hym. **1526** *Pilgr. Perf.* (W. de W. 1531) 200 b, Demaundyng & enquiryng, where is he y^t^ is borne the kyng of ye iewes. **1568** GRAFTON *Chron.* II. 226 She demaunded howe her Uncle the French king did. **1615** SIR E. HOBY *Curry-combe* 80 You should rather demand from him What likenese there is between 34 and 42. **1766** GOLDSM. *Vic. W.* xiv, The old gentleman..most respectfully demanded if I was in any way related to the great Primrose. **1845** M. PATTISON *Ess.* (1889) I. 23 All the members demanded with one voice who it was who was charged with the crime of theft.

†**10.** With cognate object: To ask (a question, etc.). *Obs.*

1502 *Ord. Crysten Men* (W. de W. 1506) I. iii. 16 Which demaundeth a questyon. **1577** NORTHBROOKE *Dicing* (1843) 62 Saye on..what you haue to demande, and I will answere you. **1602** FULBECKE *1st Pt. Parall.* 50 Then I know your opinion as touching this question, now let me demaund another. **1605** BACON *Adv. Learn.* II. Ded. §15 It asketh some knowledge to demand a question, not impertinent.

** *a person* (as to *a thing*).

†**11.** To ask (a person) authoritatively or formally to inform one (*of*, *how*, etc.). *Obs.*

c **1450** *Crt. of Love* (R.), And me demaunded how and in what wise I thither come, and what my errand was. *c* **1477** CAXTON *Jason* 18 She..demanded him how he felte him self and how he ferde. *a* **1536** *Calisto & Mel.* in Hazl. *Dodsley* I. 85 I demand thee not thereof. **1611** SHAKS. *Cymb.* III. vi. 92 When we haue supp'd Wee'l mannerly demand thee of thy Story. **1632** LITHGOW *Trav.* I. 38, I demanded our dependant, what was to pay?

b. without extension.

1490 CAXTON *How to Die* 11 Yf there be none to demaunde hym, he oughte to demaunde hymselfe. **1555** EDEN *Decades* 5 They declared the same to me when I demanded them.

c. in *passive*.

1526 *Pilgr. Perf.* (W. de W. 1531) 16 Demaunded by Pharao of what age he was, Jacob answered. **1568** GRAFTON *Chron.* II. 277 They were demaunded why they departed. **1635** SIBBES *Soul's Confl.* Pref. (1638) 9 Philip..being a long time prisoner..was demanded what upheld him all that time. **1643** PRYNNE *Sov. Power Parl.* I. (ed. 2) 91 Had our Ancestors..been demanded these few questions. **1722** SEWEL *Hist. Quakers* (1795) II. VII. 11 Being demanded in the Court why he did not tell his name.

*** *intrans.*

12. To ask, inquire, make inquiry.

a. *of*, †*at* the person asked; †**b.** *of* the object asked about.

1382 WYCLIF *Bible, Pref. Ep.* iv. 65 The Saueour.. askynge of questiouns of the lawe, more techeth, whil he prudentli demaundeth [**1388** while he askith wisely questiouns]. **1526** TINDALE *Luke* iii. 14 The soudyoures lyke wyse demaunded of hym sayinge: and what shall we do? **1568** GRAFTON *Chron.* II. 205 The king..helde her still by the right hande, demaundyng right gently of her estate and businesse. **1588** KING tr. *Canisius' Catech.* 208 Quhen God sal rise to iudge, and quhen he sal demand at me quhat sal I answer? **1611** BIBLE *Job* xlii. 4 Heare..I will demand of thee, and declare thou vnto me. **1821** SHELLEY *Prometh. Unb.* II. iv. 141 The immortal Hours, Of whom thou didst demand.

Hence **de'manded** *ppl. a.*

1552 in HULOET. **1769** *Oxford Mag.* II. 143/2 The demanded qualification is a merciful soul, if we would experience mercy. **1815** MARY PILKINGTON *Celebrity* III. 152 The demanded drugs were sold without exciting the smallest suspicion.

demandable (dɪˈmɑːndəb(ə)l, -æ-), *a.* [f. prec. + -ABLE.] That may be demanded or claimed.

1576 FLEMING *Panopl. Epist.* 62 We did no lesse..in the behalfe of our countrie, then of dutie was demaundable. **1602** FULBECKE *Pandectes* 43 Certaine ministeries or dutifull respectes were by reason of such Leagues due and demaundable. **1666** PEPYS *Diary* (1879) III. 416, £2000.. demaundable at two days' warning. **1720** *Lond. Gaz.* No. 5894/3 The..Interest..shall be demandable by the Bearers. **1818** CRUISE *Digest* (ed. 2) V. 328 Any writ by which lands are demandable. **1884** SIR R. BAGGALLAY in *Law Rep.* 28 Ch. Div. 472 A rate due and demandable at the time it was made.

demandant (dɪˈmɑːndənt, -æ-). [a. Anglo-Fr. (and Fr.) *demandant* (15th c.), sb. use of pr. pple. of *demander* to DEMAND.] One who demands.

1. *Law.* **a.** *spec.* The plaintiff in a real action; **b.** *gen.* a plaintiff or claimant in any civil action.

[**1344** *Act 18 Edw. III*, c. 7 Pour quoi tieux dismes a les demandauntz ne deivent estre restitutes—*transl.* wherefore such dismes ought not to be restored to the said demandants.] **1485** *Act 1 Hen. VII*, c. 1 The Demaundants shall not knowe ayenst whom they shall take their accion. **1495** *Act 11 Hen. VII*, c. 24 §1 The demaundaunt or playntif in the same Atteynt hath afore be nonsute. **1614** SELDEN *Titles Hon.* 234 The Earle excepted also to the Jurisdiction ..and the Demandants replie. **1641** *Termes de la Ley* 107 b, Demandant is he that sueth or complaineth in an action Reall for title of land, and he is called plaintife in an Assise, and in an action personal. **1767** BLACKSTONE *Comm.* II. 271 In such cases a jury shall try the true right of the demandants or plaintiffs to the land. **1832** AUSTIN *Jurispr.* (1879) I. vi. 295 A sovereign government..may appear in the character of defendant, or may appear in the character of demandant before a tribunal of its own appointment.

2. One who makes a demand or claim; a demander.

1590 SWINBURNE *Testaments* 62 It is to bee presumed that the testator did answer, yea, rather to deliuer himselfe of the importunitie of the demaundant, then vpon deuotion or intente to make his will. **1603** HOLLAND *Plutarch's Mor.* 204 To reproch the demandant, as though hee had little skill and discretion, to aske a thing of him who could not give the same. **1780** BURKE *Econ. Reform* Wks. 1842 I. 234 Which will give preference to services, not according to the importunity of the demandant, but the rank and order of their utility or their justice. **1888** *Co-operative News* 26 May 486 Rights equitably claimed by the demandant for himself.

3. One who questions or interrogates.

1656 J. BOURNE *Def. Scriptures* 52 Read Mr. John Deacon, a solid and sharp Questionist, Replyant and Demandant. **1826** DISRAELI *Viv. Grey* VI. vi, It was evident the demandant had questioned rather from systems than by way of security. **1854** SYD. DOBELL *Balder* Pref. 6 Perhaps it would be considered too general a reference if I were to remit my demandants to the whole history of intellect.

†**de'mandate,** *v. Obs.* [f. ppl. stem of L. *dēmandāre* to give in charge, entrust, commit: see DEMAND *v.* and -ATE.] *trans.* To commit, delegate, entrust. Hence **de'mandated** *ppl. a.*

1641 'SMECTYMNUUS' *Vind. Answ.* xiv. 174 The Church, which did first demandate this Episcopall authority to one particular person. **1640** BP. HALL *Episc.* II. i. 90 Out of his owne peculiarly demandated Authority.

de'mandative, *a. rare.* [f. ppl. stem of L. *dēmandāre* to DEMAND + -ATIVE.] Of the nature of a demand or legal claim; made by or on behalf of the demandant.

1820–27 BENTHAM *Judicial Proc.* xiii. §1 Wks. II. 74 Statements, demandative or defensive.

†**de,man'dee, demandé.** *Obs. nonce-wd.* [See -EE.] One of whom a question is demanded.

1603 HOLLAND *Plutarch's Mor.* 205 Allowing a competent space of time betweene the demand and the answere: during which silence, both the demander may have while to bethinke himselfe and adde somewhat thereto, if he list, and also the demandé time to think of an answere.

demander (dɪˈmɑːndə(r), -æ-). [f. DEMAND *v.* + -ER. Cf. F. *demandeur* (13th c.).] One who demands.

1. One who asks with authority, urgency, etc.; one who claims, requests, calls for.

a **1533** LD. BERNERS *Gold. Bk. M. Aurel.* (1546) D vij, The requeste was pitifull..and he to whom it was made, was the father, and the demaunder was the mother. **1556** *Aurelio & Isab.* (1608) A ij, Unto none of the foresayde demaunders wold he never geve her in mariage. **1638** CHILLINGW. *Relig. Prot.* I. iv. §19. 201 He hath intreated his Demander to accept of thus much in part of paiment. **1754** JOHNSON *Life of Cave*, A tenacious maintainer, though not a clamorous demander of his right.

†**2.** One who asks or inquires; one who puts a question. *Obs.*

1548 UDALL, etc. *Erasm. Par. Luke* xviii. 146 The demaunder of the question. **1583** HOLLYBAND *Campo di Fior* 157 O what an importunate asker of questions is here.. O what a troublesome demander. **1692** LOCKE *Toleration* III. i. Wks. 1727 II. 304 The Majority..shall give any forward Demander Occasion to ask, What other Means is there left?

3. One from whom there is a demand for an article of commerce; a buyer, consumer.

a **1620** CAREW (J.), And delivereth them to the demanders' ready use at all seasons. **1776** ADAM SMITH *W.N.* I. vii. (1868) I. 58 Those who are willing to pay the natural price of the commodity..may be called the effectual demanders. **1821** *New Monthly Mag.* I. 96 Demanders and not suppliers. **1885** J. BONAR *Malthus* II. i. 233 The power of buying the food that feeds new demanders.

†**de'manderess.** *Obs.* [a. F. *demanderesse*, fem. of *demandeur*: see prec.] A female demandant.

1611 COTGR., *Demanderesse*, a demaunderesse, a woman that is a Plaintife or Petitioner. **1828** WEBSTER, *Demandress.*

demanding (dɪˈmɑːndɪŋ, -æ-), *vbl. sb.* [-ING[1].] The action of the verb DEMAND.

1530 PALSGR. 212/2 Demaundyng of counsayle, *consultation.* **1556** *Aurelio & Isab.* (1608) C, Moderate demaundinges and accustomed requestes. **1642** *Protests of Lords* I. 13 The demanding by this House of some to be left to justice.

de'manding, *ppl. a.* [-ING[2].] That demands. Hence **de'mandingly** *adv.*, in a demanding manner, as a demandant.

1873 L. WALLACE *Fair God* V. v. 289 And what if the Fate had come demandingly?

de'mandingness. [f. DEMANDING *ppl. a.* + -NESS.] The quality or condition of being demanding.

1930 GWENDOLEN GREENE *Two Witnesses* i. 18 This conception he held to the last, never shrinking from its austere demandingness. **1949** M. MEAD *Male & Female* xv. 298 Conceited demandingness in a woman.

demane, obs. Sc. f. DEMEAN *v.*[1], to treat, etc.

demantoid (diːˈmæntɔɪd). [a. G. *demantoid.*] A green variety of andradite having a brilliant lustre.

1892 DANA *Syst. Min.* (ed. 6) 442 Demantoid is a grass green to emerald-green variety [of garnet] with brilliant luster. **1897** *Edin. Rev.* Oct. 346 The demantoid or Bobrovka garnet. **1957** *Encycl. Brit.* X. 29/2 The grass green demantoid is used as a gemstone and possesses high refractive and dispersive power. **1971** *Materials & Technology* II. viii. 519 By far the most valued garnet at the present time is the brilliant green demantoid.

demarcate (ˈdiːmɑːkeɪt), *v.* [Back-formation on DEMARCATION; see -ATE[3]: cf. Sp. and Pg. *demarcar.*] *trans.* To mark out or determine the boundary or limits of; to mark off, separate, or distinguish *from*; to mark or determine, as a boundary or limit; to define. **a.** *lit.* in reference to spatial limits, as of territory.

1816 KEATINGE *Trav.* (1817) I. 214 The marine deposits ..appear to demarcate its extreme undulation here. **1882** *St. James's Gaz.* Apr., The region thus demarcated is..the only part of Wales described..in Domesday. **1884** *Pall Mall G.* 9 June 11/1 An Anglo-Russian Commission will proceed.. to demarcate the northern frontier of Afghanistan.

b. *fig.* in reference to other than spatial limits.

1858 LEWES *Sea-Side Stud.* 314 How shall we demarcate Reproduction from Growth? **1883** *Athenæum* 20 Jan. 79 Sharp distinctions of national flavour which demarcate one European literature from another.

Hence **'demarcated, 'demarcating** *ppl. adjs.*

1840 GLADSTONE *Ch. Princ.* 34 For the preservation of the demarcating lines. **1862** H. SPENCER *First Princ.* II. xxi. §169 The demarcated grouping which we everywhere see.

demarcation (diːmɑːˈkeɪʃən). Also **demarkation.** [ad. Sp. *demarcacion* (Pg. *demarcação*), n. of action from *demarcar* to lay down the limits of, mark out the bounds of, f. *de-* = DE I. 3 + *marcar* to MARK. So F. *démarcation* (1752 in Hatzf.), from Spanish. First used of the *linea de demarcacion* (Pg. *linha de demarcação*) laid down by the Pope in dividing the New World between the Spanish and Portuguese.]

1. The action of marking the boundary or limits of something, or of marking it off from something else; delimitation; separation. Usually in phr. ***line of demarcation.***

a. *lit.* (*a*) originally in reference to the meridian dividing the Spanish from the Portuguese Indies.

The bull of 4 May 1493 'sobre la particion del oceano' fixed the Line of Demarcation at 100 leagues west of the Cape Verde Isles; the 'Capitulacion de la particion del Mar Oceano entre los Reyes Catolicos y Don Juan Rey de Portugal', of 7 June 1494, definitely established it at 370 leagues (17½ to an equatorial degree) west of these isles, or about 47° long. W. of Greenwich in the Atlantic, and at the anti-meridian of 133° E. long. in the East Indies. The word occurs in the latter document 'dentro de la dicha limitacion y demarcacion'. Navarrete *Viages* II. 121.)

1727–52 CHAMBERS *Cycl.*, *Line of Demarcation*, or Alexandrian Line. **1760–72** tr. *Juan & Ulloa's Voy.* (ed. 3) II. 142 Eastward it extends to Brasil, being terminated by the meridian of demarcation. **1777** ROBERTSON *Hist. Amer.* (1778) I. III. 206 The communication with the East Indies, by a course to the westward of the line of demarkation, drawn by the Pope. **1804** SOUTHEY in *Ann. Rev.* II. 6 Ruy Falero wanted to bring the Moluccas on the Spanish side of the line of demarcation. **1849** tr. *Humboldt's Cosmos* II. 655 As early as the 4th of May (1493) the celebrated bull was signed by Pope Alexander VI, which established 'to all eternity' the line of demarcation between the Spanish and Portuguese possessions at a distance of one hundred leagues to the west of the Azores.

(*b*) of other lines dividing regions.

1801 W. TAYLOR in *Monthly Mag.* XI. 646 As if the whole North of Germany, within the line of demarcation might very conveniently become a separate empire. **1809** W. IRVING *Knickerb.* (1861) 25 Nothing but precise demarcation of limits, and the intention of cultivation, can establish the possession. **1856** STANLEY *Sinai & Pal.* vi. (1858) 267 So completely was the line of demarcation observed..between Phœnicia and Palestine, that their histories hardly touch.

b. *fig.*

1776 BENTHAM *Fragm. Govt.* iv. §36 Wks. I. 290 These bounds the supreme body..has marked out to its authority: of such a demarcation, then, what is the effect? **1790** BURKE *Fr. Rev.* 43 The speculative line of demarcation, where obedience ought to end, and resistance must begin, is..not easily definable. **1875** LYELL *Princ. Geol.* II. III. xxxvii. 327 Where the lines of demarcation between the species ought to be drawn. **1883** *Century Mag.* Dec. 196/2 A strange demarkation between the sexes was enforced in these ceremonies.

2. *attrib.* ***demarcation dispute, rule,*** etc., in reference to the precise scope and kind of work laid down by trade unions for their members in their rules, a dispute occurring between two unions where such rules appear to conflict.

1930 *Monotype Recorder* XXIX. 19 The amicable settlement of demarcation problems raised by developments in machines and processes. **1931** *Economist* 14 Feb. 340/1 In engineering, as in many other British industries, the burden of labour costs has been inflated unduly by rigid demarcation rules. **1940** R. POSTGATE *Verdict of Twelve* I. vi. 82 The enforcing of the rule book had already taken out of the hands of the members their power to start continual small strikes over 'demarcation disputes'. **1963** *Ann. Reg.* *1962* 52 Demarcation dispute in the steel industry between the bricklayers' and steelworkers' unions over who should lay the dolomite blocks used to line furnaces. **1969** *Listener* 30 Jan. 157/2 David Haworth's *Observer* report on a demarcation dispute in Barrow may be read as a classic story of an employer setting two unions against each other.

demarcative (dɪˈmɑːkətɪv), *a.* [f. DEMARC(ATION + -ATIVE.] Of, pertaining to, or characterized by demarcation: used esp. in *Linguistics.*

1955 M. REIFER *Dict. New Words* 88/2 *Demarcative function*, the use of phonemic and non-phonemic features.. to mark off the boundaries of words and morphemes. **1959** *Archivum Linguisticum* XI. II. 100 The demarcative phonological features can be termed prosodies of word delimitation. **1964** R. H. ROBINS *Gen. Linguistics* 166 The phonological features in question, juncturally analysed in American phonemics, are regarded in prosodic analysis as demarcative word prosodies.

demarcator (ˈdiːmɑːkeɪtə(r)). [f. DEMARCATE *v.* + -OR.] One who marks out boundaries.

1898 *Daily News* 25 Feb. 6/3 English demarcators and French got on together excellently well. **1900** *Ibid.* 22 Dec. 7/2 The demarcators failed to agree, and there is now a tremendous question between the two countries as to the lines drawn on the map by their respective experts.

demarch (ˈdiːmɑːk). [ad. L. *dēmarchus*, a. Gr. δήμαρχος governor of the people, president of a deme, f. δῆμος district, deme, common people + ἀρχός leader, chief.] In ancient Greece: The president or chief magistrate of a deme. In modern Greece: The mayor of a town or commune.

1642 *Coll. Rights & Priv. Parl.* 10 At Lacedemonia, the Ephors: at Athens, the Demarches. *c* **1643** *Maximes Unfolded* 38 Demarchs, or popular Magistrates, to moderate their supposed Monarchy. **1838** THIRLWALL *Greece* II. xi. 74 The newly incorporated townships, each of which was governed by its local magistrate, the *demarch.* **1884** J. T. BENT in *Macm. Mag.* Oct. 431/2 These eparchs again look after the demarchs or mayors of the various towns.

‖**démarche** (demarʃ, deɪˈmɑːʃ). (In mod. Dicts. demarch.) [a. F. *démarche* (15–16th c. in Hatzf.), vbl. sb. f. *démarcher* (12th c.) to march, f. *dé-* = L. DE- I. 3 + *marcher* to MARCH. In the 18th c. nearly anglicized; now treated as a French loanword.] **a.** Walk, step; proceeding, manner of action.

1658 tr. *Bergerac's Satyr. Char.* p.v, As much deceived as those are that..expect to learne Comportment from a Comedians Demarche. **1721** *Collect. Lett. in Lond. Jrnl.* x. (T.), Imagination enlivens reason in its most solemn demarches. **1885** L. MALET *Col. Enderby's Wife* III. viii. 139 (Stanf.) Tired out, past caring whether her *démarche* had been a wise or a foolish one.

b. Esp. a diplomatic initiative, a political step or proceeding.

1678 TEMPLE *Let. Ld. Treas.* Wks. 1731 II. 479 By the French Demarches here and at Nimeguen..I concluded all Confidence irreparably broken between Us and France. **1940** *Ann. Reg.* *1939* 210 This démarche..plainly indicated to the Soviet leaders that Germany was prepared to concede to Russia more than Britain and France. **1955** *Times* 6 May 8/4 In his opinion British *démarches* against Athens radio broadcasts were unjustified. **1956** *Ann. Reg.* *1955* 228 To induce the Bonn Government to make a joint démarche to the four Foreign Ministers.

demarchy (ˈdiːmɑːkɪ). [ad. L. *dēmarchia*, a. Gr. δημαρχία the office of a DEMARCH: see -Y.] The office of a demarch; a popular government. The municipal body of a modern Greek commune.

1642 BRIDGE *Wounded Consc. Cured* §1. 9 Such..were the Ephori that were set against the Kings of Lacedemonia..or the Demarchy against the Senate at Athens. *c* **1643** *Maximes Unfolded* 38 If the people in Parliament may choose their Lawes, the Democracy will prove a Demarchy, and that spoiles and destroyes Monarchie.

demargarinated (diːˈmɑːgərɪneɪtɪd), *a.* [f. DE- + MARGARIN + -ATE[3] + -ED[1].] Of an oil, having the stearin or solid part removed.

1920 W. CLAYTON *Margarine* 10 A deposit of 'stearin' ensues.., and if this is removed a 'winter' oil is obtained... Such winter oils are also said to be 'demargarinated'. **1939** *Thorpe's Dict. Appl. Chem.* (ed. 4) III. 410/2 The filtered [cottonseed] oil, known in commerce as 'winter oil' ('demargarinated' or 'destearinated' oil).

†**de'mark, de'marque,** *v.*[1] *Obs.* [a. F. *dé-marque-r* to deprive of its mark or marks, f. *dé-*, *des-* (DE- I. 6) + *marquer* to mark. Cf. DISMARK.] *trans.* To remove the marks of, obliterate, efface.

1654 H. L'ESTRANGE *Chas. I* (1655) 168 To form their deportment in so supple a posture, as might de-marque and deface all tokens of so horrid an imputation [as rebellion].

demark (dɪˈmɑːk), *v.*[2] [Deduced from DEMARCATION after *mark* vb.: cf. Sp. and Pg. *demarcar* and DEMARCATE.] = DEMARCATE.

1834 H. O'BRIEN *Round Towers Ireland* 242 Nor are their [myriads of ages'] limits demarked by the vague and indefinite exordium of even the talented..legislator, Moses himself. **1883** F. HALL in (*N.Y.*) *Nation* XXXVII. 434/3 Distinguishing traits..such as everywhere demark the denizens of a colony from those of its mother country.

de'martialize, *v. nonce-wd.* [f. DE- II. 1 + MARTIAL *a.* + -IZE.] *trans.* To deprive of warlike character or organization.

1882 W. E. BAXTER *Winter in India* xiv. 133 The whole population being disarmed and demartialized.

dematerialize (ˌdiːməˈtɪərɪəlaɪz), *v.* [f. DE- II. 1 + MATERIAL *a.* + -IZE.] **a.** *trans.* To deprive of material character or qualities; to render immaterial. **b.** *intr.* To become dematerialized. Hence **dema'terialized** *ppl. a.*, **-izing** *ppl. a.* and *vbl. sb.*, **dema,teriali'zation.**

1884 H. SPENCER in *19th Cent.* Jan. 3 The gradual dematerialisation of the ghost and of the god. **1890** *Spectator* 11 Oct., The seeds of that spiritual development which was to culminate in the completely dematerialised God of Christianity. **1891** *Cosmopolitan* XII. 114/1 He has dematerialized everything into a memory. **1892** *Scot. Leader* 29 Jan. 4 She will gradually dematerialise, and fade away like a vapour before the eyes. **1899** *Westm. Gaz.* 1 Apr. 2/3 'The administrators of our manufacturing and commercial firms and the commercial traveller are not necessarily condemned to a barren materialism...' Perhaps when he has dematerialised the commercial traveller he will try his hand on the Stock Exchange. **1914** C. MACKENZIE *Sinister Street* II. IV. iv. 928 These abrupt dematerializations of the underworld were really very difficult to deal with. **1935** *Burlington Mag.* Aug. 53/2 It is a 'dematerialisation' which afterwards El Greco realised in another way. **1956** R. M. LESTER *Towards Hereafter* ii. 30 The clothes began to take shape, and slowly filled out until the medium was sitting in her chair again, looking just as she had done before the dematerializing. **1960** M. CECIL *Something in Common* ii. 30 She..dematerialized backwards into her office.

demath, dial. var. of DAY-MATH.

1559 *Lanc. Wills* III. 125 One demathe of hey. **1820** WILBRAHAM *Gloss. Dial. Chesh.*, *Demath*, generally used for a statute acre, but erroneously so, for it is properly one-half of a Cheshire acre..the Demath bears [the proportion] of 32 to 30¼ to the statute acre. **1887** DARLINGTON *South Chesh. Gloss.* s.v., We speak of a 'five-demath' or a 'seven-demath field'.

demaund(e, obs. form of DEMAND.

demay, obs. var. of DISMAY *v.*

†**de'mayn,** short for PAIN-DEMAINE (*panis dominicus*), bread of the finest quality: see DEMEINE.

demayn(e, obs. f. DEMEAN *v.*[1], DEMESNE.

demd, -on, obs. f. *deemed*, from DEEM *v.*

†**deme,** *sb.*[1] *Obs.* Forms: 1 dœma, 1–2 déma, 2–3 deme. [OE. *dœma*, *déma* = OHG. *tuomo*, Gothic type *dômja*:—OTeut. *dômjon-*, f. *dôm-* judgement, doom.] A judge, arbiter, ruler.

c **825** *Vesp. Psalter* xlix. [l.] 6 Forðon god doema is. *c* **1175** *Lamb. Hom.* 95 þe helend is alles moncunnes dema. *c* **1205** LAY. 9634 þerof he wes deme & duc feole ȝere. *a* **1250** *Owl & Night.* 1783 Wa schal unker speche rede And telle tovore unker deme?

deme (diːm), *sb.*[2] [ad. Gr. δῆμος district, township.]

1. A township or division of ancient Attica. In modern Greece: A commune.

[**1628** HOBBES *Thucyd.* (1822) 86 Acharnas, which is the greatest town in all Attica of those that are called *Demoi.*] **1833** THIRLWALL in *Philol. Mus.* II. 290 The procession.. is supposed to take place in the deme of Dicæopolis. **1838** —— *Greece* II. 73 The ten tribes were subdivided into districts of various extent, called *demes*, each containing a town or village, as its chief place. **1874** MAHAFFY *Soc. Life Greece* xii. 383 He was made a citizen and enrolled in the respectable Acharnian deme. **1881** *Blackw. Mag.* Apr. 542 (*Greece & her Claims*) Elementary schools in most of the demes.

2. *Biol.* Any undifferentiated aggregate of cells, plastids, or monads. (Applied by Perrier to the tertiary or higher individual resulting from the aggregate integration of merides or permanent colonies of cells.)

1883 P. GEDDES in *Encycl. Brit.* XVI. 843/1 The term colony, corm, or deme may indifferently be applied to these aggregates of primary, secondary, tertiary, or quaternary order which are not, however, integrated into a whole, and do not reach the full individuality of the next higher order. *Ibid.* 843/2 Starting from the unit of the first order, the plastid or *monad*, and terming any undifferentiated aggregate a *deme*, we have a *monad-deme* integrating into a secondary unit or *dyad*, this rising through *dyad-demes* into a *triad*, these forming *triad-demes*, etc.

3. *Ecol.* A local population of closely related plants or animals; also used as the second element of more precise terms, as in *ecodeme*, *gamodeme*, *topodeme*, etc. Hence **demo'logical** *a.*

1939 GILMOUR & GREGOR in *Nature* 19 Aug. 333/1 In the course of work on the experimental delimitation of botanical groups, the need has arisen for a term which can be applied to any specified assemblage of taxonomically closely related individuals... We propose the term *deme* (from the Greek δῆμος) for this purpose, with appropriate prefixes to denote particular kinds of demes. **1954** *Genetica* XXVII. 150 The essence of the deme terminology is the construction of a series of category-terms by the addition of one or more virtually self-explanatory prefixes to the 'neutral' suffix '-deme'. *Ibid.* 151 Sometimes, however, demological units will coincide with recognised taxa. **1961** G. G. SIMPSON *Princ. Animal Taxon.* v. 176 The smallest unit of population that has evolutionary significance is a group of individual animals (of one species or subspecies) so localized that they are in easy and more or less frequent contact with each other. .. That minimal population unit is called a deme. **1966** R. L. SMITH *Ecology & Field Biol.* xxiii. 431 Collectively, individuals within each group make up a genetical population, or deme... Individuals that make up the deme are not identical. **1969** *Nature* 22 Nov. 750/1 The patterns of polymorphisms he found in Arizona indicate that within a species there are small units, or demes, of the order of a hundred or so mice that do not mix with other demes.

deme, obs. form of DEEM *v.*, DIME.

† **de'mean**, *sb. Obs.* Also 5 demene, 6 demayne. [f. DEMEAN *v.*[1]]

1. Bearing, behaviour, demeanour.

c **1450** *Crt. of Love* 734 But somewhat strange and sad of her demene She is. **1534** MORE *On the Passion* Wks. 1292/2 For which demeane, besyde ye sentence of deth condicionally pronounced..god..declared after certeyne other punishmentes. **1590** SPENSER *F.Q.* II. ix. 40 Another Damsell..That was right fayre and modest of demayne. **1607** BEAUM. & FL. *Woman Hater* III. iv, You sewers, carvers, ushers of the court, Sirnamed gentle for your fair demean. **1692** J. SALTER *Triumphs Jesus* 2 She was a Virgin of severe demean. *a* **1756** G. WEST *On Travelling* (R.), These she..would shew, With grave demean and solemn vanity.

2. Treatment (of others).

1596 SPENSER *F.Q.* VI. vi. 18 All the vile demeane and usage bad, With which he had those two so ill bestad.

demean (dɪ'miːn), *v.*[1] Forms: 4-5 **demeyn(e, demein(e**, 4-6 **demene**, (5 **demeene, dymene**), 4-6 (chiefly *Sc.*) **demane**, 4-7 (chiefly *Sc.*) **demayn(e, demain(e**, 5 **demesne**, 5-7 **demeane**, 6 **demean**. [a. OF. *demene-r* (in Ch. de Roland 11th c.), also *deminer*, *-maner*, *-moner* (pres. t. *il demeine*, *demaine*) to lead, exercise, practise, employ, treat, direct, etc., *se demener* to carry or conduct oneself, = Pr. *demenar*, It. *dimenare*, a Romanic deriv. of DE- *pref.* + *menare*, F. *mener* to lead, conduct, etc.:—L. *mināre*, orig. (= *minārī*) to threaten, in post-cl. L. 'to drive or conduct' cattle, and, by transference, ships, men, etc. The *demaine*, *demane* forms, found chiefly in Sc., are perhaps derived from the OF. tonic form *demeine*, *demaine*. *Demesne* is taken over from the sb. so spelt.]

† **1.** *trans.* To conduct, carry on (a business, action, etc.); to manage, deal with, employ. *Obs.*

c **1315** SHOREHAM 167 Thaȝ hy[t] be thorȝ senne demeyned. *c* **1330** R. BRUNNE *Chron. Wace* (Rolls) 2196 Scheo..well couþe demeyne richeyse. *c* **1440** LYDG. *Secrees* 4 Alle his Empryses demenyd wern and lad By thavys..Of Arystotiles witt and providence. *c* **1449** PECOCK *Repr.* III. vi. 312 Cristis..abstenyng fro temporal vnmovable possessiouns lettith not preestis for to hem take..and weel demene into gode vsis. **1490** CAXTON *Eneydos* iv. 19 For to demeane this to effecte. **1523** LD. BERNERS *Froiss.* I. clxxxv. 219 So often they went bytwene the parties, and so sagely demeaned their busynesse. **1529** MORE *Comf. agst. Trib.* II. Wks. 1207/2 Euen for hys riches alone, though he demened it neuer so wel. **1613** SIR H. FINCH *Law* (1636) 21 These vses being turned into estates shall be demeaned in all respects as estates in possession. **1644** MILTON *Areop.* (Arb.) 68 As our obdurat Clergy have with violence demean'd the matter.

† **b.** To lead (one's life, days).

1413 LYDG. *Pilgr. Sowle* IV. ii. (1483) 59 How they demenen the dayes of theyr lyues.

† **c.** To express, exhibit (sorrow, joy, mirth, etc.). *Obs.* (= ME. *lead* in same sense.)

[Cf. Cotgr. *demener le dueil de*, to lament, or mourne for; *demener ioye*, to rejoyce, make merrie, be glad.]

c **1400** *Rom. Rose* 5238 For hert fulfilled of gentilnesse, Can yvel demene his distresse. *c* **1477** CAXTON *Jason* 69 They began to crye and demene the gretteste sorowe of the world. *c* **1489** —— *Blanchardyn* iv. 21 Suffryng theym to demayne theire rewthis and complayntes. **1564** HAWARD *Eutropius* III. 31 There was great myrth demeaned at Rome after theese newes. **1565** GOLDING *Ovid's Met.* VIII. (1593) 195 Then all the hunters shouting out demeaned joie ynough. **1607** HEYWOOD *Woman Killed* v. iv, With what strange vertue he demeanes his greefe.

† **d.** To produce, or keep up (a sound). *Obs.* [So in OF.]

1483 CAXTON *Gold. Leg.* 407/2 The leuys of the trees demened a swete sounde whiche came by a wynde agreable.

† **2.** To handle, manipulate, manage (instruments, tools, weapons, etc.). *Obs.*

c **1300** *K. Alis.* 663 The fyve him taught to skyrme and ride, And to demayne an horsis bride [= bridle]. *c* **1325** *Coer de L.* 456 What knyght..coude best his crafte For to demene well his shafte. *c* **1384** CHAUCER *H. Fame* 959 Lo, is it not a grete myschaunce To lat a fool han gouernaunce Of thing that he can not demeyne?

† **3.** To manage (a person, country, etc.); to direct, rule, govern, control. *Obs.*

1375 BARBOUR *Bruce* XX. 396 The kyng..Wes enterit in the land of spanȝe, All haill the cuntre till [de]manȝe. ? *a* **1400** *Morte Arth.* 1988 The Kynge..Demenys the medylwarde menskfully hyme selfene. *c* **1440** *Generydes* 4622, I am your child, demeane me as ye list. *c* **1470** HARDING *Chron.* CXL. ii, [He gave] Ierusalem to Henry.. With all Surry [= Syria], to haue and to demain. **1513** MORE in Grafton *Chron.* II. 766 To the ende that themselves would alone demeane and governe the king at their pleasure.

† **4.** To deal with or treat (any one) in a specified way. **b.** *esp.* (chiefly in Sc. writers) To treat badly, illtreat, maltreat. *Obs.*

1393 GOWER *Conf.* I. 196 And thought he wolde upon the night Demene her at his owne wille. *c* **1485** *Digby Myst.* (1882) III. 1582 Lord, demene me with mesuer! **1509-10** *Act 1 Hen. VIII*, c. 20 §1 Merchauntz denysyns..[shall] be well and honestely intreated and demeaned. **1595** SPENSER *Col. Clout* 681 Cause have I none..To quite them ill, that me demeand so well. **1682** *Lond. Gaz.* No. 1682/1 The Lords Commissioners of Justiciary..Decerne and Adjudge the said Archibald Earl of Argile to be Execute to the Death, Demained as a Traitor, and to underly the pains of Treason. **1685** *Argyll's Declar.* in Crookshank *Hist. Ch. Scotl.* (1751) II. 316 (Jam.) Demeaning and executing them..as the most desperate traitors.

b. 1375 BARBOUR *Bruce* XI. 609 Full dyspitfully Thair fais demanit thaim rycht stratly. **1483** CAXTON *Gold. Leg.* 238/2 In the fornais of fyre of fayth he was destrayned, smeton, demened and beten [L. *feriebatur* and *perducebatur*]. **1513** DOUGLAS *Æneis* IX. viii. 52 Sall I the se demanyt on sik wys? **1596** SPENSER *F.Q.* VI. vii. 39 That mighty man did her demeane With all the evill termes, and cruell meane, That he could make. *a* **1651** CALDERWOOD *Hist. Kirk* (1842-6) III. 69 Putt a barrell of powder under me, rather than I would be demained after this manner.

† **5.** To deal, distribute, hand over. *Obs.*

1439 *E.E. Wills* (1882) 114 The thirde parte to be demenyd and yoven..to pore peple. *a* **1656** USSHER *Ann.* (1658) 461 In lieu of Cyprus, to demeane unto him certain Cities with a yearly allowance of corn.

6. *refl.* [from 1] To behave, conduct or comport oneself (in a specified way). The only existing sense: cf. DEMEANOUR.

c **1320** *Sir Beues* 3651 So Beues demeinede him þat dai. *c* **1375** *Sc. Leg. Saints, Egipciane* 557 Bot I lefit nocht þane myne syned, Bot me demaynyt as I dyd are. **1413** LYDG. *Pilgr. Sowle* I. xv. (1859) 12, I haue none experyence of wysedom, how my selue to demene. *c* **1450** *Crt. of Love* 731 Demene you lich a maid With shamefast drede. **1530** PALSGR. 511/1, I demeane, or behave my selfe..*Je me porte* ..*je me demayne*. **1568** GRAFTON *Chron.* II. 349 Your subjectes have lovyngly demeaned themselves unto you. **1590** SHAKS. *Com. Err.* IV. iii. 83 Now out of doubt Antipholus is mad, Else would he neuer so demeane himselfe. **1624** CAPT. SMITH *Virginia* III. i. 43 So well he demeaned himselfe in this businesse. **1682** NORRIS *Hierocles* 31 We should..demean ourselves soberly and justly towards all. **1711** SHAFTESB. *Charac.* (1737) I. I. iii. 191 To demean himself like a Gentleman. **1821** SOUTHEY in *Q. Rev.* XXV. 305 No man who engaged in the rebellion demeaned himself throughout its course so honourably and so humanely. **1858** HAWTHORNE *Fr. & It. Jrnls.* I. 109 The Prince Borghese certainly demeans himself like a kind and liberal gentleman.

b. *fig.* of things.

1581 J. BELL *Haddon's Answ. Osor.* 150b *margin*, How will demeaneth itselfe passively and actively. **1644** MILTON *Areop.* (Arb.) 35 To have a vigilant eye how Bookes demeane themselves as well as men. **1854** J. SCOFFERN in *Orr's Circ. Sc.* Chem. 287 In many of its relations it [hydrogen] demeans itself so much like a metal, that [etc.].

† **c.** with an object equivalent to the refl. pronoun. *Obs.*

c **1375** *Sc. Leg. Saints* Prol. 81 Hou scho demanyt hir flesche, Til [= while] saule & body to-gydir ves. *c* **1400** *Destr. Troy* 3925 Troilus..demenyt well his maners & be mesure wroght. **1633** FORD *Broken H.* I. ii, How doth the youthful general demean His actions in these fortunes? **1649** JER. TAYLOR *Gt. Exemp.* Pref. §12 That man demean and use his own body in that decorum which [etc.].

† **d.** *absol.* (Cf. BEHAVE 3.) *Obs.*

1703 PENN in *Pa. Hist. Soc. Mem.* IX. 206 How to demean towards them, least there should be any alterations in their tempers. **1703** *Rules of Civility* ix, How we are to demean at our Entrance into a Noblemans House.

† **7.** *pass.* To be behaved, to behave or conduct oneself: = prec. sense. *Obs.* Cf. DEMEANED.

1375 BARBOUR *Bruce* V. 229, I wald ga se..how my men demanit are. *c* **1450** *Merlin* 79 We pray yow to yeve us counseile..how we myght beste be demened in this matere. **1586** A. DAY *Eng. Secretary* I. (1625) 60 It was affirmed (that being with loyalty demeaned) you should at length receive the reward of..glory.

¶ **8.** *app.* To bear or have in mind; to remember. *Obs.* (? Associated or confused with MEAN *v.*)

c **1460** J. RUSSELL *Bk. Nurture* 1163 [A mershall] Whensoeuer youre sovereyn a feest make shall, demeene what estates shalle sitte in the hall. **1494** FABYAN *Chron.* VII. 625 But it is to demeane and presuppose that the entent of hym was nat good. *c* **1530** H. RHODES *Bk. Nurture* 356 in *Babees Bk.* (1868) 81 Then giue good eare to heare some grace, to washe your selfe demeane.

demean (dɪ'miːn), *v.*[2] [f. DE- I. 1 + MEAN *a.*, prob. after *debase*: cf. also BEMEAN *v.*[3]

It has been suggested that this originated in a misconception of DEMEAN *v.*[1] in certain constructions, such as that of quot. 1596 in 4 b, and 1590 in sense 6 of that vb. (Johnson actually puts the latter quot. under the sense 'debase'.) It is rare before 1700, and the only 17th c. quots. (1601, 1659 below) are somewhat doubtful. Quot. 1751 in sense 2 shows how in certain contexts *demean* may be taken in either sense. See monograph on the word by Dr. Fitzedward Hall in (*New York*) *Nation*, May 7, 1891.]

1. *trans.* To lower in condition, status, reputation or character.

1601 R. ABBOT *Kingdom of Christ* 5 (L.) In his birth and life and death, far demeaned beneath all kingly state. **1715** JANE BARKER *Exilius* I. 59 By it [jealousy] we demean the Person we love, through unworthy Suspicion. **1716** M. DAVIES *Athen. Brit.* II. 140 The Author [is] demean'd, if not actively and passively ridicul'd. **1734** tr. *Rollin's Anc. Hist.* (1827) I. II. iii. 306 Without any way demeaning or aspersing poverty. **1862** HAWTHORNE *Our Old Home* (1883) I. 106 There is an elbow-chair by the fireside which it would not demean his dignity to fill.

2. esp. *refl.* To lower or humble oneself.

1659 *Burton's Diary* (1828) IV. 373, I incline rather to have Masters of Chancery attend you, and go on errands on both sides. It will cut off all debates about ceremonies, of your members going up and demeaning themselves, or of their demeaning themselves here. **1720** *Lett. fr. Mist's Jrnl.* (1722) I. 306 That Men of Honour and Estate should demean themselves by base condescension. *a* **1751** DODDRIDGE *Fam. Expos.* §169 (T.) It is a thousand times fitter that I should wash thine [feet]; nor can I bear to see thee demean thyself thus. **1754** RICHARDSON *Grandison* IV. xviii. 140 A woman is looked upon as demeaning herself, if she gains a maintenance by her needle. **1848** THACKERAY *Van. Fair* vi. (1856) 40 It was, of course, Mrs. Sedley's opinion that her son would demean himself by a marriage with an artist's daughter. **1876** BLACK *Madcap V.* xxix. 260 Could a girl so far demean herself as to ask for love?

b. Const. *to* or *to do* (what is beneath one).

1764 FOOTE *Mayor of G.* II. ii, Have I, sirrah, demean'd myself to wed such a thing, such a reptile as thee! **1767** S. PATERSON *Another Trav.* I. 427 This lesser philosophy engagingly demeans itself to all characters and situations. **1859** GEO. ELIOT *A. Bede* 15 This woman's kin wouldn't like her to demean herself to a common carpenter. **1861** *Sat. Rev.* 30 Nov. 551 They would not demean themselves to submit to this sort of paltry tutelage.

† **de'mean**, *a. Obs.* [app. an extended form of *mean* adj.; perh. from confusion of *mesne*, *demesne*.] Of middle position, middle-class, middling.

c **1380** *Sir Ferumb.* 382 Y am hir bote a demeyne kniȝt of þe realme of fraunce [*orig. draft* Y am her a meyne knyȝt].

demean, demeane, earlier forms of DEMESNE.

† **de'meanance.** *Obs.* Also 5-6 **demenaunce**. [f. DEMEAN *v.* + -ANCE. Prob. formed in Anglo-Fr.] Demeanour, behaviour.

1486 *Surtees Misc.* (1890) 48 A graduate of the Universitie of Cambridge, with record under the seal of the same Universitie testifying his demenaunce there. *a* **1529** SKELTON *Balettes* Wks. I. 25 Demure demeanaunce, womanly of porte. **1532** W. WALTER *Guiscard & S.* (1597) B ij, Your vertuous talke and carefull demeanance. **1647** H. MORE *Song of Soul* I. II. lxxxvii, Fair replying with demeanance mild.

† **de'meanant**, *a. Obs.* In 5 **demenaunt**. [ad. OF. *demenant*, pres. pple. of *demener*: see DEMEAN *v.*[1] and -ANT[1]. Cf. F. *demener marchandise*, to trade or traffique. Cotgr.] Dealing, trading.

1467 in *Eng. Gilds* (1870) 404 None other citezen withyn the seid cite demenaunt. *Ibid.* 393 No citezen resident withyn the cite and demenaunt.

demeaned (dɪ'miːnd), *ppl. a.* [f. DEMEAN *v.*[1] + -ED.] Conducted, behaved, -mannered (in a specified way). Cf. DEMEAN *v.*[1] 7.

14.. LYDG. *Temple of Glas* 1051 For so demeyned she was in honeste, That vnavised noþing hir astert. *c* **1450** *Merlin* 106 Whan thei sawgh hym thus demened. **1586** A. DAY *Eng. Secretary* I. (1625) 142 Vilde, lewd, and ill demeaned. **1634** MASSINGER *Very Woman* III. v, A very handsome fellow, And well demeaned!

demeaning (dɪ'miːnɪŋ), *vbl. sb.* [f. as prec. + -ING[1].]

† **1.** Managing, ordering, governing, directing, etc.

1429 in Rymer *Fœdera* (1710) X. 426 In Demesnyng of the which Tretie. **1432** *Paston Lett.* No. 18 I. 32 The reule, demesnyng, and governance..of the Kinges persone. *c* **1440** *Generydes* 2052 Thre thowsand knyghtes att his demening. **1450-1530** *Myrr. our Ladye* 177 They se clerely, after the demenyng of goddes sufferaunce, al thynghes that were to come.

2. Conduct, behaviour, demeanour. *Obs.* exc. in ***demeaning of oneself***, comporting oneself.

14.. LYDG. *Temple of Glas* 750 Hir sad demening, of wil not variable. **1461** *Paston Lett.* No. 405 II. 31 For cause of his lyght demenyng towards them. **1580** NORTH *Plutarch* To Rdr., The particular affairs of men..and their demeaning of themselves when [etc.]. *c* **1640** J. SMYTH *Lives Berkeleys* (1883) II. 66 Other misgovernances, and unruly demeanings.

de'meaning, *ppl. a.* [f. DEMEAN *v.*^{2} + -ING^{2}.] That demeans; lowering in character, repute, etc.

1880 *Dorothy* 70 That is uncommonly odd, very demeaning to *him!* **1889** *Pall Mall G.* 7 May 2/3 Where are the men to whose memory it would be demeaning to place their bones.. beside those of Nelson and Collingwood?

demeanour (dɪˈmiːnə(r)). Forms: 5-7 demeanure, 6 -er, (-ewr, 7 -eure), 6-9 -our, -or, (6 oure); also 6 demen-, demeinour, demain-, demaner, 6-7 demanour, (6 demesner, demeasnure, 7 demesnour). [A derivative of DEMEAN *v.*^{1}, app. of English or Anglo-Fr. formation: the corresponding OF. words are *demenement, demené, demenée*. It is not certain from the evidence whether the suffix was originally *-ure*, OF. *-eüre*:—L. *-ātūra*, as in *armour*, or the Fr. *-er* of the infinitive, taken substantively, as in *demurrer, disclaimer, dinner, supper, user*, etc. In either case the ending is assimilated to the *-our* of Anglo-Fr. words like *honour, favour*, etc., and *-or* (favoured in U.S.) a further alteration of this after *honor, favor*. Cf. BEHAVIOUR.]

1. Conduct, way of acting, mode of proceeding (in an affair); conduct of life, manner of living; practice, behaviour. Formerly often with *a* and *pl.*

1494 FABYAN *Chron.* II. xlviii. 32 The kynge disdeynynge this demeanure of Andragius. **1535** FISHER *Wks.* (1876) 419 His shameful demainer. **1543-4** *Act 35 Hen. VIII*, c. 6 §1 Mayntenaunce, imbracery, sinister labour and corrupt demeanours. **1550** CROWLEY *Way to Wealth* 185 If you be found abhominable in thy behaviour towardes thy neighboure, what shalt thou be founde.. in thy demaners to God ward? **1634-5** BRERETON *Trav.* (1844) 157 The Iunior Iudge told me of a very wise demeanour of the now mayor of Ross. **1661** BRAMHALL *Just Vind.* iv. 59 Unlesse they would giue caution by oath for their good demesnour. **1677** E. SMITH in *12th Rep. Hist. MSS. Comm.* App. v. 40 A commission is appointed to examine Lord Shaftsb[ury's] demeanours. **1783** W. F. MARTYN *Geog. Mag.* I. 34 Rewards or punishments due to its [the soul's] demeanor on earth.

†**b.** Wrong conduct, misdemeanour. *Obs. rare.*

1681 *Trial S. Colledge* 20 You cannot think we can give a priviledge to any Friend of yours to commit any Demeanor to offer Bribes to any person.

2. Manner of comporting oneself outwardly or towards others; bearing, (outward) behaviour. (The usual current sense.)

1509 FISHER *Fun. Serm. C'tess Richmond* Wks. (1876) 292 In fauour, in wordes, in gesture, in euery demeanour of herself so grete noblenes dyde appere. **1577-87** HOLINSHED *Chron.* III. 1188/2 Nine Frenchmen apparelled like women ..and counterfeiting some like demeanor to the apparell wherein they were disguised. **1640** G. WATTS tr. *Bacon's Adv. Learn.* 384 Pliant demeanure pacifies great offences. **1667** MILTON *P.L.* VIII. 59 With Goddess-like demeanour forth she went. *c* **1820** S. ROGERS *Italy, Gt. St. Bernard* 9 Two dogs of grave demeanour welcomed me. **1876** J. H. NEWMAN *Hist. Sk.* I. I. ii. 71 The Turks.. are.. remarkable for gravity and almost apathy of demeanour.

†**3.** Treatment of any one. *Obs.*

1548 HALL *Chron.* 200b, Thei were sore beaten, wounded, and very evil intreated. Good men lamented this ungodly demeanure.

†**4.** Management, direction. *Obs.*

16.. MILTON (Webster), God commits the managing so great a trust.. to the demeanour of every grown man.

demeasne, obs. form of DEMESNE.

demegoric (diːmɪˈgɒrɪk), *a.* [ad. Gr. δημηγορικ-ός, f. δημηγόρος popular orator, f. δῆμος common people + ἀγορεύειν to harangue.] Of or pertaining to public speaking.

1892 J. B. BURY in *Fortn. Rev.* 651 The controversy.. is, like most other controversies of the day.. carried on in such a demegoric atmosphere, that [etc.].

demeigne, demeine, obs. ff. DEMESNE.

demein(e, obs. form of DEMEAN *v.*^{1}

†**demeine.** *Obs.* Also demayn, -demaine. [Short for PAIN-DEMAINE, AF. *pain demeine*, L. *panis dominicus*, i.e. 'Lord's bread': see DEMESNE.] Bread of the finest quality.

1288 *Liber Albus* (Rolls) I. 353 Panis dominicus qui dicitur demeine ponderabit wastellum quadrantis. *c* **1420** *Anturs of Arth.* xxxvii, Thre soppus of demayn.. For to cumford his brayne. **1859** RILEY *Liber Albus* (Rolls) I. p. lxvii, The very finest white bread, it would seem, was that known as *Demeine* or lords' bread.

demelaunce, obs. form of DEMI-LANCE.

‖**démêlé** (demele). [Fr.; = quarrel, contest, debate; cf. *démêler* to disembroil, disengage, f. *des-, de-* (DE- I. 6) + *mesler, mêler* to mix.] Discussion between parties having opposite interests; debate, contention, quarrel.

1661 EVELYN *Land. Swed. Amb.* Diary (1892) II. 487 During this *demeslè*.. a bold and dextrous fellow.. cut the ham-strings of 2 of them. **1818** SCOTT *Br. Lamm.* xxii, At the risk of a *démelé* with a cook. **1834** GREVILLE *Mem. Geo. IV* (1874) III. xxiii. 69 (Stanf.) There is a fresh *démêlé* with Russia.

†**de'melle**, *v. Obs.* [A derivative of MELL *v.*, or OF. *mesler, meller* to mix; OF. *desmeller, -meller* was to disperse, f. *des-, dé-* = L. *dis-* + *mesler, mêler* to mix.] *trans.* To mix, mingle.

1516 *Will of R. Peke of Wakefield* 4 June, A vestement.. with myn armes and my wyffes demellede togedder.

†**de'member**, *v. Obs.* [ad. F. *démembrer* (OF. *desm-*), or med.L. *dēmembrāre*, var. of *dismembrāre* to DISMEMBER, f. L. *de-, dis-* (see DE- I. 6) + *membrum* limb.] By-form of DISMEMBER.

1491 *Sc. Acts Jas. IV*, §9 (1814) II. 225 Quhare ony man happinis to be slane or demembrit within the Realme. *c* **1575** BALFOUR *Practicks* (1754) 47 Be ressoun of the pane of deith, or demembring.

Hence **de'membrer; de'membring** *vbl. sb.*

1491 *Sc. Acts Jas. IV*, §9 (1814) II. 225/1 He sall pass and persew the slaaris or Demembraris. **1566** ed. *Sc. Acts, Jas. IV*, c. 50. 91 b *heading*, Anent slauchter or demembring.

demembration (diːmɛmˈbreɪʃən). [ad. med.L. *dēmembrātiōn-em*, n. of action f. *dēmembrāre* to DISMEMBER: see prec. Cf. OF. *demanbration* (Godef.).] The cutting off of a limb; mutilation; dismemberment. (Chiefly in *Sc. Law.*)

1597 ed. *Sc. Acts, Jas. IV*, §28 *heading*, Anent man-slayers taken, or fugitive: and of Demembration. **1609** SKENE *Reg. Maj.* Treat. 134 Mutilation and demembration is punished as slauchter. **1746-7** *Act 20 Geo. II*, Any jurisdiction inferring the loss of life or demembration is abrogated. **1857** JEFFREYS *Roxburghshire* II. iv. 269 The slaughter and demembration of a number of Turnbulls. **1861** W. BELL *Dict. Law Scotl., Demembration*.. is applied to the offence of maliciously cutting off, or otherwise separating any limb, or member, from the body of another.

fig. **1828-40** TYTLER *Hist. Scot.* (1864) I. 221 Demembration of the kingdom could not for a moment be entertained.

‖**demembré.** *Her.* [Fr.] = DISMEMBERED.

1727-51 in CHAMBERS *Cycl.*

‖**déménagement** (demenaʒmɑ̃). [Fr.] The removal of household possessions from one place to another; moving house.

1875 LADY C. SCHREIBER *Jrnl.* (1911) I. 363 They were in the course of déménagement, going to Spa. **1892** C. M. YONGE *Let.* in C. R. Coleridge *C.M.Y. Life & Lett.* (1903) xii. 312 Gertrude had to be moved into the drawing-room. .. The *déménagement* will last for another week at least. **1937** LADY FORTESCUE *Sunset House* iv. 72 Bedlam had not been let loose; it was only the *déménagement* of the Italian family. **1952** M. STEEN *Phoenix Rising* xi. 245 It would have been rather tiresome.. to have set up house.. and be faced with *déménagement* at almost any moment.

demenaunt, obs. form of DEMEANANT.

†**'demency.** *Obs.* Also -cie, -sy. [ad. L. *dēmentia* madness, f. *dēmens, -ment-em* out of one's mind, f. DE- I. 6 + *mens* mind. Cf. F. *démence* (15th c. in Hatzf.).]

1. Madness; infatuation.

1522 SKELTON *Why not to Court* 679 The kynge his clemency Despenseth with his demensy. **1559** W. CUNNINGHAM *Cosmogr. Glasse* 71 That were a poynt of demency or madnes. **1627** W. SCLATER *Exp. 2 Thess.* (1629) 225 Saint Paul.. imputes to them no lesse than franticke demency.

2. *Med.* = DEMENTIA. [tr. F. *démence* (Pinel).]

1858 COPLAND *Dict. Med.* II. 441 M. Pinel arranged mental diseases into 1st Mania.. 2d Melancholia.. 3d Demency, or a particular debility of the operations of the understanding, and of the acts of the will.

†**'demend.** *Obs.* [OE. *démend*, f. pr. pple. of *déman* to DEEM.] A judge.

Beowulf 364 Metod hie ne cuþon, dæda demend. *c* **1200** *Trin. Coll. Hom.* 171 For þat hie shulen cnowen ure demendes wraðe.

demene, obs. form of DEMEAN *v.*, DEMESNE.

demension, -tion, obs. forms of DIMENSION.

dement (dɪˈmɛnt), *a.* and *sb.* [a. F. *dément* adj. and sb., ad. L. *dēmens, dēment-em* out of one's mind, f. DE- I. 6 + *mens, mentem* mind.]

A. *adj.* Out of one's mind, insane, demented. *Obs.* or *arch.*

1560 ROLLAND *Crt. Venus* III. 290 With mind dement vneis scho micht sustene The words. **1856** J. H. NEWMAN *Callista* (1890) 248 Speak, man, speak! Are you dumb as well as dement?

B. *sb.* A person affected with dementia; one out of his mind.

1888 H. A. S[MITH] *Darwin* 43 A dement was known to the writer who could repeat the whole of the New Testament verbatim. **1890** MERCIER *Sanity & Ins.* xv. 379 An old dement begins to whimper because his posset is not ready.

dement (dɪˈmɛnt), *v.*^{1} [ad. L. *dēmentāre* to deprive of mind, drive mad (cf. OF. *démenter*, Godef.), f. *dēmens, dēmentem*, DEMENT *a.*] *trans.* To put out of one's mind, drive mad, craze.

1545 JOYE *Exp. Dan.* v. (R.), He was thus demented and bewitched with these pestilent purswasions. **1550** BALE *Apol.* 80 Minysters of Sathan, whych thus seke to demente the symple hartes of the people. *a* **1662** BAILLIE *Lett.* II. 255 (Jam.) If the finger of God in their spirits should so far dement them as to disagree. **1703** D. WILLIAMSON *Serm. bef. Gen. Assembly* 50 The Heathens used to say, whom the gods would destroy these they demented. **1890** W. C. RUSSELL *Ocean Trag.* I. viii, It would not require more than two or three incidents of this sort to utterly dement him.

Hence **de'menting** *ppl. a.*

1877 MISS YONGE *Cameos* Ser. III. xxxi. 315 The dementing demon of the Stewarts.

de'ment, *v.*^{2} *rare*$^{-1}$. [a. F. *démentir*, in OF. *desmentir*, f. *des-, dé-* (DE- I. 6) + *mentir*:—L. *mentīrī* to lie.] *trans.* To give the lie to; to assert or prove to be false.

1884 H. S. WILSON *Stud. Hist.* 330 With firmness, she demented and disproved the lie.

dementalize (diːˈmɛntəlaɪz), *v. Philos.* [f. DE- II. 1 + MENTALIZE.] To remove mind or mental characteristics from. So **de'mentalized** *ppl. a.*

1936 R. G. COLLINGWOOD *Human Nature & Human Hist.* 24 Sciences of this type tend systematically to dementalize mind and convert it into nature. **1950** *Mind* LIX. 406 Can an adequate de-mentalized psychology ever be achieved?

†**de'mentate**, *a. Obs.* [ad. L. *dēmentāt-us*, pa. pple. of *dēmentāre* to DEMENT.] Driven mad, crazed, demented.

1640 *Intentions of Armie Scotl.* 7 The plots of our dementat adversaries. **1675** J. SMITH *Chr. Relig. Appeal* II. 1 Raving and dementate Persons.

dementate (dɪˈmɛnteɪt), *v.* [f. ppl. stem of L. *dēmentāre* to DEMENT.] = DEMENT *v.*^{1} ? *Obs.*

1621 BURTON *Anat. Mel.* Democr. to Rdr. (1676) 44/1 *Daphnis insana*, which had a secret quality to dementate. **1664** H. MORE *Myst. Iniq.* 566 To.. inflame you, and dementate you to your own ruine. **1722** WOLLASTON *Relig. Nat.* v. 107, I speak not here of men dementated with wine. **1829** SOUTHEY *Sir T. More* (1831) II. 86 Those whom the Prince of this World.. dementates.

Hence **de'mentated** *ppl. a.* = DEMENTATE *a.*, DEMENTED; **de'mentating** *ppl. a.*

1652 GAULE *Magastrom.* 195 In the dementating furies of divination. **1716** M. DAVIES *Athen. Brit.* III. *Dissert. Physick* 38 Thinking the dementating Disaster of those young Ladies was caus'd.. by their being drunk. **1726** DE FOE *Hist. Devil* I. xi. (1840) 172 The blind dementated world. **1813** *Q. Rev.* IX. 419 Some.. seem to have been perfectly dementated.

dementation (ˌdiːmɛnˈteɪʃən). [ad. med.L. *dēmentātiōn-em* (Du Cange), n. of action from *dēmentāre* to DEMENT.] The action of dementing; the fact or condition of being demented; madness, infatuation.

1617 DONNE *Serm.* cxxxviii. Wks. 1839. V. 469 And then lastly.. they come to that infatuation, that Dementation, as that they lose [etc.]. **1680** BAXTER *Cath. Commun.* (1684) 35 Dementation goeth before Perdition. **1879** FARRAR *St. Paul* I. 610 *note*, The 'strong delusion' of the English version is a happy expression; it is.. judicial infatuation, the dementation before doom. **1889** GLADSTONE in *Contemp. Rev.* Oct. 486 This policy may be called one of dementation.

†**de'mentative**, *a. Obs.* [f. ppl. stem of L. *dēmentāre* + -IVE.] Characterized by madness.

1685 H. MORE *Paralip. Prophet.* 398 Their dementative Anger and Rage.

demented (dɪˈmɛntɪd), *ppl. a.* [f. DEMENT *v.* + -ED^{1}; corresp. to L. *dēmentātus* DEMENTATE.] Out of one's mind, crazed, mad; infatuated.

1644 J. MAXWELL *Sacr. Regum Maj.* 105 Who can be so demented, as.. to.. runne the hazard of totall ruine. **1726** DE FOE *Hist. Devil* II. x. (1840) 343 All their demented lunatic tricks. **1828** SCOTT *F.M. Perth* xii, Is the man demented? **1885** J. PAYN *Talk of Town* II. 248 He threw himself out of the room like one demented.

b. Affected with dementia.

1858 COPLAND *Dict. Med.* II. 462 Maniacs and monomaniacs are carried away.. by illusions and hallucinations.. the demented person neither imagines nor supposes anything. **1878** J. R. REYNOLDS *Syst. Med.* II. 33 There is a group of demented patients, in whom the mind is almost extinguished. **1883** QUAIN *Dict. Med.* s.v. *Dementia*, Fewer are left to reach the demented stage.

Hence **de'mentedly** *adv.*, **de'mentedness**.

1891 *Melbourne Punch* 4 June 365/4 Those behind.. hurled themselves dementedly against those in front. **1876** G. MEREDITH *Beauch. Career* 228 A delusion amounting to dementedness.

dementholize, -ed: see DE- II. 1.

‖**démenti** (demɑ̃ti). [Fr., f. *démentir* to give the lie.] = DEMENTIE. In modern use applied esp. to an official contradiction of a published statement. Also (*nonce-wd.*) †**dementir** = DEMENT *v.*^{2}.

1698 VANBRUGH *Prov. Wife* I. ii, The very looking-glass gives her the *démenti*. **1707** LD. RABY in Hearne *Collect.* (Oxf. Hist. Soc.) II. 42 As for his Person, he did not dementir [*sic*] ye Description I had of him. **1771** H. WALPOLE *Lett. to H. Mann* 8 May, I will run no risk of having a *démenti*. **1883** *Times* Dec. (Stanf.), That elaborate affectation of candour which distinguishes the official *démenti*. **1918** A. GRAY tr. *R. Grelling's The Crime* II. v. 228 The semi-official organ seeks to defend the reports of Pourtalès against the English *démentis*. **1921** *Contemp. Rev.* Jan. 103 My information contradicts the dementis published by the *Deutsche Tageszeitung*. **1950** M. HAY *Foot of Pride* vii. 209 They.. waited for the Vatican to publish a *démenti*.

‖**dementia** (diːˈmɛnʃɪə). [L. n. of state from *dēmens, dēmentem*: see DEMENT *a.* First used to render the term *démence* of Pinel. Formerly Englished as DEMENCY.]

1. *Med.* A species of insanity characterized by failure or loss of the mental powers; usually consequent on other forms of insanity, mental shock, various diseases, etc.

1806 D. DAVIS tr. *Pinel's Treat. Insanity* 252 To cause periodical and curable mania to degenerate into dementia or idiotism. **1840** TWEEDIE *Syst. Pract. Med.* II. 107 A state.. which French writers after Pinel have denominated *démence.* English writers have translated this term into *dementia.* **1851** HOOPER *Vade Mecum* (1858) 131 The sudden attacks of dementia produce a state of mind nearly allied to idiocy. **1874** MAUDSLEY *Respons. in Ment. Dis.* iii. 73 When his memory is impaired, his feelings quenched, his intelligence enfeebled or extinct, he is said to be suffering from dementia.

2. *gen.* Infatuation under the influence of which the judgement is as it were paralysed.

1877 MORLEY *Crit. Misc.* Ser. II. 130 Emissaries.. succeeded in persuading them—such the dementia of the night—that Robespierre was a Royalist agent.

‖**dementia præcox** (diːˈmɛnʃɪə ˈpriːkɒks). *Med.* [mod.L. (A. Pick 1891, in *Prager Med. Wochenschr.* 8 July 312/2), used to render Fr. *démence précoce* (B. A. Morel, *Traité des dégénérescences* (1857), iv. 391), f. DEMENTIA + L. *præcox* (see PRECOCIOUS *a.*).]

= SCHIZOPHRENIA.

1899 *Amer. Jrnl. Insanity* July 116 'Dementia praecox' is Kraepelin's latest designation for the three types which it includes. *Ibid.* 118 The term 'Dementia Praecox', thus bringing together with katatonia a number of these variable forms.. unifies them as belonging to one group. **1902** A. R. DEFENDORF tr. *Kraepelin's Clin. Psychiatry* 152 Dementia praecox is the name first applied by A. Pick, in 1891, to a group of cases.. characterized by maniacal symptoms followed by melancholia and rapid deterioration. **1922** tr. *Freud's Introd. Lect.* xxviii. 384 Paranoia and dementia praecox, when fully developed, are not amenable to analysis. **1926** W. MCDOUGALL *Outl. Abnormal Psychol.* ii. 41 A boy presenting a clear picture of *Dementia Praecox* of the paranoid type. **1937** J. JOYCE *Let.* 30 Aug. (1966) III. 406 He was supposed to be an absolutely hopeless case of *dementia praecox.* **1970** N. MILFORD *Zelda Fitzgerald* 256 Dr. Meyer wanted Zelda to face her sickness squarely, not passively in the fixed terms of dementia praecox and schizophrenia.

†**deˈmentie**, *sb. Obs.* [a. obs. F. *dementie* (1587 in Godef.) = mod.F. *démenti* giving of the lie, f. *démentir* = DEMENT *v.*[2] Now only as French: see DÉMENTI.] The giving any one the lie. Hence †**deˈmentie** *v. trans.*, to give the lie to, belie; = DEMENT *v.*[2]

1594 SAVIOLO *Practice* II. V j a, To come to the ende of this Treatise of Dementies or giuing the lie. *Ibid.* V ij a, I come directly to bee dementied, and so consequentlye muste become Challenger.

deˈmentify, *v. rare.* [f. L. *dēment-em* DEMENT *a.* + -FY.] = DEMENT *v.*[1]

1856 OLMSTED *Slave States* 420 Dementifying bigotry or self-important humility.

demeore, ME. form of DEMUR *vb.* and *sb.*

deˈmephitize, *v. rare*$^{-0}$. [f. DE- II. 1 + MEPHIT-IC + -IZE.] *trans.* 'To purify from foul unwholesome air' (Webster 1828). Hence **demephitiˈzation** (*Med. Repository*, cited *ibid.*).

demer, obs. form of DEEMER, judge.

1510 LOVE *Bonavent. Mirr.* xv. E vj, A presumptuous.. demer of other men.

Demerara (dɛməˈrɛərə, dɛməˈrɑːrə). The name of a region of Guyana, used to designate a kind of (raw) cane-sugar, originally and chiefly brought from Demerara, the crystals of which have a yellowish-brown colour.

1848 *Sugar Question* II. 72 With a long price of 42*s.* for Demerara sugar, and more labour, the estates could go on. **1880** *Encycl. Brit.* XI. 251/1 The 'Demerara crystals' are very popular for their purity and saccharine strength. **1895** *Army & Navy Co-op. Soc. Price List* 106/1 Sugars.. Demerara, best, per 28 lb tin 5/3. **1895** *Young Woman* Dec. 98/2 Sprinkle them with a little Demerara sugar to form a crisp brown coating. **1901** *Brit. Med. Jrnl.* 4 May 1119/2 The West India Committee have caused several grocers to be prosecuted.. for selling yellow crystals as Demerara sugar. **1959** *Which?* Oct. 134/2 Demerara sugar consists roughly of 98 per cent of sucrose, 0.7 per cent of other sugars and 0.5 per cent of moisture. In addition there are traces of some minerals and even smaller traces of a few vitamins.

demere, ME. form of DEMUR, delay.

†**demerge** (dɪˈmɜːdʒ), *v. Obs.* [ad. L. *dēmergĕre* to plunge down into, submerge, f. DE- I. 1 + *mergĕre* to plunge, dip. Cf. also OF. *de-mergier* (14–15th c.).] *trans.* To plunge, immerse.

c **1610** DONNE *Wks.* 1839 VI. 347 Our Soules demerged into those bodies are allowed to partake Earthly pleasures. **1669** BOYLE *Contn. New. Exp.* II. (1682) 23 Air breaking forth through the Water, in which it was demerged.

demerger (ˈdiːmɜːdʒə(r)). *Comm.* Also de-merger. [DE- II. 3.] The dissolution of a merger between business concerns; the separation of one or more firms or trading companies from a large group.

1948 *Sunday Times* 27 June 1/5 As from next Wednesday the oil and petrol pool, which has operated since early in the war, will go out of business. But this 'de-merger' will not mean that the public will get branded petrol from the garage pumps for a long while to come. **1968** *Socialist Leader* 21 Sept. 1/4 The Government says that it reserves the right to refer the new G.E.C.-English Electric to the Monopolies Commission... However, it is difficult to see what the Commission could do. A de-merger is, of course, out of the question. **1980** *Times* 27 Mar. 6/8 The present tax rules can in practice effectively discourage demergers of this kind, by charging the assets of the 'demerged' company to advance corporation tax and income tax as distributions.

Hence (as a back-formation) **deˈmerge** *v. intr.* and *trans.*; **deˈmerged** *ppl. a.*, **deˈmerging.**

1980 *Economist* 16 Feb. 75/1 'Demerging' is the code word in Whitehall these days. *Ibid.* 28 June 77/1 The government hit on encouraging large firms to 'demerge'. **1980** *N.Y. Times* 6 July III. 7/1 It may be time to 'demerge' his company into several smaller concerns. **1980** Demerged [see DEMERGER]. **1981** *Times* 8 May 25/2 The latest pioneer, Francis Sumner, is also attempting to demerge at a difficult period of the group's history. **1983** *Ibid.* 26 Mar. 13/3 House of Fraser directors were last night believed to be ready to recommend shareholders to vote against a proposal by Lonrho that it demerge Harrods from the rest of the.. group. **1985** *Daily Tel.* 13 Aug. 12 Hanson Trust might decide to go for Bowater Inc, America's biggest newsprint producer, and the company which was de-merged from its British parent in 1984.

demerit (dɪˈmɛrɪt), *sb.* [a. F. *démérite*, or ad. L. *dēmeritum*, f. ppl. stem of L. *dēmerērī* to merit, deserve, f. DE- I. 3 + *merērī* to deserve, *meritum* desert, merit. In Romanic the prefix appears to have been taken in a privative sense (DE- I. 6), hence med.L. *dēmeritum* fault, It. *demerito*, F. *démérite* (14th c. in Littré) 'desert, merite, deseruing; also (the contrarie) a disseruice, demerite, midseed.. (in which sence it is most commonly used at this day)', Cotgr.]

†**1.** Merit, desert, deserving (in a good or indifferent sense). Freq. in *pl. Obs.*

1399 *Rolls of Parlt.* III. 424/1 Your owne Wordes.. that ye were not worthy.. ne able, for to governe for your owne Demerites. **1447** *Will of Hen. VI* in Carter *King's Coll. Chapel* i. 13 His most fereful and last dome when every man shal.. be examined and demed after his demeritees. **1490** CAXTON *Eneydos*, xxiv. 91 A mercyfull god and pyteous wylle retrybue hym iustely alle after his demeryte. **1548** HALL *Chron.* 151 b, For his demerites, called the good duke of Gloucester. **1548** UDALL *Erasm. Paraphr. Luke* 3 a, Your demerites are so ferre aboue all prayses of man. **1603** HOLLAND *Plutarch's Mor.* 233 Worldly happines beyond all reason and demerit. **1607** SHAKS. *Cor.* I. i. 276 Opinion that so stickes on Marcius, shall Of his demerits rob Cominius. **1632** J. HAYWARD tr. *Biondi's Eromena* Ep. Ded. A iij b, Considering your known noble demerits, and princely courtesie. **1731** GAY in *Swift's Lett.* Wks. 1841 II. 665 Envy not the demerits of those who are most conspicuously distinguished.

†**b.** That by which one obtains merit; a meritorious or deserving act. *Obs.*

1548 W. PATTEN *Exped. Scotl.* Pref., What thanks then.. for these his notable demerits ought our Protector to receive of his? **1601** HOLLAND *Pliny* I. 456 It is reputed a singular demerit and gracious act, not to kill a citizen of Rome. **1655** M. CARTER *Hon. Rediv.* (1660) 8 The first atchiever in any Stock whatever, was a new man ennobled for some demerit.

2. Desert in a bad sense: quality deserving blame or punishment; ill-desert; censurable conduct: opposed to *merit.* In later use, sometimes, deficiency or want of merit.

1509 BARCLAY *Shyp of Folys* (1570) ¶¶ iij, To assemble these fooles in one bande, And their demerites worthily to note. **1643** SIR T. BROWNE *Relig. Med.* (1656) I. §53 The one being so far beyond our deserts, the other so infinitely below our demerits. **1675** TRAHERNE *Chr. Ethics* xiv. 193 The least sin is of infinite demerit; because it breaketh the union between God and the soul. **1700** DRYDEN *Fables, Meleager & Atal.* 327 Mine is the merit, the demerit thine. **1741** RICHARDSON *Pamela* (1824) I. 155 God teach me humility, and to know my own demerit! **1851** DIXON *W. Penn* xxxii. (1872) 308 It is no demerit in Penn that he did not see at once the evil. **1865** LECKY *Ration.* (1878) I. 357 The rationalistic doctrine of personal merit and demerit.

†**b.** A blameworthy act, sin, offence. (Almost always in *pl.*). *Obs.*

1485 *Act 1 Hen. VII*, c. 4 Priests.. culpable, or by their Demerits openly reported of incontinent living in their Bodies. **1494** FABYAN VII. 507 Some there were that for theyr demerytys were adiugyd to perpetuall prysone. **1549** *Compl. Scot.* iii. 27 That samyn boreau is stikkit or hangit eftiruart for his cruel demeritis. **1605** SHAKS. *Macb.* IV. iii. 226 Not for their owne demerits, but for mine Fell slaughter on their soules. *a* **1637** B. JONSON *Underwoods, Misc. Poems* lvi, There is no father that for one demerit, Or two, or three, a son will disinherit.

c. *transf.* As a quality of things: Fault, defect.

1832 LEWIS *Use & Ab. Pol. Terms* vi. 62 The merits or demerits of hereditary royalty. **1855** SINGLETON *Virgil* I. Pref. 2 Which has, it may be, the demerit of being new.

†**3.** That which is merited (*esp.* for ill doing); desert; punishment deserved. *Obs.*

1621 CADE *Serm.* 12 But Ahab.. had quickly his demerits, being destroyed, and al his seed. **1728** *Wodrow Corr.* (1843) III. 393 Many members of the Assembly thought deposition the demerit of what was already found.

4. A penalty mark awarded as a punishment for misconduct, poor work, etc., *esp.* in schools or the Services; a 'black' mark. Also ***demerit mark, point.*** orig. *U.S.*

1862 G. C. STRONG *Cadet Life at West Point* 150 The more immediate penalty is the demerit. **1877** R. J. BURDETTE *Rise & Fall of Mustache* 311 Got three demerit marks for drawing a picture of her [*sc.* a teacher]. **1903** *Daily Chron.* 20 Feb. 3/3 The smallest breach of any one of them [*sc.* military regulations] is visited by a 'demerit' mark. **1966** D. BAGLEY *Wyatt's Hurricane* ii. 40 There have been a few cases, you know, mostly among the enlisted men, and they've got shipped back to the States with a big black demerit to spend a year or two in the stockade. **1976** *N.Z. Financial Times* 10 Dec. 18/1 Demerit points are recorded against an employee for unsatisfactory work attendance. **1980** L. BIRNBACH et al. *Official Preppy Handbk.* 43/2 The process.. has its uncomfortable aspects: rules, parietals, demerits, and disciplinary action.

demerit (dɪˈmɛrɪt), *v.* [f. L. *dēmerit-*, ppl. stem of *dēmerērī* to deserve (see prec.); partly after F. *démériter* (16th c. in Hatzf.), to merit disapproval, fail to merit.]

†**1. a.** *trans.* To merit, deserve, be worthy of (good or evil; sometimes *spec.* the latter, and opposed to *merit*). *Obs.*

1538 J. HUSEE *Let. Visct. Lisle* 12 Jan. in *Lisle Papers* V. 19 The caitiff.. shall suffer such pains as he hath demerited. **1548** UDALL *Erasm. Par.* Pref. 5 If I have demerited any love or thanke. **1612** T. TAYLOR *Comm. Titus* iii. 7 Any matter or meanes demeriting the fauour of God. **1619** H. HUTTON *Follies Anat.* (1842) 26 These are the subjects which demerit blame. **1657** TOMLINSON *Renou's Disp.* 570 Those that compose.. Antidotaries.. think they demerit much praise. **1711** BP. WILSON in Keble *Life* ix. (1863) 283 Such sentence.. as the nature of your crime shall demerit.

†**b.** To obtain by merit, to earn (favour, love, etc.). *Obs.*

1555 EDEN *Decades* 25 They browght with them.. to demerite the fauour of owre men great plentie of vytayles. **1611** SPEED *Hist. Gt. Brit.* IX. xv. §110 His Princely desire to aduance their weale, and demerit their loue. **1613** T. GODWIN *Rom. Antiq.* (1674) 96 Noblemen.. sometimes, to demerit the Emperour his love endangered their lives in this fight.

†**c.** To earn favour of (a person). *Obs.*

1597 J. KING *On Jonas* (1618) 389 A Priest of Baal will cut and launce his owne flesh to demerite his idoll. **1612** T. TAYLOR *Comm. Titus* iii. 5 The likeliest things to demerit God: as workes of righteousnesse. *a* **1656** HALES *Gold. Rem.* (1688) 37 To demerit by all courtesie the men of meaner Rank.

2. †**a.** To deprive of merit, to take away the merit of, disparage. *Obs.*

1576 WOOLTON *Chr. Manual* C iv. (L.), Faith by her own dignity and worthiness doth not demerit justice and righteousness. *a* **1643** W. CARTWRIGHT *Siege* I. i, My lofty widdow, Who, if that I had dignity, hath promis'd T' accept my person, will be hence demerited.

b. To lower in status by giving an unfavourable assessment of conduct. *U.S.*

1895 *Century Mag.* Oct. 843/2 He stands a fair chance of being demerited and punished until his hope of release before he is of age is almost extinguished.

3. To fail to merit; to deserve to lose or be without.

1654 COKAINE *Dianea* III. 217 Wherein hath the unfortunate Doricia demerited thy affections? **1754** RICHARDSON *Grandison* (1781) V. xxxii. 208 A blessing that once was designed for him, and which he is not accused of demeriting by misbehaviour. **1865** TRENCH *Synon. N.T.* §47 (1876) 163 It is unearned and unmerited, or indeed demerited, as the faithful man will most freely acknowledge.

†**4. a.** *intr.* To incur demerit or guilt; to merit disapproval or blame, deserve ill. *Obs.*

1604 PARSONS *3rd Pt. Three Convers. Eng.* 122 The soules in Purgatory may meritt and demeritt; nor are sure yet of their saluation. **1605** B. JONSON *Volpone* IV. ii, I will be tender to his reputation, How euer he demerit. *a* **1677** BARROW *Serm.* (1687) I. 478 For us, who deserved nothing from him, who had demerited so much against him. *a* **1734** *North Lives* (1826) I. 96 For he was.. the kings servant already, and had not demerited.

†**b.** *trans.* To earn or incur in the way of demerit.

1635 SHELFORD *Learned Disc.* 140 (T.) Adam demerited but one sin to his posterity, viz. original, which cannot be augmented.

demeritorious (diːˌmɛrɪˈtɔərɪəs), *a.* [f. DEMERIT after *meritorious*: cf. F. *déméritoire* (15th c. in Hatzf.).]

1. Bringing demerit, ill-deserving, blameworthy; opp. to *meritorious.*

1605 T. BELL *Motives conc. Romish Faith* 92 Good works are meritorious to such as be viatores and liue in this world; and likewise euill workes demeritorious. *a* **1670** HACKET *Cent. Serm.* (1675) 229 The ill use of it.. in those that perish is demeritorious. **1871** ALABASTER *Wheel of Law* 46 The demeritorious kind is illustrated by a wilful breach of the law. **1882** L. STEPHEN *Science Ethics* 279, I deserve blame, and my conduct is de-meritorious.

†**2.** Failing to deserve, undeserving. *Obs. rare.*

a **1640** JACKSON *Creed* x. xli, Some kind of endeavours are.. as effectual, as others are idle and impertinent or demeritorious of God's grace to convert us.

Hence **demeriˈtoriously** *adv.*, according to ill-desert.

a **1703** BURKITT *On N.T.* Rom. viii. 6 The end and condition of all carnally-minded persons.. is death: always demeritoriously, that which deserves death.

†**demerlayk.** *Obs.* Forms: 3 dweomerlak, -lac, 4 demorlayk, 4–5 demerlayk(e. [f. ME. *dweomer*:—OE. *dwimer* in *ȝedwimor, -er*, illusion, phantasm, *ȝedwimere* juggler, sorcerer + ME. *layk*, LAIK play, a ON. *leikr* (= OE. *lác*).

Cf. DWEOMERCRÆFT.] Magic, practice of occult art, jugglery.

*c*1205 LAY. 270 þa sende Asscanius.. After heom ȝend þat lond, þe cuþen dweomerlakes song. *Ibid.* 11326 Tuhten to dæðe mid drenche oðer mid dweomerlace oðer mid steles bite. *c*1325 *E.E. Allit. P.* B. 1578 Deuinores of demorlaykes þat dremes cowþe rede. *a*1400-50 *Alexander* 414 All þis demerlayke he did bot be þe deuyllis craftis.

demersal (dɪˈmɜːsəl), *a.* [f. L. *demersus*, pa. pple. of *dēmergĕre* to submerge: see -AL.] Of the eggs of fishes: sinking to the bottom of the sea, deposited at or near the bottom. Of fish, etc.: living near the bottom.

1889 *Nature* 13 June 159/2 The herring with its demersal eggs, fixed firmly to the bottom. **1911** *Ann. Rept. Sea Fish.* 1909 p. vi, in *Parl. Papers* XXIV, Demersal fish landed from each 'Area' of the North Sea. **1915** A. MEEK in *Rep. Dove Mar. Lab. Cullercoats* 14 The region where the demersal fry are mainly congregated. **1925** *Public Opinion* 16 Oct. 376/1 This increase was most marked in the bottom living or demersal fish. **1936** J. T. JENKINS *Fishes Brit. Isles* (ed. 2) 9 Practically all freshwater fish lay demersal eggs. **1959** *New Scientist* 7 May 1035/1 Demersal fishes (those caught near the bottom). **1968** F. R. H. JONES *Fish Migration* ii. 13 In the Pacific Ocean, however, demersal eggs are quite common among species whose Atlantic counterparts have pelagic eggs.

†**demerse** (dɪˈmɜːs), *v. Obs.* [f. L. *dēmers-*, ppl. stem of *dēmergĕre*: see DEMERGE.] *trans.* To plunge down, immerse, submerge.

1662 J. SPARROW tr. *Behme's Rem. Wks., 1st Apol. to B. Tylcken* 73 When it demersed it self into the Center, to hide it self from the Light of God. **1669** BOYLE *Contn. New. Exp.* II. (1682) 22 The Reciever was demersed under the water all this night. **1691** E. TAYLOR tr. *Behme's Theos. Philos.* 369 And demerse itself solely into the single Love of God.

†**deˈmerse**, *a. Bot. Obs.* [ad. L. *dēmersus*, pa. pple. of *dēmergĕre*.] = next.

1793 MARTYN *Lang. Bot.*, *Demersum folium*, a demerse leaf.. frequent in aquatic plants.

demersed (dɪˈmɜːst), *ppl. a.* [f. prec. vb. + -ED.] Plunged down, immersed. In *Bot.* (repr. L. *dēmersus*): Growing beneath the water, submerged.

1866 *Treas. Bot.*, *Demersed*, buried beneath water.

demersion (dɪˈmɜːʃən). *Obs.* or *rare.* [ad. L. *dēmersiōn-em*. n. of action from *dēmergĕre*: see DEMERGE. (Occurs also in 15-16th c. French.)] Plunging in, immersion; submergence, drowning.

1692 RAY *Dissol. World* III. v. (1732) 360 This Sinking and Demersion of buildings. **1727** BAILEY vol. II, *Demersion*, (with Chymists) the putting any Medicine into a dissolving Liquor. **1807** ROBINSON *Archæol. Græca* I. xx. 93 Καταποντισμὸς, demersion, or drowning in the sea. **1820** W. TAYLOR in Robberds *Mem.* II. 507 He was.. muddled with mathematics, to whom they were always a sentence of intellectual demersion.

deˈmesmerize, *v.* [f. DE- II. 1. + MESMERIZE.] To bring out of the mesmeric state. Hence **deˈmesmerizing** *vbl. sb.* and *ppl. a.*; also **demesmeriˈzation**.

1855 SMEDLEY *Occult Sciences* 232 *note*, The eyelids.. required to be set at liberty by the demesmerizing process. **1866** *Guide Elgin Cathedral* ii. 158 The demesmerising reappearance of the sheriff released the party from their rigidity. **1870** *Eng. Mech.* 4 Feb. 508/1 He will find it very difficult to demesmerise his subjects.

demesne (dɪˈmeɪn, dɪˈmiːn). Forms: 4-7 **demeyn, -e**, 4-8 **demayn, -e**, 5 **demene, -eigne**, 5-6 **demeine**, 6- **demain(e**, 6-8 **demean(e**, 7-8 **demeasne, demesn**, 7- **demesne**. [a. Anglo-F. *demeyne, -eine, -eigne, -ene*, later *demesne* = OF. *demeine, -aine, -oine*, originally a subst. use of the adj. *demenië, demeigne, demeine, -aine, -oine*, etc., belonging to a lord, seigneurial, domanial, of the nature of private property, own, proper:—L. *dominic-us, -um* of or belonging to a lord or master, f. *dominus* lord; see in Du Cange *dominicus* 'proprius', *dominicum* 'proprietas, domanium, quod ad dominum spectat'. *Demesne* is thus a differentiated spelling of the word DOMAIN, q.v. Though the correct Latin equivalent was *dominicum*, in med.L. it was often represented by *dominium*, or by *domanium*, a latinized form of the vernacular word.

The Anglo-French spelling *demesne* of the law-books, and 17th c. legal antiquaries, was partly merely graphic (the quiescence of original *s* before a consonant leading to the insertion of a non-etymological *s* to indicate a long vowel), as in *mesne* = OF. *meien, meen, mean*, mod.F. *moyen*; partly perhaps influenced by association with *mesne* itself, in 'mesne lord', or with *mesnie*:—*mansionāta* house, household establishment. Demesne land was app. viewed by some as *terra mansionatica*, land attached to the mansion or supporting the owner and his household. Perhaps also Bracton's words (see sense 3) gave the notion that the word has some connexion with *mensa*. The prevailing pronunciation in the dictionaries and in the modern poets is (dɪˈmiːn); but (dɪˈmeɪn) is also in good legal and general use, and is historically preferable: cf. the variant form *domain*.]

I. Possession.

[In Germanic, including English, law, the primary idea in relation to property is *possession*, not *ownership* (= Roman *dominium*), as we now understand it. Hence, derivatives of L. *dominium* and *proprietas* became in mediæval law chiefly or even exclusively associated with possession. (Sir F. Pollock.)]

1. *Law.* Possession (of real estate) as one's own. Chiefly in the phrase ***to hold in demesne*** (*tenere in dominico*), i.e. in one's own hands as possessor by free tenure. (Formerly sometimes in *pl.* by confusion with senses in II.)

Applied either to the absolute ownership of the king, or to the tenure of the person who held land to his own use, mediately or immediately from the king. Opposed to 'to hold in service' (*tenere in servitio*): if A held lands, immediately or mediately of the king, part of which he retained in his own hands, and part of which were in turn held of him by B, he was said to hold the former 'in demesne', and the latter 'in service'. B, in his turn, might hold his portion wholly 'in demesne', or partly also 'in service' by admitting a tenant under him. In every case, the ultimate (free) holder, 'the person who stands at the bottom of the scale, who seems most like an owner of the land, and who has a general right of doing what he pleases with it, is said to hold the land in demesne'. Prof. F. W. Maitland.

[**1292** BRITTON III. xv. §1 Car en demeyne porrount estre tenuz terres et rentes, en fee, et a terme de vie. Mes demeyne proprement est tenement qe chescun tient severalment en fee.. Et demeyne si est dit a la difference de ceo qe est tenu en seignurie ou en service, ou en commun ovekes autres. *transl.* For in demeyne may be held lands and rents, in fee and for term of life. But demeyne is properly a tenement which is held severally in fee.. The word demeyne is also used in distinction from that which is holden in seignory or service, or in common with others.] *c*1330 R. BRUNNE *Chron.* (1810) 7 Romeyns, That wan it [Britain] of Casbalan in to þer demeyns. *c*1449 PECOCK *Repr.* III. iii. 290 Tho whiche thei helden in her owne demenys. **1523** LD. BERNERS *Froiss.* I. ccxii. 257 All other thynges comprised in this present article of Merle and of Calais we.. hold them in demayn. **1570-6** LAMBARDE *Peramb. Kent* (1826) 466 The Manor of Hethe.. which the King now hath in demeane. **1612** DAVIES *Why Ireland, etc.* (1787) 120 When the Duke of Normandy had conquered England.. he.. gave not away whole shires and counties in demesne to any of his servitors. **1655** FULLER *Ch. Hist.* IV. xiv. §32 Had not some Laws of Provision now been made, England had long since been turned part of S^t. Peters Patrimony in demeans. **1672** LEYCESTER in Ormerod *Cheshire* (1880) I. 11 The names of such towns.. as Earl Hugh held in demaine at that time. **1876** FREEMAN *Norm. Conq.* V. xxii. 8 A terrier of a gigantic manor, setting out the lands held in demesne by the lord.

b. ***in his demesne as of fee*** (*in dominico suo ut de feodo*): in possession as an estate of inheritance.

Not applied to things incapable of physical possession, such as an advowson, for which the phrase is *ut de feodo*, or *ut de feodo et jure*. (Elphinstone, etc. *Interpr. of Deeds*, 1885, 571-2.) The phrase is quite erroneously explained by Cowell, *Interp.* s.v. *Demaine*.

[**1292** BRITTON I. xxi. §4 Terres.. qe il ne avoint en lour demeyne cum de fee. *transl.* Which they held in their demesne as of fee.] **1491** *Act 7 Hen. VII*, c. 12 §5 As gode.. as if the King were seised of the premises in his demesne as of fee. **1512** *Act 4 Hen. VIII*, c. 13 Preamb., [They] enteryd into the sayd Maners.. & thereof wer seased in ther demean as of Fee in Cooparcenery. **1574** tr. *Littleton's Tenures* 4 b, Suche one was seised in his demeane as of fee. **1628** COKE *On Litt.* 17 a, In his demesne as of fee, *in dominico suo ut in feodo*. **1642** PERKINS *Prof. Bk.* ix. §612. 265 Hee.. died seised of the Land in his demeasne as of fee.

c. ***in ancient demesne***: see 4.

†**2.** *transf.* and *fig.* Possession; dominion, power.

*c*1300 *K. Alis.* 7561 That soffred theo duyk Hirkan To have yn demayn othir woman. *c*1386 CHAUCER *Monk's T.* 675 Alisandre.. That all the world weelded in his demeyne [*v.r.* demeigne, demeygne]. *c*1400 *Rom. Rose* 3310 To bidde me my thought refreyne, Which Love hath caught in his demeyne. **14..** *Epiph.* in *Tundale's Vis.* 113 Sche that hath heven in hur demeyn. **1508** *Will of Payne* (Somerset Ho.) [Goods that Jesu] hath suffred me to haue in my demayn in this worlde. *a*1541 WYATT *Poet. Wks.* (1861) 56 Since that thou hast My heart in thy demain, For service true. **1747** CARTE *Hist. Eng.* I. 32 Such was the place the Druids chose for their habitation, and they seem to have enjoyed it in demesne.

II. A possession; an estate possessed.

3. An estate held in demesne: land possessed or occupied by the owner himself, and not held of him by any subordinate tenant. **a.** In the wider sense, applied to all land not held of the owner by freehold tenants, i.e. including lands held of him by villein or copyhold tenure. **b.** In a more restricted sense, excluding the land held by the villeins or copyholders, and applied only to that actually occupied or held 'in hand' by the owner. (Cf. Vinogradoff, *Villainage in Engl.* 223-4.) Hence **c.** in modern use, The land immediately attached to a mansion, and held along with it for use or pleasure; the park, chase, home-farm, etc.

[*c*1250 BRACTON IV. iii. ix. §5 Est autem Dominicum, quod quis habet ad mensam suam & proprie, sicut sunt Bordlands Anglice. Item dicitur Dominicum Villenagium, quod traditur villanis, quod quis tempestivè & intempestivè sumere possit pro voluntate sua & revocare. **1292** BRITTON I. xix. §1 Queus demeynes nous tenoms en nostre meyn en cel counté. *transl.* What demeynes in the same county we hold in our hands.] **1398** TREVISA *Barth. De P.R.* XIV. l. (Tollem. MS.), 'Prædium' is a felde oþer demayn, þat an husbonde ordeyneþ for him selfe, and cheseþ tofore all oþer. **1523** FITZHERB. *Surv.* 2 It is to be inquered how many feldes are of the demeyns and howe many acres are in euery felde. **1541** *Act 33 Hen. VIII*, c. 32 The tenauntes.. vpon the demeanes of the saide late monasteri. **1562** *Act 5 Eliz.* c. 21 §1 Noblemen.. have imparked, environed and inclosed many Parcels of their said Demeans. **1613** SIR H. FINCH *Law* (1636) 145 Land in the Lords hands (whereof seuerall men hold by suite of Court) is termed a Mannor: the land considered apart from the seruice, is termed demesnes. **1641** *Termes de la Ley* 107 b, Demaines, or Demesnes, generally speaking according to the Law, be all the parts of any Manor which be not in the hands of freeholders of estate of inheritance, though they be occupied by Copiholders, Lessees for yeeres or for life, as well as tenant at will.. Yet in common speech that is ordinarily called Demesnes, which is neither free nor copy. **1818** CRUISE *Digest* (ed. 2) I. 47 Two material causes of a manor are demesnes and services.

b, c. **1538** LELAND *Itin.* I. 71 Sokbourne where as the Eldest House is of the Coniers, with the Demains about of it, a Mile Cumpace of exceding plesaunt Ground. **1623** COCKERAM, *Demaynes*, the Lords Manor house. **1670** COTTON *Espernon* I. III. 128 This Castle with the demean and territory belonging to it. **1732** SWIFT *Proposal for Act of Parl.* Wks. 1841 II. 123 Applying 100 acres of.. land that lies nearest his palace as a demesne for the convenience of his family. **1844** DISRAELI *Coningsby* III. iv, A grassy demesne, which was called the Lower Park. **1866** GEO. ELIOT *F. Holt* viii, Except on the demesne immediately around the house, the timber had been mismanaged. **1875** MAINE *Hist. Inst.* vii. 194 Reserving to himself only the mansion and the demesne in its vicinity.

d. ***demesne of the Crown, Royal demesne***: the private property of the Crown, Crown-lands. ***demesne of the State, State demesne***: land held by the state or nation, and of which the revenues are appropriated to national purposes.

1292 [see 4]. *c*1460 FORTESCUE *Abs. & Lim. Mon.* x, The Kyng off Ffraunce myght not sumtyme dyspende off his demaynes, as in lordeshippes, and oþer patrimonie peculier, so mich as myght tho the Kynge off England. *a*1577 SIR T. SMITH *Commw. Eng.* (1609) 69 The revenues of the crowne, as well that which came of patrimonie, which we call the demeasnes. **1580** NORTH *Plutarch* (1676) 684 Part also they [the Romans] reserved to their State as a demean. **1650** FULLER *Pisgah* II. 57 Converting them into demeans of his Crown. **1698** SIDNEY *Disc. Govt.* iii. §29 (1704) 360 According to the known maxim of the State, that the demeasnes of the Crown.. cannot be alienated. **1759** ROBERTSON *Hist. Scotl.* I. III. 226 These were part of the royal demesnes. **1832** W. IRVING *Alhambra* I. 40 The Alhambra continued a royal demesne, and was occasionally inhabited by the Castilian monarchs. **1838** ARNOLD *Hist. Rome* (1846) I. xiv. 271 The mass of the conquered territory was left as the demesne of the State. **1874** GREEN *Short Hist.* ii. §6. 89 The bulk of the cities were situated in the royal demesne.

4. ***ancient demesne***: a demesne possessed from ancient times; *spec.* the ancient demesne of the crown, i.e. that property which belonged to the king at the Norman Conquest, as recorded in Domesday-book, called in 1 Edw. VI. c. 4 'his ancient possessions'. The tenants of such lands had various privileges, hence the phrase came to be applied elliptically to their tenure, as in ***tenants in,*** or ***by ancient demesne, to plead ancient demesne.***

[**1292** BRITTON III. ii. §12 Auncienes demeynes sount terres de nos veuz maners annex a nostre Coroune, en les queles demeynes demurent acunes gentz fraunchement par chartre feffez, et ceux sount nos fraunes tenauntz. *transl.* Ancient demeynes are lands which were part of the ancient manors annexed to our Crown, in which demeynes dwell some who have been freely enfeoffed by charter,—and these are free tenants.] **1522** *Act 13 Hen. VIII, Stat. Ireland* (1621) 73 Any person.. seised of lands.. in fee simple, fee taile, or for terme of life, copyholde, and auncient demeane. **1577** HANMER *Anc. Eccl. Hist.* (1619) 177 The sundry and ancient demaines of husbandmen were quite done away. **1651** G. W. tr. *Cowell's Inst.* 94 The service of ancient Demesn is that which the tenants of the ancient Demesnes of the King performed. Now ancient Demesne is all that which was immediately held of the King St. Edward, or William the Conquerour. **1708** *Termes de la Ley* 40 Ancient demesne or demayn is a certain Tenure whereby all Mannors belonging to the Crown in the days of William the Conquerour were held. **1810** in *Risdon's Surv. Devon* App. 17 Places.. priviledged, and free from Tax and Toll.. some by *ancient Demesne*. **1817** W. SELWYN *Law Nisi Prius* (ed. 4) II. 693 Application was made for leave to plead ancient demesne. **1818** CRUISE *Digest* (ed. 2) V. 116 Tenants in ancient demesne could not sue or be sued for their lands in the King's courts.

fig. **1553** T. WILSON *Rhet.* 18 b, Custome encreaseth natures will, and maketh by auncient demeane thynges to bee justly observed whiche nature hath appoyncted.

5. By extension: **a.** The land or territory subject to a king or prince; the territory or dominion of a sovereign or state; a DOMAIN.

1387 TREVISA *Higden* (Rolls) I. 201 A lond in þe myddel bitwene þe demeynnes of Rome and Apulia. **1659** B. HARRIS *Parival's Iron Age* 53 The Low-countries, which had formerly been of the Demaynes of France. **1670** COTTON *Espernon* I. I. 3 Jane Albret Queen of Navarre, a great Fautress to those of the Reformed Religion.. desirous to draw all places within her demean into the same perswasion. **1871** BROWNING *Balaust.* 1464 And I was son to thee, recipient due Of sceptre and demesne.

b. Landed property, an estate; usually *pl.* estates, lands.

1584 POWEL *Lloyd's Cambria* 123 Borough townes with the Demeanes of the same. **1592** SHAKS. *Rom. & Jul.* III. v. 182 A Gentleman of Noble Parentage, Of faire demeanes. **1598** BARCKLEY *Felic. Man* (1631) 359 Whose house should contain no greater circuit than Cincinnatus' demaines. **1607** G. WILKINS *Mis. Enforced Marriage* in Hazl. *Dodsley* IX. 473 Our demesnes lay near together. **1735** SOMERVILLE *Chase* I. 104 By smiling Fortune blest With large Demesnes, hereditary Wealth. **1844** DISRAELI *Coningsby* II. ii, The noble proprietor of this demesne had many of the virtues of his class. **1856** EMERSON *Eng. Traits, Manners* Wks. (Bohn) II. 48 If he is rich, he buys a demesne, and builds a hall.

6. *fig.* A district, region, territory; DOMAIN.

1592 SHAKS. *Rom. & Jul.* II. i. 20 By her Fine foote, Straight leg, and Quiuering thigh, And the Demeanes, that there Adiacent lie. **1659** HAMMOND *On Ps.* lxxxiii. 12 Annot. 416 These pastures and fat demeans of God. *a* **1821** KEATS *Sonn., Chapman's Homer*, One wide expanse.. That deep-browed Homer ruled as his demesne [*rime* serene]. **1851** NICHOL *Archit. Heav.* 99 Alas! that the demesne of knowlege is so uncleared.

†7. *pl.* Estate, means. [Probably associated with the latter word.] *Obs.*

1627–77 FELTHAM *Resolves* I. liii. 84 In this fall of their melted demeans, they grow ashamed to be publicly seen come short of their wonted reuelling. **1629** MASSINGER *Picture* I. i, You know How narrow our demeans are. **1650** W. BROUGH *Sacr. Princ.* (1659) 323 Can he want demeanes that is such a Prince?

III. *attrib.* or as *adj.*

[The original OF. adjective use, = 'own', does not appear to have come into English; it was common in Anglo-Fr. (e.g. **1292** BRITTON III. xx. §3 Ne tint mie les tenementz en soen noun demeyne—*transl.* Did not hold the holdings in his own name), and it persisted down to modern times, also, in a few technical phrases, e.g. *son assault demesne*, '[it was] his [the plaintiff's] own assault', the common plea in justification on the ground of self-defence to an action for battery.

1809 TOMLINS *Law Dict.* II. 3 H. b/1 s.v. *Pleading*, In an action of assault and battery [a man with leave of Court may plead] these three [pleas]: Not guilty, *Son assault demesne*, and the Statute of Limitations.]

8. Of or pertaining to a demesne (3): demesnial.

1533 *St. Papers Hen. VIII*, IV. 634 We brynt theis townes .. with many oder by steadinges, and demayn places. **1801** STRUTT *Sports & Past.* I. i. 14 Excepting only the king's own desmean park. **1839** T. STAPLETON *Plumpton Corr.* (Camden) p. xviii, Allowed to assart the demesne woods. **1861** *Times* 10 Oct., Extensive demesne farms are occupied .. by the larger proprietors.

b. *esp.* in ***demesne lands***, lands of a demesne.

14.. *Tretyce* in *W. of Henley's Husb.* (1890) 44 Corne is sowen upon your demayn londis. **1558–9** *Act 1 Eliz.* c. 19 §2 Any the Demean Landes commonly used or occupyed with any suche Mansion or Dwelling House. **1654** FULLER *Two Serm.* 49 King William.. caused a Survey-Booke to be made of all the Demesne Lands in England. **1710** PRIDEAUX *Orig. Tithes* iv. 193 The Grant of Tithes was not only for the King's demain lands, but for all the lands of the whole Kingdom. **1846** ARNOLD *Later Hist. Rome* II. x. 275 The State never lost its right of re-entering into the possession of its demesne lands, if the tenants.. ceased to occupy them. **1861** *Times* 16 Oct., Most of the large farms, not demesne lands farmed by the proprietor, are under lease.

demesnial (dɪˈmeɪnɪəl, -ˈmiːnɪəl), *a.* [f. DEMESNE, after *manorial*, etc.: see -IAL.] Of or pertaining to a demesne; domanial.

1857 SIR F. PALGRAVE *Norm. & Eng.* II. 442 Austrasia contained the chief demesnial towns and cities.. of the Carlovingian Sovereigns.

†**deˈmess**, *v. Obs. rare.* [f. L. *dēmess-*, ppl. stem of *dēmetĕre* to mow down, reap.] To cut down (corn), to reap.

1657 TOMLINSON *Renou's Disp.* 315 Found in many fields when the segetives are demessed.

demester, obs. f. DEEMSTER, DEMPSTER.

demetallize, demetricize: see DE- II. 1.

demethylate (diːˈmɛθɪleɪt), *v. Chem.* [f. DE- II. 1 + METHYLATE *v.*] To remove a methyl group from. Hence **deˈmethylating** *ppl. a.*, **demethyˈlation**.

1911 *Chem. Abstr.* V. 2880 (*title*) Influence of caffeine on protein metabolism in dogs, with some remarks on demethylation in the body. **1933** *Ibid.* XXVII. 1624 (*title*) Demethylating the phenol ethers. **1940** *Nature* 3 Aug. 166/1 Demethylation definitely occurs in the animal body. **1967** I. L. FINAR *Org. Chem.* (ed. 5) I. xxvi. 682 Ethers that are sensitive to other demethylating reagents.

Demetian (dɪˈmiːʃɪən), *a.* and *sb.* Also **Dimetian**. [f. *Demetia*, *Dimetia*, Dyfed in S.W. Wales (Cardigan, Pembroke, and Carmarthen) + -IAN.] Of or pertaining to Demetia in South Wales; also as *sb.*, the dialect of this region.

1841 *Anc. Laws & Inst. Wales* Pref. xii, The Dimetian or West Wales Code. **1877** H. HICKS in *Q. Jrnl. Geol. Soc.* XXXIII. 230, I propose now to divide the Pre-Cambrian rocks into two distinct series under the local names of Dimetian (*Dimetia* being the ancient name for a kingdom which included this part of Wales) for the lower, and Pebidian.. for the upper series. *Ibid.* 231 The rocks which compose the Dimetian series are chiefly compact quartz schists. *Ibid.* 238 My endeavour has chiefly been to point out spots where the unconformity between them [*sc.* Pebidian rocks] and the Cambrians above, or the Dimetians below, is well marked. **1885** A. GEIKIE *Text-bk. Geol.* (ed. 2) 639 The so-called 'Dimetian' I regard as a granite which has invaded the Cambrian rocks. **1910** *Encycl. Brit.* XIII. 838/2 Three [legal] codes.. called Venedotian, Demetian and Gwentian, are said to have been written down by Bleggwryd, archdeacon of Llandaff. **1913** J. M. JONES *Welsh Gram.* 8 Demetian, the dialect of Dyfed or South West Wales. *Ibid.*, Dialectal forms, chiefly Demetian and Powysian *-e*, begin to appear in the MSS. of the 15th century.

demeuer, -meure, -mewre, etc., obs. ff. DEMURE, etc.

demeyn(e, obs. f. DEMEAN *v.*¹, DEMESNE.

demi (ˈdɛmɪ), *sb.*, *a.*, *prefix.* Also 5–6 dimi. [F. *demi*:—L. *dimidium* half: see DIMIDIATE. The Fr. word is a sb. and adj., and much used in combination. It began to be used in English in the 15th c. attrib. in *Heraldry*, and in the 16th c. in names of cannon, and soon passed to other uses. At first it was often written separately; hence it was also treated as a simple adj., and occasionally as a sb. (In certain uses the separate word survives as DEMY, q.v.) But *demi-* is now almost always hyphened to the word which it qualifies, and it has become to a large extent a living element, capable of being prefixed to almost any sb. (often also to adjs., and sometimes to verbs).]

A. As separate word. (Formerly also **demy**.)

I. *adj.* (or *adv.*) Half; half-sized, diminutive. Now *rare*.

1418 *E.E. Wills* (1882) 36 Also a bed of red and grene dimi Selour. **1486** [see B. 1]. **1556** J. HEYWOOD *Spider & F.* lii, Cannons, double and demie. **1565** JEWEL *Def. Apol.* (1611) 202 Upon these few words, M. Harding is able to build up his Dimi Communion, his Priuate Masse. **1587** M. GROVE *Pelops & Hipp.* (1878) 43 Ere that demi the way The course had ouerpast. *Ibid.* 48 Ere that The day was demi past. **1594** T. B. *La Primaud. Fr. Acad.* II. 377 From hence spring demy and double tertians and quartanes. **1603** KNOLLES *Hist. Turks* (1621) 688 The complaints of this barking demie man. **1722** DE FOE *Plague* (1884) 218 This demy Quarantine. **1891** *Daily News* 29 June 2/7 For wools of the demi class there is a good demand.. In single demi wefts there is an average turnover.

†II. as *sb.* A half. Chiefly *ellipt. Obs.* See also DEMY.

1501 *Will of Stoyll* (Somerset Ho.), A girdell callid a Demye weying ij vnce large by Troye. **1604** E. GRIMSTONE *Hist. Siege Ostend* 90 Two whole Canons and three demies. **1761** *Bill of Fare* in Pennant *London* (1813) 562, 1 Grand Pyramid of Demies of Shell fish of various Sorts.

B. **demi-** in combination.

Among the chief groups of compounds are the following:

1. In *Heraldry*, etc., indicating the half-length figure of a man or animal, or the half of a charge or bearing: e.g. ***demi-angel, -figure, -forester, -horse, -lion, -man, -monk, -moor, -ram, -virgin, -wyvern; demi-belt, †-pheon, -ship***, etc.; **demi-vol**, a single wing of a bird used as a bearing.

1486 *Bk. St. Albans, Her.* B v a, *Demy* is calde in armys halfe a best in the felde. **1882** *Academy* No. 513. 161 [Consecration] crosses.. consisting of *demi-angels holding shields. **1864** BOUTELL *Heraldry Hist. & Pop.* xxviii. §1 (ed. 3) 434 Two *demi-belts pale-wise. *Ibid.* x. 55 In the Arms of the See of Oxford are three *demi-figures. **1856** *Farmer's Mag.* Jan. 68 A pair of.. flower vases, with *demi-horses as handles, standing on square plinths. **1610** GUILLIM *Heraldry* III. xv. (1660) 193 He beareth.. a *Demy Lyon Rampand. **1696** *Lond. Gaz.* No. 3229/4 Crest a Demy-Lion Regardant. **1928** BLUNDEN *Jap. Garl.* 16 The inscrutable and dog-like grin Of demi-lions hedge me in! **1864** BOUTELL *Her.* xvii. §2. 269 A *demi-monk grasping a scourge of knotted cords. **1686** PLOT *Staffordsh.* 344 With an iron hook or *demi-pheon ingrail'd within. *a* **1661** FULLER *Worthies* II. (1662) 299 A *Demi-ramme mounting Argent, armed Or. **1792** W. BOYS *Hist. Sandwich* 797 The old seal of mayoralty [of Dover].. with four *demi-ships conjoined with four demi-lions. **1864** BOUTELL *Her.* xxi. §11. 368 *Demi virgin, couped below the shoulders. **1857** H. AINSWORTH *M. Clitheroe* II. 277 A *demi-wyvern carved in stone.

2. In *Costume*, indicating an article of half the full size or length; hence a definitely shorter or curtailed form of the article, as ***†demi-cap, †-collar, †-coronal, †-gown, -robe, †-shirt, -train***; †**demi-crown**, a coronet. See also DEMI-CEINT, -GIRDLE.

1568 NORTH *Gueuara's Diall Pr.* IV. (1679) 627/1 To see a foolish Courtier weare a *demy cappe, scant to cover the crowne of his head. **1613** SHAKS. *Hen. VIII*, IV. i. (*Order of Coronation*). Marquesse Dorset.. on his head, a *Demy Coronall of Gold. **1638** BAKER tr. *Balzac's Lett.* I. 99 And if you doe nothing but change your cloath of gold for a russet coat; and your cut-work band for a *demy collar. **1641** *Hist. Rich. III* 219 Having on his head a *demy Crown appointed for the degree of a Prince. **1480** *Wardr. Acc. Edw. IV* (1830) 124, Vj *demy gownes and a shorte loose gowne. **1721** STRYPE *Eccl. Mem.* II. i. 7 Every of their footmen in demigowns, bare-headed. **1807** in *Pall Mall Budget* 7 Oct. (1886) 30/1 A *demie robe of white Albany gauze. **1634** SIR T. HERBERT *Trav.* 146 Under this garment they weare a smocke.. in length agreeing to our *demi-shirts. **1818** *La Belle Assemblée* XVII. 36 Hessian robe of white satin, with *demi-train. **1891** *Daily News* 20 May 3/1 Demi-trains are ordained by French couturiers to be worn in the street.

3. In *Arms* and *Armour*, indicating a piece of half the size of the full piece, or a reduced variety of the latter, forming a less complete covering; as **demi-brassard, -gardebras**, a piece of plate-armour for the upper arm at the back; **demi-chamfron**, a piece covering the face of the horse less completely than the chamfron; **demi-cuirass** (see quot.); **demi-jambe**, a piece covering the front of the leg; **demi-mentonniere**, a mentonniere or chin-piece for the tilt covering the left side only; **demi-pauldron**, the smaller and lighter form of pauldron or shoulder-plate used in the end of the 15th c.; **demi-pike** = HALF-PIKE; **demi-placard, -placate**, = *demi-cuirass*; **demi-suit**, the suit of light armour used in and after the 15th c.; **demi-vambrace**, a piece of plate-armour protecting the outside of the fore-arm. See also DEMI-LANCE, -PIQUE.

1874 BOUTELL *Arms & Arm.* viii. 147 A corslet of iron, formed of two pieces.. which enclosed and protected the body, front and back, above the waist, and as low down as the hips; this may be called a **demi-cuirass*. **1883** J. HATTON in *Harper's Mag.* Nov. 849/1 The armor.. is a *demi-suit worn in the days of Henry VIII.

4. In *Artillery*, distinguishing a piece of definitely smaller size than the full-sized piece so named, as ***demi-bombard***: see also DEMI-CANNON, -CULVERIN, -HAKE.

5. In *Fortification*, as ***demi-caponier, -distance, -parallel***: see quots. Also DEMI-BASTION, -GORGE, -LUNE, -REVETMENT.

1874 KNIGHT *Dict. Mech.*, **Demi-caponniere*, a construction across the ditch, having but one parapet and glacis. **1706** PHILLIPS (ed. Kersey), **Demi-distance* of Polygons.. is the distance between the outward Polygons and the Flank. **1851** J. S. MACAULAY *Field Fortif.* 233 When arrived at about 150 yards from the enemy's covered way, he forms other places of arms, called **demi-parallels*. **1874** KNIGHT *Dict. Mech.*, *Demi-parallel*, shorter entrenchments thrown up between the main parallels of attack, for the protection of guards of the trenches.

6. In *Military tactics*, the *Manège*, etc., as ***†demi-hearse, -pesade, -pommada***; **demi-brigade**, the name given, under the first French Republic, to a regiment of infantry and artillery (Littré); see also DEMI-BATEAU, -SAP, -VOLTE.

1799 *Hist. Europe* in *Ann. Reg.* 7/1 The sons of the Mammalukes.. he brought into the *demi-brigades to supply the place of the French drummers. **1635** BARRIFFE *Mil. Discip.* lxxvi. (1643) 210 The next firing in *Front* which I present unto you, is the *Demie-hearse. **1884** E. L. ANDERSON *Mod. Horsemanship* II. xvii. 154 The Greeks.. practised their horses in leaping, in the career.. and even in the *demi-pesade. **1762** STERNE *Tr. Shandy* V. xxix, Springing into the air, he turned him about like a wind-mill, and made above a hundred frisks, turns, and *demi-pommadas.

7. In *Weights, Measures, Coins*, etc., as ***†demi-barrel, †-galonier, †-groat, -mark, -second, †-sextier, †-sovereign***; **demi-ame**, half an AAM; **demi-farthing**, a copper coin of Ceylon, of the value of half a farthing.

1494 *Act 11 Hen. VII*, c. 23 No such Merchant.. should put any Herring to Sale by Barrel, *Demy-Barrel, or Firkin. *c* **1740** SHENSTONE *Economy* I. 44 Ev'n for a *demi-groat, this open'd soul.. Revibrates quick. **1863** A. J. HORWOOD *Year-bks. 30–1 Edw. I*, Pref. 26 *note*, Mr. Booth's quære.. as to the reason for the tender of the *demy-mark in a writ of right. **1816** KIRBY & SP. *Entomol.* (1843) II. 248 Mr. Delisle observed a fly.. which ran nearly three inches in a *demi-second, and in that space made 540 steps. **1817** COBBETT *Wks.* XXXII. 142 Under the old-fashioned names of guineas and half-guineas, and not, as the newspapers told us .. under the name of sovereigns and *demi-sovereigns.

8. With names of fabrics, stuffs, etc., usually indicating that they are half of inferior material; as ***†demi-buckram, -lustre, †-worsted***. Also DEMI-CASTOR.

a **1568** ASCHAM *Scholem* (Arb.) 100 Clothe him selfe with nothing els, but a *demie bukram cassok. **1880** *Daily News* 8 Nov. 2/7 *Demi-lustres and Irish wools being relatively higher in price. **1536** A. BASSET in Mrs. Green *Lett. R. & Illust. Ladies* II. 295 Send me some *demi worsted for a robe and a collar.

9. *Music.* †**demi-cadence**, an imperfect cadence, a half-close; †**demi-crotchet**, a quaver; †**demi-ditone**, a minor third (see DITONE); †**demi-quaver**, a semi-quaver. (All *obs.* and *rare.*) See also DEMISEMIQUAVER, -SEMITONE, -TONE.

1828 BUSBY *Mus. Manual*, **Demi-Cadence*, an expression used in contradistinction to *Full-Cadence*.. so a demi-cadence is always on some other than the key-note. **1659** LEAK *Waterwks.* 28 If you will you may put on *Demi Crochets, or Quavers. **1706** PHILLIPS (ed. Kersey), **Demi-ditone*.. the same with Tierce Minor. **1753** CHAMBERS *Cycl. Supp.*, *Demiditone*, in music, is used by some for a third minor. **1669** COKAINE *Death T. Pilkington* Poems 79 Whose Loss our trembling Heart such wise lament As they like Semi- and *Demi-quavers went. **1706** PHILLIPS (ed. Kersey), *Demi-quaver*, a Musical Note; see *Semi-quaver*.

10. With names of material or geometrical figures: Half, semi-; as ***demi-canal, -column, -cylinder*** (hence ***demi-cylindrical*** adj.), ***demi-dome, †-hill, -metope, -orbit, -pillar, -plate, -tube***; †**demi-globe, -sphere** = hemisphere; **demi-octagonal, -octangular**, of the shape of half of an octagon. See also DEMI-CIRCLE.

1870 ROLLESTON *Anim. Life* 20 The place.. taken by the *demi-canal. **1879** SIR G. G. SCOTT *Lect. Archit.* II. 38 An entire pillar of this form must have suggested the *demi-column. **1781** GIBBON *Decl. & F.* (1846) III. xl. 621 The altar.. was placed in the eastern recess, artificially built in the form of a *demicylinder. **1879** SIR G. G. SCOTT *Lect. Archit.* I. 51 The most normal and readily invented vault is .. of the continuous barrel or *demi-cylindrical form. **1862** R. H. PATTERSON *Ess. Hist. & Art* 410 Beneath an apex or *demi-dome, stands the relic-shrine. **1794** G. ADAMS *Nat. & Exp. Philos.* III. xxxii. App. 327 The flat side of this *demi-globe. **1665** J. WEBB *Stone-Heng* (1725) 131 A mighty Heap in Form of a *Demi-hill. **1774** T. WEST *Antiq. Furness* (1805) 362 The ruins of the chapter-house, with four *demi-octangular buttresses in front. **1875** CROLL *Climate & T.* App. 537 The *demi-orbit, or.. the 180° comprehended betwixt the two equinoxes. **1776** *Lond. & Westm. Guide* 13 Four Gothic *Demi Pillars painted with blue Veins, and gilt Capitals. **1885** *Athenæum* 28 Feb. 284/1

A *demiplate..is never the second plate [of the ambulacra]. **1826** KIRBY & SP. *Entomol.* (1828) III. xxxv. 571 A deep channel or *demitube.

11. With ordinary class-nouns, indicating a person or thing which has half the characteristics connoted by the name; or is half this and half not, half-and-half; hence sometimes with sense 'of equivocal quality or character'; as ***demi-atheist, -Atlas, -beast, -beau, -bisque*** (BISK *sb.*), ***-brute, -cæsura, -canon, crack*** (CRACK *sb.* 11–15), ***-Christian, -critic, -dandiprat, -deity, -devil, -doctor, -gentleman, -king, -lawyer, -millionaire, -Mohammedan, -Moor, -owl, -pagan, -Pelagian*** (so ***-Pelagianism***), ***-priest, -prophetess, -savage, -urchin, -votary, -wolf***; †**demi-damsel, -lady, -lass** (rendering Sp. *semidoncella*); †**demi-male**, a eunuch. See also DEMI-GOD, -ISLAND, -ISLE, -MONDE.

1856 BOKER *Calaynos* I. i, Why talk you thus, you *demi-atheist? **1606** SHAKS. *Ant. & Cl.* I. v. 23 The *demy Atlas of this Earth. **1849** J. W. DONALDSON *Theatre Greeks* 252 The composition of demigods with *demibeasts formed a diverting contrast. *a* **1700** B. E. *Dict. Cant. Crew, Sub-beau*, or *Demibeau, a wou'd-be-fine. **1799** W. TOOKE *View Russian Emp.* II. 606 Destitute of the finer feelings of our nature, and a *demi-brute. **1824** L. MURRAY *Eng. Gram.* (ed. 5) I. 382 This semi-pause may be called a **demi-cæsura*. **1712** COOKE *Voy. to S. Sea* 396 To the Cathedral belong ten Canons..six *Demi-Canons, and six half Demi-Canons [etc.]. **1622** MASSINGER *Virg. Mart.* II. i, Herein thou shewed'st thyself a perfect *demi-Christian too. **1674** S. VINCENT *Yng. Gallant's Acad.* To Rdr. A vij b, Nay the Stationers themselves are turned *Demi-Criticks. **1756** *Gray's-Inn Jrnl.* I. 167 We the..Demi-critics of the City of London, in Coffee-houses assembled. **1620** SHELTON *Quix.* IV. xvi. II. 201 To this Hole came the two *demi-Damsels. **1622** MASSINGER *Virg. Mart.* II. iii, Adieu, *demi-dandiprat, adieu! **1640** T. RAWLINS *Rebellion* in Hazl. *Dodsley* XIV. 74 A religious sacrifice of praise Unto thy *demi-deity. **1820** BYRON *Mar. Fal.* II. i. 390 The demy-deity Alcides. **1604** SHAKS. *Oth.* v. ii. 301 Demand that *demy-Diuell, Why he hath thus ensnar'd my Soule and Body. **1823** W. IRVING in *Life & Lett.* (1864) IV. 399 What demi-devils we are to mar such scenes of quiet and loveliness with our passions! **1737** BRACKEN *Farriery Impr.* (1757) II. 90 *Demi-Doctors, who do more Mischief than all the right-knowing of the Profession do good. **1611** SPEED *Hist. Gt. Brit.* IX. vi. §14 But a *Demi-King, depriued of all Soueraignty ouer one half-deale of his Kingdome. **1742** JARVIS *Quix.* I. IV. xvi. (D.), At this hole then this pair of *demilasses [rendered by MOTTEUX and OZELL, 1757, *demy-ladies] planted themselves. **1825** T. JEFFERSON *Autobiog.* Wks. 1859 I. 45 Chicaneries..and delays of lawyers and *demi-lawyers. **1601** R. JOHNSON *Kingd. & Commw.* (1603) 235 Being a *demi Mahumetan. **1728** MORGAN *Algiers* II. v. 294 He was always called Aga, as are generally those *Demi-Males: every Eunuch is an Aga. **1614** SYLVESTER *Du Bartas, Parl. Vertues Royall* 108 Those daring *Demi-Moores. **1622** MASSINGER *Virg. Mart.* II. i, As I am a *demi-pagan, I sold the victuals. **1626** tr. *Parallel* A iij, What kindred..hath Arminius..with the *Demipelagians? *Ibid.* D ij, *Demipelagianisme is Pelagianisme. **1590** L. LLOYD *Diall Daies* 18 So inspired by god Phœbus, that she was accompted and taken for a *demie Prophetesse. **1800** HELENA WELLS *C. Neville* III. 318 The little *demi-savage gained so many friends. **1627** DRAYTON *Agincourt, etc.* 173 Other like Beasts yet had the feete of Fowles, That *Demy-Vrchins weare, and Demy-Owles. **1663** COWLEY *Complaint* vii, My gross Mistake, My self a *demy-Votary to make. **1605** SHAKS. *Macb.* III. i. 94 As..Mungrels, Spaniels, Curres..and *Demy-Wolues are clipt All by the Name of Dogges.

12. With nouns of action, condition, state; as ***demi-assignation, -atheism, -bob, -flexion, -incognito, -nudity, -premisses, -pronation, -relief, -result, -sacrilege, -translucence***; **demi-metamorphosis** (*Entom.*), partial metamorphosis, hemi-metabolism; **demi-toilet**, half evening (or dinner) dress, not full dress.

1667 G. DIGBY *Elvira* in Hazl. *Dodsley* XV. 61 Such words imply Little less than a *demi-assignation. **1710** BERKELEY *Princ. Hum. Knowl.* §155 Sunk into a sort of *Demy-atheism. **1842** BARHAM *Ingol. Leg., Auto-da-fé*, Returning his bow with a slight *demi-bob. **1808** *Med. Jrnl.* XIX. 81 *Demi-flexion becomes at length as painful as the extension at full length. **1836–9** TODD *Cycl. Anat.* II. 76/2 The fore-arm was in a state of demi-flexion. **1891** *Pall Mall G.* 5 Mar. 1/2 When a Royal personage comes to Paris in *demi-incognito. **1816** *Gentl. Mag.* LXXXVI. I. 227 Loosely attired in the *demi-nudity of the Grecian costume. **1597** HOOKER *Eccl. Pol.* v. lxxx. (1611) 400 They judge conclusions by *demipremisses and halfe principles. **1836–9** TODD *Cycl. Anat.* II. 76/2 The fore-arm was in a state of *demi-pronation. **1874** KNIGHT *Dict. Mech.*, **Demi-relief*.. half raised, as if cut in two, and half only fixed to the plane. **1612** W. SCLATER *Ministers Portion* 29 Popish *Demi-sacrilege had made seisure of tithes. **1828** SCOTT *Diary* 17 May in *Lockhart*, I contrived to make a *demi toilette at Holland House. **1880** DISRAELI *Endym.* xxii, The sisters were in demi-toilet, which seemed artless, though in fact it was profoundly devised. **1849** C. BRONTË *Shirley* v. 47 Dawn was just beginning to..give a *demi-translucence to its opaque shadows.

13. With adjectives: as ***demi-heavenly, -high, -human, -Norman, -official, -pagan, -pectinate, -savage, -simple, -unenfranchised***; **demi-equitant** (*Bot.*) = OBVOLUTE. (With most of these *semi-* is now the usual prefix.)

1616 SYLVESTER *Du Bartas, Tobacco Battered* 536 *Demi-heav'nly, and most free by Birth. **1871** *Figure Training* 120 We may go far before we meet with anything superior to the plain *demi-high button-boot now so much worn. **1822** O'CONNOR *Chron. Eri* I. p. lxvii, These wretched mortals.. considered but *demi-human, the link between man and monkey. **1876** TENNYSON *Harold* III. i, Our dear England Is *demi-Norman. **1804** W. TAYLOR in *Ann. Rev.* II. 275 These..are surely inferior to the *demi-official letters of the second volume. **1818** COBBETT *Pol. Reg.* XXXIII. 201 The publications in the demi-official newspaper of this country. **1833** CHALMERS *Const. Man.* (1835) I. i. 104 The warfare of savage or *demisavage nations. **1591** F. SPARRY tr. *Cattan's Geomancie* 168 The one is simple, the vther *demy simple. **1893** *Westm. Gaz.* 25 Feb. 2/2 Extracting verdicts from semi-disfranchised and *demi-unenfranchised constituencies.

14. With verbs and verbal derivatives: as †***demi-corpsed***, †***-deify***, †***-digested***, †***-natured***, †***-turned***.

1828 J. WILSON in *Blackw. Mag.* XXIV. 286 He [the rider] becomes *demicorpsed with the noble animal. **1784** COWPER *Task* v. 266 They *demi-deify and fume him so. **1660** FISHER *Rusticks Alarm* Wks. (1679) 229 In thy meer *demi-digested demications against them. **1602** SHAKS. *Ham.* IV. vii. 88 And to such wondrous doing brought his horse, As had he beene encorps'd and *demy-Natur'd With the braue Beast. **1793** J. WILLIAMS *Calm Exam.* 74 Has the sphere of rectitude been *demi-turned, and what was yesterday uprightness, now antipodic?

demi-Atlas: see DEMI- 11.

‖**demi-bain** ('dɛmɪbeɪn). [Fr.; = half bath.] = DEMI-BATH.

1847 in CRAIG.

†'**demi-bar**. *Obs.* [BAR *sb.*[1] 21.] Name for a kind of false dice.

1592 *Nobody & Someb.* (1878) 337 Those are called high Fulloms..low Fulloms..Those Demi-bars..bar Sizeaces.

demi-bastion ('dɛmɪ'bæstɪən). *Fortif.* [DEMI- 5.] A work of the form of half a bastion, having one face and one flank. Hence '**demi-'bastioned** *a.*, having demi-bastions.

1695 *Lond. Gaz.* No. 3100/4 The Dutch were not able to maintain themselves in the Demi-Bastion. **1813** *Chron.* in *Ann. Reg.* 198/2 Against the demy-bastion on the south-eastern angle and the termination of the curtain of the southern face. **1832** SOUTHEY *Hist. Penins. War* III. 235 Their efforts had been misdirected against the face of a demibastion. **1851** J. S. MACAULAY *Field Fortif.* 22 Of Demi-bastioned Forts.

‖**demi-bateau** (dəmibato). [Fr.; = half-boat: see BATEAU.] A half-bateau used in constructing pontoons.

1853 SIR H. DOUGLAS *Milit. Bridges* (ed. 3) 98 Those [pontoons] of greater breadth are formed by uniting two demi-bateaux at the broader ends so as to constitute an entire bateau.

demi-bath ('dɛmɪbɑːθ, -æ-), [transl. Fr. *demi-bain.*] A bath in which the body can be immersed only up to the loins.

1847 in CRAIG.

demi-bombard, -brassard, -brigade: see DEMI- 4, 3, 6.

demibranch ('dɛmɪbræŋk). *Zool.* [f. DEMI- + Gr. βράγχια gills.] = HEMIBRANCH (sense a).

1903 *Phil. Trans. R. Soc.* Ser. B. 150 A descending lamella and its corresponding ascending lamella together constitute a demibranch. The demibranchs are inner and outer, lying towards the visceral mass and the mantle respectively. **1946** *Nature* 12 Oct. 523/1 On percolation through the gills, the water passes into the interlamellar chambers..of the outer and inner demibranchs respectively.

demic ('dɛmɪk), *a. nonce-wd.* [f. Gr. δῆμ-ος district, country, people + -IC.] Belonging to or characteristic of the people.

1834 MEDWIN *Angler in Wales* II. 263 Perhaps beauty is demic or epidemic here.

demi-cadence: see DEMI- 9.

†,**demi-'cannon**. *Obs.* Also -canon. [a. F. *demi-canon* (16th c. in Littré): see DEMI- 4.] A kind of large gun formerly used, of about 6½ inches bore: see CANNON *sb.*[1] 2.

1556 [see DEMI *a.*]. **1577–87** HOLINSHED *Chron.* III. 1188/2 They were answered againe with foure or five canons, and demi canons. **1587** HARRISON *England* II. xvi. (1877) I. 281 The names of our greatest ordinance..Demie Canon six thousand pounds, and six inches and an halfe within the mouth. Cannon, seauen thousand pounds, and eight inches within the mouth. **1673** *Phil. Trans.* VIII. 6040 In the Year 1672. July 9, there was cast a Demy-canon; weighing 34 hundreds of weight. **1707** FARQUHAR *Beaux Strat.* III. ii, Her eyes.. Are demi-canons to be sure; so I won't stand their battery. **1735–6** CARTE *Ormonde* I. 341 There were three demi-canon, two sakers, and one minion.

b. *attrib.*, as in ***demi-cannon cut, drake***. (See CUT *sb.*[2] 31 a, DRAKE.)

1634–5 BRERETON *Trav.* (1844) 165 She carries 16 pieces of ordinance..four whole culverin drakes, and four iron demi-cannon drakes. **1642** in Rushw. *Hist. Coll.* III. (1692) I. The Walls..are singularly well fortified with Brass and Iron Guns, both Culverins and Demi-Cannon-Cuts.

demi-caponier: See DEMI- 5.

‖**demi-caractère** (dəmikaraktɛr), *sb.* and *a.* *Ballet.* [Fr.] (Of) a dance which retains the form of the character dance but is executed with steps based on the classical technique; also applied to a dancer.

1776 *Publ. Advertiser* 2 Nov. 1/1 New Ballet Demi-caracteres, called Les Amusemens Champetre. **1828** J. EBERS *Seven Years of King's Theatre* iii. 72 The exquisite prettiness of the *demi-caractère* steps of Fanny Bias. *Ibid.* iv. 99 Fanny Bias was a dancer of the demi-caractère, perfect in ..beautiful little half steps. **1950** *Ballet Ann.* IV. 70 A neck which is just too short for the demands of a classical ballerina. Hence she is at her best in *demi-caractère* rôles. **1957** *Times* 23 Aug. 11/3 A delightful *demi-caractère* dancer. **1963** VAN PRAAGH & BRINSON *Choreogr. Art.* 177 Really talented demi-charactère dancers are able to fill roles in either of the other categories.

†,**demi'castor**. *Obs.* Also -caster. [a. F. *demi-castor* 'chapeau de poil de castor mélangé' (Racine 17th c.): see DEMI- 8, CASTOR[1].] **a.** An inferior quality of beaver's fur, or a mixture of beaver's and other fur: usually *attrib.*, as in ***demicastor hat***. **b.** A hat made of this.

1637 *Lanc. Wills* II. 142 To Wm Nickson one demicastor hatt. *c* **1645** HOWELL *Lett.* III. xi, In that more subtill air of yours tinsell sometimes passes for tissue, Venice Beads for Perl, and Demicastors for Bevers. **1721** C. KING *Brit. Merch.* II. 236 Beaver, Demicastor, and Felt Hats, made in ..Paris.

fig. *a* **1658** CLEVELAND *Sir I. Presbyter* 58 Pray for the Mitred Authors, and defie Those Demicastors of Divinity.

demication: see DIMI-.

†'**demiceint**. *Obs.* Forms: 5–6 demycent, -sent, dymyceynt, -sent, dymisent, dymysen, -son. [a. F. *demi-ceint, demi-ceinct*, 'a halfe-girdle; a woman's girdle, whose forpart is of gold or siluer, and hinder of silke, &c.' (Cotgr.); f. *demi* half + OF. *ceint*:—L. *cinctum* girdle.] A girdle having ornamental work only in the front.

1483 in Arnolde *Chron.* (1811) 116 A dymysen with a red crosse harnossid with siluer wrought with golde. **1503** *Will of Tymperley* (Somerset Ho.), A dymysent gyrdell of siluer & gilt. *Ibid.*, A dymycent withoute any corse of siluer & gilt. *c* **1524** *Churchw. Acc. St. Maryhill, London* (Nichols 1797) 128 A demysent with a cheyne and a pommander and a pendent. **1538** *Bury Wills* (1850) 136 My best harnysid gyrdyll of gold callyd a dymysent. **1543** *Nottingham Rec.* III. 397 My dymyson gyrdylle and my coralle beydes.

demi-chamfron: see DEMI- 3.

demi-circle ('dɛmɪ,sɜːk(ə)l). [DEMI- 10.]

1. A semicircle. Now *rare*.

1654 EVELYN *Mem.* (1857) I. 308 Mathematical and magical curiosities..a balance on a demi-circle. **1662** GERBIER *Princ.* 2 How a Point, Line, Angle, Demi-circle.. must be made. **1726** CAVALLIER *Mem.* III. 185 The Hill being in the form of a Demi-Circle. **1864** BOUTELL *Heraldry Hist. & Pop.* xxi. §11. 370 A demi-circle of glory edged with clouds.

2. *Surveying.* An instrument of semicircular form used for measuring angles.

1874 KNIGHT *Dict. Mech.*, *Demi-circle*..a modest substitute for the theodolite.

Hence **demi-'circular** *a.*, semicircular.

1821 LOCKHART *Valerino* I. ix. 146 The party might consist of about twenty, who reclined along one demi-circular couch.

demi-coronal: see DEMI- 2.

†'**demi-,cross**. *Obs.* [DEMI- 1, 10.]

1. The title of one of the degrees among the Knights of Malta.

1788 *Pict. Tour thro' Part of Europe* 19 There are also some Demi-crosses, who, by express permission, are authorized to wear the golden cross with three points.

2. An instrument for taking altitudes: see quot.

1753 CHAMBERS *Cycl. Supp.*, *Demi-cross*, an instrument used by the Dutch to take the sun's altitude, or that of a star at sea..The Demi-cross is of this figure: ⊥.

demi-crotchet, -cuirass: see DEMI- 9, 3.

demi-culverin (,dɛmɪ'kʌlvərɪn). *Obs.* exc. *Hist.* [ad. F. *demi-coulevrine*: see DEMI- 4 and CULVERIN.] A kind of cannon formerly in use, of about 4½ inches bore.

1587 HARRISON *England* II. xvi. (1877) I. 281 Demie Culuerijn weigheth three thousand pounds. **1598** B. JONSON *Ev. Man in Hum.* III. i, They had planted mee three demi-culuerings, just in the mouth of the breach. **1611** CORYAT *Crudities* 104 One..was exceeding great..about sixteene foote long, made of brasse, a demy culverin. **1627** CAPT. SMITH *Seaman's Gram.* xiv. 70. **1692** LUTTRELL *Brief Rel.* (1857) II. 372 The feild train of artillery in the Tower for Flanders..are to consist of 23 pounders, 10 sakers, and 8 demiculverins. **1772** SIMES *Mil. Guide, Demi-culverin*. It is a very good field piece. **1855** MACAULAY *Hist. Eng.* III. xvi. 685 Demiculverins from a ship of war were ranged along the parapets.

attrib. **1634–5** BRERETON *Trav.* (1844) 165 She carries.. six iron demiculverin drakes. **1647** CLARENDON *Hist. Reb.* VII. (1703) II. 219 Retiring about Demy Culvering shot behind a Stone Wall.

demi-damsel, -deify, -devil: see DEMI- 11, 14.

demidiate: see DIMI-.

demi-distance, -ditone, -farthing, -galonier, -gardebras: see DEMI- 5, 9, 7, 7, 3.

demidovite (dɛmɪ'dɒvaɪt). *Min.* Also demidoffite. [ad. F. *démidovite* (N. Nordenskiold

1856, in *Bull. Soc. imp. des Naturalistes de Moscou* XXIX. I. 128), f. the name of Prince Anatoliĭ Nikolaevich *Demidov* (1813–1870), Russian patron and traveller: see -ITE[1].] (See quot. 1955.)

1868 DANA *Syst. Min.* (ed 5) 403 Demidoffite [ed. 6, demidovite] occurs at Tagilsk, Urals, in mammillated crusts of a sky-blue color. **1955** M. H. HEY *Index Min. Species* (ed. 2) 214 Demidovite. Silicate and phosphate of Cu. *Ibid.* 401 Demidoffite... Syn. of Demidovite.

demi-equitant: see DEMI- 13.

†**demi-galliot, -galleyot.** [DEMI *a.*: cf. F. *demi-galère*, It. *mezza galea* (Jal).] A small-sized galliot or brigantine formerly used in the Mediterranean.

1632 W. LITHGOW *Trav.* B. v. 180 This Tartaneta, or Demi galleyot, belonged to the Ile of Stagiro, auenciently Thasia.

†ˌ**demi-ˈgauntlet.** *Surg.*, *Obs.*

1706 PHILLIPS *Demi-gantlet*, a sort of Bandage us'd in the setting of disjoynted Fingers. **1823** in CRABBE *Techn. Dict.*

†**demi-girdle.** *Obs.* = DEMICEINT, q.v.

1501 [see DEMI A. II.]. **1533** in Weaver *Wells Wills* (1890) 155 A dymye gyrdell. **1535** *Ibid.* 170 A demye gyrdell.

‖**demi-glace** (dəmiglas). *Cookery.* [Fr.; cf. GLAZE *sb.* 2.] Half-glaze; meat stock from which the liquid has been partially evaporated. Also *attrib.*

1906 MRS. BEETON *Bk. Househ. Managem.* x. 276 *Demi-glace sauce.* Ingredients—½ a pint of Espagnole sauce..½ of a pint of good gravy, salt and pepper. **1951** *Good Housek. Home Encycl.* 438/2 *Demi-glace Sauce* (Half-glaze Sauce). Espagnole sauce to which has been added meat glaze or good gravy... Demi-glace is served with high-class meat dishes.

demigod (ˈdɛmɪgɒd). [DEMI- 11: rendering L. *semideus.*] In ancient mythology, etc.: A being partly of divine nature, as one sprung from the intercourse of a deity and a mortal, or a man raised to divine rank; a minor or inferior deity.

1530 PALSGR. 366 What so ever goddes or demye goddes that they be. **1580** NORTH *Plutarch* (1676) 278 They did sacrifice..unto the demy-gods, Androcrates..and Polyidus. **1596** SHAKS. *Merch. V.* III. ii. 115 What demie God Hath come so neere creation? **1667** MILTON *P.L.* I. 796 The great Seraphic Lords and Cherubim..A thousand Demy-Gods on golden seats, Frequent and full. **1712** POPE *Vertumnus* 75 A thousand sylvans, demigods, and gods That haunt our mountains. **1874** SAYCE *Compar. Philol.* viii. 307 The gods and demi-gods of pagan antiquity. **1878** EMERSON *Misc. Papers, Fort. of Repub.* Wks. (Bohn) III. 388 Arkwright and Whitney were the demi-gods of cotton.

ˌ**demiˈgoddess.** *rare.* [DEMI- 11 + *goddess*: rendering L. *semidea.*] A female demigod.

1603 HOLLAND *Plutarch's Mor.* 498 The most antique demi-goddesses that ever were. **1788** MRS. HUGHES *Hen. & Isab.* I. 74 Her whole appearance..reminded the beholder of a nymph or demy goddess. **1836–48** B. D. WALSH *Aristoph., Clouds* I. iv, Or am I to think that the musical maids Are certain divine demigoddesses?

Hence **demiˈgoddess-ship.**

1858 in *Grosart's Spenser* (1882) III. p. xciii, Upon Rosalinde..an affection of the demigoddess-ship..is..charged.

demi-gorge (ˈdɛmɪˌgɔːdʒ). *Fortif.* [DEMI- 5.] That part of the internal polygon from the angle of the curtain to the centre of the bastion (or point where the lines of the two adjacent curtains intersect); forming half of the gorge or entrance of the bastion.

1706 in PHILLIPS (ed. Kersey). **1755** T. FORBES in C. Gist's *Jrnls.* (1893) 151 The length of the Curtains is about 30 feet, and the Demigorge of the Bastions about eighty. **1851** J. S. MACAULAY *Field Fortif.* 29 Vauban strengthened the continued line with redans placed 260 yards apart, having 30 yards of demigorge, and 44 yards of capital. **1859** F. A. GRIFFITHS *Artil. Man.* (1862) 267 Set off 40 yards on each side of the re-entering angle of the counterscarp for their demi-gorges.

†**demigraine.** *Obs.* [a. OF. *demigraine* pomegranate: cf. F. *grenade* pomegranate, also name of a stuff.] Name of some textile fabric.

1540 *Ld. Treas. Accts. Scot.* in Pitcairn *Crim. Trials* I. *302 To be ane cote to the Fwle, vi quarteris Deme-grane and vi quarteris Frenche ʒallow.

†**demiˈgrane.** *Obs.* [a. F. *demigraine* (Cotgr.), var. of *migraine*, med.L. *demigrānia*, for L. *hēmicrānia*, a. Gr. ἡμικράνιον pain on one side of the head.] = HEMICRANIA.

c **1400** *Lanfranc's Cirurg.* 301 And for demigrania þou schalt lete blood in þe templis of his heed..I hadde a ʒong man..þat hadde demigrayn of hoot cause.

†ˈ**demigrate,** *v.* *Obs.* [f. ppl. stem of L. *dēmigrāre* to migrate from, depart, f. DE- I. 2 + *migrāre* to MIGRATE.] *intr.* To remove to another place or dwelling; to migrate.

1623 COCKERAM, *Demigrate*, to change houses. **1651** BIGGS *New Disp.* ¶ 288 Hath it demigrated to another place?

Hence †**demiˈgration.**

1623 COCKERAM, *Demigration*, a changing of places, or houses. **1628** BP. HALL *Quo Vadis?* §22 Are wee so foolish that..wee will needs bring upon our selues..the curse of Cain..that is, of demigration? **1759** STERNE *Tr. Shandy* II. v, The reason..of this sudden demigration.

demi-groat: see DEMI- 7.

†ˈ**demi-ˌhake, -haque.** *Obs.* exc. *Hist.* Also 9 demy-hag. [DEMI- 4.] A fire-arm used in the 16th c.; a smaller kind of HAQUE or HACKBUT. Also called *half-haque, half-hagg.*

1541 *Act 33 Hen. VIII*, c. 6 No person..shall shote in anie crossebowe, handgunne, hagbut or demy hake. [**1549** *Compl. Scot.* vi. 41 Hagbutes of croche, half haggis, culverenis.] **1581** LAMBARDE *Eiren.* IV. iv. (1588) 477 If any person have..used or kept..any hagbut or demyhake. **1801** STRUTT *Sports & Past.* II. i. 52 In addition to the hand-guns, I meet with other instruments of like kind..namely demy hags, or hag butts. **1834** *Penny Cycl.* II. 373/1 The *demihaque* was a kind of long pistol, the butt-end of which was made to curve so as almost to become a semicircle.

demi-hearse: see DEMI- 6.

ˌ**demi-ˈhunter.** *Watchmaking.* [DEMI- 11.]

1844 F. J. BRITTEN *Watch & Clockm.* 80 [A] Demi Hunter ..[is] a Watch case in which a glass of about half the diameter of the hunting cover is let into it.

†**demi-island.** *Obs.* Also -iland. [DEMI- 11.] A peninsula.

1600 HOLLAND *Livy* XXXII. xxi. 822 Peloponnesus is a demie island [*peninsula*]. **1614** RALEIGH *Hist. World* II. IV. vi. §8. 245 He was kept vnder sure guard in a demie-Iland. **1652–62** HEYLIN *Cosmogr.* III. (1673) 2/2 It is a demy-Island, or Peninsula, environed on all sides with waters.

Hence †**demi-ˈislander**, an inhabitant of a peninsula.

a **1649** DRUMM. OF HAWTH. *Fam. Epist.* Wks. (1711) 146 We can hardly repair unto you demi-islanders, without dancing and tossing on your arm of the sea.

†**demi-isle.** *Obs.* = prec.

1609 HOLLAND *Amm. Marcell.* XXII. viii. 200 That Biland, or demy Isle which the Sindi inhabit. **1610** —— *Camden's Brit.* I. 189 From S. Michaels mount southward..there is thrust forth a bi-land or demi-Isle. **1776** MICKLE tr. *Camoen's Lusiad* 284 Southward sea-girt she forms a demi-isle.

demi-jambe: see DEMI- 3.

demijohn (ˈdɛmɪdʒɒn). Forms: 8 demijan, 9 demijean, demi-john, demijohn. [In F. *dame-jeanne* (1694 Th. Corneille *dame-jane*, 1701 Furetière *Dame Jeanne*, lit. 'Dame Jane'); so Sp. *dama-juana* (as if *Dama Juana*); mod.Pr., in different dialects, *dama-jana*, *damajano*, *damojano*, *damejano*, *dabajano*, *debajano*; Cat. *damajana*; It. *damigiana*; mod. Arabic *damajānah*, *dāmajānah*, etc. in 19th c. lexicons.

The current Eng. form is the result of popular perversion as in 'sparrow-grass'; the earlier *demijan*, *demijean*, approach more closely to the F. and Romanic, whence the word was adopted. The original nationality and etymology of the word are disputed: see Rev. A. L. Mayhew in *Academy* 14 Oct. 1893. Some have assumed the Arabic to be the source of the Romanic forms, and have sought to explain this as of Persian origin, and derived from the name of the town *Damghān* or *Damaghān*, a commercial emporium S.E. of the Caspian. But this is not supported by any historical evidence; moreover, the word does not occur in Persian dictionaries, nor in Arabic lexicons before the 19th c., and the unfixedness of its form (*dāmijānah*, *dāmajānah*, *damajānah*, *damanjānah*) points, in the opinion of Arabic scholars, to its recent adoption from some foreign language, probably from Levantine use of It. *damigiana*. Assuming the word to be Romanic, some have taken the Provençal and Catalan forms as the starting-point, and conjectured for these either a L. type **dīmidiāna* from dīmidium half (Alart in *Rev. Lang. Rom.* Jan. 1877), or the phrase *dē mediāna* of middle or mean (size) (in illustration of which Darmesteter cites from a 13th c. tariff of Narbonne the phrase 'ampolas de mieja megeira' = L. *ampullās dē mediā mensūrā*). But these suggestions fail to explain the initial *da-* prevalent in all the langs.; on account of which M. Paul Meyer (like Littré) thinks that all the Romanic forms are simply adaptations or transliterations of the French, this being simply *Dame Jeanne* 'Dame Jane', as a popular appellation (cf. *Bellarmine*, *greybeard*, etc.). This is also most in accordance with the historical evidence at present known, since the word occurs in French in the 17th c., while no trace of it equally early has been found elsewhere.]

A large bottle with bulging body and narrow neck, holding from 3 to 10 (or, in extreme cases, 2 to 15) gallons, and usually cased in wicker- or rush-work, with one or two handles of the same, for convenience of transport.

An ordinary size is 5 gallons. Demijohns of clear glass, of ovate-quadrilateral section in the body (14 × 16 inches diam.), are employed to export vinegar and spirits to the West Indies, and are in common household use in the islands. The name is sometimes also given to vessels of earthenware or stoneware similarly cased.

1769 FALCONER *Dict. Marine* (1776), *Dame-jeanne*, a demijan, or large bottle, containing about four or five gallons, covered with basket-work, and much used in merchant-ships. **1803** CAPT. FELLOWES in *Naval Chron.* X. 183, I perceived one of the seamen emptying a demijean.. containing five gallons. [Not in TODD 1818, nor in *Pantologia* 1819.] **1828** WEBSTER, *Demijohn*, a glass vessel or bottle enclosed in wicker-work. **1842** DICKENS *Amer. Notes* (1850) 122/2 Two large stone jars in wicker cases, technically known as demi-johns. **1859** *Leisure Hour* No. 406. 626 Archy paraded round the table with a huge demijohn made of unglazed brick-earth. **1880** *Times* 7 May 3 The price paid for them was said to be a 'demijohn' of rum. **1894** *Letter fr. Messrs. Scrutton, Sons, & Co.*, We have at present 500 demijohns filled with vinegar going by one of our steamers to the West Indies.

Comb. **1884** L. OLIPHANT *Haifa* (1887) 134 Cisterns.. some of them demijohn-shaped.

demi-lance (ˈdɛmɪlɑːns, -æ-). Forms: 5 demye launce, 6 demy-, deme-, demi-, dimilaunce, dimilance, 6–7 demy-, 6–8 demilance, 7 demilaunce, 6–9 demi-lance. [a. F. *demie lance* (15th c. in Littré): cf. DEMI- 3.]

1. A lance with short shaft, used in the 15th and 16th centuries.

c **1489** CAXTON *Sonnes of Aymon* xxii. 487 Charlemagn.. helde a demye launce in hys hande. **1563–87** FOXE *A. & M.* (1596) 307/1 Who in the waie stroke the lord Gilbert Humsard such a blow with his demilance, that he feld both him and his horsse to the ground. **1598** DELONEY *Jacke Newb.* ii. 43 Fiftie tall men..demilances in their hands. **1697** DRYDEN *Virgil* VII. 1010 Light demi-lances from afar they throw, Fasten'd with leathern thongs, to gall the foe. **1877** MISS YONGE *Cameos* III. xxx. 301 He struck him such a blow with his demi-lance as to unhorse him.

attrib. **1658** J. BURBURY *Hist. Christina Alessandra* 358 His Holinesse likewise ordered that five of his demy-lance men should every day wait by turns on her Majesty.

2. A light horseman armed with a demilance. In the literal sense, obs. by 1600, exc. as *historical*; in 17th c. often used humorously like 'cavalier'.

1544 CRANMER in M. Burrows *Worthies All Souls* v. (1874) 65 To send up one demy-launce well furnished. **1560** *Diurn. Occurrents* (1833) 56 V[m] fute men and xviij[c] lycht horsemen and dimilances. **1611** SPEED *Hist. Gt. Brit.* IX. xxi. §48 Nineteene Knights, sixe hundred demi-Lances. **1631** SHIRLEY *Love's Cruelty* III. ii, Be not angry, demi-lance. **1755** CARTE *Hist. Eng.* IV. 55 The forces under his command consisting of 600 demilances, 200 archers on horsebacke, 3000 on foot. **1849** J. GRANT *Kirkaldy of Gr.* ix. 82 Kirkaldy with his troop of demi-lances accompanied this column of the army.

Hence **demi-ˈlancer** = DEMI-LANCE 2.

1552 HULOET, Dimilauncer or bearer of a dimilaunce, *lancearius.* **1625** MARKHAM *Souldiers Accid.* 40 The second Troope of Horse were called *Launciers* or *Demi-launciers.* **1767** ENTICK *London* I. 452 A large body of demi-lancers in bright armour.

demi-lass: see DEMI- 11.

deˈmilitarize, *v.* [f. DE- II. 1 + MILITARY + -IZE.] *trans.* To take away the military organization from. (In quot. 1883 referring to the organization of the Austrian 'military frontier'.) Also, to place (a sovereign state) under an obligation not to maintain armed forces in a specified region. Hence **deˌmilitariˈzation**; **deˈmilitarized** *ppl. a.*

1883 A. J. PATTERSON in *Pall Mall G.* 2 Oct. 1/2 Two out of the Croatian frontier regiments were demilitarized. But ..the Hungarians..delayed the process of demilitarization. **1905** *Westm. Gaz.* 4 Jan. 2/1 With Vladivostok demilitarised, and with Port Arthur and its entire hinterland confiscated. **1919** J. L. GARVIN *Econ. Foundations of Peace* xix. 485 If a demilitarised Germany were given a fair chance to recover..the powers of suasion and control by economic action would be paramount. **1934** H. NICOLSON *Curzon: Last Phase* 295 Ismet Pasha..made some passing reference to the possibility of establishing demilitarised zones in Thrace. **1936** *Economist* 14 Mar. 571/1 Owing to Herr Hitler's action last Saturday in reoccupying the demilitarised zone in the Rhineland the peace of Europe to-day is balancing..'on the razor's edge'. **1940** *Ibid.* 6 July 7/1 The French generals would still, it appears, resist an attack, but demilitarisation, not cession of territory or occupation, is what Italy asks of them. **1947** *Daily Tel.* 24 July, Mr. Marshall denied that the question of a 40-year Four-Power treaty guaranteeing German demilitarisation..cropped up on Monday. **1959** *Ann. Reg. 1958* 143 Israel and Jordan had agreed to try to carry out properly the July 1948 Agreement for the demilitarization of the Mount Scopus area. **1966** *Daily Tel.* 12 Oct., The draft of a treaty to keep space permanently demilitarised.

demilune (ˈdɛmɪl(j)uːn), *sb.* (*a.*) [a. F. *demilune*, in 16th–17th c. *demie lune* half moon: cf. DEMI- 10.]

†**1.** *gen.* A 'half-moon', a crescent. *Obs.*

a **1734** NORTH *Lives* (1808) I. 228 An immense mass of stone of the shape of a demilune. *a* **1734** —— *Exam.* III. vii. §95 (1740) 578 These stately Figures were planted in a Demilune about an huge Fire.

2. *Fortif.* An outwork resembling a bastion with a crescent-shaped gorge, constructed to protect a bastion or curtain.

1727–51 CHAMBERS *Cycl.*, *Demi-Lune*, *Half-Moon*, in fortification, an outwork..consisting of two faces, and two little flanks. **1870** *Daily News* 26 Sept., Demi-lunes have been constructed before the gates of Paris.

3. *Physiol.* ***demilunes*** (***crescents***) ***of Giannuzzi*** or ***Heidenhain***: certain crescent-shaped protoplasmic bodies found in the salivary glands.

1883 *Syd. Soc. Lex.*, *Demilune of Giannuzzi*, a granular mass of protoplasm, of semilunar form, which forms part of the cell-contents of the salivary cells.

B. *adj.* Crescent-shaped, semilunar.

1885 *Proc. R. Soc.* 19 Mar. 215 The demilune cells and the serous cells, which are present..in the sub-maxillary gland of the cat.

demi-lustre, -mentonnière, -metamorphosis, -metope: see DEMI- 8, 3, 12, 10.

demi-man: see DEMI *a.*

‖**demi-mondaine** (dəmimɔ̃dɛn). [Fr.; f. DEMI-MONDE.] A woman of the demi-monde.

1894 *Nation* (N.Y.) 12 July 29/1 The conclusion is irresistible that he has been fooled into believing *demi-mondaines* women of good society. **1898** W. J. LOCKE *Idols* xxi. 211 Her manner was that of the insolently luxurious demi-mondaine. **1922** *Daily Mail* 21 Nov. 6 Miss Mae Murray, most alluring of screen demi-mondaines. **1969** *Times* 25 Oct. p. iii/4 She presents a young, vivacious *demi-mondaine* who becomes steadily more tragic.

demi-monde (dəmimɔ̃d, 'dɛmɪmɒnd). [Fr.; lit. 'half-world', 'half-and-half society', a phrase invented by Dumas the younger. Cf. DEMI-REP.]

a. The class of women of doubtful reputation and social standing, upon the outskirts of 'society.' (Sometimes, though improperly, extended to include courtesans in general.)

1855 *Fraser's Mag.* LI. 579 His [Dumas'] *Demi-Monde* is the link between good and bad society..the world of compromised women, a social limbo, the inmates of which ..are perpetually struggling to emerge into the paradise of honest and respectable ladies. **1859** G. A. SALA *Twice round Clock* 30 Countesses, actresses—*demi-monde* adventuresses. **1884** MRS. C. PRAED *Zero* xiv, The *demi-Monde* overflowed the Hôtel de Paris. **1893** *N.Y. Nation* 27 Apr. 320/1 His province is the *demi-monde*, the *Bohème* of the modern Mürger, the Paris of Zola and the Naturalists.

b. *attrib.* or as *adj.*

1864 SALA *Quite Alone* I. i. 10 'Is she demi-monde?' ..'Nobody knows'.

demi-natured: see DEMI- 14.

demine (diː'maɪn), *v.* [f. DE- II. 1 + MINE *v.* 5.] In warfare: to remove mines from.

1945 *Manch. Guardian* 18 July 8/1 The time that it will take to 'de-mine' France is incalculable owing to the variety of local conditions.

demineralization (diːˌmɪnərəlaɪ'zeɪʃən). [f. DE- II + MINERALIZATION.] The removal of salts, esp. from sea or brackish water; also, any abnormal loss of salts from the body. Hence **de'mineralize** *v. trans.*, to remove salts from; **de'mineralized** *ppl. a.*; **de'mineralizer**, an apparatus or installation used for de-mineralization; **de'mineralizing** *vbl. sb.*

1903 *Med. Record* LXIII. 621/1 The demineralization is proved by an increase in the mineral residue of the urine.. and by a correlative decrease in the mineralization of the blood. **1934** WEBSTER, Demineralize v. **1943** *Industr. & Engin. Chem.* Feb. 186/2 The precise composition of this demineralized effluent depends to some extent upon the quality of the raw water. *Ibid.*, The demineralizing process does not remove silica from water. *Ibid.* 192/1 The total cost of demineralizing this water is..27 cents per 1000 gallons. **1955** *Bull. Atomic Sci.* Oct. 286/3 Recent developments in the demineralization of sea water. **1956** *Nature* 28 Jan. 183/1 The clear end was cut off and dissolved in demineralized water and the metal then recovered by electro-deposition. **1958** *New Scientist* 6 Nov. 1199/1 The new water supply scheme for Guernsey will be of this form, and some 500,000 gallons of sea water will be demineralised each day. **1960** *Farmer & Stockbreeder* 1 Mar. 137/3 She [*sc.* a sow] has been demineralized, and her bones softened. **1960** *Times* 18 Aug. p. ix/4 A special de-mineralizer to remove substances that might be harmful to the boilers. **1962** *Lancet* 2 June 1168/2 The essential defect has been recognised as a failure in the calcification of new bone and cartilage, rather than a demineralisation of existing bone.

deminish, etc.: see DIMINISH, etc.

†**demi-'ostade, -ostage.** *Obs.* Also 6 *Sc.* **damyostage.** [a. OF. *demie ostade, hostade, estade*, f. *demi*, *-e* half + *ostade, hostade, austade*, 'the stuffe worsted or woosted' (Cotgr. 1611)] A stuff: apparently half-worsted half-linen, linsey-woolsey.

1537 *Ld. Treas. Accts. Scot.* in Pitcairn *Crim. Trials* I. 290 Twa steikis of double Damyostage to hing about the Quein [at her funeral]. **1538** *Aberd. Reg.* V. 16 (Jam.), A hogtone of demyostage begareit with veluot. [**1593** tr. *Guicciardini's Descr. Low Countreys* 33 b, Sarges or Sayes, Wosteds, Demi-wosteds [It. *ostate, mezze ostate*] or Russels. **1764** ANDERSON *Orig. Commerce* (1787) II. 112 To England, Antwerp sent.. linen both fine and coarse, serges, demy ostades (quære if not worsteds?), tapestry. **1882** CAULFEILD & SAWARD *Dict. Needlework*, *Demyostage*, a description of Taminy, or woollen cloth, formerly used in Scotland.]

demiourgos (diːmɪ'aʊəgɒs). A strict transcription of Gr. δημιουργός (see s.v. DEMIURGE).

1920 T. P. NUNN *Education; Data & First Princ.* 192 The 'pure' geologist still presses for the kind of understanding of the earth's structure that we might ascribe to the demiourgos who made it. **1924** W. B. SELBIE *Psychol. Relig.* 56 The familiar conception of the demiourgos in gnostic philosophy.

demi-parallel: see DEMI- 5.

†**demi-parcel.** *Obs.* [DEMI- 7.] The half.

a **1592** GREENE *Alphonsus* (1861) 232 My tongue denies for to set forth The demi-parcel of your valiant deeds.

demi-pauldron, -pectinate, -pesade, -pike: see DEMI- 3, 13, 6.

‖**demi-pension** (dəmipɑ̃sjɔ̃). [Fr.] The price of bed, breakfast, and one other meal at a hotel, etc.: usually in reference to France or other European country.

1951 N. MARSH *Opening Night* iv. 83 Your rental, *demi-pension*, here, is two [pounds]. **1959** *Listener* 15 Jan. 128/3 Cost? Demi-pension everywhere. Bread and wine make a good third meal.

demi-pique ('dɛmɪpiːk), *a.* (*sb.*) Also 7 **-pick.** [DEMI- 10.]

A. *adj.* Of a saddle: 'Half-peaked'; having a peak of about half the height of that of the older war-saddle.

B. as *sb.* A demi-pique saddle.

1695 *Lond. Gaz.* No. 3104/4 He had on a Demy-Pick Crimson Velvet Saddle. **1761** EARL PEMBROKE *Milit. Equit.* (1778) 9 To be as firm, to work as well, and be quite as much at his ease [on the bare back] as on any demipique saddle. **1771** SMOLLETT *Humph. Cl.* (1815) 3 Send Williams thither, with my saddle-horse and the *demi pique*. **1819** SCOTT *Legend Montrose* ii, His rider occupied his demipique, or war-saddle, with an air that shewed it was his familiar seat. **1833** M. SCOTT *Tom Cringle* xvii. (1859) 450 Two stout ponies..ready saddled with old fashioned demipiques and large holsters at each of the saddle bows.

'demi-piqued (-piːkt), *a.* Also 8 **-peak'd.** [f. prec. + -ED.] = prec. A.

1759 STERNE *Tr. Shandy* I. x, He was master of a very handsome demi-peak'd saddle, quilted on the seat with green plush. **1761** EARL PEMBROKE *Milit. Equit.* (1778) 17 Nobody can be truly said to have a seat, who is not equally firm on flat, or demipiqued saddles.

demi-placard, -placate, -pommada, -premisses: see DEMI- 3, 6, 12.

†ˌ**demi-'puppet.** *Obs.* [DEMI- 10.] A half-sized or dwarf puppet.

1610 SHAKS. *Temp.* v. i. 36 You demy-Puppets, that By Moone-shine doe the greene sowre Ringlets make.

demi-quaver, -relief: see DEMI- 9, 12.

demi-rep ('dɛmɪrɛp). Also **-rip.** [f. DEMI- 11 + '*rep*, for *reputation*,' mentioned by Swift *Polite Conversation*, Introd. p. li, among 'some abbreviations exquisitely refined,' then in current use. Cf. also *reputable*, in common use in 18th c. in sense 'honourable, respectable, decent', and *disreputable*.] A woman whose character is only half reputable; a woman of doubtful reputation or suspected chastity.

1749 FIELDING *Tom Jones* xv. ix, He had yet no knowledge of that character which is vulgarly called a demirep, that is to say, a woman that intrigues with every man she likes, under the name and appearance of virtue..in short, whom every body knows to be what no body calls her. **1754** *Connoisseur* No. 4, An order of females lately sprung up.. usually distinguished by the denomination of Demi-Reps; a word not to be found in any of our dictionaries. *a* **1764** LLOYD *Poems, A Tale*, Venus..The greatest demirep above. **1831** LYTTON *Godolph.* 57 A coaxing note from some titled demirep affecting the De Stael. **1887** *Athenæum* 12 Nov. 631 His heroine appears..more of the demirep than has been commonly known.

attrib. **1784** *New Spectator* XX. 4/1 Adepts in the demi-rip language. **1841** *Edin. Rev.* LXXIII. 382 Women of the demirep genus.

transf. **1863** A. GILCHRIST *Life W. Blake* I. 99 The now dingy demi-rep street.

Hence **demi'repdom**, the domain or world of demi-reps; the demi-monde.

1839 CARLYLE in Froude *Life in London* I. vi. 158, I do not see well what good I can get by meeting him much, or Lady B. and demirepdom.

demi-reputable (dɛmɪ'rɛpjʊtəb(ə)l), *a.* [f. DEMI- + REPUTABLE; see DEMI-REP.] Of doubtful reputation. Also ˌ**demi-repu'tation.**

1897 W. J. LOCKE *Derelicts* xvii. 224 That fashionable demi-reputable world which had drawn him to his precipice. **1909** M. B. SAUNDERS *Litany Lane* x, People with doubtful histories, women of demi-reputation.

ˌ**demi-re'vetment.** *Fortif.* [a. F. *demi-revêtement*: see DEMI- 5.] A revetment or retaining wall for the face of a rampart, which is carried not to the top, but only as high as the cover in front of it, leaving the rest as an earthen rampart at the natural slope. So **demi-re'vetted** *ppl. a.* (see quot.).

1857 BIRCH *Anc. Pottery* (1858) I. 106 At Mespila and Larissa, the walls were demi-revetted, or faced with stone only half way up; namely about 50 feet from the bottom of the ditch. **1874** KNIGHT *Dict. Mech.*, *Demi-revetment.*

demisable (dɪ'maɪzəb(ə)l), *a.* [f. DEMISE *v.* + -ABLE.] Capable of being demised.

1657 SIR H. GRIMSTONE in Croke *Reports* I. 499 The land ..was..copyhold land, and demisable in fee. **1767** BLACKSTONE *Comm.* II. 97 That they have been demised, or demisable, by copy of court roll immemorially. **1818** CRUISE *Digest* (ed. 2) IV. 206 It was contended that the manor and fishery were not demisable under the power, as no rent was then paid for them.

†**de'misal.** *Obs.* [f. DEMISE *v.*] What is demised: = DEMISE 1 b.

1709 *Brit. Apollo* II. No. 53 3/2 He only got a Broken Pate, Turn'd out to Grass from all Demisals. *Ibid.* No. 56 3/1 Or on the Sex spent your Demisals, And therefore seek to make Reprizals.

‖**'demi-sang.** *Law.* [Fr.] Half-blood.

[**1575–1708** *Termes de la Ley* (as Anglo-French) Halfe blood. Demy sancke ou sangue.] **1797–1820** TOMLINS *Laws Dict.* *Demy-sangue*, half-blood [as in] brothers of the half-blood, because they had not both one father and mother. **1823** CRABBE *Tech. Dict.*

demi-sap. *Fortif.* [DEMI- 5.] A SAP, or trench of approach, with a single parapet.

1706 *Lond. Gaz.* No. 4251/2 We began the Demi-Saps on the Right and Left. **1708** *Ibid.* No. 4467/3 A Demy-Sap was begun from the Right of the Attack on the Right.

demise (dɪ'maɪz), *sb.* [app. of Anglo-Fr. origin: *démise* or *desmise* is not recorded in OF., but is regularly formed as the fem. sb. from pa. pple. of *desmettre, démettre*, to send away, dismiss, *refl.* to resign, abdicate: cf. F. *mise, remise.* In English, the prefix being identical with L. *de-*, there is a manifest tendency to treat it as DE- I. 1, as if to 'hand down' or 'lay down' were the notion.]

1. *Law.* Conveyance or transfer of an estate by will or lease.

1509–10 *Act 1 Hen. VIII*, c. 18 §2 All Dymyses, Leses, releses..made..by her or to her. **1587** LADY STAFFORD in *Collect.* (Oxf. Hist. Soc.) I. 210 Nor [shall] any hinderaunce growe to theim by this demize. **1638** SANDERSON *Serm* II. 94 In a demise a man parteth with more of his interest; he transmitteth together with the possession, the use also or fruit of the thing letten or demised. **1817** W. SELWYN *Law Nisi Prius* (ed. 4) II. 1120 Plaintiff held by virtue of a demise. **1876** DIGBY *Real Prop.* v. §1. 206 The proper mode of granting an estate for years at common law is by words of demise followed by the entry of the lessee.

†**b.** The estate demised. *Obs. rare.*

a **1660** HAMMOND *Wks.* I. 725 (R.), I conceive it ridiculous to make the condition of an indenture something that is necessarily annext to the possession of the demise.

2. Transference or devolution of sovereignty, as by the death or deposition of the sovereign; usually in phr. ***demise of the crown.***

[**1547** *Act 1 Edw. VI*, c. 7 Preamb., Which Actions..by the Death or Demise of the Kings of this Realm have been discontinued. **1660** BOND *Scut. Reg.* 58 The King hath a perpetual succession, and never dyeth; For in Law it is called the demise of the King, and there is no Inter-regnum.] **1689** EVELYN *Mem.* (1857) II. 299 That King James..had by demise abdicated himself and wholly vacated his right. **1714** SWIFT *Present State of Affairs*, The regents appointed by parliament upon the demise of the crown. **1765** BLACKSTONE *Comm.* I. 249 When Edward the Fourth..was driven from his throne for a few months..this temporary transfer of his dignity was denominated his demise. **1848** MACAULAY *Hist. Eng.* I. 534 The unexpected demise of the crown changed the whole aspect of affairs. **1857** SIR J. F. W. HERSCHEL *Essays* 615 Demise of the chair.

3. Transferred to the death or decease which occasions the demise of an estate, etc.; hence, popularly, = Decease, death.

1754 RICHARDSON *Grandison* (1781) I. ii. 7 Her father's considerable estate, on his demise..went with the name. **1799** *Med. Jrnl.* I. 206 We lament the early demise of this favourite friend of science. **1846** MCCULLOCH *Acc. Brit. Empire* (1854) I. 417 To trace their lives from the moment of their birth, marking the exact period of the demise of each individual. **1878** GLADSTONE *Prim. Homer* 43 The Odyssey does not bring us to the demise of Odusseus.

fig. **1839** *Times* 13 May, After the ostensible demise of the outward cabinet. **1860** T. L. PEACOCK *Wks.* (1875) III. 473 The demise of that periodical prevented the publication.

demise (dɪ'maɪz), *v.* [f. DEMISE *sb.*]

1. *Law.* (*trans.*) To give, grant, convey, or transfer (an estate) by will or by lease.

1480 *Bury Wills* (1850) 64 By oure chartre beryng the date of thees presentes have dimised, assigned, deliuered..to Henri Hardman clerk, William Duffeld..the forseid maner. **1495** *Act 11 Hen. VII*, c. 61 §1 To lette and demyse fermes ther for the terme of vij yere and undir. **1587** LADY STAFFORD in *Collect.* (Oxf. Hist. Soc.) I. 208 Woods..to be demized to a yong man. **1661** J. STEPHENS *Procurations* 38 Afterwards Q. Eliz...did demise the said Commandery and Rectory to Dr. Forth. **1733** NEAL *Hist. Purit.* II. 7 For demising away the Impropriations annexed to Bishopricks and Colleges. **1844** WILLIAMS *Real Prop.* (1877) 445 This word *demise* operates as an absolute covenant for the quiet enjoyment of the lands by the lessee.

b. To convey or transfer (a title or dignity); *esp.* said of the transmission of sovereignty, as by the abdication or death of the sovereign.

1670 COTTON *Espernon* I. I. 37 His Majesty would have given them in Sovereignty, and have demis'd to him the Title of the Crown. **1765** BLACKSTONE *Comm.* I. 249 When we say the demise of the crown, we mean only that..the kingdom is transferred or demised to his successor. **1892** G. B. SMITH *Hist. Eng. Parlt.* II. ix. ii. 20 He therefore recommended the Convention to declare that James II had voluntarily demised the crown.

c. *intr.* To pass by bequest or inheritance.

1823 GREVILLE *Mem.* (1874) I. 64 Now arose a difficulty —whether the property of the late King demised to the King or to the Crown.

†**2.** *gen.* To convey, transmit; to 'lease'. *Obs.*

1594 SHAKS. *Rich. III*, IV. iv. 247 What Honour, Canst thou demise to any childe of mine? *a* **1660** HAMMOND *Wks.* IV. xiv. (R.), Upon which condition his reasonable soul is at his own conception demised to him.

†**3.** To let go: to dismiss. *Obs.*

a **1541** WYATT *Defence* Wks. (1861) p. xxxiv, [What] the King and his Council thought in this matter when they demised Mason at his first examination, and for the small weight there was either against him or me. **1542** UDALL *Erasm. Apoph.* 191 a, The Thebanes he demised and let go at their libertee. *c* **1610–15** *Lives Women Saints* 141 That wearie bones may be refreshed, And wasted mindes redressed, And griefe demisd that it oppressed.

4. *intr.* To resign the crown; to die, decease. *rare.*

1727 A. HAMILTON *New Acc. E. Ind.* I. x. 103 When Shaw Abbas demised, his Son Shaw Tomas succeeded him. **1783** COWPER *Lett.* 31 May, The Kings..must go on demising to the end of the chapter.

Hence **de'mised** *ppl. a.*, **de'mising** *vbl. sb.*

1547 in *Vicary's Anat.* (1888) App. iii. 131 The orderinge, bestowinge, sellinge, dymysyng..of the late parishe churches. **1587** R. HOVENDEN in *Collect.* (Oxf. Hist. Soc.) I. 211 The demising of Alsolne Colledg Woodes. **1682** *Eng. Elect. Sheriffs* 33 It is plainly implyed in the Demised and Confirmed things and customs. **1876** DIGBY *Real Prop.* §1. 380 To pay the rent or to repair the demised premises.

'demi-'season, *a.* [ad. F. *demi-saison* (also in Eng. use), as in *robe de demi-saison*, a dress intermediate between a winter and a summer dress.] Of costume: Of a style intermediate between that of the past and that of the coming season.

[**1769** in Jesse *G. Selwyn & Contemps.* II. (1882) 380 (Stanf.), I..wish to know..if it is to be a *demi saison* or a winter velvet. **1883** *Daily Tel.* 18 Jan. 2 (ibid.), The *demi-saison* costume.] **1890** *Daily News* 24 Mar. 6/1 The demi-season cape that is most largely worn. **1892** *Ibid.* 15 Oct. 7/3 Bonnets..are still demi-season in style.

‖**demi-sec** (dəmisɛk), *a.* (*sb.*) [Fr., lit. 'half-dry'.] Of champagne and other wines: moderately sweetened; medium to medium-sweet. Also *absol.* or as *sb.* Cf. SEC *a.* and *semi-sweet* s.v. SEMI- 1 a.

1926 P. M. SHAND *Bk. Wine* v. 151 Champagne..is fortified in the sense that the *liqueur d'expédition*, which is added..so as to impart any of the degrees of dryness of flavour..(*doux, mi-doux, demi-sec, sec, dry, extra-dry, brut*.. etc.)..is made of Fine Champagne Cognac diluted with old wine. **1952** A. LICHINE *Wines of France* xviii. 247 *Demi-sec* Champagne contains up to 8 per cent, and sweet or *Doux* up to 10 [per cent of sugar]. **1965** A. SICHEL *Penguin Bk. Wines* III. 151 The degree of sweetness of a Champagne is indicated on the label, according to a formula respected by the whole trade... 'Demi-Sec' begins to taste distinctly sweet. **1978** *Washington Post* 20 Nov. E14/3 For your pumpkin pie dessert choose something less dry such as the demi-sec of Hanns Kornell. **1984** *Which?* Dec. 568/1 Both [wines] also come in sweeter *demi-sec* version. **1985** *N.Y.Times Mag.* 26 May 42/2 Gratien & Meyer's sweeter sparkling wines, its sec and demi-sec, should appeal to the vast market of Americans.

‖**demi-sel** (dəmisɛl). [Fr., lit. 'half-salt'.] (See quot. 1946.)

1946 A. L. SIMON *Conc. Encycl. Gastronomy* IX. 13/2 *Demi-sel*, a French whole-milk soft cheese, about 4 oz. in weight, similar to *Gournay*, but with 2 per cent added salt. **1966** M. KELLY *Dead Corse* vi. 98 Why do you hanker for brown skin, Amazon pirate? You're lovely creamy white, like demi-sel.

demi-semi ('dɛmɪˈsɛmɪ), *a.* [f. DEMI- 13 + SEMI- half: prob. taken from *demisemiquaver*: see next.] *lit.* Half-half, i.e. quarter; but usually a contemptuous diminutive.

1805 W. TAYLOR in *Ann. Rev.* III. 312 The demi-semi statesmen of the present age. **1842** MIALL in *Nonconf.* II. 409 Demi-semi-sacramentarianism. **1874** HELPS *Soc. Press.* vii. (1875) 98 Half men, 'demi-semi' men, were..of no use. **1901** *Contemp. Rev.* Mar. 358 England..no longer.. employed the demi-semi-educated to educate the voters. **1906** *Daily Chron.* 1 May 3/1 Among the demi-semi-educated a laugh can always be raised by sitting down upon a silk hat! **1908** *Ibid.* 13 May 7/7 In the demi-semi-rural districts on the outskirts of towns. **1929** A. HUXLEY *Holy Face* 28 Her sage-green dress was only demi-semi-evening.

demisemiquaver ('dɛmɪˈsɛmɪˌkweɪvə(r)). *Music.* [DEMI- 9.] A note of half the value of a semiquaver; the symbol for this note, resembling a quaver, but with three hooks instead of one. Also *attrib.*, as in *demisemiquaver rest.*

1706 PHILLIPS (ed. Kersey), *Demi-semi-quaver*, the least Note in Musick. **1822** T. L. PEACOCK *Maid Marian* (1837) 176 The song of the choristers died away in a shake of demisemiquavers. **1848** RIMBAULT *First Bk. Piano* 55 The Demisemiquaver Rest has three crooks turning to the left.

demi-'semitone. *Music. rare.* [DEMI- 9.] Half a semitone; a quarter-tone.

1866 ENGEL *Nat. Mus.* ii. 27 Councillor Tilesius informs us that the natives of Nukahiva..distinctly intone demi-semitones (quarter-tones) in their vocal performances.

demi-sheath ('dɛmɪʃiːθ). *Entom.* [Cf. DEMI- 3.] A half-sheath; i.e. one of the two channelled organs of which the tubular sheaths, covering the ovipositors or stings of insects, are composed.

demi-sphere, a hemisphere: see DEMI- 10.

demiss (dɪˈmɪs), *a.* [ad. L. *dēmiss-us* let down, lowered, sunken, downcast, lowly, pa. pple. of *dēmittĕre* to DEMIT. Cf. It. *demisso* 'demisse, base, submisse, faint' Florio, F. *démis* out of joint, OF. *desmis*, also 'submitted, humble, submissiue' (Cotgr.).]

1. Submissive, humble, lowly; also in bad sense, Abject, base.

1572 J. JONES *Bathes of Bath* II. 10 a, So demisse of nature. **1581** SAVILE *Tactus' Hist.* I. lii. (1591) 30 Among the seuerer sort Vitellius was thought base and demisse. **1596** SPENSER *Hymne Heavenly Love* 136 He downe descended, like a most demisse And abiect thrall. **1612** R. SHELDON *Serm. St. Martin's* 9 Spoken vnder correction of faith, and with demisse reuerence. **1649** JER. TAYLOR *Gt. Exemp.* Ad Sec. xv. §6 Sullen gestures or demiss behaviour. **1837** H. E. MANNING in J. R. S. Leslie *Life* (1921) 269, I wrote a very soft, demiss rejoinder. [**1888** cf. DEMISSNESS.] **1888** C. M. DOUGHTY *Arabia Deserta* I. 253 Not timid as the demiss Damascene Christians. **1903** J. BRYCE *Studies in Contemp. Biogr.* 53 By appearing too demiss or too unenterprising in foreign affairs.

†**2.** *lit.* Hanging down. *Obs.*

a **1693** URQUHART *Rabelais* III. xxviii. 237.

†**3.** Of the head or countenance: Hanging down, cast down, downcast. *Obs.*

1586 BRIGHT *Melanch.* xx. 121 Countenance demisse, and hanging downe. **1634** PEACHAM *Gentl. Exerc.* I. vii. 23 Giving him a demisse and lowly countenance.

†**4.** Of sound: Subdued, low. *Obs. rare.*

1646 GAULE *Cases Consc.* 129 A demisse hollow muttering.

5. *Bot.* Depressed, flattened.

demission[1] (dɪˈmɪʃən). [ad. L. *dēmissiōn-em*, n. of action from *dēmittĕre*: see DEMISS, DEMIT[1].]

1. Abasement, lowering, degradation. Now *rare.*

a **1638** MEDE *Disc. Matt.* xi. 29 Wks. (1672) I. 158 Adored with the lowest demission of mind. **1691-8** NORRIS *Pract. Disc.* 171 This Demission of the Soul. [**1883** *American* VI. 214 Their omission or their demission to a lower rank.]

†**2.** Dejection, depression, lowering of spirits or vitality. *Obs.*

1656 BLOUNT *Glossogr.*, *Demission*, an abasement, faintness, abating. **1678** NORRIS *Coll. Misc.* (1699) 141 Heaviness and demission of Spirit. **1719** WODROW *Corr.* (1843) II. 451 Temptations to demission.

†**3.** *lit.* Lowering, putting or bending down.

1708 *Brit. Apollo* No. 73. 2/1 A..Demission of his Leg. **1741** 'BETTERTON' *Eng. Stage* v. 65 The Demission or hanging down of the Head.

de'mission[2]. [a. F. *démission*, in OF. *desmission*, 'a demission, deposition, resignation, dismission, forgoing' (Cotgr.), n. of action from OF. *desmetre*, answering to late L. **dismissio*, for *dīmissio*, whence the equivalents DIMISSION, DISMISSION. From the identity of the prefix with L. *de-*, there is a tendency in English to take the literal sense as 'laying down' (DE- 1).]

1. The action of putting away or letting go from oneself, giving up, or laying down (*esp.* a dignity or office); resignation, relinquishment, abdication.

1577-87 HOLINSHED *Chron.* II. 391/1 Concerning the queenes demission of hir crowne, and resignation thereof made to hir sonne king James the sixt. *Ibid.* III. 504/2, I shall neuer repugne to this resignation, demission or yeelding vp. **16..** R. L'ESTRANGE (J.), Inexorable rigour is worse than a lasche demission of sovereign authority. **1736** CARTE *Ormonde* II. 539 Apply to his Majesty for a demission of his charge. **1855** MILMAN *Lat. Chr.* (1864) VI. XI. vi. 466 That the Cardinals were at liberty to receive that voluntary demission of the popedom.

†**b.** *fig.* Relinquishment of life; death. *Obs.*

1735 THOMSON *Liberty* III. 458 And on the bed of peace his ashes laid; A grace which I to his demission gave.

†**2.** *lit.* Letting down. *Obs.*

a **1664** F. HICKS in Jasper Mayne tr. *Lucan* II. 305 Being King of the Gods, and able, by the demission of a coard, to draw up earth and sea.

3. Sending away, dismission. *rare.*

1811 *Chron.* in *Ann. Reg.* 428 No particular period is fixed for a demission. **1824** LADY GRANVILLE *Letters* (1894) I. 296 Chateaubriand's demission was..sudden and unexpected.

†**4.** ? Order for release. *Obs.*

1554 *Churchw. Acc. Yatton* (Somerset Rec. Soc.) 166 The demyssyons of yᵉ corte for yᵉ men that where putt in there.

de'missionary, *a.*[1] *rare*—⁰. [See DEMISSION[1] and -ARY.] 'Tending to lower, depress, or degrade' (Webster 1864).

de'missionary, *a.*[2] *rare*—⁰. [See DEMISSION[2] and -ARY. Cf. F. *démissionnaire.*] Pertaining to the transfer or conveyance of an estate.

1864 in WEBSTER.

de'missionize, *v.* [DE- II. 1.] *trans.* To deprive of its character as a mission.

1883 *St. James's Gaz.* 19 Apr. 3 To prevent them from falling into foreign hands and becoming de-missionized.

†**de'missive**, *a. Obs.* [f. L. *dēmiss-*, ppl. stem of *dēmittĕre* (DEMIT *v.*[1]) + -IVE.] Downcast; humble, submissive; = DEMISS 1, 3. Hence **de'missively** *adv.*

1622 *Relat. Mogul's Kingd.* in *Harl. Misc.* (1808) I. 259 But Sir Thomas Roe..would not so much derogate from his place, to abase himself so demissively. **1630** LORD *Banians* 72 They pray with demissive eyelids. *a* **1763** SHENSTONE *Essays, A Vision*, Wks. 1764 II. 121 The subjects, very orderly, repentant, and demissive.

†**de'missly**, *adv. Obs.* [f. DEMISS *a.* + -LY[2].] Submissively, humbly; abjectly, basely.

1598 FLORIO, *Remissamente*, demislie, remislie, basely, cowardly. **1617** HIERON *Wks.* II. 390 To thinke so demissely and vnworthily of it selfe. **1610** HOLLAND *Camden's Brit.* II. 139 He most demisely beseecheth..he might now haue experience of her merciful lenity.

†**de'missness.** *Obs.* or *arch.* [f. as prec. + -NESS.] Dejectedness, submissiveness, humility, abased manner.

1603 FLORIO *Montaigne* 147 Cato..blamed them for their demissnesse. **1649** BULWER *Pathomyot.* II. v. 168 Exhibiting an humble reverence, with a sweet demisseness. **1888** BRYCE *Amer. Commw.* III. lxxxvii. 161 A kind of independence of manner..very different from the demissness of the humbler classes of the Old World.

†**de'missory**, *a. Obs.* Variant of DIMISSORY: cf. DEMIT *v.*[2]

demister (diːˈmɪstə(r)). [f. DE- II + MIST *sb.*[1] + -ER.] A device for clearing mist from the windscreen, etc., of a motor vehicle, aeroplane, etc. Also **de'mist** *v.*, **de'misting** *ppl. a.* and *vbl. sb.*

1939 *Times* 28 Mar. 20/3 A lamp under the bonnet, and provision for a heater and demister. **1950** *Engineering* 3 Feb. 139/2 Built-in heating and demisting/de-icing equipment. **1957** *Economist* 9 Nov. 499 (Advt.), The heater provides a generous flow of warm air to the readily adjustable demister nozzle. The result is supremely efficient demisting and defrosting. **1963** *Times* 28 May 15/4 An air blower for demisting the rear window. **1966** T. WISDOM *High-Performance Driving* x. 108 Make sure the outside of the screen is clean and have the demister operating at full strength. **1968** C. BURKE *Elephant across Border* iii. 102 He ..had to demist his glasses. **1968** R. PETRIE *MacLurg goes West* I. iii. 25 MacLurg turned on the blower to demist the car's windows.

demi-suit: see DEMI- 3.

demit (dɪˈmɪt), *v.*[1] [ad. L. *dēmittĕre* to send, put, or let down, to cast down, lower, sink, f. DE- I. 1 + *mittĕre* to send, etc. Cf. OF. *demetre* in same sense.]

1. *trans.* To send, put, or let down; to cause to descend; to lower.

1646 SIR T. BROWNE *Pseud. Ep.* III. xxv, If they decline their necke to the ground, they presently demit and let fall the same [their train]. **1762** FALCONER *Shipwr.* I. 226 These soon demitted stay-sails next ascend. **1885** R. W. DIXON *Hist. Ch. Eng.* III. 442 This bill seems not to have been demitted by the peers.

†**2.** *fig.* To bring down, lower; to let down, humble, abase. *Obs.*

1611 W. SCLATER *Key* (1629) 64 To whose capacitie though it haue pleased the Lord to demit himself [etc.]. *a* **1619** FOTHERBY *Atheom.* Pref. (1622) 18 The highest points, which I haue carefully indeauoured to stoop and demitte, euen to the capacitie of the very lowest. **1656** JEANES *Mixt. Schol. Div.* 103 By taking on him the nature of man..he demitted, or humbled himselfe. **1688** NORRIS *Theory Love* 173 When she, being Heaven-born, demits her noble self to such earthly drudgery.

†**3.** ? To lay down as a supposition; to suppose.

1556 J. HEYWOOD *Spider & F.* xlii. 29 Let vs here demit: one spider and ten flise All lyke honest: who seeing two sew at law, [etc.].

de'mit, *v.*[2] [ad. F. *démett-re*, in OF. *desmet-re*, *desmett-re*, f. *des-*, *dé-*:—L. *dis-* + *mettre* to send, put, etc.: taking the place of L. *dīmittĕre* to send away, dismiss, release, put away, let go, lay down (office), renounce, forsake, etc.; cf. DISMISS and DIMIT. Chiefly used by Scottish writers.]

1. *trans.* To let go, send away, dismiss. *arch.*

1529 FRITH *Ep. Chr. Rdr.* Wks. (1829) 473 That they..be compelled (as Pharaoh was) to demit thy chosen children. **1582-8** *Hist. James VI* (1804) 168 Thairefter he demittit thame frielie to pas quhair they list. **1649** BP. GUTHRIE *Mem.* (1702) 11 Mr. John was demitted, and Balmiranoch sent Prisoner to the Castle of Edinburgh. **1690** J. MACKENZIE *Siege London Derry* 47/1 Walker [was] demitted, and Hamil reduced. **1829** CARLYLE *Misc.* (1857) II. 33 Poor Longchamp, demitted, or rather dismissed from Voltaire's service.

†**b.** *fig.* To send away, remit, refer. *Obs.*

1646 S. BOLTON *Arraignm. Err.* 123 To the Scriptures doth God demit and send us for the tryall of opinions.

†**2.** To put away, part with, let go. *Obs.*

1563 WINȜET *Four Scoir Thre Quest.* Wks. 1888 I. 109 He geuis ane expres command to the innocent woman demittand hir husband, to remain vnmariit or to be reconcilit to hir husband [*marg.* 1 Cor. 7]. **1678** R. BARCLAY *Apol. Quakers* ii. §10. 45 These, though they cease not to call upon God, do nevertheless demit the Spirit.

3. To let go, resign, give up, lay down (an office or dignity); to abdicate.

1567 in Balfour *Practicks* (1754) 6 We [Mary Stewart].. haue renuncit and demittit..the gyding and gouerning of this our realme of Scotland. *c* **1610** SIR J. MELVIL *Mem.* (1735) 185 The Queen's Majesty had demitted the Government. **1678** *Trans. Crt. Spain* 26 [He] willingly demits his charge of President of Castile. **1798** DALLAS *Amer. Law Rep.* I. 107 We will..not demit any part of her sovereignty. **1855** NEIL *Boyd's Zion's Flowers* Introd. 36 His cousin..had demitted the Principalship of the University. **1876** GRANT *Burgh Sch. Scot.* 361 An Office which he demitted in 1606.

b. *absol.* To give up office; to resign.

1719 WODROW *Corr.* (1843) II. 451 Greatly tempted to demit. **1818** SCOTT *Rob Roy* ix, I advise him to get another clerk, that's all, for I shall certainly demit. **1865** CARLYLE *Fredk. Gt.* VI. XVI. ix. 238 La Mettrie had to demit; to get out of France rather in a hurry. **1880** *Daily Tel.* 30 Nov., But the Ritualists will neither submit nor demit.

†**4.** To convey by lease, demise. *Obs.*

1774 *Petit.* in A. McKay *Hist. Kilmarnock* App. iii. 304 In feu-farm let and demitted.

†**5.** To send out. *Obs.*

[Perhaps belongs to DEMIT *v.*[1], from DE- I. 2.]

1672 SIR T. BROWNE *Pseud. Ep.* III. xvi. (ed. 6/161), This..is rather generated in the head, and perhaps demitted and sent from thence by salival conducts and passages. **1756** P. BROWNE *Jamaica* 191 The rib..tapers from the base to the top..demitting its connected ribs or foliage equally on both sides.

demit (diː'mɪt), *sb. U.S. Freemasonry.* Also **dimit.** [f. DEMIT *v.*[2]] Written permission to leave a lodge, granted to a mason.

1856 R. MORRIS in A. G. Mackey *Encycl. Freemasonry* (1879) 221/2 A 'demit', technically considered, is the act of withdrawing, and applies to the Lodge and not to the individual. **1879** *Ibid.* 220/1 The granting of 'a dimit' does not necessarily lead to the conclusion that the Mason who received it has left the Lodge. He has only been permitted to do so. *Ibid.* 221/2 'A demit' is..an Americanism of very recent usage.

demi-tasse (dəmitas, 'dɛmɪtæs). Chiefly *U.S.* [Fr., lit. 'half-cup'.] A small coffee-cup; its contents. Also *attrib.* and as *adv.*

1842 *Galignani's Paris Guide* 17 To the latter [*sc.* the cafés] it is customary to retire immediately after dinner, to take a *demi-tasse* of coffee. **1870** J. MURRAY *Handbk. Paris* (ed. 4) II. 31 In the afternoon, when coffee is ordered, the waiter pours you out a small cup (demitasse). **1897** G. DU MAURIER *Martian* II. 49 Drinking our demi-tasse. **1906** 'O. HENRY' *Four Million* (1916) 94 A roasted mallard duck..with a bottle of Chablis,..a demi-tasse and a cigar. **1961** M. BEADLE *These Ruins are Inhabited* (1963) v. 71 Coffee..is served demitasse. **1966** *Daily Tel.* 18 Jan. 13/3 Add 2 gallons of hot, strong coffee and serve into demi-tasse cups.

'demi-tint. *Painting.* ? *Obs.* [DEMI- 11.] A half tint; a tint intermediate between the extreme lights and strong shades of a painting; applied also to broken tints or tertiary colour-shades.

1753 *Gray's-Inn Jrnl.* No. 59 The Touch, which so skilfully blends different Colours..is called by the Painters the Demi-tint. **1798** *Trans. Soc. Encourag. Arts* XVI. 287 Those demi-tints which conduce so much to the brilliancy of a picture. *c* **1811** FUSELI *Lect. Art* v. (1848) 467 He does not sufficiently connect with breadth of demi-tint the two extremes of his masses. **1824** *Blackw. Mag.* XV. 146 They have none of the demi-tints to study.

Hence **'demi-tinted** *a.*

1828 *Examiner* 357/1 Cream-coloured and demi-tinted city and mid-distance.

demi-toilet: see DEMI- 12.

'demi-tone. ? *Obs.* [DEMI- 9, 11: cf. Fr. *demiton.*] **a.** *Painting.* = DEMI-TINT. **b.** *Music.* = SEMITONE.

1812 R. H. in *Examiner* 4 May 283/1 The yellowish grey demi-tone which covers the trees across the middle of the canvass. **1828** in WEBSTER.

†**'demitune.** *Obs.* = DEMI-TONE b.

1598 FLORIO *Semitono*, a demitune, or halfe note in musicke.

Demiurge ('dɛmɪɜːdʒ, 'diːmɪ-). [mod. ad. Gr. δημιουργ-ός (Latinized *dēmiūrgus*), *lit.* public or skilled worker, f. δήμιος of the people, public + -εργος, -working, worker: cf. F. *demiurge.* The Gr. and Lat. forms *demiurgos, -urgus* (diːmɪ-, dɛmɪɜːgəs), were in earlier use. (So in 16th c. F. *demiourgon*, Rabelais.)]

1. A name for the Maker or Creator of the world, in the Platonic Philosophy; in certain later systems, as the Gnostic, conceived as a being subordinate to the Supreme Being, and sometimes as the author of evil.

1678 CUDWORTH *Intell. Syst.* 259 Zeus..in Plato..sometimes..is taken for the Demiurgus or Opificer of the World, as in Cratylus. **1793** T. TAYLOR *Plato, Introd. to Timæus* 402 By the demiurgus and father of the world we must understand Jupiter. **1840** BROWNING *Sordello* v. 400 'Better, ' say you, 'merge At once all workmen in the demiurge.' **1867** J. H. STIRLING tr. *Schwegler's Hist. Philos.* (ed. 8) 83 (*Plato*) Demiurgus, by model of the eternal ideas, has fashioned it [the world] in perfection. **1873** WHITNEY *Orient. Stud.* 94 The Hindu supreme God is..separated by a whole series of demiurges from all care of the universe. **1882** FARRAR *Early Chr.* II. 356 The Manichees subsequently argued, that there were two Gods—one the supreme and illimitable Deity..the other a limited and imperfect Demiurge.

2. *Gr. Hist.* The title of a magistrate in certain ancient Greek states, and in the Achæan League.

[**1600** HOLLAND *Livy* XXXII. 823 (Stanf.), He was a demiurgus.] **1844** THIRLWALL *Greece* VIII. lxi. 102 The number of the demiurges seems..to have been limited to ten.

transf. **1885** SIR H. TAYLOR *Autobiog.* II. 39 Such pressures of official work..had become frequent since the retirement of the Demiurge, James Stephen.

Hence (*nonce-wds.*) **demi'urgeous** *a.*, of the nature of a demiurge; **demi'urgism**, the doctrine of a demiurge; **demi'urgus-ship.**

1882 STEVENSON *Familiar Studies* Pref. 15 Our demiurgeous Mrs. Grundy smiles apologetically on its victims. **1880** A. GRAY *Lett.* (1893) 695, I am amused at Professor...'s substitution of demiurgism for evolution. **1886** in *Century Mag.* XXXII. 116 The prowling theosophies and demiurgisms that swarm in from the limbo of unreason. **1843** CARLYLE *Past & Pr.* IV. viii. (1872) 253 Unheard-of Demiurgus-ships, Priesthoods, aristocracies.

demiurgic (dɛmɪ'ɜːdʒɪk, diː-), *a.* [ad. Gr. δημιουργικ-ός, f. δημιουργός: see -IC.] Of or pertaining to the Demiurge or his work; creative.

1678 CUDWORTH *Intell. Syst.* 306 Amelius..supposeth these three Minds and Demiurgick Principles of his to be both the same with Plato's 'Three Kings' and with Orpheus his 'Trinity'. **1793** T. TAYLOR *Plato, Introd. to Timæus* 370 He places over the universe a demiurgic intellect and an intelligible cause. **1819** G. S. FABER *Dispens.* (1823) I. 63 Adam will have been created in the course of the sixth demiurgic day. **1869** FARRAR *Fam. Speech* i. (1873) 11 That the creation was the result of a fiat articulately spoken by the demiurgic voice. **1879** J. J. YOUNG *Ceram. Art* 86 The scarabæus was the emblem of the demiurgic god Phtha.

†**demi'urgical,** *a. Obs.* = prec.

1601 BP. W. BARLOW *Defence* 92 The demiurgical or instrumentall meanes, the word of God read or preached. **1653** H. MORE *Conject. Cabbal.* (1713) 172 These two Principles..the one Active or Demiurgical, the other Passive or Material. **1678** CUDWORTH *Intell. Syst.* 306 It is one and the same demiurgical Jupiter that is praised both by Orpheus and Plato. **1792** T. TAYLOR tr. *Comment. Proclus* I. 58 Demiurgical medicine.

Hence **demi'urgically** *adv.*

1816 G. S. FABER *Orig. Pagan Idol.* III. 67 He demiurgically renews the whole appearance of nature. **1851** —— *Many Mansions* (1862) 102 God acted demiurgically through the intervention of a Material Body.

Demiurgos, -us: see DEMIURGE.

demi-vambrace: see DEMI- 3.

‖**demi-vierge** (dəmivjɛrʒ). Also **demi-virgin.** [Fr. (*Les demi-vierges*, title of novel by M. Prévost, 1894).] A woman (esp. a young woman) of doubtful reputation or suspected unchastity, who is not a virgin except in the strict physiological sense of the word (VIRGIN 2). Also *fig.*

1908 *Westm. Gaz.* 14 Nov. 6/2 Scandal-mongering elders, vain, selfish, dissipated officers, and equally vain, selfish young ladies approximating closely to the demi-vierge. **1928** D. H. LAWRENCE *Lady Chatterley* ii. 17, I hope, Connie, you won't let circumstances force you into being a demi-vierge. **1937** *Times Lit. Suppl.* 27 Nov. 910/1 A more spiteful cat of a *demivierge* heroine has seldom adorned a novel. **1951** KOESTLER *Age of Longing* I. viii. 132 We call demi-vierges a certain category of intellectuals who flirt with revolution and violence, while trying to remain chaste liberals at the same time. **1953** R. CHANDLER *Long Good-Bye* xiii. 84 A couple of streamlined demi-virgins went by.

demi-vill. *Constit. Hist. rare.* [AF. *demie vile* half town or vill.] A half-vill or 'town'; the half of a vill (when this was divided between two lords) as a political unit.

The Anglo-French word occurs frequently in the Statute cited, but in the Record ed. is translated *half-town.*

c **1200** *Stat. Exeter* (? 14 Edw. I) Stat. I. 210 Les nuns de totes les viles, demie viles, e hamelez, ke sunt en son Wap', Hundred e Franchise [*transl.* The names of all the Towns, Half-towns, and Hamlets, within his Wapentake, etc.]. **1765** BLACKSTONE *Comm.* I. Introd. iv. 111 The statute of Exeter, which makes frequent mention of entire vills, demi-vills, and hamlets.

demi-vol: see DEMI- 1.

demi-volte ('dɛmɪvəʊlt). *Manège.* [DEMI- 6.] One of the seven artificial motions of a horse: a half-turn made with the fore legs raised.

a **1648** LD. HERBERT *Life* (1886) 74 Having a horse that was excellent in performing the demivolte. **1808** SCOTT *Marm.* IV. xxx, And making demi-volte in air. **1884** E. L. ANDERSON *Mod. Horsemanship* II. xii. 121 The horse may be made to traverse in lines and demi-voltes to the left.

†**'demi-,vowel.** *Obs. rare.* A semi-vowel.

1611 FLORIO, *Semiuocale*, a demie vowell.

demi-wolf: see DEMI- 11.

'demi-,world. *nonce-wd.* = DEMI-MONDE.

1862 *Times* 3 Sept. 5/5 The bye-world..which the French call the *demi-monde*..The demi-world or bye-world is an alluring theme.

demi-wosted: see DEMI-OSTADE.

†**de'mixture.** *Obs.* [f. DE- I. 5 + MIXTURE.] Mixture of things which are themselves formed by mixture: cf. DECOMPOSITION 1, DECOMPOUND.

1697 J. SERGEANT *Solid Philos.* 337 The Intermediate Colours are made by the Mixture and Demixture of those Extreams.

demme, obs. form of DIM *v.*

dem-me, demmy, demn: see DEM *v.*[2]

demmyt, obs. f. *dammed*: see DEM *v.*[1]

demnition (dɛm'nɪʃən). Chiefly *U.S.* Euphemistic pronunciation of DAMNATION 3 b.

1839 [see BOW-WOW 3]. **1840** POE *Business Man* in *Wks.* (1865) IV. 333 A democratic rabble is *so* obtrusive, and so full of demnition mischievous little boys. **1888** *Weekly Exam.* (San Francisco) 22 Mar. (Farmer), It was demnition hot.

Demo[1]. Colloq. U.S. abbreviation of DEMOCRAT 2.

1793 J. STEELE in *N.C. Hist. Comm. Publ.* (1924) XIII. 108 Mr. Smiley—a man who was very Popular in the State assembly, he is a great Demo(crat). **1804** FESSENDEN *Orig. Poems* 57 In vain each demo spouts and billows. **1805** —— *Democr. Unveiled* I. 117 Nothing did demos any good But syllogisms made of wood. **1948** *Chesterton* (Ind.) *Tribune* 28 Oct. 12/3 The program chairman kept peace between GOP and Demos.

demo[2] ('dɛməʊ). Colloq. abbreviation of DEMONSTRATION; so **demo-disc** (see quot. 1963); **demo tape**, a demonstration tape of music recorded by a musician or group to promote the material to potential publishers, agents, etc.

1936 J. CURTIS *Gilt Kid* iii. 28 The anti-war demo last week. **1940** *New Statesman* 16 Mar. 372 Starting as a Fundamentalist he drifts steadily through the modern heresies until he lands up talking of Moses as a militant Unionist, the Exodus as a mass demonstration, and the events in Jerusalem as another demo. **1949** A. WILSON *Wrong Set* 100 Norman's out at the demo. At Trafalgar Square. **1961** *Guardian* 15 Sept. 10/6 She was fined £1 for obstruction in an anti-nuclear 'demo' this spring. **1963** *Time & Tide* 11 Sept. 8/3 One other method of becoming known is to send an agent a 'demodisc'—a gramophone record on which the singer or musician demonstrates his ability. **1967** *Listener* 3 Aug. 130/3 What had begun as a demo..came to look as fey as any folk festival. **1968** *Ibid.* 28 Mar. 410/1 The US Embassy provided a focus for an extreme Left 'demo' against 'fascist brutality' in Vietnam. **1970** *Daily Tel.* 19 Nov. 7/2 Only the other day she was a dedicated demo-girl, but now she has settled down to exemplary bourgeois domesticity. **1971** *Sunday Times* 21 Feb. 3/1 British Rail are running 31 'Demo special' trains today to bring an estimated 30,000 people to London to take part in the trade unions' protest demonstrations against the Government's Industrial Relations Bill. **1970** *Globe & Mail* (Toronto) 26 Sept. 27/3 Danny has a demo tape he carts around, a tape with two tunes. **1986** *Sunday Express Mag.* 17 Aug. 40/3 Radio 1 DJ Janice Long was impressed by a demo tape which Owen sent and she featured him on her programme.

2. A demo-disc or demo tape (see sense 1). orig. *U.S.*

1954 *Billboard* 27 Nov. 14/4 Altho the demo is designed for distributors, it can also be used by dealers; so M-G-M's distributors will leave the demos with their retail clients for use on the customer level. **1960** WENTWORTH & FLEXNER *Dict. Amer. Slang* 144/2 *Demo*, a phonograph record made for demonstration purposes, to display the talents of a singer or musician or the merits of a new song to booking agents, bands, radio stations, and the like. **1970** *Guardian* 31 July 6/1 Frank made some demos for a fake combo..using the five-track machine to its full capacity. **1985** M. GEE *Light Years* xix. 146 He's going to be a vocalist... He's already made some demos.

demob (diː'mɒb), *sb.* and *v.* Colloq. abbrev. of DEMOBILIZATION and of DEMOBILIZE *v.* Also *attrib.*, as in ***demob suit***, a suit issued to a soldier upon demobilization.

1920 *Glasgow Herald* 2 June 11 Some young soldiers..who had been recently demobbed. **1921** *Ibid.* 5 Feb. 7 The unemployed demobbed men. **1922** W. J. LOCKE *Tale of Triona* v. 56 The impecunious demobbed. **1923** T. S. ELIOT *Waste Land* ii. 11 When Lil's husband got demobbed, I said ..Now Albert's coming back, make yourself a bit smart. **1934** M. WESEEN *Dict. Amer. Slang, Demob*, to demobilize; demobilization. **1945** *News Chron.* 17 May, No more Bevin boys will be directed to the pits, but those already there will have to remain until the time comes for them to be demobbed according to age and length of service, just as if they were soldiers. **1945** *Daily Mirror* 11 Aug. 3 (*headline*) It's 'total' demob. now—Many home by year's end. **1949** B. BOLAND in J. C. Trewin *Plays of Yr. 1948–49* 58, I know one of the places where I don't want to spend my demob. leave. **1949** G. COTTERELL *Randle in Springtime* 282 The mockery of the black Homburgs and umbrellas, the demob suits, whose patterns one often recognised [etc.]. **1959** 'B. MATHER' *Achilles Affair* 101 Jo had not long been demobbed from the Wrens.

demobilize (diː'məʊbɪlaɪz), *v.* [DE- II. 1.] *trans.* To reduce from a mobilized condition; to disband (forces) so as to make them not liable to be moved in military service.

1882 *Standard* 23 Oct. 5/3 It has been decided to demobilise those Reserve men. **1892** *Times* 15 Aug. 6/1 The mobilized ships having first been inspected, will return to their respective ports and be demobilized forthwith.

Hence **de,mobili'zation**, the action of demobilizing, reduction of forces to a peace footing.

1866 *Spectator* 14 Apr. 397/2 Austria has demanded the de-mobilization of the Prussian army. **1885** *Manch. Exam.* 26 Aug. 5/4 An order..for the demobilisation of the First-class Army Reserve.

democracy (dɪ'mɒkrəsɪ). Forms: 6–7 democracie, 6–7 (9) -cratie, 7 (9) -craty, 7- -cracy. [a. F. *démocratie* (sɪː), (Oresme 14th c.), a. med.L. *dēmocratia* (in 13th c. L. transl. of Aristotle, attrib. to William of Moerbeke), a. Gr. δημοκρατία popular government, f. δῆμος the commons, the people + -κρατια in comb. = κράτος rule, sway, authority. The latinized form is frequent in early writers, and *democratie, -craty*, in 16– 17th c.]

1. Government by the people; that form of government in which the sovereign power resides in the people as a whole, and is exercised either directly by them (as in the small republics of antiquity) or by officers elected by them. In mod. use often more vaguely denoting a social state in which all have equal rights, without hereditary or arbitrary differences of rank or privilege.

[**1531** ELYOT *Gov.* I. ii, An other publique weale was amonge the Atheniensis, where equalitie was of astate amonge the people.. This maner of gouernaunce was called in greke *Democratia*, in latine, *Popularis potentia*, in englisshe the rule of the comminaltie.] **1576** FLEMING *Panopl. Epist.* 198 Democracie, when the multitude have governement. **1586** T. B. *La Primaud. Fr. Acad.* 549 Democratie, where free and poore men being the greater number, are lords of the estate. **1628** WITHER *Brit. Rememb.* 267 Were I in Switzerland I would maintaine Democrity. **1664** H. MORE *Myst. Iniq.* 514 Presbytery verges nearer toward Populacy or Democracy. **1821** BYRON *Diary* May (*Ravenna*), What is..democracy?—an aristocracy of blackguards. **1836** GEN. P. THOMPSON *Exerc.* (1842) IV. 191 Democracy means the community's governing through its representatives for its own benefit. **1890** *Pall Mall G.* 25 Nov. 3/1 'Progress of all through all, under the leading of the best and wisest', was his [Mazzini's] definition of democracy.

b. A state or community in which the government is vested in the people as a whole.

1574 WHITGIFT *Def. Aunsw.* iii. Wks. (1851) I. 390 In respect that the people are not secluded, but have their interest in church-matters, it is a democraty, or a popular estate. **1607** TOPSELL *Four-f. Beasts* (1658) 97 Democraties do not nourish game and pleasures like unto Monarchies. **1614** BP. HALL *Recoll. Treat.* 732 Nothing..can bee more disorderlie, then the confusion of your Democracie, or popular state. **1671** MILTON *P.R.* IV. 269 Those ancient whose resistless eloquence Wielded at will that fierce democraty. **1794** S. WILLIAMS *Vermont* 342 In the ancient democracies the public business was transacted in the assemblies of the people. **1804** SYD. SMITH *Mor. Philos.* xvi. (1850) 237 In the fierce and eventful democracies of Greece and Rome. **1881** JOWETT *Thucyd.* I. 117 We are called a democracy, for the administration is in the hands of the many and not of the few.

c. *fig.*

1607 WALKINGTON *Opt. Glass* 82 Tyrannizing as it were over the Democratie of base and vulgar actions. *a* **1652** J. SMITH *Sel. Disc.* IX. xi. (1821) 410 In wicked men there is a democracy of wild lusts and passions. **1885** J. MARTINEAU *Types Eth. Th.* I. 27 All these εἴδη..are not left side by side as a democracy of real being.

2. That class of the people which has no hereditary or special rank or privilege; the common people (in reference to their political power).

1827 HALLAM *Const. Hist.* (1876) II. xii. 453 The power of the democracy in that age resided chiefly in the corporations. **1841** GEN. P. THOMPSON *Exerc.* (1842) VI. 151 The portion of the people whose injury is the most manifest, have got or taken the title of the 'democracy'. For nobody that has taken care of himself, is ever, in these days, of the democracy..The political life of the English democracy, may be said to date from the 21st of January 1841. **1868** MILL in *Eng. & Ireland* Feb., When the democracy of one country will join hands with the democracy of another.

3. Democratism. *rare.*

1856 MISS MULOCK *J. Halifax* 244 It seems that democracy is rife in your neighbourhood.

4. *U.S. politics.* **a.** The principles of the Democratic party; **b.** The members of the Democratic party collectively.

1825 H. CLAY *Priv. Corr.* 112, I am [alleged to be] a deserter from democracy. **1848** *N.Y. Herald* 13 June (Bartlett), The election of 1840..was carried by..false charges against the American democracy. **1868** in G. Rose *Gt. Country* 354 That resolution adopted by the Maine Democracy in State Convention at Augusta. **1891** *Lowell's Poems, Biglow P., Note* 301 One of the leaders of the Northern Democracy during the war, and the presidential nominee against Lincoln in 1864.

democrasian, var. of DEMOCRATIAN *Obs.*

democrat ('dɛməʊkræt). Also 8 -crate. [a. F. *démocrate* (1790 in Hatzf.), formed from *démocratie* DEMOCRACY, on the model of *aristocrate*.]

1. An adherent or advocate of democracy; *orig.* one of the republicans of the French Revolution of 1790 (opposed to *aristocrat*).

1790 *Hist. Europe* in *Ann. Reg.* 119/2 The democrates had already stripped the nobility of all power. **1791** GIBBON *Misc. Works* (1814) I. 340 Even our democrats are more reasonable or more discreet. *a* **1794** —— *Autobiog.* Wks. 1796 I. 181 The clamour of the triumphant *democrates*. **1840** CARLYLE *Heroes* vi. Napoleon, in his first period, was a true Democrat. **1851** HELPS *Comp. Solit.* ii. (1874) 15 Too affectionate a regard for the people to be a democrat.

2. *U.S. politics.* A member of the Democratic party: see DEMOCRATIC 2.

1798 WASHINGTON *Let.* Writ. 1893 XIV. 105 You could as soon scrub the blackamore white as change the principle of a profest Democrat. **1809** KENDALL *Trav.* III. lx. 5 A democrat is an anti-federalist. **1847** H. CLAY *Priv. Corr.* 544 He must say whether he is Whig or Democrat. **1888** BRYCE *Amer. Commw.* II. III. liii. 333 One of these two parties carried on, under the name of Democrats, the dogmas and traditions of the Jeffersonian Republicans.

3. *U.S.* A light four-wheeled cart with several seats one behind the other, and usually drawn by two horses. 'Originally called *democratic wagon* (Western and Middle U.S.)'. *Cent. Dict.*

1890 S. J. DUNCAN *Soc. Departure* 26 The vehicle was, in the language of the country, a 'democrat', a high four-wheeled cart, painted and varnished, with double seats, one behind the other. **1894** *Auctioneer's Catal.* (New York), Democrat Wagon in good order.

4. *attrib.* = DEMOCRATIC. *rare.*

1817 COLERIDGE *Biog. Lit.* I. x. 186 He..talked of purpose in a democrat way in order to draw me out. **1890** *Spectator* 15 Nov. 676 Whether a little farmer..is going to rule the Democrat Party in America.

†**demo'cratian**, *a.* and *sb. Obs.* Also 7 -sian. [f. med.L. *democratia* DEMOCRACY + -AN.]

A. *adj.* = DEMOCRATIC.

1574 J. JONES *Nat. Beginning Grow. Things* 33 The Democratian commen wealth..is the gouernment of the people; where all their counsell and aduise is had together in one. **1803** *Sussex Chron.* in *Spirit Public Jrnls.* (1804) VII. 248 Under the Democratian flag.

B. *sb.* = DEMOCRAT.

1658 R. FRANCK *North. Mem.* (1821) 36 When Democrasians dagger the Crown.

democratic (dɛməʊ'krætɪk), *a.* (*sb.*) [a. F. *démocratique*, ad. med.L. *dēmocratic-us*, a. Gr. δημοκρατικ-ός, f. δημοκρατία DEMOCRACY: see -IC.]

1. Of the nature of, or characterized by, democracy; advocating or upholding democracy.

1602 WARNER *Alb. Eng.* x. lvii. (1612) 250 Aristocratick gouernment nor Democratick pleas'd. **1790** MANN in *Lett. Lit. Men* (Camden) 433 All is in a flame between the Aristocratic and Democratic parties [in France]. **1837** HT. MARTINEAU *Soc. Amer.* III. 255 The most democratic of nations is religious at heart. **1874** GREEN *Short Hist.* viii. §5. 508 No Church constitution has proved in practice so democratic as that of Scotland.

2. *U.S. politics.* (With capital D.) Name of the political party originally called *Anti-Federal* and afterwards *Democratic-Republican*, initially favouring strict interpretation of the Constitution with regard to the powers of the general government and of individual States, and the least possible interference with local and individual liberty; in opposition to the party now (since 1854) called *Republican* (formerly called *Federals* and *Whigs*). **b.** Pertaining to the Democratic party, as 'a Democratic measure'.

c **1800** T. TWINING *Trav. America* in 1796 (1894) 51 One of the principal members of the opposition, or of the anti-federal or democratic party. **1812** in *Niles' Register* 96 Harford, Baltimore, Washington and Queen-Anns have returned 4 Democratic members..Federal majority [in Maryland House] 32. **1839** W. L. GARRISON in *Life* II. 312 Both the Whig and Democratic parties have consulted the wishes of abolitionists. **1860** BARTLETT *Dict. Amer.* 507 What was Whig doctrine in 1830 may be Democratic doctrine in 1850. *Ibid.* 508 The three Democratic presidents, Jackson, Van Buren, and Polk. **1888** BRYCE *Amer. Commw.* II. III. liii. 340 The autonomy of communities..has been the watch-word of the Democratic party.

†**B.** *sb.* = DEMOCRAT I. *Obs.*

1658-9 *Burton's Diary* (1828) IV. 232 The democratics of our age went upon another principle. **1681** G. VERNON *Pref. to Heylin's De Jure Paritatis Episc.*, This argument is known too well by our Anti-Episcopal Democraticks.

democratical (dɛməʊ'krætɪkəl), *a.* (*sb.*) [f. as prec. + -AL[1].] = DEMOCRATIC I.

1589 *Hay any Work* 26 It is Monarchicall, in regarde of our head Christ, Aristocraticall in the Eldership, and Democraticall in the people. **1608** D. T. *Ess. Pol. & Mor.* 4b, Ostracismes practiced in those Democraticall and Popular states of elder times. **1686** in Somers *Tracts* I. 111 The Democratical Man, that is never quiet under any Government. **1791** BOSWELL *Johnson* 21 Mar. an. 1775 I abhor his Whiggish democratical notions and propensities. **1849** GROTE *Greece* II. lxiv. (1862) V. 501 The levy was in fact as democratical and as equalising as..on that memorable occasion.

†**B.** *sb.* = DEMOCRAT I. *Obs.*

1651 HOBBES *Leviath.* II. xxii. 122 Aristocraticalls and Democraticalls of old time in Greece. **1679** —— *Behemoth* I. Wks. VI. 199 The thing which those democraticals chiefly then aimed at, was to force the King to call a parliament. **1714** E. LEWIS *Letter to Swift* 6 July, He is in with the democraticals.

democratically (dɛməʊ'krætɪkəlɪ), *adv.* [f. prec. + -LY[2].] In a democratic manner; according to the principles of democracy.

1603 HOLLAND *Plutarch's Mor.* 647 They were not summoned aristocratically..but invited democratically and after a popular manner to Supper. **1791** R. BURKE in *B.'s Corr.* (1844) III. 300 He is supposed to be very democratically inclined. **1839** *Fraser's Mag.* XIX. 149 He talked democratically with Lord Stanhope, conservatively with Mr. Pitt. **1888** BRYCE *Amer. Commw.* I. 36 Persons so democratically-minded as Madison and Edmund Randolph.

democratifiable, *a. nonce-wd.* [f. **democratify* (f. DEMOCRAT + -FY) + -ABLE.] Capable of being converted into a democrat.

1812 SHELLEY *Let.* in Dowden *Life* I. 245, I have met with no determined Republicans, but I have found some who are democratifiable.

democratism (dɪ'mɒkrætˌɪz(ə)m). [f. DEMOCRAT + -ISM.] Democracy as a principle or system.

1793 BURKE *Policy of Allies* Wks. VII. 138 Between the rabble of systems, Fayetteism, Condorcetism, Monarchism, or Democratism or Federalism, on the one side, and the fundamental laws of France on the other. **1834** *Tait's Mag.* I. 655 The red cap of democratism.

†**de'mocratist.** *Obs.* [f. as prec. + -IST.] A partisan of democracy; = DEMOCRAT I.

1790 BURKE *Fr. Rev.* 83 You will smile here at the consistency of those democratists. **1791** *Hist.* in *Ann. Reg.* 213 By the arts of the democratists they were plunged into a civil war of the most horrid kind.

democratization (dɪˌmɒkrətaɪ'zeɪʃən). [f. next + -ATION.] The action of rendering, or process of becoming, democratic.

1865 *Pall Mall G.* 24 Apr. 10 The art has not improved under this democratization. **1888** BRYCE *Amer. Commw.* II. II. xxxviii. 53 It is a period of the democratization of all institutions, a democratization due..to the influence..of French republican ideas.

democratize (dɪmɒkrətaɪz), *v.* [a. F. *démocratiser*, f. *démocrate*, *-cratie*: see -IZE.]

1. *trans.* To render democratic; to give a democratic character to.

1798 W. TAYLOR in *Monthly Rev.* XXVII. 583 Not to democratize any one of the great continental powers. **1831** *Blackw. Mag.* XXX. 398 The tendency of the measure was to democratize..the constitution. **1888** BRYCE *Amer. Commw.* II. II. xl. 85 The State Government, which is nothing but the colonial government developed and somewhat democratized.

2. *intr.* To become democratic. (*rare.*)

1840 *Tait's Mag.* VII. 506 The fact that we are democratising must be evident.

Hence **de'mocratized** *ppl. a.*; **de'mocratizing** *vbl. sb.* and *ppl. a.*; **de'mocratizer**, one who democratizes.

1859 *Sat. Rev.* 326/2 The democratizing of the House of Commons. **1882** *Pall Mall G.* 6 Oct. 3 A new and democratized Reform Club. **1882** W. JAMES *Will to Believe* (1897) 90 That element in reality..the rough, harsh, sea-wave, north-wind element, the democratizer—is banished. **1888** BRYCE *Amer. Commw.* II. II. xlii. 113 The democratizing constitution of 1846. **1893** *Nation* 21 Sept. 207/3 Nothing more democratic and democratizing..has ever emanated even from the Tories in the days of their greatest distress. **1951** D. RIESMAN in *Amer. Scholar* XX. 268 Freud..used original sin as a democratizer of men.

democraty, early variant of DEMOCRACY.

Democritean (dɪˌmɒkrɪ'tiːən), *a.* [f. L. *Dēmocritē-us* (or *-īus*, Gr. Δημοκρίτει-ος) of or pertaining to Democritus + -AN.] Of, pertaining to, or after the style of Democritus, a Greek philosopher of the 5th century B.C. (known as 'the laughing philosopher'), or of his atomistic or other theories.

So †**De'mocrital** *a.*, **Demo'critic** *a.* [L. *Dēmocritic-us*], †**Democritish** *a.*, in same sense; †**Demo'critical** *a.*, after the style or theories of Democritus; ***Democritean stories*** (*fabulæ Democriticæ*), incredible stories of Natural History; †**De'mocritism**, the practice of Democritus in laughing at everything.

a **1617** BAYNE *Diocesans Tryall* (1621) 80 As all but Morelius and such Democritall spirits doe affirme. **1650** BULWER *Anthropomet.* Ep. Ded., To summon Democriticall Atomes to conglobate into an intellectual Form. **1656** BLOUNT *Glossogr.*, *Democritick*, mocking, jeering, laughing at every thing. **1668** H. MORE *Div. Dial* I. xxvi. (1713) 53 The Existence of the ancient Democritish Vacuum. **1672** SIR T. BROWNE *Lett. Friend* xxiv. (1881) 143 His sober contempt of the world wrought no Democritism or Cynicism, no laughing or snarling at it. **1678** CUDWORTH *Intell. Syst.* Pref., The Democritick Fate, is nothing but The Material Necessity of all things without a God. **1725** BAILEY *Erasm. Colloq.* (1877) 394 (D.) Not to mention democritical stories, do we not find..that there is a mighty disagreement between an oak and an olive-tree? **1845** MAURICE *Mor. & Met. Philos.* in *Encycl. Metrop.* II. 627/1 The Democritic concourse of atoms. **1855** MILMAN *Lat. Chr.* (1864) IX. XIV. iii. 137 The Democritean notions of actual images which..pass from the object to the sense. **1888** J. MARTINEAU *Study Relig.* I. II. i. 214 A physiologist so Democritean as Haeckel.

‖**démodé** (deɪ'məʊdeɪ, ‖demɔde), *a.* [Fr., = DEMODED.] Out of fashion.

1873 *Young Englishwoman* Apr. 199/2 Light prints, when démodée, make very economical jupons for summer wear. **1896** *Westm. Gaz.* 7 Mar. 3/2 A chance of reincarnation for some demodé white satin bodice. **1900** *Daily News* 16 Oct. 6/6 There is fashion in art, as in everything else, and the démodé painter soon passes into an obscurity which he does not deserve. **1928** *Observer* 26 Feb. 15/5 Ibsen, demodé as he is, seems to have the quality of the mountain that does not move. **1930** *Time & Tide* 4 Apr. 451 This does not mean that Mr. Birrell's mind is *demodé*. **1945** R. HARGREAVES *Enemy at Gate* 61 Alarmed and incensed at the industry with which James [II] had refurbished the *démodé* mantle of 'divine right', [etc.].

de'moded, *ppl. a.* [f. F. *démodé*, pa. pple. of *démoder* to put out of fashion (f. DE- I. 6 + *mode* fashion) + -ED.] That has gone out of fashion.

1887 *Temple Bar Mag.* Mar. 436 Despite its demoded raging Romanticism. **1891** *Sat. Rev.* 17 Oct. 457/2 Anything so demoded as bustifying.

‖**Demodex** ('diːməʊdɛks). *Zool.* [mod.L.; f. Gr. δημός fat + δήξ wood-worm.] A genus of parasitic mites, of which one species, *D. folliculorum*, infests the hair follicles and sebaceous follicles of man and domestic animals.

1876 *Beneden's Anim. Parasites* 134 The dog harbours a demodex which causes it to lose its hair. **1876** DUHRING *Dis. Skin* 585.

demodulation (di:mɒdju:'leɪʃən). *Electr.* [f. DE- II. 3 + MODULATION.] The process of obtaining from a modulated wave or voltage a signal which has the same form as the signal originally used to modulate it; the recovery of modulation; cf. DETECTION (sense 3). Hence **de'modulator**, a device or circuit used to effect demodulation.

1921 *Electrician* 15 Apr. 452/1 By the term 'demodulation' is meant the process of reproducing the original low frequency modulating wave from the carrier wave upon which it has been impressed. *Ibid.*, We may determine.. the components of voice frequency in the output circuit of the demodulator by considering the interaction of the various.. frequencies. **1929** T. E. SHEA *Transmission Networks & Wave Filters* I. i. 20 In radio systems, a 'carrier frequency' and 'two sidebands' are produced. For demodulation and recognition of signals the carrier frequency and one sideband may be suppressed. **1942** *Electronic Engin.* XIV. 728 If.. it is desired to reduce the frequency modulation percentage of the broadcast signal.. this can conveniently be done by passing a portion of the signal.. through a demodulator. **1962** SIMPSON & RICHARDS *Junction Transistors* xviii. 460 The removal of the modulation from a carrier or i.f. signal is called demodulation or detection. **1963** G. TROUP *Masers & Lasers* (ed. 2) ix. 162 Demodulation of microwave-modulated light has been achieved using travelling wave tubes.

demoere, obs. form of DEMUR.

Demogorgon (ˌdi:məʊ'gɔ:gən). *Myth.* [late L. *Dēmogorgōn*, having the form of a derivative of Gr. δῆμος people + γοργός grim, terrible, whence γοργώ Gorgon; but of uncertain origin: see below.]

Name of a mysterious and terrible infernal deity.

First mentioned (so far as known) by the Scholiast (Lactantius or Lutatius Placidus, ? *c* 450) on Statius *Theb.* IV. 516, as the name of the great nether deity invoked in magic rites. Mentioned also by a scholiast on Lucan *Pharsalia* VI. 742. Described in the *Repertorium* of Conrad de Mure (1273) as the primordial God of ancient mythology; so in the *Genealogia Deorum* of Boccaccio. The latter appears to be the source of the word in modern literature (Ariosto, Spenser, Milton, Shelley, etc.).

[By some supposed to be a corruption of δημιουργός Demiurgus; but this is very doubtful. The mediæval writers connect it with *dæmon* (DEMON[1]), and explain it as meaning either *dæmonibus terror* (terror to demons), or *terribilis dæmon* (terrible demon). From its connexion with magic, it may be a disguised form of some Oriental name.]

1590 SPENSER *F.Q.* I. v. 22 O thou [Night] most auncient Grandmother of all.. Which wast begot in Dæmogorgon's hall. **1667** MILTON *P.L.* II. 965 And by them stood Orcus and Ades, and the dreaded name Of Demogorgon. **1681** DRYDEN *Sp. Friar* V. 11 He's the first begotten of Beelzebub, with a face as terrible as Demogorgon. **1705** PURSHALL *Mech. Macrocosm* 85 The Saline, and Sulphurious Vapours, I take to be the True Demogorgon of the Philosophers, or Grandfather of all the Heathen Gods, i.e. Mettals. **1821** SHELLEY *Prometh. Unb.* I. 207 All the powers of nameless worlds.. And Demogorgon, a tremendous gloom. **1850** KEIGHTLEY *Fairy Mythol.* 452 According to Ariosto, Demogorgon has a splendid temple palace in the Himalaya mountains, whither every fifth year the Fates are all summoned to appear before him, and give an account of their actions.

demographer (di:'mɒgrəfə(r)). [f. DEMOGRAPHY: see -GRAPHER.] One versed in demography.

1881 P. GEDDES in *Nature* No. 622. 524 The economic labours of the geographer.. and the demographer.

demographic (dɛməʊ'græfik), *a.* and *sb. pl.* [f. DEMOGRAPHY: see -GRAPHIC.]

A. *adj.* Of or pertaining to demography.

1882 *Lond. Med. Record* No. 86. 311 This proportion.. has no demographic interest. **1891** *Scott. Leader* 11 Aug. 4 In the demographic section there are to be investigated some social problems of more than usual intricacy.

B. *sb. pl.* Demographic statistics; the science of obtaining and interpreting these. Hence, the characteristics or composition of a population (esp. a television or other audience) so revealed. orig. *U.S.*

1967 *Time* 8 Dec. 81/3 The network feels that 'intelligent advertisers are not interested in demographics per se but in the audience's response to their product.' **1970** *Daily Colonist* (Victoria, B.C.) 28 July 7/1 Demographics is a trade name for the composition of television audiences. Until a season or two ago, numbers meant everything; the shows with the highest ratings survived. Now, advertisers appear more concerned with the quality of audiences. **1976** *National Observer* (U.S.) 22 May 8/3 The demographics have changed also. Go back to 1972, which was our best year. The largest percentage of buyers were the older middle-aged. **1978** R. LUDLUM *Holcroft Covenant* xvii. 199 When the signal came from Switzerland, the millions would be dispensed scientifically, the art of demographics employed. **1984** *Listener* 9 Feb. 14/3 They will get more precise information about the 'demographics' of the television audience.

demo'graphical, *a.* = DEMOGRAPHIC. Also **demo'graphically** *adv.*

1902 *Daily Chron.* 7 Nov. 4/2 The application of what we might almost call demographical method to departmental studies of the French Revolution. **1904** *Biometrika* Jan. 100 Buénos-Ayres is a town which is altering demographically in two very sensible ways. **1952** C. P. BLACKER *Eugenics* 175 Demographically enlightened people in Asiatic countries are appreciating the need for active measures to reduce fertility. **1965** *Math. in Biol. & Med.* (*Med. Res. Council*) II. 52 Since the Council of Trent (1545-1563), Catholic parish priests have been directed and required to register the demographical events taking place in the parishes under their jurisdiction. **1970** *Sci. Jrnl.* Apr. 84/2 Not that he neglects the demographical and social consequences of contraception.

demography (di:'mɒgrəfi). [mod. f. Gr. δῆμος people + -γραφια writing, description (see -GRAPHY): cf. F. *démographie*, *Journal des Économistes*, April 1878.] That branch of anthropology which deals with the life-conditions of communities of people, as shown by statistics of births, deaths, diseases, etc.

1880 *Libr. Univ. Knowl.* V. 560 Two sections of general anthropology, viz.: 1, anthropology proper.. 2, demography, which.. treats of the statistics of health and disease. **1882** *Athenæum* 16 Sept. 374/1 The fourth International Congress for Hygiene and Demography was held last week at Geneva.

demoid ('di:mɔɪd), *a.* [ad. Gr. δημοειδής vulgar, f. δῆμος the commons, the people: see -OID.] Used of a type of animal or plant which by its commonness or abundance characterizes a geographical region or a period of time; especially of the characteristic fossil type of a geological formation.

1884 H. G. SEELEY *Phillip's Man. of Geol.* I. 437 The abundant demoid types, which are termed characteristic fossils, for their abundance is such that strata are easily recognised by them. Every formation has its demoid types; which in the Primary rocks are generally brachiopods. **1885** W. H. HUDLESTON in *Geol. Mag.* 128 The relations of a thoroughly demoid type are pretty wide.

‖**demoi'selle.** [mod.F. (dəmwazɛl), from earlier *damoiselle*: see DAMSEL.]

1. A young lady, a maid, a girl.

Occurs in 16th c. for earlier *damoiselle, damisell* (see DAMSEL); in modern writers, in reference to France or other foreign country.

1520 *Caxton's Chron. Eng.* I. 8 b/1 A gentyl demoysell [*ed.* **1480** damisell] that was wonder fayre. **1762** STERNE *Lett.* Wks. (1839) 750/2 (Stanf.), A month's play with a French Demoiselle. **1824** BYRON *Juan* XV. xlii, A dashing damoiselle of good estate. **1884** HUNTER & WHYTE *My Ducats* iii. (1885) 38 One student, skating along with his demoiselle, has cannoned against another.

2. *Zool.* **a.** The Numidian Crane (*Anthropoides virgo*); so called from its elegance of form.

1687 *Phil. Trans.* XVI. 374 Six Demoiselles of Numidia, a Kind of Crane. **1766** *Ibid.* LVI. 210 The next I shall mention is the Grus Numidica, Numidian crane, or Demoiselle. **1862** *Chambers' Encycl.* 484 The Numidian demoiselle is remarkable.. for elegance and symmetry of form and grace of deportment.

b. A dragon-fly.

[**1816** KIRBY & SP. *Entomol.* (1818) I. 276 The name given to them in England, 'Dragon flies', seems much more applicable than 'Demoiselles' by which the French distinguish them.] **1844** GOSSE in *Zoologist* II. 709 Thus I contracted an acquaintance with these *demoiselles*.

c. = *damsel-fish* (DAMSEL III. 6).

1884 G. B. GOODE *Nat. Hist. Aquatic Anim.* 275 The Demoiselle and the Cichlid Families. **1926** C. W. BEEBE *Arcturus Adv.* xii. 315 Out from this very coral rock in its path there would shoot a diminutive demoiselle, fins erect in righteous wrath. **1931** J. R. NORMAN *Hist. Fishes* xi. 208 A little coral-reef fish (*Amphiprion*) belonging to the family of Desmoiselles (*Pomacentridae*) has a ground colour of vivid orange. **1967** *N.Z. Listener* 29 Dec. 5/1 At a depth of 160 feet, diver Jeff Pearch is surrounded by a shoal of demoiselles as he swims behind the branches of a long-armed red sponge. **1968** J. E. RANDALL *Caribbean Reef Fishes* 189 The damselfishes (or demoiselles) are small reef fishes which are often very colorful.

demolater (di:'mɒlətə(r)). *nonce-wd.* [f. δῆμο-ς people + -LATER: cf. *idolater*.] A worshipper of the common people. So **demo'maniac**, one madly attached to the common people.

1886 *Sat. Rev.* 22 May 704/2 Friendly portrait of a democracy by democrats, by demogogues, by demomaniacs even, and demolaters.

demolish (dɪ'mɒlɪʃ), *v.* [a. F. *démoliss-*, lengthened stem of *démolir* (1383) in Littré), ad. L. *dēmōlīrī* to throw down, demolish, destroy, f. DE- I. 6 + *mōlīrī* to build, construct, erect, f. *mōles* mass, massive structure.]

1. *trans.* To destroy (a building or other structure) by violent disintegration of its fabric; to pull or throw down, pull to pieces, reduce to ruin.

1570-6 LAMBARDE *Peramb. Kent* (1826) 285 The Chapell of Hakington.. was quite and cleane demolished. **1606** WARNER *Alb. Eng.* XIV. lxxxv. (1612) 353 Both twaine made hauock of their foes, demolishing their Forts. **1641** J. JACKSON *True Evang. T.* III. 181 Christ did.. demolish and breake downe that partition wall. **1776** GIBBON *Decl. & F.* I. xvi. 422 They completely demolished the remainder of the edifice. **1825** MACAULAY *Milton* Ess. 1854 I. 11/1 The men who demolished the images in cathedrals have not always been able to demolish those which were enshrined in their minds.

†**b.** To break down or ruin partially. *Obs.*

1645 EVELYN *Mem.* (1857) I. 170 Behind this stands the great altar of Hercules, much demolished. **1656** *Ibid.* I. 331 A fair town, but now wretchedly demolished by the late siege.

†**c.** *intr.* with passive sense. *Obs. rare.*

1609 BIBLE (Douay) *Joel* ii. 8 Through the windowes they shal fal and shal not demolish [Vulg. *et non demolientur*].

¶ Archaic const.: *demolishing* = *a-demolishing*, in demolition = being demolished: cf. *building* in BUILD *v.* 7.

1686 *Lond. Gaz.* No. 2118/2 The House Gulicke lived in is demolishing. **1706** *Ibid.* No. 4199/3 The Castle of Nice is demolishing.

2. *fig.* To destroy, make an end of.

1620 VENNER *Via Recta* viii. 193 They lesse resist extrinsecall and intrinsecall causes that demolish their health. **1651** BAXTER *Inf. Bapt.* 201 Demolishing the Church by division and contempt. **1735** BERKELEY *Def. Free-think. Math.* §32 It is directly demolishing the very doctrine you would defend. **1878** STEWART & TAIT *Unseen Univ.* vii. §214. 211 To demolish any so-called scientific objection that might be raised. **1882** *Athenæum* 23 Dec. 844 The author demolishes most of those fanciful etymologies.

b. *humorously.* To consume, finish up.

[**1639** MASSINGER *Unnat. Combat* III. i, As tall a trencher-man.. As e'er demolished pye-fortification.] **1756** FOOTE *Eng. fr. Paris* I. Wks. 1799 I. 106 They proceed to demolish the substantials. **1879** BEERBOHM *Patagonia* iii. 41 It is on record that he demolished the whole side of a young guanaco at one sitting.

Hence **de'molished** *ppl. a.*

1623 DONNE *Encænia* 34 That demolished Temple. **1742** YOUNG *Nt. Th.* vii. 833 Beneath the lumber of demolish'd worlds. **1840** THIRLWALL *Greece* VII. 347 On the site of the demolished theatre.

de'molishable, *a.* [f. prec. + -ABLE.] That can be demolished.

1856 RUSKIN *Mod. Paint.* III. IV. x. §10 Only a glass house, frail, hollow, contemptible, demolishable.

demolisher (dɪ'mɒlɪʃə(r)). [f. as prec. + -ER[1]: cf. F. *démolisseur* (1547 in Hatzf.).] One who demolishes.

1615 CROOKE *Body of Man* 247 Melancholy that enemy of the light and demolisher of the principles of life it selfe. **1732** BERKELEY *Alciphr.* v. §25 Whatever merit this writer may have as a demolisher, I always thought he had very little as a builder. **1798** W. TAYLOR in *Monthly Mag.* V. 354 The demolishers of the Bastille. **1827** SCOTT *Napoleon* Introd., Collot d'Herbois, the demolisher of Lyons.

demolishing (dɪ'mɒlɪʃɪŋ), *vbl. sb.* [-ING[1].] The action of the verb DEMOLISH: demolition.

1632 LITHGOW *Trav.* VI. 260, I saw many ruinous lumpes of the Wals, and demolishings of the old Towne. **1684** BUNYAN *Pilgr.* II. 159, I will therefore attempt.. the demolishing of Doubting Castle. **1691** T. H[ALE] *Acc. New Invent.* p. lxxxi, The immediate demolishing of Nusances. *Ibid.* p. lxxxii, The demolishing some particular New Encroachments.

de'molishing, *ppl. a.* [-ING[2].] That demolishes.

1726 AMHERST *Terræ Fil.* 253 The same unrelenting, demolishing spirit reigns in all monkish societies.

de'molishment. Now *rare.* [f. DEMOLISH *v.* + -MENT: cf. F. *démolissement* (1373 *desm-* in Godef.).] The act of demolishing; the state or fact of being demolished.

1602 FULBECKE *2nd Pt. Parall.* 51 Waste may bee committed in the decay or demolishment of an house. **1702** ECHARD *Eccl. Hist.* (1710) 465 The.. demolishment of fifty of their strongest cities. **1884** *Bookseller* 6 Nov. 1190 b/2 The author has succeeded in the complete demolishment of Messrs. Darwin, Huxley and Co.

†**b.** *pl.* Demolished parts or remains, ruins. *Obs.*

1627-77 FELTHAM *Resolves* I. c. 155 If no man should repair the breaches, how soon would all lye flatted in demolishments? **1670** CLARENDON *Contempl. Psalms* Tracts (1727) 372 To repair those breaches and demolishments.

demolition (dɛmə'lɪʃən, di:-). [a. F. *démolition* (14th c. in Littré), ad. L. *dēmōlītiōn-em*, n. of action from *dēmōlīrī* to DEMOLISH.]

1. a. The action of demolishing (buildings or other structures); the fact or state of being demolished.

1610 HEALEY *St. Aug. Citie of God.* 125 Before this demolition the people of Alba were all transported unto Rome. **1780** JOHNSON *Let. to Mrs. Thrale* 9 June, The outrages began by the demolition of the mass-house by Lincoln's Inn. **1852** CONYBEARE & H. *St. Paul* (1862) I. v. 136 Its demolition was completed by an earthquake.

b. *pl.* The remains of a demolished building; demolished portions, ruins. Also *fig.*

1638 BAKER tr. *Balzac's Lett.* (1654) IV. 56 Out of their demolitions, Trophies might be erected. **1641** EVELYN *Mem.* (1857) I. 20 Being taken four or five days before, we had only a sight of the demolitions [of the castle]. **1668** CLARENDON *Contempl. Psalms* Tracts (1727) 734 All the breaches and demolitions they had made in his Church.

2. *fig.* Destruction, overthrow.

1549 *Compl. Scot.* xx. 184 There querellis tendit to the demolitione of the antiant public veil. **1775** GOUV. MORRIS in Sparks *Life & Writ.* (1832) I. 49 Such controversies frequently end in the demolition of those rights and privileges which they were instituted to defend. **1871**

MORLEY *Voltaire* (1886) 243 The demolition of that Infamous in belief and in practice.

3. *attrib.* **a.**

1936 MENCKEN *Amer. Lang.* (ed. 4) vi. 289 In an Atlanta department-store the *News-Record* found..*demolition-engineers* who were once content to be house-wreckers. **1959** J. AUSTWICK *Murder in Borough Library* iii. 21, I thought the houses in Clough Street were closed under a demolition order. **1971** A. CLARKE *Mind to Murder* xii. 179, I went first to the demolition site, told the foreman I'd got to look for a room.

b. Special Comb. **demolition ball** = *wrecking ball* s.v. WRECKING *vbl. sb.*[1] 3; **demolition derby** chiefly *U.S.*, a contest in which old cars are battered into one another, the last one running being declared the winner; also *fig.*

1962 *Engin. News-Rec.* 27 Sept. 19/3 Apprehensive about putting a *demolition ball on a 200-ft-plus crane boom, decided to try the helicopter approach. **1980** *Daily Tel.* 27 Aug. 3/2 Cranes with demolition balls have moved in and destroyed the factory. **1956** *Britannica Bk. Year* (U.S.) 751 **Demolition derby*, a stock car bump-and-crash, elimination contest. **1976** *Billings* (Montana) *Gaz.* 1 July 2A/4 A demolition derby will start at 7.30 p.m. at the fairgrounds, followed by fireworks. **1982** *Listener* 20–30 Dec. 22/3 Keith Moon, the one-man demolition derby on drums, represented a physical element at the opposite end of the spectrum from Pete Townshend's lyrics.

demolitionary (dɛmə'lɪʃənərɪ), *a. rare.* [f. prec. + -ARY.] Of or pertaining to demolition; ruining.

1865 W. G. PALGRAVE *Arabia* I. 454 Too solid for the demolitionary process of hypercritical writers.

demolitionist (dɛmə'lɪʃənɪst). [See -IST.] One who aims at or advocates demolition.

1837 CARLYLE *Fr. Rev.* II. III. v, Lafayette..is marching homewards with some dozen of arrested demolitionists. **1852** *Fraser's Mag.* XLVI. 28 The Ultra-democratic party (not yet Republicans, only Demolitionists).

demomaniac: see DEMOLATER.

demon[1] ('diːmən). Also 6–9 **dæmon.** [In form, and in sense 1 a, a. L. *dæmōn* (med.L. *dēmōn*) spirit, evil spirit, a. Gr. δαίμων divinity, genius, tutelary deity. But in sense 1 b and 2, put for L. *dæmonium*, Gr. δαιμόνιον, neuter of δαιμόνιος *adj.* '(thing) of divine or dæmonic nature or character', which is used by the LXX, N. Test., and Christian writers, for 'evil spirit'. Cf. F. *démon* (in Oresme 14th c. *démones*); also 13th c. *demoygne* = Pr. *demoni*, It., Sp. *demonio*, repr. L. *dæmonium*, Gr. δαιμόνιον.]

1. a. In ancient Greek mythology (= δαίμων): A supernatural being of a nature intermediate between that of gods and men; an inferior divinity, spirit, genius (including the souls or ghosts of deceased persons, *esp.* deified heroes). Often written *dæmon* for distinction from sense 2.

1569 J. SANFORD tr. Agrippa *Van. Artes* 2 Grammarians.. doo expounde this woord Dæmon, that is a Spirite, as if it were *Sapiens*, that is, Wise. **1587** GOLDING *De Mornay* xix. 303 And vnto Cratylus again [Plato] saith, when the good man departeth this world..hee becommeth a Dæmon. **1638** MEDE *Gt. Apost.* iii. Wks. (1672) III. 627 et seq. **1680** H. MORE *Apocal. Apoc.* 252 Dæmons according to the Greek idiom, signify either Angels, or the Souls of men, any Spirits out of Terrestrial bodies, the Souls of Saints, and Spirits of Angels. **1774** J. BRYANT *Mythol.* I. 52 Subordinate dæmons, which they supposed to be emanations and derivatives from their chief Deity. **1846** GROTE *Greece* I. ii. (1862) I. 58 In Homer, there is scarcely any distinction between gods and dæmons.

b. Sometimes, particularly, An attendant, ministering, or indwelling spirit; a genius.

(Chiefly in references to the so-called 'dæmon of Socrates'. Socrates himself claimed to be guided, not by a δαίμων or *dæmon*, but by a δαιμόνιον, *divinum quiddam* (Cicero), a certain divine principle or agency, an inward monitor or oracle. It was his accusers who represented this as a personal *dæmon*, and the same was done by the Christian Fathers (under the influence of sense 2), whence the English use of the word, as in the quotations. See tr. *Zeller's Socrates* iv. 73; Riddell, *Apology of Plato*, Appendix A.)

1387 TREVISA *Higden* III. 279 We haveþ i-lerned of Socrates, þat was alway tendaunt to a spirit þat was i-cleped demon. **1603** HOLLAND *Plutarch's Mor.* 1222 The soule.. that obeieth not nor hearkeneth to her owne familiar and proper dæmon. **1606** SHAKS. *Ant. & Cl.* II. iii. 19 O Anthony!..Thy Dæmon, that thy spirit which keepes thee, is Noble, Couragious, high vnmatchable. **1758** HOME *Agis* 11, Inspiration, The guardian god, the demon of the mind, Thus often presses on the human breast. **1768–74** TUCKER *Lt. Nat.* (1852) I. 222 If the moral sense does not check, if the demon does not warn. **1865** LECKY *Ration.* (1878) I. 378 *note*, Minucius Felix thought the dæmon of Socrates was a devil.

2. An evil spirit.

a. (Representing δαιμόνιον of the LXX and N.T. (rarely δαίμων); in Vulgate *dæmonium*, *dæmon*). Applied to the idols or gods of the heathen, and to the 'evil' or 'unclean spirits' by which demoniacs were possessed or actuated.

A Jewish application of the Greek word, anterior to Christianity. Δαιμόνια is used several times by the LXX to render *shēdīm* 'lords, idols', and *sᵉʿīrīm* 'hairy ones' (satyrs or he-goats), the latter also rendered μάταια 'vain things'. It is also frequent in the Apocrypha (esp. in Tobit), and in the N.T., where in one instance (Matt. viii. 31) δαίμονες occurs in same sense. In the Vulgate generally rendered *dæmonium*, pl. *-ia*, but once in O.T. (Lev. xvii. 7), and in 10 places in N.T. (8 in St. Matthew) *dæmon*, pl. *-es*. These words are indiscriminately translated *deofol* in the Ags. Gospels, *feend* or *deuil* in Wyclif, and in all the 16–17th c. versions *devil*; the Revisers of 1881–5 substitute *demons* in Deut. and Psalms, but in the N.T. retain *devil*, *-s*, in the text, with the literal translation *demon*, *-s*, in the margin. Quite distinct from this is the word properly translated 'Devil', διάβολος, which is not used in the plural. It is owing to this substitution of *devil* in the Bible versions, that *demon* is not found so early in this, as in the popular sense b, which arose out of this identification.

1706 PHILLIPS (ed. Kersey), *Demon*..in Holy Scripture, the Word is always taken for the Devil or a Bad Genius. **1727–51** CHAMBERS *Cycl.*, *Dæmoniac* is applied to a person possessed with a spirit or dæmon. **1767** T. HUTCHINSON *Hist. Mass.* II. i. 16 A young woman..supposed to be posessed with dæmons. **1865** MOZLEY *Mirac.* 201 *note*, The relation in which these persons stood to dæmons and evil spirits. **1881** N. T. (R. V.) *John* x. 20 He hath a devil [*marg.* Gr. demon] and is mad; why hear ye him? **1885** O. T. (R. V.) *Deut.* xxxii. 17 They sacrificed unto demons, which were no God.—*Ps.* cvi. 37.

b. In general current use: An evil spirit; a malignant being of superhuman nature; a devil.

[**1398** TREVISA *Barth. De P.R.* II. xix. (1495) 45 For Demon is to vnderstonde knowynge And the deuyll hyghte soo for sharpnesse..of kyndely wytte.] *a* **1400** *Cov. Myst.* (Shaks. Soc.) 399 Blow flamys of fer to make hem to brenne, Mak redy ageyn we com to this demon. **1599** SHAKS. *Hen. V*, II. ii. 121 If that same Dæmon that hath gull'd thee thus, Should with his Lyon-gate walke the whole world. **1699** DAMPIER *Voy.* II. III. iv. 32 [They] fired their Guns to kill the old Dæmon that they say inhabits there to disturb poor Seamen. **1782** PRIESTLEY *Corrupt. Chr.* I. I. 8 A malignant dæmon had brought [them] into his power. **1813** SCOTT *Trierm.* II. Concl. vii, But wouldst thou bid the demons fly Like mist before the dawning sky. **1865** WRIGHT *Hist. Caricat.* iv. (1875) 69 The three special characteristics of mediæval demons were horns, hoofs..and tails.

c. Applied to a person (animal or agency personified), of malignant, cruel, terrible, or destructive nature, or of hideous appearance. (Cf. *devil.*)

1614 B. JONSON *Barth. Fair* III. v. Wks. (Rtldg.) 322/2 'A caveat against cut-purses!'..I' faith, I would fain see that demon, your cut-purse you talk of. **1821** T. G. WAINEWRIGHT in *Ess. & Crit.* (1880) 127 The grim demon of a bull-dog who interrupts the cat. **1822** SCOTT *Pirate* xl, The Boatswain used to be staunch enough, and so is Goffe, though an incarnate demon. **1829** CARLYLE *Misc.* (1857) II. 4 The Tartar Khan, with his shaggy demons of the wilderness.

d. *fig.* An evil passion or agency personified. *spec.* an alcoholic drink. Also *attrib.*

1712 ADDISON *Spect* No. 387 ¶11 Melancholy is a kind of Demon that haunts our Island. **1754** CHATHAM *Lett. Nephew* v. 39 Beware..of Anger, that dæmon, that destroyer of our peace. **1809** PINKNEY *Trav. France* 86 The dæmon of anarchy has here raised a superb trophy on a monument of ruins. **1884** in *Africana Notes & News* (1961) 295 A good many of them would have..made their mark in the musical history of this country, had it not been for the demon—drink. **1887** [see METHEGLIN]. *a* **1895** Led astray by the demon of intemperance. **1922** JOYCE *Ulysses* 348 Had her father only avoided the clutches of the demon drink. **1936** MENCKEN *Amer. Lang.* (ed. 4) vi. 244 An Englishman ..never uses *rum* in the generic sense that it has acquired in the United States, and knows nothing of *rum-hounds*,..the *rum-trade*, and the *rum-evil*, or of the *Demon Rum.* **1948** PARTRIDGE *Dict. Forces' Slang* 54 *Demon vino*, Italian wine of the cheaper sort.

e. Applied to a being of superhuman or 'diabolical' energy, skill, etc. (cf. 3 a *spec.*); also to an action, etc.

1876 *Coursing Calendar* 21 A demon of a hare got up for Rose and Bar Girl. *Ibid.* 315 It was hard lines indeed for Mr. Watson to meet with such a demon of a hare for the decider. **1899** *Westm. Gaz.* 6 Feb. 3/1 He is a demon of accuracy. **1961** *Times* 4 July 11/4 'Demon' services were, by custom, reserved for male opponents.

f. *Cards.* (Also ***Demon Patience.***) A simple, one-pack patience game, which rarely comes out. Also ***Racing Demon***, Demon adapted for several players, each with his own pack, but played in competition.

1893 M. WHITMORE JONES *Games of Patience* 3rd Ser. ix. 19 Demon Patience. **1900** 'L. HOFFMANN' *Patience Games* 36 The Demon. **1918** H. G. WELLS *Joan & Peter* xi. 388 A new card game, Demon Patience, a scrambling sort of game in which you piled on aces in the middle. **1919** K. MANSFIELD *Lett.* (1928) I. 245 You know how, when we get hungry, we are at last even unable to play Demon for wanting the hash-hammer to sound. **1936** 'P. QUENTIN' *Puzzle for Fools* xii. 95, I began to wonder whether she stole cards from a concealed pack... Her demon came out three times running. **1948** G. GREENE *Heart of Matter* I. III. i. 84 I've never played cards—except demon..and that's a patience.

3. *attrib.* and *Comb.* **a.** appositive (= that is a demon), as ***demon-companion, -god, -hag, -king, -lover, -mole, -snake***; *spec.* applied *colloq.* to one who seems more than human in the rapidity, certainty, destructiveness, etc. of his play or performance, as a ***demon bowler*** at cricket; **demon star**, Algol [Arab., the demon: see GHOUL], the star β Persei. **b.** simple attrib. and attrib. comb. (of, belonging, or relating to a demon or demons), as ***demon altar, -doctrine, herd, -land, life, -trap, -ship, -worship***; **demon-bird** = DEVIL-BIRD; **demon-kind** [after *mankind*], the nature of demons; the race of demons; also **c.** ***demon-like*** adj. **d.** instrumental, etc., as ***demon-infested, -scooped, -stricken.***

1863 W. PHILLIPS *Speeches* iv. 57 The *demon altar of our land. **1840** J. FORBES *11 Years in Ceylon* (1841) 353, I first heard the wild and wailing cry of the gaulawa, or *demon-bird. **1883** *Harper's Mag.* Nov. 900/1 We do not want our boys..*demon bowlers. **1814** BYRON *Corsair* II. iv, Some Afrit sprite, Whose *demon death-blow left no hope for fight. **1677** GALE *Crt. Gentiles* III. 177 Al those *demon-doctrines..introduced by Antichrist and his Sectators. **1638** MEDE *Gt. Apost.* vi. Wks. (1672) III. 635 A worshipper of *Dæmon-gods. **1814** *Prophetess* III. iv, Like the *demon-hags of Tartarus. **1774** J. BRYANT *Mythol.* I. 141 Among all the *dæmon herd what one is there of a form..so odious.. as Priapus. **1933** W. DE LA MARE *Fleeting* 169 *Demon-infested rank morass. **1890** E. H. BARKER *Wayfaring in Fr.* 15 That small *demon-insect, the mosquito. **1904** M. BEERBOHM *Around Theatres* (1953) II. 50 In the 'seventies pantomime was flourishing still. *Demon King and Fairy Queen..were familiar. **1954** 'N. BLAKE' *Whisper in Gloom* II. xi. 148 Alec Gray is..a cheap snake, a proper young Demon King. **1857** *Tait's Mag.* XXIV. 378 The sentences, on all mankind and *demonkind. **1859** G. WILSON *Life E. Forbes* i. 29 Grim or gentle visitants from *Demonland or Fairyland. **1851** MAYNE REID *Scalp. Hunt.* xi. 82 They seem endowed with *demon life. **1822** E. NATHAN *Langreath* III. 416 *Demon-like horrors. **1797** COLERIDGE *Kubla Khan* 16 Woman wailing for her *demon-lover. **1821** KEATS *Isabel* xlv, And let his spirit, like a *demon-mole, Work through the clayey soil and gravel hard. **1924** R. CAMPBELL *Flaming Terrapin* iii. 41 Sleep was a long dark tunnel *demon-scooped Out of the Night's black rock. **1895** *Funk's Standard Dict.*, *Demon star. **1909** *Daily Chron.* 1 Sept. 7/3 Algol, the Demon Star. **1936** *Discovery* June 187/2 The newly-made spirit-doctors proceed to exorcise the *pepo*.. from the scores of *demon-stricken people. **1677** GALE *Crt. Gentiles* III. 56 The *Demon-theology..was brought into the Christian Church first by the Gnostics. *Ibid.*, By this their *demon-worship.

demon[2] ('diːmən). *Austral. slang.* [Appar. ad. *Diemen* (Van Diemen's Land, early name for Tasmania).]

1. A policeman.

1889 BARRÈRE & LELAND *Dict. Slang* I. 304/1 Demons (Australian), prison slang for police. 'The *demons* put pincher on me', I was apprehended. **1933** *Bulletin* (Sydney) 15 Nov. 38/1 Those 'demons', the fools, were chasing the wrong people, as usual. **1945** BAKER *Austral. Lang.* v. 95 It was a natural development that police troopers should come to be called joes..although this use is not found often, demons and traps (1853) being more widely used. **1967** K. GILES *Death & Mr. Prettyman* ii. 61 'Tell the truth, Bert,' said the Australian, 'always help a demon in distress.'

2. (See quots.)

1909 J. R. WARE *Passing English* 107/1 *Demons*, old hands at bushranging; derived from men who arrive from Van Dieman's [*sic*] Land (Tasmania), some of whom are popularly supposed to have inaugurated bushranging in Australia. **1945** BAKER *Austral. Lang.* ii. 42 A large number of synonyms for convict became current [in the early part of the nineteenth century], among them canary, transport,.. demon (a Van Diemen's Land convict), [etc.]. *Ibid.* 51 The following synonyms for bushrangers might be noted: rangers, white Indians and stickers-up. Demon was formerly used for an old hand at the game.

3. A detective.

1926 J. DOONE *Timely Tips for New Austral.*, *Demon*, a slang word meaning a 'detective'. **1941** K. TENNANT *Battlers* viii. 96 The showers were 'demons', or plain-clothes detectives. **1967** *Sunday Mail Mag.* (Brisbane) 23 July 5/3 To the Australian criminal a demon is a..detective.

demonachize (diː'mɒnəkaɪz), *v.* [f. DE- II. 1 + L. *monach-us* monk + -IZE.] *trans.* To deprive of monks.

1820 D. TURNER *Tour in Normandy* II. 24 So thoroughly ..had the Normans demonachised Neustria.

demo'nagerie. *nonce-wd.* [f. DEMON[1], after *menagerie.*] An assemblage of demons.

1848 *Tait's Mag.* XV. 433 Slavery..unless it had been now and then checked, would have transformed the earth ere now into a demonagerie.

† de'monagogue. *Obs.* [f. as next + ἀγωγός drawing forth.] A means of expelling a demon.

1786 FERRIAR in *Mem. Lit. & Philos. Soc. Manchester* (1790) III. 74 Dr. Thoner extols *mercurius vitæ*, as remarkably useful in expelling preternatural substances from the body..Almost every man had his favourite demonagogue.

† 'demonarch. *Obs.* [f. as next + Gr. ἀρχός chief.] A ruler of demons; a chief demon.

1778 H. FARMER *Lett. Worthington* ii. (R.), The false supposition, that the Jews held only one prince of demons; and that demonarch was a term never applied by them to any but to the Devil.

† 'demonarchy. *Obs.* [f. Gr. δαίμων, δαιμον- (see DEMON[1]) + -αρχια, ἀρχή sovereignty, rule.] The rule or dominion of a demon.

c **1643** *Maximes Unfolded* 8, *Demonarchie*, or the Dominion of the Divell. **1677** GALE *Crt. Gentiles* III. 231 Al that pretended Hierarchie or Demonarchie which the Emperor, as supreme Head in al maters Civil and Ecclesiastical, assumed.

demoness ('diːmənɪs). [f. DEMON[1] + -ESS.] A female demon; a she-devil.

a **1638** MEDE *Apost. Later Times* (1641) 31 The Sichemites ..had a Goddesse or Dæmonesse under the name of Jephta's daughter. **1856** *Titan Mag.* Aug. 190/2 That smiling demoness, his mother. **1879** M. D. CONWAY *Demonol.* I. II. iv. 117 A demoness who sometimes appears just before the floods.

demonetization (dɪˌmɒnɪtaɪˈzeɪʃən). [f. next + -ATION.] The action of demonetizing, or condition of being demonetized.

1852 T. HANKEY (*title*), Faucher's Remarks..on the Production of the Precious Metals, and on the Demonetization of Gold in several Countries in Europe. **1852** A. JOHNSON *Observ. Supplies of Gold* 3 The demonetization of the Dutch Gold coin was effected at that time. **1863** FAWCETT *Pol. Econ.* III. xv. (1876) 488 Partial demonetization of silver.

demonetize (dɪˈmɒnɪtaɪz), *v.* [ad. mod.F. *démonetise-r* (Dict. Acad. 1835), f. DE- I. 6 + L. *monēta* money: see -IZE.] *trans.* To deprive of standard monetary value; to withdraw from use as money. Hence **deˈmonetized** *ppl. a.*, **-izing** *vbl. sb.*

1852 T. HANKEY tr. *Faucher's Product. Precious Metals* 31 On August 6, 1849, the Government laid before the Assembly the scheme of a law to 'demonitise' the pieces of five and ten florins. **1853** T. WILSON *Jottings on Money* 83 Merchants not understanding the demonetising of gold by the Dutch in 1850. **1876** FAWCETT *Pol. Econ.* III. xv. 487 Germany has, within the last few years, demonetised silver. **1879** *Daily News* 21 May 3/1 To keep up the price of the demonetised metal.

demonette (diːməˈnɛt). *nonce-wd.* [dim. of DEMON[1]: see -ETTE.] A little demon.

1854 CAROLINE FOX *Mem. Old Friends* (1882) 298 Baby tortoises, most exquisite black demonettes, an inch and a half long, with long tails.

demoniac (dɪˈməʊnɪæk), *a.* and *sb.* Forms: 4-5 **demoniak (-yak)**, 5-7 **-acke**, 5-8 **-ack**, 6-7 **-ake**, 7 **-aque**, **(dæ-)**, 7- **demoniac**. [ad. late L. *dæmoniac-us* (in Tertullian *c* 200), a. Gr. type *δαιμονιακ-ός, f. δαιμόνιον: see DEMON[1].]

A. *adj.* **1.** Possessed by a demon or evil spirit.

c **1386** CHAUCER *Sompn. T.* 532, I hold him certeinly demoniak. **1483** CAXTON *G. de la Tour* C vij, The lady wente oute of her wytte and was al demonyak a long tyme. **1542** BOORDE *Dyetary* xxxvii. (1870) 298 Lunatycke, or frantycke, or demonyacke. *a* **1612** DONNE *Βιαθανατος* (1644) 217 That the Kings of Spaine should dispossess Dæmoniaque persons. **1647** H. MORE *Song of Soul* I. II. xxix, Magick can onely quell natures Dæmoniake. *c* **1811** FUSELI *Lect. Art* v. (1848) 471 The demoniac boy among the series of frescoes at Grotta Ferrata. **1813** *Examiner* 15 Mar. 165/1 This..idea.. operated upon the demoniac spirit of the wretch.

b. Pertaining to demoniacal possession.

1674 MILTON *P.L.* (ed. 2) XI. 485 Demoniac phrenzy, moping melancholy, And moon-struck madness. *a* **1814** *Prophetess* II. vii, As with demoniac energy possess'd!

2. Of or pertaining to demons.

1642 MILTON *Apol. Smect.* (1851) 275 This is the Demoniack legion indeed. **1671** —— *P.R.* IV. 628 He..Shall chase thee..From thy demoniack holds, possession foul. **1669** GALE *Crt. Gentiles* I. II. vi. 71 The mourning of the Demoniac Spirits, for the death of their great God Pan. **1882** FARRAR *Early Chr.* II. 266, I agree with those who see in this vision a purely demoniac host.

3. Characteristic of or befitting a demon; devilish.

1820 HAZLITT *Lect. Dram. Lit.* 179 Wrought up to a pitch of demoniac scorn and phrensy. **1854** MRS. GASKELL *North & S.* xxii, It was as the dæmoniac desire of some terrible wild beast for the food that is withheld from his ravening. **1862** TYNDALL *Mountaineer.* i. 3 The spirit of life..is rendered demoniac or angelic.

4. Of the nature of a dæmon or in-dwelling spirit; = DEMONIC 2.

1844 MASSON *Ess., Three Devils* (1856) 171 Goethe and Niebuhr generalised in the phrase 'the demoniac [ed. 1874 p. 288 demonic] element' that mystic something which they seemed to detect in all men of unusual potency among their fellows. *Ibid.*, The demoniac element in a man..may in one case be the demoniac of the etherial and celestial, in another the demoniac of the Tartarean and infernal. **1856** W. E. FORSTER in T. W. Reid *Life* (1888) I. viii. 306 Denying.. that demoniac element in man which is the very fire of God.

B. *sb.*

1. One possessed by a demon or evil spirit.

c **1386** CHAUCER *Sompn. T.* 584 He nas no fool, ne no demoniak. **1483** CAXTON *Cato* E viij b, And helyth the demonyackes or madde folk. **1546** LANGLEY *Pol. Verg. De Invent.* I. xviii. 33 a, To banish the Spirit out of yᵉ Demoniake. **1665** BOYLE *Occas. Refl.* IV. x. (1845) 226 Possessed by it as Dœmoniacks are possessed by the Divel. **1717** BERKELEY in Fraser *Life* (1871) 580 The demoniacs of S. Andrea della Valle. **1845** DARWIN *Voy. Nat.* x. (1879) 221 They looked like so many demoniacs who had been fighting.

†**2.** *Eccl. Hist.* (See quot.) *Obs.*

1727-51 CHAMBERS *Cycl.*, *Dæmoniacs*, are also a party or branch of the Anabaptists, whose distinguishing tenet it is, that the devils shall be saved at the end of the world. **1847** in CRAIG, and later Dicts.

demoniacal (diːməˈnaɪəkəl), *a.* (*sb.*) [f. as prec. + -AL[1].] **a.** Of or pertaining to demons. **b.** = DEMONIAC 1, 1 b. **c.** Befitting or of the nature of a demon; devilish, fiendish.

demoniacal possession: the possession of a man by an indwelling demon or evil spirit, formerly held to be the cause of some species of insanity, epilepsy, etc.

1614 BP. HALL *Recoll. Treat.* 883 In the Popish Churches ..their ridiculous, or demoniacall service, who can endure? **1621-51** BURTON *Anat. Mel.* I. i. III. 35 Extaticall and dæmoniacall persons. *Ibid.* I. ii. II. vii, Imaginary dreams are of divers kinds, natural, divine, demoniacal, etc. **1681** HALLYWELL *Melampr.* 78 (T.) A notable instance of demoniacal possession. **1741** WARBURTON *Div. Legat.* IX. Notes Wks. 1811 VI. 391 The Possessions recorded in the Gospel..called demoniacal. **1856** KANE *Arct. Expl.* I. xxviii. 367 Menacing and demoniacal expressions. **1858** LYTTON *What will He do* II. xi, His quarrels with a demoniacal usher. **1877** BLACK *Green Past.* xl. (1878) 323 The temper of the mistress of the house..of such a demoniacal complexion.

Hence **demoˈniacally** *adv.*

1819 G. S. FABER *Dispens.* (1823) I. 345 Demoniacally possessed. **1865** L. OLIPHANT *Piccadilly* (1870) 102 She looked at me..demoniacally.

demoniacism (diːməˈnaɪəsɪz(ə)m). *rare*⁻⁰ 'The state of being a demoniac; the practice of demoniacs' (Craig 1847).

1848 WEBSTER cites MILMAN.

†**demoniacle**, *a. Obs.* Also **-yakyl**. [a. OF. *demoniacle*, the usual representative of L. *dæmoniac-us*: cf. OF. *triacle*, TREACLE, L. *thēriaca.*] = DEMONIAC.

c **1500** *Melusine* 314 Whiche, thrugh arte demonyacle, hath myserably suffred deth. **1503** *Kalender of Sheph.*, *Of Yre*, The man yrews ys lyk to oon demonyakyl.

deˈmonial, *a. rare.* [a. OF. *demonial*, prob. med.L. **dæmoniāl-is*, f. *dæmonium*: see DEMON[1] and -AL[1].] Of or relating to a demon or demons; also, of the nature of a demon, demoniacal.

1675 R. BURTHOGGE *Causa Dei* 310 To hear Diotima describing the Demonial Nature. **1678** CUDWORTH *Intell. Syst.* I. iv. § 14. 264 No one who acknowledges Demonial things, can deny Demons. **1849** *Sidonia* II. 287 Because of the spell which the demonial sorceress laid on them.

demoniality (dɪˌməʊnɪˈælɪtɪ). *rare.* [f. prec. + -ITY.] The nature of demons; the realm of demons, demons collectively. (Cf. *spirituality.*)

1879 (*title*), Demoniality; or Incubi and Succubi..by the Rev. Father Sinistrari, of Ameno..now first translated into English. **1891** *Sat. Rev.* 2 May 543/2 The old wives' fables ..are those of demoniality, black masses, etc.

demonian (dɪˈməʊnɪən), *a.* [f. L. *dæmoni-um* (see DEMON[1]) + -AN.] Of, relating to, or of the nature of, a demon or demons.

1671 MILTON *P.R.* II. 122 Princes, Heaven's ancient sons, ethereal thrones, Demonian spirits now. **1790** H. BOYD *Sheph. Lebanon* in *Poet. Reg.* (1808) 146 Demonian visions. **1833** THIRLWALL in *Philol. Museum* II. 582 So far as we can find our way in this truly dæmonian twilight. **1840** *Tait's Mag.* VII. 410 Against such dæmonian manifestations.

Hence †**deˈmonianism**, the doctrine of demomiacal possession.

1741 WARBURTON *Div. Legat.* IX. Wks. 1788 III. 775 An error, which so dreadfully affected the religion they were entrusted to propagate, as Demonianism did, if it were an error. **1762** —— *Doctrine of Grace* II. vii. (1763) II. 161 To ascribe both to Enthusiasm or Demonianism. [Here some modern edd. have *Demoniasm*, which has thence passed into Latham and later Dicts.]

[**demoniasm.** Error for DEMONIANISM: see note at end of prec.]

†**deˈmoniast.** *Obs. rare*⁻¹. [f. after Gr. agent-nouns in -αστης, f. -άειν, -άζειν.] One who has dealings with demons, or with the devil.

1726 DE FOE *Hist. Devil* II. x. (1840) 339 His disciples and emissaries, as witches and wizards, demoniasts, and the like.

†**deˈmoniat**, *a. Obs.* [corresp. to Pr. *demoniat*, OCat. *dimoniat*, from L. *dæmoniac-us*: see DEMONIAC.] Demoniacal, devilish.

1623 LITHGOW. *Trav.* x. 201 This grim demoniat spight.

demoniˈatic, *a. rare*⁻¹. = prec.

1880 P. GILLMORE *On Duty* 10 Tragedies as cold-blooded and demoniatic as ever occurred.

demonic (dɪˈmɒnɪk), *a.* Also **dæm-**. [ad. L. *dæmonic-us*, a. Gr. δαιμονικ-ός of or pertaining to a demon, possessed by a demon, f. δαίμων, δαιμον-: see DEMON[1] and -IC.]

1. Of, belonging to, or of the nature of, a demon or evil spirit; demoniacal, devilish.

1662 EVELYN *Chalcogr.* 68 Convulsive and even Demonic postures. **1738** G. SMITH *Curious Relat.* I. iv. 518 So many Demonick Delusions. **1840** CARLYLE *Heroes* (1858) 197 '*Jötuns*,' Giants, huge shaggy beings of a demonic character. **1886** *Q. Rev.* Oct. 53 The traditional demonic proposal, 'I will be your servant here, and you shall be mine hereafter'.

2. Of, relating to, or of the nature of, supernatural power or genius = Ger. *dämonisch* (Göthe): cf. DEMON[1] 1. (In this sense usually spelt *dæmonic* for distinction.)

1798 W. TAYLOR in *Monthly Rev.* XXVI. 491 In his immature youth he had detected within himself a something dæmonic. **1854** LOWELL *Cambridge 30 Yrs. Ago* Pr. Wks. 1890 I. 87 Shall I take Brahmin Alcott's favorite word, and call him a Dæmonic man? [**1874** see DEMONIAC 4.] **1879** FITZGERALD *Lett.* (1889) I. 447 There is enough to show the Dæmonic Dickens: as pure an instance of Genius as ever lived. **1887** SAINTSBURY *Hist. Elizab. Lit.* vii. (1890) 258 If they have not the dæmonic virtue of a few great dramatic poets, they have..plentiful substitutes for it.

demonical (dɪˈmɒnɪkəl), *a.* Now *rare* or *Obs.* [f. as prec. + -AL[1].]

1. = prec. 1.

1588 J. HARVEY *Discours. Probl.* 79 Without any..mixture of demonicall, or supernaturall Magique. **1603** HOLLAND *Plutarch's Mor.* 1299 That Typhon was some fiend or dæmonicall power. **1607** TOPSELL *Four-f. Beasts* (1658) 127 Falsly imputing this demonical illusion to divine revelation. **1652** GAULE *Magastrom.* 334 Examples of demonicall familiars. **1820** *Examiner* No. 621. 148/1 To attribute demonical properties to God. **1836** J. H. NEWMAN *Par. Serm.* (ed. 2) II. iii. 38 This divine inspiration was so far parallel to demonical possession.

†**2.** = DEMONIAC 1. *Obs.*

1626 L. OWEN *Spec. Jesuit.* (1629) 43 The people..made no more account of her words than of a Demonical creature.

demonically (diːˈmɒnɪkəlɪ), *adv.* [f. DEMONICAL *a.* + -LY[2].] In a manner befitting a demon; superhumanly.

1926 'L. MALET' *Dogs of Want* v. 124 He danced divinely. Perhaps it were more accurate to say demonically. **1962** I. MURDOCH *Unoff. Rose* xxviii. 270 Keeping pace demonically with her love for Felix.

†**demoˈnicraty.** *Obs. rare*⁻⁰

1656 BLOUNT *Glossogr.*, *Demonicratie*, the Government of divels.

deˈmoniculture. *nonce-wd.* [See CULTURE.] Demon-worship, demonolatry.

1879 M. D. CONWAY *Demonol.* I. II. x. 239 Much..is but elaborate demoniculture.

demonifuge (dɪˈmɒnɪfjuːdʒ). *nonce-wd.* [f. L. *dæmon* (DEMON[1]) + -FUGE, L. *-fugus* chasing away.] Something used to drive away demons; a charm against demons.

1790 PENNANT *London* (1813) 271 Isabella..I hope was wrapped in the friar's garment, for few stood more in need of a dæmonifuge. **1848** SOUTHEY *Comm.-pl. Bk.* III. 771 Salt a demonifuge.

demonish (ˈdiːmənɪʃ), *a. rare.* [f. DEMON[1] + -ISH.] **a.** Of the nature of a demon; demonic. So **ˈdemonishness**, devilishness.

Occurs commonly in D. H. Lawrence's works.

1863 DRAPER *Intell. Devel. Europe* vii. (1865) 159 He evoked two visible demonish imps. **1926** D. H. LAWRENCE *Plumed Serpent* iii. 55 A profound unbelief that was fatal and demonish. **1927**—— *Mornings in Mexico* 12 The penetrating, demonish mocking voices. *a* **1930** —— *Pornogr. & So On* (1936) 85 Renoir didn't try to get away from the body. But he had to..rob it of..its natural demonishness.

b. as *adv.* (*humorous.*) 'Devilish'.

1867 O. W. HOLMES *Guard. Angel* iv. (1891) 49 'It was a demonish hard case', he said.

demonism (ˈdiːmənɪz(ə)m). Also **dæ-**. [f. DEMON[1] + -ISM.] Belief in, or doctrine of, demons.

1699 SHAFTESB. *Enq. conc. Virtue* I. i. (1709) 2 Theism stands in opposition to dæmonism, and denotes goodness in the superior Deity. **1789** T. JEFFERSON *Writ.* (1859) II. 553 The comparative merits of atheism and demonism. **1865** *Spectator* 4 Feb. 130/2 The ridicule of the devil and his imps never penetrated England, demonism never having had any hold upon the masses. **1891** *Antidote* 5 May 139 A belief in demonism and witchcraft.

demonist (diːmənɪst). Also **dæ-**. [f. DEMON[1] + -IST.] A believer in, or worshipper of, demons.

1641 *Dialogue Answered* 6 One Marke a great Dæmonist. **1699** SHAFTESB. *Enq. conc. Virtue* I. i. (1709) 2 To believe the governing Mind, or Minds, not absolutely and necessarily good..but capable of acting according to mere will or fancy, is to be a dæmonist.

demonization (ˌdiːmənaɪˈzeɪʃən). [f. next: see -ATION.] The action of turning into, or representing as, a demon.

1799 W. TAYLOR in Robberds *Mem.* I. 305, I hope to atone to them for my demonizations. **1879** M. D. CONWAY *Demonol.* I. II. v. 149 The demonisation of the forces and dangers of nature belongs to the structural action of the human mind.

demonize (ˈdiːmənaɪz), *v.* [f. med.L. *dæmonizāre*: cf. Gr. δαιμονίζ-εσθαι passive, to be possessed by a demon: see -IZE.]

1. *trans.* To make into, or like, a demon; to render demoniacal; to represent as a demon.

1821 *Examiner* 579/1 That subdued superstition, espionage, and persecution..more adequately demonises active hypocrisy and oppression. **1879** M. D. CONWAY *Demonol.* I. I. iv. 26 In Persia the *asuras*—demonised in India—retained their divinity. **1888** *Morning Post* 12 Sept., Where men are brutalized, women are demonized, and children are brought into the world only to be inoculated with corruption.

2. To subject to demoniacal influence.

1864 in WEBSTER. **1888** *Sat. Rev.* 2 June 674 An alligator becomes 'demonized' and works the wicked will of a witch.

Hence **ˈdemonized**, **ˈdemonizing** *ppl. a.*

1837 CARLYLE *Fr. Rev.* II. v. iv, Black demonised squadrons. **1857-8** SEARS *Athan.* xi. 90 Demonizing passions. **1883** MONIER WILLIAMS *Relig. Th. in India* ix. 234 Tenanted by..demonized spirits of dead men, superhuman beings.

demono-, before a vowel **demon-**, repr. Gr. δαιμονο-, combining form of δαίμων DEMON[1]; occurring in various modern formations, as **demoˈnocracy**, the rule of demons; a ruling body of demons (quot. 1827). †**demoˈnomachy**, fighting with a demon. †**demoˈnomagy**, magical art relating to demons. †**ˈdemonoˌmancy**, divination by the help of demons. **demoˈnopathy**, a mental disease in which the patient fancies himself, or acts as if, possessed by a demon. ˌ**demonoˈphobia**, fear of demons. **demoˈnosopher** (*nonce-wd.*), one inspired by a demon or by the devil (controversially opposed to *theosopher*). Also DEMONOGRAPHY, etc.: see below.

1730–6 BAILEY (folio), *Demonocracy*, the government of devils. **1815** W. H. IRELAND *Scribbleomania* 282 A spirit.. By foul democracy wholly subdu'd. **1827** SIR H. TAYLOR *Isaac Comnenus* II. iii, A democracy of unclean spirits Hath govern'd long these synods of your Church. **1718** D. CAMPBELL (*title*), Dæmonomachie or War with the Devil, in a short Treatise. *a* **1808** BP. HURD (L.), The author had rifled all the stores of demonomagy to furnish out an entertainment. **1652** GAULE *Magastrom.* 165 Dæmonomancy, divining by the suggestions of evill dæmons or devils. **1865** *Cornh. Mag.* Apr. 475 But what is demonopathy the Morzinois might reasonably have asked? What was it that had come to their valley? **1883** *Syd. Soc. Lex.*, *Demonopathy*, dæmonomania. **1888** J. MURDOCH *Women of India* 16 This demonophobia was learned from their mothers. **1780** WESLEY *Wks.* (1872) IX. 518 [Behmen] ..ought to be styled a demonosopher rather than a theosopher. **1881** OVERTON *W. Law* 198 Behmen was no 'Demonosopher' (to adopt Wesley's happy phrase).

demonographer (diːməˈnɒgrəfə(r)). [f. mod.L. *dæmonograph-us*, F. *démonographe* (17th c.), answering to a Gr. type *δαιμονογράφος: see -GRAPH.] A writer on demons.

1736 BAILEY (folio) Appendix (9 N 2) *Dæmonographer.* **1877** tr. *Lacroix' Sc. & Lit. Mid. Ages* (1878) 201 Plotinus ..and his disciple Porphyrus..who may be looked upon as the first demonographers of the Middle Ages. **1883** MISS R. H. BUSK in *N. & Q.* 24 Nov. 401/2 Italian demonographers do not make any distinction between..a fairy and a witch.

So **deˈmonograph** (= prec.), **demoˈnography.**

1865 *Cornh. Mag.* XI. 485 Both these celebrated demonographs concurring in the opinion. **1889** *Cent. Dict.*, *Demonography*, the descriptive stage of demonology. *O.T. Mason.*

demonolatry (diːməˈnɒlətrɪ). [f. Gr. type *δαιμονο-λάτρεια (see -LATRY): in mod.F. *démonolâtrie* (Littré).] Demon-worship.

1668 M. CASAUBON *Credulity* 38 (T.), Nicholaus Remigius..in his books of demonolatrie, doth profess [etc.]. **1678** CUDWORTH *Intell. Syst.* 593 Creature-worship, now vulgarly called idolatry—that is, for their cosmo-latry, astro-latry, and demono-latry. **1850** ROBERTSON *Serm.* Ser. II. ii. (1864) 24 Somewhat like what we might now call demonolatry. **1879** M. D. CONWAY *Demonol.* I. II. xi. 258 The number seven holds an equally high degree of potency in Singhalese demonolatry.

So **demoˈnolater**, a demon-worshipper; **demonolaˈtriacal** *a.*, **-ˈlatric** *a.*, **demoˈnolatrous** *a.*, of, pertaining to, or of the nature of demon-worship; **demoˈnolatrously** *adv.*

1816 G. S. FABER *Orig. Pagan Idol.* I. 394 A religion..so far as its demonolatriacal part is concerned. *Ibid.* III. 290 The first authors of the great demonolatric apostasy. **1833** —— *Recapit. Apostasy* 106 The later or demonolatrously Christian Roman Empire. **1846** —— *Lett. Tractar. Secess. Popery* 240 The predicted Demonolatrous Apostasy. **1875** E. WHITE *Life in Christ* IV. xxvi. (1878) 434 Jerome and Augustine, those intolerant doctors of the demonolatrous 'apostasy', as Mr. Isaac Taylor has truly described them. **1876** BP. CALDWELL in *Contemp. Rev.* Feb. 370 Certain demonolators in the present day..display as plain signs of demoniacal possession as ever were displayed eighteen hundred years ago.

demonology (diːməˈnɒlədʒɪ). Also 7 -gie, 7–9 dæ-. [mod. f. Gr. δαίμων + -λογια -LOGY: cf. F. *démonologie* (16th c. in Littré).] That branch of knowledge which treats of demons, or of beliefs about demons; a treatise on demons.

1597 JAMES I (*title*), Daemonologie, in Forme of a Dialogue, diuided into three Bookes. *c* **1645** HOWELL *Lett.* (1650) III. 37, I return you the Manuscript you lent me of Dæmonologie. **1651** HOBBES *Leviath.* III. xl. 256 The Greeks (from whose Customes, and Dæmonology..their Religion became..corrupted). **1775** H. FARMER *Demoniacs N.T.* I. vii. 135 Demonology composed a very eminent part of the Pythagorean and Platonic philosophy. **1857** WHEWELL *Hist. Induct. Sc.* I. 215 An imaginary mythology or demonology. **1875** E. WHITE *Life in Christ* III. xxi. (1878) 310 The apostolic demonology alone explains that paradox.

So **demoˈnologer**, **demoˈnologist**, one who studies or is versed in demonology; **demonoˈlogic** *a.*, of or pertaining to demonology; **demonoˈlogical** *a.*, concerned with demonology; **demonoˈlogically** *adv.*

a **1734** NORTH *Exam.* III. ix. §7 (1740) 652 If the Devil himself..could..have supplied more livid Defamation..I am no Dæmonologer. **1749** BP. G. LAVINGTON *Enthus. Meth. & Papists* (1754) II. 36 The former suffer purely (as Dæmonologists write) from the Operation of Satan himself, or his Imps. **1801** W. TAYLOR in *Monthly Mag.* XI. 44 A metrical romance, of which his dæmonological studies were to supply the machinery. **1833** CARLYLE *Misc.* (1857) III. 194 Working quite demonologically. **1834** H. MILLER *Scenes & Leg.* xx. (1857) 291 He replied in the prescribed formula of the demonologist. **1844** *N. Brit. Rev.* I. 153 The demonologic contest, in which the Evil One is..driven off by the mystical artillery of the priest. **1886** ROGERS *Soc. Life Scotl.* III. xx. 269 Engaged in demonological inquiries.

demonomachy, -magy, -mancy: see DEMONO-.

demonomania (ˈdiːmənəʊˈmeɪnɪə). [a. med.L. *dæmonomania*, f. Gr. δαίμων, δαιμονο- + MANIA. Δαιμονομανία was used in eccles. Gr. in a somewhat different sense: see DEMONOMANIE] (See quot. 1883.)

1880 *Sat. Rev.* No. 1295. 249 Outbreaks of the epidemical demonomania to which every age is liable. **1883** *Syd. Soc. Lex.*, *Dæmonomania*, a kind of madness in which the patient fancies himself possessed by devils; it is a variety of melancholia, originating in mistaken views on religious subjects.

demonomaniac (ˌdiːmənəʊˈmeɪnɪæk). [f. DEMONOMANIA: see -AC.] One who believes himself to be possessed by a devil.

1891 C. LOMBROSO *Man of Genius* III. i. 173 For the demonomaniacs of a hundred years ago..are now substituted the modern paranoiacs. **1920** CHESTERTON *New Jerus.* ix. 177, I do not say that psychologists admit the discovery of demoniacs; and if they did they would doubtless call them something else, such as demonomaniacs.

†**demoˈnomanie.** *Obs.* [a. F. *démonomanie* (1580 in Hatzf.), ad. med.L. *demonomania*, a. eccles. Gr. δαιμονομανία foolish belief in demons, f. μανία MANIA.] Foolish belief in demons; devotion to the subject of demonology.

1623 FAVINE *Theat. Hon.* II. xiii. 208 Excelled in Demonomanie all them that had gone before them. **1638** SIR. T. HERBERT *Trav.* (ed. 2) 231 They..abolisht their celestiall worship, and (as Strabo relates) received Demonomanie, continued till Mahomet.

†**deˈmonomist.** *Obs.* [f. as DEMONOMY + -IST.] A believer in or worshipper of demons.

1638 SIR T. HERBERT *Trav.* (ed. 2) 302 The idolaters beyond all measure grosse Demonomists. *Ibid.* 329 Celebes ..well peopled, but with bad people; no place ingendring greater Demonomists.

†**demonomy** (dɪˈmɒnəmɪ). *Obs.* [app. shortened from *demononomy*, f. Gr. δαίμων DEMON[1], with ending of *astronomy*, etc.] Belief in demons, demon-worship.

1638 SIR T. HERBERT *Trav.* (ed. 2) 8 Howbeit the divell.. has infused demonomy and prodigious idolatry into their hearts. *Ibid.* 306 Drunk with abominable demonomy and superstition. **1665** *Ibid.* (1677) 365 These Javans are drunk in Demonomy.

demonopathy, -phobia: see DEMONO-.

de-monopolize (diːməˈnɒpəlaɪz), *v.* [f. DE- II. 1 + MONOPOLIZE.] *trans.* To destroy the monopoly of, withdraw from monopoly.

1878 H. A. WEBSTER in *Encycl. Brit.* VI. 154/1 Since the expiry of the contract the mines [of Colombia] have been demonopolized.

demonosopher: see DEMONO-.

demonry (ˈdiːmənrɪ). [f. DEMON[1] + -RY: cf. *devilry*.] Demoniacal influence or practices.

a **1851** JOANNA BAILLIE (O.), What demonry, thinkest thou, possesses Varus?

demonship (ˈdiːmənʃɪp). *rare.* [f. as prec. + -SHIP.] The rank or condition of a demon.

a **1638** MEDE *Apost. Later Times* (1641) 18 They commenced Heroes, who were as Probationers to a Daemonship.

demonstraˈbility. [f. next + -ITY.] The quality or condition of being demonstrable.

1825 COLERIDGE *Aids Refl.* (1873) 161 *note*, The Demonstrability required would countervene all the purposes of the Truth. **1870** M. WILLIAMS *Fuel of Sun* §170. 115 Their spectroscopic demonstrability.

demonstrable (dɪˈmɒnstrəb(ə)l, ˈdɛmən strəb(ə)l), *a.* [ad. L. *dēmonstrābil-is*, f. *dēmonstrāre*: see DEMONSTRATE and -BLE.] Capable of demonstration.

1. Capable of being shown or made evident. †**b.** *occas.* = Evident, apparent (*obs.*).

c **1400** *Rom. Rose* 4691 I wolde..Shewe thee withouten fable A thyng that is not demonstrable. **1530** PALSGR. 309/2 Demonstrable, *demonstrable.* **1604** SHAKS. *Oth.* III. iv. 142 Some vnhatch'd practise, Made demonstrable heere in Cyprus to him, Hath pudled his cleare Spirit. **1647** CLARENDON *Hist. Reb.* VI. (1843) 292/1 That it should be more demonstrable to the kingdom, than yet it was, that the war was, on his majesty's part, purely defensive. **1739** CIBBER *Apol.* (1756) I. 46 In what shape they wou'd severally come out..was not then demonstrable to the deepest foresight. **1867** J. HOGG *Microsc.* II. i. 263 This body without any demonstrable influence of a nucleus is capable of subdividing. **1875** H. C. WOOD *Therap.* (1879) 158 Upon the vaso-motor nerves..[it] has no demonstrable influence.

2. Capable of being proved clearly and conclusively

1551 RECORDE *Pathw. Knowl.* I. xxiv, This is a certaine waye to fynde any touche line, and a demonstrable forme. **1597** HOOKER *Eccl. Pol.* v. lxiii. (1611) 334 All points of Christian doctrine are either demonstrable conclusions or demonstrative principles. **1662** H. MORE *Philos. Writ.* Pref. Gen. (1712) 13 It being so mathematically demonstrable that there is that which is properly called Spirit. **1745** FIELDING *True Patriot* Wks. 1775 IX. 334 With numberless other propositions equally plain and demonstrable. **1864** BOWEN *Logic* xi. 374 Propositions are also said to be demonstrable, if they require or admit of proof.

Hence **deˈmonstrableness** = DEMONSTRABILITY.

1675 J. SMITH *Chr. Relig. Appeal* I. 30 The irrefragable demonstrableness thereof. **1706** S. CLARKE *Evid. Nat. & Rev. Relig.* 282 (L.) The natural demonstrableness both of the obligations and motives of morality.

deˈmonstrably, *adv.* [f. prec. + -LY[2].]

1. In a way which admits of demonstration; so as to be demonstrable.

1642 CHAS. I *Declar. at York* 11 June 6 Orders Evidently and Demonstrably contrary to all known Law and Reason. **1659** HAMMOND *On Ps.* xxxiii. 7 Annot. 180 Demonstrably of a gibbous, circular form. **1732** BERKELEY *Alciphr.* VII. §1 A thing demonstrably and palpably false. **1873** M. ARNOLD *Lit. & Dogma* (1876) 143 They were also demonstrably liable to commit mistakes in argument.

2. In the way of demonstration; by demonstration.

1649 JER. TAYLOR *Gt. Exemp.* II. vi. 11 He who beleeves what is demonstrably proved, is forced by the demonstration of his choice. **1754** EDWARDS *Freed. Will* II. viii. 73 It will demonstrably follow, that the Acts of the Will are never contingent, or without Necessity. **1794** SULLIVAN *View Nat.* I. 76 The calcareous and volcanic matters found in them..prove it demonstrably.

†**deˈmonstrance.** *Obs.* Also 5 -aunce. [a. OF. *demonstrance* (still in Cotgr.), orig. *demustrance*, *demostrance*, f. stem of L. *dēmonstrānt-em*, pr. pple. of *dēmonstrāre*: see -ANCE.]

1. A showing forth or pointing out; manifestation, indication; a sign.

1430 LYDG. *Chron. Troy* IV. xxxv, A fynall demonstraunce Sothfast shewing, and signifyaunce [that]..hap of olde fortune..might not contune. *c* **1430** —— *Min. Poems* (1840) 60 (Mätzn.) The hevenly signe makith demonstraunce How worldly thynges goo forwarde. *c* **1477** CAXTON *Jason* 27 b, They shewid him so many demonstraunces that he..toke upon him the charge. **1481** —— *Godfrey* 246 For demonstraunce that oure lord and his dere moder oure lady shold gyue to them vyctorye, [they] toke the baner of Tancre, and sette it on hye vpon the chirche of oure lady. **1594** CAREW *Tasso* (1881) 12 He plaine demonstrance gaue, Th' allowance longs to you, sole t' adde I haue. **1627** BP. M. WREN *Serm.* 11 What demonstrance withall he must make of the same. **1704** D'URFEY *Royal Converts* 252 Blessings sublunary prove The kind demonstrances of Gracious Love.

2. Demonstration; proof.

1481 CAXTON *Myrr.* III. xviii. 175 In lyke wyse preuyd they..by very demonstraunce and by reson, that the Sonne is gretter than alle therthe is. **1603** HOLLAND *Plutarch's Mor.* 303 (R.) Good reasons and demonstrances of how many calamities peevish obstinacy is the cause. **1646** R. JUNIUS *Cure Misprision* (L.), If one or a few sinfull acts were a sufficient demonstrance of an hypocrite, what would become of all the elect?

3. Setting forth of a plaintiff's case; = DEMONSTRATION 4.

[**1292** BRITTON III. xxvi. §6 Par variaunce del bref et de la demoustraunce seroit le bref abatable.] **1625** DARCIE *Annales* A iij [transl. from Fr.], The aduises and counsailes, the requests and demonstrances.

deˈmonstrant. [f. L. *dēmonstrānt-em*, pr. pple. of *dēmonstrāre*: see -ANT.] One who demonstrates or takes part in a public demonstration.

1868 *Pall Mall G.* 18 Aug. 3 The demonstrants would, in any case, have been obliged to seek shelter. **1887** *Scott. Leader* 14 Nov. 5 Mingling with the more respectable part of the demonstrants are a great many roughs.

ˈdemonstratable, *a. rare.* [f. DEMONSTRATE *v.* + -ABLE.] = DEMONSTRABLE.

1865 HERSCHEL in *Fortn. Rev.* July 440 (*Origin of Force*) It is a fact dynamically demonstratable.

†**deˈmonstrate,** *a.* and *sb.* *Obs.* [ad. L. *dēmonstrāt-us*, pa. pple. of *dēmonstrāre*: see prec.] Demonstrated. **a.** as *pa. pple.*

1571 DIGGES *Pantom.* IV. xxv. G g b, Manyfolde mo.. proportions than may..(I will not saye be demonstrate, but onely by Theoremes) be declared. **1605** BACON *Adv. Learn.* I. v. §2 The propositions of Euclyde..till they bee demonstrate, they seeme strange to our assent. **1671** *True Nonconf.* 305, I have already demonstrat, in the second Dialogue, that [etc.]. **1707** E. WARD *Hudibras Rediv.* I. xv, Human knowledge first commences From Things demonstrate to our Senses.

b. as *adj.*

1509 HAWES *Past. Pleas.* VIII. viii, And by scripture wyll make demonstrate Outwardly accordynge to the thought. **1632** LITHGOW *Trav.* I. 7 O! a plaine demonstrate cause, and a good resolution.

sb. A demonstrated proposition or truth.

1655–60 STANLEY *Hist. Philos.* (1701) 181/2 Of Analysis there are three kinds, one..whereby we ascend by demonstrates and subdemonstrates, to indemonstrable immediate propositions.

demonstrate (dɪˈmɒnstreɪt, ˈdɛmənstreɪt), *v.* [f. L. *dēmonstrāt-*, ppl. stem of *dēmonstrāre* to point out, show, prove, f. DE- I. 3 + *monstrāre* to show, point out. For the shifting of the stress see CONTEMPLATE. Both pronunciations appear in Shaks.]

†**1.** *trans.* To point out, indicate; to exhibit, set forth. *Obs.* Const. *simple obj.* or *obj. clause.* (So in the other trans. senses.)

1552 HULOET, Demonstrate, *indico, monstro.* **1563** SHUTE *Archit.* D ij b, In the which bodye of the pedestall is demonstrated Ichnographia. **1599** SHAKS. *Hen. V*, IV. ii. 54 Description cannot sute it selfe in words, To demonstrate the Life of such a Battaile. *a* **1633** AUSTIN *Medit.* (1635) 90 That the Starre stooped downe to Earth and sent forth greater and clearer Beames then before to demonstrate not onely the Place, but the very Child. **1650** CROMWELL *Let.* 4 Sept., Coming to our quarters at night, and demonstrating our apprehensions to some of the colonels, they also cheerfully concurred. **1684** R. H. *School Recreat.* 148 We come next to demonstrate the Time not proper, i.e. Unseasonable Angling..is when [etc.].

†**2.** To make known or exhibit by outward indications; to manifest, show, display. *Obs.*

1599 A. M. tr. *Gabelhouer's Bk. Physicke* 312/1 If..it be the Canker, it will after the third time demonstrate it selfe with a little knobbe or tumor. **1600** Shaks. *A. Y. L.* iii. ii. 400 Euerie thing about you, demonstrating a carelesse desolation. **1634** Sir T. Herbert *Trav.* 157 They be very apt on prompt occasions, to demonstrate valour and resolution. **1653** H. Cogan tr. *Pinto's Trav.* xxviii. 111 By this Figure these Idolaters would demonstrate that she was the Queen of the fiery sphear. **1734** tr. *Rollin's Anc. Hist.* (1827) I. 99 No people ever demonstrated such extent of genius. **1803** Wellington in Owen *Desp.* 224 His Highness has demonstrated the most implicit confidence in the protection of the British power.

b. To express (one's feelings) demonstratively.

1855 Thackeray *Newcomes* II. 339 Paul was a personage who demonstrated all his sentiments, and performed his various parts in life with the greatest vigour.

3. To describe and explain by help of a specimen or specimens, or by experiment, as a method of teaching a science, e.g. anatomy, chemistry; also *absol.* to teach as a demonstrator.

1683 Robinson in *Ray's Corr.* (1848) 133 Monsieur Tournefort, a Languedoc man..demonstrates now the plants in the King's Garden here. **1856** Dove *Logic Chr. Faith* Introd. §2. 2 *note*, The anatomist demonstrates, when he points out matters of fact cognisable by the senses. *a* **1859** De Quincey in H. A. Page *Life* (1877) II. xx. 307 They will do me too much honour by 'demonstrating' on such a crazy body as mine.

4. To show or make evident by reasoning; to establish the truth of (a proposition, etc.) by a process of argument or deduction; to prove beyond the possibility of doubt.

1571 Digges *Pantom.* i. xx. Fiijb, This Lemma..or proposition I minde to demonstrate. **1646** Sir T. Browne *Pseud. Ep.* i. ix, Archimedes demonstrates..that the proportion of the Diameter unto the Circumference is as 7 almost unto 22. **1691** Ray *Creation* (1701) 43 The best medium we have to demonstrate the Being of a Deity. **1754** Sherlock *Disc.* (1759) I. iv. 153 Few Workmen can demonstrate the mechanic Powers of the Instruments they use. **1814** D'Israeli *Quarrels Auth.* (1867) 355 What others conjectured, and some discovered, Harvey demonstrated. **1860** Tyndall *Glac.* ii. xxx. 404 The existence of this state of strain may be demonstrated.

b. *absol.*

1604 Shaks. *Oth.* iii. iii. 431 This may helpe to thicken other proofes, That do demonstrate thinly. **1669** Gale *Crt. Gentiles* i. Introd. 4 A Mathematician, whose office it is to demonstrate. **1867** J. Martineau *Ess.* II. 46 Euclid had to demonstrate before there could be a philosophy of geometry.

c. Of things: To prove.

1601 Shaks. *All's Well* i. ii. 47 A copie to these yonger times; Which followed well, would demonstrate them now But goers backward. **1802** Paley *Nat. Theol.* iii. (1819) 18 It is a matter which experience and observation demonstrate. **1860** Tyndall *Glac.* ii. xvii. 324 The crevassing of the eastern side of the glacier..does not..demonstrate its slower motion.

5. *intr.* To make a military demonstration; to make or take part in a public demonstration.

1827 *Examiner* 297/1 The Spanish army has been so long allowed to demonstrate on the Portuguese frontier. **1882** *Blackw. Mag.* July 13 There is not water enough for us to go and demonstrate inside the bay. **1888** Bryce *Amer. Commw.* II. iii. lxxiii. 604 The habit of demonstrating with bands and banners and emblems.

†**b.** *trans.* (*causal.*) *Obs. rare*$^{-1}$.

1803 Nelson in Nicolas *Desp.* V. 71, I have demonstrated the Victory off Brest, and am now going to seek the Admiral in the ocean.

Hence **demonstrated** *ppl. a.*, **demonstratedly** *adv.*, **demonstrating** *vbl. sb.* and *ppl. a.*

1650 B. *Discolliminium* 20 There are demonstrating and determining Providences. **1676** Newton in *Phil. Trans.* XI. 703 To examine a demonstrated proposition. **1678** Cudworth *Intell. Syst.* 145 (R.) A clear foundation for the demonstrating of a Deity distinct from the corporeal world. **1881** Froude *High Ch. Revival, Short Stud.* Ser. iv. (1883) 213 A holy life, it was demonstratedly plain to me, was no monopoly of the sacramental system. **1888** *Daily News* 4 June 3/1 Demonstrating bodies from all parts of London.. assembled on the Embankment.

demonstration (dɛmən'streɪʃən). [ad. L. *dēmonstrātiōn-em*, n. of action from *dēmonstrāre* to demonstrate: perh. immed. a. F. *démonstration* (14th c. in Oresme), a refashioning of OF. *demustreison, -aison*, intermediate form *demonstroison*.]

†**1. a.** The action of showing forth or exhibiting; making known, pointing out; exhibition, manifestation; also an instance of this. *Obs.*

1393 Gower *Conf.* II. 368 By demonstracion The man was founde with the good. **14..** *Epiph.* in *Tundale's Vis.* 117 Of a schynyng by demonstracyon Is *fanos* seyd. **1530** Palsgr. 146 Of adverbes..Some betoken demonstration & serve to shewe or poynt to a dede. **1568** Grafton *Chron.* II. 172 For the open apparaunce, and demonstracion of this godly concorde. *a* **1633** W. Austin *Medit.* (1635) 177 Christ preaching to save him [St. Thomas]..shewes himselfe (by demonstration) unto him. **1668** R. Wallis (*title*), Room for the Cobler of Gloucester and his Wife, with Several Cartloads of Abominable, Irregular, Pitiful, Stinking Priests, also a Demonstration of their Calling.

b. Outward exhibition of feeling.

1873 H. Spencer *Stud. Sociol.* xv. 358 Demonstration, be it in movements that rise finally to spasms and contortions, or be it in sounds that end in laughter and shrieks and groans.

†**c.** That by which something is shown or made known; an illustration; a sign, indication. *Obs.*

1559 W. Cunningham *Cosmogr. Glasse* Pref. Avjb, Divisinge sundry newe Tables, Pictures, demonstrations and præceptes. **1563** Shute *Archit.* Bija, Makynge demonstrations to a Latine worke with Greke letters. **1684** R. H. *School Recreat.* 130 Cock Fighting..A Scarlet Head is a Demonstration of Courage, but a Pale and Wan of Faintness..[These qualities] are Demonstrations of Excellency and Courage.

2. A display, show, manifestation, exhibition, expression. †**a.** *absol.* (*obs.*); **b.** with *of.*

a. 1556 *Aurelio & Isab.* (1608) C, With my tormented demonstrations and great boldnes..I overcame hir. **1632** J. Hayward tr. *Biondi's Eromena* 136 Beleeving those affectionate-seeming demonstrations to be really true. **1653** H. Cogan tr. *Pinto's Trav.* iv. 11 We gave them a great peal of Ordnance..beating our Drums, and sounding our Trumpets, to the end that by these exterior demonstrations they might conclude we regarded not the Turks awhit.

b. 1605 Shaks. *Lear* iv. iii. 12 Did your letters pierce the queen to any demonstration of grief? **1769** Robertson *Chas. V*, II. iv. 252 Great were the outward demonstrations of love and confidence between the two Monarchs. **1855** Prescott *Philip II*, I. ii. 14 She seemed to think any demonstration of suffering a weakness.

3. a. The action or process of demonstrating or making evident by reasoning; the action of proving beyond the possibility of doubt by a process of argument or logical deduction or by practical proof; clear or indubitable proof; also (with *pl.*) an argument or series of propositions proving an asserted conclusion.

to demonstration: to the certainty of a demonstrated and indisputable fact; conclusively.

c **1386** Chaucer *Sompn. T.* 516 In ars metrik schal þer no man fynde..of such a questioun Who schulde make a demonstracioun. **1553** Eden *Treat. New Ind.* To Rdr. (Arb.) 10 Most certayne and apparente demonstracions of Geometrye. **1563** Man *Musculus' Commonpl.* 141 a, Not meete for any wise body to beleue the word of matters vnknowen, set forth without any Syllogisticall demonstration. **1650** T. Rudd *Pract. Geom.* Biv, A Hundred Questions with their Solutions and Demonstrations. **1690** Locke *Hum. Und.* iv. ii. (1695) 305 Those intervening Ideas, which serve to shew the agreement of any two others, are called Proofs; and where the agreement, or disagreement is by this means plainly and clearly perceived, it is called Demonstration, it being shewn to the Understanding, and the Mind made see that it is so. **1730** Southall *Bugs* 25 'Tis apparent to a Demonstration, that from every Pair..about two hundred Eggs..are produced. **1876** Jevons *Elem. Logic* (1880) 335 A demonstration is either *Direct* or *Indirect*. In the latter case we prove the conclusion by disproving the contradictory, or shewing that the conclusion cannot be supposed untrue. **1878** Bosw. Smith *Carthage* 236 He proved to demonstration the soundness of the judgment he had formed.

b. That which serves as proof or evidence; an indubitable proof.

c **1374** Chaucer *Boeth.* ii. iv. 44 It haþ ben shewid and proued by ful manye demonstraciouns as I woot wel þat þe soules of men ne mowen nat dien in no wise. **1659** *Vulgar Errors Cens.* 31 The Circulation of the Blood is a Demonstration of an Eternall Being. **1696** tr. *Du Mont's Voy. Levant* 18 Found nothing..but a Book of Psalms, which was a sufficient Demonstration..that I had been a Hugonot. **1726** *Adv. Capt. R. Boyle* 269 Told me..I should have Demonstration of her Infidelity. **1804** Wellington in Owen *Desp.* 630 Additional demonstrations of those views have appeared since the renewal of the war.

4. *Rom. Law.* The statement of the cause of action by the plaintiff in presenting his case.

1864 J. N. Pomeroy *Introd. Munic. Law* i. ii. 107 The formula commenced with a part called..Demonstration (*demonstratio*) which contained a short statement of the plaintiff's cause of action. **1880** Muirhead *Gaius* iv. §40 The demonstration is that part of the formula which is inserted at the outset on purpose to show what is the matter in dispute.

5. The exhibition and explanation of specimens and practical operations, as a method of instruction in a science or art, *esp.* in anatomy. Also *attrib.*

1807 *Med. Jrnl.* XVII. 95 Mr. Taunton will resume his Winter Course of Lectures and Demonstrations on Anatomy, Physiology, Pathology, and Surgery. **1832** *Examiner* 395/1 On Monday there was a demonstration on the viscera by Mr. Grainger. **1883** *Longman's Notes on Bks.* vi. 204 (*Buckton's Food & Home Cookery*), The course consists of fifteen lessons, twelve to be given by demonstration followed by practice..Every girl who attends the whole course will have twelve Demonstration and fourteen Practice lessons. *Mod.* Miss H. will give a Cookery Demonstration.

6. *Mil.* A show of military force or of offensive movement; *esp.* in the course of active hostilities to engage the enemy's attention while other operations are going on elsewhere, or in time of peace to indicate readiness for active hostilities.

1835 Burnes *Trav. Bokhara* (ed. 2) III. 265 He made last year a demonstration against Julalabad, a district between Cabool and Peshawur. **1853** Sir H. Douglas *Milit. Bridges* (ed. 3) 205 Prince Eugene..made demonstrations to attack the post of Masi, and to cross the Adige to Badia..[He] continued his demonstrations at Masi, until he heard that Colonel Batté had succeeded in throwing 500 men across the river. **1862** Ld. Brougham *Brit. Const.* xiii. 178 The Barons having, by an armed demonstration, compelled the King to allow the appointment.

7. A public manifestation, by a number of persons, of interest in some public question, or sympathy with some political or other cause; usually taking the form of a procession and mass-meeting.

1839 *Britannia* in *Spirit Metropol. Conserv. Press* (1840) I. 421 Whig emissaries have been employed to get up what, in their own conventional cant, they call a demonstration, to mark the national joy [etc.]. **1861** *Sat. Rev.* 22 June 630 Then, besides 'ovations', there are 'demonstrations', the Q.E.D. of which is not always very easy to see. We read how the students of such an University 'made a demonstration'. This we believe means, in plain English, that the students kicked up a row. **1884** *Chr. World* 16 Oct. 781/1 The demonstration of demonstrations took place on Saturday at Chatsworth, when..about 80,000 people came together.

8. *attrib.*, chiefly in sense 5.

1883 [see sense 5 above]. **1899** *Westm. Gaz.* 16 June 4/1 The demonstration farm of the Northumberland County Council at Cockle Park. **1902** E. Lanteri *Modelling* 1 The notes of which I made use for my demonstration-classes at the Royal College of Art. **1902** *Brit. Forestry: Dept. Cttee. Rep.* 9 in *Parl. Papers* (Cd. 1319) XX, That two areas for practical demonstration be acquired... We suggest that the Alice Holt Woods in Hampshire be made available as soon as possible to serve as a Demonstration Area. **1907** *Westm. Gaz.* 22 May 12/2 The Board of Education recognises gardening as a school subject... To each school is allotted a demonstration plot, which is used by the teacher for object-lessons. **1908** J. J. Findlay (*title*) The Demonstration Schools Record. **1909** *Westm. Gaz.* 26 Jan. 4/1 To..give demonstration flights. **1943** J. S. Huxley *TVA* viii. 52 The TVA..set up five demonstration parks in the Valley. **1961** W. Vaughan-Thomas *Anzio* viii. 156 Hitler sent from Germany a special regiment, the Infantry Lehr Regiment, a demonstration unit composed of approved Nazis. **1970** J. Holt *Underachieving School* 186 It may very well be that in such schools we will have the kind of educational laboratory and demonstration centers which in your country, I guess, are supplied by many of the State schools.

demonstrational (-'eɪʃənəl), *a.* [f. prec. + -al^{1}.] Of or pertaining to demonstration.

1866 *Pall Mall G.* 1 Dec. 13 A leaning to the demonstrational view both of literature and oratory. **1886** Gurney *Phantasms of Living* II. 3 [It] connects the sleeping and the waking phenomena in their theoretic and psychological aspects, it..separates them in their demonstrational aspect.

† **demon'strationer.** *Obs. rare*$^{-1}$. [f. as prec. + -er.] One who favours or practises demonstration.

1589 *Almond for Parrat* 15 Your olde soaking Demonstrationer, that hath scrapte vp such a deale of Scripture to so lyttle purpose.

demonstrationist (-'eɪʃənɪst). [f. as prec. + -ist.] One who takes part in a demonstration.

1871 *Echo* 15 Aug., A riot between the Orangemen and the demonstrationists is considered likely. **1890** *Times* 28 Jan. 5/3 Demonstrationists nowadays dislike wet weather.

demon'strationize, *v.* [See -ize.] *intr.* To make a public demonstration.

Hence **demon'strationizing** *vbl. sb.*

1882 *St. James's Gaz.* 28 June, The history of our recent demonstrationizings.

demonstrative (dɪ'mɒnstrətɪv), *a.* and *sb.* In 5 -if. [a. F. *démonstratif, -ive* (14th c. in Hatzf.), ad. L. *dēmonstrātīv-us*, f. ppl. stem of L. *dēmonstrāre*: see -ive.]

1. Having the function or quality of clearly showing, exhibiting, or indicating; making evident; illustrative.

demonstrative legacy: see quot. 1892.

1530 Palsgr. 309/2 Demonstratyfe, *demonstratif*. **1551** T. Wilson *Logike* (1580) 27 b, A demonstrative, or shewyng reduction. **1616** R. Waller in *Lismore Papers* (1887) Ser. ii. II. 19 Some demonstrative token proportionable to the large favor wherwithall you haue vouchsafed to giue me. *a* **1700** Dryden (J.), Painting is necessary to all other arts, because of the need which they have of demonstrative figures, which often give more light to the understanding than the clearest discourses. **1892** Goodeve *Mod. Law of Real Prop.* 394 A demonstrative legacy is one which is in its nature a general legacy, but is directed by the testator to be paid out of a particular fund.

2. *Rhet.* Setting forth or describing with praise or censure.

1553 T. Wilson *Rhet.* 6 b, The oracion demonstratiue standeth either in praise or dispraise of some one man, or of some one thyng. **1576** Fleming *Panopl. Epist.* Epit. A, An epistle demonstrative consisteth in these two points, namely, commendation and dispraise. *a* **1677** Barrow *Pope's Suprem.* (1687) 72 Eloquent men do never more exceed in their indulgence to fancy, than in the demonstrative kind..in their commendations of persons. **1783** H. Blair *Rhetoric* xxvii. II. 46 The chief subjects of Demonstrative Eloquence, were Panegyrics, Invectives, Gratulatory and Funeral Orations.

3. *Gram.* Serving to point out or indicate the particular thing referred to: applied *esp.* to certain adjectives (often used pronominally) having this function.

demonstrative root: a linguistic root which appears to have had no other signification than that of pointing to a near or remote object, as the *t-* in Sanskrit *tat, tadā*, Gr. *τό, τότε*, L. *tam, tunc*, or its Teutonic representative *þ, th*, in *the, then, there*.

1520 Whitinton *Vulg.* (1527) 5 b, Whan a nowne demonstrative is referred to ye hole sentence folowynge. **1530** Palsgr. Introd. 29 Pronownes demonstratyves they have but thre *il*, *le* and *on* or *len*. **1668** WILKINS *Real Char.* III. ii. §3. 305 As *this* or *that* man or book..in these cases the Pronouns are commonly called Demonstrative. **1835** MRS. MARCET *Mary's Gram.* II. ix. 250 When we use the demonstrative pronoun, it seems as if we were pointing our finger to show the things we were speaking of. **1865** TYLOR *Early Hist. Man.* iv. 61 The demonstrative roots, a small class of independent radicals. **1892** DAVIDSON *Heb. Gram.* (ed. 10) 81 The letter *n*, having demonstrative force, is often inserted.

4. That shows or makes manifest the truth or existence *of* anything; serving as conclusive evidence.

c **1386** CHAUCER *Sompn. T.* 564 Ye shul seen..By preeue which that is demonstratif, That equally the soun of it wol wende..vn-to the spokes ende. **1570–6** LAMBARDE *Peramb. Kent* (1826) 301 The vertue of holy water (in putting the Divell to flight) was confirmed at Motindene by a demonstrative argument. **1647** N. BACON *Disc. Govt. Eng.* I. iii. (1739) 5 The first of which is cried down by many demonstrative instances. **1691** RAY *Creation* (1714) 18 A demonstrative proof..of the fecundity of His wisdom and Power. **1807** G. CHALMERS *Caledonia* I. I. iv. 117 These military works..are equally demonstrative of their skill, and creditable to their perseverance. **1855** *Ess. Intuit. Mor.* ii. 43 Another point..demonstrative of God's providence.

5. That serves to demonstrate logically; belonging to logical demonstration.

1477 EARL RIVERS (Caxton) *Dictes* 124 Galyen..in hys youth he desired greetly to knowe the science demonstratiue. **1581** MULCASTER *Positions* xli. (1887) 244 Logicke, for her demonstratiue part, plaieth the Grammer to the Mathematicalles. **1624** DE LAWNE tr. *Du Moulin's Logick* 163 A demonstrative Syllogisme as that which prooveth that the attribute of the conclusion is truely attributed unto the subject. **1736** BUTLER *Anal.* Introd. Wks. (1874) I. 1 Probable evidence is essentially distinguished from demonstrative by this, that it admits of degrees. **1864** BOWEN *Logic* ii. 34 Logic, as it proceeds from axiomatic principles,..is a purely demonstrative science.

6. Characterized or produced by demonstration; evident or provable by demonstration.

1612 T. WILSON *Chr. Dict.*, To bee infallibly assured of a thing, by demonstratiue certainety. **1665** SIR T. HERBERT *Trav.* (1677) 188 'Tis demonstrative that salt waters have much more heat than fresh waters have. **1798** MALTHUS *Popul.* (1878) 295 It is a demonstrative truth. **1863** MRS. C. CLARKE *Shaks. Char.* iv. 106 We have passed into an age of practicality and demonstrative knowledge.

7. Given to, or characterized by, outward exhibition or expression (of the feelings, etc.).

1819 *Metropolis* III. 252 No fulsomeness of public and demonstrative tenderness, on his part, ever puts me to the blush. **1832** *Examiner* 241/2 The middle party in the House have been sufficiently demonstrative of their purposes. **1863** MRS. C. CLARKE *Shaks. Char.* v. 124 The demonstrative gratitude of his heart. **1872** DARWIN *Emotions* xi. 265 Englishmen are much less demonstrative than the men of most other European nations.

8. That teaches a science by the exhibition and description of examples or experiments. *rare.* Cf. DEMONSTRATOR 2.

1814 *Philos. Mag.* XLIV. 305 (*title*) Demonstrative Course of Lectures on Drs. Gall and Spurzheim's Physiognomonical System.

B. *sb. Gram.* A demonstrative adjective or pronoun.

1530 PALSGR. 75 Demonstratives simple is only *ce*. **1591** PERCIVALL *Sp. Dict.* B iv a, Of pronounes..some are called demonstratiues, because they shew a thing not spoken of before. **1833** MᶜHENRY *Span. Gram.* 42 Possessives and demonstratives are used in Spanish both as adjectives and as pronouns. **1875** R. MORRIS *Eng. Gram.* (1877) 114 The Demonstratives are *the, that, this, such, so, same, yon.*

de'monstratively, *adv.* [f. prec. + -LY[2].] In a demonstrative manner.

†**1.** In a manner that points out, shows, or exhibits; so as to indicate clearly or plainly. *Obs.*

1571 GOLDING *Calvin on Ps.* lii. 9 The adverb behold is taken here demonstratively as if David shuld bring forth upon a stage the miserable end that remayneth for the proud despysers of God. **1676** MOXON *Print Lett.* 52 The Letters ..are..demonstratively laid down on the Plain. **1677** HALE *Prim. Orig. Man.* II. iv. 152 The new discoveries of Stars and Asterisms..by the help of the Telescope, demonstratively and to the sense.

2. In a way that makes manifest, establishes, or proves the truth or existence of anything; *spec.* by logical demonstration.

1584 FENNER *Def. Ministers* (1587) 63 What soeuer bee demonstratiuelie concluded out of the Scriptures. **1678** CUDWORTH *Intell. Syst.* 234 Able to discourse Demonstratively concerning the same. **1772** SWINTON in *Phil. Trans.* LXIII. 214 As I have elsewhere demonstratively proved. **1885** *Manch. Exam.* 22 June 5/4 The thing can be done..as..Pel has demonstratively shown.

†**3.** With clear or convincing evidence, conclusively. *Obs.*

1646 SIR T. BROWNE *Pseud. Ep.* 39 Plato and Aristotle.. demonstratively understanding the simplicity of perfection, and the indivisible condition of the first causator. **1764** WARBURTON *Lett.* (1809) 353, I was as demonstratively certain of the Author, as if I had stood behind him.

4. With strong outward exhibition of feeling.

1871 HOLME LEE *Miss Barrington* I. x. 149 Met them with a demonstratively agreeable air, and tried to engage them in talk.

de'monstrativeness. [f. as prec. + -NESS.] The quality of being demonstrative.

a **1660** HAMMOND *Wks.* II. IV. 178 (R.) [It] supersedes all demonstrativeness of proof from this text for the criminousness of will-worship. **1664** H. MORE *Myst. Iniq.* xii. 40 Nor can the demonstrativeness of this Reason be eluded. **1863** J. C. MORISON *St. Bernard* II. i. 183 There was no..weak, undisciplined demonstrativeness in their joy.

demonstrator ('dɛmənstreɪtə(r)). [ad. L. *dēmonstrātor*, agent-n. from *dēmonstrāre* to DEMONSTRATE; partly after F. *démonstrateur*, 14th c, in Hatzf. (So pronounced by Smart 1836; Walker gave *de'monstrator* in the general sense, *demon'strator* in the technical.)]

1. One who or that which demonstrates, points out, or proves.

1611 COTGR., *Demonstrateur*, a demonstrator; one that euidently shewes, plainely declares, perspicuously deliuers things. **1666** J. SMITH *Old Age* 66 (T.) The instruments of them both are the best demonstrators of human strength. **1775** JOHNSON *Tax. no Tyr.* 2 The demonstrator will find, after an operose deduction, that he has been trying to make that seen which can be only felt. **1825** COLERIDGE *Aids Refl.* (1848) I. 140 In all these demonstrations the demonstrators presuppose the idea or conception of a God.

2. One who exhibits and describes specimens, or performs experiments, as a method of teaching a science; an assistant to a professor of science, who does the practical work with the students.

1684 RAY *Corr.* (1848) 139 [A book] to facilitate the learning of plants, if need be, without a guide or demonstrator. **1758** J. S. *Le Dran's Observ. Surg.* Introd. (1771) 5 Six Demonstrators in Surgery, at the Amphitheatre of St. Cosme. **1792** A. YOUNG *Trav. France* 137 Mr. Willemet, who is demonstrator of botany, shewed me the botanical garden. **1887** *Men of the Time* 234 He [Sir Andrew Clark] was demonstrator of anatomy to Dr. Robert Knox.

3. One who takes part in a public demonstration.

1870 *Daily News* 9 Oct., Another demonstration took place to urge the Government not to make peace..An evasive answer was given to these demonstrators. **1890** *Times* 13 Feb. 5/2 The demonstrators..assembled in front of the statue of Henry IV, in order to place a wreath on it.

4. 'The index-finger'. *Syd. Soc. Lex.*

Hence **'demon,stratorship**, the office or position of a scientific demonstrator.

1870 *Athenæum* 14 May 642 A Syndicate..recommended the establishment of a Professorship and Demonstratorship of Experimental Physics.

de'monstratory, *a.* [ad. L. *dēmonstrātōrius* (Isidore), f. *dēmonstrātor*: see -ORY.] That has the property of demonstrating.

1727 BAILEY vol. II, *Demonstratory*, belonging to demonstration. **1817** COLEBROOKE *Algebra* xxvi, The gloss of Ranganátha on the Vásaná, or demonstratory annotations of Bháscara. **1880** MUIRHEAD *Gaius* IV. §60 The matter in dispute is first set forth in a demonstratory manner.

demont, obs. form of DEMOUNT, q.v.

'demo,nurgist. *rare.* [f. Gr. type *δαιμονουργός demon-working + -IST. Cf. *metallurgist*, etc.] One who practises magic by the help of demons. So **'demonurgy**, the practice of magic by the help of demons.

1797 W. TAYLOR in *Monthly Rev.* XXIV. 509 Agrippa and his friends had a taste for the occult sciences, for alchemy, divination, dæmonurgy, and astrology. **1798** *Ibid.* XXV. 502 Dæmonurgists and other professors of occult science.

demonymic (diːməʊˈnɪmɪk), *a.* and *sb.* [f. Gr. δῆμος people, DEME + -ωνυμικός adj. formative, f. ὄνομα name: cf. *patronymic.*] *adj.* Named from the deme. *sb.* The name (of an Athenian citizen) according to the deme to which he belonged.

1893 J. E. SANDYS *Aristotle's Ἀθηναίων Πολιτεία* 110 The demonymic of the former would be Ὀαθεν; of the latter Οἰῆθεν.

demoore, obs. form of DEMUR *v.*

demophil ('dɛməʊfɪl). [mod. f. Gr. δῆμ-ος people + φίλος friend.] A friend of the people.

1884 HUNTER & WHYTE *My Ducats* xxvii. (1885) 426 A man may be a democrat without being a demophile.

Hence **demophilism**.

1871 LD. HOUGHTON in *Life* (1890) II. xvii. 253 A demon not of demagoguism, but of demophilism. **1893** P. MILYOUKOV in *Athenæum* 1 July 27/2 A vague interest in the lives and habits of the masses, a sort of archæological demophilism.

demor(e, demorage, etc., obs. ff. DEMUR, DEMURRAGE, etc.

demoralization (dɪˌmɒrəlaɪˈzeɪʃən). [f. next + -ATION: so mod.F. *démoralisation*, admitted by the Acad. 1878.] The action of demoralizing; the state or fact of being demoralized.

1809 SOUTHEY in *Q. Rev.* II. 115 It would be easy to shew ..that the religion of the Koran necessarily produces this demoralization. **1877** *Daily News* 5 Nov. 5/5 His army is in a state of utter demoralisation and disorganization.

demoralize (dɪˈmɒrəlaɪz), *v.* [a. F. *démoralise-r* (f. DE- II. 1 + MORAL *a.* + -IZE), a word of the French Revolution, condemned by Laharpe, admitted by the Acad. 1798.]

1. *trans.* To corrupt the morals or moral principles of; to deprave or pervert morally.

c **1793** WEBSTER in Lyell *Trav. N. Amer.* I. 65 When.. Noah Webster..was asked how many new words he had coined, he replied only 'to demoralize', and that not in his dictionary, but long before in a pamphlet published in the last century [about 1793]. **1808** SOUTHEY *Lett.* (1856) II. 105 One of the worst principled men who ever lent his aid to debase, demoralize, and debilitate human nature. **1874** MORLEY *Compromise* (1886) 102 People..demoralised by the habit of looking at society exclusively from the juridical point of view.

b. To deprive (a thing) of its moral influence or effectiveness.

1869 *Spectator* 24 July 863 In a case where this sort of protestation of innocence,—tending to demoralize the gallows,—appeals to the passions of the people.

2. To lower or destroy the power of bearing up against dangers, fatigue, or difficulties (F. *le moral*: see MORALE): applied *esp.* to an army or a people under arms; also *transf.* to take from anything its firmness, staying power, etc.

1848 GALLENGA *Italy* II. ii. 39 Foscolo was intended for a man of action and strife: ease and fortune unnerved and demoralised him. **1874** GREEN *Short Hist.* vi. §1. 270 The long series of English victories had..demoralized the French soldiery. **1894** *Daily News* 2 June 3/7 The market became demoralized owing to foreign advices, heavy liquidations, foreign selling, and better crop news.

Hence **de'moralized, de'moralizing** *ppl. adjs.*

1808 *Crit. Rev.* Aug. (T.), The pernicious influence of their demoralizing creed. **1817** J. SCOTT *Paris Revisit.* (ed. 4) 401 The demoralized state of the public character. **1871** MORLEY *Voltaire* (1886) 133 Miracles..have necessarily a very demoralising effect.

demoralizer (dɪˈmɒrəlaɪzə(r)). [f. prec. + -ER.] A person or thing that demoralizes.

1881 *Voice* (N.Y.) 25 Aug. 1 It [rum traffic] is the general demoralizer. **1892** *Catholic News* 8 Oct. p. vi/6 Licenced demoralizers surrounded by admiring crowds.

demoralizingly (diːˈmɒrəlaɪzɪŋlɪ), *adv.* [f. DEMORALIZING *ppl. a.* + -LY[2].] In a demoralizing manner; to a demoralizing degree.

1926 W. J. LOCKE *Old Bridge* IV. xii, It seemed..so demoralizingly vicious to drink a friend's cocktails or whisky behind closed doors.

demorance, -aunce, demore: see DEMURRANCE, DEMUR.

De Morgan's laws (dəˈmɔːgən). *Logic* and *Math.* [Named after the English mathematician Augustus *De Morgan* (1806–71), but known to logicians in the Middle Ages.] Two laws of the propositional calculus, viz. that the negation of a conjunction is logically equivalent to the alternation of the negations of the conjoined expressions, and that the negation of an alternation is logically equivalent to the conjunction of the negations of the alternated expressions; also, the analogous truths in the algebra of classes. Symbolically, $\sim(p.q) \equiv \sim p \vee \sim q$ and $\sim(p \vee q) \equiv \sim p.\sim q$. Also, **De Morgan's theorem(s); De Morgan** *absol.*

1918 C. I. LEWIS *Survey Symbolic Logic* ii. 125, 3.4 and 3.41 together state De Morgan's Theorem. **1932** —— & C. H. LANGFORD *Symb. Logic* ii. 33 These always follow from their correlates by some use of De Morgan's Theorem. **1950** W. V. QUINE *Methods of Logic* (1952) §10. 53 De Morgan's laws are useful in enabling us to avoid negating conjunctions and alternations. **1957** P. SUPPES *Introd. Logic* ix. 205 Equations (23) and (24) are De Morgan's laws. **1965** P. CAWS *Philos. Sci.* xlii. 325 Which by De Morgan is seen to be equivalent.

demorlayk: see DEMERLAYK *Obs.*, magic.

‖**demos** ('diːmɒs). Occas. **demus.** *pl.* -i. [a. Gr. δῆμος district, people.]

1. One of the divisions of ancient Attica; = DEME[2] 1.

1776 R. CHANDLER *Trav. Greece* 19 (Stanford) A demos or borough-town. *Ibid.* 36 Hipparchus erected them in the demi or borough-towns.

2. The people or commons of an ancient Greek state, *esp.* of a democratic state, such as Athens; hence, the populace, the common people: often personified.

1831 *Westm. Rev.* Jan. 245 The aristocracy have had their long and disastrous day; it is now the time of the Demos. **1847** GROTE *Greece* II. xxxvi, The self-acting Dêmos assembled in the Pnyx. **1886** TENNYSON *Locksley Hall Sixty Yrs. After* 90 Celtic Demos rose a Demon, shriek'd and slaked the light with blood.

Demosthenic (dɛmɒsˈθɛnɪk), *a.* [ad. Gr. Δημοσθενικ-ός.] Of or pertaining to Demosthenes, the great Athenian orator; resembling Demosthenes or his style of oratory. So also **Demosthe'nean** [cf. Gr. Δημοσθένειος], **Demos'thenian** *adjs.*

a **1739** C. JARVIS tr. *Cervantes's Don Quixote* (1742) II. II. xv. 169 An enterprize worthy to employ..Ciceronian and Demosthenian rhetoric. **1807** J. MACKINTOSH *Jrnl.* 15 Jan. in *Life* (1835) I. 323 He [*sc.* Fox] was the most Demosthenean speaker since Demosthenes. **1821** SHELLEY *Let.* 22 Oct. (1964) II. 360, I congratulate you on your demosthenic energy. **1834** *Deb. Congress U.S.* 10 Mar. 843 This Demosthenian pouring-out of the shreds and patches of old Grecian orations. **1846** WORCESTER cites *Blackw. Mag.* for *Demosthenic.* **1874** MAHAFFY *Soc. Life Greece* xi. 343 The Demosthenic public. **1880** MᶜCARTHY *Own Times*

III. xlvi. 406 Some critics found fault with Lord Palmerston for having spoken of Cobden's as 'Demosthenic eloquence'. **1882** *Athenæum* 19 Aug. 244/3 The reviewer considers that pamphlets such as the 'Drapier Letters' and the 'Conduct of the Allies' are 'Demosthenian in style and method'.

demot ('di:mət). [a. Gr. δημότ-ης one of the (same) deme, f. δῆμος DEME², people, etc.] A member of a Greek deme.

1847 GROTE *Hist. Greece* II. xxxi. IV. 180 The inscription of new citizens took place at the assembly of the demots.

demote (di:'məʊt), *v.* orig. *U.S.* [f. DE- + PRO)MOTE.] *trans.* To reduce to a lower rank or class. Hence **de'motion**.

1893 in *Funk's Stand. Dict.* 489/2 The school children in Senator Wilson's district of Iowa 'use the word *demote* as an antithesis of promote, and..it is so used generally in that section of the country'. **1900** *Daily News* 26 May 6/7 When absentees returned to school, the masters were unwilling to 'demote' them. **1901** *Smithsonian Rep.* (1902) 75 Promotion and demotion, i.e., advancement in 'age' (rank) by common consent in recognition of prowess, etc., with correlative reducton in 'age' as the penalty for cowardice. **1919** *Daily Mail* 7 Oct. 5/4 Major-General Biddle..is shortly to be 'demoted' to brigadier. **1929** R. A. FISHER *Genet. Theory Nat. Selection* 226 The agencies controlling promotion or demotion. **1946** C. FRY *Phœnix too Frequent* (1949) 40 Demoted first and then hanged! **1954** KOESTLER *Invisible Writing* 60 Every demotion, each step down the slopes of the pyramid, is final and irrevocable. **1955** *Times Lit. Suppl.* 11 Nov. 673/1 Montesquieu has been demoted to the position of a rather disagreeable figure of fun. **1957** *Listener* 28 Nov. 881/1 Premises at the Great Central Hotel, Marylebone, now, alas, demoted to railway offices. **1958** *Economist* 22 Nov. 676/1 The demotion of the hectoring Mr. Edusei from the Ministry of Internal Affairs in Ghana to the Ministry of Communications in the course of a cabinet reshuffle. **1968** A. COWAN *Fortunately in England* 244 In any case, since they are prefects we can't very well demote them.

demotic (di:'mɒtɪk), *a.* [ad. Gr. δημοτικ-ός popular, plebeian, common, democratic, f. δημότης one of the people (the deme).]

1. a. Of or belonging to the people: *spec.* the distinctive epithet of the popular form of the ancient Egyptian written character (as distinguished from the *hieratic*, of which it was a simplification): called also *enchorial*. Also *absol.* = The demotic character or script.

1822 *Q. Rev.* XXVIII. 189 To prove, that neither the hieratic or sacerdotal, nor the demotic or vulgar, writing is alphabetic. **1880** SAYCE in *Nature* XXI. 380 The only change undergone by Egyptian writing was the invention of a running-hand, which in its earlier and simpler form is called hieratic, and in its later form demotic.

b. Of or belonging to the popular written or spoken form of modern Greek. Also as *sb.*

1927 H. NICOLSON *Some People* III. 76 And from the bridge the second officer Shouts demotic to the Company's agent. *Ibid.* VII. 172 He slowly approached Essad Pasha and addressed him in demotic Greek. **1946** R. CAPELL *Simiomata* II. 53 There are the moderate advocates of Demotic, and the advanced who are all for dropping more and more inflections. **1964** *Language* XL. 274 Here we encounter katharevusa clusters..which vary with normal demotic. **1964** J. T. PRING in D. Abercrombie et al. *Daniel Jones* 357 Now it is the partisans of demotic who are to the fore; and demotic has become the language of primary education.

2. In general sense: Of, pertaining or proper to, the common people; popular, vulgar. Also as *sb.*

1831 SYD. SMITH *Wks.* (1859) II. 220/1 Demotic habits will be more common in a country where the rich are forced to court the poor for political power. **1872** O. W. HOLMES *Poet Breakf.-t.* viii. (1885) 189 The one..does what in demotic phrase is called the 'sarsing'. **1881** *Times* 26 Apr. 4/1 There is nothing in the position that the demotic mind can apprehend. **1922** T. S. ELIOT *Waste Land* 212 Mr Eugenides, the Smyrna merchant..Asked me in demotic French To luncheon at the Cannon Street Hotel. **1958** *Times Lit. Suppl.* 17 Jan. 30/3 Mr Amis's attitudes as a writer are not so demotic as his choice of terms seems to pretend. There is a suggestion of linguistic slumming, tweedy slanginess. **1961** *Listener* 30 Mar. 573/3 In fact advertising has, of necessity, to use simple, forceful, easily understandable words—'demotic' language, as Mr Whitehead might call it. **1967** R. MABEY *Class* 110 Not only did ITV develop the popular touch—it nurtured those diverse speech tones and accents which belonged naturally to the more demotic channel. **1968** A. COWAN *Fortunately in England* 162 An occasional class of boys would do their best to add a gaiety of their own by singing unusual and demotic versions of such songs as Men of Harlech. **1969** R. HEPPENSTALL *Portrait of Artist as Professional Man* 101 To a north countryman of demotic antecedents like myself, Louis's background, manner and social attitudes were characteristically southern English upper-middle class. **1970** C. P. SNOW *Last Things* 7 At that stage, he had a knack of speaking what he thought of as American demotic.

demoticist (di:'mɒtɪsɪst). [f. DEMOTIC *a.* 1 + -IST.] A student, user, or advocate of demotic script or speech. Also **de'motist**.

1902 *Encycl. Brit.* XXVII. 726/2 Though demotic has not yet received serious attention at Berlin, the influence of that great school has made itself felt amongst demotists, especially in Switzerland, Germany, America, and England. **1911** *Year's Work Class. Stud.* 188 The use made in the syntax of the writings of the modern demoticists..is..quite fresh and very interesting. **1936** *Trans. Philol. Soc.* 50 It is very difficult to get on without them [*sc.* phrases from the purified language], as is admitted even by many of the present-day demoticists. **1964** J. T. PRING in D. Abercrombie et al. *Daniel Jones* 358 Most of the advocates of revised orthography have been demoticists.

demotivate (di:'məʊtɪveɪt), *v.* [f. DE- II. 1 + MOTIVATE *v.*] *trans.* To cause (someone) to lose motivation; to (tend to) deprive of the stimulus or incentive to continue a course of action, etc. Also *absol.*

1976 *Dun's Rev.* Nov. 42/3 Many boards today are taking a considerable interest in seeing that a line of succession is established that will not demotivate the forty-year-old tigers. **1978** *Times* 7 Nov. 4 The present tax laws demotivated people and drove them out of the country. **1981** *Tablet* 5 Dec. 1194/1 Its power to demotivate. **1984** *Times* 17 Dec. 21/3 The prospect of three years study not being appreciated by employers can demotivate one. **1986** *Financial Times* 2 Dec. 11/2 Financial rewards for good teachers would mean an artificial quota of allowances which would be 'a sure way to demotivate those who are not deemed to be "good"'.

Hence **de'motivating** *pred. a.*; **demoti'vation**, the condition or fact of being demotivated; loss of motivation.

1977 *Times* 1 June 21 A study in managerial demotivation is provided by a survey of over 500 executives. **1981** *Tablet* 5 Dec. 1194/2 The thought of doing so is..demotivating. **1986** *Times* 30 July 11/6 You ask..whether it is necessarily demotivating for an under-secretary in, say, the Scottish Office, to receive less than an under-secretary responsible for the VAT empire. **1986** *Financial Times* 12 Dec. 14/8 Both companies admit that sustained concentration on their quality problems led to demotivation and demoralisation, as more and more inadequacies were unearthed.

de'mount, *v.* Also 6 *Sc.* **demont**. [ad. F. *démonter*: cf. DISMOUNT.]

†**1.** *intr.* To dismount. *Obs.*

1533 BELLENDEN *Livy* 361 (Jam.) All horsmen..demont haistilie fra thare hors.

2. *nonce-wd.* [f. DE- + MOUNT *v.*] To descend.

1837 CARLYLE *Fr. Rev.* I. II. vi, Beautiful invention; mounting heavenward, so beautifully..Well if it do not, Pilâtre-like, explode; and demount all the more tragically!

3. *trans.* To remove from a mounting or place of support; to dismantle.

1934 in WEBSTER. **1958** *New Scientist* 24 Apr. 29/3 [The inflamed hydrogen] carried off the singularly impressive eyebrows of a scientist demounting the autoclave.

de'mountable, *a.* [f. DE- II. 3 + MOUNT *sb.*² + -ABLE; cf. F. *démontable* (1870 in Robert).] That can be taken from its mount (see MOUNT *sb.*² 3) or setting; that can be dismantled. Also as *sb.* Hence **demounta'bility**, the property of being demountable.

1909 V. LOUGHEED *Vehicles of Air* xiv. 467 *Demountable*, said of a mechanism designed with special provision for ready taking apart and reassembling. **1910** R. FERRIS *How it Flies* xx. 458 *Demountable*, a type of construction which permits a machine to be easily taken apart for transportation. **1918** WEBSTER Add., *Demountable*..said of a form of rim, for an automobile wheel, which with its tire can be removed from the wheel. **1930** *Engineering* 21 Feb. 248/1 A new form of a demountable Timken bearing idler. **1934** WEBSTER, Demountability. **1941** *Nature* 19 Apr. 481/1 Irradiation was carried out by means of a demountable X-ray tube. **1943** J. S. HUXLEY *TVA* x. 75 Its demountable house..is mass-produced in sections, which are then transported to their destination on special trailers, and erected on pre-cast concrete foundations built on the site. **1944** *Archit. Rev.* XCVI. 32/2 These [houses] were built of various types of prefabricated panels; but the degree of prefabrication and actual 'demountability'..varied considerably. **1971** *Nature* 4 June p. ix (Advt.), Demountable assemblies with photomultipliers. ..Integral assemblies for highest resolution.

demour, -oyre, demourage, -ance: see DEMUR, DEMURRAGE, -ANCE.

[**demple**: app. scribal error for *kemple* = CAMPLE *v.* to wrangle, *sb.* wordy conflict, wrangling.

c **1330** R. BRUNNE *Chron.* (1810) 196 (Petyt MS. lf. 153 b), Þe maister of þe Temple com procurand þe pes, No more of þis to demple, tak þat þat ȝe first ches. *Lambeth MS.* 131 p. 130 No more of this comple, tak þat þat ȝe first chees.]

dempne, obs. form of DAMN.

dempster ('dɛm(p)stə(r)). Forms: 4 demstere, demestre, -ter(e, demister(e, (demmepster, demaistre), 4, 7 demster, 6 demstar, 4, 8-9 dempster. See also DEEMSTER. [ME. *dēmestre*, in form fem. of *dēmere*, DEEMER, judge: see -STER. The root-vowel was originally long: cf. the modern form DEEMSTER, used in the Isle of Man; but in general use it was shortened at an early date in consequence of the elision of the short vowel of the second syllable, and the collocation of consonants in *demstre*; whence the forms *demster*, *dempster*. *Dempster* is also a surname.]

†**1.** A judge. *Obs.*

a **1300** *Cursor M.* 5585 (Cott.) Prist and demmepster sai i [*v. rr.* demestre, demister, domesman]. *Ibid.* 7005 Aioth was þan þe dempster [*v. rr.* demester, demister]. *Ibid.* 22920 [He] sal cum befor þe demstere [*v. rr.* demestere, demistere, demester]. ? *c* **1320** *Anticrist* 550 Ffor drednes o þat demster.

b. for DEEMSTER 2. (*I. of Man.*)

1823 SCOTT *Peveril* xv, One of the dempsters at the time.

†**2.** In Scotland, formerly; 'The officer of a court who pronounced doom or sentence definitively as directed by the clerk or judge' (Jamieson).

1513-75 *Diurn. Occurrents* (1833) 117 [They] creatit baillies, serjantis, clerkis, and demstaris. **1752** LOUTHIAN *Form of Process* 57 The sentence is read by the clerk to the Demster, and the Demster repeats the same to the pannel. **1753** *Stewart's Trial* 283 The court proceeded to give judgment; which, being written down in the book, and signed by the whole judges, was read by the clerk, and, in the usual manner, repeated pronounced by the dempster to the pannel as follows. **1825** JAMIESON *Dict.* s.v., As the repetition of the sentence after the judge has been of late years discontinued, the office of Dempster in the Court [Edinburgh] is also laid aside.

Hence †**'dempstery, demstary**, the office of dempster.

1551 *Aberdeen Reg.* V. 21 (Jam.), The office of demstary.

dempt, obs. pa. t. and pa. pple. of DEEM *v.*

†**'demption.** *Obs. rare*⁻¹. [ad. L. *demptiōnem*, n. of action f. *dēmere* to take away.] The action of taking away or suppressing.

1552 HULOET, Colysion, abiection, contraction, or demption of a vowel..*symphonesis*.

Dems (dɛmz). Abbrev. of *D*efensively *E*quipped *M*erchant *S*hip; a gunner on such a ship.

1943-4 *Hutchinson's Pict. Hist. War* 27 Oct.-11 Apr. 266 Defensively equipped merchant ship gunners ('Dems') taking a refresher course... A high-angle 4-in. gun being demonstrated to a 'Dems' class.

†**demulce** (dɪ'mʌls), *v. Obs.* [ad. L. *dēmulcēre* to stroke down, to soothe caressingly, f. DE- I. 1 + *mulcēre* to soothe.] *trans.* To soothe or mollify (a person); to soften or make gentle. Formerly said also of soothing medicines: cf. DEMULCENT.

1530 ELYOT *Gov.* I. xx. (*init.*), Wherwith Saturne was eftsones demulced and appaysed. **1656** BAXTER *Ref. Pastor* 301 As Seneca saith to demulce the angry. **1684** tr. *Bonet's Merc. Compit.* XIX. 690 Nervine Medicines..demulce the Part, and take away the preternatural acrimony. **1831** T. L. PEACOCK *Crotchet Castle* viii, Before I was demulced by the Muses, I was *ferocis ingenii puer*.

Hence **de'mulcing** *ppl. a.*

1619 H. HUTTON *Follies Anat.* (1842) 22 His belly is a cistern of receit, A grand confounder of demulcing meate. *a* **1670** HACKET *Abp. Williams* I. (1692) 70 The Earl's demulcing and well-languaged phrases.

†**de'mulceate**, *v. Obs. nonce-wd.* [irreg. f. L. *dēmulcēre* (see prec.) + -ATE³.] = prec. So †**demulce'ation**, *Obs.*

1627-77 FELTHAM *Resolves* II. lxxvi. 321 Those soft and smooth demulceations that insensibly do stroke us in our gliding life. **1817** *Blackw. Mag.* I. 470 Gallantry..or the exalted science of demulceating the amiable reservedness.. of the gentler sex.

demulcent (dɪ'mʌlsənt), *a.* and *sb.* Chiefly *Med.* [f. L. *dēmulcēnt-em*, pr. pple. of *dēmulcēre* to DEMULCE.]

A. *adj.* Soothing, lenitive, mollifying, allaying irritation.

1732 ARBUTHNOT *Rules of Diet* 264 All insipid inodorous Vegetables are demulcent. **1854** S. THOMSON *Wild Fl.* III. (ed. 4) 302 The linseed and the mallows, both valuable for their demulcent properties.

B. *sb.* A demulcent medicine.

1732 ARBUTHNOT *Rules of Diet* 418 Demulcents, or what abates Acrimony. **1875** H. C. WOOD *Therap.* (1879) 576.

†**de'mulcetive**, *a. Obs.* [irreg. f. DEMULCE *v.*] = DEMULCENT.

1756 P. BROWNE *Jamaica* 115 The oil is opening and demulcetive.

†**de'mulsion.** *Obs. rare*⁻¹. [f. L. **dēmuls-*, ppl. stem of *dēmulcēre*: see DEMULCE.] The action of soothing; a means of soothing.

1627-77 FELTHAM *Resolves* II. lvii. 276 Vice garlanded with all the soft demulsions of a present contentment.

demur (dɪ'mɜ:(r)), *sb.* Forms: 3-7 demure, 4 demere, demoere, 6 demoure, demourre, demoyre, demor(e, 6-7 demurr(e, 7- demur. [a. F. *demeure*, vbl. sb. from *demeurer*: see next.]

†**1.** Delay, lingering, waiting. *Obs.*

a **1300** *Floriz & Bl.* 591 Blauncheflur heo atwist þat he makede so longe demure [*v.r.* demoere: *rime* ifere]. *c* **1320** *Sir Beues* 125 Theder warde he gan gon Withouten demere. **1529** in Burnet *Hist. Ref.* II. 97 His Highness had cause.. to marvel of your long demor, and lack of expedition. **1660** HICKERINGILL *Jamaica* (1661) 51 Timely alarum'd by Jacksons Demurres, at the Harbours mouth, for four days Space. **1675** *Essex Papers* (Camden) I. 311 Causing a most unnecessary demurre.

†**b.** Stay, abode, residence. *Obs.*

1444 in *Coll. Hist. Staff.* (1891) XII. 318 During the tyme of his demurre in the presence of the seid Erle. **1524** in *Househ. Ord.* (1790) 159 In his demurre or passing from place to place. **1532-3** *Act 24 Hen. VIII*, c. 13 Comynge into the Kynges realme..and not minded to make longe or continual demoyre in the same. **1673** RAY *Journ. Low C.* 378 We saw this Town only in transitu, but it merited a little demurr.

†**c.** Continuance, duration. *Obs.*

1533 in Strype *Eccl. Mem.* I. xx. 148 Neither unjust matrymony shall have his unjust and incestuous demoure and continuance, as by delayes to Rome it is wont to have.

†**2.** Hesitation; pause; state of irresolution or doubt. *Obs.*

1581 T. Howell *Deuises* (1879) 234 No doubtfull drift whereon demurre depends. **1677** W. Hubbard *Narrative* II. 49 They were upon some demurre, whether to march directly toward Ossapy. **1683** Temple *Mem.* Wks. 1731 I. 379 He did not expect any Demurr upon such an Offer. **1824** Lamb *Elia* Ser. II. *Capt. Jackson*, You were positively at a demur what you did or did not see.

3. The act of demurring; an objection raised or exception taken to a proposed course of action, etc.

1639 Mayne *City Match* IV. ii, Sister, 'tis so projected, therefore make No more demurs. **1770** Langhorne *Plutarch* (1879) I. 154/2 Camillus..invented demurs and pretences of delay. **1791** Mad. D'Arblay *Diary* 4 June, He then said it was necessary to drink the Queen's health. The gentlemen here made no demur. **1838** Dickens *Nich. Nick.* xxii, After a little demur, he accepted the offer.

†**4.** *Law.* = demurrer[1]. *Obs.*

c **1555** Harpsfield *Divorce Hen. VIII* (1878) 36 The adversaries..made thereupon..a special demurre. *a* **1577** Sir T. Smith *Commw. Eng.* (1609) 51 If they cannot agree, then is the matter referred to a demurre in the Exchequer chamber. **1660** Willsford *Scales Comm.* A vj b, To procrastinate with Demurs, or Fines and Recoveries without end. **1713** Swift *Cadenus & V.* 120 But with rejoinders and replies..Demur, imparlance, and essoign, The parties ne'er could issue join.

demur (dɪˈmɜː(r)), *v.* Forms: 3 demeore, 4 demere, 6 demore, demoore, demour(e, 6–7 demurre, 7–8 demurr, 7– demur. [a. F. *demeurer*, in OF. *demorer*, *-mourer* (= Pr. and Sp. *demorare*, It. *dimorare*):—pop. L. *dēmorāre* = cl. L. *dēmorārī* to tarry, delay, f. de- I. 3 + *morārī* to delay. The OF. *demor-*, *demour-*, proper to the forms with atonic radical vowel, was at length assimilated to the tonic form *demeur-*; the latter gave the ME. forms *demeore*, *demere*: cf. people, and the forms *meve*, *preve* (F. *meuve*, *preuve*) of move, prove.]

†**1.** *intr.* To linger, tarry, wait; *fig.* to dwell *upon* something. *Obs.*

a **1225** *Ancr. R.* 242 Auh ȝif ich hie swuðe uorðward, demeore ȝe þe lengre. *c* **1300** *K. Alis.* 7295 He n'ul nought that ye demere [*rime* dere]. **1550** Nicolls *Thucyd.* 73 (R.), Yet durst they not demoure nor abyde vpon the campe. **1559** Baldwin in *Mirr. Mag.* (1563) 39 b, Take hede ye demurre not vpon them. **1595** Southwell *St. Peter's Compl.* 19 But ô, how long demurre I on his eyes. **1604** T. Wright *Passions* v. 213, I demurre too long in these speculative discourses. **1653** Urquhart *Rabelais* I. ii, If that our looks on it demurre.

†**b.** To stay, remain, abide. *Obs.*

1523 *St. Papers Hen. VIII*, IV. 34 She cannot demore there without extreme daunjur and peril. **1536** *Act 28 Hen. VIII*, c. 10 Any person..dwellyng, demurryng, inhabitinge or resiant within this realme. **1550** Nicolls *Thucyd.* 72 (R.) The sayde Peloponesyans demoured in the land.

†**c.** To last, endure, continue. *Obs.*

1547 Hooper *Declar. Christ* iii. Wks. (Parker Soc.) 21 This defence..shall demour for ever till this church be glorified.

†**2.** *trans.* To cause to tarry; to put off, delay.

1613 Purchas *Pilgrimage* II. xviii. 174 Whose judgement is demurred until the day of Reconciliation. **1635** Quarles *Embl.* IV. x. (1818) 239 The lawyer..then demurs me with a vain delay. **1682** D'Urfey *Butler's Ghost* 69, I swear.. Henceforth to take a rougher course, And, what you would demur to force.

†**3.** *intr.* To hesitate; to delay or suspend action; to pause in uncertainty. *Obs.*

1641 Milton *Ch. Govt.* vii. (1851) 135 This is all we get by demurring in Gods service. **1654** Codrington tr. *Hist. Ivstine* 418 He found the King to demur upon it. **1655** Fuller *Ch. Hist.* II. ii. §40 King Edwine demurred to embrace Christianity. **1699** Bentley *Phal.* 516 The Delphians demurring, whether they should accept it or no. **1743** J. Davidson *Æneid* VIII. 261 You need not demur to challenge. **1778** Miss Burney *Evelina* li, You are the first lady who ever made me even demur upon this subject. **1818** W. Taylor in *Monthly Rev.* LXXXVII. 534 All the Yorkists could thus co-operate, without demurring between their rightful sovereigns.

†**b.** To be of doubtful mind; to remain doubtful. *Obs. rare.*

1612 T. Taylor *Comm. Titus* i. 3 And demurre with the Philistines, whether God or Fortune smite vs. *a* **1628** F. Greville *Sidney* (1652) 237 To have demurred more seriously upon the sudden change in his Sonne.

†**c.** *trans.* To hesitate about. *Obs. rare.*

1667 Milton *P.L.* IX. 558 What may this mean? Language of Man pronounc't By Tongue of Brute, and human sense exprest? The first..I thought deni'd To Beasts..The latter I demurre, for in thir looks Much reason, and in thir actions oft appeers. *a* **1730** E. Fenton *Hom. Odyss.* XI. *Imit.* (Seager), Let none demur Obedience to her will.

4. *intr.* To make scruples or difficulties; to raise objection, take exception *to* (occas. *at*, *on*). (The current sense; often with allusion to the legal sense, 5.)

1639 Fuller *Holy War* II. xxxvi. (1840) 98 The caliph demurred hereat, as counting such a gesture a diminution to his state. **1751** Labelye *Westm. Br.* 93, I..gave my Directions..which being in some Measure demurred to, the Matter was brought before the Board. **1775** Sheridan *Rivals* II. ii, My process was always very simple—in their younger days, 'twas 'Jack, do this'—if he demurred, I knocked him down. **1807** Southey *Espriella's Letters* III. 29 They are so unreasonable as to demur at finding corn for them. **1855** Browning *Let. to Ruskin*, I cannot begin writing poetry till my imaginary reader has conceded licences to me which you demur at altogether. **1860** Tyndall *Glac.* I. v. 40 My host at first demurred..but I insisted. **1875** McLaren *Serm.* Ser. II. ix. 150 We can afford to recognise the fact, though we demur to the inference.

b. *trans.* To object or take exception to. *rare.*

1827 H. H. Wilson *Burmese War* (1852) 25 As the demand was unprecedented, the Mugs, who were British subjects, demurred payment. **1876** Gladstone *Homeric Synchr.* 59, I demur the inference from these facts.

5. *Law.* (*intr.*) To put in a demurrer.

[*a* **1481** Littleton *Tenures* §96 Et fuist demurre en iudgement en mesme le plee, le quel les xl. iours serront accompts de le primer iour del muster de host le Roy.] **1620** J. Wilkinson *Coroners & Sherifes* 60 It was demurred on in Law. **1628** Coke *On Litt.* 70 a, And it was demured in iudgement in the same plea, whither the 40 dayes should bee accounted from the first day of the muster of the kings host. *Ibid.* 72 a, He that demurreth in Law confesseth all such matters of fact as are well and sufficiently pleaded. **1641** in Rushw. *Hist. Coll.* III. (1692) I. 334 To which Plea Mr. Attorney-General demurred in Law, and the said Samuel Vassall joyned in Demurrer with him. **1660** *Trial of Regic.* 107, I must demur to your Jurisdiction. **1681** *Trial S. Colledge* 10 And if so be matter of Law arises upon any evidence that is given against you..you may demurr upon that Evidence, and pray Counsel of the Court to argue that demurrer. **1848** Macaulay *Hist. Eng.* II. 84 The plaintiff demurred, that is to say, admitted Sir Edward's plea to be true in fact, but denied that it was a sufficient answer.

demurante, obs. form of demurrant.

demure (dɪˈmjʊə(r)), *a.* (*sb.*) Also 4–5 dimuuir, 5 demeuer, -uere, -ewre, 6 -eure. [A derived or extended form of *meure*, *mewre*, mure *a.*, used in same sense, a. OF. *meur*, now *mûr*, 'ripe, mature, mellow; also, discreet, considerate, aduised, setled, stayed' (Cotgr. 1611). The nature and history of the prefixed *de-* are obscure.

(Palsgrave, 1530, has p. 841/1 'Sadly, wysly, *demeurement*',—p. 841/2 'Soberly, sadly, *meurement*'; but *demeurement* is not otherwise known as French.)]

A. *adj.* †**1.** Calm, settled, still. *Obs.*

1377 *Death Edw. III* in *Pol. Poems* (Rolls) I. 216 Thouȝ the see were rouȝ, or elles dimuuir, Gode havenes that schip wold geete.

2. Of persons (and their bearing, speech, etc.): Sober, grave, serious; reserved or composed in demeanour. (Cf. history of sad.)

14.. *Epiph.* in *Tundale's Vis.* 133 This Anna come demure and sad of chere. **1470–85** Malory *Arthur* XIII. i, The yonge squyer..semely and demure as a douue. **1523** Skelton *Garl. Laurel* 902 Demure Diana, womanly and sad. **1538** Bale *Thre Lawes* 238 A face demure and sage. *a* **1568** Ascham *Scholem.* (Arb.) 53 If a yong ientleman be demeure and still of nature, they say, he is simple and lacketh witte. **1632** Milton *Penseroso* 32 Come, pensive Nun, devout and pure, Sober, steadfast, and demure. **1653** H. More *Antid. Ath.* III. i. (1712) 87 Notwithstanding he fared no worse than the most demure and innocent. **1728–46** Thomson *Spring* 485 Come with those downcast eyes, sedate and sweet, Those looks demure. **1835** Marryat *Jac. Faithf.* xxiv, Her conduct was much more staid and demure. **1875** M. Pattison *Ess.* (1889) I. 320 'Like an angel, but half-dressed', thought the demure dons.

3. Affectedly or constrainedly grave or decorous; serious, reserved, or coy in a way that is not natural to the person or to one of his years or condition.

1693 Shadwell *Volunteers* III. i, This Gentleman, and his demure Psalm-singing Fellows. **1705** Stanhope *Paraphr.* II. 166 Can they pursue the demure and secret Sinners, through all the intricate mazes of their Hypocrisy. **1735** Thomson *Liberty* IV. 69 Hell's fiercest Fiend! of Saintly Brow demure. *a* **1771** Gray *Death Favourite Cat* 4 Demurest of the tabby kind, The pensive Selima. **1844** Thirlwall *Greece* VIII. lxvi. 417 The threadbare mantle of its demure hypocrisy. **1876** Black *Madcap V.* xix. 176, 'I thought he was a friend of yours', she said, with demure sarcasm.

†**B.** As *sb.* Demure look or expression. *Obs. rare.*

1766 J. Adams *Diary* 4 Nov. Wks. 1850 II. 200 He has an hypocritical demure on his face.

†**deˈmure**, *v. Obs. rare.* [f. prec. adj.]

1. *intr.* ? To look demurely, 'to look with an affected modesty' (J.). But cf. demur *v.* 3 b.

1606 Shaks. *Ant. & Cl.* IV. xv. 29 Your Wife Octauia, with her modest eyes..shall acquire no Honour Demuring vpon me.

2. *trans.* To make demure.

1651 Henshaw *Daily Thoughts* 187 (L.) Zeal mad, and voice demur'd with godly paint.

Hence **deˈmured** *ppl. a.*

1613 *Uncasing of Machivils Instr.* 11 With demured looke wish them good speede.

demure, obs. form of demur.

demurely (dɪˈmjʊəlɪ), *adv.* [f. demure *a.* + -ly[2].] In a demure manner; gravely, modestly, meekly, quietly; with a gravity, meekness, or modesty that is affected or unnatural.

c **1400** *Rom. Rose* 4627 She, demurely sad of chere. *c* **1430** *Stans Puer* 18 in *Babees Bk.* (1868) 27 Walke demurely bi streetis in þe toun. **1489** Caxton *Faytes of A.* IV. xiii. 268 The prynce or his lieutenant oughte to aduyse demewrely herupon. *c* **1500** *Consecration of Nuns* in Maskell *Mon. Rit.* II. 314 The virgyns shall demeurely arryse and make a reverence to the bisshop. **1596** Shaks. *Merch. V.* II. ii. 201 If I doe not put on a sober habite..Weare prayer bookes in my pocket, looke demurely. **1600** Dekker *Gentle Craft* Wks. 1873 I. 43 I'le looke as demurely as a Saint. **1687** Sedley *Bellamira* IV. i, He look'd so demurely, I thought butter would not haue melted in his mouth. **1768** Beattie *Minstr.* I. xvi, And now his look was most demurely sad. **1848** C. Brontë *J. Eyre* xi, Folding her little hands demurely before her. **1886** *Manch. Exam.* 27 Feb. 5/3 They sat down demurely in opposite corners of the carriage and observed a dignified silence.

†**b.** Of things: In a subdued manner. *Obs.*

1606 Shaks. *Ant. & Cl.* IV. ix. 30 Hearke the drummes demurely wake the sleepers.

demureness (dɪˈmjʊənɪs). [f. as prec. + -ness.] The state or quality of being demure.

c **1510** Barclay *Mirr. Gd. Manners* (1570) G iij, With all demurenes behaue thee in the same, As not led by malice but rather of good loue. **1582** N. T. (Rhem.) *1 Tim.* ii. 9 In like maner women also in comely attire: with demurenesse and sobrietie adorning themselves. **1659** Gauden *Tears of Ch.* 349 A most supercilious demurenesse and affected zelotry. **1821** Scott *Kenilw.* vii, The prim demureness of her looks.

deˈmurity. *rare.* In 5 demeurte. [Answers to OF. *meurté*, as demure does to OF. *meur*: cf. quot. 1483.]

1. Demure quality, demureness.

1483 Caxton *Gold. Leg.* 34/1 Joyne..demeurte to thy gladnes, and humylyte to thy demeurte [Fr. *et meurte a leesement et humilite a la meurte*]. *a* **1704** T. Brown *Wks.* (1760) II. 182 (D.) They pretend to such demurity as to form a society for the Regulation of Manners. **1889** Besant *Bell of St. Paul's* III. 271 The demurity went out of her face.

2. An embodiment of demureness; a demure character or person. (Cf. *oddity*.)

18.. Lamb *Let. to Southey* (L.), She will act after the fashion of Richardson's demurities.

†**deˈmurmurate**, *v. Obs.* [f. ppl. stem of L. *dēmurmurāre* to mutter over, f. de- I. 1 + *murmurāre* to murmur, mutter.] *trans.* To murmur, mutter.

1641 R. Baillie *Parall. Liturgy w. Mass-bk.* 43 To demurmurate a number of words on the elements.

Hence †**deˈmurmuratory** *a.*

1617 Collins *Def. Bp. Ely* II. x. 417 The demurmuratorie words, which they vse in Poperie, and call Consecration.

demurrable (dɪˈmɜːrəb(ə)l), *a.* [f. demur *v.* or *sb.* + -able. For form, cf. OF. *demorable* durable.] That may be demurred to; to which exception may be taken (*esp.* in an action at law).

1827 Hallam *Constitutional Hist.* I. i. 54 *note*, It was demurrable for a bill to pray process against the defendant, to appear before the king and his privy council. **1885** *Law Reports* Weekly Notes 219/2 The petition was demurrable, as it did not..allege that the petitioner had a complete title as executrix. **1893** J. Kekewich in *Law Times Rep.* LXVIII. 439/1 The statement of claim would be demurrable.

demurrage (dɪˈmʌrɪdʒ). Also 7 demourage, 7–8 demorage. [a. OF. *demorage*, *demourage*, f. *demorer*, *-mourer*: see demur *v.*]

†**1.** Stay; delay; hesitation; pause. *Obs.*

a **1656** Ussher *Ann.* (1658) 20 That long demourage of theirs in Kadesh. **1702** C. Mather *Magn. Chr.* II. App. (1852) 171 Powerful enemies clogged his affairs with such demurrages and such disappointments as would have wholly discouraged his designs. **1711** Addison *Spect.* No. 89 ¶3, I shall endeavour to shew the folly of Demurrage.. I would have them seriously think on the Shortness of their Time. **1823** *New Monthly Mag.* VII. 231 A demurrage, for a second, succeeded the shock, and then on we went again.

†**b.** Constrained delay, detention. *Obs. rare.*

1810 Bentham *Packing* (1821) 226 In the allowance to jury-men distinguish two parts: one for demurrage, viz. at the place of trial; the other for journeys, viz. thither and back. **1817** —— *Plan Parl. Reform* Introd. cxlvii, The expense of journeys to and from, and demurrage at, the Election town.

2. *Comm.* **a.** Detention of a vessel by the freighter beyond the time agreed upon; the payment made in compensation for such detention.

1641 *Rebels' Remonstr.* in Rushw. *Hist. Coll.* III. (1692) I. 389 A certain Summ, for the doing thereof within such a time; and if they stay'd longer, to have so much *per diem* for demurrage. **1694** tr. *Milton's Lett. State* July an. 1656, A considerable Sum of Money owing from certain Portugal Merchants..to several English Merchants, upon the account of Freightage and Demorage. **1719** De Foe *Crusoe* II. 153 If I stay more, I must pay 3*l*...*per Diem* Demorage, nor can I stay upon Demorage above eight Days more. **1755** Magens *Insurances* II. 116 If the Delay was occasioned by the Merchant, he shall be obliged to pay for the Days of Demurrage, to the Captain. **1835** Marryat *Jac. Faithf.* viii, There had already been considerable loss from demurrage. *Mod.* The Ship 'Flora' is on demurrage.

b. A charge for detention of railway trucks.

1858 Redfield *Law Railw.* (1869) II. 191 Demurrage is a claim by way of compensation for the detention of property which is subsequently restored. **1892** *Labour Commission Gloss.*, *Demurrage*, charges on overdue railway trucks.

c. A charge of 1½*d.* per ounce made by the Bank of England in exchanging gold or notes for bullion.

1875 Jevons *Money* x. 116 Including the above charge of 1½*d.* per ounce for demurrage. **1882** Bithell *Counting-House Dict.*, The metallic value of standard gold is £3 17*s.* 10½*d.* per oz. At the Bank of England £3 17*s.* 9*d.* is given for it without any delay... The difference of 1½*d.* per. oz., by which this delay is avoided, is called *demurrage*.

3. The act of demurring, or raising objection to something. *rare.*

1822 Colton *Lacon* II. 147 Without the slightest dissent or demurrage of the judgment.

demurral (dɪˈmɜːrəl). *rare.* [f. DEMUR *v.* + -AL[1]: cf. OF. *demorail, demoral,* retardation, delay.] The action of demurring; dumur.

1810 SOUTHEY in *Edin. Ann. Reg.* I. I. 413 This was a needless demurral. **1814** —— *Lett.* (1856) II. 370 Second thought in matters of feeling, usually brings with it hesitation, and demurral. **1890** *Spectator* 22 Mar., I crave a small portion of your space to express my demurral as well to the reasoning as to the accuracy of 'A Churchman', who writes to you.

†**deˈmurrance.** *Obs.* In 4 demorrance, 6 demoraunce, 7 demourance. [a. OF. *demorance* retardation, delay, f. *demorer, -mourer*: see DEMUR *v.* and -ANCE.] **a.** Delay, lingering. **b.** Abiding, abode, dwelling.

c **1300** *K. Alis.* 4123 He wolde wende, swithe snel..saun demorrance. *a* **1529** SKELTON *Bk. 3 Foles* Wks. I. 201 The man is a very fole to make his demoraunce upon such an olde wyfe. **1625** *Modell Wit* 76 b, Here is my demourance, and from hence I purpose not to part.

demurrant (dɪˈmʌrənt), *a.* and *sb.* Also 6 demurante, 9 (*erron.*) demurrent. [a. OF. *demourant*, pr. pple. of *demorer, -mourer,* now *demeurer*: see DEMUR *v.*] **A.** *adj.*

†**1.** Abiding, staying, dwelling, resident. *Obs.*

1529 *Supplic. to King* 32 To compell the same [ministers] to be demurante, abydinge, and resydent vpon their cures. **1577–87** HOLINSHED *Chron.* II. 24/3 A friend of mine, being of late demurrant in London.

†**2.** Delaying, putting off. *Obs.*

1633 T. ADAMS *Exp. 2 Peter* iii. 12 God is no judge dormant, nor demurrant, nor rampant.

3. Demurring, hesitating. *rare.*

1836 F. MAHONEY *Relig. Father Prout* (1859) 390 Why hangs he back demurrent To breast the Tiber's current?

B. *sb.* One who demurs, or puts in a demurrer, in an action at law.

1809 TOMLINS *Law Dict.* s.v. *Demurrer*, A demurrer is to be signed, and argued on both sides by counsel..The demurrant argues first. **1885** L. O. PIKE *Yearbks.* 12–13 *Edw. III*, Introd. 85 There was no complete demurrer unless the demurrant did abide judgment on the point of law.

demurrer[1] (dɪˈmʌrə(r)). Also 6 (*erron.*) demurrour, 7 demourer. [a. Anglo-Fr. *demurrer* = OF. *demourer*, pres. inf. (see DEMUR *v.*) used as sb.: cf. *refresher, user.*]

1. *Law.* A pleading which, admitting for the moment the facts as stated in the opponent's pleading, denies that he is legally entitled to relief, and thus stops the action until this point be determined by the court.

1547 *Act 1 Edw. VI*, c. 7 §1 The Process, Pleas, Demurrers and Continuances in every Action. **1565** SIR T. SMITH *Commw. Eng.* (1609) 67 If the question be of the law, that is, if both the parties doe agree vpon the fact, and each doe claime that by law hee ought to haue it..then it was called a demurrer in law. **1660** *Trial Regic.* 107 If you demur to the Jurisdiction of this Court, I must let you know that the Court doth over-rule your demurrer. **1794** GODWIN *Cal. Williams* 43 By affidavits, motions, pleas, demurrers, flaws, and appeals, to protract the question from term to term and from court to court. **1809** TOMLINS *Law Dict.* s.v., *Demurrers* are *general*, without shewing any particular causes; or *special*, where the causes of demurrer are particularly set down. **1861** MAY *Const. Hist.* (1863) II. x. 230 He pleaded Not Guilty to the first fourteen counts, and put in demurrers to the others. **1864** BOWEN *Logic* ix. 299 A Demurrer has been happily explained to be equivalent to the remark 'Well, what of that?'

b. *transf.* An objection raised or exception taken to anything; = DEMUR *sb.* 3.

1599 MARSTON *Sco. Villanie* II. vii. 205 Slowe-pac't dilatory pleas, Demure demurrers, stil striving to appease Hote zealous loue. **1873** H. SPENCER *Stud. Sociol.* ii. (ed. 6) 45 This reply is met by the demurrer that it is beside the question.

†**2.** A pause, stand-still; a state of hesitation or irresolution; = DEMUR *sb.* 2. *Obs.*

1533 MORE *Debell. Salem* Wks. 945/1 The matter is at a demurrour in this poynt, and we at your iudgement. **1627** F. E. *Hist. Edw. II* (1680) 42 The greenness of the Disgrace kept him in a long demurrer. **1645** WITHER *Vox Pacif.* 93 Not well discerning whether Griefe, Shame, or Anger, that demurrer caus'd.

†**3.** = DEMURRAGE 2 a. *Obs. rare.*

1622 MALYNES *Anc. Law-Merch.* 117 If the Master doe not stay out all his daies of demourer agreed vpon by the charterpartie of fraightment.

demurrer[2] (dɪˈmɜːrə(r)). [f. DEMUR *v.* + -ER[1].] One who demurs.

1711 ADDISON *Spect.* No. 89 ¶1, I shall distinguish this Sect of Women by the Title of Demurrers. **1742** YOUNG *Nt. Th.* IX. 1364 And is Lorenzo a demurrer still? **1812** *Examiner* 7 Sept. 565/1 It is..customary..to hear the demurrer's reasons.

demurring (dɪˈmɜːrɪŋ), *vbl. sb.* [f. DEMUR *v.* + -ING[1].] The action of the verb DEMUR, q.v.

1593 NASHE *Christ's T.* 90 b, There is no demurring, or exceptioning against his testimony. **1682** D'URFEY *Butler's Ghost* 110 Famous was he for Procuration, Demurrings, and Continuation. **1873** MISS BROUGHTON *Nancy* II. 23 But, say I with discontented demurring, you have been away often before!

deˈmurring, *ppl. a.* [-ING[2].] That demurs: see the verb.

1607 WALKINGTON *Opt. Glass* 118 His demurring judgement. **1742** YOUNG *Nt. Th.* III. 35 Are there demurring wits, who dare dispute This revolution in the world inspir'd?

Hence **deˈmurringly** *adv.*

1890 I. D. HARDY *New Othello* I. viii. 187 'But..' she observed demurringly.

demy (dɪˈmaɪ), *sb.* (and *a.*) Pl. **demies.** Also 5–6 demye, 6 demie, deamy, dymye. [An early spelling of DEMI- half, retained when this is used as a separate word. The uses are all elliptical, and quite independent of each other.]

†**1.** A gold coin current in Scotland in the 15th century: apparently, originally, the half-mark (*demi-mark*: see DEMI- 7), but rising in value with the depreciation of the silver coin from 6*s.* 8*d.* to 12*s.* (Scotch). *Obs.*

1440 J. SHIRLEY *Dethe K. James* (1818) 9 That whoso myght slee or tak hyme..shuld have iii thousand demyes of gold, every pece worth half an Englissh Noble. **1451** *Sc. Acts 8 Jas. II*, §33 (1597) The Demy that now runnis for nine shillenges. **1455** —— 13 *Jas. II*, §59 It is thocht expedient that the Demy be cryed to ten shillinges. **1489** *Ld. Treas. Acc. Scotl.*, Item to Inglis pyparis that com to the Castel ȝet and playt to the King xij demyss. **1497** *Ibid.*, Giffen to the cartes [cards] agane xxxij Franch crovnis, x Scottes crovnis and demyis, thre [ridaris], tua vnicornis.

†**2.** 'A short close vest' (Fairholt): cf. DEMI- 2. *Obs.*

a **1529** SKELTON *Bowge of Courte* 359 Of Kirkby Kendall was his shorte demye. **1540** *Lanc. Wills* I. 189 To my doughter Katheryn my best demye. **1599** NASHE *Lenten Stuffe* in *Harl. Misc.* (1808–12) VI. 166 (D.) He..stript him out of his golden demy or mandillion, and flead him.

3. *Paper Manuf.* Name of a certain size of paper. (Properly *adj.*; also *ellipt.* as *sb.* = demy paper.)

Demy printing paper measures $17\frac{1}{2}$ x $22\frac{1}{2}$ inches; demy writing paper is in Great Britain $15\frac{1}{2}$ x 20, in United States 16 x 21.

1546 LANGLEY *Pol. Verg. De Invent.* II. vi. 45 b, There be diuerse maner of papers, as paper royal, paper demy, blotting paper, marchauntes paper. **1589** *Marprel. Epit.* B, An hundred threescore and twelue sheets, of good Demie paper. **1712** *Act 10 Anne* in *Lond. Gaz.* No. 5018/3 For all Paper called..Demy fine, 4*s.* Demy second, 2*s.* 6*d.* Demy printing, 1*s.* 8*d.* **1790** WOLCOTT (P. Pindar) *Benev. Epist. Sylv. Urban* Wks. 1812 II. 251 His nice-discerning Knowledge none deny On Crown, Imperial, Foolscap, and Demy. **1878** *Print. Trades Jrnl.* xxv. 9 A demy 8vo. pamphlet of about a dozen pages.

4. A foundation scholar at Magdalen College, Oxford.

So called because their allowance or 'commons' was originally half that of a Fellow: the Latin term is *semi-communarius.*

a **1486** *Stat. Magdalen Coll.* (MS.) 6 De electione scholarium voc' Dymyes. *Ibid.*, Pro communis cujuslibet triginta pauperum scholarium, qui Demyes vulgariter nuncupantur dimidium summae illius quam pro quolibet alio socio. **1536** *Act 27 Hen. VIII*, c. 42 §1 in *Oxf. & Camb. Enactm.* 12 Felawes, Scolers, Dymyes. **1615** HEYLIN *Memoranda* 22 July in *Mem. Waynflete* (1851), I was chosen Demie of Magdalen College. **1691** WOOD *Ath. Oxon.* I. 14 William Lilye was..elected one of the Demies or Semi-commoners of St. Mary Magd. Coll. **1769** *De Foe's Tour Gt. Brit.* II. 246 Magdalen-College..has a President, 40 Fellows, a School-master, 30 Scholars called Demies. **1880** GREEN *Hist. Eng. People* IV. VIII. iii. 20 The expulsion of the Fellows was followed..by that of the Demies.

5. Short for DEMI-BAR, q.v.: A kind of false dice used in cheating.

1591 GREENE *Disc. Coosnage* (1859) 38 The name of their Cheates, Bard-dice, Flattes, Fargers, Langrets, Gourds, Demies, and many others. **1801** *Sporting Mag.* XVIII. 100 A bale of demies.

†**6.** A half-grown lad, a youth. *Obs.*

1589 WARNER *Alb. Eng.* v. xxvii, Next but demies, nor boyes, nor men, our dangerous times succeede.

demy-: see DEMI-.

demycent, -sent: see DEMI-CEINT *Obs.*

demyd, obs. pa. t. of DEEM *v.*, DIM *v.*

demyelination (diːˌmaɪəlɪˈneɪʃən). [f. DE- II. 3 + MYELINATION.] The removal or destruction of the myelin of nerve tissue. Also **deˈmyelinating** *ppl. a.*; **deˌmyeliniˈzation.**

1932 DORLAND & MILLER *Med. Dict.* (ed. 16) 362/1 *Demyelination, demyelinization*, destruction or removal of myelin. **1934** *Nature* 1 Dec. 831/1 The nerve degeneration, a demyelination of the fibres of the posterior roots, which is responsible for the inco-ordinated movements in rickets, is due to a deficiency of vitamin A in the diet. **1961** *Lancet* 9 Sept. 610/1 The Council are to set up a research group on demyelinating diseases. **1964** S. DUKE-ELDER *Parsons' Dis. Eye* (ed. 14) xxiii. 348 (*caption*) Neuromyelitis optica. Transverse section of the optic nerve showing limited area of demyelination. **1970** *Sci. Jrnl.* Apr. 38/2 Demyelination is caused by the injection in the crude [rabies] vaccines of a small basic protein derived from brain tissue and known to cause demyelinating encephalitis in experimental animals.

demyse girdle: see DEMI-GIRDLE *Obs.*

demyship (dɪˈmaɪʃɪp). Also 6 dimi-, 9 demi-. [f. DEMY 4 + -SHIP.] A scholarship at Magdalen College, Oxford.

1536 *Act 27 Hen. VIII*, c. 42 §1 in *Oxf. & Camb. Enactm.* 13 Felowshippes, Scolershippes, Dimishippes. **1687** *Royal Mandate* 18 July in *Magd. Coll.* (Oxf. Hist. Soc.) 78 Any Fellowship, Demyship, or other place..in our said College. **1869** *Echo* 11 Oct., The demyships are worth £83 per annum, and are tenable for five years. **1884** COURTHOPE *Addison* 29 Dr. Lancaster..used his influence to obtain for him a demyship at Magdalen.

demystify (diːˈmɪstɪfaɪ), *v.* [f. DE- II. 1 + MYSTIFY *v.*] *trans.* To clarify (obscure, clouded, or irrational beliefs); to reduce or remove bewilderment, irrationality, etc., in (a person).

1963 *Times Lit. Suppl.* 11 Jan. 19/2 And so he has devoted himself to 'demystifying politics'. **1967** D. COOPER *Psychiatry & Anti-Psychiatry* v. 101 People (the analytic subjects) are demystified in terms of their phantastic hopes of gratification from the therapist as a parent-figure.

Hence **deˌmystifiˈcation,** the action of demystifying.

1964 *Economist* 16 May 734/2 An attempt at demystification and therefore of human liberation. **1967** D. COOPER *Psychiatry & Anti-Psychiatry* iv. 76 Demystification of these issues is necessary before.. recommending..psycho-therapy or psycho-analysis. *Ibid.* v. 101 This avoidance is conducted in the name of a sort of demystification. **1969** *N.Y. Rev. Books* 16 Jan. 16/3 Aron talks again and again of demystification and desacralization, by which he means dissolving false or ideological constructs about the world and letting reality emerge as it really is.

demyt, obs. form of DIMITY.

demyth (diːˈmɪθ), *v.* [f. DE- II. 2 + MYTH *sb.*] Used occasionally as a synonym of DEMYTHOLOGIZE *v.*

1960 J. MACQUARRIE *Scope of Demythologizing* vii. 214 Some English writers on demythologizing..have adopted the habit of talking rather slickly of 'demything'. Apart from the fact that this word is a more than usual inelegant barbarism, it also betrays a fundamental misunderstanding of Bultmann's intention. If 'demything' meant anything, it would mean, 'the elimination of myth'.. 'Demythologizing' means 'the elimination of mythology', and this is not the same as the elimination of myth. **1961** *Times Lit. Suppl.* 14 Apr. 236/3 All three books agree that some measure of demything (if a less barbaric rendering of the German than 'demythologizing' is permissible) of the world-view and other assumptions of New Testament writers is necessary.

demythicize (diːˈmɪθɪsaɪz), *v.* [f. DE- II. 1 + MYTHICIZE *v.*] To remove the attribution of a mythical character to (a legend, etc.); = DEMYTHOLOGIZE *v.* Hence **deˌmythiciˈzation.**

1951 K. GROBEL in *Jrnl. Bibl. Lit.* 101 One may have to reject Bultmann's own attempt to de-mythicize. **1953** R. H. FULLER tr. *Bartsch's Kerygma & Myth* I. 214 Other remedies might easily be found..more efficacious than the demythicization of the Gospel. **1967** *Religious Studies* II. 171 It is especially in Greek culture that myth was submitted to a long and penetrating analysis, from which it emerged radically 'de-mythicized'.

demythify (diːˈmɪθɪfaɪ), *v.* [f. DE- II. 1 + MYTHIFY *v.*] *trans.* To deprive of mythical character; to remove the aura of reverence, sentimentality, etc., from. Cf. DEMYTHOLOGIZE *v.*

1964 S. ATTANASIO tr. *H. Fesquet's Wit & Wisdom Good Pope John* p. 19 John XXIII..by his disdain for honours, by his aversion to luxury, by his exquisite cordiality..put himself on an equal footing with the people. He 'de-mythified' the profession of pope. **1968** *Economist* 25 May 50/3 So many real names would have to be named, so many public myths demythified. **1973** *Guardian Weekly* 24 Feb. 19 Franc considers the play as a chance to demythify the politico-religious system oppressing their comrades. **1984** *Time* 30 Jan. 94/1 In his attempt to demystify and demythify 'the Bard'.., McKellen establishes two reference points between himself and Shakespeare.

demythologize (diːmɪˈθɒlədʒaɪz), *v. trans.* and *intr.* [f. DE- II. 1 + MYTHOLOGIZE *v.*] To remove the mythical elements (from a legend, cult, etc.); spec. *Theology* (cf. G. *entmythologisierung* and quot. 1953): to reinterpret the mythological elements in the Bible. Hence **demyˈthologizing** *vbl. sb.* and *ppl. a.*; **demyˌthologiˈzation.**

1950 *Scot. Jrnl. Theol.* III. 39 What it means..to be initiated into the Kingdom of Heaven, and to have religion 'de-mythologised'. **1951** F. V. FILSON tr. *Cullmann's Christ & Time* 13 A *framework*, of which we must strip the account in order to get at the kernel ('de-mythologizing' or 'myth-removal'). **1953** *Radio Times* 23 Jan. 19/2 A new word has entered into New Testament criticism since Bultmann began his exegesis: *Entmythologisierung*, best translated 'demythologising'. Bultmann claims that there are many passages in the Bible, especially those about God and his dealings with man, that have the form of mythological expressions; and if they are to be intelligible in the twentieth century they must be interpreted. **1955** J. MACQUARRIE *Existentialist Theol.* vii. 176 A demythologized Bible.. would require to use the same obscure symbolic language.. and because that language would be symbolic, it would be more accurate to speak of transmythologization than of demythologization. **1959** *Observer* 18 Jan. 20/7 Recently, there have been attempts to demythologise this highly popular saint [*sc.* St. Thérèse of Lisieux]. **1962** *Listener* 11 Jan. 68/1 Bultmann unflinchingly demythologizes, until he reaches that inner heart of Christian belief which he identifies with the *Kerygma*, the gospel truth. **1969** R. BAMBROUGH *Reason, Truth & God* ii. 37 There is no incompatibility between a refurbished, demythologized Homeric polytheism, a refurbished, demythologized Islam, and a refurbished, demythologized Christianity. **1971** *Nature* 12 Feb. 460/1 Thus, for Roszak, science, which began as a demythologizing force, by its own logic creates new and darker mysteries.

den (dɛn), *sb.*[1] Forms: 1-4 denn, 4-7 denne, (4-5 deen), 3- den. [OE. *denn* habitation of a wild beast:—OTeut. type **danjo™*, corresp. in form to OHG. *tenni* neut., MHG. *tenne* neut. fem., Ger. *tenne* f. floor, thrashing-floor, OLG. **denni*, early mod.Du. *denne* 'floor, pavement, flooring of a ship, also cave, cavern, den' (Kilian): cf. also MDu. *dan(n* m. forest, abode of wild beasts, waste place, open country. The same root *dan-* appears in *dean*, OE. *denu* (:—*dani-*) vale: the root-meaning is uncertain.]

1. The lair or habitation of a wild beast.

Beowulf 5512 Geseah [he]..wundur on wealle, and þæs wyrmes denn. **c1000** *Voc.* in Wr.-Wülcker 187/1 *Lustra*, wilddeora holl and denn. **c1220** *Bestiary* 13 Ðe leun.. driueð dun to his den ðar he him berȝen wille. **a1300** *Cursor M.* 16762 + 110 (Cott.) þe fox has his den and ilk foghel is nest. **c1380** WYCLIF *Wks.* (1880) 15 And so dide..þe prophete danyel in þe deen of lyonys. **a1400** *Octouian* 582 The lady wente.. To the tygre denne. **1585** J. B. tr. *Viret's Sch. Beastes* B ij b, It is a signe of rayne..when the Ante bringeth out of her hole and denne al her egges. **1611** BIBLE *Job* xxxvii. 8 Then the beastes goe into dennes: and remaine in their places. **1808** SCOTT *Marm.* VI. xiv, And darest thou then To beard the lion in his den, The Douglas in his hall?

2. A place hollowed out of the ground, a cavern (†*occas.* a pit). *Obs.* or blended with 1 or 3.

a1300 *Cursor M.* 4185 (Cott.) Tac we him out of yon den [Joseph in the pit]. **1382** WYCLIF *Heb.* xi. 38 Thei erringe in ..dennys and cauys of the erthe. **1387** TREVISA *Higden* (Rolls) I. 315 Þe lond of Sicilia is holow and ful of dennes [L. *cavernosa*]. **1530** PALSGR. 212/2 Den, a hole in the grounde, *cauerne.* **1548** HALL *Chron.* 191 [They] lurked in dennes and wholes secretly. **1588** SHAKS. *Tit. A.* II. iii. 215 Aaron and thou looke downe into this den. **1678** BUNYAN *Pilgr.* I. i, I lighted on a certain place, Where was a Denn; And I laid me down in that place to sleep. **1726** CAVALLIER *Mem.* I. 101, I ..had already search'd into several Denns and Caverns of the Mountains. **1847** EMERSON *Poems, Saadi* Wks. (Bohn) I. 473 No churl, immured in cave or den.

3. *transf.* and *fig.* **a.** A place of retreat or abode (likened to the lair of a beast); a secret lurking-place of thieves or the like (cf. Matt. xxi. 13).

c1275 *Pains of Hell* 176 in *O.E. Misc.* 152 Vvrþer þer beoþ olde men þat among neddren habbeþ heore den. **c1340** *Cursor M.* 14745 (Trin.) Ȝe hit make..A den to reset inne þeues. **c1430** *How wise Man taught Son* 132 in *Babees Bk.* 52 How litil her good dooþ hem availe Whanne þei be doluen in her den. **1588** SPENSER *Virgil's Gnat* 96 No such sad cares.. Do ever creepe into the shepheards den. **1719** DE FOE *Crusoe* (1840) II. viii. 186 [They would have] made the island a den of thieves. **1810** SCOTT *Lady of L.* I. iv, The Cavern, where, 'tis told, A giant made his den of old. **1860** TYNDALL *Glac.* I. xxiii. 167 The very type of a robber den.

b. A small confined room or abode; *esp.* one unfit for human habitation.

1837 DICKENS *Pickw.* ii, The musicians were securely confined in an elevated den. **1840** T. A. TROLLOPE *Summ. Brittany* I. 315 The frightful dens of some of the Manchester operatives. **1891** E. PEACOCK *N. Brendon* II. 100 The filthy den where her mother lived.

c. *colloq.* A small room or lodging in which a man can seclude himself for work or leisure; as, 'a bachelor's den'.

1771 SMOLLETT *Humph. Cl.* 5 June ¶3 So saying, he retreated into his den. **1816** SCOTT *Lett.* (1894) I. 372 A little boudoir..a good eating-room, and a small den for me in particular. **1882** *Blackw. Mag.* Dec. 709 [He] went off in the direction of his own den, a little room in which he smoked and kept his treasures.

4. The name given in the Lowlands of Scotland, and north of England, to the conventional enclosure or place of safety in boys' out-of-door games, called elsewhere the *home*, *bay*, or *base*.

1901 R. C. MACLAGAN *Games of Argyle* 22 Equal sides being chosen, a 'den'..sufficiently large to contain the whole of the side who are 'in' is fixed. **1959** I. & P. OPIE *Lore & Lang. of Schoolchildren* viii. 150 *Den* or *denny*. Occasionally used as truce term, from the 'den' or sanctuary of certain catching games. **1968** *Proc. Leeds Philos. Soc., Lit. & Hist. Section* XIII. II. 56 There is the *den*, in which players line up to take their turn in striking.

5. 'A deep hollow between hills; a dingle' (Jam.). *Sc. local.*

['Often applied to a wooded hollow' (Jam.), and then nearly synonymous with DEAN[2]; but not the same word.]

1552 ABP. HAMILTON *Catech.* (1884) 23 In the vail or den quharin thow usit to committ ydolatrie. **1785** BURNS *To W. Simpson* x, We'll sing auld Coila's..banks an' braes, her dens an' dells. **a1800** *Ballad*, 'The dowie dens of Yarrow.' **1806** SIR W. FORBES *Beattie* II. 51 (Jam.), I have made several visits of late to the Den of Rubislaw. *Note.* A *Den*, in the vernacular language of Scotland..is synonymous with what in England is called a *Dingle*.

(In many place names, as *Dura Den* near Cupar Fife, *The Den* near Kirkcaldy, *Hawthornden* in Mid Lothian; but as a termination often representing earlier *dene, dean.*)

†**6.** *Anat.* A cavity or hollow. *Obs.*

1398 TREVISA *Barth. De P.R.* III. xxii. (1495) 70 Oute of a denne of the lyfte syde of the herte comyth a veyne. **1615** CROOKE *Body of Man* 609 The implanted Ayre concluded within the dennes or cauities of the Eares. **1683** SNAPE *Anat. Horse* III. xiv. (1686) 140 The Caverns or Cavities, by some called Dens.

7. *Comb.*, as †*den-dreadful* adj. (= dreadful with dens of wild beasts).

1621 G. SANDYS *Ovid's Met.* I. (1626) 6 Now past den-dreadfull Mænalus confines [*Mænala..latebris horrenda ferarum*].

†**den**, *sb.*[2] Also dene, deyn. Obs. Sc. variant of DAN[1], sir, master.

c1375 *Sc. Leg. Saints, Egipciane* 1110 To ȝour abbot, dene Iohne, say. **c1425** WYNTOUN *Cron.* VIII. x. 92 (Jam.) The Abbot of Abbyrbrothok than, Den Henry. **c1450** HOLLAND *Howlat* 199 Gret Ganeris..That war demyt, but dowt, denyss douchty. **1552** LYNDESAY *Monarche* 4670-2 All Monkrye..Ar callit Denis, for dignite; Quhowbeit his mother mylk the kow, He man be callit Dene Androw.

den[3], in the salutation ***good den***: see GOOD EVEN.

den (dɛn), *v.*[1] [f. DEN *sb.*[1]]

1. *refl.* (or *passive*). To ensconce or hide oneself in (or as in) a den.

c1220 *Bestiary* 36 Wu he dennede him in ðat defte meiden, Marie bi name. **1613** HEYWOOD *Silver Age* III. Wks. 1874 III. 129 If he be den'd, Il'e rouze the monstrous beast. **1632** LITHGOW *Trav.* VII. 315 A pit digged to hide the Gunner..the Gunner lay denned, and durst not stirre. **1823** GALT *Entail* II. xvii. 157 'Hae ye ony ark or amrie..where a body might den himsel till they're out o' the gate and away?'

2. *intr.* To live or dwell in a den; to escape into, or hide oneself in, a den.

to den up: to retire into a den for the winter, as a hibernating animal. (*U.S. colloq.*)

1610 G. FLETCHER *Christ's Vict.* xiv, The sluggish saluages, that den belowe. **1722** DUDLEY in *Phil. Trans.* XXXII. 295 They generally den among the Rocks in great Numbers together. **1843** *American Pioneer* II. 171 In that climate [*sc.* of Canada] the bears usually den up in the winter, and lie in something of a torpid state. **c1860** TOM TAYLOR in Thornbury *Two Cent. of Song* (1867) 261 In a dingier set of chambers no man need wish to stow, Than those, old friend, wherein we denned, at Ten, Crown Office Row. **1894** *Home Miss.* (N.Y.) Jan. 463 Our people..are inclined to 'den up' in the hot weather, as certain animals.. do in the cold season. **1918** *Chambers's Jrnl.* Mar. 187/1 The brown bear usually 'dens up' early in the season.

†**3.** ***to den out***: to drive (a beast) out of its den; to unearth. *Obs.*

1571 HANMER *Chron. Irel.* (1633) 203 [They] burned their Cabbans and Cottages, and such as dwelt in caves and rockes underground (as the manner is to denne out Foxes) they fired and smothered to death.

Hence **denned** (dɛnd) *ppl. a.*, **denning** *vbl. sb.*

1622 S. WARD *Woe to Drunkards* (1627) 45 In such townes this Serpent hath no nestling, no stabling, or denning. **1854** *Tait's Mag.* XXI. 165 Arousing a denned lion.

†**den**, *v.*[2] *Obs. rare*[−1]. [Etymol. doubtful: cf. DEM *v.*[1]] *trans.* To dam up.

1375 BARBOUR *Bruce* XIV. 354 This fals tratour his men had maid..The ysche of a louch to den [*rime* men].

den, obs. form of DEAN[1] (*decanus*), DENE[2].

denaer: see DINAR.

denalagu (OE.): see DANE-LAW.

†**de'name**, *v. Obs.* [f. DE- I. 3 + NAME *v.*, after OF. *denomer*, *denommer*, L. *dēnōmināre.*] *trans.* To denominate.

1555 ABP. PARKER *Ps.* cxix. 365 These fiftene Psalmes next followyng Be songs denamd of steps or stayers. **a1640** JACKSON *Creed* x. notes, Wks. IX. 268 The exorbitance of a diseased appetite in man is therefore denamed 'caninus appetitus'.

den and strand: see DENE[2].

denar, denare ('di:nə(r), di:'nɑ:(r), -'ɛə(r)). Forms: 6 denaire, 6-8 denare, 6- denar. [Modification of ME. *dener*, *denere* (from OF. *dener*), DENIER, assimilated to L. *dēnārius*, It. *denaro*, *danaro*, and the adaptations of these in other languages.] A coin: the Roman DENARIUS; the Italian *denaro* or Spanish *dinero* of the 16-17th c.; the Persian and East Indian DINAR, q.v.

1547 BOORDE *Introd. Knowl.* 179 In Italy..in bras they haue kateryns & byokes & denares. **1597** *1st Pt. Return fr. Parnass.* I. i. 196 The villaine would not part with a denaire. **1699** BENTLEY *Phal.* xiv. 438 The Sicilian Talent was anciently Six, and afterwards Three Denares. **1701** W. WOTTON *Hist. Rome* Notes 154 Antony..promises 5000 Denares to every private Soldier. **1872** YEATS *Growth Comm.* 367 The solidi..were reckoned as equal to twelve silver denars. *Ibid.* 368 Smaller gold pieces were also coined ..under the name of gold pennies, gold denars or oboluses.

denarcotize: see DE- II. 1.

†**de'nariate**, *sb. Obs.* or *Hist.* [ad. med.L. *dēnāriāt-us* (in *Laws of Edw. Confessor*, Du Cange), f. L. *dēnārius* penny: see below.] A portion of land worth a penny a year.

1610 W. FOLKINGHAM *Art of Survey* II. vii. 58 There be also other quantities of Land taking their denominations from our vsual Coine; as Fardingdeales, Obolates, Denariates, Solidates, Librates. **1670** in BLOUNT *Law Dict.* s.v. *Fardingdeal.*

†**de'nariate**, *a. Obs.* [f. L. *dēnāri-us* (see below), in med. sense 'money': see -ATE[2].] Of or pertaining to money; monetary.

1632 LITHGOW *Trav.* x. 441 The Host perceiving their denariat charge, he entered their chamber, when they were a sleepe.

denarie, obs. form of DENARY.

‖**denarius** (dɪ'nɛərɪəs). Pl. denarii (-ɪaɪ). [L., for *dēnārius nūmus* denary coin, coin containing ten (asses), f. *dēni* every ten, ten by ten: see -ARY[1].]

1. An ancient Roman silver coin, originally of the value of ten asses (about eightpence of modern English money).

1579 NORTH *Plutarch* (1612) 862 (Stanf.), Eleuen Myriades of their Denarij. **1645** EVELYN *Diary* (1850) I. 182 (ibid.), Ten asses make the Roman denarius. **1788** PRIESTLEY *Lect. Hist.* III. xv. (R.), In the early times of Rome, the price of a sheep was a denarius, or eight pence. **1840** ARNOLD *Hist. Rome* II. 534 The silver coinage [of Rome] was first introduced in the year 485; and the coins struck were denarii, quinarii, and sestertii. **1877** C. GEIKIE *Christ* liv. (1879) 650 When they came..who were hired at the eleventh hour, they received each a denarius.

2. A gold coin (*denarius aureus*) of the ancient Roman empire, worth 25 silver denarii.

1661 LOVELL *Hist. Anim. & Min.* 8 The fourth part of a golden denarius. **1817** COLEBROOKE *Algebra* lxxxiv, We read in Roman authors of golden as well as silver denarii.

3. The weight of the silver denarius used as a measure of weight, nearly equivalent to the Greek *drachma*.

1398 TREVISA *Barth. De P.R.* XIX. cxxxi. (1495) 940 Scrupulus that is the eyghtenthe Huolus is callyd Denarius and is acountyd for ten pans. **1771** RAPER in *Phil. Trans.* LXI. 492 The Romans did not use the Denarius for a weight ..till the Greek physicians..prescribed by it, as they had been accustomed to do by the Drachm in their own country.

¶ In English monetary reckoning used for 'penny', and abbreviated *d.*; see D III. 1.

†**de'narrable**, *a. Obs.*[−0] [f. L. *dēnarrā-re* to narrate + -BLE.] 'Proper to be related, capable of being declared'.

1727 BAILEY vol. II. **1730-6** —— (folio).

So †**dena'rration**, 'a narration' (Bailey, 1727).

†**denary, denarie**, *sb.*[1] *Obs.* [ad. L. *dēnārius.*] = DENARIUS, the Roman penny.

c1449 PECOCK *Repr.* II. ii. 140 Thei offriden to him a denarie. **1548** UDALL, etc. *Erasm. Par. Matt.* xviii. 93 An hundreth denaries. **1550** LATIMER *Serm. Stamford* Wks. I. 279 'Shew me..a penny of the tribute money'..and they brought him a denari. **1615** BRIGHTMAN *Revelation* 213 Let thre such measures of barly bee sold for a denary. **1674** JEAKE *Arith.* (1696) 105 This is sometime called *Drachmal Denary* for distinction sake.

denary ('di:nərɪ), *a.* and *sb.*[2] [ad. L. *dēnāri-us* containing ten.]

A. *adj.* Relating to the number ten; having ten as the basis of reckoning; decimal.

1848 C. WORDSWORTH *Hulsean Lect. Apocalypse* 524 Being toes they must be ten..in other successive prophecies this denary number is retained. **1875** *Encycl. Brit.* II. 463 To convert 8735 of the denary into the duodenary scale. **1891** *Pall Mall G.* 4 Aug. 6/1 The ten denary symbols.

†**B.** *sb. Obs.*

1. The number ten; a group of ten, a decad.

1615 CROOKE *Body of Man* 337 Three Denaries or Decades of weekes. **a1648** SIR K. DIGBY in *Suppl. to Cabala* 248 (T.) Centenaries, that are composed of denaries, and they of units. **1682** H. MORE *Annot. Glanvill's Lux O.* 180 Suppose..Denary, is such a setled number and no other.

2. A tithing or tenth part.

1577 HARRISON *England* II. iv. (1877) I. 91 He diuided.. lathes into hundreds, and hundreds into tithings, or denaries.

de-nastification (di:nɑ:stɪfɪ'keɪʃən). *colloq.* [f. DE- II + NASTY *a.* + -FICATION.] The process or result of removing unpleasantness or of making (something) less nasty.

1983 *Economist* 24 Dec. (Wine Survey) 14/2 The result of Mr Jago's de-nastification process was Piat d'Or. **1985** *Ibid.* 8 June 15 The wider denastification of British society will succeed only if the sight of televised slaughter [among football hooligans]..has at last shocked enough decent Britons by enough.

denatality (di:nə'tælɪtɪ). [ad. F. *dénatalité*, f. DE- II. 3 + NATALITY.] A declining birthrate.

1939 *Tablet* 26 Aug. 269/2 The Daladier Government has begun to concern itself with this problem of denatality, which is far more serious even than that of the national defence. **1941** KOESTLER *Scum of Earth* iv. 238 Laziness, selfishness, alcoholism, denatality are supposed to be the clinical symptoms of decline.

denatant (di:'neɪtənt), *a.* [f. DE- + NATANT *a.*] Of fishes: swimming with the current. Hence **dena'tation**, the movement of fishes in the direction of the current.

1915 Denatant, -ation [see CONTRANATANT *a.*]. **1920** *Rep. Dove Mar. Lab. Cullercoats* 38 A consideration of our herring shoals from the standpoint of denatation. **1959** [see CONTRANATANT *a.*]. **1968** F. R. H. JONES *Fish Migration* ii. 15 Denatant means swimming, or drifting, or migrating with the current.

denationalism (di:'næʃənəlɪz(ə)m). [f. DENATIONALIZE: see -ISM.] The loss or deprivation of national character. Also **de'nationalist**, one who would deprive a people of its national identity.

1916 STANFORD & FORSYTH *Hist. Music* xvi. 305 The nationalists and the denationalists. **1923** *Glasgow Herald* 29 Mar. 9 International control of the Rhineland and the Saar meant denationalism of the people.

denationalization (dɪˌnæʃənəlaɪˈzeɪʃən). [f. next + -ATION. Also in mod.F. (*-isation*), Littré.]

1. The action of denationalizing, or condition of being denationalized.

1814 SIR R. WILSON *Diary* II. 363 Is not the advantage.. counterbalanced by the extinction of Poland and Italy, by the denationalisation of two such interesting portions of Europe? **1868** DILKE *Greater Brit.* I. I. iv. 45 Americans are never slow to ridicule the denationalization of New York.

2. The action of removing (an industry, etc.) from national control and returning it to private ownership.

1921 *Official Index to Times* Mar.-June 479/1 Russia... Textile industries—denationalization recommended. **1959** *Daily Tel.* 13 Mar. 13/4 The 13 steel companies still awaiting denationalisation. **1971** *Observer* 14 Mar. 29/3 A policy of, say, nationalisation or denationalisation of an individual industry.

denationalize (dɪˈnæʃənəlaɪz), *v.* [a. F. *dénationaliser* (a word of the French Revolution), f. DE- II. 1 + *national*, *nationaliser*.]

1. *trans.* To deprive of nationality; to take his proper nationality from (a person, a ship, etc.); to destroy the independent or distinct nationality of (a country).

1807 *Ann. Reg.* 779 By these acts the British government denationalizes ships of every country in Europe. **1841** *Blackw. Mag.* L. 773 To denationalize themselves, and to endeavour to forget that they have a country. **1880** MCCARTHY *Own Times* III. 365 New steps were taken for denationalising the country and effecting its.. subjugation.

2. a. To make (an institution, etc.) no longer national; to divest of its character as belonging to the whole nation, or to a particular nation.

1839 *Times* 29 June in *Spirit Metropol. Conserv. Press* (1840) II. 122 The attempt to.. denationalise the education of the infant poor. **1878** *N. Amer. Rev.* CXXVI. 266 That this crime against humanity [slavery].. should be denationalized.

b. To transfer (an industry, etc.) from national to private ownership. Also *intr.*

1921 *Times* 17 Jan. 10/2 The object of the.. agitation is not to improve the [telephone] service, but to get it denationalized, 'to get it handed over to private capitalists'. **1947** *Observer* 21 Dec. 5/4 It was no part of the Conservative programme to denationalise coal. **1965** *New Statesman* 7 May 714/1 All this fuss about steel would have been quite unnecessary if the Churchill cabinet had stood firm against backbench pressure to denationalise in 1951. **1970** C. N. PARKINSON *Law of Delay* 62 The Conservatives tried timidly to go into reverse over steel and road haulage. But a process by which those or other industries should be nationalised and denationalised is not technically possible.

Hence **de'nationalized** *ppl. a.*, **de'nationalizer**, **de'nationalizing** *vbl. sb.* and *ppl. a.*

1812 *Q. Rev.* VIII. 205 Those denationalised neutrals have no right to resist. **1848** *Tait's Mag.* XV. 826 A horrid system of denationalizing has roused in them terrible passions. **1860** *Sat. Rev.* X. 471/2 The cosmopolitan and denationalizing character of the Church. **1882** J. H. BLUNT *Ref. Ch. Eng.* II. 206 A long train of foreigners or denationalized Englishmen.

denaturalization (dɪˌnætjʊərəlaɪˈzeɪʃən, diː-). [f. next + -ATION. So in mod.F.] The action of denaturalizing, or condition of being denaturalized.

1811 *Chron.* in *Ann. Reg.* 347 Every person, a subject of this kingdom, who leaves it without a passport.. shall incur the punishment of denaturalisation. **1881** *Scribner's Mag.* XXII. 94 He must submit to letters of denaturalization, if he is to be passed.

b. = DENATURATION.

1882 *Chemist & Druggist* XXIV. 51/2 A Commission in Germany has reported on the processes of denaturalisation of Alcohol for manufacturing purposes.

denaturalize (dɪˈnætjʊərəlaɪz, diː-), *v.* [f. DE- II. 1 + *natural*, *naturalize*: so in mod.F. (Littré).]

1. *trans.* To deprive of its original nature; to alter or pervert the nature of; to make unnatural.

1812 SOUTHEY *Omniana* I. 34 All creatures are, more or less, denaturalized by confinement. **1853** H. ROGERS *Ecl. Faith* 140 This 'spiritual' faculty.. denaturalised and disabled. **1881** PALGRAVE *Visions Eng.* Pref. 13 The lyrical ballad.. like certain wild flowers, is almost always denaturalized by culture.

2. To deprive of the status and rights of a natural subject or citizen; the opposite of *naturalize*.

1816 KEATINGE *Trav.* (1817) II. 119 The Duque d' Aveiro, having been degraded and denaturalized previous to condemnation. **1838** PRESCOTT *Ferd. & Is.* (1846) I. Introd. 30 They also claimed the privilege, when aggrieved, of denaturalizing themselves, or, in other words, of publicly renouncing their allegiance to their Sovereign.

Hence **de'naturalized**, **-izing** *ppl. adjs.*

1800 SOUTHEY *Life* (1850) II. 45 By residing in that huge denaturalised city. **1812** *Edin. Rev.* XIX. 375 Cast off without ceremony as denaturalized beings. **1820** *Lond. Mag.* May 549/2 The practice of such denaturalizing depravities. **1847** DE QUINCEY *Schlosser's Lit. Hist.* Wks. 1862 VII. 54 In their own denaturalised hearts they read only a degraded nature.

denaturalizer (diːˈnætjʊərəˌlaɪzə(r), -tʃər-). [f. DENATURALIZE *v.* + -ER[1].] One who or that which denaturalizes.

1832 *Crisis* 19 May 31/3 Man.. the great denaturalizer of other animals, has exerted his deforming powers most remarkably.. upon himself. **1905** *Westm. Gaz.* 28 Mar. 4/2 That ideal 'de-naturaliser' which would.. solve the whole problem.

denaturant (diːˈneɪtjʊərənt, -tʃər-). Also **-ent**. [f. DENATURE *v.* + -ANT[1].] A substance added to alcohol or other substances as a denaturing agent. (Cf. DENATURE *v.* 2.)

1905 *Westm. Gaz.* 4 Apr. 5/2 Alcohol similar in purity to methylated spirits before the denaturent is added. **1906** *Daily Chron.* 15 Sept. 3/4 The problem of a cheap, available and efficient denaturant. **1920** *Auto* 4 Mar. 248/2 A real denaturant, which will leave the fuel effective for its purpose, but destroy its qualities as a substitute for drinkable spirit. **1922** *Chambers's Jrnl.* 624/2 Alcohol of 95 per cent. purity was used without denaturents. **1946** *Rep. Internat. Control Atomic Energy* II. v. 23 It is possible, both for U235 and for plutonium, to remove the denaturant.

denaturate (diːˈneɪtjʊəreɪt, -tʃər-), *v.* [f. DE- + NATURE + -ATE[3].] = DENATURE *v.* 2. So **de'naturated** *ppl. a.*

1895 G. LUNGE *Sulphuric Acid* (ed. 2) II. 14 Decomposing the salt for saltcake.. is avoided by 'denaturating' the salt under official supervision. **1904** *Daily Chron.* 4 Aug. 3/5 A proper denaturating medium is not known. **1911** *Jrnl. Physiol.* XLIII. 15 SO_4 assists the agglutination of denaturated egg-albumen much more powerfully than Cl.

denaturation (diːˌneɪtjʊəˈreɪʃən, -tʃər-). [f. DENATUR(E *v.* + -ATION.] The action of denaturing; *spec.* in *Biochem.* (see quot. 1965 and DENATURE *v.* 2 b).

1882 *Athenæum* 25 Mar. 385/1 A paper 'On the Denaturation of Alcohol by the Action of Wood-Spirit'. **1911** *Jrnl. Physiol.* XLIII. 25 Complete 'heat coagulation' of proteins.. consists of two processes: (1) the union of the protein and hot water ('denaturation'), (2) subsequent agglutination and separation of the product. **1946** *Nature* 13 July 58/1 It has not been found possible to obtain more than an insignificant amount of the protein of apple-fruits in a soluble form except by treatments so drastic as to lead, inevitably, to some degradation as well as denaturation of the protein. **1956** *Ibid.* 10 Mar. 447/2 Recent studies on the reversible denaturation of proteins. **1965** M. JOLY *Physico-chem. Approach to Denaturation of Proteins* 3 Denaturation is any modification of the secondary, tertiary or quaternary structure of the protein molecule, excluding any breaking of covalent bond.

denature (dɪˈneɪtjʊə(r), diː-), *v.* [a. F. *dénaturer*, OF. *desnaturer*, f. *des-*, *dé-* (DE- I. 6) + *nature*; a doublet of DISNATURE.]

†**1.** *trans.* To render unnatural. *Obs.*

1685 COTTON tr. *Montaigne* III. 158 Fanatick people, who think to honour their nature by denaturing themselves.

2. a. To alter (anything) so as to change its nature; e.g. to render alcohol or tea unfit for consumption.

1907 *Chem. Abstr.* I. 2009 Denaturing acetic acid... The strength of acetic acid to be denatured is not specified. **1924** H. E. FOSDICK *Mod. Use of Bible* v. 158 Unless it is willing to be denatured, religion cannot get on without this exciting aspect of its thought. **1951** E. BARKER *Princ. Soc. & Pol. Theory* II. ii. 47 We only dream; and our dream is one which denatures the State and unspheres law. **1965** *Times Lit. Suppl.* 25 Nov. 1063/3 To omit the commas.. is.. to denature or homogenize the lines.

b. *Biochem.* To modify (a protein) by heat, acid, etc., so that it no longer has its original properties.

1925 *Jrnl. Biol. Chem.* LXIV. 370 When a protein is denatured by dilute acids and alkalies.. an increase occurs in the acid- and base-binding powers. **1970** R. W. MCGILVERY *Biochem.* viii. 150 Some proteins, notably trypsin, are denatured in hot water, but return to their active form upon cooling.

Hence **de'natured** *ppl. a.*; **de'naturing** *ppl. a.* and *vbl. sb.*

1878 J. THOMSON *Plenip. Key* 7 If your liquor be.. not of the denatured nature of London milk.. chicory coffee. **1888** *Manch. Exam.* 3 July 6/5 Regulations authorising the removal from bond of what was termed denatured tea. **1907** R. F. HERRICK *Denatured or Industrial Alcohol* i. 2 A number of other substances are used as denaturing agents. *Ibid.* 3 Such denaturing was accomplished by mixing ten per cent of commercial wood alcohol with ordinary alcohol. **1971** *Sci. Amer.* June 48/2 The first step isolated the elastic fiber ..by the use of a denaturing extractant such as a concentrated solution of guanidine and enzymes that specifically break down collagen.

denaturize (diːˈneɪtjʊəraɪz, -tʃər-), *v.* [f. DE- + NATURE + -IZE.] = DENATURE *v.* 2. Hence **deˌnaturi'zation**, denaturation.

1898 *Trans. Amer. Inst. Electr. Engin.* 139 (Cent. D. Suppl.). **1905** *Westm. Gaz.* 26 Jan. 2/2 The general idea is that if the alcohol be denaturised.. it should be subject to no impost. **1969** *Physics Bull.* Jan. 8/2 Denaturization of key enzymes in the cellular structure.

denaur, var. of DINAR, an eastern coin.

denay, obs. variant of DENY *v.* and *sb.*

denazify (diːˈnɑːtsɪfaɪ), *v.* [DE- II + NAZI + -FY.] *trans.* To (attempt to) detach (Nazis, or their adherents) from Nazi allegiance, or connection; also *transf.* Hence **denazifi'cation**, the detachment of Nazis from their allegiance; the removal of Nazis from official positions; also *attrib.*

1944 *Spectator* 28 July 72/2 Whenever the problem of.. de-Nazifying the young Nazis, is being seriously approached, some encounter or incident turns up to make the.. hopelessness of the situation inescapable. **1944** *Sat. Rev. Lit.* 19 Aug. 10 His hope for a de-Nazification of Germany's killers. **1945** *Times* 16 July 3/4 The rapid progress which has been made in carrying out the allied denazification policies. **1955** *Ibid.* 26 July 7/2 Herr Gunter d'Alquen.. was ordered by a denazification court in an interim judgment to-day to pay 60,000 marks. **1957** *Economist* 28 Dec. 1136/1 The medals issued from 1939 to 1945 all carry the stigma of the swastika. They.. must give place on their holders' breasts to denazified successors. **1958** *Times Lit. Suppl.* 30 May 292/2 Denazification was a failure and so was decartelization. **1970** *Daily Tel.* 21 Feb. 8/6 In this way the casual viewer, denied the information that the anti-Jewish remark was addressed to a Jew, while the anti-Nazi remark was written during the Nazi regime, is liable to come away with the impression that here is an anti-Semite attempting to denazify himself.

dendelion, obs. form of DANDELION.

dendrachate, etc.: see under DENDRO-.

'dendral, *a. rare.* [f. Gr. δένδρ-ον tree + -AL[1].] Pertaining to or of the nature of a tree; arboreal.

1874 H. W. BEECHER in *Christian Union* 28 Jan. 72 Such trees as that dendral child of God, the elm.

dendranatomy, **-anthropology**: see under DENDRO-.

†**'dendrical**, *a. Obs.* [f. as prec. + -IC + -AL[1].] Of the nature of or resembling a tree; dendritic.

1758 MENDES DA COSTA in *Monthly Rev.* 454 The said author took a dendrites fresh dug.. scraped all the black or dendrical substance from it.

dendriform (ˈdɛndrɪfɔːm), *a.* [f. as prec. + -FORM, L. *-form-is*; after *cruciform*, etc.] Of the form of a tree; branching, arborescent.

1847 in CRAIG. **1869** NICHOLSON *Zool.* 89 A dendriform mass. **1888** ROLLESTON & JACKSON *Anim. Life* 791 A sponge may be.. leaf or fan-like, branched or dendriform.

dendrite (ˈdɛndraɪt). Also in Lat. form **dendrites** (dɛnˈdraɪtiːz), pl. **dendritæ** (-tiː). [ad. Gr. δενδρίτης of or pertaining to a tree, f. δένδρον tree: see -ITE. In F. *dendrite* (1732 in Trévoux).]

1. A natural marking or figure of a branching form, like a tree or moss, found on or in some stones or minerals; a stone or mineral so marked.

1727-51 CHAMBERS *Cycl.* s.v., In some dendrites, the figures, or signatures, penetrate quite through. **1774** STRANGE in *Phil. Trans.* LXV. 35 It is also variegated by frequent dendrites. **1825** COLERIDGE *Aids Refl.* (1848) I. 27 As dendrites derive the outlines.. from the casual neighbourhood and pressure of the plants. **1863** LYELL *Antiq. Man* vii. (ed. 3) 116 Those ramifying crystallizations called dendrites usually consisting of the mixed oxyds of iron and manganese, forming extremely delicate brownish sprigs, resembling the smaller kinds of sea-weeds.

Comb. **1856** STANLEY *Sinai & Pal.* i. (1858) 45 The older travellers.. all notice what they call Dendrite-stones,—i.e. stones with fossil trees marked upon them.

2. A crystalline growth of branching or arborescent form, as of some metals under electrolysis.

1882 A. S. HERSCHEL in *Nature* No. 642. 363 After a few hours of charging, the rough dendrites of humus-coloured substance acquired frond-like form.

3. *Anat.* Any of one or more processes from a nerve cell which are typically short and extensively branched and which conduct impulses towards the cell body.

1893, **1899** [see DENDRON]. **1900** W. S. HALL *Physiology* 535 The dendrites, or protoplasmic processes, resemble more closely in appearance the cell-body itself than does the axon. **1902** *Encycl. Brit.* XXV. 394/2 In the simplest cases the dendrites carry the sensory impulse to the nerve-cell. **1927** HALDANE & HUXLEY *Anim. Biol.* i. 40 Shorter branched outgrowths (dendrites). **1962** *Lancet* 29 Dec. 1359/2 The cell bodies and dendrites of both cerebral and cerebellar cortex are indeed conspicuously rich in protein. **1967** [see DENDRON].

Hence **den'dritiform** *a.*, having the form or appearance of a dendrite.

1890 in *Cent. Dict.*

dendritic (dɛnˈdrɪtɪk), *a.* [mod. f. DENDRITE (in F. *dendritique*): see -IC.] Resembling or of the nature of dendrite: said of various structures or formations, chiefly mineral and animal.

1. Of a branching form; arborescent, tree-like. Also in *Geogr.*

1816 P. CLEAVELAND *Mineral.* 445 This variety.. is reniform, dendritic, in membranes, &c. **1841** TRIMMER *Pract. Geol.* 74 Dendritic native silver and copper. **1870** ROLLESTON *Anim. Life* Introd. 102 This structure.. may be either dendritic or foliaceous. **1898** I. C. RUSSELL *River Devel.* vii. 204 The well-developed dendritic drainage in Lebanon valley. **1937** WOOLDRIDGE & MORGAN *Phys. Basis Geogr.* xiv. 189 The.. surface will be resolved into slopes leading down to drainage channels. In areas of homogeneous rocks such a process gives rise to a simple, tree-like or dendritic, drainage plan.

2. Having arborescent markings.

1805-17 R. JAMESON *Char. Min.* (ed. 3) 77 Steatite and dendritic calcedony. **1872** H. MACMILLAN *True Vine* iii. 110

Imitations of ferns and foliage..in moss-agates, or in what are called dendritic pebbles.

dendritical (dɛnˈdrɪtɪkəl), *a.* [f. as prec. + -AL[1].] = prec.

1822 G. YOUNG *Geol. Surv. Yorksh. Coast* (1828) 183 The dendritical impressions..observed in the parting of sandstone. **1823** FARADAY *Exp. Res.* xviii. 82 The Hydrate is produced in a crust or in dendritical crystals.

Hence **denˈdritically** *adv.*, like a dendrite.

1884 E. KLEIN *Micro-Organisms & Disease* xiii. 60 In some species [of Bacteria] the zooglæa is dendritically ramified.

dendro-, before a vowel **dendr-**, combining form of Gr. δένδρον tree, as in **ˈdendrachate** (-əkeɪt) [see ACHATE *sb.*[1]], a variety of agate with tree-like markings. †**dendraˈnatomy**, the anatomy of trees (*obs.*). **dendranthroˈpology** (*nonce-wd.*), 'study based on the theory that man had sprung from trees' (Davies). **dendroˈclastic** *a.*, breaking or destroying trees, *sb.* a destroyer of trees. **dendroˈdentine**, 'the form of branched dentine seen in compound teeth, produced by the interblending of the dentine, enamel, and cement' (*Syd. Soc. Lex.* 1883); cf. DENDRODONT below. **denˈdrography**, description of trees (*Syd. Soc. Lex.*). **dendrohelioˈphallic** *a.*, said of a symbolic figure combining a tree, a sun, and a phallus. **denˈdrolatry**, worship of trees. **ˈdendrolite**, a petrified or fossil tree or part of a tree. **denˈdrometer**, an instrument for measuring trees. **ˈdendrophil**, a lover of trees. **denˈdrophilous** *a.*, tree-loving; in *Bot.* growing on or twining round trees. **ˈdendrostyle** (*Zool.*), one of the four pillars by which the syndendrium is suspended from the umbrella in the *Rhizostomidæ*.

[**1706** PHILLIPS (ed. Kersey), *Dendrachates* (Gr.), a kind of Agate-stone, the Veins and Spots of which resemble the Figures of Trees and Shrubs.] **1865** PAGE *Handbk. Geol. Terms, Dendrachate*..moss-agate; agate exhibiting in its sections the forms or figures of vegetable growths. **1697** *Phil. Trans.* XIX. 558 *Dendranatome* may, tho' more remotely, advance even the Practice of Physick, by the Discovery of the Oeconomy of Plants. **1753** CHAMBERS *Cycl. Supp.*, *Dendranatomy*, a term used by Malpighi and others to express the dissection of the ligneous parts of trees and shrubs, in order to the examining their structure and uses. *a* **1843** SOUTHEY *Doctor* ccxv. VII. 168 He formed, therefore, no system of dendranthropology. **1856** *Chamb. Jrnl.* VI. 352 Are we not afflicted by dendroclastics? **1854** OWEN in *Circ. Sc.* (*c.* 1865) II. 96/2 We find not fewer than six leading modifications in fishes. 1. Hard or true dentine ..5. Dendrodentine. **1891** T. J. JEAKES in *N. & Q.* 7th Ser. XII. 395 The dendroheliophallic 'Tree of Life', probably. **1891** tr. *De La Saussaye's Man. Sc. Relig.* xii. 89 The impressions which have given rise to dendrolatry. **1828** WEBSTER, *Dendrolite*, a petrified or fossil shrub, plant, or part of a plant. *Dict. of Nat. Hist.* **1865** PAGE *Handbk. Geol. Terms, Dendrolite*..a general term for any fossil stem, branch, or other fragment of a tree. **1768** *Gentl. Mag.* 552 An account of the new invented Dendrometer. **1874** KNIGHT *Dict. Mech.*, *Dendrometer*, an instrument for measuring the height and diameter of trees, to estimate the cubic feet of timber therein. It has means for taking vertical and horizontal angles, and is mounted on a tripod stand. **1888** *Pall Mall G.* 21 Dec. 3/1 This is the statement of a wild dendrophil. **1886** GUILLEMARD *Cruise 'Marchesa'* II. 188 Dendrophilous plants swarmed up the tree-trunks and shrouded them with their fleshy, fenestrated leaves. **1841-71** T. R. JONES *Anim. Kingd.* (ed. 4) 88 The main trunks of the dependent polypiferous root or stem unite above into a thick quadrate disk (*syndendrium*), which is suspended by four stout pillars (*dendrostyles*), one springing from each angle.

dendrobe (ˈdɛndrəʊb). [ad. mod.L. *Dendrobium*, f. Gr. δένδρον tree + βίος life.] Anglicized form of *Dendrobium*, name of a genus of epiphytal orchids, of which many species are cultivated for the beauty of their flowers.

1882 *The Garden* 7 Jan. 9/3 One word in praise of this old and dear Dendrobe. **1891** *Pall Mall G.* 2 Nov. 3/2 The discovery of what the Anglo-German importers call the 'Elephant Moth Dendrobe'..the *Dendrobium Phalænopsis Schröderianum*.

dendrochronology (ˌdɛndrəʊkrəˈnɒlədʒɪ). [f. DENDRO- + CHRONOLOGY.] The science of arranging events in the order of time by the comparative study of the annual growth rings in (ancient) timber. Hence **ˌdendrochronoˈlogical** *a.*, **ˌdendrochronoˈlogically** *adv.*, **ˌdendrochroˈnologist**.

1928 A. E. DOUGLASS *Climatic Cycles & Tree Growth* II. 5 We are measuring the lapse of time by means of a slow-geared clock within the trees. For this study the name 'dendro-chronology' has been suggested, or 'tree-time'. This expression covers all the dating and historic problems ..as well as the study of cyclic variations and the distribution of climatic conditions. **1937** *Geogr. Jrnl.* LXXXIX. 407 A dendrochronologist is a man who investigates the climate of the past by measuring the rings of trees. **1937** *Proc. Prehist. Soc.* III. 321 The modern ways of pollen-analysis, geochronology and dendrochronology must be applied to settle geologically, once for all, the cultural correlations with Scotland. **1959** *Antiquity* XXXIII. 238 Undateable except by a rough and ready guesswork calculation from dendrochronological dates. **1969** *Nature* 15 Nov. 682/1 Radiocarbon measurements carried out on dendrochronologically dated wood samples.

dendroclastic: see under DENDRO-.

dendroclimatology (ˌdɛndrəʊklaɪməˈtɒlədʒɪ). [f. DENDRO- + CLIMATOLOGY.] The study of past climates by the examination of the annual growth rings in (ancient) timber.

1953 E. SCHULMAN in *Tree-Ring Bull.* XIX. 22 It is important in both dendro-climatology and dendro-archaeology to consider the frequency of occurrence and areal distribution of non-usable ring series in species commonly suitable for such analysis. **1978** *Nature* 4 May 40/2 This has been undertaken to obtain past climate information from the isotope ratios of the hydrogen, oxygen and carbon isotope ratios in the various constituents of wood by workers in the embryonic science of isotope dendroclimatology. **1981** *New Scientist* 19 Feb. 462/1 Dendroclimatology is a young but increasingly important branch of science. Tree rings are, in effect, a 'diary' of weather in the past.

dendrocœl, -cœle (ˈdɛndrəʊsiːl), *a. Zool.* [f. DENDRO- + Gr. κοιλία the body-cavity, abdomen.] Having a branched or arborescent intestine; belonging to the division *Dendrocœla* of Turbellarian Worms. Also **dendroˈcœlan**, **dendroˈcœlous**, in same sense.

1869 NICHOLSON *Zool.* xxiv. (1880) 242 The Nemerteans ..make a near approach to the dendrocœlous Planarians. **1877** HUXLEY *Anat. Inv. Anim.* iv. 194 Sometimes a simple sac..and occasionally branched, like that of the dendrocœle Turbellaria.

dendrocolaptine (ˌdɛndrəʊkəʊˈlæptaɪn, -ɪn), *a. Ornith.* [f. DENDRO- + κολάπτ-ειν to peck, etc.] Belonging or allied to the genus of birds *Dendrocolaptes*, or South American tree-creepers.

1892 W. H. HUDSON *La Plata* 147 There is in La Plata a small very common Dendrocolaptine bird—*Anumbius acuticaudatus*.

dendrodentine: see under DENDRO-.

dendrodic (dɛnˈdrɒdɪk), *a.* [f. Gr. δενδρώδ-ης tree-like + -IC. Cf. also mod.L. *Dendrodus*.] Having a branching or arborescent structure, as the teeth of the genus *Dendrodus* of fossil fishes: see next.

1854 H. MILLER *Footpr. Creat.* v. (1874) 78 The dendrodic or tree-like tooth was, in at least the Old Red Sandstone, a characteristic of all the Celacanth family.

dendrodont (ˈdɛndrəʊdɒnt), *sb.* and *a. Palæont.* and *Zool.* [f. DENDRO- + Gr. ὀδοντ- tooth.]

A. *sb.* A fish of the extinct fossil genus *Dendrodus*, characterized by teeth of dendritic structure. (Cf. *dendrodentine* under DENDRO-.)

1849-52 OWEN in Todd *Cycl. Anat.* IV. II. 869 The seemingly simple conical teeth of the extinct family of fishes which I have called 'Dendrodonts'. **1865** PAGE *Handbk. Geol. Terms*.

B. *adj.* Having, or consisting of, teeth of dendritic internal structure.

1872 NICHOLSON *Palæont.* 326 Dentition dendrodont. **1880** GUNTHER *Fishes* 365 Dentition dendrodont.

dendrogram (ˈdɛndrəgræm). [f. DENDRO- + -GRAM.] A branched diagram representing the apparent similarity or relationship between taxa, esp. on the basis of their observed overall similarity rather than on their phylogeny. Also in extended senses.

1953 E. MAYR et al. *Methods & Princ. Syst. Zool.* iii. 58 Figure 8..is not a phylogenetic tree, because it is not based on any information on fossil forms which might be ancestral connections of the various branches. Such a diagrammatic illustration of degree of relationship based on degree of similarity (morphological and otherwise) may be called a dendrogram. **1961** G. G. SIMPSON *Princ. Anim. Taxonomy* ii. 62 Opinions or claims regarding dendrograms vary between two extremes: that they have nothing whatever to do with phylogeny or that they do faithfully represent phylogeny. **1969** *Computers & Humanities* IV. 140 A matrix of correlation coefficients is computed and clustered and a dendrogram plotted.

dendrograph (ˈdɛndrəgrɑːf, -æ-). [cf. DENDROGRAPHY.] An instrument used to measure the periodical variations in the size of tree trunks. Hence **ˌdendroˈgraphic** *a.*

1924 D. T. MACDOUGAL (*title*) Growth in trees.. dendrographic measurements. *Ibid.* 37 Standardization of the dendrograph for measurement of daily equalizing variations... The essential feature of the instrument is a rigid metal frame surrounding the trunk with one fixed contact-point, and the second consisting of the short bearing-arm of a lever, the long arm of which carries a pen which traces the record.

dendrography, etc.: see under DENDRO-.

dendroid (ˈdɛndrɔɪd), *a.* [f. Gr. δένδρ-ον + -OID: cf. Gr. δενδρώδης, contr. from δενδροειδής.] Of the form of a tree; dendritic, arborescent.

1846 DANA *Zooph.* (1848) 544 A dendroid specimen in the coral collections of Peale's Museum. **1869** NICHOLSON *Zool.* 105 Dendroid, or tree-like, corals.

denˈdroidal, *a.* [f. as prec. + -AL[1].] = prec.

1840 *Penny Cycl.* XVIII. 372/2 (Corals) Polyparium dendroidal, dichotomous.

dendrolatry, -lite: see under DENDRO-.

dendrology (dɛnˈdrɒlədʒɪ). [f. DENDRO- + Gr. -λογια discourse, -LOGY.] The study of trees; the department of botany which treats of trees. So **dendroˈlogic**, **dendroˈlogical**, **denˈdrologous** *adjs.*, belonging to dendrology; **denˈdrologist**, one versed in dendrology, a professed student of trees.

1708 KERSEY, *Dendrology*, a Treatise, or Discourse of Trees. **1825** P. W. WATSON *Dendrol. Brit.* Introd. 1 That no person..since the time of Evelyn..should have taken up.. the Dendrologic Department of the science. *Ibid.* Introd. 10 This..work..includes about 100 Trees and Shrubs for the Dendrologist, indigenous to the British Isles. **1869** W. ROBINSON *Parks & Gardens Paris* (1878) 344 There is a school of Dendrology here. **1875** LOWELL *Lett.* (1894) II. 137 The sonnet is..'susceptible of a high polish', as the dendrologists say of the woods of certain trees. **1884** *Science* 4 July 10 Dendrological science has met with a great..loss in the death of Alphonse Lavallée.

dendrometer, -phil, -style: see DENDRO-.

dendron (ˈdɛndrɒn). *Anat.* [f. DENDR(ITE + *-on* as in *neuron, axon.*] = DENDRITE 3.

1893 E. A. SCHÄFER in *Brain* XVI. 136, I propose therefore to term the axis-cylinder or nerve-fibre processes *neurons*; and the protoplasmic processes *dendrons*. [*Note*] The latter have been known as 'dendrites', but the termination 'on' is..preferable to 'ite'. **1899** *Ibid.* XXII. 209 The protoplasmic processes are also referred to as the dendrites (His), dendrons (Schäfer) and dendritic processes. **1967** C. R. NOBACK *Human Nerv. Syst.* ii. 32/1 Neurons have two types of processes, viz., axons and dendrites (dendrons).

dene (diːn), *sb.*[1] Another spelling of DEAN *sb.*[2], a (wooded) vale.

dene (diːn), *sb.*[2] Also **den, deine, deane**. [Of uncertain derivation.

The sense seems to make it distinct from *dene*, DEAN[2], and suggests affinity to LG. *düne* (now also mod.Ger.), E. Fris. and N. Fris. *düne, dün*, Du. *duin*, sand-hill on the coast: also F. *dune* in same sense. But its relationship to these words is phonetically uncertain, and rendered more so by the existence of the form *den*. Relationship to Ger. *tenne* floor, perh. orig. 'a flat', has also been suggested; but the history of the word does not go back far enough to admit of any certain conclusion.]

1. A bare sandy tract by the sea; a low sand-hill; as in the *Denes* north and south of Yarmouth, *Dene-side* there, the *Den* at Exmouth, Teignmouth, etc.

α. in form *den*.

1278 [see 2]. **1599** NASHE *Lenten Stuffe* (1871) 26 There being aboue fiue thousand pounds worth of them at a time upon her dens a sunning. **1776** WITHERING *Brit. Plants* (1796) III. 563 On the sandy den at Teignmouth, plentiful. **1847** HALLIWELL, *Den*, a sandy tract near the sea, as at Exmouth, and other places.

β. in form *dene*.

1816 KEATINGE *Trav.* (1817) I. 7 Quitting Calais for St. Omars,—the deines or sand-hills..begin. **1845** *Blackw. Mag.* Apr. 424/2 A 'broad'..separated from the sea by a narrow strip of low sand-banks, and sandy downs or deanes as they are there termed. **1855** KINGSLEY *Westw. Ho!* xvi, Mrs. Leigh..watched the ship glide out between the yellow denes. **1857** —— *Two Y. Ago* 50 Great banks and denes of shifting sand.

†**2.** ***den and strand***:

'*Den*..is The Liberty the Ports Fishermen shall have to beet or mend, and to dry their Nets at Great Yarmouth, upon Marsh Lands there, yet called The Dennes, during.. all the Herring Season. *Strond*..the Liberty the Fishermen have to come to the Key at Great Yarmouth, and deliver their Herrings freely' (Jeake). *Obs.*

1278 *Charter Edw. I* in Jeake *Charters Cinque Ports* (1728) 12 Et quod habeant Den & Strond, apud magnam Jernemouth [*transl.* in Hakluyt *Voy.* (1598) I. 117 And that they shall haue Denne and Strande at Great Yarmouth]. **1331** *Charter Edw. III*, ibid. 13 Nous..voillouns qu'ils ayount lour eysementz en Strande & Den saunz appropriement del soil. **1706** in PHILLIPS.

†**dene**, *sb.*[3] *Obs.* A fictitious sb. made by separating the adv. BEDENE, *bydene* 'together, straight on, straightway' into ***be dene, by dene***; whence, by varying the preposition, ***with dene***.

c **1375** *Sc. Leg. Saints, Vincentius* 328 As þai had sene It þat þar downe wes done with dene. *c* **1450** *St. Cuthbert* (Surtees) 7804 Nine ȝere..And twa moneths, all' be dene. ?*c* **1475** *Sqr. lowe Degre* 272 Take thy leue of kinge and quene, And so to all the courte by dene.

†**dene**, *a. Obs. rare*[−1]. [ad. L. *dēn-i*] Ten.

c **1420** *Pallad. on Husb.* I. 587 Whenne the moone is daies dene Of age is good, and til she be fiftene.

dene, var. DAIN *sb.*, DEN *sb.*[2]; obs. f. DEAN[1], and DIN.

Deneb (ˈdɛnɛb). *Astr.* Also Denab. [ad. Arab. *ḏanab* (*ad-dajāja*) (hen's) tail.] The star α in the constellation Cygnus.

1867 SMYTH *Sailor's Word-Bk.* 243 Deneb. **1933** *S.P.E. Tract* XXXVIII. 571 Denab (α *Cygni*). **1955** *Sci. News Let.* 30 July 74/1 Just below Vega, toward the east, is the figure of Cygnus, the swan. The most familiar stars in this group form a cross, and at the head, toward the northern horizon, is the bright Deneb.

†**ˈdenegate**, *v. Obs.* [f. ppl. stem of L. *dēnegāre* to deny.] To deny.

1623 in COCKERAM. **1652** F. KIRKMAN *Clerio & L.* 124, I cannot denegate any thing unto thee.

denegation (dɛnɪˈgeɪʃən). [a. F. *dénégation* (*desn-*), 14th c. in Hatzf., ad. L. *dēnegātiōn-em*, n. of action from *dēnegāre* to deny.]

†**1.** Refusal to grant, denial of what is asked.

1489 *Will of J. Welbeke* (Somerset Ho.), Withouten any delay fraude denegacion or troble. **1548** HALL *Chron.* (1809) 849 Denegacion of Iustice. **1651** BIGGS *New Disp.* ¶273 A denegation of that, to which she hath had a strong optation.

2. Denial, contradiction.

1831 SOUTHEY in *Q. Rev.* XLV. 199 The base and beaten path of denegation. **1889** STEVENSON *Master of B.* vi. 220, I thought to interrupt him with some not very truthful denegation.

denegatory (dɪˈnɛgətərɪ), *a. rare.* [f. L. *dēnegāt-*. ppl. stem of *dēnegāre* to deny + -ORY: cf. F. *dénégatoire* (1771 in Hatzf.).] Having the effect of denying; contradictory.

1823 BENTHAM *Not Paul* 255 Denied by the opposite denegatory assertion. *Ibid.* 259 A denegatory declaration—a declaration denying the fact charged in the accusation.

†**deneger.** *Obs.* = DENIER.

(App. an error for *deneyer*, but perh. intentionally f. **denege*, ad. L. *dēnegāre*.)

1583 STUBBES *Anat. Abus.* I. (1879) 115 An infidell, and a deneger of the faith. **1592** —— *Motive Good Wks.* (1593) 117 Heathen people and infidels, denegers of the faith.

Dene-hole, Dane-hole (ˈdiːn-, ˈdeɪnhəʊl). Also 9 **Danes' hole.** [app. from the national name *Dane, Danes*, ME. *Dene*, OE. *Dęne* + HOLE.

There is no doubt that this is popularly and traditionally the local interpretation of the name: see the first quot. In various parts of the country, e.g. the county of Durham, other ancient caves and excavations are attributed to the Danes, and called *Danes' holes* or *Dane-holes*. It is not quite certain that *dene-hole* is a genuine popular form anywhere; but if so, it may possibly represent a ME. *Dene-hol(e*:—OE. *Dena-hol*, Danes' hole (cf. OE. *Dena-lagu*, ME. *Dene-lawe*, mod. *Danes' law, Dane-law*), or it may be merely a local pronunciation. But it has suggested to recent writers connexion with DENE *sb.*[1], or with other of the sbs. so spelt, or with DEN (which is phonetically impossible); and either on this account, or because it does not countenance any theory about the Danes, it has been generally adopted by the archæologists who have investigated these holes since *c* 1880. Some have very reprehensibly shortened the name *dene-hole* into *dene*, conformably to their erroneous conjectures as to its connexion with *dene* and *den*.]

The name applied to a class of ancient excavations, found chiefly in Essex and Kent in England, and in the Valley of the Somme in France, consisting of a narrow cylindrical shaft sunk through the superincumbent strata to the chalk, often at a depth of 60 or 80 feet, and there widening out horizontally into one or more chambers. Their age and purpose have been the theme of much discussion.

They are mentioned (but not named) by Lambarde 1570, by Camden 1605 as *putei*, in Plot's *Oxfordshire*, 1705, as 'the Gold-mine of Cunobeline, in Essex', and described in a letter from Derham to Ray 17 Feb. 1706. For later history see Mr. Spurrell's paper cited below, and *Trans. Essex Field Club*, 1883 III. 48, *Journal* xxviii, lvi.

1768 MORANT *Hist. Essex* I. 228 [The Dane-holes at Grays] The Danes are vulgarly reported to have used them as receptacles or hiding-places for the plunder and booty which they took from the adjoining inhabitants during their frequent piracies and descents upon this island, and hence they have been styled *Dane* or *Dene* holes. **1818** *Cambrian Reg.* III. 31 The controversy relative to the original intention of the Deneholes. **1863** *Murray's Handbk. Kent & Sussex* (ed. 2) 16 They are here called 'Daneholes' or 'Cunobeline's Gold Mines'. *Ibid.* 20 In a chalk-pit near the village of E. Tilbury are numerous excavations called Danes' Holes.. Similar excavations.. exist in the chalk and tufa on either bank of the Somme.. The tradition still asserts that these caverns were used for retreat and concealment in time of war, whence their ordinary name *Les souterrains des guerres.* **1871** R. MEESON in Palin *Stifford & its Neighbourhood* 41 The Dane-holes as they are called by the country people. **1881** F. C. J. SPURRELL in *Archæol. Jrnl.* (*title*), On Deneholes and Artificial Caves with Vertical Entrances. **1883** *Trans. Essex Field Club* III. Jrnl. 17 June 1882, An account of the Club's first visit to the 'Denes' in Hangman's Wood. **1887** T. V. HOLMES in *Essex Naturalist* I. 225 (*title*) Report on the Denehole Exploration at Hangman's Wood, Grays, 1884–1887. **1891** *Proc. Soc. Antiq.* 5 Feb. 245 On the discovery of a dene-hole containing Roman remains at Plumstead.

Denelage, -lawe: see DANE-LAW.

dener, -e, obs. form of DINNER, DENIER.

dener, var. of DEANER.

‖ˈ**denerel.** [OF. (13th c. in Godef.); in form dim. of *dener, denier*.] A measure of capacity in Guernsey: see quot.

1862 ANSTED *Channel Isl.* IV. App. A (ed. 2) 567 In Guernsey the *denerel* or dundrel is the common small unit of dry measure. Three denerels.. make one cabot; two cabots or six denerels, one bushel.

deˈnervate, *v. Med.* [f. DE- II. 1 + NERVATE *v.*] *trans.* To deprive an organ, tissue, etc. of its nerve supply. So **deˈnervated** *ppl. a.*; **denerˈvation**[2], the act of denervating or the state of being denervated.

1905 *Jrnl. Physiol.* XXXIII. 395 Considerable caution must be exercised in comparing the response of the denervated muscle with that of the normal muscle. But the results of the experiments tend to show that the responsiveness to nicotine is increased by denervation. **1948** *New. Biol.* IV. 123 The cutting of all nervous pathways to the mammary site... If under such denervated conditions the tissues were still observed to develop, [etc.]. **1962** *Lancet* 12 May 1024/2 Neurogenic hypertension, produced by denervation of the moderator nerves, required that both the nerves from the aortic arch and the carotid sinus be resected. **1963** R. P. DALES *Annelids* vi. 130 The locomotory rhythm of *Hirudo* is carried by the nerve cord and is not interrupted by denervating several segments part way down the body. **1968** *Brit. Med. Bull.* XXIV. 257/2 Electromyography is in routine clinical use for the detection of primary muscle disease and chronic partial denervation.

†**denerˈvation**[1]. *Obs. rare.* [f. DE- I. 1 + L. *nervus* string, etc., as if f. a verb **dēnervāre* to tie down with a string.] A marking or groove, such as is produced by a string tied round.

1657 TOMLINSON *Renou's Disp.* 469 Worms.. are like oblong fibres whose parts are not discriminated, save by some.. denervations.

dengerous, obs. form of DANGEROUS.

dengue (ˈdɛŋgeɪ). Also **dengue-fever, denga.** [Immediately, a. West Indian Spanish *dengue*; ultimately, according to Dr. Christie, in *Glasgow Med. Jrnl.* Sept. 1881, a Swahili word, the full name of the disease in Zanzibar being *ka dinga pepo* (*ka* partitive article, 'a, a kind of', *dinga, dyenga, denga*, 'sudden cramp-like seizure', *pepo* 'evil spirit, plague'). On its introduction to the West Indies from Africa in 1827, the name was, in Cuba, popularly identified with the Spanish word *dengue* 'fastidiousness, prudery'. In this form it was subsequently adopted in the United States, and eventually in general English use.

In the British West Indies, called by the Negroes *dandy*. Both names appear to be popular adaptations, of the 'sparrow-grass' type, of the Swahili name, with a mocking reference to the stiffness of the neck and shoulders, and dread of motion, exhibited by the patients; whence also another name of ridicule, the 'Giraffe'.— See DANDY[2].]

An infectious eruptive fever, commencing suddenly, and characterized by excruciating pains, especially in the joints, with great prostration and debility, but seldom proving fatal; it is epidemic and sporadic in East Africa and the countries surrounding the Indian Ocean, and (since 1827) in the West Indies and adjacent parts of America. Also called *dandy*, and *break-bone fever*.

(The name has apparently been sometimes given in error to other epidemic fevers.)

1828 *Charleston Courier* 15 July, The Dengue. This.. epidemic exists at this time in our city. *Ibid.* 9 Aug. **1830** *Amer. Beacon* (Norfolk, Va.) 9 Nov. 2/2 A rheumatic fever, pronounced by the physicians to be the celebrated Dengue of 1818, made its appearance. **1847** in CRAIG. **1854–60** MAYNE *Expos. Lex.*, *Dengue*, name for a fever which prevailed in Charleston, summer of 1850.. Also called.. the Break-bone fever. **1866** *Harvard Mem. Biog.* I. 37 Having had a severe attack of dengue or break-bone fever. **1881** DR. CHRISTIE *Dengue Fever* in *Glasgow Med. Jrnl.* Sept. 165 Three epidemics of dengue are reported as having occurred within the eastern hemisphere, the first during the years 1779–84, the second from 1823 to 1829, and the third from 1870 to 1875. *Ibid.* 165 In 1870 the older inhabitants [of Zanzibar] recognized the disease as one which had been epidemic about 48.. years before, and they gave to it the former designation *ka-dinga-pepo*, the name under which I described it in my first communication. *Ibid.* 169 Denga was prevalent in Zanzibar in 1823. **1885** *Times* 4 Dec. 13 What connexion there may be between the troncasa or dengue fever and the recent invasion of cholera [at Gibraltar].

Denia (ˈdiːnɪə). The name of a town in south-eastern Spain, used *attrib.* and *ellipt.* to denote the products grown in its neighbourhood.

1845 DODD *Brit. Manuf.* V. 102 The 'Lexias' produce a dry wine, the 'Denias' a sweet wine. **1904** *Westm. Gaz.* 12 Aug. 10/1 Quantities of new Denia grapes flood the market.

deniable (dɪˈnaɪəb(ə)l), *a.* [f. DENY *v.* + -ABLE.] That can be denied.

1548 GEST *Pr. Masse* 98 This is denyable. **1672** PENN *Spirit Truth Vind.* 27 The first Proposition is purely Scriptural, and therefore the consequent not deniable. **1760** LAW *Spirit of Prayer* II. 49 A maxim that is not deniable. **1865** E. LUCAS in Manning *Ess. Relig. & Lit.* 354 It is not deniable that even the inferior officers in an army.. have certain rights.

denial (dɪˈnaɪəl). [f. DENY *v.* + -AL[1] II. 5.]

1. a. The act of saying 'no' to a request or to a person who makes a request; refusal of anything asked for or desired.

1528 GARDINER in Pocock *Rec. Ref.* I. li. 122 To colour the denial of the king's purpose. **1548** UDALL, etc. *Erasm. Par. Matt.* xv. (R.), The woman was not weryed with so many repulses and denyals. **1596** SHAKS. *Tam. Shr.* II. i. 281 Neuer make deniall; I must and will haue Katherine to my wife. **1631** GOUGE *God's Arrows* iv. §8. 385 Torture.. Deniall of buriall, and other externall crosses. **1736** BUTLER *Anal.* I. v. 136 Resolution, and the denial of our passions. **1806–7** J. BERESFORD *Miseries Hum. Life* (1826) II. xl, Peremptory orders of denial to all comers whomsoever. **1847** TENNYSON *Princess* v. 324 To learn if Ida yet would cede our claim, Or by denial flush her babbling wells With her own peoples life.

b. = SELF-DENIAL.

1828 WEBSTER s.v., A *denial of one's self*, is a declining of some gratification; restraint of one's appetites or propensities. **1873** MISS J. E. A. BROWN *Thoughts thro' Year* 78 The denials of obedience.

2. The asserting (of anything) to be untrue or untenable; contradiction of a statement or allegation as untrue or invalid; also, the denying of the existence or reality of a thing.

1576 FLEMING *Panopl. Epist.* 107 Cicero laboureth in his owne purgation, and that any such thing was of him committed, maketh flat denyall. **1651** BAXTER *Inf. Bapt.* 38 That this is a Mercy.. is plain, and frequently past denyall. *a* **1704** T. BROWN *Persius* Sat. i. Prol. Wks. 1730 I. 51 Tis true, nor is it worth denial. **1841** MYERS *Cath. Th.* III. xxi. 80 The denial of these difficulties, or the ignoring of them. **1845** WHATELY *Logic* in *Encycl. Metrop.* 197/1 The denial of the suppressed premiss.. will at once invalidate the argument. **1875** JOWETT *Plato* (ed. 2) IV. 134 The denial of abstract ideas is the destruction of the mind.

3. Refusal to acknowledge a person or thing as having a certain character or certain claims; a disowning, disavowal.

1590 N. T. (L. Tomson) *Matt.* xxvi. *heading*, Peters deniall. **1651** HOBBES *Leviath.* II. xxvii. 158 All Crimes that contain not in them a denyall of the Soveraign Power. *a* **1716** SOUTH (J.), Those are the proper scenes, in which we act our confessions or denials of him.

4. *Law.* †**a.** = DENIER[2]: see quot.; **b.** The opposing by the defendant or accused party of a plea, claim, or charge advanced against him.

1628 COKE *On Litt.* 161 b, Deniall is a disseisin of a Rent Charge, as well as of a Rent secke. **1728** YOUNG *Love Fame* vii, Ev'n denials cost us dear at court. **1828** SCOTT *F.M. Perth* xx, Of course the charge will be rebutted by a denial. **1861** W. BELL *Dict. Law Scot.* s.v., Denial in law imports no more than *not confessing*. It does not amount to a positive assertion of the falsehood of that which is denied.

5. *dial.* A drawback, disadvantage, detriment, hindrance.

1736 PEGGE *Kenticisms*, A *denial* to a farm; i.e. a prejudice, a drawback, hindrance, or detriment. **1876** *S. Warwicksh. Gloss.*, *Denial*, hindrance, drawback. 'It's a great denial to him to be shut up in the house so long.' **1883** *Hampshire Gloss.*, *Denial*, an encumbrance. 'His children be a great denial to 'un'. Also in Glossaries of *Worcestersh.*, *Gloucestersh.*, *Surrey*, *Sussex*, *Leicester*, *Shropshire*, *Cheshire*.

6. *Bridge.* A bid of another suit in order to show weakness in the suit bid by one's partner.

1916 R. F. FOSTER *Auction Bridge for All* xxi. 81 Instead of continuing his denial of the major suits, and trusting his partner to protect them.. the dealer quit. **1927** G. MOTT-SMITH *Contract Bridge* viii. 117 A take-out may be a 'denial'. **1959** *Listener* 5 Mar. 434/3 On each occasion I was told that the answer should have been a denial. **1964** *Official Encycl. Bridge* 122/2 *Denial bid*, a bid that indicates lack of support for partner's bid (an obsolescent term).

†**deˈniance.** *Obs.* [f. DENY *v.* + -ANCE: cf. OF. *denoiance*, f. *denoier*, var. of *denier* to DENY.] Denial.

1548 HALL *Chron.* 244 Either for the affirmaunce or deniance of the same. **1568** GRAFTON *Chron.* II. 749.

denidation (diːnɪˈdeɪʃən). *Med.* [f. DE- + L. *nidus* nest: see -ATION.] The shedding of the superficial layer of the uterus, such as occurs during menstruation.

1874 J. H. AVELING in *Obstetr. Jrnl.* II. 212 Nidation has been likened to gestation. Denidation may be compared with parturition. **1935** *Nature* 16 Mar. 413/1 We may speculate whether some subtle distinction may not be drawn between an embryo and a mere blastocyst, between criminal abortion and permissible denidation.

denied (dɪˈnaɪd), *ppl. a.* [f. DENY *v.* + -ED.] Said not to be true or not to exist; refused.

1859 SALA *Tw. round Clock* (1861) 281 Dying of that common, but denied disease, a broken heart.

Hence **deˈniedness,** the quality of being denied; †self-denial (*obs.*).

1671 *True Non-conf.* 357 Their deniedness unto all things, their absolute resignation unto.. God.

denier[1] (dɪˈnaɪə(r)). [f. DENY *v.* + -ER.] One who denies (in various senses of the verb).

c **1400** *Apol. Loll.* 99 And ȝet þey deny to men þe understonding of þe gospel.. þei wel bi deniers [*printed* deneris]. **1530** PALSGR. 212/2 Denyer of a thynge, *escondisseur*. **1558** KNOX *First Blast* (Arb.) 46 Deniers of Christ Iesus. **1660** JER. TAYLOR *Duct. Dubit.* I. ii. rule iii. §12 He must be a despiser of the world, a great denier of himself. **1741** WARBURTON *Div. Legat.* II. Ded. 23 The Deniers of a future State. **1876** BANCROFT *Hist. U.S.* VI. xxvi. 33 One state disfranchised Jews.. another deniers of the Trinity.

†**denier**[2]. *Law. Obs.* [a. F. *dénier* pres. inf., taken subst.: cf. *disclaimer*, and see -ER[4].] The act of denying or refusing.

1532–3 *Act 24 Hen. VIII*, c. 6 Any of the kynges subiectes, to whom any denyer of sale.. shall be made. **1628** COKE *On Litt.* 153 b, Without a demand there be no denier of the rent in law. **1642** J. M. *Argt. conf. Militia* 24 This in effect was a denier of justice.

denier[3] (dɪˈnɪə(r), ‖dənje). Forms: 5–7 denere, 6 *Sc.* deneir, 6–7 deneere, 7 deneer, -eare, -ire, -iere, dinneere, 6– denier. See also DENAR. [a. OF. *dener*, later *denier* (= Pr. *dener, denier, dinier*, Cat. *diner*, Sp. *dinero*, Pg. *dinheiro*, It. *denaro, danaro*):—L. *dēnārium*: see DENARIUS.

The form *deneer(e* (cf. *musketeer*, etc.) prevailed about 1600.]

1. A French coin, the twelfth of the sou; originally, like the Roman denarius and English penny, of silver; but from 16th c. a small copper coin. Hence (*esp.* in negative phrases) used as the type of a very small sum. *Obs.* or *arch.*

Originally, from reign of Charlemagne till 12th c., a silver coin of about 22 Troy grains or rather less than a pennyweight; from the 13th c. to the reign of Chas. IX (d. 1574), usually of billon or base silver (*denier tournois*), and weighing at different times from 10 to 14 gr.; under Henry III (1574–89) it became a copper coin of about 22 gr. (less than ⅔ of the current bronze farthing), and so continued till the death of Louis XIV. (B. V. Head.)

c **1425** WYNTOUN *Cron.* VI. v. 60 To þe kyrk ilka yhere Of Rome he heycht a denere To pay (a penny þat is to say). **1580** H. GIFFORD *Gilloflowers* (1875) 132 And in his purse, to serue his neede, Not one deneere he had. **1594** SHAKS. *Rich. III*, I. ii. 252 My Dukedome to a Beggerly denier! I do mistake my person all this while. **1607** WALKINGTON *Opt. Glass* 45 Then liue in wealth and giue not a dinneere. **1611** COTGR., *Denier* a penny, a deneere; a small copper coin valued at the tenth part of an English pennie; also, a penniewleight, or 24 grains. *a* **1670** HACKET *Abp. Williams* I. (1692) 104 The Lord Treasurer, I know well, had..not drawn a denier out of the King's purse. **1706** PHILLIPS (ed. Kersey), *Denier*, a French Brass-Coin, worth three Tenths of an English Farthing, of which Twelve make a Sols. Also a Penny-weight in Silver; thus an Ounce of Silver..is of 24 Deniers. **1873** HALE *In His Name* vi. 55 A slave whom I have bought with my deniers. **1876** BROWNING *Pacchiarotto* 79 Let the blind mole mine Digging out deniers!

†**2.** Used to translate Lat. *dēnārius*: see DENARIUS 1. *Obs.*

1598 GRENEWEY *Tacitus' Ann.* I. v. (1622) 9 The Pretorian bands, which receiued two deniers a day. **1606** HOLLAND *Sueton.* 66 Gallus his scribe, had receiued 500 deniers.

†**3.** A pennyweight; = DENARIUS 3. *Obs.*

1601 HOLLAND *Pliny* II. 79 Take of wild running Thyme the weight of two deniers..Ervil floure twelue deniers or drams. *a* **1656** USSHER *Ann.* (1658) 229 Counting here, as his manner everywhere is, a deneere, for a drachma. **1706** [see sense 1 above].

4. A unit of weight used to estimate the fineness of silk, rayon, or nylon yarn.

The unit is based on a length of 450 metres of yarn weighing 0·05 gramme.

1839 URE *Dict. Arts* 1105 The first of these raw silks will have a *titre* of 20 to 24 deniers. **1858** SIMMONDS *Dict. Trade*, *Denier*,..in Italy, a small weight equal to about a grain, by which silk is weighed. **1887** *Colonial & Indian Exhib., Rep. Col. Sect.* 341 The general sizes [of silk] seem to be 16 to 20 deniers, but it will range from about 10 to 24 deniers, single thread. **1927** T. WOODHOUSE *Artifical Silk* 78 Finally the hanks are weighed..to ascertain the denier count. **1952** *Sunday Times* 15 June 8/5 Denier is the thickness of the yarn: the lower the denier number, the finer the stocking. **1957** *Times* 30 Sept. 11/3 The makers claim that these 15-denier 'Carefree' nylons will outlast several ordinary pairs. **1960** *Textile Terms & Defs.* (ed. 4) 53 *Denier*, the weight in grammes of 9,000 metres of a filament or yarn. The denier system is used as the standard count for filament silk as well as for rayon, cellulose acetate, nylon and other man-made fibres.

denigrate (ˈdɛnɪgreɪt), *v.* [f. ppl. stem of L. *dēnigrāre* to blacken, f. DE- I. 3 + *nigrāre* to blacken, f. *niger*, *nigr-*, black; cf. F. *dénigrer* (14th c. in Hatzf.). Apparently disused in 18th c., and revived in 19th c.]

1. *trans.* To blacken, make black or dark. *lit.* Now *rare.*

1623 COCKERAM, *Denigrate*, to make blacke. **1646** SIR T. BROWNE *Pseud. Ep.* VI. xii. 336 The fuliginous and denigrating humor. **1657** TOMLINSON *Renou's Disp.* 191 This Lotion will denigrate the hairs of hoary heads. **1726** AYLIFFE *Parergon* 231 Drunkenness..denigrates the Colour of the Body. **1849** CDL. WISEMAN *Ess.* (1853) III. 603 How the north wind should always drive a down-draught, with its denigrating consequences, into the drawing-room. **1857** J. RAINE *Mem. J. Hodgson* I. 89 *note*, The..smoke of pits and manufactories, with..a..dash of denigrated fog from the river.

2. *fig.* **a.** To blacken, sully, or stain (character or reputation); to blacken the reputation of (a person, etc.); to defame.

1526 *Pilgr. Perf.* (W. de W. 1531) 93 To mynysshe, denygrate, or derke his good name or fame. **1656** TRAPP *Comm. Mark* i. 24 This he spake, not to honour Christ, but to denigrate him. **1665** BOYLE *Occas. Refl.* III. v. (1845) 41 [They] do..so denigrate the Reputation of them that oppose them. **1871** MORLEY *Voltaire* (1886) 352 Napoleon ..paying writers for years to denigrate the memory of Voltaire, whose very name he abhorred. **1889** PLUMPTRE in *Antiquary* Apr. 146/2 The character he is at such pains to denigrate. **1952** *Daily Herald* 17 Nov. 4/1 Elements in this country which have always sought to denigrate the work of the United Nations. **1971** *Sci. Amer.* Sept. 237/2 They attempted to denigrate..our most crucial findings.

†**b.** To darken mentally, obscure. *Obs. rare.*

1583 STUBBES *Anat. Abus.* (1877) 78 These..smells..do rather denigrate, darken, and obscure the spirit and sences.

Hence ˈ**denigrated** *ppl. a.*, ˈ**denigrating** *ppl. a.*, **deniˈgratory** *a.*

1646, **1849**, **1857** [see 1]. **1955** *Times* 9 May 3/4 A revival of Shakespeare's *Richard III*, certainly the play most denigratory to the King. **1967** *Coast to Coast 1965–6* 179 Here Miss Silver-and-Green made an insulting shrug of great beauty, and an exquisite denigratory hand movement. **1969** *Daily Tel.* 13 Nov. 8/3 This book..is provocative and controversial..and, intentionally or not, is denigratory.

denigration (dɛnɪˈgreɪʃən). Now *rare.* [ad. L. *dēnigrātiōn-em*, n. of action from *dēnigrāre*: so in OF. (14–16th c.). As to use, see prec.]

1. The action of blackening, or process of becoming black (literally).

1646 SIR T. BROWNE *Pseud. Ep.* VI. xii. 336 These are the advenient and artificiall wayes of denigration..These are the waies wherby culinary and common fires doe operate. *a* **1691** BOYLE *Wks.* I. 714 (R.) In these several instances of denigration, the metals are worn off.

2. *fig.* Blackening of character, defamation.

1868 HELPS *Realmah* xvii, I should not care so much about this denigration, if there were not always people ready to repeat to the person blackened all the dark and unpleasant things which others have said about him or her. **1884** C. E. PLUMPTRE *G. Bruno* II. 135 The denigration of those rightfully held in esteem for their learning and virtue.

†**b.** A stain, a dark spot. *Obs. rare.*

1641 J. JACKSON *True Evang. T.* II. 149 Let [this] be the denigration, and such a spot in the..Turkish religion, as no Fullers sope can wash out.

¶ In the following (with a hyphen) app. used for '*un*blackening, whitewashing'. [See DE- II. 1.]

1868 J. H. BLUNT *Ref. Ch. Eng.* I. 290 A fallen angel whose de-nigration is beyond the power of an impartial historian.

denigrator (ˈdɛnɪgreɪtə(r)). [agent-n. in L. form from *dēnigrāre* to DENIGRATE: see -OR.]

1. Something that blackens.

1658 SIR T. BROWNE *Pseud. Ep.* VI. xii. (ed. 4) 413 Iron and Vitriol are the powerful Denigrators.

2. One who blackens another's character or reputation.

1874 HELPS *Soc. Press.* xii. 156 The denigrator had in view the abundant malice and envy of mankind. **1882** *Remin. old Bohemian* (1883) 40 Most of his denigrators and assailers.

denigrature. *rare*$^{-0}$. = DENIGRATION.

1727 BAILEY vol. II, *Denigrature*, a making black.

‖**dénigrement** (denigrəmɑ̃). *fig.* [Fr.] Blackening of character, disparagement.

1883 *Sat. Rev.* 21 Apr. 486/1 A criticism approaching to *dénigrement*. **1935** *N. & Q.* CLXVIII. 287/2 That tendency to—fundamentally futile—*dénigrement* which besets many biographers now-a-days. **1941** *Horizon* 14 Feb. 151 It shows something wrong with the whole conception of the book to treat everything in the same tone of flippancy and *dénigrement*.

denim (dɪˈnɪm, ˈdɛnɪm). [Shortened from *serge de Nim*, F. *serge de Nîmes* or *Nismes*, serge of Nismes (a manufacturing town of Southern France). See Savary des Bruslons, *Dict. gén. de Commerce* (Geneva 1742), 'serges et cadis de Nimes'. Cf. DELAINE.] A name originally given to a kind of serge; now (orig. *U.S.*) to a coloured twilled cotton material used largely for overalls, hangings, etc. In *pl.* = overalls, trousers made of denim.

1695 E. HATTON *Merchant's Mag.* 159, 18 Serge Denims that cost 6*l.* each. **1703** *Lond. Gaz.* No. 3885/4 A pair of Flower'd Serge de Nim Breeches. **1864** WEBSTER, *Denim*, a coarse cotton drilling used for overalls, etc. **1868** *Mobile Daily Tribune* 4 Nov. 4/6 Dry Goods..Blue Denims.. Brown Denims. **1875** MISS BIRD *Sandwich Isl.* (1880) 79 She wears..a scanty, loose frock of blue denim down to her knees. **1932** J. DOS PASSOS *1919* 3 He was a smiling ruddy man in blue denims. **1958** J. LODWICK *Bid the Soldiers Shoot* III. vii. 222 In the map pocket of my denims. **1959** *Manchester Guardian* 24 June 7/1 Figures in Bermuda shorts or rolled-up denims.

denitrate (diːˈnaɪtreɪt), *v.* [DE- II. 1.] *trans.* To free from nitric or nitrous acid.

1863 RICHARDSON & WATTS *Chem. Technol.* I. III. i. 94 A limited quantity of sulphurous acid passed upwards to denitrate the acid. **1893** *Brit. Jrnl. Photog.* XL. 797 Gun-cotton..loses its solubility as it becomes denitrated.

Hence **deˈnitrated** *ppl. a.*, **deˈnitrating** *ppl. a.* and *vbl. sb.*; also **deniˈtration**, the process of denitrating; **deˈnitrator**, an apparatus for denitration.

1863 RICHARDSON & WATTS *Chem. Technol.* I. III. i. 89 A close reservoir..placed..above the denitrating column. *Ibid.* 93 The denitration was then attempted. **1873** *Chemical News* XXVII. 135 There are two methods..on the Tyne for the denitration of the nitro-sulphuric acid: the Glover towers and denitration by steam. **1880** LOMAS *Alkali Trade* 73 The framework of the denitrator is formed of 10 in. square timber.

denitrification (diːˌnaɪtrɪfɪˈkeɪʃən). [f. DE- II. 1 + NITRIFICATION.] The reduction, esp. by bacteria, of simple inorganic nitrogen compounds; *spec.* the reduction of nitrates through several intermediates to gaseous nitrogen.

1883 *Jrnl. Chem. Soc.* XLIV. 230 The denitrification is effected by the organisms which are developed; for if the liquid is sterilised by heat..the liquid remains clear and the nitrate is not altered. **1932** FULLER & CONARD tr. *Braun-Blanquet's Plant Sociol.* viii. 242 Very acid soils without herbaceous cover, in conifer forests, have a decided tendency towards denitrification. **1934** G. J. FOWLER *Introd. Biochem. Nitrogen Conserv.* vi. 132 Denitrification, as the name implies, is the reverse of nitrification. **1964** M. HYNES *Med. Bacteriol.* (ed. 8) i. 8 Denitrification is effected by other bacteria which use nitrates or nitrites as hydrogen acceptors, reducing them to ammonia and thus perhaps impairing the fertility of the soil.

denitrify (diːˈnaɪtrɪfaɪ), *v.* [DE- II. 1.] *trans.* To deprive of nitrous or hyponitric acid. Hence **deˈnitrified** *ppl. a.*, **deˈnitrifying** *vbl. sb.* and *ppl. a.*; ***denitrifying bacteria*** (see quot. 1951); **deˈnitrifier**, a denitrifying agent; **deˌnitrifiˈcator**, an apparatus used in sulphuric acid works to remove the nitrous vapours (nitrous or hyponitric acids) from the sulphuric acid previously 'nitrated' in the Gay Lussac tower.

1891 G. LUNGE *Manuf. Sulphuric Acid* I. 562 Another apparatus, constructed on the same principle..is the 'Denitrificateur' proposed by Gay-Lussac himself. **1892** W. CROOKES *Wagner's Chem. Technol.* 266 Gay-Lussac's denitrificator consists of a tower of sheet lead. *Ibid.* 272 The excess of sulphuric acid acts here at the wrong place as a denitrifier. *Ibid.* 266 [This] conveys it into the denitrifying apparatus. **1902** *Encycl. Brit.* XXVI. 56/2 Fresh manure abounds in denitrifying bacteria. **1932** FULLER & CONARD tr. *Braun-Blanquet's Plant Sociol.* viii. 241 Over against the nitrate formers stand the denitrifying bacteria which destroy nitric acid. **1951** M. ABERCROMBIE et al. *Dict. Biol.* 68 *Denitrifying bacteria*, soil bacteria which in absence of oxygen break down nitrates and nitrites with evolution of free nitrogen.

denitrize (diːˈnaɪtraɪz), *v.* [DE- II. 1.] = prec. Hence **deˈnitrizing** *vbl. sb.* and *ppl. a.*

1892 W. CROOKES *Wagner's Chem. Technol.* 267 Passing out denitrised at the bottom of the tower. *Ibid.*, The denitrising apparatus devised by J. Glover of Wallsend.. used under the name of the Glover tower.

†ˈ**denizate**, *v. Law. Obs.* [f. ppl. stem of med. (Anglo-)L. *denizāre*: see DENIZE *v.*] *trans.* To constitute a denizen.

1604 in Spottiswood *Hist. Ch. Scot.* VII. (1677) 485 His Majesties Prerogative Royal to denizate, enable and prefer to such offices. **1628** COKE *On Litt.* 129 a, An alien that is enfranchised or denizated by letters patent.

denization (dɛnɪˈzeɪʃən). *Law.* [a. Anglo-F. *denization* (Littleton *Inst.*), n. of action from DENIZE *v.*: in 16–17th c. Anglo-L. *denizātio* (Du Cange).] The action of making a person a denizen, or condition of being made a denizen.

1601 *Act 43 Eliz.* c. iii, An Act for the Denization of William Myllet. **1697** EVELYN *Numism.* vi. 203 What famous Cities had Privilege of Roman denization. **1755** CARTE *Hist. Eng.* IV. 327 He..gave all the Scots in Ulster, born before the death of Q. Elizabeth, the privilege of denization. **1868** E. EDWARDS *Raleigh* I. i. 13 A merchant of Genoa, who had Letters Patent of denization from King Henry.

†**denize**, *v. Obs.* [f. DENIZ-EN, by dropping the termination: probably representing an AFr. *denizer*; in med. (Anglo-)L. *denizāre.*]

1. *trans.* To make (a person) a denizen.

1577 HANMER *Anc. Eccl. Hist.* (1619) 240 Which things when this free denized Cubricus had gotten. **1579** J. STUBBES *Gaping Gulf* C j, If he be not denized, the laws can not abide him to be myster of one foot of ground. **1602** CAREW *Cornwall* 65 a, Sundry of those now inhabiting are lately denized Cornish. **1708** J. CHAMBERLAYNE *St. Gt. Brit.* I. III. v. (1743) 181 If a foreign Lady..marry an English man and she herself be not denized, she is barred all privileges and Titles due to her husband.

2. *fig.* To admit into recognized use (as a word, a custom, etc.); to naturalize.

1577–87 HOLINSHED *Chron.* v. II. 10/2 The Irish language was free dennized in the English pale. **1594** PLAT *Jewell-ho.*, *Diverse New Exper.* 6 This secrete is as yet merely French, but it had beene long since either denized or made English if, etc.

denizen (ˈdɛnɪzən), *sb.* and *a.* Forms: 5 deynseyn, -seen, deinseyn, deynesin, 5–6 denesyn, -zen, denysen, -zen, 6 denezan, denisine, denysyn, -cen, 6–7 denisen, -zin, 6–8 denison, -zon, 7 -zan, 6– denizen. [a. AF. *deinzein*, *denzein*, *denszein* = OF. *deinzein*, f. AF. *deinz*, *denz*, *dens*, mod.F. *dans* (:—L. *dē intus*) within + *-ein*:—L. *-āneus*: cf. *foreign*, *forein*, L. *forāneus*.]

A. *sb.* **1. a.** A person who dwells within a country, as opposed to *foreigners* who dwell outside its limits. (In this, the original sense, including and mainly consisting of *citizens*.) Now *rare* in *lit.* sense.

14.. *Chalmerlain Ayr* iii. (*Sc. Stat.* I), Alswel forreyns as deynseens [*tam inhabitantes quam forinseci*]. **1488–9** *Act 4 Hen. VII*, c. 23 Coin..conveied into Flaundres..as well by merchauntes straungers as by deynesins. **1628** COKE *On Litt.* 129 a, He that is born within the king's liegeance is called sometime a *denizen*, quasi deins nee, born within... But many times *denizen* is taken for an alien born that is infranchised or denizated by letters patent. **1655** GURNALL *Chr. in Arm.* I. 53 The Charter of London..is the birth-right of its own Denisions, not Strangers. **1664** *Pennsylv. Archives* I. 25 All people shall continue free denizens and enjoy their lands. **1734** tr. *Rollin's Anc. Hist.* I. x. 388 To be a natural denizen of Athens it was necessary to be born of a father and mother both free and Athenians. **1841** JAMES *Brigand* i, The towns of that age and their laborious denizens. **1847** LYTTON *Lucretia* 374 The squalid, ill-favoured denizens, lounging before the doors.

b. *transf.* and *fig.* An inhabitant, indweller, occupant (*of* a place, region, etc.). Used of persons, animals, and plants: chiefly *poetic* or *rhetorical*.

1474 CAXTON *Chesse* II. iii. C iij, We be not deynseyns in the world but straungers, nor we ben not born in the world for to dwelle and abyde alwey therin, but for to goo and passe thrugh hit. *a* **1711** KEN *Hymns Evang.* Poet. Wks. 1721 I. 11 Bless'd Denizon of Light [an angel]. **1712-4** POPE *Rape Lock* II. 55 He summons strait his Denizens of air. **1816** SCOTT *Antiq.* viii, Winged denizens of the crag. **1860** MAURY *Phys. Geog. Sea* xix. §806 As if the old denizens of the forest had been felled with an axe.

2. a. By restriction: One who lives habitually in a country but is not a native-born citizen; a foreigner admitted to residence and certain rights in a country; in the law of Great Britain, an alien admitted to citizenship by royal letters patent, but incapable of inheriting, or holding any public office.

[**1467** in *Eng. Gilds* (1870) 391 Eny citizen or denysen. *Ibid.* 393 Yf eny citezen denesyn or foreyn departe out of the seid cite.] **1576** FLEMING *Panopl. Epist.* 151 Cæsar had made many that came from Gallia transalpina, free denizens in Rome. **1667** E. CHAMBERLAYNE *St. Gt. Brit.* I. (1684) 81 The King by his Prerogative hath Power to Enfranchise an Alien, and make him a Denison. **1719** W. WOOD *Surv. Trade* 135 In our Colonies.. all Foreigners may be made Denizons for an inconsiderable Charge. **1765** BLACKSTONE *Comm.* I. 374 A Denizen is an alien born, but who has obtained *ex donatione regis* letters patent to make him an English subject. **1830** D'ISRAELI *Chas. I*, III. vi. 94 Charles seemed ambitious of making English denizens of every man of genius in Europe. **1873** DIXON *Two Queens* I. III. iii. 133 Carmeliano, who had become a denizen, was his Latin secretary.

b. *fig.* One admitted to, or made free of, the privileges of a particular society or fellowship; one who, though not a native, is at home in any region.

1548 UDALL, etc. *Erasm. Par. Matt.* v. 36 For they be made denisens in heauen. *a* **1653** GOUGE *Comm. Heb.* xi. 21 III. (1655) 88 Naturalized by Iacob, and made free Denisons of the Church. **1857** H. REED *Lect. Eng. Poets* II. xiv. 185 He was a denizen of ocean and of lake, of Alpine regions, and of Greek and Italian plains.

c. Used of things: e.g. of foreign words naturalized in a language, etc. In *Nat. Hist.*, A plant or animal believed to have been originally introduced by human agency into a country or district, but which now maintains itself there as if native, without the direct aid of man; cf. COLONIST 2.

1578 LYTE *Dodoens* v. lviii. 623 Tarragon.. was allowed a Denizon in England long before the time of Ruelius writing. *a* **1626** BP. ANDREWES *Serm.* vi. (1661) 148 The word Hypocrite is neither English nor Latin, but as a Denison. **1878** HOOKER *Stud. Flora* Pref. 7 To the doubtfully indigenous species I have added Watson's opinion as to whether they are 'colonists' or 'denizens'. *a* **1895** *Mod. Melilotus officinalis* is widely diffused in Great Britain, but is probably only a denizen. **1933** *Shorter Oxf. Eng. Dict.* p. vii, *Denizens* are borrowings from foreign languages which have acquired full English citizenship, *aliens* are words that retain their foreign appearance and to some extent their foreign sound. **1934** *S.P.E. Tract* XLII. 35 Most words when first borrowed are *aliens*, but if they survive they are gradually accommodated to the language which borrows them and become *denizens*.

B. *adj.* or *attrib.*

1483 *Act 1 Rich. III*, c. 9 §1 All merchauntes of the nacion of Italie.. not made deinseyn. **1509-10** *Act 1 Hen. VIII* c. 20 §1 Merchaundises of every merchaunt denyseyn and alien. **1580** HOLLYBAND *Treas. Fr. Tong, Hobeine*.. the right which the prince hath vpon the goods of a stranger, not Denizen. **1613** SIR H. FINCH *Law* (1636) 41 The wife is of the same condition with her husband. Franck if he be free, Denison if he be an Englishman, though she were a nief before, or an alien borne. **1766** ENTICK *London* IV. 377 This house was.. accounted a priory alien till the year 1380, when Richard II.. made it denizen.

denizen ('dɛnɪzən), *v.* [f. prec. sb.]

1. *trans.* To make a denizen; to admit (an alien) to residence and rights of citizenship; to naturalize. Usually *fig.*

1577 B. GOOGE *Heresbach's Husb.* Ep. to Rdr. (1586) 3 They [trees, etc.] may in short time be so denisend and made acquainted with our soile, as they will prosper [etc.]. *a* **1631** DONNE *Serm.* xxxviii. 364 Can in an instant denizen and naturalize that Soule that was an alien to the Covenant. **1636** HEYWOOD *Challenge* II. Wks. 1874 V. 21 To have you denison'd in Spaine. *a* **1711** KEN *Hymnar.* Poet. Wks. 1721 II. 132 These rather might be found.. Denizon'd in a Star good Days to see. **1832** SOUTHEY *Lett.* (1856) IV. 298 The cholera is not a passing evil. It is denizened among us. **1868** LOWELL *Dryden* Pr. Wks. (1890) III. 130 note, *So few* has long been denizened.

2. To furnish with denizens; to people with settlers from another country or district. *rare.*

Hence **'denizened** *ppl. a.*

1556 SIR J. CHEKE *Let. to T. Hoby* in *Ascham's Scholem.* Introd. (Arb.) 5 If the old denisoned wordes could content and ease this neede we wold not boldly venture of vnknown wordes. **1607** CHAPMAN *Bussy D'Ambois* Plays 1873 II. 19 Some new denizond Lord.

'denizenship. [f. DENIZEN *sb.* + -SHIP.] The position or status of a denizen.

1603 FLORIO *Montaigne* III. ix. (1632) 564 An authenticke Bull, charter or patent of denizonship or borgeousship of Rome. **1807** W. TAYLOR in *Ann. Rev.* V. 568 The concession of denizenship. **1871** *Athenæum* 4 Feb. 137 Denizenship is a mongrel state, not worth preserving when the process of obtaining naturalization is so simple.

‖**denkmal** ('dɛŋkmɑːl). Pl. **-mäler.** [G.] A monument, memorial.

1877 *Echo* 31 July 1/4 A forthcoming centenary or inauguration of a 'Denkmal'. **1927** *Spectator* 26 Nov. 928/1 We raise our monuments to the fallen in lines reminiscent of the *denkmal.* **1953** W. STEVENS *Let.* 15 June (1967) 782 They [*sc.* plans] will create from this sense of things completely lost a kind of community Denkmal.

Denmark ('dɛnmɑːk). The name of one of the Scandinavian countries, used *attrib.* to designate special kinds of products, as in ***Denmark satin*** (see SATIN *sb.* I. 1 b). Also ***Denmark Street*** (see quot. 1934).

1836 DICKENS *Sk. Boz* in *Morning Chron.* 24 Sept. 3/2 A pair of Denmark satin shoes. *Ibid.*, Nor were the Denmark satins a bit behindhand. **1875** [see SATIN *sb.* I. 1 b]. **1882** CAULFEILD & SAWARD *Dict. Needlework, Denmark Satin*, a kind of worsted stuff employed for the making of women's shoes, measuring 27 inches in width. **1934** S. R. NELSON *All about Jazz* i. 29 Much knowledge of human nature is to be found in Tin Pan Alley and its English equivalent, Denmark Street, Charing Cross Road. **1967** *Guardian* 8 July 12/8 What will happen to Mick Jagger.. is not the only question .. worrying the world of 'pop' music... Denmark Street has also been exercising its mind on the identity of some ancient Greek called Euterpe.

denn (dɛn). [OE. (Kent) *denn* woodland pasture; possibly the same word as OE. *denn* habitation of a wild beast (DEN *sb.*[1]); cf. MDu. *dann* forest, haunt of wild beasts.]

An OE. word, revived by place-name scholars, which survives chiefly in place-names (see A. H. SMITH, *Eng. Place-Name Elements* (1956) I. 129), as *Halden, Tenterden*, both in Kent.

A woodland pasture, esp. for swine.

1936 E. EKWALL *Conc. Oxf. Dict. Eng. Place-Names* p. xv, Originally the *denns* belonged to the various *lathes* and were often situated far from the district to which they belonged. **1948** L. D. STAMP *Land of Brit.* iii. 46 The upland settlements had rights of feeding swine in sections or 'denns' of the great Wealden oak forests, hence such names as Tenterden and Biddenden.

dennar, -er, obs. forms of DINNER.

denne, obs. form of DIN *v.*

dennebol ('dɛnəbɒl). *S. Afr.* Also **danebol.** [Afrikaans, f. *den* pine + *bol* ball, bulb.] A fir cone.

1909 *State* II. 768 She.. began to break up a 'dennebol' between two stones. **1913** PETTMAN *Africanderisms* 139 *Danebol* or *Dennebol*.. A fir cone. **1947** L. G. GREEN *Tavern of Seas* viii. 65 Sweets made of sugar, water, eggs, naartjie peel and dennebol pits. **1953** *Cape Times* 31 Mar. 16/3 Dennebols for your fires only sixpence for 50.

dennet ('dɛnɪt). [Supposed to be from the Eng. surname *Dennet.*] A light open two-wheeled carriage akin to a gig; fashionable in England *c* 1818–1830.

1818 *Sporting Mag.* II. 193 The Dandies of our days.. Are wont to bask in fashion's blaze, In Tilbury or Dennet. **1826** *Hull Advertiser* 9 June 1/2 To be sold, a handsome light Dennet, calculated for a horse or poney. **1843** LEVER *J. Hinton* xvi, A certain gig and horse, popularly known in this city as the discount dennet.

denning: see DEN *v.*[1]

denny ('dɛnɪ), *a. Obs.* or *rare.* [f. DEN *sb.*[1] + -Y.] **a.** Having or abounding in dens, cavities, or hollows. **b.** Of the nature of a den.

1398 TREVISA *Barth. De P.R.* v. xxxvi. (1495) 148 The herte is denny and holowe. **1656** W. D. tr. *Comenius' Gate Lat. Unl.* ¶164 Hiding themselves in denny places and holes, as wilde beasts.

denominable (dɪ'nɒmɪnəb(ə)l), *a.* [f. L. *dēnōminā-re* to denominate + -BLE.] That may be denominated or named.

1658 SIR T. BROWNE *Pseud. Ep.* (ed. 4) IV. iii. 182 Inflammation.. denominable from other humours, according to the predominancy of melancholy, flegme, or choler. **1818** BENTHAM *Ch. Eng.* Introd. 165 The so often mentioned, and no otherwise denominable, T. T. Walmsley, Sec.

denominal (dɪ'nɒmɪnəl), *a.* and *sb. Gram.* [f. DE- II. 3 + NOMINAL A. 1.] = DENOMINATIVE *a.* 3, *sb.* 2.

1934 PRIEBSCH & COLLINSON *Ger. Lang.* II. iii. 225 The suffix *-ēn*..(*a*) to form durative deverbals..(*b*) to form inchoative denominals. **1959** *Archivum Linguisticum* XI. 108 *Imprison*—denominal verb.

de'nominant, *sb. rare.* [ad. L. *dēnōminantem*, pr. pple. of *dēnōmināre*: see next.] = DENOMINATOR 3.

1889 in *Cent. Dict.*

denominate (dɪ'nɒmɪnət), *ppl. a.* and *sb.* [ad. L. *dēnōmināt-us*, pa. pple. of *dēnōmināre.*]

A. *pa. pple.* Named, called, denominated. *Obs.* or *arch.*

1579 G. HARVEY *Letter-bk.* (Camden) 63 By what name or names, title or titles.. they.. may be callid, termid.. or denominate. **1665** SIR T. HERBERT *Trav.* (1677) 43 Whether Gusurat.. be denominate from Gezurat, which in the Arabick signifies an Isle. **1689** tr. *Buchanan's De Jure Regni* 10 It is no great matter how it be denominate. **1814** SOUTHEY *Roderick* xviii, The walls of Salduba.. by Rome Cæsarian and August denominate, Now Zaragoza.

†**B.** *adj. Arith.* Said of a number when used adjectivally with the name of the kind of unit treated of (= CONCRETE *a.* 4); opp. to *abstract.*

1579 DIGGES *Stratiot.* 33 These kinds of concrete or Denominate numbers. **1674** JEAKE *Arith.* (1696) 207 Abstract and.. denominate Numbers.

C. *sb.*

†**1.** That which something is called; a name, denomination, appellation. *Obs.*

1638 SIR T. HERBERT *Trav.* (ed. 2) 343 After that it varied into other denominats, as Roderigo; Cygnæa; and now, by the Hollanders, Mauritius.

†**2.** *Gram.* A word derived from another word, *esp.* from a noun; a denominative. *Obs.*

1628 T. SPENCER *Logick* 142 Aristotle.. thus.. writeth; Those [words] are called denominates, which haue the appellation of a name from some other.. as from Grammar, man is called a Grammarian. **1654** HAMMOND *Answ. Animadv. Ignat.* ii. §1. 34 The nature of the word being a denominate from a yong man, νεωτερική from νεώτεροι.

denominate (dɪ'nɒmɪneɪt), *v.* [f. L. *dēnōmināt-*, ppl. stem of *dēnōmināre* to name, specify by name, f. DE- I. 3 + *nōmināre* to name (see NOMINATE).]

1. *trans.* To give a name or appellation to; to call by a name, to name (orig. *from* or *after* something). Now usually with complement: To give (a thing) the name of.., to call.

1552 HULOET, Denominate, *denomino.* **1597** MORLEY *Introd. Mus.* 91 Quadrupla and Quintupla, they denominated after the number of blacke minimes set for a note of the plainsong. **1634** SIR T. HERBERT *Trav.* 209 The Portugals, who (not unlike a second Adam, denominating all new places and things) gave it the name. *Ibid.* 223 Americus Vespucius.. denominates that vast and spacious Continent from his owne name, America. **1639** FULLER *Holy War* II. ix. (1840) 60 From him [Guelpho] they of the papal faction were denominated Guelphes. **1774** BRYANT *Mythol.* I. 89 *Phi* is also used for any opening.. whence.. the head of a fountain is often denominated from it. **1781** COWPER *Ep. Lady Hesketh* 18 This is what the world.. Denominates an itch for writing. **1805** FOSTER *Ess.* III. iii. 51 Who have hardly words to denominate even their sensations. **1876** E. MELLOR *Priesth.* i. 16 They [the apostles] do not denominate him [the Christian minister] a priest.

†**b.** *intr.* (for *refl.*) To give oneself a name, take one's name (*from*). *Obs. rare.*

1652 SPARKE *Prim. Devot.* (1663) 336 Thou that leavest the master, and denominatest from the servant.

†**c.** To express in some arithmetical denomination. *Obs. rare.*

1788 PRIESTLEY *Lect. Hist.* III. xiv. 120 These methods of denominating time.

†**2.** Of things: To give a name to, as a quality or attribute; to give (a thing) its name or character, to characterize; to make what it is, constitute; (with complement) to constitute, give the right to be called. *Obs.*

1616 S. WARD *Coale fr. Altar* (1627) 36 The same vertue denominated Iacob a Prince with God. **1628** DONNE *Serm.* xxiii. 225 The Divine, the Physitian, the Lawyer are not qualified nor Denominated by the same Kinde of Learning. **1664** POWER *Exp. Philos.* III. 184 The numerous Rabble.. have nothing of the nobler part that should denominate their Essences. **1698** W. CHILCOT *Evil Thoughts* vi. (1851) 74 This will denominate us of the number of Christ's true disciples. **1783** JOHNSON *Let. To Susanna Thrale* (1788) II. 290 Our general course of life must denominate us wise or foolish; happy or miserable. **1816-17** BENTHAM *Chrestomathia* Wks. VIII. 19 That sort of acquaintance with the Greek and Latin classics which denominates a man a good scholar.

†**b.** *absol.*

1614 SELDEN *Titles Hon.* 126 The Abstract tastes as if it were more honorable. For that quality denominats. **1621** BURTON *Anat. Mel.* II. iii. II. (1676) 197/2 It is wealth alone that denominates, money which maintains it, gives *esse* to it ['gentry']. **1691** BAXTER *Nat. Ch.* xii. 51 The Form denominateth; and is Essential.

c. *Logic.* Of an attribute: To give a name to (a subject).

1599 [see DENOMINATOR 3]. *a* **1626** BACON *Max. & Uses Com. Law* xxiii. (1636) 84 One name and appellation doth denominate divers things. **1843** MILL *Logic* I. ii. §5 The attribute, or attributes, may therefore be said to denominate those objects, or to give them a common name.

†**3.** To point out, indicate, denote. *Obs.*

1710 in Somers *Tracts* III. 5 Our Credit in this Case.. is rightly called by some of our Writers, National Credit; the Word denominates its Original. **1756** C. LUCAS *Ess. Waters* I. 88 The portion of salt which.. suffered the greatest change, denominates the most impure water. **1792** J. BELKNAP *Hist. New Hampshire* III. 130 There is a difference sufficient to denominate the soil from the growth.

Hence **de'nominated, de'nominating** *ppl. adjs.*

1614 SELDEN *Titles Hon.* 235 At this day.. in the denominating Countie the Earle hath but only his Name. **1750** CARTE *Hist. Eng.* II. 469 They were forced to take Flemish florins at a denominated rate much higher than the intrinsick value. **1825** BENTHAM *Indic. Ld. Eldon* 83 The business of all denominated Offices.

denomination (dɪnɒmɪ'neɪʃən). [a. OF. *denominacion* (13th c. in Godef. Suppl.), ad. L. *dēnōminātiōn-em*, n. of action from *dēnōmināre* (in cl. Lat. in the sense of 'calling by another than the proper name, metonymy').]

1. The action of naming *from* or *after* something; giving a name to, calling by a name.

c **1400** *Test. Love* II. (R.), Of whiche worchings and possession of hours, yᵉ daies of the week haue take her names, after denominacion in these seven planets. **1593** NORDEN *Spec. Brit., M'sex* I. 18 To controul mine obseruations..in regarde of the vncertaine distances, vntrue denominations of places..which (I confesse) are faultes. *a* **1626** BACON *Max. & Uses Com. Law* xxv. (1636) 89 A farther sort of denomination is to name land by the attendancy they have to other lands more notorious. **1739** HUME *Hum. Nat.* I. I. vii, The reference of the idea to an object being an extraneous denomination. **1860** ABP. THOMSON *Laws Th.* §48. 76 Denomination is the imposition of a name that shall serve to recall equally the Genus or Class, and the Common Nature.

†**b.** A mentioning or specifying by name. *Obs.*

1398 TREVISA *Barth. De P.R.* II. iii. (1495) 30 By denomynacion of lymmes that ben seen, vnseen werkinges of heuenly inwyttes ben understonde. **1600** HAKLUYT *Voy.* (1810) III. 538 Vpon whose denomination I was apprehended for the same words here rehearsed.

2. A characteristic or qualifying name given to a thing or class of things; that which anything is called; an appellation, designation, title.

1432-50 tr. *Higden* (Rolls) I. 267 Storyes expresse that Gallia or Fraunce hathe denominacion of the whitenesse of peple. **1563** *Homilies* II. *Fasting* I. (1859) 284 Works..which ..are..neither good nor evil, but take their denomination of the use or end whereunto they serve. **1659** PEARSON *Creed* (1839) 1 The first word Credo..giveth a denomination to the whole confession of faith, from thence commonly called the Creed. **1778** BURKE *Corr.* (1844) II. 217, I most heartily disclaim that, or any other, denomination, incompatible with such sentiments. **1815** SCOTT *Guy M.* vii, The tribes of gypsies, jockies, or cairds—for by all these denominations such banditti were known. *a* **1871** GROTE *Eth. Fragm.* i. (1876) 17 The virtuous man or vicious man of our own age or country, will no longer receive the same denominations if trasferred to a remote climate or a different people.

†**b.** (See quot.) *Obs.*

1737 ABP. BOULTER *Lett.* II. 234 Five, six, or seven parishes (denominations we commonly call them) bestowed on one incumbent.

3. *Arith.* A class of one kind of unit in any system of numbers, measures, weights, money, etc., distinguished by a specific name.

c **1430** *Art of Nombrynge* (E.E.T.S) 8 And so oft with-draw the digit multiplying, vnder the article of his denominacioun. **1542** RECORDE *Gr. Artes* (1575) 52 Of the first ternarye, the denomination is vnities, and of the seconde ternarye, the denomination is thousandes. **1557** —— *Whetst.* Rj b, I will, for ease, turne the other into a fraction of the same denomination. **1594** BLUNDEVIL *Exerc.* I. vi. (ed. 7) 19. **1660** WILLSFORD *Scales Comm.* 9 The price by which 'twas bought, and likewise the rate at which 'twas sold must be reduced into one denomination. **1725** BRADLEY *Fam. Dict., Troy Weight*, a Weight in which the smallest Denomination is a Grain. **1868** ROGERS *Pol. Econ.* iv. (1876) 47 When..the paper money is of small denominations. *Mod.* Reduce the two quantities to the same denomination.

4. A class, sort, or kind (of things or persons) distinguished or distinguishable by a specific name.

1664 POWER *Exp. Philos.* III. 187 Civil dissention..'twixt men of the same denomination and principles. **1727** A. HAMILTON *New Acc. E. Ind.* I. xxviii. 350 The Country.. produceth good Cotton Cloth of several Qualities and Denominations. **1814** D. H. O'BRIEN *Captiv. & Escape* 154 A punishment equal to six years, with all denominations of malefactors, in the galleys.

5. A collection of individuals classed together under the same name; now almost always *spec.* a religious sect or body having a common faith and organization, and designated by a distinctive name.

a **1716** SOUTH (J.), Philosophy..has divided it into many sects and denominations; as Stoicks, Peripateticks, Epicureans, and the like. **1746-7** HERVEY *Medit.* (1818) 195 Who, when he had overcome the sharpness of death.. opened the kingdom to heaven to all generations, and to every denomination of the faithful. **1788** FRANKLIN *Autobiog.* Wks. 1887 I. 206 The multitudes of all sects and denominations that attended his sermons. **1888** BRYCE *Amer. Commw.* III. VI. civ. 496 All denominations are more prone to emotionalism in religion..than in England or Scotland.

denominational (dɪˈnɒmɪˈneɪʃənəl), *a.* [f. prec. + -AL¹.]

1. Belonging to, or of the nature of, a denomination or ecclesiastical sect; sectarian, as ***a denominational school*** or ***college***; hence ***denominational system of education***, one providing or recognizing such schools, etc.

1838 GLADSTONE *State in Rel. w. Ch.* (1839) 274 We have no fear for the Church of England in her competition with the denominational bodies around her. **1861** M. ARNOLD *Pop. Educ. France* 71 Under the dominion of the new law denominational schools are the rule. **1882** *Standard* 10 Oct. 5/1 Denominational Colleges in Universities which are now undenominational need no apology or excuse.

2. Pertaining to a denomination or name. *rare.*

1892 *Daily News* 25 Oct. 5/4 Not counters, like our silver and bronze coins, but pieces intrinsically worth their denominational value.

Hence **denomiˈnationalism**, adherence to or advocacy of denominational principles or a denominational system (e.g. of education); **denomiˈnationalist**, an adherent or advocate of these; **denominatioˈnality**, the state or condition of being denominational; **denomiˈnationalize**, *v.*, to make denominational; **denomiˈnationally**, *adv.*, according to a denominational method.

1855 TRENCH *Eng. Past & Pres.* iv. (1870) 129 We have 'inflexional', 'seasonal', 'denominational', and on this..the monstrous birth, 'denominationalism'. **1870** *Sat. Rev.* 2 Apr. 431 This plan..concedes the whole principle of Denominationalism. **1870** *Daily News* 7 Oct., In the country districts..the Denominationalists are evidently preparing to occupy the ground. **1892** E. L. STANLEY *Ibid.* 16 Nov. 5/6 Denominationality would not he believed suffer from a sudden exodus of the masses of their scholars to the Board Schools. **1869** *Nation* (N.Y.) 11 Mar. 190 (Cent.) The religious sentiment somewhat..denominationalized—to coin a new word. **1893** *Daily News* 22 June 4/7 To denationalise Trinity [College] would be, if possible, a greater calamity than to denominationalise it. **1845** *Eclectic Rev.* Dec. 622 Religious education is taken up denominationally.

denominative (dɪˈnɒmɪnətɪv), *a.* and *sb.* [ad. L. *dēnōminātīv-us*, f. ppl. stem of *dēnōmināre*: see -IVE. Cf. F. *dénominatif* (Catholicon, 15th c.).]

A. *adj.*

1. Having the quality or function of naming; characterized by giving a name to something.

1614 T. JACKSON *Comment. Apost. Creede* III. 62 The same name [Cepha] giuen vnto Simon..must imply no more then a denominatiue reference vnto the rocke. **1658** W. BURTON *Itin. Anton.* 151 The petty stream that runs thereby was denominative of the place. **1826** MRS. BRAY *De Foix* xviii. (1884) 209 High-spiced wines, that the medical monk thus fenced with the denominative armour of physic.

b. Of a word or term: Having the function of naming, denominating, or describing, as an attribute; characterized by denomination.

a **1638** MEDE *Disc.* ii. Wks. (1672) I. 6 The first we may call his Personal, the other his Denominative or Participated Name. **1674** OWEN *Holy Spirit* (1693) 9 A Name..not distinctive with respect unto His Personality, but denominative with respect unto His Work. **1843** MILL *Logic* I. ii. §5 Connotative names have hence been also called *denominative*, because the subject which they denote is denominated by, or receives a name from, the attribute which they connote.

†**2.** Having or called by a distinctive name; constituting a DENOMINATION (sense 3). *Obs. rare.*

a **1677** COCKER *Arith.* (1678) 29 The least denominative part of time is a minute, the greatest integer being a year.

3. *Gram.* Formed or derived from a noun.

[Cf. PRISCIAN *Inst.* IV. i. 'Denominativa sunt, id est, a nominibus derivantur'. The L. word was used by early translators of Aristotle to render Gr. παρώνυμος derivative.] **1783** AINSWORTH *Lat. Dict.* (Morell) v, *Denominativus*, adj. Denominative, that is, derived of a noun, as from *dens* comes *dentatus*. **1839** tr. *Gesenius' Hebr. Gram.* §85 *Denominative nouns.* 1. Such are all nouns which are formed immediately from another noun. **1875** WHITNEY *Life Lang.* vii. 131 Such *denominative* verbs, as they are called, abound in every member of our family.

†**b.** Derivative. *Obs. rare.*

1624 F. WHITE *Repl. Fisher* 236 This holinesse being only relatiue, transitorie, and denominatiue, and not inherent or durable.

B. *sb.* †**1.** A 'denominative' or attributive term: see A. 1 b. *Obs.*

1589 PUTTENHAM *Eng. Poesie* III. xvii. (Arb.), He that said thus of a faire Lady: 'O rare beautie, ô grace, and curtesie!' Whereas if he had said thus, O gratious, courteous and beautifull woman:..it had bene all to one effect, yet not with such force..to speake by the denominatiue, as by the thing it selfe. **1599** [see DENOMINATOR 3].

2. *Gram.* A word formed or derived from a noun.

a **1638** MEDE *Wks.* I. ii. (R.), For sanctity and to sanctifie being conjugates or denominatives, as logicians call them: the one openeth the way to the knowledge of the other. **1839** tr. *Gesenius' Hebr. Gram.* 45 A peculiar kind of secondary verbs..are those denominatives, one of whose consonants, originally a servile, has become a radical. **1885** tr. *Socin's Arabic Gram.* 26 Denominatives with a concealed transitive meaning.

denominatively (dɪˈnɒmɪnətɪvlɪ), *adv.* [f. prec. + -LY².] In a denominative manner; by way of denomination; †attributively, derivatively.

1563-87 FOXE *A. & M.* (1596) 1303/2 *Substantia* may be predicated denominatiuely..or in a figuratiue locution. **1656** JEANES *Fuln. Christ* 118 There is only an extrinsecall, and accidentall union betwixt a man and his garment: and the garment is predicated of the man, only denominatively. *Homo dicitur vestitus, non vestis.* **1660** T. GOUGE *Chr. Directions* xx. (1831) 108 Whatsoever in holy writ is said to be the Lord's denominatively, of that Christ is the author and institutor, as, for instance, the Lord's Supper.

denominator (dɪˈnɒmɪneɪtə(r)). [a. med.L. *dēnōminātor*, agent-n., from *dēnōmināre* to DENOMINATE. In F. *dénominateur* occurs 1484 (Hatzf.) in the arithmetical sense.]

1. One who or that which denominates or gives a name to something. Now *rare.*

1577 HARRISON *England* IV. xiv. (1878) II. 91 The Latins and Aegyptians accompted their daies after the seauen planets, choosing the same for the denominator of the daie, that [etc.]. **1641** HEYLIN *Help to Hist.* (1671) 332 In this part stands the City of Lincoln, the chief denominator of the County. **1878** *N. Amer. Rev.* 352 That inconvertible paper may serve as an accurate denominator of values.

2. *Arith.* and *Alg.* The number written below the line in a vulgar fraction, which gives the denomination or value of the parts into which the integer is divided; the corresponding expression in an algebraical fraction, denoting the divisor. (Correlative to *numerator.*) ***common denominator***, (*a*) a common multiple of the denominators of two or more fractions, i.e. a number that is a multiple of the denominator of each of them; (*b*) *fig.* something common to or characteristic of a number of things, people, etc.; also *attrib.*; so ***least*** or ***lowest common denominator***, the lowest possible common denominator; also *attrib.* and *fig.*

1542 RECORDE *Gr. Artes* (1575) 322 The Denominator doth declare the number of partes into whiche the vnit is diuided. **1557** —— *Whetst.* Fivb, Here haue I sette the lesser side as the numerator and the greatere side as the denominator. **1594** [see COMMON *a.* 16]. **1674** JEAKE *Arith.* (1696) 211 If the Numerator be given to find a Denominator. **1763** W. EMERSON *Meth. Increments* 29 Reducing them to a common denominator. **1864** BOWEN *Logic* xii. 406 The resulting fractions fall into a series, any one of which has for..its denominator the sum of the two preceding denominators. **1875** *Encycl. Brit.* II. 530/2 In practice it is usually the *least* common denominator that the fractions are compared by.

fig. **1831** CARLYLE *Sart. Res.* II. ix, The fraction of life can be increased in value not so much by increasing your Numerator as by lessening your Denominator. **1893** H. H. GIBBS *Colloq. Currency* 62 How is that capital..measured? What is the Denominator of which price is the Numerator? **1898** *Westm. Gaz.* 6 May 2/3 His speech would have to be rendered by interpreters into each of the hundred tongues .., presuming no common denominator language can be used. **1910** [see *club bore* s.v. CLUB *sb.* 19 b]. **1937** *Discovery* Mar. 75/1 All the black-and-white processes have a common denominator. **1946** R. A. KNOX *Epistles & Gospels* 56 He wants the would-be-clever people to cultivate..a lowest-common-denominator sort of mind. **1958** *Observer* 11 May 14/6 Searching among this raw material of art for the lowest common denominator on which to base a new style.

†**3.** An abstract noun denoting an attribute. *Obs.* (Cf. DENOMINATIVE A. 1 b, B. 1.)

1599 BLUNDEVIL *Art of Logick* vii. 14 Peter is said to be valiant; here valiantnes is the Denominator, valiant the Denominatiue, Peter the Denominated; for Peter is the subject whereunto the Denominator doth cleaue.

‖**de nos jours** (dənoʒur), *adj. phr.* [Fr., lit. 'of our days'.] Of our time or lifetime; contemporary.

The phrase always follows the sb. which it qualifies.

[**1864** BROWNING *Dramatis Personæ* 47 Dîs aliter visum; or, le Byron de nos jours.] **1909** BEERBOHM *Yet Again* 192, I admire the Demosthenes *de nos jours.* **1958** *Listener* 14 Aug. 249/3 The musical Robespierre *de nos jours.*

denotable (dɪˈnəʊtəb(ə)l), *a.* [f. DENOTE *v.* + -ABLE.] That can be denoted or marked.

a **1682** SIR T. BROWNE *Tracts* (1684) 25 In hot Regions, and more spread and digested Flowers, a sweet savour may be allowed, denotable from several humane expressions. **1882** *Macm. Mag.* Feb. 327 His painter's habit of presenting every motive as translated into form denotable by lines and colours.

†**denotate** (ˈdiːnəʊteɪt), *v. Obs.* [f. ppl. stem of L. *dēnōtāre* to DENOTE: cf. *connotate* vb.]

1. To note down, particularize, describe; to mark out, indicate; = DENOTE 1, 2.

1599 A. M. tr. *Gabelhouer's Bk. Physicke* Contents, In the fifth..Parte, are sett downe, and denotated vnto us certaine kindes of precious Medicamentes. **1627** SYBTHORPE *Apost. Obed.* 7 Those duties..are..denotated in this word, 'give', or 'render'. **1634** SIR T. HERBERT *Trav.* 79 And Temeriske, to denotate himselfe a thankfull person, requites with many favours such Persians as accompanied him. **1638** *Ibid.* (ed. 2) 214 More I have not to denotate, save that many severall conjectures..have passed, whence the Magi or wise men came. **1653** R. BAILLIE *Disswasive Vind.* 11 If it fitly denotated their principal position.

2. Of things: To serve as a mark, sign, or indication of; to indicate, signify; = DENOTE 3, 4.

1597 MORLEY *Introd. Mus.* 179 Short notes and quicke motions, which denotate a kind of wantonnes. **1610** W. FOLKINGHAM *Art of Survey* I. iii. 6 The high timbring Oake ..denotates a rich and battle soile. **1618** BOLTON *Florus* To Rdr., The yeeres 'from Rome built'—which these letters, A.U.C., do denotate. **1650** HUBBERT *Pill Formality* 96 All which denotate and set forth the Almighty power of God.

denotation (diːnəʊˈteɪʃən). [ad. L. *dēnōtātiōn-em*, n. of action from *dēnōtāre* to DENOTE. Cf. F. *dénotation* (15th c. in Hatzf.).]

1. The action of denoting; marking, noting; expression by marks, signs, or symbols; indication.

c **1532** DEWES *Introd. Fr.* in Palsgr. 900 Dyuers wordes, whiche for denotation or signifycation of pluralite doth ende with an *s.* **1623** COCKERAM, *Denotation*, a marking, a noting. **1631** BP. WEBBE *Quietn.* (1657) 12 A short denotation of that method which we will observe in the unfolding. **1659** PEARSON *Creed* (1839) 275 One who was called Ἐπώνυμος, because his name was used for the denotation of that year. **1803** LD. ELDON in *Vesey's Rep.* VI. 397 By that denotation of intention the Creditor has a double Fund. **1825** FOSBROKE *Encycl. Antiq.* (1843) I. 111 The idea of Julius Cæsar's building round towers out of vanity, in denotation of conquest, certainly prevailed in the middle ages.

2. (with *a* and *pl.*) A mark by which a thing is made known or indicated; a sign, indication.

1633 BP. HALL *Hard. Texts, N.T.* 97, I had no knowledge of him by any outward denotations. **1638** SIR T. HERBERT *Trav.* (ed. 2) 47 The thred tripartite hung about their neck as a mysterious denotation of the Trinity. *a* **1650** MAY *Satir. Puppy* (1657) 39 After many denotations of a troubled spirit, he charmed attention with this speech. **1837** WHITTOCK *Bk. Trades* (1842) 302 An assertion we are willing to credit as a denotation of effeminacy.

3. A term employed to denote or describe a thing; a designation.

1631 WEEVER *Anc. Fun. Mon.* 595 The Germans called an Esquire..knaue, a denotation of no ill qualitie in those dayes. **1644** HAMMOND *Of Conscience* (T.), Mind and conscience are distinguished..that former being properly the denotation of the faculty merely speculative, or intellectual; this latter, of the practical judgement. **1659** —— *On Ps.* lxxxix. 12 Annot. 446 Being here a denotation of a particular quarter of the world. **1742** FIELDING *J. Andrews* I. xi, To indicate our idea of a simple fellow we say he is easily to be seen through; nor do I believe it a more improper denotation of a simple book.

4. The meaning or signification of a term.

1614 SELDEN *Titles Hon.* 341 Time hath brought the word *knaue* to a denotation of ill qualities. **1692** J. EDWARDS *Further Enq. Texts O. & N.T.* 35 But after all that I have said, concerning this so remarkable etymology and denotation of the word, I leave every one to his liberty. **1882** *Pall Mall G.* 21 June 2 Can we limit the denotation of the term coffee to the produce of a certain berry? **1893** F. HALL in *Nation* LVII. 450/1 The term *ârya*..may have a wider denotation than that which was long attached to it.

5. *Logic.* That which a word *denotes*, as distinguished from its *connotation*; the aggregate of objects of which a word may be predicated; extension. Cf. DENOTE *v.* 5, CONNOTATION 2 b.

1843 MILL *Logic* I. viii. §7 Stripping it of some part of its multifarious denotation, and confining it to objects possessed of some attributes in common, which it may be made to connote. **1866** FOWLER *Deduct. Logic* (1887) 22 The larger the denotation or extensive capacity, the smaller is the connotation or intensive capacity. **1870** ROLLESTON *Anim. Life* Introd. 20 The quantitative relations which the corresponding divisions in almost any two of the animal sub-kingdoms hold to each other as wholes of 'extension' or of 'denotation'.

Hence **deno'tational** *a.*

1948 B. RUSSELL *Human Knowl.* 293 An example of a denotational definition is 'the tallest man in the United States'. **1957** in N. Frye *Sound & Poetry* 138 Word-repetition..repeats the..word..with the same denotational semantic spectrum. **1963** J. LYONS *Structural Semantics* iii. 38 The advantage of taking the set of colour-terms..is that they are readily shown to..cover a well-defined 'denotational field'.

denotative (dɪ'nəʊtətɪv), *a.* [f. L. *dēnōtāt-*, ppl. stem of *dēnōtāre* + -IVE: cf. *connotative.*]

a. Having the quality of denoting; designative, indicative.

1611 COTGR., *Designatif*, designatiue, denotatiue. **1751** *Lett. Physiognomy* 121 (T.), What are the effects of sickness? the alteration it produces is so denotative, that a person is known to be sick by those who never saw him in health. **1862** F. HALL *Hindu Philos. Syst.* 225 Non-difference from the subject of right notion is not here denotative of oneness with it. **1871** NAPHEYS *Prev. & Cure Dis.* II. i. 363 The half-opened eye during sleep is not necessarily denotative of any trouble.

b. *Logic.* Of a word: Having the quality of designating, as distinguished from *connotative*. Also as *sb.*

1864 LATHAM *Dict.* s.v. *Denotation*, Proper names are preeminently denotative; telling us that such an object has such a term to denote it, but telling us nothing as to any single attribute. **1869** J. MARTINEAU *Ess.* II. 327 He must have resorted to..names more purely denotative still. **1944** *Mind* LIII. 35 Roughly, empirical ties are the denotatives: demonstrative pronouns ('this', 'that'), relative adverbs ('here', 'now'), also symbols often not called linguistic, such as gestures (pointing), etc.

Hence **de'notatively** *adv.*, in a denotative manner.

1864 BOWEN *Logic* iv. 65 If used connotatively, it is called a Mark; if used denotatively, it is called a Concept. **1881** VENN *Symbolic Logic* ii. 36 The classes, whether plural or individual, are all alike represented denotatively by literal symbols, *w, x, y, z*.

denotatum (diːnəʊ'teɪtəm). *Philos.* Pl. **-tata.** [a. L. *dēnōtātum*, neut. pa. pple. of *dēnōtāre* to DENOTE.] That which is denoted by some expression; *esp.* an existent object of reference. (Cf. DESIGNATUM.)

1938 C. W. MORRIS in *Internat. Encycl. Unified Sci.* I. 83 Where what is referred to actually exists as referred to[,] the object of reference is a denotatum. It thus becomes clear that, while every sign has a designatum, not every sign has a denotatum. A designatum is not a thing, but a kind of object or class of objects—and a class may have many members, or one member, or no members. The denotata are the members of the class. **1940** [see DESIGNATUM]. **1944** M. WEITZ in P. A. Schilpp *Philos. B. Russell* 100 So to interpret the entities of physics means..that they are no longer the denotata of proper names..nor the denotata of descriptions. **1963** J. LYONS *Structural Semantics* iii. 37 The vocabulary of a language is not rightly regarded as a set of isolated symbols standing in a relation of correspondence with a set of discrete and prior concepts or denotata existing in the 'outside world'. **1968** Y. R. CHAO *Language & Symbolic Systems* 67 The word *dog* means the animal dog. The word is said to *refer to*, or *denote*, the thing and the thing is the *referent* or *denotatum*. **1968** *Language* XLIV. 40 With adjectives, it is clear that *und* is obligatory when the coördinated nouns do not refer to the same sample of the denotatum.

denote (dɪ'nəʊt), *v.* [a. F. *dénote-r* (Oresme, 14th c.), ad. L. *dēnōtāre* to mark out, f. DE- I. 3 + *nōtāre* to mark, NOTE.]

†**1.** *trans.* To note down; to put into or state in writing; to describe. *Obs.*

1612 W. PARKES *Curtaine-Dr.* (1876) 40 A most copious Regester, wherein are denoted and set downe the liues and actions of all the inhabitants of the earth. **1632** LITHGOW *Trav.* VI. 255 Which particulars, by my owne experience, I could denote. **1638** H. RIDER *Horace, Odes* II. vi, Who worthily can with his pen denote Mars? **1697** *C'tess D'Aunoy's Trav.* (1706) 32, I cannot find Words to denote to you the Horror of this Spectacle.

2. To mark; to mark out (from among others); to distinguish by a mark or sign.

1598 SHAKS. *Merry W.* IV. vi. 39 Her Mother hath intended (The better to denote her to the Doctor)..That quaint in greene, she shall be loose en-roab'd. **1646** SIR T. BROWNE *Pseud. Ep.* V. xviii, Sun Dialls, by the shadow of a stile or gnomon denoting the hours of the day. **1703** MOXON *Mech. Exerc.* 343 This line shall be the Equinoctial line, and serve to denote the Hour Distances, as the Contingent Lines does on other Dyals. *c* **1820** S. ROGERS *Italy, Luigi* 40 The latin verse, Graven in the stone that yet denotes the door Of Ariosto. **1885** *Act 48 Vict.* c. 15 Sched. II. 6 Such entry shall in the register be denoted by an asterisk.

†**b.** To point out as by a mark, to indicate, to designate. *Obs.*

1632 LITHGOW *Trav.* x. 435 The Priests as fearefull of the Ministers apprehending, or denoting them. **1701** tr. *Le Clerc's Prim. Fathers* (1702) 131 [Athanasius] had been denoted several times by this Bishop for his Successor.

3. To be the outward or visible mark or sign of, to indicate (a fact, state of things, etc.).

1592 SHAKS. *Rom. & Jul.* III. iii. 110 Thy wild acts denote The vnreasonable Furie of a beast. **1632** J. HAYWARD tr. *Biondi's Eromena* 182 The appearances which denoted her greatnesse. **1666** PEPYS *Diary* 29 July, We keep the sea, which denotes a victory. **1766** ANSTEY *Bath Guide* II. x. (1779) 90 What can a man of true fashion denote Like an ell of good ribbon ty'd under the throat? **1814** SOUTHEY *Roderick* XIII, A messenger..whose speed denoted well He came with urgent tidings. **1858** HAWTHORNE *Fr. & It. Jrnls.* (1872) I. 22 Medals..denoting Crimean service. *Mod.* A quick pulse denotes fever. A falling barometer denotes an approaching storm.

b. To indicate, give to understand, make known.

1660 WILLSFORD *Scales Comm.* 13 In this 'tis Moneths, as the Letter M denotes. *a* **1677** BARROW *Wks.* (1687) I. 423 *He hath given to the poor.* These words denote the freeness of his bounty. **1703** MAUNDRELL *Journ. Jerus.* (1732) 139 All which serve only to denote the resort which the Romans had to this place. **1749** SMOLLETT *Regicide* IV. vii, Thou hast enough Denoted thy concern. **1812–16** J. SMITH *Panorama Sc. & Art* II. 524 Horizontally [in a table] opposite the sulphuric acid is placed magnesia, to denote that it is presented to that acid.

4. To signify; to stand for as a symbol, or as a name or expression; also, **b.** (of a person) to express by a symbol.

1668 WILKINS *Real Char.* 405 The two strokes denoting an Hyphen. **1678** CUDWORTH *Intell. Syst.* 262 (R.) Deus Ipse, God himself, denotes the Supreme God only. **1711** HEARNE *Collect.* (Oxf. Hist. Soc.) III. 227 The Sun is sometimes put upon Coyns to denote Providence. **1782** PRIESTLEY *Corrupt. Chr.* II. x. 262 The word *clerk*..came to denote an officer in the law. *a* **1804** W. GILPIN *Serm.* I. xviii. (R.), The filthiness of flesh and spirit, is a general expression to denote wickedness of every kind. **1871** B. STEWART *Heat* §63 Then D V P (according to Boyle's law) will denote the mass. **1873** *Act 36–7 Vict.* c. 85 §3 The number denoting her registered tonnage shall be cut in on her main beam.

b. **1871** B. STEWART *Heat* §24 Let us denote by unity the whole volume of [etc.]. **1882** MINCHIN *Unipl. Kinemat.* 92 Denote by (*X*) the area of the path of *P*.

5. *Logic.* To designate or be a name of; to be predicated of. (Used by Mill, in distinction from *connote.*)

1843 MILL *Logic* I. ii. §5 The word white denotes all white things, as snow, paper, the foam of the sea, etc. and..connotes the attribute whiteness. *Ibid.*, A connotative name ought to be considered a name of all the various individuals which it is predicable of, or in other words *denotes*, and not of what it connotes. **1862** H. SPENCER *First Princ.* II. ii. §42 We can do no more than ignore the connotation of the words, and attend only to the things they avowedly denote.

Hence **de'noting** *ppl. a.*

1887 *Athenæum* 29 Jan. 157/3 The denoting difference between class 1 and class 3 is the same as the denoting difference between class 2 and class 4.

denotement (dɪ'nəʊtmənt). [f. DENOTE *v.* + -MENT.] The fact of denoting or making known; indication; *concr.* a means or mode of denoting; a token, sign.

1622 SHAKS. *Oth.* Qo. 1 [see DELATION 3]. **1653** E. CHISENHALE *Cath. Hist.* 128 To adde to their temporall styles, some denotement of their ecclesiasticall power. **1829** *Blackw. Mag.* XXVI. 192 These outward denotements of a perturbed spirit. **1875** M. A. LOWER *Eng. Surnames* (ed. 4) I. v. 69 *note*, Bush was formerly the common denotement, and sometimes the sign, of an inn.

denotive (dɪ'nəʊtɪv), *a.* [f. DENOTE *v.* + -IVE.] Having the quality of denoting; serving to denote; denotative; indicative.

1830 W. PHILLIPS *Mt. Sinai* II. 460 Not so aught else Of Him denotive. **1830** HERSCHEL *Stud. Nat. Phil.* II. v. (1851) 140 [Names] denotive of species too definite to admit of mistake. **1881** A. M. FAIRBAIRN in *Brit. Q. Rev.* Oct. 404 The term Church He uses..once..as denotive of a single assembly.

‖**dénouement** (de'numɑ̃). [F. *dénouement, dénoûment*, formerly *desnouement*, f. *dénouer, desnouer*, in OF. *desnoer* to untie = Pr. *denozar*, It. *disnodare*, a Romanic formation from L. *dis-* + *nodāre* to knot, *nodus* knot.]

Unravelling; *spec.* the final unravelling of the complications of a plot in a drama, novel, etc.; the catastrophe; *transf.* the final solution or issue of a complication, difficulty, or mystery.

1752 CHESTERF. *Lett.* cclxx. (1792) III. 237 Had the truth been extorted from Varon..by the rack, it would have been a true tragical *dénouement*. **1771** SMOLLETT *Humph. Cl.* (1815) 169 The particulars of the 'denouement' you shall know in due season. **1851** MAYNE REID *Scalp Hunters* xxii. 163 Up to the present time we had all stood waiting the dénouement in silence. **1871** B. TAYLOR *Faust* (1875) I. 228 These lines suggest..the moral *dénouement* of the plot.

denoumbre: see DENUMBER.

denounce (dɪ'naʊns), *v.* Also 4–5 **denounse**, 4–6 **denunce**, 5 **denouns**, *Sc.* **denwns**, 6 **denonce**. [a. OF. *denoncier*, *-noncer* (in 12th c. *denuntier*):—L. *dēnuntiāre* (*-ciāre*) to give official intimation (by a messenger, etc.), f. DE- I. 3 + *nuntiāre* (*nunciāre*) to make known, report.]

1. To give formal, authoritative, or official information of; to proclaim, announce, declare; to publish, promulgate: †**a.** a matter of fact, tidings, information, etc. *Obs.*

1382 WYCLIF *2 Thess.* iii. 10 This thing we denounsiden..to ȝou [*Rhem.* this we denounced to you; Vulg. *hoc denunciabamus vobis*] for if ony man wole not worche, nether ete he. *c* **1449** PECOCK *Repr.* I. xii. 60 The Euangelie of God..which to alle men ouȝte be denouncid. *c* **1500** *Melusine* 188 Anthony & Regnald came to theire fader & moder, and denounced to them these tydinges. **1563–87** FOXE *A. & M.* (1684) I. 488/2 The same reconcilement [was] publickly denounced in the Church of Westminster. **1609** BIBLE (Douay) *Ps.* lxxxvii. comm., When I shal be dead and buried, I can not denounce thy praises as now I can to mortal men. *a* **1677** BARROW *Wks.* (1686) II. 62 By this man remission of sins is denounced unto you. **1726** AYLIFFE *Parergon* 70 All Beadles and Apparitors..are forbidden..to denounce or publish any such Sentence.

b. an event about to take place: usually of a calamitous nature, as war or death, and thus passing into 3. *Obs.* or *arch.*

1536 BELLENDEN *Cron. Scot.* (1821) I. 53 That the king sall nothir denonce weir, nor treit peace, but advise of the capitanis of tribis. **1597** DANIEL *Civ. Wars* (1609) IV. lxxxiv, Whose Herald, Sickenes, being employd before With full commission to denounce his end. **1609** BIBLE (Douay) *Ps.* cxviii. comm., Geving thanks..at the Cocke-crowing, because at that time the coming of the day is denounced. **1631** WEEVER *Anc. Fun. Mon.* 683 An Officer at Armes, whose function is to denounce warre, to proclaime peace. *a* **1665** DIGBY *Priv. Mem.* (1827) 199 To..denounce them war. **1718** *Freethinker* No. 16 ¶6 An approaching Comet, denounced through every Street, by the noisy Hawkers. **1855** MILMAN *Lat. Chr.* (1864) II. IV. i. 197 Mohammed himself..had not only vaguely denounced war against mankind in the Koran but contemplated..unlimited conquests.

†**c.** Const. with *subord. clause. Obs.*

1388 WYCLIF *Num.* xviii. 26 Comaunde thou, and denounse to the dekenes, Whanne ȝe han take tithis of the sones of Israel..offre ȝe the first fruytis of tho to the Lord. *c* **1500** *Melusine* 19 A forester cam to denounce to the Erle Emery how there was within the fforest of Coulombyers the moost meruayllous wildbore that euer was sen byfore. **1581** J. BELL *Haddon's Answ. Osor.* 111 First of all I suppose no man will deny, but that Paule doth denounce men to be Justified by fayth. **1611** BIBLE *Deut.* xxx. 18, I denounce unto you this day, that ye shall surely perish. **1660** tr. *Amyraldus' Treat. conc. Relig.* III. v. 396 God denounced that he would cause the Deluge to come upon the Earth. **1793** *Objections to War Examined* 27 Scarcely a sitting passes..but some Department..or Town is denounced to be in a state of insurrection. **1818** JAS. MILL *Brit. India* II. v. vii. 596 To denounce to him that a failure in this respect would be treated as equivalent to an absolute refusal.

†**2.** *transf.* Of things: To make known or announce, *esp.* in the manner of a sign or portent; to portend. *Obs.*

1581 J. BELL *Haddon's Answ. Osor.* 5 Then should your three Invectives have vomited lesse slaunders and reproches, and denounced you a more charitable man & farre deeper Divine. **1595** SHAKS. *John* III. iv. 159 Meteors, prodigies, and signes, Abbortiues, presages and tongues of heauen, Plainly denouncing vengeance vpon Iohn. **1667** MILTON *P.L.* II. 106 His look denounc'd Desperate revenge, and Battel dangerous To less than Gods. **1706** ESTCOURT *Fair Examp.* III. i, A yellow or dark Spot upon the middle Finger, with me denounces Trouble, and a white one promises Joy. **1751** JOHNSON *Rambler* No. 155 ¶6 They would readily..catch the first alarm by which destruction or infamy is denounced.

3. To announce or proclaim in the manner of a threat or warning (punishment, vengeance, a curse, etc.).

1632 J. HAYWARD tr. *Biondi's Eromena* 4 He delivered the horse into his charge, as a speciall steed of the Kings: denouncing him his Majesties indignation, if he permitted any one [etc.]. **1687** T. BROWN *Saints in Uproar* Wks. 1730 I. 73 There's nothing but fire and desolation denounc'd on both sides. **1721** BERKELEY *Prevent. Ruin Gt. Brit.* Wks. III. 201 Isaiah denounced a severe judgment against the ladies of his time. **1837** W. IRVING *Capt. Bonneville* III. 121 Captain Wyeth..had heard the Crows denounce vengeance on them, for having murdered two of their warriors. **1875** E. WHITE *Life in Christ* II. xiv. (1878) 158 The Curses were to be denounced from Mount Ebal.

4. To proclaim, declare, or pronounce (a person) to be (something): **a.** usually cursed, outlawed, or something bad. ***to denounce to the horn*** (Sc. Law): publicly to proclaim a rebel with the ceremony of horning. *Obs.* or *arch.*

a **1300** *Cursor M.* 29251 (Cott.) þe [man] þat brekes kirkes grith, and es denunced cursd þar-wit. *c* **1425** WYNTOUN *Cron.* VII. ix. 534 Schyr Willame Besat gert for-þi Hys chapelane..Denwns cursyd wyth Buk and Bell All þei, þat had part Of þat brynnyn, or ony art. *c* **1555** HARPSFIELD *Divorce Hen. VIII* (1878) 182 She..was denounced..contumas, and a citation decerned for her appearance. **1579** *Sc. Acts. Jas. VI* (1597) §75 The disobedience of the processe of horning is sa great..that the persones denunced rebelles takes na feare theirof. *Ibid.*, The partie swa denunced to the Horne. **1581** J. BELL *Haddon's Answ. Osor.* 466 He accurseth and denounceth himselfe for a damned creature. **1709** STRYPE *Ann. Ref.* I. xxv. 281 He was solemnly denounced excommunicate by the President. **1802** ELIZA PARSONS *Myst. Visit.* IV. 50 Her..dislike to the late Mrs. Clifford led her to denounce her a base, false woman. **1861** W. BELL *Dict. Law Scotl.* 274/2 A messenger-at-arms..thereafter denounced the debtor rebel, and put him to the horn, as it is termed, by three blasts of a horn. **1879** DIXON *Windsor* II. vii. 76 A safer plan was to denounce him as a public enemy.

†**b.** To proclaim *king, emperor*, etc. *Obs.*

1494 FABYAN *Chron.* VI. clxiv. 159 The sayde pope..crownyd hym with y[e] imperyall dyademe and denounced hym as emperoure. *c* **1534** tr. *Pol. Verg. Eng. Hist.* (Camden) I. 102 Constantine was denounced emperowre of the Romaine soldiars. **1610** HOLLAND *Camden's Brit.* (1637) 85 (D.) His sonne Constans, whom..he had denounced Augustus or Emperor.

5. To declare or make known (an offender) to the authorities; to inform against, delate, accuse.

1485 *Bull Innoc. VIII* in *Camden Misc.* (1847), To denunce, and declare or cause to be denunced and declared alle suche contrary doers and rebelles. **1533** MORE *Apol.* Wks. 886/1 Those therfore that speake heresies, euery good man that hereth them is bounden to denounce or accuse them, and the bishoppes are bounden vpon theire wordes proued to putte them to penaunce and reforme theym. **1726** AYLIFFE *Parergon* 99 Archdeacons..shall..denounce such of them as are negligent..to the Bishop. **1883** *Times* 3 Apr. 4 She had half a mind to denounce him that she might save the lives or the liberty of the tools who might be compromised. **1887** BOWEN *Virg. Æneid* II. 83 Palamedes..Falsely denounced, and to death unjust by the Danaans done.

6. a. To declare (a person or thing) publicly to be wicked or evil, usually implying the expression of righteous indignation; to bring a public accusation against; to inveigh against openly; to utter denunciations against.

1664, 1821 [see DENOUNCER c]. **1825** J. NEAL *Bro. Jonathan* III. 443 Humanity! I forswear it— I denounce it! what have I to do with humanity? **1863** GEO. ELIOT *Romola* (1880) I. Introd. 8 Savonarola..denounced with a rare boldness the worldliness and vicious habits of the clergy. **1875** BRYCE *Holy Rom. Emp.* xvi. (ed. 5) 280 Others scorned and denounced him as an upstart, a demagogue, and a rebel.

b. *absol.* or *intr.*

1837 E. HOWARD *Old Commodore* iii, He first petitioned, then remonstrated, and, foolish boy! at last denounced. **1888** MRS. H. WARD *Robert Elsmere* xl, I went to confront, to denounce you!.. I went to denounce..and the Lord refused it to me.

7. To give formal notice of the termination of (an armistice, treaty, etc.). [So F. *dénoncer*.]

1842 ALISON *Hist. Europe* (1850) XII. lxxx. §7. 90 The armistice was denounced on the 11th, but, by its conditions, six days more were to elapse before hostilities could be resumed. **1879** *Times* 16 June, The French Government has 'denounced' the existing commercial treaties. **1885** *Manch. Exam.* 20 May 5/2 Either party would be at liberty ..to denounce the arrangement upon giving a year's notice.

8. *Mining.* (In Mexico and Spanish America.) To give formal notice to the authorities of the discovery of (a new mine) or of the abandonment or forfeiture of (an old one); hence, to claim the right to work (a mine) on the ground of such information or discovery. [= Sp. *denunciar*.]

1881 E. G. SQUIER in *Encycl. Brit.* XII. 132/1 (*Honduras*) Opals are frequent, principally in the vicinity of Erandique, where as many as sixteen mines have been 'denounced' in a single year. **1886** *Mining Circular*, One mining claim denounced and occupied in conformity with the mining laws of Mexico.

¶**9.** ? To renounce. *Obs. rare.*

c **1325** *E.E. Allit. P.* B. 106 Certez þyse ilk renkez þat me renayed habbe & denounced..Schul neuer sitte in my sale my soper to fele.

Hence **de'nounced** *ppl. a.*

1552 HULOET, Denounced, *denunciatus, indictus.* **1592** *Sc. Acts Jas. VI* (1597) §143 The denunced persones landes, gudes or geir. **1754** ERSKINE *Princ. Sc. Law* (1809) 38 He had also right..to the single escheat of all denounced persons residing within his jurisdiction. **1845** T. W. COIT *Puritanism* 521 This poor denounced Virginia.

†**de'nounce**, *sb. Obs. rare.* [f. DENOUNCE *v.* Cf. obs. F. *dénonce* in Godef.] = DENOUNCEMENT.

1705 J. ROBINS *Hero of Age* I. vi. 7 But Haughty Louis hop'd the Fate to Mock, Seems to deride her brave Denounce of War.

de'nounceable, *a. rare.* [f. DENOUNCE *v.* + -ABLE.] Capable of being denounced.

1837 CARLYLE *Fr. Rev.* II. II. ii, It is embodied; made tangible, made denounceable.

denouncement (dɪˈnaʊnsmənt). [a. obs. F. *denoncement* 'a denouncing' (Cotgr.), f. *dénoncer*: see -MENT.]

1. The action of denouncing; denunciation; †declaration; †announcement (of evil); public accusation or expression of condemnation.

1544 BALE *Chron. Sir J. Oldcastell* in *Harl. Misc.* (Malh.) I. 272 At the laufull denouncement and request of our vniuersall clergye..we proceeded against him [Oldcastell]. **1641** MILTON *Ch. Govt.* II. iii. 51 This terrible denouncement. **1646** SIR. T. BROWNE *Pseud. Ep.* I. ii. 6 Upon the denouncement of his curse. **1836** *New Monthly Mag.* XLVII. 94 Of the vengeance that overtook criminals of this sort, and of dreadful denouncements against their posterity. **1879** G. MACDONALD *P. Faber* II. xii. 236 She sat listening to the curate's denouncement of hypocrisy.

2. The fact of denouncing a mine or land; cf. DENOUNCE *v.* 8. (Mexico and Spanish America.)

1864 MOWRY *Arizona* vi. 112 The title to these deposits is a 'denouncement' as discoverer, of four *pertenencias.* **1884** *American* VII. 296 Under the law of denouncement, a species of pre-emption by which unoccupied lands are acquired [in Mexico].

denouncer (dɪˈnaʊnsə(r)). [f. DENOUNCE *v.* + -ER[1]; = OF. *denonceor, -eur.*] One who denounces, in various senses of the verb. **a.** One who announces, proclaims, declares, threatens.

1490 CAXTON *Eneydos* xxii. 82 The owle is a byrde mortalle or otherwyse denouncer of mortalite. **1611** COTGR., *Predicateur*..denouncer of things to come. **1690** DRYDEN *Don Sebastian* v. Wks. (1883) VII. 466 Here comes the sad denouncer of my fate. **1748** RICHARDSON *Clarissa* (1811) VIII. xli. 164, I undertook to be the denouncer of her doom. **1824-9** LANDOR *Imag. Conv.* (1846) II. 39 Denouncer of just vengeance, recall the sentence!

b. One who informs against, accuses, delates.

1533 MORE *Debell. Salem* Wks. 1013/1 So dooeth euery denouncer, euerye accuser, and in a maner euerye witnesse too. **1648** MILTON *Observ. Art. Peace* (1851) 576 These illiterate denouncers. **1867** SMILES *Huguenots Eng.* x. 159 Detected fugitives were..condemned to the galleys..while their denouncers were..rewarded with half their goods.

c. One who publicly inveighs against, or expresses condemnation of (a person, practice, etc.).

1664 EVELYN *Sylva* (1776) 568, I am no advocate for iron-works, but a Declared Denouncer. **1821** *Examiner* 1 Apr. 193/1 Not to be lost sight of..by the denouncers of corruption. **1878** MORLEY *Carlyle* Crit. Misc. Ser. I. 185 The chief denouncer of phantasms and exploded formulas.

d. One who denounces a mine in order to obtain possession of it. (Mexico and Spanish America.)

denounciation, obs. form of DENUNCIATION.

denouncing (dɪˈnaʊnsɪŋ), *vbl. sb.* [-ING[1].] The action of the verb DENOUNCE in various senses.

1552 HULOET, Denouncyng, *denunciatio.* **1562** J. SHUTE *Cambine's Turk. Wars* 15 b, Without any other denouncing of warres..he presented his armie. **1647** MAY *Hist. Parl.* II. vi. 100 When the first apparent denouncing of War began. **1862** CARLYLE *Fredk. Gt.* XIII. i. (1873) V. 5 Oh the pamphleteerings, the denouncings, the complainings.

de'nouncing, *ppl. a.* [-ING[2].] That denounces.

1661 COWLEY *Disc. Govt. O. Cromwel* Verses & Ess. (1669) 60 Let some denouncing Jonas first be sent To try if England can repent. **1746** COLLINS *Odes, Passions* 43 The War-denouncing trumpet.

de'nourishment. *rare.* [DE- II. 1.] = DENUTRITION

1850 *Chamb. Jrnl.* XIV. 76 On this hypothesis coffee would not nourish, but it would prevent denourishment.

de nouveau: see DE II.

de novo: see DE I. 6.

†**'densate**, *v. Obs.* [f. ppl. stem of L. *densāre* to make dense, thicken, f. *densus* DENSE.] *trans.* To thicken, condense.

1604 R. CAWDREY *Table Alph.*, Densated, made thicke. **1657** TOMLINSON *Renou's Disp.* 651 Oyl of Roses..densates, tempers the hot ventricle.

†**den'sation.** *Obs.* [ad. L. *densātiōn-em*, n. of action from *densāre*: see prec.] Thickening, condensation.

1615 CROOKE *Body of Man* 263 The Densation, Rarefaction, and Contraction of the matter of the parts. **1655-60** STANLEY *Hist. Philos.* (1701) 7/1 Densation, or rarefaction. **1729** SHELVOCKE *Artillery* IV. 261 This Densation..being a Privation of the natural property of Fire, which is Rarifaction.

‖**dens canis**, the DOG'S TOOTH VIOLET, q.v.

dense (dɛns), *a.* [ad. L. *dens-us* thick, dense, crowded. Cf. F. *dense* (Paré, 16th c., in 13th c. *dempse*), perh. the immediate source of the Eng.]

1. Having its constituent particles closely compacted together; thick, compact. **a.** Of close molecular structure. Opp. to *rare.*

1599 A. M. tr. *Gabelhouer's Bk. Physicke* 56/1 When as the Cataracte is so dense and of such a crassitude that heer-with they will not be soackede. **1671** R. BOHUN *Wind* 192 The Earth, being a dense body, retaines the Calorifique impressions. **1794** SULLIVAN *View Nat.* I. 145 It pervades all bodies, dense as well as rare. **1860** TYNDALL *Glac.* I. x. 66 Dense fog settled upon the cascade. **1878** HUXLEY *Physiogr.* 227 The dense bones resist decay longer.

b. Having its (perceptibly separate) parts or constituents closely crowded together; in *Bot.* and *Zool.* closely set.

1776 WITHERING *Brit. Plants* (1796) III. 366 Grows in dense tufts. **1793** MARTYN *Lang. Bot.*, Dense panicle. **1825** SOUTHEY *Tale of Paraguay* I. 7 Marshes wide and woodlands dense. **1836** MARRYAT *Midsh. Easy* xxv, The crowd..was so dense that it was hardly possible to move. **1846** MCCULLOCH *Acc. Brit. Empire* (1854) I. 393 Their population, which in most instances is very dense, amounts to about 45,000.

c. Crowded, 'thick' (*with*). *rare.*

1842 TENNYSON *Morte d'Arthur* 196 All the decks were dense with stately forms.

2. *fig.* **a.** *gen.*

1732 *Hist. Litteraria* III. 249 Sometimes the Author is not so properly concise, as dense, if I may use the Word. When the Subject is limpid of it self, he frequently inspissates it. **1760** FRANKLIN *Lett.* Wks. (1887) III. 42 Six weeks of the densest happiness I have met with. **1858** HAWTHORNE *Fr. & It. Jrnls.* (1872) II. 156 If his character were sufficiently sound and dense to be capable of steadfast principle.

b. *esp.* Of ignorance, stupidity, etc.: Profound, intense, impenetrable, crass.

1877 BLACK *Green Past.* vii. (1878) 55 The dense ignorance in which they have been allowed to grow up.

c. *transf.* Of persons: Stupid, 'thick-headed'.

1822 LAMB *Elia* Ser. I. *Artif. Comedy Last Cent.*, More virtuous than myself, or more dense. **1887** *Poor Nellie* (1888) 114 He will..put notions into her dense head.

3. *Photography.* Of a negative: Opaque in the developed film, so as to yield prints in which the lights and shades are well contrasted.

4. *Comb.*

1861 MISS PRATT *Flower. Pl.* V. 298 Dense-headed Rush. **1870** HOOKER *Stud. Flora* 383 Heads dense-flowered. **1874** LISLE CARR *Jud. Gwynne* I. iv. 123 How quicksighted do the most dense-minded men become when in love!

Hence (*nonce-wd.*) **dense** *v.*, to make dense; **'densing** *vbl. sb.*

1888 F. H. STODDARD in *Andover Rev.* Oct., It is the densing of the slight, the fleshing of the spiritual.

densely (ˈdɛnslɪ), *adv.* [f. DENSE *a.* + -LY[2].]

1. In a dense manner; thickly, closely, crowdedly.

1836 MACGILLIVRAY tr. *Humboldt's Trav.* xxiv. 353 Countries that have long been densely peopled. **1860** TYNDALL *Glac.* I. xxv. 184 Clouds..densely black. **1875** JOWETT *Plato* (ed. 2) III. 683 The citadel..was densely crowded with dwellings.

2. *fig.* Intensely, grossly.

1883 J. FISKE in *Harper's Mag.* Feb. 420/2 The people were densely ignorant.

'densen, *v. rare.* [f. DENSE *a.* + -EN[5].] *trans.* To make dense, or *intr.* To become dense. Hence **'densening** *vbl. sb.*, thickening, condensation.

1884 *Harper's Mag.* June 123/2 In 1800 there is some densening of population within the old lines.

'densener. *Metallurgy.* [f. DENSEN *v.* + -ER[1].] A piece of metal used as a chill in foundries.

1930 *Engineering* 11 July 57/2 A method of attaining this end has developed into the use of chills or 'denseners', which are inserted in the mould wall against certain heavy portions of castings. These consist of suitably shaped pieces of metal, generally of cast iron or steel, placed in such a manner that when the iron is poured..the chills abstract the heat. **1933** *Jrnl. Iron & Steel Inst.* CXXVIII. 554 The author deals with the use of spiral mild-steel wires as denseners in castings.

denseness (ˈdɛnsnɪs). [f. DENSE *a.* + -NESS.] The quality of being dense; density.

1669 W. SIMPSON *Hydrol. Chym.* 325 The denseness of some interposing globe. *Mod.* The denseness of the fog. The fellow's denseness tries my patience sorely.

Denshire (ˈdɛnʃə(r)), *v.* Also 7 **Devonshire, -sher, Densher, Densure,** 9 **Denshare.** [A syncopated form of *Devonshire* used as a vb.; the method having been originally practised there.

c **1630** RISDON *Surv. Devon* (1810) 2 *Devonshire*; now, by a vulgar speech, *Denshire. Ibid.* §96 (1810) 92 In our Denshire speech called *Pohill.* **1654** VILVAIN *Epit. Ess.* v. x, Two Denshire Rivers neer contermining.]

trans. To clear or improve (land) by paring off turf, stubble, weeds, etc., burning them, and spreading the ashes on the land; = BURN-BEAT. Hence **'denshiring** *vbl. sb.*

1607 NORDEN *Surv. Dial.* 228 They..call it in the West parts, Burning of beate, and in the South-East parts, Devonshiring. *c* **1630** RISDON *Surv. Devon* (1810) 11 Which kind of beating and burning..seems to be originally peculiar to this county, being known by the name of *Denshering* in other countries. **1669** WORLIDGE *Syst. Agric.* (1681) 6 About three Acres, Denshired, or Burnt-beaten. **1671** *St. Foine Improved* 8 The good husbandry of Densuring or Devonshering of Land. **1799** *Trans. Soc. Encourag. Arts* XVII. 160 The land..was denshired, and one crop of oats taken from it. **1887** ROGERS *Agric. & Prices* V. 62 The system of denssharing or devonshiring old and poor pasture had made considerable progress.

[By R. Child, 1651 (in Hartlib *Legacy*, 1655, 37) erroneously guessed to be from *Denbighshire*: thence in some Dicts.]

densify (ˈdɛnsɪfaɪ), *v. rare.* [f. L. *dens-us* DENSE + -FY.] *trans.* To make dense, condense. Hence **'densified** *ppl. a.*

1820 *Blackw. Mag.* VIII. 129 To densify the Lunar atmosphere. **1874** *Contemp. Rev.* XXIV. 421 To 'densify' into substantial existence the misty conceptions. **1900** *Westm. Gaz.* 16 Aug. 3/3 The earliest Greek manuscripts all read *Ponton Pileton*, the meaning of which is 'a densified sea'. **1944** *Electronic Engin.* XVI. 365/1 The laminated densified wood used in electrical apparatus. [**1957** *Brit. Commonw. For. Terminol.* II. 59 *Densify*, to increase the density (of wood), e.g. by compression or by impregnating with synthetic resin, as in the manufacture of improved wood.] **1960** *Farmer & Stockbreeder* 19 Jan. Suppl. 14/3 Simple lining material such as flat asbestos cement, or densified hardboard.

densimeter (dɛn'sɪmɪtə(r)). Also **den'someter.** [f. L. *dens-us* dense + -METER.] An apparatus for measuring the density or specific gravity of a solid or liquid.

1863 tr. *Ganot's Physics* (1886) 112 Rousseau's densimeter ..is of great use..in determining the specific gravity of a small quantity of a liquid. **1883** *Fisheries Exhib. Catal.* 210 Ocean salinometer and optical densometer.

densitometer (dɛnsɪ'tɒmɪtə(r)). *Photogr.* [f. DENSIT(Y 4 + -OMETER.] An instrument for the measurement of photographic density.

1901 *Camera Mag.* 23 Oct. 14 The idea at the root of the 'Densitometer' is that if it is possible to ascertain the density of a negative in a uniform and accurate manner the difficulties of bromide printing are at once overcome. **1955** *Gloss. Terms Radiology* (*B.S.I.*) 54 *Densitometer*, an instrument for measuring photographic transmission and/or reflection density. **1959** *New Scientist* 27 Aug. 283/1 The density of photographic emulsions must be accurately controlled in order to achieve the best results in colour printing. Normally this quantity is measured by means of a densitometer which successively views selected points of the image, producing a value for each position. **1961** *Printing News* 16 Feb. 9 Densitometers—particularly of the reflection type—will not always agree on a numerical value for density.

density ('dɛnsɪtɪ). [a. F. *densité* (Paré, 16th c., in 13th c. *dempsité*), ad. L. *densitās, -tātem* thickness, f. *densus* DENSE.]

1. The quality or condition of being dense; thickness; closeness of texture or consistence.

1603 HOLLAND *Plutarch's Mor.* 1187 The densitie and thicknesse of the aire. **1626** BACON *Sylva* § 592 As for the Leaves, their density appeareth in that, either they are smooth and shining..or in that they are hard and spiry. **1755** *Mem. Capt. P. Drake* I. xvii. 185 A Fogg of the greatest Density I ever remember to have seen. **1796** MORSE *Amer. Geog.* II. 311 It was..necessary to supply the defect of density by more frequent inspirations. **1864** BOWEN *Logic* xi. (1870) 361 The additional qualities of weight, attraction, impenetrability, elasticity, density.

2. a. *Physics.* The degree of consistence of a body or substance, measured by the ratio of the mass to the volume, or by the quantity of matter in a unit of bulk.

1665 *Phil. Trans.* I. 31 There is in the Air..such a variety ..both as to their density and rarity. **1696** WHISTON *Th. Earth* II. (1722) 221 More than four times the density of Water. **1726** tr. *Gregory's Astron.* I. 147 The quantity of Matter is as the Magnitude and Density conjunctly. **1831** BREWSTER *Optics* iii. 25 The bodies contained in these tables have all different densities. **1881** WILLIAMSON in *Nature* No. 618. 415 To determine the vapour densities and rates of diffusion of those which could be obtained in the gaseous state.

b. *Electr.* The quantity of electricity per unit of volume or area.

1873 CLERK MAXWELL *Electr. & Magn.* (1881) §64 The electric density at a given point on a surface is the limiting ratio of the quantity of electricity within a sphere whose centre is the given point to the area of the surface contained within the sphere, when its radius is diminished without limit. **1885** WATSON & BURBURY *Math. Th. Electr. & Magn.* I. 139 A uniform ring of electricity of density − 1.

3. a. Crowded state; degree of aggregation.

1851 NICHOL *Archit. Heav.* 154 Not..to sound depths by ordinary rules founded on the numbers of the stars, but rather to unfold densities. **1888** BRYCE *Amer. Commw.* II. xxxvi. 5 Not only these differences in size, but the differences in density of population.

b. *concr.* A dense mass or aggregation. *rare.*

1858 HAWTHORNE *Fr. & It. Jrnls.* I. 144 Stems, supporting a cloud-like density of boughs.

4. *Photogr.* Opaqueness of the developed actinized film in a negative.

1879 *Cassell's Techn. Educ.* III. 143 (*Photogr.*) A rapid acquisition of density will be the result. **1967** E. CHAMBERS *Photolitho-Offset* 271 *Density*, the quantitative measure of the blackening of a photographic emulsion.

5. *fig.* Stupidity, crassitude.

1894 A. BIRRELL in *Westminst. Budget* 27 July 48/2 The density which is sometimes..attributed to your party.

den'someter, another form of DENSIMETER.

Densure, obs. form of DENSHIRE *v.*

dent (dɛnt), *sb.*[1] [A phonetic variant or collateral form of DINT, OE. *dynt*; in sense 4 app. influenced by *indent* and its family, and thus connected with DENT *sb.*[2]]

†**1.** A stroke or blow, *esp.* with a weapon or sharp instrument: usually a blow dealt in fighting (= DINT *sb.* 1). *Obs.*

c **1325** *Coer de L.* 291 With a dente amyd the schelde. *c* **1350** *Will. Palerne* 1215 Ac he wiþ douȝti dentes defended him long. *c* **1435** *Torr. Portugal* 915 Ther schalle no knyght come nere hond, Fore dred of denttes ylle. *c* **1485** *Digby Myst.* (1882) III. 272 The dent of deth is hevyar than led. *c* **1570** PRESTON *Cambyses* in Hazl. *Dodsley* IV. 215 He shall die by dent of sword. **1596** SPENSER *F.Q.* IV. vi. 15 Plates yrent, Shew'd all his bodie bare unto the cruell dent. **1603** DRAYTON *Odes* xvii. 95 And many a cruell Dent Bruised his Helmet.

†**b.** A 'stroke' or clap of thunder; a thunderbolt. *Obs.*

a **1300** *Fragm. Pop. Sc.* (Wright) 147 The liȝting, That.. cometh after the dente. *c* **1320** *Sir Beues* 2738 A made a cri and a wonder, Ase hit were a dent of þonder. *c* **1386** CHAUCER *Miller's T.* 621 As gret as it had ben a thundir dent. *c* **1430** LYDG. *Bochas* VIII. i. (1554) 177 b, By stroke of thundre dent And fyry lightning.

†**2.** Striking, dealing of blows; vigorous wielding of the sword or other weapon (= DINT *sb.* 2).

a **1400** *Octouian* 1555 Here son was doughty knyght of dente. **1548** HALL *Chron.* 41 b, With mortal warre and dent of sworde. **1556** J. HEYWOOD *Spider & F.* lix. 32 To subdew the flies by the swoords dent. *a* **1600** *Tourn. Tottenham* 48 For to wynne my doȝter wyth dughtynesse of dent.

†**b.** Striking distance, range or reach of stroke (= DINT *sb.* 2 d). *Obs.*

1567 MAPLET *Gr. Forest* 78 There is no birde that escapeth him that commeth in his dent, but she is his owne.

†**3.** = DINT. *Obs.*

1597 J. PAYNE *Royal Exch.* 3, I am sturred by dent of Christian dutie.

4. A hollow or impression in a surface, such as is made by a blow with a sharp or edged instrument; an indentation, DINT.

1565 JEWEL *Repl. Harding* Wks. (1611) 425 We haue thrust our fingers into the dents of his nailes. **1612** BRINSLEY *Lud. Lit.* 16 Mark it with a dent with the nayle, or a pricke with a pen. **1620** SHELTON *Quix.* IV. xix. II. 233 O the most noble and obedient Squire that ever had Sword at a Girdle ..or Dent in a Nose. **1691** T. H[ALE] *Acc. New Invent.* p. viii, Taking his Hammer, he again beat out the dent. **1722** CHAMBERLAYNE in *Phil. Trans.* XXXII. 98 The fat Particles had such a Pinch, or Dent, in them, as I have shewn, that there were in the Globules of Flower of Wheat. **1848** THOREAU *Maine W.* i. (1867) 51 The rocks..were covered with the dents made by the spikes in the lumberers' boots. **1857** GEO. ELIOT *Scenes Cler. Life, Janet's Repent.* ii, Dents and disfigurements in an old family tankard.

dent, *sb.*[2] [a. F. *dent* tooth; but sense 1 perh. originated as an extension of sense 4 of prec. sb., under the influence of the Fr. word, or of *indent* and its family.]

†**1.** An indentation in the edge of anything; in *pl.* applied both to the incisions and the projections or teeth between them. *Obs.*

1552 HULOET, Dentes about a leafe lyke a saw, *crenæ.* **1660** BLOOME *Archit.* A a, *Denticuli*, a broad plinth in the cornish cut with dents. **1700** DRYDEN *Fables, Cock & Fox* 50 High was his comb, and coral-red withal, In dents embattl'd like a castle-wall.

2. A tooth, in various technical uses:

a. A burnishing tool used by gilders: sometimes an actual tooth. ? *Obs.* **b.** *Weaving.* One of the *splits* or parallel strips of metal, cane, etc. forming the reed of a loom. **c.** *Carding.* The wire staple that forms the tooth of a card. **d.** A tooth in a gear-wheel, or in the works of a lock.

1703 T. S. *Art's Improv.* 51 This is commonly practised upon Black and Coloured Wood, Polishing them with a Dent. **1831** G. R. PORTER *Silk Manuf.* 221 This saves the labour of passing the new threads through the mails and dents of the reed. **1846** G. WHITE *Treat. Weaving* 53 The reed is made to contain a certain number of *dents* or *splits* in a given space. **1894** *Textile Manuf.* 15 May 196 The satin may be reeded four in a dent if desired.

dent, *sb.*[3] *local.* A tough clay or soft claystone; *esp.* that found in the joints and fissures of sandstone or other strata.

1864 A. JEFFREY *Hist. Roxburghshire* IV. iii. 162 The walls of these houses..were cemented with pounded dent.

dent, *ppl. a.* [short for *dented.*]

†**1.** Embossed [see DENT *v.* 3]. *Obs.*

c **1450** *Golagros & Gaw.* 66 The sylour deir of the deise dayntely wes dent With the doughtyest in thair dais dyntis couth dele.

†**2.** *Her.* = INDENTED. *Obs.*

1610 GUILLIM *Heraldry* I. v. (1660) 27 Wrapt with dent bordure silver shining.

3. *dent corn*: a variety of Indian corn having a dent or depression in each kernel. Also *ellipt.* (See also quot. 1909.) *U.S.*

1853 *Trans. Mich. Agric. Soc.* V. 125 The land..was planted..with the 'Indian Yellow Dent'. **1873** *Trans. Dep. Agric. Illinois* X. 77 The Dent Corns—White and Yellow Dent, Large White, and Yellow Dent. **1909** W. BATESON *Mendel's Princ. Heredity* 264 According as the seeds [of maize] are opaque or semi-transparent, the varieties are distinguished as 'Dent' or 'Flint'. **1950** *New Biol.* VIII. 37 *Dent* or *field corns*..are flinty with soft starch extending from the base to the tip of the kernels.

dent, *v.* [A variant of DINT *v.*: see DENT *sb.*[1]]

1. *trans.* To make a dent in, as with a blow upon a surface; to mark with a dent or dents; to indent.

1388, 1398 [see DENTING *vbl. sb.* 2, 1]. *c* **1440** *Promp. Parv.* 118 Dentyn or yndentyn, *indento.* **1530** PALSGR. 511/2, I dente, *Jenfondre*..se howe it hath dented in his harnesse. **1559** SACKVILLE *Induct.* xii. 7 So dented were her cheekes with fall of teares. **1691** T. H[ALE] *Acc. New Invent.* p. viii, With which blow it was not broken but dented. **1703** T. N. *City & C. Purchaser* 161 Jumping upon it with the Heals of ones Shooes will dent it. **1845** DARWIN *Voy. Nat.* iii. (1879) 62 The fragments had been blown off with force sufficient to dent the wall. **1881** MISS BRADDON *Asph.* I. 294 Armour that had been battered and dented at Cressy.

2. To imprint, impress, implant with a stroke or impact.

c **1450** *Golagros & Gaw.* 824 Suppose his dyntis be deip dentit in your scheild. **1533** BELLENDEN *Livy* III. (1822) 246 This yoik wes maid of thre speris, of quhilkis twa war dentit in the erde. **1820** W. IRVING *Sketch Bk.* II. 407 The tracks of horses' hoofs deeply dented in the road.

†**3.** To emboss, set, inlay. *Obs.*

c **1440** *Bone Flor.* 326 The pyllers that stonde in the halle, Are dentyd wyth golde and clere crystalle. *c* **1475** *Rauf Coilȝear* 667 Dyamountes full dantely dentit betwene.

4. *intr.* **a.** To enter or sink *in*, so as to make a dent or indentation. **b.** To become indented, as a plastic surface when pressed with something pointed or edged.

1398 TREVISA *Barth. De P.R.* VII. lix. (1495) 274 Yf thou thrystest thy fyngere vpon the postume it denteth in. *Ibid.* XVII. lxxiv. 648 Yf the fynger dynteth in therto and finde it nesshe. **1611** STAFFORD *Niobe* 40 His cheekes, denting-in, as if he were still sucking at a bottle. **1869** *Eng. Mech.* 3 Dec. 271/1 You will see it dent, for it is elastic.

†**5.** To aim a penetrating blow (*at*). *Obs.*

1580 LYLY *Euphues* (Arb.) 373 So my heart..dented at with yᵉ arrowes of thy burning affections.

dental ('dɛntəl), *a.* and *sb.* [ad. mod. or ? med.L. *dentāl-is*, f. *dens, dent-em* tooth; cf. F. *dental* (1611 in Cotgr.). Ancient L. had *dentāle* (in form the neuter of *dentālis*) = 'share-beam of a plough'].

A. *adj.* **1. a.** Of or pertaining to the teeth; of the nature of a tooth.

dental arch, the arched or curved line of the teeth in the mouth; ***dental cavity***, the natural hollow of a tooth, which is filled by the ***dental pulp***. ***dental formula***, a formula or concise tabular statement of the number and kinds of teeth possessed by a mammal; the numbers in the upper and the lower row are written above and below a horizontal line, like the numerator and denominator of a fraction: see DENTITION 2.

1599 A. M. tr. *Gabelhouer's Bk. Physicke* 77/2 To vse this, and the other dentalle poulders. **1650** BULWER *Anthropomet.* Pref., To sway It downwards, and the Dental root display. **1658** SIR T. BROWNE *Gard. Cyrus* iii. 53 Dentall sockets. **1860** HARTWIG *Sea & Wond.* vi. 72 The cetaceans are either without a dental apparatus, or provided with teeth. **1894** *Times* (Weekly ed.) 16 Feb. 133/4 Dental disease..became reduced to a minimum.

b. Dealing with the teeth; of or pertaining to dentistry. ***dental apparatus, chair*** (U.S.), ***chisel, drill, file, forceps, hammer***, etc., apparatus and instruments used in dentistry. Also ***dental floss*** [FLOSS *sb.*[2] 2], ***silk***, floss silk or similar fibrous material used to clean between the teeth. ***dental surgery*** (orig. *U.S.*), dentistry.

1826 L. KOECKER (*title*) The principles of dental surgery. **1841** G. WAITE (*title*) An appeal to Parliament, the medical profession and the public, on the present state of dental surgery. **1859** J. TOMES (*title*) A system of dental surgery. **1870** (*title*), Dental Diploma Question. **1874** KNIGHT *Dict. Mech., Dental chisel..drill..file* [etc.]. *Ibid., Dental pump*, an apparatus for withdrawing the saliva from the mouth during dental operations. **1878** L. P. MEREDITH *Teeth* p. viii, Opening the doors of dental knowledge to the people. **1880** 'MARK TWAIN' *Tramp Abroad* xxiii. 222 About five hundred soldiers gathered together in the neighborhood of that dental chair waiting to see the performance. **1887** Dental surgery [see SURGERY 1]. **1890** *Times* 20 Aug. 11/2 A Dental School is attached to the Hospital. **1907** *Yesterday's Shopping* (1969) 507/2 Dental silk— reel, 0/3½; waxed 0/5. **1910** *Nat. Dent. Hosp. Gaz.* IV. xx. 42 Drill a few holes on each side of the fracture and thread them through and across with an ordinary piece of dental floss silk, finishing off with a knot on the lingual surface. **1922** JOYCE *Ulysses* 126 He took a reel of dental floss from his waistcoat pocket and.. twanged it smartly between two..of his resonant unwashed teeth. **1955** *Oxf. Jun. Encycl.* XI. 98/2 The discovery of anaesthetics was of the greatest importance in the progress of dental surgery. **1971** *Times* 12 Feb. 13/7 The decision of Johnson and Johnson to reintroduce into this country dental floss.

c. Engaged in dentistry or dental work, as **dental mechanic**, an operative who makes and repairs artifical teeth; **dental nurse**, a nurse who assists a dentist (the term is also applied to a dentist's receptionist); hence ***dental nursing*** vbl. sb.; **dental surgeon** (orig. *U.S.*), a dentist (cf. *surgeon-dentist*); hence ***dental surgeoncy***; **dental technician** = *dental mechanic*.

1840 *Amer. Jrnl. Dent. Sci.* I. 157 The objects of this Society [*sc.* the Amer. Soc. of Dental Surgeons] are to promote union and harmony among all respectable and well-informed Dental Surgeons. **1860** *Brit. Jrnl. Dent. Sci.* III. 232/2 We, the Court of Examiners, have diligently examined —— and have found him competent to exercise the art and science of a Dental Surgeon. **1881** *Jrnl. Brit. Dent. Assoc.* II. 9 The burden of a Dental Surgeoncy to a Hospital. **1916** *Daily Colonist* (Victoria, B.C.) 12 July 3/5 (Advt.), Highly skilled dentists and dental mechanics. **1921** *Act 11 & 12 Geo. V* c. 21 § 3 (1) The occupation of a dental mechanic. **1922** JOYCE *Ulysses* 571 Dental surgeon Bloom with tweezers. **1938** H. R. CULLWICK *Handbk. for Dent. Nurses* 8 The subject of the duties of a dental nurse has been sadly neglected by dental literature in England... The question of a dental nurse having a hospital training is a debatable one. *Ibid.* 11 Dental nursing as a career. **1961** *Evening Standard* 14 July 19/2 (Advt.), Dental Nurse experienced preferred. *Ibid.* 17 Aug. 15/1 (Advt.), Dental Technician... Expd. Orthodontics and simple gold work.

2. *Phonology.* Pronounced by applying the tip of the tongue to the front upper teeth, as the consonants (t, d, θ, ð, n).

In some languages, as in English, *t, d, n* are not strictly *dental*, but *alveolar*; i.e. the contact is with the gum close behind the teeth.

1594 T. B. *La Primaud. Fr. Acad.* II. 87 The Hebrewes name their letters, some gutturall, because they are pronounced more in the throat: others, dentall, because a man cannot wel pronounce them without the teeth. **1626** BACON *Sylva* § 198. *a* **1794** SIR W. JONES in *Asiat. Res.* (1799) I. 12 Each of the dental sounds is hard or soft, sharp or obtuse. **1855** FORBES *Hindūstānī Gram.* (1868) 5, ɔ is much softer and more dental than the English *d.* **1877** SWEET *Handbk. Phonetics* 31-2 This class is commonly called 'dental', but the point of the tongue is not necessarily brought against the teeth.

B. *sb.* **1.** *Phonology.* A dental consonant.

a **1794** SIR W. JONES in *Asiat. Res.* (1799) I. 11 Next came different classes of dentals. **1884** *American* IX. 105 Such a phonetic law does not account for the word under discussion, no dental being present.

2. *humorously.* A tooth.

1837 LANDOR *Pentameron* Wks. 1846 II. 344, I would not voluntarily be under his manifold rows of dentals.

3. *Arch.* = DENTIL.

1761 KIRBY *Perspect. Architect.* 39 From the dentals already drawn the others are to be taken, and also the denticles. **1857** BIRCH *Anc. Pottery* (1858) II. 195 The abacus red, the dentals yellow, with a red boss.

4. *Zool.* A mollusc of the genus *Dentalium* or family *Dentaliidæ*; a tooth-shell.

1678 PHILLIPS, *Dental*, a small Shelfish..hollow like a little tube, and acuminated. *a* **1728** WOODWARD (J.), The shell of a dental.

5. A sea fish of the Mediterranean, belonging to the genus *Dentex*.

1753 CHAMBERS *Cycl. Suppl.*, *Dentale* is a name given by some to a fish caught in the Mediterranean, and common in the markets of Italy. *a* **1850** ROSSETTI *Dante & Circ.* II. *Months* Mar., Salmon, eel and trout, Dental and dolphin.

dentalite ('dɛntəlaɪt). *Palæont.* [f. *Dentalium* (see prec. 4) + -ITE.] A fossil tooth-shell.

1828 in WEBSTER. **1847** CRAIG, *Dentalite, Dentalithe*, a fossil dentalium.

dentality (dɛn'tælɪtɪ). [f. DENTAL + -ITY: cf. *nasality*.] Dental quality.

1877 H. SWEET *Handbk. Phonet.* 38 §110, (th) is, like (r) formed by the point. The essential difference between them lies in the dentality of (th), which involves a more horizontal position of the tongue, which has to be stretched out to reach the teeth. *a* **1895** *Mod.* In Irish, the dentality of *t* and *d* is very marked.

dentalium (dɛn'teɪlɪəm). Pl. **dentalia.** [mod.L. (Linnæus *Systema Naturæ* (ed. 10, 1758) I. 785), f. L. *dentāl-is*, f. *dens, dent-em* tooth.] A tooth-shell of the genus so named (cf. DENTAL B. 4). Also *attrib.*

1864 *Proc. Zool. Soc.* 137 The value of the *Dentalium* depends upon its length. *Ibid.* 138 At one period, perhaps a remote one, in the history of the inland Indians these *Dentalia* were worn as ornaments. **1913** B. B. WOODWARD *Life of Mollusca* iv. 55 The *Dentalium*, again, buries in the sand, leaving only the apex of the shell protruding. **1926** *Daily Colonist* (Victoria, B.C.) 4 July 21/5 The effort to secure the dentalium at seacoast places, and its employment so widely by peoples far removed from the seacoast means that much more than merely ornamental value was placed upon it. **1931** *Antiquity* V. 431 Dentalium and pusiostoma shells are the most numerous. **1932** *Jrnl. R. Anthrop. Inst.* LXII. 267 Two skeletons..had head-dresses of dentalium shells. **1938** *Nature* 19 Feb. 306/2 They had necklaces, too, made of dentalium, alternating with 'twin' pendants, which seem to me to imitate the canines of deer. **1960** K. M. KENYON *Archæol. in Holy Land* ii. 38 At 'Ain Mallaha..a burial closely resembling that of Mount Carmel, with a crown of *dentalia* shells, was made in a pit lined with plaster.

dentalize ('dɛntəlaɪz), *v.* [f. DENTAL + -IZE.] *trans.* To make dental, change into a dental sound. Hence **dentali'zation.**

1861 F. HALL in *Jrnl. Asiatic Soc. Bengal* 336 The element *śri*..was probably lengthened and dentalized. **1875** —— in *N.Y. Nation* XX. 116/2 The letters *d*, *n*, and *t*, where lingual, were, we surmise, first dentalized. **1876** DOUSE *Grimm's L.* §55. 135 Cases of dentalization.

† **dentar** ('dɛntə(r)), *a. Obs. rare.* [irreg. ad. F. *dentaire*, ad. L. *dentāri-us*: see DENTARY.] = DENTAL 1.

1831 R. KNOX *Cloquet's Anat.* 39 The superior and anterior dentar canal. *Ibid.* 461 The posterior and superior dentar branches.

dentaria (dɛn'tɛərɪə). *Bot.* [mod.L. (J. P. de Tournefort *Institutiones Rei Herbariæ* (1700) I. 225), fem. sing. of L. *dentarius* pertaining to the teeth, so called from the tooth-like scales on the roots of the plant.] A plant of the cruciferous genus so named; = *pepper-root* (PEPPER *sb.* 7), PEPPERWORT 16, TOOTHWORT 3.

1818 *Mass. Hist. Soc. Coll.* 2nd Ser. VIII. 169 Among those, that flower in June, the most interesting are..the sarsaparilla, the dentaria or tooth-root,..and the mountain ash. **1886** M. ARNOLD *Lett.* (1895) II. 327 The dentarias too are beautiful.

† **dentarie.** *Obs. rare.* Anglicized form of Bot. L. *Dentaria* (Toothwort), a genus of cruciferous plants.

1578 LYTE *Dodoens* II. v. 153 The other kind [of Dames Violets or Gilofloures] is known by the name of Dentarie, and is not otherwise known to us.

dentary ('dɛntərɪ), *a.* and *sb. Zool.* and *Anat.* [ad. L. *dentāri-us* (4th c.), f. *dens, dent-em* tooth: see -ARY. (In F. *dentaire*, 1700 in Hatzf.)]

A. *adj.* Of, pertaining to, or connected with the teeth; dental. ***dentary bone***: = DENTARY *sb.*

1830 R. KNOX *Béclard's Anat.* 136 As far as the dentary papilla or pulp. **1870** ROLLESTON *Anim. Life* Introd. 44 The dentary bone of the Crocodile.

B. *sb.* A bone forming part of the lower jaw in the classes of Vertebrates below *Mammalia*, and bearing the teeth when these are present.

1854 OWEN in *Circ. Sc.* (*c* 1865) II. 67/1 The anterior piece..which supports the teeth, is called the 'dentary'. **1880** GUNTHER *Fishes* 54 The largest piece is tooth-bearing, and hence termed dentary.

‖ **dentata** (dɛn'teɪtə). *Anat.* [L. fem. of *dentātus* adj. 'toothed' (sc. *vertebra*).] The second cervical vertebra, also called *axis*: see AXIS[1] 2.

1727-52 CHAMBERS *Cycl.* s.v. *Vertebræ*, The vertebræ of the neck..The second is called..also *vertebra dentata.* **1811** HOPPER *Dict.* 852/1 The second vertebra is called *dentata.* **1847** YOUATT *Horse* ix. 211 The second bone of the neck is the dentata, having a process like a tooth, by which it forms a joint with the first bone. **1881** MIVART *Cat* 43.

dentate ('dɛnteɪt), *a.* [ad. L. *dentāt-us*, f. *dens, dent-em* tooth: see -ATE[2] 2] Having 'teeth' or tooth-like projections along the edge; toothed. Chiefly in *Zool.* and *Bot.*; in *Bot. spec.* of leaves having sharp teeth directed outwards.

1810 W. ROXBURGH in *Asiat. Res.* XI. 350 With the margin elegantly laciniate-dentate. **1828** STARK *Elem. Nat. Hist.* II. 34 Shell gibbous..outer lip generally dentate. **1835** LINDLEY *Introd. Bot.* (1848) I. 271 The leaf is merely toothed (*dentate*). **1846** DANA *Zooph.* (1848) 157 Lamellæ of the cells dentate or denticulate.

b. In comb., as ***dentate-crenate***, etc.: see DENTATO-. Hence **'dentately** *adv.*

1847 in CRAIG.

dentated ('dɛnteɪtɪd), *ppl. a.* [f. as prec. + -ED.] = prec.

1753 CHAMBERS *Cycl. Suppl.*, Dentated Leaf. **1761** GAERTNER in *Phil. Trans.* LII. 78 Nor has it a dentated margin. **1835** KIRBY *Hab. & Inst. Anim.* I. vi. 204 A beautifully dentated suture, resembling the dog's tooth of a Gothic arch. **1865** LUBBOCK *Preh. Times* 133 Saws..with their edges somewhat rudely dentated.

dentation (dɛn'teɪʃən). [n. of condition, f. stem of L. *dentāt-us*: see prec. and -ATION. Cf. L. *tabulātio*, f. *tabulāt-us*.] The condition or fact of being dentate; toothing.

1802 PALEY *Nat. Theol.* xiii, How in particular did it [the woodpecker's bill] get its barb, its dentation? **1852** DANA *Crust.* I. 253 The same species varies much in the dentation of the arm. **1880** GRAY *Struct. Bot.* iii. §4. 97 *Dentation* relates to mere marginal incision.

den'tato-, combining adverbial form of L. *dentātus*, prefixed to other adjs. in the sense 'dentately —', 'dentate and —', as ***dentato-angulate***, having dentate angles; ***dentato-ciliate***, having the margin dentate with cilia; ***dentato-costate***, having dentate or toothed ribs; ***dentato-crenate***, crenate but approaching dentate; ***dentato-serrate***, having serrations approaching the character of teeth; ***dentato-setaceous***, having the margin dentate, with setæ or bristles; ***dentato-sinuate***, 'having points like teeth on excavated borders' (*Syd. Soc. Lex.*).

In these combinations *dentate-* is often used, as *dentate-crenate, -serrate, -sinuate*, etc.

1828 WEBSTER, *Dentato-sinuate.* **1846** DANA *Zooph.* (1848) 594 Margin..with dentato-setaceous calicles. **1866** *Treas. Bot.*, *Dentato-laciniate*, when toothings are irregularly extended into long points.

dent de lion, dentdelyon: see DANDELION.

dente, obs. form of DAINTY.

dented ('dɛntɪd), *ppl. a.* [orig. f. DENT *v.* + -ED; but afterwards identified with, and assimilated in sense to, L. *dentātus*, F. *denté* toothed.]

† **1.** Bent inward; incurved, hollowed. *Obs.*

1398 TREVISA *Barth. De P.R.* XVIII. xcv. (1495) 842 The teeth [of a serpent] ben dentyd Inwarde and ben crokyd [*transfigit aculeo & dente flectitur in se*]. **1583** STANYHURST *Æneis* I. (Arb.) 28 His ships hee kenneld..vnder an angle Of rock deepe dented [*sub rupe cavata*]. **1607** TOPSELL *Four-f. Beasts* (1658) 340 This vulgar kinde of hyæna..in the middle of his back..is a little crooked or dented.

† **2.** Hollow, sunken. *Obs.*

1540 SURREY *Poems, How no age is content* 16, I saw my withered skin How it doth shew my dented chews, the flesh was worn so thin.

3. Having dents or indentations, indented, toothed; † in *Her.* = INDENTED (*obs.*).

1552 HULOET, Dented, *crenatus.* **1572** BOSSEWELL *Armorie* II. 30 Ermyne on a chiefe dented, Gules. **1578** LYTE *Dodoens* II. vi. 153 His leaves be..dented or tothed. **1692** BANISTER in *Phil. Trans.* XVII. 672 There is a small [shell] of the Land-kind, with a dented Aperture. **1776** WITHERING *Brit. Plants* (1796) II. 371 Leaves..slightly dented at the end. **1822** J. FLINT *Lett. Amer.* 87 The ragged, and dented edges of the strata.

'dentel. *Arch.* [ad. F. *dentelle* (formerly *-ele*), now used in sense of 16th c. *dentille.*] = DENTIL.

1850 LEITCH tr. *Müller's Anc. Art* §189. 170 Blending of the Ionic dentels with the Doric triglyphs. **1876** GWILT *Encycl. Archit.* Gloss., *Dentils*, or *Dentels*, the small square blocks or projections in the bed mouldings of cornices in the Ionic, Corinthian, Composite, and occasionally Doric orders.

dentelated, dentellated ('dɛntɪleɪtɪd), *ppl. a.* [Formed after F. *dentelé* 'toothed, toothie; full of iags resembling little teeth', Cotgr. (in Thierry 1564), f. OF. *dentele*, mod.F. *dentelle*, dim. of *dent* tooth.] Having small teeth, indentations, or notches; finely indented.

1797 W. TOOKE *Cath. II* (1798) III. xiv. 409 *note*, Ankarstrœm was armed with a dentelated poignard. **1824** HEBER *Jrnl.* (ed. 2) II. xxi. 398 The wall is high, with dentellated battlements and lofty towers. **1885** AGNES M. CLERKE *Pop. Hist. Astron.* 90 A very fine red band, irregularly dentelated, or as it were crevassed.

dentelle (dɛn'tɛl, Fr. dɑ̃ːˈtɛl). [a. F. *dentelle*, orig. little tooth, hence lace, a triangular facet, etc., in OF. *dentele* (14th c.), dim. of *dent* tooth.]

‖ **1.** Lace [Fr.].

1847 C. BRONTË *Jane Eyre* I. xv. 279, I..gave her..cashmeres, diamonds, dentelles, &c. **1859** SALA *Tw. round Clock* (1861) 40 That delicate border of dentelle.

2. *Bookbinding.* 'An ornamental tooling resembling notching or lace' (Knight *Dict. Mech.*). So ***dentelle binding, border, tooling.***

1890 *Catal. Exhib. Rec. Bk.-bindings Grolier Club* 11 *Dentelle Border.* A tooled pointed border with finely dotted or Gascon ornaments in imitation of lace. *Ibid.* 21 [Book] Blue morocco; doublé with blue morocco, large dentelle tooling. **1892** J. T. BENT *Ruined Cities of Mashonaland* iv. 116 Two feet below begins the dentelle pattern. **1938** *Times Lit. Suppl.* 12 Nov. 732/3 Several of the far more attractive *dentelle* bindings with which the names of Padeloup and Derome are usually associated.

dentelure ('dɛntəl(j)ʊə(r)). *Zool. rare.* [a. F. *dentelure* denticulated border, toothing, f. *dentelé* denticulated: see -URE. In quot. app. associated with *chaussure, coiffure*, etc.] Set or provision of teeth.

1877 COUES *Fur Anim.* xi. 325 The whole dentelure is modified in adaptation to a piscivorous regimen.

denter: see DENTURE.

denteuous, var. of DAINTEOUS *a. Obs.*

dentex ('dɛntɛks). [mod.L. (G. Cuvier 1815, in *Mém. Mus. Hist. Nat. Paris* I. 456, f. *Sparus dentex*, the Linnæan name of the fish), f. L. *dentex, dentix*, a kind of marine fish.] The common name of a sea bream, *Dentex dentex*, found in the Mediterranean and along the North African Atlantic coast; also used for other members of the genus.

1836 W. YARRELL *Hist. Brit. Fishes* I. 112 Duhamel..mentions a *Dentex* that weighed no less than seventy pounds. **1880** GÜNTHER *Fishes* 389 Dentex—..Marine fishes rather locally distributed in the Mediterranean. **1925** *Countries of World* IV. 2673/1 The dentex and barracada pike. **1953** tr. *Cousteau's Silent World* 10 Below I saw a big blue dentex (bream) with a bitter mouth and hostile eyes. **1957** R. CAMPBELL *Portugal* iv. 70 The Azores are as good for under-water fishing as the Berlengas... Dentex..grow to a great size there.

denti-, combining form of L. *dens, dent-em*, tooth, *dent-ēs* teeth. **'dentifactor**, a machine for making artificial teeth. **denti'labial** *a.*, having relation to both teeth and lips. **denti'lingual** *a.*, of or formed by teeth and tongue; also used as sb. (*sc.* consonant, sound, etc.). † **den'tiloquent** *a.*, speaking through the teeth (Blount, 1656); so † **den'tiloquist**, 'one that speaks through the teeth'; † **den'tiloquy**, 'the act or habit of speaking through the teeth' (Ash). † **denti'molary** *a.*, belonging to the molar teeth or grinders. **den'tiparous** *a.*, producing teeth. **'dentiphone**, an instrument for conveying sound to the inner ear through the teeth, an AUDIPHONE.

1875 WHITNEY *Life Lang.* iv. 64 A dentilabial instead of a purely labial sound. *Ibid.* 65 Real dentilinguals produced between the tongue and teeth. **1651** BIGGS *New Disp.* ¶ 284 Dentimolary operations. **1849-52** TODD *Cycl. Anat.* IV. 897/1 The vascular dentiparous membrane which lines the alveolar cavities.

† **dentiate**, *v. Obs.* [irreg. f. L. *dentīre.*]

1623 COCKERAM, *Dentiate*, to breed teeth.

† **'dentical**, *a. Obs. rare.* [f. *dens, dent-* tooth + -IC + -AL[1].] = DENTAL *a.* 1 b.

1776 'COURTNEY MELMOTH' *Pupil of Pleas.* II. 216 A Treatise on Toothpicking, wherein I show the precise method of holding, handling..and replacing the dentical instruments.

'denticate, *v. rare.* [f. late L. *denticāre* to move the teeth (Papias); cf. It. *denticāre* to pinch, to nibble, or brouse with one's teeth.] To bite or crush with the teeth.

1799 *Sporting Mag.* XIII. 37 Masticate, denticate, chump, grind and swallow.

denticete ('dɛntɪsiːt), *a.* [f. L. *dent-em* tooth + *cēt-us* whale.] Toothed (as a whale).

1885 WOOD *Whale* in *Longm. Mag.* V. 550 The two halves of the lower jaw, instead of being pressed closely against each other, as in the Denticete whale, are strongly bowed outwards, much in the form of a parenthesis ( ).

denticle ('dɛntɪk(ə)l), *sb.* (*a.*) [ad. L. *denticulus*, dim. of *dent-em* tooth. Cf. DENTICULE.]

1. A small tooth or tooth-like projection. (In quot. 1391, a pointer on the 'rete' of the astrolabe.)

c **1391** CHAUCER *Astrol.* I. §23 Thin Almury is cleped the denticle of capricorne or elles the kalkuler. **1578** LYTE *Dodoens* I. xcix. 140 Leaves dented round aboute with small denticles. **1761** GAERTNER in *Phil. Trans.* LII. 81, 5 small denticles, that surround a cavity placed in their middle. **1877** HUXLEY *Anat. Inv. Anim.* v. 237 Two powerful teeth.. besides minute accessory denticles. **1881** MIVART in *Nature* No. 615. 337 A sharp tooth, or denticle, at the inner side of the base of each claw.

2. *Arch.* = DENTIL.

1674 BLOUNT *Glossogr.*, *Denticle*..also that part of the Chapiter of a Pillar, which is cut and graven like teeth. **1723** CHAMBERS tr. *Le Clerc's Treat. Archit.* I. 40 The distances of the Columns..are adjusted by a certain number of Denticles..the first Denticle *A*, and the last *B*, being each cut..by the..Axes of the Columns. *Ibid.* 43 The Denticle is that large square Moulding underneath the Ovolo. **1761** KIRBY *Perspect. Architect.* 39 From the dentals already drawn the others are to be taken, and also the denticles.

†**B.** *adj.* Toothed, denticulated. *Obs.*

1574 EDEN tr. *Taisner's de Natura Magnetis* Ded., Turned or moued with certayne litle denticle wheeles.

denticular (dɛn'tɪkjʊlə(r)), *a.* [f. L. *denticulus* (see prec.) + -AR. Cf. mod.F. *denticulaire.*]

1. Resembling, or of the nature of, a small tooth.

1878 BELL *Gegenbauer's Comp. Anat.* 160 Converted into a gizzard by the development of denticular processes.

2. *Arch.* Characterized by having dentils.

1842–76 GWILT *Encycl. Archit.* III. i. 817 The difference between the mutular and denticular Doric lies entirely in the entablature.

denticulate (dɛn'tɪkjʊlət), *a.* [ad. L. *denticulāt-us*, f. *denticul-us*: see DENTICLE and -ATE[2] 2.]

1. Having small teeth or tooth-like projections; finely toothed.

1661 LOVELL *Hist. Anim. & Min.* Introd., Of a denticulate asperity. **1826** GOOD *Bk. Nat.* (1834) II. 41 The bill..denticulate or toothed. **1870** HOOKER *Stud. Flora* 18 Sepals denticulate.

2. *Arch.* = DENTICULAR 2.

3. In *comb.*

1856–8 W. CLARK *Van der Hoeven's Zool.* II. 383 Bill subulate..with margins denticulate-serrate. **1872** OLIVER *Elem. Bot.* App. 308 Leaves..denticulate-serrate.

Hence **den'ticulately** *adv.*, in a denticulate manner, with denticulation.

Often in *Bot.* and *Zool.*, as *denticulately serrated, ciliated*, etc.

1847 in CRAIG.

denticulated (dɛn'tɪkjʊleɪtɪd), *ppl. a.* [f. as prec. + -ED.] **1.** = prec. 1.

1665 GLANVILL *Scepsis Sci.* 48 Supposing both wheels to be denticulated, the little wheel will with its teeth describe lines. **1826** KIRBY & SP. *Entomol.* (1828) IV. xxxviii. 49 With a denticulated margin. **1869** PHIPSON tr. *Guillemin's The Sun* (1870) 244 The passage of the Sun's rays along the denticulated edge of the moon.

2. *Arch.* = prec. 2.

1823 P. NICHOLSON *Pract. Build.* 447 They are called Dentils; and the cornices are said to be denticulated.

denticulation (dɛn,tɪkju:'leɪʃən). [f. L. *denticul-us* (see DENTICLE) + -ATION: cf. *dentation.*] The condition of being denticulate or finely toothed; usually *concr.* an instance of this; a series of small teeth or tooth-like projections (mostly in *pl.*).

1681 GREW *Musæum* (J.), The denticulation of the edges of the bill, or those small oblique incisions made for the better retention of the prey. **1829** LOUDON *Encycl. Plants* 609 Branches flat, linear, leafless. Denticulations flower bearing. **1862** DANA *Man. Geol.* 477 The teeth have a smooth margin without denticulations. **1874** MOGGRIDGE *Ants & Spiders* Supp. 259 The denticulation of the tarsal claws..is similar.

denticule ('dɛntɪkju:l). *Arch.* [a. F. *denticule* (1545 in transl. of Vitruvius), ad. L. *denticul-us* little tooth, dim. of *dens*, *dent-em* tooth: see -CULE. Also used in Latin form.] = DENTIL b.

1563 SHUTE *Archit.* Cj b, In Corona, ye shal make Denticulos. *Ibid.* Civ a, They haue added Echinus, and Denticuli. **1846** WORCHESTER, *Denticule* (Arch.), the flat projecting part of a cornice, on which dentils are cut. *Francis.*

dentie, obs. form of DAINTY; *esp.* in phrase *By Gods dentie*, by God's dignity or honour.

1564–78 BULLEYN *Dial. agst. Pest.* (1888) 62 *V.* Gods dentie, Jacke sauce, whence came you? *R.* How pretely you can call verlet and sweare by Gods dentie!

†**dentient** ('dɛnʃ(ɪ)ənt), *a.* *Obs. rare.* [ad. L. *dentient-em* 'teething', pr. pple. of *dentīre* to cut the teeth.] Teething.

1651 BIGGS *New Disp.* ¶ 248 An Infant of a year old, who is dentient and febrient.

dentifactor: see under DENTI-.

dentification (,dɛntɪfɪ'keɪʃən). [f. L. *dens*, *dent-em* tooth + -FICATION. The cognate verb would be *dentify*. So in mod.F. (Littré).] Conversion into the substance of a tooth, formation of dentine. (Cf. *ossification.*)

1878 T. BRYANT *Pract. Surg.* I. 564 A change in form of the dental pulp prior to its dentification.

dentiform ('dɛntɪfɔ:m), *a.* [f. L. type **dentiform-is* (used in mod.L.), f. *dent-em* tooth: see -FORM. So F. *dentiforme* (Littré).] Of the form of a tooth, tooth-shaped, odontoid.

1708 MOTTEUX *Rabelais* v. xxi. (1737) 93 Their Dentiform Vertebra. **1843** PORTLOCK *Geol.* 213 Carbonate of lime..in prismatic, rhomboidal, and dentiform crystals.

†**'dentiformed**, *a.* *Obs.* = prec.

1578 BANISTER *Hist. Man* I. 19 The cause of the second Vertebres mouyng, and of the dentiformed Processe.

†**den'tifric**, *a.* *Obs. rare.* = next.

1760 *Lond. Mag.* XXIX. 204 The Dentifrick Elaboratory of the celebrated Professor Webb.

†**den'tifrical**, *a.* *Obs. rare.* [f. L. type **dentifric-us* (cf. DENTIFRICE) + -AL[1].] Of or pertaining to a dentifrice, teeth-cleansing.

1806 R. WINSTANLEY in *Monthly Mag.* XXI. 389 As to its dentifrical properties.

†**dentifricator** ('dɛntɪfrɪ,keɪtə(r)). *Obs.* [f. L. *dent-em* tooth + *fricātor* one who rubs, after L. *dentifricium.*] A professional cleanser of teeth.

c **1700** D. G. *Harangues of Quack Doctors* 13 Doctor, Chymist, and Dentrificator. **1752** A. MURPHY *Gray's-Inn Jrnl.* No. 12 The Profession I have taken up..is that of a Dentifricator, or what the Vulgar call a Cleaner of Teeth.

dentifrice ('dɛntɪfrɪs). [a. F. *dentifrice* (15th c. in Hatzf.), ad. L. *dentifricium*, f. *dent-em* tooth + *fricāre* to rub.] A powder or other preparation for rubbing or cleansing the teeth; a tooth-powder or tooth-paste; also applied to liquid preparations.

1558 WARDE tr. *Alexis Secr.* I. fol. 53 a, Dentifrices or rubbers for the teeth of great perfection, for to make them cleane. **1594** PLAT *Jewell-ho.*, *Diuerse New Exper.* 74 Sweet and delicate dentifrices or rubbers for the teeth. **1601** HOLLAND *Pliny* II. 591 The best dentifrices for to cleanse or whiten the teeth, be made of the pumish. **1694** *Lond. Gaz.* No. 2985/4 An excellent Dentrifice, or Powder, for cleansing Teeth. **1718** QUINCY *Compl. Disp.* 92 Myrrh is also an excellent Dentrifice. **1876** BARTHOLOW *Mat. Med.* (1879) 323 Camphor enters into the composition of many dentifrices.

dentigerous (dɛn'tɪdʒərəs), *a.* *Zool.* and *Anat.* [f. L. type **denti-ger* tooth-bearing + -OUS: in mod.F. *dentigère.*] Bearing teeth.

1839–47 TODD *Cycl. Anat.* III. 979/2 The..membrane lining the dentigerous cavity. **1847–9** *Ibid.* IV. 288/1 The teeth of the dentigerous Saurian..reptiles are..simple. **1870** ROLLESTON *Anim. Life* 6 The jaws are generally dentigerous.

dentil ('dɛntɪl). *Arch.* Also 7 **dentile**. [a. obs. F. *dentille* (16th c. in Littré); a fem. deriv. of *dent*; cf. Pr. *dentilh* masc.:—L. *denticulus*, dim. of *dens*, *dent-em* tooth. See also DENTICULE, DENTEL.]

Each of the small rectangular blocks, resembling a row of teeth, under the bed-moulding of the cornice in the Ionic, Corinthian, Composite, and sometimes Doric, orders.

1663 GERBIER *Counsel* 71 The Dentiles at three pence per foot. **1783** AINSWORTH *Lat. Dict.* (Morell) I, Dentles [in architecture], *dentuli.* **1849** FREEMAN *Archit.* 113 The dentils introduced just under the cornice..are a great source of richness. **1865** C. T. NEWTON *Trav. Levant* xxviii. 307 A stone forming the angle of a small pediment, with dentils coarsely executed.

†**b.** *transf.* That member of the entablature in which the dentils (when present) are cut. *Obs.*

1726 LEONI *Alberti's Archit.* II. 40 b, An upright cymatium; and over that a plain dentil. **1789** P. SMYTH tr. *Aldrich's Archit.* (1818) 89 A reglet divided, its parts alternately omitted, is called a dentil.

c. *attrib.*

1754 in Willis & Clark *Cambridge* (1886) I. 38 That..a Parapet Wall be erected, adorned with a Dentil Cornice. **1812–6** J. SMITH *Panorama Sc. & Art* I. 180 Under the modillions is placed an ovolo, and then a fillet and the dentil face, which is often left uncut in exterior work. **1823** P. NICHOLSON *Pract. Build.* 474 The dentil-bands should remain uncut. **1865** J. G. NICHOLS in *Herald & Geneal.* July 254 The classical dentil moulding.

dentilabial: see under DENTI-.

'dentilated, *ppl. a.* [Variant of DENTELATED, after DENTIL.] 'Formed like teeth; having teeth.' So **dentilation**, 'the formation of teeth, dentition' (Worcester, 1846); denticulation (of a margin), perforation of postage stamps.

1867 *Philatelist* I. 29 The regulation and perfection of the dentilation.

dentile ('dɛntɪl). *Conchol.* [var. of DENTIL, obs. F. *dentille*] (See quots.)

1864 WEBSTER, *Dentile* (Conch.), a small tooth like that of a saw. **1883** *Syd. Soc. Lex.*, *Dentile*, a term applied to a small sharp tooth-like projection on the border of a shell.

dentilingual, -loquent, etc.: see under DENTI-.

dentinal ('dɛntɪnəl), *a.* [f. DENTINE + -AL[1].] Pertaining to or of the nature of dentine.

1847–9 TODD *Cycl. Anat.* IV. 382/2 The calcification of the dentinal pulp. **1870** ROLLESTON *Anim. Life* Introd. 45 The dentinal tissue is free from anchylosis with the alveolus.

dentine, dentin ('dɛntɪn). *Anat.* [f. L. *dent-em* tooth + -INE.] The hard tissue, resembling bone but usually denser, which forms the chief constituent of the teeth.

1840–5 OWEN *Odontography* I. Introd. 3, I propose to call the substance which forms the main part of all teeth 'dentine'..'Dentine' consists of an organized animal basis disposed in the form of extremely minute tubes and cells, and of earthy particles. **1878** T. BRYANT *Pract. Surg.* I. 565 Well-formed dentine is uniformly dense and ivory-like.

'denting, *vbl. sb.* [f. DENT *v.* + -ING[1].]

1. The action of the verb DENT, q.v.

1398 TREVISA *Barth. De P.R.* XVII. clxii. (1495) 709 After many manere castynge, hewynge, dentynge, and planynge. **1591** PERCIVALL *Sp. Dict.*, *Abolladura*, denting in with blowes, beating in, *contusio.*

†**2.** The result of this action; an indentation.

1388 WYCLIF *Ex.* xxvi. 17 Twei dentyngis [**1382** rabitis] schulen be in the sidis of a table, bi which a table schal be ioyned to another table.

†**3.** *Arch.* = DENTIL. *Obs.*

1730 A. GORDON *Maffei's Amphith.* 367 The great Cornish, with Modilions and Dentings.

'denting, *ppl. a.* [f. as prec. + -ING[2].] That dents; †that strikes a blow.

1575 *Appius & Virginia* Epil. in Hazl. *Dodsley* IV. 155 But denting death will cause them all to grant this world as vain.

'dentinoid, *a.* [f. DENTINE + -OID.] Like or of the character of dentine.

1883 *Syd. Soc. Lex.*, *Dentinoid tumour*, a *dental osteoma* arising from the crown of the tooth; so called from its structure being like dentine covered with enamel.

dentiparous, -phone: see under DENTI-.

denti'roster. *Ornith. rare* [a. F. *dentirostre*, ad. mod.L. *dentirostr-is*, f. L. *denti-* tooth + *rostrum* beak, of which the pl. *Dentirostrēs* was introduced by Cuvier as the name of a family of birds.] A member of the *Dentirostres* or Passerine birds having a tooth or notch on each side of the upper mandible. By Cuvier applied to an immense assemblage of birds having no natural relations; by more recent naturalists restricted to the Turdoid or thrush-like *Passeres* or *Insessores*.

[**1839** JARDINE *Brit. Birds* II. 53 The first of the great tribes into which the insessorial birds are separated, the Dentirostres.] **1847** CRAIG, *Dentirosters, Dentirostres.*

Hence **denti'rostral**, **denti'rostrate** *adjs.*, belonging to the *Dentirostres*; having a toothed beak.

1841 *Proc. Berw. Nat. Club* I. 251 The Dentirostral tribe. **1847** CRAIG, *Dentirostrate.* **1876** *Amer. Cycl.* XV. 727 A very large family of dentirostral birds. **1883** *Syd. Soc. Lex.*, *Dentirostrate*, having the characters of the *Dentirostres.*

'dentiscalp. [ad. L. *dentiscalpium* toothpick, f. DENTI- + *scalp-ĕre* to scrape, scratch.]

1656 BLOUNT *Glossogr.*, *Dentiscalp*, an instrument to scrape the teeth, a tooth-picker. **1708** W. KING *Cookery* iii, Remarks from the ancients concerning dentiscalps, vulgarly called tooth-picks. **1874** KNIGHT *Dict. Mech.*, *Dentiscalp*, an instrument for scaling teeth.

[**dentise, -ize**, *v.* To cut new teeth. Error due to misreading of L. *dentire*, inf. of *dentio* to cut teeth, in Bacon *Sylva*, 1626, §755.

[**1626** BACON *Sylva* §755 They tell a Tale of the old Countesse of Desmond, who liued till she was seuen-score yeares old, that she did *Dentire*, twice, or thrice; Casting her old Teeth, and others Comming in their Place.] **1773** JOHNSON (quoting *Bacon*). Hence in some later Dicts.]

dentist ('dɛntɪst). [ad. F. *dentiste*, f. L. *dentem*, F. *dent*, tooth: see -IST.] One whose profession it is to treat diseases of the teeth, extract them, insert artificial ones, etc.; a dental surgeon.

1759 *Edin. Chron.* 15 Sept. 4 *Dentist* figures it now in our newspapers, and may do well enough for a French puffer; but we fancy Rutter is content with being called a *tooth-drawer.* **1760** *Lond. Mag.* XXIX. 204 This distinguished Dentist and Dentologist. **1808** *Med. Jrnl.* XIX. 192 Mr. Moor, Surgeon Dentist to Her Royal Highness the Duchess of York. **1855** O. W. HOLMES *Poems* 149 No! Pay the dentist when he leaves A fracture in your jaw.

den'tistic, *a.* [f. prec. + -IC.] = next.

In mod. Dicts.

den'tistical, *a. rare.* [f. as prec. + -AL[1].] Of, pertaining to, or of the nature of a dentist.

1851 H. MELVILLE *Whale* xlvii. 303 Little boxes of dentistical-looking instruments. **1853** LYTTON *My Novel* (Rtldg.) 164 The crocodile..opens his jaws inoffensively to a faithful dentistical bird, who volunteers his beak for a toothpick.

dentistry ('dɛntɪstrɪ). [f. as prec. + -RY.] The profession or practice of a dentist.

1838 *Tait's Mag.* V. 197 Dentistry, as we find it called, is growing into a profession. **1886** *Act 49–50 Vict.* c. 48 §26 Rights..to practise dentistry or dental surgery in any part of Her Majesty's dominions.

dentition (dɛn'tɪʃən). [ad. L. *dentitiōn-em* teething, n. of action from *dentīre* to teeth. (So in mod.F. in *Dict. Trev.* 18th c.)]

1. The production or 'cutting' of the teeth; teething.

1615 Crooke *Body of Man* 969 Dentition or the breeding of the Teeth begins about the seauenth yeare, sometimes sooner. **1666** J. Smith *Old Age* (ed. 2) 140 Dentition and Locution are for the most part Contemporaries. **1801** *Med. Jrnl.* V. 567 Latest Theories of difficult Dentition. **1870** Lowell *Among my Bks.* Ser. I. (1873) 365 With many constitutions it is as purely natural a crisis as dentition. *Mod.* The second dentition is to some children as critical a period as the first.

2. The arrangement of the teeth, with regard to kind, number, and order, proper to a particular animal, or to an animal at a particular age.

1849 *Sk. Nat. Hist., Mammalia* IV. 25 The dentition is as follow:—Incisors, $\frac{2}{2}$; molars, $\frac{4-4}{4-4}$. **1855** Owen *Teeth* 285 The dentition of the genus *Elephas* includes two long tusks. **1880** Haughton *Phys. Geog.* vi. 273 Of all distinguishing characters, the dentition of an animal is one of the most important.

† '**dentity**. *Obs. nonce-wd.* [f. L. *dens, dentem* tooth + -ity.] The age of teething.

1638 T. Whitaker *Blood of Grape* 43 Infancy, Dentity and another.. age, and then puberity itselfe.

dento-, an incorrect combining form of L. *dent-em* tooth, as in **dento-'lingual**, etc.: see denti-. Also in **den'tologist, den'tology**.

1760 [see dentist]. **1835** *Tait's Mag.* II. 538 The purely ornamental branch of dentology.

'**dentoid**, *a. rare.* [Bad formation, from L. *dent-em* tooth + Gr. -οειδης, -oid.] Tooth-like, dentiform, odontoid.

1828 Webster cites Barton.

dentor, dentour: see denture[1], indenture.

† '**dentulated**, *ppl. a. Obs.* = denticulated.

1796 Stedman *Surinam* (1813) II. xxiv. 220 Its leaves.. dentulated with hard prickles.

† '**denture**[1]. *Obs.* Also **dentor, dentour**. Aphetic form of indenture.

c **1400** *Beryn* 2791 An entre [þat] as a dentour wriythe. **1481-90** *Howard Househ. Bks.* (Roxb.) 348 As it perith be dentor.. lix. bales of Gene wode. **1541** *Schole-ho. Women* 837 in Hazl. *E.P.P.* IV. 137 Of you I haue no denture.

'**denture**[2]. *rare.* Also 7 **denter**. [f. dent *v.* + -ure.] Indentation, indent.

1685 *Act 1 Jas. II*, c. 22 (*Parish St. James's, Westm.*). Crossing from the south-west corner of the wall of the said house in the said Portugal Street to the middle denter thereof.. Proceeding from the said middle denter westwards. **1822** *Blackw. Mag.* XII. 532 Those clear atmospheres.. allow every denture of the chisel to be conspicuous.

denture[3] ('dɛntjʊə(r)). [a. F. *denture* (14–15th c. *denteüre* in Hatzf.), f. *dent* tooth: see -ure.] A set of teeth; *esp.* of artificial teeth.

1874 Knight *Dict. Mech.* I. 685/2 An instrument for matching the dentures of upper and lower jaw. **1882** *Worcester Exhib. Catal.* iii. 58 Specimens of dentures in wax, before vulcanizing. **1891** *Pall Mall G.* 21 Aug. 5/2 Method of preventing anterior and lateral movements in artificial dentures in edentulous cases.

denty, obs. form of dainty.

dentyuous, var. of dainteous *a. Obs.*

de'nuclearize, *v.* [f. de- II. 1 + nuclear *a.* + -ize; cf. demilitarize *v.*] *trans.* To deprive of nuclear armaments; to remove nuclear armaments from. Chiefly as *ppl. a.*, esp. with *zone*. So ˌ**denucleari'zation**.

1958 *Economist* 25 Jan. 290/1 The Polish suggestion of a 'denuclearised' area in central Europe. **1958** *Times* 20 Feb. 8/5 A denuclearized zone in central Europe would answer the vital interests of all European States. **1959** *News Chron.* 21 July 1/1 What he [*sc.* Mr. Krushchev] wanted from Scandinavia was its de-nuclearisation. **1960** *New Left Rev.* July–Aug. 1/2 A de-nuclearised, NATO-free West Germany. **1962** *Guardian* 15 Dec. 6/4 Mr. McNamara.. seems to be doing more to de-nuclearise Britian than CND has yet achieved. **1963** *Economist* 11 May 547/1 If warfare could in some way be denuclearised.

denucleate, -ed: see de- II. 1.

denudant (dɪ'nju:dənt). [f. denude *v.* + -ant[1].] That which denudes; *spec.* in *Geol.*, an agent or agency which removes disintegrated matter and lays bare the underlying rock or formation.

1894 J. Geikie *Gt. Ice Age* (ed. 3) 259 Its [*sc.* the boulder-clay's] chief denudant has evidently been running water.

denudate (dɪ'nju:dət, 'dɛnju:dət), *a.* [ad. L. *dēnūdāt-us*, pa. pple. of *dēnūdāre* to denude.] Denuded; naked, bare.

1866 *Treas. Bot., Denudate*, when a surface which has once been hairy, downy, etc., becomes naked. **1883** *Syd. Soc. Lex., Denudate*, stripped; naked. Applied to plants whose flowers have no flower-cup.

denudate ('dɛnju:deɪt, dɪ'nju:deɪt), *v.* [f. ppl. stem of L. *dēnūdāre*, to denude. All the dicts. down to Smart 1849, stress *de'nudate*: see note to contemplate.] *trans.* To strip naked or bare; = denude.

1627-77 Feltham *Resolves* II. xi. 182 Dionysia, a Noble Matron, was denudated and barbarously scourged. **1634** Sir T. Herbert *Trav.* 147 Painted.. as be their feet and legs, both which are denudated in their dances. **1657** Tomlinson *Renou's Disp.* 261 The elder.. is last denudated of its leaves. **1667** *Decay Chr. Piety* xix. §2. 363 Till he have thus denudated himself of all these encumbrances. **1816** Kirby & Sp. *Entomol.* (1843) I. 218 *note*, A perfect skeleton denudated of every fibril of muscle.

Hence '**denudated** *ppl. a.*, '**denudating** *vbl. sb.* and *ppl. a.*

1672 *Phil. Trans.* VII. 5032 In the denudated parts of the lobe. **1849** Dana *Geol.* vii. (1850) 355 The denudating agents that could scoop out valleys. **1876** Davis *Polaris Exp.* App. 661 Glacial scratches.. upon denudated surfaces.

denudation (dɛnju:'deɪʃən). [a. F. *dénudation*, in 14th c. *-acion* (Hatzf.), ad. L. *dēnūdātiōn-em*, n. of action from *dēnūdāre*: see prec.]

1. a. The action of making naked or bare; a stripping off of clothing or covering; denuded condition.

1584 R. Scot *Discov. Witchcr.* XV. xxiv. 371 Denudation and unction with holie oil. **1714** Mandeville *Fab. Bees* (1725) I. 59 To be modest, we ought.. to avoid all unfashionable denudations. **1816** Keatinge *Trav.* (1817) I. 44 The inns.. in a state of denudation of furniture. **1884** *Manch. Exam.* 10 July 5/3 Ireland, once a land of forests, has suffered enormously from the process of denudation.

† **b.** *fig.* The action of laying bare; exposure.

1593 Nashe *Foure Lett. Confut.* 62 All this he barely repeates without any disprouement or denudation. **1621** Donne *Serm.* cxviii. V. 74 The Denudation of your Souls and your Sins by a humble confession.

c. The action of divesting or depriving.

1633 T. Adams *Exp. 2 Peter* iii. 10 Such a destitution of succour, and denudation of all refuge. **1644** Bp. Hall *Devout Soul* §10 (T.) There must be a denudation of the mind from all those images of our phantasy.. that may carry our thoughts aside. **1871** Earle *Philol. Eng. Tongue* §579 The subjunctive is distinguished from the indicative merely by the denudation of flexion.

2. *Geol.* The laying bare of an underlying rock or formation through the wearing away or *erosion* of that which lies above it, by the action of water, ice, or other natural agency. Also *attrib.* So **denu'dational** *a.*

1811 Farey in *Phil. Trans.* 242 (*title*), Account of the great Derbyshire Denudation. **1823** W. Buckland *Reliq. Diluv.* 118 *note*, This gorge is simply a valley of denudation. **1845** Darwin *Voy. Nat.* xviii. (1852) 345 Considering the enormous power of denudation which the sea possesses. **1878** Huxley *Physiogr.* 149 At the present rate of denudation, it would require about $5\frac{1}{2}$ million years to reduce the British Isles to a flat plane at the level of the sea. **1913** A. Holmes *Age of Earth* iv. 60 The application of denudational statistics to the measurement of geological time will be considered. **1928** Nordenskjöld & Mecking *Geogr. Polar Regions* 58 Old denudational surfaces or raised peneplains. **1949** *Proc. Geol. Assoc.* LX. 165 (*title*) The denudation chronology of the dip-slope of the South Downs. **1954** W. D. Thornbury *Princ. Geomorphol.* iii. 35 Some geologists have used the term denudation as if it were synonymous with gradation, but as this term implies removal of material, it is hardly logical to include deposition under it. **1956** *Nature* 28 Jan. 166/1 The sequence of cyclic denudational landscapes. **1960** B. W. Sparks *Geomorphol.* i. 2 In its second sense, geomorphology is the study of the evolution of landscapes. Such study is often termed denudation chronology. **1960** L. D. Stamp *Britain's Struct.* (ed. 5) iii. 22 The cycle of denudation on the land and of sedimentation in the water is brought to a close by earth movements.

denudative (dɪ'nju:dətɪv), *a.* [f. *dēnūdāt-*, ppl. stem of L. *dēnūdāre* to denude: see -ive.] Having the quality of denuding; causing denudation (e.g. of strata).

Mod. The denudative action of water; denudative agencies.

de'nudatory, *a. rare.* [f. ppl. stem *dēnūdāt-* of L. *dēnūdāre*: see -ory.] = denudative.

1845 Newbold in *Jrnl. Asiatic Soc. Bengal* XIV. 293 This continuity.. violated by.. denudatory aqueous causes.

denude (dɪ'nju:d), *v.* [ad. L. *dēnūdā-re* to make naked, lay bare, f. de- I. 3 + *nūdāre* to make naked, *nūdus* naked. (Cf. mod.F. *dénuder* 1790 in Hatzf. The earlier F. verb is *dénuer*, OF. *denuer, desnuer*.)]

1. *trans.* To make naked or bare; to strip *of* clothing or covering; *spec.* in *Geol.* of natural agencies: To lay bare (a rock or formation) by the removal of that which lies above it.

1658 Evelyn *Fr. Gard.* (1675) 88 Some when they alter their cases, denude them of all the earth. **1691** Ray *Creation* I. (1704) 120 If you denude a Vine-Branch of its Leaves. **1845** Darwin *Voy. Nat.* (1852) 12 That any power.. could have denuded the granite over so many thousand square leagues? **1866** Livingstone *Jrnl.* (1873) I. v. 124 The long slopes are nearly denuded of trees. **1880** A. R. Wallace *Isl. Life* vii. 111 Rapidly denuded by rain and rivers.

2. *fig.* To strip, divest, deprive (*of* any possession, attribute, etc.).

1513 Douglas *Æneis* VIII. ix. 65 Nor this burgh of sa mony citesanis Left desolat and denudit. **1536** Bellenden *Cron. Scotl.* (1821) I. 95 To denude him of the Romane lady, and to adhere to his lauchfull wiffe. **1637** Gillespie *Eng. Pop. Cerem.* III. i. 6 He denudes himselfe of all right and title, which.. he might claime vnto it. **1862** Maurice *Mor. & Met. Philos.* IV. viii. §53. 492 Denuded of much of his wit and cleverness. **1874** J. Stoughton *Church of Revol.* xvii. 395 Denuding them of political rights, they denied them political duties.

b. *intr.* (for *refl.*) To divest oneself.

1880 Muirhead *Gaius* Digest 496 An heir.. fraudulently giving a secret promise to denude in favour of one to whom trust-gift was prohibited rendered himself liable to penalties. *Ibid.* 497 The heir denuding did not thereby cease to be heir.

† **3.** To lay bare to the mind, disclose, make clear. *Obs. rare.*

1572 Forrest *Theophilus* 128 in *Anglia* VII, Then approbation the case dyd denude.

Hence **de'nuded, de'nuding** *ppl. adjs.*

1639 in Maidment *Sc. Pasquil* (1868) 85 Denuding motions wer not entertained. **1813** J. Thomson *Lect. Inflam.* 467 The denuded muscles were amazingly enlarged. **1849** Murchison *Siluria* vii. 125 From the denuded valley of Wigmore. **1878** Huxley *Physiogr.* 131 Its power [tropical rain] as a denuding agent is almost incredible.

† **de'nude**, *ppl. a. Sc. Obs.* [Short for *denuded, denudit*: cf. *devoid*.] Denuded, deprived, bereft, devoid (*of*).

1552 Lyndesay *Monarche* 5430 Sonne and Mone ar, boith, denude Off lycht. **1560** Rolland *Crt. Venus* III. 512 He.. was denude of his Kingdome. **1570** *Satir. Poems Reform.* XVIII. 75 Gylouris of godlynes denude!

de'nudement. *rare.* [-ment.] = Denudation, denuded condition.

1831 Southey in *Q. Rev.* XLV. 424 He continued to live in privations and denudement.

† **de'null**, *v. Obs.* [f. de- I. 3 + L. *null-us* none, null: cf. disnull, disannul.] *trans.* To reduce to nullity; to annul, make void.

1494 Fabyan *Chron.* VII. 402 After the deth of Kynge Edwarde that banysshement was soone denulled. **1552** *Bury Wills* (Camden) 141, I denull, disalow, and sett att nothing all former wills and testaments.

† **de'number**, *v. Obs.* In 4–5 **denoumbre**. [a. F. *dénombrer* (in Littré and Hatzf. only of 16th c.), f. dé- I. 3 + *nombrer* to number, after *dēnumerāre*, erroneous scribal variant of L. *dīnumerāre* to count out, enumerate, f. *di-*, dis- + *numerāre* to count.] *trans.* To number, count, reckon up.

1382 Wyclif *Ps.* lxxxix. [xc.] 11 Who knewȝ the power of thi wrathe; and for thi drede thi wrathe denoumbren?

† **de'numberment**. *Obs.* [a. F. *dénombrement* (1376 in Hatzf.), f. *dénombrer* to denumber: see -ment.] The act of numbering or reckoning up; a reckoning, enumeration.

1455 *Paston Lett.* I. No. 263. 360 For the value and denombrement of iiij m^1 saluz of yerly rent. **1633** J. Done *Hist. Septuagint* 29 He commanded Demetrius.. to deliver him the denomberment of the Hebrew Volumes. **1657** *North's Plutarch, Addit. Lives* (1676) 47 By the denumberment of the Roman Consuls, we find that he lived long before.

denumerability (dɪˌnju:mərə'bɪlɪtɪ). *Math.* [f. next: see -ity.] The fact or quality of being denumerable.

1935 *Bull. Amer. Math. Soc.* XLI. 644 In a metrizable space the Borel theorem holds without the restriction of denumerability of the original family. **1941** Courant & Robbins *What is Math.?* ii. 79 (*title*) The denumerability of the rational numbers and the non-denumerability of the continuum. **1963** R. R. Stoll *Set Theory* ii. 91 Using the preceding theorem, the denumerability of the positive rationals can be established.

denumerable (dɪ'nju:mərəb(ə)l), *a. Math.* [f. denumerate *v.* + -able. Cf. G. *abzählbar*, Fr. *dénombrable*.] Of a set: infinite but countable; capable of being put into a one-to-one correspondence with the set of finite integers or natural numbers; also more widely, either finite or countably infinite; enumerable *a.*

C. S. Peirce used the term in a different sense.

[**1893** C. S. Peirce *Coll. Papers* (1933) IV. I. iv. 91 The dinumerable [*sic*] is to the innumerable as logarithmic infinity is to ordinary infinity.] **1902** A. N. Whitehead in *Amer. Jrnl. Math.* XXIV. 367 Imagination is very misleading, since it presents to us special aggregates which are denumerable. **1903** B. Russell *Princ. Math.* xxxvi. 296 A series of this type.. is denumerable, that is, by taking its terms in a suitable order.. we can give them a one-one correspondence with the finite integers. **1948** —— *Hum. Knowl.* IV. x. 345 Each atom may contain any one of a certain discrete denumerable series of amounts of energy. **1960** S. Körner *Philos. of Math.* iii. 63 The class of all rational numbers and the wider class of all (complex) algebraic numbers.. are denumerable. **1964** E. Bach *Introd. Transformational Gram.* vii. 151 The 'smallest' kind of infinite set is a set which is denumerable or countable. **1968** *Language* XLIV. 571 The set of all sets of integers is non-denumerable; the set of all Turing machines is denumerable; each recursively enumerable set corresponds to a Turing machine; therefore there are sets of integers which are not recursively enumerable. **1968** P. A. P. Moran *Introd. Probability Theory* v. 218 It therefore has at most a denumerable number of discontinuities.

Hence **de'numerably** *adv.*

[**1893** C. S. Peirce *Coll. Papers* (1933) IV. I. iv. 91 The innumerable is not only dinumerably [*sic*] more than the dinumerable but is innumerably more.] **1932** M. H. Stone *Linear Transformations in Hilbert Space* i. 20 Special notations for sets of elements constructed from a finite or denumerably infinite collection..of closed linear manifolds will be found..helpful. **1964** E. BACH *Introd. Transformational Gram.* vii. 153 The rules will specify the possible and denumerably infinite distributions for each of the forms of the language.

de'numerant. *Math.* [a. L. *dēnumerānt-em* pr. pple.: see next.] The number expressing how many solutions a given system of equations admits of. Hence **denumerantive**, *a.*

1859 SYLVESTER *Outl. Lect. on Partitions of Numbers* I. 2 Denumeration and Denumerant defined. *Ibid.* II. 4 To find the denumerant of $x + 2y + 4z = n$. *Ibid.* III. 4 Denumerantive function distinguished from denumerant.

† **de'numerate**, *v. Obs. rare*⁻⁰. [f. ppl. stem of L. *dēnumerāre*: see DENUMBER.]

1656 BLOUNT *Glossogr.*, *Denumerate*, to pay ready money, to pay money down.

denumeration (dɪˌnjuːməˈreɪʃən). [ad. L. *dē-, dīnumerātiōn-em*, n. of action from *dē-, dīnumerāre*: see prec.]

† **1.** A reckoning up, enumeration. *Obs.*

1623 FAVINE *Theat. Hon.* VI. ix. 152 As it is written in the denumeration of the Constables. **1651** LD. DIGBY *Lett. conc. Relig.* iv. 48 A place in their denumeration of Hereticks.

b. Reckoning by numbers, arithmetical calculation. *rare.*

1851 MANSEL *Prolegom. Logica* (1860) 115 *note*, Subtraction may be demonstrated from Addition..though it is simpler to regard Subtraction as an independent process of denumeration.

c. *Math.* The determination of the denumerant of an equation.

1859 [see DENUMERANT.]

† **2.** (See quots.) *Obs.*

1727 BAILEY vol. II, *Denumeration*, a present paying down of money. **1848** in WHARTON *Law Lex.*

‖ **denuncia** (deˈnunθia, -sia). [Sp.; = denunciation; f. *denunciar* to denounce.] In Mexico and Spanish America: The judicial proceedings by which a mine, lands, etc., are denounced, and the rights issuing from this action are secured; see DENOUNCE *v.* 8.

In mod. American Dicts.

de'nunciable, *a.* [f. L. *dēnuntiāre* (see next) + -BLE.] That can be denounced, proper to be denounced: see DENOUNCE *v.* 8.

In mod. Dicts.

denunciant (dɪˈnʌnsɪənt, -ʃɪənt), *a.* [ad. L. *dēnuntiānt-em*, pr. pple. of *dēnuntiāre* (see next) to DENOUNCE.] Denouncing.

1837 CARLYLE *Fr. Rev.* (1857) II. II. v. v. 66 Of all which things..Patriot France is informed: by denunciant friend, by triumphant foe.

denunciate (dɪˈnʌnsɪeɪt, -ʃɪeɪt), *v.* [f. ppl. stem of L. *dēnuntiāre, -nunciāre* to give official information, DENOUNCE, f. DE- I. 3 + *nuntiāre* (*nunciāre*) to make known, narrate, report.] *trans.* and *intr.* To denounce; to utter denunciation against.

1593 NASHE *Christ's T.* (1613) 46 Should I not so haue pronounst and denunciated against thee, thy blood would haue bene required at my hands. **1656** BLOUNT *Glossogr.*, *Denunciate*, to denounce or give warning, to proclaim. **1796** BURKE *Regic. Peace* i. Wks. VIII. 189 An exigent interest, to denunciate this new work. **1865** DE MORGAN in *Athenæum* No. 1987. 729/1 He only enunciated and denunciated. **1890** *Church Q. Rev.* XXX. 183 Some rabid Irish Protestant lecturer denunciating the Church of Rome.

Hence **de'nunciating** *ppl. a.*

1847 LD. G. BENTINCK in *Croker Papers* (1884) III. xxv. 161 An altar-denunciating priest [in Ireland]. **1893** *Columbus* (Ohio) *Dispatch* 15 Sept., Other denunciating expressions are employed against the special pension examiners.

denunciation (dɪˌnʌnsɪˈeɪʃən). Also 6 denunti-, 8 denounci-. [ad. L. *dēnunti-, dēnunciātiōn-em*, n. of action from *dēnuntiāre* to denounce, etc. Cf. F. *dénonciation* (13th c. in Littré), which may be the immediate source.]

† **1.** Official, formal, or public announcement; declaration, proclamation. *Obs.* (exc. in senses influenced by 2).

1548 *Act 2–3 Edw. VI*, c. 13 §13 Upon Denunciation and Publication thereof [sentence of excommunication] in the..Parish where the Party so excommunicate is dwelling. **1583** *Exec. for Treason* (1675) 37 Finding this kind of denunciation of War as a defiance. **1603** SHAKS. *Meas. for M.* I. ii. 152 She is fast my wife, Saue that we doe the denunciation lacke Of outward Order. **1649** BP. HALL *Cases Consc.* IV. ix. (1654) 366 This publique and reiterated denunciation of Bannes before matrimony. **1765** BLACKSTONE *Comm.* I. 258 Why..a denunciation of war ought always to precede the actual commencement of hostilities. **1803** JANE PORTER *Thaddeus* i. (1831) 8 Anxious to read in the countenance of my husband the denunciation of our fate. **1859** *Sat. Rev.* VII. 29/1 A denunciation of coming hostilities.

2. Announcement of evil, punishment, etc., in the manner of a warning or threat.

1563 *Homilies* II. *Rebellion* (1859) 550 With denunciation of death if he did transgress and break the said law. **1612** BRINSLEY *Lud. Lit.* xxix. (1627) 292 That severe denunciation of our Saviour for this undiscreet anger..may humble us continually. **1737** WHISTON *Josephus' Antiq.* x. vii. §4 The prophet..by the denunciation of miseries, weakened the alacrity of the multitude. **1752** JOHNSON *Rambler* No. 195 ¶6 Full of malignity and denunciations against a man whose name they had never heard. **1856** FROUDE *Hist. Eng.* I. 379 But if he still delayed his marriage, it was probably neither because he was frightened by her denunciations nor from alarm at the usual occurrence of an equinoctial storm.

† **3.** *Sc. Law.* The action of denouncing (a person) as a rebel, or to the horn. See DENOUNCE *v.* 4a.

1579 *Sc. Acts Jas. VI* (1597) §75 After their denuntiation of ony persones to the horne. **1592** *Ibid.* §138 In case onie denunciationes of Horninges, sall happen to be made at the said mercat Croce Edinburgh. **1752** J. LOUTHIAN *Form of Process* (ed. 2) 141 That..ye..relax the said ——, —— and —— from the Process of Denounciation led against them. **1861** W. BELL *Dict. Law Scotl.* 274/2 The consequences of denunciation, whether on account of civil or criminal matters, were formerly highly penal.

4. Accusation before a public prosecutor; delation.

1588 FRAUNCE *Lawiers Log.* I. xii. 53, I take a presentment to bee a meere denuntiation of the jurors themselves, or of some other officer without any other information. **1726** AYLIFFE *Parergon* 210 There are three ways of Proceeding in Criminal Causes, viz., by Accusation, Denunciation, and Inquisition.

5. The action or an act of denouncing as evil; public condemnation or inveighing against.

1842 *Mech. Mag.* XXXVI. 6 Denunciation on denunciation has been fulminated from the press—and yet the companies have adhered..to their life-and-limb-destroying practices. **1874** GREEN *Short Hist.* vii. §5. 395 A hot denunciation of the Scottish claim.

6. The action of denouncing (*v.* 7) a treaty, etc.

1885 *Act 48–9 Vict.* c. 49 Sched. Art. xvi, If one of the Signatory Powers denounce the Convention, such denunciation shall have effect only as regards that Power.

denunciative (dɪˈnʌns-, dɪˈnʌnʃɪətɪv), *a.* [f. L. *dēnuntiāt-* (see DENUNCIATE) + -IVE.] Given to or characterized by denunciation; denunciatory. Hence **de'nunciatively** *adv.*

a **1626** W. SCLATER *Three Sermons* (1629) 21 It's spoken..Denunciatiuely. **1860** *Sat. Rev.* X. 521/2 They must be of a denunciative turn of mind. **1860** FARRAR *Language* iv. (L.), The clamorous, the idle, and the ignorantly denunciative.

denunciator (dɪˈnʌns-, dɪˈnʌnʃɪeɪtə(r)). In 5 denounciatour, 6 denounciator. [a. F. *dénonciateur* (1408 in Hatzf.), ad. L. *dēnuntiātōr-em*, agent-n. from *dēnuntiāre* to denounce.] One who denounces or utters denunciations; a denouncer; in *Civ. Law*: One who lays an information against another.

1474 CAXTON *Chesse* III. i. (1860) E iij b, His accusers or denonciatours. **1563** FOXE *A. & M.* 700 a, Concerning Wylliam Lattymer and John Hooper, the pretenced denounciators of this matter. **1694** HALLE *Jersey* iv. 104 Two Denunciators, or Under-Sheriffs. **1726** AYLIFFE *Parergon* 210 The Denunciator does not inscribe himself, nor make himself a Party in Judgment as the Accuser does. **1833** LAMB *Elia* (1860) 402 The denunciators have been fain to postpone the prophecy. **1885** *Spectator* 29 Aug. 1125/1 Mr. Parnell, the denunciator of evicting landlords.

denunciatory (dɪˈnʌns-, dɪˈnʌnʃɪətərɪ), *a.* [f. L. type *dēnuntiātōri-us, f. *dēnuntiātor*: see prec. and -ORY.]

† **1.** Of or pertaining to official announcement. *letter denunciatory*: a letter or mandate authorizing publication or announcement. *Obs.*

1726 AYLIFFE *Parergon* 70 All Beadles and Apparitors..are forbidden..to denounce or publish any such sentence pronounced by Deans and Archdeacons, without the special Mandate or Letters Denunciatory of their Masters.

2. Of or pertaining to denunciation; characterized by denouncing, accusing, arraigning, condemning.

1837 CARLYLE *Fr. Rev.* II. VI. viii, Breathless messengers, fugitive Swiss, denunciatory Patriots. **1866** GEO. ELIOT *F. Holt* II. xxii. 112 His talk had been pungent and denunciatory. **1866** MRS. STOWE *Lit. Foxes* 81 Housekeepers are intolerant, virulently denunciatory concerning any departures from their particular domestic creed.

denutrition (diːnjuːˈtrɪʃən). [See DE- I. 6, or II. 3.] The opposite to nutrition; reversal of the nutritive process; in *Med.* treatment by deprivation of nourishment. Also *attrib.*

1868 W. JAMES in *North Amer. Rev.* CVII. 325 The study of those facts of elementary life, which may be summed up under the name of nutrition and denutrition. **1876** BARTHOLOW *Mat. Med.* (1879) 31 From these data we are enabled to form an estimate of the amount and kind of food necessary to maintain life in those cases of disease in which it is desirable to apply the method of denutrition. *Ibid.* 45 The hunger or denutrition cure. **1896** *Daily News* 25 Jan. 5/5 Her nervous system was a good deal shaken in consequence of an accident when out riding. Denutrition has been one of the consequences.

Denver (ˈdɛnvə(r)). Chiefly *N. Amer.* The name of the city of *Denver*, Colorado, used *attrib.* as **Denver boot, shoe**, a kind of wheel clamp used to immobilize an illegally parked vehicle (app. first used in Denver); cf. BOOT *sb.*³ 6 g.

1967 *Daily Tel.* 27 Oct. 22/3 An automatic wheel-locking device, called the Denver Shoe, which is to be used by police in Paris to 'arrest' vehicles left in streets where parking is not allowed. **1974** *Ottawa Citizen* 8 Oct. 45/1 The notice..said a large locking device had been attached to one of my wheels...This locking contraption is called a Denver Boot. **1977** *U.S. News & World Rep.* 21 Mar. 80/1 The [wheel] locks are called 'Denver boots', after the city that introduced them in 1949. **1983** *Daily Tel.* 14 July 19/1 In the first eight weeks 4,358 vehicles were clamped with the Denver shoe.

deny (dɪˈnaɪ), *v.* Forms: 4–6 denye, 6–7 denie, 4– deny; also 4–5 denoy(e, 4–7 denay(e. [a. F. *dénier* (OF. also *deneier, -noier, -neer*) = Pr. *deneyar, denegar*, Sp. *denegar*, It. *dinegare*:—L. *dēnegāre*, f. DE- I. 3 + *negāre* to say no, refuse, deny. In OF. the atonic stem-form was *denei-er, denoi-er* (:—*dēne'gāre*), the tonic *deni-e* (:—*denieie*:—*dē'negat*); by carrying each of these through, there arose two forms *denei-er* (*denoi-er*), *deni-er*, whence ME. *deney, denay* (*denoy*), and *deny*. By 16th c. writers, to whom *denay* was more or less of an archaism, it was apparently associated with *nay*: cf. the following:

1502 ARNOLDE *Chron.* (1811) 279 Yᵉ state of cardynal, whiche was naied and denayed hym by yᵉ Kyng.]

I. To say 'no' to a statement, assertion, doctrine.

1. To contradict or gainsay (anything stated or alleged); to declare to be untrue or untenable, or not what it is stated to be.

a. Const. with *simple object* (formerly sometimes *a person*).

c **1300** *K. Alis.* 3999 Antiochus saide..Thow hast denied thyself here. *c* **1330** R. BRUNNE *Chron.* (1810) 249 Þis was certified, & sikere on ilk side. It myght not be denied. *c* **1374** CHAUCER *Boeth.* III. xii. 81 (Camb. MS.) That may nat be denoyed, quod I. *c* **1400** *Apol. Loll.* 40 He liȝþ, þat..denaiþ þat, & affermiþ þe contrari. **1509** BARCLAY *Shyp of Folys* (1570) 27 And woorthy they were, what man can it denay? [*rime* betray]. **1548** HALL *Chron.* Introd. 2 b, Deniyng fiersly al the other new invencions alleged and proponed to his charge. *c* **1600** SHAKS. *Sonn.* xlvi. 7 But the defendant doth that plea deny. **1749** FIELDING *Tom Jones* VI. xi, Jones could not deny the charge. **1846** TRENCH *Mirac.* Introd. (1862) 71 Hume does not..absolutely deny the possibility of a miracle. **1875** JOWETT *Plato* (ed. 2) I. 207 You may have to deny your words.

fig. **1634** SIR T. HERBERT *Trav.* 63 The Duke was set at the very end crosse-legged like a Taylour, but his fierce aspect and bravery denied that title.

b. Const. with *that* and *clause*, or *obj.* and *infin.* (after Lat.); formerly also with *simple infin.* Formerly sometimes with *negative* or *but* in the clause.

1340 HAMPOLE *Pr. Consc.* 3572 Men shuld not denye..þat þe saules of þam þat er dede here Of payn may relesed be. *c* **1374** CHAUCER *Boeth.* II. v. 49, I denye þat þilke þing be good þat anoyeþ hym þat haþ it. *Ibid.* III. x. 88 It may nat ben denoyed þat þilke goode ne is. *c* **1400** *Apol. Loll.* 44, I denoy me not to haue seid þis. **1436** *Pol. Poems* (Rolls) II. 180 The chefare..noman may denyene, Is not made in Braban. **1513** MORE in Grafton *Chron.* II. 772 No man denieth..but that your grace..were most necessary about your children. **1542** UDALL tr. *Erasm. Apophth.* 157 b Denying the arte of geometrie..to bee to veraye litle use or purpose. **1581** PETTIE *Guazzo's Civ. Conv.* II. (1586) 49, I denie not but that there have bene amongst us..manie corrupt customes. **1589** PUTTENHAM *Eng. Poesie* III. xix. (Arb.) 218 Then is a picture not denaid, To be a muet Poesie. **1624** CAPT. SMITH *Virginia* IV. 157 Taxing the poore king of treason, who denied to the death not to know of any such matter. **1665** SIR T. HERBERT *Trav.* (1677) 310, I cannot deny but it [rice] is a solid grain. **1791** MRS. RADCLIFFE *Rom. Forest* x, You can't deny that your father is cruel. **1818** CRUISE *Digest* (ed. 2) II. 414, I beg leave to deny this to be law. **1871** MORLEY *Voltaire* 14 It is hard to deny that St. Bernard was a good man.

c. *absol.*

1382 WYCLIF *Gen.* xviii. 15 Sara denyede, seiynge, I lowȝ not. *c* **1440** *Promp. Parv.* 118 Denyyn or naytyn, *nego, denego.* *c* **1450** *St. Cuthbert* (Surtees) 5644 Ilk man for him self denyed. **15..** ? DUNBAR *Freiris of Berwik* 383 Scho saw it wes no bute for to deny.

2. *Logic.* The opposite of *affirm*; to assert the contradictory of (a proposition).

c **1425** WYNTOUN *Cron.* VIII. iii. 68 And [I] grantis, he sayd, þe antecedens; Bot I deny þe consequens. **1591** SHAKS. *Two Gent.* I. i. 84 *Sp.* Nay, that I can deny by a circumstance. *Pro.* It shall goe hard but ile proue it by another. **1596** —— *1 Hen. IV*, II. iv. 544, I deny your Maior. **1660** BARROW *Euclid* II. i. Schol., Let + A be to be multiplied into B—C; then because + A is not affirmed of all B, but only of a part of it, whereby it exceeds C, therefore AC must remain denied. **1725** WATTS *Logic* III. ii. §2 If the middle term be denied of either part of the conclusion, it may shew that the terms of the conclusion disagree, but it can never shew that they agree. **1866** T. FOWLER *Deduct. Logic* (1869) 110 If we affirm the antecedent, we must affirm the consequent, or, if we deny the consequent, we must deny the antecedent; but, if we deny the antecedent or affirm the consequent, no conclusion can be drawn.

3. To refuse to admit the truth of (a doctrine or tenet); to reject as untrue or unfounded; the opposite of *assert* or *maintain*.

1630 PRYNNE *Anti-Armin.* 137 This were to deny either the vniuersality or the equality of originall corruption. **1643** SIR T. BROWNE *Relig. Med.* I. §20 That doctrine of Epicurus, that denied the Providence of God, was no Atheism..Those that heretofore denied the Divinity of the Holy Ghost. **1681–6** J. SCOTT *Chr. Life* (1747) III. 494 To deny the Resurrection of Christ. **1733** BERKELEY *Th. Vision Vind.* §6 They who deny the Freedom and Immortality of the soul in effect deny its being. **1838** SIR W. HAMILTON *Logic* xxvi. (1866) II. 58 Those who still denied the apparition of ghosts.

b. To refuse to admit the existence of; to reject as non-existent or unreal.

1621 BURTON *Anat. Mel.* I. ii. §1. iii. (1676) 33/1 Many deny Witches at all, or [say] if there be any, they can do no harm. **1879** *Standard* 29 Nov. 5/4 The Albanian League, so often denied, has again been proved to have a real existence.

II. To say 'no' to the claims of.

4. To refuse to recognize or acknowledge (a person or thing) as having a certain character or certain claims; to disown, disavow, repudiate, renounce.

c **1340** *Cursor M.* 20871 (Trin.) Denyinge he [Petur] fel wepynge he ros. **1382** WYCLIF *Luke* xii. 9 Forsoth he that schal denye me bifor men, schal be denyed bifore the aungelis of God. *c* **1400** MAUNDEV. (Roxb.) xi. 45 Þare denyed Petre oure Lord. **1533** GAU *Richt Vay* 16 Thay that denisz thair dettis and wil noth pay thair crediturs. **1583** STANYHURST *Æneis* II. (Arb.) 46, I wyl not deny my Greecian ofspring. **1604** JAS. I. *Counterbl.* (Arb.) 100 Why do we not denie God and adore the Deuill, as they doe? **1622** WITHER *St. Peter's Day*, For if thy great apostle said He would not thee denie, Whom he that very night denayd, On what shall we relie? **1726** SHELVOCKE *Voy. round World* (1757) 232 Some of his men..happening to be taken separately, he denied them, and suffered eight of them to be hanged as pyrates. **1848** MACAULAY *Hist. Eng.* I. 176 He could not deny his own hand and seal. **1867** FREEMAN *Norm. Conq.* (1876) I. v. 289 Swegen, the godson of Cæsar, had denied his faith.

b. with complemental obj. or phrase. (Often blending with 1 b.)

1588 SHAKS. *L.L.L.* IV. iii. 119 Thou for whom Ioue would sweare..And denie himselfe for Ioue. **1595** —— *John* I. ii. 251 Hast thou denied thy selfe a Faulconbridge? **1634** SIR T. HERBERT *Trav.* 123 Letters of Credence signed by the King..who..denied them for true.

III. To say 'no' to a request or proposal, or to him who makes it; to refuse.

5. To refuse or withhold (anything asked for, claimed or desired); to refuse to give or grant.

c **1374** CHAUCER *Troylus* II. 1489 Deiphebus..Come hire to preye..To holde hym on þe morwe companye At dyner, which she wolde not denye. **1494** FABYAN *Chron.* I. cc. (R.), He asked a great summe of money of Seynt Edmundes landes, whiche the rulers denayed. *c* **1590** MARLOWE *Faust.* (Rtldg.) 98/1 Not to deny The just requests of those that wish him well. **1628** WITHER *Brit. Rememb.* 268, I will denay No more obedience then by law I may. **1697** DRYDEN *Virg. Georg.* I. 222 Trees their Forrest-fruit deny'd. **1725** POPE *Odyss.* III. 331 The royal dame his lawless suit deny'd. *a* **1839** PRAED *Poems* (1864) II. 161 Thou art very bold to take What we must still deny.

b. Const. (*a*) *To deny* a thing *to* a person, or (*b*) a person a thing. The latter connects this with sense 6; but the personal object was here originally dative, while there it appears to be accusative. In the passive either object may be made subject.

(*a*) **1398** TREVISA *Barth. De P.R.* VI. xii. (1495) 196 Auctoryte of techynge and soueraynte is graunted to men and denyed to wymmen. **1509** BARCLAY *Shyp of Folys* (1874) I. 3 To vs may no hauen in Englonde be denayd. **1509** FISHER *Fun. Serm. C'tess Richmond* Wks. (1876) 297 Mete and drynke was denyed to none of them. **1610** SHAKS. *Timon* IV. iii. 537 Giue to dogges What thou denyest to men. **1712** STEELE *Spect.* No. 278 ¶2 You will not deny your Advice to a distressed Damsel. **1875** JOWETT *Plato* (ed. 2) V. 73 Experience will not allow us to deny a place to art.

(*b*) *c* **1340** *Cursor M.* 1586 (Fairf.) He wende þat god of miȝt walde deny ham heyuen briȝt. **1576** GASCOIGNE *Philomene* (Arb.) 95 To denay His own deare child and sonne in lawe The thing that both did pray. **1593** SHAKS. *2 Hen. VI*, I. iii. 107 Then let him be denay'd the Regent-ship. **1649** H. LAWRENCE *Some Considerat.* 36 No man that considers the premises will deny me this, That [etc.]. **1652** NEEDHAM tr. *Selden's Mare Cl.* 3 It is unjust to denie Merchants or Strangers the benefit of Port, Provisions, Commerce, and Navigation. **1814** D'ISRAELI *Quarrels Auth.* (1867) 424 All the consolations of fame were denied him during his life. **1863** H. COX *Instit.* III. vii. 701 Parliament was denied its proper control over an important branch of public expenditure.

c. *fig.* (predicated of things.)

1632 J. HAYWARD tr. *Biondi's Eromena* 78 Finding no armour that..denied entrance to the fine edge of his damask blade. **1667** MILTON *P.L.* IV. 137 A steep wilderness, whose hairie sides..Access deni'd. **1736** BUTLER *Anal.* I. iii. Wks. 1874 I. 66 The known course of human things..denies to virtue its full scope. **1874** GREEN *Short Hist.* iii. §6. 146 Their [the Friars'] vow of poverty..would have denied them the possession of books.

6. To say 'no' to, to refuse (a person who makes a request or demand); †to reject (a candidate).

c **1340** *Gaw. & Gr. Knt.* 1493 For þat durst I not do, lest I denayed were. *Ibid.* 1497 Ȝif any were so vilanous þat yow denaye wolde. *c* **1400** *Destr. Troy* 7097 He denyet hym anon with a nait wille. *c* **1440** *Gesta Rom.* lxxxv. 405 (Add. MS.), I may not denye you of that ye aske. **1591** GREENE *Maiden's Dream*, The poor were never at their need denaid. *a* **1592** H. SMITH *Serm.* (1637) 508 A number that will denie a poore body of a pennie. **1676** WOOD *Life* (Oxf. Hist. Soc.) II. 338 Richard Healy..stood for Bachelor of Arts and was denied. **1697** DRYDEN *Virg. Past.* v. 141 In his Beauty's Pride; When Youth and Love are hard to be deny'd. **1773** GOLDSM. *Stoops to Conq.* III, This is but a shallow pretence to deny me. **1851** LONGF. *Gold. Leg.*, *Village Church*, Firmly to deny The tempter, though his power is strong. **1858** HAWTHORNE *Fr. & It. Jrnls.* I. 256 Where everybody begs, everybody, as a general rule, must be denied.

7. *to deny oneself*: to withhold from oneself, or refrain from, the gratification of desire; to practise self-denial, self-renunciation, or self-abnegation.

1382 WYCLIF *Matt.* xvi. 24 Ȝif eny man wole cume after me, denye he hym self, and take his crosse, and sue me. *c* **1450** tr. *De Imitatione* III. xxxvii. 107 Sonne, þou maist not haue parfit liberte, but þou denye þiself utterly. **1827** KEBLE *Chr. Y.*, *Morning* xiv, Room to deny ourselves.

†**8.** To refuse *to do* (*be*, or *suffer*) anything. *Obs.*

(Formerly sometimes with negative clause, and elliptically with pronominal substitute (*it*, *which*, etc.) for *infin.*).

a **1400** *Pistill of Susan* 140 Ȝif þou þis neodes deny. *c* **1400** *Ywaine & Gaw.* 80 Ne for us denyd noght for to rise. *a* **1450** *Knt. de la Tour* (1868) 85 The king sent vnto her onis, tuyes, thries, and she denied not to come. **1577–87** HOLINSHED *Chron.* I. 103/1 They flatlie denied to doo anie of those things. **1596** SHAKS. *Tam. Shr.* II. i. 180 If she denie to wed. **1647** MAY *Hist. Parl.* II. iii. 34 The King denied to give any other Answer. **1725** BUTLER *Serm.* vii. (1726) 125 He absolutely denyed to curse Israel. **1781** CRABBE *Poems*, *Library*, Why then denies the studious man to share Man's common good.

absol. **1805** SCOTT *Last Minstr.* II. xxix, And how she blushed, and how she sighed, And, half consenting, half denied, And said that she would die a maid.

†**9.** To refuse permission to, not to allow; to forbid (*to do* anything, *the doing* of it). *Obs.* or *arch.*

a **1533** LD. BERNERS *Huon* lxxxiv. 264 [He] herde how Gerarde offred to goo..how he had denyed hym to go. **1588** SHAKS. *Tit. A.* II. iii. 174 One thing more, That womanhood denies my tongue to tell. **1593** —— *Rich. II*, II. iii. 129, I am denyde to sue my Liuerie here. **1614** RALEIGH *Hist. World* I. 176 This place denieth dispute. **1642** CHAS. I *Answ. Declar. Both Houses* 1 July 55 Inforced..to deny a good Law, for an ill Preamble. *a* **1687** PETTY *Pol. Arith.* x. (1691) 116 The Laws denying Strangers to Purchase. **1715–20** POPE *Iliad* XVI. 463 Patroclus shakes his lance, but fate denies. **1759** JOHNSON *Rasselas* xiv, You may deny me to accompany you, but cannot hinder me from following.

†**10.** To refuse to take or accept. *Obs.*

1590 SPENSER *F.Q.* III. vii. 57 What were those three, The which thy proffred curtesie denayd? **1593** SHAKS. *Rich. II*, II. i. 204 If you..denie his offer'd homage. **1691** WOOD *Life* (Oxf. Hist. Soc.) III. 362 Dr. Beveridge did lately denie the bishoprick of Bath and Wells. **1725** POPE *Odyss.* XVII. 78 Their false addresses gen'rous he deny'd.

11. †**a.** To refuse admittance to (a visitor); to be 'not at home' to. (Akin to 6.) *Obs.*

1596 SHAKS. *1 Hen. IV*, II. iv. 544 If you will deny the Sherife, so: if not, let him enter. **1709** STEELE *Tatler* No. 89 ¶9 When he is too well to deny Company, and too ill to receive them. **1736** SWIFT *Proposal, etc.* Wks. 1824 VII. 373 At doors where they expect to be denied.

b. To refuse access to (a person visited); to announce as 'not at home'. (Akin to 5.)

1665 WOOD *Life* (Oxf. Hist. Soc.) II. 44, I was at Gasington to speake with Mrs. H...but she denied her selfe. **1689** *Ibid.* III. 317, I inquir'd after him; he denied himself. **1711** STEELE *Spect.* No. 96 ¶8 Denying my Lord to impertinent suitors and my Lady to unwelcome visitants. **1777** SHERIDAN *Sch. Scand.* v. ii, He is now in the house, though the servants are ordered to deny him. **1869** TROLLOPE *Ph. Finn* (Tauchn. ed.) III. 76, I had told the servant to deny me. **1885** *Law Times Rep.* LII. 614/2 When a debtor keeps house and denies himself to a creditor.

† **de'ny**, *sb.*[1] *Obs.* Also **denay(e.** [a. F. *déni*, OF. *desni*; also *denoi*, *desnoy*: from stem of *denier* to DENY, orig. *denei-er*, *denoi-er*.] Act of denying.

1. Denial, contradiction of a statement; negation.

1535 JOYE *Apol. Tindale* (Arb.) 6 The Saduceis in denying the lyfe aftir this, denied by the same denye but only those two.

2. Refusal (of what is asked, offered, etc.).

1530 *Proper Dyaloge* (1863) 6 Their chefe lordshippes & londes principall..Unto the clergye they gaue..Which to receiue without excepcion The courteous clergy made no denay. **1600** FAIRFAX *Tasso* XVI. xxv. (R.), Of mild denaies, of tender scornes, of sweet Repulses. **1601** SHAKS. *Twel. N.* II. iv. 127 My loue can giue no place, bide no denay. **1611** SYLVESTER *Du Bartas* II. iv. Schisme (1641) 218/1 Yet use no Threats, nor give them flat Denies. **1622** ROWLANDS *Good Newes* 35 The second widow gaue him the denie.

† **'deny, denye**, *sb.*[2] *Obs. rare*[−1]. [a. OF. *deiené*, *deené*, *dené*, mod.F. *doyenné*, orig. OF. *deienet*:—L. *decānāt-us*.] = DEANERY.

[**1292** BRITTON II. xvii. §6 Sicum dené ou thresorie ou chaunterie.] **1340** *Ayenb.* 42 Dyngnetes of holi cherche, ase byeþ bissopriches, abbayes, oþer denyes [F. *deenez*].

denying (dɪ'naɪɪŋ), *vbl. sb.* [f. DENY *v.* + -ING[1].] The action of the verb DENY; denial, refusal, abnegation.

c **1450** tr. *De Imitatione* II. ix, No better remedie þan pacience & denyeng of myself in þe wille of god. **1483** *Cath. Angl.* 95 A Deniynge, *abdicacio*..*abnegacio*..*negacio*. **1525** LD. BERNERS *Froiss.* II. cci. [cxcvii.] 613 There demaundes and denyenges were longe a debatyng. **1592** WYRLEY *Armorie* 90 He sent me the denaying. **1785** PALEY *Mor. Philos.* (1818) I. 184 There are falsehoods which are not lies..as..a servant's denying his master. **1847** EMERSON *Repr. Men*, *Montaigne* Wks. (Bohn) I. 340 Not at all of universal denying, nor of universal doubting.

de'nying, *ppl. a.* [-ING[2].] That denies.

1600 E. BLOUNT tr. *Conestaggio* 117 He was accounted sparing, giving rather than denying. **1874** MORLEY *Compromise* (1886) 190 The controversial and denying humour.

Hence **de'nyingly** *adv.*, in a way that denies or refuses.

1824 MISS MITFORD *Village* Ser. I. (1863) 51 May shakes her graceful head denyingly. **1859** TENNYSON *Vivien* 336 How hard you look and how denyingly!

† **de'nyte**, *v. Obs. rare.* [app. associated with DENY, and NAIT, NYIT, to deny.] = DENY *v.*

c **1420** *Sir Amadace* (Camden) 56 Say we haue togethir bene, I hope fulle wele he haue me sene, He wille hitte neuyr denyte [*rimes* tite, quite].

deob'struct, *v.* [f. ppl. stem *deobstruct-*, of mod.L. type **deobstruĕre*: see DEOBSTRUENT, OBSTRUCT. Cf. mod.F. *désobstruer* (Tissot 1778).] *trans.* To clear of obstruction.

1653 H. MORE *Antid. Ath.* II. vi. (1712) 57 Hypericon..is a singular good Wound-herb, as useful also for de-obstructing the pores of the Body. **1647** JER. TAYLOR *Dissuas. Popery* Pref., To de-obstruct the passages of necessary truth. **1732** ARBUTHNOT *Rules of Diet* 274 Such as carry off the Fæces and Mucus, deobstruct the Mouths of the Lacteals.

Hence **deob'structed, deob'structing** *ppl. adjs.*; also **deob'struction** *sb.* [F. *désobstruction*], the action of deobstructing; **deob'structive** *a.* [in F. *désobstructif*], having the quality of deobstructing; deobstruent.

1664 EVELYN tr. *Freart's Archit.* Ep. Ded. 9 The de-obstruction of Encounters. **1698** *Phil. Trans.* XX. 432 For rendering it more de-obstructive. **1702** SIR J. FLOYER *ibid.* XXIII. 1169 Both in its discussing quality and deobstructing. **1757** JOHNSTONE *ibid.* L. 548 From the de-obstructed duct. **1782** ELPHINSTON *Martial* III. xlvii. 153 But, above all, the deobstructive beet.

deobstruent (diː'ɒbstruːənt), *a.* and *sb. Med.* [ad. mod.L. type *deobstruent-em* (pr. pple. of **deobstruĕre*), modern f. DE- I. 6 + *obstruĕre* to obstruct. Cf. mod.F. *désobstruant* (Tissot 1778).]

A. *adj.* That removes obstructions by opening the natural passages or pores of the body.

1718 QUINCY *Compl. Disp.* 81 A subtile detergent Oil, which makes them universally deobstruent and opening. **1830** LINDLEY *Nat. Syst. Bot.* 65 Valuable on account of its aperient, deobstruent, and cooling properties.

B. *sb.* A deobstruent medicine or substance.

a **1691** BOYLE *Wks.* V. 118 (R.) A diaphoretic, a deobstruent, a diuretic. **1697** *Phil. Trans.* XIX. 403 They gave her also Vomitives and Deobstruents. **1844** T. J. GRAHAM *Dom. Med.* 14 As an alterative and deobstruent..it [calomel] is employed..in indolent inflammation of the liver.

† **de'obturated**, *pa. pple. Obs.* [DE- I. 6.]

1656 BLOUNT *Glossogr.*, *Deobturated*, shut or stopped from. Dr. Charl[eton] in his *Physiologia*.

† **de'occate.** *Obs. rare*[−0]. [f. L. *deoccāre* to harrow in, f. DE- I. 1 + *occāre* to harrow.]

1623 COCKERAM, *Deoccate*, to harrow, or clod the Land.

deoch an doris (dɒxən'dɒrɪs, djɒx-). *Chiefly Sc.* and *Irish.* Also **deoc(h)-an-doruis, deoch-an-dorris, deoch an dorus, doch-an-dorris**, etc. [Gael. *deoch an doruis*, lit. 'drink at the door'.] A parting drink, a stirrup-cup.

1682–91 J. FRASER *Chron. Frasers* (1905) 124 That ordinary farewell drink, a parting called Deoch i Dorrish, which, as it is said, Prior Dawson had invented. *Ibid.* 366 He must drink Doch in Dorris, a homely drow which the Highlanders takes [*sic*] with their familiars. **1810** W. HICKEY *Memoirs* (1925) IV. 343 Sir George..insisted upon our taking the *Dukkin Doreege* (I know not whether I spell it correctly. It means the parting glass, or glass at the door, in the Irish language). **1819** SCOTT *Br. Lamm.* II. iv. 85 The Lord Keeper, the Master, and the domestics, had drunk *doch-an-dorroch*, or the stirrup-cup, in the liquors adapted to their various ranks. **1824** —— *Redgauntlet* I. ii. 22 This was a parting cup..and..fell under the exception of *Dochan dorroch.* **1839** D. M. MOIR *Life Mansie Wauch* xxii. 283 To give Peter Farrel a dram by way of 'doch-an-dorris', as the Gaelic folk say. **1866** 'AN OLD STAGER' *Stage Reminisc.* 13 Having partaken of *deoch an doruis* with our worthy host, we left the house. **1892** W. EWING *Poems* 14 Then doch and dorus wis proposed. **1912** LAUDER & HARPER *It's Nice when you love a Wee Lassie* 3 We gave them as much as they wanted to eat, An' a wee deoch an' doris before their retreat. **1914** JOYCE *Dubliners* 96 Let us have another one as a *deoc an doruis.* **1915** A. D. GILLESPIE *Lett. from Flanders* (1916) 240 An impromptu concert, which wound up with a song from me and 'wee doch-an-dorris' from Bankier. **1920** *Glasgow Herald* 17 Nov. 9 A deoch an doris or a kindly pledge in whisky. **1931** A. J. CRONIN *Hatter's Castle* II. iv. 199 I'm wi' ye, juist a wee deoch-an-dorris to keep out the cauld. **1970** *Guardian* 2 June 12/7 The Scot['s]..last drink, the *deoch an doris*, by ancient custom must be taken standing, and..need not be paid for.

† **de'ocular**, *a. Obs.* [f. L. *de-* privative (cf. DE- I. 6, II. 3) + *oculus* eye, *oculāris* of the eyes: cf. L. *dēformis* shapeless, *dēprandis* without dinner, fasting.] Not using the eyes; blind.

1632 LITHGOW *Trav.* I. 22 It is a deocular error. *Ibid.* x. 506 Zetland, and the adjacent Iles there; have found such a sting of deoccular government within these few yeares.

de'oculate, *v. nonce-wd.* [f. DE- II. 1 + L. *oculus* eye + -ATE[3].] *trans.* To deprive of eyes, or of eyesight.

1816 LAMB *Let. to Wordsworth*, *Final Mem.* I. 188 Dorothy, I hear, has mounted spectacles; so you have deoculated two of your dearest relations in life.

deodand ('diːəʊdænd). [a. AFr. *deodande*, ad. med.(Anglo-)L. *deōdandum*, i.e. *Deō dandum* that is to be given to God.] A thing forfeited or to be given to God; *spec.* in *Eng. Law*, a personal chattel which, having been the immediate occasion of the death of a human being, was given to God as an expiatory offering, i.e. forfeited to the Crown to be applied to pious uses, e.g. to be distributed in alms. (Abolished in 1846.)

[**1292** BRITTON I. ii. §14 Volums ausi qe le vessel et quant qe leynz serra trové soit prisé cum deodande et enroule par le Corouner.] **1523** in W. H. Turner *Select. Rec. Oxford* 34 The..Chauncelor..shall have deodands. **1529** MORE *Dyaloge* III. Wks. 235/2 The kynges almoygners, to whome the goodes of such men as kyll themselfe be appoynted by the lawe..as deodandes to be geuen in almes. **1613** SIR H. FINCH *Law* (1636) 214 If a man being vpon a Cart carrying Faggots..fall downe by the mouuing of one of the horses in the Cart, and die of it; both that and all the other horses in the Cart, and the Cart it selfe, are forfeit. And these are called Deodands. **1627** SIR R. BOYLE *Diary* (1886) II. 222 [A] boat..being forfeicted to me for a deodant. **1705** HICKERINGILL *Priest-cr.* I. (1721) 42 The Sinners did bequeath these Estates..to Ecclesiastical Locusts and Caterpillars, calling them *Deodands*, or *given to God*, that's the Priest-craft Word. **1755** *Gentl. Mag.* XXV. 232 The inquest..brought in their verdict accidental death by an ox, and found the ox a deodand. **1765** BLACKSTONE *Comm.* I. 302 If a man falls from a boat or ship in fresh water, and is drowned, it hath been said, that the vessel and cargo are in strictness of law a deodand. **1827** *Gentl. Mag.* XCVII. II. 13 Apprehensive that the diamonds, if they entered the church, might be claimed as a deodand to the altar. **1845** STEPHEN *Laws Eng.* II. 551. **1882** *Times* 3 Aug. 7/4 Deodands are also things of the past.

b. *loosely.* The amount to be forfeited as the value of a deodand.

1831 TRELAWNY *Adv. Younger Son* I. 58 The master without appealing to me, laid a deodand on the gun. **1838** *Mech. Mag.* XXIX. 368 The jury levy a deodand of £1500, upon the boiler or steam engine of the Victoria. **1842** *Ibid.* XXXVI. 6 Deodand after deodand has been imposed by honest and indignant juries.

‖**deodar** (ˈdiːəʊdɑː(r)). Also in mod.L. form **deodara** (diːəʊˈdɑːrə). [a. Hindī *dē̆ōdār*, *dēwdār*:—Skr. *deva-dāra* divine tree, tree or timber of the gods. (The name occurs already in Avicenna *c* 1030 as *diūdār*. It is given in various parts of India to other trees besides this with which it has come into Europe.)]

A sub-species of cedar (*Cedrus Libani*, var. *Deodara*), a large tree closely allied to the cedar of Lebanon, found native in the Western Himālayas from Nepāl to Afghanistan, and now largely grown as an ornamental tree in England. The wood is of extreme durability.

[**1804** GOTT in Roxb. *Flora Indica* III. 652 The only account I can give you of the Devdar pine is from..enquiries..made of the natives. **1814** W. ROXBURGH *Hort. Bengal* 69 *Pinus Deodara.* Hindoostani, *Deva-daroo.* **1833** *Penny Cycl.* I. 34/1 *Abies Deodara*, the Sacred Indian Fir. The Hindoos call it the *Devadara* or God-tree, and hold it in a sort of veneration.] **1842** P. J. SELBY *Brit. Forest Trees* 539 The timber of the deodar employed in buildings. **1871** *Sat. Rev.* 29 Apr. 53 A ton of deodar seeds was ordered from India, and twelve hundred pounds' worth of deodar plants stuck into a heathy bank. **1884** Q. VICTORIA *More Leaves* 370, I afterwards planted a deodara on the lawn.

†**deodate** (ˈdiːəʊdeɪt), *sb.* and *a.* *Obs.* [ad. L. *deō datum* given to God: in sense 2, taken as = *ā deō datum* given by God.]

A. *sb.* **1.** A thing given to God.

a **1600** HOOKER *Eccl. Pol.* VII. xxii. §4 Their Corban..wherein that blessed widows deodate was laid up.

2. A thing given by God, a gift from God.

a **1633** G. HERBERT in Walton *Life* (1670) 65 All my Tythes and Church-dues are a deodate from Thee, O my God.

B. *adj.* Given by God.

1654 GAYTON *Pleas. Notes* IV. 248, I gather'd up the Deodate good Gold.

deodorant (diːˈəʊdərənt), *sb.* [Formed as if from a L. **deodōrant-em*, pr. pple. of **deodōrāre*, f. *odōr-em* smell, ODOUR, on analogy of *dēcolōrāre*: see DE- I. 6. (The long *ō* is taken over from *odour*: cf. next.)] A substance or preparation that destroys the odour of fetid effluvia, etc.; a deodorizer.

1869 ROSCOE *Elem. Chem.* 106 Employed as a disinfectant and deodorant.

deodorize (diːˈəʊdəraɪz), *v.* [f. DE- II. 1 + L. *odor* ODOUR + -IZE.] *trans.* To deprive of odour, *esp.* of offensive or noisome odour; to take away the (bad) smell of. Also *fig.*

1858 *Sat. Rev.* V. 632/1 To defecate and deodorize the sewage of London. **1870** *Observer* 13 Nov., Liquid portions of the sewage..when deodorised being allowed to flow away.

fig. **1863** *Sat. Rev.* 203 Sin and wickedness are carefully deodorised now-a-days before they can get into print.

Hence **deˈodorized, deˈodorizing** *ppl. adjs.*; also **deodoriˈzation**, removal of (bad) smell.

1856 *Engineer* II. 671/3 (Sewage of towns) The deodorising system has..achieved a perfect success at Leicester. *Ibid.* 672/1 Deodorisation, in its practical sense, does not simply mean the removal of offensive smell, but the purification of the water by the abstraction of all extraneous matter. *c* **1865** LETHEBY in *Circ. Sc.* I. 97/1 A bleaching and deodorising agent. **1875** H. C. WOOD *Therap.* (1879) 226 The deodorized tincture of opium. **1876** HARLEY *Mat. Med.* 179 The essential properties of chlorinated compounds are bleaching and deodorising.

deˈodorizer. [f. DEODORIZE + -ER.] Something that deodorizes; a deodorizing agent.

1849 J. F. JOHNSTON *Exper. Agric.* 265 Both as a fixer of ammonia, and as a deodoriser or remover of smells. **1892** *Pall Mall G.* 7 Sept. 2/1 The deodoriser is run through a six-inch pipe to the great sewer.

deol, -ful, obs. forms of DOLE, DOLEFUL.

†**deˈonerate,** *v.* *Obs.* [f. L. *deonerāre* to disburden, f. DE- I. 6 + *onerāre* to load, *onus, oner-* load.] *trans.* To disburden.

1623 COCKERAM, *Deonerate*, to unload. **1651** *Raleigh's Ghost* 80 To deonerate and disburden the body of the excrementall part of meat and food.

deontic (diːˈɒntɪk), *sb.* and *a.* *Philos.* [f. Gr. δέον, δεοντ- (see DEONTOLOGY) + -IC.]

A. *sb.* **1.** *Pl.* [After *ethics*, *eudemonics*, etc.] (See quots.)

a **1866** J. GROTE *Moral Ideals* (1876) vii. 102 A science of duty (deontics or deontology). **1906** J. S. STUART-GLENNIE in *Sociol Pap.* II. 250 The second order of ethical sciences..form the contents of three classes of sciences—Economics, Deontics, and Juridics. **1929** *Mind* XXXVIII. 275 *Deontics*..., meaning..that which, either perfectly or in a definite degree, is obligatory upon all.

2. *sing.* (See quot.)

1926 *Mind* XXXV. 395 Ethical arguments..should be able to exhibit their 'deontic' in the same way as inference reveals its 'logic'.

B. *adj.* Of or relating to duty, obligation, etc.

1951 *Mind* LX. 1 (*title*) Deontic logic. **1955** A. N. PRIOR *Formal Logic* 221 There are 'laws of movement' of deontic operators analogous to those of ordinary modal operators.

deontological (diːɒntəʊˈlɒdʒɪkəl), *a.* [f. as DEONTOLOGY + -IC + -AL[1].] Of, pertaining to, or according to deontology.

a **1832** BENTHAM *Deontology* (1834) I. i. 20 Let the moralist regard the great Deontological Law, as steadily as the Turnsole looks upon the Sun. **1867** J. H. STIRLING tr. *Schwegler's Hist. Philos.* (ed. 8) 129 The special theory of ethical action was completely elaborated by the later Stoics, who were thus the founders of all deontological schemes.

deontologist (ˌdiːɒnˈtɒlədʒɪst). [f. DEONTOLOG-Y + -IST.] One who treats of deontology.

a **1832** BENTHAM *Deontology* (1834) I. ii. 27 [It] separates the dominions of the Legislator from those of the Deontologist.

deontology (ˌdiːɒnˈtɒlədʒɪ). [f. Gr. δέον, δεοντ- that which is binding, duty (neuter of pr. pple. of δεῖ it is binding, it behoves) + -λογια discourse.] The science of duty; that branch of knowledge which deals with moral obligations; ethics.

1826 BENTHAM in *West. Rev.* VI. 448 Ethics has received the more expressive name of *Deontology*. *a* **1832** —— *Deontology* (1834) I. ii. 28 Deontology or Private Ethics, may be considered the science by which happiness is created out of motives extra-legislatorial. **1868** GLADSTONE *Juv. Mundi* vii. (1870) 214 A system which may be called one of deontology, or that which ought to be, and to be done. **1883** *Syd. Soc. Lex.* s.v., *Medical deontology*, the duties and rights of medical practitioners.

deoperculate (diːəʊˈpɜːkjʊlət), *a.* *Bot.* [f. DE- I. 6 + L. *operculātus*, pa. pple. of *operculāre* to cover with a lid: see OPERCULATE.] Having lost the operculum: see also quots.

1866 *Treas. Bot.*, *Deoperculate*, a term used in describing mosses, when the operculum will not separate spontaneously from the spore-cases. **1883** *Syd. Soc. Lex.*, *Deoperculate*..Also, without an operculum.

deoˈperculate, *v.* *Bot.* [See prec. and -ATE[3].] *intr.* To shed the operculum.

Mod. Liverworts with deoperculating capsules.

†**deoppilate** (diːˈɒpɪleɪt), *v.* *Med. Obs.* [f. DE- II. 1 + OPPILATE: in mod. medical L. *deoppilāre*, f. L. *oppilāre* to stop up.] *trans.* To free from obstruction; *absol.* to remove obstructions.

1620 VENNER *Via Recta* vii. 134 It..deoppilateth or vnstoppeth the veines. **1710** T. FULLER *Pharm. Extemp.* 214 For Raisins of the Sun..deoppilate more than Malaga. *Ibid.* 421 Aperitives ought to..deoppilate the Interstices.

So **deˈoppilant** *a.*, that removes obstructions; **deoppiˈlation**, the removal of obstructions; **deˈoppilative** *a.*, tending to remove obstructions, deobstruent; *sb.* a medicine or drug having this quality.

1625 HART *Anat. Ur.* I. ii. 31 Cordiall and deoppilatiue medicines. **1646** SIR T. BROWNE *Pseud. Ep.* III. xxii. 165 It becomes effectuall in deopilations. **1684** tr. *Bonet's Merc. Compit.* VIII. 313 An excellent deoppilative. **1712** tr. *Pomet's Hist. Drugs* I. 162 It is an universal Digestive and Deoppilative. **1854** MAYNE *Expos. Lex.* 264 Aperient, deobstruent, deoppilant; applied to medicines. **1862** MARSH *Eng. Lang.* 89 To produce that salutary deopilation of the spleen which the French hold to be so serviceable to the health of sedentary gentlemen.

deor, obs. form of DEAR, DEER.

de-ˈorbit, *v.* [f. DE- II. 1 + ORBIT *v.*] **a.** *intr.* Of a spacecraft, etc.: to leave or move out of orbit. **b.** *trans.* To send or take out of orbit.

1962 *Flight Internat.* LXXXI. 64/1 The ability to orbit, manœuvre, rendezvous, 'de-orbit', re-enter and land..and the ability to transfer men and material between spacecraft, were cited by Mr Gardner as common needs for both military and scientific/exploration types of space systems. **1963** *Atlantic Monthly* Aug. 49 Warheads de-orbited from satellites could reach their targets..quickly. **1969** *New Scientist* 27 Feb. 449 (*caption*) CSM deorbits and command module separates from service module. **1971** *Physics Bull.* Dec. 717/2 Salyut was eventually de-orbited and burnt up over the Pacific Ocean on 11 October. **1977** *Aviation Week & Space Technol.* 24 Oct. 45/2 NASA want to either reboost or deorbit the Skylab space station on that mission. **1985** *Aerospace America* Nov. 51/2 The entry capsule is separated, de-orbits, and enters the Martian atmosphere.

de-ˈorbit, *sb.* [f. the vb.] The act or process of moving out of orbit by a spacecraft. Also *attrib.*, esp. as ***de-orbit burn***.

1967 *New Scientist* 16 Nov. 424 The critical factor will be to determine the moment of de-orbit. **1976** *Times* 4 Sept. 4/3, I guess I don't know whether that deorbit burn (the rocket firing) happened or not. **1981** *Daily Tel.* 15 Apr. 1/2 A second 'de-orbit burn' three minutes later jockeyed the craft into a nose-high position for re-entry.

†**deˈordinate,** *a.* *Obs.* [ad. med.L. *deordinātus*, f. DE- I. 6 + *ordinātus* ordered. A doublet of *disordinate.*] Perverted from the natural order; inordinate.

1623 T. AILESBURY *Serm.* (1624) 13 The Idolatry consisted..in the deordinate intent of the Sacrificers. **1720** WELTON *Suffer. Son of God* II. xxiv. 641 The Principles of a Deordinate and Excessive Self-Love.

†**deˈordinate,** *v.* *Obs.* [f. med.L. verbal type **deordināre*: see prec. and -ATE[3] 5.] *trans.* To pervert from the natural order.

1688 NORRIS *Theory Love* II. ii. 107 A sensual pleasure deordinated from the end..for which it was designed.

deordination (diːɔːdɪˈneɪʃən). Now *rare* or *Obs.* [ad. med.L. *deordinātiōn-em* (Du Cange), n. of action f. verbal type **deordināre* (It. *disordinare*, OF. *desordener*) to disorder, f. DE- I. 6 + *ordināre* to order, *ordin-em* order. A doublet of *disordination.*]

1. Departure from or violation of order, *esp.* of moral order; disorder.

1596 BELL *Surv. Popery* III. ix. 378 The guilte and the deordination. **1635** SIBBES *Soules Confl.* xii. §3. 166 This sheweth us what a wonderfull deordination and disorder is brought upon mans nature. **1647** JER. TAYLOR *Dissuas. Popery* i. (1686) 99 She refuses to run into the same excess of riot and de-ordination. **1688** NORRIS *Theory Love* II. ii. 101 A deordination from the end of Nature. **1891** MANNING in *Dublin Rev.* July 157 It denotes an abuse, an excess, a de-ordination in human society.

2. Departure from ordinary or normal condition, as in physical deformity, decomposition, etc.

1686 GOAD *Celest. Bodies* III. iii. 472 A Token of the Dissolution, and as it were the Deordination of the Compound. *Ibid.* III. iv. 505 Under these years, the same Deordination is found in Animals, Lambs, Hares, Calves.

deore, obs. form of DEAR *a.* and *adv.*

de-organize, de-orientalize: see DE- II. 1.

deorling, deoreling, early ff. DARLING.

‖**deˈorsum,** *adv.* *nonce-use.* [L. = downwards.] Downward.

1770 J. CLUBBE *Physiognomy* 19 There is the same stupidity..the same deorsum tendency in the one as in the other.

deorwurðe, var. DEARWORTH *a.* *Obs.* precious.

†**deˈosculate,** *v.* *Obs.* *rare*—[0]. [f. L. *deosculārī* to kiss warmly or affectionately, f. DE- I. 3 + *osculārī* to kiss.] To kiss affectionately. Hence †**deoscuˈlation**, kissing.

1623 COCKERAM, *Deosculate*, to kiss sweetly. **1658** PHILLIPS, *Deosculation*, a kissing with eagernesse. *a* **1699** STILLINGFL. (J.), Acts of worship required to be performed to images, viz.' processions, genuflections, thurifications, and deosculations. **1755** AMORY *Memoirs* 440 *note.* **1783** AINSWORTH *Lat. Dict.* (Morell) I, Deosculation, *osculatio.*

de-ossify, -fication: see DE- II. 1.

‖**Deo volente** (ˈdiːəʊ vəʊˈlɛntiː). Also (erron.) Deo volens. [L.] God willing; if nothing prevents (the fulfilment of a promise). Abbrev. D.V. (D III. 3).

1767 GRAY *Let.* 6 June in *Wks.* (1884) III. 268 My intention is (*Deo volente*) to come to Cambridge on Friday or Saturday next. **1854** E. K. KANE *Jrnl.* 11 Sept. in *Arctic Explor.* (1856) I. xxvii. 356 *Deo volente*, I will be more lucky tomorrow. **1954** M. LOWRY *Let.* 25 Jan. (1967) 360 Deo volens, they will more than get it back in the end. **1957** B. & C. EVANS *Dict. Contemp. Amer. Usage* 131/1 The use of the phrase 'D.V.', the initials of *Deo volente*, or the English form *God willing*, as an interjection after an expressed intention is a verbal counterpart of knocking on wood and has about the same value.

deoxidate (diːˈɒksɪdeɪt), *v.* *Chem.* Also 8–9 **deoxy-**. [f. DE- II. 1 + OXIDATE *v.*] *trans.* To reduce from the state of an oxide, to remove the oxygen from (an oxide or other compound); *intr.* to undergo deoxidation. Hence **de'oxidated** *ppl. a.*; **de'oxidating** *ppl. a.*, causing or suffering deoxidation.

1799 Sir H. Davy in Beddoes *Contrib. Phys. & Med. Knowl.* 73 Phosoxygen is produced, and the metals deoxydated. **1808** —— in *Phil. Trans.* XCIX. 90 Dark brown matter was separated at the deoxydating surface. **1801** Hatchett in *Phil. Trans.* XCII. 66 The white oxide.. may be deoxidated to a certain degree. **1837** R. Bede *Pract. Chem.* 10 The latter [flame of a blow-pipe] is called oxidating, the former deoxidating.

deoxidation (diːɒksɪ'deɪʃən). [n. of action f. prec. vb.] The removal of oxygen from an oxide or other compound.

1799 Sir H. Davy in Beddoes *Contrib. Phys. & Med. Knowl.* 70 It is necessary that the temperature of de-oxydation be greater than that of oxydation. **1801** Wollaston in *Phil. Trans.* XCI. 430 The pile of Volta decomposes water, and produces other effects of oxidation and de-oxidation. **1883** G. Allen in *Nature* 8 Mar. 439 The function of a leaf is the absorption of carbonic acid from the air, and its deoxidation under the influence of sunlight.

de'oxidator. [agent-n. f. deoxidate *v.*: see -or.] A deoxidating agent or apparatus.

c **1865** J. Wylde in *Circ. Sc.* I. 396/2 The charcoal is employed as a deoxidator.

deoxidize (diː'ɒksɪdaɪz), *v. Chem.* Also 9 deoxyd-. [f. de- II. 1 + oxidize.] = deoxidate.

1794 [see deoxidizing below]. **1800** Henry *Epit. Chem.* (1808) 50 Its action is.. exerted in de-oxidizing bodies. **1810** —— *Elem. Chem.* (1826) I. 533 The silica, also.. is partly de-oxidized. **1869** E. A. Parkes *Pract. Hygiene* (ed. 3) 357 Whether disinfectants act by oxidising, or by deoxidising.

Hence **de'oxidized** *ppl. a.*, **de'oxidizing** *ppl. a.* and *vbl. sb.*; also **deoxidi'zation**, **de'oxidizement**, **de'oxidizer**.

1794 G. Adams *Nat. & Exp. Philos.* I. App. 527 The de-oxidizing power of the solar rays. **1805** Lane in *Phil. Trans.* XCV. 282 The deoxidising property of light. **1847** Craig, *Deoxydization*, deoxydation. *c* **1860** Faraday *Forces Nat.* vi. 200 *note*, A colourless deoxidised indigo. **1862** H. Spencer *First Princ.* II. viii. §70 Animals, in some of their minor processes, are probably de-oxidizers. **1877** W. Thomson *Voy. Challenger* I. iv. 279 Due to some deoxidizing process.

deoxy-, *prefix. Chem.* [f. de- II. 3 + oxy- 2.] A prefix used in forming the names of chemical compounds, indicating the loss of one or more atoms of oxygen; = desoxy- (which is less common).

1871 *Jrnl. Chem. Soc.* XXIV. 404 Deoxycodeine, $C_{18}H_{21}NO_2$. **1949** *Biochem Jrnl. Suggestions to Authors* 9 Spellings, etc., adopted.. deoxy (prefix) *not* desoxy.

deoxy,cortico'sterone. *Biochem.* Also desoxy-. [f. deoxy- + corticosterone.] A steroid compound, $C_{21}H_{30}O_3$, occuring in the adrenal cortex and also prepared synthetically.

1937 Steiger & Reichstein in *Nature* 29 May 926/1 This compound differs from corticosterone only by the absence of the fourth oxygen, and can therefore also be called desox-corticosterone. **1938** *Chem. Abstr.* XXXII. 578 The structure of the biol. active desoxycorticosterone from stigmasterol. **1941** *Ann. Reg. 1940* 344 Deoxycorticosterone was prepared artifically. **1952** G. Bourne et. al. *Cytology* (ed. 2) xi. 478 From the adrenal cortex there have been extracted two main groups of physiologically active steroids. One group, exemplified by desoxycorticosterone, acts primarily on the salt balance of the body and regulates the excretion of Na and Cl by the kidney. **1956** *Nature* 28 Jan. 189/2 Comparisons are being made of the wool growth of adrenalectomized sheep maintained on different levels of cortisone and deoxycorticosterone. **1965** *New Scientist* 1 July 33/1 The true mineralocorticoid hormone is aldosterone, but there are compounds such as deoxycorticosterone and fluorocortisol that have potent related properties.

deoxy'cortone. *Biochem.* [Shortened from prec.] = prec.

1949 *Lancet* 28 Jan. 159/1 Deoxycortone plus ascorbic acid.. seems to be an effective substitute for the naturally occurring anti-arthritic sterol hormone. *Ibid.* 26 Nov. 993/1 The patients were treated with an intramuscular injection of 5 mg. Deoxycortone (desoxycorticosterone) acetate in 1 ml. of oleum arachis. **1963** *Brit. Pharmaceutical Codex* 233 Deoxycortone is a mineralocorticosteroid which causes sodium retention and potassium excretion. It is used.. in the treatment of Addison's disease.

deoxygenate (diː'ɒksɪdʒɪneɪt), *v. Chem.* [f. de- II. 1 + oxygenate *v.*] *trans.* To deprive of (free) oxygen; also = deoxidate, deoxidize.

1799 Kirwan *Geol. Ess.* 150 By deoxygenating the vitriolic contained in the Epsom salt. **1804** T. Trotter *Drunkenness* iii. 58 Alkohol certainly deoxygenates the blood in some degree. **1808** Sir H. Davy in *Phil. Trans.* XCVIII. 336 Potassium may partially de-oxygenate the earths.

Hence **de'oxygenated** *ppl. a.*, **de'oxygenating** *vbl. sb.* and *ppl. a.*; also **deoxyge'nation**.

1799 Sir H. Davy in Beddoes *Contrib. Phys. & Med. Knowl.* 86 A deoxygenated atmosphere. **1803** —— in *Phil. Trans.* XCIII. 271 The deoxygenation of skin. **1832** Babbage *Econ. Manuf.* xxiii. (ed. 3) 239 An oxygenating or a deoxygenating flame. **1834** Mrs. Somerville *Connect. Phys. Sc.* xxiv. (1849) 224 The most refrangible extremity of the spectrum has an oxygenizing power and the other that of deoxygenating. **1878** Foster *Phys.* II. i. §2. 210 The ordinary deoxygenation of the blood.

deoxygenize (diː'ɒksɪdʒɪnaɪz), *v. Chem.* [f. de- II. 1 + oxygenize *v.*] = deoxygenate.

1881 Günther in *Encycl. Brit.* XII. 687/1 Until the air is so much deoxygenized as to render a renewal of it necessary.

de,oxyribo'nucleic 'acid. *Biochem.* Also desoxy-. [f. deoxyribo(se + nucleic *a.*] A generic term for any of the nucleic acids which yield deoxyribose on hydrolysis, which are generally found in and confined to the chromosomes of higher organisms, and which store genetic information. Also called ***deoxy-, desoxyribose nucleic acid***. Abbrev. D.N.A., DNA.

1931 Levene & Bass *Nucleic Acids* ix. 294 (*heading*) Desoxyribonucleic acids. **1938** *Jrnl. Chem. Soc.* 1722 Secondly there are deoxyribonucleic acids, in which the sugar component is d-2-deoxyribose and of which 'thymus nucleic acid' is the classical example. **1944** *Jrnl. Biol. Chem.* CLVI. 691 The key rôle of the desoxyribose type of these substances in the reproduction of inheritable characteristics has been emphasized by the identification of desoxyribose nucleic acid (DNA) as a major component of chromosomal nucleoprotein. **1947** *Thorpe's Dict. Appl. Chem.* (ed. 4) VIII. 622/1 Deoxyribonucleic acid has been identified in only a few viruses, for example those of psittacosis,.. vaccinia,.. influenza [etc.]. **1951** *Lancet* 16 June 1287/1 In normal animal and plant cells deoxyribonucleic acid (D.N.A.) is located entirely within the nucleus. **1953** *Sci. News* XXIX. 109 The structure proposed for the salts of deoxyribose nucleic acid consists of two chains coiled in the same direction about the same axis. **1955** *New Biol.* XIX. 9 DNA molecules are chains which can be broken down into nucleotides. Each nucleotide molecule can be broken down by hydrolysis into a molecule of phosphoric acid, one of deoxyribose (a five carbon sugar) and one of a purine (adenine or guanine) or of a pyrimidine (thymine, cytosine or 5-methyl cytosine, but in some phages thymine or 5-hydroxy-methyl-cytosine). **1955** *Sci. Amer.* Oct. 70/3 The chromosomes are made largely of DNA (desoxyribonucleic acid). DNA can exist in a great multitude of forms, all built of the same building blocks but with the units arranged in different sequences. The hereditary information carried by a DNA molecule is contained in the order of arrangement of these units. **1962** A. Huxley *Let.* 26 Dec. (1969) 945 He talked such nonsense ..about true intelligence residing only in the DNA molecule. **1964** *Listener* 19 Mar 493/2 The spiral of deoxyribonucleic acid. **1970** *Nature* 5 Sept. 998/2 Demolition of the hallowed idea of the molecular biologist that RNA cannot synthesize DNA has prompted a reinvestigation of other ideas.

Hence **,deoxyribo'nuclease** [-ase], any enzyme that catalyses the hydrolysis of DNA, causing it to split up into smaller nucleotide units.

1946 *Jrnl. Biol. Chem.* CLXVI. 393 (*heading*) Streptomycin and desoxyribonuclease in the study of variations in the properties of a bacterial virus. **1965** Peacocke & Drysdale *Molecular Basis Heredity* vii. 69 If.. one or other of the two nucleic acids has been eliminated from the material by digestion with a specific enzyme (deoxyribonuclease or ribonuclease), the remaining nucleic acid can be located. **1970** R. W. McGilvery *Biochem.* xx. 481 Degradation of nucleic acids begins with partial hydrolysis.. catalysed by ribonucleases or deoxyribonucleases.

de,oxyribo,nucleo'protein. *Biochem.* Also desoxy-. [f. deoxy-.] 'A nucleoprotein that yields a deoxyribonucleic acid on hydrolysis' (Webster 1961). Abbrev. D.N.A.P.

1944 *Jrnl. Biol. Chem.* CLVI. 692 Most desoxyribonucleoproteins contain very small amounts of tryptophane. **1955** *Sci. News Let.* 30 Apr. 280/3 The chemical has properties which place it in the class of biologically important substances termed deoxyribonucleoproteins... The substances are giant molecules which are found exclusively in the chromosomes and appear to be the carriers of cell heredity. **1961** *Lancet* 19 Aug. 436/2 One of these.. was probably glycoprotein in nature, and was clearly different from the desoxyribonucleoprotein (d.n.a.p.).

deoxy'ribose. *Biochem.* Also desoxy-. [f. deoxy- + ribose.] Any of the sugars derived from ribose by the replacement of a hydroxyl group by a hydrogen atom; **deoxyribose nucleic acid**: see deoxyribonucleic acid.

1931 Levene & Bass *Nucleic Acids* i. 26 This reaction is now the general method for the preparation of 2-desoxy sugars. By this procedure 2-desoxyribose [etc.].. have been prepared. **1961** *Times* 18 Aug. 12/4 The sugar component of the nucleic acid of chromosomes is known chemically as deoxyribose. **1967** *Listener* 3 Aug. 142/1 Each nucleotide is composed of a base, a sugar called deoxyribose, and phosphate.

deozonize, to deprive of ozone: see de- II. 1.

dep, obs. f. deep; (*dep.*) abbrev. of deputy.

† **de'pact**, *ppl. a. Obs.* [ad. L. *dēpact-us*, pa. pple. of *dēpangĕre* to drive down, fix into the ground, etc.] Fixed down, fastened.

1634 T. Johnson *Parey's Chirurg.* xi. xx. (1678) 293 If the Weapon be so depact and fastned in a Bone that you cannot drive it forth on the other side.

depaganize, depantheonize: see de- II. 1.

† **de'paint**, *sb. Obs. rare*⁻¹. [f. depaint *v.*] Painting, pictorial representation.

1594 *Zepheria* xvii. in Arb. *Garner* V. 73 How shall I deck my Love in love's habiliment And her embellish in a right depaint?

† **de'paint**, *ppl. a. Obs.* Forms: 3–4 depeint, 4–5 -peynt, 4–6 -paynt, 6 depaint. [ME. *depeint*, a. F. *depeint*, pa. pple. of *depeindre* (13th c. in Hatzf.), ad. L. *dēpingĕre* to depict, after F. *peindre* to paint. After the formation of the verb (see next) gradually superseded by the normal *depainted*.] Depicted, painted, delineated; ornamented; coloured: see the verb. Chiefly as *pa. pple.*

a **1225** *Ancr. R.* 396 'In manibus meis descripsi te' [Isa. xlix. 16]. Ich habbe, he seið, depeint þe in mine honden. **1303** R. Brunne *Handl. Synne* 8739 Þey shul be leyde yn toumbe of stone And hys ymage ful feyre depeynte Ry3t as he were a cors seynt. *c* **1325** *E.E. Allit. P.* A. 1101, & coronde wern alle of þe same fasoun, Depaynt in perlez & wedez qwyte. **1430** Lydg. *Chron. Troy* I. v, Vnder flowers depeynt of stablenesse. *c* **1500** *Lancelot* 1703 Bot cherice them with wordis fair depaynt. **1557** *Tottell's Misc.* (Arb.) 215 Her handes depaint with veines all blew and white.

† **depaint** (dɪ'peɪnt), *v. Obs.* or *arch.* Forms: 4–5 depeint(e, -peynt(e, -paynt(e, 6–7 depaynt (6 depant, 7–8 depeint), 6– depaint. [ME. *depeint-en*, f. *depeint* pa. pple.; taken as Eng. repr. of F. *depeindre* (3rd sing. pres. *il depeint*): see prec. *Depeint* was connected with depict by the transitional forms depeinct, *depinct*.]

1. *trans.* To represent or portray in colours, to paint; to depict; to delineate.

a **1225**, **1303** [see depaint *ppl. a.*]. *c* **1325** *Coer de L.* 2963 Off red sendel were her baneres, With three gryffouns depayntyd wel. *c* **1340** *Gaw. & Gr. Knt.* 649 Þe kny3t comlyche hade In þe more half of his schelde hir ymage depaynted. *c* **1350** *Will. Palerne* 3573, & bereth in his blasoun of a brit hewe A wel huge werwolf wonderli depeinted. *c* **1440** *Gesta Rom.* xxxix. 362 (Add. MS.) He did make a walle white, and with rede Coloure he depeynted the Image of the woman. **1570** B. Googe *Pop. Kingd.* I. (1880) 10 With crosse depainted braue upon his backe and eke his brest. **1604** T. Wright *Passions* vi. 294 The Geographers.. depaint in theyr Cardes.. the Countries and Cities adioyning. **1659** T. Pecke *Parnassi Puerp.* 77 Apelles could not depaint Motion. **1748** Thomson *Cast. Indol.* I. 326 Those pleased the most, where, by a cunning hand, Depeinten [*pseudo-archaic pa. pple.*] was the patriarchal age. *fig.* **1595** Daniel *Sonnets* 4 No colours can depaint my sorrows. **1848** J. A. Carlyle tr. *Dante's Inferno* (1849) 37 The anguish of the people who are here below, on my face depaints that pity, which thou takest for fear.

2. To depict or portray in words; to describe graphically, or by comparison.

1382 Wyclif *Bible Pref. Ep.* iii. 63 A bishop, whom in short sermoun he depeynted. **1555** Abp. Parker *Ps.* cxlii. 406 My troublouse state I did depaynt. **1664** Marvell *Corr.* Wks. 1872–5 II. 167 There are no words sufficient to depaint so real an affection. **1714** Gay *Sheph. Week* Prol. 61 Such Ladies fair wou'd I depaint In Roundelay or Sonnet quaint. **1771–2** *Batchelor* (1773) II. 13 Her lips you may in sort depaint By cherries ripe. **1808** J. Mayne *Siller Gun* II. 129 Amid the scenes, depainted here, O' love, and war, and social cheer.

b. Const. *out*, *forth*.

1553 *Short Catech.* in *Liturg. & Doc. Edw. VI* (1844) 513 Canst thou yet further depaint me out that congregation, which thou callest a kingdom or commonweal of Christians? **1578** Timme *Caluine on Gen.* 333 The state of the Church could not be more lively depainted forth. **1622** J. Reynolds *God's Revenge* II. vi. 42 In their speeches depainting forth the ioyes of heaven. **1679** G. R. tr. *Boyatuau's Theat. World* II. 147 Depainting them out in lively colours.

3. To set forth or represent, as a painting or picture does.

1598 Yong *Diana* 87 This sumptuous Palace.. that this table doth depaint vnto vs. **1607** Walkington *Opt. Glass* xv. (1664) 152 This temperature must be depainted forth of us.. according to a kind of exigency. *c* **1660** Wharton *Wks.* (1683) 357 If then success be it which best depaints A glorious Cause, Turks are the only Saints.

4. To paint or decorate with colours or painted figures; sometimes, to paint, colour (a surface).

c **1320** *Cast. Love* 704 Þis Castel is siker and feir abouten, And is al depeynted wᵗ-outen Wiþ þreo heowes þᵗ wel beþ sene. *c* **1400** Maundev. (1839) xxvii. 277 Faire chambres depeynted all with gold and azure. **14..** *Prose Legends* in *Anglia* VIII. 151 A cote.. depeynted wiþ alle maner of vertues & floryshed wiþ alle the floures of goddes gardens. **1513** Bradshaw *St. Werburge* I. 1577 Clothes of golde and arras were hanged in the hall Depaynted with pyctures. **1530** Palsgr. 512/2, I depaynte, I coloure a thynge with colours.. This terme as yet is nat admytted in comen spetche. **1605** Camden *Rem.* (1637) 129 They were wont to depaint themselues with sundry colours. **1706** [see depainted].

b. *transf.* and *fig.* To adorn as with painted figures.

c **1325** [see depaint *ppl. a.*]. *c* **1374** Chaucer *Boeth.* IV. i. 111 Þe cercle of þe sterres in alle þe places þere as þe shynyng ny3t is depeynted. **1382** Wyclif *Lev.* xi. 30 A stellioun, that is a werme depeyntid as with sterris. *c* **1450** *Crt. of Love* xv Depeinted wonderly, With many a thousand daisies, rede as rose And white also. **1509** Hawes *Past. Pleas.* (Percy Soc.) 4 A medowe both gaye and glorious, Whiche Flora depainted with many a colour. **1598** Yong *Diana* 468 Let now each meade with flowers be depainted, Of sundrie colours sweetest odours glowing.

5. To stain, distain.

c **1374** Chaucer *Troylus* v. 1611, I have eke seyn with teris al depeynted, Your lettre. **1600** Fairfax *Tasso* II. xliii. 28 Few siluer drops her vermile cheekes depaint.

Hence **deˈpainted** *ppl. a.*, painted, depicted.
1413 LYDG. *Pilgr. Sowle* II. xlvi. (1859) 53 Al this erdely fyre is but thyng depeynted in regard of that other. **1706** MAULE *Hist. Picts* in *Misc. Scot.* I. 18 By reason of their depainted bodies.

†**deˈpainter.** *Obs.* [f. DEPAINT *v.* + -ER.] One who or that which depaints, or paints.
1513 DOUGLAS *Æneis* XII. Prol. 261 Welcum depayntar of the blomyt medis.

†**deˈpair,** *v. Obs.* Also **depeyre, depeire.** [a. OF. *des-, depeire-r*, to despoil, f. *des-, dé-* (DE- I. 6) + *-peirer*:—L. *peiorāre*: cf. APPAIR, IMPAIR, and DISPAYRE *sb.*] *trans.* To impair, injure, dilapidate.
a **1460** LYDGATE *Lyfe of our Ladye* (Caxton) E. 5, c. 1 (R.) As the tryed syluer is depeired. **1501** DOUGLAS *Pal. Hon.* II. xxii, Na wretchis word may depair ȝour hie name. **1513** BRADSHAW *St. Werburge* I. 338 The corps hole and sounde was funde, verely..Nothyng depaired that ther coude be seen. **1568** T. HOWELL *Arb. Amitie* (1879) 63 Depaire no Church, nor auncient acte, in building be not sloe.

depalatalization (diːˌpælətəlaɪˈzeɪʃən). *Phonetics.* [f. DE- II. 1 + PALATALIZATION.] The loss of palatalization.
1952 *Archivum Linguisticum* IV. II. 137 The depalatalisation of the unfamiliar sounds [ɲ] and [ʎ]. **1955** *Sci. Amer.* Aug. 79/1 We should not overlook the reverse phenomenon of depalatalization: the dropping of y before vowels in words where it used to be generally pronounced.

†**deˈpalmate,** *v. Obs. rare*⁻⁰. [f. ppl. stem of L. *dēpalmāre*, f. DE- + *palma* palm of the hand.] 'To giue one a box on the eare' (Cockeram 1623).

†**deˈpance.** *Obs. rare*⁻¹. [a. F. *dépens* (in 12th c. *despans*), ad. L. *dispens-um*, or F. *dépense* (in 13th c. *despanse*), ad. L. *dispensa*: see DISPENSE *sb.*] Payment, disbursement.
c **1450** *Paper Roll* in *3rd Rep. Hist. MSS. Commiss.* 279/1 Which he complesshed withoute other payements of Fynaunce, raunceoun, or depance.

†**depaˈrayll,** *a. Obs. rare.* [a. OF. *despareil* different, dissimilar, f. *des-* = L. DIS- + *pareil* like, of the same kind = Pr. *parelh*, Sp. *parejo*, It. *parecchio*:—Rom. **pariculo-* dim. of L. *par* equal.] Unlike, dissimilar, diverse.
1413 LYDG. *Pilgr. Sowle* I. x. (1859) 7 There ben here many dyuerse pilgrymes deparayll of habyte.

†**deparˈdieu,** *interj. Obs.* [a. OF. phrase *de par Dieu*, by the authority, or in the name, of God.] In God's name; by God: used as an asseveration.
c **1290** *Beket* 1352 in *S. Eng. Leg.* I. 145 Nov de pardeus [MS. Harl. 2277 deperdeus] quath þe pope, doth ase ȝe habbeth i-þouȝt. *c* **1374** CHAUCER *Troylus* II. 1058 Quod Troylus, depardeu, y assente. *c* **1380** *Sir Ferumb.* 1452 'Wel depardieux' quaþ þe kyng 'ne schal he noȝt gon al-one.' **1634** W. CARTWRIGHT *Ordinary* II. ii. in Hazl. *Dodsley* XII. 240 [*arch.*] Depardieu, You snyb mine old years, sans fail, I wene you bin A jangler and a golierdis.

†**deˈpardon,** *v. Obs.* [f. DE- + PARDON *v.*: perh. after *part*, *depart.*] *trans.* To excuse, forgive.
1501 *Bury Wills* (1850) 90, I will that my tenaynts..be depardond of yᵉ half of all ther rents that xall be due on to me to the Mychelmesse next after my decesse.

depaˈrochialize, *v. nonce-wd.* [f. DE- II. 1 + PAROCHIALIZE *v.*] *trans.* To deprive of parochial character. Hence **depaˈrochializing** *vbl. sb.* and *ppl. a.*; also **deparochialiˈzation.**
1862 *Sat. Rev.* XIII. 211/1 We must not think of turning an impassable ditch into a passable road, for fear England should thereby be 'deparochialized'. *Ibid.* 211/2 The new formula of deparochialization. *Ibid.*, The 'deparochializing' cry will..do equally well for both.

†**depaˈrochiate,** *v. Obs. nonce-wd.* [f. DE- I. 2 + L. *parochia* parish + -ATE³; after *depatriate.*] *intr.* To depart from one's own parish.
1762 FOOTE *Orators* I. Wks. 1799 I. 196 The culture of our lands will sustain an infinite injury, if such a number of peasants were to deparochiate.

depart (dɪˈpɑːt), *v.* Also 3-6 **departe,** 5-6 **deperte,** 6-7 *Sc.* **depairt.** *Pa. pple.* 4-5 **depart(e,** 6 *Sc.* **depairt.** [a. OF. *depart-ir* (*depp-, desp-, dip-*) = Pr. *departir*, Sp., Pg. *departer, desparter*, It. *di-, dis-partire, spartire*, Rom. compound of *de-* or *dis-* (*des-*) + *partīre*, for L. *dispertīre* to divide, f. DIS- + *partīre* to part, divide. See DE- I. 6.]

I. To divide or part, with its derived senses.

†**1.** *trans.* To divide into parts, dispart. *Obs.*
1297 R. GLOUC. (1724) 394 Hii departede vorst her ost as in foure partye. **1387** TREVISA *Higden* (Rolls) I. 27 Þis werke I departe and dele in seuene bookes. *c* **1400** MAUNDEV. (Roxb.) xi. 43 Þe ȝerde of Moyses, with þe whilk he departid þe Reed See. *c* **1430** LYDG. *Min. Poems* (Percy Soc.) 219 Departe thy tyme prudently on thre. **1551** TURNER *Herbal* I. (1568) H iv a, Leues..very deply indentyd, euen to the very synewes whiche depart the mygde leues.

†**b.** *intr.* To divide, become divided. *Obs.*
1387 TREVISA *Higden* (Rolls) I. 63 Þe Rede see [*i.e.* Arabian Sea] strecceþ forþ, and departeþ in tweie mouthes and sees. Þat oon is i-cleped Persicus..þat oþer is i-cleped Arabicus. **1548-77** VICARY *Anat.* v. (1888) 37 [The sinews] depart agayne into two, and eche goeth into one eye.

†**c.** *Her.* See DEPARTED 2. *Obs.*

†**2.** *trans.* To divide or part among persons, etc.; to distribute, partition, deal out; to divide with others, or among themselves, to share; sometimes (with the notion of *division* more or less lost, as in DEAL *v.*) to bestow, impart. *Obs.*
a **1340** HAMPOLE *Psalter* xxi. 18 Þai departid to þaim my clathes. **1388** WYCLIF *Prov.* xi. 24 Sum men departen her own thingis, and ben maad richere. *c* **1430** LYDG. *Bochas* I. x. (1544) 21 a, This Kingdom..Should haue be departed of right betwene us twein. **1483** CAXTON *Gold. Leg.* 76 b/2 Yf thou haue but lytyl, yet studye to gyue and to departe therof gladly. *c* **1530** H. RHODES *Bk. Nurture* in *Babees Bk.* (1868) 103 Be content to departe to a man wylling to learne suche thinges as thou knowest. **1557** N. T. (Genev.) *John* xix. 24 They departed my rayment among them. **1582** N. LICHEFIELD tr. *Castanheda's Conq. E. Ind.* 55 a, He departed with him both money and other rewards. **1651** *Reliq. Wotton.* 22 He could depart his affection between two extremes.

†**b.** To deal (blows). *Obs. rare.*
c **1477** CAXTON *Jason* 16 b, Whan the kyng apperceyued that Jason departed suche strokes.

†**c.** *absol.* To share, partake (*with* a person *in* a thing). *Obs.*
c **1440** *Generydes* 3418, I shall..in wurchippe the avaunce, And largely departe with the also. **1499** *Plumpton Corr.* 137, I am willing to depart with him in lands & in goods. **1549** COVERDALE *Erasm. Par. 2 Cor.* viii. 14 Whyles eche of you departeth with other, so that neyther of you lacke anye thyng.

†**3.** *trans.* To put asunder, sunder, separate, part. *Obs.*
1297 R. GLOUC. (1724) 466 King Lowis..And Elianore is quene, vor kunrede departed were. **1393** GOWER *Conf.* II. 129 That deth shuld us departe attwo. *c* **1400** MAUNDEV. (1839) iii. 16 A gret Hille, that men clepen Olympus, that departeth Macedonye and Trachye. *c* **1400** *Lanfranc's Cirurg.* 265 Departe liȝtli þe tooþ and þe fleisch of þe gomis. **1483** CAXTON *G. de la Tour* D j, That god hath ioyned man may not departe. *c* **1530** LD. BERNERS *Arth. Lyt. Bryt.* (1814) 67 There began a great and a sore batayle betwene these two knightes. And Arthur dyd his payne..to depart them. **1548-9** (Mar.) *Bk. Com. Prayer, Matrimony,* Till death vs departe [*altd.* **1662** *to* do part]. **1601** *Downf. Earl Huntington* II. ii. in Hazl. *Dodsley* VIII. 134 The world shall nat depart us till we die. *a* **1677** BARROW *Serm.* (1810) I. 199 The closest union here cannot last longer than till death us depart.

†**b.** To sever or separate (a thing) *from* (another).
1340 HAMPOLE *Pr. Consc.* 3710 Þai er..Departed halely fra þe body of Criste. *c* **1400** *Lanfranc's Cirurg.* 10 It is unpossible to departe þo qualitees from bodies. *Ibid.* 142 Whanne a membre is depertid from þe bodi. **1526** TINDALE *Rom.* viii. 39 To departe [so CRANMER and **1557** *Geneva*; *Rhem.* and **1611** separate] us from Goddes love. **1574** HYLL *Planting* 78 You must translate them, and depart them farther from other. **1590** SPENSER *F.Q.* II. x. 14 Which Seuerne now from Logris doth depart.

†**c.** To separate in perception or thought; to discern apart, distinguish. *Obs.*
c **1380** WYCLIF *Sel. Wks.* III. 340 As þes þree persones of God ben o God..so alle dedes and werkes of þe Trinite mai not be departid from oþer. **1485** CAXTON *Chas. Gt.* 248 We ..had egally departed his good dedes and his euyl. *c* **1510** MORE *Picus* Wks. 2/2 Straunge tokens..departing (as it wer) and..seuering the cradles of such speciall chyldren fro the company of other of the common sorte.

†**d.** *intr.* To separate, make separation. *Obs.*
1388 WYCLIF *Isa.* lix. 2 Ȝoure wickednesses han departid bitwixe ȝou and ȝoure God. **1480** CAXTON *Descr. Brit.* 8 The Seuarn departed somtyme bitwene Englond and Wales.

†**e.** *Old Chem.* To separate a metal from an alloy or a solution.
1704 J. HARRIS *Lex. Techn.* s.v., Depart farther, and get your Silver out of the Aqua Fortis. **1751** CHAMBERS *Cycl.* s.v., The water of the first recipient serves for the first operation of departing, and the rest for the subsequent ones.

†**4.** *trans.* To sever, break off, dissolve (a connexion or the like). *Obs.*
c **1386** CHAUCER *Frankl. T.* 804, I have wel lever ever to suffre woo, Than I departe the love bytwix yow tuo. *c* **1400** *Apol. Loll* 70 Mariage mad in þrid & ferd degre..is so confermid þat it mai not be departid. **1470-85** MALORY *Arthur* VIII. xxxviii, Ye departed the loue bitwene me and my wyf. **15..** HACKET *Treas. of Amadis* 274 So sweete and so faithfull a conjunction can not be departed without a great heart breaking. **1579** TWYNE *Phisicke agst. Fortune* II. lvii. 233 b, With staues to depart their nightly conflictes.

†**b.** *intr.* (for *refl.*) Of a connexion, etc.: To be severed, dissolved, or broken off. *Obs.*
1375 BARBOUR *Bruce* II. 169 Thusgat maid thai thar aquentance That neuir syne..Departyt quhill thai lyffand war. **1377** LANGL. *P. Pl.* B. xx. 138 Thanne cam coueityse ..For a mantel of menyuere, he made lele matrimonye Departen ar deth cam, and deuors shupte. **1523** LD. BERNERS *Froiss.* I. lxxxi. 103 Than the bysshoppe sayd, Sirs, than our company shall depart.

II. To go apart or away, with its derived senses.
The perfect tenses (*intrans.*) were formerly formed with *be*: cf. *is gone.*

†**5.** *intr.* To go asunder; to part or separate from each other, to take leave of each other. *Obs.*
c **1290** *S. Eng. Leg.* I. 121/527 So departede þe court þo, and euerech to is In drouȝ. *c* **1330** R. BRUNNE *Chron.* (1810) 52 In luf þei departed, Hardknout home went. *c* **1500** *Nut-Brown Maid* 33, I here you saye farwel: nay, nay, we departe not soo sone. **1601** HOLLAND *Pliny* II. 208 The putrifaction of the flesh ready to depart from the bone. *a* **1605** MONTGOMERIE *Misc. Poems* xxxix. 12 Adeu nou; be treu nou, Sen that we must depairt. **1641** HINDE *J. Bruen* xlii. 133 So loth wee were to depart asunder.

6. *intr.* To go away (*from* a person or place); to take one's leave. (The current sense, but chiefly in literary use; *to depart from* = to leave.)
a **1225** [see DEPARTING *vbl. sb.* 3 a]. *c* **1340** *Cursor M.* 11893 (Fairf.) Be þat we fra þe depart [*earlier texts* part]. *a* **1340** HAMPOLE *Psalter* vi. 8 Departis fra me all þat wirkes wickednes. *c* **1477** CAXTON *Jason* 68 He departed out of temple and also from Athenes. **1526** TINDALE *John* xvi. 7 Yf I departe, I will sende him vnto you. **1547-8** *Ordre of Commvnion* 16 Then shall the Prieste..let the people depart. **1697** DRYDEN *Virg. Georg.* III. 818 The Learned Leaches in Despair depart. **1841** LANE *Arab. Nts.* I. 113 She then said to him, Depart, and return not hither.

b. To set out (on a journey), set forth, start. Opp. to *arrive.* (Now commonly to *leave.*)
c **1489** CAXTON *Sonnes of Aymon* i. 52 Whan the mornyng came, departed well erly from Parys the sayd Guenelon and his felawes. **1548** HALL *Chron.* 208 b, He entered the ship with the other, which were redy to depart. **1625-6** PURCHAS *Pilgrimes* II. 1081 The Negui was departed. And every man hastened to follow after. **1792** MRS. C. SMITH *Desmond.* III. 61 In case the Duke should be departed, he directs her instantly to set out for Paris. **1817** W. SELWYN *Law Nisi Prius* (ed. 4) II. 969 If the ship did not depart from Portsmouth with convoy. *Time-table.* The train departs at 6.30.

†**c.** To go away *to* or *into* (a place); to go forth, pass, proceed, make one's way. *Obs.*
c **1400** *Lanfranc's Cirurg.* (MS. A) 305 To defende þat mater schal not departe into al þe lyme. **1586** B. YOUNG *Guazzo's Civ. Conv.* IV. 227 He had a desire to depart home to his lodging. **1611** BIBLE *Matt.* ii. 12 They departed into their owne countrey another way.

†**d.** *to depart one's way*: to go one's way. *Obs.*
1535 COVERDALE *1 Esdras* ix. 51 Departe youre waye then, & eate the best, & drynke the swetest.

7. *intr.* To leave this world, decease, die, pass away. (Now only *to depart from* (*this*) *life.*)
1501 *Bury Wills* (1850) 85 My body, if it happyt me to departe wᵗin vij. myle of gret Berkehamstede, to be buryed ther. **1526** TINDALE *Luke* ii. 29 Lorde, now lettest thou thy seruaunt departe in peace. **1535** STEWART *Cron. Scot.* I. 576 Constantius depairt in Eborac throw Infirmitie. **1576** FLEMING *Panopl. Epist.* 39 That Marcellus a little before day, was departed. **1605** STOW *Annales* 39 He departed out of this life at Yorke. **1702** J. LOGAN in *Pa. Hist. Soc. Mem.* IX. 94, I went to visit him the day before he departed. *a* **1862** BUCKLE *Civiliz.* (1869) III. iv. 227 When a Scotch minister departed from this life.

8. *trans.* To go away from, leave, quit, forsake. Now *rare*, exc. in phr. *to depart this life* (= 7).
c **1340** *Cursor M.* 20266 (Br. Mus. MS.) Rewe on vs, departe vs nouȝt. **1536** in W. H. Turner *Select. Rec. Oxford* 138 Nicholas Hore paid for the wine and departed their company. **1548** HALL *Chron.* 114 All the Welshemen were commaunded..to depart the toune. **1597** HOOKER *Eccl. Pol.* v. i. (1611) 186 The soules of men departing this life. **1647** N. BACON *Disc. Govt. Eng.* I. lix. (1739) 112 No Clergyman or other may depart the Realm, without the King's Licence. **1712** ADDISON *Spect.* No. 517 ¶1 Sir Roger de Coverley is dead. He departed this life at his house in the country. **1734** tr. *Rollin's Anc. Hist.* (1827) II. II. 126 Jugurtha was commanded to depart Italy. **1839** KEIGHTLEY *Hist. Eng.* II. 33 The clergy were ordered to depart the kingdom. **1861** DICKENS *Gt. Expect.* xxxiv, Mrs. J. Gargery had departed this life on Monday last.

†**9.** To send away, dismiss. *Obs.*
1484 CAXTON *Chivalry* 73 Charite..departeth euery vyce. *c* **1500** *Chron. Gr. Friars* (Camden) 28 The Kynge..made them grete chere and so departyd them home agayne. **1614** RALEIGH *Hist. World* Pref. 17 The abolished parts are departed by small degrees.

†**10.** *intr.* To start, spring, come forth, or issue *from*; to come *of*. *Obs.*
c **1477** CAXTON *Jason* 56 b, By theyr countenaunce and habylements..they ben departed from noble and goode hous. *c* **1489** —— *Blanchardyn* xliv. 173 Of churles, bothe man and wyff, can departe noo goode fruyte.

11. *intr.* (*transf.* and *fig.* from 6.) To withdraw, turn aside, diverge, deviate; to desist (*from* a course of action, etc.). *to depart from*: to leave, abandon; to cease to follow, observe or practise.
1393 GOWER *Conf.* III. 103 The..Nile..Departeth fro his cours and falleth Into the see Alexandrine. **1535** COVERDALE *Prov.* iii. 7 Feare yᵉ Lorde and departe from euell. **1590** SPENSER *F.Q.* III. ii. 41 Shamefull lustes..which depart From course of nature. **1651** HOBBES *Leviath.* III. xl. 255 It was not with a design to depart from the worship of God. **1732** BERKELEY *Alciphr.* VII. §24 They depart from received opinions. **1867** FREEMAN *Norm. Conq.* (1876) I. App. 673 The fourth narrative departs in several important points from the Chronicles. **1893** *Law Times* XCV. 27/1 Disinclination..to depart from the long-established practice.

III. †**12. depart with. a.** To take leave of; to go away from. (Cf. 5, 6.) *Obs. rare.*
1502 *Ord. Crysten Men* (W. de W. 1506) I. iii. 22 Cursed & dampned spyrite, departe than forth with this creature. **1563** FOXE *A. & M.* 763 b, And so departed I with them.

†**b.** To part with; to give up, surrender; to give away, bestow. (Cf. 2.) *Obs.*
c **1485** *Digby Myst.* (1882) III. 102 O ye good fathyr of grete degre, thus to departe with your ryches. **1595** SHAKS. *John* II. i. 563 Iohn..Hath willingly departed with a part. **1642** PERKINS *Prof. Bk.* i. §47. 21 Shee hath departed with her right by the feoffment. **1792** CHIPMAN *Amer. Law Rep.* (1871) 41 The officer had a lien on the cattle. On receipt I do not consider that the officer wholly departs with that lien.

†**13. So depart from,** in the same sense (12 b).
1548 CRANMER *Catech.* 81 b, Neyther by threatnyng.. cause him to depart from any portion of his goodes. **1612** T. TAYLOR *Comm. Titus* i. 5 With what difficultie depart they [stones] from their naturall roughnesse? **1681** BURNET *Hist.*

Ref. II. 88 The inferior clergy departed from their right of being in the House of Commons.

†**depart**, *sb. Obs.* [a. F. *départ* (13th c. in Godef.), f. *départir* to DEPART. Partly treated as directly from the English verb; cf. the sbs. *leave*, *return*, etc.]

1. The act of departing, departure. **a.** Parting, separation. **b.** Departure from this life, death. *c* **1330** *Arth. & Merl.* 4539 For depart of his felawes, And for her men that weren y-slawe. **1590** SPENSER *F.Q.* III. vii. 20 That lewd lover did the most lament For her depart. **1591** SHAKS. *Two Gent.* v. iv. 96 At my depart I gaue this [ring] vnto Iulia. **1593** —— *3 Hen. VI*, II. i. 110 When your braue Father breath'd his latest gaspe, Tydings..Were brought me of your Losse, and his Depart. **1642** H. MORE *Song of Soul* II. II. II. xxxviii, The plantall lifes depart. **1724** RAMSAY *Tea-t. Misc.* (1733) I. 99 For her depart my heart was sair. **1840** *Sportsman in Irel. & Scotl.* II. iv. 71, The salmon having long since made his depart.

2. *Old Chem.* The separation of one metal from another with which it is alloyed. *a* **1626** BACON (J.), The chymists have a liquor called water of depart. **1686** W. HARRIS tr. *Lemery's Course Chym.* (ed. 2) 79 The Depart, or parting of Metals, is when a Dissolvent quits the Metal it had dissolved to betake itself unto another. **1704** J. HARRIS *Lex. Techn.* s.v., A certain Operation in Chymistry is called *the Depart*, because the Particles of Silver are made by it to depart from Gold when they were before melted together. **1751** CHAMBERS *Cycl.*, *Depart*, a method of refining, or separating gold from silver by means of aqua fortis...if you again filtrate this water, and pour on it the liquor of fixed nitre, you will have another *depart*, the calamine precipitating to the bottom.

†**de'partable, -ible**, *a. Obs.* [a. OF. *departable* (13–14th c. in Godef.), f. *depart-ir* vb.: see -BLE. The form in *-ible* follows L. analogy: cf. L. *partībilis* from *partīrī*.]

1. That may be parted or separated; separable. **1377** LANGL. *P. Pl.* B. XVII. 26 Þe Trinite, Thre persones in parcelles departable fro other, And alle þre but o god. *c* **1449** PECOCK *Repr.* III. ii. 282 Riȝt of vce is dyuers and departable fro the riȝt of lordschip. **1450–1530** *Myrr. our Ladye* 104 Yf eny of them were departable from other.

2. That may be, or is to be, divided or distributed; divisible. [**1292** BRITTON III. viii. §4 Qe le heretage soit departable entre touz les enfauntz.] **1483** *Cath. Angl.* 96 Departiabylle, *diuisibilis*. **1535** *Act 27 Hen. VIII*, c 26 §35 Landes..to be departed and departable amonges issues and heires males. **1574** tr. *Littleton's Tenures* 139 b, The whiche tenementes be departable among the brethren. **1741** T. ROBINSON *Gavelkind* ii. 26 They had always been departible.

†**de'partal.** *Obs. rare.* [f. DEPART *v.* + -AL[1], after *arrival*.] Departure. **1823** GALT *Entail* I. xi. 82 When my father took his departal to a better world. **1836** —— in *Tait's Mag.* III. 393 Speaking of my departal from Glasgow.

†**de'partance.** *Obs.* [a. OF. *departance*, f. *depart-ir*: see -ANCE.] Departure. **1579** *Wills & Inv. N.C.* (Surtees) 15, I will, that after the departance of this mortal liff..my bodie be buried. **1592** WYRLEY *Armorie* 61, I license craue for this departaunce.

†**de'parte.** In phrase *lay a departe* (? error) for *lay aparte*, lay aside. *c* **1489** CAXTON *Blanchardyn* iii. 17 All rewthis layde a departe, as well for his fader as for his modre.

departed (dɪ'pɑːtəd), *ppl. a.* [f. DEPART *v.* + -ED[1].]

†**1.** Divided into parts, etc.: see DEPART *v.* 1, 2. *c* **1386** CHAUCER *Pars. T.* ¶898 (H.) Eyther thay forletin her confessours al utterly, or ellis thay departen here schrifte in divers places; but sothely such departed schrifte hath no mercy of God. **1463** *Bury Wills* (1850) 36, I beqwethe..a doubyl ryng departyd of gold, with a ruby and a turkeys.

†**2.** Separated, parted; severed from the main body, schismatic, apostate; in *Her.* separated by a dividing line (cf. PARTY *a.*). *Obs.* **1439** C'TESS WARWICK in *E.E. Wills* (1883) 117 A Skochen of myn Armes departyd with my lordys. *c* **1511** *1st Eng. Bk. Amer.* (Arb.) Introd. 31/1 These ketters..is departed of the holy Romes chyrche. **1633** EARL MANCH. *Al Mondo* (1636) 14 If we consider Death aright, It is but a departed breath from dead earth.

3. That has departed or gone away; past, bygone. **1552** HULOET, Departed, *dissitus, præteritus.* **1845** J. SAUNDERS *Cabinet Pictures* 20 Antiquity and departed greatness.

4. **a.** *spec.* That has departed this life; deceased. **1503–4** *Act 19 Hen. VII*, c. 25 Pream., Lyfe [is] as uncertayne to such as survyve as to them now departed. **1599** B. JONSON *Ev. Man out of Hum.* v. iv, Shedding funereal tears over his departed dog. **1712** ADDISON *Spect.* No. 419 ¶1 Magicians, Demons, and departed Spirits. **1863** FAWCETT *Pol. Econ.* III. ii. 311 The works of a departed artist.

b. In this sense often used absolutely, *the departed* (*sing.* and *pl.*): cf. *deceased.* Also (esp. *joc.*) ***the dear departed.*** **1722** WOLLASTON *Relig. Nat.* ix. 208 The seats and circumstances of the departed. **1794** MRS. RADCLIFFE *Myst. Udolpho* ii, A prayer for the soul of the departed. **1814** JANE AUSTEN *Mansf. Park* iii. 56 Barely enough to..enable me to live so as not to disgrace the memory of the dear departed. **1838** DICKENS *Nickleby* iii. 20 The dear departed had never deigned to profit by her advice. **1868** L. M. ALCOTT *Little Women* (1871) xi. 137 Beth..sat making a winding-sheet, while the dear-departed lay in the domino-box. **1875** MANNING *Mission H. Ghost* ix. 249 The Catholic Church..cherishes with loving memory all her departed. **1887** BOWEN *Æneid* VI. 220 The departed is placed on the funeral bed. **1910** W. S. HOUGHTON (*title*) The dear departed. **1964** E. LONGFORD *Victoria R.I.* xxiv. 355 If the living Albert kept Queen Victoria and Disraeli apart, the dear departed brought them together.

departer[1] (dɪ'pɑːtə(r)). [f. DEPART *v.* + -ER[1]: probably a. OF. *departeur* (nom. case orig. *departère*, obj. *departeor*), f. *départir* to DEPART.]

†**1.** A divider, distributor; discerner. *Obs.* **1382** WYCLIF *Luke* xii. 14 A! man, who ordeynede me domesman, ether departer, on ȝou? —— *Hebr.* iv. 12 The word of God is..departer or demer of thouȝtis and intencions of hertis. *c* **1400** *Apol. Loll.* 61 He is not ordeind juge ne departar vp on men.

†**2.** *Old Chem.* One who separates a metal from an alloy; a refiner of gold or silver. Cf. PARTER. **1656** BLOUNT *Glossogr.* s.v. *Finour*, Finours of Gold and Silver..A[ct] 4 H[en.] 7. ca. 2. They be also called *Parters* in the same place; sometimes *Departers*.

3. One who separates or secedes from a body or cause; a seceder. (Now merged in sense 4.) **1586** FERNE *Blaz. Gentrie* 311 A departer from his Captaynes Banner. **1820** *Examiner* No. 652. 644/1 Lady Charlotte Lindsay, another of the departers. **1860** PUSEY *Min. Proph.* 61 They are all departers, i.e...before they were cast out visibly in the body, they departed in mind.

4. One who departs or goes away. **1673** O. WALKER *Education* 223 The Patron leaveth the rest and accompanieth the departer. **1705** *Col. Rec. Pennsylv.* II. 231 An Act about Departers out of this Province. **1747** FRANKLIN *Ess.* Wks. 1840 III. 13 The hurry and disorder of departers, carrying away their effects.

†**de'parter**[2]. *Law. Obs.* [subst. use of AF. *departer* (Britton III. iv. 25) = OF. *departir* pres. inf. to depart, departing.] = DEPARTURE 6. **1628** COKE *On Litt.* 139 a, A departer in despight of the Court..when the Tenant or Defendant after appearance..makes departure in despight of the Court..It is called a *retraxit.* **1751** CHAMBERS *Cycl.*, *Departure* or *Departer*, in law, a term properly applied to a person, who first pleading one thing in bar of an action, and that being replied to, he waves it, and insists on something different.

departible, var. form of DEPARTABLE *a. Obs.*

de'parting, *vbl. sb.* [f. DEPART *v.* + -ING[1].] The action of the verb DEPART, in various senses.

†**1.** Division (in various senses); distribution, sharing. *Obs.* *a* **1340** HAMPOLE *Psalter* cxxxv. 13 He departyd þe redd see in departynges. *c* **1380** WYCLIF *Wks.* (1880) 81 In departyng of meritis to whom þat hem likiþ. **1382** —— *1 Cor.* xii. 6 Departingis of worchingis. **1398** TREVISA *Barth. De P.R.* XV. xlvi. (1495) 504 Dalmacia is a prouynce of Grece by olde departynge of londe. *c* **1449** PECOCK *Repr.* 407 In summe cuntreis the departing was mad other wise and into iij parties. *c* **1450** *Merlin* 236 Ech man toke at his wille of that hym liked, and made noon other departynge. **1513** DOUGLAS *Æneis* VI. Prol. 90 The sted of fell turmentis, With seir departingis. **1599** HAKLUYT *Voy.* II. I. 93 In departing of the bootie.

†**2.** Separation. *Obs.* or *arch.* *c* **1300** *K. Alis.* 912 And makith mony departyng Bytweone knyght and his swetyng. *c* **1340** *Cursor M.* 895 (Fairf.) Fra þis day sal departynge be for-soþ betwix wommon and þe. *c* **1400** *Apol. Loll.* 72 Be ware of making of mariagis, & of diuorsis or departingis. **1530** PALSGR. 213/1 Departynge of man and wyfe, *repudiation, diuorse.* **1593** SHAKS. *3 Hen. VI*, II. vi. 43 A deadly grone like life and deaths departing. **1852–5** M. ARNOLD *Poems, Faded Leaves*, At this bitter departing.

†**b.** *concr.* Place of separation; division, boundary. *Obs.* **1460–70** *Bk. Quintessence* 5 And þat erþely watir wole first come out þat is in þe necke, and so til it be come out vnto þe departinge bitwixe it and þe quinte essence.

3. The action of leaving, taking one's leave or going away; departure. (In early use 'leaving each other, separation', as in 2. Now *rare* or *Obs.*; replaced by DEPARTURE.) *a* **1225** *Ancr. R.* 250 Þis was his driwerie þet he bileauede and ȝef ham in his departunge. **1340** HAMPOLE *Pr. Consc.* 6113 Þe day of departyng fra God away. *c* **1386** CHAUCER *Man of Law's T.* 162 The day is come of hire departyng. **1481–90** *Howard Househ. Bks.* (Roxb.) 186 At my Lordes departynge from London. *c* **1500** *Three Kings Sons* 73 Athis, my frende, the tyme is come now of oure departyng. **1644** MILTON *Judgm. Bucer* (1851) 335 Not..the mis-beleeving of him who departs, but the departing of him who mis-beleevs.

†**b.** = DEPARTURE 2 b; decease, death. *Obs.* **1388** WYCLIF *2 Tim.* iv. 6 The tyme of my departyng is nyȝ. **1535** STEWART *Cron. Scot.* II. 486 How King Donald was crownit..and of his worthie Deidis..and his Departing. **1633** BP. HALL *Medit. & Vows, Passing Bell* (1851) 87 It calls us..to our preparation, for our own departing. *attrib.* *a* **1618** RALEIGH *Rem.* (1664) 114 If you were laid upon your departing bed.

†**c.** *fig.* Departure from a given state or course; falling away; secession, desertion, apostasy. **1526** TINDALE *2 Thess.* ii. 3 Except there come a departynge fyrst. **1594** T. B. *La Primaud. Fr. Acad.* II. 563 The departing and declining of the soule.

†**4.** ***departing with***: parting with, giving up. **1529** WOLSEY in Ellis *Orig. Lett.* Ser. I. II. 11 Of the frankke departyng with of all that I had in thys world.

de'parting, *ppl. a.* [f. DEPART *v.* + -ING[2].] That departs, goes away, or takes leave; parting; *fig.* vanishing (often with reference to sense b). **1751** JOHNSON *Rambler* No. 187 ¶3 She stood awhile to gaze upon the departing vessel. **1855** MACAULAY *Hist. Eng.* III. 57 The opposite streams of entering and departing courtiers. **1875** JOWETT *Plato* (ed. 2) III. 155 Reflecting the departing glory of Hellas. **18..** THRING *Hymn 'The Radiant morn'*, The shadows of departing day.

b. Dying. **1603** KNOLLES *Hist. Turks* (1638) 331 It is the only sacrifice that my old departing ghost desireth of thee. **1633** BP. HALL *Medit. & Vows, Passing-bell* (1851) 87 It calls us..to our prayers, for the departing soul. **1848** MACAULAY *Hist. Eng.* II. 183 While the prayer for the departing was read at his bedside.

†**de'partingly**, *adv. Obs. rare.* [f. prec. + -LY[2].] In a divided manner; separately. **1388** WYCLIF *Num.* x. 7 Symple cry of trumpis schal be, and thei schulen not soune departyngli [**1382** not stowndmeel; Vulg. *non concise ululabunt*].

†**de'partising**, *vbl. sb. Sc. Obs.* [? from a vb. *departise* (cf. OF. *departissement*, *departisseur*), or ? corruption of *departison*.] Partition. **1478** *Act. Audit.* 86 (Jam.) The said breve of depertising of the said half landis of Blith. **1480** *Act. Dom. Conc.* 66 (ibid.) The divisioune & departising made..the xx day of Julij.

†**de'partison.** *Obs.* In 5 -ysoun, -own, -on, -isonne; also 5–6 departson. [a. OF. *departison*, f. *départer*, after *partison*:—L. *partītiōn-em*, n. of action from *partīre* to divide.] Earlier form of DEPARTITION.

1. Division into parts; distribution, partition. **1444** *Pol. Poems* (Rolls) II. 217 Make a departysoun Of ther tresours to folk in indigence. *c* **1450** *Mirour Saluacioun* 4176 And taken hire half his kyngdome be twypart departisonne.

2. Separation. *c* **1440** LYDG. *Secrees* 29 Thou must first Conceyven..unkouth divysion, Watir from Eyr by a dysseuerance, And ffyr from Eyr by a departyson.

3. Departure; *transf.* decease. *c* **1450** LONELICH *Grail* xliii. 423 Aftyr here deth and departysown. *c* **1475** *Partenay* 104 At ther departson had thay gret dolour.

†**departition** (diːpɑː'tɪʃən). *Obs.* Also 5 -ycyon, -isyon, 6 -ysion, -icion. [n. of action f. DEPART *v.*, on L. analogies: cf. L. *partītio*, *dispertītio*, f. *partīre*, *dispertīre*. The earlier form, from OF., was DEPARTISON, of which this may be considered an adaptation to the Latin type.]

1. Distribution, partition; = prec. 1. ? *c* **1530** in *Pol. Rel. & L. Poems* (1866) 33 Peraventure thei seke departysion of ther heritage.

2. Separation; severance. *c* **1400** *Test. Love* III. (1560) 294/1 The same law that joyneth by wedlocke..yeveth libel of departicion bycause of devorse. **1430** LYDG. *Chron. Troy* III. xxv, Now hast thou made a departisyon Of vs that were by hole affection Yknyt in one. **1470–85** MALORY *Arthur* XIII. vii, Hit shall greue me ryghte sore the departycyon of this felaushíp.

3. Departure. **1470–85** MALORY *Arthur* IX. xxxvi, Ye putte vpon me that I shold ben cause of his departycyon.

departitor (diːpɑː'taɪtə(r)). *rare.* [Agent-n. from DEPART *v.* with L. suffix: cf. L. *partītor*, *dispertītor*.] One who divides or distributes. **1884** J. PAYNE *1001 Nights* IX. 138, I called in a departitor from the Cadi's Court and he divided amongst us the money.

departizanize: see DE- II. 1.

department (dɪ'pɑːtmənt), *sb.* Also 5 departement. [ME. a. F. *département* (12th c. in Hatzf.) = Pr. *departe-*, *departiment*, It. *dipartemento*, a Romanic deriv. of *departire*, F. *départir*: see DEPART *v.* and -MENT. The senses in I from OF. were apparently obsolete before those in II were introduced from modern French.]

†**I.** The action of departing. *Obs.*

†**1.** = DEPARTURE, in various senses: **a.** separation; **b.** going away, leave-taking, withdrawal; **c.** decease. *c* **1450** *Mirour Saluacioun* 1890 Yt we come to thi joys with out departement. *c* **1477** CAXTON *Jason* 65 Alas Jason..prolonge ye and tarye your departement. *c* **1500** *Melusine* 97 Thanne he toke leue of them and they were sorowfull of theire departement. **1572** *Lament. Lady Scotland* in *Sc. Poems 16th C.* II. 250 Befoir her last department. **1586** A. DAY *Eng. Secretary* I. (1625) 87 By meanes whereof grew this..unkinde department betweene us. **1624** WOTTON *Archit.* (1672) 61 Our Sight is not well contented with those sudden departments from one extream to another. *a* **1677** BARROW *Wks.* (1686) II. 382 The seperation, department and absence of the soul from the body.

†**2.** Division, partition, distribution. *Obs.* **1677** GALE *Crt. Gentiles* IV. 18 Making the distributions and departments of his rayes.

II. 3. a. 'Separate allotment; province or business assigned to a particular person' (J.); hence in wider application: A separate division or part of a complex whole or organized system, *esp.* of activities or studies; a branch, province. Freq. in trivial use.

[Johnson, 1755, calls it 'a French term'.]
a **1735** ARBUTHNOT (J.), The Roman fleets.. had their several stations and departments. **1764** FOOTE *Patron* II. Wks. 1799 I. 349 The highest pitch of perfection in every department of writing but one—the dramatic. **1824** T. CREEVEY *Let.* 23 Sept. (1903) II. 83 Lady —— has two maids here—one French and the other Italian, the latter of which presides over the bonnet department. **1832** G. DOWNES *Lett. Cont. Countries* I. 528 Among the professors.. Messrs. Gautier and Picot, whose departments are severally astronomy and history. **1856** SIR B. BRODIE *Psychol. Inq.* I. v. 173 Hitherto.. little progress has been made in this department of knowledge. **1883** *Nature* 17 May 56 To judge .. whether the co-operation of scientific men would have rendered the English department more instructive than it is. **1966** *Listener* 20 Jan. 88/1 It will depend on two things: organization and performance in the field... There are limits to what may be expected of us in either department.

b. *spec.* One of the separate divisions or branches of state or municipal administration.

In the U.S. the word is used in the titles of the great branches of administration, i.e. (in 1988), the *Departments (Depts.) of State* (orig. *Foreign Affairs*), *Treasury*, *Defense*, *Justice*, *Interior*, *Agriculture*, *Commerce*, *Labor*, *Health and Human Services*, *Housing and Urban Development*, *Transportation*, *Energy*, and *Education*.

In Great Britain, the great departments of State were not so named titularly until the mid-20th c., when a number of new departments were created under that name during the administrative reorganizations of the 1960s and 1970s (alongside others which retained the title *Ministry* or *Office*); e.g. (in 1988) the Departments of *Education and Science*, *Employment*, *Energy*, *the Environment*, *Health and Social Security*, *Trade and Industry*, and *Transport*. The word is also used in naming subdivisions or branches of these, e.g. the *Prisons Dept.* of the Home Office, and for certain other branches of administration; also in the *Departments* of a local government authority, as the *Highways Department*.

1769 *Junius Lett.* i. 3 Only mark how the principal departments of the State are bestowed. **1791** WASHINGTON *Writ.* (1892) XII. 81 Statements from the proper department [of the United States] will.. apprize you of the exact result. **1863** H. COX *Instit.* Pref. 7 A general account of the British Government, of the powers and practice of its several departments. *Ibid.* III. vii. 696 The regulation of other departments subordinate to the Treasury. **1890** M. TOWNSEND *U.S.* 274 The Department of State was established by Act of Congress July 27, 1789, which act denominated it as the Department of Foreign Affairs. **1892** A. B. HART *Form. of Union* 144 In establishing the Treasury Department a strong effort was made to create a Secretary of the Treasury as an agent of Congress.

4. a. One of the districts into which France is divided for administrative purposes, and which were substituted for the old provinces in 1790. Also applied to administrative divisions in some other countries. Freq. in French form.

1792 *Explan. New Terms* in *Ann. Reg.* p. xv, *Departments*, the general divisions of France. **1793** *Objections to War Examined* 15 Its States broken up and converted into French Departments. **1841** W. SPALDING *Italy & It. Isl.* III. 383 Corsica.. is still a province of that kingdom [France]. It forms a department, called by its own name. **1846** R. FORD *Gatherings from Spain* iv. 30 The French.. introduced their own system of *départements*, by which districts were neatly squared out. **1859** JEPHSON *Brittany* xvi. 253 Situated on the confluence of the Ile and the Vilaine, from whence the modern department derives its name. **1964** *Ann. Reg. 1963* 245 From 12–16 June he visited the Charente and Poitou regions and from 24–29 September the *départements* of Vaucluse, Drôme, Ain, and Rhône.

b. A part, portion, section, region. *rare.*

1832 HT. MARTINEAU *Demerara* i. 2 In the richest regions of this department of the globe.

5. department store orig. *U.S.*, a large shop selling many different kinds of article. Cf. DEPARTMENTAL *a.* 3.

1887 in F. Presbrey *Advertising* (1929) xxxv. 314 *Evening Wisconsin*.. H. Heyn's Department Store. **1893** *Harper's Mag.* Apr. 659/2 They [*sc.* Brooklyn stores] compare favorably with the best and largest of the department stores of New York. **1910** H. G. WELLS *Mr. Polly* i. 24 One of those large, rather low-class establishments which sell everything from pianos and furniture to books and millinery—a department store. **1953** *Manch. Guardian Weekly* 30 July 7 Department stores in up-and-coming cities around the world.

de'partment, *v. nonce-wd.* [f. prec. sb.] *trans.* To divide into departments, or branches.

1885 MISS BRADDON *Wyllard's Weird* III. 261 Everything was to be classified, departmented. Organisation was to be the leading note.

departmental (diːpɑːtˈmɛntəl), *a.* [ad. mod.F. *départemental*: see prec. sb. and -AL[1].]

1. a. Of or pertaining to a French Department.

1791 MACKINTOSH *Vind. Gallicæ* Wks. 1846 III. 111 The series of three elections was still preserved for the choice of Departmental Administrators. **1862** *Fraser's Mag.* July 128 The municipal and departmental archives and public libraries in France.

b. *gen.* Of or pertaining to a particular district or region.

1883 E. CLODD in *Knowledge* 15 June 352/2 Indra.. god of the bright sky.. a departmental or tribal deity.

2. Of or pertaining to a department or branch of government, or of any organized system.

1832 SOUTHEY in *Q. Rev.* XLVIII. 256 It has found an active auxiliary in the departmental process. **1854** *Times*, *Let. War Corrospt.* 31 Mar., Needless departmental etiquette. **1883** *American* VII. 65 The new Commissioner of Internal Revenue in his first departmental report to the Secretary of the Treasury.

3. Of a store: consisting of or comprising several departments.

[**1907** *Yesterday's Shopping* (1969) p. xi/2 A list of the Society's Departmental Price Lists.. will be found on page xii.] **1911** R. STRONG in W. B. Robertson *Encycl. Retail Trading* xii. 114 Small wonder that.. the growth of a departmental store is sometimes phenomenal. **1924** *Times Trade & Engin. Suppl.* 29 Nov. 235/2 The departmental stores and the larger retail shops throughout the Western States. **1926** A. JAMES *Commerce* i. 53 Departmental stores contain under one roof many departments. It is possible to purchase groceries, boots and shoes, furniture, clothing, toilet requisites, as well as listen to the latest jazz music from the orchestra. **1955** *Times* 14 May 12/1 Perhaps the departmental stores were the most consistent in their experience.

Hence **depart'mentally** *adv.*; also **depart'mentalism**, attachment to departmental methods; **depart'mentalize** *v.*, to divide into departments; **depart'mentalized** *ppl. a.*; **depart,mentali'zation**.

1846 R. FORD *Gatherings fr. Spain* 31 It was found to be no easy matter to carry departmentalization. **1878** *Fraser's Mag.* XVIII. 636 We have.. been, geographically speaking, in the Jura, though departmentally in the Doubs. **1886** *Pall Mall G.* 1 Jan. 4/1 The.. crippling diseases of official red tape and departmentalism. **1900** *Westm. Gaz.* 6 Dec. 9/3 The Bovril business was strikingly departmentalised.. and .. the managing-director.. still occupies the position he has held from the start. **1924** W. B. SELBIE *Psychol. Relig.* 40 That tendency to departmentalize human nature from which modern psychology has at length shaken itself free. **1930** *N.Y. Times* 10 Aug. v. 2/2 Everything should be organized and departmentalized. **1931** W. ROSE *Outl. Mod. Knowl.* p. xiii, Scientific investigation is thus becoming more departmentalised; each worker finds himself compelled to devote his mind and energies to a more restricted field. **1931** A. L. ROWSE *Politics & Younger Generation* i. 11 The normal continental type of a departmentalized social life. **1933** *Jrnl. R. Aeronaut. Soc.* XXXVII. 346 In the beginning there was no departmentalisation of flying. The pioneers designed, financed, built, flew, crashed and repaired their own aircraft. **1936** *Mind* XLV. 250 The feeble-minded.. seem to be more departmentalised than normal children. **1940** *Economist* 27 July 125/1 The ultimate task of linking these 'Special' and 'Registered' accounts into an organic whole will demand more elastic methods. As a result of this departmentalisation, sterling is rapidly losing the homogeneity which is the hall-mark of a free currency. **1961** *Daily Tel.* 25 Feb. 8/2 If these negotiations fail, then President de Gaulle will have no alternative but to proceed with his interim plans for Algeria—departmentalisation, and the admission of more Moslems to office. **1962** *Listener* 5 July 19/2 Professor Haydn was arguing against departmentalization of history, the separate analysis of religious, political, and economic 'factors'.

departson, var. DEPARTISON, *Obs.*, departure.

departure (dɪˈpɑːtjʊə(r)). [a. OF. **departeüre*, *desparteüre*:—late L. type **dispartītūra*, f. *dispartīre*, F. *départ-ir* to DEPART: see -URE.]

†**1. a.** Separation, severance, parting. *Obs.*

a **1533** LD. BERNERS *Huon* clxii. 631, I shall make a departure of your two loues. **1559** SCOT in Strype *Ann. Ref.* I. App. vii. 17 The departure of Gascoygne. **1581** LAMBARDE *Eiren.* II. vii. (1588) 201 Controversies, betweene masters and servants, touching their departure. **1643** MILTON *Divorce* viii. (1851) 40 Much more can no other remedie or retirement be found but absolute departure.

†**b.** *concr.* A boundary separating two regions; a separation, division. *Obs.*

1523 LD. BERNERS *Froiss.* I. cccxxiv. 505 By the ryuer of Aude, the whiche was the departure of bothe realmes.

†**c.** *Old Chem.* Separation of a metal from an alloy or a solution. *Obs.*

1727–51 CHAMBERS *Cycl.* s.v. *Depart*, If the aqua fortis, having quitted the silver, and being united with the copper, be then filtrated, it is called *aqua secunda*; in which if you steep an iron plate some hours, you will have another departure; for the menstruum will let go the copper, and prey on the iron.

†**d.** *departure with*: parting with, giving up. (Cf. DEPARTING *vbl. sb.* 4.)

a **1563** G. CAVENDISH *Wolsey* (1893) 177 A bare and symple departure with another's right.

2. a. The action of departing or going away.

a **1533** LD. BERNERS *Huon* lxxxv. 268 After his departure Kynge Charlemayn made redy his company. **1611** SHAKS. *Wint. T.* III. ii. 78 You knew of his departure, as you know What you haue vnderta'ne to doe in's absence. **1667** MILTON *P.L.* XI. 303 Departure from this happy place. **1875** JOWETT *Plato* (ed. 2) I. 375 The hour of departure has arrived.

b. The action of departing this life; decease, death. *Obs.* or *arch.*

1558 *Bury Wills* (1850) 150 All theise.. things to him before bequeathed to be delyvered to him.. wᵗin a quarter of one yeare after my departure. **1611** BIBLE *2 Tim.* iv. 6 The time of my departure is at hand. **1752** JOHNSON *Rambler* No. 203 ¶7 The loss of our friends.. impresses.. upon us the necessity of our own departure. **1821** MAD. D'ARBLAY *Lett.* Nov., I had thought him dead, having heard.. a report that asserted his departure.

3. *transf.* and *fig.* Withdrawal, divergence, deviation (from a path, course, standard, etc.).

a **1694** TILLOTSON (J.), The fear of the Lord, and departure from evil. **1705** C. PURSHALL *Mech. Macrocosm* 122 Their.. Departure North, and South, are sometimes Greater, and sometimes Less, than that of the Sun. **1782** PRIESTLEY *Corrupt. Chr.* I. Pref. 15, I have not.. taken notice of every departure from the original standard. **1832** *Examiner* 261/2 Every departure from truth is a blemish. **1875** MAINE *Hist. Inst.* ii. 52 Partial and local departures from the Brehon Law were common all over Ancient Ireland.

4. The action of setting out or starting on a journey; *spec.* the starting of a railway train from a station. Also *attrib.* (Opposed to *arrival*.)

1540 *Stat. 32 Hen. VIII*, c. 14 [They] intende to make.. their departur from the said porte.. as soone as wynde and wether wyl serue. **1598** HAKLUYT *Voy.* I. 421 (R.) At their departure was shot off all the ordinance of the ship. **1776** GIBBON *Decl. & F.* i. (1838) I. 17 Whenever the trumpet gave the signal of departure. **1871** MORLEY *Voltaire* (1886) 101 The period of twenty years between Voltaire's departure from England and his departure for Berlin. **1887** W. E. NORRIS *Major & Minor* II. 138 Miss Huntley was standing on the departure side of the little Kingscliff station. *a* **1895** *Mod.* The Booking Office is open 15 minutes before the departure of each train.

5. *fig.* The starting or setting out on a course of action or thought. *new departure*: a fresh start; the beginning of a new course of procedure; cf. 7 b.

1839 CALHOUN *Wks.* (1874) III. 399 My aim is fixed, to take a fresh start, a new departure on the States Rights Republican tack. **1876** GLADSTONE *Homeric Synchr.* 9 To begin by stating my point of departure. **1883** CHALMERS & HOUGH *Bankruptcy Act* Introd. 9 The present Act makes a fresh departure in bankruptcy legislation.

6. *Law.* **a.** A deviation in pleading from the ground taken by the same party in an antecedent plea. †**b.** *departure in despite of the court*: see quot. 1641 (*obs.*).

1548 *Act 2–3 Edw. VI*, c. 2 §6 The Justices.. shall.. determine.. the said Offences concerning every such Departure. **1628** COKE *On Litt.* 304 b, A departure in pleading is said to be when the second Plea containeth matter not pursuant to his former. **1641** *Termes de la Ley* 110 b, Departure from a plee or matter. *Ibid.*, Departure in despight of the Court, is when the Tenant or Defendant appeareth to the action brought against him, &.. is called after.. in the same term, if he do not appeare, but make default, it is a departure in despight of the Court, and therefore he shall be condemned.

7. *Navigation.* **a.** The distance (reckoned in nautical miles) by which a ship in sailing departs or moves east or west from a given meridian; change of longitude. (Abbreviated *dep.*) **b.** The bearing of an object on the coast, taken at the commencement of a voyage, from which the dead reckoning begins.

1669 STURMY *Mariner's Mag.* bk. IV. 158 Retain the observed Difference of Latitude.. and thereby find the Departure from the Meridian. **1699** HACKE *Coll. Voy.* I. 42 Next day we took a new Departure from thence [Isle of Ascension]. **1810** J. H. MOORE *Pract. Navigator* 52 Easting or westing, in Plane Sailing, is called Departure or Meridian Distance. *Ibid.* 66 Suppose a ship takes her departure from the Lizard. **1837** *Penny Cycl.* VIII. 414 The number of miles in the course multiplied by the sine of the angle which it makes with the meridian gives the departure in miles. **1884** *Encycl. Brit.* XVII. 270 When clear of the harbor.. a bearing is taken of one known object and the distance estimated.. the result.. is entered in the log-book with the exact time. This is called the *departure* (i.e. from the land).

8. *Ellipt.* for *departure lounge* (at an airport); also, the entrance to this. Also (with cap. initial) in *colloq.* use.

1948 *Airports & Air Transportation* May 404/1 Adjoining .. the first departure lounge, is a new staff bar. **1963** 'R. ERSKINE' *Passion Flowers in Italy* iv. 48, I spent it [*sc.* the time] in the Departure Lounge. **1965** 'W. HAGGARD' *Powder Barrel* iii. 36 No trouble, sir. He's through in Departure now. **1968** A. DIMENT *Gt. Spy Race* II. ix. 165 The driver shook my hand at Departure. 'Have a good trip, sir.'

Hence (*nonce-wds.*) **de'parturism**, **de'parturist**, in the expressions *new departurism*, *new departurist*, the principle, or the advocate, of a 'new departure' in any movement or course of action.

1887 J. E. DWINELL *Side Lights* 10/2 The argument for the presence of New Departurism. **1887** G. W. VEDITZ in *Amer. Annals of Deaf* July 163, I did not mean him, but only the new departurists, Rössler, Arnold.

depascent (dɪˈpæsənt), *a. rare.* [ad. L. *dēpāscent-em*, pr. pple. of *dēpāscĕre*, *dēpāscī*, to eat down, consume, waste.] Consuming.

1651 BIGGS *New Disp.* ¶295 By the vigour of the digestible, esurine, and depascent ferment. **1727** BAILEY vol. II, *Depascent*, feeding greedily. **1755** in JOHNSON. **1822** GOOD *Stud.. Med.* (1834) II. 430 American Yaws—Depascent; and destroying progressively both muscle and bone.

depass (dɪˈpɑːs, -æ-), *v. rare.* [a. F. *dépasser*, in OF. *desp-*, f. *dé-*, *des-* (see DIS-) + *passer* to PASS.] †**a.** *intr.* To go, pass away, depart. *Obs.* **b.** *trans.* To pass beyond.

1559 in *Burgh Rec. Peebles* 5 May (Jam. Supp.), The sojarris.. to depas incontinent of the toune. **1886** *Blackw. Mag.* CXL. 505 Having depassed the height of 1800 metres .. above which fir-trees do not thrive.

†**de'pastion.** *Obs. rare.* [ad. L. *dēpāstiōn-em* eating down, feeding of cattle, n. of action from L. *dēpāscĕre*: see DEPASCENT.] Consumption.

1658 BP. REYNOLDS *Lord's Supper* xvii, A wasting depastion and decay of Nature. *Ibid.* xviii, That continual depastion of his radical moysture by vital heat.

† **de'pastor.** *Obs. nonce-wd.* [agent-noun from L. *dēpāscĕre* (see DEPASCENT), after *pastor*.] One who feeds upon, eats away, or consumes.

1583 STUBBES *Anat. Abus.* II. (1882) 91 The wicked liues of their pastors (or rather depastors). *Ibid.* 95 No more is he a good pastor or minister, but rather a depastor and minisher.

depasturage (dɪ'pɑːstjʊərɪdʒ, -æ-). [f. DEPASTURE *v.* + -AGE.] **a.** The eating down of pasture by grazing animals. **b.** Right of pasture.

1765 *Projects* in *Ann. Reg.* 144/1 The plants were all in a condition for depasturage. **1797** BURN *Eccl. Law* (ed. 6) III. 477 The value or usual price of the depasturage of such beasts per week upon such eddish or after-grass. **1807** VANCOUVER *Agric. Devon* (1813) 218 The inhabitants..have the right of a free depasturage for their sheep upon the moor. **1875** J. FISHER *Landholding in Eng.*, The profit which arose from sheep-farming led to the depasturage of the land.

depasture (dɪ'pɑːstjʊə(r), -æ-), *v.* [f. DE- I. 1 + PASTURE *v.*; cf., for sense, OF. *depaistre* (Cotgr. *desp-*), ad. L. *dēpāscĕre* to eat down, consume.]

1. *trans.* Of cattle: To consume the produce of (land) by grazing upon it; to use for pasturage.

1596 SPENSER *State Irel.* Wks. (Globe ed.) 630/1 To keepe theyr cattell..pasturing upon the mountayn..and removing still to fresh land, as they have depastured the former. *a* **1796** VANCOUVER in A. Young *Ess. Agric.* (1813) II. 284 The sheep and cow cattle, with which the primest of the grass lands through the country are generally depastured. **1799** J. ROBERTSON *Agric. Perth* 303 The cows are fed in summer on cut clover, without allowing them to depasture it. **1858** CARLYLE *Fredk. Gt.* (1865) II. VII. iii. 264 Clayey country, dirty-greenish, as if depastured partly by geese.

transf. & *fig.* **1610** G. FLETCHER *Christ's Vict.* xl, Nor Hibla, though his thyme depastured, As fast agaíne with honie blossomed. **1864** *Sat. Rev.* XVIII. 381/1 If Austria is forced to depasture the land with hordes of soldiery.

2. *intr.* To graze.

1586 *Wills & Inv. N.C.* II. Surtees (1860) 131 My cattell shall remayne and depasture, uppon my groundes..as they are at this instante. **1628** COKE *On Litt.* 96 a, To sheere all the sheep depasturing within the manor. **1785** PALEY *Mor. Philos.* (1818) I. 114 Whilst his flocks depastured upon a neighbouring hill. **1840** *Jrnl. R. Agric. Soc.* I. III. 263 Over this vast open field..no cattle can depasture.

fig. **1600** FAIRFAX *Tasso* XIII. lxxix. 250 The bait and food, Whereon his strange disease depastred long.

3. *trans.* To put (cattle) to graze; to pasture or feed (cattle).

1713 DERHAM *Phys. Theol.* V. i. 307 Depasturing their Cattel in the Desarts and uncultivated World. **1809** *Nat. Hist.* in *Ann. Reg.* 799/2 The country on which the sheep are depastured..is set out into divisions. **1844** WILLIAMS *Real Prop.* (1877) 324 A right of depasturing cattle on the land of another.

fig. **1859** I. TAYLOR *Logic in Theol.* 240 The human spirit..depasturing itself in the fat levels of the Greek literature. **1865** ALEX. SMITH *Summ. Skye* II. 147 We could pleasantly depasture our eyes on the cultivated ground.

4. Of land: To furnish pasturage to (cattle).

1805 LUCCOCK *Nat. Wool* 196 This part of the county..now..depastures flocks in whose frame and fleece are visible some strong symptoms of a more fashionable breed. **1844** *Port Phillip* (Austral.) *Patriot* 22 July 3/6 The run will depasture about 4000 sheep.

Hence **de'pastured** *ppl. a.*; **de'pasturing** *vbl. sb.* and *ppl. a.*; also **de'pasturable** *a.*, capable of being depastured; **depastu'ration**, **depasture** *sb.*, depasturing.

1794 GISBORNE *Walks Forest* v. (1796) 85 The bare worn track, and close-depastured plain. **1807** VANCOUVER *Agric. Devon* (1813) 282 The depasturable parts of the forest. **1823** SURTEES *Durham* III. 239 *note*, Bees were of so much importance that..the depasturing of bees was one article of a solemn concordat between two religious houses. **1841** *Jrnl. R. Agric. Soc.* II. II. 216 It [the winter tare] is sometimes resorted to for depasturation in the spring. **1846** J. BAXTER *Libr. Pract. Agric.* (ed. 4) I. 380 Mowing and depasturing are modes of cropping, comprehended in the term management of meadows. **1856** *Jrnl. R. Agric. Soc.* XVII. I. 282 If you watch cows on depasture, you observe them select their own food. **1858** CARLYLE *Fredk. Gt.* II. VII. iii. 183 This is memorable ground..little as the idle tourists think, or the depasturing geese, who happen to be there.

† **de'patriate,** *v. Obs.* [f. DE- I. 2 + L. *patria* fatherland: cf. med.L. *dispatriāre* in same sense.] *intr.* To leave or renounce one's native country; to expatriate oneself.

a **1688** VILLIERS (Dk. Buckhm.) *Chances* Wks. (1714) 154 If they should hear so odious a thing of us, as that we should depatriate. *a* **1797** MASON *Dean & Squire* (R.), A subject born in any state May, if he please, depatriate.

† **de'pauper,** *v. Obs.* [a. OF. *depauperer*, ad. L. *dēpauperāre*: see next.] = DEPAUPERATE *v.*

1562 WIN3ET *Cert. Tractates* Wks. 1888 I. 8 The depaupering the tennentis be 3our fewis, augmentationis and utheris exactionis. **1571** *Sc. Acts Jas. VI* (1814) 69 (Jam.) Ye haue..depaupereit the inhabitantis of the toun.

de'pauperate, *ppl. a.* Also 5–6 -at. [ad. L. *dēpauperāt-us*, pa. pple. of *dēpauperāre*: see next.] Made poor; impoverished (*obs.* in general use); **b.** *Bot.*, etc. = DEPAUPERATED.

1460 CAPGRAVE *Chron.* 103 Alle tho that were depauperat and spoiled be his predecessoure. *a* **1572** KNOX *Hist. Ref.* Wks. 1846 I. 404 The depauperat saullis that this day dwell thairin. **1670** *Lex Talionis* 26 It loses much of its vivacity, and becomes depauperate and affect. **1863** A. GRAY *Lett.* (1893) 508 Inclosed are depauperate specimens [of the seeds]. **1883** *Syd. Soc. Lex.*, *Depauperate*, impoverished; as if starved; diminished in size for want of favourable conditions of nourishment, and such like. Also..having no, or few, flowers.

depauperate (dɪ'pɔːpəreɪt), *v.* [f. ppl. stem of med.L. *dēpauperāre* to impoverish, reduce to poverty, f. DE- I. 1 + *pauperāre* to make poor, f. *pauper* poor.] *trans.* To render poor, to impoverish; to reduce in quality, vigour, or capacity.

1623 COCKERAM, *Depauperate*, to impouerish. **1647** JER. TAYLOR *Dissuas. Popery* II. II. §7 To represent God in a carved stone, or a painted Table, does depauperate our understanding of God. **1668** *Phil. Trans.* III. 891 The blood is now..depauperated of the spirituous and finer particles. **1708** MOLYNEUX *ibid.* XXVI. 59 Liming..doth not so much Depauperate the Ground. **1752** CARTE *Hist. Eng.* III. 728 Bishops..had made shameful depredations on the church and depauperated many of the sees. **1886** *Ch. Times* 5 Nov. 173/2 By depauperating the national creed.

Hence **de'pauperating** *vbl. sb.* and *ppl. a.*

1770 *Monthly Rev.* 20 In this depauperating and attenuating course the patient..persevered.

de'pauperated, *ppl. a.* [f. prec. + -ED.] Rendered poor, impoverished; reduced or deteriorated in quality, vigour, capacity, etc.

1666 J. SMITH *Old Age* (1752) 95 The best blood itself..becomes weak and much depauperated. **1756** C. LUCAS *Ess. Waters* II. 261 A languid, depauperated and broken state of the juices. **1870** C. B. CLARKE in *Macm. Mag.* Nov. 48/2 The feeble, the sickly, and the depauperated should be weeded out in the struggle for existence. **1881** HUXLEY in *Nature* XXIII. 611 The fish is left in that lean and depauperated state.

b. *Bot.*, etc. Stunted or degenerate from want of nutriment; starved; imperfectly developed from any cause that produces results analogous to innutrition.

1830 LINDLEY *Nat. Syst. Bot.* 275 Flowers hermaphrodite, surrounded by bracteæ, the outer of which are petaloid and herbaceous, the inner depauperated and coloured. **1888** *Athenæum* 1 Sept. 293/3 The rocks of this age present only a depauperated flora and fauna.

depauperation (dɪ,pɔːpə'reɪʃən). [ad. med.L. *dēpauperātiōn-em*, n. of action f. *dēpauperāre* to impoverish: see DEPAUPERATE.] The process or condition of being depauperated; impoverishment.

1664 BAXTER in *Life & Times* I. (1696) 106, I fell into another fit of Bleeding, which..after my former depauperation, did weaken me much. **1750** CARTE *Hist. Eng.* II. 320 Getting the great seal put to blank charters, to the depauperation of the Crown. **1830** LINDLEY *Nat. Syst. Bot.* 59 Flowers axillary, or in terminal spikes or racemes, in consequence of the depauperation of the upper leaves. *Ibid.* 233 A singular depauperation of the calyx..in which that organ is reduced sometimes to a mere obsolete ring.

depauperize (dɪ'pɔːpəraɪz), *v.*[1] [f. DE- I. 1 + *pauperize*, after L. *dēpauperāre*: see prec.] = DEPAUPERATE, PAUPERIZE.

1873 HUXLEY *Crit. & Addr.* 206 This immense fauna of Miocene Arctogæa is shrunk and depauperized in North Asia.

Hence **depauperi'zation**, depauperation, pauperization.

1844 LINGARD *Anglo-Sax. Ch.* (1858) I. vi. 218 *heading*, Depauperization of the Church. **1877** H. WOODWARD in *Encycl. Brit.* VI. 656/1 After such extreme retrogression, the depauperization of certain parts and organs..in the Anomoura is easily to be understood and admitted.

de-pauperize (diː'pɔːpəraɪz), *v.*[2] [f. DE- II. 1 + *pauperize*.] *trans.* To raise or free from pauperism; to DISPAUPERIZE.

1863 W. B. JERROLD *Signals of Distress* 303 The boys in this union will never be depauperized; they have to mix with the men, most of whom are gaol-birds. **1883** *19th Cent.* May 909 The neglected children..must be depauperised before they can be received into good and respectable homes.

‖ **dépaysé** (depeize), *a.* [Fr., lit. '(removed) from one's own country'.] Removed from one's habitual surroundings; = DÉRACINÉ. Also as *sb.* = EXILE *sb.*[2]

1909 in WEBSTER. **1924** *Glasgow Herald* 23 July 8 A golden eagle was discovered in the Clock Tower of the Houses of Parliament..a noble creature strangely dépaysé or out of its element! **1928** A. WAUGH *Nor many Waters* v. 208 She knew so well that drifting European life of the *depaysé*. **1938** *Times Lit. Suppl.* 9 Apr. 242/2 In those unknown countries [*sc.* romance] he would have been as completely *dépaysé* as his own Corneille or Racine. *Ibid.* 2 July 447/1 Not yet so *dépaysé* that he had forgotten the language of the village pub.

† **depe,** *v. Obs.* [OE. (Anglian) *dēpan* = OFris. *dēpa*, OS. *dôpian* (MDu. *dôpen*, Du. *doopen*, LG. *döpen*, whence Sc. *döpa*, Da. *döbe*), OHG. *toufen*, *touffan* (:—*toufjan*, MHG. *töufen*, *toufen*, Ger. *taufen*), Goth. *daupjan*, 'to baptize'; in MHG., MDu. (and Goth. *ufdaupjan*) with the wider sense 'to immerse, to dip'; OTeut. **daupjan* causal of **deupan*, *daup*, *dupan-* to be deep, **deupoz*, Goth. *diups*, deep. But in ME. this verb ran together with the cognate *depe*, DEEP, OE. *dīepan*, *dȳpan*, to make deep, to submerge.]

1. To immerse as a religious rite, to baptize.

c **960** *Rushw. Gosp.* Matt. iii. 11 Ic eowic depu *vel* dyppe wættre. *Ibid.* 13 þætte he wære depid. *Ibid.* 14 Ic sceal fram þe beon *vel* wesa deped *vel* fullwihted. *c* **1315** SHOREHAM 11 Olepi me mot hym depe ine the water. **1340** *Ayenb.* 107 Vor depe and cristni is al on.

2. To immerse, submerge, plunge deeply, dip. See also DEEP *v.* 4.

c **950** *Lindisf. Gosp.* Matt. xxvi. 23 Se ðe depeð mec mið hond in disc. **1340** *Ayenb.* 83 Efterward he depþ ine blod. **1395** PURVEY *Remonstr.* (1851) 69 Othere bisshopis that ben not so depid in errour. **1565** T. STAPLETON *Fortr. Faith* 34 Protestants are now a days so deped in darcknes. [*a* **1608** SIR F. VERE *Comment.* (1657) 34 The measure and time..which they were to observe in the deeping of their oares.]

depe, Obs. form of DEEP *a.* and *v.*

† **de'peach,** *sb. Obs.* Also 6 depesche, depech, peache, 6–7 -peche. [a. F. *dépêche*, in OF. *despeche*, *-esche* (1495 in Godef.), f. *dépêcher*: see next.] Dispatch: **a.** of messengers, messages; **b.** of business. **c.** A message or messengers sent off.

a. **1528** GARDINER in Pocock *Rec. Ref.* I. l. 116 We differed the depech of this post. **1547** *Privy Council Acts* (1890) II. 83 At their late depeache over the sees. **1577–87** HOLINSHED *Chron.* III. 918/1 Hauing his depeach, he tooke his leaue of the king at Richmond about noone. **1624** *Brief Inform. Affairs Palatinate* 34 The depeach and the instruction of the said Embassade.

b. **1568** NORTH *Gueuara's Diall Pr.* IV. 158 b, Shee onely did confirme al the prouisions & depeches of the affaires of the weale publike. *a* **1563** CAVENDISH *Wolsey* (1893) 190 Resort to hyme for the depeche of the noblemens and others patents.

c. **1552** in Strype *Eccl. Mem.* II. II. xi. 337 We send this Depeche, not by thorow Post from hence. **1568** DK. SUFFOLK in H. Campbell *Love Lett. Mary Q. Scots* App. (1824) 28 Till..they heard from the Quene their mistress by their next depeche.

† **de'peach,** *v. Obs.* Forms: 5 depesshe, 6 -peche, -peech, -peache, 6–7 -pesche, -peach; also DESPECHE q.v. [a. F. *dépêcher*, in OF. *de-*, *des-*, *peechier*, *-pechier*, *-peeschier*, *-peschier*, etc. (1225 in Godef.), repr. a late L. type *dis-*(or *de-ex-*) *pedicāre*, with the same radical as IMPEACH, F. *empêcher*, L. *impedicāre*.

The OF. forms of *dépêcher* are entirely parallel to those of *empêcher*, OF. *empeechier*, which goes back through the recorded early OF. *empedecer*, Pr. *empedegar*, to L. *impedicāre* to catch, entangle (f. *pedica* fetter, snare for the feet), used in late L. and Romanic for L. *impedīre* (Du Cange). Parallel to this is **(de-)expedicāre*, for L. *expedīre*, to free the feet, disengage, send away, dispatch. But though DISPATCH (q.v.) is synonymous, it is not etymologically connected with *depêcher*, *depeach*.

(In 16–17th c. the form *depeche*, *-peach*, was mostly English, *depesche* (rime *flesche*) Scotch.)]

trans. To send away, get rid of, dispose of, finish off expeditiously; to dispatch.

1474 CAXTON *Chesse* (1860) A ij, I dyde doo sette in enprynte a certeyn nombre of theym, whiche anone were depesshed and solde. **1523** *St. Papers Hen. VIII*, IV. 12, I..haue this daye by noone depeched hym with other letters. **1527** in Strype *Eccl. Mem.* I. App. xiv. 32 She said that our demand was reasonable and that we shold reasort unto the Chancellor therfore who shold depeache it out off hand. **1540–1** ELYOT *Image Gov.* (1549) 160 He depeached those deponentes for that time. **1556** LAUDER *Tractate* 290 All sic 3e suld frome 3ow depesche. **1566** PAINTER *Pal. Pleas.* I. 36 The Senators depeached ambassadours to the King commaunding them to say nothing of Simocharis. *a* **1651** CALDERWOOD *Hist. Kirk* (1842–6) III. 706 That the French Ambassador..may be depesched. **1655** DIGGES *Compl. Ambass.* 301 This I do depeach, without knowledge of the Queens Majestie.

b. *refl.* To rid or disembarrass oneself of (any one). Also, to make haste, to use dispatch.

1485 CAXTON *Chas. Gt.* 53 Depesshe the, or by the god on whome I byleue, I shalle smyte the there as thou lyest. **1513** DOUGLAS *Æneis* I. v. 28 Comment. Wks. 1874 II. 289 For his sone Glaucus followit Paris, he depechit him of him.

Hence † **de'peaching** *vbl. sb.*

1540–1 ELYOT *Imag. Gov.* (1549) 56 Where one man hath the depeachyng of many matters. **1552** HULOET, Depeachyng, *absolutio*.

[**depectible,** *a.* Error in Johnson's Dict. and some later Dicts. for DEPERTIBLE.]

† **de'peculate,** *v. Obs.* [f. ppl. stem of L. *dēpeculārī* to despoil, pillage, plunder, f. DE- I. 1 + *peculārī* to embezzle, peculate.] *trans.* To plunder by peculation: said of public officials.

a **1641** BP. MOUNTAGU *Acts & Mon.* (1642) 319 He..left Syria in his short Lieutenancy miserably exhausted and depeculated. **1648** C. WALKER *Hist. Independ.* I. 155 The Prætor of Sardinia being sentenced for depeculating and Robbing that Province.

† **depecu'lation.** *Obs.* [n. of action f. prec.: see -ATION.] Plunder by peculation (*esp.* by an official).

1623 COCKERAM, *Depeculation*, robbing of the commonwealth. **1651** HOBBES *Leviath.* II. xxvii. 160 Robbery and Depeculation of the Publique treasure, or Revenues. **1656** in BLOUNT *Glossogr.*

de'peditate, *v. nonce-wd.* [f. L. *pēs*, *pedis* foot, after *decapitate*.] *trans.* To deprive of one's feet (or the use of them).

1808 *Satirist* in *Spir. Publ. Jrnls.* (1809) XII. 328 Almost depeditated by the amicable contest with Thrale, in which we overleaped a Roman sellula.

So **depedi'tation.** [after *decapitation*.] Amputation of a foot.

a **1773** JOHNSON in *Tour Hebrides* 29 Aug., Dr. Johnson.. said, 'George will rejoice at the depeditation of Foote'; and when I challenged that word, laughed, and owned he had made it.

† **de'peinct, depinct,** *v.* [Intermediate forms between DEPAINT, *depeint*, and DEPICT: cf. OF. *depeinct*, var. *dépeint*, and It. *depinto*.] = DEPICT.

1579 SPENSER *Sheph. Cal.* Apr. 69 The Redde rose medled with the White yfere, In either cheeke depeincten liuely chere. **1590** —— *F.Q.* III. xi. 7 The winged boy in colours cleare Depeincted was. **1690** LEYBOURN *Curs. Math.* 356 Upon the Celestial Globe is depincted the several Constellations of the fixed Stars.

depeint, obs. form of DEPAINT *v.*

depeinten, pseudo-arch. f. *depainted*, pa. pple. of DEPAINT.

† **de'pel, depell,** *v. Obs.* [ad. L. *dēpell-ĕre* to drive out, cast down, f. DE- I. 1, 2 + *pellĕre* to drive.] *trans.* To drive away, dispel, expel.

1533 COVERDALE *Treat. Lord's Supper* Wks. 1844 I. 449 Who ought to be admitted, and who to be depelled. **1568** E. TYLNEY *Flower of Friendship*, All evill suspicions depelled, angers avoided. **1664** POWER *Exp. Philos.* II. 114 Water by its weight onely, and no innate Elatery, did depel the Succumbent Quicksilver in the Tube. **1788** *Trifler* No. 24. 324 The application.. will infallibly depell all his ills.

Hence **de'pelling** *vbl. sb.*; also **de'peller**, one who or that which drives away; a dispeller.

1597 MIDDLETON *Wisd. Solomon Par.* vi. H ij a, The very thought of her is mischiefes banne, Depeller of misdeeds. **1657** TOMLINSON *Renou's Disp.* 51 To the depelling of our distempers.

† **de'pencil,** *v. Obs.* Also 7 **depensil**. [f. DE- + PENCIL *v.*: cf. *depict, describe*.] *trans.* To inscribe with a pencil or brush; also *fig.* to depict.

1631 WEEVER *Anc. Fun. Mon.* 137 Vpon the forefront or some other places within these Abbeyes, this sentence is most commonly depensild, grauen, or painted. **1658** J. COLES *Cleopatra, 7th Pt.* 39 If mine [my astonishment] was easie to be observed in my countenance, Adallas's was no lesse depencilled out in his. **1708** E. HATTON *New View Lond.* II. 496/1 But the Decalogue, etc. are not there depencil'd. **1766** ENTICK *London* IV. 287 The names.. are depencilled in gold letters.

depend (dɪ'pɛnd), *v.*[1] [a. OF. *depend-re* (12th c. in Hatzf.), f. DE- I. 1 + *pendre* to hang, after L. *dēpendēre*, f. DE- I. 1 + *pendēre* (intr.) to hang. (The F. *pendre* in form represents L. *pendĕre* trans., to hang, suspend.)]

1. *intr.* To hang down, be suspended. (Now chiefly in literary use.)

c **1510** BARCLAY *Mirr. Gd. Manners* (1570) A ij, An olde man.. with bearde like bristles depending on his chin. **1579** SPENSER *Sheph. Cal.* Jan. 42 As on your boughes the ysicles depend. **1695** BLACKMORE *Pr. Arth.* IX. 373 Whence a deep Fring depends of Silk and Gold. **1711** POPE *Temp. Fame* 144 And ever-living lamps depend in rows. **1753** HOGARTH *Anal. Beauty* xi. 90 The drapery.. that depends from his shoulders. **1784** COWPER *Task* II. 450 With handkerchief in hand depending low. **1880** JEFFERIES *Gt. Estate* 146 The branches of the damsons depended so low.

b. *trans.* To hang down. *rare.*

1793 SOUTHEY *Lett.* (1856) I. 15 The mountain-ash.. Depends its branches to the stream below.

2. *intr. fig.* To hang *upon* or *from*, as a result or consequence is contingently attached to its condition or cause; to be contingent on or conditioned by. Const. *on, upon* (formerly *of*, rarely *from, to, in*). Also *absol.* (elliptically) in colloquial use in ***that depends***, i.e. on circumstances, or on some circumstance not expressed.

1413 LYDG. *Pilgr. Sowle* v. xiv. (1483) 108 The werk that he werketh dependeth of fortune and not of hym. **1509** HAWES *Past. Pleas.* XVI. xiv, The vii. Scyences.. Eche upon other do full well depende. **1526** *Pilgr. Perf.* (W. de W. 1531) 164 b, For in the loue of God & of our neyghbour.. dependeth all yͤ lawe & prophecyes. **1547–64** BAULDWIN *Mor. Philos.* (Palfr.) III. ii, If rulers be negligent, & looke not to small things whereunto greater doe depend. **1632** J. HAYWARD tr. *Biondi's Eromena* 153 Hee waited onely to receive her commands, whereon depended both his stay and departure. *a* **1645** FEATLY in *Fuller's Abel Rediv., Reinolds* I. 482 Howsoever the spirituall power be more excellent and noble than the temporall, yet they both are from God, and neither dependeth of the other. **1730** A. GORDON *Maffei's Amphith.* 2 From a right understanding of this, depends the Knowledge of many Places in both sacred and profane Writers. **1754** SHERLOCK *Disc.* (1759) I. iv. 141 This is a Matter depending on the Evidence of History. **1763** C. JOHNSTON *Reverie* I. 236 Forming a resolution on his steadiness, in which depends the crisis of his fate. **1847** FITZGERALD *Lett.* (1889) I. 181, I may then go to Naseby for three days: but this depends. **1848** MACAULAY *Hist. Eng.* II. 252 Whether the bond should be enforced or not would depend on his subsequent conduct. **1869** J. MARTINEAU *Ess.* II. 46 The psychological laws on which moral phenomena depend. **1886** J. R. REES *Pleas. Bk.-Worm* i. 33 The value of a book be it intrinsic or adventitious.. does not depend on its size.

† **b.** Formerly sometimes meaning little more than: To hang together with, to be connected with, to pertain or be pertinent to. *Obs.*

1525 LD. BERNERS *Froiss.* II. ccii. [cxcviii.] 623 That.. ye may write it in your Cronicle, with many other hystories that depende to the same mater. **1581** SIDNEY *Apol. Poetrie* (Arb.) 21 The.. beautie depended most of Poetrie. **1601** HOLLAND *Pliny* II. 293 And therefore this my present discourse.. howsoeuer it is in nature different, yet it dependeth of the other.

† **c.** To follow or flow from, result from. *Obs.*

1655 CULPEPPER *Riverius* x. vi. 295 A Dysentery.. with pain and torment depending upon the ulceration of the Intestines.

3. With *on, upon* († *of*, etc.: see 2): To be connected with in a relation of subordination; to belong to as something subordinate; to be a dependant of.

c **1500** *Melusine* 333 Partenay, Merment, Vouant & al theire appurtenaunces.. with the Castel Eglon with al that therof dependeth. **1578** BANISTER *Hist. Man* I. 19 Those [Vertebres] that are appertinent, or depend upon Os Sacrum. **1639** GENTILIS *Servita's Inquis.* (1676) 840 The Office of the Inquisition within these Dominions, doth not depend from the Court of Rome. *a* **1661** FULLER *Worthies* (1840) II. 419 Hereupon a story depends. **1710** WHITWORTH *Acc. of Russia* (1758) 48 They have no more freehold left, and their peasants or subjects, now immediately depend upon the Czar's officers. **1818** CRUISE *Digest* (ed. 2) V. 11 An estate tail, and all the remainders over, and the reversion depending on it.

† **b.** *absol.* To be dependent; to have or take a position of dependence. *Obs. rare.*

1673 *Ess. Educ. Gentlewom.* 26 Maids that cannot subsist without depending, as Servants, may chuse their places.

4. To rest entirely *on, upon* († *of*) for maintenance, support, supply, or what is needed; to have to rely *upon*; to be a burden *upon*, to be sustained by; to be dependent *on*.

1548 HALL *Chron.* 151 b, The whole waight and burden of the realme, rested and depended upon him. **1632** J. HAYWARD tr. *Biondi's Eromena* 151 The house not being any whit fortified, but depending altogether on the fortune of the walls below. **1691** T. H[ALE] *Acc. New Invent.* 131 The effect of depending upon forraign Countries for Hemps. **1802** MAR. EDGEWORTH *Moral T.* (1816) I. 202 A father and mother.. who depended on me for their support. **1832** HT. MARTINEAU *Life in Wilds* viii. 103 Well directed labour is all we have had to depend on. **1865** TROLLOPE *Belton Est.* xxii. 257 Clara must.. depend entirely on the generosity of some one till she was married.

5. To rely in mind, count, or reckon confidently *on, upon* († *of*, etc.). (Now chiefly in colloq. phr. ***depend upon it***, used parenthetically.)

1500–20 DUNBAR *Poems* lxxxi. 107 And on the prince depend with heuinely feir. **1563** *Homilies* II. *Faith* II. (1859) 40 Depending (or hanging) only of the help and trust that they had in God. **1638** SIR T. HERBERT *Trav.* (ed. 2) 275 The superstitious, who depended upon some supernaturall helps. **1693** *Mem. Ct. Teckely* IV. 60 If so be they had been defeated, one might have depended upon seeing the Affairs of the Ottaman Empire restored. **1738** SWIFT *Pol. Conversat.* 53 Faith Miss, depend upon it, I'll give you as good as you bring. **1745** ELIZA HEYWOOD *Fem. Spect.* (1748) 319 It may be depended on that.. we shall advertise. **1748** F. SMITH *Voy. Disc. N.-W. Pass.* I. 30 If they can eat Seal, there is such a Plenty of them.. that they may depend upon Food be their Voyage ever so long. **1855** MACAULAY *Hist. Eng.* III. 496 He could no longer depend on the protection of his master. **1885** G. ALLEN *Babylon* v, Depend upon it, Churchill, over-education's a great error.

b. *ellipt.* with following clause: To be sure or confident; = 'to depend upon it' (see 5). *colloq.*

1700 ASGILL *Argument* 95, I.. do as much depend that I shall not go hence by returning to the Dust. **1747** FRANKLIN *Plain Truth* Wks. 1887 II. 49 No man can with certainty depend that another will stand by him. **1789** *Triumphs of Fortitude* II. 150 Depend, it will not be ill conducted by one of such skill. **1791** MRS. INCHBALD *Simp. Story* II. x. 187 From the constancy of his disposition, she depended much, that sentiments like these were not totally eradicated. **1879** J. C. MORISON *Gibbon* 128 We may depend that a swift blight would have shrivelled his labours.

† **6.** To wait in suspense or expectation *on, upon*. (Cf. *to hang upon any one's lips*.) *Obs.*

c **1430** LYDG. *Bochas* VIII. i. (1554) 178 a, The heartes of men, depending in a traunce. **1500–20** DUNBAR *Poems* lxxi. 38 Off gyd and gouirnance we ar all solitair, Dependand ay vpoun thy stait and grace. **1612** *Proc. Virginia* 41 in *Capt. Smith's Wks.* (Arb.) 385 Captaine Bartholomew Gosnoll.. at last prevailed with some Gentlemen.. who depended a yeare vpon his proiects, but nothing could be effected. **1697** DRYDEN *Virg. Æneid* 4 (T.) The hearer on the speaker's mouth depends. **1704** STEELE *Lying Lover* II. i. 20 Have not I, Madam, two long Years.. depended on your Smiles?

7. To be in suspense or undetermined, be waiting for settlement (as an action at law, a bill in parliament, an appointment, etc.). (Usually in pres. pple. = pending: see also DEPENDING *ppl. a.* 5.)

c **1430** LYDG. *Story of Thebes* III. (R.), The fatall chance Of life and death dependeth in balance. **1532–3** *Act 24 Hen. VIII*, c. 12 §8 Euery matter, cause, and contention nowe dependynge.. before any of the sayde archebishops. *c* **1575** *Leg. Bp. St. Androis* 131 (*Satir. Poems Reform.*) Becaus St. Androis then dependit, To heich promotione he pretendit. **1632** *Star Chamb. Cases* (Camden) 123 The same demurrer hath been on both sides often argued, and now depends readie for the Judgement of yͤ Court. **1765** T. HUTCHINSON *Hist. Mass.* I. 185 Whilst these disputes.. were depending, the.. Indians made attacks. *a* **1859** MACAULAY *Hist. Eng.* V. 480 Bills of supply were still depending. **1883** *Law Reports* 11 Q. Bench Div. 559 The resolution was filed in the court in which the bankruptcy was depending.

† **8.** To be ready or preparing to come on; to impend, to be imminent. *Obs.*

1712 SWIFT *City Shower* 3 While rain depends, the pensive cat gives o'er Her frolicks. **1719** DE FOE *Crusoe* I. xii. (1858) 184, I had not the least notion of any such thing depending, or the least supposition of it being possible.

† **9.** To have a leaning. (Cf. *penchant*.) *Obs. rare.*

1586 *Let. Earle Leycester* 15 It might then be suspected, in respect of the disposition of such as depend that way.

† **de'pend,** *v.*[2] *rare.* [ad. L. *dēpendĕre* to pay down or away, spend, expend, f. DE- I. 1, 2 + *pendĕre* to weigh, pay. Cf. DISPEND.] *trans.* To expend, spend.

1607 *Barley-Breake* (1877) 12 To whom Dame Nature lent so rich a port, That all her glory on her was depended.

dependability (dɪpɛndə'bɪlɪtɪ). [f. DEPENDABLE: see -ILITY.] The quality of being dependable, reliability.

1901 F. T. BULLEN *Sack of Shakings* 264 Next to the Trades in dependability.. are the west winds of the regions north and south of the Tropics. **1922** *Daily Mail* 7 Nov. 8 Renowned for entire Dependability. **1928** *Daily Express* 21 Apr. 10/3 That essential solidity and dependability that every wise woman seeks in her life mate. **1960** *Farmer & Stockbreeder* 9 Feb. 103 Farmers everywhere give the 780 Special the biggest vote of confidence because they know its dependability is based on experience.

dependable (dɪ'pɛndəb(ə)l), *a.* Also **-ible**. [f. DEPEND *v.* + -ABLE.] That may be depended on; trustworthy, reliable.

1735 POPE *Let. to Gay* xxi. Wks. (1737) VI. 186 That desire was, to fix and preserve a few lasting, dependable friendships. **1840** HERSCHEL *Ess.* (1857) 92 Calculations, with more dependable data. **1842** *Murray's Handbk. N. Italy* 91 Le Quattro Nazioni, good and reasonable, and kept by very dependable people. **1864** SIR F. PALGRAVE *Norm. & Eng.* IV. 642 Flambard was thoroughly dependable. **1889** BOYD CARPENTER *Permanent Elem. Relig.* Introd. 30 We have dependable material on which to base our study.

Hence **de'pendableness; de'pendably** *adv.*

1860 PUSEY *Min. Proph.* 554 Alexander saw and impressed upon his successors the dependibleness of the Jewish people. **1862** MRS. CARLYLE *Lett.* III. 111 The accounts I get of Mr. C. from himself, and (still more dependably) from my housemaid. **1874** MISS MULOCK *My Mother & I* xi, One of his characteristics was exceeding punctuality and dependableness.

dependant, -dent (dɪ'pɛndənt), *sb.* [a. F. *dépendant* adj. and sb., properly pr. pple. of *dépendre* to DEPEND. From the 18th c. often (like the adj.) spelt *dependent*, after L. (both forms being entered by Johnson); but the spelling *-ant* still predominates in the sb.: cf. *defendant, assistant*.

1755 JOHNSON *Pref. to Dict.*, Some words, such as *dependant, dependent; dependance, dependence*, vary their final syllable, as one or another language is present to the writer.]

† **1.** Something subordinately attached or belonging to something else; a subordinate part, appurtenance, dependency. *Obs.*

1523 LD. BERNERS *Froiss.* I. clxxvii. (R.), The Frenchemen.. demaunded.. to haue the sygnorie of Guysnes.. and all the landes of Froyten, and the dependantes of Guysnes vnto the lymyttes of the water of Grauelyng. **1548** HALL *Chron.* 98 With all incidentes, circumstaunces, dependentes, or connexes. **1643** PRYNNE *Treachery of Papists* I. 32 (R.) The parliament.. repealed this parliament of 21 R. II. with all its circumstances and dependents. **1716** *Lond. Gaz.* No. 5425/9 The Lease for the.. Copper-Works.. with its Dependants. **1721** BRADLEY *Wks. Nature* 32 Monsieur de Reaumur.. discover'd certain Parts which might reasonably be esteem'd Dependants of Flowers. **1837** F. COOPER *Recoll. Europe* I. 174 [Versailles] was a mere dependant of the crown.

2. A person who depends on another for support, position, etc.; a retainer, attendant, subordinate, servant.

1588 SHAKS. *L.L.L.* III. i. 134 The best ward of mine honours is rewarding my dependants. **1632** LITHGOW *Trav.* I. 38, I demanded our dependant, what was to pay? **1647** CLARENDON *Hist. Reb.* I. (1843) 5/1 Almost all of his own numerous family and dependants. **1750** JOHNSON *Rambler* No. 28 ¶8 An error almost universal among those that converse much with dependents. **1752** *Ibid.* No. 190 ¶7 Convinced that a dependant could not easily be made a friend. **1786** BURKE *W. Hastings* Wks. 1842 II. 105 Her female dependants, friends, and servants. **1830** D'ISRAELI *Chas. I*, III. v. 76 Such a personage as Laud is doomed to have dependents, and not friends. **1855** MACAULAY *Hist. Eng.* IV. 55 Other people could provide for their dependants. **1858** FROUDE *Hist. Eng.* III. xiii. 118 The gentry were surrounded by dependents. **1875** JOWETT *Plato* (ed. 2) I. 309 A poor dependant of the family.

dependence (dɪ'pɛndəns). Forms: 6 **-aunce**, 6–9 **-ance**, 7– **-ence**. [a. F. *dépendance* (15th c. in Littré, in 14th c. *despendence*, Oresme), f. *dependant*: see prec. and -ANCE. Like DEPENDENT *a.*, subseq. assimilated to the L. type, the form in *-ance* being rare after 1800.]

† **1.** The action of hanging down; *concr.* something that hangs down. *Obs. rare.*

1697 DRYDEN *Virg. Georg.* IV. 806 Like a large Cluster of black Grapes they show, And make a large dependance from the Bough.

2. The relation of having existence hanging upon, or conditioned by, the existence of something else; the fact of depending *upon* something else.

1605 VERSTEGAN *Dec. Intell.* ii. (1628) 27 Words.. that seeme to haue dependance on the Latin. **1613** J. SALKELD *Treat. Angels* 5 Without beginning or dependence of any other cause. **1646** SIR T. BROWNE *Pseud. Ep.* I. xi. 45 There was no naturall dependance of the event upon the signe. **1677** Plot *Oxfordsh.* 196, I dare not suppose there was any dependence between the medicin and disease. **1754** Edwards *Freed. Will* I. iv. 23 The Dependence and Connection between Acts of Volition or Choice, and their Causes. **1860** Tyndall *Glac.* I. xxvii. 199 The chain of dependence which runs throughout creation. **1864** Bowen *Logic* x. 348 That which comes next it in the order of dependence.

†**b.** Connexion of successively dependent parts; logical sequence. *Obs.* (or merged in prec.).

a **1535** More *Wks.* 611 (R.) Hys woordes.. be so dark and so intriked of purpose withoute any dependence or order. **1638** Sir T. Herbert *Trav.* (ed. 2) 236 The Father next, and as they are in blood the other follow in a just dependance; the rest promiscuously. **1681-6** J. Scott *Chr. Life* (1747) III. 252 The Discourse.. from Verse to Verse runs all along in a close and continued Dependance.

†**c.** In wider sense: Relation, connexion (cf. depend 2 b). *Obs.*

a **1633** Austin *Medit.* (1635) 226 As their [St. Philip and St. Bartholomew] being of that Society of the Twelve hindred them not from being of the great Societie the Church; so their other Dependances, as being of the Church, or being of the seventy, or being married men.. hindred them not from being of the Twelve.

3. The relation of anything subordinate to that from which it holds, or derives support, etc.; the condition of a dependant; subjection, subordination. (Opp. to *independence.*)

1614 Raleigh *Hist. World* III. 72 Those two great Cities, Athens and Sparta, upon which all the rest had most dependance. **1660** R. Coke *Power & Subj.* 147 How far the Britanick Churches were from any dependence upon the Church of Rome. **1699** Bentley *Phal.* 488 A dependance upon the most Brutal of Tyrants. **1751** Johnson *Rambler* No. 101 ¶4, I lived in all the luxury of affluence without expence or dependence. **1765** Blackstone *Comm.* Introd. §4. 101 Dependence being very little else, but an obligation to conform to the will or law of that superior person or state, upon which the inferior depends. **1874** Green *Short Hist.* viii. §2. 469 To free the Crown from its dependence on the Parliament. **1886** Stevenson *Kidnapped* xviii. 172 The other four were equally in the Duke's dependance.

†**4.** *concr.* That which is subordinate to, connected with, or belonging to, something else; an appurtenance, connexion, dependency. *Obs.*

1540 *Act 32 Hen. VIII*, c. 25 To committe the state of his said mariage, with all the circumstances and dependaunce thereof vnto the prelates. **1581** Savile *Tacitus' Hist.* III. xiii. (1591) 122 As though eight Legions were to be the dependance of one nauy. **1601** Holland *Pliny* I. 127 The great riuer Indus.. issueth out of a part or dependance of the hill Caucasus. **1794** *Hist.* in *Ann. Reg.* 54 Coblentz, a dependence of the electorate of Mentz.

†**b.** A body of dependants or subordinates; a retinue. (Usually *-ance.*) *Obs.*

1606 Ford *Honor Tri.* 10 Deseruing to be beloued; of whome? Of popular opinion or unstable vulgar dependances? **1631** Weever *Anc. Fun. Mon.* 273 He feasted ..two kings, two Queenes, with their dependances, 700. messe of meate scarce seruing for the first dinner. **1638** Rawley tr. *Bacon's Life & Death* (1650) 19 A numerous Family, a great Retinue, and Dependance. **1692** South *Serm.* (1697) I. 33 Encumbred with Dependances, throng'd and surrounded with Petitioners.

5. The condition of resting in faith or expectation (upon something); reliance; assured confidence or trust.

1627 Sanderson *12 Serm.* (1632) 530 Faithful dependance vpon the providence.. of God. **1754** *Hist. Yng. Lady Distinction* II. 10 Thoroughly sensible what little dependence I ought to make on my own strength. **1763** Eliz. Carter *Mem. etc.* (1816) I. 295 The waters, I shall continue drinking, without much dependance of getting better. **1801** Gabrielli *Myst. Husb.* II. 205 There was no dependance to be placed in the word of a woman who [etc.]. **1841** Lane *Arab. Nts.* I. 68 It is the only branch of divination worthy of dependance. **1875** Jowett *Plato* (ed. 2) V. 19 Living.. in dependence on the will of God.

b. *transf.* That on which one relies or may rely; object of reliance or trust; resource. ? *Obs.*

1754 Richardson *Grandison* IV. v. 44 Your honour, your piety, are my just dependence. **1803** Wellington in Owen *Desp.* 784 The seamen from the East India fleet were the only or principal dependence for manning the navy. **1827** J. F. Cooper *Prairie* II. iv. 59 Take the Lord for your dependance.

†**c.** Reliableness, trustworthiness. *Obs. rare.*

1752 Hume *Ess. & Treat.* (1777) I. 22 So little dependance has this affair. **1790-1811** W. Combe *Devil on Two Sticks* (1817) VI. 44 The philosophy of poets.. is not of very sterling dependence.

6. The condition of waiting for settlement; pending, suspense. (Now only in legal use.)

1605 *Burgh Rec. Aberdeen* 4 Dec. (Jam. Suppl.), That anes the actioune may be put under dependance befoir onie parliament. **1679-1714** Burnet *Hist. Ref.*, After a long dependance it might end as the former had done. **1816** Shelley *Let.* in Dowden *Life* II. 8 Engagements contracted during the dependence of the late negotiation. **1861** W. Bell *Dict. Law Scot.*, *Depending Action*, an action is held to be in dependence from the moment of the citation, until the final decision of the House of Lords. **1874** *Act 37-8 Vict.* c. 94 §68 Nothing herein contained shall affect any action now in dependence.

†**b.** A quarrel or affair of honour 'depending' or awaiting settlement. *Obs.*

1598 B. Jonson *Ev. Man in Hum.* I. v, The bastinado! a most proper, and sufficient dependance, warranted by the great Caranza. **1616** —— *Devil an Ass* IV. vii, H' is friend to him, with whom I ha' the dependance. **1820** Scott *Monast.* xxi, Let us pause for the space of one venue, until I give you my opinion on this dependence. [Note. *Dependence*, a phrase among the brethren of the sword for an existing quarrel.]

dependency (dɪˈpɛndənsɪ). Also 6-7 -encie; 6 -ancye, 7 -ancie, 7-9 -ancy. [f. as prec.: see -ancy, -ency.]

1. The condition of being dependent; the relation of a thing to that by which it is conditioned; contingent logical or causal connexion; = prec. 2.

1597 Hooker *Eccl. Pol.* v. (1632) 376 That dependencie and order, whereby the lower sustaining alwayes the more excellent [etc.]. **1603** Shaks. *Meas. for M.* v. i. 62 Such a dependancy of thing, on thing, As ere I heard in madnesse. **1647** Sprigge *Anglia Rediv.* IV. vii. (1854) 286 All threaded upon one string of dependency. **1748** Hartley *Observ. Man* I. iii. 336 The Dependency of Evidences makes the resulting Probability weak. **1864** Bowen *Logic* viii. 245 In this Unfigured Syllogism.. the dependency of Extension and Intension does not subsist.

2. The relation of a thing (or person) to that by which it is supported; state of subjection or subordination; = prec. 3.

1594 Hooker *Eccl. Pol.* I. x. (1611) 26 Hauing no such dependency upon any one. **1634** W. Tirwhyt tr. *Balzac's Lett.* 251, I have no servile dependancy upon their conceptions. **1724** Swift *Drapier's Lett.* Wks. 1755 V. II. 64 Ready to shake off the dependency of Ireland upon the crown of England. **1848** C. Bronte *J. Eyre* xiv. (1873) 133 That you care whether or not a dependent is comfortable in his dependency. **1856** Froude *Hist. Eng.* (1858) II. x. 456 They found England in dependency upon a foreign power; they left it a free nation.

†**3.** Reliance; = prec. 5. *Obs. rare.*

a **1600** Hooker (J.), Their dependancies on him were drowned in this conceit. **1627-77** Feltham *Resolves* I. lx. 98 As if God.. would lead us to a dependency on Him.

4. Something dependent or subordinate; a subordinate part; an appurtenance. **a.** *gen.*

1611 Speed *Hist. Gt. Brit.* IX. xxi. (1632) 1004 Many dependancies of Story had their euents in the Acts of this man. **1690** Locke *Hum. Und.* II. xii. §4 Modes I call such complex ideas, which.. are considered as dependancies on, or affections of substances. **1741** Warburton *Div. Legat.* II. 4 The Knowledge of human Nature and its Dependencies. **1852** S. R. Maitland *Ess. Various Subj.* 155 A thorough sifting of this subject, and its dependencies.

†**b.** A body of dependants; a household establishment. *Obs.*

1615 G. Sandys *Trav.* 61 This mans Serraglio.. answerable to his small dependancie. **1670** G. H. *Hist. Cardinals* II. I. 112 The Dependencies and Relations of the Popes and Cardinals, do not suffer the poor Prelats to act according to the Dictates of Equity. **1701** Swift *Contests of Nobles & Com.*, Men, who have acquired large possessions, and consequently dependancies.

c. A dependent or subordinate place or territory; *esp.* a country or province subject to the control of another of which it does not form an integral part.

1684 *Scanderbeg Rediv.* iii. 49 The Kingdom of Poland and great Dutchy of Lyffland, together with all their Dependencies. **1684-90** T. Burnet *Th. Earth* (J.), This earth, and its dependencies. **1848** Macaulay *Hist. Eng.* I. 342 This is that Sheffield which now, with its dependencies, contains a hundred and twenty thousand souls. **1864** R. A. Arnold *Cotton Fam.* 464 There is a wide difference between a dependency and a colony. The one is held in trust, the other in absolute fee-simple.

d. An appurtenance (to a dwelling-house, etc.).

1822 W. Irving *Braceb. Hall* ii. 12 To visit the stables, dog-kennel and other dependencies.

†**5.** A quarrel 'depending' or awaiting settlement; = prec. 6 b. *Obs.*

a **1625** Fletcher *Elder Bro.* v. i, The masters of dependencies, That by compounding differences 'tween others, Supply their own necessities. **1632** Massinger *Maid of Hon.* I. i, Your masters of dependencies to take up A drunken brawl.

†**b.** *gen.* An affair pending or awaiting settlement. *Obs. rare.*

1809 W. Taylor in Robberds *Mem.* II. 279 In consequence of disagreeable commercial dependencies, which I did not succeed in liquidating.

dependent (dɪˈpɛndənt), *a.* Also 5-6 -aunt, 6-9 -ant. [Originally *dependant*, a. F. *dépendant* (14th c. in Hatzf.), pr. pple. of *dépendre* to hang down, depend: from the 16th c. often assimilated to L. *dēpendēnt-em*, and now usually so spelt, the form in *-ant* being almost obs. in the adj., though retained in the sb., q.v.]

1. Hanging down, pendent.

c **1420** *Pallad on Husb.* III. 1060 So thai be wombed wel, dependaunt, syde, That likely is for greet and mighty stoore. **1514** Barclay *Cyt. & Uplondyshm.* (Percy Soc.) p. lxxii, With glistering eyes & side dependaunt beard. **1591** Greene *Maidens Dreame* xxviii, Mourning locks dependant. **1796** Morse *Amer. Geog.* I. 378 A regular rock, from the upper part of which are dependent many excrescences. **1880** C. & F. Darwin *Movem. Pl.* 128 [The leaves] partially assume their nocturnal dependent position.

2. a. That depends *on* something else; having its existence contingent on, or conditioned by, the existence of something else. ***dependent differentiation***: see differentiation 1.

1594 Hooker *Eccl. Pol.* I. viii. (1611) 20 On these two generall heads.. all other specialties are dependent. **1623** Cockeram, *Dependant*, which hangeth vpon another thing. **1664** Power *Exp. Philos.* II. 192 Effects dependent on the same.. Causes. **1707** Norris *Treat. Humility* iii. 77 A creature is a dependent being, that is, it is essential to a creature to depend upon the author of its being. **1850** McCosh *Div. Govt.* I. i. (1874) 11 Animal life, again, is dependent on vegetable life, and vegetable life is dependent on the soil and atmosphere. **1875** Jowett *Plato* (ed. 2) I. 265 All things in nature are dependent on one another.

†**b.** Annexed, appertaining. *Obs.*

1574 tr. *Littleton's Tenures* 62 b, The reversion that is dependaunt unto the same franketenement is severed from the jointure.

3. That depends or has to rely *on* something else for support, supply, or what is needed.

a **1643** W. Cartwright *Commend. Verses* in *Fletcher's Wks.*, Whose wretched genius, and dependent fires But to their benefactors' dole aspires. **1742** Young *Nt. Th.* iii. 448 Life makes the soul dependent on the dust. **1791** Mrs. Radcliffe *Rom. Forest* ii, She found herself wholly dependent upon strangers. **1865** Trollope *Belton Est.* xxvii. 332 It was her destiny to be dependent on charity. **1874** Green *Short Hist.* ii. §6. 93 The vast estates.. were granted out to new men dependent on royal favour.

4. a. Attached in a relation of subordination; subordinate, subject; opp. to *independent.*

1616 Brent tr. *Sarpi's Counc. Trent* (1676) 574 One Bishop instituted by Christ, and the others not to have any authority but dependant from him. **1624** Fisher in F. White *Repl. Fisher* 337 Mediators subordinate vnto, and dependent of Christ. **1654** tr. *Scudery's Curia Polit.* 93 Soveraignes are not subordinate and dependant to them [the Lawes]. **1726** *Adv. Capt. R. Boyle* 364 The Assembly meet here, which is in the nature of a dependant Parliament. **1829** I. Taylor *Enthus.* vii. 178 The temper of mind which is proper to a dependant and subordinate agent. **1863** Bright *Sp. Amer.* 26 Mar., They ceased to be dependent colonies of England.

b. Math. ***dependent variable***: one whose variation depends on that of another variable (the *independent variable*).

1852 Todhunter *Diff. Calc.* i, A *dependent* variable is a quantity the value of which is determined as soon as that of some independent variable is known.

†**5.** Impending. *Obs. rare.*

1606 Shaks. *Tr. & Cr.* II. iii. 21 That me thinkes is the curse dependant on those that warre for a placket.

†**depenˈdential,** *a. Obs.* [f. med.L. *dēpendēntia* dependence + -al[1]: cf. *confidential.*] Relating to, or of the nature of, dependence.

1646 S. Bolton *Arraignm. Err.* 14 God doth it to exercise a dependentiall faith upon God.

dependently (dɪˈpɛndəntlɪ), *adv.* [f. dependent *a.* + -ly[2].] In a dependent manner; in a way depending *on* something.

1646 Sir T. Browne *Pseud. Ep.* III. xxv. 178 These.. act but dependantly on their formes. **1677** Hale *Prim. Orig. Man.* I. iii. 73 Whether there be an utter impossibility of any material Being to be either independently or dependently eternal. **1793** Beattie *Moral Sc.* I. i. §3 (R.) If we affirm.. relatively, conditionally, or dependently on something else, it is the subjunctive.

depender (dɪˈpɛndə(r)). Also 6-7 *Sc.* -ar. [f. depend *v.*[1] + -er[1].]

†**1.** A dependant. Chiefly *Sc. Obs.*

c **1565** Lindesay (Pitscottie) *Chron. Scot.* (1728) 8 Through the vain flattery of his dependers. **1577-95** *Descr. Isles Scotl.* in Skene *Celtic Scotl.* iii. App. 438 Ane dependar on the Clan Donald. *a* **1639** Spottiswood *Hist. Ch. Scot.* IV. (1677) 186 Being all vassals and dependers of Huntley. **1724** Swift *Poems, A Riddle*, I'm but a meer Depender still: An humble Hanger-on at best. **1726-31** Tindal *Rapin's Hist. Eng.* (1743) II. XVII. 78 He drew together a number of Lords of his Dependers.

2. One who depends or relies *on* something. *rare.*

1611 Shaks. *Cymb.* I. v. 58 To be depender on a thing that leanes. **1617** Hieron *Wks.* II. 306 Art thou a continuall depender vpon teaching? **1827** *Examiner* 470/2 A set of puny dependers upon a British soldiery.

dependible, var. of dependable.

deˈpending, *vbl. sb. rare.* [f. depend *v.*[1] + -ing[1]. In sense 2, perh. a subst. use of the *ppl. a.*]

1. The action of the verb depend; dependence; in quot. †waiting, suspense (see depend *v.*[1] 6, 7).

1616 B. Jonson *Epigr.*, *To William Roe*, Delay is bad, doubt worse, depending worst.

2. Something depending on or belonging to something else; an appurtenance; = dependence 4, dependency 4 a. *Obs.*

1436 *Pol. Poems* (Rolls) II. 181 Conclusion of this deppendinge of kepinge of the see. **1642** in Rushw. *Hist. Coll.* III. (1692) I. 665 The said Commissions or Writs, with all their Dependings and Circumstances.

depending (dɪˈpɛndɪŋ), *ppl. a.* (*prep.*) [f. depend *v.*[1] + -ing[2].]

A. *adj.* That depends: see the verb.

1. Hanging or inclining downwards; pendent.

1735 Somerville *Chase* III. 441 To raise the slope Depending Road. **1758** J. S. *Le Dran's Observ. Surg.* (1771) 52 To prevent the Pus from lodging in the most depending Part. **1819** Wiffen *Aonian Hours* (1820) 39 Locked in the twilight of depending boughs. **1860** Gosse *Rom. Nat. Hist.* 176 One or two depending vines.

2. That depends on something else; contingent, conditioned, etc.; dependent.

1824 L. Murray *Eng. Gram.* (ed. 5) I. 446 A number of depending circumstances distinctly and advantageously arranged.

†**3.** Subordinate, dependent, subject. *Obs.*

1705 STANHOPE *Paraphr.* I. 37 [Persons] of a mean depending Condition. **1735** BERKELEY *Querist* §419 Either kingdom or republic, depending or independent, free or enslaved.

†**4.** Relying, trusting. ? *Obs.*

1746-7 HERVEY *Medit.* (1818) 113 A lesson of heaven-depending faith. **1829** E. BATHER *Serm.* II. 372 A praying, waiting, depending frame of mind.

5. Awaiting settlement, pending.

1679 *Hist. Jetzer* 34 To hear and determine the depending cause. **1754** ERSKINE *Princ. Sc. Law* (1809) 35 Letters of diligence..granted in a depending process.

B. *prep.* [Originally the pres. pple. agreeing with the sb. in absolute construction, as in L. *pendente lite*; cf. *during, notwithstanding*.] During the continuance or dependence of; pending.

1503-4 *Act 19 Hen. VII*, c. 31 Pream., Knyghthode.. receyved, eny tyme dependyng the seid accions or suetys, shall abate the writtes. **1602** FULBECKE *1st Pt. Parall.* 61 The plaintife is put out of seruice depending the plea.

de'pendingly, *adv. rare.* [f. DEPENDING *a.* + -LY[2].] In a depending or dependent manner; with dependence on some person or thing.

1655 GURNALL *Chr. in Arm.* xi. §5 (1669) 100/1 Walk dependingly on God. **1676-7** HALE *Contempl.* II. *On Lord's Prayer* (R.), I will use it thankfully, and nevertheless dependingly.

†**de'pension.** *Obs. rare*[-0]. [ad. L. *dēpensiōn-em* expenditure, f. *dēpendĕre* to spend, expend.]

1656 BLOUNT *Glossogr.*, *Depension* (*depensio*), a weighing, a paying of money.

depeople (dɪˈpiːp(ə)l), *v. arch.* [ad. F. *dépeuple-r* (1364 in Hatzf.), *despeupler* (1611 Cotgr.); after *people*. See DE- I. 6, and cf. DISPEOPLE, DEPOPULATE.] *trans.* To deprive of people, destroy the people of, depopulate.

c **1611** CHAPMAN *Iliad* XIX. 146 Achilles in first fight depeopling enemies. **1615** —— *Odyss.* IX. 75, I depeopled it, Slew all the men, and did their wives remit. **1848** LYTTON *Harold* (1862) 297 The town, awed and depeopled, submitted to flame and to sword.

†**de'perdit, -ite**, *a.* and *sb.* Now *rare* or *Obs.* [ad. L. *dēperdit-us, -um*, corrupt, abandoned, pa. pple. of *dēperdĕre* to destroy, ruin, lose, f. DE- I. 3 + *perdĕre* to destroy, lose.]

A. *adj.* Lost, abandoned, involved in ruin or perdition.

1641 J. JACKSON *True Evang. T.* III. 198 Such miscreants, and deperdite wretches as they proved. **1642** —— *Bk. Conscience* 7 Some notable deperdite wretch.

B. *sb.* Something lost or perished.

1802 PALEY *Nat. Theol.* v. §4 (1819) 58 No reason..why, if these deperdits ever existed, they have now disappeared.

Hence **de'perditely** *adv.*

1608 J. KING *Serm.* 5 Nov. 17 The most..deperditely wicked of all others.

deperdition (diːpəˈdɪʃən). Now *rare.* [a. F. *déperdition* (Paré 16th c.), n. of action from L. *dēperdĕre*: see prec.] Loss, waste, destruction by wasting away.

1607 J. KING *Serm.* Nov. 31 Wherin was prodition, perdition, deperdition, al congested and heaped vp in on. *c* **1645** HOWELL *Lett.* I. I. xxxi, The old [flesh] by continual deperdition..evaporating still out of us. **1646** SIR T. BROWNE *Pseud. Ep.* II. v. 86 It may be unjust to deny all efficacie of gold, in the non-omission of weight, or deperdition of any ponderous particles. **1795** tr. *Mercier's Fragments* II. 63 At its horrid deperdition every citizen is alarmed. **1881** *Annihilation* 6 Alas! who will henceforth be afraid of sin, if it only..end in painless deperdition?

deperition (diːpəˈrɪʃən). *rare.* [n. of action f. L. *dēperīre* to perish, be lost utterly, f. DE- I. 3 + *perīre* to perish.] Perishing, total wasting away.

1793 EARL OF BUCHAN *Anon. Ess.* (1812) 363 That all nature was in a constant state of deperition and renovation. **1808** BENTHAM *Sc. Reform* 76 Deperition of necessary evidence, deperition of the matter of wealth, in the hands of the adverse party..deperition viz. with reference to the party in the right—by dissipation, by concealment.

deperm (diːˈpɜːm), *v.* [f. DE- II. 2 + PERM(ANENT *magnetism*.] *trans.* To demagnetize (a ship). Hence **de'perm** *sb.*, **de'perming** *ppl. a.* and *vbl. sb.* Cf. DEGAUSS *v.*

1946 *Jrnl. Inst. Electr. Engineers* XCIII. I. 508/1 The process known as 'deperming' has been developed to remove or compensate the permanent longitudinal and athwart-ship magnetisms. *Ibid.*, Deperming processes. *Ibid.* 514/1 The sequence of the flashes is of major importance since the stability of the deperm is governed by it. *Ibid.* 514/2 The model was then depermed. **1954** *Jane's Fighting Ships 1954-55* 59 Converted to special duty as mobile wiping/deperming units.

†**de'perpeyl**, *v. Obs.* [a. OF. *deparpeillier*, *desp-*, to disperse.] = DISPARPLE, to scatter.

13.. HAMPOLE *Psalter* [xliv. 11] xliii. 13 In genge þou scatird [MS. S. deperpeyld] vs.

depersonalization (diːˌpɜːsənəlaɪˈzeɪʃən). [f. DEPERSONALIZE *v.* + -ATION.] **1.** The action of depersonalizing or fact of being depersonalized.

1907 J. R. ILLINGWORTH *Doctr. Trin.* x. 191 Madness, prison, suicide may be the end, and all equally symbolise the destruction of proper personality, or, to use a modern term, the depersonalisation, to which transgression leads. **1912** F. VON HÜGEL *Eternal Life* 69 A certain depersonalization of his conception of this same Christ. **1929** *Times* 14 Aug. 6/3 That progress means the 'de-personalization' of the individual. **1942** D. JENKINS *Nature of Catholicity* iii. 74 The doctrine of transubstantiation, with its crass 'objectification' and hence its depersonalization of Christ's presence. **1953** H. READ *True Voice of Feeling* I. i. 34 We will consider..what..was lost in this particular case of 'depersonalization' of a poem. **1968** *Economist* 4 May 64/2 It is fashionable to say that despecialisation goes along with depersonalisation.

2. *spec.* in *Psychol.* [ad. F. *dépersonnalisation* (L. Dugas 1898, in *Revue philos.* XLV. 502). Cf. G. *entpersönlichung*.] A morbid state involving a loss of the sense of personal identity and a feeling of the strangeness or unreality of one's own words and actions; in extreme cases involving also an obsessive feeling of dissolution of the personality.

1904 *Amer. Jrnl. Psychol.* XV. 589 The peculiar feelings of strangeness and depersonalization. **1918** J. WARD *Psychol. Princ.* xv. 364 In some forms of so-called 'depersonalisation',..the individual doubts his own existence or denies it altogether. **1941** *Brit. Jrnl. Psychol.* XXXII. 113 This watching from without—known as depersonalization when reaching a high grade—is found in schizophrenia and also in melancholia. **1960** *Times* 15 Jan. 15/1 Three [participants in a test of isolation] showed evidence of depersonalization. **1963** H. BURN *Drugs, Med. & Man* (ed. 2) xxi. 211 The LSD intoxication stimulates an acute schizophrenia upheaval, marked by a feeling of depersonalization, of being withdrawn from reality.

de'personalize, *v.* [f. DE- II. 1 + PERSONALIZE.] *trans.* To deprive of personality; to make, or regard as, no longer personal. Hence **de'personalized** *ppl. a.*, **de'personalizing** *vbl. sb.*

1866 LOWELL *Biglow P.* Introd., He would have enabled me..to depersonalize myself into a vicarious egotism. **1889** W. S. LILLY *Century of Revol.* 170 An artificial mechanism, which destroys individuality and depersonalises man. **1901** G. B. SHAW *Capt. Brassbound* III. 277 (*stage direction*) Sir Howard (falling back on the fatalism of the depersonalized public man). **1919** C. W. EMMET in B. H. Streeter *The Spirit* v. 187 There is no substitution of the divine nature for the human, no depersonalising of man. **1950** *Mind* LIX. 419 The ego here is not a kind of depersonalised pure spectator.

†**de'personate**, *v. Obs.* [f. DE- II. 1 + PERSON + -ATE[3]. Cf. med.L. *dēpersōnāre* = *dispersōnāre*.] *trans.* To deprive of the status of a person or of personal rights.

1676 R. DIXON *Two Test.* 336 A Bond-man, a Slave.. being wholly decapitated and depersonated from the common condition of a humane person.

de'personize, *v.* [DE- II. 1 + PERSON + -IZE.] = DEPERSONALIZE.

1888 F. H. STODDARD in *Andover Rev.* Oct., The one aims to visualize the ideal, the other to depersonize the God conception itself.

deperte, obs. form of DEPART.

†**de'pertible**, *a. Obs.* [f. as if from L. vb. **dēpertīre* = *dispertīre* to divide, distribute + -BLE. The prefix follows F. *départir*, Eng. DEPART.] Capable of being divided into parts; divisible.

1626 BACON *Sylva* §857 Some Bodies have a..more Depertible Nature than others; As we see it evident in Colouration; For a small Quantity of Saffron will Tinct more then a very great Quantity of Brasil or Wine.

depesche, var. of DEPEACH, *Obs.*

†**de'pester**, *v. Obs.* [a. OF. *depestrer*, *despestrer* (13-14th c. in Hatzf.), mod. *dépêtrer*, in same sense, f. *dé-*, *dés-* (DIS-) + *-pestrer* in *empestrer*: see EMPESTER, PESTER.] *refl.* To disentangle or rid oneself (*from*).

1685 COTTON tr. *Montaigne* I. 449 One vice..so deeply rooted in us, that I dare not determine whether any one ever clearly depestred himself from it or no.

depetal (diːˈpɛtəl), *v.* [f. DE- II. 2 + PETAL.] *trans.* To remove the petals from (a flower). So **de'petalled** *ppl. a.*

1936 D. E. GASCOYNE *Man's Life is this Meat* 42 The depetalled flower. **1936** L. MACNEICE *Let.* 16 Aug. in Auden & MacNeice *Lett. fr. Iceland* (1937) iii. 33 We like to dream of..a lazy music hour by hour depetalling the daisy. **1949** E. BOWEN *Heat of Day* xi. 202 Children..engaged innocently on some act of destruction—depetalling daisies, puffing at dandelion clocks.

depeter (ˈdɛpɪtə(r)). *Building.* Also **depreter.** [Derivation obscure.

It looks like a formation of L. *de* and *petra* stone; possibly from a med.L. *dēpetrāre* to dress with stone. In that case *depreter* is an erroneous form.]

(See quots.)

1852 BREES *Gloss.*, *Depreter* or *Depeter*, plastering done to represent tooled stone. It is first pricked up and floated the same as for set or stucco, and small stones are then forced on dry from a board. **1876** *Notes on Building Constr.* (Rivington) II. 409 Depeter consists of a pricked up coat [of plaster] with small stones pressed in while it is soft, so as to produce a rough surface. **1886** SEDDON *Builder's Work* 248 *Depeter*, is somewhat similar to rough casting, except that small stones are pressed dry into the soft plaster by means of a board. *Ibid.*, *Depreter*, is a term sometimes used to denote plaster finished in imitation of tooled stone.

†**de'pex**, *v. Obs. rare*[-0]. [f. L. *dēpex-*, ppl. stem of *dēpectĕre* To comb down.] To comb down.

1623 COCKERAM, *Depex*, to kemb. [**1644** Ridiculed in *Vindex Anglicus*: see quot. s.v. DEFUST.]

depheazance, dephezaunce, obs. ff. DEFEASANCE.

1558 in *Vicary's Anat.* (1888) App. v. 183 Withoute eny maner of vse, condicion or dephezaunce.

dephilosophize: see DE- II. 1.

†**dephlegm** (dɪˈflɛm), *v. Old Chem.* [ad. mod.L. *dēphlegmāre*, F. *déflegmer* (1698) in Hatzf.): see DEPHLEGMATE.] = DEPHLEGMATE.

1660 BOYLE *New. Exp. Phys. Mech.* xxiv. 191 We took also some Spirit of Urine, carelesly enough deflegmed. **1668** —— *Ess. & Tracts* (1669) 48 We have sometimes taken of the better sort of Spirit of Salt, and having carefully dephlegm'd it [etc.]. **1683** *Phil. Trans.* XIII. 298 Very strong Vinegar, dephlegm'd by freezing.

Hence **de'phlegmed, dephlegm'd** *ppl. a.*; **de'phlegmedness.**

1660 BOYLE *New Exp. Phys. Mech.* xxx. (1682) 115 Well dephlegm'd Spirit of Wine is much lighter than Water. **1669** —— *Hist. Firmness, Ess. & Tracts* 291 The proportion.. depends..upon the strength of the former Liquor, and the dephlegmedness of the latter. **1676** —— *New Exper.* I. in *Phil. Trans.* XI. 777 We gently poured on it some highly dephlegm'd Spirit of Wine.

†**dephlegmate** (diːˈflɛgmeɪt), *v. Old Chem.* [f. ppl. stem of med. or mod.L. *dēphlegmāre*, f. DE- I. 6 + *phlegma*, a. Gr. φλέγμα (φγέγματ-) clammy humour: see PHLEGM.] *trans.* To free (a spirit or acid) from 'phlegm' or watery matter; to rectify.

1668 BOYLE *Ess. & Tracts* (1669) 65 We dephlegmated some [spirits] by more frequent, and indeed tedious Rectifications. **1686** W. HARRIS tr. *Lemery's Chym.* (ed. 2) 186 You may use either a little more, or a little less, according to the strength of the spirit, or according as it is more or less dephlegmated. **1757** A. COOPER *Distiller* I. xxiii. (1760) 95 This Ingredient cleanses and dephlegmates the Spirit considerably. **1789** J. KEIR *Dict. Chem.* 96/2 The contained matter must be dephlegmated.

b. *fig.* To rid of admixture, purify, refine.

1796 BURKE *Let. Noble Ld.* Wks. VIII. 56 The principle of evil himself, incorporeal, pure, unmixed, dephlegmated, defecated evil.

Hence **de'phlegmated** *ppl. a.*, **de'phlegmating** *vbl. sb.* and *ppl. a.*

1641 FRENCH *Distill.* v. (1651) 115 The pure dephlegmated Spirit. **1712** tr. *Pomet's Hist. Drugs* I. 162 To know whether it is truely deflegmated, or Proof-Spirit. **1807** OPIE *Lect. Art* i. (1848) 253 The ancients..produced those concentrated, dephlegmated, and highly rectified personifications of strength, activity, beauty.

†**dephlegmation** (diːflɛgˈmeɪʃən). *Old Chem.* [n. of action from prec. vb.; in mod.F. *déflegmation* (Trevoux 1732).] The process of dephlegmating a spirit or acid.

1668 BOYLE *Ess. & Tracts* (1669) 48 To separate the aqueous parts by Dephlegmation. **1718** QUINCY *Compl. Dispens.* 40 The same thing is constantly observ'd in the Dephlegmation of acid Spirit. **1758** *Elaboratory laid Open* Introd. 46 Retorts must be provided for the dephlegmation.

dephlegmator (ˈdiːflɛgmeɪtə(r)). [Agent-n. in L. form f. mod.L. *dēphlegmāre* to DEPHLEGMATE.] An apparatus for dephlegmation; a form of condensing apparatus in a still.

1828 S. F. GRAY *Operative Chemist* 767 This dephlegmator is formed of two broad sheets of tinned copper, soldered together so as to leave only ⅛th of an inch between them. **1876** *S. Kens. Mus. Catal.* No. 4376.

†**dephlogistic** (diːfləʊˈdʒɪstɪk), *a. Old Chem.* [f. DE- I. 6 + PHLOGIST-ON + -IC: cf. PHLOGISTIC.] = DEPHLOGISTICATED.

1787 DARWIN in *Phil. Trans.* LXXVIII. 52 Combination of dephlogistic and inflammable gases.

dephlo'gisticate, *v.* [f. DE- II. 1 + PHLOGISTICATE.]

†**1.** *trans. Old Chem.* To deprive of phlogiston (the supposed principle of inflammability in bodies).

1779 *Phil. Trans.* LXIX. 441 The power..of dephlogisticating common air. **1782** KIRWAN *ibid.* LXXII. 212 The nitrous acid..is well known to dephlogisticate metals as perfectly as possible. **1788** CAVENDISH *ibid.* LXXVIII. 270 We suppose that the air..was intirely dephlogisticated.

2. To relieve of inflammation. (Cf. ANTIPHLOGISTIC 2.)

1842 *Fraser's Mag.* XXVI. 452 The sheriffs..were fundamentally phlebotomised and dephlogisticated by the fragments of their own swords. **1875** GEIKIE *Life Sir R. Murchison* I. 142 Given to water-drinking and dephlogisticating.

Hence **dephlo'gisticated** *ppl. a.* (*esp.* in *dephlogisticated air*, the name given to oxygen by Priestley, who, on its first discovery, supposed it to be ordinary air deprived of phlogiston); **dephlogisticating**, *ppl. a.*; **dephloˌgisti'cation.**

1775 PRIESTLEY in *Phil. Trans.* LXV. 387 This species may not improperly be called, *dephlogisticated air*. This species of air I first produced from *mercurius calcinatus per se*. **1789** —— *ibid.* LXXIX. 146 The dephlogisticating principle. **1784** CAVENDISH *ibid.* LXXIV. 141 There is the utmost reason to think, that dephlogisticated and phlogisticated air (as M. Lavoisier and Scheele suppose) are quite distinct substances, and not differing only in their degree of phlogistication; and that common air is a mixture of the two. **1791** HAMILTON *Berthollet's Dyeing* I. I. I. i. 7 Oxygenated (dephlogisticated) muriatic acid. **1794** SULLIVAN *View Nat.* II. 86 From the greater, or less dephlogistication of the ores, or the stones in which it is contained. **1807** VANCOUVER *Agric. Devon* (1813) 459 Vegetables..again in turn, and during the daytime, exhale and breathe forth that pure dephlogisticated air, so essential to the support of animal existence.

dephosphorize (diːˈfɒsfəraɪz), *v.* [DE- II. 1.] *trans.* To deprive of or free from phosphorus.
1878 URE *Dict. Arts* IV. 451 Without attempting to dephosphorize the ore more completely. **1879** *Daily News* 31 Dec. 5/4 [This] so effectually dephosphorises the Cleveland ore as to allow it to be manufactured into steel.
Hence **deˈphosphorized** *ppl. a.*, **deˈphosphorizing** *vbl. sb.*; also **dephosphoriˈzation**, the process of freeing from phosphorus.
1878 *Rep. Annual Meeting of Iron & Steel Inst.*, The dephosphorization of iron. **1883** *Athenæum* 24 Feb. 253/1 The slag obtained in the basic dephosphorizing process. **1885** *Harper's Mag.* Apr. 819/1 The dephosphorization process, by which phosphoric pig-iron can be converted into steel.

dephosphorylation (diːˌfɒsfɒrɪˈleɪʃən). *Chem.* [f. DE- II. 1 + PHOSPHORYL + -ATION.] The removal of a phosphate group from a compound.
1931 *Jrnl. Biol. Chem.* XCII. 765 The function of such phosphorylations and dephosphorylations has..not been elucidated. **1956** *Nature* 11 Feb. 274/1 In algae it is considered that the oxidative assimilation of hexose follows the same glycolytic pathway as in higher organisms, and that these substances after dephosphorylation yield hexose phosphate. **1963** *Lancet* 5 Jan. 59/2 The free energy for sperm movement is provided by the dephosphorylation of adenosine triphosphate.
Also **dephosˈphorylate** *v. trans.*, **dephosˈphorylated** *ppl. a.*
1929 *Jrnl. Biol. Chem.* LXXXIII. 796 There occur.. others [*sc.* enzymes] capable of dephosphorylating nucleotides. **1954** *Biochem. Jrnl.* LVIII. 391/2 The dephosphorylated product was isolated by chromatography.

dephysicalize: see DE- II. 1.

†**deˈpict**, *ppl. a. Obs.* [ad. L. *dēpict-us*, pa. pple. of *dēpingĕre*: see next.] Depicted.
c **1430** LYDG. *Min. Poems* 177, I fond a lyknesse depict upon a wal. **14..** *Circumcision* in *Tundale's Vis.* 94 And letturs new depicte in every payn. **1598** STOW *Surv.* xl. (1603) 416 Embrodered, or otherwise depict upon them.

depict (dɪˈpɪkt), *v.* [f. L. *dēpict-*, ppl. stem of L. *dēpingĕre* to represent by painting, portray, depict, f. DE- I. 3 + *pingĕre* to paint: cf. DEPAINT and prec.
(Godefroy has a single example of OF. *depicter* of 1426; but the word is not recorded later, and cannot be supposed to have influenced the formation of the Eng. vb.)]
1. *trans.* To draw, figure, or represent in colours; to paint; also, in wider sense, to portray, delineate, figure anyhow.
1631 WEEVER *Anc. Fun. Mon.* 136 This old Distich, sometimes depicted vpon the wall at the entrance into the said Abbey. **1634** SIR T. HERBERT *Trav.* 10 Which Bird I have here simply depicted as you see [here is fig.]. **1639** FULLER *Holy War* IV. xii. (1840) 199 The history of the Bible as richly as curiously depicted in needle work. *a* **1667** JER. TAYLOR (J.), [They] depicted upon their shields the most terrible beasts they could imagine. **1794** SULLIVAN *View Nat.* II, The solar progress is depicted by the Hindoos, by a circle of intertwining serpents. **1867** LADY HERBERT *Cradle L.* iv. 121 The accuracy with which the painter has, perhaps unconsciously, depicted the room. **1872** YEATS *Growth Comm.* 33 Victims of the slavedealer as depicted on the earliest Egyptian monuments.
b. *transf.* To image, figure, or represent as if by painting or drawing. Also *fig.*
1817 BP. R. WATSON *Anecd.* II. 401 (R.) Why the man has ..an idea of figure depicted on the choroïdes or retina of the eye. **1834** MRS. SOMERVILLE *Connect. Phys. Sc.* xviii. (1849) 176 He..saw..a windmill, his own figure, and that of a friend, depicted..on the sea. **1839** G. BIRD *Nat. Philos.* 396 The membrane, on which the images of objects become depicted. *a* **1870** LONGFELLOW *Birds of Passage* I., *Discov. North Cape* xxi, With doubt and strange surmise Depicted in their look.
2. To represent or portray in words; to describe graphically.
a **1740** FELTON (J.), When the distractions of a tumult are sensibly depicted..while you read, you seem indeed to see them. **1856** KANE *Arct. Expl.* I. xiv. 159 No language can depict the chaos at its base. **1873** SYMONDS *Grk. Poets* ix. 294 Sophocles aims at depicting the destinies, and Shakspere the characters of men.
3. To represent, as a painting or picture does.
1871 MACDUFF *Mem. Patmos* iv. 45 Cartoons..in bold outline depicting the ever-varying and diversified features in church life and character. **1872** YEATS *Techn. Hist. Comm.* 45 Their oldest monuments depict women spinning.
Hence **deˈpicted** *ppl. a.*, **deˈpicting** *vbl. sb.*
a **1762** in H. Walpole *Vertue's Anecd. Paint.* (1786) I. 93 A depicted table of Colonia. **1885** *Athenæum* 14 Mar. 532/1 His..gay and luminous coloration, and sparkling depicting of light are not obtainable with ink.

deˈpicter, -or. [f. DEPICT *v.* + -ER; the form in -OR is after Latin.] One who depicts, portrays, or sets forth in words.
1837 LOCKHART *Scott*, Depicter (F. Hall). **1865** *Daily Tel.* 10 Aug., The mournful depicters of Calcutta life. **1892** A. HAMLYN in *Atalanta* Dec. 165/1 So brilliant a depictor of animal life.

depiction (dɪˈpɪkʃən). [ad. L. *dēpictiōn-em*, n. of action from *dēpingĕre*: see DEPICT *v.* (Cf. OF. *depiction*, 1426 in Godef., but not known later.)] The action of depicting; painted representation, picture; graphic description.
1688 R. HOLME *Armoury* III. 176/2 The true shape and depiction of a Bishop in his Pontificals. **1882** A. W. WARD *Dickens* v. 130 Dickens' comic genius was never so much at its ease..as in the depiction of such groups as this. **1884** E. FOSTER in *Elocutionist* Dec. 7/2 Mr. Denbigh had hitherto restricted his art to depictions of the fleshly school.

depictive (dɪˈpɪktɪv), *a.* [f. L. *dēpict-* ppl. stem (see DEPICT *v.*) + -IVE.] Having the function or quality of depicting.
1821 *New Monthly Mag.* II. 392 The depictive art and power with which it is written. **1892** WHITNEY *Max Müller* 40 The signs lost their pictorial or depictive character.

deˈpictment. *rare.* [f. DEPICT *v.* + -MENT.] Pictorial representation; a painting, a picture.
1816 KEATINGE *Trav.* (1817) I. 136 Hung with gay depictments, in glowing colouring..of those who have suffered. *Ibid.* II. 76 Trajan's Pillar and various depictments give the representation.

deˈpicture, *sb.* In 5 *Sc.* -our. [f. L. *dēpict-* ppl. stem of *dēpingĕre* (see DEPICT *v.*) + -URE.] = DEPICTION; depicting; painting.
1500–20 DUNBAR *To Queyne of Scottis* 14 Ma[i]stres of nurtur and of nobilnes, Of fresch depictour princes[s] and patroun. **1834** *Fraser's Mag.* X. 118 He is lost in amazement ..to see genius employed upon the depicture of such a *rascaille rabblement!* **1882** *Nature* XXVI. 534 The depicture of the..revolution which Darwin has accomplished in the minds of men.

depicture (dɪˈpɪktjʊə(r)), *v.* [f. DE- *prefix* + PICTURE *v.* (in use from 14th c.); formed under the influence of DEPICT *pa. pple.*, and of L. *dēpingĕre*, *dēpictum*.]
1. *trans.* To represent by a picture; to portray in colours, to paint; also, more widely, to draw, figure, or portray; = DEPICT *v.* 1.
1593 *Rites & Mon. Ch. Durh.* (Surtees) 40 The starre.. underneth depictured. **1631** WEEVER *Anc. Fun. Mon.* 50 The glasse-windowes wherein the effigies of..Saints was depictured. **1781** GIBBON *Decl. & F.* III. li. 183 A paradise or garden was depictured on the ground. *a* **1847** MRS. SHERWOOD *Lady of Manor* III. xviii. 9 A course of little lectures..on the subjects depictured upon the tiles.
b. To image or figure as in a painting; = DEPICT *v.* 1 b.
1742 tr. *Algarotti on Newton's Theory* I. 106 The Images ..are depictured upon the Membrane of the Eye. **1849** *Tait's Mag.* XVI. 219 The..tableau depictured itself indelibly upon the mind.
2. To set forth or portray in words; = DEPICT *v.* 2.
1798 COLERIDGE *Satyrane's Lett.* iii. in *Biog. Lit.* (1882) 268 It tends to make their language more picturesque; it depictures images better. **1844** DISRAELI *Coningsby* III. v, You have but described my feelings when you depictured your own. **1868** BROWNING *Ring & Bk.* VIII. 752 Oh! language fails, Shrinks from depicturing his punishment.
3. To represent, as a picture, figure, image, or symbol does; = DEPICT *v.* 3.
1650 *Brief Disc. Fut. Hist. Europe* 30 The Iron Leggs and the Clay Toes depictured the Roman Empire. **1834** LYTTON *Pompeii* 133 Features which but one image in the world can yet depicture and recall. **1852** J. WILSON in *Blackw. Mag.* LXXII. 151 The Outward expresses, depictures the Inward.
4. *fig.* To represent or picture to one's own mind or imagination; to imagine.
1775 ADAIR *Amer. Ind.* 209 They speedily dress a woman with the apparel of either the god, or goddess..as they depicture them according to their own dispositions. **1800** MRS. HERVEY *Mourtray Fam.* II. 213 Chowles was, in his eyes, a contemptible object; and, as such, he depictured him. **1876** MISS BRADDON *J. Haggard's Dau.* II. i. 5 Any idea about the Greeks, whom they depictured to themselves vaguely and variously.
Hence **deˈpictured** *ppl. a.*, **deˈpicturing** *vbl. sb.*; also **deˈpicturement**.
1850 MRS. BROWNING *Seraphim*, I have beheld the ruined things Only in depicturings Of angels sent on earthward mission. *a* **1866** J. GROTE *Moral Ideals* (1876) xiii. 307 We read with interest the depicturement of the lives of others. **1886** J. PAYNE tr. *Boccaccio's Decam.* III. vii. I. 321 Terrifying the mind of the foolish with clamours and depicturements.

deˌpigmenˈtation. [f. DE- II. 1 + PIGMENTATION.] The condition of being deficient or wanting in pigment (in the tissues).
1889 I. TAYLOR *Origin of Aryans* 42 Here depigmentation or albinism is very prevalent.

depilate (ˈdɛpɪleɪt), *v.* [f. L. *dēpilāt-*, ppl. stem of *dēpilāre* to pull out the hair, f. DE- I. 2 + *pilus* hair, *pilāre* to deprive of hair. Cf. F. *dépiler* (Paré, 16th c.). (Pa. t. in Sc. *depilat* for *depilatit*.)]
1. To remove the hair from; to make bare of hair.
1560 ROLLAND *Crt. Venus* III. 29 The hair..Fra hir Father throw slicht scho depilat. **1657** TOMLINSON *Renou's Disp.* 205 Which places they much desire to depilate and glabrify. **1853** HICKIE tr. *Aristoph.* (1872) II. 427, I am an old woman, but depillated with the lamp.
†**2.** To deprive of its skin, decorticate, peel. [So in Lat.] *Obs. rare.*
1620 VENNER *Via Recta* v. 90 Made of Rice accurately depilated and boyled in milke.
Hence **ˈdepilated**, **ˈdepilating** *ppl. adjs.*
1876 DUHRING *Skin Diseases*, The extraction of the diseased hairs [in *tinea sycosis*], for which purpose a pair of depilating forceps should be used.

depilation (dɛpɪˈleɪʃən). [ad. med. or mod.L. *dēpilātiōn-em*, n. of action from *dēpilāre* to DEPILATE. So in F.; in 13th c. *depilacion* (Hatzf.).]
1. The action of depriving or stripping of hair; the condition of being void of hair.
1547 BOORDE *Brev. Health* cci. 69b, Depilacion of a mannes heare. **1650** BULWER *Anthropomet.* iv. 67 [They] pluck off all the haire of their Eye-brows, taking great pride ..in that unnaturall depilation. **1861** WRIGHT *Ess. Archæol.* I. vii. 131 The practice of depilation prevailed generally among the Anglo-Saxon ladies. **1877** COUES & ALLEN *N. Amer. Rod.* 616 The depilation of the members is not always complete; younger specimens..show..hairy tail and feet.
†**2.** The action of spoiling or pillage. *Obs.*
1611 SPEED *Hist. Gt. Brit.* IX. x. (1632) 661 Orders for brideling their excessive depilations [i.e. of the Pope and his agents]. **1687** T. K. *Veritas Evang.* 37 The Depilations of Promoters, and other Under Officers.

†**depilative** (ˈdɛpɪleɪtɪv), *a. Obs.* [f. L. *dēpilāt-* ppl. stem (see DEPILATE *v.*) + -IVE. Cf. mod.F. *dépilatif*, *-ive* (1732 in Hatzf.).] = DEPILATORY.
1562 TURNER *Herbal* II. 168a, All herbes that are depilatiue or burners of hare. **1567** MAPLET *Gr. Forest* 10 They say it is vsed to Oyntments depilatiue.

depilator (ˈdɛpɪleɪtə(r)). [agent-n., on L. type, f. L. *dēpilāre* to DEPILATE.]
1. One who deprives of hair; a shaver.
1836 E. HOWARD *R. Reefer* lvi, The hungry depilator seized the razors.
2. An instrument for pulling out hairs.
1889 in *Cent. Dict.*

depilatory (dɪˈpɪlətərɪ), *a.* and *sb.* [f. L. type *dēpilātōrius*, f. *dēpilāt-*: see DEPILATE *v.* and -ORY. In F. *dépilatoire* (Paré 16th c.).]
A. *adj.* Having the property of removing hair.
1601 HOLLAND *Pliny* II, Bats bloud hath a depilatorie facultie to fetch off haire. **1766** PENNANT *Zool.* (1776) IV. 59 (Jod.) Ælian says that they were depilatory, and..would take away the beard. **1835** KIRBY *Hab. & Inst. Anim.* II. xxii. 424 It emits a milky saliva, which is depilatory.
B. *sb.* A depilatory agent or substance; a preparation to remove (growing) hair.
1606 HOLLAND *Sueton.* Annot. 12 A Depilatorie, to keepe haire from growing. **1650** BULWER *Anthropomet.* 129 Who because he would never have a Beard, used depilatories. **1830** LINDLEY *Nat. Syst. Bot.* 76 The juice of its leaves is a powerful depilatory; it destroys hair..without pain.

†**deˈpiled**, *ppl. a. Obs.* [Formed after L. *dēpilāt-us*, F. *depilé*: see DEPILATE *v.*] Depilated.
1650 BULWER *Anthropomet.* II. 48 [Shaving is] uncomely, because allied unto depiled baldnesse.

depilous (ˈdɛpɪləs), *a.* [f. assumed L. type **dēpilōs-us*: cf. L. *dēpilis* without hair, and *pilōsus* hairy.] Deprived or void of hair.
1646 SIR T. BROWNE *Pseud. Ep.* III. xiv, A quadruped corticated and depilous. *Ibid.* VI. x, How they [dogs] of some Countries became depilous and without any hair at all. **1822** T. TAYLOR *Apuleius* VII. 156 Striking me with a very thick stick, he left me [the ass] entirely depilous.

depinct *v. Obs.*: see DEPEINCT, DEPICT.

†**depinge** (dɪˈpɪndʒ), *v. Obs. rare.* [ad. L. *dēpingĕre* to DEPICT.] *trans.* To depict, portray, represent by a picture or image.
1657 TOMLINSON *Renou's Disp.* 263 That same that Garcias depinges in other lineaments.

†**deˈpinged**, *ppl. a. Obs.* (app.) Stripped of wings and legs.
1658 R. FRANCK *North. Mem.* (1821) 112 To bait for trout ..I commend the canker..or, if with a depinged locust, you will not lose your labour; nor will you starve your cause, if to strip off the legs of a grasshopper. —— 307 Let the Angler then have recourse to..the depinged grasshopper.

deˈplace, *v. rare.* [a. mod.F. *déplacer*, in OF. *desp-*.] = DISPLACE *v.*
1839 J. ROGERS *Antipopop.* xii. §5 Purgatory deplaces hell.

deplanate (ˈdiːplәneɪt), *a. rare.* [ad. L. *dēplānāt-us* levelled down, made plain.]
1883 *Syd. Soc. Lex.*, *Deplanate*, flattened, smoothened.

†**deˈplane**, *v.*[1] *Sc. Obs.* [f. DE- I. 3 + L. *plān-us* plain: cf. *de-clare*.] To make plain, show plainly, declare (to).
1572 *Satir. Poems Reform.* xxx. 136 The day is neir; as I dar weill deplane 3ow.

deplane (diːˈpleɪn), *v.*[2] [f. DE- II. 2 + PLANE *sb.*[5]] **a.** *intr.* To leave an aeroplane (after arrival at one's destination). **b.** *trans.* To remove from an aeroplane. So **deˈplaning** *vbl. sb.* and *ppl. a.*

1923 *Blackw. Mag.* July 11/2 Dudley left me, saying.. that he was to 'deplane' [*sc.* by parachute] now. **1933** *Aeroplane* 2 Aug. 218/1 The passengers..were out of the machine, which had been towed away from the passenger-deplaning area. **1948** in *Amer. Speech* (1952) XXVII. 72 A passenger under influence of liquor will be deplaned. **1967** L. JAMES *Chameleon File* (1968) iv. 57 After clearing immigration control, he..watched the crowd of deplaning passengers.

†**deplant** (diːˈplɑːnt, -æ-), *v. Obs.* [a. F. *déplant-er* (16th c. in Littré) to transplant, L. *dēplantāre* to take off a shoot, also to plant, f. DE- I. 1, 2 + *plantāre* to plant, *planta* plant.] 'To transplant' Bailey 1721. (Thence in mod. Dicts.)

Hence †**deplanˈtation**. [So in mod.F. (Littré).]

1656 BLOUNT *Glossogr.*, *Deplantation*, a taking up Plants. (Hence in BAILEY, JOHNSON, etc.)

deplenish (dɪˈplɛnɪʃ), *v.* [f. DE- II. 1 + PLENISH (*Sc.*) to furnish a house, to stock a farm; cf. DISPLENISH, REPLENISH.]

1. *trans.* To deprive (a house) of furniture, or (a farm) of stock; to DISPLENISH.

1887 *Pall Mall G.* 9 Mar. 1/1 The tenants have sold their stock, deplenished their farms.

2. *gen.* To empty of its contents: the opposite of *replenish*.

1859 SALA *Tw. round Clock* (1861) 144 Their own deplenished pockets.

depletant (dɪˈpliːtənt), *a.* and *sb. Med.* [f. DEPLETE *v.*: see -ANT[1].]

A. *adj.* Having the property of depleting (see DEPLETE *v.* 2). **B.** *sb.* A drug which has this property.

1880 *Libr. Univ. Knowl.* VIII. 13 Tonics are often of more service [in inflammation] than depletants.

deplete (dɪˈpliːt), *a.* [ad. L. *dēplēt-us* emptied out, exhausted, pa. pple. of *dēplēre*: see next.] Depleted, emptied out, exhausted.

1880 R. DOWLING *Sport of F.* III. 205 The brain was remarkably deplete of blood. **1885** L. OLIPHANT *Let.* in *Life* (1891) II. xi. 277 Creating openings in the deplete organism for access of spirits.

deplete (dɪˈpliːt), *v.* [f. L. *dēplēt-*, ppl. stem of *dēplēre* to bring down or undo the fullness of, empty out, let blood, f. DE- I. 6 + *-plēre* to fill.]

1. *trans.* To reduce the fullness of; to deprive of contents or supplies; to empty out, exhaust.

1859 SAXE *Poems, Progress* 36 Deplete your pocket and relieve your purse. **1880** *Times* 13 Oct. 5/5 The garrison is somewhat depleted of troops at the present time. **1884** *Ibid.* 8 July 11 The demand for coin..will..help to deplete the Bank's stock of gold.

2. *Med.* To empty or relieve the system or vessels when overcharged, as by blood-letting or purgatives.

1807 [see DEPLETING below]. **1858** COPLAND *Dict. Pract. Med.* I. 105/2 To deplete the vascular system. **1875** H. C. WOOD *Therap.* (1879) 465 Whenever, in inflammation, it is desired to deplete through the bowels.

Hence **deˈpleted** *ppl. a.*, **deˈpleting** *vbl. sb.* and *ppl. a.*

1807 *Med. Jrnl.* XVII. 501 Depleting and antiphlogistic remedies were continued. **1870** *Daily News* 29 Nov., To fill her depleted magazines. **1885** *Manch. Exam.* 29 June 5/2 The overcrowded village might be even worse to live in than the depleted town.

deplethoric (diːplɛˈθɒrɪk, -plɪˈθɒrɪk), *a.* [f. DE- II. 3 + PLETHORIC.] Characterized by the absence of plethora.

1837 T. DOUBLEDAY in *Blackw. Mag.* XLI. 365 In order to remedy this [plethoric state of plants], gardeners and florists are accustomed to produce the opposite, or 'deplethoric state', by artificial means. This they denominate 'giving a check'. **1882** *Pop. Sc. Monthly* Nov. 39 Doubleday attempted to demonstrate that..the deplethoric state is favorable to fertility.

depletion (dɪˈpliːʃən). [ad. L. type **dēplētiōn-em* (perh. used in med. or mod.L.), n. of action from *dēplēre*, *dēplēt-* to DEPLETE. Cf. mod.F. *déplétion* (term of medicine) in Littré. (The cl. L. equivalent was *dēplētūra*.)]

1. The action of depleting, or condition of being depleted; emptying of contents or supplies; exhaustion.

1656 BLOUNT *Glossogr.*, *Depletion*, an emptying. **1852** D. G. MITCHELL *Battle Summer* 214 With coffers in the last stages of depletion. **1889** *Spectator* 14 Sept., The depletion of London to the benefit of other English cities.

2. *Med.* The emptying or relieving of overcharged vessels of the body; reduction of plethora or congestion by medicinal agency; bleeding.

a **1735** ARBUTHNOT (J.), Depletion of the vessels gives room to the fluid to expand itself. **1803** *Med. Jrnl.* X. 471 The mode of treatment..was depletion, followed by a mercurial salivation. **1874** *Van Buren's Dis. Genit. Org.* 83 The acute symptoms..yield rapidly to local depletion and sedatives. **1890** *Times* 1 Sept. 7/2 Some blood letting was necessary and natural; but apparently it has gone on so long that a period of depletion has set in.

3. Special Comb. **depletion allowance** *U.S.*, a tax concession allowable in industries where a company's business operations diminish the value of its property assets, as in oil-drilling, etc.

1932 *Statutes at Large U.S.A.* (1933) XLVII. 202 The depletion allowance based on discovery value provided in this paragraph shall not exceed 50 per centum of the net income of the taxpayer. **1965** *McGraw-Hill Dict. Mod. Econ.* 143 The primary purpose of a depletion allowance is to prevent the imposition of a capital levy on the owners of natural resources. **1974** *Saturday* (Charleston, S. Carolina) 20 Apr. 10-A/5 By the time the well gets me in the black.. the depletion allowance will have been killed by Congress and oil fields will be taxed just like wheat fields, which, of course, can produce forever.

Hence **deˈpletionist**, an advocate of depletion.

1883 *Sat. Rev.* 14 Apr. 464 Two general views on that question [Scotch crofters]..may be summarized by the two words 'impletionist' and 'depletionist'.

depletive (dɪˈpliːtɪv), *a.* and *sb. Med.* [mod.f. L. *dēplēt-* ppl. stem of *dēplēre* to DEPLETE + -IVE. Cf. mod.F. *déplétif* (medical term) in Littré.]

A. *adj.* Characterized by depletion. **B.** *sb.* A drug having the property of producing depletion.

1835 WARDROP *Bleeding* (L.), Depletive treatment is contra-indicated..She had been exhausted by depletives. **1885** W. ROBERTS *Treat. Urin. Diseases* III. i. (ed. 4) 410 Active depletive measures are indicated.

depletory (dɪˈpliːtərɪ), *a. Med.* [f. as prec. + -ORY.] Producing depletion, depletive.

1849 CLARIDGE *Cold Water Cure* 110 Leeching and severe depletory measures are decidedly wrong. **1875** H. C. WOOD *Therap.* (1879) 535 In the one case depletory medicines are indicated, in the other case tonics are no less essential.

†**depliˈcation.** *Obs. rare.* [n. of action f. med.L. *dēplicāre* to unfold, f. DE- I. 6 + *plicāre* to fold.] Unfolding, display.

1648 W. MOUNTAGUE *Devout Ess.* I. xv. §3 (R.) An unfolding and deplication of the inside of this order. **1656** BLOUNT *Glossogr.*, *Deplication*, an unfolding.

deplorability (dɪˌplɔərəˈbɪlɪtɪ). *rare.* [f. next: see -ITY.] The quality of being deplorable; an instance of this, a deplorable matter.

1854 *Tait's Mag.* XXI. 167 It does not prevent occasional obscurities and deplorabilities. **1856** *Times* 18 Jan. (L.), The deplorability of war in general.

deplorable (dɪˈplɔərəb(ə)l), *a.* [mod.f. L. *dēplōrāre* to DEPLORE: see -BLE. Cf. F. *déplorable* (*c* 1600 in Hatzf., not in Cotgr. 1611).]

1. To be deplored or lamented; lamentable, very sad, grievous, miserable, wretched. Now chiefly used of events, conditions, circumstances.

'It is sometimes, in a more lax and jocular sense, used for contemptible; despicable: as, *deplorable* nonsense; *deplorable* stupidity' (Johnson).

1612 E. GRIMSTONE (*title*), Mathieu's Heroyk Life and Deplorable Death of The most Christian King Henry the Fourth. **1631** MASSINGER *Beleeve as you list* IV. ii, The storie of Your most deplorable fortune. *a* **1687** COTTON *Pindar. Ode, Beauty* (R.), He..does betray A deplorable want of sense. **1710** SWIFT *Tatler* No. 230 ¶2 The deplorable Ignorance that..hath reigned among our English Writers. **1759** ROBERTSON *Hist. Scotl.* I. IV. 330 The people beheld the deplorable situation of their sovereign with insensibility. **1860** TYNDALL *Glac.* I. xxii. 160 If climbing without guides were to become habitual, deplorable consequences would.. ensue.

†**b.** Formerly said of persons or things of which the state is lamentable or wretched. *Obs.*

1642 J. M. *Argt. conc. Militia* 13 Our deplorable brethren and neighbours. **1646** SIR T. BROWNE *Pseud. Ep.* VI. v. 291 A deplorable and comfortlesse Winter. **1682** BUNYAN *Holy War* 112 Thou pretendest a right to the deplorable town of Mansoul.

†**2.** Given up as hopeless; = DEPLORATE. *rare.*

1684 tr. *Bonet's Merc. Compit.* VIII. 300 That not deplorable persons, but such as have strength, be tapped.

B. as *sb. pl.* Deplorable ills.

1830 SCOTT *Jrnl.* II. 157 An old fellow, mauled with rheumatism and other deplorables.

deˈplorableness. [f. prec. + -NESS.] The state or condition of being deplorable; misery, wretchedness.

1648 HAMMOND *Serm.* x. Wks. 1684 IV. 536 The sadness and deplorableness of this estate. **1679** J. GOODMAN *Penit. Pardoned* III. iv. (1713) 321 He..hath known by sad experience the deplorableness of that condition.

deˈplorably, *adv.* [f. as prec. + -LY[2].] In a deplorable manner, or to a deplorable degree; lamentably, miserably, wretchedly.

1653 H. MORE *Antid. Ath.* III. xiv. (1712) 130 If he be not desperately wicked or deplorably miserable. **1782** V. KNOX *Ess.* 134 (R.) Editions of Greek and Latin classics.. deplorably incorrect. **1878** LECKY *Eng. in 18th C.* II. viii. 452 The defences had been so deplorably neglected.

†**deˈplorate,** *a. Obs.* [ad. L. *dēplōrāt-us* bewept, given up as hopeless, pa. pple. of *dēplōrāre* to DEPLORE.] Given up as hopeless; desperate.

1529 *Supplic. to King* 46 This deplorate & miserable sorte of blynde shepherdes. **1615** CROOKE *Body of Man* 92 In a deplorate or desperate dropsie. **1691** BAXTER *Nat. Ch.* xiii. 54 Those that..are not deplorate in Diabolism. **1695** *Phil. Trans.* XIX. 73 Many other Mysteries in Mathematicks, which were before held as deplorate.

deploration (diːplɔəˈreɪʃən). Now *rare.* In 5 -acyon, 6 -atioun. [Ultimately ad. L. *dēplōrātiōn-em*, n. of action f. *dēplōrāre* to DEPLORE; but in Caxton and early Sc. perh. from French.]

1. The action of deploring; lamentation.

1533 BELLENDEN *Livy* I. (1822) 3 The deploratioun of sic miseryis. **1582** BENTLEY *Mon. Matrones* ii. 151 The bitter deploration of mine offences. **1627** BP. HALL *Gt. Impostor* 507 The meditation and deploration of our owne danger and misery. **1831** *Examiner* 482/2 We cannot run over a tenth part of the deplorations that occur.

†**b.** Formerly, a title for elegiac poems or other compositions; a lament. [So in French.]

1537 LINDESAY (*title*), The Deploratioun of the Deith of Quene Magdalene.

†**2.** Deplorable condition, misery. *Obs. rare.*

1490 CAXTON *Eneydos* ii. 16 It sholde be an harde thynge ..to putte in forgetynge her swete firste lyf and now her deploracyon.

†**deˈplorative,** *a. Obs.* [f. *dēplōrāt-*, ppl. stem of L. *dēplōrāre* to DEPLORE + -IVE.] Characterized by or expressing deploration.

1610 HEALEY *St. Aug. Citie of God* VIII. xxvi. (1620) 315 Hermes himself in his deploratiue passage..doth plainly auerre that the Egyptian gods were all dead men.

deplore (dɪˈplɔə(r)), *v.* Also 6 *Sc.* deploir. [Ultimately ad. L. *dēplōrāre* to weep bitterly, wail, bewail, deplore, give up as lost, f. DE- I. 3 + *plōrāre* to weep, bewail. Cf. F. *déplorer*, in OF. *desplorer*, *deplourer*, *depleurer*, It. *deplorare*, to deplore, bewail (Florio). The Eng. was possibly from F. or It.]

1. *trans.* To weep for, bewail, lament; to grieve over, regret deeply.

1567 *Satir. Poems Reform.* vii. 75 Quhat duilfull mynde mycht dewlie this deploir? **1591** SPENSER *Ruines of Time* 658 He..left me here his losse for to deplore. **1659** B. HARRIS *Parival's Iron Age* 77 He was killed by a Musket bullet. He ..was much deplored, by the whole Party. **1814** CARY *Dante's Inf.* XI. 44 He.. must aye deplore With unavailing penitence his crime. **1852** TENNYSON *Ode Dk. of Wellington* ii, Where shall we lay the man whom we deplore?

†**b.** To tell with grief or lamentation. *Obs.*

1601 SHAKS. *Twel. N.* III. i. 174 Neuer more Will I my Masters teares to you deplore.

†**c.** To shed like tears, 'weep'. *Obs. rare.*

1601 CHESTER *Love's Mart., Dial.* lxv, The Turpentine that sweet iuyce doth deplore.

2. *intr.* To lament, mourn. Now *rare* or *Obs.*

1632 LITHGOW *Trav.* x. 485 My Muse left to mourne for my Liberty, deplored thus: [verses follow]. **1638** SIR T. HERBERT *Trav.* (ed. 2) 45 Bid him fulfill the ceremoniall law of deploring for ten dayes. **1776** MICKLE tr. *Camoens' Lusiad* 262 Along the shore The Halcyons, mindful of their fate deplore.

†**3.** *trans.* To give up as hopeless, to despair of. *Obs. rare.*

1559 [see DEPLORED 2]. **1605** BACON *Adv. Learn.* II. x. §7 The physicians..do make a kind of scruple and religion to stay with the patient after the disease is deplored. *a* **1729** CONGREVE *Poems, To Ld. Halifax* 29 A true Poetick State we had deplor'd.

Hence **deˈploring** *vbl. sb.* and *ppl. a.*; also **deˈploringly** *adv.*

1591 SHAKS. *Two Gent.* III. ii. 85 To their Instruments Tune a deploring dumpe. **1847** CRAIG, *Deploringly.* **1865** DICKENS *Mut. Fr.* III. xiii, Mr. Fledgeby shook his head deploringly. **1880** G. MEREDITH *Trag. Com.* xix. (1892) 256 As little was he the vanished God whom his working people hailed deploringly.

deplored (dɪˈplɔəd, -rɪd), *ppl. a.* [f. prec. + -ED[1]: rendering L. *dēplōrāt-us* DEPLORATE.]

1. Lamented, mourned for.

†**2.** Given up as hopeless; desperate; = DEPLORATE. *Obs.*

1559 KENNEDY *Lett. to Willock* in *Wodr. Soc. Misc.* (1844) 276 The maist deplorit heretykis quhilk euer wes. **1620** VENNER *Via Recta* Introd. 12 Who with deplored diseases.. resort to our Baths. **1655** GURNALL *Chr. in Arm* xiv. (1669) 300/1 His affairs were in such a desperate and deplored condition.

Hence **deˈploredly** *adv.*, **deˈploredness.**

1656 *Artif. Handsom.* 72 To be deploredly old, and affectedly young, is not only a great folly, but a grosse deformity. **1608–11** BP. HALL *Medit., Love of Christ* §2 The deploredness of our condition did but heighten that holy flame. **1675** BROOKS *Gold. Key* Wks. 1867 V. 201.

†**deˈplorement.** *Obs. rare.* [f. DEPLORE *v.* + -MENT.] The act of deploring; lamentation.

1593 NASHE *Christ's T.* (1613) 9 O that I did weepe in vaine, that your defilements & pollutions gaue mee no true cause of deplorement. **1623** COCKERAM, *Deplorement*, weeping, lamenting.

deplorer (dɪˈplɔərə(r)). [f. as prec. + -ER[1].] One who deplores.

1687 BOYLE *Martyrd. Theodora* xi. (1703) 167 All the other spectators of her sufferings, were deplorers of them too.

de'ploy, *sb. Mil.* [f. DEPLOY *v.* Cf. OF. *desploi*, *-ploy*, DISPLAY.] The action or evolution of deploying.

1796 *Instr. & Reg. Cavalry* (1813) 126 From this situation of the flank march, it is that every regiment is required to begin the deploy, when forming in line with others. **1870** tr. *Erckmann-Chatrian's Waterloo* 245 When they began to talk of the distance of the deploys.

deploy (dɪ'plɔɪ), *v.* [a. F. *déployer*, in OF. *desployer*, orig. *despleier*:—L. *displicāre* (in late and med.L.) to unfold. In its AFr. form regularly adopted in ME. as *desplay*, DISPLAY. Caxton used the forms *deploye*, *dysploye* after Parisian Fr., but the actual adoption of *deploy* in a specific sense took place in the end of the 18th c.]

† **1.** (in Caxton) *trans.* To unfold, display. *Obs.*

c **1477** CAXTON *Jason* 112 Anon they deployed their saylle. **1490** —— *Eneydos* xxvii. 96 To sprede and dysploye the sayles.

2. *Mil.* **a.** *trans.* To spread out (troops) so as to form a more extended line of small depth.

1786 *Progress of War* in *Europ. Mag.* IX. 184 His columns ..are with ease and order soon deploy'd. **1818** TODD, *Deploy*, a military word of modern times, hardly wanted in our language; for it is, literally, to *display*. A column of troops is *deployed*, when the divisions spread wide, or open out. **1863** *Life in the South* II. i. 11 Other companies were deployed along the stream.

fig. c **1829** LANDOR *Wks.* (1868) II. 206/2 But now deploy your throats, and cry, rascals, cry 'Vive la Reine'. **1865** M. ARNOLD *Ess. Crit.* ii. (1875) 97 An English poet deploying all the forces of his genius.

b. *intr.* Of a body of troops: To open out so as to form a more extended front or line. Also *fig.*

1796 *Instr. & Reg. Cavalry* (1813) 117 Before the close column deploys, its head division must be on the line into which it is to extend. **1799** WELLINGTON in Gurw *Desp.* I. 22 The right wing, having deployed into line, began to advance. **1870** DISRAELI *Lothair* lviii. 309 The main columns of the infantry began to deploy from the heights.

fig. **1848** DICKENS *Dombey* v, Mrs. Chick was constantly deploying into the centre aisle to send out messages by the pew-opener. **1873** GEIKIE *Gt. Ice Age* xix. 249 None of these [glaciers] ever got out from the mountain valleys to deploy upon the low-grounds.

Hence **de'ployed** *ppl. a.*, **de'ploying** *vbl. sb.* and *ppl. a.*

1851 MAYNE REID *Scalp Hunt.* xxxviii. 292 They behold the deploying of the line. **1863** KINGLAKE *Crimea* II. 216 Able to show a deployed front to the enemy.

de'ployment. *Mil.* [ad. F. *déploiement* (1798 in *Dict. Acad.*), f. *déployer*: see DEPLOY *v.*, and -MENT.] The action of deploying; = DEPLOY *sb.*

1796 *Instr. & Reg. Cavalry* (1813) 117 The close column of the regiment forms in line, on its front, on its rear, or on any central division, by the deployment or flank march by three's, and by which it successively uncovers and extends its several divisions. **1868** KINGLAKE *Crimea* (ed. 6) III. i. 38 Those divisions were halted, and their deployment immediately began.

deplumate (dɪ'pl(j)uːmət), *a.* [ad. med.L. *dēplūmāt-us*, pa. pple. of *dēplūmāre* to DEPLUME.] Stripped of feathers, deplumed.

1883 *Syd. Soc. Lex.*, *Deplumate*, without, or having lost, its feathers.

de'plumated, *ppl. a.* [-ED[1].] = prec.

1727 BAILEY vol. II, *Deplumated*, having the Feathers taken off. **1819** G. S. FABER *Dispens.* (1823) II. 424 Shut up in the prison of gross flesh, with deplumated wings and scanty opportunities..the soul is compelled to toil.

deplumation (diːpl(j)uː'meɪʃən). [a. F. *déplumation* (Cotgr. 1611), n. of action from *déplumer* to DEPLUME.] The action of depluming, or condition of being deplumed: loss of feathers, plumes, or *fig.* of honours, etc.

(In quot. 1834 humorously for 'plucking' in examination.)

1611 COTGR., *Deplumation*, a deplumation, pluming, vnfeathering. **1662** R. W[ALDEN] (*title*), The Deplumation of Mrs. Anne Gibbs, of those furtivous perfections whereof she was supposed a Proprietary. **1662** STILLINGFL. *Orig. Sacr.* III. iii. §15 (ed. 3) 512 Through the violence of her moulting or deplumation. **1827** G. S. FABER *Sacred Cal. Prophecy* (1844) II. 34 Notwithstanding the downfall produced by this deplumation, it [the first Wild-Beast] afterward became erect upon its feet, like a man. **1834** *Oxf. Univ. Mag.* I. 289 Lest..we recall to painful remembrance the forgotten miseries of deplumation.

¶ *Path.* (See quots.)

1706 PHILLIPS (ed. Kersey), *Deplumation*..in *Surgery*, a swelling of the Eyelids, accompany'd with the fall of the Hairs from the Eye-brows. **1883** *Syd. Soc. Lex.*, *Deplumation*..old term for a disease of the eyelids which causes the eyelashes to fall off (Gr. πτίλωσις).

deplume (dɪ'pl(j)uːm), *v.* [ad. F. *déplumer* (in OF. *desplumer*), or med.L. *dēplūmāre*, f. DE- I. 6 + L. *plūma* feather.]

1. *trans.* To strip of feathers; to pluck the feathers off.

c **1420** *Pallad on Husb.* I. 698 Twies a yere deplumed may thai be. **1575** TURBERV. *Faulconrie* 310 Ye must cast your hawke handsomly, and deplume hir head behinde..and anoynt it with butter and swynes bloud. **1651** N. BACON *Disc. Govt. Eng.* II. xxx. (1739) 141 Thus was the Roman Eagle deplumed, every Bird had its own Feather. **1651–3** JER. TAYLOR *Serm. for Year* I. xv. 188 Such a person is like Homers bird, deplumes himselfe to feather all the naked callows that he sees. **1774** PENNANT *Tour Scot. in 1772*, 237 From the circumstance of its depluming its breast. **1847** GOSSE *Birds of Jamaica* 293 [The pigeons] are..deplumed and drawn..before they are sent to market.

b. To strip off (feathers). *rare.*

1599 *Broughton's Lett.* viii. 28 There are that will.. deplume your borrowed feathers.

c. *transf.* To pluck or cut off hair from. *rare.*

1775 ADAIR *Amer. Ind.* 6 Holding this Indian razor between their fore-finger and thumb, they deplume themselves, after the manner of the Jewish novitiate priests.

2. *fig.* To strip or deprive of honour, ornament, wealth, or the like.

[**1567** DRANT *Horace Epist.* II. ii. H ij, Thence lighted I in Thessalie of fethers then deplumde.] **1651** *Fuller's Abel Rediv.*, *Andrewes* (1867) II. 174 [The bishopric] of Ely (before it was so much deplumed). *a* **1661** FULLER *Worthies* III. (1662) 168 This Scotish Demster is an arrant rook, depluming England, Ireland and Wales, of famous Writers, meerly to feather his own Country therewith. **1779** GIBBON *Misc. Wks.* (1814) IV. 588 His favourite amusement of depluming me. **1883** L. WINGFIELD *A. Rowe* I. xi. 258 [They] kept gaming-tables..where the unwary were speedily deplumed.

Hence **de'plumed** *ppl. a.*, **de'pluming** *vbl. sb.*

1638 SHIRLEY *Mart. Soldier* III. iv. in Bullen *O. Pl.* I. 219 The live taile of a deplum[e]d Henne. **1655** FULLER *Ch. Hist.* v. iii. §63 Thus on the depluming of the Pope every bird had his own feather. **1793** *Residence in France* (1797) I. 170 A fowl..dressed without any other preparation than that of depluming. **1890** H. A. HAZEN in *Science* 23 May 313/2 The most singular fact is that the fowl lives under the depluming process [in a tornado].

depnes, obs. form of DEEPNESS.

depoeticize (diːpəʊ'ɛtɪsaɪz), *v.* [DE- II. 1.] *trans.* To deprive of what is poetic; to render prosaic.

1813 *Examiner* 10 May 300/1 Pope's villa..still survives ..though much depoeticized with improvements. **1887** *Temple Bar Mag.* Sept. 73 Depressing and stale reflections upon the depoeticising influence of humanity.

depoetize (dɪ'pəʊɪtaɪz), *v.* [DE- II. 1.] *trans.* To deprive of the character of a poet; also, to deprive of poetic character; = prec.

1865 *Pall Mall G.* No. 192. 4/2 The presence of cottages ..depoetizes the scene. **1886** *Athenæum* 24 July 117 Such writing is a relief after reading the men of the decadence, the pessimists who endeavour to depoetize life for us.

depois, obs. Sc. form of DEPOSE.

depolarize (dɪ'pəʊləraɪz), *v.* [DE- II. 1.] *trans.* To deprive of polarity; to reverse or destroy the effect of polarization.

a. *Optics.* To change the direction of polarization of (a polarized ray) so that it is no longer arrested by the analyzer in a polariscope.

1819 *Edin. Rev.* XXXII. 180 The light becomes depolarised. **1854** J. SCOFFERN in *Orr's Circ. Sc.*, *Chem.* 76 The interposition of the mica must have depolarized the ray.

b. *Electr.* and *Magn.* To deprive of polarity. Also *fig.*

1860 O. W. HOLMES *Prof. Breakf.-t.* i, To depolarize every fixed religious idea in the mind by changing the word which stands for it. **1866** E. HOPKINS in *Athenæum* 22 Sept. 369/3 The iron is hard, and requires to be depolarized like a steel bar.

Hence **de'polarized** *ppl. a.*, **de'polarizing** *vbl. sb.* and *ppl. a.* Also **depolari'zation**, the action or process of depolarizing.

1815 BREWSTER in *Phil. Trans.* 29 (*title*) Experiments on the Depolarization of Light. **1818** WHEWELL in Todhunter *Acc. W.'s Wks.* (1876) II. 31 The neutral and depolarizing axes. **1860** O. W. HOLMES *Prof. Breakf.-t.* i, Scepticism is afraid to trust its truths in depolarized words. **1871** B. STEWART *Heat* §193 Forbes was able to prove the circular polarization and depolarization of heat.

depolarizer (dɪ'pəʊləraɪzə(r)). [-ER[1].] That which depolarizes; an instrument or apparatus for producing depolarization.

1846 JOYCE *Sci. Dial.* xxiii. 336 In this case the thin film is called a depolarizer. **1894** *Daily News* 22 May 5/2 Voltaic combinations with a fused electrolyte and a gaseous depolariser.

depolish (dɪ'pɒlɪʃ), *v.* [f. DE- II. 1 + POLISH, after F. *dépolir*, *dépoliss-ant* (in Furetière, 1690).] *trans.* To remove the polish from, deprive of polish. Hence **de'polished** *ppl. a.*

1873 TYNDALL *Fragm. Sc.* I. vii. *Niagara*, Glass may be depolished by the impact of fine shot. **1875** URE *Dict. Arts* II. 639 s.v. *Gilding*, The surface [prepared for gilding] should now appear somewhat depolished; for when it is very smooth, the gold does not adhere so well. **1884** *Public Opinion* 5 Sept. 305/1 A depolished bowl with cut facets.

depoliticalize: see DE- II. 1.

depoliticize (diːpə'lɪtɪsaɪz), *v.* [f. DE- II. 1 + POLITICIZE *v.*] *trans.* To render non-political, to remove from the sphere of political activity or influence. Also *absol.* So **depo,litici'zation**; **depo'liticized** *ppl. a.*

1928 *Daily Tel.* 13 Mar. 10/6 The 'depoliticisation' of the public services... The entire public services [in Jugoslavia] have come to be regarded as existing to enable political leaders to reward their followers for party services. **1937** *New Statesman* 4 Sept. 329/2 'Don't talk politics to us,' a bank clerk said to me, 'we [*sc.* the Germans] are a depoliticised people. We know we can know nothing, and anyhow knowledge is dangerous here.' *Ibid.*, For it is the intelligent of all classes who are de-politicised. **1960** *Guardian* 19 Sept. 8/2 The distribution of irrigation water is easier to 'depoliticise' than, say, the status of Kashmir. **1963** *Economist* 9 Feb. 533/3 Spokesmen of the People's Party, aware of the political dynamite involved in any large-scale attack on the nationalised empire, have stressed that their aim is to 'de-politicise' rather than de-nationalise. **1970** *Guardian* 23 Dec. 3/7 To denationalise and depoliticise Jerusalem is..the first practical step towards preparing a long-term plan for Jerusalem's future.

† **depo'lition.** *Obs. rare*$^{-0}$. [ad. L. *dēpolītiōn-em*, n. of action from *dēpolīre* to polish off.]

1656 BLOUNT *Glossogr.*, *Depolition*, a polishing, perfecting, or finishing.

depo'llute, *v.* [f. DE- II. 1 + POLLUTE *v.*] *trans.* To cleanse (land, water, etc.) of pollution. Also *absol.* and **depo'lluted** *ppl. a.*

1967 *Sunday Times* 9 Apr. 31 The cheapest desalted water in the U.S. still costs 10 times as much as depolluted fresh water in water-short areas. **1970** *Daily Tel.* (Colour Suppl.) 25 Sept. 25/1 We could depollute the Trent and take our water direct from the main river. **1977** *Forbes* (N.Y.) 1 Oct. 23/2 The steelers have been jumped on to roll back prices, up wages, pay greater taxes, modernize, depollute, compete abroad and a few other hundred contradictory things all at the same time. **1981** *N.Y. Times* 13 Sept. IV. 22/3 That the Thames is being incorporated into the majority of development plans is an outgrowth of successful efforts to depollute a waterway so dirty that in Victorian times, women sold nosegays to pedestrians by Westminster Bridge.

de'polymerize, *v.* [f. DE- II. 1 + POLYMERIZE *v.*] **a.** *trans.* To break down (a polymer) into monomers or other smaller units. **b.** *intr.* To undergo this process. So **de,polymeri'zation**; **de'polymerized** *ppl. a.*; **de'polymerizing** *vbl. sb.* and *ppl. a.*

1893 *Funk's Stand. Dict.*, Depolymerization. **1909** WEBSTER, Depolymerize v. tr. **1924** *Jrnl. Text. Inst.* XV. T. 383 The formation of dislocation marks can be ascribed to a process of twinning or gliding caused by lateral stresses in the fibre, which bring about a depolymerisation of the cellulose at these points. **1939** *Jrnl. Biol. Chem.* CXXVII. 253 The depolymerizing effect of pancreatin on the nucleic acid. *Ibid.* 257 The fully depolymerized substance has a molecular weight of 1341. *Ibid.* 258 Desoxyribonucleic acid, depolymerized by Feulgen's method.., is dephosphorylated by crude and by purified enzyme. **1962** H. HEATH in A. Pirie *Lens Metabolism Rel. Cataract* 363 This has been attributed to the consequent lack of depolymerizing peroxide and hence the accumulation of large molecules of the mucopolysaccharide. **1962** *Lancet* 12 May 1007/2 Tomkins et al. have found that the highly polymerised (tetrameric) form of the enzyme, glutamic dehydrogenase, catalyses the oxidation of glutamic acid while the depolymerised (monomeric) form catalyses oxidation of alanine. **1964** N. G. CLARK *Mod. Org. Chem.* xiv. 272 This liquid trimer is preferred to the low-boiling acetaldehyde, into which it slowly de-polymerizes under the reaction conditions. **1968** H. HARRIS *Nucleus & Cytoplasm* ii. 21 These phages induce depolymerization of the bacterial DNA. *Ibid.* 22 This phage does not depolymerize the bacterial DNA.

depone (dɪ'pəʊn), *v.* Chiefly *Sc.* [ad. L. *dēpōnĕre* to lay away or aside, to lay down, put down, depose, deposit; in med.L. to testify (Du Cange); f. DE- I. 1, 2 + *pōnĕre* to put, place; cf. DEPOSE *v.*]

† **1.** *trans.* To lay down (a burden, an office); to deposit. *Obs.*

1533 BELLENDEN *Livy* IV. (1822) 357 He had causit the maister of chevelry to depone his office. **1649–50** FOORD in M. P. Brown *Suppl. Dec.* I. 394 (Jam.) Who had deponed his money in David his hand. *a* **1843** SOUTHEY *Inscriptions* xli, The obedient element Sifts or depones its burthen.

† **2.** To remove from office; = DEPOSE *v.* 3. *Obs.*

1533 BELLENDEN *Livy* II. (1822) 106 Gif he..had deponit ony of the kingis afore rehersit fra thair empire and kingdome.

3. To state or declare upon oath; to DEPOSE. **a.** with *simple object*; also † *to depone an oath* (*serment*).

1549 *Compl. Scot.* xv. 136 Iunius brutus gart them depone ane serment that thai suld al concur. **1637–50** Row *Hist. Kirk* (1842) 26 He himself hes confessed all that they deponed. **1834** H. MILLER *Scenes & Leg.* xxi. (1857) 312 Any thing they could have to depone anent the spulzie.

b. with *clause.*

1600 *Gowrie's Conspir.* in *Select. Harl. Misc.* (1793) 198 Andrew Hendersoun..Depones, that the earle enquyred of him what he would be doing vppon the morrow. **1681** GLANVILL *Sadducismus* II. 297 Andr. Martin Servitour to the Lord of Pollock..Depones, that he was present in the house. **1830** SCOTT *Demonol.* viii. 265 Who deponed that he saw a cat jump into the accused person's cottage window. **1842** BARHAM *Ingol. Leg.*, *Dead Drummer*, One Mr. Jones Comes forth and depones That fifteen years since he had heard certain groans.

4. *intr.* To declare upon oath; to testify, bear testimony. Also *fig.*

1640 R. BAILLIE *Canterb. Self-Convict.* 34 Two witnesses ..deponing before all England to King James. **1680** G. HICKES *Spirit of Popery* 26 Prosecuted for not deponeing in the matter of Field-Meetings. **1793** *Trial of Fyshe Palmer* 66 He was the more difficulted to depone to the letter, as, etc. **1835** ALISON *Hist. Europe* (1849–50) III. xiv. §30. 164 He could not depone to one fact against the accused.

fig. **1833** CHALMERS *Bridgewater Treat.* I. i. 61 This fact or phenomenon..depones strongly both for a God and for the supreme righteousness of his nature. **1856** FERRIER *Inst. Metaph.* 414 We cannot be ignorant of what is deponed to in the opposites of the axiom.

deponent (dɪˈpəʊnənt), *a.* and *sb.* [ad. L. *dēpōnent-em*, pr. pple. of *depōnĕre* (see prec.), spec. used by the late L. grammarians as in sense 1.]

A. *adj. Gram.* Of verbs: Passive or middle in form but active in meaning: originally a term of Latin Grammar.

Both form and meaning were originally reflexive (e.g. *utor* I serve myself, *fruor* I delight myself, *proficiscor* I put myself forward, etc.), as in the Middle Voice in Greek; as, however, in ordinary verbs the reflexive form had become a passive in Latin, these verbs were erroneously regarded as having *laid aside* or dropped a passive meaning, whence the name. In reality, what was laid aside, or lost sight of, was the reflexive sense.

1528 TINDALE *Obed. Chr. Man* (1573) 130 [He] maketh a verbe passive of a verbe deponent. **1669** MILTON *Accedence* Wks. (1847) 467/1 Of verbs deponent come participles both of the active and passive form. **1859** DONALDSON *Grk. Gram.* §433 A deponent verb is one which though exclusively passive or middle in its inflexions, has so entirely *deponed* or laid aside its original meaning, that it is used in all respects like a transitive or neuter verb of the active form. **1871** GOODWIN *Grk. Gram.* (1882) 80 Deponent verbs are those which have no active voice, but are used in the middle or passive forms with an active sense.

B. *sb.*

1. A deponent verb.

1530 PALSGR. Introd. 34 All such verbes as be used in the latin tong, lyke neuters or deponentes. **1612** BRINSLEY *Pos. Parts* (1669) 36 Are Deponents and Commons declined like Passives? *c* **1790** COWPER *Comment. on P.L.* ii. 506 Wks. (1837) XV. 320 The verb *dissolve* in the common use of it is either active or passive, and we should say, either that the council *dissolved itself*, or that it was dissolved; but Milton here uses it as a deponent. **1871** GOODWIN *Grk. Gram.* (1892) 91 Deponents generally have the aorist and future of the middle form.

2. One who deposes or makes a deposition under oath; one who gives written testimony to be used as evidence in a court of justice or for other purpose.

1548 HALL *Chron.* Hen. VIII, an. 6 (R.), The sayde deponent sayeth, that on Saturdaye..he toke the charge of the pryson. **1621** ELSING *Debates Ho. Lords* (Camden) 141 The said Jarvis Unwoon told this deponent he would pull this deponent's flesh from his jawes if he wold not be conformable to theire wills. **1713** SWIFT *Poems, Cadenus & V.* 68 Witness ready to attest..That ev'ry article was true; Nor further those deponents knew. **1803** WELLINGTON in Gurw. *Desp.* II. 493 These depositions do not contain one word of truth, excepting that the deponents deserted from the service. **1878** LECKY *Eng. in 18th C.* II. vi. 165 Dean Jones himself was the deponent.

†**deˈponer.** *Obs.* [f. DEPONE *v.* + -ER[1].] One who depones: in *Sc. Law* = DEPONENT *sb.* 2.

1600 *Sc. Acts Jas. VI* (1814) 203 (Jam.) The Duik of Lennox..deponis, that..this deponar for the tyme being in Falkland..he saw maister Alexander Ruthven [etc.]. **1634** *State Trials, Ld. Balmerino* 7 June, Before he had ended it, he sayd to the deponer, Mr. John, I entreat you [etc.]. **1752** J. LOUTHIAN *Form of Process* (ed. 2) 107 That the Pannel's Presence may over-aw the Deponer.

†**deˈponible,** *a. Obs. rare*[−0]. [f. L. type **dēpōnibilis*, f. *dēpōnĕre*: see DEPONE and -BLE.] Capable of being deposed (from office, etc.). Hence †**deˌponiˈbility**. *Obs. rare.*

1635 T. PRESTON *Let.* in Foley *Eng. Province Soc. Jesus* I. 1. 257 They intend at Rome..that deponibility, which is the only chief thing denied in the oath, must not be meddled withal.

†**depoˈnition.** *Sc. Obs. rare.* = DEPOSITION 5.

1492 *Act. Dom. Conc.* 284 (Jam.) The depunitiouns of the witnes now takin.

depoost: see DEPOST.

†**deˈpopulacy.** *Obs.* [f. DEPOPULATE *ppl. a.* (see -ACY): cf. *degeneracy*.] Depopulated condition.

16.. CHAPMAN *Batrachom.* 405 O Jove, neither She nor I ..can keep depopulacy From off the Frogs!

depopularize (dɪˈpɒpjʊləraɪz), *v.* [f. DE- II. 1 + POPULARIZE *v.*] *trans.* To deprive of popularity, render unpopular.

1834 *Blackw. Mag.* XXXVI. 227 Not to depopularize a new-born power endeavouring to strengthen itself. **1849** GROTE *Greece* II. lxxii. (1862) VI. 365 But Sparta had not yet become depopularized. **1883** *Daily News* 3 July 5/7 There is nothing that tends so much to depopularise a Minister.

deˈpopulate, *ppl. a.* [ad. L. *dēpopulāt-us*, pa. pple. of *dēpopulāre* (*-ārī*), in its med.L. sense.] Laid waste; deprived (wholly or partly) of inhabitants. Used †**a.** as *pa. pple.* in which use it was at length superseded by *depopulated*; **b.** as *adj.* now *arch.* or *poet.*

a. 1531 ELYOT *Gov.* I. ii, The kynge of Mede had depopulate the countrey. **1580** NORTH *Plutarch* (1676) 377 By spoil of Wars depopulate, destroyed and disgrast.

b. 1622 F. MARKHAM *Bk. War* III. iv. 94 [A] Country that is poore and wasted or barren or depopulate. **1737** N. CLARKE *Hist. Bible* II. (1740) 127 Locusts, which left the earth as naked and depopulate. **1818** SHELLEY *Lines Euganean Hills* 127 When the sea-mew Flies, as once before it flew, O'er thine isles depopulate. **1855** CHAMIER *My Trav.* III. ii. 51 The people..are half starved, badly clothed, and depopulate.

depopulate (dɪˈpɒpjʊleɪt), *v.* [f. ppl. stem of L. *dēpopulāre* (usually deponent *-ārī*) to lay waste, ravage, pillage, spoil; f. DE- I. 3 + *populāre* (*-ārī*) to lay waste, ravage, spoil (f. *populus* people), *lit.* to spread or pour in a multitude over (a region); but in med.L. to spoil of people, depopulate, in sense associated with the Romanic parallel form **dispopulare*, whence It. *despopolare* (*dipopolare*), Sp. *despoblar*, Pr. *despovoar*, OF. *des-*, *de-peupler*, now *dépeupler*, English DISPEOPLE, DEPEOPLE.]

†**1.** *trans.* To ravage, plunder, lay waste. *Obs.*

1548 HALL *Chron.* 56 He set furth toward Caen.. depopulatyng the countrey, & destroiyng the villages. **1622** BACON *Hen. VII* (J.), He turned his arms upon unarmed and unprovided people, to spoil only and depopulate. **1641** G. FITZGERALD in *Lismore Papers* Ser. II. (1888) IV. 246 The enemy..robbed..my servants and Depopulated my Lands. **1670** MILTON *Hist. Eng.* VI. *Ethelred*, He..enter'd into Mercia..depopulating all places in their way.

2. To deprive wholly or partially of inhabitants; to reduce the population of.

1594 *Privy Council* in Arb. *Garner* I. 301 Many towns and villages upon the sea coasts are..wonderfully decayed, and some wonderfully depopulated. **1607** SHAKS. *Cor.* III. i. 264. **1634** SIR T. HERBERT *Trav.* 216 A Village..lately depopulated from her Inhabitants, by command from the Spanish King. **1690** CHILD *Disc. Trade* (1694) 50 The late Plague, which did much depopulate this Kingdom. **1777** WATSON *Philip II* (1839) 271 Depopulating the maritime provinces by the expulsion of heretics. **1837** LANDOR *Wks.* (1868) II. 339/1 The pestilence which depopulated the cities of Italy and ravaged the whole of Europe.

b. *transf.* and *fig.*

1607 TOPSELL *Four-f. Beasts* (1658) 361 [Lions] excell.. in cruelty..depopulating the flocks and herds of cattel. **1686** F. SPENCE tr. *Varilla's Ho. Medicis* 422 Whole forests and valleys were..depopulated of game. **1700** T. BROWN *Amusem. Ser. & Comic* 96 The other Knaves will.. Depopulate your Mouths..and take as much for drawing out an Old Tooth, as [etc.]. **1725** BRADLEY *Fam. Dict.* s.v. *Rabbit*, Turn 'em [Does] loose, that you may not depopulate your Warrens. **1771** GOLDSM. *Hist. Eng.* I. 282 An enterprize that..had, in a great measure, depopulated Europe of its bravest forces.

†**3.** To reduce or lessen the number of (people, etc.); to thin. *Obs.*

1545 JOYE *Exp. Dan.* xi. (1547) 182 The Iewes were euer ouerrunne and depopulated of both y[e] hostes. *c* **1611** CHAPMAN *Iliad* XI. 173 The soldier-loving Atreus' son.. Depopulating troops of men. **1798** R. P. *Tour in Wales* 24 (MS.) The modern spirit of depopulating trees having here left a gloomy house on a shaven lawn.

4. *intr.* To become less populous.

In the first two quots. prob. for *was a-depopulating* = *was being depopulated.*

[**1761** HUME *Hist. Eng.* II. App. iii. 521 The kingdom was depopulating from the increase of enclosures. **1770** GOLDSM. *Des. Vill.* Ded., An inquiry whether the country be depopulating or not.] **1882** STEVENSON *Stud. Men & Bks.* 195 Our Henry Sixth made his Joyous Entry dismally enough into disaffected and depopulating Paris.

†**5.** *trans.* To destroy, cut off. *Obs.*

1576 BAKER *Jewell of Health* 215 With this licour may you depopulate or cut of any member. **1650** BULWER *Anthropomet.* 131 With Depilatories burn up and depopulate the Genital matter thereof.

Hence **deˈpopulated, deˈpopulating,** *ppl. adjs.*

1623 SANDERSON *Serm.* (1637) 143 In these hard and depopulating times. **1632** LITHGOW *Trav.* x. 450 In that narrow depopulated street. **1643** PRYNNE *Sov. Power Parl.* III. 84 The Kings Popish depopulating Cavaleers. **1674** R. GODFREY *Inj. & Ab. Physic* 7 A depopulating Plague. **1799** J. ROBERTSON *Agric. Perth* 419 A depopulated, neglected, mountainous country. **1821** *Examiner* 1 Apr. 206/2 A depopulating war was scattering its horrors throughout all Europe. **1875** HAMERTON *Intell. Life* XII. iii. 448 The depopulated deserts of Breadalbane.

depopulation (dɪpɒpjʊˈleɪʃən). Also 5–6 **-acion.** [ad. L. *dēpopulātiōn-em*, n. of action from *dēpopulāre* (*-ārī*). In ancient L. used in sense 'devastation, pillaging'; so in French in 1500 (Hatzf.). The modern sense in Fr. and Eng. follows that of DEPOPULATE.] The action of depopulating; depopulated condition.

†**1.** Laying waste, devastation, ravaging, pillaging.

Often including the destruction of *people*, and so gradually passing into 2.

1462 EDW. IV in Ellis *Orig. Lett.* Ser. II. I. 127 Warre, depopulacion, robberye, and manslawghtar. **1543–4** *Act 35 Hen. VIII*, c. 12 The same Scottes..make..incurses, inuasions, spoyles, burnynges, murders, wastinges and depopulations in this his realme. **1655** FULLER *Hist. Camb.* (1840) 237 The Jewish law provided against the depopulation of birds' nests. **1665** MANLEY *Grotius' Low C. Warres* 68 Committing Rapes, Murthers, and daily depopulations. **1670** MILTON *Hist. Eng.* IV. Wks. (1851) 188 The Danes..infested those parts with wide depopulation. **1741** J. LAWRY in *Athenian Lett.* (1792) II. 44 Amidst tumults, depopulations, and the alarms of war. **1816** BYRON *Ch. Har.* III. xx, In vain years Of death, depopulation, bondage, fears, Have all been borne.

2. Reduction of population; depriving of inhabitants; unpeopling. In 17th c. *esp.* the clearance of the peasantry from their estates by the land-owners.

c **1460** FORTESCUE *Abs. & Lim. Mon.* v, To the grete abatynge of his revenues and depopolacion of his reaume. **1611** SPEED *Hist. Gt. Brit.* II. liv. §12. 189 For the depopulation of the Iland. **1619** JER. DYKE *Counterpoyson* (1620) 27 Extortion, inclosures, depopulations, sacriledge, impropriations. **1642** FULLER *Holy & Prof. St.* II. xiii. 100 He detests and abhorres all inclosure with depopulation. **1765** GOLDSM. *Trav.* 402 Have we not seen..Opulence, her grandeur to maintain, Lead stern Depopulation in her train. **1892** *Daily News* 7 Nov. 6/1 (*Paris*) The depopulation panic and the necessity of keeping up big armies. **1893** G. B. LONGSTAFF *Rural Depopulation* 1 'Depopulation' is often very vaguely employed, but here it will be used as denoting a diminution in the number of the inhabitants of a district, as compared with those enumerated at a preceding census.

b. The condition of being depopulated or deprived of inhabitants.

1697 DRYDEN *Virgil* (1721) I. 37 Eighteen other Colonies, pleading Poverty and Depopulation, refus'd to contribute Mony. **1721** DE FOE *Mem. Cavalier* (1840) 188 There never was seen that ruin and depopulation..which I have seen.. abroad. **1816** KEATINGE *Trav.* (1817) I. 85 Castile and Arragon realize what strangers are told concerning Spain. Denudation, depopulation, and desiccation reign throughout them. **1827** SOUTHEY *Hist. Penins. War* II. 339 The frightful silence of depopulation prevails.

deˈpopulative, *a.* [f. L. *dēpopulāt-* ppl. stem + -IVE.] Tending to depopulation.

1861 J. M. LUDLOW in *Macm. Mag.* June 170 The evidence..goes to show that American slavery is essentially wasteful and depopulative.

depopulator (dɪˈpɒpjʊleɪtə(r)). [a. L. *dēpopulātor* spoiler, marauder, pillager, agent-n. from *dēpopulāre* (*-ārī*).]

†**1.** A waster, spoiler, devastator. *Obs.*

c **1440** LYDG. *Secrees* 30 Callyd prodigus which is nat honourable, Depopulator A wastour nat tretable. **1607** TOPSELL *Four-f. Beasts* Pref., *Bestia, i. à vastando*, for that they were wilde and depopulators of other their associates. **1610** HOLLAND *Camden's Brit.* I. 427 Those wastfull depopulators did what they could..many a time to winne it by siege.

2. One who depopulates a district or country. In 17th c. *esp.* one who cleared off the rural population from his estates.

1623 T. SCOT *Highways of God & K.* 77 The Depopulator ..to inhanse his Rents, puls downe all the petty Tenements and Farmes, and will haue none dwell neere him. **1626** in Rushw. *Hist. Coll.* (1659) I. 356 Covetous Landlords, Inclosers, Depopulators. **1642** FULLER *Holy State* 237 (T.) Our puny depopulators allege for their doings the king's and country's good. **1798** MALTHUS *Popul.* II. ii. (1806) I. 339 Wars, plagues or that greater depopulator than either, a tyrannical government. **1827** SCOTT *Napoleon* Introd., Collot d'Herbois, the demolisher and depopulator of Lyons.

deˈpopulatory, *a. rare.* [f. as prec.: see -ORY.] Characterized by or tending to depopulation.

1864 G. A. SALA in *Daily Tel.* 29 Sept., The Richmond *Sentinel* calls the depopulatory decree 'an event unparalleled in the American war'..'Sherman', it continues, 'has given the war a new feature'.

†**deˈport,** *sb. Obs.* [a. OF. *deport*, *desport*, bodily manner of being, joyous manifestation, diversion, pleasure, in mod.F. *déport* action of deporting oneself; f. *deporter*, *desporter*, mod.F. *déporter* to DEPORT.]

1. Joy, pleasure; = DISPORT.

c **1477** CAXTON *Jason* 33 b, Alas my dere lady all good and honour cometh of you, and ye be all my deport and fortune.

2. Behaviour, bearing, deportment.

(The Caxton quotation doubtfully belongs here.)

1474 CAXTON *Chesse* II. ii. B v b, Whan thys emperours sone had seen and advertysed her deportes, her countenaunce, her manere, and her beaulte, he was alle ravysshed and esprysed with her loue forthwyth. **1665** J. SPENCER *Vulg. Prophecies* 22 A Doctrine, which the deport of the Soul, while a prisoner to its own house, seems a little to encourage. **1667** MILTON *P.L.* IX. 389 But Delia's self In gate [she] surpass'd and Goddess-like deport. **1716** CIBBER *Love Makes Man* IV. i, He seem'd, by his Deport, of France, or England. **1740** SOMERVILLE *Hobbinol* III. 172 Her superior Mien, And Goddess-like Deport.

deport (dɪˈpəʊt), *v.* [In branch I, a. OF. *deporter* (mod.F. *dé-*), f. *de-* (DE- I. 1 or 3) + *porter* to carry. In branch II = mod.F. *déporter* (1798 in *Dict. Acad.*), ad. L. *dēportāre* to carry off, convey away, transport, banish, f. DE- I. 2 + *portāre* to carry. The two branches are treated by Darmesteter as historically distinct words in French.]

I. †**1.** *trans.* To bear with, to be forbearing towards; to treat with consideration, to spare. *Obs.*

1474 CAXTON *Chesse* II. v. D v, Saynt Austyn de ciuitate dei sayth thus; Thou emperour..deporte and forbere thy subgettis. **1481** —— *Godfrey* 18 That ye deporte and honoure my poure lygnage.

†**2. a.** *refl.* To abstain, refrain, forbear. *Obs.*

c **1477** CAXTON *Jason* 14 b, I me deporte from hensforth for to speke ony more of this mater. **1483** —— *G de la Tour* N iij b, [I] myght wel haue deported my self of takyng of thoffyce. **1613** *Treas. Aunc. & Mod. Times* 698/1 To deport himselfe from any further mollestation of the Christians.

†**b.** *absol.* in same sense. *Obs.*

c **1477** CAXTON *Jason* 67, I shall deporte and tarye for this present tyme to speke of the faytes of Jason. **1489** —— *Faytes of A.* I. i. 9 To deporte and forbere temprsye warre.

†**3.** *trans.* ? To raise, lift up. *Obs.*

1483 CAXTON *Gold. Leg.* 33/2 Synge ye to hym in deportyng your voys [*psallite ei in vociferatione*].

4. a. *refl.* To bear or conduct oneself (with reference to manner); to behave; = COMPORT *v.* 3.

1598 BARRET *Theor. Warres* I. ii. 11 He shall deporte himselfe neither cruell nor couetous. *a* **1661** FULLER *Worthies* II. (1662) 239 He so prudently deported himself, that he soon gained the favour and esteem of the whole

Court. **1741** RICHARDSON *Pamela* (1742) IV. 62 How to deport myself with that modest Freedom and Ease. **1840** GEN. P. THOMPSON *Exerc.* (1842) V. 38 They always deported themselves like gentlemen. **1885** *Law Times* 30 May 83/2 Throughout his career he has deported himself as became The Macdermot.

†**b.** *absol.* To behave. *Obs. rare.*

1667 WATERHOUSE *Fire Lond.* 113 Mercy abused and ingratefully deported to.

II. 5. a. *trans.* To carry away, carry off, remove, transport; *esp.* to remove into exile, to banish.

a **1641** BP. MOUNTAGU *Acts & Mon.* (1642) 331 Archelaus..was..deposed and deported to Vienna. **1809** *Edin. Rev.* Apr. 237 Tronçon Ducoudray..was deported to Cayenne. **1856** GROTE *Greece* II. xcv. XII. 377 To..punish this sentiment by disfranchising or deporting two thirds of the citizens. **1886** *Manch. Exam.* 8 Jan. 6/1 Brushing the snow and slush into little mounds, from which it was easily collected into carts and deported to the Thames.

b. In Indian use, = DETAIN *v.* 1. So **depor'tation** = DETENTION 1.

1909 J. MORLEY *Indian Speeches* 144 Great uneasiness is growing in the House of Commons as to the matter of deportation. You know what deportation means. It means that nine Indian gentlemen on December 13 last were arrested and are now detained. *Ibid.* 149 If he is one of these nine deported men, he is not put into contact with criminal persons. **1910** V. CHIROL *Indian Unrest* vii. 99 The deportation struck just at that type of agitator whose influence is most pernicious because it is most subtle. **1914** MRS. BESANT *India & the Empire* 123 Harmless men like my friend Lajpat Rai, who is here, are deported or imprisoned without trial.

Hence **de'ported** *ppl. a.*, carried into exile.

a **1632** SIR D. CARLETON in *Cabbala* (R.), Better dealing then was used to the deported House of Saxe. **1880** K. JOHNSTON *Lond. Geog.* 88 A very small military force, chiefly of deported convicts.

†**de-'port**, *v. Obs. nonce-wd.* [f. DE- II. 2 + PORT *sb.*] *trans.* To deprive of the character of a port; to make no longer a port; to dis-port.

1691 BEVERLEY *Mem. Kingd. Christ* 5 Its Constantinoplitan port shall not be de-ported.

deportable (dɪ'pɔətəb(ə)l), *a.* [f. DEPORT *v.* + -ABLE.] Liable to, or punishable by, deportation.

1891 STEVENSON *Vailima Lett.* (1895) 100 This intervention would have been a deportable offence. **1957** T. P. NEILL *Common Good* xi. 182/1 No immigrant is admitted if he cannot show that he is not liable to become a public charge, and if he does so within five years, he is automatically deportable.

†**de'portate**, *v. Obs. rare.* [f. ppl. stem of L. *dēportāre.*] *trans.* To carry or convey away; = DEPORT *v.* 5.

1599 tr. *Gabelhouer's Bk. Physicke* 172/1 Akornes which the mise have deportatede into their domicilles.

†**de'portates**, *sb. pl. Obs. rare.* [cf. med.L. *deportus* in same sense (Du Cange), *déport des benefices* (Cotgr.). For the form cf. *annates.*] 'The first fruits, or one yeres reuenue of vacant benefices (due vnto the Prince, Patron, or Prelate)' (Cotgr.).

1532 *Address fr. Convoc.* in Strype *Eccl. Mem.* App. xli, Nothing at al..should bee exacted in the Court of Rome, by the reason of letters, bulls, seals, annates..first fruits, or deportates, or by whatsoever other title..they be called.

deportation (diːpɔə'teɪʃən). [ad. L. *dēportātiōn-em*, n. of action from *dēportāre* to carry off, convey away, transport: see DEPORT *v.* II. Cf. F. *déportation* (15–16th c. in Hatzf., not in Cotgr.), the modern common use of which has influenced that of the English word.]

1. The action of carrying away; forcible removal, *esp.* into exile; transportation.

1595 in Cramond *Ann. Banff* II. 21 Reservand the tua pairt to the present Viccare to his death or deportatione. **1605** G. POWEL *Refut. Epist. Puritan Papist* 112 Banishment ..among the Romanes was 3-fold, Interdiction, Relegation, and Deportation. **1633** BP. HALL *Hard Texts* Ezek. i. 2 The first deportation into Babylon. **1726** AYLIFFE *Parergon* 15 An Abjuration, which is a Deportation for ever into a foreign Land, was antiently with us, a civil Death. **1860** *Sat. Rev.* X. 510/2 Wholesale deportations to Cayenne. **1862** MERIVALE *Rom. Emp.* (1865) VI. liv. 443 The mass of the Jewish residents..had been more than once swept away by general edicts of exile or deportation. **1877** C. GEIKIE *Christ* xxxi. (1879) 364 After the deportation of the ten tribes to Assyria.

¶**2.** Deportment. *pseudo-archaism.*

1616 J. LANE *Cont. Sqr.'s T.* IX. 144 The vulgar admiration Stoode stupified att Horbills deportation.

†**depor'tator.** *Obs. rare.* [agent-n. in L. form from L. *dēportāre* to DEPORT.] One who deports or transports.

1629 T. ADAMS *Serm. Heb.* VI. 8 Wks. 1058 Oppressors, Inclosers, Depopulators, Deportators, Depravators.

deportee (diːpɔə'tiː). [f. DEPORT *v.* + -EE[1].] One who is or has been deported; *spec.* in Indian use, = DÉTENU.

1895 *Westm. Gaz.* 13 Dec. 5/1 One party of fifteen deportees from Constantinople having been massacred. **1909** J. MORLEY *Recoll.* (1917) II. 309 The failure to tell the deportee what he is arrested for. **1910** V. CHIROL *Indian Unrest* vii. 99 The grounds on which Government announced the release of these deportees last winter were even more unhappily chosen than the moment for the announcement. **1914** *Morn. Post* 3 Feb. 9/4 To intercept the Umgeni and give the deportees an opportunity of returning to their homes. **1920** *Glasgow Herald* 13 Mar. 9 The Dongola embarked yesterday at Devonport 100 Russian prisoners of war.., 9 Russian deportees, and an escort. **1939** A. TOYNBEE *Study Hist.* V. 124 The Milesian deportees were settled at the mouth of the River Tigris. **1959** *Times Lit. Suppl.* 6 Mar. 126/3 In that sparsely populated, primitive and depressed region..the deportees were more or less abandoned to fend for themselves.

deportment (dɪ'pɔətmənt). [a. OF. *deportement* (mod.F. *dé-*), f. OF. *deporter* to DEPORT.]

1. Manner of conducting oneself; conduct (*of* life); behaviour. *Obs.* or *arch.* in general sense.

1601 BP. W. BARLOW *Defence* 206 Heretickes will bee exceeding holy, both in the deportment of their life, and in [etc.]. **1603** KNOLLES *Hist. Turks* (1621) 1255 The honor and the shame that was to ensue unto them, by the different deportment of themselves in this action. **1637–50** ROW *Hist. Kirk* (1842) 385 This Antichristian deportment, How unlike it is to the Cariage of Christ's Apostles. **1719** YOUNG *Revenge* v. i, She forgives my late deportment to her. **1839** YEOWELL *Anc. Brit. Ch.* xiii. (1847) 150 Luidhard..whose saintly deportment reflected a lustre on the faith which he professed.

†**b.** *pl. Obs.* (Cf. *manners, ways.*)

1603 HOLLAND *Plutarch's Mor.* 499 By his deportments and carriage in all actions. **1665** G. HAVERS *P. della Valle's Trav. E. India* 26 The King..was slain for his evil deportments. **1751** SMOLLETT *Per. Pic.* xxiii, He humbled his deportments before her.

2. Referring to merely external manner: Carriage, bearing, demeanour, address.

1638 SIR T. HERBERT *Trav.* (ed. 2) 150 The bridge was full of women..many of them in faire deportment unmasqued their faces. **1641** BROME *Jov. Crew* I. Wks. 1873 III. 360 Provided your deportment be gentile. **1689** SHADWELL *Bury F.* II, His air, his mien, his deportment charm'd me so. **1761** CHURCHILL *Rosciad* Wks. 1767 I. 29 What's a fine person or a beauteous face, Unless deportment gives them decent grace? **1881** *Daily Tel.* 27 Dec., In the character of..a dancing-master, in which capacity he gives a comical lesson in deportment.

3. *fig.* The manner in which a substance acts under particular conditions; 'behaviour'.

1830 HERSCHEL *Stud. Nat. Phil.* 38 The identity of their deportment under similar circumstances. **1863** TYNDALL *Heat* v. 146 This is illustrated by the deportment of both ice and bismuth on liquefying.

Hence **de'portmented** *ppl. a.* (*nonce-wd.*), taught deportment.

1861 J. PYCROFT *Agony Point* I. 209 Frenched, and musicked, and deportmented.

†**deportract**, *v. Obs. rare.* [f. DE- (as in next) + *portract* var. of PORTRAIT *v.*] = next.

1611 SPEED *Hist. Gt. Brit.* IX. viii. 26 Whose Image was erected in a stately seat, wherein before the Trinitee was deportracted.

†**depor'tray**, *v. Obs.* [f. DE- (as in *depaint, describe*) + PORTRAY *v.*] *trans.* To portray, depict.

1611 SPEED *Hist. Gt. Brit.* v. vii. §13. 42 The Picture of this British woman here last deportraied.

[**deporture.** Explained as: Carriage, bearing, deportment. Error for *departure.*

[**1611** SPEED *Hist. Gt. Brit.* IX. xxiv. §285. 871/2 Her stately port and majesticall departure.] Quoted in **1775** *Gray's Poems* 34 *note*, Her stately port and majestical deporture. Hence in **1864** WEBSTER (citing *Speed*), and some later Dicts.]

deposable (dɪ'pəʊzəb(ə)l), *a.* Also 7 **-ible.** [f. DEPOSE *v.* + -ABLE.] That may be deposed; liable to be deposed.

1643 PRYNNE *Sov. Power Parl.* III. 117 Kings..deposible at the peoples pleasures. *c* **1645** HOWELL *Lett.* I. IV. viii, Keepers of the Great Seal, which, for Title and Office, are deposable. **1849** *Blackw. Mag.* LXVI. 338 One of themselves, elected by themselves, deposable by themselves.

deposal (dɪ'pəʊzəl). Also 5 **depoisale, deposayle, -ayll,** 6–7 **-all.** [prob. a. AFr. *deposaille*, f. *déposer* to DEPOSE: see -AL[1] 5, and cf. *disposal.*] The act of deposing from office; deposition.

1397 *Rolls of Parlt.* III. 379/1 It was communed and spoken in manere of deposal of my liege Loord. *c* **1470** HARDING *Chron.* CLVII. iv, By depoisale and playne coronacion. **1568** GRAFTON *Chron.* II. 405 (Rich. II) It was behovefull and necessary for the weale of the realme to proceede unto the sentence of his deposall. **1631** J. BURGES *Answ. Rejoined* 220 The places voyded by the deposall of inconformable Ministers. **1855** MILMAN *Lat. Chr.* (1864) IX. XIV. i. 7 All the acts of John XXIII till his deposal were the acts of the successor of St. Peter.

†**de'pose**, *sb. Obs.* Also 5 **depos**, *Sc.* **depois.** [f. DEPOSE *v.*]

1. The state of being laid up or committed to some one for safe keeping; custody, keeping, charge; *concr.* that which is so laid up, a deposit.

1393 GOWER *Conf.* I. 218 For God..Hath set him but a litel while That he shall regne upon depose. *c* **1430** LYDG. *Bochas* II. xxii. (1554) 58 b, The sayd herd..[and] His wyfe ..This yong child toke in their depose. *c* **1440** *Promp. Parv.* 119 Depose, *depositum.* **1488** *Inv.* in Tytler *Hist. Scot.* (1864) II. 390 The gold and silver..jowellis and uther stuff ..that he had in depois the tyme of his deceis.

2. Deposition from office or authority.

1559 FERRERS in *Mirr. Mag., Rich. II* vii, To helpe the Percyes plying my depose.

depose (dɪ'pəʊz), *v.* Also 6 *Sc.* **depois.** [a. F. *dépose-r* (12th c. in Littré), f. DE- I. 1 + *poser* to place, put down:—Rom. *posāre* = late L. *pausāre* to cease, lie down, lay down, etc.: see POSE, REPOSE. Through form-association with inflexions of L. *pōnĕre*, *posui*, *positum*, and contact of sense, this *-poser* came to be treated as synonymous with OF. *-pondre* (:—L. *pōnĕre*) and took its place in the compounds, so that *déposer* is now used instead of OF. *depondre*, L. *dēpōnĕre* to depose, and associated in idea with *deposit*, *deposition*, *depositor*, etc., which had no original connexion with *depose.*]

1. *trans.* To lay down, put down (anything material); to DEPOSIT. *arch.*

c **1420** *Pallad. on Husb.* XI. 460 Take leves..of Citur tree ..And into must..Depose, and close or faste it closed se. **1526** *Pilgr. Perf.* (W. de W. 1531) 223 b, Saynt Peter & Saynt Paule..by martyrdome deposed there the tabernacles of theyr bodyes. **1621** B. JONSON *Gypsies Metamorph.*, Face of a rose, I pray thee depose Some small piece of silver. **1658** SIR T. BROWNE *Hydriot.* 33 The ashes of Sacrifices..were carefully carried out by the Priests, and deposed in a clean field. **1718** PRIOR *Solomon* II. 607 The youthful Band depose their glitt'ring Arms. **1855** MILMAN *Lat. Chr.* (1864) III. VI. iii. 419 A paper which he solemnly deposed on the high altar.

†**b.** To put, lay, or place (somewhere) for safe keeping; to place or put in some one's charge.

1583 STUBBES *Anat. Abus.* II. (1882) 18 We must depose and lay foorth ourselues, both bodie, and goods, life, and time..into the hands of the prince. *a* **1612** DONNE *Βιαθανατος* (1644) 108 [Josephus] sayes, our Soule is, *particula Dei*, and deposed and committed in trust to us. **1750** CARTE *Hist. Eng.* II. 643 [He] left them [writings] in the monastery where they had been deposed.

†**c.** Of fluids: To deposit (as a sediment). *Obs.*

1758 HUXHAM in *Phil. Trans.* L. 524 The urine was.. turbid, and..deposed a great deal of lateritious sediment. **1816** ACCUM *Chem. Tests* (1818) 246 A blue precipitate will be deposed.

†**2.** *fig.* To put away, lay aside (a feeling, quality, character, office, etc.). *Obs.*

1526 *Pilgr. Perf.* (W. de W. 1531) 73 Depose or put from you the olde man..and be ye renewed in the spiryte of your mynde. **1620** VENNER *Via Recta* vii. 139 Being sodden.. they depose all their hurt. **1628** HOBBES *Thucyd.* II. lxv, They deposed not their anger till they had fined him in a sum of money. **1677** *Govt. Venice* 50 The General..can hardly bring himself to depose an Authority that he can so easily keep.

3. To put down from office or authority; *esp.* to put down from sovereignty, to dethrone. (The earliest and still the prevailing sense.)

c **1300** *K. Alis.* 7822 Theo kyng dude him [a justise] anon depose. *c* **1470** HARDING *Chron.* CXCVI, The parliament then for his misgouernaunce Deposed him [Richard II]. **1535** COVERDALE *Dan.* v. 20 He was deposed from his kyngly trone, and his magesty was taken from him. **1568** GRAFTON *Chron.* II. 157 The Aldermen that before were deposed, were agayne restored to their wardes and offices. **1651** HOBBES *Leviath.* III. xl. 254 In deposing the High Priest.. they deposed that peculiar Government of God. **1718** LADY M. W. MONTAGU *Lett.* 10 Mar., The late emperor..was deposed by his brother. **1848** MACAULAY *Hist. Eng.* I. 23 Shortly after the battle of Hastings, Saxon prelates and abbots were violently deposed. **1856** FROUDE *Hist. Eng.* (1858) I. ii. 108 Sir Thomas More..declared as his opinion that parliament had power to depose kings if it so pleased.

b. *gen.* To put down, bring down, lower (from a position or estate). *Obs.* exc. as *fig.* from prec.

1377 LANGL. *P. Pl.* B. xv. 514 Riȝt so ȝe clerkes for ȝowre coueityse, ar longe, Shal þei..ȝowre pryde depose. **1483** CAXTON *Gold. Leg.* 77/3, I that am an only sone to my fader and moder I shold depose theyr olde age with heuynes and sorow to helle. **1671** MILTON *P.R.* I. 413 He before had sat Among the prime in splendour, now deposed, Ejected, emptied. **1873** HOLLAND *A. Bonnic.* xviii. 281, I had never seen Mrs. Belden so thoroughly deposed from her self-possession.

†**4. a.** To take away, deprive a person of (authority, etc.); also to remove (a burden or obligation; opp. to *impose*). *Obs.*

1393 GOWER *Conf.* III. 200 In sory plite..he lay, The corone on his hede deposed. **1593** SHAKS. *Rich. II*, IV. i. 192 You may my Glories and my state depose, But not my Griefes, still am I King of those. **1617** MORYSON *Itin.* III. IV. iii. 195 Princes know well to impose exactions, and know not how to depose them.

†**b.** To divest, deprive, dispossess (a person *of* something that enhances). *Obs.*

1558 KNOX *First Blast* (Arb.) 29 If a king shulde depose himself of his diademe or crowne and royal estat. **1606** G. W[OODCOCKE] tr. *Hist. Ivstine* 98 a, He was content to depose him[self] of such a trouble as to be a soueraigne. **1649** LOVELACE *Poems* 10 Depose your finger of that Ring, And Crowne mine with't awhile. **1681** NEVILE *Plato Rediv.* 257 It would be very preposterous to believe, that the Peers would depose themselves of their Hereditary Rights.

5. To testify, bear witness; to testify to, attest; *esp.* to give evidence upon oath in a court of law, to make a deposition.

a. *techn.*

(*a*) *trans.* with *simple obj.* (usually pronominal).

?*a* **1500** *Chester Pl.* (Shaks. Soc.) 219 And blynde was borne undowtedlye And that we will depose. **1566** in Peacock *Eng. Ch. Furniture* 43 And that we will depose vpon a book. *a* **1626** BACON (J.), To depose the yearly rent or valuation of lands. **1742** YOUNG *Nt. Th.* vii. 340 Each much deposes; hear them in their turn. **1873** BROWNING *Red Cott.*

Nt.-cap 1347 And what discretion proved, I find deposed At Vire, confirmed by his own words.

(*b*) with *obj. clause* (or *obj.* and *infin.*).

1562 *Child-Marriages* (E.E.T.S.) 106 They cold not depose her to be of honest name. **1602** T. FITZHERBERT *Apol.* 20 a, [He] offred to depose that he knew that one of the prisoners..was otherwhere then was sayd in his inditement. *a* **1715** BURNET *Own Time* II. 396 The earls of Clare, Anglesey and some others..deposed what Lord Howard had said. **1802** MAR. EDGEWORTH *Moral T.* (1816) I. 236 The workman..deposed, that he carried the..Vase..to the furnace. **1871** MORLEY *Voltaire* (1886) 231 It was deposed that La Barre and D'Etallonde had passed within thirty yards of the sacred procession without removing their hats.

(*c*) *intr.* (*for* or *against* a person, *to* (†*for*) or *against* a thing or fact.)

c **1400** [see DEPOSING *vbl. sb.* 2.]

1542-3 *Act 34-5 Hen. VIII*, c. 1 Other witnes..of as good ..credence as those be whiche deposed against them. *a* **1569** KINGESMYLL *Man's Est.* xi. (1580) 74 Pilate could not but thus depose for his innocence, saying, I finde no faulte in hym. **1593** SHAKS. *3 Hen. VI*, I. ii. 26 Then seeing 'twas he that made you to depose, Your Oath..is vaine. **1623** T. SCOT *Highw. God* 57 The honest Heathen or Turke, for whose truth the Christian dares depose. **1841** D'ISRAELI *Amen. Lit.* (1867) 416 He dreaded lest the spectators of his dexterity should depose against his own witchcraft. **1848** MRS. GASKELL *M. Barton* xix, The shot, the finding of the body, the subsequent discovery of the gun, were rapidly deposed to. **1862** MRS. H. WOOD *Mrs. Hallib.* III. x, He deposed to having fastened up the house at eleven o'clock.

b. *gen.* To testify, bear witness, affirm, assert.

1529 MORE *Dyaloge* III. Wks. 211/2 Than should either the newe proues depose the same that the other did before, or els thei shoulde depose the contrary. **1634** W. TIRWHYT tr. *Balzac's Lett.* Pref. A b, [I] have knowne the Author from both our infancies, and..can depose in what fashion he effecteth his labours. **1662** EVELYN *Chalcogr.* 11 We shall not with Epigenes in Pliny, depose that this Art had its being from Eternity. *a* **1840** J. H. NEWMAN *Paroch. Serm.* Rom. iv. 23 When our memory deposes otherwise.

†**c.** To promise formally upon oath; to swear (*to do* something). *Obs.*

1610 in Picton *L'pool Munic. Rec.* (1883) I. 122 You shall depose to be true liege man unto the Queene's Majestie.

†**6.** *causally.* To examine on oath, to take the evidence or deposition of; to cite as a witness, call to give evidence. (Cf. *to swear a witness.*) *pass.* To give evidence, testify, bear witness. *Obs.*

1562 *Act 5 Eliz.* c. 9 §5 No Person..so convicted..to be ..received as a Witness to be deposed and sworn in any Court. **1593** SHAKS. *Rich. II*, I. iii. 30. **1623** MASSINGER *Dk. Milan* IV. i, Grant thou hadst a thousand witnesses To be deposed they heard it. **1642** JER. TAYLOR *Episc.* xxxvi. (1647) 225 S. Cyprian is the man whom I would choose..to depose in this cause. **1721** STRYPE *Eccl. Mem.* II. ix. 69 The said bishop got leave for certain of the clergy to be deposed on his behalf.

†**7.** To set, put, or lay down in writing. *Obs.*

1668 *Excellency of Pen & Pencil* A iij, This little Tract.. where the requisites for Limning in Water-Colours are deposed..the Colours particularly nominated [etc.]. **1698** *Phil. Trans.* XX. 287, I put here the Differences by me computed..and deposed according to the Order of the Excesses.

deposed (dɪˈpəʊzd), *ppl. a.* [f. DEPOSE *v.* + -ED[1].] Put down from office or authority.

1552 HULOET, Deposed, *abactus, depositus, depulsus.* **1790** BURKE *Fr. Rev.* 124 A deposed tyrant. **1864** BURTON *Scot Abr.* I. ii. 100 The families who had lost their estates adhered to the old title with the mournful pride of deposed monarchs.

deposer (dɪˈpəʊzə(r)). [f. DEPOSE *v.* + -ER[1].]

1. One who deposes or puts down another from office or authority.

1639 R. BAILLIE *Let.* in Macdonald *Covenanters Moray & Ross* (1875) I. 23 A deposer of godly ministers. **1699** BENTLEY *Phal.* 45 One of Phalaris's Deposers.

2. One who deposes or makes a statement on oath; a deponent.

1581 *State Trials, E. Champion* (R.), To be duly examined ..whether they be true and their deposers of credit.

deposing (dɪˈpəʊzɪŋ), *vbl. sb.* [-ING[1].] The action of the verb DEPOSE; deposition.

1. Putting down from authority.

1480 CAXTON *Chron. Eng.* ccxliii. (1482) 283 After the deposynge of kyng Rychard. **1548** HALL *Chron.* 15 When newes of kyng Richardes deposyng were reported. *c* **1630** RISDON *Surv. Devon* §68 (1810) 65 The deposing of the lord mayor. **1827** HALLAM *Const. Hist.* (1876) III. xiv. 100 The deposing of kings was branded as the worst birth of popery and fanaticism.

attrib. **1662** *Jesuit's Reasons* (1675) 117 The Popes deposing power. **1827** HALLAM *Const. Hist.* (1876) I. iii. 147 A few..disclaimed the deposing power of the Roman see.

2. Giving testimony on oath.

c **1400** *Apol. Loll.* 60 Noyþer þe deposing of þe witnes, nor þe sentens ȝeuing of þe juge, be it self makiþ a þing riȝtful. **1580** HOLLYBAND *Treas. Fr. Tong., Deposition de tesmoings*, a deposing of witnesses.

deposit (dɪˈpɒzɪt), *sb.* Also 7-9 **deposite.** [ad. L. *dēpositum*, that which is put down, anything deposited or committed for safe keeping, a deposit, sb. use of neuter of *dēpositus*, pa. pple. of *dēpōnĕre*: see DEPONE, DEPOSE.]

1. a. Something laid up in a place, or committed to the charge of a person, for safe keeping. Also *fig.*

a **1660** HAMMOND *Wks.* II. I. 677 (R.) It seems your church is not so faithful a guardian of her deposit. **1759** ROBERTSON *Hist. Scotl.* I. v. 332 To bring him this precious deposite [the casket containing Q. Mary's letters]. **1806** A. DUNCAN *Nelson's Fun.* 22 The..barge contained the sacred deposit of the body. **1865** SEELEY *Ecce Homo* ii. (ed. 8) 12 He declines to use for his own convenience what he regards as a sacred deposit committed to him for the good of others.

b. *spec.* A sum of money deposited in a bank usually at interest.

1753 HANWAY *Trav.* (1762) II. I. vii. 35 No coin or specie ..is paid out again, unless in cases of deposites. **1855** MACAULAY *Hist. Eng.* IV. 493 The bank of Saint George.. had begun to receive deposits and to make loans before Columbus had crossed the Atlantic. **1887** *Spectator* 3 Sept. 1177 The increase of 40 per cent. in Savings-Banks' deposits.

c. Something, usually a sum of money, committed to another person's charge as a pledge for the performance of some contract, in part payment of a thing purchased, etc.

1737 *Common Sense* (1738) I. 151 What is not subject to Chance is foreign to a Lottery; it is a mere useless Deposite. **1766** ENTICK *London* IV. 262 The conditions of insurance are 2*s.* per cent. premium, and 10*s.* deposit on brick houses. **1771** CUMBERLAND *West Ind.* III. iii, Not..necessary to place a deposit in my hands for so trifling a sum. **1818** M. BIRKBECK *Journ. Amer.* 37 With this they may pay the first deposit on farms of eighty or a hundred acres. **1858** LD. ST. LEONARDS *Handy Bk. Prop. Law* vii. 42 Where the deposit is considerable, and it is probable that the purchase may not be completed for a long time.

2. The state of being deposited or placed in safe keeping; in phr. *on, upon* († *in*) *deposit.*

1624 BACON *Consid. war with Spain*, They had the other day the Valtoline, and now have put it in deposite. **1701** C. LYTTELTON in Ellis *Orig. Lett.* Ser. II. IV. 220 The king's body is here at the English Benedictines in deposit, there to be kept..till they can have an opportunity to send him to Westminster to be buried. **1866** CRUMP *Banking* i. 19 No interest being allowed by [the Bank of England] for money that is placed there upon deposit. **1883** *Times* 10 July 4 The sum to be paid into Court, and invested or placed on deposit for the benefit of the infant.

3. Something deposited, laid or thrown down; a mass or layer of matter that has subsided or been precipitated from a fluid medium, or has collected in one place by any natural process.

In *Geol.*, any mass of material deposited by aqueous agency, or precipitated from solution by chemical action. In *Mining*, an accumulation of ore, esp. of a somewhat casual character, as when occurring in 'pockets'. In *Electro-plating & Electro-typing*, the film of metal deposited by galvanic action upon the exposed ground or surface.

1781 COWPER *Charity* 249 The swell of pity..throws the golden sands, A rich deposit, on the bordering lands. **1794** KIRWAN *Min.* I. 469 We now recur to the dried deposite. **1836** MACGILLIVRAY tr. *Humboldt's Trav.* vi. 80 Covered with recent deposites of sandstone, clay, and gypsum. **1870** ROLLESTON *Anim. Life* 32 A membrane laden with deposits of fat. **1872** YEATS *Growth Comm.* 39 The rich brown deposit of the Nile. *Mod.* Rich deposits of gold found in South Africa.

4. The act of depositing, laying down, placing in safe keeping, etc.: cf. prec. senses, and various senses of DEPOSIT *v.*

a **1773** CHESTERF. *Wks.* (1779) IV. App. 50 My solemn deposit of the truth. **1794** LD. AUCKLAND *Corr.* (1862) III. 273 For the deposit of all kinds of..merchandise and effects. **1823** J. BADCOCK *Dom. Amusem.* 151 A deposit of white powder soon takes place. **1841** CATLIN *N. Amer. Ind.* (1844) I. xii. 89 This cemetery or place of deposite for the dead. **1848** WHARTON *Law Lex., Deposit*..a naked bailment of goods to be kept for the bailor without recompence, and to be returned when the bailor shall require it. **1861** W. BELL *Dict. Law Scot., Depositation* or *Deposit*; is a contract, by which a subject, belonging to one person, is intrusted to the gratuitous custody of another, to be re-delivered on demand.

5. A place where things are deposited or stored; a depository, a depot. (Chiefly *U.S.*)

1719 DE FOE *Crusoe* I. xii. (1840) I. 194 After I had thus secured one part of my little living stock, I went about.. searching for another private place, to make such another deposit. **1783** J. HUNTINGTON in Sparks *Corr. Amer. Rev.* (1853) IV. 27 A safe deposit where every military article may be kept in good order and repair. **1786** T. JEFFERSON *Writ.* (1859) II. 61 The advantages of Alexandria, as the principal deposit of the fur trade. **1808** A. PARSONS *Trav.* x. 207 It is the great magazine or deposit for the goods which they bring from those parts. **1858** HAWTHORNE *Fr. & It. Jrnls.* II. 60 The Church of Santa Croce, the great monumental deposit of Florentine worthies.

6. *attrib.* and *Comb.*, as ***deposit account, -house, -money, -warrant*** (see quots.); (sense 3) ***deposit bed, gold, mine***; **deposit-receipt**, a receipt for anything deposited, *spec.* one given by a banker for money deposited with him at a specified rate of interest for a fixed time.

1795 SOUTHEY *Lett. fr. Spain* (1808) II. 216 The bodies soon after death are placed in a deposit-house. **1822** T. MITCHELL *Aristoph.* II. 129 The losing party also being obliged, beside the payment of other charges, to restore the deposit-money to his adversary. **1833** H. BARNARD in *Maryland Hist. Mag.* (1918) XIII. 346, I..hired a horse for 50 cents to go down to see the deposite mines, which are spread over the whole country. **1849** C. LANMAN *Lett. from Alleghany Mts.* i. 11 Heretofore the gold ore of Lumpkin county has been obtained from what is called the deposit beds. *Ibid.* 17 The deposit gold is extracted from the gravel by means of a simple machine called a rocker. **1851** C. CIST *Cincinnati* 89 Their average deposit account during that period was about eight hundred thousand dollars. **1866** CRUMP *Banking* iii. 77 Deposit accounts..are sums placed at stated rates of interest with a bank, for which receipts are given, called deposit receipts. **1893** BITHELL *Counting-house Dict., Deposit Warrant*, an acknowledgement, receipt, or certificate showing that certain commodities have been deposited in a certain place for safe keeping, as security for a loan, or some other defined purpose. *a* **1895** *Mod.* The deposit-receipt was returned for re-enfacement.

deposit (dɪˈpɒzɪt), *v.* Also 7 **deposite.** [a. obs. F. *depositer* 'to lay downe as a gage..to commit vnto the keeping or trust of' (Cotgr.); ad. med.L. *dēpositāre* to deposit, freq. of L. *dēpōnĕre*, used in med.L. to represent OF. *deposer*.]

1. *trans.* To lay, put, or set down; to place in a more or less permanent position of rest.

1749 FIELDING *Tom Jones* XII. x, He deposited his reckoning..mounted, and set forwards towards Coventry. **1833** L. RITCHIE *Wand. by Loire* 196 We deposit our person in the stern of a little boat. **1858** HAWTHORNE *Fr. & It. Jrnls.* (1872) I. 2 At Folkestone we were deposited at a railway station. **1891** *Law Reports* Weekly Notes 120/1 The defendants..damaged the plaintiff's land by depositing thereon dredgings from the river.

b. To lay (eggs).

1692 BENTLEY *Boyle Lect.* iv, He..observed that no other species were produced, but of such as he saw go in and deposit their eggs there. **1774** GOLDSM. *Nat. Hist.* (1776) VII. 322 She flies to some neighbouring pool, where she deposites her eggs. **1797-1804** BEWICK *Brit. Birds* (1847) I. 268 The author could never find the egg of the Cuckoo deposited in any nest but in that of a Lark. **1834** MCMURTRIE *Cuvier's Anim. Kingd.* 334 These Insects..deposit in the ground a great number of eggs.

c. Said of the laying down of substances held in solution, and of similar operations wrought by natural agencies: to form as a natural deposit.

1671 GREW *Anat. Plants* I. i. §48 (1682) 10 The greater and grosser part of the Sap may be..deposited into those [leaves]. **1794** SULLIVAN *View Nat.* I. 54 The vapours.. depositing..a slimy substance mixed with sulphur and salts. **1878** HUXLEY *Physiogr.* 53 The evaporation of any dew that may have been deposited. *Ibid.* 143 [The water] deposits more or less of the matter which it holds in suspension.

fig. **1818** JAS. MILL *Brit. India* I. II. vii. 302 Society, as it refines, deposits this [grossness] among its other impurities. **1877** L. TOLLEMACHE in *Fortn. Rev.* Dec. 855 A myth [may be] deposited from a misunderstood text.

d. *intr.* To be laid down or precipitated, to settle. *rare.*

[In its origin app. like 'the house is building' (for *a-building*) = 'being built'.]

1831 BREWSTER *Nat. Magic* vi. (1833) 155 Moisture might be depositing in a stratum of one density. **1845** DARWIN *Voy. Nat.* vi. (1873) 109 When the great calcareous formation was depositing beneath the surrounding sea. **1873** E. SPON *Workshop Receipts* I. 198/2 When no more silver deposits on the copper, the operation is completed.

†**2.** *fig.* (*trans.*) To lay aside, put away, give up; to lay down (one's life, etc.). *Obs.*

1646 SIR J. TEMPLE *Irish Rebell.* 14 Animosities..seemed now to be quite deposited and buried in a firm conglutination of their affections. **1682** *Address from Barnstaple* in *Lond. Gaz.* No. 1712/4 We are so far from any thought of..impairing..the Grandeur of this..Monarchy, that we will rather deposite our Lives in aggrandizing it. **1749** FIELDING *Tom Jones* I. x, Though..his countenance, as well as his air and voice, had much of roughness in it, yet he could at any time deposite this, and appear all gentleness and good-humour. **1804** *Miniature* No. 21 ¶3 When stripped of the buskin, he necessarily deposits his dignity.

3. To place in some repository, to commit to the charge of any one, for safe keeping; *spec.* to place (money) in a bank at interest.

1659 B. HARRIS *Parival's Iron Age* 277 [He] had.. deposited his wife in the hands of that most vertuous Princesse, the Cardinall Infanta. **1735** BERKELEY *Querist* §44 The silver supposed to be deposited in the bank. **1799** J. ROBERTSON *Agric. Perth* 365 Into this island, in times of danger, the inhabitants deposited their most valuable effects, to secure them from plunder. **1815** W. H. IRELAND *Scribbleomania* 190 The Egyptian stone relic deposited in the British Museum. **1872** GEO. ELIOT *Middlem.* xxiii, Fred had taken the wise step of depositing the eighty pounds with his mother.

b. To place in the hands of another as a pledge for the performance of some contract, in part payment of a purchase, etc.

1624 MASSINGER *Parl. Love* II. i, Let us to a notary, Draw the conditions, see the crowns deposited. **1687** in Scott *Peveril* xi. *note*, Euery person that puts in either horse, mair, or gelding, shall..depositt the sume of fiue shill. apiece. **1714** LADY M. W. MONTAGU *Lett. to W. Montagu* (1887) I. 89 The best way, to deposit a certain sum in some friend's hands, and buy some little Cornish borough. **1816** KEATINGE *Trav.* (1817) II. 70 In making agreement for hire of cattle the money was required to be deposited.

c. *fig.*

1634 'E. KNOTT' *Charity Maintained* ii. §24 The Apostles have..deposited in her [the Church], as in a rich storehouse, all things belonging to truth. **1671** MILTON *Samson* 429 To violate the sacred trust of silence Deposited within thee. **1739** BUTLER *Serm.* Matt. xxiv. 14 Christianity is..a trust, deposited with us in behalf of others..as well as for our own instruction. **1837** J. H. NEWMAN *Par. Serm.* (ed. 3) I. ix. 136 You will be depositing your good feelings into your heart, and they will spring up into fruit.

†**d.** To commit, entrust (*to* a person). *Obs. rare.*

1733 SWIFT *Advice Freemen Dublin*, Some employments are still deposited to persons born here.

4. *absol.* To make or pay a deposit. *rare.*

1799 *Piece of Fam. Biog.* III. 102 He bid, 'twas knock'd down to him, he deposited, and it was sent home.

Hence **deˈposited** *ppl. a.*, **deˈpositing** *vbl. sb.* and *ppl. a.*

1667 *Decay Chr. Piety* xix. ¶3 The greater difficulty will be, to perswade the depositing of those lusts. *a* **1693**

URQUHART *Rabelais* III. xxxiv. 285 That deposited Box. **1842** H. MILLER *O.R. Sandst.* xiv. 301 The transporting and depositing agents. **1862** M. HOPKINS *Hawaii* 420 Based upon a deposited substratum of rock. *c* **1865** G. GORE in *Circ. Sc.* I. 215/2 The depositing vessels [in electro-plating] are made of various materials.

deposit, obs. Sc. form of *deposed* (DEPOSE *v.*).

depositable (dɪˈpɒzɪtəb(ə)l), *a. rare.* [f. DEPOSIT *v.* -ABLE.] That may be deposited.

1807 W. TAYLOR in *Ann. Rev.* V. 196 Notes at hand at a long date, which, if not negotiable, are depositable.

depositary (dɪˈpɒzɪtərɪ), *sb.* [ad. L. *dēpositāri-us* one who receives or makes a deposit, F. *dépositaire* (14–15th c. in Hatzf.); f. L. *dēposit-* ppl. stem of *dēpōnere* (DEPONE, DEPOSE): see -ARY[1]. Often confounded with DEPOSITORY, when that is used of a person, or this of a thing.]

1. A person with whom anything is lodged in trust; a trustee; one to whom anything (material or immaterial) is committed or confided. In *Law*, a bailee of personal property, to be kept by him for the bailor without recompense.

1605 SHAKS. *Lear* II. iv. 254, I gaue you all.. Made you my Guardians, my Depositaries. **1712** ADDISON *Spect.* No. 495 ¶10 They [Jews]..are the Depositaries of these.. Prophecies. **1772** *Junius Lett.* Ded., I am the sole depositary of my own secret, and it shall perish with me. **1850** MRS. JAMESON *Leg. Monast. Ord.* Introd. (1863) 17 The Evangelists and Apostles are still enthroned as the depositaries of truth. **1853** C. BRONTE *Villette* xviii, I have never been the depositary of her plans and secrets. **1864** H. AINSWORTH *John Law* I. iv, Voisin was induced..to deliver up the codicil to the king's will, of which he was the depositary.

2. A place or receptacle in which something is deposited; = DEPOSITORY 1.

1797 GODWIN *Enquirer* I. v. 31 Books are the depositary of every thing that is most honourable to man. **1860** MAURY *Phys. Geog. Sea* §466 The ocean then is the great depositary of everything that water can dissolve and carry down from the surface of the continents. **1871** H. AINSWORTH *Tower Hill* II. x, Used..as a depositary for State records.

depositary, *a. rare.* [f. DEPOSIT *sb.* + -ARY[1].]

1. *Geol.* Belonging to or of the nature of a deposit. [Cf. *sedimentary.*]

1839 MURCHISON *Silur. Syst.* I. xx. 259 Before the beds entirely recover their natural depositary characters. *Ibid.* I. xxxv. 468 The other trap rocks of this district, instead of having a depositary character, have all been intruded.

2. Receiving deposits: said of a bank.

1886 *Rept. Sec. of Treasury* 88 (Cent. Dict.) A number of failures have taken place among the depositary banks.

†**deˈpositate**, *ppl. a. Sc. Obs.* [ad. med.L. *dēpositāt-us*, pa. pple. of *dēpositāre.*] Deposited.

1723 *Wodrow Corr.* (1843) III. 86 His corpse is depositate within. **1756** MRS. CALDERWOOD *Jrnl.* (1884) 298 The skilling being first depositate in a neutrall person's hand.

†**depositate**, *v. Obs.* [f. ppl. stem of med.L. *dēpositāre* to DEPOSIT; or f. obs. F. *depositer*: see -ATE[3] 7.] = DEPOSIT *v.*

1618 NAUNTON in *Fortescue Papers* 65 What teares and complaints he depositated in my bosome. **1650** HOWELL *Masaniello* I. 102 All the furniture and goods that were there depositated. **1782** A. MONRO *Anat.* 13 The Marrow is.. depositated in these cells.

depositation (dɪpɒzɪˈteɪʃən). *Chiefly Sc.* [n. of action f. med.L. *dēpositāre* to DEPOSIT: see -ATION.] The action of depositing; a deposit.

1622 MALYNES *Anc. Law-Merch.* 316 Forbidding any execution, depositation of moneys, or other courses of justice to be done thereupon. **1707** *Invent. R. Wardr.* (1815) 331 (Jam.) The delivery of the Regalia of Scotland by the Earl Marischal, and their depositation in..the castle of Edinburgh. **1754** ERSKINE *Princ. Sc. Law* (1809) 288 Depositation is a contract, by which one who has the custody of a thing committed to him (the depositary), is obliged to restore it to the depositor. **1806** FORSYTH *Beauties Scotl.* III. 205 A spontaneous depositation of ochre. **1833** *Act 3–4 Will. IV*, c. 46 §82 To deposit the same with the procurator fiscal..who shall..grant a certificate of such depositation. **1847** LD. COCKBURN *Jrnl.* II. 167 No such stream can pass through the soil of a good mind without enriching it by its depositations. **1861** [see DEPOSIT *sb.* 4].

depositee (dɪˌpɒzɪˈtiː). [f. DEPOSIT *v.* + -EE: correlative to *depositor.*] A person with whom something is deposited or placed in charge.

1676–7 HALE *Contempl.* I. (1689) 165 Thou art but an accountant, a steward, the Depositee of what thou hast received. **1891** *Law Times' Rep.* LXIII. 693/2 The deposit of this lease gave the depositee a right to its possession.

deposition (diːpəʊˈzɪʃən, dɛp-). Also 5 -ycion, 5–7 -icion, 6 -icyon. [a. OF. *deposition*, also *desp-* (12th c. in Hatzf.), ad. L. *dēpositiōn-em*, n. of action from *dēpōnĕre*: see DEPOSE. Used as the noun of action from *depone*, *depose*, and *deposit.*]

I. The action of putting down or deposing.

1. The taking down of the body of Christ from the cross; a representation of this in art.

[Cf. L. *dēpōnere* in Vulgate, Mk. xv. 46, Luke xxiii. 53.] **1526** *Pilgr. Perf.* (W. de W. 1531) 206 b, The maner of.. his deposicyon or takynge downe from the crosse. **1848** MRS. JAMESON *Sacr. & Leg. Art* (1850) 217 In the Descent or Deposition from the cross, and in the Entombment, Mary Magdalene is generally conspicuous. **1859** JEPHSON *Brittany* viii. 118 The figures..represent the Judgment of Pilate, the Bearing the Cross, the Deposition, the Entombment, the Resurrection.

†**2.** The action of laying down, laying aside, or putting away (e.g. a burden); usually *fig. Obs.*

1577 FULKE *Confut. Purg.* 116 The day of Christian mens death is the deposition of paine. **1615** HIERON *Wks.* I. 653 As it were, the quitting himselfe of a burthen, by the deposition whereof the soule is after a sort eased and lightened. **1616** CHAPMAN *Hymne to Apollo* 43 Why sit ye here..nor deposition make Of navall arms? **1748** HARTLEY *Observ. Man* II. iv. 402 The Soul is reduced to a state of Inactivity by the Deposition of the gross Body.

†**3.** *Surg.* 'Old term for the depressing of the lens in the operation of couching' (*Syd. Soc. Lex.*). *Obs.*

4. The action of deposing or putting down from a position of dignity or authority; degradation, dethronement.

1399 *Rolls of Parlt.* III. 452/1 If [they] evere be adheraunt to Richard that was Kyng and is deposed, in counsel, helpe, or comfort agayns that deposition. **1432–50** tr. *Higden* (Rolls) I. 283 After the deposicion of kynge Hildericus. **1548** HALL *Chron.* Introd. 8 To resigne..all the homages and fealties dewe to him as kyng..But er this deposicion was executed [etc.]. **1660** R. COKE *Power & Subj.* 150 Henry the Fourth his unjust usurpation, and deposition of..Richard the Second. **1726** AYLIFFE *Parergon* 206 The word Deposition properly signifies a solemn depriving of a Man of his Clerical Orders by the way of a Sentence. **1858** FROUDE *Hist. Eng.* III. xv. 287 Kings are said to find the step a short one from deposition to the scaffold.

5. The giving of testimony upon oath in a court of law, or the testimony so given; *spec.* a statement in answer to interrogatories, constituting evidence, taken down in writing to be read in court as a substitute for the production of the witness.

1494 FABYAN *Chron.* VII. 334 Mychaell Tony..was, by deposycion of the aldermen, founde gylty in the sayde cryme of periury. **1562** *Act 5 Eliz.* c. 9 §6 If any Person..commit ..Perjury, by his..Deposition in any of the Courts. **1633** T. STAFFORD *Pac. Hib.* i. (1821) 24 As well by deposition of witnesses as by all other kinde of proofes. **1726** AYLIFFE *Parergon* 149 A witness is obliged to swear pro formâ, otherwise his Deposition is not valid without an Oath. **1848** WHARTON *Law Lex.* s.v., It is a..rule at common law, that when the witness himself may be produced, his deposition cannot be read, for it is not the best evidence. **1863** H. COX *Instit.* II. x. 544 The statements of the witnesses are reduced to writing, and are then termed depositions.

b. *transf.* and *fig.* Testimony, statement (*esp.* of formal character). **c.** Allegation (*of* something).

1587 GOLDING *De Mornay* Pref. 9 Others whose depositions or rather oppositions against vs, I thinke men wil wonder at. **1648** W. MOUNTAGUE *Devout Ess.* IX. ii, The influence of Princes upon the disposition of their Courts, needs not the deposition of examples. **1699** BENTLEY *Phal.* Pref. 13, I will give a clear and full Answer to every part of their Depositions. **1885** J. MARTINEAU *Types Eth. Th.* II. 9 The depositions of consciousness on this matter.

II. The action of depositing.

6. The action of depositing, laying down, or placing in a more or less permanent or final position; *spec.* interment [med.L. *dēpositio* in liturgical language], or placing of a saint's body or relics in a new resting-place.

1659 *Vulgar Err. Censured* 78 True Christians..allow that which Christ hath redeemed a civill deposition, a decent Repose. Adam had a worthy Sepulchre. **1793** SMEATON *Edystone L.* §167 After being wrought, to be returned to its place of deposition. **1833** WHEWELL *Astron.* i. 27 The ripening of the seed, its proper deposition in order for the reproduction of a new plant. **1875** W. HOUGHTON *Sk. Brit. Insects* 130 The deposition of the eggs by these insect cuckoos. [**1894** J. T. FOWLER *Adamnan* Intr. xlv, The *depositio* or burial being in these cases commemorated rather than the *natalis* or birthday to the future life.]

7. The placing of something in a repository, or in charge of a person, for safe keeping; *concr.* a deposit.

1592 WEST *1st Pt. Symbol.*, §16 A, Deposition is a Contract reall in which a thing moueable is freelie giuen to be kept, that the selfe same thing be restored whensoeuer it shall please him that so leaueth it. **1651** C. CARTWRIGHT *Cert. Relig.* I. 140 The depositions committed to the Churches trust. **1798** MALTHUS *Popul.* (1817) III. 279 Every fresh deposition [in a savings bank].

8. The process of depositing or fact of being deposited by natural agency; precipitation.

1799 KIRWAN *Geol. Ess.* 11 The crystallization, precipitation, and deposition of these solids. **1830** HERSCHEL *Stud. Nat. Phil.* II. vi. (1851) 162 A deposition of dew presently begins. **1880** A. R. WALLACE *Isl. Life* 214 The average rate of Deposition of the Sedimentary Rocks.

b. The result of this process; a deposit, precipitate, sediment.

1797 M. BAILLIE *Morb. Anat.* (1807) 450, I have found [the pineal] gland without any deposition of earthy matter. **1831** BREWSTER *Optics* xiii. 111 A common pane of crown glass..that has on its surface a fine deposition of moisture. **1867** J. HOGG *Microsc.* I. ii. 133 The symmetrical and figurate depositions of siliceous crystals.

depositional (ˌdiːpəˈzɪʃənəl), *a.* [f. DEPOSITION 8 + -AL.] Of, relating to, or caused by deposition.

1900 *Geogr. Jrnl.* XVI. 461 Subordinate or local systems of cross-strains..are concentrated along old depositional and structural limits. **1902** [see AGGRADE *v.*]. **1967** *Oceanogr. & Marine Biol.* V. 120 Finer material is moved by longshore drift and currents to build up such depositional features as tombolos on the lee shore.

depositive (dɪˈpɒzɪtɪv), *a.* [f. DEPOSIT *v.* (or its L. etymon) + -IVE. Cf. OF. *depositif* in similar sense.] Having the quality of depositing, tending to deposit. In *Path.* see quot.

1857 DUNGLISON *Med. Lex.* 286 *Depositive*..an epithet used by Mr. Erasmus Wilson to express that condition of the membrane in which plastic lymph is exuded into the tissue of the derma.

depositor (dɪˈpɒzɪtə(r)). [In form = L. *dēpositor*, agent-n. from L. *dēpōnĕre* (DEPONE, DEPOSE); but taken as agent-n. from DEPOSIT *v.*: so mod.F. *dépositeur*, connected in sense with *dépôt* deposit.]

I. One who deposes.

†**1.** One who makes a deposition, a deponent.

1565 SIR T. SMITH *Commw. Eng.* (1623) 196 That all men may hear from the mouth of the depositors and witnesses what is said.

II. One who or that which deposits.

2. One who deposits or places something in charge of another; *spec.* one who deposits money in a bank.

1624 T. SCOTT *Votivæ Angliæ* 26 Bavaria is but Spaines Depositor, and the King of Spayne, Bavaria's Patrone and protector. **1781** SIR W. JONES *Law of Bailments* Wks. 1799 VI. 679 A depositor shall carefully enquire into the character of his intended depositary. **1832** *Examiner* 551/2 All persons were entitled to become depositors of goods. **1835** *Penny Cycl.* III. 385/2 Where a depositor has..a drawing account, the balance is struck every six months. **1880** MUIRHEAD *Gaius* Digest 486 The deposit still left the legal possession in the depositor, the depositary being merely his agent in possessing.

3. a. An apparatus for depositing some substance. **b.** A workman who coats articles with silver in electro-plating.

1834 *Brit. Husb.* I. 264 A 'depositor', which consists merely of an addition to the coulter of any common plough by wings fixed in the beam. *c* **1865** G. GORE in *Circ. Sc.* I. 216/1 The depositor should provide a large number of pieces of copper wire..for suspending the..articles to be coated.

III. †**4.** One in whose hand something is deposited; = DEPOSITARY *sb.* 1. *Obs.*

1604 E. GRIMSTONE *Hist. Siege Ostend* 145 That the sayd goods be put into the hands of the depositor of the armie.

depository (dɪˈpɒzɪtərɪ). [f. (or on the same type as) med.L. *dēpositōrium*, f. ppl. stem *dēposit-* or agent-n. *dēpositōr-em*: see -ORY.]

1. A place or receptacle in which things are deposited or placed for safe keeping; a storehouse, a repository.

1750 BEAWES *Lex Mercat.* (1752) 5 Alexandria..the depository of all merchandizes from the East and West. **1840** H. AINSWORTH *Tower of London* II. x, The Jewel Tower..the depository of the Regalia. **1858** LD. ST. LEONARDS *Handy Bk. Prop. Law* xx. 158 The Act..directs that convenient depositories shall be provided..for all such wills..as shall be deposited therein for safe custody.

fig. **1841** MYERS *Cath. Th.* III. §1. 2 [The Bible] is..a Providential Depository of certain Revelations of truth and duty which have been made at sundry times.

2. A person (a body of persons, or a thing personified) to whom something is committed for safe keeping; usually *fig.* (with reference to immaterial things); = DEPOSITARY *sb.* 1.

1656 HAMMOND *Answ. to Schism disarmed* VII. ii. ¶3 If we hold these doctrines deposited in the Church..we must hold..that the depository is so trusty, as it cannot deceive us. **1779** JOHNSON *Lett. Mrs. Thrale* 8 Nov., I think well of her judgment in chusing you to be the depository of her troubles. **1862** MERIVALE *Rom. Emp.* (1865) VI. liv. 456 The pretensions advanced..for the Roman Church..to be the sole depository of all moral principles and practice. **1878** S. COX *Salv. Mundi* viii. (ed. 3) 174 Even in those early days when one man, one family, one nation were successively chosen to be the depositories of Divine Truth.

‖**depositum** (dɪˈpɒzɪtəm). *Obs.* Pl. -a, -ums. [L. *dēpositum*; sb. use of neuter pa. pple. of *dēpōnĕre* to lay down: see DEPONE, DEPOSIT.]

1. Something placed in a person's charge or laid up in a place for safe keeping; = DEPOSIT *sb.* 1.

a. *lit.*

1592 WEST *1st Pt. Symbol.* §16 B, The thing left is called Receptum, Commendatum or depositum. **1617** COLLINS *Def. Bp. Ely* 81 Two depositums of like nature. **1669** WOODHEAD *St. Teresa* II. 272 She..had foretold of a certain Depositum, that was to be reserved in that place; and the event following declared her meaning concerning her Body. **1673** *Lady's Call.* II. §1 ¶2. 57 Testaments and other depositums of the greatest trust were usually committed to their custody. **1745** A. BUTLER *Lives of Saints* (1836) I. 527 She was to give to God an account of the least farthing of what was intrusted as a depositum in her hands.

b. *fig.* of immaterial things: *esp.* of the faith or doctrine committed to the keeping of the Church.

1582 N. T. (Rhem.) *1 Tim.* vi. 20 O Timothee, keepe the *depositum* [Vulg. *custodi depositum*]. **1583** FULKE *Defence* xxi. 569 Affected novelties of terms, such as neither English nor Christian ears ever heard in the English tongue: Scandal, prepuce, neophyte, depositum, gratis, parasceve, paraclete. **1642** ROGERS *Naaman* To Rdr., Unto whose hands, the great depositum of Truth is put. **1656** HAMMOND *Answ. to Schism disarmed* VIII. ii. §1 That depositum..that the Apostles thus deposited in all Churches, the several articles of the Apostolick faith or Creed. *a* **1711** KEN *Dedicat.* Poet. Wks. 1721 I. 7 And rather dye glad Martyrs at the Stake, Than the

Depositum he left, forsake. **1732** STACKHOUSE *Hist. Bible* (1767) III. v. iii. 348 His life was a sacred depositum of God's.

2. Something given as a pledge; = DEPOSIT *sb.* I c.

1623 COCKERAM, *Depositum*, a pledge. **1711** LUTTRELL *Brief Rel.* (1857) VI. 704 To pay down..half of that as a depositum for the remaining parts.

3. A place where things are deposited or stored; a depot, depository, 'storehouse' (*lit.* and *fig.*).

1644 EVELYN *Diary* 19 Nov., Towards the lower end of the church..is the depositum and statue of the Countess Matilda. **1646** J. HALL *Horæ Vac.* 78 It is a fit depositum of knowledge. **1756** NUGENT *Gr. Tour* II. 227 By means of these famous fairs, Leipsic is the depositum of a great part of the merchandize of Europe and the Indies. **1796** MORSE *Amer. Geog.* I. iv, The..most complete depositum of facts relating to the history of America, to be found in the United States.

depositure (dɪˈpɒzɪtjʊə(r)). *rare.* [In form corresp. to a L. type **dēpositūra*, f. ppl. stem of *dēpōnĕre* (DEPONE, DEPOSE); in sense associated with *deposit* vb.: see -URE.] The action of depositing or placing.

1635 JACKSON *Creed* VIII. xxxiii. Wks. VIII. 179 The interring or depositure of his body in the..sepulchre. **1658** SIR T. BROWNE *Hydriot.* Introd., By precious embalments, Depositure in dry Earths. **1884** ROGERS *Soc. Life Scotl.* II. x. 16 The depositure of the national records in the Register House.

† **deˈpost, depoost.** *Obs.* [a. Of. *depost* (14th c. in Littré and Hatzf.), mod.F. *dépôt*, ad. L. DEPOSITUM: see above.] An earlier equivalent of DEPOSIT *sb.* sense I.

1382 WYCLIF *1 Tim.* vi. 20 Thou Tymothe kepe the depoost, or thing bitakun to thee. —— *2 Tim.* i. 12, I woot to whom I haue bileuyd, and I am certeyn for he is myȝti for to kepe my depoost, or thing putt in keping. **1735** DYCHE & PARDON, *Depost* or *Depositum* [ed. 3, *Deposit*].

† **deˈposure.** *Obs. rare.* [f. DEPOSE *v.* + -URE: cf. *composure*, *exposure*.] The action of deposing from office; = DEPOSITION 4.

c **1630** DRUMM. OF HAWTH. *Mem. State* Wks. (1711) 130 After the deposure of king Richard II. **1648** FAIRFAX, etc. *Remonstrance* 28 An utter rejection, expulsion, and deposure ..of his whole race.

depot (ˈdɛpəʊ, dɪˈpəʊ, ˈdiːpəʊ). Also **depôt, dépôt.** [a. F. *dépôt* (depo), in OF. *depost* (14th c. in Littré and Hatzf.), (= It., Sp. *deposito*), ad. L. *dēpositum*: see DEPOSITUM, DEPOSIT, DEPOST, all forms of the same word.

As in the case of other words from modern French, the pronunciation varies widely. The French (depo), with short *e* and *o* and undefined stress, is foreign to English habits of utterance. The earlier English rendering, as shown by the dictionaries down to 1860-70, was, according to the French historical stress and quantity, or the English conception of it (cf. *bureau, chateau, Tussaud*), (diːˈpəʊ), or, with a conscious effort to reproduce the first vowel in French, (deɪˈpəʊ); these pronunciations were (1895) still heard, but the stress is now more usually on the first syllable, and the quantity of the *o* doubtful, giving (ˈdɛpəʊ, ˈdiːpəʊ), in England, (ˈdiːpəʊ, ˈdeɪpəʊ), in U.S. (where the word is much more in popular use, and (ˈdiːpɒt, diːˈpɒt), are mentioned by Longfellow, Lowell, etc., as popular vulgarisms). The form (ˈdɛpəʊ) comes as near the French (depo) as English analogies admit. The earlier Eng. spelling omitted the accent-marks, and this is now usual; the spelling *depôt* belongs especially to the pronunciation (diːˈpəʊ); the actual F. spelling *dépôt* goes together with the attempt to pronounce as in French.]

† **1.** The act of depositing; deposit, deposition. *Obs. rare.*

1794 SULLIVAN *View Nat.* I. 72 Some [mountains] have.. been formed by successive depôts in the sea.

† **2.** A deposit or collection (of matter, supplies, etc.); = DEPOSIT *sb.* 3, I. *Obs.*

1835 SIR J. ROSS *Narr. 2nd Voy.* xxxvii. 513 To fetch a third depot of fish. **1850** W. B. CLARKE *Wreck Favorite* 133 The nelleys had discovered our depôt of blubber and had eaten a portion of it.

3. *Mil.* **a.** A place where military stores are deposited. **b.** The head-quarters of a regiment, where supplies are received and whence they are distributed. **c.** A station where recruits are assembled and drilled, and where soldiers who cannot join their regiments remain. **d.** *attrib.* Applied to a portion of a regiment which remains at home when the rest are on foreign service.

1798 BERESFORD in *Ld. Auckland's Corr.* III. 412 Large quantities of arms are in their possession. Dublin is the great depôt. **1812** W. C. in *Examiner* 25 May 334/2 Barracks and Military Depots are building. **1844** *Regul. & Ord. Army* 80 By the continual transit of Officers between the Service and Depôt Companies. **1853** STOCQUELER *Milit. Encycl.* s.v., Regiments embarking for India usually leave one company at home, for the purpose of recruiting, which is called the depôt company. **1859** *Musketry Instr.* 85 When men leave a depôt battalion to join the service companies. **1861** SWINHOE *N. China Camp.* 7 The island [of Chusan]..from its central position, would form a good depôt for troops.

e. A place of confinement for prisoners of war.

The name used both in France and England during the War with Napoleon.

1806 J. FORBES *Lett. fr. France* I. 231 Prisoners of war ..[at] Fontainbleau and Valenciennes, the two principal depots appointed for that purpose. **1814** D. H. O'BRIEN *Captiv. & Escape* 87 We were safely lodged in Sarre Louis jail. This is a dépôt for seamen, and one of punishment for officers who may transgress. **1839** *36 Years Sea-faring Life* 29 Fearing death almost as little as a life of misery in a French depot.

4. a. A place where goods are deposited or stored; e.g. a ***coal depot, grain depot, furniture depot***; a store-house, depository, emporium.

1795 tr. *Moritz's Travels* 241 There was written on the sign: 'The Navigation Inn'; because it is the *depôt*, or storehouse, of the colliers of the Trent. **1802** *Edin. Rev.* I. 142 Lake Winipic..seems calculated..to become the grand depot of this traffic. **1804** H. T. COLEBROOKE *Husb. Bengal* (1806) 184 It is not practicable to render Great Britain the general dépôt of saltpetre. **1863** SIR G. G. SCOTT in *Archæol. Cant.* V. 7 *note*, The church was used as the coal depôt for the castle. **1872** YEATS *Growth Comm.* 154 Grain brought down to the maritime depots..in the Crimea.

b. *Physiol.* The site of an accumulation or deposit of a substance (esp. fat) in an animal body. So *attrib.*, applied to any substance stored for eventual absorption by the organism, or to an action or process concerned with the deposition of such a substance.

1835-6 TODD *Cycl. Anat.* I. 515/2 Depots of matter take place in the disorganized tissue. **1906** L. HILL *Rec. Adv. Physiol. & Bio-Chem.* xi. 288 The proteid metabolism.. only begins to increase in the final stage of starvation when the reserve of depôt fat is almost exhausted. **1912** E. H. STARLING *Princ. Human Physiol.* xi. 884 From the physiological standpoint the most important intracellular depôt of fat is in the liver. **1930** *Jrnl. Biol. Chem.* LXXXVII. 148 Fat obtained from the various depots. *Ibid.*, The total depot fat. **1936** *Nature* 21 Mar. 479/1 As we pass from depot fats of aquatic to those of land animals we find marked simplification in the mixed fatty acids. **1959** *Chambers's Encycl.* V. 601/1 The composition of the fat depots is practically identical with the fat in the food. **1961** *Lancet* 12 Aug. 345/1 A steroid preparation which is highly concentrated, and has a depot effect. *Ibid.* 9 Sept. 577/2 Daily injections..were replaced by a single intramuscular depot injection. **1970** PASSMORE & ROBSON *Compan. Med. Stud.* II. vi. 16/2 There are two main types of insulin in clinical use, those with a rapid onset and short duration of action, and those whose action is slow in onset and lasts longer, the depot insulins.

5. *U.S.* A railway station.

(In Great Britain formerly, and still sometimes, a goods station at a terminus: cf. sense 4 a.)

[**1830** BOOTH *L'pool & M'chester Railway* 46 This Railway will cost above £800,000 including the..stations and depots at each end. **1837** F. WHISHAW *Anal. Railways* 286 When there are warehouses attached to a station the whole is called a depôt.] **1842** LONGF. in *Life* (1891) I. 415 To borrow the expression of a fellow-traveller, we were 'ticketed through to the depot' (pronouncing the last word so as to rhyme with *teapot*). **1861** LOWELL *Biglow P.* Ser. II. i. Poems 1890 II. 232 With all ou' doors for deepot [*rime* teapot]. **1872** 'MARK TWAIN' *Innoc. Abr.* xii. 78 You cannot pass into the waiting-room of the depôt till you have secured your ticket. [**1892** *Camden Town Directory*, 71 London and North-western Goods Depôt, Chalk Farm Road.]

6. *Fortif.* (See quot.)

1823 in CRABB *Techn. Dict.* **1853** STOCQUELER *Milit. Encycl.* s.v., In fortification, the term is likewise used to denote a particular place at the trail of the trenches, out of the reach of the cannon of a besieged place. It is here that besiegers generally assemble, when ordered to attack the outworks or support the troops in the trenches.

7. *attrib.* (See *spec.* use in 3 d.)

1881 *Chicago Times* 16 Apr., The company is constructing a depot building..at Leaf River. **1884** C. R. MARKHAM in *Pall Mall G.* 20 Aug. 1/2 The party should never have been left without a depot ship wintering within accessible distance.

Also **depot** *v. trans.*, to place in a depot.

1921 H. G. PONTING *Gt. White South* 274 When near the summit, Captain Scott told off four more of the party to depôt their surplus and return.

depotentiate (ˌdiːpəʊˈtɛnʃɪeɪt), *v.* [f. DE- II. I + L. *potentia* power: cf. *potentiate*.] *trans.* To deprive of power or potency. Hence **depoˈtentiated** *ppl. a.*, **depotentiˈation.**

1841 *Fraser's Mag.* XXIII. 144 Productive powers, which unite together, combine not as dead materials by addition, but multiply into and potentiate one another, as in separating they do not merely subtract from each other, but utterly depotentiate. **1882-3** SCHAFF *Encycl. Relig. Knowl.* I. 463 A temporary self-exinanition or depotentiation of the pre-existent Logos. **1886** A. B. BRUCE *Mirac. Elem. in Gospels* viii. 275 Christ's life on earth in reference to the divine aspect was a depotentiated life.

depoulsour: see DEPULSOR.

† **deˈpoverish,** *v. Obs.* [f. DE- I. I, 3 + radical of *impoverish*: cf. OF. *apovrir, apovriss-*, F. *appauvrir*, f. *povre, pauvre* poor; also DEPAUPER, DEPAUPERATE.] *trans.* To make poor, impoverish.

1568 GRAFTON *Chron.* II. 350 So is your power depoverished, and Lordes and great men brought to infelicitie.

depper, -est, obs. comp. and sup. of DEEP.

depravable (dɪˈpreɪvəb(ə)l), *a.* [f. DEPRAVE *v.* + -ABLE.] Liable to be depraved.

1678 CUDWORTH *Intell. Syst.* I. iv. 631 Humane Nature is so mutable and depravable.

† **ˈdepravate,** *ppl. a. Obs.* [ad. L. *dēprāvātus*, pa. pple. of *dēprāvāre* to DEPRAVE.] Depraved, corrupted, demoralized.

152. BARCLAY *Sallust's Jugurth* 15 b, A great part of the Senatours were..so depravat that they contemned and set at nought þe words of Adherball. **1538** HEN. VIII in *Select. Harl. Misc.* (1793) 137 Thynges..which, nowe beinge depravate, are lyke..to be the vtter ruine of Christen relygyon. *a* **1555** BRADFORD *Wks.* 166 Seeing my corruption and depravate nature. **1665** G. HARVEY *Advice agst. Plague* 15 Contributing to the generation of depravate bloud.

Hence † **ˈdepravately** *adv.*

1666 G. HARVEY *Morb. Angl.* ii. 15 A consumption of the parts of the body, weakly, or depravately, or not at all attracting nutriment.

† **depravate** (ˈdɛprəveɪt), *v. Obs.* or *arch.* [f. L. *dēprāvāt-*, ppl. stem of *dēprāvāre* to DEPRAVE.] *trans.* = DEPRAVE.

1548 HOOPER *Declar. 10 Commandm.* vii. Wks. (Parker Soc.) 345 To depravate the use of the sacraments otherwise than they be taught in the scripture. **1581** MARBECK *Bk. of Notes* 625 The Pharesies & Saduces, which with their gloses depravated the Scriptures. **1609** J. DAVIES *Holy Roode* xxiii, The rest, in depth of scorne and hate, His Diuine Truth with taunts doe depravate. **1847** BUSHNELL *Chr. Nurt.* i. (1861) 27 The belief that a child's nature is somehow depravated by descent from parents.

depravation (diːprəˈveɪʃən, dɛp-). [ad. L. *dēprāvātiōn-em*, n. of action from *dēprāvāre* to DEPRAVE. Cf. F. *dépravation* (16th c. in Littré).]

1. The action or fact of making or becoming depraved, bad, or corrupt; deterioration, degeneration, *esp.* moral deterioration; an instance of this.

1561 T. NORTON *Calvin's Inst.* I. xiv. §16 This malice which we assigne in his [the Devil's] nature, is not by creation but by depravation. *a* **1667** COWLEY *Ess.*, *Dangers in Much Company*, The total Loss of Reason is less deplorable than the total Depravation of it. **1775** JOHNSON *Tax. no Tyr.* 48 We are as secure from intentional depravations of Government as human wisdom can make us. **1795** BURKE *Tracts on Popery Laws* Wks. 1842 II. 442 If this be improvement, truly I know not what can be called a depravation of society. **1850** H. ROGERS *Ess.* II. iv. 204 Causes of depravation..to which the language had in a measure adapted itself. **1862** ELLICOTT *Destiny of Creature* ii. (1865) 26 Depravations of instincts.

b. Deterioration or degeneration of an organ, secretion, tissue, etc.

1661 LOVELL *Hist. Anim. & Min.* 334 Trembling, which is a depravation of voluntary motion. *c* **1720** W. GIBSON *Farrier's Guide* II. xxviii. (1738) 101 The beginning of the Distemper did proceed from the Corruption or Depravation of the Blood. **1749** BP. LAVINGTON *Enthus. Methodists* (1820) 225 Some depravation of the organs of the ear. **1851-60** MAYNE *Expos. Lex.*, *Depravation*, term for a deterioration, or change for the worse; applied to the secretions, or the functions of the body.

2. The condition or quality of being depraved; corruption. Formerly, in *Theol.*, = DEPRAVITY c.

1577 tr. *Bullinger's Decades* (1592) 495 Originall sinne is the vice or depravation of the whole man. **1587** GOLDING *De Mornay* xvii. (1617) 305 Notwithstanding all this depravation, yet the soule liueth and abideth pure and cleane in God. **1633** BP. HALL *Hard Texts, Rom.* vi. 6 That by..his death the whole bulke of our maliciousness and depravation might be so far destroyed. **1725** R. TAYLOR *Disc. on the Fall* v. 122 A sense of the depravation of our nature, or of original sin which is in us. **1728** MORGAN *Algiers* I. iv. 73 Their Licentiousness and Depravation of Morals visibly increased. **1862** MERIVALE *Rom. Emp.* (1865) V. xlv. 350 Contrasting the most exquisite charms of nature with the grossest depravation of humanity.

b. (with *pl.*) An instance of this.

1621 BURTON *Anat. Mel.* I. i. III. i, Calling it [Melancholy] a depravation of the principall function. **1669** GALE *Crt. Gentiles* I. I. xii. 79 Those Leters, which the Jews now use.. being but depravations of the Syriac. **1675** TRAHERNE *Chr. Ethicks* xxvii. 429 All the cross and disorderly things..are meer corruptions and depravations of nature, which free agents have let in upon themselves. **1846** MAURICE *Relig. World* I. iii. (1861) 71 I would by no means support a paradox..that Buddhism was the original doctrine of which Brahminism was a depravation.

† **c.** A depraving influence or cause. *Obs.*

1711 ADDISON *Spect.* No. 99 ¶11 When the Dictates of Honour are contrary to those of Religion and Equity, they are the greatest Depravations of human nature.

† **3.** Perversion or corruption (of a text, writing, etc.). *Obs.*

1566 T. STAPLETON *Ret. Untr. Jewel* Epist. ij, You note that for Vntruthe, yea and for a foule depravation of holi scripture which is the very saying..of S. Hilary. **1624** GATAKER *Transubst.* 90 The next Division hee maketh entrance into with a grosse and shamelesse Depravation [substitution of '*any* thing' for '*no* thing']. **1699** BENTLEY *Phal.* xiii. 396 This is the common Reading..but if we examine it, it will be found to be a manifest Depravation. **1768** JOHNSON *Pref. to Shaks.* Wks. IX. 277 This great poet ..made no collection of his works, nor desired to rescue those that had been already published from the depravations that obscured them. **1849** W. FITZGERALD tr. *Whitaker's Disput.* 157 To persuade us of the depravation of the original scriptures.

† **4.** Vilification, defamation, detraction, backbiting, calumny. *Obs.* [So It. *depravazione*.]

(Perhaps the earliest sense in Eng.: cf. also DEPRAVE.)

1526 *Pilgr. Perf.* (W. de W. 1531) 238 All yᵉ crymes of yᵉ tonge, as sclaunders, detraccyons, depravacyons or dispraysynges. **1605** BACON *Adv. Learn.* I. ii. §8. 10 A meere depravation and calumny without all shadowe of truth. **1606** SHAKS. *Tr. & Cr.* v. ii. 132 Stubborne Criticks, apt without a theame For depravation.

† **deˈpravative,** *a. Obs.* [f. L. *dēprāvāt-* ppl. stem + -IVE.] Tending to deprave.

1682 H. MORE *Annot. Glanvill's Lux O.* 37 A debilitative, diminutive, or privative, not depravative deterioration.

†**'depravator.** *Obs. rare*⁻¹. [Agent-n. in L. form from L. *dēprāvāre* to DEPRAVE. Cf. F. *depravateur* (1551 in Hatzf.).] A depraver.
1629 T. ADAMS *Serm. Heb.* vi. 8 Wks. 1058 A great number of these Field-bryers..Oppressors, Inclosers, Depopulators, Deportators, Depravators.

†**de'prave,** *sb. Obs. rare.* [f. DEPRAVE *v.*] Detraction, slander.
1610 W. FOLKINGHAM *Art of Survey*, Author to Work 23 Whose iustly-honourd Names Shield from Depraue, Couch rabid Blatants, silence Surquedry. **1615** CHAPMAN *Odyss.* XXII. 585 That both on my head pour'd depraves unjust, And on my mother's, scandalling the court.

†**de'prave,** *a. Obs. rare.* [An extension of PRAVE = L. *prāvus*, after *deprave* vb. and its derivatives: cf. DEPRAVITY.] Depraved.
a **1711** KEN *Hymnotheo* Poet. Wks. 1721 III. 96 Ah me, even from the Womb I came deprave.

deprave (dɪ'preɪv), *v.* [ad. L. *dēprāvāre* to distort, pervert, corrupt (f. DE- I. 3 + *prāvus* crooked, wrong, perverse: perh. immediately from F. *dépraver* (14th c. in Hatzf.). Sense 4 was perh. the earliest in Eng.: cf. also the derivatives.]

1. To make bad; to pervert in character or quality; to deteriorate, impair, spoil, vitiate. Now *rare*, exc. as in 2.
a **1533** LD. BERNERS *Gold. Bk. M. Aurel.* xlvi, Olde folkes wyll depraue [*printed* depryue, L. *depravabunt*] thy mynde with their couetousnes. **1552** HULOET, Depraue, peruert, or make yll, *depravo*. **1558** WARDE tr. *Alexis' Secr.* (1568) 42 b, Sorowe, sadnesse, or melancholie corrupte the bloude..and deprave and hurt nature. *c* **1630** DONNE *Serm.* viii. 83 A good worke not depraved with an ill Ende. **1685** BOYLE *Salub. Air* 14 The air is depraved..by being impregnated with Mineral Expirations. *a* **1784** JOHNSON in *Croker's Boswell* (1831) V. 419, I believe that the loss of teeth may deprave the voice of a singer. **1802** *Trans. Soc. Encourag. Arts* XX. 222 It [sea-salt] rather depraves than improves the oils.

b. To corrupt (a text, word, etc.). *arch.*
1382 WYCLIF *Job* Prol., The thingis..bi the vice of writeris depraued. **1599** H. BUTTES *Dyets drie Dinner* G ij, Whence in tract of time the name is depraved: and B put for C. **1663** CHARLETON *Chorea Gigant.* 25 He was forced to deprave the Text. **1710** PRIDEAUX *Orig. Tithes* iv. 179 But the second Paragraph being so depraved by after Transcribers, as not to be made Sense of. **1844** LINGARD *Anglo-Sax. Ch.* (1858) II. xi. 187 Restoring the true reading where it had been depraved. **1859** F. HALL *Vāsavadattā* Pref. 9 *note*, If his text has not been depraved at the hands of the scribes.

†**c.** To debase (coinage), falsify (measures, etc.). *Obs.*
1581 W. STAFFORD *Exam. Compl.* ii. (1876) 68 And if our treasure be farre spent and exhaust..I could wish that any other order were taken for the recouery of it, then the deprauing of our coines. *a* **1632** T. TAYLOR *God's Judgem.* I. I. xxxi. (1642) 140 Among earthly princes, it is accounted a crime..to counterfeit or deprave their seales. **1650** FULLER *Pisgah* 397 The Levites were esteemed the fittest keepers of measures..which willingly would not falsifie, or deprave the same. **1733** NEAL *Hist. Purit.* II. 424 Some Ministers in our state..endeavoured to make our money not worth taking, by depraving it.

†**d.** To desecrate. *Obs. rare*⁻¹.
a **1529** SKELTON *Ware the Hauke* [42 He wrought amys To hawke in my church of Dis.] 301 Dys church ye thus depravyd.

2. *spec.* To make morally bad; to pervert, debase, or corrupt morally. (The current sense.)
1482 *Monk of Evesham* (Arb.) 59, I neuyr..hadde any suspycyon hethirto that the kynde of wemen hadde be deprauyd and defoyled by suche a foule synne. **1594** SPENSER *Amoretti* xxxi, A hart..Whose pryde depraues each other better part. **1667** MILTON *P.L.* v. 471 One Almightie is, from whom All things proceed, and up to him return, If not deprav'd from good. **1736** BUTLER *Anal.* I. v. Wks. 1874 I. 101 Vicious indulgence..depraves the inward constitution and character. **1890** *Spectator* 1 Mar., The belief that a witch was a person who leagued herself with the Devil to defy God and deprave man.

†**3.** To pervert the meaning or intention of, to pervert by misconstruing. *Obs.*
1382 WYCLIF *2 Pet.* iii. 16 Summe harde thinges in vnderstondinge, the whiche unwijse..men deprauen..to her owne perdicioun. **1526** *Pilgr. Perf.* (W. de W. 1531) 93 By..depravynge and mysiudgyng his entent in thynges that be good. **1581** J. BELL *Haddon's Answ. Osor.* 344 b, What can be spoken so sincerely, but by sinister construing may be depraved? **1643** MILTON *Divorce* II. xiii. Wks. 1738 I. 198 Our Saviour here confutes not Moses' Law, but the false Glosses that deprav'd the Law. **1660** H. MORE *Myst. Godliness* VI. xvii. 214, I must confess they have not depraved the meaning of the seventh verse. **1703** [see DEPRAVING *vbl. sb.*].

†**4.** To represent as bad; to vilify, defame, decry, disparage. *Obs.* [So It. '*depravare*..to backbite' (Florio).]
1362 LANGL. *P. Pl.* A. III. 172, I com not to chyde, Ne to depraue þi persone with a proud herte. **1388** WYCLIF *Prov.* i. 29 Thei depraueden al myn amendyng [**1382** bacbiteden]. **1432-50** tr. *Higden* (Rolls) II. 159 The peple of Englonde deprauenge theire owne thynges commende other straunge. **1581** J. BELL *Haddon's Answ. Osor.* 1 b, How maliciously and wickedly England hath bene accused and depraved by her cursed enemy Osorius. **1642** ROGERS *Naaman* 97 Perhaps I shall heare the godly depraved, jeered at. **1667** MILTON *P.L.* VI. 174 Unjustly thou deprav'st it with the name Of Servitude.

†**b.** *absol.*
1599 SHAKS. *Much Ado* v. i. 95 Fashion-monging boyes, That lye, and cog, and flout, depraue, and slander. **1816** BYRON *Monody on Sheridan* 73 Behold the host! delighting to deprave, Who track the steps of Glory to the grave.. Distort the truth, accumulate the lie, And pile the pyramid of Calumny!

†**5.** *intr.* To grow or become bad or depraved; to suffer corruption. *Obs. rare.*
1655 FULLER *Ch. Hist.* II. iii. §28 A Self-sufficiency, that soon improved into Plenty, that quickly depraved into Riot, and that at last occasioned their Ruin.

¶ Formerly often confused with, or erroneously used for, DEPRIVE.
1572 J. JONES *Bathes of Bath* Ep. Ded. 2 Sicknesse.. depriveth, deminisheth or depraveth the partes accidentally of their operations. *c* **1614** DRAYTON *Legend of Duke Robert* (1748) 194 O that a tyrant then should me deprave Of that which else all living creatures have! **1621** BURTON *Anat. Mel.* I. ii. I. iv, Lunatick persons, that are depraved [*edd.* **1660** *and later* deprived] of their wits by the Moones motion. **1632** LITHGOW *Trav.* IX. 407 John the 17. who after he was depraved his Papacy, had his eyes pulled out. **1732** ARBUTHNOT *Rules of Diet* 263 Oils entirely deprav'd of their Salts are not acrid.

depraved (dɪ'preɪvd), *ppl. a.* [f. prec. + -ED, repr. L. *dēprāvātus*, F. *dépravé*.]

1. Rendered bad or worse; perverted, vitiated, debased, corrupt. Now chiefly of taste, appetite, and the like.
1610 GUILLIM *Heraldry* III. iv. (1660) 113 We take no notice of any other forme..but onely of this depraved shape. **1656** RIDGLEY *Pract. Physick* 73 Convulsion is a depraved motion of the Muscles. *a* **1661** FULLER *Worthies* (1840) II. 363 She corrected a depraved place in Cyprian. **1712** STEELE *Spect.* No. 268 ¶4 If they would but correct their depraved Taste. **1736** BAILEY *Househ. Dict.* 34 A depraved Appetite, is when a person desires to eat and drink things that are unfit for food; as..earth, mortar, chalk, and such like things. **1807** OPIE *Lect. Art* iv. (1848) 321 A moderately lively red ..will appear brilliant, if surrounded by others of the same class but of a more depraved quality. **1816** KEATINGE *Trav.* (1817) I. 37 Fruit..every species here is dwindled in growth and depraved in flavour. **1889** J. M. DUNCAN *Lect. Dis. Women* xvi. (ed. 4) 119 The women are always in what may be vaguely called, depraved health.

2. *spec.* Rendered morally bad; corrupt, wicked.
1594 HOOKER *Eccl. Pol.* I. x. §1 Presuming man to be, in regard of his depraued minde, little better than a wild beast. **1667** MILTON *P.L.* XI. 806 So all shall turn degenerate, all deprav'd. **1736** BUTLER *Anal.* I. v. Wks. 1874 I. 102 Depraved creatures want to be renewed. **1798** FERRIAR *Illustr. Sterne* i. 11 The morals of the Court were most depraved. **1836-9** DICKENS *Sk. Boz* (C.D. ed.) 221 A place of resort for the worst and most depraved characters.

depravedly (dɪ'preɪvɪdlɪ, -'eɪvdlɪ), *adv.* [f. prec. + -LY².] In a depraved manner; perversely, corruptly.
1643 SIR T. BROWNE *Rel. Med.* To Rdr., The writings.. depravedly, anticipatively counterfeitly imprinted. **1652** J. WRIGHT tr. *Camus' Nature's Paradox* 298 So depravedly reprobate. *a* **1693** URQUHART *Rabelais* III. xxiii. 186 What moved..him to be so..depravedly bent against the good Fathers?

de'pravedness. [f. as prec. + -NESS.] Depraved or corrupt quality or condition; depravity.
1612-15 BP. HALL *Contempl., O.T.* XVIII. iv, No place could be too private for an honest prophet, in so extreame depravednesse. **1642** ROGERS *Naaman* To Rdr. §2 The depravednesse and disorder of the appetite. **1715** *Hist. Remark. Tryals* A, The Depravedness of Human Nature. **1885** L. OLIPHANT *Sympneumata* xv. 224 His unsoundness, and insaneness, and depravedness of outer structure.

depravement (dɪ'preɪvmənt). *arch.* [f. DEPRAVE *v.* + -MENT.] Depravation, perversion, corruption; †misinterpretation.
1645 MILTON *Tetrach.* Pr. Wks. (1847) 212/2 That such an irreligious depravement..may be..solidly refuted, and in the room a better explanation given. **1646** SIR T. BROWNE *Pseud. Ep.* I. x. 42 That apparitions..are either deceptions of sight, or melancholy depravements of phancy. **1677** GILPIN *Demonol.* (1867) 120 Our thoughts do not naturally delight in spiritual things, because of their depravement. **1779** SWINBURNE *Trav. Spain* xli. (R.), A period..when all arts and sciences were fallen to the lowest ebb of depravement. **1839** J. R. DARLEY *Introd. Beaum. & Fl. Wks.* I. 35 Is the *graziose* of Correggio an improvement on the *grandiose* of Raffael, or a voluptuous depravement of it?

depraver (dɪ'preɪvə(r)). Also 7 -our. [f. DEPRAVE *v.* + -ER¹.] One who depraves.

1. One who corrupts, perverts, or debases; a corrupter, perverter.
1557 [see DEPRAVERESS]. **1563-87** FOXE *A. & M.* (1596) 39/2 The deprauers of the ueritie. **1633** T. ADAMS *Exp. 2 Peter* ii. 1 The devil, that..depraver of all goodness. **1709** J. JOHNSON *Clergym. Vade M* II. 247 They that tear, or cut the books of the Old or New Testament..or sell them to Depravers of books..are excommunicated for a year. **1878** DOWDEN *Stud. Lit.* 34 The great depravers of religion.

†**2.** One who vilifies or defames; a defamer, traducer. *Obs.*
1584 WHITGIFT *Let. to Burghley*, A defender, not a depraver, of the present state and government. *a* **1634** CHAPMAN *Sonn.* xxi, So shall pale Envy famish with her food, And thou spread further by thy vain depravours [*rime* favours]. **1642** CHAS. I *Sp.* 27 Sept. in Rushw. *Hist. Coll.* III. II. 22 Brownists, Anabaptists, and publick Depravers of the Book of Common Prayer. **1709** STRYPE *Ann. Ref.* I. ii. 71 Penalties appointed for depravers of the said book, and such as should speak in derogation of anything contained in it.

†**de'praveress.** *Obs. nonce-wd.* In 6 -res. [f. prec. + -ESS.] A female depraver.
1557 *Tottell's Misc.* (Arb.) 177 (*Vnstedfast Woman*) O temerous tauntres that delightes in toyes..Iangling iestres, deprauereres [*ed.* 2 deprauers] of swete ioyes.

de'praving, *vbl. sb.* [f. DEPRAVE *v.* + -ING¹.] The action of the verb DEPRAVE in various senses.
a **1500** *Cuckow & Night.* xxxv, Thereof cometh..anger and envie, Depraving, shame, untrust, and jelousie. **1548** *Act 1 & 2 Edw. VI*, c. i. §2 If any manner of person..shall preache, declare or speake any thinge in the derogacion or depravinge of the saide Booke [of Common Prayer]. **1583** BABINGTON *Commandm.* ix. (1637) 87 Telling and hearing the depravings of the wicked. **1703** J. BARRETT *Analecta* 48 It would be a manifest depraving of that sacred Text..to turn it thus.

de'praving, *ppl. a.* [-ING².] That depraves; †defaming, traducing (*obs.*).
1606 HOLLAND *Sueton.* 152 Some depraving backe-friendes of hers. **1686** W. DE BRITAINE *Hum. Prud.* vi. 29 A clear Soul, like a Castle, against all the Artillery of depraving Spirits, is impregnable. **1881** *Athenæum* 24 Dec. 847/2 The story has not a depraving tendency.

Hence **de'pravingly** *adv.*
1665 J. WEBB *Stone-Heng* (1725) 71 His Words..as this Doctor..both inelegantly and depravingly renders them.

depravity (dɪ'prævɪtɪ). [An extension of PRAVITY (ad. L. *prāvitās*) previously used in same sense, after DEPRAVE and its derivatives. (No corresponding form in Latin or French.)] The quality or condition of being depraved or corrupt.

†**a.** Perverted or corrupted quality. *Obs.*
1643 SIR T. BROWNE *Rel. Med.* II. §7 An humorous depravity of mind. **1758** J. S. *Le Dran's Observ. Surg.* (1771) 298 A depravity in the Fluids may have a great Share in producing these Symptoms.

b. Perversion of the moral faculties; corruption, viciousness, abandoned wickedness.
1646 SIR T. BROWNE *Pseud. Ep.* VII. i, By aberration of conceit they extenuate his depravitie, and ascribe some goodnesse unto him. **1791** MRS. RADCLIFFE *Rom. Forest* i, Such depravity cannot surely exist in human nature. **1830** MACKINTOSH *Eth. Philos.* Wks. 1846 I. 232 The winding approaches of temptation, the slippery path to depravity. **1883** FROUDE *Short Stud., Origen* IV. III. 300 The conscience of the ignorant masses..was rising in indignation against the depravity of the educated.

c. *Theol.* The innate corruption of human nature due to original sin. Often ***total depravity***.
In common use from the time of Jonathan Edwards: the earlier terms were *pravity* and *depravation*.
[**1735** J. TAYLOR *Doctr. Orig. Sin* III. 184 Inquiring into the Corruption and Depravity of Mankind, of the Men and Women that lived in his Times.] **1757** EDWARDS *Doctr. Orig. Sin* i. §1 By Original Sin, as the phrase has been most commonly used by divines, is meant the innate sinful depravity of the heart. But..it is vulgarly understood in that latitude, which includes not only the depravity of nature, but the imputation of Adam's first sin. **1794** A. FULLER *Lett.* i. 3 July Wks. 302 On the total depravity of Human Nature. **1874** J. H. BLUNT *Dict. Sects* s.v. *Calvinists*, Both the elect and non-elect come into the world in a state of total depravity and alienation from God, and can, of themselves, do nothing but sin.

d. A depraved act or practice.
1641 MILTON *Reform.* I. (1851) 4 Characterizing the Depravities of the Church. **1665** GLANVILL *Sceps. Sci.* xiv. 90 As some Regions have their proper Vices..so they have their mental depravities, which are drawn in with the air of their Countrey. **1808** J. MALCOLM *Anecd. London 18th C.* (Title-p.), Anecdotes of the Depravities, Dresses and Amusements of the Citizens of London.

†**'deprecable,** *a. Obs. rare.* [In form ad. L. *dēprecābilis* that may be entreated (Vulgate); but in sense from DEPRECATE *v.*] Capable of being, or to be, deprecated.
1633 T. ADAMS *Exp. 2 Peter* ii. 19 A detestable sin, a deprecable punishment! **1648** *Eikon Bas.* 149, I look upon the Temporal Destruction of the greatest King as far less deprecable than the Eternal Damnation of the Meanest Subject.

†**'deprecant,** *ppl. a. Obs.* [ad. L. *dēprecānt-em*, pr. ppl. of *dēprecārī* to DEPRECATE.] Deprecating.
1624 F. WHITE *Repl. Fisher* 541 Meanes and causes impetrant, or deprecant, to appease Gods wrath. *Ibid.* 549 By Satisfaction he vnderstandeth deprecant Satisfaction, not compensant.

deprecate ('dɛprɪkeɪt), *v.* [f. L. *dēprecāt-*, ppl. stem of *dēprecārī* to pray (a thing) away, to ward off by praying, pray against, f. DE- I. 2 + *precārī* to pray.]

1. *trans.* To pray against (evil); to pray for deliverance from; to seek to avert by prayer. *arch.*
1628 EARLE *Microcosm., Meddling Man* (Arb.) 89 Wise men still deprecate these mens kindnesses. **1631** GOUGE *God's Arrows* ii. §3. 135 The judgements which Salomon.. earnestly deprecateth and prayeth against. **1633** BP. HALL *Medit.* (1851) 153, I cannot deprecate thy rebuke: my sins call for correction: but I deprecate thine anger. **1778** LOWTH *Transl. Isaiah* xlvii. 11 Evil shall come upon thee, which thou shalt not know how to deprecate. **1833** HT. MARTINEAU *Three Ages* ii. 47 While the rest of the nation were at church, deprecating God's judgements.

†**2.** *intr.* To pray (*against*). *Obs. rare.*
1652 GAULE *Magastrom.* 37 Where we are to deprecate.. against dangers of waters, let us commemorate the saving of Noah in the flood.

3. *trans.* To plead earnestly against; to express an earnest wish against (a proceeding); to express earnest disapproval of (a course, plan, purpose, etc.).
1641 J. SHUTE *Sarah & Hagar* (1649) 133 Saint Paul undertaketh.. that he shall return and deprecate his fault. **1646** SIR T. BROWNE *Pseud. Ep.* VII. xix. 385 Other accounts .. whose verities not onely, but whose relations honest minds doe deprecate. **1659** BP. WALTON *Consid. Considered* v. §2 Cappellus.. no where that I know affirms this, but rather deprecates is as a calumny. **1742** FIELDING *J. Andrews* IV. vi, I believe.. he'd behave so that nobody should deprecate what I had done. **1808** *Med. Jrnl.* XIX. 389, I cannot help deprecating the conduct of the other two anatomists. **1875** OUSELEY *Mus. Form* xiii. 60 Such a method of proceeding is greatly to be deprecated. **1882** *Times* 5 Dec. 7 To deprecate panic is an excellent counsel in itself.

†**4.** To make prayer or supplication to, to beseech (a person). *Obs.*
1624 F. WHITE *Repl. Fisher* Pref. 10 You haue libertie to deprecate his Gratious Maiestie to forget things past. **1715–20** POPE *Iliad* IX. 236 Much he advised them all, Ulysses most, To deprecate the chief, and save the host. **1758** JOHNSON *Idler* No. 11 ¶7 To deprecate the clouds lest sorrow should overwhelm us, is the cowardice of idleness. **1822** T. TAYLOR *Apuleius* 75 But the most iniquitous woman, falling at his knees, deprecated him as follows: Why, O my sone I beseech you, do you give [etc.].

†**b.** *absol.* To make supplication. *Obs.*
1625 DONNE *Serm.* 24 Feb. (1626) 8 He falls vpon his face .. and laments, and deprecates on their behalfe.

†**5.** To call down by prayer, invoke (evil). *Obs.*
1746 W. HORSLEY *Fool* (1748) I. No. 16. 114 Deprecating on unhappy Criminals, under Sentence of Death, all the Mischief they can think of. *a* **1790** FRANKLIN *Autobiog.* 442 Upon the heads of these very mischievous men they deprecated no vengeance.

Hence **'deprecated** *ppl. a.*, **'deprecating** *vbl. sb.*
1768 C. SHAW *Monody* vii. 61 Why.. strike this deprecated blow? **1839** *Times* 11 July in *Spirit Metropol. Conserv. Press* (1840) I. 158 To persist in such a deprecated and odious innovation.

deprecating ('dɛprɪkeɪtɪŋ), *ppl. a.* [f. DEPRECATE *v.* + -ING².] That deprecates or expresses disapproval or disavowal; deprecatory.
1871 L. W. M. LOCKHART *Fair to See* xviii, A bright, but withal deprecating, smile on her lovely face. **1919** WODEHOUSE *Damsel in Distress* xi, Albert waved a deprecating hand. **1925** M. A. LOWNDES *Some Men & Women* 199 With a queer, half-deprecating, half-humorous look on his handsome face.

deprecatingly ('dɛprɪkeɪtɪŋlɪ), *adv.* [f. DEPRECATING *ppl. a.* + -LY².] In a deprecating manner.
1837 MARRYAT *Dog-fiend* i. 10 'O Lord, sir! let me off this time, it's only a *soldier*', said S. deprecatingly. **1863** GEO. ELIOT *Romola* III. xix, She put up one hand deprecatingly to arrest Romola's remonstrance.

deprecation (dɛprɪ'keɪʃən). [a. F. *déprécation* (12th c. in Hatzf.), ad. L. *dēprecātiōn-em*, n. of action from *dēprecārī* to DEPRECATE.] The action of deprecating.

†**1.** Intercessory prayer. *Obs.* [So in L.]
1556 LAUDER *Tractate* (1864) 19 The deprecatioun of the maker for all Catholyke kyngis and prencis and thare liegis.

2. Prayer for the averting or removal (*of* evil, disaster, etc.).
1596 J. NORDEN *Progr. Pietie* (1847) 12 Deprecation, or a Prayer to prevent evils, whereby we desire God to remove sin from us and whatsoever punishment we have in justice deserved. **1631** *Star Chamb. Cases* (Camden) 87 My Lord Keeper answered with a deprecation: God forbid that Norfolke should be divided in custome from all England. **1649** ROBERTS *Clavis Bibl.* 342 His Deprecation of two things, viz. Present evils, and Future feares. **1673** *True Worship God* 8 A Confession of sin, Deprecation of Gods displeasure, Imploring his Mercy. **1754–8** T. NEWTON *Prophecies, Daniel* xiv. 221 If there shall be need of greater intercession and deprecation. **1856** J. H. NEWMAN *Callista* xvi, No reversal or respite had followed their most assiduous acts of deprecation. **1892** W. B. SCOTT *Autob.* I. xxiv. 343 The processional deprecations of the Devil Worshippers.

†**b.** Formerly: Prayer for forgiveness. *Obs.*
1604 R. CAWDREY *Table Alph.*, *Deprecation*, supplication, or requiring of pardon. **1633** T. ADAMS *Exp. 2 Peter* ii 6 They may then run on their impious courses without any repentance or deprecation.

3. Entreaty or earnest desire that something may be averted or removed; earnest expression of feeling against (a proposal, practice, etc.).
1612–5 BP. HALL *Contempl., O.T.* xx. ix, Deprecacions of evil to a malicious man are no better than advices. **1752** JOHNSON *Rambler* No. 208 ¶7 The censures of criticism, which, however, I shall not endeavour to soften by a formal deprecation. **1863** GEO. ELIOT *Romola* I. i, [He] turned his .. glassy eye on the frank speaker with a look of deprecation. **1870** DICKENS *E. Drood* ii, In a tone of gentle deprecation.

†**4.** Imprecation: curse. *Obs. rare.*
1634 BRERETON *Trav.* (1844) 48 Her sister denied, and with this deprecation, wished if she had any bread, that it might be turned into a stone. *a* **1804** W. GILPIN *Serm.* III. xi. (R.), We may.. apply to him the scriptural deprecation, 'He that withholdeth his corn, the people shall curse him.'

deprecative ('dɛprɪkeɪtɪv), *a.* [a. F. *déprécatif, -ive* (13th c. in Britton, 14th c. in Hatzf.), ad. L. *dēprecātīv-us*, f. ppl. stem of *dēprecārī* to DEPRECATE: see -IVE.] Having the quality of deprecating; of or pertaining to deprecation. †**a.** Intercessory, precative (*obs.*). **b.** Praying for deliverance from evil. **c.** Expressing earnest disapproval (of a proposal).
1490 CAXTON *Eneydos* ix. 37 To the, thenne.. I addresse my thoughte deprecatyue.. that it maye playse the to entende to the correction of the maners.. of our matrones. *a* **1617** BAYNE *Diocesans Tryall* (1621) 58 They imposed hands even on Deaconesses, where it could not be otherwise considered then a deprecative gesture. **1672–5** T. COMBER *Comp. to Temple* I. 752 (R.) The form itself is very ancient, consisting.. of two parts, the first deprecative, the second indicative; the one intreating for pardon, the other dispensing it. **1884** *Century Mag.* XXVIII. 588 It better pleased his deprecative soul to put them in an empty cigar-box.

Hence **'deprecatively** *adv.*, in a deprecative manner; in the way of entreaty for deliverance.
1638 *Penit. Conf.* viii. (1657) 270 The form of absolution is expressed in the third person deprecatively. **1879** P. R. DRUMMOND *Perthshire* I. xiv. 80 Looking up to him deprecatively, he said [etc.].

deprecator ('dɛprɪkeɪtə(r)). [a. L. *dēprecātor*, agent-n. from L. *dēprecārī* to DEPRECATE.] One who deprecates; †a petitioner (*obs.*).
1656 TRAPP *Comm. John* xiv. 16 And he shall give you another Comforter. Or, pleader, deprecator, advocate. **1794** T. TAYLOR *Pausanias* I. 220 That they should propitiate Jupiter, and employ Æacus.. as their deprecator.

deprecatory ('dɛprɪkeɪtərɪ), *a.* (*sb.*) [ad. L. *dēprecātōri-us*, f. *dēprecātor*: see prec. and -ORY. Cf. F. *déprécatoire* (15th c. in Hatzf.).]

A. *adj.* **1.** Serving to deprecate; that prays for deliverance from or aversion of evil.
1586 A. DAY *Eng. Secretary* I. (1625) 21 *Deprecatorie*, in praying for pardon of a thing committed. **1622** BACON *Hen. VII*, 190 Bishop Fox.. sent many humble and deprecatorie letters to the Scottish King, to appease him. *c* **1630** DONNE *Serm.* I. 504 All his Prayer.. is but Deprecatory, he does but pray that God will forbeare him. **1738** WARBURTON *Div. Legat.* I. II. I. 89 Deprecatory Rites to avert Evil.

2. Expressing a wish or hope that something feared may be averted; deprecating anticipated disapproval.
1704 SWIFT *T. Tub* iii. (T.), Before I had performed the due discourses, expostulatory, supplicatory, or deprecatory, with my good lords the criticks. **1838** LYTTON *Leila* I. v, The Israelite did.. seem to hear this deprecatory remonstrance. **1871** H. AINSWORTH *Tower Hill* I. viii, 'Your Grace is mistaken', observed Cromwell, in a deprecatory tone. **1872** GEO. ELIOT *Middlem.* xvi, 'Oh', said Rosamond, with a slight deprecatory laugh, 'I was only going to say that we sometimes have dancing.'

†**B.** *sb.* A deprecatory word or expression. *Obs.*
1654 GAYTON *Pleas. Notes* IV. i. 171 To convey his Consolatories, Suasories, Deprecatories. *a* **1734** NORTH *Exam.* (1740) 343 Now he is passive, full of Deprecatories and Apologetics.

Hence **'deprecatorily** *adv.*, in a deprecatory manner, in a way that expresses a prayer or desire against something.
1873 *Brit. Q. Rev.* 388, 'I do not know', said Sir William, deprecatorily, 'that it is necessary to go down so low as that.'

†**de'prece**, *v. Obs. rare.* [See note below.] *trans.* ? To set free from confinement or restraint; to release.
c **1340** *Gaw. & Gr. Knt.* 1219 Bot wolde ȝe, lady louely, þen leue me grante, & deprece your prysoun [prisoner], & pray hym to ryse.
[Of uncertain etymology. *Deprece* occurs in the same poem as a spelling of DEPRESS *v.*, but no sense of that word suits here. OF. had *despresser* to free from a press, free from pressure. OF. *despriser* to let out of prison, release from confinement, app. agrees in sense, but not in form.]

deprece, var. of DEPRESS *v.*

depreciant (dɪ'priːʃɪənt), *a.* [ad. L. *dēpretiānt-em*, pr. pple. of *dēpretiāre*: see next.] Depreciating.
1885 F. HALL in *Nation* XL. 446/2 Who is so superfluously self-depreciant and lowly-minded.

depreciate (dɪ'priːʃɪeɪt), *v.* Also depretiate. [f. L. *dēpretiāt-* (*-ciāt-*), ppl. stem of *dēpretiāre* (in med.L. commonly spelt *dēpreciāre*), f. DE- I. 1 + *pretium* price. Cf. mod.F. *déprécier* (*Dict. Acad.* 1762).]

1. *trans.* To lower in value, lessen the value of.
1646 SIR T. BROWNE *Pseud. Ep.* IV. x. 205 A method.. which much depreciates the esteeme and value of miracles. **1664** POWER *Exp. Philos.* I. 53 As these dioptrical Glasses, do heighten and illustrate the Works of Nature, so do they.. disparage and depretiate those of Art. **1739** CIBBER *Apol.* v. 102 Booth thought it depreciated the Dignity of Tragedy to raise a Smile. **1862** *Fraser's Mag.* Nov. 631 Our architectural reputation, never high, is still more depreciated by the building at South Kensington.

b. *spec.* To lower the price or market value of; to reduce the purchasing power of (money).
1656 BLOUNT *Glossogr.*, *Depretiate*, to make the price less, to make cheaper. **1719** W. WOOD *Surv. Trade* 358 That we shall.. Depretiate our Silver Standard. **1782** PAINE *Let. Abbé Raynal* (1791) 25 Every man depreciated his own money by his own consent. **1848** MILL *Pol. Econ.* III. xiii, It is true that suspension of the obligation to pay in specie, did put it in the power of the Bank to depreciate the currency. **1893** BITHELL *Counting-House Dict.* s.v. *Depreciation*, Bank Notes or State Notes are depreciated in value when issued against a small reserve of bullion.

2. To lower in estimation; to represent as of less value; to underrate, undervalue, belittle.
1666 BOYLE *Orig. Formes & Qual.* To Rdr., Where.. I do indefinitely depretiate Aristotle's Doctrine, I would be understood to speak of his Physicks. **1704** HEARNE *Duct. Hist.* (1714) I. 262 Alexander.. began to extoll his own Actions, and to depritiate those of his Father Philip. **1769** *Junius Lett.* ii. 13 His bounty.. this writer would in vain depreciate. **1865** DICKENS *Mut. Fr.* III. ix, I don't like to hear you depreciate yourself. **1875** JOWETT *Plato* (ed. 2) IV. 11 Pleasure [by Plato] is depreciated as relative, while good is exalted as absolute.
absol. **1751** JOHNSON *Rambler* No. 93 ¶13 The duty of criticism is neither to depreciate nor dignify by partial representations. **1804** *Man in Moon* No. 24. 189 He depreciates from the merits of the very man he had praised before. **1882** A. W. WARD *Dickens* iii. 54 At the bottom lay a desire to depreciate.

3. *intr.* To fall in value, to become of less worth.
a **1790** FRANKLIN *Autobiog.* (1889) 118 The wealthy inhabitants oppos'd.. all paper currency, from an apprehension that it would depreciate. **1796** MORSE *Amer. Geog.* I. 439 This breed of horses has much depreciated of late. **1858** DE QUINCEY *Wks.* (1862) V. 62 Actually to have depreciated as he grew older and better known to the world. **1884** *Manch. Exam.* 8 May 5/3 Conditions which caused property to depreciate.

depreciated (dɪ'priːʃɪeɪtɪd), *ppl. a.* [f. prec. + -ED.] Lowered in value or estimation.
1790 BURKE *Fr. Rev.* 345 Receiving in money and accounting in depreciated paper. **1796** MORSE *Amer. Geog.* I. 323 Old specie debts were often paid in a depreciated currency. **1836** H. COLERIDGE *North. Worthies* (1852) I. 38 The depreciated value of estates and personal effects. **1860** MOTLEY *Netherl.* (1868) II. ix. 33 Growing rich.. on his profits from paying the troops in depreciated coin.

de'preciating, *vbl. sb.* [-ING¹.] The action of lowering in value, price, or estimation; depreciation.
1705 STANHOPE *Paraphr.* I. 141 A wilful depretiating of one's own Worth. **1767** BLACKSTONE *Comm.* II. 282 Whatever tends to the destruction, or depreciating the value, of the inheritance. **1768–74** TUCKER *Lt. Nat.* (1852) II. 403 Open depreciatings and ridicule can do no good.

de'preciating, *ppl. a.* [-ING².] That depreciates: that lessens or seeks to lower the value of anything; that is declining in value.
1777 J. ADAMS *Wks.* (1854) IX. 463 There is so much injustice in carrying on a war with depreciating currency that we can hardly pray with confidence for success. **1796** MORSE *Amer. Geog.* I. 323 This depreciating paper currency was almost the only medium of trade. **1837** WHEWELL *Hist. Induct. Sc.* (1857) I. iii. 139 The depreciating manner in which he [Delambre] habitually speaks of.. astronomers. **1860** RUSKIN *Mod. Paint.* V. IX. xii. §4, I never heard him say one depreciating word of living man.

Hence **de'preciatingly** *adv.*, in a depreciating manner; disparagingly.
1837 *Fraser's Mag.* XV. 328 That gentleman spoke of the National Gallery very depreciatingly. **1859** F. HALL *Vâsavadattâ* Pref. 22 *note*, A poet self-depreciatingly declares [etc.]. **1868** M. PATTISON *Academ. Org.* ii. 35 Literary men.. are apt to think depreciatingly of the clergy as a class.

depreciation (dɪˌpriːʃɪ'eɪʃən) [n. of action from DEPRECIATE *v.*: so mod.F. *dépréciation* (1784 in Hatzf.).] The action of depreciating.

1. a. Lowering of value; fall in the exchangeable value (of money).
1767 FRANKLIN *Wks.* (1887) IV. 90 A depreciation of the currency. **1796** MORSE *Amer. Geog.* I. 323 The depreciation continued.. until seventy, and even one hundred and fifty nominal paper dollars, were hardly an equivalent for one Spanish milled dollar. **1829** I. TAYLOR *Enthus.* ix. 225 A great depreciation of the standard of morals among the people. **1879** H. FAWCETT in *19th Cent.* Feb. 200 Within the last few years there has been a most serious depreciation in the value of silver when compared with gold.

b. A fall in the market value of an (*esp.* durable) asset, brought about by age, wear and tear, etc.; a conventional allowance made for this in balance sheets, etc. Also *attrib.*
1900 *Pitman's Business Terms & Phrases* IV. 64 *Depreciation*.. is an annual allowance made in a balance sheet for the reduction in value, owing to wear and tear, of machinery and other tools, fixtures, and furniture, buildings, and other commercial plant. **1910** L. C. CROPPER *Book-Keeping* xvii. 310 The term 'Depreciation' includes Wear and Tear.. but it covers a much wider field, embracing.. the wastage caused by any fall in market values. **1930** *Economist* 25 Jan. 163/2 Ten or twelve modern plants would give an equal productive capacity and reduce operative costs far beyond the charges necessary for the new capital and depreciation allowances. **1934** *U.S. Supreme Courts Reports* 292 U.S. §151 Broadly speaking, the term depreciation, as applied to the property of a public utility company, means the loss, not restored by current maintenance, which is due to all the factors causing the ultimate retirement of the property; these factors include wear and tear, decay, inadequacy and obsolescence. **1953** J. L. HANSON *Textbk. Econ.* II. iv. 66 Depreciation of capital takes two forms: the wearing out of machinery, etc., and the using up of stocks. **1968** G. M. WHITEHEAD *Book-Keeping made Simple* vi. 99 Depreciation is a reduction in the book value of an asset due to fair wear and tear. **1984** HITCHING & STONE *Understanding Accounting!* iii. 18 The usual way would be to charge an equal portion to each year, so that, in the case of Andrew's car, the annual cost of depreciation would be (4,000/5 =) £800.

2. Lowering in estimation; disparagement.
1790 Bp. T. Burgess *Serm. Divin. Christ*, Note iii, Dangerous..to form comparisons..where the preference of one tends to the depreciation of the other. **1831** Lamb *Elia, Ellistoniana*, Resentment of depreciations done to his more lofty intellectual pretensions. **1872** Geo. Eliot *Middlem.* lxxxvi, She never said a word in depreciation of Dorothea.

depreciative (dɪˈpriːʃɪətɪv), *a.* [f. L. *dēpretiāt-* (see DEPRECIATE *v.*) + -IVE.] Characterized by depreciating; given to depreciation; depreciatory.
1836 in Smart, and in mod. Dicts.

depreciator (dɪˈpriːʃɪeɪtə(r)). [a. L. *dēpretiātor* (*dēprec-*) (Tertull.), agent-n. f. *dēpretiāre* to DEPRECIATE.] One who depreciates.
1799 V. Knox *Consid. Lord's Supper* (R.), The depreciators of the Eucharist. **1868** Freeman *Norm. Conq.* (ed. 3) II. ix. 387 Depreciators of Harold. **1875** Jevons *Money* vii. 66 Kings have been the most notorious false coiners and depreciators of the currency.

depreciatory (dɪˈpriːʃɪətərɪ), *a.* [f. L. type **dēpretiātōri-us*, f. *dēpretiātor*: see prec. and -ORY.] Tending to depreciate; of disparaging tendency.
1805 W. Taylor in *Ann. Rev.* III. 57 This account..is too depretiatory. **1875** Jowett *Plate* (ed. 2) V. 59, I have a word to say..which may seem to be depreciatory of legislators.

† **deˈpredable**, *a. Obs.* [f. stem of L. *dēprædāre* or F. *déprédér* (see DEPREDATE) + -BLE.] Liable to be preyed upon or consumed.
1640 G. Watts tr. *Bacon's Adv. Learn.* iv. ii. 201 The juyce and succulencies of the body, are made less depredable, if either they be made more indurate, or more dewy, and oyly. **1656** Blount *Glossogr.*, *Depredable*, that may be robbed or spoiled.

† **deˈpredar.** *Sc. Obs.* [agent-n. f. a vb. **deprede*, a. F. *déprédér*, ad. L. *dēprædāre* to DEPREDATE; perh. directly repr. a F. **déprédeur*.] = DEPREDATOR; ravager.
1535 Stewart *Cron. Scot.* II. 304 Tua vncristin kingis.. Depredaris alss of halie kirk also.

depredate (ˈdɛprɪdeɪt), *v.* [f. ppl. stem of L. *dēprædāre* to pillage, ravage, f. DE- I. 3 + *prædāre* (*-ārī*) to make booty or prey of, f. *præda* booty, prey. Cf. F. *déprédér*.]

† **1.** *trans.* To prey upon, to make a prey of; to plunder, pillage. *Obs.* (or *nonce-wd*)
1651 N. Bacon *Disc. Govt. Eng.* ii. vi. (1739) 30 That corrupt custom or practice of depredating those possessions given to a holy use. **1654** H. L'Estrange *Chas. I* (1655) 126 Such things as had been depredated and scrambled away from the Crown in his Fathers minority. **1677** Hale *Prim. Orig. Man.* iv. viii. 369 Animals..which are more obnoxious to be preyed upon and depredated. [**1886** *Pall Mall G.* 2 Oct. 4/1 These animals [tigers and leopards] are common in Corea, and depredate the inhabitants in winter.]

† **b.** *fig.* To consume by waste. *Obs.*
1626 Bacon *Sylva* §299 It [Exercise] maketh the Substance of the Body more solid and Compact; and so less apt to be Consumed and Depredated by the Spirits. **1662** H. Stubbe *Ind. Nectar* iii. 65 They do depredate, and dissolve, by way of colliquation, the flesh.

2. *intr.* To make depredations. (*affected.*)
1797 Mrs. A. M. Bennett *Beggar Girl* (1813) I. 250 If none are allowed to depredate on the fortunes of others. **1799-1805** S. Turner *Anglo-Sax.* (1836) I. iv. iii. 283 Ragnar Lodbrog depredated with success on various parts of Europe. **1888** *Boston* (Mass) *Jrnl.* 20 Oct. 2/4 Wolves.. invade farm yards and depredate upon chickens and calves.

depredation (dɛprɪˈdeɪʃən). [a. F. *déprédation*, in 15th c. *depredacion* (Hatzf.), ad. L. *dēprædātiōn-em* plundering, n. of action from *dēprædāre*: see prec.]

1. The action of making a prey of; plundering, pillaging, ravaging; also, †plundered or pillaged condition (*obs.*).
1483 Caxton *Gold. Leg.* 343/2 Somme..seyng his depredacion entryd in to his hows by nyght and robbed hym. **1494** Fabyan *Chron.* vii. 354 By yͤ depredacion & brennynge of our manours. **1618** Jas. I in *Fortesc. Papers* (Camden) 58 Touching his [Raleigh's] actes of hostilitie, depredation, abuse..of our Commission. **1783** Johnson *Lett. to Mrs. Thrale* 1 July, Till the neighbourhood should have lost its habits of depredation. **1832** Ht. Martineau *Ireland* vi. 92 When he heard of the acts of malice and depredation.

b. *Sc. Law.* (See quot.)
1861 W. Bell *Dict. Law Scot.* 278 *Depredation* or *Hership*, is the offence of driving away numbers of cattle or other bestial, by the masterful force of armed persons..The punishment is capital.

c. An act of spoliation and robbery; *pl.* ravages.
1495 *Act 11 Hen. VII*, c. 9 Preamb., Robberies, felonyes, depredacions, riottes and other greate trespaces. **1611** Speed *Theat. Gt. Brit.* xxviii. (1614) 55/1 In the depredations of the Danes. **1688** in Somers *Tracts* II. 383 For redressing the depredations and robberies by the Highland Clans. **1798** Ferriar *Illustr. Sterne* vi. 169 Sterne truly resembled Shakespeare's Biron, in the extent of his depredations from other writers. **1867** Lady Herbert *Cradle L.* vii. 202 Subject..to continual depredations at the hands of the Bedouins.

2. *fig.* † **a.** Consumption or destructive waste of the substance of anything. *Obs.*
1626 Bacon *Sylva* §91 The Speedy Depredation of Air upon Watery Moisture, and Version of the same into Air, appeareth in..the sudden discharge..of a little Cloud of Breath, or Vapour, from Glass. **1650** tr. *Bacon's Life & Death* Pref. 3 The one touching the Consumption, or Depredation, of the Body of Man; The other, touching the Reparation, and Renovation of the same. **1651** Biggs *New Disp.* ¶124 The deprædation of the strength, and very substance of our bodies.

b. *pl.* Destructive operations, ravages (of disease, physical agents).
1663 Cowley *Death Mrs. K. Philips* 4 Cruel Disease!.. the fairest Sex..thy Depredations most do vex. **1750** Johnson *Rambler* No. 74 ¶2 Peevishness..may be considered as the canker of life, that creeps on with hourly depredations. **1875** Lyell *Princ. Geol.* II. ii. xxvii. 51 [They] perished..by the depredations of the lava.

Hence **depreˈdationist**, one who practises or approves of depredations.
1828 Bentham *Wks.* (1843) X. 581 The enemies of the people may be divided into two classes; the depredationists ..and the oppressionists.

depredator (ˈdɛprɪdeɪtə(r)). [a. L. *dēprædātor*, agent-n. from *dēprædāre* (see DEPREDATE); perh. immed. ad. F. *déprédateur* (14th c. in Hatzf., not in Cotgr. 1611, in Dict. Acad. 1798).] One who, or that which, preys upon or makes depredations; a ravager, plunderer, pillager.
1626 Bacon *Sylva* §492 They be both great Depredatours of the Earth. **1646** J. Hall *Horæ Vac.* 143 Hawking..is.. a generous exercise, as well for variety of deprædators as preys. **1799-1805** S. Turner *Anglo-Sax.* (1836) I. iii. i. 154 They had been but petty and partial depredators. **1814** Scott *Wav.* xv, The depredators were twelve Highlanders. **1851** *Beck's Florist* 100 If you should be annoyed by a small black insect..use every means to encourage the plants..by brushing the depredators from the points of the shoots.

depredatory (dɪˈprɛdətərɪ, ˈdɛprɪdeɪtərɪ), *a.* [f. L. type **dēprædātōri-us*, f. *dēprædātor*: see prec. and -ORY.] Characterized by depredation; plundering, laying waste.
1651 tr. *Bacon's Life & Death* 38 That the Spirits and Aire in their actions may be the less depredatory. **1771** Macpherson *Introd. Hist. Gt. Brit.* 29 The irruption of the Cimbri was not merely depredatory. **1799-1805** S. Turner *Anglo-Sax.* (1836) I. iii. 149 More fortunate than their depredatory countrymen who had preceded them.

† **deˈpredicate**, *v. Obs. rare.* [f. DE- I. 3 + PREDICATE *v.*] To proclaim aloud; call out; celebrate.
1550 Veron *Godly Sayings* (1846) 148 Do not nowe the enemyes of the truth..as they are syttyng on theyr ale benches, depredycate and saye: Where is extortyon, bryberye and pyllynge nowe a dayes most used? **1659** Hammond *On Ps.* Annot. 1 The Hebrew..which in Piel signifies to praise, or celebrate, or deprædicate. **1674** Hickman *Quinquart. Hist.* (ed. 2) 237, I wish..that he had not depredicated the invincible constancy of Mr. Barret, as he doth.

† **deprehend** (dɛprɪˈhɛnd), *v. Obs.* [ad. L. *dēprehend-ĕre* to take or snatch away, seize, catch, detect, etc., f. DE- I. 2 + *prehend-ĕre* to lay hold of, seize.]

1. *trans.* To seize, capture; to arrest, apprehend.
1532 More *Confut. Barnes* viii. Wks. 758/1 He would.. cause them to be deprehended and taken. *a* **1572** Knox *Hist. Ref.* Wks. 1846 I. 6 About the year of God 1431, was deprehended in the Universitie of Sanctandrose, one named Paull Craw, a Bohame..accused of heresye. *a* **1639** Spottiswood *Hist. Ch. Scot.* vi. (1677) 390 With him were deprehended divers missive Letters..signed by the Earl. **1657** S. Purchas *Pol. Flying Ins.* i. v. 11 Least they should be deprehended for theeves. **1834** Hogg *Mora Campbell* 638 Two wives at once to deprehend him.

2. To catch or detect (a person) in the commission of some evil or secret deed; to take by surprise.
1529 More *Comf. agst. Trib.* i. Wks. 1148/1 [Achan] myghte wel see that he was deprehended and taken agaynst hys wyl. **1543** Grafton *Contn. Harding* 583 Yf he were deprehended in lyke cryme. **1574** Whitgift *Def. Aunsw.* ii. Wks. 1851 I. 272 Touching the woman deprehended in adultery. **1622** Donne *Serm.* i. 6 When Moses came down from God, and deprehended the people in that Idolatry to the Calfe. **1677** Cary *Chronol.* ii. ii. iii. iii. 228 Being deprehended a Confederate with Sô, King of Ægypt..this stirred up the King of Assyria against him.

b. To convict or prove guilty (*of*).
1598 Grenewey *Tacitus' Ann.* iii. xi. (1622) 80 Noting the countenance, and the feare of euerie one of such, which should be deprehended of this shamefull lauishing.

3. To detect or discover (anything concealed or liable to escape notice).
1523 in Burnet *Hist. Ref.* II. 105 The more the said Breve cometh unto light..the more falsities may be deprehended therein. **1607** Topsell *Four-f. Beasts* (1658) 430 The fraud ..is easily deprehended, for both the odour and the colour are different from the true amber. **1626** Bacon *Sylva* §98 The Motions of the Minute Parts of Bodies..are Invisible, and incurre not to the Eye; but yet they are to be deprehended by Experience. *a* **1683** Whichcote *Serm.* (1698) 22 If it [our Religion] had been a Cheat and an imposture it would have been deprehended in length of Time.

b. With *subord. cl.*
1531 Elyot *Gov.* i. xiv, In the bokes of Tulli, men may deprehende, that in hym lacked nat the knowlege of geometrye, ne musike, ne grammer. **1663** Blair *Autobiog.* vii. (1848) 89 We deprehended it to be a mere delusion. **1675** R. Vaughan *Coinage* 30 Easily deprehend if there be mixture of allay amongst it.

Hence † **depreˈhended** *ppl. a.*, caught in the act.
1655 Jer. Taylor *Unum Necess.* ix. §1 (R.) Of the thief on the cross and the deprehended adultress. **1660** —— *Duct. Dubit.* iii. i. rule 1 §12.

† **depreˈhendible**, *a. Obs.* [f. L. *dēprehendĕre* + -BLE.] Capable of being detected.
1660 H. More *Myst. Godliness* vii. ii. 288 The foolery of it [is] still more palpably deprehendible.

† **depreˈhensible**, *a. Obs.* [f. L. *dēprehens-*, ppl. stem of *dēprehend-ĕre* + -BLE.] = prec.
1653 H. More *Antid. Ath.* iii. iii. (1712) 94 His presence was palpably deprehensible by many freaks and pranks that he played. **1660** N. Ingelo *Bentivolio & Urania* ii. (1682) 61 Operations which are Regular and deprehensible by Reason.

Hence † **depreˈhensibleness**; † **depreˈhensibly** *adv.*
1664 H. More *Myst. Iniq.* i. ii. viii. ¶13 Which if they doe very grossely and deprehensibly here. **1727** Bailey vol. II, *Deprehensibleness*, capableness of being caught or understood.

† **depreˈhension.** *Obs.* [ad. L. *dēprehensiōn-em*, n. of action from *dēprehendĕre* to DEPREHEND.] The action of catching or taking in the act; detection; arrest.
1527 Knight in J. S. Brewer *Reign Hen. VIII*, xxviii. (1884) II. 199 That it be not in any wise known that the said ..deprehension should come by the King. **1612-5** Bp. Hall *Contempl., N.T.* iv. xv, To be taken in the very act was no part of her sin..yet her deprehension is made an aggravation of her shame. **1630** Sanderson *Serm.* II. 269 The next step is for deprehension, or conviction. **1649** Jer. Taylor *Gt. Exemp.* xvi. ¶9 We must conceal our actions from the surprises and deprehensions of Suspition.

† **deˈprensible**, *a. Obs.* [f. L. *dēprend-ĕre*, *dēprens-* shortened form of *dēprehendĕre*, etc.] = DEPREHENSIBLE; capable of being detected.
1648 Sir W. Petty *Advice to Hartlib* 15 Such [qualities] as are not discernible by sense, or deprensible by Certaine Experiments.

† **deˈprension.** *Obs.* [cf. prec.] = DEPREHENSION.
1654 Gayton *Pleas. Notes* iv. vi.-vii. 214 Shame and deprension is a better friend.

depresh (dɪˈprɛʃ). Now *Obs.* or *rare.* Colloq. abbrev. of DEPRESSION, esp. in sense 5.
1933 *Bulletin* (Sydney) 2 Aug. 10/4 There's no surer test of the depresh down-and-out. **1933** M. Lowry *Ultramarine* ii. 70 Forgetting depresh. of departing semester. **1942** Berrey & Van den Bark *Amer. Thes. Slang* §3/7 The depresh, the 1929-32 depression. *Ibid.* §543/4 Big bad wolf, the Big Trouble, depresh, Old Man Depression, economic depression.

depress (dɪˈprɛs), *v.* Also 4 depres(e, deprece, 5-7 depresse, (6 dyprease). [a. OF. *dépresser* (Godef.), ad. L. type **dēpressāre* (It. *depressare*), freq. of *dēprimĕre* to press down. (Cf. *pressāre* freq. of *premĕre* in L. use.) In Eng. taken as the repr. of L. *dēprimĕre*, ppl. stem *dēpress-*.]

† **1.** *trans.* To put down by force, or crush in a contest or struggle; to overcome, subjugate, vanquish. *Obs.*
c **1325** *E.E. Allit. P.* A. 777 And þou con alle þo dere outdryf, And fro þat maryag al oþer depres. *c* **1340** *Gaw. & Gr. Knt.* 6 Ennias þe aþel and his highe kinde, þat siþen depreced prouinces. **1432-50** tr. *Higden* (Rolls) I. 145 The dogges..be so greete and feerse that thei depresse bulles and peresche lyones. **1529** Frith *Pistle to Chr. Rdr.* (1829) 464 Her seed shal depress & also break thy head. **1671** Milton *Samson* 1698 So virtue..Depressed and overthrown, as seem'd..Revives, reflourishes. **1675** tr. *Machiavelli's Prince* iii. (Rtldg. 1883) 20 The kingdom of the Macedonians was depress'd and Antiochus driven out.

† **b.** To press hard; to ply closely with questions, entreaties, etc. *Obs. rare.*
c **1340** *Gaw. & Gr. Knt.* 1770 þat prince [= princess] of pris depresed hym so þikke.. þat nede hym bi-houed Oþer lach þer hir luf, oþer to-day refuse.

2. To press down (in space). Often more widely: To force, bring, move, or put into a lower position by any physical action; to lower.
1526 *Pilgr. Perf.* (W. de W. 1531) 134 b, As the belowes, the more they depresse the flame, the more the fyre encreaseth. **1646** Sir T. Browne *Pseud. Ep.* ii. ii. 61 Needles which stood before..parallel unto the Horizon, being vigorously excited, incline and bend downeward, depressing the North extreame below the Horizon. **1665** Hooke *Microgr.* 17 The globular figure..will be deprest into the Elliptico-spherical. **1692** in *Capt. Smith's Seaman's Gram.* ii. iii. 92 A Gunner's Quadrant to level, elevate, or depress his Gun. **1751** Chambers *Cycl.*, *Depression of the Pole*, So many degrees as you..travel from the pole towards the equator; so many you are said to depress the pole, because it becomes..so much lower or nearer the horizon. **1774** J. Bryant *Mythol.* I. 321 The Palm was supposed to rise under a weight; and to thrive in proportion to its being depressed. **1822** Imison *Sc. & Art* I. 184 Alternately raising and depressing the piston. **1855** Bain *Senses & Int.* ii. ii §13 The sensation of a weight depressing the hand. **1880** Gunther *Fishes* 41 The spines can be erected or depressed at the will of the fish.

3. *fig.* To lower in station, fortune, or influence; to put down, bring low, humble. Now *rare*.

1526 *Pilgr. Perf.* (W. de W. 1531) 15 b, Now they lyfte up man to honours & dignitees, & anone they depresse hym as lowe in mysery. **1648** MILTON *Tenure Kings* Wks. 1738 I. 321 By depressing..their King far below the rank of a Subject to the condition of a Captive. **1701** SWIFT *Contests Nobles & Com.* ii, Marius..used all endeavours for depressing the nobles, and raising the people. **1777** ROBERTSON *Hist. Amer.* (1778) II. VII. 280 A people depressed into the lowest state of subjection. **1857** BUCKLE *Civiliz.* I. vii. 457 Each of these vast measures has depressed a powerful party.

†**b.** To keep down, repress, restrain from activity; to put down, supress; to oppress. *Obs.*

a **1562** in G. Cavendish *Wolsey* (1818) I. 543, I request his grace..that he haue a vigilant eye to depress this newe sorte of Lutherans, that it doe not encrease. **1605** VERSTEGAN *Dec. Intell.* vi. (1628) 182 The Conqueror..had no reason by still depressing the English to prouoke them to breake all bounds of obedience. **1617** FLETCHER *Valentinian* I. iii, Pray, Depress your spirit. **1679** PENN *Addr. Prot.* I. 52 Therefore depress Vice and cherish Virtue. **1773** J. ROSS *Fratricide* IV. 544 (MS.) He..stands..Depressing the keen strugglings of his breast. **1861** O'CURRY *Lect. MS. Materials* 263 The descendants of the earlier colonists, depressed and enslaved by their conquerors.

†**4.** To bring down in estimation or credit; to depreciate, disparage. *Obs.*

1550 CROWLEY *Epigr.* 898 But other mens doynges they wyll euer dyprease, For other can do nought that may theyr mynde please. **1594** HOOKER *Eccl. Pol.* IV. vii. §1 They which disgrace or depresse the credit of others. **1659** BP. WALTON *Consid. Considered* II. xv, He..seeks to depresse the worth of the book. **1699** BENTLEY *Phal.* 423 Raise or depress the Character of a Man of Letters. **1791** MACKINTOSH *Vind. Gallicæ* 310 The frantic loyalty which depressed Paradise Lost.

†**b.** To lower in dignity, make undignified; to debase. *Obs.*

1654 GAYTON *Pleas. Notes* I. vi. 21 If such abilities depresse not themselves by meane subjects, but keep up the gravity of their stiles. **1711** ADDISON *Spect.* No. 39 ¶6, I prefer a noble Sentiment that is depressed with homely Language, infinitely before a vulgar one that is blown up with all the Sound and Energy of Expression.

5. To lower or bring down in force, vigour, activity, intensity, or amount; to render weaker or less; to render dull or languid.

Now usually in relation to trade, etc., in which use it is often associated with sense 6.

1647 MAY *Hist. Parl.* I. ix. 110 Which must needs depresse the strength of England, and keepe it from so much greatnesse. **1710** STEELE *Tatler* No. 241 ¶1 Wine..raises the Imagination, and depresses Judgment. **1802** *Med. Jrnl.* VIII. 78 That accumulation of fæces, which tends to depress and greatly impede the functions. **1831** BREWSTER *Optics* xxviii. 233 It depresses the tints in the two quadrants which the axis of the plate crosses. **1878** JEVONS *Prim. Pol. Econ.* 122 When the trade is depressed, and when wages and interest are low.

b. To lower in pitch, to flatten (the voice, or a musical note).

1530 PALSGR. 48 Whan the redar hath lyft up his voyce at the soundyng of the said vowel..he shal, whan he commeth to the last sillable, depresse his voyce agayne. **1824** SCOTT *Redgauntlet* Let. xi, He commenced his tale..in a distinct..tone of voice, which he raised and depressed with considerable skill. **1878** W. H. STONE *Sci. Basis Music* v. 53 If then we make each of the four fifths one-fourth of a comma flat, the resulting third is depressed a whole comma.

6. To bring into low spirits, cast down mentally, dispirit, deject, sadden. (The chief current use.)

1621 BURTON *Anat. Mel.* II. iii. III. (1676) 209/1 Hope refresheth as much as misery depresseth. *c* **1698** LOCKE *Cond. Underst.* § 39 Others..depress their own minds, despond at the first difficulty. **1712** ADDISON *Spect.* No. 249 ¶5 The Gloom which is apt to depress the Mind and damp our Spirits. **1806** J. FORBES *Lett. fr. France* II. 321 We came ..amidst rain and wind, and depressed by ill-forebodings. **1838** DICKENS *Nich. Nick.* xi, 'This house depresses and chills one', said Kate.

†**7.** *Alg.* To reduce to a lower degree or power.

1673 WALLIS in Rigaud *Corr. Sci. Men* (1841) II. 561 The method of depressing biquadratic equations to quadratic. **1674** JEAKE *Arith.* (1696) 372 The Quotients being depressed by Reduction in Species, may be brought to..$\frac{52}{20}$ + $\frac{20}{4}$. **1816** tr. *Lacroix's Diff. & Int. Calculus* 193 This formula furnishes the means of depressing to unity the index of the denominator.

†**de'press,** *ppl. a. Obs. rare.* [ad. L. *dēpress-us*, pa. pple. of *dēprimĕre*: see prec.] = DEPRESSED.

c **1660** HAMMOND *Wks.* I. 259 (R.) If the seal be depress or hollow, 'tis lawful to wear, but not to seal with it.

depressant (dɪ'prɛsənt), *a.* and *sb. Med.* [f. DEPRESS *v.*: see -ANT[1].]

A. *adj.* **a.** Having the quality of lowering the activity of the vital functions; sedative.

1887 *Athenæum* 13 Aug. 217/1 The depressant and narcotic action. **1892** N. MOORE in *Dict. Nat. Biog.* XXIX. 221/1 The depressant treatment of fever.

b. In ore and froth flotation: having the property of a depressant (sense c).

1945 A. F. TAGGART *Handbk. Mineral Dressing* xii. 32 Lime..present in excess in sulphide flotation..has a definite depressant effect on the copper sulphides other than chalcopyrite. **1959** *Chambers's Encycl.* X. 235/2 Alkalis are generally depressant in action on all sulphide flotations, preventing the collectors from working.

B. *sb.* **a.** A medicine or agent having this quality; a sedative.

1876 GROSS *Dis. Bladder* 267 The heart's action is reduced with aconite and other depressants. **1890** *Standard* 19 Nov. 3/6 Malaria and heat are remarkable depressants.

b. Also **depressent**. A depressing influence.

1894 STEVENSON & OSBOURNE *Ebb-Tide* I. v. 87 So strong a tonic to the merely weak, and so deadly a depressent to the merely cowardly. **1923** KIPLING *Irish Guards in Gt. War* I. 121 There are times when Extreme Unction can be a depressant. **1961** *Times* 22 Mar. 18/3 To the ambitious athlete there is really no reason why standards should not be an incentive rather than a depressant.

c. In ore and froth flotation, an agent that causes certain of the solids to sink while not affecting the others.

1934 WEBSTER, *Depressant*..*Ore Dressing*, a reagent that depresses. **1939** A. M. GAUDIN *Princ. Mineral Dressing* xv. 393 Practical depressants for sulphide flotation include alkali hydroxides. **1951** *Engineering* 19 Oct. 492/1 Agents, known as depressants, are..used to promote wetting of.. constituents, such as pyrites, which would otherwise float with the coal. **1962** *Gloss. Terms Coal Preparation* (*B.S.I.*) 24 *Depressant*, a substance which when added to a pulp prevents a particular mineral or minerals from floating.

depressed (dɪ'prɛst, *poet.* dɪ'prɛsɪd), *ppl. a.* Also 7–9 depress*t*. [f. DEPRESS *v.* + -ED[1].]

1. a. Pressed down; put or kept down by pressure or force.

1609 DANIEL *Civ. Wars* V. i, Close smothered lay the lowe depressed fire. **1774** GOLDSM. *Nat. Hist.* (1776) I. 191 The deeper any body sinks, the greater will be the resistance of the depressed fluid beneath.

b. *Her.* = DEBRUISED.

(In mod. Dicts.)

2. Lowered, sunken, or low in position; lower than the general surface: opp. to *elevated*.

1658 WILLSFORD *Natures Secrets* 71 High exalted places, and low depressed dales. **1823** CRABB *Technol. Dict.*, *Depressed Gun*, any piece of ordnance having its mouth depressed below the horizontal line. **1869** PHILLIPS *Vesuv.* ii. 13 In the centre of the old depressed crateral plain.

3. Having a flattened or hollowed form, such as would be produced by downward pressure; *spec.* said of convex things which are flattened vertically (opposed to COMPRESSED); e.g. a ***depressed arch***.

1753 CHAMBERS *Cycl. Supp.* s.v. *Leaf*, *Depressed Leaf*, one which has the mark of an impression on one side. **1828** STARK *Elem. Nat. Hist.* I. 266 Chelidones. Bill very short, much depressed. **1845** LINDLEY *Sch. Bot.* v. (1858) 56 Legumes snail-shaped, depressed-cylindrical. **1874** LUBBOCK *Orig. & Met. Ins.* i. 17 The larva of Coccinella.. is somewhat depressed.

4. *fig.* **a.** Lowered in force, amount, or degree.

1832 DE LA BECHE *Geol. Man.* 7 Alternately..under the influence of a raised and a depressed temperature.

†**b.** *Astrol.* Opposed to *exalted. Obs.*

c **1430** LYDG. *Thebes* I. (1561) Venus directe, and contrarious and depressed in Mercurious hous.

†**c.** Low in moral quality, debased. *Obs.*

1647 JER. TAYLOR *Lib. Proph.* xx. ¶7 These Propositions [e.g. 'the Pope may Dispense with all oaths'] are so deprest. **1661** BOYLE *Style of Script.* (1675) 182 That doth much more argue a depressed soul than an elevated fancy.

5. a. Brought low, oppressed, dejected, downcast, etc.; *esp.* in low spirits.

1621 BURTON *Anat. Mel.* II. ii. VI. ii, A good Orator alone ..can comfort such as are afflicted, erect such as are depressed. *c* **1790** WILLOCK *Voy.* 28 America..stands ready to receive the persecuted and depressed of every country. **1792** COWPER *Let. to Bagot* 8 Nov., My spirits have been more depressed than is common, even with me. **1818** MISS FERRIER *Marriage* xxi, Mrs. Lennox..seemed more than usually depressed. **1845** S. AUSTIN *Ranke's Hist. Ref.* II. 199 The fall of the Council of Regency, and the depressed state of the nobility in general. **1872** GEO. ELIOT *Middlem.* lxxxi, I thought he looked rather battered and depressed.

b. ***depressed area***, an area of economic depression.

1928 *Britain's Industrial Future* xx. 276 Already the local rates in the depressed areas have to shoulder too large a part of the burden of relieving unemployment. **1958** *Listener* 11 Sept. 371/2 There are no depressed areas now.

c. ***depressed class(es)***, in India, persons of the lowest castes, 'untouchables'.

1931 *Economist* 17 Oct. 696/1 The other Minorities, notably the Depressed Classes and the Anglo-Indians, have still got to be fitted into the scheme. **1957** *Encycl. Brit.* X. 13/2 He [*sc.* Gandhi] undertook several more fasts in the interests of communal tolerance and the rights of the depressed classes.

depressedly (dɪ'prɛstlɪ, -'prɛsɪdlɪ), *adv.* [f. prec. + -LY[2].] In a depressed manner.

1842 SOWERBY in *Proc. Berw. Nat. Club* II. No. x. 33 Shell clypeiform or depressedly conical. **1880** F. H. BURNETT *Louisiana* 9 'Yes', the girl replied depressedly.

depressent, var. DEPRESSANT *sb.* b.

depressible (dɪ'prɛsɪb(ə)l), *a.* [f. L. *dēpress-*, ppl. stem of *dēprimĕre* (see DEPRESS *v.*) + -BLE.] Capable of being depressed (*lit.* and *fig.*).

1860 O. W. HOLMES *Poet Breakf.-t.* v. 121 She is one of those young persons..who are impressible and of necessity depressible when their nervous systems are overtasked. **1881** GÜNTHER in *Encycl. Brit.* XII. 654/2 They [the hinged teeth of fishes] are, however, depressible in one direction only.

depressing (dɪ'prɛsɪŋ), *vbl. sb.* [f. DEPRESS *v.* + -ING[1].] The action of the verb DEPRESS; depression.

1641 WILKINS *Math. Magick* I. iv. (1648) 25 In the depressing, or elevating..of any weight. **1660** BOYLE *New Exp. Phys. Mech.* ix. 69 Upon the quick depressing of the Sucker.

de'pressing, *ppl. a.* [-ING[2].] That depresses (see the verb); usually in *fig.* senses, *esp.* 6; causing depression or lowness of spirits.

1789 W. BUCHAN *Dom. Med.* (1790) 467 Excessive fear, grief, anger, religious melancholy, or any of the depressing passions. **1814** SCOTT *Wav.* viii, The whole scene was depressing. **1882** NARES *Seamanship* (ed. 6) 205 A lower studding-sail..is a depressing sail.

Hence **de'pressingly** *adv.*

1847 in CRAIG. **1869** E. A. PARKES *Pract. Hygiene* (ed. 3) 369 The lowering of the external temperature..acts very depressingly on the very young and old. **1893** *Nat. Observer* 23 Dec. 137/2 An effect of profound isolation..depressingly real, suddenly encompassed me.

depressingness (dɪ'prɛsɪŋnɪs). [f. DEPRESSING *ppl. a.* + -NESS.] The quality of being depressing.

1923 *Glasgow Herald* 9 June 7, I wonder if he finds 'pervading depressingness' in these verses. **1927** *Chambers's Jrnl.* 3/2 More likely to stop a fellow from getting back to the mark, by its wretched 'depressingness'.

depression (dɪ'prɛʃən). [ad. L. *dēpressiōn-em*, n. of action f. *dēprimĕre* to press down, depress: perh. immed. a. F. *dépression* (14th c. in Hatzf.).] The action of depressing, or condition of being depressed; a depressed formation; that which is depressed: in various senses. (Opp. to *elevation*.)

1. *lit.* The action of pressing down, or fact of being pressed down; usually more widely: The action of lowering, or process of sinking; the condition of being lowered in position.

1656 BLOUNT *Glossogr.*, *Depression*, a pressing or weighing down. **1697** POTTER *Antiq. Greece* III. ix. (1715) 78 Flags, the Elevation whereof was a Signal to joyn Battle, the Depression to desist. **1803** *Med. Jrnl.* X. 245 With fracture, fissure, or depression of a portion of bone. **1855** LYELL *Elem. Geol.* vi. (ed. 5) 72 Movements of upheaval or depression. **1882** VINES *Sachs' Bot.* 825 The curve of growth follows all the elevations and depressions of the curve of temperature.

2. *spec.* **a.** *Astron.*, etc. (*a*) The angular distance of a star, the pole, etc., below the horizon (opp. to *altitude*); the angular distance of the visible horizon below the true horizontal plane, the DIP of the horizon; in *Surveying*, etc., the angular distance of an object below the horizontal plane through the point of observation (opp. to *elevation*). (*b*) The lowest altitude of a circumpolar star (or of the sun seen from within the polar circle), when it is on the meridian beneath the pole (opp. to *culmination*). (*c*) The apparent sinking of the celestial pole towards the horizon as the observer travels towards the equator.

c **1391** CHAUCER *Astrol.* II. §25 And than is the depressioun of the pol antartik, that is to seyn, than is the pol antartik bynethe the Orisonte the same quantite of space. **1594** BLUNDEVIL *Exerc.* III. I. xxxiii. (ed. 7) 346 The depression or lowest Meridian Altitude of the starres. **1605** BACON *Adv. Learn.* I. vi. §10 (1873) 48 He takes knowledge of the depression of the southern pole. **1667** *Phil. Trans.* II. 438 The degree of its [the Needle's] depression under the Horizon. **1727–51** CHAMBERS *Cycl.*, *Depression of the pole*.. *Depression of the visible horizon.* **1856** KANE *Arct. Expl.* I. viii. 79 The sun's lower culmination, if such a term can be applied to his midnight depression.

b. *Gunnery.* The lowering of the muzzle of a gun below the horizontal line.

1853 STOCQUELER *Milit. Encycl.*, *Depression*, the pointing of any piece of ordnance, so that its shot may be projected under the point-blank line.

c. *Surg.* The operation of couching for cataract.

1851–60 MAYNE *Expos. Lex.*, *Depression*..a term for one of the operations for cataract.

3. *concr.* A depressed or sunken formation on a surface; a hollow, a low place or part.

1665 *Phil. Trans.* I. 42 Of the Nature of the Ground..and of the several risings and depressions thereof. **1789** W. BUCHAN *Dom. Med.* (1790) 591 A dislocation of the humerus may be known by a depression or cavity on the top of the shoulder. **1855** LYELL *Elem. Geol.* xxix. (ed. 5) 520 The Curral is..one of three great valleys..a second depression called the Serra d' Agoa being almost as deep. **1884** BOWER & SCOTT *De Bary's Phaner.* 53 The leaves of the above Crassulaceæ have round spots or depressions easily seen with the naked eye. **1885** *Manch. Exam.* 13 June 5/3 The depressions, which are of course warmer..than the plateaus.

4. *fig.* **a.** The action of putting down or bringing low, or the fact or condition of being brought low (in station, fortunes, etc.). Now *rare*.

a **1533** FRITH *Wks.* 5 (R.) Aduersitie, tribulation, worldly depression. **1631** MASSINGER *Emp. of East* Ded., When the iniquity of those times laboured the depression of approved goodness. **1741** MIDDLETON *Cicero* I. v. 368 The depression of the family, and the ruin of their fortunes. **1872** YEATS *Growth Comm.* 136 The depression of the barons, during the Wars of the Roses.

†**b.** Suppression. *Obs.*

1656 HOBBES *Six Lessons* Wks. 1845 VII. 278 You.. profess mathematics, and theology, and practise the depression of the truth in both.

†**c.** Disparagement, depreciation. *Obs.*

1628 FELTHAM *Resolves* II. lxxiii, Thus depressing others, it [pride] seeketh to raise it selfe, and by this depression angers them. **1659** BP. WALTON *Consid. Considered* 286

Things which tend to the depression of the esteem of the Hebrew Text.

5. a. A lowering in quality, vigour, or amount; the state of being lowered or reduced in force, activity, intensity, etc. In mod. use *esp.* of trade; spec. ***the Depression***, the financial and industrial 'slump' of 1929 and subsequent years. Also *attrib.*

1793 VANSITTART *Refl. Peace* 57 The depression of the public funds..began long before the war. **1826** *Ann. Reg.* I A continuance of that depression in manufactures and commerce. **1837** WHITTOCK *Bk. Trades* (1842) 392 The consequence has been a general depression in price for all but the best work. **1845** STODDART in *Encycl. Metrop.* I. 64/1 There is not in actions, as there is in qualities, a simple scale of elevation and depression. **1886** (*title*), Third Report of the Royal Commission appointed to inquire into the Depression of Trade and Industry. **1934** A. HUXLEY *Beyond Mexique Bay* 233 Since the depression, books on Mexico have been almost as numerous..as books on Russia. **1935** 'J. GUTHRIE' *Little Country* xiii. 212 'I thought you had a baby.' 'No, darling,' said Carol. 'None of us are having them now. It's the depression.' **1935** *Punch* 19 June 719/1 All the wireless sets in Little Wobbly are pre-depression models. **1957** M. SHARP *Eye of Love* iii. 39 It was the Depression that had finished him off. **1963** H. GARNER in R. Weaver *Canad. Short Stories* 2nd Ser. (1968) 37 An old Scots syndicalist I'd met on a road gang..in the early years of the depression.

b. Lowering in pitch, flattening (of the voice, or a musical note).

1845 STODDART in *Encycl. Metrop.* I. 176/1 A slight degree of elevation or depression, of length or shortness, of weakness or force, serves to mark a very sensible difference in the emotion meant to be expressed. **1878** W. H. STONE *Sci. Basis Music* v. 66 The present music should be carefully gone over..and the modified notes marked..with a mark of elevation or depression, according to their specific key relationship.

c. A lowering of the column of mercury in the barometer or of the atmospheric pressure which is thereby measured; *spec.* in *Meteorol.* a centre of minimum pressure, or the system of winds around it (= CYCLONE 1 c).

1881 R. H. SCOTT in *Gd. Words* July 454 Barometrical depressions or cyclones. *Mod. Weather Report*, A deep depression is forming over our western coasts. The depression of yesterday has passed over England to the German Ocean.

d. *Path.* Lowering of the vital functions or powers; a state of reduced vitality.

1803 *Med. Jrnl.* X. 116 Great depression..has without doubt lately shewn itself in a very remarkable manner in the influenza. **1843** LEVER *J. Hinton* ii, I aroused myself from the depression of nearly thirty hours' sea-sickness. **1875** B. MEADOWS *Clin. Observ.* 38 The inflammatory nature of the local affection was much more severe, and the constitutional depression..more marked.

6. a. The condition of being depressed in spirits; dejection.

1665 *Baker's Chron.* an. 1660 (R.) Lambert, in great depression of spirit, twice pray'd him to let him escape. **1752** JOHNSON *Rambler* No. 204 ¶7 He observed their depression and was offended. **1857** MRS. CARLYLE *Lett.* II. 326 Such horrible depression of spirits. **1876** GEO. ELIOT *Dan. Der.* lxix, He found her in a state of deep depression, overmastered by those distasteful miserable memories.

b. *Psychol.* Freq. a sign of psychiatric disorder or a component of various psychoses, with symptoms of misery, anguish, or guilt accompanied by headache, insomnia, etc.

1905 *Psychol. Rev.* XII. 111 If these symptoms of depression—the motor retardation, the difficulty of apprehension and of association—become aggravated, one finds various forms of melancholia. **1934** H. C. WARREN *Dict. Psychol.* 73/1 *Depression*..the pathological usage refers to a mood of pronounced hopelessness and overwhelming feeling of inadequacy or unworthiness. **1960** KOESTLER *Lotus & Robot* II. viii. 202 Even patients with severe depression-psychosis..turned their heads slowly and worked up a mask-like smile. **1962** *Lancet* 2 June 1171/1 Even psychiatrists may profit from the reminder that 'events at the onset of depression..must be interpreted with caution for failure at work..or in a love affair may be early symptoms, rather than causes'.

†**7.** *Alg.* Reduction to a lower degree or power.

1727-51 CHAMBERS *Cycl.*, *Depression of equations.* **1823** CRABB *Technol. Dict.*, *Depression of an Equation* (*Algeb.*), the reducing an equation to lower degrees, as a biquadratic to a cubic equation, or a cubic to a quadratic.

†**de'pressity.** *Obs. rare*$^{-0}$.

1727 BAILEY vol. II, *Depressity*, a lowness.

depressive (dɪˈprɛsɪv), *a.* [f. L. *dēpress-*, ppl. stem of *dēprimĕre* to press down, DEPRESS + -IVE.]

1. Tending to press or force down. *rare.*

1620 VENNER *Via Recta* vii. 112 By reason of their compressiue and depressiue force, they protrude and driue downe the meats from the stomacke.

2. *fig.* **a.** Tending to produce depression, *esp.* of the spirits; of depressing nature.

1727 THOMSON *Britannia* 274 Even where the keen depressive North descends. **1787** *Misc.* in *Ann. Reg.* 157 A compliance..would lead her friends into some depressive sensations. *a* **1847** MRS. SHERWOOD *Lady of Manor* V. xxix. 114 In regions so depressive both to the bodily and intellectual powers. **1862** *Cornh. Mag.* VI. 607 It is a kind of stimulation..which is not followed by any unhealthy depressive reaction.

b. Involving or characterized by depression as a psychiatric illness. Hence as *sb.*, one who suffers from this condition. Cf. MANIC-DEPRESSIVE.

1905 *Psychol. Rev.* XII. 113 The German alienists are taking up again..depressive insanity, to which they rightly ascribe a great importance. **1951** R. E. MONEY-KYRLE *Psychoanalysis & Politics* iv. 84 Religion is a form of psychotherapy which promotes a belief in the existence of idealized good objects against persecutory and depressive guilt. **1962** *Lancet* 2 June 1171/2 An undiagnosed depressive illness is one of the commonest fatal mistakes in medicine. **1962** *Times* 13 Dec. 15/2 Antonio was an endogenous depressive. **1965** J. POLLITT *Depression & its Treatment* iii. 33 Guilt forms a nucleus for many delusional complaints of retarded depressives.

Hence **de'pressively** *adv.*, **de'pressiveness.**

a **1670** HACKET *Cent. Serm.* (1675) 424 If I had a thousand tongues and inventions, I should speak faintly and depressively of that supernal Palace. **1832** CARLYLE *Ess.* (1872) IV. 112 Ill-health, and its concomitant depressiveness.

depressor (dɪˈprɛsə(r)). Also 7 -er, -our. [a. L. *dēpressor*, agent-n. from *dēprimĕre*, *dēpress-* to press down, DEPRESS. In OF. *dépresseur*.]

1. One who or that which depresses (in various senses: see the verb).

1611 COTGR., *Abbaisseur*, an abaser..depresser, humbler. **1621** BP. MOUNTAGU *Diatribæ* 112 That..would haue raised it selfe against all depressors and detractors. *a* **1639** WOTTON in Gutch *Coll. Cur.* I. 219 Those that rayse stand ever in.. hazard to be thought..the fittest depressours. **1868** BAIN, The causes of pain and the depressors of vitality.

2. *Anat.* and *Phys.* **a.** A muscle which depresses or pulls down the part to which it is attached; also *attrib.* as ***depressor muscle***. **b.** ***depressor nerve***: a branch of the vagus, the stimulation of which lowers the pressure of the blood.

1615 CROOKE *Body of Man* 741 Euery leuator or lifting muscle hath a depressor or sinking muscle. **1748** HARTLEY *Observ. Man* I. ii. 148 The Depressors of the lower Jaw. **1872** HUXLEY *Phys.* ix. 234 The lower [eye-] lid has no special depressor. **1875** H. C. WOOD *Therap.* (1879) 132 The vagi and depressor nerves did not appear to be affected.

3. *Surg.* An instrument for pressing down some part or organ.

1874 KNIGHT *Dict. Mech.*, *Depressor* (*Surgery*), an instrument like a curved spatula, used for reducing or pushing into place an obtruding part. Such are used in operations on the skull..and in couching a cataract. **1883** *Syd. Soc. Lex.*, *Tongue depressor*, a flattened metallic plate for depressing the tongue, in order to see the throat.

†**depressure** (dɪˈprɛʃ(j)ʊə(r)). *Obs.* [f. L. ppl. stem *dēpress-* + -URE: cf. L. *pressūra* pressure, f. *premĕre, press-*.]

1. The action of pressing down; = DEPRESSION 1.

1699 E. TYSON in *Phil. Trans.* XXI. 432 That this depressure happened whilst the Bones were Cartilaginous.

2. *concr.* A depressed or sunken part of a surface; = DEPRESSION 3.

1621 G. SANDYS *Ovid's Met.* XIII. (1626) 278 The purple blood from that depressure fled. **1675** EVELYN *Terra* (1776) 38 To fill up the hollows and Depressures of the ground. **1677** PLOT *Oxfordsh.* 106 Those uniform eminencies and depressures, those waved and transverse lineations.

3. *fig.* The action of putting down, bringing low, or humbling; debasement; = DEPRESSION 4, 5.

1656 JEANES *Mixt. Schol. Div.* 60 Earthly mindedness, though it doth no' quite degrade the soule of its immortality yet it is a great depressure and embasement thereof. **1768-74** TUCKER *Lt. Nat* (1852) II. 137 To give them an eminence..above others, which is as well answered by the depressure of everything else above them, as by their own advancement.

de'pressurize, *v.* [f. DE- II + PRESSURIZE *v.*] *trans.* To cause an appreciable drop in the pressure of the gas inside (a container, etc.), esp. to a natural level from an artificially sustained level (in quot. 1960, to subject to decompression: cf. DECOMPRESS *v.* a). So **de'pressurized** *ppl. a.*

1944 *Aviation* July 278/3 While in action, the cabin is de-pressurized and demand oxygen employed. **1947** *Jrnl. R. Aeronaut. Soc.* LI. 972/1 This altitude was the maximum at which it was reasonably possible for a fit pilot to retain sufficient control to make a normal descent, should the cabin for any reason become de-pressurised. **1958** *Daily Mail* 12 Nov. 4/5 There was a hissing sound as Larry helped him depressurise the airlock. **1960** KOESTLER *Lotus & Robot* vi. 188 They cannot go back into the pressure chamber to dissolve the bubbles by getting gradually depressurized. **1963** *Times* 24 May 12/7 An Aer-Lingus Viscount..made an emergency dive of 12,000 ft. today after a door unfastened and the passenger cabin became depressurized.

depreter (*Building*): see DEPETER.

depretiate, obs. form of DEPRECIATE.

†**de'preve**, *v. Obs.* [a. OF. *des-*, *depreuve*, stressed stem-form of *desprover* to disprove: cf. DEPROVE.] By-form of DISPROVE.

c **1450** LONELICH *Grail* xlv. 726 What they Cowden seyn to Cristen lawe, Owther it depreven In Ony Sawe. **1465** MARG. PASTON in *Lett.* No. 506 II. 196 Ye have up an enquest to depreve ther wytnesse.

depreve, obs. form of DEPRIVE.

'depriment, *a.* (*sb.*) *rare.* [ad. L. *dēpriment-em*, pr. pple. of *dēprimĕre* to press down, DEPRESS, f. DE- I. 1 + *premĕre* to press.] **a.** Depressing; pressing or forcing down. Also *fig.*

1713 DERHAM *Phys. Theol.* IV. ii. 99 The Attollent and Depriment Muscles. **1721** BAILEY, *Depriment* [in *Anatomy*] is one of the straight Muscles which moves the Ball of the Eye. **1939** *Mind* XLVIII. 282 We have the peculiar 'depriment' emotion of reverence in the contemplation of the moral law.

b. as *sb.* Something that depresses or lowers.

a **1624** BP. M. SMITH *Serm. Job* xxix. 14 Praises they esteeme for bubbles, and applauses for bables..robes of scarlet or purple for depriments and detriments.

deprint (ˈdiːprɪnt), *sb.* ? *Obs.* [f. DE- + PRINT *sb.*] An offprint. Hence **de'print** *v.* (*Cent. Dict.* Suppl., 1909).

1885 SKEAT in *Academy* 22 Aug. 121/3 Various terms, such as 'deprint', 'exprint', &c., have been proposed to denote a separately printed copy of a pamphlet. **1895** (*title*) Modern Language Notes: Deprints of Articles by George C. Keidel, Ph.D.

depriorize: see DE- II. 1.

†**de'prise**, *v. Obs. rare.* [a. F. *dépriser* in OF. *despriser*, f. *dé-*, *des-*, L. *dis-* + *priser* to PRIZE. Cf. DISPRIZE.] *trans.* To depreciate, undervalue.

c **1550** LYNDESAY *Satyre* in Pinkerton *Sc. Poems Repr.* (1792) II. 206 Now quhill the King misknawis the veritie Be scho ressavit, then we will be deprysit.

†**de'prisure.** *Obs. rare.* [f. prec. + -URE.] Lowering in value or esteem, depreciation.

1648 W. MOUNTAGUE *Devout Ess.* vi. §2 (R.) A great abatement and deprisure of their souls in the account of God.

deprivable (dɪˈpraɪvəb(ə)l), *a.* [f. DEPRIVE *v.* + -ABLE.] Liable to be deprived; subject to deprivation.

1593 ABP. BANCROFT *Daung. Posit.* II. xii. 61 They [the Bishops]..are..depriuable. **1597** HOOKER *Eccl. Pol.* V. lxxxi. §10 The persons that enjoy them, possesse them wrongfully, and are depriuable at all howers. **1660** R. SHERINGHAM *King's Suprem.* viii. (1682) 70 They may thereby make him deprivable at their pleasure. *Mod.* Advantages of which he is not deprivable.

†**depri'vado.** *Obs. rare.* [f. DEPRIVE *v.*, or L. *dēprīvātus* deprived, after nouns in -ADO from Sp.] One deprived (of office, commission, licence, etc.).

1728 NORTH *Mem. Musick* (1846) 133, I..being for many years an alien to the faculty, and at present a deprivado.

deprival (dɪˈpraɪvəl). [f. DEPRIVE *v.*: see -AL[1] 5.] The act of depriving; DEPRIVATION.

1611 W. SCLATER *Key* (1629) 86 For argues it not a deniall, or deprivall, of grace? *a* **1638** MEDE *Disc. 1 Cor.* x. 5 Wks. (1672) I. 258 A wofull sign of..deprival of Eternal life. **1875** JOWETT *Plato* (ed. 2) V. 118 Punishing the citizen who offends with temporary deprival of his rights. **1886** L. O. PIKE *Year-bks. 13-14 Edw. III*, Introd. 66 The King..had thus the power of institution..and consequently the power of deprival.

†**'deprivate**, *ppl. a. Obs. rare.* [ad. med.L. *dēprīvāt-us*, pa. pple. of *dēprīvāre*.] Deprived.

1560 ROLLAND *Crt. Venus* I. 252 In verteous werk, scho beand depriuate..quhill I may bruik my liue, Hir from my hart I will near depriue.

'deprivate, *v. rare.* [f. med.L. *dēprīvāt-*, ppl. stem of *dēprīvāre*: see DEPRIVE.] To deprive.

1832 CARLYLE in *Fraser's Mag.* V. 257 Never..has Man been..deprivated of any faculty whatsoever that he in any era was possessed of.

deprivation (dɛprɪˈveɪʃən). [ad. med.L. *dēprīvātiōn-em*, n. of action from *dēprīvāre* to DEPRIVE.]

1. The action of depriving or fact of being deprived; the taking away *of* anything enjoyed; dispossession, loss.

1533-4 *Act 25 Hen. VIII*, c. 12 In ieopardie of loss and depriuacion of his crowne and dignitee roial. *a* **1635** NAUNTON *Fragm. Reg.* (Arb.) 15 All her deprivations either of life or liberty, being legall, and necessitated. **1731** CHANDLER tr. *Limborch's Hist. Inquis.* II. 2 Excommunication, Deprivation of Ecclesiastical Burial. **1794** G. ADAMS *Nat. & Exp. Philos.* II. xvii. 250 [Of evils] there is none more justly dreaded..than a deprivation of sight. **1830** D'ISRAELI *Chas. I* III. vi. 79 He accounted these deprivations not among the least of the many he now endured. **1875** JOWETT *Plato* (ed. 2) III. 260 The loss of a son or brother, or the deprivation of fortune.

†**b.** Const. *from*. *Obs.*

1570-1 *Act of Assembly* in Row *Hist. Kirk* (1842) 43 Also the suspension and deprivation of them therefra. **1579** FULKE *Heskins' Parl.* 317 She..was punished with depriuation from both kindes [in the sacrament]. **1586** T. B. *La Primaud. Fr. Acad.* I. (1589) 654 Danger of deprivaton from all authoritie by them.

2. *spec.* The action of depriving any one of an office, dignity, or benefice; dispossession, deposition; *esp.* the depriving an ecclesiastic of a benefice or preferment as an act of punishment or discipline.

1551 CRANMER *Answ. to Gardiner* 2 The occasion of your worthy depriuation and punishment. **1587** FLEMING *Contn. Holinshed* III. 1357/2 Sufficient force whereby the bull of hir maiesties depriuation might be publikelie executed.

1641 *Termes de la Ley* 110 b, *Deprivation* is when an Abbot, Bishop, Parson, Vicar, Prebend, &c. is deprived or deposed from his preferment for any matter in fact or in Law. *a* **1715** BURNET *Own Time* (1724) I. 192 Sheldon..seemed to apprehend that a very small number would fall under the deprivation, and that the gross of the party would conform. **1839** KEIGHTLEY *Hist. Eng.* II. 90 A sentence of deprivation ..was pronounced. **1855** MACAULAY *Hist. Eng.* IV. 49 Several months had been allowed him [Sherlock] before he incurred suspension, several months more before he incurred deprivation.

deprivative (dɪˈprɪvətɪv), *a.* [f. med.L. *dēprīvāt-* ppl. stem + -IVE: see next.] Of, pertaining to, or characterized by deprivation.
1727 BAILEY vol. II, *Deprivative*, of Deprivation. **1865** *Reader* 3 June 632/2 A man..entirely lost his sight by the excessive use of tobacco. He was..cured by adopting a mild antiphlogistic and deprivative treatment.

deprive (dɪˈpraɪv), *v.* Also 4–6 -pryve, 5 -preve, -priff. [a. OF. *depriver* (Godef.), ad. late L. **dēprīvāre* (see *dēprīvātio* in Du Cange), f. DE- I. 3 + *prīvāre* to deprive.]

I. 1. *trans.* To divest, strip, bereave, dispossess *of* (formerly †*from*) a possession. ***to deprive*** (a person) *of* (a thing) = to take it away from him.
c **1330** R. BRUNNE *Chron.* (1810) 255 Depriued þei our Kyng of alle þe tenement of londes of Gascoyn. *a* **1400–50** *Alexander* 1469 Þus was Iaudes of ioy and iolite depryued [*v.r.* depreuett]. **1426** AUDELAY *Poems* 24 These preletus of her prevelache thay deprevon. *c* **1430** LYDG. *Bochas* (ed. Wayland) 68 b, He was assented to deprive Worthy Anchus from his estate royal. **1548** HALL *Chron.* I. 17 Kyng Roberte ..firste deprived the Erle George of all his dignitees and possessions. **1586** T. B. *La Primaud. Fr. Acad.* I. 218 Henry the fift by force deprived his father from the empire. **1632** SANDERSON *Serm.* 30 For his obstinate refusall of Conformitie justly deprived from his Benefice in this Diocesse. **1660** BOYLE *New Exp. Phys. Mech.* Concl. 395, I have for diverse Yeares been deprived of His Company. **1782** PRIESTLEY *Corrupt. Chr.* I. I. 83 Arius was deprived of his office, and excommunicated. **1793** MRS. E. PARSONS *Woman as she should be* IV. 72 Your uncle..being deprived from managing your business. **1875** JOWETT *Plato* (ed. 2) IV. 283 To deprive life of ideals is to deprive it of all higher and comprehensive aims.

†**b.** with two objects, either of which might in the passive become the subject. *Obs.* Cf. sense 5, in which the personal object disappears.
c **1450** tr. *De Imitatione* III. xlv, He is depryued very vertues. **1539** TONSTALL *Serm. Palm Sund.* (1823) 45, I wyl curse him and depriue hym his kyngedome. *a* **1562** in G. Cavendish *Wolsey* (1893) 240 All is depryved me. **1621** LADY M. WROTH *Urania* 352 Why was sweet and dainty Philistella depriued mine eyes? **1667** MILTON *P.L.* IX. 857 Thee I have missed, and thought it long, depriv'd Thy presence. **1802** MARIAN MOORE *Lascelles* II. 240 To deprive themselves the pleasure of her company. **1814** MRS. JANE WEST *Alicia* III. 141 My child!.. Even in thy early infancy Deprived my care.

2. To divest of office; to inflict deprivation upon; *esp.* in reference to ecclesiastical offices.
c **1325** *E.E. Allit. P.* B. 1738 De-parted is þy pryncipalté, depryued þou worþes, Þy rengne rafte is þe fro. *c* **1400** MAUNDEV. (1839) iii. 20 The Emperour of Costantynoble maketh the Patriarks..and depryueth hem.. whan he fyndeth ony cause. **1513** MORE in Grafton *Chron.* (1568) II. 758 Edward revengyng his fathers death, deprived King Henry, and attayned the Crowne. **1630** *R. Johnson's Kingd. & Commw.* 561 He [an officer] is sometime deprived, and sometime strangled. **1706** HEARNE *Collect.* 15 Feb., The Bp. ..depriv'd him for three years. **1827** HALLAM *Const. Hist.* (1876) I. vii. 394 Archbishop Bancroft deprived a considerable number of puritan clergymen.
absol. *c* **1535** DR. LAYTON in *Lett. on Suppr. Monast.* (Camden) 76 Ye shall not deprive or visite but upon substanciall growndes.

3. To keep (a person) out *of* (†*from*) what he would otherwise have; to debar *from*.
c **1374** CHAUCER *Troylus* IV. 241 (269) Why wiltow me fro Ioye thus depryve? *c* **1590** MARLOWE *Faust.* iii. 82 In being depriv'd of Everlasting bliss. **1611** BIBLE *Isa.* xxxviii. 10, I am depriued of the residue of my yeeres. **1651** HOBBES *Govt. & Soc.* x. §2 Subjects..deprived from all possibility to acquire..by their industry, necessaries to sustain the strength of their bodies and minds. **1663** GERBIER *Counsel* B iv a, A Monster, which deprived also me from a publick imployment, during the space of seaventeen years. **1771** *Junius Lett.* lxiv. 327 The mode of trial..deprive[s] the subject of all the benefits of a trial by jury. **1884** LOWELL in *Daily News* 7 Oct. 2/7 Is it prudent to deprive whole classes of it [the ballot] any longer?

†**b.** *absol.* *Obs. rare*$^{-1}$.
1605 SHAKS. *Lear* I. ii. 4 Should I..permit The curiosity of Nations to deprive me.

†**c.** Const. with two objects. *Obs.*
1590 MARLOWE *2nd Pt. Tamburl.* v. iii, My soul doth weep to see Your sweet desires depriv'd my Company. **1671** MILTON *P.R.* III. 23 Wherefore deprive All Earth her wonder at thy acts? **1694** tr. *Milton's Lett. State* Sept. 1657, That so signal a prowess and fortitude may never..be deprived the fruit and due applause of all your pious undertakings.

†**4.** To remove (*from*) or cut off from access. *Obs.*
1542 BOORDE *Dyetary* viii. (1870) 249 Chambres the whiche be depryued clene from the sonne and open ayre. **1594** CAREW *Tasso* (1881) 42 Emaus is a Citie, which small space Doth from royall Hierusalem depriue.

†**b.** To keep off, avert. *Obs. rare*$^{-1}$.
1627 HAKEWILL *Apol.* (1630) 166 Ale was his meate, his drinke, his cloth, Ale did his death deprive; And, could hee still have drunke his ale, He had beene still alive.

II. †**5.** To take away (a possession); to carry off, remove. *Obs.*
c **1325** *E.E. Allit. P.* B. 185 For..depryue dowrie of wydoez, Man may mysse þe myrþe, þat much is to prayse. *c* **1430** LYDG. *Min. Poems* (1840) 63 This blissid name.. That, first of alle, our thraldom can deprive. *c* **1510** BARCLAY *Mirr. Gd. Manners* (1570) F iij b, He sodenly striketh with worde, or els knife, And..depriveth name or life. **1593** SHAKS. *Lucrece* 1186 (Globe) 'Tis honour to deprive dishonour'd life. **1605** STOW *Annales* 1408 His head was seuered from his body by the Axe at three stroakes, but the first deadly, and absolutely depriuing all sense and motion. **1623** COCKERAM, *Depriue*, to take away. **1654** tr. *Scudery's Curia Pol.* 96 An inheritance, which..fortune or ill events have deprived from them.

deprived (dɪˈpraɪvd), *ppl. a.* [f. DEPRIVE *v.* + -ED.] Dispossessed, divested; bereft; subjected to deprivation; *esp.* dispossessed of a benefice. In modern use freq. applied to children who lack the benefits of normal home life, parental affection, etc.
1552 HULOET, Depriued, *abactus, detectus de gradu.. priuatus.* **1710** HEARNE *Collect.* 2 Mar., No Nonjuring or depriv'd Bp. *a* **1774** GOLDSM. *Surv. Exp. Philos.* (1776) II. 168 Birds..are deprived of this apparatus. **1855** MACAULAY *Hist. Eng.* IV. 39 The deprived Archbishop showed no disposition to move. **1945** *Lancet* 3 Mar. 294/1 Many of them tell how bitter were their feelings as 'deprived children'. **1957** *Times Lit. Suppl.* 25 Oct. 637/1 The plot concerns a middle-aged spinster who was a 'deprived' child overshadowed by her brother and his tragic early death..in a search for the secret of her unhappy childhood.

†**deprivement** (dɪˈpraɪvmənt). *Obs.* [f. DEPRIVE *v.* + -MENT.] The action of depriving or fact of being deprived; deprivation.
1630 *R. Johnson's Kingd. & Commw.* 561 Five have died naturall deaths after deprivement. **1657** G. STARKEY *Helmont's Vind.* 3 The deprivement of that knowledge [is] intolerable and not to be rested in. **1691–8** NORRIS *Pract. Disc.* 223 If..by Deprivements or positive Inflictions he diminish our Happiness. **1703** D. WILLIAMSON *Serm. bef. Gen. Assembly* 48 The Deprivement of Presbyterian Ministers has been double the time of theirs [the Episcopal Clergy].

depriver (dɪˈpraɪvə(r)). [f. as prec. + -ER[1].] One who or that which deprives, or takes away possessions, rights, etc.
c **1440** *Jacob's Well* (E.E.T.S.) 62 Þise dyffoulerys & depryueres of holy cherche. *a* **1541** WYATT *Poet. Wks.* (1861) 11 Love slayeth mine heart, while Fortune is depriver Of all my comfort. *a* **1658** CLEVELAND *Poems* 38 (T.) Depriver of those solid joys Which sack creates. **1721** STRYPE *Eccl. Mem.* III. xii. 109 These deprivers were so quick..that they stayed not for the appearances of the priests to answer for themselves.

depriving (dɪˈpraɪvɪŋ), *vbl. sb.* [f. DEPRIVE *v.* + -ING[1].] The action of DEPRIVE *v.*; deprivation.
1475 *Bk. Noblesse* 74 Upon the depryvyng or yelding up of that dukedom. **1576** BAKER *Jewell of Health* 65 b, This water ..prevayleth against the Apoplexie or depriving of senses. **1621** FITZ-GEFFRAY *Elisha's Lament.* (1622) 16 Double our lamentation for him at his depriving [= our d. of him]. **1705** HEARNE *Collect.* 26 Aug., Against the Depriving of Bps. by the Civil Magistrate. **1749** FIELDING *Tom Jones* VIII. xiv, The depriving it of that power.

†**deprœliˈation.** *Obs.* [n. of action from L. *dēprœliārī* to war violently, to battle; f. DE- I. 3 + *prœliārī* to fight, *prœlium* a fight, battle.]
1623 COCKERAM, *Deprœliation*, a battell.

deprofessionalize: see DE- II. 1.

de profundis: see DE I. 7.

deˈprogramme, *v.* Chiefly *U.S.* Also *U.S.* **deprogram.** [f. DE- II. 1 + PROGRAM, PROGRAMME *v.*] *trans.* To release from apparent brainwashing (esp. by a religious cult) by the systematic reindoctrination of conventional values. So **deˈprogrammer**, a person who carries out this process; **deˈprogramming** *vbl. sb.*
1973 *Sunday Advocate-News* (Barbados) 21 Jan. 4/4 Many American parents..feel so strongly about the cults.. that they are resorting to kidnapping and brainwashing— which they call deprogramming—to bring their children home. *Ibid.* 4/7 One 23-year-old woman [screamed]..at the de-programmers that they were devils. **1973** *Newsweek* 30 Aug. 52/3 His parents..tried to push him into a rented car and take him off to be 'de-programed'. **1976** *Guardian* 13 Sept. 6/1 Deprogramming is defined as a process of constant argument and preaching which sometimes persuades a Moon Person to defect. In the United States, it has sometimes involved violence. **1979** M. TRIPP *Cruel Victim* i. 17 In America..a young member of the Hare Krishna sect brought a prosecution against a man who tried to deprogramme him. **1981** *Times* 1 Apr. 3/6 Some parents.. told how they managed to..induce back their children, and 'deprogramme' them from the Moonie doctrine. **1983** P. KURTH *Anastasia* (1985) III. xiv. 418 A blustering, seemingly unbalanced former KGB agent who had defected to the West and, in the words of one CIA deprogrammer, 'flipped his lid'.

deproletarianize (ˌdiːprəʊlɪˈtɛərɪənaɪz), *v.* Also **deproletarize.** [f. DE- II. 1 + PROLETARIANIZE *v.*] *trans.* To free of proletarian character or qualities; to cause to lose proletarian nature. Also *absol.* Hence **deproleˌtarianiˈzation**; **deproleˈtarianized** *ppl. a.*; **deproletariaˈnizable**, **deproleˈtarian** *adjs.*
1954 *Encounter* Dec. 29/2 The net effect of capitalism, then, is in the long run to deproletarise. **1957** T. KILMARTIN tr. *Aron's Opium of Intellectuals* iii. 72 In concrete terms, what would the triumph of a 'deproletarianised' working class involve? **1959** *Economist* 16 May 601 The slogan for the 1960s—more exciting perhaps than euphonic—should be to deproletarianise British society, both materially and psychologically. *Ibid.* 602/1 The social importance of what can be called the 'deproletarianisable' income groups also means..that the Conservatives should never again consider imposing restrictive controls on hire purchase. *Ibid.* 30 May 834/1 The signs of deproletarianization are as yet few and far between... A 'deproletarianized' family will surely expect to pay an economic price or rent for its house, not to have a council house provided for it. **1961** R. WILLIAMS *Long Revolution* 327 In the 'deproletarian' period since 1945. **1967** *Listener* 17 Aug. 205/1, I have never had anything but hatred and opposition for deproletarianising and back-to-the-land schemes.

†**deˈprome**, *v.* *Obs. rare.* [ad. L. *dēprōmĕre* to draw out, fetch away, f. DE- I. 2 + *prōmĕre* to bring forth, produce.] *trans.* To draw out or forth; to produce.
a **1652** BROME *City Wit* II. i. Wks. 1873 I. 297, I will only deprome, or take out a little stuffing first. **1654** Z. COKE *Logick* (1657) A viij, From it, as from a spirituall Artillery, you may deprome all weapons of reason. **1657** TOMLINSON *Renou's Disp.* 333 Both [artichocks] indeed are depromed from that tribe.

†**deˈprompt**, *v.* *Obs. rare*$^{-1}$. [f. L. *dēprompt-*, ppl. stem of *dēprōmĕre*: see prec.] = prec.
1586 FERNE *Blaz. Gentrie* 56 From a vayled and couered speech did deprompt the hidden secrets and witty sentences of philosophy.

†**deˈpromption.** *Obs. rare*$^{-0}$. [n. of action f. L. *dēprōmĕre*: see prec.]
1656 BLOUNT *Glossogr.*, *Depromption*, a drawing or bringing forth.

†**deˈproperate**, *v.* *Obs. rare*$^{-0}$. [f. ppl. stem of L. *dēproperāre* to make great haste, f. DE- I. 3 + *properāre* to make haste.]
1623 COCKERAM, *Deproperate*, to make too much speed.
Hence †**depropeˈration.**
1727 BAILEY, *Deproperation*, a making haste or speed.

†**deˈprostrate**, *a.* *Obs. rare*$^{-1}$. [f. DE- I. 3 + PROSTRATE *a.*] Extremely prostrate; grovelling.
1610 G. FLETCHER *Christ's Vict.* I. xliii, His unsmooth tongue, and his deprostrate stile.

deproteinize (diːˈprəʊtiːnaɪz), *v.* [f. DE- II. 1 + PROTEIN + -IZE.] *trans.* To remove protein from, usu. as a purification measure in a process of chemical isolation. Hence **deˌproteiniˈzation**; **deˈproteinizing** *vbl. sb.* and *ppl. a.*
1956 *Nature* 4 Feb. 237/2 The plasma was deproteinized, and the resultant liquid..desalted. **1962** J. H. KINOSHITA et al. in A. Pirie *Lens Metabolism Rel. Cataract* 405 The lens was homogenized in the deproteinizing mixture. **1963** F. HAUROWITZ *Chem. & Function of Proteins* ii. 20 This method finds extensive use in clinical laboratories in the deproteinization of biological fluids. **1967** *Oceanogr. & Marine Biol.* V. 347 Electron micrographs of cuticle deproteinized with hot potassium hydroxide.

deprotestantize, deprovincialize: see DE- II. 1.

†**deˈprove**, *v.* *Obs.* [Early var. of *desprove*, DISPROVE: cf. DEPREVE.] *trans.* To disprove, refute, contradict, disapprove.
1450–1530 *Myrr. our Ladye* 8 The more presumptuous wyll he be to fynde defaulte and to deproue..tho thynges that he vnderstondyth not.

depside (ˈdɛpsaɪd). *Chem.* [ad. G. *depsid* (Fischer & Freudenberg 1910, in *Justus Liebig's Ann. d. Chem.* CCCLXXII. 35), f. Gr. δέψ-ειν to knead (see quot. 1910) + -IDE.] Any of a group of organic compounds found principally in lichens (see quot. 1956).
1910 *Jrnl. Chem. Soc.* XCVIII. I. 266 It will no doubt be possible to prepare, by similar means, a large number of analogous substances from other hydroxybenzoic acids, and since many undoubtedly occur in nature, as, for example, tannin, it is considered advisable to classify them under the collective name *depside* (δέψειν tan). **1935** [see next]. **1956** E. H. RODD *Chem. Carbon Compounds* III. xii. 784 Depsides are substances derived from two or more molecules of phenolcarboxylic acids by esterification of a carboxyl group of one molecule..with a hydroxyl group of a second. **1959** [see next]. **1967** M. E. HALE *Biol. Lichens* viii. 111 The depsides..make up the largest group of lichen substances.

depsidone (ˈdɛpsɪdəʊn). *Chem.* [a. G. *depsidon* (Y. Asahina 1934, in *Acta Phytochimica* VIII. 34), f. prec. + -ONE.] Any of a group of compounds related to the depsides and found almost exclusively in lichens, having the benzene rings joined by an ether linkage as well as by the ester linkage.
1935 *Chem. Abstr.* XXIX. 147 The remaining compds. of the orcinol group of Zopf have, in addn. to the depside linkage, a diphenyl ether linkage between the ortho OH groups with the consequent formation of a closed-ring structure. These compds. have been termed depsidones. **1959** *New Biol.* XXIX. 86 Nineteenth-century chemists investigated the lichen acids very thoroughly... They

established that the acids are all either depsides, which are rather readily broken down by alkalis, or depsidones, which are not so broken down.

dept., abbrev. of DEPARTMENT *sb.* II.

1869 *Bradshaw's Railway Man.* XXI. 14 Supt. of Loco. Dept., C. K. Domville, Belfast. **1886** KIPLING *Departmental Ditties* (ed. 2) 3 She controlled a humble husband, who.. controlled a Dept. **1917** *Harrods Gen. Catal.* 1283/1 Vichy-Célestins..can be obtained in the Wine Dept., Harrods. **1976** *Aviation Week & Space Technol.* 1 Mar. 29 An official at the U.S. Transportation Dept. noted that a likely scenario would be that a private company..would file suit. **1985** *Los Angeles Times* 31 Dec. III. 2/4 Man Bites Dog Dept.: Cedric Maxwell, never at a loss for words, declined all interviews with the Boston media.

Deptford Pink: see PINK.

depth (dɛpθ). [In Wyclif *depthe*; not found in OE. or earlier ME.: cf. ON. *dýpt* (*dýpð*), corresp. to Goth. *diupiþa* depth, f. *diup-*, ON. *djúp-*, = OE. *déop* DEEP. But the formation might be English after *length*, etc.: cf. the similarly late *breadth*, and see -TH[1] suffix.]

I. The quality of being deep.

1. a. Measurement or distance from the top downwards (or from the surface inwards); also *fig.*

1393 GOWER *Conf.* III. 90 Geometrie, through which a man hath the sleight Of length, of brede, of depth, of height. **1413** LYDG. *Pilgr. Sowle* v. xiv. (1483) 107 Alle these thre dymensions..that is to seye lengthe, brede and depthe. **1577** B. GOOGE *Heresbach's Husb.* II. (1586) 98 Trenches of a cubite in depth and breath. **1635** N. CARPENTER *Geog. Del.* II. vii. 104 To find out the absolute depth of the Sea. **1665** HOOKE *Microgr.* 235 Filling a Glass of some depth half full with it. **1796** C. MARSHALL *Garden.* v. (1813) 64 The proper depth at which seed is to be sown. **1858** LARDNER *Handbk. Nat. Phil.* 98 It will be..necessary to find the depths at given intervals..from bank to bank. *Mod.* The arrow penetrated to a considerable depth.

b. Measurement from front to back or inward from the outer part; *spec.* (*Mil.*) the distance from front to rear of a body of soldiers as measured by the number of ranks.

1664 EVELYN *Kal. Hort.* (1729) 229 Whatsoever Length his Green-house be, the Depth should not much exceed twelve or thirteen feet. **1667** MILTON *P.L.* I. 549 Serried Shields in thick array Of depth immeasurable. **1703** MOXON *Mech. Exerc.* 127 What width and depth soever you intend your Rooms shall have. **1760–72** tr. *Juan & Ulloa's Voy.* (ed. 3) I. 157 It is furbeloed with a richer stuff, near half a yard in depth. **1832** *Regul. Instr. Cavalry* III. 46 *Depth*, distance from front to rear.

2. The quality of being deep, or of considerable extension or distance downwards, or inwards.

1526 TINDALE *Matt.* xiii. 5 Because it had no depth of erth [WYCLIF, CRANMER, depnesse]. **1697** DRYDEN *Virg. Georg.* II. 399 Requires a depth of Lodging in the Ground. **1822** SCOTT *Nigel* xvii, The frequency, strength, and depth of his potations. *Mod.* The depth of the snow prevented our passage. We could not reach it from its depth beneath the surface.

3. *fig.* **a.** Of subjects of thought: Profundity, abstruseness.

c **1590** MARLOWE *Faustus* i, Settle thy studies, Faustus, and begin To sound the depth of that thou wilt profess. **1605** BP. HALL *Medit. & Vows* II. §53 The humility of those great and profound wits, whom depth of knowledge hath not led to bypaths in judgement. **1613** SIR H. FINCH *Law* (1636) 57 A great part of the depth and learning of the Law. **1850** MᶜCOSH *Div. Govt.* IV. ii. (1874) 490 There is a great depth of meaning in the saying.

b. Of persons, or their mental faculties or actions: Profundity, penetration, sagacity.

1605 BACON *Adv. Learn* I. iv. §2 (1873) 29 Life of invention, or depth of judgement. **1711** HEARNE *Collect.* (Oxf. Hist. Soc.) III. 108 A Man of extraordinary Depth. **1781** COWPER *Charity* 392 He talks of light, and the prismatic hues, As men of depth in erudition use. **1871** MORLEY *Voltaire* (1886) 86 If it is often necessary to condemn him for superficiality, this lack of depth seldom.. proceeds from painstaking.

c. *in depth*, profoundly; with deep insight or penetration. Hence (hyphenated) as an *attrib.* phr.

1959 B. C. BROOKES in R. Quirk et al. *Teaching of English* v. 148 It takes the scientist perhaps twenty or thirty years to reach..that mature grasp of his subject which enables him to see it clearly both in depth and in relation to other disciplines. **1959** *Listener* 9 July 69/2 Dr. Waidson presumably had the choice of writing in depth about a few novelists or of skimming over as many authors as he could get into his survey. **1966** *Punch* 19 Jan. 83/3 Why haven't you asked my views on Sport? Not quite interviewing me in depth are you, Mr. Haverwood? **1967** *Electronics* XL. 35 (Advt.), He's backed by General Electric's total electronic capability—in-depth technical backup assistance. **1971** *Guardian* 20 Feb. 9/6 What I do is history plus reportage, an in-depth extension of my former journalism.

4. Of feelings, moral qualities, or states: Intensity, profundity.

1596 SHAKS. *Tam. Shr.* v. i. 141 To sound the depth of this knauerie. **1598** DRAYTON *Heroic. Ep.* xxiii. 23 The depth of Woe with words we hardly sound. **1640** GLAPTHORNE *Lady's Priv.* IV. i, This cruelty exceeds The depth of tyranny. **1738** WESLEY *Ps. & Hymns* (1765) cxxxvii, The Depth of sympathetic Woe! **1869** FREEMAN *Norm. Conq.* (1876) III. xiii. 303 Tostig alone did not stick at this depth of treason.

5. Of physical qualities or conditions, as silence, darkness, colour: Intensity. *depth of field*, *depth of focus*: see FIELD *sb.* 16 c, FOCUS *sb.* 2 e.

1624 DAVENPORT *City Nt.-Cap* 111, In depth of silence, you shall confess. *c* **1820** S. ROGERS *Italy* (1830) 132 Cedar and cypress threw Singly their depth of shadow. **1873** TYNDALL *Lect. on Light* iv. 157 A splendid azure, which.. reaches a maximum of depth and purity, and then..passes into whitish blue.

6. *Logic.* The sum of the attributes contained in a concept; = COMPREHENSION 4.

1864 BOWEN *Logic* iv. 67 This distinction of Quantity has been expressed by Logicians in various ways,.A Logical or Universal whole has Extension, Breadth, Sphere..A Metaphysical or Formal whole has Intension, Depth, Comprehension.

II. Something that is deep.

7. a. A deep water; a deep part of the sea, or of any body of water. Usually in *pl.*; now only *poetic* and *rhetorical*.

1382 WYCLIF *Ex.* xv. 5 The depe watris couerden hem; thei descendiden into the depthe as a stoon. **1388** —— *Ps.* cxlviii. 7 Herie ȝe the Lord; dragouns, and alle depthis of watris [**1382** depnessis]. *c* **1400** *Prymer* 67 Deppe clepiþ deppe, in þe vois of þi wyndowis. **1580** SIDNEY *Psalms* xviii. 5 Ev'n from the waters depth, my God preserv'd me soe. **1611** BIBLE *Ex.* xv. 5 The depths haue couered them. **1816** J. WILSON *City of Plague* II. iv. 152 But I have gazed with adoration Upon its awful depths profoundly calm. **1820** SHELLEY *Cloud* 24 In the depths of the purple sea.

†**b.** The great abyss of waters; the DEEP. *Obs.*

1382 WYCLIF *Isa* li. 10 Whether not thou driedist the se, water of the huge depthe. **1611** BIBLE *Prov.* viii. 27 When he set a compasse vpon the face of the depth.

8. A deep place in the earth, etc.; a deep pit, cavity, or valley (*obs.*); *pl.* the deep or lowest part of a pit, cavity, etc. (*rhet.*).

1523 LD. BERNERS *Froiss.* I. xviii. 20 Thus rode forthe all that daye, the yonge kyng of Inglande, by mountaignes and deptis. **1697** DRYDEN *Virg. Georg.* IV. 690 Ev'n from the depths of Hell the Damn'd advance. **1852** MRS. STOWE *Uncle Tom's C.* xv, Miss Ophelia, suddenly rising from the depths of the large arm-chair. **1871** MORLEY *Voltaire* (1886) 4 A demon from the depths of the pit.

9. A vast or unfathomable space, an abyss; the deep or remote part (*of* space, the air, the sky, etc.). Usually in *pl.* (*poet.* and *rhet.*)

1613 PURCHAS *Pilgrimage* I. ii. 6 An Earth without forme, and void, a darkened depth and waters. **1697** DRYDEN *Virg. Georg.* II. 678 The Depths of Heav'n above, and Earth below. **1712** ADDISON *Spect.* No. 420 ¶3 Those unfathomable Depths of Æther. **1849** LONGF. *Kavanagh* v. 32 Measureless depths of air around. **1883** PROCTOR *Myst. Time & Space* 57 With Briarean arms science thrust back the stars into the depths of space.

10. The inner part far from the surface or outside. Also in *pl.*

c **1400** *Lanfranc's Cirurg.* 60 (MS. B) Brennynge of hote eyren to þe deppe of the wounde ys most proffytable. *Ibid.* 91 If þat a festre perse..into deppe it is an imperfiȝt cure. **1732** POPE *Ess. Man* I. 101 Some safer world, in depth of woods embrac'd. **1774** GOLDSM. *Nat. Hist.* (1776) V. 254 In the depth of those remote and solitary forests. **1820** SHELLEY *Homer's Hymn to Merc.* xxxi, The sacred wood, Which from the inmost depths of its green glen Echoes the voice of Neptune. **1887** BOWEN *Virg. Æneid* I. 311 Compassed with trees of the forest and depths of shuddering shade.

11. The middle (of winter, of night), when the cold, stillness, or darkness is most intense.

1605 CHAPMAN *Al Fooles* I. ii, You meet by stealth In depth of midnight. **1618** BOLTON *Florus* (1636) 273 Though it were the depth of Winter. *a* **1764** LLOYD *Poems, New-River Head*, Nor finish till the depth of night. **1863** FR. A. KEMBLE *Resid. in Georgia* 19 In full leaf and beauty in the very depth of winter.

12. *fig.* **a.** A deep (i.e. secret, mysterious, unfathomable, etc.) region of thought, feeling, or being; the inmost, remotest, or extreme part. Now often in *pl.*

1382 WYCLIF *Ps.* cxxix. 1 Fro depthis I criede to thee, Lord. **1540** COVERDALE *Fruitf. Less.* v. Wks. 1844 I. 409 God's word is even as a two-edged sword, and entereth through to the depth. *c* **1592** MARLOWE *Mass. Paris* I. viii, Having a smack in all, And yet didst never sound anything to the depth. **1592** SHAKS. *Rom. & Jul.* II. iv. 104, I was come to the whole depth of my tale. **1665** J. SPENCER *Vulg. Prophecies* 96 Not a cloudy expression drops from them but it is christned a depth and a great mystery. **1813** SHELLEY *Q. Mab* VI. 187 From the depths of unrecorded time. **1874** HELPS *Soc. Press.* iii. 54 Imagine that there were no such depths of degradation.

b. Applied *attrib.* to an interview, approach, etc., that seeks to discover motives or attitudes that are not normally divulged, the results of which are used esp. as a basis for certain advertising techniques. Cf. *depth psychology* (see sense IV).

1948 *Jrnl. Appl. Psychol.* Oct. 550 To orient ourselves to the problem and sketch in its broad outlines we began with a series of a hundred 'depth interviews' of television families. **1957** *Bookseller* 28 Sept. 1216/3 No real harm can be done if, using the results brought to the surface of the human subconscious and unconscious mind by the 'depth diggers', one astute manufacturer sells more of a commodity than a rival marketing a brand of equal quality and price. **1957** *Times Lit. Suppl.* 1 Nov. 661/2 Space-salesmen have now become students of the sub-conscious mind, and advertisements are governed by the 'depth-approach'. **1970** *Guardian* 10 Apr. 7/3 Skilled depth-interviewers.

III. 13. Phr. *beyond* or *out of one's depth*: *lit.* in water too deep for one to reach the bottom without sinking; *fig.* beyond one's understanding or capacities.

1613 SHAKS. *Hen. VIII*, III. ii. 361, I haue ventur'd Like little wanton Boyes that swim on bladders..in a Sea of Glory, But farre beyond my depth. **1709** POPE *Ess. Crit.* 50 Launch not beyond your depth, but be discreet. **1712** ADDISON *Spect.* No. 403 ¶7 Finding them going out of my Depth I passed forward. **1892** *Pall Mall G.* 19 Jan. 4/3 He remained three hours in the water, afraid to move, lest he should get out of his depth.

IV. *Comb.* **depth bomb, charge**, a bomb capable of exploding under water; so **depth-charge** *v. trans.*, to attack with depth charges; **depth finder**, an apparatus for sounding the sea; *spec.* **sonic depth finder**, one in which the measurement is made by timing the echoes from the sea-bottom of sound waves transmitted from the ship; **depth-gauge**, a gauge used to measure the depth of holes; **depth-keeping** *ppl. a.* and *vbl. sb.*, the maintenance of a submarine, fishing-net, etc., at a certain depth; **depth psychologist**, one who practises or is skilled in depth psychology; **depth psychology** [tr. G. *tiefenpsychologie* (S. Freud *Das Ich und das Es* (1923) i. 17)] = PSYCHO-ANALYSIS b; hence *depth-psychological* adj.; **depth recorder**, a device for recording either how far below the surface of the sea it is or the depth of water below a vessel; so **depth-recording** *vbl. sb.*; **depth-wise** *adv.*, in the way or direction of depth.

1918 E. S. FARROW *Dict. Mil. Terms* s.v., Submarines.. are pursued and destroyed by dropping depth bombs from the observing aircraft or warship. **1944** *Jrnl. R. Aeronaut. Soc.* XLVIII. 219 Depth Bombs (D.B.)..have a very thin case and are detonated by hydrostatic fuse. **1917** *War Illustr.* 18 Dec. 361 Telegraph to seamen..who prepare to drop Depth Charges to destroy U-boat. **1920** *Blackw. Mag.* Mar. 315/2 The depth-charge thrower, which later came into common use..was as yet far from perfection. **1928** C. F. S. GAMBLE *N. Sea Air Station* 14 Lieutenant Williamson ..described how depth-charges (he said 'bombs exploding 20 feet under the surface of the water') might possibly be used to destroy submarines. **1918** *Daily Mail* 23 Sept. 2/4 From the captain of a U-boat..came to me the following description of what it is like to be depth-charged. **1940** *War Illustr.* 19 Jan. 628/3 That would find the submarine for us —and then we could depth-charge it. **1923** *Hydrographic Rev.* I. 72 Navy sonic depth finder recently developed at the Engineering Experiment Station, Annapolis, Maryland. **1948** R. DE KERCHOVE *Internat. Maritime Dict.* 232/1 *Echo sounder*... Also called depth finder. **1916** KIPLING *Tales of 'The Trade'* I. 6 Depth-keeping,..very difficult owing to heavy swell. **1923** *Blackw. Mag.* Oct. 527/1 Accurate depth-keeping being out of the question, I surfaced. **1959** H. BARNES *Oceanogr. & Marine Biol.* i. 26 Modern practice is tending more to the use of a depth-keeping device, either on the net itself or on the towing wire... The paravane principle is often employed. **1958** *Times Lit. Suppl.* 23 May p. xii/2 A sympathetic understanding of depth-psychological concepts. **1947** *Partisan Rev.* XIV. 528 Those commonplaces are too humdrum for the depth psychologist. **1957** *Observer* 27 Oct. 18/6 Motivational research took the place of market research, and the depth psychologists became the *eminences grises* of salesmanship. **1927** J. RIVIERE tr. *Freud's Ego & Id* i. 18 In the last resort the quality of being conscious or not is the single ray of light that penetrates the obscurity of depth-psychology. **1947** W. EMPSON *Seven Types of Ambiguity* (ed. 2) p. x, Some critics do not like to recognise this process because they connect it with Depth Psychology. **1960** H. READ *Forms of Things Unknown* viii. 133 Myth and dream, symbol and image—all the paraphernalia of depth-psychology—are conceived as shadow play. **1963** L. B. LEFEBRE tr. *Boss's Psychoanalysis & Daseinsanalysis* v. 87 The unconscious became so much the mark of psychoanalytic theory that psychoanalysis, and all doctrines derived from it, eventually became known as 'depth' psychologies. 'Depth' entered the picture because Freud..undertook to view mental phenomena in terms of a 'topographic' approach, and to regard the unconscious as a 'psychical locality'..'below' consciousness. **1911** *Encycl. Brit.* XIX. 295/1 Lord Kelvin's sounding machines..in the later form known as the 'depth recorder', where..results are obtained by the automatic record of the position of a piston forced upwards in a tube by..increased pressure. **1961** *Listener* 24 Aug. 269/1 After the war, echo-sounding and depth-recorders were introduced to fishing boats, and echoes were received of big shoals of fish. **1959** H. BARNES *Oceanogr. & Marine Biol.* i. 23 If the speed of the towing vessel can be accurately controlled, then the depth of the net for a given towing speed may be determined in a series of trial runs, using a depth-recording device attached to the net. **1814** W. TAYLOR in *Monthly Mag.* XXXVIII. 214 A violation of unity of scene, not sidewards, but depthwise.

ˈ**depthen**, *v. rare.* [f. DEPTH: cf. *lengthen*, *strengthen*, *heighten*, etc.] *trans.* = DEEPEN.

1587 FLEMING *Contn. Holinshed* III. 1547/1 One pent of water had so scowred and depthened the same [hauen's mouth]. **1723** *Lond. Gaz.* No. 6148/1 An Act for depthning ..and improving the Haven and Piers of Great Yarmouth.

Hence ˈ**depthening** *vbl. sb.* and *ppl. a.*; **depthening-tool** (see next).

ˈ**depthing**, *vbl. sb.* [f. assumed vb. *depth* = DEPTHEN + -ING[1].] In *depthing* or *depthening-tool*: **a.** a countersink for deepening a hole; **b.** a watchmaker's tool for gauging the distances of pivot-holes in movement plates.

1788 *Trans. Soc. Arts* VI. 188 Description of the sector depthing tool [in Horology]. **1879** *Cassell's Techn. Educ.* IV. 325/2 Supposing we place a wheel and pinion into the depthing tool, with sixty-four teeth and eight leaves respectively. **1884** F. J. BRITTEN *Watch & Clockm.* 81 Accuracy of construction is absolutely essential in the depthing tool.

depthless (ˈdɛpθlɪs), *a.* [-LESS.]

1. Of which the depth cannot be sounded; fathomless; abyssal.

1619 H. HUTTON *Follies' Anat.* 22 A sabariticke sea, a depthlesse gulfe. **1620** DEKKER *Dreame* (1860) 13 Were.. My pen of pointed adamant.. Mine inke a depthlesse sea. **1654** E. JOHNSON *Wond. wrkg. Provid.* 132 The depthlesse ditches that blind guides lead into. **1828** *Blackw. Mag.* XXIV. 159 The salt flood's limitless—depthless waters.

2. Without depth actually; shallow, superficial.

1816 COLERIDGE *Biog. Lit., etc.* (1882) 318 The depthless abstractions of fleeting phenomena, the shadows of sailing vapours. **1825** —— *Aids Refl.* (1854) 122 The breadthless lines, depthless surfaces, and perfect circles of geometry.

†**deˈpucel, -elle,** *v.* Also 5 des-, dispuselle. [a. F. *dépuceler*, in OF. *desp-* (12th c. in Littré), f. *dé-, des-*:—L. DIS- + F. *pucelle* maiden: see PUCELLE.] *trans.* To deflower.

1440 J. SHIRLEY *Dethe K. James* (1818) 5 Yn dispusellyng and defowlyng of yong madyns. **1480** CAXTON *Ovid's Met.* XIII. xv, How she was despucelled by a Gyante. **1483** —— *G. de la Tour* E vj a, Of the doughter of Iacob that was depuceled.

†**deˈpucelate,** *v. Obs. rare.* Also 7 depusilate. [f. F. *dépuceler*: see -ATE[3] 7.] = prec.

1611 COTGR., *Depuceler*, to depucelate, or deflower a virgine. **1635** BROME *Spar. Garden* IV. iv, She is depusilated by your sonne. *a* **1693** URQUHART *Rabelais* III. vi. 58 The unmaidening or depucelating of a hundred Virgins.

†**deˈpudicate,** *v. Obs. rare*—0. [f. ppl. stem of L. *dēpudīcāre* to debauch, f. DE- I. 6 + *pudīc-us* chaste.] *trans.* To violate the chastity of, deflower.

1623 in COCKERAM. **1656** in BLOUNT *Glossogr.*

†**deˈpudorate,** *v. Obs. rare.* [f. DE- II. 1 + L. *pudor* shame, modesty.] *trans.* To deprive of shame, make shameless.

1678 CUDWORTH *Intell. Syst.* I. iv. 193 Their Minds are.. Depudorated or become so void of Shame, as that [etc.].

depulluˈlation. *nonce-wd.* [noun of action f. L. DE- I. 2 + *pullulāre* to sprout out, f. *pullulus* chick, sprout.] Removal or plucking off of sprouts.

1839–40 DE QUINCEY *Casuistry* Wks. VIII. 252 It is.. by the everlasting depullulation of fresh sprouts and shoots from old boughs, that this enormous accumulation takes place.

depulper (dɪˈpʌlpə(r)). [f. *depulp vb. (in med.L. *dēpulpāre*; '*depulpo* = ἀποσαρκῶ' in *L.-Gr. Gloss.*) + -ER[1].] An apparatus for removing pulp.

1882 SPON *Encycl. Manuf.* 1839 (*Beet-sugar*) The term 'depulpers' has been applied to a class of apparatus rendered necessary by the inability of the ordinary filters to completely remove the fine pulpy matters from the juice. They are really nothing more than effective mechanical filters.

†**depulˈsation.** *Obs. rare*—0. [n. of action from L. *dēpulsāre* to thrust away: see DEPULSE.]

1727 BAILEY vol. II, *Depulsation*, a thrusting or driving away or repelling.

†**deˈpulse,** *v. Obs.* [ad. L. *dēpulsāre* to thrust away, freq. of *dēpellĕre*, f. DE- I. 2 + *pellĕre, puls-*, to drive, push: see DEPEL.] *trans.* To drive or thrust away, thrust down.

c **1555** HARPSFIELD *Divorce Hen. VIII* (1878) 87 He that married his brother's wife.. depulsed the shame and ignominy of barrenness. **1563–87** FOXE *A. & M.* (1596) 535/1 Which.. not onlie thrust into heauen.. saintes of your owne making.. but also depulse downe from heauen.. Gods welbeloued seruants. **1623** COCKERAM, *Depulse*, to driue away, to thrust one often away.

†**depulsion** (dɪˈpʌlʃən). *Obs.* [ad. L. *dēpulsiōn-em*, n. of action from *dēpellĕre* to drive away: see DEPULSE.] The action of driving or thrusting away; expulsion; repulsion.

1611 SPEED *Hist. Gt. Brit.* IX. xvi. §94 (After her Husbands depulsion from his regall Throne) her forces being vanquished at the battell of Tewksbury. **1638** WILKINS *New World* I. (1684) 163 [They] cannot have any Power of Attraction or Depulsion in them.

†**deˈpulsive,** *a. Obs.* [f. L. *dēpuls-*, ppl. stem of *dēpellĕre*: see -IVE: cf. *impulsive*.] Having the quality of driving away; averting; prophylactic.

c **1615** C. MORE *Life Sir T. More* (1828) 326 The wholesome depulsive triacle.. against this.. deadly infection.

†**deˈpulsor.** *Obs.* In 6 depoulsour. [a. L. *dēpulsor*, agent-n. from *dēpellĕre*: see DEPULSE. Cf. OF. *depulseur* (Godef.).] One who drives or thrusts away; a repeller.

1542 UDALL *Erasm. Apoph.* (1877) 130 (D.) Hercules was in olde time worshipped vnder the name of ἀλεξίκακος, that is, the depoulsour and driuer awaye of all euills.

†**deˈpulsory,** *a. Obs.* [ad. L. *dēpulsōri-us*, f. *dēpulsor*: see prec. and -ORY.] = DEPULSIVE.

1609 HOLLAND *Amm. Marcell.* XXV. ii. 263 Making supplication.. unto the gods by the meanes of certaine depulsorie sacrifices.

†**deˈpulye,** *v. Sc. Obs.* In 6 depulȝe, -uilȝie. [ad. F. *dépouiller*, in OF. *desp-*.] = DESPOIL.

1513 DOUGLAS *Æneis* IV. vii. 80 Lyk emetis.. Quhen thai depulȝe the meikle bing of quheit.

depurant (dɪˈpjʊərənt, ˈdɛpjʊ-), *a.* and *sb. Med.* [ad. med.L. *dēpūrānt-em*, pr. pple. of *dēpūrāre* (see below).]

A. *adj.* Purifying; *Med.* Having the quality of purifying the blood or other fluids of the body. **B.** *sb.* A medicine or substance which has this quality.

1875 H. C. WOOD *Therap.* (1879) 588 Water acts not only as a diluent, but also as a depurant. **1883** *Syd. Soc. Lex.*, *Depurant*, purifying; cleansing. Applied to medicines, or to any kind of diet, that purifies the fluids of the body.

†**deˈpurate,** *ppl. a. Obs.* [ad. med.L. *dēpūrāt-us*, pa. pple. of *dēpūrāre* (see next): in F. *dépuré*.] Purified, cleansed, refined, clarified.

1657 W. COLES *Adam in Eden* clxv, The said depurate juice. **1661** GLANVILL *Van. of Dogm.* xi. (R.), A material attribute, and incompatible with so depurate a nature. **1686** GOAD *Celest. Bodies* III. ii. 428 Sulfur refin'd and depurate.

depurate (dɪˈpjʊəreɪt, ˈdɛpjʊreɪt), *v.* [f. ppl. stem of med.L. *dēpūrāre*, f. DE- I. 3 + *pūrāre* to purify, *pūrus* pure. Cf. F. *dépurer* (13th c. in Hatzf.), Pr. and Sp. *depurar*, It. *depurare*.]

1. *trans.* To free from impurities, purify, cleanse.

1620 VENNER *Via Recta* Introd. 8 It [water] is the better depurated with the morning Sunne, and pure orientall Windes. **1685** BOYLE *Effects Motion* Suppl. 156 Let the Gums be depurated with the Vinegar of Squills. **1751** BAYLY in *Phil. Trans.* XLVII. 29 Sufficient to depurate the blood. **1800** HOWARD *ibid.* XC. 218 It had been depurated from excess of alkali. **1880** HAUGHTON *Phys. Geog.* iii. 78 The luxuriant Flora of the Coal period—which served to depurate the atmosphere of its Carbonic Acid.

fig. **1681** GLANVILL *Sadducismus* 148 Their Imagination is not sufficiently defecated and depurated from the filth.. of Corporeity. **1780** BURKE *Speech at Bristol* Wks. 1842 I. 263 It was long before the spirit of true piety.. could be depurated from the dregs and feculence of the contention. **1832** *Fraser's Mag.* VI. 602 Will you not feel your being depurated of its accustomed weaknesses?

2. *intr.* (for *refl.*) To become free from impurities.

1767 MONRO in *Phil. Trans.* LVII. 407 After it had stood for a month to depurate, it was again filtered.

Hence **depurated** *ppl. a.*, **depurating** *vbl. sb.* and *ppl. a.*

1651 BIGGS *New Disp.* ¶124 The depurated bloud from the *vena cava*. **1762** tr. *Busching's Syst. Geog.* I. 179 Sulphur is also found.. but the melting and depurating of it is too chargeable. **1781** *Phil. Trans.* LXXI. 41 The quantity of depurated salt they will afford. **1840** BARHAM *Ingol. Leg.*, *Spectre of Tapp.*, They had come under the valet's depurating hand. **1844–57** G. BIRD *Urin. Deposits* (ed. 5) 63 The depurating functions of [the] kidneys.

depuration (dɛpjʊˈreɪʃən). [a. F. *dépuration* (13th c. in Littré), or ad. med.L. *dēpūrātiōn-em* (It. *depurazione*, Sp. *depuracion*, Pr. *depuracio*), n. of action from *dēpūrāre* to DEPURATE.] The action or process of freeing from impurities; purification, refining; in *Med.* the removal of impurities from the humours or fluids of the body.

1603 HOLLAND *Plutarch's Mor.* 603 (R.) This manner of depuration and clarifying of it by a strainer. **1641** FRENCH *Distill.* i. (1651) 33 The depuration of Manna for this use. **1753** N. TORRIANO *Gangr. Sore Throat* p. xii, This critical Depuration of the Blood by Eruptions on the Skin. **1789** MRS. PIOZZI *Journ. France* I. 195 The depuration of gold may be performed many ways. **1880** HAUGHTON *Phys. Geog.* iii. 81 The Upper Palæozoic age, in which the chief depuration of the atmosphere took place.

depurative (dɪˈpjʊərətɪv, ˈdɛpjʊreɪtɪv), *a.* and *sb.* [f. med. or mod.L. *dēpūrātīv-us*, f. ppl. stem of *dēpūrāre*: cf. F. *dépuratif* (1792 in Hatzf.).]

A. *adj.* Having the quality of cleansing from impurities. **B.** *sb.* A purifying agent or medicine.

depurative disease, a name given by Dickinson to lardaceous disease.

1684 tr. *Bonet's Merc. Compit.* VI. 167 A depurative fermentation of the humours. **1830** LINDLEY *Nat. Syst. Bot.* 147 The depurative properties ascribed.. to Viola canina. **1861** *Technologist* II. 30 Sarsaparilla.. as a depurative and restorative in disorders of the blood.

depurator (ˈdɛpjʊreɪtə(r)). [agent-n. f. DEPURATE *v.* on Latin analogies.] An agent or apparatus that purifies or cleanses; *spec.* see quot. 1874.

1835 KIRBY *Hab. & Inst. Anim.* I. 159 Similar to what devolves upon the larves of certain insects, with regard to stagnant waters, they may be depurators. **1858** SIMMONDS, *Depurator*, a French machine for cleansing and preparing cotton for spinning. **1874** KNIGHT *Dict. Mech.*, *Depurator*, an apparatus to assist the expulsion of morbid matter by means of the excretory ducts of the skin.. The *depurator* is described in Nathan Smith's English patent, 1802. **1885** *Alien. & Neurol.* Oct. 540 The remedies indicated.. are chiefly depurators and nutrients.

depuratory (dɪˈpjʊərətərɪ), *a.* (*sb.*) [mod. f. ppl. stem of *dēpūrāre*: see -ORY.]

A. *adj.* = DEPURATIVE *a.*; formerly *spec.* 'applied to certain diseases which were supposed to carry off impurities from the system' (*Syd. Soc. Lex.*).

1676 *Phil. Trans.* XI. 569 The Continual Depuratory Feaver. **1733** CHEYNE *Eng. Malady* II. xi. §3 (1734) 233 Nervous Fevers, as distinguished from Hot and Depuratory ones. **1870** ROLLESTON *Anim. Life* 256 A water-vascular or depuratory system.

B. *sb.* = DEPURATIVE *sb.*

†**deˈpure,** *v. Obs.* [ad. F. *dépurer* or med.L. *dēpūrāre*: see DEPURATE.] *trans.* To free from impurity, cleanse, purify (*lit.* and *fig.*); = DEPURATE *v.*

a **1400–50** *Alexander* 2768 Send.. Sum pured pelloure depurid to put in oure wedis. **1447** BOKENHAM *Seyntys* (Roxb.) 246 My soule depuryd from vyce. **1599** NASHE *Lenten Stuffe* Ep. Ded., He sends for the barber to depure, decurtate, and sponge him. **1699** EVELYN *Acetaria* (1729) 156 Ingredients.. [which] depure the Blood.

Hence **deˈpured, deˈpuring** *ppl. adjs.*

1503 HAWES *Examp. Virt.* vi. 74 And lyke crystall depured was Euery wyndowe. **1508** DUNBAR *Goldyn Targe* i, With cleir depurit beims christalyne. **1545** RAYNOLD *Byrth Mankynde* 133 Confycte them with claryfied and depuryd hunny. **1546** LANGLEY *Pol. Verg. De Invent.* II. i. 35 b, Lawes promulgate by God, confirmed after the moste depured and perfecte maner. **1873** W. S. MAYO *Never Again* xxxii. 417 Spirit of Night.. Already doth thy soft depuring light Mine eyes unfilm.

†**deˈpurgatory,** *a. Obs. rare*—0. [f. ppl. stem of L. *dēpurgāre* to clean out: see -ORY.] Having the quality of purging or cleansing.

1611 COTGR., *Depurgatoire*, depurgatorie; purging.

†**deˈpurge,** *v. Obs.* [ad. L. *dēpurgāre*: see prec.] *trans.* To purge or cleanse from impurity.

1657 in *Physical Dict.*

depurit, Sc. f. DEPURED *ppl. a.*

depurition, bad form for DEPURATION.

1847 in CRAIG.

†**deˈpurse,** *v. Sc. Obs.* [f. DE- II. 2 + PURSE: cf. *deburse, disburse*.] = DISBURSE.

a **1648** *Sc. Acts Chas. I* (1814) V. 479 (Jam.), With power.. to borrow, vptak, and leavie moneyes.. and to give.. directiones for depurseing thairof. **1655** in Z. Boyd *Zion's Flowers* (1855) App. 29/1 Halfe of the expenses depursed in legall pursute. **1676** W. ROW *Contn. Blair's Autobiog.* xii. (1848) 380 Which monies Mr. Blair did most willingly depurse. **1733** P. LINDSAY *Interest Scot.* 203 The Money depurst for their Expence and Provisions.

Hence **deˈpursement** = DISBURSEMENT.

1636 RUTHERFORD *Lett.* (1862) I. 158 Write up your depursements.. and keep the account of what ye give out. **1643** *Sc. Acts Chas. I* (1870) VI. 16 Necessarie depursements bestowed be him. **1774** *Petit.* in A. McKay *Hist. Kilmarnock* 303 To.. expend the haill necessary depursement.

deputable (dɪˈpjuːtəb(ə)l, ˈdɛpjʊ-), *a.* [f. DEPUTE *v.* + -ABLE.] Capable of being, or fit to be, deputed.

1621 W. SCLATER *Tythes* (1623) 220 A fifth or tenth of Time deputable to the seruice of God. *Ibid.* 224 A sixth or eighth of time deputable to Gods seruice. **1841** CARLYLE *Baillie* Misc. (1888) VI. 207 A man deputable to the London Parliament and elsewhither.

†**ˈdeputary,** *a. Obs. rare.* [irreg. f. DEPUTE *v.* + -ARY[1].] Acting as a deputy; deputed.

1581 J. BELL *Haddon's Answ. Osor.* 391 b, His [the Pope's] Bulles of Pardons and his deputary Comissaryes.

†**ˈdeputate,** *ppl. a. Obs.* [ad. L. *dēputāt-us*, pa. ppl. of *dēputāre* to DEPUTE.] (*pple.* and *adj.*) Deputed; appointed, assigned.

a **1440** *Found. St. Bartholomew's* 32 Holy place, whiche deputat ys only to dyuyne vse. **1560** ROLLAND *Crt. Venus* III. 181 Rhamnusia, quhilk [*mispr.* quhill] was Iuge deputate.

deputation (dɛpjuːˈteɪʃən), *sb.* [f. L. type *dēputātiōn-em, n. of action from *dēputāre* to DEPUTE: cf. F. *députation* (16th c. in Littré), It. *deputazione* (*deputatione*, Florio 1598).] The action of deputing, or fact of being deputed.

†**1.** *gen.* Appointment, ordination, assignment (to an office, function, etc.). *Obs.*

1393 GOWER *Conf.* III. 178 He shall.. Ordeigne his deputation Of suche juges, as ben lerned. *c* **1449** PECOCK *Repr.* II. xii. 220 The deputacioun and the assignyng bi which the visible eukarist is ordeyned and assigned forto represente the bodi of Crist. **1509–10** *Act 1 Hen. VIII*, c. 9 The Chaunceller.. [shall] have the Deputacion and Assignement of.. Persones.. that they shall take and receyve the seid Toule and Custome. **1640** BP. HALL *Episc.* II. xxi. 207 One Bartolomæus the Bishop of the Hereticks.. taking upon him the Deputation of that week Anti-pope, yeelded unto him a wicked and abhominable reverence. *a* **1647** FILMER *Patriarcha* (1887) 32 It seems they did not like a king by deputation but desired one by succession. **1650** R. HOLLINGWORTH *Usurped Powers* 68 None can take it in hand but by deputation from him.

2. *spec.* Appointment to act on behalf of another; delegation.

[**1534** *Act 26 Hen. VIII*, c. 3 §4 Any person.. to whome any deputacion shalbe made by commission.] **1552** HULOET, Deputation, *subsortitio, substitutio, surrogatio.* **1597** HOOKER

Eccl. Pol. v. lxxxi. §7 Vnto all these..the law hath..given leaue, while themselues bear waightier burthens, to supply inferiour by deputation. **1698** NORRIS *Treat. Sev. Subjects* 280 That we Feed them our selves, and not by Proxy or Deputation. **1799** J. ROBERTSON *Agric. Perth* 44 The king.. grants this deputation to a person regularly bred to the law. **1863** A. J. HORWOOD *Year-bks. 30-1 Edw. I*, Pref. 29 An attorney might be appointed for a particular suit or generally for all suits, and the latter kind of deputation was common in Eyre.

†**b.** A document conveying such an appointment; a commission, warrant. *Obs.*

1628 DIGBY *Voy. Medit.* (1868) 4 This same day I sealed to Sir Edward Stradling a deputation of being my Vice-admirall. **1691** *Lond. Gaz.* No. 2698/4 A black Hair'd Man, who went about the Countries with a false Deputation. **1798** JANE AUSTEN *Lett.* I. 162 James Digweed called to day, and I gave him his brother's deputation.

†**3.** An appointment by the lord of the manor to the office and rights of a gamekeeper; a document conveying such appointment under statutory authority. *Obs.*

(The deputation was necessary to constitute a gamekeeper; but it was also frequently used as a means of giving to friends the privilege of shooting game over an estate.)

1749 FIELDING *Tom Jones* IV. v, The squire declared..he would give the game-keeper his deputation the next morning. *c* **1815** JANE AUSTEN *Persuas.* iii. (D.), He..had inquired about the manor; would be glad of the deputation, certainly, but made no great point of it; said he sometimes took out a gun, but never killed. **1869** *Daily News* 23 Apr., Formerly the Woods and Forests gave what were called 'deputations' to gentlemen to shoot over the Crown lands. **1880** S. WALPOLE *Hist. Eng.* III. 63 Country gentlemen who were desirous of doing a neighbour a good turn were in the habit of giving him a 'deputation' as a gamekeeper.

4. A body of persons appointed to go on a mission on behalf of another or others. Often a small company (or a single person) deputed by a society to visit various places on behalf of the society. (The chief current use.)

1732 LEDIARD *Sethos* II. IX. 344 They propos'd to send a deputation of four senators. **1828** D'ISRAELI *Chas. I*, I. vi. 186 A deputation of the Houses waited on the King. **1879** MCCARTHY *Own Times* II. xxii. 146 The deputations represented certain metropolitan parishes, and were the exponents of markedly Radical opinions.

Hence **depu'tation, depu'tationize** *v.*, to visit with a deputation; **depu'tational** *a.*, of or belonging to a deputation; **depu'tationist**, one who belongs to or supports a deputation.

1885 *Manch. Exam.* 18 Mar. 5/3 The trustees are on the side of the deputationists. **1888** *Balance Sheet Manchester Ch. of E. Temp. Soc.*, Travelling and Deputational Expenses. **1888** *Lanc. Evening Post* 3 Feb. 2/4 The Prime Minister has been deputationised by some of the most expert among our sociologists. **1891** *Scott. Leader* 12 Jan. 4 The Unionists..last week 'deputationed' Mr. Goschen.

deputative ('dɛpjʊtətɪv), *a.* [f. L. *dēputāt-*, ppl. stem of *dēputāre* to DEPUTE + -IVE.] Characterized by deputation or by being deputed; of the nature of a deputy.

1625-8 tr. *Camden's Hist. Eliz.* III. (1688) 362 A Parliament..begun by a deputative Commission granted by the Queen to the Archbishop of Canterbury, the Lord Treasurer, and the Earl of Derby. **1646** LILBURNE *Game Scotch & Eng.* 20 Wherein the joynt military interest of both Kingdomes is represented..and both thereby incorporated into one deputative body. *a* **1653** GOUGE *Comm. Heb.* ii. 5 If authority be yielded un-to Angels, yet that authority is only deputative in reference to..work which is injoyned by them.

Hence **'deputatively** *adv.*, by way of deputation.

1653 GAUDEN *Hierasp.* 472 To pay Tithes to Christ..by the hands of his Ministers, who are deputatively and ministerially himself. **1818** G. S. FABER *Hor. Mos.* II. 43 And who can have authority to send, unless God immediately, or certain of his previously appointed messengers deputatively?

deputator ('dɛpjʊteɪtə(r)). *rare.* [agent-n. from L. *dēputāre* to DEPUTE.]

1. One who deputes another to act for him.

1669 LOCKE *Laws of Carolina* §56 All such deputations.. shall be revocable at the pleasure of the deputator. **1884** *19th Cent.* Jan. 84 The deputy necessarily disappeared with the deputator.

2. A member of a deputation. (*nonce-use.*)

1894 *Nat. Observer* 6 Jan. 181/1 The philanthropic projects of Professor Stuart..and other 'deputators'.

depute ('dɛpju:t), *ppl. a.* and *sb.* Now only *Sc.* Also 5-6 deputte, 6-7 deput; see also DEBITE. [Found as pa. pple. before the appearance of any other part of DEPUTE *v.*; app. repr. OF. *depute* (mod.F. *député*) pa. pple., the final *e* having become mute, as in *assign, avowe*, etc. After the verb came into use, *depute, deput*, continued to be used as its pa. pple., and even as its pa. t. (*esp.* in Sc., where perhaps it was viewed as short for *deputit, deputed*). Only Sc. since the 17th c.]

†**A.** as *pa. pple.* Deputed; imputed, ascribed; appointed, assigned: see DEPUTE *v.*

1382 WYCLIF *Rom.* Prol. 299 The apostil..shewith..al.. to be depute to the grace of God. **1413** *Pilgr. Sowle* (Caxton) I. xxii. (1859) 24 Grace, quene and heuenly pryncesse. As depute by the souerayne kyng eterne. *c* **1440** *Gesta Rom.* liv. 235 (Harl. MS) Thei..hadde I-putte sheldes in a certeyne place deputte þerefor. **1513** DOUGLAS *Æneis* VI. ix. 180 Quhat sort of pane is deput ay For ilk trespas. **1623** CAMDEN in *Lett. Lit. Men* (Camden) 126 Some such as were deput for mee in this yeeres Visitation.

B. *sb.* One deputed; = DEPUTY. (Now only *Sc.*)

1405, 1490 [see DEPUTY 1 b, 2]. **1530** in W. H. Turner *Select. Rec. Oxford* 72 The seyd Chaunseler, hys Deputt's, and Scolers. **1563-7** BUCHANAN *Reform. St. Andros* Wks. (1892) 15 The conservatour or hys deput being present. *a* **1605** MONTGOMERIE *Misc. Poems* xxviii. 1 Melancholie, grit deput of Dispair. **1821** JOANNA BAILLIE *Metr. Leg., Lord John* xxiv, 'Twas no depute's task your guest to ask. **1868** *Act 31-2 Vict.* c. 101 §36 Such decree shall be recorded by the director of Chancery, or his depute.

C. In *comb.* (*Sc.*)

1640-1 *Kirkcudbr. War-Comm. Min. Bk.* (1855) 56 Ressaivit by the Commissar depute, the rentalles of the pretendit bischopes' rentes. **1681** *Act Secur. Peace of Kingd.* (*Scotl.*) in *Lond. Gaz.* No. 1648/4 To nominate Sheriff-Deputs, Justices of Peace, or other Commissioners. **1753** *Stewart's Trial* App. 4 Mr. Archibald Campbell of Stonefield, sheriff-depute of the shire of Argyll. **1869** *Pall Mall G.* 6 July 5 The Lord Advocate..the Solicitor-General..Subordinate to these are four advocate-deputes.

depute (dɪ'pju:t), *v.* [a. F. *députer* (1328 in Hatzf.), ad. L. *dēputāre* to consider as, destine, allot, f. DE- I. 2 b + *putāre* to think, count, consider, etc.]

†**1.** *trans.* To appoint, assign, ordain (a person or thing) to or for a particular office, purpose, or function. *Obs.*

c **1425** WYNTOUN *Cron.* VII. vi. 361 And als he depute hys Counsale The erle of Fyfe mast specyale. **1483** CAXTON *Gold. Leg.* 89 b/1 Thys chylde was taken prysoner and deputed to serue the kynge. **1489** —— *Faytes of A.* IV. xv. 274 The sygne of the Egle is deputed for the dygnyte Imperyal. **1513-4** *Act 5 Hen. VIII*, c. 1 Pream., The Kyng ..hath deputed and ordeyned in the seid Citie..divers officers and ministrees. *a* **1533** LD. BERNERS *Gold. Bk. M. Aurel.* (1546) I ij, He deputed two howres for the matters of Asie. **1631** GOUGE *God's Arrows* III. Ep. Ded. 4 Faithful.. in deputing to the Lords service men fit for their function. **1683** *Brit. Spec.* 129 Westminster..was..from its first foundation deputed for the burial of our Kings.

†**2.** To assign, impute, ascribe, attribute. *Obs.*

1382 [see DEPUTE *ppl. a.*]. **1485** CAXTON *St. Wenefr.* 10 They myght depute it to the pryde of her. *a* **1592** H. SMITH *Serm. Phil.* i. 23 The Apostle..doth depute their strange diseases and sudden death to none other cause.

†**3.** To consign, deliver over. *Obs.*

a **1440** *Found. St. Bartholomew's* 44 Lette nat me be deputid to euerlastyng flammys. **1480** CAXTON *Ovid's Met.* XI. xix, But some..seased tymbre & boordes which were broken of the shipp, whyche the flodes deputed at theyre playsire. **1483** —— *Gold. Leg.* 264/1 This blessid saint..was deputed unto an hard and strayte pryson.

4. To assign (a charge); now, *spec.* to commit, give in charge (authority, etc.) to a deputy or substitute.

1495 *Act 11 Hen. VII*, c. 35 Pream., The Kyngis Grace.. deputed to hym than and sithen offices of charge. **1526** *Pilgr. Perf.* (W. de W. 1531) 28 b, Spirituall talentes, whiche our lorde hath deputed to our credence. **1727** DE FOE *Hist. Appar.* vi. (1840) 59 The Devil may depute such and such powers and privileges to his confederates. **1833** HT. MARTINEAU *Berkeley* I. iv. 73 She could not depute it to anybody to judge when was the right time.

5. *spec.* To appoint (a person) as one's substitute, delegate, or agent; to ordain to act on one's behalf.

[**1494** FABYAN *Chron.* IV. lxiii. 42 Caraucius..was by the Senate of Rome deputed for a Substitute or a Ruler vnder the Romaynes. **1530** PALSGR. 513/1, I muste nedes departe, but I wyll depute some bodye in my romme. **1540** *Act 32 Hen. VIII*, c. 35 The Justice and Justices..shall make assigne depute and appoincte as many deputie or deputies.. as..shalbe thought convenient.] **1552** HULOET, Depute ..*surrogo, delego.* **1604** SHAKS. *Oth.* IV. ii. 226 To depute Cassio in Othellos place. **1687** in *Magd. Coll. & Jas. II*, lxviii, The vice President and others Fellows..being deputed by the rest of the Fellows of the said College, to answer. **1709** STEELE *Tatler* No. 55 ¶5 The Deputies of the Six Cantons who are deputed to determine the Affair of Tockenburg. **1833** HT. MARTINEAU *Manch. Strike* iv. 54 Allen, Clack, and Gibson were deputed to wait on the masters. **1874** GREEN *Short Hist.* iv. §2. 172 They were elected..by a few of the principal burghers deputed for the purpose.

†**b.** *absol.* To send a deputation. *Obs. rare.*

1768 *Woman of Honor* II. 94 Soon after, a borough deputed to him, with an entreaty to do it the honor of representing it.

†**6.** (See quot., and cf. DEPUTATION 3.) *Obs.*

1832 in *Pall Mall G.* 13 Aug. (1889) 3/2 There lies before me a copy of an old local newspaper of August, 1832, which contains numerous 'Notices to Sportsmen' that the game on such and such a manor is now reserved or 'deputed'.

Hence **de'puted** *ppl. a.*, **de'puting** *vbl. sb.*; also **de'puter**, one that deputes.

1548 GEST *Pr. Masse* I j, There is no sacrament which hath not..bothe hys deputed element, word, and commandement. **1603** SHAKS. *Meas. for M.* II. ii. 60 Not the Kings Crowne; nor the deputed Sword, The Marshalls Truncheon, nor the Iudges Robe. *a* **1641** BP. MOUNTAGU *Acts & Mon.* (1642) 369 No deputation depriveth the Deputer of his right. **1651** G. W. tr. *Cowel's Inst.* 41 Wee have sometimes *Tutores Dativi*, or deputed Guardians amongst us. **1742** YOUNG *Nt. Th.* ix. 228 Already is begun the grand assize..Deputed conscience scales The dread tribunal. **1795** *Fate of Sedley* II. 70 Suetonius Paulinus, the deputed Commander of Nero.

†'**deputery, deputrie.** *Obs. Sc.* [DEPUTE *sb.* + -RY.] The office of a depute, deputyship.

1584 *Sc. Acts Jas. VI* (1814) 300 (Jam.) The office of deputrie and clerkship in the said office of Thesaurarie.

deputize ('dɛpjʊtaɪz), *v.* [f. DEPUTE *sb.* or DEPUTY + -IZE.]

1. *trans.* To appoint as a deputy. Chiefly *U.S.*

1730-6 BAILEY (folio) Pref., *Députize*, to constitute or appoint one a Deputy. **1811** *Port Folio* Jan. (Bartlett), They seldom think it necessary to deputize more than one person to attend to their interests at the seat of government. **1828** WEBSTER *Deputize*, to appoint a deputy; to empower to act for another, as a sheriff. **1877** SPARROW *Serm.* xix. 248 Those who were deputized..did their master's work faithfully.

2. *intr.* To act as a deputy. *colloq.*

1869 *Athenæum* 27 Mar. 445/3 Mr. Perren deputized creditably for Mr. Sims Reeves. **1884** *Musical Times* 1 May 297/1 A London organist, who has relinquished regular work, will deputise upon nominal terms. **1900** *Westm. Gaz.* 27 Sept. 5/2 Sir Samuel Scott being absent in South Africa, has cabled the neighbouring Tory candidate, Mr. Boulnois, to deputise for him. **1904** *Daily Chron.* 15 Sept. 3/6 He was called upon at various times to deputise for other high officials. **1906** *Sat. Rev.* 30 June 807 With the exception of Mr. Stead and Mr. T. P. O'Connor, the representatives of the press were deputising in the absence of their chiefs. **1915** *Observer* 31 Jan. 9/6 Mrs. Levison..deputising for Lady Jellicoe, read to the company a letter. **1929** D. G. MACKAIL *How Amusing* 472 The parlour-maid was deputizing for the housemaid. **1955** *Times* 5 Aug. 4/1 Evans, the Kent wicketkeeper for whom McIntyre deputized in the Leeds Test, will not play again this season.

deputrie, see DEPUTERY, *Obs.*

deputy ('dɛpjʊtɪ), *sb.* Forms: 5 depute, deputee, *Sc.* depwte, 6 deputye, 6-7 deputie, 7- deputy. [a. F. *député*, subst. use of pa. pple. of *députer* to DEPUTE. Originally spelt *depute*; in one form of which the final *e* became mute (though usually retained in writing); in another form it continued to be pronounced, and then as in CITY, etc., it passed through *-ee*, *-ie* to *-y*. (Cf. †*assigne, assign, assignee.*) The ME. examples of *depute* are placed here, but might as well stand under DEPUTE *sb.* See also the corrupted forms DEBITE, DEBITY.]

1. A person appointed or nominated to act for another or others, *esp.* to hold office or exercise authority instead of another; a substitute, lieutenant, vicegerent.

c **1425** WYNTOUN *Cron.* V. x. 381 And Deputis be-hynd hym he left To keipe Brettayne. **1511** HEN. VII in Ellis *Orig. Lett.* Ser. II. I. 170 That..ye..paye unto theim, or to their deputie in their names, the summes aforesaid. **1624** LD. KENSINGTON *ibid.* Ser. I. III. 174 But the case is now different, sayd she, for there the Prince was in Person, heer is but his deputy. But a deputy, answerd I, that represents his person. **1660** WOOD *Life* (O.H.S.) I. 361 For the Greek lecture, the reader therof..got a deputy to do it. **1727** SWIFT *Gulliver* I. vi. 70 In the presence of a professor, or one of his deputies. **1818** JAS. MILL *Brit. India* II. IV. viii. 283 They sent to the army two members of council, as field deputies, without whose concurrence no operations should be carried on. **1841** W. SPALDING *Italy & It. Isl.* III. 338 The.. university of Padua..besides deputies and assistants, has 35 professors.

fig. **1717** L. HOWEL *Desiderius* 58 Those two Deputies of Pride, the Lust of the Flesh, and the Lust of the Eye. **1783** MAD. D'ARBLAY *Diary* 19 Jan., I found her..not merely free from pride, but free from affability—its most mortifying deputy.

b. *Law.* A person authorized to exercise on behalf of another the whole of his office (***general deputy***), or some special function of it (***special deputy***), but having no interest in the office.

1405 *Rolls of Parlt.* III. 605/1 Our generalls and specialls Attornes and Deputes. **1602** FULBECKE *2nd Pt. Parall.* 46 There is great difference betwixt a bailie, & a deputie. **1607-72** COWELL *Interpr.* s.v., A Deputy hath not any interest in the Office, but is onely the shadow of the Officer, in whose Name he doth all things. **1642** PERKINS *Prof. Bk.* i. §100 An assignee is such a person who doth occupie in his own right, and a deputie such a person who doth occupie in the right of another. **1833** *Act 3 & 4 Will. IV*, c. 42 §20 The Sheriff of each County..shall..name..a sufficient Deputy, who shall..have an Office within One Mile of the Inner Temple Hall, for the Receipt of Writs [etc.].

c. A person delegated or sent (alone or as a member of a deputation) to act in the place of those who send him.

1769 ROBERTSON *Chas. V*, V. I. 222 Charles artfully avoided admitting their deputies to audience. **1838** THIRLWALL *Greece* IV. 347 Three deputies were sent back with them to Sinope, to fetch the vessels. **1862** LD. BROUGHAM *Brit. Const.* vi. 87 The lesser barons were called to send deputies, instead of attending personally.

d. Phr. ***by deputy***: by another person in one's stead, by proxy.

1625 BACON *Ess., Studies* (Arb.) 11 Some Bookes also may be read by Deputy, and Extracts made of them by Others. **1764** FOOTE *Mayor of G.* II. Wks. 1799 I. 180 He is suffered to do that by deputy. **1868** FREEMAN *Norm. Conq.* (1876) II. vii. 23 His wars were waged by deputy.

2. Special applications.

†**a.** One deputed to exercise authority on behalf of the sovereign or of the sovereign power; a proconsul, a viceroy, a Lord Lieutenant (of Ireland).

c **1490** in Gairdner *Lett. Rich. III & Hen. VII* (Rolls) App. A, Our right gode lord Gerald erle of Kildare your depute lieutenaunt of this your land of Irland. **1568** BIBLE (Bishops') *1 Kings* xxii. 47 There was then no kyng in Edom, the deputie was king. —— *Acts* xviii. 12 When Gallio was the deputie of Achaia. **1613** SHAKS. *Hen. VIII*, III. ii. 260 You sent me Deputie for Ireland. **1696** *Lond. Gaz.* No. 3190/3 My Lord Capell, Lord Deputy of Ireland. **1851** ROBERTSON *Serm.* Ser. IV. (1863) I. 7 There was there a deputy, that is, a proconsul.

b. In the City of London, a member of the Common Council, who acts instead of an alderman in his absence; a deputy alderman.

1557 *Order of Hospitals* C vj b, The Alderman of the Warde or his Deputie. **1597** SHAKS. *2 Hen. IV*, II. iv. 92, I was before Master Tisick the Deputie, the other day. **1712** STEELE *Spect.* No. 503 ¶2 The deputy of the ward sat in that pew. **1772** *Ann. Reg.* 79/2 Mr. Alderman Peers, with Mr. Deputy Judd.. presented a petition. **1837** *Munic. Corp. Inq. Commission*, Every alderman, except the alderman of Bridge Without, appoints a Deputy, who must be a Common-Councilman of the Ward. **1894** *P.O. London Directory*, Common Council.—The first-named in each Ward is the Deputy.

c. An officer in a coal-mine. (See quots.)

1851 GREENWELL *Coal-trade Terms Northumb. & Durh.* 22 *Deputies*, a set of men employed in setting timber for the safety of the workmen; also in putting in brattice and brattice stoppings. They also draw the props from places where they are not required for further use. **1893** *Daily News* 20 Nov. 5/4 The deputies.. test the beams and other protective appliances put up, examine the passage walls and roofs and the state of the atmosphere, and tell the 'detallers' what to do.

d. The manager of a common lodging-house.

1851 MAYHEW *Lond. Labour* I. 249 In some places knives and forks are not provided, unless a penny is left with the 'deputy', or manager, till they are returned. **1888** *Times* 13 Oct. 12/1 She acted as deputy to the house in question [a common lodging-house].

3. A person elected to represent a constituency; a member of a representative legislative assembly. ***Chamber of Deputies***: the second house in the national assembly of France, and some other countries.

1600 E. BLOUNT tr. *Conestaggio* 76 The three estates of the Realme, that is, the Clergie, the Nobilitie, and the Deputies of the Cities and townes.. at Lisbone. **1777** WATSON *Philip II* (1839) 381 William.. meant.. to remove the assembly of the States (which was summoned to meet at Middleburgh) to a situation in which the deputies would not be so much influenced by the emissaries of Spain. **1792** *Gentl. Mag.* LXII. II. 945 Three hundred and seventy-one deputies, assembled in one of the halls of the palace of the Thuilleries. **1809** KENDALL *Trav.* I. v. 27 The deputies are now frequently denominated *representatives*. They were anciently called *committee-men*. **1837** CARLYLE *Fr. Rev.* III. II. vi, Deputy Thuriot, he who was Advocate Thuriot. **1863** MARY HOWITT *F. Bremer's Greece* I. viii. 264 The Deputies are chosen by the people for three years.

4. *attrib.* and *Comb.* Deputed; acting or appointed to act instead of..; vice-...

1548 HALL *Chron.* 211 b, Either chief Capitain of Caleis or els deputie Capitain. **1624** SANDERSON *Serm.* I. 243 The poor you shall alwayes have with you, as my deputy-receivers; but me (in person) ye shall not have always. **1645** RUTHERFORD *Tryal & Tri. Faith* (1845) 379 Christ's love to us was not deputy-love.. he loved us not by a vicar. **1695** *Lond. Gaz.* No. 3099/3 Mr. Godfrey, Deputy Governor of the Bank of England. **1805** WELLINGTON in Gurw. *Desp.* III. 659 To appoint Captain Bellingham to be Deputy Quarter Master general in Mysore. **1843** MACAULAY *Ess., Mad. D'Arblay*, Singing women escorted by deputy husbands. **1863** H. COX *Instit.* I. vii. 92 The deputy-speakers are usually the chief judges of the courts of Westminster. **1881** RT. HON. A. W. PEEL in *Times* 2 Feb. 6/4 That Standing Order is enabling only, and provides for the appointment and duties of the Deputy-Speaker during the unavoidable absence of the Speaker.

'deputy, *v. rare.* [f. prec. sb.] *trans.* To appoint or send as deputy; to depute.

1605 SYLVESTER *Du Bartas* II. iii. III. *Law* 1126 Frail Aaron, Deputi'd During his [Moses'] absence, all the Flock to guide. **1867** *Quiver* 186 Thrush, linnet, blackbird.. deputied the lark with praise to heaven.

'deputyship. [f. DEPUTY *sb.* + -SHIP]. The office, term of office, or position of a deputy.

1577–87 HOLINSHED *Chron.* III. 1079/2 Richard Beauchampe earle of Warwike.. being.. deputie for John duke of Bedford (being regent of France) did.. obteine manie castels in his deputieship. **1624** CAPT. J. SMITH *Virginia* v. 190 They would not be gouernlesse when his Deputiship was expired. **1765** COWPER *Let. to J. Hill* 8 Nov., I heartily wish him joy of his deputyship. **1881** MRS. OLIPHANT *Harry Joscelyn* II. 281 The state into which his work must have got, but for the strenuous and anxious deputyship of his clerk.

†**de'quantitate**, *v. Obs. rare*⁻¹. [f. DE- II. 1 + L. *quantitāt-em* quantity; see -ATE³ 7.] *trans.* To diminish the quantity or amount of.

1646 SIR T. BROWNE *Pseud. Ep.* II. v. 86 This we affirme of pure gold, for that which is currant.. by reason of its allay ..is actually dequantitated by fire. **1656** in BLOUNT *Glossogr.*

†**de'quass, de'quace**, *v. Obs. rare*⁻¹. [a. OF. *dequasser, decasser* to break down, crush, f. DE- I. 1 + *quasser, casser* to break: see CASS, QUASH, DECASS.] *trans.* To break down, crush.

c **1400** *Test. Love* I. (1560) 276 b/1 Thus with sleight shalt thou surmount and dequace the yvell in their herts.

de quoi, dequoy, obs. forms of DECOY *sb.*²

der, obs. form of DARE *v.*, DEAR, DEER.

deracialize (diːˈreɪʃ(ɪ)əlaɪz), *v.* [f. DE- + RACIAL + -IZE.] *trans.* To remove racial characteristics or features from. So **deraciali'zation**.

1899 S. N. PATTEN *Devel. Eng. Thought* 365 Religious leaders, no longer deracialized by education, are dissatisfied with foreign platitudes and commonplaces. **1907** *Westm. Gaz.* 21 Feb. 2/2 The good service they have rendered by deracialising (so to speak) the elections. **1931** A. KEITH *Ethnos* 27 Where Huxley went wrong was in believing that when Europeans belonging to separate racial stocks.. were planted together.. they became, if I may coin a term, deracialized. *Ibid.* 90, I am convinced that deracialization is possible.

deracinate (dɪˈræsɪneɪt), *v.* [f. F. *déracine-r* (in OF. *desr-*), f. *dé-, des-*, L. DIS- + *racine* root; see -ATE³ 7.] *trans.* To pluck or tear up by the roots; to uproot, eradicate, exterminate. *lit.* and *fig.*

1599 SHAKS. *Hen. V*, v. ii. 47 The Culter rusts, That should deracinate such Sauagery. **1606** —— *Tr. & Cr.* I. iii. 99. **1659** B. HARRIS *Parival's Iron Age* 27 But neither Arms, nor Victories.. [were] able to deracinate or root out this Doctrine. **1788** *Lond. Mag.* 477 To deracinate and annihilate the whole system of moral, historical and revealed asseverations. **1883** STEVENSON *Silverado Sq.* (1886) 80 Disembowelling mountains and deracinating pines!

b. *transf.*

1843 E. JONES *Poems, Sens. & Event* 167 Chill every river into stagnancy, Deracinate the fruitful earth of growth.

Hence **deraci'nation**, eradication, extirpation.

c **1800** tr. *Sonnini's Trav.* I. 227 (L.) Nothing can resist an extreme desire to appear beautiful. The women submit to a painful operation—to a violent and total deracination.

‖**déraciné** (derasine), *a.* [Fr.: see DERACINATE *v.*] 'Uprooted' from one's (national or social) environment. Also as *sb.*

1921 *19th Cent.* May 770 The unseen Jew *déraciné* provides munitions of argument for the revolutionary group. **1926** J. BUCHAN *Dancing Floor* I. vi, She rides well, but her manners are atrocious. Lord, how I dislike these *déracinés*! **1931** in W. Rose *Outl. Mod. Knowl.* 751 To be delocalised is not be be déraciné. **1935** AUDEN & ISHERWOOD *Dog beneath Skin* III. iv, I'm quite déraciné, as they say in Bloomsbury. **1952** D. DAVIE *Purity of Diction in Eng. Verse* ii. 24 The typical *déracinée*, Fanny Price. **1964** R. CHURCH *Voyage Home* v. 71 The dreadful self-consciousness of so many *déraciné* Americans, aping the hyper-civilized European decadents. **1967** *Listener* 22 June 832/1 Our 'dynamic' epoch has.. produced a succession of *déracinés* ranging from Bartók to Stravinsky.

†**de'rade**, *v. Obs. rare.* [ad. L. *dērād-ĕre* to scrape or shave off, f. DE- I. 2 + *rādĕre* to shave.] *trans.* To scrape off or away.

1657 TOMLINSON *Renou's Disp.* 378 Zopissa is Pitch deraded from off maritimous ships. *Ibid.* 658 Quinces.. must be.. not brayed, but deraded.

†**deradiate** (dɪˈreɪdɪeɪt), *v. Obs. rare.* [f. DE- I. 2 + L. *radiāre, radiāt-* to emit rays, f. *radius* ray.] *intr.* To radiate forth.

1650 CHARLETON *Paradoxes* Prol. 3 Those three Lines, perpetually deradiating from the Center of Truth.

Hence †**deradi'ation**, radiation from a point.

1650 CHARLETON *Paradoxes* Prol. 13 The Starres transmitting their Influence, by invisible Deradiations. **1704** J. HARRIS *Lex. Techn.* s.v. *Actinobolism*, The Diffusion or Deradiation of Light or Sound.

derai, obs. spelling of DERAY.

†**de'raign**, *sb. Obs.* In 4–5 dereyne, 5 derenȝe, -rayn, 6 derene. [a. OF. *des-, der-, deraisne, -resne, -raigne, regne, -rene*, f. *desraisnier* to DERAIGN. In Laws of William I. latinized as *disraisnia*.] The action of vindicating or maintaining one's right, *esp.* by wager of battle; hence, a challenge to single combat; a combat; a duel.

[**1292** BRITTON V. xii. §2 Ces plays soint comensables et pledables sicum en le graunt bref de dreit overt, mes nient par disreyne [*transl.* These pleas shall be commenced and tried in the same manner as the great writ of right patent, but not by dereyne].] *c* **1300** *K. Alis* 7353 This dereyne, by the barouns Is y-mad, by alle bothe regiouns. **1375** BARBOUR *Bruce* XIII. 324 On sarisenis thre derenȝeis did he; And [in-till] ilk derenȝe of thai He vencust sarisenis twa. *c* **1470** HARDING *Chron.* IX. iv, Turnus then was slayn: Eneas did that dede and that derayn With mighty strokes. *c* **1500** *Lancelot* 2313 I have o frend haith o dereyne ydoo, And I can fynd none able knycht tharto. **1513** DOUGLAS *Æneis* XII. vi. 15 Suffir me perform my derene by and by. **1658** PHILLIPS, *Derein*.. signifieth the proof of an action which a man affirmeth that he hath done, and his adversary denies. Hence in KERSEY, BAILEY, ASH, etc.

de'raign, *v.*¹ *Obs.* exc. *Hist.* Forms: 3 derenne, 3–4 dereyne, 4 derenȝe, -eine, 4–6 derayne, -aine, 5 derreyne, darreyn, darayne, 5–6 darreyne, -rayne, 5–7 darreine, 6 derene, darrein, -raine, -reigne, 6–7 dereigne, derraine, darraigne, 7 darrayne, deraigne, 7–8 darrain, 7– deraign. [a. OF. *deraisnier, -resnier, -rainier, -reiner, -regner, desr-*, to render a reason or account of, explain, defend, etc., f. *de-, des-* (see DE- I. 6) + *raisnier* to speak, discourse, declare, plead, defend:—late L. type **ratiōnāre*, f. *ratiōn-em* reckoning, account, rendering of reason. The compound may have itself been formed in late L.: cf. the med.L. forms *dē-, dī-, dirratiōnāre* in Du Cange; *disraisnāre, disrainniāre*, were latinized from OF. Cf. also ARRAIGN (OF. *araisnier*).]

1. *trans. Law.* To prove, justify, vindicate; *esp.* to maintain or vindicate (a right, claim, etc.), by wager of battle; to dispute, contest (the claim, etc., of another, asserting an opposing claim).

[**1292** BRITTON I. xxiii. §11 Si felonie, adunc doune le defendour gage a sey defendre, et le apelour gage pur la cause desreyner [*transl.* If felony, then let the defendant give security to defend himself, and the appellor security to prove the cause].] *c* **1325** *Coer de L.* 7098 That hymself agayn fyve and twenty men, In wylde field wolde fyghte, To derayne Godes ryghte. **1340–70** *Alisaunder* 124 To lache hym as Lorde þe lond for to haue, Or deraine it with dintes & deedes of armes. **1375** BARBOUR *Bruce* IX. 746 In-to playn fichting, Ʒhe suld press til derenȝe ȝour richt. *c* **1400** *Destr. Troy* 13084 There was no buerne with þat bold the batell to take, The right to derayne with the rank duke. **1539** *Act 31 Hen. VIII*, c. 1 §2 Euery of the saide ioint tenantes.. maie haue aide of the other.. to the intent to dereigne the warrantie paramount. **1628** COKE *On Litt.* 6 a. *a* **1680** BUTLER *Rem.* (1759) I. 333 You bestow much Pains to prove ..that the King is not above the Law.. And this you deraign, as you call it, so far, that at length you say, the King hath not, by Law, so much Power, as a Justice of Peace, to commit any Man to Prison. **1741** T. ROBINSON *Gavelkind* vi. 129 Who shall deraign that Warranty.

2. *trans.* To vindicate or maintain a claim to (a thing or person); to claim the possession of, *esp.* by wager of battle; to challenge.

a **1240** *Wohunge* in *Cott. Hom.* 285 Ihesu swete ihesu.. þu me derennedes wið like, and makedes of me wrecche þi leofmon and spuse. *c* **1330** R. BRUNNE *Chron.* (1810) 330 Ageyn Kyng Edward, Scotland to dereyne, With werre & batail hard. *c* **1386** CHAUCER *Knt.'s T.* 751 Thou art a worthy knycht And wilnest to darreyne [*v.r.* derreyne, darreyn, darreine, dereyne] hire by bataille. **1893** J. C. BLOMFIELD *Hist. Souldern* 12 Richard de Middelton came and deraigned that Manor in the King's Court.

3. To settle or decide (a claim or dispute) by judicial argument and decision, by wager of battle, etc.; to determine.

c **1330** R. BRUNNE *Chron. Wace* (Rolls) 12629 Ʒyf þou sette chalange þer-ynne.. þorow bataille schal hit be dereynt. **1387** TREVISA *Higden* (Rolls) VII. 241 þe cause schulde be dereynede by dent of swerd. *c* **1430** LYDG. *Bochas* II. xxii. (1554) 59 b, God and trouth was atwene them tweine Egall iudge their quarel to darayne. **1513** DOUGLAS *Æneis* XII. xi. 184 Lat me stand to my chance, I tak on hand For to derene the mater with this brand. **1601** F. TATE *Househ. Ord. Edw. II*, §89 (1876) 53 After thei have dereigned before the steward, thresorer, and the serjantes of thaccount what fee thei shal have for such a present. **1809** BAWDWEN *Domesday Bk.* 460 The jury of the Wapentake have deraigned them to the use of the King.

†**4.** *to deraign battle* (*combat*, etc.): **a.** To maintain (a wager of battle or single combat) in vindication of a claim, right, etc. *Obs.*

c **1380** *Sir Ferumb.* 265 Ʒif he miȝte ffor þat batail to dereyne profry hym forþ to fiȝte. *c* **1386** CHAUCER *Knt.'s T.* 773 Two harneys.. suffisaunt and mete to darreyne The bataille in the feeld bitwix hem tweyne. **1548** HALL *Chron.* (1809) 4 Henry of Lancastre Duke of Herfforde Appellante & Thomas Duke of Norfolke Defendante have.. been redy to darraine the batteill like two valiant Knyghtes & hardy champions. **1586** FERNE *Blaz. Gentrie* 309 To vnderstand the order of the derayning, gaging and ioyning of those battailes, or single combates. **1600** TATE in Gutch *Coll. Cur.* I. 7 Combats personal that are derrained for causes capital.

†**b.** To engage in battle, do battle; whence (in Spenser, etc.) to set the battle in array. *Obs.*

c **1534** tr. *Pol. Verg. Eng. Hist.* (Camden 1844) 88 When Duke Richard had hearde the ambassadours.. he was afeard to darraigne battaile. **1548** HALL *Chron.* 47 The Kyng of Englande.. chose a place mete and conveniente for twoo armies to darrayne battail. **1590** SPENSER *F.Q.* II. ii. 26 Three valiant knights to see.. to darraine A triple warre with triple enmitee. **1593** SHAKS. *3 Hen. VI*, II. ii. 72 Darraigne your battell, for they are at hand. **1602** CAREW *Cornwall* (1769) 125 Then darrayning a kinde of battell (but without armes) the Cæsarians got the overhand. **1608** HEYWOOD *Sallust's Iugurth.* (1609) 20 This happened towards the evening, no fit time to darraigne a battaile. **1654** VILVAIN *Epit. Ess.* I. 54 The.. Kings.. darraind battle with 4 Forreners. *a* **1756** G. WEST *Abuse Trav.* xx. 8 [imitating Spenser] As if he meant fierce battle to darrain.

†**c.** To dispose (troops, etc.) in battle array; to array; to order. (Loose applications of the word by the Elizabethan archaists.) *Obs.*

1591 SYLVESTER *Yvry* 100 Every Chief, apart, Darrains his Troups with order, speed and art. **1596** SPENSER *F.Q.* IV. ix. 4 He gan advise how best he mote darrayne That enterprize, for greatest glories gayne. **1599** NASHE *Lenten Stuffe* 50 The lesser pigmeis.. thought it meete to.. elect a King amongst them that might deraine them to battaile. **1614** SYLVESTER *Little Bartas* 472 To serve Thee, as Hee [man] is sole ordain'd; So, to serve Him, Thou hast the rest [creatures] derrain'd. **1727** J. ASGILL *Metam. Man* 45 God admitted Man to insert this Seed-Royal into the Genealogy of the World, and to deraign his Pedigree in form amongst the Descendants of Adam.

†**de'raign**, *v.*² *Obs.* Also 6 derene, derain, darrayne, 7 dereign. [a. OF. *desregner*, variant of *desrengier*, mod.F. *déranger* to put out of ranks, DERANGE.]

1. To put into disorder; to derange, disarrange.

1500–20 DUNBAR *Now Cumis Aige* 56 Befoir no wicht I did complene, So did her denger me derene. **1530** PALSGR. 506/2, I darrayne (Lydgat), I chaunge or alter a thing from one purpose to another. *Je transmue.* This worde is nat yet admytted in our comen spetche. **1706** PHILLIPS (ed. Kersey), *Deraigne*.. to disorder or turn out of Course.

2. *passive.* To be discharged from (religious) orders: see DERAIGNMENT[2].

1574 tr. *Littleton's Tenures* 42b, He that is professed monke etc. shalbe a monke, and as a monke shalbe taken for terme of his natural life, except he bee derained by the lawe of holye churche [Fr. *Sinon que il soit dereigne y la ley de saint esglise*]. **1602** FULBECKE *1st Pt. Parall.* 11 If in auncient time a Monke, Fryer, or Cannon professed, which was no Soueraigne of an house, had graunted to one an annuitie, this was a voyd graunt, though he had beene after dereigned, or made Soueraigne of the same house, or some other. **1628** [see DERAIGNMENT[2]]. **1661** J. STEPHENS *Procurations* 39 Those Religious persons being deraigned and dispersed, were not..subject to Visitation.

b. *transf.*

1778 *Love Feast* 26 Invested once, no Saint can be deraign'd.

de'raignment[1]. *Hist.* [a. OF. *desraisnement, derainement*, f. *desraisnier*: see DERAIGN *v.*[1] and -MENT.] The act of deraigning; = DERAIGN *sb.*

1706 PHILLIPS (ed. Kersey), *Deraignment*, a deraigning or proving. **1865** NICHOLS *Britton* II. 292 These pleas shall be commenced and tried in the same manner as the great writ of right patent, but not so as to admit of deraignment [AFr. *disreyne*].

†de'raignment[2]. *Obs.* [a. OF. *desrenement*, f. *desregner*: see DERAIGN *v.*[2] and -MENT.] Discharge from a religious order.

1539 *Act 31 Hen. VIII*, c. 6 The same religious persons, and euery of them shall be made able..to sue, and be sued in all manner of actions..after the time of their seueral deraignements, or departinge out of their religion. **1628** COKE *On Litt.* 136b, *Deraignment*, a displacing, or turning out of his order. So when a Monke is derained, he is degraded and turned out of his order, and become a lay man. **1668** HALE *Pref. Rolle's Abridgment* 4 Profession, Deraignment, and the several Appendixes relating thereto, made considerable Titles in the old Year Books.

derail (dɪˈreɪl), *v.* [ad. mod.F. *dérailler* (in Bescherelle's *Fr. Dict.* 1845, adm. by Académie in 1878) 'to go off the rails', f. *dé-* (= DE- II. 2) + *rail* RAIL. Introduced from French about 1850, but app. received into general use first in U.S.]

1. *intr.* To run off or leave the rails.

1850 LARDNER *Railway Economy* 326 *foot-note*, Derailment—I have adopted this word from the French..the verb *to derail* or *to be derailed* may be used in a corresponding sense. **1864** WEBSTER, *Derail*, to run off from the rails of a railway, as a locomotive. *Lardner.* **1883** A. CRANE in *Leisure Hour* 284/2 It [the locomotive] had 'derailed'. **1883** in CASSELL [the only sense given: characterized as *American*].

2. *trans.* To cause (a train, etc.) to leave the rails; to throw off the rails.

1850 LARDNER *Railway Economy* 327 On the 16th September 1847, on the Manchester and Liverpool Railway, the last carriage of the express train, having two passengers in it, was derailed. *Ibid.*, The displacement only became great enough to derail the wheels on the arrival of the last coach at the point. **1881** *Philad. Record* No. 3416. 1 [They] stopped four cars forcibly, derailed them. **1881** M. REYNOLDS *Engine-driving Life* 32 Having their engines derailed. **1892** *Daily News* 4 Apr. 2/4 The faster a train ran, the more likely would it be to derail any impediment on the track.

Hence **de'railed** *ppl. a.*, **de'railing** *vbl. sb.*

1881 *Nature* XXV. 246 A ballasted floor of sufficient strength to hold up a derailed locomotive. **1884** *Christian World* 5 June 419/5 The cause of the derailing of the carriages. **1891** *Times* 26 Sept. 5/1 The telegraph pole having been broken down..by the derailed carriages.

derailleur (dəˈreɪljə(r), dɪ-, -lə(r)). Also ‖dérailleur (derɑjœr). [ad. F. *dérailleur* (*Trésor*, 1927), f. *dérailler* DERAIL *v.*] A bicycle gear in which the ratio is changed by switching the line of the chain (while pedalling) so that it jumps to a different sprocket on the rear wheel. Also ***derailleur gear.***

1930 *Cycling* 11 Apr. 337/1 The Derailleur system of multi-speed gearing is..well-tested..on the Continent, but comparatively new to this country... The gear works by 'de-railing' the chain from one back sprocket to another of different size, thus giving a different gear. **1950** *Chambers's Encycl.* II. 307/2 The most popular variable gear in Great Britain is the 3- and 4-speed hub gear... On the Continent and in America the dérailleur-type gear is more favoured. **1959** *Elizabethan* Apr. 35/1 My lightweight bike with 4-speed hub gear, which is not so vulnerable as the derailleur. **1975** *Which?* May 140/3 All our drop handlebar bikes..had derailleur gears. **1984** *N.Y. Times* 23 Sept. v. 2/1 The whir of well-oiled machinery is interrupted only by decisive clinks as derailleurs move chains to a lower gear for the long, steady climb over the terminal moraine.

derailment (dɪˈreɪlmənt). [ad. mod.F. *déraillement* (cited by Bescherelle 1845, from F. Tourneaux 1841), f. *dérailler*: see DERAIL *v.* Introduced from French *c* 1850: at first chiefly used in U.S.] Said of a railway train, etc.: The fact of leaving or being thrown off the rails.

1850 LARDNER *Railway Economy* 326 In most cases of derailment*, it is the engine which escapes from the rails. [*Foot-note**, I have adopted this word from the French: it expresses an effect..for which we have not yet had any term in our railway nomenclature. By *déraillement* is meant the escape of the wheels of the engine or carriage from the rails.] **1864** WEBSTER, *Derailment*, the state of being off the rails of a railway, as a locomotive. *Lardner.* **1880** *Times* 20 Jan. (*Swiss Railways*), The number of accidents..was 177, of which 55 are classed as derailments, 55 as collisions. **1880** *St. James's Gaz.* 17 Aug. 12, I do not now refer to the influence of speed in producing a derailment.

†de'rain, *v. Obs. rare.* [f. DE- I. 1 + RAIN *v.*] *intr.* To rain down, fall as rain.

c **1563** CAVENDISH *Metr. Visions, Ld. Seymour*, in *Life Wolsey* (1825) II. 109 When I the teares shold se from hir face derayn.

derain(e, variants of DERAIGN *v. Obs.*

derange (dɪˈreɪndʒ), *v.* [(18th c.) a. mod.F. *déranger*, in Cotgr. (1611) *desranger* 'to disranke, disarray, disorder', in OF. *desrengier*, f. *des-, dé-*, L. *dis-* + *renc, reng*, mod.F. *rang* RANK, order. Not in Johnson; considered by him as French:—

'It is not easy to guess how Dr. Warburton missed this opportunity of inserting a *French* word, by reading,—and the wide arch Of *derang'd* empire fall!—*Ant. & Cl.* I. i, which, if *deranged* were an *English* word, would be preferable both to *ruined* and *ranged*'. *Shaks.* 1765 VII. 107.]

1. *trans.* To disturb or destroy the arrangement or order of; to throw into confusion; to disarrange.

1777 ROBERTSON *Hist. Amer.* (1778) II. VI. 173 Lest the order of the procession should be deranged, he moved so slowly, that the Spaniards became impatient. **1793** CRAUFURD in *Ld. Auckland's Corr.* III. 111 The approach of an army would..probably derange what has been decreed in regard to the Vendée. **1836** MACGILLIVRAY tr. *Humboldt's Trav.* ii. 31 A country recently deranged by volcanic action. **1848** MACAULAY *Hist. Eng.* II. 531 This letter deranged all the projects of James. **1889** *Spectator* 12 Oct., If a dancing-girl deranges her dress too much.

†b. 'To remove from place or office, as the personal staff of a principal military officer' (Webster 1828). *Obs.*

1796 MORSE *Amer. Geog.* I. 244 The officers who have been deranged by the several resolutions of Congress, upon the different reforms of the army.

2. To disturb the normal state, working, or functions of; to put into a disordered condition; to cause to act abnormally.

1776 ADAM SMITH *W.N.* IV. vii. (1868) II. 214 Both these kinds of monopolies derange more or less the natural distribution of the stock of the society; but they do not always derange it in the same way. **1789** MILLS in *Phil. Trans.* LXXX. 89 The hill Knock Renestle is a magnetic mass of rock, which considerably deranges the compass. **1804** ABERNETHY *Surg. Obs.* 130 His constitution was so deranged by the irritation of the sore. **1862** SIR B. BRODIE *Psychol. Inq.* II. ii. 39 Habits..which tend in any degree to derange the animal functions, should be scrupulously avoided.

3. To disorder the mind or brain of; to unsettle the reason of.

1825 SOUTHEY *Tale of Paraguay* IV. 60 The trouble which our youth was thought to bear With such indifference hath deranged his head. **1855** MACAULAY *Hist. Eng.* IV. 532 Minds deranged by sorrow.

4. To disturb, interrupt.

1848 *Fraser's Mag.* XXXVIII. 273, I ventured to derange your leisure. **1882** STEVENSON *New Arab. Nts.* 251, I am sorry to have deranged you for so small a matter.

Hence **de'ranging** *vbl. sb.* and *ppl. a.*

1795 *Jemina* II. 30 Her share in this deranging incident. **1870** *Daily News* 5 Oct., All kinds of deranging influences are at work.

derangeable (dɪˈreɪndʒəb(ə)l), *a.* [f. prec. + -ABLE.] Liable to derangement.

1843 SYD. SMITH *Lett.* (D.), The real impediment..is that derangeable health which belongs to old age.

deranged (dɪˈreɪndʒd), *ppl. a.* [f. DERANGE *v.*]

1. Put out of order; disordered, disarranged.

1796 MORSE *Amer. Geog.* I. 246 Measures..to recover them [commercial affairs] from their deranged situation. **1809–10** COLERIDGE *Friend* (1865) 84 A deranged state of the digestive organs. **1875** LYELL *Princ. Geol.* I. I. vii. 125 The deranged and the horizontal formations.

2. Disordered in mind; insane.

c **1790** WILLOCK *Voy.* 319 When I came to mention..they imagined I was still deranged, as there was no such place, as I described. **1856** J. H. NEWMAN *Callista* xii. 140 The few persons whom he met..thought him furious or deranged. **1875** JOWETT *Plato* (ed. 2) III. 465 A man who is deranged and not right in his mind.

derangement (dɪˈreɪndʒmənt). [a. mod.F. *dérangement* (1671 in Hatzf.), f. *déranger*: see DERANGE and -MENT.]

1. Disturbance of order or arrangement; disarrangement, displacement.

1780 T. JEFFERSON *Corr.* Wks. 1859 I. 276 A strange derangement, indeed, our riders have got into, to be nine days coming from Hillsborough. **1854** STOCQUELER *Handbk. Brit. India* 417 They could not be incorporated in their proper places without a very extensive reprint and a derangement of the entire work. **1875** LYELL *Princ. Geol.* I. I. vii. 116 Time must multiply the derangement of strata, in the ratio of antiquity.

2. Disturbance of normal or regular order or working; the condition of being out of order; disorder; disorganization.

1737 BERKELEY *Querist* §457 Whether this folly may not produce..an entire derangement of domestic life..a general corruption in both sexes? **1766** CHESTERF. *Lett.* cccxcviii. (1792) IV. 231 It is a total dislocation and *dérangement*. **1805** W. SAUNDERS *Min. Waters* 502 Without any considerable derangement in the digestive organs. **1856** FROUDE *Hist. Eng.* (1858) I. ii. 146 The derangement of the woollen trade ..was causing distress all over the country.

3. Disturbance of the functions of the mind; mental disorder; insanity.

1800 *Act 39–40 Geo. III*, c. 94 §3 (Jod.) Apprehended under circumstances, that denote a derangement of mind. **1812** G. D. COLLINSON *Law conc. Idiots* I. I. iv. (Jod.), Many actions bear too marked a character of illusion, of derangement, of alienation of mind, that a man in his senses could not by any possibility commit them. **1825** SOUTHEY *Tale of Paraguay* IV. 66 Mark of passion there was none; None of derangement. **1874** MAUDSLEY *Respons. in Ment. Dis.* vii. 233 Supplying the interpretation of the previously obscure attacks of recurrent derangement.

†de'rasion. *Obs. rare*⁻¹. [n. of action from L. *dērādĕre* to shave off.] A scraping or shaving off.

1684 tr. *Bonet's Merc. Compit.* III. 79 The derasion made at the foresaid time is sufficient.

derate (diːˈreɪt), *v.* [f. DE- II. 2 + RATE *sb.*[1]] *trans.* and *intr.* To diminish or remove the burden of rates (upon). Hence **de'rating** *vbl. sb.* and *ppl. a.*

1928 W. S. CHURCHILL in *Hansard's Parl. Deb.* Ser. v. CCXVI. 849 Twelve months will be required after that Bill is passed, to enable the new valuation to be made for the purposes of de-rating. *Ibid.* 869 The cost of the complete de-rating of agriculture is about £4,750,000. **1928** *Daily Express* 22 June 2/4 [He] asked the Government to expedite their derating scheme, which is expected to be worth £3,000,000 a year to the coal industry. **1928** *Daily Tel.* 17 July 11/4 [He] proposed to derate hospitals supported by voluntary subscriptions. **1955** *Times* 10 June 9/4 At the time they were de-rated there might have been some justification. *Ibid.* 15 June 3/1 Lord Meston said that the whole subject of derating should be reviewed.

deration (diːˈræʃən), *v.* [DE- II. 2 + RATION *sb.*] *trans.* To free (a rationed commodity) from rationing. Also **de'rationing** *vbl. sb.*

1920 *Glasgow Herald* 25 Nov. 8 The Food Controller was able to announce..last night that sugar will be derationed as from Monday. *Ibid.* 15 One substantial instalment of decontrol I can announce to you to-night—the derationing of sugar. **1945** *John o' London's* 16 Nov., Goods become derationed, only because some bureaucracy rationed them. **1955** *Times* 16 May 4/6 Withdrawal of price controls..hand in hand with derationing. **1959** *Listener* 1 Jan. 8/1 A minor news item of 1958 that strikes the fancy as one thinks back is that coal was 'derationed'.

derationalize (diːˈræʃənəlaɪz), *v.* [f. DE- II. 1 + RATIONALIZE *v.*] To deprive of reason. So **derationali'zation.**

1871 C. HODGE *Systematic Theol.* I. I. iii. 279 To call upon men to worship gravitation..is to call upon them to derationalize themselves. **1879** W. JAMES *Coll. Ess. & Rev.* (1920) 129 Further considerations..may supervene and make relative or derationalise a mass of thought. **1938** H. READ *Poetry & Anarchism* IV. 48 The dialectical method.. leaves us with an art which is not so much art as an instrument of derationalization.

deratization (diːrætaɪˈzeɪʃən). [f. DE- + RAT *sb.*[1] + -IZATION.] The expulsion or extermination of rats.

1914 *Standard* 13 Oct. in *N. & Q.* 11th Ser. X. 386 The Board of Trade communication gives a translation of the circular, in the course of which it more than once uses the curious word 'deratization', meaning, apparently, the clearing away of rats. **1921** *Glasgow Herald* 28 May 5 A discussion of 'Deratisation of Ships at British Ports'. **1929** *Stat. Rules & Orders No. 832* (*title*) The Public Health (Deratisation of Ships) Regulations. **1949** *Times* 9 Oct., The port health authority's 'measures against rodents' include 'deratization' and 'rat-proofing'.

deray (dɪˈreɪ), *sb. arch.* Also 4 derai, 4–5 derray(e, dray, 5 derei; *β.* 4–5 desray(e. See also DISRAY. [a. OF. *desrei, desrai*, later *desroi, derei, derai, deroi*, f. tonic stem of *desreer*: see DERAY *v.*, also ARRAY *v.*, DISARRAY.]

†1. Disorder, disturbance, tumult, confusion. ***to make deray***: to create a disturbance, act violently and noisily. *Obs.* (or *arch.*).

c **1300** *K. Alis.* 1177 He tok Alisaundre this deray, For to amende gef he may. *c* **1320** *Sir Tristr.* 3165 On canados sche gan crie And made gret deray. *c* **1420** *Anturs of Arth.* xl, Querto draues thou so dreȝghe, and mace suche deray? *c* **1470** HENRY *Wallace* VI. 239 The schirreff cryt: Quha makis that gret deray? **1513** DOUGLAS *Æneis* VII. x. 77 Turnus was by, and amyd this deray, This hait fury of slauchtyr, and fell afray.

β. *a* **1330** *Fragm. Alexander*, in *Rouland & V.* (1836) p. xxiii, Ther men might reuthe y-sen Muchel desray, muchel gredeing. **1485** CAXTON *Chas. Gt.* 239 Wherof they maad grete noyse and desraye.

†b. Impetuosity; display of vigour or prowess.

c **1300** *K. Alis.* 2721 Sone he say A yong knyght, also of gret deray..Ageyns him he gynneth to ride. *c* **1325** *Coer de L.* 502 The aventerous with gret deray So hard to our knyght he droff, Hys schelde in twoo peses roff.

c. Disarray, confusion. *modern archaism.*

1831 HOGG in *Fraser's Mag.* IV. 425 Whose beauty, form, and manners bland, Have wrought deray through all the land. **1850** BLACKIE *Æschylus* II. 196 Him struck dismay In wild deray. **1872** —— *Lays Highl.* 82 They rove the vest, and in deray They flung her on the floor.

†2. Disorderly action towards any one; violence, injury, insolent ill-treatment. ***to do or make deray to***: to do violence to; to disturb, molest. *Obs.*

c **1300** *Cursor M.* 23346 (Cott.) If þai suld for þaa feluns prai, It war gain godd and gret derai. *c* **1340** *Ibid.* 15568 (Trin.) þou sal se hem ȝitt to nyȝt do me gret deray. **1375** BARBOUR *Bruce* XV. 438 Lordyngis, it war my will Till mak end of the gret deray That dowglass makis vs ilk day. *c* **1440** *York Myst.* xxvii. 121 Peter I have prayed for the So that thou schall noȝt drede his dray. *c* **1450** *Guy Warw.* (C.) 4336 Who hath done þe all þys deraye. **1480** CAXTON *Ovid's Met.* XII. xix, Achylles was full of desraye and inyquyte, and drewe the body of Hector by grete woodenes. ? *a* **1550** *Freiris of Berwik* 536 In thy depairting se thow mak no deray Vnot no wicht, bot frely pass thy way.

3. Disorderly mirth and revelry as in a dance or similar festivity. Chiefly in the alliterative phrase ***dancing and deray***. *arch.*

1500–20 DUNBAR *Poems* lxxviii. 14 For din, nor danceing, nor deray, It will nocht walkin me no wise. **1513** DOUGLAS *Æneis* I. xi. *heading*, Off the bancat, and of the greit deray, And how Cupide inflambes the lady gay. *a* **1550** *Christis Kirke Gr.* i, Wes nevir in Scotland hard nor sene Sic dansing nor deray. **1807** J. STAGG *Poems* 65 Wi' lowpin', dancin' and deray. **1824** SCOTT *Redgauntlet* Let. xi, There was.. dancing and deray within. **1837** CARLYLE *Fr. Rev.* I. II. I. xii, So have we seen fond weddings..celebrated with an outburst of triumph and deray, at which the elderly shook their heads. **1892** *Daily News* 2 Dec. 5/2 The dancing and deray were so public that all classes had their share of the fun.

¶ **4.** *erron.* for ARRAY.

1538 *Aberdeen Reg.* V. 16 (Jam.) To be in thair best deray ilk persone.

† **deray** (dɪˈreɪ), *v. Obs.* Also **dray**. [a. OF. *desreer, -reier, -rayer*, later *desroier, derroyer, derayer*, = Pr. *desreiar*, It. *disredare*:— Rom. type **des-rēdāre*, f. L. DIS- + *-rēdāre*, f. **rēdo* preparation, order: see ARRAY. (The atonic stem in OF. was *desre-*, the tonic *desrei-, -rai-, -roi-*, which was afterwards extended to the inf. and other atonic forms.)] *refl.* and *intr.* To act or behave in a disorderly manner; to rage.

1340–70 *Alisaunder* 883 Nectanabus..graithes him sone Deraide as a dragoun dreedful in fight. *c* **1350** *Will. Palerne* 1210 þus despitusly þe duk drayed him þanne. *Ibid.* 2061 He deraied him as a deuel.

¶ Used for DERAIGN *v.*[1] [Confusion of *derayne* with infin. *deraye(n.)*]

c **1314** *Guy Warw.* (A.) 3915 Finde a Sarrazin oþer a kniȝt, & he schal anoþer finde, þat schal deray[ne] his riȝt kinde. *c* **1325** *Coer de L.* 5456 Wylt thou graunt with spere and scheeld Deraye the ryght in the feelde.

derayn(e, variants of DERAIGN *v. Obs.*

derb, *a. rare.* ? *nonce-wd.* [a. Ger. *derb* compact, solid, rough.] Rough, uncrystallized, massive.

1825 COLERIDGE *Aids Refl.* 329 If..I oppose transparent chrystallized Alumen to opake derb (*unchrystallized*) Alumen.

Derby (ˈdɑːbɪ, ˈdɜːbɪ). The name of a town (in OE. named by the Northmen *Déorabý, Déorbý*) and shire of England, and of an earldom named from the shire or county. See also DARBY. Hence:

1. a. Proper name of the most noted annual horse-race in England, founded in 1780 by the twelfth Earl of Derby, and run at the Epsom races, usually on the Wednesday before, or the second Wednesday after, Whitsunday (the actual date being fixed each year in connexion with those of the Newmarket and Ascot meetings, by the Jockey Club).

1844 W. H. MAXWELL *Sports & Adv. Scotl.* xxxix. (1855) 305 What care I about Oaks or Derbys? **1848** DISRAELI in *Harper's Mag.* Aug. (1883) 340/2 'You do not know what the Derby is'. 'Yes I do. It is the Blue Ribbon of the Turf'. **1871** M. COLLINS *Mrq. & Merch.* II. vi. 161, I had been to the Derby.

b. Hence *attrib.* and in *comb.*, as **Derby day**, the day on which the 'Derby' is run; **Derby dog**, the proverbial dog on the race-course, after this has been otherwise cleared; hence *allusively*, something sure to turn up or come in the way.

1838 *Observer* 26 Aug. 2/2 During last Epsom races, on the Derby day we believe, [etc.]. **1862** *Times* 6 June, It was a real Derby gathering, and, if possible, a Derby gathering exaggerated with all its queer *mélange* of high and low. **1867** *Punch* LII. 227/1 The Mystery of the Derby dog..the never-failing apparition of the Derby dog at Epsom. **1871** M. COLLINS *Mrq. & Merch.* I. vi. 190 On a Derby Day the hill at Epsom is thronged with them. **1885** *Times* 4 June 10/2 The reputation which invariably attaches to a Derby winner.

c. *transf.* Of similar important races in other countries, as ***the French Derby***.

1890 *Whitaker's Alm.* 584/1 The winner of the French Derby. **1894** *Daily News* 20 Feb. 5/3 The great 'Snowshoe Derby' took place on Sunday and yesterday at Holmenkollen near Christiania.

d. Applied to any kind of important sporting contest; also ***air Derby*** (see also *aerial Derby*, s.v. AERIAL *a.* 5); ***local Derby***, a match between two teams from the same district.

1909 *Daily Chron.* 17 June 5/6 The twenty-ninth Medway Barge Sailing Match, known locally as 'the barge Derby'. **1914** *Daily Express* 3 Oct. 3/1 A local Derby [*sc.* football match] between Liverpool and Everton. **1914** *Whitaker's Almanack 1915* 822/2 Air 'Derby' round London (94½ miles). **1919** *Sphere* 28 June 259 (*heading*) An air derby at 129 miles per hour. **1962** *BBC Handbk.* 37 It would still be right for local talent to be nursed and local derbies to be played.

2. a. Short for ***Derby hat***: a stiff felt hat with a rounded crown and narrow brim. *U.S.*

1888 *Pall Mall G.* 12 June 14/1 Girls or young ladies are seen with their hands thrust deep into the ulster pocket..the derby tipped on one side. *Ibid.* 24 Sept. 11/1 Low felt hats—Derby hats, as they are generally called here [U.S.]—were universal.

b. A kind of sporting-boot having no stiffening and a very low heel (see also quot. 1968).

1901 *Daily News* 23 Feb. 6/4 The Prince Consort is represented..as wearing low-heeled, square-toed 'Derbies', with buckles on them. **1904** *Westm. Gaz.* 15 Apr. 10/2 Russia calf Derbys for shooting-boots. **1968** J. IRONSIDE *Fashion Alphabet* 130 *Derby*,..the most common form of shoe. A tie shoe with eyelets and laces, the quarter and facings stitched *on top* of the vamp.

3. *Plastering.* = DARBY 5.

1823–42 [see DARBY 5]. **1876** W. PAPWORTH in *Encycl. Brit.* IV. 504 He is furnished with..a hand float, a quirk float, and a derby or darby, which is a long two-handled float for forming the floated coat of lime and hair.

4. Derby neck = DERBYSHIRE neck.

1769 T. PROSSER (*title*), An Account of the Method of Cure of the Bronchocele, or Derby-neck. **1771** BARRETTI *Journ. Lond. to Genoa* II. 148 Gaváys mean a Derby-neck or a man that has a Derby-neck.

5. a. Denoting a variety of porcelain made at Derby, *esp.* a soft-paste porcelain made from about 1750, Crown Derby being a variety made from 1784. Cf. *Crown Derby* s.v. CROWN *sb.* 35.

1850 [see *Crown Derby* s.v. CROWN *sb.* 35]. **1868** C. L. EASTLAKE *Hints Household Taste* ix. 194 The qualities which distinguish old Chelsea, Derby, Worcester, and Plymouth china are well known to connoisseurs. **1869** LADY C. SCHREIBER *Jrnl.* (1952) I. 1. One small Derby group. *Ibid.* 4 A small Derby statuette of Neptune. **1875** W. F. TIFFIN (*title*) A Chronograph of the Bow, Chelsea and Derby Porcelain Manufactories. **1885** *Encycl. Brit.* XIX. 641/2 The Derby under-glaze blue was remarkably fine. **1957** MANKOWITZ & HAGGAR *Encycl. Eng. Pottery* 70/2 The work of the earliest phase of Derby porcelain was nonphosphatic. .. The next phase of Derby was characterized by the use of pale delicate colours, [etc.].

b. Derby red = *chrome red* (CHROME 3).

1904 GOODCHILD & TWENEY *Technol. & Sci. Dict.* 155/1 *Derby red*, a scarlet red pigment of good covering and staining power, sometimes used as a substitute for vermilion. **1937** *Thorpe's Dict. Appl. Chem.* (ed. 4) I. 550/1 *Austrian cinnabar*. Derby red, Chinese red.

6. ***Derby*** or ***Derbyshire cheese***, a hard, pressed cheese made from partly skimmed milk, produced chiefly in the Derbyshire district. Also *ellipt.*

1902 *Encycl. Brit.* XXVII. 355/2 Derby cheese in its best forms is much like Leicester, being 'clean' in flavour and mellow. **1905** W. H. SIMMONDS *Pract. Grocer* III. 79 The true 'Derbyshire' cheese..is a small cylindrical or flat and thin cheese of pale colour, and generally of rich, buttery quality. 'Derby Goudas' are a variety shaped like the Dutch Gouda. **1955** J. G. DAVIS *Dict. Dairying* (ed. 2) 189 *Derbyshire or Derby cheese*, one of the oldest of our national cheese, but it was not until recently that a uniform method came to be adopted for its manufacture. **1970** *Listener* 12 Nov. 661 You can buy a special Derby cheese in good food shops in London that's got a green stripe in it—known as Sage-green Derby.

7. ***Derby scheme***: in the war of 1914–18, a recruiting scheme initiated in October 1915 by the seventeenth Earl of Derby. Also ***Derby recruit*** and simply *Derby*, a soldier recruited under this scheme.

1915 *Times* 4 Dec. 9/6 Last week of the Derby Scheme. *Ibid.* 20 Dec. 9/2 Men who have been attested and classified under the Derby scheme. **1917** P. GIBBS *Battles of Somme* 177 Old English regiments with new men in them, including some of the 'Derby recruits'. *a* **1918** J. T. B. MCCUDDEN *Five Yrs. R.F.C.* (1919) 198 It was at that time [Feb. & Mar. 1917] that the 'Derby' scheme was operating. **1925** FRASER & GIBBONS *Soldier & Sailor Words* s.v., Men of the 'Groups' of 'Derbies', awaiting their turn to be called up,.. wore armlets lettered 'G.R.' (General Reserve). **1927** W. S. CHURCHILL *World Crisis, 1916–18* I. x. 239 It was evident that the Derby scheme could only be a palliative.

Derbyshire (ˈdɑːbɪ-, ˈdɜːbɪʃə(r)). [In OE. *Déorbý-scír, Déorbí-scír*: see prec.] The shire or county of Derby in England. Hence

1. Derbyshire neck: a swelling of the thyroid gland; bronchocele, goitre; so called as being endemic in parts of that county.

1802 BEDDOES *Hygëia* vi. 67 The water of melted snow has been held by many authors to be the cause of the bronchocele or Derbyshire neck. **1836** SIR G. HEAD *Home Tour* 117 The malady..called the 'Derbyshire neck'—an endemic protuberance in the throat, or goitre. **1878** T. BRYANT *Pract. Surg.* I. 191 Goitre, or Derbyshire neck, is very common.

2. Derbyshire spar, †**drop**: fluor-spar.

1772 GILPIN *Lakes Cumberland* (1788) II. 217 It..is known in London by the name of the Derbyshire drop. But on the spot it is called Blue John. **1788** *Cronstedt's Min.* 26 Pieces of Derbyshire spar, through which the light of a candle formed many images. **1854** J. SCOFFERN in *Orr's Circ. Sc.* Chem. 64 Derbyshire spar (fluoride of calcium).

derche, obs. form of DIRGE.

† **der-ˈdoing**, *ppl. a. Obs. rare*$^{-1}$. A pseudo-archaism of Spenser, app. from *dare-do* taken as a compound verb, with pple. in -ING (cf. DERRING-DO) taken in the sense 'Doing daring deeds'.

Dere-doing as a legitimate combination would mean 'harm-doing, mischief-working'.

1590 SPENSER *F.Q.* II. vii. 10 Me ill befits, that in derdoing armes And honours suit my vowed daies do spend, Unto thy bounteous baytes..to attend.

† **dere**, *sb. Obs.* Forms: 3–6 **dere**, 4–5 **der**, 5 (**darr**), **deire**, **derre**, **deerre**, 5–6 **deere**, 5–7 *Sc.* **deir**, 6 **deare**, 7 *dial.* **dare**. [f. DERE *v.*: perhaps a continuation of OE. *daru* (whence ME. *darr*) with the vowel assimilated to the vb.: cf. MDu. *dere*, in Kilian *dere, deyre* 'nocumentum, offensa, noxa'. See next.] Harm, hurt, injury, mischief, *esp.* in phr. ***to do (a person) dere***.

c **1250** *Gen. & Ex.* 3214 Pharaon bannede vt his here, Israel he ðhoȝte to don dere. *c* **1330** R. BRUNNE *Chron. Wace* (Rolls) 8904 Now may ȝe lyghtly bere þe stones to schip wyþouten dere. **14..** *Grene Knt.* 401 in *Sir Gawayne* (Bannatyne Club) App. 237 If itt be poynt of any warr, There shall noe man doe you noe darr. *c* **1460** *Towneley Myst.* (Surtees) 149 Wylle ye do any dere to my chyld and me? *c* **1485** *Digby Myst.* (1882) II. 192, I shall the socor in euery dere. *c* **1570** *Pride & Lowl.* (1841) 13 Many a vice.. Which do, and have done this land mickle deere. **1603** *Philotus* lxxiii, Ȝow mon first to me sweir, That ȝe to me sall do na deir. **1674** RAY *N.C. Words* 13 *Dare*, harm or pain.. It does me no dare, i.e. no harm.

† **dere**, *v. Obs.* Forms: 1 **derian**, 2–4 **derie(n**, (4 **deri**, **derye**), 2–3 **deren**, 3–6 **dere**, 4–5 **der**, (4–7 **deere**, 5 **deire**, **dayre**, 5–6 **deyre**, 6 **dear(e**, *Sc.* **deir**, 6–7 **dare**). [OE. *dęrian, dęriȝan* = OFris. *dera*, OS. *derian*, MDu. *dēren* (*daren*), Du. *deren*, OHG. *terjan, teren*, MHG. *tern*:—WGer. **darjan*, f. WGer. **dara* str. fem., OHG. *tara*, OE. *daru*, hurt, harm, injury, damage.]

1. *trans.* To hurt, harm, injure.

In OE. intrans. with dative, 'to do harm to'.

c **888** K. ÆLFRED *Boeth.* vii. §3 þæt him ða stormas derian ne mahan. *c* **1175** *Lamb. Hom.* 13 Ne þet eou scal derien nouðer here ne hunger. *c* **1200** *Trin. Coll. Hom.* 79 Flesliche lustes þe derieð ure sowle. *c* **1300** *Havelok* 574 Leoun or wlf ..Or oþer best, þat wolde him dere. **1380** *Lay Folks' Catech.* (Lamb. MS.) 831 Fals wytnesse þow noon beere þy neyȝbore wyttyngly to dere. *c* **1470** HENRY *Wallace* IX. 164 He gert him suer Fra that day furth he suld him neuir der. *c* **1510** BARCLAY *Mirr. Gd. Manners* (1570) Div, Who is without trespasse, what can him hurt or dere. **1573** TUSSER *Husb.* ii. (1878) 8 Great charge so long did dare me. *c* **1611** CHAPMAN *Iliad* XI. 406 The wound did dare him sore. **1613** T. POTTS *Disc. Witches* (1845) Kij a, The stick nor the stake shall never deere thee.

b. *absol.* To do harm, 'hurt'.

a **1100** *O.E. Chron.* an. 1032 Gehwær hit [þat wilderfyr] derode eac on maneȝum stowum. *a* **1300** *Cursor M.* 10014 (Cott.) þat nathing mai cum in þat ders. *c* **1386** CHAUCER *Sqr.'s T.* 232 And of Achilles for his queinte spere, For he couþe wiþ it boþe hele and dere. *c* **1400** *Destr. Troy* 1293 Ffor to dere for the dethe of his dere cosyn.

2. To trouble, grieve, vex, annoy, incommode.

c **1340** *Cursor M.* 7377 (Trin.) To be king not wol him dere. *c* **1400** MAUNDEV. (Roxb.) iii. 9 Stagez..ilk ane abouen oþer, to see þe iustyng, so þat nane schall dere oþer, ne lett oþer to see. *c* **1400** *Destr. Troy* 13550 Now me bus, as a beggar, my bred for to thigge At doris vpon dayes, that dayres me full sore. **1481** CAXTON *Reynard* xxxix. (Arb.) 106 That dered hym so moche that he wyste not what to saye.. he was so angry in his herte. **1559** *Mirr. Mag., Dk. Suffolk* x, When we [envoys] shewed wherein eche other dered, we sought out meanes al quarels to haue clered. **1674** RAY *S. & E.C. Words* 64 *It dares me*, it pains or grieves me.

Hence **ˈdering** *vbl. sb.*; **ˈdering** (*derend, deriynde*) *ppl. a.*, doing harm, hurtful.

a **1325** *Prose Psalter* liv. [lv.] 3 Hij were derend to me in ire. **1340** *Ayenb.* 63 Þer byeþ leazinges helpinde, and leazinges likynde, and leazinges deriynde. *c* **1400** *Destr. Troy* 11003 Dyng hom to dethe for deyring of other. *c* **1440** *Promp. Parv.* 118 Derynge or noyynge, *nocumentum, gravamen.*

dere, obs. form of DARE *v.*[2], DEAR, DEER.

derealize (diːˈriːəlaɪz), *v. Philos.* [f. DE- II. 1 + REALIZE *v.*[2]]

To deprive of reality, make unreal. So **deˈrealizer** (see quot. 1909); **deˈrealizing** *ppl. a.*

1889 W. JAMES in *Mind* XIV. 351 Corroborated, not de-realised, by the ultimate principle of my belief. **1904** —— *Meaning of Truth* (1909) iv. 109 We have no transphenomenal absolute ready, to derealize the whole experienced world by, at a stroke. **1909** —— *Pluralistic Univ.* ii. 49 Pluralism, in exorcizing the absolute, exorcizes the great de-realizer of the only life we are at home in. **1964** B. FRECHTMAN tr. *Sartre's Saint Genet* 161 And what if, by means of this makebelieve, he drew everything—trees, plants, utensils, animals, women and men—into a derealizing whirl?

derecogˈnition. [f. DE- II. + RECOGNITION.] The withdrawal of recognition, esp. *Pol.* formally by one country, government, etc., from another.

1953 *Birmingham* (Alabama) *News* 7 Nov. 13/1 A case for the 'de-recognition' of the Soviet government has been made by the Soviet agents in this country themselves. **1977** *New Yorker* 13 June 77/1 Far more convincing..is the legitimate concern one hears expressed about the psychological as well as the material impact that derecognition could have around the world. **1979** *Time* 1 Aug. 14/1 (*heading*) Taiwan: An inauspicious beginning: disgruntlement and protest over derecognition. **1984** *Washington Financial Rep.* 26 Nov. 853 All accounting standards-setting bodies that have addressed the issue have concluded that derecognition of deposit float is inappropriate.

Hence (as a back-formation) **de'recognize** *v. trans.*, to withdraw recognition from (another country, etc.).

1961 *New Yorker* 20 May 163/1 What we have to do, then, is *not* spend money on defense, *not* pay taxes,..and, above all, derecognize Russia and it will blow away. **1972** *New Scientist* 21 Sept. 486/3 One advanced MSc course within London University has been 'derecognised'. Awards for one-year MSc studentships cannot be granted to unrecognised courses. **1980** *Economist* 31 May 50/3 The Russians suddenly discovered Genghis's 'reactionary' nature and Ulan Bator derecognised him. **1986** *Illustr. Weekly of India* 13 July 42/1 Yet another important provision in this bill was the power to derecognise degrees.

derect, obs. var. of DIRECT.

de'redden, *v. Astr.* Also **de-redden**. [f. DE- II. 1 + REDDEN *v.*] *trans.* To correct the observed spectrum of (a star, etc.) for the reddening of its light by interstellar material, so as to arrive at its intrinsic spectrum. Also with the observed spectrum as obj.

1971 *Astron. & Astrophysics* X. 270 The 41 stars..were individually dereddened by the 'Q-method' of Johnson. **1976** *Ibid.* L. 446/2 We can estimate the amount of extinction..by dereddening the observed spectrum until a smooth flux distribution..is obtained. **1978** *Nature* 5 Oct. 412/2 All the observed data are de-reddened using $E(B - V) = 0.06$..and the extinction law of Code *et al.* in the UV. **1985** *Astron. & Astrophysics* CXLIII. 455/1 H 1286 can be dereddened to a position on the ZAMS.

Hence **de'reddened** *ppl. a.*, **de'reddening** *vbl. sb.*

1971 *Astron. & Astrophysics* X. 275/2 Individual dereddened values of *B-V* were determined. **1979** *Nature* 19 Apr. 719/1 To obtain the observed (dereddened) anomalous line luminosity, we find that the particle density in the emitting region is $\sim 10^{12}\text{cm}^{-3}$. **1985** *Astron. & Astrophysics* CXLIII. 457/1 Dereddening moves H 1286 to the ZAMS.

†**'dereful**, *a. Obs.* [? f. DERE *sb.* + -FUL.] Full of grief, sorrowful.

? *a* **1400** *Morte Arth.* 4054 Thane drawes he to Dorsett.. Derefulle dredlesse with drowppande teris.

deregister (diːˈrɛdʒɪstə(r)), *v.* [f. DE- + REGISTER *sb.*¹] *trans.* To remove from a register. Hence **,deregi'stration**.

1924 *Glasgow Herald* 19 Nov. 11 Disobedience would almost certainly have caused de-registration of the union under the Arbitration Act. **1925** *Ibid.* 23 Jan. 10 Mr Justice Powers indicated plainly that he would deregister the union if he did not receive a pledge that the men would obey the award. **1928** *Daily Express* 4 Feb. 8/7 The late Dr. Axham was de-registered for assisting Sir Herbert Barker. **1951** *Here & Now* (N.Z.) May 14/1 The compulsory union officialdom is necessarily afraid of any action that may lead to 'deregistration' and with that to the possible loss of their jobs. **1971** *Daily Tel.* 15 Feb. 1/1 All unions will be automatically registered with the new Registrar, and it will be up to unions to 'de-register' themselves. *Ibid.* 13 Apr. 6/3 De-registration or non-registration will lay the unions open to heavy taxation.

deregu'lation. [f. DE- II. + REGULATION.] The removal of regulations and restrictions, esp. those fixing prices, (from an industry, etc.).

1963 *Petroleum & Chem. Transporter* Jan. 10/1 We cannot bear to think of the awful consequences of deregulation. **1964** *Economist* 23 May 838/1 The de-regulation of about two-thirds of the rates charged by the railways. **1973** *Philadelphia Inquirer* 7 Oct. 8/1 The API report said deregulation of natural gas prices would bring only minor rises in the price paid by the consumer. **1977** *National Observer* (U.S.) 1 Jan. 2 Adams is also a critic of several leading schemes for deregulation of airlines and surface carriers. **1984** *Guardian* 22 Oct. 2/7 Soon, several Conservative MPs will press ministers for a large-scale 'deregulation' of the industry.

Hence (as a back-formation) **de'regulate** *v. trans.*, to free from regulation, esp. tariff restriction; to decontrol.

1964 *Economist* 23 May 838/2 The only rates to be de-regulated were..on agricultural and fishery products transported in bulk. **1973** *Nature* 27 Apr. 550/1 President Nixon has proposed that Congress should amend the Natural Gas Act to deregulate the well-head price of gas so that the price will increase. **1980** *Times* 11 Apr. 21/5 The FCC decided to..deregulate the marketing of basic telephone equipment.

deregulatory, *a.* [f. DEREGULATE *v.* + -ORY².] Of, pertaining to, or characterized by deregulation; favouring deregulation.

1975 *Aviation Week & Space Technol.* 15 Sept. 9/2 It has also proposed a line of suggested deregulatory experimentation. **1978** *Times* 22 Mar. 23 They ran up against a team of American negotiators in full deregulatory flight, adamant that they were not going to be deflected from their main demand to have cheap fares at once, whatever the effect might be on the airlines. **1982** *Economist* 6 Mar. 11/1 The courage of their deregulatory convictions. **1984** *Sunday Times* 25 Nov. 9/2 Solicitors, who will shortly have to compete with professional house conveyancers, are already reeling from the government's de-regulatory policies.

dereign(e, dereine, var DERAIGN *v. Obs.*

derelict ('dɛrɪlɪkt), *a.* and *sb.* [ad. L. *dērelict-us*, pa. pple. of *dērelinquĕre* to forsake wholly, abandon, f. DE- I. 3 + *relinquĕre* to leave, forsake.]

A. *adj.*

1. Forsaken, abandoned, left by the possessor or guardian; *esp.* of a vessel abandoned at sea; *transf.* said of land left dry by the recession of the sea.

1649 JER. TAYLOR *Gt. Exemp.* I. i. ¶10 The affections which these exposed and derelict children bear to their mothers. **1700** LUTTRELL *Brief Rel.* (1857) IV. 640 A tryal before the barons of the exchequer..about derelict lands left by the sea in Yorkshire. **1848** HALLAM *Mid. Ages* i. Notes iii. (1855) I. 106 Gaul, like Britain..had become almost a sort of derelict possession, to be seized by the occupant. **1888** *Times* 21 Aug. 9/3 Massowah, which, having been abandoned and left derelict by Egypt..was seized by Italy as a *res nullius*.

fig. **1774** BURKE *Amer. Tax.* Wks. (1842) I. 171 They easily prevailed, so as to seize upon the vacant, unoccupied, and derelict minds of his friends.

2. Guilty of dereliction of duty; unfaithful, delinquent (*U.S.*). Hence **derelictness**.

1864 *Daily Tel.* 13 Sept., Probably you will think that United States Commissioner Newton was very 'derelict' in his duty. **1888** *The Voice* (N.Y.) 4 Oct., The derelictness of many officials in Kansas.

B. *sb.*

1. A piece of property abandoned by the owner or guardian; *esp.* a vessel abandoned at sea.

1670 *Lond. Gaz.* No. 534/1 A small Virginia ship laden with Tobacco, which they seised as a Derelict, pretending the men had forsaken the ship. **1727-51** CHAMBERS *Cycl.*, *Derelicts*, in the civil law, are such goods as are wilfully thrown away, or relinquished by the owner. **1838** DE QUINCEY *Mod. Greece* Wks. XIV. 320 Often..plague.. would absolutely depopulate a region..In such cases, mere strangers would oftentimes enter upon the lands as a derelict. **1877** W. THOMSON *Cruise Challenger* iv. 61 On the morning of March 23rd we steamed in search of the derelict.

b. A person abandoned or forsaken.

1728 SAVAGE *Bastard* Pref., I was a Derelict from my cradle. **1873** BROWNING *Red Cott. Nt.-cap* 258 To try conclusions with my helplessness,—To pounce on, misuse me, your derelict, Helped by advantage that bereavement lends?

2. One guilty of dereliction of duty (*U.S.*). Cf. A. 2.

1888 *The Voice* (N.Y.) 3 Jan., The Republicans renominated and triumphantly re-elected the derelicts.

dere'lict, *v. rare.* [f. L. *dērelict-*, ppl. stem of *dērelinquĕre*: see prec.]

†1. *trans.* To abandon, forsake. *Obs.*

1622 DONNE *Serm. John* xi. 35 Friends..must not be derelicted, abandoned to themselves. **1691** T. H[ALE] *Acc. New Invent.* lxxiii, Grants..of Lands derelicted.

2. *fig.* To fail to keep or observe; to fall short of. *nonce-use.*

1881 MACFARREN *Counterp.* iv. 9 Exceptions can only be understood by students who are thoroughly conversant with the rules they [the exceptions] derelict.

dereliction (dɛrɪˈlɪkʃən). [ad. L. *dērelictiōn-em*, n. of action from *dērelinquĕre*: see DERELICT. Cf. obs. F. (16th c.) *dereliction* (Godef.).]

1. The action of leaving or forsaking (with intention not to resume); abandonment. (Now *rare* exc. in legal use.)

a **1612** DONNE *Βιαθανατος* (1644) 123 The next species of Homicide..is Permission, which when it is toward ourselves, is by the schoolemen usually called Desertion, or Dereliction. **1649** JER. TAYLOR *Gt. Exemp.* I. viii. ¶5 Repentance and dereliction of sins. **1782** GIBBON *Decl. & F.* xxxvi. (1836) 586 This wise dereliction of obsolete, vexatious, and unprofitable claims. **1818** JAS. MILL *Brit. India* II. v. iv. 442 He recommended, if not a dereliction, at any rate a suspension of the design. **1875** BRYCE *Holy Rom. Emp.* xi. (ed. 5) 176 Imposts..by long dereliction apparently obsolete.

b. The condition of being forsaken or abandoned. Now *rare*.

1597 HOOKER *Eccl. Pol.* v. xvii. §2 Dereliction in this world, and in the world to come confusion. **1675** BROOKS *Gold. Key* Wks. 1867 V. 98 That Jesus Christ did suffer dereliction of God really; that he was indeed deserted and forsaken of God. **1771** *Junius Lett.* lxvii. 330 The unhappy baronet has no friends..you are not reduced to so deplorable a state of dereliction. **1807** VANCOUVER *Agric. Devon* (1813) 85 These mansions..whether their dereliction arises from the caprice or folly of their owners, etc.

c. *fig.* The 'abandonment' or leaving dry of land by the sea; *concr.* the land thus left dry.

1767 BLACKSTONE *Comm.* II. 261 Lands newly created.. by the alluvion or dereliction of the sea. **1804** COLEBROOKE *Husb. Bengal* (1806) 8 Land which has been gained by the dereliction of water. **1866** ROGERS *Agric. & Prices* I. iv. 106 Norfolk has gained largely on the eastern side by the dereliction of the sea.

2. In modern use implying a morally wrong or reprehensible abandonment or neglect; chiefly in the phr. *dereliction of duty*.

1778 BURKE *Corr.* (1844) II. 217 A dereliction of every opinion and principle that I have held. **1836** J. GILBERT *Chr. Atonem.* iv. (1852) 90 He will not accept of compliments paid to his power at the expense of a dereliction of his royal claims. **1840** H. AINSWORTH *Tower of London* viii, They would be answerable with their lives for any further dereliction of duty. **1860** PUSEY *Min. Proph.* Mal. ii. 11, Idolatry, the central dereliction of God. **1892** LD. ESHER in *Law Times Rep.* LXVII. 211/2 The plaintiffs have been guilty of a dereliction of duty, but for which the sewage matter would not flow into the stream.

b. Hence *absol.* Failure in duty, delinquency.

1830 HERSCHEL *Stud. Nat. Phil.* 11 In this case it was moral dereliction which gave to ridicule a weight and power not necessarily..belonging to it. **1841** EMERSON *Lect., Man the Reformer* Wks. (Bohn) II. 236 The employments of commerce..are..vitiated by derelictions and abuses at which all connive. **1881** S. H. HODGSON *Outcast Ess.* 396 What! on thy guiltless children wilt thou call Lightly the curse of such a dereliction? **1882** HINSDALE *Garfield & Educ.* I. 396 Each pupil felt..that he owed her a personal apology for any dereliction or failure on his part.

†3. Failure, cessation; *esp.* sudden failure of the bodily or mental powers, fainting. *Obs.*

1647 H. MORE *Song of Soul* III. App. lxxix, Of brasen sleep and bodi's derelictions. **1749** BP. LAVINGTON *Enthus. Methodists* (1820) 23 Derelictions, terrors, despairings. **1794** G. ADAMS *Nat. & Exp. Philos.* IV. xl. 91 The word eclipse ..signifies dereliction, a fainting away, or swooning. **1797** E. M. LOMAX *Philanthrope* 169 All at once, by some unfortunate dereliction of mind, he made a full stop.

†b. Failure, defect, shortcoming. *Obs.*

1801 FUSELI in *Lect. Paint.* ii. (Bohn 1848) 383 Michelangelo..no doubt had his moments of dereliction. **1807** OPIE *ibid.* i. 265 Michelangelo had derelictions and deficiencies too great to be overlooked.

dereligionize, -ing: see DE- II. 1.

dereling, -yng, obs. forms of DARLING.

†**dere'linque**, *v. Obs. rare*⁻⁰. = next.

1623 COCKERAM, *Derelinque*, to leaue.

†**derelinquish** (diːrɪˈlɪŋkwɪʃ), *v. Obs.* [f. RELINQUISH, after L. *dērelinquĕre*: see DERELICT. Cf. OF. *derelainquir* in same sense (Godef.).] *trans.* To relinquish utterly, forsake, abandon.

a **1612** DONNE *Βιαθανατος* (1644) 106 That it were deadly sinne in him to de-relinquish the Church. **1679** J. SMITH *Narrat. Pop. Plot* Ded. B, That you will not..both desert your Self, and de-relinquish the care of three Kingdoms. **1799** KIRWAN *Geol. Ess.* 81 This vast continental depression, whose derelinquished space was occupied by water.

derene, -renne, -reyne, variants of DERAIGN *v. Obs.*, to prove, etc.

dere'press, *v.* [f. DE- II. 1 + REPRESS *v.*¹] *trans.* To cause to be no longer repressed; to activate. So **dere'pressed** *ppl. a.*

1960 *Biochem. & Biophys. Res. Communications* III. 373 (*heading*) A 'pace-setting' phenomenon in derepressed enzyme formation. **1962** *Proc. Nat. Acad. Sci.* XLVIII. 1805 The use of leucine auxotrophs makes it possible to derepress maximally all the enzymes of isoleucine-valine biosynthesis. **1971** *Nature* 11 June 395/2 Environmentally stimulated derepressed regions of the DNA molecule. **1976** SMYTHIES & CORBETT *Psychiatry* vii. 120 Various personality traits which he had previously been able to keep under control may be derepressed. **1977** P. B. & J. S. MEDAWAR *Life Sci.* xiv. 119 Genes which operate in fetal life and are then normally switched off are somehow reawakened or 'derepressed' in tumours. **1978** *Nature* 16 Mar. 253/1 Sea urchin eggs are shed in a metabolically repressed state and are derepressed by fertilisation.

Hence **dere'pression**, the action or result of derepressing.

1960 *Biochem. & Biophys. Res. Communications* III. 373 The change from repression to derepression occurs relatively abruptly. **1971** J. Z. YOUNG *Introd. Study Man* xxii. 288 These may take many forms, perhaps by derepression of operons. **1978** *Nature* 4 May 52/2 They suggested that such reactions are due to the derepression of 'silent' genes in the tumours resulting in the expression of foreign H-2 antigens.

derequisition (diːrɛkwɪˈzɪʃən), *v.* [f. DE- II. 1 + REQUISITION *v.*] *trans.* To convey (requisitioned land, property, etc.) to its original owner. Hence as *sb.* Also **derequi'sitioning** *vbl. sb.*

1945 *News Chron.* 7 May 3/1 In the North, Blackpool's vast Olympia building, just derequisitioned, has been booked. **1946** *Ann. Reg. 1945* 3 The de-requisitioning of factory and storage space. *Ibid.* 342 Our studio space remained restricted through delays in de-requisition. **1955** *Times* 9 July 11/7 The corporation had agreed to seek authority from the Minister to derequisition the plaintiffs' premises. **1957** *Times Lit. Suppl.* 13 Dec. 753/2 The fishing inn and its stream provide a lively contrast with the de-requisitioned mansion beside the gloomy lake.

†**de'rere**, *adv. Obs.* [a. OF. *deriere*, now *derrière*, behind = Pr. *dereire*, It. *dietro*, *drieto*:—late pop. L. *de-retro* 'from backwards'.] Behind.

c **1386** CHAUCER *Reeve's T.* 181 (Harl.) This seely clerkes ronnen vp and doun, Wiþ keep, keep, stand, stand, Iossa, ware derere, Ga wightly þou and I sal keep him here.

dereserve (diːrɪˈzɜːv), *v.* [f. DE- II. 1 + RESERVE *v.*] *trans.* To deprive of exemption from military service, as in the wars of 1914–18 and 1939–45. Hence **dereser'vation**, the action of the verb; **dere'served** *ppl. a.*

1941 *Hutchinson's Pict. Hist. War* 22 Jan.–18 Mar. 247/1 We are reviewing the reserved occupations, and carrying out a great deal of dereservation. **1941** in *Amer. Speech* XVI. 277 Men in Class B who have been dereserved may be called up for civil defense in the near future. **1944** *Manpower* (*Min. of Information*) 54 We have seen..how the deferment of de-reserved men is now on an individual basis.

dere'strict, *v.* [DE- II. 1 + RESTRICT *v.*] *trans.* To remove restrictions from; *spec.* to remove a speed limit on traffic in a specified road, area, etc. So **dere'stricted** *ppl. a.*; **dere'striction** *sb.*

1935 *Punch* 29 May 634/3 Was it really necessary, for example, to add the word 'Derestriction' to our language in order to say that the speed-limit would no longer be enforced on certain roads? **1936** 'J. TEY' *Shilling for Candles* xxv. 270 Grant took full advantage of the lunchtime lull in traffic, and in derestricted areas excelled himself in the gentle art of speed with safety. **1936** *Times* 9 Jan. 7/2 In the opinion of the Minister there had been a *prima facie* case for derestriction. **1937** *Evening News* 15 Feb. 8/3 Mr. Belisha's henchmen were busy removing the derestriction signs from the lamp-posts. **1955** *Times* 24 June 4/7 The whole of the required two million tons to derestrict coal for the household market would have to come from America. **1960** *Ibid.* 9 Feb. 14/6 Few of the Ministry of Transport driving test routes include derestricted roads. **1966** J. MILES in T. Wisdom *High-Performance Driving* viii. 83 Since we've just passed a de-restriction sign, you can start motoring. **1971** *Daily Tel.* 19 May 17 De-restriction of the present broadcasting hours .. is the least independent television can reasonably expect from the Government.

†**derf**, *sb. Obs.* [app. shortened from OE. *ȝedeorf* labour, trouble, tribulation, f. *deorfan* to labour: see DERVE.] Trouble, tribuation, hurt.

[*c* **1000** ÆLFRIC *Colloquy* ⁋16 Hiȝ, hiȝ, micel ȝedeorf ys hit!] *c* **1205** LAY. 10943 Nas na man .. þæt dursten him derf makien. *a* **1225** *Ancr. R.* 80 Strong uorte drien derf ine Godes seruise. *Ibid.* 106 Heo wolde þet derf þuldeliche þolien. *Ibid.* 180 Sicnesse, meseise .. and euerich licomliche derf þet eileþ þe vlesche. *c* **1230** *Hali Meid.* 17 Abeore bliðeliche þe derf þat tu drehest.

†**derf**, *a.* (*adv.*) *Obs.* Forms: 3 (*Orm.*) **derrf, deorrf**, 3–4 **derue**, 3–6 **derf**, 4–5 **derff**, 4–6 **derfe**, 5–6 **derffe, darf(e**, 6 **dearfe**. [app. a. ON. *djarfr* (:—*derfa-z*) bold, daring, audacious, impudent: cf. OSw. *diarver, diærver*, Sw. *djerf*, Da. *diærv*; cognate with OS. *derƀi*, OFris. *derfe*; not recorded in OE. where the forms would be *deorf, dierfe*; cf. *deorrflike* in Ormin.]

1. Bold, daring, courageous, brave.

c **1200** ORMIN 16780 He [Nicodemus] nass nohht derrf inoh all opennliȝ to sekenn þe Laferrd Crist. *Ibid.* 19598 Wiþþ derrf & openn spæche. **1375** BARBOUR *Bruce* XVIII. 307 The frer .. wes derrf, stout, and ek hardy. *c* **1400** *Destr. Troy* 12800 His derf knightes. **1513** DOUGLAS *Æneis* IX. ix. 22 Turnus the prince, at was baith darf and bald.

b. In a bad sense: Bold, audacious, daringly wicked.

a **1300** *Cursor M.* 12936 (Cott.) Þat derf o ded, þat fals traitur. *Ibid.* 27749 (Cott.) Wreth .. wentes man fra goddis will and mas him derf to dedis ill. ? *a* **1400** *Morte Arth.* 3779 Thow salle be dede and undone for thy derfe dedys. *c* **1460** *Towneley Myst.* (Surtees) 305 Fulle darfe has been oure deede for-thi commen is our care. **1570** LEVINS *Manip.* 31 Darfe, stubborn, *pertinax, obduratus*.

2. Strong, sturdy, stout.

c **1340** *Gaw. & Gr. Knt.* 1233 Þe dor drawen, & dit with a derf haspe. ? *a* **1400** *Morte Arth.* 312 No more dowte the dynte of theire derfe wapyns. *c* **1450** HENRYSON *Mor. Fab.* 78 His darf oxen I compt them not a flee.

b. Vigorous, forcible, violent.

c **1440** *York Myst.* xlvi. 17 That drewe all tho domesmen derffe indignacioun. *c* **1450** *Golagros & Gaw.* 359 Delis thair full doughtely mony derf dynt. **16..** *Earl Westmorland* 291 in Furniv. *Percy Folio* I. 311 Blowes that were both derfe and dire.

3. Painful, grievous; terrible, dreadful; cruel.

a **1225** *Leg. Kath.* 565 Ich hire wule don to þe derueste deað. *c* **1325** *E.E. Allit. P.* B. 862 Dotz away your derf dyn & derez neuer my gestes. *c* **1470** HENRY *Wallace* VII. 217 Mony .. Off Wallace part, thai putt to that derff deid.

b. Troublesome, hard, difficult.

a **1225** *Leg. Kath.* 948 For nis him no derure for to adweschen feole þen fewe. *c* **1230** *Hali Meid.* 19 His reades .. derue beoð to fullen. **1535** STEWART *Cron. Scot.* III. 294 The darfast way .. Tha tuke the gait without rangat till go.

B. as *adv.* Grievously, terribly.

c **1325** *Metr. Hom.* (1862) 23 Slic wordes said Crist of thir wers That folc in werd ful derf deres.

derfde, pa. t. of DERVE *v. Obs.*

†'**derfful**, *a. Obs.* In 4 **derful**, 6 **darfful**. [? f. DERF *sb.* + -FUL.] ? Troublous, hurtful; or = DERF *a.* Hence '**derffully** *adv.*

c **1340** *Cursor M.* 22544 (Edin.) Wod and wal al doun sal draw of demster þat derful aw. [*Other MSS.* dredful.] **1535** STEWART *Cron. Scot.* 2338 The dartis flew lyke fyre out of the flint Darfful and dour. *a* **1225** *Leg. Kath.* 1090 Deien se derfliche [*one MS.* derffulliche].

†'**derfly**, *a. Obs.* [? f. DERF *a.* + -LY[1]: cf. ON. *djarfligr* bold, daring.] Grievous, terrible, dreadful; = DERF *a.* 3.

a **1300** *Cursor M.* 1143 (Cott.) Þi derfli dede has liknes nan. *Ibid.* 7182 To derfly ded þai suld him bring.

†'**derfly**, *adv. Obs.* Forms: see DERF *a.* [f. DERF *a.* + -LY[2]. Cf. ON. *djarfliga* boldly.]

1. Boldly; fiercely.

c **1200** ORMIN 9752 Forrþi toc hem Sannt Iohann Deorrf-like to begrippen. *c* **1220** *Bestiary* 411 For to winnen fode derflike wiðuten dred. *c* **1340** *Gaw. & Gr. Knt.* 2334 How þat doȝty dredles deruely þer stondez. *a* **1400–50** *Alexander* 2942 Þan has ser Dary dedeyne, & derfely [*Dublin MS.* darfly] he lokes.

2. Forcibly, violently.

c **1200** ORMIN 16195 Þatt tuss derrfliche drifesst alle þis follc ut off þiss minstre. *c* **1340** *Cursor M.* 19712 (Edin.) Þai toke þair rede derueli [*v.r.* derfli] do him to þe dede. *c* **1400** *Melayne* 1033 So darfely bothe thaire dynttis thay driste. **1535** STEWART *Cron. Scot.* I. 41 Eolus .. In Yrland cost rycht darflie did thame dryve. *a* **1605** POLWART *Flyting w. Montgomerie* 542 To dreadfull dolour dearfly or ȝe dryue him.

b. Quickly, promptly.

c **1325** *E.E. Allit. P.* B. 1641 Derfly þenne Danyel deles þyse wordes. *a* **1400–50** *Alexander* 3006 Derfly on þe toþir day a douth he assembles. *c* **1475** *Rauf Coilȝear* 798 To the Montane he maid him full boun .. Derflie ouir Daillis.

3. Grievously, terribly.

a **1225** *Ancr. R.* 114 Þus was Iesu Crist .. in alle his fif wittes derfliche ipined. ? *a* **1400** *Morte Arth.* 3278 And there-fore derflyche I am dampnede for ever!

†'**derfness.** *Obs.* [f. DERF *a.* + -NESS. Sense 1 appears to be related to DERF *sb.*]

1. Trouble, hardship; = DERF *sb.*

c **1175** *Lamb. Hom.* 21 Þes þu hefdest mare deruenesse on þisse liue of þine licome, þes þu scoldest hersumian þe bet þine leofe drihten. *a* **1300** *Cursor M.* 3996 (Cott.) Man þat þou will help in nede Thar him neuer na derfnes drede.

2. Boldness, audacity.

c **1400** *Destr. Troy* 5110 He, þat warpes thies wordes in his wild foly, Shuld degh, for his derfenes.

†'**derfship.** *Obs.* [f. DERF *a.* + -SHIP.] Audacity.

a **1225** *Leg. Kath.* 978 Þis is nu þe derfschipe of þi dusi onsware and te deopnesse.

dergie, obs. form of DIRGE.

deric ('dɛrɪk), *a. Biol.* [mod. f. Gr. δέρος skin + -IC.] Pertaining to, or constituting, the skin or outer integument of the body.

1878 BELL *Gegenbaur's Comp. Anat.* 36 The outer germinal layer (deric layer or ectoderm) forms the outer limiting layer of the body.

derick, var. spelling of DERRICK.

deridable (dɪ'raɪdəb(ə)l), *a.* [f. DERIDE *v.* + -ABLE.] That may be derided or ridiculed.

1804 JEFFREY *Let.* in Ld. Cockburn *Life* II. xliv, You .. have yet to learn that everything has a respectable, and a deridable aspect.

deride (dɪ'raɪd), *v.* [ad. L. *dērīdē-re* to laugh to scorn, scoff at, f. DE- I. 4 + L. *rīdēre* to laugh. Cf. OF. *derire* and rare *derider* (Godef.).]

1. *trans.* To laugh at in contempt or scorn; to laugh to scorn: to make sport of, mock.

1530 [see DERIDING below]. **1545** JOYE *Exp. Dan.* iii. 44 In al tymes haue the tyrants derided the godly while they paciently waited for Gods helpe. **1581** PETTIE *Guazzo's Civ. Conv.* I. (1586) 30 b, Mockers and flouters, who .. deride everie man. **1611** BIBLE *Luke* xxiii. 35 And the rulers also .. derided him. **1621** BURTON *Anat. Mel.* III. iv. I. i. (1652) 633, I knowe not whether they are more to be pitied or derided. **1667** MILTON *P.L.* XI. 817 Of them derided, but of God observ'd The one just Man alive. **1763** J. BROWN *Poetry & Mus.* v. 75 A Bagpipe (an Instrument which an Englishman derides). **1781** GIBBON *Decl. & F.* II. xxviii. 99 He justly derides the absurd reverence for antiquity. **1853** J. H. NEWMAN *Hist. Sk.* (1873) II. II. vii. 272 Doctrines which, as an orator, he does not scruple to deride.

†**2.** *intr.* To laugh contemptuously or scornfully.

1619 H. HUTTON *Follies Anat.* (Percy Soc.) 43 The hang-man .. Began to scoffe, and thus deriding said. **1663** WOOD *Life* (Oxf. Hist. Soc.) I. 466 A club .. where many pretended witts would meet and deride at others. **1675** TRAHERNE *Chr. Ethics* App. 562 When they deride at our profession.

Hence **de'rided** *ppl. a.*, **de'riding** *vbl. sb.* and *ppl. a.*; **de'rider**, one who derides, a mocker; **de'ridingly** *adv.*, in a deriding way, with derision.

1530 PALSGR. 213/2 Deridyng, laughyng to skorne, *derision*. **1543** *Necess. Doctr.* H iij, A dissembler or rather a deryder of penance. **1563–87** FOXE *A. & M.* (1596) 635 (R.) In the same epistle [he] deridinglie commendeth them. **1594** HOOKER *Eccl. Pol.* IV. i. §1 Prophane and deriding adversaries. **1672** *Life & Death J. Alleine* vi. (1837) 71 Deriding and menacing language. **1680–90** TEMPLE *Ess. Heroic Virtue* Wks. 1731 I. 221 Their decayed and derided Idolatry. **1695** WOODWARD *Nat. Hist. Earth* II. (1723) 116 His indiscreet .. Derideing .. of his Father. **1792** MAD. D'ARBLAY *Diary* Jan., 'What do you mean by going home?' cried she, somewhat deridingly. **1845** LD. CAMPBELL *Chancellors* (1857) IV. lxxiv. 8 He deridingly called the swan on his badge, 'a goose'. **1857** HUGHES *Tom Brown* I. iii. (1871) 63 [He] smote his young derider on the nose.

†**de'rident**, *a. nonce-wd. Obs.* [ad. L. *dērīdēnt-em*, pr. pple. of L. *dērīdēre* to DERIDE.]

? Deriding, or smiling.

1609 *Ev. Woman in Hum.* I. i. in Bullen *O. Pl.* IV. 308 *Bosse.* Most sweete mistriss, most derydent starre. *Acut.* Then most rydent starre faire falle ye.

derige, obs. form of DIRGE.

de rigueur: see DE II.

dering: see under DERE *v.*

derisible (dɪ'rɪzɪb(ə)l), *a.* [f. L. type **dērīsibilis*, f. *dērīs-*, ppl. stem of *dērīdēre*: see -BLE. Cf. It. *derisibile* 'that may be derided' (Florio 1611).] To be derided; worthy of derision.

1657 TOMLINSON *Renou's Disp.* 712 The Pharmacopolist that wants Sugar, is not so derisible, as he. **1885** STEVENSON *Dynamiter* 45, I was his hopeless and derisible inferior.

derision (dɪ'rɪʒən). Also 5 **dyrision**, 6 **diresioun**. [a. F. *dérision* (13th c.), ad. L. *dērīsiōn-em*, n. of action from *dērīdēre* to DERIDE.]

1. The action of deriding or laughing to scorn; ridicule, mockery.

a **1400** *Cov. Myst.* (Shaks. Soc.) 191 Of thi wurdys I have skorne and derysone. *c* **1470** HENRY *Wallace* VIII. 646 It were but derysioun To croun him king but woice off the parlyment. **1484** CAXTON *Curiall* 4 That sholde be a grete lesynge and worthy of derysion. **1590** SHAKS. *Mids. N.* III. ii. 123 Scorne and derision neuer comes in teares. **1601** ? MARSTON *Pasquil & Kath.* II. 244 Scourg'd with the whip of sharpe derision. **1624** DE LAWNE *Du Moulin's Logick* 70 Sometimes names are given by contraries, and by way of derision. As, when a dwarfe is called a Goliah. **1777** WATSON *Philip II* (1793) III. XIX. 16 She had regarded it rather as an object of derision than alarm. **1852** CONYBEARE & H. *St. Paul* (1862) I. iv. 118 The people of Antioch were notorious for inventing names of derision.

b. with *pl.* An instance of this, a deriding.

1535 COVERDALE *Jer.* xx. 10 For why I herde so many derisions and blasphemies. **1844** MRS. BROWNING *Lady Geraldine's Courtship* xci, Out of reach of her derisions.

c. Phrases. ***in, †by, †for, †to derision.***

c **1477** CAXTON *Jason* 17 And thus saide to him by derision. **1494** FABYAN *Chron.* VI. cxcviii. 205 In dyrision and despyte of the Danys. **1514** BARCLAY *Cyt. & Uplondyshm.* (Percy Soc.) 25 Than do they laughe us unto derysyon. **1526** *Pilgr. Perf.* (W. de W. 1531) 205 His tytle for derysyon wryten and set ouer his heed. **1549** *Compl. Scot.* xx. 169 He vald laucht and scorn vs be grit derisione. **1655–60** STANLEY *Hist. Philos.* (1701) 77/1 Scarce able to write, which when upon any occasion he did, it was to derision. **1747** WESLEY *Char. Methodist* 11 Those who are in Derision so called. **1847** DE QUINCEY *Sp. Mil. Nun* vii. (1853) 14 In derision of the gay colours.

d. ***to hold*** or ***have in derision***: to treat with scorn and mockery. ***to be in derision***: to be subjected to mocking ridicule, to be a laughing-stock; so ***to bring into derision***.

(With *hold, have* the action is prominent, with *be* the condition of the derided.)

1494 FABYAN *Chron.* VI. clviii. 147 Bernulphus .. hadde this Egbert in derysyon. **1527** R. THORNE in Hakluyt *Voy.* (1589) 258 Among wise men it should be had in derision. **1535** COVERDALE *Job* xxx. 1 Now they that are .. yonger then I, haue me in derision. *a* **1571** THROGMORTON *Let. to Cecil* in Froude *Hist. Eng.* (1881) VI. xxxix. 439 We begin to be in derision already for the bruit only. **1612** T. TAYLOR *Comm. Titus* ii. 8 He was in daily derision, euery one mocked him. **1770** BURKE *Pres. Discont.* (R.), British policy is brought into derision.

2. *concr.* An object of ridicule; a laughing-stock.

1539 BIBLE (Great) *Ps.* lxxix. 4 We are become .. a very scorne and derysyon to them that are rounde aboute vs. **1612** T. TAYLOR *Comm. Titus* ii. 8 His word was a reproach and derision to the profane. **1746** HERVEY *Medit.* (1818) 270 The venerable patriarch is the derision of scoundrels.

†**de'risionary**, *a. Obs.* [See -ARY.] Of the nature of derision, expressing derision, derisory.

a **1704** T. BROWN *Lett. Dead to Living* Wks. 1759 II. 215 All hell applauds you mightily for .. that derisionary festival, which you keep.

derisive (dɪ'raɪsɪv), *a.* [f. L. *dērīs-*, ppl. stem of *dērīdēre* to DERIDE + -IVE. Cf. OF. *derrisif, -ive.*]

a. Characterized by derision; scoffing, mocking.

a **1662** GAUDEN *Sacrament* 98 (L.) His derisive purple stained .. with blood. **1725** POPE *Odyss.* II. 364 Derisive taunts were spread from guest to guest. **1871** H. AINSWORTH *Tower Hill* I. ii, 'Soh! you are come!' he exclaimed, in a deep, derisive tone. *a* **1897** *Mod. Newspr. Rept. of Parlt.* The statement of the hon. member was received with derisive cheers [i.e. *Hear! hear!* uttered in derisive tones].

b. That causes derision, ridiculous.

1896 *Westm. Gaz.* 25 Feb. 2/1 In thirteen years he has brought a paper costing money to keep it going and with a derisive circulation to the front rank of the world's journalism. **1923** *Daily Mail* 15 May 8 Germany has provided only a derisive amount to make good that cruel injury.

Hence **de'risively** *adv.*, in a mocking manner, with derision; **de'risiveness**.

1665 SIR T. HERBERT *Trav.* (1677) 220 That hyperbole .. which derisively term[s] Cairo and Damascus villages. *Ibid.* 243 (R.) The Persians [were] thence called Magussæi derisively by other ethnicks. **1838** DICKENS *Nich. Nick.* xlv, 'Never you mind', retorted that gentleman, tapping his nose derisively. **1847** CRAIG, *Derisiveness*, the state of being derisive.

†**deri'sorious**, *a.* [f. as next + -OUS.] = next.

1664 H. MORE *Antid. Idolatry* 73 A derisorious Allusion to the occasion of the name of that City. **1681** —— *Postscr.* in Glanvill *Sadducismus* I. (1726) 34 His unworthy Usage of the Holy Writ, and his derisorious Interpretations of it.

derisory (dɪ'raɪsərɪ), *a.* [ad. L. *dērīsōri-us*, f. *dērīsor* derider, mocker, agent-n. from *dērīdēre*.]

a. Characterized by derision; mocking, derisive.

1618 CHAPMAN *Hesiod* II. 325 The garrulous grashopper .. Sits pouring out her derisory song. *a* **1700** B. E. *Dict. Cant. Crew, Cold Iron*, a Derisory Periphrasis for a Sword. **1791–1823** D'ISRAELI *Cur. Lit., Pol. Nicknames*, The derisory nickname [Roundhead]. **1853** GROTE *Greece* II. lxxxiii. XI. 51 Occasions for derisory cheering. **1888** *Times* 6 Sept. 7/2 They prefer decorous obscurity to a derisory notoriety.

b. = DERISIVE *a.* b.

1923 *Westm. Gaz.* 19 Mar., In comparison with what it was hoped to do the result is derisory. **1923** *Daily Mail* 5 June 8 Of the total German payments for reparations France has received in cash or kind the derisory amount of £14,500,000, and England the equally preposterous amount of £5,700,000. **1971** *Oxford Times* 23 July 1/6 Both rejected the present rate offer as 'derisory'.

deriva'bility. *rare.* [f. DERIVABLE: see -ITY.] The quality of being derivable.
1865 MASSON *Rec. Brit. Philos.* 352 The existence which each man predicates of himself is, according to Mr. Mill, derivability from that neutrum.

derivable (dɪ'raɪvəb(ə)l), *a.* [f. DERIVE *v.* + -ABLE. Cf. mod.F. *dérivable.*] Capable of being derived: in various senses of the vb.

†**1.** Capable of being transmitted or passed on from one to another; transmissible. *Obs.*
1640 BP. HALL *Episc.* II. vi. 118 Those works which are.. derivable to all successions, to the end of the world. **1649** —— *Cases Consc.* (1650) 416 This incest..was permanent, and derivable to her posterity. *a* **1716** SOUTH (J.), The eternal rule and standard of all honour derivable upon me.

2. Capable of being drawn or obtained (*from* some source); obtainable.
a **1711** KEN *Christophil* Poet. Wks. 1721 I. 521 Fill'd with all Plenitude Divine, Derivable from Godhead Trine. **1799** WELLINGTON in Owen *Desp.* 158 The collateral benefits derivable by the Company. **1869** PHILLIPS *Vesuv.* v. 150 The singular product, derivable from some organic bodies, called petroleum. **1884** *Law Times* 31 May 75/1 The income derivable from a capital sum of..twenty-six millions.

3. Capable of being obtained or drawn as a conclusion, deduction, or inference; deducible *from.*
1653 WILKINS *On Prayer* iv. (T.), The second sort of arguments, from ourselves, are derivable from some of these heads. *a* **1677** BARROW *Serm.* Wks. 1716 II. 57 The right sense thereof seemeth best derivable from..the nature of the subject he treateth on. **1873** PROCTOR *Expanse Heaven* 81 The main inference derivable from these hurricanes does not relate to their effects but to their cause.

4. Capable of being traced up to, or shown to proceed *from* (a source); traceable.
a **1682** SIR T. BROWNE *Tracts* 137 Derivable from the common Tongue diffused through them all. *a* **1716** SOUTH *Serm.* VI. 226 (T.) All these lamentable accidents were both subsequent upon, and derivable from a sin, which was fully pardoned. **1862** H. SPENCER *First Princ.* II. iii. §50 All other modes of consciousness are derivable from experiences of Force.

Hence **derivably** *adv.*, in a derivative manner.
1847 in CRAIG.

†**derivage.** *Obs. rare*⁻¹. [f. DERIVE + -AGE.] Derivation, tracing.
1610 W. FOLKINGHAM *Art of Survey* II. iii. 69 Deriuage of Pedegrees from Auncestrie.

derival (dɪ'raɪvəl). *rare.* [f. DERIVE *v.*: see -AL[2] 5.] Derivation; e.g. of one word from another.
1871 EARLE *Philol. Eng. Tongue* §533 Of the derival of a conjunction from a preposition, we have a ready instance in the old familiar '*but*'. **1878** *Ibid.* §257 Postscr., Instances of Derival rather than of Combination.

derivant (dɪ'raɪvənt), *a.* and *sb.* [a. F. *dérivant*, pr. pple. of *dériver* to DERIVE: see -ANT.]

A. *adj. Med.* Drawing off or away (inflammation, fluid, etc.); = DERIVATIVE 1 b. **B.** *sb. Math.* A term applied to derived function of a special kind.
1876 BARTHOLOW *Mat. Med.* (1879) 546 His conviction that the chief utility of cupping and leeching consists not in the blood withdrawn, but in the derivant and counter-irritant effect which they produce.

derivate ('dɛrɪvət), *ppl. a.* and *sb.* [ad. L. *dērīvāt-us, -um*, pa. pple. of *dērīvāre* to DERIVE.]

A. as *pa. pple.* and *a.* Derived.
1494 FABYAN *Chron.* VII. 293 Portgreuis, whiche worde is deriuat or made of .ii. Saxon wordis, as port and greue. *c* **1532** DEWES *Introd. Fr.* in *Palsgr.* 900 *Tenir, uenir* with all them that be derivate of them as *contenir, preuenir.* **1679** KID in G. Hickes *Spir. Popery* 9 Supremacy, and every thing Originat upon and derivate from it. **1826** J. GILCHRIST *Lect.* 44 Correlative, derivate, and hereditary holiness. **1842** SIR H. TAYLOR *Edwin the Fair* I. vii. (D.), Him From whom the rights of kings are derivate.

B. *sb.* Anything derived; a derivative.
1660 JER. TAYLOR *Duct. Dubit.* I. ii. rule iii. §22 Those things that are derivates from heauen. **1838** *Blackw. Mag.* XLIV. 550 We maintain that consciousness meets the given, the derivate in man, at every point. **1889** JACOBS *Æsop* 95 Which of them is the original, which the derivate? **1892** *Daily News* 2 Nov. 7/3 The new Ammonia derivate Piperazine.

†**'derivate,** *v. Obs. rare.* [f. ppl. stem of L. *dērīvāre* to DERIVE.] = DERIVE *v. trans.* and *intr.*
1541 R. COPLAND *Guydon's Quest. Chirurg.*, Peraduenture it wold deryuate to other membres and do more harme than was before. **1552** in HULOET. **1643** R. O. *Man's Mort.* i. 3 Thus Mortallity is derivated to all Adams posteritie.

†**'derivately,** *adv. Obs.* [f. DERIVATE *a.* + -LY[2].] In a derived capacity or way.
1636 PRYNNE *Unbish. Tim.* 106 This power is secondarily and derivately in the whole Church.

derivation[1] (dɛrɪ'veɪʃən). [a. F. *dérivation* (1377 in Lanfranc's *Chirurg.*, Littré), ad. L. *dērīvātiōnem*, n. of action from *dērīvāre* to DERIVE. (The more usual OF. word was *derivaison, -oison.*)]

†**1. a.** The action or process of leading or carrying a current of water, or the like, *from* a source, *to* another part; *concr.* a branch of a river, etc. by which such a drawing off is effected. *Obs.*
1607 TOPSELL *Four-f. Beasts* (1658) 525 They bite all the vessels reaching to the stomach, making a derivation of all those ill humors into the belly and other parts. **1612** BREREWOOD *Lang. & Relig.* xiii. 139 Pliny in the derivation of water, requireth one cubit of declining, in 240 foot of proceeding. **1691** RAY *Creation* I. (1704) 82 Plenty of Vessels for the derivation of Air to all their Parts. **1737** BRACKEN *Farriery Impr.* (1756) I. 93 This..will cause a greater Derivation..of Blood to that Leg. **1776** GIBBON *Decl. & F.* I. xxiv. 693 The fleet passed from the Euphrates into an artificial derivation of that river. **1800** E. DARWIN *Phytologia* 417 The necessary moisture..which was formerly supplied by artificial derivations of water. **1835** DE QUINCEY in *Tait's Mag.* II. 80 The great national fountain shall not be a stagnant reservoir, but by an endless derivation, (to speak in a Roman metaphor!) applied to a system of national irrigation.

b. The action of conveying or leading away (in a current); diversion; an instance of this; in *Electr.* cf. *derived circuit* (DERIVED c).
1855 BAIN *Senses & Int.* II. i. §12 The derivation of blood from the brain reduces the cerebral excitement. **1883** *Syd. Soc. Lex.*, *Derivation wire*, the wire along which a derived electric current is drawn. **1885** CULLEY *Pract. Telegr.* 41 The new path opened to the current is called a *derived* circuit or *derivation*, or, properly, a *fault.*

c. *Med.* The withdrawal of inflammation or morbid humour from a diseased part of the body, by blistering, cupping or other means.
1600 W. VAUGHAN *Direct. Health* (1633) 165 To use revulsions and derivations to withdraw some of the fumes and vapours. **1656** RIDGLEY *Pract. Physick* 85 By.. derivations, as opening a vein and Ligatures to take away the flux. **1676** R. WISEMAN *Chirurg. Treat.* 7 Derivation differs from Revulsion onely in the measure of the distance, and the force of the medicines used. **1813** J. THOMSON *Lect. Inflam.* 185 These effects of topical blood-letting are expressed in some of the older medical writings by the terms Derivation and Revulsion.

d. *Mus.* Borrowing, in an organ: see BORROW *v.*[1] 2 c.
1905 T. CASSON *Pedal Organ* 22 It is true that they often call the borrowing by another name, such as 'transmission', 'derivation' and even 'duplication', but that is not straightforward.

†**2.** A passing or handing on; transmission (from a source); communication. *Obs.*
1597 HOOKER *Eccl. Pol.* v. lvi. (1611) 309 What communion Christ hath with his Church is in him by originall deriuation. **1602** WARNER *Alb. Eng.* Epit. (1612) 387 He therefore plotted..a deriuation to himselfe of the Kingly Diademe. **1659** PEARSON *Creed* (1839) 196 In human generation the son is begotten in the same nature with the father, which is performed by derivation or decision of part of the substance of the parent. **1699** BURNET *39 Art.* ix. (1700) 108 There is both a derivation of Righteousness, and a Communication of Inward Holiness transferred to us through Christ.

3. The action of drawing, obtaining, or deducing from a source.
1660 WILLSFORD *Scales Comm.* 39 But suppose this proportion not known, but by derivation, to be collected from others. *a* **1703** BURKITT *On N.T.* Matt. v. 14 Christ himself is the light of the world, by way of original: his ministers are lights by way of derivation, and participation from him. **1835** I. TAYLOR *Spir. Despot.* v. 214 A continued derivation of doctrines from the Apostles. **1876** FREEMAN *Norm. Conq.* V. xxiv. 396 There was no real derivation of English law from Normandy.

4. Origination or coming forth from a source; extraction, origin, descent.
1599 SHAKS. *Hen. V*, III. ii. 141 As good a man as your selfe, both in the disciplines of Warre, and the deriuation of my Birth. **1608** —— *Per.* v. i. 91 My derivation was from ancestors Who stood equivalent with mighty kings. **1669** GALE *Crt. Gentiles* I. I. ii. 14 That al Languages and Leters had their derivation from the Hebrew. **1791** COWPER *Iliad* XXI. 186 Why hast thou asked My derivation? **1805–17** R. JAMESON *Char. Min.* (ed. 3) 123 If..we attend to its relation with the other crystals of the same mineral, and also to its derivation from these, it is described derivatively. **1850** ROBERTSON *Serm.* Ser. III. iv. (1872) 56 'The Son was—*of* God', showing his derivation.

5. A derived product; a derivate, a derivative.
1641 MILTON *Prel. Episc.* 17 The Father is the whole substance, but the Son a derivation, and portion of the whole. **1669** GALE *Crt. Gentiles* I. I. i. 6 Al human Arts and Sciences are but beams and derivations from the Fountain of Lights. *a* **1680** GLANVILL (J.) Most of them are the general derivations of the hypothesis they claim to. **1800** W. TAYLOR in *Monthly Mag.* X. 410 The Nicolaitans, who were a derivation from the Gnostics.

6. *Gram.* **a.** Formation of a word from a more primitive word or root in the same or another language; origination as a derivative.
1530 PALSGR. 68 Derivatyon or formation, that is to saye, substantyves somtyme be fourmed of other substantyves. **1590** SIR J. SMYTH *Disc. Weapons* 2 b, As though our language were so barren, that it were not able of it selfe, or by derivation to affoord convenient words. *a* **1704** LOCKE (J.), The derivation of the word Substance favours the idea we have of it. **1823** HONE *Anc. Myst.* 147 Better qualified to discover and explain the derivation and meaning of Hearne's word. **1875** WHITNEY *Life Lang.* 87 The relics of forgotten derivations..are scattered thickly through every part of our vocabulary.

b. The tracing of the origin of a word from its 'root' or radical elements; a statement or account (or, improperly, a conjecture) of the origin and formation of a word.
1596 SPENSER *State Irel.* Wks. (Globe) 623/2, I knowe not whether the woordes be English or Irish..the Irishmen can make noe derivation nor analogye of them. **1605** R. CAREW in *Lett. Lit. Men* (Camden) 99 His derivation of the English names doth not please me least. **1707** *Curios. in Husb. & Gard.* 10 The learned Abbot..will not allow these Derivations to be well grounded. **1823** SCOTT *Peveril* App. i. *foot-note*, [*Stipula*, a straw] Perhaps a more feasible etymology of *stipulation* than the usual derivation from *stipes.* **1851** TRENCH *Stud. Words* vii. (1869) 264 Other derivations proposed by him are far more absurd than this.

c. *Transformational Gram.* (See quots.)
1957 N. CHOMSKY *Syntactic Structures* iv. 29 Given the grammar [Σ, F], we define a derivation as a finite sequence of strings, beginning with an initial string of Σ, and with each string in the sequence being derived from the preceding string by application of one of the instruction formulas of F. **1964** E. BACH *Introd. Transformational Gram.* ii. 15 A derivation..is a sequence of strings of symbols of which the first string is an initial string and in which every string follows from the preceding one by the application of a rule.

7. *Math.* The operation of passing from any function to any related function which may be considered or treated as its derivative; *spec.* the operation of finding the derivative or differential coefficient, differentiation.
1816 tr. *Lacroix's Diff. & Int. Calc.* 608 We have already determined the law of derivation in the most common functions.

8. *Biol.* The theory of evolution of organic forms: see EVOLUTION 6 c.
1874 J. FISKE *Cosmic Philos.* I. II. ix. 442 According to the doctrine of derivation, the more complex plants and animals are the slowly modified descendants of less complex plants and animals, and these in turn were the slowly modified descendants of still less complex plants and animals, and so on until we converge to those primitive organisms which are not definable either as animal or as vegetal.

deri'vation[2]. *Gunnery.* [a. F. *dérivation*[2] (Furetière, 1690), n. of action from *dériver* (*dériver*[4] in Hatzf.) to drift, found in 16–17th c. as *driver*, and (according to Darmesteter *Dict. Gén.*) an adoption of the Eng. vb. DRIVE, in its nautical sense 'to drift with the stream or wind' (cf. Acts xxvii. 15), subseq. associated and identified in form with the pre-existing F. verb *dériver* to DERIVE. In F. applied both to the drift or driving of a ship, and (recently) to the drift or deviation of a projectile, and in the later use taken into mod.Eng.]

The deviation of a projectile from its normal course due to its form, motion, the resistance of the air, or wind; *spec.* the constant inclination of a projectile to the right due to the right-hand spin imparted by the rifling; drift.
1875 URE *Dict. Arts* II. 386 The bullet in its improved form..has no tendency to the gyrations which appear to have so puzzled French artillerists, and for which they have invented the word 'derivation' and wasted much learned disquisition. **1882–3** CASSELL'S *Encycl. Dict.*, *Derivation*, the peculiar constant deviation of an elongated projectile from a rifled gun.

derivational (dɛrɪ'veɪʃənəl), *a.* [f. DERIVATION[1] + -AL[1].] Of, belonging to, or of the nature of derivation. Also as *sb.*
1843 CAYLEY *Theory of Determinants*, Derivational functions. **1873** S. B. JAMES in *Leisure Hour* 495 'Canting arms' are..arms that..'chant'..I can think of no other derivational explanation. **1880** EARLE *Eng. Plants* Introd. 93 Weigand treats the termination..as derivational. **1953** C. E. BAZELL *Linguistic Form* 76 All morphemes which may make part of a base but which may not be stems are derivational affixes, more briefly derivationals. **1964** E. BACH *Introd. Transformational Gram.* iii. 36 Our ability to reconstruct the 'derivational history' of this terminal string depends on a process of matching succeeding lines in the derivation. **1964** R. H. ROBINS *Gen. Linguistics* vi. 258 Both these types may be illustrated from English. *-hood* is a class-maintaining derivational suffix.

Hence **deri'vationally** *adv.*, as regards derivation.
1883 E. C. CLARK *Pract. Jurispr.* 45 Derivationally, then, it [θέμις] means that which is appointed or ordained.

derivationist (dɛrɪ'veɪʃənɪst). [f. as prec. + -IST.] **1.** *Biol.* One who holds the theory of derivation or evolution of organic types. **2.** One who occupies himself with the derivation of words.
1875 DAWSON *Nature & Bible* 134 The derivationist tries to break down the line between species and varieties. **1888** —— *Geol. Hist. Plants* 266 Allied forms, some at least of which a derivationist might claim as modified descendants. **1891** ATKINSON *Moorland Par.* 242 The amateur derivationists of place names.

derivatist (dɪ'rɪvətɪst), *sb.* [f. DERIVATE *ppl. a.* + -IST.] = prec. 1. Also *attrib.* or as *adj.*
1887 E. D. COPE *Orig. Fittest* vi. 215 The doctrine of evolution of organic types is sometimes appropriately called the doctrine of derivation, and its supporters, derivatists. *Ibid.*, To accept the derivatist doctrine, and to reject the creational.

derivative (dɪ'rɪvətɪv), *a.* and *sb.* [a. F. *dérivatif, -ive* (15th c. in Hatzf.), ad. L.

dērīvātīv-us (Priscian), f. ppl. stem of *dērīvāre*: see -IVE.]

A. *adj.* †1. a. Characterized by transmission, or passing from one to another. *Obs.*

1637 LAUD *Sp. Star-Chamb.* 14 June Ded. A iv, What Honour can You hope for, either Present, or derivative to Posterity if you attend your Government no better? **1640** BP. REYNOLDS *Passions* xxx, A derivative and spreading injury..dishonouring a man..in the eyes of the world.

b. *Med.* Producing derivation; see DERIVATION[1] 1 c.

1851-60 MAYNE *Exp. Lex.*, *Derivative*, having power to turn aside, or convert, as it were, from one disease to another; applied to certain medicines which seem to act in this manner, as blisters, rubefacients, epispastics. **1881** W. B. HUNTER in *Encycl. Brit.* XII. 544 (*Hydropathy*) It is stimulative, derivative, depurative, sudorific, and alterative. **1883** *Syd. Soc. Lex.*, *Derivative bleeding*, a term applied to that method of treatment of a disease by bleeding when the blood is removed from a part of the body far away from the seat of the disease, as in bleeding from the toe in head affections.

2. a. Of derived character or nature; characterized by being derived, drawn, obtained, or deduced from another; coming or emanating from a source.

1530 PALSGR. 310/1 Deryvatyfe, *deriuatif.* **1570** DEE *Math. Pref.* in Rudd *Euclid* (1651) E ij b, The..use of Geometry: and of his second, depending, derivative commodities. **1630** PRYNNE *Anti-Armin.* 133 It must be either an acquisite, a deriuatiue, or an infused quality. **1691-8** NORRIS *Pract. Disc.* (1707) IV. 52 Not an original but a derivative Passion. **1712** STEELE *Spect.* No. 432 ¶7 They can only gain a secondary and derivative kind of Fame. **1817** BENTHAM *Parl. Ref. Catech.* (1818) 18 The distinction between a self-formed and a derivative judgment. **1866** ARGYLL *Reign Law* ii. (ed. 4) 64 The secondary or derivative senses of the word have supplanted the primary signification. **1883** *Syd. Soc. Lex.*, *Derivative circulation*, term applied to the direct communication which exists between arteries and veins in some parts of the body, so that all the blood does not necessarily pass through the capillaries of these parts.

b. Deriving authority, etc. from another.

1845 STEPHEN *Laws Eng.* I. 67 The courts of the arch-bishops and bishops and their derivative officers.

c. *Gram.* Formed from another word; not primitive.

1530 PALSGR. 79 The pronownes derivatyves have thre accidentes. **1824** L. MURRAY *Eng. Gram.* (ed. 5) I. 55 A derivative word is that which may be reduced to another word in English of greater simplicity. **1856** R. A. VAUGHAN *Mystics* (1860) I. 18 To have a distinction in the primitive and not in the derivative word is always confusing.

d. *Law.* (See quots.)

1792 CHIPMAN *Amer. Law Rep.* (1871) 21 The title of S. being void, the subsequent or derivative titles must likewise be void. **1848** WHARTON *Law Lex.*, *Derivative Conveyances*, secondary deeds which presuppose some other conveyance primary or precedent, and only serve to enlarge, confirm, alter, restrain, restore, or transfer the interest granted by such original conveyance. They are releases, confirmations, surrenders, assignments, and defeasanses. **1871** MARKBY *Elem. Law* §350 Derivative possession is the possession which one person has of the property of another. **1892** *Law Times* XCIII. 458/2 The plaintiff was a derivative mortgagee, being a mortgagee of one A. E. P——, who was a mortgagee of the defendant.

3. Of or pertaining to a theory of derivation; derivational.

1871 DARWIN *Desc. Man* I. iii. 97 Philosophers of the derivative school of morals formerly assumed that the foundation of morality lay in a form of selfishness; but more recently in the 'Greatest Happiness' principle.

4. *Geol.* a. Of fossils: occurring in rocks other than those to which they are native. b. Of rocks: formed from materials derived from older rocks.

1871 C. LYELL *Student's Elem. Geol.* Index, Derivative shells of the Red Crag. **1894** J. GEIKIE *Gt. Ice Age* (ed. 3) 371 The shells which they occasionally contain are probably, in most cases, derivative—they do not occupy the positions in which the molluscs themselves lived. **1900** J. E. MARR *Sci. Study Scenery* ii. 9 The derivative class has been formed by accumulation of material..not having been in a state of fusion immediately before its accumulation. **1904** GOODCHILD & TWENEY *Technol. & Sci. Dict.* 155/1 Conglomerates, sandstones, shales, and clays are good examples of derivative rocks.

5. Special collocation. ***derivative action*** (U.S. Law), an action brought by a shareholder in order to enforce a legal right of the corporation.

1934 *N.Y. Suppl.* CCLXIX. 361 Judgment obtained in derivative action by stockholders against directors of corporation is bar to actions by other stockholders for same relief, as to questions decided or which might have been decided. **1946** *U.S. Reports* CCCXXIV. 105 It is a misnomer to speak of the filing of the petition on behalf of the corporation as a derivative action. **1972** *N.Y. Law Jrnl.* 22 Dec. 1/7 Appeal from dismissal of shareholder's derivative action in the United States District Court for the Southern District of New York.

B. *sb.*

1. A thing of derived character; a thing flowing, proceeding, or originating from another.

1593 NASHE *Christ's T.* 81 b, The third deriuatiue of Delicacie, is sloth. **1611** SHAKS. *Wint. T.* III. ii. 45 Honor, 'Tis a deriuatiue from me to mine, And onely that I stand for. **1625** DARCIE *Annales* ¶v b, Vnskilfulnesse and her deriuatiues, Doubt and Falsity. **1665** SIR T. HERBERT *Trav.* (1677) 103 The Arabick..Howbeit, 'tis no original, but a derivative from the Hebrew. **1774** J. BRYANT *Mythol.* I. 52 Subordinate dæmons, which they supposed to be emanations and derivatives from their chief Deity. **1865** MOZLEY *Mirac.* v. 98 Testimony is thus reduced to a mere derivative of experience.

2. *Gram.* A word derived from another by some process of word-formation; any word which is not a primitive word or root.

1530 PALSGR. 74 Of pronownes some be primitives, some be derivatives. **1612** BRINSLEY *Lud. Lit.* xxi. (1627) 247 Some marke would be given under every derivative in each roote. *a* **1637** B. JONSON *Eng. Gram.* Wks. (Rtldg.) 768/2 In derivatives, or compounds of the sharp *e*..as *agreeing*, of *agree.* **1755** JOHNSON *Pref. to Dict.* §20 The derivatives I have referred to their primitives, with an accuracy sometimes needless. **1862** BURTON *Bk. Hunter* (1863) 2 The use of a Greek derivative gives notice that you are scientific. **1868** GLADSTONE *Juv. Mundi* ii. (1870) 55 When we turn from Argos to its derivative Argeioi we find [etc.].

3. *Math.* A function derived from another; *spec.* a differential coefficient.

1674 JEAKE *Arith.* (1696) 456 Derivatives of the third Sort ..are next to be exhibited. **1846** CAYLEY *Wks.* I. 95 The derivative of any number of the derivatives of one or more functions..is itself a derivative of the original functions. **1881** MAXWELL *Electr. & Magn.* I. 8 The first derivatives of a continuous function may be discontinuous.

4. *Mus.* a. A chord derived from a fundamental chord, *esp.* by inversion. b. 'The actual or supposed root or generator, from the harmonics of which a chord is derived' (Stainer & Barrett *Dict. Mus. Terms*).

1828 WEBSTER, *Derivative*..In music, a chord not fundamental. **1872** BANISTER *Music* xi. (1877) 45 These chords, with their mutations or inflexions, their inversions and their derivatives..are all the chords used in music.

5. *Chem.* A compound obtained from another, e.g. by partial replacement.

1863-72 WATTS *Dict. Chem.* I. 46 Amic acids..can decompose either as hydrates (derivatives of water), or as amides (derivatives of ammonia). **1869** PHILLIPS *Vesuvius* v. 152 Ferric oxide has been of late regarded as a derivative from ferric chloride. **1880** *Act. 43-4 Vict.* c. 24 §130 The use of methylated spirits, or any derivative thereof, in the preparation of..chloroform.

6. *Med.* A method or agent that produces DERIVATION (q.v., 1 c).

1843 *Rep. Brit. Assoc.* 78 He had..found it useful as a derivative, removing, when worn on the head, obstinate chronic ophthalmia. **1858** COPLAND *Dict. Pract. Med.* III. II. 1170 External derivatives and exutories have been advised for phthisis.

de'rivatively, *adv.* [f. prec. + -LY[2].] In a derivative manner; by derivation.

c **1630** RISDON *Surv. Devon* §145 (1810) 163 Derivatively from him is this game. **1768-74** TUCKER *Lt. Nat.* (1852) II. 252 Fundamentals are of two sorts; those essentially such.. and those derivatively fundamentals. **1837** SIR F. PALGRAVE *Merch. & Friar* Ded. (1844) 13 Thence it was acquired, either primarily or derivatively, by the Chinese.

de'rivativeness. *rare.* [f. as prec. + -NESS.] The state or quality of being derivative.

1668 WILKINS *Real Char.* II. i. §4. 35 Transcendental Relations of Quality at large..Derivativeness. **1847** in CRAIG. **1927** M. SADLEIR *Trollope: Commentary* 374 Undoubtedly *The Three Clerks* was derivative..and to the fact of its derivativeness may be attributed its popularity. **1967** *Listener* 26 Jan. 129/1 The author himself made this derivativeness perfectly clear: 'I am struggling to think other people's thoughts after them.'

†**derivator.** *Obs. rare*[−1]. [agent-n. from L. *dērīvāre* to DERIVE.] = DERIVER.

1652 GAULE *Magastrom.* 14 It may sound and signifie well, or ill; as the derivator pleases to fancy, or labours to allude.

derive (dɪˈraɪv), *v.* Forms: 5 dir-, di-, dyryve, 5-6 deryve, 6 -ryfe. [a. F. *dérive-r* (12th c. in Littré = Pr., Sp. *derivar*, It. *derivare*), ad. L. *dērīvāre* to lead or draw off (water or liquid), to divert, derive (words), f. DE- I. 2 + *rīvus* brook, stream of water.

There are 4 distinct verbs *dériver* in French. One of these, *dériver*[2], OF. *desriver*, to cause to overflow its banks, f. *rive*, L. *ripa* river-bank, possibly sometimes influenced earlier Eng. use (cf. senses 1 b and c). *Dériver*[3] to drift or drive, as a ship, with wind or current, to drift as a projectile (for earlier *driver*, from Eng. *drive*), has given DERIVATION[2], DERIVOMETER. *Dériver*[4], to *unrivet*, is not represented in English.)]

I. Transitive senses.

†1. a. To conduct (a stream of water or other fluid) *from* a source, reservoir, main stream, etc. *to* or *into* a channel, place, or destination; to lead, draw, convey down a course or through a channel. *Obs.* or *arch.*

1483 *Cath. Angl.* 96 To deryue, *deriuare.* **1530** PALSGR. 513/1, I deryve, or bringe one thynge out of another, as water is brought whan it is brought from the spring, *je deriue.* **1538** LELAND *Itin.* V. 92 The Pittes be so set abowte with Canales that the Salte Water is facily derivid to every Mannes Howse. **1555** WATREMAN *Fardle Facions* Pref. 10 From them [springes] thei deriued into cities and Tounes, the pure freshe waters a great distaunce of. **1571** DIGGES *Pantom.* I. xvii. F, Ye may conclude that this water may be deriued thither. **1606** N. BAXTER *Man Created* in Farr *S.P. Jas. I* (1848) 238 And so through conduits, secretly contriu'd, Is blood to euerie humane part deriu'd. **1632** SANDERSON *Serm.* II. 24 Little trenches, whereby.. husbandmen used to derive water from some fountain or cistern to the several parts of their gardens. **1696** BP. PATRICK *Comm. Exod.* vii. (1697) 122 Water..derived by Pipes from the River into Cisterns. **1805** W. SAUNDERS *Min. Waters* 197 Mineral springs..Externally used, either by immersing the whole body, or by deriving a stream to some particular part.

†b. with various constructions, and adverbial extensions.

1548 R. HUTTEN *Sum of Diuinitie* L viij b, Thy fountaynes shall be deriued, & the ryuers shall runne into the streetes. **1594** *2nd Rep. Dr. Faustus* in Thoms *Prose Rom.* (1858) III. 334 Danuby is derived in two arms, which..meet at length again in the same channel. **1633** BP. HALL *Hard Texts, N.T.* 411 Cyrus..drained the channell of Euphrates and derived the streames the other way. **1650** FULLER *Pisgah* IV. iii. 48 The pillar conducting them such by-ways, in levels or declivity of vales..where the water had a conveniency to be derived after them. *a* **1723** SIR C. WREN in L. Phillimore *Family & Times* (1881) App. iii. 343 They deriv'd the River when it rose, all over the Flat of the Delta. **1800** E. DARWIN *Phytologia* 417 In some parts..where rice is cultivated, they are said not to derive the water on it, till it is in flower.

†c. *refl.* To flow (*in, into, through* channels). (Chiefly *fig.*) *Obs.*

1624 DONNE *Serm.* cxiii. IV. 576 From all Eternity he derived himself into 3 Persons. *a* **1652** J. SMITH *Sel. Disc.* IX. iv. (1821) 430 When God made the world, he did not..leave it alone to subsist by itself..but he derived himself through the whole creation. *a* **1661** FULLER *Worthies* (1840) III. 120 The stream of her charity..found other channels therein to derive itself.

†2. To cause (water, etc.) to flow away; to draw off, carry off, divert the course of; *spec.* in *Med.*, cf. DERIVATION 1 c. *Obs.*

1598 STOW *Surv.* vii. (1603) 29 Intending to haue deriued the riuer of Thames..to haue flowed about it. **1601** HOLLAND *Pliny* I. 544 To water them, or to deriue & diuert water from them. *Ibid.* II. 469 To lade out the water that riseth vpon the workemen, for feare it choke vp the pits; for to preuent which inconuenience, they deriue it by other drains. **1656** RIDGLEY *Pract. Physick* 17 The matter must be derived and voided from the head. **1692** RAY *Dissol. World* iii. (1732) 37 Water the which to derive and rid away. **1771** T. PERCIVAL *Ess. Med. Exper.* (1777) I. 220 They derive the febrile matter from the brain, and assist..the other discharges.

†3. a. To carry, lead, extend (a watercourse, canal, or channel of any kind). *Obs.*

c **1534** tr. *Pol. Verg. Eng. Hist.* (Camden 1844) II. 20 After-ward, deriving a trenche from fort to fort, he environed the towne, and..beganne to annoy the same. **1600** J. PORY tr. *Leo's Africa* II. 113 So soone as the said water-conduct was derived unto the towne, he caused it to be divided, and sent into sundry places. **1623** BINGHAM *Xenophon* 16 Media, where the Channels begin, that are deriued out of the Riuer Tygris. **1777** WATSON *Philip II* (1793) II. XIII. 133 From this stream..an infinity of canals are derived.

†b. To extend by branches or ramifications; to divide by branching. *lit.* and *fig.*

c **1597** HARINGTON in *Nugæ Antiq.* (1804) I. 188 It may be derived into three kyndes. *a* **1631** DONNE *Serm.* c. IV. 322 Rooted in some one beloved Sin but derived into infinite branches of temptation. **1646** SIR T. BROWNE *Pseud. Ep.* III. xxv. 174 At the other end, by two branches [it] deriveth it selfe into the Lunges. **1677** HALE *Prim. Orig. Man.* I. ii. 65 Other ramifications of this *nervus intercostalis* are derived into the Chest and *Diaphragma.* [Cf. **1760** in 4.]

†4. *transf.* and *fig.* a. To convey from one (treated as a source) to another, as by transmission, descent, etc.; to transmit, impart, communicate, pass on, hand on. Const. *to, into, unto*, rarely *upon* the recipient. *Obs.* or *arch.* (*rare* after 1750).

1526 *Pilgr. Perf.* (W. de W. 1531) 226 This power, of byndyng & losynge of synne, is deriuyed from the apostles to yᵉ mynystres of Christes chirche. **1547** HOOPER *Declar. Christ* i. Wks. (Parker Soc.) 15 The sin of Adam..was derived into all his posterity. **1564** *Brief Exam.* B iv, The maner of prophesying..was deryued out of the Sinagoges, into our Churches. **1593** BILSON *Govt. Christ's Ch.* 6 From him God lineally derived it unto Abraham. **1607** DEKKER *Hist. Sir T. Wyatt* Wks. 1873 III. 83, I will Deriue the Crowne vnto your Daughters head. **1647** CLARENDON *Hist. Reb.* v. (1702) I. 549 His Name would be derived to Posterity, as the Preserver of his Country. **1651-3** JER. TAYLOR *Serm. for Year* Ep. Ded., That this Book is derived upon your Lordship almost in the nature of a legacy from her. *a* **1661** FULLER *Worthies* (1840) I. 208 Parents..rich enough to derive unto him the hereditary infirmity of the gout. **1681-6** J. SCOTT *Chr. Life* (1747) III. 124 Jesus.. when he ascended..derived that divine Spirit upon his Apostles. **1699** BURNET *39 Art.* xxxii. (1700) 356 The High-Priest..was to marry, and he derived to his descendents that Sacred Office. **1760** LAW *Spir. Prayer* I. 38 The life of the vine must be really derived into the branches. **1835** PAUL *Antiq. Greece* I. II. xi. §2 A festival first instituted at Athens, and from thence derived to the rest of the Ionians. **1848** HAMPDEN *Bampt. Lect.* (ed. 3) 184 The definition of Predestination, as given in the Scholastic writers, and from them derived to modern Theology.

1561 NORTON & SACKV. *Gorboduc* 86 What their fathers.. Have with great fame derived down to them. *a* **1646** J. GREGORY *Terrestrial Globe* (1650) 268 The Turkish Histories are not so completely derived down to us as to Describe the Territories by Longitude or Latitude. **1681-6** J. SCOTT *Chr. Life* (1747) III. 402 Another evident Instance of the Apostles deriving down their Apostolick Authority. **1828** SOUTHEY in *Q. Rev.* XXXVII. 208 The hatred of popery..which has..been derived down from father to son.

†c. *refl.* To pass by descent or transmission.

1597 SHAKS. *2 Hen. IV*, IV. v. 43 This Imperiall Crowne, Which (as immediate from thy Place and Blood) Deriues it selfe to me. **1654** tr. *Scudery's Curia Pol.* 126 Which Conditions did not (with his succession) derive themselves on me. **1655** FULLER *Ch. Hist.* VII. i. §35 The Womens discords derived themselves into their husbands hearts. **1678** J. PHILLIPS *Tavernier's Trav.*, *Persia* v. iv. 206 The jealousie of the Kings of Persia..derives itself to all his Subjects, who will not permit their women to be seen.

†**5.** *trans.* To cause to come; to draw, bring, turn, direct; to bring down. *Obs.*

a. Const. *to, unto, into.*

c **1534** tr. *Pol. Verg. Eng. Hist.* (Camden 1846) I. 102 Then Honorius, retaininge the Brittishe armie, did againe derive and traine the Ilande to the empire. **1601** SHAKS. *All's Well* v. iii. 265 Things which would deriue me ill will to speak of. **1613** —— *Hen. VIII*, II. iv. 32 What Friend of mine That had to him deriu'd your Anger, did I Continue in my Liking. **1647** CLARENDON *Hist. Reb.* IV. (1702) I. 270 Men.. looked upon him, as one, who could derive the King's Pleasure to them. **1678** HOBBES *Decam.* vii. 75 The force of the Sun-beams is derived almost to a point by a Burning-glass. **1772** FLETCHER *Appeal* Wks. 1795 I. 76 Those who derive putrefaction into their bones, for the momentary gratification of a shameful appetite. **1774** T. JEFFERSON *Autobiog.* App. Wks. 1859 I. 144 To undergo the great inconvenience that will be derived to them from stopping all imports whatever from Great Britain.

b. Const. *on, upon.*

1611 SPEED *Hist. Gt. Brit.* IX. xvi. (1632) 852 Hereby he deriued vpon his enemy all the enuie of the people. **1671** J. DAVIES *Sibylls* II. ii. 87 The first Persecution was raised by Nero, to derive upon the innocent Christians the Indignation of the Romanes. **1705** STANHOPE *Paraphr.* III. 65 Such Apostacy derives a double Dishonour upon Religion. **1741** RICHARDSON *Pamela* (1824) I. ix. 245 Such an example, as will derive upon you the ill-will and censure of other ladies. **1808** W. TAYLOR in *Monthly Mag.* XXVI. 224 They would derive on themselves a solid glory.

6. a. To draw, fetch, get, gain, obtain (a thing *from* a source). Const. *from*, rarely †*out of.*

1561 T. HOBY tr. *Castiglione's Courtyer* (1577) E vb, Deriuing them [newe wordes] featly from the Latins, as ye Latins, in old time, deriued from the Grecians. **1581** PETTIE *Guazzo's Civ. Conv.* Pref. (1586) A vij, If one chance to derive anie word from the Latine, which is insolent to their eares..they forthwith make a jest at it, and terme it an Inkhorne terme. **1596** SHAKS. *Merch. V.* II. ix. 42 O that estates, degrees, and offices, Were not deriu'd corruptly. **1598** B. JONSON *Ev. Man. in Hum.* II. v, Honourable worship, let me deriue a small piece of siluer from you. **1665** SIR T. HERBERT *Trav.* (1677) 140 The Romans..led Horses in honour of the Sun, a custome derived from the Persians. **1667** MILTON *P.L.* IX. 837 Sciential sap, deriv'd From Nectar, drink of Gods. **1751** HARRIS *Hermes* Wks. (1841) 234 If all minds have them [their ideas] derived, they must be derived from something, which is itself not *mind*. **1781** GIBBON *Decl. & F.* II. 32 The power of the præfect of Italy was not confined to the country from whence he derived his title. **1822** B. CORNWALL *Misc. Poems, Headland Bay Panama*, And Cheops hath derived eternal fame Because he made his tomb a place of pride. **1856** FROUDE *Hist. Eng.* (1858) I. iii. 219 The archbishop..derived no personal advantage from his courts. **1878** HUXLEY *Physiogr.* 181 The solid matter derived from the waste of the land.

b. Const. with *from* and *to*. *rare.*

1771 GOLDSM. *Hist. Eng.* I. 204 A king, from the weakness of whose title they might derive power to themselves. **1785** PALEY *Mor. Philos.* (1818) II. 404 The chief advantage which can be derived to population from the interference of law. **1844** LINGARD *Anglo-Sax. Ch.* (1858) I. v. 191 From his labours, the most valuable benefits were derived to his countrymen.

c. *to derive* (ancestry, origin, pedigree, etc.); also *refl.*

1599 H. BUTTES *Dyets drie Dinner* B viij, For Malum (an apple) deriveth his line of Ancestry from the Greeke Melon, of great antiquity. **1612** DRAYTON *Poly-olb.* xi. Notes 183 Prester John, sometimes deriuing himselfe very neere from the loines of Salomon. **1634** SIR T. HERBERT *Trav.* 10 The Mountaines of the Moone..whence seven-mouthed Nyle, derives his Origen. **1662** EVELYN *Chalcogr.* 11 Sculpture may derive its Pedegree from the infancy of the World.

d. *absol.* or *intr.*

1632 QUARLES *Div. Fancies* Ded., That like the painful Bee, I may derive From sundry Flow'rs to store my slender Hive. **1649** in *Def. Rights Univ. Oxford* (1690) 25 Erected by the city and those who derive from their title. **1796** BURKE *Let. Noble Ld.* Wks. VIII. 39 The grantee whom he derives from.

e. *Chem.* To obtain (a compound) from another, as by partial replacement.

1868 WATTS *Dict. Chem.* V. 554 This compound, derived from ethylsulphurous acid by substitution of Cl for HO.

7. To obtain by some process of reasoning, inference or deduction; to gather, deduce.

1509 HAWES *Past. Pleas.* 75 Loke what ye saye; loke it be deryfyde Frome perfyt reason well exemplyfyde. **1624** N. DE LAWNE *Du Moulin's Logik* 89 Rules to live well, derived from nature. **1690** LOCKE *Hum. Und.* II. xiv. §4 Men derive their ideas of duration from their reflections on the train of the ideas they observe to succeed one another in their own understandings. **1752** JOHNSON *Rambler* No. 203 ¶7 In age, we derive little from retrospect but hopeless sorrow. **1874** GREEN *Short Hist.* vii. §7. 426 It is difficult..to derive any knowledge of Shakspere's inner history from the Sonnets. **1875** JOWETT *Plato* (ed. 2) IV. 269 The higher truths of philosophy and religion..are derived from experience.

8. *refl.* To arise, spring, come *from* something as its source; to take its origin *from.*

1662 STILLINGFL. *Orig. Sacr.* II. ii. §9 Sem from whom he derived himself, was one of the persons who escaped it in the Ark. **1665** SIR T. HERBERT *Trav.* (1677) 127 Sheraz then probably derives it self from Sherab, which in the Persian Tongue signifies a Grape. **1690** LOCKE *Hum. Und.* II. i. §2 Experience; in that all our Knowledge is founded, and from that it ultimately derives itself. **1734** tr. *Rollin's Anc. Hist.* (1827) I. 115 Hence comedy derives itself. **1833** LAMB *Elia* Ser. II. xxiv. (1865) 404 If the abstinence from evil..is to derive itself from no higher principle.

9. a. *passive.* To be drawn or descended; to take its origin or source; to spring, come *from* (rarely †*of*, †*out of*).

c **1386** CHAUCER *Knt.'s T.* 2180 (Ellesm. & Camb. MSS.) Conuertynge al vn to his propre welle ffrom which it is dirryued sooth to telle. **1530** PALSGR. 513/1 His lynage is deryved out of the house of Melysyn. **1610** GUILLIM *Heraldry* II. vi. (1611) 58 A Couple-close is a subordinate charge deriued from a cheuron. **1701** DE FOE *Free-born Eng.* II A Race uncertain and unev'n, Deriv'd from all the Nations under Heav'n. **1737** WHISTON *Josephus' Antiq.* XIII. xiii. §5 They also reviled him, as derived from a captive. **1892** GARDINER *Student's Hist. Eng.* 6 No European population now existing which is not derived from many races.

b. *spec.* Of a word: To arise or be formed by some process of word-formation *from* (some more primitive or earlier word).

1567 MAPLET *Gr. Forest* 60 *Arundo*, sayth he, is deriued out of the Adiectiue *Aridum*, for that it so spedily drieth and withereth. **1596** SPENSER *State Irel.* Wks. (Globe) 639/2 Stirrops..being derived of the old English woord *sty*, which is, to gett up. **1676** *Port Royal Art of Speaking* 11 From one single Word many others are derived, as is obvious in the Dictionaries of such Languages as we know. **1751** WESLEY *Wks.* (1872) XIV. 48 A Participle is an Adjective derived of a Verb. **1791** *Gentl. Mag.* 27/1 The word *Tontine* is only a cant word, derived from the name of an Italian projector. **1881** SKEAT *Etym. Dict.* 150/2 From this O.F. *dars* is also derived the Breton *darz*, a dace.

10. a. *trans.* To trace or show the derivation, origin, or pedigree of; to show (a thing) to proceed, issue, or come *from*; to trace the origination of (anything) from its source; also, more loosely, to declare, assert, or state a thing to be derived *from.*

1600 E. BLOUNT tr. *Conestaggio* 4 Some derive the originall of this Count Henrie from Hungarie, others from Aragon, and from other places. **1604** *Meeting of Gallants* 4 Bastard..Thou knowest I can deriue thee. **1646** SIR T. BROWNE *Pseud. Ep.* VI. ix. 321 The observations of Albuquerque..derive this rednesse from the colour of the sand and argillous earth at the bottome. **1662** STILLINGFL. *Orig. Sacr.* III. iv. §13 Prometheus (from whom the Greeks derived themselves). **1683** *Brit. Spec.* 38 From whence Sir Edward Cook derives the Law of England at this day for burning those Women who kill their Husbands. **1749** FIELDING *Tom Jones* XVII. vii, An action which malice itself could not have derived from an evil motive. **1874** DAWSON *Nature & Bible* 202 These men derive all religion from myths.

b. *spec.* To trace the origin of (a word) *from* (†*to*) its etymological source; to establish or show the derivation of; also, less correctly, to offer a conjectural derivation for (a word).

1559 W. CUNNINGHAM *Cosmogr. Glasse* 186 Africa.. Festus saith it came of the qualitie of th' Aere..deriving it of φρίκη, as who should say, Ἀφρικὴ that is, without horrour of coldenes. **1680** H. DODWELL *Two Lett. Advice* (1691) 207 This..way of deriving unknown words to their primitive Originals. **1755** JOHNSON *Pref. to Dict.* §25 That etymologist ..who can seriously derive dream from drama, because life is a drama, and a drama is a dream. **1851** TRENCH *Stud. Words* vii. (ed. 13) 264 He derives the name of the peacock from the peak or tuft of pointed feathers on its head. **1884** *N. & Q.* 6th Ser. IX. 207, I should be much obliged if any of your readers could help me in deriving the name of the village of Allonby, in Cumberland.

II. Intransitive senses (arising out of reflexive uses in I.).

11. To flow, spring, issue, emanate, come, arise, originate, have its derivation *from*, rarely *out of* (a source). Freq. in mod. use, prob. at first as a gallicism.

c **1386** CHAUCER *Knt.'s T.* 2148 (Ellesm. MS.) Wel may men knowe but it be a fool That euery part dirryueth from his hool. **1634-5** BRERETON *Trav.* (1844) 65 A mighty revenue derives out of the excise paid for beer and wine. **1649** *Bounds Publ. Obed.* (1650) 17 We all derive from him. **1684** *Scanderberg Rediv.* i. 3 To understand the Family he derives from. **1706** DE FOE *Jure Div.* v. 11 The Right to rule derives from those that gave, And no Men can convey more Power than that they have. **1768-74** TUCKER *Lt. Nat.* (1852) II. 12 Happiness, which does not derive from any single source. **1803** SYD. SMITH *Wks.* (1859) I. 54/2 In the third class, nobility derives from the person, and not from the estate. **1850** TENNYSON *In Mem.* LV. 3. **1863** KINGLAKE *Crimea* II. 74 There was an authority not deriving from the Queen or the Parliament. **1895** tr. *P. Bourget's Outre-mer* ii. 36 How all literature derives from him [*sc.* Shakespeare] in every English-speaking country. **1899** *Daily News* 28 Nov. 6/5 As a draughtsman he derives from Charles Keene. **1901** *Ibid.* 22 Jan. 5/4 The theory of the mediæval empire derives immediately from Rome. **1907** *Daily Chron.* 18 Oct. 4/6 Thackeray derived straight from Goldsmith. **1971** *Daily Tel.* 19 Nov. 13/3 Richard Rountree..is powerful in a role that must derive from those paragons of policemen Sidney Poitier used to play.

12. To proceed, descend, pass on, come (*to* a receiver, receptacle, etc.).

1559 MORWYNG *Evonym.* Pref., The study of this Art.. derived unto the Romains and Grekes somewhat late. **1647** JER. TAYLOR *Lib. Proph.* xv. 212 If the Church meddles with them when they doe not derive into ill life. **1655-60** STANLEY *Hist. Philos.* I. I. 1 Thales..Who first introduc'd Naturall and Mathematicall Learning into Greece, from whence it derived into us. **1768** *Woman of Honor* III. 130 All that is the most excellent, in our..laws, derives to us from those very..savages. **1858** M. PATTISON *Ess.* (1889) II. 16 Puritanism..derives to this country directly from Geneva.

13. Of a word: To originate, come as a derivative (*from* its root or primitive).

1794 MRS. PIOZZI *Synon.* I. 90 *Indignant* meantime derives from a higher stock. **1804** W. TAYLOR in *Ann. Rev.* II. 632 Upholsterer is declared against as a corruption. Whence does it derive? **1866** J. B. ROSE *Virg. Ecl. & Georg.* 154 The words *Comus* and *Encomium* derive thence.

Hence **de'riving** *vbl. sb.*

1607 HIERON *Wks.* I. 420 Whosoeuer is a man by the propagation of Adams nature, the same is also a sinner by the deriuing ouer of his corruption. **1626** BACON *Sylva* §176 (R.) For our experiments are onely such as do ever ascend a degree to the deriving of causes and extracting of axiomes.

derived (dɪ'raɪvd), *ppl. a.* [f. DERIVE *v.* + -ED[1].]

a. Drawn, obtained, descended, or deduced from a source: see the verb.

1590 SHAKS. *Mids. N.* I. i. 99, I am my Lord, as well deriu'd as he, As well possest. **1638** HEYWOOD *Wise Woman* III. Wks. 1874 V. 313 A gentleman, and well deriv'd. **1661** BOYLE *Style of Script.* (1675) 157 Words and phrases, whose pithyness and copiousness, none in derived..languages can match. **1668** WILKINS *Real Char.* 353 Derived Adverbs are capable of Inflexion by degrees of Comparison. **1881** *Nature* No. 615. 352 The derived albumins noted as acid-albumins.

b. *derived function* (*Math.*): a differential coefficient (see COEFFICIENT 2 c).

1873 B. WILLIAMSON *Diff. Calc.* (ed. 2) i. §6 *note*, The method of derived functions was introduced by Lagrange.

c. *derived circuit, current* (*Electr.*): a circuit or current in part of which a second conductor is introduced so as to produce a derivation; a shunt; so *derived conductor.*

1882 *Syd. Soc. Lex.* s.v. *Current, Derived current*, the current obtained in a circuit made by the addition of a second conducting wire. **1893** *Munro & Jamieson's Pocket Bk. Electr. Form.* (ed. 9) (*Currents and Derived Circuits*) A current splits among derived circuits in proportion to their conductivities.

d. *derived fossils* (*Geol.*), fossils occurring in formations other than those to which they are native. Cf. DERIVATIVE *a.* 4 a.

1869 *Geol. Mag.* VI. 259 We must in the first place determine whether there are any derived fossils in the bed. **1940** *Cement, Lime & Gravel* Dec. 26 (*title*) Derived Upper Llandovery fossils in Bunter pebbles.

e. *Mus.* = BORROWED *ppl. a.* 2 b. Cf. DERIVATION[1] 1 d.

derivedly (dɪ'raɪvɪdlɪ), *adv.* [f. prec. + -LY[2].] In a derived way, by derivation.

1621 ARCHBOLD *Beauty Holiness* 8 Men are holy derivedly, and by participation from God. *a* **1641** BP. MOUNTAGU *Acts & Mon.* (1642) 54 By nature, derivedly from Adam.

†**de'rivement.** *Obs. rare.* [f. DERIVE *v.* + -MENT.] The fact of deriving; derivation; *concr.* that which is derived.

1593 BILSON *Govt. Christ's Ch.* Pref. 6 Much lesse anie deriuement from them. **1654** W. MOUNTAGUE *Devout Ess.* II. iv. §4. 77, I offer these derivements from these subjects, to raise our affections upward.

deriver (dɪ'raɪvə(r)). [f. DERIVE *v.* + -ER[1].] One that derives.

1613 T. MILLES *Treas. Anc. & Mod. Times* 21/2 The Children that came from Parents of such rich perfection.. must needs resemble their first Derivers. **1653** ASHWELL *Fides Apost.* 197 Such a Conveyance will argue the Church only for the Deriver..not the Originall Composer of the Creed. *a* **1716** SOUTH *Serm.* II. vi. (R.), Not only a partner of other men's sins, but also a deriver of the whole entire guilt of them to himself.

deri'vometer (dɛrɪ'vɒmɪtə(r)). [a. F. *dérivomètre*, f. *dériver* to drift (see DERIVATION[2]) + -(O)METER.] An instrument invented to show a ship's lee-way.

1842 *Mech. Mag.* XXXVII. 84 Another invention of M. Clement's, which he calls a Derivometer, is an instrument to ascertain a ship's leeway..When at anchor, the instrument will show clearly the direction of the currents. **1928** *Times* 15 Aug. 13/6 The afterpart of the cabin..contained the derivometer for measuring the airship's deviation from the straight course.

derk(e, -ly, etc., obs. ff. DARK, -LY, etc.

derling, -lyng, obs. forms of DARLING.

derm (dɜːm). *Anat.* [mod. f. Gr. δέρμα skin: cf. F. *derme* (1611 Cotgr.), mod.L. *derma* (Paré *c* 1550).] The layer of tissue (chiefly connective tissue) lying beneath the epidermis, and forming the general integument of the organs; the true skin or corium.

1835-6 TODD *Cycl. Anat.* I. 589/2 The derm or corium.. which..protects all the other parts of the skin. **1861** HULME tr. *Moquin-Tandon* II. VI. i. 317 The vesicle is beneath the derm or cutis. **1880** ORD & SEWELL in *Med. Chirurg. Trans.* LXIII. 4 Projections of the derm into the epidermis, having the appearance of distorted papillæ.

b. Comb. *derm-skeleton*: see DERMOSKELETON.

‖**derma** ('dɜːmə). *Anat.* [mod.L.: see prec.] = prec.

1706 in PHILLIPS (ed. Kersey). **1727-51** CHAMBERS *Cycl.* s.v., The derma consist of two parts; the corpus reticulare, and papillæ pyramidales. **1846** PATTERSON *Zool.* 42 The word 'derma', a coat or covering. **1875** H. WALTON *Dis. Eye* 137 A little slough or core of mortified cutaneous tissue, a portion of the substance of the derma.

dermabrasion (ˌdɜːmə'breɪʒən). *Surg.* [Blend of Gr. δέρμα skin + ABRASION.] The removal of superficial layers of the skin with a rapidly revolving abrasive tool.

1954 BLAU & REIN in *Archives of Dermatology* Dec. 758 The abrasion..should remove similar numbers of pits and pilosebaceous units... This method we have called dermabrasion. **1958** *Times* 28 Mar. 7/6 Dermabrasion—a method recently introduced for the removal of certain blemishes and lesions of the skin..consists of removing the superficial layers of the skin by 'planing' the skin with a rapidly revolving wire brush. **1967** *New Scientist* 5 Oct. 41/1 No completely satisfactory way yet exists of getting rid of unwanted tattoos... Techniques such as excision and dermabrasion at best only obscure the pattern.

dermad ('dɜːməd), *adv.* [f. Gr. δέρμα skin + *-ad* suffix applied in the sense 'toward', '-ward'.] Toward the skin or outer integument.

1803 in DR. J. BARCLAY *New Anatomical Nomencl.* **1851-60** MAYNE *Expos. Lex., Dermad*..towards the skin. **1883** *Syd. Soc. Lex., Dermad*, an adverbial term applied by Dr. Barclay to signify towards the *Dermal aspect*.

dermahæmal, bad form of DERMO-.

dermal ('dɜːməl), *a.* [f. DERM, DERMA + -AL[1]. (Not on Gr. analogies: the Gr. adj. is δερματικός.)]

1. *Anat.* Pertaining to the skin or outer integument in general; cutaneous. Rarely in restricted sense, Pertaining to the derma or true skin, as opposed to *epidermal*.

dermal muscle, a cutaneous or subcutaneous muscle, one attached to or acting upon the skin. ***dermal skeleton*** = DERMO-SKELETON.

1803 in DR. J. BARCLAY *New Anatomical Nomencl.* **1828** in WEBSTER. **1841** G. PILCHER in Dufton *Deafness* 31 The dermal membrane of the meatus auditorius. **1861** J. R. GREENE *Man. Anim. Kingd., Cœlent.* 136 An inner or dermal layer in immediate contact with the muscular substance. **1872** DARWIN *Emotions* iv. 95 Hairs, feathers, and other dermal appendages. **1875** H. C. WOOD *Therap.* (1879) 164 Producing intense dermal irritation. **1878** BELL tr. *Gegenbaur's Comp. Anat.* 493 The dermal muscles are of great functional importance in the Ophidii, as they produce a movement of the scales, which is of use in locomotion. *Ibid.*, The dermal musculature is more highly developed in the Mammalia.

2. *Bot.* Of or belonging to the epidermis, epidermal.

1874 COOKE *Fungi* 19 The dermal membrane, or outer skin. **1884** BOWER & SCOTT *De Bary's Phaner.* 135 Bodies of a nature similar to the secretions of the dermal glands..such as mucilage, and gum, resin, ethereal oils.

der'malgia. *Path.* = DERMATALGIA.

1842 BRAITHWAITE *Retrospect Med.* V. 104 Dermalgia of the skin of the pelvis. **1866** A. FLINT *Princ. Med.* (1880) 803 Neuralgia..limited to the skin..has been called dermalgia.

† **der'malogy.** *Obs.* = DERMATOLOGY.

1819 in *Pantologia*.

dermaneural, bad form of DERMO-.

‖**Dermaptera** (də'mæptərə), *sb. pl. Entom.* [mod. f. Gr. δέρμα skin, hide, leather + πτερόν wing; in mod.F. *dermaptère*: cf. Gr. δερμόπτερος having membranous wings.]

An order of orthopterous insects, comprising the Earwigs. Hence **der'mapteran** *a.*, belonging to the Dermaptera; *sb.* one of the Dermaptera; **der'mapterous** *a.*, belonging to the Dermaptera.

1835 KIRBY *Hab. & Inst. Anim.* II. xx. 318 The Dermaptera (Earwigs) have two elytra and two wings of membrane folded longitudinally. **1839** WESTWOOD *Mod. Classif. Insects* 406 Raised them to the rank of a distinct order to which the name of *Dermaptera* was misapplied.

'dermat-, 'dermato-, combining stem of Gr. δέρμα, δέρματ- skin, hide, leather (e.g. Gr. δερματοφόρος clothed in skins) entering into numerous technical terms, as ‖**derma'talgia** *Path.*, neuralgia or pain of the skin. **'dermatin** *Min.*, a variety of hydrophite, forming an olive-green crust on serpentine (1832 Shepherd *Min.* 214). **dermatine** ('dɜːmətɪn), *a.* [Gr. δερμάτινος of skin, leathern], = DERMATIC (Craig 1847). **'dermatine** *sb.*, name of an artificial substitute for leather, gutta-percha, etc. ‖**derma'titis**, inflammation of the skin. **dermato'branchia**: see DERMO-. **'dermatogen** *Bot.* [-GEN[1]], the primordial cellular layer in the embryo plant, from which the epidermis is developed. ˌ**dermato'graphia** *Path.*, = DERMOGRAPHISM (s.v. DERMO-). **derma'tography** [-GRAPHY], description of the skin. **'dermatol** *Chem.* (see quot.). **derma'tology** [-LOGY], the branch of science which treats of the skin, its nature, qualities, diseases, etc.; hence **dermato'logical** *a.*, **derma'tologist**. ‖**derma'tolysis** [λύσις loosening], a relaxed and pendulous condition of the skin in the face, abdomen, etc. ‖**dermatomy'cosis** [μύκης fungus + -OSIS], skin-disease caused by a vegetable parasite, such as ringworm. ‖**dermato'nosis** [νόσος disease], skin-disease. ˌ**dermatopa'thology**, the pathology of the skin, the subject of skin-diseases. **derma'topathy** [πάθος suffering, affection], cutaneous or skin-disease (*Syd. Soc. Lex.*). **'dermatophone** [φωνή voice], 'a kind of flexible stethoscope, the two extremities of which are covered by a tight membrane of thin india-rubber' (*Syd. Soc. Lex.*). **derma'tophony**, the use of the dermatophone applied to the surface of the living body; the observation of the sounds thus heard. **'dermatophyte** = DERMO-(*phyte*). **'dermatoˌplasty** [πλαστός moulded, formed], 'the remedying of skin defects by a plastic operation' (*Syd. Soc. Lex.*). **'dermatopsy**, 'skin vision', sensitiveness of the animal skin to light. **Derma'toptera** = DERMAPTERA. **derma'toptic** *a. Zool.* [ὀπτικός, of or for sight], having the skin sensitive to light, having 'skin vision'. ‖**dermato'rrhœa** [ῥοία flow], a morbidly increased secretion from the skin. ‖**dermatoscle'rosis** [σκλήρωσις hardening], hardening or induration of the skin; sclerodermia. ‖**derma'tosis** [-OSIS], the formation of bony plates or scales in the skin; also a skin-disease (*Syd. Soc. Lex.*). **dermato-'skeleton** = DERMO-(*skeleton*). **derma'totomy** = DERMO-(*tomy*). ‖**Dermato'zoa** [ζῷον animal], animal parasites of the skin; hence ‖**dermatozoö'nosis**, skin-disease caused by animal parasites.

1851-60 MAYNE *Expos. Lex., Dermatalgia*..neuralgia of the skin; pain of the skin; dermatalgy. **1876** DUHRING *Dis. Skin* 510 Dermatalgia is an affection characterized by pain having its seat solely in the skin..unattended by structural change. *Ibid.* 60 Dermatitis, resulting from continued exposure to a high temperature. **1882** VINES *Sachs' Bot.* 952 It is only in certain cases that the root-cap of Phanerogams is derived from the dermatogen. **1899** L. D. BULKLEY *Man. Dis. Skin* (ed. 4) xiii. 159 A name can be written on the skin with a blunt point (dermatographia, autographism). **1912** H. FRENCH *Index Diff. Diagnosis of Main Symptoms* 771 If letters or figures are marked out on the skin in this way, they appear as though they had been written in red, so that the condition has also been termed dermatographia. **1851-60** MAYNE *Expos. Lex., Dematography*, term for a description of the skin. **1893** *Brit. Med. Jrnl.* 1 Apr. 703/2 Dermatol is a yellow powder, insoluble in water and odourless; chemically it is a subgallate of bismuth. *Ibid.*, Dermatol dusting powder, a preparation intended to serve as an appropriate application to moist or irritable conditions of the skin. **1891** *Times* 14 Jan. 14/1 Read at the Dermatological Society in Paris. **1861** BUMSTEAD *Ven. Dis.* (1879) 815 This eruption has..been studied by a number of dermatologists. **1819** *Pantologia, Dermatology*, a treatise on the skin. **1847** in CRAIG. **1851-60** in MAYNE. **1876** DUHRING *Dis. Skin* 80 Dermatology, rightly viewed, is but a department of general medicine. *Ibid.* 371 Dermatolysis consists of a more or less circumscribed hypertrophy of the cutaneous structures.. and a tendency to hang in folds. **1883** *Nature* 22 Feb. 399/2 Experiments with regard to the 'skin-vision' of animals..of the earthworm, as representing the eyeless (or 'dermatoptic') lower animals, and the *Triton* as representative of the higher 'ophthalmoptic') eyed animals. **1866** FAGGE tr. *Hebra's Dis. Skin* I. ii. 33 Dermatoses..have long been divided, in reference to their etiology, into the symptomatic..and into the idiopathic.

dermatic (də'mætɪk), *a.* [ad. Gr. δερματικ-ός, f. δέρμα(τ- skin: see -IC.] Of or pertaining to the skin; dermal, cutaneous.

1847 in CRAIG. **1883** in *Syd. Soc. Lex.*

ˌ**dermato'glyphics.** [f. DERMATO- + Gr. γλυφικός (see GLYPHIC *a.* and *sb.*).] The science or study of skin markings or patterns, esp. those of the fingers, hands, and feet; also, such skin markings themselves. Hence ˌ**dermato'glyphic** *a.*, ˌ**dermato'glyphically** *adv.*

1926 CUMMINS & MIDLO in *Amer. Jrnl. Phys. Anthropol.* IX. 471 (*title*) Palmar and Plantar Epidermal Ridge Configurations (Dermatoglyphics) in European-Americans. *Ibid.*, The term 'dermatoglyphics'..is used herein for the first time... It is proposed..as a designation of the division of anatomy embracing the surface markings of skin. *Ibid.* 475 Methods of formulation are discussed..in company with the dermatoglyphic features which they symbolise. **1928** STEDMAN *Med. Dict.* (ed. 10) 276/2 *Dermatoglyphics*, the surface markings (sharply sculptured ridges) of the skin, especially of the palmar and plantar regions. **1938** *Nature* 3 Dec. 1001/1 The new quantitative method from dermatoglyphics. **1963** *Lancet* 12 Jan. 114/2 The repeated demonstration of dermatoglyphic abnormalities in the autosomal trisomies..leads us to wonder whether each autosomal trisomy syndrome will prove to be dermatoglyphically distinctive.

dermatoid ('dɜːmətɔɪd), *a.* [f. Gr. δερματ- skin: see -OID. Cf. Gr. δερματώδης, contr. for *δερματοειδής.] Like or resembling skin, skin-like; = DERMOID.

1851-60 in MAYNE *Expos. Lex.* **1857** DUNGLISON *Med. Lex.* 288 *Dermatoid*..that which is similar to the skin.

dermatome ('dɜːmətəʊm). [f. DERMAT-, DERMATO- + -TOME.]

1. *Surg.* Any of various devices for removing an intact layer of skin, often of predetermined thickness, for subsequent grafting; (see also quot. 1888[2]).

1888 J. V. SHOEMAKER *Pract. Treat. Dis. Skin* I. 87 (*caption*) The dermatome or needle-knife, with spoon upon one end. *Ibid.* 88 The integument can be depleted either by a bistoury, a tenotome, or a short pointed needle; the one which I use in my practice I have termed the 'dermatome'. **1939** E. C. PADGETT in *Surg., Gynecol. & Obstetrics* LXIX. 783/2 A mechanism consisting principally of a drum with a movable knife..was constructed. It was found..possible.. to remove a sheet of skin as large as the drum... Since the perfection of the dermatome I have had occasion to employ 83 calibrated grafts. **1958** *Immunology* I. 29 The second grafts..were 2 × 2 squares, cut with a dermatome. **1974** R. M. KIRK et al. *Surgery* v. 73 A thin sheet of the superficial part of the donor area is shaved off using a large razor-like knife, or a power-driven dermatome.

2. *Embryol.* The lateral wall of a somite, which appears to develop into connective tissue of the skin.

1910 *Amer. Jrnl. Anat.* XI. 61 The inner layer only, the *Muskellamelle* (myotome) forms muscle, whereas its outer layer *Cutislamelle* (dermatome) is converted into the connective tissue of the dermis. *Ibid.* 62, I have therefore followed with great care the history of one of the two somites of the second segment up to the time of its transformation into the sclerotome, myotome, and dermatome. **1917** L. B. AREY *Prentiss' Textbk. Embryol.* (ed. 2) x. 293 The lateral cells of the original mesodermal segment persist as a dermatome. **1968** PASSMORE & ROBSON *Compan. Med. Stud.* I. xviii. 10/2 A small, short lived cavity appears within each somite, dividing it into an outer sheet of cells, which constitutes the myotome and the so called dermatome, and an inner, more loosely-arranged collection of cells, the sclerotome. **1974** D. & M. WEBSTER *Compar. Vertebr. Morphol.* viii. 151 In the epaxial region the dermis is formed by the dermatome of the epimere.

3. *Anat.* [ad. G. *dermatom* (L. Bolk 1898, in *Morphol. Jahrb.* XXV. 468).] An area of the skin which is supplied by nerves from a single spinal root.

1915 F. A. WELBY tr. *L. Luciani's Human Physiol.* III. v. 303 There is a true segmentation of the body-surface..as well as a true segmentation of the muscles, which both correspond with the metamerism of the spinal roots... While the skin segments (Bolk's *dermatomes*) form continuous fields, the muscle segments (Bolk's *myotomes*) are compounded of portions of several muscles. **1942** T. LEWIS *Pain* ii. 21, I have compiled diagrams..from Foerster's data... They may be regarded as representing pain dermatomes with an accuracy approximating to that of touch dermatomes. **1948** A. BRODAL *Neurol. Anat.* vi. 146 On the trunk each dermatome covers an approximately circular belt-like field... The considerable degree of overlapping between neighbouring dermatomes is evident in the diagram. **1976** *Lancet* 4 Dec. 1220/2 He had a fading confluent vesicular peranal rash on both sides, with reduced pinprick sensation in the second, third, and fourth sacral dermatomes.

'dermatoˌmyo'sitis. *Path.* [ad. G. *dermomyositis* (H. Unverricht 1891, in *Deutsch. med. Wochenschr.* 8 Jan. 43/2), f. DERMATO- + MYOSITIS.] A disease of unknown origin characterized by œdema, dermatitis, and muscle inflammation.

1899 in *Index-Catal. Libr. Surgeon-General's Off.* IV. 161/1. **1905** *Med. Press & Circ.* CXXX. 207 Dermatomyositis, or acute polymyositis. **1958** WALTON & ADAMS *Polymyositis* i. 2 The terms polymyositis and dermatomyositis were used almost indiscriminately by the early authors. **1963** *Lancet* 5 Jan. 58/1 Skin lesions suggestive of dermatomyositis were never seen. **1970** J. BETHLEM *Muscle Path.* 39 If the disease is accompanied by skin involvement it is referred to as dermatomyositis.

dermatophyte ('dɜːmətəʊfaɪt). [f. DERMATO- + -PHYTE.] A pathogenic fungus that grows on skin, hair, feathers, etc. Hence **dermato'phytic** *a.*; ˌ**dermatophy'tosis**, a superficial infection caused by such a fungus; ˌ**dermato'phytid**, a secondary skin eruption caused by a dermatophyte or its toxic products.

1882 *Syd. Soc. Lex.* II, *Dermatophytic*, relating, or appertaining, to dermatophytes. **1885** H. VON ZIEMSSEN *Dis. Skin* 511 The various dermatophytes..are not so constituted as regards size, shape, and arrangement as to be microscopically differentiated from each other. **1894** F. T. ROBERTS *Theory & Pract. Med.* II. II. xcviii. 1144 This class [*sc.* Parasitic Diseases] includes all the affections produced by the various animal and vegetable parasites that infest the human skin. We shall therefore..describe, firstly, dermatozoic affections..and, secondly, dermatophytic diseases. **1894** R. QUAIN *Dict. Med.* 614/1 Epiphytic skin-diseases. Synon.: Tineae; Dermato-mycoses or Dermatophytoses; Ringworms. **1929** *Biol. Rev.* IV. 41 The name Dermatophytes is usually employed in a restricted sense, and is applied, not to all the fungi causing dermatomycoses, but only to those which cause superficial skin diseases or ringworms. **1934** *Brit. Jrnl. Dermatol.* XLVI. 139 A young man with a typical dermatophytosis of the feet and a dermatophytid of the hands was successfully treated. **1966** W. D. STEWART et. al. *Synopsis Dermatol.* xv. 312 Dermatophytid is an eruption occurring secondary to a fungal infection. **1970** REBELL & TAPLIN *Dermatophytes* (ed. 2) 4 The dermatophytes may be thought of as a group of taxonomically related fungi with affinity for cornified epidermis, hair, horn, nails, and feathers. *Ibid.* 6 Most dermatophyte thalli regularly undergo fluffy degenerative changes in laboratory culture. **1971** *Nature* 5 Feb. 435/1 In industry..there were more than 5,000 spells of incapacity attributable to dermatophytosis from June 1967 to June 1968.

‖**Dermestes** (dɜː'mɛstiːz). *Entom.* [irreg. f. Gr. δέρμα skin, leather + ἐσθίειν to eat.] A genus of beetles (the type of the family *Dermestidæ*), the larvæ of which are very destructive to leather and other animal substances. Hence **der'mestid** *a.*, belonging to the family *Dermestidæ*; *sb.* a member of this family; **der'mestoid** *a.*, resembling the genus *Dermestes*; belonging to the *Dermestidæ*.

1802 BINGLEY *Anim. Biog.* (1813) III. 111 When touched, these insects counterfeit death; but they do not contract their legs, in the manner of the Dermestes, and some other Beetles.

dermic ('dɜːmɪk), *a.* [mod. f. DERM or Gr. δέρμα + -IC: cf. F. *dermique* (Littré).] Of or relating to the skin; dermatic, dermal.

1841–71 T. R. JONES *Anim. Kingd.* (ed. 4) 388 The dermic system becomes fully developed in all its parts. **1857** DUNGLISON *Med. Lex.* 288 *Dermic*..relating to the skin.

‖**dermis** ('dɜːmɪs). *Anat.* [mod.L. deriv. of Gr. δέρμα skin, on analogy of ἐπιδερμίς *epidermis*.] The true skin; = DERM.

1830 R. KNOX *Béclard's Anat.* 142 The *Dermis, Corium*, or *Cutis vera*, is a fibro-cellular membrane, which forms the deeper and principal lamina of the skin, and of itself constitutes almost its whole thickness. **1878** T. BRYANT *Pract. Surg.* I. 172 The subjacent dermis appears of a rose colour.

der'mitis = *dermatitis*: see DERMAT-.

dermo-, repr. Gr. δερμο-, shortened combining form of δέρμα, δέρματ-, skin, etc. (as in δερμόπτερος having membranous wings), used in numerous modern formations, as **dermobranchia** (dɜːməʊ'bræŋkɪə), **-branchi'ata** *Zool.* [BRANCHIÆ; in F., *dermobranches*], a group of molluscs, having external gills in the form of dorsal membranous tufts; hence **dermo'branchiate** *a.* **dermo'gastric** *a.* [γαστήρ belly, stomach], pertaining to the skin and stomach, as in the *d. canals, pores*, which open both into the alimentary cavity and on the skin. **dermo'graphia, der'mographism** *Path.*, an irritable condition of the skin, occurring esp. in cases of urticaria, in which lines drawn on it leave a reddish elevated mark. **der'mography** = DERMATOGRAPHY. **dermohæmal** (-'hiːməl) *a.* [HÆMAL], pertaining to the skin of the hæmal or ventral aspect of the body; applied by Owen to the ventral fin rays of fishes, in their relation to the hæmal arch. **dermo'hæmia**, hyperæmia or congestion of the skin. **dermo'humeral** *a.* [HUMERAL], pertaining to the skin and humerus, as in the *d. muscle* by which in some animals the humerus is indirectly attached to the skin. **der'mology, dermomy'cosis**: see DERMATO-. **dermo'muscular** *a.*, of skin and muscle. **dermo'neural** *a.* [NEURAL], pertaining to the skin of the neural or dorsal aspect of the body; applied by Owen to the dorsal fin rays of fishes, in their relation to the neural arch. **dermo-'osseous** *a.* [OSSEOUS], of the nature of bone developed in the skin or integument, pertaining to a dermo-skeleton, exoskeletal; so **dermo-'ossify** *v.*, to ossify dermally, form a dermo-skeleton; also **dermo-ossifi'cation**. **dermo'pathic, -'opathy**: see DERMATO-. **'dermophyte** (φυτόν plant), a parasitic vegetable growth in the skin; hence **dermo'phytic** *a.* ‖**Der'moptera** *pl. Zool.* [Gr. δερμόπτερος, f. πτερόν wing], a sub-order of Insectivora, containing the *Galeopithecus* or Flying Lemur of the Moluccas (from the extension of skin, which enables them to take flying leaps from tree to tree). **der'mopterous** *a.*, having membranous wings (or fins). **dermopte'rygian** *a.*, having membranous fins. **dermo'rhynchous** *a.* [ῥύγχος snout, bill], having the bill covered by an epidermis, as in the duck. **dermo'sclerite** [σκληρός hard], a mass of calcareous or siliceous spicules in the outer layer of the tissue of some Actinozoa. **dermo'skeleton, dermskeleton**, the external bony, shelly, crustaceous, or coriaceous integument of many invertebrates and some vertebrates (e.g. crabs, tortoises); the exoskeleton; hence **dermo'skeletal** *a.* **dermo'tensor**, a tensor muscle of the skin. **der'motomy** [-τομια cutting], the anatomy or dissection of the skin.

1878 BELL tr. *Gegenbaur's Comp. Anat.* 111 In the Porifera ..The number of these pore-canals (dermo-gastric pores), which have consequently a dermal and gastric orifice, is generally very great. **1900** *Med. Rec.* (N.Y.) 4 Aug. 197/2 (*heading*) Dermographia and anidrosis. **1896** H. LELOIR in T. L. Stedman *Dis. Skin* 819 The dermographism was more marked upon the face than upon the rest of the body. **1908** *Practitioner* Feb. 252 From these individuals we get a history of attacks of urticaria, whilst they may even show dermographism. **1971** D. M. PILLSBURY *Man. Dermatol.* xv. 190 Physical agents, e.g., heat, cold, sunlight, scratching (dermographism) or heavy pressure may be responsible for urticaria in some individuals. **1851–60** MAYNE *Expos. Lex. Dermography, Dermology*, improperly used for *Dermatography, Dermatology*. **1835–6** TODD *Cycl. Anat.* I. 171/2 Pores..which traverse directly the dermo-muscular envelope. **1878** BELL tr. *Gegenbaur's Comp. Anat.* 36 Where the cœlom is present, the integument, with the muscles, forms a dermo-muscular tube. **1854** OWEN *Skel. & Teeth* (1855) 183 Both dermoneural and dermohæmal spines may present two structures. **1836–9** TODD *Cycl. Anat.* II. 880/1 The exterior of the body becomes hardened..and forms.. the Dermo-skeleton. **1854** OWEN *Skel. & Teeth* (1855) 181 The bones of the dermoskeleton..which constitute the complex skull of osseous fishes.

dermoid ('dɜːmɔɪd), *a.* and *sb.* [mod. f. Gr. δέρμα skin + -OID: in mod.F. *dermoïde*. (Not on Gr. analogies: see DERMATOID.)]

A. *adj.* Resembling or of the nature of skin. (Sometimes *loosely*, Of or belonging to the skin, dermal.)

dermoid cyst, 'a sebaceous cyst having a wall with structure like that of the skin' (*Syd. Soc. Lex.* s.v. *Cyst*).

1818 *Chron.* in *Ann. Reg.* 460 Those nations who have the dermoid system highly coloured. **1872** PEASLEE *Ovar. Tumours* 35 In the case of dermoid cysts, the more common contents are produced by the true skin, which constitutes a part or the whole of their internal surface. **1877** BURNETT *Ear* 43 The skin of the canal is extended over the drum-head, forming its dermoid or outer layer.

B. *sb.* A dermoid cyst.

1897 *Allbutt's Syst. Med.* III. 686 The intraperitoneal dermoids may be very numerous. **1906** *Practitioner* Nov. 664 These are the dermoids of the head and neck, or mediastinum; others, more complex ones, occur in the sexual organs. **1964** S. DUKE-ELDER *Parsons' Dis. Eye* (ed. 14) xxxi. 508 Sometimes a bridge of skin links the coloboma to the globe, or there is a dermoid astride the limbus at the site of the coloboma.

der'moidal, *a.* [f. prec. + -AL[1].] = prec.

1818 *Chron.* in *Ann. Reg.* 458 The instantaneous penetration of the dermoidal system by the blood.

†**dern**, *a.* and *sb. Obs.* or *arch.* Forms: 1 derne, WS. dierne, dyrne, 2 s.w. dyrne, 2–7 derne, 2–3, 7 dearne, 3 deorne, *Orm.* dærne, 3–4 durne, 4–9 dern, (*dial.* darn). [OE. *derne, dierne, dyrne* = OS. *derni*, OFris. *dern*, hidden, secret, obscure, OHG. *tarni* lying hid:—OTeut. **darnjo-*.]

A. *adj.*

†**1.** Of actions, etc.: Done or proceeding in secret or in the dark; kept concealed; hence, dark, of evil or deceitful nature. *Obs.*

Beowulf 4342 (Thorpe) Swa sceal mæȝ don, nealles inwitnet oðrum breȝdan dyrnum cræfte. *c* **897** K. ÆLFRED *Gregory's Past.* xiii. 78 Ðylæs ða smyltnesse ðes domes hine ȝewemme [oððe] se dyrna [*v.r.* dierna] æfst, oððe to hræd irre. *c* **1220** *Bestiary* 90 Old in hise sinnes derne. *c* **1250** *Gen. & Ex.* 1950 Vdas ðor quiles gaf hem red, ðat was fulfilt of derne sped. *c* **1300** *Beket* 23 The Princes douȝter..lovede him in durne love. *c* **1386** CHAUCER *Miller's T.* 14 This clerk ..Of derne love he cowde and of solas. *c* **1400** *Destr. Troy* 478 Dissyring full depely in her derne hert. *c* **1460** *Towneley Myst.* (Surtees) 310 Now bese unlokyn many dern dede. [*a* **1643** W. CARTWRIGHT *Ordinary* v. iv. in Hazl. *Dodsl.* XII. 311 [*arch.*] Hent him, for dern love, hent him.]

†**b.** Of persons: Secret in purpose or action; reserved, close; hence, underhand, sly, crafty. *Obs.*

a **1000** *Cædmon's Gen.* 490 (Gr.) Dyrne deofles boda wearp hine on wyrmes lic. *c* **1205** LAY. 13604 Uortigerne þe swike wes ful derne [**1275** deorne]. *a* **1300** *Cursor M.* 7234 (Cott.) Traitur dern and priue theif. *c* **1386** CHAUCER *Miller's T.* 111 Ye moste been ful deerne as in this cas. *c* **1400** *Destr. Troy* 13625 Deruyst & derne, myn awne dere cosyn, I graunt þe þe gouernanse of þis grete yle.

†**2.** Not made known, kept unrevealed or private; not divulged. *Obs.*

c **1000** *Ags. Gosp.* Luke viii. 47 Ða þæt wif ȝeseah þæt hit him næs dyrne, heo com forht. *c* **1200** ORMIN 9236 Forr Crist wass i þatt time ȝet All unncuþ & all dærne. *a* **1225** *Ancr. R.* 154 God his derne runes, & his heouenliche priuitez scheawede his leoue freond. *c* **1330** *Assump. Virg.* (BM. MS) 856 No man mai wite ne se What is þi derne priuete. *c* **1380** WYCLIF *Wks.* (1880) 353 Poule..herd derne wordes of God.

†**b.** Of a person: Treated as a confidant; entrusted with hidden matters; privy. *Obs.*

a **1300** *Cursor M.* 6509 (Cott.) Þis moyses was ful dern and dere To drighten..He taght him tabels of þe lai.

†**c.** Phr. *to hold, keep* (a thing) *dern*. *Obs.*

c **1000** *Ags. Ps.* cxviii. [cxix.] 19 Ne do þu me dyrne þine þa deoran bebodu. **1508** DUNBAR *Tua Mariit Wem.* 450 We dule for na euill deid, sa it be derne haldin. *a* **1575** *How Merchande dyd Wife betray* 175 in Hazl. *E.P.P.* I. 204, I pray the..As thou art my trewe weddyd fere, In thy chaumber thou woldest kepe me dern.

3. Of places, etc.: Secret, not generally known, private. *arch.*

Beowulf 4629 (Thorpe) Se guð-sceaða..hord eft ȝesceat, dryht-sele dyrnne. *a* **1000** *Elene* 1081 (Gr.) Þæt ðu funde, þa ðe in foldan ȝen deope bedolfen dierne sindon. *c* **1205** LAY. 6750 þe king hin lette don in to ane derne [*c* **1275** deorne] bure. *c* **1314** *Guy Warw.* (A.) 1289 On a dern stede he dede hem hide. *a* **1400–50** *Alexander* 4045 Darke in dennes vndire dounes & in derne holis. **1584** *Sc. Acts Jas. VI* (1814) 305 (Jam.) Gun pulder..placeit..within the voltis, laiche and darne partes and placeis thairof. **1806** FORSYTH *Beauties Scotl.* IV. 360 At the south-east corner is the darn, or private gate. **1814** SCOTT *Wav.* xii, That Davie Gellatly should meet them at the dern path. *Ibid.* xviii, There's not a dern nook, or cove, or corri, in the whole country, that he's not acquainted with.

4. Of places: Serving well to conceal, as lying out of the way, dark, etc.; hence, dark, sombre, solitary, wild, drear. *arch.*

c **1470** HENRY *Wallace* IV. 430 Fast on to Tay his buschement can he draw. In a dern woode thai stellit thaim full law. **1508** DUNBAR *Tua Mariit Wem.* 242 Thai drank, and did away dule, vnder derne bewis. **1608** SHAKS. *Per.* III. Prol. 15 By many a dern and painful perch Of Pericles the careful search..Is made. **1612** SHELTON *Quix.* III. xii. I. 240 He searching Adventures blind Among these dearn Woods and Rocks. **1647** H. MORE *Song of Soul* II. III. III. xli, Sing we to these wast hills, dern, deaf, forlorn. **1674–91** RAY *N.C. Words, Deafely*, lonely, solitary, far from neighbors. *Dearn*, signifies the same. **1813** HOGG *Queen's Wake* 96 Mid wastes that dern and dreary lie.

5. Dark, drear, dire. *arch.*

1570 LEVINS *Manip.* 211/4 Dearne, *dirus*. **1613** W. LEIGH *Drumme Devot.* 35 The light of Israel was put out for a time, Queene Elizabeth died, a dearne day to England, had it not beene presently repayred with as cleare a light from Scotland. *Ibid.* 39 Prognostications of our dearne light. **1650** B. *Discolliminium* 46 These derne, dreery, direfull dayes condunghill'd and uglified me into a darke dense lumpe. **1845** T. COOPER *Purgat. Suicides* (1877) 16 It was a crude excess Of all things dern and doleful, dark and drear. **1856** DOBELL *Eng. in Time War, Evening Dream*, The awful, twilight dern and dun.

†**6.** Deep, profound, intense. *lit.* and *fig. Obs.*

c **1400** *Destr. Troy* 3060 Hir chyn full choise was the chekys benethe, With a dympull full derne, daynté to se. *c* **1500** *Spir. Remed.* in Halliw. *Nugæ Poet.* 64 My myddelle woundys they bene derne and depe, Ther ys no plaster that persyth aryght. **1594** *Warres of Cyrus* (N.), Who, wounded with report of beauties pride, Unable to restraine his derne desire.

B. *sb.* †**1.** A hidden thing; a secret. *Obs.*

a **1000** *Gnom. Vers.* 2 (Gr.) Nelle ic þe min dyrne ȝeseċȝan. *a* **1300** *E.E. Psalter* l. 8 [li. 6] (Mätz.) Derne of þi wisdam þou opened unto me. *a* **1340** HAMPOLE *Psalter* xliii. 23 God.. knawis all þe dern in oure hert.

†**2.** Secrecy, concealment, privacy. Chiefly *in dern*, in secret. *Obs.*

a **1250** *Owl & Night.* 608 Ich can nimen mus at berne, An ek at Chirche in þe derne. *a* **1300** *Cursor M.* 2935 (Cott.) Sister, to þe in dern i sai, þou seis þe folk er all a-wai. *Ibid.* 21250 (Cott.) Marc, men sais, it wratte in dern. *c* **1420** *Avow. Arth.* lii, I am comun here loe In derne for to play. **1508** DUNBAR *Tua Mariit Wem.* 9, I drew in derne to the dyk to dirkin eftir myrthis.

†**3.** A secret place; a place of concealment.

a **1340** HAMPOLE *Psalter* xxx. 25 þou sall hide þaim in dern of þi face. *c* **1450** HENRYSON *Mor. Fab.* 27 Unto ane derne for dread hee him addrest. *c* **1500** *Leaues true Love* (W. de W.), To a derne I me droughe Her wyll to knowe.

†**4.** Darkness. *Obs.*

1500–20 DUNBAR *Ballat our Lady* 3 Haile, sterne superne ..Lucerne in derne. **15..** *Bannatyne Poems* (1770) 98 (Jam.) My dule in dern, bot gif thow dill, Doutless bot dreid I dé.

dern, a door-post: see DURN.

dern, U.S. var. DARN *sb.*

1853 *S. Lit. Messenger* XIX. 222/1 Cave said he did not care a dern for the oysters. **1874** E. EGGLESTON *Circuit Rider* (1895) 120, I tole him as how I didn't keer three continental derns fer his whole band. **1876** 'MARK TWAIN' *Tom Sawyer* vi. 56, I wouldn't give a dern for spunk-water. **1893** McCARTHY *Red Diamonds* I. 69 Ef it had been Noah I shouldn't have cared a dern.

dern, U.S. var. DARN *a.*

1853 in *D.A.E.* **1876** 'MARK TWAIN' *Tom Sawyer* ix. 97 I'd druther [rather] they was devils a dern sight. **1883** —— *Life Mississippi* xviii. 219 'Where was you born?' 'In Florida, Missouri.' 'Dern sight better stayed there!' **1919** T. K. HOLMES *Man fr. Tall Timber* xviii. 220 The dern fool! Thirty thousand against thirty millions!

†**dern, darn**, *v. Obs.* exc. *dial.* Also 2–3 dærnen, deorne. [OE. *diernan, dyrnan, dernan* = OS. *dernjan*, OHG. *tarnan, tarnen*, MHG. *ternen* to hide:—OTeut. **darnjan*, f. **darnjo-*, OE. *derne*, DERN *a.*]

†**1.** *trans.* To hide, conceal, keep secret. *Obs.*

c **893** K. ÆLFRED *Oros.* v. x, þeh hie hit ær swiþe him betweonum diernden [*later MS.* dyrndon]. *c* **1000** ÆLFRIC *Gen.* xlv. 1 Ða ne mihte Ioseph hine leng dyrnan. **1205** LAY. 7694 Alle hine grætten & heore grame dærnden [**1275** deorne]. *Ibid.* 18549 Næs þe king noht swa wis..þæt imong his duȝeþe his þoht cuðe dernen. *c* **1315** SHOREHAM 79 And he ondede hym cristendom, No lenge he nolde hyt derny.

2. *refl.* To hide, conceal oneself. *dial.*

1604 in Pitcairn *Crim. Trials Scot.* II. 428 The said George darnit him selff and his servandis in ane out-hous. **1837** R. NICOLL *Poems* (1843) 118 We dern oursel's down 'mang the fresh aiten strae. **1854** H. MILLER *Sch. & Schm.* x. (1858) 211 He..escaped them by derning himself in a fox-earth.

3. *intr.* To seek concealment; to hide. *dial.*

1584 HUDSON *Du Bartas' Judith* (1611) 31 Their courage quailed and they began to dern. **1600** J. MELVILL *Diary* (1842) 318 The enemies fled and darned. **1813** HOGG *Queen's Wake* 79 Ane nycht he darnit in Maisry's cot. **1847** J. HALLIDAY *Rustic Bard* 261 We've..dern'd amang its green.

†**4.** *trans.* To cause to hide, to run to earth.

1584 HUDSON *Du Bartas' Judith* 86 (Jam.) Holopherne, Who did a hundred famous princes derne. **1637** R. MONRO *Exped. Mackay's Reg.* II. 112 (Jam.) The cunning hunter.. giving one sweat after another, till he kill or derne, in putting the fox in the earth, and then hooke him out.

dern, obs. and dial. form of DARN *v.*[1]

dern, U.S. var. DARN *v.*[2]

1830 in *D.A.E.* **1848** J. J. HOOPER *Widow Rugby* in *Simon Suggs' Adv.*, etc. 128 Who dars to call me *hit*? Dern his old gray har, it shan't purtect him! **1883** 'MARK TWAIN' *Life Mississippi* xviii. 226 'Dod dern' was the nearest he ventured to the luxury of swearing. **1891** H. C. BUNNER *Short Sixes* 100 'Dern you,' said the keeper to Dr. Tibbitt.

†**derne**, *adv. Obs.* Also 1–3 dierne, 6 dern, 7 darne. [OE. *derne, dierne, dyrne* = OS. *darno*, adv. from *dern*, etc. adj.] 'Dernly', secretly.

a **1200** *Moral Ode* 77 in *Trin. Coll. Hom.* 222 Ne bie hit no swo derne idon. *c* **1325** *E.E. Allit. P.* B. 697, I compast hem a kynde crafte & kende hit hem derne. *c* **1440** *Bone Flor.* 1958 They..went forthe, so seyth the boke, Prevely and derne. **1631** A. CRAIGE *Pilgr. & Heremite* 5, I drew me darne to the doore, some din to heare.

† **derned**, *ppl. a. Obs.* or *dial.* Also **darned**. [f. DERN *v.*] Hidden, concealed; secret, privy.
1600 *Gowrie's Conspir.* in *Select. Harl. Misc.* (1793) 190 He privatly..took the fellow, and band him in a privie derned house, and, after lokking many durres vppon him, left him there. **1616** JAS. I, *Disc. Powder Treason* Wks. 242 That rightly-damned crew, now no more darned conspirators, but open and avowed rebels. **1631** A. CRAIGE *Pilgr. & Heremite* 7 When at the colde Caue doore darned I stood. **1725** RAMSAY *Gent. Sheph.* I. ii, A little fae Lies darn'd within my breast this mony a day.

derned, U.S. var. DARNED *a.* (= damned).
1843 *Spirit of Times* 11 Feb. 591/3 He said he would 'be *dod derned* if he'd go'! *Ibid.*, Report and be derned. **1873** J. H. BEADLE *Undevel. West* xxi. 405 [He] was rich afo' the war; derned poor now. **1898** H. S. CANFIELD *Maid of Frontier* i. 6 The derned rangers will have to make the same ride.

dernel, -al, obs. forms of DARNEL.

† **'derner.** *Obs.* Also **dirner**. [Etymology unknown: ? connected with *dern*, DURN, door-frame.] The lintel of a door.
a **1300** *Cursor M.* 6078 (Cott.) þis lamb blod..þar-wit yee mak þan takning, On aiþer post þer hus to smer, A takin o tav on þair derner [*v.r.* dernere]. *Ibid.* 6103 (Cott.) On þair post and on dirner.

† **'dernful**, *a. Obs.* [f. DERN *sb.* + -FUL. A pseudo-archaism.] Mournful, dreary.
? **1591** L. BRYSKETT *Mourn. Muse Thest.* 90 in Spenser *Astroph.*, The birds..this lucklesse chance foretold, By dernfull noise.

† **'dernhede.** *Obs.* $rare^{-1}$. [f. DERN *a.* + *-hede*: see -HEAD.] Secret matter; privity; a secret.
a **1300** *Cursor M.* 18454 (Cott.) Noght we dere O þaa dernhede tell you namar.

dernier ('dɜːnɪə(r), ‖dɛrnje), *a.* [a. F. *dernier*:—OF. *derrenier*, deriv. of *derrein*: see DARREIN. The suffix is as in *prem-ier*, L. *prim-ārius*.]
a. Last; ultimate, final.
1602 R. T. *Five Godlie Serm.* 45 The latter day..wherein we must take our dernier adewe. *a* **1688** VILLIERS (Dk. Buckhm.) *Chances*, Sir, I am in the derniere confusion to avow, that [etc.]. *a* **1734** NORTH *Lives* I. 109 While this dernier writ of error hung in the House of Lords undetermined. **1751** MRS. E. HEYWOOD *Betsy Thoughtless* I. 149 Every thing but the dernier undoing deed. **1797** MRS. A. M. BENNETT *Beggar Girl* (1813) III. 96 On how many chances did this dernier hope hang!
b. *dernier resort* (now always in F. form *dernier ressort*): last resort; *orig.* (in reference to legal jurisdiction) the last tribunal or court to which appeal can be made, that which has the power of final decision; hence, a last or final resource or refuge.
1641 ABP. WILLIAMS *Sp.* in *Apol. Bishops* (1661) 89 Here I have fixt my Areopagus, and dernier resort, being not like to make any further appeal. *a* **1709** ATKYNS *Parl. & Pol. Tracts* (1734) 97 The High Court of Parliament is the dernier Resort. **1709** *Refl. Sacheverell's Serm.* 3 The People ..were the dernier Resort of Justice and Dominion. **1711** *Vind. Sacheverell* 73 The Pretender is your *dernier Resort.* **1778** FOTHERGILL in *Phil. Trans.* LXIX. 2, I recommended, as a dernier resort, a trial of electricity. **1792** J. BELKNAP *Hist. New-Hampshire* III. 256 The dernier resort was to a court of appeals, consisting of the Governor and Council. **1893** *Nation* (N.Y.) 9 Feb. 111/1 The word *elementum*.. hithertofore, as a *dernier ressort*, has been referred in some way to *alimentum*.
c. *le* (or *the*) *dernier cri* [Fr., lit. 'the last cry']: the very latest fashion. Also in predicative use and (without article) *attrib.*
1896 *Westm. Gaz.* 10 Dec. 3/2 At a moment when cut-steel is *le dernier cri.* **1903** *Lady's Realm* XIV. 407/1 The shade *par excellence* for grey Father Thames is scarlet; in Paris this is the *dernier cri.* **1906** *Westm. Gaz.* 13 June 6/7 There was a time when the lisp was, so to speak, the 'dernier cri'. **1922** JOYCE *Ulysses* 249 Henry and James's wax smartsuited freshcheeked models, the gentlemen Henry, *dernier cri* James. **1928** *Daily Express* 16 June 5/5 That is why they wear hats and gowns that they are told are le dernier cri. *Ibid.* 9 Nov. 5/4 Any old necklace can be made modern and 'dernier cri'. **1960** *Times* 8 Jan. 13/6 The drabness of much *dernier cri* music.
d. *dernier mot*: the last word (see WORD *sb.* 25).
1834 J. S. MILL in *Monthly Repos.* VIII. 311 Propositions ..are put forth with an air of authority,..as if they were the *dernier mot* of some great question. **1905** *To-Day* 8 Mar. 175/2 One would have thought this group the *dernier mot* of singing. **1937** S. SPENDER *Forward from Liberalism* 94 Private property..and inheritance, appeared to me..the *dernier mot* of legislation.

† **'dernly**, *adv. Obs.* Also 2-3 **derneliche**, 3-6 **dernely**, *compar.* 3 **dern(e)luker**. [f. DERN *a.*: see -LY[2]. It is properly the adv. of an O.E. derived adj. **dernlic*.]
1. In a secret manner, with secrecy.
c **1175** *Lamb. Hom.* 153 Nedre smuɡeð derneliche. *a* **1225** *Ancr. R.* 128 Vorte..don derneluker þerinne flesliche fulðen. *a* **1300** *Cursor M.* 2517 (Cott.) Dernlik he did þam bide. *c* **1300** *Beket* 27 This Maide longede sore And lovede him durneliche. **1393** LANGL. *P. Pl.* C. XIV. 164 Menye of þo bryddes Hudden and heleden durneliche here egges, For no foul sholde hem fynde. *c* **1400** *Destr. Troy* 13700 þe schalke, that..so dernely hym did dere & dispit.
2. So as to be concealed or hidden.
c **1305** *St. Kenelm* 283 in *E.E.P.* (1862) 55 þe holi bodi: þat durneliche lai þere. **1513** DOUGLAS *Æneis* VIII. i. 146 So dernly hyd none wyst quhair he was gone.
3. Dismally. [A Spenserian archaism.]
1590 SPENSER *F.Q.* III. i. 14 Their puissance, whylome full dernely tryde. *Ibid.* III. xii. 34 Had not the lady..Dernly unto her called to abstaine. **1591** —— *Daphn.* xxviii, Thus dearnely plained. **1613** PURCHAS *Pilgrimage* II. xx. 223 A Lion..roared so dernely, that all the women in Rome (foure hundred miles from thence) for very horror proued abortive.

† **'dernship.** *Obs.* In 3 **darnscipe**. [f. DERN *a.* + -SHIP.] Secrecy; = DERNHEDE.
c **1205** LAY. 258 Mid darnscipe he heo luuede. *a* **1225** *Ancr. R.* 152 [Cott. MS.] Niht, ich cleopie dearneschipe [*other MSS.* priuite].

† **de'rob**, *v. Obs.* Also **derobbe, -rube, -robe**. [a. F. *dérober* (OF. also *desrober*, 13th c. in Littré), f. *de-* (*des-*), L. *dis-* + OF. *rober* to rob, take by stealth or force: see ROB. (In the second quot. perh. associated with *robe*: cf. *divest* and *derobe*.)] *trans.* To rob, plunder.
1546 *St. Papers Hen. VIII*, XI. 46 He wold preferre captaynes to Your Highnes service, but they wyl derobbe al. **1616** BUDDEN tr. *Aerodius' Parents' Hon.* Ep. Ded. 4 Methinks Lucius Brutus his seueritie well allated..that derobed himself of all respect of a Father.

derobe (dɪ'rəʊb), *v. rare.* [f. DE- II. 1 + ROBE *v.*] *trans.* To disrobe; to doff.
1841 *Tait's Mag.* VIII. 155 We quickly derobed our 'dusty apparelling'.

† **'derogant**, *a. Obs.* [ad. L. *dērogānt-em*, pr. pple. of *dērogāre* to DEROGATE.] Derogating, derogatory.
c **1620** T. ADAMS *Wks.* (1861-2) I. 12 (D.) The other is both arrogant in man, and derogant to God.

'derogate, *ppl. a.* Now *rare*. [ad. L. *dērogāt-us*, pa. pple. of *dērogāre*: see next.]
† **1.** *pa. pple.* Annulled or abrogated in part; lessened in authority, force, estimation, etc. *Obs.*
1430 LYDG. *Chron. Troy* III. xxvii, And leest through tongues to his hygh estate Through false reporte it were derogate. **1548** HALL *Chron.* 117 The chief ruler beyng in presence, the authoritie of the substitute, was clerely derogate. **1563-87** FOXE *A. & M.* (1684) III. 311 The once made oblation of Christ is hereby derogate, when this Sacramental..offering of thanksgiving is believed to be propitiatory.
2. *adj.* Deteriorated; debased.
1605 SHAKS. *Lear* I. iv. 302 And from her derogate body neuer spring A babe to honor her! **1849** *Fraser's Mag.* XL. 533 They are (like all his poetry) made derogate by vile conceits.

derogate ('dɛrəgeɪt), *v.* [f. ppl. stem of L. *dērogāre* to repeal in part, take away or detract from, diminish, disparage, f. DE- I. 2 + *rogāre* to ask, question, propose a law. Cf. prec., and see -ATE[3] 3-5.]
† **1.** *trans.* To repeal or abrogate in part (a law, sentence, etc.); to destroy or impair the force and effect of; to lessen the extent or authority of. *Obs.*
1513 BRADSHAW *St. Werburge* I. 3199 There may be no counseyll..To derogate or chaunge deuyne sentence. **1559** *Fabyan's Chron.* VII. 717 The Englishe seruice and the communion boke was derogated and disanulled, and a generalle submission..made to the sea of Roome. **1677** HALE *Prim. Orig. Man.* (J.), By severall contrary customs.. many of these civil and canon laws are controuled and derogated.
† **2.** To detract from; to lessen, abate, disparage, depreciate. *Obs.*
1526 *Pilgr. Perf.* (W. de W. 1531) 217 He dothe..as moche as is in hym, to derogate and destroy the autoritie of holy scripture. **1561** DAUS tr. *Bullinger on Apoc.* (1573) 19b, There be some at this day, which doe playnly derogate the manhode of Christ. **1570** BILLINGSLEY *Euclid* XI. Def. xii. 316 Which thing is not here spoken, any thing to derogate the author of the booke. **1642** MILTON *Apol. Smect.* (1851) 260 To derogate the honour of the State.
† **3.** To curtail or deprive (a person) *of* any part of his rights. *Obs.*
1540-1 ELYOT *Image Gov.* 24 Marcus Aurelius, whom no man can derogate of anie parte of honour and wisedome. **1570** BUCHANAN *Admonitioun* Wks. (1892) 30 Ye lordis wald not consent to put down ye quene or derogat hir of hir authoritie in ony maner.
4. To take away (something *from* a thing) so as to lessen or impair it. *arch.*
1561 T. NORTON *Calvin's Inst.* II. 105 Is that bicause their purpose is to derogate any thing from the law. **1577** HOLINSHED *Chron.* II. 134 To derogat things meerely preiudiciall to the kings roiall prerogative. **1593** ABP. BANCROFT *Daung. Posit.* I. vi. 26 [He] made Actes to derogate the free passage of the Gospell. **1623** BINGHAM *Xenophon* 141 Not to derogate credit from your owne word. **1755** YOUNG *Centaur* i. Wks. 1757 IV. 119 Nor can the diminishing imagery of our notions derogate less from Him. **1822** LAMB *Elia* Ser. I. *Mod. Gallantry*, Just so much respect as a woman derogates from her own sex..she deserves to have diminished from herself.
5. *absol.* or *intr.* To take away a part *from*; to detract, to make an improper or injurious abatement *from*. Now chiefly from an excellency; also, from a right, privilege, or possession.
c **1560** *Calvin's Com. Prayer Bk.* in *Phenix* (1708) II. 206 Other Sacrifices for Sin are blasphemous and derogate from the Sufficiency hereof. **1583** STUBBES *Anat. Abus.* II. (1882) 59 It derogateth greatly from the glorie and maiestie of God, to saye, [etc.] **1640** WILKINS *New Planet* i. (1707) 155 Fear of Derogating from the Authority of the Ancients. **1726-31** TINDAL *Rapin's Hist. Eng.* (1743) II. XVII. 124 This present Treaty shall in no way derogate from former Treaties. **1874** STUBBS *Const. Hist.* (1875) II. xiv. 88 This award is not intended to derogate from the liberties of the realm.
b. *from* a person: i.e. in respect of his excellency, eminence, authority, rights, etc. Now *arch.*
1586 WARNER *Alb. Eng.* III. xvi. (1612) 71 How captiously he derogates from me, and mine estate. *a* **1617** BAYNE *On Eph.* (1658) 78 This is a wicked Doctrin derogating from Christ. **1711** ADDISON *Spect.* No. 101 ¶3 We can now allow Cæsar to be a great Man, without derogating from Pompey. **1870** ROSSETTI *Life of Shelley* p. xiv, This vile stuff capable only of derogating from the typical Shelley.
† **c.** with *to*. *Obs. rare.*
a **1670** HACKET *Abp. Williams* II. 218 This fell into a harsh construction, derogating much to the Archbishop's credit.
6. *intr.* To do something derogatory to one's rank or position; to fall away in character or conduct *from*; to degenerate.
[Cf. F. *déroger*, *déroger à noblesse*, to do anything entailing loss of the privileges of nobility, e.g. to engage in a profession incompatible therewith.]
1611 SHAKS. *Cymb.* II. i. 48 You cannot derogate, my Lord. **1706** ESTCOURT *Fair Examp.* II. i, The World grows extravagant and derogates..from the Parsimony of our Ancestors. *a* **1830** HAZLITT (O.), Would Charles X derogate from his ancestors? Would he be the degenerate scion of that royal line? **1856** MRS. BROWNING *Aur. Leigh* III. 439, I'm well aware I do not derogate In loving Romney Leigh. **1862** TROLLOPE *Orley F.* lvii. (ed. 4) 416 In these days, too, Snow père had derogated even from the position in which Graham had first known him. **1888** *Temple Bar Mag.* Oct. 183 A nobleman derogates if he marries a lady who on her side has less than sixteen quarterings.
¶ Reproducing a barbarism of the Vulgate.
1609 BIBLE (Douay) *Ezek.* xxxv. 13 You..have derogated [**1611** multiplied] your wordes against me. [*Vulg.* derogastis adversum me verba vestra.]
Hence **'derogated** *ppl. a.*, **'derogating** *vbl. sb.* and *ppl. a.*
c **1629** LAYTON *Syon's Plea* (ed. 2) 17 Their derogating from the King, their injury to his Lawes. **1654** SIR E. NICHOLAS in *N. Papers* (Camden) II. 55 The most mischievous scandals and derogating Defamations. **1674** PRIDEAUX *Lett.* (Camden) 11 Whatsoever harsh or derogateing expression be found in any part of his booke.

† **'derogately**, *adv. Obs.* [f. DEROGATE *ppl. a.* + -LY[2].] = DEROGATORILY.
1606 SHAKS. *Ant. & Cl.* II. ii. 33 More laught at, that I should Once name you derogately.

derogation (dɛrə'geɪʃən). In 5 **-acion**. [a. F. *dérogation* (14th c. *-acion*, in Hatzf.), ad. L. *dērogātiōn-em*, n. of action from *dērogāre* to DEROGATE. In L. used only in the sense 'partial abrogation of a law': but in the mod. langs. in all the senses of the vb.]
1. The partial abrogation or repeal of a law, contract, treaty, legal right, etc.
1548 HALL *Chron. Hen. V*, An. 8. 72b, Long sufferaunce is no acquittance, nor prolongyng of tyme derogacion to right. **1628** COKE *On Litt.* 282b, New and subtile inuentions in derogation of the Common Law. **1691** RAY *Creation* I. 22 In derogation to the precedent Rule. **1692** SOUTH *Serm.* (1697) I. 430 The Scripture that allows of the Will, is neither the Abrogation, nor Derogation, nor Dispensation, nor Relaxation of that Law. **1792** CHIPMAN *Amer. Law Rep.* (1871) 13 A privilege in derogation of the common law right of the creditor. **1885** *Act 48-49 Vict.* c. 38 §1 This section shall be in addition to and not in derogation of any powers ..vested in the Committee of..Council on Education.
2. The taking away (in part) of the power or authority (*of* a person, etc.); lessening, weakening, curtailment, or impairment of authority; detraction *from*.
c **1450** tr. *De Imitatione* III. lxiii, He þat doþe hindringe to eny of my seintes, doþe derogacion to me. **1494** FABYAN *Chron.* VII. 304 One thynge he dyd to ye derogacion of ye munkys of Cantorbury. **1533** BELLENDEN *Livy* II. (1822) 195 It maid plane derogacioun to the Faderis to creat ony tribunis in times cumming, be votis of thair assessouris or clientis. **1536** *Act 28 Hen. VIII* (1621 in Bolton *Stat. Irel.* 118), Acts and Statutes made..in derogation, extirpation, and extinguishment of the Bishop of Rome. **1561** T. NORTON *Calvin's Inst.* IV. xix. (1634) 717 *marg.*, With derogation from Baptisme, force [is] given unto confirmation which doth not belong unto it. **1750** CARTE *Hist. Eng.* II. 511 Papal usurpations, to the derogation of the Crown. **1779** BURKE *Corr.* (1844) II. 269, I hope, too, that you will not think it any..derogation from the deference I ought to pay to your judgment.
3. Detraction from the honour, or reputation of; lowering or lessening in value or estimation, disparagement, depreciation.
1520 *Caxton's Chron. Eng.* IV. 31/2 Nero thought it sholde be great derogacion to his name and he were slayne of Karles. **1549** *Compl. Scot.* Epist. 5 As this nobil prelat hes dune..vytht out dirrogatione of his speritual dignite. **1596** SPENSER *State Irel.* Wks. (1862) 516/2 He is a very brave man, neither is that any thing which I speake to his derogation. **1641** MILTON *Reform.* II. (1851) 37 Clogs, and indeed derogations, and debasements to their high calling. **1656** COWLEY *Pindar. Odes* Notes (1669) 10 He does it in derogation from his adversary Bacchilides. **1690** LOCKE *Hum. Und.* I. iii. (1695) 15 This is no Derogation to their Truth and Certainty. **1713** ADDISON *Ct. Tariff* ¶8 He had heard the Plaintiff speak in derogation of the Portuguese. **1873** H. ROGERS *Orig. Bible* vii. 279, I am far from saying this in derogation.

4. Falling off in rank, character, or excellence; loss of rank; deterioration, debasement.

1838–9 HALLAM *Hist. Lit.* II. iv. II. §56. 155 He discusses also the derogation to nobility by plebeian occupation. **1847** L. HUNT *Jar Honey* (1848) 197 The sweets of the wild flowers, the industry of the bee, will continue without change or derogation. **1855** THACKERAY *Newcomes* I. 227 He might pretend surely to his kinswoman's hand without derogation. **1864** SALA in *Daily Tel.* 27 July, Men..who shudder at the derogation and degradation of the Northern American clergy.

derogative (dɪˈrɒgətɪv), *a.* [a. OF. *derogatif, -ive* (1403 in Godef.), f. L. type **dērogātīv-us*, f. ppl. stem of *dērogāre*: see -ATIVE.] Characterized by derogating; tending to derogation.

1477 in *Eng. Gilds* (1870) 305 Prejudiciall or derogatyve to the lyberties..of the bisshop. **1542–3** *Act 34–5 Hen. VIII*, c. 13 §1 Actes and statutes..derogatiue vnto the most auncient..priuileges of your said countie Palatine. **1646** SIR T. BROWNE *Pseud. Ep.* I. xi. 47 A conceit derogative unto himselfe. **1888** *Cornhill Mag.* Jan. 73 Too derogative of the intelligence of Londoners.

Hence **deˈrogatively** *adv.*

In mod. Dicts.

derogator (ˈdɛrəgeɪtə(r)). Also -our, -er. [a. L. *dērogātor*, agent-n. from *dērogāre* to DEROGATE.] One who derogates; one who diminishes or takes from the authority of anything.

1580 LUPTON *Sivqila* 120 The derogaters of Christes merits and passion. **1623** COCKERAM II, Which Diminisheth, *Derogatour*. **1684** *Vind. of Case of Indiff. Things* 9 It may be thought he is a Champion for the perfection and sufficiency of Scripture, and we the derogators from it.

derogatorily (dɪˈrɒgətərɪlɪ), *adv.* [f. DEROGATORY + -LY[2].] In a derogatory manner; with derogation or disparagement.

1603 SIR C. HEYDON *Jud. Astrol.* xxii. 481 Without speaking vnreuerently or derogatorily of God. **1648** PRYNNE *Plea for Lords* 17 He writes..derogatorily of the Commons. **1827** HARE *Guesses* (1859) 337 By speaking derogatorily and slightingly of some other power.

deˈrogatoriness. *rare.* [f. as prec. + -NESS.] Derogatory quality.

1727 in BAILEY vol. II.

†**derogaˈtorious,** *a. Obs.* [f. L. *dērogātōri-us* DEROGATORY + -OUS.] = next.

c **1555** HARPSFIELD *Divorce Hen. VIII* (1878) 234 His doings were derogatorious..to the supremacy of the Pope. **1601** DEACON & WALKER *Spirits & Divels* 186 Your speech is derogatorious to the efficacie..of Christ's death.

derogatory (dɪˈrɒgətərɪ), *a.* and *sb.* [ad. L. *dērogātōri-us*, f. *dērogātor*: see prec. and -ORY. Cf. F. *dérogatoire* (1341 in Hatzf.).]

A. *adj.*

1. Having the character of derogating, of taking away or detracting from authority, rights, or standing, of impairing in force or effect. Const. *to, from* (†*of*).

1502–3 *Plumpton Corr.* 174 Not intending to have his grant derogatorie unto justice. **1638** CHILLINGW. *Relig. Prot.* I. vi. §4. 326 If you conceive such a prayer derogatory from the perfection of your faith. **1637–50** ROW *Hist. Kirk* (1842) 501 That none be chosen, or no course be taken derogatory thereto. **1651** HOBBES *Govt. & Soc.* xiv. §12. 221 Provided there be nothing contain'd in the Law.. derogatory from his supreme power. **1730** SWIFT *Drapier's Lett.* ii. *Rep. Comm. Whiteh.*, A just..exercise of your.. royal prerogative, in no manner derogatory or invasive of any liberties. **1788** V. KNOX *Winter Even.* II. IV. x. 60 An opinion derogatory from the value of life. **1825** SCOTT *Talism.* xx, Incidents mortifying to his pride, and derogatory from his authority. **1863** H. COX *Instit.* I. vi. 34 This Act was annulled as derogatory to the King's just rights.

2. Having the effect of lowering in honour or estimation; depreciatory, disparaging, disrespectful, lowering.

1563–87 FOXE *A. & M.* (1596) 1/2 The 2nd [was] derogatorie to kings and emperors. **1592** NASHE *P. Penilesse* (ed. 2) 13 a, All holy Writ warrants that delight, so it be not derogatory to any part of Gods owne worship. **1776** SIR J. REYNOLDS *Disc.* vii. (1876) 48 Who probably would think it derogatory to their character, to be supposed to borrow. **1838–9** HALLAM *Hist. Lit.* III. iv. III. §34. 151 It would be ..derogatory to a man of the slightest claim to polite letters, were he unacquainted with the essays of Bacon. **1839** JAMES *Louis XIV*, I. 292 Conduct..derogatory to his rank. **1849** DICKENS *Dav. Copp.* (C.D. ed.) 181 To have imposed any derogatory work upon him. **1860** FARRAR *Orig. Lang.* (1865) 40 What plans are consonant to, and what are derogatory of God's..Infinite Wisdom.

†**3.** ***derogatory clause***: a clause in a legal document, a will, deed, etc., by which the right of subsequently altering or cancelling it is abrogated, and the validity of a later document, doing this, is made dependent on the correct repetition of the clause and its formal revocation. *Obs.*

1528 in Strype *Eccl. Mem.* I. App. xxx. 89 As doth appear by composition made..and also confirmed by Boniface the IV..with clauses derogatory. **1590** SWINBURNE *Testaments* 266 What maner of reuocation is to be made in the second testament, that it may suffice to reuoke the former testament, wherein is a clause derogatorie of the will of the testator. *a* **1626** BACON *Max. & Uses Com. Law* xix. (1636) 70 A derogatory clause is good to disable any latter act, except you revoke the same clause before you proceed to establish any later disposition or declaration.

†**B.** *sb. Obs. rare*⁻⁰.

1611 COTGR., *Derogatoire*, a derogatorie, or act of derogation.

†**deˈroge,** *v. Obs. rare.* [a. F. *déroge-r* (Oresme 14th c.), ad. L. *dērogāre.*] = DEROGATE.

1427 *Rolls of Parlt.* IV. 326/2 It was nought youre entent in any wyse to deroge or do prejudice unto my Lord.

derotremate (dɛrəʊˈtriːmət), *a. Zool.* [ad. mod.L. *derotrēmat-us* (in neuter pl. *Derotrēmata* name of the group), f. Gr. δέρη neck + τρῆμα(τ- hole, boring.] Of or pertaining to the *Derotremata*, a group of urodele batrachians, having gill-slits or branchial apertures, instead of external gill-tufts. So **deroˈtrematous** *a.*, **ˈderotreme** *a.* and *sb.*

1849–52 TODD *Cycl. Anat.* IV. 828/2 [Supra-renal capsules] have not been found among the Derotremate.. orders.

derout (dɪˈraʊt), *sb.* [a. F. *déroute* 'a rout, a defeature, or flight of men' (Cotgr.), f. *dérouter*: see next.] An utter defeat, a ROUT.

1644 R. BAILLIE *Lett. & Jrnls.* (1841) II. 188 We trust to heare shortly of their totall derout. *c* **1729** EARL OF AILESBURY *Mem.* (1890) 591 [Ramillies] was called a derout rather than a battle. **1803** E. HAY *Insurr. Wexf.* 150 This derout was..occasioned by the example of one of the divisional commanders.

derout (dɪˈraʊt), *v.* [a. F. *déroute-r*, OF. *desrouter* (*-roter, -ruter, -roupter*):—late L. **disruptāre*, f. *di(s)rupt-us*, pa. pple. of *dīrumpĕre* to break in pieces: cf. DISRUPT.] *trans.* To put completely to flight; to ROUT. Hence **deˈrouted** *ppl. a.*

1637 GILLESPIE *Eng. Pop. Cerem.* Ord. C iij, Untill not only all their blowes be awarded, but themselves also all derouted. **1808** J. BARLOW *Columb.* VI. 537 Till dark derouted foes should yield to flight. **1839** W. H. MAXWELL *Wellington & Brit. Armies* (1877) 147 The Spanish being utterly derouted.

derraine, -reyne, var. of DERAIGN *v. Obs.*

derrar, -ere, obs. compar. of DEAR *a.*

derre, obs. f. DEAR *a.*; obs. inflexional form of DARE *v.*

derrick (ˈdɛrɪk), *sb.* Also 7–9 derick. [from the surname of a noted hangman at Tyburn *c* 1600. The name is orig. the Du. *Dirk, Dierryk, Diederik* = Ger. *Dietrich, Theoderic.*]

†**1. a.** A hangman; hanging; the gallows. (Cf. *Jack Ketch.*)

c **1600** *Ballad Death Earl Essex* (N.), Derick, thou know'st at Coles I sav'd Thy life lost for a rape there done. **1606** DEKKER *Sev. Sinnes* I. (Arb.) 17, I would there were a Derick to hang vp him too. **1607** W. S. *Puritan* IV. i, Would Derrick had been his fortune seven years ago. **1608** DEKKER *Bellman of Lond.* (N.), He rides circuit with the devil, and Derrick must be his host, and Tyborne the inn at which he will light. **1656** BLOUNT *Glossogr.*, *Deric*..is with us abusively used for a Hang-man; because one of that name was not long since a famed executioner at Tiburn.

b. *attrib.* **derrick-jastro.**

?*a* **1610** HEALEY *Disc. New World* 174 (N.) This is inhabited only with serjeants, beadles, deputy-constables, and Derrick-jastroes.

2. A contrivance or machine for hoisting or moving heavy weights: † **a.** *orig.* A tackle used at the outer quarter of the mizen-mast. *Obs.* **b.** A spar or boom set up obliquely, with its head steadied by guys and its foot secured by lashings, or pivoted or socketed to the deck, floor, etc., and furnished with suitable tackle and purchases; orig. and chiefly used on board ship. **c.** A kind of crane (more fully ***derrick-crane***) in which the jib is pivoted to the foot of the central post, so that it may take various angles with the perpendicular; a 'jib and tie' crane. Also often applied to any outstanding jib or arm with a pulley at the end, e.g. those outside the lofts of stables, warehouses, etc. **d.** ***floating derrick***: one erected on a kind of boat, with a horizontal boom supported by stays from the top of the central post. **e.** A tall structure used to support telegraph wires. **f.** A structure erected over a deep-bored well, esp. an oil-well, to support the drilling apparatus. orig. *U.S.*

a. 1727–52 CHAMBERS *Cycl.* s.v. *Ship* (Plate), Mizon Mast ..Derrick and Spann. **1794** *Rigging & Seamanship* I. 165 *Derrick*, a tackle used at the outer quarter of a mizen-yard, consisting of a double and single block, connected by a fall.

b. 1756 *Gentl. Mag.* XXVI. 429 Lightning..cut out a piece of what they call the Derrick, at least 18 inches diameter and 15 or 16 feet long. **1800** COLQUHOUN *Comm. Thames* 626 Get up and rig a Derick for the purpose of discharging the Cargo. **1878** BESANT & RICE *Celia's Arb.* xxii. (1887) 161 They had jurymasts to serve as derricks on occasion.

c. 1856 EMERSON *Eng. Traits, Stonehenge* Wks. (Bohn) II. 126 Swinging a block of granite..with an ordinary derrick. **1881** RAYMOND *Mining Gloss.*, *Derrick*, the hoisting-tower over an artesian well-boring. **1885** DUCANE *Punishm. & Prev. Crime* 179 The construction of the large cranes and derricks in the quarries.

d. 1874 KNIGHT *Dict. Mech.* s.v., Bishop's floating-derrick ..used in 1850..is capable of self-propulsion by means of paddle-wheels, and thus removes its suspended load to a position of safety for repair or other purpose.

e. 1886 *Daily News* 28 Dec. 5/6 They have..a very large derrick here holding up an immense number of wires and a good many cables.

f. 1861 *Daily Dispatch* (Richmond, Va.) 30 Apr. 1/4 Shanties, derricks, engine-houses, and dwellings, were at once enveloped in flames. **1865** *Times* 18 Oct. 9/5 All along the last few miles to Oil City the derricks have been becoming thicker and thicker. *Ibid.* 24 Oct. 6/1 The derrick used at oil wells..is a mere tall pyramid-shaped scaffolding, about 50 ft. high. **1883, 1885** [see RIG *sb.*[4] 3 a]. **1961** H. VAN DONGEN in K. Reisz *Technique Film Editing* (ed. 9) viii. 152 It is the precise spot chosen by the oil-prospectors for drilling, and it is here that the approaching derrick will settle down.

3. *attrib.*, as ***derrick-floor, -pole***, etc.; **derrick-car,** a railroad truck on which a small derrick is mounted, for use in clearing lines from any obstruction (*U.S.*); **derrick-crane**: see 2 c.

1865 *Pall Mall G.* 21 June 9 About the same depth from their derrick floors. **1882** *Times* 27 Dec. 9/2 Unlike the derrick pole of an ordinary turret ship. **1883** ROSHER *Treat. Rating* 42 To lay down moorings and moor a derrick hulk to them.

†**ˈderrick,** *v. Obs. rare.* [f. prec. sb.] *trans.* To hang.

1600 W. KEMP *Nine Days' W.* in Arb. *Garner* VIII. 37 One that..would pol his father, derick his dad! do anything.

derricking (ˈdɛrɪkɪŋ), *vbl. sb.* and *ppl. a.* [f. DERRICK *sb.* + -ING[1], [2].] **a.** *vbl. sb.* The action of operating the jib of a derrick-crane. **b.** *ppl. a.* Operating as a derrick.

1888 *Lockwood's Dict. Mech. Engin.* s.v. *Derrick*, Portable cranes..are provided with movable jibs, whose mechanism for derricking is made in various types. **1911** C. W. HILL *Electr. Crane Constr.* iii. 31 An electric motor..was provided to drive the lifting and derricking motions. **1940** *Chambers's Techn. Dict.* 236/1 *Derricking jib crane*, a jib crane in which the inclination of the jib..can be varied by shortening or lengthening the tie-ropes between post and jib. **1958** H. H. BROUGHTON *Electr. Cranes* (ed. 3) xvii. 236 Derricking motion. The movement of a crane jib when it is pivoting in a vertical plane is known as derricking or luffing. *Ibid.* 239 Hoisting rope is taken up which prevents the load from being lowered as it would be with ordinary derricking gear.

derrid, derride (ˈdɛrɪd, -aɪd). *Chem.* [a. G. *derrid* (M. Greshoff 1890, in *Ber. d. Deut. Chem. Ges.* XXIII. 3538), f. DERR(IS: see -ID[4], -IDE.]

a. An extract of derris as obtained by Greshoff (see quots.). **b.** (See quot. 1939[2].)

1890 *Pharmaceut. Jrnl. & Trans.* XXI. 559/2 *Derris elliptica.* This plant was stated to afford the most important of several drugs passing under the name of 'tuba root'..a resinous body with an acid reaction, to which the name 'derrid' has been given... In the root it exists together with a brown colouring matter called 'derris red', derived from the tannin of derris. **1900** *Jrnl. Chem. Soc.* LXXVIII. I. 109 Derride, $C_{33}H_{30}O_{10}$, prepared from the root of *Derris elliptica, Benth.*..is a pale yellow substance. **1915** J. D. GIMLETTE *Malay Poisons* v. 93 A poisonous resin called tubain by Leonard Wray and derrid by Greshoff. **1939** MEYER & KOOLHAAS in *Rec. Trav. Chim. Pays-Bas* LVIII. 211 The name *derride* has been assigned to the new substance in memory of Greshoff, who was one of the first to isolate a substance from derris root: this substance was not examined at the time and he termed it derride. **1939** *Jrnl. Chem. Soc.* 1100 Meyer and Koolhaas have suggested the name 'derride' for this substance [*sc. l*-elliptone], somewhat unfortunately, as it has already been used by Greshoff..for a resinous extract from *D. elliptica* root.

‖**derrière** (dɛrɪˈɛə(r)). *colloq.* [Fr.] = BEHIND C. *sb.*

1774 G. SELWYN *Let.* 13 Aug. in *15th Rep. Hist. MSS. Commission* (1897) 278 *S'il fait le fier*..I shall give him several spanks upon his *derrière*. **1814** in J. Agate *These were Actors* (1943) 31 He..exposed his *derrière* to his mistress. **1933** J. MARTIN-HARVEY *Autobiogr.* vii. 83 Another poor girl with an undisguisable '*derrière*'. **1935** G. B. SHAW *Let.* 17 Mar. in *Shaw & Mrs. P. Campbell* (1952) 308 You shouldnt have left that poor young lady..with a sore derrière by dealing a quite useless parting kick.

derring do, derring-do. *pseudo-archaism.* In 4–5 dorryng, (dorynge, duryng) don (do, to do), 5 doryng(e do, 6 derrynge do, derring doe, 9 derring-do. The two words *durring, dorryng*, daring, vbl. sb. from *durran, dorren* to DARE, and *don, do*, pres. inf. of DO *v.*, literally *daring to do*, which, by a chain of misunderstandings and errors, have come to be treated as a kind of substantive combination, taken to mean, Daring action or feats, 'desperate courage'.

The words come incidentally in their ordinary sense and construction followed by the object 'that' (= what, that which) in Chaucer's *Troylus*; whence, in an imitative passage by Lydgate, in an absolute construction more liable to misunderstanding; Lydgate's *dorryng do* was misprinted in the 16th c. editions (1513 and 1555) *derrynge do*, in which form it was picked up by Spenser and misconstrued as a subst. phrase, explained in the Glossary to the *Sheph. Cal.* as 'manhood and chevalrie'. Modern romantic writers, led by Sir W. Scott, have taken it from Spenser, printed it *derring-do*, and accentuated the erroneous use.

c **1374** CHAUCER *Troylus* v. 837 Troylus was neuere vn-to no wight..in no degre secounde, In dorryng don [*v. rr.* duryng do, dorynge to do] þat longeth to a knyght..His herte ay wiþ þe firste and wiþ þe beste Stod paregal, to dorre don [*v. rr.* durre to do, dore don] that hym leste. **1430** LYDG.

Chron. Troy II. xvi. (MSS. Digby 232 lf. 56 a/2; 230 lf. 81 a/1), And parygal, of manhode and of dede, he [Troylus] was to any þat I can of rede, In dorryng [*v. rr.* doryng(e] do, this noble worþy wyght, Ffor to fulfille þat longeþ to a knyȝt, The secounde Ector..he called was. [*edd.* **1513**, **1555** In derrynge do, this noble worthy wyght.] **1579** SPENSER *Sheph. Cal.* Oct. 65 For ever who in derring doe were dreade, The loftie verse of hem was loved aye. [*Gloss.*, *In derring doe*, in manhood and chevalrie.] *Ibid.* Dec. 43, I durst in derring do [*mispr.* to] compare With shepheards swayne. **1590** —— *F.Q.* II. iv. 42 Drad for his derring doe and bloody deed. **1596** *Ibid.* VI. v. 37 A man of mickle name, Renowned much in armes and derring doe. **1820** SCOTT *Ivanhoe* xxix, Singular..if there be two who can do a deed of such derring-do. [Note. *Derring-do*, desperate courage.] **1843** LYTTON *Last Bar.* I. vi, Such wonders and derring-do are too solemn for laughter. **1866** G. W. DASENT *Gisli* 107 Such a deed of derring-do would long be borne in mind. **1885** BURTON *Arab. Nts.* (1887) III. 433 Who is for duello, who is for derring-do, who is for knightly devoir?

So †**derring doers**, daring doers; †**derring-deed**; †DER-DOING, q.v.

1596 SPENSER *F.Q.* IV. ii. 38 Dreadful derring dooers. **1633** P. FLETCHER *Purple Isl.* VI. v. 66 That Mantuan swain, who chang'd his slender reed..From Corydon to Turnus derring-deed.

Derringer (ˈdɛrɪndʒə(r)). *U.S.* Also **Deringer**. [from the surname of the inventor, Henry *Deringer* (1786–1868), a gunsmith in U.S.] A small pistol with large bore, very effective at short range. Also *attrib.*

1853 G. D. BREWERTON *Overland with Kit Carson* (1930) 188 A preventive to interference..in the shape of Bowie knives, 'Derringers', and 'six-shooters'. **1854** J. R. BARTLETT *Personal Narr. Explor. Texas* I. iii. 48 My carriage driver carried a pair of Deringer pistols. **1856** B. HARTE *Poems, Dow's Flat*, With a shovel and pick on his shoulder, and a derringer hid in his breast. **1876** BESANT & RICE *Gold. Butterfly* Prol., To have both bowie and Derringer ready to hand. **1890** *Century Mag.* Jan. 435/1 A large derringer bullet had entered the back of the head [of Pres. Lincoln].

fig. **1890** *Daily News* 4 Dec. 5/2 Tiny tomes, literary derringers for the waistcoat pocket.

derris (ˈdɛrɪs). [mod.L. (J. de Loureiro *Flora Cochinchinensis* (1790) II. 432), a. Gr. δέρρις a leather covering, membrane (referring to the pod).]

a. *Bot.* A member of the genus of woody tropical climbing plants so called, belonging to the family Leguminosæ.

1860 G. BENTHAM in *Jrnl. Linnean Soc.* IV. Suppl. 21 *Derris* has the flat pod of *Lonchocarpus*, varying likewise in consistency from thin and membranous to thick and almost woody. *Ibid.* 22, I adopted for the whole genus Loureiro's old name, *Derris*, because I could clearly identify it with his character. **1936** D. H. GRIST *Outl. Malayan Agric.* 182 Two species of derris are commonly cultivated in the Malay Peninsula. **1968** J. W. PURSEGLOVE *Tropical Crops* I. 257 Derris is propagated vegetatively by well-ripened stem cuttings.

b. A preparation, esp. the powdered root, of various species of *Derris* (and also of other genera containing rotenone), used extensively as an insecticide. Also *attrib.*

1890 [see DERRID, DERRIDE]. **1919** N. E. MCINDOO et al. in *Jrnl. Agric. Research* XVII. 199 Derris, known widely as a powerful East Indies fish poison, was found to fulfill several of the requirements of a general insecticide; it acts both as a contact insecticide and as a stomach poison. *Ibid.* 200 Derris powder..was found to be efficient against dog fleas, chicken lice, house flies. **1932** R. F. FORTUNE *Sorcerers of Dobu* iii. 174 Derris, a vegetable poison in the roots of a tall liana, is used publicly for stupefying fish. **1936** *Discovery* Feb. 42/2 The successful derris treatments for Warble Fly damage. **1958** *Times* 25 Jan. 9/1 The derris will take care of the caterpillars and the BHC, of most of the other pests that afflict our plants. **1963** H. MARTIN *Insecticide & Fungicide Handbk.* i. 8 The other principal insecticide available prior to 1939 was derris, the ground root of species of the genera *Derris* and *Lonchocarpus*. **1971** *Daily Tel.* 3 Apr. 6/4 Don't forget the dustings of derris powder round their [*sc.* daffodil bulbs'] necks to scotch the maggots of the bulb flies.

derry[1] (ˈdɛrɪ). A meaningless word in the refrains of popular songs; *hence*, a ballad or set of verses.

a **1553** UDALL *Royster D.* II. iii. (Arb.) 36 With chip and cherie Heyh derie derie. **1860** BORROW *Sleeping Bard* 50 If one can patch together any nonsensical derry, he is styled a graduate bard.

derry[2] (ˈdɛrɪ). *Austral.* and *N.Z.* [app. jocular adaptation of *derry* in the refrain *derry down.*] A 'down' (DOWN *sb.*[3] 5); esp. in phr. ***to have a derry on***, to be prejudiced against.

1896 *Argus* 19 Mar. 5/9 (Morris), Have you any particular 'derry' upon this Wendouree? **1897** D. MCK. WRIGHT *Station Ballads* 107, I ain't down on them if they ain't got a derry on me! **1900** H. LAWSON *Verses Pop. & Humorous* 185 It's orful when the p'leece has got a derry on a chap. **1915** *Bulletin* (Sydney) 15 Aug. 47/1 If you do, the Johns have a derry on yer ever after. **1918** *Chrons. N.Z.E.F.* 20 Dec. 245/1 He..[has] a particularly keen 'derry' on the parade-ground N.C.O. **1948** D. W. BALLANTYNE *Cunninghams* (1963) I. x. 58 She didn't like the Baptists though, had had a derry on that crowd ever since Hilda took her to an evening service.

derry[3] (ˈdɛrɪ). *slang.* [f. DERELICT *a.* and *sb.* + -Y[6].] A derelict building.

1968 BUSBY & HOLTHAM *Main Line Kill* v. 52 Red said it was time to kip in the derry... The derry was the second of a row of empty houses. **1969** *Guardian* 5 Aug. 4/8 Mary.. lives with her husband, two Belgian boys, three English girls, and a young Frenchman in a 'derry'—a deserted house —in Chelsea.

derth(e, obs. form of DEARTH.

dertrum (ˈdɜːtrəm). *Zool.* Also **dertron**. [mod.L., ad. Gr. δέρτρον beak.] The extremity of the upper bill of a bird when in any way distinguished from the rest of the beak.

1889 in *Cent. Dict.* **1893** A. NEWTON *Dict. Birds* I. 33 Various parts of the rostrum have received special names: *culmen*, the dorsal ridge of the upper bill; *apex* or tip; *dertrum*, in which it often terminates. **1959** VAN TYNE & BERGER *Fund. Ornith.* 566 Dertrum. Extremity of the upper mandible (maxilla); the hook of the bill. **1964** G. R. MOUNTFORT in A. L. Thomson *New Dict. Birds* 93/1 Upper mandible... may be divided into the culmen, or dorsal ridge from the tip (dertrum) of the bill to the forehead, and the upper mandibular tomia, or lateral cutting edges.

derue: see DERF *a.*, DERVE *v.*

†**de'runcinate**, *v. Obs. rare*$^{-0}$. [f. ppl. stem of L. *dēruncināre* to plane off.]

1656 BLOUNT *Glossogr.*, *Deruncinate*, to cut off or pill away that which is superfluous.

Hence †**deruncination**.

1706 PHILLIPS (ed. Kersey), *Deruncination* (in *Husbandry*), a cutting off Trees, Bushes, etc. or any thing that incumbers the Ground. Hence in BAILEY, ASH, etc.

deruralize: see DE- II. 1.

derure, compar. of DERF *a. Obs.*

derv (dɜːv). [f. the initial letters of *diesel-engined road vehicle.*] Diesel oil for road vehicles. Also *attrib.*

1948 in PARTRIDGE *Dict. Forces' Slang 1939–1945* 54. **1952** *Economist* 15 Mar. 666/2 Suggestions that 'derv' fuel might be given preferential treatment in any increase in motor fuel duty. **1958** *Oxford Mail* 17 Jan. 6/4 The fuel which supplies the motive power for buses is fuel oil (or 'derv'). **1958** *Times* 17 July 10/6 The major fuel companies yesterday announced increases of ½d. a gallon from to-day in Derv, vaporizing oil, gas oil, and light fuel oil.

†**derve**, *v. Obs.* Forms: 1 deorfan, 2–4 derue(n; *pa. t.* 3 derfde, 4 deruede; *pa. pple.* 3 idoruen, idorve, iderued, 4 deruet. [ME. *derven* str. and weak; the str. vb. app. = OE. *deorfan* (pa. t. *dearf*, *durfon*, pa. pple. *dorfen*) to labour: besides this there probably existed a causal weak vb. *dierfan* (*dierfde*) to cause to labour, afflict, grieve; confusion of this with the strong vb., as in BURN, etc. would account for the ME. forms and sense. OE. *deorfan* was app. cognate with the stem of OFris. *forderva*, and OLFrankish *fardurvon*, transl. 'perierunt' *Ps.* lxxii. 19.]

1. *intr.* To labour. (Only in OE.)

a **1000** in Thorpe *Hom.* II. 516/26 (Bosw.) Ne wiðcweðe ic to deorfenne ȝyt, ȝif ic nydbehefe eom ȝyt ðinum folce.

2. *trans.* To trouble, grieve, hurt, afflict, molest.

c **1205** LAY. 8731 Hunger him derfde. *Ibid.* 18715 Swiðe he murnede, his mod wes iderued. *a* **1225** *Ancr. R.* 106 He was idoruen in alle his oðre wittes. *a* **1240** *Lofsong* in *Cott. Hom.* 211 Þinge þat me derueð mest. *c* **1320** *Cast. Love* 676 None kunnes asaylyng Ne may him deruen. *a* **1375** *Joseph Arim.* 47 Beo þou no þing a-dred, for non schal þe derue.

absol. *a* **1225** *Ancr. R.* 112 A lutel ihurt i þen eie derueð more þen deð a muchel iðe hele.

†'**derverye**. *Obs. rare.* [a. OF. *derverie*, *desverie*, madness, f. *derver*, *desver*, to lose one's reason, go mad. (Cf. Kœrting, 2441.)] Madness.

1480 CAXTON *Ovid's Met.* x. vii, Withdrawe thyn herte fro such rage and derverye.

dervish (ˈdɜːvɪʃ). Forms: 6–9 **dervis**, 7–9 **dervise**, (7 **dervice**, **dervys**, **dervisse**, **-iche**, **dervize**, **derwis**, **darvish**, **derveesh**), 7– **dervish**, (8 **derwish**, 9 **dirvesh**, **darwesh**, **durwaysh**, **-weesh**). [a. Pers. *darvēsh*, *darvīsh* poor, a religious mendicant, a friar, in Arab. *darwēsh*, *darwīsh*, Turkish *dervīsh*, the latter being the immediate source of the European forms: cf. It. *dervis*, F. *dervis*, *derviche* (in 1559 *derviss*), Sp. *derviche*, Ger. *derwisch*. Some of the variant spellings represent Arabic and Persian forms of the word. (The native Arabic equivalent is *faqīr* poor, fakir.)]

A Mohammedan friar, who has taken vows of poverty and austere life. Of these there are various orders, some of whom are known from their fantastic practices as ***dancing*** or ***whirling***, and as ***howling dervishes***.

1585 T. WASHINGTON tr. *Nicholay's Voy.* III. xvii. 102 The thirde sect of the religious Turkes called Dervis. *Ibid.* 102 b, These devoute Dervis live of almes. **1625** PURCHAS *Pilgrims* II. IX. 1611 An order of Derueeshes, that turne round with Musike in their Diuine Seruice. **1632** LITHGOW *Trav.* VII. 316 Priests called Darvishes. **1635** PAGITT *Christianogr.* I. iii. (1636) 200 A Dervice, or religious man of theirs. **1665** SIR T. HERBERT *Trav.* (1677) 307 The Dervisse an order of begging Friar. **1728** MORGAN *Algiers* I. vi. 186 A wandering Derwish, a devout Moor. **1744** *Trav. C. Thompson* III. 267 They are not the dancing Dervises, of which Sort there are none in Egypt. **1818** JAS. MILL *Brit. India* I. III. iii. 510 A Dirvesh, or professor of piety. **1821** BYRON *Juan* III. xxix, Like dervises, who turn as on a pivot. **1832** G. A. HERKLOTS tr. *Customs Moosulmans* 206 The first class of Durwayshes is denominated *Salik*. **1847** EMERSON *Poems, Saadi* Wks. (Bohn) I. 475 Barefooted Dervish is not poor, If fate unlock his bosom's door. **1852** E. B. EASTWICK tr. *Bāgh o Bahār* 10 Adventures of the Four Darweshes. **1869** *Pall Mall G.* 7 Jan. 10 Whirling about all round you like dancing dervishes. **1877** A. B. EDWARDS *Up Nile* ii. 37 And now, their guttural chorus audible long before they arrived in sight, came the howling dervishes.

attrib. **1704** J. PITTS *Acc. Mahometans* vii. (1738) 125 Give themselves up to a Dervise sort of Life. **1882–3** SCHAFF *Encycl. Relig. Knowl.* III. 1810 This pantheistic dervish system.

Hence '**dervishhood**, the estate or condition of a dervish. '**dervishism**, the principles and practice of the dervishes; the dervish system. '**dervish-like** *a.*

1850 MRS. JAMESON *Leg. Monast. Ord.* Introd. (1863) 22 Asceticism..strangely uncouth, and dervish-like. **1865** *Sat. Rev.* 4 Feb. 144/2 Dr. Vambery wandered, because he has the genuine wild spirit of Dervishism strong within him. **1884** BROWNING *Ferishtah* 9 Half-way on Dervishhood, not wholly there.

Derwenter (ˈdɜːwəntə(r)). *Australia.* [named from the river *Derwent* in Tasmania, on the banks of which was a convict settlement.] A released convict.

1853 J. ROCHFORT *Adventures of Surveyor in N.Z.* ii. 16 Here we engaged a new steward..who I think was a Derwenter from what I have since seen of him. **1884** BOLDREWOOD *Melb. Mem.* xx. 140 An odd pair of Sawyers, generally 'Derwenters' as the Tasmanian expirees were called. **1892** in LENTZNER *Australian Word-bk.* 20.

dery, **deryge**, obs. forms of DAIRY, DIRGE.

derye, var. DERE *v. Obs.*, to hurt.

derzie, **-y**, varr. DURZEE.

des, obs. forms of DAIS, DICE.

des- in obs. words: see DEC-, DESC-, DESS-, DIS-.

des- *prefix.* Regular Romanic form of L. *dis-*, in OIt., Sp., Pg., Pr., OFr.; in mod.Fr. retained (as *dés-*) before a vowel or silent *h* (*déshabillé*), otherwise reduced to *dé-* (OF. *descharge*, mod. *décharge*). In some cases apparently representing a late L. *de- ex-*, for L. *ex-*. Partly from the frequent substitution of *dis-*, *des-*, for L. *dē-* in late L. and Romanic (see DE- prefix 6), partly through the phonetic reduction of *des-* to *dé-* in later French, the two prefixes have in that language largely fallen together under the mod.F. *dé-*. Early OF. words passed into English with the prefix in the form *des-* (*descharge*, ME. *descharge*); here it was sometimes, in conformity with later OF. pronunciation, reduced to *de-* (OF. *desmembre*, *demembre*, ME. *demembre*); but usually the *s* was retained, and the prefix at length changed back to the L. type *dis-* (*discharge*, *dismembre*, also spelt *dys-*) as was also done to some extent in French itself (*descorde*, now *discorde*).

In English, therefore, *des-* is merely the earlier form of DIS- in words from OF., e.g. *desarm*, *desblame*, *descharge*, *desclaundre*, *descolour*, *desdain*, *desembogue*, *desere* (= *desheir*), *deserite* (*disherit*), *desgyse*, *deshonour*, *desinteressed*, *desjoyne*, *desjune*, *desmail*, *desmay*, *desmesure*, *desordein*, *desordere*, *desparage*, *desparple*, *despend*, *despense*, *despeople*, *desplay*, *desport*, *despreve* (= *disprove*), *despute*, *desray*, *destempre*, *desturb*, *destribute*, etc. All these have a later form in DIS-, under which they are treated in this Dictionary. Only a few words became obsolete before *dis-* forms appeared. The prefix is exceptionally retained in *descant*, and it is occasionally found for DE- before a vowel, in chemical terms from modern French, as *desoxalic*, *desoxybenzoin*, †*desoxydate*. In *despatch*, modern var. of DISPATCH, the spelling *des-* is not historical, but originated in an 18th c. etymological error.

There are many words beginning with *des-* in which the *s* belongs to the root-word, and the prefix is *de-*, as *descry*, *describe*, *descend*, *deserve*, *despair*, *despite*, *despoil*, *destroy*. From confusion of these with words in which *des-* is the prefix, they also were in late ME. often spelt with *dis-* (*discry*, *discribe*, etc.). And, on the other hand, words in *di-* followed by *s-* were sometimes confused with words in *dis-* prefix, and so also written *des-* (*destinct*, *destress*, etc.). Both these errors have been corrected in the later orthography.

desacralization (diːˌsækrəlaɪˈzeɪʃən). [f. DE- II. 1 + SACRAL *a.*[2] + -IZ(E + -ATION.] **a.** The process of the ritual removal of a taboo. **b.** Secularization; the process of rendering something less sacred. So **de'sacralize** *v. trans.*

1911 *Encycl. Brit.* XXVI. 338/2 Temporary direct taboos, whether natural or acquired, may be removed by a process of desacralization or of purification. Thus, new crops are frequently taboo till the chief has partaken of them;..and the crops thus desacralized become free to all. **1942** H. WEBSTER *Taboo* i. 34 A state of taboo which has been formally imposed by the constituted authorities may be as formally lifted by an act of desacralization. **1959** W. R. TRASK tr. *Eliade's Sacred & Profane* 13 Desacralization pervades the entire experience of the nonreligious man of modern societies. *Ibid.*, The man who lives..in a desacralized world. **1964** M. MCLUHAN *Understanding Media* xv. 155 The visual desacralizes the universe and produces the 'nonreligious man of modern societies'. **1967** C. DAVIS *Question of Conscience* III. i. 183 Thus, nature, the State and society have all been desacralized.

†**desacrate**, *v. Obs. rare*⁻⁰. [f. L. *dēsacrāt-*, ppl. stem of *dēsacrāre* to consecrate.]

1727 BAILEY vol. II, *To Desacrate*, to consecrate or dedicate.

desai ('dɛsaɪ). *Indian Hist.* Also 7 desie, 9 desaye, dessai. [Marathi *deśāī*.] A native Indian revenue official, or petty chief.

1698 J. FRYER *Acc. E. India & Persia* 120 The Desie or Farmer, who squeezes the Countryman, as much as the Governor does the Citizen. **1800** WELLINGTON *Suppl. Desp.* (1858) II. 116 He has sent 300 horse to seize the dessays of the villages which you mention. **1835** J. BIRD tr. *Ali Mohammed Khan's Pol. & Stat. Hist. Gujarat* 408 (Y.), The Desayes..made a complaint at Court. **1883** *Pioneer Mail* 24 Jan. (Y.), The Desai of Sawantwari has arrived at Delhi on a visit. **1885** G. S. FORBES *Wild Life in Canara* 20 They were also instructed to rendezvous..under their Dessaies at any point which might be threatened.

desaife, desait(e, obs. ff. DECEIVE, DECEIT.

desalinate (diː'sælɪneɪt), *v.* [f. DE- II. 1 + SALIN(E *sb.* + -ATE³.] *trans.* To remove salt from. Hence **de'salinated** *ppl. a.*; **desali'nation**, the removal of salt.

1949 KOESTLER *Promise & Fulf.* I. xiv. 162 The strange experiment of de-salinating the soil of the barren area. *Ibid.* II. ii. 209 The blond, good-looking young man with his neutral, 'de-salinated' features. **1958** *New Scientist* 29 May 75 Desalination of desert waters. **1960** *Times* 15 Mar. 3/1 Among its present projects are..desalination studies. **1962** *Economist* 16 June 1138/1 Visions of deserts blooming under the touch of desalinated seawater. **1969** *Times* 2 May (Suppl.) p. v/1 Desalination techniques have advanced enormously since the Second World War.

desalt (diː'sɒlt, -ɔː-), *v.* [f. DE- II. 2 + SALT *sb.*¹] *trans.* To remove salt or salts from. So **de'salter**, a desalting apparatus; **de'salting** *vbl. sb.* and *ppl. a.*

1909 in WEBSTER. **1945** *Times* 29 June, The Permutit sea water de-salting apparatus for producing drinking water from sea water without the use of heat. **1956** *Nature* 14 Jan. 77/1 Active work continues on the desalting of water. *Ibid.* 83/1 A simplified form of desalter, employing ion-exchange membranes. *Ibid.*, The solution to be desalted..is separated from the anode. *Ibid.* 4 Feb. 237/2 The plasma was deproteinized, and the resultant liquid and the two specimens of urine desalted. **1965** *Listener* 2 Sept. 342/1 Tenders to build a combined nuclear-power station and de-salting plant on the shores of the Mediterranean. **1968** *Times* 22 Nov. 14/8 Desalting water by a flash distillation process.

‖**desaparecido** (desapare'siðo). [Sp., lit. 'disappeared, missing person', pa. ppl. of *desaparecer* to disappear.] Any of the many people who disappeared in Argentina during the period of military rule between 1976 and 1983, presumed killed by members of the armed services or of the police. Usu. in *pl.*

1977 *Time* 11 Apr. 45/3 Amnesty International..accused the military of arbitrary detention, torture, summary executions and the 'disappearance' of at least 500 suspects... Amnesty charges that many of the *desaparecidos* were innocent citizens abducted and murdered by soldiers and police in mufti. **1979** *N.Y. Times Mag.* 21 Oct. 45/3 The *desaparecidos* are persons who, usually after being detained by teams of well-armed men, vanish without a trace. **1985** *Newsweek* 25 Nov. 104C/1 The Official Story, made in Argentina after the downfall of the military government, raises the issue of the desaparecidos.

†**de'sarcinate**, *v. Obs. rare*⁻⁰. [f. DE- II. 1 + L. *sarcina* bundle, burden, **sarcināre* to burden (*sarcinātus* burdened).]

1656 BLOUNT *Glossogr.*, *Desarcinate*, to unload, or unburthen, to unfraught.

Hence **desarcination**.

1730-6 BAILEY (folio), *Desarcination*, a taking of baggage, an unloading. Hence in ASH.

desarde, obs. form of DICER.

1538 BALE *Thre Lawes* 1396 Counterfet desardes.

desart, obs. form of DESERT, DESSERT.

desaster, obs. form of DISASTER.

desate, desave, obs. ff. DECEIT, DECEIVE.

desaturate (diː'sætjʊreɪt), *v.* [f. DE- II. 1 + SATURATE *v.*] *trans.* To cause to become unsaturated, to make less saturated. So **de'saturated** *ppl. a.*; **desatu'ration**.

1911 *Engineer* 10 Mar. 243/1 The statement that the blood is desaturated in its passage through the lung requires proof. *Ibid.*, Desaturation of the blood in its passage through the lungs. **1931** *Brit. Jrnl. Psychol.* Jan. 285 At very low intensities, under ordinary conditions of vision..all sensations are completely de-saturated, and the spectrum is simply a band of grey. *Ibid.* 287 De-saturation is not, in fact, complete in the case of spectral colours... Even if there be no complete de-saturation, the problem of explaining a partial de-saturation is essentially the same. **1962** H. C. WESTON *Sight, Light & Work* (ed. 2) i. 17 White is thus the de-saturated 'colour' *par excellence*. **1970** *Amateur Photographer* 11 Mar. 62/3 Distant colours are desaturated by white light scattered by the atmosphere.

‖**désaxé** (dezakse), *a.* Also **-axe**. [Fr.] Of the crankshaft of a motor-car: see quot. 1908.

1906 *Daily Chron.* 14 Nov. 9/3 The setting of the crank-shaft desaxes, or out of line with the cylinders. **1908** *Westm. Gaz.* 4 June 4/2 An uncommon feature of the Metallurgique engine is the setting of the crank-shaft *desaxés*—that is to say, the centre of the crank is set slightly out of line with the centre of the cylinder. **1912** *Motor Manual* (ed. 14) iii. 66 Principle of Offset Cylinder, or Desaxe Crankshaft Setting. **1963** BIRD & HUTTON-STOTT *Veteran Motor Car* 100 It is the first known example of the *désaxé* crankshaft... *Désaxé* engines became quite the thing about ten years later.

desaxonize: see DE- II. 1.

desayue, desayvabel, obs. forms of DECEIVE, -ABLE.

desblame, var. of DISBLAME *v. Obs.*

desc-, obs. spelling of DEC-, DES-, DISC-, DISS-.

descale (diː'skeɪl), *v.* [f. DE- II. 2 + SCALE *sb.*² 5.] *trans.* To remove scale from (metal or other surfaces). So **de'scaler**, a substance or device for descaling; **de'scaling** *vbl. sb.*, the process of removing scale; also *attrib.*

1932 W. H. HATFIELD in *Jrnl. West of Scotland Iron & Steel Inst.* (*1931-32*) XXXIX. 80/2 Descaling. The removal of the scale incurred in rolling, heat-treatment, and other work operations is a very essential part of the manufacture of corrosion-resistant steels... The descaling solution has a fairly long life. **1958** *Times Rev. Industry* Feb. 19/1 To maintain output during descaling operations. **1958** *New Scientist* 31 July 526/1 It involved rotating the evaporation tubes while the de-scaler was being applied. **1959** *Design* Oct. 59/2 The heater is easy to keep clean, and descale where the water is hard.

‖**Descamisado** (deskami'sado). [Sp.; = shirtless, f. *des-* = DIS- + *camisa* shirt + -ADO. Cf. *sans-culotte*.] A nickname given to the ultra-liberals in the Spanish revolutionary war of 1820-23, and still sometimes used in an analogous sense.

1823 *Blackw. Mag.* XIV. 514 Men of liberal ideas, and..members of the Descamisados. **1827** HARE *Guesses* Ser. II. (1867) 542 What is the folly of the descamisados but man's stripping himself of the fig-leaf. **1877** WRAXALL *Hugo's Miserables* III. xxiii. 12 We are going to the abyss, and the descamisados have led us to it.

descant ('dɛskænt), *sb.* Forms: 4-5 **deschaunt**, 5-6 **dyscant**, 6-9 **dis-**, 6- **descant**. [a. OF. *deschant* (13th c. and in Cotgr.), also ONF. *descaunt*, *descant*, rarely *dis-*, mod.F. *déchant*, = Pr. *deschans*, Sp. *discante*, Pg. *descante*, ad. med.L. *discant-us* part-song, refrain, descant, f. L. *dis-* asunder, apart + *cantus* singing, song. The form directly from OF. was used by Wyclif; a form in *dis-* immediately from L. occurs from the 15th c., and would be normal for English (see DIS-).]

I. *Music.* Now only *Hist.*, or *poet.*

1. A melodious accompaniment to a simple musical theme (the *plainsong*), sung or played, and often merely extemporized, above it, and thus forming an air to its bass: the earliest form of counterpoint.

c **1380** WYCLIF *Wks.* (1880) 77 Grete crying of song as deschaunt, contre note and orgene. ? *c* **1475** *Sqr. lowe Degre* 790 Your quere nor organ songe shall wante, With countre note, and dyscant. **1501** DOUGLAS *Pal. Hon.* I. xlii, I play and sing, Fabourdoun, pricksang, discant, countering. **1591** SHAKS. *Two Gent.* I. ii. 94 You are too flat, And marre the concord, with too harsh a descant. **1595** SPENSER *Epithal.* v, The merry Larke hir mattins sings aloft; The Thrush replyes; the Mavis descant playes. **1683** CHALKHILL *Thealma & Cl.* 100 Sweet lays Wrought with such curious descant as would raise Attention in a stone. **1762** CHURCHILL *Poems, Proph. Famine*, The youth..skill'd in rustic lays, Fast by her side his am'rous descant plays. **1881** MACFARREN *Counterp.* i. 1 Descant seems to have been the art of improvising a melodic accompaniment to a fixed song. *fig.* **1641** WITHER in R. Palmer *Bk. of Praise* xxvii. 28 To this Concert when we sing Whistling winds your descants bring. **1659** ROWBOTHAM *Gate Lang. Unl.* Pref. (1664) E vij, The descant of meeter hath often corrupted the plain-song of truth. **1865** F. G. LEE *Direct. Angl.* §116. 110 Canticles (a descant of praise on the Lessons).

†**b.** ***base descant, binding descant***: see quots. ***double descant***: double counterpoint. ***plain descant***: plain or simple counterpoint. *Obs.*

1597 MORLEY *Introd. Mus.* 76 Two plainesong notes for one in the descant..is commonlie called binding descant. *Ibid.* 86 Base descant..is that kinde of descanting, where your sight of taking and vsing your cordes must be vnder the plainsong. *Ibid.* 105 Double descant..is verie neere the nature of a Canon..which being sung after diuers sortes, by changing the partes, maketh diuers manners of harmonie.

2. The soprano or highest part of the score in part-singing.

1569 J. SANFORD tr. *Agrippa's Van. Artes* 30 While the children braie the Discante. **1609** DOULAND *Ornithop. Microl.* 83 Discantus is the vppermost part of each Song. **1644** SIR E. DERING *Prop. Sacr.* C iij, Children neigh forth the descant. **1882-3** SCHAFF *Encycl. Relig. Knowl.* III. 2025 Composed for three voices—descant, tenor, and bass.

3. *gen.* A warbled song, a melodious strain.

1576 GASCOIGNE *Philomene* 6 To heare the descant of the Nightingale. **1615** WITHER *Sheph. Hunt.* i. Juvenilia (1633) 393 The cage doth some birds good, And..Will teach them sweeter descants than the wood. **1742** GRAY *Sonnet on Death of West* 3 The birds in vain their amorous descant join. **1877** BRYANT *Poems, Waiting by Gate* ii, I hear the wood-thrush piping one mellow descant more.

4. The art of singing or writing music in parts; musical composition, harmony; also, a harmonized composition.

1565-73 COOPER *Thesaurus*, *Asymphonia*, discord in descant. **1579** LYLY *Euphues* (Arb.) 93 If thou haddest learned..the first noat of Descant thou wouldest have kept thy Sol. Fa. to thyselfe. **1597** MORLEY *Introd. Mus.* Annot., The word descant signifieth, in our toung the forme of setting together of sundry voices or concords for producing of harmony..But in this signification it is seldome vsed. **1649** JER. TAYLOR *Gt. Exemp.* I. iv. 42 The whole chorus joined in descant and sang a hymn. **1674** T. CAMPION (*title*), The Art of Descant, or composing Musick in Parts. **1795** MASON *Ch. Mus.* ii. 100 A descant of thirtie-eight proportions of sondry kind. **1825** SOUTHEY *Tale of Paraguay* III. xxxix, Into a descant of her own Hath blended all their notes. **1871** *Q. Rev.* No. 261. 158 The notion of playing two different notes in successive harmony to one of longer duration, or the art of descant, had not yet occurred to any one. **1882** ROCKSTRO in Grove *Dict. Music* III. 269 [Counterpoint] was..evolved by slow degrees, from Diaphonia, Discant, and Organum.

5. An instrumental prelude, consisting of variations on a given theme.

1644 MILTON *Educ.*, *Exercise*, While the skilful Organist plies his grave and fancied descant in lofty Fugues. **1795** MASON *Ch. Mus.* i. 58 *foot-n.*, By Discant, the Musicians of Milton's time meant preluding on a given ground. **1813** SCOTT *Rokeby* v. xii, And then a low sad descant rung, As prelude to the lay he sung. **1882** SHORTHOUSE *J. Inglesant* II. 378 Mr. Inglesant being pressed to oblige the company, played a descant upon a ground bass in the Italian manner. *fig.* **1806-7** J. BERESFORD *Miseries Hum. Life* (1826) XVIII. 204 That peculiar species of prelusive flourish, or descant, with which Reviewers are accustomed to usher in the Performance under immediate examination.

II. Transferred uses: often with distinct reference to the *plainsong* or *ground*, and in the phrases ***run*** or ***sing descant***.

†**6.** Variation from that which is typical or customary; an instance of this. ***shift of descant***: a change of 'tune', i.e. of argumentative position.

1563-87 FOXE *A. & M.* (1684) III. 621 Whereas you say, they eat it spiritually, that is but a blind shift of descant. **1581** J. BELL *Haddon's Answ. Osor.* 119 Osorius lacketh not a shift of descante here, thinkyng thereby to craze the force of veritie. **1633** P. FLETCHER *Purple Isl.* VIII. xliv. 117 Runnes nimble descant on the plainest vices. **1642** FULLER *Holy & Prof. St.* III. xiii. 184 Running, Leaping, and Dancing, the descants on the plain song of walking. *a* **1661** —— *Worthies* (1840) I. 224 Their [basket] making is daily improved with much descant of art. **1712** ADDISON *Spect.* No. 543 ¶4 Providence has shewn..Wisdom..in the multiplicity of Descants which it has made on every Original Species.

7. Varied comment on a theme, amplification of a subject; a comment, criticism, observation, remark; †*occas.* censorious criticism, carping (*obs.*).

1594 SHAKS. *Rich. III*, III. vii. 49 On that ground Ile make a holy Descant. **1599** NASHE *Lenten Stuffe* (1871) 36 The wantoner sort of them sing descant on their mistress's glove. **1630** BRATHWAIT *Eng. Gentlem.* (1641) 320 Let not calumny runne descant on your tongue. **1639** FULLER *Holy War* II. xlvi. (1840) 114 Roger Hoveden's witty descant on the time. **1642** ROGERS *Naaman* 209 If thy Religion should cost thee some disgrace, scorne and descant. **1654** H. L'ESTRANGE *Chas. I* (1655) 7 It doth..render King Charles obnoxious to untoward and sinister descants. *a* **1677** BARROW *Serm.* Wks. 1716 I. 29 Neither shall I make any descant or reflection thereon. **1710** *Moderation & Loyalty of the Dissenters Exemplify'd* 3 Rendering Things worse than they were by Partiality and Discant. **1784** COWPER *Task* IV. 77 With merry descants on a nation's woes. **1820** SHELLEY *Let. to Maria Gisborne* Poet. Wks. (1891) 373/1 There are themes enough for many a bout Of thought-entangled descant.

b. A disquisition, dissertation, discourse.

1622 DONNE *Serm.* xvi. 162 The fathers have infinitely delighted themselves in this Descant, the blessed effect of holy teares. **1667** WATERHOUSE *Fire Lond.* 177 O remember the Prophetical descant of glorious King James. **1713** ADDISON *Guardian* No. 102 After this short descant on the uncertainty of our English weather. **1791** PAINE *Rights of Man* (ed. 4) 46, I have now to follow Mr. Burke through..a sort of descant upon governments. **1841** D'ISRAELI *Amen. Lit.* (1867) 196 He instructed the world by ethical descants.

III. 8. *attrib.* and *Comb.* **descant-clef**, the soprano or treble clef; **descant-viol**, the treble viol. or violin, which plays the air or soprano part.

1728 NORTH *Mem. of Musick* (1846) 67 No wonder..that organs..with the descant manner, at last entered the churches.

descant (dɪ'skænt), *v.* Also 6-9 dis- (6-7 dys-). [a. OF. *deschanter*, *descanter*, = Pr. *deschantar*, Sp. *discantar*, Pg. *descantar*, in med.L. *discantāre* (*des-*, *dē-*), f. the sb.: see prec.]

1. *Music.* **a.** *intr.* To play or sing an air in harmony with a fixed theme; *gen.* to warble, sing harmoniously; also in phr. *to descant it*.

1538 [see DESCANTER]. **1597** MORLEY *Mus.* 76 In descanting you must..seeke true cordes. **1607** TOPSELL *Serpents* (1653) 772 They will..sing so sweetly, and withall descant it so finely and tunably. **1611** COTGR. s.v. *Contre*, To

..sing the Plainesong whereon another descants. **1879** PARRY in Grove *Dict. Mus.* I. 670 This new mode of descanting. **1887** BOWEN *Virg. Eclogue* VI. 8, I with a meadow reed upon sylvan themes will descant.

†**b.** *trans.* To sing in 'descant' (words, etc.).

1538 STARKEY *England* I. iv. 134 The wordys [of Church music] be so straunge and so dyuersely descantyd.

2. *intr.* To make remarks, comments, or observations; to comment (*on*, *upon*, †*of* a text, theme, etc.).

c **1510** MORE *Picus* Wks. 15/1 The company of the court.. descanted therof to his rebuke. **1571** GOLDING *Calvin on Ps.* ii. 7 They have curiously descanted upon theis woords. **1594** SHAKS. *Rich. III*, I. i. 27 To see my Shadow in the Sunne, And descant on mine own Deformity. **1598** J. DICKENSON *Green in Conc.* (1878) 160 Nor presumptuously descant of the vnknowen proceedings of the almighty. **1624** CAPT. SMITH *Virginia* I. 13 Many began strangely to discant of those crosse beginnings. **1649** MILTON *Eikon.* B, To descant on the misfortunes of a Person fall'n from dignity is not commendable. **1738** WARBURTON *Div. Legat.* I. Ded. 23 To descant upon their very Hats and Habits. **1791** BOSWELL *Johnson* 5 Aug. an. 1763, He used to descant critically on the dishes which had been at table. **1850** KINGSLEY *Alt. Locke* vi, He ran on descanting coarsely on beauties.

b. To discourse at large, enlarge (*upon*, *on* a theme). Also with *indirect pass.*

a **1661** FULLER *Worthies* (1840) I. 68 The friar rather descanted than commented. *a* **1782** KAMES in M. Donovan *Dom. Econ.* II. 73 The young champion.. discants upon his address in catching the animal. **1791** GOUV. MORRIS in Sparks *Life & Writ.* (1832) I. 353 Abbé Syeyès.. descants with much self-sufficiency on government. **1836** *Johnsoniana* 362 Johnson never accustomed himself to descant on the ingratitude of mankind. **1878** GLADSTONE *Prim. Homer* 9 It was the bard's duty to descant upon the freshest and most interesting subjects.

†**3.** *trans.* To comment on, discourse about, discuss; *occas.* to criticize, carp at. *Obs.*

1627 F. E. *Hist. Edw. II* (1680) 53 Where they might descant their griefs. **1642** ROGERS *Naaman* 376 Such secrets as these must be.. adored, not descanted. *a* **1649** DRUMM. OF HAWTH. *Poems* Wks. (1711) 31 But who can descant right your grave aspects?

†**4.** *intr.* To work with intricate variation *on*; to fashion with artistic skill. *Obs. rare.*

a **1661** FULLER *Worthies* (1840) I. 397 Lace, costing nothing save a little thread descanted on by art and industry. *Ibid.* III. 90 The God of nature is pleased to descant on a plain hollowness with such wonderful contrivances.

descanter (dɪ'skæntə(r)). [f. prec. + -ER[1].]

1. One who sings or plays the 'descant'. *Obs.* exc. *Hist.*

1538 STARKEY *England* I. iii. 80 Curyouse descanterys and deuysarys of new songys. **1597** MORLEY *Introd. Mus.* 70 A Descanter.. [is] one that can extempore sing a part upon a playne song. **1879** PARRY in Grove *Dict. Mus.* I. 671 De Muris.. speaks with great bitterness of extempore descanters.

2. One who holds forth or discourses.

1805 FOSTER *Ess.* IV. iv. 180 A descanter on the invisible world who makes you think of a popish cathedral.

descanting (dɪ'skæntɪŋ), *vbl. sb.* [f. as prec. + -ING[1].] The action of the vb. DESCANT: **a.** singing in 'descant'; **b.** commenting, disquisition.

1538 STARKEY *England* I. iv. 137 Our Curyouse dyscantyng and conteryng [*printed* canteryng] in Churchys. **1561** DAUS tr. *Bullinger on Apoc.* (1573) 12 A wonderfull descantyng vpon letters. **1575** *Brieff Disc. Troubles Franckford* (1846) 206 The trollinge and descantinge off the Psalmes. **1680** BURNET *Rochester* (T.), The descantings of fanciful men upon them [the Scriptures]. **1851** GLADSTONE *Glean.* VI. xxi. 14, I waive descanting on personal qualities.

de'scanting, *ppl. a.* [f. as prec. + -ING[2].] Commenting, criticizing: in quot. criticizing censoriously, carping.

1594 J. DICKENSON *Arisbas* (1878) 28 To shield me from the descanting verdites of such vnfriendly readers.

descater, obs. form of DISSCATTER *v.*

descece, -ces(s, obs. forms of DECEASE.

desceit, desceiue, obs. ff. DECEIT, DECEIVE.

†**de'scence, de'scense.** *Obs.* Forms: 4 **dissence**, 5 **descens, dyscens**, 5–6 **descense**, 6 **discence**, 6–7 **descence**. [Two forms: ME. *descens*, a. OF. *descens* masc., ad. L. *dēscensus* descent, descending, f. *dēscendĕre*; also ME. *descense*, a. OF. *descense* fem., ad. late L. type *dēscensa* (*dēscēsa*), fem. sb. f. *dēscensus*, pa. pple. of *dēscendĕre*, analogous to sbs. in *-ata*, *-ada*, *-ée*: cf. It. *descesa*. The spelling *descence* app. represents the *descens* form: see DEFENCE.]

1. A going or coming down; = DESCENT 1.

1543 *Necess. Doctr.* in *Formul. Faith* 234 Iesu Christ's life, death, burial, and descense to hell. **1582–8** *Hist. James VI* (1804) 278 In his discence.. he come fornent the Colledge of Justice. **1600** ABP. ABBOT *Exp. Jonah* 219 We all do hold the article of Christ's descense into Hell.

b. Extension downwards: cf. DESCEND *v.* 2.

1578 BANISTER *Hist. Man.* I. 8 The descense of y[e] Sagittal Suture is not common either in man or woman.

2. *concr.* A downward slope; a way down; = DESCENT 2 a, 2 b.

a **1440** *Found. St. Bartholomew's* 40 From the highe descense of heuynnes.. hedir I descende. **1618** BOLTON *Florus* II. vi. 108 The very jawes of the first descence from the Alps into Italy.

3. *fig.* **a.** ? Dejection, depression of spirits.

1526 *Pilgr. Perf.* (W. de W. 1531) 166 b, In suche descense it [the mynde] is moost apte to distraccyons & waueryng fantasyes.

b. Bringing down or lowering in estimation; depreciation.

1560 ROLLAND *Crt. Venus* I. 287 That hir honour distres thoill nor ruine: Nor suffer it in na way haif discence.

4. a. Genealogical extraction; = DESCENT 7.

c **1425** WYNTOUN *Cron.* IX. xxvi. 106 In lineale Descens fra Sanct Margret. **1432–50** tr. *Higden* (Rolls) I. 281 Soe the linealle descense of the prosapy or kynrede of Feramundus faylede by men. **1513** BRADSHAW *St. Werburge* II. 1212 Son to duke Leoffwin by liniall discence. **1513** DOUGLAS *Æneis* III. iii. 39 From that ilk prince.. Is the descence of our genealogy.

b. Transmission by inheritance; = DESCENT 10.

c **1380** WYCLIF *Sel. Wks.* II. 402 Dissence of heritage.

descend (dɪ'sɛnd), *v.* Also 4 **dessende, disend, dyssente, decend**, 4–7 **discend(e**, 4–6 **descende**, (5–6 **dyscend**), (6 **desend**). *Pa. t.* and *pple.* **descended**; 4–5 **descend**, 5 **discent**, 6 **discend**. [a. F. *descend-re* (11th c. in Littré) = Pr. *deissendre*, It. *descendere*, Sp. *descender*:—L. *dēscendĕre*, f. DE- I. 1 + *scandĕre* to climb. In early times often treated as if the prefix were DES- (q.v.) and the stem *-cend*, *-send*, *-end*, whence the variant spellings in *dis-*, *dys-*, *de-*.]

I. Intransitive senses.

* *To move down or into a lower position.*

1. a. To move or pass from a higher to a lower position in space; to come or go down, fall, sink. (The general word, including all kinds of downward motion, vertical or oblique; the opposite of *ascend*.)

a **1325** *Prose Psalter* xlviii. 18 [xlix. 17] His glorie ne shal nouȝt descenden wyþ hym. *c* **1325** *E.E. Allit. P.* A. 626 As sone as þay arn borne bylyue In þe water of baptem þay dyssente. *a* **1330** *Roland & V.* 131 þan decended a liȝtnesse, Doun riȝtes fram þe heuen blis. **1393** GOWER *Conf.* III. 94 The moist droppes of the rein Descenden into middel erthe. *c* **1400** *Lanfranc's Cirurg.* 143 þat he may not discende downward. *c* **1450** *Mirour Saluacioun* 505 A man some tyme fro Jerusalem descendande. **1590** SIR J. SMYTH *Disc. Weapons* 35 b, Those furious Rebells.. descended downe their hil with such a furie. **1632** J. HAYWARD tr. *Biondi's Eromena* 193, I passed to the Nile descending on it at my leasure to the sea. **1653** H. COGAN tr. *Pinto's Trav.* xxiii. 86 The water rebounded up so high that when it came to descend again it fell as small as dew. *Ibid.* lxi. 251 The two Priests descended from their Pulpits. **1728** PEMBERTON *Newton's Philos.* 194 The earth in moving round the sun is continually descending toward it. **1790** W. WRIGHTE *Grotesque Archit.* 7 The two wings.. are each descended to by a flight of four steps. **1823** F. CLISSOLD *Ascent Mt. Blanc* 19 From the heights of the mountain.. immense avalanches often descend. **1875** BRYCE *Holy Rom. Emp.* iv. (ed. 5) 44 In the autumn of 799 Charles descended from the Alps once more.

b. *fig.* said of immaterial agents, influences, etc.

a **1300** *Cursor M.* 10884 (Cott.) And godds might in þe [sal] descend. *c* **1400** MAUNDEV. (Roxb.) ix. 36 Intill his awen heued his wikkidness schall descend. ? *a* **1500** *Wycket* (1828) p. xiv, Ye say that the manhoode of Christe descendeth into eche part of euery hoost. **1725** POPE *Odyss.* IV. 1012 And on the suitors let thy wrath descend. **1806** J. FORBES *Lett. fr. France* II. 400 The shades of evening began to descend. **1871** R. ELLIS *Catullus* l. 10 Sleep nor quiet upon my eyes descended.

†**c.** To disembark, land from a vessel; to alight from a horse, carriage, etc. *Obs.* (as a specific sense).

c **1477** CAXTON *Jason* 73 b, They ben in entencion for to descende in colchos. *c* **1489** [see DESCENDING *vbl. sb.* 1]. **1513** DOUGLAS *Æneis* VIII. i. 22 To schaw.. How Troianis war discend in Latium. **1548** HALL *Chron.* 176 b, They left their horses, & discended to flight on fote. **1600** E. BLOUNT tr. *Conestaggio* 263 Having viewed the Iland fortified on all parts where he might descend.

d. *Astron.*, etc. Of a heavenly body: (*a*) To move towards the horizon, sink. (*b*) To move southwards; see also DESCENDING *ppl. a.* 5.

c **1391** CHAUCER *Astrol.* II. §12 Than fond I the [2] degree of libra.. dessending on my west Orisonte. *c* **1500** *Lancelot* 972 The sone discending closit in the vest. **1559** W. CUNNINGHAM *Cosmogr. Glasse* 23 The signes in equall tymes do ascend and descende. **1667** MILTON *P.L.* IV. 541 The setting Sun Slowly descended. **1690** LEYBOURN *Curs. Math.* 832 Mars.. from the Northern limit.. to ☋.. is North descending. **1830** HOGG *Flodden Field*, Sol with broadened orb descending Left fierce warriors still contending. **1882** SHARPLESS *Astron.* 21 If these northern or circumpolar stars be watched.. such as are to the west of the pole will descend.

†**e.** ***to descend into*** or ***within oneself***: to betake oneself to deep meditation or consideration. *Obs.*

a **1572** KNOX *Hist. Ref.* Wks. (1846) I. 338 To move the hartis.. of the trew servandis of God.. to discend within thame selfis and deiplie to considder quhat shalbe the end of this pretended tyranny. **1594** T. B. *La Primaud. Fr. Acad.* II. 11 Those Philosophers that.. descended not into themselues, to know themselues and their nature. **1671** MILTON *P.R.* II. 111 The while her Son.. with holiest meditations fed, Into himself descended, and at once All his great work to come before him set.

2. *transf.* To have a downward extension, direction, or slope; to slope or extend downwards.

c **1391** CHAUCER *Astrol.* I. §4 A lyne þat cometh dessendinge fro the ryng down to the nethereste bordure. *c* **1400** MAUNDEV. (1839) xxv. 259 It strecchethe toward the West.. descendynge toward the litille Armenye. **1600** J. PORY tr. *Leo's Africa* II. 236 Their streetes either descend or ascend, which is verie troublesome. **1684** R. H. *School Recreat.* 120 The dash Lines.. are added only when the Notes ascend above the Staff, or descend below it. **1798** H. SKRINE *Tours Wales* 155 With a gateway at each extremity, as the hill descends. **1894** *Christian World* 27 Sep. 712/1 To your right.. the fields descend from your feet to the Chesil Beach.

fig. **1678** CUDWORTH *Intell. Syst.* 445 See, how the order and chain of this government descends down by steps and degrees, from the Supreme God to the Earth and Men.

3. a. To come down with or as a hostile force; to make an incursion or attack; to fall violently *upon*. (Cf. COME *down* g.)

c **1430** LYDG. *Bochas* I. viii. (1544) 15 b, Zisara, which was discendid doun With a great hoost. **1548** HALL *Chron.* 227 b, The kyng of England your master, is neither descended in these partes of his owne fre mocion, nor yet of us requyred. **1600** E. BLOUNT tr. *Conestaggio* 188 That the Turke woulde descend upon his realme of Naples. **1887** BOWEN *Virg. Æneid* I. 527 Not upon Libya's hearths to descend with sword and with fire.

b. to ***descend on*** or ***upon***: to visit unexpectedly; freq. applied to unwanted visitors.

1916 A. HUXLEY *Lett.* (1969) 98, I have at the moment staying with me in Balliol young Robert Nichols, who descended on me for a day or two. **1922** *Ibid.* 208 Aunt Ethel has wisely not divulged the fact that she is going to be at Como.. otherwise Aunt N would have been sure to descend upon her. **1971** R. LEWIS *Error of Judgment* i. 12 What a trial it must be for her.. to have an HMI descend on the college.

†**4.** *fig.* To submit, yield. *Obs. rare.*

c **1330** R. BRUNNE *Chron.* (1810) 134 In pes with ȝow to lyue, & at ȝour conseil descend. *Ibid.* 270 To what manere of pes þe parties wille descend.

5. To proceed (in discourse or writing) to something subsequent in time or order, or (*esp.*) from generals to particulars.

1340 *Ayenb.* 123 Erþan ich decendi to þe uirtues þet byeþ contraries to þe zeue zennes. *c* **1380** WYCLIF *Sel. Wks.* III. 513 To discende doun in specialte, fful mane articlis.. ben openly contrarie to þe apostlis reule. **1576** FLEMING *Panopl. Epist.* 406 From thence hee descendeth to particular affayres. *a* **1617** HIERON *Wks.* II. 461 By these degrees did our Sauiour discend to this speech. **1630** PRYNNE *Anti-Armin.* 79 Descend we unto Edward the VI his pious Raigne. **1657** J. SMITH *Myst. Rhet.* A b, Whereby we having spoken of a thing in general, descend unto particulars. **1797** BURKE *Regic. Peace* iii. Wks. VIII. 380 But let us descend to particulars. **1827** MACAULAY *Ess.*, *Machiavelli* (1854) 32/1 Historians rarely descend to those details from which alone the real state of a community can be collected.

6. To come down ideally, mentally, or morally; to condescend, stoop (*to do* something); usually in bad sense, to stoop to something unworthy.

1554–9 T. WATERTON in *Songs & Ball. Ph. & Mary* (1860) 9 Hath made wronge ryght, and from the truth desendyd. **1608** BP. HALL *Char. Virtues & V.* I. 54 If.. he descend to disports of chance, his games shall never make him.. pale with feare. **1626** in Rushw. *Hist. Coll.* (1659) I. 225 He hath descended to make this Explanation. **1707** NORRIS *Treat. Humility* iii. 99 To see men.. descend to the meanest and unworthiest compliances. **1752** JOHNSON *Rambler* No. 208 ¶3, I have seldom descended to the arts by which favour is obtained. **1813** BYRON *Giaour* xxxii, Not oft to smile descendeth he. **1829** *Blackw. Mag.* XXVI. 599 Wordsworth.. descends to such babyisms. **1853** LYNCH *Self-Improv.* v. 129 A man should never descend to his company, but he should condescend to it.

7. a. To go or come down, fall, or sink, in any scale.

1608–11 BP. HALL *Medit. & Vowes* II. §78 Winter comes on softly, first by colde dewes, then hoare frostes, untill at last it descende to the hardest weather of all. *a* **1625** FLETCHER *False One* v, ii, Thy glories now have touch'd the highest point, And must descend.

b. *Music.* To proceed to a lower note; to go down the scale.

1597 MORLEY *Introd. Mus.* 81 It is vnpossible to ascende or descende in continuall deduction without a discord. **1674** PLAYFORD *Skill Mus.* III. 4 If the Notes descend a second. **1706** A. BEDFORD *Temple Mus.* ix. 176 A Tune, which consisted of only Three Notes in Compass, Rising gradually in the first Part, and descending.. in the Second. **1848** RIMBAULT *First Bk. Piano* 35 In the Major Scale the two semitones retain their situations, both ascending and descending.

c. *Math.* Of series: To proceed from higher to lower quantities or powers. See DESCENDING *ppl. a.* 3.

1876 E. BROOKS *Philos. Arith.* 347 The sum of the terms of an infinite series descending equals the first term divided by 1 minus the rate.

** *To come down by generation or inheritance.*

8. To be derived in the way of generation; to come *of*, spring *from* (an ancestor or ancestral stock). **a.** simply ***to descend*** (***from*** or ***of***). Now *rare* in active voice.

1375 BARBOUR *Bruce* I. 61 Ony male That were in lyne ewyn descendand. *c* **1425** WYNTOUN *Cron.* I. xvii. 2 Fra Sem discendand lynealy. **1509** FISHER *Fun. Serm. C'tess Richmond* Wks. (1876) 290 They.. which descended of noble lygnage. **1600** SHAKS. *A.Y.L.* I. ii. 241 Thou should'st haue better pleas'd me with this deede, Hadst thou descended from another house. **1780** JOHNSON *L.P.*, *Congreve*, William Congreve descended from a family in Staffordshire. **1788** GIBBON *Decl. & F.* (1846) IV. xli. 36 Although Theodatus descended from a race of heroes.

b. Now nearly always in passive, *to be descended (from, †of).*

c **1386** CHAUCER *Reeve's T.* 64. **1399** *Rolls of Parlt.* III. 423/1, I Henry of Lancastre..am disendit by right lyne of the Blode comyng fro the gude lord Kyng Henry therde. *c* **1470** HARDING *Chron.* (Lansd. MS. 200 fol. 1) So lynyall of his generacioun, 3e bene discent. **1513** DOUGLAS *Æneis* III. ii. 54 O 3e dour pepill discend from Dardanus. **1581** PETTIE *Guazzo's Civ. Conv.* II. (1586) 82 b, Sayd to bee descended of Gentlemen. **1616** SURFL. & MARKH. *Country Farme* 674 If a dog be not wel descended..there can be little hope of his goodnesse. **1711** STEELE *Spect.* No. 78 ¶8 We are descended of ancient Families. **1818** CRUISE *Digest* (ed. 2) III. 357 Such other collateral relations as were descended from the person who first acquired it.

c. *fig.* To be derived, originate. (Const. as in a and b.)

c **1400** *Apol. Loll.* 21 Contumacy descendend of swilk crime. **1645** N. STONE *Enchir. Fortif.* 81 It would be vain to write the Etymologies of each word, much lesse those descended of the Greeke. *a* **1726** COLLIER *Agst. Despair* (J.), Despair descends from a mean original; the offspring of fear, laziness, and impatience.

†**d.** *trans.* To trace down (lineage). *Obs. rare.*

1572 J. JONES *Bathes of Bath*, Whose Genealogie..may lineally be descended to your Honour.

9. a. *intr.* Of property, privileges, etc.: To come down by way of inheritance; to pass to an heir.

1486 *Bk. St. Alban's, Her.* C viij b, Bot the possessionis & the patrimonyes descendid to other men. **1512** *Act 4 Hen. VIII*, c. 13 The premisses with ther appurtenaunces decended unto John last Duke of Norff. **1631** GOUGE *God's Arrows* iii. §93. 353 The Crowne and Kingdome by just and unquestionable title descended on her. **1667** DUCHESS OF NEWCASTLE *Life Dk. N.* (1886) 138 A good estate in the west, which afterwards descended upon my Lord. **1668** HALE *Pref. Rolle's Abridgem.* 7 Lands in Fee-simple discend to the Uncle and not immediately to the Father. **1818** CRUISE *Digest* (ed. 2) II. 445 The defendant..pleaded..that the said reversion descended.

b. *transf.* Of personal qualities, etc.: To pass by heredity; to be transmitted to offspring.

1548 HALL *Chron.* 226 Of a certayne privie canker engendered in the hartes of their forefathers..and after by lyneall succession descended into the stomackes of their nephewes. **1713** STEELE *Englishman* No. 28. 182 The eternal Mark of having had a wicked Ancestor descends to his Posterity. **1843** LEVER *J. Hinton* iv. (1878) 20 Our principles may come from our fathers; our prejudices certainly descend from the female branch.

II. Transitive senses. [Not in L.; both in Fr.]

†**10. a.** (*causal.*) To cause to descend; to bring or send down. *Obs.*

1483 CAXTON *Gold. Leg.* 21/1 Assoylle the synnars whan thou descendest into helle them of thy partye. **1509** HAWES *Past Pleas.* XXVII. xxi, I shew my power in every sundry wyse, Some to descende and on some to aryse. **1627–77** FELTHAM *Resolves* I. xiii. 22 As steps that descend us towards our Graues. **1677** HALE *Prim. Orig. Man.* III. iv. 267 The Seminal Tincture of the Herb..being again descended by Dews or Rain upon the..Earth.

fig. **1598** BARCKLEY *Felic. Man* III. (1603) 265 Christ.. descended himselfe of the greatest nobilitie that ever was in this world.

†**b.** *Old Chem.* To distil 'by descent'; see DESCENT 1 d. *Obs.*

1471 RIPLEY *Comp. Alch.* Ep. in Ashm. (1652) 115 First Calcine, and after that Putrefye, Dyssolve, Dystill, Sublyme, Descende, and Fyxe.

11. To go or come down (a hill, wall, flight of steps, etc.); to pass downwards over, along, or through (a space).

1607 TOPSELL *Four-f. Beasts* (1658) 49 Descending the lists of a second combate. **1632** J. HAYWARD tr. *Biondi's Eromena* 122 With a ladder of cords..speedily descended the walls. **1667** MILTON *P.L.* XII. 606 They both descend the Hill. **1799** COLEBROOKE in *Life* (1873) 437 Laden on canoes and small boats, to descend the Mahánadí. **1807** HUTTON *Course Math.* II. 151 To find the space descended by a body in 7 seconds. **1891** E. PEACOCK *N. Brendon* I. 221 The two women descended the steps.

†**de'scend,** *sb. Obs. rare.* In 6 **dyssende.** [f. prec. vb.] A descent; a downward slope.

1519 *Presentm. Juries* in *Surtees Misc.* (1890) 31 All wattersewers and the dyssendis þer off..be dykid.

descendable: var. of DESCENDIBLE.

descendance, -ence (dɪ'sɛndəns). Now *rare.* [a. F. *descendance* (13th c. in Littré), f. *descendre* to DESCEND: in earlier use often spelt *-ence* as in med.L. *dēscendentia*: see -ANCE, -ENCE.]

1. The action or fact of descending or springing from a particular ancestor or origin; = DESCENT 7.

1599 MINSHEU *Sp. Gram.* 12 Etymologie..this searching out of originall and descendence of words. **1630** BRATHWAIT *Eng. Gentlem.* Ep. Ded., Lineall descendence. **1875** *N. Amer. Rev.* CXX. 238 With Mr. Darwin's Theory of Descendence. **1885** H. KENDALL in *19th Cent.*, The fact that Jesus Christ had descendance from King David. **1891** *Blackw. Mag.* CL. 712/2 A descendance that is not lineal either of mind or spirit.

2. *concr.* Descendants. (App. a corruption: cf. DESCENDANT B. 1, quot. 1623, and ACCIDENCE.)

(Sir T. Elyot has *inhabitance* = *inhabitants*.)

a **1661** FULLER *Worthies* III. (1662) 60 In some descendance from the Duke of Norfolk, in the Stanhops and the Arundels.

de'scendancy, -ency. *arch.* [f. as prec. + -ANCY. Also spelt *-ency* after med.L. *dēscendentia.*] **a.** The condition or quality of being descended. **b.** A stage in lineal descent, a generation; = DESCENT 9. **c.** = DESCENDANCE.

1601 R. JOHNSON *Kingd. & Commw.* (1603) 257 The unfortunate successes hapned in his proper descendencie. **1630** *Ibid.* 251 Placentia was not granted absolutely to the house of Farnesi but only to the fourth descendencie, after which it returnes againe to the King of Spaine. *a* **1641** BP. MOUNTAGU *Acts & Mon.* (1642) 86 From Father to Son, in a continued descendency. **1661** MORGAN *Sph. Gentry* II. i. 6 To distinguish the degree of decendency. **1790** W. COMBE *Devil on Two Sticks* (1817) I. 78 Their descendancy from the common mother, Eve. **1934** DYLAN THOMAS *Let.* 9 May (1966) 124 If a poem, in the John Donne descendency, is fairly good, they print it; if very good in the Tennyson descendency, they refuse to.

descendant, -ent (dɪ'sɛndənt), *a.* and *sb.* Also 6 **discendant.** [a. F. *descendant* (13th c. in Littré), pr. pple. of *descendre* to DESCEND, used as adj. and sb. Also spelt *-ent* after L. *dēscendent-em*: see -ANT, -ENT.

Johnson gives *Descendant* sb., *Descendent* adj., and remarks 'It seems to be established that the substantive should derive the termination from the French, and the adjective from the Latin'. In the sb. sense 1, and the related sense 2 of the adj. *-ant* is now always used; in the other senses of both, *-ent* is perhaps preferable, but these are either obsolete or so rarely used as to make the distinction one of little practical moment.]

A. *adj.*

1. *lit.* Descending; coming or going down. *rare.*

1644 DIGBY *Nat. Bodies* I. (1645) 99 The aire..maketh one descendent body together with the dish. **1658** R. WHITE tr. *Digby's Powd. Symp.* (1660) 59 The ascending water becoming more heavy then the descendant on the other side. **1691** RAY *Creation* (J.), This descendent juice is that which principally nourishes both fruit and plant. **1839** BAILEY *Festus* (1848) 59/2 The descendent city of the skies.

†**b.** *Astron.* (Cf. DESCEND *v.* 1 d.) *Obs.*

1594 BLUNDEVIL *Exerc.* III. I. xi. (ed. 7) 296 The Descendent [Signs] are these, Cancer, Leo, [etc.]. **1631** WIDDOWES *Nat. Philos.* 14 The Ascendant [node] is higher where ☾..doth come nearest unto us. The descendant, when the ☾ is removing from us. **1690** LEYBOURN *Curs. Math.* 818 The Descendent Node of the Moon.

c. *Her.* Descending towards the base of the shield.

1572 BOSSEWELL *Armorie* II. 42 Their tayles.. descendante, percussed, and contercoloured.

2. Descending or originating from an ancestor; also *fig.* (See DESCEND *v.* 8.)

1594 PARSONS *Confer. Success.* II. viii. 184 Of the right discendant line of K. John. *a* **1641** BP. MOUNTAGU *Acts & Mon.* (1642) 26 His Son..descendent and extracted from his loines. **1725** POPE *Odyssey* II. 313 Were not wise sons descendent [*ed.* **1758** descendant] of the wise. **1857** RUSKIN *Pol. Econ. Art* ii. (1868) 112 The best and greatest of descendant souls.

B. *sb.*

1. One who 'descends' or is descended from an ancestor (see DESCEND *v.* 8); issue, offspring (in any degree near or remote): **a.** of persons.

1600 E. BLOUNT tr. *Conestaggio* 85 All the descendents of Beatrice. **1623** in Rushw. *Hist. Coll.* (1659) I. 86 Their Servants, Children, and Descendens. *a* **1729** S. CLARKE *On the Evidences* Prop. 14 (R.) Abraham's descendents according to the flesh. **1794** SOUTHEY *Poems, Retrospect*, The last descendant of his race. **1871** MORLEY *Voltaire* (1886) 54 A descendant of the conquering Franks. **1875** POSTE *Gaius* 265 From the rules of caducity ascendants and descendants of the testator to the third degree were excepted.

b. of animals and plants.

1866 DARWIN *Orig. Spec.* Hist. Sk. 13 The existing forms of life are the descendants by true generation of pre-existing forms. **1867** H. SPENCER *Princ. Biol.* II. vi. 431 The descendants of a wheat plant..will have become numerous.

c. *fig.* and *transf.*

1869 FARRAR *Fam. Speech* ii. (1873) 74 The Gothic language is absolutely dead..it has left no direct descendants. **1871** A. R. WALLACE *Nat. Select.* viii. 295 Are not improved Steam Engines or Clocks the lineal descendants of some existing Steam Engine or Clock? **1894** *Chr. World* 23 Aug. 629/2 The descendants of the Puritans —the Nonconformists of to-day.

†**2.** *Astron.* The part of the heavens which at any moment is descending below the horizon (opposite to the ASCENDANT). *Obs.*

1690 LEYBOURN *Curs. Math.* 385 The Descendent, or Angle of the West, or the Cuspis of the Seventh House.

†**3.** *Typogr.* A letter that descends below the line; = DESCENDER[2] b. (Cf. ASCENDANT B. 7.)

1676 MOXON *Print Lett.* 6 Descendents are those that stand lower than the Foot-line: such as are *g, p, q, y.*

descended (dɪ'sɛndɪd), *ppl. a.* [f. DESCEND *v.* + -ED[1].] **1.** Derived, sprung from a person or stock. Usually as *pa. pple.* (see DESCEND *v.* 8 b); used as *adj.* only in combination.

1640 SIR E. DERING *Carmelite* (1641) 46 Your Troy-discended Romanes. **1665** SIR T. HERBERT *Trav.* (1677) 2 A well descended Gentleman.

2. That has descended, fallen, or dropped.

1853 *Lancet* 29 Jan. 112/1 (*heading*) Excision from the inguinal canal of an imperfectly descended testicle. **1966** WRIGHT & SYMMERS *Systemic Path.* I. xxvi. 812/1 A testis that is still descending at about the end of the first year of life may fail to reach the bottom of the scrotum, remaining imperfectly descended.

descendental (di:sɛn'dɛntəl), *a. nonce-wd.* [f. L. *dēscendent-em*, pr. pple. of *dēscendĕre* to DESCEND + -AL[1]: after *transcendental.*] That descends to matter of fact; naturalistic, realistic.

1850 WHIPPLE *Ess. & Rev.* II. 342 Square, lover of Plato and Molly Segrim, with his brain full of transcendental morality, and his heart full of descendental appetites. **1860** J. YOUNG *Prov. Reason* 54 Since the days of Locke..the philosophy of England has been only descendental. **1863** *Reader* I. 376/3 Mr. Mill belongs to what has been variously named the Empirical..Sensational, or Descendental School of Philosophy.

Hence **descen'dentalism, -ist** (*nonce-wds.*).

1831 CARLYLE *Sart. Res.* I. x, With all this Descendentalism, he combines a Transcendentalism no less superlative. **1882** WHIPPLE in *Harper's Mag.* LXV. 579 He belonged to the respectable race of descendentalists, and was evidently puzzled to understand how a transcendentalist could acquire property.

†**de'scender**[1]. *Law. Obs.* Also 6 **decendre**, 6–7 **discender.** [a. F. *descendre*, pres. inf. used subst.: cf. *attainder*, *remainder*; cf. -ER[4].] Descent; title of descent.

1485 *Act 1 Hen. VII*, c. 1 Subjects having cause of Action by Formedon in the descender, or else in the remainder. **1523** FITZHERB. *Surv.* 13 To sue his pleynt in yͤ nature of the kynges writ of formdowne in decendre at the commen lawe. [**1590** SWINBURNE *Treat. Testaments* 94 If the issue do recover the same in formdon in the discent.] **1598** KITCHIN *Courts Leet* (1675) 250 Formedon in Discender lyeth where the Donee in Tail or free Marriage aliens that Land so given. **1768** BLACKSTONE *Comm.* III. 192 The heir in tail shall have this writ of formedon in the descender, to recover these lands, so given in tail, against him who is then the actual tenant of the freehold.

descender[2] (dɪ'sɛndə(r)). [f. DESCEND *v.* + -ER[1].] **a.** One who or that which descends.

1667 DENHAM *Direct. Paint.* IV. ix. 3 Horrors and Anguish of Descenders there, May teach thee how to paint Descenders here. **1855** GROTE *Greece* II. xcvi. XII. 507 An altar erected in honour of Demetrius Katabates or the Descender. **1863** MURPHY *Comm. Gen.* xiii. 10 This river [Jordan] may well be called the Descender.

b. *Typogr.* A letter or character that descends below the line; cf. DESCENDING *ppl. a.* 2 b. Also in *Printing* and *Palæography*, a descending stroke; a stroke which extends below the body of a letter.

1802 *Monthly Mag.* XIV. 70/1 Each small letter is to be without any tail-piece or descender. **1883** *Are we to read backwards?* 39 The modern Arabic figures—uniform in linage—[are] more legible than the 'old style' figures, with their many ascenders and descenders. **1938** *Times Lit. Suppl.* 30 Apr. 304/3 Where it saves space..is by very nearly eliminating the 'descenders' of the lower-case. **1954** N. R. KER in R. M. Wilson *A. Riwle* (*Caius MS.*) p. xii, The end of the descender of *r*, as of other tailed letters, often turns sharply to the left.

descendi'bility. *rare.* [f. next + -ITY.] The property of being descendible.

1765 BLACKSTONE *Comm.* I. 200 He must necessarily take the crown..with all it's inherent properties; the first and principal of which was it's descendibility.

descendible, -able (dɪ'sɛndɪb(ə)l, -əb(ə)l), *a.* [In 16th c. *descendable*, a. OF. *descendable*: subseq. conformed to L. analogies, as in *ascendibilis* from *ascendĕre.*]

1. That descends or may descend to an heir; capable of being transmitted by inheritance.

1495 *Act 11 Hen. VII*, c. 49 The Lordshippes..[shall be] descendable and discend to the heires att Commen Lawe. **1574** tr. *Littleton's Tenures* 116 a, Wher tenements bee dyscendable to the yonger sonne after the custome of borough Englishe. **1622** CALLIS *Stat. Sewers* (1647) 191 If the son had attained this Freedom by the death of his father, as a thing descendible. **1765** BLACKSTONE *Comm.* I. 404 Which title is..usually descendible to the issue male. **1822** W. TAYLOR in *Monthly Mag.* LIII. 103, I make their whole property descendable only to the first-begotten son. **1868** *Sat. Rev.* 17 Oct. 521 The Derwentwater earldom was only descendible to heirs male.

†**2.** Having the property of descending or moving downwards. *Obs. rare.*

1622 CALLIS *Stat. Sewers* (1824) 164 He may make a trench in his own grounds to let the water run downwards, and to descend upon his neighbour's grounds, for water is an element descendible *jure naturæ.*

3. Capable of being descended; down which one may go. *rare.*

1730–6 BAILEY (folio), *Descendable*, which may descend or be descended, or gone down. **1755** JOHNSON, *Descendible*, such as may be descended; such as may admit of a passage downwards. **1863** *Sat. Rev.* 418 Descendible by zigzag Indian paths, traversing the face of the rocky walls.

descending (dɪ'sɛndɪŋ), *vbl. sb.* [f. DESCEND *v.* + -ING[1].]

1. The action of the verb DESCEND (q.v.); descent, going down.

c **1489** CAXTON *Blanchardyn* xviii. 56 At the descendyng of theyr enemyes to lande. **1572** J. JONES *Bathes of Bath* Pref. 2 Some with..Descendings, Ascendings the partes wasted, etc. **1638** SIR T. HERBERT *Trav.* (ed. 2) 146 A precipice, downe which is no descending. **1690** LOCKE *Govt.* I. xi. (Rtldg.) 119 The descending and conveyance down of Adam's..dominion to posterity. **1802** SOUTHEY *Poems, Ode Astron.*, All Ether laugh'd with thy descending.

†**2.** *concr.* A downward slope, declivity, descent.

1490 CAXTON *Eneydos* lv. 152 Atte the descendynge of the hille. **1585** J. B. tr. *Viret's Sch. Beastes* B iij, The first descending..is..croked and with many turninges.

†**b.** Extension downwards. *Obs.*

1627 CAPT. SMITH *Seaman's Gram.* x. 50 The height or eleuation..should answer the descending or depth.

descending (dɪˈsɛndɪŋ), *ppl. a.* [f. DESCEND *v.* + -ING².] That descends.

1. *lit.* Moving downwards, coming down.

a **1700** DRYDEN (J.), He cleft his head with one descending blow. **1799** COLEBROOKE in *Life* (1873) 423 The resin exudes from the descending sap. **1858** LARDNER *Hand-bk. Nat. Phil.* 215 The descending column..falls..in a closed cistern.

2. *transf.* Directed or extending downwards; *esp.* in *Anat.*, *Bot.*, etc., as *descending aorta*, *colon*, *axis*, *ovule*, etc. (opp. to ASCENDING *ppl. a.* 3).

1737 BRACKEN *Farriery Impr.* (1756) I. 92 The ascending or descending Trunk of the Aorta. **1810** SOUTHEY *Kehama* XVI. viii, Descending steps, which in the living stone Were hewn. **1869** OLIVER *Indian Bot.* I. i. 15 The root being the *descending*, the stem the *ascending* portion of the axis.

b. *Typogr.* Applied to letters that have a tail or stem extending below the line. (Cf. ASCENDING *ppl. a.* 1 b.)

1676 MOXON *Print Lett.* 6 The Bottom-line is the line that bounds the bottom of the Descending Letters. **1889** T. MACKELLAR *Amer. Printer* 61 There are..descending letters in both Roman and Italic.

c. *Her.* = DESCENDANT *a.* 1 c; *esp.* having the head turned toward the base of the shield.

3. *fig.* Proceeding to what is lower in position or value, or later in order (cf. DESCEND *v.* 5); in *Math.* of series: Proceeding from higher to lower quantities or powers; thus 8, 4, 2, 1, ½, etc. is a descending series in geometrical progression.

1642 JER. TAYLOR *Episc.* (1647) 41 Schisms and Heresies ..should multiply in descending ages. **1816** tr. *Lacroix's Diff. & Int. Calculus* 234 If we wished to have a descending series with respect to *x*, we must give the proposed differential the form [etc.]. **1822** SHELLEY *Hellas* 350 To stem the torrent of descending time. **1874** MORLEY *Compromise* (1886) 28 The establishment..of an ascending and descending order among the facts.

4. Falling in pitch, stress, or other physical quality.

descending rhythm, a rhythm composed of feet in which the accented syllable is followed by the unaccented as in the trochee, dactyle, etc. ***descending diphthong*** = falling DIPHTHONG q.v.

5. ***descending node*** (Astron.): that node of a planet's orbit at which it passes from north to south of the ecliptic.

1696 WHISTON *Th. Earth* II. (1722) 188 Its descending Node was then also in..due Position. **1727-51** CHAMBERS *Cycl.*, *Descending latitude*, is the latitude of a planet in its return from the nodes to the equator. **1755** B. MARTIN *Mag. Arts & Sc.* II. vii. 159 The Descending Node, marked thus ☋. **1868** LOCKYER *Heavens* (ed. 3) 170.

Hence **de'scendingly** *adv.*

1614 SYLVESTER *Du Bartas, Bethulia's Rescue* IV. 368 Two twinkling Sparks, Two sprightfull Jetty eyes..'Twixt these two Suns, down from this liberal front, Descendingly ascends a pretty Mount. **1882** PROCTOR in *Knowledge* 24 Mar. 449 The Feast of Tabernacles was..ruled by the passage of the sun over the equator descendingly.

descens(e: see DESCENCE.

descension (dɪˈsɛnʃən). Now *rare.* Forms: 4-6 descen-, discen-, dyscen-, -cio(u)n, -cyo(u)n, -sioun, -syon, (6 decension), 6-7 descention, (7 desention), 6- descension. [a. OF. *descension* (14th c. in Godef.), ad. L. *dēscensiōn-em* going down, n. of action from *dēscendĕre* to DESCEND.]

1. The action of descending; going or coming down, descent (*lit.* and *fig.*). Now *rare.*

a **1420** HOCCLEVE *De Reg. Princ.* 31 For she knewe no lower descensioun, Save onely dethe. **1526** *Pilgr. Perf.* (W. de W. 1531) 261 The blessed descensyon of his soule to Limbo. **1549** COVERDALE *Erasm. Par. Eph.* iv. 10 The descencion is before, and the ascencion after. **1597** SHAKS. *2 Hen. IV*, II. ii. 193 From a god to a bull? a heavy descension! It was Ioves case. **1616** R. CARPENTER *Past. Charge* 54 The descension of the holy Ghost vpon the Apostles. **1652** PEYTON *Catastr. Ho. Stuarts* (1731) 16 This Bishop maintained Christ's personal Descension into Hell. **1657** AUSTEN *Fruit Trees* I. 101 As a Tree increaseth by ascension of sap, so it would decrease by its descension. **1881** RAYMOND *Mining Gloss.*, *Descension-theory*, the theory that the material in veins entered from above.

†**b.** *concr.* The alleged term for a flight of 'woodwales' (woodpeckers). *Obs.*

a **1479** in Caxton *Hors, Shepe & G.* etc. (1822) 30 A discencion of wodewalis.

†**2.** Descent from an ancestor; lineage. *Obs.*

1447 BOKENHAM *Seyntys* (Roxb.) 45 For more cler undurstondynge Of this genealogyal descencyoun. **1523** LD. BERNERS *Froiss.* I. lxiv. 86 *heading*, The duke dyed without heyre, wherby the dyscencion fell.

†**3.** A falling in dignity or importance; a coming down from dignity or high station; condescension.

1609 MIDDLETON *Shirley Ambass.* Wks. 1886 VIII. 314 Whatsoever is dishonourable hath a base descention, and sinks beneath hell. **1642** SIR E. DERING *Sp. on Relig.* 108 Wherefore is this descension from a Parliament to a People? **1692** R. L'ESTRANGE *Josephus' Antiq.* VIII. iii. (1733) 215 To treat them with Courtesy and Descension.

†**4.** *Old Chem.* = DESCENT 1 d. *Obs.*

1393 GOWER *Conf.* II. 86 Forth with the congelation, Solucion, discention. **1559** MORWYNG *Evonym.* Pref., The oyl Capnistrum..that is destilled by descention. **1612** WOODALL *Surg. Mate* Wks. (1653) 270 Descension is when the essential juyce dissolved from the matter to be distilled, is subducted and doth descend. **1657** in *Phys. Dict.*

†**5.** *Astron.* The setting, or descent below the horizon, of a celestial body. ***right descension***, ***oblique descension*** of a celestial body: the degree of the celestial equator, reckoned from the first point of Aries, which sets with it in a right, or oblique, sphere. *Obs.* (Cf. ASCENSION 3.)

1551 RECORDE *Cast. Knowl.* (1556) 209 In the Righte Sphere..the descensions or settinges vnder the Horizont are equall with the Ascensions. **1594** BLUNDEVIL *Exerc.* III. I. xxix. (ed. 7) 337, I will proceed to the ascention and descention of the starres, both right, meane, and oblique. **1658** SIR T. BROWNE *Hydriot.* v, Our longest sun sets at right descensions. **1726** tr. *Gregory's Astron.* I. 225 There will be no rising or setting at all by the diurnal Motion, and therefore no Ascension or Descension in this Sphere. **1876** G. F. CHAMBERS *Astron.* 912 Ascension, oblique..the converse word is 'descension', but it is obsolete.

†**6.** *Astrol.* The part of the zodiac in which a planet was supposed to have least influence (opp. to *exaltation*). *Obs.*

c **1391** CHAUCER *Astrol.* II. §4 That he [the lord of the ascendant] be nat in his descencioun, ne ioigned with no planete in his discencioun. **15..** '*Almanak for the Year 1386*', 2 On þe 7 syne fro þe exaltacion of euerilk a planyte, in like degre es made his descensyon.

de'scensional, *a. rare.* [f. prec. + -AL¹.] Of or pertaining to descension.

1727-51 CHAMBERS *Cycl.*, *Descensional difference*, is the difference between the right and oblique descension of the same star, or point of the heavens, etc. **1840** HERSCHEL *Ess.* (1857) 137 There must be constantly in action..a discensional force producing subaqueous currents. **1882** *Nature* XXVII. 177 The ascensional and descensional movements of the atmosphere.

descensive (dɪˈsɛnsɪv), *a.* [f. L. *dēscens-*, ppl. stem of *dēscendĕre*: see -IVE.]

1. Having the quality of descending (*lit.* and *fig.*); characterized by downward movement or tendency; the opposite of *ascensive*.

1611 COTGR., *Descensoire*, descensiue, descending. **1658** MANTON *Exp. Jude* 3 There is in man a natural desire to do his posterity good; love is descensive. **1811** W. TAYLOR in *Monthly Mag.* XXXI. 425 Either from ascensive or descensive opinion. **1882** OWEN in *Longm. Mag.* I. 68 The mammals who follow next after *Bimana* in the descensive series of mammalian orders.

2. *Gram.* Diminishing the force; cf. ASCENSIVE 2.

1854 ELLICOTT *Ep. Gal.* 39 *Kai* has also what may be termed a descensive force.

†**de'scensory**, *sb. Old Chem.* Also 6 dec-, disc-. [ad. OF. *descensoire*, *-oir*, med.L. type *dēscensōrium*, f. *dēscensōrius* adj.: see next.

(Cf. 'l'huyle du mesme bois destillé par ce que les alchemistes appellent descensoir' of 1555 in Godefroy.)]

A vessel or retort used for distillation 'by descent': see DESCENT 1 d.

c **1386** CHAUCER *Can. Yeom. Prol. & T.* 239 Sondry vessels maad of erþe and glas Oure vrinals and oure descensories. **1584** R. SCOT *Discov. Witchcr.* XIV. i. 295 Also their lamps their urinalles, discensories, sublimatories, alembicks, viols, croslets, cucurbits, stillatories, and their fornace of calcination. **1594** PLAT *Chem. Concl.* 31 Some commend the distillation..that is performed by a descensorie. **1678** R. R[USSELL] *Geber* II. I. IV. xii. 112 A chymical Descensory.

†**de'scensory**, *a. Old Chem.* [ad. L. *dēscensōrius*, f. *dēscens-*, ppl. stem of *dēscendĕre* to DESCEND: see -ORY.] Relating to, or of the nature of, distillation by descent.

1678 R. R[USSELL] *Geber* V. iv. 275 The Descensory Furnace is made as before described. **1684** tr. *Bonet's Merc. Compit.* v. 146 The specifick properties of Liquors perish in descensory distillation.

descent (dɪˈsɛnt). Also 5 dessente, 5-6 dissent, 5-7 discent, 6 discente. [a. F. *descente* (1304 in Hatzf.), formed from *descendre* after *attente*, *vente*, etc. from *attendre*, *vendre*, etc., the etymological form being DESCENCE, -ENSE.]

1. a. The action of descending; a going or coming down; downward motion (of any kind).

1590 SIR J. SMYTH *Disc. Weapons* 28 In their discents and fall. **1606** SHAKS. *Tr. & Cr.* V. ii. 175 Not the dreadfull spout ..Shall dizzie with more clamour Neptunes eare In his discent. **1659** PEARSON *Creed* (1839) 319 It is to be observed, that the descent into hell was not in the ancient creeds or rules of faith. **1698** KEILL *Exam. Th. Earth* (1734) 163 The great resistance they met with in their descent through the Air. **1866** G. MACDONALD *Ann. Q. Neighb.* vii. (1878) 125, I do not think the descent to Avernus is always easy.

b. *fig.* (of an immaterial agent or influence).

c **1374** CHAUCER *Troylus* I. 319 Lest fully the descente Of scorne fille on himself. **1875** JOWETT *Plato* (ed. 2) I. 159 The descent of a great storm may make the pilot helpless.

c. Corresp. to *trans.* sense of the verb (DESCEND *v.* 11).

1611 CORYAT *Crudities* 80 The descent of the mountaine I found more wearysome..then the ascent. **1748** F. SMITH *Voy. Disc. N.-W. Pass.* I. 95 The Sides high Marble Clifts, not difficult of Descent. *Mod.* A new descent of the Schroffspitze has been effected.

†**d.** *Old Chem.* A method of distillation: see quot. 1727. *Obs.*

1655 CULPEPPER *Riverius* VI. i. 133 The Oyl is made of Box cut in smal pieces, and then Distilled by descent, in two Vessels. **1727-51** CHAMBERS *Cycl.* s.v. *Distillation*, Distillation by descent is where the fire is applied on the top, and all around the vessel, whose orifice is at the bottom; and, consequently, the vapour not being able to rise upwards, it is forced to precipitate, and distil down to the bottom.

e. *Her.* ***in descent***: said of an animal represented as leaping or flying downwards.

1727-51 CHAMBERS *Cycl.* **1727** BAILEY vol. II. s.v., A lion in descent.

f. *Dynamics.* The downward motion of a body under the influence of terrestrial gravity.

1700 J. CRAIG in *Philos. Trans.* Abridg. IV. 542 (*title*), The Curve of Quickest Descent. **1706** PHILLIPS (ed. Kersey), *Descent of heavy Bodies* (in *Philos.*) is the tendency of them to the Center of the Earth. **1727-51** CHAMBERS *Cycl.*, s.v., Laws of the descent of bodies..*Line of swiftest Descent*, is that which a body falling by the action of gravity, describes in the shortest time; which is proved by geometricians to be the cycloid.

g. (with cap. initial.) The descent of Christ into hell.

1883 B. F. WESTCOTT *Hist. Faith* vi. 76 The eternal meaning of Christ's Descent, Resurrection, Ascension, Session in heaven, as set forth in our Creed. **1894** H. B. SWETE *Apostles' Creed* v. 56 The doctrine of the Descent had found a place in three synodical declarations. *Ibid.* 57 Cyril ..assigns great importance to the Descent, making it one of his ten primary *credenda.* **1967** *Cath. Dict. Theol.* II. 163/2 The perspective runs on from the events of Bethany to what happens at the Descent, and from there to the final judgment of the world.

2. a. *concr.* A downward slope, a declivity.

1591 SPENSER *Virgil's Gnat* 77 Spread themselves farre abroad through each descent. **1611** BIBLE *Luke* xix. 37 At the descent of the mount of Oliues. **1726** LEONI *Alberti's Archit.* I. 10/2 If it stands upon a Descent. **1887** BOWEN *Virg. Æneid* VI. 182 Massive ash-trees roll from the mountains down the descent.

b. A means of descending; a way, passage, or flight of steps leading downwards.

descent into the ditch (*Mil.*): see quot. 1803.

1634 MASSINGER *Very Woman* IV. ii, Fitting his chamber With trapdoors and descents. **1706** PHILLIPS (ed. Kersey), Descent into the Moat or Ditch. **1734** tr. *Rollin's Anc. Hist.* (1827) II. III. 144 Descents by steps to the river. **1745** POCOCKE *Descr. East* II. II. 73 There were about fourty-three degrees of seats, and eleven descents down from the top..those descents are made by dividing each seat into two steps. **1803** JAMES *Milit. Dict.* (1810) s.v., Descents into the Ditch (*descentes dans le fossé*), cuts and excavations made by means of saps in the counterscarp beneath the covert way [i.e. to enable the besiegers to cross the ditch]. **1887** RUSKIN *Præterita* II. 199 The rampart walk, unbroken except by descents and ascents at the gates.

†**c.** That to which one descends; the lowest part. *Obs.* (*nonce-use.*)

1605 SHAKS. *Lear* V. iii. 137 From th' extremest vpward of thy head, To the discent and dust below thy foote.

3. A sudden hostile invasion or attack, *esp.* from the sea, or from high ground: cf. DESCEND *v.* 3.

1600 E. BLOUNT tr. *Conestaggio* 194 Some small peeces of artillery, to hinder their descent. **1697** DRYDEN *Virg. Georg.* II. 710 He hears, but hears from far, Of Tumults, and Descents, and distant War. **1698** T. FROGER *Voy.* 26 It was determin'd to make a Descent upon the Country, to take the King prisoner. **1816** SCOTT *Old Mort.* Introd., Argyle was threatening a descent upon Scotland. **1874** GREEN *Short Hist.* vii. §8. 430 A daring descent of the English forces upon Cadiz.

4. *fig.* **a.** A coming down to a lower state or condition; fall, decline, sinking; progress downwards to that which is lower or subordinate.

1667 MILTON *P.L.* IX. 163 Oh, foul descent! that I, who erst contended With gods to sit the highest, am now constraind Into a Beast, and mixt with bestial slime. *a* **1704** LOCKE (J.), Observing such gradual and gentle descents downwards, in those parts of the creation that are beneath men. **1889** *Spectator* 26 Oct. 540 Since the descent to household suffrage.

b. A stage or step downward in any scale; a degree below. ? *Obs.*

1589 GREENE *Menaphon* (Arb.) 42 Her birth was by manie degrees greater than mine, and my woorth by manie discents lesse than hers. **1667** MILTON *P.L.* VIII. 410 Infinite descents Beneath what other Creatures are to thee. **1728** YOUNG *Love Fame* I. (1757) 84 With what a decent pride he throws his eyes Above the man by three descents less wise?

5. With reference to physical qualities: A fall, lowering (of the pitch of sound, temperature, etc.).

1581 MULCASTER *Positions* x. (1887) 58 Their perorations, and closinges, with a discent, and fall of the voice. **1836** MACGILLIVRAY tr. *Humboldt's Trav.* i. 24 The proximity of a sand-bank is indicated by a rapid descent of the temperature of the sea at its surface. *Mod.* A sudden descent of an octave in the melody.

6. †**a.** The action of proceeding in sequence, discourse, or argument, to what is subsequent; subsequent part or course; succession. *Obs.* **b.** The action of descending from generals to particulars. **c.** *Logic.* An inference from a proposition containing a higher to one containing a lower term.

1642 JER. TAYLOR *Episc.* (1647) 35 What also the faith of Christendome was concerning the Minister of confirmation

..I shall make evident in the descent of this discourse. **1655–60** STANLEY *Hist. Philos.* (1701) 73/2 These five, Thales, Anaximander, Anaximenes, Anaxagoras, Archelaus, by continul Descent succeeding one another, compleat the Ionick Sect.

7. a. The fact of 'descending' or being descended from an ancestor or ancestral stock; lineage. Also *attrib.*

c **1330** R. BRUNNE *Chron.* (1810) 249 þis ilk þre barons, þorgh descent of blode, Haf right & resons to þe coroune. **1393** GOWER *Conf.* III. 230 Which rightfull heire was by descent. *c* **1430** LYDG. *Hors, Shepe, & G.* 9 in *Pol. Rel. & L. Poems* (1866) 15 Cryste whiche lynally doune came Be dissent conveyed the pedegrewe Frome the patryarke Abrahame. **1530** PALSGR. 213/1 Descent of lynage, *descente.* **1559** *Mirr. Mag., Fall R. Tresilian* v, By discent a gentleman. **1634** W. TIRWHYT tr. *Balzac's Lett.* 123, I would draw his descent from Hector, or Achilles. **1728** YOUNG *Love Fame* III. (1757) 104 A Welch descent, which well-paid heralds damn; Or, longer still, a Dutchman's epigram. **1839** YEOWELL *Anc. Brit. Ch.* xiii. (1847) 141 A chieftain of imperial descent. **1856** FROUDE *Hist. Eng.* (1858) I. ii. 107 The descent in the female line was not formally denied. **1950** *Amer. Anthropologist* LII. 1. 2 We may differentiate unilineal descent groups from a kinship system proper. **1951** R. FIRTH *Elem. Soc. Org.* i. 8 In such a small community less importance is attached to preserving a male descent-name than to marking the establishment of a new social unit. **1957** P. WORSLEY *Trumpet shall Sound* i. 18 The framework of Fijian social organisation was a system of agnatic descent-groups. **1958** G. LIENHARDT in Middleton & Tait *Tribes without Rulers* 105 Every tribe contains descent groups from many clans of both categories.

b. *transf.* of animals and plants; in *Biol.* extended to origination of species (= EVOLUTION 6 c).

1638 SIR T. HERBERT *Trav.* (ed. 2) 192 Many Camells abound here..The Dromodarie and it are of one descent, but varie according to the Countrie. **1859** DARWIN *Orig. Spec.* (1871) 317 On the theory of descent with modification. **1871** —— (*title*), The Descent of Man and Selection in relation to Sex. **1882** VINES *Sachs' Bot.* 776 Descent determines the specific character of the growth. **1884** J. FISKE *Evolutionist* xiv. 366 The researches..into the palæontology of the horse have established beyond question the descent of the genus *equus* from a five-toed mammal not larger than a pig, and somewhat resembling a tapir.

attrib. **1871** DARWIN *Desc. Man* xi. 388 In accordance with the descent-theory, we may infer that [etc.].

c. *fig.* Derivation or origination from a particular source.

c **1530** *Remedie of Loue* (R.), Ransake yet we would..Of this worde the true orthographie, The verie discent of ethimologie. **1707** *Curios. in Husb. & Gard.* Pref. 4 Whenever I cannot fully discover the Rise and Descent of any Effect. **1803** *Med. Jrnl.* IX. 108 Its visitation..in the present year, is deducible from a similar descent.

†**8. a.** A line of descent, lineage, race, stock.

c **1330** R. BRUNNE *Chron.* (1810) 206 Elizabeth þe gent, fair lady was sche, Tuo sons of þer descent, tuo douhters ladies fre. **1605** VERSTEGAN *Dec. Intell.* iii. (1628) 63 Of whose descents are since issued the greatest Princes at this present in Germanie. **1618** CHAPMAN *Hesiod* I. 228 Then form'd our Father Jove a Third Descent, Whose Age was Brazen.

†**b.** A descendant (*lit.* and *fig.*); also, descendants collectively, offspring, issue. *Obs.*

1475 *Bk. Noblesse* (1860) 23 The noble actys of the seyd erles of Angew wyth her lyneалle dessentys. **1601** HOLLAND *Pliny* I. 67 Augusta of the Taurines, an ancient descent from the Ligurians. **1615** CHAPMAN *Odyss.* VI. 22 She went Up to the chamber, where the fair descent Of great Alcinous slept. **1667** MILTON *P.L.* x. 979 Our descent..Which must be born to certain woe, devourd By Death at last.

9. A stage in the line of descent; a generation.

1513 MORE in Grafton *Chron.* (1568) II. 809 Which house ..enjoyed the same [crown] three discentes. **1593** BILSON *Govt. Christ's Ch.* 7 Euen twelue descents after the flood. **1673** RAY *Journ. Low C.* 308 Such as can prove their Gentility for three or four Descents. **1765–9** BLACKSTONE *Comm.* (1793) 252 After a breach of the succession that continued for three descents. **1818** HALLAM *Mid. Ages* (1872) II. 67 A lineal succession of four descents without the least opposition.

10. *Law.* **a.** The passing of property (in England only of real property) to the heir or heirs without disposition by will; transmission by inheritance.

c **1330** R. BRUNNE *Chron.* (1810) 243 To haf þe scheld þorgh heritage descent. *c* **1460** FORTESCUE *Abs. & Lim. Mon.* ix, The grete lordis of þe londe, by reason off nev Dissentes ffallyng vnto ham, by reason also off mariages, Purchasses, and oþer titles, schal often tymes growe to be gretter than thay be now. **1523** FITZHERB. *Surv.* Prol., Than if the owner make a true pee degre or conueyaunce by discente or by purchace vnto the said landes. **1628** COKE *On Litt.* 13 b, Discent signifieth when lands do by right of blood fall unto any after the death of his ancestors. **1818** CRUISE *Digest* (ed. 2) I. 303 That fines should be paid upon admittance, as well upon alienation as descent. **1858** LD. ST. LEONARDS *Handy-bk. Prop. Law* xxiii. 177 No real property..can pass otherwise than by grant by deed..or by descent or devise, whereas mere personal property will pass by delivery from hand to hand.

†**b.** *descent cast*: transmission by inheritance actually effected (with special reference to its bearing on an outstanding adverse claim); cf. CAST *v.* 36. *Obs.*

[*a* **1626** BACON *Max. & Uses Com. Law* i. (1636) 3 If I make a feoffment in fee, upon condition that the feoffee shall in-feoffe over, and the feoffee be disseised, and a discent [be] cast.] *a* **1845** STEPHENS *Comment. Laws Engl.* (1868) III. 518 An Act was passed in the year 1833 (3 & 4 Will. IV. c. 27) containing..the provisions..that no descent cast or discontinuance happening after 31st Dec. 1833, should toll or defeat any right of entry or action for the recovery of land.

c. *transf.* and *fig.* Transmission of a title, dignity, personal quality, etc. to heirs or to offspring.

1413 *Pilgr. Sowle* IV. vii. (Caxton 1483) 61 The synne of Adam hath atteyned to men by..descent of kyndely herytage. *c* **1611** CHAPMAN *Iliad* II. 156 His incorrupted sceptre..his sceptre of descent. *a* **1704** LOCKE (J.), If the agreement and consent of men first gave a sceptre into any one's hand, that also must direct its descent and conveyance.

†**de'scentive,** *a. Obs. rare.* In 6 disc-. [f. prec. + -IVE.] Descending; = DESCENSIVE.

1599 NASHE *Lenten Stuffe* 7 The notable immunities, franchises, priuileges she is endowed with..by the discentiue line of Kings from the Conquest.

deceptation, obs. var. of DISCEPTATION.

†**de'scercle,** *v. Obs. rare.* [a. OF. *des-, decercler,* f. *des-, dé-* (DE- I. 6) + *cercle* circle, hoop. The mod. repr. would be *decircle.*] *trans.* To deprive of its circle or circles.

To *descercle* a helm: cf. CIRCLE *sb.* 10 b.

1485 CAXTON *Chas. Gt.* 102 Rolland..araught maradas vpon his helme, that he descerkled and departed it.

descern, desces, -ceise, descharge, descide, descipher, descition, obs. ff. DISCERN (DECERN), DECEASE, DISCHARGE, DECIDE, DECIPHER, DECISION.

1644 PRYNNE & WALKER *Fiennes' Trial* 118 The supreame Councell of the Realme to whose descition it belongeth.

deschooling (diːˈskuːlɪŋ). [f. DE- II. 1 + SCHOOL *sb.*[1] + -ING[1].] Illich's term for the action or process of transferring the function of education (within a society, etc.) from conventional schools to other, non-institutional systems of learning which are held to allow the student to develop more freely.

1970 I. ILLICH in *Sat. Rev.* (U.S.) 17 Oct. 68 The radical deschooling of society begins..with the unmasking by cultural revolutionaries of the myth of schooling. **1972** *Where* Nov. 301/1 The search for alternatives to school implicit in the issue of de-schooling. **1974** *Howard Jrnl.* XIV. 38 The 'deschooling' debate and the 'free school' movement. **1978** *Peace News* 6 Oct. 17/2 A proportion of the meeting believed passionately in de-schooling and reckoned the arguments in favour too well known and too wide ranging to need trotting out again.

Hence **de'school** *v. trans.* and *intr.*, **de'schooled** *ppl. a.*; **de'schooler**, one who advocates deschooling.

1971 I. ILLICH (*title*) Deschooling society. **1971** *Time* 7 June 33/3 His deschooled world would replace most formal classes with networks of 'learning exchanges'. **1971** *Sunday Times* 10 Oct. 17/5 Education must remember what it is for or the traditionalists in strange alliance with the de-schoolers will cut it back and start again. **1978** T. ROSZAK *Person/Planet* vii. 190 The deschoolers are up against..their stubbornest obstacles. **1982** *Times* 8 Sept. 8/1 Hardly a county council in Britain does not have its quota of de-schoolers. *Ibid.* 8/4 In the county of Hereford and Worcester..13 other families are deschooling without official objection.

†**de'scide,** *v. Obs. rare.* [f. L. *dē-scindĕre* or *dī-scindĕre* to divide, or *dis-cīdĕre* to cut in pieces.] To cut, indent.

1657 TOMLINSON *Renou's Disp.* 324 Its leafs are variously descided and serrated in their circuit.

descl-: see DISCL-.

descloizite (deɪˈklɔɪzaɪt). *Min.* [named from Descloizeaux, a French mineralogist.] A vanadate of lead and zinc, an orthorhombic mineral, of olive-green colour, occurring in small crystals on a silicious and ferruginous gangue from South America (Dana).

[**1854** A. DAMOUR in *Ann. de Chim. et de Phys.* XLI. 78 Je propose de lui donner le nom de *descloizite*, comme hommage à..M. Descloizeaux.] **1854** DANA *Syst. Min.* (ed. 4) II. 361 *Descloizite*..Trimetric..Lustre bright. Colour mostly deep black. **1951** J. R. PARTINGTON *Gen. & Inorg. Chem.* (ed. 2) xxi. 644 Vanadium is widely distributed, the principal ores being carnotite,..vanadinite,..descloizite, [etc.].

desconfite, -ure, obs. ff. DISCOMFIT, -URE.

descrial (dɪˈskraɪəl). [f. DESCRY *v.*[1] + -AL[1] II. 5.] Discovery of something obscure or distant.

1605 *Answ. Discov. Rom. Doctr.* 1 The strange Discriall of this great Discouerer.

describa'bility. [f. next: see -ITY.] Capability of being described.

a **1866** J. GROTE *Exam. Utilit. Philos.* ii. (1870) 38 A definiteness or describability as to happiness.

describable (dɪˈskraɪbəb(ə)l), *a.* [f. DESCRIBE *v.* + -ABLE.] Capable of or admitting description.

1802 PALEY *Nat. Theol.* ix. (R.), Keill has reckoned up, in the human body, four hundred and fourty-six muscles, dissectible and describable. **1877** LADY BRASSEY *Voy. Sunbeam* xv. (1878) 269 Another shade, only describable by the term molten lava colour.

de'scribble, *v. nonce-wd.* [f. *scribble* after *describe.*] *trans.* To scribble an account of.

1794 MISS GUNNING *Packet* IV. 275, I can, as you find, describble Richard and Sarah Adams; but..to describe would be absolute presumption.

describe (dɪˈskraɪb), *v.* Also 6–7 **descrybe, discrybe,** 8 **discribe.** [ad. L. *dēscrīb-ĕre* to copy off, transcribe, write down, write off, sketch off in writing or painting, mark off, etc., f. DE- I. 2 + *scrībĕre* to write. Preceded in ME. use by *descrive* (through OF.), of which *describe* may be considered as an assimilation to the orig. L. form. The spelling *dis-* arose from confusion with words having the prefix *des-, dis-*: see DES-.]

†**1.** To write down, set forth in writing or in written words; to transcribe, copy out. *Obs.*

1526 *Pilgr. Perf.* (W. de W. 1531) 233 So Peter Bercharius in his dictionary describeth it. **1607** TOPSELL *Serpents* (1653) 625 Whose verses I will here describe [*verses follow*]. **1649** JER. TAYLOR *Gt. Exemp.* Exhort. §12 Christ our Lawgiver hath described all his Father's will in Sanctions and Signatures of laws.

†**b.** To write down in a register; to enrol. *Obs.*

1535 COVERDALE *1 Chron.* iv. 41 These that are now descrybed by name. **1614** RALEIGH *Hist. World* II. IV. v. §6. 218 He was indeed gone into Ægypt..describing a royall Army. *a* **1667** JER. TAYLOR *Wks.* (1835) I. 262 (Cent. Dict.) His name was described in the book of life.

†**c.** To write down as one's opinion; to declare, state. *Obs. rare.*

1771 FLETCHER *Checks* Wks. 1795 II. 300 Is it modest to describe ecathedra, that the dead Ephesians..could not work for life?

2. To set forth in words, written or spoken, by reference to qualities, recognizable features, or characteristic marks; to give a detailed or graphic account of. (The ordinary current sense.)

1513 BRADSHAW *St. Werburge* I. 203 As auncyent Cronycles descryben it full playne. **1538** STARKEY *England* II. i. 144 Hys perfayt state..of vs before descrybyd. **1697** DRYDEN *Virg. Georg.* IV. 220 Describe we next the Nature of the Bees. **1727** SWIFT *Gulliver* II. viii. 173 Discribing the rest of his household-stuff. **1833** LAMB *Elia* Ser. II. *Wedding*, I am ill at describing female apparel. **1874** MORLEY *Compromise* (1886) 38 He was described for us..by a master hand.

b. with *complement.*

1594 HOOKER *Eccl. Pol.* I. iii. (1611) 7 The institution thereof is described as being established. **1600** E. BLOUNT tr. *Conestaggio* 314 That the Iland was no lesse fortified then had beene described unto them. **1818** CRUISE *Digest* (ed. 2) V. 71 Glanville describes a fine to be an accommodation of a..suit. **1875** JOWETT *Plato* (ed. 2) IV. 23 Pleasures as well as opinions may be described as good or bad.

3. To set forth in delineation or pictorial representation; to represent, picture, portray; in quot. 1526 *fig. Obs.* or *arch.*

1526 TINDALE *Gal.* iii. 1 To whom Jesus Christ was described before the eyes. **1535** COVERDALE *Ezek.* iv. 1 Take a tyle..and descrybe vpon the cite off Ierusalem. **1600** J. PORY tr. *Leo's Africa* II. 149 Then describe they certaine signes upon the hands and forehead. **1620** E. BLOUNT *Horæ Subsec.* 352 A Gladiatore..admirably described in Marble. **1665** SIR T. HERBERT *Trav.* (1677) 362 Accept the preceeding Map..This describing India on the other side Ganges. **1774** J. BRYANT *Mythol.* II. 123 We find the Sun to be described under the appearance of a bright star.

†**b.** Of things: To represent or stand for pictorially. *Obs.*

1643 VICARS *Looking-glass Malign.* 13 The picture of a man in a tub..to describe a Roundhead. **1703** MOXON *Mech. Exerc.* 317 These twelve Divisions are to describe the twelve Hours of the Day. **1793** SMEATON *Edystone L.* §121 A second model..to describe the external form.

4. To delineate, mark out the form or shape of, trace the outline of (a geometrical figure, etc.): **a.** said of personal agents.

1552 HULOET, Describe, *circumscribo.* **1559** W. CUNNINGHAM *Cosmogr. Glasse* 122 Describe the like arck from B to A. **1570** BILLINGSLEY *Euclid* I. i. 8 A triangle..set or described vpon a line. **1669** DRYDEN *Tyrannic Love* IV. i, With chalk I first describe a circle here. **1703** MOXON *Mech. Exerc.* 126 To measure and describe the Ground-plot. **1831** BREWSTER *Optics* i. §15 Describe arches of circles.

b. said of things.

1559 W. CUNNINGHAM *Cosmogr. Glasse* 55 A lyne, moved ..can but describe a plat forme..And a plat forme moved.. describeth a Body. **1570–6** LAMBARDE *Peramb. Kent* (1826) 239 It beginneth to divide it selfe two waies, and to describe the Ile of Thanet. **1821** CRAIG *Lect. Drawing* i. 7 Representing objects by lines which describe their contours or dimensions.

5. To form or trace by motion; to pass or travel over (a certain course or distance).

1559 W. CUNNINGHAM *Cosmogr. Glasse* 34 The most northely circle which the Sonne describeth. **1662** HOBBES *Seven Probl.* Wks. 1845 VII. 10 The arches are the spaces which these two motions describe. **1713** BERKELEY *Hylas & Phil.* i. Wks. 1871 I. 281 A body that describes a mile in an hour. **1869** PHILLIPS *Vesuv.* ix. 252 They describe parabolic curves. **1869** TYNDALL *Notes Lect. Light* 29 The white-hot particles of carbon in a flame describe lines of light.

6. To mark off or distribute into parts; to map or parcel out. *rare.*

1535 COVERDALE *Josh.* xviii. 6 Descrybe ye the londe in seuen partes [so **1611** and R.V.; WYCLIF, discryue].

†**b.** To apportion, assign under limits. [So in Lat.] *Obs. rare.*

1531 ELYOT *Gov.* I. ii, I wyll therfore kepe my penne within the space that is discribed to me.

¶**7.** = DESCRY *v.*[1] Cf. DESCRIVE *v.*[4] and the converse confusion in DESCRY *v.*[2]

1574 RICH *Merc. & Soldier* H viij, Venus was first described, sittynge in her Waggon. **1592** GREENE *Tullies Love* (1609) G, As soone as she had discribed him, and for certainty knew that it was he, yonder quoth she comes that odde man of Rome. **1620** SHELTON *Quix.* IV. xxii. 185 Over-night we described this Wharf. **1667** MILTON *P.L.* IV. 567, I describ'd his way Bent all on speed, and markt his Aerie Gate. **1781** GIBBON *Decl. & F.* xlvii. (1792) VIII. 312 The smallest blemish has not been described by..jealous..eyes.

Hence **de'scribed** *ppl. a.*

1552 HULOET, Described, *circumscriptus.* **1703** MOXON *Mech. Exerc.* 196 Their described width. **1865** TYLOR *Early Hist. Man.* iv. 64 In the described position of the three relations of speech.

describee (dɪˌskraɪˈbiː). [f. DESCRIBE *v.* + -EE.] One to whom a thing is described.

1830 DISRAELI in *Home Letters* (1885) 50 Description is always a bore, both to the describer and to the describee. **1885** *Punch* 23 May 243/2 Describee is a happy specimen of a whole series of words much required in our language.

de'scribeless, *a. nonce-wd.* [f. DESCRIBE *v.* + -LESS.] Incapable of description, indescribable.

a **1850** W. THOM in *D. Jerrold's Shilling Mag.*, Come, though no verdure on your describeless and ruined limbs.

describent (dɪˈskraɪbənt), *a.* and *sb.* [ad. L. *dēscrībentem*, pr. pple. of *dēscrībĕre* to DESCRIBE.]

A. *adj.* 'Describing, marking out by its motion' (Ash 1775). **B.** *sb. Geom.* A point, line, or surface, producing by its motion a line, surface, or solid; a generatrix.

1704 in J. HARRIS *Lex. Techn.*

describer (dɪˈskraɪbə(r)). [f. DESCRIBE *v.* + -ER[1].] One who describes, or gives a description.

1550 BALE *Apol.* 18 (R.) The descrybers of y[e] primatiue church, Egesippus and Eusebius. **1603** KNOLLES *Hist. Turks* (1638) 2 Pomponius Mela the describer of the world. **1727** DE FOE *Syst. Magic* I. ii. (1840) 47 Our wise describers of the magic of the ancients. **1878** BAYNE *Purit. Rev.* v. 160 The historical describer has always to regret that he must show events not..simultaneously..but in succession.

describing (dɪˈskraɪbɪŋ), *vbl. sb.* [f. DESCRIBE *v.* + -ING[1].] The action of the vb. DESCRIBE; description.

1559 W. CUNNINGHAM *Cosmogr. Glasse* 120 By the makinge and describyng of this onely Mappe. **1581** SIDNEY *Apol. Poetrie* (Arb.) 22 Their passionate describing of passions. **1817** COBBETT *Taking Leave* 9 Greater powers of describing.

de'scribing, *ppl. a.* [f. as prec. + -ING[2].] That describes; descriptive.

1581 SIDNEY *Apol. Poetrie* (Arb.) 29 The right describing note to know a Poet by. **1599** THYNNE *Animadv.* (1865) 66 This describinge definitione.

descrier (dɪˈskraɪə(r)). Also 7 **descryer.** [f. DESCRY *v.*[1] + -ER[1].] One who descries, or discovers.

1599–1623 MINSHEU *Span. Dict.* A Descrier, *Descubridor.* **1614** T. ADAMS *Devil's Banquet* 58 Foxes..if they bee seene stealing the Grapes, fall a biting their descryers by the shinnes. **1647** CRASHAW *Poems* 120 The glad descryer shall not miss To taste the nectar of a kiss From Venus' lips.

de'script, *ppl. a.* [ad. L. *dēscript-us*, pa. pple. of *dēscrībĕre* to DESCRIBE.] Described. Also †**a.** Properly arranged (= L. *dēscriptus*) (but perh., in quot. 1665, for L. *discriptus* divided, apportioned). **b.** Inscribed, engraved, chased (not a L. sense). **B.** as *sb.* (see quot. 1731).

1665 J. WEBB *Stone-Heng* (1725) 219 They commixt set Forms, and descript Orders in one and the same Temple. **1731** BAILEY vol. II, *Descripts* (with Botanic Writers), such plants as are described. **1775** ASH, *Descript*, described. **1820** SOUTHEY *Wesley* II. 260 Sectarians of every kind, descript and non-descript. **1863** P. S. WORSLEY *Poems & Transl.* 8 Two huge valves, embossed with graven gold..and descript with all Which earth and heaven..Foster in wave or field.

description (dɪˈskrɪpʃən). Also 4–6 **de-, discryp-, discrip-, -cion, -cioun, -cyon, -cyoun, -tyon, -tyowne, -sion,** etc. [a F. *description*, in OF. also *-cripcion, -crition, -crision*, ad. L. *dēscriptiōn-em*, n. of action from *dēscrībĕre* (ppl. stem *dēscript-*) to DESCRIBE. (See there as to the spelling *dis-*.)] The action of describing; the result or product of this action.

†**1. a.** The action of writing down; inscription. *Obs. rare.*

1480 CAXTON *Chron. Eng.* ccxxv. 231 Vnder the descripcion and writing of the name of Englond and of Fraunce.

†**b.** Writing down in a register, enrolment.

c **1380** WYCLIF *Sel. Wks.* I. 316 Syryne..bigan to make þis discripcion. **1609** BIBLE (Douay) *2 Sam.* xxiv. 9 Joab gave the number of the description of the people to the king.

2. a. The action of setting forth in words by mentioning recognizable features or characteristic marks; verbal representation or portraiture.

c **1380** WYCLIF *Last Age of Chirche* 26 þis also [he] schewiþ openly bi discripcioun of tyme. **1387** TREVISA *Higden* I. 29 (Mätz.) With descripcioun of þe lasse world. **1447** BOKENHAM *Seyntys* (Roxb.) 13 If the crafth of descrypcyoun I cowde as weel forge..As cowde Boyce. **1559** W. CUNNINGHAM *Cosmogr. Glasse* 6 Geographie is the..discriptioun of the face, and picture of th' earth. **1606** SHAKS. *Ant. & Cl.* II. ii. 203 For her owne person, It beggerd all discription. **1806** WOLCOTT (P. Pindar) *Tristia* Wks. 1812 V. 335 Description on your pencil waits. **1845** M. PATTISON *Ess.* (1889) I. 2 Writers..gifted with strong imaginations, are masters of description.

b. (with *pl.*) A statement which describes, sets forth, or portrays; a graphic or detailed account of a person, thing, scene, etc.

1340 HAMPOLE *Pr. Consc.* 8875 Yhit wille I imagyn..Ffor to gyf it a descripcion. *c* **1470** HENRY *Wallace* IX. 1911 Thai send..The discriptioune Off him tane thar. **1553** T. WILSON *Rhet.* 95 A description or an evident declaration of a thyng as though we sawe it even now doen. **1676** RAY *Corr.* (1848) 122 Clusius..had..better descriptions of them [species of birds]. **1794** SULLIVAN *View Nat.* II. 186 Polybius..takes notice of Vesuvius, in his description of Italy. **1834** MEDWIN *Angler in Wales* II. 108 An old man answering the description of Humphrey. **1878** MORLEY *Carlyle* Crit. Misc. Ser. I. 198 The more correct description of what has happened.

c. *Logic.* (See quots.)

1628 T. SPENCER *Logick* 193 A description is a sentence which setteth out a thing, even by other arguments. **1751** JOHNSON *Rambler* No. 143 ¶3 Descriptions..are definitions of a more lax and fanciful kind. **1843** MILL *Logic* I. viii. §5 The second kind of imperfect definition, in which the name of a class is defined by..attributes which are not included in its connotation..has been termed Description.

d. *Philos.* Phr. ***knowledge by description***: see ACQUAINTANCE 1 b.

3. a. The combination of qualities or features that marks out or serves to describe a particular class. Hence, **b.** A sort, species, kind, or variety, capable of being so described.

[*c* **1391** CHAUCER *Astrol.* I. §21 Shapen in maner..of a lop webbe aftur the olde descripcioun. **1535** COVERDALE *Ezek.* xliii. 11 The commynge in, the goinge out, all the maner and descripcion therof.] **1596** SHAKS. *Merch. V.* III. ii. 303 Pay him sixe thousand..Before a friend of this description Shall lose a haire. **1864** D. G. MITCHELL *Sev. Stor.* 306 The man must be a roué of the worst description.

b. 1781 T. GILBERT *Relief Poor* 6 That all Descriptions of poor Persons should be sent thither. **1785** PALEY *Pol. Philos.* (ed. 8) I. 303 The invitation, or voluntary admission, of impure thoughts..falls within the same description. **1844** MRS. HOUSTON *Yacht Voy. Texas* II. 278 The Volante..is a description of vehicle, peculiar..to Cuba.

†**4.** Pictorial representation; a picture, painting. *Obs. rare.*

1620 E. BLOUNT *Horæ Subsec.* 366 The high Altar is set out by Michael Angeloes curious description of the day of Iudgement. *a* **1646** J. GREGORY *Posthuma* 257 (T.) The description is..of the earth and water both together, and it is done by circles.

5. *Geom.* **a.** The 'describing' of a geometrical figure: see DESCRIBE *v.* 4 ? *Obs.*

1655–60 STANLEY *Hist. Philos.* (1701) 9/1 Whence may be deduced the description of a Rectangle Triangle in a Circle. **1751** CHAMBERS *Cycl., Description*, in geometry.

b. Tracing out or passing over a certain course or distance.

1706 W. JONES *Syn. Palmar. Matheseos* 294 The Times..of Description shall be as the Square Roots of the Altitudes..of the Cones. **1728** PEMBERTON *Newton's Philos.* 91 The time taken up in the description of the arch EF. **1858** HERSCHEL *Astron.* §490 Equable description of areas is itself the essential criterion of a continual direction of the acting force towards the centre.

Hence **de'scriptionate** *a.*, characterized by description, descriptive. **de'scriptionless** *a.*, without or beyond description.

1593 NASHE *Christ's T.* (1613) 164 Sutable descriptionate politures. **1852** *Fraser's Mag.* XLVI. 454 That broiling and dusty, but beautiful and quite descriptionless road.

des'criptionist. One who professes to give a description, *spec.* one who professes to give a mere or pure description, free from evaluation, prediction, or explanation; also *attrib.*

1827 *Examiner* 211/2 A mere connoisseur and descriptionist. **1838** *Fraser's Mag.* XVII. 31 These locomotive descriptionists..and thirty mile an hour travelling penmen. **1914** C. D. BROAD *Perception* ii. 91 The descriptionist view is liable to underrate it. **1950** *Mind* LIX. 423 Munro eschews all dealings with evaluation, but like so many other pure descriptionists in fact assumes a value attitude. **1953** C. E. BAZELL *Linguistic Form* viii. 103 One man is interested in city-structure, and another is interested in the description of cities... If a city is built in the form of a square, this is not more likely to escape the eye of the descriptionist than that of the structuralist.

descriptive (dɪˈskrɪptɪv), *a.* [ad. (late) L. *dēscriptīv-us* containing a description, f. *dēscript-*, ppl. stem of *dēscrībĕre*: see -IVE. Cf. F. *descriptif.*]

1. a. Having the quality or function of describing; serving to describe; characterized by description.

1751 JOHNSON *Rambler* No. 94 ¶1 The sound of some emphatical and descriptive words. **1820** HAZLITT *Lect. Dram. Lit.* 141 They are lyrical and descriptive poets of the first order. **1882** A. W. WARD *Dickens* i. 18 A descriptive power that seemed to lose sight of nothing. *Mod.* A handbook of Descriptive Anatomy.

b. const. *of.*

1794 SULLIVAN *View Nat.* II. 176 Circumstances descriptive of similar connections. **1878** HUXLEY *Physiogr.* 71 A name sufficiently descriptive of its construction.

2. *Math.* Of that branch of geometry in which the relations of lines, figures, and solids are studied, esp. in their projections on two planes. (Cf. F. *géométrie descriptive*, Monge 1794–5.)

1824–5 *Encycl. Metrop.* (1845) I. 312/2 A new species of geometry introduced..by Monge, during the period of the revolution, under the designation of descriptive geometry. **1841** T. G. HALL *Elem. Descr. Geom.* 19 The object of Descriptive Geometry is the invention of methods by which we may represent upon a plane..the form and position of a body which possesses three dimensions... The means by which descriptive geometry attains its object is the method of Projections. **1885** C. LEUDESDORF tr. *Cremona's Projective Geom.* 50 Projective Geometry..dealing with projective properties..is chiefly concerned with descriptive properties of figures. **1913** BLESSING & DARLING *Elem. Descr. Geom.* i. 1 The practical value of descriptive geometry lies in the knowledge gained in solving graphical problems which arise in engineering and architecture, and in making and reading working drawings. **1961** *New Scientist* 23 Feb. 489/1 Gaspard Monge—scientist, mathematician, father of descriptive geometry and founder of the first polytechnic school.

3. a. Consisting solely or principally of description; concerned with, or signifying, observable things or qualities, or what is the case rather than what ought to be or might or must be; not expressing feelings or valuations; relating to this type of meaning or interest. (Opp. *emotive, prescriptive, evaluative.*) Also (*rare*) as *sb.*

1885 W. JAMES in *Mind* X. 28 Our inquiry is a chapter in descriptive psychology. **1943** M. FARBER *Foundat. Phenomenol.* vii. 216 The distinctions [were] a matter of descriptive analysis. **1944** C. L. STEVENSON *Ethics & Lang.* ix. 210 In any 'persuasive definition' the term defined is a familiar one, whose meaning is both descriptive and strongly emotive. **1948** *Mind* LVII. 482 A special form of the descriptive fallacy—the fallacy of believing that all verbs are used to describe empirically distinguishable activities or states of affairs. **1951** *Ibid.* LX. 443 The traditional discussions of Free Will, confusing descriptive with prescriptive laws. **1952** R. M. HARE *Lang. of Morals* vii. 111 The descriptive properties which a particular strawberry had. **1955** J. L. AUSTIN *How to do Things* (1962) xii. 157 There is also a slide towards 'descriptives'. **1956** A. J. AYER *Probl. Knowl.* i. 7 A philosophic statement is not..like..a statement in any of the descriptive sciences..tested by observation. *Ibid.* ii. 80 There is the method of Descriptive Analysis.

b. *Linguistics.* Describing the structure of a language at a given time, avoiding comparisons with other languages or other historical phases, and free from social valuations; as in ***descriptive grammar, linguistics***, etc. (Opp. *normative, prescriptive, historical*; cf. SYNCHRONIC *a.*)

1888 H. A. STRONG tr. *Paul's Princ. Hist. Lang.* i. 2 Descriptive Grammar has to register the grammatical forms and grammatical conditions in use at a given date within a certain community speaking a common language. **1927** *Mod. Philol.* Nov. 217 (*heading*) Descriptive linguistics. *Ibid.* 218 Today descriptive linguistics is thus recognized beside historical, or rather as precedent to it. **1933** BLOOMFIELD *Lang.* i. 18 Descriptive studies did not merge with the main stream of historical work. **1933** JESPERSEN *Ess. Eng. Gram.* i. 19 Descriptive grammar..aims at finding out what is actually said and written by the speakers of the language investigated. **1944** *Amer. Speech* XIX. 211 The later directions of linguistic research: dialect geography and descriptive analysis. **1947** E. H. STURTEVANT *Introd. Ling. Sci.* vi. 51 Descriptive linguistics forms the basis for historical linguistics. *Ibid.* 53 Most of our school grammars must be classed as descriptive. **1953** J. B. CARROLL *Study of Lang.* ii. 16 Several Greek grammarians, notably Dionysius Thrax, Apollonius Dyscolus, and Herodian, developed descriptive grammars of Greek. *Ibid.* 19 The European linguist who best formulated the methodology of descriptive linguistics..was Ferdinand de Saussure. **1961** H. A. GLEASON *Introd. Descriptive Linguistics* (ed. 2) xiii. 202 A descriptive grammar..is a systematically organized set of statements about the constructional patterns that characterize grammatical statements. **1966** J. J. KATZ *Philos. Lang.* ii. 8 The philosopher of language should..draw his linguistic information from the theory of language as developed in descriptive linguistics.

4. *Gram.* Of a clause: see quot. 1903. Of adjectives, etc.: assigning a quality; not primarily restricting the application of the expression modified. (Opp. *limiting.*) ***descriptive adjective***: see quot. 1933.

1903 HALE & BUCK *Latin Gram.* IV. 260 The Volitive Subjunctive may be used..in Relative Clauses, determinative or descriptive..that is, telling *what kind* of person or thing is meant. *Ibid.* 302 A Descriptive Clause is necessarily a free one when it refers immediately to an antecedent *complete in itself*, e.g. a word denoting a person. **1927** E. A. SONNENSCHEIN *Soul of Gram.* i. 37 Descriptive genitives. **1933** BLOOMFIELD *Lang.* xii. 202 The adjectives are divided into two classes, *descriptive* and *limiting*, by the circumstance that when adjectives of both these classes occur in a phrase, the limiting adjective precedes and modifies the group of descriptive adjective plus noun. **1954** P. M. ROBERTS *Underst. Gram.* ii. 48 *A car'penter's hammer* ('a hammer customarily used by carpenters'—descriptive genitive). *Ibid.* iv. 93 Descriptive adjectives occur in three main sentence positions.

Hence **de'scriptively** *adv.*, **de'scriptiveness.**

1796 MORSE *Amer. Geog.* I 183 The Allegany..has been descriptively called the back bone of the United States. **1834** *Q. Rev.* L. 296 Represented with..lively and attractive descriptiveness. **1870** SPURGEON *Treas. Dav.* Ps. i. 1 The term 'stood' descriptively represents their obstinacy.

descriptivism (dɪˈskrɪptɪvɪz(ə)m). [f. DESCRIPTIVE *a.* + -ISM.]

1. *Philos.* The doctrine that value-words, and hence value-judgements, are equivalent in meaning to certain descriptive expressions; see also quot. 1961. (Cf. DESCRIPTIVE *a.* 3 a.)

1961 WEBSTER, *Descriptivism*, a theory of ethics according to which only descriptive or empirical statements are meaningful. **1963** R. M. HARE *Freedom & Reason* ii. 17 The thesis..that moral judgements are a kind of descriptive judgements..is descriptivism.

2. *Linguistics.* The practice or advocacy of descriptive linguistics; the belief that the descriptive part of linguistics is fundamental. (Cf. DESCRIPTIVE *a.* 3 b.)

1961 in WEBSTER. **1964** R. A. HALL *Introd. Ling.* lxxv. 442 A strict descriptivism has on occasion been preached. **1966** N. CHOMSKY *Cartesian Linguistics* 106 One of the most striking features of American descriptivism in the 1940s was its insistence on justification in terms of precisely specified procedures of analysis.

de'scriptivist. [f. as prec. + -IST.] An adherent or advocate of descriptivism. Also *attrib.* or as *adj.* So **descripti'vistic** *a.*, **descripti'vistically** *adv.* (Webster 1961).

1952 *Archivum Linguisticum* IV. I. 11 The eminent phonemicist and descriptivist W. F. Twaddell. **1960** R. M. HARE in J. O. Urmson *Conc. Encycl. West. Philos.* 141/2 Those views which hold that moral judgments are used to give some sort of information..are called 'descriptivist'. *Ibid.* 142/1 Stevenson's views did not..find favour with descriptivists. **1962** *Med. Ævum* XXXI. 149 There is some truth in the descriptivists' well-known claim: that a truly diachronic approach must be based on the comparison of descriptions of successive *états de langue*. **1963** R. M. HARE *Freedom & Reason* ii. 16 A naturalist is not the only sort of 'descriptivist'—if we may use this term for one who holds that value-words are simply one kind of descriptive word.

descriptor (dɪ'skrɪptə(r)). *Linguistics.* [a. L. *dēscrīptor* describer.] An expression or sentence-element that has the function of describing.

1933 JESPERSEN *Syst. Gram.* 12 Recently V. Brøndal..has made a very bold attempt at a completely new system ..*Relator* (R) and *Relatum* (r), *Descriptor* (D) and *Descriptum* (d). **1946** C. W. MORRIS *Signs, Lang. & Behavior* iii. 76 *Descriptors*, identifiors which describe a location. **1949** *Mind* LVIII. 27, I shall call the part of a sentence which performs the descriptive function of that sentence its 'descriptor'. **1953** W. J. ENTWISTLE *Aspects of Lang.* v. 157 The *descriptum* corresponds to quantity and has its pure expression in numerals; the *descriptor* with quality and is pure in adverbs. **1965** *Rev. Internat. Doc.* XXXII. 19/1 Any term, group of terms, or any other entity assigned to a document for the purpose of indexing it will be referred to as a descriptor.

† **de'scriptory,** *a. Obs.* [f. *dēscript-*, ppl. stem of L. *dēscrībĕre*: see -ORY.] = DESCRIPTIVE *a.* 1.

1586 A. DAY *Eng. Secretary* I. (1625) 23 Epistles meerely Descriptorie. *Ibid.* 24 A letter Descriptorie, wherein is particularly described an ancient Citie.

descriptum (dɪ'skrɪptəm). Pl. **-ta.** [a. L. *dēscrīptum*, neut. pa. pple. of *dēscrībĕre* to DESCRIBE.]

a. *Linguistics.* (Brøndal's term for) a sentence-element that has the function of numeration. **b.** *Philos.* The object for which a description, or the descriptive element of a sentence, stands; a thing given by description.

1933 [see DESCRIPTOR]. **1936** *Mind* XLV. 37 We might distinguish these two varieties..as the theories (1) that the Self is a Descriptum, and (2) that it is a Logical Construction. **1938** H. REICHENBACH *Exper. & Prediction* §25. 220 Existence is a quality not of individual things but of *descripta*. **1947** R. CARNAP *Meaning & Necessity* i. 32 The entity for which a description stands (if there is such an entity) will be called its *descriptum*. **1949** *Mind* LVIII. 29, I shall call that which is described by the descriptor, the 'descriptum'. The descriptum of an indicative sentence is what would be the case if the sentence were true; and of an imperative sentence, what would be the case if it were obeyed. **1953** [see DESCRIPTOR].

† **de'scrive,** *v. Obs.* exc. *Sc.* Forms: 3–9 **descrive, 3–5 discreve, 4–5 dyscreve, 4 descryfe, 5–6 dyscryve, discryve, -ive, descryve.** [a. OF. *descriv-re* (13th c.), later *descrire*, full stem *descriv-* (mod.F. *décrire, décriv-*) = Pr. *descriure*, Cat. *descriuer*, It. *descrivere*:—L. *dēscrībĕre*. In the course of the 16th c. gradually superseded (exc. in Sc.) by the latinized form DESCRIBE.

Descrive was in ME. reduced to *descrie* (DESCRY *v.*[2]), and thus confused in form, and sometimes in sense with DESCRY *v.*[1] Hence *descrive* also occurs as a form of the latter.]

1. To write down, inscribe; to write out, transcribe.

1382 WYCLIF *Isa.* xlix. 16 Lo! in myn hondis I haue discriued thee. **14..** *Circumcision* in *Tundale's Vis.* 90 Thys name which may not be dyscreved. *c* **1450** LYDG. *Compl. Lovers Life* xxviii, To discryve and write at the fulle The woful compleynt. **1483** CAXTON *Gold. Leg.* 284/1 Mathewe and Luke descryue not the generacion of Marye but of Joseph.

b. To write down in a register, enrol; cf. *Vulg.* Luke ii. 1 *ut describeretur universus orbis.*

1297 [see DESCRIVING *vbl. sb.*]. **1382** WYCLIF *Num.* xi. 26 There dwelten forsothe in the tentis two men..for and thei weren discryued [Vulg. *descripti fuerant*; **1611** and they were of them that were written]. —— *Luke* ii. 1 That al the world schulde be discryued. *c* **1460** FORTESCUE *Abs. & Lim. Mon.* xvi. (1714) 120 Theyr secund Emperor, comaundyd al the World to be discrivyd [*v.r.* (1885) 149 discribed.]

2. = DESCRIBE *v.* 2.

a **1225** *Ancr. R.* 10 þus seint Iame descriueð religiun & ordre. *c* **1380** WYCLIF *Serm.* Sel. Wks. II. 318 þei ben þes þat Ysay discryveþ þat þei seien good is yvel. *c* **1400** *Rom. Rose* 865, I wot not what of hir nose I shal descryve; So faire hath no womman alyve. **1552** ABP. HAMILTON *Catech.* (1884) 45 It is expedient to descrive quha is ane heretyk. **1671** *True Non-conf.* 134 Which we finde descrived in the Scriptures of the New Testament. **1785** BURNS *To W. Simpson* xvi, Let me fair Nature's face descrive. **1858** M. PORTEOUS '*Souter Johnny*' 15 Hamely chiels..Wha Tammy's haunts can weel descrive.

absol. **1393** GOWER *Conf.* III. 120 So as these olde wise men Descrive.

3. a. To represent pictorially or by delineation; also *absol.* **b.** To draw geometrically (figures, etc.). **c.** To trace out or pass over (a definite course). Cf. DESCRIBE *v.* 3–6.

c **1391** CHAUCER *Astrol.* I. §17 The plate vnder thi Riet is descriued with 3 [principal] cerclis. **1393** LANGL. *P. Pl.* C. XXI. 214 Ho couþe kyndeliche with colour discriue, Yf alle þe worlde were whit. **1398** TREVISA *Barth. De P.R.* VIII. xi. (1495) 317 Epiciclis is a lytyll cercle that a planete discryueth. **1565–73** COOPER *Thesaurus, Abacus*..a counting table such as..Astronomers descriue their figures in.

d. To map out, set forth the boundaries of.

(But also often including the general sense 2.)

1387 TREVISA *Higden* (Rolls) I. 7 þat in stories meteþ and discryueþ all þe worlde wyde. **1480** CAXTON *Descr. Brit.* 20 Kyng william conquerour made alle these..shires to be descreued and meten. **1536** BELLENDEN *Cron. Scot.* (1821) I. p. xlvi, We will discrive the samin [the Ilis] in maner and forme as followis.

¶ **4.** = DESCRY *v.*[1] [Cf. etymol. note above.]

c **1340** *Cursor M.* 6544 (Fairf.) For to discriue [*v.r.* to se] þaire cursed dede. **1377** LANGL. *P. Pl.* B. xx. 93 þenne mette þis man..ar heraudes of armes hadden descreued lordes. *c* **1440** *Gesta Rom.* xxiii. 84 (Harl. MS.) No man cowde discryve wheþer of hem shuld be Emperour. **1551** ROBINSON tr. *More's Utop.* (Arb.) 50 Also flyinge he shoulde be discriued by the roundyng of his heade.

Hence **de'scrived** *ppl. a.*

c **1449** PECOCK *Repr.* II. xvii. 248 Bi the now discriued and tauȝt maner. *Ibid.* 408 The..bifore descryued tymes.

† **de'scriving,** *vbl. sb. Obs.* [f. prec. + -ING[1].] Describing; description.

1297 R. GLOUC. (1724) 60 þis August..let make a descriuyng, þat y mad nas neuer er. **1382** WYCLIF *Luke* ii. 2 This firste discryuyng was maad of Cyryne. **1486** *Bk. St. Albans* E iv a, The discreuyng of a Bucke. **1530** PALSGR. 165 *Blasón*, a blasyng or discryvyng of ons armes. **1792** BURNS *Auld Rob Morris* v, How past descriving had then been my bliss.

descry (dɪ'skraɪ), *v.*[1] Forms: 4 **discryghe, 4–6 discrye, 5 dyscry(e, 6 descrye, 6–7 descrie, discrie, 4– descry.** [app. a. OF. *descrier* to cry, publish, decry, f. *des-, dé-*, L. DIS- + *crier* to cry.

The sense-development is not altogether clear; it was perhaps in some respect influenced by the reduction of DESCRIVE to *descry* (see next), and consequent confusion of the two words: cf. DESCRIVE *v.* 4, also DESCRIBE *v.* 7. In several instances it is difficult to say to which of the verbs the word belongs: thus

c **1300** *K. Alis.* 138 For astronomye and nygremauncye No couthe ther non so muche discryghe.]

I. To cry out, declare, make known, bewray.

† **1.** *trans.* To cry out, proclaim, announce, as a herald. *Obs. rare.*

[Cf. quot. 1377 in DESCRIVE *v.* 4.]

a **1440** *Sir Eglam.* 1178 Harowdes of armes than they wente, For to dyscrye thys turnayment In eche londys ȝende.

† **2.** To announce, declare; to make known, disclose, reveal: **a.** of persons. **b.** of things. *Obs.*

a. *c* **1460** *Towneley Myst.* (Surtees) 203 My name to you wille I descry. **1549–62** STERNHOLD & H. *Ps.* xxv. 3 Thy right waies unto me, Lord, descrye. **1621** BURTON *Anat. Mel.* I. ii. I. i, At length Jupiter descried himself, and Hercules yielded. **1655–60** STANLEY *Hist. Philos.* (1701) 290/2 Diogenes, thou..Who to content the ready way To following Ages didst descry.

b. *c* **1430** *Freemasonry* 323 Hyt [the seventhe poynt] dyscryeth wel opunly, Thou schal not by thy maystres wyf ly. **1590** SPENSER *F.Q.* I. x. 34 Whose sober lookes her wisedome well descride. *a* **1592** H. SMITH *Wks.* (1867) II. 200 This light..doth not only descry itself, but all other things round about it. **1635** COWLEY *Davideis* IV. 231 A thoughtful Eye That more of Care than Passion did descry. **1639** DRUMM. OF HAWTH. *Fam. Epistles* Wks. (1711) 140 His cheeks scarce with a small down descrying his sex.

† **c.** With a sense of injurious revelation: To disclose what is to be kept secret; to betray, bewray; to lead to the discovery of. *Obs.*

c **1340** *Cursor M.* 7136 (Trin.) þat was a greet folye hir lordes [*i.e.* Samson's] counsel to discrye. ? *c* **1475** *Sqr. lowe Degre* 110 Thy counsayl shall i never dyscry. **1596** NASHE *Saffron Walden* 131 That he be not descride by his alleadging of Authors. **1606** HOLLAND *Sueton.* 90 Hee had like to have descried them [his parents] with his wrawling. **1614** BP. HALL *Recoll. Treat.* 509 In notorious burglaries, oft-times there is..a weapon left behinde, which descrieth the authors. **1670** MILTON *Hist. Eng.* 11, His purple robe he [Alectus] had thrown aside lest it should descry him.

II. To cry out against, cry down, decry.

† **3.** To shout a war-cry upon, challenge to fight; = ASCRY *v.* 1 b.

c **1400** *Rowland & O.* 273 No kyng in Cristyante Dare.. discrye hym ther with steven. **1480** CAXTON *Chron. Eng.* cxcvii. 175 The gentil knyghtes fledden and the vileyns egrely hem discryed and grad an high 'yelde yow traytours!'

† **4.** To denounce, disparage; = DECRY *v.* 2. *Obs.*

c **1400** *York Manual* (Surtees) p. xvi, We curse and descry ..all thos that thys illys hase done. **1677** GILPIN *Dæmonol.* (1867) 407 They contemn and descry those, as ignorant of divine mysteries.

† **5.** To cry down, depreciate (coin); = DECRY.

1638 SIR R. COTTON *Abstr. Rec. Tower* 23 The descrying of the Coyne.

III. To get sight of, discover, examine.

6. To catch sight of, *esp.* from a distance, as the scout or watchman who is ready to announce the enemy's approach; to espy.

c **1340** *Gaw. & Gr. Knt.* 81 þe comlokest [lady] to discrye. *c* **1430** *Sir Tryam.* 1053, Xii fosters dyscryed hym then, That were kepars of that fee. **1569** STOCKER tr. *Diod. Sic.* III. viii. 114 He might descry a mightie and terrible Nauie.. sayling towards the citie. **1605** *Play Stucley* in Simpson *Sch. Shaks.* (1878) 190 The English sentinels do keep good watch; If they descry us all our labour's lost. **1791** COWPER *Iliad* III. 38 In some woodland height descrying A serpent huge. **1868** Q. VICTORIA *Life Highl.* 39 To meet Albert, whom I descried coming towards us. **1877** BLACK *Green Past.* xxxiii. (1878) 267 At intervals we descried a maple.

7. To discover by observation; to find out, detect; to perceive, observe, see.

c **1430** *Syr. Tryam.* 783 Hors and man felle downe..And sone he was dyscryed. **1581** J. BELL *Haddon's Answ. Osor.* 491 b, There is no man..that will not easily descry..want of Judgement..in you. **1659** HAMMOND *On Ps.* xxxiv. Paraphr. 181 Being by them descryed to be David. **1667** MILTON *P.L.* I. 290 To descry new Lands, Rivers or Mountains in her spotty Globe. **1797** SOUTHEY *Ballad K. Charlemain* 1 All but the Monarch could plainly descry From whence came her white and her red. **1812** J. WILSON *Isle of Palms* II. 582 He can descry That she is not afraid. **1862** LD. BROUGHAM *Brit. Const.* xvi. 249 The bounds which separated that school from Romanism were very difficult to descry.

absol. **1670** NARBOROUGH *Jrnl.* in *Acc. Sev. Late Voy.* (1711) 33, I could not see any sign of People..but still Hills and Vallies as far as we could descry.

† **b.** *intr.* To discern, discriminate. *Obs. rare.*

1633 P. FLETCHER *Purple Isl.* VIII. viii. 108 Pure Essence, who hast made a stone descrie 'Twixt natures hid.

† **8.** *trans.* To investigate, spy out, explore. *Obs.*

1596 DRAYTON *Legends* iii. 175 He had iudicially descryde The cause. **1611** BIBLE *Judg.* i. 23 The house of Ioseph sent to descry Bethel. **1742** SHENSTONE *Schoolmistress* 145 Right well she knew each temper to descry.

† **de'scry,** *v.*[2] *Obs.* [app. a variant of *descryve*, DESCRIVE *v.*, partly perh. originating in the later form of the Fr. infinitive *descri-re*, and pres. t. *descri, -cris, -crit*; but mainly due to confusion in Eng. of *descrive* and *descry* vb.[1])] = DESCRIVE, DESCRIBE.

c **1330** R. BRUNNE *Chron. Wace* (Rolls) 9747 Some of his þewes y wil descrye. *c* **1450** *St. Cuthbert* (Surtees) 41 In the thyrd parte ar discryed Cuthbert mirakyls. **1572** BOSSEWELL *Armorie* II. 63 b, This Serpente I haue descried, as wringled into a wreathe. **1613** WITHER *Sat., Occasion*, He..descries Elenchi, full of subtile falacies.

absol. *c* **1450** *St. Cuthbert* (Surtees) 6546 Cuthbert þai chese as bede descryse. **1571** *Damon & Pithias* Prol. in Hazl. *Dodsley* IV. 12 A thing once done indeed, as histories do descry.

† **de'scry, discry,** *sb. Obs.* [f. DESCRY *v.*]

1. Cry, war-cry; = ASCRY *sb.*

c **1400** *Rowland & O.* 1476 'Mount Joye' was thaire discrye.

2. Discovery of that which is distant or obscure; perception from a distance.

1605 SHAKS. *Lear* IV. vi. 217 The maine descry Stands on the hourely thought. **1611** SPEED *Hist. Gt. Brit.* x. i. (1632) 1253 Without danger of descry.

de'scrying, *vbl. sb.*[1] [f. DESCRY *v.*[1]] The action of the vb. DESCRY[1]; perception from a distance, discovery; also *attrib.*

1577–87 HOLINSHED *Hist. Scot.* (R.), Vpon the first descrieng of the enimies approach. *a* **1729** S. CLARKE *Serm.* I. cxiii. (R.), Now we see through a glass darkly, as through a descrying-glass.

† **de'scrying,** *vbl. sb.*[2] Description, enrolment, etc.: see DESCRY *v.*[2]

c **1400** *Three Kings Cologne* 20 þis discrying was first made vnder Cirinus. *c* **1440** *Promp. Parv.* 119 Descrynge, *descriptio.*

descure, var. *discure*, obs. f. DISCOVER *v.*

desdaine, -dayn, -deigne, obs. ff. DISDAIN.

dese, obs. form of DAIS.

deseam (diː'siːm), *v. Metallurgy.* [f. DE- II. 2 + SEAM *sb.*[1] 6.] *trans.* To remove surface defects from (metal ingots, blooms, etc.), usu. by means of a gas-torch. So **de'seaming** *vbl. sb.*

1941 D. TAYLOR in *Junior Inst. Engineers Jrnl.* LI. 263 Steel conditioning. (The deseaming process in particular.) *Ibid.*, Ingots may be..ground and chipped or deseamed. **1952** *Gloss. Terms Welding and Cutting (B.S.I.)* 115 *Deseaming*, the removal of surface defects from cold ingots, blooms, billets and slabs by means of manual gas cutting.

deseas(e, obs. form of DISEASE.

† **'desecate,** *v. Obs.* [f. L. *dēsecāre* to cut off or away, f. DE- I. 2 + *secāre* to cut. (The regular form is DESECT; but in L. *dēsecātio* for *dēsectio* is in Cassiodorus.] *trans.* To cut off, cut away; to cut free from entanglement or obstruction. Hence **'desecated** *ppl. a.*

1623 COCKERAM, *Desecate*, to mow or cut off. **1651** *Reliq. Wotton.* 334 So as the Soul hath a freer and more desecated operation. **1656** in BLOUNT *Glossogr.*; and in mod. Dicts.

So † **dese'cation.** *Obs.*

1623 COCKERAM, *Desecation*, mowing or cutting off.

desece, -es(e, -esse, -eyce, obs. ff. DECEASE, DISEASE.

desecrate (ˈdɛsɪkreɪt), *v.* [f. DE- II. 1 + stem of *con-secrate*. In L. *dēsecrāre* or *dēsacrāre* meant to consecrate, dedicate. OF. had *des-sacrer* (*des-* = L. *dis-*) still in Cotgr. (1611) 'to profane, violate, unhallow', = It. *dissacrare* 'to unconsecrate, unhallow' (Florio); these may have suggested the formation of the English word.]

trans. To take away its consecrated or sacred character from (anything); to treat as not sacred or hallowed; to profane.

a **1677** BARROW *Serm.* Wks. 1687 I. xv. 213 If we do venture to swear..upon any slight or vain..occasion, we then desecrate Swearing, and are guilty of profaning a most sacred Ordinance. [Not in PHILLIPS, COCKER, KERSEY.] **1675** [see DESECRATING *ppl. a.*]. **1721** BAILEY, *Desecrate*, to defile or unhallow. **1741** MIDDLETON *Cicero* I. VI. 416 What Licinia had dedicated..could not be considered as sacred: so that the Senate injoined the Prætor to see it desecrated and to efface whatever had been inscribed upon it. **1776** HORNE *On Ps.* lxxiv. (R.) When the soul sinks under a temptation, the dwelling-place of God's name is desecrated to the ground. **1837** J. H. NEWMAN *Par. Serm.* (ed. 2) III. xxi. 333 More plausibly even might we desecrate Sunday. **1860** PUSEY *Min. Proph.* 204 The..vessels of the Temple..were desecrated by being employed in idol-worship.

b. To divert from a sacred *to* a profane purpose; to dedicate or devote *to* something evil.

1825 *Blackw. Mag.* XVIII. 156 With a libation of unmixed water..did he devote us to the infernal gods—or..desecrate us to the Furies. **1849** SIR J. STEPHEN *Eccl. Biog.* (1850) I. 312 Particular spots..were desecrated to Satan. **1860** PUSEY *Min. Proph.* 76 Desecrating to false worship the place which had been consecrated by the revelation of the true God.

c. To dismiss or degrade from holy orders. *arch.*

1674 BLOUNT *Glossogr.*, *Desecrate*, to discharge of his orders, to degrade. **1676** in COLES. *c* **1800** W. TOOKE *Russia* (W.), The [Russian] clergy can not suffer corporal punishment without being previously desecrated.

ˈdesecrate, *ppl. a. rare.* = DESECRATED.

1873 BROWNING *Red Cott. Nt.-cap* 934 Than that her dignity be desecrate By neighbourhood of vulgar table.

desecrated (ˈdɛsɪkreɪtɪd), *ppl. a.* [f. prec. vb. + -ED.] Deprived of its sacred character; treated as unhallowed, profaned.

a **1711** KEN *Hymnarium* Poet. Wks. 1721 II. 68 Thou, O most holy, dost detest A desecrated Breast. **1833** L. RITCHIE *Wand. by Loire* 48 The desecrated temple forms the stables and coach-houses.

desecrater, var. of DESECRATOR.

ˈdesecrating, *ppl. a.* [f. DESECRATE *v.* + -ING².] That desecrates or deprives of sacredness.

1675 L. ADDISON *State of Jews* 190 (T.) The desecrating hands of the enemy. **1862** TRENCH *Poems, Visit to Tusculum* 100 The rude touch of desecrating time.

desecration (dɛsɪˈkreɪʃən). [n. of action from DESECRATE: see -ATION.] The action of desecrating, deprivation of sacred or hallowed character, profanation; also, desecrated condition.

a **1717** T. PARNELL *Life Zoilus* (T.), They sentenced him [Zoilus] to suffer by fire, as the due reward of his desecrations. **1727** BAILEY vol. II, *Desecration*, an unhallowing, a profaning. **1779** in Brand *Hist. Newcastle* (1789) II. 124 *note*, The oratory..has been..shut up to preserve it from future desecrations. *a* **1808** BP. PORTEUS *Profan. Lord's Day* (R.), Various profanations of the sabbath..threaten a gradual desecration of that holy day. **1858** FROUDE *Hist. Eng.* III. xiii. 99 The desecration of the abbey chapels. **1870** EMERSON *Soc. & Solit., Domestic Life* Wks. (Bohn) III. 55 Does the consecration of Sunday confess the desecration of the entire week?

desecrative (ˈdɛsɪkreɪtɪv), *a.* [f. DESECRATE + -IVE.] Calculated or tending to desecrate or deprive of sacred character.

a **1861** MRS. BROWNING *Lett. R. H. Horne* (1877) I. ii. 18 [Is] the union between tragedy and the gas-lights..less desecrative of the Divine theory? **1865** CARLYLE *Fredk. Gt.* IX. xx. iv. 71 Merchants' Bills were a sacred thing, in spite of Bamberg and desecrative individualities.

desecrator (ˈdɛsɪkreɪtə(r)). Also -er. [agent-n. from DESECRATE: see -OR, -ER.] One who desecrates or profanes.

1879 MORLEY *Burke* vii. 131 The desecrators of the church and the monarchy of France. **1882** *Harper's Mag.* LXV. 74 Man, the desecrater of the forest temples. **1884** *Non-conf. & Indep.* 27 Mar. 300/3 Desecrators of the Sabbath.

†**deˈsect,** *v. Obs.*$^{-0}$ [f. L. *dēsect-*, ppl. stem of *dēsecāre* to cut away or off, f. DE- I. 2 + *secāre* to cut.] *trans.* To cut away, cut down.

1604 R. CAWDREY *Table Alph.*, *Desect*, cut away from any thing.

†**deˈsection.** *Obs.*$^{-0}$ [ad. L. *dēsectiōn-em*, n. of action from *dēsecāre*: see prec.] The action of cutting off or cutting down.

1656 BLOUNT *Glossogr.*, *Desection*, a cutting down. **1663** F. HAWKINS *Youth's Behav.* 102 *Desection*, a mowing or cutting off.

desederabill, var. DESIDERABLE *Obs.*

desegmentation (ˌdiːsɛgmənˈteɪʃən). *Biol.* [f. DE- II. 1 + SEGMENT.] The process of reducing the number of segments by the union or coalescence of several of these into one, as in the carapace of a lobster, cranium of a vertebrate, etc.; the fact or condition of being thus united.

1878 BELL *Gegenbaur's Comp. Anat.* 228 A number of metameres may be united to form larger segments..This state of things results in a desegmentation of the body.

deˈsegmented, *ppl. a. Biol.* [f. as prec.] Having the number of segments reduced by coalescence; formed into one by coalescence of segments.

desegregate (diːˈsɛgrɪgeɪt), *v.* [f. DE- II. 1 + SEGREGATE *v.*] *trans.* To reunite (persons, classes, races, etc.) hitherto segregated; esp. (orig. *U.S.*) to abolish racial segregation in schools and other institutions. So **desegreˈgation**, such reunion or abolition.

1952 *N.Y. Times* 14 Dec. E9/2 A 'statement of experts'..has been filed in behalf of the NAACP, citing the 'effects of segregation and the consequences of de-segregation'. **1953** *Life* (U.S.) 13 July 36/1 It is hoped that this decision of the court will help to desegregate the white movie theaters. **1958** *Listener* 12 June 966/1 He looked forward to a day when the schools [in Rhodesia] might possibly be desegregated. **1959** *Manch. Guardian* 8 Aug. 5/1 The statement demands eight years compulsory education for African children and immediate desegregation. **1959** *Times Lit. Suppl.* 28 Aug. 491/4 The citizens of Little Rock, after a year's closure of Central High, decided that even desegregated education was better than none. **1969** *Daily Tel.* 20 Oct. 20/7 A widespread movement by White parents to beat school desegregation in the Deep South.

deseite, deseive, obs. ff. DECEIT, DECEIVE.

deseˈlect, *v.* [f. DE- II. 1 + SELECT *v.*] **1.** *trans.* To choose not to select; to remove from selection. *spec.* (*U.S.*), to dismiss (an employee). Cf. DEHIRE *v. euphem. rare.*

1968 *N.Y. Times* 24 June 7 The road from applicant to trainee to overseas volunteer is a hard one. Many individuals do not follow through. Many are 'de-selected'. **1983** *National Law Jrnl.* (U.S.) 25 July 15 The best that one can hope to achieve is to 'deselect'—to eliminate on the basis of meaningful information—the worst of the lot.

2. Of a local constituency party: to reject (a sitting Member of Parliament) as constituency candidate at a forthcoming election, esp. under the Labour party's reselection procedure. Also in extended use. Cf. RESELECT *v.*

1979 *Economist* 29 Sept. 11 Some..ideas for making the party genuinely more democratic.., involving more people in the process of selecting (and deselecting) MPs. **1981** *Times* 5 June 2/6 The party should give financial help to MPs who lost their seats through the new reselection procedure... MPs..who were 'deselected' should be helped. **1984** *Daily Tel.* 5 Oct. 2/6 He has named the MPs in an attempt to persuade them to join the SDP before they are 'deselected' by their constituency parties. **1985** *Times Educ. Suppl.* 11 Jan. 1/3 Right-wing Conservatives in Wiltshire have 'deselected' Mrs Joan Main, pro-comprehensive chairman of the education committee, for the forthcoming county council elections. **1986** *Daily Tel.* 24 Feb. 24/3 Mr Woodall, MP for 12 years.., launched a bitter attack on his opponents in the NUM and local party who, he said, had 'connived' to deselect him.

Hence **deseˈlected** *ppl. a.*; **deseˈlection.**

1978 *Serials Librarian* III. 147 Deselection, or weeding, of periodicals subscriptions has recently become a major concern. **1979** *Times* 28 Nov. 14/2 By the example of expulsion or the threat of de-selection the Labour right is to be cowed and cajoled into submission. **1983** *Daily Tel.* 9 June 11/1 Two 'deselected' Labour M.P.s are standing as independents. **1985** *Times* 30 Apr. 16/1 Michael Cocks, under serious threat of deselection.

desembogue, deseminate, obs. ff. DISEMBOGUE, DISSEMINATE.

desemiticize, desentimentalize, -ed: see DE- II. 1.

desend, desention, obs. ff. DESCEND, -CENSION.

desensitize (diːˈsɛnsɪtaɪz), *v.* [f. DE- II. 1 + SENSITIZE *v.*] *trans.* To reduce or eliminate the sensitivity of. *spec.* **a.** *Photogr.* To reduce the sensitivity to light of (a plate or film). **b.** *Med.* To render (a person or animal) insensitive to an allergen. **c.** *Psychiatry.* To free (someone) from a neurosis or complex. **d.** *Printing.* To treat (a lithographic stone or plate) with a solution which makes the areas not bearing an image repel printing-ink. Also *intr.*, to become insensitive (*rare*).

So **deˌsensitiˈzation**, the act or process of desensitizing; **deˈsensitizer**, a desensitizing agent; **deˈsensitizing** *vbl. sb.* and *ppl. a.*

1904 *Brit. & Col. Printer* 10 Mar. 15/2 Don't leave the plate too long out of the bath or it will desensitise. **1921** *Glasgow Herald* 9 Mar. 7 A single bottle contains enough solution for the desensitising of hundreds of small plates. *Ibid.* 6 Apr. 7 The discovery of phenosafranin as a desensitiser. *Ibid.* 11 May 7 The desensitising properties of pheno-safranine. **1922** *Brit. Jrnl. Photogr. Alm.* 368 The desensitising action. *Ibid.* 369 The transparent backing..acts as a powerful desensitiser. **1924** R. C. LOW *Anaphylaxis & Sensitisation* x. 197 One attack of dermatitis venenata does not produce an immunity or desensitisation to further attacks. *Ibid.*, Any attempt to desensitise patients by repeated applications of the irritant are [*sic*] not likely to be successful. **1935** HOWARD & PATRY *Mental Health* xiv. 318 The enucleation of 'sore-spots' or complex-determined topics, memories, associations and reactions which require desensitization and replacement by more wholesome resources and performances. **1937** *Sunday Dispatch* 16 May 17 Thereafter, a course of special injections (known as 'desensitisation') is given in gradually increased doses to accustom the system to the guilty factor. **1937** *Discovery* Oct. 299/1 The fixing of a photographic plate by desensitisation. **1940** A. L. M. SOWERBY *Wall's Dict. Photogr.* (ed. 15) 190 A desensitiser is a substance which, when applied to a sensitive emulsion, reduces its sensitivity to light. **1951** R. MAYER *Artist's Hand-Bk.* xii. 383 The portions of the stone that have not been drawn upon are so desensitized that..if printing ink is smeared on these areas, it may easily be washed off. **1955** E. POUND *Section: Rock-Drill* xcii. 81 For 40 years I have seen..desensitization. **1955** *Sci. News Let.* 13 Aug. 106/3 Meanwhile, for the hay fever sufferer this season, shots to desensitize, or immunize, him against the pollens are the best that can be offered. **1959** *Chambers's Encycl.* I. 709/2 On the allergic hypothesis, desensitization of the patient to the allergens to which he is sensitive seems the most rational treatment to attempt. **1961** *Lancet* 19 Aug. 413/1 Bronchoconstriction and histamine release..were followed by desensitisation. *Ibid.* 413/2 The desensitising effects of increasing small doses of a specific antigen. **1967** E. CHAMBERS *Photolitho-Offset* xiii. 198 Whereas counter-etching is to clean the plate surface to hold the image, pre-etching follows counter-etching or surface treatment and is generally known as a desensitising etch. **1968** *Listener* 15 Feb. 205/2 The patient does desensitise with a tape-recorder alone, but one patient said that without the therapist she wouldn't continue treatment.

desequestrate (ˌdiːsɪˈkwɛstreɪt), *v.* [f. DE- II. 1 + SEQUESTRATE *v.*] *trans.* To release from sequestration; to return to its owner. So **ˌdesequeˈstration.**

1959 *Times* 12 Jan. 8/5, 378 British firms and properties, and about 10,000 current bank accounts..will be desequestrated as soon as an agreement has been signed. **1959** *Daily Tel.* 13 Mar. 21/3 The first Briton to apply for desequestration papers. *Ibid.*, Desequestration will not take place until his claim has been formally admitted.

desere(n, deserite, obs. ff. DISHEIR *v.*, DISHERIT.

desert (dɪˈzɜːt), *sb.*¹ Forms: 4- desert, 3-6 deserte, 4 desserte, 4-5 decert(e, dissert, 6 dyserte, 6-7 desart. [a. OF. *desert* masc., *deserte*, *desserte* fem., derivs. of *deservir*, *desservir* to DESERVE. The Fr. words are analogous to *descent*, *descente*, etc., and belong to an obs. pa. pple. *desert* of *deservir*, repr. late L. *-servīt-um* for *-servīt-um*.]

1. Deserving; the becoming worthy of recompense, i.e. of reward or punishment, according to the good or ill of character or conduct; worthiness of recompense, merit or demerit.

1297 R. GLOUC. (1724) 253 Vor þe soþuast God..Deþe after oure deserte. *c* **1325** *E.E. Allit. P.* A. 594 Þou quytez vchon as hys desserte. **1483** CAXTON *G. de la Tour* E vij b, God rewarded eche of them after their deserte and meryte. *a* **1541** WYATT *Poet. Wks.* (1861) 168 Such sauce as they have served To me without desart. **1615** CHAPMAN *Odyss.* I. 75 Ægisthus past his fate, and had desert To warrant our infliction. **1633** G. HERBERT *Temple, Sighs & Grones* i, O do not use me After my sinnes! look not on my desert. **1752** JOHNSON *Rambler* No. 193 ¶1 Some will always mistake the degree of their own desert. **1861** MILL *Utilit.* v. 66 What constitutes desert?..a person is understood to deserve good if he does right, evil if he does wrong.

b. In a good sense: Meritoriousness, excellence, worth.

c **1374** CHAUCER *Boeth.* III. pr. vi. 78 It semeþ þat gentilesse be a maner preysynge þat comeþ of decert of auncestres. *c* **1450** *St. Cuthbert* (Surtees) 473 For þe childes hye desert, God shewed meruaile in apert. **1590** MARLOWE *2nd Pt. Tamburl.* v. iii, If you retain desert of holiness. **1655** FULLER *Ch. Hist.* III. vi. §3 The Crown..due to him, no less by desert then descent. **1704** ADDISON *Poems, Campaign*, On the firm basis of desert they rise. **1798** *Trans. Soc. Encourag. Arts* XVI. 353, I visited him as a man of desert. **1840** MACAULAY *Clive* Ess. (1854) 538/1 Ordinary criminal justice knows nothing of set-off. The greatest desert cannot be pleaded in answer to a charge of the slightest transgression.

c. personified.

c **1600** SHAKS. *Sonn.* lxvi, To behold desert a begger borne And needie Nothing trimd in iollitie. **1608** D. T. *Ess. Pol. & Mor.* 38 To hinder Desert from any place of eminencie. **1866** G. MACDONALD *Ann. Q. Neighb.* xii. (1878) 234 Desert may not touch His shoe-tie.

2. An action or quality that deserves its appropriate recompense; that in conduct or character which claims reward or deserves punishment. Usually in *pl.* (often = 1.)

c **1374** CHAUCER *Troylus* III. 1218 (1267) If thi grace passe alle oure desertis. **1393** GOWER *Conf.* III. 154 He mote..Se the desertes of his men. **1549** COVERDALE *Erasm. Par. 2 Cor.* 51 As every mans desertes have been..such shall his rewardes be. **1555** WATREMAN *Fardle of Facions* I. v. 56 Punisshing thoffendour vnder his desertes. **1606** HOLLAND *Sueton.* 42 That neither himselfe nor the olde beaten soldiers might be rewarded according to their desarts. **1782** COWPER *Lett.* 6 Mar., The characters of great men, which are always mysterious while they live..sooner or later receive the wages of fame or infamy according to their true deserts. **1861** MILL *Utilit.* v. 92 To do to each according to his deserts.

b. A good deed or quality; a worthy or meritorious action; a merit. ? *Obs.*

[*c* **1374** CHAUCER *Boeth.* II. pr. vii. 56 Or doon goode decertes to profit of þe comune.] **1563** *Homilies* II. *Rogation Week* I. (1859) 472 Alwaies to render him thanks..for his deserts unto us. **1657** J. SMITH *Myst. Rhet.* 143 It..serves for Amplification, when, after a great crime, or desert, exclaimed upon or extolled, it gives a moral note.

3. That which is deserved; a due reward or recompense, whether good or evil. Often in phr. ***to get, have, meet with one's deserts.***

1393 LANGL. *P. Pl.* C. IV. 293 Mede and mercede..boþe men demen A desert for som doynge. **1483** CAXTON *G. de la Tour* F vij, For god gyueth to euery one the deserte of his meryte. *a* **1533** LD. BERNERS *Huon* lix. 204, I shall nother ete nor drynke tyll thou hast thy dysert. **1599** *Warning Faire Wom.* II. 1508 Upon a pillory..that al the world may see, A just desert for such impiety. **1663** BUTLER *Hud.* I. ii. 40 But give to each his due desart. **1758** S. HAYWARD *Serm.* i. 10 This is the proper desert of Sin. **1756** BURKE *Vind. Nat. Soc.* Wks. 1842 I. 18 Whether the greatest villain breathing shall meet his deserts. **1853** C. BRONTE *Villette* xli. (1876) 474, I think I deserved strong reproof; but when have we our deserts? **1882** OUIDA *Maremma* I. 41 'He has got his deserts', said Joconda.

desert ('dɛzət), *sb.*^{2} Forms: 3- desert; also 3 deserd, diserd, 4 dissert, desarte, dezert, 4-5 disert, 5 dysert, 5-6 deserte, 5-9 desart (which was the regularly accepted spelling of the 18th century). [a. OF. *desert* (12th c. in Littré), ad. eccl. L. *dēsertum* (Vulgate, etc.), absol. use of neuter of *dēsertus* adj., abandoned, deserted, left waste: see DESERT *a.*]

1. An uninhabited and uncultivated tract of country; a wilderness: **a.** now conceived as a desolate, barren region, waterless and treeless, and with but scanty growth of herbage;—e.g. the *Desert of Sahara*, *Desert of the Wanderings*, etc.

a **1225** *Ancr. R.* 220 Iðe desert..he lette ham þolien wo inouh. *c* **1250** *Gen. & Ex.* 2770 Moyses was..In ðe deserd depe. *a* **1300** *Cursor M.* 5840 (Gött.) Lat mi folk a-parte Pass, to worschip me in desarte [*v. rr.* desert, dishert]. *Ibid.* 6533 (Gött.) Quen [moyses] was comen into dissert. **1484** CAXTON *Fables of Alfonce* (1889) 2 He doubted to be robbed within the desertys of Arabe. **1634** SIR T. HERBERT *Trav.* 65 Barren Mountaynes, Sand and salty Desarts. **1691** RAY *Creation* I. (1704) 94 More parched than the Desarts of Libya. **1768** BOSWELL *Corsica* ii. (ed. 2) 117 [*tr.* Tacitus] Where they make a desert, they call it peace. **1771** SMOLLETT *Humph. Cl.* 12 Sept., She fluttered, and flattered, but all was preaching to the desert. **1815** ELPHINSTONE *Acc. Caubul* (1842) I. Introd. 25 He could live in his desart and hunt his deer. **1823** BYRON *Island* II. viii. *note*, The 'ship of the desert' is the Oriental figure for the camel or dromedary. **1856** STANLEY *Sinai & Pal.* i. (1858) 64 The Desert..a wild waste of pebbly soil.

†**b.** formerly applied more widely to any wild, uninhabited region, including forest-land. *Obs.*

1398 TREVISA *Barth. De P.R.* XIV. li. (1495) 486 Places of wodes and mountayns that ben not sowen ben callyd desertes. *c* **1511** *1st Eng. Bk. Amer.* (Arb.) Introd. 33/1 In our lande is also a grete deserte or forest. **1600** SHAKS. *A.Y.L.* II. vii. 110 In this desert inaccessible, Vnder the shade of melancholly boughes. **1643** DENHAM *Cooper's H.* 186 Cities in desarts, Woods in Cities plants. **1834** MEDWIN *Angler in Wales* I. 69 Moors covered with whinberry bushes ..A more uninteresting desert cannot be conceived.

2. *transf.* and *fig.*

1725 POPE *Odyss.* IV. 748 To roam the howling desart of the Main. **1813** BYRON *Giaour* 958 The leafless desert of the mind. **1827** SOUTHEY *Hist. Penins. War* II. 752 What in monastic language is called a desert; by which term an establishment is designated where those brethren whose piety flies the highest pitch may at once enjoy the advantages of the eremite and the discipline of the coenobite life. **1871** MORLEY *Voltaire* (1886) 243 The middle age between himself and the polytheism of the Empire was a parched desert to him.

†**3.** *abstractly.* Desert or deserted condition; desolation. *Obs.*

c **1450** *Merlin* 59 He was in a waste contree full of diserte. **1523** LD. BERNERS *Froiss.* I. cclxxxiv. 424 The distructyon and conquest of the cytie of Lymoges, and how it was left clene voyde as a towne of desert.

†**4.** An alleged name for a covey of lapwings.

1486 *Bk. St. Albans* F vj b, A Desserte of Lapwyngs. **1688** in R. HOLME *Armoury.*

5. *Comb.* **a.** *attrib.*, *as desert-air, -belt, -bird, -cave, -circle, -dweller, -folk, -pelican, -ranger, -troop*; **b.** locative and instrumental, as *desert-bred, -frequenting, -haunting, -locked, -wearied, -worn* adjs.; **c.** similative, as *desert-world; desert-brown, -grey, -like, -long, looking* adjs.; also **desert boot** (see quot. 1948); **desert-chough**, a bird of the genus *Podoces*, family *Corvidæ*, found in the desert regions of Central Asia; **desert-falcon**, a species of falcon inhabiting deserts and prairies, a member of the subgenus *Gennæa*, allied to the peregrines; **desert island**, an uninhabited, or seemingly uninhabited, and remote island; also *attrib.* and *fig.*, esp. (of equipment, cultural objects, or behaviour) suited to the social isolation and limited baggage allowance of a castaway on a desert island; **desert-lemon** *Austral.*, a rutaceous tree, *Eremocitrus glauca* (*Atalantia glauca*), bearing a small acid fruit; **desert oak** *Austral.* (see OAK 3 b); **desert pea** (see PEA^1 3); **desert polish**, the polish imparted to rocks or other hard surfaces by the friction of the windblown sand of the desert; **Desert Rat** *colloq.*, a soldier of the 7th (British) armoured division, whose divisional sign was the figure of a jerboa, and which took part in the desert campaign in N. Africa (1941-2); **desert-rod**, a genus of labiate plants (*Eremostachys*) from the Caucasus (*Treas. Bot.*); **desert-ship**, 'ship of the desert', the camel or dromedary; **desert-snake**, a serpent of the family *Psammophidæ*, a sand-snake; **desert varnish**, a dark-coloured film composed of iron and manganese oxides, usually with some silica, deposited on exposed rocks in the desert and becoming polished by wind abrasion; and in various specific names of plants and animals, as ***desert-lark, -mouse, -willow.***

1750 GRAY *Elegy* xiv, And waste its sweetness on the *desert air. **1913** KIPLING *Songs from Books* 142 For he knows which fountain dries, behind which *desert-belt. **1813** BYRON *Giaour* 950 The *desert-bird Whose beak unlocks her bosom's stream To still her famish'd nestlings' scream. **1948** PARTRIDGE *Dict. Forces' Slang* 54 **Desert boots*, brown boots reaching either halfway up the ankle or to just over it and tightly laced; they had crepe soles and, made of suede or of reversed calf, they did not need to be polished. **1964** *Listener* 12 Nov. 764/2 He was wearing suede desert boots. **1862** M. L. WHATELY *Ragged Life Egypt* x. (1863) 88 It [is] hard for any who are not *desert-bred to find their way. **1923** *Daily Mail* 5 Mar. 13 Nigger, Regal Blue, Grey, *Desert Brown. **1885** W. B. YEATS in *Dublin Univ. Rev.* Sept., In gloom Of *desert-caves. **1879** DOWDEN *Southey* vii. 193 The *desert-circle girded by the sky. **1810** SCOTT *Lady of L.* III. iv, The *desert-dweller met his path. **1916** R. GRAVES *Over the Brazier* 15 Soft words of grace He spoke Unto lost *desert-folk. **1872** 'MARK TWAIN' *Roughing It* (1882) v. 28 The *desert-frequenting tribes of Indians. **1905** *Westm. Gaz.* 28 Aug. 10/2 This species (*Varanus griseus*) is a large, desert-frequenting lizard. **1906** *Ibid.* 1 Oct. 4/3 The kiang [*sc.* wild ass] is a desert-frequenting species. **1901** *Ibid.* 2 Jan. 2/1 Two stalwart sportsmen with..their *desert-grey hounds gliding near them. **1894** R. B. SHARPE *Handbk. Birds Gt. Brit.* I. 112 From its pale coloration this Pipit might be considered a *desert-haunting bird. **1607** TOPSELL *Four-f. Beasts* 13 They are driuen to a coast vnnauigable, where were many *desart Islandes inhabited of wilde men. **1690** LOCKE *Govt.* II. §14 The Promises and Bargains.. between the two Men in the Desert Island, mentioned by Garcilasso De la vega,..are binding to them, though they are perfectly in a State of Nature. **1743** F. SHERIDAN *Let.* 16 Nov. in *Private Corresp. D. Garrick* (1831) I. 17 To something worse than the desert Island. **1856** C. M. YONGE *Daisy Chain* II. i. 337 It is like having all the Spaniards and savages spoiling Robinson Crusoe's desert island! **1922** C. E. MONTAGUE *Disenchantment* xiii. 175 All castaways together, all really marooned on the one desert island. **1930** F. BRETT YOUNG *Jim Redlake* III. v. 376, I always except the Meistersinger. I think I should choose it as my desert-island opera. **1939** *Mind* XLVIII. 156, I find that desert-island morality always rouses suspicion among ordinary men. **1942** *Radio Times* 23 Jan. 15/4 '*Desert Island Discs*'... Vic Oliver discusses with Roy Plomley the eight records he would choose if he were condemned to spend the rest of his life on a desert island with a gramophone for his entertainment. **1883** MISS C. F. GORDON CUMMING in *19th Cent.* Aug. 302 *Desert-larks, wheat-ears, and other..birds do their best to diminish the locusts. **1889** J. H. MAIDEN *Useful Native Plants Austral.* 8 *Atalantia glauca*,..'Native Kumquat', '*Desert Lemon'. **1621** LADY M. WROTH *Urania* 441 In the *Desert-like wildernes. **1872** BAKER *Nile Tribut.* xxii. 384 These *desert-locked and remote countries. **1932** AUDEN *Orators* III, Spare us the numbing zero-hour, The *desert-long retreat. **1844** *Mem. Babylonian P'cess.* II. 121 A sandy *desert-looking tract. **1896** *Desert oak [see OAK 3 b]. **1903** 'T. COLLINS' *Such is Life* 91 She had revelled in the audacious black-and-scarlet glory of the *desert pea. **1929** K. S. PRICHARD *Coonardoo* 217 It was a good season, the desert pea scarlet under the mulga. **1967** A. M. BLOMBERY *Guide Native Austral. Plants* 101 (*caption*) *Clianthus formosus* (Sturt's Desert Pea). **1845** MRS. NORTON *Child of Islands* (1846) 113 A *desert-pelican whose heart's best blood Oozed in slow drops. **1903** A. GEIKIE *Text-bk. Geol.* (ed. 4) I. III. II. i. 436 On the sandy plains of Wyoming, Utah, and the adjacent territories, surfaces even of such hard materials as chalcedony are etched into furrows and wrinkles, acquiring at the same time a peculiar and characteristic glaze ('*desert-polish'). **1822** J. MONTGOMERY *Hymn, 'Hail to the Lord's Anointed'* iv, Arabia's *desert-ranger To Him shall bow the knee. **1944** in *Shorter Oxf. Eng. Dict.* Add. (1956) 2487/3 As we stewed our tea—*desert-rat style. **1945** W. S. CHURCHILL *Victory* (1946) 217 Dear Desert Rats, may your glory ever shine. **1958** *Times* 17 Apr. 11/4 The desert rat insignia will continue to be worn by all officers and men of the 7th Armoured Brigade Group. **1824** BYRON *Def. Trans.* I. i. 116 The..patient swiftness of the *desert ship, The helmless dromedary! *a* **1845** HOOD *An Open Question* xiv, That desert-ship the camel of the East. **1821** SHELLEY *Prometh. Unb.* IV. 352 The brackish cup Drained by a *desert-troop. **1903** A. GEIKIE *Text-bk. Geol.* (ed. 4) II. 1425/1 *Desert-polish or varnish. **1904** C. R. VAN HISE *Treat. Metamorphism* 547 In arid regions the hardened film has frequently been smoothed by the wind-blown sand, so as to present a polished surface. Such polished hardened films are known as 'desert varnish'. **1944** A. HOLMES *Princ. Physical Geol.* xiii. 270 The loose salts are blown away, but oxides of iron, accompanied by traces of manganese and other similar oxides, form a red, brown, or black film which is firmly retained. The surfaces of long-exposed rocks and pebbles thus acquire a characteristic coat of 'desert varnish'. **1970** R. J. SMALL *Study Landforms* ix. 294 Capillary rise is associated with the chemical breakdown of the interior of large boulders and the deposition of a hard crust of 'desert varnish'..on their surface. **1827** KEBLE *Chr. Y.* 2nd Sund. after Easter, The *desert-wearied tribes. **1833** ROCK *Hierurg.* (1892) I. 182 Pilgrimage through this *desert-world. **1890** 'R. BOLDREWOOD' *Col. Reformer* ix, Sunburned and *desert-worn passengers.

desert, obs. form of DESSERT *sb.*

desert ('dɛzət), *a.* Also 4-6 deserte, 6-8 desart. [ME. *de'sert* a. OF. *desert*, mod.F. *dé-* (11th c.) = Pr. and Cat. *desert*, Sp. *desierto*, It. *deserto*:—L. *dēsert-us* abandoned, forsaken, left or lying waste, pa. pple. of *dēserĕre* to sever connexion with, leave, forsake, abandon, etc.: in later use treated as an attributive use of DESERT *sb.*^{2}, and stressed '*desert*; but the earlier stress is found archaically in 18-19th c. in sense 1.]

1. Deserted, forsaken, abandoned. *arch.*

Sometimes as pa. pple.: cf. DESERT *v.* 4.

1480 CAXTON *Chron. Eng.* ccxxvi. 233 Wyde clothes destytut and desert from al old honeste and good vsage. **1540** HYRDE tr. *Vive's Instr. Chr. Wom.* (1592) M vj, Noemy had beene a widow and desert in deede. **1633** P. FLETCHER *Poet. Misc., Elisa* II. iv, Her desert self and now cold Lord lamenting. **1774** S. WESLEY in *Westm. Mag.* II. 654 When.. lies desert the monumented clay. **1792** S. ROGERS *Pleas. Mem.* I. 69 As through the gardens desert paths I rove. **1868** MORRIS *Earthly Par.* I. 254 In that wan place desert of hope and fear.

2. Uninhabited, unpeopled, desolate, lonely.

(In mod. usage this sense and 3 are freq. combined.)

1297 R. GLOUC. 232 þe decyples..Byleuede in a wyldernesse..þat me clepuþ nou Glastynbury, þat desert was þo. *a* **1340** HAMPOLE *Psalter* Cant. 514 He fand him in land deserte. **1494** FABYAN *Chron.* I. ii. 9 This Ile w[t] Geaunts whylom inhabyt..Nowe beynge deserte. **1577** B. GOOGE *Heresbach's Husb.* III. (1586) 127 They seeke the secretest and desartest places that may be. **1697** DRYDEN *Virg. Georg.* I. 94 When Deucalion hurl'd His Mother's Entrails on the desart World. **1711** ADDISON *Spect.* No. 85 ¶2 Fallen asleep in a desart wood. **1856** BRYANT *Poems, To a Waterfowl* iv, The desert and illimitable air.

3. Uncultivated and unproductive, barren, waste; of the nature of a desert.

1393 GOWER *Conf.* III. 158 Prodegalite..is the moder of pouerte, Wherof the londes ben deserte. *c* **1460** FORTESCUE *Abs. & Lim. Mon.* xiii, The contre..was tho almost diserte ffor lakke off tillers. **1634** SIR T. HERBERT *Trav.* 52 The Countrey..is desart, sterile and full of loose sand. **1697** DRYDEN *Virg. Georg.* IV. 147 A thirsty Train That long have travell'd thro' a Desart Plain. **1716** LADY M. W. MONTAGU *Let. to C'tess of Mar* 17 Nov., The kingdom of Bohemia is the most desert of any I have seen in Germany. **1839** THIRLWALL *Greece* VI. li. 243 A cross-road leading over a desert arid tract.

4. *fig.* Dry, uninteresting. *rare.*

a **1674** MILTON *Hist. Mosc.* Pref. (1851) 470 To save the Reader a far longer travail of wandring through so many desert Authors.

desert (dɪ'zɜːt), *v.* [a. mod.F. *déserter* to abandon, in OF. to make desert, leave desert, = Pr. and Sp. *desertar*, It. *desertare* 'to make desart or desolate' (Florio), late L. *dēsertāre* (Du Cange), freq. of *dēserĕre* to abandon.]

1. *trans.* To abandon, forsake, relinquish, give up (a thing); to depart from (a place or position).

1603 in Grant *Burgh Sch. Scotl.* II. xiii. 365 He..was resoluit to obey God calling him thairto, and to leave and desert the said school. **1651** HOBBES *Leviath.* II. xxx. 175 He that deserteth the Means, deserteth the Ends. **1715-20** POPE *Iliad* XIV. 488 His slacken'd hand deserts the lance it bore. **1784** COWPER *Task* I. 392 The languid eye, the cheek Deserted of its bloom. *c* **1790** WILLOCK *Voy.* 250 We resolved to run every risk rather than desert her [a ship]. **1798** H. SKRINE *Two Tours Wales* 6 Here deserting its banks, we climbed the hills. **1875** JOWETT *Plato* (ed. 2) IV. 8 Here ..Plato seems prepared to desert his ancient ground. **1879** LUBBOCK *Sci. Lect.* ii. 36 Such a plant would soon be deserted.

2. To forsake (a person, institution, cause, etc. having moral or legal claims upon one); *spec.* of a soldier or sailor: To quit without permission, run away from (the service, his colours, ship, post of duty, commander, or comrades).

1647 CLARENDON *Hist. Reb.* II. (1843) 44/1 His affection to the church so notorious, that he never deserted it. **1654** tr. *Martini's Conq. China* 182 Kiangus seeing himself deserted of the Tartars..returned to the City. **1700** S. L. tr. *Fryke's Voy. E. Ind.* 277 The Dutch that sometimes desert us, and go over to the King of Candi. *c* **1790** WILLOCK *Voy.* 175 The christian merchants..totally deserted him. **1791** MRS. RADCLIFFE *Rom. Forest* xii, The offence you have committed by deserting your post. **1891** SIR H. C. LOPES in *Law Times' Rep.* LXV. 603/1 A husband deserts his wife if he wilfully absents himself from her society, in spite of her wish.

b. To abandon or give up *to* something. *arch.*

1658 J. WEBB tr. *Cleopatra* VIII. ii. 53 The Princesse.. deserted her soul to the most violent effects of Passion. **1673** MILTON *True Relig.* Wks. (1847) 563/2 It cannot be imagined that God would desert such painful and zealous labourers..to damnable errours. **1812** LANDOR *Count Julian* Wks. 1846 II. 508 Gracious God! Desert me to my sufferings, but sustain My faith in Thee!

c. Of powers or faculties: To fail so as to disappoint the needs or expectations of.

1667 MILTON *P.L.* VIII. 563 Wisdom..deserts thee not. **1748** *Anson's Voy.* II. x. (ed. 4) 322 The infallibility of the Holy Father had..deserted him. **1875** JOWETT *Plato* (ed. 2) I. 260 In the presence of Socrates, his thoughts seem to desert him.

†**d.** To fall short of (a standard). *Obs. rare.*

1664 POWER *Exp. Philos.* II. 91 The Quicksilver..will not much desert nor surmount the determinate height..of 29 inches.

3. *intr.* (or *absol.*) To forsake one's duty, one's post, or one's party; *esp.* of a soldier or sailor: To quit or run away from the service in violation of oath or allegiance.

1689 *Jrnl. Ho. Lords*, The Lords Spiritual..who Deserted (not Protested) against the Vote in the House of Peers. **1693** W. Freke *Art of War* v. 247 Hannibal finding his Souldiers desert. **1792** *Gentl. Mag.* LXII. i. 561 The fourth regiment..deserted in a body with their Colonel at their head. **1802–3** tr. *Pallas' Trav.* (1812) II. 299 The Kozaks.. deserted to the Turks. **1840** Thirlwall *Greece* VII. lvii. 230 He deserted in the midst of the battle.

4. *Sc. Law.* **a.** *trans.* (with pa. pple. in 6 **desert.**) To relinquish altogether, or to put off for the time (a suit or 'diet'); to prorogue (Parliament). **b.** *intr.* To cease to have legal force, become inoperative.

1539 *Sc. Acts Jas. V* (1814) 353 (Jam.) That this present parliament proceide..quhill it pleiss the kingis grace that the samin be desert. **1569** *Diurn. Occurr.* (1833) 152 Thair foir that the saidis lettres sould desert in thameselff. **1752** J. Louthian *Form of Process* (ed. 2) 251 For deserting a Diet, or assoilizieing a Pannel. **1773** Erskine *Inst.* iv. (Jam.), If any of the executions appear informal, the court deserts the diet. **1861** W. Bell *Dict. Law Scotl.* s.v. *Desertion*, To desert the diet *simpliciter*..will..put a stop to all further proceedings.

Hence **de'serting** *vbl. sb.* and *ppl. a.*

1646 J. Whitaker *Uzziah* 23 His just deserting of them. **1700** Dryden *Palam. & Arc.* iii. 411 Bought senates and deserting troops are mine. **1883** *Times* 27 Aug. 3/6 Colonel Rubalcaba..almost single-handed, had pursued his deserting regiment.

deserted (dɪˈzɜːtɪd), *ppl. a.* [f. desert *v.* + -ed.] Forsaken, abandoned, left desolate.

1629 J. Maxwell tr. *Herodian* (1635) 413 The deserted Villages. **1667** Milton *P.L.* iv. 922 Thy deserted host. **1751** Johnson *Rambler* No. 107 ¶8 The hospital for the reception of deserted infants. **1769** Goldsmith (*title*) The Deserted Village: a Poem. **1855** Macaulay *Hist. Eng.* IV. 212 The deserted hamlets were then set on fire.

de'sertedness. [f. prec. + -ness.] Deserted condition, forlorn desolation.

1818 *Blackw. Mag.* III. 219 The..unexpected desertedness..of this romantic city. **1866** Alger *Solit. Nat. & Man* ii. 37 True desertedness and its pangs.

deserter (dɪˈzɜːtə(r)). Also 7 desertor, -our. [f. desert *v.* + -er[1]; after F. *déserteur*, L. *dēsertor* one who forsakes, abandons, or deserts, agent-noun from *dēserĕre* to leave, forsake.]

1. One who forsakes or abandons a person, place, or cause; usually with implied breach of duty or allegiance. Const. *of.*

1635 A. Stafford *Fem. Glory* (1869) 80 A base Desertour of my Mother Church. **1697** Dryden *Virg. Georg.* iv. 91 Streight to their ancient Cells..The reconcil'd Deserters will repair. **1769** *Junius Lett.* xv. 64 A submissive administration..collected from the deserters of all parties. **1885** *Act. 48–9 Vict.* c. 60 §15 The extradition of offenders (including deserters of wives and children).

2. *esp.* A soldier or seaman who quits the service without permission, in violation of oath or allegiance.

1667 *Decay Chr. Piety* iii. §7. 219 We are the same desertors whether we stay in our own camp, or run over to the enemy's. **1700** S. L. tr. *Fryke's Voy. E. Ind.* 91 These we immediately hung up..as it is the constant custom, which the Dutch observe whenever they catch any of their Deserters. **1841** Elphinstone *Hist. Ind.* II. 165 Deserters of different ranks came in from Cábul.

attrib. **1871** *Daily News* 13 Jan., The deserter officers.

desertful (dɪˈzɜːtfʊl), *a.*[1] ? *Obs.* [f. desert *sb.*[1] + -ful.] Of great desert; meritorious, deserving. Const. *of.*

1583 Golding *Calvin on Deut.* lxxxiv. 518 To shewe that God is beholden to vs, that our workes are desertfull. **1621** Fletcher *Wild-Goose Chase* v. vi, Till I be more desertful in your eye. **1638** Ford *Lady's Trial* iv. i, Therein He shews himself desertful of his happiness.

†**de'sertful,** *a.*[2] *Obs. rare.* [f. desert *sb.*[2] + -ful.] Desert, desolate.

1601 Chester *Loues Mart.* 21 Enuie, go packe thee..To some desertfull plaine or Wildernesse.

de'sertfully, *adv.* [f. desertful *a.*[1] + -ly.] By desert, deservingly, rightfully.

1598 Munday & Chettle *Downf. Earl Huntington* ii. ii. in Hazl. *Dodsley* VIII. 132 As Lacy lies, Desertfully, for pride and treason stabb'd. **1619** *Time's Storehouse* 58/2 (L.), Aristotle (and very desertfully) calleth the commonwealth of the Massilians oligarchia. **1625** *Modell Wit* 62 Wherefore desertfully..a fault of diuers conditions..ought not to bee censured with one and the same punishment.

desertic (dɪˈzɜːtɪk), *a.* [f. desert *sb.*[2] + -ic.] Characteristic of a desert. Also *fig.*

1936 *Nature* 19 Dec. 1042/1 With development of desertic conditions in North Africa and Arabia bringing increasing settlement near rivers, some degree of isolation and a high degree of long-continued local intermarriage developed. **1956** Wyndham Lewis *Red Priest* xxxiii. 286 There is nothing awaiting me but a hideous desertic existence. **1963** D. W. & E. E. Humphries tr. *Termier's Erosion & Sedimentation* 406 *Hamada*.., an Arabic term used in the Sahara to describe a bare stony plain... It is a typical feature of the desertic climate.

desertification (dɛˌzɜːtɪfɪˈkeɪʃən). [f. desert *sb.*[2] + -ification.] The process of becoming or rendering desert; the transformation of fertile land into desert or arid waste, esp. as a result of human activity.

[**1968** H. N. le Hourerou in *Annales Algériennes de Géographie* III. vi. 6 (*heading*) Désertisation ou désertification?] **1974** *Collier's Year Bk. 1974* 555/2 The governing council..established as priorities the concerns of the developing countries..health, land, water, and 'desertification'. **1977** *Observer* 28 Aug. 4/1 The small circles of desert around waterholes and settlements join up and spread outwards, until a new desert has been created... Desertification is overwhelmingly a man-made process. **1979** *Nature* 4 Jan. 2/2 As increasingly marginal land is brought under cultivation, deforestation and desertification will increase. **1980** J. Mercer *Canary Islanders* 8 The approach of the Pleistocene ice to the north and of desertification to the south brought an end to the Tethys flora. **1984** *Times* 17 Feb. 6/1 A reassessment of the areas threatened by desertification now indicates that 135 million people live in areas severely affected.

Hence (as a back-formation) **de'sertified** *ppl. a.*

1980 *Times* 5 June 25/4 Excessively low productivity of the desertified centre. **1982** *Christian Science Monitor* 28 June 6/3 Altogether, 1,490,000 square kilometers, or 15.5 percent of all China's land, is arid, and of this 328,000 square kilometers, 3.4 percent, is desertified.

desertion (dɪˈzɜːʃən). Also 7 dissertion. [a. F. *désertion* (1414 in Hatzf.), ad. L. *dēsertiōn-em*, n. of action from *dēserĕre* to forsake, abandon, f. de- I. 2 + *serĕre* to join.]

1. The action of deserting, forsaking, or abandoning, *esp.* a person or thing that has moral or legal claims to the deserter's support; sometimes simply, abandonment of or departure from a place.

1591 W. Perkins (*title*), Spiritual Desertions, seruing to Terrifie all Drowsie Protestants. **1612–15** Bp. Hall *Contempl., N.T.* iv. vi, Season, and sea, and wind, and their Master's desertion, had agreed to render them perfectly miserable. **1651** Davenant *Gondibert* ii. iii. lxiv, These scorn the Courts dissertion of their age. **1671** Milton *Samson* 632 Swoonings of despair, And sense of Heaven's desertion. **1683** *Brit. Spec.* 178 After the Desertion of this Island by the Romans. **1751** Johnson *Rambler* No. 170 ¶13 Mingled his assurances of protection..with threats of total desertion. **1856** Kane *Arct. Expl.* II. xxviii. 278 A desertion of the coast and a trial of the open water. **1875** Jowett *Plato* I. 341 He is certain that desertion of his duty is an evil.

2. *Law.* The wilful abandonment of an employment or of duty, in violation of a legal or moral obligation; *esp.* such abandonment of the military or naval service. Also, wilful abandonment of the conjugal society, without reasonable cause, on the part of a husband or wife.

1712 W. Rogers *Voy.* Introd. 18 In case of Death, Sickness or Desertion of any of the above Officers. **1811** Wellington in Gurw. *Desp.* VIII. 292 They have nearly put a stop to desertion from the enemy's ranks. **1840** Thirlwall *Greece* VII. lvii. 231 Ranks thinned by frequent desertions. **1891** Sir H. C. Lopes in *Law Times' Rep.* LXV. 603/1 To constitute desertion the parties must be living together as man and wife when the desertion takes place.

3. *Sc. Law.* ***desertion of the diet***: Abandonment of proceedings on the libel in virtue of which the panel has been brought into court; which may be *simpliciter*, altogether, or *pro loco et tempore*, temporarily. See desert *v.* 4.

1861 W. Bell *Dict. Law Scotl.* 281/1 The effect of such a [*simpliciter*] desertion of the diet is declared to be, that the panel shall be for ever free of all challenge or question touching that offence.

4. Deserted condition; desertedness.

1751 Johnson *Rambler* No. 174 ¶13, I was convinced, by a total desertion, of the impropriety of my conduct. **1821** Southey *Vis. Judgem.* iii, That long drear dream of desertion. **1876** Farrar *Marlb. Serm.* vi. 51 The College buildings will be almost melancholy in their desertion and silence.

†**b.** *Theol.* 'Spiritual despondency: a sense of the dereliction of God' (Johnson). *Obs.*

a **1716** South (J.), The spiritual agonies of a soul under desertion.

†**desertive** (dɪˈzɜːtɪv), *a. Obs. rare.* [f. desert *sb.*[1] + -ive.] Meritorious, worthy.

1596 Nashe *Saffron Walden* 124 Master Bodley, a Gentleman..of singular desertiue reckoning and industrie.

desertization (dɛsətaɪˈzeɪʃən). [ad. F. *désertisation* (1968, H. N. le Hourerou in *Annales Algériennes de Géographie* III. vi. 5), f. desert *sb.*[2] + -ization.] = desertification.

1968 H. N. le Hourerou in *Annales Algériennes de Géographie* III. vi. 5 (*Summary*) The author attempts to define *desertization* as a more or less irreversible reduction in vegetation, leading to the extension of desert lands to regions that did not show those characteristics. **1972** *Science* 1 Sept. 764/1 The process often called 'savannization' and 'desertization' of the tropical humid regions can very well be explained by these characteristics. **1976** *Daily Colonist* (Victoria, B.C.) 24 Nov. 5/4 The creation of desert by any phenomena—man-made or natural—is called desertization. **1977** A. Hallam *Planet Earth* 86 Removal of vegetation for firewood or by the grazing of domesticated animals exposes the soil to wind erosion, resulting in dune development and encroachment, and to the erosive action of the infrequent high intensity storms, which produce gully systems (arroyos) with alarming rapidity. These phenomena are known collectively as desertization.

desertless (dɪˈzɜːtlɛs), *a.*[1] [f. desert *sb.*[1] + -less.]

1. Without desert or merit: undeserving.

1601 Cornwallyes *Ess.* ii. li. (1631) 329 If desertlesse the begger and you differ but in the quantitie. **1631** Heywood *Maid of West* ii. i. Wks. 1874 II. 352 Prize me low And of desertlesse merit. **1700** Astry tr. *Saavedra-Faxardo* II. 108 He promis'd to reform the Militia, and afterwards admitted Persons wholly desertless. **1891** *Pall Mall G.* 23 Dec. 2/3 Constant to her desertless husband.

†**2.** Unmerited, undeserved. *Obs.*

1556 J. Heywood *Spider & F.* xv. 47 This augmenteth my greefe, Thus to be chargde, with desertles repreefe. **1600** Dekker *Gentle Craft* Wks. 1873 I. 74 Your Grace..Heapt on the head of this degenerous boy, Desertless favours. **1613–31** *Primer our Lady* 366 The mother wailing For her Sons desertlesse paine.

†**3.** Involving no recompense or reward; thankless.

1607 Tourneur *Rev. Trag.* iii. vi, I am allotted To that desertlesse office, to present you With the yet bleeding head. **1615** T. Adams *Lycanthropy* Ep. Ded. 1 It is no desertlesse office to discover that insatiate beast.

Hence **de'sertlessly** *adv.*, undeservedly.

1611 Beaum. & Fl. *King & no King* iii. ii, People will call you valiant; desertlessly I think.

desertless (ˈdɛzətlɪs), *a.*[2] *rare.* [f. desert *sb.*[2] + -less.] Without or devoid of desert land.

1822 *New Monthly Mag.* IV. 374 We recognize the lion as having some other relation to our desertless island.

desertness (ˈdɛzətnɪs). [f. desert *a.* + -ness.] Desert condition; barren desolation.

a **1400** *Cov. Myst.* (Shaks. Soc.) 203 In whylsum place of desertnes. **1548** Udall, etc. *Erasm. Par. Luke* v. 64 The desertenesse of the countrey liyng waste. *a* **1656** Ussher *Ann.* (1658) 773 The desertnesse of the Country..did much afflict them. **1860** Ruskin *Mod. Paint.* V. ix. i. 201 True desertness is not in the want of leaves, but of life.

†**de'sertrice.** *Obs. rare.* [f. deserter: on the type of F. feminines, e.g. *acteur, actrice*: see -trice.] A female deserter.

1645 Milton *Tetrach.* (1851) 166 Cleave to a Wife, but let her bee a wife..not an adversary, not a desertrice.

So also **de'sertress, de'sertrix.** [see -trix.] In mod. Dicts.

†**de'sertuous, de'sartuous,** *a. Obs.* [irreg. f. L. *dēsertum* desert *sb.*[2] + -ous.] Of the nature of a desert; of or pertaining to a desert.

1632 Lithgow *Trav.* vi. 253 In all this deformed Countrey, wee saw neyther house, nor Village, for it is altogether desartuous. *Ibid.* vii. 320 The Isthmus, and Confine of Desartuous Arabia. *Ibid.* ix. 378 My Desartuous wandring.

'deserty, *a.* [f. desert *sb.*[2] + -y.] Having the quality of a desert.

1891 W. S. Hawkes in *Chicago Advance* 29 Jan., The most deserty of deserts, where there is not a green thing.

†**de'servably,** *adv. Obs. rare.* [f. **deservable* (f. deserve *v.* + -able).] Deservedly, justly.

1593 Q. Eliz. *Boethius* iv. 86 Want of punishment, which deserueably thy self hast confest is the greatest yll Iniquitie can haue.

deserve (dɪˈzɜːv), *v.* Forms: 4– **deserve**; also 4 de-, des-, discerve, desserve, 4–6 disserve, 6 dyserve. [a. OF. *deserv-ir*, now (for sake of pronunciation) *desservir*:—L. *dēservīre* to serve zealously, well, or meritoriously, f. de- I. 3 + *servīre* to serve: hence, in late pop. L., to merit by service.]

†**1.** *trans.* To acquire or earn a rightful claim, by virtue of actions or qualities, to (something); to become entitled to or worthy of (reward or punishment, esteem or disesteem, position, designation, or any specified treatment). *Obs.* or *arch.*

[**1292** Britton v. x. §5 Si ele ne puisse averrer..qe ele pout dowarie aver deservi.] *c* **1325** *E.E. Allit. P.* B. 613 3yf euer þy mon vpon molde merit disserued. *c* **1340** *Cursor M.* 10350 (Trin.) Childre þat..ofte deseruen [*Laud* decervyn] muchel mede. *c* **1400** *Rom. Rose* 3093, I drede youre wrath to disserve. **1495** *Act II Hen. VII*, c. 22 §4 Artificers..waste moch part of the day and deserve not their wagis. *a* **1533** Ld. Berners *Huon* lxiii. 219 Honoure is dewe to them that dyserueth it. **1590** Shaks. *Mids. N.* ii. ii. 124 When at your hands did I deserue this scorne? **1713** Addison *Cato* i. ii, 'Tis not in mortals to Command Success, But we'll do more, Sempronius; we'll Deserve it.

†**b.** *Const.* with *inf. Obs.* or *arch.*

c **1385** Chaucer *L.G.W.* Prol. 502 That hast deseruyd sorere for to smerte. *c* **1400** Maundev. (1839) ix. 200 Men that han disserved to ben dede.

†**c.** with indirect obj. and subord. clause. *Obs.*

1529 More *Dyaloge* iv. Wks. 268/1 Nor neuer deserued we vnto him y^t he should so much doe for vs.

2. To have acquired, and thus to have, a rightful claim to; to be entitled to, in return for services or meritorious actions, or sometimes for ill deeds and qualities; to be worthy to have. (Now the ordinary sense, in which *to deserve* is the result of *having deserved* in sense 1.)

[*c* **1400** Maundev. (Roxb.) Prol. 1 He desserued neuer nane euill; for he did neuer euill, ne thoght neuer euill.] *c* **1440** *Promp. Parv.* 120 Deservyn..be worthy to havyn (K), *mereor.* *c* **1500** *New Not-br. Mayd* in *Anc. Poet. Tracts* (Percy Soc.) 46 Mercy or grace, A fore your face, He none deserueth in dede. **1599** H. Buttes *Dyets drie Dinner* G v, We have many other herbes which deserve that name. **1599** Shaks. *Much Ado* III. i. 45 Doth not the Gentleman Deserue as full as fortunate a bed? **1631** Shirley *Love Tricks* v. ii, He gave me two or three kicks, which I deserved well enough. **1651** Hobbes *Leviath.* II. xxvii. 156 All Crimes doe equally deserve the name of Injustice. **1668** Lady Chaworth in *12th Rep. Hist. MSS. Comm.* App. v. 10 Mr. Ho.. deserves a better fate than to be ever of the loosing side. **1676** Lister in *Ray's Corr.* (1848) 124, I am well pleased your Catalogue of Plants is again to be printed: it certainly deserves it. **1716** Lady M. W. Montagu *Lett.* 10 Oct. (1887) I. 128, I deserve not all the reproaches you make me. *c* **1850** *Arab. Nts.* 546 Do you think that you deserve the favour? *Mod.* The subject deserves fuller treatment than can be given to it here.

fig. or *transf.* *a* **1631** Donne *Lett., To Mrs. B. White* (1651) 6 Not to return til towards Christmas, except the business deserve him not so long.

b. *Const.* with *inf.*

1585 J. B. tr. *Viret's Sch. Beastes* A iv b, Yf the beastes do better their office.. then men doe theirs, they deserve more to be called reasonable, then men. **1612** Brinsley *Lud. Lit.* xiii. (1627) 174 Herein many a Master deserves rather to be beaten then the scholler. **1841–4** Emerson *Ess., Spir. Laws* Wks. (Bohn) I. 65 Only those books come down which deserve to last. **1856** Froude *Hist. Eng.* (1858) I. ii. 90 The clergy had won the battle then because they deserved to win it.

3. *absol.* or. *intr.* †**a.** To become entitled to the fitting recompense of action, character, or qualities. **b.** To be so entitled; to have just claims for reward or punishment; to merit, be worthy. Often in phr. ***to deserve ill*** or ***well of***.

c **1300** *Treat. Pop. Science* 140 And went wheder heo hath deserved, to joye other to pyne. *a* **1340** Hampole *Psalter* xvi. 1 Here me as my rightwisnes deserues. *c* **1400** *Destr. Troy* 12029 Ryches.. To be delt to þe dughti.. As þai sothly desseruyt. **1535** Coverdale *Eccl.* ix. 5 They yᵗ be deed, knowe nothinge, nether deserue they eny more. *a* **1669** Trapp in Spurgeon *Treas. Dav.* Ps. vii. 16 Executed at Tyburn, as he had well deserven. **1697** Dryden *Virg. Georg.* IV. 136 That he, who best deserves, alone may reign. **1709** Hearne *Collect.* (Oxf. Hist. Soc.) II. 234 He deserves well of the Publick. **1811** Genl. Floyd in Southey *Life Bell* (1844) II. 640 You would, indeed, to use the French phrase, 'Deserve well of the country.' **1840** Thackeray *Paris Sk. Bk., Fr. Fashion. Novels*, Deputies who had deserved well of their country. **1875** Jowett *Plato* (ed. 2) V. 348 Slaves ought to be punished as they deserve.

c. in implied good sense.

1608 Middleton *Trick to catch Old One* I. i, Find him so officious to deserve, So ready to supply! **1752** Young *Brothers* IV. i, While you deserved, my passion was sincere.

†**4.** *trans.* To secure by service or quality of action; to earn, win. **b.** Const. *to* (= for): To earn or win for (another). *Obs.*

1377 Langl. *P. Pl.* B. xiv. 134 Selden deieth he out of dette þat dyneth ar he deserue it. **1393** Gower *Conf.* III. 299 He.. which had his prise deserved.. Was made begin a middel borde. *c* **1440** *Gesta Rom.* x. 29 (Harl. MS.) Me most euery day nedis laboure, and deserue viij pense. *c* **1500** *Lancelot* 1027 Tharfor y red hir thonk at þow disserue. **1590** Marlowe *Edw. II*, IV. ii, But by the sword, my lord, 't must be deserv'd.

b. **1398** Trevisa *Barth. De P.R.* II. xvii. (1495) 43 And in prayenge the angel deseruyth mede to vs. *c* **1449** Pecock *Repr.* II. xix. 266 A cros.. was the instrument wher yn Crist .. deserued to us al oure good. **1628** Gaule *Pract. Th.* (1629) 10 How.. could the humane Nature of ours deserue that to vs which his own could not deserue vnto it selfe?

†**5.** To serve, do service to; to be serviceable or subservient to; to serve or treat well, to benefit. *Obs.*

c **1340** *Cursor M.* 8405 (Trin.) Þat neuer did ne disserued [*Cott.* seruid] vileny. **1382** Wyclif *Heb.* xiii. 16 By suche oostis God is disseruyd. **1501** Douglas *Pal. Hon.* Prol. 93 How lang sall I thus foruay Quhilk ȝow and Venus in this garth deseruis? **1625** Massinger *New Way* IV. ii, Of all the scum that grew rich by my riots, This.. and this.. have worst deserved me. **1634** —— *Very Woman* II. iii, You in this Shall much deserve me.

†**b.** *intr.* with *to*, *for*, or *infinitive* in same sense. *Obs.*

c **1380** Wyclif *Serm.* Sel. Wks. II. 250 Loue techiþ to forȝeue hem and disserue to hem. *c* **1450** tr. *De Imitatione* III. lv, Thou knowist.. hov muche tribulacion deseruiþ to purge þe rust of my vices. *c* **1460** *Bp. Grosseteste's Househ. Stat.* in *Babees Bk.* (1868) 330 The vessels deseruyng for ale and wyne. **1526** *Pilgr. Perf.* (W. de W. 1531) 109 b, For these vertues.. deserueth to the gyfte of pite, and thexercyse of them disposeth.. man to the perfeccyon of the same.

†**6.** *trans.* To give in return for service rendered; to pay back, requite. *Obs.*

c **1385** Chaucer *L.G.W.* 1624 *Medea*, My might, ne my labour, May nat disserve it in myn lyvys day. **1393** Gower *Conf.* III. 156 But other, which have nought deserved Through vertue.. A king shall nought deserve grace. **1470–85** Malory *Arthur* II. ix, I am moche beholdyng vnto hym, & I haue yll deserued it vnto hym for his kyndenes. **1523–5** Ld. Berners *Froiss.* II. 638 (R.) Whereof we shall thanke you, and deserve it to you and yours.

deserved (dɪ'zɜːvd, -ɪd), *ppl. a.* [f. prec. + -ed.]

1. Rightfully earned; merited.

1552 Huloet, Deserued, *meritus.* **1579** Sidney *Apol. Poetrie* (Arb.) 20 His deserued credite. **1607** Shaks. *Cor.* III. iii. 140 Giue him deseru'd vexation. **1709** Steele *Tatler* No. 9 ¶1 The Old Batchelor, a Comedy of deserved Reputation. **1828** Scott *F.M. Perth* xxxii, The day of thy deserved doom. **1859** F. Hall *Vásavadattá*, Pref. 46 Commentaries which are held in deserved esteem.

†**2.** That has deserved [L. *meritus*]; meritorious, worthy; = deserving *ppl. a.* *Obs. rare.*

1607 Shaks. *Cor.* III. i. 292 Rome, whose Gratitude Towards her deserued Children, is enroll'd.

deservedly (dɪ'zɜːvɪdlɪ), *adv.* [f. deserved + -ly².] Cf. L. *merito.*] According to desert or merit; rightfully, worthily.

1548 Thomas *Ital. Gram.*, *Meritamente*, woorthely or deseruedly. **1576** Fleming *Panopl. Epist.* 415 It may deservedly challenge immortalitie. **1671** Milton *P.R.* I. 407 Deservedly thou griev'st, composed of lies. **1709** Addison *Tatler* No. 122 ¶1 A People of so much Virtue were deservedly placed at the Head of Mankind. **1872** Jenkinson *Guide Eng. Lakes* (1879) 176 Some of the views are much and deservedly admired.

de'servedness. [f. as prec. + -ness.] The quality of having deserved; desert, worthiness; in good sense, excellence.

a **1628** F. Greville *Sidney* (1652) 24 No exterior Signe of degree, or deservedness. **1643** T. Goodwin *Aggrav. Sin* 31 Daniel would convince Balshazzar of his deservednesse to lose his Kingdome. **1889** A. P. Foster in *Chicago Advance* 28 Mar., The deservedness of his cause.

de'serveless, *a. rare.* [f. deserve *v.* + -less.] Undeserving.

1648 Herrick *Hesper.*, *To his Bk.* (1869) 79 Deserveless of the name of Paragon.

Hence **de'servelessly** *adv.*, undeservedly, unjustifiably.

1654 Vilvain *Epit. Ess.* IV. 77 Henry put to death deservelesly [*printed* deservdlesly], Two Noblemen.

deserver (dɪ'zɜːvə(r)). In 6 -our. [f. deserve *v.* + -er¹. Cf. OF. *deserveor*, *-eur* (Godef.).] One who deserves or merits; *esp.* one who deserves well.

1549 Udall, etc. *Erasm. Par. 1 Tim.* vi. 2 More is to be done for yᵉ deseruour than for the exactour, more for the louyng maister [etc.]. **1606** Shaks. *Ant. & Cl.* I. ii. 193 Whose Loue is neuer link'd to the deseruer, Till his deserts are past. **1623** Bingham *Xenophon* 139 Kinde remembrers of your well deseruers. **1631** Laud *Wks.* (1853) V. 256 The man certainly is an ill deserver. **1704** Swift *T. Tub* iii. Wks. 1760 I. 48 Other great deservers of mankind. **1829** E. Bather *Serm.* II. 364 Christ is the deserver of everything for sinners.

†**de'serveress.** *Obs.* [f. prec. + -ess.] A female deserver.

1612 Shelton *Quix.* I. I. i. 3 Make you Deserveress of the Deserts that your Greatness deserves. **1710** Steele *Tatler* No. 178 ¶1.

†**de'service.** *Obs. rare*⁻¹. In 5 -yce. [f. deserve *v.*, after *service.* (OF. had *deservice* = disservice.)] = desert *sb.*¹; deserving.

1480 Caxton *Chron. Eng.* lxxviii. 64 He reproued.. lyther tyrants and hem chastysed after hir deseruyse.

†**de'servient,** *ppl. a. Obs.* [ad. L. *dēservient-em*, pr. pple. of *dēservīre* to serve zealously, etc.] Of service, helpful.

1578 Banister *Hist. Man* I. 22 Passages.. deseruient to the transmitting of Sinewes. **1661** *Sir H. Vane's Politicks* 12 More sutable to the Time, then deservient to Necessity.

deserving (dɪ'zɜːvɪŋ), *vbl. sb.* [f. deserve *v.* + -ing¹.] Desert, merit; = desert *sb.*¹

1388 Wyclif *Ps.* vii. 5 Falle Y, bi disseruyng. **1482** *Monk of Evesham* (Arb.) 37 Aftyr ther olde merytys and deseruynges.. holpe.. or lettyd. *a* **1541** Wyatt *Poet. Wks.* (1861) 185 Chastise me not for my deserving According to thy just conceived ire. **1600** E. Blount tr *Conestaggio* 94 Striving to make knowne his better deserving. **1721** Cibber *Love in Riddle* II. i, My weak Praise would wrong his full Deservings. **1814** Mrs. J. West *Alicia de Lacy* I. 181 Was he, indeed.. ignorant of his own deserving? **1866** Kingsley *Herew.* iii, Ah, that he would reward the proud according to their deservings.

de'serving, *ppl. a.* [f. as prec. + -ing².] **a.** That deserves (good, ill, etc.); used contextually with either sense implied; but *esp.* in a good sense, meritorious, worthy. Esp. in phr. ***deserving poor.***

1576 Fleming *Panopl. Epist.* 117 Your meritorious and wel deserving behaviour. *c* **1610** Middleton, etc. *Widow* I. i, To the deservingest of all her sex. **1676** Dryden *Aurengz.* v. i. p. 77 Cease to grieve And for a more deserving Husband live. *a* **1685** Otway (J.), Courts are the places.. Where the deserving ought to rise. **1801** *Observer* 29 Nov. 4/2 [The bill] proposed to enable Overseers to relieve the deserving Poor. **1828** G. W. Bridges *Ann. Jamaica* II. xv. 224 Severer punishment upon the deserving culprits. *a* **1897** *Mod.* The problem of the relief of the deserving poor. **1971** B. Inglis *Poverty & Industrial Revolution* i. 17 The deserving poor had been issued with small badges which served as a kind of begging licence.

b. Const. *of* (rarely omitted).

1769 Goldsmith *Rom. Hist.* (1786) II. 259 He was highly deserving this distinction. **1813** J. Thomson *Lect. Inflam.* 171 Observations the more deserving of your attention. **1854** J. S. C. Abbott *Napoleon* (1855) II. xii. 206 They all appeared deserving his attention. **1855** Macaulay *Hist. Eng.* III. 405 Delinquents.. deserving of exemplary punishment.

deservingly (dɪ'zɜːvɪŋlɪ), *adv.* [f. prec. + -ly².] In a deserving manner; meritoriously.

1552 Huloet, Deseruingly, *merito.* *c* **1561** Veron *Free-will* 51 b, Iustlye and deseruinglye put from those things. **1650** R. Stapylton *Strada's Low C. Warres* VIII. 3 Had often (and deservingly) the experience of ill fortune. **1737** *Clorana* 125 Bellmont had placed his Friendship very deservingly.

de'servingness. [f. as prec. + -ness.] Deserving quality, desert, merit; worthiness.

1631 *Celestina* XII. 145 Growne to.. a better deservingnesse in your selves. **1865** J. Grote *Treat. Moral Ideas* ii. (1876) 21 That virtue consisted in moral beauty, or in deservingness of human approbation.

desese, obs. var. of disease, disseise *v.*

†**dese'speir,** *sb. Obs.* Also 5 dess-, dis-, -peyr(e. [a. OF. *desespeir* (mod.F. *désespoir*), vbl. sb. from *désespérer* to despair, q.v.] By-form of despair *sb.*

c **1374** Chaucer *Troylus* I. 605 With desespeir [*v. rr.* dessespeir, disespeyr] so sorwfully me offendeth. **1393** Gower *Conf.* II. 125 In desespeire a man to falle.

†**dese'speire,** *v. Obs.* Also disespeyre. [a. OF. *desespere-r.*] By-form of despair *v.*

c **1380** Chaucer *Compl. to his Lady* 7 So desespaired I am from alle blisse. *c* **1430** Lydg. *Min. Poems* (Percy Soc.) 236 A verray preef of his mercy, that no man disespeyre. —— *ibid.* 179 Disespeyred.

†**de'sesperance, -aunce.** *Obs.* Also dis-. [a. OF. *désespérance* (12th c. in Hatzf.) = Pr. *desesperansa*, a Romanic compound of *des-*, L. *dis-* + *esperantia*, *-za*, *-ce*, f. *esperare*, *esperer*:—L. *spērāre* to hope.] Despairing, despair.

c **1374** Chaucer *Troylus* II. 1258 (1307) That lay.. By-twixen hope and derk desesperaunce. *c* **1460** *Pol. Rel. & L. Poems* (1866) 68 His suerte he putteth in disesperaunce.

†**de'sesperat,** *a. Obs.* In 4 dis-. [ad. OF. *desesperé*, Pr. *desesperat*, = L. *dēspērāt-us* despaired, desperate.] Desperate, hopeless.

c **1384** Chaucer *H. Fame* III. 925 And wost thy selfen outtirly Disesperat of alle blys.

deseue, -seuy, -seve, obs. ff. deceive *v.*

c **1350** *Will. Palerne* 3307 A-drad to þe deth þei deseuy here wold.

desever, obs. form of dissever *v.*

de-sex, desex (diː'sɛks), *v.* [f. de- II. 2 + sex *sb.*] *trans.* **a.** To castrate or spay. **b.** To deprive of the distinctive qualities of sex; also, to remove or minimize the sexual appeal of. So **de'sexed** *ppl. a.*

1911 *Experiment Station Record* XXV. v. 474 Measurements of desexed heifers show that in conformation they approach the type of a castrated male rather than that of a normal male. **1928** *Time* 16 Jan. 18 Those who show themselves to be morons should be de-sexed before they reach the reproductive stage. **1962** A. Nisbett *Technique Sound Studio* xii. 212 Small changes of pitch therefore tend not to change the apparent sex of a voice, but rather to de-sex it. **1963** *Economist* 28 Nov. 1338/1 The desexed version of a more uninhibited.. dance.

desexualize (diː'sɛksjuːəlaɪz), *v.* [f. de- + sexual + -ize.] *trans.* **a.** To deprive of sex or sexual characters; to deprive of the distinctive qualities of a sex. So **de'sexualized** *ppl. a.*

1894 *Idler* Sept. 195 The most highly cultured, mentally most richly endowed women I have known—not *desexualised.* **1919** M. K. Bradby *Psycho-Analysis* 50 They regard all human energy as sexual, or 'libido', though Jung holds that it may become de-sexualised by turning from a sexual aim to non-sexual surrogate. **1926** *Spectator* 19 June 1038/2 The self-flatterer.. desexualizes the human form that he may pride himself on his idealization of it. **1940** *Mind* XLIX. 352 Thus the 'conclusion' that every thirst for knowledge is a 'desexualised' form of sexual curiosity is not an unwarranted generalisation but either an inexcusable linguistic eccentricity or a fruitful linguistic modification. **1958** *Times Lit. Suppl.* 14 Feb. 90/2 Later adolescent pictures show a normal interest in sex, but both boys and girls become fashion-plate types, essentially desexualized. **1969** P. A. Robinson *Freudian Left* 207 Intensification of genital sexuality.. left the body essentially desexualized.

b. To castrate.

1913 in Dorland *Med. Dict.* (ed. 7).

deseyt, -te, deseyve, obs. forms of deceit, deceive, etc.

desgise, -guise, -gyse, obs. ff. disguise.

deshabille: see dishabille.

desherit, etc., obs. form of disherit, etc.

deshese, deshight, obs. ff. disease, desight.

deshonour, obs. form of dishonour.

desi, obs. form of dizzy *a.*

desiatin, var. of dessiatine.

desiccant (dɪ'sɪkənt, 'dɛsɪkənt), *a.* and *sb.* [ad. L. *dēsiccānt-em*, pr. pple. of *dēsiccāre*: see desiccate, and note there as to stress.]

A. *adj.* Having the property of drying; serving to dry; *esp.* of a medicinal agent.

1775 Ash, *Desiccant*, drying, drying up humours. **1875** H. C. Wood *Therap.* (1879) 39 Litharge.. used as a desiccant astringent powder for ulcers. **1940** *Chambers's Techn. Dict.* 236/2 *Desiccants*, substances of a hygroscopic nature, capable of absorbing moisture and therefore used as drying agents. **1958** *Engineering* 14 Mar. 352/3 Air passing through the desiccant (activated alumina) is practically sterile when it leaves. **1967** *Times Rev. Industry* May 80/2 A hermetically sealed polythene film bag, with a quantity of desiccant enclosed within it.

B. *sb.* A drying or desiccating agent; a medicine or remedy which dries up.

1676 Wiseman *Surgery* viii. v. (R.), We endeavour by moderate detergents and desiccants, to cleanse and dry the diseased parts. **1866** *Pall Mall G.* No. 492. 739/1 Dry air is the most effective desiccant.

ˈdesiccate, *ppl. a. arch.* [ad. L. *dēsiccāt-us* dried up, pa. pple. of *dēsiccāre*: see next.] Desiccated, dried.

c **1420** *Pallad. on Husb.* iv. 179 But daies thre this seede is goode bewette In mylk or meth, and after desiccate Sette hem; thai wol be swete. **1626** Bacon *Sylva* §842 Bodies desiccate, by Heat, or Age. **1840** Browning *Sordello* ii. 313 Juicy in youth or desiccate with age.

desiccate (dɪˈsɪkeɪt, ˈdɛsɪkeɪt), *v.* [f. L. *dēsiccāt-*, ppl. stem of *dēsiccāre* to dry completely, dry up, f. de- I. 3 + *siccāre* to dry, *siccus* dry.

(For changing stress see note to contemplate: *de'siccate* is the only pronunciation in Dicts. down to 1864, and in Ogilvie 1882, Cassell 1883.)]

1. *trans.* To make quite dry; to deprive thoroughly of moisture; to dry, dry up. Also *fig.*

In U.S. applied to the thorough drying of articles of food for preservation.

1575 Turberv. *Faulconrie* 261 They doe mollifie, and desiccate the wounde or disease. **1626** Bacon *Sylva* §727 Wine helpeth to digest and desiccate the moisture. **1657** Tomlinson *Renou's Disp.* 181 This..will desiccate an ulcer. **1808** J. Barlow *Columb.* iv. 426 No..courtly art [shall] Damp the bold thought or desiccate the heart. **1832** I. Taylor *Saturday Even.* (1834) 297 Atheism in all its forms desiccates the affections. **1839** Bailey *Festus* Proem, Though we should by art Bring earth to gas and desiccate the sea. **1883** Proctor in *Knowl.* 3 Aug. 74/1 The shock was of sufficient intensity to..partially desiccate the muscular tissues.

2. *intr.* To become dry. *rare.*

1679 Rycaut *Grk. Church* 277 Bodies of such whom they have Canonized for Saints to continue unconsumed, and..to dry and desiccate like the Mummies in Egypt.

Hence **desiccating** *vbl. sb.* and *ppl. a.*

1651 tr. *Bacon's Life & Death* 7 They speak much of the Elementary Quality of Siccity or Drienesse; and of things Desiccating. **1866** J. Martineau *Ess.* I. 388 The very things which this desiccating rationalism flung off. **1871** B. Stewart *Heat* §63 The..air was..thoroughly dried by being passed through a desiccating apparatus. **1893** *Athenæum* 1 Apr. 402/2 That desiccating of the Anglo-Saxon in North America which Humboldt and others have commented upon.

desiccate (ˈdɛsɪkət), *sb.* [f. the ppl. adj.] A desiccated substance or product.

1926 *Science* 28 May 549 Some of my experiments were carried out with this desiccate. **1940** *Nature* 6 July 30/2 We decided to try desiccated 9–11 day chick embryos as a source of active principle... The desiccate was reconstituted by adding sterile distilled water.

desiccated (dɪˈsɪkeɪtɪd, ˈdɛsɪkeɪtɪd), *ppl. a.* [f. desiccate *v.* + -ed.] Deprived or freed of moisture; dried; (of food) dried for preservation.

1677 Hale *Prim. Orig. Man.* ii. vii. 193 By elevation..from the Sea or some desiccated places thereof. **1847–8** H. Miller *First Impr.* xvii. (1857) 330 The living souls..which had once animated these withered and desiccated bodies. **1884** *Health Exhib. Catal.* 9/1 Preserved Potato and Desiccated Soup. *Ibid.* 18/1 American Breakfast Cereals..hulled, crushed, steam-cooked, and desiccated.

desiccation (dɛsɪˈkeɪʃən). [ad. L. *dēsiccātiōn-em*, n. of action from *dēsiccāre*: see desiccate *v.*] The action of making quite dry; depriving or freeing of moisture; dried up condition.

1477 Norton *Ord. Alch.* vii. in Ashm. (1652) 104 Another Fier is Fire of Disiccation. **1541** R. Copland *Guydon's Formularye* T iv b, Composed woundes apostemate with venym requyreth stronge desiccacyon. **1684** T. Burnet *Th. Earth* ii. 26 A great drought and dessication of the earth. **1805** W. Saunders *Min. Waters* 352 To finish the desiccation of the residue over a water bath. **1836** Macgillivray tr. *Humboldt's Trav.* iii. 44 Mummies, reduced to an extraordinary degree of desiccation. **1865** Livingstone *Zambesi* iv. 91 The general desiccation which Africa has undergone.

b. *attrib.*, as ***desiccation-crack***, in *Geol.*, a crack produced in a bed of clay in the process of drying, and subsequently filled by a new deposit of soft matter.

1865 Page *Geol. Terms* 173 Appearances..known as desiccation cracks..not to be confounded with 'joints', 'cleavage' and similar phenomena. **1880** A. R. Wallace *Isl. Life* vi. 85 Irregular desiccation marks, like the cracks at the bottom of a sun-dried muddy pool. **1882** Geikie *Text-bk. Geol.* iv. i. 485 These desiccation-cracks or sun-cracks..prove that the surface of rock on which they lie was exposed to the air and dried before the next layer of water-borne sediment was deposited upon it.

desiccative (dɪˈsɪkətɪv, ˈdɛsɪkeɪtɪv), *a.* and *sb.* Also 5–6 **desyccatif, dyssyccatiue.** [ad. med.L. *dēsiccātīv-us*, f. L. *dēsiccāt-*: see above and -ive.]

A. *adj.* Having the tendency or quality of drying up.

1541 R. Copland *Galyen's Terap.* 2 A iv b, The faculte of medycyns ought to be desyccatyfe. **1601** Holland *Pliny* xxxi. x, Astringent it is, desiccative, binding, and knitting. **1796** Morse *Amer. Geog.* I. 60 Warm winds, as the Sirocco, Harmatan, etc., are more desiccative than cold winds. **1838** T. Thomson *Chem. Org. Bodies* 429 It is more desiccative than linseed oil.

B. *sb.* A desiccative agent: a desiccant. ? *Obs.*

c **1400** *Lanfranc's Cirurg.* 57 A moist discracie..þou schalt help wiþ desiccativis. **1541** R. Copland *Guydon's Formularye* R iij b, Medycyns that be colde, dyssycatyues, and infrigidatyues. **1601** Holland *Pliny* II. 138 Wheat is such a desiccatiue, that it wil draw and drie vp the wine or any other liquor in a barrell which is buried within it. **1708** *Brit. Apollo* No. 72. 2/1 Coffe is a very great Desiccative. **1758** J. S. *Le Dran's Observ. Surg.* (1771) 201 The Wound ..was dressed with..Desiccatives, calcined Alum [etc.].

desiccator (dɪˈsɪkətə(r), ˈdɛsɪkeɪtə(r)). [agent-n. in L. form from *dēsiccāre* to desiccate.] One who or that which desiccates or dries; a name given to a chemical apparatus used to dry substances which are decomposed by heat or by exposure to the air (= exsiccator); and, in later commercial use, to contrivances for the desiccation of fruit, milk, or other articles of food, also of tan-bark, etc.

1837 R. B. Ede *Pract. Chem.* 173 Occasionally evaporations are performed with much benefit by aid of desiccators. **1883** in *Encycl. Dict.* (Cassell).

desiccatory (dɪˈsɪkətərɪ), *a.* [f. as desiccate *v.* + -ory.] Desiccative.

c **1800** *Travels of Anacharsis* II. 467 (L.) Pork is desiccatory, but it strengthens and passes easily. **1892** *Athenæum* 30 Jan. 145/2 Beneath the desiccatory influences to which Central Asia has been subject for centuries.

deside, obs. form of decide.

†**desideraˈbility.** *Obs.* [f. next: see -ity.] The quality of being desirable; desirableness.

1635 Heywood *Hierarch.* ii. Comm. 97 Amabilitie, Desiderabilitie..Pulchritude, Iucunditie.

†**deˈsiderable,** *a. Obs.* Also 4 **deseder-, desyder-.** [ad. L. *dēsīderābil-is* desirable, f. *dēsīderāre* (see desiderate): cf. rare OF. *desiderable*, and see desirable.] To be desired; desirable.

a **1340** Hampole *Psalter* xviii. 11 Þe domes of God are desiderable abouen all riches. *c* **1340** —— *Prose Tr.* 2 Sothely, Ihesu, desederabill es thi name. *c* **1450** tr. *De Imitatione* iii. v, Verily þere is non oþer þinge here laudable ner desiderable. **1540–54** Croke *Ps.* (Percy Soc.) 33 More then gold desiderable Or stones most precious to se. **1611** Coryat *Crudities* 32 My selfe hauing had the happinesse to enjoy his desiderable commerce. **1675** *Art Contentm.* x. x. 233 'Tis sure no such desiderable guest that we should go out to meet it.

Hence †**deˈsiderably** *adv. Obs.*

1635 Quarles *Embl.* v. v. 263 O..most holy fire! how sweetly doest thou burne!..how desiderably doest thou inflame me!

desiderant (dɪˈsɪdərənt), *a.* and *sb. rare.* [ad. L. *dēsīderānt-em*, pr. pple. of *dēsīderāre* to desire.]

A. *adj.* Desiring, desirous: (implied in next adv.). **B.** *sb.* One who desires a thing.

1860 J. R. Ballantyne *Bible for the Pandits* 111 When one writes up 'The smallest donation thankfully received', it is tacitly implied that the donation shall not be what the desiderant does not care to have.

†**deˈsiderantly,** *adv. Obs. rare*$^{-1}$. [f. prec. + -ly²: cf. L. *dēsīderānter*, and OF. *desideramment*, similarly formed.] Desiringly, desirously.

c **1450** tr. *De Imitatione* iii. liv, þat þei aske so desiderantly of god.

desiderata, pl. of desideratum, q.v.

†**deˈsiderate,** *a.* and *sb. Obs.* [ad. L. *dēsīderāt-us* desired: see next.]

A. *adj.* Desired; desirable.

1640 G. Watts tr. *Bacon's Adv. Learn.* iv. ii. 199 So these are the Parts which in the knowledge of Medicine, touching the cure of Diseases, are desiderate.

B. *sb.* A thing that is desired; a desideratum.

1640 G. Watts tr. *Bacon's Adv. Learn.* Pref. 23 Where we deliver up any thing as a Desiderate. **1664** Evelyn *Sylva* (1776) 558 Those who shall once oblige our nation with a full and Absolutely Compleat Dictionary, as yet a Desiderate amongst us. **1670** —— *Mem.* (1857) III. 223 When I shall have received those other desiderates, I may proceed to the compiling part.

desiderate (dɪˈsɪdəreɪt), *v.* [f. L. *dēsīderāt-*, ppl. stem of *dēsīderāre* to miss, long for, desire, f. *dē-* (de- I. 1, 2) + a radical also found in *con-sīderāre*, perhaps connected with *sīdus, sīder-* star, constellation; but the sense-history is unknown: cf. consider.]

trans. To desire with a sense of want or regret; to feel a desire or longing for; to feel the want of; to desire, want, miss.

1645 R. Baillie *Disswasive Vind.* (1655) 29 In that pastorall freedome I desiderate these three things. **1646** Sir T. Browne *Pseud. Ep.* Pref. A vj a, If any way..wee may obtaine a worke, so much desired, at least, desiderated of truth. **1730** T. Boston *Mem.* App. xii. 453, I desiderated satisfying impressions. **1788** Gibbon *Let.* Misc. Wks. 1796 I. 679 In an evening I desiderate the resources of a family or a club. **1829** Southey in *Q. Rev.* XXXIX. 123 The great step which is now desiderated in education. **1836–7** Sir W. Hamilton *Metaph.* xxxix. (1870) II. 384 He evacuates the phænomenon of all that desiderates explanation. **1839** *John Bull* 11 Aug., We desiderate to know whether murder itself be considered one [an offence]. **1865** Trollope *Belton Est.* xxvii. 321 Incapable of enjoying the kind of life which he desiderated.

desiderated (dɪˈsɪdəreɪtɪd), *ppl. a.* [f. prec. vb. + -ed.] Desired, wanted, required.

a **1743** Cheyne (J.), Eclipses are of wonderful assistance toward the solution of this so desirable and so much desiderated problem. **1836** T. Hook *Gurney Married* (1839) 396 Kitty returned..bearing in her hand..the desiderated (I like the word, it is so long and so new) basin of broth. **1854** H. Miller *Sch. & Schm.* xxv. (1857) 550 The desiderated want was to be supplied by its writer.

desideration (dɪˌsɪdəˈreɪʃən). [ad. L. *dēsīderātiōn-em*, n. of action from *dēsīderāre*: see desiderate and -ation.] **1.** The action of desiderating; desire, with feeling of want or regret.

? *c* **1525** *Cov. Myst.* (Shaks. Soc.) 386 Yif it like youre benygnyte Nouth to ben displesid wyth my desideracyon Me longith to youre presense now conjunct to the unyte. **1633** T. Adams *Exp. 2 Peter* iii. 18 Thus it [i.e. Amen] is a note of confirmation, as well as desideration. **1813** W. Taylor *Eng. Synon.* (1856) 293 Desire is aroused by hope, while desideration is inflicted by reminiscence. **1861** G. Meredith *Evan Harrington* I. iv. 53 He will assuredly so dispose of his influence as to suit the desiderations of his family.

†**2.** Thing desired, desideratum. *Obs. rare.*

1836 Landor *Peric. & Asp.* lxxviii, Coriander-seed might correct it..The very desideration!

desiderative (dɪˈsɪdərətɪv), *a.* and *sb.* [ad. L. *dēsīderātīv-us* (in late L. grammarians), f. *dēsīderāt-* ppl. stem: see -ive. (In mod.F. *désidératif*.)]

A. *adj.*

1. Having, expressing, or denoting desire; pertaining to desire.

1655–60 Stanley *Hist. Philos.* (1701) 207/1 That to every apprehensive faculty, there might be a desiderative; to embrace what it judgeth good, to refuse what it esteemeth evil. **1816** T. Taylor *Ess.* VIII. 50 The liver signifying that he lived solely according to the desiderative part of his nature.

2. *Gram.* Of a verb or verbal form: Formed from another verb to express a desire of doing the act thereby denoted; of or pertaining to such a verb.

1552 Huloet H v b/1 It is to be noted how all verbes endyng in *Turio*..be verbes desideratyue, as desierynge or entendynge to perfourme the act of their significations. **1711** tr. *Werenfels' Disc. Logomachys* 226 Verbs..frequentative, inchoative, imitative, and desiderative. **1857** M. Williams *Sanskrit Gram.* (1864) 202 Nouns and participles derived from the desiderative base are not uncommon. **1879** Whitney *Sansk. Gram.* §1026 By the desiderative conjugation is signified a desire for the action or condition denoted by the simple root.

B. *sb. Gram.* A desiderative verb, verbal form, or conjugation: see prec.

1751 Harris *Hermes* i. vii. (1786) 127 A species of Verbs called..in Latin *Desiderativa*, the Desideratives or Meditatives. **1855** Forbes *Hindústání Gram.* (1868) 65 Desideratives, as..'to wish, *or* to be about, *or* like to speak'. **1857** M. Williams *Sanskrit Gram.* (1864) 205 Desideratives may take a passive form by adding *ya* to the desiderative base after rejecting final *a*.

‖**desideratum** (dɪˌsɪdəˈreɪtəm). Pl. **-ata.** [a. L. *dēsīderātum* thing desired, neuter of *dēsīderāt-us*, pa. pple. of *dēsīderāre*: see desiderate *v.* The subst. use belongs to med.L. Also used in the L. form in mod.F. and Sp.] Something for which a desire or longing is felt; something wanting and required or desired.

1652 N. Culverwel *Light of Nat.* 33 (Stanf.) All Desiderata shall be suppli'd. **1654** Whitlock *Zootomia* 454 Here that Desideratum my Lord Bacon speaketh of..is supplyed. **1668** Wilkins *Real Char.* Ep. to Rdr. 63 The various Desiderata, proposed by Learned men, or such things as were conceived yet wanting to the advancement of several parts of Learning. **1782** A. Monro *Compar. Anat.* Introd. (ed. 3) 6 A..technical dictionary..is one of the *desiderata* in anatomy. **1802** Playfair *Illustr. Hutton. Th.* 338 The explanation of them was still a desideratum in geology. **1807** Southey *Life* (1850) III. 105 One of the greatest desideratums in modern Oriental literature. **1875** Jowett *Plato* (ed. 2) III. 161 The fitness of the animal for food is the great desideratum. **1876** Mozley *Univ. Serm.* iii. (1877) 47 A great number of people in every age, do want morality without religion: it is a great desideratum.

‖**desiˈderium.** [L. = longing, sense of want, desire, f. stem of *dēsīderāre*: see desiderate.] An ardent desire or wish; a longing, properly for a thing once possessed and now missed; a sense of loss.

1715 Swift *Let. to Pope* 28 June, When I leave a country ..I think as seldom as I can of what I loved or esteemed in it, to avoid the *desiderium* which of all things makes life most uneasy. **1789** G. White *Selborne* (1853) II. xxxiii. 249 This strange affection probably was occasioned by that desiderium. **1883** *Sat. Rev.* 21 Apr. 485/2 Many Liberals regard the memory of Lord Beaconsfield with a *desiderium* which has not been exhibited towards that of any English political leader within the memory of living man.

†**deˈsidery.** *Obs. rare.* [a. OF. *desiderie* (11th c. in Godef.), ad. L. *dēsīderium* longing, desire: see prec.] Desire, wish.

c **1450** *Craft of Lovers* (R.), My name is True loue—of cardinal desidery..the very exemplary. **1513** Bradshaw *St. Werburge* i. 1498 To brynge his doughter to the hous of Ely

..after her desydery. *Ibid.* 2899 There to be tumylate after her desydery.

†**desidi'ose**, *a. Obs.* = next.

1727 BAILEY vol. II, *Desidiose, desidious*, idle, slothful, lazy, sluggish. **1755** JOHNSON, *Desidiose*, idle, lazy, heavy. **1822** MRS. E. NATHAN *Langreath* III. 290 From the lower orders becoming desidiose. [Used jestingly.]

†**de'sidious**, *a. Obs.* Also 7 diss-. [ad. L. *dēsidiōs-us* slothful, f. *dēsidia* sitting idle, indolence, slothfulness, f. *dēsidēre* to sit long, sit idle, f. DE- I. 3 + *sedēre* to sit.] Idle, indolent, slothful.

a **1540** [implied in next]. **1608** R. CRAKANTHORPE *Serm.* (1609) A iij a, Some..blamed both him and other Bishops, as being desidious. **1637** R. HUMPHREY tr. *St. Ambrose* ii. 5 To be desidious and defectiue in pious workes. **1647** WARD *Simp. Cobler* (1843) 75 Yee fight the battells of the Lord, bee neither desidious nor perfidious. **1656** in BLOUNT *Glossogr.*

†**de'sidiousness**. *Obs.* [f. prec. + -NESS.] Idleness, indolence, slothfulness.

a **1540** LELAND *Let. to Cromwell* in Wood *Ath. Oxon.* I. 68 The Germanes perceiving our desidiousness and negligence do send daily young Scholars hither, that spoileth them [ancient authors] and cutteth them out of libraries, returning home and putting them abroad as monuments of their own country [etc.]. **1647** N. BACON *Disc. Govt. Eng.* I. xxxviii. (1739) 58 This dissidiousness of the greater sort made one step further to the full perfection of that manner of Trial. **1651** *Ibid.* II. vi. (1739) 33 He found the People.. vexed at his Grandfather's desidiousness.

desie(n, obs. form of DIZZY.

desight (diː'saɪt). [f. DE- + SIGHT; prob. orig. a variant of *dessight*, DISSIGHT, q.v.] A thing unsightly, an ugly object to look at, an eyesore.

(But in the first quot. perhaps a misprint for *despight*.)

[**1589** PUTTENHAM *Eng. Poesie* III. xxiv. (Arb.) 292 [If he] come sodainly to be pold or shauen, it will seeme onely to himselfe, a deshight and very vndecent.] **1834** G. COX *Oxford* in 1834, v. 65 A splendid error and a grand desight, Grotesquely Gothic, blunderingly bright. **1852** MISS YONGE *Cameos* II. vi. 68 Three emeralds, three pearls, and one large rough pebble, which was such a desight to the others, that [etc.].

de'sightment. *rare*. [f. as prec. + -MENT.] The act of making unsightly; disfigurement.

a **1864** *Times* (Webster), Substitute jury-masts at whatever desightment or damage in risk.

design (dɪ'zaɪn), *sb.* Also 6 de-, des-, disseigne, disseine, 7 designe, (dessein, disseene, 8 desegn). [In 16th c. *des(s)eigne*, a. 15–16th c. F. *desseing* (in 16th c. also *dessing, desing*) 'designe, purpose, proiect, priuat intention or determination' (Cotgr.), f. *desseigner* to DESIGN. In 16th c. It. *disegno* (also *dissegno, designo*) had the senses 'purpose, designe, draught; model, plot, picture, pourtrait' (Florio). Hence the artistic sense was taken into Fr., and gradually differentiated in spelling, so that in mod.F. *dessein* is 'purpose, plan', *dessin* 'design in art'. Eng. on the contrary uses *design*, conformed to the verb, in both senses.]

I. A mental plan.

1. a. A plan or scheme conceived in the mind and intended for subsequent execution; the preliminary conception of an idea that is to be carried into effect by action; a project.

1593 HOOKER *Eccl. Pol.* I. xv. §4 (Spencer's ed. 1611 p. 46) What the lawe of God hath, either for or against our disseignes. **1596** SPENSER *F.Q.* v. viii. 25 By counterfet disguise To their deseigne to make the easier way. **1625** PURCHAS *Pilgrims* II. 1293 The Emperor vndertaketh no high design without his approvement. **1738** WESLEY *Psalms* ii. 1 Why do the Jews and Gentiles join To execute a vain Design? *a* **1843** SOUTHEY *Inscriptions* xli, What inexhaustive springs of public wealth The vast design required. **1848** MACAULAY *Hist. Eng.* I. 534 Grey..had concurred in the design of insurrection.

b. 'A scheme formed to the detriment of another' (J.); a plan or purpose of attack *upon* or *on*.

a **1704** LOCKE (J.), A sedate, settled design upon another man's life. **1704** CIBBER *Careless Husb.* II. i, To be in love, now, is only to have a design upon a woman, a modish way of declaring war against her virtue. **1848** MACAULAY *Hist. Eng.* I. 598 It was thought necessary to relinquish the design on Bristol. **1858** LYTTON *What Will he do?* I. i, He had no design on your pocket.

2. a. In weaker sense: Purpose, aim, intention.

1588 SHAKS. *L.L.L.* IV. i. 88 [Armado writes] Thine in the dearest designe of industrie. *Ibid.* v. i. 105. **1594** —— *Rich. III*, I. ii. 211 That it may please you leaue these sad designes To him that hath most cause to be a Mourner. **1659** B. HARRIS *Parival's Iron Age* 108 They who ask relief, have one designe: and he who gives it, another. **1697** DRYDEN *Virg. Past.* VI. 37 He..demands On what design the Boys had bound his hands. **1734** tr. *Rollin's Anc. Hist.* (1827) I. 344 With design to besiege it. **1736** BUTLER *Anal.* I. iii. Wks. 1874 I. 50 The design of this chapter is to inquire, how far this is the case. **1792** *B. Munchhausen's Trav.* xxx. 135 They extended an elephant's hide, tanned and prepared for the design, across the summit of the tower. **1866** G. MACDONALD *Ann. Q. Neighb.* xxxiii. (1878) 564 My design had been to go at once to London.

b. = Intention to go. (Cf. DESIGN *v.* 13.)

1725 DE FOE *New Voy.* (1840) 57 My design was to the north part of the island.

c. phr. *by* (†*out of, on, upon*) *design*: on purpose, purposely, intentionally.

1628 HOBBES *Thucyd.* (1822) 65 The man being upon design gone..into Sanctuary. **1650** FULLER *Pisgah* II. xii. 261 On design to extirpate all the smiths in Israel. **1665** MANLEY *Grotius' Low C. Warres* 141 Either out of Design, or Simplicity. *a* **1715** BURNET *Own Time* (1766) I. 4, I have, on design, avoided all laboured periods. **1867** FREEMAN *Norm. Conq.* (1876) I. App. 628 William, whether by accident or by design, was not admitted.

3. The thing aimed at; the end in view; the final purpose.

[**1605** SHAKS. *Macb.* II. i. 55 Wither'd Murther..towards his designe Moues like a Ghost.] **1657** CROMWELL in *Four C. Eng. Lett.* 86 We desire..that the design be Dunkirk rather than Grauelines. **1697** DRYDEN *Virg. Georg.* III. 604 If Milk be thy Design; with plenteous Hand Bring Clover-grass. **1711** LADY M. W. MONTAGU *Lett. to W. Montagu* 24 Mar., Happiness is the natural design of all the world. **1833** CHALMERS *Const. Man* (1835) I. iv. 187 Virtue was the design of our Creation.

4. Contrivance in accordance with a preconceived plan; adaptation of means to ends; pre-arranged purpose; *spec.* used in reference to the view that the universe manifests Divine forethought and testifies to an intelligent Creator (the ***argument from design***).

1665 MANLEY *Grotius' Low C. Warres* 141 Either out of Design, or Simplicity. **1736** [see DESIGNER 1]. **1802** PALEY *Nat. Theol.* ii. §3 The argument from design remains as it was. *Ibid.* ii. §4 The machine, which we are inspecting, demonstrates, by its construction, contrivance and design. **1831** BREWSTER *Newton* (1855) I. xiii. 359 The arrangements, therefore, upon which the stability of the system depends, must have been the result of design. **1855** TENNYSON *Maud* II. II. i, What a lovely shell..With delicate spire and whorl, How exquisitely minute, A miracle of design! **1883** HICKS (*title*), Critique of Design-Arguments.

5. In a bad sense: Crafty contrivance, hypocritical scheming; an instance of this. Cf. DESIGNING *ppl. a.* 2. *arch.*

a **1704** T. BROWN *Praise of Poverty* Wks. 1730 I. 94 Honesty (they think) design, and design honesty. **1719** DE FOE *Crusoe* I. xiv. (1858) 219 A..faithful..servant.. without passions, sullenness, or designs. **1738** WESLEY *Hymns*, '*Almighty Maker, God!*' vi, Thy Glories I abate, Or praise Thee with Design. **1796** BP. WATSON *Apol. Bible* 276 If this mistake proceeds from design you are still less fit. **1871** B. TAYLOR *Faust* (1875) I. v. 99 'Twas all deceit and lying, false design.

II. A plan in art.

6. A preliminary sketch for a picture or other work of art; the plan of a building or any part of it, or the outline of a piece of decorative work, after which the actual structure or texture is to be completed; a delineation, pattern.

1638 JUNIUS *Painting of Ancients* 270 What beauty and force there is in a good and proportionable designe. **1645** N. STONE *Enchirid. Fortif.* 78 Profile, An Italian word for that designe that showes the side..of any work. **1703** MOXON *Mech. Exerc.* 252 'Tis usual..for any person before he begins to Erect a Building, to have Designs or Draughts drawn upon Paper..in which Designs..each Floor or Story is delineated. **1793** SMEATON *Edystone L.* §278 The necessary designs for the iron rails of the balcony. **1821** W. M. CRAIG *Drawing, Painting, etc.* lect. I. 29 That these itinerant workmen had a certain set of designs, or rather patterns, handed down from generation to generation. *Mod.* The Committee appointed to report on the designs sent in for the new Corn Exchange.

7. a. The combination of artistic details or architectural features which go to make up a picture, statue, building, etc.; the artistic idea as executed; a piece of decorative work, an artistic device.

1644 EVELYN *Mem.* (1857) I. 73, I was particularly desirous of seeing this palace, from the extravagance of the design. **1670** SIR S. CROW in *12th Rep. Hist. MSS. Comm.* App. v. 15 Their ordnary designes [in tapestry]..beeing deformed and mishapen. **1797** MRS. RADCLIFFE *Italian* Prol. (1826) 3 Simplicity and grandeur of design. **1851** D. WILSON *Preh. Ann.* (1863) II. III. v. 133 A silver bracelet of rare and most artistic design. **1863** GEO. ELIOT *Romola* II. vii, To admire the designs on the enamelled silver centres. **1884** *Times* (weekly ed.) 26 Sept. 4/1 It is the design that sells the cloth.

b. *transf.* of literary work in this and prec. sense.

1875 EMERSON *Lett. & Soc. Aims, Poet. & Imag.* Wks. (Bohn) III. 153 Great design belongs to a poem, and is better than any skill of execution,—but how rare! **1879** B. TAYLOR *Stud. Germ. Lit.* 262 His design is evidently greater than his power of execution.

8. The art of picturesque delineation and construction; original work in a graphic or plastic art.

arts of design: those in which design plays a principal part, such as painting, sculpture, architecture, engraving. ***school of design***: a school in which the arts of design are specially taught.

1638 JUNIUS *Painting of Ancients* 271 [From] Designe and Proportion..we should proceed to Colour. **1735** BERKELEY *Querist* §68 The art of design, and its influence in most trades or manufactures. **1850** LEITCH *Müller's Anc. Art* §25. 9 Design or the graphic art..produces by means of light and shade the appearance of bodies on a surface. **1854** RUSKIN *Two Paths* i. (1858) 44 Design, properly so called, is human invention, consulting human capacity.

9. *attrib.* and *Comb.*, as ***design book, consultant, engineer***; **design-conscious** *a.* (see CONSCIOUS *a.* 12).

1936 *Burlington Mag.* Nov. 235/2 The silversmiths appear to have had in their minds the forms depicted in German design-books. **1955** H. READ *Grass Roots of Art* (rev. ed.) vii. 137 The buying public..was becoming design-conscious. **1960** *Guardian* 30 Sept. 10/2 Plagiarism..is a rare headache to the design-conscious Scandinavian nations. **1954** H. READ *Anarchy & Order* 226 The attempt of certain artists to adapt themselves to the modern industrial system by calling themselves 'design consultants' has had no appreciable effect on the cultural situation. **1970** J. QUARTERMAIN *Man who walked on Diamonds* iv. 23 It was a design consultant's idea of hell. **1964** F. L. WESTWATER *Electronic Computers* iii. 49 Not infrequently, a design engineer will ask the logical designer to make alterations for various reasons.

design (dɪ'zaɪn), *v.* Also 6 desyne, 6–7 designe, 7 disseigne, dissigne. [a. F. *désigner* (16th c. in Rabelais, in 14th c. *desinner* Godef. *Suppl.*) 'to denote, signifie, or shew by a marke or token, to designe, prescribe, appoint' (Cotgr.), ad. L. *dēsignāre*, *dissignāre* to mark out, trace out, denote, DESIGNATE, appoint, contrive, etc., f. DE- I. 2 and DIS- + *signāre* to mark, *signum* mark, SIGN. Cf. Pr. *designar, desegnar*, Sp., Pg. *designar*, It. *disegnare* (in 16th c. also *dissegnare, designare*, Florio). In It. the vb. had in 16th c. the senses 'to designe, contriue, plot, purpose, intend; also to draw, paint, embroither, modle, pourtray' (Florio); thence obs. F. *desseigner* 'to designe, purpose, proiect, lay a plot' (Cotgr.), and mod.F. *dessiner*, in 16th c. *designer*, 17th c. *dessigner*, to design in the artistic sense. In Eng., *design* combines all these senses.]

I. [after L. *dēsignāre*, F. *désigner*] To mark out, nominate, appoint, DESIGNATE.

†**1.** *trans.* To point out by distinctive sign, mark, or token; to indicate. Also with *forth, out*. *Obs.*

1593 SHAKS. *Rich. II*, I. i. 203 We shall see Iustice designe the Victors Chiualrie. **1594** SPENSER *Amoretti* lxxiv, Most happy letters!..With which that happy name was first desynd. **1610** DONNE *Pseudo Martyr* 313 The Sunne, which designes priesthod, is so much bigger then the Moon. **1614** SELDEN *Titles Hon.* 117 The Forme..being vsuall..with such Substantiues to designe out the subiect denominated of the Adiectiue. **1641** T. WARMSTRY *Blind Guide Forsaken* 37 Designing forth unto us the place whither hee is ascended. **1668** SEDLEY *Mulb. Gard.* I. ii, Those Cravats that design the Right Honourable.

absol. **1606** WARNER *Alb. Eng.* XIV. lxxxviii. (1612) 360 Euen so As had their Oracles of them dissigned long ago.

2. To point out by name or by descriptive phrase; in *Law*, to specify (a person) by title, profession, trade, etc.; to designate, name, style. Sometimes with *double obj.* (direct and complemental). *arch.*

1603–21 KNOLLES *Hist. Turks* 1311 Willing the Turks to designe the partie which had thrown the stone. **1614** RALEIGH *Hist. World* II. IV. iii. §1. 178 He left his Kingdom to the worthiest, as designing Perdiccas. **1794** SULLIVAN *View Nat.* II. 393 Voltaire..in designing Geneva, called it la petite République voisine de ses terres. **1814** SOUTHEY *Roderick* XVIII, The plains Burgensian..ere long To be design'd Castille. **1874** *Act 37–8 Vict.* c. 94 §38 The writer ..is not named or designed.

†**3.** Of names, signs, etc.: To signify, stand for.

1627 HAKEWILL *Apol.* (1630) Bbb iij b, The numerall.. then designeth so many hundred thousand. *a* **1631** DONNE *Serm.* (1839) IV. cvii. 466 A few lines of ciphers will design ..that number. **1642** JER. TAYLOR *Episc.* (1647) 138 Names which did designe temporary offices.

†**4.** To appoint to office, function, or position; to designate, nominate. Const. as in 2. *Obs.*

1596 BELL *Surv. Popery* III. xii. 509 The priest was designed ouer the penitents in euerie church. **1607** TOPSELL *Four-f. Beasts* (1658) 127 A perpetuall and unquenchable fire, for the watching whereof, were Dogs designed. **1611** SPEED *Hist. Gt. Brit.* IX. xvi. (1632) 862 Where Election designeth the Successor. *a* **1649** DRUMM. OF HAWTH. *Jas. V* Wks. (1711) 113 The commission..in which he is designed lieutenant. **1668** DAVENANT *Man's the Master* v. i, When you design'd your man to court her in your shape. **1701** ROWE *Ambit. Step-Moth.* II. i. 555 Great, just and merciful, such as Mankind..would have design'd a King.

5. To appoint or assign (something *to* a person); to make over, bestow, grant, give. Const. *to* or *dative*. *Obs.* exc. in *Sc. Law*.

1572 *Sc. Acts Jas. VI* (1597) §48 They haue appoynted, marked, and designed the said manse, with foure acres..to the vse of the Minister..that sall..minister at the said kirk. **1592** DAVIES *Immort. Soul* xxxiii. (R.), Three kinds of life to her designed be. **1608** J. KING *Serm. St. Mary's* 8 Afterwardes when Michal was designed to him [David]. **1650–60** TATHAM *Wks.* (1879) 169 He is the challenged and justly may Design the way of fighting. **1651** *Fuller's Abel Rediv., Musculus* 257 Designing unto Musculus one of the principallest Churches. **1681** GLANVILL *Sadducismus* II. 296 The Spirit's name which he designed her was Locas. **1784** COWPER *Task* VI. 580 Nature..when she form'd, designed them an abode. **1864** *Daily Review* 14 Nov., The minister of Dalgety in 1862..stating..that in terms of the Act 1663, chapter 21, he was entitled to have grass designed to him for the support of a horse..and praying the Presbytery to make the necessary designation accordingly.

6. Hence, with mixture of II, and ultimately fusing with 10: To set apart in thought for the use or advantage of some one; to intend to bestow or give. Const. *for*, †*to*, †*on*.

1664 DRYDEN *Rival Ladies* Ded., This worthless Present was design'd you, long before it was a Play. **1666** —— *Ann. Mirab.* lx, Their mounting shot is on our sails designed: Deep in their hulls our deadly bullets light. **1673** *Essex Papers* (Camden) I. 153 Trear. designes the place to Orrery, but I am confident it will never be. **1701** *Pennsylv. Archives*

I. 142, I fully design'd you a visit. **1725** DE FOE *Voy. round World* (1840) 245 What present I had designed for her. **1833** HT. MARTINEAU *Brooke Farm* ii. 22 Hearing what favours were designed for his boy. **1861** M. PATTISON *Ess.* (1889) I. 30 These fragments are designed for the German, rather than the English reader.

7. To appoint, destine, devote (a thing or person) to a fate or purpose. Now merged in 10.

1593 NASHE *Christ's T.* 23 a, Because I am Christ the iust, therfore you will designe me to the Crosse vniustly. **1623** MASSINGER *Bondman* IV. ii, This well-built city, not long since designed To spoil and rapine. **1662** GERBIER *Princ.* 15 The Duke..designed in his Will ten Thousand Gilders..to ..alter what he had Built amisse. **1691** RAY *Creation* (1714) 174 Neither yet need those who are designed to Divinity itself fear to look into these studies. [**1747** *Col. Rec. Pennsylv.* V. 139 The Goods design'd as a Present to the Indians.]

II. [allied to DESIGN *sb.* I, obs. F. *desseigner*] To plan, purpose, intend.

8. To form a plan or scheme of; to conceive and arrange in the mind; to originate mentally, plan out, contrive.

1548 HALL *Chron.* 215 When all thing was redy, according as he desyned. **1594** CAREW *Huarte's Exam. Wits* (1616) 218 The matters which they disseigne and worke with much wisdome. **1647** CLARENDON *Hist. Reb.* v. (1702) I. 430 That he should begin his Journey..so unfit for Travel..if his going away was design'd the day before. **1682** BUNYAN *Holy War* (Cassell) 250 If the enemy..should design and plot our ruin. **1795** SOUTHEY *Vis. Maid of Orleans* I. 170 Eternal Wisdom deals Or peace to man, or misery, for his good Alike design'd. **1812** S. ROGERS *Columbus* VII. 46 He can suspend the laws himself designed.

9. In weaker sense: To purpose, intend, mean. †Rarely, *to be designed* (obs.), like *to be purposed, resolved, determined, minded*, etc.

1660 R. COKE *Justice Vind.* Ep. Ded. 5, I designe no more than to demonstrate that [etc.]. **1701** DE FOE *True-born Eng.* 34 And yet he really designs no wrong. **1830** D'ISRAELI *Chas. I*, III. vi. 82 [Charles] designed inviting great artists to England.

b. with inf. phr.

1655–60 STANLEY *Hist. Philos.* (1701) 106/2 Great Queens, if you are design'd to speak to Mortals, Make me acquainted with your rumbling voice. **1678** BUTLER *Hud.* III. i. 1386 How does the Devil know What 'twas that I design'd to do? **1724** DE FOE *Mem. Cavalier* (1840) 162, I design to go with you. **1874** MICKLETHWAITE *Mod. Par. Churches* 224 Those objects which we design to bequeath to posterity.

c. with subord. clause as obj.

a **1704** T. BROWN *Declam. Praise Wealth* Argum., A proclamation, that she design'd her smiles should no more fall on the unworthy. **1715** DE FOE *Fam. Instruct.* I. vii. (1841) I. 125, I did not design you should have heard.

10. With complement (**a.** *inf.* or *sb.*, **b.** *prep. phr.*): To purpose or intend (a thing) *to be* or *do* (something); to mean (a thing) to serve some purpose or fulfil some plan.

a. **1703** MOXON *Mech. Exerc.* 137 So far as you design the Balcony to project. **1713** ADDISON *Cato* I. iv, Other creatures, Than what our nature and the Gods design'd us. **1733** LD. ORRERY in *Duncombe's Lett.* (1773) II. 35 The wood-walk, which I designed a labyrinth, is almost finished. **1779** COWPER *Lett.* 21 Sept., I have glazed the two frames, designed to receive my pine plants. **1802** MAR. EDGEWORTH *Moral T.* (1816) I. xiv. 116 With one..kick, designed to express his contempt. **1860** HOOK *Lives Abps.* (1869) I. i. 18 The emperors designed it to be a general council.

b. *a* **1700** DRYDEN (J.), You are not for obscurity designed, But, like the sun, must cheer all human kind. **1746** in *Leisure Hour* (1880) 23 A pewter teapot, but I believe it was designed for silver. **1756** BURKE *Vind. Nat. Soc.* Wks. 1808 I. 67 Ask of politicians the end for which laws were originally designed; and they will answer, that the laws were designed as a protection for the poor and weak. **1766** GOLDSM. *Vic. W.* xxi, The morning I designed for our departure. **1882** J. H. BLUNT *Ref. Ch. Eng.* II. 21 The palace which Somerset designed for this splendid site.

11. *intr.* To have purposes or intentions (of a specified kind). *rare.*

1749 FIELDING *Tom Jones* XIV. vii, To persuade the mother..that you designed honourably.

12. *trans.* To have in view, contemplate.

1677 HALE *Prim. Orig. Man.* I. i. 18 Before he come to the Subject it self which he designes. **1784** COWPER *Task* III. 11 So I, designing other themes, and call'd T' adorn the Sofa with eulogium. **1877** W. BRUCE *Comm. Revelation* 87 Tell him that his natural Enemies are not designed in the promise.

13. *intr.* and quasi-*pass.* (usually with *for*): To intend to go or start; to be bound *for* (a place).

1644 EVELYN *Mem.* (1857) I. 75 Within sight of Tours where we were designed for the rest of the time. **1684** LADY RUSSELL *Lett.* I. xv. 42 The question..when I design for Stratton. **1688** in Ellis *Orig. Lett.* Ser. II. IV. 141 They design to Bristol, but will take Exeter..in the way. **1691** T. H[ALE] *Acc. New Invent.* 21 Ships..designed on long Voyages. **1712** E. COOKE *Voy. S. Sea* 360 From Guam we design for Batavia. **1819** R. CHAPMAN *Life Jas. V* 129 This convinced them all that the king designed for France. **1823** SCOTT *Quentin D.* viii, On the succeeding day we were designed for Amboise. **1845** CARLYLE *Cromwell* (1871) II. 133 The new Lord Lieutenant had at first designed for Munster.

b. *transf.* To intend to start upon a certain course; to mean to enter upon a pursuit.

1694 GIBSON in *Lett. Lit. Men* (Camden) 225 And if he designs for Law, 'tis high time to begin.

III. [allied to DESIGN *sb.* II, It. *disegnare*, F. *dessiner*] To sketch, delineate, draw; to fashion artistically.

14. *trans.* †**a.** To make a sketch of (an object or scene); to sketch, draw. *Obs.* **b.** To trace the outline of, delineate.

(DESIGNMENT, implying the vb. in this sense, is quoted of 1570.)

1635 COWLEY *Davideis* I. 747 The Prophet Gad in learned Dust designs Th' immortal solid Rules of fancy'd Lines. **1638** JUNIUS *Painting of Ancients* 290 A good invention well designed and seasonably coloured. **1644** EVELYN *Diary* (1871) 69 The prospect was so tempting that I designed it with my crayon. **1699** LISTER *Journ. Paris* 53 In the Flore.. they have designed..an Universal Map. **1782** MANN in *Lett. Lit. Men* (Camden) 421 Designing, painting..and describing every Fish. **1879** STEVENSON *Trav. Cevennes* 211 The monstrous ribs and gullies of the mountain were faintly designed in the moonshine.

c. To make the preliminary sketch of (a work of art, a picture, statue, ornamental fabric, etc.); to make the plans and drawings necessary for the construction of (a building, ship, machine, etc.), which the workmen have to follow out.

1697 EVELYN *Numism.* vii. 240 Mons. Morelli, who both Designets [? designes] and Ingraves the Medals. *a* **1700** DRYDEN (J.), The prince designs The new elected seat, and draws the lines. **1743** *Peterhouse College Order* in Willis & Clark *Cambridge* (1886) I. 37 In Consideration of his Designing..the new Building. **1893** *Weekly Notes* 89/1 To design and superintend the construction of the docks in question.

15. To plan and execute (a structure, work of art, etc.); to fashion with artistic skill or decorative device; to furnish or adorn with a design.

1666 DRYDEN *Ann. Mirab.* clii, The weaver, charmed with what his loom designed. **1697** —— *Virg. Past.* v. 102 Behold, four hallow'd Altars we design. **1703** STEELE *Tend. Husb.* III. ii, However my Face is very prettily design'd today. **1853** KINGSLEY *Hypatia* v, Did Christians..design its statues and its frescoes? **1865** J. FERGUSSON *Hist. Archit.* I. I. IV. v. 346 The Roman bridges were designed on the same grand scale as their aqueducts. **1874** GREEN *Short Hist.* i. §6. 52 A lady summons him..to design a robe which she is embroidering.

16. *intr.* **a.** To trace the outline of a figure or form; to put a graphic representation on paper, canvas, etc.; to draw, sketch. **b.** To form or fashion a work of art; in a narrower sense, to form decorative figures, devise artistic patterns.

1662 EVELYN *Chalcogr.* 128 Unless he that Copies, Design perfectly himself. **1665** SIR T. HERBERT *Trav.* (1677) 149 One he knew could both design and copy well. **1854** RUSKIN *Two Paths* i. (1858) 44 A painter designs when he chooses some things, refuses others, and arranges all. **1885** H. V. BARNETT in *Mag. of Art* Sept. 454/1 She..began to design and to paint with delicacy, taste, and truth.

designable, *a.* [f. L. *dēsignā-re* (see DESIGNATE *v.*) + -BLE. In sense 2 f. DESIGN *v.* + -ABLE.]

†**1.** ('dɛsɪgnəb(ə)l) That can be distinctly marked out; distinguishable. *Obs.*

1644 DIGBY *Two Treat.* I. 85 The mover..cannot passe over all these infinite designable degrees in an instant. **1666** BOYLE *Orig. Formes & Qual.* (1667) 3 Matter..must have Motion in some or all its designable Parts. **1716** M. DAVIES *Athen. Brit.* II. 242 Book-Ware-Houses, furnish'd with such an Ideal, optable or designable Arianizing Library.

2. (də'zaɪnəb(ə)l) Capable of being designed.

designate ('dɛsɪgnət), *ppl. a.* [ad. L. *dēsignāt-us*, pa. pple. of *dēsignāre* to DESIGNATE.] Marked out for office or position; appointed or nominated, but not yet installed, as in ***bishop designate***. *spec.* in the University of Cambridge.

1646 BUCK *Rich. III*, I. 3 Richard Plantagenet..King of England, designate by King Henry the Sixth..This Duke of Yorke, and King designate. **1847** SIR W. HAMILTON *Let.* 32 *Definite*, or, more precisely, *predefinite*..is equivalent.. to *designate* and *pre-designate*. **1877** *World* VII. 11 The husband designate was present. **1878** *Cambr. Univ. Cal.* 5 There are three days of general admission to the title of Bachelor Designate of Arts in every year. **1888** *Times* 27 June 12/4 The Lord Bishop of Bedford Designate will preach. **1892** *Ordinances of Cambr. Univ.* 152 At the creation of Doctors of Law in every year, the names be arranged in order of seniority according to the seniority of the Doctors Designate as Masters of Law. **1925** *Cambr. Univ. Cal.* 85 Bachelors in Arts, Law, Medicine, Surgery, and Music remain 'Bachelors designate' until the 31st of December.

Hence **'designatehood**, the condition of being designate.

1862 *Sat. Rev.* XIV. 705/1 The period of Designatehood.

designate ('dɛs-, 'dɛzɪgneɪt), *v.* [f. ppl. stem of L. *dēsignāre* to mark out, trace out, denote by some indication, contrive, devise, appoint to an office, f. *de-* (DE- I. 3) + *signāre* to mark. Some of the senses of the L. verb, having come down through It. and Fr., are expressed by DESIGN; *designate* is a modern formation taking up the other senses: cf. F. *désigner* as distinct from *dessiner* and obs. *desseigner*.]

1. *trans.* To point out, indicate; to particularize, specify.

1801 *Brit. Crit.* July (T.), Of these [faults] so few examples occur, that it would be invidious to designate them. **1808** J. BARLOW *Columb.* VIII. 522 Its faults designate and its merits prize. **1828** WEBSTER s.v., The limits are designated on the map. **1839–40** W. IRVING *Wolfert's R.* (1855) 107 He need only designate to me the way to his chamber. **1846** TRENCH *Miracles* xxx. (1862) 430 The man ..designates the channel in which he desires that this mercy may flow. **1861** MRS. H. WOOD *East Lynne* I. xi. 170 It had four post horses..the number having been designated by Lord Mount-Severn.

2. Of things: To serve to point out; to be an indication of. With *compl.*: To point out, specify *as* being so and so.

1807 SOUTHEY *Espriella's Lett.* II. 251 A black Triton.. meant..by his crown of feathers, to designate the native Indians. *c* **1829** LANDOR *Wks.* (1868) II. 93 Her lips [in a picture] were half-open; her hair flew loosely behind her, designating that she was in haste. *a* **1831** A. KNOX *Rem.* (1844) I. 65 Those interior effects of Divine grace, which designate their nature..to the..possessor. **1870** ROGERS *Hist. Gleanings* Ser. II. 200 A man's dress designated his rank and calling. **1884** tr. *Lotze's Metaph.* II. iv. 293 The only function of the mathematical symbol is to designate *p* and *q* as absolutely equal in rank.

3. To point out by a name or descriptive appellation; to name, denominate, entitle, style.

1818 JAS. MILL *Brit. India* II. v. ix. 693 The coalition.. gave existence to the ministry which that circumstance has served to designate. **1831** CARLYLE *Sart. Res.* II. v. (1838) 161 The title Blumine, whereby she is here designated. **1868** LOCKYER *Elem. Astron.* i. (1879) 29 Clusters and nebulæ are designated by their number in the catalogues. **1871** MORLEY *Voltaire* (1886) 79 Two very distinct conceptions..equally designated by the common name of civil liberty.

b. with *double obj.* or *compl.*: To name, describe, or characterize (*as*).

1836 *Random Recoll. Ho. Lords* xvi. 397, I designate them [his ideas] as somewhat above mediocrity. **1854** MACAULAY *Misc. Writ.* (1860) II. 228 He is designated, in Mr. Ivimey's History of the Baptists, as the depraved Bunyan, the wicked tinker of Elstow. **1862** STANLEY *Jew. Ch.* (1877) I. xix. 360 Miriam is almost always designated as the 'prophetess'. **1879** M. ARNOLD *Guide Eng. Lit.* Mixed Ess. 194, I wonder at his designating Milton our greatest poet.

4. Of things: To serve as a name for, stand for; to be descriptive of.

1816 SINGER *Hist. Cards* 45 The term continued to designate hired troops. **1842** ALISON *Hist. Europe* (1849–50) X. lxix. §29. 438 The celebrated saying..'If these books [etc.]'..designates the whole system of their..government.

5. To appoint, set apart, select, nominate for duty or office; to destine or devote to a purpose or fate. Const. *for, to.*

1791 J. BARLOW *Adv. Priv. Orders* I. 27 A mere savage.. would decide the question of equality by a trial of bodily strength, designating the man that could lift the heaviest beam to be the legislator. **1828** WEBSTER s.v., This captain was designated to that station. **1853** MAURICE *Proph. & Kings* xxii. 378 Josiah..was designated to his task before his birth. **1855** MILMAN *Lat. Chr.* VII. vi. (1864) IV. 202 Men ..equally designated for perdition in this world and the next. **1855** MACAULAY *Hist. Eng.* III. 394 A clause designating the successor by name.

'designated, *ppl. a.* [f. DESIGNATE *v.* + -ED[1].]

a. = DESIGNATE *ppl. a.*

1868 FREEMAN *Norm. Conq.* (1876) II. ix. 436 Harold was virtually..the designated successor to the crown.

b. ***designated hitter*** (Baseball), a substitute named before the start of a game to hit for the pitcher anywhere in the batting order; also ***designated pinch hitter*** and *fig.*

1973 *N.Y. Times* 4 Feb. 51/1 In the baseball box scores this summer, he will be listed as the 'dh', the designated hitter for the pitcher. *Ibid.* 17 Feb. 31/2 (*caption*) Fenton, I want you to meet Ted Bolton [*sc.* a newly-appointed employee], our new designated pinch-hitter. **1973** *Newsweek* 26 Mar. 27/3 His main qualifications for office were an unswerving loyalty to Perón—who tapped him in 1972 as his own designated pinch hitter in the election. **1985** *N.Y. Times* 23 Oct. A23/1 Missouri was chosen by Congress as the designated hitter for [black] freedom and equality. **1986** *Ibid.* 11 June D29/1 He did have strong opinions on certain elements of baseball. On the designated hitter:'..it's appalling.'

designation (dɛs-, dɛzɪg'neɪʃən). [ad. L. *dēsignātiōn-em*, n. of action from *dēsignāre* (see DESIGNATE). Cf. F. *désignation* (14th c. in Hatzf., and in mod.F.; not in Cotgr. 1611).]

1. The action of marking or pointing out; indication of a particular person, place, or thing by gesture, words, or recognizable signs.

1398 TREVISA *Barth. De P.R.* XIX. cxxvi. (1495) 926 Alpha is wryte for desygnacion of letters, for amonge Grekys this letter tokenyth one. **1597** HOOKER *Eccl. Pol.* v. lxix. (1611) 374 Wherefore was it said vnto Moyses by particular designation, This very place..is holy ground. **1677** HALE *Prim. Orig. Man.* IV. vii. 357 The designation of an end in working is the great perfection of an intelligent Agent. **1731** BAILEY vol. II, *Designation*..also the marking the abutments and boundings of an estate. **1784** COWPER *Tiroc.* 640 With designation of the finger's end. **1794** PALEY *Evid.* (1825) II. 224 The designation of the time would have been more determinate. **1860** TRENCH *Serm. Westm. Abb.* xv. 164 The intention with which he thus designated Jesus unto them: they understand it..not at the first designation.

b. *concr.* A distinctive mark or indication.

1646 SIR T. BROWNE *Pseud. Ep.* IV. xiii. 224 Those stars.. were indeed but designations of such quarters and portions of the yeare, wherein the same were observed. **1831** J. DAVIES *Manual Mat. Med.* 26 The word *ana*..is placed before the designation of the quantity.

2. The action of appointing or nominating a person for a particular office or duty; the fact of being thus nominated; appointment, nomination.

1605 BACON *Adv. Learn.* II. Ded. §14 There hath not been ..any public designation of writers or inquirers. **1640** BP. HALL *Episc.* II. xvi. 176 It was in the Bishops power to raise the Clergie from one degree to another, neither might they refuse his designations. **1674** OWEN *Holy Spirit* (1693) 83

His Designation of God unto his Kingdom. *c* **1689** in Somers *Tracts* I. 315 Till the King in Designation be actually invested with the Regal Office. **1791** COWPER *Iliad.* IV. 458 By designation of the Greeks was sent Ambassador. **1868** FREEMAN *Norm. Conq.* (1876) II. ix. 378 This *quasi* designation of Eadward to the crown.

†**b.** The appointment of a thing; the summoning of an assembly. *Obs.*

a **1638** MEDE *Disc. Ezek.* xx. 20 Wks. (1672) I. 56 The designation or pitching that Seventh upon the day we call Saturday. **1649** JER. TAYLOR *Gt. Exemp.* ii. §9 By designation of Conventions for prayer. **1697** BP. PATRICK *Comm. Ex.* xvi. 5 The Designation of this seventh Day was ..from their wonderful Deliverance. **1777** BURKE *Let. Sheriffs Bristol* Wks. 1842 I. 218 At the first designation of these assemblies.

†**c.** The qualification of being marked out or fitted for an employment; vocation, bent (of mind), 'call'. *Obs.*

1657 *Burton's Diary* (1828) II. 14 That man that has a designation to that work [preaching]. **1736** BOLINGBROKE *Patriot.* (1749) 12 These are the men to whom the part I mentioned is assigned. Their talents denote their general designation. **1779–81** JOHNSON *L.P., Cowley* Wks. II. 6 That particular designation of mind, and propensity for some certain science or employment, which is commonly called Genius.

3. The action of devoting by appointment to a particular purpose or use; an act of this nature. *arch.*

1637 GILLESPIE *Eng. Pop. Cerem.* III. i. 6 Designation or deputation is when a man appoints a thing for such an use. **1767** BLACKSTONE *Comm.* II. 329 To make various designations of their profits. **1796** C. MARSHALL *Garden.* xii. (1813) 136 The designation of trees to a wall necessarily occasions cutting.

b. *Sc. Law.* The setting apart of manses and glebes for the clergy from the church lands by the presbytery of the bounds.

1572 *Sc. Acts Jas. VI* (1597) §48 Vpon the said marking and designation, the Arch-bishop..sal giue his testimoniall, bearing how he [etc.]. **1861** in W. BELL *Dict. Law Scotl.* s.v., After a designation by the presbytery. **1864** [see DESIGN *v.* 5].

c. *U.S.* The authoritative allotment of ground for oyster-culture; *concr.* the ground thus allotted.

†**4.** Purpose, intention, design. *Obs.*

1662 STILLINGFL. *Orig. Sacr.*, The end of his life in Hannahs designation. **1690** LOCKE *Hum. Und.* III. i. §7 So far is there a constant Connection between the Sound and the Idea and a Designation that the one stand for the other. **1737** WHISTON *Josephus' Antiq.* XVIII. vi. §9 God proved opposite to his designation. **1763** MRS. BROOKE *Lady J. Mandeville* (1782) II. 2 This mutual passion is the designation of heaven to restore him.

†**5.** Sketching, delineation. *Obs. rare.*

1796 JANE WEST *Gossip's Story* I. 4 A mere novice in landscape designation, I confine myself to the delineation of ..human character.

6. A descriptive name, an appellation; *spec.* in *Law*, the statement of profession, trade, residence, etc., added for purposes of identification to a person's name.

1824 LANDOR *Imag. Conv.* (1846) 8 A designation which I have no right to. **1868** GLADSTONE *Juv. Mundi* ii. (1870) 43 The name Argeioi..as a designation of the army before Troy. **1876** E. MELLOR *Priesth.* i. 15 The name 'priesthood' ..became a designation of the whole Church of God.

designative ('dɛs-, 'dɛzɪgneɪtɪv), *a.* and *sb.* [ad. med.L. *dēsignātīv-us*, f. ppl. stem *dēsignāt-*: see -IVE. In mod.F. *désignatif.*]

A. *adj.* Having the quality of designating.

1611 COTGR., *Designatif*, designatiue, denotatiue. **1812** J. HENRY *Camp. agst. Quebec* 91 Merely designative of the raw soldier. **1818** BENTHAM *Ch. Eng.* 35 Then are the words designative of the sort of act first mentioned. **1845** F. BARHAM *An Odd Medley* 8 The [Hebrew] designative preposition *ath.*

B. *sb.* Anything used to designate.

1824 J. GILCHRIST *Etym. Interpr.* 77 Perhaps the scientific purpose intended is as well accomplished by these as by any designatives that could be invented.

designator ('dɛs-, 'dɛzɪgneɪtə(r)). [a. L. *dēsignātor*, agent-n. from *dēsignāre* to DESIGNATE.]

1. One who designates or points out.

2. *Rom. Antiq.* An officer who assigned to each person his rank and place in public shows and ceremonies.

1706 in PHILLIPS (ed. Kersey). **1727–51** CHAMBERS *Cycl.* s.v., There were designators at funeral solemnities, and at the games, theatres, and shews.

'designatory, *a.* [f. L. type **dēsignātōri-us*, f. *dēsignātor*: see prec. and -ORY.] Of or pertaining to a designator or designation.

1885 SIR L. W. CAVE in *Law Times' Rep.* LII. 518/1 That the indefinite article has the same designatory force as the definite.

designatum ('dɛs-, 'dɛzɪgneɪtəm). *Philos.* Pl. -ata. [f. L. *dēsignātum*, neut. pa. pple. of *dēsignāre* to mark out, indicate (see DESIGNATE *v.*).] The object or class of objects, whether existing or not, that a sign designates. (Cf. DENOTATUM.)

1938 [see DENOTATUM]. **1940** *Jrnl. Religion* July 266 No appeal to revelation can deliver a man from responsibility for determining the designata and denotata of the words he uses. **1940** B. RUSSELL *Inquiry* vii. 109 The designatum of 'this' is continually changing. **1958** MEYER & WILKINSON tr. *Carnap's Introd. Symb. Logic* §20 The color red is the designatum of the French word 'rouge'. **1964** *Language* XL. 266 The designatum of the whole expression is a Boolean sum of the designata of the members.

designed (dɪ'zaɪnd), *ppl. a.* [f. DESIGN *v.* + -ED.] †**a.** Marked out, appointed, DESIGNATE. **b.** Planned, purposed, intended. **c.** Drawn, outlined; formed, fashioned, or framed according to design.

a. 1609 BIBLE (Douay) *Num.* viii. Comm., Their designed offices. **1622** BACON *Hen. VII*, Wks. (1860) 331 His two designed generals. **1701** W. WOTTON *Hist. Rome* ii. 28 He was designed Consul for next Year. **1751** CHAMBERS *Cycl. Suppl.* s.v. *Bishop*, Bishop designed, *episcopus designatus.* **b. 1586** B. YOUNG *Guazzo's Civ. Conv.* IV. 180b, Fortifying my designed purpose. **1660** BARROW *Euclid* Pref. (1714) 3 A Size beyond the design'd Proportion. **1717** LADY M. W. MONTAGU *Lett.* 1 Jan. (1887) I. 139 Making my designed return a mystery. **1865** MOZLEY *Mirac.* vii. 291 *note*, That this failure..should be designed. **c. 1870** EMERSON *Soc. & Solit., Art* Wks. (Bohn) III. 16 An oak-tree..being the form in nature best designed to resist a constant assailing force.

†*to be designed*, to be purposed or minded: see DESIGN *v.* 9.

designedly (dɪ'zaɪnɪdlɪ), *adv.* [f. prec. + -LY².] By design, on purpose, intentionally.

1658–9 *Burton's Diary* (1828) III. 394 You need not be their enemies, directly or designedly. **1710** STEELE *Tatler* No. 234 ¶1 An Art of being often designedly dull. **1875** JOWETT *Plato* (ed. 2) I. 343 Designedly irritating the judges.

de'signedness. [f. as prec. + -NESS.] The quality of being designed or purposed; intentional character.

1864 in LATHAM. *Mod.* The designedness of the 'coincidence' was obvious.

designer (dɪ'zaɪnə(r)). Also 7 designor. [f. DESIGN *v.* + -ER¹.] One who designs.

1. One who originates a plan or plans.

1670 G. H. *Hist. Cardinals* II. II. 151 Thoughtful and cogitative, a great designor. **1736** BUTLER *Anal.* II. Concl. Wks. 1874 I. 307 Ten thousand thousand instances of design cannot but prove a designer. **1863** J. G. MURPHY *Comm. Gen.* i. 2 The Great Designer.

2. In bad sense: One who cherishes evil designs or is actuated by selfish purposes; a plotter, schemer, intriguer.

1649 PRYNNE *Demurrer* 83 The greatest designers, plotters and lifters up of themselves against the interest of Christ. *a* **1704** T. BROWN *Praise of Wealth* Wks. 1730 I. 84 The cunning designer gets into the princes favour. **1726** in H. Campbell *Love-lett. Mary Q. Scots* (1824) 20 Where is one faithful friend to be chosen out among a thousand base designers?

3. a. One who makes an artistic design or plan of construction; a draughtsman; *spec.* one whose business is to invent or prepare designs or patterns for the manufacturer or constructor.

1662 EVELYN *Chalcogr.* 147 Where the Workman is not an accomplished Designer. **1752** JOHNSON *Rambler* No. 190 ¶10 Sculptors, painters, and designers. **1891** *Leeds Mercury* 21 May 5/1 The designers of these tank vessels. **1892** *Labour Commission* Gloss. No. 9 *Designer*, the architect who designs the enrichment for the 'modeller' in the plastering trade. *Mod.* A designer in a textile factory.

b. Freq. used *attrib.* in fashion, etc., to denote goods bearing the name or label of a famous designer, with the implication that they are expensive or prestigious. Also *transf.* and *fig.* orig. *U.S.*

1966 *N.Y. Times* 12 Feb. 31/7 (*heading*) Designer scarves join name-dropping game. **1973** E. JONG *Fear of Flying* (1974) ii. 37 She was all gotten up in designer clothes. **1977** *Washington Post* 8 Jan. C1/6 Mrs. Carter has been known to have a sharp eye for price tags, rejecting anything she feels inflated by designer labels. **1978** *Ibid.* 30 Dec. C2/1 At the moment, designer jeans are such big business that Bloomingdale's has created a department called 'Pure Jeanius'. **1979** *United States 1980/81* (Penguin Travel Guides) 321 For good buys on top-brand and designer sheets and pillowcases, New York is definitely the place. **1984** *Times* 4 Sept. 12/1 Small wonder Perrier is called Designer Water. My local wine bar has the cheek to charge 70p a glass. **1985** S. LOWRY *Young Fogey Handbk.* viii. 69 He loves seafood..and detests designer dishes. **1985** *Mail on Sunday* (Colour Suppl.) 3 Mar. 53/1 After all, this is designer-label land where the window boxes have electronic water sprinklers and the cat's manicurist is on a retainer.

c. Special Comb. **designer drug** orig. *U.S.*, a drug synthesized to mimic a legally restricted or prohibited drug without itself being subject to such restriction.

1983 *Sacramento Union* 17 Dec. E8/7 Thirty-four people have died in the last four years after using 'designer drugs', heroin look-alikes concocted in underground laboratories and hitting the streets one step ahead of government regulations. **1985** *Sunday Times* 24 Mar. 12/1 A still-growing line of what are known as 'designer drugs', new compounds that are synthetic 'analogues' of existing illegal mind-altering substances. **1985** *Times* 3 Dec. 5/8 Designer drugs were an added threat to the rising menace of heroin and cocaine addiction. **1986** *Washington Post* 2 June B4/1 The accidental discovery a few years ago of a 'designer drug' — called MPTP — that produced Parkinson's symptoms in addicts.

designful (dɪ'zaɪnfʊl), *a.* [f. DESIGN *sb.* + -FUL.] Full of design; purposed, intentional.

a **1677** [see next]. **1867** J. H. STIRLING *Crit. Ess.* (1868) 206 The ascription to Kant of designful reticence and intentional obscurity. **1890** —— *Gifford Lect.* iv. 73 The.. designful contrivance of the world.

de'signfulness. [f. prec. + -NESS.] Designful quality: **a.** craftiness, scheming; **b.** fullness of design, intentional or prearranged character.

a **1677** BARROW *Serm.* Wks. 1716 II. 83 Drawn over with ..features of base designfulness. **1890** J. H. STIRLING *Gifford Lect.* v. 94 The designfulness is but contingent.

designing (dɪ'zaɪnɪŋ), *vbl. sb.* [f. DESIGN *v.* + -ING¹.] The action of DESIGN *v.*; marking out, nomination; planning, preliminary sketching, etc.

a **1618** RALEIGH *Maxims St.* (1651) 77 Upon the designing of his successour. **1756** NUGENT *Gr. Tour* IV. 92 The designing was by Michael Angelo. **1884** *Athenæum* 12 Jan. 59/1 Both the Dublin cathedrals are of English designing.

b. Evil design, plotting, scheming.

1658–9 *Burton's Diary* (1828) III. 55 Petty designings. **1795** *Jemima* II. 18 Her suspicions were excited by his detected disguise, and probable deep designings.

c. *attrib.*

1711 SHAFTESB. *Charac.* (1737) III. 403 The designing Arts..such as Architecture. **1864** *Daily Tel.* 29 June, It has a 'designing class' at South Kensington.

designing (dɪ'zaɪnɪŋ), *ppl. a.* [-ING².]

1. That designs, plans, etc.; characterized by constructive forethought.

1653 H. MORE *Antid. Ath.* II. xi. §13 (1712) 78 A knowing and designing Providence. **1711** STEELE *Spect.* No. 43 ¶3 We are all Grave, Serious, Designing Men, in our Way. **1850** MCCOSH *Div. Govt.* III. i. (1874) 299 The order and adaptation of nature suggest a designing mind.

2. That cherishes evil designs or is actuated by ulterior motives; scheming, crafty, artful.

a **1671** LD. FAIRFAX *Mem.* (1699) 100 The sad consequences that crafty and designing men have brought to pass. **1711** ADDISON *Spect.* No. 131 ¶6 The old Knight is impos'd upon by a designing Fellow. **1887** BOWEN *Virg. Æneid* II. 196 Feigned tears and designing sorrow.

de'signingly, *adv.* [f. prec. + -LY².] Intentionally; with evil design or selfish purpose, craftily.

1684 H. MORE *Answ.* B j b, Over prone cunningly and designingly to serve their turns. **1879** BARING-GOULD *Germany* II. 239 Trades'-unions are an excellent institution, if not ignorantly or designingly misdirected.

designless (dɪ'zaɪnlɪs), *a.* [f. DESIGN *sb.* + -LESS.] Void of design or plan; purposeless.

1643 HAMMOND *Serm. at Oxf.* Wks. 1683 IV. 513 That designless love of sinning. *a* **1691** BOYLE *Hist. Air* xii. (1692) 65 These Wounds must have been made by some designless Agent. **1883** JEFFERIES *Story of my Heart* 59 The designless, formless chaos of chance-directed matter.

de'signlessly, *adv.* [f. prec. + -LY².] Without design or plan; with no specific purpose.

1648 BOYLE *Seraph. Love* xiii. (1700) 77 His [the Sun's] visits are made designlessly. *a* **1691** —— *Wks.* VI. 80 (R.) Not rashly or designlessly shuffled by a blind hazard.

†**de'signment.** *Obs.* [f. DESIGN *v.* + -MENT.] = DESIGNATION, DESIGN.

1. Indication by sign or token.

1625 GILL *Sacr. Philos.* ii. 156 No Scripture is so direct.. as this for the certaine designement of the time. *a* **1684** LEIGHTON *Comm. 1 Pet.* ii. 14 The *them that are sent*..is a very clear designment of the inferior governors of those times.

2. Appointment or nomination to office or function; consignment or destination to a fate.

1582 N. T. (Rhem.) *Luke* vi. 12 Annot., As a preparation to the designement of his Apostles. **1612** T. TAYLOR *Comm. Titus* i. 7 Designements to offices and places. **1642** JER. TAYLOR *Episc.* (1647) 93 Paul & Barnabas..went to the Gentiles, by..speciall designement made at Antioch. **1668** H. MORE *Div. Dial.* IV. xviii. (1713) 326 No designment of them to Sin and Damnation. **1732** LAW *Serious C.* xxii. (1761) 420 It is by the express designment of God, that some beings are Angels, and others are men.

3. Appointment, arrangement, or ordination of affairs; planning, designing; hence, that which is planned; an enterprise, undertaking, design.

1583 HARSNET *Serm. Ezek.* (1658) 135 Had he had freedome to haue altered Gods Designment, Adams liberty had bene aboue the designment of God. **1594** *Ord. Prayer* in *Liturg. Serv. Q. Eliz.* (1847) 654 Cruel designments so closely plotted against her innocent life. **1604** SHAKS. *Oth.* II. i. 22 The desperate Tempest hath so bang'd the Turkes, That their designement halts. **1611** CORYAT *Crudities* 205 A very disastrous accident..frustrated his whole designement. **1659** *Gentl. Calling* (1696) 139 Many hours.. intervening between the Designment and the Execution [of a Duel]. **1738** WARBURTON *Div. Legat.* I. 216 A strange Jumble as well as Iniquity in this Designment.

4. Artistic representation, delineation; an outline, sketch; an original draught or design.

1570 DEE *Math. Pref.* in Billingsley *Euclide* A j, Of all these, liuely designementes..to be in velame parchement described. **1658** DRYDEN *Death O. Cromwell* 96 For though some meaner artist's skill were shown..Yet still the fair designment was his own. **1667** —— *Ess. Dram. Poesie* (R.), Shall that excuse the ill painture or designment of them? **1703** T. N. *City & C. Purchaser* 85 A neat and full Expression of the 1st Idea or Designment thereof.

desilicate (diːˈsɪlɪkeɪt), *v.* [f. DE- II. 1.] *trans.* To deprive of silica. Hence **deˈsilicated** *ppl. a.*
In mod. Dicts.

desiˈlicify, deˈsilicize, *v.* [f. DE- II. 1.] *trans.* To free from silex or silicon; = DESILICONIZE. Hence **desiˌlicifiˈcation.**
In mod. Dicts.

desiliconize (diːˈsɪlɪkəˌnaɪz), *v.* [f. DE- II. 1.] *trans.* To deprive of or free from silicon. Hence **deˈsiliconized** *ppl. a.*; **-izing** *vbl. sb.* and *ppl. a.*; **desiliconiˈzation.**
1881 C. R. A. WRIGHT in *Encycl. Brit.* XIII. 333/1 (*Iron*) The decarbonizing and desiliconizing of iron by the action of an oxidizing atmosphere is the essential feature of the processes of refining pig iron and of making natural steel. **1891** *Times* 8 Oct. 14/6 They had suffered more from desiliconization than from desulphurization.

desilver (diːˈsɪlvə(r)), *v.* [f. DE- II. 2.] *trans.* To deprive of its silver, remove the silver from.
1864 in WEBSTER. **1886** FENN *Master of Ceremonies* I. ii. 9 The over-cleaned and de-silvered plated pot.

desilverize (diːˈsɪlvəraɪz), *v.* [f. DE- II. 1.] *trans.* To extract the silver from (lead or other metal).
1872 RAYMOND *Statist. Mines & Mining* 450 Two systems ..desilverizing and refining two charges of [lead] in twenty-four hours. **1886** A. J. BALFOUR *Question* 1239 *Gold & Silver Comm.*, The cost of desilverising the copper.
Hence **deˈsilverized** *ppl. a.*, **deˈsilverizing** *vbl. sb.* and *ppl. a.*; also **desilveriˈzation.**
1870 J. PERCY (*title*), The Metallurgy of Lead, including Desilverization and Cupellation. **1872** RAYMOND *Statist. Mines & Mining* 449 The desilverizing kettle holds 22,000 pounds of lead. **1879** *Cassell's Techn. Educ.* IV. 49/2 In lead pipes the soft desilverised lead is considered best.

desinence (ˈdɛsɪnəns). [a. F. *désinence* (16th c. in Hatzfeld) = It. *desinenza* 'a desinence or termination' (Florio), ad. med.L. *dēsinentia*, f. *dēsinent-em*: see next.] Termination, ending, close; *Gram.* a termination, suffix, or ending of a word.
1599 BP. HALL *Sat.* Postcr., Fettering together the series of the verses, with the bondes of like cadence or desinence of rime. **1623** FAVINE *Theat. Hon.* II. i. 67 The Romaine desinence or ending. **1814** BERINGTON *Lit. Hist. Mid. Ages* v. (1846) 273 The ear was thus flattered by a certain musical desinence, nor could it a moment doubt where every verse closed. **1873** BARDSLEY *Surnames* i. (1875) 13 The Saxon added 'son', as a desinence, as 'Williamson'.

desinent (ˈdɛsɪnənt), *a.* ? *Obs.* [ad. L. *dēsinent-em*, pr. pple. of *dēsinĕre* to leave off, close, f. DE- I. 1, 2 + *sinĕre* to leave.] Forming the end, terminal; ending, closing.
1605 B. JONSON *Masque Blackness*, Six tritons..their upper parts human..their desinent parts fish. **1677** CARY *Chronol.* II. II. III. iii. 227 The State was left in Confusion.. until the 38th desinent of Azariah. *Ibid.* 228 An. 39 of Uzziah desinent.

desiˈnential, *a.* [f. med.L. *dēsinentia* (see DESINENT) + -AL[1].] Pertaining to, or of the nature of, a desinence or ending.
1818 *Monthly Mag.* XLVI. 322 The desinential characteristics of the Latin noun. **1869** F. HALL in *Lauder's Tractate* 24 The desinential *-it*, for *-ed* [in Scotch pa. pples.]

desiner, var. of DECENER, *Obs.*
1591 GARRARD *Art Warre* 14 Under the charge of a Desiner or chiefe of a chamber.

desines, obs. form of DIZZINESS.

desinterressed, var. of DISINTERESSED *a. Obs.*

†**deˈsipiate,** *v. Obs.*[−0] [irreg. f. L. *dēsipĕre* (*dēsipio*) to be foolish, f. DE- I. 6 + *sapĕre* to be wise.] *intr.* To become foolish.
1623 in COCKERAM. **1663** F. HAWKINS *Youth's Behav.* 102.

desipience (dɪˈsɪpɪəns). [ad. L. *dēsipientia*, f. *dēsipient-em* DESIPIENT: see -ENCE.] Folly; foolish trifling, silliness.
1656 BLOUNT *Glossogr.*, *Desipience* is when the sick person speaks and doth idly; dotage. **1882** A. W. WARD *Dickens* ii. 24 Occasional desipience in the form of the wildest farce. **1887** *Spectator* 17 Sept. 1251 The maturity of sweet desipience.

deˈsipiency. [see prec., and -ENCY.] = prec.
1672 SIR T. BROWNE *Lett. Friend* §22 Many are mad but in..one prevalent desipiency. **1856** *Titan Mag.* Dec. 496 If the *desipere* be but *in loco*, religion itself will not forbid the seasonable desipiency.

desipient (dɪˈsɪpɪənt), *a. rare.* [ad. L. *dēsipient-em*, pr. pple. of *dēsipĕre* to be void of understanding, f. DE- I. 6 + *sapĕre* to know.] Foolish, silly; playing the fool, idly trifling.
1727 in BAILEY vol. II. **1894** STEVENSON in *Times* 2 June 17/4 In his character of disinterested spectator, gracefully desipient.

desirability (dɪˌzaɪərəˈbɪlɪtɪ). [f. next + -ITY.] The quality of being desirable; desirableness; quasi-*concr.* (with *pl.*) a desirable condition or thing.
1824 SOUTHEY *Life & Corr.* (1850) V. 189, I see possibilities and capabilities and desirabilities. **1859** FARRAR *Eric* 95 Of this school he often bragged as the acmé of desirability. **1861** BERESF. HOPE *Eng. Cathedr. 19th C.* iii. 68 Any decision upon the distinctive possibility or desirability of new cathedrals. **1873** SYMONDS *Grk. Poets* iii. 87 The desirability of consorting with none but the best company.

desirable (dɪˈzaɪərəb(ə)l), *a.* (*sb.*) Also 7-8 desireable. [a. F. *désirable* (12th c. in Hatzfeld), f. *désirer* to DESIRE, after L. *dēsīderābilis*.]
A. *adj.* **1.** Worthy to be desired; to be wished for. In early use often standing for the qualities which cause a thing to be desired: Pleasant, delectable, choice, excellent, goodly.
1382 WYCLIF *Prov.* xxi. 20 Desyrable tresor and oile in the dwelling place of the riȝtwis. *c* **1489** CAXTON *Blanchardyn* xxiii. 80 Blanchardyn..as that thinge whiche most he desyred in this world, dyde accepte this gracyouse and desyrable ansuere. **1573** G. HARVEY *Letter-bk.* (Camden) 126 Greate varietye of desirable flowers. **1611** BIBLE *Ezek.* xxiii. 12 She doted vpon the Assyrians..horsemen riding vpon horses, all of them desireable young men. **1662** STILLINGFL. *Orig. Sacr.* III. iii. §7 No evil is in its self desirable, or to be chosen. **1783** WATSON *Philip III* (1839) 169 It was surely desirable to put a period to these calamities. **1833** J. HOLLAND *Manuf. Metal* II. 301 This exceedingly convenient and desirable machine. **1891** H. MATTHEWS in *Law Times* XCII. 96/1 Some general modifications in the rules..are now desirable.
†**2.** To be regretted or desiderated; regrettable.
1650 T. FROYSELL *Gale of Opportunity* (1652) 1 He lived amiable and dyed desirable.
†**3.** Characterized by or full of desire. *Obs.*
1759 SARAH FIELDING *C'tess of Dellwyn* II. 23 With the desireable View of rendering her Smiles or Frowns of Consequence.
B. *sb.* **1.** That which is desirable; a desirable property or thing.
1645 E. WILLAN in Spurgeon *Treas. Dav.* Ps. xvi. 11 All these desirables are encircled within the compass of the first remarkable. **1721** WATTS *Serm.* ii. Wks. 1812 I. 18 He.. despises fame..pleasure and riches, and all mortal desirables. **1797** MRS. A. M. BENNETT *Beggar Girl* (1813) V. 52 Besides the desirables it would purchase [etc.]. **1873** MISS BROUGHTON *Nancy* II. 82 At that time, you see, he had not all the desirables.
2. One who is desirable.
1669 H. MORE *Antid. Idolatry* viii. 93 The highest of all desirables, that is, God himself. **1853** R. S. SURTEES *Sponge's Sp. Tour* xvi, Certainly all parties concurred in placing him high on the list of 'desirables'. **1904** *Daily Chron.* 21 Sept. 8/5 Nor did the individual who spoke proudly of 'moving in a circle'—of 'desirables'—realise the vulgarity of the expression. **1905** *Westm. Gaz.* 21 June 8/2 The real undesirables..would have to be kept back and looked after until they became 'desirables'. **1908** *Ibid.* 26 June 2/1 Could not the undesirables be got rid of, and the desirables multiplied?

deˈsirableness. [f. prec. + -NESS.]
1. The quality or fact of being desirable.
1647 CLARENDON *Hist. Reb.* I. (1843) 34/1 Discourses upon the thing itself, and the desirableness of it. *a* **1665** J. GOODWIN *Filled w. the Spirit* (1867) 125 Matters of lighter concernment or less desirableness. **1817** MALTHUS *Popul.* III. App. 229 The desirableness of a great and efficient population. **1856** FROUDE *Hist. Eng.* I. 384 To discuss..the desirableness of fulfilling the engagement into which he had entered.
†**2.** In active sense: Desirousness. *Obs.*
1649 *St. Trials, Lieut.-Col. John Lilburne* (R.), To declare my desireableness to keep within the bounds of reason, moderation, and discretion.

desirably (dɪˈzaɪərəblɪ), *adv.* [f. as prec. + -LY[2].] In a desirable manner; according to what is desirable.
1823 J. BADCOCK *Dom. Amusem.* 70 The ground where you would most desirably dig a well.

†**deˈsirant,** *ppl. a. Obs.* [a. F. *désirant*, pr. pple. of *désirer* to desire; repr. L. *dēsīderānt-em*.] Desiring, desirous of.
c **1450** *Merlin* 73 That I sholde remembre the thinge that I beste loved..and that I am moste desiraunte.

desire (dɪˈzaɪə(r)), *sb.* Forms: 4-5 desir, desyr, (desijr, dessire, dissire, -yre), 4-6 desyre, desier, (5 desyer, desere, 6 desyir), 4- desire. [ME. a. OF. *desir* (12th c. in Littré), mod.F. *désir* = Pr. *dezir*, *desire*, It. *desio*, *desire*, deriv. f. the vb. *desirare*, F. *désirer* to DESIRE: see next.]
1. The fact or condition of desiring; that feeling or emotion which is directed to the attainment or possession of some object from which pleasure or satisfaction is expected; longing, craving; a particular instance of this feeling, a wish.
1303 R. BRUNNE *Handl. Synne* 3410 Ȝyf þou haue grete desyre To be clepyd lorde or syre. *c* **1380** WYCLIF *Wks.* (1880) 147 Gret desir of heuenely þynges. **14..** *Why I can't be a nun* 303 in *E.E.P.* (1862) 146 Thy fyrst desyre and thyne entent Was to bene a nune professed. **1513** MORE in Grafton *Chron.* (1568) II. 757 The execrable desyre of sovereintie. **1632** J. HAYWARD tr. *Biondi's Eromena* 92, I have a great desire to get a sight of him. **1652** J. WRIGHT tr. *Camus' Nat. Paradox* 353 Seeing the cards thus shuffled to his own desire. **1653** H. MORE *Antid. Ath.* II. xii. §15 (1712) 83 An unsatiable desire after that just and decorous temper of Mind. **1752** JOHNSON *Rambler* No. 206 ¶4 This conflict of desires. **1759** —— *Rasselas* xxxvii, His predominant passion was desire of money. **1841** LANE *Arab. Nts.* I. 2 The elder King felt a strong desire to see his brother. **1853** J. H. NEWMAN *Hist. Sk.* (1873) II. I. i. 11 Objects of desire to the barbarian. **1856** EMERSON *Eng. Traits, Relig.* Wks. (Bohn) II. 100 The new age has new desires. **1875** JOWETT *Plato* (ed. 2) V. 51 A man should pray to have right desires, before he prays that his desires may be fulfilled.
b. *personified.*
1575 GASCOIGNE *Pr. Pleas. Kenilw.*, That wretch Desire Whom neither death could daunt [etc.]. **1821** SHELLEY *Prometh. Unb.* I. i. 734 As fleet As Desire's lightning feet. **1876** GEO. ELIOT *Dan. Der.* II. xxvii. 170 Desire has trimmed the sails, and Circumstance brings but the breeze to fill them.
2. *spec.* Physical or sensual appetite; lust.
c **1340** HAMPOLE *Prose Tr.* 3 This name Ihesu..dose away greuesnes of fleschely desyris. **1398** TREVISA *Barth. De P.R.* VII. xliv. (1495) 257 The appetyte of the stomak is callyd desyre. *a* **1400-50** *Alexander* 4289 To blemysch oure blode with bodely dissires. *a* **1535** WYATT in *Tottell's Misc.* (Arb.) 224 If thy desire haue ouer thee the power, Subiect then art thou and no gouernour. **1611** SHAKS. *Cymb.* I. vi. 47 That satiate yet vnsatisfi'd desire. **1711** STEELE *Spect.* No. 151 ¶2 A constant Pruriency of inordinate Desire. **1756** BURKE *Subl. & B.* III. i, Which shows that beauty, and the passion caused by beauty, which I call love, is different from desire. **1867** BAKER *Nile Tribut.* viii. 166 The flesh of the crocodile is eaten greedily, being supposed to promote desire. **1887** BOWEN *Virg. Æneid* IV. 91 Against enkindled desire Honour itself was feeble.
†**3.** Longing for something lost or missed; regret; DESIDERIUM. *Obs.*
c **1611** CHAPMAN *Iliad* XVII. 380 So unremoved stood these steeds, their heads to earth let fall, And warm tears gushing from their eyes, with passionate desire Of their kind manager.
4. A wish as expressed or stated in words; a request, petition.
c **1340** *Cursor M.* 10513 (Trin.) Þy desire and þy preyere Is comen to goddes ere. **1414** *Rolls of Parlt.* III. 549/1 The Kyng thanketh hem of here gode desire, willyng put it in execution als sone as he wel may. **1523** LD. BERNERS *Froiss.* I. cxiii. 135 The erle sent thyder, at their desyers, John of Norwyche, to be their Captayne. **1670** MARVELL *Corr.* clxxxvi. Wks. 1872-5 II. 377 The House hath been in conference with the Lords upon their desire, about the Addresse..concerning Popish Recusants. **1794** NELSON in *Nicolas Disp.* (1845) I. 428 The Agents have written desires from me to land everything as fast as possible. **1842** BISCHOFF *Woollen Manuf.* II. 83, I also send, at your desire, a general list of articles used in the woollen manufacture.
5. *transf.* An object of desire; that which one desires or longs for. (Originally only contextual).
1340-70 *Alisaunder* 1047 Hee hoped to haue there of his hertes desyres. **1413** *Pilgr. Sowle* I. xxxix. (Caxton, repr. 1859) 43 He sawe that he ne myght nought acheuen hys desyre. **1535** COVERDALE *Ps.* liii. [liv.] 7 So that myne eye seyth his desyre vpon myne enemies. **1611** BIBLE *Haggai* ii. 7 The desire of all nations shall come. **1699** DAMPIER *Voy.* II. II. i. We steered off to the North expecting a Sea-Breez at E.N.E. and the third day had our desire. **1709** STEELE *Tatler* No. 159 ¶5 Farewel my Terentia, my Heart's Desire, farewel. **1732** FIELDING *Mock Doctor* Ded., That politeness which..has made you the desire of the great, and the envy of the whole profession. **1863** TENNYSON *Welcome Alex.*, Welcome her, welcome the land's desire.

desire (dɪˈzaɪə(r)), *v.* Also 3-7 desyre, 4 desirre, 4-5 disire, -yre, 4-6 desir, 5 dissire, -yre, desier, desyr, disere, 5-6 dessire, -yre, dyssire, -yre, 6 dissier. [ME. a. OF. *desire-r* (earlier *desidrer*, *desirrer*) = Pr. *desirar*, It. *desiare*, *disirare*, Rom. type *desirare*:—L. *dēsīderāre* to miss, long for, desire: see DESIDERATE *v.*]
1. *trans.* To have a strong wish for; to long for, covet, crave. **a.** with *simple obj.*
c **1230** *Hali Meid.* 11 Ant þenne wile..þe king of alle kinges desire þe to leofmon. **1340** *Ayenb.* 244 Þer is..al þet herte may wylnj, and of guod desiri. *a* **1400-50** *Alexander* 922 To þe kyng he kest slik a hate, þat he desiris his deth. **1538** STARKEY *England* I. i. 21 Of al thyng best and most to be desyryd. **1607-12** BACON *Ess.*, *Empire* (Arb.) 294 It is a miserable state of minde to have few things to desier, and manie thinges to feare. **1670** MILTON *Hist. Eng.* IV. Wks. (1851) 169 Offa..a comely Person..much desir'd of the people; and such his virtue..as might have otherwise been worthy to have reigned. **1832** TENNYSON '*Of old sat Freedom on the heights*,' Her open eyes desire the truth. **1871** R. ELLIS *Catullus* lxii. 50 Many a wistful boy and maidens many desire it. **1875** JOWETT *Plato* (ed. 2) I. 201 Do not all men desire happiness?
b. with *infin.*: To wish, long (*to be, have, do*).
a **1300** *Cursor M.* 10486 (Cott.) Suilk a worthi sun..Als sco desird for to haf. *c* **1400** MAUNDEV. (Roxb.) xiv. 62 Desirand to see þare wifes and þare childer. *c* **1425** *Hampole's Psalter* Metr. Pref. 29 Who so desires it to know. **1509** HAWES *Past. Pleas.* XVIII. vi, To speke wyth her gretly desyrynge. **1602** SHAKS. *Ham.* IV. v. 140 If you desire to know the certaintie. **1697** DRYDEN *Æneid* II. *init.*, Since.. Troy's disast'rous end [you] desire to know. **1875** JOWETT *Plato* (ed. 2) IV. 30 They do not desire to bring down their theory to the level of their practice.
c. with *obj. clause.*
c **1340** *Cursor M.* 1801 (Trin.) Þenne desired þo caitifs badde þat þei had ben by noe ladde. *c* **1600** SHAKS. *Sonn.* lxi. 3 Dost thou desire my slumbers should be broken? **1784** COWPER *Tiroc.* 811 To you..Who wise yourselves, desire your sons should learn Your wisdom. **1850** TENNYSON *In Mem.* LI. 1 Do we indeed desire the dead Should still be near us? **1859** —— *Lancelot & Elaine* 1089 You desire your child to live.
2. *intr.* (or *absol.*) To have or feel a desire.
1393 GOWER *Conf.* II. 5 For she, which loveth him to-fore, Desireth ever more and more. **1611** BIBLE *Prov.* xiii. 4 The soule of the sluggard desireth, and hath nothing. **1620** SHELTON *Quix.* III. v, He that will not when he may, when he desireth shall have nay. *a* **1831** A. KNOX *Rem.* I. 37 In moral matters, to desire, and possess, differ in degree, rather

than reality. **1875** JOWETT *Plato* (ed. 2) I. 68 He who desires, desires that of which he is in want.

†**b.** Const. *after*, *to*, etc. *Obs.*

a **1300** *Holy Rode* 347 in *Leg. Rood* 46 þo desirede þe quene muche after þe nailes þre War-wiþ our lord was Inailed to þe tre. *a* **1325** *Prose Psalter* xli[i]. 1 As þe hert desiret to þe welles of waters, so de-sired my soule to þe, Lord. **1477** NORTON *Ord. Alch.* Proem in Ashm. (1652) 6 Every estate desireth after good. **1549–62** STERNHOLD & H. *Ps.* cxliii. 6 My soule desireth after thee.

†**3.** *trans.* Of things: To require, need, demand.

1577 B. GOOGE *Heresbach's Husb.* I. (1586) 29 It desyreth a moyst ground, riche and good. **1587** GOLDING *De Mornay* xxvi. 397 True beautie desireth no painting. **1591** SPENSER *Tears of Muses* 541 A doleful case desires a dolefull song. **1607** TOPSELL *Four-f. Beasts* 292 There be many kindes of Mise, and every one of them desireth a particular tractate.

4. To long for (something lost); to feel the loss of, miss, regret, desiderate. (In quot. 1614, *pass.*, to be missed, to be wanting.) *Obs.* or *arch.*

1557 NORTH tr. *Gueuara's Diall Pr.* 232 b/2 On the death of thy child Verissimus, thy sonne so much desired. **1611** BIBLE *2 Chron.* xxi. 20 He reigned in Ierusalem eight yeeres, and departed without being desired. **1614** SELDEN *Titles Hon.* 142 Otherwise . . Pharaohs discretion would have been much desired. **1658** ROWLAND *Moufet's Theat. Ins.* Ep. Ded., That the Reader . . may not desire an Epistle, or complain that there is one wanting. **1869** TENNYSON *Holy Grail* 897 And now his chair desires him here in vain.

5. To express a wish for (an object); to ask for, request.

Const. **a.** with *simple obj.*: to d. a thing; **b.** to d. a thing *of*, *from* (†*at*) a person (*arch.*); **c.** with *inf. obj.*; to d. *to know*, *have*, etc., something; **d.** with *obj. cl.*, to d. *that* . . .

a. *c* **1314** *Guy Warw.* (A.) 399 Erls, doukes of þe best . . Me [Felice] haue desired apliȝt, Þat neuer of me hadde siȝt. *c* **1350** *Will. Palerne* 4583, I desired þis damisele . . To haue hire to þi broþer . . Ac hire moder in no maner hire nold me graunte. *c* **1450** *Merlin* 27 When thei wiste that Vortiger disered the pees, they were gladde. **1656** *Burton's Diary* (1828) I. 39, I move that his Highness's advice may be desired in it. **1754** CHATHAM *Lett. Nephew* iv. 21 If you are forced to desire farther information . . do it with proper apologies. **1841** LANE *Arab. Nts.* I. 97, I had spared thee, but thou desiredst my death.

b. *c* **1400** *Destr. Troy* 7897 Þai . . sent to þat souerain . . dessirond full depely delyuerans of hir. **1535** COVERDALE *1 Kings* ii. 16 Now desyre I one peticion of the. —— *Job* xxxi. 16 When the poore desyred eny thinge at me, haue I denyed it them? **1651** SIR E. NICHOLAS in *N. Papers* (Camden) 282 What you desire from mee. **1666** PEPYS *Diary* 5 Dec., I gave him my song . . which he has often desired of me.

c. *c* **1400** *Destr. Troy* 1022 To these kynges he come . . And to haue of hor helpe hertely dissyred. **1450** W. SOMNER in *Four C. Eng. Lett.* 4 The maister desyryd to wete yf the shepmen wolde holde with the duke. **1563** ABP. PARKER *Corr.* (Parker Soc.) 191, I . . thereupon desired to have the Council's letters. **1785** *Mod. Times* I. 16 He desired never to hear any thing of me. **1828** SCOTT *F.M. Perth* xxxiii, He alighted at the Dominican Convent, and desired to see the Duke of Albany. **1887** BOWEN *Virg. Æneid* III. 358 Speech I crave of the seer, and desire his counsel to learn.

d. **1404** *Rolls of Parlt.* III. 549/1 The Comunes desiren that the Kyng shulde leve upon his owne. **1656** *Burton's Diary* (1828) I. 80, I desire it may not die. **1689** *Tryal Bps.* 19 We desire it may be read in English for we don't understand Law-Latin. **1738** SWIFT *Pol. Conversat.* 98 Run to my Lady M——; and desire she will remember to be here at Six. **1823** SOUTHEY *Hist. Penins. War* I. 176 He desired Velarde would write to the court.

6. To express a wish to (a person); to request, pray, entreat.

†**a.** with *simple object*: to make a request to (*obs.*); †**b.** to d. a person a thing, or *of* a thing (*obs.*); **c.** to d. a person *to do* something (the most freq. construction); **d.** to d. a person *that*, or *of* a person *that* . . .

†**a.** **1526–34** TINDALE *John* xii. 21 Certayne Grekes . . cam to Philip . . and desired him, sayinge: Syr we wolde fayne se Iesus. **1563–87** FOXE *A. & M.* (1596) 32/2 John spake unto him, and desired him in like maner and contestation as before.

†**b.** *a* **1555** HOOPER in Coverdale *Lett. Mart.* (1564) 127 Repente, and desyre god of forgeuenes. **1583** GOLDING *Calvin on Deut.* xviii. 105 If a Childe . . desire his Father some fond or euill thing. **1596** SHAKS. *Merch. V.* IV. i. 402, I humbly doe desire your Grace of pardon.

c. *a* **1533** LD. BERNERS *Huon* lxi. 212, I desyre you to shew me where ye have ben. *c* **1563** CAVENDISH *Metr. Vis.* in *Life Wolsey* (1825) II. 124 Desyryng me vouchesalve for to consent To wright their myshappe. **1681** TEMPLE *Mem.* III. Wks. 1731 I. 342 The Duke of Monmouth being Chancellor, I desir'd the King to speak to him. **1710** SWIFT *Lett.* 10 Oct. (1767) III. 21 He desires me to dine with him again on Sunday. **1747** *Col. Rec. Pennsylv.* V. 138 Thomas McGee . . who was desir'd to do it. **1786** SUS. HASWELL *Victoria* II. 97 Lady Wealthy . . desired her to . . desire the steward give her twelve guineas. **1833** MARRYAT *P. Simple* ix, He desired us to 'toe a line,' which means to stand in a row.

d. **1523** LD. BERNERS *Froiss.* I. cviii. 130, I desyre you that we may abyde in composicyon. **1539** CRANMER *Matt.* xvi. 1 The Pharises also with the Saduces . . desyred him that he wolde shewe them a sygne from heuen. **1585** T. WASHINGTON tr. *Nicholay's Voy.* I. xxi. 27 The Bascha sent to desire the Ambassador that the next day he would come to his solemne dynner. **1611** BIBLE *Dan.* ii. 16 Then Daniel went in and desired of the King, that hee would giue him time. **1822** SHELLEY *Chas. I*, II. 456 Go desire Lady Jane She place my lute.

†**7.** To request to know or to be told; to ask.

c **1477** CAXTON *Jason* 95 b, Iason . . desired the waye. **1708** HEARNE *Collect.* (Oxf. Hist. Soc.) II. 107 Mr. Watts came to me . . and desir'd of me whether I were a Congregation Man.

†**8.** To request the presence or attendance of; to invite. *Obs.*

c **1325** *Coer de L.* 6871 Saye, that I hym desyre, And al his cursed cumpany in fere. **1530** PALSGR. 513/2, I desyre to dynner, or to a feest, or any repast, *je semons.* **1554** BRADFORD in Strype *Eccl. Mem.* III. App. xxxi. 85, I was desyred by a neighbour . . ayenst this day to dyner. **1583** *Satir. Poem Reform.* xlv. *Leg. Bp. St. Androis* 259 This bischop, beand present thair, Desyrit him hame. **1606** SHAKS. *Tr. & Cr.* IV. v. 150, I would desire My famous Cousin to our Grecian Tents. **1606** G. W[OODCOCKE] tr. *Hist. Ivstine* 88 b, Arsinoe . . desired Phillip into her Citty Cassandria.

†**b.** To invite a course of action, etc.

c **1314** *Guy Warw.* (A.) 634, Þow dost me litel worþschipe, When þou me desirest to schenschipe. **1523** LD. BERNERS *Froiss.* I. cxv. 136 Ye haue desyred vs to a thynge that is great and weyghtie. **1588** SHAKS. *L.L.L.* v. ii. 145 But shall we dance, if they desire vs too't? **1645** CROMWELL *Lett.* 4 Aug., I sent one Mr. Lee to them, To certify the peaceableness of my intentions, and to desire them to peaceableness.

desired (dɪˈzaɪəd), *ppl. a.* [f. prec. + -ED¹.]

1. Wished for, longed for, etc.: see the vb.

1382 WYCLIF *Haggai* ii. 8 The desirid to alle folkis shal cume. *a* **1440** *Found. St. Bartholomew's* 43 To ȝeue the a ȝeifte of desirid helth. **1611** SHAKS. *Cymb.* III. v. 62 To her desir'd Posthumus. **1611** BIBLE *Ps.* cvii. 30 So he bringeth them vnto their desired hauen. **1655** EARL ORRERY *Parthen.* (1676) 21 At last, the long desired day appear'd. **1855** MACAULAY *Hist. Eng.* IV. 266 The long desired title of Elector of Hanover.

†**2.** Missed, regretted, desiderated. *Obs.*

a **1533** LD. BERNERS *Gold. Bk. M. Aurel.* (1546) Ddj a, Of the death of suche an entierly desyred husbande.

†**3.** Affected with desire; longing, desirous. [= L. *cupidus.*] *Obs.*

a **1300** *Cursor M.* 28505 (Cott.) Gerndand i haf oft ben desird o þire wymmen scen. *c* **1489** CAXTON *Blanchardyn* xlii. 158 She . . was sore desired to know of hym som gode tydynges. **1598** YONG *Diana* 318 If thy sweete voice . . might sound in our desired eares with some happie song.

Hence **deˈsiredly** *adv.*, in a desired manner; †according to one's own desire, *con amore* (*obs.*; cf. DESIROUSLY); **deˈsiredness**, the condition of being desired.

1625 BP. MOUNTAGU *App. Cæsar* 65 He being *Pater misericordiarum*, and wholly, freely, and desiredly, giving, occasioning, procuring, effecting our salvation. **1666** G. ALSOP *Maryland* (1869) 46 Every man lives quietly, and follows his labor and imployment desiredly. *a* **1866** J. GROTE *Exam. Util. Philos.* (1870) xix. 327 There being rather want in the sense of *absence* of what should be than want in the sense of desiredness. **1888** P. H. WICKSTEED *Alphabet Econ. Sc.* 8, I am not aware of any recognised word, however, which signifies the quality of being desired. 'Desirableness' conveys the idea that the thing not only is but deserves to be desired. 'Desiredness' is not English, but I shall nevertheless use it as occasion may require. **1889** *Sat. Rev.* 16 Feb. 198/1 His introduction into the English language of 'desiredness'. **1920** A. C. PIGOU *Econ. of Welfare* v. x. 771 The marginal desiredness which money has for them.

deˈsireful, *a.* Now *rare.* [f. DESIRE *sb.* + -FUL.]

†**1.** Greatly to be desired, desirable. *Obs.* or *arch.*

1382 WYCLIF *Dan.* x. 3 Y eete not desireful breede. **1435** MISYN *Fire of Love* 76 Delectabyl & desirefull it is in þi praysinge to be. *c* **1510** MORE *Picus* Wks. 15 More desirefull is it . . to be condemned of the worlde, and exalted of God, then to be exalted of the world and condemned of god. **1580** SIDNEY *Arcadia* (1622) 434 Euery thing was either vehemently desirefull, or extreamely terrible. **1877** BLACKIE *Wise Men* 68 A brood of desireful maidens immortal.

2. Full of desire; desirous; wishful, eager.

152. BARCLAY *Sallust's Jugurth* 55 a, To suche desyrefull myndes as they had, nothyng coude to fast be hasted. **1540** MORYSINE *Vives' Introd. Wysd.* Pref. A ij b, Alway helpynge some, and desyrefull to helpe mo. **1553** GRIMALDE *Cicero's Offices* I. 68 So desireful of . . learning yᵉ nature of things. **1892** C. E. NORTON *Dante's Paradise* v. 29 Beatrice . . all desireful turned herself again to that region.

Hence †**deˈsirefulness**, *Obs.*, the state or quality of being desirous; eagerness.

1548 UDALL etc. *Erasm. Par. Luke* Pref. 8 He with greate desirefulnesse useth to reade. *Ibid.* ix. 56 Toke out of their stomakes all desierfulnesse of doyng vengeaunce.

desireless (dɪˈzaɪəlɪs), *a.* [f. as prec. + -LESS.] Devoid of desire or longing.

1607 TOPSELL *Serpents* (1653) 758 Desirelesse it seeks these drinks and meats. **1640** BP. REYNOLDS *Passions* xl. 524 The Will is left Hopelesse, and therefore Desirelesse. **1856** R. A. VAUGHAN *Mystics* (1860) I. 254 Our spirit becomes desireless, as though there were nothing . . of which we stood in need.

desirer (dɪˈzaɪərə(r)). [f. DESIRE *v.* + -ER¹.] One who desires.

c **1450** tr. *De Imitatione* III. xxxvi, There are many desireres of contemplacion. **1548** R. HUTTEN *Sum of Diuinitie* A vj b, It is expedient that ther be many desirers of the office. **1579** COVERDALE *Bk. Death* xiii. 58 Earnest desirers of innocency. *a* **1613** OVERBURY *A Wife* (1638) 108 A desirer of learning. **1665** MANLEY *Grotius' Low C. Warres* 105 Yet never ceased to admonish all desirers of novelty. *a* **1691** BAXTER in Tulloch *Eng. Purit.* iii. (1861) 366 He was a great desirer of such abatements as might restore us all to serviceableness.

desiring (dɪˈzaɪərɪŋ), *vbl. sb.* [f. DESIRE *v.* + -ING¹.] The action of the verb DESIRE; longing, desire. (Now *rare* or *Obs.* exc. as gerund.)

1377 LANGL. *P. Pl.* B. XIII. 356 Þorw coueityse and vnkynde desyrynge. **1491** CAXTON *Vitas Patr.* (W. de W. 1495) II. 235 b/1 The desyrynges of the flesshe. **1593** T. WATSON *Tears of Fancie* xx. Poems (Arb.) 188 If he at first had banisht loues desiring. **1677** GILPIN *Demonol.* (1867) 63 By 'lust' I mean those general desirings of our minds after any unlawful object which are forbidden in the tenth commandment. *Mod.* One cannot gain honour merely by desiring it.

deˈsiring, *ppl. a.* [f. DESIRE *v.* + -ING².] That desires; longing, desirous.

c **1386** CHAUCER *Melib.* ¶611 A man that is to desirynge for to gete riches. *c* **1489** CAXTON *Sonnes of Aymon* xxiii. 497 They were sore desyrynge for to see theyr wyves, theyr chyldren, and theyr londes. **1552** HULOET, Desirous or desirynge, *appetens, auidus.* **1593** SHAKS. *Rich. II*, v. ii. 14 So many greedy lookes of yong and old, Through Casements darted their desiring eyes Vpon his visage. *a* **1700** DRYDEN (J.) Jove beheld it with a desiring look.

deˈsiringly, *adv.* [f. prec. + -LY².] With desire, desirously, longingly.

1552 HULOET, Desirously, or wyth desyre, or desiringly, *cupide.* **1662** J. CHANDLER *Van Helmont's Oriat.* Pref. to Rdr., My Spirit . . desiringly desiring thorowly to know the whole sacred Art. **1821** COLERIDGE *Lett. Convers. &c.* II. 35 The voice within, whenever the heart desiringly listens thereto.

desirous (dɪˈzaɪərəs), *a.* Also 5 desirouse, -rose, desyrows, dessyrous, -rus, dissyrus, dyssirus, 5–6 desyrous(e, 6 desyreous, -rus, -rowus, desierous, dissirous, 7 desireous. [a. AFr. *desirous* = OF. *desireus* (earlier *desidros*, *desirrus*, mod.F. *désireux*) = Pr. *deziros*, It. *desideroso*:—late L. or Rom. *dēsīderōs-us*, f. stem of *dēsīder-āre* to DESIRE: see -OUS. Orig. with stress on third and first syllable.]

1. Having desire or longing; characterized by or full of desire: wishful; desiring.

a. with *of*; also †*to* (obs. rare).

c **1300** *K. Alis.* 416 Olimpias stont byfore Neptanabus, Of hire neowe love wel desirous. *c* **1400** *Destr. Troy* 8003 More dessyrous to the dede, þen I dem can. **1489** CAXTON *Faytes of A.* III. i. 169 A dyscyple desyrouse of lernynge. **1508** DUNBAR *Goldyn Targe* 54 As falcounn swift desyrouse of hir pray. **1561** T. NORTON *Calvin's Inst.* III. 221 They that haue a desirous mind of amendment. **1611** BIBLE *Transl. Pref.* 4 The Grecians being desirous of learning. **1755** YOUNG *Centaur* i. Wks. 1757 IV. 125 Man is not only desirous, but ambitious too, of happiness. **1891** *Law Reports* Weekly Notes 78/2 The lessor was desirous of pulling the house down and building a new one.

b. with *inf.*

c **1374** CHAUCER *Former Age* 59 Ne nembrot desyrous To regne had nat maad his towres hye. *c* **1489** CAXTON *Blanchardyn* vii. 29 Ryght desyrouse to here tydynges of her louer. **1555** EDEN *Decades* 158 Owre men . . were desyrous to see the towne. **1651** HOBBES *Leviath.* IV. xlv. 360 He is desirous to save himselfe from death. **1752** JOHNSON *Rambler* No. 207 ¶9 We never find ourselves so desirous to finish, as in the latter part of our work. **1860** TYNDALL *Glac.* I. xvi. 66 Being desirous to learn something of its [the glacier's] general features.

c. with *obj. clause.*

1601 SHAKS. *Twel. N.* III. i. 83 My Neece is desirous you should enter. **1625** BACON *Ess.*, *Revenge* (Arb.) 503 Some . . are Desirous the party should know. **1632** J. HAYWARD tr. *Biondi's Eromena* 18 That I, desirous we might recover againe our liberty. **1828** SCOTT *F.M. Perth* iii, He averted his face, as if desirous that his emotion should not be read upon his countenance.

d. *simply.*

c **1485** *Digby Myst.* (1882) III. 1110 To shew desyrows hartes I am full nere. **1535** COVERDALE *2 Sam.* xxiii. 15 Dauid was desyrous, and sayde: Wolde God yᵗ some man wolde fetch me a drynke of water. **1667** MILTON *P.L.* v. 631 From dance to sweet repast they turn Desirous.

†**2.** Of feelings, actions, etc.: Characterized by, of the nature of, or expressing, desire or longing; sometimes in bad sense, covetous. *Obs.*

a **1420** HOCCLEVE *De Reg. Princ.* 1403 The desirous talent Ye han to goode. **1483** CAXTON *Gold. Leg.* 272/2 Thou hast brought me into a desyrous affection. **1509** BARCLAY *Shyp of Folys* (1570) 178 Alas note well thy desirous vanitie. **1580** SIDNEY *Arcadia* (1622) 166 With a desirous sigh. **1652** L. S. *People's Liberty* ii. 4 The word for *desire* . . implieth a *desirous affection.*

†**3.** Full of eagerness or spirit; eager, ardent (*esp.* in deeds of arms). *Obs.*

c **1386** CHAUCER *Sqr.'s T.* 15 Yong, fressh, strong, and in Armes desirous, As any Bacheler of al his hous. **1393** GOWER *Conf.* I. 89 Of armes he was desirous, Chivalerous and amorous. *c* **1450** tr. *De Imitatione* III. xii, Þat þou be not a louer of þiself, but a desirous folower of my wille. *c* **1470** HENRY *Wallace* II. 2 In prys of armys desirous and sauage. **1470–85** MALORY *Arthur* IV. iii, A good knyght and ful desyrous in armes. [*Modernized reprint* of **1634** desirous.]

†**4.** Longing for something lost; regretful. *Obs. rare.* (Cf. DESIRE *sb.* 3, *v.* 4.)

c **1485** *Digby Myst.* (1882) IV. 1077 My swete lorde of þe which desirose I am, and nedes must be.

†**5.** Exciting desire; desirable; pleasant, delectable. *Obs.*

1430 LYDG. *Chron. Troy* I. viii, The lusty season freshe and desyrous. **1556** in Strype *Eccl. Mem.* I. App. lxi. 219 Whiche most desirous daye of thy comfortable commynge hasten, deare Lorde. **1684** BUNYAN *Pilgr.* II. 96 They make the Woods, and Groves, and Solitary places, places desirous to be in. **1728** GAY *Begg. Op.* II. i, Wine inspires us, And fires us . . Women and Wine should Life employ. Is there ought else on Earth desirous? [**1796** cf. PEGGE *Anonym.* (1809) 434.]

desirously (dɪˈzaɪərəslɪ), *adv.* Now *rare.* [f. prec. + -LY².]

1. With desire or longing; wishfully, eagerly, longingly. (Frequent in 16–17th centuries.)

c **1400** *Test. Love* III. (1560) 301/1 By which ye be draw desirously any thyng to wilne in coveitous manner. **1504** ATKYNSON tr. *De Imitatione* III. ii, I beseche the humbly & desirously..that thou vouchesaue to speke to me thy selfe. **1556** J. HEYWOOD *Spider & F.* lxxi. *title*, Desirously deuising: by what meane to get peace. **1603** KNOLLES *Hist. Turks* (1621) 62 Which courtesie the Countie desirously embraced. **1692** SOUTH *Serm.* (1697) I. 326 Do they hasten to their Devotions..Or do they not rather come hither slowly, sit here uneasily and depart desirously? **1836** W. IRVING *Astoria* (1849) 37 It..had been..desirously contemplated by powerful associations and maternal governments.

†**b.** With earnest desire, earnestly. *Obs.*

1502 *Ord. Crysten Men* (W. de W. 1506) IV. ix. 192 The confessour ought to be well aduysed and hym enfourme desyrously. *Ibid.* IV. xxii. 291 Righte desyrously euery relygyous ought for to kepe hym from the tellynge of lesynges. **1647** F. BLAND *Souldiers March* 44 One short Observation more would I desirously commend to your Christian piety.

†**2.** Of one's own desire or wish; willingly, readily. *Obs.*

1531 ELYOT *Gov.* II. xiii, Suche one as desirously will participate with his frende all his good fortune. **1589** COGAN *Haven Health* ccxv. (1636) 233 The superfluities..with the wine, shall be drawne off the stomack..but nature doth not so desirously draw Ale. **1635** EARL STRAFFORD *Lett.* (1739) I. 399 If..I could have avoided meddling with him, I should not desirously have begun with a Gentleman..of so..turbulent a Disposition.

de'sirousness. Now *rare.* [f. as prec. + -NESS.] The quality of being desirous; wishfulness, eagerness.

1571 GOLDING *Calvin on Ps.* vii. 5 As though his desyrousenesse too reigne had moved hym too trayterous rebellion. **1665** BOYLE *Occas. Refl.* (1845) 366 My desirousness of piety in a Preacher. **1872** A. RALEIGH in Spurgeon *Treas. Dav.* Ps. cxix. 20 Dr. Chalmers..summed up his own attainments in the word 'desirousness.'

desist (dɪ'zɪst), *v.* Also 6 **-syste, -cist,** 7 **dissist.** [a. OF. *desister* (1358 in Littré; mod.F. *dé-*), ad. L. *dēsist-ĕre*, f. DE- 2 + *sistĕre* to stop, stand still.]

1. *intr.* To cease (*from* some action or procedure); to stop, leave off, give over, forbear.

1530 PALSGR. 514/1, I counsayle you desyst from this purpose. **1549** *Compl. Scot.* vi. 62, I pray the to decist fra that tideus melancolic orison. **1585** T. WASHINGTON tr. *Nicholay's Voy.* I. xv. 16 Notwithstanding [they] did not desist of their enterprise. **1632** J. HAYWARD tr. *Biondi's Eromena* 100 At last, quite wearied with kissing and weeping, they were faine to desist. **1752** FIELDING *Amelia* 121 Men should therefore desist from this enormous crime. *a* **1859** MACAULAY *Hist. Eng.* V. 51 The Peers desisted from urging a request which seemed likely to be ungraciously refused. **1866** KINGSLEY *Herew.* iii, He shouted to the combatants to desist.

†**b.** Const. *in.* *Obs.*

a **1774** GOLDSM. tr. *Scarron's Comic Rom.* (1775) II. 176 Request that he would desist in his gallantries to me. **1795** *Fate of Sedley* II. 140 He only begged me to desist..in thinking of such an union. **1842** C. WHITEHEAD *R. Savage* (1845) II. viii. 275, I desisted in the attempt; more properly to speak, I declined it.

†**c.** Const. *inf.* with *to.* *Obs.*

1539 *Act 31 Hen. VIII*, c. 12 Diuers idell..persons..haue not desisted to take egges of faucons..out of the nestes. **1597** SHAKS. *2 Hen. IV*, I. iii. 49 What do we then, but..at least, desist To builde at all? **1647-8** COTTERELL *Davila's Hist. Fr.* (1678) 19 Never desisted to persecute them. **1655-60** STANLEY *Hist. Philos.* (1701) 160/1 Gods always were, to be desisted never.

d. To cease to prefer a claim.

1673 *Pennsylv. Archives* I. 32 We doe hereby dissist off the same land.

2. To come to an end, cease, terminate. *Obs. rare.*

a **1657** SIR J. BALFOUR *Ann. Scot.* (1824-5) II. 254 The vrging of the Perth artickells must cease and desist.

†**3.** *trans.* To leave off, discontinue. *Obs.*

1509 BARCLAY *Shyp of Folys* (1570) 107 Thou foole desist thy wordes vayne. **1599** in Beveridge *Hist. India* I. I. x. 225 They shuld be required to desist their viage. **1679** OATES *Narr. Popish Plot* 53 He ordered the said Blundel, not to desist the business in hand. **1753** *Stewart's Trial* 209 The uncle desisted further inquiry. **1784** *New Spectator* xi. 6/1 Unless they desist their attacks on the fair milliner.

†**4.** To withstand (? error for *resist*). *Obs. rare*$^{-1}$.

1548 BODRUGAN (Adams) *Epit. King's Title* H iv, Who of you by reason or otherwise is able to desist my persuasion of this vnion.

Hence **de'sisting** *vbl. sb.*

1607 HIERON *Wks.* I. 270 There was no desisting from former courses, no breaking off of olde sinnes. **1709** HEARNE *Collect.* 13 Mar., Mr. Lhuyd..has carried his Point..owing to my desisting.

desistance (dɪ'zɪstəns). Also **-ence.** [f. DESIST *v.*: cf. OF. *desistance, -ence* (1300 in Godef.): see -ANCE.] The action of desisting, leaving off, or forbearing to proceed; cessation, discontinuance of action.

1632 LITHGOW *Trav.* I. 4, I partly forbeare..and reconciled times pleading desistance, moderate discretion inserteth silent patience. **1648** BOYLE *Seraph. Love* xiii. (1700) 78 Men..make it both the Motive and the Excuse of their Desistance from giving any more, That they have given already. **1768** *Women of Honor* III. 48 It is an argument the more for your desistence. **1803** S. PEGGE *Anecd. Eng. Lang.*, A word commanding cessation and desistance. **1879** H. SPENCER *Data of Ethics* vi. §33. 79 Life is maintained by persistence in acts which conduce to it, and desistance from acts which impede it. **1884** —— in *19th Cent.* Nov. 837, I must here close the discussion, so far as my own desistence enables me.

†**de'sistency.** *Obs. rare*$^{-1}$. [f. L. *dēsistent-em*, pr. pple. of *dēsistĕre*: see DESIST and -ENCY.] Cessation.

1615 *Marr. & Wiving* i. in *Harl. Misc.* (Malh.) III. 255 End of the world and desistency of all things.

de'sistive, *a.* *rare.* [f. DESIST *v.* + -IVE.] Ending, concluding.

1836 in SMART.

desition (dɪ'sɪʃən). [f. L. type **dēsitiōn-em*, n. of action f. *dēsinĕre, dēsit-* to leave off, cease: see DESINENT.] Termination or cessation of being; ceasing to be; ending.

1612 R. SHELDON *Serm. St. Martin's* 35 The consecrations, oblations, consumptions, desitions of Christ, which they make daily..vpon their prophane altars. **1645** *Souls Immortality Defended* 27 (L.) The soul must be immortal and unsubject to death or desition. **1867** BP. FORBES *Explan. 39 Art.* xxviii. (1881) 550 The plain words of Scripture, in that they freely use the word 'bread' to describe the Blessed Sacrament after consecration, go against the desition of the *signum* therein. *Ibid.* 551 Such a change..as would involve a physical desition of what before existed. **1890** A. L. MOORE *Hist. Ref.* 139 *note*, Nor does the statement..on the doctrine of the Sacrament expressly assert the desition of the natural substance of the elements.

†**desitive** ('dɛsɪtɪv), *a.* and *sb.* *rare.* *Obs.* [f. L. *desit-*, ppl. stem of *dēsinĕre* to cease + -IVE.]

A. *adj.* *Logic.* Of a proposition: Having reference to the end or conclusion of a matter.

1725 WATTS *Logic* III. ii. §4 Inceptive and desitive propositions; as, the fogs vanish as the sun rises; but the fogs have not yet begun to vanish; therefore the sun is not yet risen.

B. *sb.* A desitive proposition.

1725 WATTS *Logic* II. ii. §6 Inceptives and desitives, which relate to the beginning or ending of any thing; as the Latin tongue is not yet forgotten.

desize (diː'saɪz), *v.* [f. DE- II. 2 + SIZE *sb.*^{2} 2.] *trans.* To remove size from (textiles). So **de'sizing** *vbl. sb.*

1934 in WEBSTER. **1955** *Times* 13 July 1/7 (Advt.), Textile Chemist for work on sizing and desizing of natural and synthetic fibres. **1962** J. T. MARSH *Self-smoothing Fabrics* xi. 152 Zymolysis with the well-known products commonly employed for desizing.

desjune, var. of DISJUNE, *Obs.*, breakfast.

desk (dɛsk), *sb.* Also 5-6 **deske,** (5-7 **desque,** 6 **dexe, dext**), 6-8 *Sc.* **dask.** [ME. *deske*, app. immed. ad. med.L. *desca* 'cum descis et scamnis, et aliis ornamentis' (*c* 1250 in Du Cange). The latter is to be referred ultimately to L. *discus* (also used in med.L. in the sense 'table'), of which the regular Romanic form remains in It. *desco* 'a deske, a table, a boord, a counting boord; also a forme, a bench, a seat, or stoole' (Florio). Prob. from this It. *desco*, the med.L. *desca* fem. (like *mensa*, *tabula*) was formed.

Desk was in no way actually connected with *dish*, OE. *disc*, ME. *disch*, although OE. *disc*, WGer. *disk*, was itself an ancient adoption of L. *discus*. The OFr. repr. of L. *discus*, Rom. *desco*, Pr. *des*, was *deis*, Eng. DAIS. Thus *dais, desk, dish, disk*, all originate in the same word.]

1. An article of furniture for a library, study, church, school, or office, the essential feature of which is a table, board, or the like, intended to serve as a rest for a book, manuscript, writing-paper, etc., while reading or writing, for which purpose the surface usually presents a suitable slope.

The name is applied to articles differing greatly in details of construction and in accessories, according to their particular purpose, which is often indicated by a qualification, as ***litany-***, ***music-***, ***prayer-***, ***reading-***, ***school-***, ***writing-desk***, etc.

It may be a simple table, board, or shelf fixed at a convenient height for resting a book, etc., while reading or writing, or fitted on a small frame so as to be placed on a table, or upon a taller frame, with legs, etc., so as itself to stand on the floor, or it may be more or less elaborately provided with shelves for books, and with drawers and receptacles for papers, documents, etc., such as are required for use in a library, study, school, or office.

a. As a requisite for reading or writing on, or studying at.

c **1386** CHAUCER *Frankl. T.* 400 At Orliens in studie a book he say Of Magyk natureel, which his felawe..Hadde prively vpon his desk [*v.r.* deske] ylaft. *c* **1440** *Promp. Parv.* 299 Leterone or lectorne, deske, *lectrinum*, etc. *a* **1500** *Orol. Sap.* in *Anglia* X. 356 Lenynge hym vpon a deske. **1581** MULCASTER *Positions* v. (1887) 34 Incke and paper..a deske and a dustboxe will set them both vp [i.e. a scholar to learn to draw as well as to write]. **1594** PLAT *Jewell-ho., Diuerse Exper.* 39 You must have a deske of the cleerest and evenest glasse that is to be bought..Upon this Deske you must fasten the patterne at the foure endes with a little wax. **1615** STEPHENS *Satyr. Ess.* (ed. 2) 333 Lawyers Clarke..Hee doth relye upon his maisters practise, large indentures, and a deske to write upon. **1666** PEPYS *Diary* (1879) IV. 213, I observed the desk which he hath [made] to remove, and is fastened to one of the armes of his chayre. **1711** STEELE *Spect.* No. 109 ¶5 He sits with one Hand on a Desk writing. **1773** JOHNSON 17 Aug. in *Boswell*, Composing a Dictionary requires books and a desk: you can make a poem walking in the fields, or lying in bed. **1838** DICKENS *Nich. Nick.* ii, Nickleby closed an account book which lay on his desk. **1842** TENNYSON *Audley Court* 43 Oh! who would cast and balance at a desk, Perch'd like a crow upon a three-legg'd stool. **1847** —— *Princ.* II. 90 To Lady Psyche's..There sat along the forms..A patient range of pupils; she herself Erect behind a desk of satin-wood. **1850** —— *In Mem.* cxxviii, To cramp the student at his desk. **1871** MORLEY *Voltaire* (1886) 111 He seems to have usually passed the whole day at his desk.

b. As a repository for writing materials, letters, etc., as well as for writing on. In modern use often a portable box or case opening so as to present a sloping surface.

1548 COOPER *Bibliotheca Eliotæ, Pluteus*..a littell holowe deske lyke a coffer, whereupon men do write. **1590** SHAKS. *C. Err.* IV. i. 103 In the Deske That's couer'd o're with Turkish Tapistrie There is a purse of Duckets. **1626** BACON *Sylva* §658 Some..for Tables, Cupboards and Desks, as Walnuts. **1692** WASHINGTON tr. *Milton's Def. Pop.* Pref. (1851) 13 Your Boxes and Desks stufft with nothing but Trifles. *a* **1744** POPE (J.), I have been obliged to leave unfinished in my desk the heads of two essays. **1865** TROLLOPE *Belton Est.* xviii. 216 She got out her desk and prepared herself for her letter. *Mod.* The prisoner had forced the desk open and taken the money out of it.

†**c.** In early use, applied also to a shelf, case, or press, on or in which books stand in a library or study. *Obs.*

[*c* **1400** *Promp. Parv.* 120 Deske, *pluteum*. **1483** *Cath. Angl.* 97 A Deske; *pluteus* [a book-shelf, book-case, desk].] **1538** LELAND *Itin.* I. 55 At the Toppe of every Square was a Desk ledgid to set Bookes on Bookes on Cofers withyn them. **1557** NORTH *Gueuara's Diall Pr.* Gen. Prol. A iij, One that for his pastime is set round with deskes of bookes. **1669** HACKETT *Let.* in Willis & Clark *Cambridge* (1886) II. 554 Expended..upon the College Library, either for bookes, or desques. **1717** BERKELEY *Tour in Italy* Wks. 1871 IV. 513 The books are all contained in desks or presses, whose backs stand to the wall. These desks are all low, of an equal height, so that the highest books are within reach without the least straining.

2. a. In a church or chapel: In the general sense of 1, a sloping board on which books used in the service are laid, as the book-board in a pulpit. Hence formerly (and still in U.S.) applied to the seat, stall, or pulpit of the minister, or, (as still in Scotland) to that of the clerk or precentor; in England, to the stalls or choir-seats, and to the reading-desk in the now obsolescent arrangement of pulpit, reading-desk, and clerk's desk, one above another; where this has been abolished, and a special stall is provided for the reading of the prayers, the latter is sometimes called the 'prayer-desk'.

1449 *Churchw. Acc. St. Georges, Stamford* (Nichols 1797) 132 Making of pleyn desques and of a pleyne rodelofte. **1552** *Berksh. Ch. Goods* 32 A old clothe of baulkyn for the dexe. **1565** HARDING in Strype *Ann. Ref.* I. App. xxx. 72 Clappe me not they the bare Bible on the dext. **1604** *Vestry Bks.* (Surtees) 140 For a desk to lay the byble on. *a* **1640** W. FENNER *Christ's Alarm* (1650) 18 How reverently should ye sit in your Pewes? how sacredly should we stand in our desks? **1653** G. FIRMIN *Sober Reply* 28 My friend when he had done preaching..went downe out of the Deske. **1706** A. BEDFORD *Temple Mus.* iv. 90 Their Singers stood in the Desks. **1784** COWPER *Task* I. 94 Sweet sleep enjoys the curate in his desk, The tedious rector drawling o'er his head. **1809** KENDALL *Trav.* I. i. 4 The pulpit, or, as it is here [in Connecticut] called, the desk was filled by three, if not four clergymen; a number which, by its form and dimensions, it was able to accommodate. **1830** TENNYSON *Sonnet to J.M.K.*, The humming of the drowsy pulpit-drone..while the worn-out clerk Brow-beats his desk below. **1846** PARKER *Gloss. Archit.* (1875) 146 s.v. *Lectern*, At Debtling is one [a lectern] of Decorated date; it is made with a desk for a book on four sides. **1870** F. R. WILSON *Ch. Lindisf.* 79 The pulpit, litany desk, and stalls are oaken.

†**b.** A seat or pew in a church. Cf. DAIS 3 b. *Obs. Sc.*

1560 in Edgar *Ch. Life Scotl.* (1885) I. 15 Neither the dasks, windocks nor duris be ony wise hurt. **1603** *Ibid.*, To big ane removabill dask for his wyff. **1678** in *Old Church Life Ballingry* (1890) II. 20 Fill up with deskes the emptie roomes of the Church. **1701** in *Scott. N. & Q.* I. 12 [To farm] the haill dasks in both churches. **1885** EDGAR *Ch. Life Scotl.* I. 16 Down to about the middle of the 17th century there were very few desks or seats in Church.

3. *fig.* **a.** Used typically for the functions or office of the occupant of a desk, *esp.* in sense 2.

1581 J. BELL *Haddon's Answ. Osor.* 108 b, Luther doth not take upon him the person of a schoolemaister, nor hath challenged to himselfe the dignitie of high deske, nor ever taught any Schooles of new factions. **1821** DWIGHT *Trav.* II. 277 He [Dr. Backus, a professor of divinity] educated between forty and fifty for the desk. **1836** W. ANDREW *Hist. Winterton, etc.*, 107 At a time when the pulpit and reading-desk were generally at variance. **1838** *Brit. Critic* XXIII. 294 Their tendency is, to exalt the Pulpit too far above the Desk; to make the performance of man the very life and soul of all public worship.

b. Work at the desk in an office, etc.; clerical or office work.

1797 BURKE *Regic. Peace* III. (R.), Never can they who from the miserable servitude of the desk have been raised to empire, again submit to the bondage of a starving bureau. **1844** EMERSON *Lect., Yng. Amer.* Wks. (Bohn) II. 296 He who merely uses it [the land] as a support to his desk and ledger..values it less.

c. A specified section of a large organization, such as a newspaper office, government department, etc., responsible for a particular subject or operation. Freq. in *U.S.*, the department in a newspaper office where copy is edited. Cf. *city desk* s.v. CITY 9.

1927 U. SINCLAIR *Money Writes* 18 The reporters who write up the sensational event—each one is hoping to attract the attention of the 'desk'. **1958** E. NEWBY *Short Walk in Hindu Kush* ii. 24 [At] the Foreign Office..I was interviewed by a representative of the Asian Desk. **1966** J. BINGHAM *Double Agent* vi. 87 At the table next to Henry Blundell sat little George Patterson, in charge of the East Russian desk... At the same table was Mike Parsons, who worked at the Czech desk. **1970** R. GADNEY *Drawn Blanc* vi. 61 They gave me a desk in Soviet Counter Intelligence, it's a big outfit now.

d. The reception desk or office of a hotel, office building, etc.; the person or persons on duty at the reception desk.

1963 D. B. HUGHES *Expendable Man* vi. 200 I'll tell the desk not to put through any more calls. **1966** G. LYALL *Shooting Script* xix. 150 Room 17, I think you said? And the desk knows I'm coming? **1970** P. BAIR *Tribunal* II. iii. 76 Ask the desk to ring through to Miss Jackson's room.

4. *transf.* A meeting of those who occupy the choir desks of a cathedral.

1691 in Macray *Catal. Rawl. MSS.* D ii. 26 The sub-chanter and vicars [of Lichfield] desire to know whether he wishes to renew the lease..as the matter will be settled at the next meeting, or *deske* as they call it.

5. *attrib.* and *Comb.*, as ***desk-board, calendar, -closet, diary, -drudge, -fellow, -gong, job, lamp, -light, -officer***; **desk-book**, a book for constant use at the desk, a handbook, vade-mecum; **desk-bound** *a.*, obliged to remain at work at a desk; **desk-cloth**, a cloth to cover a reading-desk or lectern; **desk copy** orig. *U.S.*, a free copy of a book, esp. one supplied for the personal use of a teacher; **desk-knife**, a pen-knife with fixed handle, an eraser; **desk-man**, (*a*) a minister, clergyman, or preacher; (*b*) a man who works at a desk, *spec.* a journalist who works mainly at a desk; a white-collar worker; **desk-room** orig. *U.S.*, space for a desk rented in a business office; **desk sergeant** *U.S.* = *station sergeant* s.v. STATION *sb.* 29; **desk-work**, work at a desk, as clerk, book-keeper, etc.; see also DESK-TOP.

1614 SELDEN *Titles Hon.* 110 Fastned with long nailes to the *deskboards. **1892** *Literary World* 22 Jan. 82/3 This *desk-book may be highly recommended. **1944** *Time* 24 Apr. 26 Few thought he would be *desk-bound for long. **1962** *Listener* 28 June 1104/2 There were desk-bound jurists who had hatched out theories of crime 'as remote from reality as they are harmful'. **1907** *Yesterday's Shopping* (1969) p. xxxi/5 *Desk Calendar Pads. **1922** F. SCOTT FITZGERALD *Beautiful & Damned* I. iii. 100 On a desk calendar he marked the days off. **1968** H. C. RAE *Few Small Bones* II. i. 71 He ruffled the pages of his desk calendar. **1879** E. GARRETT *House by Works* I. 62 In the little oak *desk-closet at the back of the shop, stood a young woman. **1942** *Amer. Speech* XVII. 121 The teaching profession avoids the appearance of receiving forbidden favors by asking its publishers not for *free* copies but for **desk* copies. **1962** *Publishers' Weekly* 23 Apr. 39/2 Professors when they request 'desk copies' frequently also order books..for their own libraries. **1960** T. HUGHES *Lupercal* 52 Outstripping his *desk-diary at a broad desk. **1963** L. DEIGHTON *Horse under Water* xxxii. 125 He flips through the desk and finds a nice leather desk diary. **1880** BROWNING *Dram. Idylls* Ser. II. *Clive* 92 *Desk-drudge, slaving at St. David's, one must game, or drink, or craze. **1825** LAMB *Elia* Ser. II. *Superannuated Man*, To visit my old *desk-fellows. **1965** 'R. L. PIKE' *Police Blotter* (1966) vii. 105 He managed to get a soft *desk job in the war. **1833** J. HOLLAND *Manuf. Metal* II. 9 Pen-knives..fastened into the hafts, in the manner of what are now called *desk-knives. **1896** *New England Mag.* Nov. (Advt.), New designs in Dresden *desk lamps. **1922** JOYCE *Ulysses* 182 Glittereyed, his rufous skull close to his greencapped desk-lamp sought the face, bearded amid darkgreener shadow, an ollav, holyeyed. **1982** *Habitat Catal. 1982/83* 106/1 Classical desk lamp with swivelling green metal reflector cowl on a brass stem. **1929** E. WILSON *I thought of Daisy* i. 29, I turned aside the adjustable *desk-light..so that it lit only the farther wall. **1893** K. GRAHAME *Pagan Ess.* 105 The *Desk-men have a temporary majority. **1913** *Writer's Bull.* Oct. 101/1 The salaries paid..are..better than those paid to many 'desk men' in the offices of large newspapers. **1925** A. S. M. HUTCHINSON *One Increasing Purpose* I. xxx. 181 The city desk-man's feeble stoop. **1961** *Times* 8 Feb. 13/7 Millions of deskmen from an inflated officialdom have been out in the fields helping the peasants. **1967** R. J. SERLING *President's Plane is Missing* (1968) viii. 142 The IPS bureau chief was regarded as a superb deskman and a skilled writer. **1885** *Public Opinion* 9 Jan. 38/2 A scientific and what is popularly known as a *desk officer. **1868** R. B. KIMBALL *Undercurrents* 9, I occupied an office—no, I had '*desk-room' in a basement office. **1870** J. K. MEDBERY *Men & Myst. Wall Street* 117 Many of the operators, as well as the smaller brokers,..have simply desk-room. **1926** KIPLING *Debits & Credits* 337 Our War-side merely applied for desk-room in your basement. **1908** K. MCGAFFEY *Sorrows of Show Girl* 89 All he got was a clout on the head from the *desk sergeant. **1967** *Punch* 19 July 85/3 The rich having their three dollars whipped off them by the desk-sergeant and put in an envelope. **1864** TENNYSON *Sea Dreams* 78 A dozen years Of dust and *deskwork.

†**desk**, *v.* *Obs.* [f. DESK *sb.*]

1. *trans.* To fit up or furnish with desks.

a **1509** HEN. VII. *Will* in Willis & Clark *Cambridge* (1886) I. 498 That the said Chapell be desked.

2. To place in or as in a desk.

1615 *Albumazar* I. iii. in Hazl. *Dodsley* II. 311 A leaf of that small Iliad That in a walnut-shell was desk'd. **1646** J. HALL *Poems* I. 2 Then are you entertaind, and deskt up by Our Ladies Psalter and the Rosary. **1670** LASSELS *Voy. Italy* II. 164, I..saw many curious relicks desked up in the side of the wall.

3. *to desk it*: to work at a desk, do clerical work. *nonce-use.*

1846 J. MACKINTOSH *Let.* in *Mem.* (1854) 109, I have been busy, sometimes desking it 13 to 15 hours per diem.

deskater, obs. form of DISSCATTER *v.*

deskeletonize: see DE- II. 1.

deskever, obs. form of DISCOVER *v.*

deskful ('dɛskfʊl). [f. DESK *sb.* + -FUL.] As much as a desk will contain.

1877 BESANT & RICE *Harp & Cr.* ix. 67 The..letters..There was not a word of love in a deskful of them. **1894** H. TAYLOR in *Amer. Ann. Deaf* Apr. 117 The teacher finds he can get along better without a deskful of switches.

deskill (diːˈskɪl), *v.* [f. DE- II. 2 + SKILL *sb.*[1]] *trans.* To convert (a workplace, employment) from one that requires a skilled worker or workers to one that does not; to reduce the number of skilled workers in (an industry); of new technology, etc.: to render (a skilled worker) unskilled. Hence **de'skilled** *ppl. a.*, **de'skilling** *vbl. sb.*

1941 *Country Life* 1 Feb. 93/1 Civil servants are adept at the creation of composite words... One of the latest examples is the verb '*to de-skill*', which is, we believe, applied to factories and refers to the increasing [use] of unskilled labour in them. **1967** *Observer* (Colour Suppl.) 28 May 30/2 The cutlery business..needs to be 'de-skilled', because most of the highly skilled people in it are nearer 75 than 25. **1976** *Film & Television Technician* Nov. 3/3 What about the reported 'de-skilling' of television programme operations reported from the USA where the revolution is in full swing? **1982** J. NAISBITT *Megatrends* (1984) i. 31 He found that production and service jobs tended to become 'deskilled' when technology is added. **1982** *Spectator* 11 Dec. 17/2 In doing so they also deskill the typist's job and, by increasing office productivity, lead to an overall decrease in secretarial jobs in the longer term. **1985** *Guardian* 6 Apr. 4/6 It will signal a casualised and deskilled Post Office.

desk-top ('dɛsktɒp). Also **desktop**, (sense A. 1) **desk top**. [f. DESK *sb.* + TOP *sb.*[1]]

A. *sb.* **1.** The top or working surface of a desk.

1929 D. HAMMETT *Dain Curse* (1930) xiii. 144 He..returned his feet to the desk-top. **1935** R. STOUT *League of Frightened Men* xi. 137 What we are displaying on this desk-top is the soul of a man. **1959** W. MILLER *Canticle for Leibowitz* (1960) xiv. 153 His hard breathing swept a clean spot in the film of desert dust on the desktop. **1960** *Design* July 56 Several basic broad desk tops, pedestals, panels.

2. A desk-top computer. *colloq.*

1983 *Austral. Personal Computer* Sept. 69/2 The trend was for lower profile Winchester hard disk drives for the emerging desk-top and portable markets. **1985** *Personal Computer World* Feb. 13 (Advt.), If you use an HP-150 PC, IBM PC, XT or an IBM compatible you will be glad to know that the desktop and the Portable can talk to each other. **1987** *Times* 10 Feb. 24/1 (*heading*) A super desktop run by battery.

B. *attrib.* **1.** Suitable for use at or on a desk; *spec.* designating microcomputers and peripheral devices of this kind and software for them.

1958 *Computer Jrnl.* I. 101/2 The majority of design procedures..in use..were developed when 'desk top' methods of calculating were all that was available. **1965** *New Society* 7 Jan. 4/2 'Nice guys don't win' has not yet been issued as a desktop slogan for executives. **1965** [see CALCULATOR 2 c]. **1968** *Daily Tel.* 12 Nov. 22/6 Desk-top computers for use in homes..may be made possible by an invention described today. **1970** *Nature* 11 Apr. 140/1 The straight line of Fig. 1 resulted from a least squares fit to the data, with a desk-top computer. **1982** *ICL News* Nov. 1/1 The recently introduced DRS 20 model 20 and 25 desk-top terminals..offer managers direct access to the computer network. **1984** *Sunday Times* 14 Oct. 24/3 (Advt.), The new Canon PC70 desktop reader-printer produces clear crisp images. **1985** *Neat Ideas Mail Order Catal.* Spring 10 The Literature Organiser can be used either as a desk top sorter or built up in units with interlocking clips.

2. desk-top publishing, the production of printed matter similar in quality to that of typeset books by means of a printer (such as a laser printer) linked to a desk-top computer; so ***desk-top publisher***.

1984 *Financial Times* 3 Sept. 8/2 When Xerox looked for a new way to market its revolutionary but commercially unsuccessful 'Star' workstation.., it settled on what it called a 'document creation system' — in other words, a desk-top publishing unit. **1986** *Observer* 14 Sept. 41/5 Desktop publishing in one form or another has been a commercial possibility for some years. **1986** *Australian* 14 Oct. 42/4 Even commercial desk-top publishers who use the Mac-Laserwriter combination often paste graphics into gaps left in the typeset text.

deslavee, -avé, var. forms of DELAVY *a.*

†**deslay**, obs. form of DELAY *v.* [So OF. *desleer* for *deleer*.]

1393 GOWER *Conf.* II. 60 For I may say..That idel man have I be nought, For how as ever that I be deslaied, Yet evermore I have assaied. *Ibid.* 115 Every joy him is deslaied.

desma ('dɛsmə). *Biol.* Pl. **desmata, desmas.** [a. Gr. δέσμα (pl. -ατα) bond, fetter, head-band, f. δέ-ειν to bind.]

1. A bandage; a ligament.

1857 in DUNGLISON. **1883** in *Syd. Soc. Lex.*

2. A kind of spicule which unites with others to form the skeletal network in a particular group of sponges.

1887 SOLLAS in *Encycl. Brit.* XXII. 418/2 (Sponges) In the Lithistid sponges a skeleton is produced by the articulation of desmas into a network.

desmachyme ('dɛsməkaɪm). *Biol.* [f. DESMA + CHYME (Gr. χυμός animal or vegetable juice, χύμα(τ- liquid).] A suggested name (now abandoned) for the connective tissue of sponges, formed of desmacytes. Hence **desma-chymatous** (-'kɪmətəs) *a.*, of, pertaining to, or of the nature of desmachyme.

1887 SOLLAS in *Encycl. Brit.* XXII. 422/1 A layer of thickly felted desmachyme. *Ibid.* 420/2 A desmachymatous sheath surrounds the whole.

desmacyte ('dɛsməsaɪt). *Biol.* [f. DESMA + -CYTE cell.] A name suggested for one of the fusiform cells of connective tissue in sponges. Now called INO-CYTE.

1887 SOLLAS in *Encycl. Brit.* XXII. 419/2 Connective-tissue cells or *desmacytes* are present on most sponges; they are usually long fusiform bodies consisting of a clear colourless..sheath, surrounding a highly refringent axial fibre.

‖**desman** ('dɛsmən). *Zool.* [In Fr. and Ger. *desman*, from Sw. *desman-råtta* musk-rat, f. *desman* (Da. *desmer*, Icel. *des-*) musk.] An aquatic insectivorous mammal, of the genus *Myogale*, nearly allied to the shrew-mouse, but larger; esp. *M. moschata*, the musk-shrew or musk-rat, which inhabits the rivers of Russia, chiefly the Volga and Don, and secretes a sort of musk. Another species (*M. pyrenaica*) is found in parts of the Pyrenees.

1774 GOLDSM. *Nat. Hist.* (1862) I. VI. i. 454 The Desman ..has a long extended snout, like the shrew-mouse. **1861** HULME tr. *Moquin-Tandon* II. III. ii. 110 The tail of the Desman of Muscovy, or Musk Rat of Russia..is sought for as a perfume. It owes its odour to a substance which is secreted by two small follicular glands placed at its base.

desmid ('dɛsmɪd). *Bot.* [ad. Bot. L. *Desmidium* (generic name), f. Gr. type *δεσμίδιον, dim. of δεσμός band, chain.] A plant of the genus *Desmidium*, or order *Desmidiaceæ* of microscopic unicellular algæ; so called because sometimes found united in chains.

1862 DANA *Man. Geol.* 271 Desmids..are microscopic plants, consisting of one or a few cells. **1867** E. NARES (*title*), Handy Book to the Collection and Preparation of Freshwater and Marine Algæ, Desmids, etc. **1871** FARRAR *Witn. Hist.* i. 34 Look through the microscope..at some desmid gleaming like an animated opal with living iridescence.

Hence **desmidi'aceous** *a.*, of the N.O. *Desmidiaceæ*, containing the desmids; **des'midian** *a.*, of the desmids; *sb.* a desmid; **desmidi'ology**, the scientific study of desmids; **desmidi'ologist**, one who pursues this study.

desmine ('dɛsmɪn). *Min.* Also **desmin.** [f. Gr. δεσμή bundle + -INE.] A synonym of STILBITE, a zeolitic mineral occurring in tufts or bundles of crystals.

1811 PINKERTON *Petral.* II. 14 A substance in silky tufts, which he calls desmine. **1814** ALLAN *Min. Nomen.* 16. **1844** DANA *Min.* 328.

desmo- ('dɛsməʊ), combining form of Gr. δεσμός bond, fastening, chain, ligature, an element in scientific words of Greek derivation. **des'mobrya** *pl.* [Gr. βρυον; see BRYOLOGY], name for a group of ferns: hence **des'mobryoid** *a.*, belonging to or resembling the *Desmobrya*. **'desmodont** *a.* and *sb.* [Gr. ὀδοντ- tooth], belonging to, or one of, the *Desmodonta*, a group of bivalve molluscs. **des'mognathous** *a.* [Gr. γνάθος jaw], having the type of palatal structure shown in the *Desmognathæ*, a group of birds in Huxley's classification, in which the maxillopalatine bones are united across the median line; so **des'mognathism**, this type of palatal structure. **des'mography** *Anat.*, 'a description of the ligaments of the body' (Craig 1847). **des'mology**, 'the anatomy of the ligaments of the body; also, a treatise on bandages' (*Syd. Soc. Lex.*). **desmono'sology** [Gr. νόσος disease], 'the description of the diseases of the ligaments'. **desmopa'thology**, 'the doctrine of diseases of ligaments'. **des'mopathy**, 'disease of the ligaments' (Dunglison 1857). **desmo'pelmous** *a.* [Gr. πέλμα sole of the foot], *Ornith.* having the plantar tendons connected, as some birds, so that the hind toe cannot be moved independently of the front toes. **des'mostichous** (-kəs), *a.* [Gr. στίχος row, line], belonging to or having the characters of the *Desmosticha*, a group of echinoids or sea-urchins having the ambulacra equal and band-like. **des'motomy** [Gr. -τομια cutting], the dissection of ligaments (Dunglison 1857).

1854–67 HARRIS *Dict. Med. Terminol.*, *Desmology*, a treatise on the ligaments. **1875** PARKER in *Encycl. Brit.* III. 711/2 (Birds) The desmognathous type of skull. *Ibid.* 712/1 It is possible to make several important divisions in the kind and degree of desmognathism.

desmoid ('dɛsmɔɪd), *a.* [f. Gr. δεσμός band, ligament, etc. and δεσμή bundle + -OID.] Resembling a bundle. **a.** *Path.* Applied to the tissue of certain tumours which contain numerous fibres closely interwoven or arranged in bundles. **b.** *Zool.* and *Anat.* Ligamentous; tendinous.

1847 SOUTH tr. *Chelius' Surg.* II. 712 Desmoid, sarcomatous, steatomatous, chondroid and fibroid swellings, have been classed together as fibrous tumours. **1876** tr. *Wagner's Gen. Pathol.* 271 The fibrin-like appearance of this desmoid tissue.

desmoncus (dɛs'mɒŋkəs). *Bot.* [mod.L., f. Gr. δεσμός bond + ὄγκος hook.] A climbing plant of the genus of palms of this name, common in tropical America.

1899 J. RODWAY *Guiana Wilds* 14 His head grazed by the formidable hooks which hung from the horrid desmoncus.

'desmous, *a. rare*$^{-0}$. [f. as DESMOID *a.* + -OUS.] Ligamentous.

1883 in *Syd. Soc. Lex.*

‖**de'sobligeant.** *Obs.* [ad. F. *désobligeante* in same sense, fem. (sc. *voiture* carriage) of *désobligeant* disobliging.] 'A chaise so called in France from its holding but one person.' (*Note* to Sterne, in ed. 1794.) Cf. *sulky*.

1768 STERNE *Sent. Journ.* (1778) I. 20 (*Desobligeant*) An old Desobligeant.. hit my fancy at first sight, so I instantly got into it. **1770** J. ADAMS *Diary* 12 July Wks. 1850 II. 246 Got into my désobligeant to go home. **1787** ANN HILDITCH *Rosa de Montmorien* I. 48 To travel.. in the very disobligeant which Sterne celebrates in his Sentimental tour. *ibid.* I. 49. **1811** *Sporting Mag.* XXXVII. 12 Sociables, disoblegiants.

desocialize, -ation: see DE- II. 1.

‖**désœuvré** (dezœvre), *a.* [Fr.] Out of work, unemployed, unoccupied; languidly idle. So **désœuvrement**, lack of occupation.

1750 CHESTERF. *Lett.* 11 Jan. (1774) I. clxxxi. 541 If.. some charitable people.. being *desœuvré* themselves, came and spoke to me. **1794** MISS GUNNING *Packet* IV. 258 In a tone perfectly *desœuvré*.. calling her a fine old quiz. **1839** LONGF. in *Life* (1891) I. 348 Drowsy, dull, *desœuvré*, not having a book in press.

1828 *Eng. in France* II. 41 (Stanf.) The Baronne looked for a friend.. for *désœuvrement*, for amusement, not excitement. **1849** LONGF. in *Life* (1891) II. 154, I have nothing to write you, and write.. from mere *désœuvrement*.

desolate ('dɛsələt), *ppl. a.* (*sb.*) Also 4 **desolaat**, 4–5 **disolat, dissolate**, 4–6 **desolat.** [ad. L. *dēsōlāt-us* left alone, forsaken, deserted, pa. pple. of *dēsōlāre* to leave alone, desert, f. DE- I. 3 + *sōlāre* to make lonely, *sōlus* alone, lonely. The earliest uses were more or less participial.]

†**A.** as *pa. pple.* Brought to desolation, laid waste: see DESOLATE *v.*

1382 WYCLIF *Luke* xi. 17 Euery rewme departide aȝens it silf, schal be desolat [*desolabitur*]. —— *Wisd.* iv. 19 Vnto the heȝest thei shul ben desolat [*desolabuntur*].

B. *adj.* **1.** Left alone, without companion, solitary, lonely.

c **1386** CHAUCER *Merch. T.* 77 He which hath no wif.. lyveth helples, and is al desolate. *c* **1450** *Merlin* 596 Many a gentill lady be lefte wedowe, and many a gentill mayden dysolat. **1548** HALL *Chron.* 202 b, Leavyng the erle of Pembroke almoste desolate in the toune. **1657** COKAINE *Obstinate Lady* v. iv, I should live a desolater life Than e'er the strictest anchorite hath done. **1860** TYNDALL *Glac.* I. xi. 85 A position more desolate than his had been can hardly be imagined. **1863** GEO. ELIOT *Romola* III. xii, No soul is desolate as long as there is a human being for whom it can feel trust and reverence.

†**2.** Destitute or deprived *of*, lacking. Rarely with *inf.*: Without means, quite unable *to*. *Obs.*

c **1386** CHAUCER *Man of Law's T.* 838 So yong, and of armure so desolate. *c* **1430** LYDG. *Bochas* XI. i. (1554) 144 b, John Bochas.. dissolate To determine such heauenly-hid secrees. **1535** COVERDALE *Ruth* i. 5 The woman remayned desolate of both hir sonnes. **1544** PHAER *Regim. Lyfe* (1560) Q iij b, The tender babes are oftentymes affected, and desolate of remedy. **1632** LITHGOW *Trav.* x. 500 By dissolute courses.. leave themselves deservingly desolate, of Lands, Meanes, and Honesty. **1720** DE FOE *Capt. Singleton* viii. (1840) 135 The place.. was desolate of inhabitants.

†**3.** Left without a king; kingless. *Obs.*

1375 BARBOUR *Bruce* I. 40 The land vj ȝer.. Lay desolat eftyr hys day. **1393** GOWER *Conf.* I. 248 The lordes.. wolden save The regne, which was desolate.

4. Destitute of inhabitants; uninhabited, unpeopled, deserted.

(This sense and 5 are often combined in actual use.)

c **1374** CHAUCER *Anel. & Arc.* 62 So desolate stode Thebes and so bare. *c* **1450** LYDG. *Compl. Loveres Lyfe* 167 He thus lay on the grounde in place desolate. **1555** EDEN *Decades* 42 Many Ilandes very fruitefull yet lefte desolate. **1634** SIR T. HERBERT *Trav.* 138 He allured out of Babilon sixe hundred thousand soules, so that the late triumphant Citie became halfe desolate. **1735** BERKELEY *Querist* §418 Roads untrodden, fields untilled, houses desolate. **1887** BOWEN *Virg. Æneid* IV. 588 Desolate shores and abandoned ports.

5. Having the characteristics of a place deserted or uninhabited: **a.** in ruinous state or neglected condition, laid waste; **b.** without sign of life, bare of trees or herbage, barren; **c.** dreary, dismal, cheerless.

1413 *Pilgr. Sowle* III. i. (Caxton 1483) 49 A derker place, the moost wretchyd and desolate that euer men come ynne. **1559** W. CUNNINGHAM *Cosmogr. Glasse* 195 Ninivie, a great Citie, but nowe desolate. **1655** H. VAUGHAN *Silex Scint.* I. 99 Will thy secret key Open my desolate rooms. **1779** NEWTON in R. Palmer *Bk. of Praise* 86 This land through which His pilgrims go Is desolate and dry. **1838** DICKENS *Nich. Nick.* ii, No man thinks of walking in this desolate place. **1847** JAMES *Convict* ii, There was a cheerless, desolate sound about it.

†**d.** Of the head: Bare of hair, bald. *Obs.*

c **1500** *Lancelot* 366 It semyth that of al his hed ye hore Of fallith and maid desolat.

6. Destitute of joy or comfort, like one bereft of friends or relatives; forlorn, disconsolate; overwhelmed with grief and misery, wretched.

14.. *Why I can't be a Nun* 96 in *E.E.P.* (1862) 140 For now I am alle desolate, And of gode cownesayle destitute. *c* **1477** CAXTON *Jason* 45 b, Gyue confort to a desolate hert. **1598** YONG *Diana* 73 Yet did Arsenius.. leade the most sorrowfull and desolate life. **1653** H. COGAN tr. *Pinto's Trav.* xii. 36 Having heard what this desolate Queen said openly unto him. **1738** WESLEY *Ps. & Hymns* cxxxvii. 5 O England's desolate Church. **1852** MRS. STOWE *Uncle Tom's C.* ix. 67, I must feed the hungry, clothe the naked, and comfort the desolate. **1857** H. REED *Lect. Eng. Poets* II. xiii. 129 That desolate craving after the departed.

†**7.** Destitute of good quality, evil, abandoned. (Sometimes app. confounded with *dissolute*.) *Obs.*

c **1386** CHAUCER *Pard. T.* 270 A comun hasardour.. ever the heyer he is of astaat The more is he holden desolaat. **1579** TOMSON *Calvin's Serm. Tim.* 82/2 Nor glutton, nor thefe, nor man of wicked and desolate life. **1782** ? VAUGHAN *Fashionable Follies* I. 153 Unhappy men of desolate and abandoned principles.

8. *Comb.*, as ***desolate-looking*** adj.

1833 L. RITCHIE *Wand. Loire* 78 The lonely and desolate-looking wanderer. **1872** JENKINSON *Guide Eng. Lakes* (1879) 154 The barren and desolate-looking valley.. in front.

C. *absol.* or *sb.* A desolate place or person.

a **1400–50** *Alexander* 4354 Duells here in disolatis, in dennes & in cauys. **1610** G. FLETCHER *Christ's Vict.* (R.), A poor desolate, That now had measured many a weary mile. **1795** SOUTHEY *Joan of Arc* VI. 433 Travelling the trackless desolate.

desolate ('dɛsəleɪt), *v.* [f. prec., after L. *dēsōlāre*, F. *désoler* in same sense.

Wyclif has only the pa. pple. *desolat* (see prec.), and *desolatid*, immediately f. L. *dēsōlāt-us*; by the help of these a passive voice was formed; the active *to desolate* (though implied in the pa. pple. *desolated*) does not occur till much later; even in Palsgrave 1530, it is only a dictionary equivalent of F. *désoler*, without example.]

1. *trans.* To deprive of inhabitants, depopulate.

(This sense and 2 are often combined in use.)

1382 WYCLIF *Ezek.* xii. 19 That the loond be desolatid [*desoletur*] fro his multitude. **1530** PALSGR. 514/1, I desolate.. I make a countrey unhabyted, *Je desole*. **1601** R. JOHNSON *Kingd. & Commw.* (1603) 114 [Tarentum] is now by their civill dissentions almost desolated. **1791** COWPER *Iliad* v. 582 And desolate at once your populous Troy. **1875** LYELL *Princ. Geol.* II. II. xxix. 140 As if the city had been desolated by the plague.

2. To devastate, lay waste; to make bare, barren, or unfit for habitation.

1388 WYCLIF *Matt.* xii. 25 Eche kingdom departid aȝens it silf, schal be desolatid [*desolabitur*]. **1585** T. WASHINGTON tr. *Nicholay's Voy.* III. ii. 71 b, His countrie being desolated. **1606** G. W[OODCOCKE] tr. *Hist. Iustine* 104 a, All his fortunes being desolated and as it were melted from him. **1719** DE FOE *Crusoe* II. v. (1840) 106 Would quite desolate the island, and starve them. **1796** H. HUNTER tr. *St. Pierre's Stud. Nat.* (1799) III. 441 The revolutions of Nature which had desolated France. **1868** J. H. BLUNT *Ref. Ch. Eng.* I. 299 To desolate the houses.. of the monks and nuns by such plunder.

absol. **1795** SOUTHEY *Joan of Arc* I. 177 Thy bitter foes Rush o'er the land, and desolate, and kill.

3. To leave alone, forsake, abandon; to make desolate, deprive of companions or friends.

1530 PALSGR. 514/1, I desolate, I forsake one and leave hym comfortlesse.. *Je desole*. **1605** BACON *Adv. Learn.* II. xxiii. §17 (1873) 231 He did desolate him, and won from him his dependances [*i.e.* adherents]. **1809** [see DESOLATED *ppl. a.*]

†**4.** To turn *out of*, so as to leave without habitation. *Obs.*

1593 NASHE *Christ's T.* (1613) 41 A Tabernacle.. which he shall not be vndermined and desolated out of.

5. To make joyless and comfortless; to overwhelm with grief; to render wretched.

1530 [see 3]. **1535** COVERDALE *Dan.* ix. 18 Beholde how we be desolated. **1653** H. COGAN tr. *Pinto's Trav.* lxxii. 292 Altogether desolated as he was in this last affliction. **1887** *Spectator* 3 Sept. 1176 Buoyed up by constantly renewed hope or desolated by continuous despair.

desolated ('dɛsəleɪtɪd), *ppl. a.* [f. prec. + -ED.] Made or left desolate; see prec.

1580 SIDNEY *Ps.* XXII. xii, Save.. My desolated life from dogged might. *a* **1700** DRYDEN *Ovid's Metam.* I. (R.), Tell how we may.. people desolated earth. **1793** J. WILLIAMS *Mem. W. Hastings* 41, I am a stranger to the private manners of this desolated gentleman. **1806** J. FORBES *Lett. France* II. 64 The entangled walks of the desolated gardens. **1809** CAMPBELL *Gertr. Wyom.* I. xvii, In vain the desolated panther flies. **1818** BYRON *Ch. Har.* IV. xxi, Bare and desolated bosoms.

desolately ('dɛsələtlɪ), *adv.* [f. DESOLATE *a.* + -LY².] In a desolate manner; solitarily, by oneself (*obs.*); drearily, dismally, cheerlessly.

1548 HALL *Chron.* 218 b, That kyng Henry her husband, was desolately left post a lone. *a* **1699** BATES *Wks.* IV. Serm. iv. (R.), Nehemiah.. all the pleasures of the Persian court could not satisfy, whilst Jerusalem was desolately miserable. **1831** *Q. Rev.* Jan. in *Byron's Wks.* (1846) 470/2 *note*, There is.. nothing more mournfully and desolately beautiful. *a* **1851** MOIR *Poems, Des. Churchyard* vii, The wind amid the hemlock-stalks Would desolately sing.

†**b.** Abandonedly, dissolutely. *Obs.*

1608 J. KING *Serm.* 5 Nov. 17 The most abominably, desolately, deperditely wicked of all others.

'desolateness. [f. as prec. + -NESS.] The state or quality of being desolate; desertedness, dismal barrenness; cheerlessness, dreary misery.

a **1626** BACON *Wks.* VI. 38 (L.) In so great discomfort it hath pleased God some ways to regard my desolateness. **1639** BAKER in Spurgeon *Treas. Dav.* Ps. cxliii. 5 A comfort to the desolateness of my heart. **1668** H. MORE *Div. Dial.* II. xv. (1713) 135 The forlornness and desolateness of that forsaken Habitacle, the Body of a natural Fool. **1818** SHELLEY *Rev. Islam* v. xxviii, The swift fall Of one so great and terrible of yore, To desolateness. **1863** GEO. ELIOT *Romola* II. xxx, He had so weary a sense of his desolateness. **1877** H. A. PAGE *De Quincey* II. xix. 249 To face the desolateness of Wales.

desolater: see DESOLATOR.

desolating ('dɛsəleɪtɪŋ), *vbl. sb.* [f. DESOLATE *v.* + -ING¹.] The action of the verb DESOLATE.

1591 PERCIVALL *Sp. Dict.*, *Ermadura*, wasting, desolating. **1722** DE FOE *Plague* (Rtldg. 1884) 29 A mere desolating of some of the Streets.

'desolating, *ppl. a.* [f. as prec. + -ING².] That desolates (in various senses; see the verb).

1625 R. SKYNNER in *Ussher's Lett.* (1686) 361 The desolating Abomination. **1794** MATHIAS *Purs. Lit.* (1798) 429 Desolating tyranny. **1813** BYRON *Br. Abydos* II. xvii, Whose desolating tale Would make thy waning cheek more pale. **1853** TRENCH *Proverbs* 124 The desolating curse of Mohammedan domination.

desolatingly ('dɛsəleɪtɪŋlɪ), *adv.* [f. DESOLATING *ppl. a.* + -LY².] In a manner that desolates or saddens.

1888 'L. MALET' *Counsel of Perfection* xiv. 323 These desolatingly encouraging persons. **1909** H. G. WELLS *Tono-Bungay* I. iii. 81 A drab-coloured passage.. not only narrow and dirty but desolatingly empty.

desolation (dɛsəʊ'leɪʃən). [a. F. *désolation* (12th c. in Hatzf.), or ad. L. *dēsōlātiōn-em*, n. of action from *dēsōlāre* to DESOLATE.] The action of desolating; the condition of being left desolate.

1. The action of laying waste a land, etc., destroying its people, crops, and buildings, and making it unfit for habitation; utter devastation; an act or occasion of this kind. Also *personified*.

1382 WYCLIF *2 Chron.* xxxvi. 21 Alle the days of desolacioun he dide saboth. *c* **1400** *Apol. Loll.* 58 What more abhominacoun of desolacoun in holi place þan þat a swyn do vpon þe holy vestiment. **1526** TINDALE *Mark* xiii. 13 When ye se the abominacion that betokeneth desolacion [WYCLIF of discomfort]. **1599** SHAKS. *Hen. V*, III. iii. 18 All fell feats, Enlynckt to wast and desolation. **1722** WOLLASTON *Relig. Nat.* ix. 201 Wars and all those barbarous desolations which we read of. **1774** PENNANT *Tour Scotl. in 1772*, 58 The general desolation of the place by the Danes. **1814** BYRON *Lara* II. x, And Desolation reap'd the famish'd land. **1821** —— *Two Foscari* I. i, I have follow'd long Thy path of desolation.

fig. **1893** *Chicago Advance* 30 Nov., The financial panic.. the desolations of which are by no means yet overpast.

2. The condition of a place which by hostile ravaging or by natural character is unfit for habitation; waste or ruined state; dreary barrenness.

c **1430** LYDG. *Min. Poems* (1840) 144 (Mätz.) In a dirk prisoun of desolacioun. **1490** CAXTON *Eneydos* i. 14 Now was that pyetous cyte alle brent and putte in desolacyon suffretous. **1632** LITHGOW *Trav.* VII. 318 Least he impede.. the course of Nylus.. and so bring Egypt to desolation. **1667** MILTON *P.L.* I. 181 Yon dreary Plain, forlorn and wilde, The seat of desolation. **1791** MRS. RADCLIFFE *Rom. Forest* i, Such elegance.. contrasted with the desolation of the house. **1856** STANLEY *Sinai & Pal.* i. 16 The general character.. of the mountains of Sinai, is entire desolation. If the mountains are naked Alps, the valleys are dry rivers.

b. A thing or place in this condition; a desolate place; a dreary waste or ruin.

1611 BIBLE *Jer.* xxii. 5 This house shall become a desolation. **1856** EMERSON *Eng. Traits, Aristocracy* Wks. (Bohn) II. 76 Many of the halls.. are beautiful desolations.

3. Deprivation of companionship; the condition or sense of being forsaken; solitariness, loneliness.

1588 SHAKS. *L.L.L.* v. ii. 357 You haue liu'd in desolation heere, Vnseene, vnuisited. **1628** WITHER *Brit. Rememb.* VIII. 1046 Loathsome desolation, In stead of company. **1818** SHELLEY *Rev. Islam* x. xliii, As near one lover's tomb Two gentle sisters mourn their desolation. **1871** R. ELLIS *Catullus* lxiv. 57 Sand-engirded, alone, then first she knew desolation.

4. Deprivation of comfort or joy; dreary sorrow; grief.

1382 WYCLIF *Ezek.* xii. 19 Thei schulen drynke her watir in desolacioun. *c* **1477** CAXTON *Jason* 22 b, I am cause of alle the desolation of Oliferne. **1600** SHAKS. *A.Y.L.* III. ii. 400 Euerie thing about you, demonstrating a carelesse desolation. **1752** WARBURTON *Lett.* (1809) 118 Poor Foster .. is overwhelmed with desolation for the loss of his master. **1759** ROBERTSON *Hist. Scotl.* I. VI. 480 Desolation and astonishment appeared in every part of the Scottish Church. **1871** MORLEY *Voltaire* (1886) 274 The hopeless inner desolation which is the unbroken lot of myriads.

5. That which makes desolate. *rare.*

1608 *Yorksh. Trag.* I. ix, Ruinous man! The desolation of his house.

† **'desolative,** *a. Obs. rare.* [f. L. *dēsōlāt-*, ppl. stem: see -IVE.] Having the quality or tendency of desolating.

1593 NASHE *Christ's T.* (1613) 54 The full blast of this desolatiue-trumpet of Ierusalem.

desolator, -er ('dɛsəleɪtə(r)). [a. L. *dēsōlātor*, agent-n. from *dēsōlāre* to DESOLATE: see -ER[1]. Cf. F. *désolateur* (1516 in Hatzf.).] One who or that which makes desolate.

a **1638** MEDE *On Daniel* 44 (T.) A desolater, or maker of desolations. **1786** *Hist. Europe* in *Ann. Reg.* 129/2 The plunderers of mankind, the desolators of provinces. **1814** BYRON *Ode to Napoleon* v, The Desolator desolate! The Victor overthrown! **1894** EDNA LYALL *To Right the Wrong* I. 43 War is the desolater.

† **'desolatory,** *a. Obs. rare.* [ad. L. *dēsōlātōri-us* that makes lonely or desolate, f. *dēsōlātor*: see -ORY.] Characterized by causing desolation; = DESOLATIVE.

1606 BP. ANDREWES *Serm.* 5 Nov., 96 Serm. (1629) 894 This so abominable and desolatorie a plott. **1641** BP. HALL *Rem.* 55 These desolatory judgments are a notable improvement of his mercy. *a* **1656** —— *Revel. Unrev.* (R.) This desolatory abomination.

desolute, desolve: see DISS-.

‖ **de son tort** (də sɔ̃ tɔr). *Law.* [Fr., lit. 'of his wrong'.] By his own wrongdoing, without authorization; *spec.* in phrases, e.g. ***executor de son tort*** (see EXECUTOR 3 b), ***de son tort demesne*** (see quot. 1835).

1670, 1767 [see EXECUTOR 3 b]. **1835** TOMLINS *Law-Dict.* s.v. Tort, *De son tort demesne*, of his own wrong. **1874** *Law Rep. Chancery Appeal Cases* IX. 251 Responsibility may no doubt be extended in equity to others who are not properly trustees, if they are found either making themselves trustees *de son tort*, or actually participating in any fraudulent conduct of the trustee. **1959** JOWITT *Dict. Eng. Law* I. 573/1 Where B, the defendant, pleaded that what was alleged against him had been done by the order of C, his master, then A, the plaintiff, might reply that B had done it *de son tort demesne sans que C luy commande*, that is to say, of his own wrong without being ordered by C.

,deso'phisticate, *v.* [f. DE- II. 1.] *trans.* To free from sophistication, clear from sophism. Hence **deso'phisticating** *ppl. a.*, **desophisti'cation**.

1827 HARE *Guesses* (1859) 143 Selden .. in sound, sterling, desophisticating sense was far superior to him [Hobbes]. **1834** *Tait's Mag.* I. 488 The mass of the French nation has .. achieved desophistication of manners.

desorb (diː'sɔːb), *v.* [Back-formation from DESORPTION.] **a.** *trans.* To remove (a substance, etc.) from the surface upon which it is adsorbed. **b.** *intr.* Of a substance, etc.: to leave the surface upon which it is adsorbed (and pass *into*).

1924 *Proc. R. Soc.* A. CVI. 64 (*heading*) The energy required to desorb the gas-film. *Ibid.* 67 Some gases .. are desorbed from tungsten, etc., with practically zero latent heat. **1937** *Nature* 10 July 48/1 Tswett conceived the idea of making the solution flow in one direction .. through a column of the adsorbent, so that the adsorbed material might afterwards be desorbed, or 'eluted', by the same or some other more suitable solvent. **1964** *New Scientist* 26 Mar. 828/2 The free radicals were left to accumulate on the surface, from which they 'desorbed' back into the chamber. **1967** E. L. PACE in E. A. Flood *Solid-Gas Interface* I. iv. 123 The desorption was accomplished by allowing the gas to desorb into a measured volume with the simultaneous application of heat.

desordeine, -ordeynee, var. DISORDEINE *a.*

desorption (diː'sɔːpʃən). [f. DE-, after ADSORPTION.] The liberation of a substance from the surface upon which it is adsorbed or from the liquid in which it is dissolved.

1924 *Proc. R. Soc.* A. CVI. 68 The desorption of a fresh film of carbon monoxide from tungsten. **1937** *Nature* 17 July 108/1 It seems possible that the existence of a sharp transition temperature may be associated with the desorption of gas from a film originally formed under poor vacuum conditions. **1955** R. E. TREYBAL *Mass-Transfer Operations* i. 3 If air is brought into contact with an ammonia-water solution, some of the ammonia leaves the liquid and enters the gas phase, an operation known as desorption or stripping.

desoxalic (dɛsɒk'sælɪk), *a. Chem.* [ad. F. *désoxalique*: see DES- and OXALIC.] Formed by the deoxidation of oxalic acid. ***desoxalic acid***, a synonym of racemo-carbonic acid, $C_5H_6O_8$. Hence **de'soxalate**, a salt of this acid, a racemo-carbonate.

a **1868** WATTS *Dict. Chem.* V. 40 Probably formed by the deoxidation of oxalic acid, whence the name *desoxalic acid.*

desoxy-. *Chem.* [f. as prec. + OXY- combining form of *oxygen.*] Without oxygen, deoxidated; as in **desoxy-'anisoin, desoxy-'benzoin, desoxy-glu'taric acid,** etc. See DEOXY-.

1882 *Athenæum* 16 Dec. 818/2 The desoxybenzoin of phenanthrene.

† **desoxy'dation.** *Obs.* [Fr.: see DES-.] = DEOXIDATION.

1799 *Med. Jrnl.* I. 200 Pelletier .. passed over the desoxydation of that metal by tin.

despair (dɪ'spɛə(r)), *sb.* Forms: see the verb. [ME. *des-, dis-peir, -pair*, a. OF. **despeir, despoir*, vbl. sb. from *desperer* (tonic stem *despeir-, despoir-*). Cf. also F. *désespoir* (12th c.) whence DESESPEIR.]

1. a. The action or condition of despairing or losing hope; a state of mind in which there is entire want of hope; hopelessness. ***counsel of despair***: see COUNSEL *sb.* 2 c.

c **1325** *Metr. Hom.* 170 No man in dyspayr thar [= need] be .. If they wyll call on oure Lauedy. *c* **1385** CHAUCER *L.G.W.* 2557 *Phyllis*, She for dispeyr [*v.rr.* dis-, dyspayre] fordede hyre self, allas! *c* **1386** —— *Pars. T.* ⁋619 Now comeþ wanhope þat is despair [*v.rr.* dis-, despeir(e, dispeyr] of þe mercy of god. *c* **1489** CAXTON *Sonnes of Aymon* xvi. 370 He sayth it like a man that is in dyspeyre. **1503-4** *Act 19 Hen. VII*, c. 28 Pream., The seid sueters .. were .. in dispayre of expedicion of ther suetes. **1585** T. WASHINGTON tr. *Nicholay's Voy.* I. xix. 23 Seeing theyre matters too be in despaire of succour, and not able to holde out any longer. **1667** MILTON *P.L.* I. 191 What reinforcement we may gain from Hope, If not what resolution from despare. **1690** LOCKE *Hum. Und.* II. xx. (1695) 122 Despair is the thought of the unattainableness of any Good. **1726** *Adv. Capt. R. Boyle* 256 This .. drove me almost to Despair, and I lost all Hopes of ever procuring my Liberty. **1769** *Junius Lett.* xii. 48, I give up the cause in despair. **1843** PRESCOTT *Mexico* VI. viii. (1864) 400 Some .. gathering strength from despair, maintained .. a desperate fight. **1847** TENNYSON *Princ.* IV. 444 It becomes no man to nurse despair. **1887** BOWEN *Virg. Æneid* II. 298 Wails of despair broke over the town.

b. Rarely in *plural.*

1560 A. L. tr. *Calvin's Foure Serm.* ii, Our spirit is wrapped in many dispaires. **1613** SHAKS. *Hen. VIII*, II. ii. 29 Feares, and despaires, and all these for his Marriage. **1655** FULLER *Ch. Hist.* IX. vi. §40 Their hopes were .. turned into despairs.

c. *personified.*

a **1610** *Mirr. Mag.* 66 (R.), I am (quoth she) thy friend Despaire. **1667** MILTON *P.L.* XI. 489 Despair Tended the sick busiest from Couch to Couch. **1781** COWPER *Hope* 58 Hollow-eyed Abstinence, and lean Despair. **1821** SHELLEY *Prometh. Unb.* I. 576 Till Despair smothers The struggling world, which slaves and tyrants win.

2. *transf.* That which causes despair, or about which there is no hope.

1605 SHAKS. *Macb.* IV. iii. 152 Strangely-visited people, All swolne and Vlcerous .. The meere despaire of Surgery, he cures. **1821** SHELLEY *Hellas* Pref., Those faultless productions, whose very fragments are the despair of modern art. **1876** E. MELLOR *Priesth.* viii. 390 If the adult population are the despair of the priests, the children are their hope.

¶ **3.** Used by Wyclif app. for: False or mistaken hope. (Cf. DESPAIR *v.* 4.)

c **1380** WYCLIF *Serm.* Sel. Wks. I. 42 Eche man shal hope for to come to blisse; and if he lyve febly and make þis hope fals, himsilf is cause whi his hope is suche. Ffor þis fals hope, þat sum men do clepen dispeir, shulde have anoþir qualite.

† **4.** ***without any dispayre***: a metrical tag, meaning apparently 'without doubt, without fail, certainly, iwis': perhaps an alteration of '*without diswere, disware*', of earlier use.

c **1470** HARDING *Chron.* CXXX. i, Whiche Henry was erle notified Of Huntyngdon without any dispayre. *Ibid.* CXXXIV. iv, Isabell the fayre His doughter was without any dispayre.

despair (dɪ'spɛə(r)), *v.* Forms: 4-6 des-, dis-, dys-, -peir(e, -peyr(e, -payr(e, dispar(e, -paire, 5 disspare, -paire, dyspere, despeyer, 5-7 despere, -pare, -paire, -payr, 5-8 dispair, 6 dyspayer, 4- despair. [ME. *des-, dis-peiren, -payren*, a. OF. *despeir-*, stressed stem-form of *desperer*:—L. *dēspērāre* to despair, f. DE- I. 6 + *spērāre* to hope. (Displaced in F. by *dés-espérer*, a Romanic compound of *espérer* to hope: so Pr. and Sp. *desesperar*.)]

1. *intr.* To lose or give up hope; to be without hope. Const. *of* (with indirect passive *to be despaired of*); rarely †*in* (*obs.*), *to* with *inf.*

a **1340** HAMPOLE *Psalter* cxviii. 156 Of synful men peryss nane thare [= need] dispayre. **1382** WYCLIF *2 Cor.* ii. 7 Lest perauenture he that is such maner man .. dispeire. *c* **1400** *Apol. Loll.* 90 þat he despering in þe mercy of God, trust in þe cloþis of men. **1530** PALSGR. 514/1, I despayre, I am in wan hope, *je despere.* **1552** LATIMER *Serm. in Lincoln* v. 103 Phisicions had dispeired of that woman, it passed theyr cunning to helpe her. **1588** A. KING tr. *Canisius' Catech.*, *Confess.* 3 To dispaire in Gode his mercy. **1606** EARL NORTHAMPTON in *True & Perfect Relat.* Hh iv b, He dispayred in Gods protection. **1651** HOBBES *Leviath.* III. xl. 255 Despairing of the justice of the sons of Samuel, they would have a King. **1680** BURNET *Rochester* 13 He almost dispaired to recover it. **1709** STEELE *Tatler* No. 159 ⁋6 As long as you hope, I will not despair. **1718** LADY M. W. MONTAGU *Lett.* (1887) I. 241 His life was despaired of. **1770** LANGHORNE *Plutarch* (1879) I. 117/1 Tarquin, despairing to reascend the throne by stratagem, applied [etc.]. **1838** THIRLWALL *Greece* IV. 81 He did not despair of being able to find excuses. **1856** EMERSON *Eng. Traits, Times* Wks. (Bohn) II. 117 When Cobden had begun to despair, it announced his triumph.

† **b.** *refl.* in same sense. *Obs.*

c **1386** CHAUCER *Merch. T.* 425 Dispaire yow nought. —— *Pars. T.* ⁋624 He that despeireth hym, is lyke the coward campioun recreant. **1483** CAXTON *Cato* F vj b, Thou oughtest not to dyspeyre the. **1491** —— *Vitas Patr.* (W. de W. 1495) II. 242 b/2 He wolde dyspere hymselfe. **1502** *Ord. Crysten Men* (W. de W. 1506) II. x. 116 Suche lecherous people dyspeyre them whan ye houre cometh of theyr departynge.

† **c.** ***to be despaired***, in same sense: see DESPAIRED *ppl. a.* 1. *Obs.*

† **2.** *trans.* To deprive of hope, cast into despair. *Obs. rare.*

1393 LANGL. *P. Pl.* C. x. 38 That no deuel shal ȝow dere ne despeir in ȝoure deyinge. *a* **1595** SIR R. WILLIAMS *Actions Low C.* 30 (T.) Having no hope to despair the governour to deliver it [the fort] into their enemies' hands. *a* **1618** RALEIGH *Dialogue*, To despaire all his faithfull subjects.

† **3.** *trans.* To cease to hope for, to be without hope of; = *despair of* in 1. *Obs.* or *arch.*

c **1485** *Digby Myst.* (1882) v. 467 Thei that despeyer mercy haue grett conpunccion. **1597** J. KING *On Jonas* (1618) 597 Rotten members, whose cure is despaired. **1605** SHAKS. *Macb.* v. viii. 13, *Macbeth.* I beare a charmed Life .. *Macduff.* Dispaire thy Charme. **1667** MILTON *P.L.* I. 660 Peace is despaird, For who can think Submission? **1706** WATTS *Horæ Lyr.* III. 269 How are his curtains drawn For a long evening that despairs the dawn! **1732** LD. LANSDOWNE *Ess. Unnat. Flights* (T.), Love, despairing in her heart a place, Would needs take up his lodging in her face. **1773** *Hist. Ld. Ainsworth* I. 31, I had almost begun to despair ever meeting her again.

¶ **4.** Used by Wyclif app. in sense: To hope amiss, to indulge false or mistaken hope. (Cf. prec. sb. 3.)

c **1380** WYCLIF *Wks.* (1880) 339 He .. is folily disceyued in hise bileue and in hope, and þus he dispeyreþ.

† **de'spairable,** *a. Obs.* [ad. L. *dēspērābilis* to be despaired of, desperate, OF. *desperable*; assimilated to DESPAIR *v.*] To be despaired of; desperate.

1382 WYCLIF *Jer.* xv. 18 Whi mad is my sorewe perpetuel, and my wounde despeirable [**1388** dispeirid] forsoc to be cured? **1611** COTGR., *Desesperable*, despaireable, vnhopefull. **1633** T. JAMES *Voy.* 10 Pieces of Ice .. put vs into despayrable distresse.

despaired (dɪ'spɛəd), *ppl. a.* [f. DESPAIR *v.*, corresp. in use to OF. *desperé, desesperé*, L. *dēspērātus*: see DESPERATE.]

† **1.** In despair, despairing, desperate. ***to be despaired***, to be desperate or in despair, to be without hope, to despair. (Frequent 14–16th c.). *Obs.*

c **1325** *E.E. Allit. P.* C. 169 þenne bi-speke þe spakest dispayred wel nere. *c* **1386** CHAUCER *Frankl. T.* 215 He was despeyred, no thyng dorste he seye. **1483** CAXTON *Gold. Leg.* 92/1 The gloryouse vyrgyne Marye whyche is confoorte to dysconforted and hope to dispayred. *Ibid.* 425 b/2 To thende that for their synnes .. they shold not be despeyred. **1494** FABYAN *Chron.* I. xvi. 16 She beynge dyspayred of the recouery of her astate. **1525** LD. BERNERS *Froiss.* II. cxliii. [cxxxix.] 397 They shulde haue been so sore dyspayred and dyscoraged. *a* **1572** KNOX *Hist. Ref.* Wks. 1846 I. 19 He dyed .. in a phrenesye, and as one dispared. **1588** A. KING tr. *Canisius' Catech.* 27 O in hou many things haw I offended .. but ȝit I am nocht despered.

† **2.** Of conditions, circumstances, etc.: Characterized by absence of hope; hopeless, desperate.

1382 WYCLIF *Micah* i. 9 For plage, or wounde, therof is dispeirid. **1393** GOWER *Conf.* III. 376 All though the weder be despeired. **1483** CAXTON *Gold. Leg.* 104 b/1 He toke it as all dyspayred and wold haue slayn hym self. **1561** T. NORTON *Calvin's Inst.* I. 9 Men in despaired states are restored to good hope. **1581** J. BELL *Haddon's Answ. Osor.* 488 Relieving the dispeired cause of his distressed Church.

† **b.** Of persons: Desperate, reckless. *Obs. rare.*

1571 *Satir. Poems Reform.* xxv. 29 These despaired [*v.r.* dispard] birdis of Beliall.

† **3.** Despaired of; no longer hoped for; cf. DESPAIR *v.* 3. *Obs.*

1597 J. KING *On Jonas* (1618) 284 Two singular and almost despaired deliuerances. **1647** CRASHAW *Sosp. d'Hero* liv, Of th' Hebrew's royal stem, That old dry stock—a despair'd branch is sprung. **1654** R. CODRINGTON tr. *Iustine* 293 Sometimes .. more certain is a dispaired then a presumed Victory.

4. ***despaired of***: see DESPAIR *v.* 1.

1635 A. STAFFORD *Fem. Glory* (1860) 129 The fruit whereof she reaped in her dispair'd of Fertility. **1884** J. H. STIRLING in *Mind* Oct. 531 Heretofore despaired-of philosophy.

despairer (dɪ'spɛərə(r)). [f. DESPAIR *v.* + -ER[1].] One who despairs or is without hope.

1620 J. PYPER tr. *Hist. Astrea* I. II. 28 These great despairers. **1666** DRYDEN *Ann. Mirab.* ccxlii, He cheers the fearful .. And makes despairers hope for good success. *c* **1807** H. C. ROBINSON *Let.* 7 June in *Diary, etc.* (1869) I. xi. 236 A man of talent, but a political despairer, an ex-jacobin. **1867** M. ARNOLD *Poems, Thyrsis* vii, Too quick despairer, wherefore wilt thou go?

despairful (dɪˈspɛəfʊl), *a.* [f. DESPAIR *sb.* + -FUL.] Full of despair; hopeless, desperate.

Marked by Johnson as 'Obsolete'; revived in 19th c.

1580 SIDNEY *Arcadia* (1622) 72 That sweet, but sowre despairefull care. **1614** RALEIGH *Hist. World* II. 285 That despairefull worke, of joining it [Tyre] to the Continent. **1631** *Celestina* VI. 67 Peace, thou despairefull fellow, lest Calisto kill thee. **1817** J. F. PENNIE *Royal Minstrel* III. 343 Thus to raise Expectancy in my despairful breast. **1891** *Eng. Illust. Mag.* IX. 177 His short, passionate, almost despairful cry.

Hence **despairfully** *adv.*, **despairfulness**.

1604 BABINGTON *Conf. Notes Exod.* xvi. Wks. (1622) 258 To haue men depend vpon his prouidence..and not wretchedly and despairefully to mucker vp what shall neuer doe them good. **1885** W. C. RUSSELL *Strange Voy.* I. iii. 32 Thinking despairfully of the lonely hours. **1888** VEITCH in J. C. Knight *Principal Shairp & Friends* 203 His despairfulness regarding human reason in the theological sphere.

despairing (dɪˈspɛərɪŋ), *vbl. sb.* [f. DESPAIR *v.* + -ING¹.] The action of the verb; = DESPAIR *sb.*

1375 BARBOUR *Bruce* III. 194 Throw mekill disconforting Men fallis off in-to disparyng. **1633** P. FLETCHER *Pisc. Ecl.* III. xv. 17 My wants..me in despairing drown. **1749** BP. LAVINGTON *Enthus. Meth. & Papists* (1820) 23 Dereliction, terrors, despairings.

deˈspairing, *ppl. a.* [f. as prec. + -ING².] That despairs, or ceases to hope; hopeless, desperate. (Of persons, or of actions, conditions, etc.)

1591 SHAKS. *Two Gent.* III. i. 247 Hope is a louers staffe, walke hence with that, And manage it against despairing thoughts. **1697** DRYDEN *Virg. Past.* VIII. 1 The mournful Muse of two despairing Swains. **1718** *Freethinker* No. 88. 229 This Despairing Lover stood on the Bank. **1818** SHELLEY *Rev. Islam* II. xlii, I will pour For the despairing.. reason's mighty lore. **1884** J. M. GRANVILLE in *Times* 17 Apr., The physician..gives a despairing opinion.

deˈspairingly, *adv.* [f. prec. + -LY².]

1. In a despairing manner; hopelessly.

a **1633** AUSTIN *Medit.* (1635) 167 Rather prophetically than despairingly he [St. Thomas] desired to see them [Christ's wounds]. **1810** SOUTHEY *Kehama* XVI. xvi, Yielding, with an inward groan, to fate, Despairingly. **1881** MISS BRADDON *Asph.* II. 5 'How can I convince you?'..she asked despairingly.

†**2.** Hopelessly, desperately. *Obs. rare.*

1838 *New Monthly Mag.* LIII. 414 The shopman was discovered..despairingly drunk.

deˈspairingness. [f. as prec. + -NESS.] Despairing condition; hopelessness.

1727 BAILEY vol. II, *Despairingness*, a being without Hope. *a* **1729** S. CLARKE is cited by OGILVIE.

desparity, obs. form of DISPARITY.

desparple, var. DISPARPLE *v. Obs.*, to scatter.

despatch, variant spelling of DISPATCH: so **despatchful,** etc.

†**deˈspeche,** *v. Obs.* Also 6 dyspesche. [A variant of *depeche, depeach*, after 16th c. F. *despecher*, in OF. *despeechier*: see DEPEACH.] *trans.* To send away, get rid of, dispatch.

1531 ELYOT *Gov.* II. ii, The capitaynes..despeched the multitude from them. *Ibid.* III. x, Despechynge of sondry great affayres. *Ibid.* III. xxvii, Sufficient to despeche matters of weyghtye importaunce. **1542** UDALL *Erasm. Apoph.* 218 b, To have thesame Mithridates by the backe, and to despeche hym out of the waye. **1550** NICOLLS *Thucyd.* 223 (R.), They dyspesched a brigantyne [Fr. despescherent ung brigantin] by the which they aduertysed the Athenyans of that same victorie.

despecialize (diːˈspɛʃəlaɪz), *v.* [f. DE- + SPECIAL + -IZE.] **a.** *trans.* To eliminate as a specialist or specialized vocation, subject of study, etc. **b.** *intr.* To pass from a specialized to a general condition. Hence **despecialiˈzation**.

1896 F. L. D. HERBERTSON tr. *P. de Rousiers' Lab. Quest. Britain* II. iii. 190 Service is a very *despecialised* trade, at any rate in ordinary families, where a man-servant is an unknown luxury. *Ibid.* III. i. 253 The increasing despecialisation of the worker. **1898** *Edin. Rev.* Apr. 281 The whole tendency of the age of machinery has been to.. de-specialise the average workman. **1903** S. N. PATTEN *Heredity & Soc. Progr.* 61 Emotion is the same force expressed as feeling, and in conscious beings is the index of the despecialization and regeneration acting within them. *Ibid.*, The despecialized part is not restored, but a new specialization begins in the part affected by the emotion. **1967** *Times* 14 Nov. 11/5 A modest measure of despecialization would be to require all sixth formers to study four subjects at the same level. **1970** *Nature* 26 Dec. 1245/1 The report pours cold water on the idea that chemistry courses should be despecialized.

ˌ**despeˈcificate,** *v. rare.* [f. DE- II. 1.] *trans.* To deprive of its specific character. Hence **despecifiˈcation.**

1872 J. GROTE in *Jrnl. Philol.* IV. 63 Despecification (i.e. the word's becoming less specific and significant) which we might express by various metaphors, as degradation, detrition..is simply the want of point, sharpness, and definite significance which results from common..use of the word. **1873** F. HALL *Mod. Engl.* 305 *Inaptitude* and *ineptitude* have been usefully despecificated; and only the latter now imports 'folly'. **1874** —— in *N. Amer. Rev.* CXIX. 327 With exceedingly few exceptions, our so-called synonyms..are distinctly despecificated.

†**despect** (dɪˈspɛkt), *sb. Obs.* Also 7 dis-. [ad. L. *dēspectus* a looking down upon, f. ppl. stem of *dēspicĕre*: see next. Cf. OF. *despecte* contempt:—L. type **dēspecta*; also Rouchi dialect *despect* contempt, want of respect.]

1. A looking down upon; contempt.

1624 F. WHITE *Repl. Fisher* 383 The high conceit you haue of your Roman Seruice, and the partiall respect, or rather despect, you carrie against ours. **1682** SCARLETT *Exchanges* 126 Its no dispect or discredit to any to suffer a Bill to be protested for Non-acceptance. *a* **1834** COLERIDGE *Lit. Rem.* I. 357 A jeweller may devote his whole time to jewels unblamed; but the mere amateur, who grounds his task on no chemical or geological idea, cannot claim the same exemption from despect.

2. *nonce-use.* Downward view.

1663 BAXTER *Divine Life* 362 A larger prospect and vertiginous despect of the lower grounds.

†**despect** (dɪˈspɛkt), *a. Obs.* [ad. L. *dēspectus*, pa. pple. of *dēspicĕre* to look down upon, f. DE- I. 1 + **specĕre* to look.] Looked down upon; despised.

c **1450** tr. *De Imitatione* III. vi, Vile & despecte to hymself. **1447** BOKENHAM *Seyntys* (Roxb.) 280 þe more despect thyng were..And þe more contemtyble.

deˈspectant, *ppl. a. Her.* [ad. L. *dēspectāntem*, pr. pple. of *dēspectāre* to look down upon, freq. of *dēspicĕre*: see prec.] (See quot.)

1688 R. HOLME *Armoury* II. 144/1 A Beast Despectant, Dejectant, looking downwards.

†**deˈspection.** *Obs.* Also -eccyon, -exion. [ad. L. *dēspectiōn-em*, n. of action from *dēspicĕre* to look down upon, DESPISE. Cf. OF. *despection* 14th c.] A looking down upon; despising.

1482 *Monk of Evesham* (Arb.) 62 Who euer wolde haue wende that the worschyppe and fauour..sculde be turned to seche confusyon and despexion. **1526** *Pilgr. Perf.* (W. de W. 1531) 22 b, Suffrynge many wronges and despeccyons. **1654** W. MOUNTAGUE *Devout Ess.* II. ix. §1 (R.) Christian humilitie is a clear inspection into, and a full despection of ourselves. **1656** BLOUNT *Glossogr.*, *Despexion*, a looking downwards.

†**deˈspectuous,** *a. Obs. rare.* [a. OF. *despectueux*, f. L. *dēspectu-s* (*u*-stem), looking down upon, despising: see -OUS.] To be despised; contemptible.

1541 BARNES *Wks.* (1573) 243/1 Hee may recken that S. Peter and S. Paule were starke fooles & ryght mad men that liued so despectuous a lyfe.

Hence †**deˈspectuousness.** *Obs.*

1447 BOKENHAM *Seyntys* (Roxb.) 297 If ony lyf of more despecteuousnesse She coude han fondyn..She hyt wold han chosyn.

†**deˈspeed,** *v. Obs.* [f. DE- I. 2 + SPEED *v.* Perh. influenced in formation by *expede*, or *despeche*.] *trans.* To send with speed or haste; to dispatch.

1611 SPEED *Hist. Gt. Brit.* IX. viii. (1632) 548 He forthwith despeeded into England..three of the choisest men of the State. *Ibid.* IX. viii. §31 (R.) Out of hand they despeeded certaine of their crue, to craue..pardon. *Ibid.* §51 King John..despeeding his charters and safe conducts to the Archbishop and his fellow exiles, hee as speedily arriued.

despence, -pend, -pense: see DISP-.

despeple, obs. form of DISPEOPLE *v.*

†ˈ**desperacy.** *Obs.* [f. DESPERATE: see -ACY.] Desperateness, desperation.

1628 GAULE *Pract. Th.* (1629) 11 Downe to the nethermost depth beyond recouerie: Let vs there take our portion of desperacie. **1798** *Hist.* in *Ann. Reg.* 155 Such deeds of desperacy and revenge. **1800** W. E. J. *Obi* 231 Deeds of desperacy and cruelty.

desperado (dɛspəˈreɪdəʊ, -ˈrɑːd-). Also 7 (*erron.*) desparado. [In form, identical with OSp. *desperado* out of hope, desperate (:—L. *dēspērātus*), pa. pple. of *desperar* to despair:—L. *dēspērāre*. (In mod.Sp. *desesperado* from *desesperar*.) The word does not appear to have been used substantively in Spanish, and in English use it is perhaps merely a sonorous refashioning, after Sp. words in -ADO, of DESPERATE *sb.*, used in same sense.]

†**1.** A person in despair, or in a desperate condition; = DESPERATE *sb.* 1. *Obs.*

1610 G. FLETCHER *Christ's Vict.* I. lxix, The holy Desperado wip't her swollen eyes. **1686** GOAD *Celest. Bodies* III. iv. 507 Grief, Lunacy, and the Melancholly desperado are carryed forth on the same Weekly Sheet to be buryed. **1720** DE FOE *Duncan Campbell* viii. (1841) 164 Poor and miserable desperado.

2. A desperate or reckless man; one ready for any deed of lawlessness or violence; = DESPERATE *sb.* 2.

1647 WARD *Simp. Cobler* 69 Peevish Galthropes and rascall desparadoes which the Prince of lyes imployes. **1651** *Animadv. Macdonnel's Answ. Eng. Ambass.* 56 Our English Fugitives and Desperado's. *c* **1790** WILLOCK *Voy.* 95 These desperadoes had taken some rich Portuguese vessels from the Brazils, which they had plundered and sunk. **1807** T. JEFFERSON *Writ.* (1830) IV. 97 He found himself left with about thirty desperadoes only. **1818** JAS. MILL *Brit. India* I. III. iv. 606 He had associated with himself..another desperado..in a conspiracy..to assassinate the Ameer. **1877** BLACK *Green Past.* xxxii. (1878) 255 One of the wild desperadoes of Colorado.

attrib. **1805** HOLCROFT *Bryan Perdue* I. 39 The desperado bully.

Hence despeˈradoism *nonce-wd.*

1874 *Nation* (N.Y.) XIX. 207/2 The sort of sneaking desperadoism of the disguised bands of thieves infesting the rural neighborhood.

†**desperance.** *Obs.* Also dis-, -aunce. [a. OF. *desperance*, f. *desperer* to DESPAIR: see -ANCE, and cf. the by-form DESESPERANCE.] Despair.

a **1225** *Ancr. R.* 8 ȝe muhten sone uallen..in desperaunce, þet is, in unhope & in unbileaue forte beon iboruwen. *c* **1400** *Rom. Rose* (B.) 1872 So nigh I drow to desperaunce, I rought of dethe, ne of lyf. **1481** CAXTON *Godfrey* 268 They had longe don alle theyr power And the werke was not moche amended, but were falle in a desperaunce. **1560** ROLLAND *Crt. Venus* I. 183 His Name hecht Disperance. *Ibid.* I. 790 ȝone waryit wicht Hecht Desperance.

desperancy, erroneous f. DESPERACY.

desperate (ˈdɛspərət), *a.*, *sb.*, and *adv.* Also 5 dysperate, 6–7 desperat, 6 despert, 7 disperate, (*erron.*) desparate, 9 *dial.* des-, dispert. [ad. L. *dēspērāt-us*, given up, despaired of, desperate, pa. pple. of *dēspērāre* to DESPAIR. Cf. parallel use of OF. *desperé, desesperé*, It. *disperato*, Sp., Pg. *desesperado*, and of DESPAIRED *ppl. a.*]

A. *adj.*

I. †**1.** Of a person: Having lost or abandoned hope; in despair, despairing, hopeless. (Const. *of.*) *Obs.* or *arch.*

1483 CAXTON *Cato* I vij, Thenne the good man woofull and as desperate wente toward his thyrdde frende. **1489** —— *Faytes of A.* I. xviii. 55 Men thus desperate of mercy and pytie. **1529** MORE *Dyaloge* IV. Wks. 266/1 The deuil is desperate and hath not nor cannot haue faith and trust in gods promises. **1548** HALL *Chron.* 91 b, The citezens.. desperate of all aide and succor. **1591** SHAKS. *Two Gent.* III. ii. 5, I am desperate of obtaining her. **1621** BURTON *Anat. Mel.* III. iv. II. v. 781 Bede saith, Pilate died desperate eight years after Christ. **1678** SHADWELL *Timon* II, Marry'd like some vulgar creature, which Snatches at the first offer, as if she Were desperate of having any other. **1865** CARLYLE *Fredk. Gt.* VI. XV. xiv. 109 Brühl still refuses to be desperate of his bad game.

†**b.** Of actions, etc: Expressing or indicating despair, despairing. ? *Obs.*

1555 TRAVES in Strype *Eccl. Mem.* III. App. xxxiii. 87 Without desperate voices, thoughts, gronyngs or woes. **1593** SHAKS. *Lucr.* 1038 She starteth To find some desperate instrument of death. *a* **1656** HALES *Tracts* (1677) 18 If St. Paul, in this place, meant the sin against the Holy Ghost, then this were the only desperate text in the whole Bible. **1826** DISRAELI *Viv. Grey* II. xi, He was answered only with desperate sobs.

2. Of conditions, etc.: That leaves little or no room for hope; such as to be despaired of; extremely dangerous or serious.

1555 EDEN *Decades* Pref. (Arb.) 57 Th[e] expert phisitian vseth vehement remedies for desperate diseases. **1598** SHAKS. *Merry W.* III. v. 127 My suite then is desperate; You'll vndertake her no more? **1659** B. HARRIS *Parival's Iron Age* 211 The affaires of the North growing more desperate. **1683** *Brit. Spec.* 31 A Man..in a desperate Sickness. **1720** SWIFT *To Yng. Clergyman*, Younger brothers of obscure families, and others of desperate fortunes. **1747** WESLEY *Prim. Physic* (1762) 807 This has cured in a most desperate Case. **1827** POLLOCK *Course T.* I, Agony and grief and desperate woe. **1875** JOWETT *Plato* (ed. 2) V. 56 Their case seemed desperate, for there was no one to help them.

†**3.** Of things (and persons): Despaired of, given up as hopeless; whose recovery is past hope; incurable, irretrievable, irreclaimable. ***desperate debt,*** a 'bad' debt; so ***desperate debtor.*** *Obs.* (exc. as associated with 7.)

1581 MULCASTER *Positions* xxxv. (1887) 126 The Physician delivereth the desperate sicke bodie to the Diuines care. **1615** HEYWOOD *Foure Prentises* Wks. 1874 II. 223, I haue bene the meanes to saue your desperate liues. **1651** HOBBES *Leviath.* I. xi. 48 The estate of a desperate debtor. **1674** tr. *Scheffer's Lapland* 125 So as to loose all hope of recovery..When they perceived him to be desperate [etc.]. **1770** LANGHORNE *Plutarch* (1879) II. 819/2 Receiving debts which they had given up as desperate. **1819** J. GREIG *Rep. Affairs Edin.* 17 After deduction of desperate arrears. **1866** HOWELLS *Venet. Life* vi. 84 Those desperate scraps of meat which are found impracticable even by the sausage-makers.

b. Of an undertaking, etc.: That is, or may be, despaired of; which there is no hope of carrying out or accomplishing.

1642 FULLER *Holy & Prof. St.* II. xix. 126 If he throws up his desperate game, he may happily winne the next. **1647** CLARENDON *Hist. Reb.* V. (1702) I. 393 He saw his Journey into Ireland desperate. *a* **1871** GROTE *Eth. Fragm.* v. (1876) 133 Aristotle regarded the successful prosecution of ethical enquiries as all but desperate.

II. 4. Of persons: Driven to desperation, reckless or infuriated from despair. Hence, Having the character of one in this condition; extremely reckless or violent, ready to run any risk or go any length.

c **1489** CAXTON *Sonnes of Aymon* ix. 245 Reynawde setted noughte by his lyffe..for he was as a man dysperate. *c* **1535** DR. LAYTON in *Lett. on Suppress. Monast.* (Camden) 76 Thabbot is a daingerouse desperate knave and a hardy. **1563–87** FOXE *A. & M.* (1684) III. 914 Two or three desperate Villains knocked at the door. **1653** H. COGAN tr. *Pinto's Trav.* iv. 9 He used me so cruelly, that becoming even desperate..I was..upon the point to have poysoned my self. **1718** *Freethinker* No. 42 ¶5 Want makes Men desperate. **1848** MACAULAY *Hist. Eng.* I. 173 Plotters, many of whom were ruined and desperate men.

†**b.** Reckless, utterly careless (*of*). *Obs. rare.*

1601 SHAKS. *Twel. N.* v. i. 66 Heere in the streets, desperate of shame and state, In priuate brabble did we apprehend him. *a* **1625** FLETCHER *Love's Cure* v. iii, Be'st thou desperate Of thine own life? Yet, dearest, pity mine!

c. Suffering extreme need or having a great desire *for* (*colloq.*).

a **1958** M. R. RINEHART in WEBSTER (1961), The old lady was desperate for money. **1975** *Economist* 8 Feb. 95/1 Scott Lithgow..were desperate for staff throughout the crisis. **1986** *Financial Times* 21 July p. vi/2 Many New Zealanders ask why, in a world desperate for food, its most efficient dairy producers should be facing economic collapse.

5. Of actions, etc.: Characterized by the recklessness or resolution of despair; applied *esp.* to actions done or means resorted to in the last extremity, when all else fails, and the great risk of failure is accepted for the sake of the small but only chance of success; hence often connoting extreme violence of action such as is exercised in such conditions.

1579 LYLY *Euphues* (Arb.) 64 In battayles there ought to be a doubtfull fight, and a desperat ende. **1623** in Rushw. *Hist. Coll.* (1659) I. 120 According to the usual Proverb, A desperate Disease must have a desperate remedy. **1667** MILTON *P.L.* II. 107 His look denounc'd Desperate revenge, and Battel dangerous To less than Gods. *a* **1800** COWPER *Needless Alarm* 132 Beware of desperate steps. **1832** HT. MARTINEAU *Hill & Valley* ix. 134 This desperate pursuit of money. **1840** THIRLWALL *Greece* VII. 233 Alcetas made a desperate attempt to dislodge the enemy..but was repulsed. **1855** MACAULAY *Hist. Eng.* III. 225 A desperate conflict against overwhelming odds.

†**b.** Involving serious risk; very dangerous to undertake or enter upon. *Obs.*

1600 SHAKS. *A.Y.L.* v. iv. 32 This Boy..hath bin tutor'd in the rudiments Of many desperate studies, by his vnckle, Whom he reports to be a great Magitian. *a* **1654** SELDEN *Table T.* (Arb.) 69 Marriage is a desperate thing: the Frogs in Æsop..would not leap into the Well, because they could not get out again.

†**6.** Of a quality denoting recklessness; outrageous, extravagant. *Obs.*

a **1568** ASCHAM *Scholem.* (Arb.) 54 If som Smithfeild Ruffian take vp..som fresh new othe..som new disguised garment, or desperate hat, fond in facion, or gaurish in colour. **1657** J. SMITH *Myst. Rhet.* 48 Catachresis..is an improper kinde of speech, somewhat more desperate than a Metaphor. **1661** SANDERSON *Ussher's Power Princes* Pref. (1683) 19 The desparate Principles and Resolutions of Quakers..who utterly refuse to take the Oath of Supremacy.

7. Of such a quality as to be despaired of; hopelessly or extremely bad; extreme, excessive, 'awful': cf. A 3, C, and DESPERATELY 5.

1604 SHAKS. *Oth.* II. i. 22 The desperate Tempest hath so bang'd the Turkes, That their designement halts. **1615** STEPHENS *Satyr. Ess.* (ed. 2) 18 But among all base writers of this time, I cannot reckon up more desperate rime. **1709** POPE *Ess. Crit.* 271 Concluding all were desp'rate sots and fools, Who durst depart from Aristotle's rules. **1711** STEELE *Spect.* No. 113 ¶4 She is such a desperate Scholar, that no Country Gentleman can approach her without being a Jest. **1814** D. H. O'BRIEN *Captiv. & Escape* 156 It rained—blew—thundered—and lightened, I never recollect a more desperate night.

†**B.** *sb. Obs.*

†**1. a.** A person in despair. **b.** One in a desperate condition, a wretch.

1563 FOXE *A. & M.* 477 Laborious and painful to yᵉ desperats, a precher to the prisoners and comfortles. *a* **1598** BURLEIGH in *Harl. Misc.* (Malh.) II. 278 It sufficeth to weaken the discontented, but there is no way but to kill desperates. **1622** MASSINGER & DEKKER *Virg. Mart.* III. iii, Miserable tatterdemallions, ragamuffins, and lousy desperates. **1854** EMERSON *Lett. & Soc. Aims* Wks. (Bohn) III. 173 [He] who sits among the young aspirants and desperates, quite sure and compact.

†**2.** One habituated to or ready for desperate deeds; = DESPERADO 2.

c **1611** CHAPMAN *Iliad* XXIV. 159 The deadliest desperate Of all about him. **1633** J. DONE *Hist. Septuagint* 204 Theeves, and Adulterous desperates, shaken off and damned by the Word of God. **1683** *Apol. Prot. France* iii. 9 This young Desperate confessed, that he heard them say, That it was lawful to kill the King. **1718** *Freethinker* No. 32 ¶3 The Zeal of these frantick Desperates.

†**b.** In good sense: One who engages in a desperate or extremely perilous undertaking.

c **1585** ? J. POLMON *Famous Battles* 17 Three hundred..young men who for commendation gotten by extreame perill are called the Desperates, the Forlorne hopen.

C. *adv.* Desperately, hopelessly; usually (*colloq.* and *dial.*) as an intensive: Excessively, extremely, 'awfully' (cf. A. 7).

1636 SIR H. BLOUNT *Voy. Levant* (1637) 109, I noted them so desperate malicious towards one another. **1655–60** STANLEY *Hist. Philos.* (1701) 59/2, I shewed them how desperate ill I was. **1830** GALT *Laurie T.* III. ii. (1849) 86 The road..was desperate bad. **1852** DICKENS *Bleak. Ho.* II. xxvi. 341 It's a desperate sharp night for a young lady to be out in. **1860** BARTLETT *Dict. Amer.* s.v., 'I'm despert glad to see you.'

desperate ('dɛspəreɪt), *v. rare.* [f. DESPERATE *a.*] *trans.* To render or drive desperate.

1801 W. TAYLOR in Robberds *Mem.* I. 376 My ideas of perfection desperate attempt. **1842** MRS. CARLYLE *Lett.* I. 159 Desperated by the notion of confessing myself ill.

desperate, var. of DISPARATE *a.*

desperately ('dɛspərətlɪ), *adv.* [f. DESPERATE *a.* + -LY².] In a desperate manner. (See the adj.)

†**1.** In despair, despairingly. *Obs.*

1552 HULOET, Desperately, *desperanter, insolabiliter.* **1555** EDEN *Decades* 53 They had desperately consecrated them selues to death. **1605** SHAKS. *Lear* v. iii. 292 Your eldest Daughters haue fore-done themselues, And desperately are dead. **1615** G. SANDYS *Trav.* 45 Taken at length by Tamberlaine..hee desperately brained himselfe. **1634** CANNE *Necess. Separ.* (1849) 133 All these died desperately.

†**2.** In a desperate condition, wretchedly. *rare.*

1630 *R. Johnson's Kingd. & Commw.* 233 The descendants of them, that have..beene condemned by the Inquisition..live in Spaine most desperately.

3. Hopelessly, irretrievably, incurably.

1570–6 LAMBARDE *Peramb. Kent* (1826) 171 A young Child..lay desperately sicke in a cradle. **1611** BIBLE *Jer.* xvii. 9 The heart is deceitfull aboue all things, and desperately wicked [R.V. desperately sick]. **1683** BURNET tr. *More's Utopia* (1684) 187 The excluding of Men that are desperately wicked from joining in their Worship. **1766** GOLDSM. *Vic. W.* xxviii, I wounded one who first assaulted me, and I fear desperately. *a* **1808** HURD *Wks.* VI. xvi. (R.) No man becomes at once desperately and irretrievably wicked.

4. Recklessly; with utter disregard of risks or consequences, or of how far one goes; with extreme energy or violence: cf. DESPERATE *a.* 4, 5.

a **1547** SURREY *Æneid* ii. (R.), Whom when I saw..So desperately the battail to desire. **1632** LITHGOW *Trav.* III. 130 Foure French Runnagats..hearing these words, fell desperatly upon me. *Ibid.* v. 188, 20 gallies..desperatly adventured to tow her away against the wind. **1724** DE FOE *Mem. Cavalier* (1840) 179 The foot on both sides were desperately engaged. **1885** *Manch. Even. News* 23 June 2/2 The..seats for which they have fought so desperately.

5. To a desperate degree; extremely, excessively. (Cf. DESPERATE *a.* 7.) Chiefly *colloq.*

1653 H. COGAN tr. *Pinto's Trav.* lxviii. 277 She was desperately in love with him. **1697** COLLIER *Ess. Mor. Subj.* II. (1709) 136 He looks so desperately Pale and Thin. **1709** STRYPE *Ann. Ref.* I. xiii. 183 They were desperately afraid the people should have too much knowledge. **1843** FOSTER in *Life & Corr.* (1846) II. 463 How desperately rapid the flight of time. **1872** BLACK *Adv. Phaeton* xxxi. 418 She pretends to be desperately concerned about the horses.

'**desperateness.** [f. as prec. + -NESS.] The state or quality of being desperate.

†**1.** The state of being in despair. *Obs.*

1581 PETTIE *Guazzo's Civ. Conv.* III. (1586) 149 They will..be to rough..to their children..[which] driveth them to desperatenesse. *a* **1639** W. WHATELY *Prototypes* I. iv. (1640) 21 Caine was possessed with a mixture of desperatenesse and murmuring.

2. a. The state or quality of being beyond hope (or of having extremely small chance) of recovery or improvement; hopelessness, irremediableness.

1571 GOLDING *Calvin on Ps.* xxxvii. 4 When a man refuseth understanding, it is a signe of desperatenesse. *a* **1603** T. CARTWRIGHT *Confut. Rhem. N.T.* (1618) 571 You bewray the desperatenesse of your cause. **1659** HAMMOND *On Ps.* lxxxviii. 4 Paraphr. 435 The deplorablenesse and desperatenesse of my condition. **1876** BANCROFT *Hist. U.S.* V. xxi. 575 He awoke to the desperateness of his situation.

b. The state or quality of being beyond hope of attainment or accomplishment.

1667 *Decay Chr. Piety* viii. ¶5 Hope being equally outdated by the desperateness or unnecessariness of an undertaking. **1677** W. HUBBARD *Narrative* 54 The desperateness of the attempt.

3. The rashness or fury of despair; recklessness = DESPERATION 2.

1549 CHEKE *Hurt Sedit.* (R.), If for desperatenesse ye care not for yourselues, yet remember your wiues, your children, your countrie. **1600** DEKKER, etc., *Lust's Dominion* II. iv, You are too rash, you are too hot, Wild desperateness doth valour blot. **1639** FULLER *Holy War* II. xvii. (1840) 72 Loath to anger their enemies' valour into desperateness. **1677** GILPIN *Demonol.* (1867) 448 It is rashness or desperateness, and not true courage. **1963** *Times* 30 May 17/4 The people had the will and desperateness—they held out.

desperation (dɛspə'reɪʃən). Also 4–6 disperacion. [a. OF. *desperation, -acion* (Godef.), or ad. L. *dēspērātiōn-em*, n. of action and condition from *dēspērāre* to DESPAIR.]

1. The action of despairing or losing all hope (*of* anything); the condition of having utterly lost hope; despair, hopelessness. Now *rare.*

c **1366** CHAUCER *A.B.C.* 20 A greevous accioun Of verrey riht and desperacioun. *c* **1375** *XI Pains of Hell* 226 in *O.E. Misc.* App. ii, Disperacion of godis mercy, Of al þe payns in hel hit is most. *c* **1386** CHAUCER *Pars. T.* ¶983 Whiche thynges destourben penaunce..drede, schame, hope, and wanhope, that is, desperacioun. **1490** CAXTON *How to die* 4 To thende that he drawe him into disperacion. **1548** HALL *Chron.* 134 b, For feare of losyng honor, and desperacion of gain. **1551** T. WILSON *Logike* (1580) 60 Unbeleef, Desperation, whereby a man falleth from God. **1588** A. KING tr. *Canisius' Catech.* 131 Horrour of deathe..and disperation of æternal blisse. **1664** POWER *Exp. Philos.* I. 190 A diffidence and desperation..of ever reaching to any eminent Invention. **1750** JOHNSON *Rambler* No. 52 ¶5 Sunk yet deeper in the dungeon of misery..and surrounded with darker desperation. **1846** TRENCH *Mirac.* xxvi. (1862) 363 The gracious Lord..could..[not] cure him so long as there was on his part this desperation of healing.

2. *spec.* Despair leading to recklessness, or recklessness arising from despair; a desperate state of mind in which, on account of the hopelessness or extremely small chance of success, one is ready to do any violent or extravagant action, regardless of risks or consequences. (Cf. DESPERATE *a.* 4, 5.)

1531 ELYOT *Gov.* III. ix, In desperation can nat be fortitude, for that, beinge a morall vertue, is euer voluntarye. Desperation is a thinge as it were constrayned. **1581** PETTIE *Guazzo's Civ. Conv.* III. (1586) 131 She is then readie to follow, whatsoever wrath and desperation shall put in her head. **1602** SHAKS. *Ham.* I. iv. 75 The very place puts toys of desperation, Without more motive, into every brain That looks so many fathoms to the sea And hears it roar beneath. **1703** ROWE *Fair Penit.* IV. i. 1322 A Deed of Desparation. **1751** JOHNSON *Rambler* No. 150 ¶4 Strength which would be unprofitably wasted in wild efforts of desperation. **1841–4** EMERSON *Ess., Hist.* Wks. (Bohn) I. 10 Needy and hungry to desperation. **1847** JAMES *J. Marston Hall* xi, There was no use in driving him to desperation.

despere, obs. form of DESPAIR.

desperse: see DISPERSE.

†**desperview.** *Obs. rare.* [a. OF. *despourveu*, mod.F. *dépourvu*, 'vnprouided, vnfurnished, devoid of, without' (Cotgr.), f. *des-*, (L. *dis-*) + *pourvu* provided.] An indigent man, a poor beggar.

c **1600** DAY *Begg. Bednall Gr.* II. i. (1881) 32 Come, you desper-view, Deliver me the Jewell or I'll hang thee.

despetous: see DESPITOUS.

despexion, var. f. DESPECTION.

despeyr(e, obs. form of DESPAIR.

despica'bility. [f. next: see -ITY.] The quality of being despicable; despicableness,

1830 CARLYLE *Misc.* (1857) II. 122 Languishing amid boundless triviality and despicability. **1832** *Ibid.* III. 94 A life full of falsehood, feebleness, poltroonery, and despicability. **1873** WAGNER tr. *Teuffel's Hist. Rom. Lit.* I. 70 Servile covetousness and moral despicability.

b. A specimen of this; a despicable person.

1837 CARLYLE *Fr. Rev.* III. II. v, The convention..dismisses these comparative *misères* and despicabilities.

despicable ('dɛspɪkəb(ə)l), *a.* [ad. L. *dēspicābilis*, f. *dēspicārī* to look down upon, f. DE- I + **specāri*, from same root as *specĕre* to look.]

1. To be looked down upon or despised; vile, base, contemptible.

1553 EDEN *Treat. Newe Ind.* (Arb.) 14 The byldinge[s] are despicable. *Ibid.* 35 All thinges with them are despicable and vile. **1667** MILTON *P.L.* XI. 340 All th' Earth he gave thee to possess and rule, No despicable gift. **1699** DAMPIER *Voy.* II. I. viii. 162 Their insolent masters the Portuguese: than whom there are not a more despicable people now in all the Eastern Nations. **1710** LADY M. W. MONTAGU *Let. to Bp. Burnet* 20 July, There is hardly a character in the world more despicable, or more liable to universal ridicule, than that of a learned woman. **1782** ? VAUGHAN *Fashionable Follies* II. 103 A little despicable looking house honoured with the name of an inn. **1848** MACAULAY *Hist. Eng.* I. 164 The most despicable of fanatics. **1874** GREEN *Short Hist.* viii. §2. 473 The immorality of James's Court was hardly more despicable than the imbecility of his government.

†**b.** Miserable, wretched. *Obs.*

1635 PAGITT *Christianogr.* 217 These poore despicable wretches have hardly sustenance to keepe life and soule together. **1690** CHILD *Disc. Trade* (1694) 13 The people are poor and despicable, their persons ill clothed. *a* **1704** T. BROWN *Praise of Wealth* Wks. 1730 I. 85 Despicable in circumstance.

†**2.** Exhibiting or expressing contempt; contemptuous. *Obs.*

(Qualifying *opinion*, *appellation*, and the like: cf. CONTEMPTIBLE 2.)

1662 H. STUBBE *Ind. Nectar* Pref. 5, I have a very despicable opinion of the present age. **1727** FIELDING *Love in Sev. Masques* Wks. 1775 I. 34 To persuade us into so despicable an opinion of your reason. **1727** SWIFT *Gulliver* II. viii, The comparison gave me so despicable a conceit of myself. **1756** BURKE *Subl. & B.* II. v, Though we caress dogs, we borrow from them an appellation of the most despicable kind. **1775** ADAIR *Amer. Ind.* 7 Distinguished..by the despicable appellative, Tied Arse.

'**despicableness.** [f. prec. + -NESS.] The quality of being despicable; contemptibleness, vileness, worthlessness.

1653 MANTON *Exp. James* ii. 1 Apt to despise excellent things, because of the despicableness of the instrument. *a* **1691** BOYLE *Wks.* II. 13 (R.) The maker's art shines through the despicableness of the matter. **1727–1800** BAILEY, *Despicableness*, contemptibleness.

'**despicably**, *adv.* [f. as prec. + -LY².]

1. In a despicable manner; contemptibly, meanly.

a **1691** BOYLE *Wks.* II. 68 (R.) He..may, with due diligence and industry, not despicably improve his anatomical knowledge. *a* **1719** ADDISON (J.), Nor vainly rich, nor despicably poor. **1755** YOUNG *Centaur* v. Wks. 1757 IV. 228 To-day crawling out of the earth; and to-morrow more despicably still, crawling into corruption.

†**2.** With contempt; contemptuously. *Obs.*

1637 P. HEYLIN *Antidot. Lincoln.* I. 40 Since you speake so despicably of his Majesties chappell. **1665** PEPYS *Diary* 13 Feb., To see how despicably they speak of us. **1748** RICHARDSON *Clarissa* (1811) II. 243, I should think as despicably of his sense.

†**despi'cation.** *Obs. rare.* [ad. L. *dēspicātiōn-em*, n. of action from *dēspicārī*: see DESPICABLE.] Despising, contempt.

1837 WHITTOCK, etc. *Bk. Trades* (1842) 268 Senecca, who died for philosophy, and despication of Nero.

†**de'spiciency.** *Obs.* [ad. L. *dēspicientia* despising, contempt, f. *dēspicient-em*, pr. pple. of *dēspicĕre* to look down: see DESPISE, and -ENCY.] Looking down upon or despising; contempt.

1623 COCKERAM, *Despitiencie*, despite, hatred. *a* **1638** MEDE *Disc. Mark* xi. 17 Wks. (1672) I. 45 To show their despiciency of the poor Gentiles. **1658** W. BURTON *Itin. Anton.* 67 A gallant despiciency..of all human affairs. **1672** H. MORE *Brief Reply* 103 His answer is marveilous lofty and full of despiciency towards his Antagonist.

despicion, var. DISPICION, *Obs.*, discussion.

†**de'spiece,** *v. Obs.* [a. OF. *despiecer*, earlier *despecier*, mod.F. *dépecer*, *dépiécer*, f. *des-*, (L. *dis-*) + *pièce* PIECE.] To cut in pieces.

1491 CAXTON *Vitas Patr.* (W. de W. 1495) I. lxiv. 114 a/2 Many marters had ben despieced in to pyeces.

despight, etc.: see DESPITE, etc.

de-spin, despin (diː'spɪn), *v.* [f. DE- II. 1 + SPIN *v.*] *trans.* To counteract a spinning motion of, esp. of a satellite in space; to prevent from spinning. Hence **de-spun, despun** *ppl. a.*

1960 *Aeroplane* XCIX. 419/2 The H.T.P. jets...are intended to de-spin the satellite after separation. **1966** *Electronics* 3 Oct. 173 A Comsat-sponsored design study.. is developing electronically despun microwave antennas for both NASA and the Air Force. **1967** *New Scientist* 30 Nov. 527/2 The new method provides a platform on top of the satellite that is not spinning. (A 'despun platform' is the name given to it by Hughes.) **1970** *Sci. Jrnl.* Jan. 18/1 To maintain permanent radio illumination of the Earth the horn aerial mounted at one axis is mechanically despun in the opposite direction to spin stabilization.

despiritualize (dɪ'spɪrɪtjuːəˌlaɪz), *v.* [DE- II. 1.] *trans.* To deprive of spiritual character; to render material.

1868 *Contemp. Rev.* VIII. 609 Virtually de-spiritualizing that which it is the very business of literature to clearly reinvolve in the spiritual. **1874** H. R. REYNOLDS *John Bapt.* v. §1. 298 A way has been made by the perversity of man for despiritualizing Christianity.

Hence **de'spiritualized, de'spiritualizing** *ppl. adjs.*; also **deˌspirituali'zation.**

1840 *Tait's Mag.* VII. 27 Sensuality of this de-spiritualizing description. **1874** H. R. REYNOLDS *John Bapt.* iii. §1 150 A melancholy despiritualization of Christianity.

despisable (dɪ'spaɪzəb(ə)l), *a.* [In ME. *despi'sable*, a. OF. *despiç-*, *despisable*, f. stem *despis-* of *despire* to DESPISE.]

1. To be despised or treated with contempt; contemptible, despicable. Now *rare.*

a **1340** HAMPOLE *Psalter* xlviii. 19 þat is a despisabile shrift þat ese makis. *Ibid.* ciii. 24 Despisabiler fendes. **1382** WYCLIF *1 Cor.* i. 28 God chees the vnnoble thingis and dispisable thingis of the world. **1483** CAXTON *Gold Leg.* 357/1 He was of vyle habyte and despysable of chere. **1604** T. WRIGHT *Passions* v. §4. 293 Rather despiseable then commendable. **1690** *Lond. Gaz.* No. 2582/3 Ill Armed, and in a very despisable Condition. **1782** MISS BURNEY *Cecilia* IV. 269 Business is no such despiseable thing. **1873** J. M. BAILEY *Life in Danbury* 6 Brought up..to look upon a liar as the most despisable of earth's creatures.

†**2.** Contemptuous. = DESPICABLE 2. *Obs.*

1644 QUARLES *Barnabas & B.* 208, I..am now rejected by the despiseable name of a widow.

†**de'spisableness.** *Obs.* [f. prec. + -NESS.] **a.** Despicable condition. **b.** Contemptuousness.

1613 SHERLEY *Trav. Persia* 99 A direct despisablenesse of his Person and Authority. **1671** FLAVEL *Fount. of Life* xxx. 91 The outward Meanness and Despiseableness of His Condition.

despisal (dɪ'spaɪzəl). [f. DESPISE *v.* + -AL[1] 5: cf. *revisal.*] The act of despising; contempt.

1650 EARL MONM. tr. *Senault's Man become Guilty* 199 Their very looks..sufficiently witnesse their despisal. *a* **1707** BP. PATRICK *Comm. Prov.* xi. 12 (L.) No man is so mean, but he is sensible of despisal. **1887** B. FARJEON *Golden Sleep* 59 D. would look down upon him in scorn and despisal.

†**de'spisant,** *a. Obs.* [a. OF. *despisant* despising, contemptuous, pr. pple. of *despire*, used as adj.] Despising, showing contempt. Hence †**de'spisantly** *adv.*, despisingly, insolently.

1389 *Eng. Gilds* 80 If any broþer or sistere..dispisantliche lie on his broþer or on his sister.

despise (dɪ'spaɪz), *v.* Also 4-5 dispice, 4-6 des-, dispyse, 4-7 dispise, 5 dess-, disspice, 5-6 dyspyse. [f. stem *despis-* of OF. *despire* (*despisant, qu'il despise*, etc.), also *despiss-*, *despisc-*, *despiç-*:—L. *dēspicĕre* to look down (upon), f. DE- I. 1 + *specĕre* to look. (There was also a later OF. *despicer*, *despiser*, after the L. verb.) The *s* was originally spirant in F. and Eng., whence the spelling *-ice*.]

1. *trans.* To look down upon; to view with contempt; to think scornfully or slightingly of.

1297 R. GLOUC. (1724) 31 þou ne louest me noȝt..Ac despisest me in myn olde liue. **1393** LANGL. *P. Pl.* C. III. 84 To be prynces of prude and pouerte to dispice. *c* **1400** *Apol. Loll.* 6 Crist seiþ..he þat dispiciþ ȝow dispisiþ Me. **1483** *Cath. Angl.* 101 To Disspice: *contempnere.* **1590** SHAKS. *Mids. N.* III. ii. 235 This you should pitie, rather then despise. **1601** WEEVER *Mirr. Mart.*, *Sir J. Oldcastle* F iij b, Thus fooles admire what wisest men despiseth. **1611** BIBLE *Isa.* liii. 3 He is despised and reiected of men, a man of sorrows, and acquainted with griefe. **1701** DE FOE *Trueborn Eng.* I. 178 These are the Heroes that despise the Dutch. **1724** —— *Mem. Cavalier* (1840) 43 This was not an enemy to be despised. **1871** MORLEY *Voltaire* (1886) 153 The foremost men of the eighteenth century despised Joan of Arc..for the same reason which made them despise Gothic architecture. *Mod.* A salary not to be despised, as things go.

†**b.** with *inf.* or *clause.* To scorn or disdain *to do, that. Obs.*

1483 CAXTON *Gold. Leg.* 231/2 They dyspyseden to make sacrefyse. **1526** *Pilgr. Perf.* (W. de W. 1531) 285 b, You denyed and despysed to come. **1552** ABP. HAMILTON *Catech.* (1884) 32 Despisand to do as the servand of God Samuel commandit him. **1605** BACON *Adv. Learn.* II. xx. §2 Men have despised to be conversant in ordinary and common matters. **1621** LADY M. WROTH *Urania* 164 Thus the strange Princesse departed..dispising any passion but loue should dare to thinke of ruling in her.

†**2.** *intr.* To look down (*on, upon*; *up, above*).

a **1325** *Prose Psalter* liii[i] 7 Myn eȝe despised vp myn enemys [*Vulg.* = super inimicos meos despexit]. **1388** WYCLIF *ibid.*, Myn iȝe dispiside on myn enemyes. *a* **1400** *Prymer* (1891) 30 A bouen myn enemyes despisede myn eye.

†**3.** *trans.* To exhibit contempt for; to treat with contempt in word or action. *Obs.*

1377 LANGL. *P. Pl.* B. xv. 54 Aȝein such salomon speketh and dispiseth her wittes. *c* **1385** CHAUCER *L.G.W.* Prol. 135 (Fairfax MS.) To singe of him, and in hir song dispyse The foule cherl. **1483** CAXTON *Gold. Leg.* 127/2 The poure man ..began to chyde and dyspyse hym in his vysage by cause he had no more almesse. **1557** *N.T.* (Genev.) *Luke* xxiii. 11 And Herode..with his men of warre, despised him, and mocked hym. [So WYCLIF, TINDALE, etc.; *Rhem.* and **1611**, set him at naught.]

†**b.** *fig.* Of things: To set at nought, disregard.

1398 TREVISA *Barth. De P.R.* XVI. viii. (1495) 557 Though the adamas..dyspyse fyre and yren: yet it is broke wyth newe hote blode. *c* **1420** *Pallad. on Husb.* I. 170 In bareine lande to sette or foster vynes Dispiseth alle the labour and expence. **1666** STILLINGFL. *Serm. Fire Lond.* Wks. 1710 I. 6 [The fire]..despised all the resistance [which] could be made by the strength of the buildings.

['To look upon; contemplate'. An error of mod. Dicts.]

†**de'spise,** *sb. Obs.* [prob. a. OF. *despiz*, *despis*, nom. of *despit*, DESPITE, but taking the form of an Engl. deriv. of DESPISE *v.*] = DESPITE; contempt, despising.

c **1440** *Promp. Parv.* 120 Despyse [MSS. K.H.P. despyte], *contemptus, despeccio.* ? **1507** *Communyc.* A iij, Man what doost thou with all thyse..Whiche is to me a great despyse. **1586** B. YOUNG *Guazzo's Civ. Conv.* IV. 226 b, Occasion of despise and laughter.

despised (dɪ'spaɪzd), *ppl. a.* [f. DESPISE *v.* + -ED.] Looked down upon, contemned, scorned.

[*c* **1450** *St. Cuthbert* (Surtees) 750 Hated and despysyd was he.] **1592** SHAKS. *Rom. & Jul.* III. ii. 77 Dispised substance of Diuinest show. **1667** MILTON *P.L.* VI. 602 Would render them yet more despis'd. **1705** STANHOPE *Paraphr.* I. 34 A vulgar and despised Crowd. **1852** MRS. STOWE *Uncle Tom's C.* ix. 68 There was the impress of the despised race on her face.

†**de'spisedness** (-ɪdnɪs). *Obs.* [f. prec. + -NESS.] Despised condition.

1587 GOLDING *De Mornay* xxxi. (1617) 541 Jesus could not haue shewed his..glory [better] than in despisednesse. **1641** MILTON *Ch. Govt.* II. i. (1851) 151 Therefore he sent ..Despisednes to vanquish Pride.

de'spisement. *arch.* [a. OF. *despisement* (12th c. in Godef.), f. *despire*, *despis-*: see -MENT.] The action of despising; contempt, scorn.

1603 HOLLAND *Plutarch's Mor.* 155 Contempt and despisement of worldly wealth. **1886** C. A. BRIGGS *Messianic Proph.* 398 Her days of oppression and despisement are over. **1887** *Critic* X. 251/2 An uncomfortable sensation of familiarity bordering on 'despisement'.

despiser (dɪ'spaɪzə(r)). [f. DESPISE *v.* + -ER[1]. Cf. OF. *despiseor*, nom. *despisière*, *-sère.*] One who despises; a contemner, scorner.

a **1340** HAMPOLE *Psalter* Comm. Cant. 500 Y^e^ scorners & despisers of pore men. **1382** WYCLIF *Acts* xiii. 41 Se ȝe, dispiseris, and wondre ȝe, and be ȝe scaterid abrood. [TINDALE, Beholde ye despisers and wonder and perisshe ye.] **1485** CAXTON *St. Wenefr.* 20 A despysar of my wordes. **1535** COVERDALE *Prov.* xiii. 15 Harde is the way of the despysers. **1709** HEARNE *Collect.* (Oxf. Hist. Soc.) II. 252 A Despiser of modern Commentators. *a* **1745** SWIFT (J.), Atheists, libertines, and despisers of religion, usually pass under the name of free-thinkers. **1892** *Bookman* Oct. 27/2 A despiser of physical force.

de'spiseress. *rare*[−0]. [f. prec. + -ESS.] A female despiser.

1611 COTGR., *Despriseresse*, a disesteemeresse, despiseresse, or dispraiseresse of.

despising (dɪ'spaɪzɪŋ), *vbl. sb.* [f. DESPISE *v.* + -ING[1].] The action of the vb. DESPISE; contempt, scorn.

1382 WYCLIF *Ps.* cxxii[i]. 3 Myche wee be fulfild with dispising. **1535** COVERDALE *Neh.* iv. 4 Y^t^ thou mayest geue them ouer in to despisinge in the londe of their captiuite. **1659** *Gentl. Calling* (1696) 33 Flatteries and Despisings being the two contrary elements, whereof he, whom they call a Fine Gentleman, is to be compounded. **1681–6** J. SCOTT *Chr. Life* (1747) III. 391 The despising of him was a despising of God, by whom he was sent.

despisingly (dɪ'spaɪzɪŋlɪ), *adv.* [f. *despising* pr. pple. + -LY[2].] With contempt; scornfully, contemptuously.

1591 PERCIVALL *Sp. Dict.*, *Menospreciando*, despisingly. **1820** *Blackw. Mag.* VII. 251 Still speak despisingly of them. **1843** *Ibid.* LIV. 441 That son of Sparks's, as you so despisingly call him.

†**de'spisingness.** *Obs.* [f. as prec. + -NESS.] Contemptuousness.

1625 F. MARKHAM *Bk. Hon.* I. vi. §8 Riches rightly vsed, rather with a despisingnesse then a desire.

despite (dɪ'spaɪt), *sb.* Forms: 3-5 despit, (3-4 -yt, 4 despitt(e, -iit, -yt, -ijt, -iȝt, -ithe), 4-6 despyte, (5- -spyȝte), 6-8 **despight,** 4- **despite;** also 3-7 **dis-,** 3-6 **dys-** with same variants, 6 *Sc.* **dispyit.** [ME. *despit*, a. OF. *despit* (:—**despieit*), mod.F. *dépit*, = OCat. *despeit*, Sp. *despecho*, It. *dispetto*:—L. *dēspectu-m* (*u*-stem) a looking down on, f. ppl. stem of *dēspicĕre* to look down on, DESPISE. Down to 17th c. often spelt *dis-*, *dys-*, by confusion with words in the prefix *des-*, DIS-. The 16th c. *dis-*, *despight* (cf. *spight*, SPITE) was under the influence of *sight*, *right*, etc.]

1. The feeling or mental attitude of looking down upon or despising anything; the display of this feeling; contempt, scorn, disdain. *Obs.* or *arch.*

a **1300** *Cursor M.* 2037 (Cott.) If o þi fader þou haue despite [*v. rr.* -it, -ithe, -yte]. **1340** *Ayenb.* 19 þe oþer boȝ þet compþ out of þe stocke of prede zuo is onworþnesse (despit). **1375** BARBOUR *Bruce* v. 46 Persey..Wes in the castell.. Fulfillit of dispit and pride. **1382** WYCLIF *Rom.* ix. 21 Power ..to make sothli o vessel in to honour, anothir forsothe in to dispyt. *c* **1440** *Jacob's Well* (E.E.T.S.) 72 þe firste fote is dyspyȝte; þat is, in doyng no worschype to gode men dewly, but in dyspysing hem. **1483** *Cath. Angl.* 101 A Dispite, or a disspisynge, *despeccio, contemptus.* **1565** *Sc. Metr. Ps.* x. 5 He puffeth with despight. **1650** JER. TAYLOR *Holy Living* (1727) 245 Liberality..consists in the despite and neglect of money. **1651** HOBBES *Leviath.* IV. xlvi. 377 Any Attribute, that is given in despight. *a* **1845** LONGF. *King Christian* iv, Receive thy friend, who, scorning flight, Goes to meet danger with despite.

†**b.** *to hold or have in* (†*to*) *despite*: to hold in contempt; to have or show contempt or scorn for.

a **1300** *Cursor M.* 2610 (Cott.) Yone lasce..als in despit sco haldes me. *c* **1386** CHAUCER *Melib.* ¶452 Perauenture Crist hath thee in despit. *c* **1400** *Apol. Loll.* 74 Scho..haþ me to despit. **1483** CAXTON *Gold. Leg.* 162/2 He had in despyte fader and moder. **1526** *Pilgr. Perf.* (W. de W. 1531) 122 b, The good man sholde haue them in despyte..in comparyson of the thynges to come.

†**c.** The object of contempt or scorn. *Obs.*

a **1300** *Cursor M.* 18232 (Cott.) Skorning þou art o god angel, Despit [*v.r.* dis-] of al rightwis and lel. *a* **1340** HAMPOLE *Psalter* cxviii. 22 Now til proude men and enuyouse i am despite and hethynge.

2. Action that shows contemptuous disregard; contemptuous treatment or behaviour; insulting action; outrage, injury, contumely. ***to do despite to***: to treat with injury and contumely; to outrage.

1297 R. GLOUC. (1724) 464 Alle þulke, þat clerkes such despyt dude & wo. *a* **1300** *Cursor M.* 7825 (Cott.) For to do him despitte or schame. *c* **1340** *Ibid.* 6785 (Fairf.) To childer do ȝe na dispite. *c* **1385** CHAUCER *L.G.W.* 1822 *Lucretia*, Whi hast thou don despit to Chivalrye. *c* **1400** *Destr. Troy* 13700 þe schalke, that..so dernely hym did dere & dispit. **1535** COVERDALE *Lam.* iii. 47 Feare and snare is come vpon vs, yee despite and destruccion. **1631** WEEVER *Anc. Fun. Mon.* 24 Loath he was that his dead bodie should either suffer despight, or receive fauour from his enemies. **1672** MARVELL *Reh. Transp.* I. 325 There is not one Person of the Trinity that he hath not done despight to. **1803** WORDSW. *Sonn. Liberty* I. xviii, To work against themselves such fell despite. **1869** FREEMAN *Norm. Conq.* (1876) III. xiii. 319 The despite done by him to the holy relics.

b. Disregard of opposition, defiance. *Obs.*

1380–1601 [see 5 c]. **1638** SIR T. HERBERT *Trav.* 93 Chardges so furiously and so close, that in despight he mounts the wall. **1706** E. WARD *Hud. Rediv.* II. vii, That all who see..may triumph, in Despite to Rome. **1719** YOUNG *Revenge* IV. i. Wks. 1757 II. 170 What think you 'twas..But doing right in stern despite to nature?

3. (with *pl.*) An act that shows contempt, hatred, malice, or spite; an outrage, a shameful injury.

1297 R. GLOUC. (1724) 547 The Londreis ther biuore a gret despit wroȝte To the quene. **1382** WYCLIF *Rom.* i. 24 That thei ponysche with wrongis or dispitis [Vulg. *contumeliis*] her bodies. **1450–1530** *Myrr. our Ladye* 230 Herynge hys frende greued wyth repreues and dyspites. **1480** CAXTON *Cron. Eng.* ccxxv. 230 Many harmes shames and despytes they dyden vnto the Quene. **1523** LD. BERNERS *Froiss.* I. cxlvi. 174 They of Calays hathe done hym suche contraryes and dispyghtes. **1654** WHITLOCK *Zootomia* 336, I think I could not do him a greater Despite, than to bestow a woman on him. **1748** RICHARDSON *Clarissa* (1811) II. xii.

76 My declared aversion, and the unfeigned despights I took all opportunities to do him. **1820** WORDSW. *Sheep-washing*, The turmoil that unites Clamour of boys with innocent despites Of barking dogs. **1870** LONGF. tr. *Dante's Inf.* XIV. 71 His own despites Are for his breast the fittest ornaments.

4. Indignation, anger, evil feeling, especially such as arises from offended pride, vexation, or annoyance. In later use, *esp.* The entertaining of a grudge, evil feeling with a desire to harm or vex; ill-will, aversion; settled malice or hatred; SPITE.

c **1325** *E.E. Allit. P.* C. 50 What dowes me þe dedayn, oþer dispit make? **1375** BARBOUR *Bruce* II. 455 And for dispyte bad draw and hing All the prisoneris. *c* **1386** CHAUCER *Frankl. T.* 667 Sith that maydens hadde such despit To ben defouled with mannes foul delit. *c* **1400** *Destr. Troy* 10684 [He] put hym of horse, With a spar of a speire in dispit felle. **1483** *Cath. Angl.* 98 A Despite, *auersio.* **1523** LD. BERNERS *Froiss.* I. xxv. 36 The kyng had great dispyte, that the duke shuld so dele with hym. **1548** HALL *Chron.* 202 b, After many greate woordes and crakes..the Lorde Stafford..in greate dispite departed with his whole compaignie. **1579** TOMSON *Calvin's Serm. Tim.* 52/2 For they are at despite & fret, bicause they see God so against them. **1590** SPENSER *F.Q.* I. i. 50 He thought have slaine her in his fierce despight. **1598** HAKLUYT *Voy.* I. 64 A man full of all malice and despight. **1603–21** KNOLLES *Hist. Turks* 1231 Two Monkes, whom the souldiors in despight cut into many pieces. **1697** *C'tess D'Aunoy's Trav.* (1706) 27 Don Lewis had a secret Despight, in comprehending the Marquess so well satisfied. **1752** HUME *Ess. & Treat.* (1777) II. 418 Formed by the gods merely from despight to Prometheus. **1816** SCOTT *Antiq.* xxiv, He died soon after..of pure despite and vexation. **1846** TRENCH *Mirac.* xix. (1862) 326 Wounded pride, disappointed malice, rancorous despite.

5. *Phrase.* **in despite of.** †**a.** In contempt or scorn of; in contemptuous defiance of. *Obs.* ***departure in despite of the court***: see DEPARTURE 6.

[**1292** BRITTON I. v. §1 En despit et damage de nous et de noster poeple.] *c* **1290** *Beket* 1903 in *S. Eng. Leg.* I. 161 Þeos Þreo bischopus..to þe kinge heo come..And tolden..hov in despit of him, he dude swuch luþer dede. *c* **1380** *Sir Ferumb.* 5807–9 He..haþ now in dispyt of me My bysshop y-bete sore: And afterward, in þe dyspyt of crysst, Spet on þe fant. **1494** FABYAN *Chron.* cxcviii. 205 In dyrision and despyte of the Danys. **1548** HALL *Chron.* 183 b, And sent all their heddes..to be set upon poles, over the gate of the citie of Yorke in despite of them, and their lignage. *c* **1592** MARLOWE *Massacr. Paris* I. vii, In despite of thy religion, The Duke of Guise stamps on thy lifeless bulk! **1628–1641** [see DEPARTER[2]; DEPARTURE 5 b]. *a* **1735** ARBUTHNOT *John Bull* Swift's Wks. 1751 VI. 140 Let it never be said, that the famous John Bull has departed in despite of court.

†**b.** In anger or indignation at; in punishment of. *Obs. rare.*

[**1292** BRITTON II. xv. §2 En despit de lour defaute. *transl.* By way of punishment for the default of the parties.] **1528** LYNDESAY *Dreme* 1100 In dispyit of his Lycherous leuyng, The Romanis wald be subiect to no kyng.

†**c.** In open defiance of, in overt opposition to. Cf. 2 b. *Obs.*

c **1380** *Sir Ferumb.* 2192 Now haþ he my dore y-broke; ous alle in dispyte. *c* **1425** WYNTOUN *Cron.* VIII. xii. 67 A gret ost ..in þe north of Ingland past In dyspyt of þat Tyrand. **1601** BP. W. BARLOW *Serm. Paules Crosse* 40 To see Gods word alleadged in despight of Gods ordinance.

d. Notwithstanding the opposition or adverse efforts of (a person). Now rare except with reflexive pronouns (***in despite of himself***, etc.).

1570–6 LAMBARDE *Peramb. Kent* (1826) 121 They [the Danes] landed in despight of the people. **1603** KNOLLES *Hist. Turks* (1621) 1159 Collonitz in despight of the enemie, in safetie brought backe his souldiors. **1639** FULLER *Holy War* v. xii. (1647) 250 At last this warre ended it self in despite of the Pope. **1820** SHELLEY *To Mar. Gisborne* 318 We..in despite of God and of the devil Will make our friendly philosophic revel Outlast the leafless time. **1876** OUIDA *Winter City* vii. 198 The lottery tries to allure in very despite of themselves the much wider multitude.

e. Notwithstanding, in spite of (opposition, some opposing force).

a **1533** LD. BERNERS *Huon* lii. 175 In dyspyte of his teth I wyll se my nece. **1598** SHAKS. *Merry W.* v. v. 132 A receiu'd beleefe, in despight of the teeth of all rime and reason, that they were Fairies. **1600** E. BLOUNT tr. *Conestaggio* 132 To assaile the entrie of the mouth of Lisbone, in despite of all the fortresses that were there. *a* **1631** DONNE *Poems* (1650) 17 Love which in dispight of darkness brought us hither, Should in dispight of light keep us together. **1664** BUTLER *Hud.* II. i. 23 Some force whole Regions in despight O' Geography to change their site. **1747** CARTE *Hist. Eng.* I. Pref. 6 Learning..cultivated by private persons in despight of all difficulties. **1824** W. IRVING *T. Trav.* I. 116 Seized my hand in despite of my efforts to the contrary. **1868** MISS BRADDON *Dead Sea Fr.* I. i. 2 In despite of its solemn tranquility, this Villebrumeuse is not a dreary dwelling-place.

f. *archaic const.* ***in his, her, their, others', one's own despite***: in the various preceding senses.

1588 SHAKS. *Tit. A.* I. 361 What would you bury him in my despight. **1591** SPENSER *Daphn.* 442 Why doo I longer live in lifes despight. ? *a* **1600** *Beggars D. of Bednall Green* xxxiii, Thus was faire Bessey matched to the knight And then made a lady in others despite. **1681** DRYDEN *Abs. & Achit.* 539 Born to be sav'd, even in their own despight. **1725** POPE *Odyss.* IX. 250 Some rustic wretch, who lived in heaven's despight, Contemning laws, and trampling on the right. **1791** COWPER *Odyss.* III. 272 Much evil perpetrate in thy despight. **1794** BLAKE *Songs Exper., Clod & Pebble*, Love seeketh only self to please..And builds a hell in heaven's despite. **1849** SIR J. STEPHEN *Eccl. Biog. Pref.* (1850) 5, I am thus an author in my own despite. **1871** BLACKIE *Four Phases* i. 127 Bearding two of the thirty tyrants, and pursuing quietly his labours of love in their despite.

6. In later use often **despite of** (senses 5 d, e); whence by further shortening DESPITE *prep.*, rarely ***in despite*** (without *of*).

c **1590** MARLOWE *Faust* Wks. (Rtldg.) 123/2 If this Bruno ..sit in Peters chair, despite of chance. **1655** *Theophania* 181 Having, despight of all opposition..forced their way through. **1820** KEATS *Hyperion* I. 226 His Voice leapt out, despite of godlike curb. **1847** MRS. A. KERR *Hist. Servia* 420 Despite of her favouring his opponents, the guard of honour had been taken from her also. **1868** MORRIS *Earthly Par.* II. 92 Flushed and joyful in despite her fear.

despite (dɪ'spaɪt), *v. Obs.* or *arch.* [a. OF. *despite-r* (13th c.), mod.F. *dépiter*, app. f. *despit*, *dépit* DESPITE sb. Cf. Cat. *despitar*, Pr. *despeytar*, *-pechar*, Sp. *despechar*, It. *dispettare*, which may directly represent L. *dēspectāre*, freq. of *dēspicĕre* to look down on, DESPISE.]

1. *trans.* To express or show contempt for, treat with contempt, set at nought; to do despite to.

1375 BARBOUR *Bruce* IV. 596 Ynglis men, That dyspitit, atour all thing, Robert the bruce. **1481** CAXTON *Godfrey* cliii. 227 They blamed and Iniured our barons, And despyted them and alle thoost. **1594** DRAYTON *Idea* 527 Reason..Despiteth love, and laugheth at her Folly. **1614** T. ADAMS *Devil's Banquet* 181 And despiteth, which is more than despiseth the spirit..of grace. *a* **1619** FOTHERBY *Atheom.* I. iv. §1 (1622) 20 Who..both despise the Temples, and despite the gods. **1652** COTTERELL *Cassandra* VI. (1676) 555 Have you let 'scape an enemy who despites you? **1828** LANDOR *Wks.* (1868) I. 353/2 The great founder of Rome.. slew his brother for despiting the weakness of his walls. **1869** SPURGEON *Treas. Dav.* Ps. iv. 4 One reason why men are so mad as to despite Christ.

†**b.** with *inf. Obs.*

1596 DALRYMPLE tr. *Leslie's Hist. Scotl.* III. xxvii, A certane noble man dispytes to hear that edicte.

†**2.** To vex or provoke to anger; to spite. *Obs.*

1530 PALSGR. 520/2, I dispyte a person, I set hym at naught, or provoke hym to anger, *Je despite*..It dispyteth me to se his facyons. **1586** T. B. *La Primaud. Fr. Acad.* 670 Whose sonne he had murdered, and abused his wife to despite him therewith. **1586** A. DAY *Eng. Secretary* II. (1625) 49 It is not the shew you beare, but the pride wherewith you are carried that despiteth me. **1599** SHAKS. *Much Ado* II. ii. 31 Onely to despight them, I will endeauour any thing. **1655** FULLER *Ch. Hist.* III. vi. §43 A vexatious deed, meerly to despight them. **1658** *Whole Duty Man* ii. §13 We bring..a train of his enemies to provoke and despite him.

†**3.** *intr.* To show despite, contempt, or ill-will. *Obs.*

1530 PALSGR. 520/2 You neuer sawe man dispyte agaynst an other on that facyon. **1627** *Lisander & Cal.* IX. 185 Lisander despiting at Lidian's long resistance, gave him so violent a thrust. **1736** FRANKLIN *Poor Richard's Alm.* Wks. (1887) I. 461 *note*, These ill-willers of mine, despited at the great reputation I gained.

despite (dɪ'spaɪt), *prep.* [Shortened from *despite of*, orig. *in despite of*: see DESPITE *sb.* 6.] In spite of.

1593 SHAKS. *2 Hen. VI*, I. i. 179 Or thou, or I Somerset will be Protectors, Despite Duke Humfrey, or the Cardinall. **1602** MARSTON *Antonio's Rev.* IV. v. Wks. 1856 I. 130 Man will breake out, despight philosophie. **1613** HEYWOOD *Silv. Age* III. Wks. 1874 III. 159 Il'e..Ransacke the pallace where grim Pluto reignes..Despight his blacke guard. **1810** SCOTT *Lady of L.* II. xxxii, I love him still, despite my wrongs. **1876** MISS BRADDON *J. Haggard's Dau.* II. 25 The attraction that draws me to her despite myself.

despiteful (dɪ'spaɪtfʊl), *a.* [f. DESPITE *sb.* + -FUL.] Full of or abounding in despite.

†**1.** Contemptuous; insulting, opprobrious. *Obs.*

c **1450** LONELICH *Grail* xxxvii. 185 Ha, dispitful Creature ..Vnhappy aȝens al good aventure. **1533** MORE *Answ. Poysoned Bk.* Wks. 1038/2 Whoso dishonor god in one place with occasion of a false fayth..all honoure that he dooeth hym anye where beside, is odious and dispightefull, and reiected of god. **1549** COVERDALE *Erasm. Par. 1 Pet.* iv. 14 In the myddes of your dispightfull handlinge, the glorious spirite of god is kyndled againe in you. **1611** SPEED *Hist. Gt. Brit.* VI. xxix. (1632) 125 They slew them, and left their bodies to despightfull ignominy. **1676** BP. GUTHRIE in *Burton's Diary* (1828) III. 90 *note*, Having prefaced awhile with despightful exclamations, 'a pape! a pape! Antichrist! pull hid down!' threw the stools they sat on at the preachers.

2. Cruel, fierce; cherishing ill-will; malignant, malicious; spiteful.

c **1470** HENRY *Wallace* I. 207 The constable a felloun man of wer..Selbye he hecht, dispitfull and owtrage. **1500–20** DUNBAR *Poems* xx. 45 And be no wayis dispytfull to the peure. **1558** KNOX *First Blast* (Arb.) 9, I shalbe called foolishe, curious, despitefull, and a sower of sedition. **1570** LEVINS *Manip.* 187 Dispiteful, *inuidiosus.* **1600** SHAKS. *A.Y.L.* v. ii. 86 It is my studie To seeme despightfull and vngentle to you. **1663** BUTLER *Hud.* I. iii. 662 This.. Inflamed him with despightful Ire. **1667** MILTON *P.L.* x. 1 The hainous and despightfull act Of Satan done in Paradise. **1748** THOMSON *Cast. Indol.* II. lxxviii, The other was a fell despightful fiend. **1852** KINGSLEY *Poems, Andromeda* 125 False and devouring thou art, and the great world dark and despiteful.

de'spitefully, *adv.* [f. prec. + -LY[2].] In a despiteful manner.

1. Contemptuously, opprobriously, insolently, shamefully. *arch.*

1535 COVERDALE *Job* xvi. 10 They haue..smytten me vpon the cheke despitefully. **1552** HULOET, Despitefully, *contemptim, opprobriose.* **1611** BIBLE *Matt.* v. 44 Pray for them which despitefully vse you, and persecute you. **1614** RALEIGH *Hist. World* II. 335 The bodies of Saul and his sonnes: which hung despightfully over the Walls of Bethsan. **1694** F. BRAGGE *Disc. Parables* v. 197 Using those spiritual persons contumeliously and despitefully. **1872** YEATS *Growth. Comm.* 260 Members of the reformed faith, to use whom despitefully was thought to be doing God a service.

2. Angrily, maliciously, cruelly; with malicious cruelty or ill-will; spitefully.

c **1470** HENRY *Wallace* II. 193 My faithfull fadyr dispitfully thai slew. **1487** *Barbour's Bruce* XI. 608 (Camb. MS.) Full dyspitfully [Edinb. MS. dispitously] Thair fais demanit thaim rycht stratly. **1678** WANLEY *Wond. Lit. World* v. ii. §68. 471/2 His beautiful Empress, whom a young Burgundian had most despitefully mangled, cutting off both her Nose and Ears.

de'spitefulness. [f. as prec. + -NESS.] The quality of being despiteful; contemptuousness, malicious feeling or action, cruelty.

1535 COVERDALE *Ps.* cxxii[i]. 4 Oure soule is fylled..with the despitefulnesse of the proud. —— *Esther* i. 18 Thus shall there aryse despytefulnes and wrath ynough. **1611** BIBLE *Wisd.* ii. 19 Let vs examine him with despitefulnesse and torrture. **1633** G. HERBERT *Temple, Sacrifice* xxii, The Jews accuse me with despitefulnesse.

de'spitely, *adv.* In 7 despightly. [f. **despite* adj. (= OF. *despit* angry, despiteful) + -LY[2].] Despitefully.

1619 DENISON *Heavenly Banq.* i. 6 When the Lord of glory ..was despightly apprehended.

despiteous (dɪs'pɪtɪəs), *a.* Forms: 5 **dispitious, -pyteous,** 5–6 **despituous,** 5–7 **dispiteous,** 6 **dispit-, -pytuous, -pighteous, despyteous,** 6– **despiteous.** [Late ME. variant of DESPITOUS, from its spelling specially associated with *piteous* (†*pituous*), and so giving rise to a differentiated form, DISPITEOUS.]

1. *orig.* = DESPITOUS: full of despite, contempt, or ill-will; contemptuous, opprobrious. *arch.*

14.. *Chaucer's Knt.'s T.* 919 (*Harl.* MS. *a* 1425) A proud dispitious man. [6 *texts* des-, dispitous.] **1483** CAXTON *Gold. Leg.* 14/1 Derysions despituous. **1495** *Trevisa's Barth. De P.R.* VI. xi. (W. de W.) 196 Prowde and stoute and dyspiteous. **1529** MORE *Supplic. Soulys* Wks. 289/1 Despyteous and despiteful persone. **1529** —— *Dyaloge* IV. ibid. 258/1 Now is it to pyghteouse a sight to se the dispytuous dispyghtes done there..to god and al good men. **1532** —— *Confut. Tindale* ibid. 354/2 Tindalles develishe prowde dispituouse hearte. **1548** UDALL etc. *Erasm. Par. Luke* xx. 11 With much despiteous language. **1621** BP. MOUNTAGU *Diatribæ* 412 A rayling and despighteous speech of Scaliger. **1888** MORRIS *Dream of John Ball* iv. 30 The proud, despiteous rich man.

b. (*erroneous.*)

1623 COCKERAM, *Despituous*, contemptible, vile.

2. Spiteful, malevolent, cruel; passing gradually into the sense: Pitiless, merciless, DISPITEOUS.

c **1510** MORE *Picus* Wks. 25 To thy moste vtter dispiteous enemies. **1513** —— in Grafton *Chron.* II. 758 He was close and secret..despiteous & cruell. **1520** *Caxton's Chron. Eng.* v. 47 b/2 They shall..put them to dyspyteous dethe [**1480** dyspitous deth]. **1549** CHALONER tr. *Erasm. Moriæ Enc.* P ij b, Warre is so cruell and despiteous a thyng. *a* **1557** MRS. M. BASSET *More's Treat. Passion* Wks. 1372/2 The dysphighteous and horrible ende of Judas. **1568** C. WATSON *Polyb.* 92 b, The Carthaginenses having knowledge of the Crueltie shewed to their citizens..bewailed the despituous death and cruel torments they susteined. **1595** SHAKS. *John* IV. i. 34 Turning dispitious torture out of doore? **1596** SPENSER *F.Q.* I. ii. 15 Spurring so hote with rage dispiteous. **1600** HOLLAND *Livy* XXVIII. xx. 683 b, For very despiteous anger and deepe hatred. [19th c. see DISPITEOUS.]

de'spiteously, *adv.* [f. prec. + -LY[2].] In a despiteous manner, with despite: **a.** Contemptuously; insultingly. **b.** With bitter ill-will or enmity; spitefully, cruelly, pitilessly, mercilessly.

[*c* **1400** (MS. *p.* 1450) *Destr. Troy* 4744 The grekes..With speris full dispitiously spurnit at the yates.] *c* **1450** *Merlin* 257 Eche of hem hurte and wounded other dispiteously. **1500–20** DUNBAR *'Amang ther freiris'* 29 Thai.. Dispituouslie syne did him smyt. **1529** MORE *Comf. agst. Trib.* I. Wks. 1164/2 That so dispiteously put hym to hys payne. **1563** SACKVILLE *Compl. Dk. Buckhm.* xxvi, Howe Lord Hastings..Dispiteously was murdered and opprest. **1611** SPEED *Hist. Gt. Brit.* IX. viii. (1632) 561 Whom..he had caused to bee dispiteously dragged at horse-heeles. *a* **1641** BP. MOUNTAGU *Acts & Mon.* (1642) 26 The Devill, out of malice and envie, had despiteously empoysoned all mankind. **1808** SCOTT *Marm.* v. xxi, Lord Marmion said despiteously. **1885** *Sat. Rev.* 18 July 87 We should be sorry to be thought to write despiteously of Sir Philip Perring.

†**de'spiter.** *Obs.* [f. DESPITE *v.* + -ER[1]: cf. OF. *despiteur.*] One who treats with contempt or contemptuously defies.

1601 DEACON & WALKER *Spirits & Divels* 8 Pneumatomachus is as much to say, as a despiter of spirits. **1640** A. HARSNET *God's Summ.* 198 Despisers and Despighters of the Spirit of Grace.

despitesoun, -usioun, var. of DISPUTISOUN, *Obs.*, disputation.

despitiency, var. of DESPICIENCY.

de'spiting, *vbl. sb.* [f. DESPITE *v.* + -ING[1].] The action of the vb. DESPITE; a doing despite to; entertaining a grudge.

a **1529** SKELTON *Poems agst. Garnesche* III. 114 Your dyrty endytyng, And your spyghtfull despyghtyng. **1529** MORE

Dyaloge II. Wks. 198/1 It is not of worshipping, but dispityng and disworshipping of saintes. **1677** GILPIN *Demonol.* (1867) 199 The despiting and discrediting of truth.

† **despitous,** *a. Obs.* Forms: 4–7 **despitous;** 4–5 **des-, dis-, dys-pitous, -pytous, -pitus, -petous, -pytws, -pytuws.** [ME. a. AF. *despitous* = OF. *despitos, despiteus* (mod.F. *dépiteux*), f. *despit* DESPITE sb.: see -OUS. After 1400 associated with *piteous*, †*pituous*, and spelt *-uous, -ious, -eous*: see DESPITEOUS. Originally stressed on last or first syllable; subsequently on second.]

1. *orig.* Full of despite; exhibiting contempt or haughtiness; hence, insulting, vexing.

a **1340** HAMPOLE *Psalter* Comm. Cant. 517 þai þat ere proude and despitus. **1375** BARBOUR *Bruce* I. 196 Sa hawtane and dispitous. *c* **1386** CHAUCER *Prol.* 516 (Harl.) He was to senful man nought dispitous [6 *texts* He was nat to synful men despitous] Ne of his speche daungerous ne digne. —— *Pars. T.* ¶321 Despitous is he þat haþ desdayn of his neighebour. **1387** TREVISA *Higden* (Rolls) I. 241 Meny dispitous worde [*multæ contumeliæ*]. **1494** FABYAN *Chron.* VII. 410 The prouocacyon & dispytous wordes of ye Frenshmen.

2. Cruel; exhibiting ill-will, or bitter enmity, malevolent.

c **1340** *Cursor M.* 23235 Mony harde & dispitous dynt shul þe wrecches þere hynt. *c* **1374** CHAUCER *Troylus* III. 1409 (1458) Dispitous day þyn be þe pyne of helle! *c* **1400** *Rom. Rose* 2212 Keye was.. Of word dispitous and cruelle. *c* **1400** *Destr. Troy* 6494 Two speirus full dispitus he sparet to cast. **14..** HOCCLEVE *Compl. Virgin* 131 His despitous deeth with me compleyne. **1567** TURBERV. *Ovid's Ep.* 68 Then.. with dispitous nayles I rent my face. **1571** CAMPION *Hist. Irel.* II. ix. (1633) 120 Except that one despitous murther at Tartaine. **1578** T. PROCTOR in *Heliconia* I. 99, I sterve through thy dispitous fault.

b. *transf.* Violent.

c **1450** LONELICH *Grail* xii. 356 Vndir wheche ȝate ran there Ryht a wondir dyspetous ryvere.

† **despitously,** *adv. Obs.* [f. prec. + -LY².] In a 'despitous' manner, with despite.

1. Contemptuously, scornfully, despitefully; hence, shamefully, ignominiously.

c **1320** R. BRUNNE *Medit.* 615 Some dispoyle hym oute dyspetusly. *c* **1340** *Cursor M.* 16951 (Trin.) He.. Dispitusly [*earlier texts* vili, vilelik] for vs was lad buffeted & beten sare. *c* **1380** *Sir Ferumb.* 173 Myn enymys Despyseþ me her dispytously. *c* **1400** *Destr. Troy* 3889 Ector.. spake neuer dispituosly, ne spiset no man. **1523** Q. MARG. in M. A. E. Wood *Lett. R. & Illust. Ladies* I. 285 They speak right plainly & dyspytwsly.

2. Angrily, sharply; cruelly, maliciously; violently.

c **1340** *Cursor M.* 5082 (Trin.) þe coupe in to ȝoure secke put I And pursewed ȝou dispitously [*Gött.* And presuned ȝou ful spitusly]. *c* **1350** *Will. Palerne* 1137 [He] him told how despitously þe duk of þat dede him warned. **1375** BARBOUR *Bruce* II. 137 He that him in ȝhemsell had, Than warnyt hym dispitously. *c* **1374** CHAUCER *Troylus* V. 1806 (1818) Dispitously hym slough the fiers Achille. *c* **1386** —— *Reeve's T.* 354 By the throte-bolle he caught Aleyn, And he hent him dispitously ageyn. **1398** TREVISA *Barth. de P.R.* XIII. viii. (Tollem. MS.), þe ryuer aros with so gret strengþe and violence, þat he all to-brake dispitously þe brigge. **1480** CAXTON *Chron. Eng.* 2 He spak unto hem of theyr wykkednesse and despitously hem reproued. *a* **1500** *Orol. Sap.* in *Anglia* X. 338 Takynge me despiteslye & byndynge cruelye.

despituous, obs. form of DESPITEOUS.

desplay, obs. form of DISPLAY.

desplesance, var. of DISPLEASANCE, *Obs.*

despoil (dɪˈspɔɪl), *sb.* [ME. a. OF. *despoille, -pueille* (= Pr. *despuelha*), verbal sb. from *despoillier*: see next.]

1. The action of despoiling; plundering, robbery. *arch.*

1483 CAXTON *Gold. Leg.* 24 b/2 Stronge in his despoylle.. wel armed in the batayll. *a* **1530** WOLSEY *to Hen. VIII* (in *Athenæum* 12 Sept. 1840), My houses be,—by the oversight, dispoil, and euill behaviour of such as I did trust,—in ruyn and decaye. **1590** GREENE *Neuer too late* (1600) 57 Thou hast had my despoyle. **1807** WORDSW. *White Doe* VII. 18 'Tis done;—despoil and desolation O'er Rylstone's fair domain have blown.

†**2.** *concr.* Plunder, booty, SPOIL. *Obs.*

1474 CAXTON *Chesse* II. iv. C vij, So shold the dispoyle and botye be comune vnto them. **1481** —— *Godfrey* 296 Euery man laden and charged with despoylles. **1552** HULOET, Despoyle, *spolium, tropheum.* **1619** *Time's Storehouse* 55 (L.) Hercules.. covered with the despoyle of a lyon.

3. (See quot.)

1552 HULOET, Despoyle, or place where mischiefe or robberye is done, *dispoliabulum.*

despoil (dɪˈspɔɪl), *v.* Forms: 3–4 **despuile(n,** 3–7 **despoile, -oyle,** 6–7 **despoyl,** 6– **despoil;** also 4 **des-, dispoyly, dispuile, -uyle,** 4–5 **dyspoyle,** 4–7 **dispoile, -oyle,** 5 **des-, dis-, dyspoille, -oylle, dispole, disspoylle,** 6–7 **dispoil;** *Sc.* 4–5 **dispulȝe, -puilȝe.** [ME. *despuilen, -spoile-n,* a. OF. *despuillier, -oillier, -oiller* (mod.F. *dépouiller*) = Pr. *despolhar*, Cat. *despullar*, Sp. *despojar*, It. *dispogliare*:—L. *dēspoliāre* to plunder, rob, despoil, f. DE- I. 3 + *spoliāre* to strip of clothing, rob, spoil. Formerly spelt *dis-* by confusion with words in *des-* from DIS- prefix.]

1. *trans.* To strip of possessions by violence; to plunder, rob, SPOIL: **a.** a person.

1297 R. GLOUC. (1724) 212 þe oþere after vaste, And slowe & despoylede, and to grounde hem caste. **1340** *Ayenb.* 45 þe uerste [zenne] is couaytise uor to wynne and uor to dispoyly his uelaȝe. **1393** LANGL. *P. Pl.* C. XIV. 58 Robbours and reuers þat riche men dispoilen. **1484** CAXTON *Fables of Æsop* I. iv, The euylle hongry peple which.. robben and despoillen the poure folke. **1529** MORE *Dyaloge* I. Wks. 153/2 The Ebrues well dispoile the Egypcyens. **1795** SOUTHEY *Joan of Arc* III. 176 We are not yet So utterly despoil'd but we can spread The friendly board. **1871** FREEMAN *Norm. Conq.* (1876) IV. xvii. 36 To despoil those whom the Conqueror himself had spared.

b. a place; also *transf.* and *fig.*

1375 BARBOUR *Bruce* XIII. 502 Qwhen the feld.. Wes dispulȝeit, and left all bair. **1393** GOWER *Conf.* III. 371 Despuiled is the somer fare. *c* **1400** MAUNDEV. (1839) x. 114 Oure Lord descended to Helle & despoyled it. **1601** WEEVER *Mirr. Mart.* F ij, Enuie.. Despoil's his name and robs him of his merits. **1840** DICKENS *Barn. Rudge* xvi, The coach.. despoiled by highway-men. **1845** STEPHEN *Laws Eng.* (1874) II. 219 Though guilty in general of waste, if he despoils the freehold. **1873** DIXON *Two Queens* IV. XXII. viii. 215 Wolsey had set the fashion of despoiling and suppressing convents.

2. To strip or deprive (a person, etc.) violently *of* (some possession); to rob: **a.** *of* arms, clothes, or something material; also *transf.*

c **1300** *K. Alis.* 4028 That he a knyght of Grece slowgh, And dispoyled him of his armes. *c* **1386** CHAUCER *Pars. T.* ¶591 He was despoyled of al that he hadde in this lyf, and that nas but his clothis. *c* **1470** HENRY *Wallace* XI. 1396 Bot than he was dispulȝeit off his weid. **1600** FAIRFAX *Tasso* XIII. l. 244 An others hands Of these her plants the wood dispoilen shall. **1603** KNOLLES *Hist. Turks* (1638) 309 Theeues.. dispoiling him of his apparell. **1614** RALEIGH *Hist. World* II. 450 Athalia being thus dispoyled of her Son. **1659** B. HARRIS *Parival's Iron Age* 172 The Swedes, being.. despoiled of the Isle of Usedon. **1695** WOODWARD *Nat. Hist. Earth* v. (1723) 257 These formed Stones being by this Means despoil'd of their Shells. **1775** JOHNSON *Lett. to Mrs. Thrale* 12 May, You talked of despoiling his book of the fine print. **1776** GIBBON *Decl. & F.* I. xvii. 440 The cities of Greece and Asia were despoiled of their most valuable ornaments. **1870** BRYANT *Iliad* I. IV. 132 He could not despoil The slain man of his armor.

b. *of* things immaterial; also *fig.*

c **1400** MAUNDEV. (Roxb.) xxxii. 145 We bene in peess, of þe whilk þou will now dispoile vs. **1581** J. BELL *Haddon's Answ. Osor.* 212 b, We do not despoyle will of her libertye. **1593** SHAKS. *2 Hen. VI*, II. iii. 10 Despoyled of your Honor. **1667** MILTON *P.L.* IX. 411 Despoild of Innocence, of Faith, of Bliss. **1878** B. TAYLOR *Deukalion* I. iii. 30 They.. despoiled thy head Of separate honor.

†**3.** *spec.* To strip of clothes, to disrobe: **a.** *orig.* as an act of violence, spoliation, or robbery. *Obs.*

a **1225** *Ancr. R.* 260 Vor steorc naked he was despuiled oðe rode. *c* **1380** *Sir Ferumb.* 3031 To Gy tok he þat cors: 'Dispoille þis body', þan gan he saye; '& arme þe on ys wede'. **1485** CAXTON *Chas. Gt.* 88 Take these frensshe men and despoyle them.

†**b.** without the notion of spoliation: To undress; to strip *of* armour, vestments, etc. *Obs.*

c **1340** *Gaw. & Gr. Knt.* 860 þer he watz dispoyled, wyth spechez of myerþe, þe burn of his bruny, & of his bryȝt wedez. *c* **1386** CHAUCER *Clerk's T.* 318 He had That wommen schuld despoilen hir right there. *c* **1450** *Merlin* 463 Thei made dispoile the quene to go to hir bedde. **1525** LD. BERNERS *Froiss.* II. ccxlv. [ccxli.] 753 Before the aulter ther he was dispoyled out of all his vestures of estate. **1540** SURREY *Poems, Prisoner in Windsor* 13 Despoiled for the game. **1561** NORTON & SACKV. *Gorboduc* IV. ii. (1847) 142 We.. Dispoyled streight his brest, and all we might, Wyped in vaine, with napkyns next at hande. **1700** DRYDEN *Palamon & Arc.* III. 725 The surgeons soon despoiled them of their arms, And some with salves they cure, and some with charms.

†**c.** *refl.* To disrobe or undress *oneself*, put off one's clothes. *Obs.*

1388 WYCLIF *1 Sam.* xviii. 4 Jonathas dispuylide him silf fro the coote. **1470–85** MALORY *Arthur* VII. xii, Pryuely she dispoylled her & leid her doune by hym. *c* **1477** CAXTON *Jason* 106 Dispoylle you and entre in to this bathe. **1483** —— *Gold. Leg.* 85 b/1 He dyspoylled and unclad hym and gaf hys clothys unto the bochyers.

†**d.** To take *off* (clothes). *Obs.*

1483 CAXTON *Gold. Leg.* 62 b/1 Moyses toke Aaron upon the hylle & despoylled of his vesture. —— *Esope* 2 b, The lord commaunded to despoylle and take of his clothes.

†**e.** with double obj.: To strip (a person) of (clothes). *Obs.*

1632 SIR T. HAWKINS tr. *Mathieu's Vnhappy Prosp.* 1 When the play is ended.. they are dispoyled the gawdy garments of the personage represented.

†**4.** To strip of worth, value, or use; to render useless, mar, destroy; to SPOIL. *Obs.*

?*a* **1400** *Morte Arth.* 4127 Paynymes.. With speres disspetousely disspoylles our knyghttes. *c* **1539** *Plumpton Corr.* 235 A action of trespas against.. Robart Oliver for dispoyling my gras. **1685** [see DESPOILED].

†**5.** To make a spoil of (goods, etc.); to carry off by violence, rob, plunder. *Obs.*

1483 CAXTON *Cato* B iij, To despoyle and rauisshe hys neyghbours goodes. **1604** R. CAWDREY *Table Alph.*, *Dispoyle*, take away by violence.

†**b.** To remove forcibly, take away. *Obs.*

a **1533** LD. BERNERS *Gold. Bk. M. Aurel.* (1546) K ij, It is necessary to dispoyle the opilacions and leattes of the stomake.

Hence **deˈspoiled, deˈspoiling** *ppl. adjs.*

1570–6 LAMBARDE *Peramb. Kent* (1826) 146 A poore, private, and despoiled person. **1685** TRAVESTIN *Siege Newheusel* 43 The besieged.. again put in order the late dispoiled Battery. **1849** MACAULAY *Hist. Eng.* II. 130 Despoiled proprietors. **1859** C. BARKER *Associative Princ.* i. 17 The despoiling hands of the first reformers.

despoiler (dɪˈspɔɪlə(r)). [f. DESPOIL *v.* + -ER¹. Cf. OF. *despoilleur.*] One who despoils; a plunderer, spoiler.

1467 *E.E. Gilds* 389 Pillours, Robbers, dispoylers. **1592** WYRLEY *Armorie* 151 Dispoiler of my worldly pleasaunce. **1611** SPEED *Hist. Gt. Brit.* IX. ii. §57, I.. forbid that the Body of my dispoiler, be covered in my Earth. **1812** BYRON *Ch. Har.* II. lxxvi, They may lay your proud despoilers low. **1848** MACAULAY *Hist. Eng.* I. 186 The despoilers and the despoiled had for the most part been rebels alike. **1855** SINGLETON *Virgil* II. 418 A less merciful despoiler of floral beauties.

despoiling (dɪˈspɔɪlɪŋ), *vbl. sb.* [f. as prec. + -ING¹.]

1. The action of the verb DESPOIL; robbing.

1552 HULOET, Despoylinge, *despoliatio, spoliatio.* **1793** BURKE *Corr.* (1844) IV. 143 The despoiling a minister of religion.

†**2.** Spoil, plunder; esp., the arms or clothes of an enemy, the skin of a beast.

c **1374** CHAUCER *Boeth.* IV. met. vii. 147 He rafte þe despoylynge fro þe cruel lyoun, þat is to seyne he slouȝ þe lyoun and rafte hym hys skyn.

despoilment (dɪˈspɔɪlmənt). [f. DESPOIL *v.* + -MENT. Cf. OF. *despoillement*, mod.F. *dépouillement.*] The action of despoiling or fact of being despoiled; spoliation.

1822 MOIR *Stanzas on Infant* i, As yet by Earth's despoilment undefaced. **1859** LD. BROUGHTON *Italy* II. xii. 4 The first despoilment is.. to be attributed to the piety or rapacity of Stilicho. **1873** L. WALLACE *Fair God* VII. xiv. 541 The city, beautiful in its despoilment.

† **deˈspoliate,** *v. Obs.* [f. ppl. stem of L. *dēspoliāre* to DESPOIL.] = DESPOIL *v.*

1607 BP. J. KING *Serm.* Nov. 24 Excommunicate, depose, dispoliate Eagle and Falkons. **1620** VENNER *Via Recta* ii. 40 It doth.. enfeeble and dispoliate [the liver] of it's sanguifying facultie. **1656** BLOUNT *Glossogr.*, *Despoliate*, to spoil, rob, or pil.

despoliation (dɪˌspəʊlɪˈeɪʃən). [ad. L. *dēspoliātiōn-em*, n. of action from *dēspoliāre* to DESPOIL.] The action of despoiling; despoilment.

1657 PHILLIPS, *Despoliation*, a robbing or spoiling. **1658** *Ibid.*, *Dispoliation.* **1830** J. G. STRUTT *Sylva Brit.* 136 The Wallace Oak seems destined.. to share their fate of despoliation. **1894** J. BATTEN *Hist. Coll. S. Somerset* 110 The despoliation of alien priories in the time of Henry V.

despond (dɪˈspɒnd), *v.*¹ [ad. L. *dēspondē-re* to give up, yield, resign, *dēspondēre animum*, later simply *dēspondēre* to lose heart, despond; f. DE- I. 2 b + *spondēre* to promise. The form follows *respond* which came through French.]

intr. To lose heart or resolution; to become depressed or dejected in mind by loss of confidence or hope. (Distinguished from *despair* as not expressing entire hopelessness.) Sometimes with *of* (cf. *to despair of*).

1655 CROMWELL *Speech to Parlt.* 22 Jan., I did not at all despond but the stop put upon you.. would have made way for a blessing from God. **1656** BLOUNT *Glossogr.*, *Despond*.. also to fail in courage or despair. *Lord Protectors Speech.* **1696** TATE & BRADY *Ps.* cxxvi. 6 Though he despond that sows the grain. **1697** DRYDEN *Virg. Georg.* III. 819 The Learned Leaches.. shake their Heads, desponding of their Art. **1765** H. WALPOLE *Otranto* v. (1798) 79, I thought it right not to let my young lady despond. **1855** MACAULAY *Hist. Eng.* III. 686 The friends of the government desponded, and the chiefs of the opposition were sanguine. **1860** *Lit. Churchman* VI. 222/1 Are we, then, to despond of the victory?

† **deˈspond,** *v.*² *Obs.*—⁰ [f. L. *dēspondēre* (see prec.) in sense 'to promise in marriage, betroth, engage'.] (See quot. Perh. never used in Eng.).

1656 BLOUNT *Glossogr.*, *Despond*, to betroth or promise in marriage. *Ibid.*, *Despondency*, a promise in marriage.

despond (dɪˈspɒnd), *sb. arch.* Also 7 **dis-.** [f. DESPOND *v.*¹] The act of desponding; despondency.

1678 BUNYAN *Pilgr.* I. 12 This Miry slough.. called the Slough of Dispond [*called* p. 10 Slough of Dispondency]. **1684** *Ibid.* II. 21 But when Christiana came up to the Slow of Despond, she began to be at a stand. *Ibid.* II. 200 Our Disponds, and slavish Fears.

despondence (dɪˈspɒndəns). [f. L. *dēspondēre*, pr. pple. *dēspondēnt-em*: see -ENCE.] The action of desponding; also (less correctly) = DESPONDENCY.

1676 HALE *Contempl.* I. *Of Afflictions* (R.), Bear up thyself .. from fainting and despondence. **1708** *Brit. Apollo* No. 76 1/1 Affront him not.. by a Despondence of his Mercy. **1794** GODWIN *Cal. Williams* 269 My fits of despondence. **1832** LYTTON *Eugene A.* II. i, Feelings which forbid despondence. **1845** LD. CAMPBELL *Chancellors* (1857) IV. lxxvi. 34 Instead of indulging in despondence.. he employed his time with well-directed industry.

despondency¹ (dɪˈspɒndənsɪ). Also 7 **dis-.** [f. as prec. + -ENCY.] The state or condition of being despondent; depression or dejection of spirits through loss of resolution or hope.

1653 H. MORE *Conject. Cabbal.* (1662) 161 Anger, Zeal, Indignation..Despondency, Triumph or Gloriation. **1656** *Artif. Handsom.* (1662) 76 Religion is no friend..to supine and sottish despondencies of mind. **1684** BUNYAN *Pilgr.* II. 161 They fell to demolishing Doubting-Castle..and in it..they found one Mr. Dispondencie..and one Much-afraid his Daughter. **1748** *Anson's Voy.* I. ii. 16 The peevishness and despondency which..contrary winds, and a lingring voyage..create. **1838** THIRLWALL *Greece* IV. xxxiv. 326 The despondency with which the Greeks viewed the situation. **1866** GEO. ELIOT *F. Holt* I. iv. 94 In a tone of despondency.

de'spondency[2]. *Obs.*—[0] See DESPOND *v.*[2]

despondent (dɪ'spɒndənt), *a.* and *sb.* [ad. L. *dēspondēnt-em*, pr. pple. of *dēspondēre* to DESPOND: see -ENT.]

1. Characterized by loss of heart or resolution; labouring under mental depression; desponding.

a **1699** W. BATES *Fear of God* xv. (R.), For a despondent sinner to think..that God will triumph in the mere torments of his creatures..is a sin equal to atheism. **1730–46** THOMSON *Autumn* 980 Congregated thrushes..now shivering sit On the dead tree, a dull despondent flock. **1800** MRS. HERVEY *Mourtray Fam.* I. 272 She sat despondent, lamenting her own extravagance. **1849** GROTE *Greece* II. xlii. V. 215 Many..chiefs were not merely apathetic but despondent in the cause.

2. Of or belonging to despondency.

1844 DICKENS *Chimes* ii, He then made a despondent gesture with both hands. **1888** MISS BRADDON *Fatal Three* I. v, He sat in a despondent attitude.

B. *sb.* One who desponds.

1812 SOUTHEY in *Q. Rev.* VIII. 347 A war which..the despondents have pronounced hopeless. *a* **1845** MRS. BRAY *Warleigh* xxxi. (1884) 242, I am no despondent.

de'spondently, *adv.* [f. prec. + -LY[2].] In a despondent manner or state.

a **1677** BARROW *Serm.* I. ix. 112 (R. Supp.) St. Chrysostom..thus despondently concludes. **1795** LD. AUCKLAND *Corr.* III. 281, I was thought..to have talked too despondently. **1881** MISS BRADDON *Asph.* II. 117 Edgar consented to be led despondently back to the house.

desponder (dɪ'spɒndə(r)). *rare.* [f. DESPOND *v.*[1] + -ER[1].] One who desponds.

1689 EVELYN *Mem.* (1857) II. 288 More could scarce be said to encourage desponders. **1737** SWIFT *Prop. Badges Begg.* Wks. 1761 III. 344, I am a desponder in my nature.

de'sponding, *vbl. sb.* [f. as prec. + -ING[1].] The action of the verb DESPOND, q.v.

1818 *Blackw. Mag.* IV. 1 The..gloomy despondings, which deform and darken the native majesty of Byron.

de'sponding, *ppl. a.* [f. as prec. + -ING[2].] That desponds; losing or having lost heart or resolution.

1688 DRYDEN *Brit. Rediv.* 258 Desponding Peter sinking in the waves. *a* **1690** E. HOPKINS *Expos. Lord's Prayer* (R.), With no tormenting, carking, and desponding thoughts. **1746–7** HERVEY *Medit.* (1818) 195 Why should desponding fears oppress your souls? **1828** SCOTT *F.M. Perth* viii, The Glover seemed particularly desponding. **1843** J. MARTINEAU *Chr. Life* (1867) 63 The desponding are generally the indolent and useless. **1868** MILMAN *St. Paul's* 348 The weak and desponding defence of a lost cause.

b. Causing despondency, dispiriting. *rare.*

1800 *Invisible Man* I. 113 Accounts the more desponding to me, as he informs me he shall be here to-morrow.

Comb. **1803** BEDDOES *Hygeia* x. 5 His desponding-mad Ophelia, his raving-mad Lear, his jealous-mad Othello.

de'spondingly, *adv.* [f. prec. + -LY[2].] In a desponding manner; with dejection of spirits.

1656 BLOUNT *Glossogr.*, *Despondingly*, desperately, out of hope. **1706** *Lond. Gaz.* No. 4226/1 We begin to talk very despondingly of its Success. **1840** MARRYATT *Olla Podr.*, *S.W. and by W.* ¾*W.*, 'I sha'n't get any', replied Jack, despondingly. **1879** *Cassell's Techn. Educ.* IV. 7/1 A friend, who despondingly expressed his fears that the huge ship would never reach the water.

[**desponsage.** Explained as: Betrothal. Error for DESPOUSAGE.

[*a* **1587** FOXE *A. & M.* (1596) 103/2 Despousage of Athilrid his daughter.] Quoted in **1836** RICHARDSON *Dict.* as desponsage. Hence in **1864** WEBSTER (citing *Foxe*).]

† **de'sponsate,** *a. Obs.* Also dys-. [ad. L. *dēsponsāt-us*, pa. pple. of *dēsponsāre* to betroth, freq. of *dēspondēre*: see DESPOND *v.*[2]]

1. Contracted or given in marriage, betrothed, espoused.

1483 CAXTON *Gold. Leg.* 285 b/2 He shold be the man that shold be desponsate and maryed to the Vyrgyne Mary.

2. *fig.* (*Alch.*) Chemically combined.

1471 RIPLEY *Comp. Alch.* I. in Ashm. (1652) 133 Yet must theyr Elements..wyth Elements of perfyt Bodys be dysponsate. *Ibid.* VI. 167 Make them then together to be Dysponsat.

† **de'sponsated,** *ppl. a.* = prec.

1623 COCKERAM, *Desponsated*, betrothed.

† **despon'sation.** *Obs.* Also dis-, dys-. [ad. L. *dēsponsātiōn-em* (also in OF. *desponsation*) betrothal, n. of action from *dēsponsāre*: see prec.]

1. The action of contracting in marriage; betrothal.

a **1400** *Cov. Myst.* ix. (Shaks. Soc.) 89 Now xal we procede to here dissponsacion. **1649** JER. TAYLOR *Gt. Exemp.* i. §5 For all this desponsation of her..she had not set one step toward the consummation of her marriage. **1656** BLOUNT *Glossogr.*, *Desponsation*, an affiance or betrothing.

2. *fig.* (*Alch.*) Chemical combination.

1471 RIPLEY *Comp. Alch.* in Ashm. (1652) 187 The lesse of the Sprysts there be in thys dysponsation The rather thy Calcynatyon..shall thou make.

† **de'sponsion.** *Obs. rare.* [ad. L. *dēsponsiōn-em*, n. of action from *dēspondēre* to DESPOND, despair.] Desponding, despondency.

1640 BURGES *Serm.* (1641) 2 To cure them..of this desperate desponsion of mind.

† **de'sponsories,** *sb. pl. Obs.* Also 7 **desponsorios, desposories.** [ad. Sp. *desposorios* espousal, betrothal, f. *desposar* to affiance:—L. *dēsponsāre* (after which the word is modified in English). Chiefly used in relation to the proposed Spanish marriage of Charles I.]

1. Betrothal, or a ceremony in celebration of it.

c **1645** HOWELL *Lett.* I. III. xxii, The eighth of.. September is appointed to be the day of Desponsories, the day of affiance, or the betrothing day. **1659** RUSHW. *Hist. Coll.* I. 105 The delay of the Desponsorio's will grieve the Princess.

2. A document formally declaring a betrothal.

1626 in Rushw. *Hist. Coll.* (1659) I. 253 The Prince..left the powers of the Desponsories with the Earl of Bristol, to be delivered upon the return of the Dispensation from Rome, which the King of Spain insisted upon. **1647** CLARENDON *Hist. Reb.* I. (1702) I. 30 The Prince having left the Desponsorios in the hands of the Earl of Bristol. *a* **1670** HACKET *Abp. Williams* I. (1692) 155 Mr. Edward Clerke, who was sent..to the Earl of Bristol, to stop the powers he had for the dispatch of the expected desposories.

desport, obs. form of DISPORT *sb.* and *v.*

† **de'spose,** *v. Obs. rare.* [a. OF. *desposer*, occas. var. of *déposer*, from the F. confusion of *des-*, *de-*: see DE- 6.] *trans.* To depose, put down, lay down.

1587 GOLDING *De Mornay* xvi. 255 What would he thinke but that he were desposed from the Throne? **1598** E. GILPIN *Skial.* (1878) 43 And now their box complexions are despos'd. **1603** FLORIO *Montaigne* III. ix. (1632) 536 Into whose hands I might despose, and..resigne the..managing of my goods.

despose, obs. form of DISPOSE *v.*

despot ('dɛspət). Also 6 **dispotto,** 7 **despote.** [a. OF. *despot* (14th c.), modF. *despote*, ad. Gr. δεσπότης (med.L. *despota, -tus*) master, lord, despot. In sense 1 partly after It. '*dispoto*, in Florio *de'spota*, 'a lord, a lordlike governour'.]

1. *Hist.* A word which, in its Greek form, meant 'master' or 'lord' (e.g. of a household, of slaves), and was applied to a deity, and to the absolute ruler of a non-free people; in Byzantine times it was used of the Emperor, and, as representing Lat. *magister*, in various official titles, also as a form of address (= *domine* my lord) to the emperor, to bishops, and especially to patriarchs; from the time of Alexius Comnenus it was the formal title of princes of the imperial house; in the sense 'lord' or 'prince', it was borne, after the Turkish conquest, by the petty Christian rulers of dependent or tributary provinces, as the despots of the Morea or of Servia (= Servian *hospodar*). It was in this later application that the word was first known in the Western languages.

(In modern Greek, δεσπότης is the ordinary appellation of a bishop.)

1562 J. SHUTE *Cambini's Turk. Wars* (tr. from Italian) 20 Thomas Paleologo..abstained from that title..and contented himselfe with the only title of the Dispotto of Morea. **1585** T. WASHINGTON tr. *Nicholay's Voy.* III. ii. 71 b, Taken awaye from his father John Castriot Despot of Servia. **1588** GREENE *Perimedes* 11 The Despot of Decapolis and his wife..lost their way. **1603** KNOLLES *Hist. Turks* (1638) 112 He was both by the Patriarch and the yong Emperor honored with the title of the *Despot*, another step vnto the Empire. **1614** SELDEN *Titles Hon.* 122 The *Despot* was the heire or successor apparant of the Constantinopolitan Empire (vnderstand, of the times since Alexius Comnenus, though before him it were a generall name, as *My Lord*). **1656** BLOUNT *Glossogr.*, Among the ancient Greeks, he that was next to the Emperor, was, by a general name, called Despotes. **1755** JOHNSON, *Despot*, an absolute prince; one that governs with unlimited authority. This word is not in use, except as applied to some Dacian prince; as the *despot* of Servia. **1788** GIBBON *Decl. & F.* liii. V. 485 To their favourite sons or brothers, they imparted the more lofty appellation of Lord or Despot, which was illustrated with new ornaments and prerogatives, and placed immediately after the person of the emperor himself. **1819** T. HOPE *Anastasius* (1820) II. x. 203 (Stanf.), I am bearer of letters to the despots [bishops of the Greek Church] and proëstis of our different islands.

2. After ancient Greek use: An absolute ruler of a country; hence, by extension, any ruler who governs absolutely or tyrannically; any person who exercises tyrannical authority; a tyrant, an oppressor.

(The modern use, which is usually hostile, according to Mason, quoted by Todd, came into prominence at the period of the French Revolution: 'the French revolutionists have been very liberal in conferring this title'.)

[**1611** COTGR., *Despote*, a Despote; the chiefe or soueraigne Lord of a Countrey. **1755** (see sense 1).] **1781** COWPER *Expost.* 370 Hast thou..returned..A despot big with power obtained by wealth? **1784** —— *Task* v. 311 But is it fit..that a man..Should be a despot absolute, and boast Himself the only freeman of his land? **1795** SOUTHEY *Joan of Arc* x. 444 When pouring o'er his legion slaves on Greece, The eastern despot bridged the Hellespont. **1795–6** BURKE *Regic. Peace* iv. Wks. IX. 104 The friends of Jacobins are no longer despots; the betrayers of the common cause are no longer traitors! **1841** W. SPALDING *Italy & It. Isl.* II. 181 Which coincided in date with several other plots against Italian despots. **1841** ELPHINSTONE *Hist. Ind.* II. 159 The intercourse between those princes was highly characteristic of Asiatic despots. **1841–4** EMERSON *Ess.*, *Compensation* Wks. (Bohn) I. 43 Under the primeval despots of Egypt. **1848** HALLAM *Mid. Ages* ii. Note vii (1855) I. 305 Every Frank of wealth and courage was a despot within his sphere. **1857** HUGHES *Tom Brown* Pref. (1871) 12 Which divides boys into despots and slaves. **1871** MORLEY *Voltaire* (1886) 82 Voltaire..never rose above the simple political conception of an eastern tale, a good-tempered despot with a sage vizier.

3. *Comb.*

1846 C. G. PROWETT *Prometh. Bound* 34 Is not our despot-lord In all things framed to violence?

despotat ('dɛspətæt). Also **-ate.** [a. F. *despotat*, ad. med.L. type **despotātus*: see DESPOT and -ATE.] The dominion of a Greek despot under the Turks; a principality.

1866 FELTON *Anc. & Mod. Gr.* I. iii. 312 There was the despotat of Epirus. **1883** *Jrnl. Hellenic Stud.* Oct. 2 A semi-independent despotat of Epirus continued to exist for more than a hundred years after that time.

† **despo'tee.** *Obs.* [cf. OF. *despotee* court of a despot, *despotie* lordship, despotat; cf. Gr. δεσποτεία lordship, despotism.] = prec.

1656 EARL MONM. *Advt. fr. Parnass.* 361 In the Grecian Empire, whose division into several despotees..did..throw open the gates to me.

despotic (dɛ'spɒtɪk), *a.* Also 7 **despotique,** 8 **despotick.** [a. F. *despotique* (Oresme, 14th c.), ad. Gr. δεσποτικός, f. δεσπότης DESPOT: see -IC.] Of, pertaining to, or of the nature of a despot, or despotism; arbitrary, tyrannical.

1650 HOBBES *De Corp. Pol.* 58 From whence proceedeth Dominion, Paternall, and Despotique. **1720** GAY *Poems* (1745) II. 31 Where guardian laws despotic power restrain. **1751** JOHNSON *Rambler* No. 142 ¶ 10 Bluster has therefore a despotick authority in many families. **1825** LAMB *Elia* Ser. II. *Convalescent*, He lay and acted his despotic fancies. **1844** EMERSON *Lect.*, *Yng. Amer.* Wks. (Bohn) II. 298 The patriarchal form of government readily becomes despotic. **1856** GROTE *Greece* II. xciv. (1869) XII. 10 *marg.*, He becomes Asiatized and despotic. *a* **1863** AUSTIN *Jurispr.* (ed. 4) I. 283 The epithet *free* importing praise, and the epithet *despotic* importing blame, they who distinguish governments into free and despotic suppose that the first are better than the second.

Hence **de'spoticly** *adv.* = DESPOTICALLY.

169. *Ad Populum Phaleræ* I. 13 That Noah's Heirs despoticly might rule.

† **de'spotical,** *a. Obs.* Also 8 **-all.** [f. as prec. + -AL[1].] = DESPOTIC.

1608 D. T. *Ess. Pol. & Mor.* 68 Free'd themselves whollie from that Despotical kind of government. **1641** MILTON *Reform.* II. (1851) 53 Under the despoticall rule of the Monarch. **1690** LOCKE *Govt.* II. xv. §172 Despotical Power is an absolute, arbitrary Power one Man has over another. **1776** ADAM SMITH *W.N.* II. ii. (1869) I. 326 Of the most free as well as of the most despotical [governments]. **1839** J. ROGERS *Antipopopr.* IV. iii. 183 Despotical speaking and acting of the clergy.

despotically (dɛ'spɒtɪkəlɪ), *adv.* [f. prec. + -LY[2].] In a despotic manner; with absolute power.

1681 *Whole Duty Nations* 53 Despotically to command, or compel, is not of the nature of True Christian..Religion. **1765** BLACKSTONE *Comm.* I. 234 A monarchy absolutely and despotically regal. **1814** SCOTT *Wav.* xix, The great man of his neighbourhood..ruling despotically over a small clan. **1860** *Sat. Rev.* IX. 137/2 In despotically governed monarchies.

† **de'spoticalness.** *Obs.* [f. as prec. + -NESS.] The quality of being despotic; despotic mode of action; despotism.

1689 *Myst. Iniq.* 36 The eleven Judges, who gratified him with a Despoticalness over the former. **1695** *Parl. Dissolved Death Princess of Orange* 48 A Despoticalness becoming the Grand Seigniors of the Republick. **1698** R. FERGUSSON *View Eccles.* 106 Tools of Despoticalness or Democratical Demagogues in Politicks.

despotism ('dɛspətɪz(ə)m). [a. F. *despotisme* (*Dict. Acad.* 1740): see DESPOT and -ISM.]

1. The rule of a despot; despotic government; the exercise of absolute authority.

1727–51 CHAMBERS *Cycl.*, *Despotism*, despotic government. **1756** BURKE *Vind. Nat. Soc.* Wks. I. 36 The simplest form of government is despotism, where all the inferior orbs of power are moved merely by the will of the Supreme. **1817** BENTHAM *Swear not at all* Wks. 1843 V. 222 Next to the evils of anarchy, are the evils of despotism. **1857** TOULM. SMITH *Parish* 364 The worst form of despotism is the silent enslaving of a nation by Functionarism and Bureaucracy. *a* **1862** BUCKLE *Civiliz.* (1873) III. iv. 192 These very circumstances, which guarded the people against political despotism exposed them all the more to ecclesiastical despotism. **1869** RAWLINSON *Anc. Mon., Hist.* 22 Despotism is the simplest, coarsest, and rudest of all the forms of civil government. **1871** MORLEY *Voltaire* (1886) 29 In France the first effective enemy of the principles of despotism was Voltaire.

2. A political system under the control of a despot; a despotic state; an arbitrary government.

1856 SIR B. BRODIE *Psychol. Inq.* I. v. 205 It is.. dangerous suddenly to change a despotism for a free constitution. **1867** FREEMAN *Norm. Conq.* (1876) I. v. 297 A free country has greater difficulty than a despotism in the mere setting about of a war. **1879** FROUDE *Cæsar* xx. 347 They saw that a civil war could end only in a despotism. **1881** JOWETT *Thucyd.* I. 190 Your empire is a despotism exercised over unwilling subjects.

3. *fig.* Absolute power or control; rigid restraint.

1797 GODWIN *Enquirer* I. vii. 60 All education is despotism. **1807-8** W. IRVING *Salmag.* xi. (1860) 243 With what.. despotism do empty names and ideal phantoms exercise their dominion over the human mind! **1836** EMERSON *Nat., Idealism* Wks. (Bohn) II. 160 The first effort of thought tends to relax this despotism of the senses. **1859** MILL *Liberty* ii. 63 An old mental despotism had been thrown off.

'despotist. [f. as prec. + -IST.] An advocate or supporter of despotism.

1857 KINGSLEY *Life & Lett.* (1879) II. 66 And I must become as thorough a despotist and imperialist as Strafford himself. **1863** E. WARD *Captiv. Poland* I. 129 Mr. Carlyle.. a philosophical despotist.

despotize ('dɛspətaɪz), *v.* [f. as prec. + -IZE; in mod.F. *despotiser* (Littré).] *intr.* To act the part of a despot; to rule as a despot.

1799 *Chron.* in *Ann. Reg.* 288 Despotizing over those nations which will not submit. **1809** COLERIDGE *Friend* (1866) 215 He despotized in all the pomp of patriotism. **1876** MOZLEY *Univ. Serm.* i. 16 Kings and Emperors.. anxious to despotise over their brethren.

despo'tocracy. *nonce-wd.* [-CRACY.] Government by a despot; the rule of a despot.

a **1860** T. PARKER *Wks.* V. 262 (D.) Despotocracy, the worst institution of the middle ages.. came over the water.

†**despotomaniac.** *nonce-wd.* [See -MANIA.] One who has a mania in favour of despots; *attrib.* having such a mania.

1825 *Blackw. Mag.* XVIII. 690 We value liberty too highly to cram it like a nauseous potion down the throat of any Despoto-maniac patient.

†**de'spousage.** *Obs.* [f. DESPOUSE *v.* + -AGE: cf. *espousage, spousage.*] Betrothal; espousal.

a **1587** FOXE *A. & M.* (1596) 103/2 Ethelbert King of the Eastangles.. went.. to King Offa for despousage of Athilrid his daughter.

†**de'spouse,** *v. Obs.* [ad. L. *dēsponsāre* to betroth (see DESPONSATE), on the model of *spouse*:—OF. *esposer*:—L. *sponsāre.*] *trans.* To promise in marriage, to betroth; to give or take in marriage, to marry; = ESPOUSE *v.* 1, 2. Also *fig.*

1387 TREVISA *Higden* (Rolls) VII. 203 Ly wiþ me, for to day þow despousedest and weddest me. *c* **1440** CAPGRAVE *Life St. Kath.* III. 1028 She desireth þat þou shalt now wyth a ryng Despouse hir to thi-self for euere-more. **1526** *Pilgr. Perf.* (W. de W. 1531) 187, I haue despoused you to a noble man. **1543** *Necess. Doctr.* in *Formul. Faith* B iij, A virgin, which was despoused or ensured to a man, whose name was Joseph. **1609** BIBLE (Douay) *1 Macc.* x. 56 Meete me at Ptolemais, that.. I may despouse her to thee.

fig. **1526** *Pilgr. Perf.* (W. de W. 1531) 3 Whan he despoused theyr soules in fayth & ledde them in hope out of Egypt.

Hence **de'spoused** *ppl. a.*, **de'spousing** *vbl. sb.*; also **de'spouser**, one who gives in marriage.

1609 BIBLE (Douay) *Song. Sol.* iii. 11 In the day of his despousing. **1635** HEYWOOD *Hierarch.* v. 308 Chastitie the Contract, Vertue the Despouser.

despoyl(e, -poyly, -puile, obs. ff. DESPOIL.

despraise, despread, desprise: see DIS-.

de'spumate, *ppl. a.* [ad. L. *dēspūmāt-us* pa. pple. of *dēspūmāre*: see next.]

1883 *Syd. Soc. Lex., Despumate,* freed from froth and impurities; clarified; purified.

despumate (dɪ'spjuːmeɪt, 'dɛspjuːmeɪt), *v.* [f. L. *dēspūmāt-*, ppl. stem of *dēspūmāre* to skim, f. DE- I. 2 + *spūma* foam, froth, scum, *spūmāre* to froth.]

1. *trans.* To skim; to free (a liquid) of the scum, froth, or other impure part; to clarify by removing the scum.

1641 FRENCH *Distill.* iv. (1651) 95 Take of Honey well despumated as much as you please. **1718** QUINCY *Compl. Disp.* 34 The Honey is order'd to be clarify'd or despumated. **1756** P. BROWNE *Jamaica* 112 Used among the French to despumate and granulate their sugars. **1757** WALKER in *Phil. Trans.* L. 128 When it was despumated, a new cremor always succeeded.

2. *intr.* (for *refl.*) To throw off its froth or scum; to become clarified by this process.

1733 CHEYNE *Eng. Malady* 304 (L.) That discharge.. will help it the sooner and faster to despumate and purify. **1883** in *Syd. Soc. Lex.*

3. *trans.* To throw off as froth.

1733 CHEYNE *Eng. Malady* 360 (L.) They were thrown off and despumated upon the larger emunctory and open glands.

Hence **despumated** *ppl. a.*

1661 LOVELL *Hist. Anim. & Min.* 83 The sanies of it rosted, with despumated Honey, helps the Glaucoma. **1883** *Syd. Soc. Lex., Despumated honey.*

despu'mation. [ad. L. *dēspūmātiōn-em*, n. of action from *dēspūmāre*: see prec. In F. *despumation* (1616 in Hatzf.).]

1. The removal of froth or scum from a liquid; the condition of being freed from scum; clarification.

1612 WOODALL *Surg. Mate* Wks. (1653) 270 Despumation is when spume or froth floating on the top, is taken away with a spoon, feather, or by colation. **1710** T. FULLER *Pharm. Extemp.* 215 Honey.. boil'd to a perfect Despumation. **1883** in *Syd. Soc. Lex.*

2. The expulsion of impure matter from the fluids of the body; the matter thus despumated.

1684 tr. *Bonet's Merc. Compit.* VI. 164 By.. Despumation I would have nothing else understood, than the Expulsion or Separation of the febrile matter now brought under and as it were conquered. **1733** CHEYNE *Eng. Malady* II. v. §8 (1734) 164 The.. Glands become loaded with the Despumation of the whole Habit. **1802** PALEY *Nat. Theol.* xxvi, The fluids of the body appear to possess a power of separating and expelling any noxious substance which may have mixed itself with them. This they do, in eruptive fevers, by a kind of despumation, as Sydenham calls it. **1802** BEDDOES *Hygeia* viii. 158.

3. *pl.* Skimmings, scum, froth, foam.

1669 *Addr. Yng. Gentry Eng.* 51 Here you see another Cytherea born out of the despumations of our seas of wine.

†**despume** (dɪ'spjuːm), *v. Obs.* [ad. L. *dēspūmāre* (see DESPUMATE), or a. F. *despumer* (16th c.).]

1. *trans.* To skim; to clear of froth or scum.

c **1400** *Lanfranc's Cirurg.* 90 Of hony despumed [*v.r.* dispumed] oz. iiij. *c* **1553** in Hartlib *Legacy* (1655) 232 Take your Alewort.. and into it put of good Honey despumed.. a pound and a half. **1623** COCKERAM, *Despume,* to take vp the scum of a thing. **1655** in Hartlib *Ref. Commw. Bees* 36 Let the tryall be made with about a gallon of Honey, despume it. **1743** *Lond. & Country Brew.* II. (ed. 2) 146 Salting the Water, and despuming as fast as it appears.

2. *intr.* Of a liquid: To cast up a scum or froth.

1613 R. CAWDREY *Table Alph.* (ed. 3), *Despume,* fome, or cast vp a scumme.

Hence **despumed** *ppl. a.*

1601 HOLLAND *Pliny* XXII. xxiv, Made.. of despumed and clarified hony.

despute, obs. var. of DISPUTE.

despyne in *porke despyne*: see PORCUPINE.

desquamate ('dɛskwəmeɪt), *v.* [f. L. *dēsquāmāt-*, ppl. stem of *dēsquāmāre* (trans.) to remove the scales from, to scale, f. DE- I. 2 + *squāma* scale (of a fish, reptile, etc.).]

†**1.** *trans.* To take the scales off, clear from scales, peelings, or loose cuticle; to scale, peel.

1740 DYCHE & PARDON *Desquamate,* to scrape off the fins from fish; and in *Surgery,* to scale off the corrupt or shattered part of bones.

2. *intr.* To come off in the form of scales; to scale off, exfoliate, 'peel'.

1828 COMBE *Const. Man* iii. (1835) 99 As anatomists call it, desquamating; by which they mean, that the cuticle.. comes off in squamæ or scales. **1878** T. BRYANT *Pract. Surg.* I. 53 The cuticle always desquamates.

Hence **'desquamated** *ppl. a.*, scaled off; freed from scales or cuticle, peeled.

1727 BAILEY vol. II, *Desquamated,* scaled, having the Scales taken off. **1845-6** G. E. DAY tr. *Simon's Anim. Chem.* II. 107 Piutti removed all the desquamated cuticle. **1884** BOWER & SCOTT *De Bary's Phaner.* 556 They traverse and support each desquamated zone surrounding the periphery of the stem.

desquamation (dɛskwə'meɪʃən). [noun of action from prec.: see -ATION. (In French, in Dict. Trévoux, 1752).]

1. The removal of scales or of any scaly crust.

1721 BAILEY, *Desquamation* (in *Surgery*) is a scaling of foul bones. **1727-51** CHAMBERS *Cycl., Desquamation,* the act of slaking or scaling carious Bones. **1755** in JOHNSON.

2. A coming off in scales or scaly patches; *esp.* that of the epidermis, as the result of certain diseases; exfoliation, 'peeling'.

1725 HUXHAM in *Phil. Trans.* XXXIII. 389 The Desquammation was very slow, the black Crusts adhering several Days. **1805** W. SAUNDERS *Min. Waters* 105 Obstinate cases of dry desquamations. **1813** J. THOMSON *Lect. Inflam.* 147 Exfoliation or desquamation of the internal membrane. **1839** MURCHISON *Silur. Syst.* I. xxxix. 540 Granite is so prone to desquamation, that nearly all granitic chains are topped with rounded masses, which, though really in situ, have often the appearance of being bowlders. **1880** BEALE *Slight Ailm.* 28 The desquamation and falling off of a good deal of epithelium. **1888** *Times* 14 Apr. 11 Another child.. was in the stage of desquamation.

attrib. **1883** QUAIN *Dict. Med.* s.v. *Scarlet Fever,* The desquamation-period.. is also spoken of as occupying the second week.

3. That which is cast off in scales.

1565-73 COOPER *Thesaurus, Aposirmata* Phisitions call *Desquamations.* **1755** JOHNSON, *Rust,* the red desquamation of old iron.

de'squamative (dɪ'skwæmətɪv), *a.* [f. L. *dēsquāmāt-* (see above) + -IVE.] Tending to or characterized by desquamation, as in *desquamative nephritis, pneumonia,* etc.

1847 DR. G. JOHNSON in *Medico-Chirurg. Trans.* XXX. 170 To the form of renal disease here described as occurring in connection with scarlatina I propose to give the name of *acute desquamative nephritis.* **1876** tr. *Wagner's Gen. Pathol.* 285 Cheesy pneumonia.. proceeds.. from true desquamative pneumonia.

de'squamatory, *a.* and *sb.* [f. as prec. + -ORY.]

A. *adj.* Of or pertaining to desquamation.

1634 T. JOHNSON *Parey's Chirurg.* x. v. (1678) 231 This shall be done with a scaling or Desquamatory Trepan. **1837** PLUMBE *Dis. Skin* (L.), The desquamatory stage now begins.

B. *sb.* A desquamatory trepan.

1668 R. L'ESTRANGE *Vis. Quev.* (1708) 28 In the tail of these, came the Surgeons, laden with Pincers, Crane-bills, Catheters, Desquamatories. **1883** *Syd. Soc. Lex., Desquamatory,* an old form of trephine for removing exfoliations from bones.

†**de'squame,** *v. Obs.*$^{-0}$ [ad. L. *dēsquāmā-re* (see DESQUAMATE).] *trans.* = DESQUAMATE 1.

1623 COCKERAM, *Desquame,* to scale a fish. **1731** BAILEY, *Desquame,* to take off, or scrape off Scales.

desray, obs. form of DERAY.

†**dess,** *sb.*[1] *Obs.* Also **desse.** [a. OF. *deis, dais,* DAIS.] **1.** Obs. form of DAIS.

2. A desk.

1552 HULOET, Desse or lecturne to lay a boke on, *ambonus.* **1596** SPENSER *F.Q.* IV. x. 50 A bevie of fayre damzels.. Wayting when as the Antheme should be sung on hye. The first of them did seeme of ryper yeares.. And next to her sate goodly Shamefastnesse, Ne ever durst her eyes from ground upreare, Ne ever once did looke up from her desse.

dess (dɛs), *sb.*[2] *Sc.* and *north. dial.* Also **dass.** [Of doubtful origin: cf. Icel. *des* in *hey-des* hayrick; but the sense 'layer' suggests that the word is identical with prec. (OF. *deis, dais* raised platform or floor.)]

1. A stratum, a layer.

1674-91 RAY *N.C. Words* 139 First they take the mine picked from the Desse or Rock. **1795** *Statist. Acc. Stirlings.* XV. 327 (Jam.) Then 15 strata of muirstone rise above each other to the summit of the Fells.. in the face of the braes, they go by the name of *dasses* or *gerrocks.* **1818** HOGG *Brownie of B.* II. 61 (Jam.) They soon reached a little dass in the middle of the linn, or what an Englishman would call a small landing-place. **1876** ROBINSON *Whitby Gloss., Dess,* a layer of piled substances; a course in a building. 'Laid up in desses', laid tier upon tier. **1891** ATKINSON *Moorland Parish* 55 He'd getten a haill dess o' shaffs.. and was rife for another dess.

2. (See quots.)

1788 MARSHALL *Provincialisms of E. Yorksh.* in *Rural Economy* (E.D.S.), *Dess,* a cut of hay. **1875** *Lancash. Gloss., Dess* (Fylde distr.), a pile, applied to straw. **1878** *Cumbrld. Gloss., Dess,* a pile, a heap; a truss of hay.

dess, *v. north. dial.* [f. DESS *sb.*[2]]

1. *trans.* To arrange in a layer or layers; to pile up in layers.

1641 BEST *Farm. Bks.* (Surtees) 139 The usuall way for dessinge of strawe. **1674-91** RAY *N.C. Words* 20 *Desse,* to lay close together: to desse Wool, Straw, &c. **1787** GROSE *Prov. Gloss., Desse,*.. in Cumb., to put in order. **1788** MARSHALL *Provincialisms of E. Yorksh., Dess up,* to pile up neatly. **1851** *Cumbrld. Gloss., Dess,* to lay carefully together. **1855** ROBINSON *Whitby Gloss., Dess'd up,* piled up.

2. To cut (a section of hay) from a stack.

1787 GROSE *Prov. Gloss.* **1847-78** in HALLIWELL.

3. *intr.* To work in a stratum or strata; to hew out particular strata or layers from the face of a cliff.

1876 ROBINSON *Whitby Gloss.* s.v., 'They're dessing for jet', i.e. hacking it out of the layers or desses, when it occurs .. on the face of the cliff. **1882** *Good Cheer* 61 You knew he was getting jet, dessing in Helabeck Bight yonder.

'dessably, *adv. north. dial.* [Cf. DESSANTLY.]

1674-91 RAY *N.C. Words, Dessably,* constantly. **1855** ROBINSON *Whitby Gloss., Dessably,* orderly in point of arrangement.

dessait, -ate, -ayte, obs. ff. DECEIT.

†**'dessantly,** *adv. Obs. rare.* [Etymol. uncertain; cf. DESS *v.*, DESSELY.] Continuously.

c **1400** *Beryn* 790 In whose tyme sikirlich, þe vii. sagis were In Rome dwelling dessantly. *Ibid.* 1563 Ffor thre dayis dessantly þe derknes a-mong hem was.

des(s)atine, varr. DESSIATINE.

dessaue, -ayfe, -ayue, obs. ff. DECEIVE.

dessay ('dɛseɪ), repr. a form of pronunciation of (*I*) *dare say* (DARE *v.* III).

1905 H. G. WELLS *Kipps* III. i. 369 'You ought to join the volunteers, my boy.'.. 'I dessay I shall,' said Kipps.

dessayse, -seize, obs. ff. DISEASE, DISSEISE.

desse, var. of DESS *sb.*[1]

dessece, -eit, obs. ff. DECEASE, DECEIT.

† **dessely,** *adv. Obs.* Also -lic, -li. [Cf. DESS *v.*, DESSABLY.] Continuously.

a **1300** *Cursor M.* 11406 (Cott.) Did þam in a montain dern Desselic to wait þe stern. *Ibid.* 17719 (Cott.) Desseli to god praiand, Wit sacrifijs and wit offrand. *Ibid.* 19033 (Cott.) Þai .. desseli bath late and are War tentand to þe apostels lare. *Ibid.* 26881 (Cott.) Als if he desseli did ill.

dessende, -ente, obs. ff. DESCEND, DESCENT.

dessert (dɪˈzɜːt). Also 7–8 desert, 8 des-, disart, 9 desert. [a. F. *dessert* (Estienne 1539) 'removal of the dishes, dessert', f. *desservir* to remove what has been served, to clear (the table), f. *des-*, L. *dis-* + *servir* to serve.]

1. a. A course of fruit, sweetmeats, etc. served after a dinner or supper; 'the last course at an entertainment' (J.).

1600 W. VAUGHAN *Direct. Health* (1633) II. ix. 54 Such eating, which the French call desert, is unnaturall. **1666** PEPYS *Diary* 12 July, The desert coming, with roses upon it, the Duchesse bid him try. **1708** W. KING *Cookery* 261 'Tis the dessert that graces all the feast. **1739** R. BULL tr. *Dedekindus' Grobianus* 96 If the Guests may pocket the Desart. **1834** LYTTON *Pompeii* IV. iii, The dessert or last course was already on the table. **1846** J. BAXTER *Libr. Pract. Agric.* (ed. 4) II. 69 The Medlar.. when in a state of incipient decay is employed for the dessert. **1875** JOWETT *Plato* (ed. 2) III. 696 Pleasant kinds of dessert, with which we amuse ourselves after dinner.

b. 'In the United States often used to include pies, puddings, and other sweet dishes' (*Cent. Dict.*). Now also in British usage.

1789 W. MACLAY *Jrnl.* 27 Aug. (1890) iv. 138 The dessert was, first apple-pies, pudding, etc.; then iced creams, jellies, etc.; then water-melons, musk-melons, apples, peaches, nuts. **1833** H. BARNARD in *Maryland Hist. Mag.* (1918) XIII. 379 The desert was pudding—cherry pie—and strawberries, cream and sugar. **1846** J. C. PATTESON *Let.* in C. M. Yonge *Life J.C.P.* (1874) I. iii. 51, I have to give several parties.. as the pastrycook's bill for desserts will show. **1848–60** in BARTLETT *Dict. Amer.* **1864** A. V. KIRWAN (*title*) Host & guest: a book about dinners, wines, and desserts. *Ibid.* xv. 213 A dessert should above all things be simple. *Ibid.* 229 Brandied fruits, *compotes* and fruits preserved in syrup, are generally produced at a French dessert. **1887** *Scribner's Mag.* (Farmer), The pastry-cook [in Paris] is very useful. He supplies.. such dessert (I use the word in the American sense) as an ordinary cook could not be expected to make. **1935** W. CATHER *Lucy Gayheart* I. iii. 23 He might have asked her and the boys to go out to the dining-car with him and have a dessert. **1966** *Woman* 24 Sept. Pullout 1 (*heading*) A starter. A main dish. A dessert.

2. *attrib.* and *Comb.* **dessert-knife, -plate, -spoon,** etc., those used for the dessert; a *dessert-spoon* is intermediate in size between a table-spoon and a tea-spoon; **dessert-service,** the dishes, plates, and other requisites used in serving dessert.

1765 J. WEDGWOOD *Let.* 6 July (1965) 35 Mr Grants desert service will be sent today. **1769** *Ibid.* 20 Sept. (1965) 80, I have modeled you three or four sorts of desert plates. **1773** DOUGLASS in *Phil. Trans.* LXIII. 294 It is a common desert wine. **1793** W. B. STEVENS *Jrnl.* 6 June (1965) I. 86 He stabbed himself in three Places with a Desert Knife. **1808** JANE AUSTEN *Let.* 27 Dec. (1952) 243 A whole tablespoon and a whole dessert-spoon, and six whole teaspoons. **1851** MRS. GASKELL *Let.* Apr. (1966) 152 Miss Yates gives her a dessert service. **1860** *All Year Round* No. 40. 564 An eye as large as a dessert-plate. **1861** DELAMER *Kitch. Gard.* 144 Dessert apples and kitchen apples can hardly be distinguished. **1870** RAMSAY *Remin.* vi. (ed. 18) 203 The servant.. put down.. a dessert-spoon. **1875** *Fam. Herald* 13 Nov. 30/2 Take.. one dessertspoonful of allspice. **1911** *Daily Colonist* (Victoria, B.C.) 27 Apr. 3/1 (Advt.), Dessert Knives, Sheffield steel, fine handles. **1926–7** *Army & Navy Stores Catal.* 702/1 A Dessert Service consists of 12 Plates and 6 Dishes.

desseyse, -eyt, -eyue, obs. ff. DECEASE, DECEIT, DECEIVE.

‖**dessiatine, desyatin** (ˈdɛsjətiːn). Also des(s)atine, desaetine, dessjaetine. [ad. Russ. *desyatina* lit. 'tenth, tithe'.] A Russian superficial measure of 2400 sq. sazhens.

1799 W. TOOKE *View Russian Emp.* II. 345 A desaetine and a half of land was bought, with the bours upon it. **1814** W. BROWN *Hist. Propag. Chr.* II. 542 A dessatine contains 117,600 English sq. feet. **1889** tr. *Tolstoi's Anna Karénina* 166 Instead of sowing down twenty-four desyatins, they had only planted six. **1892** *Times* 3 Mar. 3/3 Some 15,761 dessiatines of grain-growing land, or.. over 40,000 acres. (A 'dessiatine' being about $2\frac{3}{4}$ acres.) **1901** *Daily Chron.* 29 Aug. 5/1 The Tsar is said.. to own in private property, mostly in the Baltic Provinces, a million desatines of land.

‖**dessous** (dəsu). [Fr., = lower part; (pl.) underclothing (of women).] **1.** Underwear.

1901 'C. HOLLAND' *Mousmé* 285 Mousmé had adopted the dainty *dessous* of Western woman. **1902** E. GLYN *Refl. Ambrosine* 237 The tiniest pink satin slippers peeped out of billows of exquisite *dessous*.

2. Phr. *dessous des cartes*: the underside of the cards as they lie face downwards when dealt; *fig.* a secret aim or object, explanation, etc. kept in reserve.

1756 LD. CHESTERFIELD *Let. to Dayrolles* 26 Nov., Misc. Wks. 1777 II. 435 There must be some *dessous des cartes*, some invisible wheels within wheels, which.. I cannot guess at. **1820** A. A. OPIE *Tales* IV. 271 Sir Walter and Arthur laughed at this *dessous des cartes*. **1885** 'L. MALET' *Col. Enderby's Wife* IV. iii, Just a little something behind, an explanation, you know, a *dessous-des-cartes*.

ˌdestabiliˈzation. [f. DESTABILIZE *v.* + -ATION.] The act or process of rendering unstable, esp. (in political contexts) of a country or government by foreign interference.

1974 *N.Y. Times* 8 Sept. 26/2 The 40 Committee authorized an expenditure of $1-million for 'further political destabilization' activities in August 1973, one month before the military junta seized control in Santiago. **1980** *Christian Science Monitor* (Midwestern ed.) 4 Dec. 1/2 At the State Department, analysts foresee a fairly rapid process of 'destabilization' in Poland. **1983** S. NAIPAUL *Hot Country* vii. 109 Alex replaced the book.. and pulled out another — a study of the destabilisation campaign waged by the United States against Allende's Chile.

destabilize (diːˈsteɪbɪlaɪz), *v.* [f. DE- II. 1 + STABILIZE *v.*] *trans.* To deprive of stability, to render unstable.

1934 in WEBSTER. **1961** *Guardian* 24 Oct. 8/4 A first strike, which would destabilise the overall strategic situation. **1965** PHILLIPS & WILLIAMS *Inorg. Chem.* I. ii. 52 It also appears to destabilize the *d* electrons slightly.

So **deˈstabilizing** *vbl. sb.* and *ppl. a.*

1924 W. M. HUGHES in *These Eventful Years* II. 285 The creation of a new political party.. seems likely to have a de-stabilising influence on Commonwealth politics. **1962** *Economist* 28 Apr. 366/1 Excessive and destabilising flows of short-term capital. **1962** W. B. THOMPSON *Introd. Plasma Physics* vi. 120 Where *I* is the total current enclosed within a cylinder of radius *r*, this de-stabilizing term is [etc.]. **1965** H. KAHN *On Escalation* xiii. 269 Ordinary technology might be almost as destabilizing as the.. 'doomsday machine'.

de'stain, *v.* Archaic variant of DISTAIN.

de-Stalinize (diːˈstɑːlɪnaɪz), *v.* [f. DE- II. 1 + *Stalin* (adopted name of Iosif Vissarionovich Dzhugashvili (1879–1953), head of government of the Soviet Union) + -IZE.] *intr.* To counteract the excesses of Stalinism or the influence of Stalin, as by reversing or amending his policies, removing monuments to him, and renaming places named in his honour; also *trans.*, to affect in some way by **de-Staliniˈzation.** So **de-ˈStalinized** *ppl. a.*; **de-ˈStalinizing** *vbl. sb.*; **de-ˈStalinizer.**

1957 *Economist* 28 Sept. 1013 The echoes of destalinisation and Hungary have reverberated among the Apennines. **1959** *Times* 7 Feb. 7/6 The GUM department store.. where.. escalators carry hopeful consumers through six floors of de-Stalinized delight. **1960** *Guardian* 20 Apr. 8/5 Russia decided to de-Stalinize in design. **1962** *Times* 6 Feb. 15/1 The so-called de-Stalinization policy. **1962** *Listener* 8 Mar. 404/1 Mr Barak's real offence was to be.. too keen a de-Stalinizer in Czechoslovakia itself. **1963** *Daily Tel.* 23 Sept. 12/2 The dismissal of the Prime Minister.. and other 'de-Stalinising' changes. **1965** *Spectator* 5 Mar. 285/1 This giant-size statue of Stalin, stationed at the end of the Volga Don Canal in Volgograd, was demolished in the wake of destalinisation.

destance, obs. f. DISTANCE, variance, disagreement.

destane, -anye, -ayne, obs. ff. DESTINE, DESTINY.

† **deˈstate,** *v. Obs.* [f. DE- II. 2 + STATE *sb.*] *trans.* To divest of state or grandeur.

16.. T. ADAMS *Wks.* (1861) I. 430 (D.) The king of eternal glory, to the world's eye destating himself.. was cast down for us that we might rise up by him.

deste, obs. pa. t. of DASH *v.*

c **1320** *Sir Tristr.* 2396 Ouer þe bregge he deste.

destemper, obs. form of DISTEMPER.

desten(e, -nie, obs. ff. DESTINE, DESTINY.

† **ˈdester.** *Obs. rare.* [a. OF. *destre* right hand:—L. *dextra.*] The right hand.

a **1300** *Body & Soul* 35 (Mätz.) Thi proude palefreys and thi stedes that thouȝ haddest in dester [OF. *en destre*] leddes.

† **desternute,** *v. Obs. rare*—⁰. [f. L. *dē*, DE- I. 3 + *sternuĕre, sternūt-*, or *sternūtāre*, to sneeze.] So **dester'nutament.**

1623 COCKERAM I 1, To sneeze, *Desternute*. A sneezing, *Desternutament*.

† **de'stert,** *v. Obs. rare*—⁰. [cf. L. *dēstertĕre* to cease snoring.]

1623 COCKERAM, *Desterting*, snorting.

destestable, obs. var. of DETESTABLE.

desteyne, -nye, obs. ff. DISTAIN, DESTINE, DESTINY.

† **ˈdesticate,** *v. Obs. rare*—⁰. [f. ppl. stem of L. *dēsticāre* to squeak as a shrew-mouse.]

1623 COCKERAM, *Desticate*. to cry like a rat.

Hence **destiˈcation,** (*rare*) squeaking.

1820 *Sporting Mag.* VII. 119 It was the destication of a mouse, who.. had got himself an unwelcome visitor in the cage of my favourite magpye.

de Stijl: see STIJL.

destill, -ation, obs. ff. DISTIL, DISTILLATION.

† **ˈdestin, destine,** *sb. Obs.* [a. F. *destin* masc. = It., Sp., Pg. *destine*, or OF. *destine* fem. destiny, f. *destiner* to DESTINE.] = DESTINY *sb.*

1575 CHURCHYARD *Chippes* (1817) 211 Makes an ende, as destine hath assignde. **1590** T. WATSON *Death Sir F. Walsingham*, Poems (Arb.) 151 By Destins fatall knife Sweet Melibœus is depriu'd of life. **1599** MARSTON *Sco. Vill.* II. viii. 211 The Destin's adamantine band. **1616** DRUMM. OF HAWTH. *Song* Poems 14 This hold to brave the skies the Destines framed. —— *Statue of Adonis*, She sighed, and said: 'What power breaks Destine's law?'

† **ˈdestinable,** *a. Obs.* [a. OF. *destinable* fatal, f. *destiner* to DESTINE: see -ABLE.

(Occurs once in MSS. of Chaucer's *Boethius*, but in 16th c. edd. is substituted five times for DESTINAL of the MS.)]

Of, pertaining to, or fixed by destiny; fated, fatal. Hence **ˈdestinably** *adv.* (in printed edd. of Chaucer).

c **1374** CHAUCER *Boeth.* IV. pr. vi. (Skeat) l. 251 He chaseth out al yvel fro the boundes of his comunalitee by the order of necessitee destinable. **1530** PALSGR. 310/1 Destynable, apoynted to be ones destenye, *destinable*. **1550–61** *Chaucer's Boeth.* IV. pr. vi. 219 b/2 (Sk. l. 70) The destinable [MS. destinal] ordinaunce is wouen and accomplished. *Ibid.* (Sk. l. 56), The order destinably [MS. destinal] proceedeth of the simplicitie of purveighaunce.

† **ˈdestinacy.** *Obs.* [f. L. *dēstināt-us, dēstināt-io*: see -ACY.] Destination, appointment.

1490 CAXTON *Eneydos* xix. 70 The successyon is unto hym due of ryghte heredytalle and by veraye destynacy after my deth.

† **ˈdestinal,** *a. Obs.* [f. DESTIN *sb.* or F. *destin* + -AL¹.] Of, pertaining to, or according to destiny or fate.

c **1374** CHAUCER *Boeth.* IV. pr. vi. (Skeat) l. 80 They surmounten the ordre of destinal moevabletee. *Ibid.* V. pr. ii. 4 Elles I wolde witen yif that the destinal cheyne constreineth the movinges of the corages of men? [And three other examples.]

(In the 16th c. printed edd. altered to DESTINABLE.)

destiˈnarian. *nonce-wd.* [f. DESTINE *v.*, after *predestinarian*.] A believer in destiny.

1838 *New Monthly Mag.* LII. 52 They seem to be destinarians—to have a dull apprehension that everything moves on in its preordained course.

† **ˈdestinate,** *ppl. a.* (*sb.*) *Obs.* or *arch.* [ad. L. *dēstināt-us*, pa. pple. of *dēstināre* to DESTINE.]

1. Fated, ordained; = DESTINED 1. **a.** as *pple.*

a **1400–50** *Alexander* 692 So was me destinate [*Ashm. MS.* destaned] to dy. **1480** CAXTON *Chron. Eng.* ccxxxii, That northeren winde that is ever ready and destynat to all evel. **1561** T. NORTON *Calvin's Inst.* III. 315 They are destinate to destruction. *c* **1611** CHAPMAN *Iliad* xxiv. 468 The Gods have destinate That wretched mortals must live sad. **1634** HABINGTON *Castara* (Arb.) 107 A small flye By a fooles finger destinate to dye.

b. as *adj.*

1605 *Lond. Prodigal* I. i, That a bad conscience may bring him to his destinate repentance. *a* **1659** BP. MORTON *Episc. Asserted* 99 (T.) Walo Messalinus, a destinate adversary to episcopacy.

2. Set apart for a particular purpose; ordained; intended; = DESTINED 2. **a.** as *pa. pple.*

1610 W. FOLKINGHAM *Art of Survey* I. xi. 38 Dry stony layers are destinate to white Saxifrage, Bugle, Lauender. **1671** F. PHILLIPS *Reg. Necess.* 199 Admitted into an Inns of Court, heretofore only destinate and appropriate to the sons of Nobility.

b. as *adj.*

1583 STANYHURST *Aeneis* II. (Arb.) 63 See that you doe folow youre moothers destinat order. *a* **1619** FOTHERBY *Atheom.* I. Pref. (1622) 8 The destinate end, and scope of this worke. **1660** GAUDEN *God's Gt. Demonstr.* 35 Wilful murther and destinate villany.

B. *sb.* That which is destined; a fated or appointed event, etc.

1675 R. BURTHOGGE *Causa Dei* 153 Destinates are said to be in vain, if either they are insufficiently, or not at all, referred to their Ends.

destinate (ˈdɛstɪneɪt), *v.* Now *rare.* [f. L. *dēstināt-*, ppl. stem of *dēstināre*: see DESTINE *v.*]

1. *trans.* To ordain, appoint: = DESTINE *v.* 1.

1490 CAXTON *Eneydos* xiii. 47 To doo sacrefyces destynated vnto the noble goddesse Ceres. **1586** FERNE *Blaz. Gentrie* 94 Vsurping that facultye and vocation at the first destinated as peculiar to gentlemen. **1638** BAKER tr. *Balzac's Lett.* I. (1654) 7 You are destinated to fill the place of that Cardinal. **1712** LD. KING *Primitive Church* II. 5 He that read the Scriptures, was particularly destinated to this office. *c* **1870** J. G. MURPHY *Comm. Lev.* i. 4 Laying the hand on is the solemn act of designating or destinating to a certain purpose.

† **b.** To doom, sentence (to a punishment); to ordain or appoint (a punishment) to be inflicted.

1579 FENTON *Guicciard.* v. (1618) 211 Destinated to a more slow, but to a greater punishment. **1611** SPEED *Hist. Gt. Brit.* VIII. i. (1632) 393 Whom the Priest by casting of lots had destinated to death. **1621** G. SANDYS *Ovid's Met.* XIII. (1626) 269 [She] Still Queen-like, destinates his punishment. **1652** L. S. *People's Liberty* x. 24 To preserve their Bishop Eusebius from banishment, to which Valens their Emperour had destinated him.

2. To appoint or predetermine in the way of fate or of a divine decree; *pass.* to be divinely appointed or fated; = DESTINE *v.* 2.

1548 UDALL, etc. *Erasm. Par. Matt.* i. (R.) That name that God.. did destinate and appoynt vnto hym, before the creation of the worlde. *a* **1617** BAYNE *On Ephes.* (1658) 156 Christ is a head of those only whom God hath destinated to convert. **1618** BOLTON *Florus* IV. i. 260 The man..to whom soveraignty was destinated in Sibylls verses. **1651** WITTIE *Primrose's Pop. Err.* II. viii. 105 The Turks..doe not regard the Pestilence, because they thinke that God hath destinated to every one his manner of death.

b. To determine the destiny of.

1839 BAILEY *Festus* viii. (1848) 91 It is love which mostly destinates our life.

3. To devote in intention to a particular purpose or use; to intend, design, allot; = DESTINE *v.* 3.

1555 EDEN *Decades* 157 Suche as they destinate to eate they geld. **1615** G. SANDYS *Trav.* 83 Decking their houses with branches of cypresse: a tree destinated to the dead. **1621** BURTON *Anat. Mel.* I. ii. III. xv, We that are bred up in learning, and destinated by our parents to this end. **1745** tr. *Columella's Husb.* II. xviii, Having plowed up..the place we have destinated for a meadow. **1826** SOUTHEY *Vind. Eccl. Angl.* 303 If they were not destinated to their profession from childhood.

†**b.** *pass.* To be designed by nature. *Obs.*

1578 BANISTER *Hist. Man* VIII. 108 Nature..prouided for the safe conduict of this Nerue, since to the midreif it was destinated. **1635** SWAN *Spec. M.* iii. §3 (1643) 53 The night ..is destinated or appointed for quiet and sleep. **1660** tr. *Amyraldus' Treat. conc. Relig.* I. vi. 91 The action of seeing, to which the eye is destinated. **1691** RAY *Creation* (1714) 262 Birds..being destinated to fly among the branches of trees. **1742** *Lond. & Country Brew.* I. (ed. 4) B, Our Mother Earth ..is destinated to the Service of Man in the Production of Vegetation.

Hence ˈ**destinating** *vbl. sb.* and *ppl. a.*

1633 PRYNNE *Histrio-Mastix* I. ii. (R.), The destinating, and denoting of vnprofitable..and vnnecessary inventions. **1652** GAULE *Magastrom.* 130 To depend upon the destinating stars.

destinated (ˈdɛstɪneɪtɪd), *ppl. a. arch.* or *Obs.* [f. prec. vb. + -ED[1].] Appointed, predetermined; destined, fated: see prec. vb.

1604 R. CAWDREY *Table Alph.*, *Destinated*, appointed. **1615** CROOKE *Body of Man* 216 The destinated corruption of the matter. *a* **1649** DRUMM. OF HAWTH. *Hist. Jas. III*, Wks. (1711) 59 The rendevouz and destinated place of meeting. **1688** BOYLE *Final Causes Nat. Things* iv. 214 That this..is the particular destinated use of such a thing.

destination (dɛstɪˈneɪʃən). [ad. L. *dēstinātiōn-em*, n. of action from *dēstināre* to DESTINE: cf. F. *destination* (12– 13th c.) perh. the immediate source, It. *destinazione*.]

1. The action of destining, appointing, foreordaining, or setting apart to a particular use, purpose, or end; the fact of being destined. (In mod. use influenced by sense 2.)

1598 FLORIO, *Destinatione*, destination. **1623** COCKERAM, *Destination*, an appointment. **1628** SPENCER *Logick* 208 The flesh of man and beasts doe differ in their proper being, and Gods destination. **1755** YOUNG *Centaur* i. Wks. 1757 IV. 114 It is said, there must be heresies..And why? There is.. no fatal necessity for them, from God's destination. **1762** KAMES *Elem. Crit.* (1763) I. ii. 246 No other branch of the human constitution shows more visibly our destination for society..than appetite for fame. **1868** M. PATTISON *Academ. Org.* v. 120 That the destination given to these endowments by their founders was wise and politic.

b. *transf.* The end or purpose for which a person or thing is destined; in quot. 1749, the profession or business for which a person is destined.

a **1656** BP. J. HALL *Rem. Wks.* (1660) II. 258 Relative, I say, not inherent in themselves but in reference to their use, and destination. **1749** CHESTERF. *Lett.* II. ccvii. 293 In your destination you will have frequent occasions to speak in public. **1755** YOUNG *Centaur* ii. Wks. 1757 IV. 160 There is not a fly, but has had infinite wisdom concern'd not only in its structure, but in its destination. **1795** CHRISTIAN in *Blackstone's Comm.* (1809) IV. 82 Sending intelligence to the enemy of the destinations and designs of this kingdom, in order to assist them in their operations against us..is high treason. **1876** MOZLEY *Univ. Serm.* xiii. 235 A destination above the objects, the employments, and the abilities of this world.

2. *spec.* The fact of being destined or bound for a particular place; hence, short for ***place of destination***, the place for which a person or thing is destined; the intended end of a journey or course. (Now the usual sense.)

1787 CANNING *Microcosm.* No. 32 ¶2 That traveller will arrive sooner at his place of destination. **1797** MRS. RADCLIFFE *Italian* vi, Anxiety as to the place of her destination. *a* **1813** SOUTHEY *Nelson* I. 199 (L.) 'It [the fleet] has as many destinations' he [Nelson] said 'as there were countries'. **1828** WEBSTER, s.v., The ship left her destination; but it is more usual to say, the place of her destination. **1832** HT. MARTINEAU *Ireland* iii. 45 She..held by his arm till they arrived at their destination. **1885** *Act 48–49 Vict.* c. 60 §20 Ships..whose last port of clearance or port of destination is in any such possession. **1891** *Leeds Mercury* 27 May 5/1 [He] has at length arrived at his destination.

3. *Sc. Law.* **a.** The nomination, by the will of the proprietor, of successors to heritable or movable property in a certain order. **b.** The series of heirs succeeding to such property, whether by will or by the course of law.

1754 ERSKINE *Princ. Sc. Law* (1809) 130 Subjects originally moveable become heritable: 1. By the proprietor's destination. Thus, a jewel, or any other moveable subject, may be provided to the heir. **1861** W. BELL *Dict. Law Scot.* s.v., A destination 'to A. and his heirs of line', carries the property to the heir in heritage, exclusive of the heir of conquest..A destination to heirs-male excludes females. **1884** *Law Reports* 9 App. Cases 325 Destinations in favour of such third persons..are presumed to be testamentary and revocable.

destinator (ˈdɛstɪneɪtə(r)). *rare.* [a. L. *dēstinātor*, agent-n. from *dēstināre* to DESTINE.] One who destines; one who fixes or pronounces a destiny; a dealer in destinies.

1579 J. JONES *Preserv. Bodie & Soul* I. xli. 94 Detestable Southsayers, and dissembling destinators. **1610** BP. WEBBE *Posie Spir. Flowers*, Time's Creator and destinator.

destine (ˈdɛstɪn), *v.* Forms: 4–5 destayn(e, 4–6 -ten, 5 -tan(e, -teyne, 5–6 -tyne, 6 -tyng, 6– destine. [a. F. *destiner* (12th c. in Hatz.-Darm.), ad. L. *dēstināre* to make fast or firm, establish, destine, f. DE- I. 3 + **stanāre*, causal deriv. of *stāre* to stand.]

†**1.** *trans.* To ordain, appoint (formally or definitely). *Obs.* (or merged in 3.)

c **1400** *Destr. Troy* 2673 It was desteynid by dome, & for due holdyn..Thay affermyt hit fully. **1613** J. SALKELD *Treat. Angels* 80 [Angels] destined for the perpetuall motion of the heavens. **1761** HUME *Hist. Eng.* I. x. 105 His appanage, which the late king had destined him. **1881** DUFFIELD *Don Quix.* I. xxv. 344 This is the place, O ye heavens! which I destine and select for bewailing the misfortune.

2. As the act of the Deity, Fate, or a supernatural power: To appoint or fix beforehand, to predetermine by an unalterable decree or ordinance. Now chiefly in *pass.*: To be divinely appointed or fated; often in weakened sense, expressing little more than the actual issue of events as ascertained by subsequent experience, without any definite reference to their predetermination. (Usually with *inf.*)

c **1300** [see DESTINING below]. *a* **1340** HAMPOLE *Psalter* lxviii. 33 þe boke of life is þe knawynge of god, in þe whilke he has destaynd all good men to be safe. *a* **1400–50** *Alexander* 518 A barne..þat driȝtyn after þi day has destaned to regne. *c* **1489** CAXTON *Sonnes of Aymon* vii. 176 Yf god destyneth hym, he shall wynne the pryse. **1583** G. BUCKE *Commend. verses, Watson's Centurie of Loue*, The starr's, which did at Petrarch's byrthday raigne, Were fixt againe at thy natiuity, Destening thee the Thuscan's poesie. *a* **1680** BUTLER *Rem.* (1759) I. 13 Since the World..prevents Our best and worst Experiments; (As if th' were destin'd to miscarry). **1719** YOUNG *Revenge* IV. i, Lovers destin'd for each other. **1816** WILSON *City of Plague* II. ii. 95 Two such souls Are not by God destined to live apart. **1856** EMERSON *Eng. Traits, Result* Wks. (Bohn) II. 134 Their [the English] speech seems destined to be the universal language of men. **1870** E. PEACOCK *Ralf Skirl.* III. 213 He was, however, not destined to escape so easily. **1874** GREEN *Short Hist.* vii. §1. 343 One who was destined to eclipse even the fame of Colet as a popular preacher.

b. quasi-*impers.* (*passive* or *active*) with indirect obj. and infin. (subject).

?*a* **1400** *Morte Arth.* 664 If me be destaynede to dye at Dryghtyns wylle. *a* **1400–50** *Alexander* 692 So was me destaned to dye. *Ibid.* 4115 þat oþer dai be desert þam destaned to ride.

3. To fix or set apart in intention for a particular purpose, use, end, course of action, etc.; to design, intend, devote, allot. (Most commonly in *pass.*)

c **1530** LD. BERNERS *Arth. Lyt. Bryt.* (1814) 408 Kyng Godyfer dyd destyng hym selfe to come on Gouernar as fast as he might; but Hector met him fyrst, and..ouerthrew him. **1541** R. COPLAND *Galyen's Terapeutyke* 2 Hij b, Hunny must be medled in all medicamentes destined & ordeyned to the vlcere of the Thorax. **1658** EVELYN *Fr. Gard.* (1675) 227 Some of these beds you must destine to be eaten young and green. **1707** *Curios. in Husb. & Gard.* 31 The little Hole..towards the..Extremity of the Bean, is destin'd for the Entrance of..aqueous Parts. **1718** LADY M. W. MONTAGU *Let. to C'tess of Bristol* 10 Apr., The apartment destined for Audiences. **1818** JAS. MILL *Brit. India* III. ii. 68 The time which was destined for re-assembling the parliament. **1822** SCOTT *Pirate* xxiii, With how little security man can reckon upon the days which he destines to happiness. **1844** LINGARD *Anglo-Sax. Ch.* (1858) II. xiv. 302 The ship destined to transport the missionaries.

4. *pass. to be destined*: to be bound (*for* a particular place): see DESTINED *ppl. a.* 2 b.

Hence †ˈ**destining** *vbl. sb. Obs.*

c **1300** *K. Alis.* 6867 Of God hit was thy destenyng. *c* **1440** *Gaw. & Gol.* 270 Dede be my destenyng.

destine, obs. f. DESTIN, DESTINY.

destined (ˈdɛstɪnd), *ppl. a.* [f. prec. vb. + -ED[1].]

1. Appointed or fixed by fate, or by a divine decree or purpose; foreordained, pre-determined, fated. (Now often in weakened sense = 'that is (or was) to be'; cf. prec. 2.)

1597 SHAKS. *Lover's Compl.* 156 But ah, who ever shunn'd by precedent The destined ill she must herself assay? **1637** MILTON *Lycidas* 20 So may some gentle Muse With lucky words favour my destined urn. **1697** DRYDEN *Virg. Æneid* I, Before he won the Latian realm, and built the destin'd town. *c* **1703** PRIOR *Ode Col. G. Villiers* 92 The infernal judge's dreadful pow'r, From the dark urn shall throw thy destin'd hour. **1810** SCOTT *Lady of L.* I. xxiv, A destined errant knight I come, Announced by prophet sooth and old. **1887** BOWEN *Virg. Æneid* III. 145 When this burden of woe to its destined end will be brought.

†**b.** 'Devoted', doomed. *Obs.*

a **1721** PRIOR (J.), May Heav'n around this destin'd head The choicest of its curses shed.

2. Fixed in human intention; intended, designed: cf. prec. 3.

1661 BRAMHALL *Just Vind.* iv. 87 Their long destined project. **1709** STEELE *Tatler* No. 58 ¶1 To restore her to her destined Husband. **1754** DODSLEY *Agric.* III. (R.), To reach the destin'd goal.

b. *spec.* Fixed or appointed to go to a particular destination; = BOUND *ppl. a.*[1] 2.

c **1790** WILLOCK *Voy.* 20 [They] proceed to whatever ship they are destined. **1853** PHILLIPS *Rivers Yorksh.* ix. 239 The troops destined for Britain, usually marched through Gaul. **1888** *Pall Mall G.* 3 Apr. 13/2 There were some railway phrases then [1838–9] introduced..You were asked the place to which you were 'destined', the place itself being your 'destination'.

destinee (ˌdɛstɪˈniː). *nonce-wd.* [see -EE.] The person for whom something (as a message, etc.) is destined.

1881 *Blackw. Mag.* Apr. 472 'Meet me at half-past seven' often reaches the destinee as 'Meet me at half-past eleven'.

destinee, destinie, obs. forms of DESTINY.

destinezite (dɛstɪˈneɪzaɪt). *Min.* [Named 1881 after M. Destinez: see -ITE.] A phosphate of iron, a variety of diadochite, from Visé in Belgium.

1882 DANA *Min.* App. iii. 36.

destinist (ˈdɛstɪnɪst). *rare.* [f. DESTINY + -IST.] A believer in destiny, a fatalist. So ˈ**destinism**, belief in destiny, fatalism. (In mod. Dicts.)

1846 WORCESTER, *Destinist*, a believer in destiny; fatalist. *Phren. Jour.*

†**destinour.** *Obs.* [a. AFr. *destinour*, OF. *destineor*, ad. L. *dēstinātōr* DESTINATOR.] He who destines; the Author of destiny.

c **1400** tr. *Secreta Secret.* (E.E.T.S.), *Govt. Lordsch.* 65 Men oghte wyth byse prayers bysek þe heghe destynour ..þat he wille oþerwyse ordeyne.

destiny (ˈdɛstɪnɪ), *sb.* Forms: 4 destine, -ene(é), -ane(e, 4–5 destyne, -ynie, -any(e, 4–6 destenie, -enye, 4–7 -eny, 5 -inee, -ynee, -eyne, -enye, -ayne, disteyne, -yne, 5–6 destyny, -onie, -onye, 6–7 destinie, 6– destiny. [ME., a. OF. *destinée* (12th c. in Littré) = Pr. *destinada*, It. *destinata*, fem. sb. from L. pa. pple. *dēstinātus*, *-a*: see -ADE suffix.]

I. As a fact or condition.

1. That which is destined or fated to happen; predetermined events collectively; = FATE *sb.* 3 a.

1340–70 *Alisaunder* 1026 Hee shall bee doluen and ded as destenie falles. *c* **1425** WYNTOUN *Cron.* VI. xiii. 134 And sua ware brokyn Destyne. *c* **1440** *Promp. Parv.* 120 Desteyne, or happe..*fatum.* **1717** tr. *Leibnitz* in Clarke & Leibnitz *Collect. Papers* v. 165 There is *Fatum Christianum*, A certain destiny of every thing, regulated by the foreknowledge and providence of God. **1849** WHITTIER *Voices of Freedom, Crisis* x, This day we fashion Destiny, our web of Fate we spin.

†**b.** A declaration or prognostication of what is fated to happen. *Obs. rare.*

1602 FULBECKE *Pandectes* 40 Æneas commeth into Italie to maintaine warre by destinies, and oracles.

2. That which is destined to happen to a particular person, country, institution, etc.; (one's) appointed lot or fortune; what one is destined to do or suffer; = FATE *sb.* 3 b.

c **1325** *E.E. Allit. P.* C. 49 ȝif me be dyȝt a destyne due to haue. *c* **1386** CHAUCER *Knt.'s T.* 250 If so be my destynee be shapen By eterne word to dyen in prisoun. *c* **1450** *Merlin* 582 On monday by goode distyne we shall meve alle to go towarde Clarence. **1548** HALL *Chron.* 91 The common people lamented their miserable destiny. **1583** STUBBES *Anat. Abus.* II. (1882) 63 Oh, I was borne to it, it was my destonie. **1596** SHAKS. *Merch. V.* II. ix. 83 The ancient saying..Hanging and wiuing goes by destinie. **1605** —— *Macb.* III. v. 17 Thither he Will come, to know his Destinie. **1665** SIR T. HERBERT *Trav.* (1677) 63 The reward and destiny due to Traytors overtakes them. **1812** J. WILSON *Isle of Palms* II. 586 Sublimely reconciled To meet and bear her destiny. **1841** MISS MITFORD in L'Estrange *Life* III. viii. 117 All literary people die overwrought; it is the destiny of the class.

3. In weakened sense (cf. DESTINE *v.* 2): What in the course of events will become or has become of a person or thing; ultimate condition; = FATE *sb.* 4. (Also in *pl.*; cf. *fortunes.*)

1555 EDEN *Decades* 58 The vnfortunate destenie of Petrus de Vmbria. **1665** SIR T. HERBERT *Trav.* (1677) 272 Jacob was murdered..and Issuff died of an Imposthume. Their Children also had little better destiny. **1716** LADY M. W. MONTAGU *Let. to Lady X—* 1 Oct., They seem worthy of another destiny. **1855** H. REED *Lect. Eng. Hist.* iv. 120 That battle which settled the destiny of Saxon independence. **1887** BOWEN *Virg. Æneid* III. 53 Troy's strength broken, her destinies waning.

II. As an agency or agent.

4. The power or agency by which, according to various systems of philosophy and popular belief, all events, or certain particular events, are unalterably predetermined; supernatural or divine pre-ordination; overruling or invincible necessity; = FATE *sb.* 1. (Often personified; see also 5.)

c **1340** *Gaw. & Gr. Knt.* 1752 How þat destine schulde þat day [dyȝt] his wyrde. *c* **1385** CHAUCER *L.G.W.* 952 *Dido*, He ..sayleth forth..Towarde Ytayle, as wolde destanee. *c* **1530** MORE *Answ. Frith* Wks. 839/2 Some ascribing all thyng to destyny without any power of mannes free wyll at all. **1600** E. Blount tr. *Conestaggio* 19 It seemed that some furious destinie lead him headlong to his end. **1610** Shaks. *Temp.* iii. iii. 53 Three men of sinne, whom destiny That hath to instrument this lower world..the..Sea Hath caus'd to belch vp. **1667** Milton *P.L.* iv. 58 Had his powerful Destiny ordaind Me some inferiour Angel. **1791** Cowper *Iliad* xviii. 678 The force Of ruthless Destiny. **1866** G. Macdonald *Ann. Q. Neighb.* i. (1878) 1 That destiny which took form to the old pagans as a gray mist high above the heads of their gods. **1887** Bowen *Virg. Eclogue* iv. 46 'Ages blest, roll onward!' the Sisters of Destiny cried.

†**b.** With possessive pronoun: The power or agency held to predetermine a particular person's life or lot. *Obs.*

c **1325** *E.E. Allit. P.* A. 757 My dere destyne Me ches to hys make al-þaȝ vnmete. *c* **1374** Chaucer *Anel. & Arc.* 339 Thus holdithe me my destenye a wrechche. *a* **1668** Denham (J.), Had thy great destiny but given thee skill To know, as well as pow'r to act her will.

5. *Mythol.* The goddess of destiny; *pl.* the three goddesses held, in Greek and Roman mythology, to determine the course of human life; the Fates: see fate *sb.* 2.

14.. *Lat. & Eng. Voc.* in Wr.-Wülcker 573/35 *Cloto*, on of thre shapsisterys *vel* shappystrys [*vel* destynyes]. **1593** Shaks. *Rich. II*, i. ii. 15 Seuen faire branches..Some..dride by natures course, Some..by the destinies cut. **1623** Lisle *Ælfric on O. & N. Test.* Ded. 27 So charge the Destinies their spindle runne. **1712** Addison *Spect.* No. 523 ¶7, I shall not allow the Destinies to have had an hand in the deaths of the several thousands who have been slain in the late war. **1814** Southey *Roderick* xxi. 345 We, poor slaves.. must drag The Car of Destiny, where'er she drives Inexorable and blind. **1857** Whewell *Hist. Induct. Sc.* I. 125 The adamantine distaff which Destiny holds.

III. *attrib.*

1552 Huloet, Desteny readers or tellers, *Fatidici.*

†**'destiny,** *v. Obs.* [f. prec. sb. Cf. *to fate.*] *trans.* To destine, foreordain, predetermine.

c **1400** *Test. Love* iii. (1560) 298/1 If in that manner bee said, God toforne have destenied both badde and her bad werkes. **1520** *Caxton's Chron. Eng.* ii. 10b/1 That lande is destenyed and ordeyned for you and for your people. **1592** Chettle *Kinde-harts Dr.* (1841) 58 Hidden treasure is by spirits possest, and they keepe it onely for them to whome it is destinied. **1652** J. Wright tr. *Camus' Nature's Paradox* 63 The high Providence of Heaven..destinying me to misfortune.

b. To devote to some fate by imprecation.

a **1450** *Knt. de la Tour* (1868) 108 It is gret perille for fader and moder to curse her children ne forto destenie hem vnto any wicked thinge.

c. To divine or prognosticate (what is destined to happen). (Cf. prec. 1 b.)

1548 Hooper *Declar. Ten Commandm.* iv, Such as give faith unto..such as destinieth what shall happen.. committeth idolatry.

†**desti'ny,** *ppl. a. Obs. rare.* In 5 destyne, 6 destany. [a. F. *destiné*, pa. pple. of *destiner* to destine.] Destined.

c **1474** Caxton *Troye* 198 (Sommer 397) Shewyng hym by certayne signes that hit was destyne that another shold make the Cyte. **1513** Douglas *Æneis* vii. iii. 36 All haill, thou ground and land, quod he in hy, By the fatis vnto me destany.

†**'destitue,** *v. Obs. rare.* Pa. t. destitut. [a. F. *destituer* to deprive (of something sustaining), ad. L. *dēstituĕre*: see next and cf. constitue.] *trans.* To deprive. (In quot. *refl.*)

c **1400** *Destr. Troy* 728 Soche a maiden to mar þat þe most louet..And dawly hir distitut [*printed* -ur] of hir dere fader.

†**de'stituent,** *a. Obs.* [ad. L. *dēstituent-em*, pr. pple. of *dēstituĕre* (see next).] Wanting, lacking.

1660 Jer. Taylor *Duct. Dubit.* ii. iii. Rule xi. §15 When any condition..is destituent or wanting, the duty it self falls.

destitute ('dɛstɪtjuːt), *a.* (and *sb.*) Also 5 destitut, -tuyt, -tud, distytute, 6 destytude, distitute. [ad. L. *dēstitūt-us* abandoned, forsaken, pa. pple. of *dēstituĕre* to forsake, abandon, desert, f. de- I. 1, 2 + *statuĕre* to set up, place.]

†**1.** Abandoned, forsaken, deserted. *Obs.*

1382 Wyclif *Rev.* xviii. 17 For in oon hour so many richessis ben destitute [*Vulg.* destitutæ sunt]. **1480** Caxton *Chron. Eng.* ccxxvi. 233 Long large and wyde clothes destytut and desert from al old honeste and good vsage. **1592** *Nobody & Someb.* (1878) 350 Great houses long since built Lye destitute and wast, because inhabited by Nobody. **1593** Shaks. *Lucr.* 441 Left their round turrets destitute and pale.

b. Of persons: Forsaken, left friendless or helpless, forlorn. (Blending at length with sense 3.)

1513 More in Grafton *Chron.* (1568) II. 757 If devision, and dissencion of their friendes, had not unarmed them, and left them destitute. **1530** Palsgr. 310/1 Destytut forsaken, *destitue*. **1632** Sherwood, To leaue destitute, *destituer, abandonner en detresse*. **1704** Cocker, *Destitute*, left forsaken. **1706** Phillips (ed. Kersey), *Destitute*, deprived, bereaved, forsaken, forlorn. **1740** Dyche & Pardon, *Destitute*, helpless, forlorn, forsaken; in want and misery. **1755** Johnson, *Destitute*..2. Abject, friendless.

2. †**a.** Deprived or bereft *of* (something formerly possessed). *Obs.* **b.** Devoid *of*, wanting or entirely lacking *in* (something desirable).

a. 1413 *Pylg. Sowle* iv. xx. (Caxton, 1483) 67 Thou art of comforte destytuyt I see And so am I. O careful now been we. **14..** *Why I can't be a Nun* 97 in *E.E.P.* (1862) 140, I am alle desolate, And of gode cownesayle destitute. **1455** Dk. of York in Ellis *Orig. Lett.* Ser. ii. I. 125 Ye stande destitut and unpourveyed of a Marshall within the town of Calyis. **1491-2** *Plumpton Corr.* 102, I am distytute of money.

b. *c* **1500** *Lancelot* 1178 Shortly to conclud, Our folk of help had ben al destitud. **1526-34** Tindale *Jas.* ii. 15 If a brother or a sister be naked or destitute of dayly food. *c* **1540** Borde *The boke for to Lerne* A ij b, Not destytude of such commodyties. **1597** Morley *Introd. Mus.* Pref., To further the studies of them who..are destitute of sufficient masters. **1608** Shaks. *Per.* v. i. 57 That..we may provision have Wherein we are not destitute for want, But weary for the staleness. **1682** Bunyan *Holy War* (Cassell) 208 If you were not destitute of an honest heart you could not do as you have done. **1718** *Freethinker* No. 27 ¶2 The Age we live in is not wholly destitute of Manly refined Spirits. **1802** Mar. Edgeworth *Moral T.* (1816) I. iv. 20 A species of fashionable dialect, devoid of sense, and destitute of..wit. **1875** Jowett *Plato* (ed. 2) III. 518 A barren waste destitute of trees and verdure.

†**c.** Bereft of power *to do* something. *Obs. rare.*

1645 Milton *Tetrach.* 60 If any therefore demand which is now most perfection..I am not destitute to say, which is most perfection.

3. Bereft of resources, resourceless, 'in want and misery'; now, without the very necessaries of life or means of bare subsistence, in absolute want.

The 16th c. quotations from the Bible have perhaps properly the sense 'forlorn' (1 b); but they appear to have led the way to the modern sense, which is not recognized by Johnson, and is only approached in other 18th c. Dictionaries.

[**1535** Coverdale *Ps.* cii. 17 He turneth him vnto the prayer of the poore destitute [**1611** He will regard the prayer of the destitute]. **1539** Bible (Great) *Heb.* xi. 37 Other.. walked vp and downe in shepes skynnes, and goates skynnes, beyng destitute [*so* **1611**, *other versions* in need], troubled, and vexed.] **1740** Dyche & Pardon [see 1 b]. **1784** Cowper *Task* iv. 455 Did pity of their sufferings..tempt him into sin For their support, so destitute. **1813** Shelley *Q. Mab* iii. 35 The deep curses which the destitute Mutter in secret. **1832** Ht. Martineau *Life in Wilds* viii. 101 He had left his companions in a destitute state. **1838** Lytton *Alice* 6, I was then so poor and destitute. **1875** Jowett *Plato* (ed. 2) III. 101 There is one class which has enormous wealth, the other is entirely destitute. *Mod.* Help for the destitute poor.

transf. **1764** Reid *Inquiry* ii. §6. 109 These ideas look pitifully naked and destitute.

†**4.** *Civil Law.* Of a will: Rendered of no effect by reason of the refusal or incapacity of the heirs therein instituted to take up the inheritance (*testamentum destitutum*); abandoned. *Obs.*

1774 Bp. Hallifax *Anal. Rom. Law* (1795) 58 If a Testator..had given freedom to slaves, and the Testament afterwards became destitute, the slaves lost their freedom.

B. as *sb.* One who is destitute, without friends, resources, or the means of subsistence.

1737 P. St. John *Serm.* 224 (R.) O, my friends, have pity on this poor destitute, for the hand of God hath touched her. **1784** *Unfort. Sensibility* II. 12 Considering them as two poor destitutes. **1863** Fr. A. Kemble *Resid. in Georgia* 7 Ask the thousands of ragged destitutes.

destitute ('dɛstɪtjuːt), *v.* Now *rare. Pa. t.* -ed; in 6 sometimes destitute. [Partly f. destitute *a.*, partly taken as Eng. repr. of L. *dēstituĕre* (ppl. stem *dēstitūt-*) to put away from oneself, forsake, abandon: see prec. adj. Cf. F. *destituer*, ad. L. *dēstituĕre.*]

†**1.** *trans.* To forsake, desert, abandon, leave to neglect. *Obs.*

1530 Palsgr. 514/1, I destytute, I forsake or leave a thyng or persone, *je destitue*. **1550** Crowley *Way to Wealth* 362 Oppressed on the one side and destituted on the other. **1627** Bacon *Ess., Plantations* (Arb.) 534 It is the sinfullest Thing in the world, to forsake or destitute a Plantation, once in Forwardnesse. **1673** *Lady's Call.* ii. §1 ¶16. 62 God, who permits not even the brutes to destitute their young ones.

2. To deprive, bereave, divest *of* (anything possessed); to render destitute, reduce to destitution.

c **1540** Borde *The boke for to Lerne* A ij b, Yf he be destytuted of any of the pryncipalles. **1545** Joye *Exp. Dan.* v. (R.), So that the chirches and ciuile ministracion be not destituted lerned men at any tyme. *c* **1561** Veron *Free-will* 44 b, The mercye of God whereof they be al together destituted. **1605** Hieron *Short Dial.* 61 That which desti[t]uteth so great a number of whole familes. **1612** T. Taylor *Comm. Titus* i. 11 Let it take any one part, and destitute it of heate and vitall spirits. **1820** Shelley *Let. to Godwin* 7 Aug., I have given you the amount of a considerable fortune, and have destituted myself..of nearly four times the amount.

3. *spec.* To deprive of dignity or office; to depose. [mod.F. *destituer.*]

1653 Baxter *Chr. Concord* 70 Where are the Cardinals and Bishops communicating with one excommunicated, instituted by one destituted? **1716** M. Davies *Athen. Brit.* I. 131 Let not the Patriarch think..to destitute or depose me. **1889** B. M. Gardiner in *Academy* 16 Nov. 314/3 He was destituted by the General Council of the Commune.

4. To leave destitute or waste, to lay waste.

1593 Nashe *Christ's T.* (1613) 40 By none shall the Sanctuary be defended, but those that wold haue none destitute or defloure it but themselues. **1890** A. Rimmer *Summ. Rambles Manchester* p. v, He would have thought that his country had been overrun by foreign foes and destituted.

†**5.** To make void, frustrate, defeat, disappoint.

c **1550** Bale *K. Johan* (Camden) 100 Examples we have in Brute, In Catilyne, in Cassius, and fayer Absolon, Whome of their purpose God alwayes destytute. **1593** Nashe *Foure Lett. Confut.* 42 If you haue anie new infringement to destitute the inditement of forgerie that I bring against you. *a* **1619** Fotherby *Atheom.* i. ii. §1 (1622) 8 Lest..he be needlesly offended, when his expectation is destituted.

Hence **'destituted** *ppl. a.*, **'destituting** *vbl. sb.*

1550 Veron *Godly Saiyngs* (1846) 139 He that seeth his brother or his syster naked or destituted of daylye fode. **1580** Hollyband *Treas. Fr. Tong*, *Destitution & delaissement*, Destituting or disappointing. **1587** Fleming *Contn. Holinshed* III. 1027/2 This monasterie for sundrie yeares was left destituted. **1662** J. Bargrave *Pope Alex. VII* (1867) 95 He was a destituted young lad, out of all conversation.

'destitutely, *adv.* [f. destitute *a.* + -ly[2].] In a destitute condition.

1548 Udall, etc. *Erasm. Par. 1 Tim.* v. (R.), She beyng destitutely lefte withoute comforte of husbande, of children ..of all the worldes solace.

'destituteness. [f. as prec. + -ness.] The state or condition of being destitute.

1657 Gaule *Sapient. Justif.* 70 The destituteness and desperateness of the Disease. **1668** H. More *Div. Dial.* ii. vi. (1713) 107 The weakness and destituteness of the Infant. **1818** Bentham *Ch. Eng.* 19 Its utter destituteness of all warrant from Scripture. **1835** Greswell *Parables* II. 293 The child, in the literal sense of the word, is the emblem of weakness, destituteness, ignorance, imperfection.

destitution (dɛstɪ'tjuːʃən). [a. F. *destitution* (1316 in Godef. *Suppl.*), ad. L. *dēstitūtiōn-em* forsaking, abandoning, n. of action from *dēstituĕre* (see above); in Romanic usually a noun of condition.]

†**1.** The action of deserting or forsaking. *Obs.*

1656 Blount *Glossogr.*, *Destitution*, a leaving or forsaking. **1678** Phillips, *Destitution*, an utter forsaking or deserting. **1727** Bailey vol. II, *Destitution*, a leaving, or forsaking, an utter abandoning; also, a being left, forsaken, etc.

2. Deprivation of office; discharge; dismissal.

1554 *Act 1-2 Phil. & M.* c. 8 §33 The Institutions and Destitutions of and in Benefices and Promotions Ecclesiastical. **1644** H. Leslie *Blessing of Judah* 27 In Law, Institution and Destitution belong both to one. **1683** Fitzwilliam in *Lady Russell's Lett.* vii. (1773) 8 Want of leisure occasioned by the destitution of a Curate by illness. **1864** Trench *Parables* 408 The man [the unjust steward] not so much as attempting a defence, his destitution [ed. 1886 dismissal] follows.

3. a. The condition of being abandoned or left helpless, of being deprived or bereft (of anything). **b.** The condition of wanting or being lacking (*of* or †*in* anything); want.

a **1440** *Found. St. Bartholomew's* 59 A certeyne woman.. was smyte with a Palsy..And yn that destitucyoun of her lymmys duryd nat a litill tyme. **1594** Hooker *Eccl. Pol.* i. x. (1611) 25 Destitution in these [food and clothing] is such an impediment. **1597** J. Payne *Royal Exch.* 12 Theire destitucion of zeale to Gods glorie. **1684** Fitzwilliam in *Lady Russell's Lett.* xii. (1773) 19 The destitution of his real self, will..cause a stronger sense of your loss. **1727** Bailey vol. II [see 1]. *a* **1768** Sterne *Lett.* xci. (R.), Thy mother and thyself at a distance from me..what can compensate for such a destitution? **1790-1810** Combe *Devil on Two Sticks* (1817) IV. 242 A destitution of all principle, honour, sentiment, and feeling. **1838** Prescott *Ferd. & Is.* (1846) I. vii. 336 This..does not necessarily imply any destitution of just moral perceptions. **1853** Kane *Grinnell Exp.* xv. (1856) 116 That..destitution of points of comparison, which make[s] the pyramids so deceptive.

4. *spec.* The condition of being destitute of resources; want of the necessaries of life.

a **1600** Hooker (J.), They..are not left in so great destitution, that justly any man should think the ordinary means of eternal life taken from them. **1659** Hammond *On Ps.* xxv. 17 Paraphr. 142 My anxieties and destitutions daily increase. **1775** Ash, *Destitution*, want, poverty. **1849** Cobden *Speeches* 33 Left in a state of destitution. **1863** Mary Howitt *F. Bremer's Greece* II. xiv. 108 The Christian inhabitants of Thessaly would be reduced to destitution. **1872** Yeats *Growth Comm.* 62 He put an end to his life as the only means of escaping destitution.

destocking (diː'stɒkɪŋ), *vbl. sb.* [f. de- II. 1 + stock *v.*[1] 15 + -ing[1].] The reduction (by a retailer, etc.) of the quantity of stock held by the re-ordering of fewer goods than are needed to replace those sold.

1959 *Economist* 31 Jan. 386/1 America ran into a destocking recession in 1949. **1963** *Ann. Reg. 1962* 474 The rate of stock-building was low and in the early months some destocking may have occurred. **1970** *Daily Tel.* 14 Jan. 16 This trend may be expected to continue as British industry swings round from de-stocking to building up its stocks.

destonie, -nye, obs. forms of destiny.

destool (diː'stuːl), *v.* [f. de- II. 2 + stool *sb.*] *trans.* To remove (an African tribal chief) from authority. Cf. stool *sb.* 1 e. Hence **de'stoolment.**

1929 R. S. Rattray *Ashanti Law & Const.* 82 Failure to accept such guidance and advice was a legitimate cause for destoolment. *Ibid.* 83 The person of a Chief was..invested with sanctity, just so long as he sat upon the Stool of his dead ancestors. This is the reason why there was a reaction the moment a Chief was destooled. **1962** *Economist* 15 Sept. 998/2 Assassination is a deplorable way of destooling a chief.

destorb, destourb, obs. forms of disturb.

‖**destour, dastur** (də'stʊə(r)). Also 7 distore(e, distoore, destoor, dustoor. [Pers. *dastūr*, prime minister, vizier:—Pahlavi *dastōbār*, prime minister, councillor of state, high priest of the Parsees.] A chief priest of the Parsees.

1630 LORD *Banians & Persees* viii. (Yule), Their Distoree or high priest. **1665** SIR T. HERBERT *Trav.* (1677) 55 The Distoore or Pope..has thirteen [precepts]. **1696** OVINGTON *Voy. Surat* 376 (Yule) The highest Priest of the Persies is called Destoor, their ordinary Priests *Daroos* or *Hurboods.* **1776** GIBBON *Decl. & F.* (1836) VIII. 81 If the destour be satisfied, your soul will escape hell. **1777** J. RICHARDSON *Dissert. East. Nations* 10 The wretched rhymes of a modern Parsi Destour. **1809** M. GRAHAM *Jrnl.* (1812) (Yule), The Dustoor is the chief priest of his sect in Bombay. **1862** M. HAUG *Ess. Sacr. Lang. Parsees* 52 The Dustoors, as the spiritual guides of the Parsee community, should take a chief part in it. **1878** —— *Relig. of Parsees* (ed. 2) 17 He bribed one of the most learned Dasturs, Dastur Dârâb, at Surat to procure him manuscripts and to instruct him in the Avesta and Pahlavi languages.

destourn, obs. form of DISTURN *v.*

destrain, -ayn, -ein, etc., obs. ff. DISTRAIN *v.*

destraught, obs. f. DISTRAUGHT *pa. pple.*, distracted.

†**de'strayt.** *Obs.* Also -te, -tte. [a. OF. *destreit* (*-ait, -oit*), mod.F. *détroit* 'a strait, a narrow place or passage, a defile, a confined place':—late pop. L. *district-um*, from *districtus* tight, strict, severe, pa. pple. of *distringĕre* to DISTRAIN: cf. DISTRICT.] A narrow pass or defile.

1481 CAXTON *Godfrey* clxv. 244 The day after passed they by a moche sharp & aspre way, & after descended by a destrayt in to a playne. *c***1500** *Melusine* lvii. 336 On the morne he passed the destraytte & mounted the mountaynes.

†**de'streche**, *v. Obs. rare*[−1]. [app. irreg. f. DE- *pref.* + STRETCH *v.*: perh. after *stroy, destroy, strain, destrain*, etc.] *intr.* To stretch out, extend.

*c***1475** *How wyse man taught Sone* 30 in *Q. Eliz. Acad.* 53 Als ferre as mesure wyll destreche.

'destrer, 'destrier ('dɛstrə(r), -ɪə(r), dɛ'strɪə(r)). *arch.* Also 4–5 destrere, 5 deistrere, dextrer(e, (9 dexter, 9 dextrier, destrière). [ME. *destrer*, a. AF. *destrer* = OF. *destrier* = Pr. *destrier*, It. *destriere, -ero*:—late L. *dextrāri-us*, in full *equus dextrārius*, f. *dextra* right hand: so called from being led by the squire with his right hand.]

A war-horse, a charger.

α. in contemporary use.

*c***1300** *K. Alis.* 801 The Knighttes hunteth after dere, On fote and on destrere. *Ibid.* 4924 The quene may lede Twenty thousande maidens upon destrers. *c***1314** *Guy Warw.* (A.) 2356 Sir Gii him smot to Gaier, And feld him doun of his destrer. *c***1330** R. BRUNNE *Chron.* (1810) 124 To ded þan gon he falle doun of his destrere. *c***1386** CHAUCER *Sir Thopas* 202 By hym baiteth his dextrer [*v.r.* destrer, dester, deistrere, dextrere]. *c***1450** LONELICH *Grail* xiii. 87 Faste preking vppon a destrere. *c***1477** CAXTON *Jason* 9 b, Two right fayr and excellent destriers or horses. *c***1500** *Melusine* xix. 82 Then descended Raymondin fro the destrer.

β. historical or archaistic. (Chiefly in Fr. spelling.)

1720 STRYPE *Stow's Surv.* (1754) I. II. ii. 354/1 So far into the Thames, as a horseman at low water, riding upon his Destrier into the river could dart his lance from him. **1803** S. PEGGE *Anecd. Eng. Lang.* 287 Dexters seem to have been what we should call Chargers. **1820** SCOTT *Ivanhoe* xl, Some palfrey whose pace may be softer than that of my destrier. **1845** T. B. SHAW in *Blackw. Mag.* LVIII. 146 The Prince pricks along on his faithful destrere. **1845** J. SAUNDERS *Pict. Eng. Life, Chaucer* 76 The war horses were led by the squires, who always keeping them in their right hand, they were called dextriers. **1858** MORRIS *Sir Galahad* Poems 51 Needs must roll The proudest destrier sometimes in the dust. **1869** FREEMAN *Norm. Conq.* (1876) III. xii. 175 The knight on his destrier. **1894** A. LANG in *Longm. Mag.* June 214 The Maiden called for her great destrier, But he lashed like a fiend when the Maid drew near.

destreyn(e, obs. forms of DISTRAIN.

destribute, obs. var. of DISTRIBUTE *v.*

†**de'striction.** *Obs. rare*[−0]. [app. f. DE- I. 1 + L. *strictio* binding, STRICTION.]

1727 BAILEY vol. II, *Destriction*, a binding.

de'strie, obs. form of DESTROY *v.*

†**de'strigment.** *Obs. rare*[−0]. [f. L. *dēstringĕre* to strip off, *strigmentum* that which is scraped or scratched off.]

1727 BAILEY vol. II, *Destrigment*, that which is scraped or pulled of any thing.

†**de'strition.** *Obs. rare.* [? a. OF. *destruision* destruction, f. *destruire* to DESTROY (cf. *destrie*).] Ravaging, ruin.

14.. *Childe of Bristowe* 328 in Hazl. *E.P.P.* I. 123 Where his fader dud destrition to man or womman in any toun..he shal make aseth therfore, and his good ayen restore.

destroer, obs. form of DESTROYER.

†**de'strouble**, *v. Obs.* [a. OF. *destroubler, detroubler* (Godef.), f. *des-*, L. *dis-* + *troubler* to TROUBLE. Cf. DISTURBLE.] *trans.* To trouble; to make it troublesome for.

*a***1450** *Knt. de la Tour* (1868) 43 Ye haue destroubled the parisshenes to here masse. **1474** CAXTON *Chesse* 94 Auarice destroubleth fayth.

destroy (dɪ'strɔɪ), *v.* Forms: 3–4 destrui-e(n, 3–5 -struy-e(n, -stru-e(n, (-stru, -striu), 4–5 -stry(e, 4–6 -stroye, (5 -stroȝe, 6 -strowe), 6–7 -stroie, 5– destroy; also 4 disstrie, dysstrye, 4–5 distruy(e, -truie, -truyȝe, -troȝe, -trou, 4–6 distroy(e, 4–7 distroie, 5 distrie, distroi, 5–6 dystroy(e, dis-, dystrow(e, -true, distrye. [ME. *destruy-en*, etc., a. OF. *destrui-re* (mod.F. *détruire* = Pr. and Sp. *destruir*, It. *distruggere*):—late pop. L. **dēstrūgĕre*, ppl. stem *dēstrūct-*, for cl. L. *dēstruĕre*, f. DE- I. 6 + *struĕre* to pile up, construct.]

1. *trans.* To pull down or undo (that which has been built); to demolish, raze to the ground.

1297 R. GLOUC. (1724) 242 Edwyne..destrude wyde aboute..Alle ys stedes, ver and ner, and to grounde caste. *a***1300** *Fall & Passion* 85 in *E.E.P.* (1862) 15 He wolde destru temple an chirche. *a***1300** *Cursor M.* 22348 (Cott.) Bath destrui þam tun and tur. *c***1380** WYCLIF *Serm.* Sel. Wks. I. 25 Þi wallis al distried. *c***1400** MAUNDEV. (Roxb.) v. 15 Þare was..a faire citee of Cristen men, but Sarzenes hase destruyd it. **1489** CAXTON *Faytes of A.* II. xxxvii. 157 The cite of rome shulde haue be dystroyed. **1513** BRADSHAW *St. Werburge* II. 694 This kyng entended by mortall enuy The cite of Chestre to spoyle and distrye. **1526–34** TINDALE *John* ii. 19 Iesus answered and sayd vnto them, destroye this temple, and in thre dayes I will reare it vp agayne. **1632** J. HAYWARD tr. *Biondi's Eromena* 78 To undergoe the brunt of destroying Epicamido's whole campe. **1760–72** tr. *Juan & Ulloa's Voy.* (ed. 3) II. 82 Another earthquake happened, by which several houses were destroyed. **1834** L. RITCHIE *Wand. by Seine* 237 The English destroyed [the monastery] and half a century afterwards rebuilt it.

b. Said of the action of water in dissolving and demolishing or washing away.

1632 LITHGOW *Trav.* VII. 317 For the nature of violent streames..[is to] destroy all that they debord upon. **1659** B. HARRIS *Parival's Iron Age* 67 Like a Torrent, which carries away, and destroies all. **1760–72** tr. *Juan & Ulloa's Voy.* (ed. 3) I. 201 The rain utterly destroys all the trenches. **1835** CRUISE *Digest* (ed. 4) I. III. ii. §24 If the banks of a river are destroyed by a sudden flood it is not waste.

†**2.** To lay waste, ravage, make desolate. *Obs.*

*a***1225** *Ancr. R.* 388 A lefdi..mid hire uoan biset al abuten, and hire lond al destrued. *c***1320** *Sir Beues* 2442 And al þe contre, saun doute, Þai distruede hit al aboute. *c***1440** *Promp. Parv.* 120 Destroyyn a cuntre (or feeldis P.), *depopulor, depredo, devasto.* **1483** CAXTON *Gold. Leg.* 202/1 That same tyme attila destroyed Italye. **1584** POWELL *Lloyd's Cambria* 11 Destroied the province of Chester. **1611** BIBLE *Ezek.* xxx. 11 The terrible of the nations shall be brought to destroy the land.

†**b.** To ruin (men), to undo in worldly estate.

1297 R. GLOUC. (1724) 376 He destrude þat pouere volc, & nom of hem hys preye. **1621** BOLTON *Stat. Irel.* 9 (an. 25 Hen. VI) The Irish enemies..destroy the common people by lodging upon them in the nights.

3. To undo, break into useless pieces, or reduce into a useless form, consume, or dissolve (any material structure or object). (Now the leading sense.)

*c***1314** *Guy Warw.* (A.) 1120 Mi bodi destrud and leyd on bere. **1382** WYCLIF *Prov.* xxi. 20 An vnprudent man schal distrie it. **1393** LANGL. *P. Pl.* C. I. 212 For meny mannys malt we mys wolde distrye. **1700** S. L. tr. *Fryke's Voy. E. India* 245 That day we destroy'd about 1100 of their Skiffs, little and great. *c***1790** WILLOCK *Voy.* 154 Plundering and destroying whatever they can lay hands on. **1798** H. SKRINE *Two Tours Wales* 155 A fire, by which most of the old houses were destroyed. **1828** AMBLER *Reports* (ed. 2) I. 147 A deed which was charged in his bill to have been destroyed and lost by Roger. **1884** GUSTAFSON *Found. Death* ii. (ed. 3) 25 All the ancient Egyptian works on alchemy..were ruthlessly destroyed by the Roman Emperor Diocletian. **1887** BOWEN *Virg. Æneid* v. 700 The vessels of Troy..are saved from flames that destroy.

b. To render useless, to injure or spoil utterly.

1542 BOORDE *Dyetary* xi. (1870) 260 God may sende a man good meate, but the deuyll may sende an euyll coke to dystrue it. **1555** EDEN *Decades* 115 Locustes whiche destrowe the fieldes of corne. **1697** DRYDEN *Virg. Georg.* IV. 468 With Blites destroy my Corn. **1774** GOLDSM. *Nat. Hist.* (1776) VII. 8 Shells assume every colour but blue; and that, sea-water..would be apt to destroy. **1806** J. FORBES *Lett. France* II. 60 The long drought and extreme heat have destroyed their vegetables.

4. To put out of existence (living beings); to deprive of life; to slay, kill.

(Now chiefly said of war, pestilence, intemperance, etc., which destroy multitudes, also of the destruction of noxious animals, and of suicide (self-destruction).)

*a***1300** *Cursor M.* 22133 (Cott.) First he sal do alle destru [*MS. Edin.* destriu, *Gött.* distrou] þat halud was of ur lauerd iesu. *a***1325** *Prose Psalter* li[i]. 5 Þer-for shal God destruen þe on ende. *a***1340** HAMPOLE *Psalter* ix. 40 When antecrist is distroid all goed sall regne. *c***1385** CHAUCER *L.G.W.* 1318 *Dido*, These lordis..Wele me distroyen only for ȝoure sake. **1473** WARKW. *Chron.* 20 The Bastarde..hade purposed to have distruyt Kynge Edwarde. **1535** COVERDALE *Bel & Dr.* 26, I shal destroye this dragon without swearde or staff. *a***1547** in *Laneham's Lett.* (Pref. 1871) 130 Haue youe drunkune any contagius drynke to dystrowe your chyld. **1700** S. L. tr. *Fryke's Voy. E. Ind.* 291 Rat-Catchers..destroy the Rats and Mice as much as any Cats would. **1712** HEARNE *Collect.* (Oxf. Hist. Soc.) III. 368 Of whose destroying himself I have made mention. **1726** *Adv. Capt. R. Boyle* 131, I was..going to destroy myself..in the height of my Despair. **1794** SULLIVAN *View Nat.* II. 252 A deluge in Friezeland covered the whole coasts, and destroyed the greatest part of the inhabitants. **1839** T. BEALE *Hist. Sperm Whale* 160 Those young bulls..are perhaps the most difficult to destroy. **1887** BOWEN *Virg. Æneid* III. 1 It had pleased the Immortals..to destroy Priam's innocent people.

5. To bring to nought put an end to; to do away with, annihilate (any institution, condition, state, quality, or thing immaterial).

*a***1300** *Cursor M.* 25239 (Cott.) Destru [*v.rr.* destruy, destroy] þou lauerd! wit pouste þin þe mightes o þis wiþerwin. **1340** HAMPOLE *Pr. Consc.* 4453 Þan sal he destroye cristen lawe. **1382** WYCLIF *Prov.* xxi. 22 [They] destroȝide [**1388** distriede] the strengthe of the trost of it. *c***1400** *Destr. Troy* 13240 All hir note of Nigromansy naitly distroyet. **1535** COVERDALE *Job* xiv. 18 So destroyest thou the hope of man. **1612** WEBSTER *Dutchesse of Malfi* IV. ii, So pity would destroy pity. **1714** MRS. CENTLIVRE *Wonder* IV. i, One tender word destroys a lover's rage. **1752** JOHNSON *Rambler* No. 193 ¶9 Every other enjoyment malice may destroy. **1833** L. RITCHIE *Wand. by Loire* 17 To wait..would destroy the little chance we appeared to have. **1841–4** EMERSON *Ess., Intellect* Wks. (Bohn) I. 143 Silence is a solvent that destroys personality. **1893** *Law Times* XCIV. 603/2 He..had been heard to express a determination to destroy his life.

†**b.** *Math.* To cancel, eliminate, cause to disappear. *Obs.*

1706 W. JONES *Syn. Palmar. Matheseos* 130 After the same manner any other Term in this..Equation may be destroyed. **1763** W. EMERSON *Meth. Increments* 123, 2 series, where all the terms destroy one another except the first.

c. *Law.* To nullify, invalidate, do away with.

1818 CRUISE *Digest* (ed. 2) II. 353 A person who has only a trust estate, cannot..destroy a contingent remainder expectant on his estate. *Ibid.* V. 217 A power collateral to the land..cannot be barred or destroyed by a fine levied [etc.]. **1892** GOODEVE *Pers. Property* (ed. 2) 361 The statutes above cited do not destroy the right.

6. To counteract or neutralize the effect of; to render of no avail.

1729 BUTLER *Serm.* Wks. 1874 II. 110 These contrary passions..do not necessarily destroy each other. **1759** W. HILLARY *Diseases Barbados* 181 If they are of opposite and contrary Natures, they must at best only destroy each other. **1760–72** tr. *Juan & Ulloa's Voy.* (ed. 3) I. 61 The medicine has destroyed the malignity of the poison. **1860** TYNDALL *Glac.* II. vi. 253 A red glass..is red because..it destroys the shorter waves which produce the other colours.

†**7.** *to destroy into* or *to* (reproducing *perdere in gehennam* of *Vulgate*): to consign or give over to perdition in. *Obs.*

*c***1380** WYCLIF *Wks.* (1880) 265 It is grett meruaile þat god ..distroieþ not alle þis cursed peple to helle. **1526–34** TINDALE *Matt.* x. 28 Which is able to destroye both soule and body into hell. [So COVERD., CRANM., *Rhemish*; WYCLIF lese in to; *Geneva* & **1611** in.]

Hence **destroyed** (dɪ'strɔɪd) *ppl. a.*, despoiled; ravaged; slain; ruined; reduced to a useless condition.

*c***1440** *Promp. Parv.* 123 Destroyyde, *destructus, dissipatus.* **1634** SIR T. HERBERT *Trav.* 76 Being a Lady of faithfull memory to her destroyed husband. **1640** (*title*), England's Petition to their King; an Humble Petition of the distressed and almost destroyed subjects of England. **1801** G. S. FABER *Horæ Mos.* (1818) I. 82 The destroyed book of the Sibyl. **1821** SHELLEY *Hellas* 494 One cry from the destroy'd and the destroyer Rose.

†**de'stroy**, *sb. Obs. rare*[−1]. In 7 distroie. [f. DESTROY *v.*] Destruction.

1616 LANE *Cont. Sqr.'s T.* IX. 476 The sweete boy, wailinge most rufullie his frendes distroie.

destroyable (dɪ'strɔɪəb(ə)l), *a.* [f. DESTROY *v.* + -ABLE.] Capable of being destroyed.

1552 HULOET, Destroyable, or able to be destroyed, *destructilis.* **1654** FULLER *Two Serm.* 41 Foundations of Religion destroyed (so farre-forth as they are destroyable). **1678** CUDWORTH *Intell. Syst.* I. ii. §ix. 70 The Accidents themselves..are all makeable and destroyable. **1851** RUSKIN *Mod. Paint.* II. III. I. iv. §9 Destroyable only by the same..process of association by which it was created.

destroyer (dɪ'strɔɪə(r)). Also 4–5 destrier. distriere, 5 distruyere, destroer. [f. DESTROY *v.* + -ER; prob. orig. a. OF. *destruiere, -eor, -eour*, f. *destrui-re* to DESTROY.]

a. A person or thing that destroys.

1382 WYCLIF *Rev.* ix. 11 Appolion, and by Latyn hauynge the name Destrier [**1388** a distriere]. **1398** TREVISA *Barth. De P.R.* II. xix. (1495) 45 Also the fende hyghte Appolyon in Grewe, A destroyer. *c***1410** *Hymn Virg.* v. in Warton *Hist. Eng. Poetry* x, Heyl distruyere of everi strisse. **1483** *Cath. Angl.* 98/1 A Destroer, *vbi* a waster. *c***1530** *Pol. Rel. & L. Poems* (1866) 30 Covetyse is distroyer of hym selfe. **1535** COVERDALE *1 Chron.* xxi. 15 The Lorde..sayde vnto the angell yᵉ destroyer: It is ynough, holde now thy hande. **1630** in *Descr. Thames* (1758) 65 They are..great Destroyers of Barbels, and other Kind of Fish. **1667** MILTON *P.L.* XI. 697 Great Conquerors..Destroyers rightlier call'd and Plagues of men. **1795** SOUTHEY *Joan of Arc* x. 54 Were it a crime if thy more mighty force Destroy'd the fell destroyer? **1807** *Med. Jrnl.* XVII. 102 A neutralizer or destroyer of contagion.

b. A type of small, fast warship armed with guns, torpedoes, etc., used for escort-work, attacking submarines, etc., orig. built for attacking torpedo-boats. Also *attrib.* and *Comb.*, *spec.* in **destroyer-escort** (chiefly *U.S.*), a small destroyer; **destroyer-leader** *U.S.*, a large destroyer.

Destroyer was the proper name of an American torpedo-boat in 1882 (see *Leisure Hour*, 1882, 637/2, quoting *Brooklyn Eagle*).

1893 Torpedo-boat destroyer [see TORPEDO BOAT b]. **1899** Torpedo destroyer [see TORPEDO *sb.* 6].
[**1893** *Revue gén. des Sciences* IV. 458 (Bonnaffé), Le *Destroyer* était amarré à 30^m, 48 d'un bassin.] **1894** *Daily News* 11 June 6/5 The torpedo-boat destroyer built by the same firm last year for the Admiralty.. This type of boiler.. is being put into most of the 'destroyers' which are being built for the Government. **1895** *Daily News* 27 July 3/1 The Rocket, another destroyer,.. will not be ready for sea until Wednesday next. **1897** *Pop. Sci. Monthly* Nov. 139 It is becoming difficult to obtain the requisite area in screws of 'destroyers' without either resorting to an abnormal width of blade or to a large diameter. **1898** KIPLING *Fleet in Being* ii. 23 Would she—and a fast cruiser can do this—try to rush her by night, destroyer-fashion? **1899** *Daily News* 25 July 6/6 She is the gunboat in charge of one of our destroyer divisions. **1914** *Sphere* 17 Oct. 74/1 She [*sc.* the submarine] discovered two German destroyers on patrol duty. **1927** *Daily Tel.* 28 June 12/1 Large cruisers, destroyer-leaders, and submarines. **1929** W. J. LOCKE *Jorico* 124 He strode up and down with the air of the Commander of a Destroyer going into his first action. **1931** [see DESTROYING *vbl. sb.* b]. **1945** *Jane's Fighting Ships 1943–4* p. vi, Most numerous of any type [of American destroyer] are the so-called destroyer-escorts the design of which corresponds with that of British frigates of the 'Captain's' class. **1952** *Ibid. 1952–3* p. vii, All five of the destroyer leaders, another new category of U.S. warship.. , have been launched and are due to be completed at the end of the year. **1969** *Daily Colonist* (Victoria, B.C.) 31 Oct. 11/1 The crippled Canadian destroyer-escort Kootenay will be towed back to Halifax for repairs.

† **de'stroyeress.** *Obs. rare.* [f. prec. + -ESS.] A female destroyer.
1662 J. SPARROW tr. *Behme's Rem. Wks., Catal. Extant Works* No. 4 The Turba or Destroyeresse of the Image.

destroying (dɪ'strɔɪɪŋ), *vbl. sb.* [f. DESTROY *v.* + -ING¹.] **a.** The action of the verb DESTROY; DESTRUCTION: now chiefly gerundial.
c **1300** *K. Alis.* 2888 Never siththe that destroying N'as in Thebes wonying. *c* **1380** WYCLIF *Wks.* (1880) 322 To telle hasty destriyng of hem. *c* **1400** *Apol. Loll.* 69 Forsoþ if he lay doun þe suerd.. he opuniþ þe distroyingis. **1659** B. HARRIS *Parival's Iron Age* 138 They.. consented to the destroying down of the fair Gardens about the Town, to begin the Fortifications. **1667** MILTON *P.L.* IX. 129 For onely in destroying I find ease To my relentless thoughts. **1805** LD. COLLINGWOOD in A. Duncan *Nelson* (1806) 271, I determined no longer to delay the destroying them.
b. *Naut. colloq.* The action of serving in a destroyer.
1931 'TAFFRAIL' *Endless Story* i. 21 Most destroyer officers, their detractors averred, went in for 'destroying' because they.. needed the extra pay.

de'stroying, *ppl. a.* [f. as prec. + -ING².] That destroys, destructive. ***destroying angel*** U.S. = DANITE 2.
1535 COVERDALE *Ezek.* xxi. 8 The destroyenge staff of my sonne, shal bringe downe all wodde. **1728** R. MORRIS *Ess. Anc. Archit.* 21 Novelty and Singleness were as destroying .. to Art, as.. Barbarism. **1781** GIBBON *Decl. & F.* II. 92 To oppose the inroad of this destroying host. **1814** SOUTHEY *Roderick* xxv, Replete with power he is, and terrible, Like some destroying Angel! **1838** *Peoria* (Ill.) *Register* 24 Nov. 1/5 They had assembled them into three different societies, called Danites, Gideonites, and the destroying Angels. **1857** [see DANITE 2]. **1872** 'MARK TWAIN' *Roughing It* (1882) xii. 71 Half an hour.. later we changed horses, and took supper with a Mormon 'Destroying Angel'. **1894** LD. WOLSELEY *Life of Marlborough* II. xci. 437 Soul-and-body-destroying debauchery. **1943** B. DE VOTO *Yr. of Decision* 83 So in 1842 O. P. Rockwell, one of the Sons of Dan (the 'Destroying Angels' of ten-cent fiction), crept up to a window in Boggs's house and shot him.

de'stroyingly, *adv.* [f. prec. + -LY².] As a destroyer, destructively.
1821 SHELLEY *Prometh. Unb.* I. i. 781 Tho' Ruin now Love's shadow be, Following him destroyingly. **1869** *Daily News* 23 Jan., Dire forms of disease which occasionally sweep destroyingly over our towns.

de'struct, *v.* [f. L. *dēstruct-* ppl. stem of *dēstruĕre* to DESTROY: cf. *construct*.] = DESTROY. Also as *sb.* and *attrib.*
Quot. *a* 1638 is an isolated use. The recent (chiefly *U.S.*) use in *Rocketry* is prob. in part a back-formation on DESTRUCTION.
a **1638** MEDE *Paraphr. 2 Pet.* iii. (1642) 12 Either wholly destructed, or marvellously corrupted from that they were before. [*So ed. 2; ed. 3* (1653) destroyed.]
1958 *Aero-Space Terms* (Air University) 9/2 *Destruct*, the deliberate action of detonating or otherwise destroying a rocket missile or vehicle after it has been launched, but before it has completed its course. Said of friendly missiles esp. during test flights. **1958** *Times* 25 Sept. 10/2 The rocket .. turned back.. towards the shore; at this point it was destroyed (or 'destructed' as the official explanation puts it) by remote control. **1963** *New Scientist* 18 Apr. 139/1 A brief stop at the 'arming tower', where the 'destruct' equipment is installed. **1969** *Guardian* 21 Jan. 2/3 He had asked for a 'destruct' system to be installed in the electronics and code area of the ship.

de'structant, *sb. rare.* [irreg. f. L. *dēstruct-* (see prec.) + -ANT.] A destroyer, a destroying agent.
1889 T. D. TALMAGE in *The Voice* (N.Y.) 25 July, There is such a thing as pretending to be *en rapport* with others, when we are their dire destructants.

de'structful, *a.* [f. L. *dēstruct-* (see prec.) + -FUL.] = DESTRUCTIVE.
1659 SPRAT *Plague of Athens* (1667) 2 We fear A dangerous and destructful War. *Ibid.* 10 The circulation from the heart, Was most destructful now. **1881** WILDE *Poems* 223 Renovated By more destructful hands. **1895** E. W. HOPKINS *Relig. India* (1896) xi. 270 She.. will be.. destructful of her husband.

destructi'bility. [f. next: see -ITY.] The quality of being destructible; capability of being destroyed.
1730–6 BAILEY (folio), *Destructibility*, a capableness of being destroyed. **1805** HATCHETT in *Phil. Trans.* XCV. 309 The varieties of tannin do not accord in the degree of destructibility. **1841** TRIMMER *Pract. Geol.* 257 The greater destructibility of the absent tribes by long immersion in water.

destructible (dɪ'strʌktɪb(ə)l), *a.* [ad. L. *dēstructibilis*, f. *dēstruct-* ppl. stem of *dēstruĕre* to DESTROY: see -BLE.] Capable of being destroyed; liable to be destroyed.
1755 JOHNSON, *Destructible* liable to destruction. **1768–74** TUCKER *Lt. Nat.* (1852) II. 667 Simple substances, not consisting of parts, nor destructible by all the powers of nature. **1783** PRIESTLEY in *Phil. Trans.* LXXIII 412 Wood, or charcoal, is even perfectly destructible, that is, resolvable into inflammable air. **1871** TYNDALL *Fragm. Sc.* (1879) I. xx. 483 Forces are convertible but not destructible. **1878** JEVONS *Prim. Pol. Econ.* 107 Destructible things, like eggs, skins, etc., are always rising or falling in value.
Hence **de'structibleness,** destructibility.
1846 in WORCESTER.

† **de'structify,** *v. rare.* [f. L. *dēstruct-us* destroyed + -FY.] *trans.* To reduce to destruction.
1841 *Fraser's Mag.* XXIV. 289 Enough to contaminate, poison, degrade, and destructify the whole race.

† **de'structile,** *a. rare*⁻⁰. [ad. L. *dēstructilis*, f. *dēstruct-* ppl. stem: see -ILE.] = DESTRUCTIBLE.
1727 BAILEY vol. II, *Destructile*, that which may be destroy'd.

destruction (dɪ'strʌkʃən). Also 4–5 destruccioun, (5 -uxion, -tyoun; 4–6 dis-, 5 dys-. [a. OF. *destructiun* (12th c.), *-cion, -tion* (mod.F. *dé-*) = Pr. *destruccio*, Sp. *destruccion*, It. *distruzione*, ad. L. *dēstructiōn-em*, n. of action from *dēstruĕre* to DESTROY.] The action of destroying; the fact or condition of being destroyed: the opposite of *construction*.
1. The action of demolishing a building or structure of any kind, of pulling to pieces, reducing to fragments, undoing, wasting, rendering useless, putting an end to, or doing away with anything material or immaterial; demolition.
1340 HAMPOLE *Pr. Consc.* 4049 Aftir þe destruccion sal be Of þe empyre of Rome. *c* **1386** CHAUCER *Man of Law's T.* 138 In destruccioun of mawmetrye And in encresse of Cristes lawe deere, They ben acordid. *c* **1400** MAUNDEV. (Roxb.) xvi. 74 He asked þe destruccioun and þe vndoyng of his order. **1481** CAXTON *Myrr.* III. xi. 158 That after the first destruxion of the world ther shold be other peple. **1520** *Caxton's Chron. Eng.* III. 19/2 He prophecyed the dystrucyon of Jerusalem. **1553** EDEN *Treat. Newe Ind.* (Arb.) 13 *marg.*, The destruction of the citie of Aden. **1604** SHAKS. *Oth.* I. iii. 177 If she confesse that she was halfe the wooer, Destruction on my head, if my bad blame Light on the man. **1651** HOBBES *Leviath.* III. xxxvii. 233 There should be no more an universall destruction of the world by Water. **1736** BUTLER *Anal.* I. i. Wks. 1874 I. 28 There is no presumption.. that the dissolution of the body is the destruction of our present reflecting powers. **1813** T. FORSTER *Atmosph. Phenom.* (1815) 3 Theory of the formation and destruction of clouds. **1875** HAMERTON *Intell. Life* I. iv. 24 The work of repairing so great a destruction of muscle.
b. The action of ravaging or laying waste; havoc, ruin. *Obs.* (as distinct from the main sense.)
c **1330** R. BRUNNE *Chron.* (1810) 202 Destruction he makes of rentes and feez. *c* **1400** *Ywaine & Gaw.* 416 He.. said, i had, ogayne resowne, Done him grete destrucciowne. **1480** CAXTON *Chron. Eng.* cxxxiv. 114 He did grete destruction to holy chirche. *c* **1500** *Lancelot* 1283 Of his realme the opin distruccioune.
c. The action of putting to death, slaughter; now chiefly said of multitudes of men or animals, and of noxious creatures.
1526 *Pilgr. Perf.* (W. de W. 1531) 4 The destruccyon of Pharao & all his hoost. **1791** MRS. RADCLIFFE *Rom. Forest* ix, I looked round for the instrument of destruction. **1837** DICKENS *Pickw.* ii, Snodgrass bore under his [cloak] the instruments of destruction. *Mod.* Rewards for the destruction of beasts of prey.
d. *personified.*
1535 COVERDALE *Job* xxviii. 20 Destruccion [WYCLIF perdicioun] & death saie, we haue herde tell of her with oure eares. **1595** SHAKS. *John* v. vii. 77 To push destruction and perpetuall shame, Out of the weake door of our fainting Land. **1810** SCOTT *Lady of L.* III. xi, Quench thou his light, Destruction dark!
2. The fact, condition, or state of being destroyed; ruin.
c **1314** *Guy Warw.* (A.) 6077 Wende we wille to þe douk Otoun, And bring him to destruccioun. **1375** BARBOUR *Bruce* I. 204 To put hym to destructione. *a* **1450** *Knt. de la Tour* (1868) 6 She thanked God humbly that had kepte her from shame and distruccion. **1535** COVERDALE *Prov.* x. 14 Y^e mouth of ye foolish is nye destruccion. **1667** MILTON *P.L.* I. 137 All this mighty Host In horrible destruction laid thus low. **1841** LANE *Arab. Nts.* I. 91 When the Prince heard their words, he felt assured of destruction.
3. A cause or means of destruction.
1526 DR. MAGNUS *Lett.* to Jas. V., 13 Feb. The Armestrongges.. had avaunted thaymselves to be the destruction of twoe & fifty parisshe churches. **1548** HALL *Chron.* 99 b, Not forseyng before, that this preferment should be his destruccion. **1611** BIBLE *Prov.* x. 15 The destruction of the poore is their pouertie. **1798** CANNING, etc. *Loves of Triangles* in *Anti-Jacobin* 7 May (1852) 126 Watch the bright destruction as it flies. **1833** HT. MARTINEAU *Fr. Wines & Pol.* iv. 58 The deplorable mistake which was likely to prove the destruction of the whole family.
†**4.** *pl.* = Ruins. *Obs. rare.*
1585 T. WASHINGTON tr. *Nicholay's Voy.* I. xxi. 26 b, Neere that are the destructions of a high tower, which in times past was.. the great temple.

† **de'structionable,** *a. Obs. rare.* [f. prec. + -ABLE in active sense.] Addicted to destruction, destructive.
c **1575** tr. *H. Nicholas' First Exhort.* (1656) 228 Possest of the seven horriblest and destructionablest devils. **1660** H. MORE *Mystery of Godliness* 269 Intimating that the rest of the Vices are Devils also, but not so destructionable.

destructional (dɪ'strʌkʃənəl), *a.* [f. DESTRUCTION + -AL.] Of or pertaining to destruction; formed by destructive agencies, *spec.* by denudation.
1900 R. T. HILL *Physical Geogr. Texas Region* (*Topogr. Atlas U.S., Folio 3*) 5 Destructional plains originate in the degradation (or planation) of older and higher surfaces down to a lower level. **1904** *Amer. Jrnl. Sci.* Jan. 38 The steep cliff is clearly in both cases a destructional surface from which material has fallen away. **1956** *Gloss. Hydrologic Terms* (U.N. Econ. Comm. Asia, ST/ECAFE/Ser. F, No. 10) 12/1 *Destructional landscape*, one resulting from action of weather, streams, glaciers, winds, waves and animal organisms.

† **de'structioner.** *Obs. rare.* [f. DESTRUCTION + -ER¹.] One that causes destruction or ruin; a destroyer.
1621 BOLTON *Stat. Irel.* 10 (*an. 25 Hen. VI*) Destructioners of the King our Souveraigne Lords liege people.

destructionist (dɪ'strʌkʃənɪst). [f. as prec. + -IST.]
1. An advocate or partisan of a policy of destruction, *esp.* that of an existing political system or constitution. (Chiefly dyslogistic.)
1841 *Blackw. Mag.* L. 407 The intestine warfare between the Destructionist and the Conservative. **1845** T. W. COIT *Puritanism* 64 Church-breakers: ecclesiastical destructionists of the straitest sect. **1888** R. DOWLING *Miracle Gold* II. xix. 107 A regular out-and-out Fire-eater, Iconoclast, Destructionist.
2. *Theol.* One who believes in the final destruction or annihilation of the wicked; an annihilationist.
1807 SOUTHEY *Espriella's Letters* II. 28 Universalists, Calvanists, Materialists, Destructionists, Brownists [etc.].

destructive (dɪ'strʌktɪv), *a.* and *sb.* [a. OF. *destructif, -ive* (1372 in Hatzf.); = Pr. *destructiu*, Sp. *destructivo*, It. *distruttivo*, ad. L. *dēstructīv-us*, f. *dēstruct-* ppl. stem of *dēstruĕre* to DESTROY: see -IVE.]
A. *adj.* Having the quality of destroying; tending to destroy, put an end to, or completely spoil; pernicious, deadly, annihilative. Const. *to, of.*
1490 CAXTON *Eneydos* vi. 22 In all destructyue of theyr personis, honoures, goodes, and chyuaunches. **1555** EDEN *Decades* 265 One of these two.. shulde be destructiue to lyuynge creatures. **1647** CLARENDON *Hist. Reb.* I. (1843) 28/2 Unpolitic, and even destructive to the services intended. **1651** HOBBES *Leviath.* I. xiv. 64 A man is forbidden to do, that, which is destructive of his life. **1651** BAXTER *Inf. Bapt.* 318 The Apostle's sence is not the same with yours (but destructive to it). **1712** STEELE *Spect.* No. 466 ¶7 Vice is in itself destructive of Pleasure. **1751** JOHNSON *Rambler* No. 163 ¶2 Destructive to happiness. **1794** SOUTHEY *Wat Tyler* I, These destructive tyrants Shall shrink before your vengeance. **1856** EMERSON *Eng. Traits, First Visit to Eng.* Wks. (Bohn) II. 1 The conditions of literary success are almost destructive of the best social power. **1875** KINGLAKE *Crimea* (ed. 6) V. i. 252 A rapid advance.. under destructive fire. **1882** *Daily Tel.* 19 May, Palmer's bowling proved extremely destructive, and he took no less than eight wickets.
b. In political and philosophical use, opposed to *constructive* and *conservative*.
1834 *Oxf. Univ. Mag.* I. 108 The two distinct lines of conservative and destructive policy. **1841–44** EMERSON *Ess., Politics* Wks. (Bohn) I. 241 The spirit of our American radicalism is destructive and aimless. **1861** F. HALL in *Journal Asiatic Soc. Bengal* 148 After so much destructive criticism, to have little of instantly helpful truth to substitute in the room of what has been swept away. **1866** J. MARTINEAU *Ess.* I. 36 His position, therefore, is simply destructive. **1878** MORLEY *Crit. Misc.* Ser. I. *Carlyle* 198 Most of us would probably find the importance of this epoch in its destructive contribution.
c. Chem. ***destructive distillation***: see quots.
1831 T. P. JONES *Convers. Chem.* xxviii. 281 When organized substances are decomposed at a red heat in close vessels, the process is called destructive distillation. **1854** RONALDS & RICHARDSON *Chem. Technol.* (ed. 2) I. 284 Distillation may involve the decomposition of the substance heated, and the condensation of the products of decomposition, when it is termed *destructive* distillation.
d. *Logic.* Applied to conjunctive (or, as they are sometimes called, conditional) syllogisms

and dilemmas, in which the conclusion negatives a hypothesis in one of the premisses.
Thus: If A is B, C is D; C is not D, ∴ A is not B. If A is B, C is D, and if E is F, G is H; but either C is not D or G is not H, ∴ either A is not B, or E is not F.
1827 WHATELY *Logic* II. iv. §7 (L.) In a destructive sorites, you go back from the denial of the last consequent to the denial of the first antecedent: 'G is not H; therefore A is not B.'

B. *sb.*

1. A destructive agent, instrument, or force; a destructive proposition or syllogism.
1640 E. DACRES tr. *Machiavelli's Prince* Ep. Ded., Poysons ..as destructives of Nature..are utterly to be abhord. **1644** BP. MAXWELL *Prerog. Chr. Kings* Ded. 3 It hath been a preparatorie destructive to Royaltie. **1646** *Burd. Issach.* in *Phenix* (1708) II. 299 Their confession of Faith..is more in Negatives and Destructives, than Affirmatives and Positives. **1674** PENN *Just Rebuke* 9 Giving, for Antidotes, Destructives to the Souls of Men. **1827** WHATELEY *Logic* II. iv. (1836) 118 Which is evidently a simple Destructive. **1856** *Chamb. Jrnl.* VI. 56 The grand destructives of nature are the winds and the waves.

2. A person whose theory or practice tends to overthrow existing institutions or systems. (Chiefly dyslogistic.)
1832 *Examiner* 786/1 The Radicals (or Destructives, as you are pleased to describe them). **1871** MORLEY *Voltaire* (1886) 4 To the critic of the schools, ever ready with compendious label, he is the revolutionary destructive.

de'structively, *a.* [f. prec. + -LY².] In a destructive manner.
1661 *Grand Debate* 122 Which lookt upon our hopes of Reformation, almost as destructively as the Papists Doctrine of Infallibility doth. **1665** MANLEY *Grotius' Low C. Warres* 255 The French Wars raged destructively, both at Sea and Land. *a* **1714** M. HENRY *Wks.* (1835) I. 37 Nothing really and destructively evil. *Mod.* Fluoric acid acts destructively upon glass.

de'structiveness. [f. as prec. + -NESS.] The quality of being destructive; tendency to destroy.
1647 SALTMARSH *Spark. Glory* (1847) 195 Far from bearing witness to any destructiveness or persecution of them. **1738** WARBURTON *Div. Legat.* I. 35 The Destructiveness of Atheism to Society. **1795** SOUTHEY *Joan of Arc* VIII. 179 A weapon for its sure destructiveness Abominated once. **1869** *Echo* 30 Oct., An epidemic fever unparalleled for destructiveness. **1875** KINGLAKE *Crimea* (1877) V. i. 335 The..rashness, or rather self-destructiveness of the charge.

b. *Phrenol.* The name of a faculty or propensity having a bump or 'organ' allotted to it.
1815 *Edin. Rev.* XXV. 235 To the Order of Feelings.. belong the following species..6. Destructiveness. **1828** COMBE *Constit. Man* ii. §5 Destructiveness serves also to give weight to indignation. *a* **1875** KINGSLEY in *Four C. Eng. Lett.* 568 These same organs of destructiveness and combativeness.

destructivity (dɪstrʌk'tɪvɪtɪ). [f. DESTRUCTIVE *a.* + -ITY.] Destructiveness. Also **de'structivism.**
1902 *Encycl. Brit.* XXVII. 609/1 With the result that seismic destructivity can be accurately expressed in mechanical units. **1927** *Times Weekly Ed.* 19 May 562/1 It [*sc.* Marxism] demolishes the foundation of an individualistic society. On the Continent this is now called destructivism. **1933** DYLAN THOMAS *Let.* July (1966) 17 The..strangled destructivism of so much modern writing.

de'structless, *a. rare.* [f. L. *destruct-* ppl. stem (see above) + -LESS.] Indestructible.
1845 T. B. SHAW in *Blackw. Mag.* LVIII. 32 The bond.. is fair and true! Destructless as the soul, and as eternal.

destructor (dɪ'strʌktə(r)). [a. L. *dēstructor* destroyer, agent-noun from *dēstruĕre* to DESTROY. In F. *destructeur* (1420 in Hatzf.).]

1. A destroyer; one who destroys.
a **1691** BOYLE *Wks.* I. 527 (R.) Helmont does somewhere wittily call the fire the destructor and the artificial death of things. **1882-3** SCHAFF *Encycl. Relig. Knowl.* II. 1212 A decree ordered..all destroyed [temples] to be rebuilt at the cost of the destructors.

2. A furnace or crematory for the burning of refuse. Also *attrib.*
1881 *Scribner's Mag.* XXII. 799 To dispose of the refuse in a quick and cleanly manner, a small cremator, or destructor, has been introduced. **1885** *L'pool Daily Post* 7 May 4/8 The abattoir will be a greater nuisance in Greenlane than the refuse destructor. **1891** *Daily News* 16 July 4/4 Reponsible for the working of the dust destructors. **1892** *Pall Mall G.* 4 Oct. 2/1 One hundred tons are extracted per week and burned in a destructor furnace.

† **de'structory,** *a.* and *sb. Obs.* [f. L. type **dēstructōri-us*, f. *dēstructor*: see prec. and -ORY.]

A. *adj.* Of the nature of a destroyer; = DESTRUCTIVE.
1614 BP. ANDREWES *Serm.* on Prov. xxiv. 21-23 IV. (1853) 312 It is destructory, a destroying sin. **1627** H. BURTON *Baiting of Pope's Bull* 13 So destructory of that most precious, and peerelesse ransome. **16..** SWINBURNE *Spousals* (1686) 228 Which impediment..is not only prohibitory, but destructory.

B. *sb.* = DESTRUCTIVE *sb.*
a **1621** S. WARD *Life of Faith* (1627) 99 Subtilties of School-men, sentences and conceits of Postilers, rosaries, destructories, Anthologies. **1644** BP. MAXWELL *Prerog. Chr. Kings* viii. 94 You have point blanke the contrary, a virtuall destructory of this imagined and conceited right.

de'structuralize, *v.* [DE- II. 1.] *trans.* To undo the structural character of; to disorganize. Hence **destructuralization.**
1880 *Libr. Univ. Knowl.* I. 494 A literal destruction (i.e. de-structuralization), an utter and final disorganization.

de'structure, *v.* [f. DE- II. 1 + STRUCTURE *v.*] *trans.* To destroy or dismantle the structure of; to deprive of structure.
1951 G. HUMPHREY *Thinking* 172 When we are told to 'find the cat' [in puzzle-pictures], and succeed in doing so, we 'destructure the tree in order to structure the cat'. **1972** R. E. ORNSTEIN *Psychol. of Consciousness* iv. 89 Our linear, analytic world is for the moment destructured. **1976** T. EAGLETON *Crit. & Ideology* iii. 98 The text..destructures ideology in order to reconstitute it on its own relatively autonomous terms. **1981** *Guardian Weekly* 6 Sept. 19 We have to get behind the missiles to the blocks which will throw them, and begin to destructure the Cold War.

destrust, -turb, -turble, obs. ff. DISTRUST, etc.

† **destuted,** *pa. pple. Obs. rare.* [perh. a corrupt form of *destituted*, f. L. *destituĕre*, which had the sense 'to neglect, omit'. But the verb DESTITUTE is not known till much later.] Omitted, left out.
c **1300** *K. Alis.* 2199 This batail destuted is, In the French, wel y-wis, Therfor I have, hit to colour, Borowed of the Latyn autour How hent the gentil knyghtis.

destyne, var. of DESTINY *ppl. a. Obs.*

destyne, -nie, -ny, obs. ff. DESTINE, DESTINY.

desubstantialize (diːsəb'stænʃəlaɪz), *v.* [f. DE- II. 1 + SUBSTANTIALIZE *v.*] *trans.* To make less substantial; to take away reality from.
1940 *Mind* XLIX. 316 A being on the lower threshold of agency would..by its tenuity, de-substantialize its objective universe towards qualitative nonentity. **1954** D. VON HILDEBRAND *New Tower of Babel* 176 We simultaneously desubstantialize that which we want to build up in the soul.

desubstantiate (diːsʌb'stænʃɪeɪt), *v.* [f. DE- II. 1 + L. *substāntia* SUBSTANCE + -ATE: after *substantiate.*] *trans.* To deprive of substance.
1884 MRS. H. WARD tr. *Amiel's Jrnl.* (1891) 255 The mind is not only unclothed but stripped of itself and so to speak de-substantiated.

† **de'subulate,** *v. Obs. rare*⁻⁰. [f. L. *dēsūbulāre* to bore in deeply, f. DE- I. 3 + *sūbula* an awl.]
1623 COCKERAM, *Desubulate*, to pierce with a nale.

desudation (diːsjuː'deɪʃən). *Med.* [ad. L. *dēsūdātiōn-em* violent sweating, n. of action from *dēsūdāre* to sweat greatly, f. DE- 3 + *sūdāre* to sweat. So in mod.F. (Littré.).]
1727-51 in CHAMBERS *Cycl.* **1857** DUNGLISON *Med. Lexicon* 289 Desudation means a profuse and inordinate sweating, a muck sweat.

† **de'sudatory.** *Obs. rare*⁻⁰. [f. L. type **dēsūdātōrium*, f. *dēsūdāre*: see prec. and -ORY.]
1727 BAILEY vol. II, *Desudatory*, an hot House or Bagnio.

† **de'suete,** *a. Obs. rare*⁻⁰. [ad. L. *dēsuēt-us* pa. pple.: see next.]
1727 BAILEY vol. II, *Desuete*, out of use.

desuetude ('dɛswɪtjuːd). [a. F. *désuétude* (1596 in Hatzf.), ad. L. *dēsuētūdo* disuse, f. *dēsuētus*, pa. pple. of *dēsuēscĕre* to disuse, become unaccustomed, f. DE- 6 + *suēscĕre* to be accustomed, to be wont.]

† **1.** A discontinuance of the use or practice (*of* anything); disuse; †protracted cessation *from*.
1623 COCKERAM, *Desuetude*, lacke of vse. **1629** tr. *Herodian* (1635) 131 A generall lazinesse and desuetude of Martiall Exercises. **1652-62** HEYLIN *Cosmogr.*, To Rdr., My desuetude from those younger studies. **1661** BOYLE *Style of Script.* (1675) 139 By a desuetude and neglect of it. **1677** HALE *Prim. Orig. Man.* II. iv. 160 Desuetude from their former Civility and Knowledge. **1706** J. SERGEANT *Account of Chapter* (1853) Pref. xv, By a desuetude of acting, expire, and be buried in oblivion.

b. The passing into a state of disuse.
1821 LAMB *Elia* Ser. I. *New Year's Eve*, The gradual desuetude of old observances.

2. The condition or state into which anything falls when one ceases to use or practise it; the state of disuse.
1637-50 ROW *Hist. Kirk* (1842) 14 To revive acts buried and brought in [= into] desuetude by Prelats. **1678** R. BARCLAY *Apol. Quakers* x. §22. 315 The weighty Truths of God were neglected, and, as it were, went into Desuetude. **1703** *Lond. Gaz.* No. 3914/4 Reviving such [Laws] as are in desuetude. **1820** SCOTT *Monast.* i, The same mode of cultivation is not yet entirely in desuetude in some distant parts of North Britain. **1826** *Q. Rev.* XXXIV. 6 This beautiful work..fell (as the Scots lawyers express it) into desuetude. **1874** GREEN *Short Hist.* iv. §2. 168 The exercise of rights which had practically passed into desuetude.

desulphur (diː'sʌlfə(r)), *v.* [f. DE- II. 2 + SULPHUR. So mod.F. *désulfurer.*] *trans.* To free from sulphur; to desulphurize.
1874 W. CROOKES *Dyeing & Calico-printing* 85 Wool deprived of naturally adhering grease, and heated to 160°, assumes a yellow tinge, which is deeper when the wool has previously been de-sulphured.

desulphurate (diː'sʌlfjʊəreɪt), *v.* [f. DE- II. 1 + SULPHURATE *v.*] = prec. Hence **de'sulphurated** *ppl. a.*, **desul'phurating** *vbl. sb.* and *ppl. a.*, **desulphu'ration.**
1757 tr. *Henckel's Pyritol.* 109 To which the pyrites-iron must, by the desulphuration, be reduced. **1791** PEARSON in *Phil. Trans.* LXXXI. 361 The difference of the times required for desulphurating the antimony. **1875** H. C. WOOD *Therap.* (1879) 619 Not really a desulphurating compound.

desulphuret (diː'sʌlfjʊərɛt), *v.* [f. DE- II. 2 + SULPHURET.] *trans.* To deprive of sulphurets or sulphides. Hence **de'sulphuretted** *ppl. a.*
1878 URE *Dict. Arts* III. 847 Soda which contains sulphides is preferred for making the mottled..soap, whereas the desulphuretted soda makes the best white-curd soap.

desulphurize (diː'sʌlfjʊəraɪz), *v.* [f. DE- II. 1 + SULPHURIZE *v.*] *trans.* To free from sulphur.
1864 WEBSTER, *Desulphurize.* **1892** *Pall Mall G.* 4 June 7/3 To induce them to desulphurize all their waste.
Hence **de'sulphurized** *ppl. a.*; **de'sulphurizing** *vbl. sb.* and *ppl. a.*; also **desulphuri'zation, de'sulphurizer.**
1854 RONALDS & RICHARDSON *Chem. Technol.* I. 106 In this sense the production of coke may also be called the desulphurization. **1870** J. ROSKELL in *Eng. Mech.* 18 Mar. 647/1 It is also a flux and a desulphuriser. **1883** *Cassell's Fam. Mag.* Dec. 59/2 Desulphurised silicates. **1892** *Daily News* 23 Sept. 3/2 A very powerful desulphurising agent. **1894** *Westm. Gaz.* 6 Feb. 6/3 The desulphurisation of Cleveland ironstone so as to convert it straightway into steel will be an accomplished fact.

desult (dɪ'sʌlt), *v. nonce-wd.* [ad. L. *dēsultāre* to leap down, f. DE- 1 + *saltāre* to leap.] *intr.* To proceed in a desultory manner.
1872 M. COLLINS *Pr. Clarice* I. vi. 95, I digress, I desult. **1873** —— *Miranda* II. 143 Having heretofore been accused of desulting and digressing. **1876** MABEL COLLINS *Blacksmith & Scholar* I. 201 We must not desult.

desultor (dɪ'sʌltə(r)). *rare.* [a. L. *dēsultor* leaper down, vaulter, agent-noun from *dēsilīre*, *dēsult-* to leap down.] A circus horse-leaper.
[**1727** BAILEY vol. II, *Desultores, desultorii*, Persons of agility of body, who used to leap from one horse to another, at the Horse Races in the Circensian Games.] **1880** M. COLLINS *Th. in Garden* I. 183 Clowns and desultors in ragged jackets were hanging about.

desultorily ('dɛsəltərɪlɪ), *adv.* [f. DESULTORY + -LY².] In a desultory or random manner; unmethodically.
1664 EVELYN *Mem.* (1857) III. 146 Or else he had not passed so desultorily our Universities and the Navy. **1803** *Med. Jrnl.* X. 306 The late influenza..proceeded desultorily in some cases, in others it was more regularly progressive. **1812** SHELLEY *Let.* in Hogg *Life* (1858) II. v. 140 Have I written desultorily? **1891** T. HARDY *Tess* I. vi, They had spent some time wandering desultorily. **1891** ATKINSON *Moorland Par.* 324 Birds hopping slowly and desultorily about.

'desultoriness. [f. as prec. + -NESS.] The quality of being desultory; scrappy discursiveness; disconnectedness; lack of method.
1661 BOYLE *Style of Script.* Pref. (1675) 10 The Seeming Desultorinesse of my Method. **1727** BAILEY vol. II, *Desultoriness*, the Skipping from one Thing to another. **1788** REID *Act. Powers* II. iii. 538 There is a desultoriness of thought in man. **1816** BUCHAN in Singer *Hist. Cards* 360 Excuse the desultoriness of these observations. **1870** *Pall Mall G.* 9 Aug. 12 Accidental defects of desultoriness and sketchiness.

desultorious (dɛsəl'tɔərɪəs), *a.* [f. L. *dēsultōri-us* DESULTORY + -OUS.] = DESULTORY *a.* I.
1637 GILLESPIE *Eng. Pop. Cerem.* II. ix. 52 O desultorious Declamation! O roving Rethorike! *a* **1638** MEDE *Rem. Apoc.* Wks. (1672) III. 582 Our desultorious and shifting Interpreters. **1703** BP. PATRICK *Comm. 2 Sam.* vi. 10 David danced with composed and decent, not desultorious and light motions, such as vain fellows are wont to use. **1719** WATERLAND *Vind. Christ's Divinity* 459 Fixing the Sense of Scripture, and preventing its being ill-used by desultorious Wits. **1819** H. BUSK *Vestriad* III. 525 Tripping with loose and desultorious toe.

desultory ('dɛsəltərɪ), *a.* (*sb.*) [ad. L. *dēsultōri-us* of or belonging to a vaulter, superficial, desultory, f. *dēsultor*: see DESULTOR.] **A.** *adj.*

1. Skipping about, jumping or flitting from one thing to another; irregularly shifting, devious; wavering, unsteady. *lit.* and *fig.*
1581 MULCASTER *Positions* xxxix. (1887) 220 Not resting vpon any one thing, but desultorie ouer all. **1594** BP. ANDREWES *Serm.* II. 68 'Winter brooks' as Job termeth flitting desultory Christians. **1655** FULLER *Ch. Hist.* III. ii. §31 The Crown, since the Conquest, never observed a regular, but an uncertain and desultory motion. **1699** BENTLEY *Phal.* 86 Persons of a light and desultory temper, that skip about, and are blown with every wind, as Grass-hoppers are. **1699** BURNET *39 Art.* xx. (1700) 195 All men ought to avoid the Imputations of a desultory Levity. **1748** J. MASON *Elocut.* 19 To cure an uneven, desultory Voice.. do not begin your Periods..in too high or too low a Key. **1754** EELES in *Phil. Trans.* XLIX. 132 That desultory motion, by which it flies off from an electrified body. **1784** H. ELLIOTT in *Dk. of Leeds's Pol. Mem.* (1884) 259 There is also a peculiar desultory motion in His Royal Highnesses eye. **1789** G. WHITE *Selborne* xv. (1853) 63, I shot at it but

it was so desultory that I missed my aim. **1825** SOUTHEY *Paraguay* Proem., Ceasing here from desultory flight.

2. Pursuing a disconnected and irregular course of action; unmethodical.

1740 WARBURTON *Let.* 2 Feb. (R.), This makes my reading wild and desultory. **1773** BURKE *Corr.* (1844) I. 427 Writing ..not in a desultory and occasional manner, but systematically. **1779** MAD. D'ARBLAY *Diary* 14 June, She is a very desultory reader. **1827** HARE *Guesses* (1859) 146 Desultory reading is indeed very mischievous, by fostering habits of loose, discontinuous thought. **1855** MILMAN *Lat. Chr.* (1864) IV. VII. i. 3 A desultory and intermitting warfare. **1872** GEO. ELIOT *Middlem.* xxix. (1873) 104 Guests whose desultory vivacity makes their presence a fatigue. **1876** STUBBS *Med. & Mod. Hist.* ii. 41 The temptation to desultory research must in every case be very great, and desultory research, however it may amuse or benefit the investigator, seldom adds much to the real stock of human knowledge.

b. Of a single thing: Coming disconnectedly; random.

a **1704** R. L'ESTRANGE (J.), 'Tis not for a desultory thought to attone for a lewd course of life. **1822** HAZLITT *Table-t.* Ser. II. vi. (1869) 131 He no sooner meditates some desultory project, than [etc.].

c. Irregular and disconnected in form or appearance; motley. *rare.*

1842 ALISON *Hist. Europe* (1849-50) XIII. lxxxviii. §42. 148 They..shuddered when they gazed on the long and desultory array of Cossacks..sweeping by. **1866** HOWELLS *Venet. Life* ii. 19 A beggar in picturesque and desultory costume.

B. *sb.* A horse trained for the 'desultor' in a circus. *Obs. rare*$^{-1}$.

1653 URQUHART *Rabelais* I. xxiii, These horses were called desultories.

†**de'sulture.** *Obs. rare*$^{-0}$. [ad. L. *dēsultūra*, leaping down, vaulting.]

1727 BAILEY vol. II, *Desulture*, a vaulting from one horse to another.

†**de'sume,** *v. Obs.* [ad. L. *dēsūm-ĕre* to take from a mass, pick out, cull, f. DE- 2 + *sūmĕre* to take.] *trans.* To take or obtain (*from* some source); to derive, borrow, deduce.

1564 HAWARD *Eutropius* To Rdr. 7 A language more rife and familiare than those from whence he [Tully] desumed them. **1623** HART *Arraignm. Ur.* Ep. to Rdr. A ij, Some things desumed from mine owne experimentall knowledge. **1646** SIR T. BROWNE *Pseud. Ep.* III. xiv. 140 Nor is this Salamanders wooll desumed from any Animal, but a Minerall substance. **1697** POTTER *Antiq. Greece* II. xiii. (1715) 304 From this Species, those, whose profession it was to interpret Dreams, have desumed their Names.

†**de'sumption.** *Obs. rare.* [n. of action f. L. *dēsūmĕre*, ppl. stem *desumpt-*.] Taking (from some source).

1656 BLOUNT *Glossogr.*, *Desumption*, a chusing, or taking out. **1775** ASH, *Desumption*, the act of taking from others.

desuperheat (diːˈs(j)uːpəhiːt), *v.* [f. DE- II. 1 + SUPERHEAT *v.*] *trans.* To reduce the temperature of (superheated steam). So **de'superheated** *ppl. a.*, **de'superheating** *vbl. sb.*

1931 CRAIG & ANDERSON *Steam Power* viii. 201 It is often necessary to desuperheat steam when the pressure and temperature..are too high. **1959** C. D. SWIFT *Steam Power Plants* xvii. 429 The desuperheating water must be broken up into a fine mist in order to get a large and intimate contact surface with the steam to be desuperheated. *Ibid.*, The element which feels the desuperheated steam temperature must be carefully located.

Hence **de'superheater**, an apparatus which desuperheats steam.

1931 CRAIG & ANDERSON *Steam Power* viii. 201 A desuperheater is sometimes used as a feedwater heater. **1951** *Engineering* 23 Nov. 643/2 Steam..is passed through desuperheaters..which reduce the temperature to..above saturation.

desupernaturalize: see DE- II. 1.

†**des'voy,** *v. Obs. rare*$^{-1}$. [a. OF. *desvoy-er*, var. of *desvier*:—late L. type **disviāre* for L. *dēviāre*: see DE- I. 6.] *intr.* To go out of the way, to deviate.

1481 CAXTON *Myrr.* III. xiv. 166 By which they desuoy and goo out of the waye.

deswade, obs. form of DISSUADE *v.*

†**deswarré,** *ppl. a. Obs.* [a. AFr. **deswaré*, OF. **desguaré*, **desgaré* = OF. *esguaré*, *esward*, *esgaré*, mod.F. *égaré*.] Gone out of the way; that has lost his way, gone astray, stray. Another form of the word is in the title *Sir Dégarré* = *knight deswarré*, in the quotation.

c **1314** *Guy Warw.* (A.) 6003 A kniȝt icham deswarre, þat in [*v.r.* herborough] y bid þar charite.

desy, obs. var. of DIZZY.

de'synchronize, *v.* [DE-.] *trans.* The reverse of SYNCHRONIZE *v.* (esp. sense 2 b). So **de'synchronized** *ppl. a.*

1896 *Bootle Times* 18 Jan. 6/6 One of the machine doctor's principal uses is in desynchronising looms. **1956** D. E. CHARLWOOD *No Moon Tonight* ii. 15 A bomber passed overhead, its desynchronized engines droning through the night.

desynonymization (diːsɪˌnɒnɪmaɪˈzeɪʃən). [n. of action f. next: see -ATION.] The process by which words originally synonymous come to be differentiated in use.

1862 H. SPENCER *First Princ.* II. xix. §153 It has been remarked..that with the advance of language, words which were originally alike in their meanings acquire unlike meanings—a change which he [Coleridge] expresses by the formidable word, 'desynonymization'. *Ibid.*, The desynonymization of words is the ultimate effect.

desynonymize (diːsɪˈnɒnɪmaɪz), *v.* [f. DE- II. 1 + SYNONYM + -IZE.]

1. *trans.* To differentiate in meaning words previously synonymous.

1817 COLERIDGE *Biog. Lit.* iv. (1870) 42 In all languages there exists an instinct of growth..working unconsciously to desynonymize those words originally of the same meaning. **1827** HARE *Guesses* Ser. I. (1873) 220 His [Coleridge's] word to *desynonymise*..is a truly valuable one, as designating a process very common in the history of language. **1882** FARRAR *Early Chr.* I. ix. 205 There had been a rapid tendency to desynonymize the words 'bishop' and 'presbyter'.

b. To free from synonyms.

1873 F. HALL *Mod. Eng.* 169 To form an idea of the extent to which our language has been desynonymized.

2. *intr.* To cease to be synonymous.

a **1862** BUCKLE *Misc. Wks.* (1872) I. 547 Remarks on the tendency of words to desynonymize.

Hence **desy'nonymized** *ppl. a.*, **-izing** *vbl. sb.* and *ppl. a.*

1833 J. C. HARE in *Philolog. Museum* II. 224 From the desynonymizing tendency before spoken of. **1851** TRENCH *Study of Words* vi. (1869) 225 The process of 'desynonymizing'. **1884** FARRAR *Luke* 359 'Ανάθεμα is only a desynonymised form of the same word [ἀνάθημα].

†**desyte,** *v. Obs. rare.* [? f. L. *dēsit-*, ppl. stem of *dēsinĕre* to cease: cf. DESITION.] ? To leave off.

a **1529** SKELTON *Col. Cloute* 8 Eythyr for to endyte or else for to desyte.

det, earlier spelling of DEBT *sb.* and *a.*

detach (dɪˈtætʃ), *v.* In 5 distache. [a. F. *détache-r*, earlier *destacher*, *destachier* (12th c. in Godef.) = Pr., Sp. *destacar*, It. *distaccare*, f. Rom. *des-*, L. *dis-* (DIS-) + Rom. *tacca*, F. *tache* nail, tack, fixed point, spot. Cf. ATTACH. Used by Caxton in form *distache* from OF. *des-* (see DES-); but the existing word appears to have been adopted from modern F. late in the 17th c.]

1. *trans.* To unfasten and separate; to disconnect, disengage, disunite. *lit.* and *fig.*

[*c* **1477** CAXTON *Jason* 115 b, He distached and ripte it of.] **1686** F. SPENCE tr. *Varilla's Ho. Medicis* 75 Coglione detach'd himself out, for the viewing him the better. **1691-8** NORRIS *Pract. Disc.* IV. 219 We must now Detache and disingage our Hearts from the Creatures. **1736** BUTLER *Anal.* II. vii. 333 The testimony of S. Paul is to be considered as detached from that of the rest of the Apostles. **1794** SULLIVAN *View Nat.* II. 6 The flints..I can readily conceive to have been detached from mountains very distant from them. **1797** MANN in *Lett. Lit. Men* (Camden) 446 The French have long sought to detach Austria from England. **1798** LAMB *Rosamund Gray* xi, [It] only tends to soften and tranquillise my mind, to detach me from the restlessness of human pursuits. **1800** tr. *Lagrange's Chem.* I. 335 The caloric endeavours to detach carbonic acid from the lime. **1847** MRS. A. KERR *Hist. Servia* 258 Nor could Kara George venture to detach himself from the Russians. **1868** FREEMAN *Norm. Conq.* (1876) II. App. 575 Northamptonshire and Huntingdonshire were afterwards again detached from Northumberland. **1874** KNIGHT *Dict. Mech.* I. 314 A failure to detach both hooks simultaneously may lead to the swamping of the boat.

2. *Mil.* and *Naval.* To separate and send off (a part from a main body) for a special purpose; to draw off (a regiment, a ship, or the like) for some special mission. Also *transf.*

1684 *Scanderbeg Rediv.* vi. 145 A Body of Foot and Dragoons was Detached to Attacque their Cannon. **1697** POTTER *Antiq. Greece* I. xxvi. (1715) 181 The Chivalry shall be detacht out of the most puissant and wealthy Athenians. **1706** PHILLIPS (ed. Kersey), *To detach* (Fr. in the Art of War), to make a Detachment, to send away a Party of Soldiers upon a particular Expedition. **1727** H. BLAND *Milit. Disc.* xix. 287 When Battalions are Detach'd for the covering of the General's Quarters, it only goes for a Tour of Fatigue. **1748** SMOLLETT *Rod. Rand.* (1845) 148 She was immediately detached to look out for a convenient place. **1796-7** *Instr. & Reg. Cavalry* (1813) 257 During this the front line detaches skirmishers. **1855** MACAULAY *Hist. Eng.* III. 678 Several regiments..detached from the army which had lately besieged Limerick.

absol. **1809** WELLINGTON in Gurw. *Desp.* IV. 400 If they should venture to detach, they will lose both kingdoms.

3. *intr.* (for *refl.*) To disengage and separate oneself, to become disconnected.

1842 TENNYSON *Vision of Sin* iii, Detaching, fold by fold, From those still heights, and slowly drawing near.

Hence **de'taching** *vbl. sb.* and *ppl. a.*

1865 CARLYLE *Fredk. Gt.* (1873) VI. xv. xi. 62 Stronger than they by their detachings. **1874** KNIGHT *Dict. Mech. Boat-detaching Hook*, one adapted to be suddenly cast loose when a boat lowered from the davits touches the water. **1884** *Pall Mall G.* 25 July 11/1 The detaching shaft springs back. **1890** *Athenæum* 21 June 795/3 That detaching and absorbing interest which from time to time is necessary to physical and mental well-being.

detacha'bility. [f. next: see -ITY.] Capability of being detached.

1825 COLERIDGE *Aids Refl.* (1861) 255 Its singleness, its detachability for the imagination. **1878** *Scribner's Mag.* XVI. 434/1 We only realize the detachability of things when we see a baby at work.

detachable (dɪˈtætʃəb(ə)l), *a.* [f. prec. vb. + -ABLE.] Capable of being detached or separated.

1818 BENTHAM *Ch. Eng.* 406 This detachable mass of pay. **1834** *Fraser's Mag.* X. 700 Poetry yet intrudes in separate and detached or detachable passages. **1867** MACGREGOR *Voy. Alone* (1868) 22 The chart frame is also detachable from its place. **1878** DOWDEN *Stud. Lit.* 241 Many good things in particular passages of her writings are detachable. **1883** *Standard* 6 Apr. 5/2 The detachable spear point of the Fraser River savage.

de'tachableness. [f. prec. + -NESS.] Capability of being detached.

1855 H. SPENCER *Princ. Psychol.* (1870) I. 564 The detachableness which distinguishes ideas that are fully developed.

detached (dɪˈtætʃt), *ppl. a.* [f. DETACH *v.* + -ED.]

a. Disconnected, disengaged, separated; separate, unattached, standing apart, isolated.

1706 PHILLIPS (ed. Kersey), *Bastion detached or cut off*, that which is separated from the Body of the Works. **1712** J. JAMES tr. *Le Blond's Gardening* 29 The House stands detached. **1727-51** CHAMBERS *Cycl.* s.v., In painting, the figures are said to be well detached, or loosened, when they stand free, and disengaged from each other. **1791** BOSWELL *Johnson* Advt., Innumerable detached particulars. **1794** SULLIVAN *View Nat.* II. 77 Ore found in large detached masses. **1801** MRS. CH. SMITH *Solitary Wanderer* II. 38, I took a small, but elegant, detached house. **1860** TYNDALL *Glac.* I. vii. 47 In the centre..stands a detached column of granite. **1868** FREEMAN *Norm. Conq.* (1876) II. ix. 409 A few detached events must be mentioned. **1879** SIR G. G. SCOTT *Lect. Archit.* I. 149 Attached and detached shafts may be used alternately. **1879** *Cassell's Techn. Educ.* IV. 27/2 The villa stands alone, or as it is termed 'detached'.

b. Of persons, their conduct, etc.: characterized by detachment (see DETACHMENT 4 b).

1913 D. H. LAWRENCE *Sons & Lovers* xii. 322 He was pale and detached-looking. **1924** A. D. SEDGWICK *Little French Girl* II. xi, She might be detached, and even callous; but she was not brazen. *Ibid.* IV. i, Someone quite, quite detached and devoted must fall in love with her. **1948** D. CECIL *2 Quiet Lives* II. ii. 127 Gray's maturity appears in the detached clear-sightedness with which he could observe his own character.

de'tachedly, *adv.* [f. prec. + -LY².] In a detached manner; disconnectedly; apart from others of the same kind, or from context, etc.

1797 E. M. LOMAX *Philanthrope* 252 The tree, the rock, or the meadow, considered detachedly from one another. **1824** SIR E. BRYDGES *Lett. on Byron*, Some of the sentiments [in 'Cain'], taken detachedly..are..dangerous. **1847** LD. LINDSAY *Chr. Art* I. 122 We are at liberty..to consider them detachedly.

detachedness (dɪˈtætʃtnɪs, -ɪdnɪs). [f. as prec. + -NESS.] The quality of being detached or of standing apart; separation; isolation.

1768 *Wom. of Honor* III. 214 So complete had his detachedness been from his family. **1892** *Athenæum* 17 Sept. 392/2 It may be that this 'detachedness'—unkind persons call it selfishness..is an element of a noble strain.

detacher (dɪˈtætʃə(r)). [f. DETACH *v.* + -ER¹.] A person or thing that detaches; an apparatus or instrument for detaching.

1884 *Bath Herald* 27 Dec. 6/5 After being carried through certain apparatus called detachers, the wheat passes through centrifugal dressers.

detachment (dɪˈtætʃmənt). [a. F. *détachement* (1642 in Hatzf.), f. *détacher*: see -MENT.]

1. The action of detaching; unfastening, disconnecting, separation.

1669 WOODHEAD *St. Teresa* I. Pref. 35 A perfect Detachment, and clearing of our affections from the friendships of the creature. **1699** J. WOODWARD in *Phil. Trans.* XXI. 208 So continual an Emission and Detachment of Water, in so great Plenty from the Parts of Plants. **1783** POTT *Chirurg. Wks.* II. 17 A detachment of fibres from the *fascia lata* of the thigh. **1876** W. H. POLLOCK in *Contemp. Rev.* June 55 The growth of the drama has..gone hand in hand with its detachment from the service of its parent. **1880** CARPENTER in *19th Cent.* No. 38. 612 Bergs which show least signs of change since their first detachment from the parent mass.

2. *Mil.* and *Naval.* The separating and dispatching of part of a body of troops, etc., on special service.

1678 PHILLIPS, *Detachment*, a word now very much brought into use, in relations of the affairs of the French Army, and signifies a drawing off of a party from one place for the relief or assistance of some party, upon occasion, in another place. **1693** LUTTRELL *Brief Rel.* (1857) III. 116 They confirm the detachment of the dauphine with 25,000 men to the Rhine. **1724** DE FOE *Mem. Cavalier* (1840) 107 The army, after so many detachments, was not above nineteen thousand men. **1748** CHESTERF. *Lett.* II. clx. 75 Which would have..caused a great detachment from their army in Flanders. **1841** ELPHINSTONE *Hist. Ind.* I. 143 [They] had become tenants on condition of service instead of mere officers on detachment.

3. *concr.* A portion of an army or navy taken from the main body and employed on some separate service or expedition; any party similarly separated from a main body.

1678 Butler *Hud.* III. iii. 35 Haunted with detachments, sent From Marshal Legion's regiment. **1681** Luttrell *Brief Rel.* (1857) I. 89 He has sent out a detachment of six witnesses, to confound Fitzharris's discovery. **1724** De Foe *Mem. Cavalier* (1840) 68 Detachments were made out of every regiment to search among the dead. **1739** Cibber *Apol.* x. 273 A Detachment of Actors from Drury-Lane. **1781** Gibbon *Decl. & F.* III. lii. 256 A detachment of cavalry intercepted his march. **1838** Thirlwall *Greece* II. xv. 291 He sent a detachment of his fleet to seize the island of Cythera. **1859** F. A. Griffiths *Artil. Man.* (1862) 112 A gun detachment consists of one non-commissioned officer and nine gunners.

attrib. **1881** J. Grant *Cameronians* I. i. 3 The smartest officers are usually selected for detachment duty. **1881** Mrs. Alexander *Freres* iii, He was almost immediately told off for detachment duty.

4. a. A standing apart or aloof from objects or circumstances; a state of separation or withdrawal from connexion or association with surrounding things.

1862 Maurice *Mor. & Met. Philos.* IV. iii. §36. 88 This detachment from Italian feelings might have led one to expect [etc.]. **1871** Tyndall *Fragm. Sc.* (1879) I. iv. 126 The mountain sprang forth with astonishing solidity and detachment from the surrounding air. **1874** Morley *Compromise* (1886) 115 Oxford, 'the sweet city with her dreaming spires', where there has ever been so much detachment from the world. **1883** *Brit. Q. Rev.* Oct. 392 An apartness or detachment from self. **1888** Bryce *Amer. Commw.* II. III. liii. 335 The detachment of the United States from the affairs of the Old World.

b. A condition of spiritual separation from the world. (Cf. 1669 in 1.) More widely, freedom or aloofness from ordinary concerns or emotional commitments.

1798 Lamb *Rosamund Gray* xi, The stronger I feel this detachment, the more I find myself drawn heavenward. **1853** M. Kelly tr. *Gosselin's Power of Pope* I. 91 To inspire all the faithful with the spirit of detachment. **1856** J. H. Newman *Callista* 199 A most heroic faith, and the detachment of a saint. **1865** T. F. Knox *Life Henry Suso* 152 Let all who suffer with detachment rejoice. **1888** H. James in *Harper's Mag.* Feb. 342/2 Her detachment, her air of having no fatuous illusions, and not being blinded by prejudice, seemed to me at times to amount to an affectation. **1891** *Daily News* 3 Apr. 5/2 There is no such excellent cure for 'detachment' as an attachment. **1915** R. Brooke *Let.* 6 Apr. (1968) 677 One just hasn't, though, the time and detachment to write, I find. **1924** A. D. Sedgwick *Little French Girl* II. xi, 'C'était un bien méchant homme,' Madame Vervier remarked in a tone of surpassing detachment. **1926** W. S. Churchill in W. R. Inge *Lay Thoughts of a Dean* 166 That sense of detachment and impartiality, that power of comprehending the other man's point of view. **1935** W. S. Maugham *Don Fernando* x. 201 This person seems to preserve a strangely ironic detachment: it would never occur to you that he was a mystic.

¶ Erroneously for attachment 1–2.

1706 Phillips (ed. Kersey), s.v. *Detachiare*, To seize or take into custody another man's goods or person by writ of Detachment or other course of law. **1727** Bailey vol. II, *Detachment*, in Law, a sort of Writ.

detail (dɪˈteɪl, ˈdiːteɪl), *sb.* [a. F. *détail* (12th c. in Hatzf.) the action of detailing, the result of this action, retail, f. stem of *détailler*: see next. App. first adopted in the phrase *in detail*, F. *en détail*, opposed to *en gros* in the gross, wholesale. Sense 5 represents the F. *détail du service*, *distribuer l'ordre en détail*, Feuquieres, *a.* 1711.]

1. a. The dealing with matters item by item; detailed treatment; attention to particulars. Esp. in phrase ***in* (†*the*) *detail***, item by item; part by part; minutely; circumstantially. So *to go into detail*, i.e. to deal with or treat a thing in its individual particulars.

1603 Holland *Plutarch's Mor.* 306 (R.) As if a man would say, that necessary it is for him to offer wrong in detaile, who mindeth to do right in the gross. **1706** Phillips *Detail* (Fr.), the particular Circumstances of an Affair; as These advantages need not be offered in Detail to your View. **1734** Pope *Ess. Man*, Introd., I was unable to treat this part of my subject more in detail. **1769** Goldsm. *Rom. Hist.* (1786) I. 320 They..perhaps condemned them in the gross for defects, which they thought it not worth while to mention in the detail. **1785** Cowper *Wks.* (1837) XV. 163 The consequences need not, to use the fashionable phrase, be given in detail. **1840** Gladstone *Ch. Princ.* 69 The fear of punishment in the gross or in the detail. **1847** Emerson *Repr. Men, Swedenborg* Wks. (Bohn) I. 332 His revelations destroy their credit by running into detail. **1868** M. Pattison *Academ. Org.* iv. 110 Relieved from the drudgery of detail. **1870** Freeman *Norm. Conq.* (ed. 2) I. App. 558 The tale, which is told in great detail, is doubtless mythical in its details. **1884** *Law Times Rep.* 16 Feb. 773/2 We had to go into detail, so as to make the case clear.

b. *Mil. in detail*: by the engagement of small portions of an army or force one after another. ***war of detail***, a war carried on after this fashion, instead of by general engagements. (Often *fig.*)

1841 Miall *Nonconf.* I. 1 Their war has been one of detail, not of principle. **1842** H. Rogers *Introd. Burke's Wks.* 85 Pursuing a war of detail instead of acting on some uniform scheme. **1845** Ford *Handbk. Spain* 2 Being without union [it] is also without strength and has been beaten in detail. **1858** Froude *Hist. Eng.* III. xiii. 116 Without concert..without a leader they would be destroyed in detail. **1886** Stokes *Celtic Ch.* 293 He [Brian Boru] defeated his enemies in detail.

2. A minute or circumstantial account; a detailed narrative or description of particulars.

1695 Woodward *Nat. Hist. Earth* IV. (1723) 238 But I must be forced wholey to wave and supersede the Detail of these. **1726** *Adv. Capt. R. Boyle* Pref. A iv, The following Sheets are a detail of Fortunes I have run through. **1810** (*title*), A Chronological detail of events in which Oliver Cromwell was engaged, from 1642 to 1658. **1815** T. Forster *Atmosph. Phænom.* p. ix, Aristotle..appears to have given a more minute detail of the various appearances of clouds..and other phænomena. **1825** Lytton *Falkland* 9 But my detail must be rather of thought than of action.

3. a. An item, a particular (of an account, a process, etc.); a minute or subordinate portion of any (*esp.* a large or complex) whole. (See also 4 a.)

'But that is a detail!' was (*c* 1897) a current phrase humorously making light of what was perhaps really an important element in the matter in question.

1786 T. Jefferson *Writ.* (1859) I. 560 It has given me details..which are very entertaining. **1832** Ht. Martineau *Demerara* ii. 16 The details of the management of a plantation. **1851** J. S. Macaulay *Field-Fortif.* 267 Hedges ..skirted by details of ground that may render them obstacles. **1853** J. H. Newman *Hist. Sk.* (1873) I. i. iv. 194 In the details of dress, carriage, and general manners, the Turks are very different from Europeans. **1863** Fr. A. Kemble *Resid. in Georgia* 17, I shall furnish you with no details. **1868** Dickens *Lett.* (1880) II. 393 Be particular in the minutest detail.

b. *collective sing.* The particulars or items of any whole considered collectively.

1861 Mill *Utilit.* v. 71 Nobody desires that laws should interfere with the whole detail of private life. **1886** *Law Times* LXXX. 193/2 Legal questions..full of dry and uninteresting detail.

4. *Fine Arts.* **a.** A minute or subordinate part of a building, sculpture, or painting, as distinct from the larger portions or the general conception. **b.** *collective sing.* Such minute parts collectively, or the manner of treatment of them. (Also *transf.* in reference to natural objects.)

1823 P. Nicholson *Pract. Build.* 309 The detail of both sculpture and masonry on the building. **1846** Ruskin *Mod. Paint.* I. II. II. v. §15 The detail of a single weedy bank laughs the carving of ages to scorn. **1870** F. R. Wilson *Ch. Lindisf.* 85 There are no architectural details of interest. **1882** Hamerton *Graphic Arts* iv. 29 The most careful study of antiquarian detail is united to an artist's vivid recollection of the colour and sunshine of the South. **1865** J. Fergusson *Hist. Archit.* I. I. III. ii. 232 The Assyrian honeysuckle.. forms as elegant an architectural detail as is anywhere to be found.

c. *Arch.* Short for ***detail drawing(s***, working drawings.

1819 P. Nicholson *Archit. Dict.* I. 383 *Detail*, the delineation of all the parts of an edifice, so as to be sufficiently intelligible for the execution of the work. The detail is otherwise denominated *the working drawings.* **1876** Gwilt *Encycl. Archit.* Gloss., *Details*, a term usually applied to the drawings on a large scale for the use of builders, and generally called *working drawings.* **1892** *Archit. Publ. Soc. Dict.* VIII. s.v. *Working Drawings*, Working drawings..consist of plans, elevations, sections, details of construction..many being to the full size.

5. *Mil.* **a.** The distribution in detail, to the different officers concerned, of the Daily Orders first given in general, with apportionment to each division and subdivision of the force (and finally to individual officers and men) of the share of duty falling upon them in their order; hence, the list or table showing the general distribution of duty for the whole force (***general*** or †***grand detail***), or the particular distribution of that falling upon any division or subdivision of it (***particular detail***).

office of detail (in U.S. Navy Dept.), the office where the roster of officers is kept, and from which orders as to duty are issued.

1703–8 *Order Dk. Marlborough* in Kane *Camp Disc.* (1757) 4 The Adjutant-General is to keep all the Details and an account of all things that happen in the Army. **1708** —— *Order* ibid. 4 Of Details, Whereas great Inconveniences have happened in changing the Details after made, it is agreed..by all the Generals of the Army, that all Details made at orderly Time should stand, though several other Details came afterwards; and that they should march accordingly, though the others made before did not march. *a* **1711** *Ibid.* 3 The Brigadier of the Day is to distribute the Orders he received immediately to the Majors of Brigade; and see that all the Details are made upon the Spot. **1727** H. Bland *Milit. Discip.* 281 (ch. xix, *Title*) Of the Method in Flanders for the Receiving and Distributing of the Daily Orders; General Detail of the Army (by which is meant the General Duty to be perform'd by the Officers and Soldiers) with the Form of a Roster, or Table, by which the Duty of Entire Battalions, and the Officers, is regulated. *Ibid.* in Simes *Milit. Medley* (1768) 69 Our late Monarch, the glorious King William..was perfectly knowing in the small as well as the grand detail of an army. *c* **1745** Kane *Camp. Disc.* (1757) 16 Whenever the Quarter-master General demands a Detachment, to go along with him to reconnoitre, they are to be furnished immediately from the nearest Troops, and it will be allowed them in the next Detail. **1778** *Orderly book, Maryland Loyalists*, 28 Aug., Detale for outline pickett this evening. **1779** *U.S. Army Regulation*, [The adjutant] must assemble the first serjeants of the companies, make them copy the orders, and give them their details for the next day. **1779** Capt. G. Smith *Univ. Milit. Dict.* s.v., *Detail of Duty* is a roster or table for the regular..performance of duty, either in the field, garrison, or cantonments. The general detail of duty is the proper care of the majors of brigade, who are guided by the roster for the officers, and by the tables for the men to be occasionally furnished. The adjutant of a regiment keeps the detail of duty for the officers of his regiment. **1781** T. Simes *Milit. Guide* (ed. 3) 9 The Major of Brigade is charged with the particular detail in his own brigade in much the same way as the Adjutant-general is charged with the general detail of the army. **1853** Stocqueler *Milit. Encycl.* s.v. *Detail of Duty.* **1894** *Brigade Orders, Aldershot* (MS.) 1. *Detail*, 14.10.94. Brigade Captain, Adjutant and Picquet: 2nd Worc. R. Special Picquet Hospital Hill: 2nd Lein. R. Brigade Quartermaster: 2nd Ches. R. Drums: 2 Lein. R. Company for Fire Screen Drill: none. Duties No. 1 Canteen: 2nd Ches. R. Duties No. 2 Canteen: 2nd Lein. R. Visitor to Bde. Schools (a Captn.): 2nd Ches. R.

b. The detailing or telling off a small party for a special duty. **c.** *concr.* A small body detached for a particular service or duty; a small detachment. Originally military, but extended to the police, etc.

[**1708** see under a above.]

1780 Gen. Washington *Order* 14 Mar., The fatigue party for finishing the new orderly room is to be furnished by detail from the line of the army. **1828** Webster, *Detail* 2, A selecting of officers or soldiers from the rosters. **1862** Beveridge *Hist. India* II. v. vii. 458 A small body of cavalry, and a detail of European artillery. **1884** *Daily News* 3 Mar., The ground..was explored..by the Mounted Infantry and by details from the regular Cavalry. **1885** Gen. Grant *Pers. Mem.* I. xx. 278 Details that had gone to the front after the wounded. **1888** *Troy Daily Times* 6 Feb., An extra detail of police is always made..and the crowd is not allowed to block the exit.

6. *attrib.* and *Comb.*, as ***detail work***; **detail man** *U.S.* (see quot. 1961).

1928 *Proc. 17th Ann. Meeting Amer. Drug Mfrs. Assoc.* I. 96 With the detail man, we tell our message through the human ambassador. **1961** Webster, *Detail man*, a representative of a drug manufacturer who introduces new drugs to professional users (as physicians or pharmacists). **1964** *New Statesman* 12 June 906/3, I..became a drug pedlar, or more politely a medical representative. The American-owned company I joined preferred the term 'detailman', because it indicated the essential purpose of the work: to persuade the General Practitioner to prescribe the company's drugs by serving him with suitably tempting details. **1907** *Daily Chron.* 8 June 3/4 The parish councils would..be competent to relieve the controlling authorities of much detail work. **1922** H. Crane *Lett.* (1965) 97 The infinite and distasteful detail work I have been doing at the office. **1937** *Burlington Mag.* May 251/2 Inscription and detail-work are examples of the best Netherlandish engraving.

detail (dɪˈteɪl, ˈdiː-), *v.*[1] [a. F. *détailler* (12th c. in Hatz.-Darm.), to cut in pieces, retail, deal with or relate circumstantially, f. de- I. 3 + *tailler* to cut in pieces. Adopted in English only in the transferred uses.]

1. *trans.* To deal with, give, relate, or describe minutely or circumstantially; to give particulars of; to enumerate, mention, or relate in detail.

1637–50 Row *Hist. Kirk* (1842) p. xliii, The proceedings ..are too long to be here detailed. **1751** Johnson *Rambler* No. 177 ¶3 When I delivered my opinion, or detailed my knowledge. **1802** Mrs. E. Parsons *Myst. Visit* I. 1 He was too modest to..detail news and scandal from house to house. **1875** Lyell *Princ. Geol.* II. II. xxvii. 62 From the whole of the facts above detailed, it appears [etc.]. **1875** Scrivener *Lect. Text N. Test.* 10 Certain peculiarities to be detailed hereafter. **1879** *Cassell's Techn. Educ.* IV. 90/1 We have now detailed all the various coverings ordinarily put upon books.

absol. **1841** D'Israeli *Amen. Lit.* II. 7 There were occasions when they [monastic writers] were inevitably graphic,—when they detail like a witness in court.

2. *Mil.* To appoint or tell off for a particular duty. (See detail *sb.* 5.)

1793 *Laws of Mass.* c. 1 §32 Whenever a detachment is made, the officers, non-commissioned officers and privates, being able of body, shall be detailed from the rosters or rolls for the purpose. **1810** *Ibid.* c. 107 §31 The officers, ordered to be detailed to serve on courts martial shall be detailed in the following manner. **1828** Webster, *Detail*, to select, as an officer or soldier from a division, brigade, regiment, or battalion. **1861** Swinhoe *N. China Camp.* 329 The First Division, under General Michel, was detailed for this work of destruction. **1861** W. H. Russell in *Times* 14 May 10/3 His cartridges were out, and he was compelled to detail some of his few men to make them out of shirts, stockings and jackets. **1868** Sir R. Napier in *Morn. Star* 30 June, I trust she is now recovering under the care of the medical officer.. who has been detailed by me to provide for her comfort. **1885** Gen. Grant *Pers. Mem.* I. xxi. 293 Soldiers who had been detailed to act with the navy. **1886** *Manch. Exam.* 19 Jan. 5/6 The field officers of the Royal Horse Guards detailed for the escort of Her Majesty.

b. *transf.*

1837–40 Haliburton *Clockm.* (1862) 248 We propose detailing you to Italy to purchase some originals for our gallery. **1868** *Daily News* 2 Sept., The dry dock..will start on its..voyage across the Atlantic, being towed by five vessels to be detailed for the purpose. **1874** M. Collins *Transmigr.* III. xviii. 269 A trim little waiting-maid..whom I detailed to wait upon Grace.

3. *Arch.* ***to detail on the plane***: to be exhibited in profile by abutting against the plane; said of a moulding. (Ogilvie.)

1875 *Encycl. Brit.* II. 403/2 At the base they detail on the pavement or floor of the stylobate. *Ibid.* 404/1 The glyphs detail on the tænia of the architrave, but are variously finished above.

¶ **4.** ? Confused with entail *v.*[2] (sense 4).

1794 Godwin *Cal. Williams* 289 Who had..sworn to detail upon me misery without end.

de-tail, detail (diːˈteɪl), *v.*^{2} [f. De- II. 2 a + Tail *sb.*^{1}] *trans.* To deprive of its tail or tails.

1837 Marryat *Snarleyyow* III. i. 14 The dog had been *detailed*. **1900** G. Swift *Somerley* 148 His de-tailed coat looked like a ragged Eton jacket.

detailed (dɪˈteɪld, ˈdiː-), *ppl. a.* [f. Detail *v.*^{1} + -ed^1.] Related, stated, or described circumstantially; abounding in details; minute, particular, circumstantial.

1740 Warburton *Div. Legat.* iv. 83 *note* (R.) In a professed and detailed poem on the subject. **1855** Macaulay *Hist. Eng.* IV. 419 No detailed report of the evidence has come down to us. **1857** Ruskin *Pol. Econ. Art* 6, I will not lose time in any detailed defence. **1867** Freeman *Norm. Conq.* (1876) I. iv. 254 In my more detailed narrative of English affairs.

b. *Fine Arts.* Executed in detail; furnished with all its details.

1867 A. Barry *Sir C. Barry* viii. 283 A fully detailed cornice of the order.

c. *transf.* Of a writer: Given to detail, circumstantial.

1871 Freeman *Norm. Conq.* (1876) IV. xviii. 153 Described by the most detailed historian of this campaign.

Hence **deˈtailedly** *adv.*, **deˈtailedness**.

1806 J. Pytches in *Monthly Mag.* XXII. 210 He regrets that I have not gone more detailedly into my design. **1842** J. Sterling *Ess. & Tales* (1848) I. 439 Its positiveness, shrewdness, detailedness, incongruity. **1887** Benson *Laud* 104 The..extent and detailedness of the criticism.

detailer (dɪˈteɪlə(r)). [f. Detail *v.*^{1} + -er^1.] One who details or relates circumstantially.

1794 *Crit. Rev.* Jan., The detailers of anecdotes. *a* **1809** Seward *Lett.* VI. 135 (T.) Individuality was sunk in the number of detailers.

deˈtailing, *vbl. sb.* **a.** The action of the verb; also *attrib.*

1810 *Laws of Mass.* c. 107 §31 In case of inability..of any officer..to serve..the detailing officer shall certify such circumstance to the officer who ordered the court martial. **1866** Carlyle *Edw. Irving* 94 Considerable gossiping and quizzical detailing. **1883** Clodd in *Knowl.* 7 Sept. 147/2 [These] need no detailing here.

b. *Fine Arts* = Detail *sb.* 4.

1931 C. H. Reilly in W. Rose *Outl. Mod. Knowl.* 976 Fine craftsmanship, such as the detailing of the Maison Carrée at Nîmes. **1958** *Listener* 20 Nov. 827/1 The timber detailing..seems to me not so satisfactory. **1960** *House & Garden* Dec. 31/1 Its warm colour..looks well with white detailing.

ˈdetailism. *nonce-wd.* [f. Detail *sb.* + -ism.] A system of attention to details.

1865 Lewes in *Fortn. Rev.* I. 588 There has been a reaction against conventionalism which called itself Idealism, in favour of detailism which calls itself Realism.

detain (dɪˈteɪn), *v.* Forms: 5–7 deteyn(e, 6–7 detein(e, deteign(e, detayn(e, detaine, (7 deten), 7– detain. [Late ME. *deteine, deteyne*, a. OF. *detenir* (12th c. in Littré), *detener* (Britton) = Pr. and Sp. *detener*, Cat. *detenir*, It. *ditenere*:—Rom. type **dē-tenēre* for L. *dētinēre*, to hold off, keep back, detain, f. De- I. 2 + *tenēre* to hold. For the root-vowel cf. *contain, maintain, sustain, retain.*]

1. a. *trans.* To keep in confinement or under restraint; to keep prisoner. *spec.* To place (a political offender) in confinement.

[**1292** Britton i. v. §3 Ou si maliciousement le fet detener.] **1485** Caxton *Chas. Gt.* 145 The peres of fraunce beyng thus assyeged and deteyned. **1548** Hall *Chron.* 10 A traytor..whiche is apprehended and deteigned in prisone for his offence. **1605** Camden *Rem.* 16 When King Richard first was deteined prisoner. **1761** Hume *Hist. Eng.* III. lix. 279 He was detained in strict confinement. **1884** Miss Braddon *Flower & Weed* 139 'Beg your pardon, sir,' said the constable..'I shall be obliged to detain you till this business is settled.' **1918** *Rep. Comm. Rev. Conspiracies* 86 in *Parl. Papers* (Cd. 9190) VIII, Such men are the leaders and organizers of the movement. They are now detained or their arrest is intended under Regulation III of 1818. **1940** J. Anderson in *Hansard Commons* 23 May 277, I have found it my duty, in the exercise of my powers under Regulation 18B of the Defence (General) Regulations, 1939, to direct that Captain Archibald Henry Maule Ramsay, Member of Parliament, be detained.

†**b.** *pass.* To be 'holden' or possessed *with* (infirmity, disease, etc.). *Obs.*

a **1440** *Found. St. Bartholomew's* 18 With this so grete A sykenes was he deteynyd. **1549** Chaloner *Erasmus on Folly* T iij b, To be deteigned with suche a specie of madnesse. **1660** Bloome *Archit.* C b, A Maide of the City Corinthia.. detained with sicknesse, dyed.

2. a. To keep back, withhold; *esp.* to keep back what is due or claimed. ? *Obs.*

c **1535** in Froude *Short Stud.* (1876) I. 422 The said abbot hath detained and yet doth detain servants wages. *a* **1625** Fletcher & Massinger *Elder Bro.* v. i, My sword forced from me too, and still detained. **1670** Marvell *Let. to Mayor of Hull* Wks. I. 153 To call to account such persons as detained money in their hands given charitably. **1710** Prideaux *Orig. Tithes* v. 221 These Tithes..have been granted by the King..but afterwards by the instinct of the Devil many have detained them. **1715–20** Pope *Iliad* xxiv. 172 No longer then..Detain the relics of great Hector dead ..restore the slain. **1768** Blackstone *Comm.* III. 855 The form of the writ..is sometimes in the *debet* and *detinet*, and sometimes in the *detinet* only: that is, the writ states..that the defendant *owes* and unjustly *detains* the debt or thing in question, or only that he unjustly *detains* it. **1849** Macaulay *Hist. Eng.* iii. I. 288 The interest of the sum fraudulently detained in the Exchequer by the Cabal.

†**b.** To keep (a person) *from* his right. *Obs.*

1583 Stubbes *Anat. Abus.* ii. (1882) 80 Hereby the poore pastors are deteined from their right, and almost beggered.

†**3. a.** To keep, retain (in a place or position, in a state or condition, or in one's possession). *Obs.* (exc. as associated with 4.)

1541 Wyatt *Defence* Wks. (1861) p. xxv, That in all accusations the defendant might detain unto him counsel. **1578** Banister *Hist. Man* v. 66 Some [glandules] are strewed as beddes vnto Veynes, and Arteries, to deteine them from hurt. **1606** Birnie *Kirk-Buriall* xix. (Jam. Suppl.), To dedicate the same thing a Kirk, and yet deteene it a buriall. **1632** Lithgow *Trav.* v. 195 Rivers mentioned in the Scriptures, which to this day detayne their names. **1635** Pagitt *Christianogr.* i. ii. (1636) 41 The inhabitants of Spaine are detained in superstition, by the vigilancy of the Inquisition. **1774** Goldsm. *Nat. Hist.* (1776) II. 159 When we fix and detain them [our eyes] too long upon the same object.

†**b.** To hold, hold down: transl. *dētinēre* of the Vulgate. *Obs.*

1582 N. T. (Rhem.) *Rom.* i. 18 Those men that deteine the veritie of God in iniustice [**1611** hold: Wycl., Tind., Cranm., *Geneva*, withhold: *Rev. V.* hold down: Gr. κατεχόντων]. **1593** Bilson *Govt. Christ's Ch.* 100 That..they might learne not to detaine the trueth of God in unrighteousnes. *a* **1694** Tillotson *Serm.* (1743) VII. 1846 Men have a natural knowledge of God; if they contradict it by their life and practice, they are guilty of 'detaining the truth of God in unrighteousness'.

†**c.** To hold or occupy with an armed force. *Obs.*

1632 Lithgow *Trav.* III. 103 A large and strong Fortresse..now detained by a Garison of Turkes. **1642** *Lanc. Tracts* (Chetham Soc.) 56 Thus the Lord hath preserved an unwalled Towne from being destroyed or detained by a great Armie.

†**d.** To hold, engage, keep the attention of. *Obs.* (or merged in 4.)

c **1585** C'tess Pembroke *Ps.* lxxiii. 7 No good on earth doth my desires detaine. **1621–51** Burton *Anat. Mel.* ii. ii. vi. iii. 301, I am mightily detained and allured with that grace and comeliness. **1780** Harris *Philol. Enq.* Wks. (1841) 429 It wants those striking revolutions, those unexpected discoveries, so essential to engage and to detain a spectator.

†**e.** To constipate, 'bind'; also *absol.* to cause constipation. *Obs.*

1580 Frampton *Dial. Yron & Steele* 158 The water that cooleth the yron, doeth detayne the bellie. *Ibid.* 158 b, It is byndyng, and therefore it doeth deteyne.

4. To keep from proceeding or going on; to keep waiting; to stop. (The ordinary current sense.)

1592 Shaks. *Ven. & Ad.* 577 For pity now she can no more detain him. **1644** Milton *Educ.* Wks. (1847) 99/2, I shall detain you no longer in the demonstration of what we should not do. *a* **1665** Sir K. Digby *Private Mem.* (1827) 89 Here Theagenes resolved to detain him self some time. **1790** Paley *Horæ Paul.* Rom. ii. 12 The business which then detained him. **1825** Cobbett *Rur. Rides* 424, I was detained ..partly by the rain, and partly by company that I liked very much. **1861** Dutton Cook *P. Foster's D.* i, Don't let me detain you. **1891** E. Peacock *N. Brendon* I. 113 We will not detain our readers. **1892** *Times* (Weekly Ed.) 21 Oct. 2/4 The vessel..is detained in quarantine.

†**5.** To keep back or restrain from action; to hinder; to delay. *Obs.*

1600 E. Blount tr. *Conestaggio* 54 But he resolved not any thing, deteined by his blinde commission, and the advise of some other Capteines. **1621–51** Burton *Anat. Mel.* iii. ii. iii. (1676) 326/1 Modesty would detain them from doing amiss. **1681** Dryden *Abs. & Achit.* 244 How long wilt thou the general joy detain: Starve, and defraud the People of thy Reign?

†**deˈtain,** *sb. Obs. rare*$^{-1}$. [f. Detain *v.*] the action of detaining, or fact of being detained; detention.

1596 Spenser *F.Q.* v. vi. 15 And gan enquire of him with mylder mood The certaine cause of Artegals detaine.

detainable (dɪˈteɪnəb(ə)l), *a.* [f. Detain *v.* + -able.] Capable of being detained.

1801 W. Taylor in *Monthly Mag.* XII. 581 It seems.. detainable, like water, by an attraction of cohesion, on the surface of certain bodies.

deˈtainal. *rare.* [f. Detain *v.* + -al^1 5.] The act of detaining; detention.

1806 W. Taylor in *Ann. Rev.* IV. 116 The injustice of the detainal is a disgrace to Bonaparte.

†**detainder.** *Obs.* Also deteinder, detaindor. Variant of Detainer^2, perhaps influenced by *attainder, remainder*.

1672 *Essex Papers* (Camden) I. 35 Ye deteinder of moneys by ye Farmers upon pretence of defalcations. **1701** Beverley *Apoc. Quest.* 32 There is also..in it the Detaindor of a Disease, a *Catochus*, and a *Catoche*, a Dead Sleep, or Insensibility with Pungency, or Vexation.

detainee (diːteɪˈniː). [f. Detain *v.* + -ee^1; cf. Détenu.] A person detained in custody, usually on political grounds and in an emergency, without or pending formal trial.

1928 in M. H. Weseen *Crowell's Dict. Eng. Gram.* 118. **1940** *Times* 11 Dec. 9/4 There were other varieties of detainees with whom he had the greatest sympathy. **1957** *Times* 10 Sept. 6/6 The [Mau Mau] detainees were.. employed on constructive development work. **1959** *Listener* 26 Feb. 359/1 Within hours of the return to the island [*sc.* Cyprus] of Sir Hugh Foot, the Governor, came the mass release of the detainees.

detainer^1 (dɪˈteɪnə(r)). Also 6 deteiner, -our, deteynour, 7 detayner. [f. Detain *v.* + -er^1: perh. orig. a. AF. **detenour* = OF. *deteneor, -eur.*] One who or that which detains; see the verb.

1531–2 *Act 23 Hen. VIII*, c. 5 §3 To punisshe the dettours and deteiners of the same by fines. **1547** *Act 1 Edw. VI*, c. 3 §2 To punish..the deteinour. **1586** J. Hooker *Girald. Irel.* in *Holinshed* II. 51/1 The deteiners of the kingdome of England against the lawfull heire. **1647** R. Baillie *Lett. & Jrnls.* (1842) III. 14 It pleased God to make his detainers let him goe. **1689** *Def. Liberty agst. Tyrants* 120 He..is..an unjust detainer which takes another Mans goods against the Owners will. **1850** Chubb *Locks & Keys* 10 This lock.. contains..several independent moveable detainers of the motion of the bolt, any one of which would alone prevent that motion; the key was adapted to move and arrange all those detainers simultaneously.

deˈtainer^2. *Law.* Forms: 7 deteiner, deteigner, deteyner, 7– detainer; *erron.* 7 -or, 8 -our. [a. Anglo-Fr. *detener* inf. used subst. Cf. *cesser, disclaimer, retainer*: see -er^4.]

The action of detaining, withholding, or keeping in one's possession; *spec.* **a.** The (wrongful) detaining of, or refusal to restore, goods taken from the owner for distraint, etc.

1619 Dalton *Countr. Just.* vii. (1630) 27 By distress or deteyner of the defendant's goods. **1768** Blackstone *Comm.* III. 150 Deprivation of possession may also be by an unjust detainer of another's goods, though the original taking was lawful. **1817** W. Selwyn *Law Nisi Prius* (ed. 4) II. 1123 If the tenant, before distress, tender..the arrears of rent, the taking of the distress becomes wrongful..but if the distress has been made, and before impounding the arrears are tendered, then the *detainer* only is unlawful. **1865** Nichols *Britton* II. 249 In like manner shall widows recover damages for the wrongful detainer of dower.

b. *forcible detainer*: see quot. 1769.

1619 Dalton *Countr. Just.* xxii. (1630) 61 One Justice of Peace may proceed in..cases of forcible entry or Deteiner. **1769** Blackstone *Comm.* IV. 147 An eighth offence against the public peace is that of a forcible entry or detainer; which is committed by violently taking or keeping possession, with menaces, force, and arms, of lands and tenements, without the authority of law. **1800** Addison *Amer. Law Rep.* 41 Indicted for a forcible entry and detainer.

c. The detaining of a person; *esp.* in custody or confinement.

1640 in Rushw. *Hist. Coll.* (1692) iii. I. 20 That the Cause of their Detainer may be certified. *a* **1719** Bp. Smallridge (J.), St. Paul sends him back again, that Philemon might have no reason to be angry at his longer detainour. **1795** Christian in *Blackstone's Comm.* (1809) I. 425 Lord Mansfield granted a habeas corpus, ordering the captain of the ship to bring up the body of James Somersett, with the cause of his detainer. **1884** *Law Times Rep.* 16 Aug. 759/2 There was no evidence..of the detainer of the child either by force or fraud.

d. A process authorizing the sheriff to detain a person already in his custody; *spec.* a writ whereby a prisoner arrested at the suit of one creditor might be detained at the suit of another.

1836–9 Dickens *Sk. Boz* (1850) 274/1 Unless the gen'lm'n means to go up afore the court, it's hardly worth while waiting for detainers, you know. **1848** Wharton *Law Lex.* s.v., A process lodged with the sheriff against a person in his custody is called a detainer. **1855** Thackeray *Newcomes* I. 248 The detainers against him were trifling.

deˈtaining, *vbl. sb.* [f. Detain *v.* + -ing^1.] The action of the verb Detain; detention, withholding, †seizure, etc. (Now usually gerundial.)

a **1535** More *Wks.* 386 (R.) That their paine in the fire wer but a detaining therin by some strenger power then themselfe. **1572** *Sc. Acts Jas. VI* (1597) §50 Taking and deteining of prisoners, ransounes, buitinges. **1600** E. Blount tr. *Conestaggio* 125 He then conceived the cause of his detaining. **1632** tr. *Bruel's Praxis Med.* 97 Catalepsis is a sudden detaining both of soule and body. **1768** Blackstone *Comm.* III. ix. (R.), To shew the cause of his detaining in prison. **1795** *Jemima* I. 165 He scorned your detainings.

deˈtaining, *ppl. a.* [f. as prec. + -ing^2.] That detains; see the verb.

1822 T. Taylor *Apuleius* vi. 121 The detaining earth. **1865** Bushnell *Vicar. Sacr.* Introd. (1868) 25 The detaining power of a dogmatizing effort.

Hence **deˈtainingly** *adv.*

1856 *Titan Mag.* Aug. 119/2 He gazed at her entreatingly and detainingly. **1880** *Argosy* XXIX. 388 Laying her hand detainingly upon his arm.

detainment (dɪˈteɪnmənt). Now *rare.* [f. Detain *v.* + -ment: cf. OF. *detenement.*] The fact of detaining, or of being detained; detention.

1586 *Death Earl Northumberl.* in Somers *Tracts* (1751) iv. III. 422 As well of the Cause of the Earl's Detainment, as of the Manner of his Death. **1622** Malynes *Anc. Law Merch.* 159 The danger of generall or particular Embargos of Ships, the likelihood of detainements of Kings and Princes. **1641** *Jrnls. Ho. Com.* II. 151 His Detainment close Prisoner. **1755** Magens *Insurances* I. 456 The unjust..Detainment of their Ships. **1883** Ld. Blackburn in *Law Reports* 8 App. Cases 398 Arrests, restraints and detainments of princes..involve such a taking of the subject insured out of the control of the owners.

detainor, -our, erron. ff. Detainer^2.

† **detainure** (dɪ'teɪnjʊə(r)). *Obs.* [f. DETAIN *v.* + -URE: cf. OF. *deteneure.*] = DETAINER² (of which it may be a refashioning).

1641 in Rushw. *Hist. Coll.* (1692) III. I. 340 Unlawful Seisure and Detainure. **1710** PRIDEAUX *Orig. Tithes* v. 315 A Sacrilegious detainure of that which is.. due unto God.

detane, -nie, -ny, obs. ff. DITTANY.

detant (dɪ'tænt). [A variant of DETENT, affected by the pronunciation of mod.F. *détente* (detɑ̃t) trigger; established in this sense in gunsmiths' use.] In the mechanism of a gun-lock, an oscillating tongue pivoted over the half-cock notch in the tumbler, to prevent the sear from catching therein when the cock falls.

1884 T. SPEEDY *Sport* v. 60 Rifles which are generally made with a very light pull not exceeding two or three pounds, and on the tumbler of which a detant is attached, in order to carry the scear over the half-cock. **1894** W. A. GREENER (*in letter*), *Detant* not *Detent* is the usual spelling.. the German technical word for the gun-lock *detant* is *Schleuder.*

† **de'tard,** *v. Obs.* [a. OF. *detarder,* also *des-,* to retard, delay, f. *des-* (L. *dis-*) + *tarder* to delay:—L. *tardāre,* f. *tardus* slow.] *trans.* To retard, delay.

1675 TEONGE *Diary* (1825) 46 Leave to com on shoare.. was detarded. **1693** W. FREKE *Art of War* ix. 264 Let them detard their pursuers, and save their lives by scattering their Treasures.

† **detaste,** *v. Obs. rare.* [var. of DISTASTE: see DE- I. 6.] = DISTASTE; to dislike, loathe.

1614 EARL STIRLING *Doomes-day* VII. ciii, Who now in darkness do detaste the day.

† **det-bound,** var. of DEBT-BOUND, *ppl. a. Obs.* Mortgaged, pledged.

1541-2 *Burgh Rec. Edin.* 20 Jan. (Jam. Suppl.), The hous .. wes detbound to the said Jhone.

dete, obs. form of DEBT, DITTY.

detect (dɪ'tɛkt), *ppl. a.* [ad. L. *dētect-us,* pa. pple. of *dētegĕre* to DETECT. After the formation of DETECT *v.,* used for some time as its pa. pple.] Detected; disclosed; discovered; open, exposed.

† **a.** as *pa. pple. Obs.* **b.** as *adj. arch.*

a. 1387 TREVISA *Higden* (Rolls) V. 243 Thei were detecte by the olde moneye y-schewede. **1460** CAPGRAVE *Chron.* 134 He was that same day detect that a strumpet was in his chaumbir. **1526** *Pilgr. Perf.* (W. de W. 1531) 273 b, [I] haue detecte & declared the errours. **1555** ABP. PARKER *Ps.* cxix. 346 Detect I haue my wayes to thee.

b. 1661 LOVELL *Hist. Anim. & Min.* Introd., Their gills are detect. **1854** SYD. DOBELL *Balder* xix. 81 Detect, disowned, detested, and despised, There is no power to which ye can be true.

detect (dɪ'tɛkt), *v.* [f. ppl. stem *dētect-* of L. *dētegĕre* to uncover, discover, detect, f. DE- I. 6 + *tegĕre* to cover. The earlier ppl. adj. DETECT (see prec.) was retained as pa. pple. of the verb, till gradually displaced by *detected.*]

† **1.** *trans.* To uncover, lay bare, expose, display (something covered up or hidden). *Obs.*

1447 BOKENHAM *Seyntys* (Roxb.) 7, I preye.. that ye detecte It in no wyse wher that vylany It myht haue. **1526** *Pilgr. Perf.* (W. de W. 1531) 34 b, Whiche illusyon.. as soone as it was detected & brought to lyght.. anone it auoyded. **1563-87** FOXE *A. & M.* (1684) II. 73/2 Secret Confession, wherein Men do detect their sins in the Priests ear. **1594** *Ord. of Prayer* in *Liturg. Serv. Q. Eliz.* (1847) 664 Detect and reveal still the foundations and buildings of all treasons and conspiracies. **1668** CULPEPPER & COLE *Barthol. Anat.* I. iii. 5 On one side the Fat besprinkled with its Vessels, and on the other side certain Muscles Detected. **1691** *Case of Exeter Coll.* Pref. A ij, The badness of his cause was sufficiently detected by the weakness of his defence. **1739** LABELYE *Short Acc. Piers Westm. Bridge* 41, I cannot Answer this Objection, without detecting a gross Ignorance in those that proposed it.

† **2. a.** To expose (a person) by divulging his secrets or making known his guilt or crime; to inform against, accuse. *Obs.*

c **1449** PECOCK *Repr.* I. xvi. 88, I detecte here no man in special. **1577-87** HOLINSHED *Chron.* I. 41/1 Whose last words.. detected him of manifest ambition. **1594** HOOKER *Eccl. Pol.* (1676) 342 The Gentlewoman goeth forward, and detecteth herself of a crime. **1603** SHAKS. *Meas. for M.* III. ii. 129, I neuer heard the absent Duke much detected for Women. **1604** R. CAWDREY *Table Alph., Detect,* bewray, disclose, accuse. **1645** PAGITT *Heresiogr.* (1646) 9 And he also cut a young wenches throat, lest she should detect him.

† **b.** To divulge, reveal, give information of (a thing). *Obs.*

c **1465** *Hist. Doc. Roch.* (E.E.T.S.) 7 But if it shall hap so to know any such [heresies], I shall detecte them to myn ordinarie. **1725** DE FOE *Voy. round World* (1840) 314 One of the lieutenants discovered and detected this villanous contrivance.

3. To find out, discover (a person) in the secret possession of some quality, or performance of some act; to find out the real character of.

1581 PETTIE *Guazzo's Civ. Conv.* I. (1586) 28 b, In processe of time she was detected to be one of a naughtie slanderous tongue. **1711** *Medley* No. 39 If he is detected of the grossest Calumnies, he goes on to repeat them again, as if nothing had happen'd. **1774** GOLDSM. *Grecian Hist.* I. 99 Cleomenes.. being detected of having suborned the priestess, slew himself. **1789** BENTHAM *Princ. Legisl.* xi. §24 You have detected a baker in selling short weight, you prosecute him for the cheat. **1870** E. PEACOCK *Ralf Skirl.* III. 214 Like a schoolboy detected in robbing an orchard. **1875** JOWETT *Plato* (ed. 2) III. 209 Your dishonesty shall do you no good, for I shall detect you.

4. To discover, find out, ascertain the presence, existence, or fact of (something apt to elude observation).

1756 C. LUCAS *Ess. Waters* III. 263 The former obstacles must be abolished as soon as detected. **1797** GODWIN *Enquirer* I. vi. 43 We detect all the shades of meaning. **1823** J. BADCOCK *Dom. Amusem.* 25 It is a capital good test for detecting arsenic in any liquid whatever. **1835** BROWNING *Paracelsus* ii, What use were punishment, unless some sin Be first detected? **1847** EMERSON *Repr. Men, Napoleon* Wks. (Bohn) I. 373 Napoleon examined the bills of the creditors himself, detected overcharges and errors. **1849** MURCHISON *Siluria* iii. 45 Sandstone in which no other remains but fucoids have been detected. **1882** PEBODY *Eng. Journalism* xvi. 120 He was a man.. with an eye that detected a false note in an article.

5. *intr.* To be engaged in work of detection; to act as a detective.

1926 D. L. SAYERS *Clouds of Witness* iv. 105 Parker.. was paid to detect and to do nothing else. **1930** M. KENNEDY in D. L. Sayers *Great Short Stories of Detection, Mystery & Horror* (1931) 2nd Ser. 276 (title) Mr. Truefitt detects. **1957** A. CHRISTIE *4.50 from Paddington* xviii. 178 'Good evening, Inspector Craddock.' 'Coming to detect in the kitchen?' asked Bryan with interest.

Hence **de'tected** *ppl. a.,* **de'tecting** *vbl. sb.*

1602 SHAKS. *Ham.* III. ii. 95 Well my Lord. If he steale ought the whil'st this Play is Playing, And scape detecting, I will pay the Theft. **1654** CODRINGTON tr. *Hist. Ivstine* 518 To collect the detected Oar [= ore]. **1660** MILTON *Free Commw.* (1851) 449 The detected Falshood and Ambition of som. **1694** tr. *Milton's Lett. State* Aug. 1656 The vilest and most openly detected Assassinates. **1836** J. GILBERT *Chr. Atonem.* ii. (1852) 52 Who would not.. frown it away as a detected cheat?

detecta'bility. Formerly *rare.* Also detectibility. [f. next: see -ITY.]

1805 W. TAYLOR in *Monthly Mag.* XIX. 219 With far feebler detectability. **1972** *Nature* 17 Mar. 99/2 Both systems have changed dramatically since their discovery.. β Lyrae having faded below the level of detectability and β Persei now showing irregular variations and flaring. **1978** *Ibid.* 23 Nov. 374/1 The limiting detectibility for our discussion is $W(3727) \sim 0.6$Å equivalent width. **1983** *Defense Industry Rep.* (U.S.) 4 Apr. 150 Rockwell is working with Lockheed Corp. on an effort to apply stealth technology to the bomber to reduce the radar detectibility to one square meter or less. **1984** *Christian Science Monitor* 4 Dec. 36 It may not even be possible to reduce pollutant concentrations below the level of detectability.

detectable (dɪ'tɛktəb(ə)l), *a.* Also **-ible.** [f. DETECT *v.* + -ABLE. The spelling *-ible* is according to L. analogies, but L. *-tectibilis* does not occur.] Capable of being detected.

1655 FULLER *Ch. Hist.* VII. ii. 419 More were concealed by parties not detectable. **1831** *Blackw. Mag.* XXX. 122 No heel-tap was detectable. **1845-6** G. E. DAY tr. *Simon's Anim. Chem.* II. 151 The amount of phosphates.. is extremely minute, and no longer detectible by the ordinary tests. **1871** R. H. HUTTON *Ess.* I. 340 The real link not being detectable without a special and individual insight. **1888** BRYCE *Amer. Commw.* II. 124 Where illegitimate expenditure is more frequent and less detectible.

Hence **de'tectably** *adv.*

1887 *Standard* 1 June 5/3 The result is a 'detectably' different liquid.

detection (dɪ'tɛkʃən). [ad. L. *dētectiōn-em* (Tertullian), n. of action from *dētegĕre* to DETECT.] The action of detecting.

† **1.** Exposure, revelation of what is concealed; criminal information, accusation. *Obs.*

1471 RIPLEY *Comp. Alch.* Rec. xi. in Ashm. (1652) 189 That Oylysh substance.. Raymond Lully dyd call Hys Basylyske, of whyche he made never so playne deteccyon. **1529** MORE *Dyaloge* III. iv. Wks. 211/1 Wherfore it were not reason in a detection of heresy, to suffer,.. the crime wel proued, any new witnesses to be receyued. **1541** PAYNEL *Catiline* xxxvi. 54 b, The Senate decreed Tarquinius detection to be false. **1547** A. GILBY (*title*), An answer to the devillish detection of Stephane Gardiner, Bishoppe of Wynchester. **1564** *Brief Exam.* A ij b, The detection and detestation.. of the whole Antichrist of Rome. **1570-6** LAMBARDE *Peramb. Kent* (1826) 209, I will not sticke to bestow a few wordes for the detection thereof. **1691** *Case of Exeter Coll.* 30 But this fallacy.. must not escape without a detection. **1709** STEELE *Tatler* No. 76 ¶4 When by a publick Detection they fall under the Infamy they feared. **1807** CRABBE *Par. Reg.* I. 710 In all detections Richard first confessed.

2. a. Discovery (of what is unknown or hidden); finding out. *Obs.* exc. as in b.

1623 COCKERAM, *Detection,* a discouerie. **1702** C. MATHER *Magn. Chr.* I. i. 3 Americus Vesputius, a Florentine, who in the year 1497, made a further Detection of the more Southern Regions in this Continent.

b. *spec.* The finding out of what tends to elude notice, whether on account of the particular form or condition in which it is naturally present, or because it is artfully concealed; as crime, tricks, errors, slight symptoms of disease, traces of a substance, hidden causes, etc.

1619 NAUNTON in *Fortesc. Papers* 105 Whether.. safe for him to attend him selfe in person, without danger of detection. **1751** JOHNSON *Rambler* No. 183 ¶7 It is easy for the author of a lie, however malignant, to escape detection. **1791** MRS. RADCLIFFE *Rom. Forest* viii, She wondered to what part of the abbey these chambers belonged, and that they had so long escaped detection. **1798** FERRIAR *Illustr. Sterne* vi. 175 One of the most curious detections of his imitations. **1856** DOVE *Logic Chr. Faith* v. i. §2. 278 The utmost stars of our present faint detection. **1874** MORLEY *Compromise* (1886) 29 The detection of corresponding customs, opinions, laws, beliefs, among different communities. **1884** GUSTAFSON *Found. Death* i. (ed. 3) 2 Adulteration, now perfected almost beyond the possibility of detection.

3. *Electr.* The process of obtaining a required electrical signal from a carrier wave or current that contains it; demodulation.

1906 J. A. FLEMING *Princ. Electr. Wave Telegr.* vi. 353 (*heading*) Detection and measurement of electric waves. **1922** GLAZEBROOK *Dict. Appl. Physics* II. 1040/2 All the above methods of detection are appropriate for the reception of damped wave signals but not for continuous wave signals. **1953** F. LANGFORD-SMITH *Radio Designer's Hand-bk.* (ed. 4) xxxvi. 1292 There are three main methods of performing the functions of F-M detection and A-M rejection in commercial F-M receivers. **1959** K. HENNEY *Radio Engin. Handbk.* (ed. 5) xii. 18 Detection is the process of removing desired information from a composite signal which conveys it through a communication or a processing system. **1962** SIMPSON & RICHARDS *Junction Transistors* xviii. 460 The removal of the modulation from a carrier or i.f. signal is called demodulation or detection.

detective (dɪ'tɛktɪv), *a.* and *sb.* [f. L. *dētect-* ppl. stem: see DETECT *v.* and -IVE. (The sb. has been adopted in mod.F. from English.)]

A. *adj.* Having the character or function of detecting; serving to detect; employed for the purpose of detection. ***detective camera,*** a term formerly used for a hand camera adapted for taking instantaneous photographs.

1843 *Chamb. Jrnl.* XII. 54 Intelligent men have been recently selected to form a body called the 'detective police' .. at times the detective policeman attires himself in the dress of ordinary individuals. **1862** SHIRLEY *Nugæ Crit.* vii. 303 Every author now looks after his mind, as if he were a member of the detective police. **1881** *Brit. Jrnl. Photogr.* 28 Jan. 44/2 A form of the detective camera, in which the finding arrangement and the stock of slides are omitted, is in progress. **1882** E. P. HOOD in *Leisure Hour* Apr. 227 Instances of the detective power of ridicule. **1882** SPURGEON *Treas. Dav.* Ps. cxxii. 1 [It] is detective as to our character. **1882** *Year Bk. Photogr.* 27 Among novel apparatus we may mention.. Mr. Bolas' so-called 'Detective Camera'. **1888** *Brit. Jrnl. Photogr.* 18 May 305 The subject of detective cameras is capable of considerable subdivision. **1893** T. BENT *Ethiopia* 62 Regardless of.. strangers, and my wife's detective camera.

B. *sb.* One whose occupation it is to discover matters artfully concealed; particularly (and in the original application as short for *detective policeman,* or the like) a member of the police force employed to investigate specific cases, or to watch particular suspected individuals or classes of offenders. ***private detective,*** one not belonging to the police force, who in his private capacity, or as attached to a Detective Agency or Bureau, undertakes similar services for persons employing him. Also *attrib.,* as ***detective agency, anecdote, fiction, film, force, -inspector, novel, novelist, -sergeant, service, story.***

1850 DICKENS in *Household Words* 13 July 368/1 To each division of the Force is attached two officers, who are denominated 'detectives'. *Ibid.* 369/1 The two Detectives of the X division. **1852** —— *Bleak Ho.* xxv. 251 Detective Mr. Bucket. **1856** *Ann. Reg.* 185 Some London detectives were despatched, to give their keen wits to the search. **1871** B. TAYLOR *Faust* (1875) I. Pref. 12 There are critical detectives on the track of every author. **1875** JOWETT *Plato* (ed. 2) III. 39 The criminal turned detective is wonderfully suspicious and cautious. **1876** D. R. FEARON *School Inspection* §59. 90 If the inspector is to be anything more than a mere detective of faults.

attrib. **1872** E. CRAPSEY *Nether Side N.Y.* 56 All the large commercial cities are now liberally provided with 'Detective Agencies', as they are called. **1959** *Encounter* XII. v. 30 The detective agency girls. **1850** DICKENS in *Household Words* 14 Sept. 577/1 (*title*) Three 'detective' anecdotes. **1922** 'SAPPER' *Black Gang* ii. 28 What I'm going to tell you now .. may seem extraordinary and what one would expect in detective fiction. **1928** R. A. KNOX *Footsteps at Lock* iii. 26 The Muse of detective fiction.. cannot tell a plain unvarnished tale. **1958** *Times Lit. Suppl.* 6 June 316/5 This is one of the tales in which M. Simenon indulges his characteristic inquisitiveness about people while preserving the 'puzzle' convention of detective-fiction. **1911** C. N. BENNETT et al. *Handbk. Kinematography* xiii. 100 Moreover, the bulk of modern motion picture detective films are of the Nick Carter and Sexton Blake variety. **1849** *Alta California* (San Francisco) 24 Dec. 3/3 The badge is of such a character that, when it becomes necessary to employ any of them [*sc.* policemen], as a detective force, they can be removed. **1850** DICKENS *Repr. Pieces* in *Wks.* (1858) VIII. 307 I'm an Officer in the Detective Force. **1888** A. C. GUNTER *Mr. Potter of Texas* xx, Sergeant Brackett, of the British detective force. **1898** *Westm. Gaz.* 17 Nov. 7/2 Detective-inspector Egan said that he arrested the prisoner upon the charge. **1938** *Times Lit. Suppl.* 8 Oct. 649/2 Some long-suffering detective-inspector at Scotland Yard. **1924** *19th Cent.* May 718 We note that the plot of a detective novel is, in effect, an argument conducted under the guise of fiction. **1942** 'N. BLAKE' in H. Haycraft *Murder for Pleasure* p. xxii, The detective-novel proper is read almost exclusively by the upper and professional classes. **1926** E. M. WRONG *Crime & Detection* p. xx, One temptation the detective novelist does well to avoid. **1850** DICKENS in *Household Words* 13 July 369/2 The Detective sergeant.. fairly owned.. that he could afford no hope of elucidating the mystery. **1969** *Listener* 24 Apr. 583/2 Interest centres on the man sent in to investigate, Detective-Sergeant Demosthenes de Goede. **1848** MRS. GASKELL *Mary Barton*

II. iii. 31 A well-known officer in the Detective Service. **1883** ANNA K. GREEN (*title*) XYS, a Detective Story. **1905** G. K. CHESTERTON *Club of Queer Trades* iii. 96 The detectives in the detective stories. **1911** F. SWINNERTON *Casement* ii. 75 'Douse the glim'..that old phrase in the detective stories he had read. **1963** AUDEN *Dyer's Hand* 153 The detective-story society is a society of apparently innocent individuals.

Hence **de'tectiveship**, the office or function of a detective; **de'tectivist**, *nonce-wd.*, one who professedly treats of detectives.

1877 J. HAWTHORNE *Garth* III. IX. lxxv. 184 In my amateur detectiveship. **1892** W. WALLACE in *Academy* 24 Sept. 261/1 It may be hoped that Dick Donovan is the last of the detectivists in fiction.

detectivism (dɪ'tɛktɪvɪz(ə)m). [f. DETECTIVE + -ISM.] The activities of a detective; detective work.

1894 *Academy* 23 June 514/2 An incredible piece of detectivism. **1896** *Athenæum* 15 Aug. 225 Literary detectivism of a high order. **1905** *Book Lover* 10/2 A sea story with a little detectivism and plenty of humour in it.

detector (dɪ'tɛktə(r)). Also -er. [a. L. *dētector* (Tertull.), agent-n. from L. *dētegĕre* to DETECT.] He who or that which detects.

†**1.** A person or thing that discloses, brings to light, or reveals; one who informs against or accuses; a revealer; an informer, an accuser. *Obs.*

1541 PAYNEL *Catiline* xxxiv. 52 The detectour is false and corrupted with mede. **1611** COTGR., *Encuseur*, a detecter, discloser, appeacher, accuser. **1614** RALEIGH *Hist. World* v. iii. §18 (R.) As a reward unto the detectors of lands concealed. **1637** BASTWICK *Litany* IV. 3 Those should be punished, that were detectors and manifesters of them. **1680** BAXTER *Cath. Commun.* (1684) 30 This is to comply with the World, that taketh the detecter only for the sinner. **1742** YOUNG *Nt. Th.* ii. 641 A deathbed's a detector of the heart. Here tir'd dissimulation drops her masque.

2. One who finds out that which is artfully concealed, or which tends to elude observation.

1605 SHAKS. *Lear* III. v. 14 O Heauens! that this Treason were not; or not I the detector! **1657** EVELYN *Diary* 7 Jan., Dr. Joyliffe..first detector of the lymphatic veins. **1755** JOHNSON, *Detecter*, a discoverer, one that finds out what another desires to hide. **1791** BOSWELL *Johnson* (1887) I. 407 Rev. Dr. Douglas, now Bishop of Salisbury, the great detector of impostures. **1840** MILL *Diss. & Disc.*, *Bentham* (1859) I. 352 The keenest detector of the errors of his predecessors.

3. An instrument or device for detecting the presence of anything liable to escape observation, for indicating any deviation from normal conditions, or the like.

a. An arrangement in a lock by which any attempt to tamper with it is indicated and frustrated. **b.** A low-water indicator for a boiler. **c.** A small portable galvanometer, which indicates the flow and direction of a current of electricity, used for testing purposes. **d.** An apparatus for detecting the presence of torpedoes under water, a torpedo-detector. **e.** *attrib.* in various senses, as *detector-bar*, *-galvanometer*, *-lock*, *-pad*, *-spring*, etc.

1833 J. HOLLAND *Manuf. Metal* II. 275 His success in this attempt was not better than before, for he overlifted the detector of each lock. **1850** CHUBB *Locks & Keys* 13 *F* is the detector-spring. **1860** *Encycl. Brit.* XXI. 114/2 A 'detector' or common telegraphic galvanometer. **1874** KNIGHT *Dict. Mech.* s.v., Chubb had a detector in his lock of 1818. **1889** G. FINDLAY *Eng. Railway* 75 'Detector Bars' are employed on parts of the line which cannot be seen by the signalman, to prevent the signals being lowered when the line is occupied by a train. *Ibid.*, 'Detector Locks' are applied to facing points, and are worked by the wire that works the signals. **1893** MUNRO etc. *Pocket Book of Electrical Rules* (ed. 9) 395 Cells should be tested on the thick wire of a detector. *Ibid.* 396 For fault inspection, a detector or galvanometer, a battery, knife, etc. **1894** *Catalogue*, Galvanometers and Measuring Instruments:—Detector Galvanometer, wound for intensity, resistance up to 500 Ohms. **1940** *Illustr. London News* CXCVI. 192/1 Imagine that two vehicles are converging on the crossing, the one on the Twyford road being nearer the junction... The former would reach his detector-pad first, and cause the lights to change in his favour.

f. Any of various devices or circuits designed to carry out detection (sense 3).

1894 O. LODGE *Work of Hertz & Successors* 29 We can easily see the detector respond to a distant source of radiation now..separated from the receiver, therefore, by several walls and some heavily gilded paper, as well as by 20 or 30 yards of space. **1898** *Science Siftings* 11 June 117/2 A Hertz-wave 'detector' resistance included in the circuit. **1902** *Encycl. Brit.* XXXIII. 232/2 The coherer, or detector, is inserted between the earth and the outer end of this last wire. **1924** *Wireless Weekly* 8 Oct. 744/2 Seven valves (all 'peanuts'), used successively as first detector, oscillator valve, three stages of intermediate frequency, second detector valve, and one stage of transformer-coupled note-magnification. **1928** *Morning Post* 6 Feb. 3/4 The nature of the circuit connected to the detector helps to determine the amplification. **1957** D. G. FINK *Telev. Engin. Handbk.* xvi. 148 The separation of the luminance signal, the chrominance subcarrier, and the sound carrier is carried out at the second detector.

detei(g)n(e, etc., obs. forms of DETAIN, etc.

detemporalize (di:'tɛmpərəlaɪz), *v.* [f. DE- II. 1 + TEMPORALIZE *v.*] *trans.* To make timeless in character; to remove the impression of passage of time from; to detach from a particular time.

1914 *Philos. Rev.* XXIII. 144 The very intensity of his vision detemporalizes what he sees. **1954** K. TILLOTSON *Novels of Eighteen-Forties* I. 97 In *Wuthering Heights* the past..is not only..a means of detemporalizing the action.

detend (di:'tɛnd), *v.* [f. DE- II. 1 + TEND *v.*[2]; cf. F. *détendre* to relax, slacken.] *trans.* To reduce the tension or intensity of.

1930 H. READ *Wordsworth* vii. 243 The philosopher begins with his intuitive apprehension and *detends* it—resolves it into that lower tension of expression which is *prose*. **1949** KOESTLER *Insight & Outlook* xx. 282 Self-transcending emotions de-tend the body as no action is required.

†**de'tenebrate**, *v. Obs. rare.* [f. DE- II. 1 + L. *tenebræ* darkness, *tenebrāre* to darken.] *trans.* To free from darkness or obscurity.

1646 SIR T. BROWNE *Pseud. Ep.* VI. vi. 296 To detenebrate and cleare this truth. **1656** BLOUNT *Glossogr.*, *Detenebrate*, to dispel or drive away darkness, to bring light.

detenewe, obs. form of DETINUE.

de-tension (di:'tɛnʃən), *sb.* A reduction of anxiety; a relaxation.

1949 KOESTLER *Insight & Outlook* v. 58 The delight in laughing is one of the many variants of catharsis or de-tension.

Hence **de-'tension** *v.*, **de-'tensioning** *vbl. sb.* and *ppl. a.*

1952 A. HUXLEY *Let.* July (1969) 649 This process of remembering will induce a complete detensioning. **1958** *Times* 29 Sept. 5/4 A substitute 'detensioning' agent, something less harmful than smoking. **1961** *New Statesman* 10 Mar. 376/2 Macmillan's attempt to de-tension the conference and work for some face-saving compromise. **1966** *Observer* 3 Apr. 13/1 Detensioning had already set in before the first Labour gain.

detent (dɪ'tɛnt), *sb.*[1] (Also 7 detton.) [a. F. *détente*, OF. *destente* (Froissart, 14th c.), deriv. of *détendre* 'to slacken, unstretch, undo', in OF. *destendre*, f. *des-*, L. *dis-* privative (cf. DE- 6) + *tendre* to stretch. (In L. *distendĕre* the prefix had a different force: see DISTEND.)

The earliest application of the word in French was to the *destente* of the arbalest or cross-bow, whereby the strained string was released and the bolt discharged; hence it was transferred to the analogous part in fire-arms. In English, the word seems to have been viewed as connected with L. *dētinēre*, *dētent-*, and so with *detain*, *detention*, and to have been modified in meaning accordingly. The fact that the same part which allows of the escape of that which is detained or held tense, is also often the means of detention, favoured this misconception of the word.]

1. *gen.* A stop or catch in a machine which checks or prevents motion, and the removal of which brings some motor at once into action.

1831 BREWSTER *Nat. Magic* xi. (1833) 283, When a spring was touched, so as to release a detent, the figure immediately began to draw. **1832** BABBAGE *Econ. Manuf.* viii. (ed. 3) 59 Leaves a small dot of ink on the dial-plate whenever a certain stop or detent is pushed in. **1860** *Proc. Amer. Philol. Soc.* VII. 339 A detent shoots the slate back and a new record begins. **1869** *Daily News* 16 Mar., The handle, on being pulled, releases a detent in the guard's van, which allows a weighted lever to drop and pull up the slack of a chain which communicates with the engine whistle. **1869** *Athenæum* 25 Dec. 874 A Christmas recollection..more than fifty years old..These boxes..had each a little slit, into which, a halfpenny being dropped, a detent was let go, the box would open, and the pipe might be filled. **1871** TYNDALL *Fragm. Sc.* (1879) I. xx. 488 An engineer..loosing a detent, can liberate an amount of mechanical motion [etc.]. *Ibid.* II. vii. 97 When these crystals are warmed, the detent is lifted, and an outflow of light immediately begins.

2. *spec.* **a.** In a gun-lock: see DETANT.

b. In clocks and watches: The catch which regulates the striking.

1688 R. HOLME *Armoury* III. 374/1 In the Clock..the two Dettons with their Notches, that strike into two Wheel Detton Latches. **1704** J. HARRIS *Lex. Techn.*, *Detents*, in a Clock, are those stops, which by being lifted up, or let fall down, do lock and unlock the Clock in striking. **1825** J. NICHOLSON *Operat. Mechanic* 509 When the oil thickens, the spring of the pivot-detents become so affected by it, as to prevent the detent from falling into the wheel quick enough, which causes irregular time, and ultimately a stoppage of the watch. **1884** F. J. BRITTEN *Watch & Clockm.* 85 The detent of a chronometer escapement is the piece of steel carrying the stone which detains or locks the escape wheel.

c. In locks.

1850 CHUBB *Locks & Keys* 28 If any one of the tumblers was lifted too high, it overset the detector detent, which by a spring action fastened the bolt.

3. *attrib.* and *Comb.*, as *detent-wheel*, *-catch*, *-work*; **detent-joint**, the 'trigger-joint' by which the pectoral spine of a siluroid fish is kept erect.

1704 J. HARRIS *Lex. Techn.*, s.v. *Watch-work*, The Detent-wheel moves round every Stroke the Clock striketh or sometimes but once in two Strokes. **1822** IMISON *Sc. & Art* I. 93 Regard need only be had to the count-wheel, striking-wheel, and detent-wheel. **1874** KNIGHT *Dict. Mech.* I. 690/2 A detent-catch falls into the striking-wheel of a clock, and stops it from striking more than the right number of times. **1881** GREENER *Gun* 244 The furniture filer also fits the detent work for the hair-triggers.

detent, *sb.*[2] [? f. L. *dētent-* ppl. stem of *dētinēre* to DETAIN.] ? Restraint; holding back or inhibition.

c **1465** *Pol. Rel. & L. Poems* (1866) 10 Gabull of the chancery begynyth 'heu mihi!' that is his preve bande, and detent of treson. **1907** W. JAMES *Mem. & Studies* (1911) 256 They are forces of detent in situations in which no other force produces equivalent effects, and each is a force of detent only in a specific group of men. **1929** R. BRIDGES *Test. Beauty* IV. 150 A pinprick or a momentary whiff or hairbreadth motion freeth the detent of force.

†**de'tent**, *ppl. a. Obs.* [ad. L. *dētent-us*, pa. pple. of *dētinēre* to DETAIN.] DETAINED; kept back; 'holden' (with infirmity, etc.).

(In quot. 1494 perhaps past tense.)

1432-50 tr. *Higden* (Rolls) I. 361 After that thei be detente with longe infirmite thei be brouȝhte to another yle. **1494** FABYAN *Chron.* VII. 591 And yet for that his mynde nothynge detent All goostly helthe for his soule to prouyde.

‖**détente** (detɑ̃t). [Fr., = loosening, relaxation.] The easing of strained relations, esp. in a political situation.

1908 *Times* 17 Aug. 5/4 A change in the European situation..had..set in... The characteristic feature of this transformation may be called a *détente*. **1921** VON HÜGEL in L. S. Hunter *John Hunter* 213 The profound impression of a comforting *détente* made upon my mind by my first contact with his spirit. **1928** *Daily Tel.* 29 May 9/5 To bring about an early détente in Turco-Persian relations. **1940** *Ann. Reg.* *1939* 182 The very slight *détente*..which had followed the signature of the Franco-German accord..had brought her [*sc.* France] no real tranquillity. **1955** *Times* 6 June 7/7 The sense of *détente* is not to the liking of the party zealots who cry for more revolutionary fervour under the leadership of the party.

detention (dɪ'tɛnʃən). [? a. F. *détention* (13th c. in Godef. *Suppl.*, = Pr. *detention*, Sp. *detencion*, It. *detenzione*), ad. L. *dētentiōn-em*, n. of action from *dētinēre* to DETAIN. The word is late in Eng. and may have been taken immed. from L.] The action of detaining, or condition of being detained.

1. a. Keeping in custody or confinement; arrest. Used *spec.* of the confinement of a political offender. Cf. *preventive detention*.

house of detention, a place where arrested persons are kept in custody, before being committed to prison; a lock-up.

? **1570** in Spottiswood *Hist. Ch. Scot.* (1655) 247 Her [Q. Mary's] detention under safe custody. **1793** VANSITTART *Refl. Peace* 37 The state of detention in which the King and Royal Family of France were. **1831** LYTTON *Godolph.* 12 Offering twenty guineas reward for his detention. **1871** MORLEY *Voltaire* (1886) 204 The detention of a French citizen by a Prussian agent in a free town of the Empire was a distinct..illegality. **1909** J. MORLEY *Indian Speeches* 146 There is no fixed limit of time of detention. **1920** *Statem. Moral & Mat. Progr. India 1919* 26 in *Parl. Papers* (Cmd. 950) XXXIV. 744 The continued detention of dangerous characters already under control or in confinement. **1940** J. ANDERSON in *Hansard Commons* 5th Ser. CCCLXI. 290 Regulation 18 B of the Defence Regulations was last night amended by the addition of a provision enabling me to order the detention of members of organizations which have had associations with the enemy.

†**b.** Bodily restraint by infirmity, etc. *Obs. rare.*

1650 FULLER *Pisgah* IV. v. 86 Darkness for three days, not ..from the suspension of the sun-beams, or detention of the Egyptians eyes.

c. At schools: keeping in as a punishment. Also *concr.* and *attrib.*

1882 *Boy's Own Paper* 3 June 574/3 Mr. Rastle..set them each twelve propositions of Euclid to learn by heart, and two hours a-piece in the detention-room, there to meditate over their evil ways. **1909** WODEHOUSE *Mike* xliii. 243 There is only one thing to be said in favour of detention on a fine summer's afternoon, and that is that it is very pleasant to come out of. **1931** 'R. CROMPTON' *William's Crowded Hours* ii. 34 He was unable to answer two very simple questions that the Latin master asked him, and was given a detention.

2. The keeping back or withholding of what is due or claimed.

1552 HULOET, Detencion or witholdinge, *detentio*. **1607** SHAKS. *Timon* II. ii. 39 The detention of long since due debts. **1640-1** *Kirkcudbr. War-Comm. Min. Bk.* (1855) 21 Such monie..shall be frie of any common burden by detentione of any pairt of the annual rent. **1727-51** CHAMBERS *Cycl.*, *Detention*..is chiefly used in an ill sense, for an unjust withholding, etc. **1861** STANLEY *East. Ch.* vii. (1869) 238 We can hardly suppose that his opponents really believed him guilty of the..detention of the corn.

3. Keeping in a place; holding in one's possession or control; retention. ? *Obs.* exc. in *Law*.

1626 BACON *Sylva* § 343 In Bodies that need Detention of Spirits, the Exclusion of the Air doth good. **1788** PASQUIN *Childr. Thespis* II. (1792) 139 With ditties and puns he holds thought in detention. **1809-10** COLERIDGE *Friend* (1866) 173 Had the First Consul acquiesced in our detention of Malta. **1871** MARKBY *Elem. Law* §365 Possession sometimes means the physical control simply, the proper word for which is detention. **1875** POSTE *Gaius* IV. Comm. (ed. 2) 643 The depositary has mere detention, the depositor has possession.

4. A keeping from going on or proceeding; hindrance to progress; compulsory delay.

1600 HAKLUYT *Voy.* III. 150 (R.) Minding to proceede further south without long detention in those partes. **1793** R. HALL *Apol. Freedom Press* Pref. 1 The accidental detention of the following pamphlet in the press longer than was expected. **1818** M. BIRKBECK *Journ. Amer.* 83 Benighted, in consequence of accidental detention, at the foot of one of these rugged hills. **1835** SIR J. ROSS *Narr. 2nd Voy.* vi. 81 In spite of all the detention we had suffered.

5. *attrib.*, as **detention barrack**, a military prison; **detention camp**, in the war of 1914-18, a camp in which aliens and others were kept under restraint; also applied to other places of incarceration; **detention centre**, an institution in which young offenders are detained for short periods.

1906 *Act 6 Edw. VII* c. 2 §6. 5 A soldier sentenced to imprisonment..may be confined in a detention barrack. **1916** J. BUCHAN *Greenmantle* v. 62 The lieutenant discoursed a lot about prisoners and detention-camps. **1958** *New Statesman* 25 Jan. 93/1 The new governor, by..his dramatic gesture of a Christmas amnesty for 100 prisoners from the detention camps, has provided a much needed tonic. **1948** *Act 11 & 12 Geo. VI* c. 58 §48 Detention centres, that is to say places in which persons not less than fourteen but under twenty-one years of age who are ordered to be detained in such centres under this Act may be kept for short periods under discipline suitable to persons of their age and description. **1961** *Listener* 19 Oct. 612/1 Mr. Sewell Stoke's talk on detention centres..paints a rosy picture of this comparatively new method of dealing with boys and young men of fourteen to twenty-one.

de'tentive, *a. rare.* [f. L. *dētent-*, ppl. stem of *dētinēre* to DETAIN: see -IVE.] Having the quality or function of detaining.

1881 PATRICK GEDDES in *Encycl. Brit.* XIII. 139/1 The detentive surface [of the pitcher in *Nepenthes*] is represented by the fluid secretion.

‖**détenu** (detəny). [Fr.; subst. use of *détenu* detained, pa. pple. of *détenir* to detain. (The Fr. fem. is *détenue*.)] A person detained in custody.

Applied especially to the English subjects detained as prisoners in France, and the French subjects detained in England during the Wars 1793–1815.

1803–1810 JAMES *Military Dict.* s.v., That these *detenus* (we are borne out by the public prints for using the term) would remain as hostages to secure to men in open rebellion all the rights and privileges of fair warriors. **1815** *Sporting Mag.* XLVI. 84 He was a *detenu* for eleven years at Verdun. **1819** B. E. O'MEARA *Exp. Trans. St. Helena* 139 The inhabitants..are in general greatly benefitted by the arrival of the *detenus*. **1862** *Times* 8 July 12/4 If detention in its carriages is frequent, it is a reason for making the *détenus* as comfortable as possible. **1889** *Athenæum* 13 July 65/3 Down to the release of the *détenus* at Verdun. **1918** *Parl. Papers* (Cd. 9198) VIII. 105 (*title*) Report of Sir N. Chandavarka and Mr. Justice Beachcroft on Detenus and Internees in Bengal. **1920** H. V. LOVETT *Hist. Indian Nat. Movem.* vii. 196 The Committee recommended the release of six only of all the above enumerated *détenus*. **1956** M. COLLIS *Last & First in Burma* xxiii. 209 He had passed through Uganda and was able to secure for the *détenu* some extra comforts. **1969** *Hindusthan Standard* (Calcutta) 5 Aug. 8/1 The High Court asking for production of the detenus.

deter (dɪ'tɜː(r)), *v.*[1] [ad. L. *dēterrēre* to frighten from or away, f. DE- I. 2 + *terrēre* to frighten. (Cf. rare OF. *deterrer*, in Godef., which does not appear to have influenced the Eng. word.)]

1. *trans.* To discourage and turn aside or restrain by fear; to frighten from anything; to restrain or keep back from acting or proceeding by any consideration of danger or trouble.

1579 LYLY *Euphues* (Arb.) 106 If the wasting of our money might not dehort vs, yet the wounding of our mindes should deterre vs. **1646** SIR T. BROWNE *Pseud. Ep.* I. i. (1686) 2 He..had thereby Example and Punishment to deterr him. **1748** *Anson's Voy.* III. x. 405 They [sailors] were rather animated than deterred by the flames and falling buildings amongst which they wrought. **1766** tr. *Beccaria's Ess. Crimes* xxviii. (1793) 101 That degree of severity which is sufficient to deter others. **1832** HT. MARTINEAU *Ella of Gar.* ix. 113 The farmer..was not deterred by the dreary weather. **1855** MILMAN *Lat. Chr.* (1864) II. III. vii. 141 *note*, Maurice..had been deterred by the alarming prophecy of a monk. **1877** J. D. CHAMBERS *Div. Worship* 308 To deter instead of to invite communicants.

b. Const. *from* a place, purpose, action, doing anything; †formerly, *to do*.

1594 HOOKER *Eccl. Pol.* I. x. (1611) 28 Punishments which may more deterre from euill, than any sweetnesse thereto allureth. **1599** HAKLUYT *Voy.* II. II. 9 Whereby other may be deterred to doe the like, and vertuous men encouraged to proceed in honest attempts. **1667** MILTON *P.L.* II. 449 If aught propos'd And judg'd of public moment, in the shape Of difficulty or danger, could deterre Me from attempting. **1696** BP. PATRICK *Comm. Exod.* xxiii. (1697) 437 The Judges were not to be deterred..to pronounce a false judgment. **1709** PRIOR *Celia to Damon* 55 When my own Face deters me from my Glass. **1759** JOHNSON *Rasselas* 34 Do not seek to deter me from my purpose. **1777** WATSON *Philip II* (1839) 9 This undutiful behaviour did not deter the emperor from resolving to resign to his son all the rest of his dominions. **1858** FROUDE *Hist. Eng.* III. xvi. 411 Superstition had become powerless to deter from violence.

†**2.** To terrify, alarm.

1604 DANIEL *Civ. Wars* v. cvi, Who, to deter The state the more, named himself Mortimer. **1634** WITHER *Emblems* Ep. Ded., The storms which late these Realmes deterred.

†**de'ter**[2], **de'terre**, *v. Obs.* [a. F. *déterrer*, OF. *desterrer* (11th c. in Hatz.-Darm.), f. *dé-*, *des-* (DE- I. 6) + *terre* earth: cf. INTER *v.*] *trans.* To disinter.

1632 LITHGOW *Trav.* IX. 407 To deterre his dead body.

deterge (dɪ'tɜːdʒ), *v.* [ad. L. *dētergē-re* to wipe off or away, f. DE- I. 2 + *tergēre* to wipe: perhaps after F. *déterger* (Paré 16th c., not in Cotgr.; in Dict. Acad. from 1740).]

trans. To wipe away; to wash off or out, cleanse; chiefly, in Medical use, to clear away foul or offensive matter from the body, from an ulcer, etc.

1623 COCKERAM, *Deterge*, to rub out. **1634** T. JOHNSON *Parey's Chirurg.* XXVI. xiv. (1678) 638 Detersive is defined to be that which doth deterge or cleanse an ulcer. **1651** WITTIE tr. *Primrose's Pop. Err.* IV. 268 They further the working of the purge, and deterge and cleanse the stomach from humours. **1727** BRADLEY *Fam. Dict.* I. U ij, If externally used, it [Balm of Gilead] gently deterges and incarnates. *a* **1734** NORTH *Exam.* I. ii. §133 (1740) 104 To deterge some of the frothy foul slaver he has spit at it. **1787** J. COLLINS in *Med. Commun.* II. 364 The fauces were deterged with gargles. **1857** DUNGLISON *Med. Lex.* 289 Medicines which possess the power to deterge or cleanse parts.

Hence **de'terging** *ppl. a.*; also **de'terger** = DETERGENT *sb.*

1651 WITTIE tr. *Primrose's Pop. Err.* I. v. 20 A Surgeon, who in an Ulcer..did daily apply a strong deterger, viz., Verdigrease. *Ibid.*, A deterging Medicine. **1732** ARBUTHNOT *Rules of Diet* I. 250 Barley is deterging, tho' viscous in a small degree.

de'tergency. [f. next: see -ENCY.] Detergent quality; cleansing power. Also, the process of cleansing a solid by means of a liquid, the action of a detergent.

1710 T. FULLER *Pharm. Extemp.* 3 Ale, by reason of its.. Detergency..is not adviseable. **1748** *De Foe's Tour Gt. Brit.* II. 290 (D.) Bath water..possesses that milkiness, detergency, and middling heat, so friendly adapted to weakened animal constitutions. **1943** *Industr. & Engin. Chem.* Jan. 110/1 Detergency is not completed until the soil has been suspended in the detergent solution with sufficient stability so that it can be rinsed away rather than redeposited. **1950** *Thorpe's Dict. Appl. Chem.* (ed. 4) X. 803/1 Use of Launderometer... Detergency is measured either by the increase in the whiteness of the soiled cloth on washing..or by the dirt content of the detergent solution. **1959** *Times* 14 Sept. 2/6 Chemistry problems associated with detergency. **1965** R. D. & M. J. VOLD *Colloid Chem.* v. 96 These effects may..contribute to effective detergency by helping to maintain the separated dirt in colloidal suspension.

detergent (dɪ'tɜːdʒənt), *a.* and *sb.* [ad. L. *dētergēnt-em*, pr. pple. of *dētergēre*: see DETERGE. Cf. mod.F. *détergent* (1611 in Cotgr., in Dict. Acad. from 1835).]

A. *adj.* Cleansing, purging.

1616 SURFL. & MARKH. *Country Farme* 581 By vertue and force of a detergent facultie, wherewith barley is greatly furnished. **1718** QUINCY *Compl. Disp.* 80 Sage is undoubtedly a very good Cephalick, of the detergent kind. **1805** W. SAUNDERS *Min. Waters* 434 Sufficient to give it a very soft soapy feel, and to render it more detergent than common water. **1875** H. C. WOOD *Therap.* (1879) 648 A detergent antiseptic in various ulcerated..conditions of the mouth.

B. *sb.* A cleansing agent; anything that cleanses. Now esp., any of various synthetic solids or liquids which are soluble in or miscible with water, which resemble soap in their cleansing properties, but which differ from it in not combining with the salts present esp. in hard water; also, any of various oil-soluble substances which have the property of holding dirt in suspension in lubricating oils; so ***detergent oil***, an oil containing such a substance. Also *attrib.* and *Comb.*

1676 WISEMAN *Surgery* II. vi. (R.), If too mild detergents caused the flesh to grow lax and spongy, then more powerful driers are required. **1718** QUINCY *Compl. Disp.* 127 Detergents differ only in Degree of Efficacy from the former Class. **1888** CAVE *Inspir. O. Test.* v. 274 He believes in a possible Divine detergent. **1938** *Encycl. Brit. Bk. of Yr. 1938* 331/1 Word came of a new process for rapid saponification; the 'Igepals' are new detergents of German origin. **1941** *Ann. Rep. Prog. Chem. 1940* 102 A large number of synthetic substances used during recent years as detergents. **1941** *Jrnl. R. Aeronaut. Soc.* XLV. App. 141 [It] has a viscosity index of approximately 100—nearly twice that previously available in special detergent oils. **1951** *Good Housek. Home Encycl.* 45/2 Once a week use hot water and soapless detergent to remove all traces of grease. **1952** M. LASKI in *Observer* 26 Oct. 5/2 Detergent-packets..almost always fall over and spill. **1957** G. I. BROWN *Introd. Org. Chem.* xviii. 223 Synthetic detergents..are usually more soluble in water than soap is; they do not form a scum in hard water; they enable water to spread and penetrate more fully over or through an article being cleaned. **1957** *Technology* July 168/4 Detergents usually contain a surface active agent, alkylbenzenesulphonate, which influences surface adsorption and, incidentally, causes the familiar foaming (of doubtful utility). **1958** *Engineering* 21 Mar. 353/3 Detergent powders..which are bought by a large section of the population. **1958** *Spectator* 4 July 12/1 Like detergent foam in a millrace. **1958** *Sunday Times* 23 Nov. 28/3 He's..detergent-white and very cuddly. **1959** *Engineering* 16 Jan. 96/1 Improved performance has followed the use of heavy-duty and detergent oils. **1959** *Which?* Sept. 105/1 'Detergent' is often used—loosely—as a synonym for 'synthetic detergent'. *Ibid.*, A good detergent is one which removes dirt easily from the clothes, holds the dirt in suspension in the washing-water, so that it can be rinsed away and will not get re-deposited on the clothes, and —in the process—does them no damage. **1960** V. B. GUTHRIE *Petroleum Products Handbk.* II. 34 The use of detergents in oils has introduced additional demands on oxidation inhibitors. **1966** *McGraw-Hill Encycl. Sci. & Technol.* IV. 81/2 Soap..was the principal detergent until superseded in production in 1954 by synthetic detergents.

deterior (dɪ'tɪərɪə(r)), *a. rare.* [a. L. *dēterior* worse, meaner, poorer, compar. of an obs. adj. **dēter*, f. *dē* down.] Inferior in quality, worse.

1839 BAILEY *Festus* (1848) 64/2 Some of downward and deterior lot.

†**de'terior**, *v. Obs.* [a. F. *détériorer* (1411 in Hatz.-Darm.), L. *dēteriōrāre* to make worse, f. *dēterior*: see prec.] *trans.* To make worse, deteriorate.

1646 BP. MAXWELL *Burd. Issach.* in *Phenix* (1708) II. 270 He will..deterior his condition.

†**de'teriorate, -at**, *pa. pple. Sc.* [ad. L. *dēteriōrāt-us*, pa. pple. of *dēteriōrāre* (see prec.).] Made worse, deteriorated.

1572 *Sc. Acts Jas. VI* (1814) 76 (Jam.) That all houses, &c., rewinit, cassin doun, distroyit, or deteriorat, within.. the said burghe—sall be reparit. **1598** in Row *Hist. Kirk* (1842) 190 If he hes meliorat or deteriorat his benefice any way to the prejudice of his successor.

deteriorate (dɪ'tɪərɪəreɪt), *v.* [f. ppl. stem of L. *dēteriōrāre* to make worse: see prec.]

1. *trans.* To make worse or of inferior quality; to lower in character or excellence; to worsen.

1572–98 [See prec.]. **1644** BP. MAXWELL *Prerog. Chr. Kings* i. 10 How much more they deteriorate and depresse Kings. **1673** O. WALKER *Educ.* 46 Not onely not bettered, but much deteriorated. **1784** COWPER *Let.* 10 Feb., A long line of grandsires, who from generation to generation have been employed in deteriorating the breed. **1813** WELLINGTON in Gurw. *Desp.* X. 380 Maintained by means ..which will deteriorate the discipline of the troops. **1847** C. G. ADDISON *Law of Contracts* II. iii. §2 (1883) 603 To deteriorate the value of the property. **1879** M. ARNOLD *George Sand* Mixed Ess. 343 Equality, as its reign proceeded, had not deteriorated but improved them.

2. *intr.* To grow worse in character; to become lowered or impaired in quality or value; to degenerate.

1758–65 GOLDSM. *Ess.* (L.), Under such conditions the mind rapidly deteriorates. **1841** D'ISRAELI *Amen. Lit.* (1867) 269 Elyot had a notion that, for the last thousand years, the world had deteriorated. **1856** FROUDE *Hist. Eng.* (1858) I. i. 22 The condition of the labourer was at this period deteriorating rapidly. **1892** KATH. TYNAN in *Speaker* 3 Sept. 290/1 The roses..will deteriorate year after year, returning gradually to wildness.

Hence **de'teriorated** *ppl. a.*, **de'teriorating** *vbl. sb.* and *ppl. a.*

1656 BLOUNT *Glossogr.*, *Deteriorated*, made worse, impaired; spoiled. *a* **1691** BOYLE *Wks.* IV. 367 (R.) Which we concluded to have proceeded from the deteriorated metal. **1836** J. GILBERT *Chr. Atonem.* vi. (1852) 170 Classical story has imperceptibly lent its deteriorating influence. **1837** SYD. SMITH *Let. to Singleton* Wks. 1859 II. 292/2 Judging, that the Church is a very altered and deteriorated profession. **1883** F. HALL in *Nation* (N.Y.) XXXVII. 434/3 The deteriorating, if not debasing, mode of existence.

deterioration (dɪˌtɪərɪə'reɪʃən). [a. F. *détérioration* (15th c. in Godef. *Suppl.*), n. of action f. *détériorer*, L. *dēteriōrāre* to DETERIORATE.]

The action or process of deteriorating, a growing or making worse; a deteriorated condition.

1658 PHILLIPS, *Deterioration*, a making worse. **1727–51** CHAMBERS *Cycl.* s.v., When the deterioration of a commodity, seized by an officer, arises from the fault of the keeper, he is answerable for the same. **1823** J. BADCOCK *Dom. Amusem.* 28 To preserve the article from deterioration. **1841** W. SPALDING *Italy & It. Isl.* I. 24 In our floating notions of Italian character, we grievously exaggerate the extent of its deterioration. **1842** MANNING *Serm.* (1848) I. i. 7 (Except in penitents) the whole life of a man from birth to death is a deterioration. He is ever becoming worse. **1875** SCRIVENER *Lect. Text N. Test.* 5 The process of deterioration may be carried on for many generations [of MSS.].

Hence **deterio'rationist**, one who holds that deterioration, not progress, is the order of things.

1816 T. L. PEACOCK *Headlong Hall* i, Mr. Escot, the deteriorationist. **1861** *Westm. Rev.* Apr. 591 In the true tone of the deteriorationist who amused everyone so much thirty years since. **1875** *Contemp. Rev.* XXV. 740 Mr. Foster..the perfectibilist, and Mr. Escot..the deteriorationist, take sides so opposite on the subject of human life.

deteriorative (dɪ'tɪərɪərətɪv), *a.* [f. L. *dēteriōrāt-*, ppl. stem of *dēteriōrāre* (see above) + -IVE.] Causing or tending to deterioration.

1800 BENTHAM *Wks.* (1838–43) X. 346 The deteriorative expedient of removal of moisture by heat. **1808** G. EDWARDS *Pract. Plan* ii. 13 Pretended plans of improvement..which are actually ruinous, or deteriorative. **1879** RICHARDSON in *Nature* 23 Oct. 618/2 The whole course of life had undergone a deteriorative change.

deteriorator (dɪ'tɪərɪəreɪtə(r)). [agent-n. in L. form, from *dēteriōrāre* to DETERIORATE.] One who or that which deteriorates.

1857 H. MILLER *Test. Rocks* vi. 234 It is man..that is the deteriorator of man. **1883** *Daily Tel.* 25 Apr. 3 Cities are great deteriorators of physical strength.

de'teriorism. *nonce-wd.* [f. L. *dēterior* (see above) + -ISM.] The doctrine that the tendency of things is to grow worse.

1880 GOLDW. SMITH in *Atl. Monthly* No. 268. 212 Meliorism and the opposite theory, which we suppose must be called deteriorism.

deteri'ority. *rare.* [f. L. *dēterior* + -ITY: cf. *superiority*.] The being of worse or inferior quality; poorer or lower quality; worseness.

1692 RAY *Dissol. World* 43 Their holding out for some Generations against the inconveniences of the Air, or deteriority of Diet. **1719** W. WOOD *Surv. Trade* 358 The

Exchange to all the Parts of the World would alter in proportion to the Deteriority of our Standard.

†**de'term**, *v. Obs.* [f. DE- prefix + TERM, after L. *dētermināre*: cf. also OF. *termer* to end, fix. determine.] By-form of DETERMINE *v.*

1423 JAS. I *Kingis Q.* xiii, Determyt furth therewith in myn entent..I tuke conclusion Sum new thing to write. **1513** DOUGLAS *Æneis* x. v. 62 Bot Turnus hes determit, as certane thing, Gret garnysonys to send betwix thame sone. **1533** BELLENDEN *Livy* v. (1822) 418 The Faderis..determit to abide on the returning of thare legatis fra the tempil of Delphos. **1535** COVERDALE *Dan.* ix. 24 LXX wekes are determed ouer thy people and ouer thy holy cite. **1551** TURNER *Herbal* I. (1568) D vj b, I dare not plainly determe, that it was the right clematitis. **1573** TWYNE *Æneid* XII. Kk iv b, Therwith I am determd. **1647** H. MORE *Song of Soul* II. I. II. lix, For to determ The hid conditions of vitalitie.

Hence **de'terming** *vbl. sb.*

1535 COVERDALE *1 Esdras* ix. 17 And so the matter was a determynge..vntill the new moone.

determa (dɪ'tɜːmə). Also 8 **tetermer**. [Native name.] A native wood of Guyana.

1769 E. BANCROFT *Nat. Hist. Guiana* 80 The Tetermer Tree grows to near fifty feet in height. **1851** *Illustr. Catal. Gt. Exhib.* IV. I. 984/2 Determa, transverse and vertical sections, from River Demerara. **1858** SIMMONDS *Dict. Trade, Determa*, a native wood of Guiana, which is used for masts, booms, and planking for colonial craft.

determent (dɪ'tɜːmənt). [f. DETER *v.*[1] + -MENT.] The action or fact of deterring; *transf.* a means of deterring, a deterring circumstance.

1646 SIR T. BROWNE *Pseud. Ep.* VI. viii. 319 Nor will the ill successe of some be made a sufficient determent unto others. **1653** HAMMOND *On 1 Cor.* i. 23. 542 A mighty determent and discouragement. **1661** BOYLE *Style of Script.* Pref., But these, Sir, are not all the Deterrments that Oppos'd my Obeying You. **1684** BUNYAN *Pilgr.* II. 111 That also shall be so far from being to my Determent. **1764** *Mem. G. Psalmanazar* 24 Rather a determent than an effectual means. **1876** J. GRANT *Hist. India* I. lvi. 284/1 Cornwallis executed nine for the determent of others.

determina'bility. [f. next: see -ITY.] The quality of being determinable.

1825 COLERIDGE *Aids Refl.* (1848) I. 195 The power of proposing an ultimate end, the determinability of the will by ideas. **1877** E. CAIRD *Philos. Kant* II. xviii. 624 Beyond this mere formal principle of determinability, there is a transcendental principle of complete determination.

determinable (dɪ'tɜːmɪnəb(ə)l), *a.* and *sb.* [In ME., a. OF. *determinable* fixed, determinate, ad. L. *dētermīnābilis* (Tertull.) that has an end, finite. In later use, following the ordinary analogy of adjs. in *-able*, in which sense it has also been revived in mod.F. (Not in Cotgr.; 1878 in Dict. Acad.)]

A. *adj.* †**1.** Fixed, definite, determined. *Obs.*

c **1325** *E.E. Allit. P.* A. 593 In sauter is said a verce ouerte þat spekez a poynt determynable. **1486** *Bk. St. Albans, Her.* A v a, Ther be ix. vices contrary to gentilmen of the wiche v. ben indetermynable and iiij. determynable. **1525** LD. BERNERS *Froiss.* II. ccxxii. [ccxviii.] 686 The kynge hath commaunded me to gyue you a determynable answere to your requestes. **1646** SIR T. BROWNE *Pseud. Ep.* VI. i. 280 Yet were there no small difficulty to set downe a determinable Chronology.

2. Capable of being determined; proper to be determined. **a.** Capable of being, or proper to be, legally or authoritatively decided or settled.

1485 *Act 1 Hen. VII*, c. 7 The same Rescous and Disobeysance shall be Felony, enquirable and determinable as is aforesaid. **1570–6** LAMBARDE *Peramb. Kent* (1826) 165 Certaine principall points concerning the Port townes, be determinable at Shipwey onely. **1594** HOOKER *Eccl. Pol.* II. (1632) 110 Affairs..which were not determinable one way or other by the Scripture. *c* **1645** HOWELL *Lett.* (1655) IV. IV. xvi. 39 A Forest hath her Court..where matters are as pleadable and determinable, as at Westminster-Hall. **1685** *Col. Rec. Pennsylv.* I. 248 All Causes not Determinable by y[e] Respective County Courts. **1827** HALLAM *Const. Hist.* (1876) III. xvii. 307 To prepare all matters determinable in parliament. **1845** LD. CAMPBELL *Chancellors* (1857) I. xix. 281 Matters determinable by your common law.

b. Capable of being definitely limited, fixed, assigned, or laid down.

1581 MULCASTER *Positions* xlii. (1887) 261 The Elementarie time, determinable not by yeares, but by sufficiencie. **1611** R. FENTON *Usury* I. iii. 15 Every intention ..is determinable by the act it selfe to be good or bad. **1794** G. ADAMS *Nat. & Exp. Philos.* III. xxvi. 96 Standards of space and velocity are also determinable.

c. Capable of being definitely ascertained (*a*) as to fact or identity, (*b*) as to meaning or character.

1658 SIR T. BROWNE *Gard. Cyrus* Wks. II. 522 What is the most lasting herb or seed, seems not easily determinable. **1748** HARTLEY *Observ. Man* I. iii. 274 These words being determinable only by means of the known words to which they are joined. *Ibid.* 348 Relations..not determinable with Certainty and Precision. **1846** ELLIS *Elgin Marb.* I. 29 One remarkable little spot is also determinable with certainty. **1846** GROTE *Greece* I. xviii. (1862) II. 447 Whether Sidon or Tyre was the most ancient, seems not determinable. **1880** GUNTHER *Fishes* 314 Some of the earliest determinable fish remains.

3. Liable to be terminated or to come to an end; terminable (*esp.* in *Law*).

1584 R. SCOT *Discov. Witchcr.* VIII. iii. 130 The divels death, whose life he held to be determinable and mortall. **1677** HALE *Prim. Orig. Man.* IV. viii. 376 It presents all our enjoyments as determined or determinable in a short time. **1707** *Lond. Gaz.* No. 4382/4 In Lease for 99 Years, determinable on one, two and three Lives. **1815** T. JEFFERSON *Writ.* (1830) IV. 260 A truce determinable on the first act of impressment. **1848** WHARTON *Law Lex.*, *Determinable Freeholds*, estates for life, which may determine upon future contingencies before the life for which they are created expires. **1876** DIGBY *Real Prop.* v. 229 *note*, Here the estate would be an estate determinable upon the specified event.

B. *sb. Philos.* [*tr. G. das bestimmbare.*] That which is capable of being given a more determinate form or of being more precisely specified; *spec.* (in W. E. Johnson's use) a general term or concept (e.g. colour) under which several specific terms or concepts fall (e.g. red, yellow, green). Also as *adj.*

1878 S. H. HODGSON *Philos. of Reflection* I. iv. 272 Maimon adds [in *Die Kathegorien des Aristoteles*: *Propädeutik* 248] that since the critical philosophy has already fixed the meaning of the expressions, matter and form, he will use expressions of his own instead of them, namely, the ***determinable*** and its ***determination***. *Ibid.*, Space is therefore the matter, the determinable (*bestimmbare*). **1906** W. JAMES *Let.* 3 Apr. in R. B. Perry *Thought & Char. W. J.* (1935) II. 392 Taking 'experience' concretely..seems to me the only way in which to leave all its determinations real so far as they are attained, and at the same time to leave always a *determinable*..that provides for what is fertile and developable in the process. **1921** W. E. JOHNSON *Logic* I. xi. 174, I propose to call such terms as colour and shape determinables in relation to such terms as red and circular which will be called determinates. **1949** G. RYLE *Concept of Mind* ii. 44 Many disposition-concepts are determinable concepts. **1960** S. KÖRNER *Philos. of Math.* viii. 167 Perceptual characteristics which in the philosophical literature are sometimes called 'determinables' or 'respects of likeness', such as 'colour', 'shape', etc., are all internally inexact.

Hence **de'terminableness.** *rare.*

1727 BAILEY vol. II, *Determinableness*, capableness of being determined or decided. **1775** in ASH; and in mod. Dicts.

determinably (dɪ'tɜːmɪnəblɪ), *adv.* [f. prec. + -LY[2].] In a determinable manner. †**a.** Definitely, precisely. **b.** In a way or to a degree that can be determined; ascertainably.

1375 BARBOUR *Bruce* IV. 677 It wes vounderfull, perfay, How ony man throu steris may Knaw the thingis that ar to cum Determinabilly. **1609** SIR E. HOBY *Let. to T. Higgins* 60 Augustine..doth plainly and determinablie conclude that they are not *Diuini Canonis*. *Mod.* A substance of which the granules are determinably smaller.

de'terminacy. [f. DETERMINATE *a.*: see -ACY.] The quality of being determinate; determinateness, definiteness.

1873 ATKINSON tr. *Helmholtz's Pop. Sci. Lect.* 80 Yet the ear solves its problem with the greatest exactness, certainty, and determinacy. **1953** C. E. BAZELL *Linguistic Form* 108 It is the fact that different postulates tend to lead to similar solutions which guarantees the relative determinacy of phonemic as opposed to componential analysis. **1958** *Listener* 18 Dec. 1019/2 The determinacy which exists in events where large numbers of atoms are involved.

determinandum (dɪ,tɜːmɪ'nændəm). *Logic* and *Philol.* [a. L. *dētermīnandum* 'thing to be determined', neut. of gerundive of *dētermināre* to DETERMINE.] That part of a proposition (or an expression) which is to be made determinate by a thought-process (or by another part of the expression).

1921 W. E. JOHNSON *Logic* I. i. 9 The determinandum is defined as what is presented *to be* determined or characterised by thought or cognition; the determinans as what *does* characterise or determine in thought that which is given to be determined. **1924** JESPERSEN *Philos. Gram.* xi. 146 At the outset indefinite and indeterminate,..the subject is..a determinandum which only by means of the predicate becomes a determinatum. **1961** [see DETERMINANS].

determinans (dɪ,tɜːmɪ'nænz). *Logic* and *Philol.* [a. L. *dētermīnans*, pres. pple. of *dētermināre* to DETERMINE.] The limiting or qualifying part of a proposition or expression.

1921 [see DETERMINANDUM]. **1961** *Brno Studies* III. 13 Syntagmatic relations of the type 'determinans—determinandum'.

determinant (dɪ'tɜːmɪnənt), *a.* and *sb.* [ad. L. *dētermīnānt-em*, pr. pple. of *dētermināre* to DETERMINE: cf. F. *déterminant* (Trevoux 1752).]

A. *adj.* Determining; that determines; determinative.

1610 W. FOLKINGHAM *Art of Survey* IV. v. 84 Determinant Valuation concludes and determines the Right and Interest of the Possident by Alienation of the Fee or Possession. **1686** GOAD *Celest. Bodies* II. i. 152 The Sun and Moon alone..cannot be the Causes preparatory or determinant of a Showre. **1825** COLERIDGE *Aids Refl.* 280 Some other Principle which has been made determinant of his Will. **1860** RUSKIN *Mod. Paint.* V. VIII. iv. §8 His usual drawings from nature..being both commemorative and determinant..determinant, in that they record an impression received from the place there and then, together with the principal arrangement of the composition in which it was afterwards to be recorded. **1888** J. MARTINEAU *Study of Relig.* I. II. i. 211 He rightly appropriates the word Cause to the determinant act. **1892** *Current Hist.* (Detroit, Mich.) II. 73 A new determinant factor of unknown power.

B. *sb.* One who or that which determines.

1. In *University Hist.* (repr. med.L. *dētermīnāns*). A determining Bachelor: see DETERMINE *v.* 13, DETERMINATION 4.

[**1449** (2 Jan.) in *Registr. Univ. Oxf.* (O.H.S.) I. 2 Magistri determinantium. **15..** *Ibid.* II. I. 52 (*Title of Official List*) Nomina determinantium.] **1864** D. LAING in *Pref. to Lauder's Dewtie of Kyngis* 6 Two years later, in due course of his academical studies, this Guillelmus Lauder appears among the Determinants in that College; which shows that he had qualified himself for taking his Master's degree. **1887** A. CLARK *Reg. Univ. Oxf.* II. I. 53, 12 Mar. 1586 this Committee decided that..Whereas in times past collectors had exacted unfairly large sums from the determinants, they should in future exact only 12*d.* from each determinant.

2. a. A determining factor or agent; a ruling antecedent, a conditioning element; a defining word or element.

1686 GOAD *Celest. Bodies* II. i. 150 Not because they have no determinant, but because 'tis unknown. **1809–10** COLERIDGE *Friend* (1865) 173 We should..make Malta the direct object and final determinant of the war. **1825** —— *Aids Refl.* 67 His own will is the only and sufficient determinant of all he is, and all he does. **1836–7** SIR W. HAMILTON *Metaph.* xxxiii. (1859) II. 266 Considering the Representative Faculty in Subordination to its two determinants, the faculty of Reproduction, and the faculty of Comparison or Elaboration. **1882** PALGRAVE in Grosart *Spenser's Wks.* IV. p. cvii, Points..taken as determinants of date. **1887** F. HALL in *Nation* (N.Y.) XLIV. 97/3 Good usage—the sole determinant, in general, of what is acceptable in language. **1894** *Pop. Sci. Monthly* June 180 Amphimixis alone could never produce a multiplication of the determinants.

b. *Logic.* = CONJUNCT *sb.* 5.

1887 J. N. KEYNES *Formal Logic* (ed. 2) IV. i. 335 We may speak of the elements combined in a conjunctive term as the determinants of that term. **1892** W. E. JOHNSON in *Mind* I. 237 The separate constituents *a*, *b*, are called the determinants of the determinative synthesis *a.b.* **1949** *Mind* LVIII. 3 We find..a marked difference between the use of the word 'determinant' by symbolic logicians of the late 19th century, and the medieval use of its Latin equivalent. For such writers as Schroeder and J. N. Keynes a 'determinant' is any one of the elements combined in a logical conjunction.

c. *Philol.* A limiting or qualifying expression; *esp.*, in a compound word, the element that limits or qualifies the meaning of the other element.

1869 FARRAR *Fam. Speech* iii. 89 In Aryan the determinant precedes the thing determined. **1934** PRIEBSCH & COLLINSON *German Lang.* II. v. 258 Composite words consisting of a determinant word (*Bestimmungswort*) and a nucleus (*Grundwort*). The determinant may be an adjective ..or a substantive. **1960** [see DETERMINATUM]. **1962** A. MARTINET *Functional View Lang.* ii. 51 Some determinants are lexical (an adjective like *great*), and others grammatical (an adjective like *my*, the article *the*, or the 'plural' moneme).

3. *Math.* The sum of the products of a square block or 'matrix' of quantities, each product containing one factor from each row and column, and having the plus or minus sign according to the arrangement of its factors in the block.

A determinant is commonly denoted by writing the matrix with a vertical line on each side, thus—

$$\begin{vmatrix} a_1 & a_2 & a_3 \\ b_1 & b_2 & b_3 \\ c_1 & c_2 & c_3 \end{vmatrix}$$

Originally applied (in Latin form), in 1801, by Gauss (*Disquis. Arithmet.* 180 §v. §154) to a special class of these functions on the nature of which the properties of certain quadratic forms depend; thence adopted in French by Cauchy.

1843 CAYLEY (*title*), On the Theory of Determinants. **1853** SYLVESTER in *Phil. Trans.* CXLIII. I. 543–4 *Determinant.*—This word is used throughout in the single sense, after which it denotes the alternate or hemihedral function the vanishing of which is the condition of the possibility of the coexistence of a certain number of homogeneous linear equations of as many variables. **1885** SALMON *Higher Algebra* 338 Cauchy introduced the name 'determinants', already applied by Gauss to the functions considered by him, and called by him 'determinants of quadratic forms'.

4. *Biol.* In Weismann's theory of heredity, each of the hypothetical units in the germ-plasm supposed to determine the character and development of a cell or group of cells (hence called a *determinate*) in the organism; also, a gene or other hereditary 'factor'.

1893 PARKER & RÖNNFELDT tr. *Weismann's Germ-Plasm* I. i. 57, I shall designate the cells or groups of cells which are independently variable from the germ onwards as the 'hereditary parts' or 'determinates', and the particles of the germ-plasm corresponding to and determining them, as the 'determining parts' or 'determinants'. *Ibid.* 59 A determinant is always a group of biophors. **1905** *Westm. Gaz.* 30 Mar. 2/1 Selection acts on the determinants and produces the variations once so plausibly attributed to the Lamarckian principle of acquired characters. **1920** *Cambr. Bulletin* Feb. 16 Germ-cell Determinants. **1944** C. D. DARLINGTON in *Nature* 5 Aug. 165/1 How far are we justified in assuming the same kind of determinant in the cytoplasm where determinants are not fastened to the immediate products of their activity? **1971** *Nature* 19 Mar. 185/1 Factors in the cytoplasm of many eggs can influence the development of the cells, part of which they eventually constitute. This is most clearly seen in the case of the germ cell determinants.

determi'nantal (dɪ,tɜːmɪ'næntəl). *a. Math.* [f. prec. + -AL[1].] Relating to determinants;

consisting of or expressed as a determinant: see DETERMINANT B. 3.

1867 C. L. DODGSON *Elem. Treat. Determinants* 12 The determinantal coefficient of any Element of a square Block is the Determinant of its complemental Minor. 1879 THOMSON & TAIT *Nat. Phil.* I. I. §337 Roots..of a determinantal equation. 1892 *Daily News* 24 Mar. 3/5 Essay on 'Determinantal Theorems'. 1968 FOX & MAYERS *Computing Methods for Scientists & Engineers* v. 95 Finding a zero of some function expressed in determinantal form.

determinate (dɪˈtɜːmɪnət), *ppl. a.* and *sb.* [ad. L. *dētermināt-us*, pa. pple. of *dētermināre* to DETERMINE.] That has been or is determined: in the chief senses of the verb.

A. as *pa. pple.* = DETERMINED. *Obs.* or *arch.*

c1391 CHAUCER *Astrol.* I. §21 Sterres fixes with hir longitudes & latitudes determynat. *Ibid.* II. §18 *heading*, To knowe the degrees of the longitudes of fixe sterres after that they ben determinat in thin astrolabie. 1471 RIPLEY *Comp. Alch.* Ep. in Ashm. (1652) 111 By Raymond and others determynate. 1560 in Strype *Ann. Ref.* I. xvii. 216 So that their causes be determinate within three weeks. c1600 SHAKS. *Sonn.* lxxxvii, My bonds in thee are all determinate. 1885 BRIDGES *Nero* II. iii. 8/2 The seasons, lady, Of divination are determinate By stars and special omens.

B. *adj.*

1. a. Definitely bound or limited, in time, space, extent, position, character, or nature; definite, fixed; clearly defined or individualized; distinct, as opposed to *vague*, *undefined*, or *indefinite*.

c1386 CHAUCER *Friar's T.* 161 Han ye figure thanne determinat In helle ther ye been in youre estat? 1398 TREVISA *Barth. De P.R.* XIII. i. (Tollem. MS.), Water haþ no determinate qualite, noþer coloure, noþer sauoure. 1432-50 tr. *Higden* (Rolls) I. 287 A determinate place in the ryuer that is abowte Lincoln. 1532 MORE *Confut. Tindale* Wks. 721/2 The saluacion of any determinate persone yet liuying. 1548 HALL *Chron.* 245 b, Taken and concluded for a determinate season. 1613 J. SALKELD *Treat. Angels* 22 They seeme to define some determinate number of Angels. 1626 BACON *Sylva* §602 Plants are all figurate and determinate, which inanimate Bodies are not. 1662 HOBBES *Seven Prob.* Wks. 1845 VII. 16 A certain and determinate distance. 1705 BERKELEY *Commonpl. Bk.* Wks. 1871 IV. 443 The clear and determinate meaning of my words. 1767 BLACKSTONE *Comm.* II. 140 The possession of lands or tenements, for some determinate period. 1777 PRIESTLEY *Matt. & Spir.* (1782) I. I. 11 [It] must be..round, or square, or of some other determinate form. 1818 HALLAM *Mid. Ages* (1841) I. vii. 522 Consecrated bishop without any determinate see. 1845 H. ROGERS *Ess.* I. iii. 102 He has clothed the determinate quantities of arithmetic in the universal symbols of algebra. 1852 —— *Ecl. Faith* (1853) 201 In time, my doubts, as usual, assumed a determinate shape. 1871 B. STEWART *Heat* §112 Determinate vapour pressure corresponds to determinate temperature. 1875 MAINE *Hist. Inst.* xii. 351 The sovereign is a determinate human superior.

b. Limited, restricted, finite: opposed to *infinite*, *unbounded*.

1586 FERNE *Blaz. Gentrie* 33 The determinate glory of an earthly prince. 1604 T. WRIGHT *Passions* II. i. 50 Our soule being of a determinate power and activitie cannot attend exactly to twoo vehement and intensive operations together. 1608 J. KING *Serm. St. Mary's* 6 A superiority..over limited and determinate chardges.

c. *Math.* Having a fixed value or magnitude. (Opp. to *indeterminate*); ***determinate number***, ***problem***: see quots.

1722 WOLLASTON *Relig. Nat.* i. 13 As determinate and immutable as any ratio's are in mathematics. 1727-51 CHAMBERS *Cycl.*, *Determinate problem*, is that which has but one, or at least but a certain number of solutions, in contradistinction to an indeterminate problem, which admits of infinite solutions. *Ibid.* s.v. *Number*, A *determinate Number* is that referred to some given unit; as a ternary, or three; which is what we properly call a *number*. 1879 THOMSON & TAIT *Nat. Phil.* I. I. §327 This problem is essentially determinate, but generally has multiple solutions. 1885 WATSON & BURB. *Electr. & Magn.* 59 There exists one determinate function *u* which has the given value at each point of *S*.

d. *Bot.* Of inflorescence: In which the terminal flower bud opens first, followed by those on the lateral branches; definite, centrifugal.

1880 GRAY *Struct. Bot.* v. 144 The kinds of Inflorescence are all reducible to two types..Indeterminate and Determinate.

2. Settled, fixed, so as not to vary.

1526-34 TINDALE *Acts* ii. 23 The determinat counsell and foreknoweledge of God. 1543-4 *Act 35 Hen. VIII*, c. 9 The which order..shall stande..for a full determinate order. 1559 *Primer* in *Priv. Prayers* (1851) 10 A determinate fourme of praiyng. 1581 PETTIE *Guazzo's Civ. Conv.* I. (1586) 21 There can be no certaine and determinate science, from particular to particular. 1625 K. LONG tr. *Barclay's Argenis* II. xvii. 120 To what end is the freedome of man, if he cannot avoid the determinate order of the starres? 1726 BUTLER *Serm. Hum. Nat.* ii, Virtue and religion..require.. that every action be directed by some determinate rule. 1855 BRIMLEY *Ess.* 22 (Tennyson) Smitten with a determinate aversion to popularity. 1861 MILL *Utilit.* i. 4 There should be a determinate order of precedence among them.

3. Finally determined upon or decided; expressing a final decision; definitive; conclusive, final.

1533-4 *Act 25 Hen. VIII*, c. 12 The determinate and plaine iudgementes of the said sondrie vniuersitees. 1540-1 ELYOT *Image Gov.* 25 Not onely myne opinion herein, but also my determynate sentence. 1566 PAINTER *Pal. Pleas.* I. 29 To consulte vppon some determinate aunswere. 1589 NASHE in *Greene's Menaphon* Pref. (Arb.) 14, I had rather referre it, as a disputatiue plea to diuines than set it dcwne as a determinate position. 1609 BIBLE (Douay) *Jer.* xv. Comm., He confirmeth the same determinate sentence of their punishment. 1711 SHAFTESB. *Charac.* (1737) III. v. iii. 303 The Reasonableness of a proportionate Taste, and determinate Choice. 1803 WELLINGTON in Gurw. *Desp.* II. 151 *note*, No determinate reply could be given to the letter.

4. Determined upon, intended.

1586 T. B. *La Primaud. Fr. Acad.* I. 235 To drive him from his determinat purpose. 1601 SHAKS. *Twel. N.* II. i. 11 My determinate voyage is meere extrauagancie.

5. Fixed in mind or purpose, determined, resolved, resolute.

1587 HOLINSHED *Chron. II. Hist. Scot.* 316/1 That thing the heart thought and was determinat to do. 1598 BARRET *Theor. Warres* I. i. 8 Men..of determinate minds and courage. 1686 F. SPENCE tr. *Varillas' Ho. Medicis* 309 The most active and determinate adventurer of his age. 1727 FIELDING *Love in Sev. Masq.* Wks. 1775 I. 46 Nor am I perfectly determinate what species of animals to assign him to. 1779-81 JOHNSON *L.P.*, *Prior* Wks. III. 143 A Tory so ardent and determinate that he did not willingly consort with men of different opinions. 1827 CARLYLE *Misc.* (1857) I. 58 Men of cool judgment, and determinate energetic character.

C. *sb.* **1.** *Biol.* (See DETERMINANT B. *sb.* 4.)

1893 PARKER & RÖNNFELDT tr. *Weismann's Germ-Plasm* I. i. 58 Similar hereditary parts or determinates may be observed in butterflies, in which the colours on the wings often form very complicated lines and spots of slight extent but of great constancy.

2. *Philos.* (See quot.)

1921 [see DETERMINABLE *sb.*].

†**de'terminate**, *v.* *Obs.* [f. ppl. stem of L. *dētermināre*: see prec.]

1. *trans.* To determine in time, space, or compass; to terminate, end, bound, limit.

1563 WINȜET *Four Scoir Thre Quest.* Wks. 1888 I. 125 Gif we..limitatis and determinatis nocht the wisdom of God be our phantasie. 1593 SHAKS. *Rich. II*, I. iii. 150 The slye slow [Fol. 2, flye slow] houres shall not determinate The datelesse limit of thy deere exile. a1638 MEDE *Rem. Apoc.* Wks. (1672) III. 602 Who would have them [prophetic months] taken for bare days, and determinated in the persecution of Antiochus. 1671 CROWNE *Juliana* Ep. Ded., I have nothing to determinate my sight, but a bright and serene sky.

2. To determine or decide (a controversy or issue).

1647 H. MORE *Song of Soul* II. III. IV. vii, But let more hardy wits that truth determinate. 1653 —— *Antid. Ath.* I. ix. §4. 27 They do plainly determinate the controversy. 1715 MRS. J. BARKER *Exilius* I. 83 Sent for..to give my determinating Voice before the Senate.

b. *intr.* To decide, come to a decision.

1639 MRQ. OF HAMILTON *Explan. Oath & Covenant* 15 To treat, consult, or determinate in any matter of state. 1652 EARL MONM. tr. *Bentivoglio's Hist. Relat.* 6 The absolute authority of determinating residing in the chief magistracies of every City.

3. *trans.* To ordain, appoint.

1636 E. DACRES tr. *Machiavel's Disc. Livy* I. 83 The free government propounds honours and rewards upon some worthy and determinated occasions. 1652 GAULE *Magastrom.* 151 Although nature and every naturall agent be..determinated to one effect.

4. To direct to some end; to determine the course of; to guide authoritatively or decisively.

1626 FENNER *Hidden Manna* (in Spurgeon *Treas. Dav.* Ps. xxv.), A determinating of the very will. 1653 H. MORE *Antid. Ath.* I. xi. (1662) 35 To determinate the course of the Spirits into this or that part of the Body. 1659 PEARSON *Creed* I. 43 If we should apprehend more Gods than one, I know not what could determinate us in any instant to the actual adoration of any one. a1683 WHICHCOTE *Disc.* (1703) III. 36 'Tis no disparagement to the Highest and wisest to be ruled and determinated by the reason of things. 1686 GOAD *Celest. Bodies* I. xii. 61 This Aspect, apt to cause Winds, is apt also to determinate them to the West and to the South.

5. To fix upon definitely, define, individualize, identify.

1681 H. MORE *Exp. Dan.* iv. Notes 123 The person is determinated in Artaxerxes. 1681 GLANVILL *Saddducismus* II. 237 Though the Sir-name of the party be wanting, yet he is determinated so by other circumstances.

6. To render determinate or definite.

1672 GREGORY in Rigaud *Corr. Sci. Men* (1841) II. 236 The most ready general method..for determinating all equations.

7. To ascertain definitely.

1665-6 *Phil. Trans.* I. 297 The more precise determinating of the Difference of Meridians. 1788 PRIESTLEY *Lect. Hist.* II. xii. 96 As nearly..as their coarse observations would enable them to determinate.

Hence **de'terminated** *ppl. a.*, **de'terminating** *vbl. sb.* and *ppl. a.*

1626 [See sense 4]. 1635 PAGITT *Christianogr.* I. iii. (1636) 137 A prefixed and determinated time of monthes or yeeres. a1693 URQUHART *Rabelais* III. xliii. 353 His final judging and determinating of Suits of Law, by the meer Chance..of the Dice. 1715 [See sense 2].

de'terminately, *adv.* [f. DETERMINATE *a.* + -LY².] In a determinate manner.

1. By way of final decision; conclusively, finally.

1509 FISHER *Fun. Serm. C'tess Richmond* Wks. (1876) 293 She sholde the morowe after make answer of her mynde determynatly. 1669 WOODHEAD *St. Teresa* I. xxxv. (1671) 260, I did never determinately conclude. 1729 BUTLER *Serm.* Wks. 1874 II. 24 Conscience..pronounces determinately some actions to be in themselves just, right, good. 1736 —— *Anal.* II. vii. 270 Those Persons..insist upon it as determinately conclusive. 1792 R. BURKE in *Burke's Corr.* (1844) III. 489 The ministers had made up their minds determinately to a strict neutrality.

2. Definitely, distinctly, exactly, precisely.

1529 MORE *Comf. agst. Trib.* III. Wks. 1225/2 Yet can not the vse of them lightly stand indifferent, but determinately must either be good or bad. 1551 T. WILSON *Logike* (1580) 21 b, Wordes, whiche..determinatly doe betoken some one certaine thyng. a1653 GOUGE *Comm. Heb.* xiii. 8, 1. Indefinitely, time after time. 2. Determinatly, to the end of the world. 1759 WARNER in *Phil. Trans.* LI. 307 A discovery of the fact, could it be determinately made, would prove of very little consequence. 1830 GLEIG *Country Curate* I. xiv. 274, I cannot pronounce the night..the most determinately miserable which it has been my lot to spend.

b. With a definite purpose, purposely.

1862 DARWIN *Fertil. Orchids* v. 203 All these parts seemed determinately contrived that the plant should never be fertilised.

3. With settled purpose; resolutely, determinedly; with determination.

1556 J. HEYWOOD *Spider & F.* xiv. 69 When he sawe.. The spider, thus bent determinately, He thought it foly him to contrary. 1653 H. MORE *Antid. Ath.* III. xvi. (1712) 140 Observed to fight determinately over such and such a City. 1724 SWIFT *Wood's Execution*, Determinately bent to take revenge upon him. 1755 FOX in H. Walpole *Mem. Geo. II* (1847) II. App. 386 The Duke of Devonshire is.. determinately against it. 1860 FROUDE *Hist. Eng.* V. 69 A servant determinately idle. 1881 E. COXON *Basil Pl.* II. 176 For all her weakness, she spoke determinately.

de'terminateness. [f. as prec. + -NESS.] The quality of being determinate.

1. Definiteness, distinctness, preciseness.

1692 *Covt. Grace Conditional* 14 No way evacuating either the efficacy or determinateness of God's Election. 1846 POE *N.P. Willis* Wks. 1864 III. 30 The word fancy is used with very little determinateness of meaning. 1884 tr. *Lotze's Metaph.* 31 Each of their marks..has been limited to a completely individual determinateness.

2. Decidedness of judgement or choice; resoluteness; determination.

1652 GAULE *Magastrom.* 22 He reprooves..their.. peremptory determinatenes, 'Ye say, it will be to day'. 1814 JANE AUSTEN *Mansf. Park* (1851) 83 His determinateness and his power seemed to make allies unneccessary.

determination (dɪˌtɜːmɪˈneɪʃən). [a. F. *détermination* (Oresme 14th c.), or ad. L. *dēterminātiōn-em*, n. of action from *dētermināre* to DETERMINE.] The action of determining, the condition of being determined.

1. A bringing to an end; a coming to an end; ending; termination. *arch.* (exc. as in b).

1483 *Cath. Angl.* 98 A Determynacion, *determinacio, diffinicio*. 1526 *Pilgr. Perf.* (1531) 93 b, A conclusyon or a full determinacyon of the mater. 1584 R. SCOT *Discov. Witchcr.* VII. xv. 123 The determination and ceasing of oracles. 1586 A. DAY *Eng. Secretary* I. (1625) 63 By reason of the over-hasty determination of his life. 1634-5 BRERETON *Trav.* (1844) 153 After the determination of the thirteen years. 1659 *Burton's Diary* (1828) IV. 324 After the end or other determination of this Parliament. 1668 CULPEPPER & COLE *Barthol. Anat.* IV. i. 336 All other Bones save the Teeth have a certain determination of their growth: but the Teeth grow continually. 1794 PALEY *Evid.* II. vi. (1817) 151 A date subsequent to the determination of Pilate's government. 1874 STUBBS *Const. Hist.* II. xvi. 465 The war continued..seeming year by year further removed from a determination.

b. *Law.* (esp. in *Conveyancing*) The cessation of an estate or interest of any kind.

1495 *Act 11 Hen. VII*, c. 54 §4 After the.. dettermynacions of the states..by deth without heires male or eny other wise. 1581 W. STAFFORD *Exam. Compl.* i. (1876) 18 Such landes as come to our handes..by determination, and ending of such termes of yeares. 1818 CRUISE *Digest* (ed. 2) VI. 465 To take effect on the determination of the estate tail. 1827 JARMAN *Powell's Devises* II. 321 A devise of real estate to the heirs of a person living at the determination of the prior estates. 1875 *Act 38-9 Vict.* c. 92 §4 Determination of tenancy means the cesser of a contract of tenancy by reason of effluxion of time or from any other cause. 1891 *Law Reports* Weekly Notes 79/1 Immediately after the determination of defendant's tenancy.

2. The ending of a controversy or suit by the decision of a judge or arbitrator; judicial or authoritative decision or settlement (*of* a matter at issue).

1494 FABYAN *Chron.* VII. 396 To abyde all suche determynacion and iudgement. 1553 T. WILSON *Rhet.* 6 The Judges before whom he knoweth the determinacion of his cause resteth. 1652 NEEDHAM tr. *Selden's Mare Cl.* 22 The Nations to whose determination the matter was committed. 1737 *Col. Rec. Pennsylv.* IV. 187 Upon the final Determination of our Disputes. 1875 JOWETT *Plato* (ed. 2) I. 116 In the determination of this question the identity of virtue and knowledge is found to be involved. 1891 SIR R. V. WILLIAMS in *Law Times' Rep.* LXV. 609/1 The general question of the right of the licensee was not essential to the determination of that case.

b. The decision arrived at or promulgated; a determinate sentence, conclusion, or opinion.

1395 PURVEY *Remonstr.* (1851) 73 That ech determinacioun of the chirche of Rome is trewe on ech side. 1460 CAPGRAVE *Chron.* 306 The determinacion of the Cherch and the Doctouris..ar pleynly ageyn Holy Scripture. 1552 ABP. HAMILTON *Catech.* (1884) 5 The decisiouns and determinatiouns of general counsallis. 1648 MILTON *Tenure Kings* (1650) 59 The cleer and positive determination of all who have writt'n on this argument. 1711 ADDISON *Spect.* No. 122 ¶5 They were neither of them dissatisfied with the Knight's Determination. 1785 T. BALGUY *Disc.* 75 To listen to our Saviour's determination,—'He that is without sin'. 1875 JOWETT *Plato* (ed. 2) V. 180 We must run a risk..in coming to any determination about education.

†**3.** The settlement of a question by reasoning or argumentation; discussion. *Obs.*

c **1400** *Test. Love* I. (R.), These clerkes sain, and in determinacion shewen, that three things hauen the names of Goddes been cleaped. **1593** Bp. Andrewes (*title*), A Determination concerning Oaths.

†**4.** The resolving of a question or maintaining of a thesis in a scholastic disputation; *spec.* in University history, the name of certain disputations which followed admission to the degree of Bachelor of Arts, and completed the taking of that degree, qualifying the student for proceeding to the residence and exercises required for the Master's degree. *Obs.* exc. *Hist.*

Determination took place regularly in the Lent following presentation for the B.A., and consisted originally in the determining by disputation of questions in grammar and logic. 'It was originally, it would appear, a voluntary disputation got up by the Bachelors themselves in imitation of the magisterial INCEPTION, but it was early recognized and enforced by the Universities.' (Rev. H. Rashdall.)

[**1408** in *Munim. Acad. Oxon.* (Rolls) I. 241 Quia per solemnes determinationes Bachillariorum in facultate artium nostra mater Oxoniæ universitas multipliciter honoratur. **1517** *Statutes of Corpus Chr. Coll., Oxon.*, c. xxiv, Baccalaurei artium, completo prius post gradum baccalaureatus et determinationes triennio..ad gradum magistratus..promoveantur.] **1665** J. Buck in Peacock *Stat. Cambridge* (1841) App. B 79 The Vice-Chancellor dismisseth the Answerer..then he beginneth his Determination. **1693-4** Gibson in *Lett. Lit. Men* (Camden) 219 There is a Statute..which upon extraordinary occasions allows twice Austins instead of Determinations. **1726** Amherst *Terræ Fil.* xlii. 223 The manner of this determination is as follows. All persons, that have taken their bachelor of arts degree since the Lent preceding, are obliged to dispute twice in one of the public schools..and go to prayers at St. Mary's Church every Saturday morning. **1822** in Fowler *Hist. Corpus Chr. Coll.* 302 The whole business and ceremony of Determination having been now by competent authority abolished in the University. **1866** Rogers *Agric. & Prices* I. v. 121 The Determination Feast, that is the festival following the assumption of the Bachelor's Degree, generally took place on Shrove Tuesday. **1868** H. Anstey *Munim. Acad. Oxon.* (Rolls) Introd. 82 It was undoubtedly from the superior importance attached to logical studies that the name 'determination' took its rise, the examination for the bachelor's degree consisting mainly of questions to be determined by the candidate. **1887** A. Clark *Regr. Univ. Oxf.* (O.H.S.) II. I. 63 All traces of determination have now disappeared from the procedure of the University. The last relic of it was abolished in 1855... To such a base end had 'determining' come.

5. The determining of bounds or fixing of limits; delimitation; definition; a fixing of the extent, position, or identity (*of* anything).

1594 Hooker *Eccl. Pol.* I. x. (1611) 28 The particular determination of the reward or punishment. **1606** Shaks. *Tr. & Cr.* II. ii. 170 To make vp a free determination 'Twixt right and wrong. **1651** Hobbes *Leviath.* IV. xlvi. 373 The Circumscription of a thing, is..the Determination, or Defining of its Place. **1665** Hooke *Microgr.* 54 A determination of Light and shadow. **1744** Harris *Three Treat.* i. (1765) 27 Is our Account still too loose and in need of stricter Determination? **1794** S. Williams *Vermont* 283 The determination made by Congress of the boundary lines. **1860** Mansel *Proleg. Logica* iv. 112 Under such determinations as the conditions of my sensibility require. **1866** J. G. Murphy *Comm. Exod.* xii. Introd., The determination of the parties who are admissible. **1877** E. Caird *Philos. Kant* I. 165 The determinations of space are not consequences, but reasons, of the positions of different parts of matter in relation to each other.

b. *Logic.* (*a*) The rendering of a notion more determinate or definite by the addition of characters or determining attributes. (*b*) A determining attribute.

1644 Digby *Nat. Bodies* I. (1645) 87 To be a Quality is nothing else but to be the determination or modification of the thing whose quality it is. **1838** Sir W. Hamilton *Logic* xi. (1866) I. 194 Every series of concepts which has been obtained by abstraction, may be reproduced in an inverted order, when..we, step by step, add on the several characters from which we had abstracted in our ascent. This process..is called Determination. **1860** Mansel *Proleg. Logica* vi. 209 Determination..consists in the reunion of attributes previously separated by definition. **1864** Bowen *Logic* v. 107 Unless one is regarded as an attribute or determination of the other. **1875** Jowett *Plato* (ed. 2) III. 595 The finite and infinite of Philolaus have become logical determinations in the Philebus. *Ibid.* IV. 266 A multitude of abstractions are created..which become logical determinations.

6. The action of definitely ascertaining the position, nature, amount, etc. (*of* anything).

1677 Hale *Prim. Orig. Man.* III. iii. 263 The determination of Insects in their several Species. **1717** J. Keill *Anim. Œcon.* Pref. (1738) 48 The Determination of the *Vis Elastica* was the Thought of the learned John Bernouli. **1793** Englefield (*title*), On the Determination of the Orbits of Comets. **1845-6** G. E. Day tr. *Simon's Anim. Chem.* II. 181 The quantitative determination of earthy-phosphate sediments. **1882** L. B. Carll *Treat. Calculus Variation* 61 The determination of these constants is not..difficult.

b. The result ascertained by this action; that which has been determined by investigation or calculation; a conclusion, a solution.

1570 Billingsley *Euclid* I. i. 9 The determination, which is the declaration of the thing required. **1646** Sir T. Browne *Pseud. Ep.* IV. vi. 194 That persons drowned arise and float the ninth day..is a questionable determination. **1807** T. Thomson *Chem.* (ed. 3) II. 162 The differences between their determinations were too great. **1831** Brewster *Optics* iii. 25 As philosophers have determined the index of refraction for a great variety of bodies, we are able, from those determinations, to ascertain the direction of any ray. **1857** Whewell *Hist. Induct. Sc.* I. 105 Generally founded on astronomical determinations.

7. Fixed direction towards some terminal point; decisive or determining bias. *lit.* and *fig.*

1660 Boyle *New Exp. Phys. Mech.* i. 35 Others, whose motion has an opposite determination. **1710** J. Clarke *Rohault's Nat. Phil.* (1729) I. 78 When a Body moves any particular way, the Disposition that it has to move that way, rather than any other, is what we call its Determination. **1713** Addison *Guardian* No. 100 ¶7 The whole tribe of oglers gave their eyes a new determination. **1727-51** Chambers *Cycl.* s.v., Heavy bodies have a determination towards the centre of the earth. **1754** Edwards *Freed. Will* I. ii. 5 When we speak of the Determination of motion, we mean causing the Motion of the Body to be such a Way, or in such a Direction, rather than another. **1798** Malthus *Popul.* (1806) II. III. x. 253 The real price of corn varies during periods sufficiently long to affect the determination of capital. **1836** Sir W. Hamilton *Discuss.* (1852) 336 The determination given to the Church of Scotland..was not one of erudition. **1881** *Daily News* 10 Mar. 5/3 An increasing determination of historic and genre painters towards landscape.

b. *spec.* A tendency or flow of the bodily fluids, now *esp.* of the blood, to a particular part.

1737 Bracken *Farriery Impr.* (1757) II. 203 The Distempers which proceed from an irregular and disorderly Determination of the animal Spirits. **1805** W. Saunders *Min. Waters* 242 On account of the property of this natural water..and from its rapid determination to the kidnies. **1831** Scott *Let. to A. Dyce* 31 Mar. in *Lockhart*, Threatened with a determination of blood to the head. **1883** *Syd. Soc. Lex.*, *Determination*, the active direction to a part; as of blood to a special organ with increased vascular action.

†**8.** The final condition to which anything has a tendency. *Obs.*

1646 Sir T. Browne *Pseud. Ep.* II. i. 50 The determination of quick-silver is properly fixation, that of milke coagulation, and that of oyle and unctious bodies onely incrassation. **1707** *Curios. in Husb. & Gard.* 340 Each Corpuscle of Salt returns into the primitive Determination which it holds from Nature.

9. *Metaph.* The definite direction of the mind or will toward an object or end, by some motive, regarded as an external force.

c **1685** South *Serm.*, *Will for Deed* (1715) 389 Homage which Nature commands all Understandings to pay to it, by necessary Determination. **1690** Locke *Hum. Und.* II. xxi. 50 The determination of the will, upon inquiry, is following the direction of that guide: and he that has a power to act or not to act, according as such determination directs, is a free agent; such determination abridges not that power wherein liberty consists. **1727-51** Chambers *Cycl.*, Determinations, again, are either moral or physical: a moral determination is that proceeding from a cause which operates morally. **1788** Reid *Act. Powers* III. II. vi. 571 Dr. Hutcheson, considering all the principles of action as so many determinations or motions of the will.

10. The mental action of coming to a decision; the fixing or settling of a purpose; the result of this; a fixed purpose or intention.

1548 Hall *Chron.* an. 8 Edw. IV. 203 Havyng a sure determinacion, fixed in their myndes. **1570-6** Lambarde *Peramb. Kent* (1826) 237 King Alfred was in Kent when he made determination of this journey. **1577** B. Googe *Heresbach's Husb.* I. (1586) 8 Cato would have a man long in determination to builde, but to plant and sowe out of hand. **1630** *R. Johnson's Kingd. & Commw.* 107 The English had no determination to leave them. **1794** Mrs. Radcliffe *Myst. Udolpho* xxvi, Agitated with doubts and fears and contrary determinations. **1883** Sir T. Martin *Ld. Lyndhurst* xvii. 416 Lord Lyndhurst left office with the determination never again to return to it. *Mod.* From this determination no reasoning could move her.

11. The quality of being determined or resolute; determinedness, resoluteness.

1822 Scott *Nigel* xxvii, Elizabeth possessed a sternness of masculine sense and determination which rendered even her weaknesses..respectable. **1829** Lytton *Devereux* II. xi, If I had less determination in my heart, I could not love you so well. **1853** Sir H. Douglas *Milit. Bridges* (ed. 3) 145 Never was..operation executed with greater intelligence and determination. **1866** Geo. Eliot *F. Holt* (1868) 32 There was an expression of acuteness and determination about him. **1875** F. Hall in *Lippincott's Mag.* XV. 345/2 In the same spirit of determination.

determinative (dɪˈtɜːmɪnətɪv), *a.* and *sb.* [a. F. *déterminatif, -ive* (15th c. in Godef. *Suppl.*), f. ppl. stem of L. *dētermināre* to DETERMINE: see -IVE.] **A.** *adj.*

1. a. Characterized by determining, deciding, or fixing; serving or tending to determine or decide.

1655 Bramhall *Agt. Hobbes* (J.), That individual action ..cannot proceed from the special influence and determinative power of a just cause. **1678** Gale *Crt. Gentiles* III. 23 This efficacious concurse, as it determines and applies the second cause to act, is..termed determinative. **1682** Luttrell *Brief Rel.* (1857) I. 205 The day appointed for pronouncing the determinative sentence in the cause. **1725** tr. *Dupin's Eccl. Hist.* I. III. vi. 120 The determinative Voice of the Head of the Church. **1865** Holland *Plain T.* v. 183 Determinative of the character of life. **1884** Fairbairn in *Contemp. Rev.* Mar. 360 The underlying conception, the determinative principle or idea.

†**b.** Characterized by being determined or fixed.

a **1677** Hale *Contempl.*, *Christ Crucif.* (R.), Our Lord Christ's body could not be longer detained under the power of death, then the determinative time of three days.

2. a. Serving to limit or fix the extent, or the specific kind or character of anything: said of attributes or marks added with this purpose. Cf. B. 2.

1697 J. Sergeant *Solid Philos.* 310 The one..is Common or Determinable properly by the other, and the other is Particular or Determinative of it. **1711** Shaftesb. *Charac.* (1737) III. VI. vi. 385 If..we wou'd needs add some exteriour marks, more declaratory and determinative of..Virtue and Pleasure. **1725** Watts *Logic* II. ii. §5 The term..is determinative and limits the subject to a particular part of its extension. **1865** Tylor *Early Hist. Man.* v. 99 The Egyptians do not seem to have got rid of their determinative pictures. **1881** —— *Anthropol.* vii. 171 These examples..give some idea of the principles of its [Chinese writing] sound-characters and keys or determinative signs.

b. Gram. ***determinative adjective, pronoun,*** etc. (see quots.); ***determinative compound*** = TATPURUSHA.

1921 E. Sapir *Lang.* vi. 135 The words of the typical suffixing languages (Turkish, Eskimo, Nootka) are 'determinative' formations, each added element determining the form of the whole anew. **1924** H. E. Palmer *Gram. Spoken Eng.* II. 24 To group with the pronouns all determinative adjectives..shortening the term to *determinatives*. **1933** Bloomfield *Lang.* xiv. 235 One can ..distinguish..determinative (attributive or subordinative) compounds (Sanskrit *tatpurusha*). **1961** R. B. Long *Sentence & its Parts* 486 *The, a,* and *every* are exceptional among the determinative pronouns in requiring stated heads.

B. *sb.*

1. A determinative agent; that which determines, decides, or impels in a given direction.

1832 Austin *Jurispr.* (1879) I. xxvii. 521 A right of action is not merely considered as an instrument or means of redress but as a restraint or determinative from wrong.

2. That which serves to determine or define the character or quality of something else. **a.** In *hieroglyphic writing*, an ideographic sign annexed to a word phonetically represented, for the purpose of defining its signification. Thus in the ancient Egyptian hieroglyphics there were ***generic determinatives*** which indicated the class of notions to which the word belonged, ***determinatives of number***, etc. **b.** In *Science of Language*, a spoken syllable having an analogous function in some languages; also, a determinative or demonstrative word.

1862 Marsh *Eng. Lang.* iv. 67 Very many of the native Mono-syllables are mere Determinatives. **1862** Rawlinson *Anc. Mon.* I. iv. 81 The 'determinative' of a god—the sign, that is, which marks that the name of a god is about to follow. **1875** Renouf *Egyptian Gram.* 11 Plural nouns and adjectives usually..take the sign ⁝ or ııı after them as a determinative of plurality. **1881** Tylor *Anthropol.* vii. 173 Even where they spelt words by their sounds, they had a remarkable way of adding what are called determinatives, which are pictures to confirm or explain the spelt word. **1883** Sayce *Fresh Light Anc. Mon.* i. 18 Determinatives..characters which have no phonetic value, but which determine the class to which the word they accompany belongs.

deˈterminatively, *adv.* [f. prec. + -LY[2].] **a.** In a determinative manner; so as to determine. †**b.** = DETERMINATELY.

1641 *Argument Law* in *Harl. Misc.* (Malh.) V. 63 Such things as are intended immediately, directly, and determinatively against the life and person of the King. **1643** Marshall *Let.* 14 To judge every person..in the Nation determinatively and conclusively, so as from that judgement there is no appealing. **1662** Evelyn *Chalcogr.* 124 For the symmetrically conducting of his hatches, determinatively, and with certitude.

deˈterminativeness. [f. prec. + -NESS.] **a.** The quality of being determinative. **b.** = DETERMINATENESS 2; determination.

1821 *Blackw. Mag.* X. 76 A due proportion of the organ of determinativeness in our peasantry and mechanics might make our subjugation a matter of absolute impossibility. **1851** I. Taylor *Wesley* (1852) 121 [Wesley] whose letters are eminent samples of succinct determinativeness.

determinator (dɪˈtɜːmɪneɪtə(r)). [a. L. *dētermīnātor*, agent-noun from L. *dētermināre* to DETERMINE: with quot. 1556 cf. obs. F. *déterminateur.*] He who or that which determines (in various senses of the verb); a determiner.

1556 *Aurelio & Isab.* (1680) D v, Of that they ware the juges, and determinateurs. **1642** Sir E. Dering *Sp. on Relig.* xiv. 44 The proper determinators of this point. **1646** Sir T. Browne *Pseud. Ep.* III. v. 115 Three determinators of truth, Authority, Sense and Reason. **1855** *Ess. Intuit. Mor.* 146 If a man set forth Moral pleasure as the determinator of his Will. **1879** H. George *Progr. & Pov.* 18 To make the ratio with production, and not the ratio with capital, the determinator of wages.

determinatum (dɪˌtɜːmɪˈneɪtəm). *Logic* and *Philol.* [a. L. *dētermīnātum* 'thing determined', neut. of pa. pple. of *dētermināre* to DETERMINE.] A qualified or limited element of a phrase or proposition; the part determined.

1924 [see DETERMINANDUM]. **1960** S. Potter *Lang. in Mod. World* v. 67 In English the determinant (*air*) always precedes the determinatum (*man*).

determine (dɪˈtɜːmɪn), *v.* [a. OF. *determine-r* (12th c. in Littré), = Pr., Sp., It. *determinar*, ad. L. *dētermināre* to bound, limit, determine, fix, f. L. DE- I. 3 + *termināre* to set bounds to.]

I. To put an end or limit to; to come to an end.

1. *trans.* To put an end to (in time); to bring to an end; to end, conclude, terminate. (Now chiefly in *Law.*)

1483 *Cath. Angl.* 98 To Determyn, *determinare, diffinire, distinguere, finire.* **1494** FABYAN *Chron.* 5 At the Conquest I haue eke determyned The vi. part. *c* **1510** MORE *Picus* Wks. 9/1 Death determineth the manifolde incommodities..of this life. *a* **1533** LD. BERNERS *Huon* lviii. 199 It behoueth vs shortely to determyne oure besynes. **1651** SMITH in *Fuller's Abel Rediv., Willet* 573 Here also God determined his travails. **1709** STEELE *Tatler* No. 167 ¶5 Her Husband's Death.. would certainly have determined her Life. **1785** PALEY *Mor. Philos.* (1818) I. 326 To determine a connexion which is become odious to both. **1818** CRUISE *Digest* (ed. 2) IV. 444 A warranty..may be defeated, determined, or avoided, in all or in part. **1845** STEPHEN *Laws Engl.* (ed. 6) I. 298 The lessee..hath determined his estate by his own default. **1874** STUBBS *Const. Hist.* (1875) II. xvi. 441 The death of Edward III determined the crisis.

†**b.** To cause to end *in* (some conclusion). *Obs.*

a **1668** DENHAM *Poems* 98 The people join'd In glad consent, and all their common fear Determine in my fate. **1673** TEMPLE *Observ. United Prov.* Wks. 1731 I. 25 Albert bent the whole Force of the War upon France, till he determined it in a Peace with that Crown.

2. *intr.* (for *refl.*) To come to an end; to cease to exist or be in force; to expire, to die. (Now chiefly in *Law.*)

c **1374** CHAUCER *Troylus* III. 330 (379) That rather dye I wold, and determyne, As thinkith me, stokkid in prisoun. **1571** *Ludlow Churchw. Acc.* (Camden) 147 His interest in the said pewe to determyne. **1607** SHAKS. *Cor.* III. iii. 43 Must all determine heere? **1615** G. SANDYS *Trav.* 73 His life was to determine with his fathers. **1677** CARY *Chronol.* II. I. I. v. 104 The Year..was that in which the 4th of the 6th Olympiad did Determine. **1770** LANGHORNE *Plutarch* (1879) I. 422/2 The changes we have to experience only determine with our lives. **1794** MATHIAS *Purs. Lit.* (1798) 289 The custom ceased and determined at Sir Matthew Mite's election. **1818** CRUISE *Digest* (ed. 2) V. 56 In fact the estate of Martin did not determine by his death, surrender, or forfeiture, but by the death of King Charles II. **1883** GLADSTONE *Sp. in Parl.* 19 July, The privileges..do not determine with the life of M. de Lesseps.

b. To end *in* (a termination, conclusion, or result); 'to end consequentially' (J.). *Obs.* or *arch.*

1605 CAMDEN *Rem.* (1637) 143/4 As long as issue male continued, which determined in John Moubray Duke of Norfolke. *a* **1631** DONNE in Spurgeon *Treas. Dav.* Ps. lxvi. 3 As long as their rage determined in his person, he opened not his mouth. **1654** TRAPP *Comm. Job* xxi. 13 Their merry dance determineth in a miserable downfall. **1684** *Contempl. State of Man* I. vii. (1699) 71 The Misery wherein all the Felicity of this World is to determin. *a* **1716** SOUTH *Serm.* (1744) X. 78 But that which begins in vanity, must needs determine in vexation of spirit. **1767** *Byron's Voy. r. World* 114 The head is small..and determines in a snout. **1875** STUBBS *Const. Hist.* III. xviii. 4 The crisis..is to determine in that struggle between the crown and the commons which the last two centuries have decided.

†**3.** *trans.* To set bounds to; to bound, limit.

1398 TREVISA *Barth. De P.R.* XIX. i. (1495) 861 Colour is the vttermest party..that is determyned fro the vtter party of a bodily thynge. **1571** DIGGES *Pantom.* I. Elem. Bij, A Circle is a plaine figure, determined with one line, which is called a Circumference. **1601** HOLLAND *Pliny* I. 128 Many of the Geographers set not downe Indus the riuer, for to determine the marches of the Indians Westward. **1654** CROMWELL *Sp.* 22 Jan. (Carlyle), It determines his power. **1689** *Col. Rec. Pennsylv.* I. 311 The Two Countyes shall have the Moors of the sayd Countyes otherwise determined. *a* **1732** ATTERBURY (J.), That hill which thus determines their view at a distance.

b. *Logic.* To limit by adding differences; to limit in scope.

[**1555** WATREMAN *Fardle Facions* II. iv. 141 Determinyng the Tradicions of Moyses, by certein ordenaunces and decrees, whiche thei them selues [Phariseis] sette vp.] **1838** SIR W. HAMILTON *Logic* xi. (1866) I. 194 When we determine any notion by adding on a subordinate concept, we divide it. **1842** ABP. THOMSON *Laws Th.* lxxxvii. (1860) 158 Some mark may be added..which narrows the extent of both, but renders them more definite—better determined.

†**c.** To limit *to*, restrict *to. Obs.*

1450–1530 *Myrr. our Ladye* 101 Soche a fredome as is determyned to nothynge in certeyne, but yt may be applyed generally. **1659** HAMMOND *On Ps.* xix. 11 Annot. 115 The context seems rather to determine it to the first..sense. **1690** LOCKE *Hum. Und.* III. ix. §17 No one has Authority to determine the signification of the word Gold..more to one Collection of Ideas..than to another. **1691** RAY *Creation* II. (1704) 380 Not..necessarily determined to one manner of Respiration.

II. To bring to an end a dispute, controversy, or doubtful matter; to conclude, settle, decide, fix.

4. *trans.* To settle or decide (a dispute, question, matter in debate), as a judge or arbiter.

c **1380** WYCLIF *Sel. Wks.* III. 345 þat ȝif þe pope determine ouȝt, þanne it is soiþ & to bileue. *c* **1440** *Generydes* 1695 To determyne [*MS.* -mytte] this mater, Generydes was brought owt. **1526** TINDALE *Acts* xix. 39 Itt may be determined in a lawfull congregacion. **1530** PALSGR. 514/2, I determyne, I make a conclusion in a mater. **1576** FLEMING *Panopl. Epist.* 246 Sitting in his long gowne, or riche robe, is occupied in suche matters as are of him to be determined. **1588** SHAKS. *Tit. A.* I. i. 407 Let the lawes of Rome determine all. **1660** *Trial Regic.* 9 Authorized by the King's Majestie to hear, and determine, all Treasons, Felonies, and other Offences. *c* **1710** C. FIENNES *Diary* (1888) 260 Matters of Life and death are not here tryed or determined. **1868** MILMAN *St. Paul's* vii. 133 The Dean presided in all causes brought before the Chapter, and determined them. **1868** M. PATTISON *Academ. Org.* iv. 114 This ambiguity should be determined in one direction or in the other.

b. with an object expressing the sentence, conclusion, or issue.

1647 CLARENDON *Hist. Reb.* I. (1843) 6/1 He would undertake..that his presence would in a moment determine the restitution of the palatinate to his brother and sister. **1751** JOHNSON *Rambler* No. 181 ¶3 The time at which every man's fate was to be determined. **1752** HUME *Ess. & Treat.* (1777) I. 108 The laws will..determine the punishment of the criminal. **1832** HT. MARTINEAU *Each & All* v. 67 The circumstances which determine the recompense of each. **1853** J. H. NEWMAN *Hist. Sk.* (1873) II. I. ii. 86 It was an era which determined the history of the world. **1875** JOWETT *Plato* (ed. 2) V. 63 The law will determine all our various duties towards relatives.

c. with subordinate clause, expressing the matter at issue.

1399 *Pol. Poems* (Rolls) I. 385 And whedir the grounde of ȝiste were good other ille, trouthe hathe determyned. **1561** DAUS *Bullinger on Apoc.* (1573) 192 Lucius the third.. determineth playnly, that heretickes are stricken with an euerlastyng curse. **1568** GRAFTON *Chron.* II. 227 To determine what was meetest to be done in this matter. **1589** R. HARVEY *Pl. Perc.* (1590) 15 As senseles, as they which determine vpon an Ale bench whether the passenger..be a Saint or a Diuell. **1611** BIBLE *Acts* xxvii. 1 When it was determined [*earlier vv.* demed, concluded, decreed] that we should saile into Italy. **1747** *Col. Rec. Pennsylv.* V. 105 It might now be determin'd whether the Council's Speech to the Assembly..shou'd be Printed. **1834** SOUTHEY *Doctor* lxv. (1862) 137 Far happier are they who always know what they are to do, than they who have to determine what they will do. **1887** RUSKIN *Præterita* II. 179, I determined that the Alps were, on the whole, best seen from below.

5. *intr.* To come to a judicial decision; to give a decision; to decide. †Const. *of* (*on*).

c **1384** CHAUCER *H. Fame* I. 343 Wayte vpon the conclusyon, And eke how that ye determynen, And for the more part diffynen. *c* **1477** CAXTON *Jason* 72 Smale thinges of which they shall haue the knowleche for to determine. **1579** TOMSON *Calvin's Serm. Tim.* 41/2 Suche men.. although they affirme, yet can they certeinely determine of nothing. **1598** HAKLUYT *Voy.* I. 68 Neither..to speake of any affaires, after they haue beene determined of by the Emperour. **1613** SHAKS. *Hen. VIII*, I. i. 214 You shall to th' Tower, till you know How he determines further. **1634** W. TIRWHYT tr. *Balzac's Lett.* 244 Who have reason enough to doubt, but not science sufficiently to determine rightly. **1709** STRYPE *Ann. Ref.* I. xxxix. 447 Cox, Bishop of Ely, determined on both questions. **1751** JOHNSON *Rambler* No. 155 ¶4 The general inability of man to determine rightly concerning his own. **1759** FRANKLIN *Ess.* Wks. 1840 III. 268 The representatives of the people have an undoubted right to judge and determine..of the sum to be raised. **1767** *Junius Lett.* xxxv. 166 What..remains, but to leave it to the people to determine for themselves?.. They alone ought to determine.

†**b.** To decide *for. Obs.*

1624–25 BP. MOUNTAGU *Corr. J. Cosin* (1869) I. 42, I determine next weke for Pettworth. **1750** BP. HURD in *Warburton's Lett.* (1809) 52 He has determined for the Law.

c. To decide or fix *upon, on.* (Blending with 18 c, q.v.)

†**6.** To lay down decisively or authoritatively; to pronounce, declare, state. (Const. as in 4, 5.)

1393 GOWER *Conf.* III. 86 Of theorique principall The philosophre in speciall The propretes hath determined. *c* **1400** *Rom. Rose* 4885 Of ech synne it is the rote..As Tulius can determyne. **1486** *Bk. St. Albans, Her.* Aj a, Here in thys booke folowyng is determyned the lynage of Coote armuris.

†**b.** To decide or declare to be; to term. *Obs.*

1653 H. MORE *Antid. Ath.* II. xi. (1712) 161 This he determines primogenious moisture.

†**7.** *trans.* To settle or fix beforehand; to ordain, decree; to ordain what is to be done. *Obs.*

1382 WYCLIF *Acts* xvii. 26 Determynynge tymes ordeyned, and termes of habitacioun. **1535** COVERDALE *Isa.* x. 23 Ye Lorde..shal perfectly fulfil the thinge, that he hath determyned. **1586** A. DAY *Eng. Secretary* I. (1625) 121 His houre was come, so was it determined, which way could he shun it? **1611** BIBLE *1 Sam.* xxv. 17 For evil is determined against our master. **1677** HALE *Prim. Orig. Man.* III. iii. 263 Some superintendent Intellectual Nature, that by certain election and choice determined things. **1758** S. HAYWARD *Serm.* xiv. 408 God..determined holiness to be the way to everlasting happiness.

8. *trans.* To fix or decide causally; to condition as a cause or antecedent.

1651 HOBBES *Leviath.* I. x. 42 As in other things..not the seller, but the buyer determines the Price. **1751** JOHNSON *Rambler* No. 141 ¶2 The whole tenor of his life has been determined by some accident of no apparent moment. **1839** MURCHISON *Silur. Syst.* I. xxxvi. 505 These divergences have..been determined by the eruptive forces which evolved the trap rocks. **1856** EMERSON *Eng. Traits, Wealth* Wks. (Bohn) II. 72 The wealth of London determines prices all over the globe. **1874** SAYCE *Compar. Philol.* ii. 73 Dante has determined classical Italian. **1883** GILMOUR *Mongols* xviii. 213 His religion..determines for him the colour and cut of his coat.

9. To decide upon (one of several); to fix (which or what it is to be).

1659 PEARSON *Creed* (1662) 195 The apertion of the wombe determineth the first-born. **1720** OZELL *Vertot's Rom. Rep.* II. x. 155 To rob his Enemy of the cruel Pleasure of determining the kind of..Death. **1771** MRS. GRIFFITH tr. *Viaud's Shipwreck* 37 Let us then determine the first passengers by lot. **1850** MCCOSH *Div. Govt.* III. i. (1874) 269 It is the will which determines what is to be preferred or rejected. **1886** SIR J. STIRLING in *Law Times' Rep.* LV. 283/2 Determining what particulars of objections ought to be allowed.

b. *with alternative clause.*

1772 *Hist. Rochester* 33 Whether in this tower..I cannot determine. **1818** CRUISE *Digest* (ed. 2) VI. 325 To determine whether he should or should not consider it as his own.

†**10.** To conclude from reasoning, investigation, etc. (a thing *to be*, or *that* it is). *Obs.*

1494 FABYAN *Chron.* IV. lxxv. 53 Whiche length of tyme is of some Auctour determyned to be longe and of some but shorte. **1526** *Pilgr. Perf.* (W. de W. 1531) 163 b, Rosell, Angelus, & other doctours determyneth & concludeth that [etc.]. **1559** W. CUNNINGHAM *Cosmogr. Glasse* 26 Stadium.. which length Plinie determineth to be 125 pases. **1621** BURTON *Anat. Mel.* II. ii. III. (1676) 162/2 Thus Clavius and Maginus, etc., with their followers, vary and determine of these celestial orbs and bodies. **1788** PRIESTLEY *Lect. Hist.* III. xvi. 139 Bishop Fleetwood has determined..that five pounds in this reign was equivalent to twenty eight, or thirty, now. **1814** MRS. JANE WEST *Alicia de Lacy* IV. 218 Hereford determined him to be an audacious knave.

11. *trans.* To ascertain definitely by observation, examination, calculation, etc. (a point previously unknown or uncertain); to fix as known.

1650 FULLER *Pisgah* I. vii. 18 It is hard to determin their exact habitation. **1696** WHISTON *Th. Earth* II (1722) 121 The entire Circle may still be describ'd, and its Original Situation determin'd. **1715** DESAGULIERS *Fires Impr.* 24 We shall in the third Book determine the..Bigness..and Situation of those Cavities. **1737** WHISTON *Josephus's Hist.* Pref. §10 The measures of those edifices..all accurately determined. **1806** HUTTON *Course Math.* I. 367 Having given the Area..of a Rectangle, inscribed in a given Triangle; to determine the Sides of the Rectangle. **1811** PINKERTON *Petral.* I. 357 A rock very difficult to determine. **1824** DE QUINCEY *Pol. Econ. Dial.* v. (1860) 553 As when I say that the thermometer determines the heat, viz., that it determines or ascertains it to my knowledge. **1860** TYNDALL *Glac.* I. viii. 60 We also determined both the velocity and the width of the Glacier. **1861** F. HALL in *Jrnl. Asiat. Soc. Bengal* 147 He has determined him to A.D. 490. **1878** BOSW. SMITH *Carthage* 201 Some difficulty in determining the route by which he approached it.

12. *Geom.* (*trans.*) To fix or define the position of.

1840 LARDNER *Geom.* xiii. 159 To determine a similar system of points. **1885** LEUDESDORF *Cremona's Proj. Geom.* 175 Two projective ranges of points determine an involution; for they determine the straight line *s*, which determines the involution.

b. *intr.* To be defined as to position.

1885 LEUDESDORF *Cremona's Proj. Geom.* 285 All straight lines passing through *U* determine on the circumference.

13. To discuss and resolve a disputed question (*determinare quæstionem*), or maintain a thesis against an opponent in a scholastic disputation, especially in a disputation by which a student entered upon the degree of B.A.; hence, *absolutely*, To perform the exercises of DETERMINATION (sense 4) which completed the degree of Bachelor of Arts, and enabled the student to proceed to qualify himself for the Master's degree. *Obs.* exc. *Hist.*

[**1267** in *Munim. Acad. Oxon.* (Rolls) I. 34 Ut certa forma provideretur sub qua Bachillarii artium determinaturi ad determinandum forent admittendi.] **1570–6** LAMBARDE *Peramb. Kent* (1826) 193 That a young Novesse should thus boldly determine at their disputations. **1649** *Order* 26 Jan. in Wood *Life* (Oxf. H.S.) I. 149 That all Bachelaurs of this University who have not determined the last yeare do determine this Lent. **1691** —— *Ath. Oxon.* II. 413 After he had taken the degree of Bach. of Arts and determined. *a* **1695** —— *Life* II. 517 Every bachelor was to determine twice between the 17 Feb. to 7 March. **1708** J. CHAMBERLAYNE *St. Gt. Brit.* I. III. xi. (1743) 281 He is obliged..to propose a question in the publick Schools within a Year after he hath taken the said Degree [D.D.], and to determine upon the same. **1878** A. CLARK *Reg. Univ. Oxf.* (O.H.S.) II. I. 50 In some cases the University bound over the 'admissi' to determine next Lent under a money penalty. *Ibid.*, On 17 Feb. 1599 a committee was apppointed to provide a scheme by which bachelors presented might be compelled to determine.

III. To direct to some end or conclusion; to come to some conclusion.

14. *trans.* To give a terminus or aim to; to give tendency or direction to; to direct; to decide the course of; to impel *to* (some destination).

a **1430** LYDG. *Bochas* IX. xxxii. (1554) 211 b, He..Gan his compleint to Bochas determine. **1711** ADDISON *Spect.* No. 121 ¶1 Such an Operation..as..determines all the Portions of Matter to their proper Centres. **1751** JOHNSON *Rambler* No. 151 ¶4 Accidental impulses determine us to different paths. **1753** N. TORRIANO *Gangr. Sore Throat* 71 Determining the morbific Matter from the internal to the.. external Parts. **1798** MALTHUS *Popul.* (1806) II. III. x. 252 Thus determining a greater quantity of capital to this particular employment. **1842** GROVE *Corr. Phys. Forces* 80 A power..of determining the oxygen of the liquid to its surface.

b. *fig.* To direct, impel, give a direction or definite bias to.

1529 MORE *Dyaloge* I. Wks. 164/2 Ye shoulde not haue wyste on which parte to determine your byleue. **1613** J. SALKELD *Treat. Angels* 221 Are by reason of the same beatitude so prevented and determined to all good..that in no wise they can sinne. **1662** STILLINGFL. *Orig. Sacr.* III. iii. §7 If this power of determining its self either way must be taken away. *a* **1670** RUST *Disc. Truth* (1682) 189 It is no imperfection in God to be determined to Good. **1690** LOCKE *Hum. Und.* II. xxi. §50 We are endowed with a power to suspend any particular desire, and keep it from determining the will, and engaging us in action. **1772** W. CULLEN *Inst. Med.* IV. §202 Animals are determined to take in aliment by the appetites of hunger and thirst. **1836–7** SIR W. HAMILTON *Metaph.* (1877) I. ii. 23 Speculative truth is valuable only as it determines a greater quantity of higher power into activity. **1842** GROVE *Corr. Phys. Forces* 86 It only determines or facilitates the action of chemical force.

15. *intr.* To take its course, go, tend *to* (a particular terminus or destination). *arch.*

1651 *Life Father Sarpi* (1676) 61 Until it might be discerned whether the malady would determine to life, or death. 1656 SANDERSON *Serm.* (1689) 542 They all determine and concentre there. 1805 W. SAUNDERS *Min. Waters* 293 A dose of this water..will generally determine pretty powerfully to the kidneys. 1839 BAILEY *Festus* xxi. (1848) 272 To these they all determine. 1858 SEARS *Athan.* III. IV. 290 When the separating judgment shall come on, and each [human being] determines to the place he loves.

†**b.** *intr.* To be directed *upon* (anything) as a goal or final object. *Obs.*

1649 JER. TAYLOR *Gt. Exemp.* II. Ad §12. 94 The hopes of a Christian ought not to determine upon any thing lesse than heaven. *Ibid.* iv. §18 To suffer corporal austerities with thoughts determining upon the external action or imaginations of sanctity inherent in the action.

16. *trans.* To decide the course of (a person); to bring to the determination, decision, or resolution (*to do* something).

1672 WILKINS *Nat. Relig.* 29 He..shall not be able to determine himself to the belief or practice of any thing. 1712 STEELE *Spect.* No. 278 ¶2 A distressed Damsel, who intends to be determined by your Judgment. 1741 MIDDLETON *Cicero* (1742) III. IX. 56 All these informations determined him at last not to venture to the Senate. 1788 T. JEFFERSON *Writ.* (1859) II. 520 Determining the fishermen to carry on their trade from their own homes. 1818 MRS. SHELLEY *Frankenst.* vi. (1865) 97 These reflections determined me and I resolved to remain silent. 1821 SCOTT *Kenilw.* xx, A step to which Janet by farther objections only determined her the more obstinately. 1886 DOWDEN *Shelley* II. i. 7. [She] took credit to herself for having determined Shelley to travel abroad.

†**17.** *refl.* To bring oneself to a decision; to come to the resolve (*to do* something). [= F. *se determiner*.] *Obs.*

1393 GOWER *Conf.* I. 267 They upon this medicine Appointen hem and determine That..They wolde [etc.]. 1477 EARL RIVERS (Caxton) *Dictes* 1, I determyned me to take that voyage. 1490 *Act 7 Hen. VII*, c. 1 Preamb., The King..hath determined himself to pass over the Sea. 1701 tr. *Le Clerc's Prim. Fathers* (1702) 57 Tis the part of a Witty Man, to Determine himself speedily upon all sorts of Questions.

18. *intr.* (for *refl.*) To come to the decision, resolve definitely (*to do* something). †In early use often ***to determine with oneself***.

1450–1530 *Myrr. our Ladye* 226 The moste meke wylle of the Vyrgyn vtterly determyned to sarue god. 1509 HAWES *Past. Pleas.* II. vi, I have determyned in my judgement, For La Bell Pucell..To passe the waye of so greate jeopardy. 1526–34 TINDALE *Acts* xx. 16 Paul had determined [WYCLIF, *Rhem.*, purposed] to leave Ephesus as they sailed. 1530 PALSGR. 514/2 Whan I determyne with my selfe to do a thyng. 1548 HALL *Chron.* 187b, He in the meane season determined to make hys abode in Scotland. *Ibid.* 194b, He determined with him selfe clerely to marye with her. 1590 MARLOWE *2nd Pt. Tamburl.* II. ii, Determines straight To bid us battle for our dearest lives. 1769 ROBERTSON *Chas. V*, V. IV. 375 He determined to set the highest price upon Francis's freedom. 1808 *Med. Jrnl.* XIX. 437 The obstinacy ..of the fever made me determine..to administer some remedy. 1891 E. PEACOCK *N. Brendon* I. 310 Narcissa determined to go at once.

b. with subordinate clause or equivalent.

1582 N. LICHEFIELD, tr. *Castanheda's Conq. E. Ind.* i. 3 Taking order and determining with Pedro.., that at a time appointed they shuld meet. 1594 MARLOWE & NASHE *Dido* v. i, That have I not determin'd with myself. 1736 BUTLER *Anal.* I. i. Wks. 1874 I. 24 A man determines, that he will look at such an object.

c. To resolve *upon*, *on*, †*of* (some course of action). With indirect passive, ***to be determined on*** or ***upon***.

This appears to combine senses 5 and 18, and to pass imperceptibly from the sense *decide* to that of *resolve*.

1607 SHAKS. *Cor.* IV. i. 35 Determine on some course. 1636 tr. *Ariana* 307, I could not as yet determine of what I was to doe. 1754 J. SHEBBEARE *Matrimony* (1766) I. 19 [This] seduced him to determine on the Life of a Gentleman, when his Uncle should die. 1801 MRS. CH. SMITH *Solitary Wand.* I. 33 Unable to determine on what answer they were to give. 1883 FROUDE *Short Stud.* IV. I. vi. 69 The bishops..determined on a further appeal to the pope. 1885 *Manch. Exam.* 26 June 5/4 Not at present definitely determined on.

d. *impersonal passive.*

1852 MRS. STOWE *Uncle Tom's C.* xxix, It was determined to sell the place.

19. ***to be determined***, to have come to a decision or definite resolve (*to do* something); to be finally and firmly resolved. (Cf. DETERMINED *ppl. a.*)

1513 MORE in Grafton *Chron.* (1568) II. 771 If she finally were determined to kepe him. 1529 —— *Dyaloge* I. Wks. 161/2 One, whom she is determined neuer to mary. 1594 SHAKS. *Rich. III*, I. i. 30 Therefore, since I cannot proue a Louer..I am determined to proue a Villaine. 1601 —— *Jul. C.* v. i. 100 What are you then determined to do? 1725 DE FOE *Voy. round World* (1840) 19 If I had been otherwise determined. 1793 SMEATON *Edystone L.* §208 Being now determined as to the composition of the mortar for the Edystone. 1866 GEO. ELIOT *F. Holt* (1868) 17 No; I'm determined not to sleep up-stairs.

†**b.** To be bound *for*. *Obs.*

1784 R. BAGE *Barham Downs* I. 222 Sir George is determined for Switzerland in a few days.

determined (dɪˈtɜːmɪnd), *ppl. a.* [f. prec. + -ED[1].]

1. Terminated, ended.

1581 J. BELL *Haddon's Answ. Osor.* 444 Albeit the thing itselfe..be past, and ye tyme thereof determined.

2. Limited, restricted: **a.** as to extent; **b.** as to freedom of action or choice; conditioned.

1603 SHAKS. *Meas. for M.* III. i. 70 Perpetual durance, a restraint..To a determin'd scope. 1805 WORDSW. *Prelude* I. 641 'Tis a theme Single and of determined bounds. 1871 R. H. HUTTON *Ess.* (1877) I. 53 Fails to render such a fact as free-will in the offspring of absolutely determined natures even conceivable.

3. Decided, settled, fixed; decided or resolved upon.

1561 T. NORTON *Calvin's Inst.* II. 113 Let vs hold for determined, that the life of man is instructed in the law. 1576 FLEMING *Panopl. Epist.* 193 He mangled him selfe to cloake his determined mischiefe. 1602 T. FITZHERBERT *Apol.* 21 a, So farre as my determined breuity wil permit. 1603 OWEN *Pembrokeshire* (1891) 197 [I] fall into my determyned matter to speake of Pembrokshire. 1650 J. TAYLOR *Holy Living* iii. §4 (1727) 173 It is a determined rule in divinity. 1836 J. GILBERT *Chr. Atonem.* ix. (1852) 261 Some determined bias must have existed.

4. Appointed, ordained; fixed beforehand.

?*a*1500 *Wycket* (1828) 3 The chosen..shalbe made whyte tyll a tyme determined. 1559 W. CUNNINGHAM *Cosmogr. Glasse* 25 Not any determined, or appointed measure, as a yarde, a furlong. 1580 LYLY *Euphues* (Arb.) 284 Caused al the company to breake off their determined pastimes. 1591 SHAKS. *1 Hen. VI*, IV. vi. 9 To my determin'd time thou gau'st new date. 1612 T. TAYLOR *Comm. Titus* i. 3 They are so by the determined counsell of God.

5. Defined, definite, exact; distinctly marked or laid down; fixed.

1570 DEE *Math. Pref.* 3 If a Poynt moue from a determined situation. 1582 BATMAN *Trevisa's Barth. de P.R.* III. xx. 21 If it had a determined savour..it might not take the savour of another thing. 1690 LOCKE *Hum. Und.* III. v. §14 Names..when they have any determin'd Signification. 1726 LEONI *Alberti's Archit.* II. 55 a, Others set apart a certain determined place of burial. 1733 NEAL *Hist. Purit.* II. 375 Oaths ought to be explicit, and the words as clear and determined as possible. 1789 GILPIN *Wye* 10 A body of water..wearing any determined form. 1796–7 *Instr. & Reg. Cavalry* (1813) 77 The determined line on which the pivots of the column are to stand. 1891 ROSEBERY *Pitt* xi. 194 Some cynical offer..of his interest for a determined price.

6. Definitely ascertained or identified.

1817 CHALMERS *Astron. Disc.* i. (1852) 21 A round ball of a determined magnitude. 1882 *Entomol. Mag.* Mar. 235 Specimens..either determined or undetermined.

7. a. Of persons: Characterized by determination or final and fixed resolve; resolute; not to be moved from one's purpose.

1772 *Ann. Reg.* 26/2 Because they were determined deists. 1803 G. ROSE *Diaries* (1860) II. 46 The King..is a determined Antigallican. 1847 EMERSON *Repr. Men, Goethe* Wks. (Bohn) I. 391, I meet the eyes of the most determined of men. 1883 FROUDE *Short Stud.* IV. I. ii. 24 Intimating that the king would find him a most determined antagonist. 1885 F. TEMPLE *Relat. Relig. & Sc.* i. 4 Science and Religion seem very often to be the most determined foes to each other. 1887 *Times* 10 Oct. 3/3 Two determined looking men, were charged with being suspected persons.

b. Of personal properties, actions, etc.: Showing determination, unflinching, unwavering.

1604 SHAKS. *Oth.* II. iii. 227 Cassio following him with determin'd Sword To execute vpon him. 1765 STERNE *Tr. Shandy* VII. ix, With as determined a pencil as if I had her in the wettest drapery. 1792 *Anecd. W. Pitt* I. xvii. 277 There was a determined resolution..against any vigorous exertion of the national power. 1837 DISRAELI *Venetia* I. ii, Gave a determined ring at the bell. 1856 EMERSON *Eng. Traits, Times* Wks. (Bohn) II. 119 Courage, not rash and petulant, but considerate and determined.

c. (For the predicative use in *to be determined*, see DETERMINE *v.* 19.)

deˈterminedly, *adv.* [f. prec. + -LY[2].] In a determined, decided, or resolute manner.

*c*1540 *Deposit.* in *Old Ways* (1892) 100 Her mynde was determynedly fyxitt that she wolde not marrye with hym. 1790 *Hist. Europe* in *Ann. Reg.* 20/1 The..club, so determinedly inimical to monarchy. 1811 *Chron.* ibid. 7 After fighting 25 minutes most determinedly. 1849 RUSKIN *Sev. Lamps* v. §6. 141 In every style that is determinedly progressive. 1870 MISS BRIDGMAN *Ro. Lynne* II. xiii. 268 She tied on her bonnet grimly and determinedly.

deˈterminedness. [f. as prec. + -NESS.] The quality of being determined or resolute.

1748 RICHARDSON *Clarissa* (1811) I. iii. 12 So much determinedness; such a noble firmness in my sister. 1771 T. HULL *Sir W. Harrington* (1797) IV. 25 With a determinedness, in his looks, that made me tremble. 1883 *Chicago Advance* 15 Mar., A persistent determinedness that has known no discouragement.

determiner[1] (dɪˈtɜːmɪnə(r)). [f. DETERMINE *v.* + -ER[1].]

1. He who or that which determines, in various senses. **a.** He who or that which decides.

1530 PALSGR. 213/1 Determyner, *determineur.* 1584 FENNER *Def. Ministers* (1587) 59 Anie other determinors of the issue. 1653 A. WILSON *Jas. I*, 167 The Sword, as it is the best determiner, so it is the most honourable Treater. 1659 MILTON *Civ. Power* Wks. 1738 I. 547 No Man or body of Men in these times can be the infallible Judges or Determiners in matters of Religion. 1754 RICHARDSON *Grandison* (1781) III. xvi. 125 Miss Grandison must be the sole determiner on this occasion. 1884 *Century Mag.* XXVIII. 122 The determiner of the future policy of the Church.

b. That which decides the course of action, or determines the result.

1754 EDWARDS *Freed. Will* I. ii. (1762) 5 If the Will be determined, there is a Determiner. This must be supposed to be intended even by them that say the Will determines itself. *Ibid.* II. vii. 90 The opportunity that is left for the Will itself to be the determiner of the act.

c. One who ascertains definitely.

1846 GROTE *Greece* I. xviii. II. 18 The original determiner of this epoch.

d. *Biol.* = DETERMINANT B. *sb.* 4.

1909 W. BATESON *Mendel's Princ. Heredity* 79 Hitherto we have spoken of the determiner for such a colour as grey in rabbits and mice as 'dominant' over the colours lower in the scale, such as black or chocolate... We shall then speak of the determiner for grey as epistatic to that for black. 1922 R. C. PUNNETT *Mendelism* (ed. 6) 113 A female determiner incapable of carrying sex-limited factors. 1926 J. S. HUXLEY *Ess. Pop. Sci.* 236 The future symmetry of the embryo is not influenced by anything that one could call a 'determiner' in the cytoplasm. *Ibid.* 246 It then became an obvious task to discover more precisely where this structure-determiner was situated and how it acted.

†**2.** A determining bachelor of arts; = DETERMINANT B 1. *Obs.* (exc. *Hist.*)

1574 M. STOKYS in Peacock *Stat. Cambridge* (1841) App. A. 6 [The bell shall] be tolled in every Colledge, Howse, Hall or Hostell where eny Determiners be. 1726 AMHERST *Terræ Fil.* xlii. 224 The collectors..draw a scheme..in which the names of all determiners are placed in several columns, and over against them, in other columns, the days when, and the schools where, they are to respond.

3. *Gram.* A class of limiting expressions modifying nouns (see quot. 1933). Also *attrib.*

1933 BLOOMFIELD *Lang.* xii. 203 Our limiting adjectives fall into two sub-classes of determiners and numeratives... The determiners are defined by the fact that certain types of noun expressions (such as *house* or *big house*) are always accompanied by a determiner (as, *this house, a big house*). 1961 R. B. LONG *Sentence & its Parts* ii. 39 The most characteristic modifiers of nouns in positions in front of the nouns are (1) determiners, such as *the* and possessives, and (2) adjectives. *Ibid.* 40 Determiner modifiers, pronounal in function, normally precede adjectival modifiers. 1964 *Language* XL. 37 Traditionally, grammarians have recognized two kinds of determiners: *the*, usually called the definite determiner, and *a*, usually called the indefinite determiner. It is now common to regard other elements as determiners, or as parts of determiners... Further, it is convenient to regard *all, any*, and the like as part of the determiner (these items are frequently called predeterminers). And finally, prenominal genitives such as *his* and *John's* are shown to behave as determiners by transformational criteria.

†**determiner**[2]. *Law.* [subst. use of F. *déterminer* pres. inf.] The final determining of a judge or court of justice: in ***oyer and determiner***, a variant of *oyer and terminer*. (*Obs.* exc. *Hist.*)

1450 *Paston Lett.* No. 103 I. 138 That ye hadde sued hym for an especiall assise, and an oier and determiner. 1548 HALL *Chron.* 169b, A commission of oyer and determiner, for the punishment of this outragious offence & sedicious crime. 1583 STUBBES *Anat. Abus.* II. (1882) 106 Iustices of Assises, Ewer, Determiner, and the lyke. 1633 T. STAFFORD *Pac. Hib.* i. (1821) 16 Of Oyer, Determiner, and Goale deliverie. 1848 WHARTON *Law Lex.*, Oyer and Terminer.. sometimes written *determiner.*

determining (dɪˈtɜːmɪnɪŋ), *vbl. sb.* [f. DETERMINE *v.* + -ING[1].] The action of the verb DETERMINE; determination. (Now chiefly gerundial.)

1530 PALSGR. 213/1 Determynyng, *terminance, determination.* 1580 HOLLYBAND *Treas. Fr. Tong, Determinance*..the determining or ending of a thing. 1607 HIERON *Wks.* I. 117 The determining of all cases and questions in religion. 1670 EACHARD *Cont. Clergy* 22 The.. inconsiderate determining of youths to the profession of learning. 1726 LEONI tr. *Alberti's Archit.* I. 9a, We must have regard to the..Use of every Edifice in the determining of its Situation. [1772 C. HUTTON *Bridges* 4 Their spans are still necessary for determining their figure.]

b. In academic use = DETERMINATION 4.

1675 (25 Feb.) in A. Wood *Life & T.* (O.H.S.) II. 309 Officers that have fees for determining. 1887 [see DETERMINATION 4].

deˈtermining, *ppl. a.* [f. as prec. + -ING[2].]

1. That determines; *esp.* that decides, or leads to a decision; that fixes the course or issue.

1711 STEELE *Spect.* No. 158 ¶3 A certain positive and determining manner in which you talk. 1842 GROVE *Corr. Phys. Forces* 45 The force of heat seems more a determining than a producing influence. 1856 FROUDE *Hist. Eng.* (1858) I. ii. 110 The determining principle of their action. 1884 *Athenæum* 23 Feb. 241/1 What was the determining motive?

b. Terminating, ending.

1893 *Daily News* 21 Feb. 7/8 What is called the determining school year (that is the school year ended last before the 1st Jan. 1891).

†**2.** Performing the academic exercise of DETERMINATION: ***determining bachelor***, a bachelor of arts who had to determine in the Lenten disputations of the year. *Obs.* exc. in *University Hist.*

1649 *Order* 26 Jan., in Wood *Life & T.* (O.H.S.) I. 149 That all determining Bachelaurs do meet at St. Marie's at 12 of the clock..and be conducted to the Schooles by the bedells. 1709 STEELE & SWIFT *Tatler* No. 71 ¶8 Not a Senior Fellow [will] make a Pun, nor a determining Batchelor drink a Bumper. 1721 AMHERST *Terræ Fil.* No. 42 (1726) 232 The collectors..are chosen out of the determining batchelors by the two proctors. 1887 A. CLARK *Registr. Univ. Oxf.* II. I. 52 To arrange the determining bachelors into groups, so that each determining bachelor might dispute twice at least.

Hence **determiningly** *adv.*

a **1641** Bp. Mountague *Acts & Mon.* (1642) 489 We dare not determiningly resolve, wee ought not boysterously to rush upon it.

determinism (dɪˈtɜːmɪnɪz(ə)m). [f. determine *v.* + -ism.]

1. The philosophical doctrine that human action is not free but necessarily determined by motives, which are regarded as external forces acting upon the will.

1846 Sir W. Hamilton *Reid's Wks.* 87 *note*, There are two schemes of Necessity—the Necessitation by efficient—the Necessitation by final causes. The former is brute or blind Fate; the latter rational Determinism. **1855** W. Thomson in *Oxford Essays* 181 The theory of Determinism, in which the will is regarded as determined or swayed to a particular course by external inducements and formed habits, so that the consciousness of freedom rests chiefly upon an oblivion of the antecedents to our choice. **1860** Mansel *Proleg. Logica* App. Note D. 334 The latter hypothesis is Determinism, a necessity no less rigid than Fatalism. **1866** *Contemp. Rev.* I. 465 He arrived at a system of absolute determinism, which entirely takes away man's free will, and with it his responsibility. **1880** W. L. Courtney in Abbot *Hellenica* (1880) 257 Epicurus..was an opponent of Fatalism, not of Determinism.

2. *gen.* The doctrine that everything that happens is determined by a necessary chain of causation.

1876 Martineau *Materialism* 71 If man is only a sample of the universal determinism. **1944** G. Bateson in J. McV. Hunt *Personality & Behavior Disorders* II. xxiii. 714 The phrase 'economic determinism' has..become a slogan. *Ibid.* 716 It is this sort of cultural 'genetics' and cultural 'physiology' which I have tried to sum up with the phrase 'cultural determinism'. **1945** K. R. Popper *Open Society* II. xxii. 196 *Sociological determinism* [is the view that]..all our opinions..depend upon society and its historical state. **1950** C. D. Darlington in Darlington & Mather *Genes, Plants & People* p. xvii, Mendel directed his enquiries with a rigorous determinism. He assumed that every property of every seedling was determined by something that happened in its two parents. **1957** N. Frye *Anatomy of Criticism* 6 The fallacy of what in history is called determinism, where a scholar with a special interest in geography or economics expresses that interest by the rhetorical device of putting his favorite subject into a causal relationship with whatever interests him less.

deˈterminist, *sb.* and *a.* [f. as prec. + -ist.]

A. *sb.* One who holds the doctrine of determinism.

1874 Mivart in *Contemp. Rev.* Oct. 784 The objections of our modern Determinists. **1881** *Spectator* 30 Apr. 574 He is an Agnostic and a Determinist, with no reserves. **1887** J. C. Morrison *Service of Man* ix. 298 The determinist is not less but more resolute in teaching morality than his free-will opponent.

B. *adj.* Of or pertaining to the theory of determinism.

1860 Mansel *Proleg. Logica* App. Note E. 348, I believe the scheme of liberty is inconceivable only if the determinist argument is unanswerable. **1874** Sidgwick *Meth. Ethics* v. 55 A Determinist scheme of morality. **1885** R. H. Hutton in *Contemp. Rev.* Mar. 388 The necessarian or determinist theory of human action. **1887** Fowler *Princ. Morals* II. ix. 308 The theory of Hobbes [on Volition] may most appropriately be called Determinist. The actions of men, he holds, are, like all other events, determined, and determined wholly, by antecedent circumstances..The will is 'the last desire in deliberation', and our desires are the necessary result of their various antecedents.

deterministic (dɪtɜːmɪˈnɪstɪk), *a.* [f. prec. + -ic.] Of or pertaining to determinism or determinists.

1874 W. G. Ward *Ess.* (1884) I. vi. 248 That which motives—to use deterministic language—affect is most evidently the will's spontaneous inclination. **1880** W. G. Ward in *Dublin Rev.* Oct. 300 Mr. Hodgson maintains that the Deterministic theory is by no means inconsistent with 'the existence of guilt and sin'.

deterministically (dɪtɜːmɪˈnɪstɪkəlɪ), *adv.* [f. deterministic *a.* + -ly[2].] In a deterministic manner; inevitably.

1885 W. James *Let.* 5 Feb. (1920) I. 238 Since such activity has failed to be universally realized, it was (deterministically) impossible from eternity. **1935** *Mind* XLIV. 85 The relation of the part to the deterministically unfolding pattern of the whole.

†**determission.** *Obs.* ? Corrupted form of *determinacion* or OF. *determineson*: see determination.

c **1400** *Test. Love* II. (1561) 291 b/1 This dualitie, after Clerkes determission, is founden in every creature.

deterrable (dɪˈtɜːrəb(ə)l), *a.* Chiefly *U.S. Law.* [f. deter *v.*[1] + -able.] That may be deterred from a course of action, esp. by fear of legal punishment.

1955 *Univ. Chicago Law Rev.* XXII. 374 The problem is to differentiate between the wholly non-deterrable and persons who are more or less susceptible to influence by law. **1970** *N.Y. State Misc. Rep.* LXIII. 2nd Ser. (1971) 221 *Is he deterrable*, i.e., despite any mental illness, is his present motivation such that anticipation of consequences can decisively influence his behavior? **1980** *U.S. Supreme Court Rec. & Briefs* CXXI. *Petitioner's Opening Brief* 34 This statement..plainly reflects the Court's conclusion that..illegal searches and seizures that are deterrable..will be successfully deterred by the knowledge that [etc.]. **1984** *Washington Q.* Spring 76/2 For all its military robustness, the Soviet Union remains eminently deterrable.

†**deteˈrration.** *Obs.* [f. L. *dē* down + *terra* earth + -ation. (Not connected with mod.F. *déterrer*, OF. *desterrer* to disinter.)] The carrying down or descent of the surface of the earth from hills and higher grounds into the valleys, by the action of rain, landslips, or other physical process: a frequent term of physiographers about 1700; cf. degradation[1] 6.

1686 Plot *Staffordsh.* 113 By the deterration or sinking of a hill between the Church and place of view. **1686** *Phil. Trans.* XVI. 210 A Marish..being buried in Earth, by those frequent Deterrations from the adjoyning Hills. **1695** Woodward *Nat. Hist. Earth* I. (1723) 57 *Deterrations*, or the Devolution of Earth down upon the Valleys, from the Hills and higher Grounds. **1704** J. Harris *Lex. Techn.*, *Deterration* is a Removal of the Earth, Sand, &c., from the Mountains and higher Grounds down into the Valleys and Lower Parts: This is occasioned by Rains.

deterred, pa. t. and pa. pple. of deter *v.*

deterrement, obs. form of determent.

deterrence (dɪˈtɛrəns). [f. next: see -ence.] Deterring or preventing by fear. *spec.*, the reduction of the likelihood of war by the fear that nuclear weapons will be used against an aggressor; so ***graduated deterrence*** (see quot. 1966).

1861 T. B. L. Baker in *War with Crime* (1889) 124 That punishment is to be preferred which combines the greatest deterrence with the least pain. **1875** Poste *Gaius* I. Intr. (ed. 2) 8 The deterrence of future wrongdoers by..punishment of a past offender. **1884** F. Peek in *Contemp. Rev.* July 77 The main objects of imprisonment should be..deterrence from crime and the reformation of offenders. **1955** *Economist* 5 Nov. 457 (*heading*) Graduated Deterrence? **1958** *New Statesman* 19 July 90/1 The argument about self-preservation and deterrence is trivial and thoughtless. At the moment the nuclear powers will probably not start war against each other except in the event of an accident. **1959** *Times Lit. Suppl.* 9 Jan. 17/3 The present state of passive deterrence (in which each side could retaliate devastatingly if attacked, so neither side can afford to attack) provides a framework of insurance. **1962** *Observer* 13 May 15/2 The 'deterrence only' school include most of the adherents of finite deterrence (or minimum deterrence)... If each side can be certain of inflicting terrible damage on the other with its strategic forces, then neither side will use them. **1966** Schwarz & Hadik *Strategic Terminology* 59 *Graduated deterrence*, a strategy threatening a whole range of countermoves, each of which is designed not so much to punish the enemy and to destroy his war-making capacity or to change the local balance of power, as to demonstrate the will to inflict greater punitive damage, to escalate the conflict, in the hope of convincing the enemy to refrain from pursuing his objective.

deterrent (dɪˈtɛrənt), *a.* and *sb.* [ad. L. *dēterrēnt-em*, pr. pple. of *dēterrēre* to deter: see -ent.]

A. *adj.* Deterring; that deters, or has the power or tendency to deter.

1829 *Bentham's Ration. Punishments* (L.), The deterrent effect of such penalties. **1861** W. L. Clay *Mem. J. Clay* 210 The influence of a deterrent policy is the greatest on professional criminals. **1884** *Times* 16 Oct. 10 The influence of favourable or deterrent weather.

B. *sb.* Something that deters; a deterring agent. Esp. the nuclear weapons of any one country or alliance; *spec.*, the hydrogen bomb. Freq. ***the (great) deterrent***. Also *attrib.* and *Comb.*

1829 *Bentham's Ration. Punishments* (L.), No deterrent is more effective than a punishment which..is sure, speedy, and severe. **1829** Southey in *Q. Rev.* XLI. 196 Operating as a provocative to many—as a deterrent, perhaps, to none. **1855** H. Spencer *Princ. Psychol.* I. II. ix. (1872) 281 Feelings that serve as incentives and deterrents. **1892** *Speaker* 3 Sept. 277/1 The death penalty is no deterrent of adventure, nor even of pastime. **1954** *Statement on Defence* p. 4 in *Parl. Papers 1953–54* XXII. 474 The primary deterrent, however, remains the atomic bomb and the ability of the highly organised and trained United States strategic air power to use it. **1954** *New Statesman* 14 Aug. 173/2 The theory and practice of the Great Deterrent is in fair way to becoming the theory and practice of the Great Bluff. **1955** *Ibid.* 26 Feb. 271/1 The Government has concurred in the Nato decision to rely on nuclear weapons and begun itself to manufacture a British H-bomb. It admits..that this leaves the United Kingdom well-nigh defenceless if the deterrent fails. **1957** J. Slessor (*title*) The great deterrent. **1958** *Punch* 27 Aug. 275/1 A lot of good that would do the human race, with..the stockpile of deterrents rising as high as the Empire State Building. **1959** *Times Lit. Suppl.* 9 Jan. 17/3 The theory of the H-bomb as a deterrent. **1959** *Observer* 14 June 16/2 Britain should also be prepared to give up her independent deterrent and stop the manufacture of nuclear weapons. **1962** *Listener* 29 Mar. 548/1 There is no sign..to suggest that the Great Powers will be able to abandon deterrent strategy in the forseeable future. **1963** *Economist* 12 Oct. 101/1 Restraint on German 'deterrent-mongers'.

deterring (dɪˈtɜːrɪŋ), *vbl. sb.* [f. deter *v.*[1] + -ing[1].] The action of hindering through fear.

1642 in Clarendon *Hist. Reb.* IV. (1843) 161/2 The deterring of others from discharging their duties. **1648** W. Mountague *Devout Ess.* I. x. §1 (R.) The deterrings and disabuses appeare together with the delectations.

deˈterring, *ppl. a.* [f. as prec. + -ing[2].] That deters; that keeps off through fear.

1638 Sir T. Herbert *Trav.* (ed. 2) 323 A new deterring name, of Kill abundance. **1774** Goldsm. *Nat. Hist.* (1862) I. ii. 10 The internal parts of the country are still more desolate and deterring. **1872** Geo. Eliot *Middlem.* lxxiii. 188 Their highest qualities can only cast a deterring shadow over the objects.

†**deˈterse,** *v.* *Obs. rare.* [f. L. *dēters-*, ppl. stem of *dētergēre*.] By-form of deterge.

1684 tr. *Bonet's Merc. Compit.* III. 84 The matter being thus incided, detersed and attenuated..may more easily be carried off.

detersion (dɪˈtɜːʃən). [a. F. *détersion* (Paré 16th c.) or ad. L. *dētersiōn-em*, n. of action from *dētergēre* to deterge.] The action of cleansing (a sore or the like).

1607 Topsell *Four-f. Beasts* (1658) 22 The substance of it is fitter for detersion then nutriment. **1684** tr. *Bonet's Merc. Compit.* I. 13 A Gargarism of Hydromel used often is good for Detersion. **1775** Sir E. Barry *Observ. Wines* 294 Leave to others the active parts of the perfusions, detersions, etc.

detersive (dɪˈtɜːsɪv), *a.* and *sb.* [a. F. *détersif*, *-ive* (1545 in Hatzf.), ad. medical L. *dētersīv-us*, f. *dēters-*, ppl. stem of *dētergēre*: see prec. and -ive.]

A. *adj.*

1. Having the quality of cleansing or scouring; tending to cleanse.

1601 Holland *Pliny* II. 37 The same pouder is detersiue and scouring, and therefore put into sope and washing-balls. **1756** P. Browne *Jamaica* 226 The foliage of the tree is of a very detersive character, and frequently used to scour and whiten the floors. **1835** F. Mahoney *Rel. Father Prout* (1859) 509 The recording angel..no doubt dropped a detersive tear on an oath the decided offspring of monomania. **1886** *Pall Mall G.* 7 Aug. 3/2 Without experience of the detersive influences of common soap.

2. *Med.* and *Surg.* Having power to cleanse or purge the body, or to remove corrupt matter from a sore; detergent.

1586 Bright *Melanch.* xli. 276 No detersive medicine is able to pare and wipe away the blemish. **1704** J. Harris *Lex. Techn.*, Detersive Medicines, are such as are used to cleanse the Body from sluggish, viscous, and glutinous Humours. **1782** W. F. Martyn *Geog. Mag.* I. 734 Laying open the wound, and applying a detersive plaister. **1818** Cooper & Travers *Surg. Ess.* I. (ed. 3) 167 Stimulant detersive applications which have been made to the part.

B. *sb.* A cleansing agent: in the general and medical senses.

1634 T. Johnson *Parey's Chirurg.* xxvi. xiv. (1678) 638 Neither..with a painful and drie ulcer doth any other than a liquid detersive agree. **1665** G. Harvey *Adv. agst. Plague* 26 A Dysentery is stopt by a Detersive mixt with a Narcotick. **1756** P. Browne *Jamaica* 199 The pulp is a warm pungent detersive. **1843** *Blackw. Mag.* LIII. 228 Serving as detersives of the grosser humours of commercial life. **1862** S. Lucas *Secularia* 114 *note*, Bristol was celebrated for its soap..Richard of Devizes refers in his history to its manufacture of this famous detersive.

Hence **deˈtersively** *adv.*, **deˈtersiveness.**

1727 Bailey vol. II, *Detersiveness*, cleansing Quality. [Also **1775** in Ash]. **1742** Bailey, *Detersively*, cleansingly. [Also **1864** in Webster, etc.]

†**deˈtersory,** *a.* and *sb.* *Obs. rare.* [f. L. *dēters-*: see prec. + -ory.] = detersive *a.* and *sb.*

1657 Tomlinson *Renou's Disp.* 97 From the commission of these two will proceed one moderate detersory.

detest (dɪˈtɛst), *v.* [a. F. *déteste-r* (Villon, 15th c.), ad. L. *dētestāre* (*-ārī*) to execrate while calling God to witness, to denounce, abhor, renounce, f. de- I. 1, down + *testārī* to bear witness, call to witness.]

†**1.** *trans.* To curse, calling God to witness; to express abhorrence of, denounce, execrate. *Obs.*

1533–4 *Act 25 Hen. VIII*, c. 12 The saide mariage..was prohibited and detested by the lawes of almighty god. **1536** Bellenden *Cron. Scot.* (1821) I. 62 He..began, be lang orisone, to detest the insolence, avarice and unnatural hatrent of the kingis sonnis. **1563–87** Foxe *A. & M.* (1684) I. 733/2 All that were about him being amazed, utterly detested the fact. **1627** Hakewill *Apol.* II. vii. §5 The fearefull inhabitants of Putyole flying through the dark..crying out and detesting their Calamities. **1632** Le Grys tr. *Velleius Paterc.* 254 All posteritie shall..with execrations detest thy fact. **1653** H. Cogan tr. *Pinto's Trav.* xxxvii. 147 We did not a little detest amongst ourselves both the Fonsecas and the Madureyras, but much more the Devil, that wrought us this mischief. *a* **1745** Swift *Hen. I* Wks. 1768 IV. 275 With bitter words, detesting the pride and insolence of Henry.

2. To feel abhorrence of; to hate or dislike intensely; to abhor, abominate.

a **1535** More *Wks.* 422 (R.), I find in Erasmus my derlyng y[t] he detesteth and abhorreth the errours and heresies that Tyndall plainly teacheth. **1535** Stewart *Cron. Scot.* II. 528 To caus all man for to detaist sic thing. **1550** Crowley *Last Trump.* 1292 A vile slaue that doth all honestie deteste. **1579** Lyly *Euphues* (Arb.) 111 Learn..of Diogenes to detest women, be they neuer so comely. **1601** Shaks. *Twel. N.* II. v. 220 A colour she abhorres, and..a fashion shee detests. **1638** Sir T. Herbert *Trav.* (ed. 2) 240 His owne pallat detested them. **1792** Burke *Corr.* (1844) III. 391 My party principles..must lead me to detest the French revolution, in the act, in the spirit, in the consequences, and most of all, in the example. **1833** Ht. Martineau *Tale of Tyne* vii. 130, I detest the very name. *Mod.* To marry a man whom she detests!

b. with *infin.* or *clause. rare.*

a **1553** Philpot *Wks.* (1842) 410 Why dost thou so much detest to grant that we obtain the divine justice through faith. **1647** G. Palmer *Sectaries Unm.* 52, I detest to think of it. 1655 FULLER *Ch. Hist.* IX. vi. §51 The Justice of the Land detesteth that the Judge should himself be an Accuser.

†3. To renounce solemnly or under oath; to abjure. *Obs. rare.*

1688 *Answ. Talon's Plea* 23 They openly detested their faults either by themselves or by their Ambassadours.

¶ Misused for *attest, protest, testify.*

1562 PHAER *Æneid.* VIII. Y iij b, He shewd also the sacrid groue of Argilethus heath, Detesting in that place where Greekish gest was done to death. 1598 SHAKS. *Merry W.* I. iv. 160 But (I detest) an honest maid as euer broke bread. 1606 *Sir G. Goosecappe* I. ii. in Bullen *O. Pl.* III. 17, I detest, Sir Cutt, I did not thinke he had bin halfe the.. scholler he is.

Hence **de'testing** *vbl. sb.* and *ppl. a.*

1591 PERCIVALL *Sp. Dict., Abominacion,* detesting. *a* 1622 AINSWORTH *Annot. Ps.* lxix. 25 Powre out upon them thy detesting ire. 1625 BP. MOUNTAGU *App. Cæsar* 57 In their Abhorring and Detesting of it. 1711 SHAFTESB. *Charac.* (1737) III. VI. iii. 366 Virtue wou'd.. be seen with this Hand, turn'd.. downwards.. as in a detesting manner, and with abhorrence.

†**de'test**, *sb. Obs. rare.* [f. prec. vb.] Detestation, hearty hatred.

1638 R. BAILLIE *Lett. & Jrnls.* (1841) I. 74 With the increase of detest of the authors. 1671 *True Nonconf.* 33 One cause, sufficient to produce a just detest.

detesta'bility. [f. next: see -ITY. In med.L. *dētestābilitās* (Du Cange).] The quality of being detestable; detestableness.

1831 CARLYLE *Sart. Res.* II. iv, As young ladies are to mankind precisely the most delightful in those years.. so young gentlemen do then attain their maximum of detestability. 1868 BROWNING *Ring & Bk.* VI. 1943 There let.. Both teach, both learn detestability!

detestable (dɪ'tɛstəb(ə)l), *a.* [a. F. *détestable* (1380 in Hatzf.), ad. L. *dētestābilis*, f. *dētestārī*: see -BLE. Originally *dete'stable*; in Spenser and Shaks. '*detestable*.]

1. To be detested; intensely hateful or odious; execrable, abominable.

1461 *Liber Pluscardensis* XI. viii. (1877) I. 387 To mak ws till oure Makare detestabile. *c* 1477 CAXTON *Jason* 75 The terrible dragon cast upon me a gobet of the most detestable infeccion that euer was. *c* 1489 —— *Sonnes of Aymon* xiv. 331 What saist thou, fole destestable? 1526 *Pilgr. Perf.* (W. de W. 1531) 34 Theyr presumpcion is to god moost detestable & hatefull. 1548–9 (Mar.) *Bk. Com. Prayer*, Litany, The bishop of Rome and all his detestable enormities. 1588 SHAKS. *Tit. A.* V. i. 94 Oh detestable villaine! Call'st thou that Trimming? 1590 SPENSER *F.Q.* I. i. 26 That detestable sight. 1702 PENN in *Pa. Hist. Soc. Mem.* IX. 132 Busy at that detestable work, privateering. 1771 *Junius Lett.* xlix. 256 That detestable transaction.. ended in the death of Mr. Yorke. 1851 RUSKIN *Stones Ven.* (1874) I. App. 396 The detestable ornamentation of the Alhambra. 1860 TYNDALL *Glac.* I. xii. 89 Along edges of detestable granular ice.

2. quasi-*adv.* Detestably.

1610 *Histrio-m.* II. 108 O detestable good!

de'testableness. [f. prec. + -NESS.] The quality of being detestable; extreme hatefulness or odiousness.

1612 T. TAYLOR *Comm. Titus* ii. 11 Oh these sinnes cannot be brooked for the foulenesse and detestablenesse of them. 1681 H. MORE *Exp. Dan.* Pref. 80 To instruct the people touching the Solidity of our Reformed Religion and of the Detestableness of Popery. *a* 1729 CLARKE *Serm.* I. xl. (R.), The unfitness and abominableness, and detestableness and profaneness of any uncleanness or impurity appearing in the Temple of God. 1883 H. KENNEDY tr. *Ten Brink's E. Eng. Lit.* 280 Now the theme is the baseness, the detestableness, of this earthly world.

de'testably, *adv.* [f. as prec. + -LY².] In a detestable manner; execrably, abominably.

1531–2 *Act 23 Hen. VIII*, c. 3 Periurie is.. detestably vsed to the disheritaunce and great damage of many. 1593 NASHE *Christ's T.* (1613) 14 It would sauour so detestably in Gods nostrils, hee were neuer able to endure it. *a* 1716 SOUTH (J.), A temper of mind rendering men so detestably bad, that [etc.]. 1863 GEO. ELIOT *Romola* III. 61 God grant you are mad! else you are detestably wicked!

†**de'testant**, *a.* and *sb. Obs.* [f. DETEST *v.* after F. *détestant*, L. *dētestānt-em* pr. pple.: see -ANT.]

A. *adj.* Detesting, full of detestation.

1650 W. BROUGH *Sacr. Princ.* (1659) 16 He that is detestant of the corruption.

B. *sb.* One who detests; a detester.

1648 T. HILL *Truth & Love* Ep. Ded., He is a Detestant of divers Opinions of Rome. *a* 1670 HACKET *Abp. Williams* I. (1692) 121 (D.) Detestants of the Romish idolatry.

†**de'testate**, *v. Obs. rare.* [f. L. *dētestāt-*, ppl. stem of *dētestāre* (*-ārī*) to DETEST: see -ATE³ 5.] By-form of DETEST *v.*

1548 UDALL, etc. *Erasm. Par. John* Pref. 6 a, This worlde, whiche as a mortall enemy the doctrine of the Ghospel dooeth detestate and abhorre. 1649 *State Trials, Col. J. Lilburne* (R.), Well therefore might the lord president.. detestate star-chamber examinations.

detestation (diːtɛ'steɪʃən). [a. F. *détestation* (14th c. in Godef. *Suppl.*), ad. L. *dētestātiōn-em*, n. of action from *dētestārī* to DETEST.]

†1. Public or formal execration (of a thing); formal testifying against anything. *Obs.*

1432–50 tr. *Higden* (Rolls) I. 285 For the detestacion of that dede, the Frenche men made a statute that noo woman after here scholde reioyce the realme of Fraunce. 1590 SWINBURNE *Testaments* 274 In these cases the testament is void, in detestation of such odious shiftes and practises. *a* 1633 AUSTIN *Medit.* (1635) 216 St. Paul rent his Garments in detestation of it. 1658 T. WALL *Charac. Enemies Ch.* (1659) 50 The unreasonable creature.. in detestation of the sinner whom it serves, is made obnoxious to temporal punishment. 1683 *Brit. Spec.* 108 [Galgacus] by his rough Oratory in detestation of Servitude and the Roman Yoke, having [etc.].

2. a. The feeling or mental state of detesting; intense dislike or hatred; abhorrence, loathing.

1526 *Pilgr. Perf.* (W. de W. 1531) 12 To the great detestacyon & uttermost despysyng of all the transitory goodes.. of this worlde. 1553 T. WILSON *Rhet.* 40 Induce theim to the feare of God, and utter detestation of al synne. 1660 R. COKE *Justice Vind.* Pref. 15, I did in detestation of the thing.. set myself to make these observations upon it. 1688 in Gutch *Coll. Cur.* I. 436 Something.. which he had.. sometime call'd a Dislike, sometime an Abhorrence, sometime a Detestation of the Pr. of Orange's proceedings. 1779–81 JOHNSON *L.P., Rowe* Wks. III. 30 The fashion.. of the time was, to accumulate upon Lewis all that can raise horrour and detestation. 1834 MACAULAY *Ess., Pitt* (1854) 296 The object of the Duchess of Marlborough's fiercest detestation. 1875 JOWETT *Plato* (ed. 2) III. 189 His detestation of priests and lawyers.

b. *to hold* or *have in detestation*: to regard with hatred or abhorrence, to abominate. *to be in detestation*: to be held in abhorrence, to be detested.

1576 FLEMING *Panopl. Epist.* 65, I have the state of these times in great detestation. *Ibid.* 155 Such as told you truth.. were in contempt, disdain, hate, and detestation. 1607 ROWLANDS *Famous Hist.* 46 Let God and man hold me in detestation. 1777 ROBERTSON *Hist. Amer.* (1778) I. I. 6 They held all sea-faring persons in detestation. 1847 MARRYAT *Childr. N. Forest* xii, One who is joined to a party which I hold in detestation.

3. *concr.* That which is detested; the object of intense dislike.

1728 SWIFT *Mullinix & Timothy*, Thou art grown the detestation of all thy party. 1792 T. JEFFERSON *Writ.* (1859) III. 343 This.. business is becoming more and more the public detestation. 1849 C. BRONTE *Shirley* I. 10 As if he were the darling of the neighbourhood.. being, as he is, its detestation.

de'tested, *ppl. a.* [f. DETEST *v.* + -ED.] Intensely disliked or hated; abominated; held in abhorrence; odious.

1552 HULOET, Detested, *abominatus.* 1588 SHAKS. *L.L.L.* IV. i. 31 Guiltie of detested crimes. 1634 SIR T. HERBERT *Trav.* 73 With such heathenish and detested Oratory. 1791 COWPER *Iliad* VI. 438 Both Paris and my most detested self. 1805 SOUTHEY *Madoc in Azt.* xx, Let a curse.. For ever follow the detested name.

Hence **de'testedly** *adv.*, with detestation.

1836 E. HOWARD *R. Reefer* xxxiii, Who viewed the West India station.. detestedly.

de'tester. [f. as prec. + -ER¹.] One who detests; a cordial hater; an abhorrer, abominator.

1611 COTGR., *Abhorrant*, an abhorrer, detester, loather. 1651 FULLER *Abel Rediv.* (1867) II. 99 A detester of controversies. 1779 SHERIDAN *Critic* I. ii, A detester of visible brickwork. 1863 SALA *Capt. Dangerous* I. ix. 254 Known as stanch detesters of the House of Hanover.

de'testful, *a. rare.* [f. DETEST *v.* (or ? *sb.*) + -FUL.] Hateful, odious.

1654 COKAINE *Dianea* II. 116 Thou hast tormented them with a Ghost, with a Phantasme so noyous, so detestfull.

†**detestine**, †**detestiue**, *a. Sc. Obs.* [irreg. f. DETEST *v.*] Detestable.

1560 ROLLAND *Crt. Venus* II. 975 But bad me sone pas hine Vnto the nine nobillis of excellence, Quhair I gat not be ansueir detestine. *Ibid.* III. 369 The law positiue It did suspend, and haldis as detestiue.

†**de'text**, *ppl. a. Obs.* —⁰ [In form, ad. L. *dētextus*, pa. pple. of *dētexĕre* to weave off, finish weaving; but with the prefix taken as DE- I. 6.]

1623 COCKERAM, *Detext*, vnwouen.

deteyn(e, -nour, obs. ff. DETAIN, DETAINER.

detful(l, obs. form of DEBTFUL.

deth(e, obs. form of DEATH *sb.*; also of DEATH *a.* and *v.* = deaf.

detheorize: see DE- II. 1.

dethronable (dɪ'θrəʊnəb(ə)l), *a.* [f. next + -ABLE.] Liable to be dethroned.

1644 BP. MAXWELL *Prerog. Chr. Kings* Introd. 3, Kings are.. censurable, punishable, and dethronable. *Ibid.* i. 11 They are deposable and dethronable by the people.

dethrone (dɪ'θrəʊn), *v.* [f. DE- II. 2 + THRONE: cf. F. *détrôner*, in 16th c. *detroner* (Littré), Cotgr. *desthroner* 'to disthronize'; cf. also DISTHRONE, DISTHRONIZE.]

trans. To remove from the throne; to deprive of royal or sovereign authority and dignity; to depose (a ruling prince).

1609 BP. W. BARLOW *Answ. Nameless Cath.* 153 Authoritie to de-Throan and de-Crowne Princes. *a* 1649 DRUMM. OF HAWTH. *Poems.* Wks. (1711) 15 Then let them do their worst, since thou art gone! Raise whom they list to thrones, enthron'd dethrone. 1790 BURKE *Fr. Rev.* 43 The question of dethroning, or, if these gentlemen like the phrase better, 'cashiering', kings. 1839 THIRLWALL *Greece* VI. 121 That Artaxerxes whom Cyrus attempted to dethrone.

b. *transf.* and *fig.*

1648 BOYLE *Seraph. Love* vi. (1700) 42 Love, by dethroning Reason.. doth kill the Man. 1761 HUME *Hist. Eng.* III. lxi. 319 That republicans being dethroned by Cromwell. 1879 FARRAR *St. Paul* (1883) 604 Dethrone the sin that would rule over your frail nature.

Hence **de'throned** *ppl. a.*, **de'throning** *vbl. sb.*

1648 PRYNNE *Speech in Parlt.* 4 Dec. (1649) 75 By a speedy publique dethroning and decolling of the King.. as the Army-Remonstrants advise. 1705 J. PHILIPS *Blenheim* (R.), His dethron'd compeers. 1809–10 COLERIDGE *Friend* (1865) 136 Compensations for dethroned princes. 1892 *Athenæum* 27 Aug. 299/1 The story.. is that Nero's wife Poppæa.. is the head of a plot for her husband's dethroning and slaughter.

dethronement (dɪ'θrəʊnmənt). [f. prec. vb. + -MENT: cf. mod.F. *détrônement.*] The action of dethroning, or fact of being dethroned; deposition from kingly authority.

1707 *Lond. Gaz.* No. 4365/1 The News.. of the Dethronement of the Grand Signior. 1820 KEATS *Hyperion* II. 315 In midst of this dethronement horrible. 1849 H. ROGERS *Ess.* (1860) III. 179 The boasted prerogative of Reason is also that of a limited monarch; and its attempt to make itself absolute can only end in its own dethronement. 1852 GROTE *Greece* II. lxxvi. X. 66 The frequent dethronements and assassinations of Kings.

dethroner (dɪ'θrəʊnə(r)). [f. DETHRONE + -ER¹.] One who dethrones (a king, etc.).

1649 ARNWAY *Tablet* (1661) 176 (T.) The hand of our dethroners.. hath prevailed. 1817 SOUTHEY *Fun. Song Princess Charlotte*, Passive as that humble spirit, Lies his bold dethroner too. 1833 MRS. BROWNING *Prometh. Bound* Poems 1850 I. 186 The name of his dethroner who shall come.

†**dethro'nize**, *v. Obs. rare.* [See DETHRONE and -IZE, and cf. DISTHRONIZE.] = DETHRONE. Hence †**dethroni'zation** = DETHRONEMENT.

1611 SPEED *Hist. Gr. Brit.* IX. xi. (1632) 682 The Queene.. aduertised of her husbands dethronization. 1656 S. HOLLAND *Zara* (1719) 66 We are in daily danger of dethronizing by the malevolent combinations of Cursed spirits. 1691 WOOD *Ath. Oxon.* (R.), To persuade the king.. to consent to the 4 votes of dethronizing him.

detie, obs. form of DITTY.

detin (diː'tɪn), *v.* [f. DE- II. 2 + TIN *sb.*] *trans.* To remove the tin from (scrap tin plate).

1909 in *Cent. Dict.* Suppl. 1923 *Glasgow Herald* 15 Aug. 7 The major portion of the old tins was disposed of after being detinned and pressed into billets. 1929 *Times* 21 Sept. 7/4 Scrap metal.. suitable for detinning. 1960 E. S. GYNGELL *Appl. Chem. Engineers* (ed. 3) xiii. 207 The well-known process used for detinning metal cans.

detinue ('dɛtɪnjuː). *Law.* Also 5 detenewe, detunue, -now, detynu(e, 7 detinu (detiny). [a. OF. *detenue* (1313, Godef.) detention, (:—Rom. type **dētenūta*) f. pa. pple. of *detenir* to detain.]

The act of detaining or withholding what is due (see DETAIN *v.* 2); *spec.* unlawful detention of a personal chattel belonging to another. *Obs.* exc. as in b.

1563–87 in Foxe *A. & M.* (1596) 348/1 Philip de Valous.. we haue gently requested you.. to that intent you should haue rendered unto us our lawfull right and inheritance to the Crowne of Fraunce, which from us.. you haue by great wrong and force deteined.. we well perceiue you meane to perseuere in the same your purpose and iniurious detinue. 1598 KITCHIN *Courts Leet* (1675) 148 Detinue of Goods may be sued. 16.. T. ADAMS *Wks.* (1861–2) I. 145 (D.) There are that will restore some, but not all.. let the creditors be content with one of four. But this little detiny is great iniquity. 1643 PRYNNE *Sov. Power Parl.* III. 46 [citing *Act 11 Rich. II* c. 1] Taking, leading away, or detinue of any horses or of any other beasts. 1727–51 CHAMBERS *Cycl.* s.v., The damages sustained by the detinue.

b. *action of detinue*: an action at law to recover a personal chattel (or its value) wrongfully detained by the defendant. So *writ of detinue.*

1467 in *Eng. Gilds* (1870) 376 Accicuns of dette, trespass an detenewe. 1514 FITZHERB. *Just. Peas* (1538) 123 Every man maye sue for the same by accion of detinue. 1602 FULBECKE *2nd Pt. Parall.* 20 One of the parties may haue an action of dette for the money, and the other a writte of Detinue for the wares. 1677 WYCHERLEY *Plain Dealer* III. (Routl.) 123/2 I'll bring my action of detinue or trover. 1768 BLACKSTONE *Comm.* III. 151 If I lend a man a horse, and he afterwards refuses to restore it.. the regular method for me to recover possession is by action of *detinue.* 1845 LD. CAMPBELL *Chancellors* (1857) VI. cxxviii. 143 The remedy was at law by an action of trover or detinue.

c. Also *detinue* = action or writ of detinue.

a 1626 BACON *Max. & Uses Com. Law* iii. (1636) 20 In a detinue brought by a feme against the executors of her husband. 1803 J. MARSHALL *Const. Opin.* i. (1839) 21 The judgment in detinue is for the thing itself or its value. 1875 POSTE *Gaius* IV. Comm. (ed. 2) 650 Trover and Detinue, which were brought to recover movable property.. were kinds of Trespass, that is of action on delict.

†**de'tithonize**, *v. Obs.* [f. DE- II. 1 + TITHONIC (f. Gr. Τιθωνός, the spouse of Eos or Aurora) + -IZE.] *trans.* To deprive (light) of actinic or chemical power.

1843 *Mech. Mag.* XXXIX. 170 As if the light, being dethithonized in passing through the larger mass, lost its energy in producing chemical action.

† **de'tomb**, *v. Obs. nonce-wd.* [f. DE- II. 2 b + TOMB *sb.*] *trans.* To deliver from the tomb.

1607 SIR R. AYTON *Pref. Verses* in *Earl of Stirling's Monarch. Trag.*, Crownes, throwne from Thrones to Tombes, detomb'd arise To match thy Muse with a Monarchicke theame.

detonable ('dɛtənəb(ə)l), *a.* [f. L. *dētonāre* (see next) + -BLE.] Capable of detonation.

1884 EISSLER *Mod. High Explosives* iii. 68 These grades of dynamite are only rendered detonable by the admixture of explosive salts.

detonate ('dɛtəneɪt, diː-), *v.* [f. L. *dētonāt-*, ppl. stem of *dētonāre* to thunder down or forth (f. DE- I. 1, 2 + *tonāre* to thunder), after F. *détoner* (1680 in Hatz.-Darm.) in the modern sense.]

1. *intr.* To produce a loud noise by the sudden liberation of gas in connexion with chemical decomposition or combination; to explode with sudden loud report (as when heated or struck).

1729 SHELVOCKE *Artillery* II. 89 Saltpeter.. detonates, or makes a Noise in the Fire. **1807** T. THOMSON *Chem.* (ed. 3) II. 140 Hydrogen gas and nitrous oxide gas detonate violently.. when a strong red heat is applied, or when the electric spark is made to pass through the mixture. **1859** R. F. BURTON *Centr. Afr.* in *Jrnl. Geog. Soc.* XXIX. 78 Metals are ever rusty;.. percussion caps.. will not detonate; gunpowder.. refuses to ignite. **1864** H. SPENCER *Biol.* I. 8 Iodide of nitrogen detonates on the slightest touch.

b. *fig.* To give vent to sudden anger or other violent feeling; to 'explode'. (Also *trans.*).

1836 *Blackw. Mag.* XXXIX. 309 He.. is notoriously choleric, and detonates upon the object nearest to him like one of his own chlorides. **1859** *Chamb. Jrnl.* XI. 258 It seemed to me that it would be quite a natural conclusion.. that Blodger should detonate: 'Committed as a rogue'.

c. To make a thundering noise, to 'thunder'. *rare.*

1853 MISS E. S. SHEPPARD *Ch. Auchester* III. 190 The drum detonated and was still.

2. *trans.* To cause to explode with sudden loud report, in the act of chemical decomposition or combination.

1801 *Phil. Trans.* XCI. 378 By detonating sulphuret of antimony and nitrate of potash, in a crucible, he obtained a mass, which [etc.]. **1808** HENRY *ibid.* XCVIII. 290 Detonate the mixture, and observe the amount of the diminution after the explosion. **1880** *Daily News* 27 Mar. 5/4 The destruction of the reef known as Hell Gate, in East River, New York, when something like 49,915 lb. [of dynamite] was detonated at once. **1890** NOBLE in *Nature* 18 Sept., One.. cause which has made gunpowder so successful an agent for the purposes of the artillerist is that it is a mixture, not a definite chemical combination; that it is not possible to detonate it.

† **3.** To convert (a flint gun) into a 'detonator'. *Obs. nonce-use.*

1824 COL. P. HAWKER *Instr. Y. Sportsm.* 69, I have since had a double gun *detonated* to my order.

detonating ('dɛtəneɪtɪŋ), *ppl. a.* [f. prec. + -ING[2].] That detonates. **a.** That explodes with sudden loud report, explosive, as ***detonating gas***; **b.** That causes, or is used in producing, detonation, as ***detonating primer, tube***; **c.** *esp.* That explodes by a blow, or is used in explosion by percussion, as ***detonating hammer, powder.***

detonating ball, a toy ball filled with a fulminating powder, exploding on percussion; ***detonating bulb***, the small glass bulb also called *Prince Rupert's drop*, which flies to pieces on a slight scratch; ***detonating gun***, a fire-arm which is fired by means of a detonating agent (as a percussion-cap) instead of by the application of a match or spark.

1808 HENRY *Epit. Chem.* (ed. 5) 131 By firing it in a detonating tube over mercury. *Ibid.* 224 A new detonating compound of silver. **1814** *Ann. Reg.* 324 These detonating-balls were calculated to effect abundant mischief. **1817** *Sporting Mag.* L. 257, I got from Joseph Manton a detonating gun. **1824** COL. P. HAWKER *Instr. Y. Sportsm.* 67 To fire with detonating powder, the gun requires to be much stronger than that used for a flint. **1840** BLAINE *Encycl. Sports* (1870) 752 The Percussion or Detonating System of Gun Firing. **1856** *Engineer* 428/2 (*heading*) Detonating Arms. *Ibid.*, A cap containing detonating powder, covered by a preparation of shellac. **1869** *Echo* 9 Oct., 'It is dangerous to play with edged', and still more with detonating 'tools'. **1879** LOCKYER *Elem. Astron.* iii. 138 At times meteors.. are heard to explode with great noise; these are called detonating meteors.

detonation (dɛtə'neɪʃən, diː-). [a. F. *détonation*, noise of explosion, n. of action from *détoner* to DETONATE.] The action of detonating.

1. a. *Chem.* 'The noise accompanying the sudden decomposition or combination of substances, and due to the concussion of the air resulting from the sudden production of a large quantity of gas' (Watts *Dict. Chem.*); hence, explosion accompanied with a sudden loud report.

1677–86 W. HARRIS *Lemery's Chym.* (ed. 2) 41 Detonation is a noise that is made when the Volatile parts of any mixture do rush forth with impetuosity: it is also called Fulmination. **1686** PLOT *Staffordsh.* 55 Common Niter in its detonation or alcalisation with coales, acquires a green colour. **1704** J. HARRIS *Lex. Techn.*, Detonation is a Chymical word expressing the Thundring Noise that is often made by a mixture being enkindled in the containing Vessel. **1800** tr. *Lagrange's Chem.* I. 107 This experiment is dangerous, as it is often accompanied with violent detonations. **1864** SPENCER *Biol.* I. 8 Percussion produces detonation in sulphide of nitrogen.

b. In an internal combustion engine, the rapid and premature combustion of the mixture in the cylinder before it is ignited by the spark or the flame from the spark, producing a rattling or thumping noise (cf. KNOCK *sb.*[1]).

1912 *Motor Manual* (ed. 14) vi. 201 With super-compression of the charge instead of a gradual expansion of the ignited gases a 'detonation' occurs. **1937** *Autocar Handbk.* (ed. 13) v. 91 Should the charge be fired off too early, detonation, or, as it is more popularly known, 'pinking', will result. **1968** *Practical Motorist* Oct. 205 The detonation causes a distinctive knock ('pinking') when the engine is under load.

2. *gen.* **a.** A loud noise as of thunder; a violent explosive report, e.g. in a volcanic eruption.

1830 LYELL *Princ. Geol.* (1875) II. II. xxvi. 28 The great Crater.. testified by its loud detonations [etc.]. **1834** MRS. SOMERVILLE *Connex. Phys. Sc.* xxvi. (1849) 283 The detonations [from the eruption in Sumbawa 1815] were heard in Sumatra. **1869** PHILLIPS *Vesuv.* iv. 112 After each detonation globes of white vapour were formed. **1875** *Wonders Phys. World* II. ii. 201 They attribute the movements and detonations to the expansion of the ice.

b. The action of causing a substance to detonate.

1727–51 CHAMBERS *Cycl.*, *Detonation* denotes the.. operation, of expelling the impure, volatile, and sulphureous part, out of antimony. **1758** *Elaboratory laid Open* Introd. 58 The chemists have called the operation, detonation, or deflagration. **1827** FARADAY *Chem. Manip.* xvii. 433 A tube for detonation.

3. *fig.* A sudden utterance or expression of anger or other violent feeling; an 'explosion'.

1878 BROWNING *La Saisiaz* 79 As Rousseau, then eloquent, as Byron prime in poet's power,—Detonations, fulgurations, smiles. **1882** STEVENSON *New Arab. Nts.* (1884) 296 Detonations of temper were not unfrequent. **1891** ROSEBERY *Pitt* xi. 179 It was impossible for Pitt after his detonations and activity of the autumn to prevent the agitation of the Catholic Question.

detonative ('dɛtəneɪtɪv), *a.* [f. L. *dētonāt-*, ppl. stem of *dētonāre* to DETONATE + -IVE.] Having the property of detonating; of the nature of a detonation.

1875 C. F. CHANDLER in Eissler *Mod. High Explosives* (1884) iii. 69 When the gunpowder is exploded by nitroglycerine, its explosion becomes instantaneous; it becomes detonative; it occurs at a much higher temperature. **1888** *Evening Standard* 11 Feb. 4/4 The water which runs through the factory is highly detonative.

detonator ('dɛtəneɪtə(r)). [Agent-noun, in L. form, f. *dētonāre* to DETONATE: see -OR.] Something that detonates; a contrivance for producing detonation, as a percussion-cap; a railway fog-signal. † *spec.* A detonating gun (*obs.*): see DETONATING.

1822 *Sporting Mag.* IX. 156 Somewhat of a contrast this, to our expensive detonators. **1825** COL. P. HAWKER *Diary* (1893) I. 283 An old flint gun which put me out, after the detonators. **1845** FORD *Handbk. Spain* I. 104 Bringing his own double barrel detonator with a good supply of caps and cut wadding. **1871** TYNDALL *Fragm. Sc.* (1879) I. x. 319 By the ignition of a fuse associated with a detonator, the gun-cotton should be fired. **1887** *Pall Mall G.* 10 Jan. 6/1 When the signal is placed on the railway plate the ends of the band are drawn out and bent under the surface of the rail, upon which the detonator (as the fog signal is also called) then rests securely.

† **de'tond**, *v. Obs. rare*$^{-0}$. [ad. L. *dētondē-re*, f. DE- I. 2. + *tondēre* to clip.] *trans.* To shave, poll.

1623 COCKERAM, *Detonded*, poled.

† **'detonize**, *v. Obs.* [f. F. *détoner* to detonate + -IZE.] = DETONATE (*trans.* and *intr.*). Hence † **detonization** = DETONATION.

1731 S. HALE *Stat. Ess.* I. 277 The fumes of detonized nitre. **1804** tr. *Fourcroy* (Webster 1828), This precipitate.. detonizes with a considerable noise. **1828** WEBSTER, *Detonization*, the act of exploding, as certain combustible bodies.

de'tonsure. *nonce-wd.* [f. L. *dētons-*, ppl. stem of *dētondēre*: see DETOND and -URE.] Shaving, polling. (*affected* or *humorous.*)

1819 *Blackw. Mag.* V. 639 That able-bodied barber.. insisting upon the immediate detonsure of you.

detorsion, var. of DETORTION.

† **detort** (dɪ'tɔt), *v. Obs.* [f. L. *dētort-*, ppl. stem of *dētorquēre* to twist or turn aside, twist or turn out of shape, distort, f. DE- I. 2 + *torquēre* to twist. Cf. F. *détordre.*]

1. *trans.* To turn aside from the purpose; to twist, wrest, pervert (*esp.* words or sayings). (Common in 17th c.)

c **1555** HARPSFIELD *Divorce Hen. VIII* (1878) 54 How miserably doth Tertullian wrest and wring the Levitt: to detort it to the confirmation of his heresy. **1609** BP. W. BARLOW *Answ. Nameless Cath.* 41 Schoolemen blasphemously detorting Scriptures. **1620** BRINSLEY *Virgil* 39 Detorting to that purpose those things which Sibyl had prophecied. **1632** LITHGOW *Trav.* I. 1 And Lorets Chappell ..On Angells backes, from Nazareth detorted. **1682** DRYDEN *Relig. Laici* Pref. (Globe) 187 The Fanatics.. have detorted those texts of Scripture. **1829** SOUTHEY *Sir T. More* I. 87 In these days good words are so detorted from their original and genuine meaning.

b. To extract (by perversion of the sense).

a **1612** DONNE *Βιαθανατος* (1644) 185 The Donatists.. racked and detorted thus much from this place, That [etc.]. **1824** SOUTHEY *Bk of Ch.* (1841) 355 Conclusions as uncharitable as ever were detorted from Scripture.

2. To derive by perversion of form; *pa. pple.* perverted, corrupted (of words).

1605 CAMDEN *Rem.* 54 Garret, for Gerard, and Gerald: see Everard, for from thence they are detorted, if we beleeve Gesnerus. **1657** TOMLINSON *Renou's Disp.* 705 *Ἄγριππον* is wilde succe, whence its nomenclature is detorted.

Hence **de'torted** *ppl. a.*, **de'torting** *vbl. sb.*

1550 BALE *Apol.* 129 Nowe wyll I shewe some of hys detorted scriptures. **1579** FULKE *Heskins' Parl.* 306 By miserable detorting of a worde or two. **1692** WAGSTAFFE *Vind. Carol.* Introd. 2 Under the false detorted Names of Law, Justice, and Honour of the Nation.

detortion, -sion (dɪ'tɔːʃən). [n. of action f. L. *dētorquēre*, ppl. stem *dētort-* and *dētors-*: see DETORT. Cf. OF. *detorsion.*]

† **1.** The action of 'detorting'; twisting, wresting, perversion of meaning. Now *rare* or *Obs.*

1598 *Ord. for Prayer* in *Liturg. Serv. Q. Eliz.* (1847) 681 By a blasphemous application or rather detortion of that excellent Scripture *Unum necessarium*, One thing is necessary. **1652** GAULE *Magastrom.* 69 A depraving adulteration, a sacrilegious detorsion. **1728** EARBERY tr. *Burnet's St. Dead.* I. 135 A rash and bold Detorsion of the sacred Scriptures.

2. In physical sense: Distortion. Now *rare* or *Obs.*

1853 KANE *Grinnell Exped.* (1856) 512 Refracted detortion very great.

3. *Biol.* (Spelt **detorsion.**) Evolutionary reversion to a primitive linear anatomical organization in a species of organisms, esp. gastropod molluscs, whose intermediate ancestors underwent torsion through 180°

1902 *Encycl. Brit.* XXX. 796/2 Not an absence of torsion, but an actual detorsion of the visceral commissure. **1930** G. R. DE BEER *Embryol. & Evol.* vii. 54 That intermediate stages are not *a priori* impossible is proved by the fact that intermediate stages in detorsion in later Gastropods are not wanting. **1968** R. D. PURCHON *Biol. Mollusca* i. 25 The penis is situated on the right side of the head.. and has evidently been 'left behind' when the mantle cavity retreated posteriorly during the process of detorsion.

detour, ‖ **détour** (dɪ'tʊə(r), now freq. 'diːtʊə(r); ‖detur), *sb.* [a. mod.F. *détour* turning off, change of direction, in OF. *destor, -tour*, orig. **destorn*; f. *destorner* now *détourner* turn away, f. *des-*, L. *dis-* + *tourner* to turn.] A turning or deviation from the direct road; a roundabout or circuitous way, course, or proceeding. In 18th c. mostly *fig.*

1738 WARBURTON *Div. Legat.* I. 63 After many *Detours*, Mr. Bayle is at length brought to own [etc.]. **1780** H. WALPOLE *Let. to W. Mason* 1 Nov., We are above *détours*. **1794** R. H. LEE in *Washington's Writ.* (1891) XII. 417 *note*, Upon our guard against all the arts and *détours* of the subtlest policy. **1807** SIR R. C. HOARE *Tour in Ireland* 237, I was amply recompensed for this *detour*. **1809** SCOTT *Fam. Lett.* 14 June (1894) I. 137, I ought in conscience to have made ten thousand pretty détours about all this. **1825** *Ibid.* 22 Jan. II. 230 Perhaps they may make a détour in their journey to see you. **1870** LOWELL *Study Wind.* (1871) 242 Rhyming [words].. sometimes.. have driven the most straightforward of poets into an awkward *détour*. **1877** BLACK *Green Past.* xliv. (1878) 357 To avoid these ruts we made long detours. **1922** JOYCE *Ulysses* 237 Better turn down here. Make a detour. **1923** E. O'NEILL *Hairy Ape* 50 They make wide detours to avoid the spot where he stands in the middle of the pavement. **1966** 'J. HACKSTON' *Father clears Out* 26 It's no use travelling by the compass if one has to make wide detours.

detour, *v.* [f. DETOUR *sb.*]

a. *intr.*, to make a detour; to turn aside from the direct way; to go round about.

1836 *Tait's Mag.* III. 481 This has been a busy week; rambling and climbing, touring and detouring. **1837** *New Monthly Mag.* LI. 192 We.. detoured again to the right. **1937** D. ALDIS *Time at her Heels* x. 225 Mary detoured to pick up her bag from the table. **1955** E. BOWEN *World of Love* ii. 41 A stranger, who detoured to drop them at the Montefort gates.

b. *trans.* To send by a detour. *U.S.*

1905 *N.Y. Even. Post* 18 Sept., The Missouri Pacific is detouring its St. Louis—Kansas City trains over the Burlington Railway via Chillicothe. **1967** *Boston Globe* 18 May 12/2 (*caption*) Workman carries signs detouring motorists off Cambridge st. and Broadway.

de'tox, *v.* [Colloq. abbrev. of DETOXIFY *v.*]

1. *trans.* To treat (a motor vehicle or its engine) in order to remove or limit the noxious fumes emitted through the exhaust system, etc.

1970 *Daily Tel.* 9 Dec. 12/5 Manufacturers find it necessary to incorporate 'detoxing' equipment such as exhaust 'mufflers' or afterburners to meet increasingly stringent standards. *Ibid.* 7 June 13/2 In certain very sunny conditions the amount of noxious fumes emitted from the petrol tank while a car is being refuelled can exceed the emissions through the exhaust of a 'detoxed' engine. **1976** *New Motorcycling Monthly* Oct. 26/4 What Yamaha's weight-paring has done is give their new, mildly tuned, detoxed and over-silenced 500cc single a chance to show its teeth.

2. Chiefly *U.S.* To subject (an alcoholic, drug addict) to detoxification.

1972 *N.Y. Times* 24 Dec. IV. 10 We can detox a heroin addict on an outpatient basis in three weeks. **1978** *N.Y.*

Times Mag. 6 Aug. 38 They did get me detoxed and clean. They told me I was an alcoholic. **1982** *Time* 8 Nov. 82/3 Gaetano's goodly impulse is to detox Hud. **1986** *Nursery World* 18 Dec.–1 Jan. 10/2 Mothers who are heroin addicts can pass the addiction on to the baby and..the art of safely 'detoxing' newborn infants has come to be recognised as an essential medical expertise in many parts of the country.

'detox, *sb.* Chiefly *U.S.* Colloq. abbrev. of DETOXIFICATION; also, a detoxification centre. Freq. *attrib.*, esp. of a place used for the treatment of alcoholics or drug addicts.

1975 *Canadian* 18 Oct. 7/1 I'm looking at a very shaky scrawl that tells me of my first day there, in the detox area where everybody—drunk or sober—starts off. **1978** *N.Y. Times Mag.* 6 Aug. 11, I went to detox again..and it's been five years since I came out and I haven't had a drink or pill since. **1978** *Tucson Mag.* Dec. 20/3 KL collars will be brought to 'Dick of the Jungle's' de-tox center. **1979** *Arizona Daily Star* 5 Aug. (Advt. Section) 2/4 Requires knowledge of group dynamics as it relates to the treatment of alcoholics in the detox stages of recovery. **1986** *Washington Post* 25 Mar. (Weekend Suppl.) 30/1 After waking up in detox, he's spoiling to redeem himself.

de'toxicate (diːˈtɒksɪkeɪt). *v.* [f. DE- II. 1 + L. *toxic-um* poison, after *intoxicate.*] *trans.* To deprive of poisonous qualities.

1867 *Pall Mall G.* No. 729. 2043/2 Defecated, detoxicated, and deodorized. **1906** *Practitioner* Nov. 590 Focalisation of the infection in the liver, with disturbance of its detoxicating mechanism. **1927** *Observer* 7 Aug. 3 It detoxicates the blood and keeps it clean and free-running. **1964** *Economist* 14 Mar. 1020/3 A toxic amine, which ordinarily is detoxicated in the liver.

Hence **detoxi'cation**, the action of depriving of poisonous qualities; **de'toxicator**, that which detoxicates; also **de,toxifi'cation** and **de'toxify** *v.*

1905 GOULD *Dict. New Med. Terms* 213/1 *Detoxification*, the power of reducing the poisonous properties of a substance. *Ibid.*, *Detoxify*, to deprive a substance of its poisonous attributes. **1906** *Practitioner* Nov. 586 A reducer and detoxicator of toxic substances. *Ibid.* 593 The detoxication of the poisons found in the blood. **1948** W. W. PIGMAN *Chem. Carbohydrates* xi. 509 Many phenols and alcohols when injected into animals are detoxified by conjugation as glucuronides. **1955** *Sci. News Let.* 9 Apr. 229/3 The vaccine for this is made by detoxifying the toxin, or poison, produced by the diphtheria germs. **1956** *Nature* 4 Feb. 219/1 Biochemical aspects of mechanisms of detoxication. *Ibid.* 25 Feb. 357/2 The conversion of insecticides to harmless metabolites or detoxification. **1961** *New Scientist* 7 Sept. 601/1 Many tumours do not have the ability of detoxifying drugs. **1963** *Guardian* 22 Jan. 8/5 You give the impression that detoxification of ordinary coal gas is neither a practical nor an economic proposition. **1967** *New Scientist* 16 Nov. 410/1 Resistance mechanisms often involve detoxication—that is, the resistant individuals are able to convert the insecticide into relatively harmless products. **1970** *Daily Tel.* 20 Jan. 14/1 This is Cocteau's second attempt at detoxication, the first having failed owing to lack of medical knowledge about withdrawal. **1971** *Ibid.* 2 Mar. 2/7 People with a serious drink problem may be detained in the 'detoxification centres' for 10 days while they receive medical treatment.

†**de'tract,** *sb. Obs. rare.* [ad. L. *dētractus* a taking away, f. *dētrahĕre*: see DETRACT *v.*] Protraction, delay: cf. DETRACT *v.* 6.

1563–87 FOXE *A. & M.* (1596) 353/1 Without delay and other detract of time.

†**de'tract,** *ppl. a. Obs.* [ad. L. *dētract-us*, pa. pple. of *dētrahĕre* to draw off or away: see next.] Extracted, taken out.

c **1420** *Pallad. on Husb.* XII. 171 The bonys Detracte of Duracyne.

detract (dɪˈtrækt), *v.* Also 6 *Sc.* **detrack.** [f. L. *dētract-* ppl. stem of *dētrahĕre* to draw off or away, take away, pull down, disparage, etc, f. DE- I. 2 + *trahĕre* to draw. Cf. F. *détracter* (1530 in Hatz.-Darm.). In some senses app. directly representing L. *dētractāre* or *dētrectāre*, to decline, refuse, pull down violently, depreciate, freq. of *dētrahĕre*.

(The chronological order of the senses in English is not that of their original development; sense 3 being the earliest)]

I. To take away, take from, take reputation from.

1. *trans.* To take away, withdraw, subtract, deduct, abate: **a.** some part *from* (rarely † *to*) a whole. (Now usually with a quantitative object, as *much*, *something*, etc.)

1509 BARCLAY *Shyp of Folys* (1874) I. 17 Some time addynge, somtyme detractinge and takinge away such thinges as semeth me necessary and superflue. **1571** DIGGES *Pantom.* II. xxiii. P ij b, Then 36 detracted from 48 leueth 12. **1591** SHAKS. *1 Hen. VI*, V. iv. 142 Shall I..Detract so much from that prerogatiue, As to be call'd but Viceroy? **1622** S. WARD *Christ is All in All* (1627) 25 All defects detract nothing to the happiness of him that [etc.]. **1677** HALE *Prim. Orig. Man.* IV. iv. 326 To which there can be nothing added, nor detracted, without a blemish. *a* **1696** E. SCARBURGH *Euclid* (1705) 207 Let the magnitude AB be equimultiple of CD, as the part detracted AE is of the part detracted CF. **1870** DISRAELI *Lothair* lxix, That first great grief which..detracts something from the buoyancy of the youngest life.

†**b.** something *from* a possessor, etc. *Obs.*

1607 *Schol. Disc. agst. Antichr.* I. ii. 97 They vilifie it and detract much authoritie from it. **1709** STEELE *Tatler* No. 13 ¶1 A Lady takes all you detract from the rest of her Sex to be a Gift to her. **1710** PRIDEAUX *Orig. Tithes* i. 17 We rob him, whenever we detract from his Ministers any part of that Maintenance.

2. *absol.* or *intr.* To take away a portion. Usually ***to detract from***: to take away from, diminish, lessen (a quality, value, authority, etc.).

a **1592** H. SMITH *Wks.* (1866–7) I. 65 To the testament of him that is dead, no man addeth or detracteth. **1699** BURNET *39 Art.* vi. (1700) 89 This may be urged to detract from its Authority. **1799** COLEBROOKE in *Life* (1873) 446 The sight ..detracted from the pleasure with which the landscape might be viewed. **1827** JARMAN *Powell's Devises* II. 101 These circumstances detract from the weight of the decision. **1863** D. G. MITCHELL *My Farm Of Edgewood* 47 This alteration was of so old a date as not to detract from the venerable air of the house.

b. Connoting depreciation: cf. 3 c.

1593 HOOKER *Eccl. Pol.* III. viii. (1611) 100 To detract from the dignity thereof, were to iniury euen God himselfe. **1603** KNOLLES *Hist. Turkes* (1638) 212 Our late Historiographers..detracting from his worthy praises. **1765** BLACKSTONE *Comm.* I. 5 Without detracting..from the real merit which abounds in the imperial law, I hope I may have leave to assert [etc.]. **1882** B. D. W. RAMSAY *Recoll. Mil. Serv.* I. viii. 172 There were always some ready to detract from his fair fame.

†**c.** quasi-*trans.* (in loose const.) *Obs. rare.*

1654 WHITLOCK *Zootomia* 452 In Revenge he would have Detracted, and lessen'd his Territories. **1785** JEFFERSON *Corr.* Wks. 1859 I. 417 To detract, add to, or alter them as you please.

3. *trans.* To take away from the reputation or estimation of, to disparage, depreciate, belittle, traduce, speak evil of. Now *rare.*

c **1449** PECOCK *Repr.* IV. i. 417 Thei bacbiten and detracten the clergie. **1533** GAU *Richt Vay* 91 Lat wsz forgiff thayme quhilk detrackis and spekis euil of wsz. **1603** B. JONSON *Sejanus* I. i, To..detract His greatest actions. **1618** BOLTON *Florus* IV. ii. 265 Cato..detracted Pompey, and found fault with his actions. **1632** MASSINGER & FIELD *Fatal Dowry* I. ii, Such as may Detract my actions and life hereafter. **1890** [see DETRACTED below]. **1891** SMILES *Jasmin* vii. 93 Jasmin, like every person envied or perhaps detracted, had his hours of depression.

†**b.** *absol.* To speak disparagingly; to use or practise detraction. *Obs.*

1605 BP. HALL *Medit. & Vows* I. §7 So would there not be so many open mouthes to detract and slaunder. **1610** SHAKS. *Temp.* II. ii. 96 To vtter foule speeches, and to detract. **1777** SHERIDAN *Sch. Scand.* Portrait, Adepts..who rail by precept, and detract by rule.

†**c.** *intr.* with *from* (†*of*).

c **1590** GREENE *Fr. Bacon* vii. 66 Dar'st thou detract and derogate from him? **1609** BIBLE (Douay) *Num.* xiii. 33 They detracted from the Land, which they had viewed. **1683** D. A. *Art Converse* 106 They detract generally of all Mankind.

†**II.** To draw away, off, out.

†**4.** *trans.* To draw away or aside, withdraw, divert (*from* an action or undertaking); *refl.* and *intr.* To withdraw, refrain. *Obs.*

1548 PATTEN *Exped. Scotl.* in Arb. *Garner* III. 110 My Lord Marshal..whom no danger detracted from doing his enterprise. **1637** GILLESPIE *Eng. Pop. Cerem.* Ep. C, There are too many Professours who detract themselves from undergoing lesser hazards for the Churches liberty. **1643** SLINGSBY *Diary* (1836) 104 Long experience hath taught their General wisely to detract from fighting. **1802** *Hatred* I. 211 [To] detract their attention from every thing foreign.

†**5.** To draw or pull off. *Obs. rare.*

1607 TOPSELL *Four-f. Beasts* (1658) 486 The skins of sheep..when the wool is detracted and pulled off from them.

†**6.** To draw out, lengthen in duration, protract, delay; usually in phr. ***to detract time.*** *Obs.*

1569 SIR J. HAWKINS in *Hawkins' Voy.* (1878) 73 To detract further time. **1579** CHURCHYARD in Arb. *Garner* IV. 206 The French Horsemen..offered a skirmish, to detract time. **1604** EDMONDS *Observ. Cæsar's Comm.* 59 To linger and detract the war. **1605** *Play Stucley* in Simpson *Sch. Shaks.* (1878) 188 Some let or other to detract our haste. **1641** *Life Wolsey* in *Select. Harl. Misc.* (1793) 132, I would not have you to detract the time, for he is very sick.

†**b.** *absol.* or *intr.* To delay. *Obs.*

1584 POWEL *Lloyd's Cambria* 333 Willing the Prince to come thither, and doo him homage, which when the Prince detracted to doo, the king gathered an army to compell him thereto. *a* **1592** GREENE *James IV* I. i, My zeal and ruth.. Make me lament I did detract so long.

III. = DETRECT.

†**7.** *trans.* To draw back from, decline, refuse, shun; to give up, relinguish, abandon. *Obs.*

1572 [see DETRACTING *vbl. sb.*] **1577** HOLINSHED *Chron.* II. B b vij (N.), The English men..minding not to detract the battel, sharply encounter their enimies. **1595** *Locrine* III. iv, And if Thrasimachus detract the fight..Let him not boast that Brutus was his eam. **1600** ABP. ABBOT *Exp. Jonah* 634 Ionas detracting his Masters businesse. **1600** HAKLUYT *Voy.* (1810) III. 135 The winde comming faire, the captaine and the master would by no means detract the purpose of our discovery. **1606** HOLLAND *Sueton.* 25 Neither held he off, and detracted fight.

Hence **de'tracted** *ppl. a.* (see the various senses above); also as *sb.* a calumniated person.

1552 HULOET, Detracted, *detractus, rosus, suggillatus.* **1890** T. J. DUNCAN *Social Departure* 289 The detracted's enemies follow him.

detrac'tation (diːtrækˈteɪʃən). *rare.* [f. DETRACT *v.* + -ATION: perhaps ad. L. *dētractātio* or *dētrectātio*, from *dētractāre*, *-trectāre* to decline, refuse, also to detract from, depreciate, freq. of *dētrahĕre.*] = DETRACTION 2.

1563–87 FOXE *A. & M.* (1596) 283/1, I cannot speake unto you, but to your detractation. **1646** J. MAINE *Serm.* (1647) 8 So much Libell, or holy Detractation. **1888** H. S. SALT *Shelley* 141 Against Shelley he never uttered a word of detractation.

de'tractatory, *a. rare.* [f. DETRACT *v.*, or L. *dētractāre*: see prec. and -ORY.] Of detracting or disparaging nature or tendency.

1860 *Chamb. Jrnl.* XIV. 251 It is harsh and detractatory towards the author's equals and superiors.

detracter, var. of DETRACTOR.

detracting (dɪˈtræktɪŋ), *vbl. sb.* [f. DETRACT *v.* + -ING[1].] The action of the verb DETRACT, q.v.; †protraction (*obs.*); †shunning, avoiding (*obs.*); disparagement, detraction.

1572 BOSSEWELL *Armorie* II. 83 b, Fabius..so tempered Prudence with..prowesse, that by detracting of battayle, and trayning Anniball from place to place, and.. skirmishing with hym, he minished hys puissaunce. **1581** SAVILE *Tacitus' Hist.* I. i. (1591) 1 Detracting and envyous carping. **1581** STYWARD *Mart. Discipl.* II. 164 The detracting of time shall enforce vs to take counsaile when it is to late. **1599** HAKLUYT *Voy.* II. II. 135 The detracting of the time of our setting out. **1613** JACKSON *Creed* I. 331 The Iewes detractings of our Sauiour.

detracting (dɪˈtræktɪŋ), *ppl. a.* [f. as prec. + -ING[2].] That detracts; given to detraction; disparaging, depreciative.

1530 PALSGR. 310/1 Detractyng, belongyng to detractyon, *detractoire.* **1599** MARSTON *Sc. Villanie* II. vi. 201 Hence ye big-buzzing, little-bodied Gnats..With your malignant, weake, detracting vaine. **1674** tr. *Scheffer's Lapland* v. 14 They are..of a censorious and detracting humor. **1718** PRIDEAUX *Connection* II. II. 78 He had criticised in a very biting and detracting style. **1824** L. MURRAY *Eng. Gram.* (ed. 5) I. 398 A man who is of a detracting spirit, will misconstrue the most innocent words.

Hence **de'tractingly** *adv.*

1598 FLORIO, *Prauamente*, wickedly..detractingly. **1761** MURPHY *All in Wrong* v. i, I am not fond of speaking detractingly of a young lady. **1818** COLERIDGE *Treat. Method* in *Encycl. Metrop.*, *Mental Philos.* (1847) 16 Why Bacon should have spoken detractingly of such a man.

detraction (dɪˈtrækʃən). [a. F. *détraction*, in 12th c. *detractiun* (Ph. de Thaun), ad. L. *dētractiōn-em*, n. of action from *dētrahĕre*: see DETRACT *v.*] The action of detracting.

†**1.** A taking away, subtraction, deduction, withdrawal. *Obs.* or *arch.* exc. as in b. (Cf. DETRACT *v.* 1, 2.)

1528 GARDINER in Pocock *Rec. Ref.* I. li. 130 Wherein.. we saw the additions, detractions, and corrections. **1541** R. COPLAND *Galyen's Terapeutyke* 2 G iv, The detraction of blode..ought to be doone in the partye..moste dystaunt, & then in the vlcerate parties. **1648** BOYLE *Seraph. Love* xx. (1700) 127 With less detraction from their true Magnitude. **1684** tr. *Bonet's Merc. Compit.* VI. 243, I approve..rather of Incision, than of Detraction of the Callus. **1817** SCORESBY in *Ann. Reg.* Chron. 555 A detraction of vapour from the circumpolar regions.

b. A detracting, or part to be detracted *from* (merit, reputation, or the like); cf. sense 2.

1633 MILTON *Arcades* 11 Fame..We may justly now accuse Of detraction from her praise: Less than half we find expressed. **1809** PINKNEY *Trav. France* 263 There is one heavy detraction..from the excellence of the Avignonese climate. **1848** DICKENS *Dombey* v, Let it be no detraction from the merits of Miss Tox.

2. The action of detracting from a person's merit or reputation; the utterance of what is depreciatory or injurious to his reputation; depreciation, disparagement, defamation, calumny, slander. (The earliest and the prevalent sense: cf. DETRACT *v.* 3.)

1340 *Ayenb.* 10 þo þet misziggeþ guode men behinde ham ..þet me clepeþ þe zenne of detraccion. *c* **1400** *Rom. Rose* 5531 With tonge woundyng..Thurgh venemous detracciouun. *c* **1440** *Gesta Rom.* xxxvi. 145 Lesynges, & bacbitinges, and detracciouns. *c* **1510** BARCLAY *Mirr. Gd. Manners* (1570) G. j, Be no tale bearer, vse not detraction. **1599** MARSTON *Sco. Villanie* 165 Enuies abhorred childe, Detraction. **1659** B. HARRIS *Parival's Iron Age* 53 By occasion of petty envies, and shamefull detractions. **1709** ADDISON *Tatler* No. 102 ¶5 Females addicted to Censoriousness and Detraction. **1827** HARE *Guesses* Ser. II. (1873) 527 Flattery and detraction or evil speaking are, as the phrase is, the Scylla and Charybdis of the tongue. **1875** MANNING *Mission H. Ghost* v. 139 To listen to detraction is as much an act of detraction as to speak it.

†**3.** Protraction (*of time*); delay. *Obs.* (Cf. DETRACT *v.* 6.)

1579 FENTON *Guicciard.* III. (1599) 141 Mens..mindes [began] to grow cold for the detraction and negligence which the king used. **1588** HOWARD *Let. to Walsyngham* 14 June, The Commissioners cannot perceive whether they..use the same to detract a time for a further device; and if our Commissioners do discover any detraction in them [etc.]. **1637** R. HUMPHREY tr. *St. Ambrose* I. 138 Lest through detraction of time, those sugred baits..ingage too far.

†**4.** Withdrawal, declinature, relinquishment. *Obs. rare.* (Cf. DETRACT *v.* 7.)

1655–60 STANLEY *Hist. Philos.* (1701) 620/2 For want of this renouncing or detraction.

†**detractious** (dɪˈtrækʃəs), *a. Obs.* [f. DETRACTION: see -TIOUS.] Given to detraction; disparaging, calumnious.

1626 T. H[AWKINS] *Caussin's Holy Crt.* 202 Giue detractious tongues leaue..to li[c]ke up dust. **1755** JOHNSON, *Derogatory*, detractious.

detractive (dɪˈtræktɪv), *a.* [a. OF. *detractif, -ive*, f. L. type **dētractīv-us*, f. *dētract-*: see DETRACT *v.* and -IVE.]

1. Conveying, of the nature of, or given to, detraction; disparaging, depreciative, defamatory, calumnious.

1490 CAXTON *Eneydos* vi. 23 To saye wordes detractiues. **1618** CHAPMAN *Hesiod, Bk. of Days* 40 Whispering out detractive obloquies. **1633** T. MORTON *Discharge* 276 (T.) An envious and detractive adversary. **1767** GOLDSM. *Rom. Hist.* (1786) II. 342 Envious and detractive. **1822** *Examiner* 154/1 Walpole shines more in the detractive and satirical, than in the candid and urbane.

2. Tending to detract *from*: see DETRACT *v.* 2.

1654 W. MOUNTAGUE *Devoute Ess.* II. iii. §2 (R.) Admitting the being of evil not at all detractive from God. **1830** *Examiner* 5/2 Looked upon as detractive from the merits of a production.

†**3.** 'Having the power to take or draw away' (T.). *Obs.*

1580 E. KNIGHT *Triall of Truth* 28 (T.) [The surgeon] straightway will apply a detractive plaister.

Hence **detractively** *adv.*, **deˈtractiveness**.

1727 BAILEY vol. II, *Detractiveness*, detracting Quality or Humour. *Mod.* A review detractively written.

detractor (dɪˈtræktə(r)). Also 4-7 -tour, 5 -towre, 6-8 -ter, 6 *Sc.* detrakker. [a. AFr. *detractour* = OF. *detracteur*, ad. L. *dētractor*, agent-noun from *dētrahĕre* (see DETRACT *v.*): see -OR.]

1. One who detracts from another's merit or reputation by uttering things to his prejudice; a person given to detraction; a defamer, traducer, calumniator, slanderer.

1382 WYCLIF *Rom.* i. 30 Detractouris, or opyn bacbyteris. **1474** CAXTON *Chesse* II. v. D viij b, They ben..right mordent and bytyng detractours. **1537** *Inst. Chr. Man* in *Formul. Faith* M iv, The detractour is not glad to tell, but to hym, that is glad to here. **1549** *Compl. Scot.* Prol. 9 To confound ignorant detrakkers. **1563-87** FOXE *A. & M.* (1596) 108/1 A malicious detractor of Gregorie. **1598** BARCKLEY *Felic. Man* IV. (1603) 287 Instead of favourers he shall have detracters. **1633** J. DONE *Hist. Septuagint* 147 You will not suffer your selfe to be perswaded by the reports of detractors. **1720** WELTON *Suffer. Son of God* II. xxi. 577 That which a Friend would excuse..or Wink at..the Detractor publishes without sparing or Reserve. **1755** JOHNSON, *Detracter*. **1858** DORAN *Crt. Fools* 51 Every fashion has its detractors. **1860** PUSEY *Min. Proph.* 281 The detractor preys on his brother's flesh.

†**b.** Const. *from. Obs.* (Cf. DETRACT *v.* 3 c.)

1599 MARSTON *Sco. Villanie* iv. 151 Vaine enuious detractor from the good. *a* **1610** HEALEY *Epictetus* (1636) Life, Lucian..a perpetual detractor from all the Philosophers. **1660** R. COKE *Power & Subj.* 141 If Sabinianus were so malitious a detractor from the works of St. Gregory. **1829** LANDOR *Wks.* (1868) I. 160/2 It exhibits him as a detractor from Shakspeare.

‖**2.** *Anat.* A DEPRESSOR muscle. [prop. mod.L.] ? *Obs.*

1811 HOOPER *Med. Dict.* s.v. **1823** CRABBE *Technol. Dict.*, *Detractor*..a muscle whose office it is to draw down the part to which it is attached. **1883** *Syd. Soc. Lex.*, *Detractor*..old name for a muscle whose office is to draw the part to which it is attached away from some other part.

detractory (dɪˈtræktərɪ), *a.* [ad. L. *dētractōri-us* disparaging, slanderous, f. *dētractor*: see prec. and -ORY. Cf. OF. *detractoire* 15th c. in Godef.] Tending to detract; depreciatory, disparaging, defamatory; = DETRACTIVE 1.

1585 PARSONS *Chr. Exerc.* II. i. 157 An excuse most dishonourable and detractorie to the force of Christe hys grace. **1646** SIR T. BROWNE *Pseud. Ep.* I. v. 17 This is not only derogatory unto the wisdome of God..but also detractory unto the intellect. **1712** SWIFT *Art Political Lying*, The detractory, or defamatory, is a lie which takes from a great man the reputation that justly belongs to him. **1805** *Miniature* No. 26 ¶3 Others..have divided them [lies] into the Additory, Detractory, and Translatory.

b. Const. *from*: cf. DETRACT *v.* 2, 3 c, DETRACTIVE 2.

1648 BOYLE *Seraph. Love* xx. (1700) 126, I use the expressions I find less detractory from a Theme, as much above our Praises, as the Heav'n..is above our Heads.

detractress (dɪˈtræktrɪs). [f. DETRACTOR: see -ESS.] A female detractor.

1716 ADDISON *Freeholder* No. 23 The said detractress shall be..ordered to the lowest place of the room. **1788** PASQUIN *Childr. Thespis* II. (1792) 141 With a terrific tongue to assist a detractress.

†**deˈtrain**, *v.*[1] *Obs.* In 6 detrayne. [Cf. OF. *detrainer* to drag away, draw.] *trans.* To draw.

1587 M. GROVE *Pelops & Hipp.* (1878) 112 If that thou list ..with pensell to detrayne A picture that all other shews of pictures aye should stayne.

detrain (dɪˈtreɪn), *v.*[2] [f. DE- II. 2 b + TRAIN *sb.*, after *debark*, etc.]

1. *trans.* To discharge from a railway train: the converse of *entrain*. (Orig. a military term.)

1881 *Globe* 9 July 5 The corps travelling by the Great Northern and Great Eastern railways..are 'detrained' at Ascot. **1882** *Times* 20 Nov. 7 The horses were rapidly and safely detrained. **1892** *Whitby Gaz.* 26 Aug. 4 A grand total of 4794 persons were detrained at the Town Station.

2. *intr.* To alight from a railway train.

1881 *Graphic* 3 Sept. 1 The Regiment detraining. **1882** *W. Chester* (Pa.) *Republican* V. No. 142 The English are using a new word. Soldiers going out of railway cars 'detrain'. **1888** *Times* 31 Mar., These Easter manœuvres give great practice to the Volunteers in entraining and detraining. **1890** *Daily Tel.* 18 July, The train..was blocked [by a flood] and the passengers had to detrain.

Hence **deˈtraining** *vbl. sb.* (also *attrib.*).

1885 A. FORBES in *19th Cent.* XVII. 635 Their trained labourers are deftly building detraining platforms. **1887** *Times* 8 Apr. 4/3 Strict silence is to be maintained during entraining and detraining.

detrainment (dɪˈtreɪnmənt). [f. DETRAIN *v.*[2] + -MENT.] The action of discharging (persons, esp. troops) from a train, or of alighting from a train.

1899 *Westm. Gaz.* 9 Dec. 6/1 Three trains of mounted troops have been detrained at Arundel,..being covered in their detrainment by the New Zealand Mounted Infantry. **1916** LD. E. HAMILTON *First 7 Div.* 142 On October 11th the detrainment of the 2nd A.C. was completed. **1923** W. S. CHURCHILL *World Crisis, 1911-1914* I. xvi. 363 His detrainments at St. Omer, etc., were not completed till the 19th. **1928** *Observer* 18 Mar. 13/1 All detrainments of the assault divisions were made well back on a wide front. **1963** *Times* 24 May p. vii/4 London Transport has done everything it can to..explain why these detrainments are occasionally necessary.

‖**détraqué** (detrake), *sb.* and *a.* Also fem. détraquée. [Fr., pa. pple. of *détraquer* to put out of order, derange.] **A.** *sb.* A deranged person; a psychopath.

1902 W. JAMES *Var. Relig. Exper.* i. 7 From the point of view of his nervous constitution, [George] Fox was a psychopath or *détraqué* of the deepest dye. **1936** D. BARNES *Nightwood* iii. 80 Those who love a city..become the shame of that city, the *détraqués*, the paupers. **1969** *Daily Tel.* (Colour Suppl.) 25 Apr. 58/4 The *detraquées*—or potential nymphomaniacs—with their desires inflamed by concealment and repression.

B. *adj.* Deranged; crazy; psychopathic.

1925 A. HUXLEY *Those Barren Leaves* IV. v. 307 German romanticism, a little détraqué, turns..into expressionismus. **1930** *Times Lit. Suppl.* 13 Mar. 209/2 Here too are Augusta Leigh, refined, plaintive and *détraquée*, [etc.]. **1958** A. WILSON *Middle Age of Mrs Eliot* II. 255 She may be *détraquée*, as they say, but she's strictly U.

†**deˈtray**, *v. Obs.* [ad. OF. *detrai-re* (*detrayant*) = Pr. *detraire*, Pg. *detrahir*, It. *detrarre*:—L. *dētrahĕre* to draw off or away, DETRACT *v.*]

1. *trans.* To take away, subtract, remove; = DETRACT *v.* 1, 2.

1509 HAWES *Past. Pleas.* 56 The walles..dyd..expres, With golde depaynted, every perfyte nombre, To adde, detraye, and to devyde asonder. *Ibid.* XXX. xx, That she your sorow may detray or slake. *c* **1520** WOLSEY in Burnet *Hist. Ref.* II. 90, Ye be put at liberty to add, detray..chuse or mend, as ye shall think good.

2. To disparage, calumniate; = DETRACT *v.* 3.

c **1475** *Babees Bk.* 205 (1868) 8 Prayyng..Of this labour that no wihte me detray.

3. To withdraw; = DETRACT *v.* 4.

1517 H. WATSON *Shyppe of Fooles* A ij, And you be of the nombre of the fooles moundaynes that ye may lerne somwhat for to detraye you out of the shyp stultyfere.

†**deˈtrect**, *v. Obs.* [ad. L. *dētrectā-re* (also *-tractāre*) to decline, refuse, also to detract from, depreciate, freq. of *dētrahĕre*: see DETRACT *v.*]

1. *trans.* To draw back from, decline, refuse; = DETRACT *v.* 7. (With *simple obj.* or *inf.*)

1542 HENRY VIII *Declar. Scots* D ij b, They detrected the doing of theyr duetie. **1543** BECON *Policy of War* Early Wks. (1843) 235 Whosoever detrecteth and refuseth to do for his country whatsoever lieth in his power. *a* **1619** FOTHERBY *Atheom.* II. i. §8 (1622) 194 Hee detrected his going into Egypt, vpon a pretence, that he was not eloquent. **1629** H. BURTON *Babel no Bethel* 75 We detrect not to hold communion with her. **1661** G. RUST *Origen* in *Phenix* (1721) I. 85 A Testimony of that great Power your Commands have over me, which you see I have not detrected.

absol. **1630** B. JONSON *New Inn* II. vi, Doe not detract: you know th' authority Is mine.

2. To disparage, depreciate, speak evil of, blame; = DETRACT *v.* 3.

1563 WINȜET *Four Scoir Thre Quest.* §64 Wks. 1888 I. 116 Quhy detrect ȝe and rebukis ws Catholikis for the obseruatioun thairof.

detrectation (diːtrɛkˈteɪʃən). *rare.* [ad. L. *dētrectātiōn-em*, n. of action from *dētrectāre*: see prec.] A drawing back, refusal, declinature.

1623 COCKERAM, *Detrectation*, a refusing to doe a thing. *a* **1647** BP. HALL *Rem. Wks.* (1660) II. 308 The more hateful is the detrectation of our observance. **1789** BENTHAM *Princ. Legisl.* xvi. §27 (1879) 237 If he was [in possession], it may be termed *wrongful abdication* of trust; if not, *wrongful detrectation* or *non-assumption*.

†**deˈtrench**, *v. Obs.* [a. OF. *detrenchier, -cher* (also *-tranchier*) to cut, cut away, cut off, f. DE- I. 2 + *trencher, trancher* to cut.]

1. *trans.* To cut asunder or through.

1398 TREVISA *Barth. De P.R.* v. lx. (1495) 176 A synewe whyche is kytte asondre and detrenchyd growyth neuer after. **1491** CAXTON *Vitas Patr.* (W. de W. 1495) I. xxxvi. 39 a/1 Wyth his teeth he detrenched and bote his tonge. *c* **1500** *Melusine* xxii. 146 He detrenched & cutte the two maister vaynes of his nek.

2. To cut up, cut or hew in pieces; to inflict severe slaughter upon, 'cut to pieces' in battle.

1470-85 MALORY *Arthur* V. vi, Sir Launcelot with suche knyghtes as he hadde..slewe and detrenchid many of the Romayns. *c* **1477** CAXTON *Jason* 111 We shall rendre to the thy sone slayn and detrenched by pieces. *c* **1489** —— *Blanchardyn* xx. 63 He detrenched and kutte bothe horses and knyghtes, he cloue and rent helmes and sheldes.

3. To cut off, sever by cutting.

1553 T. WILSON *Rhet.* 38 b, If your hande were detrenched, or youre bodie maimed with some soubdaine stroake.

4. *fig.* To cut away, cut down, retrench, curtail.

1654 H. L'ESTRANGE *Chas. I.* (1655) 183 Had the king yeelded to a detrenching some luxuriances of his Prerogative. *Ibid.* 216 Many would detrench from them their secular power.

†**deˈtressed**, *ppl. a. Obs.* [f. F. *détressé*, OF. *destrecié* (13th c.), f. *de-, des-* (DE- I. 6) + *tressé* arranged in a tress or tresses, f. *tresse* TRESS.] Of hair: Out of 'tress' or plait; hanging loose.

1500-20 DUNBAR *Poems* lxxvii. 43 Syne come thair four and twentie madinis ȝing..With hair detressit, as threidis of gold did hing. **1603** HOLLAND *Plutarch's Rom. Quest.* (1892) 22 With their haires detressed and hanging downe loose.

detribalization (diːˌtraɪbəlaɪˈzeɪʃən). [f. next.] The process of becoming detribalized (see next).

1928 R. L. BUELL *Native Probl. Afr.* II. 1064/1 Detribalization, Belgian Congo. **1941** G. WILSON (*title*) Essay on the economics of detribalization in Northern Rhodesia (Rhodes-Livingstone Papers No. 5). **1959** *Times Lit. Suppl.* 6 Mar. 131/3 It is their [*sc.* West Indians'] detribalization and assimilation into White life which has paradoxically made them more self-aware..of their African-ness.

detribalize (diːˈtraɪbəlaɪz), *v.* [f. DE- + TRIBAL *a.* + -IZE.] *trans.* To render (a person) no longer a member of a tribe; to destroy the tribal habits of. So **deˈtribalized** *ppl. a.*

1920 *Contemp. Rev.* Sept. 397 Numbers of natives who, through living in close contact with the settlers have become quite detribalised. **1925** *Glasgow Herald* 25 Apr. 8 The African National Congress..is a very small body composed principally of detribalised natives. **1927** *Public Opinion* 272/1 White men have detribalised him. **1944** *Archit. Rev.* XCVI. 106/4 There is the Bantu tradition—the cultural unity of a tribal society which still persists or to which the detribalized African is still close, if only in time. **1955** *Times* 20 Aug. 7/4 It is not only the intelligentsia who are detribalized, but thousands of men, of all levels of education and intelligence, who have left their reserves to seek employment in Nairobi and elsewhere. **1969** *Guardian* 7 July 9/5 Tom Mboya chose..to detribalise himself.

detriment (ˈdɛtrɪmənt), *sb.* Also 5-6 **detryment**. [a. F. *détriment* (1236 in Hatzf.-Darm.), ad. L. *dētrīmentum* loss, damage, detriment, f. *dēterĕre* (*dētrīvi, dētrīt-*) to wear away, impair.]

1. Loss or damage done or caused to, or sustained by, any person or thing.

a **1440** *Found. St. Bartholomew's* 24 Dumme he was know ..berynge heuyly the detrimente of his tonge. **1529** *Act 21 Hen. VIII*, c. 16. §11 To the great Detriment of our own natural Subjects. **1533** ELYOT *Cast. Helthe* II. iii. (1539) 17 a, Nature shulde systeyne treble detriment. **1542** BOORDE *Dyetary* vii. (1870) 243 Yf he..lese hym selfe, and bryng hym selfe to a detryment. **1548** STAUNFORD *King's Prerog.* v. (1567) 25 b, Note that somtymes the king is to take a detriment by the liuere with yᵉ particion. **1616** R. C. *Times' Whistle* iii. 1032 Thinkst thou Peeters chaire..Can free thee from eternall detriment? **1663** BUTLER *Hud.* I. ii. 929 Sole author of all Detriment He and his Fiddle underwent. **1756-7** tr. *Keysler's Trav.* (1760) III. 419 Lest any detriment might accrue to the heirs. **1859** MILL *Liberty* iii. (1865) 40/1 The luxury of doing as they like without detriment to their estimation. **1875** LYELL *Princ. Geol.* II. III. xl. 393 [Seeds] may be carried without detriment through climates where the plants themselves would instantly perish.

b. That which causes or embodies a loss; something detrimental.

1504 ATKYNSON tr. *De Imitatione* I. iv, Those thynges that be the hurt of theyr owne soules & the detriment of theyr neyghboure. **1548** LD. SOMERSET *Epist. Scots* B vj b, This forein helpe is your confusion, that succour is your detriment. **1664** EVELYN *Kal. Hort.* (1729) 187 Some of them must of Necessity be neglected..which is the greatest Detriment to this Mystery. **1855** HT. MARTINEAU *Autobiog.* I. 400 Their advocacy of Woman's cause becomes mere detriment.

2. *Astrol.* The position or condition of a planet when in the sign opposite its house; a condition of weakness or distress.

1632 MASSINGER *City Madam* II. ii, Saturn out of all dignities, in his detriment and fall, combust. **1660** H. MORE *Myst. Godliness* VII. xv. 342 Saturn, Jupiter and Mars from their conjunction to their opposition with the Sun are Oriental, and gain two fortitudes; but from their Opposition to their Conjunction are Occidental, and incur two detriments.

3. *Her.* Eclipse (of sun or moon); also, the invisible phase of the moon at her change.

1610 GUILLIM *Heraldry* III. iii. (1660) 110 [see DECREMENT 1 c]. *Ibid.* 112 He beareth, Argent, a Moon in her detriment or Eclipse, Sable. **1688** R. HOLME *Armoury* II. 22/1 This is ..a Moon in her detriment or Eclipse. **1839** BAILEY *Festus* (1872) 121 Nor moon's dim detriment.

4. *pl.* The name of certain small charges made by colleges and similar societies upon their members.

The 'detriments' at Cambridge corresponded to the 'decrements' at Oxford, and appear to have been originally deductions from the stipends of foundation members on account of small extras for the table, etc., not included in their statutory or customary commons; the charge was afterwards extended to all members and students of the colleges. See Fowler *Hist. C.C.C.* (O.H.S.) 354.

1670 EACHARD *Cont. Clergy* 20 A solemn admission, and a formal paying of Colledge-Detriments. **1686** *Kenyon MSS.* in 14th *Rep. Hist. MSS. Comm.* App. iv. 185 His bill of June 24 [16]85 £11:09:11. His detriments, De. to June 24 [16]86 £02:17:03½. **1705** *Order-book of Christ's Coll. Camb.* (MS.) 6 Nov., The Schollars to be eased in their detriments from 1 June to 1 November. We'll think of a Method in the meantime.

5. *pl.* Ruins (of buildings).

1632 LITHGOW *Trav.* v. 200 The stony heapes of Jericho, the detriments of Thebes, the relicts of Tyrus. *Ibid.* IX. 402 We came..to the detriments of Messina.

'detriment, *v.* [f. prec. sb.] *trans.* To cause loss or damage to; to damage, injure, hurt.

1621 W. SCLATER *Tythes* (1623) 226 His losse of reserued time, already so detrimented in his hallowed substance. **1659** FULLER *App. Inj. Innoc.* I. 7 That others might be detrimented thereby. **1678** MARVELL *Growth Popery* 35 Upon the Ballance of the French Trade, this Nation was detrimented yearly 900000*l.* or a Million. **1743** *Lond. & Country Brew.* II. (ed. 2) 112 This ill forceable usage..clogs and detriments the fine penetrating Particles. **1841** D'ISRAELI *Amen. Lit.* (1867) 122 The disuse of the French would detriment their intercourse abroad.

detrimental (dɛtrɪ'mɛntəl), *a.* and *sb.* [f. DETRIMENT *sb.* + -AL[1].]

A. *adj.* Causing loss or damage; harmful, injurious, hurtful.

1656 BLOUNT *Glossogr.*, *Detrimental*, hurtful, dangerous, full of loss. *a* **1661** FULLER *Worthies* (1840) I. 281 A gift indeed..loaded with no detrimental conditions. **1719** W. WOOD *Surv. Trade* 84 That the Trade..is most detrimental to the Nation. **1801** *Med. Jrnl.* V. 1 Particularly detrimental to the constitution. **1872** YEATS *Growth Comm.* 271 Their admission was detrimental to French industry. **1875** JOWETT *Plato* (ed. 2) IV. 53 Paradoxes..which [are]..detrimental to the true course of thought.

B. *sb.* A person or thing that is prejudicial; in *Society slang*, a younger brother of the heir of an estate; an ineligible suitor.

1831 *Westm. Rev.* XIV. 424 The eldest son is pursued by ..damsels, while the younger are termed 'detrimentals'.. and avoided by 'mothers and daughters' as more dangerous company than the plague. **1832** MARRYAT *N. Forster* xxv, These *detrimentals* (as they have named themselves) may be provided for. **1854** LADY LYTTON *Behind the Scenes* I. II. iii. 188 There were also plenty of detrimentals, such as younger brothers, unpaid red tapeists, heiress-seekers, and political connection-hunters. **1870** C. F. GORDON-CUMMING in *Gd. Words* 137/1 The sisters of the wife being considered detrimentals, are placed in Buddhist convents. **1886** *Househ. Words* 13 Mar. 400 (Farmer) A detrimental, in genteel slang, is a lover, who, owing to his poverty is ineligible as a husband; or one who professes to pay attentions to a lady without serious intention of marriage, and thereby discourages the intentions of others. **1893** MRS. C. PRAED *Outlaw & Lawmaker* II. 80 Mrs. Valliant..thought that the detrimentals kept off desirable suitors.

Hence **detrimen'tality, detri'mentalness.**

1727 BAILEY vol. II, *Detrimentalness*, prejudicialness. **1873** *Daily News* 5 Aug., When you are hinting to your fair daughter the detrimentality of Charlie Fraser..who has his subaltern's pay and about 50*l.* a year thrown in.

detrimentally (dɛtrɪ'mɛntəlɪ), *adv.* [f. prec. + -LY[2].] In a manner causing detriment or harm; hurtfully.

1879 H. SPENCER *Data of Ethics* iv. §22. 60 The loss of character detrimentally affects his business. **1886** *Law Times' Rep.* LIII. 674/1 The exercise of the franchise by its servants cannot prejudicially or detrimentally affect the Crown.

detri'mentary, *a. rare.* [f. DETRIMENT *sb.* + -ARY. Cf. ELEMENTARY.] = DETRIMENTAL *a.*

1841 *Fraser's Mag.* XXV. 27 An internal commotion.. detrimentary to the high trust he held.

†detri'mentous, *a. Obs.* [f. as prec. + -OUS.] = DETRIMENTAL *a.*

1648 J. GOODWIN *Right & Might* 24 It..would be detrimentous and destructive to it. *Ibid.* 40 Counsels.. detrimentous and destructive to the generall..interest.

detrital (dɪ'traɪtəl), *a. Physiogr.* [f. DETRITUS + -AL[1].] Of or pertaining to detritus; consisting of particles worn away from some solid body.

1832 DE LA BECHE *Geol. Man.* (ed. 2) 249 The detrital deposits of the country. **1853** KANE *Grinnell Exp.* xlviii. (1856) 455 The valleys were studded with..rocks, and a detrital paste resembling till. **1869** PHILLIPS *Vesuv.* vii. 173 Where atmospheric vicissitudes have produced detrital slopes. **1878** HUXLEY *Physiogr.* 132 The detrital matter which is worn away from the land and carried along by rivers.

†de'trite, *ppl. a. Obs.*[−0] [ad. L. *dētrītus*, pa. pple. of *dēterĕre* to wear away.] Worn down, worn away.

1656 BLOUNT *Glossogr.*, *Detrite*, worn out, bruised, or consumed.

detrited (dɪ'traɪtɪd), *ppl. a.* [as prec. + -ED.]

1. Worn down.

1697 EVELYN *Numism.* iv. 10 Some of our worn-out and detrited Harry Groats. **1887** *N. & Q.* 7th Ser. 3 Sept. 194/2 A halfpenny detrited.

2. *Geol.* Disintegrated; formed as detritus.

1853 KANE *Grinnell Exp.* xlviii. (1856) 448 A long earthen stain, garnished probably with detrited rubbish, extended down like the lines of a moraine. **1856** —— *Arct. Expl.* II. xv. 157 Impregnated throughout with detrited matter.

de'tritic, *a. rare.* [f. DETRIT-US + -IC.] = DETRITAL.

1843 PORTLOCK *Geol.* 514 The stream..runs through a deep detritic ravine.

detrition (dɪ'trɪʃən). [n. of action f. L. *dēterĕre*, ppl. stem *dētrīt-*, to wear away, rub away. Cf. mod.F. *détrition* (in Cuvier).] The action of wearing away by rubbing.

1674 PETTY *Disc. Dupl. Proportion* 125 Gross tangible Bodies being very mutable by the various Additions and Detritions that befal them. **1741** MONRO *Anat. Bones* (ed. 3) 55 The Uses of Cartilages..are, to allow..Bones..to slide easily without Detrition. **1890** *Nature* 27 Nov. 90 Detrition has made it as smooth as the shingle pebbles on our shores. **1893** *Dublin Rev.* July 733 What remains after centuries of detrition and denudation.

detritus (dɪ'traɪtəs). *Physiogr.* [a. L. *dētrītus* (*u*-stem) rubbing away.

The proper meaning of the L. word appears in sense 1. The etymologically improper sense 2 may have been taken from French, in which *détritus* is cited of date 1780 by Hatz.-Darm. Earlier in the century, according to the *Dict. de Trévoux*, the more correct *détritum* was used in F.]

†1. Wearing away or down by detrition, disintegration, decomposition. *Obs.*

1795 HUTTON *Theory of Earth* (1797) I. 115 Such materials as might come from the *detritus* of granite. *Ibid.* 206, I have nowhere said that *all* the soil of this earth is made from the decomposition or detritus of these stony substances. **1802** PLAYFAIR *Illustr. Hutton. Th.* Wks. 1822 I. 63 The effects of waste and *detritus*. *Ibid.* 113 Proofs of a *detritus* which nothing can resist. *Ibid.* 123 The waste and *detritus* to which all things are subject.

2. Matter produced by the detrition or wearing away of exposed surfaces, especially the gravel, sand, clay, or other material eroded and washed away by aqueous agency; a mass or formation of this nature.

1802 PLAYFAIR *Illustr. Hutton. Th.* Wks. 1822 I. 409 The quantity of detritus brought down by the rivers. *Ibid.* 425 The distance to which the *detritus* from the land is confessedly carried. **1802** —— in *Edin. Rev.* I. 207 When the detritus of the land is delivered by the rivers into the sea. **1823** W. BUCKLAND *Reliq. Diluv.* 26 Deposits of diluvial detritus, like the surface gravel beds of England. **1832** DE LA BECHE *Geol. Man.* (ed. 2) 210 The whole is evidently a detritus of the Alpine rocks, and in it organic remains are by no means common. **1851** MAYNE REID *Scalp Hunt.* xli, We entered the cañon, and galloped over the detritus. **1862** DANA *Man. Geol.* 643 The fine earthy material deposited by streams or their sediment, is called *silt* or *detritus*. **1876** PAGE *Adv. Text-bk. Geol.* xix. 389 That broad valley..covered to an immense depth with an angular detritus.

3. *transf.* and *fig.* Waste or disintegrated material of any kind; debris.

1834 J. FORBES *Laennec's Dis. Chest* (ed. 4) 189 The walls of this abscess had..no surface, the pus being observed gradually to pass into a purulent detritus, and this into a firmer tissue. **1849** H. ROGERS *Ess.* II. vi. 306 The loose detritus of thought, washed down to us through long ages. **1851** SIR F. PALGRAVE *Norm. & Eng.* I. 701 The detritus of languages covering the Northern Gauls. **1876** tr. *Wagner's Gen. Pathol.* 192 The red blood-corpuscles and fibrinous detritus..are reabsorbed.

b. An accumulation of debris of any sort.

1851 LAYARD *Pop. Acc. Discov. Nineveh* vii. 134 We found ourselves at the foot of an almost perpendicular detritus of loose stones. **1866** R. CHAMBERS *Ess.* Ser. I. 185 There is a detritus of ruin in every corner, composed of broken toys, sofa-pillows, foot-stools.

de trop: see DE II.

detrude (dɪ'tru:d), *v.* [ad. L. *dētrūdĕre* to thrust away or down, f. DE- I. 1, 2 + *trūdĕre* to thrust.]

1. *trans.* To thrust, push, or force down. (*lit.* and *fig.*)

1548 HALL *Chron., Rich. III*, an. 3 (R.) And theim to cast and detrude sodaynly into continual captiuitie and bondage. **1638** SIR T. HERBERT *Trav.* (ed. 2) 216 His wife Semiramys detruded him into prison. **1644** H. PARKER *Jus Pop.* 51 This want detrudes them into a condition below beasts. **1728-46** THOMSON *Spring* 567 The torpid sap, detruded to the root By wintry winds. **1885** W. ROBERTS *Treat. Urinary Dis.* III. xiv. (ed. 4) 673 The right kidney..could be detruded downwards.

2. To thrust out or away; to expel or repel forcibly. (*lit.* and *fig.*)

1555 ABP. PARKER *Ps.* xxxviii. 109 Detrude me not. *a* **1575** *Diurn. Occurrents* (1833) 152 [They] detrudit the ministerie of Goddis word. **1627-77** FELTHAM *Resolves* II. lvi. 274 To be detruded Heaven for his meerly pride and malice. **1664** POWER *Exp. Philos.* II. 138 The included Ayr ..striving to dilate itself, detrudes the Quicksilver. **1751** HARRIS *Hermes* II. iii. (1786) 266 Not a word..is detruded from its proper place. **1847** TODD *Cycl. Anat.* IV. 83/2 Tartar..sometimes detrudes this [tooth] from its socket.

detruncate (dɪ'trʌŋkeɪt), *v.* [f. ppl. stem of L. *dētruncāre* to lop off, f. DE- I. 2 + *truncāre* to cut off, maim.] *trans.* To shorten by lopping off a portion (*lit.* and *fig.*); to cut short, 'cut down'. Hence **de'truncated** *ppl. a.* = TRUNCATED.

1623 COCKERAM, *Detruncate*, to cut or lop boughs. **1727** BAILEY vol. II, *Detruncated*, cut or chopped off; beheaded. **1846** LANDOR *Wks.* (1868) I. 537/2 Which..would detruncate our rank expenditure. **1877** BURNETT *Ear* 46 In the wide end of a detruncated cone. **1885** H. CONWAY *Family Affair* vi, He had not yet detruncated a [china] Chelsea figure.

detruncation (di:trʌŋ'keɪʃən). [ad. L. *dētruncātiōn-em* a lopping off, n. of action f. *dētruncāre*: see prec. Cf. mod.F. *détroncation.*] The action of cutting off or cutting short; the fact or condition of being cut short. (*lit.* and *fig.*)

1623 COCKERAM, *Detruncation*, a lopping or cutting. **1651** BIGGS *New Disp.* ¶287 Detruncation or diminution of their strength. **1751** JOHNSON *Rambler* No. 88 ¶11 This detruncation of our syllables. **1845** *Blackw. Mag.* LVII. 523 Not a perilous gash, but a detruncation fatal to the living frame. **1877** BURNETT *Ear* 43 Two detruncated cones placed together at their points of detruncation.

b. *Obstetric Surg.* (See quot.)

1847 CRAIG, *Detruncation*, The separation of the trunk of the fœtus from the head, the latter remaining *in utero*. **1883** in *Syd. Soc. Lex.*

†de'trunk, *v. Obs.* [ad. L. *dētruncāre* to lop off; after TRUNK.] *trans.* To cut off, lop off.

1566 DRANT *Horace' Sat.* iii. G vj b, When she of dolefull chylde The head detruncte dyd beare about. **1654** H. L'ESTRANGE *Chas. I* (1655) 80 This Petition they thought would detrunck too much and some thought strike at the very root of that Prerogative.

†de'truse, *v. Sc. Obs.* [f. L. *dētrūs-* ppl. stem of *dētrūdĕre.*] By-form of DETRUDE.

1571 *Sempill Ballates* (1872) 126 Gif ye neglect, than God ..Will from yat rowme thoill you to be detrusit.

detrusion (dɪ'tru:ʒən). [ad. late L. *dētrūsiōn-em*, n. of action f. *dētrūdĕre*, ppl. stem *dētrūs-*, to thrust down or away.] The action of thrusting down or away (*lit.* and *fig.*); cf. DETRUDE.

force of detrusion in *Mech.* = downward thrust.

1620 BP. HALL *Hon. Mar. Clergie* III. §6 Insolent detrusion of imperiall authority. **1635** SWAN *Spec. M.* v. §2 (1643) 180 By..violent detrusion from the cloud wherein it was enclosed. **1707** NORRIS *Humility* vii. 306 A detrusion into the bottomless pit. **1855** MILMAN *Lat. Chr.* (1864) IX. XIV. i. 51 The detrusion from its autocratic..throne.

detrusor (dɪ'tru:sə(r)). Also 6 *Sc.* **-ar.** [agent-noun from L. *dētrūdĕre, dētrūs-* to DETRUDE.]

†1. One who thrusts away or rejects. *Obs.*

1571 *Sempill Ballates* (1872) 121 Detrusaris, refuisaris Of hir authoritie.

2. *Anat.* [mod.L.; in full *detrusor urinæ.*] Name for the muscular coat of the bladder, by the contraction of which the urine is expelled.

[**1706** in PHILLIPS (ed. Kersey), *Detrusor Urinæ.*] **1766** PARSONS in *Phil. Trans.* LVI. 215 The detrusor muscle of the..urinary bladder. **1876** GROSS *Dis. Bladder* 55 The internal fibres of the detrusor muscle.

†detruss (dɪ'trʌs), *v. Obs.* Also 5 **destruss.** [a. OF. *destrousser, detroucer*, mod.F. *détr-*, to despoil one of his *trousses*, i.e. baggage, to rob, pillage, f. *dé-, des-*, L. *dis-* + *trousse* bundle, pl. baggage.] *trans.* To spoil, plunder (of baggage).

1475 *Bk. Noblesse* 65 Wyth grete aventur he scapyth..but he levyth hys felyshyp destrussed. **1598** BARRET *Theor. Warres* IV. i. 100 That the enemy detrusse him not thereof [munition]. *Ibid.* v. ii. 142 To detrusse the enemies conuoy.

dette, detter, -our, etc., obs. ff. DEBT, DEBTOR.

Dettol ('dɛtɒl, -əl). Also **dettol.** [Invented name.] A proprietary name for germicidal liquids and lotions based on chloroxylenol and used esp. as disinfectants for the skin and surgical instruments; *spec.* a brown liquid household disinfectant.

1931 *Trade Marks Jrnl.* 25 Feb. 280/2 *Dettol*... Chemical substances used for agricultural, horticultural, veterinary and sanitary purposes. Reckitt & Sons, Limited. **1938** 'J. BELL' *Port of London Murders* x. 176 'All doctors have lysol.' 'Mine doesn't,..he has Dettol. He says lysol's out of date. It doesn't smell so bad as lysol - Dettol, I mean... And it goes a thick white with water.' **1959** H. PINTER *Birthday Party* I. 12, I scrubbed the place out with Dettol. **1960** G. BUTLER *Death lives Next Door* vii. 151 Another smell, something faintly medicinal and disinfectant, as if the lady had been having a bath in dettol. **1977** *Martindale's Extra Pharmacopoeia* (ed. 27) 513/2 Skin sensitivity to Dettol.

detton, obs. var. of DETENT *sb.*

†'detty, *a. Obs.* [a. OF. *deté, detté*, f. *dete*: L. type **dēbitātus*, f. *dēbita* debt.]

1. Owed, due.

1387 TREVISA *Higden* (Rolls) V. 7 To ȝelde nouȝt what is detty [*quod debetur*]. *Ibid.* VI. 225 þe detty travaylle of service and of psalmes [*debitum psalmodiæ pensum.*] **1483** CAXTON *Gold. Leg.* 392 b/2 Detty trauayle of seruise.

2. Indebted.

1398 TREVISA *Barth. De P.R.* XV. lvii. (1495) 509 She shewyth herselfe detty to wise men and vnwise.

†de'tumefy, *v. Obs.* [DE- II. 1.] *intr.* To lose swollen condition, subside from being swollen.

1684 tr. *Bonet's Merc. Compit.* XIV. 485 If it be fomented with very cold Water, it will detumefie.

detumescence (di:tju:ˈmɛsəns). [f. L. *dētumēscĕre* to cease or subside from swelling (f. DE- I. 6 + *tumēscĕre* to begin to swell): see -ENCE. So in mod.F. (1792 in Hatzf.-Darm.)] Subsidence from swelling, or (*fig.*) from tumult.
1678 CUDWORTH *Intell. Syst.* 581 The Wider the Circulating Wave grows, still hath it the more Subsidence and Detumescence. **1704** W. COWPER in *Phil. Trans.* XXV. 1584 Unfitness for its retraction till there is a detumescence of its Glans. **1883** FARRAR & POOLE *Gen. Aims Teacher* 10 The School was in the detumescence of a most ruinous rebellion. **1883** *Syd. Soc. Lex.*, *Detumescence*, the subsidence of a swelling, or the absorption of a tumour.

deˈtune, *v.* [f. DE- II. 1 + TUNE *v.*] *trans.* **a.** To alter or adjust (an oscillatory system, as a resonant circuit or a microwave cavity) so that its resonant frequency no longer coincides with the frequency of some other oscillation with which it interacts. **b.** (See quot. 1963[1].) Hence **deˈtuned** *ppl. a.*; **deˈtuning** *vbl. sb.*
1924 S. R. ROGET *Dict. Electr. Terms* 60/2 *Detuning* (or Mistuning), the alteration of the period of oscillation of a circuit from that of the waves being dealt with. **1958** *Oxf. Mail* 23 Aug. 3/6 A new Hillman Husky powered by a detuned version of the overhead valve Minx engine. **1962** SIMPSON & RICHARDS *Junction Transistors* xiv. 358 Detuning also occurs in the external-gain control method described below. **1963** R. F. WEBB *Motorists' Dict.* 75 *Detune*, to deliberately tamper with an engine to reduce its performance or efficiency... A high-powered racing engine that has been slightly 'detuned' will stand up to normal wear and tear better than a fully tuned engine. Detuning consists normally of fitting lower compression pistons, etc. **1963** G. TROUP *Masers & Lasers* (ed. 2) vi. 105 Detuning the cavity centre pulls the oscillation frequency away from the molecular frequency. **1970** *Daily Tel.* 17 June 13/5 The engine is a detuned version of Rover's aluminium, 3½ litre V8.

detunow, -nue, obs. ff. DETINUE.

detur (ˈdi:tə(r)). [L. *dētur* let there be given (*dare* to give).] A prize of books given annually at Harvard College, U.S., to meritorious students: so called from the first word of the accompanying Latin inscription.
(The prizes are provided from the bequest of the Hon. Edward Hopkins who died in 1657.)
1836 LOWELL *Lett.* (1894) I. 10 The 'deturs' have been given out, and I have got Akenside's Poems. **1883** *Harvard Univ. Catal.* 110 A distribution of books called Deturs is made..near the beginning of the Academic Year, to meritorious students of one year's standing. Deturs are also given to..members of the Junior Class who..have made decided improvement in scholarship. Last year twenty-nine Deturs were given in the Sophomore Class and five in the Junior Class.

†**deˈturb**, *v. Obs.* [ad. L. *dēturb-āre* to thrust down, f. DE- I. 1 + *turbāre* to disturb, disorder.] *trans.* To drive or beat down; to thrust out.
1609 BP. W. BARLOW *Answ. Nameless Cath.* 243 That thou be..deturbed or tumbled out of the possession of thy Kingdome. **1620** VENNER *Via Recta* ii. 24 They deturbe the meats from the stomacke. **1636** BRATHWAIT *Lives Rom. Emp.* 303 Hee deturbed the aforesaid Pope from the seate. **1652** BP. HALL *Invisible World* IV. (L.) As soon may the walls of heaven be scaled and thy throne deturbed, as he can be foiled that is defenced within thy power. **1657** TOMLINSON *Renou's Disp.* 640 These Trochisks..potently deturb such humours.

†**deˈturbate**, *v. Obs. rare*[-1]. [f. L. *dēturbāt-* ppl. stem of *dēturbāre*: see prec.] = prec.
1563-87 FOXE *A. & M.* (1684) I. 662/1 This your rejecting, expelling..deturbating and thrusting out of Anatholius.
So †**deturˈbation** *Obs. rare*[-0].
1727 BAILEY vol. II, *Deturbation*, a casting or throwing down from on high; also a troubling or disturbing.

†**deturn** (dɪˈtɜ:n), *v. Obs.* [a. F. *détourne-r* (in OF. *desturner*, whence DISTURN), f. *dé-*, *des-*:—L. *dis-* (DIS- 1) + *tourner* to TURN.] *trans.* To turn away or aside; to divert, cause to deviate.
a **1450** *Knt. de la Tour* ci. 134 To deturne hym from eueri euelle dede. **1607** *Sc. Act Jas. VI* (1816) 388 (Jam.) To alter and deturne a litill the said way to the..better travelling for the lieges. **1644** DIGBY *Nat. Bodies* xi. (1658) 117 The force that can deturn a feather from its course downwards, is not able to deturn a stone. **1745** CHESTERF. *Lett.* I. cii, Let nothing deturn you from the thing you are about.

†**deˈturpate**, *ppl. a. Obs.* In 6 -at. [ad. L. *dēturpāt-us*, pa. pple. of *dēturpāre*.] Defiled.
c **1532** DEWES *Introd. Fr.* in *Palsgr.* 1046 The sayd glasse is nat deturpat nor made foule.

†**deturpate** (dɪˈtɜ:peɪt), *v. Obs.* [f. ppl. stem of L. *dēturpāre* to disfigure, f. DE- I. 3 + *turpāre* to make unsightly, pollute, deform, disgrace, f. *turpis* foul, disgraceful.]
1. *trans.* To defile, pollute; to debase.
1623 COCKERAM, *Deturpate*, to defile. **1628** PRYNNE *Lovelockes* 52 These Vnchristian cultures, which Defile, Pollute, Deturpate and deforme our Soules. **1647** JER. TAYLOR *Dissuas. Popery* i. (1686) 99 The heresies and impieties which had deturpated the face of the Church. **1657** TOMLINSON *Renou's Disp.*, Nigritude deturpates them [the Teeth].
2. *intr.* To become vile or base.
1691 WOOD *Ath. Oxon.* II. 484 He did nothing but deturpate, and so continued worse and worse till his death. **1833** *Fraser's Mag.* VII. 635 He afterwards deturpated, and became idle, dissipated, and reckless.

†**deturˈpation.** *Obs.* [n. of action f. prec.: see -ATION.] Defilement, debasement.
1490 CAXTON *Eneydos* xxviii. 110 Alle the deturpacyons and the hardenesse of olde age. **1660** JER. TAYLOR *Duct. Dubit.* II. iii. rule xiv. §29 The corrections and deturpations and mistakes of transcribers.

detynu(e, obs. form of DETINUE.

deu, obs. form of DEW, DUE.

deubash, obs. form of DUBASH.

†**ˈdeubert.** *Obs.* [? f. DEW.] One of the old appellations given to the hare.
a **1325** *Names of Hare* in *Rel. Ant.* I. 133 The scot, the deubert, the gras-bitere, the goibert.

deuce[1] (dju:s). Forms: 5-6 **deux**, 6 **dewse, deuis**, 6-7 **dewce, deuse**, 7 **dews, deus**, 7-9 **duce**, 6- **deuce**. [a. F. *deux*, OF. *deus* two. The *-ce* regularly represents earlier *-s*, as in *peace*, *pence*, *defence*, etc.]
1. The *two* at dice or cards. **a.** *Dice.* That side of the die that is marked with two pips or spots; a throw which turns up this side.
1519 HORMAN *Vulg.* 280 b, Deuce and synke were nat in the olde dyce. **1598** FLORIO, *Duini*, two dewses at dice. **1605** CAMDEN *Rem.* 148 Two in a garret casting dews at dice. *a* **1680** BUTLER *Rem.* (1759) I. 81 Or settling it in Trust to Uses, Out of his Pow'r, on Trays and Deuses. **1772** FOOTE *Nabob* II. Wks. 1799 II. 301 Tray, ace, or two deuces.
b. *Cards.* That card of any suit which is marked with two spots.
1680 COTTON *Gamester* in Singer *Hist. Cards* 343 They.. carry about..treys, deuces, aces, &c. in their pockets. **1775** GOUGH in *Archæologia* (1787) VIII. 154 On the duce of acorns besides the card-maker's arms is [etc.]. **1853** LYTTON *My Novel* I. xii, My partner has turned up a deuce—deuce of hearts.
2. *Tennis.* [= It. *a due*, F. *à deux de jeu*.] A term denoting that the two sides have each gained three points (called 40) in a game (or five games in a set), in which case *two* successive points (or games) must be gained in order to win the game (or set). (See ADVANTAGE *sb.* 2.) Also *attrib.* **deuce-game** (see quot. 1897); **deuce-set**, a set in which the sides are level, each having won five or more games.
1598 FLORIO, *Adua*..a dewce, at tennice play. **1816** *Encycl. Perth.* XXII. 221 Instead of calling it 40 at all, it is called *deuce*. **1878** JUL. MARSHALL *Annals of Tennis* 134 Scaino [in 1555] then tells his readers that [the scoring is] 'at two (*a due*)' as it is called when the game is reduced or 'set' to two strokes to be gained, in order to win it. The term..*a due* is still preserved in the French form *à deux*, corrupted in English into *deuce*. **1882** *Daily Tel.* 18 July 2 The game ran to 30 all, and then deuce was called twice. **1885** *Pall Mall G.* 12 May 11/1 The concluding game was so close that deuce and advantage were repeatedly called, and the set more than once hung on a single difficult stroke. **1886** *Cassell's Fam. Mag.* Oct. 704/2 It also scores back to deuce points and deuce games. **1897** *Encycl. Sport* I. 621/2 *Deuce-game*, the game won, which makes the score in games level when each side has won more than five. **1908** *Westm. Gaz.* 16 Nov. 14/1 Losing the first game after a deuce set. **1969** *New Yorker* 14 June 67/1 Games are five-all. It is a so-called deuce set.
†**3.** *Mus.* The interval of a second. *Obs. rare.*
1829 R. H. FROUDE *Rem.* (1838) I. 237, I also can acknowledge a discord in a deuce and a seventh.
4. *slang.* Twopence.
a **1700** B. E. *Dict. Cant. Crew*, *A Duce*, two Pence. **1851** MAYHEW *Lond. Labour* I. 256 Give him a 'deuce' and 'stall him off'.
5. *Comb.* **deuce-ace**, two and one (i.e. a throw that turns up deuce with one die and ace with the other); hence, a poor throw, bad luck, mean estate, the lower class (cf. Ger. *daus es*, s.v. *Daus* in Grimm); **deuce-point**, the second point from either end of the board at backgammon.
1481 CAXTON *Reynard* (Arb.) 47 He was a pylgrym of deux aas [Fl. *een pellegrym van doys aes*]. **1588** SHAKS. *L.L.L.* I. ii. 49 You know how much the groase summe of deus-ace amounts to..Which the base vulgar call three. **1596** GOSSON in Hazl. *E.P.P.* IV. 254 Deuse-ace fals still to be their chance. **1609** *Ev. Woman in Hum.* IV. i. in Bullen *O. Pl.* IV, Twere better, by thrice deuce-ace, in a weeke [etc.]. **1658** J. JONES *Ovid's Ibis* 75 Deuce Ace cannot pay scot and lot, and Sice Sink will not pay: Be it known to all, what payments fall must light on Cater Tray [i.e. the middle classes]. **1766** GOLDSM. *Vic. W.* ii, I threw deuce-ace five times running. **1778** C. JONES *Hoyle's Games Impr.* 179 Suppose, that 14 of his Men are placed upon his Adversary's Ace Point, and one Man upon his Adversary's Deuce Point. **1894** F. S. ELLIS *Reynard the Fox* 336 That which is likened to deuce ace Hath in esteem the lowest place.

deuce[2] (dju:s). *colloq.* or *slang.* Also 7 **dewce**, 7-8 **deuse**, 7-9 **duce**, 8 **dewse**, 9 *dial.* **doose**. [Prob. from LG. in 17th c.: cf. Ger. *daus*, LG. *duus*, used in precisely the same way, in the exclamatory *der daus! was der daus...!* LG. *de duus! wat de duus!*
The derivation of German *daus* is disputed: but there is reason to think that it is the same word as *das daus* = the DEUCE[1] at dice (where 'two' is the lowest and most unlucky throw), the gender being changed when the gambler's exclamation of vexation 'the deuce!' was metamorphosed into a personal expletive. A parallel development is known in Danish where the plural sb. *pokker* 'pocks, pox', has come to be felt as a singular, and to be taken for 'the devil', from its use in imprecations such as *Gid pokker havde det!* Would that a pox had that!, *Pokker staa i det!* A pox on that! *Hvad pokker er det?* What the pox (devil) is that? (See POX.) (On other conjectural identifications see Rev. A. L. Mayhew in *Academy* 30 Jan. 1892, p. 111.)]
a. Bad luck, plague, mischief; in imprecations and exclamations, as ***a deuce on him! a deuce of his cane!*** **b.** The personification or spirit of mischief, the devil. Originally, in exclamatory and interjectional phrases; often as a mere expression of impatience or emphasis: as, ***what the*** (†***what a***) ***deuce?***, so, ***who, how, where, when the deuce?*** (***the***) ***deuce take it!***, ***the deuce is in it!*** Later, in other phrases parallel to those under DEVIL: ***to play the deuce*** (***with***), ***the deuce and all***, ***the deuce to pay***, ***a deuce of a mess***, etc.
In the quotations under a (to which the earliest instances belong), 'plague' or 'mischief' is evidently the sense: cf. the parallel and earlier 'A mischief (a pox, or a plague) on him!' 'Mischief (or plague) take you!' 'What a mischief (pox, plague)!' This meaning is also possible in those under b[1]: cf. the parallel 'What the mischief (or the plague)!' But *mischief* was personified already before 1700, and 'the Mischief' was in the late 18th c. a frequent euphemism for 'the devil'; that *deuce* was already taken in this sense in 1708 is evident from Motteux's use of it as = F. *diantre*, in b[2]. In the other quotations in the same group, 'deuce' plainly takes the place of 'devil' in well-known phrases; but such clearly personified uses as 'the deuce knows', 'to go to the deuce', appear late.
a. **1651** RANDOLPH, etc. *Hey for Honesty* I. i, But a deuce on him, it does not seem so. **1677** OTWAY *Cheats of Scapin* III. i, A dewce on't. *a* **1679** LD. ORRERY *Guzman* II, Who, a duce, are those two fellows? **1708** MRS. CENTLIVRE *Busie Body* (1732) 41 A Duce of his Cane! **1719** D'URFEY *Pills* (1872) II. 66 A-duce take their chat! *a* **1721** PRIOR *Poems, Thief & Cordelier*, What a duce dost thou ayl? **1796** BURNS *Let. to Cunningham* 7 July, The deuce of the matter is this; when an excisemen is off duty, his salary is reduced.
b[1]. **1694** CONGREVE *Double Dealer* I. i, The deuse take me, if there were three good things said. **1726** SWIFT *To a Lady*, Duce is in you, Mr. Dean. **1757** SMOLLETT *Reprisal* I. viii, What the deuce are you afraid of? **1776** S. J. PRATT *Pupil of Pleasure* II. 34 How the duce came she to marry? **1826** DISRAELI *Viv. Grey* V. xii, What the deuce is the matter with the man? **1861** HUGHES *Tom Brown at Oxf.* iii. (1884) 28 How the deuce did you get by the lodge, Joe?
b[2]. **1708** MOTTEUX *Rabelais* V. xix, The Dewse take 'em [F. *Mais quoy diantre!*]; (they flatter the Devil here, and smoothifie his Name, quoth Panurge). **1762** STERNE *Tr. Shandy* V. xxviii, There has been..the deuce and all to do. **1763** COLMAN *Deuce is in Him* Prol., If our author don't produce Some character that plays the deuce; If there's no frolick, sense, or whim, Retort! and play the dev'l with him! **1793** COWPER *Let.* Wks. 1837 XV. 250 If the critics still grumble, I shall say the very deuce is in them. **1824** BYRON *Juan* XV. lvii, He had that kind of fame Which sometimes plays the deuce with womankind. **1830** LADY GRANVILLE *Lett.* 9 Nov. (1894) II. 65 An unpopular one..would have been the deuce to pay. **1840** THACKERAY *Catherine* ii, Love is a bodily infirmity..which breaks out the deuce knows how or why. **1848** DICKENS *Dombey* ii, The child is..Going to the Deuce. **1851** D. MITCHELL *Fresh Gleanings* 19 Tearing away at a deuce of a pace. *a* **1860** G. P. MORRIS *Poems* (ed. 15) 251 Here'll be the deuce to pay! **1861** DUTTON COOK *P. Foster's D.* iii. A gipsy, rollicking, deuce-may-care sort of bird. **1862** THACKERAY *Four Georges* iv. 196 To lead him yet farther on the road to the deuce.
c. As an expression of incredulous surprise; also, as an emphatic negative, as in (***the***) ***deuce a bit!***, etc. (Cf. *plague*, *sorrow*, *devil*, *fiend*.)
1710-11 SWIFT *Lett.* (1767) III. 89 We were to dine at Mr. Harley's alone, about some business of importance..but the deuce a bit, the company staid, and more came. **1712** —— *Jrnl. to Stella* 22 Mar., The deuce he is! married to that vengence! **1728** VANBR. & CIB. *Prov. Husb.* I. i. 26 *Man.* He has carried his Election..*L. Town.* The Duce! what! for—for—. **1774** FOOTE *Cozeners* II. Wks. 1799 II. 171 Me? ha, ha, ha! the deuce a bit. **1789** MRS. PIOZZI *Journ. France* II. 26 At Florence and Milan, the deuce a Neapolitan could he find. **1805** S. & HT. LEE *Canterb. T.* V. 56 The old lady glanced at her..but deuce a bit did she desire her to sit down. **1831** *Examiner* 354/1 'Lord Eldon was not one of those'..The deuce he's not!

deuced (dju:st, ˈdju:sɪd), *a. colloq.* or *slang.* Also 8 **duced**, 9 (*humorously*) **doosed**, **doosid**. [f. DEUCE[2] + -ED[2]; app. after ppl. adjs. like *confounded*, *cursed*, *damned*, etc.] Plaguy, confounded; 'devilish'; expressing impatient dislike, or as a mere emphatic expletive.
1782 MRS. E. BLOWER *G. Bateman* II. 215 Wife puts me into sitch a duced passion sometimes. *Ibid.* III. 21 What a duced pother thee art in, Captain! **1791** MAD. D'ARBLAY *Diary* 4 June, If it was not for that deuced tailor, I would not stir. **1819** BYRON *Juan* I. clxvii, When we call our old debts in At sixty years..And find a deuced balance with the devil. **1876** F. E. TROLLOPE *Charming Fellow* I. ii. 18 She's a deuced deal cleverer than lots of men. **1887** *Poor Nellie* 57 That's why I came off in such a deuced hurry.
b. Often adverbially: = next.
1779 MAD. D'ARBLAY *Diary* 20 Oct., A clever fellow..got a deuced good understanding. **1840** THACKERAY *Bedford-Row Consp.* i, She's a deuced fine woman! **1866** A. TROLLOPE *Claverings* xi, 'Upon my word she's a doosed good-looking little thing', said Archie. **1881** LADY HERBERT *Edith* 245 She's so deuced obstinate.

deucedly (ˈdju:sɪdlɪ), *adv.* [f. prec. + -LY[2].] In a deuced manner; plaguily, confoundedly; excessively.
1819 *The Provincials* I. 17 Deucedly lucky. **1844** THACKERAY *Little Travels* i, Why people..should get up so

deucedly early. **1884** E. L. BYNNER in *Harper's Mag.* Aug. 467/1 Bile does upset a man deucedly.

† **'deuding.** *Obs.* One of the appellations anciently given to the hare.

a **1325** *Names of Hare* in *Rel. Ant.* I. 133 On oreisoun In the worshipe of the hare.. The deudinge, the deu-hoppere.

deue, obs. form of DEAF (pl.), DEAVE.

deuedep, var. of DIVEDAP, *Obs.*

deuel, obs. form of DEVIL.

deuel, deul, -e, obs. var. (assimilated to later Fr.) of *dule*, DOLE, DOOL, grief, mourning.

deuers, obs. form of DIVERS, DIVERSE.

deuice, deuis(s, obs. ff. DEVICE, DEVISE.

deuin(e, obs. form of DIVINE.

deuis, obs. form of DEUCE[1].

† **deuit**, *pa. pple. Sc. Obs.* [f. *deu*, DUE + *-it*, -ED.] Owed, due.

1587 HOLINSHED *Chron.* II. Hist. Scot. 296/2 For deuit & postponit justice to our lieges.

deuitie, deulie, obs. forms of DUTY, DULY.

deurbanize (diː'ɜːbənaɪz), *v.* [f. DE- + URBANIZE *v.* 2.] *trans.* To deprive (a district) of its urban character. Also *fig.*

1924 *Public Opinion* 15 Feb. 154/3 Its work is to deurbanise the minds of British rulers. **1927** *Observer* 29 May 7 Can we de-urbanise England? Or will all our efforts to empty the towns merely result in urbanising the countryside?

deure, obs. form of DEAR *a.*[1], DEER.

† **deus.** *Obs.* Also 5 **dewes.** [OF. *deus*, nom. of *deu* God, in common use as an exclamation: cf. *Chanson de Roland* xxv, 'Dient Franceis: Deus! que pourrat-ce estre?' (Littré); *Horne* and *Rimenh.* 2848 'Ohi! deus'.]

The French interjectional *deus!*, *ohi! deus*, God!, ah God! occasionally retained in translation, or ascribed to foreigners, fiends, etc., but not apparently in native English use.

c **1300** *Havelok* 1930, and 2096 'Deus!' quoth ubbe, 'hwat may þis be!' *Ibid.* 1312, 1650, 2114. *c* **1330** R. BRUNNE *Chron.* (1810) 254 Philip seysed Burdews, þorgh Sir Edward scrite, þe toþer, as so say deus! ȝald þam also tite. *c* **1440** *York Myst.* i. 92 Owe! dewes! all goes downe!

‖ **deus absconditus** ('diːəs æb'skɒndɪtəs). [L., 'hidden god'; cf. *Isaiah* xlv. 15.] A god who is hidden from man. Also *fig.*

1932 *Character & Personality* Sept. 51 Where..in the annals of Victorianism is the sentimental God of the nineteenth century ever faced with a *deus absconditus* as in Luther's teaching? **1960** AUDEN *Homage to Clio* 21 Pray to a *Deus Absconditus*. **1965** S. MARCUS *Dickens: from Pickwick to Dombey* vi. 217 The novelist has become a *deus absconditus*, asserting his godhead by his apparent indifference to his creation.

† **deusan, deuzan.** *Obs.* Also **dewsant, dewzin, deux ans.** [for F. *deux ans* two years.] A kind of apple said to keep two years; = APPLE-JOHN.

1570 in Gutch *Coll. Cur.* II. 8 For xx Dewsants..viij*d.* For xij Pippines..xij*d.* **1609** N. F. *Fruiterers' Secr.* 24 Especially Pippins, John Apples, or as some call them Dewzins. **1620** VENNER *Via Recta* vii. 109 Such are our Queene-apples..and next our Rosiars, Pear-maines and Pippins, Deusans, &c. **1635** QUARLES *Embl.* v. ii, 'Tis not the lasting deuzan I require, Nor yet the red-cheek'd queening. **1741** *Compl. Fam. Piece* II. iii. 377 Apples [June], Oaken Pin, Deux Ans or John Apple.

deus(e), obs. forms of DEUCE.

‖ **deus ex machina** ('diːəs ɛks 'mækɪnɑː). Also (*nonce-wd.*) fem. **dea ex machina.** [mod.L., tr. Gr. θεὸς ἐκ μηχανῆς, lit. 'god from the *machina*' (the device by which gods were suspended above the stage in the Greek theatre): cf. MACHINE *sb.* 6.] A power, event, person, or thing that comes in the nick of time to solve a difficulty; providential interposition, esp. in a novel or play.

1697 J. SERGEANT *Solid Philos.* 136 Nor is it at all allowable in Philosophy, to bring in a *Deus è Machinâ* at every turn, when our selves are at a loss to give a Reason for our *Thesis*. **1840** BARHAM *Ingol. Leg.* 135 This was, however, no less a personage than the *Deus ex machinâ*,—the illustrious Aldrovando himself. **1857** TROLLOPE *Barchester T.* II. xv. 292 Doctor Gwynne was the *Deus ex machina* who was to come down upon the Barchester stage, and bring about deliverance from these terrible evils. **1873** HOTTEN *Slang Dict.* 223 *Mary Ann*, the title of the dea ex machinâ evolved from trades-unionism at Sheffield. **1889** A. E. HAIGH *Attic Theatre* iv. 190 The mêchanê was used under various circumstances; but the most ordinary occasion for its employment was to introduce the 'deus ex machina' at the end of a play, when affairs had reached such a complicated condition that only divine interference could put them right again. **1896** W. CALDWELL *Schopenhauer's System* ii. 62 If you assume in every brain a spirit like a sort of *deus ex machinâ*, you ought to concede a spirit to every stone. **1928** C. DAWSON *Age of Gods* p. xiv, The dominant fashion is to look to the racial factor as the *deus ex machina* of the human drama. **1937** M. SHARP *Nutmeg Tree* ix. 108 Her function at Les Sapins was that of a *dea ex machina*; and the make of her car would not bear examining. **1962** W. NOWOTTNY *Lang. Poets Use* vi. 145 Fruitful Ambiguity, that popular *deus ex machina* of the contemporary critical scene. **1970** T. HILTON *Pre-Raphaelites* v. 133 The accepted interpretation, that he [*sc.* Ruskin] descended to the Brotherhood like some *deus ex machina*, ignores the real similarity of artistic purpose that bound him to the group.

deusing: see DOUSING, divining.

deuteragonist (djuːtə'rægənɪst). [ad. Gr. δευτεραγωνιστής one who plays the second part in a drama, f. δεύτερο-ς DEUTERO- second + ἀγωνιστής combatant, actor.] The second actor or person in a drama: distinguished from the *protagonist*.

1855 LEWES *Goethe* I. III. viii. 290 In the first scene [of the *Prometheus*] the protagonist would take Power and the deuteragonist Vulcan. **1893** ZIMMERN *Home Life Anc. Greeks* xii. 422 The next [part] in importance—viz. the one which was brought into the closest connection with the chief person, fell to the deuteragonist.

† **'deuteral**, *a. Obs. rare.* [f. Gr. δεύτερ-ος second + -AL[1].] Of or pertaining to the second; second-class.

1656 BLOUNT *Glossogr.*, *Deuteral*, pertaining to a weak or second sort of Wine, or to the second of any kind. *Dr. Br.*

deuteranomalous (ˌdjuːtərə'nɒmələs), *a. Ophthalmology.* [f. DEUTERO- + ANOMALOUS *a.*] Of, pertaining to, or exhibiting partial deuteranopia.

1932 W. S. DUKE-ELDER *Textbk. Ophthalmology* I. xxv. 976 Holmgren (1880) reported 2 protanopes..and Reichert (1915) and v. Kries (1918) deuteranomalous cases. **1952** *Brit. Jrnl. Psychol.* Nov. 312 A study made upon..19 protanomalous and 32 deuteranomalous subjects.

deuteranope ('djuːtərənəʊp). *Ophthalmology.* [a. G. *deuteranope* (J. von Kries 1897, in *Zeitschr. f. Psychol. d. Sinnesorgane* XIII. 248), f. DEUTERO- + Gr. priv. ἀν- + ὤψ eye.] One who is green-blind. So **deutera'nopia**, green-blindness.

1901 BALDWIN *Dict. Philos.* I. 274 *Deuteranopia*,..the name proposed by v. Kries for what was formerly called green-blindness. **1902** *Ibid.* II. 787 The wave-length which corresponds to the colourless sensation, *W*, is different for the two sorts of colour-defectives, proteranopes and deuteranopes. **1937** *Nature* 10 July 49/1 A diagnosis can be made from the tables of dichromasy in general, and of protanopia, deuteranopia, and tritanopia in particular. **1962** H. C. WESTON *Sight, Light & Work* (ed. 2) i. 18 The green-blind are called 'deuteranopes'.

deuterated ('djuːtəreɪtɪd), *a.* [f. DEUTER(IUM + -ATE[2] + -ED[2].] Containing deuterium; having had an atom of ordinary hydrogen replaced by one of heavy hydrogen (deuterium). So **deute'ration**, the process of substituting a deuterium atom for an ordinary hydrogen atom in a molecule.

1947 *Nature* 11 Jan. 62/2 The Raman spectra of deuterated methyl halides. **1955** *Trans. Faraday Soc.* LI. 620 Data are given for all the partially deuterated species of methyl cyanide and methyl acetylene. **1956** *Nature* 31 Mar. 629/1 The effects of deuteration on biological activity. **1967** *New Scientist* 29 June 780/2 As such catalysts are normally used to promote reaction between hydrogen and organic molecules their efficiency in deuteration is not surprising. **1971** *Nature* 7 May 30/2 All the samples of lunar fines examined release CD_4 when treated with deuterated acids.

deuteric ('djuːtərɪk), *a. Petrol.* [f. Gr. δεύτερ-ος DEUTERO- + -IC.] Pertaining to or resulting from the changes that take place in igneous rock during the later stages of consolidation of the magma (see quots.).

1916 J. J. SEDERHOLM in *Bull. Comm. Géol. Finlande* IX. XLVIII. 142 It would be advisable to discriminate between.. metasomatic changes which belong to a later period of metamorphism, i.e. are secondary in the strictest sense of the word, and those which have taken place in direct continuation of the consolidation of the magma of the rock itself. I propose to call the latter deuteric, as distinct from secondary changes. **1929** *Econ. Geol.* XXIV. 101, I thus conclude that the term deuteric is established as covering those metasomatic changes in igneous rocks caused by the reaction between the minerals already formed and the emanations..which have been given off from the same magma from which the rock itself crystallized. **1946** *Nature* 10 Aug. 206/2 In the deuteric or late stage there was a development of concentrations of titaniferous magnetite, apatite and other accessory minerals. **1967** K. D. WATSON in P. J. Wyllie *Ultramafic & Related Rocks* IX. v. 319/2 Some of the calcite in the kimberlite at Bachelor Lake is probably deuteric.

deuterium (djuː'tɪərɪəm). *Chem.* [mod.L., f. Gr. δεύτερ-ος second + -IUM.] One of the isotopes of hydrogen, differing from the commonest isotope in having a neutron as well as a proton in the nucleus and present to about 1 part in 6000 in naturally occurring hydrogen (elemental and combined); also called *heavy hydrogen*. Symbols ^2H (also H^2), D.

1933 H. C. UREY et al. in *Jrnl. Chem. Physics* I. 513/1 We wish to propose that the names for the H^1 and H^2 isotopes be protium and deuterium. **1934** *Times Educ. Suppl.* 18 Aug. p. i/2 The newly discovered 'heavy water' or deuterium oxide in Antarctic snow. **1935** *Discovery* June 179/2 'Heavy water'..is rich in deuterium, the hydrogen isotope of mass 2. **1958** *Engineering* 31 Jan. 134/3 The deuterium or heavy-hydrogen content of seawater is calculated to be sufficient to sustain present energy consumption for a thousand million years.

'deutero-, before a vowel **deuter-**, a. Gr. δευτερο- combining form of δεύτερος second, as in δευτεραγωνιστής one who plays second, δευτερο-νόμιον second law. Hence in Eng. in DEUTERAGONIST, DEUTERONOMY, and several words of modern formation, as DEUTEROCANONICAL, etc. Also **'deuterocol** *nonce-wd.* [after *protocol*], a second dispatch. **'deuterocone**, the inner or lingual cusp of an upper premolar tooth of certain mammals. **ˌdeutero'conid**, the corresponding cusp of a lower premolar. **'deuterodome** (*Crystallogr.*), a secondary dome. **deutero'genic** *a.* [Gr. γένος race], of secondary origin: in *Geol.* applied to the rocks of secondary formation derived from the primary or protogenic rocks. **'deuterograph**, a duplicate written or printed passage. **Deutero-Isaiah**, a second or later Isaiah; a later writer to whom c. xl–lxvi of the book of Isaiah are by some critics attributed. **deute'romerite**, a deutomerite. **deutero'mesal** *a. Entom.* [Gr. μέσος middle], applied to certain cells in the wings of hymenopterous insects, now usually called the first and third discoidal and first apical cells. **Deutero-Nicene** *a.*, belonging to the second Nicene council. **Deutero-Pauline**, of or pertaining to a second or later Paul, or later writer assuming the character of St. Paul. **deute'rostoma** *Biol.* [Gr. στόμα mouth], a secondary blastopore; hence **deutero'stomatous** *a.*, characterized by having a secondary instead of a primary blastopore. **deuterosyste'matic** *a.*, belonging to a secondary system. **'deuterotheme** (see quot. 1897). **deute'rotoky** [Gr. τόκος bringing forth], that form of parthenogenesis in which the virgin female produces offspring of both sexes; amphitoky. **ˌdeutero'toxin** (see quots.). **ˌdeutero'zoic** (see quots.). **deutero'zooid** (*Biol.*), a secondary zooid, produced by gemmation from a zooid.

1858 HOGG *Life Shelley* I. 477 Diplomatic notes without stint; protocols, deuterocols, and chiliostocols. **1892** W. B. SCOTT in *Proc. Acad. Nat. Sci. Phil.* 412 As early as the Puerco, however, we find that p^4 in every known genus is complicated by the addition of a second cusp upon the inner or lingual side of the protocone, which may be called the deuterocone. **1922** W. K. GREGORY *Orig. & Evol. Human Dentition* II. i. 104 A similarly situated, but better developed, basal cingulum in later mammals may be traced from the premolars, where it gives rise to the so-called 'deuterocone' or internal spur, backward to the 'protocone' of the molars. **1968** R. ZANGERL tr. *Peyer's Compar. Odontology* 188 W. B. Scott thus proposed a special terminology for the description of the premolars, in which the cusps are simply numbered as protocone, deuterocone, tritocone, tetracone, and '-conid' respectively. **1892** W. B. SCOTT in *Proc. Acad. Nat. Sci. Phil.* 415 In the premolars, therefore, when a cusp occurs occupying the position taken by the metaconid in the molars, it cannot be regarded as homologous with that element, but rather with the deuterocone of the upper premolar and may consequently be called the deuteroconid. **1907** H. F. OSBORN *Evol. of Mammalian Molar Teeth* viii. 199 There appears a cuspule on the inner side of the crown of the protoconid... (This is the deuteroconid of Scott's terminology.) **1878** GURNEY *Crystallog.* 52 The latter [dome is] known as the deuterodome. **1894** R. B. GIRDLESTONE (*title*) Deuterographs. Duplicate Passages in the Old Testament. **1896** *Expositor* Jan. 36 We can explain..the repeated occurrence in the same book of deuterographs. **1844** MOSES STUART *O.T. Canon* IV. (1849) 102 Did we know that such a person lived and wrote, we might call him Deutero-Isaiah. **1891** DRIVER *Introd. Lit. O. Test.* (ed. 2) 210 There are features in which it is in advance not merely of Isaiah, but even of Deutero-Isaiah. **1888** Deuteromerite [see *protomerite* s.v. PROTO- 2 b]. **1859** *Lit. Churchman* 43/1 The Deutero-Nicene defence of images. **1885** tr. *Pfleiderer's Influence Paul Chr.* vi. 256 The authors of the Deutero-Pauline and the Ignatian Epistles. **1877** HUXLEY *Anat. Inv. Anim.* xii. 684 The resulting organism would be a deuterostomatous gastrula. **1897** W. G. SEARLE *Onomasticon Anglo-Saxonicum* p. xii, The Anglo-Saxon personal names may be divided into several classes. 1. The first and chief class consists of names that may be termed dithematic names, as they consist of two elements or themes, mostly monosyllabic, a first element or prototheme, and a second element or deuterotheme. **1937** H. G. H. HALVORSON in *Harvard Univ. Summary Theses 1937* (1938) 271 (*title*) A study of Old English dithematic personal names: deuterothemes. **1895** *Cambr. Nat. Hist.* V. 141 It is a curious fact that the result of parthenogenesis in some species is the production of only one sex, which in some Insects is female, in others male; the phenomenon in the former case is called by Taschenberg Thelyotoky, in the latter case Arrhenotoky; Deuterotoky being applied to the cases in which two sexes are produced. **1965** F. A. E. CREW *Sex-determination* (ed. 4) v. 76 Deuterotoky or amphitoky in which both impaternate males and females are produced. *Ibid.* 77 Deuterotoky is found in several species of moths. **1900** DORLAND *Med. Dict.* 200/1 *Deuterotoxin*, any one of the second of the four groups of diphtheria-toxins. **1904** Deuterotoxin [see *prototoxin* s.v. PROTO- 2 b]. **1898** J. E. MARR *Princ. Stratigr. Geol.* vi. 59 Another suggestion was to split the Palæozoic age into an earlier Proterozoic and later

Deuterozoic division. **1904** GOODCHILD & TWENEY *Technol. & Sci. Dict.* 156/2 *Deuterozoic rocks*, the group of rocks comprising the Devonian Rocks, Old Red Sandstone, and Carboniferous System. **1870** ROLLESTON *Anim. Life* Introd. 126 A sexual protozooid has been observed to give origin by gemmation to a sexual deuterozooid.

deuterocanonical (djuːtərəʊkəˈnɒnɪkəl), *a.* [f. mod.L. *deutero-canonicus* (used by Sixtus Senensis 1566: see quot.); see DEUTERO- and CANON, CANONICAL.]

Of, pertaining to, or constituting a second or secondary canon: opposed to *protocanonical*.

Applied historically to those books of the Scripture Canon as defined by the Council of Trent which are regarded by Roman Catholic divines as constituting a second Canon, accepted later than the first, but now of equal authority. In the Old Testament they include Esther and most of the 'Apocrypha' of English Bibles; in the New Testament the Epistle to the Hebrews, the Epistles of James, 2nd of Peter, 2nd and 3rd of John, Jude, and the Revelation, and certain verses of Mark, Luke, and John.

[**1566** A. F. SIXTUS SENENSIS *Bibl. Sancta* I. §1 (1575) 14 Canonici secundi ordinis (qui olim Ecclesiastici vocabantur, nunc a nobis Deutero-canonici dicuntur) illi sunt, de quibus, quia non statim sub ipsis Apostolorum temporibus, sed longe post ad notitiam totius Ecclesiæ peruenerunt, inter Catholicos fuit aliquando sententia anceps.] **1684** N. S. *Crit. Enq. Edit. Bible* App. 263 In the other Classis he places those which he calls Deutero Canonical, or Canonical of the second Order. **1727–51** CHAMBERS *Cycl.* s.v., The deuterocanonical books are, with them [Roman Catholics] as canonical as the proto-canonical. **1859** F. HALL *Vâsavadattâ* 11 Among orthodox records, the deutero-canonical *Revámáhátmya*..consents to this aberration. **1864** PUSEY *Lect. Daniel* vi. 295 This describes a portion of the deuterocanonical books of the Old Testament; books held in estimation among the Jews as well as by Christians, but not received by the Jews into their Canon. **1882** FARRAR *Early Chr.* I. 99 The Catholic Epistles..regarded..as being at best deutero-canonical—authentic (if at all) in a lower sense, and endowed with inferior authority. **1893** F. X. REICHART *Convert's Catech.* iii. 12 This list includes the so-called deutero-canonical books of both Testaments ..*Deutero-canonical* does not mean *Apocryphal* but simply 'later added to the Canon'.

deuterogamist (djuːtəˈrɒgəmɪst). [f. next + -IST.] One who marries a second time, or who upholds second marriages.

1766 GOLDSM. *Vic. W.* xviii, He had published for me against the Deuterogamists of the age.

deuterogamy (djuːtəˈrɒgəmɪ). [ad. Gr. δευτερογαμία second marriage, n. of state f. δευτερογάμος marrying a second time, f. DEUTERO- + γάμος marriage.] **1.** Marriage a second time; marriage after the death of a first husband or wife.

1656 BLOUNT *Glossogr.*, *Deuterogamy*, second marriage, or a repetition of it. **1766** GOLDSM. *Vic. W.* xiv, That unfortunate divine who has so long..fought against the deuterogamy of the age. **1869** *Echo* 7 Sept. 6/1 We do not allow deuterogamy until the primal spouse is disposed of by death or divorce.

2. *Bot.* The condition in which fertilization by the fusion of gametes is replaced by other processes, as in some fungi, the higher algæ, and flowering plants.

1898 P. GROOM in *Trans. Bot. Soc. Edinb.* 8 Dec. 140 Bearing in mind the analogy to the sexual act, we may describe these nuclear unions as being cases of deuterogamy. **1928** C. W. DODGE tr. *Gäumann's Compar. Morphol. Fungi* iv. 12 Copulation of the gametes is suppressed and replaced by many secondary processes... All these secondary processes are called deuterogamy (secondary pairing). **1952** F. L. WYND tr. *Gäumann's Fungi* 60 Copulation therefore does not occur between true sexual cells, but between the gametangia. This secondary type of sexuality is called deuterogamy.

deuteron (ˈdjuːtərɒn). Also †ˈdeuton. [f. Gr. δεύτερ-ος second + -ON, after PROTON.] The nucleus of an atom of deuterium, consisting of a proton and a neutron in combination.

1933 H. C. UREY et al. in *Jrnl. Chem. Physics* I. 513/2 Lewis (private communication) proposed the name deuton for the deuterium nucleus... It would appear to us that the name deuteron would follow the Greek definition better. **1933** *Times* 9 Dec. 9/3 In heavy hydrogen the nucleus is about double the weight of that of ordinary hydrogen. It is this nucleus of heavy hydrogen which is called the deuteron. **1934** *Physical Rev.* XLV. 612/1 Fortunately deutons have very long free paths in an atmosphere of deuterium. **1936** *Discovery* Feb. 36/1 Protons and deuterons are to be introduced into this magnetic field and directed under the accelerating chamber. **1942** *Ann. Reg. 1941* 352 Two processes of fission induced by deuteron bombardment. **1963** *New Scientist* 17 Oct. 159 Produced in the Institute's cyclotron by bombarding copper with deuterons.

Deuteronomic (djuːtərəʊˈnɒmɪk), *a.* [f. DEUTERONOMY (or its Gr. elements) + -IC.] Of or pertaining to, or possessing the literary or theological character of, the book of Deuteronomy.

1857 J. W. DONALDSON *Chr. Orthodoxy* 202 The Deuteronomic view of the matter was the only tradition..at that time, recognised as Mosaic and divine. **1867** MARTINEAU tr. *Ewald's Israel* I. 162 Sins against Jahveh, repentance, and amendment, are the three pivots on which the Deuteronomic scheme turns. **1882** SEELEY *Nat. Relig.* 133 We have even framed for ourselves a sort of Deuteronomic religion which is a great comfort to us. **1891** DRIVER *Introd. Lit. O. Test.* (ed. 2) 180 Deuteronomic phraseology.

Deuteroˈnomical, *a.* [f. as prec. + -AL[1].] = prec.

1533 MORE *Let. to T. Cromwell* Wks. 1425/1 Concerning the woordes in the law leuitycall and the lawe deuteronomicall. **1681** H. MORE in *Glanvill's Sadducismus* I. Postcr. (1726) 20 This Deuteronomical List of abominable Names. **1887** MIVART in *19th Cent.* July 39 This is the second code, and is called the Deuteronomical Code, because it makes up the bulk of the book of Deuteronomy.

Deuteˈronomist. [f. as prec. + -IST.] The writer of the book of Deuteronomy, or of the parts of that book which do not consist of earlier documents.

1862 S. DAVIDSON *Introd. to O. Test.* I. 370 The Deuteronomist's style is diffuse, and his language unlike that of the other writings traditionally ascribed to the same individual. **1867** MARTINEAU tr. *Ewald's Israel* I. 117 The work of an author whom we may briefly call 'the Deuteronomist'. **1882–3** SCHAFF *Encycl. Relig. Knowl.* III. 1792 The final compiler is not to be identified with the Deuteronomist. **1888** CHEYNE *Jeremiah* 70 The Deuteronomist (if we may so for convenience term the author, or joint-authors, of the original Deuteronomy).

Hence **Deuteronoˈmistic** *a.*, of the nature or style of the writer of Deuteronomy.

1862 S. DAVIDSON *Introd. to O. Test.* I. 363 Let us now compare the Deuteronomistic with the Jehovistic legislation. **1881** ROBERTSON SMITH *O.T. in Jewish Ch.* (1892) 425 Judges, Samuel, and Kings, in the Deuteronomistic redaction. **1888** CHEYNE *Jeremiah* 71 A Deuteronomistic writer composed Deut. i–iv. 40 as a link between his own and the earlier work.

Deuteronomy (djuːtəˈrɒnəmɪ, ˈdjuːtərəʊnɒmɪ). Also 4–5 **Deutronomye, -ie**, 6 **Deutronome**. [ad. eccl. L. *Deuteronomium*, a. Gr. Δευτερονόμιον, f. δεύτερος second + νόμος law, etc.: in 13th c. OF. *deutronome*, F. *deutéronome*.

The name is taken from the words of the LXX in Deut. xvii. 18 το δευτερονόμιον τοῦτο, a mistranslation of the Heb. *mishnēh hattōrāh hazzōth* 'a copy or duplicate of this law', for which the Vulgate has *Deuteronomium legis hujus*.]

The name or title of the fifth book of the Pentateuch, which contains a repetition, with parenetic comments, of the Decalogue, and most of the laws contained in Exodus xxi–xxiii, and xxxiv.

1388 WYCLIF *Prol. to Deut.*, In this book of Deutronomye ben contened the wordis which Moises spak to al Israel. *Rubric.* Here begynneth the bok of Deutronomie. **1549** *Compl. Scotl.* (1872) 24 It is vrityne in the xxviii. of deutronome, thir vordis. **1609** BIBLE (Douay) *Deut.* xvii. 18 He shal copie to him selfe the Deuteronomie of this Law in a volume. **1649** ROBERTS *Clavis Bibl.* 63 *Deuteronomie*.. Thus denominated by the Greek, because this book containeth a Repetition of Gods Law given by Moses to Israel. *c* **1878** *Helps to Study of Bible* 17 Deuteronomy consists mainly of three addresses by Moses to the people who had been born in the wilderness, and had not heard the original promulgation of the Law. **1891** DRIVER *Introd. Lit. O. Test.* (ed. 2) 85 Deuteronomy may be described as the prophetic re-formulation, and adaptation to new needs, of an older legislation.

b. *transf.*

1827 SOUTHEY in *Q. Rev.* XXXVI. 306 A fourth volume, containing her latter writings and certain new developements..being the papers which M. Genet speaks of as a kind of Deuteronomy.

deuteropathy (djuːtəˈrɒpəθɪ). [f. DEUTERO- + Gr. -πάθεια suffering: cf. -PATHY.]

†**1.** *gen.* A being affected at second hand. *Obs.*

1647 H. MORE *Song of Soul* Notes 161/1 Deuteropathie, Δευτεροπάθεια, is a being affected at second rebound, as I may so say. We see the sunne not so properly by sympathie as deuteropathie. *Ibid.* 163/2 If the air be struck aloof of, I am sensible also of that but by circulation or propagation of that impression into my eare; and this is Deuteropathy. **1650** CHARLETON *Paradoxes* 60 The body also cannot but submit to compassion and deuteropathy.

2. *Med.* A secondary affection, sympathetic with or consequent upon another, that is, 'where the second part suffers from the influence of the part originally affected'. *Syd. Soc. Lex.*

1651 BIGGS *New Disp.* ¶248 Whether or no there be a Deuteropathy or consent of the head with the part wounded. [**1657** G. STARKEY *Helmont's Vind.* 128 The Gout properly ..is an Arthritical pain affecting the joynts immediately, and some nerves sometimes by a Deuteropatheia.] **1669** W. SIMPSON *Hydrol. Chym.* 88 Either by a deuteropathy..or by an idiopathy.

Hence **deuteroˈpathic** *a.*, of or pertaining to deuteropathy.

deuteroscopy (djuːtəˈrɒskəpɪ). [f. DEUTERO- + Gr. -σκοπία, σκοπιά look-out, watch, view.]

†**1.** The second view; that which is seen upon a second view; an ulterior meaning. *Obs.*

1646 SIR T. BROWNE *Pseud. Ep.* I. iii. 9 Not attaining the deuteroscopy and second intention of the words. **1650** CHARLETON *Paradoxes* 49 Truth itself interprets this..text literally, and without enfolding any mystery or deuteroscopy. **1656** BLOUNT *Glossogr.*, *Deuteroscopy*, the second end, aim, or intention, a second consideration or thought.

2. 'Second sight'; clairvoyance. *rare.*

1822 SCOTT *Nigel* Introd. Ep., The Highland seers, whom their gift of deuteroscopy compels to witness things unmeet for mortal eye.

Hence **deuteroˈscopic** *a.*, of or pertaining to second sight.

1841 *Fraser's Mag.* XXV. 270 The deuteroscopic, or thanatomantic faculty.

†**deuterosy.** *Obs. rare.* [ad. Gr. δευτέρωσις repetition, iteration, a name of the Jewish traditions. The Gr. form also occurs.] A 'tradition of the elders' among the Jews.

a **1641** BP. R. MOUNTAGU *Acts & Mon.* (1642) 477 Those Deuterosies, those Traditions of the Elders, and Additions to the Law. **1650** J. TRAPP *Clavis Bible* iii. 83 The Iews have added their Deuteroseis.

deutery, obs. var. of DEWTRY Datura.

deuto-, before a vowel **deut-**, a shortened form of DEUTERO-, used

1. In Chemistry to distinguish the second in order of the terms of any series. Thus **deuˈtoxide**, the second of the series of oxides of a metal, etc., that which comes next to the *protoxide*, containing the next smallest quantity of oxygen. So ***deut-iodide***, ***deuto-bromide***, ***deuto-carbonate***, ***deuto-chloride***, ***deuto-sulphide***, etc. The prefix has sometimes been improperly used to indicate the *constitution* of a compound, as compared with that of the *proto-* or *mono-* compound of the same series; but it is now obsolescent, being usually replaced by such prefixes as *sesqui-*, *di-*, *tri-*, etc., which properly indicate the constitution.

1810 HENRY *Elem. Chem.* (1826) I. 263 Deutoxide or Peroxide of Hydrogen. *Ibid.* 310 This gas..examined by Dr. Priestly, and called by him *nitrous air*, a term afterwards changed to *nitrous gas*, then to *nitric oxide*, and more lately to *deutoxide of azote*, or *deutoxide of nitrogen*, which last appears to be its most appropriate title. **1822** IMISON *Sc. & Art* II. 20 The smallest quantity of oxygen forms the protoxide of the metal, the second quantity of oxygen makes the deutoxide. **1854** J. SCOFFERN in *Orr's Circ. Sc.* Chem. 489 *Binoxide*, sometimes called *deutoxide* of copper ($Cu\ O_2$). **1857** BULLOCK *Cazeaux' Midwif.* 137 Precipitated by the deuto-chloride of mercury. **1864** H. SPENCER *Illust. Univ. Progr.* 40 Later in the Earth's history, are the deutoxides, tritoxides, etc. **1864** —— *Biol.* I. 6 Deutoxide of nitrogen is a gas hitherto uncondensed.

2. In many terms of *Biology*; as **deutenˈcephalon** [Gr. ἐγκέφαλος brain], the second of the three primary cerebral vesicles of the embryo. Hence **deutenceˈphalic** *a.* ‖**deutoˈmala** [L. *māla* jaw], the second pair of jaws of the Myriapoda; hence **deutoˈmalar** *a.* **deuˈtomerite** [Gr. μέρος part], the second or posterior cell of a dicystid gregarine, as distinguished from the smaller anterior cell or *protomerite*. **ˈdeutoplasm** [Gr. πλάσμα anything formed], term applied by Reichert to the food-yolk of the mero-blastic egg, e.g. the yellow yolk of a bird's egg; also, the special form of protoplasm which composes the granules seen in the centre of the protamœba (*Syd. Soc. Lex.*); hence **deutoˈplasmic**, **-ˈplastic** *a.*, of, pertaining to, or of the nature of deutoplasm; **ˌdeutoplaˈsmigenous** *a.*, producing deutoplasm; **deutoˈplasmogen**, that which forms or is converted into deutoplasm. **deutoˈsclerous** *a.*, [σκληρός hard], in ***deutosclerous tissue***, Laurent's term for osseous tissue. **deutoˈscolex** [σκώληξ worm], a secondary scolex, or daughter-cyst of a scolex or cystic worm; the cysticercus of the *Tæniæ*. **deutoˈtergite** [L. *tergum* back], the second dorsal segment of the abdomen of insects. **deuˈtovum** [L. *ovum* egg] *pl.* **-ova**, a secondary egg-cell, as contrasted with the protovum or normal and usual egg-cell; also called *metovum*, and after-egg.

1881 MIVART *Cat* 358 The fore-brain, called also the deutencephalon. **1884** SEDGWICK tr. *Claus' Zool.* I. 111 The contents of every egg consist..(1) Of a viscous albuminous protoplasm; and (2) of a fatty granular matter, the deutoplasm or food yolk. **1886** *Jrnl. R. Microsc. Soc.* Apr. 224 In the young unfertilized ova a small 'protoplasmic' and larger 'deutoplasmic' portion are readily distinguished. **1881** *Smithsonian Report* 425 The development alike of excretory and deutoplasmigenous functions, at certain times of the year, of the genital glands. **1872** E. R. LANKESTER *Adv. Science* (1890) 265 The others disappear as deutoplasmogen or vitellogenous cells. **1877** HUXLEY *Anat. Inv. Anim.* vii. 383 The proper vitelline membrane bursts into two halves..and the deutovum emerges. **1881** *Athenæum* 31 Dec. 904/2 The occurrence of a deutovum stage in the egg is recorded.

3. In some other words; as **deutosysteˈmatic** *a.*, of or pertaining to a secondary system; DEUTEROSYSTEMATIC.

1878 GURNEY *Crystallogr.* 72 The deutosystematic planes which bisect the angles between the [protosystematic].

deuton: see DEUTERON.

deutoxide: see DEUTO- 1.

deutro, deutroa: see DEWTRY.

Deutsche mark, Deutschemark (ˈdɔɪtʃə ˌmɑːk). Also **Deutschmark**. [G., 'German mark'.] The monetary unit of the German Federal Republic, instituted in June 1948; also, a coin representing one Deutsche mark. Abbrev. *D.M.* or *D-mark.*

1948 *Sunday Times* 27 June 1/2 He will..take stock of the first week of economic life with the new Deutsche mark. **1948** *Economist* 27 Nov. 868/1 The future of the D-mark was a matter for considerable alarm. **1957** *Ibid.* 7 Sept. 817/2 A half-world that has to learn to live with the D-mark. **1958** *Spectator* 27 June 840/1 The Federal German Republic, whose gold and currency reserves have reached the record total of DM 23,926,000,000. **1959** *Times* 15 May 13/6 They are Germans on a *Drang nach Osten*..dutifully getting their Deutschmark's worth. **1969** *Listener* 22 May 723/1 It wasn't until the Deutschmark crisis that we began to suffer on our exchanges.

‖**Deutzia** ('djuːtsɪə, 'dɔɪtsɪə). *Bot.* [mod.Bot. L.; named in 1781 after J. Deutz of Amsterdam.] A genus of shrubs (N.O. *Saxifragaceæ*), natives of China and Japan, cultivated for the beauty of their white flowers. *D. gracilis* is a well-known spring flowerer.

1837 *Penny Cycl.* VIII. 444/2 Deutzia..inhabiting the north of India, China, and Japan. **1880** Miss Bird *Japan* I. 5 Deutzias with their graceful flowers. **1882** *Garden* 11 Feb. 104/2 Where Deutzias are forced there will be a fine crop of young shoots.

deux, deux ans: see DEUCE[1], DEUSAN.

‖**deux-chevaux** (døʃəvo). [Fr.] A two-horse-power motor vehicle; a small French car. Also *attrib.*

1962 *Harper's Bazaar* Dec. 76/2 The French Director-General who arrived..in a workaday Deux Chevaux. **1963** V. Canning *Limbo Line* xiv. 189 They used a *deux-chevaux* with the top rolled back. **1964** 'J. Welcome' *Hard to Handle* ix. 93 A *deux chevaux* van was drawn up on a path outside the door.

‖**deux-temps** (døtɑ̃). [F.; in full, *valse à deux temps* lit. 'two-time waltz'.] A kind of waltz, more rapid than the ordinary or trois-temps waltz, the step consisting of two movements, a *glissade* and a *chassé*.

1860 *All Year Round* No. 74. 568 O golden-haired, but yet hungry heroine of a thousand deux-temps! **1862** Calverley *Verses & Tr.* 17 But oh! in the deuxtemps peerless, Fleet of foot, and soft of eye!

deuyce, deuys(e, obs. ff. DEVICE, DEVISE.

deuzan, var. DEUSAN, *Obs.*, a kind of apple.

dev, variant of DIV, a demon or evil spirit in Persian mythology.

‖**deva** ('deɪvə). [Skr. *dēva* a god, *orig.* 'a bright or shining one' from **div-* to shine.] A god, a divinity; one of the good spirits of Hindu mythology.

1819 T. Hope *Anast.* (1820) III. x. 251 (Stanf.) A palace, a mosque, and a bath, whose architecture, achieved as if by magic, seemed worthy of the Devas. **1834** *Baboo* II. viii. 157 (*ibid.*) By the Deva, who is enshrined in this temple! **1878** Max Müller *Orig. Relig.* (1891) 280 When the poets of the Veda address the mountains to protect them, when they implore the rivers to yield them water, they may speak of rivers and mountains as *devas*, but even then, though *deva* would be more than bright, it would as yet be very far from anything we mean by divine. **1879** E. Arnold *Lt. Asia* I. 2 The Devas knew the signs, and said, 'Buddha will go again to help the World'. **1888** Geldner in *Encycl. Brit.* XXIV. 821 In the older *Rig-Veda*..a god is spoken of as *dêva*, but not every *dêva* is an *asura*... *Asura* is ethically the higher conception, *deva* the lower: *deva* is the vulgar notion of God, *asura* is theosophic.

attrib. and *Comb.* **1878** Haug *Religion of Parsis* (ed. 2) 287 A vital struggle between the professors of the Deva and those of the Ahura religion. *Ibid.*, The Deva-worshippers combated by the Zoroastrians.

‖**devadasi** (deɪvə'dɑːsɪ). [a. Skr. *devadāsī*, lit. 'a female servant of a god' (cf. DEVA).] A nautch girl in a Hindu temple.

1817 tr. *Dubois' Manners & Customs of India* III. iii. 401 Next to the Sacrificers, the most important persons about the temple are the dancing girls, who call themselves *Devadasi*, Servants or slaves of the gods. **1886** in Yule & Burnell *Hobson-Jobson* 237/2. **1913** J. N. Farquhar *Crown of Hinduism* (1919) 397 To this day troops of dancing-girls, who are called *devadasis*, servants of the god, and who now and then do take part in the ritual, but whose real occupation is prostitution, are connected with most of the great temples of the South and West. **1931** *Times Educ. Suppl.* 8 Aug. 313/3 Legislation to abolish brothels and the system of dedication to temple uses of *devadasis*. **1958** E. Linklater *Position at Noon* i. 16 His sublime, inspired, and supernacular tart (or *devadasi*).

devalgate (dɪ'vælgət), *a. rare*—°. [ad. mod.L. *dēvalgātus*, f. *valgus* bow-legged.]

1851–60 Mayne *Expos. Lex.*, *Devalgatus*, having bowed legs; bandy-legged; devalgate. **1883** in *Syd. Soc. Lex.*

devall (dɪ'vɔːl), *v. Now only Sc.* Forms: 5–6 **deuale**, 6 **deuaill**, **dewall**, 7–9 **devall**, 9 **deval**, **devaul**, **devawl**. [a. F. *dévaler*, OF. *devaler* to descend = Pr. *devalar*, *davalar*, It. *divallare*:—Rom. **devallare*, f. L. DE- I. 1 down + *vallis* valley: cf. AVALE *v.*] Hence **devalling** *vbl. sb.* and *ppl. a.*

†**1.** *intr.* To move downwards, sink, fall, descend, set (as the sun). *Obs.*

c **1477** Caxton *Jason* 25 b, The sonne began to deuale in to the Weste. **1481** —— *Myrr.* II. ix. 88 He..deualeth down into the water. **1501** Douglas *Pal. Hon.* I. vi, Thy transitorie plesance quhat auaillis? Now thair, now heir, now hie, and now deuaillis. **1597** Montgomerie *Cherrie & Slae* 83, I saw an river rin..Dewalling and falling Into that pit profound. **1632** Lithgow *Trav.* IX. 392 *marg.*, The combustious devalling of Ætnæs fire. *Ibid.* x. 506 Devalling floods.

†**b.** To lower the body, stoop. *Obs.*

1513 Douglas *Æneis* x. vii. 58 As onwar he stowpyt, and devalyt.

†**c.** To slope downwards: as a line or surface.

1632 Lithgow *Trav.* v. 210 This Petrean Countrey..devalling even downe to the limits of Jacob's bridge. *Ibid.* VIII. 365 The..devalling faces of two hills. **1645** *Siege of Newcastle* (1820) 14 A number of narrow devalling lanes.

†**2.** *trans.* To lower. *Obs.*

1501 Douglas *Pal. Hon.* II. liii, And euerie wicht..Thankand greit God, their heidis law deuaill.

3. *intr.* To cease, stop, leave off. *mod.Sc.*

a **1774** Fergusson *Poems* (1789) II. 99 (Jam.) Devall then, Sirs, and never send For daintiths to regale a friend. **1822** Galt *Sir. A. Wylie* II. x. 92 She ne'er devauls jeering me. **1827** Scott *Let.* 26 Apr. in *Lockhart*, I have not till to-day *devauled* from my task. **1891** H. Halliburton *Ochil Idylls* 20 Sair dings the rain upon the road, It dings,—an nae devallin' o't.

Hence **devall** *sb. Sc.*, 'a stop, cessation, intermission' (Jamieson).

1802 Sibbald *Gloss.*, *Without devald*, without ceasing.

devalorize (diː'vælərɑɪz), *v.* [f. DE- + VALOR + -IZE: see VALORIZATION.] *trans.* To lower the value of; to devalue. Hence **devalori'zation**.

1925 *Glasgow Herald* 1 Apr. 8 To face honestly the question of devalorising the franc. **1928** *Observer* 15 July 12/2 So that he and they may equally share the devalorisation. **1931** *Daily Express* 16 Oct. 8/4 The French currency had been devalorised by eighty per cent.

devaluate (diː'væljuːeɪt), *v.* [f. DE- + VALUE *sb.* + -ATE[3].] *trans.* = DEVALUE *v.*

1898 W. J. Locke *Idols* xiii. 128 He is relying on his speech to-morrow to devaluate the evidence. **1924** *Glasgow Herald* 1 Mar. 8 The country has gone a great length in the direction of devaluating the vote by conferring it on men whose politics are as immature as themselves.

devaluation (diːvæljuː'eɪʃən). [f. prec. or next: see -ATION.] The process of devaluing or fact of being devalued; *spec.* the reduction of the official value of a currency in terms of gold or of another currency. Hence **devalu'ationist**, one who advocates or supports devaluation.

1914 *Eng. Hist. Rev.* Jan. 140 The devaluation of the ancient Merovingian pence. **1921** *Glasgow Herald* 10 Dec. 8 Devaluation has an important bearing on Lord Inchcape's criticism of teachers' salaries. **1922** *Ibid.* 12 May 9 The probable further devaluation of the mark. **1935** *New Statesman* 1 June 793/1 Events in Belgium showed plainly the practicability of limited and controlled devaluation of the currency, and strengthened the hands of the devaluationists in France. **1961** D. Woodward tr. *Simenon's Premier* iii. 84 After the disastrous experiments made by previous governments..the only solution was a large-scale devaluation. **1969** *Daily Tel.* 14 Mar. 3 The 1968 balance of payments figures..must make the devaluationists think twice about the effectiveness of their remedy.

devalue (diː'væljuː), *v.* [f. DE- II. 2 + VALUE *sb.*] *trans.* To reduce or annul the value of; to deprive of value; *spec.* to effect the devaluation of (a currency). Also *absol.* Hence **de'valued** *ppl. a.*

1918 *Guardian* 24 Oct. 847/3 The chemist has succeeded in devaluing the ruby. **1925** *Glasgow Herald* 29 Apr. 10 To return to the gold standard on the basis of a devalued sovereign. **1956** C. Wilson *Outsider* v. 133 Hegel..devalued life, failed to recognize that thought is only an instrument to 'more abundant life'. **1957** *Times* 18 Nov. p. iii/1 The pound would have to be devalued. **1965** *New Statesman* 23 Apr. 631/1 Wilson missed his chance to devalue last October.

‖**Devanagari** (ˌdeɪvə'nɑːgəriː), *a.* and *sb.* [Skr., Hindī, Marāthī *dēvanāgarī* (in Bengālī *devanāgar*), a compound app. of Skr. *dēva* god + *Nāgarī* an earlier or a more generic appellation of the same alphabet; lit. 'Nāgarī (? town-script) of the gods'.

Nāgarī is app. the fem. adj. meaning 'of the city or town, urban, urbane, refined' (sc. *lipi* writing, script), f. Skr. *nagara* city. Its application to a particular written character can be traced back to the 11th c., when Albirūnī mentions an alphabet called *Nāgara*, and of a derivative from it called *Ardha-nāgarī*, i.e. 'half-Nāgarī'. The actual origin and history of the compound *Dēva-nāgarī* has not been ascertained, any more than that of *Nandi-nāgarī*, applied to the South-Indian form of the Nāgarī. It has been noted that the terms *dēva-lipi* 'writing of the gods', and *nāga-lipi* 'writing of the serpents', occur side by side in a list of 64 kinds of writing enumerated in the Buddhistic *Lalitavistara* of the 7th c.; but whether these terms have any connexion with *dēva-nāgarī* is unknown. The 18th c. European scholars who adopted the word, have variant forms from Bengālī or other Indian vernaculars.]

The distinctive name of the formal alphabet in which, throughout northern, western and central India, Cashmere, and Nepāl, the Sanskrit has, for some centuries, been written, as are also the vernacular languages of those regions. Also called simply *Nagari*, though the latter is often used in a wider sense, to embrace various local forms taken by the same original alphabet. Used both as *adj.* and absolutely as *sb.*

1781 Sir C. Wilkins in *Asiatic Res.* (1799) I. 294 It differs but little from the Dewnagur. **1784** W. Chambers *Ibid.* I. 152 It resembles neither the *Devya-nâgre* nor any of the various characters connected with..it. **1785** Sir C. Wilkins *Ibid.* I. 279 In the modern Dēwnāgăr character. **1786** Sir W. Jones *Ibid.* I. 423 The polished and elegant Dévanágarí. **1789** *Ibid.* I. 13 We may apply our present alphabet so..as to equal the Dévanágarí itself in precision and clearness. **1801** Colebrooke *Ibid.* (1803) VII. 224 *foot-note*, Prácrit and Hindí books are commonly written in the Dévanágarí. **1820** W. Yates *Gram. Skr. Lang.* vii, The character in which Sunscrit works are usually printed is called Daivŭ-nāgŭree. **1845** Stocqueler *Handbk. Brit. India* (1854) 55 The translation to be written..both in Persian and Deva Nagree. **1876** *Times* 15 May (Stanf.), His alphabet was founded on the Devanagari, which he accommodated to the needs of the Tibetan tongue. **1879** Burnell *S. Indian Palæog.* (ed. 2) 52 The South-Indian form of the Nāgarī character..the Nandināgarī is directly derived from the N. Indian Devanāgarī of about the eleventh century. **1886** Eggeling in *Encyc. Brit.* XXI. 272/2 The character..is the so-called *Devanâgarî*, or *nâgarî* ('town-script') of the gods.

devance (dɪ'vɑːns, -æ-), *v.* [a. F. *devancer* to arrive before, precede, outstrip, f. *devant* before, on the model of *avancer* (ADVANCE). Became obs. early in 17th c., but has been again used by some in the 19th c.] *trans.* To anticipate, forestall; to get ahead of; to outstrip.

1485 Caxton *Chas. Gt.* viii. 72 Olyuer whyche sawe the stroke comyng deuaunced hym in such wyse that he gaf two euyl strokes to Fyerabras. **1598** Barckley *Felic. Man* v. (1603) 489 In his owne conceit he lacketh so much as he seeth himselfe devaunced by another that hath more. **1615** *Trade's Incr.* in *Harl. Misc.* (Malh.) III. 293 Our neighbours [the Dutch]..have devanced us so far in shipping. **1863** R. F. Burton *Abeokuta* II. 72 So far from 'caving in', he devanced me on one occasion. **1864** —— *Dahome* Pref. 9 Commodore Wilmot, R.N...accompanied by Capt. Luce..devanced me. **1880** *Ginevra* 86 My wish devanced the hour.

¶ Catachrestic uses.

1646 J. Hall *Horæ Vac.* 123 Tis hard to keepe these two equally ballanc't, especially those that devance. **1653** —— *Paradoxes* 108 Some Crazy Phylosophers..have endeavoured to devance them [women] from the same Species, with men.

†**de'vant, de'vaunt**, *adv.* and *sb. Obs.* [a. F. *devant* prep. and adv., before, in front, = Pr. *davan*, *devant*, Cat. *devant*, *davant*, It. *davanti*, f. L. *dē* prep., from, of + late L. *abante* before: see AVAUNT *adv.*]

A. *adv.* Before, in front.

1609 Holland *Amm. Marcell.* xxv. vi. 270 His beard..was shagged and rough, with a sharpe peake devant.

B. *sb.* Front; e.g. of the body or dress.

1411 *E.E. Wills* (1882) 19 A boorde clope with .ij. towelles of deuaunt of oo sute. **1599** B. Jonson *Cynthia's Rev.* v. ii, Come, sir, perfume my devant.

devant, *v. Obs.*: see DEVAUNT.

†**de'vaporate**, *v. Obs.* [f. DE- II. 1 + L. *vapōrem* vapour, after EVAPORATE.] **a.** *trans.* To bring out of the state of vapour; to condense. **b.** *intr.* To become condensed, or deprived of vapour. Hence †**devapo'ration**.

1787 E. Darwin in *Phil. Trans.* LXXVIII. 49 The privation of heat may be esteemed the principal cause of devaporation. *Ibid.* 50 The deduction of a small quantity of heat from a cloud or province of vapour..will devaporate the whole. *Ibid.* 52 The air..by its expansion produces cold and devaporates. **1789** *Ann. Reg.* 127 The vapour..is brought to the summit of mountains by the atmosphere, and being there devaporated slides down between the strata.

de'vast, *v.* Now *rare.* [a. F. *dévaster* (1499 in Hatzf.-Darm.), ad. L. *dēvastāre* to lay waste, f. DE- I. 1, 3 + *vastāre* to lay waste, *vastus* waste. Frequent in 17th c.; not recognized by Johnson, and said by Todd to be 'not now in use'; but occurring in end of 19th c.] *trans.* To lay waste, DEVASTATE.

1537 *St. Papers Hen. VIII*, I. 553 The yere soo ferre spent, and the countrey soo devasted. **1613** Heywood *Silver Age* III. i, An uncouth, savage boar Devasts the fertile plains of Thessaly. *a* **1751** Bolingbroke *Study of Hist.* vi, The thirty years war that devasted Germany. **1887** *Voice* (N.Y.) 13 Jan. 5 A statute..which, in prohibiting an injurious business, devasts property previously existing. **1890** W. F. Rae *Maygrove* III. vii. 254 The mountain slopes have been devasted by lava.

absol. **1652** Gaule *Magastrom.* 6 To devast according to the prædictions of vain humane art.

†**b.** To waste (time, etc.). *Obs. rare.*

1632 Lithgow *Trav.* II. 44 After my returne from Padua to Venice and 24 days attendance devasted there for passage.

Hence **de'vasted, de'vasting** *ppl. adjs.*

1632 Lithgow *Trav.* v. 214 Time..running all things to devasted desolation. **1659** T. Pecke *Parnassi Puerp.* 39 Love prudent Laws; devasting Arms neglect. **1789** [see DEVASTER].

devastate ('dɛvəsteɪt), *v.* [f. L. *dēvastāt-* ppl. stem of *dēvastāre* (see DEVAST). Used by Sir T. Herbert and in Bailey 1727, but not recognized by Johnson 1755, and app. not in common use till the 19th c.] *trans.* To lay waste, ravage, waste, render desolate.

1638 Sir T. Herbert *Trav.* (ed. 2) 77 Jangheer..subjects Berar, and devastates the Decan Empire unto Kerky. **1727**

BAILEY vol. II, *To Devastate*, to lay waste, to spoil. [Omitted in ed. 2, 1731, and not in *Folio* 1730.] **1818** TODD s.v. *Devast*, Not now in use. But *devastate* supplies its place. **1842** MACAULAY *Fredk. Gt.* Ess. (1854) 683/2 A succession of cruel wars had devastated Europe. **1847** EMERSON *Poems, Blight* Wks. (Bohn) I. 483 We invade them impiously for gain; We devastate them unreligiously. **1874** GREEN *Short Hist.* v. §4. 241 [Black Death] devastating Europe from the shores of the Mediterranean to the Baltic.

fig. **1856** DOVE *Logic Chr. Faith* v. i. §2. 298 Kant completely devastates the cobwebs and sophistries. **1864** LONGF. in *Life* (1891) III. 31 Went to town, which devastated the day.

Hence **'devastated** *ppl. a.*

1813 SHELLEY *Queen Mab* IV. 112 The bloodiest scourge Of devastated earth.

devastating, *ppl. a.* That devastates. Freq. *fig.*, esp. in trivial or hyperbolical use: very effective or upsetting; astounding, overwhelming, 'stunning'. Cf. next.

1634 SIR T. HERBERT *Trav.* 81 Those devastating and mercilesse Infidels. **1815** SHELLEY *Alastor* 613 Thou, colossal Skeleton, that..In thy devastating omnipotence Art king of this frail world. *a* **1859** MACAULAY *Hist. Eng.* V. 105 An exhausting and devastating struggle of nine years. **1889** A. JAMES *Diary* 4 Aug. (1965) 50 The somewhat devastating episode of July 18th when Harry after a much longer absence than usual presented himself, doubled by William! **1910** *Daily Chron.* 22 Mar. 1/3 It is expected that a devastating strike will be declared. **1924** G. W. HILLYARD *40 Yrs. Lawn-Tennis* iii. 83 No man who ever walked on to a court was equipped with more perfect style, greater physical advantages, or more devastating strokes. **1925** *New Yorker* 8 Aug. 4/2 Not since the Tango provided luscious livelihoods for many svelte youths has so devastating a dance agitated the town. **1926** S. JAMESON *Three Kingdoms* ii. 63 She was struggling with a devastating shyness. **1927** H. T. LOWE-PORTER tr. *Mann's Magic Mountain* v. 378 Everything, whether in jest or earnest, was 'devastating', the bob-run, the sweet for dinner, her own temperature. **1933** E. SHANKS *Enchanted Village* ix. 133 Oh yes, poor old Julian—I think, to be honest, that he's a devastating bore. **1936** R. LEHMANN *Weather in Streets* i. 11 Oh, darling have you got to *go*? How *devastating*. **1957** I. MURDOCH *Sandcastle* ix. 150 From the very depths of his being the knowledge came to him, suddenly and with devastating certainty. **1971** *Sunday Times* 28 Mar. 32/6 Ludovic Kennedy published his devastating analysis of the Christie murders and established the innocence of Timothy Evans.

devastatingly ('dɛvəsteɪtɪŋlɪ), *adv.* [f. DEVASTATING *ppl. a.* + -LY².] In a devastating manner; so as to devastate: freq. in trivial or hyperbolical use (cf. prec.).

1905 *Daily Chron.* 28 Sept. 4/6 The devastatingly tidy housemaid. **1915** J. C. POWYS *Visions & Revisions* 96 The stripping from human beings of their characteristic 'outer garments' makes them so dreadfully, so devastatingly, alike! **1927** *Observer* 15 May 8 A man in whom a natural violence of lust and temper is restrained by the unnaturally strict taboos of his childhood's environment, but breaks loose all the more devastatingly when his inhibitions are removed by drink. *Ibid.* 21 Aug. 5 The devastatingly betraying sentences of Theodore Parker. **1928** *Daily Tel.* 15 May 8 His conversation..is positive, narrow-minded, egregiously self-satisfied, impregnably commercial, but it is devastatingly entertaining. **1966** *Listener* 20 Oct. 578/3 The final sequence ..is devastatingly lovely in its sadness.

devastation (dɛvə'steɪʃən). [prob. a. F. *dévastation*, n. of action f. *dévaster*, and L. *dēvastāre*, used in 1502, but not in Cotgr. 1611; Florio, 1599 and 1611, has It. *devastatione*, 'a wasting, spoiling, desolation, or destruction'.] The action of devastating, or condition of being devastated; laying waste; wide-spread destruction; ravages.

1603 HOLLAND *Plutarch's Mor.* 1190 The ruine and devastation [*sic*] of so many..great cities. **1677** HALE *Prim. Orig. Man.* II. ix. 213 The great Devastations made by the Plague..in Forein Parts. **1770** GOLDSM. *Des. Vill.* 395 E'en now the devastation is begun And half the business of destruction done. **1794** MRS. RADCLIFFE *Myst. Udolpho* xv, Over the beautiful plains of this country the devastations of war were frequently visible. **1809–10** COLERIDGE *Friend* (1865) 72 Devastation is incomparably an easier work than production. **1878** HUXLEY *Physiogr.* 188 The terrible devastation wrought by the great tidal wave which followed the earthquake at Lima.

b. *Law.* (See quot. 1848.)

1670 BLOUNT *Law Dict.* s.v. *Devastaverunt*, The orderly payment of Debts and Legacies by Executors, so as to escape a *Devastation*, or charging their own Goods. **1848** WHARTON *Law Lex.*, *Devastavit*, a devastation or waste of the property of a deceased person by an executor or administrator being extravagant or misapplying the assets.

devastative ('dɛvəsteɪtɪv), *a.* [f. L. *dēvastāt-* ppl. stem (see above) + -IVE.] Having the quality of devastating; wasting, ravaging.

1802 *Triads of Bardism* in Southey *Madoc* I. §2 (note) To collect power towards subduing the adverse, and the devastative. **1839** CARLYLE *Chartism* v. (1858) 24 Devastative, like the whirlwind. **1884** J. G. PYLE in *Harper's Mag.* Sept. 619/2 The devastative power of floods.

devastator ('dɛvəsteɪtə(r)). [a. late L. *dēvastātor* (Cassiodorus), agent-n. from *dēvastāre* to devastate.] He who or that which devastates; a waster, ravager.

1818 E. BLAQUIERE tr. *Pananti's Algiers* vi. 136 All is to no purpose with these devastators. **1829** LANDOR *Imag. Conv.* (1846) II. 6/1 This devastator of wines and olives. **1855** MACAULAY *Hist. Eng.* III. 437 He marched against the devastators of the Palatinate.

‖**devastavit** (di:væ'steɪvɪt). *Law.* [L. *dēvastāvit* he has wasted, 3rd sing. perf. of *dēvastāre*: see DEVASTATE.] A writ that lies against an executor or administrator for waste or misapplication of the testator's estate.

[**1579** RASTELL *Exp. termes lawes, Deuastauerunt bona testatoris*, is when Executours wyl deliuer the legacyes that their Testatour hath geeuen, or make restytutyon for wronges done by him, or pay hys det due vpon contracts or other detes vpon specialties, whose dayes of paymentes are not yet come, etc.] **1651** in Picton *L'pool Munic. Rec.* (1883) I. 176 The Sheriffe shall be solizited for a Devastavit. **1729** GILES JACOB *Law Dict.* s.v., His Executor or Administrator is made liable to a *devastavit*, by Stat. 4 & 5 W. & M. c. 24. **1817** W. SELWYN *Law Nisi Prius* (ed. 4) II. 743 A writ of *fi. fa.* having been sued out on the judgment, to which the sheriff had returned a devastavit.

b. The offence of such waste or misapplication.

1729 GILES JACOB *Law Dict.* s.v., Where an executor, &c. payeth legacies before debts, and hath not sufficient to pay both, 'tis a *devastavit*. Also where an Executor sells the Testator's Goods at an Undervalue, it is a *Devastavit*. **1893** ROMER in *Law Times* XCV. 54/2 The rule that an executor who pays a statute-barred debt is not thereby committing a devastavit.

de'vaster. *rare.* [f. DEVAST *v.* + -ER¹.] = DEVASTATOR.

1789 MRS. PIOZZI *Journ. France* I. 127 In eight hours no trace was left either of the devasters or devasted.

[**devastion, devastitation, devastor,** errors for DEVASTATION, DEVASTATOR, in some editions and Dicts.]

†**de'vaunt,** *v. Obs.* [app. a. OF. *desvanter* to vaunt excessively, make one's boast, f. *des-*, L. *dis-* + *vanter* to vaunt, boast.] To vaunt, boast.

c **1540** *Surr. Northampton Priory* in Prance *Addit. Narr. Pop. Plot* 36 To the most notable slaunder of Christs Holy Evangely, which..wee did ostentate and openly devant to keepe most exactly. [**1655** quoted by FULLER *Ch. Hist.* VI. 320 with spelling *devaunt*, mod. ed. *advaunte.*]

deve, obs. f. DEAVE *v.* to deafen and of DIVE *v.*

†**de'vection.** *Obs. rare*⁻⁰. [n. of action from L. *dēvehĕre* to carry down.]

1656 BLOUNT *Glossogr.*, *Devection*, a carrying away or down.

deveer, obs. form of DEVOIR, duty.

de'vehent, *a.* [ad. L. *dēvehent-em*, pr. pple. of *dēvehĕre* to carry down.] (See quot.)

1883 *Syd. Soc. Lex.*, *Devehent*, carrying away, efferent.

devel ('dɛv(ə)l), *sb. Sc.* Also devvel, devle. [Derivation unknown.] A severe or stunning blow. Hence **'devel** *v.*, to strike or knock down with a stunning blow; **'develler**, a boxer; also 'a dextrous young fellow' (Jamieson).

1786 BURNS *Tam Samson's Elegy* iii, Death's gien the Lodge an unco devel, Tam Samson's dead. **1807** TANNAHILL *Poems* 116 (Jam.) Guile soud be devel'd i' the dirt. **1816** SCOTT *Antiq.* xxv, Ae gude downright devvel will split it.

†**'develing,** *adv. Obs.* Also 3 duvelunge. [f. *duve, deve*, DIVE *v.* + -LING.] Headlong, as with a dive.

a **1225** *Juliana* 77 Ha beide hire & beah duuelunge adun. *a* **1225** *St. Marher.* 20 Ant te meiden duuelunge feol dun to þe eorðe. *c* **1320** *Sir Beues* 648 Into his chaumber he gan gon, and leide him deueling on þe grounde. *c* **1330** *Arth. & Merl.* 7762 (Mätz.) Mani threwe doun deueling riht.

develop (dɪ'vɛləp), *v.* Also 7 devellop, 7– develope. [a. F. *développe-r*, OF. (12–13th c.) *desvoleper, -volosper, -voloper*, 14th c. *desvelopper* (whence an earlier Eng. form DISVELOP), = Pr. *desvolopar, -volupar*, It. *sviluppare* 'to unwrap, to disentangle, to rid free' (Florio), f. *des-*, L. *dis-* + the Rom. verb which appears in mod.It. as *viluppare* 'to enwrap, to bundle, to folde, to roll up, to entangle, to trusse up, to heape up', *viluppo* 'an enwrapping, a bundle, a fardle, a trusse, an enfolding' (Florio).

The oldest form of the radical appears to have been *volupare, volopare*; its derivation is uncertain: see also ENVELOP.]

†**1. a.** *trans.* To unfold, unroll (anything folded or rolled up); to unfurl (a banner); to open out of its enfolding cover. *Obs.* (in general use.)

1592–1611 [see DISVELOP]. **1656** BLOUNT *Glossogr.*, *Developed* (Fr. *desvelopé*), unwrapped, unfolded, undone, displaied, opened. Ed. **1670** [adds] It is the proper term for spreading or displaying an Ensign in war. **1692** COLES, *Developed*, unfolded. **1730–6** BAILEY (folio), *Developed*, unwrapped, unfolded, opened. **1775** ASH, *Developed*, disentangled, disengaged, cleared from its covering. **1794** MISS GUNNING *Packet* I. 32, I must suppose he returned to the contents of the packet in the same hurry of spirits with which he first developed them. **1814** MRS. JANE WEST *Alicia de Lacy* III. 94 The red rose banner was developed in front of the Lancasterian army. **1868** CUSSANS *Her.* xx. 265 So depicted on the Standard as to appear correct when it was developed by the wind.

b. *Geom.* To flatten out (a curved surface, e.g. that of a cylinder or cone) as it were by unrolling it; also, in wider sense, to change the form of (a surface) by bending. See DEVELOPABLE b.

1879 THOMSON & TAIT *Nat. Phil.* I. I. §139 The process of changing the form of a surface by bending is called 'developing'. But the term 'Developable Surface' is commonly restricted to such inextensible surfaces as can be developed into a plane, or, in common language, 'smoothed flat'.

†**2. a.** To lay open by removal of that which enfolds (in a fig. sense), to unveil; to unfold (a tale, the meaning of a thing); to disclose, reveal. *Obs.* (exc. as passing into 3.)

1742 POPE *Dunc.* IV. 269 Then take him to devellop, if you can, And hew the Block off, and get out the Man. **1756** *Monitor* No. 35 Flattering his sagacity in developing the concealed meaning. **1789** T. JEFFERSON *Writ.* (1859) II. 554 To appeal to the nation, and to develop to it the ruin of their finances. **1812** J. J. HENRY *Camp. agst. Quebec* 156 The steam would search for a vent through the crevices of the door..and develop our measures. **1837** DICKENS *Pickw.* xvii, Nathaniel Pipkin determined that, come what might, he would develope the state of his feelings.

†**b.** To unveil or lay bare to oneself, to discover, detect, find out. *Obs.*

1770 C. JENNER *Placid Man* I. 53 This circumstance was of singular use to me in helping me to develope her real character. **1785** MRS. A. M. BENNETT *Juvenile Indiscretions* (1786) I. 172 No great penetration was required to develope the writer of this friendly billet. **1787** ANN HILDITCH *Rosa de Montmorien* I. 74 His principles were unimpeached, because none could ever develope their real tendency. **1796** J. MOSER *Hermit of Caucasus* I. 27 'Here,' said Ismael, 'is a recess which I hope is impossible to be develop'd.' **1802** tr. *A. La Fontaine's Reprobate* I. 153 To live amidst men whose real characters you will find it difficult, sometimes impossible, to develop. **1822** MRS. E. NATHAN *Langreath* I. 202 He did not possess the tact of developing in an instant the weakness of the human heart.

†**c.** To unroll or open up that which enfolds, covers, or conceals. *Obs.*

1779 *Sylph* I. 192 Nor will the signature contribute to develop the cloud behind which I chuse to conceal myself. *Ibid.* II. 41 If he should have..developed the thin veil I spread over the feelings I have laboured..to overcome. **1785** MRS. A. M. BENNETT *Juvenile Indiscretions* (1786) III. 41 Nor is it necessary they should have the trouble of developing the obscurity of my character.

3. a. To unfold more fully, bring out all that is potentially contained in.

1750 WARBURTON *Julian* Wks. 1811 VIII. xxviii, To instruct us in the history of the human mind, and to assist us in developing its faculties. **1790** SIR J. REYNOLDS *Disc.* xv, To develope the latent excellencies..of our art. **1827** HARE *Guesses* (1859) 285 One may develope an idea..But one cannot add to it, least of all in another age. **1864** BOWEN *Logic* ix. 268 To ascertain, develop, and illustrate its meaning. **1873** M. ARNOLD *Lit. & Dogma* v. (1876) 129 Learned religion elucidates and developes the relation of the Son to the Father. **1885** *Manch. Exam.* 10 July 5/3 The trade might be developed to almost any extent.

b. *Mil.* To open gradually (an attack).

1883 STEVENSON *Treas. Isl.* IV. xxi, The attack would be developed from the north.

c. *Mus.* See DEVELOPMENT 10.

1880 STAINER *Composition* ix. §161 A melody is rarely developed without frequent changes of key, or of harmony. *Ibid.* §162 A fragment of melody is said to be developed when its outline is altered and expanded so as to create new interest. *Ibid.*, Exercises. Develope by various methods the following subjects, as if portions of a Pianoforte Sonata.

d. *Chess.* Phrases: ***to develop one's game***, to move one or more men from the original position into positions more useful for attack or defence; ***to develop a piece***, to bring that piece towards or into a position where it is of greatest service.

1847 H. STAUNTON *Chess-Player's Handbk.* 22 In chess, this is attempted by the first player putting a Pawn en prise of the enemy early in the game, by which he is enabled more rapidly and effectually to develop his superior Pieces. *Ibid.* 147 Leaving him the option of exchanging Knights or of protecting his K.P., either of which would afford you an opportunity of developing your game. **1864** *Chess Player's Mag.* 52 Black, it seems, had no other chance of developing his game than to give up Rook for Knight at this point. **1952** E. LASKER *Chess Secrets* 41 He has developed one more piece than White.

e. To show the details of (a piece of work) in a drawing (cf. DEVELOPMENT 7 d).

1888 [see DEVELOPMENT 7 d].

f. To realize the potentialities of (a site, estate, property, or the like) by laying it out, building, mining, etc.; to convert (a tract of land) to a new purpose or to make it suitable for residential, industrial, business, etc., purposes.

1890 SIR R. ROMER in *Law Times' Rep.* LXIII. 685/2 For working and developing the property to the best advantage. **1901** *Times* 6 Nov. 5/1 Hogarth's house in Chiswick..will probably be purchased by a builder who will do what is called develop the property; we all know pretty well what that means. **1931** *Economist* 20 June 1312/1 It was unjust to apply this burden to 'developed' land, that is, to land the value of which has been raised by the energy or enterprise of its owner in putting it to good use. **1932** *Times Lit. Suppl.* 26 May 392/2 The tenants will be turned out as soon as possible and the whole estate 'developed' as a site for a factory.

4. *Math.* To change a mathematical function or expression into another of equivalent value or meaning and of more expanded form; *esp.* to expand into the form of a series.

1871 E. OLNEY *Infinit. Calc.* 67 It is proposed to discover the law of development, when the function can be developed in the form $y = f(x) = A + Bx + Cx^2 + Dx^3 + Ex^4 +$ etc.

5. a. To bring forth from a latent or elementary condition (a physical agent or condition of matter); to make manifest what already existed under some other form or condition.

1813 SIR H. DAVY *Agric. Chem.* (1814) 66 Acids are generally developed. **1831** BREWSTER *Optics* vii. 73 Such a white light I have succeeded in developing. **1834** MRS. SOMERVILLE *Connex. Phys. Sc.* xxx. (1849) 350 The same mechanical means which develope magnetism will also destroy it. **1839** G. BIRD *Nat. Phil.* 279 This mode of developing electricity was discovered.. by Prof. Seebeck. **1842** GROVE *Corr. Phys. Forces* 59 Heat is developed in some proportion to the disappearance of light. **1860** TYNDALL *Glac.* I. xx. 144 We thus develop both attraction and repulsion.

b. *Photogr.* To bring out and render visible (the latent image produced by actinic action upon the sensitive surface); to apply to (the plate or film) the chemical treatment by which this is effected. Also *absol.*

1845 *Athenæum* 22 Feb. 203/1 It is evident then, that all bodies are capable of photographic disturbance, and might be used for the production of pictures—did we know of easy methods by which the pictures might be developed. *Ibid.* 14 June 593/1 The paper used by Mr. Fox Talbot is the iodide of silver, and the picture is developed by the action of gallic acid. **1859** JEPHSON & REEVE *Brittany* 48 He went to and fro to develope the plates and prepare new ones. **1861** *Photogr. News Alm.* in *Circ. Sc.* I. 160/2 The plate can be developed for hours or days. **1863–72** WATTS *Dict. Chem.* II. 693 In order to develop the latent image, the [Daguerreotype] plate was exposed to the action of the vapour of mercury. **1873** TRISTRAM *Moab* xi. 203 All our photographs.. have failed, from an accident before they were developed. **1876** G. F. CHAMBERS *Astron.* 719, I prefer to develope with an iron solution. **1893** ABNEY *Photogr.* i. (ed. 8) 3.

c. *intr.* for *refl.*

1861 *Photogr. News Alm.* in *Circ. Sc.* I. 160/1 A plate well washed.. developes cleaner than one washed insufficiently.

d. *intr.* To come to light, become known. *U.S.*

1864 WEBSTER 366/1 The plans of the conspirators develop. **1903** *N.Y. Even. Post* 17 Sept., A new feature of the shooting developed to-day, when it was discovered that [etc.]. **1927** *N.Y. Times* 29 Sept. 1/6 It developed that Beach had been pressed for money.

e. *trans.* To reveal, bring to light. *U.S.*

1889 *Kansas Times & Star* 8 May, A census of Kansas City's saloons develops the startling fact that there are about 1,000. *Ibid.* 16 July, A search for the pioneer bicyclist hereabouts developed Dr. Henderson, who proudly rode a wheel on our streets in 1880. **1932** T. J. GRAYSON *Leaders & Periods of Amer. Finance* v. 95 He did develop the fact that enormous lump sum appropriations had been made.

6. *trans.* To cause to grow (what exists in the germ). **a.** Said of an organ or organism.

1857 HENFREY *Bot.* §40 In the Banyan tree adventitious roots are frequently developed on the outstretched woody branches. **1863** HUXLEY *Man's Place Nat.* 65 In the floor of which a notochord is developed. **1866** ARGYLL *Reign Law* ii. (ed. 4) 106 They grow, or, in modern phraseology they are developed. *a* **1871** GROTE *Eth. Fragm.* i. (1876) 15 Ethical sentiment tends to develop the benevolent impulses. **1878** BROWNING *Poets Croisic* 19 We need.. benevolence Of nature's sunshine to develop seed So well.

b. Said of a series of organisms showing progression from a simpler or lower to a higher or more complex type; to evolve.

1839 *Penny Cycl.* XIII. 281 He [Lamarck] supposed that all organized beings, from the lowest to the highest forms, were progressively developed from similar living microscopic particles. This may be called the theory of metamorphosis. **1857** H. MILLER *Test. Rocks* v. 200 The Lamarckian affirms that all our recent species of plants and animals were developed out of previously existing plants and animals of species entirely different. **1880** HAUGHTON *Phys. Georg.* vi. 273 Forces have been at work, developing in each great continent animal forms peculiar to itself.

7. *transf.* **a.** To evolve (as a product) from pre-existing materials; to cause to grow or come into active existence or operation.

1820 SHELLEY *Witch of Atlas* xxxvi, In its growth It seemed to have developed no defect Of either sex. **1834** HT. MARTINEAU *Moral* I. 5 Fresh powers.. which.. develop further resources. **1841–4** EMERSON *Ess.*, *Politics* Wks. (Bohn) I. 242 Wild liberty developes iron conscience. Want of liberty.. stupefies conscience. **1847** —— *Repr. Men, Napoleon* ibid. I. 369 The times.. and his early circumstances combined to develop this pattern democrat. **1866** ROGERS *Agric. & Prices* I. xxiii. 601 In the hope that a new set of customers might be developed. **1868** BAIN *Ment. & Mor. Sc.* Ethics (1875) 630 The situations of different ages and countries develop characteristic qualities.

b. To exhibit or display in a well-formed condition or in active operation.

1834 MEDWIN *Angler in Wales* II. 180 His organ of veneration was strongly developed. **1874** HELPS *Soc. Press.* iv. 63 It is astonishing what ambulatory powers he can develop. **1878** HUXLEY *Physiogr.* 169 The hardest rocks of Britain are developed in the western and northern parts of the island. **1885** *Manch. Exam.* 6 Apr. 5/3 Indignant jurymen have recently developed a quite unusual tendency to write letters to the newspapers.

8. *refl.* To unfold itself, come gradually into existence or operation.

1793 W. ROBERTS *Looker-on* (1794) III. No. 67. 36 This prominent part of their character began to develope itself. **1830** D'ISRAELI *Chas. I*, III. ii. 16 The faculties of Charles developed themselves. **1841** TRENCH *Parables*, *Tares* 96 We learn that evil.. is ever to develop itself more fully. **1847** L. HUNT *Jar Honey* x. (1848) 132 New beauties successively developed themselves. **1860** RUSKIN *Mod. Paint.* V. VII. iii. §8. 130 The quiet, thoroughly defined, infinitely divided and modelled pyramid [of cloud] never develops itself. **1875** BUCKLAND *Log-bk.* 276 A serious fault had developed itself. **1879** MᶜCARTHY *Own Times* II. xxii. 122 Our constitutional system grows and developes itself year after year.

9. *intr.* (for *refl.*) **a.** To unfold itself, grow from a germ or rudimentary condition; to grow into a fuller, higher, or maturer condition.

a **1843** SOUTHEY *Inscriptions* xxxv, How differently Did the two spirits.. Develope in that awful element. **1845** J. H. NEWMAN *Ess. Developm.* I. i. (1846) 37 An idea.. cannot develope at all except either by destroying, or modifying and incorporating with itself, existing modes of thinking and acting. **1859** KINGSLEY *Misc.*, *Swift & Pope* (1860) I. 285 The man.. goes on.. developing almost unconsciously. **1874** GREEN *Short Hist.* vii. §5. 387 London developed into the general mart of Europe. **1880** MᶜCARTHY *Own Times* IV. liv. 179 It seems certainly destined to develope rather than fade. **1884** L. MALET *Mrs. Lorimer* 11 Such women.. do not develop very early either spiritually or mentally.

b. Of diseases: To advance from the latent stage which follows the introduction of the germs, to that in which the morbid action manifests itself.

1891 *Law Times* XCII. 131/2 The time swine fever takes to develop.

developable (dɪˈvɛləpəb(ə)l), *a.* and *sb.* [f. prec. vb. + -ABLE: in mod.F. *développable.*]

A. *adj.* **a.** Capable of being developed or of developing.

1835 R. F. WILSON in *Newman's Lett.* (1891) II. 139 Principles.. only developable under one form. **1865** WILKINS *Pers. Names Bible* 360 It is the nature of symbolical names used sacramentally to possess a developable significance. **1875** WHITNEY *Life Lang.* xiv. 292 Instinctive gesture, developable into a complete system of expression. **1879** JEVONS in *Contemp. Rev.* Nov. 537 It now becomes a moving and developable moral sense.

b. *Math.* (*a*) Of a function or expression: Capable of being expanded. (*b*) Of a curved surface: Capable of being unfolded or flattened out: (see DEVELOP *v.* 1 b).

1816 tr. *Lacroix' Diff. & Int. Calc.* 479 If $f(\Delta)$ be a function of Δ developable in a series of powers of Δ.. then [etc.]. **1840** LARDNER *Geom.* 247 Two developable surfaces will intersect in a right line, if the right lines, by the motion of which they are generated, coincide in any one position. **1865** ALDIS *Solid Geom.* ix. §146 Ruled surfaces in which consecutive generating lines lie in one plane are called *developable surfaces*, while all other ruled surfaces are called *skew surfaces.* **1866** PROCTOR *Handbk. Stars* 16 *note*, In reality.. even such narrow strips of a globe are not developable, and the chord and arc of five degrees are not equal, as they are assumed to be.

c. *Photogr.* Capable of being developed (see DEVELOP *v.* 5 b).

1878 ABNEY *Treat. Photogr.* iv. 30 An exposure in the camera to produce a developable image would have to be very prolonged. **1907** *Westm. Gaz.* 26 Oct. 13/2 They take only a short time to produce a developable condition in the emulsion. **1958** *Amateur Photographer* 31 Dec. 393/2 The need for one quantum (the unit of energy) to strike each grain of silver to make it developable.

B. *sb.* (*Math.*) A developable surface; a ruled surface in which consecutive generators intersect.

1874 SALMON *Geom. three Dimens.* §305 The locus of points where two consecutive generators of a developable intersect is a curve.. which is called the cuspidal edge of that developable.

deˈveloped, *ppl. a.* [f. DEVELOP *v.* + -ED] In senses of the vb. *spec.* economically advanced, industrialized; esp. as ***developed country***. Cf. *developing country* s.v. DEVELOPING *ppl. a.* and UNDER-DEVELOPED *a.* b.

1656 BLOUNT *Glossogr.*, *Developed* [see DEVELOP *v.* 1]. **1859** MILL *Liberty* iii. (1865) 37/2 To show, that these developed human beings are of some use to the undeveloped. **1945** *Ann. Reg. 1944* 137 Fully urbanised natives, native farm-workers, 'relatively developed' and dependent on regular earnings. **1962** J. K. GALBRAITH *Econ. Devel. in Perspective* iii. 31 In the modern and developed economy there is a certain choice as to how resources.. will be organized for productive purposes. **1968** *New Statesman* 19 July 82/2 The advance of the developed countries today and the nature and rate of change in modern technology are such as constantly to widen the gap between the rich and the poor. **1971** *Nature* 11 June 341/1 The sad condition of Bengal will remain as a sombre reproach to developed nations for many years to come. **1978** *Internat. Rel. Dict.* (U.S. Dept. State Library) 11/2 Developed countries were asked to provide 1 percent of their national incomes as financial aid to developing countries. **1986** *Times* 15 Apr. 24/2 The drift of mineral production, smelting, refining and even fabrication from developed industrial countries to developing and industrializing competitors.

developer (dɪˈvɛləpə(r)), *sb.* [f. DEVELOP *v.* + -ER.] He who or that which develops.

1833 WHEWELL in Todhunter *Acc. Whewell's Writ.* (1876) II. 164 That you should think I have done any injustice to the mathematical developers. **1846** G. S. FABER *Lett. Tractar. Secess.* 98 A developer of the Adoration of the Host from the unestablished doctrine of Transubstantiation. **1850** MAURICE *Mor. & Met. Philos.* (ed. 2) 85 Developers of a certain set of theories about gods, men, and nature. **1894** *Chicago Advance* 4 Jan., The home is the great developer of individuality and character.

b. *Photogr.* A chemical agent by which photographs are developed.

1869 *Eng. Mech.* 3 Dec. 281/3 By judicious management of the developer, an over-exposed and under-exposed plate can be made to work equally well. **1879** *Cassell's Techn. Educ.* IV. 323/2 The iron developer and the pyrogallic acid solution for intensifying. **1890** ABNEY *Photogr.* (ed. 6) 20 The chemical agents which are utilized in order to allow the development of the latent image to take place.. are technically called developers, a term which, critically speaking, is a misnomer, as in the majority of cases the part they play is a secondary one.

c. *Photogr.* An operative who develops photographs.

1899 *Daily News* 28 Apr. 5/2 We had two men on the train—our regular developer and his assistant. **1921** in *Dict. Occup. Terms* (1927) §527.

d. An apparatus for developing a person's muscles, etc.

1900 E. SANDOW *Strength* (rev. ed.) 41 The great value of the Developer lies in the fact that it serves to render the muscles pliable. *Ibid.*, Exercise with the rubber Developer affords a welcome change from work with the dumb-bells. **1907** *Westm. Gaz.* 17 Jan. 4/2 With regard to the use of grip dumb-bells and the developer, they are not intended for the abnormal development of any one muscle. **1971** *Woman* 13 Mar. 45 (Advt.), The world's most successful bustline developer.

e. With defining word prefixed: a person who develops or matures at a specified time or speed, as ***late*** or ***slow developer*** (see also quot. 1961).

1930 R. LEHMANN *Note in Music* VI. 249, I was a very slow developer. By the time I started to wake up and think for myself, it was too late. **1936** A. THIRKELL *August Folly* vi. 166 He is one of those late developers, trying to himself and to others. **1942** F. J. SCHONELL *Backwardness in Basic Subjects* iii. 53 They subscribe to the doctrine that dull children are frequently slow developers. **1953** R. FULLER *2nd Curtain* vi. 103 How frightful I must have been at thirteen... I was a late developer. **1961** *Where?* III. 15 *Late developer*, a term used to describe a child whose mental capacity matures notably later than that of most children. It is often used of a pupil who shows increasing evidence of higher ability than was apparent at 11 plus. **1971** *T.V. Times* 11 Mar. 7/3, I have loved my 30's. I am a late developer.

f. One who develops (see DEVELOP *v.* 3 f) a site, etc.; a speculative builder.

1938 N. L. NORTH *Real Estate Selling* xvii. 257 The result was no sales, defaulted contracts, 'busted' developers. **1958** *Observer* 2 Mar. 8/4 As 'developers' and L.P.T.B. leap-frogged over each other.. far into the Home Counties. **1971** M. RUSSELL *Deadline* ix. 103 A developer who was.. putting in a bid for the airfield with a view of erecting.. a shopping precinct.

deˈveloping, *vbl. sb.* [f. DEVELOP *v.* + -ING¹.] In senses of the vb. Also *attrib.*, as ***developing cup***, ***room***, ***solution***; **developing circle** *Spiritualism*, a group of people who meet for the purpose of developing the latent psychic abilities they may possess; **developing (out) paper** (see quot. 1918).

1775 ASH, *Developing*, disentangling, disengaging, uncovering. *c* **1865** J. WYLDE in *Circ. Sc.* I. 148/2 The result of developing depends.. on the strength of the silver solution.

attrib. **1870** *Spiritualist* 15 Oct. 111/1 A Developing Circle... Mr. A. C. Swinton.. has favoured us with the following details about the gradual development of mediumship in the circle held at his house. **1960** H. EDWARDS *Spirit Healing* i. 16, I received a number of messages from mediums stating that I possessed the healing gift. So I attended two church developing circles, where I again received encouragement to utilise my gift of healing. **1967** *Psychic News* 22 Apr. 8/3 In my view, would-be healers should sit in a developing circle to receive knowledge from competent spirit guides before attempting to treat patients. **1878** ABNEY *Treat. Photogr.* xvi. 118 The solution should be flowed back into the developing cup. **1884** T. C. HEPWORTH *Photogr. Amat.* 149 Wavy markings on a developed plate may generally be traced to dirty dishes or developing-cups. **1918** *Photo-Miniature* Mar. 15 *Developing Out Papers* (*D.O.P.*), papers requiring to be developed, but of such sensitiveness that they can be printed by exposure to gaslight, yet developed by the same, placed at a greater distance. **1890** *Anthony's Photogr. Bull.* III. 166 Any one who has ever manipulated developing paper. **1882** TYNDALL in *Longm. Mag.* I. 32 The photographer.. illuminates his developing room with light transmitted through red or yellow glass. **1861** *Photogr. News Alm.* in *Circ. Sc.* I. 160/1 Take a sufficient quantity of the.. developing solution.

deˈveloping, *ppl. a.* [f. DEVELOP *v.* + -ING².] In senses of the vb. Esp. in ***developing country***, ***nation***, a poor or primitive country which is developing higher economic, industrial, and social conditions.

1879 *Athenæum* 83/2 Developing animals may at any stage in embryonic history become more or less profoundly modified. **1880** A. WILSON in *Gentl. Mag.* CCXLVI. 45 It.. might be ranked as a developing snail. **1964** H. MYINT (*title*) The economics of the developing countries. **1969** R. BLACKBURN in Cockburn & Blackburn *Student Power* 208 Bourgeois economists once talked about the economically 'backward' countries; then 'underdeveloped' was felt to be a kinder adjective. They now prefer to refer to poor capitalist countries as 'developing nations'. **1971** *Times* 17 Mar. 4/6 Many developing countries are facing growing unrest among young people.

deˈvelopist. *nonce-word.* [f. as DEVELOPER *v.* + -IST.] An evolutionist.

1854 H. STRICKLAND *Travel Thoughts* 12 You are a Vestiges of Creation developist, and think that a Frenchman may, by cultivation, be developed into an Englishman.

development (dɪˈvɛləpmənt). Also 8–9 develope-. [f. DEVELOP *v.* + -MENT, after F. *développement*, in 15th c. *desv-*.] **I.** The process or fact of developing; the concrete result of this process.

1. A gradual unfolding, a bringing into fuller view; a fuller disclosure or working out of the details of anything, as a plan, a scheme, the plot of a novel. Also quasi-*concr.* that in which the fuller unfolding is embodied or realized.

[**1752** CHESTERF. *Lett.* cclxxvi. (1792) III. 263 A *développement* that must prove fatal to Regal and Papal pretensions.] **1756** J. WARTON *Ess. Pope* I. 49 (T.) These observations on Thomson..might still be augmented by an examination and developement of the beauties in the loves of the birds, in Spring; a view of the torrid zone in Summer; [etc.]. **1759** STERNE *Tr. Shandy* I. xiii. (R.), A map..with many other pieces and developements of this work will be added to the end of the twentieth volume. **1786** *Francis the Philanthropist* I. 155 Congratulations..on the developement, so much to his honour, of this intricate and confused affair. **1851** GLADSTONE *Glean.* IV. v. 5 Essential to the entire development of my case.

2. Evolution or bringing out from a latent or elementary condition; the production of a natural force, energy, or new form of matter.

1794 SULLIVAN *View Nat.* I. 176 How slow is the developement of heat. **1863** E. V. NEALE *Anal. Th. & Nat.* 214 The development discernible in nature, is only the bringing to light a new manifestation of forces already existing, with the same characters, under some other manifestation. **1863** TYNDALL *Heat* i. §6. (1870) 5 Experiments which illustrate the development of heat by mechanical means.

3. The growth and unfolding of what is in the germ; the condition of that which is developed: **a.** of organs and organisms.

1796 JEFFERSON in Morse *Amer. Geog.* I. 92 The developement and formation of great germs. **1813** SIR H. DAVY *Agric. Chem.* (1814) 213 The various stages of the development and decay of their organs. **1835** KIRBY & SP. *Entomol.* Let. iii, The transformations of insects..strictly, they ought rather to be termed a series of developments. **1846** DANA *Zooph.* (1848) 686 The latter also differ in their modes of developement. **1862** SIR B. BRODIE *Psychol. Inq.* II. i. 5 Watching the development of buds and flowers. **1875** BENNETT & DYER tr. *Sachs' Bot.* 327 As the development progresses the cells..become differentiated. **1877** HUXLEY *Anat. Inv. Anim.* iii. 111 The development of the sponges has been carefully investigated. **1880** HAUGHTON *Phys. Geog.* i. 16 Some are now in their infancy; others in the full vigour of their development.

b. Of races of plants and animals: The same as EVOLUTION; the evolutionary process and its result. ***development theory*** or ***hypothesis*** (*Biol.*): the doctrine of Evolution; applied especially to that form of the doctrine taught by Lamarck (died 1829).

1844 R. CHAMBERS *Vestiges of Creation* 191 (*title*), Hypothesis of the Development of the Vegetable and Animal Kingdoms. *Ibid.* 202 The whole train of animated beings..are then to be regarded as a series of *advances of the principle of development*, which have depended upon external physical circumstances to which the resulting animals are appropriate. **1849** H. MILLER *Footpr. Creat.* xiii. (1874) 243 The development visions of the Lamarckian. **1851** G. F. RICHARDSON *Introd. Geol.* 306 The theory of progressive development receives no support from the facts unfolded by the history of fossil reptiles. **1866** ARGYLL *Reign Law* i. (ed. 4) 32 All theories of Development have been simply attempts to suggest..the physical process by means of which, this ideal continuity of type and pattern has been preserved. **1871** TYLOR *Prim. Cult.* I. 1 Its various grades may be regarded as stages of development or evolution, each the outcome of previous history. **1878** STEWART & TAIT *Unseen Univ.* iv. §151. 156 Creation belongs to eternity and development to time.

c. The bringing out of the latent capabilities (of anything); the fuller expansion (of any principle or activity).

1865 R. W. DALE *Jew. Temp.* xii. (1877) 131 A promise the final developement and fulness of which we are still waiting for. **1874** GREEN *Short Hist.* v. §2. 225 A yet larger development of their powers was offered to the Commons by Edward himself. *Ibid.* ix. 697 A mightier and more rapid development of national energy. **1878** LECKY *Eng. in 18th C.* II. v. 50 The real development of Scotch industry dates from the Union of 1707. **1879** LUBBOCK *Addr. Pol. & Educ.* iv. 85 Natural science, as a study is perhaps the first in development of our powers. **1879** *Cassell's Techn. Educ.* IV. 34/2 This extraordinary development of the iron manufacture.

d. The act or process of developing (see DEVELOP *v.* 3 f) a mine, site, estate, property, or the like; also, a developed tract of land. Freq. *attrib.*, esp. in ***development work*** (see also sense 11 below). Cf. *ribbon development*.

1885 *Pall Mall G.* 12 Feb. 5/2 No development work has been done whatever, not a shaft has been sunk. **1897** *Daily News* 4 Jan. 2/1 During the year an unusual amount of development work was done on the producing mines. **1898** *Westm. Gaz.* 21 Apr. 4/3 Advance moneys for development purposes. **1900** *Daily News* 11 June 2/1 Development operations have been carried out upon the Le Roi, No. 2 Property. **1904** CONRAD *Nostromo* II. iii. 126 The new loan connected with railway development. **1936** P. NASH *Dorset* 6 All those courageous enemies of 'development' to whom we owe what is left of England. **1947** S. J. TRUSCOTT *Mine Econ.* (ed. 2) ii. 8 Sampling for the establishment of reserves is conducted primarily upon the exposures along the roads by which the deposit is explored and the property developed, this being development sampling. **1957** W. H. WHYTE *Organization Man* 274 The little developments that encircle some towns. **1962** A. CHRISTIE *Mirror Crack'd* i. 16 All the people from the Development doing their shopping. *Ibid.* 17 Where once there had been meadows with cows, there was the Development.

e. The economic advancement of a region or people, esp. one currently under-developed (sense b).

1902 *Daily Chron.* 25 Nov. 4/5 This consideration leads us to what is the supreme need for all parts of that country, namely, economic development. 'Development first' was the formula for the moment used by Lord Milner in his latest speech. What South Africa..needs above all is..the primary plant of civilised development. **1945** *Political Q.* Oct.–Dec. 359 Economic development has benefited large sections of the people in Anatolia. **1966** *New Statesman* 11 Mar. 355/3 (Advt.), The Institute of Development Studies the University of Sussex..Professorial fellow in Development Economics. **1982** *Dædalus* Spring 133 All African countries lack sufficient managerial, administrative, and technical skills to undertake the massive task of development contemplated at independence.

4. Gradual advancement through progressive stages, growth from within.

1836 J. GILBERT *Chr. Atonem.* iv. (1852) 104 Only where those means exist..is there a development of holy character. **1845** J. H. NEWMAN *Ess. Developm.* I. i. (1846) 37 The development of an idea, being the germination, growth, and perfection of some living..truth. **1861** GARBETT *Boyle Lect.* 46 This scheme..exhibits a progressive development, in which there is not a missing link. **1862** S. LUCAS *Secularia* 6 Nations proceed in a course of Development, their later manifestations being potentially present in the earliest elements. **1867** FREEMAN *Norm. Conq.* (1876) I. iv. 251 Gradual developement without any sudden change.

5. A developed or well-grown condition; a state in which anything is in vigorous life or action.

1851 G. F. RICHARDSON *Introd. Geol.* 258 The genus Serpula..attained its greatest development in the oolitic seas. **1851** MANSEL *Proleg. Log.* (1860) 18 His disciple..has carried the doctrine to its fullest development. **1870** ROLLESTON *Anim. Life* Introd. 49 The great development of the sternum whence the muscles of flight take origin. **1871** SMILES *Charac.* xii. (1876) 366 The highest development of their genius. **1875** JOWETT *Plato* (ed. 2) I. 76 The Laches has more play and development of character.

6. The developed result or product; a developed form of some earlier and more rudimentary organism, structure, or system.

1845 J. H. NEWMAN *Ess. Developm.* I. iii. (1846) 58 The butterfly is the development..of the grub. **1856** FROUDE *Hist. Eng.* (1858) I. i. 2 The last orders of Gothic architecture were the development of the first. **1871** R. W. DALE *Commandm.* Introd. 4 The Christian Faith may be spoken of as, in some sense, the development of Judaism. **1873** M. ARNOLD *Lit. & Dogma* Pref. (1876) 22 Attacking Romish developments from the Bible, which..were evidently..false developments. **1877** E. R. CONDER *Bas. Faith* i. 5 Natural to man only as a development, not as an original element in his nature.

II. Technical uses.

7. a. *Geom.* The action of unrolling a cylindrical or conical surface, the unbending of any curved surface into a plane, or of a non-plane curve into a plane curve. †**b.** Applied to the unrolling of a papyrus or other roll which has become rigid (*obs.*).

1800 J. HAYTER *Herculanean & Pompeian MSS.* 12 About thirty years ago, His Sicilian Majesty ordered the Developement, the Transcription, and the printing of the Volumes [rolls]..to be undertaken. **1817** (*title*), Herculaneum Rolls.—Correspondence Relative to a Proposition made by Dr. Sickler, of Hildburghausen, upon the Subject of their Development. **1878** HUXLEY *Physiogr.* xix. 333 Let the outline of the country be projected on this cone: then on unfolding the paper, it may be spread out on a flat surface: hence the method is known as that of conical development. *Ibid.* 336 The polar regions are not brought within Mercator's projection, for the poles are supposed, by the cylindrical development to be indefinitely distant.

c. See quots.

1874 KNIGHT *Dict. Mech.*, *Development*, The process of drawing the figures which given lines on a curved surface would assume, if that surface were a flexible sheet and were spread out flat upon a plane without alteration of area and without distortion. **1879** *Cassell's Techn. Educ.* IV. 195/1 To draw the various forms required in 'development'—that is the covering of surfaces.

d. The indication of the full details of a piece of work, esp. in a technical drawing.

1888 *Lockwood's Dict. Mech. Engin.* 107 *Development.* A drawing is said to be developed when certain working details are drawn in full. Thus a propeller blade is developed when the various transverse sections are shown. **1904** GOODCHILD & TWENEY *Technol. & Sci. Dict.* 156/2 *Development*, giving full details of some part of a piece of work.

8. *Math.* The process by which any mathematical expression is changed into another of equivalent value or meaning, and of more expanded form; the expanded form itself.

1816 tr. *Lacroix' Diff. & Int. Calc.* 148 This developement has been obtained by first putting $x + h$ instead of x. **1837** *Penny Cycl.* VIII. 445/1 The mathematical use of an expression is frequently facilitated by employing its development. —— *Ibid.*, The usual form of development is into infinite series.

9. The action of developing a photograph; the process whereby the latent image on the exposed film is rendered visible by the chemical precipitation of new material on the surface.

1845 *Athenæum* 29 Mar. 312/3 If an impressed Daguerreotype plate..be exposed to the vapour of chlorine, iodine, or bromine..the nascent picture is obliterated, so as to be no longer capable of developement by the vapour of mercury. **1861** *Photogr. News Alm.* in *Circ. Sc.* I. 160/2 Add more silver, till the development is complete. **1881** *Eng. Mech.* No. 874. 382/1 The exposed plates, after development and before fixing, should be put [etc.].

10. a. *Mus.* The unfolding of the qualities or capacities of a musical phrase or subject by modifications of melody, harmony, tonality, rhythm, etc., esp. in a composition of elaborate form, as a sonata; the part of a movement in which this takes place. Also *attrib.*

1880 PARRY in Grove *Dict. Mus.* s.v., The most perfect types of development are to be found in Beethoven's works, with whom not seldom the greater part of a movement is the constant unfolding and opening out of all the latent possibilities of some simple rhythmic figure. **1880** STAINER *Composition* ix. §156 This splendid musical form [sonata-form] differs..chiefly in having a Development-portion. *Ibid.* §166 A figure, or rhythmic motive, or melodic phrase from any part preceding the double bar [of a movement in sonata-form] may be chosen for development. **1889** H. A. HARDING *Analysis of Form* 5 The Coda begins with a development of the figure taken from the 1st subject. *Ibid.*, The development commences in C major.

b. *Chess.* The disposition of the forces for attack or defence at an early stage of a game.

1864 *Chess Player's Mag.* 195 The difficulty..of meeting the many new developments of the attack, especially those resulting from 9 Q.Kt. to B.3rd, has led to a reaction in favour of the move Q.Kt. to R.4th. **1865** *Ibid.* 48 In order to fix a Pawn at his Q. fifth, and so obstruct the development of Black's cavalry. **1889** FREEBOROUGH & RANKEN *Chess Openings* 13 There are two styles of development; the attacking and the defensive. In one the pieces are spread about to secure the greatest possible command of the board. In the other they are kept together mutually supporting or defending each other. *Ibid.* 14 When you cannot see your way to an attacking move, play a development move. **1970** B. LARSEN *Larsen's Selected Games of Chess 1948–69* 181 Severe cases of neglected development are rare in master games.

11. *attrib.* **development area**, any of several areas designated by the Distribution of Industry Act of 1945 as places suffering or liable to suffer from unemployment, where new industries, etc., are encouraged. See also 3 d.

1945 *Act 8 & 9 Geo. VI* c. 36 §1 In any area specified in the First Schedule to this Act (hereinafter referred to as a 'development area') the Board of Trade may for the purpose of facilitating the provision of premises needed for meeting the requirements of industrial undertakings (including requirements arising from the needs of persons employed or to be employed therein)..acquire..land for the provision..of such premises. **1948** *Times Rev. Industry* Aug. 28/3, 117 new factory buildings and extensions were completed in the development areas. **1961** E. A. POWDRILL *Vocab. Land Planning* iv. 65 Industrial estates should not necessarily be confused with the Government's programme for inducing industry to occupy sites in Development Areas.

Hence **developmen'tarian**, **de'velopmentist**, *nonce-wds.*, one who holds a theory of development or evolution in biology, theology, etc.; an evolutionist.

1865 *Morn. Star* 2 Sept., The most curious part of the business is that some polygenists are also developmentarians. **1870** *Sat. Rev.* XXIX. 807 If Mr. Proctor were a developmentist, and boldly laid it down that out of elementary substances of proved identity with those of our earth..life..must of necessity be engendered in forms much the same as those we know. **1888** *Indian Churchman* 26 May 144 No loophole of escape is here left for the 'developmentarians'.

developmental (dɪˌvɛləp'mɛntəl), *a.* [f. prec. + -AL[1].] Of, pertaining, or incidental to development; evolutionary.

developmental disease, a disease which is associated with a stage or process in the development of the body.

1849 OWEN *Parthenogenesis* 8 So much of the primary developmental processes. **1859** DARWIN *Orig. Species* xiv. (1873) 390 Sometimes it is only the earlier developmental stages which fail. **1864** *Daily Tel.* 27 July, Deaths by convulsions rose from 38 to 71..by developmental diseases of children from 24 to 42. **1883** *Birm. Weekly Post* 11 Aug. 3/6 One of the diseases, so called, of the developmental class—viz., senile decay. **1884** *Knowledge* No. 160. 421 They are interesting from a developmental point of view. **1890** HUMPHRY *Old Age* 5 A developmental or physiological death terminates the developmental or physiological decay.

Hence **develop'mentalist**, an evolutionist. Also *attrib.*

1862 *Temple Bar Mag.* V. 215 According to the developmentalists..the various races of men..gradually developed themselves in the progress of ages, from lower forms of animal life. **1936** M. T. HODGEN *Doctrine of Survivals* iii. 72 All developmentalists were committed to the search for social origins. **1936** *Times Lit. Suppl.* 20 June 524/1 Questions for which the current developmentalist methodology has no answer. **1957** *Antiquity* XXXI. 215 Opposition to the independent developmentalists came from those who could demonstrate..the diffusion of certain traits.

develop'mentalism. [f. DEVELOPMENTAL *a.* + -ISM.] Belief in development or evolution; evolutionism.

1934 *Mind* XLIII. 393 Bartlett's notion of a 'Schema'..incorporates developmentalism. **1936** M. T. HODGEN *Doctrine of Survivals* vi. 188 Developmentalism may well suffer defeat. **1947** C. S. LEWIS *Miracles* xiv. 146 A certain degree of 'evolutionism' or 'developmentalism' is inherent in Christianity.

develop'mentally, *adv.* [f. DEVELOPMENTAL *a.* + -LY[2].] In relation or reference to development.

1849–52 OWEN in Todd *Cycl. Anat.* IV. 873/1 The investigation..of this vast subject zootomically, developmentally, and microscopically. **1863** HUXLEY *Man's Place Nat.* iii. 148 The base of the skull may be demonstrated developmentally to be its relatively fixed part. **1874** CARPENTER *Ment. Phys.* II. xv. (1879) 571 The retina may be developmentally regarded as a kind of off-shoot from the optic ganglion.

‖**développé** (devlɔpe). *Ballet.* Also **développée.** [Fr., pa. pple. of *développer* to stretch out, unwind, develop.] A movement in which one leg is raised and then fully extended.

1913 C. D'ALBERT *Dancing* 61 *Développé*... A temps, signifying the slow unfolding of the leg to its full length, whilst placing it in the position demanded. **1953** *Ballet Ann.* VII. 127/2 Some stunning développées growing out of incredible *pirouettes.* **1959** *Times* 10 Sept. 6/3 Miss Svetlana Beriosova..generously expressive in the sweep of her *développés.*

†**de'venerate,** *v. Obs.*—⁰. [ad. L. *dēvenerārī* to reverence, f. DE- 3 + *venerārī* to worship.]

1623 COCKERAM, *Deuenerate,* to worship.

†**deve'nustate,** *v. Obs. rare*—¹. [f. late L. *dēvenustāre* (Gellius) to disfigure, deform, f. DE- 6 + *venustāre* to beautify, *venustus* beautiful: see -ATE³.] *trans.* To deprive of beauty or comeliness; to disfigure, deform.

1653 WATERHOUSE *Apol. Learning* 245 (L.) To see what yet remains of beauty and order devenustated, and exposed to shame and dishonour.

†**dever,** *sb. Obs.* ME. form of DEVOIR, duty.

deverbal (dɪ'vɜːbəl), *sb.* and *a. Gram.* [f. DE- + VERB + -AL¹.] **A.** *adj.* Derived from a verb. **B.** *sb.* = DEVERBATIVE *sb.*

1934 PRIEBSCH & COLLINSON *German Lang.* II. iii. 225 The suffix *-ēn* had two specific functions: (*a*) to form durative deverbals, e.g. *hangēn* 'to be hanging'. **1946** *Ibid.* (ed. 2) 256 The deverbal derivatives. **1959** *Archivum Linguisticum* XI. 108 Runner—deverbal noun.

deverbative (dɪ'vɜːbətɪv), *sb.* and *a. Gram.* [f. DE- + VERB, after *denominative.*] **A.** *sb.* A word formed on or derived from a verb. **B.** *adj.* Derived from a verb.

1913 J. M. JONES *Welsh Gram.* 381 Other Aryan stem-forms, mostly deverbatives and denominatives. **1949** *Archivum Linguisticum* I. 167 The verbal base is either radical or thematic, the first being monosyllabic and primary, i.e. neither deverbative nor denominative. **1951** *Trans. Philol. Soc. 1951* 116 Secondary formations, perhaps deverbatives based on the common verbs. **1970** *Language* XLVI. 381 The three morphemes are mutually exclusive, and each of them is related..to large sets of nominal roots and deverbative nouns.

†**de'vergence.** *Obs. rare*—⁰. [ad. late L. *dēvergentia* (Gellius) an inclining downward, a sloping, f. *dēvergĕre,* f. DE- I + *vergĕre* to incline, turn.] Downward slope, declivity.

1727 BAILEY vol. II, *Devergence,* a devexity or declivity, by which any thing tends or declines downward. **1755** JOHNSON, *Devergence,* declivity, declination. (*Dict.*) **1847** CRAIG, *Devergence, Devergency,* declivity; declination. *Obs.* [**1864** WEBSTER, *Devergence, Devergency,* the same as *Divergence.*]

devers, deversion, -itie: see DIVERS-.

†**de'versary.** *Obs. rare.* [? ad. L. *dēversōrium* lodging-house, inn.] ? A lodging-house, inn, tavern: see DIVERSORY.

c **1485** *Digby Myst.* (1882) III. 754, I was drynchyn In synne deversarye.

devest (dɪ'vɛst), *v. arch.* [a. OF. *devester* (13th c.), also *desvestir* (12th c. in Hatzf.), f. *des-, dé-* = L. *dis-* (see DE- 6, DIS-) + *vestir,* mod.F. *vêtir*:—L. *vestīre* to clothe. The Latin dictionaries cite a single instance of *dēvestīre* to undress, from Appuleius; but in Romanic, the prefix is *dis-, des-*: cf. Pr. *desvestir, devestir,* It. *divestire,* med.L. *dis-, dī-, dē-vestire,* from OFr. In later English the prefix is conformed to classical L. analogies as DIVEST, q.v., and *devest* now survives only in sense 5 (in which *divest* also occurs).]

†**1.** *trans.* To unclothe, undress, disrobe (a person); *refl.* to undress oneself. *Obs.*

1598 YONG *Diana* 13 If that she was alone, deuesting her. **1599** SHAKS. *Hen. V,* II. iv. 78 That you deuest your selfe, and lay apart The borrowed Glories. **1604** —— *Oth.* II. iii. 181 Like Bride and Groome Deuesting them for Bed. **1623** COCKERAM, *Deuest,* to vncloath one. *a* **1625** FLETCHER *Woman's Prize* I. ii, Leave it Maria: Devest you with obedient hands; to bed! **1649** *Alcoran* 417 Whose filthy nakedness must appear When he is devested.

†**b.** *fig.* To dismantle, reduce to a defenceless state.

1652 GAULE *Magastrom.* 335 The City of Rome being mightily devested by the Gaules, the Senators began to deliberate, whether they should repaire their ruined walls, or flee to Vejus.

†**2.** To strip (a person) *of* clothes, armour, etc.; to strip or deprive of anything that clothes or covers, or is *fig.* considered to do so. *Obs.*

1583 STANYHURST *Æneis* I. (Arb.) 33 Troilus hee marcked running, deuested of armour. **1683** GADBURY in *Wharton's Wks.* Pref., Left naked, and devested of every thing. **1687** DRYDEN *Hind & P.* I. 187 And Aaron of his Ephod to devest. **1722** WOLLASTON *Relig. Nat.* v. 122 Thoughts in their naked state, devested of all words. **1809** KENDALL *Trav.* II. xlvii. 148 One crab devested of its shell.

†**3.** *fig.* To strip (a person or thing) *of* (*from*) possessions, rights, or attributes; to denude, dispossess, deprive; rarely in good sense, to free, rid.

1563 SACKVILLE in *Mirr. Mag., Buckingham* xxix, The royall babes deuested from theyr trone. **1640** SANDERSON *Serm.* II. 155 We will speak of things..considered in themselves, and as they stand devested of all circumstances. **1641** MILTON *Ch. Govt.* II. iii. (1851) 158 With much more reason..ought the censure of the Church be quite devested and disintal'd of all jurisdiction. **1647** WARD *Simp. Cobler* 15 What a Cruelty it is to devest Children of that onely externall priviledge! **1647** JER. TAYLOR *Dissuas. Popery* II. I. §11 How to devest it from its evil appendages. **1660** —— *Duct. Dubit.* II. i, To say that God..had devested them of their rights. **1671** *True Nonconf.* 268 To devest Preaching of this Authority. **1686** GOAD *Celest. Bodies* I. xviii. 117 The Aspects are not wholly devested of Influence when under the Horizon.

†**4. a.** To take or pluck off (the clothing of any one). **b.** To put off (clothing, anything worn, borne, possessed, or held); to throw off, give up, lay aside, abandon. *Obs.*

1566 DRANT *Horace* To Rdr. 2 Few or none doo attempt to deuest or pluck of her vaile of hypocrisie. **1625** DONNE *Serm.* lxvi. 667 As those Angels doe not devest Heaven by coming, so there, Soules invest Heaven in their going. **1626** *Ibid.* iv. 33 No man that hath taken Orders can..devest his orders when he will. *a* **1631** *Ibid.* i. (1634) 5 The highest cannot devest mortality. —— *Poems* (1650) 252 Who..made whole townes devest Their wals and bulwarks. **1673** S. C. *Art of Complaisance* 5 Perswading them that we have devested our own enmity. **1675** *Art Contentm.* ix. §4. 224 That ugly form..by use devests its terror. **1765** BLACKSTONE *Comm.* I. 370 This natural allegiance..cannot be devested without [etc.].

†**c.** refl. *to devest oneself of*: to strip or dispossess oneself of; to put or throw off, lay down, lay aside. *Obs.*

1633 J. DONE *Hist. Septuagint* 2 His Father..devested himselfe of all Authority. **1651** HOBBES *Leviath.* II. xxvi. 147 To be able..to devest himselfe of all fear. **1672** MARVELL *Reh. Transp.* I. 239 The same day that they took up Divinity, they devested themselves of humanity. **1707** *Curios. in Husb. & Gard.* 330 Salt..cannot devest it self of the Impression it had received from Nature. **1791** BOSWELL *Johnson* an. 1783 (1816) IV. 273 The Reverend Mr. Shaw, a native of the Hebrides..devested himself of national bigotry.

5. *Law.* **a.** To take away (a possession, right, or interest vested in any one), to alienate; to annul (any vested right), to convey away. *to devest out of*: the opposite of to 'vest in'.

1574 tr. *Littleton's Tenures* 32 a, They cannot deveste that thing in fee which hath beene vested in theire house. **1613** SIR H. FINCH *Law* (1636) 43 If a woman hauing chattels personall take a husband, the Law deuesteth the property out of her, and vesteth it in her husband onely. **1767** BLACKSTONE *Comm.* II. 184 The interest, which the survivor originally had, is clearly not devested by the death of his companion. **1818** CRUISE *Digest* (ed. 2) II. 364 Where..the freehold is not conveyed away or devested. **1840** S. WARREN *10,000 a Year* IX. in *Blackw. Mag.* XLVIII. 92 The estate had once been vested, and could not subsequently be devested by an alteration or blemish in the instrument. **1842** STEPHEN *Laws Eng.* (1874) II. 687 The title of any person instituted..to any benefice with cure of souls will be afterwards devested unless he shall publicly read..the 39 articles. **1848** ARNOULD *Mar. Insur.* (1866) I. I. iii. 104 A mere pledge of the property, as a collateral security, does not devest all his insurable interest out of the property originally insured.

†**b.** To dispossess (a person) of any right, authority, etc., with which he is invested. *Obs.*

1644 H. PARKER *Jus Pop.* 17 It invests the grantee without devesting the grantor. **1661** CRESSY *Refl. Oathes Suprem. & Alleg.,* He [Hen. VIII] devested the Pope, and assumed to himself the power of Excommunication. **1672** in Picton *L'pool Munic. Rec.* (1883) I. 268 Persons which beare..offices..and are not legally devested. **1810** J. MARSHALL *Const. Opin.* (1839) 133 The same power may devest any other individual of his lands.

Hence **de'vested** *ppl. a.*, **de'vesting** *vbl. sb.*; also **de'vestment.**

1603 HOLLAND *Plutarch's Mor.* 1303 The devesting of trees, which..begin to shed and lose their leaves. **1647** M. HUDSON *Div. Right Govt.* Introd. 6 By the Generall devestment of the creature of all its native graces and blessings. **1660** BOYLE *New Exp. Phys. Mech.* xxii. 164 They..lay aside the disguise of Air, and resume the devested form of Liquors. **1672** PETTY *Pol. Anat.* 42 The people of Ireland are all in Factions..called English and Irish, Protestants and Papists: Though indeed the real distinction is vested and devested of the Land belonging to Papists, ann. 1641.

devestiture, obs. var. of DIVESTITURE.

de'vesture. *rare.* [a. OF. *des-, devesture, -eure* (14th c. in Godef.):—Rom. type **desvestitūra,* f. *desvestire*: see DEVEST and -URE; cf. DIVESTURE.] The action of devesting: putting off (as clothes); dispossession (of property).

1648 W. MOUNTAGUE *Devout Ess.* I. xiv. §3 (R.) The very disadvantage we have..in the devesture of self-respects. **1798** COLEBROOKE tr. *Digest Hindu Law* (1801) III. 52 Devesture of property happens three ways; by degradation, by abdication or renunciation, and by natural death.

†**de'vex,** *a.* and *sb. Obs.* [ad. L. *dēvex-us* inclined or sloping downwards, pa. pple. of *dēvehĕre,* f. DE- I. 1 + *vehĕre* to carry, convey.]

A. *adj.* Bent or bending down, inclined or sloping downward.

c **1420** *Pallad. on Husb.* III. 920 Thai love lande devexe and inclinate. **1669** BADDILY & NAYLOR *Life T. Morton* To Rdr., In his devex old age. **1727** BAILEY vol. II, *Devex,* hollow like a valley; bowed down, bending. **1775** in ASH.

B. *sb.* Downward slope, declivity; DEVEXITY.

1627 MAY *Lucan* x. 47 Vpon the Westerne lands (Following the worlds deuexe) he meant to tread.

Hence †**de'vexness.**

1727 BAILEY vol. II, *Devexness,* devexity, bendingness downwards.

†**de'vexed,** *ppl. a. Obs.* [f. prec. + -ED.] Bent or bowed down.

1562 *Wills & Inv. N.C.* (Surtees 1835) 205 Yf he shalbe by aidg or other wyse devexed or blynd.

†**de'vexion.** [irreg. f. L. *devex-us*: see DEVEX.]

1727 BAILEY vol. II, *Devexion,* devexity, bendingness or shelvingness. **1775** in ASH.

†**de'vexity.** *Obs.* Also 7 **di-.** [ad. L. *dēvexitās,* f. *dēvexus*: see DEVEX and -ITY.] Downward slope or incline; concavity: see quots.

1601 HOLLAND *Pliny* I. 32 No man doubteth that the water of the sea came euer in any shore so far as the deuexitie would have suffered. *Ibid.* 34 So far as the other deuexitie or fall of the earth. **1611** COTGR., *Devexité,* deuexitie; a hollownesse, bowing, bending, hanging double. *a* **1618** DAVIES *Wittes Pilgrimage* (1876) 30 (D.) His haire..Doth glorifie that Heau'n's Divexity, His head. **1656** BLOUNT *Glossogr., Devexity,* the hollowness of a valley, a bending down. **1678** in PHILLIPS. **1775** in ASH.

devey, var. DEEVY *a.*

†**de'veyn.** *Obs. rare.* In phrase *in deveyn(e,* in vain.

c **1400** *Lanfranc's Cirurg.* (MS. B) 17 þat he traveylle noȝt in deveyne [MS. A, in veyn]. *Ibid.* (MS. A) 120 þei speken in devyn [MS. B, deveyn].

deviability (ˌdiːvɪə'bɪlɪtɪ). [f. DEVIATE *v.*: see -BILITY.] Capability of being caused to deviate or of being deflected. So **'deviable** *a.*, that can be caused to deviate; deflectable.

1902 [see BETA 2 f]. **1904** S. BOTTONE *Radium* iii. 25 These experimental demonstrations of the deviability of the α and β rays. **1913** J. COX *Beyond Atom* iii. 50 The α rays bear a positive charge... Though deviable by magnetic and electric fields, the amount of deviation is minute compared with that of kathode rays or β rays. **1938** R. W. LAWSON tr. *Hevesy & Paneth's Man. Radioactivity* (ed. 2) ii. 33 The deviability of the α-rays in strong magnetic fields.

deviance ('diːvɪəns). [f. DEVIANT *ppl. a.* + -ANCE.] Deviant state or quality; the behaviour or characteristics of a deviant. So **'deviancy.**

1944 G. BATESON in J. McV. Hunt *Personality & Behavior Disorders* II. xxiii. 722 The term 'deviance' implies standardization; and..deviance *is* allowed for and expected to occur in all cultures. **1954** W. J. H. SPROTT *Sci. & Social Action* vi. 104 Deviance is the departure on the part of participants from culturally expected rules of conduct. *Ibid.* 106 Different societies put different pressures upon their members, and therefore every society provides its own deviancy hazards. **1956** J. KLEIN *Study of Groups* x. 134 If deviance is displayed not by one member, but a set of members sharing a set of norms, control by group pressure is less possible. **1968** FREEDMAN & DOOB (*title*) Deviancy: the psychology of being different. **1970** *New Society* 31 Dec. 1150 (Advt.), Crime, deviance and social sickness.

'deviant, *ppl. a.* [ad. late L. *dēviānt-em,* pr. pple. of *dēviāre*: see DEVIATE *ppl. a.* and -ANT.]

1. Deviating; divergent. *spec.* Deviating from normal social, etc., standards or behaviour.

c **1400** *Rom. Rose* 4789 From youre scole so devyaunt I am. **1623** COCKERAM, *Deuiant,* farre out of the way. **1935** M. MEAD *Sex & Temperament* xviii. 302 Because it is believed marriage must be based upon contrasting personalities, deviant men often choose deviant women. **1944** G. BATESON in J. McV. Hunt *Personality & Behavior Disorders* II. xxiii. 722 A character structure which is normal among us may be deviant among the Kwakiutl. **1957** *Observer* 3 Nov. 10/5 Even among experimental groups, there is always a certain percentage of deviants who do not conform to standard norms, and in social terms these deviant groups are most necessary. **1959** B. WOOTTON *Social Sci.* x. 314 Elaborate studies of deviant behaviour have been..undertaken which make no attempt to establish the norms from which the subjects are presumed to be deviating.

†**2.** That diverts or causes to turn aside. *Obs. rare.*

1471 RIPLEY *Comp. Alch.* Pref. in Ashm. (1652) 121 O deviaunt fro danger, O drawer.

deviant ('diːvɪənt), *sb.* [f. the ppl. adj.]

a. Something that deviates from normal. **b.** = DEVIATE *sb.* 1.

1927 *Jrnl. Amer. Med. Assoc.* 5 Feb. 376 Omental bands or deviants, when extensive, are prone to contain a great deal of fibrous tissue. **1928** M. MEAD *Coming of Age in Samoa* (1929) xi. 169 These girls all represented the deviants from the pattern in one direction... At any time, they, like all deviants, might come into real conflict with the group. **1950** B. WOOTTON *Test. Social Sci.* vi. 126 The fact that there are always many individual deviants shows that a strong-minded (or weak-willed) individual can substitute purely personal choices of his own for those favoured by the community in which he lives. **1952** M. MCCARTHY *Groves of Academe* (1953) iv. 74 Seasoned nonconformists and dissenters, sexual deviants, feather-bedders. **1957** [see prec.]. **1959** *Listener* 28 May 947/2 Our attitudes to offenders and other 'deviants'.

†'**deviate**, *ppl. a. Obs. rare.* [ad. late L. *dēviāt-us*, pa. pple. of *dēviāre* to turn out of the way: see next.] Turned out of the way; remote.

1560 ROLLAND *Crt. Venus* I. 208 Thow art far deuiat For to conforme thy lufe to sic estait. **1638** SIR T. HERBERT *Trav.* (ed. 2) 196 In the way no doubt, or not farre deviat to Rages.

deviate ('diːvɪeɪt), *v.* [f. L. *dēviāt-* ppl. stem of *dēviāre* (Augustine and Vulgate), to turn out of the way, f. DE- I. 2 + *via* way. Cf. F. *dévier* (Oresme, 14th c.).]

1. *intr.* To turn aside from the course or track; to turn out of the way; to swerve.

1635 QUARLES *Embl.* IV. iii. (1718) 199 Neither stand still, nor go back, nor deviate. **1675** OGILBY *Brit.* Pref., Some have deviated more than a whole Degree. **1748** *Anson's Voy.* III. vi. 348 Nor did they deviate in the least from their course. **1749** FIELDING *Tom Jones* XII. xi, Our travellers deviated into a much less frequented track. **1860** TYNDALL *Glac.* I. xviii. 127 We hewed our steps..but were soon glad to deviate from the ice.

2. *fig.* To turn aside *from* a course, method, or mode of action, a rule, standard, etc.; to take a different course, diverge.

a **1633** AUSTIN *Medit.* (1635) 8 We had not onely deviated, and like Sheepe gone astray, but were become Enemies. **1659** B. HARRIS *Parival's Iron Age* 28 They had deviated from their duty. **1682** DRYDEN *Mac Flecknoe* 20 The rest to some faint meaning make pretence, But Shadwell never deviates into sense. **1777** WATSON *Philip II* (1839) 165 Those who deviated, or whom he suspected of deviating, from the Catholic faith. **1824** MACAULAY *Ess., Mitford's Greece* Wks. 1866 VII. 684 By resolutely deviating from his predecessors he is often in the right. **1860** TYNDALL *Glac.* I. xvi. 108 Why I deviated from my original intention.

b. To digress from the subject in discourse or writing.

1638 SIR T. HERBERT *Trav.* (ed. 2) 241, I have deviated, this was discourse at dinner, not yet ended. **1823** BYRON *Juan* IX. xli, I am apt to grow too metaphysical..And deviate into matters rather dry.

c. To diverge or depart in opinion or practice.

1660 BARROW *Euclid* Pref. (1714) 3 It seem'd not worth my while to deviate..from him. **1811** L. M. HAWKINS *C'tess & Gertr.* II. 79, I say nothing of sectaries: as they profess to deviate from us, they do not belong to us.

d. Of things (usually abstract): To take a different course, or have a different tendency; to diverge or differ (*from* a standard, etc.).

1692 BENTLEY *Boyle Lect.* v. 149 If ever Dead Matter should deviate from this Motion. **1770** *Junius Lett.* xxxvii. 181 As far as the fact deviates from the principle, so far the practice is vicious and corrupt. **1801** STRUTT *Sports & Past.* I. ii. 33 Particulars..deviating from the present methods of taking fish. **1870** MAX MÜLLER *Sc. Relig.* (1873) 301 Sanskrit and Greek have deviated from each other.

3. *trans.* To turn (any one) out of the way, turn aside, divert, deflect, change the direction of. (*lit.* and *fig.*)

1660 WILLSFORD *Scales Comm.* A viij b, None shall be.. deviated with doubtfull directions. **1685** COTTON tr. *Montaigne* xxxv. (D.), To let them deviate him from the right path. **1879** NEWCOMB & HOLDEN *Astron.* 63 The eye-lens..receives the pencil of rays, and deviates it to the observer's eye. **1894** *Pop. Sci. Monthly* June, If the angle of vision in one eye be deviated even to a slight degree..we see two images.

†**4.** *trans.* To depart from. *Obs. rare.*

1757 MRS. GRIFFITH *Lett. Henry & Frances* (1767) II. 222 This primitive reason is the great criterion, which may be deviated, according as reason or conscience instructs the.. mind.

Hence '**deviating** *ppl. a.*

1883 *Pall Mall G.* 13 Sept. 11/2 Ten batteries, ten deviating points, and ten induction coils have about six times the power of one battery.

deviate ('diːvɪət), *sb.* [f. the vb.] **1.** A person who, or thing which, deviates; esp. one who deviates from normal social, etc., standards or behaviour; *spec.* a sexual pervert.

1912 *Pedagogical Seminary* XIX. 186 To analyze and diagnose mental deviates whose deviation has caused social maladjustment. **1940** *School & Society* 20 Apr. 503 (*title*) Contribution to the IQ controversy from the study of superior deviates. **1947** OGBURN & NIMKOFF *Handbk. Sociol.* ix. 180 Group pressure tends to cut off extreme deviates. **1952** W. J. H. SPROTT *Social Psychol.* i. 8 He was a 'social deviate'. *Ibid.* vi. 92 We do not expect uniformity, of course; there are plenty of eccentrics or 'deviates'.

2. *Statistics.* The value of a variate measured from some standard point of a distribution, usu. the mean, and usu. expressed in terms of the standard deviation of the distribution.

1925 R. A. FISHER *Statistical Methods* iii. 47 Table I. shows that the normal deviate falls outside the range $\pm 1{\cdot}598193$ in 10 per cent of cases. **1937** C. BURT *Backward Child* ii. 22 He works out the 'mean variation' by taking the deviates about the general average and then averaging in turn the deviates themselves. **1967** CONDON & ODISHAW *Handbk. Physics* (ed. 2) I. xii. 179/1 If X is normally distributed with parameters m and σ, then $Y = (X-m)/\sigma$, termed a standardized normal deviate, is normally distributed with parameters 0 and 1.

deviation (diːvɪ'eɪʃən). [n. of action from L. *dēviāre* to DEVIATE: cf. med.L. *dēviātio*, F. *déviation* (1461 in Godef. *Suppl.*; not in Cotgr.; in *Acad. Dict.* only from 1762).]

1. a. The action of deviating; turning aside from a path or track; swerving, deflexion.

1646 SIR T. BROWNE *Pseud. Ep.* VI. iv. 288 The dayes encrease or decrease according to the declination of the Sun; that is, its deviation Northward or Southward from the Æquator. **1697** DAMPIER *Voy.* I. x. 287 According as the Ship deviated from its direct course..such deviation is.. exprest by N. or S. **1781** COWPER *Friendship* 113 They manifest their whole life through The needle's deviations too. **1831** BREWSTER *Optics* iv. 29 The angle..representing its angular change of direction, or the *angle of deviation*, as it is called.

†**b.** *Astron.* The deflexion of a planet's orbit from the plane of the ecliptic: attributed in the Ptolemaic astronomy to an oscillatory motion of the deferent. *Obs.*

1727–51 CHAMBERS *Cycl.*, *Deviation*, in the old astronomy, a motion of the deferent, or eccentric, whereby it advances to, or recedes from, the ecliptic. The greatest deviation of Mercury is sixteen minutes; that of Venus is only ten.

c. *Comm.* Voluntary departure from the intended course of a vessel without sufficient reason.

1809 R. LANGFORD *Introd. Trade* 131 *Deviation*, a departure from the regular course of a voyage without cause, which renders the assurance irrecoverable if the ship is lost.

2. a. Divergence from the straight line, from the mean, or standard position; variation, deflexion; the amount of this; †the declination or variation of the magnetic needle (*obs.*).

1675 OGILBY *Brit.* Pref. 3 Measuring even the smallest Deviations of the Way. **1690** LEYBOURN *Curs. Math.* 607 This Deviation of the Needle is called by the Mariners, the North-Easting or North-Westing of the Needle.

b. *spec.* The deflexion of the needle of a ship's compass, owing to the magnetism of the iron in the ship or other local cause.

1821 A. FISHER *Jrnl. Voy. Disc.* 3 An experiment..for.. ascertaining the effect of local attraction on the compasses; or, to use the term that has been lately adopted, to determine the deviation of the compass, or magnetic needle, with the ship's head brought to the different points of the compass. **1834** *Nat. Philos., Navigation* III. lxiii. 30 (Useful Knowl. Soc.) The deviation of the compass was first observed by Mr. Wales, the astronomer of Capt. Cook.

c. *Path.* Divergence of one or both of the optic axes from the normal position. ***conjugate deviation***: see CONJUGATE *a.* 5.

d. *Statistics.* The amount by which one of a set of measurements, numerical observations, etc. differs from the arithmetical mean of the whole set; ***standard deviation***, a common measure of the scatter or dispersion of a set of measurements, equal to the square root of the mean of the squares of the deviations.

1858 GREENER *Gunnery* 375 The mean deviation on the target from the centre of the group of 10 hits being only ·85 of a foot at 500 yards' range. **1875** F. GALTON in *Phil. Mag.* 4th Ser. XLIX. 35 Medium values will occur very much more frequently than extreme ones, the rarity of the latter rapidly increasing as the deviation slowly increases. **1894** K. PEARSON in *Phil. Trans. R. Soc.* A. CLXXXV. 80 Then σ will be termed its standard-deviation (error of mean square). *Ibid.* 104 We have no less than three measurements deviating by more than four times the standard-deviation from the mean. **1925** R. A. FISHER *Statistical Methods* iii. 46 A deviation exceeding the standard deviation occurs about once in three trials. Twice the standard deviation is exceeded only about once in 22 trials. **1946** F. J. SCHONELL *Backwardness in Basic Subjects* (ed. 3) v. 80 This is at a point 1·6 standard deviations from the mean of the normal population group. **1968** J. H. BURN *Lect. Notes Pharmacol.* (ed. 9) 135 The standard deviation usually makes the scatter look greater than the average deviation makes it look. Thus for the cocaine figures, using the standard deviation we have $57{\cdot}5 \pm 23{\cdot}1$ mg. per kg., instead of $57{\cdot}5 \pm 16{\cdot}2$ mg. per kg. **1970** *Nature* 12 Dec. 1081/1 In VLF data handling we usually assume a normal distribution of deviations.

3. *fig.* **a.** Divergence *from* any course, method, rule, standard, etc.; with *a* and *pl.*, an instance of this. (The earliest and most frequent sense.) *spec.* the behaviour or characteristics of a deviate.

1603 HOLLAND *Plutarch's Mor.* 1307 The obscuration or ecclipse of the sunne, the defect of the moone..be as it were the excursions, deviations out of course. **1651** HOBBES *Leviath.* II. xxvii. 151 All manner of deviation from the Law. *a* **1665** J. GOODWIN *Filled w. the Spirit* (1867) 236 To walk in ways of righteousness..without any scandalous or self-allowed deviation. **1713** STEELE *Englishman* No. 3. 18 His Ministers are responsible for all his Deviations from Justice. **1793** *Trial of Fyshe Palmer* 14 This trifling deviation in the spelling could not possibly be of any consequence. **1842** GROVE *Corr. Phys. Forces* (ed. 2) 27 A deviation from the plain accepted meaning of words. **1860** TYNDALL *Glac.* I. xviii. 129 There was no deviation from the six-leaved type. **1872** J. G. MURPHY *Comm. Lev.* v. 1 Iniquity, that is deviation from equity. **1881** WESTCOTT & HORT *Grk. N.T.* Introd. §7 Inherited deviations from the original. **1912** [see DEVIATE *sb.* 1]. **1934** R. BENEDICT *Patterns of Culture* viii. 272 He [*sc.* the unsupported individual] may gradually achieve a ..less tortured attitude toward his deviations. *Ibid.* 273 Much more deviation is allowed to the individual in some cultures than in others. **1960** HINSIE & CAMPBELL *Psychiatric Dict.* (ed. 3) 683/1 Sexual deviation—such as homosexuality, transvestism, pedophilia, fetishism, sexual sadism. **1962** R. COOK *Crust on its Uppers* ii. 29 Every single person one knows seems to be mixed up in some kind of deviation or other.

†**b.** Formerly sometimes *absol.* = Deviation from rectitude, moral declension, or going astray.

1625 SIR S. D'EWES *Jrnls. Parl.* (1783) 32 He [Jas. I] had his vices and deviations. **1748** RICHARDSON *Clarissa* (J.), Worthy persons..inadvertently drawn into a deviation. *a* **1831** A. KNOX *Rem.* (1844) I. 79 A feeling..which years of subsequent deviation did not wholly destroy.

†**c.** A turning aside from the subject, a digression. *Obs. rare.*

1665 SIR T. HERBERT *Trav.* (1677) 159 Fearing I have made too large a deviation. *a* **1713** SHAFTESB. *Misc. Refl.* i. Wks. 1749 III. 10 To vary..from my propos'd Subject, and make what Deviations or Excursions I shall think fit.

d. *spec.* (*a*) ***deviation of the complements***, in *Biochem.*, the prevention of the complements from acting upon the receptors. (*b*) *Embryol.* Divergence in the development of an animal from the ontogenetic stages of its ancestor.

1906 *Practitioner* Dec. 748 Another and much more important and serious cause of failure comes about by means of the phenomenon described by Neisser and Wechsburg, and known as the 'deviation of the complements'. **1930** G. R. DE BEER *Embryol. & Evol.* xv. 102 The appearance of characters in the early stages of development is caenogenesis, and these characters which loom so largely in neoteny and deviation are flies in the Haeckelian ointment of recapitulation.

e. *Politics.* Departure or divergence from the principles, policies, or directives of a government or political party, used esp. of such actions in a Communist society. Also *transf.*, any deliberate divergence from prescribed rules or standards. So **devi'ationism; devi'ationist** *sb.* and *a.*

1930 W. H. CHAMBERLIN *Soviet Russia* iii. 78 The Right Deviationists..favored a larger production of goods for immediate consumption. **1931** *Economist* 5 Sept. 425/1 That need may cause a further change in the plan as striking as the recent deviations from the pure doctrines of Communism. **1937** tr *Lenin's Sel. Wks.* IX. 92 A slight syndicalist or semi-anarchist deviation would not have been terrible. *Ibid.* 126 A deviation is not yet a finished trend. A deviation is something that can be rectified. People have just wandered somewhat from the path, or are beginning to wander from the path, but they can still be put right. This, in my opinion, is what the Russian word *uklon* means. **1937** 'G. ORWELL' *Road to Wigan Pier* xiii. 253 To them, the whole Socialist movement is no more than a kind of exciting heresy-hunt —a leaping to and fro of frenzied witch-doctors to the beat of tom-toms and the tune of 'Fee, fi, fo, fum, I smell the blood of a right-wing deviationist!' **1938** H. G. WELLS *Brothers* iii. 47 We know of their groups and their—what is your word?—deviations. **1940** *Economist* 31 Aug. 271/1 Lenin tried to reconcile his conscience to the existing degree of governmental control by talking of 'bureaucratic deviationism'. **1947** L. HASTINGS *Dragons are Extra* i. 23 No deviation from the Party line. **1952** *Scottish Jrnl. Theol.* V. 186 The Church cannot submit to any other, cannot flirt with any other. Deviationism is nothing less than unfaithfulness, adultery, harlotry. **1955** H. HODGKINSON *Doubletalk* 45 Deviationist is a Communist who, whether with good or evil intentions, strays from the path of the official party line. **1959** *Times* 7 Feb. 7/7 Such deviationist diversions as 'rock 'n roll'. *a* **1963** L. MACNEICE *Astrology* (1964) v. 156 Here Kepler appears to be what orthodox astrologers might call a mystical deviationist.

deviative ('diːvɪətɪv), *a.* [f. L. *dēviāt-* ppl. stem + -IVE.] Causing or tending to deviation or deflexion.

1878 LOCKYER *Stargazing* 400 A crown-glass prism is cemented on a flint one of sufficient angle that their deviative powers reverse each other.

deviator ('diːvɪeɪtə(r)). [a. late L. *dēviātor* (Augustine), agent-n. f. *dēviāre* to DEVIATE.]

1. One who deviates, goes astray, digresses, etc.; see the verb.

1651 FULLER *Abel Rediv.* 220 Though Latimer was in his heedlesse youth A deviator. **1756** W. TOLDERVY *Hist. 2 Orphans* III. 48 Here we are obliged to be, in some measure, deviators. **1851** P. FAIRBAIRN tr. *Hengstenberg's Revel. S. John* i. 7 The deviators are quite at variance among themselves.

2. An appliance for altering the course of a balloon.

1886 *Pall Mall G.* 14 Sept. 8/2 Their deviator had ceased to act.

deviatory ('diːvɪətərɪ), *a.* [f. L. type *dēviātōri-us* from *dēviātor*: see prec. and -ORY.] Characterized by deviation.

1702 S. PARKER tr. *Cicero De Finibus* 20 The Deviatory Motions of the Atoms.

device (dɪ'vaɪs). Forms: 3–5 deuis, 4 *Sc.* deuiss, 4–5 deuys, *Sc.* dewis(e, -ys(s, -ice, -yce, 4–6 deuyse, diuis(e, dyuys(e, 4–7 deuise, devise, 5–6 deuyce, 6 *Sc.* devyiss, 6–7 divice, 5– device. [Here two original OF. and ME. words *devis* and *devise* have run together. The actual form *device* represents phonetically ME. *devīs*, *devȳs*, a. OF. *devis* masc., 'division, partition, separation, difference, disposition, wish, desire, will' (Godefroy); 'speech, talke, discourse, a conference, or communication; deuising, conferring, or talking together; also, a deuice, inuention; disposition or appointment of' (Cotgr.); in mod.F. 'action of discoursing, conversation, talk, specification (of work to be done)'. But the form *devise* (when not a mere variant spelling of *device*: see below) represents OF. *devise* fem. 'division, separation, difference, heraldic device, will, testament, plan, design, wish, desire, liking, opinion, conversation, conference, manner, quality, kind' (Godefroy); 'a deuice, posie, embleme, conceit, coat or cognizance borne; an inuention; a diuision; bound, meere, or marke diuiding land' (Cotgr.); in mod.F. 'action of dividing, that which divides or distinguishes, the motto of a shield, seal, etc., an adage'. The two French words correspond to Pr. *devis*, *devisa*, It. *diviso*, *divisa*, Romanic derivs. of *dīvīs-* ppl. stem of *dīvĭdĕre* to divide: see DEVISE *v.*

The older word in ME. appears to have been *devis*, *devys*, but *devise* also appears from Caxton onward, and prob. earlier, at least in the phrase, *to devise* = F. *à devise* (sense 12). It is however very difficult to distinguish the two words, since *devise*, *devyse* occurs not only as the proper spelling of the repr. of OF. *devise*, but also, in northern and late ME., and in the 16th c., as a frequent spelling of ME. *devis*, mod. *device*. In rimes it is generally possible to separate *devise* = *devis*, *device*, from *devise* proper, but in other positions it is often impossible; nor does the sense give much help, because in OF. *devis* and *devise* partly coincided in meaning, while the English distinctions do not always agree with the French. In later times *device* gradually became the accepted form in all senses, except in that of 'testamentary bequest', which still remains DEVISE, q.v. There is also some reason to think that in the 17th c. *devises* (-aɪzɪz) was, in the south of England, used in the plural, when *device* (-aɪs) was written or at least pronounced in the singular: cf. *house* sing., *houses* (-zɪz) pl. The sense-development had to a great extent taken place before the words were adopted in English, so that here the historical and logical orders do not agree.]

1. The action of devising, contriving, or planning; the faculty of devising, inventive faculty; invention, ingenuity. Now *arch.* and *rare.* (orig. *devis*).

c **1400** *Rom. Rose* 1413, I ne can the nombre telle Of stremes smale, that by devys Mirthe had don come through condys. **1513** MORE *Rich. III*, Wks. 58 The deuise of some convenient pretext. **1563** SHUTE *Archit.* B j b, A pillour of their owne deuise. **1568** BIBLE (Bishops') *Acts* xvii. 29 Golde, siluer, or stone grauen by art and mans deuice. **1594** SPENSER *Amoretti* xxx, That fire, which all thing melts, should harden yse; And yse, which is congeald with sencelesse cold, Should kindle fyre by wonderful devyse! **1600** SHAKS. *A.Y.L.* I. i. 174 Hee's gentle..full of noble deuise. **1601** HOLLAND *Pliny* II. 459 As touching the deuise and inuention of mony. **1611** BIBLE *Eccles.* ix. 10 There is no worke, nor deuice, nor knowledge, nor wisedome in the graue whither thou goest. **1634** SIR T. HERBERT *Trav.* 196 By device, tis so made to open, that [etc.]. **1858** T. PARKER *Historic Americans* (1871) 15 Much of our social machinery ..is of his [Franklin's] device.

b. The manner in which a thing is devised or framed; design. *arch.*

c **1400** *Destr. Troy* 1576 The sydes..of sotell deuyse. **1611** SHAKS. *Cymb.* I. vi. 189 'Tis Plate of rare deuice. **1810** SCOTT *Lady of L.* I. xxvi, It was a lodge of ample size, But strange of structure and device. **1870** BRYANT *Iliad* I. v. 136 Who knew to shape all works of rare device. *a* **1881** ROSSETTI *Rose Mary*, A chiming shower of strange device.

†**c.** A contrived shape or figure. *Obs.*

a **1400-50** *Alexander* 359 þis grete god..In a dredfull deuys, a dragons forme.

†**2.** Purpose, intention. *Obs.* (orig. *devis*).

c **1320** *Sir Beues* 1887 To sire Beues a smot therwith A sterne strok..Ac a failede of his diuis And in the heued smot Trenchefis. *c* **1440** *Promp. Parv.* 120 Devyce, purpose, *seria*. **1548** HALL *Chron.* 75 b, When he had thus ordered his affaires accordyng to his device and ordre.

3. Will, pleasure, inclination, fancy, desire. In earlier use chiefly in phr. ***at one's (own) device*** [OF. *à mon, ton*, etc. *devis*]; later only in pl.; now only in phr. ***left to one's own devices***, etc., where it is associated with sense 6. (orig *devis*).

a **1300** *Cursor M.* 11576 (Cott.) þat he ne suld rise, Al at his aun deuise. **1303** R. BRUNNE *Handl. Synne* 11786 Hyt ys sloghenes and feyntes To take penaunce at þy dyuys. *c* **1450** *Crt. of Love* xii, No sapphire of Inde, no ruby rich of price There lacked than..ne thing to my devise. **1523** LD. BERNERS *Froiss.* I. cccxcviii. 691 They..toke a place of grounde at their deuyse, abyding their enemyes. **1552** *Bk. Com. Prayer* Gen. Conf., We haue folowed to much the deuyses [*ed.* **1607** devices] and desyres of our owne heartes. **1599** SANDYS *Europæ Spec.* (1632) 38 Loosing and knitting marriages, by devise at pleasure. **1611** BIBLE *Jer.* xviii. 12 We will walk after our own deuices. **1648** MILTON *Ps.* lxxxi. 52 Their own conceits they follow'd still, Their own devises blind. **1870** MRS. H. WOOD *G. Canterbury's Will* xv, What would you do, if left to your own devices?

†**b.** Will or desire as expressed or conveyed to another; command, order, direction, appointment. Chiefly in phr. ***at*** (some one's) ***device***. *Obs.* (Cf. DEVISE *v.* 3.) (ME. *devis*; OF. *devise*.)

1307 *Elegy Edw. I* iv, That hit he write at mi devys [*rime* pris]. *c* **1325** *Coer de L.* 1439 Lokes that ye doo be my devys. *c* **1440** *Ipomydon* 716 Full feyre he dyd his servyse, And servyd the quene at hyr devyse. *c* **1470** HENRY *Wallace* VIII. 1150 Scho graithit hir apon a gudlye wis, With gold and ger and folk at hir dewis. *Ibid.* x. 473 The Bruce askyt; 'Will thow do my dewyss?' **1523** LD. BERNERS *Froiss.* I. cxlv. 173, I am natte determynedde to folowe his deuyse and ease [*faire à sa devise ne à son aise*]. **1535** STEWART *Cron. Scot.* II. 396 God..At his devyiss all thing in erth is done. **1535** COVERDALE *Dan.* iv. 24 It is the very deuyce of him yt is hyest of all.

†**4.** Opinion, notion; what one thinks about something. Sometimes it may mean 'opinion offered, advice, counsel'. *Obs.* (In 15th c. *devis* and *devise*. OF. *devise*, opinion, sentiment.)

c **1325** *E.E. Allit. P.* A. 199 Bounden bene Wyth þe myryeste margarys at my deuyse þat euer I seȝ ȝet with myn yȝen. **1393** GOWER *Conf.* I. 278 As thou shalt here my devise, Thou might thy self the better avise. *c* **1400** *Rom. Rose* 651 For certes at my devys Ther is no place in Paradys So good. *c* **1420** *Sir Amadace* (Camden) xxix, Thenne iche mon sayd thayre deuise. *c* **1430** LYDG. *Hors, Shepe, & G.* 86 Pees to profyr, as to my Devyce, Makythe no delaye. *c* **1435** *Torr. Portugal* 779 Now wolle ye telle me your devyce, That how I may govern me? *c* **1450** *St. Cuthbert* (Surtees) 2698 As a woman war vnwyse þus sho spird him hir deuyse. **1568** GRAFTON *Chron.* II. 395 When the Duke of Norffolk had heard fully his device, he tooke it not in good parte. **1594** *2nd Pt. Contention* (1843) 125, I prethe Dicke let me heare thy deuise.

†**5.** Familiar conversation, talk, chat. *Obs.* [OF. and mod.F. *devise*.]

c **1489** CAXTON *Blanchardyn* xli. 153 Blanchardyn..talked wyth the kynge..his fader And as they were thus in deuyses [etc.]. *c* **1500** *Melusine* lix. 348 After many playsaunt deuyses and joyfull wordes, they wesshed theire handes and sette them at dyner. **1581** PETTIE *Guazzo's Civ. Conv.* III. (1586) 127 To entertaine them with familiar device, as the fashion in Fraunce and other places is. **1600-10** in *Shaks. C. Praise* 40 What for your businesse, news, device, foolerie and libertie, I never dealt better since I was a man.

6. Something devised or contrived for bringing about some end or result; an arrangement, plan, scheme, project, contrivance; an ingenious or clever expedient; often one of an underhand or evil character; a plot, stratagem, trick.

c **1290** *S. Eng. Leg.* I. 381/156 'Sire,' he seide, 'mi deuis þou schalt here i-seo: þe halle ichulle furst arere.' **1494** FABYAN *Chron.* VII. 358 All was done according to theyr former deuyse. **1535** COVERDALE *Ps.* xxi. 11 They.. ymagined soch deuyces, as they were not able to perfourme. **1548** HALL *Chron.* 12 This devise so much pleased the sedicious congregation. *Ibid.* 48 b, This device of fortifying an armye was at this tyme fyrst invented. *Ibid.* 158 b, To set open the fludde gates of these devises. **1553** T. WILSON *Rhet.* 7 His pollicies and wittie devises in behove of the publique weal. **1568** BIBLE (Bishops') *2 Cor.* ii. 11 We are not ignorant of his deuises [**1611** deuices]. **1601** SHAKS. *Twel. N.* II. iii. 176 Excellent, I smell a deuice. **1603** KNOLLES *Hist. Turks* (1638) 140 The Captaine..declared to him his whole deuise. **1782** PRIESTLEY *Corrupt. Chr.* I. I. 104 By this happy device..[they] screen themselves. **1843** MACAULAY *Lays Anc. Rome* Pref. (1864) 25 The device by which Elfleda was substituted for her young mistress.

7. *concr.* The result of contriving; something devised or framed by art or inventive power; an invention, contrivance; *esp.* a mechanical contrivance (usually of a simple character) for some particular purpose.

c **1325** *E.E. Allit. P.* A. 139, I hoped þe water were a deuyse Bytwene myrþez by merez made. **1570** DEE *Math. Pref.* 35 He alone, with his deuises and engynes..spoyled and discomfited the whole Army. **1577** B. GOOGE *Heresbach's Husb.* I. (1586) 41 b, The devise was, a lowe kinde of Carre with a couple of wheeles, and the Front armed with sharpe Syckles, which forced by the beast through the Corne, did cut downe al before it. **1665** SIR T. HERBERT *Trav.* (1677) 120 To remedy which they have devices like Turrets upon the tops of their Chimneys to suck in the air for refreshment. **1874** KNIGHT *Dict. Mech.* I. 218/1 The devices for baling cut hay. **1884** [See DEVIL *sb.* 8].

b. Used of things non-material.

1529 MORE *Supplic. Soulys* Wks. 326/2 This exposicion is nether our deuise nor ani new founden fantasy, but a very trueth well perceiued. **1587** GOLDING *De Mornay* Ep. Ded. 5 It is not a deuise of man as other Religions are. **1614** BP. HALL *Recoll. Treat.* Ep. Ded. A iij, It was a mad conceit.. That an huge Giant beares up the earth..If by this devise he had meant onely an Embleme of Kings.

8. Something artistically devised or framed; a fancifully conceived design or figure.

1399 LANGL. *Rich. Redeles* iii. 178 In quentise of clothinge ffor to queme sir pride..and iche day a newe deuyse, it dulleth my wittis. **1465** *Mann. & Househ. Exp.* 490 My master bout of Arnold gooldsmythe a dyvyse of goold for mastres Margret. **1555** EDEN *Decades* 159 Curiously buylded with many pleasaunt diuises. **1665** SIR T. HERBERT *Trav.* (1677) 119 The glass..curiously painted with such knots and devices as the Jews usually make for ornament. **1821** CRAIG *Lect. Drawing* i. 21 A practice of painting, in curious devices and figures, the coffins destined for the dead. **1879** H. PHILLIPS *Notes Coins* 1 The most modern [coins] present complicated and intricate devices.

9. *spec.* An emblematic figure or design, *esp.* one borne or adopted by a particular person, family, etc., as a heraldic bearing, a cognizance, etc.: usually accompanied by a motto.

c **1350** *Will. Palerne* 3222 þat i haue a god schel[d]..& wel & faire wiþ-inne a werwolf depeynted..þe quen þan dede comaunde to crafti men i-nowe, þat deuis him were diȝt er þat day eue. *c* **1385** CHAUCER *L.G.W.* 1272 *Dido*, And beryn in hise devysis for hire sake, N'ot I nat what. **1489** CAXTON *Faytes of A.* IV. xv. 276 They take armes att theyre owne wylle and suche a deuyse as them plaiseth, wherof som grownde..the same upon theyre name. **1581** PETTIE *Guazzo's Civ. Conv.* II. (1586) 108 b, A Carcanet of golde.. whereon..is bravelie set forth the devise or armes of the Academie. **1602** MARSTON *Ant. & Mel.* v. Wks. 1856 I. 55, I did send for you to drawe me a devise, an Imprezza, by Sinecdoche a Mott. I wold haue you paint me for my device a good fat legge of ewe mutton. **1608** SHAKS. *Per.* II. ii. 19 The deuice he beares vpon his shield Is a blacke Ethyope, reaching at the sunne. The word, *Lux tua vita mihi.* **1651** HOBBES *Leviath.* I. x. 45 Shields painted with such Devises as they pleased. **1790** PENNANT *London* 116 (R.) With the hart couchant under a tree, and other devices of Richard II. **1862** BURTON *Bk. Hunter* (1863) 63 The devices or trade emblems of special favourites among the old printers.

b. A motto or legend borne with or in place of such a design.

1724 SWIFT *Drapier's Lett.* vi, I observed the device upon his coach to be *Libertas et natale solum.* **1759** ROBERTSON *Hist. Scot.* VII. (an. 1587), Repeating..sentences which she borrowed from some of the devices then in vogue: *aut fer, aut feri* [etc.]. **1851** LONGF. '*Excelsior*', A banner with the strange device, 'Excelsior!'

10. A fanciful, ingenious, or witty writing or expression, a 'conceit'. *Obs.* or *arch.*

1576 GASCOIGNE *Notes making of verse* §1 in *Steele Gl.* (Arb.) 31 By this *aliquid salis*, I meane some good and fine deuise, shewing the quicke capacitie of a writer. **1576** FLEMING *Panopl. Epist.* 342 In versifying..his devises are not darkened with mystie cloudes..the conveiaunce of his matter is manifest. **1645** *Kingdom's Weekly Post* 16 Dec. 76 This is the man who would have his device alwayes in his sermons, which in Oxford they then called conundrums. **1768** BEATTIE *Minstr.* I. lii, Ballad, jest, and riddle's quaint device. **1834** MEDWIN *Angler in Wales* II. 193 Some droll and merry device.

11. Something devised or fancifully invented for dramatic representation; 'a mask played by private persons,' or the like. *arch.* or *Obs.*

1588 SHAKS. *L.L.L.* v. ii. 669 But I will forward with my deuice. **1590** —— *Mids. N.* v. i. 50 The riot of the tipsie Bachanals..That is an old deuice, and it was plaid When I from Thebes came last. **1607** —— *Timon* I. ii. 155 You haue ..entertain'd me with mine owne deuice. **1635** SHIRLEY *Coronat.* (T.) Masques and devices, welcome! **1789** BURNEY *Hist. Mus.* III. iv. 273 Baltazar de Beaujoyeux..having published an account of his devises in a book. **1812** BYRON *Ch. Har.* I. lxvii, Devices quaint, and frolics ever new.

†**12.** Phrases. ***at device, to device*** [OF. *à devis, à devise*]: at or to one's liking or wish; perfectly, completely, entirely, certainly. ***at all device***, in all respects, completely, entirely (cf. *point-device*) *Obs.*

1375 BARBOUR *Bruce* IV. 264 For mynerfe ay wes wont to serfe Hym fullely at all deuiss. *Ibid.* XI. 348 The king..wes vicht and viss And richt vorthy at all deuiss. *c* **1375** *Sc. Leg. Saints, Clemens* 628 Clement..empleysit wele in godis serwice In althinge, at al dewise. *c* **1385** CHAUCER *L.G.W.* 1206 *Dido* (Tanner), Up on a courser..Sit Eneas lik phebus to deuyse So was he freish arayed in his wise. *a* **1420** HOCCLEVE *De Reg. Princ.* 404 He is a noble prechour at device. *c* **1450** *Mirour Saluacioun* 4141 With thire Armures this knyght faght so wele at devis. *c* **1475** *Partenay* 479 A litel his colour cam, vnto deuise. *c* **1500** *Melusine* xxi. 126 He is moche fayre & wel shapen of membres, & hath a face to deuyse, except that one of his eyen is hyer sette than the other is. **1513** DOUGLAS *Æneis* x. ix. 85 The Troiane prynce ..with his brand hym brytnys at devys, In maner of ane offerand sacryfys.

device, obs. form of DEVISE *v.* and *sb.*

de'viceful, *a.* Now *rare.* [f. prec. + -FUL.] Full of, or characterized by, device, ingenuity or invention; ingenious, 'cunning', 'curious'.

1590 SPENSER *Teares of Muses* 385 The devicefull matter of my song. **1596** —— *F.Q.* v. iii. 3 To tell the glorie of the feast..The goodly service, the devicefull sights..Were worke fit for an herauld. **1606** MARSTON *Parasitaster* III. i, Oh quick, deviceful, strong-brain'd Dulcimel, Thou art too full of wit to be a wife. **1615** CHAPMAN *Odyss.* I. 206 A carpet, rich and of deviceful thread. **1621** QUARLES *Argalus & P.* (1656) 24 The quaint Impresas their deviseful shows. **1681** H. MORE in Glanvill *Sadducismus* I. Postcr. (1726) 18 In his deviceful imagination.

Hence **de'vicefully** (†**devisefully**) *adv.*, ingeniously, 'cunningly'; **devicefulness.**

a **1631** DONNE *Poems* (1650) 77 The Alphabet Of flowers, how they devisefully being set And bound up, might.. Deliver errands mutely, and mutually. **1894** *Liberal* 17 Nov. 3/2 It was from the Germans that the Japs derived all their discipline and devicefulness.

de'viceless, *a.* [f. as prec. + -LESS.] Without a device (in various senses: see the sb.). Also [after Gr. ἀμήχανος], against which no device avails.

1851 M. ARNOLD *Lett.* (1932) 118 We are growing old, and advancing towards the deviceless darkness. **1866** RUSKIN *Crown Wild Olive* Pref. 27 To teach that there is no device in the grave may..make the deviceless person more contented in his dulness. **1884** TRAILL *New Lucian* 130 That coin of language which..has been worn down to an unmeaning counter, deviceless and legendless.

†**de'vict**, *ppl. a. Obs.* [ad. L. *dēvict-us*, pa. pple. of *dēvincĕre* to subdue, f. DE- I. 3 + *vincĕre* to conquer.] Subdued, overcome.

1432-50 tr. *Higden* (Rolls) I. 205 A region..where the Wandalynges were devicte. **1541** BECON *News out of Heaven* Early Wks. (1843) 46 Ready to be devict and overcome. *c* **1550** *Knighthood & Battle* (MS. Cott. Titus, A. xxiii. 1) 6 For mightily what man may renne and lepe, May well devicte and saf his party kepe. [But here perhaps a verb].

devide, devident, etc., obs. ff. DIVIDE, etc.

devil ('dɛv(ə)l, 'dɛvɪl), *sb.* Forms: 1 diobul, díoful, déoful, 1-2 déofol, 2-3 deofel, 2-5 deouel, 3-5 deuel, 4-7 deuil, devel, 6-7 divel, 6- devil. Also 1 díoful, déoful, *north.* diowul, diowl, dioul, diwl, deuil), 3 diefel, *Orm.* de(o)fell, 3-4 dieuel, 4 dyevel, 5 dewill, -elle, dyuell, 5-6 devell, devyl, -yll(e, deuyl(l, 5-7 deuill, 6 diuill, 6-7 diuel(l, divel(l, 8-9 *dial.* divul, *Sc.* deevil; *monosyllabic* 4-5 deul, dele, del, 5 dewle, dwill, dwylle, delve, 5-6 dule, 7 de'el, 8-9 *Sc.* deil, *Exmoor* doul, *Lancash.* dule. *Plural* 1 déoflu, 2 deofle, deoflen, deflen, 2-3 deulen, 5 develyn; 1 *north.* diules, 2 deofles, deoules, deuules, deules, doules, 3 *Orm.* de(o)fless, 4 devles, devels, etc.; *gen. pl.* 1-3 déofla, 3-4 devele; *dat. pl.* 1 déoflum, 2 deoflan,

-en. [OE. *déofol*, etc., corresponding to OFris. *diovel*, OS. *diubul*, *-ðal*, *diobol*, *diabol*, *diuvil* (MDu. *düvel*, *dievel*, Du. *duivel*, MLG., LG. *düvel*), OHG. *tiuval*, *tioval*, *tiufal* (Notker), *diuval*, *diufal* (Tatian, Otfrid), MHG. *tiuvel*, *tievel*, *tiufel*, *tiefel*, Ger. *teufel*; ON., Icel. *djöfull* (Sw. *djefvul*, Da. *djævel*); Goth. *diabaulus*, *diabulus*, immediately a. Gr. διάβολος, in Jewish and Christian use 'the Devil, Satan', a specific application of διάβολος 'accuser, calumniator, slanderer, traducer', f. διαβάλλειν to slander, traduce, *lit.* to throw across, f. διά through, across + βάλλειν to cast. The Gr. word was adopted in L. as *diabolus*, whence in the mod. Romanic langs., It. *diavolo*, Sp. *diablo*, Pg. *diabo*, Pr. *diablo*, *diable*, F. *diable*; also in Slavonic, OSlav. *diyavolŭ*, *dĭyavolŭ*, etc. In Gothic the word was masc., as in Greek and Latin; the plural does not occur; in OHG. it was masc. in the sing., occasionally neuter in the plural; in OE. usually masculine, but sometimes neuter in the sing., regularly neuter in the plural *deofol*, *deoflu*; but the Northumbrian Gospel glosses have masculine forms of the plural.

The Gothic word was directly from Greek; the forms in the other Teutonic langs. were partly at least from Latin, and prob. adopted more or less independently of each other. Thus ON. *djöfull* regularly represents an original *diabulz*. OE. *díobul*, *déoful*, *déofol* can also be referred to an earlier *diabul*, *diavol* (cf. It. *diavolo*), *éo* coming, through *ío*, from earlier *ía*. The OE. *déo-* would normally give modern *dē-*, exemplified in 15th c., and in mod. Sc. and some Eng. dialects, but generally shortened at an earlier or later date to *dev-* or *div-*. In some, especially northern, dialects, the *v* was early vocalized or lost, leaving various monosyllabic forms, of which mod. Sc. *deil*, and Lancashire *dule* are types.

The original Greek διάβολος was the word used by the LXX to render the Heb. *sāṭān* of the O.T.; in the Old Latin version it was regularly retained as *diabolus*; but Jerome substituted *Satan*, which is thus the reading of the Vulgate everywhere in the Canonical books, except in Ps. cviii. (cix.) 6 (the Psalter in the Vulgate being the Gallican version from the LXX). Wyclif translating the Vulgate, has in this place 'the deuell', but elsewhere in O.T. 'Sathan'; the 16–17th c. Eng. versions have 'Satan' throughout after the Hebrew.]

1. ***the Devil*** [repr. Gr. ὁ διάβολος of the LXX and New Test.]: In Jewish and Christian theology, the proper appellation of the supreme spirit of evil, the tempter and spiritual enemy of mankind, the foe of God and holiness, otherwise called Satan.

He is represented as a person, subordinate to the Creator, but possessing superhuman powers of access to and influence over men. He is the leader or prince of wicked apostate angels, and for him and them everlasting fire is prepared (Matt. xxv. 41).

Besides the name *Satan*, he is also called *Beelzebub*, *Lucifer*, *Apollyon*, *the Prince of darkness*, *the Evil One*, *the Enemy of God and Man*, *the Arch-enemy*, *Arch-fiend*, *the Old Serpent*, *the Dragon*; and in popular or rustic speech by many familiar terms as *Old Nick*, *Old Simmie*, *Old Clootie*, *Old Teaser*, *the Old One*, *the Old lad*, etc.

(In this the original sense the word has no plural.)

a **800** *Corpus Gloss.* 1457 (O.E.T) *Orcus*, hel diobul. *c* **825** *Vesp. Hymns* xiii. 4 Ðone dioful biswac. *a* **1000** *Juliana* 460 (Gr.) Hyre þæt deofol oncwæð. *a* **1000** *Solomon & Sat.* 122 (Gr.) Him bið þæt deofol laþ. *c* **1000** *Ags. Gosp.* John viii. 44 Ge synd deofles bearn. *c* **1160** *Hatton Gosp.* Matt. iv. 5 Ða ȝebrohte se deofel hine on þa halȝan ceastre. *a* **1175** *Cott. Hom.* 237 Al folc ȝede in to þes diefles muðe. *c* **1200** *Trin. Coll. Hom.* 35 To luste þe defles lore. *Ibid.*, þa wurhliche weden þe þe dieuel binom ure forme fader adam. *c* **1250** *Moral Ode* 98 in *E.E.P.* (1862) 28 Dieð com in þis middenerd þurh þe ealde deofles onde. *c* **1290** *S. Eng. Leg.* I. 62/294 þat was þe Deuel of helle. *a* **1310** in Wright *Lyric P.* xxxix. 111 Ichot the cherl is def, the Del hym todrawe! *c* **1380** Wyclif *Sel. Wks.* III. 442 þen God and þe devell were weddid togedre. **1382** —— *Ps.* cviii. [cix.] 6 Sett vp on hym a synere; and the deuell stonde at his riȝt side [**1535** Coverdale, Let Satan stonde at his right hande; **1611** Satan, *marg.* or, an aduersary; **1885** (R.V.) adversary, *marg.* Or Satan, or *an accuser*]. —— *Matt.* xxv. 41 Euer-lastynge fijr, the which is maad redy to the deuyl and his angelis. —— *Rev.* xii. 9 And the ilke dragoun is cast doun, the greet olde serpent, that is clepid the Deuel. *c* **1400** *Destr. Troy* 4392 þe folke.. vnder daunger of þe dule droupet full longe. *c* **1450** Myrc 364 Hyt ys a sleghþe of the del. *c* **1450** *St. Cuthbert* (Surtees) 7170 Ôft to gydir þai did euill, And gaf occasion to þe deuill. *a* **1535** Fisher *Wks.* (1876) 402 To forsake the diuel and all his works. **1571** Campion *Hist. Irel.* iv. (1633) 13 So wee say.. *dile* for *divill*. **1576** Fleming *Panopl. Epist.* 277 As mad as the divel of hell. **1577** B. Googe *Heresbach's Husb.* I. (1586) 46 b, Where a man must deale with the Devil. **1596** Shaks. *Merch. V.* I. iii. 99 The diuell can cite Scripture for his purpose. **1604** Jas. I *Counterbl.* (Arb.) 100 Why do we not denie God and adore the Deuill as they doe. **1638** Sir T. Herbert *Trav.* (ed. 2) 302 The Samoreen.. black as the devill, and as treacherous. *a* **1652** Brome *Queene's Exch.* II. iii. Wks. 1873 III. 490 He looks So damnably as if the Divel were at my elbow. **1738** Swift *Polite Convers.* 97 That would have been a Match of the Devils making. **1817** Cobbett *Wks.* XXXII. 150, I defy the Attorney General, and even the Devil himself, to produce from my writings any one essay, which is not written in the spirit of peace. **1828** Carlyle *Misc.*, *Burns* (1857) I. 212 The very Devil he cannot hate with right orthodoxy. **1846** Trench *Mirac.* v. (1862) 159 All gathers up in a person, in the devil, who has a kingdom, as God has a kingdom.

b. According to mediæval notions: cf. 3.

c **1290** *S. Eng. Leg.* I. 245/165 In fourme of a fair womman þe deuel cam heom to. *Ibid.* 372/174 And þe Aungel heom scheuwede al a-brod þene deuel ase huy stude, þe fourme of a grislich man þat al for-broide were And swarttore þane eueri ani blouȝman.. Fuyrie speldene al stinkende out of is mouth he blaste And fuyr of brumston at his nose. **1563** W. Fulke *Meteors* (1640) 10 b, There was newes come to London, that the Devill.. was seene flying over the Thames. **1603** Shaks. *Meas. for M.* II. iv. 16 Let's write good Angell on the Deuills horne 'Tis not the Deuills Crest. **1681** Glanvill *Sadducismus* II. 111, The Devil.. appeared to her in the shape of a handsome man, and after of a black dog. *Ibid.* xxviii, Declares that the Devil in the shape of a black man lay with her in the Bed.. that his feet were cloven. **1805** Nicholls *Let.* in *Corr. w. Gray* (1843) 45 He thought that Milton had improved on Tasso's devil by giving him neither horns nor a tail. *c* **1850** J. W. Croker in *Croker Papers* (1884) III. xxvii. 215 By his bad character and ill-looking appearance, like the devil with his tail cut off. **1868** Browning *Ring & Bk.* IV. 1296 The devil appears himself, Armed and accoutred, horns and hoofs and tail!

c. In plural applied to 'the Devil and his angels', the host of fallen and evil spirits for whom hell was prepared: see 3.

2. From the identification of the *demons*, δαιμόνια, δαίμονες, of the Septuagint and New Testament with Satan and his emissaries, the word has been used from the earliest times in English, as equivalent to or including DEMON[1] (sense 2), applied **a.** (in Scripture translations and references) to the false gods or idols of the heathen; **b.** (in Apocrypha and N. Test.) to the evil or unclean spirits by which demoniacs were possessed; **c.** in O. Test. translating Heb. *sheʿîrîm* hairy ones, 'satyrs'.

In the Vulgate, as in Gr., *diabolus* and *dæmon* are quite distinct; but the Gothic of Ulfilas already uses *unhulþa* (Ger. *unhold*) to render both words, and in all the modern languages, *devil*, or its cognate, is used for *dæmon* as well as for *diabolus*: see DEMON[1].

a. *c* **825** *Vesp. Psalter* xcv[i]. 5 Forðon alle godas ðioda ðioful, dryhten soðlice heofenas dyde. *a* **1175** *Cott. Hom.* 227 An meȝie cynn þe nefer ne abeah to nane deofel ȝyld. *c* **1340** *Cursor M.* 11759 (Trin.) Alle þo deueles [*Cott.* idels; *Fairf.* mawmettes] in a stounde Grouelynge fel to þe grounde. **1382** Wyclif *Ps.* cvi. 37 Thei offriden ther sones and ther doȝtris to deuelis. [**1611** deuils, **1885** (R.V.) demons. So *Deut.* xxxii. 17]. —— *Acts.* xvii. 18 A tellere of newe deuelis [**1388** of newe fendis; **1526** Tindale, a tyddynges brynger off new devyls; **1557** *Geneva* of newe Gods; **1611** of strange gods; **1881** (R.V.) strange gods (Gr. demons)]. —— *Rev.* ix. 20 Thei worschipeden not deuels, and simulacres golden, treenen, the whiche nether mowen see, nether heere, nether wandre. **1555** Watreman *Fardle Facions* II. x. 210 He.. abolished all worshippe of deuilles. **1638** Sir T. Herbert *Trav.* 335 This Devill (or Molech) is of concave copper.. double guilded. *Ibid.*, 70 Temples, wherein they number 3333.. little guilded Devils. **1667** Milton *P.L.* I. 373 Devils to adore for deities. **1881** N.T. (R.V.) *1 Cor.* x. 20 The things which the Gentiles sacrifice, they sacrifice to devils [*marg.* Gr. *demons*], and not to God.

b. *c* **950** *Lindisf. Gosp.* Matt. ix. 34 In aldormenn diowbla [he] fordrifes diowlas. *c* **975** *Rushw. G.* ibid., In aldre deofla he ut-weorpeð deoful. *c* **1000** *Ags G.* ibid., On deofla ealdre he drifð ut deoflu. *c* **1200** *Trin. Coll. Hom.* 39 Ure drihten drof fele deules togedere ut of a man.. and þe swin urnen alse deulen hem driuen. **1382** Wyclif *Matt.* ix. 34 In the prince of deuelis he castith out deuilis. —— *John* x. 20 He hath a deuel, and maddith, or wexith wood. —— *1 Tim.* iv. 1 Ȝyuynge tent to spiritis of errour, and to techingis of deuels. —— *Rev.* xvi. 14 Thre vncleene spirites.. sotheli thei ben spirites of deuelis, makinge signes. **1548** Udall etc., *Erasm. Par. John* 73 b, He hathe the Deuell (say they) and is madde. **1604** *Canons Ecclesiastical* lxxii. Neither shal any Minister not licensed.. attempt.. to cast out any deuill or deuils. **1611** Bible *John* x. 20 He hath a deuill and is mad. *a* **1656** Bp. Hall *Rem. Wks.* (1660) 18 The ejection of Divells by fasting and prayer. **1881** N.T. (R.V.) *Matt.* ix. 34 By the prince of the devils casteth he out devils [*marg.* Gr. *demons*].

c. **1382** Wyclif *Isa.* xxxiv. 14 And aȝen come shul deueles [**1388** fendis], the beste party an asse, and a party a man. —— *Rev.* xviii. 2 Greet Babilon fel doun fel doun, and is maad the habitacioun of deuelis [**1611** deuils]. (Cf. Isa. xiii. 2.) [**1607** Topsell *Four-f. Beasts* 11 The Satyre, a most rare and seldome seene Beast, hath occasioned others to thinke it was a Deuill.. and it may be that Deuils haue at some time appeared to men in this likenes.]

d. *fig.* A baleful demon haunting or possessing the spirit; a spirit of melancholy; an apparition seen in *delirium tremens*: see BLUE DEVIL.

3. Hence, generically, A malignant being of angelic or superhuman nature and powers; one of the host of Satan, as 'prince of the devils', supposed to have their proper abode in hell, and thence to issue forth to tempt and injure mankind; a fiend, a demon. Also, applied to the malignant or evil deities feared and worshipped by various heathen people (cf. 2 a).

In mediæval conception, devils (including Satan himself) were clothed with various hideous and grotesque forms; their usual appearance, however (still more or less retained in art), was derived from the satyrs of Roman mythology, or from the figure attributed to Pan, being a human form furnished with the horns, tail, and cloven foot of a goat.

Beowulf 757 Wolde on heolster fleon, secan deofla ȝedræȝ. *Ibid.* 1680 Hit on æht ȝehwearf aefter deofla hryre, Deniȝea frean. *a* **1000** *Crist* 1531 (*Cod. Exon.* 30 b) On þæt deope dæl deofol·ȝefeallað. *c* **1175** *Lamb. Hom.* 87 Ure ifan þet beoð þa deofles beoð bisencte in to helle. *c* **1200** *Trin. Coll. Hom.* 69 Witeð ȝe.. in þat eche fur þat is ȝarked to deuules and here fereden. *Ibid.* 173 Hie iseð bineðen hem deflen þe hem gredeliche kepeð. *c* **1200** Ormin 1403 Alle þa þatt fellenn swa þeȝȝ sinndenn laþe deofless. *Ibid.* 10565 Deofle flocc. *c* **1290** *S. Eng. Leg.* I. 37/104 þere nis no deuel þat dorre nouþe neiȝ þe come, for drede. *c* **1380** Wyclif *Sel. Wks.* III. 450 A veyn blast of a fool, and, in cas, of a devyl. **1393** Langl. *P. Pl.* C. xxII. 21 For alle deorke deoueles dreden hit to huyre. *c* **1430** *Hymns Virg.* (1867) 121 Develyn schall com oute off helle. **1530** Palsgr. 214/2 Divell she, *diablesse*. *a* **1535** Fisher *Wks.* (1876) 428 Thou shalt paye thine owne debtes amongest the diuils in hell. **1563** Winȝet *Four Scoir Thre Quest.* §70 Wks. 1888 I. 118 Ane terribill cumpany of dewlis hastalie apperand to him. **1602** *Narcissus* (1893) 330 The haire of the faire queene of devills. **1605** Z. Jones tr. *De Loyer's Specters* title-p., The Nature of Spirites, Angels, and Divels. **1632** Lithgow *Trav.* IX. 404 The Italians swore, I was a Divell and not a man. *a* **1646** J. Gregory *Posthuma* (1649) 96 This Lilith was.. a kinde of shee-divel which killed children. **1698** Fryer *Acc. E. India & P.* IV. v. 180 The visible appearance of a Devil or Dæmon which they say is common among them. **1842** Tennyson *St. Simeon Stylites* 4 Scarce meet For troops of devils. **1879** M. D. Conway *Demonol.* I. I. iv. 36 A devil.. a being actuated by simple malevolence.

4. *transf.* Applied to human beings. **a.** A human being of diabolical character or qualities; a malignantly wicked or cruel man; a 'fiend in human form'; in ME. sometimes a man of gigantic stature or strength, a giant.

c **960** *Lindisf. Gosp.* John vi. 70 Ic iuih tuelfo ȝeceas & of iuh an diul [*Rushw.* diowul] is. *a* **1154** *O.E. Chron.* an 1137 þa fylden hi mid deoules & yuele men. *c* **1205** Lay. 17669 He .. wende anan rihte in to Winchæstre swulc hit weore an hali mon, þe hæðene deouel. *c* **1400** *Rom. Rose* 4288 An olde vecke.. The which devel, in hir enfaunce Hadde lerned of Loves arte. *c* **1470** Henry *Wallace* IV. 407 At thus with wrang, thir dewillis suld bruk our land. *c* **1500** *Melusine* xxxvi. 256 Ayeynst this strong dyuell I ne may withstand. **1509** Hawes *Past. Pleas.* xxix. (Percy Soc.) 136 Some develles wyll theyr husbandes bete. **1604** Shaks. *Oth.* v. ii. 132 Thou do'st bely her, and thou art a diuell. **1608–11** Bp. Hall *Medit. & Vows* I. § 6 That olde slaunder of early holiness: A young Saint, an olde Devill: sometimes young Devils have prooved olde Saints: never the contrary. **1611** Bible *John* vi. 70 Haue not I chosen you twelue, and one of you is a deuill? **1642** Fuller *Holy & Prof. St.* v. xvii. 426 Devils in flesh antedate hell in inventing torments. **1726** *Adv. Capt. R. Boyle* 82 Thou Devil! said he to Susan, and hast thou betray'd me. **1867** Parkman *Jesuits N. America* xxii. 319 He was a savage still, but not so often a devil.

b. In later use, sometimes, merely a term of reprobation or aversion; also playfully connoting the qualities of mischievous energy, ability, cleverness, knavery, roguery, recklessness, etc., attributed to Satan.

1601 Shaks. *Twel. N.* II. v. 226 Thou most excellent diuell of wit. **1651** *Life Father Sarpi* (1676) 29 An Angel in his behaviour, and a Devil.. in the Mathematicks. **1774** Goldsm. *Retal.* 57 So provoking a devil was Dick. **1775** Sheridan *Rivals* III. iv, An ill-tempered little devil! She'll be in a passion all her life. **1849** Thackeray *Pendennis* lvi, A man of great talents, who knew a good deal.. and was a devil to play. **1854** Warter *Last of Old Squires* xvi. 151 In our forefathers' days the term *devil* (for instance, 'queer devil', 'rum devil') had a modified signification, intimating more of the knave than of the fool, but not without a strong dash of the humourist.

c. Applied in contempt or pity (chiefly with *poor*): A poor wretched fellow, one in a sorry plight, a luckless wight. [So in It., Fr., etc.]

1698 T. Froger *Voy.* 160 The poor Devil was condemned to have his head chopped off. **1768** Sterne *Sent. Journ.* (1775) 36 (*Montriul*), I am apt to be taken.. when a poor devil comes to offer his service to so poor a devil as myself. **1816** Scott *Antiq.* xxi, 'What can we do for that puir doited deevil of a knight-baronet?' **1850** Ld. Beaconsfield *Let.* 16 Nov. in *Corr. w. Sister* (1886) 250 Riding the high Protestant horse, and making the poor devils of Puseyites the scapegoats. **1876** F. E. Trollope *Charming Fellow* I. xiii. 167 Why should he do anything.. for a poor devil like me?

d. Applied also to a vicious, evil-tempered, or mischievous beast.

1834 Medwin *Angler in Wales* II. 44 He was the fastest trotter in the cantonment, but a restive devil. **1884** *Bath Jrnl.* 26 July 6/5 That tusker there (pointing to the large elephant).. is a devil. He has killed three keepers already.

5. *spec.* **a.** ***printer's devil***: the errand-boy in a printing office. Sometimes the youngest apprentice is thus called. (In quot. 1781 a girl or young woman.)

1683 Moxon *Mechanic Exercises* II, The Press-man sometimes has a Week-Boy to Take Sheets, as they are Printed off the Tympan: These Boys do in a Printing-House, commonly black and Dawb themselves: whence the Workmen do Jocosely call them Devils; and sometimes Spirits, and sometimes Flies. **1709** Steele *Tatler* No. 31 ¶13 Mr. Bickerstaff's Messenger, or (as the Printers call him) Devil, going to the Press. *a* **1764** Lloyd *Dialogue* Poet. Wks. 1774 II. 4 And in the morning when I stir, Pop comes a Devil 'Copy Sir'. **1781** Johnson 20 Apr. in *Boswell*, He had married a printer's devil... I thought a printer's devil was a creature with a black face and in rags... Yes, sir: but I suppose he had her face washed and put clean clothes on her. **1836** Smart s.v. *Sematology*, Mr. Woodfall's men, from the devil up to the reader. **1849** E. E. Napier *Excurs. S. Africa* I. p. xxviii, As neither space, time, nor printers devils are under control, I must therefore content myself with the above brief.. review.

b. A junior legal counsel who does professional work for his leader, usually without fee. ***Attorney-General's Devil***, a familiar name of the Junior Counsel to the Treasury.

1849 Ld. Campbell *Lives Chief Justices* II. xxxiv. 437 He [Lord Mansfield] had signed and forgotten both opinions, —which were, perhaps, written by devils or deputies. **1872** *Echo* 14 Nov. (Farmer), Sir James Hannen, we are told, was a Devil once. **1884** *Bath Jrnl.* 12 July 8/1 Mr. Clarke was offered the post of 'devil' to the Attorney General, and his declining may be said to have been without precedent. **1888** *Pall Mall G.* 29 Dec. 3/1 It is by no means an uncommon thing for an Attorney-General's 'devil', or point and case hunter, to be offered a judgeship.

c. One employed by an author or writer to do subordinate parts of his literary work under his direction; a literary 'hack'; and generally one who does work for which another receives the credit or remuneration or both.

1888 *Star* 8 Aug., Certain societies, the Early English Text, Chaucer, Shakspere, etc., though large employers of 'devils', pay the highest wages. **1891** [see DEVIL *v.* 3 c].

6. *fig.* Applied to qualities. **a.** The personification of evil and undesirable qualities by which a human being may be possessed or actuated. (Usually with some fig. reference to sense 2.)

1604 SHAKS. *Oth.* II. iii. 297 It hath pleas'd the diuell drunkennesse, to giue place to the diuell wrath. **1606** —— *Tr. & Cr.* II. iii. 23, I haue said my prayers and diuell, enuie, say Amen. *Ibid.* v. ii. 55 How the diuell Luxury..tickles these together. **1701** DE FOE *True-born Eng.* 104 Ingratitude, a Devil of Black Renown. **1819** SHELLEY *Cenci* II. i. 45 The devil was rebuked that lives in him. **1828** SCOTT *F.M. Perth* xxx, The devil of sophistry, with which thou art possessed. **1842** TENNYSON *Walking to Mail* 13 Vex'd with a morbid devil in his blood. **1855** —— *Sailor Boy* 24 A devil rises in my heart, Far worse than any death to me. **1884** H. BROADHURST in *Fortn. Rev.* Mar. 347 The devil of short-sighted greed is powerful enough if left alone.

b. *colloq.* Temper, spirit, or energy that can be roused; fighting spirit; perplexing or baffling strategy of attack (as in cricket).

1780 T. PASLEY *Private Sea Jrnl.* 5 Mar. (1931) 69 He has many good qualities, but as the old adage says, has not Divil enough in him. **1823** *Gentl. Mag.* Nov. 434/2 They must have *Devil* enough..to do gallant things. **1847** LD. G. BENTINCK in *Croker Papers* (1884) III. 156 That any nation was so without 'devil' in it as to have laid down and died as tamely as the Irish have. **1884** HON. I. BLIGH in *Lillywhite's Cricket Ann.* 5 Evans bowled steadily, but without much 'devil'.

7. Used (generally with qualifications) as the name of various animals, on account of their characteristics, e.g. ***Tasmanian devil,*** a carnivorous marsupial of Tasmania (*Sarcophilus ursinus*); ***sea devil,*** the DEVIL-FISH: cf. also SEA-.

1686 RAY *Willoughby's Hist. Piscium* III. III. i. 85 heading, *Rana piscatrix*, the Toad-fish or Frog-fish or Sea-Divel. **1700** S.L. tr. *Fryke's Voy. E. Ind.* 286 There is a sort of Creature here..called..by the Dutch, The Devil of Negombo..because of its qualities.. It hath a sharp Snout, and very sharp Teeth. **1799** *Naval Chron.* I. 67 The Lophius..or Sea Devil, is a genus of the branchiostegious order. **1829** H. WIDOWSON *Pres. State Van Dieman's Land* xviii. 180 The devil, or as the naturalists term it '*dasyurus ursinus*', is very properly named... It is as great a destroyer of young lambs as the hyena; and, generally speaking, is as large as a middling-sized dog. **1832** BISCHOFF *Van Dieman's Land* ii. 29 The devil, or as naturalists term it 'dasyurus ursinus' is very properly named. **1857** THOREAU *Maine W.* (1894) 381 'Devil [that is, Indian Devil, or cougar] lodges about here—very bad animal.' **1862** JOBSON *Australia* vii. 186 Colonists in Tasmania..called it the 'devil' from the havoc it made among their sheep and poultry.

b. A local name of the Swift (*Cypselus apus*); formerly also of the Coot.

1580 HOLLYBAND *Treas. Fr. Tong, Foulque*, a bird called a Coute, & because of the blackenesse, is called a Diuell. **1885** SWAINSON *Prov. Names Brit. Birds* 95 From its impetuous flight, and its dark colour, it is called *Devil* (Berks).. *Swing Devil* (Northumb.), *Skeer Devil* (Devon, Somerset), *Devil's screecher* (Devon), *Devil shrieker* (Craven).

c. A collector's name of a tropical shell, *Cynodonta turbinellus. Obs.*

1776 DA COSTA *Elem. Conchol.* 291 (Plate V, fig. 5), A Murex, *The Devil.*

8. A name of various instruments or mechanical contrivances, *esp.* such as work with sharp teeth or spikes, or do destructive work, but also applied, with more or less obvious allusion, to others. Among these are

a. A machine used for tearing open and cleaning wool, cotton, flax, and other fibres, preparatory to spinning; also called *willow, willower, willy.* **b.** A machine used to tear up old cloth and reduce it to 'shoddy', to be worked up again into cloth; also one used to tear up linen and cotton rags, etc., for manufacture into paper. **c.** An instrument used for feloniously cutting and destroying the nets of fishermen at sea. **d.** An instrument of iron wire used by goldsmiths for holding gold to be melted in a blow-pipe flame. **e.** An iron grate used for fire in the open air.

1831 J. HOLLAND *Manuf. Metal*, Certain implements acting with a boss and a slit block of iron, called a devil. **1836** SIR G. HEAD *Home Tour* 144 The town of Dewsbury.. celebrated for..grinding old garments into new; literally tearing in pieces fusty old rags..by a machine called a 'devil', till a substance very like the original is reproduced. **1851** MAYHEW *Lond. Labour* (1861) II. 30 'Shoddy'.. consists of the second-hand wool manufactured by the tearing up, or rather grinding, of woollen rags by means of coarse willows, called devils. **1860** *All Year Round* No. 57. 160 Where the 'devil' first beats the cotton from the bale. **1867** O. W. HOLMES *Guard. Angel* xxv. (1891) 304 To the paper factory, where they have a horrid machine they call the devil, that tears everything to bits. **1870** *Eng. Mech.* 31 Dec. 610/1 The machine..is called a willow, or willey, vulgarly a devil; it is used principally for opening raw cotton. **1872** *Manch. Guardian* 24 Sept. (Farmer), Mr. Powell's Bill contains abundant powers for suppressing the vile nuisance known as the American Devil [steam whistle or hooter]. **1874** KNIGHT *Dict. Mech., Devil*, a machine for making wood screws. *a* **1877** KNIGHT *Dict. Mech.* I. 691/1 *Devil*, a machine for making wood screws. **1879** *Cassells Techn. Educ.* IV. 349/2 [He] dives into the recesses of his skin for the 'devil' which is a bunch of matted iron wire. **1880** *Times* 13 Dec., An instrument called 'the Devil' used by foreign fishermen for destroying the fishing nets of English boats on the East coast. **1883** *Stonemason* Jan., Dried by means of sundry coke fires kept burning in iron grates called 'devils', similar to those used by the Gas Company's men in our streets. **1884** *Sat. Rev.* 12 July 61/1 'Devils'..are used to catch sea-trout in Wales, but Mr. Fitch justly regards 'devils' as an unsportsmanlike device. **1886** *Pall Mall G.* 7 Dec. 10/1 There were exhibited in the court room three Belgian 'devils' and three Belgian grapnels which had been captured by Lowestoft fishermen. **1887** *Harper's Mag.* June 119/1 The devil, a hollow cone with spikes projecting within, against which work the spikes of a drum, dashing the rags about at great speed. **1890** W. J. GORDON *Foundry* 72 A herculean metallic disk, grimly named the 'devil', armed with steel cutters on its circumference that takes off a pound of shavings at every revolution. **1893** *Star* 15 July 3/2 The machine for unloading grain..not inaptly named a 'devil', will..do the work of four gangs of dock laborers of 12 men each. **1895** *Daily Chronicle* 7 Jan. 8/3 The match was only brought off at Cardiff by the extraordinary precautions for warming the ground by means of 'devils'. **1901** *Farm, Field & Fireside* 13 Dec. 362/2 Large surfaces are dealt with by burning, an instrument called a 'devil' being generally employed by painters for 'burning off' doors, panels, etc.

9. a. A name for various highly-seasoned broiled or fried dishes; also for hot ingredients.

1786 CRAIG *Lounger* No. 86 Make punch, brew negus, and season a *devil.* **1788** WOLCOTT (P. Pindar) *Peter to Tom* Wks. 1812 I. 530 By Devil..I mean a Turkey's Gizzard So christen'd for its quality, by man Because so oft 'tis loaded with Kian. **1820** W. IRVING *Sketch-bk., L'Envoy* (1865) 458 Another holds a curry or a devil in utter abomination. **1828** SMEATON *Doings in London* (Farmer), The extract of Capsicums or extract of Grains of Paradise is known in the gin-selling trade by the appellation of the Devil. **1830** G. GRIFFIN *Collegians* xiii, The drumstick of a goose or turkey, grilled and highly spiced, was called a devil. *c* **1844** THACKERAY *Mr. & Mrs. Berry* ii, The devilled fowl had.. no devil in it. **1848** *Paddiana* (ed. 2) I. 50 Devils were his forte: he imparted a pungent relish to a gizzard or a drumstick that set the assuaging power of drink at defiance. **1889** BOLDREWOOD *Robbery under Arms* (1890) 327 Let's.. have a devil and a glass of champagne.

b. ***devils on horseback,*** angels on horseback (see ANGEL *sb.* 7); also, a similar dish consisting of a prune or plum wrapped in a bacon-rasher and served on fried bread.

1909 in *Cent. Dict.* Suppl. **1963** R. McDOUALL *Cookery Book* 228 Devils on horseback are much the same [as canapés diane], except that a stoned prune is substituted for the chicken-livers.

10. The name of various forms of fireworks; also 'a sort of priming made by damping and bruising gunpowder' (Smyth *Sailors' Word-bk.*).

1742 FIELDING *J. Andrews* III. vii, The captain..pinned a cracker or devil to the cassock. **1807** W. IRVING *Salmag.* (1824) 135 Like a nest of squibs and devils in a firework. **1809** *Naval Chron.* XXII. 203 Rockets, infernals, fire-devils. **1836** T. HOOK *G. Gurney* vii, Four devils or wild-fires, such as we were in the habit of making at school.

11. The name given to sand-spouts or moving columns of sand in India and Eastern countries. Also, a dust-storm in South Africa.

1835 BURNES *Trav. Bokhara* (ed. 2) III. 40 Whirlwinds, that raised the dust to a great height, and moved over the plain like water-spouts at sea. In India these phenomena are familiarly known by the name of *devils.* **1886** BURTON *Arab. Nts.* I. 99 *note*, Devils, or pillars of sand, vertical and inclined, measuring a thousand feet high, rush over the plain. **1889** *Daily News* 8 July (Farmer), Clouds of dust.. went whirling across the common in spiral cones like desert Devils. **1893** EARL DUNMORE *Pamirs* I. 269 The amount of devils we saw was surprising. (*Note*) Common in the plains of India, where they are called by the natives Bagoola. English people in India call them 'devils'. **1897** BADEN-POWELL *Matabele Camp* 284 A 'Devil' with its roaring pillar of dust and leaves, comes tearing by. **1900** *Daily News* 3 Apr. 3/1 The 'dust devils' that sweep across the blustering plain. **1901** *Westm. Gaz.* 16 Mar. 3/1 The 'devil' in South Africa will pick up boots and tins of sardines, even bottles of whisky and saddle bags.

12. Short for *devil-bolt*: see 24.

1873 PLIMSOLL *Our Seamen, an Appeal* 37 'Oh, devils are sham bolts, you know; that is, when they ought to be copper, the head and about an inch of the shaft are of copper, and the rest is iron'.. Seventy-three devils were found in one ship by one of the surveyors of Lloyd's.

13. *Naut.* 'The seam which margins the waterways on a ship's hull' (Smyth *Sailor's Word-bk.*); 'a seam between the garboard-strake and the keel' (Funk and Wagnall).

Hence various writers derive the phrase 'the devil to pay and no pitch hot'; but this is prob. only a secondary and humorous application of 'the devil to pay': cf. 22 j.

14. ***a devil of a***... : a diabolical example or specimen of a..., one (of the things in question) of a diabolical, detestable, or violently irritating kind; passing into a mere intensive, = a deuced, confounded, very violent. [So F. *diable de.*]

[**1749** FIELDING *Tom Jones* XII. vii, You don't know what a devil of a fellow he is.] **1767** S. PATERSON *Another Trav.* I. 345 Running downhill at the devil of a rate. **1794** SCOTT *Let. to Miss Rutherford* 5 Sept. in *Lockhart*, Both within and without doors, it was a devil of a day. **1819** BYRON *Juan* II. xi, A devil of a sea rolls in that bay. **1822** SHELLEY in *T.L. Peacock's Wks.* (1875) III. 477 A devil of a nut it is to crack. **1826** J. WILSON *Noct. Ambr.* Wks. 1855 I. 180 What an outlandish toozy-headed wee sunburnt deevil o' a lassie that. **1852** R. S. SURTEES *Sponge's Sp. Tour* liv. 313 We had a devil of a run—I don't know how many miles. **1869** TROLLOPE *He Knew, etc.* liv. (1878) 299 Lead him the very devil of a life. **1890** BESANT *Demoniac* v. 53 There will be a devil of a fight when the time comes.

15. *predicatively*: Something as bad as the devil, as bad as can be conceived, the worst that can happen or be met with. [F. *c'est bien le diable, le diable est que..*]

1710 *Brit. Apollo* III. No. 60. 2/2 To quit a Yielding Mistress is the Devil. *a* **1735** GRANVILLE (J.), A war of profit mitigates the evil; But to be tax'd, and beaten, is the devil. **1798** SOUTHEY *Ballad of Cross Roads* 7 In such a sweltering day as this A knapsack is the devil. **1827** SCOTT *Jrnl.* 28 June, To be cross-examined by those who have seen the true thing is the devil. **1885** *Scribner's Mag.* XXX. 734/2 These Southern girls are the very devil.

16. ***like the devil, like devils*** [F. *comme le diable, comme tous les diables*], beside the more literal sense, sometimes means: With the violence, desperation, cleverness, or other quality attributed to the devil; extremely, excessively: cf. DIABOLICALLY. So in similes, e.g., ***as drunk as the d.***, diabolically drunk.

1599 SHAKS. *Hen. V.* III. vii. 162 They will eate like Wolues, and fight like Deuils. **1632** LITHGOW *Trav.* VIII. 345 The distressed Protestants..over whom they domineered like Divells. **1791** 'G. GAMBADO' *Ann. Horsem.* ix. (1809) 106 My horse..pulls like the devil. **1816** *Sporting Mag.* XLVIII. 39 A man is said to be..when he is very impudent, as drunk as the devil. **1847** EMERSON *Repr. Men, Napoleon* Wks. (Bohn) I. 378 He disputed like a devil on these two points.

II. In imprecations, exclamations, proverbs, and phrases.

17. In imprecations, wishes of evil, and the like, as ***the devil take him***, etc. (Cf. similar uses with *deuce, mischief, pest, plague, pox*, etc.) ***devil take the hindmost***: see HINDMOST *a.* 1 b.

c **1300** *Havelok* 1188 Godrich hem hatede, þe deuel him hawe! *c* **1410** *Sir Cleges* 515 The styward seyd..the dewle hym Born [= burn] on a lowe! *c* **1460** *Towneley Myst.* (Surtees) 175 The dwille he hang you highe to dry! *c* **1500** *Robin Hood & Potter* lxxvii. in Child *Ballads* III. v. cxxi. 113/2 The deyell spede hem, bothe bodey and bon. **1513** DOUGLAS *Æneis* I. *Prol.* 260 A twenty devill mot fall his werk at anis. **1548** HALL *Chron.* 14 b, Saiyng, the devill take Henry of Lancastre and the together. **1600** SHAKS. *A.Y.L.* III. ii. 225 Nay, but the diuell take mocking: speake sadde brow, and true maid. *a* **1652** BROME *Queene's Exch.* II. ii. Wks. 1873 III. 485 Now the Dee'l brast crag of him. **1738** SWIFT *Polite Conv.* 129 Here take it, and the D——l do you good with it. **1749** FIELDING *Tom Jones* VII. xii, The devil take my father for sending me thither. **1833** TENNYSON *The Goose*, 'The Devil take the goose, And God forget the stranger!'

18. ***to go to the devil***: to go to ruin or perdition. In the imperative, expressing angry impatience, and desire to be rid of the person addressed. So ***to wish*** any one ***at the devil***, etc. [F. *aller, envoyer, donner, être au diable.*]

[*c* **1394** J. MALVERNE *Contn. Higden* (Rolls) IX. 33 Excanduit rex [Rich. II] et..dixit ei [comiti Arundel], 'Quod si tu mihi imponas..vadas ad diabolum'.] *c* **1460** *Towneley Myst.* (Surt.) 10 Go to the deville, and say I bad. *c* **1489** CAXTON *Sonnes of Aymon* iii. 102 Lete theym go to a hundred thousand devils! **1553** T. WILSON *Rhet.* (1580) 178 All his Superstition and Hypocrisie, either is or should be gone to the devill. **1568** GRAFTON *Chron.* II. 367 They cursed them betwene their teeth, saiyng: Get ye into England, or to the devill. **1634** SIR T. HERBERT *Trav.* 102 Ere they could strangle him, he sent three of them to the Devill. **1822** HAZLITT *Table-t., Disagreeable People* (1852) 121 Whether they are demons or angels in themselves, you wish them..at the devil. **1823** BYRON *Juan* x. lxvi, When a man's country's going to the devil. **1859** H. KINGSLEY *G. Hamlyn* xxxii, Tom..having told her..to go to the devil. **1881** W. H. MALLOCK *Rom. 19th Cent.* I. 219, I wish..the little animal was at the devil.

†**19.** ***a devil way*** (*adv.*): originally an impatient strengthening of AWAY (*a* being the prep., varying with *on, in*, and *devele* the genitive pl., OE. *deofla*); further intensified as ***a twenty devil way, on aller*** or ***alther*** (corrupted to ***all the***) ***devil way, on aller twenty devil way.*** *Obs.*

c **1290** *S. Eng. Leg.* I. 203/124 Þov worst lif and soule a deuele wei al clene i-nome. *c* **1320** *Seuyn Sag.* (W.) 2298 And bad hire go, that ilche dai, On alder twenti deuel wai! *c* **1385** CHAUCER *L.G.W.* 2177 *Ariadne*, A twenty develewey the wynd hym dryue. *c* **1386** —— *Reeve's T.* 337 And forth he goth a [3 *MSS.* on, *Harl.* in] twenty deuel way. *c* **1460** *Towneley Myst.* (Surt.) 130 Go hens, harlottes, in twenty dewille way, Fast and belyfe! *Ibid.* 176.

†**b.** In later times it appears to have been taken more vaguely, as an expression of impatience, and sometimes = 'in the devil's name.' *Obs.*

c **1386** CHAUCER *Miller's Prol.* 26 Tel on, a deueleway [*v.r.* a delewey]. —— *Sompn. T.* 534 Lat hym go honge hymself a [*Harl.* on] deuel way. —— *Miller's T.* 527. —— *Can. Yeom. Prol. & T.* 229. *a* **1440** *Sir Degrev.* 776 Go and glad thi gest, In alther [*printed* all the] devyl way! *c* **1460** *Towneley Myst.* (Surt.) 10 Sit downe in the dewille way, With thi vayn carpyng. *Ibid.* 18 Com downe in twenty deville way. ? *a* **1500** *Chester Pl., Deluge* 219 Come in, wife, in 20 devills waye, or els stand there without. *a* **1529** SKELTON *Wks.* I. 336 That all the worlde may say, Come downe, in the devyll way. **1530** PALSGR. 838 In the twenty devyll way, *au nom du grant diable.*

20. As an expression of impatience, irritation, strong surprise, dismay, or vexation. **a.** After an interrogative word, as *who, what, how, where, when.*

[App. taken directly from Fr.; cf. 12th c. OF. *comment diables! dist li rois au vis fier*; *diables* being in the nominative (= vocative case); mod.F. *que diable faire!*; in ME. also *what devil*, about 1600 often *what a devil.* Also in Ger., Du., Da. and other langs.]

c 1385 CHAUCER *L.G.W.* 2694 *Hypermestre*, What devel have I with the knyfe to doo? c 1440 *York Myst.* xxxi. 237 What the deuyll and his dame schall y now doo? c 1460 *Towneley Myst.* (Surtees) 114 What the deville is this? he has a long snowte. 1470–85 MALORY *Arthur* x. xlviii, What deuylle doo ye in this Countrey? c 1489 CAXTON *Sonnes of Aymon* xix. 408 How the devyll dare ye thus speke? 1529 MORE *Dyalogue* III. v. Wks. 214 Why, quod he, what deuill rigour could thei more haue shewed? 1562 J. HEYWOOD *Prov. & Epigr.* (1867) 183 When the diuell will ye come in? 1568 GRAFTON *Chron.* II. 355 Who the devill hath sente for them? 1589 PUTTENHAM *Eng. Poesie* III. xxiii. (Arb.) 274 What a diuell tellest thou to me of iustice? 1596 SHAKS. *1 Hen. IV*, I. ii. 6 What a diuell hast thou to do with the time of the day? 1670 G. H. *Hist. Cardinals* I. II. 40 How a Devil will the Pope observe the Decrees of a Councel? 1692 WASHINGTON tr. *Milton's Def. Pop.* viii. (1851) 184 What the Devil is it to you? 1749 FIELDING *Tom Jones* XV. v, Why, who the devil are you? 1803 tr. *Lebrun's Mons. Botte* I. 155 What the devil business had she in the store-room? 1819 BYRON *Juan* I. c, And wonders why the devil he got heirs. a 1845 HOOD *Lullaby* ii, What the devil makes him cry?

b. Used interjectionally, or prefixed to a predication.

c 1460 *Towneley Myst.* (Surt.) 67 Dwylle! what may this be? Out, harow, fulle wo is me!.. A, fy, and dewyls! whens cam he That thus shuld reyfe me my pawste. 1589 *Pappe w. Hatchet* B iij, She is dead: the diuell shee is. 1590 SHAKS. *Com. Err.* IV. iv. 130 Will you be bound for nothing, be mad good Master, cry the diuell. 1709 STEELE *Tatler* No. 107 ¶13 The Devil! He cried out, Who can bear it? 1832 *Blackw. Mag.* Jan. 63/1 'The Pacha has put twelve ambassadors to death already.' 'The devil he has! and I'm sent here to make up the baker's dozen!' 1854 EMERSON *Lett. & Soc. Aims, Comic* Wks. (Bohn) III. 209 'That is W,' said the teacher. 'The Devil!' exclaimed the boy, 'is that W?'

21. Expressing strong negation: prefixed to a substantive, as ***the devil a bit, the devil a penny***.

1508 KENNEDIE *Flyting w. Dunbar* 441 The deuill a gude thou hais! 1542 UDALL *Erasm. Apoph.* (1877) 132 The Deuill of the one chare of good werke they doen. 1579 FULKE *Confut. Sanders* 697 'Godly images leade vs to spirituall deuotion.' The Diuel they doe. But if they did, yet not more then the ceremonies of the olde law. c 1590 MARLOWE *Faust.* Wks. (Rtldg.) 90/1 The devil a penny they have left me, but a bare pension. 1601 SHAKS. *Twel. N.* II. iii. 159 The diu'll a Puritane that hee is, or any thing constantly. a 1661 FULLER *Worthies* (1811) I. 386 We have an English expression, 'The Devil he doth it, the Devil he hath it'; where the addition of Devil amounteth only to a strong denial, equivalent to, 'He doth it not, he hath it not.' 1708 MOTTEUX *Rabelais* (1737) V. 221 The Devil-a-Bit he'll see the better. 1710 *Brit. Apollo* III. No. 78. 3/1 The D——l was Sick, the D——l a Monk would be, the D——l was Well, the D——l a Monk was he. 1828 SCOTT *F.M. Perth* xxvii, The deil a man dares stir you within his bounds. 1832 *Examiner* 349/1 Devil another word would she speak.

22. In proverbs and proverbial phrases.

a. ***the devil and all***: Everything right or wrong (especially the wrong); the whole confounded lot; all or everything bad: cf. also g below. (But sometimes a strengthened form of sense 15.)

1543 BALE *Yet a Course*, Baptyzed bells, bedes, organs.. the devyll and all of soche idolatrouse beggery. 1592 NASHE *P. Penilesse* A iij, Masse thats true: they say the Lawyers haue the deuill and al. 1606 WARNER *Alb. Eng.* XVI. ciii, Be Lawyers, get the Diuell and all. 1689 HICKERINGILL *Ceremony-Monger* Wks. 1716 II. 507 He may get the Devil and all of Money, and a Purse as large as his Conscience. 1703 MRS. CENTLIVRE *Love's Contriv.* v, If she cou'd steal a husband, she'd have stole the Devil and all of Gallants. 1811 EARL GOWER 18 Dec. in *C.K. Sharpe's Corr.* (1888) I. 508, I begin to fear that the rheumatism has taken possession of your right arm.. which would be the devil and all, as the vulgar would say. 1838 DICKENS *O. Twist* xx, I needn't take this devil-and-all trouble to explain matters to you.

b. ***between the d. and the deep*** (formerly also ***Dead***) ***sea***.

1637 MONRO *Exped.* II. 55 (Jam.), I, with my partie, did lie on our poste, as betwixt the devill and the deep sea. 1690 W. WALKER *Idiomat. Anglo-Lat.* 394 Between the devil and the dead sea. 1721 KELLY *Sc. Prov.* 58 (Jam.) *Between the Deel and the deep sea*; that is between two difficulties equally dangerous. 1816 [see DEIL 1]. 1894 H. H. GIBBS *Colloquy on Currency* 199 You must remember that he was between the devil and the deep sea.

c. ***black as the d., to paint the d. blacker than he is***, and kindred expressions. ***give the devil his due***: see DUE.

1596 LODGE *Margarite Amer.* 84 Divels are not so blacke as they be painted.. nor women so wayward as they seeme. 1642 HOWELL *For. Trav.* (Arb.) 65 For the Devill is not so black as he is painted, no more are these Noble Nations and Townes as they are tainted. 1654 WHITLOCK *Zootomia* 271 They use their Adversary according to the Proverb, painting the Devill blacker then he is. 1837 A. FONBLANQUE *Eng. under 7 Administ.* I. 226 That the Devil of Charles X could be painted blacker than his complexion would prove.

d. ***when the d. is blind***: at a date infinitely remote, at the Greek calends, or 'latter Lammas'.

1662 *Rump Songs* (1874) I. 9 But when this comes to passe, say the Devil is blind. c 1702 *Bagford Ballads* (1876) 74 For we will be Married, When the Devil is Blind. 1725 BAILEY *Erasm. Colloq.* (1877) 216 (D.) They will bring it when the devil is blind [*id fiet ad Calendas Græcas*]. 1738 SWIFT *Polite Convers.* i. (D.), *Nev.* I'll make you a fine present one of these days. *Miss.* Ay, when the Devil is blind, and his eyes are not sore yet.

e. The devil's hostility to the *Cross*; sometimes with a play upon 'cross' as a coin.

a 1529 SKELTON *Bowge of Courte* 365 The deuyll myghte daunce therin for any crowche. 1612 SHELTON *Quix.* I. I. vi. 44 It is a common saying—'The Devil lurks behind the Cross'. 1627 DRAYTON *Agincourt* 82 Ill's the precession (and foreruns much losse,) Wherein men say, the Deuill beares the Crosse. 1636 MASSINGER *Bashf. Lover* III. i, The devil sleeps in my pocket: I have no cross To drive him from it. 1726 *Adv. Capt. R. Boyle* 209 Leaving Room in all our Pockets for the Devil to Dance a Saraband, for we had not one Cross to keep him out.

†**f.** ***the date of the devil*** is opposed to the date of our Lord; but ***in the devil's date*** is also = 'in the devil's name'. *Obs.*

1362 LANGL. *P. Pl.* A. II. 81 In þe Date of þe deuel þe Deede was a-selet. 1526 SKELTON *Magnyf.* 954 What needed that, in the devyls date? a 1529 —— *Sp. Parrot* 439 Yet the date of ower Lord And the date of the Devyll dothe shrewdlye accord. —— *Bowge of Courte* 375 In the devils date, What arte thou?

g. ***the d.*** (***and all***) ***to do***: much ado, a world of trouble or turmoil.

1708 MOTTEUX *Rabelais* v. iii, There was the Devil and all to do. 1711 SWIFT *Jrnl. to Stella* 17 Nov., This being queen Elisabeth's birthday, we have the d——and all to do among us. 1712 ARBUTHNOT *John Bull* III. v, Then there was the devil and all to do: spoons, plates, and dishes flew about the room like mad. 1716 SWIFT *Phillis* 39 See here again the devil to do. a 1774 GOLDSM. tr. *Scarron's Comic Rom.* (1775) I. 42 Here had been the devil and all to do.

h. The devil's aversion to *holy water*.

1570–6 LAMBARDE *Peramb. Kent* (1826) 301 The olde Proverbe how well the Divell loveth holy water. 1738 SWIFT *Polite Convers.* 149, I love Mr. N—, as the Devil loves Holy Water. *Mod.* To hate——, as the devil hates holy water.

i. ***as the devil looked over Lincoln***.

(Popularly referred to a grotesque sculpture on the exterior of Lincoln Cathedral.)

1562 J. HEYWOOD *Prov. & Epigr.* (1867) 75 Than wold ye looke ouer me, with stomake swolne, Like as the diuel lookt ouer Lincolne. a 1661 FULLER *Worthies* Oxf. & Linc. Prov. (D.). 1737 POPE *Hor. Epist.* II. ii. 245 Yet these are wights who fondly call their own Half that the Devil o'er-looks from Lincoln town. 1738 SWIFT *Polite Convers.* 86 She looked at me, as the Devil look'd over Lincoln.

j. ***the devil to pay***.

Supposed to refer to the alleged bargains made by wizards, etc., with Satan, and the inevitable payment to be made to him in the end. It has also been attributed to the difficulty of 'paying' or caulking the seam called the 'devil', near a ship's keel, whence the expanded form 'the devil to pay and no pitch hot'. But there is no evidence that this is the original sense, and it has never affected the general use of the proverb.

1711 SWIFT *Jrnl. to Stella* 28 Sept. (Farmer), And then there will be the devil and all to pay. 1728 VANBR. & CIB. *Prov. Husb.* v. i. 93 In comes my Lady Townly here.. who ..has had the Devil to pay yonder. 1738 SWIFT *Polite Convers.* 179, I must be with my Wife on Tuesday, or there will be the Devil and all to pay. 1820 BYRON in Moore *Life & Lett.* (1833) III. 63 There will be the devil to pay, and there is no saying who will or who will not be set down in his bill. 1837 MRS. CARLYLE *Lett.* I. 72 Had he been laid up at present, there would have been the very devil to pay. 1892 A. BIRRELL *Res Judic.* xii. 272 Then, indeed—to use a colloquial expression—there would be the devil to pay.

k. ***to play the devil*** (***the very d., the d. and all***): to act diabolically, do mischief, make havoc or ruin.

1542 BOORDE *Dyetary* ix. (1870) 250 The malt worme playeth the deuyll so fast in the heade. a 1592 GREENE *Alphonsus* I, Burning towns, and sacking cities fair, Doth play the devil wheresome'er he comes. 1594 SHAKS. *Rich. III*, I. iii. 338 Seeme a Saint, when most I play the deuill. 1656 JEANES *Mixt. Schol. Div.* 119 The word was incarnate, and shall we play the incarnate Divels? 1811 in Col. Hawker *Diary* (1893) I. 35, I should have played the devil with his pheasants. 1826 SCOTT *Jrnl.* 15 Apr., A bad report from that quarter would play the devil. 1833 MARRYAT *P. Simple* xxxviii, Salt water plays the devil with a uniform. 1838 DICKENS *Nich. Nick.* xvi, Your firm and determined intention.. to play the very devil with everything and everybody.

l. ***speak*** or ***talk of the d., and he will appear***. Freq. shortened to ***talk of the devil***; esp. used in reference to a person who appears unexpectedly when one is talking about him.

[1591 LYLY *Endimion* I. iii. 3, O that we had Sir Tophas.. in the midst of our myrth, & *ecce autem*, wyl you see the deuill?] 1666 G. TORRIANO *Piazza Universale* 134 The English say, Talk of the Devil, and he's presently at your elbow. 1672 *Cataplus, a mock Poem* 72 (in Hazlitt *Prov.*) Talk of the Devil, and see his horns. a 1721 PRIOR *Hans Carvel* 71 Forthwith the Devil did appear, For name him and he's always near. 1721 J. KELLY *Sc. Prov.* 299 *Speak of the Dee'l, and he'll appear*, spoken when they, of whom we are speaking, come in by Chance. 1738 SWIFT *Polite Conv.* I He's just coming towards us. Talk of the Devil! 1853 TRENCH *Proverbs* vi, To talk as little about the devil.. as they can; lest he appear. 1893 G. ALLEN *Scallywag* I. 10 'Talk of the devil!—Here comes Thiselton!' 1922 E. O'NEILL *Anna Christie* (1923) I. 9 Speak of the devil. We was just talkin' about you. 1958 G. GREENE *Our Man in Havana* III. iii. 136 'What's the matter, Hasselbacher?' 'Oh, it's you, Mr. Wormold. I was just thinking of you. Talk of the devil,' he said, making a joke of it.

m. ***the d. among the tailors***: a row going on (see Farmer *Slang Dict.* s.v.); also a game.

1834 LD. LONDONDERRY *Let.* 27 May in *Court Will. IV & Victoria* (1861) II. iv. 98 Reports are various as to the state of the enemy's camp, but all agree that there is the devil among the tailors. 1851 MAYHEW *Lond. Labour* (1861) II. 17 A game known as the 'Devil among the tailors'.. a top was set spinning on a long board, and the result depended upon the number of men, or 'tailors', knocked down by the 'devil' (top) of each player.

n. In other expressions (mostly self-explanatory).

to pull the devil by the tail (F. tirer le diable par la queue): to be in difficulties or straits. ***to whip the devil round the stump*** (U.S.): 'to get round or dodge a difficulty or dilemma by means of a fabricated excuse or explanation' (*Cent. Dict.*) See also DRIVE *v.* 1 b, NEEDS *adv.* d, SPOON *sb.* 3 a.

1553 T. WILSON *Rhet.* (1580) 26 Every man for himselfe, and the Devill for us all, catche that catche maie. a 1555 RIDLEY *Wks.* 10 It is also a true common proverb, that it is even sin to lie upon the devil. 1562 J. HEYWOOD *Prov. & Epigr.* (1867) 60, I will not beare the diuels sacke, by saint Audry. 1581 PETTIE *Guazzo's Civ. Conv.* II (1586) 79 The Proverbe, That the divell is full of knowledge, because he is olde. 1593 *Pass. Morrice* 74 Like will to like, quoth the Devell to the Collier. 1599 MINSHEU *Dial. Sp. & Eng.* (1623) 35/2 Let us not give the divell his dinner. 1606 J. DAY *Isle of Guls* sig. D4v, You were worse then the deuil els, for they say hee helps his seruants. 1611 COTGR. s.v. *Retirer*, To giue a thing and take a thing; to weare the diuells gold-ring. 1615 SWETNAM *Arraignm. Wom.* (1880) p. xvi, They will finde that they haue but the Deuill by the foote. 1661 A. BROME *Songs & Other Poems* 136 The Devil's ever kind to his own. 1687 CONGREVE *Old Bach.* I. iv, Ay there you've nicked it—there's the devil upon devil. 1690 W. WALKER *Idiomat. Anglo-Lat.* 49 What is got over the devil's back is spent under his belly. a 1704 T. BROWN *Wks.* (1760) II. 194 (D.) We became as great friends as the Devil and the Earl of Kent. —— *Ibid.* III. 245 (D.) The devil and nine-pence go with her, that's money and company, according to the.. adage. 1708 MOTTEUX *Rabelais* IV. xxxiii. (1737) 138 There will be the Devil upon Dun. This is a worse Business than that t'other Day. c 1708 W. KING *Art of Love* III. 82 She'd run, As would the Devil upon Dun. 1709 *Brit. Apollo* II. No. 56. 3/2 At Play 'tis often said, When Luck returns —*The Devil's dead.* 1720 DE FOE *Capt. Singleton* i. (1840) 8 He that is shipped with the devil must sail with the devil. 1738 SWIFT *Polite Conv.* 182 Well, since he's gone, the Devil go with him and Sixpence; and there's Money and Company too. *Ibid.* 13 It rain'd, and the Sun shone at the same time .. Why, then the Devil was beating his Wife behind the Door, with a Shoulder of Mutton. *Ibid.* 159, I beg your Pardon: but they say, the Devil made Askers. *Ibid.* 200 As great as Cup and Can.. Ay, Miss; as great as the Devil and the Earl of Kent. 1806 [see GOOD *a.* 7 a]. 1822 BYRON *Werner* v. i. 427 Father, do not raise The devil you cannot lay between us. a 1832 BENTHAM *Wks.* (1838–43) X. 25 So fond of spending his money on antiquities, that he was always pulling the devil by the tail. 1837 F. CHAMIER *Arethusa* II. i. 13 Weazel was the only midshipman saved besides myself: the devil always takes care of his own. 1840 BARHAM *Ingol. Leg.*, '*St. Dunstan*', The Devil, they say, 'Tis easier at all times to raise than to lay. 1846 WHATELY *Rhetoric* (ed. 7) Additions 14 Various evasions and equivocations, such as are vulgarly called 'cheating the Devil'. 1855 TENNYSON *Maud* I. i. xix, I will bury myself in myself, and the Devil may pipe to his own. 1857 TROLLOPE *Barchester T.* II. vii. 123 'Better the d—— you know than the d—— you don't know,' is an old saying. 1857 *N.Y. Evening Post* (Bartlett), There, you are now whipping the devil around the stump! 1892 HON. E. BLAKE in *Daily News* 5 Aug. 3/4 Time enough to bid the Devil good morning when you meet him. 1940 R. A. J. WALLING *Why did Trethewy Die?* vii. 195 The devil looks after his own. 1960 *Times* 30 Jan. 3/3 They are probably wise to leave well alone on the devil-you-know principle.

o. Other phrases see under leading words, as *to hold a* CANDLE *to the d., the d. and his* DAM, *the d. in the* HOROLOGE, etc.

III. *attrib.* and *Comb.*

23. General combinations. **a.** 'devil' *in apposition*, as ***devil-god, -jailor, -monk, -porter***, etc. Hence as vb. ***to devil-porter it***, to be devil-porter.

1605 SHAKS. *Macb.* II. iii. 19 Ile Deuill-Porter it no further. 1610 HEALEY *St. Aug. Citie of God* IV. xvi, Such a rable of divill-gods. 1613 SHAKS. *Hen. VIII*, II. i. 21 That Diuell Monke, Hopkins. 1625–6 SHIRLEY *Maid's Rev.* v. iii, My eldest devil-sister! 1629 —— *Wedding* III. i, Thy devil jailor May trust thee without a waiter. 1892 B. F. C. COSTELLOE *Church Catholic* 13 A Devil-giant coercing hapless lives.

b. *attrib.* and *objective genitive*, as ***devil-hive, -master, -work; devil-conjurer, -drawer, -driver, -extractor***.

1535 COVERDALE *Dan.* ii. 27 The sorcerer, the charmer nor the deuell coniurer. 1682 HICKERINGILL *Black Non-Conf.* Wks. 1716 II. 42 The Pope would be a Devil-driver too. a 1700 B.E. *Dict. Cant. Crew, Devil-drawer*, a sorry Painter. 1727 DE FOE *Syst. Magic* I. ii. (1840) 51 Any sorcery or devil-work. 1749 BP. LAVINGTON *Enthus. Meth. & Papists* (1820) 319 These men, who are called enchanters, devil-drivers, and prophesiers. 1823 BENTHAM *Not Paul* 321 Fear of the more skilful devil-master. 1849 SOUTHEY *Comm.-pl. Bk.* Ser. II. 400 They struggled till fire issued from eyes, nostrils, and mouth of the poor devil-hive. 1886 *Pall Mall G.* 29 Dec. 6/2 A refusal to pay the fee charged by a 'devil extractor' for the cure of a mental disease.

c. *instrumental* and *parasynthetic*, as ***devil-born, -driven, -haired, -haunted, -inspired, -possessed -ridden***, etc. adjs.

1607 TOPSELL *Four-f. Beasts* (1658) 17 The Asse.. is.. phrased with many epithets.. as slow.. idle, devil-haired. 1829 SOUTHEY *Sir T. More* II. 108 Men become priest-ridden or devil-ridden. 1850 TENNYSON *In Mem.* xcvi, You tell me, doubt is devil-born. 1860 LD. LYTTON *Lucile* II. v, Scorn and hate.. are devil born things. 1888 *Catholic Press* 16 June 125/1 A devil-inspired cult. 1898 KIPLING in *Spectator* 2 July 15/2 Afraid of the devil-haunted beach of noises. 1899 *Daily News* 20 Sept. 3/3 Then came the famous devil-possessed district. 1906 R. WHITEING *Ring in New* ix. 59 The devil-driven and purposeful way in which people do most things in this part of the world. 1922 W. B. YEATS *Trembling of Veil* II. viii. 108 The only Young Ireland politician who had music and personality, though rancorous and devil-possessed. 1926 M. LEINSTER *Dew on Leaf* II. i, Jack is lonely, wretched, devil-driven.

d. *objective*, as ***devil-driving***, etc.

1707 J. STEVENS *Quevedo's Com. Wks.* (1709) 327 There is a Devil ferking Priest.

24. Special combinations. **devil-bolt**, a sham bolt (see 12); 'a bolt with false clenches, often introduced into contract-built ships' (Smyth *Sailor's Word-bk.*); **devil-carriage, -cart**, a carriage for moving heavy ordnance; †**devil-cleper** (*obs.*), one who invokes the devil, an enchanter; **devil-crab**, the velvet crab, *Portunus puber*; = *lady-crab* (LADY *sb.* 16); **devil dance**, the dance of a devil-dancer; **devil-dancer**, an Indian votary, akin to the Dancing Dervishes; so **devil-dancing**; **devil-dare** *a.* = DARE-DEVIL; **devil-dealer**, one who has dealings with the devil, a sorcerer; **devil-devil**, (*a*) in Australian folk-lore, a devil, an evil spirit; (*b*) *Austral. slang* (see quot. 1933); **devil float**, a tool for roughening the surface of plaster; **devil-in-a-bush**, a garden flower, *Nigella damascena*, so called 'from its horned capsules peering from a bush of finely-divided involucre' (Prior); **devil liquor** (see quot. 1912); **devil-monger** = *devil-dealer*; **devil-on-both-sides**, a local name of the corn crowfoot (*Ranunculus arvensis*), in allusion to its prickly horned capsules; **devil-on-the-coals** *Austral. slang*, a small damper hastily baked in hot ashes; **devil on two sticks**, a wooden toy in the form of an hour-glass or double cone, which is made to spin in the air by means of a string attached to two sticks held in the hands; cf. DIABOLO; **devil-shrieker**, **-skriker**, local name of the Swift: see sense 7 b; **devil-tree**, an apocynaceous tree (*Alstonia scholaris*) of India, Africa, and Australia, having a powerfully bitter bark and milky juice; **devil-ward** *a.* and *adv.*, towards or in the direction of the devil; **devil-wise** *adv.*, after the manner of a devil; **devil-wood**, *Osmanthus americanus*, N.O. *Oleaceæ*, a small N. American tree with wood of extraordinary toughness and heaviness; **devil-worship**, the worship or cult of the devil, or of a demon or malignant deity; so **devil-worshipper**, **-worshipping**; **devil-wort**, a plant. Also, DEVIL-BIRD, -DODGER, -FISH, etc.

1894 *Daily News* 30 Nov. 7/5 The '*devil-bolt' swindle must have been the death of many a brave crew. **1828** J. M. SPEARMAN *Brit. Gunner* 50 *Devil Carriages, large, limber, small. *Ibid.* 426 Devil carriage, 7 ft.; Sling cart, 5 ft. 6 in. **1797** NELSON in Nicolas *Disp.* VII. p. cxxxix, I want..two or three artillerymen to fix the fusees, and a *devil-cart. **1382** WYCLIF *Isa.* xlvii. 9 The huge hardnesse of thi *deuel-cleperes. **1871** C. DARWIN *Desc. Man* II. ix. 269 When a *Devil-crab (Portunus puber) was seen..fighting with a *Carcinus mænas*, the latter was soon thrown on its back. **1899** *Strand Mag.* June 655/2 Prickly devil-crabs. **1849** R. CALDWELL *Tinnevelly Shanars* 19 The musical instruments ..chiefly used in the *devil-dance are the tom-tom..and the horn. **1901** KIPLING *Kim* ix. 212 He had seen devil-dance masks at the Lahore Museum. *Ibid.* x. 248 Devil dances, and spells and charms. **1930** G. KNIGHT *Intim. Glimpses Myster. Tibet* 29 The Devil Dances of Tibet..represent either some historical, legendary, or mythological event. **1887** *Pall Mall G.* 14 Sept. 14/1 They were followed by the *devil-dancers, who were terribly affected. **1871** MATEER *Travancore* (1872) 214 Connected with this is what is called *devil-dancing, in which the demoniacal possession is sought. **1857** tr. *Dumas' Three Musketeers* ii. 14/2 His soldiers formed a *devil-dare legion. **1727** DE FOE *Syst. Magic* I. i. (1840) 32 The magicians were not all sorcerers and *devil-dealers. **1900** H. LAWSON *Over Sliprails* 108 Black Jimmie shifted away from the hut [of the dead woman]..for the '*devil-devil' sat down there. **1933** *Bulletin* (Sydney) 20 Dec. 34/1 The alternation of wet seasons or floodings on the one hand and of droughts on the other induces characteristic alternations of depressions and rises in heavy soils. These have received various local names, of which melonhole, gilgai, Bay of Biscay, devil-devil and crab-hole are the most frequently met. **1954** B. MILES *Stars my Blanket* xvii. 117 It's full of skulls, that cave is. Can't get a blackfella near it. They say the devil-devil's in it. **1939** *Devil float [see DEVIL *v.* 6]. **1767** J. ABERCROMBIE *Ev. Man his own Gardener* Index, *Devil-in-a-bush. **1815** ELPHINSTONE *Acc. Caubul* (1842) I. 95 A plant very common about Peshawer, which much resembles that..called Devil in the bush. **1912** THORPE *Dict. Appl. Chem.* (ed. 2) I. 149/1 The aqueous condensate obtained by cooling the waste gases [from ammonium sulphate manufacture] is a very noxious-smelling liquid, and is hence termed '*devil-liquor'. It contains sulphuretted hydrogen, pyridines, and similar substances, and hydrocyanic acid, and is also difficult to dispose of. **1930** *Engineering* 5 Sept. 311/3 The evaporation of the devil liquor or the aqueous condensates. **1843** LYTTON *Last Bar.* I. vii, Those *devil-mongers can bake ye a dozen such every moment. **1878** BRITTEN & HOLLAND *Plant-n.* 148 *Devil on both sides or Devil o' both sides, *Ranunculus arvensis* L. *Bucks.*, *Durh.*, *Warw.* **1862** A. POLEHAMPTON *Kangaroo Land* 77 Instead of damper we occasionally made what is colonially known as '*devils on the coals'. **1864** ATKINSON *Prov. Names Birds*, *Devil-skriker (Yorks.). **1866** *Treas. Bot.* 45 *Alstonia scholaris*, called *Devil-tree or Pali-mara about Bombay. **1837** CARLYLE *Fr. Rev.* (1857) I. II. i. iv. 250 And tended either godward or else *devilward. **1631** CORNWALLYES *Ess.* II. xlix. 308 And *devill-wise labour for nothing but to make all soules levell with theirs. **1818** A. L. HILLHOUSE tr. *Michaux's N. Amer. Sylva* II. 153 *Olea Americana*.. belongs exclusively to the Southern States, the Floridas and Lower Louisiana;..it has hitherto received no name from the inhabitants of the country, except on the banks of the river Savannah, where it is called *Devil Wood. **1832** D. J. BROWNE *Sylva Amer.* 225 The wood..when perfectly dry —is excessively hard and very difficult to cut and split— hence is derived the name of Devil Wood. **1938** W. R. VAN DERSAL *Native Woody Plants U.S.* 175 Devilwood..often occurs in sandy soil. **1719** DE FOE *Crusoe* (1840) II. vi. 138 Idolatry and *devil-worship. **1727** —— *Syst. Magic* I. iii. 69 To introduce Devil-worship in the world. **1879** M. CONWAY *Demonology & Devil-lore* I. 137 The *devil-worshippers of Travancore to this day declare that the evil power approaches them in the form of a Dog. **1726** DE FOE *Hist. Devil* II. xi. 353 Wormwood, storax, *devil-wort, mandrake, nightshade.

25. The possessive, **devil's**, has somewhat specialized uses as expressing things supposed to belong to or be in the power of the devil; hence it is used in opposition to *God's*, as *devil's martyr*, MATINS, PATERNOSTERS; and sometimes, like DEVILISH, as an intensive qualification of that which is evil, violent, or excessive. [Cf. F. *un froid de diable, un vent de tous les diables.*]

It is also used of natural or prehistoric works attributed to Satanic agency, as *Devil's bridge, dike, punch-bowl*, etc.

?**12..** *Charter* in *Cod. Dipl.* IV. 231 þurgh ðes defles lore. **1297** R. GLOUC. (1724) 475 Foure of the deueles limes, [h]is kniȝtes hurde this. **1530** PALSGR. 214/2 Divelles worke, *diablerie.* **1675** BROOKS *Gold. Key* Wks. 1867 V. 592 Balaam ..who was the devil's hackney. **1820** SCOTT *Ivanhoe* xx, What devil's matins are you after at this hour? **1827** —— *Jrnl.* 16 Mar., I had the devil's work finding them. **1854** WHYTE MELVILLE *Gen. Bounce* xv. (Farmer), His wives.. yowlin', and cryin', and kickin' up the devil's delight. **1859** H. KINGSLEY *G. Hamlyn* v, We had better be as comfortable as we can this devil's night. **1863** READE *Hard Cash* I. 278 (Farmer) What business have you in the Captain's cabin, kicking up the devil's delight? **1884** E. M. BEAL in *Gd. Words* May 323/1 The newly discovered 'devil's liquor', starch.

b. Special phrases. **devil's advocate** (L. *advocatus diaboli*), one who urges the devil's plea against the canonization of a saint, or in opposition to the honouring of any one; hence, one who advocates the contrary or wrong side, or injures a cause by his advocacy; so **devil's advocacy**; **devil's bedpost** (see quots.); **devil's bones**, an appellation of dice; **devil's cow**, a black beetle; **devil's darning-needle** (*U.S.*) = *devil's needle* (see also c); **devil's dirt**, **devil's dung**, asafœtida; **devil's dozen**: see DOZEN; **devil's finger**, a belemnite; **devil's fingers**, the star-fish; **devil's grip** *colloq.*, pleurodynia; **devil's horse** *U.S.*, the praying mantis; **devil's mint**, a succession of things hurtful or offensive, as if the devil himself were at work coining them (Forby); †**devil's missionary** *N.Z.* (see quots.); **devil's needle**, provincial name of the dragon-fly; **'Devil's Own'**, a pet name of the 88th Foot (*the Devil's own Connaught boys*); also of the Inns of Court Rifle Corps of Volunteers; **devil's picture(d)-books**, **picture-gallery** or **pictures** *colloq.* = DEVIL'S BOOKS; **devil's sheaf**: see quot.; **devil's tattoo**: see TATTOO; **devil's toe-nail**, a belemnite. Also DEVIL'S-BIRD, CLAW, etc.

1760 *Impostors Detected* II. 128 By..playing the true part of the *Devil's advocate. **1885** J. BONAR *Malthus* I. i. 7 The father made it a point of honour to defend the *Enquirer*; the son played devil's advocate. **1887** R. BUCHANAN *Heir of Linne* ii, Even the Socialist party regarded him as a devil's advocate, and washed their hands of him. **1854** MAURICE *Philos. First Six Cent.* (ed. 2) v. 119 The claims of Proclus to canonisation in spite of our *devil-advocacy. **1892** A. BIRRELL *Res Judic.* iv. 108 There is just enough of..truth in it, to make it one of the most powerful bits of devil's advocacy ever penned. **1873** *Slang Dict.*, *Devil's bed-posts*, the four of clubs. **1879** *N. & Q.* 5th Ser. XII. 473, I have always heard the four of clubs called the devil's bed-post, and also that it is the worst turn-up one could have. **1664** ETHEREDGE *Comical Revenge* II. iii (Farmer), I do not understand dice..hang the *devil's bones. **1822** SCOTT *Nigel* xxiii, A gamester, one who deals with the devil's bones. **1688** R. HOLME *Armoury* II. 213/1 Blind Beetles.. are generally known to us by the name of..*Devils cows. **1854** *Putnam's Monthly* June (Bartlett), Now and then..a *devil's-darning-needle would pertinaciously hover about our heads. **1578** LYTE *Dodoens* II. cxii. 304 Called..in Englishe also *Assa fetida*; in high Douche Teufels dreck, that is to say *Deuilles durt. **1604** DEKKER *Honest Wh.* Wks. 1873 II. 40 The *Divels dung in thy teeth! **1799** G. SMITH *Laboratory* I. 237 Asafœtida is sometimes called by the name of devil's dung. **1888** *Amer. Jrnl. Med. Sci.* XCVI. 400 So agonizing was this pain that it was nicknamed the '*devil's grip' by a sufferer from the disease in Rappahannock County, Virginia, and this name became a common one there afterwards. **1924** *Ibid.* CLXVIII. 569 Devil's grip..is certainly due to an acute infection, and the recurrences seem like those of a protozoan infection. **1962** *Daily Tel.* 21 Nov. 1/3 Mr. Duncan Sandys..has Bornholm disease, it was said last night. The disease is also known as 'Devil's Grip'. **1883** SWEET & KNOX *Through Texas* (1884) xliv. 629 Another of the most peculiar and interesting insects in Texas is called the '*devil's horse'. **1937** *Nature* 14 Aug. 264/1 Less graceful but fascinating are the devil's-horses, a showy grasshopper commonly six inches long which travels over the land by the million devouring vegetation as it goes. **1837** E. G. WAKEFIELD *Brit. Colonization N.Z.* ii. 31 [The lawless renegade Englishmen] really deserve a name which has been given them—that of '*Devil's missionaries'. **1839** *Colonial Gaz.* XXIX. 474 [Low types, vagabonds, etc.,] devil's missionaries as they are appropriately called. **1857** THOREAU *Maine W.* (1894) 316 On Moosehead I had seen a large *devil's-needle half a mile from the shore. **1871** STAVELEY *Brit. Insects* 128 The swift approach of one of these glittering 'devil's needles'. **1864** MARK LEMON *Jest Bk.* 211 (Farmer) At a review of the volunteers..the *devil's own walked straight through. **1893** *Pall Mall G.* 21 Jan. 2/3 'What! what!' exclaimed his Majesty [George III. in 1803], 'all lawyers! all lawyers! Call them the Devil's Own—call them the Devil's Own'..the fighting gentlemen of the long robe have been the 'Devil's Own' ever since. **1786** BURNS *Twa Dogs* 226 They..wi' crabbit leuks Pore ower the *devil's pictur'd beuks. **1913** D. H. LAWRENCE *Sons & Lovers* i. 20 Morel never in his life played cards,..'the devil's pictures', he called them! **1927** W. E. COLLINSON *Contemp. Eng.* 31 My father..jocularly referred to the cards as the Devil's picture-gallery. **1964** A. WYKES *Gambling* vii. 161 Some old shipmasters won't allow 'the devil's picture-books' aboard. **1496** *Dives & Paup.* (W. de W.) v. Introd. 25/1 Make ye the poore men your frendes of the *deuyllessheyf eyther richesses of wyckednesse. **1847** ANSTED *Anc. World* ix. 190 The Belemnite has..various local names (such as thunderbolt, *devil's toe-nail).

c. *esp.* in popular names of plants; **devil's apple**, the thorn apple (*Datura Stramonium*); **devil's apron**, a popular name in the United States of species of *Laminaria* and other olive-brown sea-weeds with a large dilated lamina; **devil's brushes**, a general name for ferns in the 'Black Country' (Britt. & Holl.); **devil's candlestick**, the fungus *Phallus impudicus*; the ground-ivy (Midland Counties); **devil's club**, a prickly araliaceous plant, *Fatua horrida*, found in the north-western U.S.; **devil's coach-wheel**, **d. curry-comb**, corn crowfoot (Hants); **devil's cotton**, an East Indian tree, *Abroma*, the fibres of which are made into cordage; **devil's darning-needle**, *Scandix Pecten Veneris*; **devil's ear** (*U.S.*), a species of wake-robin (*Arum*); **devil's fig**, the prickly pear; **devil's garter**, the bindweed, *Convolvulus sepium*; **devil's horn**, *Phallus impudicus*; **devil's leaf**, a very virulent species of stinging nettle, *Urtica urentissima*, found in Timor; **devil's oatmeal**, **d. parsley**, wild chervil, *Anthriscus sylvestris*; **devil's posy**, ramsons, *Allium ursinum*; **devil's snuff-box**, the puff-ball; **devil's stink-pot**, *Phallus impudicus*. Also DEVIL'S-BIT, CLAWS, MILK.

1846 SOWERBY *Brit. Bot.* VI. 104 *Devil's Apple. **1858** O. W. HOLMES *Aut. Breakf.-t.* vii. (1883) 142 Washed up on one of the beaches in company with *devil's-aprons, bladder-weeds, dead horse-shoes. **1891** *Proc. R. Geog. Soc.* Feb. 78 That unpleasant plant, growing to the height of a man's chest, known as the *devil's club, and covered with fine loose barbed prickles. **1851** S. JUDD *Margaret* (ed. 2) II. v. 66 There are berries in the woods, the scarlet *devil's ear and blue dracira. **1795** SOUTHEY *Lett. fr. Spain* (1808) II. 38, I saw the prickly pear, or as it is called here the *devil's fig. **1830** LINDLEY *Nat. Syst. Bot.* 94 A nettle called *daoun setan*, or *devil's leaf, in Timor; the effects of which are said..to last for a year, and even to cause death. **1883** R. TURNER in *Gd. Words* Sept. 589/2 The puff-balls are known in Scotland as 'de'il's sneeshin' mills' (*devil's snuff-boxes). **1884** *Cheshire Gloss.*, *Devil's snuff-box*, puff-ball.

devil ('dɛv(ə)l, 'dɛvɪl), *v.* [f. DEVIL *sb.*]

†**1.** *to devil it*: to play the devil, to act like the devil. *Obs.*

1593 NASHE *Christ's T.* (1613) 158 In the euillest of euill functions, which is, in diuelling it simply.

†**b.** *trans.* To play the devil with, to ruin. *Obs.*

1652 BENLOWES *Theoph.* II. xv, The Serpent devil'd Eve.

c. *allusive nonce-wd.*

1698 VANBRUGH *Prov. Wife* IV. iv. 89 *Lady B.* The devil's hands! Let me go! *Sir J.* I'll devil you, you jade you!

2. *trans.* To grill with hot condiments.

1800 [see DEVILLED 2]. **1817** T. L. PEACOCK *Melincourt* xxiii, If the carp be not caught, let me be devilled like a biscuit after the second bottle. **1831** TRELAWNY *Adv. Younger Son* I. 291 Come Louis, devil us a biscuit. *a* **1845** HOOD *Tale of Temper* vi, He..felt in his very gizzard he was devill'd! **1870** RAMSAY *Remin.* iv. (ed. 18) 83 One of the legs should be *deviled.*

3. *intr.* To act as 'devil' to a lawyer or literary man; to do professional work for another without fee, or without recognition.

1864 *Athenæum* No. 1921. 232/2 He devils for the counsel on both sides. **1880** *Social Notes* 20 Nov. 243/2 This unjust system is termed 'devilling', and those who appear in cases for which others are retained, at the sole request of the latter, are called 'devils', whilst the original holders of transferred briefs may be styled 'devilees.'..As long as briefless barristers consent to 'devil', so long will the abuse flourish, to the disadvantage of the public and the Bar. **1889** *Sat. Rev.* 9 Feb. 159/2 He must have chambers and a clerk, or a share of both. He must be ready and willing to 'devil'.

b. *trans.* To do (work) as a 'devil'.

1887 *Cornh. Mag.* Jan. 62 Allowing me to devil his work for him for ten years.

c. To entrust to a 'devil' or private deputy.

1891 LEACH *Southwell Minster* (Camden) 22 *note*, Of course he 'devilled' his duties, and equally of course the 'devil' neglected them.

4. *trans.* To tear to pieces (rags, old cloth, etc.) with a machine called a devil. See DEVILLING 2.

5. To worry (someone) excessively; to harass, annoy, tease. Chiefly *U.S. colloq.*

1823 W. FAUX *Mem. Days* 216 Go..tell our great Father, the President, how we are deviled and cheated. **1883** SWEET & KNOX *Through Texas* (1884) iii. 47 They devilled the poor fellow almost to death. **1940** C. MCCULLERS *Heart is Lonely Hunter* (1943) I. iii. 42 Sometimes it was fun to devil Portia. **1946** K. TENNANT *Lost Haven* (1947) iii. 48 A man with any push would form a progress association and devil the shire council about the roads.

6. To scratch or score the surface of (plaster) to provide a rough surface for the next coat.

1939 *Archit. Rev.* LXXXV. 212 All these materials.. should be covered with a pricking-up coat, well scratched, a floating coat, 'devilled' with a 'devil float', and a finishing coat, hard trowelled.

†**devi'lade.** *Obs. nonce-wd.* after *masquerade.*

1775 GARRICK *Bon Ton* 4 Coteries, Masquerades, and all the Devilades in this town.

ˈdevil-bird. A name popularly given to various birds, from their appearance, flight, cry, etc.; especially **a.** A local English name of the Swift; = DEVIL 7 b.

1885 SWAINSON *Prov. Names Brit. Birds* 95 It is called.. Devil bird (West Riding).

b. The Brown Owl of Ceylon (*Syrnium Indrani*).

1849 PRIDHAM *Ceylon* 737 (Y.) Devil's Bird.. The wild and wailing cry of this bird is considered a sure presage of death and misfortune, unless [etc.]. **1860** in Tennent *Ceylon* I. 167 *Note*, The brown owl, which, from its hideous yell, has acquired the name of the '*Devil-Bird*'. **1876** *Ceylon* II. 145 The 'oolanna', or devil bird of the Sinhalese, whose horrid shriek at night terrifies the natives.. some think it is not an owl, but a black night-raven.

c. A name of the East Indian drongo-shrikes, family *Dicruridæ*.

ˈdevil-dodger. *humorous.* [See DODGE *v.*] One who tries to dodge the devil (see quot. 1893); also, a nickname for ranting preachers, or preachers generally. So **ˈdevil-dodging** *vbl. sb.* and *ppl. a.*

1791 LACKINGTON *Mem.* vi (D.), These devil-dodgers happened to be so very powerful (that is, noisy). **1861** *Under the Spell* III. 111 So you have taken to 'devil-dodging', sermonizing, or whatever you call it. **1886** G. ALLEN *Maimie's Sake* i, He has a rabid objection to the clergy—the black brigade and the devil-dodgers, he calls them. *Ibid.* v, A pack of trumpery superstitious devil-dodging nonsense. **1893** M. WEST *Born Player* 202 Unbiassed people who went to church in the morning and to chapel in the evening—*devil-dodgers* as they were coarsely called, who were determined to be right one way or another.

devildom (ˈdɛv(ə)ldəm). [f. DEVIL + -DOM.]

1. The dominion, rule, or sway of the (or a) devil; exercise of diabolic power.

1694 S. JOHNSON *Notes Past. Lett. Bp. Burnet* I. 5 The true Art of spelling all the Oppressions and Devildoms in the World out of the pregnant word King. **1856** MRS. BROWNING *Aur. Leigh* II. Poems 1890 VI. 73 A commination, or, at best, An exorcism against the devildom Which plainly held me. **1893** R. KIPLING *Many Invent.* 207 It was witchcraft,—witchcraft and devildom.

2. The domain of the devil; the realm or estate of devils; the condition of devils.

1825 COLERIDGE in *Pall Mall G.* 27 May (1887) 5/2 Depressed by day and wandering all night thro' the Swedenborgian Devildom. **1828** FR. A. KEMBLE *Let.* in *Record of Girlhood* (1878) I. viii. 226, I have been revelling in that divine devildom, 'Faust'. **1847** O. BROWNSON *Two Brothers* Wks. VI. 268 All motleydom and all devildom had broken loose. **1892** T. WRIGHT *Blue Firedrake* 197 Never surely were more repulsive hags in all devildom.

deviˈlee. *nonce-wd.* See DEVIL *v.* 3 quot. 1880.

deviless (ˈdɛv(ə)lɪs). [f. DEVIL + -ESS: cf. F. *diablesse*.] A she-devil.

a **1693** URQUHART *Rabelais* IV. xxvii. 226 There was not Angel, Man, Devil, nor Deviless, upon the place, who would not [etc.]. **1761** STERNE *Tr. Shandy* (1802) III. xx. 318 Though we should abominate each other ten times worse than so many devils or devilesses. **1881** *Athenæum* 9 July 45/3 But a commonplace woman, with little of either the saint or the 'deviless' in her composition.

devilet (ˈdɛv(ə)lɪt). [f. DEVIL + -ET[1].]

1. A little devil, in various senses.

1794 MATHIAS *Purs. Lit.* (1798) 135 To meet the Printer's dev'let face to face. **1841** DE QUINCEY *Homer* Wks. 1862 V. 297 To the derision of all critics, compositors, pressmen, devils, and devillets. *a* **1845** BARHAM *Ingol. Leg.*, *Truants*, And pray now what were these devilets call'd? These three little fiends so gay! *c* **1876** SIR R. BURTON in Lady Burton *Life* (1893) I. 21 We boys became perfect devilets.

2. The Swift; = DEVILING 2.

1828 WILSON in *Blackw. Mag.* XXIV. 277 The long-winged legless black devilet, that, if it falls to the ground, cannot rise again. **1828** SOUTHEY in *Q. Rev.* XXXVIII. 238 The merry Dominican.. continued to eat devilets on fast days.

ˈdevil-fish. A name popularly given to various large and formidable fishes or other marine animals; especially **a.** In Great Britain, a large pediculate fish (*Lophius piscatorius*) also called ANGLER (q.v.), frog-fish, sea-devil, toad-fish. **b.** In U.S., a gigantic species of eagle-ray, *Ceratoptera vampyrus*, having expanded sides gradually passing into flappers or pectoral fins, the expanse of which is sometimes 20 feet. Less commonly, **c.** The Californian grey whale. **d.** The piranha of Uruguay. **e.** The octopus, cuttle-fish, or other cephalopod.

1814 *Sporting Mag.* XLIV. 94 That species, called by Dr. Goldsmith the Devil Fish. **1839** T. BEALE *Nat. Hist. Sperm Whale* 351 Enormous sting-rays, or 'devil fish'.. from five to six feet across. **1860** *Merc. Marine Mag.* VII. 213 They ['California Grey' Whale] have a variety of names among whalemen, as.. 'Hard-head', 'Devil-fish'. **1861** HULME tr. *Moquin-Tandon* II. IV. i. 214 The Piranha or Devil-fish discovered by M. de Castelnau in Uruguay.. When any object is thrown into the water inhabited by the Piranhas, these fish immediately attack it. **1863** RUSSELL *Diary North & South* I. 208, I heard much of the mighty devil-fish.. The fish.. possesses formidable antennæ-like horns, and a pair of huge fins, or flappers, one of which rises above the water as the creature moves below the surface. **1867** *Chronicle* 5 Oct. 669 The Devil Fish.. This giant of the Cephaloptera is simply a monstrous Ray; and though Sea-Devil and Vampire are assigned to it as trivial names, it.. is in no way formidable save from its enormous strength and bulk. **1883** G. L. FABER *Fisheries Adriatic* 185 *Myliobalis aquila* L... Devil fish, Sea-Devil, Toad-fish. **1885** C. F. HOLDER *Marvels Anim. Life* 162 [The squid] was found.. to fully justify its popular name of devil fish. **1889** *Catholic News* 15 June 5/5 The octopus, popularly known as 'the devil fish'.

ˈdevilhead. [See -HEAD.] = DEVILHOOD.

a **1350** *Life of Jesus* (ed. Horstm.) 499 (Mätz.) No deuelhede I ne habbe in me. **1870** MORRIS *Earthly Par.* III. IV. 300 A swallowing dread, A curse made manifest in devilhead.

devilhood (ˈdɛv(ə)lhʊd). [f. DEVIL + -HOOD.] The condition and estate of a devil.

1618 WITHER *Motto, Nec Habeo* Wks. (1633) 521 Except the Devill, and that cursed brood Which have dependance on his Devilhood. **1880** SWINBURNE *Study Shaks* iii. 173 Her imperious and dauntless devilhood. **1894** J. BRAND in *Chicago Advance* 24 May, A downward development toward devilhood.

†**ˈdevilified,** *ppl. a. Obs.* [see -FY.] Made into or of the nature of a devil.

1645 PAGITT *Heresiogr.* Ep. Ded, Unpure Familists, who blasphemously pretend to be godified like God, whereas indeed they are devillified like their Father the Devil. **1647** J. HEYDON *Discov. Fairfax* 2 Devils and devilified men would be glad to have any thing against him.

So **ˈdevilifier.**

1793 *Regal Rambler* 37 The emendator, corrector, and Devilifier.. of my bank.

deviling (ˈdɛv(ə)lɪŋ). [f. DEVIL *sb.* + -LING or -ING; the suffixes being here confounded.]

1. A young devil; an imp or mischievous little creature.

[**1575** G. HARVEY *Letter-bk.* (Camden) 98 Close to the britche like a Divelinge.] *a* **1616** BEAUM. & FL. *Knt. of Malta* v. ii, And engender young devillings. **1672** R. WILD *Declar. Lib. Consc.* 9 His Divelings, the Officers and Clarks of that wondrous Kitchin. **1806** SOUTHEY in *Ann. Rev.* IV. 540 He received the little deviling in a basket. **1849** SIR J. STEPHEN *Eccl. Biog.* (1850) I. 310 The deviling.. was about twelve years old and looked exactly like any other boy.

2. A local name of the Swift; also of the Pied Wagtail. (See quots.)

a **1825** FORBY *East Ang. Voc.*, *Devilin*, the species of swallow, commonly called the swift. **1826** *Sporting Mag.* XVIII. 312 The bird called a Swift.. more commonly a Devilin. **1837** MACGILLIVRAY *Hist. Brit. Birds* III. 614 Black Marten, Swift, Develing. **1885** SWAINSON *Prov. Names Brit. Birds* 45 *Pied Wagtail*.. Devil's bird or deviling (Ireland). From the constant uncanny motion of its tail. *Ibid.* 95 *Swift*.. It is called Deviling (E. Angl., Lanc., Westm.).

3. The third or lowest vat used in the manufacture of indigo; called in French *diablotin*.

1731–7 MILLER *Gard. Dict.* (ed. 3) s.v. *Anil*, The second is call'd the Battery.. And the third, which is much less than the second, is call'd the Deviling. As for the Name.. I do not see how it agrees with it; unless it be because this Vat is deeper colour'd than the others.

devilish (ˈdɛv(ə)lɪʃ), *a.* [f. DEVIL + -ISH.]

1. Of persons: Having the nature or character of the devil; like a devil in character or actions.

1494 FABYAN *Chron.* IV. lxv. 44 By styrynge of disclaunderous and deuylysshe persones. *a* **1555** LATIMER *Serm.* (1845) 301 What marvel is it, if they call you devilish persons and heretics? **1587** TURBERV. *Trag. T.* (1837) 151 The divilish Queenes devise. **1604** SHAKS. *Oth.* II. i. 249 A diuelish knaue! **1634** SIR T. HERBERT *Trav.* 8 A Monster not a little esteemed of amongst these Divellish Savages. **1653** H. COGAN tr. *Pinto's Trav.* xxviii. 113 Who.. censed those two divelish Monsters. **1868** BROWNING *Ring & Bk.* I. 247 We pronounce Count Guido devilish and damnable.

2. Of things, actions, or qualities: Characteristic of the devil; worthy of or befitting the devil; diabolical; execrable.

c **1496** *Serm. Episc. Puer.* (W. de W.) B iij, Euyll fasshened garmentes, & deuyllysshe shoon & slyppers of frensmen. **1526** *Pilgr. Perf.* (W. de W. 1531) 93 Whiche is moost deuyllysshe synne. **1553** EDEN *Treat. Newe Ind.* (Arb.) 18 They make certayne deuylishe gestures lyke vnto madde men. **1631** GOUGE *God's Arrows* iii. §94. 360 The matchlesse, merciless, devilish, and damnable gun-powder-treason. **1663** F. HAWKINS *Youth's Behav.* 87 'Tis of humane frailty to erre, but 'tis devilish to persevere in it. **1790** BURNS *Tam O'Shanter* 127 By some devilish cantrip slight. **1827** POLLOK *Course T.* IX. 266 Indistinct and devilish whisperings.

b. Expressing the speaker's strong detestation.

1694 R. L. ESTRANGE *Fables* cccxxxii. (ed. 6) 345 The Develish People would keep such a Snearing and Pointing at me. **1800** MRS. HERVEY *Mourtray Fam.* II. 101 Hold your devilish tongue.

3. Of or belonging to the devil.

1526–34 TINDALE *1 Tim.* iv. 1 Geue hede vnto spretes of erroure and dyuelysshe doctrine. **1548** HALL *Chron.* 135 b, Therto by devilishe instigacion incensed and procured. **1562** BULLEYN *Bk. Sicke Men* 75 b, Ingratitude [is] sprong of a deuelishe petigree. **1864** BURTON *Scot Abr.* I. v. 287 So skilled in devilish arts of magic.

4. *loosely.* Violent, virulent, terrible; extremely bad; enormous, excessive.

1612 WOODALL *Surg. Mate* Wks. (1653) 241 It is a divellish, deadly, coarse medicine. **1688** R. HOLME *Armoury* II. 198/2 [Lice] are devilish Biters, especially the little ones. **1738** SWIFT *Polite Convers.* 187 Mr. N— got the devilishest Fall in the Park To-day. **1831** FONBLANQUE *Eng. under 7 Administ.* (1837) II. 93 The Six Acts, hurried, with such devilish speed, through Parliament. **1849** THACKERAY *Pendennis* xl, She has a devilish deal more than ten thousand pound.

5. *Comb.*

1705 HICKERINGILL *Priest-Cr.* Wks. 1716 III. 110 Such a Devilish-like Black-guard.

B. *adv.* = DEVILISHLY 2; excessively, exceedingly, enormously: originally of things bad, but in later use a mere coarse intensive.

1612 ROWLANDS *Knaue of Harts* 14 Because we finde.. Mony makes fooles most diuellish proud in mind. **1631** MASSINGER *Beleeve as you list* IV. iii, The cur is divelishe hungrie. **1719** DE FOE *Crusoe* (1840) I. xx. 353 Taking devilish long strides. **1768** FOOTE *Devil on 2 Sticks* I. Wks. 1799 II. 251 They are *devilish* rich, *devilish* poor, *devilish* ugly, *devilish* handsome. **1807** BYRON *Let. to Miss Pigot* 11 Aug., I should be devilish glad to see him. **1843** LEVER *J. Hinton* viii, Devilish pretty girl, that she is. **1886** STEVENSON *Dr. Jekyll* ii, I have seen devilish little of the man.

†**ˈdevilished,** *ppl. a. Obs. rare.* [f. prec. + -ED; or (?) with the suffix *-ish* = *-ise*, *-ize*, as in *anentish*, ANIENTISE: cf. also *publish*.] Demonized, possessed with a demon or 'devil'.

1601 DEACON & WALKER *Answ. to Darel* 13 *Dæmonizomenos*.. one Diuellished, or one afflicted, tormented, or vext with a Diuell. *Ibid.* 20 A man, hauing the spirit of an vncleane diuell.. a diuelished vncleane spirit. **1601** —— *Spirits & Divels* 39 Demoniakes, or diuellished persons.

devilishly (ˈdɛv(ə)lɪʃlɪ), *adv.* [f. prec. + -LY[2].]

1. In a devilish manner, diabolically.

1531 TINDALE *Exp. 1 John* (1537) 18 We synne not diuellishlye agaynst the holy goost. **1642** FULLER *Holy & Prof. St.* v. xi. 405 None but devils and men devilishly minded. **1830** ARNOLD *Let. to Hare* 24 Dec. in Stanley *Life* I. vi. 236 A devil's doctrine, certainly, and devilishly applied. **1878** E. JENKINS *Haverholme* 47 The declaration.. has a touch of the devilishly humorous about it.

2. Excessively, exceedingly: originally of things bad, but becoming at length a strong intensive.

1668 SHADWELL *Sullen Lovers* IV, How devillishly impertinent is this. **1687** SETTLE *Refl. Dryden* 13 The Poet lyes Divellishly if he tells you [etc.]. **1782** MRS. E. BLOWER *Geo. Bateman* II. 140 She's devilishly pretty. **1845** MRS. CARLYLE *Lett.* I. 360, I think it devilishly well done.

devilishness (ˈdɛv(ə)lɪʃnɪs). [f. DEVILISH + -NESS.] The state or quality of being devilish; diabolical or infernal character.

1530 PALSGR. 214/2 Divellysshnesse, *diablerie*. **1549** ALLEN *Jude's Par. Rev.* 13 Very wicked and abhominable supersticions and diuillyshnes. **1620** MELTON *Astrolog.* 80 The diuellishnesse of your Diuination. **1733** LORD M. in *Swift's Lett.* (1766) II. 185, I have betrayed to you the devilishness of my temper. **1844** MASSON *Ess.*, *The Three Devils* iii. (1856) 74 Mephistophiles's nature.. complete, confirmed, irrevocable devilishness.

devilism (ˈdɛv(ə)lɪz(ə)m). [f. DEVIL *sb.* + -ISM.]

1. A system of action or conduct proper to a devil; devilish quality.

1652 BP. HALL *Rem. Wks.* II. (1660) 150 Did ever any seek for the greatest good in the worst of evils? This is not heresie, but meer Divilisme. **1691–8** NORRIS *Pract. Disc.* (1711) III. 173 To the highest pitch of Impiety, to the very ridge of Devilism. **1726** DE FOE *Hist. Devil* (1822) 203 Such a perfection of devilism as that of the Inquisition. **1820** *Examiner* No. 619. 113/1 The deliberate devilism of the tortures. **1892** PEYTON *Memorab. Jesus* xvi. 451 The devilism in human nature is that which wants bread by which to live in the body, and seeks not the interest of the soul.

2. A system or cult, the object of which is the Devil; devil-worship.

1773 E. IVES *Voy. Eng. to India* 317 The Sanjacks.. once professed Christianity, then Mahometanism, and last of all Devilism.

†**deˈvility.** *Obs.* In 6–7 divil(l)itie. [f. DEVIL *sb.* + -ITY: formed with mocking reference to *civility* and *divinity*.] Devilism, devilry.

1589 *Marprel. Epit.* F iij, Whom the D. of diuillitie.. affirmeth to haue beene Arch. of Creet. **1598** R. BARCKLEY *Felic. Man* IV. (1603) 317 A formal kind of strangers civilitie.. which.. may rather bee called Divillitie. **1601** DEACON & WALKER *Answ. to Darel* 113 These are but quick-sands wherewith you doe grauell your deepe skill of Diuillitie. **1609** BP. W. BARLOW *Answ. Nameless Cath.* 39 [He] must also bee his Diuilitie Reader or Schoole-man.

devilize (ˈdɛv(ə)laɪz), *v.* [f. DEVIL *sb.* + -IZE.]

1. *trans.* To make a devil of; to render devilish in character. (Cf. *canonize*.)

1624 BP. HALL *Rem. Wks.* (1660) 13 He that should deify a Saint should wrong him as much as he that should Divellize him. **1888** *Chicago Advance* 12 Apr. 232 The native heathenism of the Dark Continent devilized by rum from the lands of Christendom.

†**2.** *intr.* To play the devil; to act as a devil.

1647 WARD *Simp. Cobler* 48 The worst they [Englishmen] doe, is to keep their Kings from Divelizing, and themselves from Assing. **1720** T. GORDON *Cordial for Low Spirits* 69 Let loose his inclinations, and devilized with all his might.

Hence **ˈdevilized** *ppl. a.*, converted into a devil, rendered devilish.

1701 FLAVEL *Husb. Spirit.* (1770) 282 How full of devils and devilized men is this lower world. **1726** DE FOE *Hist. Devil* (1822) 208 To consider human nature devilized. **1890** J. PULSFORD *Loyalty to Christ* I. 238 The highest and most reputable members of society.. have come through a devilized line of ancestry.

devilkin ('dɛv(ə)lkɪn). [f. DEVIL *sb.* + -KIN.] A little devil; an imp. Also *fig.*

1748 RICHARDSON *Clarissa* (1811) VI. 14 That a Beelzebub has his devilkins to attend his call. **1833** T. HOOK *Widow & Marquess* iii, Attendant devilkins of an inferior class, with hoofs, horns, talons and tails. **1851** D. JERROLD *St. Giles* xxii, Now shout, ye imps! Scream, ye devilkins.. for it is done! **1893** *Pall Mall Mag.* II. 118 Black itching marks, left by the stings of these imperceptible little devilkins.

¶ The following is an example of DEVIL 20 a, with *what-kins* of what kind, what kind of.

c **1510** *Robin Hood* 290 in Arb. *Garner* VI. 430 What devilkyns draper, sayd litell Much, Thynkyst thou to be.

devilled ('dɛv(ə)ld), *ppl. a.* [f. DEVIL + -ED.]

1. Possessed or afflicted with a devil: see DEVIL *sb.* 2 b.

c **1550** CHEKE *Matt.* viii. 16 In ye evening yei brought him mani y^t was develled. *Ibid.* viii. 28 Yeer mett him ij develds ..veri fiers men. *Ibid.* xv. 22 Mi doughter is veri evel develled. **1645** RUTHERFORD *Tryal & Tri. Faith* (1845) 47 *Kakos daimonizetai*, she is exceedingly devilled.

2. Grilled with hot condiments.

1800 *Oracle* in *Spir. Publ. Jrnls.* (1801) IV. 253 At half past two [I] ate a devil'd kidney. **1845** DISRAELI *Sybil* IV. x, His table cleared, a devilled biscuit placed before him, a cool bottle and a fresh glass. **1855** MRS. GASKELL *North & S.* xlii, The devilled chicken tasted like saw-dust. **1881** J. GRANT *Cameronians* I. xviii. 276 An aroma of coffee and devilled bones.

3. Prepared by a devil, or unrecognized professional helper: see DEVIL *sb.* 5 b, c.

1893 *Athenæum* 5 Aug. 182/1 We imagine that Mr. Robinson got his authors 'devilled' for him, for hardly any single brain could have extracted all this material.

deviller ('dɛv(ə)lə(r)). [f. DEVIL + -ER[1].] **a.** The workman who attends to the machine called a 'devil' in a cotton or other factory. **b.** The name of a machine used for the shaking of rags. **c.** A 'devil' or literary hack.

1874 *Manch. Guardian* 3 Aug. 6 The term is applied to those persons who tend hard-waste breakers in cotton manufactories. The machines are termed devils, and in this district the person who tends them a deviller. **1885** *Leeds Mercury* 23 June 3 A rag-shaking machine called a 'deviller'. **1893** *Athenæum* 5 Aug. 182/1 Sometimes the delver, or 'deviller', nods.

'devil-like, *a.* and *adv.* [See LIKE: cf. DEVILLY.]

A. *adj.* Like a devil; diabolical.

c **1470** HENRY *Wallace* VIII. 895 His dewyllyk deid he did in to Scotland. **1610** HEALEY *St. Aug. Citie of God* IV. xxxii, Devil-like Princes perswaded their people to their owne vaine inventions. **1722** MRS. E. HAYWOOD *Brit. Recluse* 73 With more than Devil-like cruelty. **1869** W. P. MACKAY *Grace & Truth* (1875) 225 What a devil-like intention!

B. *adv.* Like, or after the manner of a devil; diabolically.

1688 BUNYAN *Jerusalem Sinner Saved* (1886) 129 Who has ..thus horribly and devil-like contemned and trampled upon Him. **1717** L. HOWEL *Desiderius* 104 Themselves, Devil-like, are never the better for doing us this Mischief.

devilling ('dɛv(ə)lɪŋ), *vbl. sb.* [f. DEVIL *v.* + -ING[1].]

1. Working as a devil or hack: see DEVIL *sb.* 5 b, c; *v.* 3.

1880 BESANT & RICE *Seamy Side* xiv. 114 The young barrister was engaged in some devilling. **1888** *Star* 8 Aug., Devilling is the term used in the literary trade for sweating. **1894** *Westm. Gaz.* 7 Feb. 8/1 After all, devilling at the Bar has the same consolation as fagging at school. First, you fag for others; but in the end you have other devils to fag for you.

2. Tearing to pieces by the machine called a devil.

1891 *Labour Commission* Gloss., *Devilling*, the same process as willeying.

† **'devilly, devily,** *a. Obs.* [OE. *déofollíc*, f. *déofol* devil + *-líc* (-LY[1]), contr. *déoflíc*, whence in ME. *deoflich*, later *devily*: rarely in ME. with second *l*, *develly*. Cf. OHG. *tiufallîh*, MHG. *tiuvellich*, ON. *djöfulligr*.] = DEVILISH.

c **1000** ÆLFRIC *Hom.* (Thorpe) I. 102 (Bosw.) Mid deofellicum wiȝlungum. *Ibid.* I. 62 Underȝeat se apostol ðas deoflican facn. *c* **1175** *Lamb. Hom.* 105 Þenne maȝe we fordon swa þa deofliche ȝitsunge. **1481** CAXTON *Reynard* (Arb.) 73 Alway to mysdo and trespace..that is euyl, and a deuely lyf [*Flem.* een duuelic leven]. **1483** —— *Cato* H iv b, Certaynly suche thought is wycked and deuylly. *c* **1485** *Digby Myst.* v. ii. *heading*, Entreth lucyfere in a deuely a-ray. *a* **1628** F. GREVILLE *Sidney* x. (1652) 131 The devily characters of so tyrannical a deity.

† **'devilly, devily,** *adv. Obs.* [f. as prec. + -LY[2].] Devilishly, diabolically, excessively (in a bad sense).

a **1300** *Cursor M.* 14392 (Cott.) Ful deueli [*v.r.* deuelly] war þai Iuus thra, þair blisced lauerd for to sla. *c* **1400** *Sowdone Bab.* 265 The Dikes were so develye depe..Ouer cowde thai nother goo nor crepe. *Ibid.* 2193 Ther to he was devely stronge, His skynne was blake and harde.

'devil-may-'care, *a.* (and *sb.*) Also erroneously **devil-me-care.** [The exclamation *devil may care!* used as an attribute.] Wildly reckless; careless and rollicking. Hence as *sb.*, a devil-may-care person, attitude, etc.

[**1793** *Regal Rambler* 95 Deel care, said Dr. Leveller, loud enough to be heard.] **1837** DICKENS *Pickw.* xlix, He was a mighty free and easy, roving, devil-may-care sort of person. **1857** G. W. THORNBURY *Songs of Cavaliers* 120, I and some seventy devil-may-cares Rode to Bristol. [**1858** M. PORTEOUS *Souter Johnny* 8 But deil-ma-care! my facts are clear.] **1858** LYTTON *What will he do* II. ii, He..looked altogether as devil-me-care, rakehelly, handsome, good-for-nought as ever swore at a drawer. **1861** HUGHES *Tom Brown at Oxf.* xi. (1889) 103 A face radiant with devil-may-care delight. **1870** MISS BROUGHTON *Red as a Rose* i. 3 The salt of a racy, devil-me-care wit. **1887** W. M. ROSSETTI *Life of Keats* vi, Without any aggressive or 'devil-may-care' addenda. **1928** *Manch. Guardian Weekly* 21 Sept. 230/3 An air of devil-may-care.

Hence **devil-may-'careness** (*erron.* **-'care-lessness**); **devil-may-'carish** *a.*, **-'carishness, -'carism,** *nonce-wds.*

1833 *Fraser's Mag.* VII. 693 Similar attempts at a jaunty devil-me-carishness. **1841** *Tait's Mag.* VIII. 221 From them he dates that devil-may-carism, that recklessness of the world and the world's law. **1842** LYTTON *Zanoni* IV. v, A devil-me-carish air. **1890** M^cCARTHY *Fr. Rev.* I. 22 The wantonness, the licence, the devil-may-careness of the Regency. **1891** *Blackw. Mag.* CXLIX 510/1 There was more of Hibernian devil-may-care-lessness than of Saxon foresight.

devilment ('dɛv(ə)lmənt). [f. DEVIL *v.* + -MENT.]

1. Action befitting a devil, or of devilish character; mischief: also humorously like DEVILRY 4 b.

1771 *Contemplative Man* I. 130, I thought some Devilment or other would befal us. **1840** THACKERAY *Paris Sk-bk.* (1869) 64 So little sign of devilment in the accomplishment of his wishes. **1843** LEVER *J. Hinton* xxxi, Courtship, fun, frolic, and devilment. **1886-7** *Proc. Amer. Convent. on Instruct. Deaf* 220 A certain amount of superfluous animal spirits—devilment I have heard it called.

2. *concr.* **a.** A devilled dish. **b.** A devilish device or invention.

1775 GARRICK in *G. Colman's Posth. Lett.* (1820) 309 Hot cakes and devilments at breakfast. **1871** *Standard* 20 Jan., Greek fire and fifty other molten devilments may be coruscating among her chimney pots.

† **'devilness.** *Obs. rare.* [f. DEVIL *sb.* + -NESS.] A thing diabolical or of demonic character, a demon: = DEVILRY 1.

a **1300** *E. E. Psalter* xcv. 5 For alle goddes of genge develnesses ere þa. *a* **1448** *Note* in *R. Glouc. Chron.* (MS. Coll. Arms) (1724) 415 The monekes toke holywater, and drof a way the maner deuelnesse.

devilry ('dɛv(ə)lrɪ). Also 4 **dewilry,** 7 **deuillary.** [f. DEVIL *sb.* + -RY.]

† 1. A demon; a demoniacal possession. (Cf. F. *diablerie.*) *Obs.*

c **1380** WYCLIF *Last Age of Chirche* p. xxiv, Chaffare walkynge in derkenessis and myddais deuylrye þat is to seye antecrist. **14..** *Prose Legends* in Anglia VIII. 143 Temptyd of þe deuelry þat walkes in derknesse. *Ibid.* 144 Þis maner of deuilry myghte not anoon be casten oute. *c* **1450** *Mirour Saluacioun* 2023 Fforto cast out Dyvelleres he gaf the auctoritee. **1483** *Cath. Angl.* 98 A Devylry..*demonium.*

2. Magical operation performed by the supposed help of Satan; dealing with the Devil; diabolical art.

1375 BARBOUR *Bruce* IV. 690 Throu thair gret clergy, Or ellis throu thair deuilry. *c* **1425** WYNTOUN *Cron.* IX. xxiv. 48 Be Wichcraft or Devilry. **1583** STUBBES *Anat. Abus.* II. (1882) 5 Art magike, witchcraft, and all kind of diuelrie. **1596** DALRYMPLE tr. *Leslie's Hist. Scot.* I. 287 The king throuch the arte of Magik, Witchcraft, and deuilrie was consumet. **1795** SOUTHEY *Joan of Arc* VII. 556 Witch though she be, methinks Her devilry could neither blunt the edge Of thy good sword, or mine. **1867** MISS BRADDON *Rupert Godwin* III. iii. 44 By what devilry did he stumble upon the truth.

3. Works or operation of the devil.

1533 TINDALE *Supper of Lord* Wks. (1573) 463 They be proued starke lyes and very deuelry. **1581** *Satir. Poems Reform.* xliv. 316 Double sonnis of Deuilrie! *a* **1876** G. DAWSON *Biog. Lect.* 38 He fought for light against darkness, for God's truth against Devilry.

4. Devilish action or conduct; extreme wickedness, cruelty, or perversity; wicked mischief.

1637 BASTWICK *Litany* I. 19 Greater cruelty..(to say nothing of deuillary, atheisme and popery) I know no where. **1831** CARLYLE *Sart. Res.* II. viii, What devilry soever Kings do, the Greeks must pay the piper! **1851** HELPS *Comp. Solit.* x. (1874) 180 Finding that such is the devilry of circumstances. **1852** THACKERAY *Esmond* I. xiv, I took to all sorts of devilries out of despair and fury. **1870** *Daily News* 24 Sept., A sight of misery, chaos, disorganisation, and general devilry.

b. *humorously.* Reckless indulgence in mischief, hilarity, or daring.

1840 DICKENS *Barn. Rudge* lxvii, A fellow..who has the daring and devilry in him of twenty fellows. **1842** S. C. HALL *Ireland* II. 340 The reckless 'devilry' of a former time, and the decent hilarity of the present. **1843** LYTTON *Last Bar.* I. i, Too sober and studious for such men-at-arms' devilry. **1887** MISS BRADDON *Like & Unlike* ix, What devilry has brought you here, in that get-up.

5. A system of devils; demonology.

1844 MASSON *Ess., The Three Devils* iii. (1856) 80 The second part of Faust is devilry all through, a tissue of bewilderments and devilries. **1871** TYLOR *Prim. Cult.* II. 230 The evil demon Aeshma Daeva..becoming the Asmodeus of the book of Tobit, afterwards to find a place in the devilry of the middle ages.

6. Devils collectively, a company of devils. (Cf. *cavalry, yeomanry.*)

1832 *Examiner* 453/2 The carrying-off of Don Juan was managed by the same identical red-and-yellow gauze winged devilry. **1856** R. A. VAUGHAN *Mystics* VIII. ix, The swarming devilry that everywhere attends him.

'devil's-bird. A name popularly given to various birds. (See also DEVIL-BIRD.)

† 1. The Stormy Petrel. [app. transl. Fr. *oiseau du diable.*] *Obs.*

1634 SIR T. HERBERT *Trav.* 18 Upon view of this Bird (which Sea-men improperly call Devils Bird) an infallible tempest and storme in lesse than two dayes, assailes the ship. **1832** A. WILSON *Amer. Ornith.* II. 383 They have been called Witches, Stormy Petrels, the Devil's Birds, Mother Carey's Chickens.

2. The Yellow Hammer.

1837 MACGILLIVRAY *Hist. Brit. Birds* I. 445 Yellow-Hammer..Skite, Devil's-Bird.

3. The Pied Wagtail.

1885 SWAINSON *Prov. Names Brit. Birds* 44 Pied Wagtail ..Devil's bird or Deviling (Ireland). From the constant uncanny motion of its tail.

devil's-bit. *Herb.* [A transl. of med.L. *morsus diaboli*, devil's bite, in Ger. *Teufels-abbisz.*]

1. A species of Scabious (*Scabiosa succisa*), a common meadow plant with blue flowers, having a thickish premorse root; also ***devil's-bit scabious.***

c **1450** *Alphita* (Anecd. Oxon) 121 Morsus diaboli..ang. *deue[le]sbite.* **1568** TURNER *Herbal* III. 43 The devils bite is called in common Latine *Morsus diaboli & succisa.* **1578** LYTE *Dodoens* I. lxxiv. 110 Deuels bit groweth in dry medowes. **1616** SURFL. & MARKH. *Country Farme* 203 Diuels-bit (so called, because it sheweth as though the middle, or the heart of the root, were gnawed or bitten by some Diuell..as though the Diuell did enuie the good which it bringeth vnto men by the incredible vertues that are therein). **1672-3** GREW *Anat. Roots* I. i. (1682) 61 That Plant superstitiously called *Devils-bit*: because the end of it [i.e. the Root] seems to be bitten off. **1747** WESLEY *Prim. Physic* (1762) 78 Half a Pint of strong Decoction of Devil's bit. **1854** S. THOMSON *Wild Fl.* III. (ed. 4) 247 The root which seems to be 'bitten' off is the natural appearance..and..has given rise to the appellation 'devil's bit scabious'.

2. ***yellow devil's-bit,*** a composite plant, *Apargia autumnalis*, also called ***autumnal hawk-bit***, frequent in meadows in autumn.

1758 PULTNEY in *Phil. Trans.* L. 514 Hawkweed with bitten roots, or Yellow Devil's-bit. **1779** LIGHTFOOT *Fl. Scot.* (1789) I. 433.

3. Transferred in U.S. to several American plants, having roots of similar shape, as *Chamælirium luteum*, the Blazing Star, N.O. *Liliaceæ*; *Liatris spicata*, the Button Snakeroot, N.O. *Compositæ.* **swamp d.**, *Ptelea trifoliata*, a shrub or small tree, so called from its bitterness.

devil's books. An appellation of Playing Cards (also called by Swift *Pluto's books*). Cf. *devil's picture(d)-books* s.v. DEVIL *sb.* 25 b.

1729 SWIFT *Intelligencer* No. 4 ed. 2) 43 (Farmer) Cards are the devil's own invention, for which reason, time out of mind, they are and have been called the devil's books. [**1730** —— *Death & Daphne* 80 For cards, we know, are Pluto's books.] **1738** —— *Polite Convers.* iii. 194 Damn your Cards, said he, they are the Devils Books. **1801** *Sporting Mag.* XVII. 144 They all voluntarily declared they would never more touch the *Devil's Books* on the *Lord's Day.* **1861** THACKERAY *Four Georges* iv. (1876) 119 What hours, what nights, what health did he waste over the devil's books!

devil's claw.

1. *Naut.* **a.** 'A very strong kind of split hook made to grasp a link of a chain cable, and used as a stopper' (Smyth *Sailor's Wd.-bk.*). **b.** A grapnel.

2. *Conchol.* A species of Scorpion shell (*Pteroceras Scorpio*) from the Indian Ocean.

3. **devil's claws,** *Herb.* **a.** The Corn Crowfoot; **b.** The Bird's-foot Trefoil.

1878 BRITTEN & HOLLAND *Plant-n.* 148 *Devil's Claws*, (1) *Ranunculus arvensis*, so called from the dislike which farmers have for one of the worst of weeds and from the hooks which terminate each seed. *Wight.* (2) *Lotus corniculatus. Somerset.*

devil's coach-horse. A popular name of the large rove-beetle (*Goerius olens*), from the rearing and defiant attitude which it assumes when disturbed. The name is sometimes extended to other cock-tail beetles.

1840 WESTWOOD in *Cuvier's Anim. Kingd.* 506 Well known under the name of the Devil's coach horse. **1850** KAVANAGH *Jrnl.* in *Biog.* (1891) 86 Lots of scorpions, devil's coach-horses, and large spiders. **1869** BLACKMORE *Lorna D.* (1889) 25 This atrocious tale of lies turned up joint by joint before her like a devil's coach-horse. **1881** W. E. NORRIS *Matrim.* III. iii. 51 One of those little beetles known to children as the devil's coach-horses.

devil's dust. 1. The flock to which old cloth is reduced by the machine called a devil; shoddy. (Originally the dust made in this process.)

1840 CARLYLE *Misc.* (1857) IV. 239 (D.) Does it beseem thee to weave cloth of devil's dust instead of true wool? **1851** GLADSTONE *Let. Ld. Aberdeen* 7 Apr., Very like the cloth made in this country from what is called devil's dust. **1851** MAYHEW *Lond. Labour* (1861) II. 30 The operation..sends forth choking clouds of dry pungent dirt and floating fibres —the real and original 'devil's dust'. **1864** *Athenæum* No. 1925. 364/3 Made up of as much devil's dust as flax.

2. Applied rhetorically to dust or powder of devilish invention or use.

1856 FROUDE *Hist. Eng.* I. 42 [They] were to take care.. that cloth put up for sale was true cloth, of true texture and weight.. wine pure.. flour unmixed with devil's dust. **1883** H. SMART *Hard Lines* i. (Farmer) The snow-white walls.. what a mess the devil's dust, as used by modern artillery, would make of them in these days.

† **devil's gold ring.** *Obs.* Popular name of a destructive caterpillar.

1552 HULOET, Canker worme which creapeth.. on colewortes. Some do call them the deuyls goldrynge, & some the colewort worme. **1601** HOLLAND *Pliny* I. 547 *margin.* **1611** COTGR., *Vrbec*, the Vine-Fretter, or Devill's Gold-ring; a worm. **1693** EVELYN *De la Quint. Compl. Gard.* Gloss., *Devils Gold Ring*, in French, *Lisette*, a sort of a Worm or Cater-pillar infesting the young shoots of Vines. **1783** AINSWORTH *Lat. Dict.* (Morell) I. s.v. *Devil*, The devil's gold ring (a caterpillar).

devil's-guts. *Herb.* **a.** A popular name of the Dodder (*Cuscuta*), from its pale slender stems which wind round and strangle other plants.

1670 RAY *Catalog. Pl. Angl.* 88 In Sussexia rustici et agricolæ eam execrantur, odiosis nominibus *Hellweed* et *Devils guts* appellantes. **1878** BRITTEN & HOLL. *Plant-n.* 149 Devil's Guts, *Cuscuta*, various species, especially *C. europæa.*

b. Transferred to the Bindweeds, *Convolvulus arvensis* and *sepium*, and the creeping Crowfoot, *Ranunculus repens.*

1879 MISS JACKSON *Shropshire Wordbk.*

c. An Australian plant of the genus *Cassytha.* Also called *devil's twine.*

1889 J. H. MAIDEN *Useful Native Plants* 14 This and other species of *Cassytha* are called 'Dodder-laurel'. The emphatic name of 'Devil's guts' is largely used. It frequently connects bushes and trees by cords, and becomes a nuisance to the traveller. **1962** N. C. W. BEADLE et al. *Handbk. Vasc. Plants Sydney Distr.* 133 *Cassytha* L., Devil's Twine. **1965** *Austral. Encycl.* II. 279/2 There are 12 indigenous species [of *Cassytha*].. one species, *C. glabella* (devil's twine), being found in all the states.

† **'devilshine.** *Obs.* [In Ormin *deofellshine*, repr. OE. *déofolscín*, f. *déofol* devil + *scíne* a phantom, in comp. magic art, illusion.] A demon; demonic power or skill: = DEVILRY I, 2.

a **1050** *Liber Scintill.* vii. (1889) 35 Deofulscinnu [*demonia*] þurh ȝebed beoð oferswyþede. *c* **1200** ORMIN 8110 And ȝet he dide mare inoh off deofellshine o life. *c* **1290** *S. Eng. Leg.* I. 294/13 All false godes so beoth deuelschine, i-wis.

devilship ('dɛv(ə)lʃɪp). [f. DEVIL *sb.* + -SHIP.] **a.** The office, condition, or quality of a devil.

1644 SIR E. DERING *Prop. Sacr.* C ij b, It were a devilship of mind to forge such report. **1871** H. MARSHALL *For very Life* I. v, Cleverness is an attribute of devilship as well as of Godhood.

b. *humorously.* As a title: cf. *lordship.*

1624 GEE *Foot out of Snare* 63 His Deuil-ship raues and struggles. **1668** DRYDEN *Evenings Love* v. i, Bless his devilship, as I may say. **1760** *Impostors Detected* I. 52 If her devilship of a wife of his was in such a hurry. **1885** J. HAWTHORNE *Miss Cadogna* iv. 45 His delectable little devilship, Señor Asmodeus.

devil's milk. *Herb.* [tr. by Lyte of Ger. *Teufelsmilch*, Du. *Duyvels melck.*] A name given to plants with acrid milky juice. **a.** The Sun-Spurge (*Euphorbia Helioscopia*) and Petty Spurge (*E. Peplus*).

1578 LYTE *Dodoens* III. xxxii. 363 We may cal it after the Greke Peplos, or following the Douche, Dyuels milke. **1611** FLORIO, *Pepilio*, Wilde-purcelaine, some take it for Diuelsmilke or Pety-spurge. **1783** AINSWORTH *Lat. Dict.* (Morell) I, Devil's milk (herb), *Tithymallus.* **1878** BRITTEN & HOLL. *Plant-n.*, Devil's milk.. *Euphorbia Helioscopia.* Middlesex.

b. The Celandine, *Chelidonium majus.*

1878 BRITTEN & HOLLAND *Plant-n.* (Yorkshire.)

deviltry ('dɛv(ə)ltrɪ). [Corruption of DEVILRY: perh. after such words as *harlotry, gallantry,* etc.] = DEVILRY. (Dial. Eng. and U.S.)

1788 *Massachusetts Spy* 28 Aug. (Th.), His shoes were made of the leather of hypocrisy, tanned with the bark of presumption, and curried in the shop of deviltry. *a* **1825** in FORBY *Voc. E. Anglia.* **1825** J. NEAL *Bro. Jonathan* III. 257 All sorts of bloated she things attracted by the sharp odour of his deviltry. **1827** J. F. COOPER *Prairie* II. i. 3 The imps will lie for hours.. brooding their deviltries. **1863** READE *Hard Cash* liii, Dr. Sampson rushed in furious. 'There is some deviltry afloat.' **1876** HOLLAND *Sev. Oaks* xxiii. 324 What deviltry there is in it, I don't know. **1893** *Cath. News* 5 Aug. 4/6 Imposture combined with a good deal of deviltry.

devily, var. of DEVILLY *a.* and *adv. Obs.*

devin(e, -al, -or, etc., obs. ff. DIVINE, etc.

† **de'vinct**, *ppl. a. Obs. rare.* [ad. L. *dēvinctus* obliged, devoted, greatly attached, pa. pple. of *dēvincīre* to bind fast, lay under obligations, f. *dē* (DE- I. 3) + *vincīre* to bind.] Bound, bounden.

1573 *Sc. Acts Jas. VI* (1814) 81 (Jam.) The said lady being.. obleist and devint to be cairfull of his hienes preseruatioun. **1614** R. WILKINSON *Paire Serm.* Ep. Ded. A iij b, His majesties euer deuoted, and now of late more deuinct and obliged Chaplaine. **1643** SIR J. SPELMAN *Case of Affairs* 21 Devinct and obliged to the person of the King.

devious ('diːvɪəs), *a.* [f. L. *dēvi-us* out of the way (f. *dē* = DE- I. 2 + *via* way) + -OUS.]

1. Lying out of the way; off the high or main road; remote, distant, retired, sequestered.

1599 H. BUTTES *Dyets drie Dinner* i vij, They [wild swine] pigge, in desart, streyte, craggie and devious places. **1667** MILTON *P.L.* III. 489 A violent cross wind.. Blows them transverse ten thousand Leagues awry Into the devious Air. **1771** MRS. GRIFFITH tr. *Viaud's Shipwreck* 256 Where I thought.. to provide myself.. better than in so devious and desolate a place as St. Marks. **1826** SCOTT *Woodst.* xi, Showing.. upon how many devious coasts human nature may make shipwreck. **1856** KANE *Arct. Expl.* I. xx. 250 These devious and untrodden ice-fields.

2. Departing from the direct way; pursuing a winding or straying course; circuitous.

1628 MAY in Le Grys tr. *Barclay's Argenis* 181 The foes disranked fled Through deuious paths. *a* **1633** AUSTIN *Medit.* (1635) 61 Neither had they, so devious a Journey, nor so long a time, to travell in. **1727–46** THOMSON *Summer* 80 The wildly-devious morning-walk. **1817** COLERIDGE *Poems*, '*The Picture*', Alone, I rise and trace its devious course. **1874** L. MORRIS *To an Unknown Poet* i, Along thy devious Usk's untroubled flow. **1887** STEVENSON *Underwoods* I. xx. 42 The river of your life I trace Up the sun-chequered, devious bed To the far-distant fountain-head.

b. Of persons or moving bodies: Following a winding or erratic course; rambling, roving.

1735 SOMERVILLE *Chase* III. 344 But whither roves my devious Muse? **1744** AKENSIDE *Pleas. Imag.* I. 197 The long career Of devious comets. **1868** LOWELL *Willows* v, A shoal Of devious minnows wheel from where a pike Lurks balanced.

3. *fig.* Deviating or swerving from the straight way; erring, straying.

1633 PRYNNE *Histrio-M.* I. VI. xii. (R.), Whose heart is so estranged from reason, so devious from the truth through perverse error. **1638** COWLEY *Love's Riddle* iv, Yet still this devious Error draws me backward. **1650** *Caussin's Ang. Peace* 53 Those men.. precipitate themselves into devious enormities. **1847** LONGF. *Ev.* II. iii. 143 Like the sweet thoughts of love on a darkened and devious spirit.

4. quasi-*adv.* With wandering or straying course.

1782 COWPER *Progr. Err.* 60 Seek to.. lead him devious from the path of truth. **1784** —— *Tiroc.* 309 To pitch the ball into the grounded hat, Or drive it devious with a dext'rous pat. **1848** C. BRONTË *J. Eyre* xxvii, I sought the Continent, and went devious through all its lands.

Hence **'deviously** *adv.*, in a devious manner or course, with deviation; **'deviousness.**

1727 BAILEY vol. II, *Deviousness*, swervingness, or going out of the way. **1742** WARBURTON *Comm. Pope's Ess. Man* Wks. 1811 XI. 34 God.. deviously turns the natural bias of its malignity to the advancement of human happiness. **1791** J. WHITAKER *Gibbon's Decl. & F.* 252 (R.) No words can fully expose the astonishing deviousness of such a digression as this. **1842** C. WHITEHEAD *R. Savage* (1845) II. ix. 288 Money that comes deviously into a man's pocket goes crookedly out of it. **1870** LOWELL *Study Wind., Good word for Winter* (1871) 40 A nuthatch scaling deviously the trunk of some hard-wood tree.

devire, obs. form of DEVOIR.

† **de'virginate**, *pa. pple. Obs. rare.* [ad. L. *dēvirgināt-us*, pa. pple. of *dēvirgināre*: see next.] Deprived of virginity, deflowered.

c **1470** HARDING *Chron.* LXIII. xx, And for they would not be deuirgynate, They slewe theim all. **1600** CHAPMAN *Musæus* III. Argt., Fair Hero, left devirginate, Weighs, and with fury wails her state.

† **de'virginate**, *v. Obs.* [f. L. *dēvirgināt-* ppl. stem of *dēvirgināre* to deprive of virginity, deflower, f. DE- I. 6 + *virgin-em* virgin, maid.] *trans.* To deprive of virginity; to deflower, violate. Also *fig.* Hence **de'virginated** *ppl. a.*

1583 STUBBES *Anat. Abus.* I. (1879) 145 To deverginat Mayds, to deflour honest Wyues. **1624** DONNE *Serm.* ii. 19 That Virgin Soule devirginated in the blood of Adam but restored in the blood of the Lamb. *a* **1639** W. WHATELY *Prototypes* II. xxxiv. (1640) 157 Though Shechem had done the Maiden this wrong to devirginate her. **1654** GAYTON *Pleas. Notes* III. viii. 120 Her devirginated Daughter. *a* **1680** R. ALLESTREE *Serm.* (1684) II. 96 (L.) To make use of watchfulness over ourselves, that sin do not devirginate us.

devirgi'nation. [ad. L. *dēvirginātiōn-em*, n. of action from L. *dēvirgināre*: see prec.] The action of devirginating; deflowering of a virgin.

1606 HOLLAND *Sueton.* 192 Maidens, when they bee forced and suffer devirgination. **1650** BULWER *Anthropomet.* 226. **1704** D'URFEY *Nt. Advent.* 187 A devirgination Was justice upon this occasion. **1883** *Syd. Soc. Lex.*, *Devirgination*, the loss of the signs of virginity from sexual connection.

de'virginator. *rare.* [a. L. agent-n. from *dēvirgināre* to DEVIRGINATE.] A deflowerer, ravisher. In quot *fig.*

1889 R. ELLIS *Comment. on Catull.* lxii. 32 An attack on *Night*, the Devirginator, the foe of sun and daylight.

devirilize (diː'vɪrɪlaɪz), *v.* [f. DE- + VIRILE *a.* + -IZE.] *trans.* To deprive of virility or manly qualities; to devitalize. So **devirili'zation**; **de'virilized** *ppl. a.*

1901 *Amer. Jrnl. Psychol.* XII. 277 The devirilized effects of transcendental and idealistic habits of thought. **1920** W. J. LOCKE *House of Baltazar* v, These new women are out for the devirilisation of man.

devisable (dɪ'vaɪzəb(ə)l), *a.* Also 6 devysable, diuisable, 6–9 deviseable. [a. OF. *devisable*, that can be divided; in AF. that can be assigned by will; f. *deviser* to DEVISE.]

1. *Law.* That can be devised or bequeathed, as real property: see DEVISE *v.* 4.

[**1292** BRITTON III. xx. §7 Si.. le tenement soit devisable par usage et custume del lu, sicum est de burgages.] **1535** *Act 27 Hen. VIII*, c. 10 §1 By the common lawes.. landes, tenementes and hereditamentes, be not diuisable by testamente. **1590** SWINBURNE *Testaments* 91 Whether corne growing on lande morgaged, bee deuiseable. **1628** COKE *On Litt.* 322 Tenements deuisable to another for life, or for yeares. **1755** MAGENS *Insurances* II. 369 The Shares in the capital Stock shall be transferrable and devisable. **1818** CRUISE *Digest* (ed. 2) I. 405 Uses were devisable, although at that time lands were not. **1847** *Tait's Mag.* XIV. 192 Genius and talent are not devisable possessions. **1875** POSTE *Gaius* III. Comm. (ed. 2) 422 Land held in emphyteusis was alienable, devisable, descendible by intestacy.

2. That can be devised or contrived; contrivable.

1649 SADLER *Rights of Kingdom* 189 (T.) If there be no records, there is scarce devisable a legal traverse or a trial. *a* **1677** BARROW *Serm.* Wks. 1686 II. 36 Exceptions or cavils devisable by curious or captious wits. **1795** *Jemima* II. 39 Every devisable method for obtaining her. **1889** MRS. LYNN LINTON *Thro' Long Night* II. ix, Any folly devisable by man.

† **3.** Of deceitful contrivance, of feigned nature.

1659 MILTON *Civ. Power* Wks. 1848 II. 547 The more they will.. find how false and deviseable that common saying is, which is so much relied upon.

devisal (dɪ'vaɪzəl). *rare.* [f. DEVISE *v.* + -AL[1]. Cf. OF. *devisaille* device.] The act of devising; contrivance, invention.

1854–6 PATMORE *Angel in Ho.* I. II. VI. (1879) 201 If aught of your devisal prove Too hard or high to do or be. **1875** WHITNEY *Life Lang.* xiv. 309 Each word.. has its own place, mode, and circumstances of devisal.

deviscerate (dɪ'vɪsəreɪt), *v. rare.* [f. DE- II. 1 + L. *viscera* entrails + -ATE[3].] To disembowel, eviscerate. Hence **de'viscerated** *ppl. a.*, **devisce'ration**, 'the removal of the abdominal viscera' (*Syd. Soc. Lex.*).

1727 BAILEY vol. II, *Deviscerated*, imbowelled.

devise (dɪ'vaɪz), *v.* Forms: 4–5 deuise-n, 5– devise; also 4 deuis, -iss, 4–5 dyuyse, 4–6 deuyse, diuise, -yse, deuice, 5 dyuise, *Sc.* dewice, dyuys, 5–6 deuys, dewyss(e, *Sc.* dewyse, 6 devize, *Sc.* dewyiss, diwyse. [a. OF. *devise-r* to divide, etc. = Pr. and OSp. *devisar*, It. *divisare*:—late pop.L. **dīvīsāre*, freq. of *dividĕre* to DIVIDE, which by dissimilation became *devisare* in Romanic. The sense-development was far advanced before the word was taken into English; OF. had the senses, 'to divide, distribute, dispose in portions, arrange, array, dispose of, digest, order, form a plan or design, invent, contrive, express or make known one's plan or will', whence in later use, 'to confer, discourse, commune, talk, chat', the last the chief sense in modern French. It. *divisare* has in Florio, 1611, the senses 'to deuise, to invent; also, to deuide or part a sunder; to discource, to talke or confer together; to blazon armes; also, to surmise, to thinke, to seeme vnto'.]

† **1.** *trans.* To divide; to separate, part; to distribute. *Obs.*

c **1330** R. BRUNNE *Chron.* (1810) 187 In þre parties to fight his oste he did deuise. **1340** HAMPOLE *Pr. Consc.* 349 þis buk.. In seven partes divised es. ? *a* **1400** *Morte Arth.* 1389 The knyghte one þe coursere he clevede in sondyre, Clenlyche fro þe croune his corse he dyvysyde. *c* **1400** MAUNDEV. (Roxb.) xvii. 79 Inde es diuised in three partys. **1483** CAXTON *Cato* E v, A waye whyche is deuysed in thre wayes.

† **b.** To separate mentally, distinguish. *Obs.*

c **1340** *Cursor M.* 22929 (Fairf.) Wele can he deuise þe tane fra þe toþer. **1483** CAXTON *Gold. Leg.* 237/2 Thou hast thought in thy corage.. how thou myghtest deuyse the reliques of eche.

† **2.** To arrange, set in battle array. *Obs.*

c **1325** *Coer de L.* 3928 Kyng Richard.. devysyd hys hoost in the feeld. (Cf. quot 1330 in sense 1.)

† **3.** To assign, appoint, order, direct. (*absol.* or *trans.* with simple obj. or obj. clause.) *Obs.*

1303 R. BRUNNE *Handl. Synne* 9510 But he were.. In fonte stone and watyr baptysede As Iesu cryst haþ dyuysede. *c* **1325** *E.E. Allit. P.* B. 238 Þer pryuely in paradys his place watz devised. **1375** BARBOUR *Bruce* VII. 265 As scho deuisit, thai haue done. *c* **1420** *Pallad. on Husb.* III. 21 Chiches sowe afore as I devysed. *c* **1450** *Merlin* 58 What wilt thow that I do, for I will do euen as thow wilte devise. *c* **1450** *St. Cuthbert* (Surtees) 374 He him baptysyd, And to him his name dyuysid. **1548** HALL *Chron.* 11 For.. this enterprise he devised a solempne justes to be.. at Oxforde. **1597** MONTGOMERIE *Cherrie & Slae* 927 Cum on.. And do as we deuyse. **1606** G. W[OODCOCKE] tr. *Hist. Ivstine* 26 b, They were forced to deuise and let out their Citty vnto strangers.

4. *Law.* To assign or give by will. Now technically used only of realty, but formerly of all kinds of property that could be disposed of by will, = bequeath.

[In med.L. *dividĕre* = testamento disponere: see Du Cange. The primary sense was literally 'to divide or distribute one's possessions', but the word had apparently passed into that of 'assign or ordain by will' before its adoption in English. Cf. quot. 1375 in sense 5 b.]

[1347 *Test. Ebor.* (Surtees) I. 44 (Will of Earl Warenne) Jeo devys a Isabelle de Holland ma compaigne mon anel dor.] 1395 *E.E. Wills* (1882) 4, I deuyse to Thomas my sone, a bed of tapicers werk. c 1422 HOCCLEVE *Min. Poems* (1892) 219 Y to thee dyuyse Iewelles .iij . a ryng brooch & a clooth. 1574 tr. *Littleton's Tenures* 35 b, A man may devise by his testament hys lands and tenementes. 1647 N. BACON *Disc. Govt. Eng.* I. lxii. (1739) 126 Richard the first devised the Crown to King John. 1748 RICHARDSON *Clarissa* (1811) I. xix. 136 Giving up to my fathers controul the estate devised me. 1818 CRUISE *Digest* (ed. 2) VI. 17 Persons under the age of twenty-one years are incapable of devising their lands. 1827 JARMAN *Powell's Devises* II. 12 Lands or goods cannot be devisd to superstitious uses, within stat. 23 Hen. VIII. c. 10, by any means whatsoever. 1837 *Act 7 Will. IV & 1 Vict.* c. 26 §33 Any person.. to whom any real or personal estate shall be devised or bequeathed. a 1845 STEPHEN *Laws Engl.* (ed. 6) I. 620 Where a man devises lands to his heir at law. 1862 TROLLOPE *Orley F.* i. (ed. 4) 2 This codicil.. devised a sum of two thousand pounds to a certain Miriam Elsbech. 1895 POLLOCK & MAITLAND *Hist. Eng. Law* II. 336 The modern convention which sets apart 'devise' for 'realty' and 'bequeath' for 'personalty'.

5. To order, appoint, or arrange the plan or design of; to plan, contrive, think out, frame, invent; **a.** something material, as a work of art or a mechanical contrivance. (Formerly including the notion 'to construct, frame, fashion'; now expressing only the mental process of inventing or contriving.)

a 1300 *Cursor M.* 9960 (Cott.) Suilk a hald.. neuer bes wroght wijt mans wijt, For godd him-self deuised it. c 1340 *Ibid.* 8311 (Fairf.) þis werk.. þou salle deuise hit in þi þoȝt And þoru salamon hit sal be wroȝt. 1393 LANGL. *P. Pl. C.* XXII. 331 Grace deuysede A cart.. to carien home peers sheues. c 1400 *Rom. Rose* 923 In his honde holdyng Turke bowes two, fulle wel devysed had he. 1486 *Henry VII at York* in *Surtees Misc.* (1890) 55 A convenient thing divisid wherby.. schall rayne rose water. 1526 *Pilgr. Perf.* (W. de W. 1531) 17 b, The moost.. delicate dysshes, that can or may be deuysed for a kynge. 1548 HALL *Chron.* 131 b, To tel.. what engynes were devised, what harneis was provided. 1577 B. GOOGE *Heresbach's Husb.* I. (1586) 9 b, This Court I thus devised mee selfe. *Ibid.* IV. 173 Ponds for Oysters, were first devised by Sergius Orata. 1603 KNOLLES *Hist. Turks* (1638) 187 More ingenious than his father in deuising warlike engines. 1784 COWPER *Task* I. 211 The artist whose ingenious thought Devised the Weatherhouse, that useful toy! 1860 TYNDALL *Glac.* II. xxx. 404 [An] instrument.. exceeding in accuracy any hitherto devised. 1863 GEO. ELIOT *Romola* I. iii, Marble inlaying and statued niches, which Giotto had devised a hundred and fifty years before. 1879 *Cassell's Techn. Educ.* IV. 62/2 The ingenuity with which he devised tools for.. lock-making.

b. something immaterial or abstract, or a product of the mind. (The chief current sense.)

a 1300 *K. Horn* 930 A writ he dude deuise, Aþulf hit dude write. 1375 BARBOUR *Bruce* XX. 309 His testament deuisit he, And ordanit how his land suld be Gouernit. 14.. LYDG. *Temple of Glas* 927 þi woordis so deuyse, That she on þe haue compassioun. 1530 PALSGR. 523/2, I can devyse a thing wel, but I can nat penne it. 1538 STARKEY *England* I. i. 12 Meruelus gud lawys.. deuysyd by man. 1555 EDEN *Decades* (Arb.) 49 The mynde of man.. taketh pleasure in diuisynge or excogitatynge sume honest thynge. 1601 SHAKS. *Jul. C.* III. i. 246 Speake all good you can deuise of Cæsar. 1661 BRAMHALL *Just Vind.* iv. 63 Then Pope Paschalis the second had devised a new Oath for Arch-Bishops. 1791 COWPER *Odyss.* XIV. 600 So I.. the remedy at once Devised. 1833 HT. MARTINEAU *Briery Creek* v. 115 Whatever occupation might have been devised for their leisure evening hours. 1862 SIR B. BRODIE *Psychol. Inq.* II. iii. 105 It is impossible to devise any sanitary measures which would do all that is required. 1870 LUBBOCK *Orig. Civiliz.* iv. (1875) 167 Having devised words for father and mother.

c. *absol.* or with clause: To contrive, plan (*that ..., how ...*, etc., or *to do* something).

c 1325 *E.E. Allit. P.* B. 1100 Wel clanner þen any crafte cowþe deuyse. c 1400 *Rom. Rose* 7362 At the last they devysed, That they wolde gone in tapinage. c 1420 *Pallad. on Husb.* I. 784 Dyversed wittes dyversely devyse. 1568 GRAFTON *Chron.* II. 313 He.. devysed to set great taxes and impositions upon the people. 1598 SHAKS. *Merry W.* IV. iv. 27 Deuise but how you'l vse him when he comes, And let vs two deuise to bring him thether. 1667 MILTON *P.L.* VIII. 207 How suttly to detaine thee I devise. 1725 POPE *Odyss.* IX. 377 Thus.. I thought, devis'd, and Pallas heard my prayer. 1832 TENNYSON '*Love thou thy land*' x, For Nature also, cold and warm.. devising long.. Matures the individual form.

†**d.** To design, draw, represent by art. *Obs.*

a 1400-50 *Alexander* 280 In þis oþir draȝt ware deuysid a dusan of bestis. c 1400 *Destr. Troy* 1678 Twenty pase vp pight all of pure cristall, þat were shynyng full shene shalkes to deuyse. 1590 SPENSER *F.Q.* II. i. 31 That deare Crosse uppon your shield devizd.

†**6. a.** *refl.* To plan, determine, resolve. *Obs.*

1393 GOWER *Conf.* III. 248 He all hole the cite lad Right as he wolde him self devise. c 1450 *St. Cuthbert* (Surtees) 6342 þe seruand sees many penys Lig on the toumbe, he him deuys To stele of þaim belyue.

†**b.** *intr.* To resolve or decide *upon*. *Obs.*

1548 UDALL, etc. *Erasm. Par.* Pref. 18 Lyke a man that had deuised upon it afore. 1598 BARCKLEY *Felic. Man* III. (1603) 161 Devising upon a man that might see this treason punished.

†**c.** with *inf.* To design. *Obs.*

1714 GAY *Sheph. Week* v. 19 Of Patient Grissel I devise to sing.

7. *trans.* In a bad sense: **a.** To plot, scheme, lay plans to bring about (evil). *arch.* (Const. with simple obj. or infin.)

c 1400 *Destr. Troy* 9478 To deire hym with dethe he duly deuyset, With an arow. 1513 MORE in Grafton *Chron.* II. 788 Under pretext of her dutie to Godward, she divised to disturbe this mariage. a 1533 LD. BERNERS *Huon* lxv. 223 These .ii. traytours deuysyd and concludyd the deth of Huon. 1633 G. HERBERT *Temple, Sacrifice* v, For thirtie pence he did my death devise. 1791 COWPER *Iliad* VIII. 533 Devising.. calamity to Troy. 1864 TENNYSON *Aylmer's Field* 783 And knew not what they did, but sat Ignorant, devising their own daughter's death!

b. To contrive or make up deceitfully or falsely; to feign, forge, invent. *arch.*

1513 MORE *Rich. III*, Wks. 56 Much mater was ther.. deuised to the slaunder of yᵉ lord Chamberlain. 1605 *Play Stucley* in Simpson *Sch. Shaks.* (1878) 166, I cannot tell what to do. I'll devise some 'scuse. 1719 *Freethinker* No. 109. ¶2 The Eldest.. devised a monstrous Calumny to ruin his Brother. 1820 SOUTHEY *Ode St. George's Day* 1 The tales which fabling monks of old Devised. 1887 BOWEN *Virg. Æneid* IV. 51 Devise fair pleas for delay.

†**c.** with *obj. cl.*, or *absol.* To feign, pretend.

1600 E. BLOUNT tr. *Conestaggio* 208 Incouraging them, sometimes devising that the French succours were on the way, sometimes shewing the.. forces to bee greater then they were. 1609 HOLLAND *Amm. Marcell.* xxx. iv. 386 If thou shouldest devise [*finxeris*] and say, That wilfully thou hadst murthered thine owne mother. 1610 —— *Camden's Brit.* (1637) 8 He.. deviseth first that this Brutus was a Consul of Rome.

†**8.** *trans.* (or *absol.*) To 'contrive' successfully; to achieve, accomplish, 'manage'. *Obs.*

1340-70 *Alex. & Dind.* 670 Hercules.. Diuisede here.. a dosain of wondrus. 1415 HOCCLEVE *To Sir J. Oldcastle* 511 Thee hie as faste as þat thou canst dyuyse. 1553 T. WILSON *Rhet.* (1580) 214 [He] could not devise the makyng of some Letters, in his Crosse rowe.. whereas before.. he wrote both fast and faire. c 1592 MARLOWE *Mass. Paris* I. viii, Could we devise To get those pedants from the King Navarre, That are tutors to him.

†**9.** To prepare with skill, make ready, provide, purvey. (Also *absol.*) *Obs.*

c 1385 CHAUCER *L.G.W.* 1453 *Hypsipyle*, Anoon Argus his shippes gan devyse. c 1400 *Lanfranc's Cirurg.* 87 It sufficiþ þat a man diuise þe medicyn after þe complexioun mai bee. c 1500 *Three Kings Sons* 182 The kynge was the best diuiser that any man coude fynde: he deuised not as a pore caitif, but as a kynge.

†**10.** *trans.* (or *absol.*) To conceive, imagine; to conjecture, guess. *Obs.*

c 1325 *E.E. Allit. P.* B. 1046 Also red & so ripe & rychely hwed, As any dom myȝt device of dayntyez oute. 1340 *Ayenb.* 73 Ine helle þou sselt yzi mo zorȝes þanne me moȝe deuisy. c 1350 *Will. Palerne* 2985 Makende þe most ioye þat man miȝt deuise. c 1440 *Ipomydon* 94 Full riche, I wot, were hyr seruice, For better myght no man devyse. 1592 SHAKS. *Rom. & Jul.* III. i. 72, I do protest I neuer iniur'd thee, But lou'd thee better then thou can'st deuise: Till thou shalt know the reason of my loue. 1754 EDWARDS *Freed. Will* II. v. 53 If Liberty don't consist in this, what else can be devised that it should consist in. 1814 MAD. D'ARBLAY *Wanderer* V. 358 Little enough devizing I should ever meet with [etc.].

†**11.** *intr.* (or *trans.* with *obj. cl.*) To think, meditate, consider, deliberate. *Obs.*

c 1400 *Destr. Troy* 4938 Ses now your seluyn.. And deuys of þis dede as you dere think. c 1450 *St. Cuthbert* (Surtees) 4411 He deuysed what he suld do. c 1533 LD. BERNERS *Huon* cxxii. 435 Thus as ye haue harde Huon deuysyd by hymselfe at the fountayne. 1548 HALL *Chron.* 105 Vieuyng the cite and devisyng in what place it was best assautable. 1598-9 E. FORDE *Parismus* I. (1661) 34 Thus by devising what should be become of him she could enjoy no quiet nor content.

†**12.** *trans.* To consider, scan, survey, examine, look at attentively. *Obs.*

c 1320 *Sir Beues* 3872 þe castel ase he ȝede aboute, For to diuise þe toures stoute. 1377 LANGL. *P. Pl.* B. XIX. 273 He shulde ar he did any dede deuyse wel þe ende. a 1400-50 *Alexander* 5099 Sone as þis princes of pris þis pistyll had deuysid. c 1470 HENRY *Wallace* III. 101 The worthi Scottis.. Dewysyt the place. 1509 BARCLAY *Shyp of Folys* (1570) 9 Beholde vnto your prince: Consider his sadnes, his honestie deuise.

†**b.** To perceive, discern, observe. *Obs.*

a 1300 *Cursor M.* 9895 (Gött.) Baylis has þis castel thre, wid wallis thrinne, semly to se, As ȝe sal siþen here diuyse. a 1400-50 *Alexander* 3053 Sone as ser Dary it deuysid, and seȝis his foke faile. c 1430 *Syr Gener.* (Roxb.) 1148 That no man youre counsel devise. 1620 SHELTON *Quix.* IV. vii. II. 88 We Phœbus may devise Shine thro' the rosal Gates of th' Orient bright.

†**13.** To set forth in detail, recount, describe.

a 1300 *Cursor M.* 8979 (Cott.) Salamon þe wys, His dedes coth naman deuis. c 1300 *K. Alis.* 7377 N'is no nede heore armes to devyse. 1393 GOWER *Conf.* I. 206 And tho began he to devise, How he the childis moder fonde. 1481 CAXTON *Myrr.* I. iv. 16 We shal deuise to yow herafter the fourme of the world and the facyon. 1513 DOUGLAS *Æneis* XIII. ix. 110 Lang war to devys Thair hasty fair, thair revellyng and deray. c 1570 *Pride & Lowl.* (1841) 18 And foorth they went, as I shall you devise.

†**b.** *intr.* or *absol.* To give an account. *Obs.*

c 1400 *Rom. Rose* 888 His beaute gretly was to preyse: But of his robe to devise I drede encombred for to be. c 1430 *Pilgr. Lyf Manhode* I. c. (1869) 54 Ryght as grace dieu spak and diuised of these belles. 1601 R. JOHNSON *Kingd. & Commw.* (1603) 194 Hitherto have we devised of Siam and Pegu (as they stood) before the comming of the Portugals into India. *Ibid.* (1603) 207 Of whose originall and fortunes.. it shall not bee amisse to devise.

†**14.** To confer, commune, discourse, converse, talk. *Obs.* [So in mod.F.] **a.** *refl.*

c 1477 CAXTON *Jason* 34 b, And we shall deuise us to geder of oure auentures. c 1489 —— *Blanchardyn* xvi. 52 The proude pucelle.. talked and deuysed her self sore harde and angerly wyth her maystres.

†**b.** *intr.*

c 1477 CAXTON *Jason* 51 b, Knowyng that he was moche pensif.. he deuised to him of many thinges and meruailes. 1530 PALSGR. 514/2, I devyse, I talke or fynde comunycacion. a 1533 LD. BERNERS *Huon* xx. 54 After they had dynyd and deuysed too gether a grete space. 1596 SPENSER *State Irel.* 2 Let us.. a little devise of those evils, by which that country is held in this wretched case. 1600 HOLLAND *Livy* XLV. xii. 1208 He answered that he would devise with.. his friends and consider what was best to be don. 1614 RALEIGH *Hist. World* v. iii. §1 His father, and other friends, had long time deuised of this businesse.

†**c.** *trans.* with cognate obj.

1538 STARKEY *England* I. i. 25, I schal now at thys leser.. some thyng wyth you, Master Lvpset, deuyse, touchyng the ordur of our cuntrey and commyn wel.

devise (dɪˈvaɪz), *sb. Law.* Also 6-7 device. [a. OF. *devise*, *devis* (in same sense):—Romanic *devīso*, *devīsa*, for L. *dīvīsus*, and (late) *dīvīsa*, from ppl. stem of *dīvidĕre* to divide, distribute, apportion, also, in med.L., = *disponere testamento*, to dispose by will. In med.L., *dīvīsa* was in common use = *dīvīsio*, originally 'division of goods by testament', 'whence also the testament itself is called *dīvīsa* [and *dīvīsio*]' (Du Cange). The same word as DEVICE *sb.*, and formerly also sometimes spelt *device*; the eventual victory of the form *devise* may be partly due to the influence of the med.L. *dīvīsa* in wills, but is prob. more owing to the influence of the verb, and the close association of the sb. with it in this special sense.]

The act of devising, apportioning, or assigning, by will; a testamentary disposition of real property; the clause in a will conveying this.

'A gift by will of freehold land, or of such rights arising out of or connected with land as are by English law classed with it as *real property*, is called a *devise*. A gift by will of *personal property* is called a *bequest*.' (Sir F. Pollock; *Land Laws* (1887) v. 126) But this distinction is modern: cf. quot. 1641, and DEVISE v. 4.

[1182 HENRY II *Will* in Gervase of Cant., Notum facio quod apud Waltham.. feci Divisam meam de quadam parte pecuniæ meæ.]

1542-3 *Act 34-5 Hen. VIII*, c. 5. §9 Any suche person, that shall make any.. deuise by his last will in writing. 1574 tr. *Littleton's Tenures* 35 b, He to whom such devise ys made after the death of the devisour, may enter in the tenementes. 1641 *Termes de la Ley* 114 Devise is where a man in his testament giveth or bequeatheth his goods or his lands to another after his decease. 1709 *Case of Heirs at Law to G. Monke* 12 The Devise in that Will, by Christopher to his Dutchess. 1765 BLACKSTONE *Comm.* I. II. vii. 84 It does not extend to devises by will. 1817 W. SELWYN *Law Nisi Prius* II. 813 The devisor wrote upon a sheet of paper a devise of land, and subscribed the paper, but did not seal it. 1841 STEPHEN *Laws Engl.* (ed. 6) I. 609 The law of testamentary disposition.. as it affects estates of freehold duration and tenure; or as it is commonly expressed, the law of *devises*. 1858 LD. ST. LEONARDS *Handy Bk. Prop. Law* xx. 151 A general devise or bequest.. will pass any real or personal estate which you have power to appoint in any manner you think proper. 1876 FREEMAN *Norm. Conq.* V. xxiii. 329 For the first time in our story, a devise of the Crown made before the actual vacancy took effect. 1895 POLLOCK & MAITLAND *Hist. Eng. Law* II. 332 In the year 1182.. the king made, not indeed his testament, but his division or devise (*divisam suam*) of a certain portion of his fortune.

β. 1589 PUTTENHAM *Eng. Poesie* III. xix. (Arb.) 241 No man can say its his by heritage, Nor by Legacie, or Testatours deuice. 1618 BOLTON *Florus* II. xx. 157 The people.. entring upon the whole estate, retained it.. by vertue of his device, and Testament. a 1626 BACON *Max. & Uses Com. Law* xiv. (1636) 58 If I devise the mannour of D.. of which at that time I am not seised.. this device is void.

devised (dɪˈvaɪzd), *ppl. a.* [f. DEVISE *v.* + -ED[1].] Planned, contrived, invented, feigned, etc.: see the verb.

1552 HULOET, Deuised, *cogitatus*.. Deuised in thought, or purposed precisely, *meditatus*. 1553 T. WILSON *Rhet.* (1580) 179 Allegories, and darke devised sentences. 1611 BIBLE *2 Pet.* i. 16 Wee have not followed cunningly deuised fables. 1634 CANNE *Necess. Separ.* (1849) 82 Worthily speaketh M. Perkins.. when men set up a devised worship, they set up also a devised God. a 1850 CALHOUN *Wks.* (1874) IV. 26 What is it but a cunningly devised scheme, to replenish the treasury of some of the states.

devisee (dɪˌvaɪˈziː). *Law.* [f. DEVISE *v.* + -EE.] The person to whom property is devised by will: see DEVISE *v.* 4. (Correlative to *devisor*.)

1542-3 *Act 34-5 Hen. VIII*, c. 5 §17 The right and title of the donees, feoffes, lessees, and deuisees therof. 1602 FULBECKE *2nd Pt. Parall.* 33 The deuisee cannot take the goodes without the deliuerie of the executor. 1767 BLACKSTONE *Comm.* II. 108 If the devise be to a man and his assigns, without annexing words of perpetuity, there the devisee shall take only an estate for life. 1813 *Examiner* 8 Feb. 95/2 The nephew was to be heir or devisee and legatee of.. the uncle's property. 1875 POSTE *Gaius* II. Comm. (ed. 2) 227 In the language of English jurisprudence, Heir denotes a successor to real estate by descent, Devisee denotes a successor to real estate under a will.

devisely, obs. var. DIVISELY *adv.*

deˈvisement. *rare.* [a. OF. *devisement*, f. *deviser* to DEVISE: see -MENT.]

1. Description. (Cf. DEVISE *v.* 13.)

c 1325 *E.E. Allit. P.* A. 1019, I knew hit by his deuysement, In þe apocalyppez þe apostel Iohan. As Iohan deuysed ȝet saȝ I þare.

2. The act of devising or contriving; a device.

1541 WYATT *Defence* Wks. (1861) p. xxvi, For the inventing, for the setting forth, for the indictment, for devisement of the dilating of the matters. 1879 [S. MOSES] *Spirit-Identity* 97 App. II. §5 Cunning devisements of curious brains.

deviser (dɪˈvaɪzə(r)). Also 4 *Sc.* dewisowr, 4–6 deuysour, 4–7 diviser, 6 deuisour, deuysar, -er, 6–7 (9) devisor. [ME. *devysour*, a. AF. *devisour* = OF. *deviseor*, *-eur*, f. *deviser* to DEVISE. In mod.Eng. (exc. in a special sense: see DEVISOR) the suffix is changed into the common agent-ending -ER.]

One who devises; a contriver, inventor, framer, forger, plotter, schemer, etc.: cf. the verb.

1523 LD. BERNERS *Froiss.* I. ccxxxi. 316 The prince of Wales was a mean bytwene them, and chefe deuysour therof. **1538** STARKEY *England* II. iii. 80 Curyouse descanterys and deuysarys of new songys. **1571** GOLDING *Calvin on Ps.* vii. 16 Devisers of mischeefe perish through their own devises. **1577** NORTHBROOKE *Dicing* (1843) 116 Who was the firste deuisour of dyce playing? **1614** RALEIGH *Hist. World* III. 24 The deviser of the mischiefe against Cyrus. **1646** SIR T. BROWNE *Pseud. Ep.* I. iii. 11 They are daily mocked into errour by subtler devisors. **1672** EACHARD *Hobbes's State Nat.* (1705) 11 As very a deviser, as if you had found out gun-powder or printing. **1791** COWPER *Iliad* IV. 398 And thou, deviser of all evil wiles! **1867** FREEMAN *Norm. Conq.* (1876) I. App. 629 The first deviser of the scheme.

†**b.** One who makes ready, plans, or arranges (a feast, etc.): cf. DEVISE *v.* 9. *Obs.*

1375 BARBOUR *Bruce* XX. 72 Devysouris of that fest till be. *c* **1500** *Three Kings Sons* 182 The kynge was the best diuiser that any man coude fynde.

†**c.** One who prepares the plans of a building, etc.; an architect. *Obs.*

1548 PATTEN *Exped. Scotl.* in Arb. *Garner* III. 76 Sir Richard Lee Knight, Devisor of the fortifications to be made. **1581** MULCASTER *Positions* xli. (1887) 242 What should..maryners, deuisours, architectes..do with latin. **1647** HAWARD *Crown Rev.* 23 Devisor of the Buildings.

devising (dɪˈvaɪzɪŋ), *vbl. sb.* [f. DEVISE *v.* + -ING[1].] The action of the verb DEVISE; contriving, planning, invention, etc.

c **1400** *Lanfranc's Cirurg.* (MS. B) 106 Aftere þe devysinge of my symple wytt. **1530** PALSGR. 213/2 Devisyng, *deuis.* **1594** HOOKER *Eccl. Pol.* II. viii, That in them God hath..left his intent to be accomplished by our diuisinges. *a* **1610** HEALEY *Theophrastus, Newes forging* (1636) 32 A devising of deeds and words at the fancy or pleasure of the Inventor. **1879** MCCARTHY *Own Times* II. xxiii. 190 He sometimes rode in a curious little cab of his own devising. **1885** BRIDGES *Nero* I. i. 2/2 The curse of life is of our own devising, Born of man's ignorance and selfishness.

†**b.** Conversation, talking (DEVISE *v.* 14). *Obs.*

1586 B. YOUNG *Guazzo's Civ. Conv.* IV. 178 He thought.. such a companie..would have passed the time in some manner of devising, and discourses, but now perceaved himselfe to be rather in a..silent place.

c. *Law.* The bequeathing of real property (DEVISE *v.* 4).

1868 ROGERS *Pol. Econ.* xvii. (1876) 228 That which relates to the letting, devising, and settlement of land.

devision, obs. form of DIVISION.

devisor (dɪˈvaɪzɔː(r)). *Law.* Also 6–7 -our. [a. AF. *devisour*, = OF. *deviseor*, *-eur*, f. *deviser* to DEVISE. Formerly used in all senses of the vb., for which DEVISER is now the general form.] One who devises (real property) by will; one who makes a devise. (Correlative to *devisee.*)

1542–3 *Act 34–5 Hen. VIII*, c 5 §11 After the death of any such owner or deuisour which shall make any such..deuice by his last will in writing. **1574** [see DEVISE *sb.*]. **1657** SIR H. GRIMSTONE in *Croke's Rep.* I. 476 The intent of the devisor. **1767** BLACKSTONE *Comm.* II. 379 No after-purchased lands will pass under such devise, unless, subsequent to the purchase or contract, the devisor re-publishes his will. **1876** DIGBY *Real Prop.* viii. 351 No liability attached to the lands in the hands of the devisee for the debts of the devisor.

devisor, -our, obs. forms of DEVISER.

†**devitable**, *a. Obs.*[—0] [f. L. *dēvītāre* DEVITE *v.* + -BLE.]

1727 BAILEY vol. II, *Devitable*, easy to be shunned or avoided.

devitalize (dɪˈvaɪtəlaɪz), *v.* [f. DE- II. 1 + VITALIZE.] *trans.* To deprive of vitality or vital qualities; to render lifeless or effete.

1849 I. TAYLOR *Loyola & Jes.* (1857) 359 The philosophy which is propounded to youth must be devitalized. **1861** H. MACMILLAN *Footnotes Page Nat.* 223 Those [persons].. being devitalized by other noxious influences, such as vitiated air, defective sewerage, bad water, or an inadequate supply of food. **1869** [see DEVIVE]. **1876** *Contemp. Rev.* XXVIII. 729 This one incontestable fact of itself overthrows or devitalizes the entire doctrine. **1883** H. DRUMMOND *Nat. Law in Spir. W.* (ed. 2) 86 The biologist cannot devitalise a plant or an animal and revivify it again.

Hence **deˈvitalized, deˈvitalizing** *ppl. adjs.*; also **deˌvitaliˈzation**, the action of devitalizing.

1866 *Reader* 1 Sept. 770 Fungi..flourish on..surfaces.. which belong to devitalized beings. **1871** *Sat. Rev.* 1 Apr. 398/2 New preparations of concentrated food..to meet the 'devitalization' which seems increasing in what we suppose to be the well-nourished class of families. **1875** H. C. WOOD *Therap.* (1879) 349 The poison exerts no destructive chemical or devitalizing influence upon the tissues. **1875** B. W. RICHARDSON *Dis. Mod. Life* 385 Devitalized air finds its entrance into human habitations.

†**deviˈtation.** *Obs. rare.* [ad. L. *dēvītātiōn-em*, n. of action f. *dēvītāre*: see next.] Shunning, avoiding; exhortation to shun: the opposite of *invitation.*

1614 T. ADAMS *Devil's Banquet* 45 If there be any here that..will venture himselfe a guest at the Deuils Banket, maugre all devitation, let him stay and heare the Reckoning. **1623** COCKERAM, *Deuitation*, an eschuing.

†**deˈvite**, *v. Obs. rare*[—1]. [f. L. *dēvītāre* to shun, avoid, f. DE- I. 3 + *vītāre* to shun. Cf. INVITE.] *trans.* To shun.

1549 CHALONER *Erasm. Moriæ Enc.* R iij a, I exhorte you ..to devite or shonne the company of heretikes.

¶ *nonce-use.* To ask not (*to do*): the opposite of *invite.*

1832 LAMB *Let. to Cary* in *Life & Lett.* Wks. (1865) 174 I am de-vited to come on Wednesdays.

devitrification (dɪˌvɪtrɪfɪˈkeɪʃən). [a. mod.F. *dévitrification* (1803 in Hatz.-Darm.), f. *dévitrifier*: see next.] The action or process of devitrifying; deprivation of vitreous character; *esp.* change (of rocks) from a glassy to a crystalline condition.

1832 G. R. PORTER *Porcelain & Gl.* xvi. 317 *heading*, On the Devitrification of Glass. *Ibid.* 326 The devitrification was by no means perfect. **1865** *Ecclesiologist* XXVI. 269 The process of de-vitrification in ancient painted glass. **1879** RUTLEY *Stud. Rocks* x. 163 The development of micro-liths is one of the causes of devitrification in glassy rocks and in artificial glass. **1881** JUDD *Volcanoes* ix. 258 These glassy rocks easily undergo 'devitrification'.

devitrify (dɪˈvɪtrɪfaɪ), *v.* [f. DE- II. 1 + VITRIFY; app. after F. *dévitrifier* (1803 in Hatz.-Darm.).] *trans.* To deprive of vitreous qualities or properties; to cause (glass or a vitreous substance) to become opaque, hard, and crystalline in structure. Hence **deˈvitrified** *ppl. a.*

1832 G. R. PORTER *Porcelain & Gl.* 325 Experiments made to devitrify stained glass taken from church windows. *Ibid.* 326 Glass, when devitrified, becomes a much more perfect conductor of heat and electricity. *Ibid.* xvi. *heading*, Power of devitrified glass to bear sudden changes of temperature. **1879** RUTLEY *Stud. Rocks* x. 170 In most instances this impure or devitrified matter is opaque.

deˈvive, *v. nonce-wd.* [f. DE- II. 1, after *revive.*] *trans.* To render lifeless, devitalize.

1869 OWEN in *Microsc. Jrnl.* May 294 Organisms which we can devitalise and revitalise—devive and revive—many times.

devize, obs. form of DEVISE.

devocalize (dɪˈvəʊkəlaɪz), *v.* [f. DE- II. 1 + VOCALIZE.] *trans.* To make (a vowel or voice consonant) voiceless or non-sonant.

1877 SWEET *Phonetics* 142 [*W*] often becomes (*bh*) and even (*v*), which, when a voiceless consonant follows, is devocalised [to *f*]. **1888** —— *Eng. Sounds* 18 The more primitive Sanskrit usage..devocalizes finally only before a pause or a breath consonant.

Hence **devocaliˈzation.**

1879 SWEET in *Trans. Philol. Soc.* 484 Before voiceless stops there is always devocalization.

†**ˈdevocate**, *v. Obs. rare.* [f. L. *dēvocāt-* ppl. stem of *dēvocāre* to call off, away, or down, f. DE- I. 1, 2 + *vocāre* to call.] *trans.* To call down.

(In quot. 1570 perhaps 'to make calls or demands', if not a misprint for *derogate.*)

c **1570** PRESTON *Cambyses* in Hazl. *Dodsley* IV. 188 The Commons of you do complain, From them you devocate. **1633** W. STRUTHER *True Happiness* 52 Superstitious worshippers thinke by their prayers, as charmes, to devocat and draw God out of heaven.

†**devoˈcation.** *Obs.* [n. of action f. L. *dēvocāre*: see prec. and -ATION.] A calling down or away.

1623 COCKERAM II, A *Calling* downe, deuocation. **1661** RUST *Origen* in *Phenix* (1721) I. 33 All corporeal Pleasure having something of Confusion and Disturbance in it, together with a strong magical Devocation of the Animadversion of the sense of it. **1680** HALLYWELL *Melampr.* 97 (T.) To be freed and released from all its [sorcery's] blandishments and flattering devocations.

devoice (diːˈvɔɪs), *v.* [f. DE- + VOICE *v.* 8.] *trans.* = DEVOCALIZE *v.* Hence **deˈvoicing** *vbl. sb.* and *ppl. a.*

1932 D. JONES *Outl. Eng. Phonetics* (ed. 3) v. 21 The voiced sound is commonly said..to become unvoiced or to be devocalized or better devoiced. **1950** —— *Phoneme* p. xv, Devoicing..voicing. **1951** TRAGER & SMITH *Outl. Eng. Structure* 31 The voiced spirants show marked devoicing. **1964** E. BACH *Introd. Transformational Gram.* vi. 132 The North German pronunciation will result automatically from the general devoicing rule for word final consonants. **1965** W. S. ALLEN *Vox Latina* 69 A voiced velar plosive..is devoiced before the *t.*

devoid (dɪˈvɔɪd), *a.* Also 5–6 devoide, -voyde, 5 -vode, 6 -voyd. [Originally pa. pple. of DEVOID *v.*, short for (or collateral variant of) *devoided*: see next.]

With *of*: Empty, void, destitute (*of* some attribute); entirely without or wanting. (Originally participial, like *bereft*, and, like the latter, only used predicatively, or following its substantive.)

c **1400** *Rom. Rose* 3723 Devoid of pride certaine she was. **1430** LYDG. *Chron. Troy* I. v, So is my meaning cleane devoyde of syn. *c* **1465** *Pol. Rel. & L. Poems* (1866) 2 Devode of vices. **1509** HAWES *Conv. Swearers* 47 Go lytell treatyse deuoyde of eloquence. **1530** PALSGR. 310/1 Devoyde, without or delyvered of a thyng, *vuyde.* **1603** KNOLLES *Hist. Turks* (1638) 101 He lay speechlesse, deuoid of sence and motion. **1660** BOYLE *New Exp. Phys. Mech.* xxxiii. (1682) 126 Though it be not quite devoy'd of all body whatsoever. **1762** FALCONER *Shipwr.* III. 181 A wretch deform'd, devoid of ev'ry grace. **1865** W. G. PALGRAVE *Arabia* I. 410 A very simple style of dress, devoid of ornament or pretension.

b. without *of*: Void, empty. *rare.*

1590 SPENSER *F.Q.* I. ix. 15 When I awoke, and found her place devoyd, And nought but pressed gras where she had lyen, I sorrowed all so much as earst I joyd.

†**devoid**, *v. Obs.* or *rare.* Forms: 4–7 devoyde, 4–6 -vode, 5–6 -voyd, -vyde, 5–7 -void(e, (4–5 dewoyde, 5 -voyede, 6 -wod, -woyd, -wid). [a. OF. *de-*, *desvoidier*, *-vuidier*, *-voyder*, in mod.F. *dévider*, f. *de-*, *des-* (L. *dis-*) + *vuide*, mod. *vide*, empty. Cf. med.L. *disvacuāre*, in same sense.

(In 15–16th c. sometimes confused in form with DIVIDE.)]

†**1.** *trans.* To cast out, get rid of, do away with, remove, expel; to void. *Obs.*

c **1325** *E.E. Allit. P.* A. 15 Wyschande þat wele þat wont watz whyle deuoyde my wrange. *Ibid.* B. 544 De-voydynge þe vylanye þat venkquyst his þewez. *c* **1400** *Rom. Rose* 2929 Right so is al his woo fulle soone Devoided clene. *a* **1400–50** *Alexander* 4327 Auyrice & errogaunce & all we devoide. *c* **1420** *Liber Cocorum* (1862) 45 Devoyde þo worme-etone alle bydene. *c* **1485** *Digby Myst.* III. 787 We xal gete yow leches, ȝower peynes to devyde. **1508** DUNBAR *Tua Mariit Wem.* 166, I sall the venome devoid with a vent large, And me assuage of the swalme, that suellit wes gret. **1509** HAWES *Past. Pleas.* 45, 61, 63, 64.

†**b.** To destroy, annihilate. *Obs.*

c **1325** *E.E. Allit. P.* B. 908 For we schal tyne þis toun & trayþely disstrye, Wyth alle þise wyȝez so wykke wyȝtly deuoyde. *a* **1400–50** *Alexander* 3875 To be deuowrid & devoidid and vencuste for euire.

†**c.** To empty out, pour out, discharge. *Obs.*

c **1450** *Bk. Curtasye* 718 in *Babees Bk.* (1868) 323 For a pype þer is insyde so clene, þat water deuoydes, of seluer schene. **1513** DOUGLAS *Æneis* XIII. i. 10 The Latyn pepyll.. gan devoid [*v. r.* devode], and hostit owt full cleyr Deip from thar brestis the hard sorow smart.

†**2.** To vacate; to leave. *Obs.*

c **1325** *Coer de L.* 1228 He took hys doughter by the hand, And bad her swythe devoyde hys land. *a* **1450** *Le Morte Arth.* 1167 There-fore devoyede my companye. **1545** *Aberdeen Reg.* V. 19 (Jam.) He is ordanit to dewid the tovnn within xxiiij houris.

†**b.** *refl.* To withdraw (oneself). *Obs.*

a **1400** *Cov. Myst.* (Shaks. Soc.) 243, I am with ȝow at alle tymes whan ȝe to councel me calle, But for a short tyme myself I devoyde. **1535** STEWART *Cron. Scot.* II. 123 Or tha culd diuyde thame of that land, Tha war baith tane and fast bund fit and hand.

†**c.** *intr.* (for *refl.*) To go away, withdraw.

c **1485** *Digby Myst.* v. 380 Here lucyfere devoydeth, and commyth in ageyne as a goodly galaunt. **1497** in *Phil. Trans.* XLII. 421 That they devoyd and pass with thame.

†**3.** *trans.* To avoid, shun; to get out of the way of. *Obs.*

1509 HAWES *Past. Pleas.* xxxv. xviii, I ful swyftly dyd geve back ful oft, For to devoyde his great strokes unsoft. **1530** PALSGR. 515/1 It shalbe harde to devoyde this mater: *ce seroyt forte chose de euiter ceste matiere.*

†**4.** To empty; to make void or empty. *Obs.*

a **1400–50** *Alexander* 2938 Alexander..clekis vp þe coupe & putis in his bosom. Anoþire boll was him broȝt & bathe he deuoydid. *c* **1430** LYDG. in Turner *Dom. Archit.* III. 39 The canell scoured was so clene, And deuoyded into secrete wyse.

†**b.** To empty, clear, rid, free (*of*). *Obs.*

c **1450** HOLLAND *Howlat* 519, I sal devoid the of det, Or de in the place. *c* **1500** *Lancelot* 1022 Now help thi-self at neid, And the dewod of euery point of dred. **1535** STEWART *Cron. Scot.* III. 163 To devoid Scotland Of Inglismen. **1548** GEST *Pr. Masse* 80 Howe coulde the bread and wyne serve to hys purpose, yf they were utterly divoided of theyr accostumed nature?

†**5.** To render void or of none effect. *rare*[—1].

1601 BP. W. BARLOW *Defence* 225 Least..the Apostles labour, by their carelesse leuitie, or carnall securitie, should bee deuoyded and abased.

6. To make devoid; to divest. *rare. nonce-wd.*

1878 *N. Amer. Rev.* CXXVI. 372 In any minds, so devoided of their religious sentiments.

†Hence **ˈdeˈvoided** *ppl. a.*, divested, made void.

c **1430** LYDG. *Bochas* I. ii. (1544) 4 b, As a prince devoyded of all grace Against God he gan for to compasse. **1605** TIMME *Quersit.* I. iii. 10 Those things which are made by arte..are deuoided of all sense and motion.

†**deˈvoider.** *Obs. rare*[—1]. [f. DEVOID *v.* + -ER = OF. type *desvuideor*, of which the fem. *desvuideresse*, *devoyderesse*, is recorded by Godefroy.] An expeller, a driver out.

14.. LYDG. *Temple of Glass* 329 O blisful sterre.. deuoider of derknes.

devoir (see below), *sb.* Forms: α. 3–6 dever, (4 deverre), 4–5 devere, (5 deveer, -yr, -ire, -yer, deyver, deffere, 6 debuer). β. 4–6 devor, 4–7 devour, 5 divour, 5–6 devoure, 5–7 *Sc.* devore, 6–7 deavour. γ. 5– devoir, 5–7 devoire, devoyr(e, devoyer, 6–7 devoier. [ME. *dever*, a. OF. *deveir* (= Pr. *dever*, Sp. *deber*, It. *devere*, *dovere*), substantive use of pres. inf. of verb:—L. *dēbēre* to owe. In Eng. the stress was shifted from (dɛ'vɛːr) to ('dɛvər, 'dɛːvər), and this subsequently often spelt *devour, devor, deavour*: cf. ENDEAVOUR. In the 15th c., and *esp.* by Caxton, the spelling was often conformed to Parisian Fr. *devoir*, though, even thus, the stress was still often on the first syllable, *'devoir* being treated merely as a variant spelling of *'devor, 'devour*. *'Dever* occurs as late as the Psalms of Sternhold and Hopkins; but the English tradition of the word died out before 1600, leaving *devoir*, in 16–17th c. often anglicized as *devoyer*, but now commonly treated as if adopted from modern French, and pronounced (də'vwɑː(r), də'vwɔː(r), 'dɛvwɔː(r)); though it would be more correct, historically, to pronounce it ('dɛvə(r)) as in *endeavour*.]

1. That which one ought to do, or has to do; (one's) duty, business, appointed task. (Chiefly in phr. ***to do one's devoir***). *arch.*

α. *a* **1300** *Cursor M.* 21901 (Cott.) All liueand thing on sere maners dos þair deuer [*v.r.* deuerre]. *c* **1315** SHOREHAM 54 And ȝyf hy [clerkes] douth wel hare dever Ine thysse heritage. *c* **1330** R. BRUNNE *Chron.* (1810) 71 Als knyght did his deuere [*rime* austere]. *c* **1400** *Destr. Troy* 234 Do þi deuer duly as a duke nobill. *c* **1430** *Pilgr. Lyf Manhode* I. xli. (1869) 25 To do alwey my deueer. **1462** DAUBENEY in *Paston Lett.* No. 452 II. 103 The Lords..thynk they do ryght well her devyer, and be worthey moche thanke of the Kyng.

β. **1377** LANGL. *P. Pl.* B. XIV. 136 Til he haue done his deuor and his dayes iourne. *a* **1470** TIPTOFT *Cæsar* iv. (1530) 5 Doyng the devoure of myne offyce. **1489** (MS.) BARBOUR *Bruce* XI. 430 Thai stalwardly sall stand, And do thair deuour as thai aw. **1552** ABP. HAMILTON *Catech.* (1884) 35 Do your devore and dewtie. *a* **1605** MONTGOMERIE *Flyting* 443 Whan thae dames deuoutly had done their devore..Of that matter to make remained no more. **1606** HOLLAND *Sueton.* 56 In the Cirque he brought forth to doe their devour Charioteers, Runners and Killers of savage beasts.

γ. *a* **1430** (MS.) CHAUCER *Man of Law's T.*, Head-link 38 (Ellesm.) Thanne haue ye do your deuoir atte leeste [so Hengwrt, *devoire* Petw., *deuer* Corp. & Lansd., *deuyr* Camb., *deuour* Harl.]. **1485** CAXTON *Chas. Gt.* 29 He faylled not to doo gretely hys deuoyr. **1573** *Satir. Poems Reform.* xxxix. 236 And Drurie deulie did his ful deuoir. **1589** GREENE *Menaphon* (Arb.) 90 Democles commanded the deathsman to doo his devoyre. **1608** L. MACHIN *Dumbe Knight* I, What devoyre Drawes you within these lists? **1682** N. O. *Boileau's Lutrin* II. 16 The Rhine shall first his streams mix with the Loire, E're I forget the sence of my Devoire. **1738** WARBURTON *Div. Legat.* I. 28 Exactly perform to one another the Devoirs of Citizens. **1828** SCOTT *F.M. Perth* viii, I think the Knight of Kinfauns will do his devoir by the burgh in peace or war. **1875** W. S. HAYWARD *Love agst. World* 37 Did my worthy brother do his devoir as a gallant knight should?

†**2.** That which one can do, (one's) utmost or best; endeavour, effort. Chiefly in phr. ***to do one's devoir, to put oneself in devoir*** = to do what one can, to endeavour (*to do* something). *Obs.*

α. **1362** LANGL. *P. Pl.* A. XII. 2, I have do my deuer þe dowel to teche. *c* **1460** J. RUSSELL *Bk. Nurture* 659 in *Babees Bk.* (1868) 162 þus y shalle do my devere To enforme yow. **1482–8** *Plumpton Corr.* 59, I shall put me in dever to fullfill your intent. **1537** T. CUMPTUN in Ellis *Orig. Lett.* Ser. II. II. 91, I have..don my debuer accordyng to the teneur of hit. **1549–62** STERNHOLD & H. *Ps.* xxii. 26 And those that doe their deuer To know the Lord shall prayse his name.

β. *c* **1400** *Song Roland* 498 Trist us neuer If we in this mater do not our deuour. **1451** *Paston Lett.* No. 114 I. 154, I..wol put me in devour for to execute your comaundements. **1502** ARNOLDE *Chron.* (1811) 240 Lerne of me and do thy besy deuor From my folke al rauen to disseuor. **1513** MORE *Rich. III*, Wks. 66/2 He woold doe his vttermost deuor to set the realm in good state. **1533** —— *Answ. Poysoned Bk.* ibid. 1072/2 Wening that his owne deuour wer in vaine. **1664** *Flodden F.* iii. 22 Your deavours here are all in vain.

γ. **1470–85** MALORY *Arthur* VII. xxiii, I am moche beholdynge vnto that knyght, that hath put soo his body in deuoyre to worshippe me and my courte. **1509** BARCLAY *Shyp of Folys* (1874) II. 251 Doynge his deuoyr for the same ay to prouyde. *c* **1534** tr. *Pol. Verg. Eng. Hist.* (Camden 1844) 15 The Duke of Bedford exhorted them to defend with all their devoire the dignitie and high reputation of King Henry. **1602** MARSTON *Ant. & Mel.* II. Prol., May we be happie in our weake devoyer. **1671** MRS. BEHN *Forc'd Marriage* I. iv, No, my Erminia, quit this vain devoir, And follow Love that may preserve us all.

†**3.** Service due or rendered to any one. *Obs.*

c **1386** (MSS. after 1400) CHAUCER *Pars. T.* ¶690 (Ellesm.) As Reson is and skile it is that men do hir deuoir ther as it is due [*v. rr.* deuoire, devoyre, deuere, deuyr]. **1502** *Ord. Crysten Men* (W. de W. 1506) II. v. 98 Yf..she yeldeth the deuoure of maryage ayenst her wyll. **1590** MARLOWE *Edw. II*, v. i, To do your highness service and devoir.. Berkeley would die. **1642** CHAS. I in Rushw. *Hist. Coll.* III. (1692) I. 633 [They] shall in no wise be excused of their Service and Devoiers due of their said Lands and Possessions. **1698** FRYER *Acc. E. India & P.* 46 It may be wondred why the French did not assist us..the reality is, they offered their Devoirs, but we must equip their Ships. **1742** YOUNG *Nt. Th.* vi. 292 Monarchs, and ministers, are aweful names; Whoever wear them, challenge our devoir.

4. A dutiful act of civility or respect; usually in *pl.*, dutiful respects, courteous attentions, addresses; chiefly in phr. ***to do*** or ***pay one's devoir(s*** (*to* some one). (The current sense.)

α, β. **14..** *Epiph.* in *Tundale's Vis.* 107 That he hym selffe [Herod] wold after goo Vnto the chyld and hys deyver doo. *a* **1845** HOOD *Faithless Nelly Gray* iv, He went to pay her his devours, When he'd devoured his pay!

γ. **1513** BRADSHAW *St. Werburge* I. 655 This royall maryage was solempnysed..Theyr frendes, cosyns redy on euery syde To do theyr deuoyre. **1669** DRYDEN *Wild Gallant* IV. i, I beseech your ladyship instruct me where I may tender my devoirs. **1673** —— *Marr. à la Mode* II. i, O, my dear, I was just going to pay my devoirs to you. **1676** SHADWELL *Virtuoso* I. i, He's come to pay his devoir to you. **1754** RICHARDSON *Grandison* Let. 14 Oct., I am come down to pay my devoirs to Miss Byron. I hope for acceptance. **1782** *European Mag.* I. 248 She..resisted the devoirs of the tender and pious Lord George Gordon. **1816** J. SCOTT *Vis. Paris* 37 In the inn-yards of our great North-road, when the passing coachmen pay their devoirs to the expectant chambermaids. **1873** BROWNING *Red Cott. Nt.-cap* 141 When he paid devoir To Louis Quatorze as he dined in state. **1880** DISRAELI *Endym.* lxiv, Prince Florestan paid his grave devoirs, with a gaze which seemed to search into Lady Roehampton's inmost heart.

†**5.** *pl.* Moneys due; dues; duties. *Obs.*

[**1360** *Act 34 Edw. III*, c. 18 Paiant lour custumes & autres devoirs au Roi. **1378** *Act 2 Rich. II*, Stat 1 c. 3 Custumes, subsides et autres devoirs de Calays.] **1502** ARNOLDE *Chron.* (1811) 125 The said William Herris sued a plee from the courte Xp̄ian too the court of Rome in a cause of deuors hanging bewixt oon Alis Doughtirlawe of R. S. and the said William. **1503–4** *Act 19 Hen. VII*, c. 27 §1 The Kinges duetie called the devours or Custume of Calays. **1641** *Termes de la Ley* 116b, [tr. quot. 1378] Customes and subsidies, and other devoires of Caleis.

†**6.** A school exercise or piece of home-work. *Obs.*

c **1845** C. BRONTË *Professor* (1857) I. xvi. 264 One day I gave, as a devoir, the trite little anecdote of Alfred tending cakes..to be related with amplifications. *Ibid.* 270, I made a report of the other devoirs. **1849** —— *Shirley* III. iv. 100 Were the faults of that devoir..grammatical errors, or did you object to the substance? **1857** MRS. GASKELL *Let.* 13 Aug. (1966) 464, I should be glad if some one would look over the French dévoirs [*sic*], please.

†**devoir**, *v. Obs. rare.* In 6 dever, devoyre. [f. prec. sb.] *intr.* and *refl.* = ENDEAVOUR *v.*

1530 PALSGR. 514/2 I dever, I applye my mynde to do a thing..I shall devoyre my selfe to the best that I maye.

devoit, obs. Sc. form of DEVOUT.

de'voke, *v. Obs. rare*—⁰. [ad. L. *dēvocāre* (see DEVOCATE): after *convoke, invoke*, which go back to French originals.]

1623 COCKERAM, *Deuoke*, to call downe.

devolatilize: see DE- II. 1.

†**de'volt, -'voult**, *pa. pple. Obs.* [a. Anglo-Fr. *devolt* = F. *dévolu*, repr. L. *dēvolūtus*, pa. pple. of *dēvolvĕre*.] = DEVOLVED.

1531 *Dial. on Laws Eng.* II. xxxvi. (1638) 124 If he.. present not, then the presentment is devolt [*ed.* 1721 devoulte] to the Patriark.

†**'devolute**, *ppl. a. Obs.* [ad. L. *dēvolūt-us* pa. pple. of *dēvolvĕre*: see DEVOLVE.] Devolved, transmitted down.

1460 CAPGRAVE *Chron.* 53 Alisaundre rejoysed the kyngdam of Babilon, that was thanne..devolute to the kyngdam of Perse. **1513** MORE *Rich. III*, Wks. 63 Yᵉ right and title of [the crown of England]..is..deuolute & comen vnto yᵉ most excellent prince yᵉ lord protector. **1531** *Dial. on Laws Eng.* xxxi. (1638) 54 If a Title..be once devolute to the heire in the taile. **1621** R. JOHNSON *Way to Glory* 41 The monarchie of the Romans..became devolute to Julian the apostate. [**1721** *St. German's Doct. & Stud.* 261 Specially if the collation be devolute to the Pope.]

devolute ('dɛvəl(j)uːt), *v. rare.* [f. L. *dēvolūt-* ppl. stem of *dēvolvĕre*: see DEVOLVE.]

1. *trans.* To pass or transfer by devolution; to DEVOLVE.

c **1534** tr. *Pol. Verg. Eng. Hist.* (Camden 1846) I. 127 At the lengthe the monarchie was devoluted to one onlie. **1548** HALL *Chron.* 182 The saied Crowne..should immediatly bee divoluted to the Duke of Yorke. **1570–6** LAMBARDE *Peramb. Kent* (1826) 229 The right of the Advowson was devoluted unto him. **1586** FERNE *Blaz. Gentrie* 31 The coat deuoluted to the bearer from his auncestours. **1891** *Pall Mall G.* 28 July 2/2 The House will devise means of devoluting some of its work to more leisured bodies.

2. *intr.* To lapse.

1893 A. KENEALY *Molly & Man* 24 Some dusky potentate, whose entity and powers had devoluted through the ages.

devolution (dɛvəʊ-, diːvə'l(j)uːʃən). [ad. med.L. *dēvolūtiōn-em*, n. of action f. L. *dēvolvĕre* to roll down: see DEVOLVE and -ION¹.]

I. From the intrans. senses of the verb.

1. *lit.* Rolling down; descending or falling with rolling motion. *arch.*

1623 COCKERAM *Deuolution*, a rolling downe. **1695** WOODWARD *Nat. Hist. Earth* I. (1723) 57 Deterrations, or the Devolution of Earth down upon the Valleys, from the Hills. *Ibid.* (1723) 257 This Deterration..or Devolution of Earth and Sand from the Mountains.

2. *fig.* The rolling or passing on of time; descent or passing on through a series of revolutions or stages, in time, order, etc.

c **1630** JACKSON *Creed* VI. xviii, The possible devolutions or alternations of the reasonable creatures from his antecedent will to his consequent. **1651** *Raleigh's Ghost* 157 After a long devolution of years fulfilled. **1826** C. BUTLER *Life Grotius* I. 3 *heading*, Boundaries and Devolution of the Empire of Germany during the Carlovingian Dynasty. **1841** *Blackw. Mag.* L. 400 Everybody's price of corn must depend on this descent, or devolution as we call it, through ranges of different machinery. **1843** *Ibid.* LIV. 541 The 'devolution' of foreign agriculture upon lower qualities of land and consequently its permanent exaltation in price.

3. Descent by natural or due succession from one to another, of property, or *fig.* of qualities, etc.

1545 UDALL, etc. *Erasm. Par.* Pref. 11 By a moste just and right deuolucion, and dyscent of inheritaunce of the crounes of Englande, Fraunce, and Irelande. **1590** SWINBURNE *Testaments* 291 The legacie is lost without hope of deuolution thereof to the executors or administrators. *a* **1631** DONNE in *Select.* (1840) 130 Now for the riches themselves..he may have them by devolution from his parents. **1706** DE FOE *Jure Div.* IX. 194 If Kings by Jus Divinum wear the Crown, By nat'ral Devolution handed down. **1827** HALLAM *Const. Hist.* (1876) III. xiv. 95 The party of lord Danby..asserted a devolution of the crown on the princess of Orange. **1842** GROVE *Corr. Phys. Forces* (ed. 6) 10 A force cannot originate otherwise than by devolution from some pre-existing force or forces.

4. a. The passing of any unexercised right to the one upon whom it devolves if allowed to lapse.

1593 BILSON *Govt. Christ's Ch.* 349 To loose their right.. by devolution, when they neglected their time aboue sixe monethes. **1656** BLOUNT *Glossogr.*, *Devolution*..a falling into lapse. **1661** BRAMHALL *Just. Vind.* vi. 129 A thousand other artifices to get money. As provisions, Collations, Exemptions, Canonisations, Divolutions, Revocations. **1707** HEARNE *Collect.* (Oxf. Hist. Soc.) I. 337 An Empty Fellow..whom the Archbp. of Cant. Dr. Tennison, put into the Society upon the Devolution to him of that Power. **1712** *Ibid.* III. 331 If it [election of Warden of New Coll.] be not determin'd within 12 Days there will be a Devolution. **1769** BLACKSTONE *Comm.* IV. 62 Vacating the place or office, and a devolution of the right of election for that turn to the crown. **1818** HALLAM *Mid. Ages* (1872) II. 212 The popes soon assumed not only a right of decision, but of devolution; that is, of supplying the want of election..by a nomination of their own. **1872** JERVIS *Gallican Ch.* I. Introd. 23 *note*, 'Devolution' signifies the lapse of a benefice to the Pope, by reason of failure on the part of the patron to present a clerk duly qualified.

†**b.** The passing of jurisdiction upon appeal. *Obs.*

1593 BILSON *Govt. Christ's Ch.* 11 All matters without exception pertaine to Christ's tribunal originally, and not by way of devolution. *a* **1676** HALE (J.), The jurisdiction exercised in those courts is derived from the crown of England, and the last devolution is to the king by way of appeal. **1706** tr. *Dupin's Eccl. Hist. 16th C.* II. IV. xx. 363 Nor shall any Devolution or Appeal be lodged with the Apostolical See. **1726** [see DEVOLVE 3 b].

c. *Sc. Law.* (See quot.)

1861 W. BELL *Dict. Law Scotl.*, *Devolution* is a term sometimes applied to the reference made by two or more arbiters who differ in opinion, to an oversman or umpire, to determine the difference. To confer this power on arbiters, an express clause in the submission is necessary. The term is also applied to the devolution of a purchase made under articles of roup upon the next highest offerer, on the failure of the highest offerer to find caution for payment of the price within the time limited by the articles.

5. The passing of the power or authority of one person or body to another.

1765 BLACKSTONE *Comm.* I. 162 This devolution of power, to the people at large, includes in it a dissolution of the whole form of government established by that people. **1875** BRYCE *Holy Rom. Emp.* xiv. (ed. 5) 236 The complete exclusion.. of any notion of a devolution of authority from the sovereign people.

6. *Biol.* (opposed to EVOLUTION): Degeneration.

1882 H. S. CARPENTER in *Homilet. Monthly* Sept. 688 If there be e-volution, there surely is de-volution, a degradation of the species. **1892** *Pop. Sc. Monthly* XLI. 709 Psychical disease, the progress of which in contrast with evolution is called devolution.

II. From the transitive senses of the vb.

†**7.** The action of throwing down. *Obs.*

1663 BP. PATRICK *Paral. Pilgr.* 303 In those submissions and devolutions of ourselues before our Lord.

8. *fig.* The causing of anything to descend or fall *upon* (any one); the handing (of anything) on to a successor.

1621 SANDERSON *Serm.* I. 169, 2. The suspension of his judgment for his time; 3. And the devolution of it upon Jehoram. **1702** C. MATHER *Magn. Chr.* v. II. (1852) 255 A devolution of certain burdens on the heads of such as were treated with it. **1858** GLADSTONE *Homer* I. 489 A devolution of sovereignty either partial or total, by aged men upon their heirs.

9. a. The causing of authority, duties, or the like to fall upon a substitute or substitutes; *esp.* the delegation or leaving of portions or details of duties to subordinate officers or committees.

1780 T. JEFFERSON *Lett.* Writ. (1893) II. 305 Disappointments which flowed from the devolution of his duties on Deputies acting without a head. **1878** *N. Amer. Rev.* CXXVII. 189 To lighten the cares of the central Legislature by judicious devolution. **1880** GLADSTONE *Sp. in Parlt.* 28 Feb., The day when there may be wisely devised, and successfully carried through the House an important and effectual measure for the devolution of such portions of its powers as may be safely devolved, with the view of lightening its duties. **1888** —— in *Daily News* 6 Nov. 6/2 They were passed by the Grand Committees—passed by the method of what is called devolution. **1889** G. FINDLAY *Eng. Railway* 15 The management of this great service is nothing more than a carefully arranged system of devolution combined with watchful supervision.

b. In Irish politics, with reference to a scheme proposed as a substitute for Home Rule.

1898 J. REDMOND in *Hansard Commons* 4th Ser. LIII. 379 Liberal popular opinion in England is in the direction..of the diminution of the magnitude of the Home Rule question, from 1886 and 1893, down to some scheme of devolution and federalism. **1907** A. S. T. GRIFFITH-BOSCAWEN *14 Yrs. Parl.* 323 In the middle of the summer holidays [1905] the country had been startled by the promulgation by Lord Dunraven and his friends of a plan of 'devolution' of Irish Government, which was neither Unionism nor Home Rule, but a sort of half-way house, in which Irishmen of all persuasions were to live in happiness for ever after. **1907** *Daily Chron.* 9 May 4/6 The vehement language in which some of the Orange Members spoke of resistance to Mr. Birrell's Irish Council scheme might.. almost justify fears of another 'Devolution War'. **1971** *Times* 19 Mar. 21/3 The form of devolution that is peculiar to that corner of the United Kingdom [*sc.* Northern Ireland] will have to be changed.

c. The transfer of some powers from Parliament at Westminster to proposed Scottish and Welsh assemblies; also, the delegation of certain administrative functions from central government to provincial offices in Scotland and Wales.

1889 G. B. CLARK in *Hansard Commons* 72, I think the only solution of the present state of affairs in this House is to have devolution upon the lines of nationality. **1904** W. S. CHURCHILL in *Times* 19 Oct. 5/5 The Irish demand and the Welsh demand for devolution ought not to go forward separately, but together hand in hand. **1929** J. BARR in *Hansard Commons* 10 July 957, I am not emphasising particularly Scottish Home Rule, because I recognise that in all parts of this House there are those who think that some measure of devolution is necessary. **1954** *Rep. R. Comm. Scottish Affairs* 109 in *Parl. Papers 1953–54* (Cmd. 9212) XIX. 1 In 1939 the opening of St. Andrew's House as the headquarters of Scottish administration marked the culmination of a steady process of administrative devolution and transfer of staff from London. **1973** LD. KILBRANDON et al. *Rep. R. Comm. Constitution* xxi. 296 in *Parl. Papers 1973–4* (Cmnd. 5460) XL. 1 We have found it convenient to use the term administrative devolution to cover all arrangements for the conduct of central government business in Scotland, Wales and the English regions. **1978** *Guardian Weekly* 17 Sept. 3 The demand for devolution.. was conceded by the Labour Government not out of conviction but to stem the threatening tide of nationalism.

†**10.** *Math.* = EVOLUTION 4 b. *Obs.*

1690 LEYBOURN *Curs. Math.* 343 Eduction of the Lesser Root by Devolution.

devolutionary (diːvəˈl(j)uːʃənərɪ), *a.* [f. DEVOLUTION + -ARY².] Of, pertaining to, or characterized by devolution.

1896 *Daily News* 1 June 8/3 The symptoms of a coming devolutionary change. **1920** *Glasgow Herald* 17 Apr. 6 He has arresting ideas of the Clyde Valley as a devolutionary unit.

devolutionist (diːvəˈl(j)uːʃənɪst), *sb.* (and *a.*) [f. DEVOLUTION + -IST.] One who believes in or advocates the principles of (political) devolution. Hence as *adj.*

1905 *Westm. Gaz.* 20 Feb. 1/2 Sir West Ridgeway, now a Devolutionist. **1920** *Glasgow Herald* 17 Apr. 6 Everyone is a convinced devolutionist to-day. **1968** *Economist* 11 May 9/2 The Tories' private plans seem more devolutionist than anything yet accepted by Labour.

devoˈlutive, *a.* [f. L. *dēvolūt-* (see DEVOLUTE) + -IVE.] Of, pertaining, or tending to devolution.

1872 JERVIS *Gallican Ch.* I. Introd. 76 Whether the *appel comme d' abus* had a 'suspensive', or only a 'devolutive' effect.

devolve (dɪˈvɒlv), *v.* [ad. L. *dēvolv-ĕre* to roll down, f. DE- I. 1 + *volvĕre* to roll.]

I. *trans.*

1. To roll down; to cause to descend with rolling motion; also to unroll (something rolled up), to unfurl (a sail). *arch.*

c **1420** *Pallad. on Husb.* XI. 497 Thenne hem to the presses they devolve. **1623** COCKERAM, *Deuolue*, to role downe. **1641** MERVIN in Rushw. *Hist. Coll.* III. (1692) I. 217 These like Straws and Chips play'd in the Streams, until they are devolved in the Ocean of their deserved Ruine. **1700** PRIOR *Carmen Seculare* 283 His Thames, With gentle course devolving fruitful Streams. **1758** MURPHY *Orphan of China* II. ii. 18 Where the Tanais Devolves his icy tribute to the sea. **1765** BEATTIE *Judgm. of Paris* lix, Who.. All to the storm the unfetter'd sail devolve. **1846** DE QUINCEY *Syst. Heavens* Wks. III. 171 Where little England.. now devolves so quietly to the sea her sweet pastoral rivulets.

fig. **1610** BARROUGH *Meth. Physick* Pref. (1639) 2 Whose names are devolved and brought unto us by the succession of ages. **1830** TENNYSON *Character*, He spake of virtue.. And with.. a lack-lustre dead-blue eye, Devolved his rounded periods.

†**b.** To roll over so as to cause to fall; to overturn, overthrow. *Obs.*

c **1470** HARDING *Chron.* XCVIII. iv, All his nacyon Deuolued were, and from theyr ryght expelled. **1608** HEYWOOD *Rape of Lucrece* v. iv, They behind him will devolve the bridge. *a* **1658** CLEVELAND *Wks.* (1687) 215 That pious Arch whereon the building stood, Which broke, the whole's devolv'd into a Flood.

†**c.** To roll away (*from* a person). *Obs.*

1654 GATAKER *Disc. Apol.* 10 He was solicitous to devolv and depel from himself.. the note of avarice.

†**d.** To roll (to and fro). *Obs. rare.*

1725 POPE *Odyss.* xx. 35 Ulysses so, from side to side devolv'd, In self-debate the Suitors doom resolv'd.

2. *fig.* To cause to pass down by the revolution of time (*into* some state or condition).

1533 BELLENDEN *Livy* II. (1822) 145 All the soumes, quhilkis war afore devolvit in dett, war commandit to be restorit to thair creditouris. **1545** JOYE *Exp. Dan.* xi. (R.) Thus was the worlde 47 yeris before Crystis birthe deuolued into the fourth monarchie called the Romane and last empyre. **1644** HUNTON *Vind. Treat. Monarchy* viii. 57 That State was then devolved into a Monarchy by Conquest.

3. *fig.* To cause to pass *to* or fall *upon* (a person). **a.** To cause to pass down by inheritance or legal succession (*to* another).

1538 LELAND *Itin.* VI. 31 The Dykes Landes by Heyres generalles is devolvid now to Mr. Goring and to Mr. Deringe. **1590** SWINBURNE *Testaments* 291 The legacie is not devolved to his executors. **1631** WEEVER *Anc. Fun. Mon.* 569 The inheritance diuolued by marriage vnto the Maynards. **1659** B. HARRIS *Parival's Iron Age* 20 They grew to be devolved under the House of Burgundy. **1751** JOHNSON *Rambler* No. 121 ¶5 Students.. can seldom add more than some small particle of knowledge, to the hereditary stock devolved to them from ancient times.

†**b.** To cause to pass (*to* or *into* the hands of another); especially through the failure or forfeiture of the previous holders. *Obs.*

1579 FENTON *Guicciard.* I. (1599) 6 They were diuolued to the sea Apostolike by the disposing of the lawes. **1602** FULBECKE *Pandectes* 32 The State being now.. deuolued to the dregges of the people. **1603** KNOLLES *Hist. Turks* (1621) 1239 Pronouncing their lives, their goods.. to be confiscate and devolved unto the Emperour his cofers. **1622** DONNE *Serm.* clv. VI. 212 By their connivence that power was devolved into a foreign prelate's hand. **1690** LOCKE *Govt.* II. viii. (Rtldg.) 108 War.. naturally devolves the command into the king's.. authority. **1726** AYLIFFE *Parergon* 74 The Appeal operates the Effect of a Devolution; because it devolves the cause to a Superiour Judge.

†**c.** To cause to fall or alight (*on* or *upon* an object). *Obs.*

1601 HOLLAND *Pliny* II. 460 The denomination of these criminall Iudges.. being thus deuolued vpon them, there continued. **1649** MILTON *Eikon.* 30 The King envying to see the peoples love devolv'd on another object. **1667** —— *P.L.* x. 135 Least on my head both sin and punishment.. be all Devolv'd. *a* **1682** SIR T. BROWNE *Tracts* 172 The last excuse devolveth the errour.. upon Crœsus. **1703** DE FOE *Shortest Way w. Dissenters* Misc. 429 When our Government shall be devolv'd upon Foreigners.

d. To cause (a charge, duty, or responsibility) to fall *upon* (any one); *esp.* to throw upon or delegate to deputies duties for which the responsibility belongs to the principal. (Now a chief sense.)

1633 BP. HALL *Hard Texts* 316 All affaires.. of the King's household.. shall be devolved upon his fidelity. **1641** SMECTYMNUUS *Vind. Answ.* x. (1653) 42 He gives this charge not to his Chancellor or Commissary, or any other man upon whom hee had devolved his power. **1754** HUME *Hist. Eng.* I. xiv. 352 He was obliged to devolve on others the weight of government. **1777** ROBERTSON *Hist. Amer.* (1783) I. 183 The Spanish court.. was extremely willing to devolve the burden of discovery upon its subjects. **1818** JAS. MILL *Brit. India* II. v. ii. 354 The master.. becomes too weak to resume the power which he has imprudently devolved. **1847** ADDISON *Law of Contracts* I. i. §2 (1883) 114 A mere honorary churchwarden who.. devolves all the duties of this office upon a paid colleague. **1880** C. H. PEARSON in *Victorian Rev.* 2 Feb. 540 Those who, because they are too busy or too ignorant to discharge the higher duties of self-government, have been glad to devolve them upon their representatives.

†**4.** To throw (a person) *upon* (some resource).

1636 WILSON alias KNOTT *Direction to be observed by N.N.* ii. 17 If the true Church may erre.. we are still deuolued either vpon the private Spirit.. or else vpon naturall wit and judgement. *a* **1672** WREN in Gutch *Coll. Cur.* I. 252, I am now devolved upon that unparalleled villainy. **1675** BURTHOGGE *Causa Dei* 166 He.. then intirely devolves himself on Jesus Christ for it.

II. *intrans.*

5. To roll or flow down *from* (a source). *arch.*

1630 LORD *Banians* 18 (L.) Streams that had in rolling currents, from the tops of the mountains, devolved into the rivers below. **1725** POPE *Odyss.* IV. 34 Two youths whose semblant features prove Their blood devolving from the source of Jove. **1771** SMOLLETT *Ode to Leven-Water* 17 Devolving from thy parent lake, A charming maze thy waters make. **1783** W. F. MARTYN *Geog. Mag.* II. 320 The quantities of snow which devolve from the superior parts of the mountain have sometimes proved fatal to travellers. **1847** R. CHAMBERS *Traditions Edin.* 188 It was a goodly sight to see the long procession devolve from the close.

6. *fig.* To roll or flow on *to* or *into* (some condition).

1579 FENTON *Guicciard.* v. (1618) 197 That the matters.. would with speed diuolue to their perfection. *Ibid.* (1618) 299 The affaires of the Pisans.. did daily diuolue into greater straits. **1678** MARVELL *Growth Popery* Wks. 1875 IV. 300 To raise, betwixt the King and his people, a rational jealousy of Popery and French government, till he should insensibly devolve into them. *a* **1859** DE QUINCEY *Theban Sphinx* Wks. X. 238 Four separate movements through which this impassioned tale devolves.

7. To pass to the next in natural or conventional order. **a.** To pass or fall *to* another, *esp.* through the failure or forfeiture of the earlier holder.

c **1555** HARPSFIELD *Divorce Hen. VIII* (1878) 184 That it should not devolve from himself and his colleague to the court of Rome. **1683** *Brit. Spec.* 66 Yet does not the Supremacy devolve to the multitude, who never yet had right to Rule, or choose their Rulers. **1754** HUME *Hist. Eng.* III. lxi. 322 To him the benefit of all forfeiture devolved. **1765** BLACKSTONE *Comm.* I. 22 Being then entirely abandoned by the clergy.. the study and practice of it [civil law] devolved.. into the hands of laymen. **1786** BURKE *Warren Hastings* Wks. (1842) II. 145 By the death of Colonel Monson, the whole power of the government of Fort William devolved to the governour and one member of the council.

b. To pass down, descend, or fall in course of succession *to* (*on*, *upon*) anyone.

1611 SPEED *Hist. Gt. Brit.* VI. xliv. 150 The Empire thus deuolued to Dioclesian. **1655–60** STANLEY *Hist. Philos.* (1701) 38/2 He had a Brother, who dying without Issue, his Estate devolved to Pittacus. **1689** in Somers *Tracts* II. 341 If a King dies, he hath a Successor, and the Right devolves upon him. *a* **1713** ELLWOOD *Autobiog.* (1765) 3 This Friendship devolving from the Parents to the Children. **1752** JOHNSON *Rambler* No. 198 ¶13 He died without a will, and the estate devolved to the legal heir. **1806** SURR *Winter in Lond.* III. 25 A considerable estate in the Cape of Good Hope, which had devolved to us through a relation of my wife's mother. **1885** *Law Times* LXXIX. 175/1 A service of plate bequeathed by a baronet to devolve with his baronetcy.

c. To fall as a duty or responsibility *on* or *upon* anyone.

1769 ROBERTSON *Chas. V*, V. IV. 418 After Bourbon's death, the command.. devolved on Philibert de Chalons. **1791** COWPER *Odyss.* II. 440 To us should double toil ensue, on whom the charge To parcel out his wealth would then devolve. **1819** J. MARSHALL *Const. Opin.* (1839) 208 By the revolution, the duties.. of government devolved upon the people of New Hampshire. **1860** TYNDALL *Glac.* I. xvi. 107, I knew that upon him would devolve the chief labour. **1884** *Manch. Exam.* 9 May 5/2 They recognise the obligation which devolves upon them.

8. Of persons: **a.** To have recourse *to* (for support); come *upon* as a charge. **b.** To fall or sink gradually, to degenerate. ? *Obs.*

1748 JOHNSON *L.P.*, *Savage* Wks. III. 348 His conduct had.. wearied some.. but he might.. still have devolved to others whom he might have entertained with equal success. **1751** —— *Rambler* No. 149 ¶9 Multitudes are suffered by relations equally near to devolve upon the parish. **1830** J. BEE *Ess. on Foote* Foote's Wks. p. ii, A gentleman and scholar devolving into the buffoon.. is an unseemly sight.

Hence **deˈvolving** *vbl. sb.*

1675 TRAHERNE *Chr. Ethics* xxvii. 427 Tidings of his father's death, and the devolving of his crown and throne on himself.

devolvement (dɪˈvɒlvmənt). [f. DEVOLVE *v.* + -MENT.] The action of devolving; devolution.

1847 in CRAIG. **1892** MISS BROUGHTON *Mrs. Bligh* xv. 336 Arrangements for the temporary devolvement of her philanthropical labours upon a fellow-worker.

Devon (ˈdɛvən). The name of a county in the south-west of England, used *attrib.* or as *sb.* to designate (*a*) a breed of cattle noted for the quality of their milk; (*b*) a breed of sheep.

1834 W. YOUATT *Cattle* iii. 15 The skin of the Devon, notwithstanding his curly hair, is exceedingly mellow and elastic. **1837** *Penny Cycl.* VIII. 454 The North Devon oxen are famed for their docility. *Ibid.*, A cow bred from a North Devon by a Yorkshire bull. *Ibid.*, South Devon nott, brown face and legs, long wool, pure. **1844** H. STEPHENS *Bk. Farm* II. 172 The Devons may perhaps be classed among the Galloways and Angus. **1851** *Ibid.* (ed. 2) II. 144/1 Lord Farnham's Devon ox, slaughtered in Dublin in 1828. **1960** *Farmer & Stockbreeder* 1 Mar. 15/1 Main beef breeds include Shorthorns, Herefords, Devons, [etc.]. *Ibid.*, Other types [of sheep] include Cluns, Kerries, Devon Closewool and pure Down breeds.

b. *Angling.* The name of an artificial fly.

1924 *Blackw. Mag.* Apr. 492/1, I.. fished out across the stream with a heavy Devon. **1960** *Times* 30 Apr. 9/4 Indifference sometimes shown by new run, settled-down salmon, to fly, prawn or devon pulled across their nebs.

Devonian (dɪˈvəʊnɪən), *a.* (*sb.*) [f. med.L. *Devonia*, latinized form of *Devon*, OE. *Defena-*, *Defna-scir* Devonshire.]

1. Of or belonging to Devonshire.

1612 DRAYTON *Poly-olb.* I. 284 Easely ambling downe through the Deuonian dales. **1880** MISS BRADDON *Just as I am* ii, A younger branch of a good old Devonian family tree. **1887** —— *Like & Unlike* xi, The hedgerows were budding in the soft Devonian air.

b. as *sb.* A native or inhabitant of Devonshire.

1882 C. E. MATHEWS in *Athenæum* 23 Dec. 848/1 A treasure not only to Devonians, but to book lovers generally.

2. *Geol.* Name given to a geological formation or 'system' of rocks lying below the Carboniferous and above the Silurian formations; hence, of or pertaining to this formation and the geological period during which it was deposited.

The name was given in reference to the great development of these rocks as a marine formation in Devonshire. The rocks called 'Old Red Sandstone' in Scotland, West of England, and South Wales, are held to be lacustrine deposits of contemporary age, and included in the Devonian System; and the term is applied all over the world to a system of rocks having the same stratigraphical position, and containing organic remains similar to those of the Devonshire strata.

1837 SEDGWICK & MURCHISON in *Trans. Geol. Soc.* Ser. II. V. 701 We purpose therefore for the future to designate these groups [the Cornish *Killas* and the Devonian slates] collectively by the name *Devonian system*, as involving no hypothesis and being agreeable to analogy. **1846** *Expos. Outline of Vestiges Nat. Hist. Creation* 24 The Old Red Sandstone or Devonian System comes next. **1871** LYELL *Stud. Elem. Geol.* 421 The name Devonian was given by Sir R. Murchison and Professor Sedgwick to marine fossiliferous strata which, in the South of England, occupy a similar position between the overlying coal and the underlying Silurian formation. **1873** DAWSON *Earth & Man* v. 84 The Devonian, or, as it may be better called in America, from the vast development of its beds on the south side of Lake Erie, the Erian formation. **1885** *Lyell's Stud. Elem. Geol.* 418 The number of American Devonian plants has now been raised.. to 160. *Ibid.* 419 There were no.. Reptilia during the Devonian age.

Devonic (dɪˈvɒnɪk), *a. Geol. rare.* [f. as DEVONIAN + -IC.] = DEVONIAN 2.

1876 DAVIS *Polaris Exp.* xv. 339 The slaty overhanging layers of Devonic limestone.

devonite (ˈdɛvənaɪt). *Min.* [f. *Devon* + -ITE.] A synonym of WAVELLITE, from its having been first discovered near Barnstaple in Devonshire.

1826 EMMONS *Min.* 214.

devonport: see DAVENPORT.

Devonshire (ˈdɛvənʃə(r)). = DEVON; used *attrib.* to designate various articles produced or animals reared in Devonshire, or characteristic of Devonshire, as ***Devonshire cake, cider, pie, pottery, sheep, tea***; **Devonshire cream** (see CREAM *sb.*[2] 1); **Devonshire slipper** (see quot. 1921); **Devonshire wainscot**, a species of moth, *Leucania putrescens* (see WAINSCOT *sb.* 4).

1747 H. GLASSE *Art of Cookery* viii. 72 A Devonshire squab-pye. **1791** [see REGALE *sb.*[2] 2]. **1807** [see NOT *a.* and *sb.* 3 a]. **1825** H. WILSON *Mem.* III. 113 She gave us most excellent Devonshire cream, and hot Devonshire cakes. **1837** YOUATT *Sheep* vii. 253 The Devonshire notts, or polled sheep used, forty or fifty years ago, to be at least middle-woolled, if not short-woolled sheep. **1845** DODD *Brit. Manuf.* V. 176 Straw-plait... There are several descriptions of plait made in England— such as..the 'Devonshire'. **1858** GEO. ELIOT *Scenes Cler. Life* I. 167 The respective merits of the Devonshire breed and the short-horns. **1881** *Instr. Census Clerks* (1885) 57 Devonshire Slipper Maker. **1893** YONGE & COLERIDGE *Strolling Players* xxxvi. 336 On the mantelpiece some Devonshire pottery. **1907** R. SOUTH *Moths Brit. Isles* I. 310 The Devonshire Wainscot (Leucania (Cirphis) putrescens). So far as the British distribution of this species is known, it seems to be confined to the coasts of South Devon and South Wales. **1909** *Bradshaw's Railway Guide* Apr. p. i (Advt.), Symons' prize medal Devonshire Cyder. **1921** *Dict. Occup. Terms* (1927) §344 *Devonshire slipper maker*; a brown saddler who makes the fitting known as a slipper for one type of lady's side saddle. **1928** E. WAUGH *Decline & Fall* II. vi. 199 The sale of brass toasting forks, picture post-cards and 'Devonshire teas'. **1959** *Listener* 8 Oct. 599/2 Another tasty and satisfying dish is Devonshire pie. **1959** R. D. MACLEOD *Key to Names Brit. Butterflies & Moths* 32/1 L[eucania] putrescens, Devonshire W[ainscot]. **1970** D. CLARK *Sweet Poison* i. 29 Devonshire ice cream. Devonshire cider—Devonshire everything.

Devonshire, *v.*: see DENSHIRE.

devor, obs. form of DEVOIR.

†**devoˈration.** *Obs.* [a. obs. F. *devoration, -acion*, ad. L. *dēvorātiōn-em* (in Vulgate), n. of action from *dēvorāre* to DEVOUR.] The action of devouring or consuming.

1528 ROY *Rede me* (Arb.) 94 [Poverty]..is the goulfe of devoracion And fountayne of desolacion. **1614** T. ADAMS *Devil's Banquet* 72 The decoration of the body is the deuoration of the Substance.

†**devoratory**, *a. Obs. rare.* [ad. L. *dēvorātōri-us* (Tertull.), f. *dēvorātor* DEVOURER: see -ORY.] Of devouring or consuming quality.

1647 TRAPP *Comm. Matt.* vi. 13 Deliver us from those devoratory evils. **1650** —— *Comm. Pentat.* III. 112 These devoratory evills, as Tertullian calleth them.

devorce, -vors(e, obs. ff. DIVORCE.

devore, obs. ff. DEVOIR, DEVOUR.

devoste, devot, obs. ff. DEVOUT.

devot, obs. var. of DIVOT, a sod.

‖**dévot, dévote**: see DEVOTE *sb.* β.

‖**deˈvota.** *Obs.* [It. and Sp., fem. of DEVOTO, q.v.] A female devotee, a *dévote*.

1644 EVELYN *Mem.* (1879) I. 134 The church of St. Prudentia in which is a well..visited by many devotas. **1685** EVELYN *Mrs. Godolphin* 63 This Act of those Devotas.

†**deˈvotary.** *Obs.* [ad. med.L. *dēvōtārius, -āria* (Du Cange), f. *dēvōt-* ppl. stem: see DEVOTE *v.*, and cf. VOTARY.] A votary; a devotee.

1646 J. GREGORY *Notes & Obs.* (1650) 50 Diana..to whose shrine there went up a more famous..pilgrimage of devotaries. *a* **1670** HACKET *Cent. Serm.* (1675) 149 Religious honour is done unto them by some superstitious devotaries.

devote (dɪˈvəʊt), *a.* and *sb.*[1] *arch.* [ad. L. *dēvōt-us* devoted, consecrated or dedicated by vow, pa. pple. of *dēvovēre* to DEVOTE. In Eng. it appears partly as a continuation of ME. *devot, -te*, variant of DEVOUT, OF. *devot, devote*. As a sb. it was generally superseded 1675–1725 by DEVOTEE, and when retained later is usually identified with mod.F. *dévote* fem., and applied only to a female devotee, the corresponding F. *dévot* masc., being occasionally used of the male.]

A. *ppl. a.* = DEVOTED. **a.** with *to*.

1596 SHAKS. *Tam. Shr.* I. i. 32 So deuote to Aristotle's Ethickes [*printed* checkes]. **1597** HOOKER *Eccl. Pol.* v. (1632) 209 The places where Idols have beene worshipped are.. deuote to vtter destruction. **1613** SHERLEY *Trav. Persia* 4 The glory of God, to which his excellent religious mind was evermore devote. **1667** MILTON *P.L.* III. 208 To destruction sacred and devote. **1747** COLLINS *Passions* 105 Where is thy native simple heart Devote to Virtue, Fancy, Art? **1839** BAILEY *Festus* (1854) 107, I am devote to study.

b. without *to*.

1599 HAKLUYT *Voy.* I. 148 We..as your perpetual and deuote friends. **1599** *Warn. Faire Wom.* II. 750, I will be to you a husband so devote. **1621** BURTON *Anat. Mel.* III. i. II. i. (1651) 417 He is thy slave, thy vassall, most devote, affectioned, and bound in all duty.

B. *adj.* = DEVOUT.

[**1225–1552**: see DEVOUT *a.*] *a* **1625** BOYS *Wks.* (1630) 124 By meditation and deuote prayer. **1651** *Serm. Coron. Chas. II*, in *Phenix* I. 244 Trajan the Emperor was, I. Devote at home. II. Courageous in war. **1839** *New Monthly Mag.* LV. 550 The deep drawn sigh—the devote interjection.

C. *sb.* A devotee. †*a.* in form *devote. Obs.*

1630 DAVENANT *Just Italian* IV. Wks. 1872 I. 252 Two faces more allied In all devotes of view I have not seen. **1660** BLOUNT *Boscobel* 8 Sectaries, who through a Fanatique zeal were become Devotes to this great Idol. **1662** J. BARGRAVE *Pope Alex.* VII. (1867) 71 He is a devote of the house of Austria. **1673** *Lady's Call.* I. v. §18 Those who from great voluptuaries have turned devotes. **1717** LADY M. W. MONTAGU *Let. to C'tess Mar* 18 Apr., The difference between an old devote and a young beauty. **1720** WELTON *Suffer. Son of God* I. x. 255 He who seeks to do his Own Will ..has no Claim..to the Peace or Merit of a Devote.

β. in mod.F. form *dévot*, fem. *dévote*.

1702 W. J. *Bruyn's Voy. Levant* xl. 156, I..saw a great many of those Devots pass along the Streets. **1746** LADY M. W. MONTAGU *Let. to W. Montagu* 24 Nov., I know not how to acknowledge enough my obligations to the countess; and I reckon it a great one from her who is a *dévote*, that she never brought any priest to me. **1779** J. ADAMS *Diary* 14 Dec. Wks. 1851 III. 232 Numbers of *dévots* upon their knees. **1808** SCOTT *Lett.* 22 Jan. (1894) I. 92 In her own character as a sort of *dévote*. **1866** MRS. H. WOOD *St. Martin's Eve* xxxi. (1874) 395 Maria, poor thing, had no hand in it; she is not a *dévote*.

†**devote**, *sb.*[2] *Obs.* [f. DEVOTE *v.*] Act of devoting, devotion.

1659 R. EEDES *Christ's Exalt.* Ep. Ded., Some manifestation of a reciprocation in this devote.

devote (dɪˈvəʊt), *v.* [f. L. *dēvōt-*, ppl. stem of *dēvovēre* to vow, dedicate by a vow, devote, f. DE- I. 2 + *vovēre* to vow, dedicate: cf. also the L. frequentative *dēvōtāre*, in med.L. much used for *dēvovēre*.]

1. *trans.* To appropriate by, or as if by, a vow; to set apart or dedicate solemnly or formally; to consecrate (*to*).

1586 A. DAY *Eng. Secretary* I. (1625) 16 Yours devoted till death. **1599** H. BUTTES *Dyets drie Dinner* A iv, Love and friendship..urgeth mee particularly to devote my selfe unto you. **1611** BIBLE *Lev.* xxvii. 28 No deuoted thing that a man shall deuote vnto the Lord. **1665** SIR T. HERBERT *Trav.* (1677) 262 A chalice of gold also he devoted. **1732** LAW *Serious C.* iv. (ed. 2) 48 All Christians are by their Baptism devoted to God. **1802** LD. ELDON in *Vesey's Rep.* VII. 73 The Will..devoting the property to charity was producible. **1856** STANLEY *Sinai & Pal.* i. (1858) 53 Each of the thirty-six chapels was devoted to the worship of a separate sect.

2. To give up, addict, apply zealously or exclusively (*to* a pursuit, occupation, etc., or *to* a particular purpose); *esp.* refl. ***to devote oneself***.

1604 SHAKS. *Oth.* II. iii. 321 He hath deuoted, and giuen vp himselfe to the Contemplation..of her parts and Graces. **1703** ROWE *Fair Penit.* I, Devote this day to mirth. **1798** H. SKRINE *Two Tours Wales* 72 Having devoted some days to the objects in the neighbourhood of Swansea, we left that place. **1868** M. PATTISON *Academ. Org.* 3 Had these endowments..been devoted to national education. **1875** JOWETT *Plato* (ed. 2) III. 672 [He] who devotes himself to some intellectual pursuit. **1894** J. T. FOWLER *Adamnan* Introd. 66 Hill sides now devoted to pasturage.

3. To give over or consign to the powers of evil or to destruction; to doom; to invoke or pronounce a curse upon.

1647 *Power of Keys* vi. 133 The Senate..did devote or Anathematize even a whole Country or Region at once. *a* **1718** ROWE (J.), Let her..Devote the hour when such a wretch was born. **1776** GIBBON *Decl. & F.* I. IX. 181 The hostile army was devoted with dire execrations to the gods of war and of thunder. **1821** LOCKHART *Valerius* II. ix. 267 May Jove devote me, if I had [etc.]. **1871** B. TAYLOR *Faust* (1875) I. xxiii. 206 A witches' guild. They scatter, devote, and doom!

†**b.** To invoke or pronounce (a curse). *Obs.*

1749 FIELDING *Tom Jones* XVI. i, A hearty curse hath been devoted on the head of that author.

Hence **deˈvoting** *vbl. sb.*

1640 O. SEDGWICKE *Christ's Counsell* 222 What was our baptisme but a devoting..of our selves to be faithfull to Christ? **1677** GILPIN *Demonol.* (1867) 434 'Sons of Belial', a name very significant, shewing..their devoting of themselves to the devil's service.

†**devoté.** *Obs.* [An erroneous form of DEVOTE *sb.*[1], or of DEVOTEE, with pseudo-French spelling.]

1729 FIELDING *Love Sev. Masques* III. vi, We must all be proud of so elegant a devoté! **1824** MISS L. M. HAWKINS *Mem.* I. 231 My father was a devoté of Titian.

devoted (dɪˈvəʊtɪd), *ppl. a.* [f. DEVOTE *v.* + -ED[1].]

1. Vowed; appropriated or set apart by a vow or formally; under a vow; dedicated, consecrated.

1594 SHAKS. *Rich. III*, I. ii. 35 To stop deuoted charitable deeds. **1611** HEYWOOD *Gold. Age* II. Wks. 1874 III. 27 All deuoted To abandon men, and chuse virginity. **1623** COCKERAM, *Deuoted*, vowed. **1638** BAKER tr. *Balzac's Lett.* II. 113 A Societie of devoted persons, who continued in meditation so many houres a day. **1663** J. SPENCER *Prodigies* (1665) 381 The Ethnick Temples and devoted places at Rome. **1829** N. WORCESTER *Atoning Sacr.* iv. (1830) 16 Laying the hands on the head of the devoted sacrifice.

2. Characterized by devotion; zealously attached or addicted to a person or cause; enthusiastically loyal or faithful. (Of persons, their actions, etc.)

1600 E. BLOUNT tr. *Conestaggio* 261 Being a devoted servant to the Prior. **1606** MARSTON *Parasitaster* III. i, When you vow a most devoted love to one, you swear not to tender a most devoted love to another. **1777** SHERIDAN *Sch. Scand.* I. i, Sir, your very devoted. **1888** BRYCE *Amer. Commw.* III. xcvi. 348 These democratic institutions have cost the life work of thousands of devoted men.

b. with *to*.

1600 E. BLOUNT tr. *Conestaggio* Ded. A ij, A Gentleman most sincerely devoted to your Honor. **1634** PEACHAM *Gentl. Exerc.* 13 A Gentleman of this Land wholly devoted to Puritanisme. **1791** MRS. RADCLIFFE *Rom. Forest* i, Her heart was devoted to La Motte. **1848** MACAULAY *Hist. Eng.* II. 115 Devoted as Queensberry had always been to the cause of prerogative.

3. Formally or surely consigned to evil or destruction; doomed.

1611 BIBLE *Deut.* xiii. 17 There shall cleave nought of the cursed [*marg.* deuoted] thing to thine hand. **1667** MILTON *P.L.* v. 890 These wicked Tents devoted. **1700** DRYDEN *Theodore & Hon.* 124 He cheered the dogs to follow her who fled, And vowed revenge on her devoted head. **1718** PRIOR *Solomon* II. 543 Round our devoted heads the billows beat. **1741** MIDDLETON *Cicero* II. VI. (ed. 3) 59 He leaves him..a devoted victim to Milo. **1777** PRIESTLEY *Philos. Necess.* 183 All your violent declamation falls upon..my devoted head. *a* **1862** BUCKLE *Civiliz.* (1869) III. i. 16 Another storm burst on the devoted land. **1862** TROLLOPE *Orley F.* xiii, Though the heaven should fall on her devoted head.

deˈvotedly, *adv.* [f. prec. + -LY[2].] In a devoted manner; zealously, enthusiastically.

1812 SHELLEY in Hogg *Life* (1858) II. 137 Believe how devotedly and sincerely I must now remain yours. **1820** SOUTHEY *Ode Portrait Bp. Heber* 4 For this great end devotedly he went, Forsaking friends and kin. **1840** MISS MITFORD in L'Estrange *Life* III. vii. 109 Mary Duff, one of the Maries to whom Lord Byron was so devotedly attached. **1875** JOWETT *Plato* (ed. 2) I. 47 He is a lover, and very devotedly in love.

deˈvotedness. [f. as prec. + -NESS.] The quality of being devoted or zealously addicted.

1668 H. MORE *Div. Dial.* I. xii. (1713) 23, I have very much wondred at the devotedness of some Mens Spirits to the pretence of pure Mechanism in the solving of the Phænomena of the Universe. *a* **1714** M. HENRY in Spurgeon *Treas. Dav.* Ps. xxv. 5 To live a life of devotedness to God. **1827** HOOD *Nat. Tales, Fall of Leaf*, [She] cherished him with all a woman's devotedness. **1872** LIDDON *Elem. Relig.* i. 19 This idea of religion as personal devotedness to God.

devotee (dɛvəʊˈtiː). [An Eng. formation, from DEVOTE *v.* or *a.* + -EE, after words like *assignee, refugee*, etc., in which this suffix came historically from Fr. *-é* of the pa. pple. *Devotee* may be looked upon as a re-fashioning of the sb. DEVOTE, which was formerly used in the same sense: *devote* and *devotee* were used indifferently from *c* 1675 to 1725. (Cf. *assign* and *assignee*.) In early instances, writers or printers sometimes made *devotée*, as if a French feminine: cf. DEVOTÉ.]

1. *gen.* A person zealously devoted to a particular party, cause, pursuit, etc.; a votary.

1657–83 EVELYN *Hist. Religion* (1850) I. 22 Our atheistical devotees to Dame Nature. **1669** HACKET *Let.* in Willis & Clark *Cambridge* (1886) II. 553, I was once an vnworthy member of your Bodie, and will be euer a most affectionat deuotee vnto it. *a* **1670** —— *Abp. Williams* II. §212 (1693) 230 A great Devotee to publick and private Prayer. **1676** D'URFEY *Mad. Fickle* v. ii, Come, my witty Devotees of Venus. **1691** WOOD *Ath. Oxon.* (R.) He [Edward Dyer] was esteemed by some a Rosie-crucian, and a great devotee to Dr. Job Dee. **1788** REID *Aristotle's Log.* iv. §6. 98 A devotee of Aristotle. **1862** BURTON *Bk. Hunter* (1863) 284 As fanatical a devotee of vegetarianism. **1878** H. M. STANLEY *Dark Cont.* II. xiii. 377 He was a devotee to his duty.

2. *spec.* One zealously devoted to religion, or to some form of worship or religious observance; one characterized by religious devotion, *esp.* of an extreme or superstitious kind.

1645 EVELYN *Diary* (1879) I. 208 As much trudging up and downe of devotees. **1698** FRYER *Acc. E. India & P.* 220 Those Vessels set out to carry Devotees to Mahomet's Tomb. **1712** STEELE *Spect.* No. 354 ¶ 1 You have described most sorts of Women..but I think you have never yet said anything of a *Devotée*. A *Devotée* is one of those who disparage Religion by their indiscreet and unseasonable introduction of the Mention of Virtue on all Occasions. **1748** SMOLLETT *Rod. Rand.* xxv. (1812) I. 171 A set of devotees in some parts of the East Indies who never taste flesh. **1780** HARRIS *Philol. Enq.* Wks. (1841) 503 He grew older, became..from a profligate a devotee. **1852** ROBERTSON *Serm.* Ser. III. xvi. 202 The highest form of religion was considered to be that exhibited by the devotee who sat in a tree until the birds had built their nests in his hair.

Hence **devoˈteeism**, the principles or practice of a devotee.

1828 J. HUNTER in C. More *Life Sir T. More* Pref. 56 The spirit of religious devoteeism which appears in his work. **1852** STONE *A. Ballou's Spirit Manif.* vii. 93 Victims of these popular devoteeisms.

†**de'voteless,** *a. Obs.* [f. DEVOTE *v.* (? or *sb.*) + -LESS.] Without devotion; undevout.

1650 W. BROUGH *Sacr. Princ.* (1659) 169 He shall do God and thee good service in these devote-lesse times. **1738** G. SMITH *Curious Relat.* II. 216 To..bend thy knees twice in thy Prayer, with a hundred devoteless wandring Thoughts.

devotely, obs. form of DEVOUTLY.

devotement (dɪ'vəʊtmənt). [f. DEVOTE *v.* + -MENT.]

1. The action of devoting, or fact of being devoted; devotion, dedication.

[**1604** SHAKS. *Oth.* II. iii. 322 He hath deuoted, and giuen vp himselfe to the Contemplation, marke, and deuotement of her parts and Graces. (So Fol. 1; Qq. and Fol. 2 denotement.)] **1621** AINSWORTH *Annot. Pentat.* Lev. xxvii. 29 A devotement was more than a simple vow, whereof there might be redemption, but things devoted had no redemption. *a* **1678** WOODHEAD *Holy Living* (1688) 217 A devotement and a dedication of themselves..to God is then made. **1749** HURD *Notes on Hor. Art. of Poetry* (T.), Her [Iphigenia's] devotement was the demand of Apollo. **1809** SOUTHEY in *Q. Rev.* I. 223 The self-denial and the self-devotement of apostles. **1827** SIR W. HAMILTON in *Life* I. 272 A moderate devotement of time. **1852** WAYLAND *Mem. Judson* (1853) I. i. 29 His own personal devotement to the missionary cause.

†**2.** *concr.* Something devoted; a votive offering. *Obs. rare.*

1799 E. KING *Munimenta Antiq.* I. Pref. 19 Ἀναθήματα, consecrated devotements..inscribed with Greek Letters.

†**de'voteness.** *Obs.* [f. DEVOTE *a.* + -NESS.] Devoutness, devotedness.

1606 G. W[OODCOCKE] tr. *Hist. Ivstine* Ggj a, There are two things which are desired of excellent Princes, Deuotenesse at home, valor in Warre.

devoter (dɪ'vəʊtə(r)). [f. DEVOTE *v.* + -ER[1].]

†**1.** A votary, a devotee. (Cf. DEVOTRESS.) *Obs. rare.*

[**1599** SANDYS *Europæ Spec.* (1632) 4 Where one doth professe himselfe a *Devoto* or peculiar servant of our Lord; whole Townes..are the *Devoti* of our Ladie.] **1634** SIR M. SANDYS *Ess.* 196 [Quoting the above] Where one doth professe himselfe a Devoter, or peculiar Servant of our Lord, whole Towns..are Devoters of our Lady.

2. One who devotes.

1828 in WEBSTER; and in later Dicts.

devoterer, corrupted form of *advoterer*, ADULTERER. (Cf DEVOUTOUR.)

1550 BECON *Gov. Virtue* Early Wks. (1843) 450 The man that breaketh wedlock with another man's wife..let him be slain, both the devoterer [ed. 1566 advoterer] and the advouteress.

†**devo'tesse.** *Obs. rare.* [f. DEVOTE *sb.*[1] + -ESS: cf. DEVOTA, DÉVOTE.] A female devotee.

1658 BRAMHALL *Consecr. Bps.* viii. 193 Are not Governants, and Devotesses, besides ordinary maidservants, women?.. Let themselves be Judges whether a Woman a wife, or a Woman a Governant or a Devotesse, be more properly to be ranged under the name.

devotion (dɪ'vəʊʃən), *sb.* Also 3-6 -cion, -oun, -un, -cyon, etc., 5-6 -tioun(e, 6 -syon. [a. OF. *devocion, -ciun, -tiun* (12th c. in Littré), mod.F. *dévotion* = Pr. *devotio*, Cat. *devoció*, Sp. *devocion*, It. *devozione*, all early ad. L. *dēvōtiōn-em*, n. of action from *dēvovēre* to devote.

The order of development of the senses in L. was (1) the action of devoting or consecrating (to good or evil) by vow, (2) the condition of being devoted (to something good), devotedness, loyalty, fealty, allegiance, (3) (in Christian use) devotion to God and his service, piety, religious zeal. Only the Christian use passed from ecclesiastical L. into the Romanic langs. in the Middle Ages, and appears (with various extensions) in ME. from OF. After the Renascence, the etymological sense 'action of devoting' appeared in It., Fr., and Eng., at first only in reference to religious matters; in the 16th c. the word was extended to secular persons and things; this is specially noticed as a novelty in French in 1578 by H. Estienne (see Hatz.-Darm.). As all the senses are now in Eng., a logical arrangement without regard to history would follow the order, 8 (including 4); 5 (with 6); 1 (with 2, 3); 7.]

I. In religious use: appearing in ME. from ecclesiastical L., through OF.

1. The fact or quality of being devoted to religious observances and duties; religious devotedness or earnestness; reverence, devoutness.

a **1225** *Ancr. R.* 368 Þet oðer þing is heorte þeauwes, deuociun, reoufulnesse, merci..and oðre swuche uertuz. *a* **1300** *Cursor M.* 10123 *heading* (Gött.) Listens now wid gode deuocion. **1340** HAMPOLE *Pr. Consc.* 3459 When þou says praier or orison With over litel devocion. *a* **1400** MAUNDEV. (Roxb.) x. 40 Þai syng þaire messez with grete deuocioun. *c* **1400** *Rom. Rose* 5147 But unto Love I was so thralle..So that no devocioun Ne hadde I in the sermoun Of dame Resoun. **1559** W. CUNNINGHAM *Cosmogr. Glasse* 195 The Sepulcher of Mahomet, which the Turkes go to visite wyth great devotion. **1602** SHAKS. *Ham.* III. i. 47 With Deuotions visage, And pious Action, we do sugar o're The diuell himselfe. **1710** PRIDEAUX *Orig. Tithes* iv. 171 Ethelwulf took a journey of Devotion to Rome. **1848** MACAULAY *Hist. Eng.* I. 199 The austere devotion which..gave to his court the aspect of a monastery. **1854** FABER *Growth in Holiness* xxii. (1872) 421 In theology, 'devotion' means a particular propension of the soul to God, whereby it devotes itself to the worship and service of God.

b. Const. *to, toward* a deity, etc.

c **1384** CHAUCER *H. Fame* II. 158 In somme recompensacion Of labour and devocion That thou hast had ..To Cupido. **1483** CAXTON *G. de la Tour* H vj, This good lady had grete deuocion toward this hooly man and prophete. **1685** H. MORE *Paralip. Prophet.* 244 Extravagant Devotion towards the Martyrs and their Reliques. **1852** ROCK *Ch. of Fathers* III. I. 241 Nothing could be warmer than Catholic England's devotion to the Blessed Virgin Mary.

†**c.** A feeling of devout reverence or awe. *Obs.*

a **1225** *Ancr. R.* 286 Amidde þe redunge..þeonne cumeð up a deuocium & tet is wurð monie bonen. **1601** HOLLAND *Pliny* I. 91 All is still and silent, like the fearfull horror in desert wilderness: and as men come neerer and neerer vnto it, a secret deuotion ariseth in their hearts.

†**d.** A devout impulse or desire. *Obs.*

c **1489** CAXTON *Sonnes of Aymon* vii. 156 Charlemagne was at Parys, and cam to hym a devocyon for to goo in pilgrymage to saynt James in Gales. *a* **1533** LD. BERNERS *Huon* cxvii. 419 A deuosyon toke me to go a pylgremage to the holy sepulture.

2. Religious worship or observance; prayer and praise; divine worship. **b.** *spec.* (*R.C. Ch.*) Worship directed to a special object, e.g. the Sacred Heart, Precious Blood, etc. **c.** An act of worship; now only in *pl.*, worship, 'prayers'. **d.** A form of prayer or worship, intended for private or family use.

1340 HAMPOLE *Pr. Consc.* 7252 For na devocyone Of prayer, ne almusdede, ne messe, May þam help. *c* **1385** CHAUCER *L.G.W.* 1017 *Dido*, Ther Dido was in hire devocyoun. *a* **1450** *Knt. de la Tour* (1868) 137 Her saulter or other bokes of deuocion. *c* **1470** HENRY *Wallace* VI. 127 Quhen sadly thai had said thar deuotioune. **1493** [See DEVOTIONER]. **1548** HALL *Chron.* 126 The churches were seldome used for devocion. **1592** SHAKS. *Rom. & Jul.* IV. i. 41 God sheild: I should disturbe Deuotion. **1624** DONNE (*title*) Devotions upon Evangelical Occasions. **1632** LITHGOW *Trav.* IV. 143 At their devotion, they will not tollerate any women. **1678** LADY CHAWORTH in *12th Rep. Hist. MSS. Comm.* App. v. 52 The Queen..goeing to Somersett House to her devotions. **1710** *Lond. Gaz.* No. 4671/1 To assist at an established Devotion. **1711** STEELE *Spect.* No. 79 ¶8 If they..read over so many Prayers in six or seven Books of Devotion. **1763** J. BROWN *Poetry & Mus.* xii. 211 Church Music in Italy..is considered more as a Matter of Amusement than Devotion. **1858** HAWTHORNE *Fr. & It. Jrnls.* (1872) I. 8 We saw several persons kneeling at their devotions. **1867** FREEMAN *Norm. Conq.* (1876) I. vi. 456 He sent him a splendid book of devotions. **1876** J. P. NORRIS *Rudim. Theol.* I. iv. 70 Devotion, by which we mean the soul's communion with God. **1879** E. WATERTON *Pietas Mariana Brit.* II. 156 The Bead-Psalter..was the popular devotion to our Ladye. **1885** *Cath. Dict.* 393/1 The special and formal devotion to the Heart of Jesus..owes its origin to a French Visitation nun.

†**e.** An object of religious worship. *Obs.*

(But this sense is not very certain, the meaning of the quots. being in every case doubtful.)

1580 SIDNEY *Arcadia* (1622) 277 Dametas began to speake his loud voice, to looke big, to march vp and downe.. swearing by no meane deuotions, that the walles should not keepe the coward from him. **1611** BIBLE *Acts* xvii. 21 As I passed by and beheld your deuotions [*margin* Or, gods that you worship; Gr. σεβάσματα, *Vulg.* simulachra, WYCLIF symulacris, maumetis, *Rhem.* Idols]. *a* **1625** FLETCHER *Double Marriage* IV. iv, Churches and altars, priests, and all devotions, Tumbled together into one rude chaos.

†**3.** An offering made as an act of worship, an oblation; a gift given in charity, alms. *Obs.*

[*c* **1400** *Beryn* 134 To make hir offringis Riȝte as hir devocioune was of sylvir broch and ryngis.] **1542** UDALL *Erasm. Apoph.* II. (1877) 325 To contribute..towardes a sacrifice..other folkes geuing their deuocion towardes it. **1552** *Bk. Com. Prayer* Communion, Then shal the Churche wardens..gather the deuocion of the people. **1581** PETTIE *Guazzo's Civ. Conv.* I. (1586) 43 There commeth on a time ..to crave his devotion, a poore old man. **1626** L. OWEN *Running Reg.* 68 In the lid there is a hole, for people to put their Deuotion in. **1662** *Bk. Com. Prayer* Communion, The alms for the poor, and other devotions of the people.

4. The action of devoting or setting apart to a sacred use or purpose; solemn dedication, consecration.

[A Renascence sense, but connecting itself with the earlier religious uses.]

1502 *Ord. Crysten Men* (W. de W. 1506) v. vi. 408 Deuocyon is as moche to say as dedycacyon, or to be ordeyned to serue god and hym prayse. **1657–61** HEYLIN *Hist. Ref.* II. 55 He built two Altars, the one..by the Lord's appointment, the other..of his own devotion. **1879** LOFTIE *Ride in Egypt* 145 Sometimes the inscription records the devotion of some town or place to a divinity.

II. In non-religious use; introduced in 16th c. from ancient L. through It. and Fr.

5. The quality of being devoted to a person, cause, pursuit, etc., with an attachment akin to religious devotion; earnest addiction or application; enthusiastic attachment or loyalty.

a **1530** WOLSEY in Foxe *A. & M.* (1583) 990/2 For the singular deuotion, whych you beare towardes the kynge and hys affaires. **1577** HARRISON *England* II. v. (1877) I. 117 But vnto this also I haue no great deuotion. **1593** SHAKS. *Rich. II*, I. i. 31 In the deuotion of a subiects loue. **1604** —— *Oth.* v. i. 8, I haue no great deuotion to the deed. **1607** —— *Cor.* II. ii. 21 Hee seekes their hate with greater deuotion, then they can render it him. **1726** LEONI tr. *Alberti's Archit., Life* 5 Lewis..had a very great devotion for the Annuntiata of Florence [a church]. **1830** D'ISRAELI *Chas. I*, III. vi. 100 This fervid devotion to art in Charles. **1865** MISS BRADDON *Only a Clod* I. 9 To attach themselves with slavish devotion to some brutal master.

†**6.** Devoted or attached service; command, disposal. ***to be at the devotion of, at*** a person's ***devotion***, etc. [F. *être à la dévotion de quelqu'un*, 16th c. in Littré], to be entirely devoted to him or her. *Obs.*

1558 in Strype *Ann. Ref.* I. II. App. iv. 5 Men known to be sure at the queen's devotion. **1568** GRAFTON *Chron.* II. 1300 Considering the multitude of them which is come to his majesties devotion. **1581** MULCASTER *Positions* xix. (1887) 80 When they had their whirling gigges under the devotion of their scourges. **1600** E. BLOUNT tr. *Conestaggio* 92 He drew all he coulde to the Catholique Kings devotion. **1623** BINGHAM *Xenophon* 94 Shipping is readie now, and at your deuotion. **1635** R. BOLTON *Comf. Affl. Consc.* i. 139 He stood now before them in bonds, at their mercy and devotion as they say. **1709** STEELE & SWIFT *Tatler* No. 68 ¶5 A little of which [wax] he puts upon his Fore-finger, and that holds the Die in the Box at his Devotion. **1759** ROBERTSON *Hist. Scotl.* I. I. 64 The eight ecclesiastics..were entirely at the king's devotion. **1794** BURKE *Pref. to Brissot's Address* Wks. VII. 315 The *sans culottes*, or rabble..were wholly at the devotion of those incendiaries, and received their daily pay. **1839** *Times* 13 May in *Spirit Metrop. Conserv. Press* (1840) I. 337 Such channels as were at the devotion of the minister.

†**b.** quasi-*concr. Obs.*

1570–6 LAMBARDE *Peramb Kent.* (1826) 215 Such as were of the devotion of the Earle.

†**7.** That to which a person's action, or a thing, is devoted; object, purpose, intent. *Obs.*

1594 SHAKS. *Rich. III*, IV. i. 9 Whither away? *Anne.* No farther then the Tower, and as I guesse, Vpon the like deuotion as your selues. **1646** J. GREGORY *Notes & Obs.* (1650) 27 The devotion of the Reverse [of the Coyne] is to celebrate the..victory of Augustus over all Ægypt.

8. The action of devoting or applying to a particular use or purpose.

1861 M. PATTISON *Ess.* (1889) I. 31 The devotion of a few pages to it. **1885** *Pall Mall G.* 19 Mar. 5/1 The devotion of half a million to the carrying out of railway construction.

†**devotionair.** *Obs. rare.* A variant of DEVOTIONARY with Fr. ending *-aire*.

a **1734** NORTH *Lives* II. 195 Chief Justice Hales, a profound common lawyer, and both devotionair and moralist.

devotional (dɪ'vəʊʃənəl), *a.* (and *sb.*) [f. DEVOTION *sb.* + -AL[1].]

1. Of, pertaining to, of the nature of, or characterized by, religious devotion, or the exercise of worship (see DEVOTION 1, 2).

1648 *Eikon Bas.* 117 Apt for that Devotional compliance and juncture of hearts, which I desire to bear in those holy Offices. **1664** H. MORE *Myst. Iniq.* 257 That high act of Religion and devotional Love which is due to him. **1678** CUDWORTH *Intell. Syst.* 364 There is another Devotional Passage, cited out of Euripides, which conteins a clear acknowledgment of One Self-existent Being. **1769** J. GILLIES (*title*) Devotional Exercises on the New Testament. **1841** W. SPALDING *Italy & It. Isl.* II. 247 The devotional spirit of the older masters. **1859** (*title*) Devotional Helps for the Seasons of the Christian Year. **1860** FROUDE *Hist. Eng.* VI. 244 Contrasting the vexations of the world with the charms of devotional retirement.

2. Belonging to, or arising from, devotion or enthusiastic attachment to a person, etc. *rare.*

1677 GILPIN *Demonol.* (1867) 168 Men are apt to subscribe to anything he shall say, from a blind devotional admiration of the parts wherewith he is endowed.

†**B.** *sb.* A devotional composition; a form of prayer or worship. *Obs. rare.*

1659 GAUDEN *Tears of Church* 87 In their disputings against the Devotionals of the Church of England.

Hence **de'votionalism**, devotional character; **de'votionalist**, one given to (religious) devotion, a devotee; **devotio'nality, de'votionalness**, the quality of being devotional.

1673 H. MORE *App. Antid.* 25 This Image was the Object of the kissing, with all the exteriour devotionalness used therein. **1736** H. COVENTRY *Phil. to Hyd.* Conv. I. (T.) The complete image of a French devotionalist. **1829** *Blackw. Mag.* XXV. 600 Lord Pitsligo was of the first class of devotionalists. *c* **1849** CLOUGH *Poems & Prose Rem.* (1869) I. 299 To believe that religion is, or in any way requires, devotionality, is, if not the most noxious, at least the most obstinate form of irreligion. **1850** ROBERTSON *Life & Lett.* I. 327, I should not say that devotionality was the characteristic of Channing's mind. **1859** *Sat. Rev.* VII. 31/2 Mr. Gladstone's particular variety of sentimental devotionalism. **1883** J. HATTON in *Harper's Mag.* Nov. 833/1 To take in the eclecticism of Greek art, the devotionalism of the Mediæval.

devotionally (dɪ'vəʊʃənəlɪ), *adv.* [f. DEVOTIONAL *a.* + -LY[2].] In a devotional manner; in the way of (religious) devotion.

1668 H. MORE *Div. Dial.* II. xiv. (1713) 131 By studiously and devotionally quitting..his own animal desire thro' an intire purification of his Spirit. **1694** KETTLEWELL *Comp. Persecuted* 135 Read, not only for Instruction, but Devotionally, as Hymns to God. **1891** T. MOZLEY *The Son* xxxii. 206 If people would..read portions of Scripture carefully, thoughtfully, and devotionally, every day of the year.

†**de'votionary,** *a.* and *sb. Obs.* [f. DEVOTION *sb.* + -ARY[1].]

A. *adj.* Pertaining to (religious) devotion; devotional.

1631 J. BURGES *Answ. Rejoined* App. 108 Such priuate deuotionary prayers. **1715** M. DAVIES *Athen. Brit.* I. 219 The first Popish..Confessor..that liv'd in Private Families, and regulated their Devotionary Conduct. **1808** SOUTHEY *Lett. fr. Spain* I. 264 This was a fashionable devotionary receipt.

B. *sb.* A person characterized by religious devotion; = DEVOTEE 2.

1660 WATERHOUSE *Arms & Arm.* 116 [They] haue rifled Academies, and disbanded Convents of Devotionaries. *a* **1670** HACKET *Abp. Williams* II. (1692) 51 A crew of bawds and gamesters might have set up a standing with less prejudice than these devotionaries.

b. *gen.* One devoted or addicted to something; = DEVOTEE I.

1671 *True Nonconf.* 26 The great Devotionaries of ease.

de'votionate, *a. rare.* [f. DEVOTION, after *affectionate, compassionate*, etc.: see -ATE².] Full of devotion, devout.

1864 SIR J. K. JAMES *Tasso* (1865) II. XIII. lxx, To God raised up devotionate appeal.

de'votioner. *rare.* [f. DEVOTION + -ER²: cf. *missioner*.] A member of a guild of devotion; a devotionary.

1883 *Ch. Times* 21 Sept. 655/4 The wives of the devotioners [Brethren of 'the devocyon of the Masse of Ihu.', at Reading, 1493] were honoured with the highest seats or pews next to the mayor's wife's seat.

de'votionist. [f. DEVOTION + -IST.] One who formally professes or practises devotion.

a **1656** BP. HALL *Soliloq.* 73 (T.) There are certain zealous devotionists, which abhor all set forms and fixed hours of invocation. **1676** R. DIXON *Two Test.* To Rdr. 12 Whining Devotionists, floating in their blind and zealous Formalities. **1755** T. AMORY *Mem.* (1769) II. 193 Those doating devotionists of Christendom.

de'votionize, *v. nonce-wd.* [See -IZE.] *trans.* To convert to devotional use.

1894 *Scott. Leader* 1 Mar. 3 Another great fault is the author's tendency to devotionize everything.

†**de'votious,** *a. Obs. rare.* [a. F. *dévotieux*, in 15th c. *devocieus, -eux*, f. *dévotion*: see -OUS.] Full of devotion, devoted. Hence †**de'votiously** *adv.*, †**de'votiousness.**

1583 in Sir J. Melvil *Mem.* (1735) 303 By secret and mutual Conference of devotious and discreet Instruments. **1621** LADY M. WROTH *Urania* 124 Our affectionate seruices ..shall euer..bee most deuotiouslie obseruing to your commands. *a* **1660** HAMMOND *Wks.* I. 234 (R.) By which 'tis clear what notion they had of ἐθελοθρησκεία, to wit, that of devotiousness, piety.

†**de'votist.** *Obs.* [f. DEVOTE *a.* + -IST: cf. *devotee*.] A devotee.

1641 J. JOHNSON *Acad. Love* 85 All such Devotists we enlist in the Hall of Musicke. **1675** OGILBY *Brit.* 52 Shaftsbury..here King Edward 2d..was Interr'd..his Shrine afterwards was so visited by Devotists that the Town for a time bore his Name.

†**de'votive,** *a.* and *sb. Obs. rare.* [f. L. *dēvōt-* ppl. stem: see DEVOTE *v.* and -IVE.]

A. *adj.* Characterized by devotion; ready to devote (himself).

1608 W. WILKES *2nd Memento Mag.* 9 A King..so respectiue of publike good, and deuotiue to the seruice of God.

B. *sb.* A person who devotes himself, a DEVOTEE.

1608 W. WILKES *2nd Memento Mag.* 11 The holy consort of Gods deuotiues.

†**devoto** (di:'vəʊtəʊ), *sb. Obs.* Pl. -oes, -o's, -os; also (as in It.) -i. [a. It. or Sp. *devoto*, devoted, devout:—L. *dēvōtus*; cogn. with OF. *devot*, F. *dévot*, and thus with DEVOUT and DEVOTE *a.* and *sb.* The corresp. feminine is DEVOTA.]

A person zealously devoted to religion or religious observances, or to the service of a cause, person, etc.; a devotee.

1599 SANDYS *Europæ Spec.* (1605) A iv, Where one professeth himself a *devoto* or perculiar servant to [*ed.* 1632, of] our Lord, whole towns sometimes..are the *Devoti* of our Ladie. **1655** GURNALL *Chr. in Arm.* XV. (1669) 163/1 As doubtfully..as the Devil did [speak] in his Oracles to his Devoto's. **1678** CUDWORTH *Intell. Syst.* I. iii. 138 Such Devotoes to the heavenly bodies as look upon all other stars as petty deities, but the Sun as the supreme Deity. *a* **1694** J. SCOTT *Wks.* (1718) II. 375 The Devotos of all religions. **1712** ARBUTHNOT *John Bull* II. ii, Which gave rise to two great parties among the wives—the Devotoes..and the Hitts.

†**de'votor.** [Cf. DEVOTER.] = prec. (for which it may be a misprint).

1648 JOS. BEAUMONT *Psyche* IX. 123 This done: His sacred Hand He lifted up, And round about on his Devotor's dealt His bounteous blessing. [Quoted by R. as *devoto's*.]

†**de'votory,** *a. Obs. rare.* [ad. L. type **dēvōtōri-us*, f. *dēvōtor* he who devotes: see DEVOTE *v.* and -ORY.] Having the function of devoting: see DEVOTE *v.* 3.

1652 GAULE *Magastrom.* 279 Thereupon the Chaldæans set up an imprecatory and devotory libell.

devotour, corrupt f. ADULTER: see DEVOUTOUR.

†**de'votress.** *Obs.* [f. DEVOTER: see -ESS.] A female devotee; a votaress.

1624 *Gag for Poe* 68 Nuns and other deuotresses. **1662** EVELYN *Chalcogr.* 20 Aristotle mentions Daphne a certain Devotresse of Apollo. **1689** J. CARLISLE *Fortune Hunters* 35 Cruel Devotress, will you rob the World Of the but one sweet Angel they have left To add to those vast Millions are above?

†**devouation.** *Obs.* In 5 -acioun. [app. f. F. *dévouer* to devote by a vow: see -ATION.] The act of vowing, a vow.

1428 *E. E. Wills* (1882) 81 Y woll thet myne Executours.. parfourme forth my deuouaciouns forth as I was wonte.

†**devouement.** *Obs.* [a. F. *dévouement* (15-16th c. in Hatz.-Darm.), f. *dévouer*: see DEVOW.] The act of devoting; devotion.

1611 SPEED *Hist. Gt. Brit.* ix. xii. 108 The worthy devouement of some Calisian Townesmen to that certaine perill.

devour (dɪ'vaʊə(r)), *v.* Also 4-6 **devoure,** 5 **-vowre, -vowryn, -vouir, -wore,** 6 **devore, -vower, -voir(e.** [a. OF. *devorer* (stressed stem *devur-, devour-*) = Pr. and Sp. *devorar*, It. *devorare*, ad. L. *dēvorāre* to swallow down, f. DE- I. 1 + *vorāre* to swallow, gulp.] (Formerly often with *up*.)

I. properly.

1. To swallow or eat up voraciously, as a beast of prey; to make a prey of, to prey upon.

c **1315** SHOREHAM 29 He soffreth noȝt to be to-trede, And of bestes devoured. *c* **1400** MAUNDEV. (Roxb.) xiii. 55 Of Babiloyne sall a nedder comme, þat sall deuoure all þe werld. *c* **1430** LYDG. *Chichev. & Byc.* in Dodsley *O. Pl.* XII. 334 Wherfor Bycorn this cruel beste will us devouren at the lest. **1494** FABYAN *Chron.* vii. 12 He..was of wylde bestes or Woluys slayne or deuouryd. **1559** *Mirr. Mag., J. Cade* xxi, Set aloft for vermine to deuower. **1588** A. KING tr. *Canisius' Catech.* Prayers 36 The dragon with his mouthe oppin reddy to deuoire ws. **1650** TRAPP *Comm. Pentat.* I. 70 Like enough to devour up both men and beasts. **1722** SEWEL *Hist. Quakers* (1795) I. II. 120 Turned as a wolf to devour the lambs. **1869** TENNYSON *Coming of Arthur* 27 And ever and anon the wolf would steal The children and devour.

absol. **1610** SHAKS. *Temp.* III. iii. 84 Brauely the figure of this Harpie hast thou Perform'd (my Ariell): a grace it had, deuouring.

2. Of human beings: **a.** To eat greedily, eat up, consume or make away with, as food. **b.** *spec.* To eat like a beast, to eat ravenously or barbarously.

a. **1382** WYCLIF *Rev.* x. 9 He seide to me, Take the book and deuoure it. **1480** CAXTON *Chron. Eng.* ccxxxix. 265 Than they wente vnto the dukes place of lancastre..that was callyd the sauoy, and ther they deuoured and destroyed al the goodes. **1586** B. YOUNG tr. *Guazzo's Civ. Conv.* IV. 187 On Shroftuesdaie night I devoured so much, that yᵉ next daie I had no stomacke to eate anie thing at all. **1833** HT. MARTINEAU *Manch. Strike* x. 110 To devour their meals hastily, as if their time were not their own. **1842** A. COMBE *Physiol. Digestion* (ed. 4) 240 *We* never eat more than enough. *We* never devour lobsters, or oysters, or salmon. **b.** **1603** KNOLLES *Hist. Turks* (1621) 442 A great feeder, so that he seemed rather to devour his meat than to eat it. **1611** BIBLE *Ecclus.* xxxi. 16 Eate as it becommeth a man..and deuoure not, lest thou be hated. **1719** DE FOE *Crusoe* II. ii. 28 The poor creatures rather devoured than ate it.

II. *transf.* With *consume* as the main notion.

3. Of a person or personal agent: To consume destructively, recklessly, or wantonly; to make away with, waste, destroy (substance, property or *fig.* its owners). *Obs.* exc. in bibl. language.

a **1340** HAMPOLE *Psalter* Cant. 511 Him þat deuours þe pore in hidil. **1382** WYCLIF *Ps.* xxxiv. 25 Ne sei thei, wee shal devouren hym. **1382** —— *Luke* xv. 30 This thi sone, which deuouride his substaunce with hooris. *c* **1386** CHAUCER *Reeve's T.* 66 He wolde his joly blood honoure, Though that he schulde holy chirche deuoure. **1393** LANGL. *P. Pl.* C. XVII. 280 Lightliche þat þei leue loseles hit deuouren. *c* **1460** FORTESCUE *Abs. & Lim. Mon.* iii. (1885) 115 The reaume of Englonde..wolde be than a pray to all oþer nacions þat wolde conqwer, robbe, and deuouir it. **1655** STANLEY *Hist. Philos.* I. (1701) 23/1 If any one maintain not his Parents, let him be infamous, as likewise he that devours his patrimony. **1657** J. SMITH *Myst. Rhet.* 19 So we say of some Guardians, They have devoured the Orphans, intimating the Orphans' patrimony.

b. with the sense *swallow up* more or less present: cf. 5.

1382 WYCLIF *Mark* xii. 40 Scribis..whiche deuouren the housis of widewis. **1526** *Pilgr. Perf.* (W. de W. 1531) 140 Ye ..rape and deuour the almes and sustenaunce of the poore seruauntes of god. **1602** MARSTON *Ant. & Mel.* I. Wks. 1856 I. 11 She..Inticeth princes to devour heaven, Swallow omnipotence, out-stare dread fate. **1697** DRYDEN *Virg. Past.* III. 6 Thou, Varlet, dost thy Master's gains devour. **1836** HOR. SMITH *Tin Trump.* (1876) 144 Wherever Religion has been the mother of wealth the daughter has invariably devoured the parent.

†**c.** To make a prey of, treat with rapine. *Obs.*

1530 PALSGR. 515/1 He hath devoured twenty maydens and wyves agaynst their wylles in his dayes. *c* **1540** in Knox *Hist. Ref.* Wks. 1846 I. 73 Seikand Christes peple to devoir. **1547** SALESBURY *Welsh Dict.*, *Teisio morwyn*, devoure a mayden.

†**d.** To despoil (a person) *of* (substance) by consuming it. *Obs. rare*⁻¹.

1545 BRINKLOW *Compl.* iv. (1874) 17 Let them make good defence, that their poore neyhbors..be not deuouryd of their corne and grasse.

4. Of inanimate agencies: To consume, destroy. Said esp. of fire, sword, pestilence, or other agencies which claim numerous victims.

c **1374** CHAUCER *Anel. & Arc.* 14 This old story..That eild..hath nigh devoured oute of my memory. **1382** WYCLIF *Joel* ii. 3 Before the face of hym fijr deuourynge, and after hym brenyng flawme. **1393** GOWER *Conf.* I. 339 So that no life shall be socoured, But with the dedely swerd devoured. **1538** STARKEY *England* I. ii. 46 Etyn away, dayly deuouryd and consumyd by commyn syknes and dysease. **1579** GOSSON *Sch. Abuse* (Arb.) 39 Stir Iupiter to anger to send vs a Stroke that shal deuoure vs. **1652** NEEDHAM tr. *Selden's Mare Cl.* 266 The Earth did not bring forth its Fruits..but devoured very many people by famine. **1665** SIR T. HERBERT *Trav.* (1677) 210 But the Monument..is not now to be seen, for Time has devoured it. **1667** MILTON *P.L.* XII. 183 Haile mixt with fire must rend th' Egyptian Skie And wheel on th' Earth, devouring where it rouls. *a* **1711** KEN *Hymnotheo* Poet. Wks. 1721 III. 300 Their Beings no Corruption can devour, Annihilable by sole boundless Power. **1863** FR. A. KEMBLE *Resid. in Georgia* 69 The flames devouring the light growth. **1874** STUBBS *Const. Hist.* I. iv. 61 Whom the sword spared famine and pestilence devoured.

III. With *swallow* as the main notion.

5. Of water, the earth, etc.: To swallow up, engulf.

1555 EDEN *Decades* 92 He had seene many Culchas deuoured of whirlepoles. **1590** SHAKS. *Mids. N.* I. i. 148 The iawes of darknesse do deuoure it vp. **1602** MARSTON *Antonio's Rev.* IV. iv. Wks. 1856 I. 128 The very ouze, The quicksand that devours all miserie. **1614** RALEIGH *Hist. World* II. IV. i. §4. 135 Those that tooke the Sea, were therein deuoured ere they recouered them. **1783** CRABBE *Village* I. Wks. 1834 II. 79 The ocean roar Whose greedy waves devour the lessening shore.

6. Of persons: **a.** To take in greedily and with eagerness the sense of (a book, discourse, or the like).

1581 PETTIE tr. *Guazzo's Civ. Conv.* II. (1586) 63 They have devoured all sortes of bookes. **1604** SHAKS. *Oth.* I. iii. 150 She'l'd come againe, and with a greedie eare Deuoure vp my discourse. **1647** TRAPP *Comm. Epistles* 530 Ministers must so devour and digest the holy Scriptures, that [etc.]. **1753** A. MURPHY *Gray's-Inn Journ.* No. 40 ¶2 Miss Vainlove devoured up these Expressions of Admiration with a greedy Ear. **1823** SCOTT *Quentin D.* Introd., He devoured the story of the work with which he was engaged. **1831** BREWSTER *Newton* (1855) I. i. 15 Devouring some favourite author. **1850** KINGSLEY *Alt. Locke* i. (1876) 11 Missionary tracts..how I devoured them. **1878** R. H. HUTTON *Scott* ii. 19 He learned Spanish and devoured Cervantes.

b. To take in eagerly with the eyes; to look upon with avidity.

1621 BURTON *Anat. Mel.* III. ii. III. (1676) 312/1 Drink to him with her eyes, nay drink him up, devour him, swallow him as Martial's Mammurra is remembered to have done. **1697** DRYDEN *Virg. Georg.* II. 645 Early Visitants, With eager Eyes devouring..The breathing Figures of Corinthian Brass. **1718** PRIOR *Solomon* II. 381 With an unguarded look she now devour'd My nearer face. **1870** MORRIS *Earthly Par.* II. III 57 His eyes devoured her loveliness. **1891** I. ZANGWILL *Bachelors Club* 186 The Doctor devoured her with his eyes.

c. To absorb greedily or selfishly.

1647-8 COTTERELL *Davila's Hist. Fr.* (1678) 11 The House of Guise in a manner devoured all the Chief Employments of the State.

d. To swallow or suppress within one's own breast (chagrin, grief, etc.).

1650 TRAPP *Comm. Pentat.* I. 262 To persevere in prayer, and to devour all discouragements. **1820** SCOTT *Abbot* xxxviii, Catherine Seyton devoured in secret her own grief. **1850** PRESCOTT *Peru* II. 182 Devouring his chagrin as he best could.

7. Of things: **a.** To occupy (a person) so as to engross the attention; to absorb.

(Sometimes including the notion of consuming (4) or of swallowing up (5))

1500-20 DUNBAR *Poems* xiv. 81 Devorit with dreme, devysing in my slummer. **1608** SHAKS. *Per.* IV. iv. 25 Pericles, in sorrow all devour'd, With sighs shot through, and biggest tears o'ershower'd, Leaves Tarsus and again embarks. **1715-20** POPE *Ep. Addison* 41 Poor Vadius, long with learned spleen devour'd, Can taste no pleasure since his Shield was scour'd. **1863** MRS. OLIPHANT *Sal. Ch.* xxi. 25 She walked home with Beecher, devoured by feverish hopes and fears. **1865** M. ARNOLD *Ess. Crit.* ii. (1875) 79 Not to hold ideas of this kind a little more easily, to be so devoured by them, to suffer them to become crotchets.

b. To absorb so as to do away with.

1625 E. TILMAN in Ellis *Orig. Lett.* Ser. II. III. 244 The joy of the people devoured their mourning. **1875** HELPS *Ess., Pract. Wisd.* 5 The large hands and feet of a dwarf seem to have devoured his stature.

8. Phrases. †**a.** *to devour difficulties* [F. *dévorer les difficultés*]: to tackle and overcome difficulties with spirit. *Obs.* **b.** *to devour the way, course*, etc. [F. *dévorer l'espace*]; to get over the ground with great rapidity.

1597 SHAKS. *2 Hen. IV*, I. i. 47 He seem'd in running, to deuoure the way, Staying no longer question. **1642** ROGERS *Naaman* 128 She will hold close to her own tacklings and devour a great deale of difficulty. **1648** SANDERSON *Serm. Ad Aulam* xvi. §25 (1674) 230 He that setteth forth for the goal, if he will obtain, must resolve to devour all difficulties, and to run it out. *a* **1661** FULLER *Worthies* (1840) III. 190 Wat Tyler was woundly angry with Sir John Newton, Knight.. for devouring his distance, and not making his approaches mannerly enough unto him. **1725** POPE *Odyss.* VIII. 102 None..swifter in the race devour the way. **1772** PEGGE tr. *Fitzstephen's Descr. London* 38 The signal once given, they [the horses] strike, devour the course [*cursum rapiunt*], hurrying along with unremitting velocity. **1883** HOLME LEE *Loving & Serving* II. xiii. 271 The strong black horse was very fresh, and devoured the road before him.

de'vourable, *a.* [f. DEVOUR *v.* + -ABLE: cf. 16th c. F. *devor-, devourable*, L. *dēvorābilis*.] Capable of being devoured; consumable.

1603 HOLLAND *Plutarch's Mor.* II. 116 (L.) A clear and undebauch'd appetite renders every thing sweet and delightful to a sound body, and devourable. **1615** HIERON *Wks.* I. 602 Fier burnes vp..such as is deuourable by it. **1725** SLOANE *Jamaica* II. 2 Any papers or other goods devourable by them are put up in chests of this wood. **1826** *Blackw. Mag.* XIX. 335 The editors..seized on the devourable parts, and gave both islands a feast.

devourer (dɪˈvaʊərə(r)). Also 5 -our, -ar. [ME. *devourour*, a. AF. *devorour* = OF. *devoreor*, *devoreeur* (12th c. in Godef.):—*dēvorātōr-em*, agent-n. from *dēvorāre* to DEVOUR.]

1. One who devours; one who eats greedily or voraciously.

1382 WYCLIF *Matt.* xi. 19 A man deuourer, or glotoun. **1398** TREVISA *Barth. De P.R.* XVIII. lxvi. (1495) 822 The lyon is a deuourer of meete wythout chewynge. **1399** LANGL. *Rich. Redeles* III. 371 Devourours of vetaile. **1555** EDEN *Decades* 48 Men which are deuourers of mans fleshe. **1664** EVELYN *Kal. Hort.* (1729) 209 Earwigs..are cursed Devourers. **1796** MORSE *Amer. Geog.* I. 219 They..move slowly, but reluctantly, towards the yawning jaws of their devourers. **1884** G. F. BRAITHWAITE *Salmonidæ of Westmorland* vi. 26 It is a devourer of the spawn of salmon.

2. *transf.* and *fig.* One who or that which consumes, destroys, swallows up, or absorbs.

c **1385** CHAUCER *L.G.W.* 1369 *Hypsip.*, Duk Iason Thou sly [*v.r.* sleer] deuourere.. Of tendere wemen. *c* **1470** HENRY *Wallace* x. 492 Thou renygat deuorar off thi blud. **1580** BARET *Alv.* D 624 An vnsatiable reader: a deuourer of bookes. **1586** T. B. *La Primaud. Fr. Acad.* I. 622 Achilles offering great injuries to Agamemnon..called him Devourer of the people. **1659** *Gentl. Calling* (1696) 82 Gaming, like a Quick Sand, swallows up a Man in a moment ..Hawks, and Hounds and Horses, &c. are somewhat slower devourers. **1698** WANLEY *Wond. Lit. World* III. xliv. §30. 228/1 The Eye that is the devourer of such beautiful Objects. **1890** *Spectator* 7 June 799 The shallowest novel-devourer will find in it excitement enough.

† **deˈvouress.** *Obs.* [short for *devoureress*, a. OF. *devoureresse*, *-voreresse*, fem. of *devorere*, *devoreor* DEVOURER.] A female devourer.

1382 WYCLIF *Ezek.* xxxvi. 13 Thou art a deuouresse of men. **1598** YONG *Diana* 428 The fierce deuouresse of my life approoued..As fell in hart, as she is faire in face. **1611** FLORIO, *Diuoratrice*, a deuouresse.

deˈvouring, *vbl. sb.* [f. DEVOUR *v.* + -ING[1].] The action of the verb DEVOUR.

1382 WYCLIF *Tobit* xii. 3 Me myself fro the deuouring of the fish he delyuerede. **1398** TREVISA *Barth. De P.R.* XIII. xxvi. (1495) 457 They byte other wyth vnresonable swalowynge and deuourynge. **1577** B. GOOGE *Heresbach's Husb.* IV. (1586) 187 b, Many times, they [bees] die of a disease that they call the great devouring. **1659** *Gentl. Calling* (1696) 70 The more ravenous devourings of the Vulture.

devouring, *ppl. a.* [f. DEVOUR *v.* + -ING[2].] That devours, in various senses of the word.

1382 WYCLIF *Isa.* xxix. 6 Gret vois of whirlewind, and of tempest, and of flaume of fijr deuourende [**1388** fier deuowrynge]. **1590** SPENSER *F.Q.* I. vii. 48 His biting Sword, and his devouring Speare. **1634** SIR T. HERBERT *Trav.* 140 Where the two famous Rivers Tygris..and Euphrates..become one with the same devouring Gulph. **1724** R. FALCONER *Voy.* (1769) 63 For fear some devouring Creature should come and seize me. **1751** JORTIN *Serm.* (1771) VII. i. 21 Avoid the devouring deep. **1810** SOUTHEY *Kehama* I. xiv, Devouring flames have swallow'd all. **1818** SHELLEY *Rev. Islam* VIII. xix, Ye are the spoil Which Time thus marks for the devouring tomb.

Hence **deˈvouringly** *adv.*; **deˈvouringness.**

1552 HULOET, Deuouryngiye, *voraciter.* **1600** F. WALKER *Sp. Mandeville* 23 a, It was a thing of admiration, to see how deuouringly he eat and drank. **1611** FLORIO, *Diuoracità*, deuouringnesse, greedinesse. **1837** CAMPBELL in *Athenæum* 11 Mar. 173/3 My Mauritanian beauties are devouringly fond of puppies. They gobble them up by litters in their couscousou. **1887** MRS. C. PRAED *Bond of Wedlock* I. vii. 184 His eyes fixed devouringly upon her.

devourment (dɪˈvaʊəmənt). [f. DEVOUR *v.* + -MENT.] The action of devouring or consuming.

1828 *Blackw. Mag.* XXIII. 601 His faculties of devourment were next to boundless. **1841** J. T. HEWLETT *Parish Clerk* II. 77 Supper announced to be ready for their 'devourment'. **1891** *Fun* 3 June 233/2 We approached the devourment of this book with the keenest relish.

devout (dɪˈvaʊt), *a.* and *sb.* Forms: α. 3–5 (6 *Sc.*) devot, 3–7 (9 *arch.*) devote, (4 devoste), 6 *Sc.* devoit, divoit, divot. β. 3– devout, 4–5 devowt(e, 4–6 devoute. [ME. *devot*, *devout*, a. OF. *devot*, *devote* (12th c. in Littré), = Pr. *devot*, Sp. *devoto*, It. *divoto*, ad. L. *dēvōt-us* devoted, given up by vow, pa. pple. of *dēvovēre* to DEVOTE. The close OF. *ō* became the vowel *ou* (uː) in ME., whence the modern diphthong *ou*; but a form in *ō*, Sc. *oi*, was also in use: see DEVOTE *a.*]

1. Devoted to divine worship or service; solemn and reverential in religious exercises; pious, religious.

α. *a* **1225** *Ancr. R.* 376 þuruh aromaz, þet beoð swote, is understonden swotnesse of deuot heorte. *c* **1325** *E.E. Allit. P.* A. 406 Be dep deuote in hol mekenesse. *c* **1400** MAUNDEV. (Roxb.) viii. 30 þai er deuote men and ledez pure lyf. **1535** STEWART *Cron. Scot.* II. 567 Diuoit he wes with mony almous deid. **1549** *Compl. Scot.* (1872) 4 The deuot Kyng, Numa pompilius. **1651** [see DEVOTE *a.*].

β. **1297** R. GLOUC. (1724) 369 In chyrche he was deuout ynou. **1382** WYCLIF *Ex.* xxxv. 29 Alle men and wymmen with a deuowt mynde offerden ȝiftis. *c* **1440** *Promp. Parv.* 120 Devowte, *devotus.* *a* **1450** *Knt. de la Tour* (1868) 7 A shorte orison, saide with good devouute herte. *c* **1511** *1st Eng. Bk. Amer.* (Arb.) Introd. 31/2 These people be very deuoute. **1530** PALSGR. 310/1 Devoute, holy disposed to praye, *deuot.* **1636** SIR H. BLOUNT *Voy. Levant* (1637) 87 All the devouter sort (which are not many) goe to Church, and say their prayers. **1732** LAW *Serious C.* i. (ed. 2) 1 He..is the devout Man who lives no longer to his own will..but to the sole will of God. **1865** M. ARNOLD *Ess. Crit.* ix. (1875) 398 The devoutest of your fellow Christians. **1883** FROUDE *Short Stud.* IV. II. ii. 185 Keble was a representative of the devout mind of England.

†**b.** *gen.* Devoted, religiously or reverently attached (*to* a person or cause). *Obs.*

c **1380** WYCLIF *Serm.* Sel. Wks. I. 113 God wolle have oure herte devoute to him wiþouten ende. *c* **1450** *St. Cuthbert* (Surtees) 6953 To saint cuthbert he was deuoute. **1609** BIBLE (Douay) *Comm.* 201 Isaac was..devout to God. **1659** B. HARRIS *Parival's Iron Age* 205 Sir Thomas Wentworth..became the most devout friend of the Church.

2. Of actions and things: Showing or expressing devotion; reverential, religious, devotional.

α. *a* **1340** HAMPOLE *Psalter*, Cant. 502 þe deuot ȝernyngis of his halighis. *c* **1500** *Blowbol's Test.* in Halliwell *Nugae Poet.* 3 He wold syng Foure devoite masses at my biryng. *a* **1541** BARNES *Wks.* 318 (R.), To help mee wyth his deuote prayer. **1552** ABP. HAMILTON *Catech.* (1884) 8 Faithful and devoit prayar. **1625**– [see DEVOTE *a.*].

β. *c* **1340** HAMPOLE *Prose Tr.* 24 Deuoute prayers, feruent desires, and gostely meditacions. **1526** (*title*), The Pylgrymage of Perfeccyon, a devoute Treatyse in Englysshe. **1603** KNOLLES *Hist. Turks* (1621) 78 The devout warre, taken in hand for the reliefe of the poore Christians in Syria. **1667** MILTON *P.L.* XI. 863 With uplifted hands, and eyes devout. **1763** JOHN BROWN *Poetry & Mus.* xii. 214 Our parochial Music..is solemn and devout. **1841** ELPHINSTONE *Hist. Ind.* II. 347 In his writings, he affects the devout style usual to all Mussulmans.

3. Earnest, sincere, hearty.

1828 WEBSTER *s.v.*, You have my devout wishes for your safety. **1880** MRS. LYNN LINTON *Rebel of Family* I. v, The sanctity of caste, in which she..was so devout a believer.

B. as *sb.* †**1.** A devotee. *Obs.*

[*c* **1440** *Gesta Rom.* xcii. 419 (Add. MS.) This knyght had a good woman to wife, and a deuoute to oure ladie.] **1616** R. SHELDON *Miracles Antichrist* 247 (T.) Not..the ordinary followers of Antichrist, but..his special devouts. **1675** tr. *Machiavelli's Prince* xv. (Rtldg. 1883) 98 One a devout, another an atheist.

2. That which is devout; the devotional part.

1649 MILTON *Eikon.* i. (1851) 344 This is the substance of his first Section, till we come to the devout of it, model'd into the form of a privat Psalter.

† **deˈvout,** *v. Obs.* Variant of DEVOTE *v.*

1605 STOW *Chron.* an. 1603 (R.) Hee shewed himselfe a well deuouted Christian. **1639** DRUMM. OF HAWTH. *Libraries* Wks. (1711) 223 How much is Florence adebted.. to Bessarion..who at his death devouted to it a library. **1651** tr. *Bacon's Life & Death* 15 A Man peaceable, Contemplative and much devouted to Religion.

‖**deˈvoutement,** *adv. Obs. rare.* [a. OF. *devotement* (in AF. *devou-*).] Devoutly.

a **1400** *Octouian* 63 The holy pope Seynt Clement.. prayede God deuoutement..That [etc.].

† **deˈvoutful,** *a. Obs.* [irreg. f. DEVOUT *a.* + -FUL: (a suffix properly added to a sb.).] Full of devoutness; devout, pious.

1597 DANIEL *Civ. Wars* I. xiv, Richard..who..all his fathers mighty treasure spent, In that devoutfull Action of the East. **1598** TOFTE *Alba* (1880) 28 As painfull Pilgrim in deuoutfull wise. **1604** MARSTON & WEBSTER *Malcontent* I. i, To make her his by most devoutful rites.

† **deˈvoutless,** *a. Obs. rare*[−0]. [irreg. f. as prec. + -LESS; cf. DEVOTELESS.] Without devoutness, undevout. Hence † **deˈvoutlessness.**

1576 R. CURTIS *Two Serm.* C vj b (T.), The darts of devoutlessness, unmercifulness, and epicurisme..fly abrode.

devoutly (dɪˈvaʊtlɪ), *adv.* Also 4–6 deuote-: see DEVOUT *a.* [f. DEVOUT *a.* + -LY[2].]

1. In a devout manner; reverently, piously, religiously.

α. *c* **1325** *Metr. Hom.* 160 And ilke day deuotely, Herd scho messe of our Lefdye. *c* **1380** WYCLIF *Wks.* (1880) 319 To preye deuoteliche. *c* **1400** MAUNDEV. (Roxb.) xv. 69 ȝe serue ȝour Godd wele and deuotely. ? *c* **1500** *How Plowman lerned Pater Noster* 42 in Hazl. *E.P.P.* I. 211 Late me here The saye devotely thy pater noster. **1588** A. KING tr. *Canisius' Catech.* 34 Prayers..quhan thay in yͤ name off Iesus Christ, ar humblie and deuotlie desyrit, helpis mony.

β. *c* **1325** *E.E. Allit.* P. B. 814 His two dere doȝterez deuoutly hem haylsed. *c* **1400** MAUNDEV. (Roxb.) xvii. 76 He serued Godd full deuoutely. *c* **1489** CAXTON *Blanchardyn* xxxvii. 137 They sholde deuoutly do baptyse hem self. **1568** *Knt. of Curtesy* 451 She confessed her devoutly tho, And shortely receyved the Sacrament. *c* **1611** DONNE *Poems* (1633) 275 Who dream'd devoutlier then most use to pray. **1781** GIBBON *Decl. & F.* II. 137 Julian most devoutly ascribes his miraculous deliverance to the protection of the Gods. **1849** JAMES *Woodman* iv, She crossed herself devoutly.

2. Earnestly, sincerely, fervently.

1602 SHAKS. *Ham.* III. i. 64 'Tis a consummation Deuoutly to be wish'd. **1605** CAMDEN *Rem.* (1637) 349 His devote minde to his Lady hee devoutly, though not religiously shewed. **1795** SOUTHEY *Joan of Arc* I. 219 Childhood..Listening with eager eyes and open lips Devoutly in attention. **1814** SCOTT *Wav.* lxvii, Let us devoutly hope, that..we shall never see the scenes..that were general in Britain Sixty Years since. **1874** MORLEY *Compromise* (1886) 113 Men were then devoutly persuaded that their eternal salvation depended on their having true beliefs.

devoutness (dɪˈvaʊtnɪs). [f. as prec. + -NESS.] The quality of being devout; reverential spirit or character; religiousness, piety.

1377 *Pol. Poems* (Rolls) I. 217 Nou is devoutnes out icast. **1530** PALSGR. 213/2 Devoutnesse, *deuotion.* *a* **1680** GLANVILL *Serm.* 52 (T.) There are some who have a sort of devoutness and religion in their particular complexion. **1840** CARLYLE *Heroes* (1858) 221 What devoutness and noblemindedness had dwelt in these rustic thoughtful peoples. **1874** MORLEY *Compromise* (1886) 178 Religiosity or devoutness of spirit.

devoutour, -trour, corrupted forms of *advoutour*, *advoutrer*, ADULTER, -ERER. (Cf. DEVOTERER.) So **devoutrie** for *advoutrie*, ADULTERY.

1377 LANGL. *P. Pl.* B. II. 175 Owre synne to suffre, As deuoutrie [*other MSS.* aduoutrie] and deuo[r]ses and derne vsurye. **1393** *Ibid.* C. III. 184 And ich my-self cyuyle and symonye my felowe Wollen ryden vp-on rectours and riche men deuoutours [*v. rr.* deuotours, deuoutrours].

† **deˈvove,** *v. Obs.* [ad. L. *dēvovēre* to vow or devote, f. DE- I. 2 + *vovēre* to vow.] *trans.* To devote. Hence † **deˈvoved** *ppl. a.*, devoted.

1567 DRANT *Horace's Epist.*, *Julius Florus* C vj, I haue agaynste your home comminge A long deuoued cowe Which graseth here..And fattes her selfe for you. **1618** BOLTON *Florus* I. xiii. (1636) 37 Such of the Senatours, as had borne highest offices..devove themselves, for their Country's safty, to the gods infernall. **1656** COWLEY *Davideis* IV. 1063 'Twas his own Son..that he devov'd. **1808** J. BARLOW *Columb.* III. 852 Receive, dread Powers (since I can slay no more), My last glad victim, this devoved gore.

devovement: see DEVOUEMENT.

† **deˈvow,** *v. Obs.* [a. 16th c. F. *devouer* to dedicate or consecrate by a vow, f. DE- I. 2, 3 + *vouer* to vow, after L. *dēvovēre*, *dēvotāre*: see DEVOTE.]

1. *trans.* To dedicate or give up by a vow.

1579 J. STUBBES *Gaping Gulf* E iij b, A deuowed enemy to our Queene. **1600** HOLLAND *Livy* VIII. ix. 287 Come and say afore me that forme of words, wherby I may devow and betake myselfe for the legions. **1601** —— *Pliny* XXII. v, P. Decius,..devowed and yeelded himselfe to all the divels of hell for the safety of his armie. **1609** —— *Amm. Marcell.* 226, I have devowed my selfe to the Roman Empire.

2. To devote, give up.

1621 G. SANDYS *Ovid's Met.* xv. (1626) 317 By Step-dames fraud, and fathers credulous Beliefe deuow'd to death. **1632** B. JONSON *Magn. Lady* I. i, To the inquiry And search of which, your mathematical head Hath so devow'd itself.

3. To disavow, give up, renounce. *rare.*

1610 G. FLETCHER *Christ's Vict.* in Farr *S. P. James I* (1848) 54 There too the armies angelique devow'd Their former rage, and all to Mercy bow'd.

Hence **deˈvowed** *ppl. a.*: see in 1.

devowt(e, obs. form of DEVOUT.

devoyer, devoyr(e, obs. forms of DEVOIR.

devulcanize (diːˈvʌlkənaɪz), *v.* [f. DE- + VULCANIZE *v.*] *trans.* To restore (vulcanized rubber, etc.) to its former unvulcanized condition.

1899 *Eng. Mechanic* 19 May 316 Any one who can devulcanise indiarubber 'so as to make it soluble in benzine' will assuredly take out a patent for the process.

deˈvulgarize, *v.* [f. DE- II. 1 + VULGARIZE.] *trans.* To free from vulgarity. Hence **deˈvulgarizing** *ppl. a.*

1868 ABBOTT in *Macm. Mag.* May 38/2 Shakespeare, and Plutarch's 'Lives', are very devulgarizing books.

devulgate, -vulge, obs. ff. DIVULGATE, -VULGE.

devy, var. DEEVY *a.*

devyde, obs. form of DIVIDE.

devyer, devyr, obs. forms of DEVOIR.

devyn(e, -al, -or, -our, etc., obs. ff. DIVINE, -AL, -ER, etc.

dew (djuː), *sb.* Forms: 1 déaw, 2 dáw, 2–4 deu, deuȝ, 3 dæw (*Orm.*), 4 deew, dewȝ, deau, 4–6 dewe, deaw(e, 6 deow(e, due, 3– dew. [Common Teut.: OE. *déaw*, OFris. *daw*, OS. *dau*, MLG. *dau*, Du. *dauw*, OHG., MHG. *tou* (*touwes*), Ger. *thau*, *tau*, ON. *dögg*, gen. *döggvar*, Sw. *dagg*, Da. *dug*, Goth. **daggwa-*:—OTeut. **dauwo-*, Aryan **dhāwo-*: cf. Skr. *dhāw* to flow, run.]

1. a. The moisture deposited in minute drops upon any cool surface by the condensation of the vapour in the atmosphere; formed after a hot day during or towards night, and plentiful in the early morning.

Formerly supposed to fall or descend softly from the heavens, whence numerous current phrases, figures, and modes of speech: cf. DEWFALL.

a **800** *Corpus Gloss.* 1752 Roscido, deawe. *c* **825** *Vesp. Psalter* cxxxii[i]. 3 Swe swe deaw se astigeð in munt. *c* **1000** ÆLFRIC *Exod.* xvi. 13 On morȝen wæs þ deaw abutan þa fyrdwic. *a* **1175** *Cott. Hom.* 233 His sonne, mone, sterren, rien, daw, wind. *c* **1175** *Lamb. Hom.* 159 þe sunne drach up þene deu. *c* **1200** *Trin. Coll. Hom.* 256 On þe liȝte þe heouene deuȝ. *c* **1250** *Gen. & Ex.* 3325 Knewen he noȝt ðis dewes cost. **1340** *Ayenb.* 91 Bote a drope of deau..þe drope of þe deawe. *c* **1380** WYCLIF *Sel. Wks.* III. 27 Weetynge of hevenly deew. **1382** —— *Daniel* iv. 30 With dewe of heuen his body was enfourmed. **1398** TREVISA *Barth. De P.R.* VIII. xvii. (1495) 326 The more clere that the mone is in the Somer tyme the more plente of dewe is seen vpon the grasse and herbes. *a* **1400** *Minor Poems Vernon MS.* 618 Softur þen watur or eny licour, Or dewȝ þat liþ on þe lilie flour, Was cristes bodi. *c* **1440** *Promp. Parv.* 120 Dewe, *ros.* **1508** DUNBAR *Tua Mariit Wemen* 10 The dew donkit the daill, and dynarit the foulis. **1549** *Compl. Scot.* vi. 59 The deu.. is ane humid vapour, generit in the sycond regione of the ayr. **1596** SPENSER *Astroph.* 191 All the day it standeth full of deow. **1601** SHAKS. *Jul. C.* v. iii. 64 Our day is gone, Clowds, Dewes, and Dangers come. **1609** HOLLAND *Amm. Marcell.* XXIII. vi. 238 These pearles, within strong and bright shels of the sea-fishes, conceived.. by a commixtion of deaw. **1665** SIR T. HERBERT *Trav.* (1677) 372 Pearls.. generated.. of the morning dew of Heaven, which in serenes falls into the gaping Shell-fish. **1784** CAVENDISH in *Phil. Trans.* LXXIV. 129 Almost all the inflammable air, and near one-fifth of the common air, lose their elasticity, and are condensed into dew. **1795** SOUTHEY *Joan of Arc* II. 9 As the dews of night Descended. **1800** WORDSW. *Pet-lamb* 1 The dew was falling fast, the stars began to blink. **1840** DICKENS *Old C. Shop* xvii, She walked out into the churchyard, brushing the dew from the long grass with her feet. **1848** LYTTON *Harold* I. i, Arch and blooming faces bowed down to bathe in the May dew. **1878** HUXLEY *Physiogr.* 51 Moisture which is thus deposited upon any cold surface, without production of mist, is termed *dew.* **1887** BOWEN *Virg. Eclogue* v. 77 While bee sucks from the thyme, and cicalas drink of the dew.

†**b.** *pl.* ? Damp places. *Obs.*

1377 LANGL. *P. Pl.* B. xv. 289 And also Marie Magdeleyne by mores lyued and dewes.

2. *fig.* Something likened to dew in its operation or effect: **a.** as coming with refreshing power or with gentle fall; **b.** as characteristic of the morning of life, of early years, like the 'early dew'.

a. *c* **1200** ORMIN 9883 All wiþþutenn dæw Off Haliz Gastess frofre. **1508** FISHER *Wks.* (1876) 176 Make them moyst with the due of thy grace. **1559** *Bk. Com. Prayer, Morning Prayer,* The continuall deawe of thy blessinge. **1607** SHAKS. *Cor.* v. vi. 23 He watered his new plants with dewes of Flattery. **1667** MILTON *P.L.* IV. 614 The timely dew of sleep.. inclines Our eye-lids. **1738** POPE *Epil. Sat.* I. 69 The gracious Dew of Pulpit Eloquence. **1819** SHELLEY *Cenci* IV. i. 178 Sleep, that healing dew of heaven. **1821** —— *Ginevra* 115 The dew of music more divine Tempers the deep emotions. **1839** YEOWELL *Anc. Brit. Ch.* vi. (1847) 52 Hearts baptized with the heavenly dews of the Gospel.

b. **1535** COVERDALE *Ps.* cix. [cx.] 3 Yᵉ dewe of thy birth is of yᵉ wombe of the mornynge. **1849** ROBERTSON *Serm.* Ser. I. iii. (1866) 53 Dried up the dew of fresh morning feeling. **1858** LONGF. *M. Standish* I. 18 Having the dew of his youth, and the beauty thereof.

3. *transf.* **a.** Applied to moisture generally, especially that which appears in minute drops on any surface or exudes from any body.

a **1300** *Cursor M.* 17682 (Cott.) Wit a deu mi face he wette. **1586** A. DAY *Eng. Secretary* I. (1625) 139 Whom furres must fence.. and dew of nappie Ale cherish. **1607** TOPSELL *Four-f. Beasts* (1658) 316 Pare his [the horse's] hinder-feet thin, untill the dew come out. **1610** MARKHAM *Masterp.* II. c. 382 Raze both the quarters of the hoofe with a drawing-knife.. so deepe that you may see the dew come foorth. **1631** WIDDOWES *Nat. Philos.* 56 Dew is a humor contained in the hollownesse of the members, and joyned to their substance. **1674** N. FAIRFAX *Bulk & Selv.* 126 That cold and dew and clamminess, that goes to the hatching of a snails [egge]. **1756–7** tr. *Keysler's Trav.* (1760) III. 210 Ballani do not feed on the gross parts of the sea-water, but as it were on the subtile dew that penetrates through the stone. **1822** SHELLEY *Triumph Life* 66 The fountains, whose melodious dew Out of their mossy cells for ever burst.

b. Moisture glistening in the eyes; tears. Hence *funeral dew.*

1588 SHAKS. *L.L.L.* IV. iii. 29 The night of dew that on my cheekes downe flowes. **1612–5** BP. HALL *Contempl., O.T.* XX. iii, These expostulations might have fetched some dewes of pitie from the eyes. **1649** DAVENANT *Love & Honour* III. Dram. Wks. 1873 III. 134 Sure I could weep, but that my eyes Have not enough of funeral dew to melt Away. **1662** COKAINE *Ovid* IV. vii, Shed no more tears! You have.. Spent too much of that precious dew. **1814** SCOTT *Ld. of Isles* IV. xvi, Those poor eyes that stream'd with dew. **1847** TENNYSON *Princ.* VII. 120 The dew Dwelt in her eyes, and softer all her shape And rounder seem'd.

c. Perspiration, sweat.

1674 S. VINCENT *Yng. Gallant's Acad.* 33 Thou feelest the fat Dew of thy body.. run trickling down thy sides. **1795** SOUTHEY *Joan of Arc* VIII. 211 The dews of death Stood on his livid cheek. **1814** SCOTT *Ld. of Isles* V. xxvi, Cold on his brow breaks terror's dew. **1859** TENNYSON *Enid* 568 The dew of their great labour.. flowing, drained their force.

d. With qualifying words, as ***Bacchus' dew***, the juice of the grape, wine, or other fermented or distilled drink; ***mountain-dew***, a fanciful term for whisky illicitly distilled on the mountains; ***dew of Glenlivat***, Glenlivat whisky; †***dew of vitriol*** (*ros vitrioli*).

1559 *Mirr. Mag., Dk. Clarence* iii, Sowst in Bacchus dewe. **1706** PHILLIPS (ed. Kersey) *Dew of Vitriol,* a Name given by some Chymists to a kind of Phlegm or Water drawn from that Mineral Salt, by Distillation in Balneo Mariæ, or with a gentle Heat. **1800** tr. *Lagrange's Chem.* II. 84 There remains a whitish-grey mass, which formerly was called *Vitriol Calcined to Whiteness.* If you distil it in a retort, and collect the product, you will have first, a water slightly acid, called *Dew of Vitriol.* **1822** SHELLEY *Zucca* ix, Full as a cup with the vine's burning dew. **1826** P. P. in Hone *Every-day Bk.* II. 610 Whiskey, or mountain dew. **1836** E. HOWARD *R. Reefer* xxxv, Then came the whiskey—the real dew. **1840** *Chamb. Jrnl.* IX. 94 The discomfited gaugers fled.. leaving the victorious chief in undisturbed possession of the much coveted mountain-dew. **1884** *Daily News* 23 May 5/7 [They] cannot compete with the dew of Glenlivat.

4. Applied with qualification to surface deposits formed on plants, etc. (as by exudation, insects, parasitic vegetation), formerly imagined to be in origin akin to dew: see HONEY-DEW, MILDEW.

1563 W. FULKE *Meteors* (1640) 53 b, There is another kind of sweet dewes, that falleth in England, called the Meldewes, which is as sweet as honey.. There is also a bitter kind of dew, that falleth upon herbs, and lyeth on them like branne or meale. **1660** JER. TAYLOR *Worthy Commun.* Introd. 10 It will not be impossible to find honey or wholesome dewes upon all this variety of plants. **1821** T. DWIGHT *Trav.* II. 341 When it first exudes, it is very sweet to the taste; and has hence been commonly supposed to be the residuum of a particular kind of dew, called by the farmers honey-dew.

5. *attrib.* and *Comb.* (Especially frequent in poetical use.) **a.** attrib., 'of dew,' as ***dew-bead, -blob, -damp, -gem, -globe, -mist, -star, -water, -web***; 'characterized by' or 'characterizing dew', as ***dew-locks, -prime, -silence, -wind.*** **b.** locative and originative, as ***dew-dance, -light.*** **c.** similative, 'like' or 'as dew', as ***dew-burning, -cold, dew-grey*** adjs. **d.** objective and obj. genitive, as ***dew-brusher, -dropping*** adj. **e.** instrumental, as ***dew-bedabbled, -bediamonded, -bespangled, -besprent, -bright, -clad, -dabbled, -damp, -drenched, -gemmed, -laden, -pearled, -soaked, -sprent, -sprinkled, -wet*** adjs. **f.** parasynthetic, as ***dew-lipped*** adj.

1832 MOTHERWELL *Poet. Wks.* (1847) 85 In every *dew-bead glistening sheen. **1868** GEO. ELIOT *Sp. Gipsy* I. (Cent. Dict.), The dew-bead, Gem of earth and sky begotten. **1887** STEVENSON *Underwoods,* Every fairy wheel and thread Of cobweb *dew-bediamonded. *a* **1748** THOMSON *Hymn to Solitude* 26 Just as the *dew-bent rose is born. **1634** MILTON *Comus* 540 The savoury herb Of knot-grass *dew-besprent. **1727–38** GAY *Fables* I. 14 (Jod.) As forth she went at early dawn To taste the *dew-besprinkled lawn. **1727–46** THOMSON *Summer* 86 Aslant the *dew-bright earth and coloured air. **1854** J. WARTER *Last of Old Squires* v. 51 He was what the Persians call a *dew-brusher.. Ten to one but the labourer met him as he was going to his work. **1590** SPENSER *F.Q.* I. xi. 35 His bright *deaw-burning blade. **1847** *Mischief of Muses* 35 The moisture of the *dew-clad grass. **1817** MOORE *Lalla R., Fire Worshippers* (1854) 235 She who leans.. pale, sunk, aghast, With brow against the *dew-cold mast. **1818** KEATS *Endym.* I. 683 The poppies hung *Dew-dabbled on their stalks. **1798** COLERIDGE *Sibyl. Leaves* Poems (1864) 265 She the *dew-damp wiped From off her brow. **1899** A. R. COWAN *Hist. Kiss* 86 The grass, still *dew-damp in the glade. **1906** T. S. MOORE *Poems* 29 She.. ordered the dew-damp hair. **1885** W. B. YEATS in *Dublin Univ. Rev.* Apr. 56/2 And from the *dew-drench'd wood I've sped. **1919** V. WOOLF *Night & Day* xvi. 206 Her rather pale, dew-drenched look. **1812** G. COLMAN *Br. Grins, Lady of Wreck* II. xxiii, *Dew-dript evening. **1592** SHAKS. *Rom. & Jul.* I. iv. 103 The *dew-dropping South. **1893** LE GALLIENNE in *Westm. Gaz.* 16 Feb. 2/3 See how yonder goes, *Dew-drunk.. Yon Shelley-lark. **1832** TENNYSON *Lotos-Eaters* 75 Sun-steep'd at noon, and in the moon Nightly *dew-fed. **1823** JOANNA BAILLIE *Poems* 228 *Dew-gemm'd in the morning ray. **1821** SHELLEY *Prometh. Unb.* IV. 432 As the dissolving warmth of dawn may fold A half unfrozen *dew-globe, green and gold, And crystalline. **1932** W. FAULKNER *Light in August* (1933) vii. 149 Against the *dewgray earth.. fireflies drifted. **1603** DRAYTON *Sonnets* liii, (T.) Where nightingales in Arden sit and sing Amongst the dainty *dew-impearled flowers. **1830** TENNYSON *Ode to Memory* ii, The dew-impearled winds of dawn. **1859** GEO. ELIOT *A. Bede* 41 The *dew-laden grass. **1647** HERRICK *Noble Numb., Star Song,* Spangled with *deaw-light. **1818** KEATS *Endymion* II. 408 Just as the morning south Disparts a *dew-lipp'd rose. **1856** BRYANT *Poems, Ages* v, When the *dew-lipped spring comes on. **1830** TENNYSON *Adeline* 47 Those *dew-lit eyes of thine. **1648** HERRICK *Hesper.* I. 92, *Corinna's Maying,* The light Hangs on the *dew-locks of the night. **1821** SHELLEY *Prometh. Unb.* III. iii, The *dew-mists of my sunless sleep. **1841** BROWNING *Pippa Passes* I. (1889) 24 The hill-side's *dew-pearled; The lark's on the wing. **1872** —— *Fifine* xxxiii, Though *dew-prime flee. **1850** MRS. BROWNING *Poems* II. 165 Descend with sweet *dew silence on my mountains. **1941** W. DE LA MARE *Bells & Grass* 139 *Dew-soaked shoes. **1850** BLACKIE *Æschylus* I. 13 My *dew-sprent dreamless couch. **1884** SYMONDS *Shaks. Predecessors* vii. §3. 263 Abroad in dew-sprent meadows. **1733** SHENSTONE *Past. Ballad* IV. 33 The sweets of a *dew-sprinkled rose. **1821** SHELLEY *Prometh. Unb.* II. i. 168 As *dew-stars glisten, Then fade away. *c* **1200** *Trin. Coll. Hom.* 151 Ðe teares.. ben cleped rein water oðer *deu water. **1813** HOGG *Queen's Wake* ii. Wks. (1876) 22 And *dew-webs round the helmets weave.

6. Special combs.: **dew-beam** (*poetic*), a ray of light reflected from a dewdrop; **dew-bit** (*dial.*), a small meal or portion of food taken in the early morning, before the regular breakfast; **dew-board,** a board used as a cover to keep off the dew; **dew-cap** (see quot.); **dew-drink** (see quot., and cf. *dew-bit*); †**dew-hopper,** a name for the hare (see DEUDING); †**dew-pear,** name of a delicate kind of pear (*obs.*); †**dew-piece** *Sc.* = *dew-bit*; **dew-plant,** (*a*) a name for the ice-plant (*Mesembryanthemum*), and for the sundew (*Drosera*); (*b*) a plant nourished with dew (*nonce-use*); **dew-ripen** *v.* = DEW-RET; **dew-shoe,** translation of ON. *döggskor* (see quot.); **dew-stone,** 'a species of limestone, found in Nottinghamshire, which collects a large quantity of dew on its surface' (O.).

1824 SHELLEY *Witch* xvi, Woven from *dew-beams while the moon yet slept. **1863** BARNES *Dorset Gloss.,* **Dew-bit,* the first meal in the morning, not so substantial as a regular breakfast. Also in *Berksh., Hampsh., W. Somerset Gloss.* **1800** R. WARNER *Walk West. Count.* 64 [We] were obliged to sleep for several weeks in the shell of the tenement, with no other covering (for it was not roofed) than a *dew-board. **1879** PROCTOR *Pleas. Ways Sc.* xvi. 364 A cylinder of tin or card, called a *dew-cap, is made to project beyond the glass [of the telescope], and thus to act as a screen, and prevent radiation. *a* **1825** FORBY *Voc. E. Anglia,* **Dew-drink,* the first allowance of beer to harvest men, before they begin their day's work. **1616** SURFL. & MARKH. *Country Farme* 417 Tender or delicate peare.. such as *dew peare. **1685** SINCLAIR *Satan's Invis. World* (1769) 48 When I was eating my *due piece this morning. **1869** RUSKIN *Q. of Air* §81 You are to divide the whole family of the herbs of the field into three great groups—Drosidæ, Carices, Gramineæ—*dew-plants, sedges, and grasses. **1884** MILLER *Plant-n.,* Dew-plant, *Mesembryanthemum glabrum.* **1805** R. W. DICKSON *Pract. Agric.* (1807) II. 218 What is called *dew ripen or ret the produce. **1880** STALLYBRASS tr. *Grimm's Teut. Mythol.* I. 387 When the godlike Sigurðr strode through the.. corn, the *dew-shoe of his seven-span sword was even with the upright ears. *Note. Döggskôr,* Sw. *doppsko,* the heel of the sword's sheath, which usually brushes the dew.

dew (djuː), *v.* Forms: 3 dæwwenn, 4–5 dewen, (4 dewey), 5–7 dewe, (6–7 deaw), 6– dew. [ME. *dewen,* in Ormin *dæwwenn,* implying an OE. **déawian* (entered by Somner) = OFris. *dawia* (WFris. *dauwjen*), OS. **daujan* (MDu. *dauwen,* LG. *dauen*), OHG. *towôn, towên* (MHG. *touwen,* Ger. *thauen, tauen*), ON. *döggva* (Sw. *dagga*):—OTeut. **dauwôjan,* f. *dauw-* DEW.]

†**1.** *intr.* To give or produce dew; *impers.* to fall as dew (cf. *it rains, snows,* etc.). *Obs.* or *arch.*

c **1300** [implied in DEWING *vbl. sb.*]. **1382** WYCLIF *Isa.* xlv. 8 Deweth ȝee heuenus fro aboue [**1388** Sende ȝe out dew]. *c* **1440** *Promp. Parv.* 120 Dewyn or yeve dewe, *roro.* **1450–1530** *Myrr. our Ladye* 148 *Rorate,* dew heuens from aboue. **1552** HULOET, Dew or droppe lyke dewe, *roro.* **1663** in T. Birch *Hist. R. Society* I. 246 It did not dew upon those parts where trees lay buried under ground. **1726** *Nat. Hist. Irel.* 93 It deweth exceedingly in the hot and dry countries.

†**b.** To distil or exude as dew. *Obs.*

1652 BENLOWES *Theoph.* Epistle, When This Manna dew'd from your inspired pen. *Ibid.* IV. xxv, Meat came from the Eater, from the strong did dew Sweetnesse.

2. *trans.* To wet with or as with dew; to bedew; to moisten.

c **1200** ORMIN 13848 To wattrenn & to dæwwenn swa þurrh beȝȝske & sallte tæress þatt herrte. *a* **1325** *Prose Psalter* vi. 6 Ich shal dewey my couertour wyth min teres. **1544** PHAER *Regim. Lyfe* (1560) F iij, Take a sponnefull of hote ashes, dewe them wyth good wyne. **1590** SPENSER *F.Q.* I. xi. 48 Overflowed all the fertile plaine, As it had deawed bene with timely raine. **1593** SHAKS. *2 Hen. VI,* III. ii. 340 Giue me thy hand, That I may dew it with my mournfull teares. **1615** CROOKE *Body of Man* 821 To water or dew some partes that stoode need of moysture. **1680** OTWAY *Orphan* II. iv. 598 Cold sweat Dew'd all my face. **1821** W. C. WELLS *Ess. Dew* (1866) 7 Grass after having been dewed in the evening, is never found dry until after sunrise. **1830** HERSCHEL *Stud. Nat. Phil.* II. vi. (1838) 162 The cooling.. of the body dewed. *a* **1851** MOIR *Castle of Time* xxi, Moloch's monstrous shrines are dew'd with human blood.

b. *fig.* (Cf. 'bedew', 'steep' in fig. use.)

c **1510** BARCLAY *Mirr. Gd. Manners* (1570) A iij, As fruitfull nutriment To dewe them in vertue, as plantes to augment. **1610** G. FLETCHER *Christ's Vict.* xxv, While deaw'd in heavie sleepe, dead Peter lies. *a* **1631** DONNE *Serm.* CV. IV. 413 But infected and dewed with these frivolous, nay pernicious apparitions and revelations. **1810** SCOTT *Lady of L.* I. xxxi, Fairy strains of music fall, Every sense in slumber dewing. **1865** BUSHNELL *Vicar. Sacr.* III. iii. 233 Mercy.. dewing it thus with her tender mitigations.

†**3.** To cause to descend or drop as dew; to distil, instil. *Obs.*

1572 FORREST *Theophilus* in *Anglia* VII. 92 The devill in the harte of the busshoppe did dewe His divillishe stirringis. **1591** *Troub. Raigne K. John* II. (1611) 89 The heauens dewing fauours on my head. **1593** NASHE *Christ's T.* (1613) 1 O dew thy spirit plentiful into my inke.

†**4.** *intr.* To become moist, to exude moisture.

1658 A. FOX *Wurtz' Surg.* I. viii. 34 Wounds that are thus compelled to dew, will hardly come to healing.

Hence **dewed, 'dewing** *ppl. adjs.*

1552 HULOET, Dewed or wete wyth dewe, *roratus.* **1593** SOUTHWELL *Peter's Compl.* 33 Dew'd eyes, and prostrate prayers. **1635** SWAN *Spec. M.* (1670) 101 Which can have no existence or being, but in a dewing or distilling cloud. **1830** HERSCHEL *Stud. Nat. Phil.* II. vi. (1838) 163 The cooling of the dewed surface by radiation.

dew, obs. or dial. pa. t. of DAW *v.*[1]

dew, dewfull, obs. ff. DUE, DUEFUL.

Dewalee, Dewali (diːˈwɑːliː). Also 7 Dually, 9 Divali, Diwali, Dewallee. [Hind. *dīwālī,* ad. Skr. *dīpāvalī* (*dīpālī*) row of lights, f. *dīpa* light, lamp.] A Hindu festival with illuminations held on the day of the new moon in the month Asvina or Kārttika.

1698 FRYER *Acc. E. India & P.* 110 The first New Moon in October, is the Banyans Dually. **1820** T. COATS in *Trans. Lit. Soc. Bombay* (1823) III. 211 The Dewallee, Deepaullee, or Time of Lights, takes place twenty days after the Dussera, and lasts three days. **1849** E. B. EASTWICK *Dry Leaves* 84 The Diwálí happening to fall on this day, the whole river was bright with lamps. **1883** MONIER-WILLIAMS *Religious Thought & Life in India* 432 The Dīvālī is celebrated with splendid effect at Benares. **1952** J. MASTERS *Deceivers* xiv. 142 It was the Dewali, the festival dedicated to lights and gambling, which fell always on the twentieth day after Dussehra. **1969** *Eve's Weekly* (Bombay) 20 Dec. 33/1 It is not Divali, but Christmas.

‖**dewan** (diːˈwɑːn). Also duan, diwan, deewaun, dewaun, dēwān. [Arab. and Pers. *dīwān, dīvān,* Pers. formerly *dēvān,* the same word as DIVAN, of which an early sense was 'register'. Through the application to a register of accounts, and the financial department of a state, the word has in India been individualized and applied to the minister or officer over this department.]

In India: **a.** The head financial minister or treasurer of a state under former Mohammedan governments. **b.** The prime minister of a native state. **c.** The chief native officer of certain Government establishments, such as the Mint. **d.** In Bengal, a native servant in charge of the affairs of a house of business or a large domestic establishment, a steward. (Yule and Burnell.)

1690 J. CHARNOCK, etc. *MS. Lett. to Mr. Ch. Eyre at Ballasore* (Y.), Fearing miscarriage of y Originall ffarcuttee we have herewth Sent you a Coppy Attested by Hugly Cazee, hoping ye Duan may be Sattisfied therewth. **1766** HOLWELL *Hist. Events* I. 74 (Y.) A Gentoo named Allum Chund, who had been many years Dewan to Soujah Khan. **1771** in Gleig *Mem. W. Hastings* (1841) I. 221 (Y.) Divesting him of the rank and influence he holds as Naib Duan of the Kingdom of Bengal. **1786** BLANE in *Phil. Trans.* LXXVII. 297 Making the enquiries I wished..from his Dewan or Minister. **1804** in Owen *Wellesley's Desp.* 632 The English Company..has forfeited its rights as dewan and treasurer of the Empire. **1806** WELLINGTON *Ibid.* p. cii, Scindiah's minister..was the Peshwah's dewan. **1818** JAS. MILL *Brit. India* V. v. (1848) IV. 226 He sent on a commission to Calcutta his dewan or treasurer. **1835** BURNES *Trav. Bokhara* (ed. 2) I. 235 The Hindoo Dewans of Sinde now transact the entire pecuniary concerns of the state. **1862** BEVERIDGE *Hist. India* I. I. vi. 142 Subordinate to the subahdar..was an officer, with the title of dewan or diwan, who had the superintendence of all matters of revenue and finance. **1871** MATEER *Travancore* 22 Colonel Munro.. acted for about three years in the capacity of Dewan, or Prime Minister.

Hence **de'wanship** = next.

1789 *Seir Mutaqherin* II. 384 (Y.) [Lord Clive] visited the Vezir..and asked that the Company should be invested with the Divanship of the three provinces. **1818** JAS. MILL *Brit. India* V. iv. (1848) IV. 149 Procuring for the donor the dewanship of the Zamindari.

‖**dewani, dewanny, dewaunee** (di:ˈwɑːnɪ). Also dûanny, dewauny, dīwānī. [a. Pers. *dīwānī*, *dīvānī*, the office or function of *dīwān*: see prec.]

The office of dewan; *esp.* 'the right of receiving as *dewān*, or finance minister, the revenue of Bengal, Behar, and Orissa, conferred upon the E.I. Company by the Great Mogul Shāh 'Alam in 1765. Also used sometimes for the territory which was the subject of that grant' (Yule and Burnell).

1783 BURKE *Report Affairs India* Wks. XI. 141 The acquisition of the Dûanny opened a wide field for all projects of this nature. *Ibid.* 196 Under the jurisdiction of the Dewanny Courts. **1801** R. PATTON *Asiat. Mon.* 178 *note*, The officers of the dewanny, the revenue department. **1862** BEVERIDGE *Hist. India* I. III. xii. 671 An offer of the dewaunee had..been made to Clive. **1876** GRANT *Hist. India* I. xx. 106/2 The Mogul ceded the dewaunee, or collection of the revenues in Bengal, Behar, and Orissa.

Dewar, dewar ('djuːə(r)). The name of Sir James *Dewar* (1842–1923), British physicist and chemist, used *attrib.* or *absol.* to designate a double-walled vessel or flask, usu. of glass or copper, having the space between the walls empty of air to prevent conduction and convection of heat to and from the inner container. Cf. *vacuum-bottle*, *-flask*, and *-vessel* s.v. VACUUM 4.

1899 T. O'C. SLOANE *Liquid Air* xi. 246 The Dewar vacuum bulb consists of a double or treble walled glass vessel, with the space or spaces between the vessels hermetically sealed and with a nearly perfect vacuum therein. *Ibid.* 248 Various shapes and modifications of Dewar bulbs. **1902** *Encycl. Brit.* XXX. 281/2 Vacuum or 'Dewar' vessels. **1930** *Engineering* 5 Sept. 314/1 A calorimeter consisting of a wide-necked Dewar flask, [etc.]. **1964** N. G. CLARK *Mod. Org. Chem.* vii. 112 The reaction is carried out in a Dewar vessel. **1966** *New Scientist* 21 July 138/3 A replenisher that automatically maintains the level of liquefied gas in a dewar has been developed.

dewater (diːˈwɔːtə(r)), *v.* [f. DE- II. 2 + WATER *sb.*] *trans.* To remove the water from. So **de'watered** *ppl. a.*, **de'watering** *vbl. sb.* and *ppl. a.*

1909 in WEBSTER. **1923** *Glasgow Herald* 10 Oct. 10 There is now more hope of getting through 'dewatered' roadways. **1929** *Times* 10 May 22/3 The Lagan Navigation Company shall..dewater such portion of the canal. **1930** *Engineering* 4 Apr. 436/1 These will be employed when de-watering of the culvert is necessary. **1960** E. L. DELMAR-MORGAN *Cruising Yacht Equip. & Navig.* vi. 81 This type of dewatering protective was used very widely on flooded machinery. **1962** *Times* 1 Feb. 3/4 Construction of and dewatering inside a cofferdam. **1969** *Washington Post* 22 Feb. B1/4 Water consumption drops and the tunnel can be, in the jargon of the engineers, 'dewatered'. That means drained. **1970** *Fremdsprachen* XIV. 135 The carbon slurry is drawn off the bottom of the column to one of the dewatering bins.

'dew-beater. [f. DEW *sb.* + BEATER.]

1. One who beats or shakes off the dew in front of others in the same path; an early pioneer.

a **1670** HACKET *Abp. Williams* I. (1692) 57 The dew-beaters have trod the way for those that come after them. **1883** *Hampshire Gloss.*, *Deaw-bitter*, a dew-beater, one who has large feet, or who turns his toes out so that he brushes the dew off the grass in walking.

2. *pl.* The feet. *slang.*

1811 in *Lexicon Balatron.* **1823** SCOTT *Peveril* xxxvi, First hold out your dew-beaters till I take off the darbies.

3. (See quot.)

a **1825** FORBY *Voc. E. Anglia*, *Dew-beaters*, coarse and thick shoes which resist the dew. **1847–78** in HALLIWELL.

dew-berry ('djuːbɛrɪ). [f. DEW *sb.* + BERRY. Cf. mod.Ger. *thau-beere* dew-berry, Oberdeutsch *taub-ber*, *tauben-ber*, i.e. dove-berry. The origin of the first element is thus doubtful, but it is, in English use, associated with DEW *sb.*]

A species of blackberry or bramble-berry, the name being applied both to the fruit and the shrub: in Great Britain *Rubus cæsius*, a low-growing procumbent species, the black fruit of which has a bluish bloom; in N. America *R. canadensis*, resembling the British plant in its low growth and trailing habit, but differing in the fruit. In some earlier English writers, and mod. dialects, the name is applied to the GOOSEBERRY (DAYBERRY).

Shakspere's dew-berry, which is mentioned among delicate cultivated fruits, is supposed by some to have meant the gooseberry; Hanmer conjectured the raspberry. In some books dewberry is erroneously given as the cloud-berry, *Rubus Chamæmorus.*

1578 LYTE *Dodoens* VI. iv. 661 The fruite is called a Dewberie, or blackberie. **1655** MOUFET & BENNET *Health's Improv.* (1746) 304 When Mulberries cannot be gotten, Blackberries or Dewberries may supply their room. **1674** tr. *Scheffer's Lapland* 141 Some Dew-berries, or the Norway Berry, whose species is the same that grows on Brambles. **1750** ELLIS *Mod. Husbandman* IV. i. 77 (E.D.S.) *Dew-berry-brier.* **1829** JESSE *Jrnl. Nat.* 116 The root of an ancient beech, its base overgrown with the dewberry. **1859** W. S. COLEMAN *Woodlands* (1862) 106 Dewberry, or Grey Bramble..The fruit..is generally less than that of a fullsized Blackberry; but the grains of which it is composed are usually much larger, and..covered with fine bloom. **1881** *Scribner's Mag.* XXII. 642 Overrun with dewberry-briars.

b. **1590** SHAKS. *Mids. N.* III. i. 169 Feede him with Apricocks and Dewberries With purple Grapes, greene Figs, and Mulberries. **1652** CULPEPPER *Eng. Physic.* (1656) 117 Goos-berry Bush, called in Sussex Dewberry Bush, and in some Countries Wine-berries. **1657** W. COLES *Adam in Eden* clxxiv. 271 In some Countries of England it is called the Feaberry in others Dewberry..but most commonly the Gooseberry.

dew-blown, -bole: see next.

†**dew-bolne,** *a. Obs.* exc. *dial.* Also 6 -bole, 7–9 -blown(e, 8 -born. [f. DEW *sb.* + BOLNE *ppl. a.* The second element became corrupted into *-bole*, *-born*, *-blown*, and the last survives in dialects, associated with BLOWN puffed up.] Of cattle: Swollen with eating too freely of fresh moist grass or clover. Sometimes used subst. as the name of the affection.

1523 FITZHERB. *Husb.* §60 Dewbolne..commeth whan a hungry beaste is put in a good pasture full of ranke grasse, he wyll eate soo moche that his sydes wyll stande as hygh as his backebone. **1587** MASCALL *Govt. Cattle* (1627) 33 The Dew-bole in Oxe, or Cow, or other beast..is gotten by eating of the trifoyle grasse in a deawy morning. **1601** HOLLAND *Pliny* XXVIII. i, If kine or oxen were dew-blowne or otherwise puffed up. **1614** MARKHAM *Cheap Husb.* (1623) 98 Some of our English writers are opinioned, this Dewbolne or generall Gargill is a poysonous and violent swelling. **1730–6** BAILEY (folio), *Dew-born*, a distemper in cattle. **1884** *Chesh. Gloss.*, *Dewblown*, said of cows which are swelled from eating green clover.

dew-bow ('djuːbəʊ). [f. DEW *sb.*, after *rainbow.*] An arch resembling a rainbow, occurring on a dew-covered surface.

1873 R. JOHNSON in Tristram *Moab* 387 A lunar rainbow on the ground, or to speak more correctly a lunar dew-bow. **1920** *Conquest* May 346/1 That curious phenomenon known as the dew bow. *Ibid.* 346/2 The..author may have seen a dew bow effect at his feet. **1960** *New Scientist* 31 Mar. 792/3 Dewbows..are rainbow effects of moonlight shining on dew-pearled grass.

dewce, obs. form of DEUCE.

dew-clap, obs. erron. form of DEWLAP.

dew-claw ('djuːklɔː). [App. f. DEW *sb.* + CLAW *sb.*

(Perhaps referring to the fact that while the other claws come in contact with the soil, or press the grass to the ground, this only brushes the dewy surface.)]

1. The rudimentary inner toe or hallux (answering to the great toe in man) sometimes present in dogs.

In Newfoundland dogs, and St. Bernards, it is sometimes abnormally double.

1576 TURBERV. *Venerie* 23 Some other haue taken marke by the hynder legges by the dewclawes. **1580** HOLLYBAND *Treas. Fr. Tong*, *Herigote*, dew clawes. **1611** COTGR., *Controngle*, the Deaw-claw, or water-claw of dogs. **1690** *Lond. Gaz.* No. 2548/4 Lost..a little white Spaniel Dog.. with dew Claws upon the hind Feet. *c* **1785** G. WHITE *Let. to D. Barrington* in *Selborne*, The bitch has a dew claw on each hind leg. The dog has none. **1854** E. MAYHEW *Dogs* (1862) 248 The dew-claws, as they are termed, grow high upon the inner side of the leg, nearer to the foot than the elbow. **1884** *Sat. Rev.* 15 Nov. 626 The monks liked their dogs [St. Bernards] to have these double dew-claws, because they offered more resistance in soft, newly-fallen snow. **1883** W. H. FLOWER in *Encycl. Brit.* XV. 438/1 *note*, In domestic dogs a hallux is frequently developed, though often in a rudimentary condition, the phalanges and claw being suspended loosely in the skin, without direct connection with the other bones of the foot; it is called by dog-fanciers the 'dew-claw.'

2. The false hoof of deer and other ungulates, consisting of two rudimentary toes.

1576 TURBERV. *Venerie* 97 The shinne bones large, the dew clawes close in port..An hart to hunt, as any man can seake. **1611** COTGR., *Les gardes d'un sanglier*, the deawclawes or hinder-clawes of a wild Bore. **1630** [see ABATURE]. **1678** PHILLIPS, *Dew-claw*, among Hunters the Bones or little Nails behind the Foot of the Deer.

Hence **dew-clawed,** †**'dew-cleyd** *a.*, having dew-claws. (Formerly applied sometimes to the feet of bees.)

1576 TURBERV. *Venerie* 8 Those whiche are well ioynted and dewclawed are best to make bloudhoundes. **1609** C. BUTLER *Fem. Mon.* i. (1634) 8 Her rough and dew-claw'd feet, apt to take hold at the first touch, are in number six. **1611** COTGR., *Ergoté*..hauing spurres; deaw-clawed. **1616** SURFL. & MARKH. *Country Farme* 679 Round feete, strong cleys, high dewcleyd. **1647** WARD *Simp. Cobler* 11 *note*, By Brownists I mean not Independents, but dew clawd Seperatists. **1657** S. PURCHAS *Pol. Flying Ins.* I. iii. 7 Her feet are six, dew-clawed..full of joynts. **1818** KEATS *Endym.* IV. 685 Sorrel untorn by the dew-claw'd stag.

'dew-cup. [f. DEW *sb.* + CUP.]

1. The early morning allowance of beer to harvest-men.

1847–78 HALLIWELL s.v. *Dew-drink*, Called the dew-cup in Hants. **1883** in *Hampsh. Gloss.*

2. The plant called Lady's Mantle (*Alchemilla vulgaris*).

1799 *Ess. Highl. Soc.* III. 389 (Jam.) Giving them a decoction of the Dewcup and Healing leaf boiled in buttermilk. **1813** HOGG *Queen's Wake* ii. Wks. (1876) 21 He thought..of sleeping in the dew-cups eye. **1818** —— *Brownie of Bodsbeck* II. 183 They [fairies] 'll hae to..gang away an' sleep in their dew-cups..till the gloaming come on again.

dewdrop ('djuːdrɒp). [f. DEW *sb.* + -DROP. Cf. Ger. *thau-tropfen*, Du. *dauw-droppel.*] **a.** One of the rounded 'drops' or globules in which dew collects on surfaces on which it is deposited.

[*a* **1310** in Wright *Lyric P.* xli. 114 Ase fele sythe ant oft as dewes dropes beth weet.] **1590** SHAKS. *Mids. N.* II. i. 14, I must go seeke some dew drops heere, And hang a pearle in euery cowslips eare. **1667** MILTON *P.L.* V. 746 Starrs of Morning, Dew-drops, which the Sun Impearls on every leaf, and every flouer. **1788** COWPER *Stanzas for Year* 31 Dew-drops may deck the turf that hides the bones. **1810** SCOTT *Lady of L.* III. ii, The lawn Begemmed with dew-drops. **1847** TENNYSON *Princ.* VII. 53 When two dewdrops on the petal shake To the same sweet air. **1871** TYNDALL *Fragm. Sc.* (1879) I. xi. 342 The little pearly globe which we call a dew-drop.

transf. & *fig.* **1781** COWPER *Truth* 144 The shivering urchin, bending as he goes, With slip-shod heels, and dew-drop at his nose. **1807–8** W. IRVING *Salmag.* (1824) 161 And feel the dew-drop in my eye. **1826** HOOD *Wee Man* xiv, On every brow a dew-drop stood. **1831** CARLYLE *Sart. Res.* II. vi, The heart..unvisited by any heavenly dew-drop.

b. A glass bead resembling a drop of dew.

1880 *Harper's Mag.* June 31/1 'Grass-work' consists in the fastening of small glass beads or 'dew-drops' to the artificial blades.

Hence **dew-dropped** *a.*, covered or bespangled with dew-drops.

1756 W. TOLDERVY *Hist. Two Orphans* IV. 201 The dew-dropp'd rose. **1762** J. WARTON *Enthusiast* Poems 82 Bladed grass perfumed with dewdropped flowers. **1811** W. R. SPENCER *Poems* 161 How bright it's dewdropp'd tint appears!

dewe, obs. form of DUE *a.* and *sb.*

dewe(n, obs. f. DEAVE *v.*, to become deaf.

dewes: see DEUS.

†**'dewess.** *rare.* [a. OF. *deuesse, *dieuesse*, f. *deu*, *dieu* god: see -ESS. Cf. DEESS.] A goddess.

a **1400–50** *Alexander* 3555 All driȝtens and dewessis ere dute of my name.

dewey, dewy, ME. pres. inf. of DEW *v.*

Dewey ('djuːɪ). The surname of Melvil *Dewey* (1851–1931), American librarian, applied *attrib.* to designate a decimal system of library classification developed by him. (See *decimal classification* s.v. DECIMAL A. 1 a.)

1879 *Library Jrnl.* IV. 139 The books on the shelves were numbered and arranged according to the 'Dewey system'. **1885** *Ibid.* X. 26 The scheme looks like a modification or improvement of the Dewey Decimal System. **1931** *Times Educ. Suppl.* 27 June 250/1 Classification of books—Dewey system. **1959** *Observer* 14 June 19/5 If anthropologists wrote with a little more levity, those of us who have to cook would be constantly at the shelves numbered 572 (Dewey classification) of the public libraries. **1970** E. MCGIRR *Death pays Wages* iii. 59, I suppose they have some sort of Dewey System master index.

Deweyism ('djuːɪɪz(ə)m). [f. *Dewey* (see below) + -ISM.] The tenets of the American philosopher and educationist John Dewey (1859–1952); pragmatism in philosophy or education. So **Deweyite** ('dju:ɪaɪt), a follower of Dewey or of his philosophy.

1904 W. JAMES in *Mind* XIII. 464 How can a Deweyite discriminate sincerity from bluff? **1906** —— in *Jrnl. Philos., Psychol. & Sci. Methods* III. 337 The style of article that has usually discussed pragmatism, Deweyism, or radical empiricism. **1954** D. RIESMAN *Individualism Reconsidered* p. x, A renewed drive against 'Deweyism' and progressive education generally.

deweylite ('dju:ɪlaɪt). *Min.* [Named 1826 after Prof. Dewey, U.S. see -LITE.] An amorphous resinous-looking mineral of yellowish colour, consisting of a hydrated silicate of magnesium.

1826 EMMONS *Min.* 133. **1868** DANA *Min.* 470.

dew-fall ('dju:fɔ:l). [f. DEW + FALL *sb.*: cf. Dan. *dugfald.*] The formation or deposition of dew; the time when this begins, in the evening.

1622 R. TISDALE *Lawyer Philos.* in Farr *S.P. Jas. I* (1848) 316 Shake off the dewfalls of the night. **1798** COLERIDGE *Sibyl. Leaves* Poems (1864) 115 The gentle dewfall. **1820** SHELLEY *Witch Atlas* xxix, She past at dewfall to a space extended. **1828** MOORE *Before the Battle* i, 'Midst the dew-fall of a nation's tears. *c* **1850** WHITTIER *Call of Christian* vii, Noiseless as dew-fall. **1878** HUXLEY *Physiogr.* 65 The temperature after dewfall. **1892** *Daily News* 1 Mar. 5/4 The rainfall is.. supplemented by.. excessive dewfalls.

So **'dewfalling**.

1868 HOLME LEE *B. Godfrey* xix. 109 The time of the dew-falling.

dewgard, -gar, Sc. forms of DIEUGARD. *Obs.*

† **dew-grass** ('dju:grɑ:s, -græs). *Obs.* [f. DEW *sb.* + GRASS, suggested by L. G. *Himmeldau*, med.L. *ros cæli*, 'dew of heaven', manna.] A name given by Gerarde and other early herbalists to an esculent grass of Central Europe, the cultivated form of *Panicum sanguinale*, Manna-grass.

1597 GERARDE *Herbal* I. xx. 25 The Germanes call it Himeldau, that is to say *Cæli ros*, whereupon it was called *Gramen Mannæ*.. Lobel calleth it *gramen mannæ esculentum*, for that in Germany and other parts, as Bohemia, and Italy, they use to eat the same as a kind of bread corne, and also make potage therewith as we do with oatmeale.. In English it may be called *manna grasse* or *Dew grasse*; but more fitly *rice-grasse*. **1610** W. FOLKINGHAM *Art of Survey* I. vii. 14 Panick, Amilcorne, Spelt-corn, Garences, Dewgrasse, Jobs teares. **1640** PARKINSON *Theat. Bot.* 1180 The Dew grasse is said to discusse the hardnesse of womens breasts, the seede is food for small birds, and Pidgeons and Hens and for men also.

[Erroneously taken by Prior, *Plant Names*, for the Cock's-foot grass, *Dactylis glomerata*; whence in later Dictionaries and lists].

dewice, dewis(e, obs. Sc. ff. DEVICE, DEVISE.

dewid, obs. form of DIVIDE.

dewille, obs. form of DEVIL.

dewily ('dju:ɪlɪ), *adv.* [f. DEWY + -LY[2].] After the manner of dew.

1818 *Blackw. Mag.* III. 32 The song Dropp'd dewily from that sweet tongue. **1872** S. MOSTYN *Perplexity* III. viii. 212, I will make my love fall dewily on your heart. **1887** BOWEN *Virg. Æneid* IV. 699 So upon saffron wings came Iris, dewily bright.

dewindtite (dɪ'wɪntaɪt). *Min.* [a. F. *dewindtite* (A. Schoep 1922, in *Compt. Rend.* CLXXIV. 625), f. the name of Jean *Dewindt*, Belgian geologist: see -ITE[1].] A hydrated basic phosphate of lead and uranium (see also quot. 1956).

1922 *Jrnl. Chem. Soc.* CXXII. II. 305 Dewindtite, a new radioactive mineral... This occurs at Kasola, Katanga, Belgian Congo, as a canary-yellow powder intimately mixed with torbernite and a white, powdery material. **1956** *Amer. Min.* XLI. 921 The validity of 'dewindtite' as a separate species is in doubt, as it appears to be structurally identical to renardite, but chemically different.

dewiness ('dju:ɪnɪs). [f. DEWY + -NESS.] The quality of being dewy; *fig.* freshness, vigour.

1627 tr. *Bacon's Life & Death* (R.), A dewinesse dispersed, or.. radicall in the very substance of the body. **1817** KEATS '*I Stood Tiptoe*' iv, Ye ardent marigolds!.. again your dewiness he kisses. **1863** TYNDALL *Heat* v. §186 (1870) 150 [This] caused a dewiness on the external surface. **1868** BROWNING *Ring & Bk* IX. 242 Farewell to dewiness and prime of life!

'dewing, *vbl. sb.* [f. DEW *v.* + -ING[1].]

1. Deposition of dew.

13.. *K. Alis.* 914 Theo sunne ariseth, and fallith the dewyng; Theo nessche clay hit makith clyng. **1398** TREVISA *Barth. de P.R.* XI. v. (Tollem. MS.), þerof comeþ a litel dewynge. *Ibid.* XVI. lxii. (Tollem. MS.), þe more dewynge is founde, þe more and þe gretter þe margarite is gendrid of þe dewe. **1838** JEFFREY in Ld. Cockburn *Life* II. Let. cxl, After the dewing of yesterday, everything is so fresh and fragrant.

2. A wetting with or as with dew; a gentle sprinkling; moistening, bedewing.

14.. HOCCLEVE *Compl. Virgin* 158 They by taast of swich dewynge, Hem oghte clothe ageyn. **1513** DOUGLAS *Æneis* VI. iii. 143 With clene watter.. Strinkland a litle dewing.. With the branche of ane happy olive thrise. **1565-73** COOPER *Thesaurus, Aspergo*, a sprinckling or dewing. **1646** RUTHERFORD *Lett.* II. xlvii. (1881) 455 A night's dewing of grace and sweetness. **1882** *Garden* 28 Jan. 65/3 An occasional dewing over with the syringe.

dewing, *ppl. a.*: see DEW *v.*

† **'dewish**, *a. Obs.* [f. DEW *sb.* + -ISH.] Of the nature of or akin to dew; moist, damp.

1589 FLEMING *Georg. Virg.* III. 48 And dewish moone doth new refresh the woods. **1620** MARKHAM *Farew. Husb.* (1625) 117 A more moist place.. which euer is vomiting wet and dewish humours. **1656** RIDGLEY *Pract. Physick* 141 The dew or dewish moisture.

dewite, obs. form of DUTY.

† **Dewitt, De-Witt** (dɪ'wɪt), *v. Obs.* [From the surname of the two brothers John and Cornelius *De Witt*, Dutch statesmen, opponents of William III as Stadtholder of the United Provinces, who were murdered by a mob in 1672.] *trans.* To kill by mob violence; to lynch.

1689 *Modest Enquiry into Present Disasters* (1690) 32 It's a wonder the English Nation have not in their fury *De-Witted* some of those men. **1690** ABP. SANCROFT *Protestation*, Such a fury, as may end in *Dewitting* us (a bloody Word, but too well understood). **1695** (*title*), Gallienus Redivivus; or, Murther Will Out, &c., being a true account of the De-Witting of Glencoe, Gaffney, &c. **1711** *Vind. of Sacheverell* 69 King William deserved to be De-Witted. **1724** in *Lockhart Papers* II. 162 Had Mr. Campbell himself been in town, they had certainly De-witted him. **1824** SOUTHEY *Bk. of Ch.* (1841) 544. **1855** MACAULAY *Hist. Eng.* III. 660. **1888** PLUMPTRE *Life Ken* II. xviii. 1 Men.. were stirring up the people to that form of 'lynching' which was then knowne as 'De Witting.'

dewlap ('dju:læp). Also 6 **dew lop**, *erron.* **dew-clap**. [The second element LAP is OE. *læppa*, pendulous piece, skirt, lappet, lobe; the first is uncertain: the equivalent Da. *doglæb*, Norw. *doglæp*, Sw. *dröglapp*, in which the first element is not the word for 'dew', suggest that the original form has been altered under the influence of popular etymology.

The English form may be explained as the 'lap' or pendulous piece which touches the dewy surface; but that is not likely to have been the original notion.]

1. a. The fold of loose skin which hangs from the throat of cattle.

1398 TREVISA *Barth. De P.R.* XVIII. xiii. (*MS. Bodl.* 3738) In Siria beþ oxen þat haue no dewe lappis nother fresche lappes vnder þrote [*palearia sub gutture*]. *c* **1420** *Pallad. on Husb.* IV. 711 The kyen.. Wel hered eres, and dewlappes syde [= hanging low]. *c* **1440** *Promp. Parv.* 120 Dew lappe, syde skyn' vndur a bestys throte, *peleare*. **1523** FITZHERB. *Husb.* §59 To cutte the dewlappe before. **1565** GOLDING *Ovid's Met.* VII. 155 Their dangling dew-claps with his hand he coid unfearefullie. **1579** SPENSER *Sheph. Cal.* Feb. 74 His deuelap as lythe as lasse of Kent. **1589** GREENE *Menaphon* (Arb.) 74 White.. as the dangling deawlap of the silver Bull. **1621** G. SANDYS *Ovid's Met.* II. (1626) 43 His broad-spred brest, long dangling dew-laps deck. **1872** MIVART *Elem. Anat.* 237 Folds of skin hang freely in some animals, as the dewlap of cattle.

b. Transferred to similar parts in other animals, as the loose skin under the throat of dogs, etc., the pendulous fleshy lobe or wattle of the turkey and other fowls, and humorously to pendulous folds of flesh about the human throat.

1590 SHAKS. *Mids. N.* II. i. 50 When she drinkes, against her lips I bob, And on her wither'd dewlop poure the Ale. **1654** GAYTON *Pleasant Notes* II. iii. 42 The dulapes and the jawy part of the face. **1668** WILKINS *Real Char.* 161 Described to have a dew-lap under the throat.. Senembi, Iguana. **1690** W. WALKER *Idiomat. Anglo-Lat.* 222 Dew-laps hang down from his chaps. **1774** GOLDSM. *Nat. Hist.* (1862) I. I. iii. 267 The skin hangs loose.. in a kind of dewlap. **1859** J. BROWN *Rab. & F.* (1862) 9 He [mastiff].. has the Shaksperian dewlaps shaking as he goes. **1863** WHYTE MELVILLE *Gladiators* I. 3 Gelert is down, torn and mangled from flank to dewlap.

2. 'A brand used in marking cattle, being a cut in the lower part of the neck' (Farmer, *Americanisms*, 1889).

3. Comb., ***dewlap-deep*** adj.

1916 A. HUXLEY *Burning Wheel* 28 Great oxen, dewlap-deep In meadows of lush grass. **1922** BLUNDEN *Shepherd* (ed. 2) 21 Where milch cows dewlap-deep may wade.

Hence **'dewlapped**, having a dew-lap.

c **1420** *Pallad. on Husb.* IV. 679 [699] Compact, a runcle necke, dewlapped syde Unto the kne. **1590** SHAKS. *Mids. N.* IV. i. 127 My hounds are bred out of the Spartan kinde.. Crooke-kneed, and dew-lapt, like Thessalian Buls. *a* **1732** GAY (J.), The dewlapt bull now chafes along the plain. **1806** SOUTHEY *Lett.* (1856) I. 355 He is a fat, dew-lapped, velvet-voiced man. **1887** RUSKIN *Hortus Inclusus* 11 Dew-lapped cattle.. feeding on the hillside above.

dewle, obs. f. *dule*, DOLE, DOOL, grief, mourning.

dewless ('dju:lɪs), *a.* [f. DEW + -LESS.] Devoid of or without dew.

a **1618** SYLVESTER *Maiden's Blush* 1322 Both solstices like deawless and adust. **1799** CAMPBELL *Pleas. Hope* I, When the sea-wind wafts the dewless day. **1832** TENNYSON *Miller's Dau.* 246 On the chalk-hill the bearded grass Is dry and dewless. **1865** E. BURRITT *Walk to Land's End* 36 What a dewless Sahara would be the walk of life without the companionship of children!

Dew line, D.E.W. line: see D III. 3.

dew-point ('dju:pɔɪnt). **a.** That point of atmospheric temperature at which dew begins to be deposited.

1833 N. ARNOTT *Physics* (ed. 5) II. 47 The degree of heat at which the dew begins to appear is called the *dew-point*, being an important particular in the meteorological report of the day. **1854** HOOKER *Himal. Jrnls.* I. i. 14 This indicated a dew-point of 11½°. **1878** HUXLEY *Physiogr.* 52 When the temperature is sufficiently lowered, the dew-point is reached.

b. *attrib.*, as ***dew-point apparatus, depression, front, hygrometer, meter***.

1843 *Proc. Amer. Phil. Soc.* II. 249 Professor Baebe described a dew-point hygrometer. **1933** *Discovery* Dec. 360/1 The dew-point apparatus.. is designed to discover the temperature to which a metal must be cooled before dew will deposit upon it. **1956** W. A. HEFLIN *U.S. Air Force Dict.* 165/1 *Dew point depression*, the lowering of the dew point by decreasing water content or pressure. **1958** *Engineering* 4 Apr. 422/1 A dew point meter for use with any gases that are not corrosive to brass or copper. **1960** *Aeroplane* XCIX. 624/1 The dew-point front is the boundary between moist 'maritime tropical' air.. and dry 'tropical continental' air.

dew-pond ('dju:pɒnd). [DEW *sb.*] A shallow pond, usually of artificial construction, occurring on downs where there is no adequate water-supply from springs or surface-drainage.

These ponds were originally thought to be fed by the condensation of water from the atmosphere, but it is now generally thought that dew plays little or no part in supplying the water.

1865 *Jrnl. R. Agric. Soc.* 2nd Ser. I. 273 *Dew-ponds*. These ponds are chiefly constructed on the highest ridges of the chalk range. **1877** H. P. SLADE (*title*) A short practical treatise on dew ponds, the farmers' summer water suppliers. **1879** *Athenæum* 14 June 757/1 The Wiltshire farmers, having learned the value of 'cloud ponds' or 'dew ponds', have formed them at much expense on the tops of the hills. **1903** KIPLING *Five Nations* 71 Only the dewpond on the height Unfed, that never fails. **1905** A. J. & G. HUBBARD *Neolithic Dew-ponds* 2 The gang of dew-pond makers commence operations by hollowing out the earth for a space far in excess of the apparent requirements of the proposed pond. They then thickly cover the whole of the hollow with a coating of dry straw. The straw.. is covered by a layer of well-chosen, finely puddled clay, and the upper surface of the clay is then closely strewn with stones. **1919** *Chambers's Jrnl.* Apr. 268/2 Every one must have heard of the famous dew-ponds of Sussex.

dew-rake ('dju:reɪk). [f. DEW *sb.* + RAKE *sb.*] A rake for the surface of grass or stubble.

1659 GAUDEN *Tears of Ch.* 381 Like dew-rakes and harrowes, armed with so many teeth. **1806-7** A. YOUNG *Agric. Essex* (1813) I. 108, 4 dew rakes, 20s. each. **1886** *Daily News* 24 Sept. 7/2 Where stubble is much infested it should be brushed off with poles.. and collected as closely as possible for burning by means of 'dew rakes'.

Hence **'dewrake** *v.*

1797 A. YOUNG *Agric. Suffolk* 55 The stubbles are dew-raked, by men drawing a long iron-toothed rake.

dewrance, obs. form of DURANCE.

dewre, var. of DURE *v. Obs.*

dew-ret ('dju:rɛt), *v.* Also **-rot, -rate**. [f. DEW *sb.* + RET *v.*[2]] *trans.* To ret or macerate (flax, hemp, etc.) so as to detach the fibre from the woody stem, by exposure to the dew and atmospheric influence instead of by steeping in water. Hence **'dew-retting** *vbl. sb.*

1710 HILMAN *Tusser Redivivus*, There is a Water-retting and a Dew-retting, which last is done on a good Rawing, or aftermath of a Meadow Water. **1807** VANCOUVER *Agric. Devon* (1813) 208 The flax is always dew-rotted. *a* **1825** FORBY *Voc. E. Anglia*, *Dew-retting*, which is spreading the crop on the grass, and turning it now and then to receive the dew. **1846** J. BAXTER *Libr. Pract. Agric.* (ed. 4) I. 274 In Dorsetshire and the neighbourhood the flax growers have generally adopted the practice of dew retting. **1849** *Jrnl. R. Agric. Soc.* X. I. 180 It takes perhaps six weeks to dew-ret hemp. **1877** *N.W. Linc. Gloss.*, *Dew-rated*, said of flax, which is retted on the ground, not by steeping in water.

dewry, obs. form of DOWRY.

dews, -e, obs. form of DEUCE.

dewsant, var. DEUSAN *Obs.*, a kind of apple.

dew-snail ('dju:sneɪl). *Obs.* exc. *dial.* [f. DEW *sb.* + SNAIL.] A slug. (So called from appearing while the dew is on the herbage.)

1548 THOMAS *Ital. Gram.*, *Lumaca*, the dewe snayle that hath no house. **1611** COTGR., *Limace*, (properly) the dew Snaile, or Snaile without a shell. **1699** ROBERTS *Voy. Levant* 15 All the sustenance we had there was three Dew snails, and some Roots. **1725** BRADLEY *Fam. Dict.* s.v. *Diseases of Trees*, Those Animals call'd Earwigs and Dew-snails, eat the finest Fruits on the Trees. **1783** AINSWORTH *Lat. Dict.* (Morell) II, *Līmax*, A snail, a dew-snail, or slug. **1880** *W. Cornwall Gloss.* s.v., As slippery as a dew-snail. **1888** ELWORTHY *W. Somerset Word-bk.*, *Dew-snail*, the large black slug.

† **dewtry**. *Obs.* Forms: 6-7 **deutroa**, 7 **deutro, doutro, doutry, dutry, dutra, deutery**, 7-8 **dewtry**. [From Western Indian vernacular forms of Skr. *dhattūra*, DATURA: e.g. Marāṭhī *dhutrā, dhotrā*, dialectally *dhutrō*.] The Thorn-apple, *Datura Stramonium*, and other Indian species of the

genus; a drug or drink prepared from this, employed to produce stupefaction.

1598 W. PHILLIPS tr. *Linschoten* 60 (Y.) An hearbe called *Deutroa*, which beareth a seede, whereof bruising out the sap, they..give it to their husbands, eyther in meate or drinke, and presently therewith the Man is as though hee were halfe out of his wits. **1662** J. DAVIES tr. *Mandelslo's Trav.* 104 A drug which..stupefies his senses..The Indians call this herb *Doutro, Doutry*, or *Datura*. **1678** BUTLER *Hud.* III. i. 321 Make lechers and their punks, with dewtry, Commit phantastical advowtry. **1691** SHADWELL *Scowrers* v, Some rogue that had a mind to marry me gave me deutery last night. **1696** OVINGTON *Voy. Suratt* 235 (Y.) Mixing Dutra and Water together to drink..which will intoxicate almost to Madness. **1698** FRYER *Acc. E. India & P.* 33 They give her Dutry; when half mad she throws herself into the Fire, and they ready with great Logs keep her in his Funeral Pile. *a* **1711** KEN *Hymnotheo* Poet. Wks. 1721 III. 192 As Indian Dames, their Consorts to abuse, Dewtry by Stealth into their Cups infuse.

dew-worm ('djuːwɜːm). [f. DEW *sb.* + WORM. OE. *deaw-wyrm*, Du. *dauwworm*, are known only in the sense 'ring-worm'; E.Fris. *dauwurm* is 'earth-worm' and 'ring-worm'; Da. *dugorm* 'a dew-snail'.] The common earth-worm; in OE. a name of the disease ring-worm.

c **1000** *Sax. Leechd.* II. 122 Wið..deaw wyrmum ʒenim doccan oððe clatan. **1599** MARSTON *Sco. Villanie* II. vii. 206 Cling'd so close, like deaw-worms in the morne. **1653** WALTON *Angler* 92 The Dew-worm which some call the Lob-worm. **1675** TEONGE *Diary* (1825) 83 Earth..like that which dew-wormes throe up. **1829** *Sporting Mag.* XXIII. 222 The small dew-worm is an excellent bait. **1875** M. G. PEARSE *Daniel Quorm* 27 Like to a dew-worm that hears you a comin' an' starts back into his hole in a minute. **1875** 'STONEHENGE' *Brit. Sports.* I. v. §3. 312 The dew-worm, or large garden-worm..six to twelve inches in length.

dewy ('djuːɪ), *a.* [OE. *déawiʒ*, f. *déaw* DEW: see -Y. Not recorded in ME.; prob. formed anew in Mod.Eng. (Cf. MHG. *touwec*, Ger. *thauig*, Sw. *daggig*).]

1. a. Characterized by the presence of dew, abounding with dew; covered or wet with dew.

a **1000** *Cædmon's Exod.* 344 (Gr.) Guþcyste onþrang deawiʒ sceaftum. *a* **1533** LD. BERNERS *Gold. Bk. M. Aurel.* (1546) S ij b, After the night cometh the dewy mornyng. **1579** SPENSER *Sheph. Cal.* May 316 The deawie night now doth nye. **1667** MILTON *P.L.* I. 743 From Noon to dewy Eve. **1699** POMFRET *Past. Ess. Death Q. Mary* 4 He found Cosmelia weeping on the dewy ground. **1762** FALCONER *Shipwr.* I. 267 Decking with countless gems the dewy lawn. **1834** HT. MARTINEAU *Demerara* iv. 48 However dewy the evening, she must stand in the grass. **1893** *Westm. Gaz.* 15 July 2/1 Water-hens were hurriedly gathering dewy slugs.

b. Affected by the influence of dew.

1725 POPE *Odyss.* XVII. 688 The sun obliquely shot his dewy ray. **1792** S. ROGERS *Pleas. Mem.* I. 215 Twilights dewy tints deceived his eye. **1795** SOUTHEY *Joan of Arc* VIII. 133 O'er the landscape spread The dewy light. **1833** HT. MARTINEAU *Cinnamon & P.* iii. 42 The dewy radiance of a morning in paradise.

2. *transf.* Wet or moistened, as with dew. In *Bot.* Appearing as if covered with dew.

1577 B. GOOGE *Heresbach's Husb.* I. (1586) 44 b, Newe grounde for Meddowe..take such as is ritche, dewye, levell, or a little hanging. **1590** SPENSER *F.Q.* III. ii. 34 And her faire deawy eies with kisses deare Shee ofte did bathe. **1853** LYNCH *Self-Improv.* ii. 40 His eye..will be clear and calm, and sometimes dewy. **1856** MISS YONGE *Daisy Chain* I. xxiv. (1879) 250 Pulling off the spectacles that had become very dewy.

3. Of the nature or quality of dew, dew-like, moist.

c **1000** *Sax. Leechd.* II. 258 þara breosta biþ deawiʒ wætung swa swa sie ʒespat. **1563** W. FULKE *Meteors* (1640) 36 b, Already resolved into dewy drops of rayne. **1594** SHAKS. *Rich. III*, V. iii. 283, I would these dewy teares were from the ground. **1598** FLORIO, *Nebbiarella*, a deawie exhalation, thinner then a cloud. **1635** SWAN *Spec. M.* vi. §2 (1643) 197 Sea-water, when it is boyled, doth evaporate a dewie or waterie humour. **1650** W. BROUGH *Sacr. Princ.* (1659) 124 What is my deawy sweat to Thy bloody agony. **1794** MRS. RADCLIFFE *Myst. Udolpho* iv, The vales below were still wrapped in dewy mist.

4. Of dew, made or consisting of dew. *poetic.*

1820 KEATS *Isabella* xxiv, Ere the hot sun count His dewy rosary on the eglantine. **1821** SHELLEY *Music* 15 When the hot noon has drained its dewy cup. **1827** HOOD *Mids. Fairies* lxxix, The buds were hung with dewy beads.

5. *fig.* **a.** Likened in some quality to dew, dew-like; falling gently, vanishing, as the dew. *poetic.*

1611 W. SCLATER *Key* (1629) 188 Those ἐφήμεροι, diary dewy Christians, whose goodnesse is dissipate as soone as euer the Sunne beholds it. **1667** MILTON *P.L.* IX. 1044 Till dewie sleep Oppress'd them. *a* **1670** HACKET *Abp. Williams* II. (1692) 144 Some of their Ministers that were softened with the dewy drops of his tongue. **1791** COWPER *Iliad* II. 41 Awaking from thy dewy slumbers. **1830** TENNYSON *Ode to Memory* i, Strengthen me, enlighten me!.. Thou dewy dawn of memory.

b. Innocent and trusting; naïve.

1958 *Times* 20 Oct. 3/1 The street-walker..should surely not be played..like the dewy ingenue from *Stage Struck*. **1962** *John o' London's* 8 Feb. 139/2 Once as dewy-innocent as the great director.

6. *Comb.* (poetic). **a.** *adverbial*, as ***dewy-bright***, ***-dark***, ***-fresh***, ***-warm***, etc. **b.** *parasynthetic*, as ***dewy-eyed*** (also *fig.* = sense 5 b above.), ***-feathered***, ***-pinioned***, ***-swarded***, etc. OE. had ***déawiʒ-feðere*** = dewy-pinioned.

a **1000** *Cædmon's Gen.* 1984 (Gr.) Sang se wanna fuʒel, deawiʒ-feðera. —— *Exod.* 163. **1632** MILTON *Penseroso* 146 Entice the dewy-feathered sleep. **1730–46** THOMSON *Autumn* 961 The dewy-skirted clouds imbibe the sun. **1777** ELIZ. RYVES *Poems* 36 Dewy-pinioned twilight's shadowy reign. **1796** T. TOWNSEND *Poems* 69 Some dewy-feather'd herald send. **1820** KEATS *Isabella* xxxvii, Its eyes..all dewy bright with love. **1832** TENNYSON *Œnone* 47 Aloft the mountain lawn was dewy-dark, And dewy-dark aloft the mountain pine. **1833** —— *Poems* 40 Upon the dewy-swarded slope. **1842** —— *Gardener's Dau.* 45 The fields between Are dewy-fresh. **1847** —— *Princ.* I. 93 Green gleam of dewy-tassell'd trees. **1864** —— *En. Ard.* 611 November dawns and dewy-glooming downs. **1938** 'E. QUEEN' *Four of Hearts* (1939) i. 9 Hollywood agents, fat or thin, tall or short, dewy-eyed or soiled by life. **1960** *Guardian* 7 Nov. 6/6 He is not..dewy-eyed about young people, but he feels that promotion should come early.

dewy, ME. inf. of DEW *v.*

dewyce, -ys, -yss(e, obs. ff. DEVICE, DEVISE.

dewzin, var. DEUSAN *Obs.*, a kind of apple.

dexamethasone (ˌdɛksə'mɛθəsəʊn, -zəʊn). *Pharm.* [f. *dexa-* (blend of *hexa-* and *deca-* in *hexadecadrol* (see quot. 1958[2]), representing the number 16 in the systematic names) + METH(YL + *-a* + CORTI)SONE.] A synthetic steroid, $C_{22}H_{29}FO_5$, which resembles cortisone in its effects and is used in the treatment of some blood disorders and as an anti-inflammatory agent.

1958 *Arthritis & Rheumatism* Aug. 330 Preliminary results of..investigations on the effect of dexamethasone in rheumatoid arthritis are encouraging. **1958** *Ann. Rheumatic Dis.* Dec. 376 In December, 1957, four separate 16a-methylated derivatives of hydrocortisone were made available for clinical trial... 16a-methyl 9a-fluoroprednisolone first received the generic name of 'hexadecadrol', but this was later changed to 'dexamethasone'. **1961** *Lancet* 12 Aug. 348/2 The therapy was changed from triamcinolone to dexamethasone. **1968** J. H. BURN *Lect. Notes Pharmacol.* (ed. 9) 95 Dexamethasone is a derivative of hydrocortisone, which is very much more active than hydrocortisone.

dexamphetamine (ˌdɛksæm'fɛtəmiːn, -ɪn). *Pharm.* [f. DEX(TRO- + AMPHETAMINE.] The dextro-rotatory isomer of AMPHETAMINE, used in the form of the sulphate and phosphate and having effects similar to those of amphetamine sulphate but more marked. Also called ˌ**dextro-am'phetamine**.

1949 *Brit. Med. Jrnl.* 17 Dec. 1394/1 (*title*) Acute psychosis caused by dextro-amphetamine. **1952** *Martindale's Extra Pharmacopœia* (ed. 23) I. 516 The action of dexamphetamine sulphate is similar to that of amphetamine sulphate but it is effective in smaller dosage. **1958** *Spectator* 24 Jan. 103/2 A similar list of dangers can be made out for dexamphetamine (dexedrine). **1964** *Economist* 9 May 576/1 Dexamphetamine amylobarbitone *alias* 'purple hearts'.

dexe, dext, obs. forms of DESK.

Dexedrine ('dɛksədriːn). Also **dexedrine**. [prob. f. DEX(TRO- + *-edrine* as in BENZEDRINE.] The proprietary name of a preparation of dexamphetamine sulphate.

1942 *Trade Marks Jrnl.* 4 Nov. 458/1 *Dexedrine*, pharmaceutical preparations and substances for human use and for veterinary use; sanitary substances;..Smith, Kline & French Laboratories. **1949** *Lancet* 21 May 888/2, I have used 'Dexedrine' (*d*-amphetamine sulphate) in the treatment of twenty-two cases of chronic skin disease. **1955** *Sci. News Let.* 9 Apr. 232/3 Only brain stimulants such as caffeine and Dexedrine ('pep pill' ingredient)..are able to keep tired aircrews working efficiently. **1958** [see prec.]. **1970** *Sci. Jrnl.* Feb. 7/1 Amphetamines, better known to most people as benzadrine [*sic*] and dexedrine—or as 'speed' in the drug subculture—have acquired a dirty name in the medical profession.

dexiocardia (ˌdɛksɪəʊ'kɑːdɪə). *Path.* [a. Gr. δεξιό-ς on the right side + καρδία heart.] An anomaly of development in man in which the heart is on the right side; sometimes applied to cases in which the heart is displaced to the right side in consequence of disease.

1866 T. B. PEACOCK *Malformations of Heart* I *Transposition, Dexiocardia*..when the heart is placed in a position on the right side corresponding to that which it should occupy on the left. **1875** HAYDEN *Dis. Heart* 105 Hope has also noted, in a case of dexiocardia, the existence of systolic murmur, which ceased on the return of the heart to its normal position. **1883** *Syd. Soc. Lex.*

dexiotrope ('dɛksɪəʊtrəʊp), *a.* [f. Gr. δεξιό-ς on or to the right + -τροπος turning.] = next.

1883 *Syd. Soc. Lex.*, *Dexiotrope*, a term signifying turning or turned to the right, as the spire of some shells.

dexiotropic (ˌdɛksɪəʊ'trɒpɪk), *a.* [f. as prec. + -IC: cf. Gr. τροπικός having a turning, inclined.] Turning or turned to the right: said *spec.* of those 'reversed' Gastropod Molluscs in which the spire turns to the right; opposed to *leiotropic*.

The terms *leiotropic* and *dexiotropic* as used by Ray Lankester refer to the left and right sides *of the animal*, not *of the spectator* as is the case with *dextral* and *sinistral*. Hence *dexiotropic* is the opposite of *dextral*.

1883 RAY LANKESTER in *Encycl. Brit.* XVI. 661 (*Mollusca*) In Planorbis, which is dexiotropic (as are a few other genera or exceptional varieties of Anisopleurous Gastropods) instead of being leiotropic, the osphradium is on the left side ..the whole series of unilateral organs being reversed. This is..what is found to be the case in all 'reversed' Gastropods.

†'**dexter**, *sb. Obs. rare.* [app.:—OE. **deaʒestre*, *deʒestre*, *deʒstre*, f. *deaʒian* to DYE: cf. DYESTER.] A dyer.

14.. *Pueritia vel Infancia Christi* 569 in Horstmann *Altengl. Leg.* (1878) 119/2 A dyer yn hys dore he stode..þe dexter on Jhesu dede calle: Knowst þou owte of mystere? *Ibid.* 613 þe dexter toke vp a fyre-brond.

dexter ('dɛkstə(r)), *a.* (*sb.*[1] and *adv.*) [a. L. *dexter* on the right hand or right side, right, a comparative form from root *dex-* cognate with Gr. δεξιός, and Goth. *taihswa*, Skr. *daksha*, *daksh-ina*, from a primitive form **dekswo-*.]

A. *adj.* **1.** Belonging to or situated on the right side of a person, animal, or object worn on the body; right; *esp.* in *Her.* the opposite of SINISTER.

The dexter side of a person, animal, shield, etc., is to the *left* of the spectator facing it, which is important in Heraldry: see quot. 1882.

1562 LEIGH *Armorie* (1597) 64 b, Seing you call this a Bende Sinister, wherfore did you not call the other dexter bend? Because it is knowne to all..if it bee named a bend and no more to be a bende dexter. **1572** BOSSEWELL *Armorie* II. 33 b, At the Dexter angle of the shielde. **1600** DYMMOK *Ireland* (1843) 33 There was loste in the retreyte of the dexter winge of the forlorne hope, capten Boswell. **1705** *Lond. Gaz.* NO. 4110/4 A Dexter Hand holding a Branch of Acorns. **1762** FALCONER *Shipwr.* I. 766 The imperial trident graced her dexter hand. **1878** BROWNING *Poets Croisic* cxv, [He] pressed to heart His dexter hand. **1882** CUSSANS *Handbk. Her.* 45 The right-hand side..[of the shield] would be towards the left of a spectator; and in a representation of a coat of arms, that part of the shield which appears on the *left* side is called the Dexter, and that on the *right*, the Sinister.

fig. **1581** MARBECK *Bk. of Notes* 270 Aristotle in Politices, admonisheth that men which haue learned to do sinister things, ought not be compelled to doe thinges dextere.

†**b.** Situated on the side which is to the right of the spectator. *Obs.*

1674 JEAKE *Arith.* (1696) 210 The dexter Figure of the Quotient shall be Primes.

†**c.** Of omens: Seen or heard on the right side; hence, auspicious, favourable, propitious. *Obs.*

1646 SIR T. BROWNE *Pseud Ep.* IV. v. 191 Sinister and dexter respects. **1676** HOBBES *Iliad* (1677) 203 This said, an eagle dexter presently Flew over them. **1715–20** POPE *Iliad* XIII. 1039 On sounding wings a dexter eagle flew.

d. Belonging to the right hand; right; straightforward, fair. *rare.*

a **1734** NORTH *Exam.* III. vii. §53 (1740) 542 The managers of these Petitions used all Manner of Arts, *dexter* and *sinister*, to gain People's Hands or Marks.

†**2.** = DEXTEROUS. *Obs.*

1597 LOWE *Chirurg.* (1634) 320 A man of great learning and experience, most fortunate and dexter in this operation. **1622** F. MARKHAM *Bk. War* II. i. §6. 43 He is..more swift, more dexter, and more seruiceable. **1659** TORRIANO, *Fiero*, nimble, lively, dexter either of body or mind.

B. *sb.* The right (hand or side).

1814 CARY *Dante, Paradise* XV. 18 The horn That on the dexter of the cross extends.

C. *adv.* On the right side, to the right.

1715–20 POPE *Odyss.* XV. 184 The bird majestic flew Full dexter to the car. *Ibid.* 573 Yon bird that dexter cuts the aërial road, Rose ominous.

D. *Comb.* **dexterways, -wise**, on the right side, to the right.

1610 GUILLIM *Heraldry* IV. xiv. (1611) 224 Foure speares in bend garnished with Penoncels dexterwaies.

Dexter ('dɛkstə(r)), *sb.*[2] Also **dexter**. [Said to have originated from the name of a Mr. *Dexter*, who is credited with having established the breed.] One of a breed of small hardy Irish cattle originating from the Kerry breed. Also called ***Dexter Kerry***.

1880 *Encycl. Brit.* XIII. 225/2 The variety known as the 'Dexter', a cross between the 'Kerry' and some unknown breed, is shorter and plumper than the pure 'Kerry'. **1894** *Country Gentlemen's Catal.* 17/2 If the capacity to make good beef is..a *sine quâ non* in the perfect dairy cow.., it must actually be conceded that..the little Dexter-Kerry..presents the nearest approach of any! **1899** *Daily News* 20 June 9/5 The best dexter animal in the show. *Ibid.* 21 June 9/1 The dainty Jersey or pigmy Dexter and Kerry. **1902** *Encycl. Brit.* XXV. 192/2 The Dexter breed... Until recently it was called the Dexter Kerry. **1953** D. D. C. P. MOULD *Ireland of Saints* ii. 23 The typical cow of Celtic Ireland was rather like the modern dexter.

†**dex'terical**, *a.* [irreg. f. L. *dexter* (see DEXTER *a.*) + -IC + -AL[1].] Dexterous, adroit, skilful.

1607 WALKINGTON *Opt. Glass* (N.), Those have most dexterical wits. *Ibid.* 27 It is called..the right hand of the minde, because it makes any conceit dexterical. **1644** BULWER *Chiron.* 10 A smirke, quick and dextericall wit.

†**dex'terious**, *a. Obs.* A 17th c. variant of DEXTEROUS.

1629 SYMMER *Spir. Posie* I. iv. 15 His dexterious histrionicall acting of his part. **1644** BULWER *Chirol.* 134 Which if it once grow dexterious by habituall theeving. *Ibid.* 179 To scrape and get by such dexterious endeavours. **1653** *Cloria & Narcissus* I. 248 By his dexterious valour.

†**dex'teriously**, *adv. Obs.* [see prec.] A 17th c. variant of DEXTEROUSLY.

1601 SHAKS. *Twel. N.* I. v. 66 *Ol.* Can you do it? *Clo.* Dexteriously, good Madona. **1605** BACON *Adv. Learn.* II. xxii. §15 [The Sophist] he calleth Left-handed, because with all his rules..he cannot form a man so Dexteriously.. as loue can do. *a* **1635** NAUNTON *Fragm. Reg.* (Arb.) 28 To play his part well, and dexteriously. **1663** F. HAWKINS *Youths' Behav.* 102 Dexteriously, quickly.

dexterity (dɛkˈstɛrɪtɪ). [ad. L. *dexteritās*, f. *dexter*: see above and -ITY. Cf. F. *dexterité* (1539 in Hatz.-Darm.), perh. the immediate source.]

1. Manual or manipulative skill, adroitness, neat-handedness; hence, address in the use of the limbs and in bodily movements generally.

1548 UDALL, etc. *Erasm. Par.* Pref. (R.), A prince..of inuincible fortitude, of notable actiuitee, of dexteritee wonderfull. **1578** T. N. tr. *Conq. W. India* 279 They have great dexteritie and skill in swimming. **1591** GARRARD *Art Warre* 2 Able to handle his Peece with due dexteritie. **1603** HOLLAND *Plutarch's Mor.* 107 A Chirurgian when he maketh incision.. had need to use great dexteritie. **1703** MOXON *Mech. Exerc.* 214 Some Turners to shew their Dexterity in Turning..Turn long and slender Sprigs of Ivory, as small as an Hay-stalk. **1776** GIBBON *Decl. & F.* i. (1838) I. 12 To dispute with them the prize of superior strength or dexterity. **1848** MACAULAY *Hist. Eng.* I. 382 His dexterity at sword and pistol made him a terror to all men.

2. Mental adroitness or skill; 'readiness of expedient, quickness of contrivance, skill of management' (J.); cleverness, address, ready tact. Sometimes in a bad sense: cleverness in taking an advantage, sharpness.

1527 *Chron. Calais* (Camden 1846) 114 (Stanf.) Expedyente that she by her greate wisdom and dexteryte do cause the kyng her sonne to write to such cardynelles as be at lyberte. *c* **1529** WOLSEY in Ellis *Orig. Lett.* Ser. I. II. 8 Aftyr your accustomable wysdom and dexteryte. **1549** *Compl. Scot.* (1872) 4 Comparit to the deuot Kyng, Numa pompilius..for his prudens ande dixtirite. **1598** SHAKS. *Merry W.* IV. v. 120 My admirable dexteritie of wit. **1647** CLARENDON *Hist. Reb.* VIII. (1703) II. 467 The dexterity that is universally practiced in those parts. **1656** BRAMHALL *Replic.* iv. 177 Persons of great maturity of judgement, of known dexterity in the Cannon Laws. **1677** GALE *Crt. Gentiles* II. III. 99 Al manner of Calliditie or dexteritie to cheat and deceive. **1732** BERKELEY *Alciphr.* v. §15, I admire his address and dexterity in argument. **1807–8** SYD. SMITH *Plymley's Lett.* Wks. (1859) II. 161/1 It is not..that the dexterity of honest Englishmen will ever equal the dexterity of French knaves. **1874** GREEN *Short Hist.* vii. §6. 404 Elizabeth trusted to her dexterity to keep out of the storm.

†**b.** *with pl.* A dexterous or clever act; in bad sense, a piece of 'sharp practice'. *Obs.*

1577–87 HOLINSHED *Chron.* III. 1104/2 Being acquainted with the citizens, knowing the corruptions and dexterities of them in such cases. **1621** G. HELLIER in *Lismore Papers* (1888) Ser. II. III. 29 By dextereaties I shall retayne them. **1635** R. BOLTON *Comf. Affl. Consc.* iv. 176 In pressing the law, besides other dexterities. **1805** FOSTER *Ess.* I. vii. 92 All these accommodating dexterities of reason.

†**3.** Handiness, conveniency, suitableness. *Obs.*

1611 CORYAT *Crudities* Oration 5 He..trauelleth..for the commodity of his studies, and the dexterity of his life. **1614** T. ADAMS *Devil's Banquet* 18 A full belly is not of such dexteritie for the Deuils imployment, as a full braine.

4. *lit.* Right-handedness; the using of the right hand in preference to the left. *rare* and *late.*

a **1882** *Lancet* (O.), Dexterity appears to be confined to the human race, for the monkey tribes use the right and left limbs indiscriminately. **1885** *Science* V. June 460 In the drawings of the cave-men of France..the proportion of left-hand drawings is greatly in excess of what would now be found; but there is still a distinct preponderance of the right hand, which, however originated, has sufficed to determine the universal dexterity of the whole historic period. **1891** D. WILSON *Right Hand* 39 To determine the preference for one hand over the other, and so to originate the prevalent law of dexterity.

dexterous, dextrous (ˈdɛkstərəs, ˈdɛkstrəs), *a.* Also 7 DEXTERIOUS. [f. L. *dexter, dextr-* right, handy, dexterous, *dextra* the right hand + -OUS. If an analogous word had been formed in L., it would have been *dextrōsus*; hence *dextrous* (cf. *sinistrous*) is the more regular form; but *dexterous* appears to prevail in 19th c. prose.]

†**1.** Situated on the right side or right-hand; right, as opposed to *left*; = DEXTER 1, DEXTRAL.

1646 SIR T. BROWNE *Pseud. Ep.* IV. v. 190 The dextrous and sinistrous parts of the body. **1678** CUDWORTH *Intell. Syst.* 221 The Contrarieties and Conjugations of things, such as..Dextrous and Sinistrous, Eaven and Odd, and the like.

†**2.** Handy, convenient, suitable, fitting. *Obs.*

1605 BACON *Adv. Learn.* II. xv. §2 The Art..is barren, that is, not dexterous to be applyed to the serious vse of businesse and occasions.

3. Deft or nimble of hand, neat-handed; hence skilful in the use of the limbs and in bodily movements generally.

1635–56 COWLEY *Davideis* IV. 353 So swift, so strong, so dextrous none beside. **1650** FULLER *Pisgah* I. 423 Though skilfull in the Mathematicall..so dexterous in the manual part. **1697** DRYDEN *Virg. Georg.* III. 570 The dext'rous Huntsman wounds not these afar. **1776** GIBBON *Decl. & F.* I. xviii. 483 He was a dextrous archer. **1801** SOUTHEY *Thalaba* III. xviii, With dexterous fingers. **1818** JAS. MILL *Brit. India* II. IV. i. 13 The flagellants in India are said to be so dextrous, as to kill a man with a few strokes of the chawbuck.

4. Having mental adroitness or skill; skilful or expert in contrivance or management; clever.

1622 MABBE tr. *Aleman's Guzman d'Alf.* II. * * iv a, As dextrous in Letters as disciplin'd in Armes. **1642** FULLER *Holy & Prof. St.* IV. ix. 281 Generally the most dexterous in spirituall matters are left-handed in temporall businesse. **1672** MARVELL *Reh. Transp.* I. 194 A dexterous Scholastical Disputant. *a* **1720** SHEFFIELD (Dk. Buckhm.) *Wks.* (1753) II. 25 To which, that dexterous Minister replied something haughtily. **1838** THIRLWALL *Greece* IV. 433 A dexterous politician of Lysander's school. *a* **1843** SOUTHEY *Doctor* clxxiv. (1862) 457 She was devout in religion, decorous in conduct..dextrous in business. **1850** MRS. JAMESON *Leg. Monast. Ord.* (1863) 333 Dexterous in the management of temporal affairs.

†**b.** In a bad sense: 'Clever', crafty, cunning.

1701 tr. *Le Clerc's Prim. Fathers* (1702) 154 Eusebius.. was a dextrous Person which made no scruple to subscribe to Terms which he did not like. *a* **1715** BURNET *Own Time* (1823) I. 332 Ward..was a very dexterous man if not too dexterous; for his sincerity was much questioned.

5. Of things: Done with or characterized by dexterity; skilful, clever.

a **1625** BEAUM. & FL. *Bloody Brother* IV. ii, He..cuts through the elements for us..In a fine dextrous line. **1627–77** FELTHAM *Resolves* I. lxxxviii. 136 A dexterous Art shows cunning and industry; rather than judgment and ingenuity. **1748** *Anson's Voy.* II. xiv. 287 Trained to the dexterous use of their fire-arms. **1808** SYD. SMITH *Wks.* (1859) I. 115/1 An uninterrupted series of dexterous conduct.

6. Using the right hand in preference to the left; right-handed.

In mod. Dicts.

ˈdexterously, ˈdextrously, *adv.* [f. prec. + -LY[2]. (See also DEXTERIOUSLY.)]

1. In a dexterous manner, with dexterity; adroitly, cleverly. **a.** With manual dexterity.

1646 SIR T. BROWNE *Pseud. Ep.* IV. v. 191 Many women, and some men, which though they accustome themselves unto either hand, do dexterously make use of neither. **1659** B. HARRIS *Parival's Iron Age* 139 And so neately, and dexterously retorted the ball. **1685** BOYLE *Effects of Mot.* ix. 109 A glass being dexterously inverted and shaken. **1766** GOLDSM. *Vic. W.* xxvii, Observing the manner in which I had disposed my books..he very dextrously displaced one of them. **1856** KANE *Arct. Expl.* II. xv. 163 So dexterously has this thrust to be made.

b. With mental dexterity.

1605 BACON *Adv. Learn.* I. viii. §2 The good parts he hath he will..use..dexterously. **1648** BOYLE *Seraph. Love* vi. (1700) 42 The Condition of Lovers..so dexterously and delightfully described. **1699** BENTLEY *Phal.* 287 He explains very dextrously..the expression of Phalaris. **1798** FERRIAR *Illust. Sterne, Eng. Hist.* 248 The small chasms of private history are so dextrously supplied. **1849** MACAULAY *Hist. Eng.* II. 24 Dexterously accommodating his speech to the temper of his audience. **1856** DOVE *Logic Chr. Faith* Introd. §6. 23 Scepticism dextrously fights one department against the other.

2. With the right hand. *rare.*

1830 *Blackw. Mag.* XXVIII. 888 We often stand.. dexterously, and sinistrously fingering the string.

ˈdexterousness, ˈdextrousness. [f. as prec. + -NESS.] The quality of being dexterous or adroit in mind or body; dexterity.

1622 MABBE tr. *Aleman's Guzman d'Alfar.* II. **va, The modesty and dextrousnes of his style. **1674** tr. *Scheffer's Lapland* xxvi. 124 Olaus Magnus..wonderfully extols their dextrousness herein. **1677** W. HUBBARD *Narrative* 66 The subtlety and dexterousness of these Natives. **1866** MRS. WHITNEY *L. Goldthwaite* ix. (1873) 153 With dexterousness and pains and sacrifice.

dextrad (ˈdɛkstræd), *adv.* and *a.* [f. L. *dextra* right hand + *-ad* suffix proposed by Barclay in sense *toward.*] To or toward the right side of the body; dextrally.

1803 J. BARCLAY *New Anatomical Nomencl.* 165–6 The new terms by a change of termination, may be used adverbially..*Dextrad* will signify towards the dextral aspect. **1882** WILDER & GAGE *Anatom. Technol.* 27 Barclay proposed that the various adjective forms should be converted into adverbs by substituting for the ending *-al* the letters *-ad*, the Latin equivalent of the English *-ward*. Thus *dorsal, ventral, dextral, sinistral,* and *lateral* become *dorsad, ventrad, dextrad, sinistrad,* and *laterad.* **1883** *Syd. Soc. Lex.*, *Dextrad aspect.*

dextral (ˈdɛkstrəl), *a.* (and *sb.*) [f. L. *dextra* right hand + -AL[1]. Late L. has *dextrālis, dextrāle* as sbs.]

1. a. Situated on the right side of the body; right, as opposed to *left.*

1646 SIR T. BROWNE *Pseud. Ep.* IV. v. 188 Which should hinder the Liver from enabling the dextrall parts. **1794** MATHIAS *Purs. Lit.* iv. 452 Throw wide that portal; let no Roman wait, But march with Priestly through the dextral gate.

†**b.** Of omens: Auspicious, favourable. *Obs.*

1774 *Poetry* in *Ann. Reg.* 203 No eastern meteor glar'd beneath the sky, No dextral omen.

c. That uses the right hand in preference to the left; right-handed: see DEXTRALITY 2. Hence as *sb.*, a (predominantly) right-handed person.

1871 *Lancet* I. 49 On Dextral Pre-eminence by William Ogle M.D. **1904** *Westm. Gaz.* 6 Aug. 11/3 As if fate had chosen to make it a dextral child. **1927** *Amer. Jrnl. Psychol.* XXXVIII. 327 People fall into four groups, pure or crossed dextrals, and pure or crossed sinistrals... In the pure dextral there is right-handedness and a dominant right eye. **1964** M. CRITCHLEY *Developmental Dyslexia* viii. 54 A fair number of dyslexics are unequivocal dextrals with no family history of left-handedness or ambidexterity.

2. *Conchol.* Of a gastropod shell: Having the spire or whorl ascending from left to right (i.e. of the external spectator), which is the prevalent form.

1847 CRAIG, s.v., A dextral shell, as in mostly all univalves, has its turns or convolutions from left to right when placed in a perpendicular position. **1851** RICHARDSON *Geol.* viii. 241 In the first instance the shell is termed *dextral*; in the latter it is called *sinistral* or *reversed.* **1854** WOODWARD *Mollusca* (1856) 46 Left-handed, or reversed, varieties of spiral shells have been met with in some of the very common species, like the whelk and garden snail. *Bulimus citrinus* is as often sinistral as dextral. **1866** TATE *Brit. Mollusks* iii. 45 When the aperture of the shell is on the right-hand side it is said to be dextral.

dextrality (dɛkˈstrælɪtɪ). [f. prec. + -ITY.]

1. The condition of having the right side differing from the left.

1646 SIR T. BROWNE *Pseud. Ep.* IV. v. 187 If there were a determinate prepotency in the right..wee might expect the same in other animals, whose parts are also differenced by dextrality. *Ibid.* 191 This doth but peti[ti]onarily inferre a dextrality in the heavens.

2. The use by preference of the right hand, and the limbs of the right side generally; right-handedness.

1646 SIR T. BROWNE *Pseud. Ep.* IV. v. 187 Did not institution, but Nature determine dextrality, there would be many more Scevolaes then are delivered in story. **1881** LE CONTE *Monoc. Vision* 94 There is no doubt that dextrality affects the whole side of the body.

†**ˈdextralize,** *v. Obs. rare.* [f. DEXTRAL *a.* + -IZE.] *trans.* To make a 'right' hand or 'right' side of; hence to use in preference to the other.

1651 BIGGS *New Disp.* ¶196 Dextralize and preferre it before their laxatives.

dextrally (ˈdɛkstrəlɪ), *adv.* [f. DEXTRAL *a.* + -LY[2].] In a dextral way or direction; to the right, as opposed to the left.

1881 LE CONTE *Monoc. Vision* 19 To rotate it on its axis outward, i.e. dextrally—or like the hands of a watch. **1883** *Journ. Bot. Brit. & For.* 237 The spathes..are rolled up indifferently either way—either dextrally or sinistrally—in about equal numbers.

dextran (ˈdɛkstræn). [a. G. *dextran* (C. Scheibler 1874, in *Zeit. Ver. Rübenz.-Ind.* XXIV. 321), f. DEXTRO- + -AN.] **a.** *Chem.* An amorphous, gummy substance produced by the fermentation of sucrose and some other organic materials, and now known to include many structurally related branched polysaccharides of glucose and to be produced only by a few micro-organisms, notably bacteria of the genus *Leuconostoc.* **b.** *Med.* A preparation of degraded, partially hydrolysed dextran in a suitable solvent (as saline solution), used as a substitute for blood plasma.

1879 *Jrnl. Chem. Soc.* XXXVI. A. 912 Beetroot Gum..is converted..after some days' boiling with a solution of potash into dextran. **1939** *Thorpe's Dict. Appl. Chem.* (ed. 4) III. 567/2 Dextran, $C_6H_{10}O_5$, or viscose, is a gum which occurs in the unripe sugar beet... An animal dextran..is found in the galls produced on elms by the louse. **1946** *Adv. Carbohydrate Chem.* II. 209 The term 'dextran' has been applied to carbohydrate slimes originating from sugar sirups, fermenting vegetables and dairy products. **1948** *Daily Express* 24 Feb. 3/2 Synthetic blood..is known as dextran. **1963** *Brit. Pharm. Codex* 239 Dextran injection is used as a plasma substitute. It is not, however, a complete substitute. **1970** R. W. MCGILVERY *Biochem.* xxviii. 707 A column packed with beads of dextran, available under the trade name *Sephadex*, can be used to separate molecules of varying size.

dextrane, var. DEXTRAN.

dextrer(e, dextrier: see DESTRER, a war-horse.

dextrin (ˈdɛkstrɪn). *Chem.* Also (*less correctly*) -ine. [a. F. *dextrine*, f. L. *dextra* right-hand: see -IN. Named by Biot and Persoz in 1833, from the optical property mentioned below.

1833 BIOT & PERSOZ in *Ann. de Chimie et de Physique* [2] lii. 72 Nous la nommons dextrine, pour la designer par le caractère spécial que lui donne le sens et l'energie de son pouvoir rotatoire.]

A soluble gummy substance into which starch is converted when subjected to a high temperature, or to the action of dilute alkalis or acids, or of diastase. Called also *British gum*, and *leiocome.*

It has the same chemical composition as starch, but is not coloured blue by iodine, and has the property of turning the plane of polarization 138·68° to the right; whence its name.

1838 T. THOMSON *Chem. Org. Bodies* 653 Amidin.. caused a deviation of the rays to the right, about three times as great as common sugar—a deviation which is sensibly the same with that of his [M. Biot's] *dextrine.* **1838** *Ann. Reg.* 374 List of patents, For improvements in the manufacture of dextrine. **1863–72** WATTS *Dict. Chem.* II. 313 Dextrin is an uncrystallizable, solid, translucent substance having the aspect of gum arabic..It is employed..for the adhesive layer at the back of postage-stamps. **1870** BENTLEY *Bot.* 29 If starch be exposed to heat for a prolonged period it is converted into a solid gummy substance, called dextrin or British gum.

dextro-, combining form of L. *dexter, dextra*, used in the sense '(turning or turned) to the right', in physical and chemical terms, chiefly having reference to the property possessed by certain substances of causing the plane of a ray of polarized light to rotate to the right. Among these are:

a. dextrogyre ('dɛkstrəʊdʒaɪə(r)) *a.* [L. *gȳrus*, Gr. γῦρος circuit], gyrating or circling to the right. **dextro'gyrate** *a.* [L. *gyrāt-us*, pa. pple. of *gȳrāre* to wheel round], characterized by turning the plane of polarization to the right, as a ***dextrogyrate crystal***. **dextro'gyrous** *a.* = DEXTROGYRE. **dextro-ro'tation**, rotation to the right. **dextro-'rotatory** *a.*, having or producing rotation to the right; dextrogyrous.

b. dextro-'compound, a chemical compound which causes dextro-rotation. **dextro-'glucose**, the ordinary variety of GLUCOSE or grape-sugar, DEXTROSE. **dextro-ra'cemic, dextro-tar'taric acid**, the modifications of racemic and tartaric acid which cause dextro-rotation. Hence **dextro-racemate, -tartrate**, the salts of these.

a. **1876** HARLEY *Mat. Med.* 366 Called mycose, because it is rather less dextrogyre than cane sugar. **1878** FOSTER *Phys.* II. i. 197 The solutions of both acids have a dextro-rotatory action on polarized light. **1882** *Nature* XXV. 283 With each electrode, diverging currents produce dextro- and converging ones lævo-rotation. **1883** *Athenæum* 29 Dec. 871/1 The dextrorotatory and optically inactive gums. **1891** *Lancet* 3 Oct. 751 The dextro-rotatory tartaric acid. b. **1853** *Pharmac. Jrnl.* XIII. 111 Pasteur discovered that racemic acid is a compound of two acids, one of which turns the plane of polarization of a ray of light to the right, and the other to the left; he therefore called them *Dextro-racemic-acid* and *Levo-racemic-acid*. *Ibid.* 112 A solution of dextro-racemate of soda and ammonia. *Ibid.* 377 The dextro-tartrate crystallizes out. **1863–72** WATTS *Dict. Chem.* II. 855 Dextro-glucose occurs abundantly in sweet fruits, frequently together with cane sugar. **1873** *Fownes' Chem.* (ed. 11) 731 Dextrotartaric Acid is the acid of fruits.

dextro-amphetamine: see DEXAMPHETAMINE.

dex'trorsal, *a. rare.* [f. L. *dextrorsum* (see next) + -AL[1].] (See quot.)

1828 WEBSTER, *Dextrorsal*, rising from right to left, as a spiral line or helix.

dextrorse (dɛk'strɔːs), *a.* [ad. L. *dextrorsum*, *-sus*, for *dextrovorsum*, *-versum*, turned to the right.] Turned towards the right hand.

Used by botanists in two opposite senses. The earlier authors, Linnæus, the De Candolles, etc., used it as = 'to the right-hand of the observer'; modern botanists generally use it as = 'to the right hand of the plant, or of a person round whom the plant might be twining', which is to the left of the external observer.)

1864 in WEBSTER. **1880** GRAY *Struct. Bot.* iv. §2. 140 Direction of Overlapping. It may be to the right (*dextrorse*).

dextrose ('dɛkstrəʊs). *Chem.* [f. L. *dexter*, *dextra* (see above), with the ending of *glucose*: see -OSE[2].] The form of GLUCOSE which is dextro-rotatory to polarized light; dextro-glucose; ordinary glucose or grape-sugar.

1869 ROSCOE *Elem. Chem.* 396 Dextrose, or right-handed glucose. **1872** THUDICHUM *Chem. Phys.* 7 It polarises to the right four times more intensely than dextrose sugar. **1878** M. FOSTER *Phys.* (1879) App. 673 Dextrose is soluble in alcohol, but insoluble in æther.

dextrous: see DEXTEROUS.

dey[1] (deɪ). *Obs.* exc. *dial.* Forms: 1 dæᵹe, 3 daie, 4, 8 deie, 4–5 deye, 5–9 dey, 9 dai, dei (*dial.*). [OE. *dǽᵹe*, corresp. to ON. *deigja*, maid, female servant, house-keeper (whence Sw. *deja* dairy-maid):—OTeut. **daigjôn*, from ablaut-stem of the vb. (in Gothic) *deigan*, *daig*, *dig-un*, *digan-*, to knead; whence Goth. *daigs*, OE. *dáᵹ*, *dáh*, dough.

The primitive meaning 'kneader', 'maker of bread', appears in OE. in the first quotation; in ON. and in early ME. we find the wider sense of 'female servant', 'woman employed in a house or farm'. Cf. also ON. *bú-deigja* (*bú*, house, household) and mod. Norw. *bu-deia*, *sæter-deia*, *agtar-deia*. The same word, or a cognate derivative of the same root, is understood to form the second element in OE. *hlæfdiᵹe*, *hlæfdiᵹe* now LADY. See also DAIRY.]

1. A woman having charge of a dairy and things pertaining to it; in early use, also, with the more general sense, female servant, maid-servant. Still in living use in parts of Scotland.

a **1000** *Ags. Gloss.* in Wr.-Wülcker 277/2 *Pristris* [for *pistrix*] dæᵹe. *a* **1087** *Record of Contract* in Earle *Land-Charters* 268 Her swutelað..þ Godwiᵹ se bucca hæfð ᵹeboht Leofgife þa dæᵹean æt norðstoke..mid healfan punde æt Ælsiᵹe abbod to ean freote. [**1086** *Domesday Bk.* lf. 180 b, [In Biseley, Worcestershire] Ibi viij inter servos & ancillas & vaccarius & daia.] *c* **1200** *Trin. Coll. Hom.* 163 He awlencð his daie mid cloðes more þan him seluen. *c* **1325** *Poem Times Edw. II.* 81 in *Pol. Songs* (Camden) 327 And leveth thare behinde..A serjaunt and a deie that leden a sory lif. *c* **1386** CHAUCER *Nun's Pr. T.* 26 She was as it were a maner deye. **14..** *Lat. & Eng. Voc.* in Wr.-Wülcker 563/42 *Anadrogia*, a deye. *Ibid.* 564/6 *Androchia*, a deye. **1483** in *Cath. Angl.* **16..** in Maidment *Sc. Pasquils* (1868) II. 262 An old dey or dairy maid at Douglas Castle. **1721** RAMSAY *To Gay* xvii, Dance with kiltit dees, O'er mossy plains. *c* **1820** *Lizie Lindsay* in Child *Ballads* VIII. (1892) 524/1 My father he is an old shepherd, My mither she is an old dey. *Ibid.* To the house o' his father's milk-dey. **1863** MORTON *Cycl. Agric.* Gloss., *Dey* (Perthsh.) a dairymaid. [**1866** ROGERS *Agric. & Prices* I. ii. 14 This part of the medieval farm was under the management of a deye, or dairy-woman.]

2. Extended to a man having similar duties.

[**1351** *Act 25 Edw. III* (*Stat. Labourers*) Stat. II. c. 1 Chescun charetter, Caruer, Chaceour des carues, Bercher, Porcher, Deye, et touz autres servantz. **1363** *Act 37 Edw. III*, c. 14 Bovers, vachers, berchers..Deyes, et touz autres gardeinz des bestes.] **1483** *Cath. Angl.* 94 A Deye (Dere, deire A.); Androchius, Androchea, genatarius, genetharia. **1492** *Will of Hadley* (Somerset Ho), William Bayly my dey. **1764** BURN *Poor Laws* 9 [citing 25 Ed. III] Shepherds, swineherds, deies and all other servants. **1770–4** A. HUNTER *Georg. Ess.* (1803) III. 262 Thus would the careful dai be able on all occasions to observe the particular quality of each individual cow's milk. (*Note. Dai* or *dei*, in Aberdeenshire, denotes the person who has the superintendence of a dairy, whether that person be male or female.)

3. *Comb.* **dey-girl, dey-maid**, a dairy-maid. Also DAY-HOUSE, -WIFE, -WOMAN.

1828 SCOTT *F.M. Perth* xxxii, This happened so soon as the dey-girl..was about to return.

‖**dey**[2] (deɪ). Forms: 7 dye, dij, dei, 7–9 dey, [a. F. *dey*, Turkish *dāī* 'maternal uncle'. Also 'a friendly title formerly given to middle-aged or old people, *esp.* among the Janissaries; and hence in Algiers appropriated at length to the commanding officer of that corps'.]

The titular appellation of the commanding officer of the Janissaries of Algiers, who, after having for some time shared the supreme power with the pasha or Turkish civil governor, in 1710 deposed the latter, and became sole ruler. There were also deys at Tunis in the 17th c., and the title is found applied to the governor or pasha of Tripoli.

'The title of dey was not lately used at Algiers: the sovereign was styled *pacha* and *effendi*; the Moors called him Baba "Father"' (*Penny Cycl.* 1833).

1659 B. HARRIS *Parival's Iron Age* 294 General Blake..set sayl for Tunnis, where he fired a castle, and nine Turkish ships in Portferino, upon the disdainful refusal of the Dye of that place, to give satisfaction. **1676** *Lond. Gaz.* No. 1102/1 The late Dey of Tripoli being fled, those People have made choice of Mustaphe Grande to succeed him. **1678** DRYDEN *Limberham* I. i, By corrupting an Eunuch, [he] was brought into the Seraglio privately, to see the Dye's Mistress. **1679–88** *Secr. Serv. Money Chas. II & Jas. II* (Camden) 91 Sent, the one to the Alcade of Alcazar, the other to the Dij of Algiers. **1688** *Lond. Gaz.* No. 2313/1 The Dey of Tunis sent his Grace the usual Present. **1833** *Penny Cycl.* I. 329/2 An insult offered by Hassein Pacha, the last dey, to the French consul in April 1827, induced the French government to send an expedition..to take possession of Algiers..in June 1830. **1843** *Ibid.* XXV. 366/2 Of twenty-three deys who reigned [in Tunis], all were strangled or otherwise assassinated, with the exception of five. During these tumultuous times, the beys, who were the second officers of that state, gained the influence, and eventually the succession. **1847** MRS. A. KERR *Hist. Servia* 104 Of all the Janissaries..none were more opposed to the Sultan than those at Belgrade..Already did their commanders designate themselves Dahis, after the example of the Deys of Barbary.

dey, obs. f. DIE *sb.* and *v.*

†**'deyar.** *Obs.* [A transl. of AF. *deye* in Acts of Edward III: see DEY[1] 2.] A dairy man.

15.. transl. 37 *Edw. III*, c. 14 Oxherds, Cowherds, Shepherds, Deyars, and all other Keepers of Beasts. **1764** BURN *Poor Laws* 19 (citing the same act).

deyde, obs. form of DEAD, DIED.

deye, -en, ME. form of DIE *v.*, DYE *v.*

deye-nettle: see DEA-NETTLE.

deyer, obs. form of DYER.

deyery, obs. form of DAIRY.

deyf(fe, obs. form of DEAF.

dey-house ('deɪhaʊs). Now *local.* Forms: 4 deyhus, 6 dayhowse, deahouse, deyhowse. [f. DEY[1] + HOUSE.] A dairy or dairy-house.

1342–74 *Roll* in *Scriptores tres* (Surtees) App. cxli, Item unam stabulam et unam deyhus de Petynton. *a* **1547** *Surv. Tykford Priory* in *Monast. Anglic.* V. 206 On the northside the gate is a howse called the dayhowse. **1565–73** COOPER *Thesaurus*, *Casearia taberna*..A dayhouse where cheese is made. **1578** *Lanc. Wills* III. 101 Item belongyng to ye deahouse xij brasse pannes vij skelletes two ladles and a scomer. **1825** BRITTON *Beauties of Wiltsh.* (E.D.S. 1879), *Deyhouse*, *Da'us*, *Dayus*, a dairy, or room in which the cheese is made. **1883** COPE *Hampsh. Gloss.*, *Dey-hus.* **1890** *Glouc. Gl.*, *Dey-house* (pronounced dey'us), the dairy.

deyite, obs. form of DEITY.

deyl, -lle, obs. ff. DOLE, DOOL, grief, mourning.

deyle, deyll, obs. form of DEAL, part.

deyme, obs. form of DEEM *v.*

deyn, obs. Sc. variant of DAN[1]: see DEN *sb.*

deyn, for *deyen*, obs. inf. of DIE *v.*, DYE *v.*

deyn, deyne, obs. ff. DEAN *sb.*[1] and [2].

deyne, obs. f. DEIGN *v.*, var. of DAIN *sb.*, *a.*, *v.*, DIGNE, *a.*

1500–20 DUNBAR *Poems* (1893) xlii. 28 To luke on me he thocht greit deyne.

deynous, obs. form of DEIGNOUS *a.*

deynt, deynte, -tie, deynteous, deynteth, etc.: see DAINT-.

deype, obs. form of DEEP.

deyr, deyre, obs. ff. DEAR, DERE, hurt.

c **1470** HENRY *Wallace* IV. 561 Wallace persauit his men tuk mekill deyr.

deyrie, -ry, obs. ff. DAIRY.

deys, obs. f. DICE: see DIE *sb.*[1]

deys, -e, deysie, -sy, obs. ff. DAIS, DAISY *sb.*

deyship ('deɪʃɪp). [f. DEY[2] + -SHIP.] The state or dignity of a dey (of Algiers, etc.).

1704 J. PITTS *Acc. Mahometans* viii. (1738) 174 Succeeded him in the Deyship. **1863** CHALLICE *Heroes*, etc. *Louis XVI*, II. 20 He would have sent your Deyship a he-goat.

deyster, obs. var. of DYESTER, dyer.

deyte, deyyte, obs. ff. DEITY.

deythe, deyver, obs. ff. DEATH *sb.*, DEVOIR.

deytron, obs. pl. DAUGHTER.

†**'dey-wife.** *Obs.* [f. DEY[1].] A dairy woman.

1398 TREVISA *Barth. De P.R.* XIX. lxxiv. (1495) 904 Chese ..slydeth oute bytwene the fyngres of the Deye wyfe. **1530** PALSGR. 212/2 Dey wyfe, *meterie.* **1547** SALESBURY *Welsh Dict.*, *Hanodwraic*, deywyfe.

†**'dey-woman.** *Obs.* exc. *dial.* [f. DEY[1] + WOMAN.] A dairy woman.

1588 SHAKS. *L.L.L.* I. ii. 136 For this Damsell I must keepe her at the Parke, shee is alowd for the Day-woman. **1828** SCOTT *F.M. Perth* xxxii, The dey or farm-woman entered with her pitchers to deliver the milk for the family. *Ibid.*, The warder..averred he saw the dey-woman depart. **1890** *Glouc. Gloss.*, *Day-woman*, Dairymaid.

dezincation (ˌdiːzɪŋ'keɪʃən). [f. DE- II. 1 + ZINC.] The removal or abstraction of zinc from an alloy or composition in which it is present. So **de-'zinc** *v.*, **de-'zinced** *ppl. a.*, **de-'zincing** *vbl. sb.*

1891 EISSLER *Metall. Argentiferous Lead* 277 Abstrich from dezincation of poor lead. **1892** W. CROOKES *Wagner's Chem. Technol.* 183–4 Zinkiferous poor lead for de-zinking. .. The de-zinking can at once begin... The total de-zinking process, from running the poor lead into the refining process to letting off the de-zinked lead, requires..nine hours.

deˌzincifi'cation. The separation of zinc from an alloy or composition in which it is present.

a. *spec.* Used in connection with Parkes' process for desilvering lead by means of zinc.

1874 J. A. PHILLIPS *Elem. Metallurgy* 586 The dezincification of the de-silverised lead is effected by the aid of chloride of lead. **1891** EISSLER *Metall. Argentiferous Lead* 304 As only minute quantities of antimony are contained in the lead, dezincification is sufficient.

b. A type of corrosion that causes copper-zinc alloys to become soft and porous as a result of the leaching out of the zinc.

1898 *Engineer* 15 Apr. 363/3 The deterioration in the strength of Muntz metal bolts was due to a partial dezincification of the metal. **1939** *Jrnl. R. Aeronaut. Soc.* XLIII. 616 In untreated glycol brass was found to suffer attack by 'dezincification'. **1960** U. R. EVANS *Corrosion & Oxidation of Metals* xii. 474 It is today common practice to add 0·02 to 0·06% arsenic to brass condenser alloys..; since this plan has been adopted, dezincification has ceased to be a serious menace.

dezincify, dezinkify (dɪ'zɪŋkɪfaɪ), *v.* [f. DE- II. 1 + ZINCIFY.] *trans.* To separate zinc from an alloy or composition in which it is present. Chiefly used in connexion with Parkes' process for desilverizing lead by means of zinc. Hence **de'zinkified** *ppl. a.*

1892 W. CROOKES *Wagner's Chem. Technol.* 181 The pan for the de-zinkified poor lead.

dezymotize (dɪ'zaɪmətaɪz), *v.* [f. DE- II. 1 + ZYMOT-IC + -IZE.] *trans.* To free from disease-germs.

1884 *Chr. World* 31 July 578/3 Each [traveller]..is to 'disinfect and dezymotise his own drinking water'.

dghaisa ('daɪsə). Also **dghajsa**, **dhiassa.** [Maltese.] A boat resembling a gondola, used in Malta.

1893 'S. GRAND' *Heavenly Twins* I. II. i. 214 A rainbow fleet of dghaisas..propelled by oarsmen who stood to their work. **1923** *Blackw. Mag.* Dec. 744/2 Not my business the fare—ask dghaisa-man. *Ibid.* 750/2 Innumerable dghaisas skated about the surface of the harbour. **1940** M. DICKENS *Mariana* ix. 339 Wireless messages from Aunt Annabelle telling them to jump into a *dhiassa* and come ashore. **1964** *House & Garden* Dec. 28/1 The Maltese dghajsa..is first cousin to the gondola of Venice.

dgiahour, obs. form of GIAOUR.

dh- is not an English combination, but, in the English spelling of (East) Indian words, is used to represent the Indian dental sonant-aspirate, in the Devanāgarī alphabet *dha*, also the lingual or cerebral sonant-aspirate, more exactly written *ḍha*. In earlier spelling by Europeans these sounds were commonly represented by simple *d*, and in the general rectification of this to *dh*, the latter has been erroneously extended to several words having simple *da* dental or *ḍa* lingual, or to words not really Indian, apparently under the notion that an oriental appearance is given to a word by spelling it with *dh*. Words thus erroneously spelt with *dh* are *dhooly*, *dhow*, *dholl*, *dhoney*, *dh(o)urra*, *dhurrie*.

dha (dɑː). [Burmese.] A Burmese measure of length.

1821 P. KELLY *Univ. Cambist* (ed. 2) I. 115 The Dha, or Bamboo, consists of 7 royal Cubits; 1000 Dhas make 1 Dain, or Birman League, equal to 2 English Miles 2 Furlongs. **1888** *Encycl. Brit.* XXIV. 490/1 Burmah.—..dha 154 inches.

‖**dhak** (dhɑːk). Also **dhawk**. *E. Ind.* [Hindī *ḍhāk*.] An East Indian tree *Butea frondosa*, N.O. *Leguminosæ*, growing in the jungles in many parts of India, and noted for its brilliant flowers.

[**1799** COLEBROOKE in *Life* (1873) 407 *Note, Butea frondosa*, named Palás, or Dhák.] **1825** HEBER *Jrnl.* (1828) II. 487 The most common tree, or rather bush, in these forests, is the dhâk. **1866** *Treas. Bot.* 183 Dr. Hooker states that when in full flower the Dhak tree is a gorgeous sight, the masses of flowers resembling sheets of flame, their 'bright orange-red petals contrasting brilliantly against the jet-black velvety calyx.' The Dhak tree supplies the natives of India with several articles of a useful nature.

dhall, variant of DAL, Indian pulse.

dhaman ('dɑːmən). *India*. Also **dhamin**. [Hindī (Skr. *dharmaṇa*).] **1.** The rat-snake, *Ptyas mucosus*.

1878 P. ROBINSON *In my Indian Garden* 92 A pair of gorgeous dhaman snakes. **1927** *Chambers's Jrnl.* 2 July 495/1 The local natives all think that the dhaman or 'rat snake', is the female of the cobra. **1960** *Times* 26 Aug. 12/7 That's our resident dhamin—rat-snake.

2. The grass *Cenchrus ciliaris*, used for fattening cattle. **b.** The dhamnoo, *Grewia tiliæfolia*, and other trees of the same genus.

1887 C. A. MOLONEY *Forestry W. Afr.* 248 Dhaman of Punjab. **1889** W. COLDSTREAM *Illustr. Grasses S. Punjāb* Pl. xi, no. 11, (*caption*), Dhaman is..equivalent to the English clover. **1923** ZON & SPARHAWK *Forest Resources of World* I. iii. 432 The *Grewias*, known indiscriminately as 'dhamin' (*Grewia asiatica, G. tiliaefolia, G. vestita*). Wood tough and elastic. **1932** PEARSON & BROWN *Commercial Timbers of India* I. 175 Dhaman timber as a beam is about 10 per cent. stronger than teak.

‖**dhamma** ('dɑːmə). [Pali.] = DHARMA (esp. among Hinayana Buddhists).

1912 C. A. F. R. DAVIDS *Buddhism* ii. 32 Dhamma, more familiar perhaps to us in its Vedic and Sanskrit form, *Dharma*, is an ancient Indian word. **1924** W. B. SELBIE *Psychol. Rel.* xii. 227 Infractions of the moral law or Dhamma are the result of folly based on ignorance. **1966** D. FORBES *Heart of Malaya* xi. 130 The *Dhamma* is the Doctrine or Law. **1971** *Illustr. Weekly India* 11 Apr. 15/4 It has been stated in *Acharanga Niryukti* that the essence of the world is religion (*dhamma*). **1982** C. DE SILVA *Winds of Sinhala* xxii. 219 The Venerable Rahula..physically beat me with his staff..to leave the mark of *dhamma* on me.

dhamnoo ('dæmnuː). [Hind.] An Indian tree, *Grewia tiliæfolia*, of the family Tiliaceæ, or the timber therefrom; = DHAMAN 2 b.

1839 J. F. ROYLE *Illustr. Bot. Himal. Mts.* I. 104 *Grewia elastica*,..called *dhamnoo* by the natives,..affords timber which is highly valued for its strength and elasticity. **1846** J. LINDLEY *Veget. Kingd.* 372 The wood of Grewia elastica, called Dhamnoo, affords timber highly valued for its strength and elasticity.

dhan (dɑːn). *India*. [Hind. *dhān*, ad. Bengali *dhāna* rice, grain, *dhānā* fried barley, rice, etc. (Skr. *dhānā*).] Rice in the husk.

a **1815** W. ROXBURGH *Flora Indica* (1832) II. 201 Dhan the Bengalee name of the plant, and the unhusked rice, and Chaul the clean rice. **1858** SIMMONDS *Dict. Trade, Dhan*, a vernacular name in parts of Hindustan for rice. **1908** *Animal Managem.* 299 In Burma, unhusked rice (*dhan*), and in Madras, koolthi, is issued instead of gram or barley.

dhandh (dænd). Also **dandh, dhand**. [Sindhi.] A lake or swamp of the territorial division of Sind in India.

1851 R. F. BURTON *Sindh* i. 11 Numerous channels.. carry off the surplus water, feeding and refilling the lakes and dandhs, whose moisture has evaporated during the cold season. **1887** *Encycl. Brit.* XXII. 91/1 In the cold season the lakes or *dhandhs* are covered with wild geese, *kulang*, ducks, teal, curlew, and snipe. **1926** *Blackw. Mag.* Dec. 807/1 Any swamp or overflow water or tank or jhil in Sind is a dhand. **1928** *Ibid.* Mar. 389/1 In that year the dhand extended more than a hundred miles north and south, and ten to thirty miles east and west. *Ibid.* 389/2 Several canals took off from the dhand.

dhani ('dʌnɪ). Also **dhunny**. A kind of palm, the leaves of which are often used for making thatch in the tropics.

1926 *Chambers's Jrnl.* 9 Jan. 85/2 Bamboo matting, jungle-wood boards, and dhunny thatch make ready prey for flames. **1926** *Blackw. Mag.* June 731/2 She arrived soon after seven at the steamer anchorage, beyond the flat islands of dhani palm and mangrove swamp. *Ibid.* Dec. 718/1 Huts ..squalid and filthy and stinking, but for the most part newly roofed with dhani thatch against the rains. *Ibid.* 732/2 There was a sampan with a hooped covering of dhani leaves.

dhao, var. DAO.

dharma ('dɑːmə). Also **dharm, dharmma, dherma, dhurm**. [Skr., = decree, custom.] In India, social or caste custom; right behaviour; law; esp. in Buddhism and Hinduism: moral law, truth. Cf. DHAMMA. So **dharma'kaya, dharma'sastra, dharma'sutra** (see quots.).

1796 W. JONES tr. *Inst. Hindu Law* p. viii, Our Menu with his divine Bull, whom he names as Dherma [ed. 3 (1863), *dharma*] himself, or the genius of abstract justice. *Ibid.* p. xii, A number of glosses or comments on Menu were composed by the Munis, or old philosophers, whose treatises, together with that before us, constitute the Dhermasastra, in a collective sense, or Body of Law. **1849** M. MÜLLER *Let.* 29 July in *Sacred Bks. East* (1879) II. p. x, Complete Sûtra works are divided into three parts..the third (Sâmayâ-karika or Dharma-sûtras), treating on temporal duties, customs, and punishments. **1850** R. S. HARDY *Eastern Monachism* i. 5 Expositions of the doctrines of Budha..are called bana, or the Word; and the system itself is called dharmma, or the Truth. **1862** M. MÜLLER *Chips* (1867) I. ix. 196 The second and third baskets [*sc.* canonical books of the Buddhists] are sometimes comprehended under the general name of *Dharma*, or law. **1884** S. BEAL *Buddhism in China* x. 102 Here was the germ from which proceeded the idea or formula of an invisible presence; the teaching and power of the law (*dharma*) represented the *dharmakāya*, or law-body of Buddha. **1886** *Encycl. Brit.* XXI. 287/2 The *Dharmasûtras*, or 'rules of (religious) law'. **1938** B. L. SUZUKI *Mahayana Buddhism* ii. 46 The general explanation is that Dharmakaya..is the permanent, undifferentiated, comprehending Truth, but the detailed explanation differs according to the different schools of Buddhism. **1958** J. KEROUAC *Dharma Bums* i. 5 An oldtime bhikku in modern clothes wandering the world ..to turn the wheel of the True Meaning, or Dharma. **1961** *Listener* 31 Aug. 316/3 Everything was composed of these six elements, they were the origin of all things and were the *Dharmakaya*, the body and consciousness of Dainichi the Great Illuminator, the primordial and eternal Buddha. **1963** *Ibid.* 28 Mar. 548/1 By religion I am translating the Sanskrit word *dharma*... For Hindus it acquired a special meaning of sacred law, the law of the *Dharma-sastras* or law books... *Dharma* is eternal.

dharmsala ('dɑːmsɑːlə). *India*. Also **dharma sala, dhormsal, dhurmsal(l)a, durhm sallah**. [Hind. (Skr. *dharmasālā*, f. *dhārma* custom, decree, *sālā* house).] A building devoted to religious or charitable purposes, *esp.* a resthouse for travellers.

a **1805** in WELLINGTON *Dispatches* (Stanford). **1826** W. B. HOCKLEY *Pandurang Hari* I. 255, I then proceeded to the *durhm sallah*, or place where travellers put up, and where I had left the two females. **1838** *Penny Cycl.* XII. 233/2 A *Dharma Sala*, one or more sheds or buildings for the accommodation of the mendicants or travellers who are constantly visiting the math. **1920** *Chambers's Jrnl.* 434/1 Even the precincts of the regimental mosque and *dharmsala* (Sikh temple) were examined. **1922** *Blackw. Mag.* Oct. 550/2 At the door of the *dhormsal* I was met by some of the priests.

‖**dharna, dhurna** (dhʌrna). *E. Ind.* Also **dherna**. [Hindī *dharnā* placing, act of sitting in restraint, f. Skr. *dhṛ* to place.] A mode of extorting payment or compliance with a demand, effected by the complainant or creditor sitting at the debtor's door, and there remaining without tasting food till his demand shall be complied with; this action is called 'sitting in dharnā' or 'sitting dharnā', and the person on whom it is practised is said to be 'put in dharnā'.

c **1793** SIR J. SHORE in *Asiat. Res.* (1799) IV. 332 The practice called Dherna [which] may be translated Caption, or Arrest. **1824** HEBER *Jrnl.* (1828) I. 433 To sit 'dhurna'.. till the person against whom it is employed consents to the request offered. **1837** *Indian Penal Code* Act XLV (1860) c. 22 §508 (Y.) A. sits dhurna at Z.'s door with the intention [etc.]. **1842** W. MILES tr. *Hist. Hydur Naik* 41 (Y.) His troops, for want of their pay, placed him in Dhurna. **1844** H. H. WILSON *Brit. India* II. 175 Detaining their commanders in the sort of arrest termed dharna. **1875** MAINE *Hist. Inst.* 40 (Y.) The institution is..identical with one widely diffused throughout the East, which is called by the Hindoos 'Sitting dharna'.

dhatura, dhutoora, E. Indian forms of DATURA, DEWTRY.

1848 G. WYATT *Revelations of Orderly* (1849) 16 A gang of poisoners..rifling some travellers to whom they had administered dhutoora. **1892** *Daily News* 5 Aug. 5/3 A professional dhatura poisoner.

Dhimini, var. DIMINI.

dhobeying, var. DOBEYING.

dhobi ('dəʊbɪ). Also **dhobie, dhoby, dobee, -ie**. [Hindī *dhōbī*, f. *dhōb* washing, Skr. *dhāv-* to wash.]

1. A native washerman in India. Also **dhobi-man**.

1816 'QUIZ' *Grand Master* VIII. 230 Dobies, and burrawa's, and coolies. *a* **1847** MRS. SHERWOOD *Lady of Manor* II. xiii. 127 Linen as white and delicate as an Indian dobee could make it. **1860** W. H. RUSSELL *Diary in India* I. 110 The 'dhoby-man' was waiting outside, and in a few moments made his appearance—a black washerman, dressed in cotton. **1886** YULE *Anglo-Ind. Gloss.* 242/2 A common Hind. proverb runs..Like a dhoby's dog belonging neither to the house nor to the riverside. **1891** R. KIPLING *Plain Tales fr. Hills* 183 Adored by every one from the dhoby to the dog-boy.

2. dhobie('s) itch, ring-worm affecting the arm-pit and groin in hot moist climates; also, a form of contact dermatitis (see quot. 1967).

1890 BILLINGS *Med. Dict.*, *Dhobie's itch*, Tinea circinata tropica of scrotum, thighs, and perineum; so called in India. **1910** *Practitioner* Jan. 16 The name 'Dhobie itch' is used to denote several kinds of troublesome eczema generally first appearing on the covered hairy regions of the body. **1964** M. HYNES *Med. Bacteriol.* (ed. 8) xxvii. 417 Ringworm of the groin (dhobie itch). **1967** A. C. ALLEN *Skin* (ed. 2) vii. 241 (*caption*) Contact eczematous dermatitis (so-called 'dhobie itch') produced by contact with the ink from the betel nut used for marking laundry.

dhol (dəʊl). [ad. Skr. *ḍhola*.] A large Indian drum. Also **dholuck, dholak, 'dholuk, 'dholkee**, drums similar to the dhol, but varying in size or shape.

1837 A. CAMPBELL in *Jrnl. Asiatic Soc. Bengal* VI. 956 *Dholuck*, differs from the *dhol* in having one end only covered with leather. **1865** *Proc. R. Irish Acad.* IX. I. 116 (*Dhôl*)..(*Dhôlkee*).—Ordinary Drum and Little Drum. Both played by hand as accompaniment to the voice, or struck with a stick when in concert with pipes or loud instruments. **1891** C. R. DAY *Mus. & Musical Instr. S. India* vii. 140 The Dhol..is a species of drum chiefly employed in the native bands that are usually heard at weddings and other festivities. *Ibid.*, The Dholkee is a smaller dhol, much used by women in the Deccan. *Ibid.*, The Dholuk and Dâk are drums somewhat similar to the dhol, but are generally rather larger and vary slightly in shape in different parts of India. **1954** *Grove's Dict. Mus.* (ed. 5) IV. 459/2 The typical drums are the *tabla* (right, and left hand, wedged in the crook of the knee) and the *dhol* (slung like a muff). **1955** R. P. JHABVALA *To whom she Will* 292 *Dholak*, a kind of small drum, oblong in shape, with skin at both ends. **1971** *Illustr. Weekly India* 4 Apr. 6/1 The girls of the bridegroom's family dance and sing to the accompaniment of dholak (small drum). **1983** *Washington Post* 30 May D9 Asha's songs were..played with unbelievable precision by the eight-piece orchestra that included Indian tabla and dholak drums.

‖**dhole** (dhəʊl). *Zool.* [Origin unknown.

Given by Hamilton Smith in 1827, as the name 'in various parts of the East'; but not included among the native Indian names by Blanford (*Fauna of British Ind.* (1888), *Mammals* 143), and unknown to Indian Scholars. (In Canarese, *tôḷa* is the wolf: can this be, through some confusion, the source of *dhole*?)]

The wild dog of the Deccan in India.

1827 COL. C. H. SMITH in E. Griffith *Cuvier's An. Kingd.* II. 326 The Dhole, or Wild Dog of the East Indies, is made like the Dingo, but the hairs of the tail are not bushy. It is of a uniform bright red colour, and is found in South Africa, and in various parts of the East, where it is named Dhole. **1837** T. BELL *Brit. Quadrup.* in *Penny Cycl.* IX. 58/1 Of dogs in such a state of wildness..two very remarkable ones are the Dhole of India and the Dingo of Australia. **1866** WOOD *Pop. Nat. Hist.* I. 89 The Kholsun, or Dhole as it is often called, of British India. *Ibid.* 90 The sanguinary contests between the Dholes and their prey.

‖**dholl**, variant of DAL, the Cajan pea, Indian pulse.

1878 E. A. PARKES *Pract. Hygiene* I. vi. (ed. 5) 253 Mr. Cornish mentions that in the Sepoy Corps, the men are much subject to diarrhœa from the too great use of the 'dholl' (*Cajanus indicus*).

‖**dhoney, doney** ('dəʊnɪ). Also 6–7 **doni, tonee, tony**. [ad. Tamil, *thōṇi* (pronounced *dōni*): perh. a foreign word; cf. Pers. *dōnī* a yacht. (Spelt *donny* by the French writer Pyrard de la Val *c*1610.)] A small native sailing vessel of Southern India.

1582 N. LICHEFIELD tr. *Castanheda's Conq. E. Ind.* lxi. 125 a, Coching, from whence they were minded to send the Tone which carried the pepper, laden with merchandise. **1660** F. BROOKE tr. *Le Blanc's Trav.* 70 Near to Zeilan, where they use flat-bottome boats, called Tune, because they have little bottome. **1803** R. PERCIVAL in *Naval Cron.* X. 26 Boats and donies employed in the fishery. **1859** TENNENT *Ceylon* II. 103 (Y.) Amongst the vessels at anchor lie the dows of the Arabs, the patamars of Malabar, the dhoneys of Coromandel. **1880** *Standard* 15 May 5/3 His Wardian cases will cumber the decks of Arab dhows, Coromandel dhoneys. **1894** *Monthly Circ. Lloyd's Reg.*, Abbreviations..Dhy. Dhoney.

dhooley, -lie, -ly, erron. ff. DOOLIE, a litter.

dhoon (duːn). Also **dhun, doon, dun**. [Hind. *dūn*, ad. Hindī *dūna* valley.] Any of the flat valleys lying parallel to the base of the Himalayas dividing the sub-Himalayan hills into two ranges; *spec.* the valley of Dehra.

1814 R. R. GILLESPIE *Let.* 29 Oct. in *Asiatic Jrnl.* (1816) II. 151/1 *Me voici* in the far-famed Dhoon, the Tempè of Asia; and a most beautiful valley it is. **1877** *H. M. Elliot's Hist. India* VII. 106 Khalilu-lla Khán..having reached the Dún. **1879** MEDLICOTT & BLANFORD *Geol. India* II. xxii. 521 They consist of two ranges, separated by a broad flat valley, for which the native name 'dun' (doon) has been adopted in India. **1922** *19th Cent.* Jan. 46 In the lower valleys and hollows, or *dhuns*.

dhoona ('duːnə). [Hind. *dhūna*.] A resin obtained from the Indian tree *Shorea robusta*.

1846 J. LINDLEY *Veget. Kingd.* 394 The dhoona or dammer pitch, generally used in India for marine purposes, and as incense. **1924** *Public Opinion* 20 June 582/1 The odour of dhoop (incense) and dhoona greeted our breath.

dhoop, erron. f. DOOB an Indian grass.

dhoop (du:p). [Hindī, Bengali *dhūp* incense, resin, gum.] An Indian plant, *Vateria indica*; also the pitch obtained therefrom.

1851 *Illustr. Catal. Gt. Exhib.* IV. I. 877/1 Piney resin of dhoop tree..from Canara... Different sorts of dhoop, a perfume, from Nepal, Bhotan. **1924** [see DHOONA].

dhormsal, var. DHARMSALA.

‖**dhoti, dhootie** (ˈdəʊtɪ, ˈdu:tɪ; also dh-). Also 7 **duttee**, 9 **dote, dhotee, -ty, dhootie, dhooty.** [Hindī *dhōtī*.] The loin cloth worn by Hindus; a long narrow cloth which is wound round the body, passed between the thighs, and tucked in under the waist-band behind.

1622 in W. N. Sainsbury *Cal. State Papers E. Ind.* (1878) III. 24 (Y.) Price of calicoes, duttees fixed. **1810** T. WILLIAMSON *Vade Mecum* I. 247 (Y.) A dotee or waist-cloth. **1845** STOCQUELER *Handbk. Brit. Ind.* (1854) 277 He must..leave the house with nothing on but his gombong and dhootie. **1881** *Manch. Guard.* 18 Jan., Shirtings, dhooties, mulls and jacconets are all very firm. **1883** F. M. CRAWFORD *Mr. Isaacs* x. 203 Clad simply in a dhoti or waist-cloth. **1891** *Daily News* 16 Nov. 3/1, I never remember seeing him in anything but a delicate pink silk dhotee. **1894** *Longm. Mag.* Dec. 213 Ordinary coolies dressed only in their 'dhotis' or loin-cloths.

dhourra, dhurra, = DURRA, Indian millet.

‖**dhow, dow** (daʊ). Also **daou, daw.** [Original language unknown; now in use all round the coast of the Arabian Sea from Western India to E. Africa, also on Lake Nyanza. The Marāthī form is *ḍāw*, and the word exists in mod. Arabic as *dāw* (Johnson 1852). See DH-.

If the word *tava* occurring of date 1470 in Athanasius Nikitin (India in 15th c., Hakl. Soc. 1858) be, as it appears to be, the same word, it would tend to localize the word at Ormus or Hormuz in the Persian Gulf.]

A native vessel used on the Arabian Sea, generally with a single mast, and of 150 to 200 tons burden; but the name is somewhat widely applied to all Arab vessels, and has become especially well known in connexion with the slave trade on the East coast of Africa.

1799 J. JACKSON *Journ. from India* 3 Observed a dow in chase of us. *Ibid.* 5 A large Arab dow. **1802** *Naval Chron.* VIII. 255 A fleet of piratical Dows. **1803** *Ibid.* IX. 216 The navigation of the Red Sea is confined to vessels which they call *daous*..They carry a single square sail. **1809** *Q. Rev.* Aug. 108 At Mocha they hired a dow. **1831** TRELAWNEY *Adv. Younger Son* I. 178 On board a small and very singular craft, called a dow. **1860** KRAPF *Travels E. Africa* 117, I left ..Takaungu in a small boat, called a 'Daw' by the Suahilis ..the smallest sea-going vessel. **1862** *Illustr. Melbourne Post* 26 July, The boats..captured a large number of slave dhows off the eastern coast. **1865** LIVINGSTONE *Zambesi* Pref. 9 The general effect is to drive the independent native chiefs to the Arab dhow slave trade. **1875** BEDFORD *Sailor's Pock. Bk.* vi. (ed. 2) 227 The Slave Dhows on the East Coast of Africa are specially rigged for running with the Monsoons. **1883** *Bombay Gazetteer* XIII. 717–8 (Y.) Dhau is a large vessel which is falling into disuse..Their origin is in the Red Sea. The word is used vaguely, and is applied to baghlas. **1886** YULE *Anglo-Ind. Gloss.* 243/1 *Dhow, Dow*..used on the E. African coast for craft in general; but in the mouths of Englishmen on the western seas of India it is applied specially to the old-fashioned vessel of Arab build, with a long 'grab' stem, *i.e.* rising at a long slope from the water, and about as long as the keel, usually with one mast and lateen rig.

dhrupad (ˈdru:pæd). [ad. Skr. *dhraupada* kind of dance.] A classical form of north Indian vocal music, consisting of a prelude and four sections developing various parts of the raga, usually sung in a slow tempo.

1898 B. A. PINGLE *Indian Mus.* (ed. 2) ii. 63 There are certain fixed modes of rendering the Rágas or Ráginis and Jilhás or Dhuns, in vocal as well as instrumental music... The principal among these are the Alápa or Joḍa and Dhrupada, [etc.]. **1921** H. A. POPLEY *Music of India* vi. 88 The *Dhrupad* is usually in slow time and in selected tālas such as Āditāla, Rūpaka tāla, Chantāla, and Dhīma tāla. **1959** A. N. SANYAL *Ragas & Raginis* 1 The present work chiefly concerns the materials representing the classical forms, namely Dhrubapada and Khyal forms. *Ibid.* (*index*) 275/1 Dhrubapada, (colloquial 'Dhrupad'). **1968** *Indian Mus. Jrnl.* V. 54 Translations of Sanskrit treatises, original treatises, *dhrupada* collections..and the like.

dhudheen, var. DUDEEN.

dhuine-wassel, var. DUNIWASSAL.

dhun, var. DHOON.

dhunny, var. DHANI.

dhurrie, durrie (ˈdʌrɪ). [Hindī *darī*. See DH-.] A kind of cotton carpet of Indian manufacture, usually made in rectangular pieces with fringes at the ends, and used for sofa-covers, curtains, and similar purposes.

1880 ELIOT JAMES *Indian Industries* iv. 19 Dhurries are made in squares, and the ends often finished off with fringe; the colours are not bright, but appear durable. **1891** COTES *Two Girls on a Barge* 21 Curtains to hang..and dhurries to be draped over the fresh-scented pine of the little cabins. *Ibid.* 22 The dhurries to be arranged æsthetically on either crosswise beam. **1921** E. M. FORSTER *Let.* 17 May in *Hill of Devi* (1953) 80 The gifts were dumped on a durry..where sat H.H., among clerical assistants. **1924** *Chambers's Jrnl.* July 472/2 He returned with a roll of Kashmir *durries*, and one by one each *durrie* became a fatter roll than it had been. **1934** M. L. DARLING *Wisdom & Waste in Punjab Village* i. 11 The durry in my room was impregnated with dirty foot-marks.

dhu stone (dju:, dʒu:). [ad. Welsh *du* black + STONE *sb.*] A type of dolerite found in Shropshire.

1879 G. F. JACKSON *Shropshire Word-Bk.* 117 *Dhu-stone*, basalt, of a black or very dark colour, quarried at Titterstone Clee. **1902** C. G. HARPER *Holyhead Road* II. xx. 99 Had his road not been one of the best in the world..and constructed of hard dhu-stone—he could not have kept that excellent time. **1938** P. T. JONES *Welsh Border Country* vii. 79 The Clee Hills..are crowned with deep caps of basalt that provide the valuable road-metal known as *dhu* stone. **1963** L. F. CHITTY in Foster & Alcock *Culture & Environment* vii. 172 Professor Shotton has found no evidence for the use of Clee Hill dolerite ('Dhu Stone') for stone implements.

dhyana (di:ˈɑ:nə). *Hinduism* and *Buddhism.* [Skr. *dhyāna*.] Profound meditation; the penultimate (seventh) stage of yoga (see quot. 1850).

1850 R. S. HARDY *Eastern Monachism* xxi. 255 By the power of nimitta the thoughts that prevent the exercise of dhyána will be restrained. *Ibid.* 270 The word dhyána is said to mean, 'that which burns up evil desire, or the cleaving to existence'. It is sometimes used in the sense of meditation, and at other times is allied to samádi; in some places it is a cause, and in others an effect. **1871** S. BEAL *Catena Buddhist Scriptures* I. 90 Next come the eighteen heavens... Their general collective title is 'the Worlds of the Brahmas', because of their purity. The distinctive title is 'the Heavens of the four Dhyânas', because all disturbing influences are removed from them, and those who dwell in them are employed in contemplation (dhyâna). **1902** W. JAMES *Var. Relig. Exper.* 401 'Dhyâna' is their [*sc.* Buddhists'] special word for higher states of contemplation. There seem to be four stages recognized in dhyâna. **1962** A. HUXLEY *Island* vi. 76 The operations are called yoga, or dhyana, or Zen. *Ibid.* 79 *Dhyana* is contemplation.

dhye, var. DAYE.

di- (dɪ, daɪ) *pref.*[1], repr. L. *dī-*, reduced form of *dis-*, used in L. before the consonants *b*, *d*, *g* (usually), *l*, *m*, *n*, *r*, *s* + cons., *v*, and sometimes before *j*, as in *dī-būcināre*, *dī-dūcĕre*, *dī-gestio*, *dī-gressio*, *dī-jūdicāre*, *dī-jungĕre* and *dis-jungĕre*, *dī-lātāre*, *dī-minuĕre*, *dī-missio*, *dī-numerāre*, *dī-rectus*, *dī-ruptio*, *dī-spersus*, *dī-stinguĕre*, *dī-strictus*, *dī-vertĕre*. Often changed back in late L. and Romanic popular words to the full form *dis-*, whence *dismiss*, *disrupt*; but in mod. Eng. generally *di-*. In OF. and ME. often varying with *de-*, whence *defer*, *demission* sb.[2], *devise*, from L. *differre*, *dīmissio*, *dīvīsa*. This took place especially before a radical beginning with *s* + cons., where *di-* was phonetically identified with *dis-*, and shared in the alternation of *dis-*:—*des-* (DE- 6, DES-, DIS-). Thus in ME. *desperse*, *destinct*, *destill*, *destrain*, *destress* for *dis-*; and per contra *dispair*, *dispise*, *dispite*, *dispoil*, *distroy* for *de-*. For its force in composition, see DIS-: it is not, like the latter, a living prefix. The historical pronunciation in an unstressed syllable is (dɪ-); cf. *divide*, *diversion*, *diminish*; but in cases where there is a parallel word in *de-*, as *delate*, *dilate*, it is usually pronounced (daɪ-) for the sake of distinction, and the present tendency is to extend (daɪ-) to other words, as *digest*, *dilute*, *diluvium*, *diradiation*, *direct*, *diverge*, *diverse*, *divest*. This seems due partly to analysis of the compound, partly to the influence of stressed forms as ˈ*digest* sb. ˈ*divers*, in which the *i* is long and diphthongal.

di- (daɪ, dɪ), *pref.*[2], repr. Gr. *δι-* for *δίς* twice, as in *δίγαμος* twice married, *δίγλωττος* double-tongued, bilingual, *δίδραχμος* worth two drachmas, *δίπτυχος* double-folded. Hence:

1. Entering into numerous Eng. words, mostly technical, as *dichromic*, *dicotyledon*, *digamma*, *digamy*, *diglot*, *digraph*, *dilemma*, *diphthong*, *diptych*, *distich*, *disyllable*; also in the nomenclature of Natural History as *Diadelphia*, *Diandria*, *Didelphia*, *Diptera*: which see in their alphabetical places. So in Crystallography, as in ***di-tetrahedron*** a crystal having twice four sides or planes; so ***di-hexahedron***, etc.

2. As a living prefix, used in *Chemistry*, with the names of compounds and derivatives, in the general sense 'twice, double', but with various special applications.

a. With the names of classes of compounds, as *bromide*, *oxide*, *sulphide*, *cyanide*, *acetate*, *chlorate*, *nitrate*, *sulphate*, *amide*, *amine*, etc., expressing the presence of two atoms or combining equivalents of the element or radical, as *carbon dioxide* CO_2, *manganese dichloride* $MnCl_2$.

¶ In the earlier part of the 19th c. the use was different: the Latin prefix *bi-* was then used, where *di-* is now, to express two proportions of the chlorous constituent, as in *bi-chloride of mercury* = corrosive sublimate; while the Greek *di-* was used to express two proportions of the basic constituent; thus calomel, when supposed to contain two of mercury to one of chlorine, was called a *di-chloride*.

b. With the names of specific compounds (chiefly organic), indicating a body having twice the formula of a given compound; used chiefly with the names of hypothetical radicals, to indicate the free state of these (supposed to be that of a double molecule), as in *di-allyl*, *dibenzyl*, *dicyanogen*.

In *diphenol*, the use is less exact, since this substance has not exactly the constitution of two molecules of phenol.

c. With the name (or combining form of the name) of an element or radical, expressing the presence of two atoms or molecules of that body, as in *di-hydr(o)-*, *di-oxy-*, *di-carbon-*, *di-carb(o)-*, *di-nitr(o)-*, *di-az(o)-*, *di-chlor(o)-*, *di-brom(o)-*, *di-iod(o)-*, *di-sulph(o)-*, *di-phosph(o)-*, *di-bor(o)-*, *di-arsen(o)-*, *di-ammoni(o)-*, *di-amm(o)-*, *di-amid(o)-*, *di-cyan(o)-*, *di-methyl-*, *di-ethyl-*, *di-propyl-*, *di-amyl-*, *di-allyl-*. Used especially in organic chemistry, to indicate that two atoms or molecules of the body take the place of two atoms of hydrogen, as in *dibromomethane*, *dichlorobenzene*.

d. These formations (c) are sometimes used attributively or adjectively as separate words, as *di-azo* compounds, *di-carbon* series, *di-phenyl* group. So with other adjectives, as *diacid*, *dihydric*, *diphenic*.

e. On the preceding classes of words derivatives are formed, as *diazotize*, *diazotype*, *dichromated*.

di-, *pref.*[3], the form of DIA- used before a vowel, as in *di-acoustic*, *di-æresis*, *di-esis*, *di-ocese*, *di-optric*, *di-orama*.

dia-, *pref.*[1], before a vowel di-, repr. Gr. *δια-*, *δι-*, the prep. *διά* through, during, across, by. [orig. **δϝιγα*, from root of **δϝο*, *δύο* two, and so related to *δίς*, **δϝίς* twice (DI-[2]) and L. *dis-* a-two, asunder (DIS-, DI-[1]).] Much used in Greek in composition, in the senses 'through, thorough, thoroughly, apart', as in *διάδρομος* running through, *διάλεκτος* discourse, *διάμετρος* measure through or crosswise, diameter, *διατριβή* wearing through or away, pastime, *δίοπτρον* a thing for looking through, a spyglass. Hence in English, in a few old words through Latin and French, or Latin only, and in many modern scientific and technical words formed directly from Greek, or on Greek analogies.

dia-, *pref.*[2], in medical terms. In Greek such phrases as *διὰ καρύων*, *διὰ κωδειῶν*, *διὰ μίσυος*, *διὰ μόρων*, *διὰ τριῶν πεπερέων*, *διὰ τεσσάρων*, *διὰ πέντε*, meaning 'made or consisting of nuts, of poppy-heads, of vitriol, of mulberries, of three peppers, of four or of five (ingredients)', etc., were applied to medicaments of which these ingredients were the chief constituents, the full form implied being *τὸ διὰ τριῶν πεπερέων φάρμακον* medicament made up of three peppers, etc. By the Latin physicians these phrases were treated as words, thus *diachȳlōn*, *diacissōn*, *diacōdīōn*, *diaglauciōn*, *diagrydiōn*, *dialibanōn*, *diamelilōtōn*, *diamelitōn*, *diamisyos*, *diamorōn*, *diapente*, *diatessarōn*; and their number was increased by many later formations of the same kind. Their grammatical character tended to be forgotten, final *-ōn* (Gr. *-ων*) being taken for *-on* (Gr. *-ον*), and then latinized as *-um*, e.g. *diachȳlum*, *diaglaucium*, *dialibanum*, *dihæmatum* (*δι'-αἱμάτων*); or a nominative was otherwise formed, as *diapentes*. The *New Sydenham Society's Lexicon* gives about eighty of these in mediæval and early modern Latin.

Several of these are given in French form by Cotgrave; many were formerly in English use, either in their mediæval-Latin form or partly anglicized. Phillips 1678–1706 has '*Dia*, a Greek Preposition..set before the names of many medicinal compositions, to which that of the principal Ingredient is usually joined, by Physicians and Apothecaries, as *Diaprunum*, *Diascordium*, *Diasenna*, etc.' Only a few, e.g. DIACHYLUM, survive in modern use: see also, in their alphabetical places, DIACATHOLICON, DIACODIUM, DIAGRYDIUM, DIAMBER, DIAMORON, DIAPALMA, DIAPRUNE, DIASCORD, DIASENNA, DIATESSARON. Among others, are the obsolete **diaˈcarthami (-amy)** [F. *diacartami* Cotgr.], a preparation of carthamus or bastard saffron; **diaˈcassia**, of cassia or bastard cinnamon; **diaˈcissum** [Gr. *κισσῶν*], of ivy leaves;

diaco'rallion, composed of red coral; **diacy'minon, diaci'minon** [F. *diaciminon* Cotgr.; Gr. κυμῖνον], composed of cumin; **diaga'langa** [F. *diagalange*], made of galanga or galingale; **diamarga'riton** [also in OF.; Gr. μαργαρίτων of pearls]; †**diape'nidion** *Obs.* [med.L. *pēnidion, -um* (F. *penide* 'a pennet, the little wreath of sugar taken in a cold') = Gr. *πηνίδιον, dim of πήνη thread. (See Skeat *Notes to P. Pl.*, E.E.T.S. 110.).] **dia'phœnic(-on)** [F. *diaphenicum* Cotgr.; Gr. φοινίκων of dates]; **di'arrhodon** [F. *diarrodon* Cotgr.; Gr. ῥόδων of roses, διάρροδον (*sc.* κολλύριον a salve) compound of roses]; **dia'rhubarb**, a preparation of rhubarb; **dia'tragacanth** [OF. *diadragant*, etc. Godef.], preparation of tragacanth; **diatrion-pipereon, -santalon**, a preparation consisting of three kinds of pepper, or of sanders or sandal-wood; **dia'zingiber, -'zinziber**, a confection of ginger.

The 17–18th c. English Dictionaries, Phillips, Bailey, Chambers, Ash, etc., give also ***dia'botanum***, a plaster made of herbs, ***diacala'minthe***, ***dia'capparis*** (of capers), ***dia'caryon*** (of walnuts), ***diaca'storeum***, ***diachal'citis***, ***diacinna'momum***, ***diaci'tonium***, ***diaco'præg ia*** (of goats' dung), ***diacorum*** (of acorus or calamus), ***dia'costum*** (of costmary), ***dia'crommyon*** (of onions), ***diacy'donium*** (conserve of quinces, marmalade), ***diadama'scenum*** (of damsons), ***dia'glaucion*** (of glaucium), ***dia'hexapla*** (a drink for horses of six ingredients), ***dia'hyssopum***, ***dia'lacca*** (of gum lac), ***dial'thæa*** (of marsh mallow), ***dia'merdes*** (of ordure), ***dia'moschum*** (of musk), ***dia'nisum*** (of anise), ***dia'nucum*** (of walnuts), ***diaoli'banum***, ***diapa'paver*** (of poppies), ***diapom'pholygos*** (of pompholyx), ***diasa'tyrion***, ***diase'besten***, ***dia'tribus*** (of three sorts of sanders), ***diaxy'laloes*** (of wood of aloes), etc. Cf. also **1621** BURTON *Anat. Melanch.* II. iv. I. v.

1471 RIPLEY *Comp. Alch.* Ep. in Ashm. (1652) 113 Use *Diacameron. **1544** PHAER. *Regim. Life* (1553) A viij a, A potion.. made of halfe an ounce of *diacartamy dissolved in ..iij ounces of betonie. **1565–73** COOPER *Thesaurus*, *Cnicos*, an herbe called Carthamus, wherof is made an notable confection named Diacarthami to purge fleume. **1671** SALMON *Syn. Med.* III. lxxxiii. 762 First sufficiently cleanse with *Diacassia with Turpentine. **1545** *Nottingham Rec.* III. 224 Duas pixides de conserves vocatis *'diacitrin'. **1741** *Compl. Fam. Piece* I. i. 53 Take.. *Diacorallion a Dram and a half. **1362** LANGLAND *P. Pl.* A. v. 101 May no Suger so swete aswagen hit vnneþe, No no Diopendion [*v.rr.* dyapendyon, diapenydion, B. diapenidion] dryve it from myn herte. **1625** HART *Anat. Ur.* II. xi. 127 A certaine portion of the Electuarie **Diaphœnicon*, mingled with.. powder of *Diagridium*. **1646** SIR T. BROWNE *Pseud. Ep.* III. xii. 133 Diaphænicon a purging electuary.. which receiveth that name from Dates. **1727–51** CHAMBERS *Cycl.*, *Diaphoenic*.. a soft purgative electuary. **1789** *Archaeol.* IX. 233 Diarhodon ad servorum seems a salve or water of roses for inflammations in the eyes. *c* **1400** *Lanfranc's Cirurg.* 229 Trociscus de turbit maad wiþ *diarubarbe. **1657** *Physical Dict.*, **Diatraganth*, a confection.. good against hot diseases of the breast. *c* **1400** *Lanfranc's Cirurg.* 238 ȝeve him *diatrion piperion or anoþer hoot eletuarie. *Ibid.*, He schal take *diazinziberum of oure makinge. **1600** W. VAUGHAN *Direct. Health* (1602) 63 If you be troubled with rheumes.. vse diatrion piperion.

†**dia, dya**, *sb. Obs.* The pharmaceutical prefix DIA-², used as a separate word: A medical preparation or compound.

goats' milk dia, a specific preparation of which goats' milk was the chief ingredient: see DIA-².

1377 LANGL. *P. Pl.* B. xx. 173 And dryuen awey deth with dyas and dragges [*v. rr.* dias, drogges]. *c* **1430** LYDG. *Min. Poems* (Percy Soc.) 40 Drugge nor dya was none in Bury towne. **1562** BULLEYN *Def. agst. Sickness* I. *Bk. Simples* 22 b, Eaten, either in Goates milk Dia, or Syruppe.

diabantite (daɪə'bæntaɪt). *Min.* [irregularly f. DIABASE (as if the latter represented Gr. διάβας, διαβαντ- having crossed over) + -ITE. Substituted by Hawes 1875 for the Ger. name *diabantachromyn*.] A chlorite-like mineral occurring in diabase and giving to this rock its green colour.

1875 *Amer. Jrnl. Sc.* Ser. III. IX. 454 On Diabantite.

diabase ('daɪəbeɪs). *Min.* [a. F. *diabase*, erroneously formed, since (according to Littré) it was meant to signify 'rock with two bases' (for which *dibase* would have been a proper form), and subsequently abandoned by its author, Brongniart, for Haüy's name *diorite*; but in 1842 re-introduced by Hausmann, perhaps with an intended affiliation to Gr. διάβασις a crossing over, transition.]

The name originally given by A. Brongniart to the rock afterwards called DIORITE; now applied to a fine-grained, compact, crystalline granular rock, consisting essentially of augite and a triclinic feldspar, with chloritic matter in varying amount; a variety of the class of rocks called greenstone and trap, being an altered form of basalt.

[**1816** CLEAVELAND *Min.* 609 *Greenstone* (note), *Diabase* of some French mineralogists.] **1836** MACGILLIVRAY tr. *Humboldt's Trav.* xiv. 166 They observed two large veins of gneiss in the slate, containing balls of granular diabase or green-stone. **1862** DANA *Man. Geol.* ix. 79 *Diabase*, a massive hornblende rock.. It is like diorite in composition, except that the feldspar is less abundant, and is either labradorite or oligoclase. **1882** GEIKIE *Text-bk. Geol.* 145 The main difference between diabase and basalt appears to be that the rocks included under the former name have undergone more internal alteration, in particular acquiring the 'viridite' so characteristic of them.

b. *attrib.*, as in **diabase-aphanite**, a very fine-grained variety of quartz-diabase in which the separate constituents are not distinguishable by the naked eye; **diabase-porphyrite, -porphyry**, the dark-green antique porphyry, containing hornblende in its compact diabase-like mass; **diabase-schist**, a schistose form of diabase-aphanite.

1868 DANA *Min.* 343 If the diabase contains distinct crystals of porphyry, it is a diabase porphyry, the green porphyry or oriental verd-antique of Greece.. being of this nature. **1879** RUTLEY *Stud. Rocks* 247 Diabase aphanite.. Diabase schist.

diabasic (daɪə'beɪsɪk), *a.* [f. prec. + -IC.] Of, pertaining to, or of the nature of diabase.

1884 *Science* 20 June 763/1 Limestones, well proved to be of carboniferous age, cut by diabasic eruptives.

‖**di'abasis.** *Obs. rare.* [a. Gr. διάβασις, from διαβαίνειν to pass over.] A passing over.

1672 H. MORE *Brief Reply* 234 This Diabasis or passing of the Worship to the Prototype.

diabaterial (ˌdaɪəbə'tɪərɪəl), *a. rare.* [f. Gr. διαβατήρια (*sc.* ἱερά) offerings before crossing the border, or a river (f. διαβατός to be crossed, διαβαίνειν to go through, cross) + -AL¹.] Pertaining to the crossing of a frontier or river.

1784–90 MITFORD *Hist. Greece* XVII. iv. (1829) III. 112 There, according to the constant practice of the Greeks.. the diabaterial or border-passing sacrifice was performed.

diabeah, var. DAHABEEYAH.

1864 J. A. GRANT *Walk across Africa* 366 Baker led us to his 'diabeah', or Nile pleasure-boat.

†**'diabete.** *Med. Obs.* [a. F. *diabète* (1611 in Cotgr., but prob. earlier in medical use), ad. L. *diabētēs*, a. Gr. διαβήτης: see next.] = next.

1541 COPLAND tr. *Guydon's Chirurg.* Y iij b, Auycen graunteth in diabete the water of the clere mylke of a shepe. **1598** SYLVESTER *Du Bartas* II. i. III. *Furies* (1608) 279 As opposite the Diabete.. Distills vs still. **1625** HART *Anat. Ur.* I. ii. 23 *Diabete* or *Potdropsy*, an extraordinarie fluxe of the vrine. **1647** J. BIRKENHEAD *Assembly Man* (1662–3) 19 Ever sick of a Diabete.

diabetes (daɪə'biːtiːz). *Med.* [a. L. *diabētēs*, a. Gr. διαβήτης, *lit.* 'a passer through; a siphon', also, in Aretæus as the name of the disease, f. διαβαίνειν to pass through.]

†**1.** A siphon. *Obs.*

1661 BOYLE *Spring of Air* (1682) 107 If a Glass *Diabetes* or Syringe be made of a sufficient length.

2. *Med.* A disease characterized by the immoderate discharge of urine containing glucose, and accompanied by thirst and emaciation.

Sometimes called *Diabetes mellitus*, to distinguish it from *Diabetes insipidus* which is characterized by an absence of saccharine matter. (In 18th c. usually with *the* or *a*.)

1562 TURNER *Baths* 7 a, It is good for the flixe to the chamber pot called of the beste Physicianes Diabetes, that is when a man maketh water oft and much. **1649** CULPEPPER *Phys. Direct.* 70[It] helps the Diabetes, or continual pissing. **1690** LUTTRELL *Brief Rel.* (1857) II. 106 The earl of Gainsborough died lately of a diabetes. **1769** ALEXANDER tr. *Morgagni's Seats and Causes of Diseases* II. III. 465 A certain Count, who had laboured under a diabetes. **1845** G. E. DAY tr. *Simon's Anim. Chem.* I. 327 Rollo was.. the first who proved the presence of sugar in the blood during diabetes. **1875** T. TANNER *Pract. Med.* (ed. 7) I. 28 A temporary diabetes can occasionally be produced by the excessive consumption of sugar or starch. **1879** KHORY *Princ. Med.* 59 In diabetes the skin is dry and harsh.

b. *transf.* and *fig.*

1686 GOAD *Celest. Bodies* II. viii. 273 What is the reason of this Diabetes Celestial, when the Clouds are so often dropping, and can't hold? **1839** LANDOR *Wks.* (1846) I. 375/2 Knowing your diabetes of mind.

diabetic (daɪə'bɛtɪk), *a.* [a. F. *diabétique* (14th c. in Hatz.-Darm.), ad. L. *diabēticus*, f. *diabetes*: see prec. and -IC. The older pronunciation (daɪə'biːtɪk) is now only rarely used.]

A. *adj.*

1. Of or pertaining to diabetes or its treatment.

1799 *Med. Jrnl.* II. 88 Dr. Lubbock began to suspect it was connected with the diabetic diathesis. **1819** J. G. CHILDREN *Chem. Anal.* 308 The sugar of diabetic urine. **1845** tr. *Simon's Anim. Chem.* I. 66 Diabetic sugar.. is identical in its chemical composition with sugar of grapes.

2. Affected with diabetes.

1799 *Med. Jrnl.* II. 209 The body of my diabetic patient. **1876** tr. *Wagner's Gen. Pathol.* 579 This.. explains the remarkable vulnerability of the tissues of diabetic persons. **1880** MACCORMAC *Antisept. Surg.* 107 Some.. diseased states of the body, the diabetic for instance.

fig. **1831** CARLYLE *Sart. Res.* III. v, Society, long pining, diabetic, consumptive, can be regarded as defunct.

B. *sb.* One who suffers from diabetes.

1840 A. TWEEDIE *Libr. Med.* IV. 259 Exaggerated notions .. of the quantity of food which diabetics consume. **1880** BEALE *Slight Ailm.* 74 Many a diabetic can consume one pound.. of rump steak at a sitting.

diabetical (daɪə'biːtɪkəl), *a.* [f. as prec. + -AL¹.] = DIABETIC 1.

1603 SIR C. HEYDON *Jud. Astrol.* xxi. 458 He was affected with the Diabeticall passion. **1625** HART *Anat. Ur.* II. ii. 58 The Diabeticall disease, called by some a *Pot-dropsie*.

diabetogenic (ˌdaɪəbiːtəʊ'dʒɛnɪk, -bɛt-), *a.* [f. DIABET(ES + -O + -GENIC.] Giving rise to or produced by diabetes.

1903 DORLAND *Med. Dict.* (ed. 3) 210/2 *Diabetogenic*, producing diabetes. **1938** *Encycl. Brit. Bk. of Yr. 1938* 227/2 The full diabetogenic effect—namely excretion of sugar and ketones in the urine. **1946** *Nature* 26 Oct. 589/1 The intravenous injection of high diabetogenic doses of alloxan ..in the dog produces a very severe diabetic-uræmic syndrome. **1970** W. B. YAPP *Introd. Anim. Physiol.* (ed. 3) vi. 165 Probably the 'diabetogenic hormone' and 'ketogenic hormone' that have been described were simply impure preparations of it [*sc.* growth hormone].

‖**diable** (djɑbl(ə)), *int.* [Fr.] = DEVIL *sb.* 20 b.

1598 SHAKES. *Merry W.* I. iv. 70 O *Diable, Diable*: vat is in my Closset? **1765** STERNE *Tr. Shandy* VII. viii. 28 What's wrong now?—Diable!—a rope's broke! **1867** 'OUIDA' *Under Two Flags* I. xiii. 302 They were fine men—*diable*!—they were fine men. **1937** LADY FORTESCUE *Sunset House* vi. 113, I feel it all in my arms and down to my toes. *Diable*! there is enough of it.

‖**diable au corps** (djɑbl o kɔr). [Fr., lit. 'devil in the body'.] = DEVIL *sb.* 6 b; restless or inexhaustible energy; devilment.

1895 G. B. SHAW *Our Theatres in Nineties* (1932) I. 197 Miss Lottie Collins.. has still her Tarararesque *diable au corps*. **1916** G. SAINTSBURY *Peace of Augustans* vii. 276 But in *diable au corps*—that quality which Voltaire declared to be necessary in everything—Congreve and Sheridan are nearer to each other. **1959** *Manchester Guardian* 24 July 4/5 Skiffle has a diable au corps, which is denied to some profounder forms of art.

diablerie (dɪ'ɑːblərɪ). Also **-ery.** [a. F. *diablerie* (djɑbləri), in 13th c. *deablerie*, f. *diable* devil + *-erie*: see -ERY.]

1. Business belonging to or connected with the devil, or in which the devil is employed or has a hand; dealings with the devil; sorcery or conjuring in which the devil is supposed to assist; wild recklessness, devilry.

1751 WARBURTON in Pope's Wks. (1757) IV. 235 *note*, The diablerie of witchcraft and purgatory. **1809** *Q. Rev.* May 347 We are no defenders of ghost seeing and diablerie. **1812** SOUTHEY *Omniana* I. 270 The night mare has been a fruitful source of miracles and diablery in the Romish mythology. **1852** MRS. STOWE *Uncle Tom's C.* xx. 211 Miss Eva.. appeared to be fascinated by her wild diablerie, as a dove is sometimes charmed by a glittering serpent. **1868** GEO. ELIOT *Sp. Gipsy* I. 59 Diablerie that pales the girls and puzzles all the boys.

2. That part of mythology which has to do with the devil or devils; devil-lore; the description or representation of devils.

1824 SCOTT *St. Ronan's* viii, The devil, in the old stories of *diablerie*, was always sure to start up at the elbow of any one who nursed diabolical purposes. **1837** LOCKHART *Scott* ix, Erskine showed Lewis Scott's version of 'Lenore' and the 'Wild Huntsman'; and.. mentioned that his friend had other specimens of the German Diablerie in his portfolio. **1882** T. MOZLEY *Remin.* I. x. 76 An extraordinary figure that might have stepped out of a scene of German *diablerie*.

3. The realm, world, or assemblage of devils.

1852 MRS. STOWE *Uncle Tom's C.* xx. 205 She might have fancied that she had got hold of some sooty gnome from the land of Diablerie. **1880** W. LEIGHTON *Shaks. Dream* 50 Out of sin's diablery We arise, the fateful three.

di'ablerist. *nonce-wd.* [f. prec. + -IST.] A painter or drawer of pictures in which devils are represented (called in Fr. *diableries*).

1859 *Eminent Men & Pop. Bk.* 72 Caricature after the manner of Gilray or the French Diablerists.

‖**diablotin** (djɑblotɛ̃). [F. *diablotin*, dim. of *diable* devil.] **1.** A little devil; an imp.

1812 SCOTT *Fam. Lett.* 1 Jan. (1894) I. viii. 237 A whole hive of these little diablotins. **1821** —— *Kenilw.* xxiv, The little diablotin again thrust in his oar. **1828** *Blackw. Mag.* XXIV. 746 The mischievous diablotin who had cut so principal a figure among his tormentors.

2. a. In the West Indies, the rare black-capped petrel, *Pterodroma hasitata*. **b.** A name in Trinidad for the guacharo.

1823 J. LATHAM *Gen. Hist. Birds* VII. 366 They [*sc.* Trinidad Goatsuckers] were served up without the heads or feet, under the name of Dumpy Ducks, or Diablotins. **1891** *Ibid.* 6th Ser. III. 131 The Capped Petrel or Diablotin (*Œstrelata hæsitata*) formerly bred on the tops of the mountains of Dominica. **1958** J. C. GREENWAY *Extinct & Vanishing Birds of World* 151 If, as is supposed, the diablotin nests somewhere in this vicinity [*sc.* Hispaniola], it must be considered to be in great danger in that part of its range. **1961** G. A. C. HERKLOTS *Birds of Trinidad & Tobago* 131 Guachero or Oilbird or Diablotin.

diabolarch (daɪ'æbəlɑːk), *sb.* [f. Gr. διάβολος devil + -αρχός ruler.] The ruler or prince of the devils, the arch-fiend.

1845 J. OXLEE *Three Lett. Archbp. Canterb. & Confut. Diabolarchy* I. 27 The universal belief not only in the existence, but in the pluripresence and prepotency of a Diabolarch, commonly called, The Devil. *Ibid.* 32 Such an antagonist of the Almighty as a Diabolarch or the Devil.

diabolarchy (daɪ'æbəlɑːkɪ). [f. as prec. + Gr. -αρχία, f. ἀρχή rule.] The position of a diabolarch; the rule of the devil (as 'prince of the powers of the air').

1845 J. OXLEE *Three Lett. Archbp. Canterb. & Confut. Diabolarchy* I. 29, I must distinguish between *a* devil and *the* devil..as the whole error of the Diabolarchy. *Ibid.* 35 The dogma of a Diabolarchy could have been first revealed to the world neither by Moses nor by Christ. **1879** M. D. CONWAY *Demonol.* II. IV. xix. 212 A great deal might be plausibly said for this atmospheric diabolarchy.

di'abolepsy. *nonce-wd.* [f. Gr. διάβολος devil, after *catalepsy, epilepsy*, from Gr. -ληψία = -ληψις taking, seizure.] Diabolical seizure or possession. So **diabo'leptic**, one possessed with a devil.

1886 H. MAUDSLEY *Nat. Causes* 315 Neither theolepsy nor diabolepsy nor any other lepsy in the sense of possession of the individual by an external power.

dia'boliad. [f. Gr. διάβολος, L. *diabolus* devil + -AD I c, after *Iliad*, and the like.] An epic of the devil; a tale of the devil's doings.

1777 W. COMBE (*title*), The Diaboliad, a poem. **1838** G. S. FABER *Inquiry* III. v. 339 To believe all the Manichean Diaboliads ascribed to the old Paulicians and the later Albigenses.

diabolic (daɪə'bɒlɪk), *a.* and *sb.* [a. F. *diabolique* (13th c. in Hatz.-Darm.), ad. L. *diabolicus* (in Vulgate), a. Gr. διαβολικός, f. διάβολος devil.]

A. *adj.* **1.** Of or pertaining to the devil; belonging to, having to do with, or under the influence of the devil.

1399 LANGL. *Rich. Redeles* III. 199 Alle deabolik doeris dispise hem ichone. **1491** CAXTON *Vitas Patr.* (W. de W. 1495) II. 292 a/1 To knowe by what moyen his doughter myght ben preserued from this vexacyon dyabolyke. **1533–4** *Act 25 Hen. VIII.* c. 12 To vse the said Elizabeth, as a diabolike instrument, to stirre, moue, and prouoke the people of this realme. *a* **1555** LATIMER *Serm. & Rem.* (1845) 290 But not the church which you call catholic, which sooner might be termed diabolic. **1667** MILTON *P.L.* IX. 95 Doubt..of Diabolic pow'r, Active within beyond the sense of brute. **1669** GALE *Crt. Gentiles* I. III. i. 13 Suitable to many Ecstatic Diabolic Enthusiasts. **1822** BYRON *Vis. Judgment* xxxvii, Satan..merely bent his diabolic brow An instant. **1831** CARLYLE *Sart. Res.* II. vii. A Hell..without Life, though only diabolic Life, were more frightful. *c* **1850** NEALE *Hymns East. Ch.* (1866) 118 Diabolic legions press thee. **1871** M. COLLINS *Mrq. & Merch.* II. ii. 48 Theories..about lunacy and diabolic possession.

b. Pertaining to witchcraft or magic as attributed to Satanic influence.

1727 DE FOE *Hist. Appar.* vi. (1840) 59, I have already entered my protest against all those arts called magical and diabolic. **1863** GEO. ELIOT *Romola* l, His belief in some diabolic fortune favouring Tito.

c. Like or resembling the devil.

1843 CARLYLE *Past & Pr.* II. iii. (1845) 71 A..more or less Diabolic-looking man. **1862** H. TAYLOR *St. Clement's Eve* I. iii, Some I daily met Of aspect diabolic.

2. Partaking of the qualities of the devil; devilish, fiendish; inhumanly wicked.

1483 CAXTON *Cato* B ij, Lesyng is a synne dyabolyque. **1546** BALE *Eng. Votaries* II. 10 (R.) Of these most hellish and diabolick frutes, holy S. Paule admonished the Romains, in the first chaptre of his Epistle. **1642** MILTON *Apol. Smect.* viii. (1851) 306 He does not play the Soothsayer but the diabolick slanderer of prayers. **1871** MORLEY *Carlyle* (1878) 193 A diabolic drama of selfishness and violence. **1876** GEO. ELIOT *Dan. Der.* III. xlviii. 363 No diabolic delight.

†**B.** as *sb.* An agent of the devil. *Obs.*

1502 *Ord. Crysten Men* (W. de W. 1506) IV. xv. 214 Of inuocacyons of the deuyll..or of paccyons with hym & with his dyabolykes. **1638** SIR T. HERBERT *Trav.* 215 Witches..Hydro and Pyro-mantiques and other Diaboliques.

diabolical (daɪə'bɒlɪkəl), *a.* and *sb.* [f. as prec. + -AL[1].]

1. Of or pertaining to the devil; actuated by or proceeding from the devil; of the nature of the devil.

1503 HAWES *Examp. Virt.* v. 59 Be neuer taken in dyabolycall engyne. **1548** HALL *Chron.* 114 b, [They] adiudged the same Jone [of Arc] a sorceresse, and a diabolical blasphemeresse of God. **1603** *Adv. Don Sebastian* in *Harl. Misc.* (Malh.) II. 400 He began to suspect the same apparition to be diabolical or merely fantastical. **1651** HOBBES *Govt. & Soc.* xii. §10. 175 The most ancient of all diabolicall tentations..Yee shall be as Gods, knowing good and evill. **1651** —— *Leviath.* IV. xlvi. 370 Hee was commonly thought a Magician, and his Art Diabolicall. **1796** H. HUNTER tr. *St.-Pierre's Stud. Nat.* (1799) I. 409 If a God..governs Nature, diabolical spirits direct and confound at least the affairs of the children of men. **1862** H. SPENCER *First Princ* I. i. §6 (1875) 21 That Religion is divine and Science diabolical, is a proposition..implied in many a clerical declamation.

b. Resembling a devil in outward appearance.

1752 FOOTE *Taste* I. Wks. 1799 I. 9 Daubing diabolical angels for ale-houses. **1839** W. CHAMBERS *Tour Holland* 34/1 An old fantastical-looking dwelling..literally covered with diabolical figures.

2. Characteristic of or befitting the devil; devilish, fiendish, atrociously wicked or malevolent.

1546 LANGLEY tr. *Pol. Verg. De Invent.* VII. vii. 141 b, Of al these supersticiouse sectes afore rehersed there is not one so diabolical as the sect of Mahometaines. **1664** H. MORE *Myst. Iniq.* iv. 10 This Mystery..that is so horrid, and Diabolical, and so Antipodal to both the Person and Spirit of Christ. **1709** STEELE & SWIFT *Tatler* No. 68. ¶1 This Malevolence does not proceed from a real Dislike of Virtue, but a diabolical Prejudice against it. **1789** GOUV. MORRIS in Sparks *Life & Writ.* (1832) I. 321 To collect the various papers found in the Bastile, and then..to write the annals of that diabolical castle. **1818** SCOTT *Rob Roy* xii, I shall never forget the diabolical sneer which writhed Rashleigh's wayward features. **1882** B. M. CROKER *Proper Pride* I. vii. 134 Such diabolical vengeance, uprooting my home and estranging my wife. **1884** A. R. PENNINGTON *Wiclif* vi. 193 Their so-called poverty is nothing else but a diabolical lie.

3. *slang.* In weakened sense: outrageous, disgraceful; disgracefully bad. Also, used as an intensive, esp. in ***diabolical liberty***.

1958 B. BEHAN *Borstal Boy* III. 231 Why ain't I given a chance to follow my trade in 'ere, eh?..It's a diabolical liberty. Geezers get no chance to follow their trade. **1965** *Listener* 30 Sept. 507/2 A parody piece..which took diabolical liberties with Eurovision song contests, British Beatlemania and other suitable themes. **1972** MITTON & MORRISON *Community Project in Notting Dale* 69 The names he called those kids round there was diabolical for any vicar. **1982** S. TOWNSEND *Secret Diary A. Mole* 94 Asked our postman about communications between Tunisia and England. He said they were 'diabolical'. **1986** *Observer* 16 Feb. 50/4 From my point of view that pitch was dangerous. In fact, it was diabolical.

†**B.** *sb.* A person possessed by a devil; one of diabolical character. *Obs.*

1547 LATIMER *Serm. & Rem.* (1845) 426 As your naturals and diabolicals would have you to do. **1829** SOUTHEY *Sir T. More* I. 127 That devilish [doctrine] concerning infants, which so many divines (more fitly they might be called diabolicals!) have repeated after St. Augustine.

Hence **diaboli'cality**, diabolicalness.

1839 J. ROGERS *Antipopopr.* Introd. 16 Then we should see..diabolicality..overwhelm everything good.

diabolically (daɪə'bɒlɪkəlɪ), *adv.* [f. prec. + -LY[2].] **1.** In a diabolical manner; devilishly, very wickedly or badly, atrociously.

1599 *Life Sir T. More* in Wordsworth *Eccl. Biog.* (1853) II. 164 If onlie these odious terms maliciouslie, traiterouslie, diabollicallie were put out of the inditement. **1633** PRYNNE *Histriom.* I. II. Chorus (R.), So diabolically absurd, so audaciously impious, so desperately prophane. **1681** N. N. *Rome's Follies* 37 By'r Lady the Woman grows Diabollically Impudent. **1756** FOOTE *Eng. fr. Paris* II. Wks. 1799 I. 113 You look divinely, child. But..they have dressed you most diabolically. **1853** J. H. NEWMAN *Hist. Sk.* (1873) II. I. ii. 81 A place as diabolically wicked as it was wealthy.

2. *slang.* In weakened sense: exceedingly, excessively; often of things bad, but now used as a gen. intensive. Cf. DIABOLICAL *a.* 3 and DEVILISHLY *adv.* 2.

1958 L. VAN DER POST *Lost World of Kalahari* (1968) i. 19, I can remember my grandfather saying..'Yes! he [the Bushman] was clever, diabolically clever.' **1977** *Washington Post* 29 May A2/3 The whole idea is 'diabolically simple', notes Drake. **1981** H. SECOMBE *Welsh Fargo* iv. 48 The process was diabolically slow and it seemed an eternity before he reached the bushes. **1983** *Washington Post* 22 Aug. B1/1, I see this as diabolically funny.

dia'bolicalness. [f. as prec. + -NESS.] The quality of being diabolical; devilishness; atrocity.

1727 BAILEY vol. II, *Diabolicalness*, devilish Nature. *a* **1800** J. WARTON *Sat. Ranelagh House*, I wonder he did not change his face as well as his body, but that retains its primitive diabolicalness.

ˌdiabo'licity. *nonce-wd.* Diabolic quality.

1865 DE MORGAN *Budget Paradoxes* (1872) 294 If the Apostolicity become Diabolicity.

†**dia'bolicly,** *adv.* *Obs. rare.* [-LY[2].] = DIABOLICALLY *adv.* 1.

1683 E. HOOKER *Pref. Ep. Pordage's Mystic Div.* 21 Sin is ..autoritativly, exemplarily and Diabolicly, in public, countenanced.

di'abolifuge. *nonce-wd.* [f. L. *diabolus* devil + -FUGE, L. *fugium*, after *febrifuge*.] Something that drives away the devil.

1872 O. W. HOLMES *Poet Breakf.-t.* xi. (1885) 279 Odor as potent as that of the angel's diabolifuge.

diabolify (daɪə'bɒlɪfaɪ), *v.* [f. L. *diabolus* devil + -FY.] *trans.* To make a devil of; to figure as a devil.

1647 FARINGDON *Serm.* 59 (L.) The Lutheran [turns] against the Calvinist, and diabolifies him. **1813** J. FORSYTH *Excurs. Italy* 222 Dante's devils, his Minos and his Charon diabolified.

Hence **diabolifi'cation**.

1893 *Pall Mall Mag.* II. 346/1 Apotheosis is still with us, and diabolification (if I may coin such a word).

di'abolish, *adv.* *nonce-wd.* Humorous substitute for 'devilish'.

1858 O. W. HOLMES *Aut. Breakf.-t.* v. (1891) 121 The Professor said it was a diabolish good word. **1860** —— *Prof. Breakf.-t.* xi. 251 This was a diabolish snobby question.

diabolism (daɪ'æbəlɪz(ə)m). [f. Gr. διάβολ-ος devil + -ISM: cf. DIABOLIZE.]

1. Action in which the devil has, or is supposed to have, a share; dealing with the devil; sorcery, witchcraft.

1614 JACKSON *Creed* III. xxx. Wks. II. 559 Diabolism or symbolizing with infernal spirits. **1762** WARBURTON *Doctr. Grace* II. xii, The Farce of Diabolisms and Exorcisms. **1855** SMEDLEY *Occult Sciences* 82 Any compact savouring of diabolism. **1879** FARRAR *St. Paul* (1883) 466 Ephesus was the head-quarters of diabolism and sorcery.

2. Action or conduct worthy of the devil; diabolical or devilish conduct, devilry.

1681 BAXTER *Answ. Dodwell* Introd. C iij, If you had rather, call it Church-Tyranny, Cruelty, or Diabolism. **1683** E. HOOKER *Pref. Ep. Pordage's Mystic Div.* 18 Speculativ Infidelitie, practicous Atheism, horrid Blasphemies, and all manner of Diabolism. **1777** T. CAMPBELL *Surv. S. Ireland* (1778) 298 A degree of diabolism, not to be found in the human heart. **1826** *Gent. Mag.* I. 636/1 The mob are stimulated by harangues to new acts of diabolism. **1884** J. PARKER *Apost. Life* III. 75 To put an end to their censure, their malice, their diabolism of spirit.

†**b.** A doctrine of devils; a devilish system of belief. *Obs.*

1608 T. JAMES *Apol. Wyclif* 66 [He] taught..[that] there was an equalitie of al men, and communion of al things, which is pure Anabaptisme, or Diabolisme rather.

3. Doctrine or system of opinions as to devils; belief in or worship of the devil.

1660 FISHER *Rusticks Alarm* Wks. (1679) 557 Delusion, Fanaticism, Enthusiasm, Quakerism, Diabolism. **1822** LAMB *Lett.* xii. *To B. Barton* 114, I do not know whether diabolism is part of your creed. **1874** WOOD *Nat. Hist.* 4 Putting aside the terrors of diabolism, which are engrained in the native African mind.

4. The character or nature of a devil.

1754 FIELDING *J. Wild* I. i, Only enough [goodness] to make him partaker of the imperfection of humanity, instead of the perfection of diabolism. **1778** T. HARTLEY *Pref. Swedenborg's Heav. & H.* (1851) 48 Now the very idea of diabolism carries in it a repugnance and hatred to God and goodness. **1838** *Blackw. Mag.* XLIII 770 The brutal vulgar ruffian, who makes as close an approach to pure diabolism as the imperfect faculties of human nature will permit.

diabolist (daɪ'æbəlɪst). [mod. f. as prec. + -IST.] A professor or teacher of diabolism; a writer who deals with diablerie.

1895 *Westmin. Gaz.* 8 Mar. 2/1 These..are written under the inspiration of the French school of Diabolists. That school..is possessed with ideas of black magic, spirits of evil, devils become incarnate, and numerous other nightmares of corruption.

diabolize (daɪ'æbəlaɪz), *v.* [f. Gr. διάβολος devil + -IZE. (Du Cange has *diabolizāre* = *dæmonizāre* for Gr. δαιμονίζεσθαι to be possessed by a demon or 'devil'.)]

1. *trans.* To make a devil of, turn into a devil; to make like the devil; to render diabolical.

1702 C. MATHER *Magn. Chr.* II. App. (1852) 216 The mixt Paganry and Popery which hitherto diabolized them. *a* **1711** KEN *Hymns Festiv.* Poet. Wks. 1721 I. 296 The jealous Fears which Tyrants seize Diabolize them by degrees. **1889** *Cornh. Mag.* Sept. 268 The devil, only less than archangel ruined, retaining much of his former beauty, and almost all his former power, though now diabolised. **1890** *Chicago Advance* 24 July, Manufacturing rum to..debauch and diabolize the..natives of Africa.

2. To represent or figure as diabolical.

a **1883** O. W. HOLMES *Jonathan Edwards* in *Pages fr. Old Vol. Life* 400 It is a less violence to our nature to deify protoplasm than it is to diabolize the Deity.

3. To subject to diabolical influence.

1823 [see DIABOLIZED below]. **1860** O. W. HOLMES *Prof. Breakf.-t.* viii. 170 There were two things..that diabolized my imagination,—I mean, that gave me a distinct apprehension of a formidable bodily shape.

Hence **di'abolized** *ppl. a.*; **diaboli'zation**, the action of diabolizing, or representing as a devil.

1823 BENTHAM *Not Paul* 319 A man in his sound senses counterfeiting a diabolized man or a madman. **1879** M. D. CONWAY *Demonol.* II. IV. xi. 120 The diabolisation of Asteria (the fallen star) was through her daughter Hecate.

diabolo (diː-, daɪ'æbələʊ). [It., = devil.] The game of the devil-on-two-sticks revived under this name. Also, the wooden top with which the game is played. Hence **di'abolist**, a player of the game.

The game consists in balancing and spinning a double-headed top on a string (which is supported on two sticks), throwing it into the air, and catching it again.

1907 *C.B. Fry's Mag.* Mar. 582 The Devil Game: Diabolo. *Ibid.* 586/2 It is not difficult to learn to spin the diabolo. *Ibid.* 587/2 The diabolo game can be played by sides of almost any number. **1907** *Westm. Gaz.* 25 Sept. 12/1 The inventor of the modern Diabolo is M. Gustave Phillipart, a French engineer, well known in the automobile world. **1922** C. E. M. JOAD *Highbrows* iv. 135 They invent some quaint form of amusement like diabolo or roller-skating. **1964** W. L. GOODMAN *Hist. Woodworking Tools* 196 The curiously small, diabolo-shaped mallet.

diabo'locracy. *nonce-wd.* [see -CRACY.] Government by the devil.

1814 SOUTHEY in *Q. Rev.* XII. 195 Bruce has marked out a certain part of Africa as the dominion of the Devil, believing that the people there are actually under a species of diabolocracy, as much as the Jews were under a divine government.

†**di'abologue.** *Obs. nonce-wd.* A discussion or dialogue of devils.

a **1713** ELLWOOD *Autobiog.* (1885) 260 These dialogues, shall I call them, or rather diabologues.

diabology (daɪə'bɒlədʒɪ). [euphonic abbreviation of *diabolology*: see next.] The doctrine of the devil; devil-lore. Hence **diabo'logical** *a.*

a **1693** URQUHART *Rabelais* III. xxiii. 191 To speak in the true Diabological Sense. *Ibid.* 192 According to the Doctrine of the said Diabology [*some edd.* diabolology]. **1869** O. W. HOLMES *Med. Ess.* (1891) 355 Remember the theology and the diabology of the time.

diabolology (ˌdaɪəbɒ'lɒlədʒɪ). [f. Gr. διάβολος devil + -LOGY, Gr. -λογία speech. See also prec.] The doctrine of the devil as a branch of science or study; devil-lore.

1875 KINGLAKE *Crimea* (1877) VI. vi. 67 What, in diabolology, has often been called a snare.

diabolonian (ˌdaɪəbɒ'ləʊnɪən), *a.* and *sb.* [f. L. *diabolus*, in imitation of such forms as *Babylonian, Thessalonian.*] Bunyan's name in the *Holy War* for: One of the host of Diabolus (the Devil) in his assault upon Mansoul; also, as *adj.* Of the party of Diabolus or the Devil.

1682 BUNYAN *Holy War* Ded., When the Diabolonians were caught. **1869** SPRUGEON *Treas. Dav.* Ps. xix. 9 Till.. every corner of the town of Mansoul is clean rid of the Diabolonians who lurk therein. **1894** EGGLESTON in *Harper's Mag.* Feb. 469/1 Vile diabolonians all of them.

‖**dia'brosis.** *Med. Obs.* [a. Gr. διάβρωσις, f. διά through + βρῶσις eating, f. βιβρώσκειν to eat.] Corrosion, ulceration.

1706 in PHILLIPS (ed. Kersey). **1883** in *Syd. Soc. Lex.*

†**dia'brotic,** *a.* and *sb. Obs.* [ad. Gr. διαβρωτικός able to eat through, corrosive; f. as prec.]

A. *adj.* Corrosive. **B.** *sb.* A corrosive agent.

1775 in ASH.

diacalorimeter (daɪəkælə'rɪmɪtə(r)). [f. Gr. διά through + CALORIMETER.] An instrument to measure the resistance which liquids offer to the passage of heat.

1876 *Catal. Sci. App. S. Kens.* 151.

diacanthous (daɪə'kænθəs), *a. Bot.* [f. DI-[2] + Gr. ἄκανθα thorn.] Having two spines.

1883 *Syd. Soc. Lex., Diacanthous*.. in Botany, having two spines under each leaf.

†ˌ**diaca'tholicon.** *Obs.* [So in OF. (Cotgr.) and med.L., repr. Gr. διὰ καθολικῶν composed of general or universal (ingredients).] Old term for a laxative electuary; so called from its manifold composition, or, according to some, from its general usefulness: hence, a universal remedy or appliance.

As prescribed by Nicolaus, it was made of senna leaves, pulp of cassia and tamarinds, roots of male fern, rhubarb, and liquorice, aniseed, sweet fennel, and sugar. (Quincy.)

1562 in BULLEYN *Bk. Simples* (Blount). **1621** BURTON *Anat. Mel.* II. iv. II. iii. (1676) 237/2 Solid purgers are.. Diacatholicon, Weckers Electuarie de Epithymo.. of which divers receipts are daily made. **1656** BLOUNT *Glossogr., Diacatholicon*.. so called because it serves as a gentle purge for all humours. **1657** in *Physical Dict.* **1665** J. WILSON *Projectors* I. Dram. Wks. (1874) 226 Certainly nature and art .. could not produce such another diacatholicon that shall equally serve to all purposes,—roast, bake, boil.

‖**diacausis** (daɪə'kɔːsɪs). *Med.* [Gr. διάκαυσις burning heat: cf. next.]

1883 *Syd. Soc. Lex., Diacausis*.. excessive, intense heat of body.

diacaustic (daɪə'kɔːstɪk), *a.* and *sb.* [f. Gr. διά through, across + καυστικός burning, f. καίειν to burn. Cf. F. *diacaustique*.]

A. *adj.*

1. *Math.* Of a surface or curve: Formed by the intersection of refracted rays of light. (Opp. to *catacaustic*: see CAUSTIC *a.* 3.)

1704 J. HARRIS *Lex. Techn.* Pref. A iij, The Nature and Properties of Catacaustick and Diacaustick Figures. **1727–51** CHAMBERS *Cycl., Diacaustic Curve*, or *Caustic by refraction*.. the curve line, which touches all the refracted rays, is called the *diacaustic*. **1868** *Chambers' Encycl.* II. 693/1 When the caustic curve is.. formed by refraction, it is called the Diacaustic Curve.

†**2.** *Med.* 'Formerly applied to a double convex lens or burning glass, such having been used to cauterize parts' (Mayne, *Exp. Lex.* 1851–60). *Obs.*

B. *sb.* **1.** *Math.* A diacaustic curve or surface; a caustic by refraction.

1727–51 CHAMBERS *Cycl.* s.v. *Caustics*, Caustics are divided into catacaustics, and diacaustics. **1841** *Penny Cycl.* XIX. 356 The caustics formed by the continued intersections of refracted rays emanating from a luminous point, are called diacaustics. **1869** TYNDALL *Notes Lect. Light* §166 Spherical lenses have their caustic curves and surfaces (diacaustics) formed by the intersection of the refracted rays.

†**2.** *Med.* A double convex lens used to cauterize. *Obs.*

diacenous (daɪ'æsɪnəs), *a.* [f. Gr. διάκεν-ος quite empty or hollow (DIA-[1]) + -OUS.] (See quot.)

1883 *Syd. Soc. Lex., Diacenous*.. porous, like a sponge or pumice stone.

di-'acetamide. *Chem.* See DI-[2] 2 and ACETAMIDE.

1866 E. FRANKLAND *Lect. Notes for Chem. Stud.* 373.

di'acetate. *Chem.* [f. DI-[2] 2 + ACETATE.] A salt with two equivalents of acetic acid (or its radical acetyl, C_2H_3O), as ***diacetate of ethylene*** $(C_2H_4)''\cdot Ac_2\cdot O_2$.

1825 THOMSON *First Princ. Chem.* II. 373 Diacetate of lead. **1826** HENRY *Elem. Chem.* II. 121 A diacetate or compound of 2 atoms of acetic acid with 1 atom of base. **1863–72** WATTS *Dict. Chem.* I. 24 The diacetates are produced by the action of acetate of silver on the chlorides, bromides, or iodides of the several diatomic alcohol-radicles. **1876** HARLEY *Mat. Med.* 133 Acetate and diacetate of lead.

diacetic (daɪə'siːtɪk), *a.* [See DIACETATE.] ***diacetic acid***: = ***acetoacetic acid.*** So **diace'turia**, the presence of this acid in the urine.

1882 *Brit. Med. Jrnl.* 6 May 665/2 As the ferric chloride reaction points to the presence of a compound allied to ethyl-aceto-acetate,.. he [*sc.* A. Deichmüller] concludes that the compound is free diacetic acid. **1885** *Med. News* 3 Oct. 367/2 Diabetic patients suffering from diaceturia are liable.. to develop coma and die. **1908** *Practitioner* Feb. 197 Urine did not contain acetone nor diacetic acid. **1953** E. P. JOSLIN *Diabetic Man.* (ed. 9) xxxii. 285 The simplest method for the detection of acidosis by urinary examination is Gerhardt's ferric chloride reaction for diacetic acid.

diacetin (daɪ'æsɪtɪn). *Chem.* [f. DI-[2] 2.] Diacetic glycerin; a liquid with a biting taste, formed by the action of acetic acid upon glycerin, so that two of the three hydrogen atoms are replaced by acetyl. See ACETIN.

1855 WATTS tr. *Gmelin's Chem.* IX. 426. **1866** E. FRANKLAND *Lect. Notes for Chem. Stud.* 362 Acetic salts of a triacid alcohol:—Monacetin, Diacetin, Triacetin.

Also **di-'acetona,mine** *Chem.* See DI-[2] and ACETONAMINE. **diace'tonic** *a. Chem.* See DI-[2] + ACETONIC; in ***diacetonic alcohol***, a syrupy liquid $2(CH_3)C(OH)\cdot CH_2\cdot CO\cdot CH_3$, obtained by the action of potassium nitrite on diacetonamine.

di'acetyl. *Chem.* See DI-[2] 2, and ACETYL.

1872 WATTS *Dict. Chem.* VI. 30 [He] has obtained a colourless pungent liquid, which is probably free acetyl or diacetyl $(C_2H_3O)_2$. **1883** *Syd. Soc. Lex., Diacetyl carbamide* $CO(NH.C_2H_3O)_2$, a product of the action of carbonyl-chloride on urea at 50°C.; it crystallises from hot alcohol in rhombic needles.

diˌacetyl'morphine. *Chem.* [f. DIACETYL + MORPHINE *sb.*] An acetyl derivative of morphine, more commonly called HEROIN. (Cf. DIAMORPHINE.)

1875 *Jrnl. Chem. Soc.* XXVIII. 315 Isomeric diacetylmorphines. **1884** *Ibid.* XLVI. 613 Morphine dissolves easily in excess of acetic anhydride at 85°, to form diacetylmorphine. **1912** *Chem. Abstr.* VI. 2287 Descriptions and tests are given for diacetylmorphine hydrochloride. **1951** A. GROLLMAN *Pharmacol. & Therapeutics* iv. 89 In heroin (diacetylmorphine), acetyl (CH_3CO-) groups replace H in the OH groups at positions 3 and 6 of morphine. **1965** ALSTEAD & MACARTHUR *Clin. Pharmacol.* (ed. 21) xii. 299 *Diamorphine hydrochloride* (heroin). This is diacetylmorphine and its actions resemble those of morphine.

‖**diachænium** (daɪə'kiːnɪəm). *Bot.* [mod.L., f. DI-[2] + L. *achænium* ACHENE.] A 'fruit' or seed-vessel consisting of two mericarps resembling achenes; = CREMOCARP.

1870 BENTLEY *Bot.* 313 Each portion of the fruit resembles the achænium, except in being inferior, hence the name diachænium has been given to this fruit.

‖**dia'chalasis.** *Surg. Obs.* [a. Gr. διαχάλασις, f. διαχαλάειν to cause to open or gape.] (See quots.) Hence †**diacha'lastic** *a. Obs.*

1751 CHAMBERS *Cycl. Supp., Diachalasis*, in the medicinal works of the antients, a term used to express a solution of continuity in the bones of the cranium at the sutures. **1851–60** MAYNE *Expos. Lex., Diachalasis*.. a former term for the separation or opening of the cranial sutures. **1883** *Syd. Soc. Lex., Diachalastic*, relating to a Diachalasis.

‖**diacho'resis.** *Med. Obs.* [Gr. διαχώρησις excretion.] (See quot.) Hence **diacho'retic** *a.*

1706 PHILLIPS (ed. Kersey), *Diachoresis*, the act or faculty of voiding excrements. **1721** in BAILEY. **1883** *Syd. Soc. Lex., Diachoretic*.. promoting the excretion of fæces; laxative.

diachronic (daɪə'krɒnɪk), *a.* [f. Gr. διά throughout, during + χρόν-ος time + -IC.]

1. Lasting through time, or during the existing period.

1857 GOSSE *Creation* 87 The two creations—the extinct and the extant—or rather the prochronic and the diachronic —here unite.

2. *Linguistics.* [tr. F. *diachronique* (F. de Saussure *a* 1913, in *Cours de linguistique générale* (1916) iii. 120).] Pertaining to or designating a method of linguistic study concerned with the historical development of a language; historical, as opposed to descriptive or synchronic. Also *transf.*, in Anthropology, etc. Hence **dia'chronically** *adv.*; **di'achrony**.

1927 *Mod. Philology* No. 218 De Saussure.. outlines the relation of 'synchronic' to 'diachronic' linguistics. **1937** JESPERSEN *Analytic Syntax* xvii. 60 A view which is historically (diachronically) impeccable. **1938** R. H. LOWIE *Hist. Ethnol. Theory* xii. 228 We.. ought to study the changes going on before our eyes: a 'synchronic' approach must be combined with a 'diachronic' one. **1951** E. E. EVANS-PRITCHARD *Social Anthropol.* iii. 61 Social anthropologists generally study synchronic problems while historians study diachronic problems. **1957** R. W. ZANDVOORT *Handbk. Eng. Gram.* p. v, Contemporary and historical (or, in the terminology of modern linguistics, synchronic and diachronic) grammar are.. best treated separately. **1959** W. BASKIN tr. *F. de Saussure's Course in Gen. Linguistics* I. iii. 81 Everything that has to do with evolution is diachronic. Similarly, synchrony and diachrony designate respectively a language-state and an evolutionary phase. **1963** *Canadian Jrnl. Linguistics* Fall 54 The synchrony and diachrony of language are reflected in the synchrony and diachrony of grammatical theory. **1967** C. L. WRENN *Word & Symbol* 13 So too must the whole cultural significance of a country be examined with a minute appreciation of its language seen diachronically if its literature is to be fully apprehended. **1968** *Assoc. Teachers of Russian Jrnl.* XVII. 8 Diachronic study.. is concerned with the movement of a language through time, with the changes that occur in all its planes and the reasons for them.

diachronism (daɪ'ækrənɪz(ə)m). [f. as DIACHRONIC *a.*: see -ISM.] **1.** *Geol.* The existence of a geological feature that transgresses palæontological zones (see quot. 1929).

1926 W. B. WRIGHT in *Rep. Brit. Assoc. 1926* 354 (*title*) Stratigraphical diachronism in the millstone grit of Lancashire. **1929** L. J. WILLS *Physiographical Evol. Brit.* xiv. 164 The sediments.. do not represent the deposits of a given epoch of time... There is a great divergence between the lithological and chronological classification. This is another example of diachronism. **1966** D. T. DONOVAN *Stratigr.* v. 119 It is likely.. that diachronism is the rule, not the exception, for formations.

2. *Linguistics.* A diachronic method of linguistic study; diachronic treatment.

1962 Y. MALKIEL in Householder & Saporta *Problems in Lexicography* i. 15 The fundamental dimension (diachronism versus synchronism).

So **diachro'nistic** *a.*; **diachro'nistically** *adv.*

1933 *Publ. Mod. Lang. Assoc. Amer.* XLVIII. 616 The diachronistic investigation of the great linguists of the nineteenth century. **1951** S. ULLMANN *Princ. Semantics* i. 36 It is not language that is synchronistic or diachronistic, but the approach to it, the method of investigation, the science of language. **1957** *Archivum Linguisticum* IX. 26 The term *langue* should be applied only to a language considered diachronistically.

diachronous (daɪ'ækrənəs), *a.* [f. as DIACHRONIC *a.*: see -OUS.] **1.** *Geol.* Exhibiting or characteristic of diachronism (see prec., sense 1); not of a uniform geological age.

1926 W. B. WRIGHT in *Rep. Brit. Assoc. 1926* 355 The Haslingden Flag Marine Band was not contemporaneous in the north-east and south-west.. analogous phenomena are demonstrable in almost every highly fossiliferous formation. It is now proposed to introduce the term diachronous to describe a bed having such relations to the zonal succession. **1929** L. J. WILLS *Physiographical Evol. Brit.* xxiv. 322 The grit facies must therefore transgress the time-zones, i.e. the grits are diachronous. **1966** D. T. DONOVAN *Stratigr.* v. 125 There is a recurring tendency among stratigraphers to be alarmed when a formation is discovered to be diachronous. **1969** *Proc. Geol. Soc. Lond.* Aug. 146 Once the marker-points are adequately defined, subsequent demonstrations of facies-changes, diachronous boundaries, lacunae or similar phenomena do not affect their validity.

2. *Linguistics.* = DIACHRONIC *a.* 2.

1936 *English Studies* XVIII. 93 Since de Saussure and Bally we have learnt to distinguish diachronous and synchronous linguistics.

diachylon, -lum (daɪ'ækɪlən, -ləm), **diaculum** (daɪ'ækjʊləm). Forms: α. 4–6 **diaquilon**, 7– **diachylon**, 8– **diachylum** (9 **diaclum**); β. 4–9 **diaculon**, 6 **dyaculome**, 6– **diaculum**. [a. med.L. *diachylum, diaculon*, and OF. *diaculon* (14th c.), *diaquilon, dyachilon, diachilon* (Paré, 16th c.), L. *diachȳlōn* (Celsius), repr. Gr. διὰ χυλῶν (a medicament) composed of juices; cf. also Gr. διάχυλος very juicy, succulent. The pronunciation with shortened penult comes through Fr. and med.L.]

Originally, the name of a kind of ointment composed of vegetable juices; now a common name for lead-plaster, *emplastrum plumbi*, an adhesive plaster made by boiling together litharge (lead oxide), olive oil, and water; prepared on sheets of linen as a sticking-plaster which adheres when heated.

α. **1313** in *Wardr. Acc. Edw. II* 20/15 Diaquilon 1 lb. 10*d.* *c* **1400** *Lanfranc's Cirurg.* 238 Diaquilon maad of litarge and oile and juys of mustard seed. **1541** R. COPLAND *Guydon's Formul.* Sj b, Diaquilon of Rasis. **1660** BOYLE *New Exp. Phys. Mech.* Proem 8 The Common Plaister call'd Diachylon. **1725** BRADLEY *Fam. Dict.* s.v. *Plaister*, Let the Grease be first well melted, add the Diachylum and Wax to it. **1786** *Phil. Trans.* LXXVI. 156 I took some diachylum which had been bought at Apothecaries Hall. **1797** BURKE *Regic. Peace* iii. Wks. VIII. 272 Half a yard square of balmy diplomatick diachylon. **1836** MARRYAT *Japhet* i. 4 Did a bull gore a man, Mr. Cophagus appeared with his diachylon and lint. **1842** S. LOVER *Handy Andy* iv, Your sympathy is better than diachylon to my wounds.

β. **1322** in *Wardr. Acc. Edw. II* 23/20 Dyaculon 4*d.* per lb. **1530** PALSGR. 729 Splette this dyaculome upon a lynen clothe. **1541** R. COPLAND *Guydon's Formul.* Y ij b, Emplayster the place with diaculum. **1671** SHADWELL *Humourist* I, To set up with Sixpenny-worth of Diaculum. **1821** PRAED *Gog* Poems (1866) I. 92 Diaculum, my story says, Was not invented in those days. *a* **1839** *Ibid.* (1864) I. 35 The skin was rubbed from off her thumb, And she had no Diaculum. **1836** GEN. P. THOMPSON *Exerc.* (1842) IV. 92 Will.. your druggists sell more rhubarb and diaculon?

b. *Comb.*, as ***diachylum-plaster***.

1599 A. M. tr. *Gabelhouer's Bk. Physicke* 249/2 Applye as then theron a Diaquilon playster. 1676 I. Coniers in *Phil. Trans.* XI. 718 The ends..I closed up with Diachylon Plaster. *a* 1692 Mountford *Faustus* I. ad fin., I..devour'd Three Yards of Diaculum Plaister instead of Pancake. 1794 Scott *Let. to Miss C. Rutherford* 5 Sept. in *Lockhart*, To hint the convenience of a roll of diaculum plaister.

† **di'achyma.** *Bot. Obs.* [f. Gr. διa- through + χύμα that which is poured out, liquid: cf. διαχέ-ειν to diffuse, etc.] 'A synonym of PARENCHYMA, especially such as occupies the space between two surfaces, as in a leaf'. *Syd. Soc. Lex.* 1883.

1866 *Treas. Bot.* 397 *Diachyma*, the green cellular matter of leaves.

diacid (daɪ'æsɪd), *a. Chem.* [f. DI-[2] 2 + ACID, on the analogy of DIBASIC.] Capable of combining with two acid radicals.

diacid alcohol, a diatomic alcohol containing two hydroxyl groups both replaceable by an acid radical. Thus ethene alcohol or glycol $C_2H_4{\cdot}(OH)_2$ is *diacid*, and when acted on by acetic acid may form either a mono-acetate or a di-acetate.

1866 E. Frankland *Lect. Notes for Chem. Stud.* 241 The monad radicals give monacid alcohols, the dyad radicals diacid alcohols. 1877 Watts *Fownes' Chem.* 166 In the diacid glycol ethers, the two radicles by which the hydrogen is replaced may belong either to the same or to different acids. 1883 C. L. Bloxam *Chem.* (ed. 5) 546 The diamines ..are capable of combining with 2 molecules of hydrochloric or any similar acid, which is implied by stating that they are diacid.

‖ **di'aclasis.** [a. Gr. διάκλασις f. διακλάειν to break in twain.] (See quots.)

1730–6 Bailey (folio), *Diaclasis* a fracture. 1883 *Syd. Soc. Lex.*, *Diaclasis*, refraction of light rays.

Hence **dia'clastic** *a.*

1883 *Syd. Soc. Lex.*, *Diaclastic*..relating to *Diaclasia* [a method of amputation], or to *Diaclasis*.

diaclasite (daɪ'ækləsaɪt). *Min.* [f. Ger. *diaklas* (Breithaupt, 1823), f. Gr. διακλάειν to break through or asunder; on account of its easy cleavage.] A bisilicate of iron and magnesium; a brassy yellow or greenish grey mineral of the pyroxene group, which is orthorhombic in crystallization.

1850 Dana *Min.* 268.

† **'diacle.** *Sc. Obs.* [? related to DIAL; the *-cle* appears to be as in *receptacle*, *spiracle*, and other reprs. of L. instrumental *-culum*, as in *gubernāculum* rudder.] A small portable dial or compass; a pocket-dial.

1488 *Ld. Treas. Acc. Scot.* I. 83 A fare diacle. 1612 *Rates & Customs Scot.* in *Halyburton's Ledger* (Scot. Rec. Ser. 1867) 297 Diacles of wode, the dozen, xijs; of bone, the dozen, xlviijs. 1794 *Scot. Agric. Surv., Shetland* 87 (Jam.), Every boat carries one compass at least, provincially a diacle.

diaclinal (daɪə'klaɪnəl), *a. Geol.* [f. Gr. διά through + κλίν-ειν to bend + -AL.] Of a valley, river, etc.: crossing a fold; passing through an anticline or syncline.

1874 J. W. Powell in *Bull. Philos. Soc. Washington* I. 50 Still other valleys were found cutting across folds. These were called diaclinal valleys. 1875 —— *Explor. Colorado River* xi. 160 Three varieties [of transverse valleys] are noticed: (*a*) diaclinal, those which pass through a fold, [etc.]. 1963 D. W. & E. E. Humphries tr. *Termier's Erosion & Sedimentation* v. 107 Valleys are classified by their relationship to the dip of the beds. These are: monoclinal or homoclinal rivers..; diaclinal..which cross folds.

‖ **diacodium** (daɪə'kəʊdɪəm). *Obs.* Also 6 diacodion, 8–9 diacode. [med. and mod.L. *diacōdion*, *-cōdium*, in ancient L. *diacōdīōn*, from Gr. διὰ κωδειῶν (a preparation) made from poppy-heads: see DIA-[2]. Cf. also French *diacodion* (16th c.), *diacodium* (17–18th c.), *diacode* (adm. by Academy 1762); the last is of rare use in English. So It. *diacodione* (Florio 1599), now *diacodio*.]

A syrup prepared from poppy-heads, used chiefly as an opiate.

1564–78 Bulleyn *Dial. agst. Pest.* (1888) 51 Drinke your Diacodion at night to reconcile slepe again. 1681 tr. *Willis' Rem. Med. Wks.* Vocab., *Diacodium*, a syrup to procure sleep, made off the tops of poppy. 1695 Congreve *Love for L.* III. xiii, You had best take a little Diacodion and Cowslip-Water. 1817 W. Taylor in *Monthly Mag.* XLIV. 313 His favourite medicine was a diacodium, consisting of opium administered in honey. 1820 *Blackw. Mag.* VII. 328 [It] puts one to sleep more effectually than a double dose of diacodium. 1829 J. Togno tr. *Edwards' & Vavasseur's Mater. Med.* 323 Calming Mixture..Diacode Syrup.

Hence † **dia'codiate** *sb.*: cf. *opiate*. *Obs.*

1684 tr. *Bonet's Merc. Compit.* XIV. 488 We may sometimes use Diacodiates if the Patients strength hold out.

‖ **diacœlosis** (ˌdaɪəsiː'ləʊsɪs). *Biol.* [f. Gr. δια- (DIA-[1]) + κοίλωσις hollow, belly.] The separation of the cœlome or body-cavity into several sinuses in some Vermes, as leeches.

1888 Rolleston & Jackson *Anim. Life* 579. *Ibid.* 630 The coelome is much restricted by a growth of connective tissue, which splits it up into sinuses and channels, a process termed *diacoelosis*.

diacon, -e, obs. forms of DEACON.

diaconal (daɪ'ækənəl), *a.* [ad. late L. *diācōnāl-is*, f. *diāconus* DEACON: cf. F. *diaconal* (14th c. in Hatz.-Darm.).] Of or belonging to a deacon (in various senses of the word).

1611 Cotgr., *Diaconal*, Diaconall; of, or belonging to a deacon. 1656 in Blount *Glossogr.* 1725 tr. *Dupin's Eccl. Hist. 17th C.* I. v. 176 The Matter of the Diaconal Ordination. 1863 J. M. Ludlow *Sisterhoods* in *Gd. Words* 494 A large development..of what I may call the natural diaconal functions of women. 1866 F. G. Lee *Direct. Angl.* (ed. 3) 3 Being about to execute a diaconal function.

diaconate (daɪ'ækənət), *sb.* [ad. late L. *diāconāt-us*, f. *diāconus* DEACON: see -ATE[1]. Cf. F. *diaconat*.]

1. The office or rank of deacon.

1727–51 Chambers *Cycl.*, *Deaconry, Diaconate*, the order or ministry of a deacon or deaconess. [Not in Johnson, Todd, Richardson, Webster 1828, Craig 1847.] *a* 1846 Worcester cites *Eclectic Rev.* 1849 (*title*) The Diaconate and the Poor. 1852 Conybeare & H. *St. Paul* (1862) I. xiii. 408 If..we explain these intimations by what we know of the Diaconate in the succeeding century. 1884 D. Hunter tr. *Reuss's Hist. Canon* iii. 34 A vocation quite as special as that of the apostleship or the diaconate.

2. The time during which any one is a deacon.

1880 *Sunday School Times* 3 Apr. 212 During his diaconate the Rev. Thos. Gaulandet was assistant to Dr. Pierce. 1891 E. W. Gosse *Gossip in Library* v. 59 The English divines . were accustomed to stupendous efforts of endurance from their very diaconate.

3. A body of deacons.

1891 Stoughton in *Wesl. Meth. Mag.* May 347 A deputation from our diaconate called upon him.

† **di'aconate,** *a. Obs. nonce-wd.* [f. L. *diācon-us* DEACON + -ATE[2].] Having, or managed by, deacons.

a 1679 T. Goodwin *Wks.* IV. IV. 189 (R.), This one great diaconate church (as we may, in a parallel allusion, to that other name of presbyterial, call it).

diaconess, -isse, obs. forms of DEACONESS.

‖ **dia'conicon.** *Eccl. Antiq.* and *Mod. Gk. Ch.* Also in Lat. form **diaconicum.** [Gr. διᾱκονικόν, neut. adj. pertaining to a deacon, f. διάκονος a servant, a DEACON.] A building or room adjoining the church, where vestments, ornaments, and other things used in the church service are kept; a sacristy, a vestry.

1727–51 Chambers *Cycl.*, *Diaconicon, Sacristy*, a place adjoining to the antient churches, where the sacred vestments, with the vessels, and other ornaments of the altar, were preserved. 1794 *Archæol.* XI. 331 Thus, among the Greeks, is always placed the sacristy, or *diaconicon*. 1850 Neale *East. Ch.* I. I. ii. 191 On the opposite side of the bema was the diaconicon or sacristy. 1876 in Gwilt *Encycl. Archit.* Gloss. s.v.

† **di'aconize,** *v. Obs.* [f. Gr. διάκονος, L. *diāconus* DEACON + -IZE. Cf. F. *diaconiser* 'conférer le diaconat.'] *intr.* To act as deacon; to minister.

1644 Bulwer *Chiron.* 130 The Left Hand..in the more accomplish'd and plenary exhibition of this sacred rite [benediction] hath oft Diaconiz'd unto the Right.

† **di'acony.** *Obs. rare.* [ad. med.L. *diāconia*, a. Gr. διακονία office, etc. of a deacon. Cf. F. *diaconie* 'a deaconrie, the place of a deacon' (Cotgr.).] The place or office of a deacon.

1636 Abp. J. Williams *Holy Table* (1637) 79 The very Altar it self..hath been termed, in the ancient Councells, The Diaconie, as a place belonging (next after the Bishop) to the care and custodie of the Deacon only.

‖ **diacope** (daɪ'ækəʊpiː). [a. Gr. διακοπή cleft, gash, f. διακόπτ-ειν to cut through.]

† **1.** *Gram.* and *Rhet.* 'A figure by which two words that naturally stand together, especially two parts of a compound word, are separated by the intervention of another word; tmesis' (Webster 1864). *Obs.*

1586 A. Day *Eng. Secretary* II. (1625) 83 *Tmesis* or *Diacope*, a division of a word compound into two parts, as, What might be so ever..for, whatsoever might be, &c. 1678 Phillips (ed. 4), *Diastole*, this figure is otherwise called *Diacope*, and by Ruffinianus by a Latin term *Separatio*.

2. *Surg.* (See quots.)

1706 Phillips (ed. Kersey), *Diacope*, a Cutting or dividing asunder, a deep Wound, especially one made in the Scull by a sharp Instrument. 1851–60 in Mayne *Expos. Lex.* 1883 *Syd. Soc. Lex.*, *Diacope*, a cut, incision, fissure, or longitudinal fracture. It generally signifies an oblique incision made in the cranium by a sharp instrument, without the piece being removed.

diacoustic (daɪə'kaʊstɪk), *a.* [f. DI-[3] + ACOUSTIC *a.*] Pertaining to diacoustics.

1775 in Ash: and in mod. Dicts.

diacoustics (daɪə'kaʊstɪks). [mod. f. DI-[3] + ACOUSTICS: in F. *diacoustique*. Cf. DIOPTRICS.] A name for the science of refracted sounds. Also termed *diaphonics*.

1683 *Phil. Trans.* XIV. 473 Hearing may be divided into direct, refracted and reflex'd..which are yet nameless unless we call them Acousticks, Diacousticks and Catacousticks. 1704 J. Harris *Lex. Techn.*, *Diacousticks* or *Diaphonicks* is the consideration of the properties of Refracted sound, as it passes through different mediums. 1803 Cavallo *Nat. Philos.* II. 309 *Diacoustics*, viz. of refracted sound.

diacran'teric, *a. Anat.* [f. Gr. διά through, apart + κραντῆρες the wisdom teeth + -IC.]

1883 *Syd. Soc. Lex.*, *Diacranteric*, a term applied to describe the dentition of those snakes in which the posterior teeth are separated by longer intervals than the anterior.

So **diacran'terian** *a.*, in same sense.

1889 in *Cent. Dict.*

‖ **di'acre.** *Obs. rare.* In 6 dyacre. [a. F. *diacre* for OF. *diacne*, ad. L. *diāconus*.] A deacon.

1523 Ld. Berners *Froiss.* I. ccccxlii. 779 There came..a byshop, a dyacre, and two knightes.

‖ **di'acrisis.** *Med.* [mod.L. *diacrisis*, a. Gr. διάκρισις, f. διακρίνειν to separate; *spec.* to mark a crisis in a fever. Cf. F. *diacrise*.] **a.** 'A term for the act of separation or secretion.' **b.** 'A critical evacuation.' **c.** = DIAGNOSIS. Hence **diacrisi'ography,** 'a description of the organs of secretion' (*Syd. Soc. Lex.*).

1684 tr. *Bonet's Merc. Compit.* VI. 200 The Fermentation causes such a diacrisis..in the mass of bloud. 1706 Phillips (ed. Kersey), *Diacrisis*, a separating, severing or dividing; the Faculty of discerning, Judgment. In the Art of *Physick*, a judging of and distinguishing Diseases with their respective Symptoms. 1721 in Bailey. 1851–60 Mayne *Expos. Lex.*, *Diacrisis*..synonymous with *Diagnosis*, which is the term generally used.

diacritic (daɪə'krɪtɪk), *a.* and *sb.* [ad. Gr. διακριτικός, that separates or distinguishes, f. διακρίνειν to separate. In mod.F. *diacritique*.]

A. *adj.* Serving to distinguish, distinctive; *spec.* in *Gram.* applied to signs or marks used to distinguish different sounds or values of the same letter or character; e.g. è, é, ê, ë, ė, ē, ĕ, ę, etc.

[1677 Gale *Crt. Gentiles* III. 87 Plato in his Repub. 9. makes a Philosopher to be ὄργανον διακριτικόν, a diacritic or very critic instrument.] 1699 Wallis *to Bp. Lloyd* in *Nicolson's Epist. Corr.* I. 123 (T.), The Arabick *ha* or *cha* —distinguished only by the diacritick points. 1875 T. Hill *True Ord. Studies* 106 Printed with diacritic signs. 1892 *Nation* (N.Y.) 21 July 49/2 Printing 'hī snōs'..'brôt,' 'twilīt,' 'ẽarlier,' and other diacritic novelties.

B. *sb. Gram.* A diacritic sign or mark.

1866 A. J. Ellis *On Palæotype* in *Trans. Phil. Soc.* 1867 App. I. 6 Lepsius's *Standard Alphabet* in which..as many as two or three diacritics are applied to a single body. 1877 Sweet *Phonetics* 174 Even letters with accents and diacritics ..being only cast for a few founts, act practically as new letters. *Ibid.* 175 We may consider the *h* in *sh* and *th* simply as a diacritic written for convenience on a line with the letter it modifies. 1888 *Athenæum* 1 Sept. 287/1 A system which requires several new types and makes constant use of diacritics.

diacritical (daɪə'krɪtɪkəl), *a.* [f. as prec. + -AL[1].]

1. *Gram.* = DIACRITIC *a.*

1749 B. Martin (*title*), Lingua Britannica Reformata: or a universal English Dictionary..Universal, Etymological, Orthographical, Orthoepical, Diacritical. 1755 Johnson *Dict.* Gram. Eng. Tongue, From *f* in the Islandick alphabet, *v* is only distinguished by a diacritical point. 1840 Malcom *Trav.* 42/1 [In Siamese] there are thirty-four consonants.. and twelve vowels, with several diacritical marks. 1867 A. J. Ellis *E.E. Pronunc.* I. i. 21 In quite recent days, the innovation of diacritical signs arose as in French and German.

b. *gen.* Distinguishing, distinctive.

1857 Birch *Anc. Pottery* (1858) II. 343 The diacritical marks of this ware are a paste of red coralline colour, [etc.]

c. *Electr.* (See quot.)

1884 S. P. Thompson *Dynamo-Electr. Mach.* (1888) 307 This number of ampère-turns he named the diacritical number; and the current producing half-saturation he called the diacritical current.

2. Capable, or showing a capacity, of distinguishing or discerning.

1856 Alexander *Life Dr. Wardlaw* xix. 477 His intellect was eminently dialectic and diacritical. 1865 *Athenæum* 24 June 837/2 Where is his diacritical power?

Hence **dia'critically** *adv.*

1820 *Blackw. Mag.* VII. 198 Masoretically print it, diacritically compose it.

diact ('daɪækt). *Zool.* Shortened form of next.

1887 tr. *F. E. Schulze* in *Challenger Rep., Zool.* XXI. 36 The two rays of a diact belong either to the same or to different axes. *Ibid.*, A..typical diact structure.

diactine (daɪ'æktɪn), *a.* (and *sb.*) *Zool.* [f. DI-[2] + ACTINE 2.] Of a monaxon sponge spicule: having two rays, growing in both directions. Also as *sb.*, a spicule of this type. Hence **di'actinal** *a.*

1888 Sollas in *Challenger Rep.* XXV. p. liii, Diactine (*diactina*).—A monaxon in which growth proceeds in both directions along the axis. 1900 E. A. Minchin in E. R. Lankester *Treat. Zool.* II. 116 A simple monaxon rod, which may be either diactinal (*rhabdus*), or monactinal (*style*). 1940 L. H. Hyman *Invertebrates* I. vi. 297 Monaxons that develop by growth in both directions from a central point are named diactinal monaxons, diactines, or, briefly, rhabds.

diactinic (daɪæk'tɪnɪk), *a. Optics.* [f. DI-[3] = DIA-[1] + Gr. ἀκτίν- a ray + -IC.] Having the property of transmitting the actinic rays of light.

1867 W. A. Miller *Elemen. Chem.* I. (ed. 4) 230 Rock-salt, fluor-spar, water..are almost as diactinic..as quartz. 1880 *19th Cent.* Mar. 529 Substances which are chemically transparent are said to be *diactinic*. 1880 *Athenæum* 11 Dec. 781/3 Experiments which prove the diactinic character of substances constructed on an open chain of carbon compounds.

So di'actinism, 'the condition of transparency for chemical or actinic rays' (*Syd. Soc. Lex.* 1883).

diaculum, a popular variant of DIACHYLUM.

diad, obs. form of DYAD.

diadelph ('daɪədɛlf). *Bot. rare*⁻⁰. [f. next; cf. *didynam.*] A plant of the class *Diadelphia*.
1828 in WEBSTER; whence in later Dicts.

‖**Diadelphia** (daɪə'dɛlfɪə). *Bot.* [mod.L. (Linnæus 1735) f. Gr. δι-, DI-² + ἀδελφός brother + -IA.] The seventeenth class in the Linnæan Sexual system, including plants with stamens normally united in two bundles. Hence **dia'delphian** *a.*
1762 HUDSON *Flora Anglica*, Diadelphia. **1794** MARTYN *Rousseau's Bot.* ix. 93 In the seventeenth class diadelphia, the filaments are united at bottom. **1828** WEBSTER, *Diadelphian.* **1857** HENFREY *Bot.* ii. §385 The Class Diadelphia includes a large number of Papilionaceous genera.

diadelphic (daɪə'dɛlfɪk), *a.* [f. as prec. + -IC.] **a.** *Bot.* = DIADELPHOUS. **b.** *Chem.* Of a compound: Having the elements combined in two groups.
1847 CRAIG, *Diadelphic*, pertaining to the class Diadelphia. **1866** E. FRANKLAND *Lect. Notes for Chem. Stud.* 201 Non-nitrogenous organic compounds.. 1. The monadelphic, or marsh-gas type. 2. The diadelphic, or methyl type.

diadelphous (daɪə'dɛlfəs), *a. Bot.* [f. as prec. + -OUS.] Of stamens: United by the filaments so as to form two bundles. Of plants: Having the stamens so united.
1807 J. E. SMITH *Phys. Bot.* 442 The plants of this section are really not diadelphous but monadelphous. **1870** BENTLEY *Bot.* (1882) 248 When the filaments unite so as to form two bundles, the stamens are termed diadelphous, as in the Pea, Milkwort and Fumitory.

diadem ('daɪədɛm), *sb.* [a. F. *dyademe* (13th c. in Godef.), mod.F. *diadème*, ad. L. *diadēma*, Gr. διάδημα band or fillet, *esp.* the regal fillet of Persian kings, adopted by Alexander of Macedon and his successors; f. διαδέειν to bind round, f. δια- across, through + δέειν to bind.]

1. A crown; an ornamental cincture or covering for the head, worn as a symbol of honour, *esp.* of royal dignity. (In quot. 1290, applied to the aureola or crown of a martyr. Now chiefly *poetic* and *rhetorical.*)
c **1290** *S. Eng. Leg.* I. 167/2125 Al round it orn a-boute is heued, ase it were a dyademe. **1382** WYCLIF *Rev.* xii. 3 And lo! a greet reed dragoun, hauynge seuene heedes.. and in the heedis of him seuen diademes. **1415** HOCCLEVE *To Sir J. Oldcastle* 232 O Constantyn.. O cristen Emperour.. Wel was byset on thee thy diademe! **1513** MORE in Grafton *Chron.* (1568) II. 807 In habite royall with Scepter in hande and Diademe on his head. **1602** SHAKS. *Ham.* III. iv. 100 A vice of kings.. That from a shelfe, the precious Diadem stole, And put it in his Pocket. **1785** WILKINS *Bhagvat* 69, I wish to behold thee with the diadem on thy head. *a* **1839** PRAED *Poems* (1864) II. 433 Many a gem Fit for a Sultan's diadem.

b. *spec.* A band or fillet of cloth, plain or adorned with jewels, worn round the head, originally by Oriental monarchs, as a badge of royalty. (The original sense of the word in Gr. and L.)
1579–80 NORTH *Plutarch* (1612) 518 He had sent her his Diademe or royall band and called her by the name and title of Queene. **1656** COWLEY *Pind. Odes, Praise of Pindar* ii. *Notes*, Diadems (which were used by the ancient Kings.. for the mark of Royalty).. were Bindings of white Ribband about the Head, set and adorn'd with precious stones. **1776** GIBBON *Decl. & F.* I. 388 Diocletian.. ventured to assume the diadem.. It was no more than a broad white fillet set with pearls, which encircled the emperor's head. **1882** FARRAR *Early Chr.* II. 226 *note*, A diadem.. this badge of Oriental autocracy—a purple silken fillet embroidered with pearls.

c. A wreath of leaves or flowers worn round the head.
1530 PALSGR. 213/2 Diademe of laurell, *laureole.* **1883** *Myra's Jrnl.* Aug., Diadems of orange-flowers have been more worn lately.

d. *Her.* (See quots.)
1727–51 CHAMBERS *Cycl.*, *Diadem*, in heraldry, is applied to certain circles, or rims, serving to bind or inclose the crowns of sovereign princes; and to bear the globe, and cross, or the flower-de-luces, for their crest. **1787** PORNY *Elem. Heraldry* Gloss., *Diadem*.. is now frequently used to signify the Circles, which close on the top of the Crowns of Sovereigns, and support the Mound.

2. *fig.* The authority or dignity symbolized by a diadem; royal or imperial dignity, sovereignty; = CROWN *sb.* 3.
a **1300** *Cursor M.* 22357 (Cott.) Þan sal he fare to iursalem .. and yeild up þare his diademe. *a* **1400–50** *Alexander* 3240 Don aȝayne þe dignite, þe diademe of Pers, And all þe riȝtis of þi rewme resayue as before. **1548** HALL *Chron.* 224 That the Erle of Richemond, should once attein to the Crowne and diademe of the realme. **1602** FULBECKE *Pandectes* 10 Such things can not be seuered from the princely Diadem. **1789** BELSHAM *Ess.* I. xviii. 348 A diadem could not.. raise the personal character of the Protector. **1821** BYRON *Mar. Fal.* I. ii. 173 Old Dandolo Refused the diadem of all the Cæsars.

3. *fig.* A distinction or adornment conferring glory or dignity, figured as a crown.
1526 *Pilgr. Perf.* (W. de W. 1531) 7 b, They shall receyue of the hande of god the crowne of glory and diademe of honour. **1605** CAMDEN *Rem.* 3 One of the fairest.. Plumes in the triumphant Diademe of the Roman Empire. **1825** J. NEAL *Bro. Jonathan* III. 370 The name of Yankee was a reproach here; it was a diadem there.

4. *transf.* Something that surmounts and adorns like a crown; a crowning ornament.
1781 COWPER *Retirement* 82 The crescent moon, the diadem of night, Stars countless, each in his appointed place, Fast anchored. **1817** BYRON *Manfred* I. i. 64 Mont Blanc is the monarch of mountains; They crown'd him long ago On a throne of rocks, in a robe of clouds, With a diadem of snow. **1845–75** MACKAY *Seven Angels of Lyre* iii, A rainbow is her diadem.

5. Short for *diadem-monkey*.

6. *Surg.* In Lat. form *diadema*: a bandage for the head.
1811 in HOOPER *Med. Dict.*

7. *attrib.* and *Comb.*, as ***diadem-shaped*** adj.; **diadem-lemur**, a species of *Indris*; **diadem-monkey**, *Cercopithecus diadematus*; **diadem-spider**, the garden spider, *Epeira diadema*.
1851 D. WILSON *Preh. Ann.* (1863) II. III. v. 143 Diadem, and coronet shaped ornaments. **1854** H. MILLER *Sch. & Schm.* (1858) 67 The large diadem spider, which spins so strong a web.

'diadem, *v.* [f. prec. sb.] *trans.* To place a diadem upon; to adorn with or as with a diadem; to crown. Chiefly in *pa. pple.*: cf. next.
1362 LANGL. *P. Pl.* A. III. 268 Dauid schal ben dyademed and daunten hem alle. **1738** POPE *Epil. to Sat.* II. 232 When diadem'd with rays divine.. Her Priestless Muse forbids the Good to die. **1777** SIR W. JONES *Turkish Ode* Poems 91 And every stalk is diadem'd with flowers. **1826** H. H. WILSON tr. *Uttara Râma Cheritra* 46 Hills, whose towering peaks Are diademed with clouds. **1858** NEALE *Bernard de M.* (1865) 13 The Judge that comes in mercy.. To diadem the right.

Hence **diademed** ('daɪədɛmd) *ppl. a.*, wearing or adorned with a diadem; crowned.
1790 J. WILLIAMS *Shrove Tuesday* (1794) 9 Where Despots diadem'd and toga'd stride. **1805** SOUTHEY in *Ann. Rev.* III. 556 One of the three diademed princes. **1840** CARLYLE *Heroes* iii. (1891) 79 Is he not obeyed, worshipped after his sort, as all the Tiaraed and Diademed of the world .. could not be? **1892** *Athenæum* 19 Mar. 380/1 Draped diademed bust of the empress.

diademated ('daɪədɪmeɪtɪd), *ppl. a.* ? *Obs.* [f. L. *diadēmāt-us* (f. Gr. διάδημα DIADEM) + -ED.] Wearing a diadem; diademed.
1727 BAILEY vol. II, *Diadémated*, wearing a Diadem, Crown or Turbant. **1763** SWINTON in *Phil. Trans.* LIV. 99 The first of these medals presents to our view a diademated head. **1770** *Ibid.* LX. 84 *note*, Coins.. with diademated heads upon them.

‖**dia'dexis.** *Med. Obs.*⁻⁰. [a. Gr. διάδεξις, n. of action f. διαδέχεσθαι to relieve one another, succeed.] A transposition of humours in the body from one place to another.
1811 in HOOPER *Med. Dict.* **1847** in CRAIG.

‖**diadoche** (daɪ'ædəkiː). [a. Gr. διαδοχή succession, f. διαδέχεσθαι: see prec.] Succession; *spec.* in *Med.* (see quots.).
1706 PHILLIPS (ed. Kersey), *Diadoche*, in the Art of Physick, the succeeding or progress of a Disease, to its change call'd Crisis. **1883** *Syd. Soc. Lex.*, *Diadoche*, the exchange of one disease into another of different form or character and in a different situation. **1884** *Church Q. Rev.* XVIII. 258 The diadoche of early Greek scholars.. was but a broken and fitful succession.

Diadochian (daɪə'dəʊkɪən), *a.* [f. Gr. διάδοχ-ος succeeding, successor (see prec.) + -IAN.]

Belonging to the *Diadochi* or Macedonian generals among whom the empire of Alexander the Great was divided after his death, or to their time.
[**1855** GROTE *Greece* XII. 362 The interests of these Diadochi—Antigonus, Ptolemy, Seleucus, Lysimachus.] **1881** J. T. CLARKE *Rep. Invest. Assos* in *Papers Archæol Inst. Amer.* Class. Ser. I. 40 A monument of small dimensions and lavish Diadochian ornamentation.

diadochite (daɪ'ædəkaɪt). *Min.* [mod. f. Gr. διάδοχος (see prec.) + -ITE. Named by Breithaupt in 1837, from his belief that phosphorus had succeeded arsenic in its composition.] Hydrous phosphate and sulphate of iron, of brown or yellowish colour and resinous appearance.
1850 DANA *Min.* 454. **1851** WATTS tr. *Gmelin's Chem.* V. 246 Diadochite.. Resembles iron-cinder in.. appearance.

‖**diadosis** (daɪ'ædəsɪs). *Med.* [a. Gr. διάδοσις, f. διαδιδόναι to hand over, distribute.]

a. Distribution of nutritive material to the body. **b.** Remission or decline of a disease.
1721 in BAILEY. **1811** in HOOPER *Med. Dict.*

†**'diadrom, -ome.** *Obs.* [ad. Gr. διαδρομή a running through or across, f. διά + δρομ- ablaut stem of δραμεῖν to run.] A vibration of a pendulum.
1661 BOYLE *Examen* v. (1682) 55 In Water the Diadromes are so much more slow [than in air]. **1690** LOCKE *Hum. Und.* IV. x. §10. 293 A Pendulum, whose Diadroms.. are each equal to one Second of Time.

diæresis (daɪ'ɛrɪsɪs, -'ɪərɪsɪs). Also dieresis. [a. L. *diæresis*, a. Gr. διαίρεσις, n. of action f. διαιρέ-ειν to divide, separate.]

1. The division of one syllable into two, *esp.* by the separation of a diphthong into two simple vowels.
1656 BLOUNT *Glossogr.* s.v. *Dieretic*, The figure Diæresis, whereby one syllable is divided into two parts, as *Evoluisse* for *Evolvisse*. **1755** JOHNSON, *Diæresis*, the separation or disjunction of syllables; as *aër*. **1887** ROBY *Lat. Gram.* (ed. 5) I. 478 *Diæresis*, 'separation' of one vowel sound into two; e.g. *Orphĕus* for *Orpheus* also the treatment of a usually consonantal *v* as a vowel; e.g. *sĭlŭae* for *silvae*.

b. The sign [¨] marking such a division, or, more usually, placed over the second of two vowels which otherwise make a diphthong or single sound, to indicate that they are to be pronounced separately.
1611 COTGR. N n n n, Diæresis is when two points ouer a vowell diuide it from another vowell, as *bouë*, *queuë*. **1706** PHILLIPS (ed. Kersey) s.v. *Diæresis*, An ë, ï or ü Diæresis, to show that such a vowel is sounded by it self and not joyn'd with any other, so as to make a Diphthongue. **1767** G. SHARPE *Grk. Tongue* 16 (R.) If any two vowels are to be read as two distinct syllables, the latter is marked with a diæresis, or two dots over it; παϊς, boy, and αϋπνος, sleepless. **1824** J. JOHNSON *Typogr.* II. xi. 284 The diæresis [¨] separates two vowels, that they may not be taken for a diphthong.

2. *Prosody.* The division made in a line or a verse when the end of a foot coincides with the end of a word.
1844 BECK & FELTON tr. *Munk's Metres* 39 From the coincidence and disagreement of verse-series and word-series springs the idea of the diæresis and cæsura (διαίρεσις and τομή), abscission and incision.

3. *Surg.* Separation of parts normally united, as by a wound or burn, the lancing of an abscess, etc.
1706 in PHILLIPS (ed. Kersey). **1727–51** CHAMBERS *Cycl.* s.v. *Diæresis*, There are five manners of performing the diæresis viz. by cutting, pricking, tearing, drawing and burning. **1883** *Syd. Soc. Lex.*, *Diæresis*, a division of parts from a wound, or burn; a solution of continuity, produced by mechanical means.

4. *gen.* (*nonce-use.*) Division, separation.
1856 ALEXANDER *Life Wardlaw* xiii. 331 This diæresis of opinion has separated ethical writers into two sections.

diæretic (daɪɪ'rɛtɪk), *a.* and *sb.* Also dieretic. [ad. Gr. διαιρετικός divisible, of or by division, f. διαιρετός, vbl. adj. f. διαιρεῖν: see prec.; cf. F. *diérétique* (Littré).]

A. *adj.* Of, pertaining to, or by means of diæresis or division.
1640 G. WATTS tr. *Bacon's Adv. Learn.* VI. ii. 231 The others [methods], as the analytic, systatic, diæretic, etc. **1656** BLOUNT *Glossogr.*, *Dieretick*, pertaining to a division, or the figure Diæresis. **1851–60** MAYNE *Expos. Lex.* 269/1 Having power to divide, dissolve, or corrode; escharotic, corrosive, dieretic. **1883** *Syd. Soc. Lex.*, *Diæretic*.

B. *sb. Med.* A caustic or corrosive agent. *Obs.*
1721 BAILEY, *Diæretics*, medicines which corrode and eat. **1883** *Syd. Soc. Lex.*, *Diæretic*, an old term for a caustic.

diafragma, -fragme, obs. ff. DIAPHRAGM.

diagenesis (daɪə'dʒɛnɪsɪs). [mod. f. Gr. δια- across + γένεσις generation, origination: -GENESIS.] Transformation by dissolution and recombination of elements. Hence **diage'netic** *a.*, of or pertaining to diagenesis.
1886 T. S. HUNT *Mineral Physiol. & Physiogr.* 173 The reactions.. resulting not only in the conversion of amorphous into crystalline bodies, but in the breaking up of old combinations, as well as in the union of unlike matters mechanically mingled to form new crystalline species, are instructive examples of what Gümbel has termed *diagenesis*. *Ibid.*, An instructive phase in this diagenetic process is that of the gradual conversion of smaller crystalline grains or crystals into larger ones. **1965** *New Scientist* 30 Dec. 893 Diagenesis—the chemical alteration that takes place in sediments, turning them into rocks for posterity. **1965** G. J. WILLIAMS *Econ. Geol. N.Z.* vi. 65/2 Barium and strontium were concentrated by lowgrade diagenesis during the consolidation of 28,000 ft. of Triassic sediments.

diageotropic (daɪədʒiːəʊ'trɒpɪk), *a. Bot.* [f. Gr. διά across + γῆ, γεο- the earth + τροπικός belonging to turning.] Characterized by diageotropism.
1880 C. & F. DARWIN *Movem. Pl.* 189 The rhizomes of Sparganium ramosum grow out horizontally in the soil to a considerable length, or are diageotropic. **1882** F. DARWIN in *Nature* XXV. 600 A diageotropic organ is one which possesses the power of growing at right angles to the line of gravitation.

diageotropism (ˌdaɪədʒiː'ɒtrəpɪz(ə)m). *Bot.* [f. prec.: see -ISM.] The tendency in parts of plants to grow transversely to the earth's radius.
1880 C. & F. DARWIN *Movem. Pl.* 5 Diageotropism, a position more or less transverse to the radius of the earth.

diaglyph ('daɪəglɪf). *rare.* [f. stem of Gr. διαγλύφειν to carve through, carve in intaglio, f.

διа- through + γλύφειν to carve: in mod.F. *diaglyphe* (Hatz.-Darm.).] A sculpture or engraving in which the figures are sunk below the general surface; an intaglio. Hence **dia'glyphic** *a.*, pertaining to, or of the nature of, such sculpture.

Evelyn's name for the art is after Gr. γλυφική (*sc.* τέχνη).

[**1662** EVELYN *Chalcogr.* (1769) 16 *Diaglyphice*, when hollow, as in seals and intaglias. **1819** P. NICHOLSON *Archit. Dict.* I. 9 The *Diaglyphice* where the strokes [of the figures] are indented.] **1864** WEBSTER, *Diaglyphic.* **1889** *Century Dict.*, *Diaglyph.*

diagnosable (daɪəg'nəʊzəb(ə)l), *a.* [f. next + -ABLE.] Capable of being diagnosed.

1891 *Scot. Leader* 24 Sept. 6 Before it [tubercular disease] became in the individual diagnoseable.

diagnose (daɪəg'nəʊz), *v. Med.* [f. next; cf. *anastomose*, *metamorphose* (immediately after F. verbs in *-oser* from a sb. in *-ose*).] *trans.* To make a diagnosis of (a disease), to distinguish and determine its nature from its symptoms; to recognize and identify by careful observation.

1861 WYNTER *Soc. Bees* 339, I was enabled to diagnose the complaint at once. **1877** ROBERTS *Handbk. Med.* (ed. 3) I. 231 Articular rheumatism has also to be diagnosed from the other forms. **1887** *Homeop. World* 1 Nov. 497, I diagnosed chronic jaundice.

fig. **1879** TOURGEE *Fool's Err.* ii. 11 Her heart had diagnosed the symptoms. **1885** *Times* 13 Aug. 4/1 It is not difficult for me to diagnose..the name of the 'former house-surgeon' who wrote to you.

b. *absol.* or *intr.*

1882 ATTFIELD in *Standard* 23 Aug. 2/2 The pharmacist.. attempting to diagnose while knowing nothing about the human frame.

diagnosis (daɪəg'nəʊsɪs). Pl. -oses. [a. L. *diagnōsis*, Gr. διάγνωσις, n. of action f. διαγιγνώσκειν to distinguish, discern, f. δια- through, thoroughly, asunder + γιγνώσκειν to learn to know, perceive. In F. *diagnose* in Molière: cf. prec.]

1. a. *Med.* Determination of the nature of a diseased condition; identification of a disease by careful investigation of its symptoms and history; also, the opinion (formally stated) resulting from such investigation.

1681 tr. *Willis' Rem. Med. Wks.* Vocab., *Diagnosis*, dilucidation, or knowledg. **1791** P. P. PRICE (*title*) A Treatise on the Diagnosis and Prognosis of Disease. **1834** J. FORBES *Lænnec's Dis. Chest* (ed. 4) 199 It is in the diagnosis ..of pneumonia..that the greatest practical benefit of auscultation will be found. **1855** O. W. HOLMES *Poems* 274 The diagnosis was made out, They tapped the patient; so he died. **1872** BAKER *Nile Tribut.* i. 8 The crows can form a pretty correct diagnosis upon the case of a sick camel. **1878** H. S. WILSON *Alp. Ascents* iv. 132 Then came the diagnosis —to wit a severe contusion and strain of right knee.

b. *transf.* and *fig.*

1855 H. SPENCER *Princ. Psychol.* (1872) II. VI. xviii. 253 Perception is essentially a diagnosis. **1868** T. G. DUFF *Pol. Surv.* 113 Our diagnosis of the character of a person. **1892** *Spectator* 1 Oct. 438/1 [Swindlers] seem to possess, in an extraordinarily high degree, the power of moral diagnosis, —of telling what are the weak spots in the mind of the ordinary man.

2. *Biol.* etc. Distinctive characterization in precise terms, (*of* a genus, species, etc.).

1840 W. WHEWELL *Phil. Inductive Sci.* I. VIII. ii. 492 The Characteristick has been termed by some English Botanists the Diagnosis of plants; a word which we may conveniently adopt. **1853** J. LINDLEY *Veget. Kingd.* 371 *Tiliaceæ*, Linden-blooms..Diagnosis.—Malval Exogens, with free stamens on the outside of a disk, albuminous seeds, and straight embryo. **1854** BADHAM *Halieut.* 235 Specimens..in a fit condition for diagnosis. **1858** WHEWELL *Nov. Org. Renov.* 23 The Diagnosis, or Scheme of the Characters, comes, in the order of philosophy, after the Classification. **1874** JEVONS *Prin. Science* (1877) 708 This operation of discovering to which class of a system a certain specimen or case belongs, is generally called Diagnosis. **1880** GUNTHER *Fishes* 10 The 'Genera Piscium' contains well-defined diagnoses of 45 genera.

diagnost ('daɪəgnɒst). *rare*$^{-0}$. [ad. Gr. διαγνώστης one who examines and decides, agent-n. from διαγιγνώσκειν: see DIAGNOSIS.] = DIAGNOSTICIAN.

diagnostic (daɪəg'nɒstɪk), *a.* and *sb.* [ad. Gr. διαγνωστικός able to distinguish, ἡ διαγνωστική (*sc.* τέχνη) the art of distinguishing diseases, f. διαγιγνώσκειν: see DIAGNOSIS. Cf. F. *diagnostique* (17th c. in Hatz.-Darm.).]

A. *adj.*

1. Of or pertaining to diagnosis.

1625 HART *Anat. Ur.* I. i. 13 Physicke diagnosticke or semioticke..teacheth vs to know the nature..of the disease by the signes..of the same. **1654** WHITLOCK *Zootomia* 46 The Diagnostick and disease-discovering Part. **1775** SIR E. BARRY *Observ. Wines* 394 The diagnostic knowledge..of these symptoms. **1884** E. SHEPPARD in *Law Times* 4 Oct. 373/2 The judgment and diagnostic skill of the..medical practitioner.

2. Of value for purposes of diagnosis, discrimination, or identification; specifically characteristic, distinctive: **a.** in *Med.*; **b.** in *Biol.*; **c.** *gen.*

a. **1650** BULWER *Anthropomet.* 4 As to the signes Diagnostick, a vitious figure of the head is known by sight. **1737** BRACKEN *Farriery Impr.* (1756) I. 306 The Diagnostick Signs of a Dog truly mad. **1885** *Lancet* 26 Sept. 562 The most important diagnostic signs of pleural effusion.

b. **1862** SIR H. HOLLAND *Ess., Life & Organization* 79 The teeth..so important a diagnostic mark. **1872** OLIVER *Elem. Bot.* II. 124 The brief characters which..distinguish these species from each other are said to be diagnostic. **1875** BUCKLAND *Log-bk.* 244 Much has been said as to the tail being a diagnostic mark between the wild and tame cat.

c. **1669** *Address Yng. Gentry Eng.* 17 Necessary aphorisms to regulate their own lives by, and be diagnostic of all others. **1803** *Edin. Rev.* I. 256 *note*, The *self-reviewing* philosophy would have been a term more diagnostic. **1888** *Pall Mall G.* 28 Apr. 11/2 The *Times* cannot regard the Mid Lanark election as possessing any particular diagnostic value.

3. *Computing.* Of a program or sub-routine: designed to identify program errors or system faults and give information about them.

[**1950** W. W. STIFLER et al. *High-Speed Computing Devices* xvii. 437 In the computer proposed by the Raytheon Company, self-checking and diagnostic equipment is provided throughout.] **1953** *Proc. IRE* XLI. 1320/1 We discuss the use of three types of diagnostic and servicing programs which enable us to use the computer to diagnose its own troubles. **1967** A. BATTERSBY *Network Analysis* (ed. 2) viii. 140 Diagnostic routines are able to detect obvious errors in the input and print out comments on them—I THINK I HAVE A LOOP is one. **1985** *Sci. Amer.* July 13/1 This program, which will run only in the graphics mode, is diagnostic.

B. *sb.*; sometimes in *collect. pl.* **diagnostics**.

1. = DIAGNOSIS 1.

1625 HART *Anat. Ur.* I. ii. 13 Diagnosticke whose most common scope is to discerne..the sick and infirme from the whole. **1669** W. SIMPSON *Hydrol. Chym.* 94, I fear the Doctor mistakes in his diagnosticks. **1753** N. TORRIANO *Gangr. Sore Throat* 10 From this Appearance of the Blood, no Diagnostic can be formed of the Disease. **1803** *Med. Jrnl.* IX. 126 The disease, the diagnostic of which he found difficult to determine. **1855** MACAULAY *Hist. Eng.* IV. 530 Radcliffe..had raised himself to the first practice in London chiefly by his rare skill in diagnostics.

fig. **1769** BURKE *Late St. Nat.* Wks. 1842 I. 89 The false diagnostick of our state physician. **1874** L. STEPHEN *Hours in Libr.* (1892) I. ix. 335 May be described as a system of religious diagnostics.

2. A distinctive symptom or characteristic, a specific trait: **a.** in *Med.* **b.** *Biol.* and *gen.*

a. **1651** WITTIE *Primrose's Pop. Err.* 225 That Physitian.. having fully found out the diagnosticks, and prognosticks of a disease. **1751** SMOLLETT *Per. Pic.* (1779) II. lvii. 158 From these diagnostics [the physician] declared that the *liquidum nervosum* was intimately affected. **1764** REID *Inquiry* vi. §23. 194 An unusual appearance in the colour of familiar objects may be the diagnostic of a disease in the spectator. **1853** READE *Chr. Johnstone* 15 You have the maladies of idle minds, love, perhaps, among the rest; you blush, a diagnostic of that disorder.

b. **1646** S. BOLTON *Arraignm. Err.* 144 What are the Diagnosticks or marks whereby we may..discern of errour from truth. **1748** RICHARDSON *Clarissa* (1811) VII. ix. 53 Oaths, and curses, the diagnostics of the rakish spirit. **1818** *Blackw. Mag.* II. 404 The diagnostics (if so technical a term may be allowed) of his conduct, deportment, and conversation. **1826** KIRBY & SP. *Entomol.* (1828) IV. xlvii. 405 We cannot point out any certain diagnostic.

3. *Computing.* A message produced by a computer that helps a user to identify an error or malfunction. Also, a facility or routine for producing such a message. Usu. in *pl.*

1963 P. M. SHERMAN *Programming & coding Digital Computers* xix. 404 Following is a partial list of the comments (called diagnostics) provided by Fortran during a compilation. *Ibid.* 405 A number of these diagnostics would apply to any algebraic-language program. **1964** FISHER & SWINDLE *Introd. Computer Programming Syst.* I. i. 4 Programming systems..employ extensive error diagnostics, which check for and announce both clerical and logical errors. **1973** C. W. GEAR *Introd. Computer Sci.* iv. 160 If the programmer attempts to assign a value of B(I) in an assignment statement, the compiler will detect an error at the time it translates that statement and produce a diagnostic that says something about incorrect usage of functions. **1985** *Computing Equipment* Sept. 27/3 (Advt.), Operation of the network is completely automatic and supported by full diagnostics.

diag'nostically, *adv.* [f. prec. + -AL[1] + -LY[2].] By means of diagnosis, with reference to diagnosis.

1657 G. STARKEY *Helmont's Vind.* 51 By Rules set down to finde out the disease Diagnostically. **1891** *Pall Mall G.* 21 Oct. 5/2 Diagnostically and therapeutically it was only the amount of the dose which determined the effect.

diagnosticate (daɪəg'nɒstɪkeɪt), *v.* [f. as prec. + -ATE[3]: cf. F. *diagnostiquer.*] = DIAGNOSE *v.*

1846 T. CALLAWAY *Dislocations* (1849) Could it [a complication] be clearly diagnosticated. **1863** LYTTON *Caxtoniana* I. 44 It assumes to diagnosticate in cases that have baffled the Fergusons. **1871** HAMMOND *Dis. Nervous Syst.* 47 From thrombosis cerebral congestion is diagnosticated by the circumstances that, [etc.].

So **diagnosti'cation** = DIAGNOSIS.

1883 in *Syd. Soc. Lex.*

diagnostician (ˌdaɪəgnɒ'stɪʃən). [f. as prec. + -IAN.] One who is skilled in diagnosis.

1866 A. FLINT *Princ. Med.* (1880) 108 The mental qualifications of the skilful diagnostician. **1894** *Pop. Sci. Monthly* XLIV. 478 By the skilled teacher I now mean the one who is an expert diagnostician of powers.

dia'gometer. *Electr.* [ad. F. *diagomètre*, f. Gr. διάγειν to carry across, conduct + μέτρον measure.] An instrument designed to measure the electro-conductive power of various substances.

1863–72 WATTS *Dict. Chem.* II. 314 *Diagometer*, an electrical apparatus, intended for the detection of adulterations in olive oil, this oil being said to have less electric conducting power than other fixed oils. **1886** WORMELL tr. *Von Urbanitzky's Electr. in Serv. Man* (1890) 109 In the construction of his diagometer, an instrument which makes use of the different conducting powers of substances for the determination of their chemical combination.

†**'diagon**, *sb. Obs.* [ad. mod.L. *diagōnus*, ad. Gr. διαγώνιος: see DIAGONAL.] = DIAGONAL *sb.* 1.

[**1563** SHUTE *Archit.* Diva, A strike ouerthwarte the greate square from corner to corner, that line is named Diagonus.] **1656** BLOUNT *Glossogr.*, *Diagon* or *Diagonal.*

†**'diagon**, *v. Obs. rare.* [f. prec.; cf. *paragon* vb.] *trans.* ? To join by a diagonal line.

1610 W. FOLKINGHAM *Art of Survey* II. v. 55 To Rectifie the Plot: diagone alternate angles.

diagonal (daɪ'ægənəl), *a.* and *sb.* [ad. L. *diagōnālis* (Vitruvius), f. Gr. διαγών-ιος from angle to angle, f. διά across + γωνία angle: see -AL[1] I. 2. Cf. F. *diagonal* (13th c. in Littré).]

A. *adj.*

1. *Geom.* Extending, as a line, from any angular point of a quadrilateral or multilateral figure to an opposite or non-adjacent angular point. (Also applied to a plane extending from one edge of a solid figure to the opposite edge.) Hence *gen.* Extending from one corner of anything to the opposite corner.

1541 [implied in DIAGONALLY]. **1563** SHUTE *Archit.* Civa, The diagonall line marked B. **1570** BILLINGSLEY *Euclid* XI. xxxix. 354 Diagonall lines drawen from the opposite angles. **1660** BLOOME *Archit.* Ab, The square..crossed with two Diagonall lines. **1823** H. J. BROOKE *Introd. Crystallogr.* 12 The diagonal plane of a solid..is an imaginary plane passing through the diagonal lines of two exterior parallel planes. **1859** R. F. BURTON *Centr. Afr.* in *Jrnl. Geog. Soc.* XXIX. 156 From east to west the diagonal breadth of Mgunda Mk'hali is 140 miles.

2. More loosely: Having an oblique direction like the diagonal of a square or other parallelogram; lying or passing athwart; inclined at an angle other than a right angle (usually about 45°).

1665 [see 4]. **1796** *Instr. & Reg. Cavalry* (1813) 57 By the diagonal march of divisions either to front or rear. **1821** CRAIG *Lect. Drawing* vi. 350 A supposed diagonal line from the outer corner of each eye. **1831** LARDNER *Pneumat.* iv. 257 Every change in the position of the surface of the mercury.. will be three times as great in the diagonal barometer as it would be in the vertical one. **1851** DE LA BECHE *Geol. Obs.* 612 Diagonal arrangements of the minor parts..are very common in many sandstones. **1867** SMYTH *Sailor's Word-bk.*, *Diagonal* braces, knees, planks, etc. are such as cross a vessel's timbers obliquely. **1876** MATHEWS *Coinage* i. 7 On some English coins of last century the milling is diagonal to the edge.

3. Marked with diagonal or oblique lines, or having some part placed diagonally or obliquely.

diagonal bellows: a bellows (in an organ) having its sides inclined at an angle. ***diagonal cloth***: a twilled fabric having the ridges diagonal, i.e. running obliquely to the lists. ***diagonal couching*** (in needlework): couching in which the stitches form a zig-zag pattern. ***diagonal scale***: a scale marked with equidistant parallel lines crossed at right angles by others at smaller intervals (e.g. $\frac{1}{10}$ of the larger), and having one of the larger divisions additionally crossed by parallels obliquely placed; used for measurement of small fractions (e.g. hundredths) of the unit of length.

a **1679** SIR J. MOORE *Math.* (1681) 224 Then taking 1 or 10 from any line of equal parts or Diagonal Scale, prick it on AD six times. **1824** *Gill's Techn. Repos.* VI. 199 The proposed Diagonal Pavement in the streets of London. **1876** HILES *Catech. Organ.* viii. (1878) 52 Afterwards diagonal or wedge-shaped bellows came into use. **1879** MOSELEY *Naturalist on Challenger* 473 A wide patch of diagonal ornamentation upon the abdomen. **1882** CAULFEILD & SAWARD *Dict. Needlework* 152 Diagonal couching..is chiefly employed in Church Work. **1883** A. E. SEATON *Mar. Engineering* 55 Any engine whose cylinders are not perfectly horizontal may..be called Diagonal.

4. *Comb.*, as **diagonal-built** *a.*, (a boat or ship) having the outer skin consisting of two layers of planking making angles of about 45° with the keel in opposite directions; **diagonal-planed** *a.* (see quot. 1805–17); **diagonal-wise** *adv.* = DIAGONALLY.

1665 *Phil. Trans.* I. 84 They may make up a Cylinder cut Diagonal wise. **1805–17** R. JAMESON *Char. Min.* (ed. 3) 212 A crystal is said to be diagonal planed, when it has facets.. situated obliquely. **1869** R. W. MEADE *Naval Archit.* 416 In diagonal-built boats the skin consists of two layers of planking.

B. *sb.*

1. *Geom.* A diagonal line; a straight line joining any two opposite or non-adjacent angles of a rectilineal figure (or of a solid contained by planes).

[**1563** SHUTE *Archit.* Cijb, A lyne ouerthwart from the one corner to the other, which line is called *Dyagonalis.*] **1571** DIGGES *Pantom.* IV. v. V iv, Wherby the diagonal exceedeth the side pentagonal. **1662** HOBBES *Seven Prob.* Wks. 1845 VII. 62 You pitched upon half the diagonal for your foundation. **1827** HUTTON *Course Math.* I. 322 The rectangle of the two diagonals of any quadrangle inscribed in a circle. **1831** CARLYLE *Sart. Res.* I. vii. 33 A square Blanket, twelve feet in diagonal. **1847** TENNYSON *Princ.* Concl. 27 Betwixt them both, to please them both, And yet to give the story as it rose, I moved as in a strange diagonal, And maybe neither pleased myself nor them. **1871** TYNDALL *Fragm. Sc.* (1879) I. iv. 115 The short diagonal of the large Nicol [prism] was in the first instance vertical.

b. A diagonal 'line' or row of things arranged in a square or other parallelogram (e.g. of squares on a chess-board).

c. A part of any structure, as a beam, plank, etc., placed diagonally.

1837 GORING & PRITCHARD *Microgr.* 112 The light stopped by the diagonals of the engiscope. **1853** SIR H. DOUGLAS *Milit. Bridges* 330 The diagonals *b c*, *b' c'*, having the quality of ties. **1874** KNIGHT *Dict. Mech.* I. 691 *Diagonal*, a timber brace, knee, plank, truss, etc., crossing a vessel's timbers obliquely.

2. = *diagonal cloth* (see A. 3): **a.** a soft material used for embroidery; **b.** a black coating for men's wear.

1861 URE *Cotton Manuf.* (ed. 2) II. 259 A fustian, with a small cord running in an oblique direction..is called diagonal. **1878** A. BARLOW *Hist. Weaving* Gloss, *Diagonals*, fancy lozenge pattern cloths. **1883** *Daily News* 19 Sept. 6/6 Thin meltons, diagonals, and serges. **1890** R. BEAUMONT *Colour in Woven Design* 268 Diagonals are but plainly coloured.

diago'nality. *rare.* [f. prec. + -ITY.] The quality of being diagonal or having an oblique position.

1859 R. F. BURTON *Centr. Afr.* in *Jrnl. Geog. Soc.* XXIX. 290 The Katonga river..is supposed to fall into the Nyanza ..This diagonality may result from the compound incline produced by the northern counterslope of the mountains.. and the south-eastward depression.

di'agonalize, *v. rare.* [f. as prec. + -IZE.] *intr.* To move in a diagonal.

1884 TENNYSON *Becket* II. ii, His Holiness, pushed one way by the Empire and another by England, if he move at all, Heaven stay him, is fain to diagonalise. *Herbert.* Diagonalise! thou art a word-monger! Our Thomas never will diagonalise. [Cf. DIAGONAL B. I quot. 1847.]

diagonally (daɪ'ægənəlɪ), *adv.* [f. as prec. + -LY[2].] In a diagonal direction; so as to extend from one angle or corner to the opposite. Also: In a slanting direction or position, obliquely.

1541 R. COPLAND *Guydon's Quest. Chirurg.*, Two longe wayes that descende fro the kydnees that entre by the sydes of the bladder dyagonelly. **1653** URQUHART *Rabelais* I. viii. (1694) I. 29 Six hundred Ells..of blew Velvet..diagonally purled. **1774** PENNANT *Tour Scotl. in* 1772, 23 The upper part being set diagonally within the lower. **1837** GORING & PRITCHARD *Microgr.* 121 A coarse piece of canvas, with the fibres running diagonally. **1855** H. SPENCER *Princ. Psychol.* (1870) I. v. ii. 518 The diagonally opposite angle.

†**dia'gonial,** *a.* and *sb. Obs.* [f. Gr. διαγώνιος DIAGONAL + -AL[1].] = DIAGONAL; also diagonally opposite; *fig.* diametrically opposed. Hence †**dia'gonially** *adv.*

1624 WOTTON *Archit.* (1672) 41 The Diagonial or overthwart Line, from Angle to Angle, of the said Square. **1643** MILTON *Divorce* II. iii. (1851) 64 Both diagonial contraries. **1646** SIR T. BROWNE *Pseud. Epid.* III. v. 115 The shortnesse being affixed unto the legs of one side, which might have been more tolerably placed upon the thwart or Diagoniall movers. *Ibid.* 190 Which..stands a thwart or diagonially unto the other. **1668** H. MORE *Div. Dial.* I. xx. (1713) 44 A Quadrate whose Diagonial is commensurate to one of the Sides is a plain Contradiction. **1678** CUDWORTH *Intell. Syst.* I. v. 728 The diameter or diagonial of a square.

diagonic (daɪə'gɒnɪk), *a. rare.* [ad. L. *diagōnicus* (Vitruvius), a. Gr. διαγωνικός: see DIAGONAL and -IC.] = DIAGONAL.

1592 R. D. *Hypnerotomachia* 7 Meeting together over the Diagonike line. **1881** J. MILNE in *Nature* 8 Dec. 126 This particular earthquake..might therefore be called a transverse or diagonic shock.

†**di'agonite.** *Min.* [Named by Breithaupt in 1832 from its oblique crystallization.] An obsolete synonym of BREWSTERITE.

1844 DANA *Min.* 325.

†**di'agony.** *Obs.* [ad. L. *diagōnius*, Gr. διαγώνιος DIAGONAL.] = DIAGONAL *sb.*

1690 LEYBOURN *Curs. Math.* 325 [The Proportion] of the Hexaedron's..Side to its Basial Diagony. *Ibid.* 326 Their Axes or Diagonies.

†**di'agorize,** *v. Obs. rare*$^{-1}$. [f. Gr. διά through + ἀγορά public assembly, forum, market-place + -IZE.] *trans.* To proclaim in the market-place.

1633 T. ADAMS *Exp. 2nd Peter* iii. 4. 1174 Let their pains ..be employed in weeding up those Diagoriz'd opinions.

diagram ('daɪəgræm), *sb.* [a. F. *diagramme*, or ad. L. *diagramma*, Gr. διάγραμμα that which is marked out by lines, a geometrical figure, written list, register, the gamut or scale in music, f. διαγράφειν to mark out by lines, draw, draw out, write in a register, f. δια- through + γράφειν to write.]

1. *Geom.* A figure composed of lines, serving to illustrate a definition or statement, or to aid in the proof of a proposition.

polar diagram: a spherical polygon, *i.e.* one traced on the surface of a sphere, whose sides are arcs joining the poles of the sides of a given spherical polygon.

1645 N. STONE *Enchir. Fortif.* 68 The Diagram on the Table directs for the making of it thus. *Ibid.* 74 Diagram, a word used by the Mathematicks for any thing that is demonstrated by lines. **1734** BERKELEY *Analyst* §50 The diagrams in a geometrical demonstration. **1879** THOMSON & TAIT *Nat. Phil.* I. I. §134 Another closed or open polygon, constituting what is called the polar diagram to the given polygon.

2. An illustrative figure which, without representing the exact appearance of an object, gives an outline or general scheme of it, so as to exhibit the shape and relations of its various parts.

Hence applied to such different designs as a map of the heavens, a delineation of a crystal, a representation of microscopic forms, etc. ***floral diagram*** (Bot.): a linear drawing showing the position and number of the parts of a flower as seen on a transverse section.

1619 BAINBRIDGE *Descr. Late Comet* 16, I must entreat you to examine this following diagram. **1635** N. CARPENTER *Geog. Del.* I. v. 111 To set downe in a Diagram both the number and order of all the heauenly Orbs. **1727** BRADLEY *Fam. Dict.* s.v. *Building*, If the Workman be well skill'd in perspective more than one face may be represented in one Diagram, scenographically. **1831** BREWSTER *Newton* (1855) II. xxii. 394 A scroll, on which is drawn a remarkable diagram relative to the solar system. **1855** THACKERAY *Newcomes* I. xvii. 165 Illustrated by diagrams the interview which he had with that professor. *c* **1860** FARADAY *Forces Nat.* 175, I have shown in this diagram..the rays of a candle. **1875** BENNETT & DYER *Sachs' Bot.* II. v. 524 Diagram of the flower of Liliaceæ.

transf. **1860** EMERSON *Cond. Life, Consid.* Wks. (Bohn) II. 420 We learn geology the morning after the earthquake on ghastly diagrams of cloven mountains. **1876** GEO. ELIOT *Dan. Der.* III. xlii. 226 Turning himself into a sort of diagram instead of a growth.

3. A set of lines, marks, or tracings which represent symbolically the course or results of any action or process, or the variations which characterize it; e.g. the intensity of action or quality, the rise and fall of temperature or pressure, of the death-rate, rate of emigration, rate of exchange, the derivation and mutual relation of languages, etc. **b.** A delineation used to symbolize related abstract propositions or mental processes.

Often with defining word prefixed, as ***indicator-diagram*** (in the steam-engine), ***acceleration-***, ***force-***, ***velocity-diagram***.

1839 R. S. ROBINSON *Naut. Steam Eng.* 157 The diagram points out that the steam port was now closed. **1876** *Daily News* 30 Sept. 2/2 Five successive shots..within a few feet of each other..In small-arm parlance, the gun has made a wonderfully 'good diagram'. **1885** WATSON & BURBURY *Math. Th. Electr. & Magn.* I. 242 We may represent the thermoelectric powers of different metals at different temperatures by a diagram. **1893** MINTO *Logic* I. I. ii. 64 The relations between the terms in the four forms are represented by simple diagrams known as Euler's circles.

†**4.** After Greek usage: A list, register, or enumeration; a detailed inscription; also, 'the title of a booke' (Cockeram 1623). *Obs.*

1631 WEEVER *Anc. Fun. Mon.* 8 An Epitaph is..an astrict pithie Diagram, writ..vpon the tombe..declaring..the name, the age..and time of the death of the person therein interred. **1662** STILLINGFL. *Orig. Sacr.* III. iv. §9 In only one Family..he makes a Diagramme consisting of almost an innumerable company of men.

†**5.** *Mus.* A musical scale, a gamut. *Obs.*

1656 BLOUNT *Glossogr.*, *Diagram*..in Musick is called a proportion of measures distinguished by certain notes. **1727–51** CHAMBERS *Cycl.* s.v., Guido Aretine improved this scale, or diagram, very greatly.

'diagram, *v.* Chiefly *U.S.* [f. prec. sb.] *trans.* To represent by a diagram, make a diagram of. Hence **'diagramed** *ppl. a.*, **'diagraming** *vbl. sb.*

1840 CARLYLE *Heroes* i. (1872) 23 They are matters which refuse to be theoremed and diagramed. **1880** *New Eng. Jrnl. Educ.* 20 May 327/3 The specimens of diagraming sent us. **1884** *Health Exhib. Catal.* 144/1 Diagrammed results of experiments. **1884** F. V. IRISH *Gram. or Anal. by Diagram* Pref. 3 To diagram a few easy sentences. **1936** M. H. BRADLEY *Five-minute Girl* xii. 221 What else was she doing but winding the net about him, diagramming the ignominy of every exit? **1938** S. CHASE *Tyranny of Words* vii. 67 The ..Ogden and Richards analysis can be diagrammed by a triangle. **1964** C. CHAPLIN *Autobiogr.* xxi. 354, I had read Major H. Douglas's *Social Credit*, which analysed and diagrammed our economic system. **1970** *Nature* 14 Nov. 685/2 These two reactions can be diagrammed according to two schemes.

diagramic (daɪə'græmɪk), *a. rare.* [f. prec. sb. + -IC.] Of the nature of a diagram; diagrammatic. Hence **dia'gramically** *adv.*, in the manner of a diagram.

1839 *Tait's Mag.* VI. 701 Referring our readers now to the diagramic wood-cuts. **1885** *Philad. Times* 18 Apr. (Cent. Dict.), The folds of her skirts hanging diagramically and stiffly.

diagrammatic (ˌdaɪəgrə'mætɪk), *a.* [f. Gr. διαγραμματ- stem of διάγραμμα DIAGRAM + -IC, after Gr. γραμματικός.] Having the form or nature of a diagram; of or pertaining to diagrams.

1853 SIR W. HAMILTON *Discuss.* (ed. 2) App. ii. 667 Aristotle undoubtedly had in his eye, when he discriminates the syllogistic terms, a certain diagrammatic contrast of the figures. *Ibid.* 671 *note*, The several diagrammatic figures are also each in a different position. **1854** J. SCOFFERN in *Orr's Circ. Sc.* Chem. 305 The appended diagrammatic scheme. **1862** H. SPENCER *First Princ.* II. x. §87 (1875) 268 Diagrammatic representations of births, marriages, and deaths. **1873** GEIKIE *Gt. Ice Age* xviii. 242 Diagrammatic view of drift deposits of the basin of the Forth. **1884** BOWER & SCOTT *De Bary's Phaner.* 522 This arrangement appears with quite diagrammatic regularity in..bast.

diagra'mmatical, *a.* [See -AL[1].] = prec.

1880 *Sat. Rev.* 15 May 637 In a diagrammatical form.

diagra'mmatically, *adv.* [f. prec. + -LY[2].] In the form of a diagram; with diagrammatic representation.

1853 SIR W. HAMILTON *Discuss.* (ed. 2) App. ii. 671 *note*, For the first syllogistic figure, the terms, without authority from Aristotle, are diagrammatically placed upon a level. **1875** CROLL *Climate & T.* xix. 313 The variations of eccentricity..are represented to the eye diagrammatically in Plate iv. **1881** F. O. BOWER in *Jrnl. Microsc. Sc.* 15 Jan., The tissues of the root cap are more diagrammatically arranged.

diagrammatize (daɪə'græmətaɪz), *v.* [f. Gr. διαγραμματ- stem of διάγραμμα DIAGRAM + -IZE; cf. Gr. διαγραμμίζειν.] *trans.* To put into the form of a diagram; to exhibit in a diagram.

1884 W. JAMES in *Mind* Jan. 18 It can be diagrammatised as continuous with all the other segments of the subjective stream. **1893** *Athenæum* 2 Dec. 773/3 There is not a single *picture* of a section; they have all been diagrammatized.

diagrammeter (daɪə'græmɪtə(r)). [f. DIAGRAM *sb.* + -METER.] (See quot.)

1876 *Catal. Sci. App. S. Kens.* §270 Holt's Diagrammeter. This instrument is specially made for measuring the ordinates of indicator-diagrams..and is used much after the manner of a parallel rule.

diagraph ('daɪəgrɑːf, -græf), *sb.*[1] [f. Gr. διαγραφή diagram, description, etc. f. δια- through + γραφή writing: cf. med.L. *diagraphum* 'descriptio census' (Du Cange).]

†**1.** A description. *Obs.*

1727 in BAILEY vol. II.

2. = DIAGRAM 3 b. *rare.*

1853 SIR W. HAMILTON *Discuss.* App. ii. (ed. 2) 671 *note*, What is indeed noticed and acknowledged..as a variation from 'Aristotle's diagraph'..the Major Term is not, in any way, placed 'nearer to' and 'further from the Middle,' for the Second and Third Figures.

diagraph ('daɪəgrɑːf, -græf), *sb.*[2] [a. F. *diagraphe*, f. stem of Gr. διαγράφ-ειν to mark out by lines, draw; cf. DIAGRAM.]

1. An instrument used for drawing mechanically projections of objects, enlarged copies of maps, etc.; it consists of a pencil governed by cords and pulleys, and guided by the application of a pointer to the object to be copied.

1847 CRAIG, *Diagraph*, a certain instrument used in perspective drawing, invented by M. Gavard, Paris. **1851** *Exhib. Catal.* III. 1187 Diagraphs and pantographs, for copying maps. **1878** BARTLEY tr. *Topinard's Anthrop.* II. iii. 269 The diagraph of Gavard. *Note.* Instrument by the help of which drawings [of the skull] by projection are obtained.

2. A combined protractor and scale used in plotting.

'diagraph, *v. rare.* [f. Gr. διαγράφειν: see next.] *trans.* To represent diagrammatically; = DIAGRAM *v.*

1889 J. M. ROBERTSON *Ess. Crit. Method* 54 A set of formulas supposed to describe or diagraph the dramatic practice of Shakspere.

diagraphic (daɪə'græfɪk), *a.* [f. Gr. διαγράφ-ειν to mark out by lines, διαγραφή marking out by lines, geometrical figure, diagram + -IC, after Gr. γραφικός.] Of or pertaining to drawing or graphic representation. Hence also **dia'graphical** *a. Obs.*, in same sense. **dia'graphics**, the art of drawing.

[**1601** HOLLAND *Pliny* II. 537 The art Diagraphice, that is to say, the skill to draw and paint in box-tables.] **1623** COCKERAM, *Diagraffical art*, the art of painting, or caruing. **1656** BLOUNT *Glossogr.*, *Diagraphick Art*, the art of painting or graving. **1801** FUSELI in *Lect. Paint.* i. (1848) 353 The diagraphic process..is the very same with the linear one we have described.

diagrid ('daɪəgrɪd). [f. DIA(GONAL *a.* + GRID.] A supporting structure consisting of diagonally intersecting ribs of metal, concrete, etc.

1943 *Westinghouse Wartime Engin.* Jan. 30 Construction engineers resorted to a new type of structure..known as Diagrid... The walls were built around the old plant, and the Diagrid roof framing erected. **1954** *Archit. Rev.* CXV. 424 A stressed concrete diagrid with in situ concrete joints cast between short precast units. **1963** *Engineering* 13 Dec. 764/2 The stress relieving of the diagrid in a French nuclear reactor.

‖**dia'grydium.** *Pharm.* Also 5 -gredie, 7 -gredium. [L. *diagrydium* (Cælius Aurelianus ?5th c.), according to Littré a corruption, through association with names of drugs in *dia-*, of Gr. δακρυδίον 'a kind of scammony', dim. of δάκρυ tear, drop. In F. *diagrède.*] An old name for a preparation of scammony, used in pharmacy.

1436 *Pol. Poems* (Rolls) II. 173 Wee shulde have no nede to skamonye, Turbit, euforbe, correcte, diagredie. *a* **1600** *Customs Duties* (Brit. Mus. Add. MS. No. 25697), Digredum, the pounde. vis. viijd. **1625** HART *Anat. Ur.* II. xi. 127 Mingled with..powder of Diagridium. **1651** BIGGS *New Disp.* ¶106 They hide *Scammony* under the name of *diagredium.* **1741** *Compl. Fam. Piece* I. i. 66 Take.. Diagridium and Tartar-Vitriolate a Dram. **1825** BRANDE *Man. Pharmacy* 157 In some old Pharmacopœiæ..methods of correcting the acrimony of scammony are described, and to such preparations they gave the name of diagridia.

Hence **dia'grydiate** *a.*, made with diagrydium. Also as *sb.*: see quots.

1657 *Phys Dict, Diagridiates,* medicines that have scammony or diagridium in their composition. **1684** tr. *Bonet's Merc. Compit.* III. 99 With diagrydiate Purges. *a* **1734** FLOYER J., All cholerick humours ought to be evacuated by diagrydiates. **1755** JOHNSON, *Diagrydiates,* strong purgatives made with diagrydium.

diaheliotropic (daɪəˌhiːlɪəʊ'trɒpɪk), *a. Bot.* [f. Gr. διά across + ἥλιος sun + τροπικός pertaining to turning.] Growing or moving transversely to the direction of incident light; of or pertaining to diaheliotropism.

1880 F. DARWIN in *Nature* No. 582. 179 A diaheliotropic organ has an inherent tendency to place itself at right angles to the direction of the light. **1880** C. & F. DARWIN *Movem. Pl.* 441 Diaheliotropic movements.

diaheliotropism (daɪəhiːlɪ'ɒtrəpɪz(ə)m). *Bot.* [f. as prec.: see -ISM.] A tendency in leaves and organs of plants to grow transversely to the direction of incident light.

1880 C. & F. DARWIN *Movem. Pl.* 5 Diaheliotropism may express a position more or less transverse to the light and induced by it. **1882** F. DARWIN in *Nature* 27 Apr. 600 The power..called *Transversal Heliotropismus* by A. B. Frank, we have called diaheliotropism.

dia'hydric, *a.* [f. DIA-[1] + Gr. ὕδωρ water + -IC.]

1883 *Syd. Soc. Lex., Diahydric,* through water; a term applied by C. J. Williams to the percussion note obtained from an organ separated from the parieties by a layer of fluid.

diakinesis (ˌdaɪəkaɪ'niːsɪs). *Cytology.* [mod.L., ad. G. *diakinese* (V. Häcker 1897, in *Biol. Centralbl.* XVII. 701), f. DIA-[1] + Gr. κίνησις motion.] The last stage of meiotic prophase, immediately preceding the disappearance of the nuclear membrane.

1902 E. B. WILSON *Cell* (ed. 2) 440 *Diakinesis* (διά, through), the segmented-spireme-stage, following the synapsis, in the primary oöcyte or spermatocyte, during which the chromosomes persist for a considerable period in the form of double rods. **1922** *Encycl. Brit.* XXX. 784/1 The nuclear wall is dissolved and the chromosomes separate as if repelled from one another: this process is known as 'diakinesis'. **1939** *Nature* 8 July 81/1 The number of bivalents attached to the nucleolus at zygotene to diakinesis. **1970** AMBROSE & EASTY *Cell Biol.* x. 326 The final stage of the first prophase of meiosis is sometimes called diakinesis (or 'moving apart').

dial ('daɪəl), *sb.*[1] Also 5 **dyale, dyel,** 5–7 **dyal(l, diall.** [Presumably a derivative of L. *dies* a day, through a med.L. adj. *diāl-is* daily (repr. in Du Cange by *diāle* = *diurnāle* 'as much land as could be ploughed in a day', and *diāliter* adv. daily.) Outside Eng., however, *dial* is known only from a single OF. instance in Froissart, in which the *dyal* in clockwork is said to be 'the daily wheel (*roe journal*) which makes a revolution once in a day, even as the sun makes a single turn round the earth in a natural day'. This would answer to a med.L. *rota diālis*: the transition from 'diurnal wheel' to 'diurnal circle' is easy. But more evidence is wanted.]

1. An instrument serving to tell the hour of the day, by means of the sun's shadow upon a graduated surface; a SUN-DIAL.

1430 LYDG. *Chron. Troy.* I. v, For by the dyal the hour they gan to marke. *c* **1440** *Promp. Parv.* 120 Dyale, or dyel or an horlege (dial or diholf of an horlage). **1530** PALSGR. 213/2 Diall to knowe the houres by the course of the sonne, *quadrant.* **1535** COVERDALE *2 Kings* xx. 11 The shadowe wente backe ten degrees in Achas Dyall. **1552** HULOET, Diall set vpon a chymney or wall to knowe what is a clocke by the sunne, *sciotericon.* **1593** SHAKS. *3 Hen. VI,* II. v. 24 To carue out Dialls queintly, point by point, Thereby to see the Minutes how they runne. **1647** WARD *Simp. Cobler* 39 Where clocks will stand, and Dials have no light. **1719** YOUNG *Busiris* v. i, How, like the dial's tardy-moving shade, Day after day slides from us unperceiv'd. **1720** GAY *Poems* (1745) I. 151 Here to sev'n streets sev'n dials count the day. **1799** VINCE *Astron.* iv. (1810) 56 A clock or watch may..be regulated by a good dial. **1878** B. TAYLOR *Deukalion* I. vi. 50 The Hour shall miss its place, And the shadow recede on the dial's face.

b. *fig.* **1513** DOUGLAS *Æneis* I. Prol. 347 Venerable Chaucer..Hevinlie trumpat, horleige and reguleir..condit, and diall. **1854** J. FORBES *Tour Mt. Blanc* Introd. 11 The stately march of the glacier is yet a stage more slow, months and even years are but the units of division of its dial.

2. a. With qualifying words descriptive of the various forms of the sun-dial: e.g. *declining, horizontal, primary, reflecting, universal, vertical* (etc.) *dial.*

1688 R. HOLME *Armoury* III. 373/1 Pendant Dials which are hung by the hand..commonly called Equinoctial or Universal Dials, are most used by Sea-Men and Travellers that oft shift Latitudes. **1706** PHILLIPS (ed. Kersey), *Erect declining Dials,* Dials whose Planes are not directly opposite to any of the Four Cardinal Points, but decline from the Meridian or prime Vertical Circle. **1782** *Archæologia* VI. 143 Vitruvius says they had horizontal, vertical, and declining dials. **1819** P. NICHOLSON *Architect. Dict.* I. 332 Deinclining Dials, such as both decline and incline, or recline.

b. With various qualifying words, as ***night-*** or ***nocturnal dial*** (= MOON-DIAL), RING-DIAL, SUN-DIAL.

1605 CAMDEN *Rem.* 165 Which bare a Sunne-diall and the Sun setting. **1667** *Phil. Trans.* II. 435 A large Ring-Dial.. having a Box with a Compass or Needle. **1727–51** CHAMBERS *Cycl., Moon-Dial* or Lunar Dial, is that which shews the hour of the night by means of the light, or shadow, of the moon. *Ibid., Nocturnal* or *Night-Dial,* is that which shews the hours of the night. **1820** W. IRVING *Sketch Bk.* I. 66 The neighbours could tell the hour by his movements as accurately as by a sun dial.

†**3.** A timepiece or chronometer of any kind; a clock or watch. *Obs.* Also with qualifying words as WATER-DIAL, etc.

1552 HULOET, Diall, *clepsydra, horologium.* **1580** BARET *Alv.* D 651 A diall measuring houres by running of the water ..*clepsydra.* **1585** T. WASHINGTON tr. *Nicholay's Voy.* i. xvii. 19 b, The Ambassadour sent his presents..one small clocke or dyall. **1600** SHAKS. *A.Y.L.* II. vii. 20 And then he drew a diall from his poake, And..Sayes, very wisely, it is ten a clocke. **1611** COTGR., *Horloge d'eau,* a Clepsydra, or water Dyall. **1660** BOYLE *New Exp. Phys. Mech.* xli. 329 One of those accurate Dyals that go with a Pendulum. **1662** GERBIER *Princ.* 40 Motions..no more to be discovered, than that of the Hand of a Diall. **1676** *North's Plutarch 765 note,* Like a water Diall or Clepsydra.

b. *fig.* **1556** J. JONES (*title*), The Dial of Agues. **1557** NORTH (*title*), Gueuara's Diall of Princes. **1582** BENTLEY *Mon. Matrones* Pref. B j b, A delectable diall for to direct you to true deuotion. *c* **1600** in C. B. MARKHAM *Fighting Veres* (1888) 345 He was the very dial of the army, by which we knew when we should fight.

4. The face of a clock or watch; the surface which bears the graduations and figures marking the hours, etc. Cf. DIAL-PLATE.

1575 LANEHAM *Let.* (1871) 54 Too Dyallz ny vnto the battilments ar set aloft vpon too of the sidez of Cezarz toour ..to sheaw the oourz too the tooun and cuntree. **1632** SHERWOOD s.v. *Dial,* The hand of a clock-dyall, *la monstre d'un Horloge.* **1747** *Gent. Mag.* 224 Varnished, and silvered in all respects as a clock-dial. **1750** JOHNSON *Rambler* No. 42 ¶8, I walk in the great hall and watch the minute hand upon the dial. **1823** P. NICHOLSON *Pract. Build.* 569 The part where the dials of the clock are placed is of an octagonal form. **1884** F. J. BRITTEN *Watch & Clockm.* 85 Sir Edmund Beckett advocates a concave form for the dials of public clocks.

b. *fig. a* **1680** BUTLER *Rem.* (1759) II. 214 The Face is the Dial of the Mind.

5. †**a.** A mariner's compass. *Obs.*

1523 FITZHERB. *Surv.* xx. 38 It is necessarie that he haue a Dyall with hym for els..he shall nat haue perfyte knowlege whiche is Eest West Northe and Southe. **1559** W. CUNNINGHAM *Cosmogr. Glasse* 85 Whan the nedle standeth stedfastlye in the right Line wythin the Diall, it dothe as it were poynte directlye North and South. **1591** SYLVESTER *Du Bartas* I. iii. 986 For first inuenting of the Sea-man's Diall. **1600** J. PORY tr. *Leo's Africa* I. 34 Cabo das Agulhas, or the cape of Needles, because there the needles of dialles touched with the loadstone, stand directly North. **1642** ROGERS *Naaman* 830 The needle of the Diall set just on the North point..shakes not.

b. *Mining.* A miner's compass for underground surveying.

1669 E. MONTAGU tr. *Barba's Metals, etc.* (1740) 286 Having provided yourself of a Dial in a square Box. **1778** W. PRYCE *Min. Cornub.* 207 Apply the side of the dial to the string, and take the degree the needle stands on. **1875** URE *Dict. Arts* II. 18 The compass used in underground surveying is called a miner's dial, and is essentially the same instrument as the circumferentor used by the land-surveyor.

6. a. An external plate or face on which revolutions, pressure, etc. are indicated by an index-finger or otherwise, as in a gas-meter, telegraphic instrument, steam or water-gauge, etc.

1747 *Gentl. Mag.* 223 Move one tooth every revolution of the wheel, thereby discovering the true distance of places by the index on the dial. **1842** *Penny Cycl.* XXIV. 154/1 For communication..this object may be effected by a mechanical connection, by chains or wires, between two dials with revolving indexes or pointers. **1875** URE *Dict. Arts* II. 233 Let us now turn to the face of the instrument. Here we have a dial and an index, which is on the same axis as the magnetised needle.

b. With qualifying words, as *tide-, wind-dial.*

1792 *Archæologia* X. 174 This machine of Varro's may be considered as the first wind-dial at Rome.

c. *slang.* The human face.

1811 in *Lexicon Balatronicum.* **1889** *Bird o' Freedom* 7 Aug. 3 (Farmer) An absinthe tumbler which caught him a nasty crack across the dial. **1933** *Punch* 5 Apr. 384/3 The major hesitated, and then a grin lamped up his dial. **1958** L. A. G. STRONG *Light above Lake* xxi. 146 You should have seen the solemn dials on all the Gardas and officials.

d. On a telephone, a circular plate marked with letters, numbers, etc., above which is a disc which can be rotated by means of finger-holes to establish connection with another telephone. Cf. DIAL *v.* 4.

1879 *U.S. Pat. 222, 458* Automatic Telephone-Exchanges. ..each station comprises..a dial instrument.. to make intermittent breaks in the electric current, the number and character of which are successively indicated on a dial. **1903** *Daily Mail Yr. Bk.* 164/1 A moveable dial is attached to the instrument, and by manipulating this..the connection is completed and conversation becomes possible. **1914** W. ATKINS *Princ. Automatic Telephony* 8 To call, a finger is placed in the hole of the appropriate figure and the dial revolved until the stop-piece is reached. The dial is then let go and revolves back. **1921** [see DIAL *v.* 4]. **1931** [see sense 8 b below].

e. (See quot. 1940.)

1922–3 *T. Eaton's Catal.* Fall & Winter 401/1 *Radio Supplies...* Dials and Knobs. **1928–9** *Ibid.* Fall & Winter 245/2 One knob 'selects' the stations. The dial is illuminated by a miniature light within and geared control gives fine adjustments. **1940** *Chambers's Techn. Dict.* 239/2 *Dial* (*Radio*), the mechanism for adjusting, and for indicating the adjustment, of the tuning controls. **1960** *Which?* May 100/1 BBC and ITA channel numbers could be read easily on most sets, though the DECCA dial could be misread.

7. A lapidary's instrument for holding a gem while exposed to the wheel.

It has markers indicating degrees in adjustment, so as to portion out the circumference of the stone in facets.

1875 URE *Dict. Arts* III. 42 An important instrument called a dial, which serves to hold the stone during the cutting and polishing.

8. *attrib.* and *Comb.* **a.** General, as *dial-foot, -hand, -maker, -motto, -stone, -work.*

1884 F. J. BRITTEN *Watch & Clockm.* 87 In common watches pins falling out of the *dial feet is a fruitful source of trouble. *c* **1600** SHAKS. *Sonn.* civ, Yet doth beauty, like a *dial-hand, Steal from his figure and no pace perceived. **1599** MINSHEU *Sp. Dict., Relogero*..a *diall-maker. **1875** LANIER *Poems, Symphony* 157 Each *dial-marked leaf and flower-bell. **1822** LAMB *Elia, Decay of Beggars,* The standing *dial-mottos. **1874** KNIGHT *Dict. Mech.,* **Dial-work* (Horology), the motion work between the dial and movement plate of a watch.

b. Special comb., as **dial-less** *a.*, without a dial, having no dial; **dial-like** *a.*, like a dial; **dial-lock**, a lock furnished with dials, having hands or pointers, which must be set in a determinate way before the bolt will move; **dial-moth**, *Tortrix gnomana* (Samouelle, *Entomol. Compend.* 1819); **dial-piece** = DIAL-PLATE; **dial-plane**, the flat-surface of a sun-dial; **dial-ring**, a finger-ring in the form of a ring-dial; **dial telegraph** (orig. *U.S.*), a telegraph having a dial marked with letters, numbers, etc., and operated in such a way that the needle on the dial at the receiving station copies the movements of that at the transmitting station; **dial (tele)phone**, a telephone operated by means of a dial; **dial tone** (orig. *U.S.*), = *dialling tone*; **dial-wheel** (in a watch), one of the wheels placed between the dial and pillar-plate; **dial-writer**, a type-writer with a dial. Also DIAL-PLATE.

1865 *Athenæum* 8 July 49 The tower remained *dial-less as before. **1851** MAYNE REID *Scalp-Hunt.* i. 10 Where the helianthus turns her *dial-like face to the sun. **1659** D. PELL *Improv. Sea* To Redr., Upon a *Dial-peece of a Clock in the Colledge Church of Glocester. **1690** LEYBOURN *Curs. Math.* 699 The number of *Dial Plains are 25. **1703** MOXON *Mech. Exerc.* 310 A Dyal Plane is that Flat whereon a Dyal is intended to be projected. **1868** *Chambers' Encycl.* III. 531/1 A dial consists of two parts—the stile or gnomon..and the dial-plane. **1877** W. JONES *Finger-ring* 453 A *dial-ring consisting of two concentric rings moving one within the other. **1860** G. B. PRESCOTT *Telegraph* 160 The *dial telegraphs are those in which a needle traverses a dial, upon the margin of which are placed the letters of the alphabet. **1886** WORMELL tr. *Von Urbanitzky's Electr. in Serv. Man* (1890) 804 Of *A B C* systems where a battery is employed to furnish the current, Bréguet's Dial Telegraph is a good example. **1930** U. PARROTT *Strangers may Kiss* II. iii. 59 The first *dial telephone exchange was opened. **1931** *Punch* 27 May 564/2, I like the dial telephone. Bless its funny little dial! *Ibid.,* One can do such a lot with the dial phone without getting into a hot exchange of snappy come-backs. **1923** *Bell System Techn. Jrnl.* II. ii. 62 The subscriber will first remove his receiver from the hook and will hear the so-called ..'*dial tone', which indicates that the apparatus is ready to receive the call. **1727–51** CHAMBERS *Cycl.* s.v. *Watch-work,* The *dial-wheel..serves to carry the hand. **1883** *Pall Mall G.* 5 May 6/2 The last thing in type-writers, called a '*dial writer'.

'dial, *sb.*[2] A name given in commerce to a superior kind of Kauri gum of a clear pale colour.

1893 *Times* 14 July 4/4 Gums, Kowrie..Dial—pale yellowish, £11.

Dial, dial ('daɪəl), *sb.*[3] *Pharm.* [Proprietary name, first registered in Switzerland in 1918, a shortened form of *diallylbarbituric acid.*] A preparation of diallylbarbituric acid, used as a sedative.

1922 *Chem. Abstr.* XVI. 4299 Veronal, phenobarbital and dial condense readily in AcOH soln. **1931** *News Chron.* 19 Mar. 9/6 The opinion that dial, a preparation of veronal often taken by sufferers from sleeplessness, should be scheduled under the Dangerous Drugs Act. **1942** E. WAUGH *Put out more Flags* 142 She..returned to bed, took two tablets of Dial and slept, gently.

dial ('daɪəl), *v.* [f. DIAL *sb.*[1]]

1. *trans. fig.* To measure as with a dial; to indicate the degree of.

1821 CAMPBELL in *New Monthly Mag.* I. 10 Experienced sensibility is like the gnomon. It measures the altitude and dials the light of inspiration. **1839** BAILEY *Festus* (1852) 201 To teach us how to dial bliss. *a* **1854** TALFOURD (Webster), Hours of that true time which is dialled in heaven.

2. To survey or lay out with the aid of a dial or miner's or surveyor's compass.

1653 MANLOVE *Lead Mines* 164 To make inquiry, and to view the Rake, To plum and dyal. **1747** HOOSON *Miner's Dict.* s.v. *Boring*, Having exactly dialed it, to the place where you would have your Shaft to come through, and laid it out at the Day upon the Surface. **1778** W. PRYCE *Min. Cornub.* 203 Most of our Mines and Adits were dialled for in this manner. **1853** *Jrnl. R. Agric. Soc.* XIV. I. 153 To cut the gutters with the plough used by him after being dialled out.

3. To mark as the plate of a dial.

1817 [see DIALLED *ppl. a.*].

4. To manipulate a telephone dial (DIAL *sb.*[1] 6 d) so as to establish connection with (another telephone). Also *intr.*, to manipulate a telephone dial. Also *transf.* See also DIALLING *vbl. sb.* 2 b.

1921 *Conquest* Jan. 124/3 The operator's attention is obtained.. by dialling 'o' usually. *Ibid.* 125/1 In order to dial a number, say 7, the finger is put in the hole above 7, and the dial is rotated to the stop and let go. *Ibid.* 126/3 The subscriber begins to dial by putting his finger in hole 5. **1928** *Daily Tel.* 28 Feb. 15 She goes to the 'central supply conveyor', at which, by dialing on an indicating switchboard, she lets the store know her requirements. **1930** *Punch* 21 May 579/1, I keep meeting people who are quite worn out with dialling all day. **1932** E. BOWEN *To North* xxv. 276 Very clumsily, slowly, she dialled a number. **1938** L. MACNEICE *Earth Compels* 52 Dial her number, None will reply. **1966** *Listener* 21 July 103/1 This one dialled the safe's vital combination.

b. As *imp.*, in ***dial-a-bus***, etc., used chiefly of an agency or service that is accessible by telephone. (Freq. in *attrib.* collocations.)

1963 *Daily Tel.* 6 Sept. 23/5 Britain's first 'Dial-a-prayer' system comes into operation on Birmingham's subscriber trunk dialling telephones next Tuesday. **1966** *Economist* 19 Mar. 1127/3 The Boston-to-Washington system, 'dial-a-stop' and all, could be built and operating within ten years. **1969** *Nature* 15 Feb. 601/2 The later introduction of a development in transport called 'dial-a-bus' or 'telebus' is also recommended. **1969** *Daily Mail* 5 Apr. 5/1 A 24-hour dial-an-expert service has been set up to give advice to farmers. **1971** *Times* 8 Jan. 3/8 The organisation also offered the public a 'dial-a-chat' service, where anyone could telephone its central switchboard.. and speak to one of its members.

c. ***to dial up*** (trans. and intr.): to gain access to (a computer, etc.), or transmit (data), over a telephone line, orig. by manipulating a telephone dial or keypad; to ring up (a person, place, etc.) on the telephone. Cf. DIAL-UP *a.* and *sb.*

1977 *Times* 30 Sept. 23/3 A much larger range of information.. will be available for transmission when dialled up (via a calculator-like keypad—not the telephone dial—to be precise). **1982** *New Scientist* 9 Dec. 654/1 High-bandwidth cable could be vital in services in which people 'dial up' their banks from home to conduct financial transactions. **1984** *Guardian* 16 Aug. 13/5 With BBS's, users dial up, read the messages on the board, and leave their own comments. There are over 2,000 such systems in the United States, with about a dozen in the UK. **1984** *Listener* 15 Nov. 38/2 Dial up directory inquiries and you find that whereas local inquiries are free, you are charged for those in other telephone areas. **1984** *Which?* Dec. 539/2 You simply dial up Prestel and type in the recipient's Mailbox number. **1985** *Inmac Catal.* Spring/Summer 83/2 You can dial-up using the single stored number, or direct from your keyboard. **1986** *Guardian* 15 May 15/2 You just dial up Easynet, like any other telephone service, and enter a password. You're then offered a menu of choices or subjects on which to search.

dialatik, obs. f. DIALECTIC *sb.*[1]

dial-bird. [ad. Hindī *dahiyāl* or *dahēl*, the native name in Upper India.] An Indian bird (*Copsichus saularis*), also called Magpie-robin; hence sometimes extended to the genus *Copsichus*.

1738 E. ALBIN *Nat. Hist. Birds* III. 17 These Birds were brought from Bengall in the year 1734, and are called by the Natives the Dial-Bird. **1812** SMELLIE & WOOD *Buffon's Nat. Hist.* XI. 261 The East India bird which the English that visit the coasts of Bengal term the Dial-bird. **1859** TENNENT *Ceylon* II. VII. vii. 254 The songster that first pours forth his salutation to the morning is the dial-bird.

dialdane (daɪ'ældeɪn). *Chem.* [f. DI-[2] + ALD(OL + -ANE.] 'A compound, $C_8H_{14}O_3$, formed by the condensation of two molecules of aldol, with elimination of one molecule of water'. Hence **dial'danic** *a.* in *dialdanic acid.*

1879 WATTS *Dict. Chem. 3rd Suppl.* 631.

dialect ('daɪəlɛkt). [a. F. *dialecte* (16th c. in Hatz.-Darm.), or ad. L. *dialectus*, Gr. διάλεκτος discourse, conversation, way of speaking, language of a country or district, f. διαλέγεσθαι to discourse, converse, f. δια- through, across + λέγειν to speak.]

1. Manner of speaking, language, speech; *esp.* a manner of speech peculiar to, or characteristic of, a particular person or class; phraseology, idiom.

1579 E. K. *Ded. to Spenser's Sheph. Cal.*, Neither.. must .. the common Dialect and manner of speaking [be] so corrupted thereby, that [etc.]. **1599** NASHE *Lenten Stuffe* (1599) 41 By corruption of speech they false dialect and missesound it. **1638** *Penit. Conf.* vii. (1657) 191 Such a dialect which neither Men nor Angels understand. **1663** BUTLER *Hud.* I. i. 93 A Babylonish Dialect, Which learned Pedants much affect. **1740** J. CLARKE *Educ. Youth* (ed. 3) 172 The Lawyer's Dialect would be too hard for him. **1805** FOSTER *Ess.* IV. iv. 163 Naturalized into the theological dialect by time and use. **1831** CARLYLE *Sart. Res.* III. vii. (1858) 155 Knowest thou no Prophet, even in the vesture, environment, and dialect of this age? **1857** H. REED *Lect. Eng. Poets* iii. 87 They lay aside the learned dialect and reveal the unknown powers of common speech.

fig. **1603** SHAKS. *Meas. for M.* I. ii. 188 In her youth There is a prone and speechlesse dialect, Such as moue men. **1860** EMERSON *Cond. Life, Behaviour* Wks. (Bohn) II. 384 The ocular dialect needs no dictionary.

2. a. One of the subordinate forms or varieties of a language arising from local peculiarities of vocabulary, pronunciation, and idiom. (In relation to modern languages usually *spec.* A variety of speech differing from the standard or literary 'language'; a provincial method of speech, as in 'speakers of dialect'.) Also in a wider sense applied to a particular language in its relation to the family of languages to which it belongs.

1577 HANMER *Anc. Eccles. Hist.* 70 Certaine Hebrue dialectes. **1641** RALEIGH *Hist. World* II. 496 The like changes are very familiar in the Aeolic Dialect. **1635** PAGITT *Christianogr.* 73 The Slavon tongue is of great extent: of it there be many Dialects, as the Russe, the Polish, the Bohemick, the Illyrian.. and others. **1716** *Lond. Gaz.* No. 5497/1 He made a Speech.. which was answered by the Doge in the Genoese Dialect. **1794** S. WILLIAMS *Vermont* 200 A language may be separated into several dialects in a few generations. **1841** ELPHINSTONE *Hist. Ind.* I. iv. 203 Páli, or the local dialect of Maghada, one of the ancient kingdoms on the Ganges. **1847** HALLIWELL *Dict.* Eng. Dialects (1878) 17 The Durham dialect is the same as that spoken in Northumberland. **1873** HALE *In His Name* viii. 71 That dialect of rustic Latin which was already passing into Italian.

b. *attrib.*, as ***dialect speech, speaker, poems, specimens***; **dialect atlas, geography**: see quots. 1933; hence ***dialect-geographer, dialect-geographical*** adj.

1932 *Missouri Alumnus* Apr. 232/1 The American Council of Learned Societies is financing a Dialect Atlas of the United States and Canada. **1933** BLOOMFIELD *Lang.* iii. 51 Dialect atlases, collections of maps of a speech area with isoglosses drawn in, are an important tool for the linguist. **1948** *South. Folklore Q.* Dec. 231 The project was.. inspired by the great European dialect atlases. **1929** *Germanic Rev.* I. 291 In 1898 Carl Haag introduced the term 'Kernland-schaften'.. into the treatment of dialect geography. **1933** BLOOMFIELD *Lang.* xix. 321 The study of local differentiations in a speech-area, dialect geography, supplements the use of the comparative method. **1936** *Language* XII. 245 The dialect-geographers.. have found variations. **1948** *Neophilologus* XXXII. 183 The results of the English dialect-geographical inquiry.

†**3.** = DIALECTIC *sb.*[1] I. *Obs.*

1551 T. WILSON *Logike* (1580) 2 b, Logike otherwise called Dialecte (for thei are bothe one) is an Arte to trie the corne from the chaffe. **1677** GALE *Crt. Gentiles* II IV. 223 We may draw forth the force of this Platonic Argument, in Plato's own dialect thus. **1691** WOOD *Ath. Oxon.* I. 395 He had a Tutor to teach him Grammar, and another Dialect. **1698** J. FRYER *Acc. E. Ind. & P.* 362 [They] teach Aristotle's Dialect, and the Four Figures of Syllogism.

attrib. **1761** STERNE *Tr. Shandy* IV. 35 The learned.. busy in pumping her [Truth] up thro' the conduits of dialect induction.

[**dialect**, *v.* Explained as: To speak a dialect.

[**1599** NASHE *Lenten Stuffe* 41 By corruption of speech they false dialect and misse-sound it.] Here *false* is a vb. meaning to 'falsify', and *dialect* a sb. But **1881** DAVIES *Suppl. Eng. Gloss.* (quoting the above) has erron. entered *dialect* as a vb. Hence in some later Dicts.]

dialectal (daɪə'lɛktəl), *a.* [f. prec. + -AL[1]: cf. mod.F. *dialectal.*] Belonging to or of the nature of a dialect.

1831 *For. Q. Rev.* VII. 380 We cannot consider them mere dialectal variations. **1834** H. O'BRIEN *Round Towers Irel.* 121 It was a mere dialectal distinction, appertaining to the court-language.. of the times. **1873** A. J. ELLIS *President's Address* in *Trans. Philol. Soc.* 208 Their historical relations [are] considered, and their dialectal differences explained. **1880** J. E. C. WELLDON in *Academy* 24 July 58 Dialectal peculiarities might still creep into the Homeric text. **1885** *Ibid.* 29 Aug. 134/2 August Corrodi's dialectal poetry is remarkable for its humour and naturalness.

Hence **dialec'tality**, dialectal quality.

1864 FURNIVALL in *Reader* 22 Oct. 514/2 The dialectality or provinciality of the prefixed *h.*

dia'lectally, *adv.* [f. prec. + -LY[2].]

a. In a dialectal manner; in dialect. **b.** = DIALECTICALLY I.

1840 G. S. FABER *Regeneration* 391 The two have no dialectally necessary connection. **1890** F. HALL in *Nation* (N.Y.) L. 316/3 An archaism still existent dialectally.

'dialected, *a. nonce-wd.* [see -ED[2].] (In *comb.*) Having or speaking a (specified) dialect.

1836 E. HOWARD *R. Reefer* lv, The.. cockney-dialected Josh.

dialectic (daɪə'lɛktɪk), *sb.*[1] Forms: 4 **dialatik**, 5-(**dialiticus**), **dialetike, -yk, dyaletyque**, 6 **dialectik(e**, 6–7 **-ique**, 7–9 **-ick**, 7– **-ic**. [a. OF. *dialectique, -etique* (12th c. in Hatz.-Darm.), ad. L. *dialectica* fem. sing., ad. Gr. ἡ διαλεκτική (sc. τέχνη) the dialectic art, the art of discussion or debate, fem. sing. of διαλεκτικός adj.: see next. The L. *dialectica* was also treated as a neuter pl., whence the later Eng. *dialectics.*]

1. a. The art of critical examination into the truth of an opinion; the investigation of truth by discussion: in earlier English use, a synonym of LOGIC as applied to formal rhetorical reasoning; logical argumentation or disputation.

Originally, the art of reasoning or disputation by question and answer, 'invented', according to Aristotle, by Zeno of Elea, and scientifically developed by Plato, by whom the term διαλεκτική was used in two senses, (*a*) the art of definition or discrimination of 'ideas', (*b*) the science which views the inter-relation of the ideas in the light of a single principle 'the good'; corresponding broadly to logic and metaphysic. By Aristotle the term was confined to the method of probable reasoning, as opposed to the demonstrative method of science. With the Stoics, rhetoric and dialectic formed the two branches of λογική, logic, in their application of the term; and down through the Middle Ages *dialectica* was the regular name of what is now called 'logic', in which sense accordingly *dialectic* and *dialectics* were first used in English.

1382 WYCLIF *Bible* Pref. Ep. Jerome 68 Job.. determyneth alle the lawes of dialatik, in proposicoun, assumpcoun, etc. [*a* **1400–50** *Alexander* 1583 (Ashm. MS.) Prestis of þe lawe, Of dialiticus [*v.r.* dialeticus], and decre, doctours of aythir.] *c* **1440** CAPGRAVE *Life St. Kath.* I. 372 Sche lerned þan þe liberall artes seuen.. The thyrde sciens call þei dialetyk.. þe trewth fro þe falsned þat techeth for to know. **1481** CAXTON *Myrr.* I. viii. 34 The seconde science is logyke whiche is called dyaletyque. **1586** T. B. *La Primaud. Fr. Acad.* 72 Dialectike or Logike, which is to learn the truth of al things by disputation. **1656** STANLEY *Hist. Philos.* v. (1701) 174/2 Dialectick is the Art of Discourse, whereby we confirm or confute any thing by Questions and Answers of the Disputants. **1865** GROTE *Plato* I. ii. 96 Zeno stands announced as the inventor of dialectic.. the art of cross-examination and refutation. **1874** W. WALLACE *Logic of Hegel* vi. 127 The Platonic philosophy first gave the free scientific, and thus at the same time the objective, form to Dialectic. **1882** FARRAR *Early Chr.* II. 22 He has nothing of the Pauline method of dialectic. **1889** COURTNEY *Mill* 27 The Platonic ideal of Dialectic.. the giving and receiving of reasons.

b. Also in pl. form **dialectics** (cf. *mathematics*).

1641 MILTON *Animadv.* i. (1851) 192 Bishop Downam in his Dialecticks will tell you [etc.]. **1781** GIBBON *Decl. & F.* III. lii. 263 The human faculties are fortified by the art and practice of dialectics. **1796** BP. WATSON *Apol. Bible* 224 You will pardon my unskilfulness in dialectics. **1853** MARSDEN *Early Purit.* 336 The dialectics of those times afford no specimens of reasoning more acute than the examinations of the martyrs. **1873** DIXON *Two Queens* III. XIV. viii. 112 If Henry wearied of dialectics.

2. In modern Philosophy: Specifically applied by Kant to the criticism which shows the mutually contradictory character of the principles of science, when they are employed to determine objects beyond the limits of experience (i.e. the soul, the world, God); by Hegel (who denies that such contradictions are ultimately irreconcilable) the term is applied (*a*) to the process of thought by which such contradictions are seen to merge themselves in a higher truth that comprehends them; and (*b*) to the world-process, which, being in his view but the thought-process on its objective side, develops similarly by a continuous unification of opposites.

1798 WILLICH *Elem. Critical Philos.* 65, 3. Of the division of general Logic, into Analysis and Dialectic. 4. Of the division of transcendental Logic, into transcendental Analysis and Dialectic. **1819** J. RICHARDSON tr. *Kant's Logic* 17 It would become a dialectic, a logic of appearance.. which arises from a mere abuse of the analytic. **1838** [F. HAYWOOD] tr. *Kant's Crit. Pure Reason* 267 There is therefore a natural and unavoidable dialectick of pure reason .. which irresistibly adheres to human reason, and even when we have discovered its delusion, still will not cease to play tricks upon reason, and to push it continually into momentary errors. **1856** FERRIER *Inst. Metaph.* IV. xvi. 134 This reduction.. could not have been effected upon any principle of psychological strategy. It is a manœuvre competent only to the dialectic of necessary truth. **1874** W. WALLACE *Logic of Hegel* i. 14 That dialectic is the very nature of thought.. forms one of the main lessons of logic. *Ibid.* vi. 126 By Dialectic is meant an indwelling tendency outwards and beyond.. Dialectic is.. the life and soul of scientific progress, the dynamic which alone gives an immanent connexion and necessity to the subject-matter of Science. **1880** J. CAIRD *Philos. Relig.* viii. 229 An idea which expresses the inner dialectic, the movement or process towards unity, which exists in and constitutes the being of the objects themselves. **1888** WATSON *Philos. Kant* 137 Transcendental Dialectic must.. be satisfied with bringing to light the illusion in transcendent judgments, and guarding us against its deceptive influence.

b. In more general use, the existence or working of opposing forces, tendencies, etc. Also in pl. form (const. sing. vb.).

1925 tr. *Bukharin's Historical Materialism* iii. 75 For Marx, dialectics means evolution by means of contradictions. **1939** *Nature* 21 Jan. 97/1 He [*sc.* J. B. S. Haldane] does not succeed in dispelling the fog that surrounds the uses of the term 'dialectic'. The mildest use seems only to imply that in any complex system of things, people, or thoughts, opposing forces or tendencies are at work, so that processes are likely to oscillate first one way then another between extremes. **1953** *Times Lit. Suppl.* 25 Dec., 'Dialectics', that magic word which nowadays too often gives an aura of perfection to the most outrageous obscurities and rhapsodizings.. and not only among Marxists. **1965** *Listener* 25 Nov. 837/2 Schofield presents only one half of the dialectic and virtually ignores the other half, namely the counter-pressures which parents, and adult society in general, must bring to bear on rebellious youth. **1967** *Ibid.* 3 Aug. 140/3 Attempts to formulate the rules of dialectics usually result in arid scholasticism. Dialectics is indeed the grammar of Marxist thinking. *Ibid.* 14 Sept. 321 He [*sc.* J. K. Galbraith] suggested that for every apparently dominant force in modern capitalism, an equal and opposite force existed or could be conjured up: big trade unions to oppose monopolies, the state to oppose both, and so on, in an endless dialectic.

dialectic (daɪəˈlɛktɪk), *a.* and *sb.*[2] [ad. L. *dialectic-us*, a. Gr. διαλεκτικός of or pertaining to discourse or discussion, f. διάλεκτος: see DIALECT. Cf. mod.F. *dialectique*.]

A. *adj.*

1. a. Of, pertaining to, or of the nature of logical disputation; argumentative, logical.

1650 B. *Discolliminium* 35 If I should read this Dialectique straine to my Mare. **1669** GALE *Crt. Gentiles* I. I. ii. 14 Their several Modes of Philosophizing, both Symbolic, and Dialectic. **1843** GLADSTONE *Glean.* V. lxxix. 68 A more artful and constant resort to dialectic subtleties. **1846** tr. *F. Von Schlegel's Philos. Hist.* 89 This question cannot be settled..by mere dialectic strife.

b. In Marxist theory used specifically in relation to materialism. Cf. next.

1892 E. AVELING tr. *Engels's Socialism Utopian & Scientific* 39 Modern materialism is essentially dialectic. **1926** M. EASTMAN *Marx, Lenin & Sci. of Revolution* I. ii. 24 That is the philosophy of 'dialectic materialism', the intellectual background of scientific socialism, and..the official state philosophy of the Union of Soviet Socialist Republics. **1952** W. J. H. SPROTT *Social Psychol.* x. 208 Marxists..have always accepted the reaction of ideas on..economic processes. This is, indeed, a field of 'dialectic' operation. **1961** P. USTINOV *Loser* viii. 138 Those impregnated with the spirit of dialectic materialism.

2. Addicted to or practising logical disputation.

1831 CARLYLE *Sart. Res.* II. v. (1858) 87 Of which dialectic marauder..the discomfiture was visibly felt as a benefit. **1838** THIRLWALL *Greece* II. xii. 138 A metrical vehicle did not so well suit Zeno's dialectic genius. **1844** *Ibid.* VIII. 95 Engaged in a learned conversation with the dialectic philosopher Aristoteles.

3. [f. DIALECT + -IC.] Belonging to or of the nature of a dialect; = DIALECTAL.

1813 W. TAYLOR *Eng. Synonyms* (1856) 51 Is it [*prodezza*] a mere dialectic variation of *prudenza*? **1828** WHATELY *Rhet.* in *Encycl. Metrop.* 303/1 An indistinct, hesitating, dialectic, or otherwise faulty, delivery. **1850** H. TORRENS in *Jrnl. Asiat. Soc. Bengal* 13 Another alphabet, dialectic of the Hebrew. **1851** D. WILSON *Preh. Ann.* II. IV. i. 185 The close dialectic affinities between Celtic Scotland and Ireland.

B. *sb.*[2] [The adj. used absolutely.]

A dialectic philosopher, one who pursues the dialectic method; a critical inquirer after truth; a logical disputant.

1640 G. WATTS tr. *Bacon's Adv. Learn.* Pref. 25 As for Induction, the Dialectiques seem scarce ever to have taken it into any serious consideration. **1677** GALE *Crt. Gentiles* III. 91 Thou callest a Dialectic one who considers the reason of every Being: for he that accurately discerneth things is a Dialectic. **1801** MOORE *Nature's Labels* 20 As learned dialectics say, The argument most apt and ample For common use, is the example.

diaˈlectical, *a.* (*sb.*) [f. as prec. + -AL[1].]

A. *adj.* **1. a.** = DIALECTIC *a.* 1.

1548 GEST *Pr. Masse* 116 Theyr argumentation is nothing dialectical. **1656** STANLEY *Hist. Philos.* v. (1701) 164 Speech ..Dialectical, used by such as discourse in short questions and answers. **1657** *North's Plutarch* Add. Lives (1676) 39 Instructed in the Rhetorical, Dialectical, and Astrological Arts. **1850** GROTE *Greece* II. lxvii. VIII. 460 Dialectical skill in no small degree is indispensable. **1876** A. M. FAIRBAIRN in *Contemp. Rev.* June 132 The dialectical pot in which ecclesiastical dogma had been cooked.

b. Belonging to, or of the nature of, dialectic in its later philosophical developments of meaning. spec. ***dialectical materialism***, the theory propagated by Karl Marx and Friedrich Engels according to which political events or social phenomena are to be interpreted as a conflict of social forces (the 'class struggle') produced by the operation of economic causes, and history is to be interpreted as a series of contradictions and their solutions (the thesis, antithesis, and synthesis of Hegelian philosophy). So ***dialectical materialist***. See DIALECTIC *sb.*[1] 2.

1788 REID *Aristotle's Log.* v. §1. 106 When the premises are not certain but probable only, such syllogisms are called dialectical. **1838** [F. HAYWOOD] tr. *Kant's Crit. Pure Reason* 64 Universal Logic, *considered as Organon*, is always a Logic of Appearance, that is, is dialectical. **1874** W. WALLACE *Logic Hegel* vi. 128 The physical elements prove to be Dialectical. The process of meteorological action is the appearance of their Dialectic. **1877** E. CAIRD *Philos. Kant* II. xviii. 633 The Cosmological argument is a nest of dialectical assumptions. **1888** WATSON *Philos. Kant* 289 Pure reason is always dialectical. [**1891–92** G. PLECHANOW in *Neue Zeit* X. I. 278 Die dialektische Methode—das war das wichtigste wissenschaftliche Vermächtniss, das der deutsche Idealismus seinem Erben, dem modernen Materialismus, hinterlassen hat... Der moderne dialektische Materialismus weiss..besser als der Idealismus, dass die Menschen ihre Geschichte unbewusst machen.] **1927** D. KVITKO tr. *Lenin's Materialism* ii. 107 As far as dialectical materialism is concerned there does not exist a fixed immutable boundary between relative and absolute truth. **1934** *Discovery* Feb. 31/2 This conversion of the quantitative into the qualitative..is stressed by dialectical materialists today. **1934** V. ADORATSKY (*title*) Dialectical materialism. The theoretical foundation of Marxism-Leninism. **1936** M. PLOWMAN *Faith called Pacifism* 26 They pride themselves on being dialectical materialists, unencumbered by any ethical humbug. **1939** 'G. ORWELL' *Coming up for Air* III. i. 185 A lot of stuff that nobody else understood, such as dialectical materialism and the destiny of the proletariat and what Lenin said in 1918. **1963** V. NABOKOV *Gift* iv. 237 Such methods of knowledge as dialectical materialism curiously resemble the unscrupulous advertisements for patent medicines, which cure all illnesses at once.

2. = DIALECTIC *a.* 2.

1876 C. M. DAVIES *Unorth. Lond.* 356, I entertained pleasant recollections from certain experiences at the Dialectical Society.

3. = DIALECTAL.

1750 HODGES *Job* Prel. Disc. (T.) At that time the Hebrew and Arabick language was the same, with a small dialectical variation only. **1847** HALLIWELL *Dict.* Pref. (1878) 7 Separating mere dialectical forms. **1861** MAX MÜLLER *Sc. Lang.* v. 199 A language, not yet Sanskrit or Greek or German, but containing the dialectical germs of all.

B. *sb.* = DIALECTIC *sb.*[1] 1.

a **1529** SKELTON *Replyc.* 96 In your dialecticall And principles sillogisticall If ye to remembrance call.

diaˈlectically, *adv.* [f. prec. + -LY[2].]

1. By means of dialectic; in dialectic fashion; argumentatively, logically.

a **1665** J. GOODWIN *Filled w. the Spirit* (1867) 458 You may argue..dialectically or with probability. **1692** SOUTH *Serm.* (1718) IV. 51 He discoursed, or reasoned dialectically. **1847** GROTE *Greece* I. xxxvii. (1862) III. 331 Discussed dialectically, or by reasonings expressed in general language. **1878** HUXLEY in *N. Amer. Rev.* CXXVII. 48 The most reverend prelate might dialectically hew M. Comte in pieces.

2. As regards dialect; = DIALECTALLY.

1868 G. STEPHENS *Runic Mon.* I. 86 A rune may dialectically..vary in power, according to locality. **1884** R. S. POOLE in *Encycl. Brit.* XVII. 641/1 Two coins, differing dialectically in their inscriptions, were found in the Tigris.

dialectician (ˌdaɪəlɛkˈtɪʃən). [a. F. *dialecticien* (Rabelais, 16th c.), f. L. *dialectic-us* DIALECTIC *a.*: see -ICIAN.]

1. One who is skilled in dialectic; a master of argument or disputation; a logician.

a **1693** URQUHART *Rabelais* III. xix. 155 According to the Dialecticians. *a* **1751** BOLINGBROKE *Author. in Relig.* xli. (R.), An art that..might help the subtile dialectician to oppose even the man he could not refute. **1791** S. PARR *Seq. to Print. Paper* (R.), The great poetical dialectician [Dryden]. **1827** HALLAM *Const. Hist.* (1876) I. iv. 218 The terseness or lucidity which long habits of literary warfare.. have given to some expert dialecticians. **1851** LONGF. *Gold. Leg.* VI. 73 For none but a clever dialectician Can hope to become a great physician. *a* **1862** BUCKLE *Civiliz.* (1869) III. v. 287 They were acute dialecticians, and rarely blundered in what is termed the formal part of logic.

2. A professed student of dialects.

1848 CLOUGH *Bothie*, Lindsay the ready of speech, the Piper, the Dialectician..Who in three weeks had created a dialect new for the party. **1882** MISS POWLEY in *Trans. Cumbld. & Westmld. Antiq. Soc.* VI. 272 However well established [his] opinion among dialecticians may be.

dialecticism (daɪəˈlɛktɪsɪz(ə)m). [f. DIALECTIC + -ISM.] **1.** The characteristic tendency or influence of dialect.

1888 *Academy* 14 Jan. 27 Dialecticism, phoneticism, ellipsis.

2. *Philos.* Dialectical philosophy or practice.

1901 *Pop. Sci. Monthly* Jan. 298 A man..may be determined to do nothing not pronounced reasonable, either by his own cogitations (rationalism), or by public discussion (dialecticism), or by crucial experiment. **1936** H. READ *Surrealism* 81 Blake labours in hope that Enthusiasm and Life may not cease. In the whole of his writings I feel the presence of an instinctive dialecticism. **1948** *Theology* LI. 30 A world in which dialecticism and existentialism are the desperate and tortured answers that faith must grasp at.

diaˈlectics, *sb. pl.*: see DIALECTIC *sb.* 1 b.

ˈdialecˌtize, *v. rare.* [f. DIALECT + -IZE.] *trans.* To make into a dialect, or make dialectal.

1883 G. STEPHENS *S. Bugge's Stud. N. Mythol.* 23 It has even had time to become dialectized.

dialectology (daɪəlɛkˈtɒlədʒɪ). [f. Gr. διάλεκτο-ς DIALECT + -LOGY.] The study of dialects; that branch of philology which treats of dialects.

1879 *President's Addr. Philol. Soc.* 32 Materials for the dialectology of a single province. **1888** SWEET *Eng. Sounds* Pref. 12 The obscure and tortuous paths of Old English dialectology.

Hence **dialecˈtologer**, **dialecˈtologist**, one versed in dialectology; **dialectoˈlogical** *a.*, pertaining to dialectology.

1879 *President's Addr. Philol. Soc.* 32 A dialectological introduction. **1881** *Athenæum* 23 Apr. 554/3 The county [Cornwall] presents to the dialectologer two varieties of an English dialect. **1883** A. M. ELLIOTT in *Amer. Jrnl. Philol.* IV. 490 The dialectologist must be fastidious indeed who would not be satisfied with this extraordinary mass of material.

ˈdialector. *rare*⁻⁰. [f. DIALECT + -OR.]

1847 CRAIG, *Dialector*, one learned in dialects. Hence in mod. Dicts.

diaˈlectual, *a. rare.* [irreg. f. DIALECT; cf. *effect*, *effectual*.] = DIALECTAL.

1854 R. G. LATHAM *Native Races Russian Emp.* 256 Dialectual varieties increase as we go westwards. **1856** KITTO & ALEXANDER *Cycl. Bibl. Lit.* (1863) 188/2 Dialectual varieties of pronunciation.

dialer, dialing: see DIALLER, DIALLING.

dialetike, -yk, obs. forms of DIALECTIC.

dialist (ˈdaɪəlɪst). [f. DIAL *sb.*[1] + -IST.] A maker of dials; one skilled in dialling.

1652 T. STIRRUP (*title*), Horometria; or the Complete Diallist. **1703** MOXON *Mech. Exerc.* 346 Helps to a young Dyalist for his more orderly and quick making of Dyals. **1776** G. CAMPBELL *Philos. Rhet.* (1801) I. Introd., The architect, the navigator, the dialist.

di-ˈalkalamide. *Chem.* See DI-[2] and ALKALAMIDE.

1866 E. FRANKLAND *Lect. Notes Chem. Stud.* 375 Secondary and tertiary monalkalamides, dialkalamides, and trialkalamides, are known.

‖**diallage**[1] (daɪˈælədʒiː). *Rhet.* [mod.L. *diallagē*, a. Gr. διαλλαγή interchange, f. διαλλαγ- aorist stem of διαλλάσσειν to interchange, f. διά through, across + ἀλλάσσειν to change, make other than it is, f. ἄλλος other.]

A figure of speech by which arguments, after having been considered from various points of view, are all brought to bear upon one point.

1706 in PHILLIPS (ed. Kersey). **1831** *Crayons from Commons* 44 And when a whole diallage was rear'd, Chagrined he found that no one member cheer'd.

diallage[2] (ˈdaɪəlɪdʒ). *Min.* [a. F. *diallage*, f. Gr. διαλλαγή (see prec.), named by Haüy 1801, from its dissimilar cleavages.] A grass-green variety of pyroxene, of lamellar or foliated structure: formerly applied more widely to similar minerals, such as hypersthene, bronzite, etc.

1805 R. JAMESON *Char. Min.* II. 605 Smaragdite, Saussure..Diallage, Hauy. **1811** PINKERTON *Petral.* I. 353 Metallic diallage, from Saxony. **1865** L'ESTRANGE *Yachting round W. Eng.* 222 Some Serpentine is permeated by veins of golden diallage. **1879** RUTLEY *Stud. Rocks* x. 121 Some of the so-called diallages belong rather to enstatite than to pyroxene, since the crystallisation is rhombic.

attrib. **1843** PORTLOCK *Geol.* 211 Hypersthene..passes into a greyish-green diallage, and, with a greenish felspar, forms the very beautiful diallage rock of those localities [Athenry]. **1855** J. D. FORBES *Tour Mt. Blanc* xi. 237 The boulders here seemed to be gabbro or diallage rock.

Hence **diallagic** (daɪəˈlædʒɪk), *a.* [F. *diallagique*], **diallagoid** (daɪˈæləgɔɪd), *a.*, containing or resembling diallage.

1847 CRAIG, *Diallagic.* **1879** RUTLEY *Stud. Rocks* x. 125 The diallagic augite sections are broad. *Ibid.* x. 132 The diallagoid augite of Boricky.

dialled (ˈdaɪəld), *ppl. a.* [f. DIAL *sb.*[1] or *v.* + -ED.] Measured or marked by a dial.

1817 T. L. PEACOCK *Melincourt* III. 50 The careless hours ..Still trace upon the dialled brass The shade of their unvarying way. **1891** W. TUCKWELL *Tongues in Trees* 145 Six hours to toil, the rest to leisure give, In them—so say the dialled hours—live.

†**ˈdiallel.** *Obs.*⁻⁰. [ad. Gr. διάλληλος through one another.] (See quot.)

1656 BLOUNT *Glossogr.* s.v., As parallels are lines running one by the other without meeting: so *Diallels* are lines which run one through the other, that is, do cross, intersecate, or cut. [Hence in BAILEY, ASH, etc.].

‖**diallelon** (daɪəˈliːlɒn). *Logic.* [mod.L. f. Gr. δι' ἀλλήλων through or by means of one another: see prec.] Definition in a circle, i.e. definition by means of a term which is itself defined by the defined word.

1837–8 SIR W. HAMILTON *Logic* xxiv. (1860) II. 17 The ancients called the circular definition by the name of *Diallelon*, as in this case we declare the *definitum* and the *definiens* reciprocally by each other (δι' ἀλλήλων).

‖**diallelus** (daɪəˈliːləs). *Logic.* [mod.L. f. Gr. (τρόπος) διάλληλος reasoning in a circle: see prec. (In mod.F. *diallèle*.)] Reasoning in a circle; i.e. endeavouring to establish a conclusion by means of a proposition which is itself dependent on the said conclusion.

1837–8 SIR W. HAMILTON *Logic* xxvi. (1860) II. 51 The proposition which we propose to prove must not be used as a principle for its own probation. The violation of this rule is called the *Orbis vel circulus in demonstrando,—diallelus.*

Hence **diaˈllelous** *a.*, involving reasoning or defining in a circle.

In mod. Dicts.

dialler, dialer (ˈdaɪələ(r)). [f. DIAL *sb.*[1] + -ER[1].]

1. One who makes a survey of mines by the aid of a 'dial' or compass.

1747 HOOSON *Miner's Dict.* R iij, This Roofing..if done by a skillful Dialer, and by a Dial that he is acquainted with ..is certain enough. **1778** W. PRYCE *Min. Cornub.* 204 In the same manner the Dialler takes his second measurement.

2. A device for dialling telephone-numbers automatically.

1969 *Daily Tel.* 3 Feb. 4/5 The first batch of 'card diallers' —numbers prestored on cards which automatically dial a number when 'punched'—is also due for field trials shortly. *Ibid.*, The automatic diallers are expected to benefit businesses mainly with a large volume of regular calls. **1971** *Sci. Amer.* June 90/3 As a prototype for a bubble mass-memory we have designed and built a 'telephone repertory dialer', a device for storing 50 to 100 frequently called telephone numbers.

dial-less, dial-like: see DIAL *sb.*[1] 8 b.

dialling, dialing ('daɪəlɪŋ), *vbl. sb.* [f. DIAL *sb.*[1] and *v.* + -ING[1].]

1. a. The art of constructing dials. †**b.** The measurement of time by a dial (*obs.*).

1570 DEE *Math. Pref.* 37 Horometrie..in Englishe, may be termed Dialling. **1593** FALE (*title*), The Art of Dialling; teaching an easie and perfect way to make all kinde of Dialls vpon any plaine platte, howsoeuer placed. **1703** MOXON *Mech. Exerc.* 307 These Rules of adjusting the Motion of the Shadow to the Motion of the Sun, may be called Scientifick Dyalling. **1727-51** CHAMBERS *Cycl.*, *Dialling*, the art of drawing sun, moon, and star-dials, on any given plane, or on the surface of any given body. **1837** WHEWELL *Hist. Induct. Sc.* (1857) I. 122 Another result of the doctrine of the sphere was Gnomonick or Dialling.

2. a. The use of a 'dial' or compass in underground surveying.

1670 SIR J. PETTUS *Fodinæ Regalis* 2 He is directed toward the Shaft by a Needle touch'd with a Loadstone, the using whereof is called Dialling. **1778** W. PRYCE *Min. Cornub.* 202 Dialling is requisite in almost every shaft.

b. The act or process of DIAL *v.* 4.

1931 *Punch* 27 May 564/1 Those who think they can understand dialling but can't. **1965** C. FREMLIN *Jealous One* xxi. 169 After four or five minutes of fruitless dialling..she allowed herself to admit that there were no taxis available.

†**3.** *concr.* Apparatus of the nature of dials. *rare.*

1756 NUGENT *Gr. Tour* I. 258 A handsome garden, in which there is a variety of dialling.

4. *attrib.* and *Comb.*, as (sense 2 b) ***dialling apparatus***, ***code***; **dialling-globe** (see quot.); **dialling-scale**, graduated lines on rulers, the edge of quadrants, etc., to facilitate the construction of dials; **dialling-sphere**, a variety of *dialling-globe*; **dialling tone**, the sound produced by a telephone where automatic exchanges are in operation, indicating that the line is in order and the caller can start dialling.

1933 *Discovery* Apr. 132/1 Mechanical equipment is required to pilot the call through each successive stage from the *dialling apparatus to the final selector. **1962** A. NISBETT *Technique Sound Studio* x. 176 Dialling is rather more of a performance than being on the receiving end of a phone call, simply because most *dialling codes are much too long. **1706** PHILLIPS (ed. Kersey), **Dialling-Globe*, an Instrument made of Brass or Wood, with a Plane fitted to the Horizon, and an Index particularly contrived to draw all sorts of Dials, and to give a clear demonstration of that Art. **1767** *Phil. Trans.* LVII. 389 A new Method of constructing Sun-Dials..without the Assistance of *Dialing Scales. **1666** COLLINS in Rigaud *Corr. Sci. Men* (1841) II. 462 A *dialling scheme of Mr. Foster's. **1922** *Telegr. & Teleph. Jrnl.* VIII. No. 84, 82/1 As soon as a connexion has been made with an idle final selector, a '*Dialling tone' is transmitted to the subscriber. **1927** *Daily Express* 28 Oct. 3/1 The dialling tone is heard as soon as you place the receiver to your ear—if your line is in order. **1966** A. PRIOR *Operators* v. 47 'Hello, hello!' But there was just the dialling tone.

diallogite: see DIALOGITE.

di-'allyl. *Chem.* [DI-[2].] **A.** *sb.* The organic radical allyl in the free state, $C_6 H_{10} = C_3H_5{\cdot}C_3H_5$: see ALLYL. **B.** *attrib.* and *Comb.* Containing two equivalents of allyl.

1869 ROSCOE *Elem. Chem.* 389. **1880** E. CLEMINSHAW tr. *Wurtz' Atomic Th.* 265 Free allyl or diallyl, has doubled its molecule.

dialogic (daɪə'lɒdʒɪk), *a.* [ad. med.L. *dialogicus*, a. Gr. διαλογικός, f. διάλογος DIALOGUE: see -IC. In mod.F. *dialogique* (18th c.).] Of, pertaining to, or of the nature of dialogue; sharing in dialogue.

1833 THIRLWALL in *Philol. Mus.* II. 560 The dialogic form had not then become so indispensable with Plato. **1850** BLACKIE *Æschylus* I Pref. 44 The iambic or dialogic part of ancient tragedy. **1886** *Harper's Mag.* Sept. 642 Several dialogic personages.

dialogical (daɪə'lɒdʒɪkəl), *a.* [f. as prec. + -AL[1].] = prec.

1601 DEACON & WALKER (*title*), Dialogicall Discourses of Spirits and Divels. **1621-51** BURTON *Anat. Mel.* II. ii. III. (1651) 258 That dialogicall disputation with Zacharias the Christian. **1880** E. OPPERT *Forbid. L.* Pref. 9 For the sake of a more vivid description, especially in the dialogical parts.

Hence **dia'logically**, *adv.*

1766 GOLDSM. *Vic. W.* vii, If you are for a cool argument ..are you for managing it analogically or dialogically?

dialogism (daɪ'ælədʒɪz(ə)m). [ad. L. *dialogismus* the rhetorical figure (see sense 1), a. Gr. διαλογισμός balancing of accounts, reasoning, conversation, debate, f. διαλογίζεσθαι to DIALOGIZE: see -ISM. In F. *dialogisme* (1557 in Hatz.-Darm.).]

1. *Rhet.* The discussion of a subject under the form of a dialogue, to the personages of which the author imputes ideas and sentiments.

1580 FULKE *Retentive* 306 (T.) His foolish dialogism is a fighting with his own shadow. [**1589** PUTTENHAM *Eng. Poesie* III. xix. (Arb.) 243 This manner of speech is by the figure *Dialogismus*, or the right reasoner.] **1609** R. BERNARD *Faithfull Shepheard* 67 Dialogisme..is, when a question is made, and forthwith readily answered, as if two were talking together. **1659** D. STOKES *Twelve Minor Proph.* Pref. (L.), Enlarging what they would say..by their dialogisms and colloquies.

2. A conversational phrase or speech; a DIALOGUE, spoken or written.

1623 COCKERAM *Eng. Dict.* II, A Talking together.. Dialogisme. **1647** TRAPP *Comm. Matt.* xxv. 37-9 Not that there shall be then any such dialogism (say divines) at the last day. **1651** *Life Father Sarpi* (1676) 74 Such Dialogisms as these past betwixt them. **1822** *Blackw. Mag.* XI. 444 Byron will never write a tragedy, though he sent ten dialogisms to the Albemarle-street Press.

3. *Logic.* A term introduced for a form of argument having a single premiss and a disjunctive conclusion.

The kind of argument is as follows: 'A B is an unimaginative man; therefore either he is not a true poet, or true poets may be men without imagination.' The name implies a parallelism to the syllogism.

1880 C. S. PEIRCE *Algebra of Logic* in *Amer. Jrnl. Math.* III. 20 In this way any argument may be resolved into arguments, each of which has one premiss an two alternative conclusions. Such an argument, when completed, may be called a Dialogism.

dialogist (daɪ'ælədʒɪst). [ad. L. *dialogista*, ad. Gr. διαλογιστής, f. διάλογος; see DIALOGUE and -IST: in F. *dialogiste* (17th c.). See also DIALOGUIST.]

1. One who takes part in a dialogue; one of the personages in an imaginary dialogue.

a **1677** BARROW *Serm.* Wks. 1686 II. 114 The like doth Cicero [assert] ..in the person of his Dialogists. **1761** STERNE *Tr. Shandy* III. xxxvii, The dialogist affirmeth, That a long nose is not without its domestic conveniences also. **1847** DE QUINCEY *Milton v. Southey* Wks. XII. 176 The two dialogists are introduced walking out after breakfast.

2. A writer of dialogues.

a **1660** HAMMOND *Wks.* II. 232 (R.) If we will believe the dialogist's reasonings. **1711** SHAFTESB. *Charac.* (1737) III. v. ii. 292 The Characters, or Personages, employ'd by our new orthodox Dialogists. **1839** MAGINN in *Fraser's Mag.* XX. 271 The doctor had never read the Greek dialogist.

dialogistic (daɪələʊ'dʒɪstɪk), *a.* [ad. Gr. διαλογιστικός of or for discourse: see prec. and -IC.] Having the nature or form of dialogue; taking part in dialogue; argumentative.

1677 GALE *Crt. Gentiles* II. III. 92 In their disputes or Dialogistic ratiocinations. **1882-3** SCHAFF *Encycl. Relig. Knowl.* II. 1390 The form of the book [Malachi] is dialogistic,—an assertion of the prophet followed by an excuse of the people, which in turn is refuted.

dialo'gistical, *a.* [f. prec. + -AL[1].] = prec.

1715 M. DAVIES *Athen. Brit.* I. 185 Two dialogistical conjurers, with their dramatick enchantments, change the scene.

dialo'gistically, *adv.* [f. prec. + -LY[2].] In dialogistic fashion; in manner of a dialogue.

a **1654** J. RICHARDSON *On Old Test.* 449 (T.) In his prophecy he [Malachi] proceeds most dialogistically.

dialogite (daɪ'ælədʒaɪt). *Min.* Erron. diall-. [Named by Jasche about 1817 from Gr. διαλογή 'doubt, selection': see -ITE.] A rose-red carbonate of manganese; a synonym of *rhodochrosite*.

1826 EMMONS *Min.* 215 Dialogite. **1835** SHEPARD *Min.* 134 Diallogite.

dialogize (daɪ'ælədʒaɪz), *v.* See also DIALOGUIZE. [mod. ad. Gr. διαλογίζεσθαι to converse, debate, f. διάλογος DIALOGUE; in F. *dialogiser*, 16–17th c.: see -IZE.] *intr.* To converse, discuss, or carry on a dialogue (*with*). Hence **di'alogizing** *vbl. sb.* and *ppl. a.*

1601 DEACON & WALKER *Spirits & Divels* To Rdr. 12 This dialogizing manner of dealing. **1677** GALE *Crt. Gentiles* II. IV. 402 Plato..brings in Socrates dialogising with young Alcibiades. **1689** *Col. Rec. Pennsylv.* I. 254 He did not think it was their work to dialogize with any man without dores. **1854** LOWELL *Lett.* (1894) I. 211 In them also there are dialogizing and monologizing thoughts, but not flesh and blood enough.

dialogous (daɪ'æləgəs), *a. rare.* [f. L. *dialog-us*, Gr. διάλογ-ος DIALOGUE + -OUS.] Of or belonging to dialogue; in quot. = dialogue-writing.

1737 FIELDING *Hist. Reg.* Ded., The iniquitous surmises of a certain anonymous dialogous author.

dialogue ('daɪəlɒg), *sb.* Forms: 3–7 dialoge, (4 dialoke, -logg, -log), 5–6 dyalogue, 6– dialogue. [a. F. *dialoge* (13th c. in Hatz.-Darm.), mod.F. *dialogue*, ad.L. *dialogus*, Gr. διάλογος conversation, dialogue, f. διαλέγεσθαι to speak alternately, converse: see DIALECT.]

1. a. A conversation carried on between two or more persons; a colloquy, talk together.

(The tendency is to confine it to two persons, perhaps through associating *dia-* with *di-*: cf. *monologue*.)

1401 *Pol. Poems* (Rolls) II. 109 To make with the a dialogge, I holde it bot wast. **1509** FISHER *Fun. Serm. C'tess Richmond* Wks. (1876) 289 A dyalogue, that is to saye a comynycacyon betwyxt..Martha, and our sauyour Jhesu. **1599** SHAKS. *Much Ado* III. i. 31 Feare you not my part of the Dialogue. **1749** FIELDING *Tom Jones* VI. XVI. ii, A short dialogue..then passed between them. **1865** DICKENS *Mut. Fr.* I. ix, Bella had closely attended to this short dialogue.

b. (without *pl.*) Verbal interchange of thought between two or more persons, conversation.

c **1532** DEWES *Introd. Fr.* (in Palsgr. 1052) By way of dyalogue betwene the lady Mary & her servant Gyles. **1595** SHAKS. *John* I. i. 210 In Dialogue of Complement. **1651** HOBBES *Leviath.* II. xxv. 133 To enter into Dispute, and Dialogue with him. **1725** POPE *Odyss.* xv. 532 So passed in pleasing dialogue away The night. **1859** GEO. ELIOT *A. Bede* 87 That is the great advantage of dialogue on horse-back; it can be merged any minute into a trot or canter.

c. In *Politics*, discussion or diplomatic contact between the representatives of two nations, groups, or the like; hence *gen.*, valuable or constructive discussion or communication.

1953 *Times* 13 May, M. Mayer went on to speak of the 'dialogue' which was tending to establish itself between east and west. **1961** L. MUMFORD *City in History* vi. 181 He would have turned the urban dialogue into the sterile monologue of totalitarian power. **1962** *Listener* 29 Nov. 896/2 The Hungarian Communist party congress was another sounding-board for the increasingly acrimonious but still largely oblique dialogue between Peking and Moscow. **1963** *Ibid.* 31 Jan. 191/2 The essential working basis within the Community is provided by the 'dialogue' between the Commission and the Ministers. **1966** *Rep. Comm. Inquiry Univ. Oxf.* I. iv. 264 We would expect a continuing dialogue between the Hebdomadal Council and the Council of the Colleges on the working of Oxford's part in the Universities Central Council on Admissions. **1970** *Guardian* 25 Sept. 3/2 The new society, based on dialogue between all sections of society. **1971** *Times* 27 Feb. 13/5 May I comment on Professor Rahner's plea..for a strengthening of dialogue between religious believers and non-believers?

d. ***dialogue of the deaf*** [tr. F. DIALOGUE DE SOURDS], a discussion, meeting, etc., in which neither side understands or makes allowance for the point of view of the other.

1970 *New Yorker* 17 Oct. 171/1 This lack of understanding..has made the Paris talks a dialogue of the deaf for many months. **1974** *Times* 15 Feb. 14 Better communication is no panacea for every industrial dispute... But English reserve does seem to lead, all too often, to a muted dialogue of the deaf. **1979** H. KISSINGER *White House Years* xxi. 880 The Nixon-Gandhi conversation thus turned into a classic dialogue of the deaf. **1980** *Ghanaian Times* 23 Jan. 4 The PFP are conducting a dialogue of the deaf among themselves. **1985** *Financial Times* 10 July 4/1 The talks were little more than a dialogue of the deaf and broke down essentially over the vexed issue of sovereignty over the islands.

2. a. A literary work in the form of a conversation between two or more persons.

a **1225** *Ancr. R.* 76 þis beoð sein Gregories wordes, in his dialoge. *c* **1325** *E.E. Allit. P.* B. 1157 Danyel in his dialokez devysed sum tyme. **1493** *Dives & Paup.*, Here endith a.. dyalogue of Dives & pauper. *a* **1531** *Pol. Rel. & L. Poems* (1866) 35 A Dyalog betwixt the gentylman and the plowman. **1588** SHAKS. *L.L.L.* v. ii. 895 Wil you heare the Dialogue that the two Learned men haue compiled, in praise of the Owle and the Cuckow? **1751** JOHNSON *Rambler* No. 156 ¶7 Tragedy was a Monody..improved afterwards into a dialogue by the addition of another speaker. **1838** THIRLWALL *Greece* IV. 275 Plato, in one of his dialogues, introduces Anytus as vehemently offended with Socrates. **1882** *Temperance Mirr.* Mar. 63 Uncle Job's Theory, A Dialogue [between 5 persons].

b. (without *pl.*) Literary composition of this nature; the conversation written for and spoken by actors on the stage; hence, in recent use, style of dramatic conversation or writing.

1589 PUTTENHAM *Eng. Poesie* I. xi. (Arb.) 41 Others who ..by maner of Dialogue, vttered the priuate and familiar talke of..shepheards, heywards and such like. **1656** STANLEY *Hist. Philos.* v. (1701) 174/2 The Writings of Plato are by way of Dialogue. **1779-81** JOHNSON *L.P.*, *Smith* Wks. II. 468 The diction..is too luxuriant and splendid for dialogue. **1829** LYTTON *Disowned* 98 Your book is very clever, but it wants dialogue. **1841** ELPHINSTONE *Hist. Ind.* I. 283 The plots are generally interesting; the dialogue lively. **1880** GROVE *Dict. Mus.* II. 531/1 [In *Opéra comique*] the dénouement is happy, and the Dialogue spoken.

†**3.** Such a composition set to music for two or more voices. *Obs.*

1653 J. PLAYFORD (*title*), Select Musical Ayres and Dialogues. **1657** J. GAMBLE (*title*), Ayres and Dialogues to be sung to the Theorbo-Lute or Bass Viol. **1659** —— (*title*) (in Grove *Dict. Mus.* I. 580) Ayres and Dialogues for One, Two, and Three Voices.

4. *attrib.* and *Comb.*, as ***dialogue-author***, ***-novel***, ***-piece***, ***-writer***; **dialogue-wise** *adv.*, in the form of a dialogue.

1561 VERON (*title*), The Hvntynge of Purgatorye to Death, made Dialogewyse. **1612** WOODALL *Surg. Mate* Wks. (1653) 19* Explained Dialogue wise, betwixt the Authour and a Military Surgeon. **1711** SHAFTESB. *Charac.* (1737) III. 317 The form or manner of our dialogue-author. **1732** FIELDING *Covent Gard. Trag.* Prolegom., A Tragedy is a thing of five acts, written dialoguewise. **1768** FOOTE *Devil on 2 Sticks* III. Wks. 1799 II. 280 A kind of circulating library, for the vending of dialogue novels. **1783** *Hist. Miss Baltimores* I. 211, I will write it dialogue fashion. **1861** J. M. NEALE in *Lit. Churchman* VII. 375/1 It is a poem written dialoguewise.

dialogue ('daɪəlɒg), *v.* [f. prec. sb.; cf. F. *dialoguer* (1717 in Hatz.-Darm).] Hence also **'dialogued** *ppl. a.*, **'dialoguing** *vbl. sb.*

1. *intr.* To hold a dialogue or conversation.

1607 SHAKS. *Timon* II. ii. 52 *Var.* How dost Foole? *Ape.* Dost Dialogue with thy shadow? **1685** *Trial of H. Cornish, etc.*, 28 You must not stand to Dialogue between one another. **1741** RICHARDSON *Pamela* II. 45 Thus foolishly dialogued I with my Heart. **1817** COLERIDGE *Biog. Lit.* (1882) 286 Those puppet-heroines for whom the showman contrives to dialogue without any skill in ventriloquism. **1858** CARLYLE *Fredk. Gt.* I. IV. v. 426 Much semi-articulate questioning and dialoguing with Dame de Roucoulles.

b. *transf.* and *fig.*

1628 EARLE *Microcosm., Tobacco-seller* (Arb.) 59 Where men dialogue with their noses, and their communication is smoak. 1892 *Sat. Rev.* 18 June 709/2 With oboe obbligato dialoguing now with sopranos, now with tenors.

†2. *trans.* To converse with. *Obs.*

1699 F. BUGG *Quakerism Exposed* 9 To dialogue the Bishops, and call them Monsters. *Ibid.* 27 The Quakers dialogu'd the Bishops.

3. To express in the form of a dialogue; to furnish with dialogue.

1597 SHAKS. *Lover's Compl.* 132 And dialogu'd for him what he would say. 1781 MAD. D'ARBLAY *Diary* May, Our conference grew very grave.. I have not time to dialogue it. 1885 *Academy* 16 May 356 A tale full of human interest, brightly dialogued. 1887 *Contemp. Rev.* May 717 The prodigious skill of his dialogued argumentation.

‖**dialogue de sourds** (dialɔg də sur). Also *erron.* with des. [Fr.] = *dialogue of the deaf* s.v. DIALOGUE *sb.* 1 d.

1963 *Atlantic Monthly* Sept. 55/1 The dialogue between Christians became increasingly the *dialogue des sourds*, the exchanges of men deaf to each other, drowning the voice of conciliation in cries and countercries of 'Antichrist' and in the clash of arms. 1966 *Economist* 24 Sept. 1237/3 The members present agreed with fine accord that the present *dialogue de sourds* between the poor, who parrot the need for aid, and the rich, who parrot the need for efficiency, is quite artificial.

dialoguer ('daɪəlɒgə(r)). *rare.* [f. DIALOGUE *v.* + -ER[1].] One who takes part in a dialogue; = DIALOGIST 1.

1879 G. MEREDITH *Egoist* I. xvii. 314 A polished whisperer, a lively dialoguer, one for witty bouts.

dialoguist ('daɪəlɒgɪst). [f. DIALOGUE *sb.* + -IST.] A writer of dialogue; = DIALOGIST 2.

1739 ELIZ. CARTER tr. *Algarotti on Newton's Philos.* (1742) II. 60 The Azolian Dialoguists. 1888 *Pall Mall G.* 3 July 11/1 The whimsical dialoguist of the Happy Islands.

'dialo,guize, *v.* ? *Obs.* See DIALOGIZE. [f. as prec. + -IZE.] *intr.* To take part in dialogue; to converse. Hence **'dialo,guizing** *vbl. sb.*

1599 *Broughton's Lett.* xii. 42 Euripides and Menander, Socrates and Epicurus dialoguising and conferring together. 1603 HARSNET *Pop. Impost.* xxiii. 166 Upon questioning and Dialoguizing with the Devil. *a* 1619 FOTHERBY *Atheom.* I. xii. §3 (1622) 126 These interlocutorie and dialoguising dreames.

'dial-plate. [f. DIAL *sb.*[1] + PLATE.] The face-plate of a dial; *spec.* (in *Clock-making*) the sheet of metal, glass, etc. on the face of which the hours, etc. are marked; = DIAL *sb.*[1] 4.

1690 *Lond. Gaz.* No. 2603/4 A little Gold Watch with a white Enamell Dial-Plate, made in France. 1781 COWPER *Conversation* 380 The circle formed.. Like figures drawn upon a dial-plate. 1816 J. SCOTT *Vis. Paris* (ed. 5) 63 Niches ..in which different.. names might be slid..in the same way as the ever-changing days of the month are slid into the dial-plates of our clocks. 1840 CARLYLE *Heroes* iii. (1858) 263 His characters are like watches with dial-plates of transparent crystal.

fig. 1829 LYTTON *Disowned* 59 Every stroke upon the dial-plate of wit was true to the genius of the hour. 1836 EMERSON *Nature, Lang.* Wks. (Bohn) II. 153 The visible world..is the dial plate of the invisible.

b. A graduated plate used with a lapidary's dial.

1875 URE *Dict. Arts* III. 42 A needle..marks by its points the divisions on the dial-plate.

dial-up ('daɪəlʌp), *a.* and *sb.* [f. DIAL *v.* + UP *adv.*[1]: see DIAL *v.* 4 c and *to ring up*, RING *v.*[2] 10 b.] **A.** *adj.* Pertaining to or designating a data transmission link that is part of a public telephone network, access to it being gained by dialling or keying manually or automatically.

1961 *Proc. Eastern Joint Computer Conf.* Dec. 214/1 More recent developments are magnetic tape-to-tape transmission over telephone lines, either private or dial-up. 1969 G. B. DAVIS *Computer Data Processing* xvi. 400 TELEX...A dial-up network for low-speed communications. 1972 *AFIPS Conf. Proc.* XL. 114/1 It is implemented on a DEC PDP9 computer..and a dial-up 2000 bit/sec link to the local big machine. 1972 *New Scientist* 26 Oct. 218/1 The market for cheap desk-top 'dial-up' [facsimile] units for the executive will increase from today's $17 million to $110 million by 1980. 1975 *Rep. Computer Board Managem.* (Univ. Coll., London) 2 Of the initial 32 lines, half are hardwired and the rest dial-up. 1979 J. E. ROWLEY *Mechanised In-House Information Syst.* i. 63 The user may use private leased lines or rely on the public telephone network, using dial-up lines. 1984 *Listener* 20 Sept. 7/2 Access to that database was through a telephone dial-up system and was used by thousands of subscribers all over the United States.

B. *sb.* The action of dialling up.

1978 W. S. DAVIS *Information Processing Systems* xvi. 351 Dial-up can get expensive if the call is long distance. 1979 *Financial Times* 17 Sept. 14/2 Information can be transmitted (via automatic dialup) by ordinary telephone lines.

dia'luric, *a. Chem.* [f. DI-[2] + AL(LOXAN) + URIC.] In ***dialuric acid***, $C_4N_2H_4O_4$, an acid obtained by hydrogenizing alloxan, which crystallizes in needles, and forms, with metals, salts called **dia'lurates.** Hence **dia'luramide**, the primary amide in which the replacing radical is that of dialuric acid.

1845 G. E. DAY tr. *Simon's Anim. Chem.* I. 60 On treating alloxan with sulphuretted hydrogen, we obtain..dialuric acid. 1856 WATTS tr. *Gmelin's Chem.* X. 158 Dialurate of Potash. Deposited on mixing a potash-salt with aqueous dialuric acid. 1868–77 WATTS *Dict. Chem.* V. 958 Dialuric and uric acids may be regarded as tartron-ureide and tartron-diureide respectively.

dialy- (ˌdaɪəlɪ), ad. Gr. διαλυ-, stem (but not regular combining form) of διαλύ-ειν to part asunder, separate, used as the first element in many botanical terms, with the sense of 'separated', or 'non-united'. Synonymous terms are usually found in APO- and POLY-. Thus **dialycarpel** (-'kɑːpəl) [see CARPEL], 'an ovary or fruit with ununited carpels' *Syd. Soc. Lex.* **dialycarpous** (-'kɑːpəs), *a.* [Gr. καρπός fruit], having the carpels distinct. **dialypetalous** (-'pɛtələs) *a.*, having the petals distinct. **dialyphyllous** (-'fɪləs) *a.* [Gr. φύλλον a leaf], having the leaves distinct. So **dialy'sepalous, dialy'staminous** *adjs.*, having the sepals, the stamens, distinct.

1849 HENFREY *Rudim. Bot.* (1858) 100 More correctly called dialypetalous, with the petals distinct. 1859 C. DRESSER *Rudim. Bot.* 346 It is said to be apocarpous..or dialycarpous. 1866 *Treas. Bot.*, *Dialyphyllous*, the same as Polysepalous. 1880 GRAY *Struct. Bot.* vi. §5. 244 Dialypetalous (used by Endlicher) has the same meaning, polypetalous. 1883 *Syd. Soc. Lex.*, *Dialyphyllous*, having separate leaves. *Ibid.*, *Dialysepalous*, having the sepals distinct; same as *Polysepalous*. *Ibid.*, *Dialystaminous*, having separate, distinct stamens.

'dia,lysable, -zable, *a.* [f. DIALYSE *v.* + -ABLE. So F. *dialysable*.] Capable of separation by dialysis.

In mod. Dicts.

dialysate (daɪ'ælɪzət). *Chem.* [f. DIALYSE + -ATE[1].] That portion of a mixture that remains after dialysis.

1867 J. ATTFIELD *Chem.* (1885) 811 The portion passing through the septum is termed the diffusate, the portion which does not pass through is termed the dialysate.

di'aly,sator. *Chem. rare.* [f. DIALYSE, with L. agent-suffix *-ator*.] = DIALYSER.

1891 *Daily News* 16 Jan. 2/3 It does not belong to the group of so-called toxalbumins, as it can withstand high temperatures, and in the dialysator passes quickly and easily through the membrane.

dialyse, -ze ('daɪəlaɪz), *v. Chem.* [f. DIALY-SIS, after *analyse*.] **a.** *trans.* To separate the crystalloid part of a mixture from the colloid, in the process of chemical dialysis.

1861 GRAHAM in *Phil. Trans.* 186 The mixed fluid to be dialysed is poured into the hoop upon the surface of the parchment-paper. *Ibid.* 205 The solution is the more durable the longer it has been dialysed. 1885 A. W. BLYTH in *Leisure Hour* Jan. 23/1 Salt dialysed through the walls into the distilled water.

b. *spec.* in *Med.* To subject (blood) to dialysis (see DIALYSIS 5 b).

1914 *Jrnl. Pharmacol. & Exper. Therap.* V. III. 277 An apparatus made of celloidin or other dialysing membrane. 1944 *Acta Medica Scandinavica* CXVII. 122 One might try to remove these substances from the blood by dialysis. For this purpose the blood must be dialysed..through a system of tubes or membranes outside the body, and then brought back again into the patient's body. 1963 *Lancet* 12 Jan. 82/2 The dialysing area of the particular hæmodialyser employed is given, together with the urea clearance achieved by its use.

Hence **'dialysed** *ppl. a.*, that has undergone the process of dialysis; ***dialysed iron***, a soluble ferric hydroxide, prepared by dialysis, used in medicine; **'dialysing** *vbl. sb.* and *ppl. a.*

1867 [see DIALYTIC 1]. 1875 H. C. WOOD *Therap.* (1879) 96 Dialyzed Iron..is a clear, neutral, nearly tasteless, dark-red liquid, prepared by dialyzing a solution of the chloride of iron. 1884 W. G. STEVENSON in *Pop. Sc. Monthly* XXIV. 771 Membranes possessing dialyzing power.

dialyser, -zer ('daɪəlaɪzə(r)). *Chem.* [f. DIALYSE + -ER[1].] **a.** An apparatus for effecting dialysis; a vessel formed of parchment or animal membrane floated on water into which the crystalloids pass through the membrane, leaving the colloids behind.

1861 GRAHAM in *Phil. Trans.* 186 The vessel described (dialyser) is then floated in a basin containing a considerable quantity of water. 1861 *N. & Q.* 7 Dec., The Dialyser, invented by Thomas Graham, Esq., F.R.S., Master of the Mint, is an Apparatus for effecting Chemical Analysis by means of Liquid Diffusion. 1863–72 WATTS *Dict. Chem.* I. 316 A sheet of this parchment stretched on a hoop of thin wood or gutta percha forms a very convenient dialyser. 1864 H. SPENCER *Biol.* I. 20 Combined substances between which the affinity is feeble, will separate on the dialyzer.

b. *spec.* in *Med.* = HÆMODIALYSER.

1944 *Acta Medica Scandinavica* CXVII. 123 (*heading*) The artificial kidney: a dialyser with a great area. *Ibid.* 125 Blood may be let into or out of the patient and into or out of the dialyser. 1966 DUNLOP & ALSTEAD *Textbk. Med. Treatment* (ed. 10) 755 This device allows periodic access to blood vessels so that they may be connected to a suitable dialyser.

dialysis (daɪ'ælɪsɪs). Pl. dialyses. [a. Gr. διάλυσις separation, dissolution; f. διαλύειν to part asunder, f. δια- through, asunder + λύειν to loose.]

†1. *Rhet.* **a.** A statement of disjunctive propositions. **b.** = ASYNDETON. *Obs.*

1586 DAY *Eng. Secretary* II. (1625) 98 *Dialisis*, a separation of one thing from another, both being absolved by a severall reason, in the nature of a Dilemma, as thus.. If you remember it, I have said enough, if not, my words will not provoke you. 1589 PUTTENHAM *Eng. Poesie* III. xix. (Arb.) 230 A maner of speach [Dialisis, or the Dismembrer] not so figuratiue as fit for argumentation, and worketh not vnlike the dilemma of the Logicians. 1823 CRABB *Technol. Dict.*, *Dialysis*, (Rhet.)..i.e. asyndeton, a figure of speech in which several words are put together without being connected together by a conjunction, as *veni, vidi, vici*.

†2. *Gram.* = DIÆRESIS 1. *Obs.*

1727–51 CHAMBERS *Cycl.*, *Dialysis*, in grammar, a character, consisting of two points ¨ placed over two vowels of a word, which would otherwise make a diphthong; but are hereby parted into two syllables. As in Mosaïc. 1818 E. V. BLOMFIELD tr. *Matthiæ's Gram.* (1829) p. xlviii, 'Εέλπετο is not a dialysis of ἤλπετο but comes from ἐέλπομαι.

†3. *Med.* Dissolution of strength. *Obs.*

1823 CRABB *Technol. Dict.*, *Dialysis*..a dissolution of the strength, or a weakness of the limbs. 1883 *Syd. Soc. Lex.*, *Dialysis*, an old term for weakness of the muscles of the limbs.

4. *Path.* Solution of continuity.

1811 HOOPER *Dict.*, *Dialysis*, a solution of continuity, or a destruction of parts.

5. **a.** *Chem.* A name given by Graham to a process of separating the soluble crystalloid substances in a mixture from the colloid by filtration through a parchment membrane floating in water. In wider use: any process in which particles of different kinds are selectively removed from a liquid as a consequence of differences in their capacity to pass through a membrane into another liquid.

1861 GRAHAM in *Phil. Trans.* 186 It may perhaps be allowed me to apply the convenient term *dialysis* to the method of separating by diffusion through a septum of gelatinous matter. 1864 *Reader* 22 Oct. 516 (*heading*), On the Detection of Poisons by Dialysis. 1878 FOSTER *Phys.* II. i. 194 By dialysis it may be still further purified. 1950 KIRK & OTHMER *Encycl. Chem. Technol.* V. 15 The most important field for dialysis today is the recovery of caustic soda from industrial wastes and the refining of crude caustic.

comb. 1869 E. A. PARKES *Pract. Hygiene* (ed. 3) 197 Place the filtered brine in a bladder or vessel of the prepared dialysis-parchment.

b. *spec.* in *Med.* The process of allowing blood to flow past a suitable membrane on the other side of which is another liquid, so that certain dissolved substances in the blood may pass through the membrane and the blood itself be purified or cleansed in cases of renal failure, poisoning, etc.; the dialysis may take place outside the body in an artificial kidney or inside it using a natural membrane such as the peritoneum. Also, an occasion of undergoing this process.

1914 *Jrnl. Pharmacol. & Exper. Therap.* V. III. 276 We have devised a method by which the blood of a living animal may be submitted to dialysis outside the body, and again returned to the natural circulation. 1944 [see DIALYSE *v.* b]. 1953 J. A. LUETSCHER in Smith & Wermer *Mod. Treatment* xix. 414 Potassium Intoxication... Efforts may be made to eliminate potassium from the body by dialysis (artificial kidney or intestinal or peritoneal dialysis) if the situation is urgent. 1966 DUNLOP & ALSTEAD *Textbk. Med. Treatment* (ed. 10) 750 Such patients may require several dialyses with the artificial kidney. 1968 *Listener* 11 July 42/1 The system of treatment is known as haemodialysis, or more simply dialysis. It is a way of cleaning the blood by external means. 1970 R. W. MCGILVERY *Biochem.* xxvii. 669 The accumulation [of urea in the blood] can be relieved by dialysis, now sometimes performed by simply flushing large volumes of fluid through the peritoneal cavity.

dialytic (daɪə'lɪtɪk), *a.* [ad. Gr. διαλυτικός able to dissolve, f. διάλυτος separated, dissolved, f. διαλύειν: see DIALYSIS.]

1. *Chem.* Of the nature of or pertaining to chemical dialysis.

1861 GRAHAM in *Phil. Trans.* 186 The most suitable of all substances for the dialytic septum appears to be the commercial material known as vegetable parchment or parchment paper. 1867 J. ATTFIELD *Chem.* (1885) 813 Dialysed iron or dialytic iron. 1876 *Catal. Sci. App. S. Kens. Mus.* §2546 Experiments on absorption and dialytic separation of gases by colloid septa.

†2. *Med.* 'Relating or pertaining to dialysis (sense 3); relaxing.' *Syd. Soc. Lex.* 1883. *Obs.*

3. *Geol.* and *Min.* (See quot.)

1877 A. H. GREEN *Phys. Geol.* iii. §1. 93 Those derivative rocks, which have been formed not by the mechanical wear and tear of pre-existing rocks, but by the chemical decomposition of their constituents, are sometimes called Dialytic.

4. *Math.* Of or pertaining to the differentiation of equations by the process of dissolution described in the quotation.

1853 SYLVESTER in *Phil. Trans.* CXLIII. I. 544 *Dialytic.* If there be a system of functions containing in each term different combinations of the powers of the variables in number equal to the number of the functions, a resultant may be formed from these functions, by, as it were, dissolving the relations which connect together the different combinations of the powers of the variables, and treating them as simple independent quantities linearly involved in the functions. The resultant so formed is called the Dialytic

Resultant of the functions supposed; and any method by which the elimination between two or more equations can be made to depend on the formation of such a resultant is called a dialytic method of elimination.

5. *dialytic telescope*: a telescope in which achromatism is effected by means of two lenses separated and placed at some distance from each other.

1846 E. WEST tr. *Peschel's Elem. Physics* II. 136 Prof. Littrow of Vienna in 1827..proposed that the telescope should be fitted up with its proper object glass of crown glass; and that a flint glass lens, of much smaller diameter, should be placed at a proper distance behind the former, to counteract the prismatic dispersion of the rays. The name of dialytic telescopes was given to these instruments.

dia'lytically, *adv.* [f. DIALYTIC + -AL[1] + -LY[2].] By way of dialysis; by the dialytic method of elimination in mathematics.

1873 G. SALMON *Higher Plane Curves* 29 The actual elimination of λ is easily performed dialytically.

†**di'alyton.** *Rhet. Obs.* [L., a. Gr. τὸ διάλυτον, subst. use of διάλυτος: see DIALYTIC.] = DIALYSIS 1 b.

1657 J. SMITH *Myst. Rhet.* 182 Dialyton..is all one with Asyndeton. **1706** PHILLIPS (ed. Kersey), *Dialyton*, a Rhetorical Figure, when several Words are put together without any Conjunction Copulative. **1721** in BAILEY.

diamagnet (ˌdaɪəˈmægnɪt). [f. DIA- *pref.*[1] + MAGNET; cf. next.] = DIAMAGNETIC *sb.*

1864 in WEBSTER. **1871** TYNDALL *Fragm. Sc.* (1879) I. xiii. 380 Each man walking over the earth's surface is a true diamagnet.

diamagnetic (ˌdaɪəmægˈnɛtɪk), *a.* and *sb.* [f. Gr. δια- DIA- *pref.*[1] through, across + MAGNETIC.

Introduced by Faraday in 1846, first as sb., and then as adj.]

A. *adj.*

1. Of a body or substance: Exhibiting the phenomena of DIAMAGNETISM; the opposite of *magnetic* or *paramagnetic*.

A *diamagnetic* substance in the form of a bar or the like, when suspended freely and exposed to magnetic force, takes an *equatorial* position, i.e. at right angles to the lines of the force; a *paramagnetic* (or *magnetic*) substance takes an *axial* position, i.e. in the direction of those lines.

1846 FARADAY *Exper. Res. in Electr.* in *Phil. Trans.* I. 42 §2348 The metals which are magnetic retain a portion of their power after the great change has been effected, or in what might be called their diamagnetic state. **1849** MRS. SOMERVILLE *Connect. Phys. Sc.* xxxiii. 369 Substances affected after the manner of bismuth [when suspended between the poles of an electro-magnet] are said to be diamagnetic. **1863–72** WATTS *Dict. Chem.* III. 777 The same body may appear magnetic or diamagnetic, according to the medium in which it is placed. **1892** *Suppl. to Lightning* 7 Jan. 9 Diamagnetic substances are those through which magnetic effects are transmitted less readily than through air.

2. Belonging or relating to diamagnetic bodies, or to diamagnetism.

1846 FARADAY *Exper. Res. Electr.* in *Phil. Trans.* I. 26 §2270, As I have called air, glass, water, etc. diamagnetics (2149), so I will distinguish these lines by the term *diamagnetic curves*, both in relation to and contradistinction from the lines called magnetic curves. **1851** H. MAYO *Pop. Superst.* (ed. 2) 190 Od-force, which its discoverer now holds to be the same with the diamagnetic influence. **1855** H. SPENCER *Princ. Psychol.* (1872) I. I. iv. 69 Altering the direction of diamagnetic polarity in metals.

B. *sb.* A body or substance exhibiting the phenomena of DIAMAGNETISM.

1846 FARADAY *Exper. Res. Electr.* in *Phil. Trans.* I. 2 §2149 By a *diamagnetic*, I mean a body through which lines of magnetic force are passing, and which by their action does not assume the usual magnetic state of iron or loadstone. *Ibid.* 3 §2152 A piece of this glass, about two inches square and 0·5 of an inch thick, having flat and polished edges, was placed as a *diamagnetic* between the poles. **1871** TYNDALL *Fragm. Sc.* (1879) I. xiii. 375 The body used to excite this diamagnetic.

diamag'netically, *adv.* [f. prec. + -AL[1] + -LY[2].] In the manner of a diamagnetic body, or of diamagnetism. Also *fig.*

1850 GROVE *Corr. Phys. Forces* (ed. 2) 88 Their optic axis points diamagnetically or transversely to the lines of magnetic force. **1871** TYLOR *Prim. Cult.* II. 338 The influence of the divine Sun..still subsists as a mechanical force, acting diamagnetically to adjust the axis of the church and turn the body of the worshipper.

diamagnetism (ˌdaɪəˈmægnɪtɪz(ə)m). [f. DIA-[1] + MAGNETISM, after *diamagnetic.*] **a.** The phenomena exhibited by a class of bodies, which, when freely suspended and acted on by magnetism, take up a position transverse to that of the magnetic axis, i.e. lie (approximately) east and west; the force to which these phenomena are attributed; the quality of being diamagnetic. **b.** That branch of the science of magnetism which treats of diamagnetic bodies and phenomena.

1850 W. GREGORY *Lett. Anim. Magnetism* p. xv, He does indeed propose to include under the general term Magnetism two forms of it; viz. Paramagnetism..and Diamagnetism. **1854** J. SCOFFERN in *Orr's Circ. Sc.* Chem. 273 The..beginning of the science of dia-magnetism. **1873** WATTS *Fownes' Chem.* (ed. 11) 88 Diamagnetism must be regarded as a force distinct from magnetism. **1877** LE CONTE *Elem. Geol.* (1879) 184 Apparent diamagnetism of cleaved slates under certain conditions.

diamagnetize (ˌdaɪəˈmægnɪtaɪz), *v.* [f. DIA-[1] + MAGNETIZE, after *diamagnetic.*] *trans.* To render diamagnetic; to cause to exhibit diamagnetism.

1877 MILLER & MCLEOD *Elem. Chem.* I. (ed. 6) 677 The bismuth bars..will become diamagnetized.

Hence **diaˌmagneti'zation**, the action of diamagnetizing, or condition of being diamagnetized.

In mod. Dicts.

diaˌmagne'tometer. [f. DIAMAGNET(ISM) + Gr. μέτρον, after *magnetometer.*] An instrument for measuring diamagnetic force.

1886 WORMELL tr. *Von Urbanitzky's Elect. in Serv. Man* (1890) 180 Weber constructed an instrument, the diamagnetometer, by means of which he measured the magnetic moment of bismuth.

diamand(e, -mant, -maund(e, etc., obs. ff. DIAMOND.

‖**diamanté** (diːəˈmɑ̃te). [Fr., pa. pple. of *diamanter* to set with diamonds, to make shine like diamonds.] Material to which a sparkling effect is given by the use of paste brilliants, powdered glass or crystal, etc. Also *attrib.*

1904 *Daily Chron.* 3 May 6/4 The duchess was in black with diamanté wings in her hair. **1909** *Ibid.* 20 Mar. 4/6 A long stole-like panel of crystal and diamanté embroidery. *Ibid.* 18 Aug. 4/5 Garnitures of pale blue silk embroidery and diamanté. **1923** *Weekly Dispatch* 29 Apr. 15 The gown being draped Greek fashion and trimmed with bands of diamanté. **1955** *Times* 20 May 12/5 A high-necked fitted bodice fastened with diamanté buttons.

diamantiferous (ˌdaɪəmænˈtɪfərəs), *a.* [f. after mod.F. *diamantifère*, f. F. *diamant* DIAMOND: see -FEROUS.] Diamond-producing.

1878 in *Academy* 14 Sept., The diamantiferous sands of the valleys. **1880** CLERKE in *Fraser's Mag.* 822 The diamantiferous districts of Brazil.

diamantine (daɪəˈmæntɪn), *a.* and *sb.* [a. F. *diamantin* (16th c. in Littré), f. *diamant* DIAMOND: see -INE.] **A.** *adj.*

1. Consisting of, or of the nature of, diamond; containing or producing diamonds.

1605 TIMME *Quersit.* I. xii. 49 That he might reduce the more pure and ethereall mercury..into a christalline and dyamantine substance. **1676** *Phil. Trans.* XI. 755 Iron-hooks, with which they fetch out the Diamantin-oar. **1827** MONTGOMERY *Pelican Isl.* IX. 149 Day after day he pierced the dark abyss..Till he had reach'd its diamantine floor.

†**2.** Hard as diamond, adamantine. *Obs.*

1591 SYLVESTER *Du Bartas* I. iv. (1641) 35/2 Destinies hard Diamantine Rock. *a* **1649** DRUMM. OF HAWTH. *Poems* Wks. (1711) 29 Doors of eternity, With diamantine barrs.

B. *sb.*

1. A preparation of adamantine or crystallized boron, used as a polishing powder for steel work.

1884 F. J. BRITTEN *Watch & Clockm.* 86 A name may be removed from an enamel dial by gently rubbing it with a little fine diamantine on the point of the finger. **1889** *Ibid.*, *Diamantine*, a preparation of crystallized boron much esteemed as a polishing powder for steel work.

2. ? A fabric with diamond-shaped pattern.

1832 *East Anglian* 21 Feb. (in *Queen* 19 May 1883), Corderetts, diamantines, chiveretts.

†**di'amber.** *Pharm. Obs.* Also **diambre, diambar.** [a. F. *diambre*, in med.L. *diambra*: see DIA-[2] and AMBER.] An old stomachic and cordial containing ambergris, musk, and other aromatics.

1558–68 WARDE tr. *Alexis' Secr.* 10 a, He made her also eate the confection of Diambre. **1608** MIDDLETON *Mad World* III. ii, Mixed in a stone or glass mortar with the spirit of diamber.

diamesogamous (ˌdaɪəmɪˈsɒgəməs), *a. Bot.* [f. Gr. διάμεσον the intervening part (f. διά through + μέσο-ς middle) + γάμ-ος marriage + -OUS.] Of flowers: Fertilized by the intervention of some external agency, as that of insects or the wind.

[**1883** D'ARCY THOMPSON tr. *Müller's Fertil. Flowers* 14 Plants which require external aid to bring their reproductive elements together are termed 'Diamesogamæ'.]

diametarily, erroneous f. DIAMETRALLY.

diameter (daɪˈæmɪtə(r)). Also 4–6 **diametre.** [a. OF. *dia-*, *dyametre* (13th c. in Littré; mod.F. *diamètre*), ad. L. *diametrus*, *-os*, a. Gr. διάμετρος (*sc.* γραμμή line) diagonal of a parallelogram, diameter of a circle, f. διά through, across + μέτρον measure.]

1. *Geom.* A straight line passing through the centre of a circle (or sphere), and terminated at each end by its circumference (or surface). Hence extended to a chord of any conic (or of a quadric surface) passing through the centre; and further, to a line passing through the middle points of a system of parallel chords (or through the centres of mean distances of their points of intersection with the curve), in a curve of any order. **b.** The DIAGONAL of a parallelogram. (*obs.*) **c.** *gen.* A line passing from side to side of any body through the centre.

1387 TREVISA *Higden* (Rolls) VII. 71 Þe dyameter [of] a figure [is] þe lengest even lyne þat is devysed þerynne, take who þat may. **1551** RECORDE *Pathw. Knowl.* I. Def., And all the lines that bee drawen crosse the circle, and goe by the centre, are named diameters. **1551** —— *Cast. Knowl.* (1556) 18 Euery right lyne that passeth from side to syde in a globe, and toucheth the centre, is aptely called a diameter. **1635** N. CARPENTER *Geog. Del.* I. v. 110 All the Diameters of the world concurre, and cut one the other in the Center. **1660** BARROW *Euclid* I. Def. xxxvi, In a parallelogram, when a diameter..[is] drawn. **1726–7** SWIFT *Gulliver* II. iv. 129, I paced the diameter and circumference several times. **1796** HUTTON *Math. Dict.* s.v., *Diameter, of any Curve*, is a right line which divides two other parallel right lines, in such manner that, in each of them, all the segments or ordinates on one side, between the diameter and different points of the curve, are equal to all those on the other side. This is Newton's sense of a Diameter. But, according to some, a diameter is that line, whether right or curved, which bisects all the parallels drawn from one point to another of a curve. **1831** R. KNOX *Cloquet's Anat.* 35 The Thorax..is measured by means of certain ideal lines, named its diameters, which pass from the sternum to the vertebral column, or from one side to the other. All the diameters are greater below than above. **1885** LEUDESDORF *Cremona's Proj. Geom.* 217 If any number of parallel chords of a conic be drawn, the locus of their middle points is a straight line..This straight line is termed the diameter of the chords which it bisects.

¶ In some editions of Lydgate's *Balade of our Ladie* 87 'dyametre' is misprinted for 'dyamaunt': see Skeat *Chaucerian Pieces* 278, MacCracken *Minor Poems of Lydgate* I. 258.

2. The transverse measurement of any geometrical figure or body; the length of a straight line drawn from side to side through the centre, *esp.* of a circle or body of circular, spherical, or cylindrical form; width; thickness.

c **1391** CHAUCER *Astrol.* II. §38 Let this pyn be no lengere than a quarter of the diametre of thi compas. **1557** RECORDE *Whetst.* iv. b, A Gonne of sixe inches diameter in the mouthe. *a* **1635** CORBET *Poems* 192 The just proportion..Of the diameter and circumference. **1703** MOXON *Mech. Exerc.* 273 A Chimny, whose Diameter between the Jambs is eight feet. **1774** GOLDSM. *Nat. Hist.* (1776) VIII. 106 [A wasp] boring a hole..not much wider than the diameter of its own body. **1812–6** J. SMITH *Panorama Sc. & Art* I. 312 The power and the weight will balance each other, when the power bears the same proportion to the weight that the diameter of the axis bears to the diameter of the wheel. **1868** LOCKYER *Elem. Astron.* ii. (1879) 39 The diameter of the Sun is 853,380 miles.

†**b.** *ellipt.* with numeral expressions: = *of* (such a) *diameter*, or = *in diameter* (4 a). *Obs.*

1663 GERBIER *Counsel* 69 Balls twelve inches Diameter. **1718** LADY M. W. MONTAGU *Let. to C'tess Bristol* 10 Apr., The dome..is said to be one hundred and thirteen feet diameter. **1825** J. NICHOLSON *Operat. Mechanic* 191 Some ..were not more that $3\frac{1}{2}$ inches diameter.

†**c.** *Geom.* The length of the diagonal of a parallelogram. *Obs.* †**d.** *Arith.* A number that is the square root of the sum of the squares of the two factors of a DIAMETRAL number (and hence may be represented by the diagonal of a rectangle whose sides are proportional to these factors, the rectangle itself representing the 'diametral number'). *Obs.*

1557 RECORDE *Whetst.* Dj, 17 is the diameter to that diametralle number 120 [= 8 × 15]. *Ibid.*, 5 is the diameter of that platte forme.

e. *Arch.* The transverse measurement of a column at its base, taken as a unit of measurement for the proportions of an order.

1604 DRAYTON *Owle* 629 Of Columnes the Diameters doth tell. **1727–51** CHAMBERS *Cycl.* s.v., *Diameter of a Column*, is its thickness just above the base. From this the module is taken, which measures all the other parts of the column. *Diameter of the Diminution*, is that taken from the top of the shaft. *Diameter of the Swelling*, is that taken at the height of one-third from the base. **1842–76** GWILT *Archit.* III. i. §2556 Vitruvius in this order [the Tuscan] forms the columns six diameters high, and makes their diminution one quarter of the diameter. **1850** LEITCH *Müller's Anc. Art* §54 The columns in the temple of Ephesus were eight diameters high.

f. As a unit of linear measurement of the magnifying power of a lens or microscope. (Cf. also quot. 1665 in 4 a.)

1856 EMERSON *Eng. Traits, First Visit* Wks. (Bohn) II. 3 His microscopes, magnifying two thousand diameters.

g. Whole extent from side to side or from end to end.

1602 SHAKS. *Ham.* IV. i. 41 [Slander], whose whisper o'er the world's diameter, As level as the cannon to his blank, Transports his poison'd shot. *c* **1645** HOWELL *Lett.* I. VI. xxxviii. 261, I have traversed the Diameter of France more than once.

†**3.** The diametrical or direct opposite; contrariety, contradiction. Also *ellipt.* = *in diameter* 4 b. *Obs.*

1579 J. STUBBES *Gaping Gulf* A v, What a diameter of religion were it for vs dwelling among Christians, to admit from ouer sea, the sons of men in mariage? **1661** GLANVILL *Vanity of Dogmatizing* 76, I shall not undertake to maintain the Paradox, that stands diameter to this almost Catholic opinion.

4. Phrases. ***in diameter.*** **a.** *lit.* in sense 2 (with numerals, etc.): In measurement across through the centre; in width or thickness. (Formerly also ***in the diameter.***)

1577 DEE *Relat. Spir.* I. (1659) 356 A trunk of fire, which ..seemeth to be 4 foot over in the Diameter. **1665** *Phil. Trans.* I. 60 It would magnifie but 600 times in Diameter. *a***1719** ADDISON *Italy* (T.), The bay of Naples..lies in almost a round figure of about thirty miles in the diameter. **1858** HOGG *Veg. Kingd.* 110 The fruit hangs from the tree [baobab] by a stalk two feet long and an inch in diameter.

†**b.** Diametrically, directly (with words denoting opposition or contrariety); in direct opposition. [After Gr. ἐκ διαμέτρου ἀντικεῖσθαι to lie diametrically opposite.] (Usually *fig.*) Also (in lit. sense) ***by a diameter***. *Obs.* (Cf. DIAMETRICAL 2, 2 b.)

1543 TRAHERON *Vigo's Chirurg.* VI. i. 181 By flebothomie on the contrary syde by a diameter. **1598** B. JONSON *Ev. Man in Hum.* IV. vii, To come to a publike schoole..it was opposite (in diameter) to my humour. **1643** MILTON *Divorce* II. xxi. (1851) 122 To hinder..those deep and serious regresses of nature..is in diameter against both nature and institution. **1643** SIR T. BROWNE *Relig. Med.* I. §3 To stand in diameter and swords point with them. *Ibid.* I. §51 It is not worthy to stand in diameter with Heaven.

†**c.** ***in a diameter***: in a direct line, directly. *Obs.* (Cf. DIAMETRICALLY 3.)

*a***1681** J. LACY *Sir H. Buffoon* I. Dram. Wks. (1875) 228 Deriving our pedigree in a diameter from the best blood of Europe.

Hence **di'ametered** *a.*, of a (specified) diameter.

1707 SLOANE *Jamaica* I. 57 A two or three inch long diameter'd broad woody pedestal. *Ibid.* 63 A foot diameter'd, large, broad, roundish root.

†**di'ameterly,** *adv. Obs. rare.* [f. prec. + -LY[2].] = DIAMETRICALLY 2 b.

1603 FLORIO *Montaigne* III. ix. (1632) 560 Libertie and idlenesse..are qualities diameterly contrary to that mysterie. **1633** AMES *Agst. Cerem.* II. 518 So diameterly contrary to it.

†**di'ameter-wise,** *adv. Obs.* = prec.

1600 W. VAUGHAN *Direct. Health* (1633) 133 Being diameter-wise repugnant to our Makers commandment.

diametral (daɪ'æmɪtrəl), *a.* and *sb.* [a. OF. *dyametral* (14th c. in Godef. *Suppl.*; mod.F. *diamétral*), ad. med.L. *diametrālis*, f. *diametrus* DIAMETER: see -AL[1].] **A.** *adj.*

1. Of or relating to a diameter; of the nature of or constituting a diameter.

diametral plane: (*a*) *Geom.* a plane passing through the centre of a sphere or other solid; (*b*) *Cryst.* a plane passing through two of the axes of a crystal (see DIAMETRIC 1).

1555 EDEN *Decades* 6 An other Ilande..whose *Diametral* syde extendynge frome the Easte to the weste, they iudged to bee a hundreth and fyftie myle. **1668** CULPEPPER & COLE *Barthol. Anat.* II. iii. 90 The Diametral wideness of the lower Belly. **1676** MOXON *Print Lett.* 46 Through this Circle draw a..Diametral line. **1833** HERSCHEL *Astron.* iii. 151 In the orthographic projection, every point of the hemisphere is referred to its diametral plane or base. **1865** W. S. ALDIS *Elem. Solid Geom.* vi. (1886) 85 The locus of the middle points of a system of parallel chords of a surface is called the diametral surface of the system. **1877** HUXLEY *Anat. Inv. Anim.* iii. 162 The diametral folds of the oral aperture. **1881** MAXWELL *Electr. & Magn.* I. 12 A diameter of an ellipsoid and its conjugate diametral plane.

†**b.** Forming, or situated in, a straight line. *Obs.*

1594 BLUNDEVIL *Exerc.* III. I. xv. (ed. 7) 307 When the Sunne, the Earth, and the Moone be met in one selfe diametrall line. **1647** H. MORE *Song of Soul* I. I. xlvii, The Sunne and Moon combine, Then they're at ods in site Diametrall.

†**2.** *Arith.* ***diametral number***: one that is the product of two factors the sum of whose squares is a square. (Cf. DIAMETER 2 d.) *Obs.*

Thus $3^2 + 4^2 = 5^2$; then $3 \times 4 = 12$ is a diametral number.

1557 RECORDE *Whetst.* C iv b. **1674** JEAKE *Arith.* (1696) 179 Diametral numbers..are produced as Oblongs, by multiplying their proper parts together. *Ibid.* 181 All Diametral Numbers do set forth a Plain Rectangled Triangle, having all 3 Sides known.

†**3.** = DIAMETRICAL 2. *Obs.*

1628 DONNE *Serm.* lxxii. 726 There is not so direct and Diametrall a contrariety between the Nature of any Sinne and God, as betweene him and Pride. **1641** LD. J. DIGBY *Sp. in Ho. Com.* 21 Apr. 11, I see the best Lawyers in diametrall opposition. **1666** SANCROFT *Lex Ignea* 22 Your own Oppositions direct and Diametral to God. **1768** *Life Sir Barth. Sapskull* I. 56 The genius of pleasure is a diametral contradiction to the spirit of trade and commerce.

†**B.** *sb. Obs.*

1. A diametral line, diameter.

1658 SIR T. BROWNE *Gard. Cyrus* iii. 56 The incession or locall motion of animals is made..by decussative diametrals, Quincunciall Lines and angles. **1676** MOXON *Print Lett.* 47 Through the Diametral *c, d,* draw another Diametral line.

2. A diametral number: see A. 2.

1674 JEAKE *Arith.* (1696) 184 If 540, or 432, etc. be Diametrals, then 54,000 and 43,200 be the like.

di'ametrally, *adv.* [f. prec. + -LY[2].]

1. In the way of a diameter; in a line passing through the centre.

[**1486** *Bk. St. Albans, Her.* F iv b, The lawiste parte extendys to the lawist parte of the shelde dyametralit[er].] **1589** PUTTENHAM *Eng. Poesie* II. (Arb.) 111 Ouerthwart and dyametrally from one side of the circle to the other. *a***1638** MEDE *View Apoc.* Wks. v. 917 Which Beasts are here said to be 'in the midst of the Throne' and 'round about the Throne', that is, diametrally placed round about the Throne. **1882** PROCTOR in *Longm. Mag.* Dec. 193 Meteoric streamers extending apparently diametrally from the sun.

†**2.** Directly, in a straight line. *Obs.* (Cf. DIAMETRAL 1 b.)

1604 E. G. *D'Acosta's Hist. Indies* I. 6 When as the roundnesse of the earth opposeth itselfe diametrally betwixt her [the moon] and the sunne. **1616** MARLOWE *Faust.* iv. 73 Let thy left eye be diametrally [Q. **1604** diametarily] fixed on my right heel.

†**3. a.** *lit.* = DIAMETRICALLY 2 a. *Obs.*

1563 FULKE *Meteors* (1640) 376 The center..of the Rayne-bow is Diametrally opposite to the center [of the Sun]. **1594** BLUNDEVIL *Exerc.* III. I. xv. (ed. 7) 307 The Moone [is] said to be diametrally opposite to the Sunne.. When a right line drawne from the Center of the Sunne, to the Center of the Moon, passeth thorow the Center of the earth. **1652** GAULE *Magastr.* 4 a, There are yet in Heaven two Stars Diametrally opposite one to the other.

†**b.** *fig.* = DIAMETRICALLY 2 b. *Obs.*

*c***1532** DEWES *Introd. Fr.* in *Palsgr.* 1077 Coldenes and drinesse..ben diametrally opposite and contrary to hete and moisture. **1630** PRYNNE *Anti-Armin.* 2 Diametrally repugnant to the anciently established..Doctrine. **1647** CUDWORTH *Serm. on 1 S. John* ii. 3-4 One that should encourage that..which is diametrally opposite to God's.. Being.

diametric (daɪə'mɛtrɪk), *a.* [ad. Gr. διαμετρικός, f. διάμετρος DIAMETER: see -IC.]

1. Relating to or of the nature of a diameter; diametral.

1868 DANA *Min.* Introd. (1880) 20 By a diametric plane or section..is meant a plane passing through any two of the crystallographic axes.

2. Of opposition or the like: = DIAMETRICAL 2.

1802 H. MARTIN *Helen of Glenross* IV. 51 She is..the diametric reverse of her sister Lady Clavington. **1886** J. A. ALDIS in *Academy* 3 July 2/2 The diametric, the irreconcilable, discord between James Hinton and 'Church teaching'.

diametrical (daɪə'mɛtrɪkəl), *a.* [f. as prec. + -AL[1].]

1. Of, pertaining to, or of the nature of a diameter; passing through or along a diameter; diametral.

1553 EDEN *Treat. Newe Ind.* Ep. to Rdr. (Arb.) 10 They were..antipodes, walking feete to feete one agaynste the other, almost as directly as a diametrical lyne. **1615** MARKHAM *Pleas. Princes, Angling* iii. (1635) 16 He should have knowledge in proportions of all sorts, whether Circular, square, or Diametricall. **1730** A. GORDON *Maffei's Amphith.* 291 The diametrical Passage following cross-ways. **1864** H. SPENCER *Illustr. Univ. Progr.* 282 A current proceeding in a diametrical direction from the equator to the centre.

2. Of opposition or the like: Direct, entire, complete (like that of two points on a circle at opposite ends of a diameter: cf. DIAMETER 4 b). Usually *fig.*

1613 JACKSON *Creed* II. 221 The Diametricall opposition betwixt the spirit of God and the Spirit of the Papacie. **1642** FULLER *Holy & Prof. St.* III. xx. 207 The East and West Indies..whose names speak them at diametricall opposition. **1753** SMOLLETT *Ct. Fathom* (1784) 29/1 Advice improperly administered generally acts in diametrical opposition to the purpose for which it is supposed to be given. **1874** H. R. REYNOLDS *John Bapt.* iv. §1. 247 The diametrical difference between the Talmud and Christianity.

†**b.** Directly or completely opposed, either in nature or result. *Obs.*

1647 SALTMARSH *Sparkl. Glory* (1847) 117 When Christians are under several forms and administrations, and these diametrical, or opposite to each other. **1670** G. H. *Hist. Cardinals* I. II. 55 The two profest diametrical Enemies of those virtues. *a***1734** NORTH *Exam.* I. ii. §31 (1740) 46 The Revolution was very quick and diametrical.

†**c.** quasi-*adv.* = DIAMETRICALLY 2. *Obs.*

1653 J. CHETWIND *Dead Speaking* 16 Such diametrical opposite effects..from the same cause.

dia'metrically, *adv.* [f. prec. + -LY[2].]

1. In the manner or direction of a diameter; along the diameter; straight through.

1695 WOODWARD *Nat. Hist. Earth* III. i. (1723) 137 The Vapour..cannot penetrate the Stratum diametricaly. **1794** T. TAYLOR *Pausanias* III. 95 Its breadth, measured diametrically, may be conjectured to be about four cubits. **1826** SCOTT *Mal. Malagr.* i. 53 This true course cannot always be followed out straight and diametrically. **1889** *Nature* 7 Nov. 13 The molecules, which he represents diametrically.

2. In the way of direct or complete opposition. Usually with ***opposite***, ***opposed***, ***contrary***: Directly, exactly, entirely, completely. (Cf. prec. 2.) **a.** *lit.* of physical opposition.

*c***1645** HOWELL *Lett.* (1650) I. I. xxvii. 44 Two white keen-pointed rocks, that lie under water diametrically opposed. **1726** tr. *Gregory's Astron.* I. 13 This Planet will not always attend the Sun, but sometimes be diametrically opposite to it. **1870** R. M. FERGUSON *Electr.* 32 These points are not diametrically opposite each other.

b. *fig.* (The usual sense.)

1633 T. ADAMS *Exp. 2 Peter* ii. 10 Vice cannot consist with virtue, because it is diametrically opposite. **1672** CLARENDON *Ess.* Tracts (1727) 241 That men of equal learning..integrity and..piety, should differ so diametrically from each other. **1799** J. ROBERTSON *Agric. Perth* 397 It is diametrically contrary to the genius of the British constitution. **1856** FROUDE *Hist. Eng.* I. 118 That the positions of England and Spain toward the papacy would be diametrically changed. **1872** MINTO *Eng. Prose Lit.* I. i. 51 Two kinds of emotion..diametrically antagonistic.

†**3.** Directly, in an exact line (*with*); in the way of complete agreement. *Obs. rare.*

1661 *Sir H. Vane's Politics* 6 My Judgement runs diametrically with his.

†**diamictonic** (ˌdaɪəmɪk'tɒnɪk), *a.* and *sb. Min. Obs.* [f. Gr. *διαμικτός, vbl. adj. from διαμιγνύναι to mix up (cf. μικτός, f. μιγνύναι); after *plutonic*, etc.] Applied by Pinkerton to a 'domain' or division of minerals consisting of various substances intimately combined. **b.** as *sb.* A mineral belonging to this 'domain'.

1811 PINKERTON *Petral.* I. Introd., The remaining six domains, derived from circumstances or accidences, are..8. The Diamictonic, or rocks in which the substances are so completely mingled, that it is difficult..to pronounce which preponderates. **1814** *Edin. Rev.* XXIII. 73 The gross error which led to the foundation of the eighth Domain, or the Diamictonic as it is entitled. *Ibid.* 74 Forming an essential character in a system of Diamictonics.

diamide ('daɪəmaɪd). *Chem.* [f. DI-[2] + AMIDE.] An amide formed on the type of two molecules of Ammonia, the hydrogen of which is replaced partly or wholly by one or more acid radicals.

1866 E. FRANKLAND *Lect. Notes Chem. Stud.* 374 The diamides may be regarded as derived from two molecules of ammonia.

diamidine (daɪ'æmɪdiːn). *Chem.* [f. DI-[2] + AMIDE + -INE[5].] Any compound having a structure based on two amidine, $-C(NH)(NH_2)$, groups; usually, a compound in which these groups are joined by a chain of carbon atoms or two benzene rings or both.

1931 *Jrnl. Chem. Soc.* 2992 We have..tested the hypoglycæmic action of a series of diamidines of basic fatty acids of varying length of chain. **1956** *Nature* 31 Mar. 604/2 An entirely new group of chemotherapeutic drugs, the diamidines. **1968** J. H. BURN *Lect. Notes Pharmacol.* (ed. 9) 120 The early stage of infection by either species is treated by injections of diamidines.

dia'mido-. *Chem.* [DI-[2] + AMIDO-.] Having two atoms of hydrogen replaced by two of the radical Amidogen NH_2, as ***diamido-'benzene*** $C_6H_4(NH_2)_2$.

1880 FRISWELL in *Soc. of Arts* 446 We have thus produced diamidobenzene.

dia'midogen. *Chem.* See DI-[2] and AMIDOGEN.

1887 *Athenæum* 9 July 57/2 The preparation of a new compound of nitrogen and hydrogen..He [Curtius] terms it hydrazine or diamidogen. It has the composition expressed by the formula N_2H_4.

diamine ('daɪəmaɪn). *Chem.* [f. DI-[2] + AMINE.] An amine, or compound derived from two molecules of ammonia the hydrogen of which is replaced partly or wholly by one or more basic radicals, as ***ethene-diamine*** $\left.\begin{matrix}NH_2\\NH_2\end{matrix}\right\}C_2H_4$.

1866 E. FRANKLAND *Lect. Notes Chem. Stud.* 367 The diamines are formed by the coupling together two atoms of nitrogen in two molecules of ammonia. **1869** ROSCOE *Elem. Chem.* 362 Ethylene diamines are volatile bases obtained by acting with ammonia on ethylene dibromide.

diammo-, diammonio-. *Chem.* See DI-[2] 2, AMMO-, AMMONIO-.

1873 WATTS *Fownes' Chem.* (ed. 11) 424 The Diammonio-platinous and Tetrammonio-platinic Compounds. *Ibid.*, These tetrammonio-platinous compounds may also be regarded as salts of diammoplatoso-diammonium.

diamond ('daɪəmənd, 'daɪmənd), *sb.* Forms: *α.* 4-5 **dia-, dyamawnte,** 4-6 **-maunt,** 5-6 **dyamant,** 5-7 **diamant;** *β.* 4-5 **dia-, dya-, -maund(e, -mawnde, -mounde, -mownde,** 4-6 **-mand(e,** 5 **dyamonde, -mount, -monthe, deamond(e,** 5-6 **dyamont(e, diamonde,** 5-7 **dyamond,** 6 **diamont, -munde,** 6- **diamond;** *γ.* 7 **dimond,** 8 **di'mond.** [ME. *diamant, -aunt,* a. OF. *diamant* (= Pr. *diaman,* Cat. *diamant,* It. *diamanto,* OHG. *demant*), ad. late L. *diamas, diamant-em* (med.Gr. διαμάντε), an alteration of L. *adamas, -antem,* or perh. of its popular variant *adimant-em* (whence Pr. *adiman, aziman, ayman,* OFr. *aïmant*), app. under the influence of the numerous technical words beginning with the prefix DIA-, Gr. δια-.

The differentiation of form in late L. was probably connected with the double signification acquired by *adamas* of 'diamond' and 'loadstone' (see ADAMANT); for, in all the languages, *diamant* with its cognates was at length restricted to the gem, as *aimant* was in F. to the loadstone. In English the *dyamaund* and *adamaund* are distinguished from and opposed to each other *c* 1400 in Maundevile, ed. 1839, xiv. 161, ed. Roxb. Soc. xvii. 80; but *adamant* long retained the double sense of late L. *adamas*: thus Sherwood, 1623, has 'An Adamant stone, (F.) *aimant, diamant, calamite, pierre marinière*.' See ADAMANT.

The *a* of the middle syllable has tended to disappear since the 16th c., as shown by the spelling *di'mond, dimond.* Sheridan and other early orthoepists recognize the dissyllabic pronunciation, but most recent authorities reckon three syllables. In Shakspere the word is more frequently a trisyllable; but it is very generally dissyllabic in Pope, Thomson, Young, Cowper, Keats, and Tennyson.]

I. 1. a. A very hard and brilliant precious stone, consisting of pure carbon crystallized in regular octahedrons and allied forms (in the native state usually with convex surfaces), and either colourless or variously tinted. It is the most brilliant and valuable of precious stones, and the hardest substance known.

Diamonds are commonly cut in three forms, called TABLE, ROSE, and BRILLIANT: see these words. *plate diamond*, *point diamond*, *scratch diamond*: see quots. 1854, 1880, 1883.

a **1310** in Wright *Lyric P.* v. 25 A burde in a bour ase beryl so bryht, Ase diamaunde the dere in day when he is dyht. *c* **1386** CHAUCER *Knt.'s T.* 1289 Of fyne Rubyes and of dyamauntz [*v.r.* dyamauntis, diamantz]. *c* **1400** MAUNDEV. (Roxb.) xvii. 79 Men fyndez dyamaundes gude and hard apon þe roche of þe adamaund in þe see. *c* **1475** *Sqr. lowe Degre* 844 in Ritson *Romances* III. 180 Wyth dyamondes set and rubyes bryght. **1501** *Bury Wills* (Camden) 87 A ryng wt a dyamond therin. **1553** EDEN *Treat. Newe Ind.* Table (Arb.) 12 Of the Adamant stone, otherwise called the Diamant. **1593** SHAKS. *3 Hen. VI*, III. i. 63 My Crowne is in my heart, not on my head: Not deck'd with Diamonds, and Indian stones. **1607** —— *Timon* III. vi. 131 One day he giues vs Diamonds, next day stones. **1673** RAY *Journ. Low C.* 127 Diamants and other pretious Stones. **1727–46** THOMSON *Summer* 142 The lively diamond drinks thy purest rays. **1734** POPE *Ess. Man* IV. 10 Deep with di'monds in the flaming mine. **1750** D. JEFFRIES *Diamonds & Pearls* 58 The manufacture of Table and Rose Diamonds. **1833** N. ARNOTT *Physics* (ed. 5) II. I. 189 Diamond has nearly the greatest light-bending power of any known substances, and hence comes in part its brilliancy as a jewel. **1854** J. SCOFFERN in *Orr's Circ. Sc.* Chem. 9 The operation of scratching on glass may be conducted..with a variety of diamond, known as the *scratch diamond*, sold by this name on purpose. **1861** C. W. KING *Ant. Gems* (1866) 71 The diamond..has the peculiarity of becoming phosphorescent in the dark after long exposure to the rays of the sun. **1880** BIRDWOOD *Indian Arts* II. 30 When the natural crystal is so perfect and clear that it requires only to have its natural facets polished..jewellers call [it] a point diamond. **1883** M. F. HEDDLE in *Encycl. Brit.* XVI. 381/2 The cleavage of certain of the African diamonds is so eminent that even the heat of the hand causes some of them to fall in pieces. Such diamonds, generally octahedra, may be recognized by a peculiar watery lustre; they are called plate diamonds.

†**b.** As a substance of extreme hardness; = ADAMANT. *Obs.*

c **1400** *Rom. Rose* 4385 Herte as hard as dyamaunt, Stedefast, and nought pliaunt. **1590** SPENSER *F.Q.* I. vi. 4 As rock of Diamond stedfast evermore. **1642** MILTON *Apol. Smect.* ii, Zeal, whose substance is ethereal, arming in complete diamond, ascends his fiery chariot. **1656** HOBBES *Lib. Necess. & Chance* (1841) 304 Laid down upon the hardest body that could be, supposing it an anvil of diamant. **1667** MILTON *P.L.* VI. 364 On each wing Uriel and Raphael his vaunting foe, Though huge, and in a Rock of Diamond Armd, Vanquish'd.

c. *Her.* In blazoning by precious stones, the name for the tincture *sable* or black.

1572 BOSSEWELL *Armorie* II. 55 b, The field is parted per pale Nebule, Carboncle and Diamonde. **1766–87** PORNY *Her.* 19.

d. *pl.* Shares in a diamond-mine.

1905 *Daily Report* 22 Mar. 1/2 Lace Diamonds have been bought from Johannesburg. **1907** *Daily Chron.* 28 Oct. 1/7 In Mines diamonds declined. **1964** *Financial Times* 3 Mar. 19/4 Gold shares were irregular, while Diamonds were strong.

2. *transf.* Applied (usually with distinguishing epithet) to other crystalline minerals, resembling the diamond in brilliancy; as ***Bristol diamond***, ***Cornish diamond*** (see BRISTOL, CORNISH), ***Matura diamond***, ***Quebec diamond*** (see quots.).

1591 NASHE in Arber's *Garner* I. 501 If one wear Cornish diamonds on his toes. **1610** HOLLAND *Camden's Brit.* I. 239 St. Vincent's rock so full of Diamants that a man may fill whole strikes or bushels of them. **1665** HOOKE *Microgr.* 79 *Striæ* of Crystal, or like the small Diamants I observ'd in certain Flints. **1802** R. BROOKES *Gazetteer* (ed. 12), Piseck.. Bohemian diamonds are found here. **1886** S. M. BURNHAM *Precious Stones* 319 The variety [of zircon] obtained from Matura, Ceylon, where it is called 'Matura diamond,' is often sold in the bazaars of India for the genuine diamond. *Ibid.* 350 Rock Crystal..is recognized by various names, as Bristol, Welsh, Irish, Cornish, and California diamonds. **1890** G. F. KUNZ *Gems N. Amer.* 262 Small, doubly terminated crystals [of rock-crystal] found in the Limestone of the Levis and Hudson River formations, and locally called Quebec diamonds.

3. *fig.* **a.** Something very precious; a thing or person of great worth, or (in mod. use) a person of very brilliant attainments. (Cf. 7.)

c **1440** *York Myst.* xxv. 518 Hayll! Dyamaunde with drewry dight. **1526** *Pilgr. Perf.* (W. de W. 1531) 183 The diamonde moost precyous to mankynde, thy swete sone Jesus. **1597** *1st Pt. Return fr. Parnass.* III. i. 1043, I will bestowe upon them the precious stons of my witt, a diamonde of invention. **1651** *Reliq. Wotton.* 20 His second son, Walter Devereux..was indeed a dyamond of the time, and both of an hardy and delicate temper and mixture. **1888** FROUDE *Eng. in W. Ind.* 112 There are many diamonds, and diamonds of the first water, among the Americans as among ourselves.

b. Something that shines like a diamond; a glittering particle or point.

1814 SCOTT *Ld. of Isles* IV. xiii, Each puny wave in diamonds roll'd O'er the calm deep. **1862** SHIRLEY *Nugæ Crit.* i. 75 The grass is..covered with minute diamonds of white frost, which sparkle keenly in the winter light.

4. A tool consisting of a small diamond set in a handle, used for cutting glass; called distinctively ***glazier's diamond*** or ***cutting diamond***.

1697 *Lond. Gaz.* No. 3331/4 [He] took with him a valuable Glasier's Diamond. **1816** *Phil. Trans.* 266 Having procured a common glazier's diamond. **1831** J. MURRAY *Diamond* 37 Points are those minute fragments which are set in what are called glazier's cutting diamonds. **1875** URE *Dict. Arts* II. 28 The irregular octahedrons with round facets are those proper for glazier's diamonds.

5. a. A diamond-shaped figure, i.e. a plane figure of the form of a section of an octahedral diamond; a rhomb (or a square) placed with its diagonals vertical and horizontal; a lozenge. (In early use, a solid body of octahedral or rhombohedral form.)

1496 in *Ld. Treas. Acc. Scot.* I. 293 Item for a waw of irne, to be dyamondis for guncast, xxv. s. *Ibid.* 310 Item, giffin to Johne Smyth, for hedis to xij speris, and dyamandis to xxiiij justing speris xvj s. **1651** T. RUDD *Euclid* 11 Rombus, or a Diamond, is a figure having four equal sides, but is not right angled. **1831** BREWSTER *Nat. Magic* xi. (1833) 289 The rows were placed so that the flowers formed what are called diamonds. **1842** S. C. HALL *Ireland* II. 462 'The Diamond', a term frequently used in the Northern Counties, to indicate an assemblage of buildings which, taken together, are diamond-shaped. **1889** KENNAN in *Century Mag.* XXXVIII. 167/2 Convicts in long gray overcoats with yellow diamonds on their backs. *Mod.* (*Mercantile Letter*) 'We send you Bill of Lading of 2 bales Wool, mark L in a diamond.'

b. *spec.* A figure of this form printed upon a playing-card; a card of the suit marked with such figures.

1594 LYLY *Moth. Bomp.* III. iv, My bed-fellow..dreamt that night that the king of diamonds was sick. **1598** FLORIO, *Quadri*, squares, those that we call diamonds or picts upon playing cards. **1680** COTTON *Gamester* in Singer *Hist. Cards* 340 The ace of diamonds. **1710** *Brit. Apollo* III. No. 71. 2/2 The Nine of Diamonds is..call'd the Curse of Scotland. **1712–14** POPE *Rape Lock* III. 75 Clubs, Diamonds, Hearts, in wild disorder seen. **1820** PRAED *To Julia* 78 As if eternity were laid Upon a diamond, or a spade. **1870** HARDY & WARE *Mod. Hoyle* 150 Single Besique is composed of a Knave of Diamonds and a Queen of Spades laid upon the table.. together. This scores 40.

c. A kind of stitch in fancy needlework.

1882 CAULFEILD & SAWARD *Dict. Needlework* 152 *Diamond*, a stitch used in Macramé lace to vary the design.. There are three ways of making Diamonds; The Single.. The Double..and the Treble.

d. The square figure formed by the four bases in the game of base-ball; also, by extension, applied to the whole field. (*U.S.*)

1875 *Cincinnati Enquirer* 6 July 4/5 In the last seven innings the ball hardly got outside the diamond. **1894** *Boston* (Mass.) *Jrnl.* 25 Feb. 3/7 Rulers of the Diamond. The National Base Ball League.

e. In a bicycle, the diamond-shaped frame of steel tubing. More fully ***diamond frame***. (Now disused.)

1891 *Young Man* Apr. p. ii/2 (Advt.), Safety bicycle.— Diamond frame. **1897** *Outing* (U.S.) XXIX. 488/2 Those had canvas luggage-cases in the diamond of their wheels. **1898** *Cycling* 26 Valises which fit into the 'diamond' of the frame. **1917** *Cycling Man.* 2 Diamond frame, with horizontal top tube.

f. *Gliding.* (See quot. 1960[1].) Also *attrib.*

1960 *Times* 16 May 5/6, I was trying for my diamonds (a premier award in gliding)... I failed, but got my diamond heights over Newcastle. **1960** *Sunday Times* 6 Nov. 23/6 Diamond height had suddenly become a possibility. *Ibid.* 23/8 Diamond distance remains to be achieved. **1971** *Daily Tel.* 21 July 4/3 (*heading*) Burton third in gliding 'diamond'. *Ibid.*, The 'diamond distance' is considered one of the highest achievements in international gliding.

6. *Printing.* The second smallest standard size of roman or italic type, a size smaller than 'pearl', but larger than 'brilliant'. Also *attrib.* [ad. Du. *diamant*: so named by its introducer Voskens.]

1778 MORES *Dissert. Eng. Typog. Founders* 26 Minion, Nonpareil, Pearl, Ruby and Diamond, so named from their smallness and fancied prettiness. **1808** C. STOWER *Printer's Gram.* 43 Diamond is only pearl face upon a smaller body, and seldom used. **1824** J. JOHNSON *Typogr.* II. v. 83. **1829** CARLYLE *Misc.* (1857) II. 6 The very diamond edition of which might fill whole libraries. **1843** *Penny Cycl.* XXV. 455/2 Diamond..is the smallest type used in this country. *Ibid.* 456 The Dutch were the first in Europe to cut Diamond type. **1856** *Book and its Story* (ed. 9), 206 The value of the type for a Diamond Bible..is several thousand pounds. **1889** H. FROWDE in *Pall Mall G.* 26 Nov. 2/3 We specially cast the type for the book [the 'Finger Prayer-Book'], which is printed, you will see, in 'diamond' and 'brilliant'.

II. 7. Phrases. **a.** ***black diamond***: (*a*) a diamond of a black or dark brown colour, *esp.* a rough diamond as used by lapidaries, etc.; (*b*) *pl.* a name playfully given to coal, as consisting, like the diamond, of carbon. **b.** ***rough diamond***: a diamond in its natural state, before it is cut and polished; hence *fig.* a person of high intrinsic worth, but rude and unpolished in manners. **c.** ***diamond cut diamond***: an equal match in sharpness (of wit, cunning, etc.).

a. 1763 W. LEWIS *Comm. Philos.-Techn.* 321 A black diamond cut and set in a ring. **1849** T. MILLER in *Gabarni in London* 43 (Farmer) Were he even trusted with the favourite horse and gig to fetch a sack of black diamonds from the wharf. **1860** EMERSON *Cond. Life, Power* (1861) 53 Coal..We may well call it black diamonds. Every basket is power and civilizaton. **1867** *Jrnl. Soc. Arts* XV. 349 The boring machine..is composed of a steel ring set with black diamonds.

b. 1624 FLETCHER *Wife for Month* IV. ii, She is very honest, And will be hard to cut as a rough diamond. **1685** BOYLE *Effects of Mot.* Suppl. 148 Having at the Diamond-Mine purchased..a rough Diamond. **1700** DRYDEN *Pref. Fables* (Globe) 503 Chaucer, I confess, is a rough diamond. **1875** URE *Dict. Arts* II. 24 The value of a cut diamond is esteemed equal to that of a similar rough diamond of double weight. **1890** T. KEYWORTH in *Cassell's Fam. Mag.* Dec. 49 He was a rough-looking man, and somebody called him a rough diamond.

c. 1628 FORD *Lover's Mel.* I. iii, We're caught in our own toils. Diamonds cut diamonds. **1642** FULLER *Holy & Prof. St.* IV. xi. 293 Then Gods diamonds often cut one another. *a* **1700** B. E. *Dict. Cant. Crew, Diamond cut Diamond*, bite the Biter. **1863** READE *Hard Cash* xxv, He felt..sure his employer would outwit him if he could; and resolved it should be diamond cut diamond. **1891** J. WINSOR *Columbus* xi. 256 In the game of diamond-cut-diamond, it is not always just to single out a single victim for condemnation.

III. *attrib.* and *Comb.*

8. *attrib.* **a.** Made or consisting of diamond, as ***diamond lens***, ***diamond stone*** (= sense 1).

1553 EDEN *Treat. Newe Ind.* (Arb.) 14 *marg.* The diamonde stone. **1617** MINSHEU *Ductor in Ling.*, A Diamond or Picke at Cards, because he is picked and sharpe pointed as the Diamond stone. **1771** ELIZ. GRIFFITH *Lady Burton* III. 270 The diamond eyes of the Indian idol. **1827** GORING in *Q. Jrnl. Sc. & Arts* XXII. 280 *note*, Diamond lenses I conceive to constitute the ultimatum of the perfection of single microscopes. **1830** *Optics* 39 (Libr. Useful Knowl.) Mr. Pritchard finished the first diamond microscope in 1826. **1831** J. MURRAY *Diamond* 39 If the power of the glass lens be 24, that of the diamond would be 64. **1841** LONGF. *Elected Knight* v, A lance that was.. sharper than diamond-stone.

†**b.** Hard or indestructible as diamond, adamantine. (Cf. 1 b.) *Obs.*

1580 NORTH *Plutarch* (1656) 800 Those strong diamond chains with which Dionysius the elder made his boast that he left his tyranny chained to his son. **1586** T. B. *La Primaud. Fr. Acad.* I. 224 Making men hir slaves, and chaining them..with diamond chains. **1633** P. FLETCHER *Purple Isl.* III. x, With such a diamond knot he often souls can binde. **1659** B. HARRIS *Parival's Iron Age* 101 To trye if luck would turn, and whether Fortune would be alwayes fixed with a Diamant-Nayle.

†**c.** ? Brilliant, shining. *Obs.*

1579 G. HARVEY *Letter-bk.* (Camden) 81 Delicate pictures ..of most beautifull and diamond wenches. **1583** STUBBES *Anat. Abus.* I. (1879) 63 To heare their dirtie dregs ript vp and cast in their diamond faces.

9. *attrib.* Set or furnished with a diamond or diamonds, as ***diamond button***, ***clasp***, ***ring***, ***signet***.

1642 FULLER *Holy & Prof. St.* III. xxii. 213 Some hold it unhappy to be married with a diamond ring. **1717** LADY M. W. MONTAGU *Let. to C'tess. of Mar* 1 Apr., This smock..is closed at the neck with a diamond button. **1827** E. TURRELL in *Gill's Techn. Repos.* I. 195 Diamond turning-tools. **1837** CARLYLE *Fr. Rev.* II. viii, Consider that unutterable business of the Diamond Necklace..Astonished Europe rings with the mystery for ten months. **1880** CLERKE in *Fraser's Mag.* 819 The diamond clasp which fastened the imperial mantle of Charlemagne. **1891** *Law Times* XC. 283/1 Two diamond rings which he wished to dispose of.

10. *attrib.* or *adj.* **a.** Of the shape of a diamond (see 5); lozenge-shaped, rhombic; forming a design consisting of figures of this shape, as ***diamond couching***, ***fret***, ***netting***, ***pattern***, ***work***; having a head or end of this shape, as ***diamond dibber***, ***nail***.

1598 BARRET *Theor. Warres* III. ii. 77 The nearest..vnto the square of men, is the Diamant battell. **1663** WOOD *Life* (Oxf. Hist. Soc.) I. 481 A larg diomond hatchment with Canterbury and Juxon impaled. **1667** PRIMATT *City & C. Build.* 160 A Diamond Figure, whose sides are parallel, but not at right Angles. **1840** *Penny Cycl.* XVIII 215 s.v. *Planting*, The *diamond-dibber*, a pointed plate of steel with a short iron handle. **1840** DICKENS *Barn. Rudge* i, Its windows were old diamond-pane lattices. **1858** *Archit. Publ. Soc. Dict.*, *Diamond fret*, a species of checker work in which..a diamond..is interlaced by the prolongations of the diameters of the square. **1874** KNIGHT *Dict. Mech.*, *Diamond-nail*, a nail having a rhombal head. *Ibid.*, *Diamond-work* (*Masonry*), reticulated work formed by courses of lozenge-shaped stones, very common in ancient masonry. **1882** CAULFEILD & SAWARD *Dict. Needlework* 152 Diamond couching [is] one of the Flat Couchings used in Church Work. *Ibid.* 359 Fancy Diamond Netting is worked in three different ways.

b. Having a surface hewn or cut into facets, formed by low square-based pyramids placed close together.

1717 BERKELEY *Jrnl. Tour Italy* 27 Jan. Wks. 1871 IV. 551 Church of the Carmelites..in the front a little diamond work. **1870** A. BEAZELEY *Specif. Flamboro' Lighth.*, The Gallery-course is to be..cast with a neat diamond pattern as shewn, to give a safe foot-hold.

11. General combs. **a.** attributive. Of or relating to diamonds, as ***diamond-bort*** (see BORT), ***-broker***, ***-carat***, ***-factory***, ***-merchant***, ***-trade***; containing or producing diamonds, as ***diamond-bed***, ***-conglomerate***, ***-deposit***, ***-gravel***, ***-mine***. **b.** objective and obj. genitive, as ***diamond-bearing*** adj., ***-digging***, ***-polisher***, ***-producing*** adj., ***-seeker***, ***-setter***, ***-splitter***. **c.** instrumental, as ***diamond-paved***, ***-pointed***, ***-tipped*** adjs. **d.** similative, as ***diamond-bright***, ***-distinct*** adjs.; also ***diamond-like*** adj. **e.** parasynthetic, as ***diamond-headed***, ***-paned***, ***-shaped***, ***-tiled*** adjs.

a **1618** SYLVESTER *Woodman's Bear* lxxiii, Diamond-headed darts. **1628** in *Archæologia* (1883) XLVII. 392 Dyamond boart and divers other materialls for the Cutting and finishing of our Armes in a Dyamond. **1632** LITHGOW *Trav.* III. 85 The goodliest plot, the Diamond sparke, and the Honny spot of all Candy. **1685** Diamond-mine [see 7 b]. **1704** *Phil. Trans.* XXV. 1548 Such a Diamond-like Sand. **1820** KEATS *Hyperion* I. 220 Diamond-paved lustrous long arcades. **1835** WILLIS *Pencillings* I. xiv. 108 The diamond-shaped stones of the roof. **1842** TENNYSON *Vision of Sin* ii, Till the fountain spouted, showering wide Sleet of diamond-drift and pearly hail. **1863** I. WILLIAMS *Baptistery* I. vii. (1874) 79 Writ.. With a diamond-pointed pen, On a plate of adamant. **1871** M. COLLINS *Mrq. & Merch.* II. x. 300 Casements diamond-paned. **1876** J. B. CURREY in *Jrnl. Soc. Arts* XXIV. 375 The diamond-bearing soil. *Ibid.* 377 Keen-faced diamond brokers. **1880** CLERKE in *Fraser's Mag.* 818 It is said there were diamond-polishers at Nuremberg in 1373. *Ibid.* 821 The conditions of diamond-digging. **1883** *Archæologia* XLVII. 396 Tavernier, a diamond merchant and jeweller, who visited Persia in .. 1664.

12. Special combs.: **diamond-bird**, an Australian shrike of the genus *Pardalotus*, esp. *P. punctatus*, so called from the spots on its plumage; **diamond-borer, d. boring machine** = *diamond-drill* (b); **diamond boron**, an impure form of boron obtained in octahedral crystals nearly as hard and brilliant as the diamond; **diamond-breaker** = *diamond-mortar*; **diamond-broaching**, broached hewn-work done with a diamond-hammer; **diamond cement**, cement used in setting diamonds; **diamond-crossing**, a crossing on a railway where two lines of rails intersect obliquely without communicating (see DIAMOND-POINT 2); **diamond-drill**, (*a*) a drill armed with one or more diamonds used for boring hard substances; (*b*) a drill for boring rocks, having a head set with rough diamonds, a diamond-borer; **diamond dust** = *diamond-powder*; **diamond-ficoides**, the ice-plant, *Mesembryanthemum crystallinum*; **diamond-field** [cf. *coal-field*], a tract of country yielding diamonds from its surface strata; **diamond file, fish** (see quots.); **diamond-hammer**, a mason's hammer having one face furnished with pyramidal pick points for fine-dressing a surface on stone; **diamond hitch**, a method of fastening ropes in packing heavy loads; **diamond-knot** (*Naut.*), a kind of ornamental knot worked with the strands of a rope; **diamond-mill** (see quot.); **diamond-mortar**, a steel mortar used for crushing diamonds for the purposes of the lapidary; **diamond-plaice**, a local name (in Sussex) for the common plaice (*Pleuronectes platessa*), from its lozenge-shaped spots; **diamond-plough**, (*a*) a diamond-pointed instrument for engraving upon glass; (*b*) a small plough having a mould-board and share of a diamond or rhomboidal shape (Knight); **diamond-powder**, the powder produced by grinding or crushing diamonds; **diamond rattlesnake**, a rattlesnake (*Crotalus adamanteus*) having diamond-shaped markings; **diamond-spot**, collector's name for a moth (*Botys tetragonalis*); **Diamond State** *U.S.*, the state of Delaware (see quot. 1934); **diamond stitch**, an embroidery stitch producing a diamond pattern (see quot. 1964); **diamond-tool**, a metal-turning tool whose cutting edge is formed by facets; **diamond wedding** [after *silver w.*, *golden w.*], a fanciful name for the celebration of the 60th (or according to some, the 75th) anniversary of the wedding-day; **diamond-weevil** = DIAMOND-BEETLE; **diamond-wheel**, a metal wheel used with diamond-powder and oil in grinding diamonds or other hard gems. See also DIAMOND-BACK, etc.

1840 *Penny Cycl.* XVIII. 179/2 s.v. *Piprinæ, Pardalotus punctatus*.. Mr. Caley states that this species is called *Diamond Bird by the settlers, from the spots on its body. **1865** GOULD *Handbk. Birds Austral.* I. 157 No species.. is more widely and generally distributed than the spotted Diamond-bird. **1875** URE *Dict. Arts* I. 445 In soft strata it is somewhat difficult to obtain a core by the *diamond borer. **1867** *Jrnl. Soc. Arts* XV. 349 *Diamond boring machine. **1875** URE *Dict. Arts* I. 442 *The Diamond Boring Machine*.. The boring bit is a steel thimble, about 4 inches in length, having two rows of Brazilian black diamonds.. in their natural rough state firmly imbedded therein. **1863–72** WATTS *Dict. Chem.* I. 628 *Adamantine* or **Diamond Boron*.. extremely hard, always sufficiently so to scratch corundum with facility, and some crystals are nearly as hard as diamond itself. **1880** J. C. BRUCE in *Archæologia* XLVI. 165, I have most frequently found the *diamond-broaching in camps which have been repaired by Severus. **1884** G. W. COX *Cycl. Com. Things* 117 A *Diamond cement.. used by Armenian jewellers in setting diamonds, is composed of gum mastic and isinglass dissolved in spirits of wine. **1881** E. MATHESON *Aid Bk. Engineer. Enterp.* 252 Where a siding crosses a main road without connecting it, what is known as a *diamond crossing is used. **1891** *Morning Post* 20 Feb. 3/4 Major Marindin strongly recommends.. that there should be no diamond crossing worse than one to eight. **1827** E. TURRELL in *Gill's Techn. Repos.* I. 129 Pierced by very fine *diamond drills. **1881** E. MATHESON *Aid Bk. Engineer. Enterprise* 391 Diamond drills.. will pierce the hardest known rocks. *c* **1702** C. FIENNES *Journeys* (1947) III. ix. 239 The true diamond.. cannot be divided nor cut but by some of it self *diamond dust. **1844–57** G. BIRD *Urin. Deposits* (ed. 5) 221 A white powder.. of a glistening appearance, like diamond-dust. **1767** 'MAWE' [J. ABERCROMBIE] *Ev. Man own Gardener* Feb. 50 *Diamond ficoides, or ice plant. **1811** MRS. M. STARKE *Beauties of C.M. Maggi* 48 The Ice-plant, properly called, the Diamond-Ficoides. **1876** J. B. CURREY in *Jrnl. Soc. Arts* XXIV. 379 The discovery of the *diamond-fields. **1884** F. J. BRITTEN *Watch & Clockm.* 88 A *Diamond file is formed of a strip of copper with diamond powder hammered into it. **1854** ADAMS, BAIKIE & BARRON *Nat. Hist.* 93 Family.. *Diamond Fishes (also called Bony-Pikes) *Lepisosteidæ*. **1858** *Archit. Publ. Soc. Dict.*, **Diamond hammer*, a tool used by masons in the Isle of Man and in parts of Scotland for 'fine pick dressing' limestone and granite. **1883** *Specif. N. East. Railw., Alnwick & Cornhill Br.* Contr. No. 2. 5 The face is to be either tooled, or broached with a diamond hammer. **1769** FALCONER *Dict. Marine* (1789) s.v. *Knot*, There are several sorts, which differ in.. form and size: the principal of these are the *diamond-knot, the rose-knot, the wall-knot. **1867** SMYTH *Sailor's Word-bk.*, *Diamond-knot*, an ornamental knot worked with the strands of a rope, sometimes used for bucket-strops, on the foot-ropes of jib-booms, man-ropes, etc. **1884** F. J. BRITTEN *Watch & Clockm.* 87 [In a] *Diamond Mill.. for cutting and polishing ruby pallets and other hard stones, discs charged with diamond powder and rotated at a high speed are used. **1853** SOYER *Pantroph.* 237 The flounder, the brill, the *diamond and Dutch plaice. **1827** J. LUKENS in *Gill's Techn. Repos.* I. 76 On an improved *Diamond Plough.. for cutting Circular Lines upon Glass. —— E. TURRELL *ibid.* 195 On Diamond ploughs for Engravers. **1753** CHAMBERS *Cycl. Supp.* s.v., *Diamond Powder is of great use for grinding hard substances. **1802** T. THOMSON *Chem.* I. 47 Diamond powder can only be obtained by grinding one diamond against another. **1883** *Times* 26 Mar. 7/6 Of all the snake varieties.. the *diamond rattlesnake.. seems to be the most deadly. **1819** G. SAMOUELLE *Entomol. Compend.* 436 The *diamond spot. **1866** *Galaxy* 15 Oct. 386 Without other significance than such.. as attaches to the '*Diamond State', 'the Empire State', [etc.]. **1934** G. E. SHANKLE *State Names* 107 Delaware gets the nickname, the Diamond State, from the fact that it is small in size but great in importance. *c* **1926** 'MIXER' *Transport Workers' Song Bk.* 10 You should also learn to crochet, *Diamond stitch and centre tuck. **1964** *McCall's Sewing* xiii. 243/1 *Diamond* or *chevron stitch*. This looks like the honeycomb stitch except that the thread between the rows is carried on top of the fabric instead of under the fabric. **1872** *Punch* 23 Nov. 210/2 *Diamond Wedding. **1892** HAYDN *Dict. Dates* 1058 Diamond weddings after a union of 60 years, some apply it to 75 years.

'diamond, *v.* [f. prec. sb.]

1. *trans.* To furnish or bedeck with diamonds.

1751 H. WALPOLE *Lett. H. Mann* (1891) II. 241 He plays, dresses, diamonds himself, even to distinct shoe-buckles for a frock.

2. *fig.* To adorn as with diamonds. (Cf. *impearl*.)

1839 BAILEY *Festus* xvi. (1852) 211 Wreathed round with flowers and diamonded with dew. **1845** JAMES *A. Neil* III. xvi, The tears rolled over the long lashes, and diamonded her cheek. **1878** LOWELL *Lett.* (1894) II. 216 Just as we got there, it cleared, and all the thickets.. were rainbowed and diamonded by the sun.

b. To make glittering like a diamond.

1839 BAILEY *Festus* xiii. (1852) 157 The first ray Perched on his [a bard's] pen, and diamonded its way.

3. *nonce-use.* To call or name (diamonds).

1859 TENNYSON *Idylls, Elaine* 503 'Advance and take your prize The diamond'; but he answer'd, 'diamond me No diamonds! for God's love, a little air'.

Hence **'diamonding** *vbl. sb.*, adornment with or as with diamonds; brilliant ornamentation.

c **1818** KEATS *Notes on Milton* in Ld. Houghton *Life* (1848) I. 277 The light and shade, the sort of black brightness, the ebon diamonding.. of the following lines. *a* **1821** —— *Castle Builder*, Their glassy diamonding on Turkish floor.

'diamond-back, *a.* and *sb.* [Short for next.]

A. *adj.* = Diamond-backed, having the back marked with one or more lozenge-shaped figures.

1887 *Lippincott's Mag.* Sept. 456 Baltimore,.. the home of the soft-shell crab, the diamond-back terrapin. **1894** G. W. CABLE *J. March* xxvii, Di'mon'-back rattle-snake hisself cayn't no mo' scare me 'n if I was a hawg. **1931** H. F. PRINGLE *T. Roosevelt* I. v. 58 People of the blue blood dined nightly on diamond-back terrapin. **1956** C. H. POPE *Reptile World* 219 The diamond-back rattlers.. are the giants among rattlesnakes.

B. *sb.* **a.** The Diamond-back Moth (see quots.). **b.** The Diamond-backed Turtle. **c.** A rattlesnake, *Crotalus adamanteus* or *C. atrox*, having diamond-shaped markings on its back. *U.S.*

1819 G. SAMOUELLE *Entomol. Compend.* 436 The testaceous Diamond-back, *Tortrix trapezana*. **1891** MISS E. A. ORMEROD in *Jrnl. R. Agric. Soc.* 30 Sept. 599 The pale patterns along these edges form diamond-shaped marks, whence the English name 'diamond-back moth'. *Ibid.* 611 These showed unmistakable signs of diamond-back caterpillar ravage. **1895** *Lippincott's Mag.* Jan., The diamond-back [turtle] is undeniably and unspeakably ugly. **1907** R. L. DITMARS *Reptile Bk.* xlv. 449 The flattened trails of the big Diamond-backs across the dry sandy roads. **1908** *Daily Chron.* 28 Aug. 7/4 The fangs of a big diamond-back are three-quarters of an inch long. **1956** C. H. POPE *Reptile World* 219 The western diamond-back (*Crotalus atrox*) is a reptile of dry country and deserts.

'diamond-backed, *a.* [f. DIAMOND *sb.* + BACKED 1.] Having the back marked with lozenge-shaped figures.

diamond-backed turtle or ***terrapin***, the fresh-water tortoise of the Atlantic coast of N. America, *Malaclemmys palustris*.

1895 *Daily News* 14 Jan. 5/3 Diamond-backed terrapin are the newest pets of fashionable folk in the States. They.. are chiefly adopted by artists at present, but are to be found in some boudoirs as well as studios.

diamond-beetle. A South American beetle *Curculio* (*Entimus*) *imperialis*, of which the elytra are studded with brilliant sparkling points; also applied to other species of Curculio, and (with qualifications) to other beetles with splendid markings.

1806 G. SHAW *Gen. Zool.* VI. I. 65 The most brilliant and beautiful is the Curculio imperialis.. commonly known by the name of the Diamond Beetle. **1839** J. O. WESTWOOD *Mod. Classif. Insects* I. 340 The various species of diamond beetles surpassing (in their colours) the majority of Coleopterous insects. **1860** W. S. DALLAS *Anim. Kingd.* 219 Few insects can boast of greater magnificence than the well-known Diamond-beetle of Brazil. **1860** G. BENNETT *Nat. in Austral.* 273 The Diamond beetle of Australia of green and gold tints (*Chrysolopus spectabilis*).

'diamond-cut, *a.* and *sb.*

A. *adj.* **1.** Cut into the shape of a diamond or rhomb.

1637 *Bursar's Bk. Gonville & Caius Coll.* in Willis & Clark *Cambridge* (1886) I. 194 Paveing the chappell with stones diamond cut. *c* **1710** C. FIENNES *Diary* (1888) 238 Ye windows.. are all diamond Cut round the Edges.

2. Cut with facets like a diamond; cut in relief in the form of a low square-based pyramid, pointed or truncated.

diamond-cut glass, thick glass cut into grooves or channels of V-shaped section crossing one another obliquely so as to leave pyramid-shaped projections; a common style of ornamentation in cut glass.

1703 *Lond. Gaz.* No. 3973/4 A Diamond cut Steel-headed Cane. **1717** BERKELEY *Jrnl. Tour Italy* Wks. 1871 IV. 541 Well-built streets, all hewn stone, diamond-cut, rustic.

†**B.** *sb.* *Obs.*

1691 tr. *Emilianne's Frauds Romish Monks* 27 A magnificent Structure, all of hewn Stone of a Diamond-Cut. **1698** FRYER *Acc. E. India & P.* 214 If it be very fair and cut Diamond-Cut.. The second sort of Ruby is White.. which also is of good esteem, if cut of a Diamond-Cut.

'diamond-cutter. A lapidary who cuts and polishes diamonds. So **'diamond-cutting** *sb.*, the art of the diamond-cutter.

1722 *Lond. Gaz.* No. 6100/4 Moses Langley.. Diamond-Cutter. **1827** *Gill's Techn. Repos.* I. 4 The diamond-cutter seats himself in front of his work-board. **1872** YEATS *Growth Comm.* 213 The art of diamond-cutting intruduced by Jews driven from Lisbon to Amsterdam.

'diamonded, *a.* [f. DIAMOND *sb.* or *v.* + -ED.]

1. Adorned with or wearing diamonds.

1860 EMERSON *Cond. Life, Behaviour* (1861) 111 As when, in Paris, the chief of the police enters a ballroom, so many diamonded pretenders shrink, and make themselves as inconspicuous as they can. **1885** A. J. C. HARE *Russia* iii. 143 Diamonded saddle-cloths and trappings.

b. *fig.* Adorned as with diamonds.

1830 TENNYSON *Poems* 144 The diamonded night. **1831** J. WILSON *Unimore* I. 26 Dew-diamonded daisies. **1860** LD. LYTTON *Lucile* I. iv. §6 The scarp'd ravaged mountains.. Were alive with the diamonded shy salamander.

2. Marked or furnished with lozenge-shaped figures or parts; having the figure of a diamond.

1642 FULLER *Holy & Prof. St.* v. vi. 382 Break a stone.. or lop a bough.. and one shall behold the grain thereof.. diamonded or streaked in the fashion of a lozenge. **1820** KEATS *Eve St. Agnes* xxiv, A casement high and triple-arch'd.. And diamonded with panes of quaint device. **1880** *Dorothy* 25 Came through the diamonded panes.

†**3.** *fig.* ? Endowed with the characteristics of the diamond; brilliant and keen. *Obs.*

1641 J. JACKSON *True Evang. T.* II. 138 These pointed and diamonded speeches, which doe indeed leave a sting.. in the mind of the pious Auditor.

diamon'diferous, *a.* [f. DIAMOND + -(I)FEROUS, in imitation of *diamantiferous*, F. *diamantifère*, from med.L. *diamant-em*.]

Diamond-producing.

1870 *Echo* 14 Oct., Those who have rushed to the diamondiferous region [of S. Africa]. **1870** *Daily News* 21 Dec., A new diamondiferous track had been discovered. **1877** W. THOMSON *Voy. Challenger* II. vi. 116 Sufficient diamondiferous country is already known to provide many years' employment for a large population. **1885** *Times* 20 Apr. 4/4 Filled.. with a blue diamondiferous mud.

'diamondize, *v.* [f. DIAMOND *sb.* + -IZE.]

1. *trans.* To bedeck with, or as with, diamonds.

1599 B. JONSON *Ev. Man out of Hum.* III. iv, Modellizing, or enamelling, or rather diamondizing of your subject. **1863** OUIDA *Held in Bondage* (1870) 52 Diamondized old ladies.

2. To convert into diamond.

1893 E. L. REXFORD in Barrows *Parl. Relig.* I. 516 The diamondizing of soot.

diamond-point. [f. DIAMOND *sb.* + POINT *sb.*]

1. A stylus tipped with a fragment of diamond, used in engraving, etc.

1874 KNIGHT *Dict. Mech.* I. 698/1 Wilson Lowry introduced the diamond-point into engraver's ruling-machines. **1881** *Every Man his own Mechanic* §569 The diamond point.. is used for roughing very small and delicate work that will not bear the gouge.

2. *Railways.* Usually in *pl.* The set of points at a diamond crossing, where two lines of rails intersect obliquely without communicating, forming a diamond or rhombic figure; in *sing.*

one of the acute angles formed by two rails at such a crossing.
1881 *Daily News* 15 Sept. 3/2 It [a train] had to pass over a diamond point. **1890** *Morning Post* 24 Oct. 6/7 A North British mineral train, while crossing a set of diamond points, ran off the line. **1894** *Westm. Gaz.* 24 July 5/2 On reaching the diamond point the guard's van next the engine jumped the metals.

3. *attrib.*, as ***diamond-point chisel***, a chisel having the corners ground off obliquely.
1874 KNIGHT *Dict. Mech.* s.v. *Chisel.*

diamond-snake. A name given to various snakes or serpents having diamond-shaped markings, *esp.* **a.** a large Australian serpent, *Morelia spilotes*; **b.** a venomous Tasmanian serpent, *Hoplocephalus superbus*.
1814 *Sporting Mag.* XLIV. 93 A snake of the diamond species was lately killed at St. George's River..New South Wales. **1847** LEICHHARDT *Jrnl.* iii. 78 Charley killed a diamond snake, larger than any he had ever seen before. **1850** J. B. CLUTTERBUCK *Port Phillip* iii. 43 The diamond snake is that most dreaded by the natives. **1863** WOOD *Nat. Hist.* 117 It is called the Diamond snake on account of the pattern of its colours..arranged so as to produce a series of diamonds along its back. **1882** MISS C. C. HOPLEY *Snakes* 423 The Diamond snake..on the mainland is the harmless *Python molurus*, and in Tasmania the venomous *Hoplocephalus superbus*, with very broad scales.

diamond-spar. *Min.* [ad. Ger. *demantspath* (Klaproth 1786), so called from its extreme hardness.] (See quot.)
1804 R. JAMESON *Min.* I. 93. **1807** J. MURRAY *Syst. Chem.* III. 593 The Diamond spar, which has been distinguished from corundum, appears to be a variety of it.

'diamond-wise, *adv.* [see -WISE.] In the manner or form of a diamond or lozenge.
1530 PALSGR. 799 Dyamant wyse, lyke or in maner of a dyamant. **1582** N. LICHEFIELD tr. *Castanheda's Conq. E. Ind.* lxxvi. 154b, Of sundrye coulours, the which was wrought Diamond wise. **1688** R. HOLME *Armoury* III. 100/1 Diamond wise..is..anything set or hung having one corner of the square set upwards, the other downwards. **1698** FRYER *Acc. E. India & P.* 158 His Effigies..upon it Escutcheon, or Diamond-wise.

diamond-work: see DIAMOND 10.

†**di'amoron.** *Pharm.* Also 5 **diameron.** [L. *diamorōn*, a. Gr. διὰ μόρων 'made from black mulberries.'] A preparation of syrup and mulberry juice, used as a gargle for a sore throat.
c **1400** *Lanfranc's Cirurg.* 218 þan make him a gargarisme wiþ a decoccioun..wiþ þe which be distemperid þerwiþ diameron. *Ibid.* 262 þan þou muste make consumynge þingis as diameron & sappa michum. **1647** WARD *Simp. Cobler* 10 [It] will be found a farre better *Diamoron* for the Gargarismes this Age wants.

diamorphine (daɪə'mɔːfiːn). *Chem.* [Shortened form of DIACETYLMORPHINE.]
= DIACETYLMORPHINE.
1914 *Chemist & Druggist* LXXXV. 819/2 Diamorphinæ Hydrochloridum... The name 'diamorphine' cannot be regarded as satisfactory, as it gives no indication of the presence of the acetyl radicle on which the special properties of the compound depend. **1916** P. W. SQUIRE *Comp. Brit. Pharmacopœia* 551 Diamorphine Hydrochloride..is described officially as the hydrochloride of an alkaloid obtainable by the action of acetic anhydride on morphine. **1920** *Act 10 & 11 Geo. V* c. 46 §8 The drugs to which this Part of this Act applies are morphine, cocaine, ecgonine and diamorphine (commonly known as heroin). **1965** [see DIACETYLMORPHINE].

‖**diamorphosis** (daɪə'mɔːfəsɪs, -mɔː'fəʊsɪs). *Biol.* [mod.L., a. Gr. διαμόρφωσις, n. of action f. διαμορφό-ειν to form, shape, f. δια- through, thoroughly, asunder (see DIA-[1]) + μορφή form.]
1. 'The building up of a body to its proper form' (*Syd. Soc. Lex.* 1883).
¶ **2.** *erroneously* for DIMORPHISM.
1861 H. C. WOOD in *Quart. Jrnl. of Micr. Sc.* I. No. 3, 157 (title) On the Diamorphosis of Lyngbya, Schizogonium, and Prasiola.

di'amyl. *Chem.* [DI-[2].] **A.** *sb.* The organic radical AMYL in the free state, $C_{10}H_{22}$ = $C_5H_{11}{\cdot}C_5H_{11}$. **B.** *attrib.* and *Comb.* Containing two equivalents of amyl, as ***diamylaniline***.
1850 DAUBENY *Atom. Th.* viii. (ed. 2) 241 Diamylaniline, where 2 atoms [of hydrogen] are replaced by amyle and 1 by aniline. **1869** ROSCOE *Elem. Chem.* 333 Diamyl..is obtained by acting on amyl iodide with sodium.

di'amylene. *Chem.* See DI-[2] and AMYLENE.

†**'dian.** *Obs.* Also 6 **diana.** [a. F. *diane* (16th c. in Littré), Sp. *diana*, a beating of the drum at day-break, It. *diana* 'a kind of march sounded by trumpetters in a morning to their generall and captaine' (Florio 1598), f. *dia* day. Cf. L. *quoti-diānus*, etc.] A trumpet call or drumroll at early morn. Also *attrib.*, as ***dian-sounding***.
1591 GARRARD *Art Warre* 29 Even until the Diana be sounded through all the Campe. **1652** URQUHART *Jewel* Wks. (1834) 180, I warn them with the first sound of the trumpet..but if, after this Diansounding [etc.]. *a* **1678** MARVELL *Appleton House* 292 Poems 208 The bee through these known allies hums Beating the dian with its drums.

Diana (daɪ'ænə, daɪ'eɪnə). Anglicized 4- **Dian** ('daɪən). Also 3-6 **Diane,** 6 **Dyane, Dean.** [a. L. *Diāna* in F. *diane*, whence Eng. *Diane*, *Dian*, retained as a poetic form.]
1. a. An ancient Italian female divinity, the moon-goddess, patroness of virginity and of hunting; subsequently regarded as identical with the Greek Artemis, and so with Oriental deities, which were identified with the latter, e.g. the Artemis or Diana of the Ephesians.
c **1205** LAY. 1145 A wifmonnes liche, Diana [*c* **1275** Diane] wes ihaten. **1382** WYCLIF *Acts* xix. 24 Makinge siluerene housis to Dian. *a* **1400-50** *Alexander* 2299 To Dyanaas temple. **1508** DUNBAR *Goldyn Targe* 76 Dyane the goddesse chaste of woddis grene. **1590** SHAKS. *Mids. N.* I. i. 89 Or on Dianaes Altar to protest For aie, austerity, and single life. *Ibid.* IV. i. 78 Dians bud or [= o'er] Cupids flower, Hath such force and blessed power. **1791** COWPER *Odyss.* IV. 153 Dian, goddess of the golden bow.
b. *poet.* The moon personified as a goddess.
1398 TREVISA *Barth. De P.R.* VIII. xvii. (1495) 328 The mone is callyd Dyana, goddes of wodes and of groues. **1660** SHIRLEY *Andromana* II. v, Pale-fac'd Dian maketh haste to hide Her borrow'd glory in some neighb'ring cloud. **1818** BYRON *Ch. Har.* IV. xxvii, Meek Dian's crest Floats through the azure air.
†**c.** Alluding to *Acts* xix. 24: Source of gain.
1640 SOMNER *Antiq. Canterb.* 237 So loth were they to forgo their Diana. **1681** J. HOUGHTON *Coll. Husb. & Trade* 28 April, No. 353 They..are prohibiting our wollen manufactures which is our *Diana*.
d. *attrib.* or *adj.* Virgin, unsullied.
1870 J. ORTON *Andes & Amazons* ix. (1876) 144 Snow of Dian Purity.
e. *transf.*
1784 COWPER *Task* IV. 517 Nymphs were Dianas then, and swains had hearts That felt their virtues. **1897** *Westm. Gaz.* 25 Oct. 2/1 Some of these fair Dianas are clad in divided skirts. **1931** [see ASTRIDE *a.*].
2. In early Chemistry a name for silver.
(By the astro-alchemists also called *Luna*, from the 'silver' light of the moon: cf. the other planetary names of the metals *Sol*, *Mercury*, *Venus*, *Mars*, *Jupiter*, and *Saturn*, i.e. gold, quicksilver, copper, iron, tin, and lead.)
Hence **Tree of Diana,** *Arbor Dianæ*: the dendritic amalgam precipitated by mercury from a solution of nitrate of silver.
1706 PHILLIPS (ed. Kersey), Diana's Tree..whereby a Mixture of Silver, Quick-silver and Spirit of Nitre may be Crystallized in shape of a Tree, with little Balls at the end of its Branches representing Fruit. **1798** G. GREGORY *Œcon. Nature* (1804) II. 247 *note*, Diana's tree, from the whim of the alchemists..who appropriated silver to the Moon, or Diana. **1849** J. R. JACKSON *Minerals* 287 A pretty metallic vegetation in glass jars:..called the Tree of Diana.
3. Diana monkey, *Cercopithecus Diana*, a large African monkey, so named from a crescent-shaped white marking on its forehead.
1812 SMELLIE & WOOD *Buffon's Nat. Hist.* X. 190 This monkey..is the same animal that Linnæus has called Diana. **1860** WOOD *Illustr. Nat. Hist.* I. 49 The most conspicuous feature in the Diana Monkey is the long and sharply pointed beard.

[**dianatic,** misprint in Phillips (ed. Kersey) 1706 for DIANOETIC.]

†**di'ander.** *Bot. Obs.* [ad. F. *diandre*, ad. mod.L. *diandrus*, f. as next.] A plant bearing flowers with two stamens.
1828 in WEBSTER.

‖**Diandria** (daɪ'ændrɪə). *Bot.* [mod.L. (Linnæus, 1735), f. Gr. type *δίανδρος, mod.L. *diandrus*, δι- twice, + ἀνδρ-, stem of ἀνήρ, man, male: see MONANDRIA, POLYANDRIA.] The second class in the sexual system of Linnæus, comprising all plants having two stamens.
1753 CHAMBERS *Cycl. Supp.* s.v. Diandria..of this class of plants are the jessamine, phillerea, olive, rosemary, etc.
Hence **di'andrian** *a.*, of or pertaining to the class *Diandria*.
1828 in WEBSTER.

diandrous (daɪ'ændrəs), *a.* Also 8 **-ious.** [f. mod.L. *diandrus* (see prec. and MONANDROUS).]
1. *Bot.* Belonging to the class Diandria; two-stamened.
1770 GRAY *Lett.* Wks. 1884 III. 383 Sage-tea..is a poly-dynamious plant, take my word; though your Linnaeus would persuade us it is merely diandrious. **1806** J. GALPINE *Brit. Bot.* 38 Bromus..flor. lanceolate, nerved, furrowed, diandrous. **1830** LINDLEY *Nat. Syst. Bot.* 229 Irregular diandrous or didynamous stamens.
2. *Zool.* Having two male mates.
1885 C. TROTTER in *Academy* 6 June 395/3 He also records a polyandrous, or rather diandrous, species among the birds.

†**diane'metic,** *a. Obs. rare*$^{-1}$. [ad. Gr. διανεμητικός distributive, f. διανέμειν to distribute.] = DISTRIBUTIVE.
1675 R. BURTHOGGE *Causa Dei* 72 In Distributive (or as Aristotle calls it, Dianemetic) Justice.

dianetics (daɪə'nɛtɪks), *sb. pl.* [Alteration of DIANOETIC *sb.*] A system, developed by the American writer L. Ron Hubbard, that has as its aim the relief of psychosomatic illnesses by a process of cleansing the mind of harmful mental images. Hence **dia'netic** *a.*, of or pertaining to dianetics.
1950 *Time* 24 July, A new cult is smouldering through the U.S. underbrush. Its name: dianetics. Last week its bible, *Dianetics: The Modern Science of Mental Health*, was steadily climbing the U.S. bestseller lists. **1950** A. HUXLEY *Let.* 10 Dec. (1969) 634 We have been looking into dianetics. **1951** L. R. HUBBARD *Dianetics* p. xii, The main contributions of dianetic theory to the field of psychology and psychotherapy are seven fundamental assumptions. *Ibid.* i. 6 Dianetics..contains a therapeutic technique with which can be treated all inorganic mental ills and all organic psycho-somatic ills. **1954** J. CHRISTOPHER *22nd Cent.* 140 A group of pseudo-scientific mystical fanatics..who went in for a thing called dianetics. **1955** A. HUXLEY *Let.* 24 Oct. (1969) 769 Dianetic procedures were tried..but there was absolutely no recall. **1960** *Guardian* 1 July 9/4 A series of cod psychoanalytic scenes and 'dianetic' games are then evolved.

dianite ('daɪənaɪt). *Min.* Name given by Von Kobel in 1860 to a variety of COLUMBITE, supposed to contain a new metal called by him *dianium*.
1861 *Amer. Jrnl. Sc.* Ser. II. XXXI. 360.

'Dianize, *v. nonce-wd.* [f. DIANA + -IZE.] *intr.* To 'moon' (with an allusion to the myth of Endymion).
1834 MEDWIN *Angler in Wales* II. 49 If our Endymion had been Dianizing, I should not have been surprised.

dianodal (daɪə'nəʊdəl), *a. Math.* [f. DIA-[1] + NODE + -AL[1].] Passing through nodes. ***dianodal curve*** or ***surface***: one passing through the nodes of a given curve or surface.
1870 CAYLEY in *Proc. Lond. Math. Soc.* III. 199 The ninth node of the Sextic may be any point whatever on the dianodal curve.

dianoetic (daɪənəʊ'ɛtɪk), *a.* and *sb. Metaph.* [ad. Gr. διανοητικός of or pertaining to thinking, f. διανοητός, vbl. adj. from διανοέ-εσθαι to think, subst. the process of thought, f. δια- through, thoroughly + νοέ-ειν to think, suppose.]
A. *adj.* Of or pertaining to thought; employing thought and reasoning; intellectual.
1677 GALE *Crt. Gentiles* II. III. 92 Dianoetic Philosophie, which is the assent to conclusions by discourse from first principes. **1732** BERKELEY *Alciphr.* VII. §34 A Dianoetic Academy, or seminary for free-thinkers. **1829** SIR W. HAMILTON *Discuss.* (1852) 4 The dianoetic or discursive faculty..the faculty of relations or comparison. **1885** J. MARTINEAU *Types Eth. Th.* II. II. iii. §1. 518 The theories of the dianoetic moralists.
B. *sb. Metaph.* (See quot.)
1836-7 SIR W. HAMILTON *Metaph.* (1877) II. xxxviii. 350, I would employ the word *noetic*..to express all those cognitions that originate in the mind itself, *dianoetic* to denote the operations of the Discursive, Elaborative, or Comparative Faculty.

†**diano'etical,** *a. Obs.* [f. as prec. + -AL[1].] = prec. adj.
1570 DEE *Math. Pref.* 2 The Mercurial fruite of Dianoeticall discourse. **1588** FRAUNCE *Lawiers Log.* II. ix. 97 The disposition dianoeticall is when one axiome by reason is inferred of another. **1682** H. MORE *Annot. Glanvill's Lux O.* 253 As if the one were Noematical, the other Dianoetical.

diano'etically, *adv.* [f. prec. + -LY[2].] In a dianoetic manner; by or with the reasoning faculty; intellectually.
1822 T. TAYLOR *Apuleius* 365 The Demiurgus..is said to energize dianoëtically, and to reason.

dianoialogy (ˌdaɪənɔɪ'ælədʒɪ). *Metaph.* [f. Gr. διάνοια intelligence, understanding, thinking + -LOGY. The analogically regular form would be *dianæology*.] Term proposed by Sir W. Hamilton for: That portion of logic which deals with dianoetic or demonstrative propositions. So also **ˌdianoia'logical** *a.*
1846 SIR W. HAMILTON *Dissert.* in *Reid's Wks.* 770.

dianome ('daɪənəʊm). *Math.* [f. Gr. διανομή distribution: so called as having nodes of determinate distribution.] A surface, generally a quartic surface, having all its nodes, if in excess of the number which can be arbitrarily assumed, situated on a surface, called dianodal, which is determined by the arbitrary points.
1874 SALMON *Analyt. Geom. of three Dimens.* (ed. 3) 507.

‖**Dianthus** (daɪ'ænθəs). *Bot.* [f. Gr. Διός of Jupiter + ἄνθος flower (Linnæus).] A genus of caryophyllaceous flowering plants, which includes the pinks and carnations; a flower of this kind. Hence **di'anthine,** name of an aniline dye.
1849 *Florist* 289 The three florists' species of Dianthus, the Carnation, Picotee, and Pink. **1869** RUSKIN *Q. of Air* §84 Later in the year, the dianthus..seems to scatter, in multitudinous families, its crimson stars far and wide. **1860** *Sunday Times* 5 Aug. 7/1 Another new colour..called Dianthine..extracted from gas tar. The shades range from a deep purple to a brilliant rose.

† **di'antre, -ter**, *int. Obs.* [a. F. *diantre* (16th c. in Littré), euphemism for *diable*.] Devil!

1751 *Female Foundling* I. 151 Dianter! what Strength you have, when you please! *Ibid.* I. 181 Diantre, you have been prudent.

‖**dia'palma.** *Pharm.* [med. or mod.L. f. DIA-² + L. *palma* palm: in F. *diapalme*.] A desiccating or detersive plaster composed originally of palm oil, litharge, and sulphate of zinc, now of white wax, emplastrum simplex, and sulphate of zinc.

1646 SIR T. BROWNE *Pseud. Ep.* IV. iv. 186 We as highly conceive of the practice in Diapalma, that is in the making of that plaister, to stirre it with the stick of a Palme. **1660** BOYLE *New Exp. Phys. Mech.* xxii. 176 We stopt the mouth of the Glass with a flat piece of Diapalma, provided for the purpose. **1741** *Compl. Fam. Piece* I. i. 30 Take of Diapalma melted down very thin, with Oil of Chamomile 1 Ounce. **1883** in *Syd. Soc. Lex.*

'diapase. Anglicized form of DIAPASON, used by the poets.

1591 SPENSER *Tears of Muses* 549 Melodious measures, With which I..make a tunefull Diapase of pleasures. **1647** H. MORE *Song of Soul* I. II. xv, From this same universall Diapase Each harmony is fram'd. **1652** BENLOWES *Theoph.* VI. lxv, On the trembling cords his swift hand strayes, And clos'd all with full Diapaze. **1880** MRS. WHITNEY *Odd or Even?* xxiv. 255 The ceaseless soft crush of the waterfall kept up its gentle diapase.

diapasm ('daɪəpæz(ə)m). *Obs.* or *arch.* [ad. L. *diapasma*, a. Gr. διάπασμα, f. διαπάσσ-ειν to sprinkle over. In mod.F. *diapasme*.] A scented powder for sprinkling over the person.

1599 B. JONSON *Cynthia's Rev.* v. ii, There's an excellent diapasm in a chain, too, if you like. **1657** G. STARKEY *Helmont's Vind.* 121 Chymistry is larger then to be totally comprehended by the Art of Medicine, for by it are prepared Diapasmes. [**1706** PHILLIPS (ed. Kersey), *Diapasma*, a Pomander or Perfume.] **1863** SALA *Capt. Dangerous* I. i. 21 She had an exquisitely neat and quick hand for..confecting of diapasms, pomanders, and other sweet essences.

diapason (daɪə'peɪzən, -sən), *sb.* Also 4-5 **dyapason(e, 6 dio-, dyopason, 7 diapazon.** [a. L. *diapāsōn*, a. Gr. διαπᾱσῶν, or divisim διὰ πασῶν (sc. χορδῶν), more fully ἡ διὰ πασῶν χορδῶν συμφωνία, the concord through, or at the interval of, all the notes of the scale, f. διά through + πασῶν, genit. pl. fem. of πᾶς all. Cf. ἡ διὰ τεσσάρων the interval of a fourth, ἡ διὰ πέντε of a fifth, etc. Cf. also F. *diapason* (12th c. in Hatz.-Darm.), whence, in 16-17th c., accented by poets *di'apason*, but already before 1600 with stress on penult.]

†**1. a.** The interval of an octave; the consonance of the highest and lowest notes of the musical scale.

Spoken of by early musicians as 'a Consonance of eight sounds and seuen Interuals' (Dowland) in reference to the intermediate notes of the diatonic scale: cf. sense 3.

1398 TREVISA *Barth. De P.R.* XIX. cxxvi. (1495) 926 Musyk hath names of nombres as it faryth in Dyatesseron Dyapente and in Dyapasone and in other Consonanciis and accordes. **1413** [see DIAPENTE 1]. **1509** HAWES *Past. Pleas.* XVI. ii, The lady excellent, Played on base organs expedient, Accordyng well unto dyopason, Dyapenthe, and eke dyetesseron. **1629** BACON *Sylva* §183 It discovereth the true Co-incidence of Tones into Diapasons, which is the return of the same Sound. **1787** HAWKINS *Johnson* 376 *note*, Answering to the unison, the diapente, the diatessaron, and the diapason, the sweetest concords in musick.

†**b.** In ancient music, in names of compound intervals, as ***diapason-diapente***, an octave and a fifth, a twelfth: so ***diapason-diatessaron***, ***diapason-ditone***, etc.; cf. Chambers *Cycl.* (1727-51) s.v.

[**1694** HOLDER *Treat. Harmony* v. (1731) 84 These are the mean Rations comprehended in the Ration of 6 to 2, by which *Diapason cum Diapente*, or a 12th, is divided into the aforesaid Intervals.] **1727-51** CHAMBERS *Cycl.* s.v., The *diapason-diapente* is a symphony made when the voice proceeds from the 1st to the 12th tone. The word is properly a term in the Greek music: we should now call it a *twelfth*. [**1880** STAINER & BARRETT *Dict. Mus. Terms, Diapason cum diapente*, the interval of a 12th. *Diapason cum diatessaron*, the interval of an 11th.]

†**c.** A part in music that produces such a consonance; an air or bass sounding in exact concord, i.e. in octaves. Chiefly *fig. Obs.*

1593 SHAKS. *Lucr.* 1132 So I at each sad strain will strain a tear, And with deep groans the diapason bear. **1740** DYER *Ruins Rome* 355 While winds and tempests sweep his various lyre How sweet thy diapason. **1814** SCOTT *Ld. of Isles* I. i, The diapason of the Deep. **1844** LONGF. *Arsenal at Springfield* vii, I hear..in tones of thunder the diapason of the cannonade.

†**2.** *fig.* Complete concord, harmony, or agreement. *Obs.*

1591 GREENE *Maidens Dreame* xxiii, Her sorrows and her tears did well accord; Their diapason was in self-same cord. **1621** BURTON *Anat. Mel.* III. i. II. iii, A true correspondence, perfect amity, a diapason of vows and wishes..as between David and Jonathan. **1630** MILTON *At a Solemn Music* 23 Their great Lord, whose love their motion swayed In perfect diapason. **1647** H. MORE *Song of Soul* I. I. lvi, In her there's tun'd a just Diapason. **1719** D'URFEY *Pills* (1872) I. 343 Contentment..tunes the Diapason of our souls.

3. More or less vaguely extended, with the idea of 'all the tones or notes', to: **a.** The combination of parts or notes in a harmonious whole, properly in concord. **b.** A melodious succession of notes, a melody, a strain; now *esp.* a swelling sound, as of a grand burst of harmony: perhaps in this sense also associated with the organ-stop (sense 7). **c.** The whole range of tones or notes in the scale; the compass of a voice or instrument.

a. 1501 DOUGLAS *Pal. Hon.* I. xli, Fresche ladyis sang.. Concordis sweit, divers entoned reportis..Diapason of many sindrie sortis. **1580** LYLY *Euphues* (Arb.) 387 In Musicke there are many discords, before there can be framed a Diapason. **1601** HOLLAND *Pliny* I. 14 Thus are composed seuen tunes; which harmonie they call Diapason, that is to say, the Generalitie, or whole state of consent and concord, which is perfect musicke. **1604** R. CAWDREY *Table Alph., Diapason*, a Concord in Musicke of all parts. **1878** H. M. STANLEY *Dark Cont.* II. vii. 197 A deep and melodious diapason of musical voices chanting the farewell song.

b. 1599 MARSTON *Sco. Villanie* III. xi. 228 When some pleasing Diapason flies From out the belly of a sweete touched Lute. **1646** CRASHAW *Music's Duel* Poems 92 A full-mouth'd diapason swallows all. **1776** SIR J. HAWKINS *Hist. Music* IV. I. x. 148 When all the stops are drawn, and the registers open..we hear that full and complete harmony.. which..is what the ancient writers mean to express by the term Diapason. **1804** J. GRAHAME *Sabbath* 66 The organ.. swells into a diapason full. **1860** C. SANGSTER *Into the Silent Land* 139 Tune the lyre To diapasons worthy of the theme. **1880** OUIDA *Moths* II. 263 His voice, is rising in its wonderful diapason clearer and clearer.

c. 1687 DRYDEN *St. Cecilia's Day* 15 From Harmony to Harmony Through all the compass of the Notes it ran, The Diapason closing full in Man. **1748** THOMSON *Cast. Indol.* I. xli, Who up the lofty diapason [of an Aeolian harp] roll Such sweet, such sad, such solemn airs divine? *c* **1800** K. WHITE *To my Lyre* iii, No hand, thy diapason o'er, Well skilled, I throw with sweep sublime. **1806** MOORE *Vis. Philos.* 27 To him who traced upon his typic lyre The diapason of man's mingled frame.

4. *transf.* and *fig.* **a.** A rich, full, deep outburst of sound.

1589 GREENE *Menaphon* (Arb.) 82 The Diapason of thy threates. **1596** NASHE *Saffron Walden* 115 By your leaue they said vnto him (in a thundring yeoman vshers diapason). **1840** BARHAM *Ingol. Leg., St. Nicholas*, Full many an Aldermanic nose Rolled its loud diapason after dinner.

b. Entire compass, range, reach, scope.

1851 HELPS *Comp. Solit.* viii. (1874) 141 In marriage the whole diapason of joy and sorrow is sounded. **1888** *Daily News* 23 Apr. 6/4 Those who run up to the topmost note of the diapason of dress. **1893** *Ibid.* 9 June 5/8 Not..above the diapason of this Protectionist Chamber of Deputies.

5. A rule or scale employed by makers of musical instruments in tuning.

1727-51 CHAMBERS *Cycl., Diapason*, among musical instrument-makers, is a kind of rule, or scale, whereby they adjust the pipes of their organs, and cut the holes of their flutes..There is a particular kind of diapason for trumpets ..there is another for sackbuts and serpents..The bell-founders have likewise a diapason, or scale. **1828** in WEBSTER.

6. A fixed standard of musical pitch; as in Fr. ***diapason normal***. Also *fig.*

1875 HAMERTON *Intell. Life* x. v. 392 Tuning his whole mind to the given diapason, as a tuner tunes a piano. **1876** tr. *Blaserna's Theory Sound* iv. 70 An international commission fixed as the normal pitch (usually called the *diapason normal*) a tuning fork giving 435 vibrations per second.

7. The name of the two principal foundation-stops in an organ, the ***Open Diapason***, and the ***Closed*** or ***Stopped Diapason***, so called because they extend through the whole compass of the instrument; also the name of other stops, e.g. ***Violin Diapason***.

1519 *Organ Specif. Barking* in Grove *Dict. Mus.* II. 588/1 *Diapason*, containing length of x foot or more. **1613** *Organ Specif. Worcester Cathedral*, 2 open diapasons of mettall CC faut, a pipe of 10 foot long. **1791** HUDDESFORD *Salmag.* 12 When the vast Organ's breathing frame Echoes the voice of loud acclaim, And the deep diapason's sound Thunders the vaulted iles around. **1876** HILES *Catech. Organ* ix. (1878) 67 *Violin Diapason*, a..manual stop, with a crisp, pungent tone, very like that of the Gamba. **1880** E. J. HOPKINS in Grove *Dict. Mus.* II. 597/1 The second Open Diapason has ..stopped pipes and 'helpers'.

8. *attrib.*

1549 *Compl. Scot.* vi. 37 In accordis of mesure of diapason prolations. **1613-16** W. BROWNE *Brit. Past.* I. iv, And lastly, throwes His Period in a Diapazon Close. **1851** A. A. WATTS *Evening* ii, The echoes of its convent bell..With soft and diapason swell. **1880** E. J. HOPKINS in Grove *Dict. Mus.* II. 594/2 The larger open diapason pipes.

†**dia'pason**, *v. Obs.* [f. prec. sb.]

1. To resound sonorously. (*intr.* and *trans.*)

1608 HEYWOOD *Rape Lucrece* I. i, What diapasons more in Tarquins name Than in a subjects? **1611** —— *Golden Age* III. Wks. 1874 III. 48 Th' amazed sounds Of martiall thunder (Diapason'd deep).

2. *intr.* To maintain accord *with*.

1617 WITHER *Fidelia* Juvenilia (1633) 479 In their chime, Their motions Diapason with the time.

diapasonal (daɪə'peɪsənəl, -'peɪz-), *a.* [f. DIAPASON *sb.* + -AL.] Of or pertaining to the diapason or melody. Also **diapa'sonic** *a.*

1928 *Daily Tel.* 31 Jan. 8 There was no 'diapasonal excess', which a distinguished Mus. Doc. has declared to be the abuse of modern organ-playing. **1928** *Observer* 8 Apr. 9/4 The trills, roulades, cascades, and diapasonic fertility of 'Zampa'.

diapause ('daɪəpɔːz). *Ent.* [f. DIA-² + PAUSE *sb.*] A period of retardation or suspension of development in some insects. Also *transf.*

1893 W. M. WHEELER in *Jrnl. Morphology* VIII. 68, I shall designate..the intervening resting stage as the diapause. **1934** *Times* 18 Sept. 17/2 The duration of the life-cycle depends on the absence or presence or a diapause in the adult stage. **1956** *New Biol.* XXI. 106 Many species [of Earthworms] survive unfavourable conditions by going into a state of diapause in which they roll themselves up into a tight ball in spherical earthen cells which are lined with mucus. **1969** R. F. CHAPMAN *Insects* xxxv. 717 Diapause is a delay in development which, although its effect is usually to facilitate survival during unfavourable periods, is not immediately referable to the adverse environmental conditions.

diaped ('daɪəpɛd). *Geom.* [as if ad. Gr. *διάπεδον, f. διά through + πεδ- in πέδον ground, πεδίον plain, ἐπίπεδος plane.] The line in which any two non-contiguous planes of a polyhedron intersect.

In mod. Dicts.

‖**diapedesis** (ˌdaɪəpiː'diːsɪs). *Path.* [mod.L., a. Gr. διαπήδησις, f. διαπηδά-ειν to ooze through, f. δια- through + πηδά-ειν to leap, throb. In mod.F. *diapédèse* (Paré 16th c.).] The oozing of blood through the unruptured walls of the blood-vessels.

1625 HART *Anat. Ur.* II. iv. 68 Such an excretion of bloud ..is..called *Diapedesis*: that is, as much as a streining through. **1634** T. JOHNSON *Parey's Chirurg.* IX. i. (1678) 216 That solution of Continuity..which is generated by sweating out and transcolation, [is termed] Diapedesis. **1866** A. FLINT *Princ. Med.* (1880) 27 When the red blood corpuscles are pressed through the unruptured vascular wall, it is denominated hemorrhage by diapedesis. **1885** *Lancet* 26 Sept. 589 It is possible..that the mercury gains access to the circulation by a sort of diapedesis.

So **diape'detic** *a.*, pertaining to or of the nature of diapedesis.

In mod. Dicts.

†**diapente** (daɪə'pɛntiː). *Obs.* [= OF. *diapenté* (Godef.), a. L. *diapente*, Gr. διὰ πέντε, in sense 1 short for ἡ διὰ πέντε χορδῶν συμφωνία the harmony through five strings or notes; in sense 2 for τὸ διὰ πέντε φάρμακον the medicament composed of five (ingredients): see DIA-².]

1. In ancient and mediæval *Music*: The consonance or interval of a fifth.

1398 [see DIAPASON 1]. **1413** *Pilgr. Sowle* (Caxton) v. i. (1859) 72 The fayre dyapente, the swete Dyapason. **1579** TWYNE *Phisicke agst. Fort.* II. xcvii. 290 a, By what tunes of numbers Diapente, or Diapason consisteth..a deafe man may vnderstande. **1609** DOULAND *Ornith. Microl.* 18 *Diapente*, is a Consonance of fiue Voyces, and 4. Interuals.. Or it is the leaping of one Voyce to another by a fift, consisting of three Tones, and a semitone. **1694** *Phil. Trans.* XVIII. 70 A Diapente added to a Diatessaron makes a Diapason. **1787** [see DIAPASON 1]. **1876** HILES *Catech. Organ* ix. (1878) 69.

2. In old *Pharmacy*: A medicine composed of five ingredients.

Originally, an electuary formed by adding ivory shavings to the diatessaron.

1610 MARKHAM *Masterp.* I. xcvii. 192 This word Diapente is as much as to say, a composition of fiue simples. **1614** —— *Cheap Husb.* I. i. (1668) 7 Give him..2 spoonfuls of Diapente..which is called Horse-Mitridate. **1678** PHILLIPS, *Diapente*, also a Composition consisting of five ingredients, viz. Myrrh, Gentian, Birthwort, Ivory and Bay-berries..it is given by Farriers to Horses that want purging. **1721-1800** in BAILEY.

b. *transf.* A beverage composed of five ingredients; punch.

[**1698** FRYER *Acc. E. India & P.* 157 That enervating Liquor called *Paunch* (which is Indostan for Five) from Five Ingredients; as the Physicians name their Composition *Diapente*.] **1706** PHILLIPS (ed. Kersey), *Diapente*, also, a kind of strong Water, made of five several Simples. **1721-1800** in BAILEY. **1741** LINING in *Phil. Trans.* XLII. 497 The Punch, or Diapente..is made thus: Take Water 2 Pounds, Sugar $1\frac{1}{4}$ Ounce, recent Juice of Limes $2\frac{1}{2}$ Ounces, Rum $3\frac{1}{4}$ Ounces.

diaper ('daɪəpə(r)), *sb.* Forms: 4-6 **diapre, dyapre, 5 dyapere, 6 dyoper, dieper, dyeper, 6-7 dyaper, (7 dipar, dibar), 6- diaper.** [ME. a. OF. *dyapre, diapre*, orig. *diaspre* (Godef.), Pr. *diaspre, diaspe*, in med.L. *diasprus* adj., *diaspra, diasprum* (*c* 1023), sb. (Du Cange); in Byzantine Gr. δίασπρος adj., f. δια- (DIA-¹) + ἄσπρος white.

Early French references mention *diaspre* 'que fu fais en Costantinoble' and 'dyaspre d'Antioch', and associate it with other fabrics of Byzantine or Levantine origin. Thus, the *Roman de la Rose* l. 21193 (Meon III. 294) has 'Cendaux, molequins arrabis, Indes, vermaux, jaunes et bis, Samis, diapres, camelos'. The word occurs in mediæval Greek, *c* 959, in Constantine Porphyrogenitus *De Ceremoniis Aulæ Byzant.* (Bonn 1829-40, p. 528) where the ἱμάτιον or robe used in the investment of a Rector is described as δίασπρον. On the analogy of διάλευκος, δίασπρος may mean 'white at intervals, white interspersed with other colour'; though the sense might also be 'thoroughly' or 'pure white.' In OF., *diaspre* is often described as *blanc*. (The It., Sp., and Pg. *diaspro* 'jasper' appears to be unconnected with F. and Prov. *diaspre* 'diaper'. Du Cange has mixed up the two. A gratuitous guess that the name was perhaps derived from Ypres in Flanders has no etymological or historical basis.)]

I. 1. The name of a textile fabric; now, and since the 15th c., applied to a linen fabric (or an inferior fabric of 'union' or cotton) woven with a small and simple pattern, formed by the different directions of the thread, with the different reflexions of light from its surface, and consisting of lines crossing diamond-wise, with the spaces variously filled up by parallel lines, a central leaf or dot, etc.

In earlier times, esp. in OFr. and med.L., the name was applied to a richer and more costly fabric, apparently of silk, woven or flowered over the surface with gold thread. See Francisque Michel, *Recherches sur les Etoffes de Soie, d'Or et d'Argent* (Paris 1852) I. 236–244.

a **1350** *Syr Degarre* 802 In a diapre clothed ȝhe was. **13..** *Minor Poems fr. Vernon MS.* xlvi. 200 Til a Nonnerie þei came; But I knowe not þe name: þer was mony a derworþe dame In Dyapre dere. **1466** *Mann. & Househ. Exp.* 364 Paid for xj. Flemyshe stykes of fyne dyapere..xxvij. vj.*d.* **1502** ARNOLDE *Chron.* (1811) 244 A borde cloth of dyaper, a towell of dyaper. **1513** *Bk. Kervynge* in *Babees Bk.* 268 Couer thy cupborde and thyn ewery with the towell of dyaper. **1513** BRADSHAW *St. Werburge* I. 1667 The tables were couered with clothes of Dyaper Rychely enlarged with syluer and with golde. **1552–3** *Inv. Ch. Goods Staff.* in *Ann. Litchfield* IV. 50 One vestement of red sylke, one vestement of lynen dyoper. **1591** SPENSER *Muiopotmos* 364 Nor anie weauer, which his worke doth boast In dieper, in damaske, or in lyne. **1623** COCKERAM, *Diaper*, a fine kinde of Linnin, not wouen after the common fashion, but in certaine workes. **1624** *Will* in *Ripon Ch. Acts* 364 One suite of damaske and another of diaper for his table. **1662** *Vestry Bks.* (Surtees) 198 For Dyaper for a Communion table cloth and napkin, 12*s.* 6*d.* **1721** *Lond. Gaz.* No. 6020/4 Diapers, Damasks, Huckabacks. **1840** BARHAM *Ingol. Leg., Jackd. Rheims*, A napkin.. Of the best white diaper fringed with pink. **1888** J. WATSON *Art Weaving* (ed. 3) 101 [This] makes by far the best bird-eye Diaper.

2. A towel, napkin, or cloth of this material; a baby's napkin or 'clout'.

1596 SHAKS. *Tam. Shrew* I. i. 57 Let one attend him vvith a siluer Bason Full of Rose-water, and bestrew'd with Flowers, Another beare the Ewer: the third a Diaper. **1837** HT. MARTINEAU *Soc. Amer.* II. 245 Table and bed-linen, diapers, blankets. **1889** J. M. DUNCAN *Lect. Dis. Women* ix. (ed. 4) 54.

II. 3. The geometrical or conventional pattern or design forming the ground of this fabric.

1830 *Edin. Encycl.* VI. 686 A design of that intermediate kind of ornamental work which is called diaper. **1882** BECK *Draper's Dict.* 97 Some of the diapers are very curious. One of them consists of a series of castles; in each are two men holding hawks; the size of each diaper being about six inches, and the date the fourteenth century.

4. A pattern or design of the same kind, or more florid, in colour, gilding, or low relief, used to decorate a flat surface, as a panel, wall, etc.

1851 TURNER *Dom. Archit.* I. vi. 305 There are still some remains of good distemper diaper on the walls. **1863** SIR G. G. SCOTT *Westm. Abbey* (ed. 2) 61 The glass..is decorated on its face with gold diaper. **1866** *Athenæum* 17 Nov. 645/2 The diaper, composed of a raised pattern, decorating the background. **1884** *Pall Mall G.* 11 Sept. 5/1 The ground is most beautifully carved in a minute hexagonal diaper.

b. *Heraldry.* A similar style of ornamentation, in painting or low relief, used to cover the surface of a shield and form the ground on which the bearing is charged. See DIAPRE.

1634 PEACHAM *Gentl. Exerc.* III. 159 Some charge their Scotcheons..with diaper as the French. **1882** CUSSANS *Handbk. Her.* v. 81 To represent the Diaper by a slightly darker tint of the same tincture as that on which it is laid.

c. *fig.* Applied to the floral variegation of the surface of the ground.

1600 *Maides Metam.* II. in Bullen *O. Pl.* I. 118 This grassie bed, With summers gawdie dyaper bespred.

III. 5. *attrib.* **a.** Of or made of diaper (see 1).

(In quot. 1497 perh. for F. *diapré*, diapered.)

1497 *Old City Acc. Bk.* in *Archæol. Jrnl.* XLIII, Itm a table cloth diapre. **1538** *Bury Wills* (1850) 134 A dyeper towell of vij yarde longe. **1599** *Nottingham Rec.* IV. 250 Halfe a dosen of diaper napkins..one diaper table cloathe. **1604** *Vestry Bks.* (Surtees) 140 A poulpit clothe of silke, one owld dipar tablecloth. **1676** *Lond. Gaz.* No. 1124/4 One Damask and two Diaper Table Cloaths, three dozen of Diaper Napkins. **1812** J. SMYTH *Pract. Customs* (1821) 130 Diaper Tabling, of the manufacture of the kingdom of the United Netherlands. **1863** MISS BRADDON *J. Marchmont* I. ii. 30 Her brown-stuff frock and scanty diaper pinafore.

b. Having a pattern of this kind, diapered; as ***diaper-work, -pattern, -couching.***

1480 *Wardr. Acc. Edw. IV* (1830) 131 Table clothes off dyaper werk ij. **1602** CAREW *Cornwall* (1811) 303 Two moor stones..somewhat curiously hewed, with diaper work. **1769** *De Foe's Tour Gt. Brit.* I. 392 Both of them were curiously wrought by Diaper-work Carvings. **1838** *Archæol.* XXVII. 421 What the older Diaper-work was—a small regular pattern—we may gather from its appearance as borrowed in Heraldry. **1859** TURNER *Dom. Archit.* III. ii. 29 The spandrel of the arch is carved with a sort of diaper pattern. **1874** PARKER *Illustr. Goth. Archit.* I. v. 175 The surface of the wall is often covered with flat foliage, arranged in small squares called diaper-work. **1876** GWILT *Archit.* Gloss. 1231 *Diaper Work*, the face of stone worked into squares or lozenges, with a leaf therein; as over arches and between bands. **1882** CAULFEILD & SAWARD *Dict. Needlework* 153 *Diaper couching*, a variety of couching used in Church Work. **1886** RUSKIN *Præterita* I. 335 The diaper pattern of the red and white marbles.

diaper ('daɪəpə(r)), *v.* [prob. a. F. *diaprer*, OF. *diasprer*, f. *diapre, diaspre*: see prec. sb.]

1. *trans.* To diversify the surface or ground of (anything) with a small uniform pattern; now *spec.* with one consisting of or based upon a diamond-shaped reticulation.

c **1375** *Sc. Leg. Saints, Eugenia* 711 And cled hyr wele..In clath, dyopret of gold fyne. *c* **1386** CHAUCER *Knt.'s T.* 1300 Couered in clooth of gold dyapred weel. *c* **1400** *Rom. Rose* 934 And it [the bow] was peynted wel and thwiten, And over-al diapred and writen With ladies and with bacheleres. ?*c* **1475** *Sqr. lowe Degre* 744 With damaske white, and asure blewe, Wel dyapred with lyllyes newe. **1680** MORDEN *Geog. Rect.* (1685) 150 Excellent Artists in Diapring Linnen-Cloaths. **1842–76** GWILT *Archit.* §302 The practice of diapering the walls, whereof an instance occurs in Westminster Abbey.

2. *transf.* and *fig.* To adorn with diversely coloured details; to variegate.

1592 GREENE *Upst. Courtier*, Fragrante flowres that diapred this valley. **1603** FLORIO *Montaigne* II. xii. (1632) 300 The wheelings..of the celestiall bodies diapred in colours. **1613** W. BROWNE *Brit. Past.* I. i, The rayes Wherewith the sunne doth diaper the seas. **1665** SIR T. HERBERT *Trav.* (1677) 380 Such flowres as Nature usually diapers the Earth with. **1862** SALA *Seven Sons* I. ix. 209 Tall chimneys, from whose tops smoke curled and diapered the woodland distance. **1865** CARLYLE *Fredk. Gt.* IX. xx. v. 97 Six coffee-cups, very pretty, well diapered, and tricked-out with all the little embellishments which increase their value.

3. *intr.* To do diaper-work; to flourish.

1573 *Art of Limming* 8 How to florishe or diaper with a pensel over silver or goulde. *Ibid.* (1588) 8 If thou wilt diaper upon silver, take Cerius with a pensill and draw or florish what thou wilt over thy silver. **1634** PEACHAM *Gentl. Exerc.* I. xiv. 46 If you Diaper upon folds, let your worke be broken.

diapered ('daɪəpəd), *ppl. a.* [f. prec. + -ED: = F. *diapré*, OF. *diaspré*.]

1. Having the surface or ground diversified and adorned with a diaper or fret-work pattern.

?*a* **1400** *Morte Arth.* 3252 A duches dere-worthily dyghte in dyaperde wedis. *c* **1400** MAUNDEV. (1839) xxii. 233 All clothed in clothes dyapred of red selk all wrought with gold. **1656** BLOUNT *Glossogr., Diaperd* or *Diapred*, diversified with flourishes or sundry figures, whence we call Cloth that is so diversified, Diaper. **1664** POWER *Exp. Philos.* I. 50 The backside of a..sweet Brier Leaf, looks diaper'd most excellently with silver. **1871** B. TAYLOR *Faust* (1875) II. III. 211 Bind ye in precious diapered stuffs. **1873** FERGUSON in Tristram *Moab* 371 The same diapered brick-wall that is now seen. **1881** *Every Man his own Mechanic* §798 A blue, green, or scarlet ground with a fleur-de-lys, or cross, or small diapered pattern.

b. *Heraldry*: see DIAPER *sb.* 4 b.

1610 GUILLIM *Heraldry* I. v. (1660) 31 That Field or bordure is properly said to be diapered, which being fretted all over, hath something quick or dead, appearing within the Frets. **1864** BOUTELL *Heraldry Hist. & Pop.* xix. 303 The seal of Jaspar Tudor also has the field of the seal itself diapered with the *Planta Genista*.

c. *transf.* and *fig.*

1595 SPENSER *Epithal.* 51 And let the ground..Be strewd with fragrant flowers all along, And diapred lyke the discolored mead. **1597** *Pilgr. Parnass.* III. 305, I like this grassie diapred greene earth. **1650** R. MASON in *Bulwer's Anthropomet.* Let. to Author, Any vegitable on the diaper'd earth. *a* **1849** J. C. MANGAN *Poems* (1859) 426 Our diapered canopy, the deep of the sky.

'diapering, *vbl. sb.* [f. as prec. + -ING[1].]

1. The production of a diaper pattern; the covering of a surface with such a pattern.

1606 PEACHAM *Art of Drawing* 34 Diapering..is..a light tracing or running over with your pen your other work when you have quite done (I mean folds shadowing and all); it chiefly serveth to counterfeit cloth of Gold, Silver, Damask-brancht, Velvet, Chamlet, &c., with what branch you list. **1882** BECK *Draper's Dict.* 97 The application of diapering to linen cannot definitely be traced. **1882** CUSSANS *Handbk. Her.* 78 Diapering was a device much practised by the Mediæval armorists..This was usually effected by covering the shield with a number of small squares, or lozenges, and filling them with a variety of simple figures.

2. A diaper pattern; diaper-work collectively.

1875 FORTNUM *Majolica* viii. 72 Covered with the most elegant arabesque diapering of foliage and flowers intertwined. **1882** CUSSANS *Handbk. Her.* 81 Diapering being merely a fanciful embellishment, does not..enter into the Blazon of a Coat of Arms.

† **'diapery, 'diapry,** *sb. Obs.* [f. DIAPER, after collective nouns in -ERY; in sense 1 perh. ad. OF. *diaspré, diapré* 'diapered (stuff)'.]

1. = DIAPER *sb.* 1.

c **1460** J. RUSSELL *Bk. Nurture* 193 Cover þy cuppeborde of thy ewery with the towelle of diapery.

2. Diaper-work; *fig.* variegated face (of the earth).

1633 EARL MANCH. *Al Mondo* (1636) 119 The little Bee, so soone as flowers spring, goes abroad, views the gay Diapery.

† **'diapery, 'diapry,** *a. Obs.* [f. DIAPER *sb.* + -Y[1]: cf. *papery, wintry*.] Of the nature of diaper or diaper-work; chequered with various colouring.

1598 SYLVESTER *Du Bartas* II. i. *Handie-crafts* 654 The diapry mansions where man-kinde doth trade Were built in six dayes. *Ibid.* II. ii. *Colonies* 428 They lie neerer the diapry verges Of tear-bridge Tigris swallow-swifter surges.

† **di'aphanal,** *a.* and *sb. Obs. rare.* [f. mod.L. and Romanic stem *diaphan-* (see DIAPHANE) + -AL[1].]

A. *adj.* = DIAPHANOUS.

1607 B. JONSON *Entertainment to K. & Q. at Theobalds* (22 May), Divers diaphanal glasses filled with several waters, that shewed like..stones of orient and transparent hues. *a* **1645** W. BROWNE *Love Poems* Wks. (1869) II. 276 By thy chaster fire will all be so wrought diaphanall.

B. *sb.* A diaphanous or transparent body.

1653 SHIRLEY *Court Secret* I. i, If you find Within that great diaphanal [the Soul] an atom Look black as guilty.

diaphane ('daɪəfeɪn), *a.* and *sb.* [a. F. *diaphane* (14th c. in Hatz.-Darm.); cf. Pr. *diafan*, It., Sp., Pg. *diafano*, med. and mod.L. *diaphan-us*; f. Gr. διαφανής transparent, f. δια- through + -φανης showing, appearing, from φαίνειν to show, cause to appear.]

† **A.** *adj.* = DIAPHANOUS, transparent. *Obs.*

1561 EDEN *Arte of Nauig.* I. i, Diaphane or transparent bodyes. **1594** CAREW *Huarte's Exam. Wits* vi. (1596) 77 Some haue colours, and some are diaphane and transparant. **1824** *Ann. Reg.* 270* A new manufacture of stuffs, with transparent figures, which he calls Diaphane Stuffs.

B. *sb.* **1.** A transparent body or substance; a transparency.

[**1677** HALE *Prim. Orig. Man.* IV. ii. 296 Frequently both in the Language of the Holy Scripture, and of divers of the ancient Heathen Authors, the whole *Diaphanum* of the Air and *Æther* is in one common appellation called Heaven; which is the denomination here given to this *Expansum*.] **1840** MRS. BROWNING *Drama of Exile* Poems (1889) I. 100 Through the crystal diaphane.

2. A silk stuff: see quot.

1824 [see A]. **1882** CAULFEILD & SAWARD *Dict. Needlework* 153 *Diaphane*, a woven silk stuff, having transparent coloured figures.

† **'diaphaned,** *ppl. a. Obs.* [repr. F. *diaphané*, pa. pple. of *diaphaner* to make transparent (Cotgr.).] Made diaphanous; transparent.

1626 tr. *Boccalini* 53 (T.) Drinking of much wine hath the virtue to make bodies diaphaned or transparent.

diaphaneity (daɪ,æfə'niːɪtɪ). Also 7 -iety. [mod. f. Gr. διαφανής, stem διαφανε-, transparent, or διαφάνεια transparency: see -ITY. Perhaps originating in a med. or mod.L **diaphaneitās*. Occurring in F. (*diaphanéité*) in 14th c. (Hatz.-Darm.); in Eng. late in 17th c., an earlier synonym being DIAPHANITY (q.v.). The corresponding form of the adj. is *diaphaneous*.]

The quality of being freely pervious to light; transparency.

1660 BOYLE *New Exp. Phys. Mech.* xxxvii. 311 The Diaphaneity of the Air. **1661** —— *Examen* vii. (1682) 83 The difficulty of explaining the Diaphaneity of glass or crystal. **1662** MERRETT tr. *Neri's Art of Glass* xxxvi, Until the Sea-green lose it's transparencie and diaphanietie. **1671** *Phil. Trans.* VI. 3046 The different Diaphanieties of the Humors of the Eye. **1678** HOBBES *Decam.* ix. 121 The Causes of Diaphaniety and Refraction. **1825** *New Monthly Mag.* XIII. 206 The diaphaneity of the material. **1837** WHEWELL *Hist. Induct. Sc.* (1857) II. 399 The diaphaneity of bodies is very distinct from their power of transmitting heat.

diaphaneous, obs. var. DIAPHANOUS.

† **dia'phanic,** *a. Obs.* [irreg. f. Gr. διαφανής, or f. Romanic stem *diaphan-* (see DIAPHANE) + -IC.] = DIAPHANOUS.

1614 RALEIGH *Hist. World* I. i. §6 Vast, open, subtile, diaphanicke, or transparent body.

‖ **diaphanie** (diafani). [mod.F. *diaphanie*, f. *diaphane*: see DIAPHANE.] The name given to a process for the imitation of painted or stained glass.

1859 *Ecclesiol.* XX. 122 A French invention called Diaphanie—a transparent coloured paper..intended to be applied to plain glass. **1869** *Eng. Mech.* 3 Dec. 289/1, I have ..decorated a window in diaphanie. **1874** (*title*), Designs for Windows to be executed in Diaphanie.

† **dia'phanity.** *Obs.* [ad. obs. F. *diaphanité* (Palissy, 16th c.) = Sp. *diafanidad*, It. *diafanità*, f. F. *diaphane*, It. *diafan-o*, med.L. *diaphan-us*: see DIAPHANE and -ITY.] = DIAPHANEITY.

1477 NORTON *Ord. Alch.* iii. in Ashm. (1652) 42 A goodly stone glittering with perspecuitie, Being of wonderfull and excellent Diaphanitie. **1577** DEE *Relat. Spir.* I. (1659) 9 The Stone was of his natural Diaphanitie. **1646** SIR T. BROWNE *Pseud. Ep.* II. i. 55 If it be made hot in a crusible..it will grow dim, and abate its diaphanity. **1664** POWER *Exp. Philos.* I. 55 It was like a thin horn something diaphanous.. which diaphanity might perchance hinder the appearance both of its cavity and angularity.

diapha'nometer. [f. Gr. διαφανής transparent, or rather its med.L. and Romanic adaptation *diaphano-* + -METER, Gr. μέτρον measure.] A measurer of transparency; *spec.* an instrument for measuring the transparency of the atmosphere.

1789 *Tilloch's Philos. Mag.* III. 377 (*Article*) Description of M. de Saussure's Diaphanometer..The diaphanometer is..designed to show the greatness of the evaporation existing in any limited part of the atmosphere which surrounds us. The measure of transparency..is founded on the proportion of the distances at which determined objects cease to be visible. **1807** T. YOUNG *Lect. Nat. Phil. & Mech. Arts* II. 74. **1857** J. P. NICHOL *Cycl. Phys. Sc.*

diaphanoscope (daɪ'æfənəʊskəʊp). [f. as prec. + Gr. -σκοπ-ος observing.]

† **1.** A contrivance for viewing transparent positive photographs. *Obs.*

1868 *Chambers' Encycl.* III. 538/1 *Diapha'noscope*, a dark box constructed for exhibiting transparent photographs.

2. An instrument used in obstetrical surgery for the examination of internal organs through the translucent walls of the abdomen when internally illuminated by electricity. Hence **diapha'noscopy**, the clinical use of the diaphanoscope.

1883 *Q. Rev.* July 82 The long promised but never perfected diaphanoscope. **1883** *Syd. Soc. Lex.*, *Diaphanoscopy*, a term applied by Lazarewitch to the exploration of the genital organs by means of an electric light introduced into the vagina in a glass tube.

diaphanous (daɪ'æfənəs), *a.* Also 7 diaphaneous. [f. med.L. *diaphan-us* (see DIAPHANE) + -OUS. The form *diaphaneous* more closely represented the Gr.: cf. DIAPHANEITY.]

Permitting the free passage of light and vision; perfectly transparent; pellucid.

1614 RALEIGH *Hist. World* I. i. §7 Aristotle calleth light a quality inherent, or cleauing to a Diaphanous body. **1633** T. ADAMS *Exp. 2 Peter* ii. 4 In hell there shall be nothing diaphanous, perspicuous, clear. *c* **1645** HOWELL *Lett.* I. I. xxix, To transmute Dust and Sand to such a diaphanous pellucid dainty body as you see a Crystal-Glasse is. **1669** W. SIMPSON *Hydrol. Chym.* 10 The diaphaneous texture of the particles in the vitrioline solution. **1680** BOYLE *Scept. Chem.* v. 326 The one substance is Opacous, and the other somewhat Diaphanous. **1794** MARTYN *Rousseau's Bot.* xxxii. 500 The fructifications are in a diaphanous membrane. **1833** *Penny Cycl.* I. 450/2 The crystals of the amethyst vary from diaphanous to translucent. **1868** DUNCAN *Insect World* ii. 59 The wings are whitish, not diaphanous. **1895** *The Lady* 31 Jan. 133 With this was worn a diaphanous white picture hat caught up with .. white ribbons.

Hence **di'aphanously** *adv.*, in a diaphanous manner, transparently; **di'aphanousness**, diaphanous quality, transparency.

1683 E. HOOKER *Pref. Epist. Pordage's Mystic Div.*, Most Diaphanously, perspicuously, no less clearly .. than the Sun Beams upon a Wall of Crystall. **1710** T. FULLER *Pharm. Extemp.* 220 As here order'd 'twill be diaphanously clear. **1727** BAILEY vol. II, *Diaphaneity, Diaphanousness*, the property of a diaphanous Body. **1969** A. GLYN *Dragon Variation* i. 4 A pot-bellied shah was reclining on cushions .. while a diaphanously veiled maiden knelt before him, offering a cup.

diaphemetric (daɪ,æfiː'mɛtrɪk), *a.* [mod. f. Gr. δια- apart (DIA-[1]) + ἁφή touch + -METRIC.]

Relating to the measurement of the comparative tactile sensibility of parts.

diaphemetric compasses, 'an instrument, consisting of a pair of compasses with a graduated scale, used for the same purpose as the ÆSTHESIOMETER.' (*Syd. Soc. Lex.*)
18.. in DUNGLISON.

diaphone[1] ('daɪəfəʊn). [f. DIA-[1] + PHONE *sb.*[2]] A low-pitched fog signal operated by compressed air and characterized by the 'grunt' which ends each note. Also *attrib.*

1906 *Daily Colonist* (Victoria, B.C.) 20 Jan. 6/5 The fog alarm will consist of a diaphone, operated by compressed air. **1950** *Engineering* 29 Dec. 570/1 Three types of sound signal compared were a diaphone with a fundamental frequency of about 180 cycles p. second, [etc.]. **1970** *Motor Boat & Yachting* 16 Oct. 36/1 The fog horn was one of the diaphone type and I can't beat the description in Reed's—'a strong note of low tone ending with a well-defined "grunt"'.

diaphone[2] ('daɪəfəʊn). *Linguistics.* [f. DIA-[1] + PHONE *sb.*[1]] All the different forms of a phoneme that collectively occur in all the dialects of a language (see quot. 1932).

1932 D. JONES *Outl. Eng. Phonet.* (ed. 3) xi. 52 The term diaphone is used to denote a sound used by one group of speakers together with other sounds which replace it in the pronunciation of other speakers. **1950** [see DIAPHONIC *a.*[2]]. **1953** W. J. ENTWISTLE *Aspects of Lang.* iv. 114 The diaphones are also found in the speech of a single individual. **1961** KURATH & MCDAVID *Pronunc. Eng. in Atlantic States* iii. 101 (*heading*) The regional and social dissemination of the diaphones of stressed vowels.

diaphoneme (daɪə'fəʊniːm). *Linguistics.* [f. DIA-[1] + PHONEME.] The collective dialectal variants of a phoneme; = prec. Hence **diapho'nemic** *a.*; **diapho'nemically** *adv.*

1939 D. JONES in *Proc. Third Internat. Congr. Phonetic Sci.* 6 As long as the divergences are not wide enough to interfere with intelligibility, we get higher degrees of abstractions which might be termed diaphonemes. **1939** H. E. PALMER *Ibid.* 7 It might be appropriate to divide each degree of abstraction into .. the phonemic and .. the diaphonemic aspects of the abstraction. **1959** *Amer. Speech* XXXIV. 266 The core contrasts .. can also be reached by way of the diaphonemic pattern, but a smaller set will emerge because of the phonetic integrity that is built into the diaphoneme. The criterion for assigning diaphonemically different entities to a single slot in the phonemic inventory is dialectal complementation among the contrasts.

diaphonic (daɪə'fɒnɪk), *a.*[1] [f. as DIAPHON-Y + -IC.] Also **diaphonical**.

1. Of or pertaining to diaphony: see DIAPHONY 2.

1822 *New Monthly Mag.* VI. 201 To give a concert with a full orchestra upon the diaphonic principle.

2. = DIACOUSTIC.

1775 ASH, *Diaphonic.* **1846** WORCESTER, *Diaphonic, Diaphonical.*

diaphonic (daɪə'fɒnɪk), *a.*[2] *Linguistics.* [f. DIAPHONE[2] + -IC.] Of or relating to a diaphone or diaphones. Hence **dia'phonically** *adv.*

1932 D. JONES *Outl. Eng. Phonet.* (ed. 3) xv. 108 There exist .. diaphonic variants; that is to say, there are English speakers who use a somewhat different diphthong. **1950** —— *Phoneme* xxvii. 198 Overlapping of diaphones is .. especially liable to happen when a sound lies near the limit of a diaphonic 'area'. *Ibid.* 202 The ʔ belongs diaphonically to *k* and *p* as well as to *t*. **1965** *Amer. Speech* XL. 227 The pronunciation (tagə·) .. is phonologically unlikely in the diaphonic variations before (g).

diaphonics. ? *Obs.* [f. as pl. of DIAPHONIC *a.*[1]: see -ICS.] = DIACOUSTICS.

1683 *Phil. Trans.* XIV. 473 Three parts of our Doctrine of Acousticks; which are yet nameless, unless we call them Acousticks, Diacousticks, and Catacousticks, or (in another sense, but to as good purpose) Phonicks, Diaphonicks, and Cataphonicks. **1704** J. HARRIS *Lex. Techn.*, *Diacousticks*, or *Diaphonicks*, is the consideration of the properties of Refracted sound, as it passes through different mediums.

† **di'aphonist.** *Obs. rare*—0. [f. next + -IST.]

1656 BLOUNT *Glossogr.*, *Diaphonist*, he that makes divers sounds.

diaphony (daɪ'æfənɪ). *Mus.* [ad. late L. *diaphōnia* dissonance, discord, a. Gr. διαφωνία discord, f. διάφωνος dissonant, f. δια- apart + φωνεῖν to sound. Cf. F. *diaphonie*, 18th c. in Hatz.-Darm.]

† **1.** In etymol. sense: Discord. *Obs.*—0

1656 BLOUNT *Glossogr.*, *Diaphony*, a divers sound, a discord.

2. In mediæval music (as usually understood): The most primitive form of harmony, in which the parts proceeded by parallel motion in fourths, fifths, and octaves: the same as ORGANUM.

But some suppose it to have meant a system in which the parts were sung *responsively* at these intervals.

1834 A. MERRICK *Albrechtsberger's Theoret. Wks.* 154 *note.* **1871** *Q. Rev.* No. 261. 158 We might add no harmony, for the diaphony employed .. is to our ears most terrible discord. **1880** C. H. H. PARRY in Grove *Dict. Mus.* I. 391 The supposed first form of harmony, which was called Diaphony, or Organum. **1881** MACFARREN *Counterp.* i. 1 Diaphony .. may have meant alternation or response .. the parts .. were sung in succession and not together.

diaphorase (daɪ'æfəreɪs, -eɪz). *Biochem.* [a. G. *diaphorase* (Adler, von Euler & Günther 1938, in *Arkiv f. Kemi* XII. B. LIV. 4), f. Gr. διάφορ-ος different + -ASE.] A flavoprotein enzyme reported to catalyse the reduction of dyes by diphosphopyridine nucleotide.

1938 *Brit. Chem. Abstr.* 1048 Diaphorase... Top and bottom yeasts have the same diaphorase activity. **1939** E. ADLER et al. in *Nature* 15 Apr. 641/2 We have used the name 'diaphorase' to designate the enzyme which catalyses the transport of hydrogen from dihydrocodehydrogenase I (CoH_2I) to acceptors like methylene/blue or cytochrome. **1966** S. P. COLOWICK et al. in Florkin & Stotz *Comprehensive Biochem.* XIV. i. 78 The biological significance of the diaphorase activity .. is vague, at best, but it may prove useful in understanding the mechanism of hydrogen transfer. **1968** A. WHITE et al. *Princ. Biochem.* (ed. 4) xvii. 366 The diaphorase activity initially reported has proved to be the lipoyl dehydrogenase described above; diaphorase activity, therefore, is entirely artifactual.

‖ **diaphoresis** (,daɪəfɒ'riːsɪs). *Med.* [L. *diaphorēsis*, a. Gr. διαφόρησις a sweat, perspiration, f. διαφορεῖν to carry off, *spec.* to throw off by perspiration, f. δια- through + φορεῖν to carry.] Perspiration; especially, that produced by artificial means.

1681 tr. *Willis' Rem. Med. Wks.* Vocab., *Diaphoresis*, evaporation, as by sweating. **1710** T. FULLER *Pharm. Extemp.* 101 This sort of Cure by a Diaphoresis is not always certain. **1718** QUINCY *Compl. Disp.* 93 In the Height of Fevers .. it is very effectual .. to forward a Diaphoresis. **1876** BARTHOLOW *Mat. Med.* (1879) 53 When active diaphoresis is the object to be accomplished, the patient must be well enveloped in blankets.

diaphoretic (,daɪəfɒ'rɛtɪk), *a.* and *sb. Med.* [ad. L. *diaphorēticus*, a. Gr. διαφορητικός promoting perspiration, f. διαφόρησις: see prec. So F. *diaphorétique*, in 14th c. *diaforetique* in Hatz.-Darm.]

A. *adj.* Having the property of inducing or promoting perspiration; sudorific.

1563 T. GALE *Antidot.* I. iv. 3 The simples Diaphoretik are these. **1631** H. SHIRLEY *Mart. Souldier* III. iv. in Bullen *O. Pl.* I. 219 Diophoratick Medicines to expell Ill vapours from the noble parts by sweate. **1680** MORDEN *Geog. Rect.* (1685) 253 Baths and Hot Springs that are very Diaphoretick. **1725** BRADLEY *Fam. Dict.* s.v. *Antimony*, To prepare Diaphoretick Antimony. **1883-4** *Med. Ann.* 44/1 It is diuretic but not diaphoretic.

B. *sb.* A medicinal agent having this property.

1656 RIDGLEY *Pract. Physick.* 19 Then diaphoreticks at first, and colder diureticks. **1672** *Phil. Trans.* VII. 4029 He commends Spirit of Hartshorn, as an excellent Diaphoretick. **1732** ARBUTHNOT *Rules of Diet* 273 Diaphoreticks or Promoters of Perspiration. **1877** ROBERTS *Handbk. Med.* (ed. 3) I. 35 The only diaphoretic that is of much practical value is some form of bath which promotes perspiration.

† **diapho'retical,** *a. Obs.* [f. as prec. + -AL[1].] = DIAPHORETIC *a.*

1601 HOLLAND *Pliny* II. 341 The ashes of a goats horn incorporat into an vnguent with oile of myrtles, keeps those from diaphoretical sweats who are anointed therwith. **1605** TIMME *Quersit.* II. vii. 141 Why it should be diaphoretical, that is to say, apt to prouoke sweates. **1657** W. COLES *Adam in Eden* 329 By its dryness and diaphoretical quality.

diaphoric (daɪə'fɒrɪk), *a. Math.* [f. Gr. διάφορος different + -IC.] Of or pertaining to difference; in ***diaphoric function***, a function of the differences of variables.

1883 CAYLEY in *Camb. Phil. Trans.* XIII. 12 The function .. is a function of the differences of the variables .. Any such function is said to be 'diaphoric': and it is easy to see that taking for the variables any inverts whatever, a diaphoric function is always curtate. **1893** LLOYD TANNER in *Proc. Lond. Math. Soc.* XXIV. 264.

diaphorite (daɪ'æfəraɪt). *Min.* [f. Gr. διάφορος different, διαφορά difference, distinction + -ITE.]

† **a.** A name formerly used for an altered rhodonite related to allagite. **b.** A name given by Zepharovich to the orthorhombic form of Freieslebenite.

1868 DANA *Min.* Index, Diaphorite, *v.* Allagite. **1871** *Amer. Jrnl. Sc.* Ser. III. I. 381 He retains the original name for the monoclinic species, and gives the name *diaphorite* to the orthorhombic.

diaphototropic (,daɪəfəʊtəʊ'trɒpɪk, -'trəʊpɪk), *a. Bot.* [f. DIA-[1] + PHOTOTROPIC *a.*] Of a plant, leaf, etc.: turning at right angles to incident light. So **,diapho'totropism**. Cf. DIA-HELIOTROPIC *a.*, -ISM.

1901 D. T. MACDOUGAL *Pract. Text-bk. Plant Physiol.* viii. 127 Leaves .. place their surfaces at right angles to the direction of the rays in response to their diaphototropism. *Ibid.* 138 The leaves of *Taraxacum* are diaphototropic, apogeotropic, and epinastic. **1929** J. C. BOSE *Growth & Tropic Movem. Plants* xiii. 133 (*title*) Dia-phototropism and negative phototropism. *Ibid.*, The seedling .. assumed a diaphototropic position under intense and long-continued action of light.

diaphragm ('daɪəfræm), *sb.* Also 7- agme. [ad. L. *diaphragma*, a. Gr. διάφραγμα, the midriff, primarily 'partition-wall, barrier', f. δια- through, apart + φράγμα fence, f. φράσσειν to fence in, hedge round. Long used in L. form. Cf. F. *diaphragme*, in 13-14th c. *diaffragme* (Hatz.-Darm.).]

I. 1. *Anat.* The septum or partition, partly muscular, partly tendinous, which in mammals divides the thoracic from the abdominal cavity; the midriff.

Its action is important in respiration, and it is also concerned in laughter, sneezing, and hiccough; hence *to move the diaphragm*, to excite laughter.

1398 TREVISA *Barth. De P.R.* VII. lv. (1495) 269 Diafragma is a skynne that departyth and is sette bitwene the bowels and the spirytuall membres. *c* **1400** *Lanfranc's Cirurg.* 161 þis diafragma departiþ þe spirituals from þe guttis. **1594** T. B. *La Primaud. Fr. Acad.* II. 220 There is a partition called diaphragma by the Græcians, which separateth the instruments of the vital partes, from the nourishing parts. **1626** BACON *Sylva* §697 It is true that they [*Insecta*] have (some of them) Diaphragm and an Intestine. **1629** GAULE *Holy Madn.* 293 It still moues my Diaphragme, what once mou'd the Spleene of Cyrus. **1685** BOYLE *Enq. Notion Nat.* 326 Divers of the Solid Parts, as the Heart and Lungs, the Diaphragma. **1767** GOOCH *Treat. Wounds* I. 369 The Diaphragm is a muscle of the greatest importance in respiration. **1872** DARWIN *Emotions* viii. 202 The sound of laughter is produced by a deep inspiration, followed by short, interrupted spasmodic contractions of the chest, and especially of the diaphragm. **1875** BLAKE *Zool.* 1 Inspiration is performed chiefly by the aid of the diaphragm.

II. Transferred uses.

2. a. *generally.* Applied to anything natural or artificial which in its nature or function resembles the diaphragm of the animal body, or similarly serves as a partition.

1660 BOYLE *New. Exp. Phys. Mech.* xxiv. 192 Certain Diaphragmes, consisting of the coats of the bubbles. **1862** M. HOPKINS *Hawaii* 27 That this fiery bottom was only a roof or diaphragm, of no great thickness, the upper and solidified portion of the incandescent matter of the volcano. **1891** *Pall Mall G.* 21 Aug. 6/2 A real advance in cartography was made when Dicæarch of Messena (390-290 B.C.) introduced the parallel of Rhodes. This 'diaphragm' was intersected at right angles by parallel lines representing meridians.

b. A thin rubber or plastic contraceptive cap with a flexible metal rim which fits over the cervix.

1933 G. M. COX *Clinical Contraception* ix. 120 The patient may be fitted with a diaphragm or vault pessary if she so desires. **1948** N. MAILER *Naked & Dead* (1949) III. ii. 490 They wanted a baby, but now he cannot afford another one, and he is wondering if her diaphragm has been set properly. **1968** M. RICHLER *Cocksure* xvi. 96 He found himself buying tubes of vaginal jelly, diaphragms in all available sizes, prophylactics. **1970** *Contraceptives* (Suppl. to *Which?*) 47 There are basically three types of cap that can be used by women—diaphragm, cervical cap and vault cap. All fit in the vagina, over the cervix.

3. a. *Zool.* A septum or partition separating the successive chambers of certain shells. Also applied to the operculum of a gastropod.

1665 HOOKE *Microgr.* 111 These shells which are thus spirallied and separated with Diaphragmes, were some kind of Nautili. **1728** WOODWARD *Fossils* (J.), Parted into numerous cells by means of diaphragms. **1858** GEIKIE *Hist. Boulder* v. 68 The same thin diaphragms..marked the successive stages of the animal's growth. **1880** A. R. WALLACE *Isl. Life* v. 76 Some..which close the mouth of the shell with a diaphragm of secreted mucus.

b. *Bot.* A septum or partition consisting of one or more layers of cells, occurring in the tissues of plants; a transverse partition in a stem or leaf.

1665 HOOKE *Microgr.* 115 Not to consist of abundance of long pores separated with Diaphragms, as Cork does. **1874** COOKE *Fungi* 35 The mouth being for some time closed by a veil, or diaphragm, which ultimately disappears. **1884** BOWER & SCOTT *De Bary's Phaner.* 217 The air-passages in the internodes, petioles, and leaves of most Monocotyledons ..the internodes and petioles or conical leaves of the Marsiliaceæ, the leaves of the Isoeteæ, etc., are partitioned by diaphragms. *Ibid.* 219 The one-layered diaphragms..in the leaf of Pistia.

4. *Mech.* A thin lamina or plate serving as a partition, or for some specific purpose; sometimes transferred to other appliances by which such purpose is effected: e.g.

a. A thin plate or disk used as a partition, especially in a tube or pipe; in optical instruments, an opaque plate or disk pierced with a circular hole to cut off marginal beams of light; *spec.* in *Photography*.

1665 HOOKE *Microgr.* Pref., The Ray..passes also perpendicularly through the Glass diaphragme. **1669** BOYLE *Contn. New Exp.* II. (1682) 19 A Diaphragma or Midriff of Tin whose edges are so polished on both sides that [etc.]. **1682** *Weekly Mem. Ingen.* 250 Two tin pipes, with a diaphragm pierced in the middle, and stopped with a sucker. **1773** *Phil. Trans.* LXIII. 203 Several diaphragms of pasteboard..to be applied to the object-glass externally. **1800** *Ibid.* XC. 557 A diaphragm, whose aperture was ½ an inch, was then put over the object-glass of the transit telescope. **1850** CHUBB *Locks & Keys* 35 In a line with the plane of the plate, or diaphragm of the lock. **1872** HUXLEY *Phys.* ix. 229 To have what is termed a diaphragm (that is an opaque plate with a hole in the centre) in the path of the rays. **1878** W. ABNEY *Treat. Photogr.* xxix. 205 In the doublet lens the position of the diaphragm is important. **1892** *Photogr. Ann.* II. 38 The diaphragm case. *Ibid.* 39 A flare spot is..really the reflection of the diaphragm aperture. **1918** *Photo-Miniature* Mar., *Diaphragm shutter*, one working approximately in the position of the diaphragm in the doublet lens. Constructed of leaves or blades which open and then close the aperture in the exposure shutter.

transf. **1860** TYNDALL *Glac.* I. xxvii. 207 The clouds.. had, during the night, thrown vast diaphragms across the sky. **1867** A. J. ELLIS *E.E. Pronunc.* I. iii. 161 The lips which form a variable diaphragm. **1878** FOSTER *Phys.* III. ii. 397 The iris serving as a diaphragm.

b. The porous cup of a voltaic cell.

1870 R. M. FERGUSON *Electr.* 136 Taking 1[d]. for diaphragm or porous cell. **1885** WATSON & BURBURY *Math. Th. Electr. & Magn.* I. 234 The hydrogen H_2 does not as in that case remain free. It passes through the diaphragm and displaces an equivalent of copper in the sulphate of copper.

c. A membrane stretched in or on a frame; a vibrating membrane or disk in an acoustic instrument; the vibrating disk of a telephone.

1853 KANE *Grinnell Exp.* l. (1856) 483 The kayack itself is a mere diaphragm of skin, stretched on a wooden frame. **1866** *Reader* 15 Sept. 796 An ear-trumpet, across the mouth of which was stretched a diaphragm of Indian rubber. **1879** G. PRESCOTT *Sp. Telephone* p. iii, In 1861 Reiss discovered that a vibrating diaphragm could be actuated by the human voice. **1879** *Cassell's Techn. Educ.* IV. 155/1 When the sound vibrations impinge upon the mica diaphragm the needle-point will indent the tinfoil.

d. The assemblage of lines of reference in the focus of a telescope, whether ruled upon glass, or formed of spider webs stretched in a frame.

1829 W. PEARSON *Pract. Astron.* II. 133 The first reticulated diaphragm that was used in making astronomical observations was by the Parisian astronomer Cassini. **1844** SMYTH *Cycle Celest. Objects* (1860) 215 Reticulated diaphragms..useful in mapping stars, and differentiating them. **1879** NEWCOMB & HOLDEN *Astron.* 76 Fine spider lines tightly stretched across a metal plate or diaphragm.

5. *attrib.*, as ***diaphragm current, eyepiece, nerve, plate***, etc.

1667 R. LOWER in *Phil. Trans.* II. 546 A dog, whose Diaphragme-nerves are cut. **1859** F. A. GRIFFITHS *Artill. Man.* (1862) 89 One inch in length for diaphragm shells. **1883** *Syd. Soc. Lex.*, *Diaphragm currents*, electric currents caused by forcing a liquid through a porous diaphragm.

Hence ‖**diaphrag'malgia, diaphragma'talgia** [Gr. ἄλγος, -αλγια pain], pain in the diaphragm; ‖**diaphragma'titis, -'mitis**, inflammation of the diaphragm; **dia'phragmatocele**, hernia of the diaphragm (*Syd. Soc. Lex.* 1883).

1835-6 TODD *Cycl. Anat.* II. 6/2 The diaphragm is subject to attacks of inflammation..termed diaphragmitis. **1854-67** C. A. HARRIS *Dict. Med. Terminol.*, Diaphragmalgia, Diaphragmatocele. **1857** DUNGLISON *Med. Lex.* 293 Diaphragmatalgia, Diaphragmalgia. *Ibid.*, The essential symptoms of diaphragmitis.

'diaphragm, *v.* [f. prec.] *trans.* To fit or act upon with a diaphragm. ***to diaphragm down***, in *Optics*: to reduce the field of vision of (a lens, etc.) by means of an opaque diaphragm with a central aperture (see prec. sb. 4a).

1879 H. GRUBB in *Proc. R. Dubl. Soc.* 181 Even after shutting one eye and diaphragming the other down. **1894** *Brit. Jrnl. Photogr.* XLI. 1 If both [lenses] are diaphragmed down to the same aperture.

dia'phragmal, *a.* [f. DIAPHRAGM + -AL[1].] Of the nature of a diaphragm; diaphragmatic.

1890 *Darwin's Expr. Emotions* (ed. 2) iii. 85 *note*, The diaphragmal respiration.

diaphragmatic (ˌdaɪəfræg'mætɪk), *a.* [mod. f. Gr. διάφραγματ-, stem of διάφραγμα DIAPHRAGM: see -IC. Cf. F. *diaphragmatique* (Paré 16th c.).] Of or pertaining to the diaphragm; of the nature of a diaphragm.

1656 BLOUNT *Glossogr.* s.v. *Vein*, *Diaphragmatick veins*, the midriff veins. **1755** SPRY in *Phil. Trans.* XLIX. 478 The diaphragmatic upper mouth of the stomach. **1836** *Blackw. Mag.* XXXIX. 167 The diaphragmatic convulsion, which, in the expressive language of our nation, is called a guffaw. **1878** FOSTER *Phys.* II. ii. § 1. 259 That movement in the lower part of the chest and abdomen so characteristic of male breathing, which is called diaphragmatic. **1881** MIVART *Cat* 462 A complete diaphragmatic partition.

diaphrag'matically, *adv.* [f. prec. + -AL[1] + -LY[2].] In a diaphragmatic manner; by means of the diaphragm.

1888 *Cassell's Fam. Mag.* Dec. 14/1 The important point in breathing is to do so diaphragmatically and not clavicularly.

'diaphragmed, *ppl. a.* [f. DIAPHRAGM *v.* or *sb.* + -ED.] Furnished with a diaphragm or diaphragms.

1665 HOOKE *Microgr.* 114 The pores..were they diaphragm'd like those of Cork, would afford us..ten times as many little cells.

diaphysis (daɪ'æfɪsɪs). [ad. Gr. διάφυσις a growing through, also a point of separation, f. δια- through, apart + φύειν to produce, bring forth.]

1. *Anat.* 'The shaft of a long bone, as distinct from the extremities' (*Syd. Soc. Lex.*).

1831 R. KNOX *Cloquet's Anat.* 11 Their extremities are enlarged, and their middle part, which is named body or diaphysis, is contracted. **1890** W. J. WALSHAM *Surgery* (ed. 3) III. 184 Twenty-one years of age, the period at which nearly all the epiphyses have united with their diaphyses. **1891** *Lancet* 3 Oct. 768 When amputation is done in the diaphysis the bone keeps on growing from its upper epiphysis.

2. *Bot.* 'A præternatural extension of the centre of the flower, or of an inflorescence' (*Treas. Bot.* 1866).

Hence **dia'physial** *a.*, of or pertaining to the diaphysis.

In mod. Dicts.

diapir ('daɪəpɪə(r)). *Geol.* [f. Gr. διαπειρ-αίνειν to pierce through.] An anticlinal fold in which overlying rocks are pierced by a mobile rock core. Also *attrib.* Hence **dia'piric** *a.*; **'diapirism**.

1918 *Economic Geol.* XIII. 467 A peculiar characteristic.. is the tendency of the Miocene beds, and especially the salt formation, to pierce through the overlying rocks at certain points on anticlinal axes, thus giving rise to a structure so common that Mrazec [in 1906 *Bull. Soc. Sci. Bucarest*] has coined the term 'diapir fold' to describe it. **1923** *Bull. Amer. Assoc. Petrol. Geologists* VII. 581 Mrazec..has written, in French, considerably in detail on the subject of diapirism, and has found this interpretation applicable to many folds. **1932** *Ibid.* XVI. 1062 The conception of diapiric structure, that is, folds in which the core unconformably penetrates overlying beds. **1942** M. P. BILLINGS *Struct. Geol.* iii. 54 Piercing or diapir folds are anticlines in which a mobile core has been able to break through the more brittle overlying rocks. *Ibid.* xiv. 257 In Rumania..the salt, forced upward by orogenic pressure, has penetrated the sediments at the crest of the anticlines to form diapir folds. **1949** *Q. Jrnl. Geol. Soc.* CIV. 475 Diapiric upswelling and doming is, in fact, a regular phenomenon in the intrusion of granitic magma. **1956** *Ibid.* CXII. 263 (*title*) The Ardara granitic diapir of County Donegal. **1970** *Nature* 25 July 351 Deep seismic reflexion surveys have revealed diapiric structures in deep water. *Ibid.*, The diapirs described by Ewing *et al.* were salt domes.

‖**diaplasis** (daɪ'æpləsɪs). *Surg.* [mod.L., a. Gr. διάπλασις a putting into shape, setting of a limb, f. διαπλάσσειν to form, mould.] (See quots.)

1704 J. HARRIS *Lex. Techn.*, *Diaplasis*, is the setting of a Limb which was out of joynt. **1706** PHILLIPS (ed. Kersey). **1857** DUNGLISON *Med. Lex.* 232 In French surgery.. Diaplasis and Anaplasis mean also, restoration to the original form—as in fractures, etc. **1883** in *Syd. Soc. Lex.*

† **dia'plastic,** *a.* and *sb.* *Obs.* [f. same etymon as prec.: see PLASTIC.]

1721 BAILEY, *Diaplasticks* (in *Pharmacy*), medicines which are good for a Limb out of joint. **1883** in *Syd. Soc. Lex.*

‖**di'apnoe.** *Med. Obs.* [mod.L., a. Gr. διαπνοή in Galen, perspiration.] An insensible perspiration, or gentle moisture on the skin.

1681 tr. *Willis' Rem. Med. Wks.* Vocab., *Diapnoe*, a breathing forth. **1706** PHILLIPS, *Diaphoresis* or *Diapnoe*.

Hence **diap'nogenous, diap'noic** *adjs.*, producing a moderate perspiration.

1857 DUNGLISON *Med. Lex.* 699 The perspiratory fluid is secreted by an appropriate glandular apparatus termed by Breschet, *diapnogenous*.

diapophysis (daɪə'pɒfɪsɪs). *Anat.* Pl. **-physes.** [f. Gr. δια- through, apart + ἀπόφυσις offshoot, APOPHYSIS.] A term applied by Owen to a pair of exogenous segments of the typical vertebra, forming lateral processes of the neural arch.

In the cervical vertebræ of man and other mammals it is represented by the posterior part of the ring enclosing the vertebral artery; in the dorsal vertebræ by the transverse process; in the lumbar and sacral vertebræ by short processes of the centrum (*Syd. Soc. Lex.*).

1854 OWEN *Skeleton* in *Circ. Sc.* Organ. Nat. I. 168 The neural arch..also sometimes includes a pair of bones, called 'diapophyses'. **1872** MIVART *Elem. Anat.* vi. (1873) 220 We may thus distinguish two series of paraxial parts on each side, one made up of tubercular processes (or diapophyses) and ribs, and the other made up of capitular processes (or parapophyses) and ribs.

Hence **diapo'physial** *a.*, of or belonging to a diapophysis.

1854 OWEN in *Circ. Sc.* Organ. Nat. I. 206 The bones.. manifest more of their diapophysial character than their homotypes do in the occipital segment.

‖**diaporesis** (ˌdaɪəpɒ'riːsɪs). *Rhet.* [mod.L., a. Gr. διαπόρησις a being at a loss, doubting.] A rhetorical figure, in which the speaker profeses to be at a loss, which of two or more courses, statements, etc., to adopt.

1678 PHILLIPS, *Diaporesis*, a doubting, a Rhetorical figure, in which there seems to be a doubt proposed to the audience before whom the Oration is made. [So in later Dicts.] **1844** J. W. GIBBS *Philol. Studies* (1857) 215 *Aporia*..called also *diaporesis*. The Latin term is *addubitatio*.

† **di'aporous,** *a.* *Obs. rare.* [f. Gr. δια- through + -πορος passing through, f. πόρος passage, pore: cf. εὔπορος easy to pass through.] Having the quality of penetrating or passing through.

1682 EVELYN *Mem.* 24 Mar., A discourse of..the difficulty of finding any red colour effectual to penetrate glass..that the most diaporous, as blue, yellow, &c., did not enter into the substance of what was ordinarily painted, more than very shallow..other reds and whites not at all beyond the superfices.

diapositive (daɪə'pɒzɪtɪv). *Photogr.* [f. Gr. δια- through + POSITIVE.] A transparent positive photographic picture, such as those used as lantern slides.

1893 *Voice* (N.Y.) 30 Nov., An ordinary negative..is first made, then placed in contact with another sensitive (dry) plate and a diapositive made from it.

† **'diapre,** *a.* *Her. Obs.* [a. F. *diapré* diapered.] = DIAPERED 1 b.

1562 LEIGH *Armorie* (1597) 93 The field Geules, a Frette engrailed Ermine. If this Fret be of mo peeces then ye here see, then altereth it from the same name, & is blazed dyapre. **1586** FERNE *Blaz. Gentrie* I. 190 A coat-armour Diapre may be charged with any thing, either quick or dead; but plants, fruits, leaues, or flowres, be aptest to occupy such coates. **1727-51** CHAMBERS *Cycl.*, *Diapre* or *Diapered*, in heraldry, a dividing of a field into planes, or compartments, in the manner of fret-work; and filling the same with variety of figures.

† **'diaprize,** *v.* *Obs. nonce-wd.* [f. F. *diapr-er* to DIAPER + -IZE.] = DIAPER *v.*

1626 LISLE *Du Bartas, Noe* 116 The diaprized ridges [*marges diaprez*] And faire endented banks of Tegil bursting bridges. [Cf. DIAPERY *a.*, second quot.]

† **dia'prune.** *Obs.* Also **diaprunum.** [ad. med.L. *diaprūnum*, f. DIA-[2] + L. *prūnum* plum. In F. *diaprun* (1700 in Hatz.-Darm.) formerly *diaprunum*.] 'An electuary made of damask prunes and divers other simples, good to cool the body in hot burning feavers' (*Physical Dict.* 1657).

1625 HART *Anat. Ur.* II. i. 55 They had purged him..with Diaprunum. **1639** J. W. tr. *Guibert's Char. Physic* I. 23 Mixe with it two drammes of diaprunes.

diapry, *sb.* and *a.*: see DIAPERY.

† **'diapsalm.** *Obs.* In 4 diasalm, 8 diapsalma. [a. L. *diapsalma* (Jerome), a. Gr. διάψαλμα, used by the LXX in the Psalms for the Heb. *Selah*.] (See quots.)

1382 WYCLIF *Ps.* Prol. iii, The deuyseoun of salmys that ben clepid diasalmys ben in noumbre of seuenti and fiue. **1706** PHILLIPS (ed. Kersey), *Diapsalma*, a Pause or change of Note in Singing. [**1877** JENNINGS & LOWE *Ps.* Introd. 28 Διάψαλμα then means probably a musical interlude, perhaps of a *forte* character.]

diapsid (daɪ'æpsɪd), *a.* (and *sb.*) [f. mod.L. *Diapsida* (H. F. Osborn 1903, in *Mem. Amer. Mus. Nat. Hist.* I. 455), f. DI-[2] + Gr. ἀψίς, ἀψιδ- arch.] Of a reptile skull: having two pairs of temporal arches, as in reptiles once grouped in the subclass Diapsida. Also as *sb.* Also **di'apsidan** *a.* and *sb.*

1903 *Mem. Amer. Mus. Nat. Hist.* I. 460 In all the Diapsidan types without exception the supratemporal fenestra is relatively small. **1933** A. S. ROMER *Vertebr. Paleont.* vi. 128 It was once thought that all reptiles originally had two temporal openings, and hence forms with two openings (or two bars across the temple, which amounts to the same thing) were termed 'diapsid' (two-arched). **1956** —— *Osteol. Reptiles* II. 473 It is very possible that all diapsids and diapsid derivatives have sprung from a common ancestor. **1969** A. BELLAIRS *Life of Reptiles* I. ii. 24 In many reptiles there are in fact two such openings in the skull on each side, one above the other, and hence an upper and a lower arch. This condition is known as diapsid.

‖**diapy'esis.** *Path.* [mod.L., a. Gr. διαπύησις, f. διαπυεῖν to suppurate.] Suppuration. Hence **diapy'etic** *a.* and *sb.*, **diapy'etical** *a.*

1657 TOMLINSON *Renou's Disp.* 699 Both of them [greater and lesser Basilicum] are Diapyetical. 1706 PHILLIPS (ed. Kersey), *Diapyeticks*, Medicines that cause Swellings to suppurate or run with Matter, or that ripen and break Sores. 1883 *Syd. Soc. Lex.*, Diapyesis.

diaquilon, obs. form of DIACHYLON.

diarch ('daɪɑːk), *a. Bot.* [f. Gr. δι- twice + ἀρχή beginning, origin.] Proceeding from two distinct points of origin: said of the primary xylem (or wood) of the root.

1884 BOWER & SCOTT *De Bary's Phaner.* 362 Its xylem is in the great majority of cases..diametrally diarch. *Ibid.* 363 Triarch and tetrarch bundles sometimes occur in thick roots of species, which are usually diarch. 1887 HILLHOUSE *Strasburger's Pract. Bot.* 188 The roots of..ferns are generally diarch.

diarchal (daɪ'ɑːkəl), *a.* Also **diarchial, dyarchal, -ial.** [f. DIARCHY + -AL.] Of or pertaining to a diarchy; *spec.* (see DIARCHY).

1921 *Glasgow Herald* 11 Mar. 10 Among the Ministers recently elected under the new 'Dyarchal' system was an Indian who had been previously convicted on charges of conspiracy. 1921 *Evening Standard* 20 May 4/3 Mr...Sastri ..took a prominent part in the dyarchal reforms in India. 1924 *Observer* 3 Aug. 5/1 In Bengal, the Diarchal plan is in suspense. 1927 *Ibid.* 27 Mar. 11/2 The diarchial system had to be suspended. *Ibid.* 13 Nov. 18/2 The dyarchial system [in India]. 1932 *Times Educ. Suppl.* 1 Oct. 375/3 In a total population in the existing dyarchial provinces (excluding Burma) there are roundly 131,000,000 adults.

diarchic (daɪ'ɑːkɪk), *a.* Also **dyarchic.** [f. DIARCHY: see -IC.] = prec. So **di'archical** *a.*

1920 *Edin. Rev.* Oct. 386 The diarchic character of the Swiss Government. 1921 *Spectator* 5 Feb. 161/2 The preposterous dyarchical constitution forced upon India by Mr. Montagu. 1926 *Contemp. Rev.* Feb. 240 He broke every rule of the diarchic principle. *Ibid.* Mar. 274 The dyarchic executives. 1963 *Times* 28 Jan. 9/3 The new dyarchic central government would presumably deal with 'national' issues.

diarchy ('daɪɑːkɪ). Also (*erron.*) **dyarchy.** [f. Gr. δι- twice + -αρχία rule: cf. μοναρχία rule of one; f. ἀρχός chief.] A government by two rulers. Also *spec.* the system of provincial government in India established by the Government of India Act of 1919 (9 & 10 Geo. V c. 101) (see also quot. 1917).

1835 THIRLWALL *Greece* I. viii. 318 A *diarchy*, though less usual than a monarchy, was not a very rare form of government. 1885 *Academy* 10 Oct. 231/2 The imperial government is a Dyarchy, says Dr. Mommsen. 1886 *Eng. Hist. Rev.* I. 350 The 'dyarchy' of senate and emperor is taken for granted. 1917 L. CURTIS *Let.* 6 Apr. in *Papers Princ. Dyarchy* (1920) III. 105 Self-government in any large country thus involves the operation of two authorities with separate mainsprings side by side. The word 'dyarchy'..has been coined to denote this principle. 1919 *Let. Govt. India Const. Reform* 55 in *Parl. Papers* (Cmnd. 123) XXXVII, The only method by which this can be attained is one which involves the division of the functions of government between two different sets of authorities, a method which has been compendiously styled 'dyarchy'. 1920 H. V. LOVETT *Hist. Indian Nat. Movement* vi. 163 In the Government of India there was to be no dyarchy, but the Indian element in the Viceroy's Executive Council was to be increased. 1959 *Times* 24 Feb. 11/2 The proposed constitution is essentially a diarchy. It comprises the two communal chambers, as well as very extensive communal self-government at municipal and local level. 1964 A. SWINSON *Six Minutes to Sunset* i. 9 Montagu proposed..a system known as diarchy, whereby some functions of government should be taken over by the Indians, while others should be retained by the British.

diaria, obs. form of DIARRHŒA.

diarial (daɪ'ɛərɪəl), *a.* [f. L. *diāri-um* DIARY *sb.* + -AL[1].] Of, pertaining to, of the nature of, a diary.

1845 W. L. ALEXANDER *Mem. J. Watson* Pref. 6 A series of detached notes and diarial jottings. 1885 G. MEREDITH *Diana* I. i. 2 The diarial record. 1888 A. G. DRAPER in *Amer. Ann. Deaf* Apr. 124 Letters and diarial extracts.

diarian (daɪ'ɛərɪən), *a.* and *sb.* [f. as prec. + -AN.] **A.** *adj.* Of or pertaining to a diary or journal; †journalistic (*obs.*).

1774 (*title*) The Diarian Repository or Mathematical Register, containing a complete collection of all the Mathematical Questions, published in the Ladies' Diary, from 1704 to 1760. 1785 CRABBE *Newspaper* Wks. 1834 II. 137 Diarian sages greet their brother sage. 1794 WOLCOTT (P. Pindar) *Rowl. for Oliver* Wks. II. 392 His strength in fields diarian dares he try?

B. *sb.* The author or writer of a diary; †a journalist. *rare.*

1800 *Morn. Her.* in *Spirit Publ. Jrnls.* (1801) IV. 148 A Diarian [an article is so signed].

'diariness. *nonce-wd.* [f. DIARY *sb.* + -NESS.] The quality characteristic of a diary.

1891 *Murray's Mag.* Sept. 464 The 'diariness' of his writing makes us regret that..he should have sought publication.

diarist ('daɪərɪst). [f. DIARY *sb.* + -IST.] One who keeps a diary; the author of a diary.

1818 in TODD. 1826 SCOTT *Rev. Pepys' Mem.* (1849) 107 The characters of the two diarists were essentially different. 1854 LOWELL *Jrnl. in Italy* Prose Wks. 1890 I. 121 The English language..can show but one sincere diarist, Pepys. 1856 *Sat. Rev.* II. 36/2 In these volumes, he [T. Moore] is only a remarkably dull diarist.

diaristic (daɪə'rɪstɪk), *a.* [f. prec. + -IC.] Of the style of a diarist; of the nature of a diary.

1884 *Manch. Even. News* 2 Apr., Lady Brassey's diaristic account of her visit to Egypt after the war. 1891 *Murray's Mag.* Oct. 616 His letters and diaristic fragments.

diarize ('daɪəraɪz), *v.* [f. DIARY *sb.* + -IZE.] *intr.* To write a record of events in a diary. Hence **'diarizing** *vbl. sb.* and *ppl. a.*

1827 MOORE *Diary* 6-31 Mar. V. 161 [I] have not had time to diarize, so must record by wholesale what I remember. 1853 LOCKHART in *Croker Papers* (1884) III. xxviii. 295, I had to spare Tories about as often as Whigs the castigation of diarizing Malagrowther. 1854 *Fraser's Mag.* XLIX. 443 Where is the man who, when he diarizes frankly and fairly, does not write himself vain?

diarrhœa (daɪə'riːə). Also 4-5 **diaria**, 6- **diarrhea.** [a. L. *diarrhœa*, a. Gr. διάρροια a flowing through, diarrhœa, f. διαρρέ-ειν to flow through.]

1. A disorder consisting in the too frequent evacuation of too fluid fæces, sometimes attended with griping pains.

In the 17th c. usually with *the*, in 18th with *a*, now (in literary and educated use) without article.

1398 TREVISA *Barth. De P.R.* VII. li. (1495) 265 Diaria is a symple flyxe of the wombe. 1544 PHAER *Regim. Lyfe* (1545) H viij b, The sayde fluxe is named diarrhea. 1564 SIR W. CECIL in Ellis *Orig. Lett.* Ser. II. II. 291 The Quenes Majesty fell perillosly sick on Saturday last, the accident cam to that which they call diarrhœa. 1569 R. ANDROSE tr. *Alexis' Secr.* IV. I. 12 To remedie the diseases called Dissinteria and Diarrhea. 1598 SYLVESTER *Du Bartas* II. i. *Furies*, The diarrhœa and the burning-fever In Sommer-season doo their fell endeavour. 1658 ROWLAND *Moufet's Theat. Ins.* 1104 They stay also the Dyarrhœa..kill and drive out all Belly-worms. *c* 1723 POPE *Let. to Gay* (1735) I. 323 To wait for the next cold Day to throw her into a Diarrhœa. 1732 ARBUTHNOT *Rules of Diet* 269 A cholera Morbus, or incurable Diarrhœas. 1800 *Med. Jrnl.* IV. 60 These medicines caused diarrhœa. 1811 A. T. THOMSON *Lond. Disp.* (1818) 240 Celebrated in Ireland as a remedy in diarrhœa. 1866 A. FLINT *Princ. Med.* (1880) 525 The term diarrhœa is used to denote morbid frequency of intestinal dejections which are, also, liquid or morbidly soft, and often otherwise altered in character.

attrib. 1890 B. A. WHITELEGGE *Hygiene & Public Health* xii, The diarrhœa death-rate..Density of buildings upon an area increases the tendency to diarrhœa mortality.

2. *transf.* An excessive flow (of words, etc.).

1698 F. B. *Modest Censure* 15 This sort of Medicaments hath cured his Pen of the Diarrhæa. *a* 1797 H. WALPOLE *Mem. Geo. III.* (1845) II. ii. 47 He..was troubled with a diarrhœa of words. 1883 *Contemp. Rev.* Dec. 937 We allude ..to the diarrhœa of emendations.

diarrhœal (daɪə'riːəl), *a.* [f. prec. + -AL[1].] Of or pertaining to diarrhœa.

1651 BIGGS *New Disp.* ¶ 248 The diarrheall porraceous flux. 1871 *Daily News* 16 Aug., Diarrhœal infection. 1883 E. A. PARKES *Pract. Hygiene* xviii. (ed. 6) 479 Diarrhœal and dysenteric evacuations. 1890 B. A. WHITELEGGE *Hygiene* xii. 303 High temperature of the air has long been observed to be associated with high diarrhœal mortality.

diarrhœic (daɪə'riːɪk), *a.* [f. as prec. + -IC.] Of, pertaining to, or of the nature of diarrhœa.

1876 *Wagner's Gen. Pathol.* (ed. 6) 86. 1894 *Daily News* 25 July 5/4 It is in diarrhœic complaints that the increase was most marked.

diarrhœtic, -rhetic (daɪə'rɛtɪk, -'riːtɪk), *a.* [f. DIARRHŒA, in loose imitation of Gr. verbal adjectives in -τικός. (The actual verbal adj. from διαρρέ-ειν is διάρρυτ-ος, which would have given *diarrhytic*.] = DIARRHŒIC.

Also confused with *diuretic*.

1656 BLOUNT *Glossogr.*, *Diarrhoetick*, that hath a Lask or loosness in the belly without inflammation. *a* 1735 ARBUTHNOT (J.), Millet is diarrhœtick, cleansing, and useful in diseases of the kidneys. 1883 *Syd. Soc. Lex.*, *Diarrhetic*, *Diarrhœtic*, same as *Diarrhœic*.

diarthrodial (ˌdaɪɑː'θrəʊdɪəl), *a. Anat.* [f. DI- *pref.*[3] (Gr. δια-) + ARTHRODIAL.] Pertaining to or characterized by diarthrosis.

'*Diarthrodial cartilages*: the cartilages which cover the joint-ends of bones' (*Syd. Soc. Lex.*).

1830 R. KNOX *Béclard's Anat.* 285 The diarthrodial cartilages..have disappeared. 1845 TODD & BOWMAN *Phys. Anat.* I. 88 The bones entering into the composition of diarthrodial joints. 1876 QUAIN *Elem. Anat.* (ed. 8) I. 132 Certain forms of diarthrodial joint have received special names.

diarthrosis (ˌdaɪɑː'θrəʊsɪs). *Anat.* [f. DI- *pref.*[3] (Gr. δια-) + ἄρθρωσις ARTHROSIS, articulation.] The general term for all forms of articulation which admit of the motion of one bone upon another; free arthrosis.

1578 BANISTER *Hist. Man.* 3 b, Not vnder the kynde of Diarthrosis, but Synarthrosis: for asmuch as the mouyng of these bones is most obscure. 1634 T. JOHNSON *Parey's Chirurg.* XVI. xxxv. (1678) 365 The wrist..consisting of a composure of eight bones knit to the whole cubit by Diarthrosis. 1658 SIR T. BROWNE *Gard. Cyrus* iii. 59 The Diarthrosis or motive Articulation. 1830 R. KNOX *Béclard's Anat.* 283 The rotatory diarthrosis..is that which allows only motions of rotation. 1842 E. WILSON *Anat. Vade M.* (ed. 2) 92 Diarthrosis is the movable articulation which constitutes by far the greater number of the joints of the body.

diary ('daɪərɪ), *sb.* [ad. L. *diāri-um* daily allowance, also (later) a journal, diary, f. *die-s* day: in form, a subst. use of the neuter of *diārius* adj. (see next), which, however, is not recorded in ancient L. See -ARIUM, -ARY[1] B. 2.]

1. A daily record of events or transactions, a journal; specifically, a daily record of matters affecting the writer personally, or which come under his personal observation.

1581 WM. FLEETWOOD in Ellis *Orig. Lett.* Ser. I. II. 288 Thus most humbly I send unto yor good Lo. this last weeks Diarye. 1605 BACON *Adv. Learn.* II. ii. §11. 14 It is..an vse well received in enterprises memorable..to keepe Dyaries of that which passeth continually. 1642 *Answ. to Printed Bk.* 14 A diary..of the Parliament held 1 Hen. 4. 1652-62 HEYLIN *Cosmogr.* Introd. (1674) 17/2 A Diary or Journal, as the name imports, containing the Actions of each day. 1677 PLOT *Oxfordsh.* 228 Diaries of wind and weather, and of the various qualifications of the air. 1684 PETER (*title*), A Relation or Diary of the Siege of Vienna. 1765 T. HUTCHINSON *Hist. Mass.* I. ii. 213 Goffe kept a journal or diary. 1791-1823 D'ISRAELI *Cur. Lit.*, *Diaries*, We converse with the absent by letters, and with ourselves by diaries. 1803 *Med. Jrnl.* X. 305 As I kept no diary during the prevalence of the influenza, I send what I can recollect. 1889 JESSOPP *Coming of Friars* iii. 130 In the thirteenth century men never kept diaries or journals..but monasteries did. *Mod.* The entries of a private diary.

attrib. 1891 *Pall Mall G.* 25 Apr. 2/3 The plaintiff gave peculiar diary accounts of about fifty meetings with the defendant.

2. A book prepared for keeping a daily record, or having spaces with printed dates for daily memoranda and jottings; also, applied to calendars containing daily memoranda on matters of importance to people generally, or to members of a particular profession, occupation, or pursuit.

A *diary* in this sense may vary in size from a folio volume, large enough to hold a detailed daily record in sense 1, to a small pocket-book with daily spaces only for the briefest notes, or merely with printed memoranda for daily reference.

1605 B. JONSON *Volpone* IV. i, This is my diary, Wherin I note my actions of the day. 1642 HOWELL *For. Trav.* (Arb.) 20 He must alwayes have a Diary about him..to set down what..his Eyes meetes with most remarquable. 1662 J. NEWTON (*title*), A Perpetual Diary; or, Almanac. 1800 W. ROBSON (*title*), The Persian Diary; or, Reflection's Oriental Gift of Daily Counsel. 1879 *Print. Trades Jrnl.* XXVIII. 7 The left hand pages form a perpetual poetical diary. *Ibid.* XXIX. 6 The diary before us..is a stout quarto. 1883 *Whitaker's Alm.* 456 The English Citizen's Diary..showing the days when certain Official Duties are to be performed; also the days when Inland Revenue Licences expire and must be renewed.

†**3.** Short for *diary fever*: see DIARY *a.* 1. *Obs.*

1639 HORN & ROB. *Gate Lang. Unl.* xxiv. §310 A diary is of one daies continuance, and runs not beyond that time. 1657 G. STARKEY *Helmont's Vind.* 164 The disease at the first taking in hand was but a plain Diary. 1684 tr. *Bonet's Merc. Compit.* VI. 155 Hippocrates..thought that all Fevers, Diaries excepted, have their rise from choler.

diary ('daɪərɪ), *a.* [ad. med.L. *diāri-us* daily, f. *dies* day: cf. F. *diaire* ('fievre ephemere ou diaire') 16th c. in Hatz.-Darm.]

1. Lasting for one day; ephemeral.

1610 BARROUGH *Meth. Physick* IV. ii. (1639) 218 All Diarie feavers be ingendred of an outward Cause. 1611 W. SCLATER *Key* (1629) 188 Those ἐφίμεροι, diary dewy Christians, whose goodnesse is dissipate as soone as euer the Sunne beholds it. 1658 ROWLAND *Moufet's Theat. Ins.* 948 These diary creatures break forth out of certain husks of putrefied grapes. 1693 *Phil. Trans.* XVII. 660 A Diary Period..may be hence expected. 1707 FLOYER *Physic. Pulse-Watch* 122 Obstructions produce a diary Fever if small, but if great a continent Fever. 1834 J. M. GOOD *Study Med.* (ed. 4) I. 596 There are few persons who have not felt this species of diary fever at times. 1883 *Syd. Soc. Lex.*, *Diary-fever*, a fever lasting one day; also called *Ephemera.*

†**2.** Daily. *Obs.*

1592 UNTON *Corr.* (Roxb.) 322, I doe kepe a diary memoreall of all the places of our marchinge and incampinge. 1603 SIR C. HEYDON *Jud. Astrol.* V. 147 Almanack-writers foretelling the diarie state of the weather. 1623 COCKERAM, *Diarie*, daily.

disceuast, var. of DIASKEUAST.

diaschisis (daɪ'æskɪsɪs). *Path.* [mod.L., a. G. *diaschisis* (K. von Monakow 1906, in *Neurologisches Centralblatt* XXV. 1030), ad. Gr. διάσχισις division, f. διασχίζ-ειν (see DIASCHISMA).] A loss of functional activity in a region of the nervous system, resulting from injury to some other connected region of the system.

1915 H. C. THOMSON *Dis. Nervous Syst.* (ed. 2) xlii. 401 Temporary attacks in which a patient has difficulty in speaking..may be caused by 'diaschisis' (Monakow), i.e. by a temporary loss of function produced by the shock of a lesion some distance away. 1942 *Brit. Jrnl. Psychol.* Apr. 284 The lowering of vigilance produced by cortical damage would seem to be comparable to the incidence of '*Diaschisis*' postulated by von Monakow.

‖**diaschisma** (daɪə'skɪzmə). *Mus.* Also in 8 in anglicized form **diaschism.** [a. Gr. διάσχισμα, f. διασχίζ-ειν to cleave asunder, split.]

a. In ancient Greek music, a small interval equal to about half a DIESIS. **b.** In modern music, an interval equal to the difference of the common comma (80:81) and the enharmonic diesis (125:128), or to 10 schismas.

1753 CHAMBERS *Cycl. Supp.* s.v., The octave contains 61 Diaschisms nearly. **1880** STAINER & BARRETT *Dict. Mus. Terms, Diaschisma* (Gk.), an approximate half of a limma.

diascope ('daɪəskəʊp). [f. DIA-[1] + -SCOPE.] A magic lantern or projector by which the image on a transparent slide or the like is projected on to a screen, wall, etc. Cf. EPIDIASCOPE, EPISCOPE[1]. So **dia'scopic** *a.*

1911 [see EPISCOPE[1]]. **1937** *Nature* 27 Feb. 380/2 A classroom epidiascope..has a 500-watt lamp, and the change-over from episcope to diascope is instantaneous. **1951** *Engineering* 2 Nov. 564/1 An exhibition of 'Visual Aids to Industry'..includes diascopes.

† **'diascord.** *Pharm. Obs.* Usually in L. form **dia'scordium.** [medical L. *diascordium* (also mod.F.), for *diascordiōn*, from Gr. διὰ σκορδίων (a preparation) of σκόρδιον scordium, a strong-smelling plant mentioned by Dioscorides, 'perhaps water-germander *Teucrium Scordium*': see DIA-[2].] A medicine made of the dried leaves of *Teucrium Scordium*, and many other herbs.

1605 BACON *Adv. Learn.* II. x. §8 (1873) 140 Except it be treacle..diascordium..and a few more. **1654** WHITLOCK *Zootomia* 121 What think you Sir of your what-sha' come Water and Diascord, sure it could not be amisse. **1797** J. DOWNING *Disorders Horned Cattle* 50 The diascordium has its share in accomplishing the cure. **1820** SCOTT *Abbot* xxvi, With their sirups, and their julaps, and diascordium, and mithridate, and my Lady What-shall-call'um's powder.

† **dia'senna.** *Pharm. Obs.* Also 6–7 diasene. [medical L., f. DIA-[2] + SENNA. Also a. F. *diasène*, *diasenne* (Paré, 16th c.).] A purgative electuary of which senna formed the base; the confection of senna.

1562 TURNER *Baths* 10 Let the patient be purged with electuarye lenitiuo or diasene. **1621** BURTON *Anat. Mel.* II. v. I. iv. (1651) 388 Polypody, Sene, Diasene, Hamech, Cassia. **1657** *Physical Dict.*, *Diasena*, a purging electuary, good against quartan agues.

diaskeuast (daɪə'skjuːæst). Also **diasceuast, -scevast.** [ad. Gr. διασκευαστής reviser of a poem, interpolator, f. διασκευάζειν, f. διά through + σκευάζειν to make ready.] A reviser; used *esp.* in reference to old recensions of Greek writings.

1822 CAMPBELL in *New Monthly Mag.* IV. 195 They gave the world materials which were capable of being moulded by future diascevasts into grand and interesting poems. **1871** tr. *Lange's Comm. Jer.* 244 The oversight of a diaskeuast who added this verse of the prophecy against Elam as a postscript. **1886** *Athenæum* 30 Jan. 162/3 He has taken upon himself..the part of a diasceuast, stringing together a number of 'older lays'.

So ‖**dia'skeuasis** [Gr. διασκεύασις], revision (of a literary work), recension.

1886 EGGELING in *Encycl. Brit.* XXI. 281 The authorship of this work [Mahâbhârata] is aptly attributed to Vyâsa, 'the arranger', the personification of Indian diaskeuasis.

† **di'asper.** *Obs.* Also 6–7 diasprie. [ad. med.L. *diasprum*, It., Sp., Pg. *diaspro* jasper.] = JASPER.

1582 HESTER *Secr. Phiorav.* I. lxv. 78 The other stone was of Diasper, but bright and through shinyng with certaine white vaines. **1592** R. D. *Hypnerotomachia* 53b, Not of Marble, but of rare and hard Diasper of the East. **1638** SIR T. HERBERT *Trav.* (ed. 2) 108 Agats, Cornelians, Diaspries, Calcedons.

‖**diaspora** (daɪ'æspərə). [a. Gr. διασπορά dispersion, f. διασπείρ-ειν to disperse, f. διά through + σπείρειν to sow, scatter.]

The Dispersion; i.e. (among the Hellenistic Jews) the whole body of Jews living dispersed among the Gentiles after the Captivity (John vii. 35); (among the early Jewish Christians) the body of Jewish Christians outside of Palestine (Jas. i. 1, 1 Pet. i. 1). Hence *transf.*: see quots.

(Originating in Deut. xxviii. 25 (Septuagint), ἔσῃ διασπορὰ ἐν πάσαις βασιλείαις τῆς γῆς, thou shalt be a diaspora (or dispersion) in all kingdoms of the earth.)

1876 C. M. DAVIES *Unorth. Lond.* 153 [The Moravian body's] extensive *diaspora* work (as it is termed) of evangelizing among the National Protestant Churches on the continent. **1881** tr. *Wellhausen* in *Encycl. Brit.* XIII. 420/1 s.v. *Israel*, As a consequence of the revolutionary changes which had taken place in the conditions of the whole East, the Jewish dispersion (diaspora) began vigorously to spread. **1885** *Encycl. Brit.* XVIII. 760 s.v. *Philo*, The development of Judaism in the diaspora differed in important points from that in Palestine. **1889** *Edin. Rev.* No. 345. 66 The mental horizon of the Jews of the Diaspora was being enlarged.

diaspore ('daɪəspɔə(r)). *Min.* [mod. f. Gr. διασπορά scattering, dispersion: see prec. So called by Haüy, 1801, from its strong decrepitation when heated.] Native hydrate of aluminium, an orthorhombic, massive, or sometimes stalactitic mineral, varying in colour from white to violet, commonly associated with corundum in crystalline rocks.

1805 DAVY in *Phil. Trans.* XCV. 161 The diaspore..is supposed to be a compound of alumine and water. **1873** *Fownes' Chem.* (ed. 11) 371 The monohydrate is found native, as diaspore.

diasporometer (daɪ,æspɒ'rɒmɪtə(r)). [mod. f. Gr. διασπορά dispersion (see above) + -(O)METER.] An instrument for measuring the dispersion of rays of light.

1807 T. YOUNG *Lect. Nat. Phil.* II. 282 His [Rochon's] diasporometer is a compound prism.

diasprie, var. DIASPER, *Obs.*, jasper.

diastaltic (daɪə'stæltɪk), *a.* [f. Gr. διασταλτικός serving to distinguish, in Music 'able to expand or exalt the mind', f. διαστέλλειν to separate, put asunder, f. διά apart + στέλλειν to set, place, dispatch, send. Cf. F. *diastaltique.*]

1. In ancient Greek music: **a.** Dilated, extended: applied to certain intervals. **b.** Applied to a style of melody fitted to expand or exalt the mind.

1774 BURNEY *Hist. Mus.* (1789) I. v. 61 Melopœia was divided into three kinds..the second, Diastaltic or that which was capable of exhilarating.

2. *Phys.* 'A term applied by Marshall Hall to the actions termed reflex, inasmuch as they take place through the spinal cord' (*Syd. Soc. Lex.*).

diastaltic nervous system, term for the spinal nervous system.

[*Diastaltic* appears to be here taken as = *transmissive.*]

1852 M. HALL (*title*), Synopsis of the Diastaltic Nervous System. **1855** GARROD *Mat. Med.* (ed. 6) 238 A reduction and final abolition of the diastaltic function of the spinal cord. **1879** *Cornh. Mag.* June 700 Is there anything in your essay about our diastaltic nerves?

diastase ('daɪəsteɪs). *Chem.* [a. mod.F. *diastase*, ad. Gr. διάστασις separation: see next.

1833 PAYEN ET PERSOZ *Ann. Chim. et Phys.* LIII. 76 Cette singulière propriété de séparation nous a determinés à donner à la substance qui la possède le nom de *diastase* qui exprime précisément ce fait.]

A nitrogenous ferment formed in a seed or bud (e.g. in barley and potatoes) during germination, and having the property of converting starch into sugar.

It is obtained as a white amorphous substance, of unknown analysis (Watts *Dict. Chem.*). It is found throughout the vegetable kingdom, in the infusoria, and in various secretions, etc., in the higher animals (*Syd. Soc. Lex.*).

1838 T. THOMSON *Chem. Org. Bodies* 666 Diastase..is a name given by MM. Payen and Persoz, to a substance which they extracted from malted barley. **1846** J. BAXTER *Libr. Pract. Agric.* (ed. 4) I. 19 During the germination, some of the elements..in the grain form a fresh compound, which acts as a ferment. This compound is called..diastase, the effect of which is..to turn all the starch..first, into gum, and then into sugar. **1863–72** WATTS *Dict. Chem.* II. 319 Neither potatoes nor cereals contain diastase before germination. **1894** *Lancet* 3 Nov. 1045 An extremely active poison, delicate, resembling the diastases or venoms.

Hence **dia'stasic**, *a.* = DIASTATIC.

1886 W. JAGO *Chem. Wheat* 128 The bacteria cause more or less change in albuminoids, but exert no diastasic action.

‖**diastasis** (daɪ'æstəsɪs). *Path.* [mod.L., a. Gr. διάστασις separation, f. διά apart + στάσις placing, setting, f. root στα- stand.] Separation of bones without fracture, slight dislocation; also, separation of the fractured ends of a bone.

1741 MONRO *Anat. Bones* (ed. 3) 39 A Diastasis, or other violent Separation of such disjoined Pieces of a Bone. **1883** in *Syd. Soc. Lex.*

diastatic (daɪə'stætɪk), *a.* [ad. Gr. διαστατικός separative, f. διά apart + στατικός causing to stand, f. root στα- stand.] Pertaining to or of the nature of diastase.

1881 ATKINSON in *Nature* No. 622. 510 The opinion that the diastatic property is connected with the degree of solubility of the albuminoid matter. **1883** *Athenæum* 10 Nov. 606/3 Lacquer contains..a peculiar diastatic body containing nitrogen.

Hence **dia'statically** *adv.*, after the manner of diastase.

1882 tr. *Thausing's Beer* 291 (Cent. Dict.) The diastatically acting albuminous substances.

† **dia'statical**, *a. Obs. rare*[−1]. [f. as prec. + -AL[1].] Characterized by transplantation.

1656 S. BOULTON (*title*), Medicina Magica, tamen Physica: Magical, but Natural Physick; or, a Methodical Tractate of Diastatical Physick; containing the general Cures of all Infirmities, by way of Transplantation.

diastatite (daɪ'æstətaɪt). *Min.* [mod. f. Gr. διάστατ-ος divided, separated + -ITE.] A black variety of Hornblende, so called (by Breithaupt 1832) as differing in the form of its crystals.

1850 DANA *Min.* 273.

diastem ('daɪəstem). [ad. Gr. διάστημα: see next. Cf. F. *diastème* (1732 Trévoux).] In ancient Greek music, an interval; *esp.* an interval forming a single degree of the scale.

1694 HOLDER *Treat. Harmony* vi. 110 *Diastem* signifies an Interval or Space; *System*, a Conjunction or Composition of Intervals. So that, generally speaking, an Octave, or any other System, might be truly call'd a Diastem..Tho'..strictly, by a Diastem they understood only an Incomposit Degree. **1727–51** CHAMBERS *Cycl., Diastem, Diastema*, in music, a name the antients gave to a simple interval; in contradistinction to a compound interval, which they called a *system.*

‖**diastema** (daɪə'stiːmə). Pl. **diastemata.** [L. *diastēma*, a. Gr. διάστημα space between, interval.]

1. *Mus.* = prec.

1398 TREVISA *Barth. De P.R.* XIX. cxxxi. (1495) 941 Dyastema is couenable space of two voyces other of moo accordynge. **1727–51** [see prec.].

2. *Zool.* and *Anat.* An interval or space between two consecutive teeth, or two kinds of teeth, occurring in most mammals except man.

1854 OWEN in *Orr's Circ. Sc.* Organ. Nat. I. 235 A long diastema is not..peculiar to the horse. *Ibid.* 298 In all the apes and monkeys of the Old World..the same number and kinds of teeth are present as in man; the first deviation being the disproportionate size of the canines and the concomitant break or 'diastema' in the dental series for the reception of their crowns when the mouth is shut. **1871** DARWIN *Desc. Man* II. xix. 324 Canine teeth which project above the others, with traces of a diastema or open space for the reception of the opposite canines.

diastematic (,daɪəstiː'mætɪk), *a. rare.* [ad. Gr. διαστηματικ-ός separated by intervals: see prec. and -IC.] Characterized by intervals.

1798 HORSLEY in *Monthly Rev.* XXVI. 288 Ask Aristoxenus [etc.] in what the difference consists between speaking and singing; they tell you..'That the one is a continuous motion; the other diastematic. That the continuous is the motion of the voice in discourse; the diastematic, in singing'. **1952** *Latin Liturg. MSS.* (Exhib. Guide, Bodl. Lib.) 11 An important step towards the development of a 'diastematic' notation was the method of scratching or tracing a line in the parchment.

diaster (daɪ'æstə(r)). *Biol.* Also **dy-.** [mod. f. Gr. δι-, DI-[2] twice + ἀστήρ star.] The double star of chromatin filaments which forms the penultimate stage in the division of a single cell-nucleus into two.

1882 J. T. CUNNINGHAM in *Jrnl. Microsc. Soc.* Jan. 43 The threads travel towards the poles, forming a dyaster (*note*, This term I take from Klein in his *Atlas of Histology*, 1880). **1885** E. R. LANKESTER in *Encycl. Brit.* XIX. 833 A polar star is seen at each end of the nucleus-spindle, and is not to be confused with the diaster.

Hence **di'astral** *a.*

1894 *Athenæum* 24 Nov. 719/3 As to the spindle fibres..during the diastral stage of the division they [etc.].

dia'stimeter. [irreg. f. Gr. διάστασις interval, distance + -METER.] An instrument for measuring distances.

1851 *Official Catal. Exhib.* III. 1115 Improved diastimeter for the use of the army.

‖**diastole** (daɪ'æstəʊliː). [med.L., a. Gr. διαστολή a putting asunder, separation, expansion, dilatation, f. διαστέλλειν, f. διά asunder (DIA-[1]) + στέλλειν to put, place, send, etc. Cf. F. *diastole* (14th c. in Hatz.-Darm.).]

1. *Phys.* The dilatation or relaxation of the heart or an artery (or other pulsating organ in some lower animals), rhythmically alternating with the *systole* or contraction, the two together constituting the *pulse.* (Formerly sometimes applied also to the dilatation of the lungs in inspiration.)

1578 BANISTER *Hist. Man* VII. 93 Diastole [is] when the hart in his dilatation receiueth in of spirit. **1615** DANIEL *Queen's Arcadia* Poet. Wks. (1717) 187 The Systole and Dyastole of your Pulse Do shew your Passions most hysterical. **1660** BOYLE *New Exp. Phys. Mech.* Digress. 350 The Systole and Diastole of the Heart and Lungs, being very far from Synchronical. *a* **1711** KEN *Hymnotheo* Poet. Wks. 1721 III. 79 His Heart a sudden gentle opning feels; It seem'd no more by Systole compress'd, But in a fix Diastole at rest. **1835** KIRBY *Hab. & Inst. Anim.* I. v. 174 Nutrition seems carried on by a kind of systole and diastole, the sea water being alternately absorbed and rejected by the tubes composing the substance of the sponge. **1880** HUXLEY *Crayfish* ii. 74 When the systole is over the diastole follows.

fig. **1831** CARLYLE *Sart. Res.* II. iii, As in longdrawn Systole and longdrawn Diastole, must the period of Faith alternate with the period of Denial. **1849** DE QUINCEY *Eng. Mail-coach* Wks. 1862 IV. 298 The great respirations, ebb and flood, systole and diastole, of the national intercourse. **1872** GEO. ELIOT *Middlem.* lxiii, There must be a systole and diastole in all inquiry.

2. *Gr.* and *Lat. Prosody.* The lengthening of a syllable naturally short.

1580 SPENSER *To Master G.H.* Wks. (Globe) App. ii. 709/1 *Heaven* being used shorte as one sillable, when it is in verse stretched out with a Diastole, is like a lame dogge that holdes up one legge. **1657** J. SMITH *Myst. Rhet.* 177. **1704** J. HARRIS *Lex. Techn., Diastole*..'Tis also the making long a Syllable which is naturally short.

3. *Gr. Gram.* A mark (originally semicircular) used to indicate separation of words; still occasionally used, in the form of a comma, to distinguish ὅ,τι, ὅ,τε, neut. of ὅστις, ὅστε, from ὅτι (that), ὅτε (when).

1704 J. HARRIS *Lex. Techn.* **1833** E. ROBINSON tr. *Buttman's Grk. Gram.* 45 From the comma must be distinguished the Diastole or Hypodiastole—which serves more clearly to separate some short words connected with enclitics, in order that they may not be confounded with other similar words.

diastolic (daɪə'stɒlɪk), *a. Phys.* and *Med.* [f. prec. + -IC.] Of or pertaining to diastole.

a **1693** URQUHART *Rabelais* III. iv, By its [the heart's] agitation of Diastolick and Systolick motions. **1861** T.

GRAHAM *Pract. Med.* 365 A second or diastolic sound, synchronous with the diastole of the heart. **1877** HUXLEY *Anat. Inv. Anim.* ii. 77 This systolic and diastolic movement usually occurs at a fixed point in the protoplasm.

diastral: see DIASTER.

diastrophism (daɪ'æstrəʊfɪzm). *Geol.* [f. Gr. διαστροφή distortion, dislocation, διάστροφος twisted, distorted, f. διαστρέφειν to turn different ways, twist about, f. διά (DIA-[1]) + στρέφειν to turn: see -ISM, and cf. *catastrophism.*]

A general term for the action of the forces which have disturbed and dislocated the earth's crust, and produced the greater inequalities of its surface. Hence **diastrophic** (daɪə'strɒfɪk), of or pertaining to diastrophism. (Also, otherwise employed in quot. 1881.)

1881 J. MILNE in *Nature* XXV. 126 Other [earthquake shocks] again are compounded of direct and transverse motions, and might therefore be called diastrophic. **1890** G. K. GILBERT *Lake Bonneville* i. 3 *note* (Funk) It is convenient also to divide diastrophism into orogeny..and epeirogeny. **1895** J. W. POWELL *Physiogr. Processes*, in *Nat. Geogr. Monogr.* I. I. 23 Regions sink and regions rise and the upheaval and subsidence may be called *diastrophism*, and we have *diastrophic* processes.

diastyle ('daɪəstaɪl), *a.* and *sb. Arch.* Also 6–8 in L. and Gr. form **diastylos**. [mod. ad. L. *diastȳlos*, Gr. διάστῡλος 'having a space between the columns'; also ad. Gr. διαστύλιον the intercolumnar space; f. διά through + στῦλος pillar.]

A. *adj.* Of a colonnade or building: Having the intervals between the columns each of three (or four) diameters (in the Doric order, of 2⅔). **B.** *sb.* Such a colonnade or building, or such an interval between columns.

1563 SHUTE *Archit.* Fja, Diastylos, whose..distaunce betwene the .2. pillers ought to be .3. Diameters or .4. at ye furdest. **1704** J. HARRIS *Lex. Techn.*, *Diastyle*, is a sort of Edifice, where the Pillars stand at such a distance one from another, that three Diameters of their thickness are allow'd for Intercolumniation. **1725** HENLEY tr. *Montfaucon's Antiq. Italy* (ed. 2) 18 The ancient Colonnade..is a Diastylos of sixteen fluted Columns. **1842–76** GWILT *Archit.* §2605 The ancient names..of the different intercolumniations..are—the *pycnostyle*..the *systyle*..the *eustyle*..the *diastyle*..and the *aræostyle*. **1856** M. LAFEVER *Archit. Instructor* 358 A colonnade..is designated..as.. pycnostyle when the space between the columns is a diameter and a half of the column, systyle when it is two diameters..diastyle when three.

diasyrm ('daɪəsɜːm). *Rhet.* [ad. Gr. διασυρμός, Latinized *diasyrmus*, disparagement, ridicule, the rhetorical figure expressing this, f. διασύρειν to disparage, ridicule, f. διά through, apart + σύρειν to drag.] A figure of rhetoric expressing disparagement or ridicule.

1678 PHILLIPS, *Diasyrmus* (Grk.), a figure in Rhetorick, in which we elevate any person or thing by way of derision. **1757** W. DODD *Beauties Shaks.* I. 97 (Jod.) We have a beautiful passage in Richard the Third (act I, sc. i) on this topick in that fine diasyrm he speaks on himself.

diasystem ('daɪəsɪstɪm). *Linguistics.* [f. DIA-[1] + SYSTEM.] A linguistic macro-system constructed by treating variants between dialects as part of a continuum of variations.

1954 U. WEINREICH in *Word* X. 390 Structural linguistic theory now needs procedures for constructing systems of a higher level out of the discrete and homogeneous systems that are derived from description and that represent each a unique formal organization of the substance of expression and content. Let us dub these constructions 'diasystems'... A 'diasystem' can be constructed by the linguistic analyst out of any two systems which have partial similarities. **1963** T. A. SEBEOK in J. A. Fishman *Readings Sociol. of Lang.* (1968) 24 Crows free to migrate between the two regions construct a diasystem which enables them to understand both local dialects. **1968** *Language* XLIV. 485 But all languages and all dialects are dia-systems as well, so this does not constitute a special characteristic of proto-languages. **1982** *Amer. Speech* LVII. 14 What we see, then, is an attempt to define the limits of a diasystem which is open to considerable vagueness and arbitrary delimitation when examined in detail.

Hence **diasyste'matic**, **diasy'stemic** *adjs.*; **diasy'stemically** *adv.*

1976 *Language* LII. 267 T[rudgill] posits a model which includes a diasystemic phonological system,.. morphological alternation rules,..phonological realization rules, [etc.]. **1977** *Word 1972* XXVIII. 326 Before discussing the phonological similarities and differences among these dialects as they are brought into prominence diasystemically, I should like to describe briefly the importance of the *Atlas Linguistique de la France* in the history and development of dialect studies. **1981** *Amer. Speech 1977* LII. 227 A diasystematic base from which all observable dialect variants could be derived.

diat(e, obs. form of DIET.

†**dia'tactic**, *a. Obs.* [ad. Gr. διατακτικός distinguishing, distinctive, f. διατάσσειν to dispose severally, appoint, ordain, f. διά apart + τάσσειν to set in order.] Of or pertaining to order or arrangement, *spec.* as exercised by the Church; ordaining. Also †**dia'tactical** *a.* in same sense.

1646 S. BOLTON *Arraignm. Err.* 284 The Diatactick power. *Ibid.*, The severall branches laid down by Holy and learned men, viz. Dogmaticall, Diatacticall and Critical. The first hath relation to Doctrine; the second to Order; the third to Censure. **1673** T. FORRESTER in Wodrow *Hist. Suff. Ch. Scot.* (1829) II. II. ix. 253 All power or jurisdiction in its assemblies either diatactic, critic, or dogmatic. **1688** RENWICK *Serm., etc.* (1776) 538 The diatactick power, whereby the courts of Christ are to discern the circumstances of the worship of God as to time, place, etc.

‖**diatessaron** (daɪə'tɛsərən). Also 5–6 **dya-**, 5–7 **diatesseron**, 6 **diathesaron**. [a. OF. *diatessaron* (Godfr.), a. L. *diatessarōn*, Gr. διὰ τεσσάρων through or composed of four.]

†**1.** In Greek and mediæval music: The interval of a fourth. (Cf. DIAPASON, DIAPENTE.) *Obs.*

1398 [see DIAPASON 1]. **1413** *Pilgr. Sowle* (Caxton) v. i. (1859) 72 Ofte amonges other, the lusty Dyatesseron felle in they songes. **1549** *Compl. Scot.* vi. 37 Mony smal birdis.. singand..in accordis of mesure of diapason prolations, tripla ande dyatesseron. **1626** BACON *Sylva* §107 The Concords in Musick..the Fourth which they call Diatesseron. **1694** *Phil. Trans.* XVIII. 70 A Diapente added to a Diatessaron makes a Diapason. **1857** MAURICE *Mor. & Met. Philos.* III. v. §27. 183 The circle..the diatessaron in music, and the like are certain stable forms.

†**2.** In old *Pharmacy*, a medicine composed of four ingredients: see quot. 1883. *Obs.* [DIA-[2].]

c **1400** *Lanfranc's Cirurg.* 264 He shal holde in his mouþ tiriacum diatesseron. **1577** FRAMPTON *Joyful News* (1580) 119a (Stanf.) The triacle Diathesaron. **1698** FRYER *Acc. E. India & P.* 157 That enervating Liquor called *Paunch*.. from Five Ingredients; as the Physicians name their Composition *Diapente*; or from Four things, *Diatesseron*. **1883** *Syd. Soc. Lex.*, *Diatessaron*, old name for a medicine of gentian and *Aristolochia rotunda* roots, laurel berries, and myrrh, made into a confection with honey and extract of juniper; anciently used as alexipharmic.

3. A harmony of the four Gospels.

From the title of the earliest work of the kind, the 2nd century Εὐαγγέλιον διὰ τεσσάρων, i.e. 'gospel made up of four', of Tatian.

1803 T. THIRLWALL (*title*), Diatessaron; or the History of our Lord Jesus. **1805** R. WARNER (*title*), The English Diatessaron; or the History of Christ, from the compounded Texts of the Four Evangelists. **1831** MACAULAY *Ess., Boswell's Johnson* (1854) 174/2 Who would lose, in the confusion of a Diatessaron, the peculiar charm which belongs to the narrative of the disciple whom Jesus loved? **1887** *Dict. Chr. Biog.* IV. s.v. *Tatianus*, Tatian's Diatessaron found acceptance in the West as well as in the East.

Hence †**diate'ssarial** *a. Obs.*, belonging to a diatessaron (sense 1).

1501 DOUGLAS *Pal. Hon.* I. xli, Proportionis fine with sound celestiall, Duplat, triplat, diatesseriall.

dia'thermacy. [ad. F. *diathermasie* (Melloni, 1841), ad. Gr. διαθερμασία a warming through, f. διά through + θερμασία heat. This Eng. form, which would regularly have been *diathermasy*, is conformed to words in -ACY.] The quality of being diathermic; = DIATHERMANCY 2.

1867 W. A. MILLER *Elem. Chem.* I. (ed. 4) 296 Scarcely superior to pure water in diathermacy. **1870** MATT. WILLIAMS *Fuel of Sun* §113 Any degree of diathermacy permitting radiation to take place..across the flame. **1877** WATTS *Dict. Chem.* V. 61 [see DIATHERMIC *a.* 1].

diathermal (daɪə'θɜːməl), *a.* [f. Gr. διά through (DIA-[1]) + THERMAL (Gr. θερμ-ός warm, θέρμ-η, θερμ-όν heat): rendering F. *diathermane*; see next.] = DIATHERMIC *a.* 1, DIATHERMANOUS. Also *fig.*

1835 FARADAY tr. Melloni in *L. & E. Phil. Mag.* VII. 475 (*title*), On the Immediate transmission of Calorific Rays through Diathermal Bodies. **1923** *Blackw. Mag.* Nov. 584/2 The Diplomatic Body's process of diathermal hibernation.

diathermancy (daɪə'θɜːmənsɪ). *Physics.* [ad. F. *diathermansie*, formed by Melloni, 1833, from Gr. διά through + θέρμανσις heating, f. θερμαίνειν to heat. The French ending follows the analogy of *paralysie* for Gr. παράλυσις. The Eng. ending simulates the *-ncy* of *transparency*, *buoyancy*.

Melloni's original term was *diathermanéïté*, from *diathermane* adj. (*Ann. Chim. et Phys.* 1833, LIII. 59, LV. 396, *Phil. Mag.* 1835 VII. 476); the latter was, according to him, 'f. διά + θερμαίνω, in imitation of *diaphane*, f. διά + φαίνω to show.' But the analogy was not exact: *diaphane* is not derived from διά and φαίνω, only from the same root; and in θερμαίνω, -αίνω does not belong to the root, but is a verbal suffix, the stem being θερμ-. *Diathermane* was first rendered in Eng. *diathermal*, but after 1837 generally *diathermanous*. To express the notion of 'coloration ou teinte calorifique', Melloni introduced *diathermansie*, f. Gr. διά + θέρμανσις heating (*Ann. Chim. et Phys.* LV. 377). But the distinction between *diathermanéïté* and *diathermansie* appears not to have been generally appreciated; in the Eng. translation of Melloni's paper in Taylor's *Scientific Memoirs*, 1837, I. 72, *diathermancy* is used for both F. words, and English writers generally have used it in the sense of Melloni's *diathermanéïté*. For these and other reasons, Melloni afterwards (*Comptes Rendus*, 1841, XIII. 815) abandoned his original terms, and gave a new nomenclature: viz. *diathermique* adj., instead of *diathermane*; *diathermasie* (ad. Gr. διαθερμασία) in place of *diathermanéïté*; and *thermochrose* for *diathermansie* 'colouring or tint of heat', with corresponding adj. *thermochroïque*. But, though some English writers have thence used *diathermic* and *diathermacy*, most have continued to employ *diathermanous* and *diathermancy*, the latter in the sense not of Melloni's *diathermansie*, but of his *diathermanéïté* or *diathermasie*.]

†**1.** *orig.* The property, possessed by radiant heat, of being composed of rays of different refrangibilities, varying in rate or degree of transmission through diathermic substances; THERMOCHROSY; also called *heat-colour*. *Obs.*

[**1833** MELLONI in *Ann. Chim. et Phys.* LV. 377 Les rayons calorifiques..possèdent, pour ainsi dire, la *diathermansie* propre à chaque substance qu'ils ont traversée. (Note) Je prends *diathermansie* comme l'équivalent de *coloration* ou *teinte calorifique*.] **1837** transl. in Taylor's *Scientific Mem.* I. 61 The calorific rays..possess (if we may use the term) the *diathermancy* peculiar to each of the substances through which they have passed. (Note) I employ the word *diathermancy* as the equivalent of *calorific coloration* or *calorific tint*. —— *Ibid.* 69 They diminish the quantity of heat transmitted by the glass without altering its diathermancy [*diathermansie*].

2. Now: The property of being diathermic or diathermanous; perviousness to radiant heat; = DIATHERMANEITY.

[**1833** MELLONI in *Ann. Chim. et Phys.* LV. 396 Les couleurs introduites dans un milieu diaphane diminuent toujours plus ou moins sa diathermanéïté.] **1837** transl. in Taylor's *Scientific Mem.* I. 72 The colours introduced into a diaphanous medium always diminish its diathermancy in a greater or less degree. **1843** A. SMEE *Sources Phys. Sc.* 194 The extent to which interposed bodies allow radiation is called the extent of diathermancy. **1857** WHEWELL *Hist. Induct. Sc.* (ed. 3) II. 399 Their power of transmitting heat, which has been called diathermancy. **1863** TYNDALL *Heat* ix. 296 Diathermancy bears the same relation to radiant heat that transparency does to light. **1893** *Brit. Med. Jrnl.* 1 Apr. 684/1 Perhaps the diathermancy is the most striking feature of mountain climates, as it affords an explanation of the great solar temperatures which prevail during the day..and of the great nocturnal radiation.

diatherma'neity. *rare.* [ad. F. *diathermanéité*, f. *diathermane*, with the ending of *diaphanéité* DIAPHANEITY.] The quality of being diathermanous; = prec. 2, and DIATHERMACY.

1835 FARADAY tr. Melloni in *L. & E. Phil. Mag.* VII. 476 According to the diathermaneity [*diathermanéïté*] of the substance of which the plate consists. **1837** tr. Melloni in Taylor's *Scient. Mem.* 69 Variations produced in the diathermaneity [*diathermanéïté*] of white glass. **1854** J. SCOFFERN in *Orr's Circ. Sc.* Chem. 276 The transmissibility of heat (diathermaneity) of various laminæ. **1877** WATTS *Dict. Chem.* V. 61 [see DIATHERMIC *a.* 1].

†**dia'thermanism**. *Obs.* [a. F. *diathermanisme* (Larousse), f. *diathermane*.] = DIATHERMANCY.

1858 LARDNER *Hand-bk. Nat. Phil.* 372 (*Title of section*).

diathermanous (daɪə'θɜːmənəs), *a.* [f. F. *diathermane* (Melloni 1833) + -OUS. For history of the Fr. word see DIATHERMANCY.]

Having the property of freely transmitting radiant heat; pervious to heat-rays; = DIATHERMIC *a.* 1. (Corresp. to *transparent* or *diaphanous* in relation to light.)

1834 E. TURNER *Elem. Chem.* 107 Melloni has.. introduced a distinct name *diathermanous*, to denote free permeability to heat. **1854** J. SCOFFERN in *Orr's Circ. Sc.* Chem. 103 We have transcalent and not-transcalent substances—otherwise called diathermanous and a-diathermanous. **1858** LARDNER *Hand-bk. Hydrost., etc.* 371 The only substance found to be perfectly diathermanous was rock salt. Plates of this crystal transmit nearly all the heat which enters them..Certain media which are nearly opaque are highly diathermanous, while others which are highly transparent are nearly athermanous. **1874** HARTWIG *Aerial W.* vi. 75 The great diathermanous power of dry air. **1881** O. J. LODGE in *Nature* XXIII. 265 The ice, being less diathermanous than the vapour, will get heated first.

†**dia'thermant**, *a. Obs.* [f. DIATHERMANCY, after *transparent*, *buoyant*, etc.] = prec.

1871 J. C. WARD *Nat. Phil.* 179 Rock-salt..may be said to be transparent to heat, or as it is called diathermant.

diathermic (daɪə'θɜːmɪk), *a.* [ad. F. *diathermique* (f. Gr. διά through + θέρμ-η, θερμ-όν heat: see -IC), substituted by Melloni for his earlier term *diathermane*: see DIATHERMANCY.]

1. = DIATHERMANOUS.

1840 T. THOMSON *Heat & Electr.* (ed. 2) 132 To bodies which transmit heat well, Melloni has given the name of diathermic or transcaloric bodies. **1867** W. A. MILLER *Elem. Chem.* (ed. 4) I. 296 A solution of alum is equally diathermic with a solution of rock salt. **1869** MRS. SOMERVILLE *Molec. Sc.* I. I. ii. 37 Bi-sulphide of carbon..of all liquids is the most diathermic. **1877** WATTS *Dict. Chem.* V. 61 Bodies which..afford a more or less free passage to rays of heat, are called by Melloni *diathermic*; while those which..entirely obstruct the passage of radiant heat, are called *adiathermic*; the corresponding properties..being called *diathermacy* and *adiathermacy*, sometimes also *diathermaneity* and *adiathermaneity*.

2. Of or pertaining to diathermy. Also **dia'thermically** *adv.*, by means of a diathermic current.

1910 F. NAGELSCHMIDT in *Proc. R. Soc. Med.* (Electro-Therapeutic Sect.) IV. 2, I have designed a special diathermic apparatus. **1910** *Brit. Med. Jrnl.* 12 Nov. 1547/2 During diathermic operations the blood vessels and lymph channels are securely sealed. **1929** C. C. MARTINDALE *Risen Sun* 100 They were sure I liked heat, and pumped an incredible amount, diathermically, into me each day. **1949** E. B. CLAYTON *Electrotherapy & Actinotherapy* xvii. 284 All diathermic treatments to the head should be given with the patient reclining on a couch.

diather'mometer. [f. Gr. διά through + θερμ-όν heat + μέτρον measure.] (See quot.)

1883 *Syd. Soc. Lex., Diathermometer*, an instrument designed to measure the thermal resistance of a body by registering the amount of transmitted heat.

dia'thermous, *a.* [f. Gr. διά through + stem of θερμός hot + -OUS.] = DIATHERMIC *a.* 1.

1843 A. SMEE *Sources Phys. Sc.* 194 As a specimen of a diathermous body, air is a capital example. 1885 MCGEE in *Amer. Jrnl. Sc.* 3rd Ser. XXIX. 390 The solar accession of the east half of the assumed ice-stream will be freely dissipated through the diathermous forenoon atmosphere.

diathermy ('daɪəθɜːmɪ). [ad. G. *diathermie* (F. Nagelschmidt 1909, in *Münch. med. Wochenschr.* 14 Dec. 2575/1), f. Gr. διά through + θερμός heat + -Y[3].] The therapeutic passing of high-frequency electric currents through the body by means of external electrodes in order to generate heat within the body; ***medical diathermy***, diathermy in which the tissues are warmed but not sufficiently to change their nature; ***surgical diathermy***, diathermy in which there is sufficient heating to produce a local change such as destruction of tissue or coagulation of bleeding vessels.

1910 F. NAGELSCHMIDT in *Proc. R. Soc. Med.* (Electro-Theropeutic Sect.) IV. 1 Diathermy is one effect of high-frequency currents of all kinds. 1910 *Archives Roentgen Ray* June 19 Diathermy is but one phase of d'Arsonvalisation, which, besides the production of heat, has other physiological effects dependent on the tension, length, form and frequency of the waves. 1911 *Brit. Med. Jrnl.* 14 Oct. 900/1 The now familiar diathermy apparatus. 1918 *Proc. R. Soc. Med.* (Electro-Therapeutic Sect.) XI. 39 *(heading)* Practical difficulties in performing surgical diathermy of malignant growths. 1929 *Times* 19 Apr. 16/3 Dr. F. D. Howitt visited Craigweil House and again applied the diathermy treatment to the King. 1930 D. MCKENZIE *Diathermy in Oto-Laryngology* i. 10 When we are giving medical diathermy we begin the current at zero and raise it gradually. 1957 B. O. SCOTT *Princ. & Pract. Diathermy* v. 55 Short-wave diathermy with its higher frequency as compared to long-wave diathermy is more convenient to apply to a patient since it can be used with air-spaced electrodes. 1966 *Listener* 13 Jan. 62/3 When a third subject was heated by diathermy—which is a kind of heat treatment sometimes given in hospitals—his speed of counting was increased too.

dia'thesic, *a. rare.* [f. DIATHES-IS + -IC.] = DIATHETIC.

1883 in *Syd. Soc. Lex.* 1884 L. BRACHET *Aix-les-bains* i. 69 Their retrograde action on diathesic affections.

‖**diathesis** (daɪ'æθɪsɪs). Pl. **diatheses** (-iːz). [mod.L., a. Gr. διάθεσις disposition, state, condition, f. διατιθέναι to arrange, dispose.]

Med. A permanent (hereditary or acquired) condition of the body which renders it liable to certain special diseases or affections; a constitutional predisposition or tendency.

1681 tr. *Willis' Rem. Med. Wks.* Vocab., *Diathesis*, the affection or disposition. 1727-51 CHAMBERS *Cycl.*, *Diathesis*, a term used by some writers in the same sense with constitution. 1789 A. CRAWFORD in *Med. Commun.* II. 349 The..barytes is..calculated to correct the scrophulous diathesis. 1879 FARRAR *St. Paul* I. 490 The epileptic diathesis which was the qualification of the Pythonesses of Delphi. 1885 F. WARNER *Phys. Expression* xvi. 275 The tendencies in the development of a child or adult may be studied by determining the diathesis, as it is called.

b. *fig.*

1651 BIGGS *New Disp.* ¶236 An exotick Diathesis of corruption. 1861 MAINE *Anc. Law* ix. (1876) 340 Enormous influence on the intellectual diathesis of the modern world. 1874 BLACKIE *Self-Cult.* 90 Practically, there is no surer test of a man's moral diathesis than the capacity of prayer. 1877 F. HALL *Eng. Adj. in -able* 173 Helpless slaves of what a metaphysician might call the sequacious diathesis.

Hence **di,athesi'sation**, 'the rendering general or systemic of an originally local disease; as the development into pyæmia of a simple abscess'. *Syd. Soc. Lex.* 1883.

diathetic (daɪə'θɛtɪk), *a.* [f. DIATHESIS, on Greek analogies: cf. *antithesis, antithetic*: see -THETIC.]

Of, pertaining to, or arising from diathesis: constitutional.

1866 FLINT *Princ. Med.* (1880) 92 Diseases..involving a constitutional predisposition, or diathesis, are sometimes distinguished as diathetic diseases. 1880 J. EDMUNDS in *Med. Temp. Jrnl.* July 184 Diathetic conditions need.. appropriate medical treatment.

Hence **dia'thetically** *adv.*, in a diathetic manner, constitutionally.

1883 E. C. MANN *Psychol. Med.* 346 They are related to each other nutritionally and diathetically.

diatom ('daɪətəm). [ad. mod.L. *Diatoma*, f. Gr. διάτομ-ος cut through, cut in half, f. διατέμνειν to cut through.] A member of the genus *Diatoma*, or, in a wider sense, of the *Diatomaceæ*, an order of microscopic unicellular Algæ, with silicified cell-walls, and the power of locomotion, on which account they were formerly placed by many naturalists in the Animal kingdom. They exist in immense numbers at the bottom of the sea, as well as in fresh water; and their siliceous remains form extensive fossil deposits in many localities.

The genus *Diatoma* is distinguished by having the frustules, or individual cells, connected by their alternate angles so as to form a kind of zig-zag chain: hence the name.

1845 GRAY *Lett.* (1893) 332 Then the low, minute forms and Confervæ come..ending with diatoms, transitions to corallines through sponge, etc. 1853 W. SMITH *British Diatomaceæ* 25 During the healthy life of the Diatom the process of self-division is being continually repeated. 1858 C. P. SMYTH *Astron. Exper. Teneriffe* 6 The countless millions of diatomes that go to make a feast for the medusæ. 1862 DANA *Man. Geol.* §74 Microscopic siliceous shields of the infusoria called diatoms, which are now regarded as plants. [1865 GOSSE *Land & Sea* (1874) 158 The name Diatoma..has reference to the readiness with which the strings or chains in which most of the forms are aggregated may be separated.] 1882 VINES *Sachs' Bot.* 260 The movements of Diatoms are not altogether dissimilar to those of Desmids, and even the silicification of the cell-wall..is found, though to a smaller extent, in *Closterium* and other Desmids.

attrib. 1880 CARPENTER in *19th Cent.* No. 38. 605 Their exquisitely sculptured cases, accumulating on the bottom, form a siliceous 'Diatom-ooze', which takes the place in higher latitudes of the white calcareous mud resulting from the distintegration of foraminiferal shells. 1893 A. H. S. LANDOR *Hairy Ainu* 74 Beds of lignite, coal of inferior quality, and diatom earth.

diatomaceous (,daɪətə'meɪʃəs), *a.* [f. mod.L. *Diatomăceæ* (f. *Diatoma*) + -OUS: see prec. and -ACEOUS.] **a.** Of or pertaining to the order *Diatomaceæ*, containing the diatoms and their allies. **b.** *Geol.* Consisting or formed of the fossil remains of diatoms, as in ***diatomaceous earth, deposits***, etc.

1847 J. D. HOOKER in *Brit. Assoc. Rept.* II. 83 *(Paper)* On the Diatomaceous Vegetation of the Antarctic Ocean. 1853 KANE *Grinnell Exp.* xlviii. (1856) 455 Filled with slimy diatomaceous life. 1878 HUXLEY *Physiogr.* xvii. 292 In diatomaceous deposits the individual diatoms run into a sort of opal. 1883 *Cassell's Fam. Mag.* 507/1 The best diatomaceous earth is the 'Kieselguhr' of Hanover, which serves for the preparation of dynamite.

So **diato'macean**, a member of the *Diatomaceæ*; = next.

In mod. Dicts.

dia'tomean. [f. mod.L. *Diatome-æ* (f. *Diatoma*) + -AN.] A diatomaceous plant, a diatom.

1853 HENFREY *Ray Society's Bot. & Physiol. Mem.* 360 Every Diatomean is formed by a siliceous shield and a soft substance therein contained.

diatomic (daɪə'tɒmɪk), *a. Chem.* [f. DI-[2] twice + ἄτομ-ος ATOM *sb.* + -IC.] Consisting of, or having, two atoms; specifically applied to compounds containing two replaceable atoms of hydrogen; sometimes used as = divalent.

1869 ROSCOE *Elem. Chem.* xxxiv. *heading*, Diatomic acids, resulting from the oxidation of the glycols. *Ibid.* 417 It..is monobasic but diatomic. 1869 *Eng. Mech.* 12 Nov. 198/3 Elements..classified as..diatomic or bivalent, having two attractions, as sulphur. 1880 CLEMENSHAW *Wurtz' Atom. Th.* 119 *note*, The term diatomic molecules clearly and correctly expresses molecules formed of two atoms.

,diato'miferous, *a.* [f. mod.L. *Diatoma* DIATOM + -FEROUS.] Producing or yielding diatoms.

In mod. Dicts.

diatomin (daɪ'ætəmɪn). [f. as prec. + -IN.] The yellowish-brown or buff-coloured pigment, which colours diatoms and the brown algæ.

1882 VINES *Sachs' Bot.* 260 [In diatoms] the green colouring matter is concealed, as in the chlorophyll-granules of the Fucaceæ, by a buff-coloured substance, Diatomin or Phycoxanthin.

diatomist (daɪ'ætəmɪst). [f. as prec. + -IST.] One who studies diatoms.

1881 *Jrnl. Quekett Microsc. Club* No. 46. 191, I should like the attention of Diatomists to be drawn..towards the elucidation of the true sexual generation in these plants.

diatomite (daɪ'ætəmaɪt). [f. as prec. + -ITE.] Diatomaceous or infusorial earth.

1887 *Sci. Amer.* 12 Mar. 161/1 The fossil meal, diatomite, or infusorial earth of the English. 1905 *Chambers's Jrnl.* Aug. 622/1 Diatomite is an excellent non-conductor of heat. 1939 J. G. D. CLARK *Archaeol. & Soc.* ii. 51 Among the more specialized minerals the digging of which has benefited archaeology, one may mention diatomite, a freshwater silt used for insulation purposes. 1957 G. E. HUTCHINSON *Treat. Limnol.* I. i. 41 Deposits of diatomite are frequently found at the sites of such lakes.

diatomous (daɪ'ætəməs), *a. Min.* [f. Gr. διάτομ-ος cut through (see DIATOM) + -OUS.] 'Having crystals with one distinct diagonal cleavage'.

1847 in CRAIG; and in later Dicts.

diatonic (daɪə'tɒnɪk), *a.* [a. F. *diatonique* (14th c. in Hatz.-Darm.), ad. L. *diatonic-us*, a. Gr. διατονικός, f. διάτονος, f. διά through, at the interval of + τόνος tone.]

1. The name of that genus or scale of ancient Greek music (the others being CHROMATIC and ENHARMONIC) in which the interval of a tone was used, the tetrachord being divided into two whole tones and a semitone (as in each half of the modern diatonic scale).

1603 HOLLAND *Plutarch's Mor.* 1252 Before his time, al Musické was either Diatonique or Chromatique. 1694 HOLDER *Treat. Harm.* (1731) 102 The Diatonick had two Colours; it was Molle and Syntonum. 1763 J. BROWN *Poetry & Mus.* v. 64 In the ancient Diatonic Scale..one Semitone and two whole Tones are ordained to succeed each other invariably.

2. In modern music, denoting the scale which in any key proceeds by the notes proper to that key without chromatic alteration; hence, applied to melodies and harmonies constructed from such a scale.

[1597 MORLEY *Introd. Mus.* Annot., *Diatonicum* is that which is now in vse.] 1694 HOLDER *Treat. Harm.* (1731) 114 In Diatonic Music there is but one sort of Hemitone.. whose Ration is 16 to 15. 1726 SWIFT *It cannot rain but it pours*, He sings..with equal facility in the chromatick, inharmonick, and diatonick stile. 1774 BURNEY *Hist. Mus.* (ed. 2) I. ii. 23 In modern music the Genera are but two: Diatonic and Chromatic. 1848 RIMBAULT *First Bk. Piano* 91 *Diatonic*, the natural scale; ascending by notes, containing five tones and two semitones. 1856 COMSTOCK & HOBLYN *Nat. Philos.* (ed. 6) 234 What is called the gamut, or diatonic scale. 1876 MACFARREN *Harmony* (ed. 2) ii. 39 The word *Diatonic*,—rendered *through the tones* by etymologists—must have been intended to signify *through the uninflected notes*. 1879 G. MEREDITH *Egoist* xxi. (1889) 198 Crossjay's voice ran up and down a diatonic scale.

b. *fig.* Of a normal or natural sort; free from fancies or crotchets.

1871 *Contemp. Rev.* XVI. 649 The healthy diatonic nature of Mr. Hutton's chief preferences in literature.

Hence †**dia'tonical** *a. Obs.* = DIATONIC; **dia'tonically** *adv.*, in a diatonic manner.

1597 MORLEY *Introd. Mus.* Annot., This diuision is false in the diatonicall kind of musicke. 1727-51 CHAMBERS *Cycl.* s.v. *Diapente*, The diapente is a simple concord; yet, if considered diatonically, it contains four terms. 1774 BURNEY *Hist. Mus.* I. iv. 57 Taking..two or more perfect chords of the same kind diatonically.

diatonicism (daɪə'tɒnɪsɪz(ə)m). *Mus.* [f. DIATONIC *a.* + -ISM.] The quality or state of being diatonic; music the tonality of which is predominantly diatonic; a diatonic system.

1931 *Times Lit. Suppl.* 23 July 580/4 Returning from Schönbergian wanderings to a 'sincere diatonicism'. 1938 *Scrutiny* VII. II. 173 Even his most complex departures from diatonicism can be referred back to some scale system or chordal structure. 1959 *Listener* 20 Aug. 297/1 Frank added-note diatonicism is allied to blatantly nautical-English melody.

diatonism (daɪ'ætənɪz(ə)m). *Mus.* [f. DIATONIC *a.*: see -ISM.] = prec.

1927 *Music & Lett.* July 325 An insipid diatonic scheme which lacks the primitive freshness of Beethoven's diatonism. 1928 G. COOKE *Theory of Music* 19 Recent attacks upon conventional and arbitrary Diatonism.

diatory, obs. form of DIETARY.

diatribe ('daɪətraɪb), *sb.* Formerly also in L. form **diatriba**. [a. F. *diatribe* (15th c. in Hatz.-Darm.), ad. L. *diatriba* a learned discussion, a school, a. Gr. διατριβή a wearing away (of time), employment, study, and (in Plato) discourse, f. διατρίβ-ειν to rub through or away. The senses in F. and Eng. exactly correspond.]

1. A discourse, disquisition, critical dissertation. *arch.*

1581 J. BELL *Haddon's Answ. Osor.* 246b, I heare the sounde of an Argument from the Popish Diatriba. 1643 R. BAILLIE *Lett. & Jrnls.* (1841) II. 65 Some parergetick Diatribes of that matter. 1672 *Mede's Wks.* Gen. Pref. A, That excellent Diatriba upon S. Mark i. 15. 1683 *Lond. Gaz.* No. 1820/4 The constant Communicant; a Diatribe, proving that Constancy in receiving the Lords Supper is the indispensable Duty of every Christian. 1703 J. QUICK *Dec. Wife's Sister* Lett., Possibly this poor Diatribe may contribute something thereunto. 1816 KIRBY & SP. *Entomol.* (1828) II. xxiv. 397, I shall conclude this diatribe upon the noises of insects. 1875 LOWELL *Spenser* Prose Wks. 1890 IV. 273 A diatribe on the subject of descriptive poetry.

2. In modern use: A dissertation or discourse directed against some person or work; a bitter and violent criticism; an invective.

1804 SCOTT *Let. Ellis* in Lockhart *Life* xiii, One must always regret so very serious a consequence of a diatribe. 1830 CUNNINGHAM *Brit. Paint.* II. 132 On the appearance of this bitter diatribe in 1797. 1850 KINGSLEY *Alt. Locke* xxviii, A rambling, bitter diatribe on the wrongs and sufferings of the labourers. 1854 THACKERAY *Newcomes* II. 293 Breaking out into fierce diatribes. 1877 MORLEY *Carlyle* Crit. Misc. Ser. I. (1878) 201 The famous diatribe against Jesuitism in the Latter-Day Pamphlets.

Hence **'diatribe** *v. intr.*, to utter a diatribe; to inveigh bitterly.

1893 *National Observer* 6 May 630/1 Why diatribe against the tradesmen of Liskeard?

'diatribist. [f. prec. + -IST.] One who writes or utters a diatribe; †the writer of a critical dissertation.

a 1660 HAMMOND *Wks.* II. IV. 134 (R.) The same I desire may introduce my address to this diatribist. 1678 CUDWORTH *Intell. Syst.* I. iv. 190 Against a modern Diatribist.

diatrion: see DIA-[2].

‖**diaty'posis.** *Rhet.* [L., a. Gr. διατύπωσις vivid description, f. διατυπό-ειν to form or represent perfectly.] (See quot.)

1657 J. SMITH *Myst. Rhet.* 251 *Diatyposis*.. A figure when a thing is so described by mere words, that it may seem to be set.. before our eyes. **1706** in PHILLIPS (ed. Kersey).

diaulic (daɪ'ɔːlɪk), *a.* [f. Gr. δίαυλος (see next) + -IC.] Of or pertaining to, or of the nature of, the diaulos or double course.

1837 WHEELWRIGHT tr. *Aristophanes* I. 225 Come they thus arm'd to the diaulic course.

‖**diaulos** (daɪ'ɔːlɒs). *Gr. Antiq.* [Gr. δίαυλος double pipe, channel, or course, f. δι- (DI-²) + αὐλός pipe.]

1. A double course, in which the racers turned round a goal and returned to the starting point.

1706 PHILLIPS (ed. Kersey), *Diaulon*, a kind of Race among the Ancients, two furlongs in length, at the end of which they return'd back along the same Course. *a* **1859** DE QUINCEY *Post. Wks.* (1891) I. 165 Eight days for the *diaulos* of the journey. **1884** R. C. JEBB in *Encycl. Brit.* XVII. 766 (*Olympia*) Beside the foot-race in which the course was traversed once only, there were now the diaulos or double course and the long foot-race.

2. An ancient Greek musical instrument; the double flute.

di'axial, *a. rare.* [f. Gr. δι- (DI-²) twice + AXIAL.] Having two (optic) axes; = BIAXIAL *a.* 1.

1843 J. PEREIRA *Lect. Polarized Light* 69 Another kind.. is called by mineralogists prismatic, or diaxial mica.

‖**diaxon** (daɪ'æksən), *a. Zool.* [mod. f. Gr. δι- (DI-²) + ἄξων axis.] Of sponge spicules: Having two axes.

1886 VON LENDENFELD in *Proc. Zool. Soc.* (1886) 560 When one of the rays of this tri-act spicule becomes rudimentary, *Diaxonia* can theoretically be produced. It is, however, advantageous to consider the diaxon spicules as part of the *Triaxonia*.

diaxon (daɪ'æksɒn), *sb. Anat.* Also -one. [f. DI-² + AXON.] A nerve-cell having two axons.

1900 in DORLAND *Med. Dict.*

diazepam (daɪ'æz-, daɪeɪzəpæm). *Pharm.* [f. BENZO)DIAZEP(INE + *-am*, of unkn. origin.] A minor tranquillizer of the benzodiazepine group with sedative, anticonvulsant, and amnesic properties, given orally and by injection to treat anxiety, muscle spasm, status epilepticus, etc., and sometimes giving rise to withdrawal symptoms when it is discontinued.

1961 L. O. RANDALL et al. in *Current Therapeutic Res.* III. 405 (*caption*) Valium (LAIII) (diazepam). **1968** [see LIBRIUM]. **1977** *Sci. Amer.* Mar. 53/3 Alcohol, barbiturates and antianxiety drugs, such as chlordiazepoxide (Librium) or diazepam (Valium) seem to share brain mechanisms for tolerance and dependence. **1979** *Daily Tel.* 29 Nov. 8/8 The big winner at the benzodiazipine tables has been the Swiss firm Roche, which introduced the first drug of this group, chlordiazepoxide, under the brand name Librium in 1960, followed by a variant, diazepam, brand named Valium, three years later. **1981** M. C. GERALD *Pharmacol.* (ed. 2) xvi. 344 In 1977, 54 million prescriptions were written for diazepam.

diazeuctic (daɪə'zjuːktɪk), *a.* [ad. Gr. διαζευκτικός disjunctive, f. διαζευγνύναι to disjoin, f. διά apart + ζευγνύναι (stem ζευγ-) to join.] Disjunctive; applied, in ancient Greek Music, to the interval of a tone separating disjunct tetrachords; also to the tetrachords (= DISJUNCT). So ‖**dia'zeuxis** [Gr. διάζευξις], the separation of two tetrachords by a tone.

1698 WALLIS in *Phil. Trans.* XX. 250 The Difference of which, is *La mi*. Which is, what the Greeks call, the *Diazeuctick Tone*; which doth Dis-join two Fourths.. and, being added to either of them, doth make a Fifth. **1760** *Ibid.* LI. 709 The position of the diazeuctic tone. **1874** CHAPPELL *Hist. Music* I. 129 At the base of each Octave was a 'diazeuctic', or Major tone. **1880** STAINER & BARRETT *Dict. Mus. Terms*, Diazeuxis.

diazingiber, -zinziber: see DIA-².

diazo (daɪ'æzəʊ), abbrev. of DIAZOTYPE (see DIAZO-).

1948 *Jrnl. Documentation* Dec. 184 An important advantage of the diazo system of reproduction.. is that there is no need to decide beforehand what the eventual demand will be. **1953** *Library Assoc. Rec.* LV. 10 (*title*) Progress in reflex copying; Diazo and after. **1964** *Economist* 9 May 618/2 The most important of these [*sc.* sensitized papers] is diazo paper.

diazo- (daɪ'æzəʊ). *Chem.* [f. DI-² + AZO-.] A formative used in chemical nomenclature to denote the substituent $=\overset{+}{N}=\overset{-}{N}$ (as in ***diazomethane***, CH_2N_2) and also the group $-N=N-$ when one bond only is to a carbon atom of an organic group (as in ***benzenediazochloride***, $C_6H_5-N=N-Cl$). Also used *attributively*, as in ***diazo compounds, derivatives, reaction***. †Formerly also used in naming compounds in which the group $-N=N-$ has both bonds attached to carbon atoms in organic groups (now replaced by *azo-*) and compounds containing the diazonium group, $-N_2^+$. (***Diazo compound*** is also used *loosely* to denote azo and diazonium compounds as well as true diazo compounds.)

1859 P. GRIESS in *Proc. R. Soc.* IX. 595 The new body, for which I propose the provisional name diazodinitrophenol, is soluble in alcohol and ether. **1873** *Fownes' Chem.* (ed. 11) 797 Whereby they were converted into diazotoluenes. **1878** *Law Reports* 29 Ch. Div. 367 Naphthylamine is converted into its diazo compound by the action of nitrous acid. **1880** FRISWELL in *Soc. Arts Jrnl.* 446 The diazobenzene formed at once attacks the free aniline salt. **1880** *Athenæum* 13 Nov. 645/2 Action of Diazonaphthalin on Salicylic Acid. **1890** *Lancet* 23 Aug. 413/1 The so-called diazo reaction of urine .. A bright or carmine red colouration denotes the diazo action. **1908** J. C. CAIN *Chem. Diazo-Compounds* xviii. 133 Hantzsch.. adopted Blomstrand's formula for the diazo-salts. He preferred also to call these 'diazonium' salts. **1940** S. MIALL *New Dict. Chem.* 169/1 The diazonium salts are by far the most important diazo-compounds. **1951** I. L. FINAR *Org. Chem.* xxiv. 489 Diazo-compounds have the structure Ar−N=N−Y... Azo-compounds, on the other hand, have the structure Ar−N=N−Ar. **1951** C. R. NOLLER *Chem. Org. Compounds* xiii. 258 Compounds containing the characteristic group $>CN_2$ are known as aliphatic diazo compounds. **1959** *Chambers's Encycl.* IV. 690/1 Azo dye synthesis depends on two reactions discovered by Griess (1858): first, diazo compound formation..; secondly, adding this diazo component to an aromatic amino or hydroxy compound, called the coupling component. **1965** *Nomencl. Org. Chem.* (I.U.P.A.C.) C. 217 Compounds RN=NX are named by adding, after the name of the parent compound RH, the syllables 'diazo' joined to the designation of the atom or group X.

Hence **di'azotype**, a method of photographic copying or colouring, using paper or textile materials impregnated with a diazonium compound.

1890 *Photogr. News* 28 Nov. 934/2 Feer's process is not a primuline process, although it is a diazotype process. **1891** *Art Jrnl.* Feb. 54 The Diazotype process, a method of photographic dyeing and printing. **1967** *Times Rev. Industry* May 117/1 (Advt.), Diazotype printing processes have endless permutations.

‖**diazoma** (daɪə'zəʊmə). [L. *diazōma* space between the seats in a theatre, a. Gr. διάζωμα girdle, partition, or diaphragm, lobby in a theatre, f. διά through, over + ζῶμα that which is girded, f. ζωννύναι to gird round.]

1. In the ancient Greek theatre: A semicircular passage through the auditorium, parallel to its outer border, and cutting the radial flights of steps at right angles at a point about half way up.

1706 PHILLIPS (ed. Kersey), *Diazoma*, a Girdle or Waste-belt; also a broad Footstep on the Stairs of an Amphi-theater. **1820** T. S. HUGHES *Trav. Sicily* I. xi. 335 (Stanf.) It is of small dimensions, containing only one diazoma or corridor.

†**2.** *Anat.* The diaphragm or midriff. *Obs.*

1706 PHILLIPS (ed. Kersey), *Diazoma*.. in Anatomy the same with the Diaphragm or Midriff. **1883** *Syd. Soc. Lex.*, *Diazoma*, an old name.. for the diaphragm.

diazonium (daɪə'zəʊnɪəm). *Chem.* [a. G. *diazonium* (A. Hantzsch 1895, in *Ber. d. Deut. Chem. Ges.* XXVIII. 1735), f. DIAZ(O- + -ONIUM.] A formative used in chemical nomenclature to denote the ion $-N_2^+$ attached to a carbon atom in an organic compound (usu. an aromatic one, as ***benzenediazonium chloride***, $C_6H_5N_2^+Cl^-$). Hence used *attrib.*, as ***diazonium compound***, any of the compounds containing this group, some of which are commercially important, being prepared by diazotization and used in the manufacture of azo dyes and in chemical synthesis.

1895 *Jrnl. Chem. Soc.* LXVIII. I. 516 (*title*) Diazonium Compounds and Normal Diazo-compounds. *Ibid.*, The salts of diazobenzene with oxy-acids.. contain the radicle N⋮NPh, which is strictly analogous to ammonium, behaving in all respects as a compound alkali-metal, and may therefore be termed 'diazonium'. *Ibid.* 517 Benzenediazonium mercurochloride, $PhN_2 \cdot HgCl_3$. **1908** [see DIAZO-]. **1938** G. H. RICHTER *Textbk. Org. Chem.* xxiv. 509 For most purposes the diazonium salts are not isolated; the solution is employed for whatever purpose is required. .. The pure *dry* diazonium salts are quite explosive. **1964** N. G. CLARK *Mod. Org. Chem.* xxii. 460 On adding a diazonium salt solution to a solution of a phenol in aqueous sodium hydroxide, an azo-compound is formed... Compounds of this type are highly coloured, and are used as dyes. **1965** *Economist* 22 May 942/3 Ultra-violet light shone on the original, passes through the plain bits and decomposes a diazonium compound coating on the copy paper beneath.

‖**dia'zoster.** [a. Gr. διαζωστήρ the twelfth vertebra in the back, f. διά through, over + ζωστήρ girdle, belt, f. ζωννύναι to gird.] (See quots.)

1811 HOOPER *Med. Dict.*, *Diazoster*, a name of the twelfth vertebra of the back. **1883** *Syd. Soc. Lex.*, *Diazoster*, old name for the twelfth vertebra of the spinal column; because a belt girding the body is usually placed over it (Gorræus).

di,azoti'zation. *Chem.* [f. DIAZOTIZE *v.* + -ATION.] The process of converting a compound or a group of atoms into a diazo or diazonium compound or group; *esp.* the conversion of an aromatic primary amine into a diazonium compound by the action of nitrous acid in ice-cold acid solution.

1893 in *Funk's Stand. Dict.* **1902** *Chem. News* 18 July 32/1 This compound, on diazotisation in acetic acid in presence of sulphuric or nitric acid, behaves normally, and forms a dinitrodiazonium salt. **1939** *Thorpe's Dict. Appl. Chem.* (ed. 4) III. 580/2 These diazo-derivatives are generally.. prepared from aromatic amines, and the process.. is termed *diazotisation*. **1949** N. G. HEATLEY in H. W. Florey et al. *Antibiotics* iii. 152 The nitrite content of each is then estimated photometrically by the diazotization of the *p*-aminobenzoic acid. **1963** A. J. HALL *Textile Sci.* iv. 179 A number of disperse dyes are of a type which contain amino (NH_2) groups capable of diazotisation.

diazotize (daɪ'æzətaɪz), *v. Chem.* [f. DI-² + AZOTE + -IZE: cf. *azotize*.] *trans.* To convert into a diazo compound. Hence **di'azotizable** *a.*, capable of being converted into a diazo or diazonium compound or group; **di'azotized** *ppl. a.*

1889 M'GOWAN tr. *Bernthsen's Org. Chem.* 361 The conversion of amido- into diazo-compounds is termed diazotizing. **1892** *Nature* 28 July, The number of amidogen groups which have been diazotized can be determined. **1890** THORPE *Dict. Appl. Chem.* I. 247 *Flavophenin*.. prepared by the action of diazotised benzidine (one molecule) on two molecules of salicylic acid in alkaline solution. **1899** *Jrnl. Soc. Chem. Industry* 31 May 488/1 With diamines such as *m*- or *p*-phenylene diamine.. compounds are obtained which are still diazotisable. **1963** A. J. HALL *Textile Sci.* iv. 181 The components of an insoluble azoic dye are a base having at least one diazotisable amino (NH_2) group in its molecule and a coupling component.

dib, *sb.*¹ *dial.* [A variant of DIP *sb.*: cf. DIB *v.*¹] A dip; a small hollow in the ground.

1847–78 HALLIWELL, *Dib*, a valley. *North.* **1869** *Lonsdale Gloss.*, *Dib*, a dip. **1876** F. K. ROBINSON *Whitby Gloss.*, *Dib*, a slight concavity on the ground's surface.

2. *Comb.* **dibboard**, the dip or inclination of a seam of coal. *Northumbld. Gloss.* 1892.

dib, *sb.*² Generally in *pl.* dibs. [*Dibs*, found in the 18th c., was prob. a familiar shortening of *dibstones*, mentioned by Locke. Prob. a deriv. of DIB *v.*²: cf. the names DABBERS, and (*dial.*) *dabs*, applied to a similar game, f. DAB *v.*]

1. a. *pl.* A game played by children with pebbles or the knuckle-bones of sheep; also the name of the pebbles or bones so used; see ASTRAGAL, CHECK-STONE¹, COCKAL.

1730–6 BAILEY (folio), *Dibbs*, a play among children. **1810** E. D. CLARKE *Trav.* I. 177 This game is called 'Dibbs' by the English. **1867** H. KINGSLEY *Silcote of S.* xiii, His dibbs and agate taws. **1888** *Berksh. Gloss.*, *Dibs*, a game played with the small knuckle bones taken from legs of mutton; these bones are themselves called dibs. **1890** J. D. ROBERTSON *Gloucestersh. Gloss.*, *Dibs*, pebbles.

b. A children's word used to express a claim or option on some object (freq. *int.*); chiefly in phr. ***to get*** (etc.) ***dibs on*** (something), to have first claim to. Cf. BAGS I, DUBS. *U.S. colloq.*

1932 *Amer. Speech* VII. 401 *Dibs*, *interj.*, an interjection giving option on first chance or place. 'Dibs on that magazine when you're through.' 'Dibs on going with the team if there's room.' **1943** *Amer. N. & Q.* III. 139/1 If a sprout came out of the house with some candy or an apple and saw a couple of friends who might have an interest in his prize, the only sensible thing for him to do was to cry 'No dibs!' before they could say 'I/We got dibs!' **1953** L. M. URIS *Battle Cry* III. i. 197 Two bottles of beer were issued to all enlisted men... 'Dibs on your beer, Mary'. 'Two lousy bottles, can they spare it?' **1954** E. EAGER *Half Magic* iv. 69 You always get dibs on first 'cause you're the oldest. **1985** *New Yorker* 29 Apr. 71/3 Patterson took care to remember ..which upstream banks had dibs on which borrowers.

2. A counter used in playing at cards, etc. as a substitute for money.

3. *pl.* A slang term for money.

1812 H. & J. SMITH *Rej. Addr.*, *G. Barnwell*, Make nunky surrender his dibs. **1867** SMYTH *Sailor's Word-bk.*, *Dibbs*, a galley term for ready money. **1868** MISS BRADDON *Run to Earth* III. ix, 'You are the individual what comes down with the dibbs.' **1883** BESANT *Garden Fair* II. iii, To make other beggars do the work and to pocket the dibs yourself.

4. = DIBBLE. (In various Eng. dialects.)

1891 *Leicestersh. Gloss.*, *Dib*, *Dibber or Dibble*, a pointed instrument often made of a broken spade-handle, for making holes for seeds.

dib, *sb.*³ A local Sc. var. of DUB, a puddle.

1821 GALT *Ann. of Parish* 312 (Jam.) The dibs were full, the roads foul. **1821** —— *Ayrsh. Legatees* 100 (Jam.) He kens the loan from the crown of the causeway, as well as the duck does the midden from the adle dib.

dib, *v.*¹ *Obs.* exc. *dial.* [App. an onomatopœic modification of DIP *v.*, expressing the duller sound caused by broader contact. Cf. DIB. *sb.*¹] *trans.* = DIP *v.*

c **1325** *Metr. Hom.* 121 Jesus.. bad thaim dib thair cuppes alle, And ber tille bern best in halle. *c* **1570** *Durham Deposit.* (Surtees) 100 Dib the shirt in the water, and so hang it upon a hedge all that night. **1580** BARET *Alv.* D 653 To Dibbe or dippe. **1617** MINSHEU *Ductor*, To Dibbe, *vi.* to Dippe. **1868** ATKINSON *Cleveland Gloss.*, *Dib*, To dip.

dib, *v.*² [A derivative form from DAB *v.*¹, expressing an action of the same kind but weaker or lighter: cf. the forms *sip*, *snip*, *tip*, and the reduplicating element in *bibble-babble*, *tittle-*

tattle, *pit-pat*, *zig-zag*, which expresses a weakened phase of the notion expressed by the radical.

Sense 3 is also expressed by DAP, another derived form from *dab*, in which the consonant is lightened; also by DOP. Here there may also be association with DIP.]

1. *trans.* To dab lightly or finely: cf. DAB *v.*[1] 2.

1609 *Ev. Woman in Hum.* I. i. in Bullen *O. Pl.* IV, Mistris that face wants a fresh Glosse. Prethee, dib it in well, Bos.

2. *intr.* To tap or pat lightly: cf. DAB *v.*[1] 1 d.

1869 BLACKMORE *Lorna D.* x, It is a fine sight to behold.. the way that they dib with their bills.

3. *intr.* To fish by letting the bait (usually a natural insect) dip and bob lightly on the water; = DAP *v.* 1, DIBBLE *v.*[2] 2.

1681 CHETHAM *Angler's Vade-m.* iv. §8 (1689) 37 Put one on the point of a Dub-fly Hook, and dib with it, or dib with the Ash-fly. **1827** *Mirror* II. 118/1 It is customary to dib for them, or to use a fly. **1880** *Boy's own Bk.* 265 House-crickets are also good, to dib with, for chub. *Ibid.* 277 The hawthorn-fly.. is used to dib in a river for Trout.

4. To dibble.

Known in actual use only in mod. dial., but implied in DIBBER, DIBBING-STICK: see also DIBBLE.

1891 EVANS *Leicestersh. Gloss.*, *Dib* and *Dibble* vb., to use a 'dibble'. Dibble is the commonest form, both of the *sb.* and *v.*

Hence **ˈdibbing** *vbl. sb.*; **ˈdibbing-stick**, a dibble.

1681 CHETHAM *Angler's Vade-m.* xxxiii. §1 (1689) 174 Angling with a natural Fly (called dibbing, dapeing or dibbling). *Ibid.* §2. 174 Dibbing is always performed on the very surface.. or permitting the Bait to sink for 2 inches. **1833** BOWLKER *Angling* 27 The natural flies best adapted for dibbing or bobbing at the bush. **1863** H. C. PENNELL *Angler Nat.* 154 A natural caterpillar, cockchafer, or grasshopper, used with a short line by dibbing over the bushes. **1886** *Chesh. Gloss.*, *Dibbin-stick*, a stick used for planting cabbages, etc. or making holes for sowing seed.

dibar, obs. form of DIAPER.

dibasic (daɪˈbeɪsɪk), *a. Chem.* [f. DI-[2] + BASE *sb.*[1] + -IC.] Having two bases, or two atoms of a base. ***dibasic acid***: one which contains two atoms of displaceable hydrogen. See BIBASIC.

1868 *Chambers' Encycl.* X. 462/2 When an acid admits of the displacement of two atoms of hydrogen, it is termed dibasic. **1869** ROSCOE *Elem. Chem.* (1874) 365 The acids.. of the second series are *dibasic*. **1880** CLEMENSHAW *Wurtz' Atom. The.* 204 Oxygen and sulphur, the 'dibasic' character of which was demonstrated by Kekulé.

Hence **dibaˈsicity**, dibasic quality.

1880 CLEMENSHAW *Wurtz' Atom. The.* 179 The dibasicity of tartaric acid.

dibatag (ˈdɪbətæg). [Native name.] A species of antelope, *Ammodorcas clarkei*, found in Somaliland, having recurved horns ringed at the base.

1891 *Proc. Zool. Soc.* II. 210 The new Gazelle.. Somali name 'Debo Tag', which means 'carries tail high'. **1894** *Ibid.* II. 318 The Dibatag is common enough where it is found at all, but it is very local in its distribution. **1945** F. HARPER *Extinct & Vanishing Mammals of Old World* 675 Dibatag; Clarke's Gazelle... This.. gazelle is confined to the interior of British and Italian Somaliland and southeastern Ethiopia. **1970** DORST & DANDELOT *Field Guide Larger Mammals Afr.* 234 Very shy and alert, Dibatag move around a great deal.

dibb, var. of DIB.

dibber (ˈdɪbə(r)). [f. DIB *v.*[2] (sense 4) + -ER[1].]

1. An instrument for dibbling; a dibble; especially, an implement having a series of dibbles or teeth for making a number of holes at once.

1736 PEGGE *Kenticisms*, *Dibble*, I think they call it *dibber* in Kent. **1783** *Trans. Soc. Encourag. Arts* I. 112, I.. ploughed the land very deep, dressed the ground down, and planted with hand-dibbers. **1797** A. YOUNG *Agric. Suffolk* 48 A man .. with a dibber of iron, the handle about three feet long, in each hand, strikes two rows of holes. **1847** RAYNBIRD in *Jrnl. R. Agric. Soc.* VIII. I. 215 By using a drop-drill, or a larger dibber for making the holes. **1848** *Ibid.* IX. II. 548 Five cut sets [of hops] should be planted to make a hill, which should be put in with a dibber around the stick.

2. *Mining.* The pointed end of an iron bar used for making holes. *U.S.*

1871 W. MORGANS *Man. Mining Tools* 158 The pointed ends of bars are often slightly bent, to facilitate getting a pinch and levering in certain positions. The end is called a 'dibber', for making holes.

dibbin, dibben. *Obs.* or *dial.*

†**1.** In the leather trade: Part of a hide; perh. the shank. *Obs.*

1603-4 *Act 1 Jas. I*, c. 22 §35 The Neckes, Wombes, and Dibbins, or other peeces of Offall cut of from the saide Backes or Buts of Leather.

2. *dial.* (See quot.)

1847-78 HALLIWELL, *Dibben*, a fillet of veal. *Devon.*

dibble (ˈdɪb(ə)l), *sb.* Forms: 5 **debylle**, 6 **dybbil**, 6-7 **dible**, 6- **dibble**. [In form belonging app. to DIB *v.*[2] (sense 4), -LE being instrumental as in *beetle*, or diminutive: cf. *dibber*, *dibbing-stick* in same sense. *Dibble* is however evidenced much earlier than DIB *v.*[2], which leaves the nature of their relation doubtful.]

An instrument used to make holes in the ground for seeds, bulbs, or young plants. In its simplest form, a stout pointed cylindrical stick with or without a handle; but it may also have a cross bar or projection for the foot (*foot-dibble*), or be forked at the point, or furnished with several points to make a number of holes at once.

c **1450** *Nominale* in Wr.-Wülcker 713 *Hoc subterrarium*, a debylle. **1483** *Cath. Angl.* 92 A Debylle, *pastinacum*, *subterratorium*. **1563** HYLL *Art Garden.* 128 With your forked dibble, put vnder the head, loose it so in the earth, that [etc.]. **1570** LEVINS *Manip.* 124/42 A dybbil. **1573** TUSSER *Husb.* (1878) 101 Through cunning with dible, rake, mattock, and spade, By line and by leauell, trim garden is made. **1611** SHAKS. *Wint. T.* IV. iv. 100 Ile not put The Dible in earth, to set one slip of them. **1674** RAY *S. & E.C. Words* 64 A *Dibble*, an instrument to make holes in the ground with for setting beans, pease or the like. **1727** BRADLEY *Fam. Dict.* s.v. *Dibble*, There is a Dibble of a modern Invention with several Teeth, the Body of it is made of a light Wood, and the Teeth of a Wood that is somewhat harder. **1818** KEATS *Endym.* III. 153 In sowing-time ne'er would I dibble take, Or drop a seed. **1859** R. F. BURTON *Centr. Afr.* in *Jrnl. Geog. Soc.* XXIX. 397 The people use a msaha or dibble, a chisel-shaped bit of iron, with a socket to receive a wooden handle. **1861** DELAMER *Fl. Gard.* 48 To plant them with the trowel or dibble.

†**b.** ? A moustache. *Obs. slang.*

1614 B. JONSON *Barth. Fair* II. iii, Neuer tuske, nor twirle your dibble, good Iordane.

dibble (ˈdɪb(ə)l), *v.*[1] [f. DIBBLE *sb.*]

1. *trans.* To make a hole in (the soil) with or as with a dibble; to sow or plant by this means. ***to dibble in*** (***into***): to put in or plant by dibbling.

1583 STANYHURST *Æneis* IV. (Arb.) 110 So far is yt crampernd with roote deepe dibled at helgats. **1791** COWPER *Yardley Oak* 26 A skipping deer, With pointed hoof dibbling the glebe. **1797** A. YOUNG *Agric. Suffolk* 47 One farmer near Dunwich.. dibbled 258 acres. **1799** *Gentl. Mag.* I. 392 A woman employed.. dibbling beans. **1847-8** H. MILLER *First Impr.* ix. (1857) 145 The clayey soil around it was dibbled thick.. by the tiny hoofs of sheep. **1855** M. ARNOLD *Balder Dead* III. 312 The soft strewn snow Under the trees is dibbled thick with holes. **1872** BAKER *Nile Tribut.* iv. 54 The seeds of the dhurra are dibbled in about three feet apart.

transf. **1883** SIR E. BECKETT in *Knowl.* 31 Aug. 140/2 The printer's passion for dibbling in a comma between every two adjectives.

2. *intr.* To use or work with a dibble; to bore holes in the soil.

Mod. He was dibbling in his garden.

Hence **ˈdibbled** *ppl. a.*; **ˈdibbling** *vbl. sb.*; also in *Comb.*, as ***dibbling-machine***.

1795 *Hull Advertiser* 10 Oct. 3/3 If Dibbling, instead of Broadcast, was wholly practised, it would produce a saving. **1832** *Veg. Subst. Food* 38 Depositing the seed in holes.. at regular intervals.. is called drilling, or dibbling. **1846** J. BAXTER *Libr. Pract. Agric.* II. 210 It appears.. that drilling with the hoe is much preferable to dibbling. *Ibid.* There was .. one quarter more of produce from the drilled crop than from the dibbled. **1874** KNIGHT *Dict. Mech.*, *Dibbling-machine*, one used for making holes in rows for potato sets, for beans, or other things which are planted isolated in rows.

dibble (ˈdɪb(ə)l), *v.*[2] [Perhaps a derived form from DABBLE with lighter vowel: but cf. DIB *v.*[2] 3.]

1. *intr.* = DABBLE *v.* 2.

1622 DRAYTON *Poly-olb.* xxv. (1748) 366 And near to them you see the lesser dibbling teale.

2. = DIB *v.*[2] 3, DAP *v.* 1.

1658 R. FRANCK *North. Mem.* (1821) 60 Dibble lightly on the surface of the water. **1676** COTTON *Angler* (T.), This stone-fly.. we dape or dibble with, as with the drake. **1681** CHETHAM *Angler's Vade-m.* vii. §2 (1688) 75 When you angle at ground in a clear Water, or dibble with natural Flies. **1833** *Fraser's Mag.* VII. 54 He.. bobs and dibbles till he hooks his prey.

Hence **ˈdibbling** *vbl. sb.*

1676 COTTON *Angler* II. v. 295 This way of fishing we call *Daping* or *Dabbing*, or *Dibling* wherein you are always to have your Line flying before you up or down the River as the Wind serves. **1858** *Sat. Rev.* V. 569/2 Dibbling for trout he considers a high achievement.

ˈdibble-ˈdabble. *colloq.* or *dial.* [Reduplication of DABBLE, the form expressing repetition with alternation of intensity, as in *bibble-babble*, *tittle-tattle*, *zig-zag*, etc.] *lit.* An irregular course of dabbling or splashing; *fig.* rubbish; also, uproar with violence.

c **1550** BALE *K. Johan* (Camden) 7 They are but dyble dable I marvell ye can abyd such byble bable. **1767** C'TESS. COWPER in *Mrs. Delany's Life & Corr.* Ser. II. (1862) I. 99 It turned out such a dibble-dabble... We have had March weather before March came. **1825** JAMIESON, *Dibble-dabble*, uproar, accompanied with violence. **1847-78** HALLIWELL, *Dibble-dabble*, rubbish. *North.*

dibbler (ˈdɪblə(r)). [f. DIBBLE *v.*[1] + -ER[1].]

1. One who dibbles.

1770-4 A. HUNTER *Georg. Ess.* (1804) II. 356 One dibbler generally undertakes the business of one gang. **1797** A. YOUNG *Agric. Suffolk* 49 *note*, A one-horse roll to level the flag, or furrow, for the dibblers.

2. An agricultural implement used in dibbling; a machine dibble.

1847 *Illustr. Lond. News* 24 July 58/1 For the best horse seed-dibbler, £15. **1874** KNIGHT *Dict. Mech.* I. 699/1 Dibblers [figured]. **1884** *Athenæum* 6 Dec. 736/2 Drills, seed planters and dibblers.

3. A species of opossum: see quot.

1850 A. WHITE *Pop. Hist. Mammalia* 166 The *Antechinus apicalis* of Mr. Gray, which is called the 'Dibbler' at King George's Sound. **1967** *Times* 15 Nov. 7/8 An animal thought to have become extinct at some time in the past 83 years has come to light again in Western Australia—the rat-sized carnivorous marsupial popularly known as the dibbler. **1970** *Wildlife in Austral.* Sept. 67/1 The re-discovery of.. the dibbler, the noisy scrub-bird and the shortnecked tortoise.

dibbler, dial. f. DOUBLER, large plate.

dibbuk, var. DYBBUK.

dibchick: see DABCHICK β.

dibenzanthracene (ˌdaɪbɛnˈzænθrəsiːn). *Chem.* [f. DIBENZ(O- + ANTHRACENE.] Any of several hydrocarbon derivatives of anthracene with a molecular structure consisting of five fused benzene rings and the formula $C_{22}H_{14}$; *spec.* ***1, 2, 5, 6-dibenzanthracene***, a colourless crystalline compound, present in coal tar and tobacco smoke, and having carcinogenic properties.

1918 *Jrnl. Chem. Soc.* CXIV. I. 494 (*title*) Synthesis of the isomeric hydrocarbons 1:2:5:6-dibenzanthracene and 3:4:5:6-dibenzphenanthrene. **1944** *Ann. Reg. 1943* 352 Ethyl mercuric chloride proved to be a polyploidogenic agent, dibenzanthracene facilitating its action. **1962** D. B. CLAYSON *Chem. Carcinogenesis* iii. 65 Magnus (1939) introduced 1:2:5:6-dibenzanthracene into mice by forced feeding and obtained lung tumours. **1964** R. SCHOENTAL in E. Clar *Polycyclic Hydrocarbons* xviii. 141 For example, 1,2,5,6-dibenzanthracene.. is a potent carcinogen, but the 1,2,3,4-dibenzanthracene.. is inactive.

diˈbenzo-. *Chem.* See DI-[2] and BENZO-.

diˈbenzoyl. *Chem.* A synonym of BENZILE $C_{14}H_{10}O_2$, as having the formula of two molecules of the radical BENZOYL. Also in *Comb.*

diˈbenzyl. *Chem.* [f. DI-[2] + BENZYL.] An aromatic hydrocarbon crystallizing in large colourless prisms, having the formula of two molecules of the radical benzyl. Also in *Comb.* and *attrib.*, as ***dibenzyl-methane***, ***dibenzyl ketone***.

1873 *Fownes' Chem.* (ed. 11) 763.

dib-hole. *Mining.* [app. f. *dib*, variant of DUB + HOLE.] The hole at the bottom of the shaft, which receives the drainage of a mine, in order to its being pumped to the surface; also called SUMP.

1883 *Pall Mall G.* 2 Oct. 8/2 As the cage was being brought up the rope broke.. The cage was precipitated into the dibhole and the scaffolding smashed. **1892** *Daily News* 11 Jan. 3/6 Examining the dib hole at the bottom of the pit shaft.

diblastula (daɪˈblæstjʊlə). *Embryol.* [f. DI-[2] + mod.L. *blastula* BLASTULE.] That stage of the embryo of multicellular animals at which it consists of a vesicle inclosed by a double layer of cells; = GASTRULA.

1890 E. R. LANKESTER *Adv. Science* 348 The term 'diblastula' has more recently been adopted in England for the 'gastrula' of Haeckel.

diborane (daɪˈbɔəreɪn). *Chem.* [f. DI-[2] + BORANE.] A borane containing two atoms of boron; *spec.* B_2H_6, a colourless poisonous gas having a disagreeable odour.

1926 *Brit. Chem. Abstr.* 227/2 Structure of ethane and diborane, B_2H_6. **1956** *Chem. & Engin. News* 6 Feb. 560/2 The names of some of the boron hydrides are: BH_3, borane (3), or simply borane; B_2H_4, diborane (4); B_2H_6, diborane (6); [etc.]. **1962** P. J. & B. DURRANT *Introd. Adv. Inorg. Chem.* xvii. 516 Diborane, B_2H_6, is made by the action of a metallic hydride on a halide of boron. **1968** *Materials & Technol.* I. xii. 517 Diborane is of interest as a fuel for rockets to be launched under a water surface.

dibrach (ˈdaɪbræk). *rare.* [ad. L. *dibrachys*, ad. Gr. δίβραχυς of two short syllables, f. δι- two + βραχύς short.] In Gr. and L. prosody: A foot consisting of two short syllables; a pyrrhic.

In mod. Dicts.

dibranch (ˈdaɪbræŋk). *Zool.* [ad. F. *dibranche(s*, f. Gr. δι- (DI-[2]) + βράγχια gills of fishes.] A dibranchiate cephalopod; see next.

1877 LE CONTE *Elem. Geol.* II. (1879) 305 If we divide all known Cephalopods into Dibranchs (two-gilled) and Tetrabranchs (four-gilled).. The naked or Dibranchs are decidedly higher in organization.

dibranchiate (daɪˈbræŋkɪət), *a.* and *sb. Zool.* [f. mod.L. *dibranchiāta*, f. as prec.: see -ATE[2].]

A. *adj.* Belonging to the *Dibranchiata*, an order of cephalopods having two branchiæ or gills. **B.** *sb.* A cephalopod belonging to this order.

1835-6 TODD *Cycl. Anat.* I. 520/1 The Dibranchiate Order of Cephalopods. *Ibid.* 528/2 The.. suckers with which the.. arms of the Dibranchiates are provided. **1875** BLAKE *Zool.* 244 In the dibranchiate Cephalopods, the animal is swimming.

So **diˈbranchious** *a.*, 'having two branchiæ or gills.' *Syd. Soc. Lex.* 1883.

dibromide (daɪˈbrəʊmaɪd, -mɪd). *Chem.* [f. DI-² + BROMIDE.] A compound of two atoms of bromine with a dyad element or a radical, as ***ethine dibromide*** $C_2H_2Br_2$.
1869 ROSCOE *Elem. Chem.* 362 Ethylene diamines.. obtained by acting with ammonia on ethylene dibromide. **1873** *Fownes' Chem.* (ed. 11) 560 Ethine unites with bromine, forming a dibromide.

dibromo-, before a vowel **dibrom-**. *Chem.* [f. DI-² + BROMO-.] A combining element, expressing the presence in a compound of two atoms of bromine, which have replaced two of hydrogen, as ***dibromaldehyde*** $CH\ Br_2{\cdot}CHO$.
1873 *Fownes' Chem.* (ed. 11) 680 Dibromacetic Acid is obtained by the further action of bromine upon bromacetic acid. *Ibid.* 759 Dibromobenzene exhibits two modifications. **1880** CLEMENSHAW *Wurtz' Atom. Th.* 285 Dibromopropyl alcohol.. which is the result of the direct action of bromine upon allyl alcohol.

dibs (dɪbz). [colloq. Arab. *debs* = Heb. *deḇaš* honey, wine syrup.] A thick sweet syrup made from grape-juice in Eastern countries; also, a similar syrup made from dates.
1757 B. PLAISTED *Jrnl. Calcutta to Busserah* 112 The inspissated Juice of the Grape, called here Dibbs. **1841** E. ROBINSON *Bibl. Res. Palestine* II. 442 The finest grapes are dried as raisins; and the rest being trodden and pressed, the juice is boiled down to a syrup, which under the name of *Dibs* is much used by all classes wherever vineyards are found. **1864** W. K. TWEEDIE *Lakes & Rivers of Bible* 62 He will fetch fresh-baked bread, and a supply of dibs—a kind of honey made from grapes. **1946** N. GLUECK *River Jordan* 96 Dibs, something like honey, usually made of dates.

dibs (plural): see DIB *sb.*²

ˈdibstones, *sb. pl.* [See DIB *sb.*²] The name of a children's game: the same as *dibs* or *dabstones.*
1692 LOCKE *Educ.* §152, I have seen little Girls exercise whole Hours together and take abundance of Pains to be expert at Dibstones as they call it. **1775** ASH, *Dibstone*, a play among children, a little stone to be thrown at another stone. *Addison.*

diˈbutyl, dibutyro-. *Chem.* See DI-² and BUTYL.

†**diˈcacious**, *a. Obs.*—⁰ [f. L. *dicāx, dicāci-* talking sharply + -OUS.] Pert of speech, saucy.
1830 MAUNDER *Treas. Knowl.*, *Dicacious*, talkative, pert.
Hence †**diˈcaciousness**.
1727 BAILEY vol. II, *Dicaciousness*, talkativeness.

dicacity (dɪˈkæsɪtɪ). *Obs.* or *arch.* [f. L. *dicāx, dicāc-em*, sarcastic (f. *dic-* stem of *dīcĕre* to say, speak) + -ITY.] A jesting or mocking habit of speech; raillery, banter; pertness. (Sometimes after L. *dīcĕre*: Talkativeness, babbling.)
1592 BACON *Confer. Pleasure* (1870) 8 Vespasian, a man exceedinglie giuen to the humor of dicacitie and iesting. **1637** HEYWOOD *Dial.* iv. Wks. 1874 VI. 185 His quicke dicacitie Would evermore be taunting my voracitie. *a* **1670** HACKET *Abp. Williams* II. (1692) 133 Lucilius, a centurion, in Tacitus Annal. lib. 1, had a scornful name given him by the military dicacity of his own company. **1751** BYROM *Enthusiasm* Poems 1773 II. 23 To remit the freedom of inquiry.. for their dicacity. **1840** *New Monthly Mag.* LX. 55 Between human eloquence, and the dicacity of the parrot.. there is all the difference in the world.

†**dicæarch.** *Obs. rare*—⁰. In 7 dice-. [f. Gr. δίκαι-ος just + -αρχος ruler.] (See quot.) So also †**dicæarchy.**
1656 BLOUNT *Glossogr.*, *Dicearchy* (*dicæarchia*), just government. *Dicearck* (*dicæarchus*), a just Prince. **1658** PHILLIPS, *Dicearch.*

dicæology (daɪsiːˈɒlədʒɪ). Also 7 dice-. [ad. L. *dicæologia*, a. Gr. δικαιολογία a plea in defence, f. δίκαιο-ς righteous, just + λογία account, speech.]
†**1.** A description or account of jurisdiction. *Obs.*
1664 J. EXTON (*title*), The Maritime Dicæologie, or Sea-jurisdiction of England.
2. *Rhet.* Justification.
[**1589** PUTTENHAM *Eng. Poesie* III. xix. (Arb.) 237 *Dichologia*, or the Figure of excuse.] **1656** BLOUNT *Glossogr.*, *Diceology*..justification by, or in talk. [**1830** MAUNDER *Treas. Knowl.*, *Dicæology*, self-vindication.]

dicage, dicar: see DIKAGE, DICKER.

dicalcic (daɪˈkælsɪk), *a. Chem.* [f. DI-² 2 + CALCIC.] Containing two equivalents of calcium.
1863–72 WATTS *Dict. Chem.* I. 719 Dicalcic phosphide. **1884** F. J. LLOYD *Science Agric.*

dicarbo-, before a vowel dicarb-. *Chem.* [See DI-² and CARBO-.] In composition: Containing two atoms or equivalents of carbon.
1881 *Nature* XXIII. 243 The acid..was probably identical with dicarbopyridenic acid.

dicarbon (daɪˈkɑːbən), *a. Chem.* [DI-².] Containing or derived from two atoms of carbon, as the *dicarbon* series of hydrocarbons.
1869 ROSCOE *Elem. Chem.* xxx, Dicarbon or Ethyl series. The starting point of this important series is common alcohol or spirits of wine C_2H_6O.

dicarbonate (daɪˈkɑːbənət). *Chem.* See DI-² and CARBONATE.

diˈcarpellary, *a. Bot.* [f. DI-² + CARPELLARY.] Having or consisting of two carpels.
1876 HARLEY *Mat. Med.* 501 Distinguished by a dicarpellary fruit.

dicaryon, var. DIKARYON.

dicast (ˈdɪkæst). *Gr. Antiq.* Also **dikast.** [ad. Gr. δικαστής judge, juryman, agent-noun f. δικάζ-ειν to judge, pass judgement on, f. δίκη right, justice, judgement, trial.] One of the 6000 citizens chosen annually in ancient Athens to try cases in the several law-courts, where their functions combined those of the modern judge and jury.
[**1708** MOTTEUX *Rabelais* V. xi. (1737) 46 The Statues of their *Dicastes.*] **1822** T. MITCHELL *Aristoph.* I. p. cxlv, Nearly one-third of the population of Athens were, in part, supported by their attendance upon the courts of law in the quality of dicasts, an office something between the judge and juryman of modern times. **1873** SYMONDS *Grk. Poets* Ser. I. i. (1877) 30 The whole Athenian nation as dikasts and ecclesiasts, were interested in Rhetoric. **1874** MAHAFFY *Soc. Life Greece* vii. 215 The contemptible old dicast in the *Wasps.* **1875** JOWETT *Plato* (ed. 2) I. 215 This art acts upon dicasts and ecclesiasts and bodies of men.

dicastery (dɪˈkæstərɪ). Also **dikastery.** [ad. Gr. δικαστήριον a court of justice.]
One of the courts of justice in which the dicasts sat; the court or body of dicasts.
[**1656** J. HARRINGTON *Oceana* 147 (Jod.) The dicasterion ..in Athens..the comitia of that commonwealth. **1822** T. MITCHELL *Aristoph.* II. 179 The very essence of the Athenian democracy..was centered in its Dicasteria, or courts of justice.] **1846** GROTE *Greece* I. xii. I. 304 It was unlawful to put to death any person, even under formal sentence by the dicastery. **1866** FELTON *Anc. & Mod. Gr.* II. vi. 99 The people in the country..were as likely to be drawn into the senate and dicasteries, as the people..of the town.

dicastic (dɪˈkæstɪk), *a.* Also **dikastic.** [ad. Gr. δικαστικ-ός of or for law or trials: see DICAST.] Of or belonging to a dicast or dicasts.
1849 GROTE *Greece* II. xlvi. V. 484 The archon..retained only the power of..presiding over the dikastic assembly by whom peremptory verdict was pronounced. **1874** MAHAFFY *Soc. Life Greece* vi. 176 The wrangling and dicastic habit of his countrymen. **1884** *Q. Rev.* Oct. 348 Citizens each furnished with his dicastic badge and staff.

dicatalectic (ˌdaɪkætəˈlɛktɪk), *a. Pros.* [ad. Gr. δικαταληκτικ-ός: see DI-² and CATALECTIC.] Of a verse: Doubly catalectic; wanting a syllable both in the middle and at the end, as e.g. the dactylic pentameter.
In mod. Dicts.

†**diˈcation.** *Obs. rare*—⁰. [ad. L. *dicātiōn-em* formal declaration, n. of action f. *dicāre* to proclaim.]
1656 BLOUNT *Glossogr.*, *Dication*, a vowing, submitting, promising, or dedicating.

dicayue, obs. form of DECEIVE.

dice, *sb.* (properly pl.): see DIE *sb.* and in Combs. below.

dice (daɪs), *v.* [f. *dice*, pl. of DIE *sb.*]
1. a. *intr.* To play or gamble with dice. In extended use (*fig.*): to take great risks, esp. in phr. ***to dice with death.*** Freq. in Motoring contexts.
c **1440** *Promp. Parv.* 121 Dycyn, or pley wythe dycys, *aleo.* **1519** *Presentm. Juries* in *Surtees Misc.* (1890) 32 Latt no manservauntes dysse nor carde in ther howsses. **1548** LATIMER *Ploughers* (Arb.) 25 Thei hauke, thei hunt, thei card, thei dyce. **1596** SHAKS. *1 Hen. IV*, III. iii. 18, I was.. vertuous enough, swore little, dic'd not aboue seuen times a weeke. **1647** R. STAPYLTON *Juvenal* 253 If th' old man dice, th' heire in long coats will doe The like. **1855** MACAULAY *Hist. Eng.* IV. 97 The Dick Talbot who had diced and revelled with Grammont.
fig. **1941** PRINCE CHULA CHAKRABONGSE *Dick Seaman* xiv. 357 Racing motorists usually referred to driving in a race as either 'cracking' or 'dicing', the latter word having been derived from the journalists' former habit of writing about their being 'speed demons dicing with death'. **1969** *Observer* (Colour Suppl.) 23 Mar. 24/1 On the M1 or the M4 a lot of them try to dice with us... You'll get the bod who will come up behind you, an Aston Martin, a Sprite, a Mini Cooper, and they'll be flashing their lights to get by you. **1971** *Daily Tel.* 29 Jan. 3/8[He] had been 'dicing' along the road with the driver of another car. They were trying to 'carve each other up' after a motoring incident a mile away.
b. *trans.* To lose or throw *away* by dicing; to gamble away. Also *fig.*
1549 [see DICING-HOUSE]. **1618** N. FIELD *Amends for Ladies* I. i. in Hazl. *Dodsley* XI. 94 Have I to dice my patrimony away? **1871** TOM TAYLOR *Jeanne Darc* II. i, How cheerily a king and kingdom May be diced, danced, and fiddled to the dogs! **1881** BLACKIE *Lay Serm.* i. 79 The conscript boy, torn from his father..to dice away his sweet young life in a cause with which he has no concern.
c. *trans.* To bring by dice-play (*into, out of*, etc.).
1843 MACAULAY *Ess., Addison* (1889) 721 When he diced himself into a spunging house.

d. To reject, throw away; to leave alone. *Austral. slang.*
1944 L. GLASSOP *We were Rats* I. i. 5 It's me name, but it's too cissy, so I dices it and picks up 'Mick'. **1953** K. TENNANT *Joyful Condemned* xxii. 214 I'll dice it—for now.
2. To cut into dice or cubes: *esp.* in cookery.
?*c* **1390** *Forme of Cury* in *Warner's Culin. Antiq.* 5 Take Funges [mushrooms], and pare hem clene, and dyce hem. *c* **1440** *Promp. Parv.* 121 Dycyn, as men do brede, or other lyke, *quadro.* **1769** MRS. RAFFALD *Eng. Housekpr.* (1778) 95 Make a ragoo of oysters and sweetbreads diced.
3. To mark or ornament with a pattern of cubes or squares; to chequer; *spec.* **a.** *Needlework.* (See quot. 1808–80.) **b.** *Book-binding.* To ornament (leather) with a pattern consisting of squares or diamonds: see DICED *ppl. a.* 2.
1688 J. CLAYTON in *Phil. Trans.* XVIII. 126 The young Ones [snakes] have no Rattles..but they may be known.. being very regularly diced or checker'd, black and gray on the backs. **1808–80** JAMIESON, *Dice*, 1. Properly, to sew a kind of waved pattern near the border of a garment..2. To weave in figures resembling dice.
†**4.** To mark with spots or pips, like dice. *Obs.*
1664 POWER *Exp. Philos.* I. 8 The Butter Fly. The eye is large and globular, diced or bespeck'd here and there with black spots.

dice, obs. Sc. f. DAIS, pew or seat in a church.

dice, *adv. Naut.*: see DYCE.

dice-box. The box from which dice are thrown in gaming, usually of the form of a double truncated cone.
1552 HULOET, Dice boxe, *fimum, fritillum.* **1617** MINSHEU *Ductor*, A Dice box..a saucer, porringer, or some other such like dish, out of which they cast the dice. **1713** ADDISON *Guardian* No. 120 ¶1 Thumping the table with a dice-box. **1784** COWPER *Task* IV. 221 What was an hourglass once, Becomes a dicebox. **1833** HT. MARTINEAU *Three Ages* ii. 47 Charles and the Duke of Ormond were rattling the dice-box. **1849** MACAULAY *Hist. Eng.* II. 50 Welcome at the palace when the bottle or the dicebox was going round.
b. Used typically for dice-play, dicing, gaming.
1857 MAURICE *Ep. St. John* xi. 179 The only resources left for either are the dice-box and the bottle. **1859** MACAULAY *Life Pitt*, Fox, a man of pleasure, ruined by the dice-box and the turf.
c. *attrib.* Of the form of a dice-box. ***dice-box insulator***, a hollow porcelain insulator of this shape for supporting a telegraph wire, which passes through the axis.
1841 W. SPALDING *Italy & It. Isl.* I. 296 A smaller lake.. backed by a range of rocks and a rude dice-box tower. **1895** W. PREECE (*in letter*), The 'dice-box' insulator was invented by the late Mr. C. P. Walker; it was used on the South-Eastern Railway.

diced (daɪst), *ppl. a.* [f. DICE *v.* + -ED¹.]
1. Formed or cut into dice or cubes; see DICE *v.* 2.
1671 J. WEBSTER *Metallogr.* xvii. 246, I have by me very many sorts of these squared or diced golden Marchasites. **1741** *Compl. Fam. Piece* I. ii. (ed. 3) 147 Make Sauce with some of the Liquor, Mushrooms, diced Lemon, etc.
2. Marked or ornamented with figures of cubes or squares; chequered; see DICE *v.* 3.
1725 RAMSAY *Gentl. Sheph.* I. ii, He kaims his hair..And spreads his garters diced beneath his knee. **1880** W. SMITH *Catal.* No. 6, 4 vols, royal 8vo, diced calf. **1893** W. F. CLAY *Catal.* 16, 4to, diced russia, neatly rebacked.

dicellate (daɪˈsɛlət), *a.* [f. Gr. δίκελλα, a two-pronged hoe + -ATE².] Two-pronged: said *spec.* of sponge-spicules.

‖**Dicentra** (daɪˈsɛntrə). *Bot.* [mod.L., f. Gr. δίκεντρος, f. δι- two + κέντρον sharp point, spur.] A genus of plants (N.O. *Fumariaceæ*) having drooping heart-shaped flowers; the species are natives of North America and Eastern and Central Asia, and several are in cultivation in the flower-garden, esp. *D. spectabilis* (also called *Dielytra*).
1866 in *Treas. Bot.* **1883** *Century Mag.* Sept. 726/2 The beautifully divided leaves of the dicentra. **1884** E. P. ROE in *Harper's Mag.* May 932/1 Clumps of bloodroot, hepaticas, dicentras, dog-tooth violets, and lilies-of-the-valley.

dicentric (daɪˈsɛntrɪk), *a.* (and *sb.*) *Biol.* [f. DI-² + -CENTRIC.] Of a chromosome or chromatid: having two centromeres. Hence as *sb.*, a dicentric chromosome or chromatid.
1937, etc. [see ACENTRIC *a.*]. **1956** *Nature* 18 Feb. 325/1 Breakage of chromosomes is followed by reunion to give dicentrics. **1970** *Ibid.* 15 Aug. 707/2 Chromosome fragments and structural abnormalities (for example, dicentrics and acentrics) were rare.

dicephalous (daɪˈsɛfələs), *a.* [f. Gr. δικέφαλος (f. δι-, DI-² + κεφαλή head) + -OUS. In mod.F. *dicéphale.*] Having two heads, two-headed.
1808 *Edin. Rev.* XII. 487 A dicephalous monster.

dice-play. [f. *dice*, pl. of DIE *sb.*] The action or practice of playing with dice; the game of dice.
c **1440** *Promp. Parv.* 120 Dyce play, *aleatura.* **1551** ROBINSON tr. *More's Utop.* (Arb.) 84 Dice-playe, and suche other folishe and pernicious games they know not. **1577** NORTHBROOKE *Dicing* Introd. 2 If a man can dice-play. **1580**

LUPTON *Sivqila* 94 To get greedie gain by diuellish and detestable Diceplaye. **1606** HOLLAND *Sueton.* 60 For giving himselfe much to dice play.

†**b.** *fig.* Trickery, deceit, sleight. *Obs.*

1633 ROGERS *Treat. Sacraments* I. 159 Not easily carried away by each Doctrine and dice-play of men [cf. *Eph.* iv. 14 ἐν τῇ κυβείᾳ τῶν ἀνθρώπων].

So **dice-playing.**

c **1490** *Promp. Parv.* (MS. K.) 120 Dicepleyinge, *aleatura.* **1551** ROBINSON tr. *More's Utop.* (Arb.) 19 The Poete likeneth..the life of man to a diceplaiyng or a game at the tables. **1606** HOLLAND *Sueton.* 70 The rumour that ran of his dice-playing.

dice-player. [See prec.] One who plays or gambles with dice; a dicer.

1377 LANGL. *P. Pl.* B. VI. 73 Iakke þe iogeloure..And danyel þe dys-playere. **1577** tr. *Bullinger's Decades* (1592) 183 We doe vtterly forbid all bishops..to keepe companie with dice players. **1660** JER. TAYLOR *Duct. Dubit.* II. 471 (L.) A common gamester or dice-player may call himself Christian, but indeed he is not.

dicer (ˈdaɪsə(r)). Forms: 5-6 **dyser, dysar,** 6 **dysour, disar, dycer, dicear, desard,** 6- **dicer.** [f. DICE *v.* (or as pl. of DIE *sb.*) + -ER[1]. The suffix was sometimes changed to AFr. -OUR, and -AR.] One who plays or gambles with dice; a person addicted to dicing.

1408 *Nottingham Rec.* II. 62 Rogerus Mokyngton est communis hospitator, contra Assisam, scilicet, [hospitat] dysers. *c* **1460** *Towneley Myst.* (Surtees) 242 Thise dysars and thise hullars, Thise cokkers and thise bollars. **1500-20** DUNBAR *Poems* xxxiv. 71 Ane dysour said..The Devill mot stik him with a knyfe, Bot he kest vp fair syisis thre. **1531** ELYOT *Gov.* I. xxvi, Suche a reproche, to be sayde that they had made aliaunce with disars. **1602** SHAKS. *Ham.* III. iv. 45 Such an Act, That..Makes marriage vowes As false as Dicers Oathes. **1654** GATAKER *Disc. Apol.* 3 The better Dicer, the wors man. **1837** DE QUINCEY *Revolt Tartars* Wks. 1862 IV. 130 Upon the hazard of a dicer's throw. **1844** J. T. HEWLETT *Parsons & W.* xix, A deep drinker, and a dicer.

dicerate (ˈdaɪsərət), *a.* [f. Gr. δίκερας, δικερατ- double horn.] 'Having two horns'. *Syd. Soc. Lex.* 1883.

dicerous (ˈdaɪsərəs), *a. Entom. rare.* [irreg. (for *dicerote*) f. Gr. δίκερως two-horned, f. δι- two + κέρας horn.] Having two 'horns', antennæ, or tentacles.

1826 KIRBY & SPENCE *Introd. Entom.* IV. 316 *Dicerous*, insects that have two antennæ.

dicese, dicesse, obs. forms of DECEASE.

dicetyl (daɪˈsiːtɪl). *Chem.* [See DI-[2].] The free form of the hydrocarbon radical CETYL, q.v.

dicey (ˈdaɪsɪ), *a. slang* (orig. *Air Force*). [f. *dice*, pl. of DIE *sb.* + -Y[1].] Risky, dangerous; uncertain, unreliable.

1950 'N. SHUTE' *Town like Alice* x. 303 He..made a tight, dicey turn round in the gorge with about a hundred feet to spare. **1959** P. CAPON *Amongst those Missing* 139 The river got a little dicey. I thought we'd wait for the moon. **1959** 'J. BELL' *Easy Prey* xi. 117 What d'you say we..get a bit more information? That sketch map looks dicey to me.

†**dich.** *Obs. rare.* A corrupt or erroneous word, having apparently the sense *do it*:

1607 SHAKS. *Timon* I. ii. 73 Much good dich thy good heart. **1630** *R. Johnson's Kingd. & Commw.* 87 So mich God dich you with your sustenancelesse sauce. [Cf. **1542** UDALL tr. *Erasm. Apoph.* (1877) 112 Biddyng much good do it him.]

dich, obs. form of DITCH.

dichasial (daɪˈkeɪzɪəl), *a. Bot.* [f. next + -AL[1].] Belonging to or of the nature of a dichasium.

1876 J. H. BALFOUR in *Encycl. Brit.* IV. 124/1 In the natural order *Caryophyllaceæ*, the dichasial cymose form of inflorescence is very general.

‖**dichasium** (daɪˈkeɪzɪəm). *Bot.* Pl. **-ia.** [mod.L., f. Gr. δίχασις division.] A form of cymose inflorescence, apparently but not really dichotomous, in which the main axis produces a pair of lateral axes, each of which similarly produces a pair, and so on; a biparous cyme.

1875 BENNETT & DYER *Sachs' Bot.* 158 False dichotomies of this kind, which occur abundantly in the inflorescences of Phanerogams, are termed by Schimper Dichasia. *Ibid.* 521 The dichasium easily passes, in the first or a succeeding order of lateral axes, into a sympodial mode of development. **1876** J. H. BALFOUR in *Encycl. Brit.* IV. 124/1 In some members of the tribe *Caryophyllaceæ* the inflorescence has the form of a contracted dichasium.

‖**dichastasis** (daɪˈkæstəsɪs). [mod. f. Gr. δίχα asunder, apart + στάσις standing.] 'Spontaneous subdivision' (Webster 1864).

a **1864** WEBSTER cites DANA. **1883** in *Syd. Soc. Lex.*

dichastic (daɪˈkæstɪk), *a.* [mod. f. Gr. *διχάστος divided, f. διχάζ-ειν to divide: see -IC.] 'Capable of subdividing spontaneously' (Webster 1864).

a **1864** WEBSTER cites DANA. **1883** *Syd. Soc. Lex.*, *Dichastic*, capable of undergoing dichastasis.

diche(n, obs. forms of DITCH.

dichlamydeous (daɪkləˈmɪdiːəs), *a. Bot.* [f. mod. Bot.L. *dichlamydeæ*, f. Gr. δι- two + χλαμύς, χλαμυδ- cloak: see -EOUS.] Having both the floral envelopes (calyx and corolla); having a double perianth. Also said of a plant bearing such flowers.

1830 LINDLEY *Nat. Syst. Bot.* Introd. 26 If the corolla is present, a plant is said to be dichlamydeous. **1882** G. ALLEN in *Nature* 17 Aug. 373 Our English species have no true petals; but some exotic forms are truly dichlamydeous.

dichlor-, dichloro-. *Chem.* [f. DI-[2] + CHLOR(O)-.] A formative element in names of compounds formed by the substitution of two atoms of chlorine for hydrogen atoms, as ***dichlora'cetic acid, dichlor'hydrin***: see CHLOR- and CHLORO-; **ˌdichlorodiˌfluoro-ˈmethane**, a colourless, easily liquefied gas, CCl_2F_2, used as a refrigerant and as a propellant in aerosols, etc.

1873 *Fownes' Chem.* (ed. 11) 627 Dichlorhydrin is treated with potash, it gives up a molecule of hydrochloric acid. *Ibid.* 679 Dichloracetic acid is produced by the action of chlorine and iodine on boiling acetic acid. *Ibid.* 759 Of dichlorobenzene, two modifications are known. **1876** HARLEY *Mat. Med.* (ed. 6) 346 Allyl-chloroform is unstable, and breaks up into hydrochloric acid and dichlorallylene. [**1930** *Engineering* 13 June 776/2 Dichlorofluoromethane as a refrigerant.] **1958** *Times Rev. Industry* Feb. 68/3 The liquid refrigerant used in the compression cycle may be dichlorodifluoromethane. **1964** N. G. CLARK *Mod. Org. Chem.* ix. 171 Dichlorodifluoromethane..is used as a propellant in insecticide sprays, hair lacquers, shaving lather, etc.

dichloride (daɪˈklɔəraɪd, -rɪd). *Chem.* [f. DI-[2] + CHLORIDE.] A compound of two atoms of chlorine with an element or radical, as mercury dichloride $HgCl_2$.

†Formerly, a compound of chlorine with two atoms of another body: see DI-[2] 2 a ¶.

1825 T. THOMSON *First Princ. Chem.* II. 44 Dichloride of antimony. **1826** HENRY *Elem. Chem.* II. 75. **1854** J. SCOFFERN in *Orr's Circ. Sc.* Chem. 508 Dichloride of gold remains. *c* **1865** LETHEBY in *Circ. Sc.* I. 120/1 A solution of dichloride of copper. **1873** *Fownes' Chem.* (ed. 11) 437 The dichloride is produced, together with the trichloride.

dicho-, a. Gr. διχο-, combining form of adv. δίχα in two, asunder, apart, as in διχοτομία cutting in two. A first element in several scientific words, with the meaning, 'asunder, separately, in two parts or halves'.

(The ι is short in Greek, so that the usual English pronunciation is not etymological.)

dicho'gamic, *a. Bot.* = DICHOGAMOUS.

in mod. Dicts.

dichogamous (daɪˈkɒgəməs), *a. Bot.* [mod. f. Gr. type *διχόγαμος (f. διχο-, DICHO-, asunder, separately + -γαμος wedded, married, γάμ-ος wedding) + -OUS.] Said of those hermaphrodite plants in which the stamens and pistils (or analogous organs) become mature at different times, so that self-fertilization is impossible.

1859 DARWIN *Orig. Spec.* iv. (1873) 78 These so-named dichogamous plants have in fact separated sexes, and must habitually be crossed. **1882** VINES *Sachs' Bot.* 906 Insects are the main agents in the conveyance of the pollen to the stigma of other flowers of dichogamous Phanerogams.. Whether the Algæ named above and some Muscineæ are dichogamous is doubtful. **1894** DRUMMOND *Ascent Man* vi. 303 The subtle alliance with Space in Diœcious flowers; with Time in Dichogamous species.

dichogamy (daɪˈkɒgəmɪ). *Bot.* [mod. f. Gr. type *διχογαμία, n. of state from *διχόγαμος: see prec. and -Y: in mod. Ger. and F. *dichogamie.*] The condition of being dichogamous, i.e. in which the stamens and pistils (or analogous organs) of a hermaphrodite plant mature at different times.

1862 DARWIN in *Life & Lett.* (1887) III. 303 What old C. K. Sprengel called dichogamy and which is so frequent in truly hermaphrodite groups. **1882** VINES *Sachs' Bot.* 906 One of the simplest and commonest means for ensuring cross-fertilisation is *Dichogamy*, i.e. the arrangement by which the two kinds of reproductive organs, when.. contiguous, are mature at different times.

di'chopterous, *a. Entom.* [f. DICHO- + Gr. πτερ-όν wing + -OUS.] 'Having cut or emarginate wings' (*Syd. Soc. Lex.* 1883).

dichoptic (daɪˈkɒptɪk), *a. Zool.* [f. DICHO- + OPTIC *a.*] Of certain dipterous insects: having the eyes widely separated.

1899 D. SHARP in *Camb. Nat. Hist.* VI. 440 When the eyes of the two sides meet in a co-adapted line of union the Insect is said to be 'holoptic', and when the eyes are well separated 'dichoptic'. **1949** *Handbks. Identification Brit. Insects* (R. Ent. Soc.) IX. I. 5 In many families [of Diptera] the males have the eyes approaching or meeting (holoptic) and the females have them well separated (dichoptic).

dichord (ˈdaɪkɔːd). [ad. Gr. δίχορδος two-stringed, f. δι- two + χορδή string (of a lyre), chord.] **a.** An instrument having two strings. **b.** An instrument having two strings to each note. (Stainer & Barrett *Dict. Mus. Terms.*)

1819 *Pantologia*, *Dichord*, in music, the name given to the two-stringed lyre, said to have been invented by the Egyptian Mercury.

dichoree (ˌdaɪkɒˈriː). *Pros.* [a. F. *dichorée* (1736 in Hatz.-Darm.), ad. L. *dichorē-us*, a. Gr. διχόρειος, f. δι-, DI-[2] + χορεῖος: see CHOREE.] A metrical foot consisting of two chorees or trochees.

1801 D. IRVING *Elem. Composition* x. (1828) 109 Its music consisted in the dichoree with which it is terminated. **1885** R. C. JEBB *Œdipus Tyrannus* p. lxxxi, When the ionic -- ◡◡ ..is interchanged with the dichoree - ◡ - ◡.

dichostasy (dɪˈkɒstəsɪ). *nonce-wd.* [ad. Gr. διχοστασία a standing apart, dissension, f. διχο-, DICHO- + στάσ-ις standing.] A standing separate.

c **1859** BP. SHORT *Sp.* in *Academy* 30 July (1892) 86 His orders are irregular..and his Church system—he would not say schism—but dichostasy.

di'chotomal, *a.* [f. as DICHOTOMOUS + -AL[1].] Of or pertaining to dichotomy.

In mod. Dicts.

dichotomic (daɪkəʊˈtɒmɪk), *a.* [mod. f. as DICHOTOM-OUS + -IC: in F. *dichotomique.*] Relating to or involving dichotomy; dichotomous.

1873 *Brit. Q. Rev.* Jan. 301 The Scriptural representation is as often dichotomic as it is trichotomic..The dichotomic must be radically and essentially wrong. **1881** LINCOLN tr. *Trousseau & Pidoux, Treat. Therapeutics* I. 278 The followers of Brown and Broussais, after a long struggle with the arguments which were ruining their dichotomic doctrine, were at last forced to recognise special diseases. **1882-3** SCHAFF *Encycl. Relig. Knowl.* III. 2231 A decidedly dichotomic expression, as 1 Pet. ii. 11, where the soul is regarded simply according to her spiritual determination as the bearer of the divine life-principle.

dicho'tomically, *adv.* [f. prec. + -AL[1] + -LY[2].] = DICHOTOMOUSLY.

1880 GUNTHER *Fishes* 40 Branched rays are dichotomically split.

dichotomist (daɪˈkɒtəmɪst). [f. DICHOTOM-Y + -IST.] One who dichotomizes, or classifies by dichotomy.

c **1592** MARLOWE *Massacre Paris* I. viii, He that will be a flat dichotomist..Is in your judgment thought a learned man. **1597** MORLEY *Introd. Mus.* Pref., The booke, although ..not such as may in euery point satisfie the curiositie of Dichotomistes. *c* **1630** JACKSON *Creed* IV. i, Curious dichotomists never allotting more than two branches to one stock. **1882** W. OGLE tr. *Aristotle's Parts Anim.* 13 Privative terms..which are not available to the dichotomist.

Hence **di,choto'mistic** *a.*, pertaining to a dichotomist, or to dichotomy.

1847 BUCK tr. *Hagenbach's Hist. Doctr.* II. 248 Most writers adopted the dichotomistic principle, according to which man consists of body and soul.

dichotomization (daɪˌkɒtəmaɪˈzeɪʃən). [f. DICHOTOMIZE + -ATION.] The action of dichotomizing, or condition of being dichotomized: in quot. of the moon (see DICHOTOMIZED 2).

1867 G. F. CHAMBERS *Astron.* I. v. 68 A discrepancy.. between the first, or last, appearance of the dichotomisation.

dichotomize (daɪˈkɒtəmaɪz), *v.* [f. Gr. διχότομος (see DICHOTOMOUS) + -IZE.]

1. *trans.* To divide into two parts or sections; *esp.* in reference to classification: cf. DICHOTOMY 1 a.

1608-11 BP. HALL *Epist.* I. v, That great citie might well be dichotomized into cloysters and hospitals. **1639** FULLER *Holy War* IV. i. (1647) 166 Not a city of note..which was not dichotomized into the sect of the Guelfes..and Gibellines. **1678** CUDWORTH *Intell. Syst.* I. iii. 139 The Four forementioned Forms of Atheism may be again Dichotomized..into such as [etc.]. **1866** *St. James's Mag.* Oct. 367 So far as they were concerned the University was dichotomized in 'Christ Church men' and 'squibs'.

†**b.** *loosely.* To divide (into several parts). *Obs.* (In first quot. humorously as a blunder.)

1631 T. POWELL *Tom All Trades* 144 Then dicotomize the whole portion of his wife into several shares. **1650** CHARLETON *Paradoxes* 56 They againe dichotomize..the influxive spirit into the naturall, vitall, and animall. **1667** *Decay Chr. Piety* ix. ¶10 When they came to be dichotomiz'd, and canton'd out into curious aerial notions.

2. *intr.* (for *refl.*) To divide or become divided into two continuously; *spec.* used of the branching of a stem, root, leaf-vein, etc.: see DICHOTOMOUS 2, DICHOTOMY 3.

1835 [see DICHOTOMIZING below]. **1846** DANA *Zooph.* (1848) 652 Stem dichotomising and bearing..nearly simple erect branchlets. **1875** BENNETT & DYER *Sachs' Bot.* II. iv. 406 The roots of Lycopodiaceæ are..the only ones known to dichotomise. **1884** M. BOOLE in *Jrnl. Educ.* 1 Sept. 342 Elements which..tend to dichotomize into pairs of evils.

Hence **di'chotomizing** *vbl. sb.* and *ppl. a.*; **di'chotomizer,** one who dichotomizes.

1606 BRETON *Sidney's Ourania*, He has no fine Dichotomizing Wit. **1621** BP. MOUNTAGU *Diatribae* 393 These two great Dichotomisers, being at odds with all others, and with themselues. **1639** FULLER *Holy War* V. xv. (1647) 255 The Turks, who in the dichotomizing of the world fall under the Northern part. **1835** KIRBY *Hab. & Inst. Anim.* II. xiii. 11 Surrounded by dichotomizing articulated organs. **1881** G. BUSK in *Jrnl. Microsc. Soc.* Jan. 5 Numerous, long, sparsely dichotomising, biserial branches.

di'chotomized, *ppl. a.* [f. prec. + -ED[1].]

1. Divided into two branches: see prec.

1884 BOWER & SCOTT *De Bary's Phaner.* 61 Stellate hairs ..with 3-4 rays once or twice dichotomised. **1892** CLERKE *Stud. Homer* iv. 87 Beyond the rising-places of the sun, where one branch of his dichotomised Ethiopians dwelt.

2. *Astron.* Said of the moon in the phase at which exactly half her disk appears illuminated (the 'half-moon').

1727-51 CHAMBERS *Cycl.* s.v. *Dichotomy*, She appears dichotomized at least for the space of a whole hour: in which time any moment may be taken for the true point of the dichotomy, as well as any other. **1834** *Nat. Philos., Hist. Astron.* vi. 24/1 (Useful Knowl. Soc.) The difficulty of determining exactly the instant at which the moon is dichotomized. **1866** AIRY *Pop. Astron.* v. (1868) 167 Observation of the place of the moon when it is 'dichotomized'.

dichotomous (daɪ'kɒtəməs), *a.* [f. L. *dichotomos, -mus*, a. Gr. διχότομος cut in half, equally divided: see DICHO- and -OUS. Cf. F. *dichotome* (1752 in Hatz.-Darm.).] Divided or dividing into two; characterized by dichotomy.

†1. *Astron.* = DICHOTOMIZED 2; of the form of a half-moon. *Obs.*

1690 LEYBOURN *Curs. Math.* 448 Mercury..in its greatest digression from the Sun..appears Dichotomous.

2. *Bot.*, etc. Dividing into two equal branches; *esp.* so branched that each successive axis divides into two; relating to, or of the nature of, such branching.

1752 SIR J. HILL *Hist. Anim.* 23 (Jod.) The short, dichotomous, horned monoculus. **1753** ELLIS in *Phil. Trans.* XLVIII. 116 These stretch out into many regular dichotomous branches. **1794** MARTYN *Rousseau's Bot.* xvii. 226 The Lesser Centaury..is distinguished by its dichotomous stalk. **1842** E. WILSON *Anat. Vade M.* 262 The division of arteries is usually dichotomous. **1872** OLIVER *Elem. Bot.* II. 185 Common Mistletoe..a dichotomous parasitical shrub, with opposite leathery leaves. **1882** VINES *Sachs' Bot.* 170 Dichotomous branching is very common among Thallophytes, especially Algæ and the lower Hepaticæ.

3. *Logic*, etc. Of classification: Involving division (of a class or group) into two (lower groups); proceeding by dichotomy; dichotomic.

1838 SIR W. HAMILTON *Logic* xxv. (1866) II. 30 The division may be not only dichotomous but polytomous, as for example,—angles are right, or acute, or obtuse. **1864** *Reader* 3 Sept. 304/2 The unities or molecules..are either isovoluminous or in what I have called dichotomous ratio.

di'chotomously, *adv.* [f. prec. + -LY[2].] In a dichotomous manner; by division into twos or pairs: see prec.

1806 J. GALPINE *Brit. Bot.* §102 Stem herbaceous, dichotomously panicled. **1846** DANA *Zooph.* (1848) 530 Branches..dichotomously subdivided. **1866** A. FLINT *Princ. Med.* (1880) 160 A bronchus, after it enters a lobule ..divides dichotomously once or twice and terminates in the alveolar passages. **1870** H. MACMILLAN *Bible Teach.* vii. 143 The dichotomously-veined leaves, representing the cryptogamia.

dichotomy (daɪ'kɒtəmɪ). [ad. Gr. διχοτομία a cutting in two, f. διχότομ-ος (see DICHOTOMOUS): cf. F. *dichotomie* (1754 in Hatz.-Darm.).]

1. Division of a whole into two parts. **a.** *spec.* in *Logic*, etc.: Division of a class or genus into two lower mutually exclusive classes or genera; binary classification.

1610 HEALEY *St. Aug. Citie of God* 303 This Trichotomy ..doth not contradict the other Dichotomy that includeth all in action and contemplation. **1725** WATTS *Logic* I. vi. §8 Some.. have disturbed the Order of Nature..by an Affectation of Dichotomies, Trichotomies, Sevens, Twelves, &c. Let the Nature of the Subject, considered together with the Design which you have in view, always determine the Number of Parts into which you divide it. **1864** BOWEN *Logic* iv. 97 Convenience often requires what Logicians call division by dichotomy, in which a Genus is divided into two Species having Contradictory Marks. **1877** E. CAIRD *Philos. Kant* II. vi. 302 The whole sphere of reality may be divided in relation to any predicate..in what is called dichotomy by contradiction, e.g. that 'everything must either be red or not red'.

b. *gen.* Division into two. Something divided into two or resulting from such a division; something paradoxical or ambivalent.

1636 FEATLY *Clavis Myst.* xxi. 277 Whose day after a ramisticall dichotomy being divided into forenoone and afternoone. **1668** WILKINS *Real Char.* II. vii. §3. 190 The way of Dichotomy or Bipartition being the most natural and easie kind of Division. **1868** *Contemp. Rev.* Apr. 598 Popular theology is rather founded on the dichotomy of man into body and soul, than on the Christian trichotomy of body, soul, and spirit. **1942** *N.Y. Times* 28 Nov. 12/4 'An absolute dichotomy between science and reason on the one hand and faith and poetry on the other.' In other and simpler days people spoke of the conflict between science and religion, or the clash between the two, or the wide gulf between the two. **1950** *Listener* 28 Sept. 430/1 The questions of thinking in one language and writing in another, the doubtful dichotomy of east and west. **1957** 'J. WYNDHAM' *Midwich Cuckoos* xiii. 105 By a dichotomy familiar to us all, a woman requires her own baby to be perfectly normal, and at the same time superior to all other babies. **1966** *Listener* 3 Mar. 323/2 Their uncritical use of the 'Communist' versus 'free world' dichotomy.

2. *Astron.* That phase of the moon (or of an inferior planet) at which exactly half the disk appears illuminated; the 'half-moon'.

1686 GOAD *Celest. Bodies* I. xv. 81 This Quadrate or Quartile in its Dichotomy, as the Greeks call it. **1797** *Encycl. Brit.* II. 419/1 Aristarchus..gave a method of determining the distance of the sun by the moon's dichotomy. **1878** NEWCOMB *Pop. Astron.* 551 *Dichotomy*, the aspect of a planet when half illuminated.

3. *Bot., Zool.*, etc. A form of branching in which each successive axis divides into two; repeated bifurcation: see DICHOTOMOUS 2.

1707 SLOANE *Jamaica* I. 264 From the middle of the leaves rise one or two stalks..always divided into two, or observing a Dichotomy. **1835** KIRBY *Hab. & Inst. Anim.* II. xiii. 13 The last [Encrinus] seems to differ..in the dichotomies and length of the arms. **1880** GRAY *Struct. Bot.* iii. §3. 47 *note*, *Dichotomy* or *forking*, the division of an apex into two. **1882** VINES *Sachs' Bot.* 169 Dichotomy..never produces structures..dissimilar to the producing structure; the divisions of a root produced by dichotomy are both roots, those of a leaf-bearing shoot both leaf-bearing shoots.. dichotomy hence always falls under the conception of branching in the..narrower sense. *Ibid.* 464.

dichotriæne (ˌdɪkəʊtraɪ'iːn). *Zool.* [f. DICHO- + Gr. τρίαινα trident: see TRIÆNE.] A dichotomous triæne; a three-forked sponge spicule, having each fork dividing into two.

1887 SOLLAS in *Encycl. Brit.* XXII. 417/1 The arms of a triæne may bifurcate (*dichotriæne*) once, twice, or oftener, or they may trifurcate.

dichro-. [f. Gr. δίχρο-ος: see next.] In combination = DICHROIC.

1889 I. REMSEN *Inorg. Chem.* 709 $Co(NH_3)_3\ Cl_3 + H_2O$ which is known as dichro-cobaltic chloride.

dichroic (daɪ'krəʊɪk), *a.* [ad. Gr. δίχροος, -ως two-coloured (f. δι- two + χρώς colour, complexion) + -IC.] Having or showing two colours; *spec.* applied to doubly-refracting crystals that exhibit different colours when viewed in different directions; or to solutions that show essentially different colours in different degrees of concentration.

a **1864** DANA cited in WEBSTER. **1878** GURNEY *Crystallogr.* 112 Tourmaline is strongly dichroic. **1879** DANA *Man. Geol.* (ed. 3) 67 This mineral..being dichroic.

dichroiscope: see DICHROSCOPE.

dichroism ('daɪkrəʊɪz(ə)m). [mod. f. Gr. δίχροος, -ως two-coloured (see DICHROIC) + -ISM. In F. *dichroïsme.*] The quality of being dichroic; *spec.* as exhibited by certain crystals and solutions: see prec.

1819 BREWSTER in *Phil. Trans.* 17 This dichroism, as it may be called..so far as I know, has never been observed in any other minerals than iolite and mica. **1843** *Rep. Brit. Assoc.* 14 The dichroism of a solution of stramonium in æther. **1884** *Chamb. Jrnl.* 15 Nov. 731/2 This stone [sapphire] possesses the singular property known as dichroism—that is, it shines with two colours, blue and red.

Hence **dichro'istic,** *a.* = DICHROITIC.

In mod. Dicts.

dichroite ('daɪkrəʊaɪt). *Min.* [mod. f. Gr. δίχροος (see DICHROIC) + -ITE. In F. *dichroite* (1809 Cordier).] A synonym of IOLITE, from its often exhibiting dichroism.

1810 *Nicholson's Jrnl.* XXVII. 231 Description of the Dichroit, a new Species of Mineral. **1831** BREWSTER *Optics* xxx. §148. 249 M. Cordier observed the same change of colour in a mineral called iolite, to which Haüy gave the name of *dichroite*. **1881** *Sat. Rev.* 23 Apr. 518/1 The great ball of dichroite which seems crystal white when looked at from one point of view, rich blue from another, and straw-colour from another, is perhaps the most entertaining object.

b. *Comb.*

1875 DAWSON *Dawn of Life* vi. 145 The gneiss..is chiefly grey and very silicious, containing dichroite, and..known as dichroite-gneiss.

dichroitic (daɪkrəʊ'ɪtɪk), *a.* [f. prec. + -IC.] Of, or of the nature of dichroite; characterized by dichroism; dichroic.

1831 BREWSTER *Newton* (1855) I. viii. 190 The relation of the colours of dichroitic crystals to their axes of double refraction. **1855** J. D. FORBES *Tour Mt. Blanc* xi. 248 By transmitted light it is dichroitic—brown orange in one direction and bright green in another. **1881** TYNDALL *Floating-Matter of Air* 95 The dichroitic action which produces the colours of the sky.

dichromasy (daɪ'krəʊməsɪ). *Ophthalmology.* [ad. mod.L. *dichromasia*, f. DI-[2] + Gr. χρῶμα colour.] = DICHROMATISM 2.

1909 in WEBSTER. **1937** *Brit. Jrnl. Psychol.* Oct. 218 The tables of dichromasy in general, and of protanopia, deuteranopia and tritanopia in particular. **1969** [see next].

'dichromat. *Ophthalmology.* Also 'dichromate. [f. DI-[2] + Gr. χρωματ-ικός (see DICHROMATIC *a.*): see -ATE[1].] A person affected with dichromatism.

1908 A. DUANE tr. *Fuch's Textbk. Ophthalmology* (ed. 3) II. xi. 538 The man with partial color blindness recognizes only two colors in the spectrum, while for the man with normal sight at least three fundamental sensations may be assumed to exist... Hence, we call the former dichromates, the latter trichromates. **1937** *Brit. Jrnl. Psychol.* Oct. 218 'Hidden' figures which are visible only to the dichromate. **1959** *New Scientist* 30 Apr. 972/2 There are three types of dichromat, known as protanopes, deuteranopes and tritanopes respectively. **1969** *Nature* 26 July 414/2 For human dichromats the presence of a restricted region in the visible spectrum that cannot be discriminated from white light..is considered to be diagnostic of dichromacy.

dichromate (daɪ'krəʊmət). *Chem.* [f. DI-[2].] A double CHROMATE (q.v.), as ***potassium dichromate*** $K_2{\cdot}CrO_4{\cdot}CrO_3$. (Also *bichromate.*)

1864 in WEBSTER. **1876** HARLEY *Mat. Med.* (ed. 6) 71 Potassic dichromate. **1883** *Athenæum* 27 Oct. 538/1 [He] recommends potassium dichromate as an exceedingly useful disinfecting agent.

Hence **di'chromated** *ppl. a.*, treated with a dichromate.

1890 ABNEY *Treat. Photogr.* (ed. 6) 178 The insolubility of dichromated gelatine.

dichromatic (daɪkrəʊ'mætɪk), *a.* (and *sb.*) [f. Gr. δι- two + χρωματικός of or relating to colour, f. χρῶμα colour.] **1. a.** Having or showing two colours; *spec.* of animals: Presenting, in different individuals, two different colours or systems of coloration.

1847 CRAIG, *Dicromatic.* **1864** in WEBSTER. **1884** COUES *Key to N.A. Birds* (ed. 2) 504 Plumage dichromatic in some cases; i.e. some individuals of the same species normally mottled gray, while others are reddish. **1889** G. A. BERRY *Dis. Eye* xi. 340 Why in the case of the partially colour-blind the absence of the perception of two complementary hues should leave the individual only a dichromatic spectrum.

b. *fig.*

1962 *Listener* 28 June 1128/3, I am not sure that he [*sc.* a novelist] presents his world with justice; his characterization is too dichromatic.

2. *Ophthalmology.* Of, pertaining to, or affected with dichromatism.

1897 NORRIS & OLIVER *Syst. Dis. Eye* I. 654/2 Dichromatic color-blindness. **1905** J. W. BAIRD *Color Sensitivity of Peripheral Retina* 21 The color sensitivity of the periphery is so weak as to approximate in some degree the condition of the dichromatic, or even of the monochromatic retina. **1907** *Smithsonian Inst. Rep. 1907* 620 In dichromatic vision color perception is so limited that all of the shades perceived may be made by combining two of the spectral colors. *Ibid.*, The ordinary color blindness is dichromatic. **1959** *Chambers's Encycl.* V. 552/2 Subjects who have what is called two-colour (dichromatic) vision.. could be of three varieties: red-blind subjects, green-blind subjects and blue-blind subjects.

Hence as *sb.*, = DICHROMAT.

1897 W. THOMSON in Norris & Oliver *Syst. Dis. Eye* I. 600 We find people who can see only two colors in the whole spectrum. They are called dichromatics.

dichromatism (daɪ'krəʊmətɪz(ə)m). [f. as prec.: see -ISM.] **1.** The quality or fact of being dichromatic.

1884 COUES *Key to N.A. Birds* (ed. 2) 656 Remarkable differences of plumage in many cases, constituting dichromatism, or permanent normal difference in color.

2. *Ophthalmology.* Defective colour vision in which only two (rather than three) pure colours, in different combinations, are sufficient to produce a colour indistinguishable from any perceived.

1909 in WEBSTER. **1910** *Proc. R. Soc.* B. LXXXII. 463 The defect which has caused the non-perception of certain red rays has not caused the dichromatism. **1959** *New Scientist* 30 Apr. 972/2 In dichromatism, the colour-blind subject requires only two primaries in order to match any spectral colour.

dichromic (daɪ'krəʊmɪk), *a.* [f. Gr. δίχρωμ-ος two-coloured (see DICHROMATIC) + -IC.]

1. Relating to or including (only) two colours; applied, in connexion with the theory of three primary colour-sensations, to the vision of colour-blind persons including only two of these.

1854 *Fraser's Mag.* L. 559 Such Dichromic visionaries must lose a great deal. The harmonies of colour cannot touch them. **1881** LE CONTE *Monoc. Vision* 63 Herschel regarded normal vision as trichromic, but the vision of Dalton as dichromic, the red being wanting.

2. Exhibiting in different positions or circumstances two different colours; DICHROIC.

1877 MILLER & MCLEOD *Elem. Chem.* I. (ed. 6) 179 In dichromic media, or solutions which, under certain circumstances, appear to the unaided eye to transmit light of one tint, and, under certain other circumstances, to transmit light of a different tint.

dichronous ('daɪkrənəs), *a.* [f. late L. *dichronus*, a. Gr. δίχρον-ος of two prosodic quantities, either long or short (f. δι-, DI-[2] + χρόνος time) + -OUS.]

1. *Gr.* and *Lat. Prosody.* Having two times or quantities; sometimes short and sometimes long.

In mod. Dicts.

2. *Bot.* 'Having two periods of growth in the year'. *Syd. Soc. Lex.* 1883.

dichroous ('daɪkrəʊəs), *a.* [f. Gr. δίχρο-ος two-coloured + -OUS.] Of two colours; dichromatic; dichroic.

1864 in WEBSTER; and in mod. Dicts.

dichroscope ('daɪkrəʊskəʊp). Also dichroiscope, dichroöscope. [f. Gr. δίχρο-ος two-coloured + -σκοπ-ος observing.

(The etymologically regular form is *dichroöscope*, but *dichroscope* is more convenient.)]

An instrument for observing or testing the dichroism of crystals, etc. Hence **dichro'scopic** *a.*, of or pertaining to a dichroscope.

1857 NICHOL *Cycl. Phys. Sc.* (1860) 582 Dichroscopic lens, or dichroscope. **1876** *Catal. Sci. Appar. S. Kens.* §3469 Dichroiscope. **1879** ROOD *Chromatics* x. 137 A..piece of apparatus contrived by Dove, for mixing the coloured light furnished by stained glass, and called by him a dichroöscope. **1888** *Proc. R. Geog. Soc.* May 273 The ruby ..when examined by the dichroscope, exhibited two tints. **1890** M. D. ROTHSCHILD *Handbk. Prec. Stones* 15 When a stone is examined by means of the dichroiscope, it will show two images of the same hue, or of different hues.

dichrotal, -tism, erron. ff. DICROTAL, -TISM.

dicht, etc., Sc. forms of DIGHT, etc.

† **'dicible,** *sb. Philos. Obs.* [ad. med.L. *dīcibilis* (Du Cange), f. *dīcĕre* to say: see -BLE.] That which is capable of being said; a notion or idea expressible in words.

1656 STANLEY *Hist. Philos.* VIII. xviii. 40 *Dicible* is that which consisteth according to rationall phantasy. *Ibid.*, Dicibles are notions, that is, νοήματα, but not meerly and simply notions..being ready for expression, they are called dicibles, and pertain to the enunciative faculty of the soule.

dicing ('daɪsɪŋ), *vbl. sb.* [f. DICE *v.* + -ING[1].]

1. The action or practice of playing or gambling with dice; dice-play.

1456 *How wise man taught Son* 60 in Hazl. *E.P.P.* I. 171 Dysyng I the forbede. **1535** *Act 27 Hen. VIII*, c. 25 Any open..place for common bowling, dising, carding, closhe, tenys, or other unlawfull games. **1550** CROWLEY *Epigr.* 669 Diceynge hath brought many wealthye menne to care. *a* **1648** LD. HERBERT *Life* (1886) 79 The exercises I wholly condemn, are dicing and carding. **1708** MRS. CENTLIVRE *Busie Body* II. i, These young fellows think old men get estates for nothing but them to squander away in dicing. **1861** M. PATTISON *Ess.* (1889) I. 47 Severer penalties awaited drunkenness, dissipation, or dicing.

2. *Book-binding.* A method of ornamenting leather in squares or diamonds: see DICE *v.* 3 b.

Done originally by ruling with a blunt awl or edging-tool; the effect is imitated by pressure or stamping with a block.

3. *attrib.* and *Comb.* (in sense 1), as ***dicing-board, -box, -chamber, -money, -table.***

1571 *Wills & Inv. N.C.* (Surtees 1835) 366 A round dyssenge table. **1586** T. B. *La Primaud. Fr. Acad.* I. 128 [Thou] dost set downe as it were on a dicing boord in the hazard of one houre, both thy kingdome and life. **1586** A. DAY *Eng. Secretary* II. (1625) 44 It was in an Inne..in a dicing Chamber. *a* **1634** RANDOLPH *Muses' Looking-Gl.* I. iv, A niggard churl Hoarding up dicing-moneys for his son. **1655** MRQ. WORCESTER *Cent. Inv.* §90 A most dexterous Dicing Box..that with a knock..the four good Dice are fastened, and it looseneth four false Dice.

'dicing, *ppl. a.* [f. as prec. + -ING[2].] Playing with dice.

1884 H. D. TRAILL *Coleridge* iii. 54 The skeleton ship, with the dicing demons on its deck [*Anc. Mar.* III. xii.]

† **dicing-house.** *Obs.* [f. DICING *vbl. sb.*] A house for dice-play; a gambling-house.

1549 LATIMER *6th Serm. bef. Edw. VI* (Arb.) 161 Dysynge howses also..where yong Gentlemenne dyse away their thrifte. **1555** *Act 2-3 Phil. & M.* c. 9 Every Licence..for the having..of any Bowling-Allies, Dicing-houses, or other unlawful Games. **1649** MILTON *Eikon.* iii. (1851) 357 The spawn and shiprack of Taverns and Dicing Houses. **1660** JER. TAYLOR *Duct. Dubit.* II. 470 (L.) The public peace cannot be kept where public dicing-houses are permitted.

dicion, var. DITION, *Obs.*, dominion.

Dick (dɪk), *sb.*[1] [A playful alteration of *Ric-*, contraction of Norman Fr. and Anglo-Norman *Ricard*, L. *Ricardus* = *Richard*.]

1. a. A familiar pet-form of the common Christian name *Richard*. Hence generically (like *Jack*) = fellow, lad, man, especially with alliterating adjectives, as *desperate, dainty, dapper, dirty*. ***Tom, Dick and Harry***: any three (or more) representatives of the populace taken at random; see also TOM *sb.* 1 a; ***clever Dick***: a clever or smart person; usu. ironical: a 'know-all'; also *attrib.*

1553 T. WILSON *Rhet.* (1580) 192 Desperate Dickes borowes now and then against the owners will all that ever he hath. **1581** STUDLEY *Agamemnon* I, Whom with the dint of glittering sword Achilles durst not harme, Although his rash and desperat dickes the froward Knight did arme. **1588** SHAKS. *L.L.L.* v. ii. 464 Some Dick That smiles his cheeke in yeares, and knowes the trick To make my Lady laugh. **1589** *Marprel. Epit.* E, The desperat Dicks, which you.. affirm to be good bishops. **1592** GREENE *Upst. Courtier* in *Harl. Misc.* (Malh.) II. 227 A braue dapper Dicke, quaintly attired in veluet and sattin. **1822** GALT *Sir A. Wylie* II. viii. 75 He's a gone dick, a dead man. **1864** *Standard* 13 Dec. *Review Slang Dict.* (Farmer), [He] replied, 'Oh yes, in the reign of queen dick', which, on inquiry we found to be synonymous with 'Never', or 'Tib's eve'. **1887** in H. BAUMANN *Londinismen* 27/1 **1891** *Daily News* 17 Nov. 2/4 The only bears still extant are the Tom, Dick, and Harry of the Bourses. **1895** J. T. CLEGG *Works* I. 238 There's olez tuthri cliverdicks to smile At owt they thinken rayther eaut-o'th'-road. **1933** J. B. PRIESTLEY *Wonder Hero* vi. 222 One o' these clever Dicks from London bought it. **1957** J. BRAINE *Room at Top* xxiv. 197 'Clever Dick,' she said. 'Think yer knows everythink, doncha?' **1957** *Observer* 29 Sept. 12/5 He wrote an article for the *Radio Times*, accompanied by a picture of two actors with funny hats and cutlasses, to disarm all clever-dick criticism. **1969** I. & P. OPIE *Children's Games* iv. 154 There is bound to be some clever-dick who has hidden in a coal-hole and refuses to show himself.

b. Rarely applied to a female.

1814 *Watch-house* II. i, It's all over wi' you, madam; ye're a gone dick: ye hear he's confessing.

2. *dial.* or *local.* (See quots.)

1847–78 HALLIWELL, *Dick*, a kind of hard cheese. *Suffolk.* **1883** *Almondbury & Huddersfield Gloss.*, *Dick*, plain pudding. If with treacle sauce, *treacle dick*. *Mod.* '*Spotted dick*', currant or raisin pudding.

3. *slang.* **a.** A riding whip.

1873 *Slang Dict.*, *Dick*, a riding whip; gold-headed dick, one so ornamented. **1891** FARMER *Slang*, *Dick*, 2. (coachman's) a riding whip.

b. The penis. *coarse.*

1891 in FARMER *Slang*. **1929** F. MANNING *Middle Parts of Fortune* I. v. 95 Dost turn thysen to t'wall, lad, so's us 'ns sha'n't see tha dick? **1934** H. MILLER *Tropic of Cancer* 68 That circumcised dick of his. **1963** J. T. STORY *Something for Nothing* ii. 42 At a time when sex was being introduced into the school curriculum as something entirely new, they were already playing 'dicks and bums' with boisterous enjoyment. **1969** P. ROTH *Portnoy's Complaint* 79 You might have thought that..my dick would have been the last thing on my mind.

4. *Phr.* and *Comb.* (chiefly dial. or local.) ***Dick-a-dilver***, the periwinkle. ***Dick-a-Tuesday***, a will-o'-the-wisp. ***Dick-ass***, a jack-ass. ***Dick-dunnock***, a local name of the hedge-sparrow. ***dick-head*** *coarse slang*, (*a*) the glans penis; (*b*) *transf.*, esp. a stupid person. Also ***long-tailed Dick***, the long-tailed titmouse.

1636 SAMPSON *Vow Breaker* (N.), Ghosts, hobgoblins, Will-with-wispe, or Dick-a-Tuesday. *a* **1825** FORBY *Voc. E. Anglia*, *Dick-a-dilver*, the herb periwinkle..It is so called from its rooting (*delving*) at every joint, and spreading itself far and wide. **1832** COL. P. HAWKER *Diary* (1893) II. 47 Found in the garden the nest of a 'long-tailed Dick', with 3 eggs. **1847–78** HALLIWELL, *Dickass*, a jack-ass. *North. Ibid.*, *Dick-a-tuesday*, the ignis fatuus. **1969** L. MICHAELS *Going Places* 73 Tito screamed, 'I tell her you got it, dick-head.' **1972** W. LABOV in T. Kochman *Rappin' & Stylin' Out* 289 The originator will search for images that would be considered as disgusting as possible: 'Your mother eat fried dick-heads.' **1983** A. BLEASDALE *Shop thy Neighbour* xl. 141 But I lost that job, it was alright, I deserved to lose it, I was a dickhead—but haven't we all been at one time or another—haven't we all woken up the next mornin' an' gone 'oh Jesus, did I do that'?

dick, *sb.*[2] *dial.* [Perh., like prec., merely an arbitrary application of the proper name *Dick*; but a possible connexion with Du. *dek* 'covering, cover, horse-cloth' has been suggested. Cf. DICKY *sb.* III.] A leather apron.

1847–78 HALLIWELL, *Dick*, a leather apron and bib, worn by poor children in the North. **1883** *Almondbury & Huddersfield Gloss.*, *Dick*, a kind of apron such as worn by shoemakers, especially a leather one, which was called a 'leather dick'. **1888** *Sheffield Gloss.*, *Dick*, a leather apron for children.

dick, *sb.*[3] *dial.* [Cf. DIKE and DITCH.] **a.** A ditch. **b.** The bank of a ditch; a dike.

1736 PEGGE *Kenticisms*, *Dick*, a ditch. **1787** MARSHALL *E. Norfolk*, Gloss., *Dick*, the mound or bank of a ditch. **1875** *Sussex Gloss.*, *Dick*, a ditch. **1893** *Field* 25 Feb. 295/1 Most fences should be on banks with 'dicks' where the ground requires them.

dick, *sb.*[4] *slang.* Abbreviation of *dictionary*; hence, 'Fine language, long words' (*Slang Dict.*).

1860 HALIBURTON (Sam Slick) *Season Ticket* xii. (Farmer), Ah, now you are talking 'DIC.', exclaimed Peabody, and I can't follow you. **1873** *Slang Dict.* s.v., A man who uses fine words without much judgment is said to have 'swallowed the dick'.

dick, *sb.*[5] *slang.* [Short for *declaration*: cf. DAVY for *affidavit*.] In phr. ***to take one's dick*** = to take one's declaration.

1861 D. COOK *P. Foster's Dau.* xxvi. (Farmer), I'd take my dying dick he hasn't got a writ in his pocket. **1878** YATES *Wrecked in Port* I. 1 I'll take my dick I heard old Osborne say so!

¶ To this (in the commercial sense of 'declaration' as to the value of goods) is perhaps to be referred the vulgar phrase ***up to dick***: as *adj.* up to the proper standard, excellent, 'proper'; as *adv.* properly, suitably, fittingly.

(It has however been referred by some to DICK *sb.*[4])

1871 *Daily News* 7 Sept., The capital of the West is up to dick in the matter of lunches. **1877** J. GREENWOOD *Blue Blanket* (Farmer), 'Ain't that up to dick, my biffin?' **1877** *Punch* 10 Sept. 111/1.

dick, *sb.*[6] *slang.* [? Arbitrary contraction of DETECTIVE *sb.*] A detective; a policeman.

1908 J. M. SULLIVAN *Crim. Slang.* 8 *Dick*, a cop, detective (Canadian slang). **1912** A. H. LEWIS *Apaches of N.Y.* 95 Still, those plain-clothes dicks did not despair. **1924** *Amer. Speech* I. 151/2 'Dick' and 'bull' and 'John Law' have become established as names for the police. **1928** E. WALLACE *Gunner* xxix. 234 They'd persuaded a couple of dicks—detectives—to watch the barriers. **1956** J. D. CARR *P. Butler for Defence* xiii. 140 Plain-clothes C.I.D. men..are currently known as bogeys, busies, dicks, and scotches.

dickcissel (dɪk'sɪsəl). [Imitative of the bird's cry.] The black-throated bunting or little meadowlark, *Spiza americana*, of North America.

1886 R. RIDGWAY *Man. N. Amer. Birds* 452 Dickcissel,.. dark grey, becoming whitish on belly and lower tail-coverts. **1961** *New Scientist* 6 July 16/2 Nesting success of redwing blackbirds, dickcissels and other ground-nesting birds was very low on treated areas in Louisiana and Texas.

† **dicken.** *Obs.* or *dial.* Some water-bird.

1579 J. JONES *Preserv. Bodie & Soule* I. xiv. 26 Snipe, Godwipe, Dicken, Poppel, Bitter, Hearon white and gray.

dicken, dickin ('dɪkən), *int. Austral.* and *N.Z. slang.* Also **dickon, dikkon.** [var. DICKENS.] An interjectional exclamation expressing disgust or disbelief: come off it!, cut it out! Also const. *on.*

1894 *Bulletin* (Sydney) 5 May 13/3 'And did yer stouch him back?' 'No.' 'Dicken!' 'Swelp me.' **1906** E. DYSON *Fact'ry 'Ands* v. 53 'Well, what price goin' inter trainin' fer er livin' skelington?' 'Dicken! Skeletons is low.' *Ibid.* viii. 98 To all iv which ther murmur is dickin. **1918** *Chrons. N.Z.E.F.* 10 Apr. 101 'Say, Kiwi, some coot told me you were a wingless bird.' 'Dicken, Yank, yer gotter have arms when there's a war on.' **1937** N. MARSH *Vintage Murder* xxi. 238 Aw dikkon, Mr. Alleyn... I suppose it's N.Z. digger slang 'Dikkon'. It's the same as if you'd say 'Come off it'. Used to hear it on the Peninsula. 'Aw dikkon, dig.' **1949** D. M. DAVIN *Roads from Home* III. iii. 237 Dicken on that for a joke. **1950** *Evening Post* (Wellington) 6 Nov. 8/2 The accused said, 'Murder..dicken on that, me murder anyone!' **1970** *N.Z. Listener* 12 Oct. 13/5 'You don't lie and cheat the way my mother does.' 'Ah, dicken.'

dickens ('dɪkɪnz). *slang* or *colloq.* Also 7–8 **dickins,** 8–9 **dickons,** 9 **dickings.** [App. substituted for 'devil', as having the same initial sound. It has been suggested to be worn down from *devilkin* or *deilkin*, but no evidence of this has been found. *Dickin* or *Dickon*, dim. of *Dick* (cf. *Wilkin, Watkin, Jankin* or *Jenkin, Simkin*) was in use long before the earliest known instance of this, and *Dickens* as a surname was probably also already in existence.]

The deuce, the devil. **a.** ***the dickens!*** (formerly also ***a dickens!***) an interjectional exclamation expressing astonishment, impatience, irritation, etc.; usually with interrogative words, as *what, where, how, why*, etc. (Cf. DEUCE, DEVIL.)

1598 SHAKS. *Merry W.* III. ii. 19, I cannot tell what (the dickens) his name is. **1600** HEYWOOD *1 Edw. IV*, III. Wks. 1874 I. 40 What the dickens? is it loue that makes ye prate to me so fondly? **1676** D'URFEY *Mad. Fickle* II. i, Oh have I found you at last? I wonder where the Dickins you ramble! **1687** CONGREVE *Old Bach.* II. i, What, a dickens, does he mean by a trivial sum? **1728** VANBR. & CIB. *Prov. Husb.* IV. i. 72 The dickens! has the Rogue of a Count play'd us another Trick then? **1794** WOLCOTT (P. Pindar) *Rowl. for Oliver* Wks. II. 308 Then what a dickens can I do or say? **1842** S. C. HALL *Ireland* II. 402 Why the dickons don't you let us serve them all out at once?

b. in imprecations, as ***the dickens take you!***; also in phr. ***to go to the dickens***, to go to ruin or perdition; ***to play the dickens***, to cause mischief or havoc.

1653 URQUHART *Rabelais* I. Prol., Hearken joltheads..or dickens take ye. **1656** BLOUNT *Glossogr.*, *Dickins*, a corruption of Devilkins, i. little Devils; as tis usually said, the Dickens take you. **1771** SMOLLETT *Humph. Cl.* 3 June ¶4 He [the lion] would roar, and tear, and play the dickens. **1831** MOORE *Summer Fête* 822 Like those Goths who played the dickens With Rome and all her sacred chickens. **1861** SALA *Dutch Pict.* xiii. 199 They played the very dickens with Doctor Pantologos. **1877** BLACK *Green Past.* xlii. (1878) 336 Business went to the dickens.

c. as a strong negative (= DEVIL 21).

1842 S. LOVER *Handy Andy* xxiii, The dickings a mind he minded the market. **1884** *Illustr. Lond. News* Christm. No. 19/3 'The dickens you are', thought Fred.

Dickensian (dɪ'kɛnzɪən), *a.* and *sb.* **A.** *adj.* Of or pertaining to the English novelist Charles *Dickens* (d. 1870), or his style; marked by conditions or features resembling those described by Dickens.

1881 *Athenæum* 19 Mar. 390/3 He [Bret Harte] has a touch of Dickens in his style..he observes with a Dickensian eye. **1892** *Spectator* 16 Jan. 93/2 The quiet old city has, of course, personal as well as literary Dickensian associations. **1928** *Daily Express* 16 Apr. 10/2 It makes foreigners wonder whether the comfort and the good fare of the old Dickensian type of inn were purely mythical. **1955** *Times* 11 May 6/7 It ..has reverted to the Dickensian standard of longer hours, less pay, and poorer conditions. **1962** *Daily Tel.* 6 Dec. 12/2 Fog as dense, if not as black, as anything that Dickensian London ever knew.

B. *sb.* An admirer or student of Dickens or his works.

1903 *Westm. Gaz.* 24 Nov. 2/3 A keen Dickensian like Mr. Pett Ridge. **1905** (*title*) The Dickensian, a magazine for Dickens lovers. **1964** *English Studies* XLV. 336 Dickensians will find it of interest.

So **Dicken'sesque (Dickenesque), 'Dickensish, 'Dickensy (Dickeny),** *adjs.*; **'Dickensite** = DICKENSIAN *sb.* Also **Dickensi'ana** (see ANA *suff.*). (All more or less nonce-wds.)

1856 *Sat. Rev.* II. 196/1 A Dickenesque description of an execution. **1859** MRS. GASKELL *Let.* 9 Mar. (1966) 538 My story..is fated to go to this new Dickensy periodical. **1880** *Athenæum* 25 Sept. 399/2 The Dickenesque portion..is poor beside its prototype. **1885** *Ibid.* 17 Oct. 503 His is a Dickensesque manner, but he has not the local knowledge nor humour of his master. **1886** *Century Mag.* XXXII. 937 My ideas of London were ..preeminently Dickeny. **1886** F.

G. Kitton (*title*) Dickensiana, a bibliography of the literature relating to Charles Dickens and his writings. **1888** A. Lang in *Good Words* Apr. 233/1 One is a Dickensite pure and simple. **1890** *Spectator* 30 Aug. 281 Disraeli never descended even into Dickensish depths of human nature. **1892** Kate D. Wiggin in *Atlantic Monthly* May 616 It would be so delightful and Dickensy to talk..with a licensed victualer by the name of Martha Huggins. **1905** *Daily Chron.* 12 July 4/7 A correspondent..assures us that he is..a Dickensite. **1949** D. G. Smith *I capture Castle* vi. 75, I had hoped the lawyers' office would be old and dark, with a Dickensy old lawyer. **1958** *Listener* 18 Dec. 1046/1 There may soon be a special department in public libraries devoted to Dickensiana.

dicker ('dɪkə(r)), *sb.*[1] Forms: α. 4–5 **dyker**, 5–6 dycker, 6 deker, diker, -ar, dickar, dikkar, 7 dicar, 6– dicker. β. 6– dacre, daker, (6 daiker, dakir, 8 dakker). [The form *dicker*, ME. *dyker*, etc., with the latinized forms *dicora*, *dikera*, *dicra*, point to an OE. **dicor*, corresponding to MLG. *dêker*, MHG. *decher*, *techer*, mod.G. *decher*, LG. *diekr* (Westphal.), *dǣkr* (Pomerania), Icel. *dekr*, Da. *deger*, Sw. *däcker*; all evidently from a WGer. **decura*, **decora*, ad. L. *decuria*, a company or parcel of ten: cf. OE. *sicor* for L. *securis*. This WGer. form must be the source of the med.L. *decora*, *decara*, *dicara*, *dacora* (Du Cange), and of the OF. *dacre*, *dakere*, and corresp. med.L. *dacra*, *dacrum*, whence the Sc. and northern forms in β.

The word has been used from ancient times in the reckoning of skins or hides; a letter of the Roman Emperor Valerian (A.D. 253–260) preserved by Trebellius Pollio, directs Zozimion, procurator of Syria, to furnish to Claudius, among other supplies, 'pellium tentoriarum decurias triginta', i.e. 30 dickers of skins for tents. Kluge points out that the early adoption of the Latin word by the Germans is explained by the tribute of skins which the latter had to pay to the Romans (Tacitus *Ann.* iv. 72), as well as by the fact that skins formed a leading item in the frontier trade between the Romans and the northern barbarians, as they have in the traffic between white men and the Indians in North America in modern times (see DICKER *v.*).]

The number of ten; half a score; being the customary unit of exchange in dealing in certain articles, *esp.* hides or skins; hence a package or lot of (ten) hides.

Its use in the skin trade appears to be the only one in continental languages; in English it has been extended to some other goods; the dicker (*dicra* or *dacra*) of iron in Domesday is generally held to have been ten rods, each sufficient to make two horse-shoes.

α. [**1086** *Domesday* I. lf. 162 a, T.R.E. reddebat civitas de Glowecestre...xxxvi. d icras ferri. **1275** *Placita in Curiis Magnat. Angliæ*, Per iij diker' de coriis bovinis.] **1266–1307** *Assisa de Pond. et Mensur.* (Stat. Realm I. 205), Item Last Coriorum ex xx Dykeres, et quodlibet Dacre constat ex x coreiis. Item Dacre Cirotecarum ex x paribus. ¶ Dacre vero ferrorum equorum [viginti] ferris. *Transl.* ex *Lib. Horw. Lond.* lf. 123 A Last of Leather doth consist of Twenty Diker, and every Diker consisteth of Ten Skins. And a Diker of Gloves consisteth of Ten Pair of Gloves. Item a Diker of Horse-shoes doth consist of [Ten *v.r.* twenty] Shoes. **1428** *Will of Tanner* (Somerset Ho.), j dyker de Rigges et neckes. **1467** in *Eng. Gilds* (1870) 384 Payinge for the custome of euery dyker j d. **1526** *Tolls* in Dillon *Calais & Pole* (1892) 81 A dycker of hydes tanned, ten hydes a dyker. **1535** *Act 27 Hen. VIII*, c. 14 §1 Two persons.. nombre all suche lether by the hide, accomptinge ten hides to the deker. **1553–54** *Trinity Coll. Accts.* in Willis & Clark *Cambridge* (1886) III. 610 It' to John Barbour for a dikkar of knives. **1579** in Wadley *Bristol Wills* (1886) 227 Fower diker of Rawe leather. **1679** Blount *Anc. Tenures* 33 A Dicar of Iron contained ten Barrs. **1691** *Lond. Gaz.* No. 2661/4 Also 16 Dickers of Butts in the Fatts near Tanned. **1799** S. Freeman *Town Off.* 146 The sealer of leather's fee shall be 6*d.* per dicker. **1812** J. Smyth *Pract. of Customs* (1821) 51 Bracelets, or necklaces, of Glass. The Gross to contain 12 Bundles or Dickers, and each Bundle or Dicker being 10 Necklaces. **1835** P. Kelly *Universal Cambist* II. Index, Dicker, or dacre of leather, 10 hides; of necklaces, 10 bundles, each bundle ten necklaces.

β. [**1286** in Rogers *Agric. & Prices* II. 458/3 (Iron & Steel). *c* **1300** *Fleta* II. xii. §4 (Jam.) Item lastus coriorum consistit ex decim dakris, & quodlibet dacrum ex decim coriis.. Dacrum vero ferrorum equorum ex viginti ferris.] **1531** *Aberdeen Burgh Rec.* XIII. 248 The dakir of hidis. **1548** *Wills & Inv. N.C.* (Surtees) 130, ij daker off lether off daker wayre iij[l]. vj[s]. viij[d]. **1588** *Will of Willison* (Somerset Ho.), Dacre of leather. **1609** Skene *Reg. Maj.* Stat. of Gild 147 In halfe ane daker of hydes. **1732** in Cramond *Ann. Banff* (1891) I. 206 For each dakker of leather freemen shall pay 3*s.* 4*d.* **1835** (see α.) Dacre.

†**b.** *transf.* A considerable number; a 'lot', a 'heap'. *Obs.*

1580 Sidney *Arcadia* III. (1622) 393 Behold, said Pas, a whole dicker of wit. **1596** Nashe *Saffron Walden* 2 Such a huge dicker of Dickes in a heape altogether. **1602** *Narcissus* (1893) 686 On my love kisses I heape a dicker. **1641** Brathwait *Engl. Intelligencer* I, Newes, Althea, I have a whole dicker of newes for thee. **1676** Marvell *Mr. Smirke* 33 But if the Dean foresee that 'tis a very vendible Book, he ..sends up for a whole Dicker of 'em to retaile.

dicker ('dɪkə(r)), *sb.*[2] *U.S.* [f. DICKER *v.*] The action or practice of dickering; barter; petty bargaining. Also, a deal, bargain; articles or commodities as a medium of exchange or payment.

1823 J. F. Cooper *Pioneer* xiv. (1869) 61/1 You have sold your betterments. Was it cash or dicker? **1831** *Boston Evening Transcript* 22 Dec. 1/1 His 'dicker' was begun, And by aid of solemn face, He closed a bargain soon. **1833** J. Neal *Down-Easters* I. v. 81 A dicker's a dicker I allays concate, where people's upon honor, but not where they aint. **1856** Whittier *Panorama* 270 Selfish thrift and party held the scales For peddling dicker, not for honest sales. **1880** *Harper's Mag.* May 907/1 An old watch and shot-gun ..that he had taken as 'dicker' on accounts. **1888** *N.Y. Weekly Times* 28 Mar. (Farmer *Amer.*), Considering the advisability of making a dicker with his old political opponents. **1940** Wodehouse *Eggs, Beans & Crumpets* 57 It was his intention to..make a dicker with it [*sc.* a dog] by means of the slab [of cheese] which he had just purchased.

dicker, *v.* *U.S.* [? f. DICKER *sb.*[1]

Quotation 1848 refers to the barter traffic on the Indian frontier in N. America. As skins have always formed a chief item in that trade, it has been suggested with much probability that the verb arose, in the sense 'to deal by the dicker, to deal in skins', among the traders with the Indians, and has thence extended in U.S. to trade by barter generally. If this be the fact, it is interesting that a word which passed from Latin into Germanic in special connexion with dealing in skins, and which has ever since in Europe been associated with this trade (see DICKER *sb.*[1]), should, in America, through similar dealings between a civilized and uncivilized race, have received another development of use.]

a. *intr.* To trade by barter or exchange; to truck; to bargain in a petty way, to haggle. Also in extended use (*intr.*): to dither, vacillate, hesitate. **b.** *trans.* To barter, exchange. Hence '**dickering** *vbl. sb.*; also '**dickerer**, one who dickers.

1802 *Port Folio* (Phila.) ii. 268 (Th.), *Dickering* signifies all that *honest* conversation, preliminary to the sale of a horse, where the parties very laudably strive in a sort of gladiatorial combat of lying, cheating, and overreaching. **1824** *Woodstock* (Vermont) *Observer* 15 June 4/5 (Advt.) (Th.), The subscriber has for sale the following property which he wishes to dicker for. **1845** J. T. Headley *Lett. fr. Italy* xx. 99, I had acquired quite a reputation in dickering with the thieving Italian landlords and vetturini. **1848** J. F. Cooper *Oak Openings* (Bartlett), The white men who penetrated to the semi-wilds [of the West] were always ready to dicker and to swap. **1864** Sala in *Daily Tel.* 7 July, The required needle was dickered for the egg, and the Yankee was going away. **1888** Bryce *Amer. Commw.* II. III. lxiii. 457 By a process of dickering (i.e. bargaining by way of barter)..a list is settled on which the high contracting parties agree. **1891** Goldw. Smith *Canadian Question*, Government, in the persons of the Parliamentary heads of departments, is on the stump, or dickering for votes. **1891** *Columbus* (*Ohio*) *Dispatch* 2 Apr., Bargains that would do credit to London East End dickerers. **1891** Stevenson & Osbourne *Wrecker* (1892) iv. 63 To this romance of dickering I would reply with the romance..of art. **1947** D. M. Davin *Gorse blooms Pale* 78 Phyllis dickers a bit but of course she finishes by getting up and saying she's going to play. **1960** *Sunday Express* 6 Nov. 17/5 He withdrew it [*sc.* a play] angrily when A.-R. dickered over the production date. **1961** *John o'London's* 25 May 589/2 Dickering on the edge of adulthood. **1962** *Sunday Express* 30 Sept. 4/5 The large stores who dicker and dither before they take a cheque. **1963** B. Pearson *Coal Flat* ix. 159 Henderson, though he dickered, usually came round to the majority opinion.

dickinsonite ('dɪkɪnsəˌnaɪt). *Min.* [Named 1878 after the Rev. J. Dickinson: see -ITE.] A hydrous phosphate of manganese, calcium, and sodium, usually micaceous in structure and green in colour.

1878 *Amer. Jrnl. Sc.* Ser. III. XVI. 115 Distinct crystals of dickinsonite are not often found.

dicky, dickey ('dɪkɪ), *sb. colloq.*, *slang*, and *dial.* Also dickie. [The senses here included may belong to two or more words of distinct origin. Some of them are evidently applications of *Dicky*, dim. of *Dick* (cf. Tommy, Willy, Bobby, etc.); another group is probably closely related to DICK *sb.*[2]; of others the relationship is obscure.

Many other applications of 'dicky' may be found in the dialect and slang dictionaries.]

I. As applied to persons.

1. *Naut.* (See quot.)

1867 Smyth *Sailor's Word-bk.*, *Dickey*, an officer acting in commission.

II. As a name applied to animals.

2. A donkey; properly, a he-ass.

First noted in East Anglia and Essex, now widely known.

1793 *Gentl. Mag.* II. 1083 A Donky, or a Dicky. An ass. Essex and Suffolk. **1818** Moore *Fudge Fam. Paris* II. 25 When gravely sitting Upon my dickey. *a* **1825** Forby *Voc. E. Anglia*, *Dicky-ass*, a male ass; the female being usually called a Jenny ass, or a Betty ass. **1876** E. FitzGerald *Lett.* (1889) I. 388 About Sancho's stolen Dicky.

attrib. **1801** Bloomfield *Rural T.*, *Richard & Kate* (1802) 8 Time to begin the Dicky Races, More fam'd for laughter than for speed. **1883** Jessopp in *19th Cent.* Oct. 602 Ridin' in a dickey cart's enow for him and me.

3. A small bird (also DICKY-BIRD). **a.** A tame (caged) bird. **b.** *dial.* The hedge-sparrow.

1851 *Florist* Nov., There was..dicky's cage on its old nail. **1868** *Daily Tel.* 29 May, We should not like to trust a canary bird near the picture. Mr. Radford's monk would surely spring from the canvas..and crunch the dickey to splinters. **1878** *Cumbld. Gloss.*, *Dickey*, the hedge-sparrow, *Accentor modularis.* **1881** Black *Beautiful Wretch* xviii. (Farmer), 'The dicky-laggers are after them too.' 'The what?' 'The bird-catchers, Miss.' **1885** Swainson *Prov. Names Birds* 29 Hedge Sparrow..Dickie (Lancashire)..Blue dickie (Renfrew). **1887** *Kentish Gloss.*, *Dicky-hedge-poker*, a hedge-sparrow. **1888** *Sheffield Gloss.*, *Dicky-dunnock*, the hedge-sparrow.

c. See DICKY-BIRD, DICKEY-BIRD 2.

III. As a name of articles of clothing: cf. DICK *sb.*[2]

†**4.** An under petticoat. *Obs.*

1753 *Songs Costume* (Percy Soc.) 231 With fringes of knotting your Dickey cabod [? cabob], On slippers of velvet, set gold a-la-daube. **1787** *Minor* I. 99 Of all her splendid apparel not a wreck remained..save her flannel dicky. **1800** Wolcott (P. Pindar) *Ld. Auckland's Tri.* Wks. 1812 IV. 311 The hips ashamed forsooth to wear a dicky. **1847–78** Halliwell, *Dicky*, a woman's under-petticoat.

†**5.** A worn-out shirt. (*Obs. slang.*)

1781 G. Parker *View of Society* I. 82 *note* (Farmer), Dickey, cant for a worn-out shirt.

6. A detached shirt-front.

1811 *Lex. Balatronicum*, *Dickey*, a sham shirt. **1843** Thackeray *Crit. Rev.* Wks. 1886 XXIII. 29 If not a shirt-collar at least a false collar, or by possibility a dicky. **1848** —— *Bk. Snobs* xxvii, Wretched Beaux..who sport a lace dickey. **1886** Baring-Gould *Court Royal* I. vi. 87 Paper collars, cuffs, and dickies. **1889** J. M. Barrie *Window in Thrums* iii, 'Come awa doon..an' put on a clean dickey.'

7. A shirt collar. (*New England.*)

1858 Holland *Titcomb's Lett.* iii. 36 A beautiful cravat, sustaining a faultless dicky. **1864** Lowell *Biglow P.* Poems 1890 II. 283. **1864** Thoreau *Cape Cod* vi. (1894) 130 Cockles..looking..like a flaring dickey made of sand-paper. **1887** M. E. Wilkins *Humble Romance, etc.* (1891) 50 David Emmens, arrayed in his best clothes, with his stiff white dickey.

8. A covering worn to protect the dress or upper part of it during work, etc.; variously applied (according to time and place) to **a.** A leather apron or pinafore. **b.** A child's bib. **c.** A 'slop' or loose over-jacket of coarse linen coming down to the waist, worn by workmen in the north. **d.** An oil-skin suit.

1847–78 Halliwell, *Dicky*..a common leather apron. **1879** *Cumbld. Gloss.* Suppl., *Dicky*, a short upper garment of coarse linen till lately worn by working men. **1883** Mrs C. Garnett in *Sunday Mag.* Dec. 751/2 To the office..we walked to be arrayed in our dickies.

IV. In other applications.

9. a. The seat in a carriage on which the driver sits. (Also **dicky-box.**) **b.** A seat at the back of a carriage for servants, etc., or of a mail-coach for the guard.

1801 Gabrielli *Myst. Husb.* IV. 260 The farmer..came down upon the dicky in front of the chaise, to save a horse. **1803** *Times* 17 Jan., Hammer-cloths, except on state occasions, are quite out of date, and the dickey-box is following their example. **1803** *Lit. Jrnl.* in *Spirit Publ. Jrnls.* (1804) VII. 5 The style which has changed a tub into a chariot, and a coach-box into a dicky. **1806** Surr *Wint. in Lond.* (ed. 3) II. 210 She..ventured to introduce a plain black leather chair for the driver, which was called a dicky. **1812** *Ann. Reg.* 131 The guard travelled by the side of the coachman on the box, and on returning to the dickey he discovered the robbery. **1823** Byron *Juan* XIII. xlvii, The valet mounts the dickey. **1837** Dickens *Pickw.* xlvi, A hackney cabriolet..three people were squeezed into it besides the driver, who sat..in his own particular little dickey at the side. **1862** Sala *Seven Sons* I. iv. 72 He had seen him..in the dickey of a phaeton. **1886** Ruskin *Præterita* I. vi. 185 We carried our courier behind us in the dickey with Anne.

c. An extra seat at the back of a two-seater motor car which can be closed down when not in use.

1912 *Motor Manual* (ed. 14) iv. 139 On most two-seaters a light, detachable, rear single or dickey seat can be arranged for if specially desired. **1926** W. Deeping *Sorrell & Son* v, I'll take it round to a garage for you, sir. Luggage in the dicky?

d. In other extended uses.

1907 Masefield *Tarpaulin Muster* iv. 57, I..went to the leadsman's dicky, or little projecting platform, on the starboard side. *a* **1922** T. Burt *Autobiogr.* (1924) 94 The hauling-engine, called the 'dickey', was at the surface.

10. *Comb.*: **dicky-box** (see 9 a); **dicky-daisy** (*local*), a nursery name for the common daisy (*Bellis perennis*), also applied to other wild flowers; **dicky dilver**, a local name of the periwinkle (Britten & Holl.) = *dick-a-dilver* (DICK *sb.*[1]); **Dicky Sam** [understood to be a corruption of *Dick o'Sam's*, an example of the Lancashire form of patronymic], a nickname for a Liverpool man.

1870 *Athenæum* 10 Sept., We cannot even guess why a Liverpool man is called a Dickey Sam. **1884** *Book Lore* Dec. 27 (Farmer), The natives of Liverpool call themselves, or are called by others, Dicky Sams.

'**dicky, dickey**, *a.* *slang* or *colloq.* [Etymol. not ascertained.] Of inferior quality, sorry, poor; in bad condition, unsound, shaky, 'queer'.

1812 J. H. Vaux *Flash Dict.*, *Dicky*..very bad or paltry; any thing of an inferior quality, is said to be a dicky concern. *a* **1845** Hood *Conveyancing* iv, At last to find Your dinner is all dickey. **1883** *Standard* 8 Jan. 2/4 Without doubt Iroquois has been very 'dickey' on his pins. **1889** D. C. Murray *Danger. Catspaw* 24 The very honestest tradesman..must run the risk of meeting very dicky people now and then. **1894** Sir J. D. Astley *My Life* I. 312 Poor 'Curly' was uncommon dicky for several days from concussion of the brain.

b. *all dicky with*: 'all up' or 'all over' with.

1810 *Morning Post* 26 June in *Spirit Pub. Jrnls.* (1811) XIV. 278 At one time he thought it was all dicky with Sir Francis. *a* **1845** Barham *Ingol. Leg.*, *Bros. Birchington* xl, 'Tis all dickey with poor Father Dick—he's no more! **1880** Mrs. Parr *Adam & Eve* xxxvi. 490 'Ah, poor old Zebedee! ..'tis all dickey with he.'

c. *Comb.*, as *dicky-legged*.

1894 Sir J. D. Astley *My Life* II. 2 The trainer of some dicky-legged racer.

'dicky-bird, dickey-bird. *colloq.* [DICKY 3.]
1. a. In nursery and familiar speech: A little bird, such as a sparrow, robin, or canary-bird.
1781 H. WALPOLE *Let.* 2 Jan. (1904) XI. 354 The Sphinx was a harmless dicky-bird in comparison. **1820** T. CREEVEY *Let.* 23 Jan. in *Creevey Papers* (1903) I. xiii. 296 Lady Jersey ..is like one of her numerous gold and silver musical dickey birds. *a* **1845** BARHAM *Ingol. Leg.*, *Knight & Lady*, On tree-top and spray The dear little dickey-birds carol away. **1852** R. S. SURTEES *Sponge's Sp. Tour* lxv, Others take guns and pop at all the little dickey-birds that come in their way. *a* **1869** KINGSLEY in *Life* (1879) II. 41 Gladly would I throw up history, to think of nothing but dicky-birds. **1886** J. K. JEROME *Idle Thoughts* 121 We do not sigh over dead dicky-birds with the bailiffs in the house.
b. Applied *dial.* to particular birds: see quots., and cf. DICKY *sb.* 3.
1879 *Cumbld. Gloss.* Suppl., *Dicky-bird*, a general name for a canary. **1885** SWAINSON *Prov. Names Birds* 188 Oyster Catcher (*Hæmatopus ostrilegus*). Dickie bird (Norfolk).
2. Rhyming slang for 'word'. Also in shortened form *dick(e)y*.
1932 'P. P.' *Rhyming Slang* 15 Word... Dicky bird. **1936** 'M. BENNEY' *Low Company* ii. 48 Didn't say a dicky bird, the poor girl didn't. **1943** M. HARRISON *Reported Safe Arrival* 61, I give yer me dicky. **1963** J. PRESCOT *Case for Hearing* vii. 108 Never said a dicky-bird about doing the place myself. **1970** A. DRAPER *Swansong for Rare Bird* ix. 76 George didn't say a dicky bird when I ambled in.

‖**diclesium** (daɪˈkliːzɪəm). *Bot.* [mod.L., f. Gr. δι- twice (DI-[2]) + κλῇσις a shutting up, closing.] A dry indehiscent fruit consisting of an achene enclosed within the indurated base of the adherent perianth.
1857 HENFREY *Bot.* I. ii. 140 The Diclesium only differs from the utriculus in having the indurated perianth adherent to the carpel, and forming part of the shell (*Mirabilis*, *Salsola*).

diclinic (daɪˈklɪnɪk), *a. Cryst.* [f. Gr. δι- two + κλίν-ειν to incline + -IC.] Having the lateral axes at right angles to each other, but both oblique to the vertical axis: applied to a hypothetical system of crystals. Also **'diclinate** *a.*
1864 WEBSTER cites DANA.

diclinism (ˈdaɪklɪnɪz(ə)m). *Bot.* [mod. f. as next + -ISM: in F. *diclinisme*.] The condition of being DICLINOUS.
1882 VINES *Sachs' Bot.* 920 The arrangements.. manifested in polygamy, diclinism, dichogamy, dimorphism..are different means for promoting the cross-fertilisation of individuals belonging to the same species.

diclinous (ˈdaɪklɪnəs), *a. Bot.* [f. F. *dicline* (1793 in Hatz.-Darm.) or Bot.L. *Diclines* pl. (Jussieu 1779), f. Gr. δι- twice, double (DI-[2]) + κλίνη bed, couch: see -OUS.
(A. L. de Jussieu gave the name *Diclines irregulares* to the 15th class of his arrangement of the Natural Orders.)]
Having the stamens and pistils on separate flowers, either on the same plant (*monœcious*), or on separate plants (*diœcious*). Also said of the flowers (= unisexual).
1830 LINDLEY *Nat. Syst. Bot.* Introd. 27 Even Ranunculaceæ contain hermaphrodite and diclinous genera. **1876** DARWIN *Cross-Fertil.* x. 409 All plants which have not since been greatly modified, would tend still to be both diclinous and anemophilous. **1880** GRAY *Struct. Bot.* vi. §7. 270 The flowers in all Gymnosperms are diclinous, either diœcious or monœcious.

dicoccous (daɪˈkɒkəs), *a. Bot.* [f. DI-[2] + Gr. κόκκ-ος grain + -OUS.] 'Splitting into two cocci' (*Treas. Bot.*): see COCCUS 2.
1819 *Pantologia* s.v., Dicoccous, or two-grained capsule. **1870** BENTLEY *Bot.* (ed. 2) 298 The fruit is described as dicoccous. **1878** MASTERS *Henfrey's Bot.* 266 Bruniaceæ differ in their dicoccous fruit.

dicœlious (daɪˈsiːlɪəs), *a.* [f. DI-[2] + Gr. κοιλί-α a hollow + -OUS.] Having two cavities.
1836-9 TODD *Cycl. Anat.* II. 631/2 The dicœlious heart of Hunter..exists at a very early period of the development of the Mammiferous embryo.

dicœlous (daɪˈsiːləs), *a.* [f. DI-[2] + Gr. κοῖλ-ος hollow, κοίλη a hollow + -OUS.] = prec.; *spec.* Of a vertebra: Cupped or hollowed at each end.
1864 WEBSTER cites OWEN.

dicolic (daɪˈkəʊlɪk), *a. Gr. Rhet.* and *Pros.* [f. Gr. δίκωλος (f. δι- twice + κῶλον limb, clause) + -IC.] Consisting of two cola: see COLON[2] I.
1885 T. D. GOODELL in *Trans. Amer. Philol. Ass.* XVI. 85 The first two lines..resemble the two cola of a Greek dicolic line.

dicondylian (daɪkɒnˈdɪlɪən), *a. Zool.* [f. Gr. δικόνδυλ-ος double-knuckled (cf. CONDYLE) + -IAN.] Of a skull: Having two occipital condyles.
1883 W. H. FLOWER in *Encycl. Brit.* XV. 370/2 The *Amphibia* are the only air-breathing *Vertebrata* which, like mammals, have a dicondylian skull.

dicot, dicotyl. Abbreviations of DICOTYLEDON.
1877 J. D. HOOKER *Let.* 8 Feb. in L. Huxley *Life & Lett. of J.D.H.* (1918) II. xxxix. 236, 1. Monocots. 2. Dicots. *a.* Angiosp. *b.* Gymnosp. **1877**, **1890** [see MONOCOT, MONOCOTYL]. **1903** *Amer. Jrnl. Sci.* Dec. 416 The main development of the early Dicotyls and other plants constituting the best horizon markers took place in the late Jurassic. **1907** J. D. HOOKER *Let.* 13 May in L. Huxley *Life & Lett. of J.D.H.* (1918) II. xxix. 22 You ask why 'in the British Flora of Mr. Bentham and myself I begin Dicots with Ranunculaceae'! **1967** *Kew Bull.* XXI. 342 Finally the monocots and dicots must be equally old, as is also apparent from the fossil record.

dicotyledon (ˌdaɪkɒtɪˈliːdən). *Bot.* [f. mod. Bot.L. *dīcotylēdones* (plural), f. Gr. δι- twice + κοτυληδών cup-shaped hollow or cavity: see COTYLEDON.
(The term *Dicotyledones* was employed by Ray, but its practical introduction into botanical classification dates from Jussieu 1779.)]
A flowering plant having two cotyledons or seed-lobes: the Dicotyledons (in Bot.Lat. *Dicotyledones*) constitute one of the great classes of flowering plants, characterized by an exogenous mode of growth (hence also called EXOGENS), and usually by having the parts of the flower in fives or fours, and the veins of the leaves reticulated.
[**1703** RAY *Methodus Plant.* (ed. 2) 1 Floriferas dividemus in *Dicotyledones*, quarum semina sata binis foliis anomalis, *Seminalibus* dictis, quæ *Cotyledonum* usum præstant, è terra exeunt.] **1727** BAILEY vol. II, *Dicotyledon* (with Botantists), a Term used of Plants, which spring with two Seed Leaves opposite to each other, as the generality of Plants have. **1830** LINDLEY *Nat. Syst. Bot.* Introd. 15 Two great divisions.. Monocotyledons and Dicotyledons. **1839** *Penny Cycl.* XIII. 157 In his 'Genera Plantarum' Jussieu divided the vegetable kingdom into classes, subclasses, orders, and genera..hence his classes *Acotyledons*, *Monocotyledons*, and *Dicotyledons*. **1875** BENNETT & DYER *Sachs' Bot.* II. v. 564 In the great majority of Dicotyledons the parts of the flower are arranged in whorls..the whorls are usually pentamerous, less often tetramerous.

dicotyledonary (ˌdaɪkɒtɪˈliːdənərɪ), *a. rare.* [f. prec. + -ARY[2].] = next.
1870 in *Eng. Mech.* 11 Mar. 629/2 The seeds have..four or more cotyledons instead of the usual dicotyledonary structure.

dicotyledonous (ˌdaɪkɒtɪˈliːdənəs), *a.* [f. as prec. + -OUS.] Having two cotyledons; belonging to the class of Dicotyledons.
1794 MARTYN *Rousseau's Bot.* xiii. 131 The body of the seed does not split into two lobes, but continues entire. Such plants are called *monocotyledonous*, the others *dicotyledonous*. **1845** LINDLEY *Sch. Bot.* (1858) i. 19 If the embryo has two cotyledons it is called *dicotyledonous*, as in the Bean. **1861** MISS PRATT *Flower. Pl.* I. 13 Dicotyledonous plants have a distinct deposition of pith, cellular tissue, spiral vessels, wood, and bark. **1872** H. MACMILLAN *True Vine* iii. 87 Its dicotyledonous seed expands in germinating into two lobes. **1872** OLIVER *Elem. Bot.* I. iv. 46 The Buttercup is dicotyledonous..the character expressed by this term (the possession of a pair of cotyledons, or, more strictly, the simple fact that the first leaves of the plant are opposite).
b. Of or belonging to a dicotyledonous plant.
1870 BENTLEY *Bot.* 39 In the inner bark or liber of Dicotyledonous stems. **1876** PAGE *Adv. Text-bk. Geol.* ix. 185 The reticulated venation of a dicotyledonous leaf.

dicoumarin (daɪˈkuːmərɪn). *Chem.* [ad. G. *dicumarin* (R. Fittig 1885, in *Ber. d. Deut. Chem. Ges.* XVIII. 2525), f. DI-[2] + COUMARIN.] Orig., any compound with a structure based on two coumarin molecules joined together; now *spec.* the compound 3,3′-methylenebis-(4-hydroxycoumarin), $C_{19}H_{12}O_6$, a white powder first isolated from spoiled sweet clover as the cause of hæmorrhage in sweet clover poisoning of cattle and later prepared synthetically and used as an anti-coagulant.
1886 *Jrnl. Chem. Soc.* L. 47 Salicylaldehyde and succinic aldehyde yield a dicoumarin..very similar in chemical behaviour to coumarin. **1941** *Jrnl. Biol. Chem.* CXXXVIII. 526 The hemorrhagic agent..present in improperly cured hay made from the common sweet clovers..is the dicoumarin, 3,3′-methylenebis (4-hydroxycoumarin). **1943** *Acta Physiol. Scand.* VI. 28 The author has presented data on the prothrombin depressing effect in animals and man of a dicoumarin..first isolated from moulded sweet clover hay. **1947** tr. *Schmidt's Textbk. Org. Chem.* (ed. 5) II. xi. 475 The clinical value of dicoumarin is enhanced by its lasting effect and the fact that it can be taken orally. **1965** [see ANTICOAGULANT *a.* and *sb.*].

dicoumarol, dicumarol (daɪˈkuːmərɒl). *Chem.* [f. prec. + -OL.] = prec. (in its specific sense).
Dicumarol is a proprietary term in the U.S. (see quot. 1942).
1942 *Official Gaz. U.S. Pat. Off.* 28 July 721/2 Wisconsin Alumni Research Foundation... Dicumarol for anti-coagulants. Claims use since May 15, 1942. **1943** *Lancet* 14 Aug. 195/1 The work on the anticoagulant drug 3:3-methylenebis-(4-hydroxycoumarin) was done in America;..the Americans have adopted 'dicoumarol' as its short name. *Ibid.* 28 Aug. 276/2 'Dicoumarol'..should be spelled 'dicumarol'. **1948** *Reader's Digest* Nov. 32/1 From the Mayo Clinic, where dicumarol was used postoperatively in 1686 cases. **1949** *Sci. News* VII. 63 Dicoumarol is now being used in medicine in conditions where it is desirable deliberately to decrease the clotting power of the blood. **1952** *Ibid.* XXV. 113 Dicoumarol is the only naturally occurring anti-vitamin. **1970** JUBB & KENNEDY *Path. Domestic Anim.* (ed. 2) I. 361/1 Dicoumarol is the toxic factor responsible for sweetclover poisoning of livestock.

dicres, obs. Sc. form of DECREASE.

dicrotal (daɪˈkrəʊtəl), *a.* [f. as next + -AL[1].] = next.
1867 J. MARSHALL *Phys.* II. 237 A subsidiary wave occurs after the principal one, producing the phenomena named dichrotism or the dichrotal pulse.

dicrotic (daɪˈkrɒtɪk), *a. Phys.* and *Path.* [f. Gr. δίκροτ-ος double-beating (f. δι- twice + κρότ-ος rattling noise, beat) + -IC: in mod.F. *dicrote*, med. or mod.L. *dicrotus*.]
Of the pulse (or a sphygmographic tracing of its motion): Exhibiting a double beat or wave for each beat of the heart; applied *esp.* to a pathological pulse in which the secondary wave which follows the primary is more marked than usual.
(Etymologically 'dicrotic' might be applied to any double-beating pulse, whether the secondary wave occurs in the rise or in the fall of the main wave; it is, in use, restricted to the latter case, the former being called ANACROTIC.)
[**1706** PHILLIPS (ed. Kersey), *Dicrotus*, a Pulse that beats twice. (So in BAILEY; in ASH *dicrotos*). **1741** JAS. NIHELL *Crises of the Pulse* 1 The *Pulsus Dicrotus* of the Ancients, which in English may be properly called the Rebounding Pulse.] **1811** HOOPER *Med. Dict.*, *Dicrotic*, a term given to a pulse in which the artery rebounds after striking, so as to convey the sensation of a double pulsation. **1822** GOOD *Stud. Med.* II. 26 When..we come to a distinction between the free and dilated pulse..the quick and the frequent..the dicrotic, coturnising, and inciduous..proposed by Solano, as mere subvarieties of the rebounding, or redoubling. **1857** DUNGLISON *Med. Dict.* 772 *Pulse, dicrotic*..that in which the finger is struck twice at each pulsation, once lightly, the other time more strongly. **1865** *New Syd. Soc. Year-bk. Med.* 11 On the other hand, increase in the heart's force.. makes the pulse dicrotic. **1875** H. C. WOOD *Therap.* (1879) 140 Some of his sphygmographic tracings are markedly dicrotic.
b. Of or pertaining to a dicrotic pulse or tracing, as a ***dicrotic notch***, or ***wave***.
1869 *New Syd. Soc. Retrospect Med.* 149 The correspondence between the depth of the dicrotic notch and the severity of the pyrexia. **1878** FOSTER *Phys.* I. iv. §3. 137 The dicrotic wave occurring towards the end of the descent. **1883** *Syd. Soc. Lex.*, *Dicrotic wave*, a secondary wave which follows more or less quickly the primary wave of the pulse in sphygmographic tracings.

dicrotism (ˈdaɪkrətɪz(ə)m). [f. as prec. + -ISM.] The condition of being dicrotic.
1864 *New Syd. Soc. Year-bk.* 121 Duchek..contends that dicrotism of the pulse is in no way dependent on the heart or great vessels. **1867** J. MARSHALL *Phys.* II. 236 When the pulse is very accurately examined, a subsidiary wave occurs after the principal one, producing the phenomena named *dichrotism*. **1875** H. C. WOOD *Therap.* (1879) 139 Decided therapeutic doses of digitalis..produce great reduction and sometimes dicrotism of the pulse.

dicrotous (ˈdaɪkrətəs), *a.* [f. F. *dicrote*, Gr. δίκροτ-ος (see DICROTIC) + -OUS.] = DICROTIC.
1867 *New Syd. Soc. Retrospect Med.* 165 At the one extreme..lies the paralytic pulse, at the other the fully developed dicrotous pulse. **1877** ROBERTS *Handbk. Med.* (ed. 3) II. 21 The aortic wave prominent, the pulse is called dicrotous.

dict (dɪkt), *sb. Obs.* or *arch.* [ad. L. *dictum*, a saying, a word, f. *dīcĕre* to say: cf. also OF. *dict*, var. spelling of *dit*. (OE. had *diht* from same source.)] A saying or maxim.
1388 WYCLIF *Prol.* x. 34 Grostede declarith wel this in his dicte. **1460** CAPGRAVE *Chron.* 153 Robert Grostede..mad eke a noble book thei clepe his Dictes. **1477** EARL RIVERS (Caxton) *Dictes* 2 The saynges or dictis of the philosophers. **1483** CAXTON *Gold. Leg.* 112/1 He had in his dictes grete obscurete and profoundnes. *a* **1536** *Calisto & Mel.* in Hazl. *Dodsley* I. 53 According to their dicts rehearsed. **1860** READE *Cloister & H.* xxxvi, The old dict was true after all.

dict, *v. Obs.* or *arch.* [f. L. *dictāre* to DICTATE.] *trans.* To put into words; to dictate.
a **1626** BACON *Max. & Uses Com. Law* Pref. (1636) 4 The concordance between the lawes penn'd, and as it were dicted verbatim. **1642** R. BAILLIE *Lett.* 796, I have dicted already my primiel lesson..I hope to dict before June a little compend of the chief controversies. **1860** READE *Cloister & H.* lxii, Dict to me just what you would say to him.

dicta, pl. of DICTUM.

dictam, -amen, -amne, obs. ff. DITTANY.

dic'tamen. ? *Obs.* [a. late and med.L. *dictāmen*, pl. *dictāmina*, saying, precept, decree, f. *dictāre* to prescribe, dictate.] Dictate, pronouncement.
1626 C. MORE *Life Sir T. More* (1828) 131 The true dictamen of his conscience. **1638** CHILLINGW. *Relig. Prot.* I. Answ. Pref. §27 All Protestants according to the *Dictamen* of their Religion should doe so. **1652** URQUHART *Jewel* Wks. (1834) 276 He will regulate his conscience by the..true dictamen of reason. **1787** HAWKINS *Johnson* 67 All the world knows that the Essay of Man was composed from the dictamen of Lord Bolingbroke. **1826** *Blackw. Mag.* XX. 223 The business of the echo..to repeat the dictamina of his master.

†**dictament.** *Obs.* [ad. assumed L. *dictāment-um, f. *dictāre* to pronounce, DICTATE: see prec. and -MENT.] **a.** Diction. **b.** A dictate.
a **1572** KNOX *Hist. Ref.* Wks. (1846) I. 8 We translait according to the barbarousnes of thair Latine and dictament. **1644** DIGBY *Nat. Bodies* I. xviii. (1645) 198 Sense is not easily quieted with such Metaphysicall contemplations, that seem to repugne against her dictaments. **1652** tr. *Cassandra* II. 95 To follow the

Dictaments of an Inclination that already began to be powerfull.

dictamnus (dɪk'tæmnəs). [L. : see DITTANY. Adopted as a genus name by Linnæus in his *Hortus Cliffortianus* (1737) 161.] A perennial herb of the genus so called, belonging to the family Rutaceæ, esp. the cultivated species *D. albus* (= FRAXINELLA); or the sub-shrub *Origanum dictamnus* (= DITTANY 1).

1551 [see DITTANY 3]. **1603** HOLLAND tr. *Plutarch's Mor.* 569 To finde out the herbe Dictamnus, for to feed on it. **1728** R. BRADLEY *Dict. Bot.* s.v., The true Dictamnus is usually housed in Winter. **1846** J. LINDLEY *Vegetable Kingdom* 470 Dictamnus is found in the south of Europe. **1922** *Glasgow Herald* 5 Aug. 6 The dictamnus is easily raised from seeds. **1962** *Amateur Gardening* 31 Mar. 4/2 Dictamnus or 'dittany'..is absolutely reliable once established.

Dictaphone ('dɪktəfəʊn). Also **dictaphone**. [f. DICTA(TE *v.* + -PHONE.] The proprietary name of a machine which records and subsequently reproduces for transcription words spoken into it. Also *attrib.*

1907 *Trade Marks Jrnl.* 15 May 840 *Dictaphone.* Philosophical instruments, Scientific Instruments, and Apparatus for Useful Purposes. Instruments and Apparatus for Teaching. Columbia Phonograph Company General.. New York. **1907** *Daily Chron.* 3 July 3/5 The 'dictaphone', an adaptation of the phonograph. **1920** *Chambers's Jrnl.* 264/2 A familiar object in many business and editorial offices is the dictaphone, an instrument which records on wax cylinders letters or articles spoken into it. **1920** *Glasgow Herald* 22 May 5 Typing for half an hour an aggregate of 3991 words for dictaphone records. **1926** 'J. J. CONNINGTON' *Death at Swaythling Court* xvi, You know he's an expert on gramophones and dictaphones and all that kind of truck... He got a dictaphone record of a telephone message from Hubbard to his clerk. **1961** *Evening Standard* 14 July 20/2 Dictaphone Typist urgently required. **1967** *Times Rev. Industry* Mar. 41/1 One of Dictaphone's directors..doubts whether a 'generic' name has any specific advantage 'for people may call it a Dictaphone, but they will not necessarily come to us'.

dictate ('dɪkteɪt, -ət), *sb.* [ad. L. *dictāt-um* 'thing dictated', subst. use of neuter pa. pple. of *dictāre* to dictate (see next); in Lat. usually in pl. *dictāta* things dictated, lessons, rules, precepts, dictates.]

†**1.** That which is orally expressed or uttered in order to be written down; a dictated utterance.

1617 MINSHEU *Ductor in Ling.*, Dictates or lessons which the master enditeth for his schollers to write. **1621** BURTON *Anat. Mel.* Democr. to Rdr. (1651) 12 Six or seven Amanuenses to write out his dictats. **1691** tr. *Emilianne's Obs. Journ. Naples* 21 They are not made to Write, that is, to take Dictates. **1807** CRABBE *Library* 74 Skill and power to send, The heart's warm dictates to the distant friend. **1826** (*title*), Dictates, or Selections in Prose and Verse for dictating as exercises in Orthography.

†**b.** The action of dictating; DICTATION. *Obs.*

1642 JER. TAYLOR *Episcopacie* xxiii. 132 Many were actually there long after S. Pauls dictate of the Epistle. **1678** *Lively Orac.* ii. §41 Said to have wrote by dictat from him, as Mark did from Saint Peter.

†**2.** An authoritative utterance or pronouncement; a DICTUM. *Obs.*

1627–77 FELTHAM *Resolves* I. xxii. 41 It was the Philosophers dictate. **1651** C. CARTWRIGHT *Cert. Relig.* I. 164 According to the late Roman dictates. **1728** NEWTON *Chronol. Amended* 19 This gives a beginning to Oracles in Greece: and by their dictates the Worship of the Dead is every where introduced.

†**b.** A saying commonly received; a current saying, a maxim. *Obs.*

1650 HOBBES *De Corp. Pol.* 37 This Rule is very well known and expressed in this Old Dictate, *Quod tibi fieri non vis, alteri ne feceris.* **1682** SIR T. BROWNE *Chr. Mor.* III. §11 If, according to old dictates, no man can be said to be happy before death [etc.].

3. An authoritative direction delivered in words; an order given by one in authority.

1618 DONNE *Serm.* cxxxiii. V. 387 A faithful executing of his commission and speaking according to his Dictate. **1645** WITHER *Vox Pacif.* 3 By Gods immediate dictates, I indite. **1651** BAXTER *Inf. Bapt.* 42 Themselves give us but their Magisteriall Dictates. **1751** JOHNSON *Rambler* No. 95 ¶9, I could not receive such dictates without horror. **1876** MOZLEY *Univ. Serm.* i. 12 They speak at the dictate of a higher power, whose word is law.

b. Often applied to the authoritative words or monitions of a written law, of scripture or revelation, and to those attributed to or derived from inspiration, conscience, reason, nature, experience, self-interest, and other ruling or actuating principles.

1594 HOOKER *Eccl. Pol.* I. vii. (1597) 60 The lawes of well doing are the dictates of right reason. **1644** BULWER *Chiron.* 137 He might have followed the dictate of his owne Genius. **1656** BRAMHALL *Replic.* i. 56 Contrary to the dictate of his conscience. **1692** BENTLEY *Boyle Lect.* Serm. ix. 315 He should constantly adhere to the dictates of Reason and Nature. **1781** GIBBON *Decl. & F.* II. xliv. 659 Every man will obey the dictates of his interest. **1798** MALTHUS *Popul.* (1817) I. 19 Pursuing the dictate of nature in an early attachment to one woman. **1874** CARPENTER *Ment. Phys.* I. vi. §1 (1879) 238 He seems to have followed the dictates of his artistic feelings.

dictate (dɪk'teɪt, 'dɪkteɪt), *v.* [f. L. *dictāt-* ppl. stem of *dictāre* to say often, pronounce, prescribe, dictate, freq. of *dīcĕre* to say, tell.

The pronunciation *dic'tate* is now usual in England, though unrecognized by the dictionaries, with the exception of Cassell's *Encyclopædic*, 1884. The poets from G. Herbert to Byron and Shelley have only '*dictate*.]

1. *trans.* To put into words which are to be written down; to utter, pronounce, or read aloud *to* a person (something which he is to write).

1612 BRINSLEY *Lud. Lit.* 151 You are to dictate, or deliuer vnto them word by word, the English of the sentence. **1661** BRAMHALL *Just Vind.* vi. 130 A book..not penned, but dictated by such as know right well the most secret Cabales, and Intriques of the Conclave. *a***1783** MRS. WILLIAMS in *Boswell's Johnson* (1831) I. 240 He dictated them while Bathurst wrote. **1853** J. H. NEWMAN *Hist. Sk.* (1873) II. II. v. 262 He [Cicero] used to dictate his thoughts to his scribes. **1856** SIR B. BRODIE *Psychol. Inq.* I. iv. 126 During his last illness..he dictated an account of some scientific observations.

b. *absol.* (the object being left out) To practise or use dictation.

1592 DEE *Comp. Rehears.* (Chetham Soc.) 7, I did also dictate upon every proposition beside the first exposition. **1633** G. HERBERT *Temple, Posie* ii, Whether I sing, Or say, or dictate, this is my delight. **1667** MILTON *P.L.* IX. 23 My Celestial Patroness who..dictates to me slumbring. **1724** SWIFT *Drapier's Lett.* Wks. 1755 V. II. 91 My custom is..to dictate to a prentice, who can write in a feigned hand. **1871** B. TAYLOR *Faust* (1875) I. iv. 78 Yet in thy writing as unwearied be, As did the Holy Ghost dictate to thee.

2. *trans.* To prescribe (a course or object of action); to lay down authoritatively; to order, or command in express terms: **a.** of persons.

Not now used of prescribing medicine, as in quot. 1637.

1637 SHIRLEY *Gamester* III. i, Your learned physician dictates ambergrease. **1699** C. HOPKINS *Crt. Prosp.* i. 14 He meditates, and dictates Europe's Fate. **1725** WATTS *Logic* II. v. §6 God can dictate nothing but what is worthy of himself. **1752** JOHNSON *Rambler* No. 196 ¶6 He will..dictate axioms to posterity. **1781** GIBBON *Decl. & F.* II. xxxiv. 264 They dictated the conditions of peace. **1838** THIRLWALL *Greece* V. xliv. 355 Thus both were decreed..on the terms dictated by Philip. **1891** *Speaker* 2 May 532/2 The Socialist no longer thinks of dictating to society what it ought to be.

b. of things that have acknowledged authority, or that determine action.

1621 BURTON *Anat. Mel.* III. iv. I. ii. (1676) 394/1 Our own conscience doth dictate so much unto us. **1651** HOBBES *Leviath.* II. xxx. 185 The same Law, that dictateth to men.. what they ought to do. **1766** GOLDSM. *Vic. W.* xxxi, I find his present prosecution dictated by tyranny, cowardice, and revenge. **1781** COWPER *Truth* 513 Of all that Wisdom dictates, this the drift. **1791** BURKE *Corr.* (1844) III. 304 Wisdom and religion dictate that we should follow events. **1795** S. ROGERS *Words by Mrs. Siddons* 47 Her prudence dictates what her pride disdained. **1819** SHELLEY *Cenci* V. ii. 96 Which your suspicions dictate to this slave. **1878** HUXLEY *Physiogr.* Pref., It appeared to me to be plainly dictated by common sense.

3. *intr.* To use or practise dictation; to lay down the law, give orders.

1651 HOBBES *Govt. & Soc.* vii. §8. 125 We have seen how Subjects, nature dictating, have oblig'd themselves..to obey the Supreme Power. **1728** POPE *Dunc.* II. 377 To cavil, censure, dictate, right or wrong. **1755** YOUNG *Centaur* iii. Wks. 1757 IV. 176 Did this poor, pallid, scarce-animated mass dictate in the cabinet of pleasure? **1807–8** W. IRVING *Salmag.* (1824) 55 He is the oracle of the family, dictates to his sisters on every occasion. **1872** GEO. ELIOT *Middlem.* ix, A woman dictates before marriage in order that she may have an appetite for submission afterwards.

†**4.** *trans.* To express, indicate. *Obs. rare.*

1638 SIR T. HERBERT *Trav.* (ed. 2) 95 A letter..dictating nothing save hypocrisie and submission. *Ibid.* 182 Left them with a frowne, dictating their base carriage and my impatience.

Hence **dic'tated, dic'tating,** *ppl. adjs.*

1611 COTGR., *Dicté*, dictated, indicted. **1709** STEELE & SWIFT *Tatler* No. 71 ¶9 You rival your Correspondent Lewis le Grand, and his dictating Academy. **1830** *Westm. Rev.* XII. 3 Under the controlling and dictating power of truth and nature. **1874** TYRWHITT *Sketching Club* 47, I have worked very hard, and by strict dictated method.

dictating, *vbl. sb.* [f. DICTATE *v.* + -ING[1].]

a. The action of the verb (esp. in sense 1).

1631 *Star Chamber Cases* (Camden) 5 Sr Arthur denyed the dictating of the letter. **1815** SCOTT *Guy M.* xxxix, He'll write to my dictating three nights in the week without sleep.

b. Special Comb. **dictating machine**, a machine on which dictated matter is recorded for subsequent audio playback and typing; cf. DICTAPHONE; formerly, a telephone apparatus by which letters could be dictated directly to a secretary elsewhere in an organization (see DICTOGRAPH).

1907 *Sci. Amer. Suppl.* 11 May 26208/1 Messrs. Kelley M. Turner and William F. H. Germer..have been granted a United States patent (No. 843,186) on a telephone *dictating machine which they term a 'dictograph'. **1957** *Economist* 19 Oct. 205/1 (Advt.), Most people like Stenorette Dictating Machines... A Stenorette takes an average day's dictation on one spool of magnetic tape that can be used over and over again indefinitely. **1980** *Brit. Med. Jrnl.* 29 Mar. (Advt. between pp. 924 & 925), Sony dictating-machines are made by people who make hi-fi systems as well.

dictation (dɪk'teɪʃən). [ad. late L. *dictātiōn-em*, n. of action from *dictāre* to DICTATE.] The action of dictating.

1. a. The pronouncing of words in order to their being written down.

1727 BAILEY vol. II, *Dictation*, a pronouncing or dictating of any Thing to another Man to be written by him. **1784** JOHNSON Dec. in *Boswell*, Dictation..would be performed as speedily as an amanuensis could write. **1842** H. ROGERS *Introd. Burke's Wks.* (1842) I. 8 Sketches, either actually written by himself or at his dictation. **1868** FREEMAN *Norm. Conq.* (1876) II. viii. 272 Some evident slip of dictation or copying. **1875** JOWETT *Plato* (ed. 2) I. 12, I will write out the charm from your dictation.

attrib. **1870** DICKENS *E. Drood* iv, My style became traceable in the dictation-exercises of Miss Brobity's pupils. **1894** *Westm. Gaz.* 23 Feb. 6/3 A dictation cylinder will contain from 1,000 to 1,200 words.

b. [Cf. Fr. *dictée*.] The school exercise of transcribing a dictated passage, esp. one in a foreign language; an instance of such transcription.

1789 E. WYNNE in *Wynne Diaries* 18 Aug. (1935) I. 1 Mademoiselle Eberts gave us our dictation as Mons. Fries is away. **1854** E. RUSKIN *Let.* 4 Feb. in M. Lutyens *Millais & Ruskins* (1967) 133, I hear Sophie practise an hour, then her spelling, Dictation, arithmetic. **1892** *School Inspector's Rep.* in S. E. Ellacott *Everyday Things in England 1914–68* vi. 86 Dictation in the second and fourth Standards needs attention. **1969** N. FREELING *Tsing-Boum* xix. 138 Four large horrible faults in your dictation... Write it out again.

2. a. Authoritative utterance or prescription.

*a***1656** BP. HALL *Rem.* 148 (T.) Heresies..maintained to the death under the pretence of the dictation and warrant of God's spirit! *a***1805** PALEY (Webster, 1828), It affords security against the dictation of laws. **1844** DISRAELI *Coningsby* II. i, The terms were at his own dictation.

b. Arbitrary command; the exercise of dictatorship.

1856 FROUDE *Hist. Eng.* I. 188 It would have probably been unsafe for the crown to attempt dictation or repression. **1858** *Ibid.* III. xiii. 88 The proud English nobles had now for the first time to..submit to the dictation of a lay peer. **1861** MAY *Const. Hist.* (1863) II. x. 220 No sooner has the dictation of any journal..become too pronounced, than [etc.].

3. Something dictated.

1841 MYERS *Cath. Th.* III. §32. 116 Had they been the very dictations of the Almighty.

4. *attrib.*, as **dictation speed**, the speed of speech (as) of a person dictating.

1957 H. NICOLSON *Let.* 21 Feb. (1968) III. 332 'Has your husband joined you,' asked Vita at dictation-speed, 'or is he still in Formosa?' **1971** M. RUSSELL *Deadline* v. 51 Larkin recounted the incident at dictation speed.

dic'tational, *a. rare.* [f. prec. + -AL[1].] Of or belonging to dictation.

1885 G. W. CABLE in *Century Mag.* XXIX. 409 The popular mind..has retreated from its uncomfortable dictational attitude.

dictative (dɪk'teɪtɪv, 'dɪktətɪv), *a.* [f. DICTATE *v.* + -IVE.] Of the nature of dictation; characterized by dictating or saying what must be done.

1768–74 TUCKER *Lt. Nat.* (1852) II. 684 Not striving to force attention with a dictative authority. **1823** J. F. COOPER *Pioneer* xxiii, Such other dictative mandates as were necessary.

dictator (dɪk'teɪtə(r)). [a. L. *dictātor*, agent-n. from *dictāre* to DICTATE. Cf. F. *dictateur*.]

1. A ruler or governor whose word is law; an absolute ruler of a state. **a.** *orig.* The appellation of a chief magistrate invested with absolute authority, elected in seasons of emergency by the Romans, and by other Italian states.

1387 TREVISA *Higden* (Rolls) II. 273 After consuls, tribunes plebis and dictatores rulede the comounte. **1470–85** MALORY *Arthur* v. i, The Emperour Lucyus whiche was called at that tyme Dictatour or procurour of the publyke wele of Rome. **1592** GREENE *Upst. Courtier*, Was he not called to be dictator from the plough? **1607** SHAKS. *Cor.* II. ii. 93 Our then Dictator..saw him fight. **1621** BURTON *Anat. Mel.* I. ii. III. iv, As in old Rome, when the Dictator was created, all inferiour magistracies ceased. **1735–8** BOLINGBROKE *On Parties* 164 A Dictator was a Tyrant for six Months. **1874** MORLEY *Compromise* (1886) 11 Our people.. have long ago superseded the barbarous device of dictator and Cæsar by the manly arts of self-government.

b. A person exercising similar authority in a mediæval or modern state; *esp.* one who attains to such a position in a republic. Also *transf.*

*c***1592** MARLOWE *Massacre Paris* II. vi, Guise, wear our crown..And, as dictator, make or war or peace. **1671** MILTON *P.R.* I. 113 To him their great Dictator, whose attempt At first against mankind so well had thriv'd. **1840** *Penny Cycl.* XVII. 227 After some changes in the government, Doctor Gaspar Rodriguez de Francia became dictator [of Paraguay]. **1863** KINGLAKE *Crimea* (1876) I. xiv. 235 Numbers in France..would have been heartily glad to see the Republic crushed by some able dictator.

2. A person exercising absolute authority of any kind or in any sphere; one who authoritatively prescribes a course of action or dictates what is to be done.

1605 BACON *Adv. Learn.* I. iv. §12 The overmuch credit that hath been given unto authors in sciences, in making them dictators. **1625** B. JONSON *Staple of N.* III. ii, Say that you were the emperor of pleasures, The great dictator of fashions, for all Europe. *a***1654** SELDEN *Table-t.* (Arb.) 4 He ..was usually stiled the great dictator of learning of the

English nation. **1700** TYRRELL *Hist. Eng.* II. 893 Arbitrators, who are sometimes called *Assessors*, sometimes *Dictators* of *Amends*. **1720** SWIFT *Mod. Educ.* Wks. 1755 II. II. 34 The dictators of behaviour, dress, and politeness. **1875** STUBBS *Const. Hist.* III. xxi. 525 The medieval church of England stood before the self-willed dictator [Henry VIII]. **1892** F. LAWLEY *Pref. to Racing Life Ld. G. C. Bentinck* 7, I inquired who was now the Dictator of the Turf.

3. One who dictates to a writer.

1617 MINSHEU, *Ductor in Ling.*, A Dictator, or inditer. **1721** BAILEY, *Dictator*, he that tells another what to write. **1873** J. RAINE *Lett. fr. N. Registers* Pref. 18 Marks of interest which delineate to a certain extent both the dictator and his amanuensis. **1883** *Athenæum* 16 June 759/1 Reminiscences ..dictated to a scribe and checked here and there by reference to documents in the dictator's possession.

4. *attrib.*

1825 J. WILSON *Noct. Ambr.* Wks. 1855 I. 22 Certainly these are not dictator times.

dic'tatorate. [f. DICTATOR + -ATE[1].] The office of a dictator.

1866 CARLYLE *Inaug. Addr.* 179 Oliver Cromwell's Protectorate, or Dictatorate if you will let me name it so. **1868** GOLDW. SMITH in *Macm. Mag.* Apr. 531/1 Cicero accepted and..served under the dictatorate of Cæsar.

dictatorial (dɪktə'tɔərɪəl), *a.* [f. L. *dictātōri-us*, of or belonging to a dictator + -AL[1]. So mod.F. *dictatorial* (adm. by Academy 1835).]

1. Of, pertaining, or proper to a dictator.

1701 W. WOTTON *Hist. Rome* vii. 118 The whole Dictatorial Power within the City. **1741** MIDDLETON *Cicero* II. VII. 119 He [Cæsar] was created Dictator..and by his Dictatorial power declared himself Consul. **1795** *Ann. Reg.* Pref., The late metamorphosis of the [French] Republic into a dictatorial or military government. **1818** BYRON *Ch. Har.* IV. lxxxiv, Thou didst lay down With an atoning smile.. The dictatorial wreath. **1849** MACAULAY *Hist. Eng.* I. 542 A captain who has been entrusted with dictatorial power.

2. Pertaining to or characteristic of dictation; inclined to dictate or prescribe the actions of others; imperious; overbearing in tone.

a **1704** T. BROWN *Sat. Persius* Wks. 1730 I. 53 A dictatorial youth does envy draw. **1724** SWIFT *Drapier's Lett.* Wks. 1841 II. 26 By violent measures, and a dictatorial behaviour. **1748** RICHARDSON *Clarissa* (1811) VI. 107 Sally was laying out the law, and prating away in her usual dictatorial manner. **1818** MISS MITFORD in L'Estrange *Life* (1870) II. 36 He is..very learned, very dictatorial, very knock-me-down. **1873** BLACK *Pr. Thule* xxiv. 389 The dictatorial enunciation of his opinions.

dicta'torialism. [f. prec. + -ISM.] A dictatorial practice, mode of action, or system.

1863 MISS BRADDON *Eleanor's Vict.* I. v. 99 Under the sheltering dictatorialism of a paternal government. **1863** MRS. C. CLARKE *Shaks. Char.* ii. 60 The ostentatious moralising and sententious dictatorialism of Jaques.

dicta'torially, *adv.* [f. as prec. + -LY[2].] In a dictatorial manner; imperiously; with the tone or manner of authority.

a **1797** H. WALPOLE *Mem. Geo. II* (1847) II. viii. 277 Lord Hardwicke still took the lead very dictatorially. **1832** *Examiner* 538/1 Why should the state dictatorially step in and forbid the transaction? **1880** MRS. FORRESTER *Roy. & V.* I. 13 'You will come to-morrow', repeats Netta dictatorially.

dicta'torialness. [f. as prec. + -NESS.] Dictatorial quality or manner; imperiousness.

1876 GEO. ELIOT *Let.* 29 Oct. in Cross *Life* III. 294 A spirit of arrogance and contemptuous dictatorialness is observable. **1880** MRS. FETHERSTONHAUGH *A. Dering* I. i. 18 'You never spoke to any one else!'..adds Mary, with sisterly dictatorialness. **1888** *Times* 25 Dec. 3/2 The Cabinet crisis in Bulgaria has been brought about through the dictatorialness of M. Stambouloff.

†**dicta'torian,** *a. Obs.* [f. L. *dictātōri-us* of or belonging to a dictator + -AN.] Of, proper to, or characteristic of, a dictator.

c **1642** *Contra-Replicant's Compl.* 19 A kind of a dictatorian power is to be allowed to her. **1659** J. HARRINGTON *Lawgiving* II. iii. (1700) 415 Samuel, distinguishing to perfection between Dictatorian and Royal Power. **1709** L. MILBOURNE *Melius Inq.* 6 Took all the power into his own hand, govern'd in the dictatorian way. **1711** DENNIS *Reflect. on 'Ess. Criticism'* 2 While this little Author struts and affects the Dictatorian Air.

dictatorily ('dɪktətərɪlɪ), *adv.* [f. DICTATORY *a.* + -LY[2].] = DICTATORIALLY.

1788 BURNS *Let. to Clarinda* Sunday Noon (Globe) c. 383 They must also be so very dictatorily wise. **1867** *Hare's Guesses* 226 An academy will lay down laws dictatorily. **1890** J. C. JEFFERY *J. Vraille* II. viii. 203 Ordering his 'daddee' about so dictatorily.

†**dic'tatoring,** *vbl. sb. Obs. rare.* [f. DICTATOR + -ING[1]: cf. *tailoring, soldiering*.] Acting as dictator.

1644 J. GOODWIN *Danger Fighting agst. God* 48 Diametrally bent against all dictatoring, and law-giving by men.

dic'tator-like, *a.* and *adv.*

A. *adj.* Like or befitting a dictator.

1641 R. BROOKE *Eng. Episc.* 34 If they only took a Dictatorlike power. **1644** J. GOODWIN *Danger Fighting agst. God* 47 Any ambitious or Dictator-like designe. **1680** HICKERINGILL *Wks.* (1716) I. 261 A Style and Language more Magisterical, Dictator-like.

B. *adv.* Like or after the manner of a dictator.

1581 MULCASTER *Positions* xlv. (1887) 293, I do not herein take vpon me dictatorlike to pronounce peremptorily. **1646** SIR T. BROWNE *Pseud. Ep.* To Rdr. A vj a, Nor have wee Dictator-like obtruded our conceptions.

dictatorship (dɪk'teɪtəʃɪp). [See -SHIP.]

1. The office or dignity of a dictator.

1586 T. B. *La Primaud. Fr. Acad.* 176 Bicause he would not have the dictatorship, and the other the consulship. **1636** E. DACRES tr. *Machiavel's Disc. Livy* I. 129 If any one were made Dictatour, he got most honour by it, that layd downe his Dictatourship soonest. **1665** MANLEY *Grotius' Low C. Warres* 167 They advised him [Leicester] also to a too hasty..hope of the Dictatorship, after the Example of the Prince of Aurange. **1796** H. HUNTER tr. *St. Pierre's Stud. Nat.* (1799) I. 331 Attilius-Regulus, who was called from the plough to the Dictatorship. **1835** ALISON *Hist. Europe* III. xv. §59. 323 A dictatorship is the last step in the despair of nations. **1838** ARNOLD *Hist. Rome* I. 446 A dictatorship is the most natural government for seasons of extraordinary peril, when there appears a man fit to wield it.

2. Absolute authority in any sphere.

16.. DRYDEN (J.), This is that perpetual dictatorship which is exercised by Lucretius, though often in the wrong. **1741** WATTS *Improv. Mind* I. v. §9 Where an author.. assumes an air of sovereignty and dictatorship. **1869** *Daily News* 22 Dec., The whole movement was an attempt to set up an illegal dictatorship in the Church. **1892** LOUNDSBURY *Stud. Chaucer* III. vii. 100 His [Dryden's] literary dictatorship..remained unshaken.

attrib. **1839** *Times* 4 July, The House..rejected the first, or dictatorship clause of the bill.

†**dic'tatory,** *sb. Obs. rare.* In 6 -oury. [a. OF. *dictatorie, -urie* (Bersuire's transl. of Livy, 14th c. in Godef.), f. L. *dictātor*.] Dictatorship.

1533 BELLENDEN *Livy* II. (1822) 151 The Faderis..thocht expedient to gif the empire and dictatoury to ane man of mair soft ingine.

dictatory ('dɪktətərɪ), *a.* [ad. L. *dictātōri-us*, f. *dictātōr-em* DICTATOR. Cf. OF. *dictatoire*, Sp. *dictatorio*.] = DICTATORIAL.

1644 MILTON *Areop.* (Arb.) 40 Our English..will not easily finde servile letters anow to spell such a dictatorie presumption. **1823** *New Monthly Mag.* IX. 52/2 The three dictatory nations, to whom Europe must bow. **1863** M. LEMON *Wait for End* xviii. (1866) 223 A solemn dictatory letter. **1872** DE MORGAN *Budget of Paradoxes* 378 When he obtrudes his office in a dictatory manner.

dictatress (dɪk'teɪtrɪs). [f. DICTATOR + -ESS. Cf. next.] A female dictator. *lit.* and *fig.*

1784 R. BAGE *Barham Downs* II. 1 Vanity was the universal dictatress. **1809** BYRON *Bards & Rev.* li, Earth's chief dictatress, ocean's lovely queen. **1827** SCOTT *Napoleon* lxxvi, Paris..the dictatress..of taste..to..Europe. **1874** HELPS *Ivan De Biron* v. vi. 290 She was a dictatress in all matters that related to the dress, scenery, and general arrangements.

dictatrix (dɪk'teɪtrɪks). [a. L. *dictātrix*, fem. of *dictātor*: see -TRIX. In F. *dictatrice*.] A female dictator: = prec.

1623 COCKERAM, *Dictatrix*, a woman commanding things to be don. **1647** JER. TAYLOR *Lib. Proph.* Ep. Ded. 42 The Church of Rome which is the great dictatrix of dogmaticall resolutions. **1789** BENTHAM *Wks.* (1838-43) X. 206 A Dictatrix on the seas. **1848** LYTTON *Caxtons* I. II. ix, Mrs. Primmins..housekeeper, and tyrannical dictatrix of the whole establishment.

dictature (dɪk'teɪtjʊə(r)). [ad. L. *dictātūra* the office of a DICTATOR: see -URE. Cf. F. *dictature* (15th c. in Godef. *Suppl.*).]

1. = DICTATORSHIP.

1553 GRIMALDE *Cicero's Offices* II. (1558) 84 The other who in the dictature had been secretarie. **1605** BACON *Adv. Learn.* I. vii. §29. 40 What strange resolution it was in Lucius Scylla, to resign his Dictature. **1640** G. WATTS tr. *Bacon's Adv. Learn.* Pref. 10 Autors, who have usurp't a kind of Dictature in Sciences. *c* **1810** L. HUNT *Blue-Stocking Revels* II. 152, I can't see..why love should await dear good Harriet's dictature! **1867** *Contemp. Rev.* VI. 413 A temporal dictature took the place of the former..combination of the spiritual and temporal powers. **1875** BROWNING *Aristoph. Apol.* 101 Choosing the rule of few, but wise and good, Rather than mob-dictature.

2. A collective body of dictators.

1759 *State Papers* in *Ann. Reg.* 203/2 An imperial decree of commission was carried to the dictature against that resolution. **1855** M. BRIDGES *Pop. Mod. Hist.* 435 Nine individuals were chosen out of it to form a Dictature.

†'**dictery.** *Obs. rare*[−1]. [ad. L. *dictērium* a witty saying, bon-mot, in sense associated with L. *dictum*, but in form like Gr. δεικτήριον a place for showing, a pulpit.] A witty saying.

1632 BURTON *Anat. Mel.* III. ii. v. v. 589 In a publike auditory..I did heap up all the dicteries I could against women, but now recant.

dictical, var. form of DEICTICAL, *Obs.*

diction ('dɪkʃən). [a. F. *diction* (12th c. in Hatz.-Darm.), or ad. L. *dictiōn-em* saying, diction, mode of expression; in late L., a word; n. of action from *dīcĕre* to say.

Apparently not in English Dictionaries before Johnson.]

†1. A word. *Obs.*

1542 UDALL *Erasm. Apophth.* I. (1877) 136 Two sondrie wordes, albeit by reason of the figure called *Synalephe*, it seemeth in maner no more but one diction. **1549** *Compl. Scot.* Prol. 17 The quhilkis culd nocht be translatit in oure Scottis langage, as..pretours, tribuns, and mony vthir romane dictions. **1652** GAULE *Magastrom.* Liva, Dictions, syllables, letters, numbers. **1697** tr. *Burgersdicius his Logick* I. xxv. 99 In Dictions are first to be consider'd their Etymology and Conjugation, and then their Synonymy and Homonymy, and Acception Words.

†2. A phrase, locution, mode of speech. *Obs.*

a **1660** HAMMOND *Wks.* I. 425 (R.) We are not wont to require the dictions of the New Testament..to be tryed by Attical heathen Greek writers. **1709** STEELE *Tatler* No. 62 ¶7 An easy Flow of Words, without being distracted (as we often are who read much) in the choice of Dictions and Phrases.

†3. Expression of ideas in words; speech; verbal description. *Obs.*

(In Shakspere in an intentionally Euphuistic passage.)

1581 SIDNEY *Apol. Poetrie* (Arb.) 68 Now, for the out-side of it..which is words, or..Diction. **1602** SHAKS. *Ham.* v. ii. 123 To make true diction of him, his semblable is his mirror.

4. The manner in which anything is expressed in words; choice or selection of words and phrases; wording; verbal style: a. of writings.

1700 DRYDEN *Fables* Pref. (Globe) 496 The first beauty of an Epick poem consists in diction, that is, in the choice of words and harmony of numbers. **1709** POPE *Let. to Cromwell* 7 May, It would be very kind in you to observe any deficiencies in the diction or numbers [of my translation]. **1791** BOSWELL *Johnson* (1816) I. 201 Sir Thomas Brown.. was remarkably fond of Anglo-Latin diction. **1827-48** HARE *Guesses* Ser. II. (1873) 368 Almost all fancy the diction makes the poet. **1868** STANLEY *Westm. Abb.* iii. 195 A grace and accuracy of diction worthy of the scholarship for which the exiled chief..was renowned. **1880** L. STEPHEN *Pope* iii. 69 It is, I think, impossible to maintain that the diction of poetry should be simply that of common life.

b. of speech or oratory.

1748 J. MASON *Elocut.* 5 Elocution: By which they always meant, what we call, Diction; which consists in suiting our Words to our Ideas, and the Stile to the Subject. **1750** JOHNSON *Rambler* No. 27 ¶8 The celebrated orator renowned equally for the..elegance of his diction, and the acuteness of his wit. **1855** MACAULAY *Hist. Eng.* III. 134 Tyrconnel..with his usual energy of diction, invoked on himself all the vengeance of heaven if the report was not a cursed, a blasted, a confounded lie. **1886** RUSKIN *Præterita* I. vii. 208 My mother..resolved that I should learn absolute accuracy of diction and precision of accent in prose.

dictio'narial, *a. rare.* [f. med.L. *dictiōnāri-um* DICTIONARY + -AL[1] I. 3.] Of, pertaining to, or characteristic of a dictionary; lexicographical.

1750 BEAWES *Lex Mercat.* (1752) p. viii, As every subject is placed by itself the chain of reading is not broke through, as it is in the dictionarial and some other methods.

†**dictio'narian.** *Obs. rare.* [f. as prec. + -AN.] The maker of a dictionary; a lexicographer.

1846 WORCESTER cites DR. DAWSON.

†**dictionarist.** *Obs. rare.* [f. next + -IST.] The maker of a dictionary.

1617 COLLINS *Def. Bp. Ely* II. vi. 238 One of the Dictionarists aforenamed [viz. Budæus, Crispinus] quotes the place.

dictionary ('dɪkʃənərɪ). [ad. med.L. *dictiōnārium* or *dictiōnārius* (sc. *liber*) lit. 'a repertory of *dictiōnēs*, phrases or words' (see DICTION) in F. *dictionnaire* (R. Estienne 1539), It. *dizionario*, Sp. *diccionario*.]

1. a. A book dealing with the individual words of a language (or certain specified classes of them), so as to set forth their orthography, pronunciation, signification, and use, their synonyms, derivation, and history, or at least some of these facts: for convenience of reference, the words are arranged in some stated order, now, in most languages, alphabetical; and in larger dictionaries the information given is illustrated by quotations from literature; a word-book, vocabulary, or lexicon.

Dictionaries proper are of two kinds: those in which the meanings of the words of one language or dialect are given in another (or, in a polyglot dictionary, in two or more languages), and those in which the words of a language are treated and illustrated in this language itself. The former were the earlier.

Dictionarius was used *c* 1225 by Joannes de Garlandia, a native of England, as the title of a collection of Latin vocables, arranged according to their subjects, in sentences, for the use of learners; e.g.

'In horto magistri Johannis sunt herbe scilicet iste: salvia, petroselinum, dictamnus, ysopus, celidonia, feniculus, piret[r]um, columbina, rosa, lilium, et viola; et a latere crescit urtica, carduus, et saliunca.'

In the following century Peter Berchorius (died Paris, 1362) wrote a *Dictionarium morale utriusque Testamenti*, consisting of moralizations on the chief words of the Vulgate for the use of students in theology. In 1538 Sir Thomas Elyot published his Latin-English 'Dictionary'; and in 1556 J. Withals published 'A shorte dictionarie for yonge beginners' in English and Latin, in which the words were arranged not alphabetically, but under subject-headings, e.g. 'the names of Byrdes, Byrdes of the Water, Byrdes about the house, as cockes, hennes, etc., of Bees, Flies, and others,' etc. In 1539 R. Estienne published his *Dictionaire Francois-latin*. Dictionaries (so entitled) of English and various modern languages appeared in England from 1547 onward; in the 17th c. the name was gradually extended to works explaining English words, only 'hard words' being admitted into the earliest English Dictionaries.

Vocabulary is now generally limited to a smaller and less comprehensive collection of words, or to a word-book of technical, or specific terms. *Lexicon* is the name usually given to dictionaries of Greek, Hebrew, Arabic, Syriac, Ethiopic, and some other literary languages.

1526 *Pilgr. Perf.* (W. de W. 1531) 233 And so Peter Bercharius in his dictionary describeth it. **1538** (*title*), The Dictionary of syr Thomas Eliot knyght. —— *Preface* A ij *bk.*,

About a yere passed I beganne a Dictionarie, declaryng latine by englishe. **1547** SALESBURY (*title*), A Dictionarie in Englyshe and Welshe, moche necessary to all such Welshemen as will spedly lerne the Englyshe tongue. **1556** WITHALS *Shorte Dictionarie* (1568) *Colophon*: ¶ Thus endeth this Dictionarie, very necessary for children: compiled by J. Withals. *a* **1568** ASCHAM *Scholem.* (Arb.) 27 As the Grammer booke be euer in the Scholers hand, and also vsed of him, as a Dictionarie, for euerie present vse. **1580** J. BARET (*title*), An Alvearie or Quadruple Dictionarie, containing foure sundrie tongues: namelie English, Latine, Greeke, and French. **1588** *Marprel. Epist.* (Arb.) 42 His Lordship of Winchester is a great Clarke, for he hath translated his Dictionarie, called Co[o]pers Dictionarie verbatim out of Robert Stephanus his Thesaurus, and ilfauored to, they say. **1598** FLORIO (*title*), A Worlde of Wordes, or most copious, and exact Dictionarie in Italian and English, collected by Iohn Florio. *c* **1616** WEBSTER *Duchess of Malfi* v. ii, A.. disease.. they call lycanthropia. *Pes.* What's that? I need a dictionary to't. **1623** H. COCKERAM (*title*), The English Dictionarie: or an Interpreter of hard English Words. **1656** T. BLOUNT (*title*), Glossographia or a Dictionary Interpreting all such Hard Words.. as are now used in our refined English Tongue. **1665** BOYLE *Occas. Refl.* v. vii. (1845) 322 A man must have ..learn'd an Hebrew Grammar, and turn'd over Buxtorf's, Schindler's, and other Dictionaries. **1721** N. BAILEY (*title*), An Universal Etymological English Dictionary. **1752** FIELDING *Amelia* Wks. 1775 X. 129 All the major's words are not to be found in a dictionary. **1755** JOHNSON *Dictionary* Preface ¶3, I have, notwithstanding this discouragement, attempted a dictionary of the English language, which, while it was employed in the cultivation of every species of literature, has itself been hitherto neglected. **1849** *Lond. Jrnl.* 12 May 149 Morrison mentions a dictionary in the Chinese language of 40,000 hieroglyphical characters, as having been compiled 1100 years before Christ. **1857** TRENCH *On some Deficiencies in our English Dictionaries* 4 A Dictionary, according to that idea of it which seems to be alone capable of being logically maintained, is an inventory of the language. **1870** EMERSON *Soc. & Solit., Books* Wks. (Bohn) III. 87 Neither is a dictionary a bad book to read.. it is full of suggestion,—the raw material of possible poems and histories. **1878** R. W. DALE *Lect. Preach.* vi. 181 A dictionary is not merely a home for living words; it is a hospital for the sick; it is a cemetery for the dead.

†**b.** *fig.* The vocabulary or whole list of words used or admitted by any one. *Obs.*

1579 FULKE *Heskins' Parl.* 58 If I may vse that tearme vnder correction of M. Heskins dictionarie. **1646** SIR T. BROWNE *Pseud. Ep.* I. x. 41 Not only in the dictionary of man, but the subtiler vocabulary of Satan. **1727** SWIFT *Gulliver* III. ii. Wks. 1883 XI. 197, I much enlarged my dictionary; and when I went next to court, was able to understand many things the king spoke.

c. Colloq. phr. ***to have swallowed the*** (or ***a***) ***dictionary***: to use long or recondite words.

1934 'G. ORWELL' *Burmese Days* ii. 29 Have you swallowed a dictionary?.. We shall have to sack this fellow if he gets to talk English too well. **1966** M. TORRIE *Heavy as Lead* x. 124 'The whole point is that my Society deprecates, as much as you do...' The voices began again, 'Aw, cut it out!' 'Put a sock in it!' ''Ev've swallered the dictionary!'

d. An ordered list stored in and used by a computer; *spec.* (*a*) a list of contents, e.g. of a database; (*b*) a list of words acceptable to a word-processing program, against which each word of text is checked.

1957 *IBM Jrnl. Res. & Devel.* I. 150/1 The dictionary for language translation by a computer.. and many other problems which are essentially table look-up require a system like those described. **1964** *AFIPS Conf. Proc.* XXVI. 353/1 A separate dictionary is maintained for each disk area. Each dictionary entry contains the following information for each subroutine within that area: 1. subroutine name. 2. disk address of the subroutine. 3. length of the subroutine. 4. date the subroutine was filed. **1969** P. B. JORDAIN *Condensed Computer Encycl.* 286 A load module usually contains three principal subdivisions: an external symbol dictionary (ESD), a text section (TXT), and a relocation dictionary (RLD)... The ESD contains the names and locations within the module of all entry points. **1975** J. MARTIN *Computer Data-Base Organiz.* xxxiii. 481 Each entry in the dictionary points to an occurrence list giving every occurrence in the document file of the word in question. **1975** *Nature* 16 Oct. 556/2 The present practice is for computers to store an 'exception' dictionary, the routine being to search the dictionary for the word and use the recorded hyphenation break if it is there, or otherwise to hyphenate by logic. **1980** *New Scientist* 3 July 31/3 The Displaywriter has a dictionary of 50 000 common words and space for another 500 which can be added by the typist. **1984** J. HILTON *Choosing & using your Home Computer* 115/2 Some sophisticated word processing programs can perform useful extra functions. The automatic dictionary, or spelling checker, is among the most popular inclusions.

2. a. By extension: A book of information or reference on any subject or branch of knowledge, the items of which are arranged in alphabetical order; an alphabetical encyclopædia: as a Dictionary of *Architecture*, *Biography*, *Geography*, of *the Bible*, of *Christian Antiquities*, of *Dates*, etc.

(Here the essential sense 'word-book' is supplanted by the accidental one of 'reference book in alphabetical order' arising out of the alphabetical arrangement used in modern word-books.)

1631 MASSINGER *Emp. East* I. ii, I have composed a dictionary, in which He is instructed how, when, and to whom, To be proud or humble. **1712** ADDISON *Spect.* No. 499 ¶2 The story.. which I have since found related in my historical dictionary. **1871** MORLEY *Voltaire* (1886) 299 Minutiæ ought to be collected by annalists, or in some kind of dictionaries where one might find them at need.

b. *fig.* A person or thing regarded as a repository of knowledge, convenient for consultation.

1774 GOLDSM. *Nat. Hist.* (1776) I. Pref. 7 A system may be considered as a dictionary in the study of nature. **1837** EMERSON *Addr., Amer. Schol.* Wks. (Bohn) II. 181 Life is our dictionary. **1849** MACAULAY *Hist. Eng.* II. 180 Burnet was eminently qualified to be of use as a living dictionary of British affairs. **1893** SELOUS *Trav. S.E. Africa* 359 Mr. Edwards is a perfect walking dictionary concerning all matters connected with sport and travel in the interior of South Africa.

3. *attrib.* and *Comb.*, as ***dictionary English***, ***meaning***, ***order***, ***phraseology***, ***word***, ***work***; ***dictionary-maker***, ***-making***, ***-writer***, ***-writing***; ***dictionary-tutored*** adj.; **dictionary-monger**, one who deals much with dictionaries; **dictionary-proof** *a.*, proof against the informing influence of a dictionary.

1632 J. HAYWARD tr. *Biondi's Eromena* A iv, I would not.. be taken (or rather mistaken) for a Dictionary-tutred Linguist. **1668** WILKINS *Real Char.* Ded. A iij, This Work of Dictionary-making, for the polishing of their Language. **1727** SWIFT *Gulliver* IV. xii. Wks. 1883 XI. 355 Writers of travels, like dictionary-makers, are sunk into oblivion by the weight and bulk of those who come last, and therefore lie uppermost. **1742** ARBUTHNOT & POPE, etc., *Note* on *Dunciad* IV. 231 The first [Suidas] a dictionary-writer, a collector of impertinent facts and barbarous words. **1759** GOLDSM. *Polite Learn.* ii, Dictionary writing was at that time much in fashion. **1794** W. B. STEVENS *Jrnl.* 19 Nov. (1965) 206 He seems to be quandaryed (that's not a dictionary word I believe). **1806** *Oracle* in *Spirit Pub. Jrnls.* (1807) X. 43 The dictionary-monger in the *Blind Bargain.* **1818** MISS MITFORD in L'Estrange *Life* (1870) II. 27 After the fashion of certain dictionary-mongers who ring the changes upon two words. **1819** *Sporting Mag.* V. 122 Grose.. was even dictionary-proof. **1830** GALT *Lawrie T.* VII. iii. (1849) 318 Miss Beeny was an endless woman with her dictionary phraseology. **1831** CARLYLE *Sart. Res.* I. iv, He.. calls many things by their mere dictionary names. **1837** MILL in *Westm. Rev.* XXVII. 19 A few phrases,.. by adding up the dictionary meanings of which, we may hunt out a few qualities. **1854** W. C. ROSCOE in *Prospective Rev.* X. 398 [Shakespeare] leaves his meaning to rest in great measure on the atmosphere that hangs about his language, rather than on its dictionary meaning and grammatical construction. **1858** R. S. SURTEES *Ask Mamma* i. 1 His fine dictionary words and laboured expletives. **1880** GRANT WHITE *Every-Day Eng.* 100 Trying to speak dictionary English. **1882** FREEMAN in *Longm. Mag.* I. 97 Did anybody, even a dictionary-maker, really fancy that the last three letters of 'neighbour' had anything in common with the last three letters of 'honour'? **1887** *Trans. Philol. Soc. 1885–6* p. ix. The main difficulty in the Dictionary work is to trace the history of the development of the meanings of a word. **1929** C. I. DODD *Apples & Quinces* II. iv. 146 It was over the Dictionary work that Amanda made the acquaintance of Mr. Jasper Stafford. *Ibid* v. 156 Amanda went back to Oxford and Dictionary-making.

Hence **ˈdictionaryless** *a.*, without a dictionary.

1854 *Fraser's Mag.* L. 317 Battling, grammarless and dictionaryless, with a work in a strange idiom.

dictioˈneer. *nonce-wd.* [f. DICTION + -EER[1]; cf. *auctioneer.*] One who makes it his business to criticize diction or style in language. (*contemptuous.*)

1848 *Tait's Mag.* XV. 557 Taking a high tone against the decision of the 'dictioneers' generally.

†**ˈdictitate,** *v. Obs. rare.* [f. L. *dictitāre* to say often or emphatically, freq. of *dictāre*: see DICTATE.] *trans.* To declare.

1615 A. STAFFORD *Heav. Dogge* 44 No doubt the old man did dictitate thinges, the knowledge wherof would haue beautified all happy wits.

Dictograph (ˈdɪktəgrɑːf, -græf). Also **dictograph.** [f. DICT(ATION + -O + -GRAPH, after *phonograph.*] The proprietary name of a device used as an internal telephone without mouthpiece or earpiece, by means of which speech in one room is picked up by a sensitive microphone and reproduced through a loudspeaker elsewhere in the building. Also *attrib.*

1907 K. M. TURNER & W. DONNAN *U.S. Pat. 843,186* 1/1 Our invention relates to what we shall term a 'dictograph', being a telephonic system or apparatus by which a person —for example, the manager of an office—may dictate letters to any one of his corps of stenographers without requiring them to leave their places at their own desks. **1907** *Times* 26 June 12/4 Mr. [K. M.] Turner of New York.. had the honour of exhibiting the Dictograph before the King and Queen. **1912** *Times* (weekly ed.) 23 Feb., Indianapolis advices.. say that a 'dictograph' which was concealed in the office soon after John McNamara's arrest enabled Government stenographers in the room below to take the daily conversations. **1921** *Trade Marks Jrnl.* 27 Apr. 852 *Dictograph.* Telephone Instruments and Apparatus (all included in Class 8). Dictograph Telephones, Limited, Dictograph House.. London S.E. 1. **1926** *Spectator* 20 Mar. 520/1 Among inventions for great captains of industry, I looked with awe upon the Dictograph Telephone. **1962** *Punch* 3 Oct. 498/2 Those status-creating Dictograph telephones.

†**ˈdictour.** *Obs. rare*[−1]. [a. Anglo-Fr. **dictour* = OF. *dicteor*, *diteor*, author, dictator, arbiter:—L. *dictātōr-em*: see DICTATOR.] (?) A spokesman.

? *a* **1400** *Morte Arth.* 712 Syr Mordrede.. Salle be thy dictour, my dere, to doo whatte the lykes.

‖**dictum** (ˈdɪktəm). Pl. **dicta, dictums.** [L. *dictum* thing said, saying, word, f. *dict-us*, pa. pple. of *dīcĕre* to say.] A saying or utterance: sometimes used with emphasis upon the fact that it is a mere saying; but oftener with the implication of a formal pronouncement claiming or carrying some authority. (In the latter case probably transferred from the legal use in b.)

1706 PHILLIPS (ed. Kersey), *Dictum* (Lat.) a Word, a Saying, a Proverb; an Order or Command. **1787** SIR J. HAWKINS *Life of Johnson* 542 This dictum carries the more weight with it, as it comes from a man whose sentiments, respecting sectaries, may be inferred from the following passage. **1787** *Gentl. Mag.* Nov. 947/1 The above quoted sentence is a dictum of Johnson's after reading these several opinions. **1809** *Edin. Rev.* XIV. 452 He concludes his remarks, or rather *dicta* upon this topic, with the following passage. **1821** CRAIG *Lect. Drawing* vii. 365 We will not take for our guide the dictum of any professor in the art. **1828** COMBE *Const. Man* ii. (1835) 66 The collective dicta of the highest minds illuminated by the greatest knowledge. **1861** *Court Life at Naples* II. 148 His dictums were not regarded with the same awe to which he had been used. **1874** HELPS *Social Press.* viii. 104, I will.. allow Milverton's dicta to pass unquestioned.

b. In *Law*, An expression of opinion by a judge on matter of law, which is not the formal resolution or determination of a court.

1776 BURROW *Reports* IV. 2294 He intimated that long contrary Usage ought to go a great way towards overturning any old *Dictum*. **1827** JARMAN *Powell's Devises* II. 62 Against these authorities may be adduced the solitary dictum of Lord Rosslyn, who, in *Walker* v. *Denne* doubted whether there was any equity between the real and personal representatives. *Ibid.* 299 The doctrine appears to rest solely on the *dicta* of the Lords Commissioners. **1863** H. COX *Instit.* I. ix. 215 The dicta of judges concerning privilege of Parliament have been very conflicting. **1892** *Law Jrnl.* Notes of Cases XXVII. 4/2 The statement in Maure v. Harrison that he is so entitled is a *dictum* only, and cannot be supported.

c. A thing that is generally said; a current saying; a maxim or saw.

1826 SYD. SMITH *Wks.* (1852) II. 110/2 Of all false and foolish *dicta*, the most trite and the most absurd is that which asserts that the Judge is counsel for the prisoner. **1848** MILL *Pol. Econ.* v. xi. §5 The popular dictum, that people understand their own interests better.. than government does, or can be expected to do. **1859** —— *Liberty* ii. 52 The *dictum* that truth always triumphs. **1871** BLACKIE *Four Phases* i. 36 The famous dictum that 'the natural state of man is a war of all men against all men.'

†**d.** In old Logic, the statement in a modal proposition.

1697 tr. *Burgersdicius his Logick* I. xxviii. 113 Modal Enunciation consists of a Dictum and Mood: The Dictum of which is as it were the Subject, and the Mood the Predicate ..'It is necessary that God be good': that is, *Deum esse bonum*; the Dictum is, *that God be good*; the Mode, *Necessary*.

e. In some historical and other phrases: ***dictum of Kenilworth***, an award made in 1266 between King Henry III and the barons who had taken arms against him. ***dictum of Aristotle***, ***dictum de omni et*** (***de***) ***nullo*** i.e. 'concerning every and none', the name given by the Schoolmen to the canon of direct syllogism, given by Aristotle (λέγομεν δὲ τὸ κατὰ παντὸς κατηγορεῖσθαι.. καὶ τὸ κατὰ μηδενός, *An. Pr.* I. i.): see quots. ***obiter dictum***: see OBITER.

1670 BLOUNT *Law Dict.* s.v., *Dictum de Kenelworth* was an Edict or Award between Henry III and all those Barons.. who had been in Armes against him. **1697** tr. *Burgersdicius his Logick* II. viii. 32 If the Dictum of All and None be Paraphrastically propounded. **1761** HUME *Hist. Eng.* (1763) I. 233 Knights and esquires, says the dictum of Kenelworth, who were robbers, if they have no land, shall pay the half of their goods. **1827** WHATELY *Logic* 38 The object of Aristotle's dictum is precisely analogous. **1843** MILL *Logic* I. v. §3 These views.. are the basis of the celebrated *dictum de omni et nullo*. **1864** BOWEN *Logic* vii. 187 The famous Dictum of Aristotle, usually called the *Dictum de omni et nullo*, that whatever is predicated (affirmed or denied) universally of any Class (i.e. of any whole), may be also predicated of any part of that Class.

dicty (ˈdɪktɪ), *a. U.S. slang.* [Origin unknown.] **a.** Conceited; snobbish. **b.** Elegant, stylish, high-class.

1926 A. NILES in W. C. Handy *Blues* 22 Gay-cattin' 'roun' with dicty cats. *Ibid.* 33 *Dicty*, uppish and conceited. **1926** C. VAN VECHTEN *Nigger Heaven* 12 'Winter Palace?' she inquired... 'Naw.. too many ofays and jig-chasers.' 'Bowie Wilcox's is dicty.' 'Too many monks.' **1944** A. ROSE in G. Myrdal *Amer. Dilemma* xliv. 966 These are only a few dozen words and phrases that are uniquely Negro.. such as 'dicty' which means trying to put on airs and act upper class without having the basis for doing so. **1959** R. GANT *World in Jug* 162 Nice boy, Julian.. from one of those dicty schools and Oxford too, who had surprisingly turned to jazz.

dictyogen (ˈdɪktɪəʊdʒɛn, dɪkˈtaɪədʒɛn). *Bot.* [f. Gr. δίκτυο-ν net + -γενης born, produced: see -GEN[1]. Formed to match *endogen*, *exogen*, and other terms of the same classification.]

The name applied by Lindley to those plants which have a monocotyledonous embryo, and reticulated leaf-veins (in the latter respect resembling the Dicotyledons).

1846 LINDLEY *Veg. Kingdom* 4 The separation by me of Endogens into 1. Endogens proper, and 2. Dictyogens. **1855**

—— in *Circ. Sc., Botany* 184 Dictyogens are Endogens, but with the peculiarity that the root is exactly like Exogens without concentric circles, and the leaves fall off the stem by a clean fracture, just as in that class. **1857** BERKELEY *Cryptog. Bot.* §39. 52 Dictyogens are supposed to approach Exogens in their leaves and in the arrangement of their tissues, but their embryo and the development of their wood are distinctly monocotyledonous. **1860** J. DARBY *Bot. Southern States* 600 Dictyogens, monocotyledonous plants, with net-veined leaves, as smilax and trillium.

Hence **dicty'ogenous** *a.*, belonging to this group of plants.

dictyospore ('dɪktɪəʊspɔə(r)). *Bot.* [f. Gr. δίκτυο-ν net + SPORE.] (See quot. 1940.) So **dictyo'sporic** *a.*

1933 E. W. MASON *Annotated Account Fungi* (Imp. Bur. Mycol.) List II. Fasc. 2. 12 In the classical species of this little understood genus the thallus breaks up into dictyosporic elements. **1940** *Chambers's Techn. Dict.* 243/1 *Dictyospore*, a multicellular spore divided into segments by both transverse and longitudinal walls. **1962** C. J. ALEXOPOULOS *Introd. Mycology* (ed. 2) xviii. 394 Conidia are also named in accordance with their shape or structure. Thus we have *dictyospores*.., which possess both vertical and horizontal septa.

dictyostele ('dɪktɪəʊstiːl, dɪk'taɪəstiːl). *Bot.* [f. Gr. δίκτυο-ν net + STELE 2.] In some ferns and dicotyledons, a stele which is so interrupted by leaf-gaps as to resemble a network of strands. Hence **dictyo'stelic** *a.*

1902 G. BREBNER in *Ann. Bot.* XVI. 521 *Dictyostele*, a vascular tube with large overlapping leaf gaps, so that the whole structure becomes a network of vascular strands. **1911** *Encycl. Brit.* XXI. 736/2 It is better to call.. a segment of a broken-up stele a *meristele*, the whole solenostele with overlapping leaf-gaps being called a *dictyostele*. **1934** WEBSTER, Dictyostelic. **1955** *Ann. Bot.* XIX. 495 The vascular structure of the attenuated specimens was dictyostelic.

dicumarol: see DICOUMAROL.

di'cyan-, di'cyano-. *Chem.* [f. DI-² + CYAN(O-.] Combined with two equivalents of the radical cyanogen, CN, replacing two of hydrogen, chlorine, etc. (See CYAN- 2.)

dicyanide (daɪ'saɪənaɪd). *Chem.* [f. DI-² + CYANIDE *sb.*] A compound containing two equivalents of cyanogen (CN) united to an element or dyad radical, as ***mercuric dicyanide*** $Hg(CN)_2$.

1863-72 WATTS *Dict. Chem.* II. 221 Dicyanide and tricyanide of iron have not yet been obtained in very definite form.

dicy'anogen. *Chem.* See DI-² and CYANOGEN. Cyanogen in the free form.

dicycle ('daɪsɪk(ə)l). [f. DI-² + Gr. κύκλος wheel, CYCLE. (A more regularly formed word than the hybrid *bicycle*.)] The name given to a form of velocipede in which the two wheels are parallel to each other, instead of being in the same line as in a bicycle.

[**1870** *Belgravia* Feb. 441 Bicycle should be either *dicycle* .. or *birota*.] **1887** *Cycl. Tour. Club Gaz.* Jan. 14/1 They will exhibit.. a new tricycle, a new bicycle, and a dicycle on the lines of the 'Otto.' **1892** *Cycl. Tour. Club Handbk.* 49 'Otto' and other Dicycles, same rate as Tricycles.

Hence **'dicyclist**, one who rides a dicycle.

1887 *Bicycling News* 11 June 145/1.

dicynodont (daɪ'sɪnədɒnt), *sb.* and *a.* *Palæont.* [mod. f. Gr. δι- two + κυν- dog + ὀδοντ- tooth.]

A fossil reptile characterized by the absence of all teeth except two long canines in the upper jaw. **b.** *adj.* Having this character.

The typical genus is *Dicynodon*, order *Dicynodontia*.

1854 OWEN in *Circ. Sc.* (c 1865) II. 97/2, I have called them 'Dicynodonts', from their dentition being reduced to one long and large canine tooth on each side of the upper jaw. **1876** PAGE *Adv. Text-Bk. Geol.* xvi. 292 The Dicynodont reptiles from the red sandstones of South Africa.

Hence **dicyno'dontian** *a.*

1873 HUXLEY *Critiques & Addresses* ix. 213 The supposition that the Dinosaurian, Crocodilian, Dicynodontian, and Plesiosaurian types were suddenly created at the end of the Permian epoch may be dismissed. **1875** BLAKE *Zool.* 162 The evidences of this most singular dicynodontian family of reptiles have hitherto been found only in South Africa.

did, past tense of DO *v.*, q.v.

‖**Didache** ('dɪdəkiː). [English form of Gr. διδαχή teaching, first word of the title of the treatise Διδαχὴ τῶν δώδεκα ἀποστόλων Teaching of the twelve apostles.] The name of a Christian treatise of the beginning of the second century. Hence **'Didachist, Dida'chographer**, the writer or compiler of the *Didache*.

1885 SCHAFF in *Jrnl. Soc. Bibl. Lit.* June & Dec. 3 The great interest and significance of the Didache consists in filling the gap between the Apostolic age and the Church of the second century. *Ibid.* 6 The Didachographer seems also to have some slight acquaintance with Luke and Acts and some epistles of Paul. **1888** *Dublin Rev.* Jan. 141 This would give about A.D. 120, as the latest date at which the Didache could have been published. **1891** F. H. CHASE *Lord's Prayer in Early Church*, Against this correction either of the text of the Didaché or of the Didachist's report of his original.

2. (With small initial.) The instructional or didactic element in early Christian theology, as distinct from 'kerygma' or preaching.

1936 C. H. DODD *Apostolic Preaching* i. 6 For the early Church.. to preach the Gospel was by no means the same thing as to deliver moral instruction or exhortation... It was by *kerygma*, says Paul, not by *didaché*, that it pleased God to save men. **1953** *Scottish Jrnl. Theol.* VI. 435 *Didache* was an expanded version of the *kerygma*, embracing Christian life and conduct, but including also instruction in the 'historical facts' as well as the 'saving facts', in the sacraments and eschatology. **1960** *Times Lit. Suppl.* 15 Apr p. xii/1, The 'kerygma' is not of course opposed to the 'didache': the messsage must imply the teaching.

didactic (dɪ'dæktɪk), *a.* and *sb.* [mod. ad. Gr. διδακτικ-ός apt at teaching, f. διδάσκειν to teach. Cf. F. *didactique* (1554 in Hatz.-Darm.)]

A. *adj.* Having the character or manner of a teacher or instructor; characterized by giving instruction; having the giving of instruction as its aim or object; instructive, preceptive.

1658 R. FRANCK *North. Mem.* (1821) 54 Must I be didactick to initiate this art? **1661** WORTHINGTON *To Hartlib* xvi. (T.), Finding in himself a great promptness in such didactic work. **1756** J. WARTON *Ess. Pope* (1782) I. iii. 101 A poem of that species, for which our author's genius was particularly turned, the didactic and the moral. **1824** DIBDIN *Libr. Comp.* 682 The dullest of all possible didactic and moral poetry. **1830** MACKINTOSH *Eth. Philos.* Wks. 1846 I. 59 A permanent foundation of his [Hobbes'] fame remains in his admirable style, which seems to be the very perfection of didactic language. **1878** Bosw. SMITH *Carthage* 130 Polybius.. is too didactic—seldom adorning a tale but always ready to point a moral. **1878** R. W. DALE *Lect. Preach.* viii. (ed. 2) 226, I do not mean that sermons addressed to Christian people should be simply didactic.

absol. **1754** A. MURPHY *Gray's-Inn Jrnl.* No. 90 ¶6 Both [Eloquence and Poetry].. have occasionally strengthened themselves with Insertions of the Didactic.

B. *sb.* †**1.** A didactic author or treatise. *Obs.*

1644 MILTON *Educ.* Wks. (1847) 98/2 To search what many modern Januas and Didactics.. have projected, my inclination leads me not. **1835** SOUTHEY *Doctor* III. 162 Acknowledged in the oldest didactics upon this subject.

2. *pl.* **didactics** [see -ICS]: The science or art of teaching.

1846 WORCESTER cites *Biblical Repos.* **1856** MRS. BROWNING *Aur. Leigh* I. Poems 1890 VI. 38 Didactics, driven Against the heels of what the master said. **1860** EMERSON *Cond. Life, Consid.* Wks. (Bohn) II. 412 Life is rather a subject of wonder, than of didactics. **1881** J. G. FITCH *Lect. Teach.* ii. 36 The art of teaching, or Didactics as we may for convenience call it, falls under two heads.

di'dactical, *a. rare.* [f. as prec. + -AL¹.] Of instructive nature or tendency; = DIDACTIC.

1604 R. CAWDREY *Table Alph.*, *Didacticall*, full of doctrine or instruction. **1649** ROBERTS *Clavis Bibl.* 382 Amongst the Didacticall or Doctrinall Books. **1711** J. GREENWOOD *Eng. Gram.* 255 Never any man labour'd more at the didactical Art, or the Art of teaching than he did.

Hence **didacti'cality**, didactic quality.

1827 CARLYLE *Misc.* (1872) I. 230 For a like reason of didacticality.. Wieland could affect me nothing.

didactically (dɪ'dæktɪkəlɪ), *adv.* [f. DIDACTICAL + -LY².] In a didactic manner; in the form or with the purpose of giving instruction.

a **1626** BP. ANDREWES *Answ. Cdl. Perron* 50 (L.) Books of the Fathers, written dogmatically or didactically. **1822-56** DE QUINCEY *Confess.* (1862) 226, I will give it not didactically but wrapped up. **1868** GLADSTONE *Juv. Mundi* xi. (1870) 436 He might have done this didactically, or by way of narrative.

didactician (dɪdæk'tɪʃən). [f. DIDACTIC + -IAN: cf. *tactician*, etc.] One who follows a didactic method, a didactic writer; one who writes with the aim of instructing.

1875 STEDMAN *Victorian Poets* (1887) 100 He [M. Arnold] thus becomes a better prose-writer than a mere didactician ever could be.

didacticism (dɪ'dæktɪsɪz(ə)m). [f. DIDACTIC *a.* + -ISM.] The practice or quality of being didactic or aiming at the conveyance of instruction.

1841 CARLYLE in Froude *Life in Lond.* (1884) I. viii. 223 Harriet Martineau full of didacticism. *a* **1849** POE *Longfellow* Wks. 1864 III. 365 Didacticism is the prevalent tone of his song. **1888** *Spectator* 28 July 1036/1 The hardly veiled didacticism of novels like those of Miss Edgeworth.

didacticity (dɪdæk'tɪsɪtɪ). *rare*⁻¹. [f. DIDACTIC *a.* + -ITY.] Didactic quality.

1827-48 HARE *Guesses* Ser. II. (1874) 362 The German professors, of whose uninterrupted didacticity their literature bears too many marks.

didactive (dɪ'dæktɪv), *a.* [irreg. f. Gr. διδακτ-ός taught, or that can be taught + -IVE: after words from L. like *act-ive*.] = DIDACTIC.

1711 SHAFTESB. *Charac.* (1737) I. 258 The way of form and method, the didactive or preceptive manner. **1768** *Misc.* in *Ann. Reg.* 168/2 Either drily didactive.. or triflingly volatile. **1821** *Blackw. Mag.* X. 330 So enchanted was the didactive muse with the verses. **1821** LAMB *Elia* Ser. I. *Old & New Schm.*, He is under the restraint of a formal or didactive hypocrisy in company, as a clergyman is under a moral one.

didactyl, -yle (daɪ'dæktɪl), *a.* *Zool.* [f. DI-² + Gr. δάκτυλ-ος finger: cf. Gr. διδάκτυλ-ος of two fingers.] Having two fingers, toes, or claws.

1819 G. SAMOUELLE *Entomol. Compend.* 157 Didactyle claws. **1826** KIRBY & SP. *Entomol.* (1828) III. xxxv. 676 The generality of insects have a didactyle or tridactyle hand or foot. **1852** DANA *Crust.* I. 600 This last pair [of legs] being didactyle. **1854** OWEN in *Circ. Sc.* (c 1865) II. 74/2 The toes in the didactyle ostrich have respectively four and five phalanges. **1886** A. WINCHELL *Walks in Geol. Field* 256 The bovine foot.. its didactyle structure.

didactylous (daɪ'dæktɪləs), *a.* *Zool.* [f. as prec. + -OUS.] = prec.

1828 in WEBSTER. **1870** ROLLESTON *Anim. Life* Introd. 51 The foot is reduced to the didactylous condition. **1875** BLAKE *Zool.* 297 The palps are large, terminated by a didactylous hand, or chela.

didakai, didakei: see DIDICOI.

didal(l, obs. ff. DIDLE.

didapper ('daɪˌdæpə(r)). Forms: 5 dydoppar, 6-7 dydopper, 7 didopper, dydapper, dy-dapper, 6-9 diedapper, 6- didapper. [A reduced form of DIVE-DAPPER, in same sense.]

1. A small diving water-fowl; = DABCHICK.

c **1440** *Promp. Parv.* 121/1 Dydoppar, watyr byrde. **1565-73** COOPER *Thesaurus, Collimbris*, the birde called a Douker, or Didapper. **1591** PERCIVALL *Sp. Dict.*, *Somorgujo*, ducking, diuing, a diedapper. **1591** SYLVESTER *Du Bartas* I. v. 775 The nimble Teal, the Mallard strong in flight, The Di-dapper, the Plover and the Snight. **1621** BURTON *Anat. Mel.* I. ii. II. i. (1651) 67 All fenny Fowl.. as Ducks.. Didappers, Waterhens. **1699** R. L'ESTRANGE *Colloq. Erasm.* (1711) 11 One while up, and another while down, like a Didapper. **1837** WHEELWRIGHT tr. *Aristophanes* II. 142 Daws, chickens, coots, wrens, ducks and didappers. **1885** SWAINSON *Prov. Names Bird.* 216 From its diving propensities this bird [little grebe] is called Diver (Renfrew); Diedapper (Dorset, Hants, Norfolk); Divedapper, or Divedop (Lincolnshire); Divy duck (Norfolk); Dive an' dop (Norfolk).

2. Applied ludicrously to a person.

1589 *Pappe w. Hatchet* 3 Such dydoppers must be taken vp, els theile not stick to check the king. **1612** R. CARPENTER *Soules Sent.* 20 Thou art a Didapper peering vp and downe in a moment. **1727** POPE, etc. *Art Sinking* 83 The didappers are authors, that keep themselves long out of sight, under water, and come up now and then, where you least expected them. **1851** COLTON *Lacon* I. 163 Wilkes was one of those didappers, whom, if you had stripped naked, and thrown over Westminster bridge, you might have met on the very next day, with.. a laced coat upon his back, and money in his pocket.

didascalic (dɪdæ'skælɪk), *a.* [ad. L. *didascalic-us*, a. Gr. διδασκαλικός fit for teaching, instructive, f. διδάσκαλος teacher, f. διδάσκειν to teach.] Of the nature of a teacher or of instruction; didactic; pertaining to a teacher. Hence **dida'scalics** *sb. pl.*: = DIDACTICS.

1609 R. BARNERD *Faithf. Sheph.* 42 This of some is called the Didascalike or Doctrinall part of a Sermon. **1638** A. SYMSON in Spurgeon *Treas. Dav.* Ps. xxxii. II. 94 This is a Didascalic Psalm, wherein David teacheth sinners to repent by his doctrine. **1718** PRIOR *Solomon* Pref., Under what species it may be comprehended, whether didascalic or heroic, I leave to the judgment of the critics. **1813** T. BUSBY (*title*), Lucretius' Nature of Things, a Didascalic Poem. **1833** LYTTON *England & Eng.* IV. iv, They have no toleration for the didascalic affectations in which academicians delight. **1866** *Elgin & Cathedral Guide* I. 110 The didascalic power of the drama.

So **di'dascalar** *a.*, of or pertaining to a teacher, didactic. *nonce-wd.*

a **1846** WORCESTER cites BULWER for *Didascalar*. *a* **1873** LYTTON *Ken. Chillingly* ix, Give off chaffing.. said Bob, lowering the didascular intonations of his voice.

di'dascaly. *Gr. Antiq.* [mod. ad. Gr. διδασκαλία instruction, teaching; in pl. as in quot. So mod.F. *didascalie*.] In *pl.* The Catalogues of the ancient Greek Dramas, with their writers, dates, etc., such as were compiled by Aristotle and others.

1831 T. L. PEACOCK *Crotchet Castle* vi. (1887) 79 Did not they give to melopoeia, choregraphy, and the sundry forms of didascalies [*printed* -ics], the precedence of all other matters, civil and military? **1849** GROTE *Greece* II. lxvii. (1862) VI. 26 The first, second and third [tetralogies] are specified in the Didaskalies or Theatrical Records.

didder ('dɪdə(r)), *v.* Now only *dial.* Forms: 4 diddir, 5 didir, dyder, dedir, -ur, 6 dydder, 7- didder. See also DITHER. [Found in the 14th c. related to DADDER and DODDER; the form in all being frequentative as in *totter, flutter*, etc.

It is not certain whether they belong to an ablaut stem *did, dad, dod*, (*dud*), or whether they are entirely onomatopœic, *didder* e.g. being a natural imitation of tremulous motion, and *dadder, dudder, dodder*, variations expressing clumsier or heavier forms of it. *Didder* is chiefly northern; DITHER, which appears later, is also midl. and southern, the *-ther* arising out of *-der*, as in *father, mother, hither*, etc.]

intr. To tremble, quake, shake, shiver.

c **1375** *Sc. Leg. Saints, Johannes* 264 Cald [*frigus*].. þat makis wrechis ful chel to diddir. *c* **1420** *Avow. Arth.* xxv, Dyntus gerut him to dedur. *c* **1440** *York Myst.* xxviii. 2 My flesshe dyderis & daris for doute of my dede. *c* **1460** *Towneley Myst.* (Surtees) 28, I dase and I dedir For ferd of that taylle. *c* **1550** *Hye Way to Spyttil Hous* 118 in Hazl. *E.P.P.* IV. 28 Boyes, gyrles, and luskysh strong knaues, Dydderyng and dadderyng, leaning on their staues. *a* **1693**

URQUHART *Rabelais* III. xx. 167 Diddering and shivering his Chaps, as Apes use to do. **1783** AINSWORTH *Lat. Dict.* (Morell) I, To didder (shiver with cold), *algeo.* **1790** MRS. WHEELER *Westmld. Dial.* (1821) 34, I quite didderd for fear. **1869** *Lonsdale Gloss., Didder*, to shiver, to tremble.

Hence **'diddering** *vbl. sb.* and *ppl. a.*

c **1440** *Promp. Parv.* 121/1 Dyderynge for colde, *frigitus.* **1687** A. LOVELL tr. *Bergerac's Com. Hist.* i. 18 By his extraordinary chattering and diddering, one half of his Teeth dropt out. **1785** HUTTON *Bran New Wark* (E.D.S.) 347 Her knocking knees, and diddering teeth melted my heart. **1869** *Lonsdale Gloss., Didderin'-girse*, quaking grass.

diddest, rare f. *didst*, 2nd sing. pa. t. of DO *v.*

diddle ('dɪd(ə)l), *v.*[1] *colloq.* or *dial.* [app. a parallel form to DIDDER, the formative suffixes -LE and -ER being somewhat akin in their force, though the former is more strictly diminutival. Cf. DADDLE, DAIDLE; there are evident analogies both of form and sense between *didder, dadder, diddle, daddle.*]

†**1.** *intr.* To walk unsteadily, as a child; to toddle; = DADDLE. *Obs.*

1632 QUARLES *Div. Fancies* I. iv. (1660) 3 And when his forward strength began to bloom, To see him diddle up and down the Room!

2. *intr.* To move from side to side by jerks; to shake, quiver.

1786 BURNS *Ep. to Major Logan* iii, Hale be your heart, hale be your fiddle; Lang may your elbuck jink and diddle. *a* **1810** TANNAHILL *Poems* (1846) 60 You..wi' your clairon, flute, an' fiddle, Will gar their southern heart-strings diddle. **1835** D. WEBSTER in *Harp Renfrewsh.* Ser. II. (1873) 154 Wi fiddling and diddling and dancing The house was in perfect uproar.

3. *trans.* To jerk from side to side.

1893 STEVENSON *Catriona* 173 A fiddler diddling his elbock at the chimney side.

4. a. *intr.* and *trans.* To copulate or have sexual intercourse (with), esp. with woman as obj. **b.** *intr.* and *refl.* To masturbate (now chiefly *U.S.*). *slang.*

1879 in G. Legman *Limerick* (1979) 131 There was a young man from Toulouse Who thought he would diddle a goose. **1889** BARRÈRE & LELAND *Dict. Slang* I. 308/2 *Diddle, to* (vulgar), to have sexual commerce. **1940** W. FAULKNER *Hamlet* II. ii. 134 'I'll find all three of them. I'll—' 'What for? Just out of curiosity to find out for certain just which of them was and wasn't diddling her?' **1960** WENTWORTH & FLEXNER *Dict. Amer. Slang* 146/2 There was a man from Racine Who invented a diddling machine; Both concave and convex, It could fit either sex. **1966** [see POLACK *a.*]. **1974** K. MILLETT *Flying* (1975) III. 348 Paraphernalia with the scarf. .. Supposed to diddle herself with it. Male fantasy of lonely chick masturbating in sad need of him. **1983** M. GEE *Sole Survivor* vi. 60 'I used to get erections on parade in the school cadets.' 'What did you do?' He shrugged. 'Do you diddle yourself?' That was hard for me to admit. He waited until I said yes.

'diddle, *v.*[2] [app. onomatopœic, representing the effect of singing, without uttering connected words. Dialectally *deedle* and *doodle* are used in a similar sense.] *trans.* To sing without distinct utterance of words.

1706 E. WARD *Hud. Rediv.* I. VI. 3 So all sung diff'rent Tunes and Graces, Such as they us'd to lull and diddle To froward Infants in the Cradle.

diddle ('dɪd(ə)l), *v.*[3] *colloq.* [A recent word, of obscure origin.

It is possible that sense 1 was transferred from DIDDLE *v.*[1], and was the source of the name DIDDLER, and that sense 2 was back-formation from that word. Sense 2 might however, as far as form and meaning go, be related to OE. *didrian, dydrian* to deceive, delude (cf. what is said of the suffixes *-er*, and *-le*, under DIDDLE *v.*[1]); but there is an interval of eight or nine centuries between the known occurrences of the words. It is worthy of note also that *doodle* occurs in the sense 'to befool', and that *doodle* sb. 'simpleton, noodle' goes back to *c* 1600.]

1. 'To waste time in the merest trifling' (Forby *a* 1825). Hence *to diddle away*: to trifle away (time), to waste in a trifling manner.

1826 SCOTT *Jrnl.* (1890) I. 250 A day diddled away, and nothing to show for it! **1829** *Ibid.* 17 Feb., I was at the Court, where there was little to do, but it diddled away my time till two.

2. *trans.* **a.** To cheat or swindle; to victimize; to 'do'. **b.** To do for, undo, ruin; to kill.

1806 SURR *Winter in Lond.* II. 127 That flashy captain.. may lay all London under contribution..but he can't diddle me. **1809** *European Mag.* LX. 19 We shall soon find ourselves completely diddled and undone. **1810** W. B. RHODES *Bomb. Fur.* iv. (1822) 22 O Fusbos, Fusbos, I am diddled quite [*He dies*]. **1817** LADY GRANVILLE *Letters* (1894) I. 111 He..exclaimed, 'Then you are diddled!' Think of the effect of this slang upon incroyable ears! **1823** BYRON *Juan* XI. xvii, Poor Tom was..Full flash, all fancy, until fairly diddled. **1829** MARRYAT *F. Mildmay* xvii, I suppose we diddled at least a hundred men. **1859** SALA *Tw. round Clock* (1861) 145 The labourer..invariably finds himself at the end of the week victimised, or, to use a more expressive, though not so genteel a term, diddled, to a heart-rending extent. **1879** *Public Opinion* 12 July 42 He may diddle his tradesmen.

c. *to diddle out of*: to do out of, swindle out of.

1829 SCOTT *Jrnl.* 27 Mar., I am diddled out of a day all the same. **1833** LAMB *Lett.* (1888) II. 285 What a cheap book is the last Hogarth you sent me! I am pleased now that Hunt diddled me out of the old one. **1886** A. GRIFFITHS *Pauper Peer* i, You were robbed, euchred, diddled out of fifty thousand pounds.

Hence **'diddling** *vbl. sb.* and *ppl. a.*

a **1849** POE *Diddling* Wks. 1864 IV. 268 Diddling, rightly considered, is a compound, of which the ingredients are minuteness, interest, perseverance, ingenuity, audacity, nonchalance, originality, impertinence and grin. **1894** *Westm. Gaz.* 10 May 2/3 No Interference with the Diddling of the Public.

'diddle, *sb. slang* and *vulgar*. [Three different words: cf. prec. vbs.]

1. The sound of the fiddle; cf. next.

1806 J. TRAIN *Poet. Reveries* (Jam.), In their ears it is a diddle Like the sounding of a fiddle.

2. A swindle, a deception.

1885 *Punch* 5 Sept. 110 (Farmer) And something whispered me—in diction chaste—It's all a diddle!

3. A slang name for gin, and in U.S. for liquor generally. Hence **diddle-cove** (*slang*), a keeper of a gin or spirit shop.

c **1700** *Street Robberies Consider'd, Diddle*, Geneva. **1725** *New Cant Dict., Diddle*, the Cant Word for *Geneva*. **1858** MAYHEW *Paved with Gold* III. i. 252 (Farmer) And there's a first-rate 'diddle-cove' keeps a gin-shop there.

diddle- in comb. [Connected with DIDDLE *v.*[1], *v.*[3]] **diddle-daddle**, 'stuff and nonsense', 'fiddle-faddle': cf. *tittle-tattle.* **diddle-dee**, a name for the shrub *Empetrum rubrum* in the Falkland Islands. **diddle-diddle**, used to denote the sound of a fiddle, or the action of playing it. **diddledum** (in 6 **-dome**), used contemptuously for, or in reference to, something trifling.

1523 SKELTON *Garl. Laurel* 741 What blunderar is yonder, that playth didil diddil He fyndith fals mesuris out of his fonde fiddill. **1599** BRETON *Dreame Strange Effects* 17 When thou findest a foole for thy diet, feede him with a Dish of Diddledomes, for I have done with thee. *c* **1670** (*title of song*), 'Diddle-diddle, or the kind country lovers.' **1778** MAD. D'ARBLAY *Diary* Sept., *Mrs. Thrale.* Come, let us have done now with all this diddle-daddle. **1797** CANNING, etc. in *Anti-Jacobin* No. 5. 19 Reason, philosophy, 'fiddledum diddledum'. **18..** *Nursery Rime*, Hey! diddle diddle! The cat and the fiddle. **1847** SIR J. C. ROSS *Voy. S. Seas* II. 249 A roaring fire of 'diddle-dee' ready to cook our supper. **1893** *Times* 27 May 14/1 The open country [Falkland Islands] is clothed with short scrub called diddle-dee (*Empetrum rubrum*).

diddler ('dɪdlə(r)). [Of obscure origin.

Found first in the name of 'Jeremy Diddler', the chief character in Kenney's farce, 'Raising the Wind', brought out in 1803. The name was of course intended to be contemptuous and ludicrous, and it seems probable that it was formed on DIDDLE *v.*[2] sense 1, or on the first element of the earlier *diddle-daddle, diddle-dum* (see DIDDLE-); it is also probable that Jeremy Diddler's characteristic methods of 'raising the wind', by continually borrowing small sums which he does not pay back, and otherwise sponging upon people, gave rise to the current sense of the verb (DIDDLE *v.*[3] sense 2), of which 'diddler' is now naturally viewed as the agent-noun.]

A mean swindler or cheat; one who diddles people out of what belongs to them.

1803 J. KENNEY *Raising Wind* I. i, in Inchbald's *Coll. Farces* (1815) I. 113 Oh, it's Mr. Diddler trying to joke himself into credit at the bar. *Ibid.* 114, I wasn't born two hundred miles north of Lunnun, to be done by Mr. Diddler, I know. *Ibid.* 116 [Diddler *loquitur*] This it is to carry on trade without a capital. Once I paid my way..but thou art now, Jerry Diddler, little better than a vagabond. *a* **1849** POE *Diddling* Wks. 1864 IV. 268 Your diddler is guided by self-interest. **1863** HOLLAND *Lett. Joneses* iii. 48, I think you are a diddler and a make-believe.

diddums ('dɪdəmz). Also **didums.** [= *did 'em*, i.e. did they (tease you, etc.)?, with addition of plural *s.*] An expression of commiseration addressed to a child and jocularly to an adult; hence used as a meaningless term of address to children, etc. Hence **'diddum** *v. trans.* (*rare*), to say 'diddums' to.

1893 E. F. BENSON *Dodo* I. vii. 142 Women who were content to pore on their baby's face..saying 'Didums' occasionally. **1908** *Magnet* I. 1, Poor little thing! He misses his mammy, you know! Diddums! **1926** *Spectator* 1 May 795/1 On being 'diddumed' when sleeping..it [*sc.* a cat] opened its eyes crossly. **1928** *Internat. Jrnl. Psycho-Analysis* IX. 17 Where an hysteric will spend endless time consciously rejecting, say, an obscene word, the obsessional will spend the same time in an agony of confusion over a simple nursery phrase, e.g. 'Diddums' or 'Ducky'. **1928** R. MACAULAY *Keeping Up Appearances* viii, Sometimes they inquire..as to the past life in general of the object of their solicitude, as 'Was he?' or 'Diddums?' **1961** M. KELLY *Spoilt Kill* ii. 109 Mr Luke gave it to me... That was his way of saying diddums to baby. **1970** B. TURNER *Another Little Death* iv. 31 'Diddums,' I said soothingly, and booted him in the backside to land headlong at her feet.

diddy ('dɪdɪ). *slang* or *dial.* Also **deddy, diddey.** [Alteration of TITTY[3].] A woman's breast or nipple, or her milk; the teat of an animal.

1788 GROSE *Dict. Vulg. Tongue* (ed. 2), *Diddeys*, a woman's breasts or bubbies. **1841** C. H. HARTSHORNE *Salopia Antiqua* 393 The cow's got a sore diddy. *Ibid.*, Gie th' lickle un a drop o' the diddy. **1876** T. E. BROWN *Doctor* 48 Take a baby from the deddy Just when the mother's gettin' it reddy! **1922** JOYCE *Ulysses* 610 Cuts off their diddies when they can't bear no more children. **1961** S. BECKETT *Happy Days* i. 32 What's she doing? he says—What's the idea? he says—stuck up to her diddies in the bleeding ground.

dide, obs. f. DEED, *died* (see DIE *v.*), *did* (see DO *v.*).

†**di-deca'hedral**, *a. Crystal. Obs.* [f. F. *didécaèdre* (Haüy) + -AL[1]: see DI- *pref.*[2] I.]

Having the form of a ten-sided prism with five-sided bases, making twenty faces in all.

1805–17 R. JAMESON *Char. Min.* (ed. 3) 204 Di-decahedral felspar.

didelphian (daɪ'dɛlfɪən), *a. Zool.* [f. mod.L. *Didelphia* (F. *Didelphes*, Cuvier 1795), f. Gr. δι-, DI-[2] twice + δελφύς womb: see -AN.] Belonging to the subclass *Didelphia* of the class *Mammalia*, characterized by a double uterus and vagina, and comprising the single order of Marsupials. So **di'delphic, di'delphine, di'delphous** *adjs.*, in same sense; **didelph, di'delphid**, an animal of the subclass *Didelphia*, or of the family *Didelphidæ* (opossums); **di'delphoid** *a.*, double, as the uterus in the *Didelphia.*

1847 ANSTED *Anc. World* ix. 197 Insectivorous didelphine animals like the opossum. **1847** CRAIG, *Didelphoid.* [**1851** RICHARDSON *Geol.* viii. 314 The didelphia have special bones, called Marsupial, for supporting the pouch.] **1872** MIVART *Elem. Anat.* 17 Didelphous mammals.

didgeridoo (ˌdɪdʒərɪ'duː). Also **didjeridoo, didjeridu, dijiridu**, etc. [Imitative.] A musical instrument of the Australian Aborigines, consisting of a long tube made from bamboo or a hollow sapling which is blown into to produce a resonant sound.

1924 F. T. MACARTNEY in *Bulletin* (Sydney) 18 Dec., Didjeridoo—didjeridoo! A blackfellow blows through a length of bamboo To the regular beat of an ironwood stick. *Ibid.*, And all..Is dark while you hark to the didjeridoo. **1936** F. D. DAVISON *Children of Dark People* i. 10 He would make music on his didjeridoo. **1938** F. D. MCCARTHY *Austral. Aboriginal Decorative Art* 36 The chanting tubes or *didjeridu* are painted with red, yellow, white and black dashes on a red or plain field. **1944** W. E. HARNEY *Taboo* (ed. 3) 80 From the river bank came the droning of the didgeredoo. **1959** S. H. COURTIER *Death in Dream Time* iv. 38 Only the didgeridoo, the native hollow-log trumpet, could produce that galvanising noise. **1965** *Sunday Mirror* 5 Sept. 23/1 A didgeridoo blown by Australian entertainer Rolf Harris. **1971** *Times Lit. Suppl.* 19 Nov. 1453/2 The everlasting drone of the dijiridu.

didicoi, didicoy ('dɪdɪkɔɪ). *slang* or *dial.* Also **didakai, -kei, diddekai, diddicoy, didekei, -ki, -kie, -ky, didikai, -koi, didycoy.** [Romany.] A gipsy (see also quot. 1966).

1853 'E. R.' in M. Carpenter *Juvenile Delinquents* iv. 126 Gipseys, romaneys, didycoys, 'our people', as they call themselves. **1907** *Daily Chron.* 5 Oct. 6/2 Making raids on gipsy encampments with the object of getting them to send their young 'didekies' (children) to school. **1936** G. GREENE *Journey without Maps* I. iii. 79 A didicoi..was the name they gave in Gloucestershire to gipsies. **1936** *Punch* 18 Mar. 321/3 Dappled with mire, By the didakai's fire. **1959** 'O. MILLS' *Stairway to Murder* iv. 37 What's a man of your age and education doing wandering the country..? You don't strike me as a natural diddicoy type. **1960** W. ROBERTSON *Shadow of Rope* xiii. 131 Them there diddicoys is wholly afeard o' the ma'sh. **1961** *Guardian* 23 May 5/5 These were the dreaded scrap-metal Didakeis. **1966** *Ibid.* 3 Nov. 4/6 'Didicoys'—the Irish tinkers and other nomads around London who far outnumber the true Romanies.

didimist: see DIDYMIST.

didine ('daɪdaɪn), *a. Zool.* [f. mod.L. *didus* the dodo + -INE.] Belonging to the family *Didida* of birds, akin to the dodo.

1885 C. F. HOLDER *Marvels Anim. Life* 158 On the island of Rodriguez lived a didine bird, the *Pezophaps solitarius* of Leguat.

ˌdi-di'urnal, *a.* [f. DI-[2] twice + DIURNAL.]

Occurring twice a day.

1854 WOODWARD *Mollusca* (1856) 32 Some water-breathers require only..a di-diurnal visit from the tide.

didle ('daɪd(ə)l), *sb. local.* Also 5–8 **didal(l**, 9 **dydle.** [Derivation unascertained: see the vb.] A sharp triangular spade, used for clearing out ditches and water-courses; also a metal scoop or dredge fixed to the end of a long pole, used for a similar purpose. Hence **didle-man**, a didler.

1490 *Chamberl. Acc.* in Kirkpatrick *Relig. Orders Norwich* (1845) 316 Paid to the didalmen and other labourers, for carrying the muck out of the said ditch [of Norwich Castle]. **1573** TUSSER *Husb.* (1878) 38 A didall and crome for draining of ditches. **1688** R. HOLME *Armoury* III. 244/1 A Didall and Crome to drain Ditches. **1710** HILMAN *Tusser Redivivus, Didal*, a triangular spade, as sharp as a knife, excellent to bank ditches, where the earth is light and pestered with a sedgy weed. **1787** in GROSE *Provinc. Gloss.* **1883** G. C. DAVIES *Norfolk Broads* xx. (1884) 148 We have ice 'dydles'. They are large nets made of wire, at the end of a pole, with which we can scoop the broken pieces of ice up.

didle ('daɪd(ə)l), *v. local.* Also **dydle.** [Cf. prec.

A suggestion is that *didle* is worn down from *dike-delve.*]

a. *trans.* To clean out the bed of (a river or ditch). **b.** *intr.* To work with a didle or didling scoop. Hence **'didling** *vbl. sb.*, **'didler.**

1803 W. TAYLOR in Robberds *Mem.* I. 471 The older theology of the reformers is so gone by..that I should despair of the patience to didle in their mud for pearl-muscles. *a* **1825** FORBY *Voc. E. Anglia, Didle*, to clean the bottom of a river. **1835** *Municip. Corp. 1st Rept.* App. IV. 2465 The Surveyor of Didlers [of Norwich] superintends the persons employed in cleansing the river. **1842** *Ann. Reg.*

195 Messrs. Culley and Cossey lately built a didling boat. **1863** MORTON *Cycl. Agric.* Gloss., *Didle* (Norf., Suff.), to clean the bottom of a river with a didling scoop. **1865** W. WHITE *East. Eng.* I. 81, I..saw only a man who appeared to be hoeing the river bottom. He..was the dydler. **1883** G. C. DAVIES *Norfolk Broads* xv. (1884) 112 The dykes are kept clear, and the channel of the river deepened, by 'dydling'... At the end of a long pole is a metal scoop, in the shape of a ring, with a network..attached. This is plunged into the river, and scraped along the bottom to the side, where it is lifted out and the semi-liquid mud poured on to the rond. *Ibid.* xvii. 124 The reach had been dydled out.

didn't: see DO *v.* 29.

† **'dido**[1]. *Obs.* [Skeat suggests 'a tale of Dido', an old story.] ? An old story, a thrice-told tale.

1377 LANGL. *P. Pl.* B. XIII. 172 'It is but a dido', quod þis doctour, 'a dysoures tale'. [C. has the *v.rr.* a dydo, a dico, a dede, abido.]

dido[2] ('daɪdəʊ). *dial.* and *U.S. slang.* [Origin uncertain.] A prank, a caper; a disturbance, 'row', 'shindy'; *esp.* in phr. ***to cut (up) didoes.***

1807 J. R. SHAW *Life* ix. 140 A jolly Irishman, who cut as many didos as I could for the life of me. **1843-4** HALIBURTON *Sam Slick in Eng.* (Bartlett), Them Italian singers recitin' their jabber..and cuttin' didoes at a private concert. **1851** *New York Tribune* 10 Apr. (Farmer *Amer.*), We should have had just the same didoes cut up by the chivalry. **1869** MRS. STOWE *Oldtown Folks* 106 They will be a consultin' together, and cuttin' up didos. **1880** L. PARR *Adam & Eve* I. vi 151, I thought..you'd be cuttin' up a Dido with everything. **1891** 'Q.' *Noughts & Crosses* 76 There was a pretty dido goin' on atween the dree. **1893** Q. [COUCH] *Delectable Duchy* 271 What a dido he do kick up, to be sure. **1919** H. JENKINS *John Dene of Toronto* (1920) v. 84 'Well, you can't,' snapped John Dene, 'receiver's off. Your boys have been playing dido all morning on my phone.'

† **di,dodeca'hedral**, *a. Crystal. Obs.* [f. F. *didodécaèdre* (Haüy) + -AL[1]: see DI- *pref.*[2] I.] Having the form of a twelve-sided prism, with six planes in each base, or twenty-four faces in all.

1805-17 R. JAMESON *Char. Min.* (ed. 3) 204 Di-dodecahedral asparagus-stone..is a six-sided prism, truncated on the lateral edges, and acuminated on the extremities with six planes.

didonia (daɪ'dəʊnɪə). *Math.* [From the story of Dido, who bargained for as much land as could be covered with a hide, and cut the hide into a long narrow strip so as to inclose a large space.] (See quot.) Hence **di'donian** *a.*

1873 TAIT *Quaternions* (ed. 2) 191 If we give the name of 'Didonia' to the curve..which, on a given surface and with a given perimeter, contains the greatest area, then for such a Didonian curve [etc.].

didopper, obs. form of DIDAPPER, dabchick.

didrachm ('daɪdræm). Also 6 **didragme, didramme**, 6-7 **didrachme, didram**. [ad. L. *dīdrachma* or *didrachmon*, Gr. δίδραχμον a double drachma; f. δι-, DI-[2] + δραχμή DRACHMA. Cf. mod.F. *didrachme.*] An ancient Greek silver coin, of the value of two drachmæ: see DRACHMA.

1548 UDALL, etc., *Erasm. Par. Matt.* xvii. 24 Doth your master (quoth they) pay a Didram for trybute? **1582** N. T. (Rhem.) *Matt.* xvii. 24 Your maister doth he not pay the didrachmes? **1649** JER. TAYLOR *Gt. Exemp.* III. xiv. 45 A Sicle or didrachme the fourth part of an ounce of Silver. **1656** BLOUNT *Glossogr.*, *Didram*..an ancient coyn..of our money, it values 15*d.* **1807** ROBINSON *Archæol. Græca* v. xxvi. 550, 2 drachmæ or didrachm = 1*s.* 3½*d.* **1879** H. PHILLIPS *Notes Coins* 8 A didrachm of Velia in Lucania presents on the reverse a lion destroying a stag.

didrachmal (daɪ'drækməl), *a.* [f. prec. + -AL[1].] Of the weight of two drachmæ: applied to the stater, a gold coin.

1771 RAPER in *Phil. Trans.* LXI. 466 The didrachmal gold of Philip and Alexander is about 4 grains heavier than our guinea.

didst, 2nd sing. pa. t. of DO *v.*

† **di'duce**, *v. Obs.* [ad. L. *dīdūcĕre* to pull asunder or apart, pull in two, f. DI-[1], DIS- + *dūcĕre* to lead, draw. Used in 16-17th c., and sometimes confused in form with DEDUCE.]

1. *trans.* To pull or draw away or apart.

1578 BANISTER *Hist. Man* I. 26 By this yᵉ arme is distaunt, and deduced from the ribbes. **1650** BULWER *Anthropomet.* 118 It is moved and diduced outward and foreward. *a* **1696** SCARBURGH *Euclid* (1705) 8 The extreams of any crooked line may..be further and further diduced, till the crooked line be stretched to a strait line.

2. To dilate, expand, enlarge.

1605 BACON *Adv. Learn.* II. xxv. §11. 124 The exposition is diduced into large comentaries. **1657** TOMLINSON *Renou's Disp.* 307 Its seed brayed and drunk in passum..diduces its passages.

diduce, -ment, obs. (erron.) ff. DEDUCE, -MENT.

† **di'duct**, *v. Obs.* [f. L. *dīduct-* ppl. stem of *dīdūcĕre*: see prec.] = DIDUCE 1.

1676 GREW *Anat. Leaves* I. iv. (1682) 155 The lesser Threds, being so far diducted, as sometimes to stand at Right-Angles with the greater.

† **di'duction.** *Obs.* [ad. L. *dīductiōn-em*, n. of action f. *dīdūcĕre*: see DIDUCE and -TION.]

1. Drawing or pulling apart, separation.

a **1640** JACKSON *Creed* XI. v, By whose diduction or rent a place was opened for this future edifice to be erected in Him. **1649** BULWER *Pathomyot.* II. ii. 107 This Diduction of the Lips. **1661** BOYLE *Spring of Air* III. iv. (1682) 70 The strings ..must draw as forcibly as those within the bladder so as to hinder the diduction of the sides.

2. Dilatation, expansion.

1634 JACKSON *Creed* VII. xxv, By a gentle diduction or dilatation, of that sense which was included in the Apostles' Creed. **1664** H. MORE *Myst. Iniq.* 214 The 1260 days being but the Diduction of those larger measures of three times and a half or of forty two months in more numerous parts.

diductively, obs. (erron.) f. DEDUCTIVELY.

didy ('daɪdɪ). *U.S. colloq.* Also didie. [Infantile alteration of DIAPER *sb.*] = DIAPER *sb.* 2.

1902 in *Dialect Notes* II. 232. **1942** O. NASH *Good Intentions* 62 There are few spectacles..more untidy Than 1914 or something in a didy. **1945** B. MACDONALD *Egg & I* (1947) xvi. 175, I gathered up my baby..and the didy bag.

didymate ('dɪdɪmət), *a. Zool.* and *Bot.* [f. mod.L. *didym-us*, a. Gr. δίδυμ-ος twin + -ATE.] Paired, twinned; = DIDYMOUS. So **'didymated** *a.*

1843 HUMPHREYS *Brit. Moths* I. 70 Near the apex is a faint didymated brown spot. **1876** HARLEY *Mat. Med.* (ed. 6) 365 The stems are sometimes 1 inch in length, and the spherical heads $\frac{1}{10}$ inch in diameter and didymate.

‖ **'didymis.** *Anat. Obs.* Pl. **-es.** [f. Gr. δίδυμοι testicles, orig. 'twins'.] = EPIDIDYMIS.

[*c* **1400** *Lanfranc's Cirurg.* 169 þoruȝ þis dindimi goiþ arterijs and veynes to þe ballokis.] **1543** TRAHERON *Vigo's Chirurg.* 10 The didymes ben thin skynnes, which compasse the stones, and holde them hangyng. **1547** BOORDE *Brev. Health* cccxxii. 104 Of this Siphac the two dydymes be ingendred the which doth discend to the Stones. **1883** *Syd. Soc. Lex.*, *Didymis*, a synonym of *Epididymis*.

† **'didymist.** *Obs.* In 7 didimist. [f. *Didymus*, Gr. Δίδυμος twin, surname of the apostle Thomas, + -IST: cf. John xx. 24-27.] A doubter, sceptic.

1607 R. C. tr. *Estienne's World of Wonders* Ep. Ded., Those Didymists, who will beleeue nothing except their senses say Amen. **1631** R. H. *Arraignm. Whole Creature* x. §3. 87 If any bee a doubtfull Didimist in this poinct, or a disputefull Scepticke. *Ibid.* xii. §4. 134 Didimists, Sceptecks, or Athists.

didymite[1] ('dɪdɪmaɪt). = prec.

1822 *Blackw. Mag.* XI. 465 His Lordship is a Dydimite in politics and religion..he must put forth his finger to touch, ere he be convinced.

'didymite[2]. *Min.* Also erron. didrimite. [Named 1843 from Gr. δίδυμ-ος twin, being thought to be one of two minerals containing calcium carbonate in combination with silica.] A micaceous schist found in the Tyrol, nearly allied to Muscovite.

1863-72 WATTS *Dict. Chem.* II. 321 *Didrimite* or *Didymite.* **1868** DANA *Min.* 311.

didymium (dɪ'dɪmɪəm). *Chem.* [mod. f. Gr. δίδυμ-ος twin, with ending -IUM used with new metals. The name referred to its close association ('twin-brotherhood') with *lanthanium* previously discovered, both metals being found associated with cerium.] A rare metal, discovered by Mosander in 1841; found only in association with cerium and lanthanium. Symbol Di.

1842 *Chemical Gaz.* I. 4 Mosander, the discoverer of lanthanium, has found that these metals are always mixed with a third new element (didymium), from which at present it is impossible to separate them. **1867** W. A. MILLER *Elem. Chem.* I. (ed. 4) 166 Small quantities of didymium in solutions of lanthanium and cerium. **1892** *Daily News* 11 Feb. 3/6 A method of separating cerium from didymium.

didymous ('dɪdɪməs), *a. Bot.* and *Zool.* [f. mod.L. *didym-us*, a. Gr. δίδυμ-ος twin + -OUS. In mod.F. *didyme.*] Growing in pairs, paired, twin.

1794 MARTYN *Rousseau's Bot.* xxxi. 483 The outer ones [nectaries] being..didymous or twinned. **1870** HOOKER *Stud. Flora* 171 Araliaceæ..anthers didymous.

‖ **Didynamia** (dɪdɪ'neɪmɪə) *Bot.* [mod.L. (Linnæus, 1735) f. Gr. δι-, DI-[2] twice, two + δύναμις power, strength; fancifully referring to the superior length of two of the stamens.] The fourteenth class in the Linnæan Sexual System of plants, containing those with four stamens in pairs of unequal length, and comprehending the Natural Orders *Labiatæ*, *Scrophulariaceæ*, and other smaller groups.

Hence **'didynam**, a plant of this class; **didy'namian** *a.*, **didy'namic** *a.*, of or pertaining to the class Didynamia; didynamous.

1753 CHAMBERS *Cycl. Supp.* s.v., Didynamia..of this class of plants are thyme, lavender, basil, etc. **1794** MARTYN *Rousseau's Bot.* ix. 91 The fourteenth class, didynamia, signifying that two of the stamens are stronger than the others. **1828** WEBSTER, *Didynam..Didynamian.* **1882** OGILVIE. *Didynamic.*

didynamous (daɪ'dɪnəməs, dɪd-), *a. Bot.* [f. as prec. + -OUS.] Of stamens: Arranged in two pairs of unequal length. Also of a flower or plant: Having four stamens thus arranged; belonging to the Linnæan class *Didynamia.*

1794 MARTYN *Rousseau's Bot.* xxii. 314 The corolla.. personate with four didynamous stamens. **1830** LINDLEY *Nat. Syst. Bot.* 202 *Globularineæ*, stamens 4..somewhat didynamous. **1857** HENFREY *Bot.* 355 *Orobanchaceæ*.. Flowers monopetalous, didynamous. *Ibid.* 357 A general resemblance exists between the..other didynamous monopetalous Orders.

didynamy (daɪ'dɪnəmɪ, dɪd-). *Bot.* [f. prec. + -Y: cf. *autonomous, autonomy.*] Didynamous condition or structure.

1830 LINDLEY *Nat. Syst. Bot.* 234 The didynamy of Acanthaceæ is frequently different from that of Scrophularineæ in the posterior pair of stamens being the longest.

die (daɪ), *sb.*[1] Pl. dice (daɪs), dies (daɪz). Forms: 4-5 dee, 6-8 dye, dy, 6- die. *Plur.* 4 des, 4-5 dees, deys, dys, 4-6 dyse, dyce, 5-6 dis(e, (dysse, 6 dyyss), 5- dice; also 5-6 dyes, 5- dies. Also *Sing.* 4- 5 dyse, 5-6 dyce, 5-7 dice; *Plur.* 4-5 dyces, 5 dises, dices, dycys. [Early ME. *dē*, *dee*, pl. *dēs*, *dees*, a. OF. *de* (nom. sing. and obl. pl. 12-14th c. *dez*), mod.F. *dé*, pl. *dés* = Pr. *dat*, *datz*, Cat. *dau*, Sp., It. *dado*; in form:—L. *datum*, subst. use of *datus*, *-um* 'given', pa. pple. of *dare* to give. It is inferred that, in late pop. L., *datum* was taken in the sense 'that which is given or decreed (sc. by lot or fortune)', and was so applied to the dice by which this was determined. Latinized mediæval forms from It. and Fr. were *dadus*, *decius*.

In late OF. the form *dey* occurs in 14th c.; and *dez* was sometimes used in sing. down to 17th c.: cf. the 14-17th c. Eng. use of *dice* as sing. The remarkable point in the history of the Eng. word is the change of *dē*, *dēs*, to *dȳ*, *dȳs*, (*dyse*, *dyce*, *dice*), in the ME. period. The oldest Chaucer MSS., Harl., Ellesm., Hengwrt, have *dees*, which also survived as late as 1484 in Caxton, but *dys* occurs in the other Chaucer MSS., and in rime in the Bodleian MS. of *Kyng Alisaunder*, part of which is in the Auchinleck MS., attributed to the middle of the 14th c. Before 1500, *dȳ*, *dȳs* seem to have completely passed from the *ē* into the *ī* class, the fortunes of which they have since shared. As in *pence*, the plural *s* retains its original breath sound, probably because these words were not felt as ordinary plurals, but as collective words; cf. the orig. plural *truce*, where the collective sense has now passed into a singular. This pronunciation is indicated in later spelling by *-ce*: cf. the umlaut plurals *lice*, *mice*, the inflexional forms *hence*, *once*, *twice*, *since*, and the words *ice*, *nice*, *advice*, *device*, *defence*, in all which *-ce* represents a phonetic and original *-s*. In the newer senses where the plural is not collective, a form (daɪz) of the ordinary type has arisen; cf. the non-collective later plural *pennies*.]

I. With plural *dice.* (The form *dice* (used as *pl.* and *sing.*) is of much more frequent occurrence in gaming and related senses than the singular *die.*)

1. a. A small cube of ivory, bone, or other material, having its faces marked with spots numbering from one to six, used in games of chance by being thrown from a box or the hand, the chance being decided by the number on the face of the die that turns uppermost. Also, a cube bearing other devices on its faces, or a solid with more or less than six faces (see quots.). **b.** *pl.* The game played with these; *esp.* in phr. ***at (the) dice.***

α. *singular.* dee, dye, dy, die.

1393 GOWER *Conf.* II. 209 The chaunce is cast upon a dee, But yet full oft a man may see [etc.]. *c* **1430** *Pilgr. Lyf Manhode* I. cv. (1869) 56 Nouht so gret as a as in a dee. **1570** LEVINS *Manip.* 96/41 A dye, *alea.* **1589** *Pappe w. Hatchet* (1844) 23 Hee'le cogge the die. **1610** B. JONSON *Alch.* II. i, You shall no more deale with the hollow die, Or the fraile card. **1656** STANLEY *Hist. Philos.* VIII. 85 So to cast the dy that it may chance right. **1680** COTTON *Gamester* in Singer *Hist. Cards* 336 He puts one dye into the box. **1705** MRS. CENTLIVRE *Gamester* I. i, To teach you the management of the die. **1779-81** JOHNSON *L.P.*, *Butler* Wks. II. 191 To throw a dye, or play at cards. **1822** HAZLITT *Table-t.* II. vii. 156 Dependent on the turn of a die, on the tossing up of a halfpenny. **1838** DE MORGAN *Ess. Probab.* 74 The real probability that 6000 throws with a die shall give exactly 1000 aces. **1872** F. HALL *Exempl. False Philol.* 68 The cast of a die is absolutely impossible of prediction.

β. *plural.* des, dees, deys, dys, dyse, dyce, dise, dice.

c **1330** R. BRUNNE *Chron. Wace* (Rolls) 11392 Somme pleide wyþ des and tables. **1340** *Ayenb.* 45 þe gemenes of des, and of tables. **13..** *K. Alis.* (MS. Laud Misc. 622) 3297 þe rybaude pleieþ at þe dys [*ed. Weber*, deys] Swiþe selde þe fole is wys. *c* **1386** CHAUCER *Pard. T.* 5 They daunce and pleyen at dees [so *Harl.*, *Heng.*; *Camb.* deis, *Petw.* dys, *Corp.* dyse, *Lansd.* dise] bothe day and nyght. **1387** TREVISA *Higden* (Rolls) VII. 75 Pleyenge wiþ dees of gold. *c* **1400** *Destr. Troy* 1622 (MS. *a* 1500) The draghtes, the dyse, and oþer dregh gaumes. **1474** CAXTON *Chesse* 127 In his lift hand thre dyse. **1477** EARL RIVERS (Caxton) *Dictes* 109 His maistre pleyed gladly atte dise. **1479** in *Eng. Gilds* (1870) 422 The towne clerke to fynde theym Dice. **1481-90** *Howard Househ. Bks.* (Roxb.) 327 For a bale of dysse. **1484** CAXTON *Fables of*

Avian (1889) 21 Whiche doo no thynge but playe with dees and cardes. **1495** *Act 11 Hen. VII*, c. 2 §5 The Tenys, Closshe, Dise, Cardes, Bowles. **1536** R. BEERLEY in *Four C. Eng. Lett.* 35 Sume at cardes and sume at dyyss. **1556** *Chron. Gr. Friars* (Camden) 73 Wych playd wyth kynge Henry the viij^te at dysse. **1576** FLEMING *Panopl. Epist.* 340 In casting a paire of dyce. **1580** BARET *Alv.* D 656 The life of a man is like a game at the dice. **1603** HOLLAND *Plutarch's Rom. Quest.* (1892) 57 Playing at dice with cokall bones. **1697** DRYDEN *Æneid* IX. 452 From Dice and Wine the Youth retir'd to Rest. **1784** R. BAGE *Barham Downs* II. 54 Lord Winterbottom is ruined by the dice. **1821** BYRON *Mar. Fal.* IV. ii, They Have won with false dice. **1871** T. TAYLOR *Jeanne Darc* III. i, Rough soldiers left their oaths, and dice, and lewdness. **1874** *Macomb* (Ill.) *Eagle* 23 Nov. 1/5 'Now, gentlemen,' said she, 'we will throw poker dice.' **1910** *Encycl. Brit.* VIII. 176/2 Eight-sided dice have comparatively lately been introduced in France as aids to children in learning the multiplication table. **1927** W. E. COLLINSON *Contemp. Eng.* 32 Crown and Anchor is played by means of dice marked with crowns, anchors, hearts, etc. and a board similarly marked. **1960** R. C. BELL *Board & Table Games* v. 125 Games with two-sided dice. *Ibid.* 141 Three special dice are used marked with a crown, an anchor, a heart, a spade, a diamond, and a club.

γ. singular *dice*, plural *dices*: cf. obs. F. sing. *dez*.

1388 *Act 12 Rich. II*, c. 6 §1 Les..jeues appellez coytes dyces, gettre de pere. *c* **1425** *Voc.* in Wr.-Wülcker 666 *Hic talus*, dyse. *c* **1440** *Promp. Parv.* 121/1 Dycyn, or pley wythe dycys, *aleo*. *c* **1450** *Bk. Curtasye* 228 in *Babees Bk.* 306 Ne at the dyces with him to play. **1474** CAXTON *Chesse* 132 He caste thre dyse and on eche dyse was a sise. **1483** *Cath. Angl.* 99/1 A Dice, *taxillus, alea*. **1552** HULOET, Dice or die, *alea, talus, thessera*. **1677** GALE *Crt. Gentiles* III. 100 Amongst the Grecians κυβεια signifies a Dice..the cast of a Dice was most casual and incertain. **1751** MRS. E. HEYWOOD *Hist. Betsy Thoughtless* IV. 202 Protesting never to touch a card or throw a dice again.

2. a. In figurative and allusive use; thus sometimes = Hazard, chance, luck.

1548 HALL *Chron., Hen. V* 56b, When kyng Henry perceived that the dice ranne not to his purpose, he abstained from the assaulte. **1590** SPENSER *F.Q.* I. ii. 36 His harder fortune was to fall Under my speare; such is the dye of warre. **1594** SHAKS. *Rich. III*, v. iv. 10, I haue set my life vpon a cast, And I will stand the hazard of the Dye. **1676** D'URFEY *Mad. Fickle* IV. i, The uncertain Dice of Fate thus far runs well. **1693** DENNIS *Imp. Crit.* ii. 8 If that was his design, the Author has turn'd the Dice upon him, I gad. **1742** YOUNG *Nt. Th.* vi. 37 When..th' important dye Of life and death spun doubtful, ere it fell, And turn'd up life. **1844** DISRAELI *Coningsby* VI. vi, The immensity of the stake which he was hazarding on a most uncertain die. **1871** MORLEY *Voltaire* (1886) 169 France and Austria were both playing with cogged dice.

b. Phrases. †(*a*) ***to make dice of*** (a person's) ***bones***: see quot. 1646. †(*b*) ***to set (put) the dice upon*** (any one): see quot. 1598. (*c*) ***the die is cast***: the decisive step is taken; the course of action is irrevocably decided. (*d*) ***upon a*** or ***the die***: depending upon a chance or contingency, in a critical position, at stake; so ***to set upon the die***. (*e*) ***in the dice***: liable to turn up, as a contingent possibility (cf. *on the cards*, CARD *sb.*^{2} 2 e). (*f*) In comparisons: ***as smooth, true, straight as a die***. (*g*) Colloq. phr. ***no dice***: (it is or was) useless, hopeless, unsuccessful, profitless, etc; nothing; 'nothing doing' (orig. *U.S.*).

a. 1591 R. TURNBULL *Exp. St. James* 103 They wil make dice of their bones, but they will haue the extremitie of them. **1621** BURTON *Anat. Mel.* III. i. III. iii. (1676) 268/1 We will not relent..till we have confounded him and his, made dice of his bones, as they say, see him rot in prison. **1646** J. COOKE *Vind. Law* 22 We say proverbially 'make dice of his bones', the meaning whereof is, that if a prisoner die in execution, after the Crowner has viewed his body, the creditor hath dice delivered him at the Crowne Office as having all that he is likely to have.

b. 1598 FLORIO, *Stancheggiare*..to set the dice vpon one, to tyrannize ouer one. **1658** *Whole Duty Man* xii. §6. 94 Thou..takest this opportunity to set the dice upon him. **1699** BENTLEY *Phal.* Introd. 2 He will put the Dice upon his Readers, as often as he can.

c. 1634 SIR T. HERBERT *Trav.* A iij b, Is the die cast, must At this one throw all thou hast gaind be lost? **1720** OZELL *Vertot's Rom. Rep.* II. XIII. 287 Cæsar..throws himself into the River..saying..It is done: The Die is thrown. **1879** G. MEREDITH *Egoist* xxvii. (1889) 262 The die is cast—I cannot go back.

d. *c* **1659** D. PELL *Impr. Sea* 230 To recover her young when they are upon a dye. *Ibid.* 393 Ah poor soul..It will not now bee granted thee, when thou art upon thy dye. **1821** BYRON *Sardan.* II. i. 139 But here is more upon the die—a kingdom. **1832** SOUTHEY *Hist. Penins. War* III. 859 When Rochejaquelein..set life and fortune thus upon the die.

e. 1858 DE QUINCEY *Greece under Rom.* Wks. VIII. 317 It is hardly 'in the dice' that any downright novelty of fact should remain in reversion for this nineteenth century.

f. 1530 PALSGR. 629 Make this borde as smothe as a dyce, *comme vng dez*. **1600** HAKLUYT *Voy.* (1810) III. 256 Goodly fields..as plaine and smoothe as any die. *c* **1710** C. FIENNES *Diary* (1888) 151 Y^e tide was out all upon the sands at Least a mile, wch was as smooth as a Die. *a* **1732** GAY *Songs & Ball., New Song on New Similies*, You'll know me truer than a die. **1877** SPRY *Cruise Challenger* xiii. (ed. 7) 226 Arums climbing fifty feet up large trees as straight as a die.

g. 1931 D. RUNYON *Guys & Dolls* (1932) 136 He is a guy I consider no dice. *a* **1939** R. CHANDLER *Trouble is my Business* (1950) 62 The old man's had a stroke... No dice there. *Ibid.* 222 No dice, sister. I'm putting the pressure on. **1943** P. CHEYNEY *You can always Duck* iv. 67 'She can come back here and go on driving a car.' 'No, sir,' I tell him. 'No dice. That dame has started bein' Mrs. Cara Travis an' she's goin' on bein' Mrs. Travis.' **1952** WODEHOUSE *Barmy in Wonderland* viii. 81, I was around at her bank this morning trying to find out what her balance was, but no dice. Fanny won't part. **1959** 'H. HOWARD' *Deadline* iv. 47 She was on her way back to report that it was no dice. **1959** M. PUGH *Chancer* 10 Nothing doing. I'm not going. No dice. **1968** *Globe & Mail* (Toronto) 10 July 1/4 'It's no dice as far as I'm concerned,' said one picket who made a derisive gesture.

3. a. A small cubical segment formed by cutting anything down. †Also, a small cubical bullet (cf. *die-shot*).

?*c* **1390** *Form of Cury* in Warner *Antiq. Culin.* 6 Take the noumbles of a calf, swyne, or of shepe, parboile hem, and skerne [? kerue] hem to dyce. **1496** *Ld. Treas. Acc. Scotl.* I. 295 For cutting of viij^xx and ix dis of irne to the pellokis. **1549** *Privy Council Acts* (1890) II. 350 Dyce of yron. ijm^l; shott of stone, v^c. *a* **1628** F. GREVILLE *Sidney* (1652) 139 Wounded..with a square die out of a field-piece. **1769** MRS. RAFFALD *Eng. House-kpr.* (1778) 141 Dish them up..with turnips and carrots cut in dice. **1889** B. WHITBY *Awakening M. Fenwick* II. 166 She hacked her buttered toast into dice.

γ. with *dice* in singular.

14.. *Anc. Cookery* in *Househ. Ord.* (1790) 466 Take fresshe braune of a bore sothen, and cut hit in grete dices. *c* **1420** *Liber Cocorum* (1862) 38 Square as dises þou shalt hit make. **1557** RECORDE *Whetst.* R ij, I haue a dice of Brasse of .64. vnces of Troye weighte.

†**b.** With negative: ***never a dyse*** = not a bit, not in the least. *Obs.*

c **1400** *Destr. Troy* 808 þai..shall..neuer dere hym a dyse.

II. with plural *dies*.

4. a. A cubical block; in *Arch.* a cubical or square block of stone forming part of a building; *spec.* the cubical portion of a pedestal, between the base and cornice; = DADO 1. †**b.** A square tablet.

1664 EVELYN tr. *Freart's Archit.* 123 The Italians call it the Zoccolo, Pillow or Die (because of its Cubique and solid figure). **1726** LEONI *Alberti's Archit.* I. 13/1 A kind of little Wall, which we shall call the Plinth, others perhaps may call it the Dye. **1730** A. GORDON *Maffei's Amphith.* 240 Some Plinths, or rather Dyes, seen upon the second Cornish. *Ibid.* 265 Marble, cut thin in small square Dyes. *a* **1748** WATTS (J.), Young creatures have learned spelling of words by having them pasted upon little flat tablets or dies. **1832** GELL *Pompeiana* I. vi. 109 The figures stand..upon little square plinths or dies. **1854** E. DE WARREN tr. *De Saulcy's Dead Sea* II. 224 The coping..is composed, first, of a cube, or die, measuring nearly six yards on each side.

5. An engraved stamp used for impressing a design or figure upon some softer material, as in coining money, striking a medal, embossing paper, etc.

Often used in pairs, which may be dissimilar, for impressing unlike designs on opposite sides of the thing stamped (as in coining), or corresponding, one in relief and one countersunk (as in an embossing stamp).

1699 in M. Smith *Mem. Secret Service* App. 19 To bring or send to him some Deys..to coin some Mill'd Money. *c* **1724** SWIFT *Consid. Wood's Coinage* Wks. 1761 III. 164 There have been such variety of dyes made use of by Mr. Wood in stamping his money. **1787** T. JEFFERSON *Writ.* (1859) II. 123 The workman..brought me..the medal in gold, twenty-three in copper, and the dye. **1862** T. MORRALL *Needle-making* 16 Making sail and packing needles..by means of dies fixed in a stamp, after the manner of making buttons. **1879** H. PHILLIPS *Addit. Notes Coins* 1 The portrait is reduced..to the size it is to occupy on the die. **1879** *Cassell's Techn. Educ.* IV. 263/1 The die..is a block of steel welded in a larger block of iron, the impression of the intended work cut in its face.

6. The name of various mechancial appliances:

spec. **a.** One of two or more pieces (fitted in a *stock*) to form a segment of a hollow screw for cutting the thread of a screw or bolt. **b.** The bed-piece serving as a support for metal from which a piece is to be punched, and having an opening through which the piece is driven. **c.** *Forging.* A device consisting of two parts which act together to give to the piece swaged between them the desired form. **d.** *Brick-making.* A mouth-piece or opening through which the clay is forced, serving to mould it into the required form. **e.** A part of the apparatus used in crushing ore: see quot. 1881. **f.** *Shoe-making*, etc. A shaped knife for cutting out blanks of any required shape and size: cf. DIE *v.*^{2}

1812-6 J. SMITH *Panorama Sc. & Art* I. 39 The best outside screws are..cut with what are called stocks or dies. **1833** HOLLAND *Manuf. Metal* II. 197 The interstices are then filled by the insertion of the hardened steel dies. **1856** *Farmer's Mag.* Nov. 406 (*Brick-making*) The mouthpiece or die is about half-an-inch deeper and half an inch broader than the stream of clay after it passes through the moulding rollers to the cutting apparatus. *a* **1875** CHAMBERLAIN in Ure *Dict. Arts* I. 529 As soon as it has..forced the clay of one box through the die..the plunger returns and empties [the other] box of clay through a die on the opposite side. **1881** RAYMOND *Mining Gloss., Die*, a piece of hard iron, placed in a mortar to receive the blow of a stamp, or in a pan to receive the friction of the muller. Between the die and the stamp or muller the ore is crushed. **1885** *Harper's Mag.* LXX. 282 By means of 'dies', or sole-shaped knives, in a die-machine, required shapes, sizes, and widths are cut out. Before the use of dies, soles were 'rounded out' by hand..Steam-power and revolving die-block [were] applied in 1857.

7. *Sc.* 'A toy, a gewgaw' (Jamieson).

(Also in nursery language *die-die*. Identity with this word is doubtful.)

1808 JAMIESON, *Die*, a toy, a gewgaw, *Loth.* **1816** SCOTT *Antiq.* xxi, 'The bits o' weans wad up..and toddle to the door, to pu' in the auld Blue-Gown that mends a' their bonny dies.' **1816** —— *Old Mort.* x, 'Ye hae seen the last o' me, and o' this bonny die too', said Jenny, holding between her finger and thumb a splendid silver dollar.

III. 8. *attrib.* and *Comb.* **a.** ***die-like, -shaped*** adjs.; ***die-block, -machine*** (see 6 f); †**die-bone**, the cuboid bone of the tarsus; †**die-shot**, shot of cubical form, dice-shot; **die-sinker**, an engraver of dies for stamping (see 5); so **die-sinking; die-stake**: see quot. 1874; **die-stock**, the stock or handle for holding the dies used in cutting screws (see 6 a); **die-wise** *a.* and *adv.*, in the manner of a die, in a cubical form.

1634 T. JOHNSON *Parey's Chirurg.* 234 It is knit by Synarthrosis to the *Die-bone. **1875** URE *Dict. Arts* II. 29 This must..be left to the experience of the *die-forger. **1688** R. HOLME *Armoury* III. 378/1 A..*Die-like figure four square every way; a square solid. **1875** URE *Dict. Arts* II. 29 The very cross-grained, or highly crystalline steel..acquires fissures under the *die-press. **1878** HUXLEY *Physiogr.* 148 A huge *die-shaped mass of stone. **1581** STYWARD *Mart. Discipl.* II. 143 Such as haue *die shot..contrarie to the Cannons & lawes of the field. **1815** *Chron.* in *Ann. Reg.* 317/2 Employed by..*dye sinkers and ornamental engravers. **1893** *Daily News* 3 July 2/7 Medallists and die-sinkers have been very busy..in view of the Royal wedding. **1874** KNIGHT *Dict. Mech.* I. 592 s.v. *Coining-press*, The lower die is on what is termed the *die-stake, and gives the reverse impression. **1863** SMILES *Indust. Biogr.* 238 He..seems to have directed his attention to screw-making..and [made] a pair of very satisfactory *die-stocks. **1674** N. FAIRFAX *Bulk & Selv.* 128 In *die wise or cubically. **1702** THORESBY in *Phil. Trans.* XXV. 1864 The heads not Die-wise, as the large Nails now are, but perfectly flat.

b. Combs. with the pl. form *dice*, as ***dice-cogging, -gospeller, -maker***; **dice-board**, a board upon which dice are thrown; **dice-coal** (see quot.); **dice-headed** *a.*, having a cubical boss or stud (of nails used for strengthening doors, etc.); **dice holes** (see quot.); **dice-man**, a sharper who cheats with dice; **dice-shot** = *die-shot* (see DIE); **dice-top**, a top of polygonal form with numbers marked on its faces, a teetotum. Also DICE-BOX, -PLAY, etc.

1844 THIRLWALL *Greece* VIII. 453 Mummius..had as little eye for them as any of his men, who made *dice-boards of the finest master-pieces of painting. **1842** BRANDE, **Dice-coal*, a species of coal easily splitting into cubical fragments. **1852** THACKERAY *Esmond* I. xiii, I played a *dice-cogging scoundrel in Alsatia for his ears. **1550** LATIMER *Serm. at Stamford* Wks. I. 269 Among so great a number of gospellers, some are card-gospellers, some are *dice-gospellers, some are pot-gospellers; all are not good. **1497** *Ld. Treas. Acc. Scot.* I. 357 V^c ȝet nalis *dis hedit to Dunbar. **1593** in Willis & Clark *Cambridge* (1886) I. 74, 100 dicheaded nailes pro ostio. **1882** CAULFEILD & SAWARD *Dict. Needlework* 153 *Dice Holes..a stitch..used in Honiton..lace. **1530** PALSGR. 213/2 *Dice maker, *dessier*. **1714** MANDEVILLE *Fab. Bees* (1725) I. 81 Card and dice-makers..are the immediate ministers to a legion of vices. **1871** *Echo* 14 Mar., *Dice-men and thimble-rigs were scattered here and there, making a fine harvest. **1588** LUCAR *Colloq. Arte Shooting* App. 57 Chaine shot..*dice shot. **1668** J. WHITE *Rich Cab.* (ed. 4) 124 Square pieces of iron, called dice-shot. **1894** MASKELYNE *Sharps & Flats* 257 That well-known device, the '*dice-top' or 'teetotum'.

die, *sb.*^{2} *slang.* [f. DIE *v.*^{1}] Only in phr. ***to make a die (of it)*** = to die.

1611 COTGR., *Fouïr aux taupes*, to turne vp the heeles; goe feed wormes, make a dy. *Ibid.*, *Tirer les chausses*, to kicke vp the heeles; to make a dye. **1819** *Metropolis* I. 58 I thought he was going to make a die of it! Why, he's as old as the Hills. **1883** *Century Mag.* XXVI. 238/2, 'I believe you're trying to make a die of it', said the doctor.

die (daɪ), *v.*^{1} Pa. t. and pple. **died** (daɪd); pr. pple. **dying** ('daɪɪŋ). Forms α. 2–4 **deȝ-en, dei-e(n**, 3 **deiȝ-en, deaiȝ-e**, 4 **day-e**, 4–5 **deghe**, 4–6 **dei(e, dey(e**, (5 **deyn**), 4–6 (*north.*) **de**, 4– **dee**. β. 4–5 **diȝ-en, dyȝ-en, digh-e, dygh-e, dy-en, di-en**, 4–7 **diy**, (5 **dyi**), 4–8 **dye**, 4– **die**. Pa. t. α. 3 **deiȝede, dæide, deaide**, 3–5 **deid(e**, 4 **daide, dayed, deȝed, deied(e**; *north.* **deyt, ded**, 4–5 **deyd(e, deyed**, 5 **deghit, -et, -t**, 5– *north.* **deed, deit, deet**. β. 4 **dyede**, 4–5 **dyde**, 4–6 **dide**, (5 **dyet**), 4–8 **dyed**, 4– **died**. [Early ME. *dēȝen, dēghen*, corresp. to ON. *deyja* (orig. *døyja*, OSw. and ODa. *döia*, Da. *döe*, Sw. *dö*), OFris. *deia, deja*, OS. *dōian*, OHG. *touwan*, MHG. *töuwen*; these represent an OTeut. strong verb of the 6th ablaut class **daw-j-an*, pa. t. *dôw*, pa. pple. *dawan-*, the strong inflexions being retained in ON. (*dó-*:—**dów*, *dáinn*:—**dawans*). In the other langs. and in Eng. a regular weak verb. No instance of the word is known in OE. literature (its sense being expressed by *steorfan, sweltan*, or the periphrastic *wesan déad*, pa. t. *wæs déad*: see DEAD 1 d) hence it is generally held to have been early lost in OE. (as in Gothic, and as subsequently in all the continental WGer. langs.), and re-adopted in late OE. or early ME. from Norse; but some think that the facts point rather to the preservation of an OE. *diēȝan, dēȝan*, in some dialect; the word appears to have been in general use from the 12th c., even in the s.w. dialects (see Napier in *Hist. Holy Rood*, E.E.T.S., 1894). The ME. *dēȝen, dēghen* came regularly down to 1500 as *deye*, which was retained in the North as *dey, dē, dee* (still current from Lancashire to Scotland); but in standard English *dēghe* was in 14th c. (in conformity with the common phonetic history of OE. *eh, eah, eoh*, as in *dye, eye, fly, high, lie, nigh, thigh*, etc.) narrowed to *diȝe, dighe*, whence the later *dye, die*.

The oldest text of Cursor M. (Cotton) has only *dey*; in the later texts this is frequently altered to *dighe, dye*, when not in rime, in the late Trinity MS. sometimes even in rime, with change of text. Chaucer used both *dey* and *dye*, the C.T. (Ellesm. MS.) contains in the rimes 22 examples of *deye* and 50 of *dye*. Both forms are also used in the Wyclifite version, and both occur in Caxton's works.

The stem *dau-* appears also in Gothic in the ppl. a. *dauþs*, OE. *dēad* (:—*daud-oz*) DEAD, and the sb. *dauþus*, OE. *dēaþ*, DEATH *sb.*; also in *afdôjan* (:—*afdôwjan*), pa. pple. *afdauid-* (:—*afdôwid-*) vexed, worried. (The relationship of Gothic *diwanô*, *undiwanei*, etc. is uncertain.) The simple verb has shown a notable tendency to die out, and leave its place to be taken by derivatives: thus in Gothic *dauþnan* to die.]

I. Of man and sentient beings. * *literally.*

1. a. *intr.* To lose life, cease to live, suffer death; to expire.

The proper word for this, and more especially for the cessation of life by disease or natural decay (to which it is often restricted dialectally), but also used of all modes of death, as 'to die in battle', 'at the stake', 'at the hands of justice'.

α. Forms deȝe(n, dey-e(n, deiȝ-e(n, dei-e(n, day, de, dee. (After 1500, north. Eng. and Sc.)

c **1135** *Holy Rood* (1894) 14 Forþan ðe ic nu deȝen sceal. *c* **1205** LAY. 28893 þe alde king deȝede. *Ibid.* 31796 Al folc gon to deȝen. *a* **1225** *Ancr. R.* 108 Me schal er deien. *Ibid.* 110 He þolede sundri pine, & deiȝede. *c* **1290** *S. Eng. Leg.* I. 62/311 Heo deide þane þridde day. *a* **1300** *Cursor M.* 24139 (Edin.) Latte vs deien samin [*Cott.* dei, *Fairf.* deye]. **13..** *Ibid.* 16762 + 119 (Cott.) Him was not geue..plas, War-on he miȝt dee fayre..but deed heȝe in þe air. **13..** *Ibid.* 11323 (Gött.) þat heo dede suld neuer dei, Til he suld se crist self wit ei [*Trin. MS.* deȝe, eȝe]. **13..** *Sir Beues* 3135 þat emperur ne ȝ daide, His wif confortede him & saide. **1375** BARBOUR *Bruce* I. 430 Hys fadyr..deyt tharfor in my presoun. *c* **1380** *Sir Ferumb.* 5738 Ech man schal rysen on such aray As he dayeþ ynne. *c* **1380** WYCLIF *Wks.* (1880) 296 Crist deyede to destrie þis heresye & alle his martyrs aftir deyeden. **1382** —— *Rom.* xiv. 8 Where we deien, we deien to the Lord. *c* **1386** CHAUCER *Prioress' T.* 82 And eek hire for to preye To been oure help and socour when we deye. *c* **1400** *Destr. Troy* 921 All dropet the dule as he degh wold. *Ibid.* 9551 The buerne deghet. *a* **1420** *Sir Amadace* (Camden) lxxii, Thenne sone aftur the kinge deet. *c* **1440** *Promp. Parv.* 117 Deyyn, *morior*. *c* **1460** *Towneley Myst.* (Surtees) 40 It gars me quake for ferd to dee. *c* **1470** HENRY *Wallace* II. 127 Than wist he nocht of no help, bot to de. **1483** CAXTON *Gold. Leg.* 142/2 Hys fader and moder deyden. *c* **1489** —— *Sonnes of Aymon* iii. 79 Noble knyghtes deyeng full myserably vpon the erthe. *a* **1500** *Nutbrown Maid* xxiv. in *Arnolde's Chron.* (1811) 202, I [shal] dey sone after ye be gone. **1552** LYNDESAY *Monarche* 6114 Neuer to de agane. *a* **1605** MONTGOMERIE *Sonn.* lix. 5 To see Sa many lovers, but redemption, dee. *a* **1800** W. DOUGLAS *Song*, For bonnie Annie Lawrie, I'd lay me down and dee. **1861** E. WAUGH *Birtle Carter's Tale* 11 Yo desarven a comfortable sattlement i'th top shop when yo dee'n.

β. Forms diȝ-e(n, dy-e(n, di-e(n, dye, dy, die.

c **1330** R. BRUNNE *Chron. Wace* (Rolls) 14306 He was so wounded, he most dye. **13..** *Cursor M.* 7959–60 (Gött.) For þu sal witt þat i sal noght lye þe son of barsabe he sal die [*Cott.* lei, dei, *Fairf.* legh, degh, *Trin.* lyȝe, diȝe]. **13..** *Guy Warw.* (A.) 630 Felice said to Gij, þou dost folie þatow wilt for mi loue dye. **13..** *E.E. Allit. P.* A. 306 þaȝ fortune dyd your flesch to dyȝe. **13..** *Song of Yesterday* 87 in *E.E.P.* (1862) 135 A mon þat nou parteþ and dis [*rime* wys]. **1382** WYCLIF *Rev.* xiv. 13 Blessid the deede men, that dien in the Lord. *c* **1386** CHAUCER *Miller's T.* 627 And for the smert he wende for to dye, As he were wood for wo he gan to crye. *a* **1400–50** *Alexander* 1260 (Ashm. MS.) To do as driȝten wald deme & dyi [*MS.* D. dye] all togedire. **1477** SIR J. PASTON in *Paston Lett.* No. 806 III. 207 Yf I dyghe ny the Cyte of London. **1483** *Cath. Angl.* 99 To Die, *mori*. **1523** LD. BERNERS *Froiss.* I. cccxv. 485 To dye in prison. **1553** T. WILSON *Rhet.* (1567) 19 b, Undoubtedly, the lawier neuer dieth a begger. **1556** *Chron. Gr. Friars* (Camden) 3 Thys yere this kynge Henry the thirde dyde. **1633** EARL MANCH. *Al Mondo* (1636) 142 He that will live when he dyes, must dye while hee lives. **1635** A. STAFFORD *Fem. Glory* (1869) 147 Her armes express the Crosse whereon He dide. **1651** HOBBES *Leviath.* II. xix. 99 Not onely Monarchs, but also whole Assemblies dy. **1667** MILTON *P.L.* VII. 544 In the day thou eat'st, thou di'st. **1695** WOODWARD *Nat. Hist. Earth* (1723) 28 The Shell-fish..live and dye there. **1712** POPE *Spect.* No. 48 ¶6 Little Spirits that are born and die with us. **1727–38** GAY *Fables* I. xxvii. 50 So groaned and dy'd. **1728** NEWTON *Chronol. Amended* 37 Some of these Archons might dye before the end of the ten years. **1769** JOHNSON in Boswell *Life* (1847) 211 It matters not how a man dies, but how he lives. **1807** WORDSW. *White Doe* VII. 315 At length, thus faintly, faintly tied To earth, she was set free, and died. **1847** TENNYSON *Princ.* VI Song 4 She must weep or she will die.

b. Const. To die *of* a malady, hunger, old age, or the like; *by* violence, the sword, his own hand; *from* a wound, inattention, etc.; *through* neglect; *on* or *upon* the cross, the scaffold, *at* the stake, *in* battle; *for* a cause, object, reason, or purpose, *for* the sake of one; formerly also *with* a disease, the sword, etc.; *on* his enemies (i.e. falling dead above them). In earlier use the prepositions were employed less strictly.

c **1200** ORMIN 8656 Siþþenn shule witt anan Off hunngerr deȝenn baþe. *c* **1330** R. BRUNNE *Chron. Wace* (Rolls) 850 Of his burþe his moder deide. *c* **1340** *Cursor M.* App. ii. 887 (B.M. Add. MS.) No womman..dien ne schal of hure childe. *c* **1400** *Destr. Troy* 6528 All þat met hym..dyet of his dynttes. **1483** CAXTON *G. de la Tour* D v, Yf they ete of that fruyte they shold deye of it. **1580** BARET *Alv.* D 643 To die of the plague. **1590** SHAKS. *Mids. N.* II. i. 130 She being mortall, of that boy did die. **1597** —— *2 Hen. IV* Epil. 31 Falstaffe shall dye of a Sweat. **1658–9** E. BODVILE in *Hatton Corr.* (1878) 17 Like to diy of the small pox. **1716** ADDISON *Drummer* v. i, The wound of which he dy'd. **1796** BURNS *Lett. Mr. Cunningham* 7 July, If I die not of disease, I must perish with hunger. **1892** DU MAURIER *Peter Ibbetson* 247 I thought I must die of sheer grief.

1382 WYCLIF *Ezek.* v. 12 The thridde part of thee shal die bi pestilence. *a* **1631** DONNE *Poems* (1650) 10 We can dye by it, if not live by love. **1643** DENHAM *Cooper's H.* 315 Disdains to dye By common hands. **1683** *Col. Rec. Pennsylv.* I. 95 A Calfe that Dyed, as they thought by Witchcraft.

c **1340** *Cursor M.* 26847 (Fairf.) Oft man deys þoru [*Cott.* of] an wounde. **1382** WYCLIF *Num.* xvi. 29 If thurȝ vsid deeth of men thei dien. *Ibid.* xxiii. 10 Dye my soule thurȝ the deeth of riȝtwise men. *Mod.* If the child had died through neglect.

13.. *Cursor M.* 17153 (Cott.), I haf..ded on þis rode tre. *Ibid.* 9039 (Gött.) God þat dide apon þe rode. *c* **1400** *Destr. Troy* 427 Whan Criste on the crosse for our care deghit. **1675** BROOKS *Gold. Key* Wks. 1867 V. 90 He that died on the cross was long a-dying. **1820** T. KELLY *Hymn*, We sing the praise..Of him who died upon the cross.

a **1300** *Cursor M.* 16762 + 89 (Cott.) When þou deed for drede. *c* **1300** *Havelok* 840, I wene that we deye mone For hunger. *c* **1380** WYCLIF *Wks.* (1880) 8 Redy to dye for cristin mennus soulis. *c* **1489** CAXTON *Blanchardyn* vii. 27 *heading*, The whiche deyde for sorowe. **1552** HULOET, Dye for the loue of a womanne, *Perire feminam*. **1553** T. WILSON *Rhet.* (1580) 177, I can not chappe these textes in Scripture, if I should die for it. **1580** BARET *Alv.* D 643 Willing to die for ones safetie. **1581** PETTIE *Guazzo's Civ. Conv.* III. (1586) 129, I should die for verie shame. **1599** HAKLUYT *Voy.* II. II. 73 Shortly after they all die for hunger and cold. **1600** SHAKS. *A.Y.L.* IV. i. 108 Men haue died from time to time, and wormes haue eaten them, but not for loue. **1654** WHITLOCK *Zootomia* 121 Though he dye for it, he cannot think of it. **1655** H. VAUGHAN *Silex Scint.* I. Ded. (1858) 15 My God! thou that didst dye for me. **1713** STEELE *Guardian* No. 17 ¶7 But child..can you see your mother die for hunger. **1832** TENNYSON *May Queen* 21 They say he's dying all for love. *Mod.* To die for one's opinions.

1382 WYCLIF *Jer.* xvi. 4 With dethes of siknyngus thei shul die. *c* **1386** CHAUCER *Monk's T.* 711 The place in which he schulde dye With boydekyns. *c* **1400** *Destr. Troy* 8273 Thow dowtles shall dye with dynt of my hond. *a* **1612** DONNE *Βιαθανατος* (1644) 52 Annibal..dyed with poyson which he alwaies carryed in a ring. *a* **1672** WOOD *Life* (1848) 8 His grandmother Penelopie..died with grief. **1692** E. WALKER *Epictetus' Mor.* xvi, To dye with Thirst and Hunger.

1591 SHAKS. *Two Gent.* II. iv. 114 Ile die on him that saies so but your selfe. **1712–14** POPE *Rape Lock* v. 78 Nor fear'd the Chief th' unequal fight to try, Who sought no more than on his foe to die.

c. To die *in* a state or condition.

a **1300** *Cursor M.* 25850 (Cott.) Qua þat dees in dedli sin sal duell in bale. **1382** WYCLIF *Jer.* xxxi. 30 Eche in his wickednesse shal die. **1549** *Compl. Scot.* iii. 25 Cleopatra vas lyike to dee in melancolie. **1552** HULOET, Dye in great debte, *Relinquere debitum*. **1703** MAUNDRELL *Journ. Jerus.* (1732) Lett. ii. 3 To dye in the Romish Communion. **1784** COWPER *Tiroc.* 150 Would die at last in comfort, peace, and joy. *Mod.* He died in poverty and neglect.

d. To die *poor*, *a beggar*, *a martyr*, *a millionaire*, etc.

a **1225** *Ancr. R.* 108 Heo ouh for to deien martir in hire meseise. **1393** GOWER *Conf.* II. 55 Lo, thus she deiede a wofull maide. **1553** [see 1 β.]. **1671** MILTON *P.R.* III. 422 But so dy'd Impenitent. **1683** SALMON *Doron Med.* I. 17 They dye (as it were) laughing. **1781** COWPER *Retirement* 14 Having lived a trifler, died a man. **1842** TENNYSON *Vision of Sin* iv. 144 Yet we will not die forlorn. **1883** *Century Mag.* XXV. 765/1 Her old friend had died a bankrupt. **1894** WOLSELEY *Marlborough* I. 246 He was every inch a sailor, and died an Admiral.

e. *to die on* (someone): (*a*) to die in the presence of or while in the charge or care of (someone); (*b*) to cease to function for or be of use to (someone); to cease to interest.

1907 J. M. SYNGE *Aran Islands* I. 47 A farmer was in great distress as his crops had failed, and his cow had died on him. **1930** KIPLING *Limits & Renewals* (1932) 243, I decided to drive in on a gust under the spitfire-sprit—and, if she answered her helm before she died on us, to humour her a shade to starboard. **1931** *Times Lit. Suppl.* 10 Dec. 1002/4 Carruthers drank all New York could give him for thirty-six hours and..the 'drink died on him'. Well, sometimes the novel dies on Mr. Waugh. That happened this time. **1934** A. THIRKELL *Wild Strawberries* iii. 53 Let Weston know that the horn died on us this morning, so he'd better fix it up. **1936** J. TICKELL *See how they Run* iv. 44 'I want to look after her while she's in England.' 'Suppose she died on you?' **1936** C. DAY LEWIS *Friendly Tree* vi. 80 That was one thing which had not died on her—the love of birds.

2. *to die a* (specified) *death*: to die by or suffer a particular death.

Death prob. represents the OE. *dēaþe* instrumental, in *dēaþe sweltan*, L. *morte mori*: it was in ME. also preceded by various prepositions, *on*, *in*, *a*, *o*, *of*, *by*, *with*; but is now generally treated as a cognate object. In *die a death*, *a* was prob. originally the preposition = *on*, *o* (see quots. *c* 1200, *c* 1386) but came to be treated as the indefinite article.

a. with instrumental case, or equivalent preposition.

[*c* **900** *Ælfred's Laws* 14. 15 in Thorpe I. 48 (Bosw.) He sceal deaþe sweltan. *a* **1175** *Cott. Hom.* 221 þu scealt deaðe sweltan. *c* **1200** *Trin. Coll. Hom.* 181 þu shalt a deðe swelte.] **13..** *Cursor M.* 660 (Cott.) O [*Fairf.* Wit, *Gött.* Of, *Trin.* On] dulde ded þan sal ȝee dei. **1382** WYCLIF *Gen.* ii. 17 In what euer day sotheli thow etist there of, with deth thow shalt die [**1388** Thou schalt die by deeth [Vulg. *morte morieris*]]. —— *Judg.* xiii. 22 Bi deeth die we [Vulg. *morte moriemur*], for we han seen the Lord. —— *Ezek.* xxviii. 10 In deeth of vncircumcydid men, thou shalt die. *c* **1386** CHAUCER *Melib.* ¶606 Bettre it is to dye of [*so 5 MSS.*; *Harl.* on, *Petw.* a] bitter deeth. *c* **1450** *Merlin* 52, I knowe not what deth this fole shall on dye. *c* **1477** CAXTON *Jason* 42 If I dye not of bodily deth I shal dye of spirituel deth. **1483** —— *G. de la Tour* G v, Your sone deyd this nyght of a good dethe. *c* **1500** *Melusine* 247 To deye of an euyl deth. **1625–6** PURCHAS *Pilgrims* II. 1041 He died of his naturall death.

b. without preposition.

13.. *Sir Beues* 341, I ne reche, what deþ he diȝe, Siþþe he be cold. **13..** *Cursor M.* 952 (Gött.) And siþen dobil dede to dei [*Cott.*, *Fairf.* wit, *Trin.* on doubel deþ]. *Ibid.* 10917 (Gött.) He þat first na dede miht die [*Cott.* na ded moght drei]. *c* **1460** *Towneley Myst.* (Surtees) 6 Thou shalle dye a dulfulle dede. *a* **1533** LD. BERNERS *Huon* cxxv. 453 He wolde cause the emperour to dye an yll dethe. **1535** COVERDALE *Num.* xxiii. 10 My soule die yᵉ death of yᵉ righteous, and my ende be as the ende of these. **1598** SHAKS. *Merry W.* IV. ii. 158 He shall dye a Fleas death. **1602** WARNER *Alb. Eng.* IX. xlv. (1612) 212 But twentie two a naturall death did die. **1610** SHAKS. *Temp.* I. i. 72, I would faine dye a dry death. **1611** BIBLE *John* xviii. 32 Signifying what death he should die. **1687** SETTLE *Refl. Dryden* 85 I'le die a thousand deaths before I'le do so or so. **1832** TENNYSON *Miller's Dau.* xii, Love dispell'd the fear That I should die an early death.

c. *to die the death*: to suffer death, to be put to death.

Dr. Johnson (*Shaks.* (1765) I. 311) says '"die the death" seems to be a solemn phrase for death inflicted by law.'

1535 COVERDALE *Judg.* xiii. 22 We must dye the death, because we haue sene God [WYCLIF Bi deeth die we]. **1581** LAMBARDE *Eiren.* II. vii. (1588) 269 If one do burne a dwelling house maliciously, he shall die the death for it. **1590** SHAKS. *Mids. N.* I. i. 65 Either to dye the death, or to abiure For euer the society of men. **1611** —— *Cymb.* IV. ii. 97 Dye the death: When I haue slaine thee with my proper hand, Ile follow those that euen now fled hence. **1801** SOUTHEY *Thalaba* IX. xxxix, And in that wild and desperate agony Sure Maimuna had died the utter death. **1859** TENNYSON *Lancelot & Elaine* 866 [He] had died the death In any knightly fashion for her sake.

3. a. In various phrases, describing the manner or condition of death. (Sometimes *fig.*: cf. 10.)

to die game, to maintain a bold and defiant bearing to the last, i.e. like a gamecock; whence by contrast ***to die dunghill***; ***to die hard***, i.e. with difficulty, reluctantly, not without a struggle; ***to die in one's bed***, i.e. of illness or other natural cause, the opposite of which is ***to die in one's shoes***; ***to die in one's boots*** or ***shoes*** or ***with one's boots on***: to die a violent death, *spec.* to be hanged; so ***to die with one's boots off***: to have a peaceful or unspectacular death or end; ***to die in harness***, i.e. in full work; ***to die in the last ditch***, i.e. in defending the last ditch of an entrenchment, to fight to the last extremity; and in other similar phrases.

1523 LD. BERNERS *Froiss.* I. lxxxiv. 107 We shall not forsake you to dye in the quarrell. *Ibid.* I. ccvi. 243 Tyll he had made an ende of his warr..or els to dye in the payne. **1631** RUTHERFORD *Lett.* II. ix. (1881) 384 It cannot stand with his honour to die in the burrows. **1663** *Flagellum, or O. Cromwell* Pref. (1672) 3 He had the fortune..to dye in his bed. **1694**, etc. [see SHOE *sb.* 2 d]. *a* **1700** B. E. *Dict. Cant. Crew*, *Die like a Dog*, to be hang'd..*Die on a Fish-day*, or *in his shoes*, the same. *Die like a Rat*, to be poysoned. **1712** HEARNE *Collect.* (Oxf. Hist. Soc.) III. 341 He dy'd in his Shoes; his Domesticks say of an Apoplexie. *a* **1715** BURNET *Own Time* (1766) I. 457 There was a sure way never to see it lost, and that was to die in the last ditch. **1784** *Gentl. Mag.* LIV. I. 19/1 The only solicitude too many of them discover is, whether the criminals *die hard*, according to the Tyburn phrase. **1805** *Ann. Reg.* 370 Declaring, in cant terms, that they would 'die game'. **1811** SYD. SMITH *Wks.* (1867) I. 203 Nothing dies so hard..as intolerance. **1825** *On Bull-baiting* II. (*Houlston Tracts* I. xxviii. 5), I don't intend to die dunghill. **1863** FAWCETT *Pol. Econ.* II. xi. (1876) 294 Reform is slow, and abuses die hard. **1867** *Homeward Mail* 16 Nov. 951/2 Mr. P. A. Dyke has died in harness at his post as Government agent. **1868** M. PATTISON *Academ. Org.* v. 129 Learning in Oxford died hard and yielded up its breath not without many a struggle. **1870** SPURGEON *Treas. Dav.* Ps. x. 15 Very few great persecutors have ever died in their beds. **1871** FREEMAN *Norm. Conq.* (1876) IV. xvii. 42 Men who..had actually died in arms against him. **1873** J. H. BEADLE *Undevel. West* xxxi. 435 It will be said in Western dialect. 'They died in their Boots'. **1873** J. MILLER *Life amongst Modocs* vi. 75 If you keep on slinging your six-shooter around loose..you will..die with your boots on. **1875** STUBBS *Const. Hist.* III. xxi. 544 Like most medieval workers they all died in harness. **1888** [see HARD *adv.* 3]. **1895** W. RYE *E. Angl. Gloss.* 21 Died with his *boots on*, viz. died a violent death. **1903** MASEFIELD *Ballads* 22 So I'm for drinking honestly, and dying in my boots. **1946** B. SUTTON *Jungle Pilot* 99 An aircraft which ends its career by dying with its 'boots off' and being deliberately burnt to ashes on the ground is a sight at once undignified and pathetic. **1959** *Listener* 6 Aug. 200/1 They died with their boots on; they hardly ever surrendered.

b. ***never say die***: never consent or resign oneself to death; never give in.

1837 DICKENS *Pickw.* ii, Never say die—down upon your luck. **1880** PAYN *Confid. Agent* III. 161 Never say die while there's a shot in the locker.

c. (***I***) ***hope*** (or ***wish***) ***I may die***, (***I***) ***hope to die***, etc.: colloq. asseverations of the truth of what one says.

1865 DICKENS *Mut. Fr.* II. III. xi. 100 'Wish I may die,' cried Mr. Riderhood, with a hoarse laugh, 'if I warn't a goin' to say the self-same words to you.' **1899** R. WHITEING *No. 5 John St.* xxiv. 244, I see it in the piper. Wish I may die! **1912** MULFORD & CLAY *Buck Peters* xvii. 160 'There's a Witch's Ring right here on the range!' 'Nonsense!' 'Hope I may die! I'll show you, to-morrow.' **1926** [see CROSS *v.* 3 b]. **1927** I. GERSHWIN *Let's Kiss & Make Up* 2, I didn't mean to start any scene to make you sigh. Hope to die! **1968** M. ALLINGHAM *Cargo of Eagles* xi. 133 'Off the record?' 'Never a word, may I die.'

4. To suffer the pains or dangers of death; to face death.

1382 WYCLIF *1 Cor.* xv. 31 Ech day I deie for ȝoure glorie, britheren. **1526–34** TINDALE *ibid.*, By oure reioysinge which I have in Christ Iesu oure Lorde, I dye dayly. **1633** [see 1 β].

** *transf.* and *fig.*

5. *Theol.* To suffer spiritual death; 'To perish everlastingly' (J.): cf. DEATH *sb.* 5.

1340 HAMPOLE *Pr. Consc.* 8159 þai salle ay deghand lyf, and lyfand dyghe, And ever-mare payns of ded þus dryghe. **1382** WYCLIF *Ezek.* xviii. 4 The soule that shal synne, the ilk shal die. **1552** *Bk. Com. Prayer* Burial of Dead, And whosoever liveth, and believeth in him, shall not die eternally. **1627** HAKEWILL *Apol.* (1630) 512 So long as God shall liue, so long shall the damned die.

6. *to die unto*: to cease to be under the power or influence of; to become dead unto: cf. Rom. vi. 2.

1648 *Westm. Assembly's Shorter Catech.* Q. 35 Sanctification..whereby we..are enabled more and more to die unto sin, and live unto righteousness.

7. a. To suffer pains identified with those of death; (often hyperbolical) to languish, pine away with passion; to be consumed with longing desire; *to die for*, to desire keenly or excessively.

1591 LYLY *Endym.* I. iv, The lady that he delights in, and dotes on every day, and dies for ten thousand times a day. 1593 NASHE *Christ's T.* 33 a, He saw him swallow downe a bitte that he dyde for. 1599 SHAKS. *Much Ado* III. ii. 69 And in despight of all, dies for him. 1610 —— *Temp.* III. i. 79 And much lesse take What I shall die to want. *a* 1631 DONNE *Poems* (1650) 14 Deare, I die As often as from thee I goe. 1711 ADDISON *Spect.* No. 86 ¶2 Nothing is more common than for lovers to..languish, despair, and dye in dumb show. 1832 TENNYSON *Eleänore* 141–8, I die with my delight..I would be dying evermore, So dying ever, Eleänore. *Mod. colloq.* I am dying for a drink.

b. *to be dying to do* (something): to long greatly.

1709 PRIOR *Celia to Damon* 8 That durst not tell me, what I dy'd to hear. 1711 STEELE *Spect.* No. 254 ¶3 She dies to see what demure and serious Airs Wedlock has given you. 1780 MAD. D'ARBLAY *Diary* May, Mrs. Bowdler has long been dying to come to the point. 1786 *Ibid.* 17 July, Miss P—, who was..dying with impatience to know..everything about me. 1832 L. HUNT *Sir R. Esher* (1850) 83 The secret was dying to escape him. 1893 G. ALLEN *Scallywag* I. 20 The pretty American's dying to see you.

c. Used hyperbolically to indicate extreme feelings of amusement, embarrassment, etc.; esp. in phr. *to die with* or *of laughing*.

1596 SHAKS. *Tam. Shr.* III. ii. 243 Went they not quickly, I should die with laughing. 1606 —— *Tr. & Cr.* I. iii. 176 At this sport Sir Valour dies; cries..giue me ribs of Steele, I shall split all In pleasure of my Spleene. 1778 MAD. D'ARBLAY *Diary* 23 Aug., An account he gave us..would have made you die with laughing. 1796 JANE AUSTEN *Pride & Prej.* vi. (1813) 194, I was ready to die of laughter. 1820 M. WILMOT *Let.* 12 Jan. (1935) 50 Once in a tender love speech, I thought I should have died, when Lady Grace..told him *audibly* he had turned over *two leaves!* *a* 1930 D. H. LAWRENCE *Phoenix II* (1968) 84 He looked like a positive saint: one of the noble sort, you know, that will suffer with head up and with dreamy eyes. I nearly died of laughing. 1949 D. SMITH *I capture Castle* xi. 190 She knew some of the manaquins [*sic*] at a dress show—I could have died. 1969 WIDDOWSON & HALPERT in Halpert & Story *Christmas Mumming in Newfoundland* 162 He was dressed up, you know, and he was like an old shepherd. Well I nearly died.

d. To experience a sexual orgasm. (Most common as a poetical metaphor in the late 16th and 17th cent.)

1599 SHAKES. *Much Ado* III. ii. 70 *Claudio.* Nay, but I know who loues him..and in despight of all, dies for him. *Prince.* Shee shall be buried with her face vpwards. *a* 1631 DONNE *Elegies Songs & Sonnets* (1965) 39 Once I lov'd and dyed; and am now become Mine Epitaph and Tombe. Here dead men speake their last, and so do I; Love-slaine, loe, here I lye. 1673 DRYDEN *Marriage a-la-mode* IV. ii, Now die, my Alexis, and I will die too. 1680 ROCHESTER *Poems* 71 In love, 'tis equal measure. The Victor lives with empty pride, The Vanquisht dye with pleasure. 1714 POPE *Rape of Lock* v. 45 Nor fear'd the Chief th'unequal Fight to try, Who sought no more than on his Foe to die. 1923 D. H. LAWRENCE *Birds, Beasts & Flowers* 20 That's how the fig dies..Like a prostitute, the bursten fig, making a show of her secret. That's how women die too. 1961 R. AMATO in *Landfall* Sept. 200 You're nice, though. You make me die every time. 1974 J. DENVER *Annie's Song* (sheet-music) 4 Come let me love you... Let me die in your arms.

II. Of non-sentient objects, substances, qualities, actions.

8. a. Of plants, flowers, or organized matter: To lose vegetative life; to cease to be subject to vital forces; to pass into a state of mortification or decomposition.

1382 WYCLIF *1 Cor.* xv. 36 That thing that thou sowist, is not quykenyd, no but it deie first. *c* 1420 *Pallad. on Husb.* III. 642 Thai wol multiplie There as all other treen and herbes deye. 1513 DOUGLAS *Æneis* IX. vii. 149 Lyke as the purpour flour..Dwynis away, as it doith faid or de. 1573 TUSSER *Husb.* (1878) 85 Good quickset bie, Old gatherd will die. 1599 SHAKS. *Hen. V*, v. ii. 42 Her Vine..Vnpruned, dyes. 1607 TOPSELL *Four-f. Beasts* (1658) 477 The same part of his tail which is beneath the knot will die after such binding, and never have any sense in it again. 1707 *Curios. in Husb. & Gard.* 62 The Plant, grown dry and withered..must dy. *c* 1820 SHELLEY *Autumn* 2 The pale flowers are dying. 1855 TENNYSON *Maud* VI. i. 6 The shining daffodils die. 1869 HUXLEY *Phys.* i. (ed. 3) 22 Individual cells of the epidermis and of the epithelium are incessantly dying and being cast off.

b. Said of the heart: To cease to beat; to sink as in swooning.

1611 BIBLE *1 Sam.* xxv. 37 His heart died within him, and he became as a stone. 1771 SMOLLETT *Humph. Cl.* 26 June ¶18 My heart seemed to die within me. 1795 SOUTHEY *Joan of Arc* I. 290 It might be seen..by the deadly paleness which ensued, How her heart died within her.

9. *fig.* Of substances: To lose force, strength, or active qualities, to become 'dead', flat, vapid, or inactive.

1612 WEBSTER *White Devil* IV. i, Best wine, Dying, makes strongest vinegar. 1823 P. NICHOLSON *Pract. Build.* 390 Plaster is said to die when it loses its strength.

10. a. Of actions, institutions, states, or qualities: To come to an end, pass out of existence; to go out, as a candle or fire; to pass out of memory, to be utterly forgotten.

a 1240 *Lofsong* in *Cott. Hom.* 211 þine pinen buruwen me..from þene deað ðet neuer ne deieð. 1387 TREVISA *Higden* (Rolls) I. 7 (Mätz.) Dedes þat wolde deie, storye kepeþ hem euermore. *c* 1420 *Pallad. on Husb.* I. 600 As cornes that wol under growe her eye, That but thou lete hem oute, the sight wol die. 1548 HALL *Chron., Edw. IV*, 240 In whose person died the very surname of Plantagenet. 1577 B. GOOGE *Heresbach's Husb.* II. (1586) 110 The coles that are made of the Pine tree..die not so fast as the other. 1580 BARET *Alv.* D 643 Loue vtterly dieth, or decaieth. 1593 SHAKS. *3 Hen. VI*, II. vi. 1 Heere burnes my Candle out; I, heere it dies. 1599 —— *Much Ado* v. i. 301 So dies my reuenge. 1710 PRIDEAUX *Orig. Tithes* v. 237 But he dying the same year he published them [Laws], they also dyed with him. 1711 ADDISON *Spect.* No. 26 ¶5 When I look upon the Tombs of the great, every Emotion of Envy dies in me. 1820 SHELLEY *Ode Liberty* ix. 13 Art, which cannot die. 1847 TENNYSON *Princ.* III. 189 Speak, and let the topic die. 1871 MORLEY *Voltaire* (1886) 7 A fragile and secondary good which the world is very willing to let die. 1892 DU MAURIER *Peter Ibbetson* 247 It is good that my secret must die with me.

b. Sometimes more directly fig. from 1.

1594 HOOKER *Eccl. Pol.* I. xvi. (1611) 50 All these controuersies might have dyed, the very day they were first brought foorth. 1596 SHAKS. *1 Hen. IV*, I. iii. 74 What euer Harry Percie then had said..May reasonably dye, and neuer rise To do him wrong. 1601 —— *Twel. N.* I. i. 3 The appetite may sicken, and so dye. 1610 —— *Temp.* II. i. 216 Thou let'st thy fortune sleep: die rather.

11. To pass gradually away (*esp.* out of hearing or sight) by becoming fainter and fainter; to fade away.

[1581 PETTIE *Guazzo's Civ. Conv.* II. (1586) 58b, The fault of some, who suffer the last letters to die betweene their teeth.] 1704 POPE *Windsor For.* 266, I hear sweet music die along the grove. 1715–20 —— *Iliad* II. 126 Fainter murmurs dy'd upon the ear. 1826 DISRAELI *Viv. Grey* v. xii, The words died on Vivian's lips. 1832 TENNYSON *Miller's D.* 74, I watch'd the little circles die. 1859 —— *Elaine* 323 The living smile Died from his lips.

12. a. To pass by dying (*into* something else); to change (*into* something) at death or termination.

1633 EARL MANCH. *Al Mondo* (1636) 27 The brightest dayes dye into dark nights, but rise againe a mornings. 1645 BP. HALL *Remedy Discontents* 20 The day dyes into night. 1742 YOUNG *Nt. Th.* vi. 697 The world of matter, with its various forms, All dies into new life. 1755 —— *Centaur* ii. 87 He that lives in the kingdom of Sense shall die into the kingdom of Sorrow. 1784 COWPER *Task* II. 96 The rivers die into offensive pools. 1842 TENNYSON *Day-Dream* 188 The twilight died into the dark.

b. *Archit.* To merge *into*, lose itself by passing *into*; to terminate gradually *in* or *against*. Cf. 13c.

1665 J. WEBB *Stone-Heng* (1725) 88 A Parapet..is let into, or made to die against the Columns. 1859 JEPHSON *Brittany* xviii. 291 The mouldings of the arches die into the pillars. 1870 F. R. WILSON *Ch. Lindisf.* 116 There is a staircase turret which dies into the tower.

III. With adverbs, forming compound verbs.

13. die away. a. To pass away from life gradually; to faint or swoon away.

1707 *Curios. in Husb. & Gard.* 62 We see several Plants grow dry, and dy away. 1711 ADDISON *Spect.* No. 3 ¶7 She fainted and died away at the sight. 1713 —— *Cato.* IV. i, I die away with horror at the thought. 1725 POPE *Odyss.* XIV. 401 Oh! had he..in his friend's embraces dy'd away! 1821 SHELLEY *Prometh. Unb.* II. ii. 21 Droops dying away On its mate's music-panting bosom. 1853 R. W. BROWNE *Grk. Classical Lit.* (1857) 138 My feeble pulse forgot to play, I fainted, sank, and died away.

b. To diminish gradually in force or activity and so come to an end; to fade away, cease or disappear gradually.

1680 HACKE *Collect. Voy.* (1699) II. 15 The wind in the mean time dying away, I was becalmed. 1706 A. BEDFORD *Temple Mus.* ix. 172 The Voices..seem to die away. 1712 STEELE *Spect.* No. 427 ¶2 Thus groundless Stories die away. 1792 S. ROGERS *Pleas. Mem.* II. 91 At his feet the thunder dies away. 1837 DISRAELI *Venetia* III. vii, The day died away, and still he was wanting. 1840 R. H. DANA *Bef. Mast* xxv. 81 The breeze died away at night. 1860 TYNDALL *Glac.* I. xxiv. 175 The direct shock of each avalanche had died away.

c. *Archit.* and *Carpentry.* To pass or merge gradually into the adjacent structure. Cf. 12b.

1869 SIR E. J. REED *Ship-build.* v. 76 To be 2 feet deep amidships and to extend across until they die away with rise of floor. 1873 FERGUSON in Tristram *Land of Moab* 373 The arch must have died away against the towers.

†**d.** *trans.* To cause to die or come to an end. *rare*⁻¹.

1748 RICHARDSON *Clarissa* (1811) VIII. 33 By little and little, in such a gradual sensible death..God dies away in us, as I may say, all human satisfaction, in order to subdue his poor creatures to himself.

14. die back. Said of the recent shoot of a plant: To die from the apex back to the woody or perennial part.

Cf. *die down*; herbaceous plants die down to the ground, tender shoots die back to the old wood.

1850 *Beck's Florist* Nov. 265 The shrub..will in a manner prune itself, or at least those shoots that require removing will die back, and there will be only the dead wood to cut away. 1928 F. T. BROOKS *Plant. Dis.* xii. 201 Stone fruit trees often die back in association with the presence of various fungi.

15. die down. a. To subside gradually into a dead or inactive state; to die away.

1834 KEBLE in *Lyra Apost.* (1849) 58 The deep knell dying down. 1859 TENNYSON *Elaine* 179 Laughter dying down as the great knight Approach'd them. 1874 GREEN *Short Hist.* vi. §1. 267 The war died down into mere massacre and brigandage. 1894 *Antiquary* May 222 The tin trade of Cornwall died down. *Mod.* The fire was left to die down of itself.

b. Of plants: To die down to the ground, while the underground stem and roots survive.

1895 *Home Garden* 40 To secure perfect blooms [of Crocus], the foliage must be left to die down of its own accord. *Mod.* This Polygonum attains a height of ten feet, and yet dies down entirely in the winter.

16. die off. a. To go off, be removed or carried off, one after another, by death.

1697 DAMPIER *Voy.* I. 113 It is usual with sick men coming from the Sea Air to dye off as soon as ever they come within the view of the Land. 1741 RICHARDSON *Pamela* (1742) III. 292 A Gentleman's Friends may die off. 1807 SOUTHEY *Espriella's Lett.* III. 100 The Russian soldiers..sickened and died off like rotten sheep. 1840 DICKENS *Barn. Rudge* vii, Accustomed to wish with great emphasis that the whole race of women could but die off. 1857 BUCKLE *Civiliz.* I. xi. 649 That generation having died off. *Mod.* If the cattle and other stock are not sold off, they will die off. The cuttings in the frames damped off, the plants in the greenhouse died off.

b. *transf.* Of sounds, etc.: To die away, to pass away.

1722 DE FOE *Plague* (1884) 10 This Rumour died off again. 1805 FLINDERS in *Phil. Trans.* XCVI. 245 On the wind dying off..it descended quickly to 30 inches. 1878 BROWNING *La Saisiaz* 45 If the harsh throes of the prelude die not off into the swell. 1886 SIR F. H. DOYLE *Reminiscences* 175 So the debate died off.

17. die out. a. Of a family or race (of animals or plants): To be (gradually) extinguished by death; to become extinct.

1865 SEELEY *Ecce Homo* iv. (1866) 38 His house soon dies out. 1866 MRS. CARLYLE *Lett.* III. 306 So sad that one's family should die out. 1875 JOWETT *Plato* (ed. 2) III. 163 Barbarous nations when they are introduced by Europeans to vice die out. 1887 F. B. ZINCKE *Hist. Wherstead* 173 They never bore any more fruit, and gradually died out.

b. To go out, or come to an end (gradually); to pass away or become extinct by degrees.

1853 KANE *Grinnell Exp.* xxvii. (1856) 219 The lard-lamp died out in the course of the night. 1872 FREEMAN *Gen. Sketch* xii. §21. 232 In England villainage was on the whole dying out. 1885 *Truth* 11 June 936/2 Public interest had flagged and gradually died out. 1887 *Athenæum* 7 May 603/3 To tell how the religions of Greece and Rome died out. 1892 DU MAURIER *Peter Ibbetson* 43 The last red streak dies out of the wet west.

†**18. die up.** To die off entirely, to perish. *Obs.*

a 1300 *Cursor M.* 4703 (Cott.) þan deid þe bestes vp biden, Thoru þe hunger þat was sa kene. *c* 1340 *Ibid.* 4831 (Trin.) þe folke deȝeþ vp al by dene. 1475 *Bk. Noblesse* (1860) 42 His peple died up by gret mortalite of pestilence. 1563–87 FOXE *A. & M.* (1596) 76/1 Most part of the husbandmen..died up with the famine and pestilence.

die, *v.*[2] [f. DIE *sb.*[1]] *trans.* To furnish with a die; to mould or shape with a die.

1703 T. N. *City & C. Purchaser* 213 The Sheathing-nail ought not to go through the Plank..and the Head must be well clasped, or died, so as it may sink into the Wood. 1885 *Harper's Mag.* LXX. 282 Every machine-made shoe also has an 'inner sole' died out or moulded, to correspond in shape with the 'outer sole'.

die, obs. form of DYE *v.* and *sb.*

'die-away, *a.* [from the verbal phr. *to die away*: see DIE *v.*[1] 13.] That dies away or has the air of dying away; languishing.

1802 MARIAN MOORE *Lascelles* II. 196 If I thought you liked that die-away Miss. 1832 *Examiner* 229/2 He sang a die-away love-ditty. 1840–1 S. WARREN *10,000 a Year* I. 124 The die-away manner in which she moved her head. 1871 G. MEREDITH *H. Richmond* xxv. (1889) 227 The Margravine groaned impatiently at talk of such a die-away sort.

‖**dieb** (di:b). *Zool.* [a. Arab. *ðīb*, 'wolf', also in some districts 'jackal', = Heb. *zĕ'ēb* wolf.] A species of Wild Dog or Jackal (*Canis anthus*) found in Northern Africa.

1829 FISCHER *Synopsis Mammal.* 181 'Dieb' of the Arabs. 1869 GRAY *Cat. Carnivora in Brit. Mus.* 189.

'die-back, *sb.* [from the phrase *to die back*: see DIE *v.*[1] 14.] The progressive dying of a shrub or tree shoot from the tip backwards, caused by disease or unfavourable conditions, esp. a disease of fruit trees.

1886 in S. FALLOWS *Suppl. Dict.* 1895 *Dept. Agric. Yearbk. 1894* (U.S.) 199 Die-back manifests itself by a number of striking characters. The foliage becomes very dark green, [etc.]. *Ibid.* 200 Finally a reddish brown resinous substance exudes on the twigs, forming the so-called die-back stain. 1910 G. MASSEE *Dis. Cultivated Plants & Trees* 430 Die back of willow shoots..attacks the tips of willow shoots and causes them to die back. 1916 B. D. JACKSON *Gloss. Bot. Terms* (ed. 3) 112/2 *Die-back*, of *Salix*, a disease due to *Diplodina salicina*; ~ of *Citrus*, some uncertain condition of health; ~ of *Prunus*, from *Naemospora crocea*. 1928 *Forestry* II. 27 Out in the forest die-back or canker due to frost is only likely to occur in particular areas. 1933 *Discovery* Feb. 66/2 *Phytopthora cambivora* has been isolated from dying beech in two separate woods in Somerset, and has been found to be the undoubted cause of the die-back. 1938 *Nature* 2 Apr. 612/1 Trees may be killed [by elm disease] in a single year, or the dieback may be more gradual. 1949 E. HYAMS *Not in our Stars* i. 8 The Morello plantation has very bad die-back. 1957 *Country Life* 8 Aug. 248/1 Slight lightning discharges may do no more than cause dieback in a few of the topmost twigs. 1968 *Punch* 27 Mar. 466/3 The central brown stain from dieback disease.

ˈdie-cast, *v.* [f. DIE *sb.*¹ 6 c + CAST *v.* 50.] *trans.* To make by casting hot metal in a die or mould. Hence **die-cast** *ppl. a.*

1909 *Daily Chron.* 7 Aug. 6/7 The frames are now die-cast instead of moulded. **1960** *Times Rev. Industry* Feb. 16/1 The first diecast radiator grilles were fitted.

die-casting, *vbl. sb.* [f. prec. + -ING¹.] The action of DIE-CAST *v.*; also *concr.*, a piece of metal cast in a die or mould. Also *attrib.*

1911 *Machinery* (N.Y.) May 715/2 (*heading*) Die-casting and die-casting machines. **1930** *Engineering* 14 Feb. 196/3 The association has also continued its support of the researches in die-casting and die-casting alloys. **1942** J. N. GREENWOOD *Gloss. Metallographic Terms* (ed. 2) 17 *Die casting*, the casting of alloys in metal moulds or dies. There are pressure and gravity die castings, according to whether the metal is forced into the die or not. **1955** *Times* 6 July 16/7 A reorganization of their facilities for producing gravity die-castings and high pressure die-castings is contemplated.

diecious, etc., var. DIŒCIOUS, etc.

‖**diectasis** (daɪˈɛktəsɪs). *Pros.* [a. Gr. διέκτασις a stretching: see DI-³ and ECTASIS] Lengthening by the interpolation of a syllable.

1894 *Athenæum* 29 Dec. 884/1 From the scientific point of view there is..not a word to be said in favour of such grammatical monsters as ἔῃς and ἐράασθε. But it is perfectly easy to see how they arose from a misunderstanding of the 'Epic diectasis.'

diedapper, obs. f. DIDAPPER, dabchick.

diederik, diedrik (ˈdiːdərɪk, ˈdiːdrɪk). *S. Afr.* Also didric, diedrick. [Imitative.] A small African cuckoo, *Chrysococcyx caprius* (see quot. 1790).

1790 E. HELME tr. *Le Vaillant's Trav. Afr.* I. 347 The green-golden cuckoo of the Cape... Perched on the tops of large trees, it continually repeats, and with a varied modulation, these syllables, *di, di, didric*, as distinctly as I have written them; for this reason I have named it the *didric*. **1853** *Edin. New Philos. Jrnl.* LV. 82 The pretty notes of the ..*diedrick* further enliven the growing day. **1939** S. CLOETE *Watch for Dawn* ix. 122 The intermittent calls of michi and diedrik. **1959** GILL & WINTERBOTTOM *First Guide S. Afr. Birds* (ed. 6) 109 *Didric* or *Diederik Cuckoo*, Diedrikkie; *Chrysococcyx caprius*.

diedral, var. DIHEDRAL.

†**diegeˈmatical,** *a. Obs.* [f. Gr. διηγηματικ-ός descriptive + -AL¹.] Of the nature of a narrative or descriptive; descriptive.

1624 BP. MOUNTAGU *Invocation Saints* 184 That which he [Nazianzen] hath is diegematicall, not by way of conclusion, or of approbation.

‖**diegesis** (daɪɪˈdʒiːsɪs). [a. Gr. διήγησις narration, narrative; in a speech, the statement of the case, f. διηγέομαι to describe, narrate.] A narrative; a statement of the case.

1829 R. TAYLOR (*title*), The Diegesis, being a Discovery of the Origin, Evidences, and Early History of Christianity.

†**diego** (ˈdjeːgəʊ). *Obs.* [Sp. *Diego*, the Christian name James, being that of the patron saint of Spain; see also *Don Diego* s.v. DON.]

1. A name for a Spaniard: cf. DAGO. (Also *attrib.*)

c **1611** J. TAYLOR (Water P.) *Laugh & be Fat*, Wks. (1630) 72/1 Next followes one, whose lines aloft doe raise Don Coriat, chiefe Diego of our daies. To praise thy booke, or thee, he knowes not whether, It makes him study to praise both, or neither. **1659** DAVENANT *Play-House to Let* III. Dram. Wks. 1873 IV. 55 The Diegos we'll board to rummage their hold. **1667** DRYDEN *Sir Martin Mar-all* II. ii. This hungry Diego rogue. **1687** M. CLIFFORD *Notes Dryden* (N.), That were as Diego said of the poor of his parish, All the parish.

2. A Spanish sword, or one of the same sort.

1709 STEELE *Tatler* No. 39 ¶40 Insulted by a Bully with a long Diego. **1867** SMYTH *Sailor's Word-bk.*, *Diego*, a very strong and heavy sword.

3. Name of a variety of pear.

1664 EVELYN *Kal. Hort.* (1729) 21 Pears..Bing's Pear, Bishop's Pear (baking), Diego [etc.].

ˈdie-hard, *sb.* and *a.* [from the phrase *to die hard*: see DIE *v.*¹ 3.]

A. *adj.* That dies hard, resisting to the last. Cf. sense B. 2.

1922 *Weekly Dispatch* 5 Nov. 1/1 The splitting away of the great masses of the Conservative Party—of the Die-hard section. **1923** E. A. ROSS *Russian Soviet Republ.* 395 The die-hard Tories. **1955** *Times* 19 May 10/1 There were also some diehard Mau Mau leaders who were doing everything in their power to prevent their followers from giving themselves up. **1971** *Internat. Affairs* (Moscow) Apr. 39/2 Diehard British chauvinism, rich with anti-Sovietism, was expressed back in October 1970, when the Conservative Party held its first conference..after it came to power.

B. *sb.* **1.** One that dies hard; *spec.* an appellation of the 57th Regiment of Foot in the British Army.

1844 W. H. MAXWELL *Sports & Adv. Scotl.* x. (1855) 100 The Die-hards (57th regiment). **1856** J. W. COLE *Brit. Gen. Penins. War* I. v. 200 *note.* **1871** *Standard* 28 Jan., Ducrot, who is a good die-hard general of brigade. **1871** *Daily News* 1 Feb., Some 20,000 die-hards are determined to get up into that keep and hold out for a spell longer. **1892** W. R. LLUELLYN in *Dict. Nat. Biog.* XXIX. 8/1 At Albuera the 57th occupied a position as important as it was deadly. 'Die hard! 57th', said Inglis, 'die hard!' They obeyed, and the regiment is known as the 'Die-hards' to this day.

2. A person who is extremely conservative, stubborn, or irreconcilable, esp. on a political or other issue; *spec.* (*a*) one of those who were prepared to 'die in the last ditch' in their resistance to the Home Rule Bill of 1912; (*b*) one of those members of the Conservative Party who followed the leadership of the Marquess of Salisbury in 1922. Also *transf.*

1857 HUGHES *Tom Brown* I. v. 114 They [*sc.* Rugby football players] are 'the fighting brigade', the 'die-hards' larking about at leap-frog..and playing tricks on one another. **1912** *Tatler* 9 Oct. 32a (*caption*) One of the 'Die-hards'. Lord Willoughby de Broke speaking recently at Ballyroney against Home Rule for Ireland. **1920** *Studies* June 197 The heroes of Marathon were conservative 'diehards': the modern Athenian..was a Socialist or Spartacist. **1922** *Times* 18 Oct. 14/2 Diehards demand freedom. Lord Salisbury on Coalition. **1922** *Daily Mail* 25 Oct. 10 Mr. Chamberlain said: Politics have many vicissitudes. A few days ago I was orthodox; to-day I am a 'Die-hard'. *Ibid* 3 Nov. 13 Die hard, the section of Conservatives led by Lord Salisbury who were hostile to Mr. Lloyd George's Premiership and Home Rule. **1927** A. T. HAGG *Labour Community Song Bk.* 6 The Tory Die-hards in their clubs They sing this plaintive song. **1957** *New Yorker* 29 June 60/2 The few million white Algerian French citizens, who the diehards declare must not be abandoned. **1963** F. T. VISSER *Hist. Syntax* I. iv. 365 It would seem to have been a linguistic die-hard.

3. The Scottish terrier.

1900 *Westm. Gaz.* 9 July 3/1 To anyone in doubt as to a suitable dog to take up as household guard or companion the Scottish terrier, often called the 'Die-hard', or Aberdeen terrier, and the Dandie Dinmont, immortalised by Sir Walter Scott, are strongly recommended. **1921** *Melbourne Argus* 13 Sept. 5 The name 'Die-Hards' has been given to the well-known black or brindle Scottish terrier.

Hence **die-hardism** (ˈdaɪhɑːdɪz(ə)m), the principles, tenets, or spirit of a die-hard.

1922 *Glasgow Herald* 8 Mar. 8 If the atmosphere of cooperation can be created, 'die-hardism' will be painlessly asphyxiated. **1923** *Ibid.* 28 July 8 There is a core of 'die-hardism' in all sincerely held convictions, and its language does not consist only of 'outworn shibboleths'. **1926** *Manch. Guardian Weekly* Sept. 181/1 Mr. Churchill has reversed his former die-hardism and struck out boldly. **1934** A. J. TOYNBEE *Study Hist.* III. 77 The most remarkable feat of Spartan 'Diehardism' was the attempt of the Royal Martyrs ..to reclothe the dry bones of the 'Lycurgean' system in flesh.

dieidism (daɪˈaɪdɪz(ə)m). *Biol.* [f. Gr. δι- two + εἶδ-ος form + -ISM.] The condition of having two different forms at different stages of life.

1874 LUBBOCK *Orig. & Met. Ins.* iv. 80 Those cases in which animals or plants pass through a succession of different forms might be distinguished by the name of dieidism or polyeidism.

die-in (ˈdaɪɪn). [-IN³.] A political demonstration in which people play dead, esp. in order to protest about the development or use of nuclear and other fatal weapons.

1970 *Time* 8 June 53/1 A petition to stop the shipment [of nerve gas] collected 200,000 signatures; various groups staged 'die-ins' to simulate the effects of the gas. **1978** *Peace News* 1 Dec. 5/2 They (Le Monde à Bicyclette) recently held a series of 'die-ins' at which cyclists blocked traffic during rush-hour. **1983** *Daily Tel.* 16 Nov. 32/6 In Norwich police arrested five demonstrators who staged a 'die-in' in a centre street.

dieldrin (ˈdiːldrɪn). *Chem.* [f. the name of O. *Diels* (1876–1954), German chemist + *-drin*, after ALDRIN: so called because the Diels-Alder reaction (the *diene synthesis*) was used in preparing it.] A crystalline solid, $C_{12}H_8Cl_6O$, white when pure and light brown in commercial preparations, which is an epoxide of aldrin and is used as an insecticide.

1949 *Dieldrin* (Interdepartmental Comm. Pest Control, Bur. Entomol. & Plant Quarantine, U.S. Dept. Agric.) 1 The coined generic name 'dieldrin' is announced for an insecticidal product..meeting the specifications set forth in the attached statement. **1950** *Adv. Chem. Series* (Amer. Chem. Soc.) I. 177 The most interesting oxidation of aldrin ..is the oxidation with per acids. This oxidative process.. produces 6, 7-epoxy-6, 7-dihydroaldrin, the compound now called dieldrin. **1956** *Nature* 17 Mar. 532/2 In connexion with the..Malaria Control Pilot Project, an area of about 300 square miles has been set aside for treatment with dieldrin. **1957** *New Scientist* 23 May 25/1 Dieldrin, used as a sheep dip in Australia as a protection against blowflies, was found to impregnate the wool fibres almost irremovably. **1969** *Times* 24 Mar. 4/5 There are severe restrictions on the use of the persistent insecticide dieldrin.

dielectric (daɪɪˈlɛktrɪk), *sb.* and *a.* [f. DI- *pref.*³ = Gr. δι-, δια- through + ELECTRIC.]

A. *sb.* A substance or medium through or across which electric force acts without conduction; a non-conductor; an insulating medium.

1837 FARADAY in *Phil. Trans.* (1838) I. 25 The particular action described occurs in the shell-lac..as well as in the *dielectric* used within the apparatus. **1838** —— *Exp. Res.* (1839) 364 My view that electric induction is an action of the contiguous particles of the insulating medium or dielectric. *Note.* I use the word dielectric to express that substance through or across which the electric forces are acting. (Dec. 1838.) **1881** MAXWELL *Electr. & Magn.* I. 462 The resistance of the greater number of dielectrics diminishes as the temperature rises. **1885** WATSON & BURBURY *Math. Th. Electr. & Magn.* I. 184 The dielectric, in Faraday's language, has *inductive capacity*. It is less for air and the permanent gases than for any solid dielectrics, and rather less for vacuum than for air.

B. *adj.*

1. Having the property of transmitting electric effects without conduction; non-conducting.

1871 *Athenæum* 10 June 723 He supposes..that the sheaths of the muscular fibres are dielectric. **1885** WATSON & BURBURY *Math. Th. Electr. & Magn.* I. 77 Such a medium, considered as transmitting these electrical effects without conduction, is called a *Dielectric* medium, and the action which takes place through it is called..*Induction*.

2. a. Relating to a dielectric medium, or to the transmission of electricity without conduction.

1863 ATKINSON tr. *Ganot's Physics* (1886) 685 The action is..analogous to that of the pole of a magnet on a piece of soft iron; and Faraday called it *dielectric polarisation*. **1881** MACFARLANE in *Nature* No. 620. 465 By the dielectric strength of a substance I mean the ratio of the difference of potential required to pass a spark through air under the same conditions. **1881** *Athenæum* 5 Feb. 203/2 [A paper on] 'Dielectric Capacity of Liquids', by Dr. Hopkinson.

b. ***dieletric constant***: one of the physical parameters of a non-conducting medium, equal to the ratio of the electric displacement at any point in the medium to the displacement an identical charge distribution would produce in a vacuum, measured at the same point; the relative permittivity. (Some writers call this the *relative dielectric constant*, using *dielectric constant* for the ratio of electric displacement to electric field strength: cf. PERMITTIVITY.)

1875 *Jrnl. Chem. Soc.* XXVIII. 38 (*heading*) Experimental determination of the dielectric constants of insulators. **1893** E. ATKINSON tr. *Ganot's Elem. Treat. Physics* (ed. 14) IX. iii. 734 In crystallised bodies the dielectric constant varies with the direction of the axes. **1936** HAUSMANN & SLACK *Physics* xxiii. 445 The dielectric constant..is very nearly unity (1·000586) for air at normal temperature and pressure. **1943** *Electronic Engin.* XVI. 206 The physical constant associated with a dielectric is called the dielectric constant. This is generally defined as the ratio of the capacitance of a condenser with the dielectric material between the electrodes to the capacitance of the electrodes alone when placed in vacuo. **1955** C. P. SMYTH *Dielectric Behavior & Struct.* i. 1 In the m.k.s. system the dielectric constant of free space is $8{\cdot}854 \times 10^{-12}$ farad per m. **1959** B. I. & B. BLEANEY *Electr. & Magn.* xvi. 454 The dielectric constant of a substance affords some valuable information as to the structure of its constituent molecules. **1967** M. NELKON *Fund. Physics* xxxvi. 673 Mica has a higher dielectric constant of 7.

dieˈlectrically, *adv.* [f. prec. + -AL¹ + -LY².] In a dielectric manner; by dielectric action.

1881 *Athenæum* 16 Apr. 529/3 On the Internal Forces of Magnetized and Dielectrically Polarized Bodies.

die-link (ˈdaɪlɪŋk). *Numism.* [f. DIE *sb.*¹ 5 + LINK *sb.*² 3 a.] A relationship established between two or more coins made or stamped by the same die. Hence as *v. trans.* (used *pass.*). Also **die-linked** *ppl. a.*, **die-linking** *vbl. sb.*

1941 C. H. V. SUTHERLAND in *Numismatic Chron.* 6th Ser. I. 99 The consideration of die-axes, and of die-linkings, which can be achieved only by the study of very numerous examples. *Ibid.* 104 The small thunderbolt accompanying the obverse portrait on the 'Seater Livia' series is not found on any other group; we cannot therefore hope for die-links between one group and another. *Ibid.* 105 A twin die-linked series, forming a parallel to the twin die-linked *Clementiae-Moderationi* series. *Ibid.*, The twin *Clementiae-Moderationi* series, being so closely die-linked. **1958** *Times* 11 Feb. 11/5 The hoard included coins of Edward the Elder..which were die-linked, 20 being from the same die of one moneyer. **1958** *Oxf. Univ. Gaz.* 7 Mar. 678/1 Such die-links serve to confirm that issues for both Titus and Domitian were produced in the same establishment.

dielytra (daɪˈɛlɪtrə). *Bot.* [mod.L. (Chamisso & Schlechtendal 1826, in *Linnæa* I. 556), f. Gr. δι- DI-² + ἔλυτρον sheath.] A plant belonging to the genus once so called, now included in the genus DICENTRA.

1864 C. M. YONGE *Trial* II. vi. 122 Do you know this Dielytra? I think it is the prettiest of modern flowers. **1872** G. M. HOPKINS *Jrnl.* 29 June (1959) 220 Dielytras—in the full-blown flower there are at least four symmetrical 'wards'. **1900** J. M. ABBOTT in W.D. Drury *Bk. Gardening* viii. 269 Dicentras (Dielytras) are lovely spring- or early summer-flowering plants.

diem [L. = day], in phr. *per diem*: see PER.

‖**diencephalon** (daɪɛnˈsɛfəlɒn). *Anat.* [mod.L., f. Gr. δι-, δια- through (DI-³) + ἐγκέφαλον brain: see ENCEPHALON. Representing Ger. *zwischenhirn*.] The middle brain; that division of the brain between the mesencephalon and prosencephalon; also called *deutencephalon* or *thalamencephalon*. Hence **dienceˈphalic** *a.*, pertaining to the diencephalon.

1883 *Syd. Soc. Lex.*, *Diencephalon.*

diene (ˈdaɪiːn). *Chem.* [f. DI-² + -ENE.] **a.** Any organic compound containing two double bonds between carbon atoms.

1917 *Chem. Abstr.* XI. 3031 (*title*) The melting points of hydrocarbons, especially dienes, having a system of conjugated double bonds. **1929** *Ibid.* XXIII. 3232 Dienes such as isoprene in relatively pure condition. **1961** L. F. &

M. Fieser *Adv. Org. Chem.* v. 197 Butadiene is significantly more stable..than dienes with isolated (nonconjugated) double bonds.

b. *attrib.*, esp. in **diene synthesis**, an addition reaction in which two carbon atoms joined by a double or triple bond in an unsaturated compound become attached to the first and fourth carbon atoms of a conjugated diene, forming a ring of six carbon atoms in the resulting molecule; the Diels-Alder reaction; **diene value**, a number expressing the degree of unsaturation in fatty compounds.

1928 *Chem. Abstr.* XXII. 1144 (*heading*) Addition of 'diene' hydrocarbons. **1930** *Ibid.* XXIV. 356 (*heading*) The 'diene-syntheses'. An ideal method for the synthesis of organic compounds. **1957** *Encycl. Brit.* I. 549/2 The diene synthesis consists essentially of the addition of substances containing two conjugate double bonds, such as the butadienes, to substances such as maleic acid or quinones. **1936** *Rep. Prog. Applied Chem.* 433 Linseed oil itself shows a definite 'maleic' or 'diene value', equivalent to about 5-7% of conjugated triene glycerides.

diener, var. DEANER.

dieng, obs. form of *dying*: see DIE *v.*

† **diennial**, *a. Obs. rare*⁻⁰. = BIENNIAL.

1656 Blount *Glossogr.*, *Diennial*, of or pertaining to two years.

diep(e, obs. form of DEEP.

dier ('daɪə(r)). *rare.* Also 6 **dyer**. [f. DIE *v.*[1] + -ER[1].] One who dies; one who suffers, or is liable to, death.

1570 *Piththy Note to Papists* (1862), Many sundry deaths doo bring the dyers endles shame. **1638** Suckling *Brennoralt* I. i, Dead, as I live; Well, goe thy wayes, for a quiet drinker and dier. **1887** Jessopp in *19th Cent.* Dec. 839 'I suppose I am a dier', she said..'I used to think I should never die'.

dier, obs. form of DEAR, DEER, DYER.

dieresis, dieretic, var. DIÆRESIS, -ETIC.

diervilla (ˈdɪəvɪlə). *Bot.* [mod.L. (Tournefort 1707, in *Acta Acad. 1706* VII. 85), f. the name of *Dierville*, a French surgeon, who discovered a species of the plant in Acadia 1699-1700.] A plant of the genus so named, comprising deciduous shrubs having pink, crimson, yellow, or white flowers; some species are also called WEIGELA or *bush-honeysuckle* (see HONEYSUCKLE 3 b).

1806 B. McMahon *Amer. Gardener's Cal.* 293 Flowering shrubs..may now be planted with good success, such as.. St. Peter's-wort, Diervilla, roses, and all kinds of hardy deciduous shrubs. **1816** *Curtis's Bot. Mag.* XLIII. 1796 (*heading*) Yellow-flowered Diervilla. **1884** G. Nicholson *Illustr. Dict. Gardening* I. 475/1 The gracefully spreading form of Diervillas renders them remarkably well adapted for shrubberies. **1924** A. J. Macself *Flowering Trees & Shrubs* x. 134 Formerly known as Weigelas, a name indeed still familiarly used, the Diervillas are worthily held in high esteem. **1951** *Good Housek. Home Encycl.* 117/1 Other favourite flowering shrubs and trees that will grow in most soils are..Weigelias or Diervillas, Heaths, [etc.]. **1959** *Times* 31 Jan. 9/4 The forsythias, diervillas, pyracanthas.

‖ **dies** (ˈdaɪiːz). The Latin word for 'day'; used in certain phrases.

a. dies iræ, 'day of wrath', the first words, and hence the name, of a Latin hymn on the Last Judgement ascribed to Thomas of Celano (*c* 1250).

b. dies non (short for *dies non juridicus*), in *Law*, a day on which no legal business is transacted, or which is not reckoned in counting days for some particular purpose. Also in other legal phrases: see quot. 1848. Also *transf.*, a day that does not count or on which there is no activity.

1607-72 Cowell *Interpr.*, *Dies*..A legal day, and that is of two sorts, 1. *Dies Juridicus*, and 2. *Dies non Juridicus. Dies Juridici* are all dayes..given in Term to the Parties in Court. *Dies non Juridici* are all Sundayes in the year, besides, in the several Terms particular dayes. **1805** Scott *Last Minstr.* vi. xxx, And far the echoing aisles prolong The awful burthen of the song,—Dies iræ, dies illa, Solvet sæclum in favilla. **1825** Hone *Every-day Bk.* I. 156 A Sunday..is a *dies non*, or no day in law. **1848** Wharton *Law Lex.*, *Dies amoris* (the day of love), the appearance day of the Term on the fourth day, or *quarto die post.* It was the day given by the favour and indulgence of the court to the defendant for his appearance, when all parties appeared in court, and had their appearance recorded by the proper officer. *Dies datus*, the day of respite given to a defendant... *Dies juridicus*, a court day... *Dies non juridicus*, not a court day. **1860** Thackeray *Round. Papers* (1863) 196 The idea (*dies iræ*!) of discovery must haunt many a man. **1887** Ruskin *Præterita* II. 213 Men have been curiously judging themselves by always calling the day they expected, 'Dies Iræ', instead of 'Dies Amoris'. **1897** *Daily News* 19 Apr. 2/1 This has been almost a 'dies non' in the city, owing to the Stock Exchange being closed. **1937** *N. & Q.* CLXXIII. 369/2 Thursdays are a *dies non* in the players' week.

Diesel, diesel (ˈdiːzəl). **a.** The name of Rudolf *Diesel* (1858-1913), German engineer, used *attrib.* to designate a type of internal-combustion engine invented by him, in which air alone is drawn into the cylinder, this air being so highly compressed that the heat generated ignites the fuel-oil when it enters the combustion space. Also *ellipt.*, a diesel engine; a locomotive, motor diesel etc., driven by a diesel engine (also *attrib.*).

1894 S. B. Donkin *Text-bk. Gas, Oil, & Air Engines* Index 413 Diesel engine. **1894** —— tr. *Diesel's Rational Heat Motor* 53 The three vertical cylinders of the Diesel motor. **1928** J. K. Roberts *Heat & Thermodynamics* xiv. 284 The use of a Diesel engine results in considerable fuel economy as compared with an engine working on a 'constant-volume' cycle. **1930** *Engineering* 16 May 623/3 The first two Diesel locomotives in the world were built by The General Electric Company in 1917 and 1918. **1934** T. E. Lawrence *Lett.* (1938) 806 The new four-cylinder Gardner 60 bhp light Diesel is having its gear box fitted for test in 159 hull. **1957** [see sense b below]. **1966** J. Betjeman *High & Low* 15 Through the midlands of Ireland I journeyed by diesel. **1970** *Railway Mag.* Oct. 584/2 A number of class '47' diesels have been noted working under the wires in the London area recently.

b. *attrib.* and *Comb.*, as ***diesel-driven, -engined, -hauled, -hydraulic*** adjs.; **diesel-eletric** *a.*, driven by electric motors powered by current from a generator, which in turn is driven by a diesel engine; also *absol.*, a diesel-electric engine, locomotive, or vehicle; **diesel oil**, a petroleum fraction used as fuel in diesel engines.

1905 H. Allen *Gas & Oil Eng.* 267 Test of a 500 B.H.P. Diesel Oil Engine. **1916** *Motor Ship & Motor Boat* 30 Nov. 379, 1200 h.p. Diesel-engined Auxiliaries. **1921** *Sci. Amer.* 2 Apr. 267 Advantages of the Diesel-Electric System over the Straight Diesel Drive. *Ibid.*, The advantage is decidely with the Diesel-electric, since the engine runs continuously in one direction... A Diesel-electric operated boat can change from full speed ahead to full speed reverse in.. seconds. **1926** *Marine Engineer* Mar. 113/2 The primary valuation of a Diesel oil is obtained from the specific gravity and viscosity. *Ibid.* Apr. 145/2 Below are shown microphotographs of Diesel oil and boiler oil, before and after treatment in a..centrifuge. **1930** *Engineering* 16 May 624/2 The Diesel electric locomotive for the London and North Eastern Railway. **1935** *Hansard Commons* 18 June 236 Diesel oil used for the purpose of road vehicles. **1936** *Discovery* Mar. 89/1 Diesel-driven parcels vans. **1955** A. Ross *Australia 55* iii. 43 The train is..diesel-hauled. **1957** *Economist* 30 Nov. 799/2 The 52 diesel-hydraulic locomotives ordered..bring the total number of main-line diesels ordered so far..to 282, of which all except 66 are diesel electrics. **1958** *Listener* 12 June 964/1 The experimental diesel car service introduced between Banbury and Bletchley. **1958** 'N. Shute' *Rainbow & Rose* i. 7 They've got a diesel-engined boat.

dieselize (ˈdiːzəlaɪz), *v.* orig. *U.S.* [f. DIESEL, DIESEL + -IZE.] *trans.* To equip with a diesel engine or with diesel-electric locomotives. So **ˌdieseliˈzation**; **ˈdieselized** *ppl. a.*

1946 in *Amer. Speech* (1947) XXII. 158/2 The Burlington's main line passenger trains are largely dieselized. **1949** *Time* 30 May 38/1 He..hopes to cut costs more by dieselizing the entire [railway] line. **1950** *Engineering* 24 Mar. 328/1 In the U.S.A., where 'dieselisation' has gained..a foothold for long hauls. **1958** *Economist* 1 Feb. 381/2 The area needs an integrated system of road transport and dieselised railways. **1958** *New Statesman* 15 Nov. 668/3 Priority must be given to those schemes bringing quickest results, e.g., dieselisation before electrification. **1970** *Railway Mag.* Oct. 550/2 Some interesting combinations of locomotives could be observed on this train before dieselisation. *Ibid.* 553/1 The North Island system has been entirely dieselised for some years.

‖ **diesis** (ˈdaɪɪsɪs). Pl. **dieses** (-iːz). [a. L. *diesis*, Gr. δίεσις a quarter-tone, lit. a sending through or apart, f. διϊέναι to send through, f. διά through + ἱέναι to send.]

1. *Mus.* **a.** In ancient Greek music, a name given to several different intervals smaller than a tone; *esp.* the Pythagorean semitone, equal to the difference between two major tones and a perfect fourth (ratio 243:256). **b.** In modern music, the interval equal to the difference between three major thirds and an octave, or between the chromatic and diatonic semitones (ratio 125:128); usually called ***enharmonic diesis.***

1398 Trevisa *Barth. De P.R.* xix. cxxxi. (1495) 941 Diesis is the space and doynge of melodye and chaungynge out of one sowne in to a nother. **1597** Morley *Introd. Mus.* Annot., Diesis is the halfe of the lesse halfe note. **1694** Holder *Harmony* (1731) 121 The Ditone, made by these two Degrees, is too much by a Diesis (128 to 125). *a* **1734** North *Lives* (1826) II. 210 He makes great ado about dividing tones major, tones minor, dieses and commas. **1867** Macfarren *Harmony* i. 8 The effect of the Enharmonic diesis is employed by no means rarely in.. musical performances.

2. *Printing.* The sign ‡, usually called 'double dagger'.

[Formerly used to denote a diesis in Music: cf. 1727-51 Chambers *Cycl.* s.v., 'The chromatic, or double diesis, denoted by a double cross.' In French, the sign of the 'sharp' ♯ is called *dièse*.]

1706 Phillips (ed. Kersey), *Diesis*..among Printers it is taken for a Mark, otherwise call'd a *Double-dagger* ‡. **1874** Knight *Dict. Mech.* I. 701/1 *Diesis* (*Printing*), the double dagger (‡), a reference-mark.

diet (ˈdaɪət), *sb.*[1] Forms: 3-6 **diete**, (5 **diat, dyette**, 5-6 **dyete, diette**), 5-8 **dyet**, (6 **diot, dyot, dyat, dieat, dyeat**), 5- **diet**. [a. OF. *diete* (13th c. in Hatz.-Darm.), = Sp., Pg., and It. *dieta*, ad. L. *diæta* (in med.L. *diēta*), a. Gr. δίαιτα 'mode of life'. (Supposed to be connected with ζάειν to live: see Meyer *Gr. Gram.* §261.)]

† **1.** Course of life: way of living or thinking. ***of the same diet, of a different diet, both of a diet***, i.e. sort or kind.

c **1400** *Beryn* 1431 Ech day our diete Shall be mery & solase, & this shall be for-ȝete. **1567** *Triall Treas.* (1850) 31 Behold howe a lie can please some folkes diet! **1612-5** Bp. Hall *Contempl.*, *O.T.* x. ii, Either this was the Sonne himselfe, or else one..of the same diet. *Ibid.* xiv. vi, Worldly mindes think no man can bee of any other then their owne dyet. **1618** —— *Serm.* v. 104 Francis of Assise and he were both of a diet. *a* **1656** —— *Rem. Wks.* (1660) 255 The minds of men may be of a different diet.

2. *esp.* Customary course of living as to food: way of feeding.

c **1386** Chaucer *Pard. T.* 188 He wolde been the moore mesurable Of his diete sittynge at his table. *c* **1470** Henry *Wallace* iv. 333 Off dyet fayr Wallace tuk neuer kepe; Bot as it come, welcum was meit and sleip. **1531** Elyot *Gov.* i. xiii, He wyll..enquire what skyll he hath in feedyng, called diete, and kepyng of his hauke from all sickenes. **1635** N. Carpenter *Geog. Del.* ii. xv. 259 Scarcity inuites the mountaine dwellers to a more sparing and wholesome diet. **1774** J. Bryant *Mythol.* II. 261 He brought mankind from their foul and savage way of feeding to a more mild and rational diet. **1838** Prescott *Ferd. & Is.* (1846) II. v. 360 He maintained the same abstemious diet amidst all the luxuries of his table. **1866** Livingstone *Last Jrnl.* 23 Dec. (1873) I. vii. 162 A meat diet is far from satisfying.

3. Prescribed course of food, restricted in kind or limited in quantity, *esp.* for medical or penal reasons; regimen. Hence ***to put to a diet*** (F. *mettre à la diète*), ***to keep*** or ***take diet*** (F. *observer une diète*).

c **1386** Chaucer *Nun's Pr. T.* 18 No deyntee morsel passed thurgh hir throte..Attempree diete was al hir phisik. *c* **1400** *Lanfranc's Cirurg.* 72 Þe firste tretis is of gouernaunce & diete of men þat ben woundid. *c* **1440** *Gesta Rom.* xix. 334 (Add. MS.), There was a man-sleer taken, and put into prison, and put to his diete. **1495** *Act 11 Hen. VII*, c. 2 §1 He to be sette..in Stokkis by the space of vj daies with like diete as is before reherced. *a* **1533** Ld. Berners *Gold. Bk. M. Aurel.* (1546) M vij b, The ydeotte kepeth diete from bookes and resteth on his meate. **1591** Shaks. *Two Gent.* ii. i. 25 To fast, like one that takes diet. **1603** —— *Meas. for M.* ii. i. 116 Past cure of the thing you wot of, vnlesse they kept very good diet. **1655** Moufet & Bennet *Health's Improvem.* (1746) 68, I define Diet..to be an orderly and due Course observed in the Use of bodily Nourishments. *a* **1735** Arbuthnot *John Bull* Postscr. Swift's Wks. 1751 VI. 166 He..by Diet, Purging, Vomiting, and Bleeding, tried to bring them to equal Bulk. **1741** Johnson *L.P.*, *Morin*, To preach diet and abstinence to his patients. **1841** Elphinstone *Hist. Ind.* I. 455 They rely most on diet and regimen, and next, on external applications.

4. Food; the provisions or victuals in daily use, viewed as a collective whole, especially in relation to their quality and effects.

a **1225** *Ancr. R.* 112 Vnderstondeð, hwuc was his diete þet dei, iðen ilke blodletunge! So baluhful & so bitter! **1398** Trevisa *Barth. De P.R.* vii. lv. (1495) 268 In chyldern the vryne is thycke by cause of gleymy diete. *c* **1420** *Anturs of Arth.* xv, With alle dayntethis on dese, thi dietis are diȝte. *c* **1555** Harpsfield *Divorce Hen. VIII* (1878) 202 Kept in prison with coarse and thin diet. **1579** Lyly *Euphues* (Arb.) 129 That the babe be..not fedde with counterfaite dyet. *a* **1682** Sir T. Browne *Tracts* (1684) 17 The Athletick Diet was of Pulse. **1718** Lady M. W. Montagu *Let. to C'tess Bristol* (1887) I. 241 Herbs or roots (without oil) and plain dry bread. That is their lenten diet. **1856** Kane *Arct. Expl.* II. xiv. 144 The dogs were too much distended by their abundant diet to move. **1868** Gladstone *Juv. Mundi* v. (1870) 128 Nay, even a change of diet confronts us..the ox ceases to be used as food.

b. *fig.* **1579** Gosson *Sch. Abuse* (Arb.) 41 Yet are they [plays] not fit for euery mans dyet. **1823** Lamb *Elia* Ser. ii. *Some Sonnets of Sydney*, A thin diet of dainty words.

† **5. a.** An allowance or provision of food. *Obs.*

1533 *Ord. Hen. VIII* in Ellis *Orig. Lett.* Ser. i. II. 30 We ..commaunde you to alloue dailly from hensforth unto.. the Lady Lucye..the dyat and fare herafter ensuyng. **1611** Bible *Jer.* lii. 34 And for his diet, there was a continuall diet [Coverd. lyuynge] giuen him..euery day a portion [Cov. a certayne thinge alowed him]. **1663** Evelyn *Diary* 20 Aug., It was said it should be the last of the public diets or tables at Court. **1671** F. Phillips *Reg. Necess.* 370 The young Lords or Nobility had a constant Table or dyet in the Court.

† **b.** Board. *Obs.* exc. *Hist.*

1455 *Rolls of Parlt.* 293 The said Prince shall sojorne and be at dietteз with the Kyng. **1596** Shaks. *1 Hen. IV*, iii. iii. 84 You owe Money here besides, Sir John, for your Dyet. **1602** —— *Ham.* i. i. 99 Young Fortinbras..Hath..Shark'd vp a List of Lawlesse Resolutes, For Foode, and Diet. **1621-51** Burton *Anat. Mel.* i. ii. iii. xv, He shall have..ten pound per annum, and his diet. **1645** Evelyn *Mem.* (1857) I. 204 Here many of the merchants..have their lodging and diet as in a College. **1792** Chipman *Amer. Law Rep.* (1871) 27 The bond was taken for the prisoner's..diet and to secure the gaoler's fees. **1878** Simpson *Sch. Shaks.* I. 74 The king..gave him 3,000 ducats more, besides the daily expenses of his lodging and diet.

† **6.** Allowance for the expenses of living. *Obs.*

a **1483** *Liber Niger* in *Househ. Ord.* 24 This must cause her comyn diette to be the more for the high estate of her proper person. **1535** *Act 27 Hen. VIII*, c. 27 Suche like diettes, rewardes, profites and commodities..for their attendance vpon the saide Chauncellour. *c* **1540** Bp. Bonner in *Wyatt's Poems* Pref. (1854) 41 If he were a good husband, the diets of iiij marks would find his house..after a far other sort than it is kept. **1551** Sir R. Moryson *Lett. to Cecil* Jan. 20 (Record Off.) Is my land so increast sins my cummyng out..that men do thynke I may serue the Kyng without my dyettes? **1651** Hobbes *Leviath.* ii. xxiv. 236 Common-wealths can endure no diet; seeing their expense is not limited by their own appetite, but by external accidents. [1885 R. W. Dixon *Hist. Ch. Eng.* (1893) III. xix. 338 The allowances of the ambassador, or, as they were called, his diets, were ever unpaid.]

7. a. *Comb.*, as ***diet-bag, -list, -money***; also **diet-bread**, special bread prepared for invalids or persons under dietetic regimen; **diet-kitchen** (see quot.); †**diet-pot**, a pot by which to measure diet-drink; **diet-sheet**, a paper showing a daily diet, esp. for the inmates of an institution; †**diet-wood** (see quot.). Also DIET-BOOK, -DRINK.

1669 W. Simpson *Hydrol. Chym.* 162 Heaps of plants by some physicians are ordered to stuff *diet-bags withal. 1617 Collins *Def. Bp. Ely* II. ix. 357 To feede them with such dirt for *diet-bread. 1824 Miss Mitford *Village* Ser. I. (1863) 223 Drinking her green tea, eating her diet-bread, begging her gowns. 1880 Webster *Suppl.*, **Diet-kitchen*, a charitable establishment which provides proper food for the helpless poor. 1856 Kane *Arct. Expl.* I. i. 19 A very moderate supply of liquors..made up the *diet-list. 1519 Sir T. Boleyn in Ellis *Orig. Lett.* Ser. I. I. 161 Send me such *dyett-money as shall best please your Grace. 1551 Sir R. Moryson *Lett. to Cecil* Jan. 7, I mervayl my dieat mony cummith not. 1727 A. Hamilton *New Acc. E. Ind.* I. vii. 74 Allow them as much Diet money as their own Soldiers receive. 1612 Woodall *Surg. Mate* Wks. (1653) 23 The *Dyet Pot is not alone to be used in cases of dyet drink. *c*1863 Florence Nightingale in C. Woodham-Smith *F. Nightingale* (1950) xvii. 397 Revised *diet sheets for Troop-Ships. 1902 J. H. M. Abbott *Tommy Cornstalk* 182 We all lay in, or upon, our beds with our board-mounted diet-sheets in our hands. 1918 W. Owen *Let.* 22 July (1967) 566, I see an old Diet Sheet on the table. 1967 *Vogue* Jan. 51/1 This is the Diet sheet. Vary meat, eggs, chicken and fish.. to avoid boredom. 1568 Turner *Herbal* III. 34 Guiacum.. Some call it the *Diet woode because they that kepe a diet for the French poxe..most commonly drinke the broth of this woode.

b. Used *attrib.* of (esp. carbonated soft) drinks with reduced sugar content sold commercially, as ***diet cola, Pepsi***, etc. orig. *U.S.*

1963 *Newsweek* 8 July 76/3 Pepsi introduced its Patio Diet Cola..and Coke its Tab..only days apart this year. 1964 *Business Week* 27 June 90/3 Patio Diet Cola was not the success Pepsi had hoped, so it has rushed to market a new drink, Diet Pepsi. 1966 *Official Gaz.* (U.S. Patent Office) 29 Nov. TM237 PepsiCo, Inc., New York... *Diet Pepsi.* 1969 *New Yorker* 25 Oct. 58/2 She loves diet cola spiked with a spoonful of chocolate syrup. 1970 *Ibid.* 24 Oct. 58 (*caption*) They open flip-top can..Diet Pepsi. 1985 *Washington Post* 18 Sept. E21/6 The third- and fourth-fastest-growing items were breakfast sandwiches and diet colas.

diet ('daɪət), *sb.*[2] [ad. med.L. *diēta* in same senses, or a. F. *diète* in sense 5 (Cotgr. 1611): cf. also It. *dieta* 'a parliament or generall assembly of estates' (Florio, 1598), Sp. *dieta* the (Germanic) diet.

Med.L. *diēta* had the various senses 'day's journey', 'day's work', 'day's wage', 'space of a day', as well as that of 'assembly, meeting of councillors, diet of the empire'. The same senses, more or less, are (or have been) expressed by Ger. *tag*, and F. *journée* day. *Diēta* has therefore been viewed as a simple derivative of L. *dies* day, distinct from *diæta*, Gr δίαιτα, DIET *sb.*[1] But it seems more likely that one or other of the senses developed from *diæta* was associated with *dies*, and led to the application of the word to other uses arising directly from *dies*. One of the senses given by Du Cange is 'the ordinary course of the church': this seems naturally transferred from δίαιτα, *diæta*, in the sense 'ordinary or prescribed course of life', which might be understood to mean 'daily office', and so lead to the use of *diēta* for other daily courses, duties, or occasions.]

†**1.** A day's journey; 'an excursion, a journey' (Jamieson). *Obs.* chiefly *Sc.* (So F. *journée.*)

[*c*1290 *Fleta* IV. xxviii. §13 (Du Cange) Omnis rationabilis dieta constat ex 20 miliaribus.] *c*1440 *Gesta Rom.* xix. 67 (Harl. MS.) Also how many daies iourneys... This terme or this dyet, is not ellis but the terme of thi lyfe. *c*1565 Lindesay (Pitscottie) *Chron. Scot.* (1814) 212 (Jam.) Sum of the conspiratouris, who hard tell of the kingis dyett, followed fast to Leith eftir him. 1609 Skene *Reg. Maj.* 143 Twa or thrie gude men of the Gilde sall travell with him for twa dyets. *a*1651 Calderwood *Hist. Kirk* (1678) 248 (Jam.) The king..prayeth him to waken up all men to attend his coming..for his diet would be sooner perhaps than was looked for.

†**2.** A day's work. *Sc. Obs.* (So F. *journée.*)

1494 *Ld. Treas. Accts. Scot.* I. 246 Item, to Thome Red and Jhone of Schipe, for vj diet at the wod, vj s.

3. *Sc.* A day fixed for a particular meeting or assembly; an appointed date or time. **b.** *spec.* The day on which a party in a civil or criminal process is cited to appear in court. More fully ***diet of appearance, compearance***. (So OF. *journée.*)

1568 *Satir. Poems Reform.* xlvii. 80 Gif he cumis nocht thair, I wald we tuke, To keip oure dyet, Maister Dauid Makgill. 1640–1 *Kirkcudbr. War Comm. Min. Bk.* (1855) 93 To compeir befoire the said Committie of Estaites..and that to anie day or diet the said Commissares or Collectores shall pleis to charge thame to. 1692 *Will. III. Instr. to Sir T. Livingston* 16 Jan. (*Highland Pa.*, Maitl. Cl. 1845) Those who have not taken the benefit of our indemnity within the diet prefixt by our proclamation. 1708 J. Chamberlayne *St. Gt. Brit.* II. II. vi. (1743) 391 Having obtained a Dyet, i.e. a set day for his publick trial. 1752 Louthian *Form of Process* (ed. 2) 9 All the Diets of Court are peremptory. 1810 *Act 50 Geo. III*, c. 112 §27 In actions at present requiring two diets of appearance against persons within Scotland, there shall be only one diet of twenty-seven days. 1823 Symson *Descr. Galloway* 26 (Jam.) A market for good fat kine [is] kept on the Friday..this market being ruled by the dyets of the nolt-market of Wigton.

†**c.** Date, day of date. *Obs.*

1588 A. King tr. *Canisius' Catech.* 9 To raise [= erase] the diett off an instrumente.

4. *Sc.* A session or sitting of a court or other body on an appointed day; a single session of any assembly occupying a day or part of one.

1587 *Sc. Acts Jas. VI* (1599) §82 Called..before the justice or his deputes at iustice aires, or particular diettes. 1637 Gillespie *Eng. Pop. Cerem.* III. i. 13 At the diets of weekly and ordinary preaching. 1643 Row *Hist. Kirk* (1842) p. xxi, I attendit many dayes and dyetts, and in end..a decreit was gifine thereupon. 1854 *Phemie Millar* II. 21 He's put on his Sabbath day claes..and sat out the haill diet. 1854 H. Miller *Sch. & Schm.* iii. (1857) 48, I began to dole out to them by the hour and the diet, long extempore biographies. 1876 Grant *Burgh Sch. Scotl.* II. iv. 147 In the week preceding, the classes shall be tried at two different diets by examiners appointed by the town Council. 1894 Crockett *Raiders* 25 Who met statedly for their diets of worship at Springholm.

b. ***to call the diet***: to call the parties to an action in court on the appointed day. ***to desert the diet***: see DESERT *v.* 4.

1753 *Scots Mag.* Sept. 469/1 The diet was deserted as to Cameron. 1850 Blackie *Æschylus* I. 217 Herald, proclaim the diet, and command The people to attention. 1893 *Daily News* 28 Dec. 5/4 Outlawry is a sentence pronounced in the Supreme Criminal Court of Scotland in the absence of the accused at the calling of the diet, that is, the day on which he is summoned to appear and stand his trial.

5. A meeting by formal appointment for conference or transaction of national or international business; a conference, congress, convention. (In later use generally influenced by b.) (So OF. *journée.*)

*c*1450 Holland *Howlat* 280 Thai counsall the Pape to writ in this wyss To the Athile Empriour..To adress to that dyet, to deme his awyss. 1471 in Rymer *State Papers* 717 It is Appointed..that the Twenty fourth Day of September next comeyng, at the Towne of Alnewyke, shall be kept a Dyet, by the grete Commissioners of both Landes, for Reformyng of the said Wrongs and Injuries. 1494 Fabyan *Chron.* VII. 453 A daye of dyet was atwene the two kynges [of England and France] appoyntyd. *Ibid.* 611 After Easter was a daye of diot holden bytwene Grauenynge and Calays, for the matyers touchynge the kynge and the duke of Burgoyne. 1598 Hakluyt *Voy.* I. 156 There was demaunded in the first dyet or conuention holden at Dordract, a recompense at the handes of the sayd English ambassadors. 1600 Holland *Livy* XXXV. xxv. 902 The Achæans..published a Diet and generall Counsell at Sicyone. 1879 Froude *Cæsar* xiv. 209 A diet of chiefs was held under Cæsar's presidency.

b. *spec.* Applied to the regular meeting of the estates of a realm or confederation; hence also collectively to the estates or representatives so meeting (cf. CONGRESS). The English name (from end of the 16th c.) of the former *Reichstag* of the (German) Roman Empire, and of the federal or national assemblies of Switzerland, Poland, Hungary, etc.; later of the *Bundestag* of the Germanic Confederation (1815–66); applied also to the existing *Reichstag* or Imperial Parliament of the Austro-Hungarian and German Empires, and the *Landtag* or local parliament of their constituent states, and sometimes to the parliamentary assemblies of other states of Eastern Europe, of Japan, etc.

1565 T. Stapleton *Fortr. Faith* 140a, They haue had diets and assembles in Germany by the force and procurement of the Catholike Emperours. 1586 T. B. *La Primaud. Fr. Acad.* 632 In Switzerland..if any greate matter fall out, that is common to all the leagues, they hold their generall councell, called a Journey, or a Diet. 1611 Speed *Hist. Gt. Brit.* IX. vii. §48 At an assembly or dyet, where the greatest Princes and States of the Empire were in person. 1656 Blount *Glossogr.*, *Diet* (diæta) in Germany it is the same thing as a Parliament in England, a great Assembly or Council of the States and Princes of the Empire. 1687 Dryden *Hind & Panther* II. 407 Thus would your Polish Diet disagree, And end, as it began, in anarchy. 1698 *Lond. Gaz.* No. 3377/2 Several Deputies from the Palatinates in Lithuania..seem very desirous of a Dyet on Horseback. 1709 Steele *Tatler* No. 21 ¶19 To assist at the Diet of the States of Hungary. 1756–7 *Keysler's Trav.* (1760) IV. 422 Possibly a few of the most powerful princes might find their account in the dissolution of the diet. 1814 tr. *Klaproth's Trav.* 66 The Poles assembled at the diet held in 1573 for the election of a new sovereign. 1838 *Penny Cycl.* XI. 192/2 The three colleges formed the diet of the empire, whose ordinary meetings were formerly summoned by the emperors twice a year. *Ibid.* 191/1 The central point and organ of the present Germanic Confederation is the Federative Diet, which sits at Frankfort on the Main. 1838 *Murray's Handbk. N. Germ.* 446 The Diet meets to deliberate..in the building, formerly the palace of the Prince of Thurn and Taxis. 1849 Macaulay *Hist. Eng.* I. 261 The meeting at Oxford resembled rather that of a Polish diet than that of an English parliament. 1871 *Outl. Mod. Geog.* 68 Frankfürt-on-the-Main, formerly a free city and seat of the Germanic Diet. 1895 *Times* (Weekly Ed.) 29 Mar. 1/4 The Japanese Diet was closed on Wednesday. *Ibid.* 2/4 The Lower House of the Prussian Diet..authorized its President to convey its congratulations to Prince Bismarck. *Ibid.*, There is..no intention of dissolving the Imperial Diet.

6. The metal scraped or cut from gold and silver plate assayed day by day at the Mint, and retained for the purpose of trial.

1700–1 *Act 12–13 Will. III*, c. 4 §4 It shall..be lawfull to detain Eight Grains only from every Pound Troy of Silver he shall assay, Four Grains whereof shall be put into the Box of Dyett. *Ibid.* §5 That the Box or Boxes wherein the Diet of all such Plate as shall be tryed by the Assayers aforesaid shall be locked up with Three different Locks..And the said Diet therein contained shall be tryed as the Pix of the Coin of this Kingdom is tryed. 1772–3 *Act 13 Geo. III*, c. 52 §6. 1883 Roberts & Hill in *Encycl. Brit.* (ed. 9) XVI. 491/2 Another operation..performed in the mint is the assay of the 'diet' or metal scraped from the gold and silver plate manufactured at Sheffield and Birmingham. 1889 *19th Rep. Deputy-Master of Mint* 53 These diets, consisting of scrapings from gold and silver wares which have been hall-marked at the Assay offices.

b. *attrib.* as ***diet-box***.

1835 P. Kelly *Univ. Cambist* i. (ed. 2) 219 The cuttings and scrapings of the articles assayed..are kept in what is called the Diet-box, in order to be melted into a mass and proved like the Pix, before the proper officers.

'diet, *v.* Forms: 4 diȝete, 5 diete, dyatt, 5–7 dyet, 6 diate, 7 dyat, diett, diot, 5– diet. [a. OF. *diete-r* to feed, order the diet of (Godef.), f. *diete* DIET *sb.*[1]: cf. med.L. *diætāre* to live according to a certain plan (*a* 1087 in Du Cange), f. *diæta.*]

I. *trans.*

1. To feed, *esp.* in a particular way, or with specified kinds of food; to put (a person) to a specified diet.

1362 Langl. *P. Pl.* A. VII. 255 And ȝif þou diȝete þe þus I dar legge boþe myn Eres, þat Fisyk schal his Forred hod, for his foode sulle. *c*1400 *Lanfranc's Cirurg.* 98 Voide him a litil and diete him with colde metis and stiptik. 1483 *Cath. Angl.* 99 To Diet, *dietare.* 1535 Coverdale *Ecclus.* xxxvii. 34 He that dyeteth him self temperatly prolongeth his life. 1583 Stanyhurst *Æneis* III. (Arb.) 91 My self I dieted with sloas. 1655 Moufet & Bennet *Health's Improv.* (1746) 69 He that taught Abel how to diet Sheep. 1667 Milton *P.L.* IX. 803 Dieted by thee I grow mature In knowledge as the Gods who all things know. 1742 Fielding *J. Andrews* II. xvii, He diets them with all the dainty food of holiness. 1860 Emerson *Cond. Life, Consid.* Wks. (Bohn) II. 425 It makes no difference, in looking back five years, how you have been dieted and dressed.

†**b.** (predicated of the food). *Obs.*

1638 Sir T. Herbert *Trav.* (ed. 2) 17 Dead Whales, Seales, Pengwins, grease or raw Puddings diet them.

c. *fig.*

1602 Warner *Alb. Eng.* Epit. (1612) 375 Only his golden thoughts would not be worser Dioted than with a Diademe. 1611 Shaks. *Cymb.* III. iv. 183 Thou art all the comfort The Gods will diet me with. 1670 Eachard *Cont. Clergy* 6 You diet him with nothing but with rules and exceptions. 1816 Coleridge *Lay Serm.* 327 That vast company..whose heads and hearts are dieted at the two public ordinaries of literature, the circulating libraries, and the periodical press.

2. To fix, prescribe, or regulate the food of (a person, etc.) in nature or quantity, for a purpose. *spec.* **a.** as a regimen of health.

*c*1400 *Lanfranc's Cirurg.* 213, I dietide him as a man þat hadde a fever agu. 1533 Bellenden *Livy* v. (1822) 400 Eftir that the sick man has sufferit himself to be diet fra metis and drinkis. 1590 Shaks. *Com. Err.* v. i. 99, I will attend my husband, be his nurse, Diet his sicknesse. 1641 Milton *Animadv.* (1851) 188 You are not dieted, nor your loynes girt for spiritually valour. 1768 Foote *Devil on 2 Sticks* III. Wks. 1799 II. 275 Full power..to pill..diet..and poultice all persons. 1849 R. A. Vaughan in *Brit. Q. Rev.* May 312 Goethe..having dieted himself for hard work, was busy at Weimar with his 'Faust'.

fig. 1647 N. Bacon *Disc. Govt. Eng.* I. lxxi. (1739) 188 These must be purged by dieting the State. 1705 Hickeringill *Priest-cr.* II. iv. 44 The Archbishopric of York and..the Bishopric of Ely (being both of them thought needlessly gross)..were dieted, some say, pinch'd and impaired too much.

b. as a punishment, etc.

1530 Tindale *Pract. Prelates* Wks. (Parker Soc.) II. 348 After they had dieted and tormented him. 1712 Addison *Spect.* No. 440 ¶6 The President immediately ordered him to be..dieted with Water-gruel, till such time as he should be sufficiently weakened for Conversation. 1862 Burton *Bk. Hunter* (1863) 12 The simple privilege of locking him up, dieting him [etc.].

†**3.** *fig.* To order, regulate. *Obs. rare.*

1576 Woolton *Chr. Manual* (Parker Soc.) 125 In dieting all our words and works to his honour and glory.

4. To provide with daily meals; to board.

1635 J. Sadler in *Verney Papers* (1853) 160 His men maye ..be taken of his hande and dyeted for theyre worke for the first yeare. *a*1661 Fuller *Worthies* (1840) II. 362 Tower prisoners were not dieted on their own, but on the king's charges. *a*1713 Ellwood *Autobiog.* (1714) 235, I..was dieted in the House of a Friendly Man. 1732 *Acc. Workhouses* 111 We have 20 men and women..lodg'd and dieted here. 1778 *Eng. Gazetteer* (ed. 2.) s.v. *Thingdon*, A charity-school for 20 girls, who are cloathed, lodged, and dieted.

II. *intr.*

5. To take one's ordinary food, or meals; to feed (*on*).

1566 Drant *Horace Sat.* iii. D iv, Haste thou a frende that dyets harde? 1600 J. Pory tr. *Leo's Africa* I. 23 Where the Canons live togither, they go each man to diet at his owne house. 1647 Fuller *Good Th. in Worse T.* (1841) 118 At what ordinary, or rather extraordinary do they diet? *a*1734 North *Lives* I. 192 He kept no house in town, but ordinarily dieted in the Temple. 1791 Cowper *Iliad* XXIV. 522 Neither worm, which diets on the brave In battle fall'n, hath eaten him, or taint Invaded. 1843 Carlyle *Past & Pr.* II. xv. (1845) 150 Those four-and-twenty young bloods dieted all that day with the Lord Abbot.

b. To board (*with* a person, *at*, *in* a house, etc.).

1581 L. Aldersey in Hakluyt *Voy.* (1589) 181 There we lay and dieted of free cost. 1617 Moryson *Itin.* I. III. i. 205 They were to diet at the Carriers charge. 1656 J. Hammond *Leah & R.* (1844) 15 To dyet and quarter in another mans house. 1703 Thoresby *Diary* I. 411 We lodged and dieted with him at Mr. Lamplugh's. 1802 *Chron.* in *Ann. Reg.* 370/2 A young man..who dieted and lodged in the house, has been apprehended on suspicion.

6. To regulate oneself as to diet; to eat according to prescribed rules, i.e. as to the kind of food, the quantity and time of eating, and the like.

1660 STANLEY *Hist. Philos.* IX. (1701) 348/2 He first taught Wrestlers..to diet with flesh. **1749** WESLEY *Acct. School* 5 They diet thus: Breakfast, Milk-porridge and Water-gruel, by Turns. **1893** *Strand Mag.* VI. 215/1 She dieted as carefully as if she had been a dyspeptic in ruins.

Hence **'dieted** *ppl. a.*, subjected to a regimen of diet.

1605 BACON *Adv. Learn.* I. ii. §3 There will bee seldome vse of..Phisicke in a sound or well dieted bodie. **1655** MOUFET & BENNET *Health's Impr.* (1746) 75 Idle Heads have made these addle Proverbs; 1. Dieted Bodies are but Bridges to Physicians Minds.

dietal (daɪ'i:təl), *a.* [f. med.L. *diēta* DIET *sb.*² + -AL¹.] Of or belonging to a diet.

1885 LOWE *Bismarck* II. App. B. 568 Until the putting in execution of the consequent Dietal decree, this port [is] to be made use of by the ships of war of both Powers.

dietarian (daɪə'tɛərɪən), *a.* and *sb. rare*⁻⁰. [f. as next + -AN.] (See quot.)

1880 WEBSTER *Suppl.*, *Dietarian*, one who lives in accordance with prescribed rules for diet; dieter.

dietary ('daɪətərɪ), *sb.* and *a.* Also 5 diatorie. [ad. L. *diætāri-us*, in med.L. *diētāri-us* adj. and sb., also *diētārium* sb., in various applications, f. L. *diæta*, *diēta*: see DIET *sb.*¹ and ², and -ARY.]

A. *sb.*

1. A course of diet prescribed or marked out; a book or treatise prescribing such a course.

c **1430** *A Diatorie* in *Babees Bk.* (1868) 54 To be rulid bi þis diatorie do þi diligence, For it techiþ good diete & good gouernaunce. **1542** BOORDE (*title*), A Compendyous Regyment or a Dyetary of Helth. —— (1870) 231 Here foloweth the dyetary or the regyment of helth. **1570** LEVINS *Manip.* 104/1 A Dietarie, *dietarium.* **1860-1** FLO. NIGHTINGALE *Nursing* 52 Careful observation of the sick is the only clue to the best dietary. *fig.* **1879** G. MEREDITH *Egoist* iv. (1889) 26 Patience..is a composing but a lean Dietary.

2. An allowance and regulation of food, as for the inmates of a hospital, workhouse, or prison.

1838 DICKENS *O. Twist* ii, Do I understand that he asked for more, after he had eaten the supper allotted by the dietary? **1861** WYNTER *Soc. Bees* 202 It is clear, then, that the prevalent sea-dietary is a degrading dietary; it is deficient in the albumen, the soluble phosphates..necessary to sustain vigorous life. **1884** *Daily News* 19 Dec. 3/3 The introduction of fish dinners into the workhouse dietaries appears..to have been eminently successful.

B. *adj.* Of or pertaining to diet, of the nature of a diet. **b.** Of or belonging to a dietary.

1614 W. B. *Philosopher's Banquet* (ed. 2.) 19 There are dietary times and hours. **1655** MOUFET & BENNET *Health's Improv.* (1746) 71 Albeit there lived no dietary Physicians before the Flood. **1844** DISRAELI *Coningsby* III. iii, Lord Henry would not listen to statistics, dietary tables. **1863** HAWTHORNE *Our Old Home* (1879) 208 The ancient fishing-ponds..of vast dietary importance to the family. **1889** J. BARR in *Times* 9 Mar. 16/1 Dietary punishment..inflicted for breaches of prison discipline.

'diet-book. [f. DIET *sb.*¹ and ².]

†**1.** A journal or diary. *Obs.*

1624 *Epistle Christian Brother* 25 (Jam.) It is a diet-booke, wherein the sinnes of everie day are written.

2. A book in which a course of diet is laid down.

1651 WITTIE tr. *Primrose's Pop. Err.* III. 139 Lessius..in his Eloquent Diet-booke, hath so endeavoured to mete out every mans course of Diet, that he would have twelve ounces to be a sufficient quantitie of meat for any man.

'diet-drink. [f. DIET *sb.*¹ + DRINK.] A drink prescribed and prepared for medicinal purposes.

1600 ROWLANDS *Let. Humours Blood* vi. 76 We gaue the Brewers Diet-drinke a wipe. **1601** HOLLAND *Pliny* II. 317 As for the diet drink made of cow milk..I have written already in my treatise of herbs. **1693** OLIVER in *Phil. Trans.* XVII. 909 A pleasant..soft Water..which the Country People use in Fevers as their ordinary Diet-drink. **1744** BERKELEY *Siris* §9 The leaves and tender tops of pine and fir are..used for diet drinks. **1844-57** G. BIRD *Urin. Deposits* 455 The host of apozems, diuretic decoctions, and diet-drinks, in which renal stimulants abound. **1854-67** C. A. HARRIS *Dict. Med. Terminol.* 214 *Diet Drink*, a decoction of sarsaparilla and mezereon. The Lisbon diet drink, or compound decoction of sarsaparilla, which it resembles, is the most celebrated.

'dieter. [f. DIET *v.* + -ER¹.] *Now rare.* **a.** One who regulates the diet of himself or others. †**b.** A feeder. *Obs.*

1577 B. GOOGE *Heresbach's Husb.* III. (1586) 122 The best dyeter of horses, that ever I knewe in England. **1603** H. CROSSE *Vertue's Commw.* (1878) 147 He that feedeth but of one dish, liueth longer..then those accidentall dieters..that glutte themselues with euerie kinde artificially compounded. **1611** SHAKS. *Cymb.* IV. ii. 51 As Iuno had bin sicke, And he her Dieter. **1617** MARKHAM *Caval.* III. 25 In his daies of rest..let him be his own dieter.

dietetic (daɪə'tɛtɪk), *a.* and *sb.* Also 6 dia-, 7-8 diæ-. [ad. L. *diætētic-us*, a. Gr. διαιτητικός of or for diet, f. δίαιτα DIET *sb.*¹; in F. *diététique.*]

A. *adj.* Of or pertaining to diet, or to the regulation of the kind and quantity of food to be eaten, especially as a branch of medical science.

1579 J. JONES *Preserv. Bodie & Soule* I. xxxiii. 64 Tutors ought to haue the knowledge of the Diatetike part of Phisicke. **1684** tr. *Bonet's Merc. Compit.* XVI. 562 A diætetick regiment extends to divers things. **1799** W. TOOKE *View Russian Emp.* II. 282 Not so salutary and dietetic is the command which enjoins abstinence from all manner of food. **1869** E. A. PARKES *Pract. Hygiene* (ed. 3) 180 The dietetic treatment of disease is destined to be the great work of the future. **1874** MCCARTHY *Linley Rochford* ix. (1878) 90, I think..I would rather dine with a gourmand than with a dietetic reformer.

B. *sb.* [In sense 1, repr. L. *diætēticus*, the adj. used abs.; in 2 repr. Gr. ἡ διαιτητική (sc. τέχνη) the dietetic art, in mod.L. *diætētica*, F. *diététique* (Paré 16th c.): see -ICS.]

1. One who studies dietetics.

1759 B. STILLINGFL. tr. *Linnæus on Travelling* Misc. Tracts (1762) 23 The curious diætetic, whose business it is to inquire into the various ways of living.

2. dietetics, less usually **dietetic**: The part of medicine which relates to the regulation of diet.

1541 R. COPLAND *Galyen's Terap.* 2 A j b, The parties of the art of Medycyne (yᵗ is to wyt dyetityke, pharmaceutyke, and cyrurgery)..can not be seperated one fro the other. **1720** POPE *Iliad* III. 208 Celsus says expressly that the diætetic was long after invented. **1799** *European Mag.* 247 Dietetics..comprise the doctrine of health. **1875** JOWETT *Plato* (ed. 2) III. 283 He must go through a course of dietetics. **1881** *Med. Temp. Jrnl.* XLIX. 23 The former is a question of dietetics, the latter of therapeutics.

†**die'tetical,** *a. Obs.* [f. as prec. + -AL¹.] Of or pertaining to dietetics; = DIETETIC *a.*

1620 VENNER *Via Recta* (1650) 295 Divers necessary Dieteticall observations. **1646** SIR T. BROWNE *Pseud. Ep.* I. x. 41 Caracalla..received no other counsell then to refraine cold drinke, which was but a dieteticall caution. **1802** T. BEDDOES *Hygëia* I. 48 Many generally received maxims, medical and diætetical. **1822** LAMB *Elia* Ser. I. *Chimney-Sweepers*, Palates..not uninstructed in dietetical elegancies.

die'tetically, *adv.* [f. prec. + -LY².] In the way of diet or dietetics.

a **1846** *N. Amer. Rev.* cited in WORCESTER. **1852** *Fraser's Mag.* XLVI. 96 Fish were formerly much used in medicine as well as dietetically.

dietetics, *sb. pl.*: see DIETETIC *sb.*

die'tetist. *rare*⁻⁰. [f. DIETET-IC + -IST.] 'A term applied to one who treats disease by a systematic course of diet.' *Syd. Soc. Lex.* 1883.

a **1846** in DUNGLISON (Worc.).

diethene- (daɪ'ɛθi:n). *Chem.* [See DI-².] Combined with two equivalents of ethene (C_2H_4), as *diethene-diamine.* Hence **die'thenic** *a.*, as in ***diethenic alcohol*** $(C_2H_4)_2H_2O_3$.

1873 *Fownes' Chem.* (ed. 11) 621 The first products of this reaction are diethenic alcohol..and water. **1877** WATTS *Ibid.* (ed. 12) II. 172, 224.

†**dietheroscope** (daɪi:'θɛrəskəʊp). *Obs.* [ad. It. *dieteroscopio* (G. Luvini 1874, in *Atti d. R. Accad. d. Scienze Torino 1873–74* IX. 389), f. Gr. δι- DI-² + αἰθήρ ETHER + -O + -SCOPE.] An instrument for measuring variations in atmospheric refraction, usually consisting of a telescope having additional lenses or mirrors which bring two images of any object into the field of vision.

1877 *Q. Jrnl. Meteorol. Soc.* III. 414 The dietheroscope serves to show every little change of position, apparent or real, of any distant object. Its principal application is the measurement of the variations of atmospheric refraction. **1889** *Times* 21 Mar. 3/3 There are also Luvini's dietheroscope for observing the changes of atmospheric refraction optically; [etc.].

diethyl (daɪ'ɛθɪl). *Chem.* [f. DI-² + ETHYL.]

1. as *sb.* A name for the group C_4H_{10} (*butyl hydride* or *butane*), considered as a double molecule of the radical ethyl.

1877 WATTS *Fownes' Chem.* (ed. 12) II. 47 Normal Butane, Diethyl, or Methyl-propyl, occurs in natural petroleum, and in the distillation-products of Cannel and Boghead coal.

2. in *Comb.* Denoting two equivalents of the monad radical ethyl (C_2H_5), replacing two atoms of hydrogen in a compound, as ***di'ethyla,mine*** $NH(C_2H_5)_2$, ***diethyl carbinol*** $COH{\cdot}H{\cdot}(C_2H_5)_2$, ***diethylstilbœstrol*** (or ***-bestrol***), $C_{18}H_{20}O_2$, a synthetic compound having œstrogenic properties; = STILBŒSTROL.

1850 DAUBENY *Atom. Th.* viii. (ed. 2) 241 Diethylamine, in which 2 atoms of hydrogen are replaced by 2 of ethyle. **1869** ROSCOE *Elem. Chem.* (1874) 330 A hydrocarbon called diethyl or butyl hydride. *Ibid.* 350 Acetal is isomeric with diethyl glycol. **1877** WATTS *Fownes' Chem.* (ed. 12) II. 218 Diethylamine behaves with cyanic acid like ammonia and ethylamine, giving rise to diethyl-urea, $CH_2(C_2H_5)_2N_2O$. **1880** *Boston Jrnl. Chem.* Dec. 137/2 The monethyl and diethyl phosphines have been prepared. **1938** E. C. DODDS et al. in *Nature* 5 Feb. 248/2 In this way 4:4'-*dihydroxy-αβ-diethylstilbene* (diethylstilbœstrol) was obtained. **1943** *Thorpe's Dict. Appl. Chem.* (ed. 4) VI. 272/2 Diethylstilbœstrol..confers the mating instinct on ovariectomised animals. **1944** *Ann. Reg. 1943* 359 Carcinoma of the prostate was successfully treated by oral administration of the synthetic œstrogen diethylstilbœstrol. **1969** *Daily Tel.* 18 Dec. 15/8 Heavy doses of the synthetic oestrogen diethylstilbestrol are being given to prevent pregnancy in rape victims.

dietic (daɪ'ɛtɪk), *a.* and *sb.* [f. DIET *sb.*¹ + -IC: cf. med.L. *diēticus* keeping a daily course.]

A. *adj.* Of or pertaining to diet; = DIETETIC *a.*

1716 M. DAVIES *Athen. Brit.* III. *Diss. Physick* 39 Whence came the Dietick and Gymnastick Physick. *Ibid.* 52 This regular Diætick Branch of the most natural kind of Physick. **1775** SIR E. BARRY *Observ. Wines* 356 The best dietic rules for preserving health. **1883** *Syd. Soc. Lex.*, *Dietic diseases*, diseases caused by inattention to wholesome rules of diet.

†**B.** *sb.* A dietetic article or application. *Obs.*

1659 GAUDEN *Tears Church* 397 If it be not drawn away by ..gentle dieticks or healing applications. —— *Slight Healers of Public Hurts* (1660) 28.

di'etical, *a.* [f. as prec. + -AL¹.]

†**1.** = DIETETIC, DIETETICAL. *Obs.*

1634 R. H. *Salernes Regim.* Pref. 3 Some violent Disease, which they might happily have prevented by Dieticall Observations. **1640** FERRAND *Love Melancholy* 237 (T.) The three fountains of physick, namely, dietical, chirurgical, and pharmaceutical. **1657** G. STARKEY *Helmont's Vind.* Ep. to Rdr., I..oppose your Diaeticall prescriptions.

†**2.** [after med.L.: see DIETIC.] *Obs.*

1656 BLOUNT *Glossogr.*, *Dietical* (*dieticus*), keeping from day to day, regular.

3. [f. DIET *sb.*²] Pertaining to the Germanic Diet.

1854 *Tait's Mag.* XXI. 451 The Lichtenstein, sovereign and subject at once; octopartite possessor of a vote dietical.

dietie, obs. form of DEITY.

dietine ('daɪəti:n). [a. F. *diétine* lit. 'little diet', spec. the Polish provincial diet, f. *diète* DIET *sb.*²: see -INE.] A subordinate diet; in Polish Hist., a provincial diet which elected deputies for the national diet; called in Polish *sejmik.*

1669 *Lond. Gaz.* No. 412/1 The King has given Power to the Dietine [*printed* -ive] of Cracovie to Assemble themselves within 4 Leagues of this place. **1753** *Scots Mag.* Jan. 3/1 The nuncios of a general diet of Poland were chosen in August last, when disputes ran very high in some dietines. **1773** *Gentl. Mag.* XLIII. 245 The dietine of Lenczy was still more unruly, for there more than thirty of the Members were cut to pieces. **1800** W. TAYLOR in *Monthly Mag.* VIII. 599 This order is governed by a descending oligarchy, the over-ruling synod or diet deputing assessors to the subordinate synods or dietines. **1887** LECKY *Eng. in 18th C.* V. xx. 545 All the Dietines ratified the new Constitution.

dieting ('daɪətɪŋ), *vbl. sb.* [f. DIET *v.* + -ING¹.] The action of the verb DIET: **a.** Subjection to a diet or regimen. **b.** Taking of daily food, feeding (*rare*). †**c.** *concr.* Food (*obs.*).

c **1400** *Lanfranc's Cirurg.* 61 Norissche hym with dyetynge þat fattyth hym. *Ibid.* 72 Of dietynge of men þat ben wounded. **1599** T. M[OUFET] *Silkwormes* 74 The dieting of these my spinning bands. **1641** MILTON *Ch. Govt.* I. i, Those maiden dietings and set prescriptions of baths and odours. *c* **1819** SHELLEY in Dowden *Life* II. 256 How delicate the imagination becomes by dieting with antiquity day after day.

dietist ('daɪətɪst). [f. DIET *sb.*¹ + -IST.] One who professes or practises dietetics or some theory of diet.

1607 WALKINGTON *Opt. Glass* 16 Reasonable appetite, the *Cynosura* of the wiser dietist. **1655** MOUFET & BENNET *Health's Improv.* (1746) 227 Not lately devised by our Country Pudding-wrights, or curious Sauce-makers, as..foolish Dietists have imagined. **1842** F. PAGET *Milf. Malv.* 181 Mr. Clemmalive..an inexorable dietist on the water-gruel system at the Union work-house.

die'titian. Also dietician. [prop. *dietician*, f. DIET *sb.*¹, after *physician*, *politician*, etc.] = prec.

1846 WORCESTER, *Dietitian*, one skilled in diet; a dietist. *Qu. Rev.* **1905** *Springfield Weekly Republ.* 29 Dec. 16 The dietitian's work consists in ordering food and preparing the dietary for the patients. **1906** *Daily Chron.* 14 Aug. 5/3 An ex-graduate of Harvard, and an experienced dietician. **1928** *Daily Express* 2 Aug. 2/3 An outline of each day's menu is supplied to the steward's department by the dieticians on board. **1960** *Act 8 & 9 Eliz. II* c. 66 §1 Chiropodists, dietitians, medical laboratory technicians. **1971** *Daily Tel.* 18 June 4/5 His team includes dieticians, nutrition experts and engineers.

Dietl's crisis ('di:t(ə)lz 'kraɪsɪs). *Path.* [f. the name of Joseph *Dietl* (1804–1878), physician of Cracow.] (See quots.) Freq. pl., *Dietl's crises.*

1897 *Internat. Clinics* IV. 94 The symptoms..—sudden, great abdominal pain, vomiting, distention of the belly, tenderness, and signs of collapse—were strongly suggestive of Dietl's crises. **1907** *Practitioner* Dec. 750 In such cases [of movable kidney] as present symptoms, the severity of these may present every gradation from a dull aching pain in the back to the acutest paroxysms of renal pain. To the latter the name of Dietl's crises is commonly applied. **1910** E. L. KEYES *Dis. Genito-Urinary Organs* xliv. 494 The tumor..is usually very painful and tender, and its growth is often attended by renal colic (Dietl's crises). **1953** A. W. BADENOCH *Man. Urol.* xii. 349 The so-called Dietl's crisis due to twisting of the pedicle producing torsion of the kidney is also very rare and I have not seen a case.

dietrichite ('di:trɪkaɪt). *Min.* [Named 1878 after Dietrich, a German chemist.] A fibrous alum containing zinc and other bases.

1882 DANA *Min.* App. iii. 38.

diety, obs. form of DEITY.

†**dieugard(e.** *Obs.* Also 5 dugarde, 5-6 *Sc.* dewgar(d, 7 due gard. [French (in full *Dieu vous*

garde, in OF. *dieu vous gard*), 'God keep (you)!'] The salutation 'God preserve you!'; a polite or formal salutation; a spoken salutation or word of recognition, as contrasted with a mere 'beck' or nod.

c **1380** *Antecrist* in Todd 3 *Treat. Wyclif* (1851) 149 Ne wiþ beckus ne wiþ dugardes as ypocritis usen. *c* **1470** HENRY *Wallace* VI. 132 He salust thaim, as it war bot in scorn; 'Dewgar, gud day, bone Senȝhour, and gud morn!' **1565** JEWEL *Def. Apol.* (1611) 172 In the end you conclude, A becke is as good as a Dieugard. **1568** H. CHARTERIS *Pref. to Lyndesay's Warkis* ✠ ij b, He cummis to the King, and efter greit dewgard & salutationis, he makis him as thocht he war [etc.]. **1598** FLORIO Epist. Ded., So in your studies to attend, as your least becke may be his dieugarde. **1600** J. MELVILL *Diary* (1842) 263 The cheiff commanders mak sic dewgard and curtessie. **1605** CHAPMAN *All Fooles* Plays 1873 I. 168 Their winckes, their beckes, due gard, their treads a' the toe. *a* **1656** BP. HALL *Wks.* IX. 278 (D.) His master Harding could not produce..any vow anciently required or undertaken, whether by beck or Dieu-gard.

dieve, obs. (? dial.) form of DIVE *v.*

dieve, erron. form of DEAVE *v.* to deafen.

diew, obs. form of DUE.

die-wise, -work: see DIE *sb.*[1]

dif, diff, *sb.* and *a.* *colloq.* A. *sb.* Abbrev. of DIFFERENCE *sb.*

1896 ADE *Artie* 24 He said he didn't know her. 'What's the diff?' I says. **1909** J. R. WARE *Passing Eng.* 108/2 There is a great diff between a dona and a mush. You *can* shut up a mush (umbrella) sometimes. **1910** O. JOHNSON *Varmint* iv. 58 'What's the diff?' said the Tennessee Shad, yawning. **1914** S. LEWIS *Our Mr. Wrenn* vi. 62 It wouldn't make any dif. what they met as long as they was fighting together. **1919** *Punch* 28 May 417/1 But Lallie couldn't see the dif between a man and a novelist. **1967** 'H. CALVIN' *Nice Friendly Town* ix. 123 Here today gone tomorrow. What's the diff, duckie?

B. *adj.* Abbrev. of DIFFERENT *a.*

1908 *Punch* 10 June 416/3 They're not *really* a bit like themselves, but are something quite dif.! **1924** LAWRENCE & SKINNER *Boy in Bush* v. 61 'He's different from the rest of you, and his lingo's rotten.' 'He's not dif!' said Tom.

dif-, prefix of L. origin, being the assimilated form of *dis-* before *f*, as in *dif-ferre, dif-fūsio*. In Romanic it became *def-*, which in OF. was subsequently reduced to *de-*; this occasionally appears in Eng., as *defer* from L. *differre*, OF. *defferer*, mod.F. *déférer*, *defy* from L. type *diffīdāre*, It. *diffidare*, *disfidare*, OF. *desf-, deff-, defier*, mod.F. *défier*. Usually, however, the Latin form of the prefix is used in Eng.: cf. *differ, difficult, diffidence, diffuse*. For its force, see DIS-: it is not, like the latter, a living prefix.

difalt, difame, difence: see DEF-.

diffame, -famation, etc., etymol. form of DEFAME, -FAMATION, etc., generally obsolete, but still occasionally used.

1894 R. BRIDGES *Feast of Bacchus* IV. 1263 Diffame my own daughter.

diffarreation (dɪfæriːˈeɪʃən). *Rom. Antiq.* [ad. L. *diffareātiōn-em*, f. DIF- + *farreum* a spelt-cake: see CONFARREATION.] An ancient Roman mode of dissolution of marriage, the undoing of the ceremony of confarreation.

1623 COCKERAM, *Diffarreation*, a sacrifice done betwixt a man and his wife at a diuorcement. **1727-51** CHAMBERS *Cycl.* s.v., Diffarreation was properly the dissolving of marriages contracted by confarreation, which were those of the pontifices. Festus says it was performed with a wheaten cake.

diffaute, diffeature, diffence, -ens(e, diffend(e, etc.: see DEF-.

differ (ˈdɪfə(r)), *v.* Also 6 dyffer (defer), 6-7 differre. [a. F. *différer* (in Froissart 14th c.), ad. L. *differ-re* to carry or bear apart, spread abroad, distract, protract, delay, defer; also *intr.* to tend apart or diversely in nature or character, to differ. The verb was used with both senses in F. in 14th c., and has continued to be so used till the present day. In English, it was taken first in the transitive sense, with stress *di'ffer* (cf. *confer, refer, prefer*), which led at length to the transitive senses being written *defer*: see DEFER *v.*[1]; the intrans. use, being closely related in sense to *different, difference*, apparently followed these words in stressing the first syllable. (*Offer, suffer*, which have the same stress, have a distinct form in French and Romanic.) And one transitive use, closely associated with the intrans., and with *different, difference*, has gone with these. In this way L. *differre*, F. *différer*, ME. *di'fferre*, has been split into the two verbs *defer* to put off, and *differ* to make or be unlike. The pr. pple. *differing* occurs in Chaucer's *Boethius*; but instances of the verb in the form *differ* are rare before 1500.]

1. The earlier form of DEFER *v.*[1] in all senses.

2. *trans.* To put apart or separate from each other in qualities; to make unlike, dissimilar, different, or distinct; to cause to vary; to distinguish, differentiate. Now *unusual.*

a **1400-50** *Alexander* 4223 Ȝour manars fra all othire mens so mekill ere deffirrid. **1562** LEIGH *Armorie* (1597) 32 b, This is not vnlike the other Crosse. The pyke which it hath to pitch into the ground, onely differeth it. **1603** SIR C. HEYDON *Jud. Astrol.* v. 158 Homo, and Brutum..differ the whole kind. **1633** EARL MANCH. *Al Mondo* (1636) 120 Why is the winter harder to the Grashopper than to the Ant? Prudencie in one, and imprudencie in the other differs them. **1656** R. ROBINSON *Christ all* 44 Garments..differ one sex from another. **1713** J. PETIVER in *Phil. Trans.* XXVIII. 213 Its glaucous Leaves and pale Flowers, differ it from the yellow Split. **1818** CRUISE *Digest* (ed. 2) IV. 510 That differed it from the cases wherein the Court had gone some lengths. **1867** BUSHNELL *Mor. Uses Dark Th.* 36 All which differs the landscape in beauty from mere wild forest.

†**b.** *Her.* To distinguish by the addition of a DIFFERENCE. *Obs.*

1586 FERNE *Blaz. Gentrie* 98 Til then it was permissiue for eche brother to differ his coat after his fancye.

3. *intr.* To have contrary or diverse bearings, tendencies, or qualities; to be not the same; to be unlike, distinct, or various, in nature, form, or qualities, or in some specified respect: two (or more) things are said to differ (absolutely, or *from each other*), one thing differs *from* another.

1374 [see DIFFERING *ppl. a.* 1]. *a* **1400-50** *Alexander* 4617 Bot we þat..has a fre will Differris as in oure fraunches fere fra ȝoure kynde. **1526** *Pilgr. Perf.* (W. de W. 1531) 234 This differeth from that other, as..the rose differeth from the budde. **1526-34** TINDALE *1 Cor.* xv. 41 One starre differth from another in glory. *a* **1568** ASCHAM *Scholem.* II. (Arb.) 139 These differre one from an other. **1570** LEVINS *Manip.* 77/29 To Defer, *differre, discrepare*. **1600** SHAKS. *A. Y. L.* I. i. 10 Call you that keeping for a gentleman of my birth, that differs not from the stalling of an Oxe? **1651** HOBBES *Leviath.* I. xv. 79 The same man, in divers times, differs from himselfe. **1689-90** TEMPLE *Misc., Pop. Discontents* Wks. 1720 I. 270 'Tis hard to find any point wherein they differ. **1774** GOLDSM. *Nat. Hist.* (1776) III. 324 It [the fox]..differs still more from the dog in its strong offensive smell. **1823** H. J. BROOKE *Introd. Crystallogr.* 98 Which individual forms..will be found to differ from each other in the measurement of some of their angles. **1847** HELPS *Friends in C.* (1851) I. 28 Even the leaves of the same tree are said to differ, each one from all the rest. **1859-74** TENNYSON *Merlin & Vivien* 812 Men at most differ as Heaven and earth, But women, worst and best, as Heaven and Hell. **1875** JOWETT *Plato* (ed. 2) IV. 32 Man is not man in that he resembles [brutes], but in that he differs from them.

4. *intr.* To be at variance; to hold different opinions concerning any matter; to disagree. Const. *with*; also *from* (esp. when followed by *in*, as in quot. 1843).

1563 WINȜET *Four Scoir Thre Quest.* Wks. 1888 I. 135 Sen ȝe..differris fra ws..tweching the said day of the moneth. **1647** CLARENDON *Hist. Reb.* III. (1843) 79/1 A latitude that honest and wise men may safely and profitably differ [in]. **1653** WALTON *Angler* ii. 42 The question has been debated among many great Clerks, and they seem to differ about it. **1716** ADDISON *Freeholder* (J.), To irritate those who differ with you in their sentiments. **1735-8** BOLINGBROKE *On Parties* 81 To think They [the Tories]..had only differ'd with the Whigs about the Degree of Oppression..in order to sanctify Resistance. **1749** FIELDING *Tom Jones* III. v, Many people differed from Square and Thwackum, in judging [etc.]. **1791** BURKE *Corr.* (1844) III. 351, I can never for a moment differ from you and your brother in sentiment. **1809** W. GIFFORD in Smiles *Mem. John Murray* I. 158, I differ with him totally. **1833** J. H. NEWMAN *Lett.* (1891) I. 466 To unite with those who differ with us. **1843** *Ibid.* II. 430 She may..differ from me in opinion. **1869** SIR J. T. COLERIDGE *Mem. Keble* (ed. 2) 186, I differed with him in the conclusion he drew. **1885** *Law Rep. 10 App. Cases* 379 The appellant and respondents differ as to when the gate was erected.

†**b.** To express or give vent to disagreement or difference of opinion; to dispute; to have a difference, to quarrel (*with*). *Obs.*

1625 BACON *Ess., Unity in Relig.* (Arb.) 429 A man..shall sometimes heare Ignorant Men differ, and know well..that those which so differ, meane one thing. **1709** HEARNE *Collect.* (Oxf. Hist. Soc.) II. 245 As they went out of Town they happen'd to differ. *a* **1718** ROWE (J.), Here uncontroll'd you may in judgment sit; We'll never differ with a crowded pit. **1737** BRACKEN *Farriery Impr.* (1757) II. 118 As to his Size, I would have him full Fifteen Hands, nay, I would not differ for his being Sixteen, provided he was strong in proportion.

c. *trans.* To cause disagreement between; to set at variance. *Sc.*

1814 *Saxon & Gael* I. 79 (Jam.) If Maister Angis and her mak it up, I'se ne'er be the man to differ them.

ˈ**differ**, *sb.* *Sc.* and *dial.* [f. DIFFER *v.*] = DIFFERENCE *sb.*

1627 P. FORBES *Eubulus* 94 (Jam.) No such material points are in differ betwixt vs. **1639** *Declar. Tumults Sc.* 340 The generall assembly..would remove any doubt and differ which might arise. **1786** BURNS *Addr. to Unco Guid* iii, Cast a moment's fair regard, What maks the mighty differ. **1842** S. LOVER *Handy Andy* ix, But I'll pay you the differ out of my wage. **1873** LOWELL *Lett.* (1894) II. 94 So far as I understood your 'differ' with your electors I thought you were right. **1893** STEVENSON *Catriona* 94 Either come to an agreement, or come to a differ.

differ, obs. form of DEFER *v.*[1] and [2].

difference (ˈdɪfərəns), *sb.* Also 4 differense, 4-6 differens, defference, 5 deference, 5-6 dyfference, -ens, 6 differance, diffrence, diference. [a. F. *différence*, OF. also *-ance* (12th c. in Hatz.-Darm.), ad. L. *differentia*, abstr. sb. f. *different-em*: see DIFFERENT and -ENCE.]

1. **a.** The condition, quality, or fact of being different, or not the same in quality or in essence; dissimilarity, distinction, diversity; the relation of non-agreement or non-identity *between* two or more things, disagreement.

1340 *Ayenb.* 210 Zuyche difference is betu[e]ne þe rearde of þe bene and þe deuocioun of þe herte. *c* **1470** HENRY *Wallace* IV. 7 The changing courss quhilk makis gret deference. **1535** COVERDALE *2 Chron.* xiv. 11 Lorde, it is no difference with yᵉ, to helpe by fewe or by many. **1611** SHAKS. *Wint. T.* I. i. 4 You shall see..great difference betwixt our Bohemia, and your Sicilia. **1699** BURNET *39 Art.* xxv. (1700) 266 In all this Diversity there is no real difference. **1734** POPE *Ess. Man* IV. 56 All nature's diff'rence keeps all nature's peace. **1739** HUME *Human Nat.* I. v. (1874) I. 323 Difference is of two kinds as oppos'd either to identity or resemblance. **1824** MACAULAY *Athenian Orators* Misc. Writ. 1860 I. 135 If he miss the mark, it makes no difference whether he have taken aim too high or too low. **1844** EMERSON *Lect. Yng. Amer.* Wks. (Bohn) II. 298 Difference of opinion is the one crime which kings never forgive. **1847** TENNYSON *Princ.* VII. 162 Not like to like, but like in difference. **1851** RUSKIN *Mod. Paint.* I. Pref. to ed. 2. 15 Not so much by the resemblance of his works to what has been done before, as by their difference from it.

†*Various obs. and archaic constructions.*

1526 TINDALE *Doctr. Treat.* (1848) 389 Note the difference of the law and of the gospel. **1557** NORTH *Gueuara's Diall Pr.* 150 a/2 There is a greate difference to teache the chyldren of Prynces, and to teache the chyldren of the people. *Ibid.* 210 b/1 There is great difference from the cares and sorowes of women, to that of men. **1671** H. M. tr. *Colloq. Erasmus* 354 There is also another difference of divine and humane laws. **1778** MISS BURNEY *Evelina* lii, Let me observe the difference of his behaviour..to that of Sir Clement Willoughby. **1792** *Elvina* I. 6 The difference with us is most striking. **1820** WHEWELL in *Life* (1881) 61 Some idea of the difference of French and English manners.

b. (with *a* and *pl.*) A particular instance of unlikeness; a point in which things differ.

1393 GOWER *Conf.* III. 20 There is non evidence, Wherof to knowe a difference Betwene the drunken and the wode. *c* **1430** LYDG. *Min. Poems* 23 (Mätz.) A difference betwix day and night. **1513** MORE in Grafton *Chron.* (1568) II. 787 There is not betwene a Marchant and his mayde so great a difference as betwene a king and his subject. **1688** *Vox Cleri Pro Rege* 47 It seems his Power is absolute, but, not arbitrary, which is, like a Dear-Joy's Witticism, a distinction without a difference. **1847** TENNYSON *Princ.* v. 173 You clash them all in one, That have as many differences as we. **1856** FROUDE *Hist. Eng.* (1858) I. i. 15 While the differences of social degree were enormous, the differences in habits of life were comparatively slight. **1875** JOWETT *Plato* (ed. 2) IV. 243 There is a great difference between reasoning and disputation.

2. **a.** *Math.* The quantity by which one quantity differs from another; the remainder left after subtracting one quantity from another. **b.** *spec.* The increment produced in a function of a variable by increasing the variable by unity.

ASCENSIONAL, DESCENSIONAL *difference*: see these words. *c* **1391** CHAUCER *Astrol.* II. §43 The diff[e]rense be-twen 1 and 2..is 1. **1559** W. CUNNINGHAM *Cosmogr. Glasse* 103 Subtract the lesser time, from oute of the greater, and the difference turn into degrees, and mi. of the Equinoctial. **1593** FALE *Dialling* 19 Which you shall find least subtract that from the greater, and that which remaineth keep, (for it shall be called the difference kept). **1719** DE FOE *Crusoe* I. xvi. (1858) 204 The difference of that price was by no means worth saving. **1774** M. MACKENZIE *Maritime Surv.* iii. 13 The greater the Difference of Latitude of the two Places is. **1807** J. BRINKLEY (*title*), An Investigation of the General Term of an important Series in the Inverse Method of Finite Differences. **1821** J. Q. ADAMS in C. Davies *Metr. Syst.* III. (1871) 115 The difference between them was but of about half an ounce. **1827** HUTTON *Course Math.* I. 12 *note*, If the difference of two numbers be added to the less, it must manifestly make up a sum equal to the greater. **1837** *Penny Cycl.* VIII. 487 s.v. *Difference*, It is a very wide branch of pure mathematics which must be considered under this term, namely, the method or calculus of differences. *Ibid.* 488 The symbol [$\Delta^n a$] is called the nth difference of *a*.

c. *spec.* The amount of increase or decrease in the price of stocks or shares between certain dates; in phrase *to pay* (etc.) *the difference*.

1717 MRS. CENTLIVRE *Bold Stroke for Wife* IV. i, Hark ye, Gabriel, you'll pay the difference of that stock we transacted for t'other day. **1814** *Stock Exchange Laid Open* 11 Every man must either take, deliver, or pay his difference. **1885** *Pall Mall G.* 31 Mar. 8/2 He had paid all his 'differences' previous to his departure. **1887** *Daily News* 12 Oct. 2/2 The differences to be met and liquidated are enormous.

d. phr. *to split the difference*: to divide the difference equally between the two parties so that they meet half-way; to come to a compromise by equal mutual concession.

a **1778** PITT *Sp.* (1806) I. 85 The common course, when parties disagreed, was what the vulgar phrase called 'to split the difference'. **1787** *Generous Attachment* I. 213 My Aunt, coming in, began to split the difference, by seriously advising me to think of neither. **1846** WHATELY *Rhet.* Addit. (ed. 7) 23 The result will usually be, after much debate, something of what is popularly called 'splitting the difference'. **1885** *Pall Mall G.* 9 June 3/1 A Cabinet of Compromise is of necessity a Cabinet of Split the Difference.

3. **a.** A diversity or disagreement of opinion, sentiment or purpose; hence, a dispute or

quarrel caused by such disagreement: used in various shades of intensity from a simple estrangement or dispute to open hostility. †*in difference*, in dispute (*obs.*).

1387 TREVISA *Higden* (Rolls) III. 423 (Mätz.) Touching þe cause þerof is no differens bytwene us. **1484** CAXTON *Æsop* II. xviii, The ape.. made theyr dyfference to be acorded. **1556** *Aurelio & Isab.* (1608) A v, We cast lottes betwene us, by the which our difference shall finishe. **1596** SHAKS. *Merch. V.* IV. i. 171 Are you acquainted with the difference That holds this present question in the Court? **1606** G. W[OODCOCKE] tr. *Hist. Ivstine* 40b, They encountred in battell, in which difference..they were ouercome. **1641** J. JACKSON *True Evang. T.* I. 41 Who was the chiefe..remaines in some difference. **1652** NEEDHAM tr. *Selden's Mare Cl.* 1 In the year 1508, there began certain slight differences, which concluded in a notable..war. **1774** GOLDSM. *Grecian Hist.* I. 253 With full power to concert all matters in difference. **1791** BOSWELL *Johnson* (1831) IV. 229 In the course of this year there was a difference between him and his friend Mr. Strahan. **1849** MACAULAY *Hist. Eng.* II. 143 He had never, he said, in his life, had any difference with Tyrconnel, and he trusted that no difference would now arise. **1893** *Leeds Mercury* 17 May 5/1 The speedy.. settlement of trade differences.

†**b.** phr. *to be* (etc.) *at difference*: to have a controversy, be at variance; to quarrel.

1525 LD. BERNERS *Froiss.* (1812) II. 349 The duke of Bretayne was in great difference with the realme of Fraunce. **1607** SHAKS. *Cor.* V. iii. 201 Thou hast set thy mercy, & thy Honor At difference. **1641** J. SHUTE *Sarah & Hagar* (1649) 170 We..are at such deadly differences amongst our selves. **1654** WHITLOCK *Zootomia* 391 He is doubtlesse his own best Friend, that is oft at difference with himselfe, for his miscarriages. **1677** YARRANTON *Eng. Improv.* 53, I fear their neighbouring Gentlemen will fall at Difference. **1737** WHISTON *Josephus' Hist.* I. xi. §1 The great men were mightily at difference one with another.

4. a. A mark, device, or characteristic feature, which distinguishes one thing or set of things from another. Now *rare* or *Obs.* exc. as in b and c.

1481 CAXTON *Myrr.* II. xiii. 94 Pictagoras..by his grete entendement fonde the poyntes and the difference of musyque. **1513** DOUGLAS *Æneis* X. vii. 81 Markyt 3ou swa with sic rude differens, That by hys keyll 3e may be knaw fra thens. **1602** SHAKS. *Ham.* V. ii. 112 An absolute gentleman, full of most excellent differences. **1631** WEEVER *Anc. Fun. Mon.* 149 The foure Deacons, for a difference from the Priests, carried a round wreath of white cloth. **1842** TENNYSON *Two Voices* 41 Will one beam be less intense, When thy peculiar difference Is cancell'd in the world of sense?

b. *Her.* An alteration of or addition to a coat of arms, to distinguish a junior member or branch of a family from the chief line.

c **1450** HOLLAND *Howlat* 600 He bure the said Dowglass armis with a differens. **1489** CAXTON *Faytes of A.* IV. xv. 275 The hed of the lordship bereth the playne armes without difference and thoo that are of his linage they putte therunto dyuerse dyfferences. **1564–78** BULLEYN *Dial. agst. Pest* (1888) 96 My name is Mendax, a yonger brother linially descended of an auncient house..We giue three Whetstones in Gules with no difference. **1602** SHAKS. *Ham.* IV. v. 183 Ther's Rew for you, and heere's some for me..Oh you must weare your Rew with a difference. **1610** GUILLIM *Heraldry* I. vi. (1611) 22 The sonne of an Emperour cannot beare a difference of higher esteeme during the life of his father. **1864** BOUTELL *Heraldry Hist. & Pop.* xiv. 137 When the Heir succeeds, he inherits the Arms of his Father without any Difference. **1882** CUSSANS *Handbk. Heraldry* x. (ed. 3) 150 Devices called Marks of Difference..In the early days of Heraldry, Differences were effected by a variety of arbitrary arrangements—such as changing the tinctures of the Coat.

c. *Logic.* A quality, mark, or characteristic, that distinguishes a thing from all others in the same class; the attribute by which a species is distinguished from other species of the same genus; more fully *specific difference*: = DIFFERENTIA.

1551 T. WILSON *Logike* (1567) 39 a, When the propertie or difference is graunted, then the kinde straight foloweth. **1656** HOBBES *Lib. Necess.* Wks. 1841 V. 371 He requires in a definition so exactly the genus and the difference. **1697** J. SERGEANT *Solid Philos.* 387 Not by the old beaten way of Genus and Difference. **1706** PHILLIPS (ed. Kersey) s.v., The difference of a Body is impenetrable Extension, and the difference of a Spirit is Cogitation or Thought. **1857** WHEWELL *Hist. Induct. Sc.* I. 208 The Predicables are the five steps which the gradations of generality and particularity introduce;—genus, species, difference, individual, accident. **1860** ABP. THOMSON *Laws Th.* §69. 112 The difference, or that mark or marks by which the species is distinguished from the rest of its genus.

†**d.** *transf.* A division, class, or kind. *Obs.*

c **1532** DEWES *Introd. Fr.* in *Palsgr.* 920 There ben two dyfference of perspectyves. **1541** R. COPLAND *Galyen's Terap.* 2 A iv, The flowyng of humours is dyuyded in two dyfferences. **1610** HOLLAND *Camden's Brit.* (1637) 34 (D.) There bee of times three differences: the first from the creation of man to the Floud or Deluge..the second from the Floud to the first Olympias. **1668** WILKINS *Real Char.* 441 The several Species are to be learned, belonging to each Difference. *a* **1682** SIR T. BROWNE *Tracts* (1684) 36 The Sycamore..is properly but one kind or difference of Acer.

5. A discrimination or distinction viewed as conceived by the subject rather than as existing in the objects. Now only in phr. *to make a difference*: to distinguish, discriminate, act or treat differently.

1382 WYCLIF *1 Esdras* iv. 39 To taken persones and differences is not anent it [truth]. **1393** GOWER *Conf.* III. 10 In making of comparison There may no difference be Betwen a drunken man and me. **1483** CAXTON *Gold. Leg.* 427/1 He vysyted the seek folke without dyfference. **1598** SHAKS. *Merry W.* II. i. 57 I shall thinke the worse of fat men, as long as I haue an eye to make difference of mens liking. **1611** BIBLE *Lev.* xi. 47 To make a difference betweene the vncleane and the cleane. **1662** STILLINGFL. *Orig. Sacr.* II. ii. §2 To make them more capable of putting a difference between truth and falshood. **1716** ADDISON *Freeholder* (J.), Our constitution does not only make a difference between the guilty and the innocent, but, even among the guilty, between such as are more or less criminal. **1819** SHELLEY *Cenci* V. iv. 82 No difference has been made by God or man ..'Twixt good or evil, as regarded me.

6. *attrib.* and *Comb.*, as **difference-engine**, a machine for calculating arithmetical differences; **difference-equation**, an equation expressing a relation between functions and their differences (sense 2 b); **difference limen** or **threshold** [tr. G. *unterschiedsschwelle* (G. T. Fechner *Elemente der Psychophysik* (1860) I. x. 239)], the amount by which two stimuli or sensations must differ for the difference to be perceived; also, the degree of ability to perceive differences between stimuli; **difference-tone**, see TONE *sb.*

1876 *Catal. Sci. App. S. Kens.* §23 The mode in which the Difference Engine calculates tables is, by the continual repetition of the simultaneous addition of several columns of figures to other columns, in the manner more particularly described below, and printing the result. **1876** J. WARD in *Mind* I. 459 This 'relativity' between difference-threshold and stimulus [may] be due to something not in any sense psychical. **1895** E. B. TITCHENER tr. *Kuelpe's Outl. Psychol.* 160 With an area of contact of 1 mm. diameter, the difference limen on the index finger of the right hand was $\frac{1}{10}$ to $\frac{1}{20}$. **1902** W. JAMES *Var. Relig. Exper.* vi. 135 When one is sensitive to small differences in any order of sensation, we say he has a low 'difference-threshold'—his mind easily steps over it into the consciousness of the differences in question. **1953** C. E. OSGOOD *Method & Theory Exper. Psychol.* (1956) I. ii. 73 Absolute and difference thresholds are correlated in hearing, however, both varying concomitantly as functions of frequency.

'difference, *v.* [f. DIFFERENCE *sb.*: cf. F. *différencier*, in Cotgr. 1611.]

†**1.** *intr.* To be different, to differ. *Obs. rare.*

c **1450** *Mirour Saluacioun* 3026 So differences fire werldly fro thilk purgatoriale. **1474** CAXTON *Chesse* 72 The ryght lawe of nature defferenceth ofte tymes fro custom. **1483** —— *Gold. Leg.* 347 b/2 They difference as moche as is bitwene not to synne and to do well.

†**2.** *trans.* To make (something) different from what it was (or from what it is in another case); to change, alter, vary. *Obs. rare.*

1481 CAXTON *Myrr.* II. xxi. 111 In the londe of Samarye is a wel that chaungeth and differenceth his colour four tymes in the yere. **1572** BOSSEWELL *Armorie* 8, I wil not here speake how well thys Lyon is differenced. **1593** NASHE *Christ's T.* 72 b, God shall reply..Thou hast so differenced and diuorced thy selfe from thy creation, that I know thee not for my creature. **1675** EVELYN *Terra* (1729) 11 How far Principles might be..differenced by Alteration and Condensation.

b. *Her.* To make an alteration in or addition to (a coat of arms) for the purpose of distinguishing members or branches of the same family.

1708 J. CHAMBERLAYNE *St. Gt. Brit.* II. II. v. (1743) 379 The king at arms..has power to give and difference arms. *c* **1710** C. FIENNES *Diary* (1888) 96 Like Mullets that they have in an Eschuteon to difference the third son from the first and second in a family. **1882** CUSSANS *Handbk. Heraldry* x. (ed. 3) 152 The third son differences his paternal coat with a Mullet..The Arms of the sixth son are differenced by a Fleur-de-lys. *Ibid.* 153 All the members of the Royal Family—the Sovereign excepted—difference their Arms with a silver Label of three points, charged with some distinguishing mark, specially assigned to them by the crown.

3. To make different, cause or constitute a difference in, differentiate, distinguish (*from* something else). Usually predicated of a quality or attribute: frequently in *passive*.

1598 BARRET *Theor. Warres* V. i. 124 The artillery is deuided and differenced into greatnesse or Sizes royall, and into lesser sizes. **1627–77** FELTHAM *Resolves* I. xxv. 45 This differenceth a wise man and a fool. **1628** PRYNNE *Love-lockes* 17 A desire of singularitie, or differencing our selues from others. *c* **1698** LOCKE *Cond. Underst.* §31 Every individual has something that differences it from another. *c* **1710** C. FIENNES *Diary* (1888) 223 They have Little or noe wood and noe Coale wch differences it from Darbyshire. **1851** TRENCH *Study of Words* vi. (1869) 221 Synonyms..differenced not by etymology..but only by usage. **1871** TYLOR *Prim. Cult.* II. 300 That theologic change which differences the Jew of the Rabbinical books from the Jew of the Pentateuch. **1888** M. BURROWS *Cinque Ports* vi. 162 The..corporation..was differenced off from all others by its military service, its special functions, etc.

4. To perceive or mark the difference in or between; to make a distinction between, discriminate, distinguish (in the mind, or in speech). Const. *from*. (Now *rare*.)

1570–6 LAMBARDE *Peramb. Kent* (1826) 131 One called it Dorobrina, differencing it from Canterbury (which he termeth Doroborni). *c* **1611** CHAPMAN *Iliad* v. 130 From thy knowing mind..I have remov'd those erring mists..That thou may'st difference Gods from men. **1646** FULLER *Wounded Consc.* (1841) 291 Thus these two kinds of repentance may be differenced and distinguished. **1755** S. WALKER *Serm.* viii, He is known and differenced from never-so-many, who presume, without Title, to be of equal Birth with him. **1878** GLADSTONE *Prim. Homer* 149 The Nestor of the Odyssey is carefully differenced from the Nestor of the Iliad, yet in just proportion to the altered circumstances.

†**b.** *intr.* or *absol.* To perceive or mark the difference, distinguish (*between*). *Obs.*

1646 S. BOLTON *Arraignm. Err.* 166 You cannot difference between false and true. **1647** TRAPP *Comm. Matt.* xix. 20 Aristotle..differencing between age and youth, makes it a property of young men to think they know all things. **1685** *Case of Doubting Conscience* 65 St. Paul saith, that he that doubteth or differenceth, is damned or condemned, if he eat.

5. *Math.* **a.** To take or calculate the difference of. †**b.** To take the differential of; = DIFFERENTIATE *v.* 4 (*obs.*).

1670 NEWTON in Rigaud *Corr. Sci. Men* (1841) II. 307 I thank you for your intimation about the limits of equations and differencing their homogeneal terms. **1727–51** CHAMBERS *Cycl.*, *Differential calculus*..is a method of differencing quantities; that is, of finding a *differential*, or infinitely small quantity, which, taken an infinite number of times, is equal to a given quantity. **1788** HOWARD *Cycl.* I. 424 To difference quantities that mutually divide each other.

Hence **'differenced** *ppl. a.*; †**'differencer**, one who or that which differences or distinguishes.

1638–48 G. DANIEL *Eclog.* II. 252 Shall looke at Glorie.. with a differenced Light To those, who liveing saw that flame more bright. **1633** D. ROGERS *Treat. Sacraments* I. 81 Circumcision..to be the Differencer of all other Nations from the Jews.

†**difference,** *a. Obs.*, representing L. *deferens*: see DEFERENT B. 2.

1398 TREVISA *Barth. De P.R.* VIII. xi. (1495) 317 The cercle that hyghte *Difference* is the cercle of a planete and highte *Difference*..for it beryth the cercle Epiciclis.

differencing ('dɪfərənsɪŋ), *vbl. sb.* [f. prec. vb. + -ING[1].] The action of the verb to DIFFERENCE (in various senses).

1610 GUILLIM *Heraldry* I. i. (1660) 4 Names were instituted for differencing of each person from other severally. **1659** FULLER *App. Inj. Innoc.* (1840) 617 Writers of civil dissentions are sometimes necessitated, for differencing of parties, to use those terms they do not approve. **1809–10** COLERIDGE *Friend* (1866) 340 The mechanism of the understanding, the whole functions of which consist in individualization, in outlines and differencings by quantity, quality, and relation. **1865** *Edin. Rev.* Apr. 339 Differencing is..a far more important part of Scottish than of English heraldry.

'differencing, *ppl. a.* [f. as prec. + -ING[2].] That differences or makes a difference; distinguishing, differentiating; discriminating: see the verb.

1652 J. PAWSON *Vind. Free Grace* 24 Differencing grace. **1657** BAXTER *Acc. Pres. Th.* 5 Augustine who rose up against Pelagius..in defence of differencing free grace. **1660** W. SECKER *Nonsuch Prof.* 16 Differencing mercy calls for differencing duty. **1768** *Phil. Trans.* LIX. 499 There is in each [Chinese] character a distinctive or differencing *Pou.* **1845** *Blackw. Mag.* LVII. 398 The differencing conditions which qualify the rule.

Hence **'differencingly** *adv.*

a **1640** W. FENNER *Christ's Alarm* (1650) 28 To preach differencingly, to distinguish between the precious and the vile.

†**'differency.** *Obs.* [ad. L. *differentia* DIFFERENCE: see -ENCY.] = DIFFERENCE *sb.*

1607 SHAKS. *Cor.* V. iv. 11 There is a differency between a Grub & a Butterfly; yet your Butterfly was a Grub. **1640** SIR E. DERING *Proper Sacrifice* (1644) 21 The differencie of Editions. **1707** *Lond. Gaz.* No. 4333/1 All Jealousies and Differencies being removed. **1812** HENRY *Camp. agst. Quebec* 3 Many differencies of style corrected.

different ('dɪfərənt), *a.* (*sb.*, *adv.*) [a. F. *différent* (14th c. in Hatz.-Darm.), ad. L. *different-em* differing, different, pr. pple. of *differ-re* trans. to bear or carry asunder, etc., *intr.* to tend asunder, have opposite bearings, DIFFER.]

A. *adj.*

1. a. Having characters or qualities which diverge from one another; having unlike or distinguishing attributes; not of the same kind; not alike; of other nature, form, or quality.

c **1400** *Lanfranc's Cirurg.* 90 To heele boþe þe ulcus and þe festre wiþ medicyns different þat longen to þem boþe. **1477** EARL RIVERS (Caxton) *Dictes* 1 Largely and in many diffirent maners. *c* **1500** *Sc. Poem Her.* 43 in *Q. Eliz. Acad., etc.* 95 The fader the hole, the eldest son deffer[e]nt, quhiche a labelle; a cressent the secound. **1581** PETTIE *Guazzo's Civ. Conv.* I. (1586) 21 b, Persons different in state and condition. **1607** SHAKS. *Lear* IV. iii. 37 Mate and mate could not beget Such different issues. **1651** HOBBES *Leviath.* I. xv. 79 Appetite, and Aversions..in different tempers..are different. **1711** STEELE *Spect.* No. 114 ¶4 Their Manners are very widely different. **1802** MAR. EDGEWORTH *Moral T.* (1816) I. viii. 50 With what different eyes different people behold the same objects. **1860** TYNDALL *Glac.* I. xxii. 154 Different positions of the limb require different molecular arrangements. **1875** JOWETT *Plato* (ed. 2) IV. 29 Principles as widely different as benevolence and self-love. **1887** RUSKIN *Præterita* II. 248 We both enjoyed the same scenes, though in different ways.

b. Const. *from*; also *to*, *than* (†*against*, †*with*).

The usual construction is now with *from*; that with *to* (after *unlike*, *dissimilar to*) is found in writers of all ages, and is frequent colloquially, but is by many considered incorrect. The construction with *than* (after *other than*), is found in Fuller, Addison, Steele, De Foe, Richardson, Goldsmith, Miss Burney, Coleridge, Southey, De Quincey, Carlyle, Thackeray, Newman, Trench, and Dasent, among others: see F. Hall *Mod. English* iii. 82.

1526 *Pilgr. Perf.* (W. de W. 1531) 125b, His lyght is moche different and vnlyke to the lyght of the holy goost. **1588** R. PARKE tr. *Mendoza's Hist. China* 257 If..they could write any other language that were different vnto theirs. [*Ibid.* 271, 291.] **1590** SHAKS. *Com. Err.* v. i. 46 This weeke he hath beene..much different from the man he was. **1603** DEKKER, &c. *Grissil* (1841) 72 Oh, my dear Grissil, how much different Art thou to this curs'd spirit here! **1624** HEYWOOD *Gunaik.* I. 15 Humane wisdome, different against the divine will, is vaine and contemptible. **1644** DIGBY *Nat. Bodies* II. (1645) 45 We make use of them in a quite different manner then we did in the beginning. **1649** EARL MONM. tr. *Senault's Passions* (1671) 245 She [hatred] hath this of different with love, that she is much more sensible. **1711** ADDISON *Spect.* No. 159 ¶2 Tunes..different from anything I had ever heard. **1737** FIELDING *Hist. Reg.* II. Wks. (1882) X. 218 It's quite a different thing within to what it is without. **1769** GOLDSM. *Rom. Hist.* (1786) I. 105 The consuls..had been elected for very different merits than those of skill in war. **1790** COLEBROOKE in *Life* (1873) 38 The different prosperity of the country which they conquered..with that of the countries under English rule. **1848** J. H. NEWMAN *Loss & Gain* 306 It has possessed me in a different way than ever before. **1852** THACKERAY *Esmond* II. ii. (1869) 169 The party of prisoners lived..with comforts very different to those which were awarded to the poor wretches there. **1861** M. PATTISON *Ess.* (1889) I. 44 Warehouses and wharves no way different from those on either side of them.

c. *colloq.* Out of the ordinary, special, *recherché*.

1912 D. F. CANFIELD *Squirrel Cage* iii, What a perfectly lovely couch... Why, it is so beautifully *different*! *Ibid.* xviii, To avoid being 'queer' and 'different' one had to play a good hand [at Bridge]. **1930** *Publishers' Weekly* 8 Feb. 709/1 They are always striving to write a piece of copy that will be 'different', that 'will hit the reader right between the eyes'. *Ibid.* 15 Mar. 1554/1 A 'different' book ad appeared in the Sunday, March the 9th, New York *Herald Tribune.* **1930** *Week-end Rev.* 7 June 467 Ireland this year! For a 'different' holiday, with all the charms of foreign travel and none of the disadvantages. **1965** *New Statesman* 7 May 712/2 The *Mail*'s bold, different typography.

2. In a weaker sense, used as a synonym for *other*, as denying identity, but without any implication of dissimilarity; not the same, not identical, distinct.

1651 HOBBES *Leviath.* II. xxvi. 138 Civill, and Naturall Law are not different kinds, but different parts of Law. **1711** ADDISON *Spect.* No. 35 ¶3 At different times he appears as serious as a Judge, and as jocular as a Merry-Andrew. **1802** PALEY *Nat. Theol.* v. §2 (1819) 52 To different persons, and in different stages of science. **1860** TYNDALL *Glac.* I. i. 3 Some..may be split with different facility in different directions. **1867** FREEMAN *Norm. Conq.* (1876) I. App. 717 Eadwig King of the Churls is quite a different person from Eadwig the Ætheling. **1868** LOCKYER *Elem. Astron.* iii. (1879) 145 The daily motion of the Earth is very different in different parts. *Mod.* I suspect this is a different coin from the other, though, being both new sovereigns of this year, they are quite indistinguishable.

3. *Comb.*, as ***different-minded, -coloured.***

1680 ALLEN *Peace & Unity* 13 If this..will not reconcile the different-minded to our judgement. **1768–74** TUCKER *Lt. Nat.* (1852) II. 455 We may have different heights..or wear different-coloured clothes. **1831** BREWSTER *Optics* x. 91 The different-coloured spaces of the spectrum.

B. *sb.*

†1. A disagreement, dispute; = DIFFERENCE *sb.* 3. *Obs. rare.* [OF. *différent*, written by the Academy *différend.*]

1483 CAXTON *Cato* C iij b, The whych deuyll myght not fynde the manere for to..brynge them to dyscencion and dyfferente. **1484** —— *Fables of Æsop* IV. vi, Whan a lygnage or kyndred is in dyfferent or in dyuysyon. *Ibid.* v. x, We praye the that thow vouchesauf to accorde our dyferent so that pees be made betwene vs. **1606** G. W[OODCOCKE] tr. *Hist. Ivstine* Ll ij a, Whereupon arose cruell differents betweene the Genooise and the Venetians.

2. That which is different; a contrary or opposite. *rare.*

1581 LAMBARDE *Eiren.* IV. Epil. (1602) 589 To shew things by their contraries and differents. **1890** J. H. STIRLING *Philos. & Theol.* iii. 49 The fairest harmony results from differents.

C. as *adv.* = DIFFERENTLY. Now only in uneducated use.

1744 SARAH FIELDING *David Simple* I. 253, I spent my Infancy..very different from what most Children do. **1775** MAD. D'ARBLAY *Early Diary* (1889) II. 131 He pronounces English quite different from other foreigners. **1803** tr. *Lebrun's Mons. Botte* III. 9 They had..acted perfectly different from those parties who [etc.]. **1863** KINGSLEY *Water Bab.* viii. 374 'Oh dear, if I was but a little chap in Vendale again..how different I would go on!'

different, obs. form of DEFERENT.

‖**differentia** (dɪfəˈrɛnʃɪə). *Logic.* Pl. **-iæ** (-iiː). [L. = difference, diversity; a species.] The attribute by which a species is distinguished from all other species of the same genus; a distinguishing mark or characteristic; = DIFFERENCE *sb.* 4 c.

1827 WHATELY *Logic* ii. I. §4 (ed. 2) 62 Either the material part [of their essence] which is called the Genus, or the formal and distinguishing part, which is called Differentia, or in common discourse, characteristic. **1850** KINGSLEY *Tennyson* Misc. I. 218 This deep, simple faith in the divineness of Nature..which, in our eyes, is Mr. Tennyson's differentia. **1851** MANSEL *Proleg. Logica* i. (1860) 54 The concept whiteness, as a species of colour, is capable of definition by its optical differentia. **1889** A. LANG *Introd. Romilly's Verandah N.G.* 17 To be inconsistent and incoherent and self-contradictory is the very differentia and characteristic of myth. **1889** R. L. OTTLEY in *Lux Mundi* (1890) xii. 476 To arrive at the true differentiæ of Christian morals.

differentiability (dɪfərɛnʃɪəˈbɪlɪtɪ). [f. DIFFERENTIAB(LE *a.* + -ILITY.] Capability of being differentiated.

1909 in *Cent. Dict.* Suppl. **1925** G. A. BLISS *Calculus of Variations* v. 144 Hilbert's differentiability condition. **1947** *Mind* LVI. 48 The *f*'s must be single-valued, but no restrictions of continuity or differentiability are implied. **1964** E. A. POWER *Introd. Quantum Electrodynamics* vi. 78 The usual differentiability conditions of the calculus of variations are required.

differentiable (dɪfəˈrɛnʃɪəb(ə)l), *a. rare.* [f. med.L. *differentiā-re* differentiate: see -BLE.] Capable of being differentiated.

1863 E. V. NEALE *Anal. Th. & Nat.* 219 So as to produce a new differentiable material from the crash of ancient integrations. **1867** H. SPENCER *Princ. Biol.* II. vii. §296. 309 Undeniable proof that they [the tissues] are easily differentiable. *Mod.* (*Math.*) All functions of a variable are differentiable, but not all are integrable.

differential (dɪfəˈrɛnʃəl), *a.* and *sb.* [ad. med. or mod.L. *differentiāl-is*, f. *differentia* DIFFERENCE: see -AL[1]. Cf. mod.F. *différentiel* (Dict. Trev. 1732).] A. *adj.*

1. Of or relating to difference or diversity; exhibiting or depending on a difference or distinction; *esp.* in *Comm.* used of duties or charges which differ according to circumstances.

1647 H. MORE *Song of Soul* I. II. xii, This be understood Of differentiall profunditie. **1841** MYERS *Cath. Th.* III. xxiv. 90 This testimony does not decide..the differential amount of sacredness between Substantial Divinity and Literal Infallibility. **1845** MCCULLOCH *Taxation* II. v. (1852) 222 To reduce the present differential or prohibitory duties on the sugar of foreign countries. **1868** ROGERS *Pol. Econ.* xix. (1876) 5 Differential duties in favour of colonial timber. **1894** JESSOPP *Rand. Roam.* ii. 60 They compounded for murder according to a differential tariff.

2. a. Constituting a specific difference or *differentia*; distinguishing, distinctive, special.

1652 GAULE *Magastrom.* 77 Any quality of sympathy or antipathy (which doe follow naturally the specifick or differentiall forms). **1733** CHEYNE *Eng. Malady* II. xi. §1 (1734) 227 The great differential Marks of the Distemper will appear. **1851** DE QUINCEY *Carlisle on Pope* Wks. XIII. 24 Every case in the law courts..presents some one differential feature peculiar to itself. **1893** F. HALL in *Nation* (N.Y.) LVII. 449/3 One of the differential peculiarities of a highly important division of the Hindus of olden times.

b. Relating to specific differences. ***differential diagnosis***: the distinguishing between two similar species of disease, or of animals or plants.

1875 B. MEADOWS *Clin. Observ.* 29 Any system of specific treatment governed by differential diagnosis. **1877** ROBERTS *Handbk. Med.* I. 19 In others the diagnosis has to be more or less differential. **1883** in *Syd. Soc. Lex.*

3. *Math.* Relating to infinitesimal differences (see B. 1).

differential analyser, a machine designed for solving differential equations. ***differential calculus***: a method of calculation invented by Leibnitz in 1677, which treats of the infinitesimal differences between consecutive values of continuously varying quantities, and of their rates of change as measured by such differences. (Newton's method of FLUXIONS was another way of treating the same subject.) ***differential coefficient***: a function expressing the rate of change, or the relation between consecutive values, of a varying quantity: see COEFFICIENT B. 2c. ***differential equation***: an equation involving differentials (see B. 1).

1702 RALPHSON *Math. Dict.* s.v. *Fluxions*, A different way ..passes..in France under the Name of Leibnitz's Differential Calculus, or Calculus of Differences. **1706** H. DITTON *Instit. Fluxions* 17 The Fundamental Principles [of Fluxions]..appear to be more accurate, clear, and convincing than those of the Differential Calculus. **1727–51** CHAMBERS *Cycl.* s.v., Mr. Leibnitz..calls it *differential calculus*, as considering the infinitely small quantities..as the differences of the quantities; and, accordingly, expressing them by the letter *d* prefixed: as the *differential* of *x* by *dx*. **1763** W. EMERSON *Meth. Increments* 75 A differential equation. **1808** *Edin. Rev.* Jan. 256 The general methods of integrating the differential equations above mentioned. **1816** tr. *Lacroix's Diff. & Int. Calculus* 4 The limit of the ratio of the increments, or the differential coefficient, will be obtained. **1819** G. PEACOCK (*title*), Comparative view of the fluxional and differential Calculus. **1835** MACAULAY *Ess.*, *Mackintosh's Hist. Rev.* (1854) 321/1 We submit that a wooden spoon of our day would not be justified in calling Galileo and Napier blockheads, because they never heard of the differential calculus. **1931** D. BUSH in *Jrnl. Franklin Inst.* CCXII. 447 The differential analyzer. A new machine for solving differential equations. **1957** *Technology* July 188/1 The analogue laboratory contains a large electro-mechanical differential analyser. **1962** *Gloss. Terms Automatic Data Proc.* (*B.S.I.*) 8 *Differential analyser*, (1) an analogue computer using interconnected integrating gears to solve differential equations; (2) by extension, any computer designed primarily for solving differential equations.

4. *Physics* and *Mech.* Relating to, depending on, or exhibiting the difference of two (or more) motions, pressures, temperatures, or other measurable physical qualities: a. of physical actions or effects. ***differential tone*** (in *Acoustics*) = *difference-tone*: see TONE *sb.*

1768–74 TUCKER *Lt. Nat.* (1852) I. 406 Weight is made by the differential, not the absolute pressure of ether. **1868** LOCKYER *Elem. Astron.* 318 As the Sun's distance is so great compared with the diameter of the Earth, the differential effect of the Sun's action is small. **1873** B. STEWART *Conserv. Energy* iv. §136. 97 Wherever in the universe there is a differential motion, that is to say, a motion of one part of it towards or from another. **1877** LE CONTE *Elem. Geol.* I. (1879) 55 The centre of the glacier moved faster than the margins. This differential motion is the capital discovery in relation to the motion of glaciers. **1880** E. J. PAYNE in Grove *Dict. Mus.* I. 726 Two notes..sounded together..generate a third..tone, whose vibrational number equals the difference of their several vibrational numbers..These tones Helmholtz calls differential tones.

b. of instruments or mechanical contrivances. *spec.* Applied to mechanisms devised for imparting differing velocities, e.g. to the two halves of the driving axle of a motor vehicle (so that the wheels revolve at different rates when turning a corner).

differential gear, gearing: a combination of toothed wheels communicating a motion depending on the difference of their diameters or of the number of their teeth. ***differential pulley***: a pulley having a block with two rigidly connected wheels or sheaves of different diameters, the chain or rope unwinding from one as it winds on the other. ***differential screw***: a screw having two threads of different pitch, one of which unwinds as the other winds. ***differential thermometer***: a thermometer consisting of two air-bulbs connected by a bent tube partly filled with a liquid, the position of the column of liquid indicating the difference of temperature between the two bulbs. ***differential winding***: the method of winding two insulated wires side by side in an electric coil, through which currents pass in opposite directions.

1804 J. LESLIE *Heat* 9 The instrument most essential in this research..was the differential thermometer. **1834** *Mech. Mag.* XXI. 3 Saxton's differential pulley. *Ibid.* 6 The 'locomotive differential pulley' can never be made to answer the expectations of the inventor. **1881** MAXWELL *Electr. & Magn.* I. 433 The differential galvanometer, an instrument in which there are two coils, the currents in which are independent of each other. **1884** MINCHIN *Statics* (ed. 3) I. 188 A Differential Wheel and Axle is sometimes employed. **1888** *Encycl. Brit.* XXIII. 559 In 1877 Mr. James Starley, it is believed without any knowledge of the gear used by Fowler for traction engines, re-invented the same differential gear for tricycles. **1902** A. C. HARMSWORTH *Motors & Motor-Driving* x. 213 The differential gear acts on the principle of the action of the pair-horse whippletree and equalising bar. **1903** *Sci. Amer.* 7 Feb. 91/2 Single-chain drives are more popular than ever, although..it looked as if the double outside chain drive to both rear wheels from a differential countershaft would supplant this form. **1904** A. B. F. YOUNG *Compl. Motorist* iii. 62 A separate shaft, parallel with the rear axle, called the differential shaft, driven by bevel gearing from the secondary shaft in the gear case. **1925** *Morris Owner's Man.* 26 If any adjustments to the differential bearings are required. *Ibid.*, This adjusting sleeve is easily accessible through an opening on the upper side of the differential carrier. **1967** E. RUDINGER *Consumer's Car Gloss.* (ed. 2) 32 The differential gears are in the middle of the rear axle.

B. *sb.*

1. *Math.* a. (In the differential and integral calculus) The infinitesimal difference between consecutive values of a continuously varying quantity (corresponding to a MOMENT or FLUXION in Newton's method); either of the two quantities (usually considered to be infinitesimal) whose ratio constitutes a differential coefficient.

1704 J. HARRIS *Lex. Techn.* s.v. *Fluxion*, This Method is much..shorter than..the French one with the Differential *d* multiplied into the Flowing Quantity, to denote the Fluxion. **1730–6** BAILEY (folio), *Differential* of any quantity, is the fluxion of that quantity. **1788** HOWARD *Cycl.* I. 424 Multiply the differential of [each] factor into the other factor, the sum of the two [products] is the differential sought. **1819** G. PEACOCK *View Fluxional & Diff. Calc.* 25 The Differential is but the measure of the rate of increase. **1880** BUCKINGHAM *Elem. Diff. & Int. Calc.* (ed. 2) 42 The function which Leibnitz terms 'differential' and which Newton designates as a 'fluxion' is the concrete symbol which represents the rate of change in the variable.

†b. A logarithmic tangent. *Obs.*

1727–51 CHAMBERS *Cycl.*, *Differential*, in the doctrine of logarithms. Kepler calls the logarithms of tangents, *differentiales*; which we usually call artificial tangents. **1845** CAYLEY *Wks.* I. 145 Logarithmic differential.

2. *Biol.* A distinction or distinctive characteristic of structure: opp. to *equivalent*.

1883 A. HYATT in *Proc. Amer. Assoc. Adv. Sci.* XXXII. 358 During their subsequent history, characteristics are divisible into two categories: those which become morphological equivalents and are essentially similar in distinct series, and those which are essentially different in distinct series and may be classed as morphological differentials.

3. a. *Comm.* A differential charge: see A. 1.

1890 *Spectator* 20 Sept. 383 The morality of American Railway Companies as regards..differentials and commissions.

b. The difference in wages between one class of workmen and another (esp. between skilled and unskilled workmen) or between one industry, etc., and another; a difference in prices of similar products, services, etc.

1941 *Economist* 8 Feb. 178/2 The present economic differentials between one occupation and another and one status and another are, over a wide field, calculated to make people stay where they are. **1950** D. W. BROGAN *Era of F. D. Roosevelt* v. 100 Controversy arose over wage differentials between North and South. **1955** *Times* 17 June 4/4 This trend would lift the skilled differential and the future might show a relative improvement in payment for skill. **1959** *Punch* 19 Aug. 30/2 The rise of Oundle's fees to £435 puts the school within £25 of Eton... What does Eton do now? Does it preserve its status by leaping ahead.., or does it get the Headmasters' Conference to negotiate a national agreement on differentials? **1965** *New Statesman* 23 Apr. 634/2 The major companies have reacted with countrywide cuts of 1d., 1½d. or 2d. off certain grades [of petrol]. Some..cut-price companies have followed suit, to try to keep their 3d. differential.

4. A differential gear, *spec.* of a motor vehicle.

1902 *Daily Chron.* 30 June 6/2 He broke the differential of his 70 h.-p. Panhard car 50 kilometres from the finish. **1905** *Westm. Gaz.* 17 Feb. 8/2 A motor-boat requires no differential. **1930** J. B. PRIESTLEY *Angel Pavement* ii. 72 Wanted new plugs and mag. and brakes re-lining and something doing to the differential, and just cleanin' up a bit. **1959** *Motor Man.* (ed. 36) iv. 94 When a rigid rear axle is used, the differential naturally moves up and down in relation to the chassis whenever the wheels meet a bump.

diffe'rentialize, *v.* [f. prec. + -IZE.] *trans.* To make differential; to differentiate.

1862 *Sat. Rev.* XIV. 601/1 Words..more or less modified or, as some philosophers would say, differentialized in meaning.

differentially (dɪfəˈrɛnʃəlɪ), *adv.* [f. as prec. + -LY².] In a differential manner.

1. Distinctively, specially, by way of difference: see DIFFERENTIAL A. 2.

1644 J. STRICKLAND in Spurgeon *Treas. Dav.* Ps. xlvi. 7 God is said to be in heaven differentially, so as he is not anywhere else. **1646** SIR T. BROWNE *Pseud. Ep.* VI. xxviii. (R.) When biting serpents are mentioned in the Scripture they are not differentially set down from such as mischief by stings. **1846** DE QUINCEY *Antigone of Sophocles* Wks. XIV. 207 These persons will.. wish to know..what there is differentially interesting in a Grecian tragedy, as contrasted with one of Shakspere's or of Schiller's. **1880** STUBBS *Med. & Mod. Hist.* ix. (1886) 210, I will..state next what sorts of rights, forces, and ideas I consider, mark differentially the three periods at which I have been looking.

2. In relation to the difference of two measurable quantities; in two different directions: see DIFFERENTIAL A. 4.

1862 H. SPENCER *First Princ.* x. (L.), Whether.. everything is explicable on the hypothesis of universal pressure, whence what we call tension results differentially from inequalities of pressure in opposite directions. **1883** *Nature* XXVII. 275 The magnets..being in both these patterns of lamp wound differentially. **1892** *Gloss. Electrical Terms* in *Lightning* 7 Jan. (Suppl.), Differentially-wound dynamo machine, a compound-wound machine in which currents flow in opposite directions in the coils on the field magnets.

differentiant (dɪfəˈrɛnʃɪənt). *Math.* Also **differenciant.** [f. pr. ppl. stem of med.L. *differentiā-re* or F. *différentier*: see next and -ANT¹.] A rational integral function of elements a, b, c,.., which elements multiplied by binomial coefficients are the coefficients in a binary quantic, which remains unchanged when for them are substituted the elements of the new quantic obtained by putting $x + hy$ for x in the original quantic (Sylvester).

1878 SYLVESTER in *Phil. Mag.* March, I propose to give a systematic developement of the Calculus of Invariants, taking a differentiant as the primordial germ or unit.

differentiate (dɪfəˈrɛnʃɪeɪt), *v.* [f. ppl. stem of med.L. *differentiāre*, f. *differentia* DIFFERENCE: cf. F. *différentier*, *-encier*.]

1. *trans.* To make or render different; to constitute the difference in or between; to distinguish.

1853 DE QUINCEY *Autobiog. Sk.* Wks. I. 199 *note*, Genius differentiates a man from all other men. **1872** YEATS *Techn. Hist. Comm.* 22 The use of fire..constitutes one of the great distinctions by which man is differentiated from the lower animals. **1874** L. STEPHEN *Hours in Libr.* (1892) II. ii. 48 His language..is sufficiently differentiated from prose by the mould into which it is run.

2. *Biol.*, etc. To make different in the process of growth or development; to make unlike by modification, *esp.* for a special function or purpose; to specialize. (Chiefly used in *passive*.)

1858 HUXLEY *Oceanic Hydrozoa* (Ray Soc.) 22 The substance of the spermarium..becomes differentiated into minute, clear, spherical vesicles. **1869** SEELEY *Lect. & Ess.* i. 15 We have heard..of the power which all organisms possess of differentiating special organs to meet special needs. **1871** DARWIN *Desc. Man* II. xx. 365 The power of sexual selection in differentiating the tribes. **1874** H. R. REYNOLDS *John Bapt.* iii. §1. 127 The office of priest..is ultimately differentiated from that of the prophet and the prince. **1874** CARPENTER *Ment. Phys.* I. ii. §43 'Protoplasm' or living jelly, which is not yet differentiated into 'organs'. **1885** J. BALL in *Jrnl. Linn. Soc.* XXII. 26 A very long period of..isolation during which a large number of separate species, and not a few genera, have been differentiated. **1893** F. HALL in *Nation* (N.Y.) LVII. 229/2 As being distinctly differentiated from *practiser*, it [*practitioner*] has.. unquestionable utility.

b. *intr.* (for *refl.*) To become differentiated or specialized.

1874 LEWES in *Contemp. Rev.* Oct. 692 Nebulæ which differentiate into a solar system. **1884** BOWER & SCOTT *De Bary's Phaner.* 155 Their walls become thickened as they differentiate from the meristem.

3. *trans.* To observe, note, or ascertain the difference in or between; to discriminate between, distinguish.

1876 G. F. CHAMBERS *Astron.* 915 *Differentiate*, to fix the position of one celestial object by comparing it with another. **1878** MISS BRADDON *Open Verd.* xxxv. 239 Typhus and typhoid, which two fatal diseases..Jenner was just then seeking to differentiate. **1880** R. C. DRYSDALE in *Med. Temp. Jrnl.* Oct. 3, I have known some difficulty in differentiating such attacks from those of epilepsy.

b. *intr.* To recognize the difference.

1891 J. JASTROW in *Educat. Rev.* I. 258 One important use of child study is to differentiate between functions that in the adult have become merged.

4. *Math.* To obtain the differential or the differential coefficient of.

1816 tr. *Lacroix's Diff. & Int. Calculus* 18 The differential coefficient being a new function..may itself be differentiated. **1882** MINCHIN *Unipl. Kinemat.* 229 Differentiate this equation first with respect to ξ and then with respect to η.

Hence **diffe'rentiated** *ppl. a.*, **diffe'rentiating** *vbl. sb.* and *ppl. a.*; also **diffe'rentiator**, he who or that which differentiates.

1861 H. MACMILLAN *Footn. Page Nat.* 203 In the fungi, however, there is little or nothing of this specializing or differentiating process. Their entire structure is uniform. **1864** H. SPENCER *Illust. Univ. Progr.* 3 Each of these differentiated divisions..begins itself to exhibit some contrast of parts. **1871** TYNDALL *Fragm. Sc.* (1879) I. xx. 490 The differentiating influence of 'environment' on two minds of similar natural cast. **1888** R. F. LITTLEDALE in *Academy* 7 July 6/1 No impression of conscious imitation.. but only that of differentiated heredity. *Mod.* (*Math.*) The result can be obtained by differentiating.

differentiation (dɪfərɛnʃɪˈeɪʃən). [n. of action f. DIFFERENTIATE: so in mod.F.]

1. a. The action of differentiating, or condition of being differentiated (see prec. 1, 2); any change by which like things become unlike, or something homogeneous becomes heterogeneous; *spec.* in *Biol.*, etc., the process, or the result of the process, by which in the course of growth or development a part, organ, etc. is modified into a special form, or for a special function; specialization; also the gradual production of differences between the descendants of the same ancestral types. Esp. ***dependent differentiation*** and ***self-differentiation*** (see quot.).

1855 H. SPENCER *Princ. Psychol.* (1870) I. I. iii. 49 In the rudimentary nervous system, there is no such structural differentiation. **1863** E. V. NEALE *Anal. Th. & Nat.* 217 The differentiation of a diffused material substance into the opposite forms of suns and planets. **1865** GOSSE *Land & Sea* (1874) 213 The lower the rank of an organism..the less of differentiation we find, the less of specialty in the assignment of function to organ. **1871** DARWIN *Desc. Man* I. ii. 61 He [the naturalist] justly considers the differentiation and specialisation of organs as the test of perfection. **1874** SWEET *Eng. Sounds* 23 The Roman alphabet has been further enriched by the differentiation of various forms of the same letter, of which the present distinction between *u* and *v*, *i* and *j*, are instances. **1875** LYELL *Princ. Geol.* II. III. xliii. 480 We cannot so easily account for the differentiation of the Papuan and the Malay races. **1880** A. R. WALLACE *Isl. Life* 278 Long continued isolation would often lead to the differentiation of species. **1926** J. S. HUXLEY *Ess. Pop. Sci.* xviii. 269 The future differentiation of a particular region at a particular moment may be of two kinds. It may be entirely independent of other organs, in which case we speak of self-differentiation, or it may depend upon some other organ, when it is called dependent differentiation.

b. *Philol.* The action of differentiating or fact of being differentiated: used of two adjacent phonemes, the meanings of synonyms, etc.

1925 P. RADIN tr. *Vendryès's Language* I. iii. 60 The two contiguous phonemes..take advantage of their differences to exaggerate them until they no longer have anything in common. This is the process of *differentiation* as opposed to accommodation. **1926** FOWLER *Mod. Eng. Usage* 114/1 *Differentiation.* In dealing with words, the term is applied to the process by which two words that can be used indifferently in two meanings become appropriated one to one of the meanings & one to the other. **1928** *S.P.E. Tract* XXXI. 323 Differentiation..consists in giving deliberate help to that natural process of language which is always tending to give different meanings to..synonyms. **1934** M. K. POPE *From Lat. to Mod. Fr.* II. i. 64 Differentiation is at times due to the same instinct, as for instance when plosive + plosive is differentiated to fricative + plosive. **1939** L. H. GRAY *Found. Lang.* iii. 69 Dissimilation..may be..either contiguous (differentiation) or incontiguous (dissimilation proper).

2. The action of noting or ascertaining a difference (see prec. 3); discrimination, distinction.

a **1866** WHEWELL in *Macm. Mag.* XLV. 142 Men rush.. to differentiation on the slightest provocation. **1875** G. H. LEWES *Prob. of Life & Mind* Ser. I. II. VI. iv. 504 The logical distinctions represent real differentiations, but not distinct existents. **1876** BARTHOLOW *Mat. Med.* (1879) 114 A careful differentiation of the causes.

3. *Math.* The operation of obtaining a differential or differential coefficient.

1802 WOODHOUSE in *Phil. Trans.* XCII. 123 *note*, Processes of evolution, differentiation, integration, &c. are much more easily performed with the former expression. **1816** tr. *Lacroix's Diff. & Int. Calculus* 21 The principles of differentiation having been deduced. **1885** WATSON & BURBURY *Math. Th. Electr. & Magn.* I. 31 Performing the differentiations and substituting, we get [etc.].

differentiator (dɪfəˈrɛnʃɪeɪtə(r)). [f. DIFFERENTIATE *v.* + -OR.] One who or that which differentiates; *spec.* (*a*) *Biol.* an organ, part, etc., that stimulates or controls differentiation; (*b*) a device that produces an output proportional to the rate of change (with respect to time or another variable) of the input.

1889 *Cent. Dict.* s.v., The radicals of written Chinese serve as differentiators of the sense. **1894** *Times* 11 Aug. 11/1 It was..advisable to have a 'differentiator'..and this was difficult to construct, because any irregularities in a curve were magnified in its differential coefficients. **1924** *Discovery* June 77/1 Some influence..made the tissues of the host build themselves up in the special and orderly way of differentiation. It was a differentiator. **1969** P. B. JORDAIN *Condensed Computer Encycl.* 156 An ordinary transformer produces an output voltage proportional to the rate of change of the input current, but its use as a differentiator is not common.

†**differentio-differential,** *a. Math. Obs.*

1727–51 CHAMBERS *Cycl.*, *Differentio-differential Calculus* is a method of differencing differential quantities..the same, in effect, with the *differential*.

differently (ˈdɪfərəntlɪ), *adv.* [f. DIFFERENT *a.* + -LY².] In a different manner, or to a different degree; diversely.

1398 TREVISA *Barth. De P.R.* II. viii. (1495) 35 Not alle lyke but defferently. *c* **1400** *Lanfranc's Cirurg.* 124 Wounded in þe heed differentliche. **1450–1530** *Myrr. our Ladye* 292 To the sonne ys sayde, Christeleyson dyfferentely from them, for he ys not only god wyth them, but also man. **1618** BOLTON *Florus* IV. viii. 305 And now his Navie wafted up and down..O how differently from his Father! hee rooted out the Cilicians, but this man stirred Pyrats to take his part. *a* **1622** R. HAWKINS *Hawkins' Voyages* (1878) 124 Those..have recounted this mysterie differently to that which is written. **1651** HOBBES *Leviath.* I. iv. 17 When we conceive the same things differently, we can hardly avoyd different naming of them. **1665** J. SERGEANT *Sure-footing* 182 Reason acts much differently now then formerly. **1713** BERKELEY *Guardian* No. 70 ¶5 Philosophers judge of most things very differently from the vulgar. **1770** MAD. D'ARBLAY *Early Diary* 10 Jan. (1889) I. 64 How very differently do I begin this year to what I did the last! **1844** C. C. SOUTHEY *Andrew Bell* III. 135 He seems to have spent his time somewhat differently than was usual with him. **1860** TYNDALL *Glac.* I. vi. 45 Two surfaces, differently illuminated. **1865** RUSKIN *Sesame* 25 He will think differently from you in many respects.

'**differentness.** [f. as prec. + -NESS.] The quality of being different; difference.

1727 BAILEY vol. II, *Differentness*, difference. **1862** F. HALL *Hindu Philos. Syst.* 95 In the twenty-four qualities, they include differentness, contact, separation, remoteness. **1934** F. SCOTT FITZGERALD *Tender is Night* I. vi. 36 His manner was softer than at the studio, as if his differentness had been put on at the gate. **1966** G. N. LEECH *Engl. in Advertising* xxii. 200 These deviant styles derive their power mainly through their 'differentness'. **1967** *Economist* 19 Aug. 657 A demonstration of differentness? A badge of his unhappiness?

'**differing,** *vbl. sb.* [f. DIFFER *v.* + -ING¹.]

1. The action of the verb DIFFER, q.v.; difference.

1822 MRS. E. NATHAN *Langreath* I. 151 You must excuse so material a differing in our opinions.

†**2.** *Her.* = DIFFERENCE *sb.* 4 b. *Obs.*

1592 WYRLEY *Armorie* 7 Another matter..to be reformed, is the maner of differings.

†**3.** A disagreement; = DIFFERENCE *sb.* 3.

1660 R. COKE *Power & Subj.* 266 [To] decide our differings in Church and State. **1690** W. WALKER *Idiomat. Anglo Lat.* 220 Hence grow great differings (*magnæ discordiæ*). **1709** CHANDLER *Eff. agst. Bigotry* 16 Their little Differings should not occasion the abating of their mutual Love.

'**differing,** *ppl. a.* [f. as prec. + -ING².] That differs: see the verb.

1. in gen. sense: = DIFFERENT *a.* Very common in 17th and early 18th c.; now *rare* or *Obs.*

c **1374** CHAUCER *Boeth.* v. Pr. v. 131 Dyuerse and differyng substaunces. **1598** MANWOOD *Lawes Forest* x. §7 (1615) 79/1 An especiall manner of proceeding..which is differing from the proceeding [etc.]. **1605** BACON *Adv. Learn.* I. iv. §2 (1873) 28 Whose writings were in a differing style and form. *c* **1645** J. HOWELL *Lett.* II. xii, Which makes me to be of a differing opinion to that Gentleman. **1666** BOYLE *Orig. Formes & Qual.*, Very differing from that pure whitenesse to be observ'd in the neighbouring Snow lately fallen. **1702** POPE *Sappho* 43 Turtles and doves of diff'ring hues unite. **1719** DE FOE *Crusoe* II. xii. (1858) 547 A differing name from that which our Portuguese pilot gave it. **1763** SIR W. JONES *Caissa* Poems (1777) 128 A polish'd board, with differing colours grac'd. **1802** H. MARTIN *Helen of Glenross* II. 126, I was so changed by dress..as to appear..essentially differing to what I had ever been.

2. Disagreeing in opinion or statement; discrepant, discordant.

1581 SIDNEY *Apol. Poetrie* (Arb.) 31 Hauing much a-doe to accord differing Writers. **1677** W. HUBBARD *Narrative* 68 There are differing accounts about the manner of his taking and by whom. **1858** MARTINEAU *Stud. Chr.* 280 The differing voices of the intellect and the soul.

†**3.** At variance, disputing, quarrelling. *Obs.*

c **1611** CHAPMAN *Iliad* IX. 543 Then sent they the chief priests of Gods with offer'd gifts t' atone His differing fury. **1700** DRYDEN *Pal. & Arc.* Ded. to Duchess Ormond 152 O daughter of the Rose, whose cheeks unite The differing titles of the Red and White.

†'**differingly,** *adv. Obs.* [f. prec. + -LY².] In a differing manner, differently.

1602 WARNER *Alb. Eng.* (1612) 364 More diffringly and doubtingly than of the other sixe. **1666** BOYLE *Orig. Formes & Qual.* (1667) 27 Each organ of Sense..may be it selfe differingly affected by external Objects. **1688** —— *Final Causes Nat. Things* ii. 58 Organs of sight that are very differingly framed and placed. *a* **1691** —— *Hist. Air* xix. (1692) 163 These differingly colour'd sorts of Vitriol.

† **di'fferrence.** *Obs.* [f. *differ*, obs. form of DEFER *v.*[1] + -ENCE.] The action of deferring or putting off, delay.

1559 CROSRAGUELL *Let. Willock* in Keith *Hist. Ch. Scotl.* App. 198 The hail warld may se that it is bot difference that ye desyre, and not to haif the mater at ane perfyte tryall.

diffet, obs. var. DIVOT, a sod.

† **di'ffibulate**, *v. Obs. rare*—0. [f. ppl. stem of L. *diffībulāre*, f. *dif-*, DIS- + *fībula* clasp, buckle, FIBULA.] to unclasp. unbuckle.

1656 BLOUNT *Glossogr., Diffibulate*, to unbutton, open or ungird.

† **diffi'cacity.** *Obs. rare*—0. [ad. med.L. *difficācitās*, f. *difficāx* difficult (*Catholicon*).] Difficulty.

1656 BLOUNT *Glossogr., Difficacity*, hardness or difficulty.

‖ **difficile, -il** (dɪ'fɪsɪl, 'dɪfɪsɪl), *a. Obs.* (exc. as Fr.) [a. late OF. *difficile* (15th c. in Littré), ad. L. *difficil-is*, f. *dif-*, DIS- + *facilis* able to be done, easy. Cf. Pr. *difficil*, Sp. *dificil*, It. *difficile*.] The opposite of *facile*.

†**1.** Not easy, hard to do or accomplish, troublesome; = DIFFICULT *a.* 1 a, b (q.v. for constructions). *Obs.*

1477 EARL RIVERS (Caxton) *Dictes* 143 It is a difficile thing to a man to be long in helth. **1489** CAXTON *Faytes of A.* I. x. 29 Al thinges seme dyfficyle to the dysciple. **1500–25** *Dunbar's Poems* (1803) 309 Thocht luve be grene in gud curage, And be difficill till asswage. **1533** BELLENDEN *Livy* II. (1822) 205 The Romanis..finalie wan the difficillest and maist strate parte of the said montane. **1566** PAINTER *Pal. Pleas.* I. 45 b, To adventure anye hard and difficile exploit. **1573** *New Custom* II. ii. in Hazl. *Dodsley* III. 30 No matter so difficile for man to find out. **1621** BURTON *Anat. Mel.* II. i. IV. ii. 302 They..make it most dangerous and difficill to be cured. **1663** BUTLER *Hud.* I. i. 53 That Latine was no more difficile Than to a Blackbird 'tis to whistle. **1665** SIR T. HERBERT *Trav.* (1677) 88 Hope oft fancies that to be facile in the attainment, which reason in the event shews difficile.

†**2.** Hard to understand; = DIFFICULT *a.* 1 c.

c **1546** JOYE in Gardiner *Declar. Art. Joye* (1546) p. xv, Isai prophecied of Christ that..he shoulde not be darke and dyffycyle or harde in his doctrine. **1552** ABP. HAMILTON *Catech.* (1884) 46 Ane exposition of difficil & obscuire placis. **1637** GILLESPIE *Eng. Pop. Cerem.* III. viii. 196 If the matter be doubtfull and difficille.

‖**3.** Of persons: Hard to persuade or satisfy; unaccommodating, making difficulties; awkward, troublesome to deal with; = DIFFICULT *a.* 2.

In modern use as nonce-wd. from French (difi'sil).

1536 in Strype *Eccl. Mem.* I. App. lxxvi. 183 The Kings highnes..wold not shew himself very difficile. **1622** BACON *Hen. VII*, Wks. (Bohn) 448 This cardinal..finding the pope difficile in granting thereof. **1633** J. DONE *Hist. Septuagint* 146 Some race of Women are deficile and troublesome. **1855** CAROLINE FOX *Mem. Old Friends* (1882) 301 The most difficile and bizarre body in Christendom. **1881** MALLOCK *Romance 19th Cent.* I. 248 No jealousy..made her in the least cold or *difficile*.

† **difficilely, -illy**, *adv. Obs.* [f. DIFFICIL(E + -LY[2].] In a difficult manner; with difficulty.

1613 SHERLEY *Trav. Persia* 99 Princes difficilly speak of peace while they feele themselues able to make warres.

difficileness (dɪfɪ'siːlnɪs). [f. prec. + -NESS.] The quality of being 'difficile'; see above. (In modern use from DIFFICILE 3.)

1607–12 BACON *Ess., Goodness* (Arb.) 204 A Crosnes, or frowardnes, or aptnes to oppose, or difficilenes. **1632** LITHGOW *Trav.* VIII. 373 Doubting of his passage, and the difficilnesse of the Countrey. **1886** R. A. KING *Shadowed Life* III. iii. 58 In love..with her person, her pleasantness, her fortune..and last, though not least, her difficileness.

diffi'cilitate, *v. rare* or *Obs.* [f. L. *difficil-is* difficult: cf. DIFFICULTATE.] *trans.* To render difficult: the opposite of *facilitate*.

1611 COTGR., *Difficulter*, to difficultate, or difficilitate; to make difficult. **1640** QUARLES *Enchirid.* I. lxxviii, The boldnesse of their resolution will disadvantage the assaylants, and difficilitate their design. **1648** W. MOUNTAGUE *Devout Ess.* I. xv. §4 (R.) The inordinateness of our love difficilitateth this duty.

† **difficul**, *a. Obs.* Also 5 deffykel, 6 difficull. [? a. OldLat. *difficul* (cited by Nonius from Varro): the Eng. word may however have been deduced from *difficul-ty*, or pronounced after the latter, instead of with sibilant *c* as in *difficile*.] = next. Hence † **difficully** *adv. Obs.*

c **1400** *Lanfranc's Cirurg.* 99 Olde woundys which þat beþ diffykel to be consowdyde. **1552** HULOET, Difficull reason, *obscuratio, obscurum argumentum.* Diffuse or difficull, *obscurus. Ibid.*, Difficullye, *difficile. c* **1645** HOWELL *Lett.* (1650) II. 112 Certain..words..accounted the difficulst in all the whole Castilian language.

difficult ('dɪfɪkəlt). *a.* Also 5 dyficulte, 5–6 difficulte. Comp. **difficulter**, sup. **difficultest** (now *rare*). [An English formation, of which the ending *-cult* is not etymologically regular: cf. L. *difficil-is*, F. *difficile*. It has been regarded as deduced from the sb. *difficult-y*; and it may have arisen under the joint influence of *difficul* (see prec.) and *difficulty*. It appeared earlier than the adoption of *difficile* from French, which it has also outlived.]

1. Not easy; requiring effort or labour; occasioning or attended with trouble; troublesome, hard. **a.** of actions, etc.: Hard to do, perform, carry out, or practise. Often with *inf.* subject.

1586 T. B. *La Primand. Fr. Acad.* I. (1594) 42 Good beginnings in all great matters are alwaies the difficultest part of them. **1598** HAKLUYT *Voy.* I. 212 (R.) Things difficulte [they] haue made facile. **1600** J. PORY tr. *Leo's Africa* II. 149 Necromancers..their arte is exceeding difficult. **1608** D. T. *Ess. Pol. & Mor.* 19 b, How difficult a thing it is, to love, and to be wise, and both at once. **1666** BOYLE *Orig. Formes & Qual.*, The greatest and difficultest Changes. **1676–7** MARVELL *Corr.* cclxxv. (1872–5) II. 504 It is much difficulter for you to have obtained an injunction, than to retain it. **1751** JOHNSON *Rambler* No. 172 ¶ 14 Virtue is sufficiently difficult with any circumstances. **1799** KIRWAN *Geol. Ess.* 10 [Their] difficult solubility in water. **1860** MOTLEY *Netherl.* (1868) I. i. 1 It is difficult to imagine a more universal disaster. **1876** MOZLEY *Univ. Serm.* ix. (1877) 195 Generosity to an equal is more difficult than generosity to an inferior.

b. of the object of an action. Const. *inf.* (now usually *act.*, less freq. *pass.*), or with *of* or *in* before a noun expressing the action; also with the action contextually implied (=hard to pass, reach, produce, construct, or otherwise deal with.)

c **1400** *Lanfranc's Cirurg.* 99 To consowde olde woundes whiche þat ben difficult [*MS.* B. deffykel] to be consowded. *Ibid.* 105 þe cheke be constreyned and difficulte of mevynge. **1509** HAWES *Past. Pleas.* x. iv, If apparaunce Of the cause.. Be hard and difficulte in the utteraunce. **1651** HOBBES *Leviath.* III. xxxvii. 233 The thing..is strange, and the naturall cause difficult to imagine. **1734** tr. *Rollins's Anc. Hist.* (1827) VII. XVII. vii. 203 A river very difficult, as well in regard to its banks as to the marshes on the sides of it. **1749** FIELDING *Tom Jones* VII. vi, The real sentiments of ladies were very difficult to be understood. **1793** SMEATON *Edystone L.* Ded. 4 A plain and simple building, that has nevertheless been acknowledged to be, in itself, curious, difficult, and useful. **1814** WORDSW. *Excursion* v. 492 Knowledge..is difficult to gain. **1850** MCCOSH *Div. Govt.* I. ii. (1874) 29 This is a difficult question to answer. **1860** TYNDALL *Glac.* I. viii 58 In some places I found the crevasses difficult. **1870** YEATS *Nat. Hist. Comm.* 89 Markets are so difficult of access.

c. Hard to understand; perplexing, puzzling, obscure.

1556 *Aurelio & Isab.* (1608) G vj, If youre difficulte speakinge overcome me. **1612** BRINSLEY *Lud. Lit.* 46 The difficultest things in their Authours. **1661** BOYLE *Style of Script.* (1668) 53 Leaving out all such difficulter matters. **1858** BUCKLE *Civiliz.* (1869) II. v. 217 Butler, one of the most difficult of our poets. **1885** BIBLE (R.V.) *Jer.* xxxiii. 3 Great things, and difficult, which thou knowest not.

2. Of persons. **a.** Hard to please or satisfy; not easy to get on with; unaccommodating, exacting, fastidious. In mod. use after F. *difficile*). Cf. DIFFICILE *a.* 3.

1589 PUTTENHAM *Eng. Poesie* I. xii. (Arb.) 44 To make him ambitious of honour, iealous and difficult in his worships. **1663** HEATH *Flagellum or O. Cromwell* (ed. 2) 7 Being in his own nature of a difficult disposition..and one that would have due distances observed towards him. **1734** tr. *Rollin's Anc. Hist.* (1827) III. 32 Children were early accustomed not to be nice or difficult in their eating. **1773** GOLDSM. *Stoops to Conq.* I. i, I'll..look out for some less difficult admirer. **1855** THACKERAY *Newcomes* II. 87 My temper is difficult. **1889** LOWELL *Walton* Lit. Ess. (1891) 81 He [Cotton] also wrote verses which the difficult Wordsworth could praise. **1904** *Westm. Gaz.* 20 Jan. 3/2 Lady Verona refers to her husband as 'rather difficult'. **1929** *Times* 2 Feb. 10/1 A letter from a 'difficult' customer. **1960** J. FINGLETON *Four Chukkas* 2 A touring team is infinitely better off without the 'difficult' player.

b. Hard to induce or persuade; unwilling, reluctant, obstinate, stubborn.

a **1502** in Arnolde *Chron.* (1811) 81 That such persones which were difficulte [*printed* difficultie] ageynst the sayd ordre be callid afore my Lorde Mayr and Aldirmen to be reformed bi their wise exortacions. *c* **1645** HOWELL *Lett.* I. vi. 8, I attended him also with the Note of your Extraordinaries, wherein I find him something difficult and dilatory yet. **1691** RAY *Creation* I. (1701) 56 In particular I am difficult to believe, that [etc.]. **1749** FIELDING *Tom Jones* XIV. ii. Lady Bellaston will be as difficult to believe any thing against one who [etc.]. **1891** L. KEITH *The Halletts* I. xiii. 248 Sir Robert had been rather a difficult husband—that is to say, he had occasionally taken his own way.

† **difficult**, *sb. Obs. rare.* [f. DIFFICULT *a.*] Difficulty.

1709 tr. *Sir J. Spelman's Alfred Gt.* 95 What Difficult Ælfred had to recover the Land. *Ibid.* 118 *bis*, 120.

'**difficult**, *v.* Now *local.* [a. obs. F. *difficulter* to make difficult, f. med.L. *difficultāre*, f. *difficultās* difficulty: see DIFFICULTATE, DIFFICILITATE.]

†**1.** *trans.* To render difficult, impede (an action, etc.). The opposite of *to facilitate*. *Obs.*

a **1608** [see DIFFICULTING below]. **1678** TEMPLE *Let. to Ld. Treasurer* Wks. 1731 II. 506 Those which intended to difficult or delay the Ratification with France. *a* **1698** *Ibid.* II. 484 (L.), Having desisted from their pretensions, which had difficulted the peace. **1818** TODD s.v. *Difficultate*, The late lord chancellor Thurlow was fond of using the verb *difficult*; as, he difficulted the matter; but he was pronounced unjustifiable in this usage.

2. To put in a difficulty, bring into difficulties, perplex, embarrass (a person). Usually *pass.* (*Sc.* and *U.S.*)

1686 [see DIFFICULTING below]. **1713** WODROW *Corr.* (1843) I. 464, I would be difficulted to read the King of France 'the most Christian king' to my people. **1718** *Ibid.* II. 410 How far the alterations..may straiten and difficult some ministers who have formerly sworn the oath. **1782** J. BROWN *Address to Students* (1858) 62 If you be difficulted how to act. **1813** J. BALLANTYNE in Lockhart *Ballantyne-humbug Handled* (1839) 29 This business has always been.. difficulted by all its capital..being lent the printing-office. **1845** BUSH *Resurrection* 51 (Bartlett) We are not difficulted at all on the score of the relation which the new plant bears to the old. **1861** W. E. AYTOUN *N. Sinclair* I. 155 The poor lads might be difficulted to find meal for their porridge.

Hence '**difficulting** *vbl. sb.* and *ppl. a.*

a **1608** SIR F. VERE *Comm.* 119 Lest..[this] might give the enemy an alarm, to the difficulting of the enterprise. **1686** RENWICK *Serm.* xviii. (1776) 212 There is not a case that can put Him to a non-plus or difficulting extremity.

† '**difficultate**, *v. Obs. rare.* [f. ppl. stem of med.L. *difficult-āre* to render difficult, f. *difficult-ās* difficulty.] *trans.* To make difficult: = prec. 1.

1611 COTGR., *Difficulter*, to difficultate or difficilitate. **1829** SOUTHEY *Lett.* (1856) IV. 161 The circumstances which facilitated or difficultated (if I may make such a word for the nonce) the introduction of Christianity.

difficultly ('dɪfɪkəltlɪ), *adv.* [f. DIFFICULT *a.* + -LY[2]. Formerly very frequent in literary use; now rather avoided, and in speech rarely used; in sense 1, 'with difficulty' is usually substituted.]

1. In a difficult manner, not easily, hardly; with difficulty.

1558 in Strype *Ann. Ref.* I. App. iv. 4 Ireland..will be very difficultly stayed in their obedience. **1624** SCOTT *Vox Coeli* 6 Our posterity will difficultly beleeue it. **1646** S. BOLTON *Arraignm. Err.* 47 Castles, and forts, and strong holds, they are hardly conquered, difficultly overcome. **1654** H. L'ESTRANGE *Chas. I* (1655) 1 He..was none of the gracefullest of Orators, for his words came difficultly from him. *a* **1677** BARROW *Serm.* Wks. 1716 I. 5 A possession of trifles..difficultly acquired and easily lost. **1685** BOYLE *Effects of Mot.* vi. 66 The Mountain Carpathus..said to be much more steep and difficultly accessible than any of the Alps. **1718** PRIDEAUX *Connect. O. & N.T.* II. iv. 219 Gorgias difficultly escaping fled to Marisa. **1784** J. KEIR *Dict. Chem.* 97 The vapours..are very elastic, and difficultly condensable. *a* **1843** SOUTHEY *Doctor* ccxxi. (1862) 594 Diseases..difficultly distinguishable by their symptoms. **1875** RUSKIN *Fors Clavig.* V. 37 No. 50 The difficultly reconcileable merits of old times and new things. **1879** RUTLEY *Study Rocks* x. 87 Labradorite fuses readily.. anorthite is more difficultly fusible.

b. In a way hard to understand; obscurely.

1581 PETTIE *Guazzo's Civ. Conv.* II. (1586) 62 It is a thing as blame worthie to speake dissolutelie, as to speake difficultlie. **1875** A. J. SWINBOURNE *Picture Logic* ix. 58 Things seem to me to be put so difficultly in books.

c. To a difficult degree; so as to be difficult of access, passage, etc.

1872 C. KING *Mountain. Sierra Nev.* iv. 88 We found the ice-angle difficultly steep; but made our way successfully along its edge.

d. In a difficult position; in a condition of embarrassment. (Cf. DIFFICULTY 2 c.)

1886 P. O. HUTCHINSON *Diary T. Hutchinson* II. 430 These unfortunate people were very difficultly placed.

†**2.** Unwillingly, reluctantly. *Obs.*

1551 ROBINSON tr. *More's Utop.* II. (Arb.) 99, I knowe howe difficultlie and hardelye I meselfe would haue beleued. **1614** LODGE *Seneca* 2 Hath..either..denied, or promised but difficultly..with strained and reproachful words. **1677** OTWAY *Cheats of Scapin* II. i, How easily a miser swallows a load, and how difficultly he disgorges a grain.

'**difficultness.** *rare.* [f. as prec. + -NESS.] The quality of being difficult; difficulty.

1560 P. WHITEHORNE tr. *Macchiavelli's Arte of Warre* (1573) 70 b Such difficultnesse is necessarie. **1580** FRAMPTON *Dial. Yron & Steele* 170 It toke away the difficultnesse of the swallowing downe. **1644** DIGBY *Two Treatises* (1645) II. 77 The difficultnesse of this subject.. would not allow us that liberty. **1934** C. S. FORESTER *Peacemaker* 19 He was experienced now in Mary's 'difficultness'. **1947** *Trans. Philol. Soc. 1946* 195 The growth in more serious shape of that difficultness—at times almost suggestive of nascent 'persecution-mania'—which prevented any happy relationships with almost all of his academic colleagues.

difficulty ('dɪfɪkəltɪ). Also 4–6 dyff-, -te, 5–6 -tee, -tye, 6–7 -tie. [ad. L. *difficultās, -tātem* (f. *dif-*, DIS- + *facultas* FACULTY), perh. immed. through OF. or AF. *difficulté*.

In OF. the word is as yet recorded only of 15th c.; it may have been in earlier use in Anglo-Fr.; but the English word, which was common before 1400, may have been formed directly from L., on the type of the many existing words in *-té* corresponding to L. words in *-tas*, e.g. *povreté, pureté*.]

1. The quality, fact, or condition of being difficult; the character of an action that requires labour or effort; hardness to be accomplished; the opposite of *ease* or *facility*.

1382 WYCLIF *Num.* xx. 19 No difficulte shal be in the prijs. **1398** TREVISA *Barth De P.R.* XII. ii. (1495) 409 Yf..the Egle hath thre byrdes, she throwyth oute one of her neste for dyffyculte of fedyng. *c* **1450** *St. Cuthbert* (Surtees) 7969 His sonn with grete difficulte Gart his fader monke to be. **1513** MORE in Grafton *Chron.* (1568) II. 786 He speedily without any difficultie..brought the matter to a good conclusion.

1667 MILTON *P.L.* II. 449 If aught..in the shape Of difficulty or danger could deterre Me. **1719** DE FOE *Crusoe* (1840) I. viii. 139, I had no great difficulty to cut it down. **1759** ROBERTSON *Hist. Scot.* I. II. 134 Nor was this reconcilement a matter of difficulty. **1770** *Junius Lett.* xli. 208, I have been deterred by the difficulty of the task. **1797** MRS. RADCLIFFE *Italian* i, She walked with difficulty. **1860** TYNDALL *Glac.* II. x. 283 The difficulty of thus directing a chain over crevasses and ridges. **1875** JOWETT *Plato* (ed. 2) I. 261 Socrates has no difficulty in showing that virtue is a good.

b. Said of the object of an action (the nature of which is contextually implied: cf. DIFFICULT *a.* 1 b).

1747 *Col. Rec. Pennsylv.* V. 103 The Length and Difficulty of the Bay. *Mod.* The steepness and difficulty of the direct path. A route of considerable difficulty.

c. The quality of being hard to understand; perplexing character, obscurity.

1529 MORE *Supplic. Soulys* Wks. 321/1 Because that of the difficultie of his [St. Paul's] writing thei catch some-time some matter of contencion. **1644** MILTON *Educ.* Wks. (1847) 100/1 If the language be difficult..it is not a difficulty above their years. **1860** FARRAR *Orig. Lang.* i. 21 The difficulty and obscurity of the phrase.

2. with *a* and *pl.* A particular instance of this quality; that which is difficult. **a.** A thing hard to do or overcome; a hindrance to action.

a **1619** DANIEL *Funeral Poem* (R.), Nor how by mastering difficulties so..He bravely came to disappoint his foe. *a* **1716** SOUTH (J.), They mistake difficulties for impossibilities. **1775** BURKE *Corr.* (1844) II. 53, I see, indeed, many, many difficulties in the way. **1856** FROUDE *Hist. Eng.* (1858) I. ii. 130 As difficulties gathered round him, he encountered them with the increasing magnificence of his schemes. **1880** GEIKIE *Phys. Geog.* iv. 232 A difficulty may sometimes be felt in understanding how [etc.]. **1893** *Westm. Gaz.* 13 Feb. 1/2 To parade difficulties is the delight of the pedant; to grapple with them is the task of the statesman. *Mod.* The children, I admit, are a difficulty.

b. Something hard to understand; a perplexing or obscure point or question.

c **1385** CHAUCER *Friar's T.* Prol. 8 Ye han her touchid..In scole matier gret difficulte. *a* **1500** *Chester Pl.* (1892) 118 Discussing this difficulty. **1577** tr. *Bullinger's Decades* (1592) 29 There is no cause for anye man by reason of a few difficulties, to dispaire to attaine to the true vnder-standinge of the Scriptures. **1692** R. L'ESTRANGE *Fables* No. 494 (1708) I. 540 When People have been Beating their Brains about a Difficulty, and find they can make Nothing on't. **1770** BEATTIE *Ess. Truth* II. i. §1 (R.), Let us see, then, whether..we can make any discovery preparatory to the solution of this difficulty. *a* **1843** J. H. NEWMAN *Par. Serm.*, *Chr. Myst.* (1868) I. 211 Difficulties in revelation are especially given to prove the reality of our faith.

c. An embarrassement of affairs; a condition in which action, co-operation, or progress is difficult; a trouble; often *spec.* a pecuniary embarrassment. (Usually in *pl.*)

1705 ADDISON *Italy* (J.), They lie under some difficulties, by reason of the emperour's displeasure, who has forbidden their manufactures. *a* **1715** BURNET *Own Times* I. 346 The king was under no difficulties by anything they had done. **1831** FR. A. KEMBLE *Jrnl.* in *Rec. Girlhood* (1878) III. 68 Mr Brunton..is in 'difficulties' (civilized plural for debt). **1861** SMILES *Engineers* II. 142 A serious difficulty occurred between him and his wife on this very point, which ended in a separation. **1885** *Law Times* LXXIX. 173/2 In Dec. 1867 the company fell into difficulties. **1886** *Tip Cat* xix. 254 Come to me if you..are in any difficulty or trouble.

3. Reluctance, unwillingness (see DIFFICULT *a.* 2 b); demur, objection. *Obs.* exc. in phr. ***to make a difficulty*** or ***difficulties***, now associated with 2 a; formerly † ***to make difficulty***, i.e. to show reluctance.

1513 MORE in Grafton *Chron.* (1568) II. 795 The Protector made great difficultie to come to them. **1548** HALL *Chron., Hen. V*, 70 b, To obeye us without opposicion, contradiccion or difficultee. *a* **1608** SIR F. VERE *Comm.* 119 Her Majesty..with some difficulty (as her manner was) granted the men to be levied. **1687** T. SMITH in *Madg. Coll.* (Oxf. Hist. Soc.) 18 Hee making severall difficultyes. **1769** ROBERTSON *Chas. V.* II. VI. 95 This she granted with some difficulty. **1769** GOLDSMITH *Rom. Hist.* (1786) II. 355 Apollonius..made no difficulty of coming from Greece to Rome. **1873** TRISTRAM *Moab* xiii. 239 They..never made any difficulties or demands.

diffidation (dɪfɪˈdeɪʃən). *Hist. Instit.* [ad. med.L. *diffīdātiōn-em* (Du Cange), n. of action from med.L. *diffīdāre* to distrust, f. *dif-*, DIS- + **-fīdāre* to trust, keep faith: see DEFY *v.*[1]] The undoing of relations of faith, allegiance, or amity; declaration of hostilities; = DEFIANCE 1.

1731 CHANDLER tr. *Limborch's Hist. Inquis.* II. 24 Diffidation declares Hereticks to be enemies of their Country and the Empire..When any one is declared an Heretick by the Sentence of the Judge, any Man..may seize, plunder, and kill him. **1807** COXE *Hist. Ho. Austria* (Bohn) I. xxx. 454 They sent a..letter of diffidation, in which they renounced their allegiance. **1818** HALLAM *Mid. Ages* (1872) II. 58 The ceremony of diffidation, or solemn defiance of an enemy. **1845** S. AUSTIN *Ranke's Hist. Ref.* I. 81, The evils attendant on the right of diffidation or private warfare (*Fehderecht*). **1857** SIR F. PALGRAVE *Norm. & Eng.* II. i. 27 According to modern principles, the Subject's allegiance is indefeasible..but the primeval legislation of the Teutons permitted to the vassal..the right of diffidation—he might undo his faith.

diffide (dɪˈfaɪd), *v.* Now *rare.* [f. L. *diffīdĕre* to distrust, be distrustful, f. *dif-*, DIS- + *fīdĕre* to trust. Cf. DEFY *v.*[1] sense 7.] *intr.* To want faith or confidence; to have or feel distrust; *to diffide in* (†*of*), to distrust. (The opposite of *confide*.)

1532 BONNER *Let.* in Burnet *Hist. Ref.* II. 180, I diffided in the justness of the matter. *c* **1565** LINDESAY (Pitscottie) *Chron. Scot.* (1728) 55 Never diffiding of good fortune. **1606** J. HYND *Eliosto Libidinoso* 30, I..wish thee not to diffide. **1624** FISHER in F. White *Repl. Fisher* 115 Not to seeme to diffide..of your Maiesties iudgement. **1697** DRYDEN *Æneid* XI. 636 If in your arms thus early you diffide. *a* **1806** C. J. FOX *Reign James II.* (1808) 32 With regard to facts remote ..wise men generally diffide in their own judgment. **1829** J. DONOVAN *Catech. Council of Trent* (1855) 517 And diffiding entirely in ourselves, we shall seek refuge..in the mercy of God. **1845** R. W. HAMILTON *Pop. Educ.* i. 7 We speak not now of certain affirmed calculations. We diffide in them.

†**b.** with *clause. Obs.*

1647 H. MORE *Cupid's Conflict* lxxvii, To..diffide Whether our reasons eye be clear enough. *a* **1713** ELLWOOD *Autobiog.* (1885) 257 Which of us can now diffide That God will us defend?

†**c.** *trans.* To distrust, doubt. *Obs.*

1678 R. BARCLAY *Apol. Quakers* ii. §14. 62 So would I not have any reject or diffide the Certainty of that Unerring Spirit. **1678** CUDWORTH *Intell. Syst.* 779 Alwaies fluctuating about them [Incorporeals] and diffiding them. **1686** HORNECK *Crucif. Jesus* xxii. 658 How basely hast thou diffided this providence!

Hence **diˈffiding** *vbl. sb.*, distrusting.

1657 G. STARKEY *Helmont's Vind.* 149 It is a great diffiding in God's mercy.

†**diffiˈdelity.** *Obs. rare*$^{-1}$. [f. *dif-*, DIS- + FIDELITY, after *infidelity*.] Disbelief, unbelief.

1659 FULLER *App. Inj. Innoc.* I. 61 Parcel-Diffidelity in matters of such nature, I am sure is no sin.

diffidence (ˈdɪfɪdəns). [ad. L. *diffīdentia* want of confidence, mistrust, distrust, f. *diffīdent-em*, pr. pple. of *diffīd-ĕre* to distrust: see DIFFIDE and -ENCE. Cf. obs. F. *diffidence*, *-ance*, 16–17th c. in Godef.] (The opposite of CONFIDENCE *sb.*)

1. Want of confidence or faith; mistrust, distrust, misgiving, doubt. Now *rare* or *Obs.*

1526 *Pilgr. Perf.* (W. de W. 1531) 94 Bycause we put diffedence or mistrust in God. **1548** HALL *Chron., Edw. IV*, 208 b, King Edward beyng..in diffidence of reysyng any army..departed. **1595** SHAKS. *John* I. i. 65 Thou dost shame thy mother, And wound her honor with this diffidence. **1614** BP. HALL *Recoll. Treat.* 684 Away with these weake diffidences. **1614** T. JACKSON *Comment. Creede* II. 251 Distrust or diffidence to God's promises. **1641** J. SHUTE *Sarah & Hagar* (1649) 33 Diffidence in the promise of God. **1649** MILTON *Eikon.* xii. (1851) 436 Hee had brought the Parlament into so just a diffidence of him, as that they durst not leave the Public Armes at his disposal. **1712** POPE *Let. to Steele* 15 July, Sickness..teaches us a diffidence in our earthly state. **1741** RICHARDSON *Pamela* (1742) IV. 271 Since that Time, I have always had some Diffidences about her. **1818** JAS. MILL *Brit. India* II. v. v. 549 A diffidence.. of his judgment or his virtue. **1823** LINGARD *Hist. Eng.* VI. 65 His former refusal..proceeded..from diffidence in the sincerity of his ally. **1838** EMERSON *Addr., Lit. Ethics* Wks. (Bohn) II. 206 The diffidence of mankind in the soul has crept over the American mind.

2. Distrust of oneself; want of confidence in one's own ability, worth, or fitness; modesty, shyness of disposition.

[**1651** HOBBES *Leviath.* I. vi. 25 Constant Despayre, Diffidence of our selves. *a* **1683** SIDNEY *Disc. Govt.* iii. §40 (1704) 394 Every one ought to enter into a just diffidence of himself.] **1709** POPE *Ess. Crit.* 567 Speak, tho' sure, with seeming diffidence. **1798** FERRIAR *Illustr. Sterne* i. 12 The diffidence of Erasmus prevented him from assuming that title. **1841** MACAULAY *Ess., W. Hastings* (1854) 646/1 With great diffidence, we give it as our opinion. **1862** TROLLOPE *Orley F.* xxxii. (ed. 4) 229 She had aid aside whatever diffidence may have afflicted her earlier years, and now was able to speak out her mind.

†**ˈdiffidency.** *Obs.* [f. as prec.: see -ENCY.] = DIFFIDENCE; distrust, mistrust.

1604 EDMONDS *Observ. Cæsar's Comm.* 6 So doth diffidencie wait vpon indirect and perfidious designements. **1676** WYCHERLEY *Pl. Dealer* I. i, He has the courage of men in despair, yet the diffidency and caution of Cowards. **1694** F. BRAGGE *Disc. Parables* xiii. 450 He..prays with great diffidency, and distrust of prevailing. **1748** RICHARDSON *Clarissa* (1811) III. i. 3 All diffidencies, like night-fogs before the sun, disperse at her approach.

diffident (ˈdɪfɪdənt), *a.* [ad. L. *diffīdent-em*, pr. pple. of *diffīdĕre* to mistrust; see DIFFIDE, and -ENT. (The opposite of CONFIDENT.)]

1. Wanting confidence or trust (*in*); distrustful, mistrustful (*of*).

1598 FLORIO, *Diffidénte*, mistrustful, diffident. *a* **1618** RALEIGH *Mohomet* (1637) 207 In the constancie of his people he was somewhat diffident. *a* **1631** DONNE *Serm.* xii. 114 A fainting and a diffident Spirit. **1667** MILTON *P.L.* VIII. 562 Be not diffident Of Wisdom, she deserts thee not, if thou Dismiss her not, when most thou needst her nigh. **1691** RAY *Creation* I. (1704) 159, I am somewhat diffident of the truth of those Stories. **1734** WATTS *Reliq. Juv.* (1789) 131 A feeble man and diffident had need to pray daily, Lord, lead us not into temptation. **1802** H. MARTIN *Helen of Glenross* III. 330 Had I been more diffident in its effects, I had not trusted.. to it. **1873** SYMONDS *Grk. Poets* v. 141 The English are not musicians, and are diffident in general of the artist class.

2. Wanting in self-confidence; distrustful of oneself; not confident in disposition; timid, shy, modest, bashful. (The usual current sense.)

[**1648** *Eikon Bas.* xi. (1824) 88, I am not so diffident of My selfe, as brutishly to submit to any men's dictates.] **1713** ADDISON *Cato* II. i, Let us appear nor rash nor diffident. **1785** MAD. D'ARBLAY *Lett.* 3 Jan., He [Dr. Johnson] never attacked the unassuming, nor meant to terrify the diffident. **1835** W. IRVING *Newstead Abbey* Crayon Misc. (1863) 362 She was shy and diffident. **1882** B. M. CROKER *Proper Pride* I. ii. 42 She little knew that the apparently diffident young man was the life and soul of his mess.

diffidently (ˈdɪfɪdəntlɪ), *adv.* [f. prec. + -LY[2].] In a diffident manner, with distrust or self-distrust.

?**1613** *State Trials, C'tess of Essex* (1816) II. 831 He found it to be uncertainly and diffidently set down. **1730–6** BAILEY (folio), *Diffidently*, distrustfully, suspiciously. **1741** RICHARDSON *Pamela* (1742) III. 169, I looked, I suppose, a little diffidently. **1856** EMERSON *Eng. Traits, Manners* Wks. (Bohn) II. 46 Don't creep about diffidently; make up your mind.

†**ˈdiffidentness.** *Obs. rare*$^{-0}$. [f. as prec. + -NESS.] = DIFFIDENCE.

1727 in BAILEY vol. II. **1775** in ASH.

diffie, obs. form of DEFY.

†**diˈffind,** *v. Obs. rare*$^{-0}$. [ad. L. *diffind-ĕre* to cleave asunder, f. *dif-*, DIS- + *findĕre* to cleave.]

1727 BAILEY vol. II, To *Diffind*, to cut or cleave asunder. **1775** in ASH.

diffine, -ition, etc., obs. ff. DEFINE, etc.

†**diffinish, -isse,** *v. Obs.*: see DEFINISH.

†**diˈffission.** *Obs. rare*$^{-0}$. [ad. L. *diffissiōn-em*, n. of action f. *diffindĕre* to cleave asunder.]

1727 BAILEY vol. II, *Diffission*, a cleaving asunder.

†**diˈffixed,** *pa. pple. Obs. rare*$^{-0}$. [f. *dif-*, DIS- + L. *fixus*, FIXED.]

1727 BAILEY vol. II, *Diffixed*, loosened, unfastened.

†**diˈfflate,** *v. Obs.* [f. L. *difflāt-* ppl. stem of *difflāre* to blow apart, disperse by blowing, f. *dif-*, DIS- + *flāre* to blow.] *trans.* To blow apart or away.

1620 VENNER *Via Recta* (1650) 311 Thereby..vaporous and rheumatick superfluities are discussed and difflated.

†**diˈfflation.** *Obs.* [n. of action f. L. *difflāre*, *difflāt-*: see prec. Cf. obs. F. *difflation* Cotgr.] Blowing asunder, or dispersing by blowing.

1568 SKEYNE *The Pest* (1860) 18 Purgation is perfitit..be ..fasting, and difflatioun. **1574** NEWTON *Health Mag.* 76 Convenient refrigeration and difflation of vapoures. **1620** VENNER *Via Recta* (1650) 301 Hindering the difflation and dissipation of vaporous fumes.

b. In early Chemistry: see quot. 1706.

1662 J. CHANDLER *Van Helmont's Oriat.* 247 A substance scarce capable of diflation or blowing away. **1706** PHILLIPS (ed. Kersey) *Difflation*..a Term us'd by some Chymists, when Spirits raised by heat, are blown with a kind of Bellows, into the opposite Camera or Arch of the Furnace, and there found congealed. **1763** W. LEWIS *Commerc. Phil. Techn.* 211 Difflation of the antimonial metal.

diffloryssh, var. of DEFLOURISH *v. Obs.*

diffluan (ˈdɪfluːæn). *Chem.* Also **difluan.** [mod. f. L. *difflu-ĕre* to flow away, dissolve + -AN I. 2.] A chemical compound, obtained, as a loose white very soluble powder of bitter saline taste, by the action of heat on a solution of alloxanic acid.

1847 *Turner's Elem. Chem.* (ed. 8) 787 *Difluan*, this compound is found in the liquid which has deposited the leucoturic acid. **1863–72** WATTS *Dict. Chem.* I. 138 s.v. *Alloxanic Acid*, An aqueous solution of alloxanic acid is decomposed by boiling, carbonic anhydride being abundantly evolved, and two new bodies formed, one of which..diffluan, remains in solution, but may be precipitated by alcohol. *Ibid.* II. 322 Diffluan.

diffluence (ˈdɪfluːəns). [f. DIFFLUENT, or its L. source: see -ENCE. Cf. mod.F. *diffluence*.]

1. The action or fact of flowing apart or abroad; dispersion by flowing. Also *fig.*

1633 FLETCHER *Purple Isl.* VIII. xvi, Their violence 'Fore danger spent with lavish diffluence, Was none, or weak in time of greatest exigence. **1656** BLOUNT *Glossogr.*, *Diffluence*, a looseness, a flowing forth or abroad. **1816** G. S. FABER *Orig. Pagan Idol.* I. 292 Such a confluence and diffluence make, he supposes, the four heads mentioned by Moses. **1853** READE *Chr. Johnstone* x. 128 The loose, lawless diffluence of motion that goes by that name [dancing].

2. Dissolution into a liquid state; deliquescence; *spec.* in *Biol.* the peculiar mode of dissolution or disintegration of Infusoria, called by Dujardin 'molecular effusion'.

1847–9 TODD *Cycl. Anat.* IV. 712/1 Softening may vary from simple flabbiness to a state approaching diffluence. **1861** J. R. GREENE *Man. Anim. Kingd., Cœlent.* 52 Such amœboid particles occasionally become detached by the method denominated 'diffluence'.

†**ˈdiffluency.** *Obs. rare*$^{-1}$. [f. as prec.: see -ENCY.] Diffluent condition; quality of flowing out in all directions, fluidity.

1646 SIR T. BROWNE *Pseud. Ep.* II. i. 50 Ice is only water congealed by the frigidity of the ayre, whereby it acquireth no new forme, but rather a consistence, or determination of its diffluency.

diffluent (ˈdɪfluːənt), *a.* [ad. L. *diffluent-em*, pr. pple. of *difflu-ĕre* to flow apart or away, f. *dif-*, DIS- 1 + *fluĕre* to flow. Cf. mod.F. *diffluent*.]

Characterized by flowing apart or abroad; fluid; deliquescent. Also *fig.*

a **1618** SYLVESTER *Tobacco Battered* 626 Yet over-moist [Brain], againe Makes it [Memory] so laxe, so diffluent and thin, That nothing can be firmly fixt there-in. **1642** ANNE BRADSTREET *Poems* (1678) 33 What's diffluent I do consolidate. **1647** TRAPP *Comm. Luke* xvii. 8 A loose, discinct, and diffluent mind is unfit to serve God. **1811** W. TAYLOR in *Monthly Rev.* LXV. 228 Speech is confluent, rather than diffluent. **1851-9** OWEN in *Man. Sc. Enq.* 365 Their soft organic substance is commonly diffluent. **1880** GRAY in *Nat. Sc. & Relig.* 14 A formless, apparently diffluent and structureless mass.

† **'diffluous,** *a. Obs. rare*$^{-0}$. [f. L. *difflu-us* flowing asunder, overflowing (f. *difflu-ĕre*: see DIFFLUENT) + -OUS.] = DIFFLUENT.

1727 BAILEY vol. II, *Diffluous*, flowing forth, abroad or several Ways.

† **di'ffluxive,** *a. Obs. rare*$^{-1}$. [f. L. *difflux-* ppl. stem of *difflŭere* (see DIFFLUENT) + -IVE.] That flows in different or all directions.

1653 H. MORE *Antid. Ath.* III. ix. (1712) 166 What the Wind, join'd with no statick power but loose and diffluxive, can do in shaking houses.

† **di'ffode,** *v. Obs. rare.* [ad. med.L. *diffod-ĕre* (Joannes de Janua *Cathol.*) to dig out, f. L. *dif-*, DIS- 1 + *fodĕre* to dig. (Thence OF. *desfouir*, *défouir* to dig out.)] *trans.* To dig out, excavate.

1657 TOMLINSON *Renou's Disp.* 91 When a ditch is diffoded in the earth. **1657** *Physical Dict.*, *Diffoded*, digged, as a hole or ditch is digged in the earth.

† **difform** (dɪ'fɔːm), *a. Obs.* Also 6 **dyfforme.** [ad. med. or mod.L. *difform-is* dissimilar in form, f. *dif-*, DIS- 4) + *forma* shape.]

1. Of diverse forms; differing in form.

1547 RECORDE *Judic. Ur.* 14 b, The dyfforme facyon of the urinall. **1548** —— *Urin. Physick* ix. (1651) 68 Other difform contents there be also. **1660** BOYLE *New Exp. Phys. Mech.* xxxvi. 300 The dif-form consistence . . of the Air at several distances from us. **1672** NEWTON in *Phil. Trans.* VII. 5087 A confused Mixture of difform qualities. **1677** GALE *Crt. Gentiles* IV. 38 The pleasures of the multitude are difforme and repugnant to each other.

2. Without symmetry or regularity of parts; not uniform; of irregular form.

1644 DIGBY *Nat. Bodies* I. xvii. (1658) 193 What a difform net with a strange variety of mashes wou'd this be? **1693** *Phil. Trans.* XVII. 929 A difform or Papilionaceous Flower. **1707** S. CLARKE *3rd & 4th Defence* (1712) 7 If the Parts be dissimilar, then the Substance is difform or Heterogeneous. **1845** *Whitehall* iv. 19 A huge difform mass of steel and adamant.

† **difform,** *v. Obs. rare.* Also 5 **defourme.** [a. OF. *differmer* (16th c. in Godef.), or ad. med.L. *difformāre*, f. med.L. *difformis*: see prec.] *trans.* To bring out of conformity or agreement: the opposite of CONFORM *v.* 2.

c **1380** WYCLIF *Serm.* Sel. Wks. II. 150 Hereinne shulde ech man sue Crist . . and ȝif he be contrarie herto, he synneþ, difformed [*v.r.* defourmyd] fro Cristis wille.

difform(e, -ourme, etc., obs. ff. DEFORM, etc.

† **di'fformed,** *ppl. a. Obs. rare.* [f. as DIFFORM *a.* + -ED.] Diversely or irregularly shaped.

1665 WEBB *Stone-Heng* (1725) 145 Tumuli were . . set about . . with petty and difformed Blocks of broken Craggs.

† **difformity** (dɪ'fɔːmɪtɪ). *Obs.* [a. F. *difformité* (1520 in Hatz.-Darm.), ad. med.L. *difformitās*, f. *difformis* differing in form: see DIFFORM *a.*]

1. Difference or diversity of form; want of uniformity between things.

1530 PALSGR. *Introd.* 18 To avoyde all maner difformyte. **1580** HOLLYBAND *Treas. Fr. Tong*, *Absurdité*, difformitie, vnlikenesse. *c* **1630** JACKSON *Creed* IV. II. v. Wks. III. 273 This difformity was most apparent in their works . . for destitute of all good works most of them were not, but only of uniformity in working. **1646** JER. TAYLOR *Extemp. Prayer* (T.), There must [thus] needs be infinite difformity in the publick worship. **1748** HARTLEY *Observ. Man* I. i. 17 The Difformity of Texture. **1857** WEBB *Intellectualism Locke* vii. 126 Locke . . resolves all knowledge into a perception of the 'conformity' or 'difformity' of Ideas.

2. Divergence in form *from*, want of conformity *with* or *to* (a standard).

1565 T. STAPLETON *Fortr. Faith* 138 b (T.), In respect of uniformity with the primitive church, as of difformity. **1640** P. DU MOULIN *Lett. Fr. Prot. to Scotchm. Covt.* 4 Among all the reformed Churches . . there is neither deformity nor difformity in that point. **1641** MAISTERTON *Serm.* 7 To judge of their conformity or difformity thereunto. **1646** SIR T. BROWNE *Pseud. Ep.* I. xi. 48 They . . doe tacitely desire in them a difformitie from the primitive rule. **1677** GALE *Crt. Gentiles* IV. 45 In their conformitie to . . or difformitie from . . the perfect measure of morals.

† **di'fformness.** *Obs. rare.* [f. DIFFORM *a.* + -NESS.] = prec.

1548 RECORDE *Urin. Physick* xi. 70/1 The difformenes [ed. **1651** difforments] and disagreing of the partes of it together.

difforse, obs. f. DEFORCE *v.* (sense 4).

c **1375** *Sc. Leg. Saints, Theodera* 569 Theodorus . . Our childe difforsit & it [þe barne] gat.

diffoule, diffowl, var. DEFOUL *Obs.*

diffound, obs. form of DIFFUND.

di'ffract, *a. Bot.* [ad. L. *diffract-us* broken in pieces: see next.] Of lichens: 'Broken into *areolæ* with distinct interspaces.' *Syd. Soc. Lex.* 1883.

diffract (dɪ'frækt), *v.* [f. L. *diffract-*, ppl. stem of *diffring-ĕre* to break in pieces, shatter, f. *dif-*, DIS- 1 + *frangĕre* to break.] *trans.* To break in pieces, break up; in *Optics*, To deflect and break up (a beam of light) at the edge of an opaque body or through a narrow aperture or slit; to affect with DIFFRACTION. Also *fig.*

1803 YOUNG in *Phil. Trans.* XCIV. 2 These fringes were the joint effects of the portions of light passing on each side of the slip of card, and inflected, or rather diffracted, into the shadow. **1839** CARLYLE *Chartism* i. (1858) 7 It is . . for some obscure distorted image of right that he contends; an obscure image diffracted, exaggerated, in the wonderfullest way.

Hence **di'ffracted, di'ffracting** *ppl. adjs.*

1849 H. ROGERS *Ess.* (1860) III. 222 The diffracted appearance of various parts. **1873** TYNDALL *Lect. Light* ii. 92 The diffracting particles were becoming smaller. **1876** J. MARTINEAU *Hours Th.* (1877) 292 The devout [mind] ascends beyond all diffracted or intercepted rays to the primal light that flings them.

diffraction (dɪ'frækʃən). [ad. mod.L. *diffractiōn-em* (Grimaldi 1665), n. of action from *diffringĕre*: see prec. So F. *diffraction* 1666 in Hatz.-Darm.]

1. *Optics.* The breaking up of a beam of light (in the case of monochromatic light) into a series of light and dark spaces or bands, or (in that of white or other composite light) of coloured spectra, due to interference of the rays when deflected from their straight course at the edge of an opaque body or through a narrow aperture or slit.

(These phenomena were formerly denoted by the name INFLEXION; cf. also DEFLEXION 5.)

1671 *Phil. Trans.* VI. 3068 Light is propagated . . also by diffraction . . when the parts of Light, separated by a manifold dissection, do in the same medium proceed in different ways. **1803** YOUNG *Ibid.* XCIV. 13 The observations on the effects of diffraction and interference. **1830** HERSCHEL *Stud. Nat. Phil.* III. ii. (1838) 252 The diffraction or inflection of light, discovered by Grimaldi, a Jesuit of Bologna. **1855** H. SPENCER *Princ. Psych.* (1872) II. VI. xi. 138 Only on the theory of undulations can . . diffraction be accounted for. **1860** TYNDALL *Glac.* I. xxii. 154 All the hues produced by diffraction were exhibited in the utmost splendour. **1878** J. D. STEELE *Physics* 126 If we hold a small needle close to one eye and look toward the sun we see several needles. This is caused by diffraction.

b. *Acoustics.* An analogous phenomenon occurring in the case of sound-waves passing round the corner of a large body, as a house.

2. In etymol. sense: Breaking in pieces, breakage. *nonce-use.*

1825 COLERIDGE *Aids Refl.* (1848) I. 286 There being . . no facts in proof of the contrary, that would not prove equally well the cessation of the eye on the removal or diffraction of the eye-glass.

3. *attrib.* (in sense 1), as ***diffraction band, fringe, spectrum***, etc.; **diffraction grating**, a plate of glass or polished metal ruled with very close equidistant parallel lines, producing a spectrum by diffraction of the transmitted or reflected light.

1863-72 WATTS *Dict. Chem.* III. 608 Barton's buttons, which are metallic buttons having very fine lines engraved on their surfaces . . exhibit magnificent diffraction spectra. **1867** G. F. CHAMBERS *Astron.* x. iii. (1877) 847 A diffraction grating. **1868** LOCKYER *Guillemin's Heavens* (ed. 3) 496 Observing the image of a large star out of focus. If . . the diffraction rings are not circular, the screws of the cell should be carefully loosened [etc.] **1873** TYNDALL *Lect. Light* ii. 91 The street-lamps . . looked at through the meshes of a handkerchief, show diffraction phenomena. **1890** C. A. YOUNG *Elem. Astron.* vi. §193 The essential part of the apparatus [spectroscope] is either a prism or train of prisms, or else a diffraction 'grating'.

diffractive (dɪ'fræktɪv), *a.* [f. L. *diffract-* ppl. stem (see DIFFRACT *v.*) + -IVE. In mod.F. *diffractif, -ive.*] Tending to diffract.

1829 CARLYLE *Misc.*, *Voltaire* (1872) II. 120 Through whatever dim, besmoked and strangely diffractive media it may shine.

Hence **di'ffractively** *adv.*, in a diffractive manner; by diffraction.

1883 W. B. CARPENTER in *Encycl. Brit.* XVI. 268/2 s.v. *Microscope*, A marked distinction between . . objectives of low or moderate power . . worked dioptrically, and those of high power . . worked diffractively.

diffractometer (dɪfræk'tɒmɪtə(r)). [f. DIFFRACT *v.* + -O + -METER.] An instrument for measuring diffraction; esp. an instrument used in diffraction analysis in Crystallography.

1909 in WEBSTER. **1926** *Proc. R. Soc.* B. XCIX. 275 Certain size changes of erythrocytes have been followed under the 'diffractometer'. **1954** *Philips Techn. Rev.* XVI. 123 The new instrument, which from now on will be termed an X-ray diffractometer . . comprises . . a basic diffraction unit . . a Geiger counter goniometer, and an electronic circuit panel with automatic recorder. **1955** *Gloss. Terms Radiol.* (*B.S.I.*) 29 *Neutron diffractometer*, an instrument . . for measuring with a neutron beam . . the intensities of the diffracted beams at different levels. **1960** *Times Rev. Industry* May 31/1 Crystal structure can be examined by means of a diffractometer. **1961** *Engineering* 15 Sept. 333 Our instrument, known as the linear X-ray diffractometer, incorporates an analogue computer, which computes the crystal and detector settings for each of the many thousands of X-ray reflections that have to be measured for a complete determination of atomic structure. **1970** *New Scientist* 21 May 383/1 A new type of neutron diffractometer—the 'hedgehog' neutron diffraction spectrometer—has been developed.

diffractometry (dɪfræk'tɒmɪtrɪ). [f. prec.: see -METRY.] The measurement of diffraction; the use of a diffractometer.

1956 *Jrnl. Applied Physics* XXVII. 1215 (*heading*) Comparison of X-ray wavelengths for powder diffractometry. **1965** W. PARRISH *X-ray Analysis Papers* p. vii, Specialized topics such as . . automatic single crystal diffractometry.

[**diffranchise, -ment.** Errors for DISFRANCHISE, -MENT, due to reading ſ as f.

1755 JOHNSON. (No quotation.) **1828-32** WEBSTER, *Diffranchise*, *Diffranchisement*: see *Disfranchise*, which is the word in use. Hence in **1864** WEBSTER, and some later Dicts.]

diffrangible (dɪ'frændʒɪb(ə)l), *a. rare*$^{-0}$. [f. L. *diffring-ĕre*, changed to *diffrang-ĕre* + -BLE.] Capable of being diffracted. Hence **diffrangi'bility**, capacity of being diffracted.

1882 C. A. YOUNG *Sun* iii. 98 The refrangibility of a ray and its diffrangibility, if we may coin the word, both depend upon the number of pulsations per second with which it reaches the diffracting or refracting surface.

† **di'ffude,** *v. Obs. rare.* [irreg. f. L. *diffundĕre* (perf. *diffūdi*) to pour forth: see DIFFUSE.]

1. *trans.* To pour away.

1599 A. M. tr. *Gabelhouer's Bk. Physicke* 61/2 Diffude . . that wyne & take other.

2. *trans.* and *intr.* = DIFFUSE *v.* I.

1638 SIR T. HERBERT *Trav.* 125 The clouds . . sometimes breake, and . . diffude to some purpose. *Ibid.* 343 The benevolent heaven daily diffudes a gentle shower.

3. *trans.* To dissolve, liquefy.

1657 TOMLINSON *Renou's Disp.* 74 Fatness, marrow . . which with little heat [are] diffuded.

diffugient (dɪfjuːdʒɪənt), *ppl. a. rare*$^{-1}$. [ad. L. *diffugient-em*, pr. pple. of *diffugĕre* to flee in different directions, disperse, f. *dif-*, DIS- 1 + *fugĕre* to flee.] Fleeing away, dispersing.

1860 THACKERAY *Round. Papers* (1861) 102 To-morrow the diffugient snows will give place to Spring.

† **'diffugous,** *a. Obs. rare*$^{-0}$. [f. L. *dif-*, *dis-* + *fug-us* fleeing (in *refugus*, etc.): cf. prec.]

1727 BAILEY vol. II, *Diffugous*, that flieth divers Ways.

† **di'ffund,** *v. Obs.* Also 5-6 **diffound(e.** [a. OF. *diffond-re*, *-fundre* (15th c. in Godef.) to shed, pour out, diffuse, ad. L. *diffundĕre*, f. *dif-*, DIS- 1 + *fundĕre* to pour.] *trans.* To pour out or abroad, to diffuse.

1447 BOKENHAM *Seyntys* (Roxb.) 257 For the kynde of lyht ys . . That . . It dyffoundyth the self wyth owte inquy-nacyoun. **1533** BELLENDEN *Livy* II. (1822) 156 It diffoundis the blude be quhilk we lief . . throw all the vanis. **1574** J. JONES *Nat. Beginning Grow. Things* 8 It is the mouinge of the harte diffunded or spreade by the arteries.

diffusable: see DIFFUSIBLE.

diffusate (dɪ'fjuːzət). *Chem.* [f. DIFFUSE *v.* + -ATE[1].] The amount of salt diffused in a solution; the crystalloid portion of a mixture which passes through the membrane in the process of chemical dialysis.

1850 GRAHAM in *Phil. Trans.* CXL. 806 The diffusate or quantity of acid diffused was determined by precipitating the liquid. **1863-72** WATTS *Dict. Chem* III. 706 The amount of salt diffused, called the diffusion-product, or diffusate, is ascertained [etc.]. **1867** J. ATTFIELD *Chem.* (1885) 811 The portion passing through the septum is termed the diffusate, the portion which does not pass through is termed the dialysate.

diffuse (dɪ'fjuːs), *a.* Also 5-6 **dyf-**, 5-7 **de-**. [ad. L. *diffūs-us*, pa. pple. of *diffundĕre*: see DIFFUND. Cf. F. *diffus*, *-use* (15th c. in Hatz.-Darm.) perh. the immediate source; also It. *diffuso*.]

I. †**1.** Confused, distracted, perplexed; indistinct, vague, obscure, doubtful, uncertain. *Obs.*

[This sense (as if 'poured forth in divers contrary directions'), is not recorded in ancient L., but is found in all the Romanic langs.: thus, It. *diffuso*, defused, confused, scattred (Florio), Sp. *difuso*, defused, out of order (Minsheu), obs. F. *diffuse*, dyffuse, harde to be understande (Palsgr.), *diffusément*, disorderedly (Cotgr.).]

a **1400** *Cov. Myst.* (Shaks. Soc.) 93 This matere is dyffuse and obscure. **1413** *Pilgr. Sowle* (Caxton) v. xiv. (1859) 82 I haue nat translated worde for word . . because of some thynges that were diffuse and in some place ouer derk. **1494** FABYAN *Chron.* 213 Whan he had longe whyle lyen at the siege of a castel . . and sawe it was defuse to wynne by strength. *Ibid.* VII. ccxxviii. 257 The pope gaue such a defuse sentence in this mater y[t] he lyfte y[e] stryfe vndetermyned. *a* **1529** SKELTON *P. Sparrowe* 806 It is dyffuse to fynde The sentence of his mynde. *c* **1560** *Dial. Secretary & Jealousy* iii. (Collier), A mater to me doubtfull and diffuse. **1572** BOSSEWELL *Armorie* II. 55 The hounde . . hath mind of diffuse and longe waies: so that if they loose their masters, they goe by furre space of Lands . . to theire maisters houses againe. **1584** R. SCOT *Discov. Witchcr.* xv.

xlii. 393 Their strange names, their diffuse phrases. **1594** CAREW *Huarte's Exam. Wits* xi. (1596) 159 Men..of.. feeble memory..retaine a certaine diffuse notice of things. **1602** —— *Cornwall* 74 b, The hurling to the Countrey, is more diffuse and confuse, as bound to few of these orders.

II. 2. a. Spread out in space; spread through or over a wide area; widespread, scattered, dispersed: the reverse of *confined* or *concentrated*.

a **1711** KEN *Hymnotheo* Poet. Wks. 1721 III. 319 Our Empire o're the Universe diffuse. **1737** WHISTON *Josephus Hist.* III. x. §7 [The water is] cooler than one would expect in so diffuse a place as this. **1759** JOHNSON in *Boswell's Life* note, The pomp of wide margin and diffuse typography. **1831** BREWSTER *Optics* xiv. 119 Diffuse masses of nebulous light. **1871** TYNDALL *Fragm. Sc.* (1879) I. v. 131 Floating matter..invisible in diffuse daylight. **1872** HUXLEY *Phys.* viii. 188 They are not only diffuse, but they are subjective sensations.

†**b.** *fig.* Having a wide range, extensive. *Obs.*

1643 MILTON *Divorce* To Parl. Eng., Men.. of eminent spirit and breeding, joined with a diffuse and various knowledge of divine and human things.

c. *Bot.* 'Applied to panicles and stems which spread and branch indeterminately, but chiefly horizontally' (*Syd. Soc. Lex.* 1883).

1775 H. ROSE *Elem. Bot.* 71 A panicle is said to be diffuse when the partial footstalks diverge. **1861** MISS PRATT *Flower. Pl.* IV. 132 Diffuse Toad-flax. **1870** HOOKER *Stud. Flora* 18 Fumaria officinalis..diffuse.

d. *Path.* Applied to diseases which widely affect the body or organ, in contradistinction to those which are circumscribed.

1807–26 S. COOPER *First Lines Surg.* (ed. 5) 57 To some cases..the name of diffuse inflammation in the cellular membrane has been lately applied. **1874** ROOSA *Dis. Ear* (ed. 2) 120 Diffuse inflammation of the external auditory canal. **1877** ERICHSEN *Surg.* I. 14 Tendency to erysipelas, Pyæmia, and low and diffuse inflammations generally.

e. *Embryol.* Applied to a form of non-deciduate placenta in which the villi are scattered.

1888 ROLLESTON & JACKSON *Anim. Life* 367 The non-deciduate placenta is either diffuse, when the villi are scattered..or cotyledonary, when they are aggregated into patches.

f. In Forestry, ***diffuse-porous*** adj., applied to woods in which the pores are scattered evenly throughout the growth ring.

1902 F. ROTH *First Bk. Forestry* III. 222 The diffuse-porous woods, like maple, yellow poplar, and cherry, where pores are usually very small and evenly scattered through the annual ring. **1928** *Forestry* II. 65 Under sub-alpine conditions woods which are normally diffuse-porous tend to become ring-porous. **1953** H. L. EDLIN *Forester's Handbk.* ii. 27 In some trees, those with diffuse-porous wood, they [*sc.* the vessels] are scattered evenly through the tissues.

3. a. Of a style of writing or speech: Using many words to convey the sense; extended, wordy, verbose: the opposite of *concise* or *condensed*.

1742 GRAY *Let.* Poems (1775) 146 [This] is no commendation of the English tongue, which is too diffuse, and daily grows more and more enervate. **1783** POTT *Chirurg. Wks.* II. 194 Some parts of them will appear prolix and diffuse. **1815** JANE AUSTEN *Emma* I. vii, Too strong and concise, not diffuse enough for a woman. **1842** H. ROGERS *Introd. Burke's Wks.* 47 His style is always full..and in many places even diffuse. **1868** *Pref. to Digby's Voy. Medit.* 22 Digby, who as a writer is always diffuse, dwells upon the wonder.

diffuse (dɪˈfjuːz), *v.* Also 6–7 defuse. [f. L. *diffūs-*, ppl. stem of *diffundĕre* to pour out or away: see DIFFUND. Cf. F. *diffuser* (15th c. in Hatz.-Darm.)]

I. †**1.** *trans.* To pour out as a fluid with wide dispersion of its molecules; to shed. *Obs.*

1598 FLORIO, *Diffondere*, to defuse, to shed. **1610** SHAKS. *Temp.* IV. i. 79 Who, with thy saffron wings, vpon my flowres Diffusest hony drops, refreshing showres. **1634** W. TIRWHYT tr. *Balzac's Lett.* 400 A place whereon Heaven defuseth all its Graces. **1734** tr. *Rollin's Anc. Hist.* (1827) I. Pref. 4 [This] diffuses great light over the history of those nations.

2. To pour or send forth as from a centre of dispersion; to spread abroad over a surface, or through a space or region; to spread widely, shed abroad, disperse, disseminate. **a.** (material things, or physical forces or qualities).

1590 SPENSER *F.Q.* II. ii. 4 The..veneme..Their blood.. infected hath, Being diffused through the senceless tronck. **1601** HOLLAND *Pliny* I. 312 The vitall vertue in them..is.. spred and defused throughout the whole body. **1627** MAY *Lucan* IX. (1631) 606 Those trees no shadow can diffuse. **1654** WARREN *Unbelievers* 95 The Head diffuseth nerves to the several members. **1669** GALE *Crt. Gentiles* I. I. v. 27 The Phenicians..began to diffuse themselves throughout the whole of the Midland Sea. **1711** POPE *Temp. Fame* 308 From pole to pole the winds diffuse the sound. **1752** JOHNSON *Rambler* No. 190 ⁋6 Diffuse thy riches among thy friends. **1791** HAMILTON *Berthollet's Dyeing* II. II. iii. ii. 142 Hot water in which cow's dung has been diffused. **1815** SHELLEY *Demon World* 227 Ten thousand spheres diffuse Their lustre through its adamantine gates. **1860** TYNDALL *Glac.* II. vii. 260 The colours of the sky are due to minute particles diffused through the atmosphere.

b. (immaterial or abstract things).

1526 *Pilgr. Perf.* (W. de W. 1531) 31 The charite of God is diffused & spred in our hertes. **1656** BRAMHALL *Replic.* vi. 279 The true Catholick Church, diffused over the World. **1689** SHADWELL *Bury F.* II, His fame is diffus'd throughout the town. **1814** D'ISRAELI *Quarrels Auth.* (1867) 363 Diffusing a more general taste for the science of botany. **1839** JAMES *Louis XIV*, III. 114 A general rumour began to diffuse itself through the court. **1852** MASSON *Ess.* i. (1856) 32 A heartless man does not diffuse geniality and kindness around him, as Goethe did.

c. *fig.* The reverse of *collect* or *concentrate*: to dissipate.

1608–11 BP. HALL *Medit. & Vows* I. §79 The one gathers the powers of the soule together..the other diffuses them. **1752** JOHNSON *Rambler* No. 190 ⁋9 Determined to avoid a close union..and to diffuse himself in a larger circle. **1887** RUSKIN *Præterita* II. 274 He diffused himself in serene scholarship till too late.

3. To extend or spread out (the body or limbs) freely; in *pa. pple.*, Extended or spread out. *arch.* and *poetic.*

1671 MILTON *Samson* 118 See how he lies at random, carelessly diffused. **1706** WATTS *Horæ Lyr.* (1779) 284 Beneath your sacred shade diffused we lay. **1806–7** J. BERESFORD *Miseries Hum. Life* (1826) II. xxxiii, After having ..diffused yourself on the sopha. **1815** SHELLEY *Alastor* 636 His limbs did rest, Diffused and motionless, on the smooth brink Of that obscurest chasm.

4. *intr.* (for *refl.*) To be or become diffused, to spread abroad (*lit.* and *fig.*).

a **1653** [see DIFFUSING below]. **1700** S. PARKER *Six Philos. Ess.* 51 It [the Chimist's Fire] does not merely sustain it self, but propagates too, and diffuses upon the ruins of its neighbours. *a* **1711** KEN *Hymnarium* Poet. Wks. 1721 II. 12 Love..Will all diffuse in Extacy. **1785** *Eugenius* II, 192 In several other parts..the same benevolent spirit and moral improvement are diffusing. **1814** SOUTHEY *Roderick* XXI, The silver cloud diffusing slowly past.

5. *Physics.* **a.** *trans.* To cause (gases or liquids) to intermingle by diffusion; to disperse by diffusion. **b.** *intr.* Said of fluids: To intermingle or interpenetrate each other by diffusion; to pass by diffusion. See DIFFUSION 5.

a. 1808 DALTON *New Syst. Chem. Philos.* I. 150 Gases always intermingle and diffuse themselves amongst each other, if exposed ever so carefully. *Ibid.* 191 When two equal measures of different gases are thus diffused. **1831** T. GRAHAM in *L. & E. Phil. Mag.* (1833) II. 179 The ascent of the water in the tube, when hydrogen is diffused, forms a striking experiment. **1849** —— in *Phil. Trans.* (1850) 5 The phial was filled up with the solution to be diffused.

b. 1831 GRAHAM in *L. & E. Phil. Mag.* (1833) II. 189 The air does not diffuse out against so strong a pressure. **1849** —— in *Phil. Trans.* (1850) 4 The carbonic acid found in the upper bottle, and which had diffused into it from the lower. **1854** *Ibid.* 178 Water appears to diffuse four times more rapidly than alcohol. **1869** E. A. PARKES *Pract. Hygiene* (ed. 3) 127 Every gas diffuses at a certain rate.

II. †**6.** *trans.* To distract, perplex, disorder, render confused or indistinct. *Obs.* (Cf. DIFFUSE *a.* 1; and see also DIFFUSED 1.)

1605 SHAKS. *Lear* I. iv. 2 If but as well [*1st Folio* will] I other accents borrow, That can my speech defuse.

Hence **diˈffusing** *ppl. a.*

a **1653** GOUGE *Comm. Heb.* i. 9 The Spirit is as Oyl, of a diffusing nature. **1887** *Poor Nellie* (1888) 286 She had told her, with diffusing circles of surprise.

diffused (dɪˈfjuːzd, *poet.* -ɪd), *ppl. a.* Also 6–7 defused. [f. DIFFUSE *v.* + -ED¹.]

I. †**1.** Confused, distracted, disordered, obscure.

[Cf. DIFFUSE *a.* 1, DIFFUSE *v.* 6.]

1535 COVERDALE *Isa.* xxxiii. 19 So diffused a language, that it maye not be vnderstonde. **1591** GREENE *Farew. Folly* C iij b, I have seene an English gentleman so defused in his sutes, his doublet being for the weare of Castile, his hose for Venice, his hat for France. **1594** SHAKS. *Rich. III*, I. ii. 78 Defus'd infection of man. **1599** —— *Hen. V*, v. ii. 61 Sterne Lookes, defus'd Attyre, And euery thing that seemes vnnaturall. **1608** ARMIN *Nest Ninn.* (1842) 6 The whole lumpe of this defused chaios. **1614** BP. HALL *Recoll. Treat.* 845 There is no divine word (as Tertullian speaketh..) so dissolute and defused, that onely the words may be defended, and not the true meaning of the wordes set downe.

II. 2. Spread abroad, widespread; dispersed over a large area; †covering a wide range of subjects (*obs.*). ***diffused lighting*** (see quot. 1926).

1610 HEALEY *St. Aug. Citie of God* XVI. ii. (1620) 541 Christ..in whose houses, that is, in whose Churches, the diffused Nations shall inhabite. For Iaphet is *diffused*. **1644** DIGBY *Nat. Bodies* (1645) II. 123 Able to exempt themselves from defused powers. **1699** BENTLEY *Phal.* Introd. 15 Galen, with all his vast and diffused Learning. *a* **1715** BURNET *Own Time* (1766) I. 81 He had a most diffused love to all mankind. **1849** MRS. SOMERVILLE *Connect. Phys. Sc.* xxxvii. 413 The diffused light of myriads of stars. **1882** VINES *Sachs' Bot.* 748 Within two hours in direct sunlight, within six hours in diffused daylight. **1926** *Gloss. Terms Electr. Engin.* (*B.S.I.*) 146 *Diffused lighting*, a system of lighting in which the luminous flux, after passing through a diffusing medium, reaches the area to be illuminated, in part directly and in part indirectly. **1933** *Discovery* Aug. 251/2 Strip-lighting which flood-lights the walls and gives a diffused lighting to the room.

†**3.** = DIFFUSE *a.* 3. *Obs.*

1579 LYLY *Euphues* (Arb.) 64 In pleadinge [there ought to be]..a difficulte enteraunce, and a defused [**1636** diffused] determination.

diffusedly (dɪˈfjuːzɪdlɪ), *adv.* [f. prec. + -LY².] In a diffused manner.

I. †**1.** Confusedly, obscurely; disorderly. *Obs.*

[See DIFFUSE *a.* 1.]

1567 MAPLET *Gr. Forest* 16 In this stone is..seene..the verie forme of a Tode, with bespotted and coloured feete, but those vglye and defusedly. **1588** PARKE tr. *Mendoza's Hist. China* 395 Whose memorie doth remain vnto this day amongst the..people, although diffusedly. *a* **1625** FLETCHER *Nice Valour* III. iii, Goe not so diffusedly.

II. 2. With diffusion or spreading abroad; dispersedly; with interpenetration.

1591 PERCIVALL *Sp. Dict.*, *Difusamente*, diffusedly. **1611** COTGR., *Ça & là*, diffusedly, scatteringly. *a* **1711** KEN *Hymnotheo* Poet. Wks. 1721 III. 303 Till from thy powerful Word to rule dull Mass, Life energetick should diffus'dly pass. **1813** T. BUSBY *Lucretius* IV. 101 Each, widely scattered, and diffusedly, flies. **1884** *Pall Mall G.* 13 Sept. 5/1 The heavy metals..are present, though far more diffusedly.

†**b.** In the wider or extended sense. *Obs.*

a **1641** BP. MOUNTAGU *Acts & Mon.* 100 Talking Iudah either restrainedly, for the Tribe..or diffusedly, for the nation.

†**3.** Diffusely; with much fullness or prolixity of language; at large. *Obs.*

1594 BLUNDEVIL *Exerc.* Cont. (ed. 7) A iv, As Monte Regio wrote diffusedly, and at large, so Copernicus wrote of the same briefly. **1604** T. WRIGHT *Passions* v. iv. 218 Of this more diffusedly in my third booke. **1730** A. GORDON *Maffei's Amphith.* 193 Those who have diffusedly wrote on Amphitheatres. **1805** *Ann. Reg.* 1054 [They] have also diffusedly written on Brasil. **1817** J. LAWRENCE in *Monthly Mag.* XLVII. 38 Many..will descant most ably, diffusedly, and elegantly, upon the superstructure.

diˈffusedness. [f. as prec. + -NESS.] The condition or quality of being diffused.

†**1.** Confusedness, perplexity, obscurity. *Obs.*

1611 COTGR., *Obscurité*, obscuritie..diffusednesse.

2. The quality of being widely dispersed.

a **1626** BP. ANDREWES *Serm.* (1856) I. 378 Willing to reduce the diffusedness of our repentance at large to the certainty of some one set time. **1681–2** BOYLE *New Exp. Icy Noctiluca* 46 A conjecture I had made about the great diffusedness of the Noctilucal Matter. **1747** EDWARDS *Canons Crit.* xxii. (1765) 211 It is the diffusedness, or extent of her infection which is here described.

diffusely (dɪˈfjuːslɪ), *adv.* [f. DIFFUSE *a.* + -LY².] In a diffuse manner.

†**1.** Confusedly, obscurely. *Obs.*

1515 BARCLAY *Egloges* II. (1570) B iv b, Diffusely thou speakest to vnderstande.

2. In a diffused or widespread manner; with wide dispersion.

1552 HULOET, Diffuselye, *diffuse*. **1718** ROWE tr. *Lucan* VI. 936 (Seager), Pleas'd that her magic fame diffusely flies. *c* **1839** LANDOR *Wks.* (1846) I. 464 The sun colours the sky most deeply and most diffusely when he hath sunk below the horizon. **1870** HOOKER *Stud. Flora* 189 Centaurea calcitrapa ..diffusely branched. **1874** *Lommel's Light* 12 The light is diffusely reflected from their surface.

3. In many words, verbosely, copiously; fully, at large: the opposite of *concisely*.

c **1380** WYCLIF *Serm.* cxvii. Sel. Wks. I. 391 It sufficide to Mathew to telle..biginnynge at Abraham. But Luk..tellip more diffuseli how man stieþ up to God, from Adam to þe Trinite. **1662** GLANVILL *Lux Orient.* xi. (R.), These places have been more diffusely urged in a late discourse to this purpose. **1783** H. BLAIR *Lect.* xviii. (R.), A sentiment, which, expressed diffusely, will barely be admitted to be just, expressed concisely, will be admired as spirited. **1837** HALLAM *Hist. Lit.* iv. III. §106 That great branch of ethics.. has been so diffusely handled by the casuists..that Grotius deserves..credit for the brevity with which he has laid down the simple principles.

diffuseness (dɪˈfjuːsnɪs). [f. as prec. + -NESS.] The quality of being diffuse; *esp.* in speech or literary style, the opposite of *conciseness*.

1797 *Monthly Mag.* III. 46 He..spreads out his conceptions with tedious diffuseness. **1845** S. AUSTIN *Ranke's Hist. Ref.* III. 283 People dreaded their violence and their diffuseness. **1875** JOWETT *Plato* (ed. 2) V. 23 The apology for delay and diffuseness which occurs not unfrequently in the Republic. **1892** *Speaker* 22 Oct. 505/2 Notes..written with intolerable diffuseness, dullness, and obscurity.

diffuser (dɪˈfjuːzə(r)). [f. DIFFUSE *v.* + -ER¹.]

1. One who or that which diffuses or spreads abroad.

a **1679** T. GOODWIN *Wks.* V. I. 19 (R.) The Holy Ghost.. being the author and diffuser of them into our hearts. **1681** MANNINGHAM *Disc. conc. Truth* 32 (T.) Diffusers of secular learning. **1797** W. TAYLOR in *Monthly Rev* XXII. 545 The diffusers, not the inventors, of their unprincipled principles. **1807** SOUTHEY *Espriella's Lett.* III. 96 Women..become the most useful diffusers of their own faith. **1893** *Arena* (Boston) Nov. 707 Promoter of purity, diffuser of sweetness and light.

2. a. *spec.* A contrivance for diffusing air, light, heat, etc.

1884 *Health Exhib. Catal.* 114/1 Patent Inlets and Air Diffusers for Buildings. **1891** *Truth* 10 Dec. 1242/1 The burners were shaded with the new bead ray diffusers. **1894** *Harper's Mag.* July 216/2 Patents have been granted for 'diffusers', whereby the lightning is to be distributed over a larger area than, presumably, it could find unassisted.

b. *Engin.* A duct in a centrifugal pump, compressor, wind tunnel, etc., so shaped that it reduces the velocity of a fluid by increasing the cross-sectional area of flow.

1926 W. J. KEARTON *Turbo-Blowers & Compressors* vii. 186 The diffusers are of the 'free vortex' type, no guide vanes being fitted. **1946** J. G. KEENAN *Gas Turbines & Jet Propulsion* iv. 68 The diffuser is the name given to a ring of fixed guide vanes..surrounding the impeller. *Ibid.* 70 One object of the diffuser is to provide a smooth canalization of the flow from the impeller. **1959** D. D. WYATT in *High-Speed Aerodyn. & Jet Propul.* XII. E. §33. 350 The jet diffuser..consists of a divergent shroud attached to the outlet end of the jet nozzle.

diffusibility (dɪfjuːzɪˈbɪlɪtɪ). [f. DIFFUSIBLE + -ITY.] Capacity of being diffused; *esp.* in *Physics*, as a measurable quality of gases or fluids.

1813 J. THOMSON *Lect. Inflam.* 489 On account of their greater diffusibility in the atmosphere. **1849** [see DIFFUSIBLE]. **1861** GRAHAM in *Phil. Trans* 183 Low diffusibility is not the only property which the bodies.. possess in common. **1883** *Fortn. Rev.* 1 Oct. 598 Influenza ..is remarkable for its amazing diffusibility.

diffusible (dɪˈfjuːzɪb(ə)l), *a.* Also **-able**. [f. L. *diffūs-* ppl. stem of *diffundĕre* to pour out, DIFFUSE + -IBLE: so in mod.F.] Capable of being diffused; *spec.* in *Physics*, having the capacity, as a fluid, of spreading itself between the molecules of a contiguous fluid.

1782 CLARK in *Med. Commun.* I. 64 *note*, The infection.. being of an exceedingly diffusable nature. **1794** J. HUTTON *Philos. Light, etc.* 151 The moveable or diffusible heat in bodies, by which we are made to feel. **1811** PINKERTON *Petral.* II. 425 It is not diffusible in cold water. **1830** LINDLEY *Nat. Syst. Bot.* 65 The volatile oil of Cajeputi is.. a highly diffusable stimulant. **1849** GRAHAM in *Phil. Trans.* (1850) 1 A diffusibility like that of gases, if it exists in liquids, should afford means for the separation and decomposition even of unequally diffusible substances. **1864** H. SPENCER *Biol.* I. 19 Hydrochloric acid is seven times as diffusible as sulphate of magnesia.

Hence **di'ffusibleness** = DIFFUSIBILITY.

1847 CRAIG, *Diffusibleness*, diffusibility.

†**di'ffusile**, *a. Obs. rare*$^{-0}$. [ad. L. *diffūsil-is* diffusive, f. *diffūs-* ppl. stem of *diffundĕre* to DIFFUSE.] = DIFFUSIBLE.

1727 BAILEY vol. II, *Diffusile*, spreading.

diffu'simeter = next.

diffusi'ometer. [f. L. *diffūsio* diffusion + -METER.] An apparatus for measuring the rate of diffusion of gases.

1866 GRAHAM in *Phil. Trans.* CLVI. 399 The diffusiometer, consisting of a plain glass tube..closed at the upper end by a thin plate of stucco, and open below. **1879** *Nature* XXI. 191 The diffusiometer which I have constructed.

diffusion (dɪˈfjuːʒən). Also 6 defusion. [ad. L. *diffūsiōn-em*, n. of action from *diffundĕre* to pour out: see DIFFUND. Also in mod.F. (1610 in Hatz.-Darm.)]

†**1.** The action of pouring or shedding forth; outpouring, effusion. *Obs.*

c **1374** [see 4]. **1626** BACON *Sylva* §268 The Diffusion of Species Visible. *a* **1631** DONNE in *Select.* (1840) 49 Diffusion of yᵉ Holy Ghost.

2. a. The action of spreading abroad; the condition of being widely spread; dispersion through a space or over a surface; wide and general distribution.

1591 DRAYTON *Harmonie of Church, Song of Faithfull*, He stood aloft and compassed the land, and of the nations doth defusion make. [Cf. Habakkuk iii. 6.] **1642** HOWELL *For. Trav.* (Arb.) 46 The bloud gathering up by an unequall diffusion into the upper parts. **1665** *Phil. Trans.* I. 50 A Medium..much less disposed to assist the diffusion of Cold. **1797–1803** FOSTER in *Life & Corr.* (1846) I. 166 A stream spread into listless diffusion. **1821** CRAIG *Lect. Drawing* iii. 168 To the painter..the diffusion of light..is of high importance. **1842** BISCHOFF *Woollen Manuf.* II. 261 The propagation and diffusion of that breed of sheep.

b. The condition of branching out on all sides.

a **1682** SIR T. BROWNE *Tracts* (1684) 34 This diffusion and spreading of its Branches. **1712** ADDISON *Spect.* No. 414 ¶5 A Tree in all its Luxuriancy and Diffusion of Boughs.

c. quasi-*concr.* That which is extended, a diffused extension or extent. *rare.*

a **1696** SCARBURGH *Euclid* (1705) 2 Space is an Infinite, and Unmoveable Diffusion every way. **1750** JOHNSON *Rambler* No. 36 ¶11 The Sea is..an immense diffusion of waters.

†**d.** *in diffusion*: in distribution among the members of a body generally; = DIFFUSIVELY b; cf. DIFFUSIVE 3. *Obs.*

1642 JER. TAYLOR *Episc.* (R.), And therefore the determination of councils pertains to all, and is handled by all, not in diffusion but in representation.

e. Formerly used as a semi-technical term in psychological writings: the arousal of a widespread response by a stimulus; the dissemination of nervous energy.

1859 A. BAIN *Emotions & Will* I. 10 Where feeling exists there must be a free diffusion of nervous energy over the brain and its outlying connexions. **1890** W. JAMES *Princ. Psychol.* II. xxiii. 373 There are probably no exceptions to the diffusion of every impression through the nerve-centres. **1918** J. WARD *Psychol. Princ.* I. iv. 79 This 'diffusion' or 'irradiation'..diminishes as we pass from the class of organic sensations to the sensations of the five senses.

3. a. *fig.* Spreading abroad, dispersion, dissemination (of abstract things, as knowledge).

1750 JOHNSON *Rambler* No. 101 ¶2 The writer..receives little advantage from the diffusion of his name. **1752** HUME *Ess. & Treat.* (1777) I. 224 The universal diffusion of learning among a people. **1834** J. BOWRING *Minor Morals, Story Perseverance* 146 This diffusion of enjoyment. **1862** SIR B. BRODIE *Psychol. Inq.* II. I. 14 The effect which the general diffusion of knowledge produces on society. **1874** GREEN *Short Hist.* viii. §2. 461 The rapid diffusion of the new doctrines in France. **1875** GLADSTONE *Glean.* VI. xlv. 133 There is a wider diffusion of taste among the many.

b. *Anthropol.* The spread of elements of a culture or language from one region or people to another; also, the simultaneous existence of such elements in two or more places.

1871 E. B. TYLOR *Prim. Culture* I. i. 8 How good a working analogy there really is between the diffusion of plants and animals and the diffusion of civilization, comes well into view when we notice how far the same causes have produced both at once. **1937** R. H. LOWIE *Hist. Ethnol. Theory* xii. 223 Repudiating the notion that contact automatically precipitates diffusion. *a* **1942** B. MALINOWSKI *Sci. Theory Culture* (1944) iii. 17 The other dominant tendency of older anthropology laid primary stress on diffusion, that is, the process of adopting or borrowing by one culture from another various devices, implements, institutions, and beliefs.

4. Of speech or writing: Diffuseness; prolixity, copiousness of language.

In quot. 1374 (which stands quite alone in point of date) the sense is rather 'use of diffuseness, copious outpouring' of speech.

c **1374** CHAUCER *Troylus* III. 247 (296) Nere it that I wilne as now tabregge Diffusioun of speche, I coude almost A thousand olde stories thee alegge. **1779–81** JOHNSON *L.P., Akenside*, The reader wanders through the gay diffusion, sometimes amazed, and sometimes delighted. **1782** V. KNOX *Ess.* (1819) I. xliv. 244 Attributing to the former [Demosthenes] conciseness, and to the latter [Tully] diffusion. **1791** BOSWELL *Johnson* an. 1772 (1816) II. 184, I love his knowledge, his genius, his diffusion, and affluence of conversation. **1870** LOWELL *Study Wind.* 278 The power of diffusion without being diffuse would seem to be the highest merit of narration.

5. *Physics.* The permeation of a gas or liquid between the molecules of another fluid placed in contact with it; the spontaneous molecular mixing or interpenetration of two fluids without chemical combination.

1808 DALTON *New Syst. Chem. Philos.* I. 191 The diffusion of gases through each other is effected by means of the repulsion belonging to the homogeneous particles. **1831** T. GRAHAM *L. & E. Phil. Mag.* (1833) II. 175 (On the Law of the Diffusion of Gases.) The diffusion or spontaneous intermixture of two gases in contact is effected by an interchange in position of indefinitely minute volumes of the gases..These replacing volumes of the gases may be named *equivalent volumes of diffusion*. **1863–72** WATTS *Dict. Chem.* II. 323 *Diffusion*..takes place both when the fluids are in immediate contact, and when they are separated by porous membranes or other partitions. **1878** A. H. GREEN *Coal* i. 11 A portion of the carbonic acid is dissipated by diffusion. **1882** VINES *Sach's Bot.* 718 The sugar is the migratory product which takes part in the diffusion; the starch-grains are the temporarily stationary product.

6. *attrib.* and *Comb.* (chiefly sense 5), as ***diffusion-apparatus, -bulb, -cell, -circle, -coefficient, -instrument, -phial, -tube, -volume.***

1831 GRAHAM in *L. & E. Phil. Mag.* (1833) II. 178 A simple instrument which I shall call a Diffusion-tube was constructed. *Ibid.* 179 When such a diffusion-tube..was filled with hydrogen over mercury, the diffusion or exchange of air for hydrogen instantly commenced, through the minute pores of the stucco. *Ibid.* 186 The first time a diffusion-bulb is tried, it generally gives the diffusion volume of hydrogen below the truth. **1849** —— in *Phil. Trans.* (1850) 5 The saline solution in the diffusion cell or phial thus communicated freely with about 5 times its volume of pure water. **1858** —— *Elem. Chem.* II. 612 Another method of determining the diffusion-coefficient of a salt has been devised by Jolly. **1874** KNIGHT *Dict. Mech.*, *Diffusion-apparatus*, a mode of extracting the sugar from cane or beet-root by dissolving it out with water. **1878** FOSTER *Phys.* III. ii. 399 If the object be..removed farther away from the lens, the rays..will be brought to a focus in front of the screen, and, subsequently diverging, will fall upon the screen as a circular patch composed of a series of circles, the so-called diffusion circles. **1883** *Syd. Soc. Lex.*, *Diffusion apparatus*, a cell divided into two parts by a porous septum or diaphragm.

di'ffusionist. [f. DIFFUSION + -IST.] One who adheres to a theory of diffusion. Also *attrib.* or as *adj.* Cf. DIFFUSION 3b.

1893 *Athenæum* 25 Nov. 736/3 The most strenuous advocate of the diffusionist theory [of folk-tales]. **1926** *Encycl. Brit.* III. 566/2 As substitutes for the 'evolutionary' syntheses.., several 'diffusionist' schemes have been elaborated. **1931** *Times Lit. Suppl.* 5 Mar. 167/2 The diffusionist school..has done good work..by attempting the stratigraphical analysis of a given 'culture-complex'. **1934** *Nature* 12 May 707/2 Other schools, the 'diffusionists', the 'functionalists', [etc.]. **1946** J. S. HUXLEY *Unesco* ii. 46 The diffusionists on the one hand and on the other their opponents who believe in parallel and independent evolution of cultural patterns. **1951** E. E. EVANS-PRITCHARD *Social Anthropol.* iii. 46 The so-called evolutionary theories ..were attacked from two directions, the diffusionist and the functionalist. *Ibid.*, Those who became known as diffusionist anthropologists. *Ibid.* 47 Diffusionist anthropology is still predominant in America. **1961** L. MUMFORD *City in History* iii. 91 The old diffusionists, like G. Elliott Smith, who jumped too quickly at an answer, cast discredit on the question.

Hence **di'ffusionism** *Anthropol.*, the theory that all or most cultural similarities are due to diffusion.

1937 R. H. LOWIE *Hist. Ethnol. Theory* xi. 186 We.. concede..some of the strong points of German diffusionism. *a* **1942** B. MALINOWSKI *Sci. Theory Culture* (1944) iii. 21 The basis of diffusionism must be a correct identification of cultural realities plotted on the map.

diffusive (dɪˈfjuːsɪv), *a.* Also 7 defusive. [f. L. *diffūs-* ppl. stem of *diffundĕre* to DIFFUSE + -IVE. Cf. F. *diffusif, -ive*, found 15–16th c., but app. unused in 17–18th c. (Hatz.-Darm.)]

1. Having the quality of diffusing (*trans.*); dispensing or shedding widely or bountifully.

1614 T. ADAMS in Spurgeon *Treas. Dav.* Ps. cxxxiii. 2 Christ's grace is so diffusive of itself, that it conveys holiness to us. **1641** MILTON *Ch. Govt.* ii. (1851) 104 So diffusive of knowledge and charity. **1648** BOYLE *Seraph. Love* xiii. (1700) 77 It is his [the sun's] Nature to be diffusive of his Light. **1700** DRYDEN *Fables* Ded., Diffusive of the goods which they enjoy'd. **1714** BERKELEY *Serm. 1 Tim.* i. 2 Wks. 1871 IV. 613 The most ardent and diffusive charity. **1742** R. BLAIR *Grave* 611 The big-swoln inundation, Of mischief more diffusive. **1816** KEATINGE *Trav.* (1817) I. 149 *note*, Matters diffusive of such an extent of moral good.

2. Having the quality of diffusing itself or of being diffused; tending to be widely dispersed or distributed; characterized by diffusion. **a.** *lit.* of material things, or physical qualities, etc.; *spec.* in *Physics* (cf. DIFFUSION 5).

a **1631** DONNE in *Select.* (1840) 89 So are these spices, and incense, and spikenard, of a diffusive and spreading nature, and breathe even over the walls of the garden. *a* **1656** BP. HALL *Rem. Wks.* (1660) 187 Leaven hath..a diffusive faculty. **1683** *Lond. Gaz.* No. 1856/5 Cherished..by the diffusive beams of the Sun. **1684** T. BURNET *Th. Earth* I. 26 All liquid bodies are diffusive. **1712** ADDISON *Spect.* No. 411 ¶1 Our Sight..may be considered as a more delicate and diffusive kind of Touch. **1727** THOMSON *Britannia* 144 Far as the sun rolls the diffusive day. *c* **1750** SHENSTONE *Ruin'd Abbey* 197 His less'ning flock In snowy groups diffusive scud the vale. **1851** GRAHAM in *Phil. Trans.* CXLI. 483 The diffusive relation of the two bases. **1869** ROSCOE *Elem. Chem.* 31 This important property is called the diffusive power of gases.

b. *fig.* of immaterial or abstract things.

1634 HABINGTON *Castara* (Arb.) 100 A common courtier ..hath his love so diffusive among the beauties, that man is not considerable. **1677** GALE *Crt. Gentiles* IV. 190 Democratie hath a diffusive facultie, as it takes in the concernes and interests of each individual. **1781** GIBBON *Decl. & F.* III. 43 The diffusive circle of his benevolence was circumscribed only by the limits of the human race. **1832** TENNYSON '*You ask me why*' iv, The strength of some diffusive thought Hath time and space to work and spread. **1871** SMILES *Charac.* iii. (1876) 71 The good character is diffusive in its influence.

†**3.** Of a body of people: As consisting of members in their individual capacity. The 'diffusive body' is contrasted, by the notion of individually diffused or distributed action, with the 'collective body', and, by that of universal participation, with a 'representative body'. The action of the 'diffusive body' is that in which every member of the body shares directly. (Common in 17th c.) *Obs.*

1642 *Answ. to Printed Bk.* 11 The election of the diffusive, not of any representative body. **1647** JER. TAYLOR *Lib. Proph.* ix. 161 The incompetency of the Church in its diffusive Capacity to be Judge of Controversies. **1647** DIGGES *Unlawf. Taking Arms* iii. 66 If actions of this nature were unwarrantable in the diffusive body, they are so in the representative. **1660** FULLER *Mixt Contempl.* i. (1841) 259 The diffusive nation was never more careful in their elections. **1691** T. H[ALE] *Acc. New Invent.* p. lxxxii, His Majesty and all his People, both representative and diffusive. *a* **1694** TILLOTSON *Serm.* (1743) I. 259 They are not agreed..where this infallibility is seated; whether in the pope..or a council..or in the diffusive body of Christians. **1718** HICKES & NELSON *J. Kettlewell* III. x. 212 That the Supreme Power was Fundamentally in the whole Body Diffusive of the People.

4. Prolix in diction or speech; = DIFFUSE *a.* 3. (Sometimes in good sense: Copious, full.)

1699 BURNET 39 *Art.* Pref. (1700) 2 The heaviness..of Stile, and the diffusive length of them, disgusted me. **1734** tr. *Rollin's Anc. Hist.* (1827) VIII. XVIII. viii. 57 Polybius.. generally is diffusive enough. **1794** SULLIVAN *View Nat.* V. 257, I have..been unavoidably, and I am afraid tiresomely, diffusive. **1874** L. STEPHEN *Hours in Lib.* (1892) I. i. 34 He is less diffusive and more pointed than usual.

†**5.** *Bot.* = DIFFUSE *a.* 2c. *Obs.*

1756 WATSON in *Phil. Trans.* XLIX. 815 The rigid leaved Bell-flowers, with a diffusive panicle and patulous flowers.

†**6.** Difficult to understand, obscure: = DIFFUSE *a.* I. *Obs.*

1709 STRYPE *Ann. Ref.* I. xxii. 266 Whereas Turcopolier was so diffusive a name as not worthy the pains of pronouncing.

diffusively (dɪˈfjuːsɪvlɪ), *adv.* [f. prec. + -LY².] In a diffusive manner or condition; see the adj.

1628 T. SPENCER *Logick* 54 It is diffusiuely good, in as much as it is fit..to bestow good vpon others. **1677** HALE *Prim. Orig. Man.* II. vii. 198 Whether the primitive.. Animals..were diffusively created over the habitable or dry Ground as Vegetables were. **1710** *Managers' Pro & Con* 67 May the Influence of good Examples..be.. diffusively prevailing. **1773** J. ALLEN *Serm. St. Mary's Oxford* 18 So diffusively hath this doctrine descended to posterity. **1787** HAWKINS *Johnson* 129 Rhapsodically and diffusively eloquent. **1816** *Chron.* in *Ann. Reg.* 543 It branches more diffusively. **1868** GLADSTONE *Juv. Mundi* iii. (1869) 75 Probably Thracians existed diffusively, like Pelasgians, among the Greeks. **1869** MRS. SOMERVILLE *Molec. Sc.* I. iii. 110 The particles of the crystals unite diffusively with the water.

†**b.** In, or with respect to, the individual members; individually, severally; cf. DIFFUSIVE 3. *Obs.*

1644 *Narr. Beginnings & Causes War* 19 The Subjects of the Kingdome of England diffusively considered cannot take up Armes against the King, and how then can their Representatives assembled in Parliament? **1644** BP.

Maxwell *Prerog. Chr. Kings* ii. 25 The people all and every one, diffusively, collectively, representatively. 1710 Bentley *Phil. Lips.* §35 (T.), *Εκκλησία*..means diffusively the whole community of the Christian name.

diffusiveness (dɪˈfjuːsɪvnɪs). [f. as prec. + -ness.] The quality or condition of being diffusive.

1630 Donne *Serm.* lxxii. 726 The extent and Diffusivenesse of this Sinne. 1648 Boyle *Seraph. Love* iii. (1700) 19 Those..Excellences, which the Diffusiveness of his Goodness, makes him pleased to communicate. 1702 Addison *Dial. Medals* iii. 154 The first fault..that I shall find with a modern legend, is its diffusiveness. 1831 Graham in *L. & E. Phil. Mag.* (1833) II. 356 A certain proportion of each of the mixed gases..corresponding to its individual diffusiveness. 1848 Hallam *Mid. Ages* viii. *note* xi, An Essay..written with remarkable perspicuity and freedom from diffusiveness. 1884 W. H. Rideing in *Harper's Mag.* June 68/1 The natural buoyancy and diffusiveness of smoke.

diffusivity (dɪfjuːˈsɪvɪtɪ). *Physics.* [f. diffusive + -ity. Cf. *activity*, *conductivity*.] Diffusive quality; capacity of diffusion (as a measurable quality of liquids, gases, heat, etc.); = diffusibility.

1876 Tait *Rec. Adv. Phys. Sc.* xi. 280 We may speak of the diffusivity of one substance in solution in another. 1881 Everett *Deschanel's Nat. Philos.* xxxv. 413 'Diffusivity' (to use the name recently coined by Sir Wm. Thomson) measures the tendency to equalization of temperature. 1882 *Nature* XXVI. 567 'Diffusivity', that is..conductivity divided by thermal capacity of unit volume.

diffusor, var. of diffuser.

difluan: see diffluan.

difoil (ˈdaɪfɔɪl), *a. nonce-wd.* [f. di-[2], after *trefoil*, etc.] (See quot.)

1860 Ruskin *Mod. Paint.* V. vi. iii. 20 The elementary structure of all important trees may, I think..be resolved into three principal forms: three-leaved..four-leaved..and five-leaved..Or, in well-known terms, trefoil, quatrefoil, cinqfoil..The simplest arrangement..in which the buds are nearly opposite in position..cannot, I believe, constitute a separate class..If it did, it might be called difoil.

dify(e, obs. form of defy.

dig (dɪg), *v.* Forms: 4–6 **dygge(n**, 4–7 **digge**, (5 **degge**), 6– **dig**. Pa. t. and pple. **digged** (4 **-ide**, 5 **dygged, deggyd, deghit**); also **dug** (pa. t. 8–, pa. pple. 6–; in 7 **dugg**). [Found since 14th c.; prob. a. F. *diguer*, according to Darmesteter properly 'creuser la terre', to dig or hollow out the ground, by extension = 'piquer' to prick or prod, as now used in Normandy; also, in the Manège, *diguer un cheval* to dig the spur into a horse; related to F. *digue* dike, also to F. *digon*, *digot*, iron prongs for catching fish and shell-fish, *digonner* 'to dig, or pricke (Norm.)' Cotgr. Cf. also Da. *dige* dike, ditch, trench, *vb.* to raise a dike.

Dig cannot be derived from, or in any way directly related to, OE. *díc* dike, ditch, and *dícian* to dike, embank, from which it differs both in vowel and final consonant; but if the French derivation be correct, it goes back through F. to the same Teutonic root. It is properly a weak verb, pa. t. and pple. *digged*, but in 16th c. received a strong pa. pple. *dug*, analogous to *stuck*, which since 18th c. has also been used as pa. t.]

I. *intr.*

1. a. 'To work in making holes or turning the ground' (J.); to make an excavation; to work with a spade or other tool similarly employed. *spec.* To make an archæological excavation.

Locally the word was, and in some cases still is, the technical term for working with a mattock as distinguished from a spade, the latter being 'graving' or 'delving'. Cf. quots. 1530, 1691; also 1611, 1888 in sense 4.

*c*1320 *Orfeo* 239 in Ritson *Met. Rom.* II. 258 Now he most bothe digge and wrote, Er he have his fille of rote. *c*1380 Wyclif *Serm.* Sel. Wks. I. 99 Digge about þe vyne rotis. 1387 Trevisa *Higden* (Rolls) III. 159 (Mätz.) þey founde a mannis hede in þat place while þey digged. *c*1400 Maundev. (1839) xxvi. 267 Thei schullen dyggen and mynen so strongly. *c*1440 *Promp. Parv.* 121/1 *Dyggyn*, supra in delvyn. *c*1440 *Gesta Rom.* iii. 7 (Harl. MS.) He toke a shoville, and dyggyd in the erthe. *c*1500 *Ballad on Money* in Halliw. *Nugae Poet.* 48 The plowman hymselfe dothe dyge and delve In storme, snowe, frost and rayne. 1526 *Pilgr. Perf.* (W. de W. 1531) 120b, They that dygge for water. 1530 Palsgr. 516/1, I dygge in the grounde with a mattocke. 1607 Dekker *Wh. of Babylon* Wks. 1873 II. 197 When mines are to be blowne vp men dig low. 1611 Bible *Exod.* vii 24 The Egyptians digged round about the riuer. 1691 Brokesby in Ray *N.C. Words*, s.v. *Dig*, In Yorkshire, they distinguish between digging and graving; to dig is with a Mattock; to grave, with a Spade. 1740 W. Stukeley *Stonehenge* x. 43 (*heading*) How the body is posited. What has been found in digging into these barrows. *c*1755 Johnson *Review Blackwell's Mem. Crt. Augustus* Wks. X. 185 Mr. Blackwell has neither digged in the ruins of any demolished city, nor [etc.]. 1836 Emerson *Nat.*, *Spirit* Wks. (Bohn) II. 168 If labourers are digging in the field hard by. 1873 C. Robinson *N.S. Wales* 35 He went so far as to recommend the unemployed miners of Cornwall to come out here and dig for it [gold]. 1907 E. Wharton *Fruit of Tree* I. iii. 32 As an archaeologist..I should really like to come here and dig. 1911 T. E. Lawrence *Lett.* (1938) 125 My orders are to..bring out Woolley (new chief), and the stores and dig for three months. 1912 *Ibid.* 136, I would like to dig in the Persian gulf.

b. Said of animals: to excavate the ground with snout or claws.

1388 Wyclif *Isa.* xxxiv. 15 There an irchoun hadde dichis ..and diggide aboute [1382 dalf, deluede]. 1535 Coverdale *Ibid.*, There shall the hedghogge buylde, digge..and bringe forth his yonge ones. 1774 Goldsm. *Nat. Hist.* (1776) VIII. 122 They [ants] dug deeper and deeper to deposite their eggs.

c. *fig.* with allusion to the general sense; also *spec.* to study hard and closely at a subject (*U.S.*). Hence, to understand (cf. sense 6c) (*slang* (orig. *U.S.*)).

1789 *Trifler* No. 43. 549 Youths who never digged for the rich ore of knowledge thro' the pages of the Rambler. 1801 Southey *Thalaba* iv. xv, 'Tis a well of living waters, Whose inexhaustible bounties all might drink, But few dig deep enough. 1827–8 *Harvard Reg.* 303 Here the sunken eye and sallow countenance bespoke the man who dug sixteen hours per diem. 1869 Louisa M. Alcott *Little Women* II. xii. 165 Laurie 'dug' to some purpose that year. 1936 *N.Y. World Telegram* 6 Oct. 16/1 'You dig?' is a short cut for 'You understand?' 1952 B. Ulanov *Hist. Jazz Amer.* 344 The man who really 'digs' can more often than not describe the next development in jazz before the musicians have reached it. 1957 C. MacInnes *City of Spades* I. xi. 89 Twist now —you dig?

d. To have 'diggings'; to lodge. *colloq.*

1914 C. Mackenzie *Sinister St.* II. iii. xi. 717 Soon it would come to the point of declaring outright that he did not want to dig with him. 1919 W. T. Grenfell *Labrador Dr.* (1920) iv. 64 Two or three classmates would 'dig' together.

e. To make incisions with action resembling digging.

1930 W. A. Thorpe in *Connoisseur* Oct. 226/2 To produce relief motives the operator has to 'dig' with his wheel at a steep angle to the surface.

2. With various prepositional constructions: To penetrate or make one's way *into* or *through* something by digging; to make an excavation or loosen the soil *under* anything.

1535 Coverdale *Ezek.* viii. 8 Thou sonne off man, dygge thorow the wall. 1580 Baret *Alv.* D. 697 To digge vnder an hill, *suffodere montem*. 1611 Bible *Job* xxiv. 16 In the darke they digge through houses. 1628 Hobbes *Thucyd.* (1822) 76 They united themselves by digging through the common walls between house and house. 1705 Addison *Trav.* (J.), The Italians have often dug into lands described in old authors, as the places where statues or obelisks stood, and seldom failed of success. 1832 *Examiner* 709/2 He seemed to dig into his subject. 1865 Gosse *Land & Sea* (1874) 5 The little boat ploughed and dug through the green and foaming waves. 1877 *Holderness Gloss.*, *Dig-into*, to set about a job of work in earnest and with energy.

II. *trans.*

3. a. To penetrate and excavate or turn up (the ground, or any surface) with a spade or similar tool. *spec.* to excavate archæologically.

*c*1340 *Cursor M.* 6747 (Trin.) þeof hous breking or diggyng ground If mon him smyte [etc.]. 1382 Wyclif *Ezek.* viii. 8 Sone of man, dig the wal; and whanne Y hadde thurȝ diggide the wal, o dore aperide. 1608 Shaks. *Per.* i. iv. 5 Who digs hills because they do aspire. 1697 Dryden *Æneid* vi. (R.), A rav'nous vulture..still for the growing liver digg'd his breast. 1743 W. Stukeley *Abury* xvi. 92 The very same appearances as I had so often seen, in digging the barrows about Stonehenge and Abury. 1912 T. E. Lawrence *Lett.* (1938) 134 The right way to dig a temple. 1949 W. F. Albright *Archaeol. of Palestine* ii. 41 The initial plan to dig the great site systematically..had to be abandoned because of the prohibitive expense. 1968 R. L. S. Bruce-Mitford *Sutton Hoo Ship-Burial* 18 It was the richest treasure ever dug from British soil.

b. Said of an animal penetrating and turning up (the ground) with its snout, etc.

1398 Trevisa *Barth. De P.R.* xviii. cii. (1495) 847 The molle hathe a snowte..and dyggeth therwyth the erthe and castyth vpp that he dyggyth. 1697 Dryden *Virg. Georg.* ii. 398 The bristled Boar..New grinds his arming Tusks, and digs the Ground.

4. a. *spec.* To break up and turn over (the soil) with a mattock, spade, or the like, as an operation of tillage. (See sense 1 as to technical use in quot. 1888.)

1388 Wyclif *Isa.* v. 6 It [a vineyard] schal not be kit, and it schal not be diggid, and breris and thornes schulen growe vp on it. 1552 [see digging *vbl. sb.* 1]. 1580 Baret *Alv.* D 697 That the ground should be dug three foote deepe. 1611 Bible *Isa.* vii. 25 And on all hilles that shalbe digged with the mattocke. 1715 Desaguliers *Fires Improv.* 114 Suppos'd to have been digg'd four Inches deep. 1888 Elworthy *W. Somerset Word-bk.*, *Dig*, v.t., to work ground with a mattock. Ground is never said to be *dug* with a spade. 1889 H. H. Romilly *Verandah in N. Guinea* 200 The first moon is spent in digging the ground.

†**b.** To till (a plant) by this operation. *Obs.*

1526 *Pilgr. Perf.* (W. de W. 1531) 54 We..sholde not onely dygge our vyne wele by compunccyon. 1577 B. Googe *Heresbach's Husb.* ii. (1586) 83 The plants of a yeere ..must bee discretely digged and dounged. 1626 Bacon *Sylva* §622 The Vines..are..so much digged and dressed, that their Sap spendeth into the Grapes.

†**c.** with *together*. *Obs.*

1398 Trevisa *Barth. de P.R.* xiii. xxix. (Tollem. MS.), On his rigge pouder and erþe is gaderid, and so digged to gederes, þat herbes and smale tren and busches groweþ þeron, so þat þe gret fische semeþ an ylonde.

5. To make (a hole, hollow place, mine, etc.) by the use of a mattock, spade, or the like; to form by digging; to hollow out; to excavate.

1387 Trevisa *Higden* (Rolls) I. 159 (Mätz.) Some diggeþ caues and dennes. 1388 Wyclif *Num.* xxi. 18 The pit which the princes diggiden [1382 delueden, doluen]. *c*1400 *Destr. Troy* 11363 þai droppe in the dike þai deghit have for vs. *c*1430 Lydg. *Min. Poems* 113 (Mätz.) To here hys dyrge do, and se hys pet deggyd. 1535 Coverdale *Gen.* xxi. 30, I haue dygged this well. 1579–80 North *Plutarch*, *Lucullus* 569 (Wright *Bible Word-bk.*) So did Xerxes..cause..a channell to be digged there to passe his shippes through. 1597 Shaks. *2 Hen. IV*, iv. v. 111 Then get thee gone, and digge my graue thy selfe. 1606 *Proc. agst. Late Traitors* 7 To digge a certain mine under the sayd House of Parliament. 1653 Holcroft *Procopius* ii. ix. 49 Anciently there was no passage through, but in time a way was dig'd through it. 1697 W. Dampier *Voy.* I. 85 In working their Canoas hollow, they cannot dig them so neat and thin [with stone hatchets]. —— *Ibid.* 215 Making a Canoa. Then again they turn her, and dig the inside. 1796 H. Hunter tr. *St. Pierre's Stud. Nat.* (1799) I. 2 The child, who, with a shell, had dug a hole in the sand, to hold the water of the Ocean. 1853 Sir H. Douglas *Milit. Bridges* (ed. 3) 17 Torrents..dig for themselves beds approaching to that form. 1864 H. Ainsworth *John Law* i. iv. (1881) 91 He..is ever digging mines under our feet.

6. a. To obtain or extract by excavation; to exhume, unearth; = *dig out* or *up* (13, 14). Const. *from*, *out of*.

*c*1350 *Will. Parlerne* 2243 þat werkmen forto worche ne wonne þidere sone, Stifly wiþ strong tol ston stifly to digge. 1387 Trevisa *Higden* (Rolls) I. 271 (Mätz.) In Gallia beþ many good quarers and noble for to digge stoon. 1565–73 Cooper *Thesaurus*, *Argilletum*..a place where clay is digged. 1601 Holland *Pliny* xviii. xvii. (Wright *Bible Word-bk.*), This same toad must be digged out of the ground againe. 1610 Shaks. *Temp.* ii. ii. 172, I with my long nayles will digge thee pig-nuts. *a*1661 Fuller *Worthies*, *Wales* (R.), Metalls elsewhere are digged..out of the bowells of the land. 1663 Gerbier *Counsel* D iv a, Chalk..is daily digged here at home. 1678 Cudworth *Intell. Syst.* 681 To declare out of what Quarry the Stones were dugg. 1682 R. Burton *Curios.* (1684) 30 Rocks out of which the Tinn is digged. 1726 Leoni *Alberti's Archit.* I. 31 We are..not to make our Bricks of Earth fresh dug, but to dig it in the Autumn. 1837 W. Irving *Capt. Bonneville* II. 221 The Indians..come to it in the summer time to dig the camash root. *Mod.* The cottagers were busy digging their potatoes.

b. ***to dig a badger.***

1706 Phillips (ed. Kersey), *To Dig a Badger* (in the Hunter's Language) is to raise or dislodge him. 1721–1800 in Bailey. 1869 *Lonsdale Gloss.*, *Dig*, to start a badger.

c. *slang* (orig. *U.S.*). (*a*) To understand, appreciate, like, admire; (*b*) to look at or listen to; to experience. Cf. sense 1 c.

1935 *Hot News* Sept. 20/2 If you listen enough, and dig him enough, you will realise that that..riff is the high-spot of the record. 1941 *Life* 15 Dec. 89 Dig me? 1943 M. Shulman *Barefoot Boy with Cheek* 90 Awful fine slush pump, I mean awful fine. You ought to dig that. 1944 C. Calloway *Hepsters Dict.*, *Dig* v.—(1) Meet. (2) Look, see. (3) Comprehend, understand. 1944 M. Zolotow *Never whistle in Dressing Room* iii. 52 When they see a pretty girl they shout, 'Dig the chick.' 1947 R. de Toledano *Frontiers of Jazz* p. x, I recognize it when I see it, the same as I dig good Jazz when I hear it. 1949 L. Feather *Inside Be-Bop* iii. 28 Dizzy didn't dig the band's kind of music and the band didn't dig Dizzy. 1958 *Punch* 8 Jan. 92/1 The lines of communication get tangled. In other words the people don't quite 'dig' you. 1958 *Listener* 29 May 912/1 He wants to 'dig' the whole of life, and is convinced that experience comes only to the irresponsible. 1958 *Punch* 25 June 853/3 Does the beat generation really dig such crazy old-world catch-phrases? 1959 C. MacInnes *Absolute Beginners* 60 If you *like* the other number, I mean like the looks of them, really dig them sexually. *Ibid.* 62 Everything you learned, you hadn't learned until you'd really dug it: i.e., made it part of your own experience. 1960 N. Mitford *Don't tell Alfred* xviii. 192 Of course he's a man's man, you might not dig him like we do. 1969 *New Yorker* 29 Nov. 48/1, I just don't dig any of these guys. I don't understand their scenes.

†**7.** To put and cover up (in the ground, etc.) by digging or delving; to bury. Cf. *dig in*, 11 b.

1530 Palsgr. 516/1, I wyll dygge this dogge in to the grounde somwhere for feare of stynkyng. 1607 Topsell *Serpents* (1658) 797 All the Winter time they dig themselves into the earth. 1647 Trapp *Comm. Matt.* v. 15 Such idle servants as..dig their talents into the earth.

8. To thrust, plunge, or force (something) *in* or *into*.

1553 T. Wilson *Rhet.* 107 As though a sworde were ofte digged and thrust twise or thrise in one place of the bodie. 1832 L. Hunt *Sir R. Esher* (1850) 258 Delighting, as he went over the noble Lord, to dig his knuckles in his back. 1860 Tyndall *Glac.* i. xi. 77 We..dug our feet firmly into the snow. 1883 F. M. Peard *Contrad.* i, He dug his hands into his pockets, and lounged off. 1893 Selous *Trav. S.E. Africa* 37, I dug my spurs into my horse's ribs.

9. To spur (a horse) vigorously [= F. *diguer un cheval*]; to thrust, stab, prod; to give (any one) a sharp thrust or nudge (in the ribs, etc.).

1530 Palsgr. 516/1, I dygge my horse in the sydes with my spores. 1551 Robinson tr. *More's Utop.* (Arb.) 102 You shoulde haue sene children..digge and pushe theire mothers under the sides. 1875 Tennyson *Q. Mary* ii. iii, Gamble thyself at once out of my sight, Or I will dig thee with my dagger. 1881 Mrs. P. O'Donoghue *Ladies on Horseback* 68, I dug him with my spur, and sent him at it. 1889 Farmer *Americanisms*, *To dig a man in the ribs*, is to give him a thrust or blow in the side.

III. In comb. with adverbs.

10. dig down. a. *trans.* To bring down or cause to fall by digging.

1526–34 Tindale *Rom.* xi. 3 Lorde, they haue..dygged doune [so 1611 and 1881 R. V.] thyn alters. 1580 Baret *Alv.* D. 688 To digge downe, *defodio*. *a*1619 Fotherby *Atheom.* ii. vii. §4 (1622) 268 Wicked Citizens..doe overthrow their owne Cities, and digge downe their Walls.

b. To lower or remove by digging or excavating.

1591 Spenser *Virg. Gnat* 46 Mount Athos..was digged downe. 1778 Bp. Lowth *Transl. Isa.* (ed. 12) Notes 313 She ordered the precipices to be digged down.

c. *intr.* To pay money from one's own pocket. *U.S. colloq.*

1942 in BERREY & VAN DEN BARK *Amer. Thes. Slang* §550/3. **1951** J. STEINBECK *Log from 'Sea of Cortez'* (1958) p. xxvi, She was a wise and tolerant pushover for any hard-luck story... Even when she knew it was a fake she dug down.

11. dig in. †**a.** *trans.* To pierce, stab, penetrate. *Obs.* (Cf. 9.) **b.** To put in and cover up by digging. (Cf. *dig into* in 7.)

1530 PALSGR. 516/1, He hath dygged hym in nat withstandyng his almayne ryvettes. **1839** *Penny Cycl.* XIV. 402/2 The dung.. may be dug in without fermentation for most kitchen-garden crops.

c. To cause to penetrate, to drive in deeply. (Cf. 8.) Colloq. phr. ***to dig in one's feet, heels, toes***: to adopt a firm position; to keep resolutely or obstinately to one's decision, opinion, attitude, etc.

1885 *Sat. Rev.* 6 June 765/2 [Dæmons].. laughing with glee if the.. rider cursed or dug in the spurs. **1933** *Punch* 16 Aug. 174/1, I am prepared to declare mosques open and to grace the inaugurations of new caravanserais, though I personally have no taste for ritual. But at that point I dig in my toes. **1941** L. A. G. STRONG *Bay* 179 One thing I had dug in my heels over was the church I went to. **1956** N. COWARD *South Sea Bubble* I. i. 8 You jumped at him before he had time to get his breath and now he's dug his feet in.

d. *intr.* or *refl.* To fix oneself firmly in a position; *spec.* (*a*) *Mil.*, to excavate a trench or the like in order to withstand an attack or consolidate a position; (*b*) *Cricket*, to consolidate one's position as a batsman.

1851 *Knickerbocker* XXXVIII. 183 [The crab] pinched, scratched, 'dug in', and held on. **1917** A. G. EMPEY *From Fire Step* 145 The machine-gunners went over with the fourth wave to consolidate the captured line, or 'dig in', as Tommy calls it. **1919** J. B. MORTON *Barber of Putney* xvi. 263 Word came back that they [*sc.* a platoon] were to go to a certain point and dig in. **1922** *Daily Mail* 21 Nov. 8 The most alarming of Sir Percival Phillips's disclosures is that our 'limpets' in Mesopotamia are digging themselves vigorously in. **1934** C. DAY LEWIS *Hope for Poetry* vii. 41 D. H. Lawrence dug himself in in the Unconscious. **1944** BLUNDEN *Cricket Country* iv. 49 Such a side is free from the solemn rule of 'digging in' which big cricket prescribes. **1949** *Manch. Guardian Weekly* 14 July 2/4 The policy of stimulating expansion rather than digging in to protect the status quo. **1959** *Times* 29 May 4/4 Watson was bowled by the second ball he received. But.. Phillips dug in with gallant determination.

e. *intr.* To set to work earnestly and energetically; to work hard. *dial.* and *U.S. colloq.*

[**1877** F. ROSS et al. *Gloss. Holderness* 53/2 *Dig-intiv* it, lads, and you'll seean get it deean.] **1884** 'MARK TWAIN' *Huck. Finn* xxxviii, We got to dig in like all git-out. **1951** F. S. ANTHONY *Me & Gus* (1953) 26 We'll dig in like niggers, Mark, and show those old jokers over the fence how to smack up wood.

f. To begin eating, esp. heartily. *colloq.*

1912 *Dialect Notes* III. 574 Dig in and help us eat the rest of this turkey. **1952** A. BARON *With Hope* IV. ii. 119 Sit down and dig in. Your grub's getting cold.

12. dig off. *trans.* To cut off by digging. *rare.*

1655 STANLEY *Hist. Philos.* I. (1701) 46/1 He attempted to dig the Isthmus off from the Continent.

13. dig out. a. *trans.* To take out, thrust out, extract or remove by excavation. (Cf. 6.) *fig.* to obtain, get hold of, or get out by search or effort.

1388 WYCLIF *Job* iii. 21 As men diggynge.. out [**1382** deluende out] tresour. **1526** TINDALE *Gal.* iv. 15 Ye wolde have digged [**1534** plucked] out youre awne eyes, and haue geven them to me. **1580** BARET *Alv.* D 697 To digge out ones eies, *elidere alicui oculos*. **1667** MILTON *P.L.* I. 690 Soon had his.. crew Op'nd into the Hill a spacious wound And dig'd out ribs of Gold. **1772** HUTTON *Bridges* 94 The sand having been previously digged out for that purpose. **1847–78** HALLIWELL, *Dig out*, to unearth the badger.

fig. **1864** R. B. KIMBALL *Was he successful?* II. xi. 259 It was their habit to go over their lessons together, after Chellis had 'dug out' his. **1877** *Gentl. Mag.* CCXL. 596 This last-named prince.. had hidden himself in a cupboard in the midst of a roll of carpet, and was with difficulty dug out to be girt with the sword of Othman. **1887** *Harper's Mag.* May 884/2, I don't believe it is worth while to dig out the glasses. **1929** 'P. WILLIAMS' *Jacob's Ladder* xix. 269 It was Carolyn who.. dug out two old volumes of eighteenth century pictures lying forgotten in a cupboard. **1930** *Daily Express* 30 July 3/7 England.. may need more batsmen of the type who have to be dug out. **1968** *Globe & Mail* (Toronto) 3 Feb. B2/2 The Europeans.. can dig out many reasons for their shortcomings.

b. To excavate, to form by excavation. Cf. DUG-OUT (canoe).

1748 *Relat. Earthq. Lima* Pref. 9 These usually were Caves, or Hollows dug-out in the Mountains.

c. *intr.* To depart, elope. (*U.S. colloq.*)

1884 S. L. CLEMENS (Mark Twain) *Adv. Hucklebury Finn* (Farmer *Amer.*), Then I jumped in a canoe, and dug out for our place.. as hard as I could go. **1888** *Detroit Free Press* 21 July (Farmer *Amer.*), She dug out last night with a teamster.

14. dig up. a. *trans.* To take or get out of the ground, etc., by digging or excavating; to exhume, disinter, unearth. Also *fig.* to obtain, find, search out (cf. 13 a) (now *colloq.*) ***to dig up the hatchet***, to renew strife: see HATCHET. (Cf. 6.)

c **1400** MAUNDEV. (1839) ix. 107 He [John the Baptist] was.. buryed at Samarie. And there let Julianus Apostata dyggen him vp. *c* **1425** *Seven Sag.* (P.) 1126, I se a gras of grete solas, Were hyt dyggyd uppe by the rote, Of many thyngs hit myght be bote. **1535** COVERDALE *Job* iii. 21 Those that dygge vp treasure. **1588** SHAKS. *Tit. A.* v. i. 135 Oft haue I dig'd vp dead men from their graues. **1695** WOODWARD *Nat. Hist. Earth* II. (1723) 81 There are dig'd up Trees.. in some Northern Islands, in which there are at this Day growing no Trees at all. **1726–7** SWIFT *Gulliver* II. vii. 160 Huge bones and skulls, casually dug up in several parts of the kingdom. **1858** GLENNY *Gard. Everyday Bk.* 267/1 *Jerusalem Artichokes*, Dig them up if it be not done already. **1889** FARMER *Amer.*, *To dig up the hatchet*, a phrase decidedly Indian in origin.. This [the hatchet] was buried to signify the putting away of strife; and digging up the hatchet, meant a renewal of warfare.

fig. **1611** BIBLE *Prov.* xvi. 27 An vngodly man diggeth vp euill: and in his lips there is a burning fire. **1861** BRIGHT *Sp. India* 19 Mar., A Committee to dig up all the particulars of our supposed perils. **1895** *Century Mag.* Sept. 674/1, I heard he was tryin' to dig up a trade with a man who's got a mine over in the Slocan country. **1909** 'O. HENRY' *Options* 50 Ogden digs up a deck of cards, and we play casino. **1959** I. & P. OPIE *Lore & Lang. Schoolchildren* iii. 53 'Tell us news, not history.' 'Where did you dig that up?'

b. To excavate, break up or open by digging.

1551 ROBINSON tr. *More's Utop.* II. (Arb.) 73 Kyng Utopus.. caused. xv. myles space of vplandyshe grounde.. to be cut and dygged vp and so brought the sea rounde aboute the land. **1593** SHAKS. *3 Hen. VI*, I. iii. 27 If I digg'd vp thy forefathers Graues, And hung their rotten Coffins vp in Chaynes. **1855** MACAULAY *Hist. Eng.* IV. 132 The English government would be unable to equip a fleet without digging up the cellars of London in order to collect the nitrous particles from the walls.

c. To break up and loosen the soil of, by digging: said esp. of a place not previously or recently dug.

1377 LANGL. *P. Pl.* B. VI. 109 Dikeres & delueres digged vp þe balkes. *a* **1698** TEMPLE (J.), You cannot dig up your garden too often. **1799** J. ROBERTSON *Agric. Perth* 247 He directs the moss to be delved or dug up with spades. **1889** BOLDREWOOD *Robbery under Arms* (1890) 7 He dug up a little garden in front.

Hence **digged** (dɪgd), **'digging** *ppl. adjs.*

c **1394** *P. Pl. Crede* 504 þat was þe dygginge devel þat dreccheþ men ofte. **1552** HULOET, Dygged, *fossitius*. **1616** SURFL. & MARKH. *Country Farme* 302 In a well husbanded and digd ground. **1617** *Janua Ling.* 170 Souldiers.. lie in digged trenches.

dig, *sb.*[1] Also 9 (*Sc.*) **deg.** [f. prec. vb.]

1. a. An act of digging; the plunging or thrusting (of a spade, or the like) into the ground.

1887 *Pall Mall G.* 15 Oct. 11/1 The price which is obtained for the excavated sand.. just meets the expense of the dig out. **1894** *Contemp. Rev.* Jan. 66 At each 'dig' four sets of forks are thrust into the ground.

b. *colloq.* An archæological excavation; an expedition for the purpose of an archæological excavation.

1896 A. J. EVANS in *Academy* 13 June 494/1 He showed me several clay bulls.. obtained through his dig. **1908** *Chambers's Jrnl.* July 527/1 They [*sc.* tomb-hunters] speak of the different excavations as 'digs'. **1911** T. E. LAWRENCE *Lett.* (1938) 112 We are only two on this dig. **1940** 'M. INNES' *Secret Vanguard* vi. 56 The dig at Dabdab must be completed before the rains. **1957** K. M. KENYON *Digging up Jericho* 39 The first stages of a dig.. start long before one actually gets down to excavating. **1969** *Times* 23 Jan. 13/1 The many archaeological digs that have been going on since the beginning of the Aswan Dam project.

2. A definite depth or quantity to be dug out.

1890 *Daily News* 4 Sept. 6/4 For every 'dig' 30*s.* is to be paid to the gang. The 'dig' is to be 9 ft. measured from where the crane plumbs in the hatchway.

3. A tool for digging; a mattock, pick-axe, etc.

1674–91 RAY *N.C. Words*, *Dig*, a Mattock. **1877** *Holderness Gloss.*, *Dig*, a mattock; a navvy's pick. **1877** *N.W. Linc. Gloss.*, *Dig*, an instrument used for stubbing up roots, more commonly called a *stub-dig*. 'As straight as a dig' is a common proverbial expression.

4. a. A thrust, a sharp poke, as with the elbow, fist, or other part of the body.

1819 MOORE *Tom Crib's Mem.* 51 While *ribbers* rung from each resounding frame, And divers *digs*, and many a ponderous *pelt*. **1823** GALT *R. Gilhaize* I. 127 (Jam.) Winterton, when he lay down, gave him a deg with his elbow, and swore at him to be quiet. **1843** J. T. HEWLETT *College Life* xxxi. (Stratm.) Brunt gave him a hard dig in the ribs. **1855** BROWNING *Holy-Cross Day* v, Somebody deal him a dig in the paunch. **1860** TYNDALL *Glac.* I. xvi. 117 A vigorous dig of leg and hatchet into the snow was sufficient to check the motion.

b. *fig.* (Cf. *hit* sb.)

1840 HOOD *Miss Kilmansegg, Her Fancy Ball* iii, Thus Tories like to worry the Whigs.. Giving them lashes, thrashes and digs. **1884** *Pall Mall G.* 15 Mar. 1/2 The Opposition.. caring absolutely for nothing except how to get a dig at the fellows who are in. **1887** E. J. GOODMAN *Too Curious* ix, This, of course, was a sly dig at Frank.

5. A diligent or plodding student. (*U.S. Students' slang.*)

1849 *Let. to Yng. Man* 14 The treadmill.. might be a useful appendage to a college, not as a punishment, but as a recreation for digs. **1851** *N.Y. Lit. World* 11 Oct. (Bartlett) There goes the dig.. How like a parson he eyes his book! **1894** *N.Y. Weekly Witness* 12 Dec. 2/2 The student who earnestly pursues his scholastic studies is held to be a scrub, or grind, or dig.

6. *pl.* Lodgings (cf. DIGGING *vbl. sb.* 5); also occas. as *sing.* (and *Comb.*). *colloq.*

1893 *Stage* 11 May 16/2 'Being in the know' regarding the best 'digs' can only be attained by experience. **1905** *Varsity* 16 Nov. 79/1 An invitation from a friend in digs. **1908** A. S. M. HUTCHINSON *Once Aboard the Lugger* I. i. 27, I have heard that one can work far better by living near the hospital in digs. **1916** W. OWEN *Let.* 6 Nov. (1967) 414, I like this digs far better than the Queen's Hotel life. **1959** A. LEJEUNE *Crowded & Dangerous* vii. 78 His old digs.. where he lived when he used to work for us. **1959** *Times* 6 Mar. 12/6 Dig-hunting is a serious business... The good woman is offering you a room in her home for a whole year.

dig, *sb.*[2] *Obs.* exc. *dial.* A duck.

c **1420** *Liber Cocorum* (1862) 9 þandon for wylde digges, swannus, and piggus. ? *a* **1500** *Chester Pl., Deluge* 189 Heare are doves, diggs, drakes, Redshankes, runninge through the lakes. **1611** COTGR., *Anette*, a Ducke, or Dig. **1616** *Inventory* in Earwaker *Powltrey, &c., Sandbach* (1890) 135 Three Digs and a Drake. **1884** *Cheshire Gloss.*, *Dig*, a duck.

b. *Comb.*, as **dig-bird**, *Lancash.*, a young duck (Halliwell); **dig-meat**, duckweed (*Chesh. Gloss.*).

dig (dɪg), *sb.*[3] *Austral.* and *N.Z. colloq.* Abbrev. of DIGGER 2 f.

1918 *Chrons. N.Z.E.F.* 21 June 221/2 Be shrewd, sweet Dig. *Ibid.* 22 Nov. 198/1 'How far's the war, Dig?' was the first question we asked. **1933** *Bulletin* (Sydney) 18 Oct. 10/3 He gave his verdict: 'That's good, Dig.; that's strong.' **1946** E. G. WEBBER *Johnny Enzed in Italy* 4 The war has finished and a large number of Old Digs have bustled their way down various gangways. **1965** G. MCINNES *Road to Gundagai* ii. 25 Often they shouted at us.. 'Howsit up in the dress circle, dig?'

digallic (daɪ'gælɪk), *a. Chem.* [f. DI-[2] + GALLIC *a.*[2]] In ***digallic acid***, which has the composition of two molecules of gallic acid, minus one equivalent of water.

1877 WATTS *Fownes' Chem.* (ed. 12) II. 547 Gallotannic Acid, Digallic Acid or Tannin.. occurs in large quantity in nut-galls.. and many other plants.

digamist ('dɪgəmɪst). [f. as DIGAMY + -IST.] A man or woman who has married a second time.

1656 BLOUNT *Glossogr.*, *Digamist*,.. one that marries after his first wives death. *a* **1660** HAMMOND *Wks.* I. 597 (R.) The digamist, or he that hath had two wives successively, one after another. **1706** HEARNE *Collect.* 9 Nov., I can say no more of this Bp. than y^{t} in complyance wth y^{e} Fashion of y^{e} Age he is a *digamist*. **1869** LECKY *Europ. Mor.* (1877) II. 327 'Digamists', according to Origen, are saved in the name of Christ, but are by no means crowned by him.

†**b.** = BIGAMIST. *Obs.* (So F. *digame*, Cotgr.)

1656 BLOUNT *Glossogr.*, *Digamist*, one that hath had two Wives together.

†**'digamite.** *Obs.* [f. as prec. + -ITE.] = prec.

1616 T. GODWIN *Moses & Aaron* (1655) 238 Persons marrying after such divorcements, were reputed digamites, that is, to have two husbands or two wives. **1674–81** BLOUNT *Glossogr.*, *Digamist* or *Digamite*.

digamma (daɪ'gæmə). [a. L. *digamma*, Gr. δίγαμμα the digamma, f. δι- twice + γάμμα the letter gamma: so called by the grammarians of the first century, from its shape ϝ or **F**, resembling two gammas (Γ) set one above the other.]

The sixth letter of the original Greek alphabet, corresponding to the Semitic *waw* or *vau*, which was afterwards disused, the sound expressed by it having been gradually lost from the literary language.

It was a consonant, probably equivalent to English *w*; in the Italian alphabets derived from Greek, it appears to have passed through the power of consonantal *v*, to that of *f*, its value in the Roman alphabet: see F. It was lost in Ionic and Attic before the date of the earliest known monuments, but it occurs in inscriptions in all the other dialects down to late times, and it was also retained in the literary remains of Æolic, whence the appellation *Æolic digamma* or *letter*. Though not written in classical Greek, it can be restored on linguistic and metrical grounds in the Homeric and other ancient forms of Greek words, as ϝέργον, work, Διϝί dative of Ζεύς, etc.

[**1552** HULOET, F letter among the latines is called *Digamma*. **1565–73** COOPER *Thesaurus*, *Digamma*, the letter F. Cicero useth it for his maner of Formium beginning with F.] **1698** M. LISTER *Journ. Paris* (1699) 50 (Stanford) His new invented Letter the Digamma, which he instituted or borrowed from the Eolique to express V Consonant. **1727–51** CHAMBERS *Cycl.* s.v., This letter *F* is derived to us from the Romans, who borrowed it from the Æolians; among whom it is called digamma, or double gamma, as resembling two Γ's, one over the other. **1742** POPE *Dunc.* IV. 218 Tow'ring o'er your Alphabet, like Saul, Stands our Digamma, and o'ertops them all. **1814** JAMIESON *Hermes Scyth.* I. iv. 41 It has been thought that the Aeolic digamma approached nearly to the sound of W. **1845** STODDARD in *Encycl. Metrop.* (1847) I. 94/1 The Æolic digamma is described by Dionysius of Halicarnassus, in the 1st book of his Antiquities. **1857** BIRCH *Anc. Pottery* (1858) II. 17 The use of the digamma.. is continued on Doric vases both of this [the second year of the 94th Olympiad] and even of a later age.

digammate (daɪ'gæmət), *a.* [ad. mod.L. *digammāt-us*, f. *digamma*: see -ATE[2].] = next.

1864 in WEBSTER.

digammated (daɪ'gæmətɪd), *ppl. a.* [f. as prec. + -ATE[3] + -ED.]

1. Spelt with or having the digamma.

1803 *Edin. Rev.* July 315 The conjunction ἰδὲ, *and*,.. is a digammated word. **1805** VALPY *Grk. Gram.* (1818) 151 A short Syllable is often made long when the next word begins with a digammated vowel. **1863** J. HADLEY *Ess.* (1873) iv. 56 It is more than forty years since Richard Payne Knight published in 1820 his famous digammated Iliad. **1882** R. C. JEBB *Life Bentley* 152 The number of digammated roots in Homer is between thirty and forty.

2. Formed with a figure like the digamma, as the digammated cross, a phallic symbol.

† **di'gammic,** *a. Obs.* [f. DIGAMMA + -IC.] Of or belonging to a digamma.

1817 G. S. FABER *Eight Diss.* (1845) I. 134 The Anakim or (with the digammic prefix) Fanakim.

digamous ('dɪgəməs), *a.* [f. L. *digam-us*, a. Gr. διγαμος that has been married twice (f. δι-, DI-² twice + γάμος marriage) + -OUS.]

1. Married a second time; that contracts a second marriage after the death of the first spouse; of the nature of digamy.

1864 in WEBSTER. **1868** MILMAN *St. Paul's* xi. 302 A digamous Bishop could hardly be more odious to Elizabeth.

2. *Bot.* = ANDROGYNOUS.

1883 *Syd. Soc. Lex.*, *Digamous*, having both sexes on the same flower-cluster.

digamy ('dɪgəmɪ). [ad. L. *digamia*, a. Gr. διγαμία a marrying twice, f. δίγαμ-ος: see DIGAMOUS and -Y.]

1. Digamous condition or state; second marriage; re-marriage after the death of the first spouse.

1635 PAGITT *Christianogr.* App. 17 The ordinary Priests marry once, Digamy is forbidden them. **1672** CAVE *Prim. Chr.* II. v. (1673) 83 Three sorts of Digamy or Second Marriages. **1672-5** COMBER *Comp. Temple* (1702) 220 Digamy, as well as Marrying after a Divorce while the former Wife lives, are forbid under the Gospel. **1755** JOHNSON, *Digamy*, second marriage; marriage to a second wife after the death of the first: as *bigamy*, having two wives at once. **1869** LECKY *Europ. Mor.* II. v. 346 Digamy, or second marriage, is described by Athanagoras as 'a decent adultery'.

† **2.** = BIGAMY 1; having two wives at the same time. *Obs.*

1638 SIR T. HERBERT *Trav.* (ed. 2) 39 The Antick Romans, who..so hated Digamy (both in enjoying two wives at one time, and being twice married). **1761-66** BAILEY, *Digamy*, a being married to two Wives at the same Time.

digastric (daɪ'gæstrɪk), *a.* and *sb. Anat.* [ad. mod.L. *digastric-us*, f. Gr. δι-, DI-² + γαστήρ, γαστρ- belly: cf. GASTRIC. In F. *digastrique* 'hauing two bellies' Cotgr. 1611.]

A. *adj.*

1. Having two parts swelling like bellies; *spec.* applied to muscles having two fleshy bellies with an intervening tendinous part, as that of the lower jaw; see B.

1721 BAILEY, *Digastric*, that has a double belly. **1732** MONRO *Anat. Bones* 102 Where the digastric Muscle of the lower Jaw has its Origin. **1872** HUXLEY *Phys.* vii. 175 There are muscles which are fleshy at each end and have a tendon in the middle. Such muscles are called digastric or two-bellied.

2. Of or pertaining to the digastric muscle of the lower jaw: see B.

1831 R. KNOX *Cloquet's Anat.* 53 On the inside of, and behind, the mastoid process, is a longitudinal depression named the Digastric Groove, on account of its giving attachment to the muscle of that name. **1840** J. ELLIS *Anat.* 82 The digastric nerve, the largest of the three branches of the portio dura..is distributed by many filaments to the under surface of the posterior belly of the digastric. **1842** E. WILSON *Anat. Vade M.* (ed. 2) 49 Upon the inner side of the root of the mastoid process is the digastric fossa.

B. *sb.* (Also in L. form *digastricus.*) A muscle of the lower jaw, thick and fleshy at its extremities, thin and tendinous at its middle.

It arises from the back part of the skull, and is inserted into the mandible. Its action is to depress the lower jaw, or to raise the hyoid bone and carry it backwards or forwards as in deglutition. (*Syd. Soc. Lex.*)

1696 PHILLIPS, *Digastric*, a double-bellied Muscle, which ..ending in..the Chin, draws it downward. **1746** J. PARSONS *Hum. Physiognomy* i. 30 It serves..to assist the Digastric in opening the Jaws. **1872** MIVART *Elem. Anat.* 286 The digastric is a muscle with two fleshy bellies, with a median tendon. **1881** *Athenæum* 9 Apr. 496/1 On the Tendinous Intersection of the Digastric.

Digby ('dɪgbɪ). [The name of a seaport of Nova Scotia.] A dried or cured herring of a type caught at Digby. In full ***Digby chicken*** or ***chick.***

1829 G. HEAD *Forest Scenes Wilds N. Amer.* 40 A small species of herring... They are extremely delicate, and are salted in great quantities every year. They have gained the nick-name of Digby chickens. **1862** *Chambers's Encycl.* III. 557/2 A variety of small herrings or pilchards, which are smoked and dried for export; they have a high flavour, and are known in trade as Digbies. **1883, 1887** [see CHICK *sb.*¹ 4]. **1958** *Encycl. Canadiana* III. 267/1 Digby is noted..for fish, including cured herrings known as 'Digby chickens'.

digeneous (daɪ'dʒiːniːəs), *a.* [f. Gr. διγενής of double or doubtful sex (f. δι-, DI-² + γένος, γενε- kind, race, sex) + -OUS.]

1. Of two sexes, bisexual. *Syd. Soc. Lex.* 1883.

2. Of or pertaining to the *Digenea*, a division of the trematode worms or flukes.

digenesis (daɪ'dʒɛnɪsɪs). *Biol.* [mod.L., f. Gr. δι-, DI-² + γένεσις generation.] Successive generation by two different processes, as sexual and asexual.

1876 *Beneden's Anim. Parasites* 102 This phenomenon has been known by the name of alternate generation; we have called it digenesis. **1883** in *Syd. Soc. Lex.*

digenetic (daɪdʒɪ'nɛtɪk), *a.* [f. as prec. + Gr. -γενετικός, f. γένεσις.] Relating to or characterized by digenesis.

1883 *Syd. Soc. Lex.*, *Digenetic worms*, parasitic worms which at different periods of life have different forms. **1890** E. R. LANKESTER *Adv. Science* 265 Whether the female.. belonged to a parthenogenetic or digenetic brood. *Ibid.* 266 In Artemia salina parthenogenetic alternate with digenetic broods.

digenite ('dɪdʒɪnaɪt). *Min.* [mod. f. Gr. διγενής of doubtful sex or kind + -ITE.] A variety of CHALCOCITE or copper-glance.

1850 DANA *Min.* 509. **1863-72** WATTS *Dict. Chem.* II. 323.

digenous ('dɪdʒɪnəs), *a.* [irreg. f. Gr. δι- two + γένος kind, race + -OUS.] Of two sexes, bisexual.

1884 SEDGWICK tr. *Claus' Zool.* I. 97 The digenous or sexual reproduction depends upon the production of two kinds of germinal cells, the combined action of which is necessary for the development of a new organism.

Hence **'digeny**, digenous reproduction.

1883 in *Syd. Soc. Lex.*

† **di'ger,** *v. Obs. rare.* [a. F. *digér-er* (14th c. in Hatz.-Darm.), ad. L. *dīger-ĕre* to DIGEST.] *trans.* = DIGEST *v.*

1541 R. COPLAND *Guydon's Quest. Chirurg.*, A pyt wherin the nourysshynge blode commynge fro the lyuer is dygered. **1597** LOWE *Chirurg.* (1634) 103 Such things as have the virtue to discusse, diger, and dry lightly, and not humect.

† **'digerate,** *v. Obs. rare.* [f. as prec. + -ATE³.] *trans.* To digest. Hence **'digerating** *ppl. a.*

1634 T. JOHNSON *Parey's Chirurg.* XVIII. xvii. (1678) 426 They must be strengthened with hot and digerating things.

† **'digerent,** *a.* and *sb. Obs. rare.* [ad. L. *dīgerent-em*, pres. ppl. of *dīger-ĕre* to DIGEST.]

A. *adj.* Digesting.

1477 NORTON *Ord. Alch.* v. in Ashm. (1652) 62 But our cheefe Digestiue [*printed* -ure] for our intent, Is virtuall heate of the matter digerent. **1755** JOHNSON, *Digerent*, adj., that which has the power of digesting, or causing digestion.

B. *sb.* A medicine or agent that promotes digestion or suppuration.

1731 BAILEY, *Digerents* (with Physicians) Medicines which digest or ripen. **1854-67** C. A. HARRIS *Dict. Med. Terminol.* 215 *Digerents*..medicines which promote the secretion of proper pus in wounds and ulcers.

digest ('daɪdʒɛst), *sb.* Also 5 **dy-**, 7 **dis-**. [ad. L. *dīgesta* 'matters digested', a name given to various collections of writings arranged and distributed under heads; n. pl. of *dīgest-us*, pa. ppl. of *dīgerĕre*: see DIGEST *v.* The appearance of the senses in English, does not correspond in order to the original development.]

1. a. A digested collection of statements or information; a methodically arranged compendium or summary of literary, historical, legal, scientific, or other written matter.

1555 BRAHAM *Address to Reader* in *Lydgate's Chron. Troy*, The verye trouthe therof is not to be had in theyr dygestes. **1605** BACON *Adv. Learn.* II. xv. §1. 58 The Disposition..of that Knowledge..consisteth in a good Digest of Common Places. **1789** T. JEFFERSON *Writ.* (1859) III. 14 This is a very elegant digest of whatever is known of the Greeks. **1825** MACAULAY *Ess., Milton* (1854) I. 2/1 His digest of scriptural texts. **1854** H. MILLER *Sch. & Schm.* (1858) 313 Those popular digests of geological science which are now so common.

b. *spec.* A periodical composed wholly or mainly of condensed versions of articles, stories, etc., previously published elsewhere. Also *attrib.*

1922 (*title*) Reader's Digest. **1946** (*title*) The Literary Digest. A monthly magazine of popular literary interest. **1957** *Times Lit. Suppl.* 11 Oct. 604/4 The Chaplain's loving biography has been edited on the principles of 'condensed reading', as popularized by the 'digest' kind of magazine. **1958** J. CANNAN *And be a Villain* i. 6 Mad ideas they'd got from medical articles in Digests. **1967** G. STEINER *Lang. & Silence* 258 A time of fantastic intellectual cheapness,..the century of the book club, the digest, and the hundred great ideas on the instalment plan.

2. *Law.* **a.** An abstract, or collection in condensed form, of same body of law, systematically arranged.

a **1626** BACON (*title*) An Offer to King James, of a Digest to be made of the Laws of England. **1652** NEEDHAM tr. *Selden's Mare Cl.* 38 The Digests of the Jewish Law. **1681** W. ROBERTSON *Phraseol. Gen.* (1693) 471 Digests, gathered out of the 37 civilians. **1724** A. COLLINS *Gr. Chr. Relig.* 14 A Digest of System of Laws for the Government of the Church. **1765** BLACKSTONE *Comm.* I. 66 Out of these three laws..king Edward the confessor extracted one uniform law or digest of laws. **1792** J. WILSON in Sparks *Corr. Amer. Rev.* (1853) IV. 388 A digest of the laws of the United States. **1818** CRUISE *Digest* (ed. 2) I. 126 Lord Chief Baron Comyn, in his Digest, states the case in Dyer as having decided that [etc.]. **1869** RAWLINSON *Anc. Hist.* 357 The code of the Twelve Tables..was a most valuable digest of the early Roman law.

b. *spec.* The body of Roman laws compiled from the earlier jurists by order of the Emperor Justinian. (The earliest use in English.)

1387 TREVISA *Higden* (Rolls) III. 255 Iustinianus..made and restored þe lawes of digest. **1530** PALSGR. 213/2 Digest, a boke in lawe, *digeste.* **1577** tr. *Bullinger's Decades* (1592) 427 The lawes and constitutions of princes..founde either in the Code, in the booke of Digestes, or Pandectes. **1660** BURNEY Κέρδ. Δῶρον (1661) 115 All they read in the Pandects, Digests and Codes in the Statute and common Law-books. **1845** GRAVES *Roman Law* in *Encycl. Metrop.* 762/1 Notes on the laws of the Twelve Tables according to the order of the Institutes and the first part of the Digest. **1882** STUBBS *Med. & Mod. Hist.* xiii. (1886) 306 If you take any well-drawn case of litigation in the middle ages..you will find that its citations from the Code and Digest are at least as numerous as from the Decretum.

† **3.** = DIGESTION. *Obs.*

1398 TREVISA *Barth. De. P.R.* XVII. ii. (*MS. Bodl.* 3738) Yf a plante shall be durable: it nedyth that it haue humour wᵗ good dygest and fatty. So plantes yᵗ haue humour w[ythou]t good digestion wydre sone in grete colde. **1602** CAREW *Cornwall* 29 b, Some giue meate, but leaue it no disgest, Some tickle him, but are from pleasing farre.

† **di'gest,** *ppl. a. Obs.* Also 6 *Sc.* **de-**. [ad. L. *dīgest-us*, pa. ppl. of *dīgerĕre* to DIGEST.]

1. as *pa. pple.* and *adj.* Digested.

1398 TREVISA *Barth. De P.R.* XVII. lxxiv. (1495) 648 Grene frute and rawe and not dygest greue bodies and make them swell. **1430** LYDG. *Min. Poems* (1840) 195 (Mätz.) Whan Phebus entrith in the Ariete, Digest humoures upward doon hem dresse. **1460-70** *Bk. Quintessence* 6 Take þe beste horse dounge þat may be had þat is weel digest.

2. *adj.* Composed, settled, grave. *Sc.*

1500-20 DUNBAR *Poems* x. 30 Sing In haly kirk, with mynd degest. *Ibid.* xxiv. 3 Quhair no thing ferme is nor degest. **1513** DOUGLAS *Æneis* XII. i. 45 Kyng Latyn tho with sad and degest mynd To hym answeris. **1585** JAS. I *Ess. Poesie* (Arb.) 67 With gracis graue, and gesture maist digest. *a* **1605** MONTGOMERIE *Misc. Poems* l. 21 Sa grave, sa gracious, and digest.

digest (dɪ'dʒɛst, daɪ-), *v.* Forms: α. 5-6 **degest(e**, 5- **digest**, (6 **dejest, dygest**, *Sc.* **degeist**). β. 5 **desgest(e**, 6-7 (9 *dial.*) **disgest**, 7 **disjest**. [f. L. *dīgest-*, ppl. stem of *dīger-ĕre* to carry asunder, separate, divide, distribute, dissolve, digest, f. *dī-* = *dis-* (DI-¹) apart, asunder + *gerĕre* to carry. Cf. OF. *digester* (15th c. in Godef.). A parallel form with the prefix as *dis-* was frequent in the 16th and 17th c. (and is still dial.); in earlier times, the French modifications *des-*, *de-*, are found.]

† **1.** *trans.* To divide and dispose, to distribute.

α. **1578** BANISTER *Hist. Man* v. 71 Two Nerues..are digested into the bottome of the ventricle. **1610** *Mirr. Mag.* 763 (T.), I did digest my bands in battell-ray. *c* **1611** CHAPMAN *Iliad* XVI. 187 All these digested thus In fit place by the mighty son of royal Peleus. **1650** FULLER *Pisgah* III. xi. 341 That Jerusalem was digested and methodized into severall streets is most certain. **1675** tr. *Machiavelli's Prince* xii. (Rtldg. 1883) 84 They changed their militia into horse, which, being digested into troops [etc.].

β. **1579** FENTON *Guicciard.* III. (1599) 116 Afore this nauie could be disgested into order and point.

† **b.** To disperse, dissipate. *Obs.*

α. **1513** BRADSHAW *St. Werburge* I. 1264 Some of his louers ..Gaue hym theyr counseyll..unto melody all thoughtes to degest. *a* **1547** HENRY VIII in *Laneham's Let.* Pref. (1871) 149 Company me thynkes then best, All thoughtes & fancys to deiest. **1549** *Compl. Scot.* Prol. 9 The quhilkis humours nocht beand degeistit, mycht be occasione to dul their spreit. **1727** BRADLEY *Fam. Dict.* s.v. *Bath*, It does by insensible transpiration digest and dissipate superfluous humours.

β. **1565** *Satir. Poems Reform.* i. 25 Some meane that may thie greves disgest. **1604** T. WRIGHT *Passions* v. ii. 160 Musicke..[to] rectifie the blood and spirits, and consequently disgest melancholy.

2. To dispose methodically or according to a system; to reduce into a systematic form, usually with condensation; to classify.

α. **1482** *Monk of Evesham* (Arb.) 28 He told thees thynges the whiche here after be digestyd and wreten. **1562** *Act 5 Eliz.* c. 4 §1 The Substance of..the said Laws..shall be digested and reduceed into one sole Law and Statute. **1668** HALE *Pref. to Rolle's Abridgm.* 8 The Civil Law is digested into general Heads. **1704** SWIFT *Mech. Operat. Spirit* Misc. (1711) 275, I have had no manner of Time to digest it into Order, or correct the Stile. **1791** BOSWELL *Johnson* an. 1738, The debates in Parliament, which were brought home and digested by Guthrie. **1862** LD. BROUGHAM *Brit. Const.* xix. §1. 301 Every government is bound to digest the whole law into a code. **1875** E. WHITE *Life in Christ* II. xiii. (1876) 152 To digest these testimonies into definite forms.

β. **1576** GASCOIGNE *Steele Gl.* (Arb.) 68 A strange deuise, and sure my Lord wil laugh To see it so desgested in degrees. **1676** WOOD *Life* (Oxf. Hist. Soc.) II. 358 Purposely to disgest some notes for the press.

3. To settle and arrange methodically in the mind; to consider, think or ponder over.

α. *c* **1450** HENRYSON *Test. Cres.* (R.), Than thus proceeded Saturne & the Mone Whan they the mater ripely did degest. *c* **1470** HENRY *Wallace* VIII. 1430 Wer or pes, quhat so yow likis best, Lat your hye witt and gud consaill degest. **1548** HALL *Chron.* 20 When the kyng had long digested and studied on this matter. **1614** BP. HALL *Recoll. Treat.* 934 When he had somwhat digested his thoughts, and considered. **1793** SMEATON *Edystone L.* §130 I digested a plan for the keeping our accounts and correspondence. **1855** PRESCOTT *Philip II*, I. II. xi. 261 The regent was busy in digesting the plan of compromise.

β. **1494** FABYAN *Chron.* VI. ccvii. 221 Whanne kynge Henry had well desgested in his mynde the wrongful trouble that he..hadde put the duke vnto. **1637** HEYWOOD *Royal King* I. Wks. 1874 VI. 11 Come to horse, And, as we ride, our farther plots disgest.

4. To prepare (food) in the stomach and intestines for assimilation by the system; see DIGESTION 1.

α. **1483** *Cath. Angl.* 99/2 To Digeste, *digerere.* **1526** *Pilgr. Perf.* (W. de W. 1531) 192, XII baskettes of breedes that they coude not eate and digest. **1580** LYLY *Euphues* (Arb.)

468, I digested the Pill which had almost choakt me. **1661** LOVELL *Hist. Anim. & Min.* Introd., The skinne..even of rosted pigge..can hardly be well digested of a strong stomach. **1789** MRS. PIOZZI *Journ. France* I. 7 The cattle.. cannot digest tobacco. **1842** A. COMBE *Physiol. Digestion* (ed. 4) 363 To diminish the food to such a quantity as the system requires and the stomach can digest.

β. *a* **1536** TINDALE *Wks.* 234 (R.) That thy stomacke shall disgeste the meate that thou puttest into it. **1592** NASHE *P. Penilesse* (ed. 2) 10a, It is..a hard matter to disgest salt meates at Sea. **1600** ROWLANDS *Let. Humours Blood* vi. 75 Blowne drinke is odious, what man can disiest it? **1681** W. ROBERTSON *Phraseol. Gen.* (1693) 482 To disgest or digest what one eats. **1877** *N.W. Linc. Gloss.*, *Disgest*, to digest. **1892** *Northumbld. Gloss.*, *Disgest*.

b. *absol.*

1530 PALSGR. 516/1 He maye boldely eate well, for he dygesteth well. *c* **1532** DEWES *Introd. Fr.* in *Palsgr.* 1054 A body..may nat degeste without holdyng that mete. **1667** MILTON *P.L.* v. 412 Every lower facultie..whereby they hear, see, smell..digest, assimilate. **1707** FLOYER *Physic. Pulse-Watch* 85 Fishes and Birds want a Diaphragm, and yet Digest well. **1840** CLOUGH *Amours de Voy.* II. 39 Each has to eat for himself, digest for himself.

c. Applied to the action of insectivorous plants.

1875 DARWIN *Insectiv. Pl.* xiii. 311 Mrs. Treat..informs me that several leaves caught successively three insects each, but most of them were not able to digest the third fly. **1884** BOWER & SCOTT *De Bary's Phaner.* 100 The power..of digesting animal substance and absorbing it as nourishment ..known in the case of the peculiarly-formed leaves of Droseraceæ.

d. *intr.* (for *refl.*) Of the food: To undergo digestion.

1574 HYLL *Conject. Weather* iv, Weathers over olde are to be refused in eating in that they..smally nourish and hardly disgest. **1586** MARLOWE *1st Pt. Tamburl.* IV. iv, Fall to, and never may your meat digest. **1677** HALE *Prim. Orig. Man.* I. i. 30 My Blood circulates, my Meat digests..without any intention of mind to assist their actings. **1854-6** PATMORE *Angel in H.* I. IX. Prol. iii, The best [fare], Wanting this natural condiment.. will not digest.

e. *trans.* To cause or promote the digestion of (food).

1607 MIDDLETON *Five Gallants* II. iii, It comes like cheese after a great feast, to digest the rest. *c* **1645** HOWELL *Lett.* (1650) II. 76 French wines may be said but to pickle meat in the stomach; but this is the wine that disgests. **1725** POPE *Odyss.* IX. 409 Drain this goblet, potent to digest.

†**f.** ***to digest the stomach***: to promote the action of the stomach in digestion. Cf. DEFY *v.*[2] 1 b.

c **1460** J. RUSSELL *Bk. Nurture* 947 Youre soueraynе aftir mete his stomak to digest yef he wille take a slepe hym self þere for to rest. **1596** SIR J. SMYTHE in *Lett. Lit. Men* (Camden) 91 Dryncking wynes dyvers tymes to disgest and comforte my stomacke.

5. *fig.* and *transf.* (from the digestion of food).

1576 FLEMING *Panopl. Epist.* 341 He maketh suche to love learning..as before coulde by no meanes digest it. **1601** SHAKS. *Jul. C.* I. ii. 305 This Rudenesse is a Sawce to his good Wit Which giues men stomacke to disgest his words. **1614** BP. HALL *Recoll. Treat.* 994 The fire digests the rawnesse of the night. **1691** RAY *Creation* I. (1704) 61 This Opinion, I say, I can hardly digest. **1835** I. TAYLOR *Spir. Despot.* v. 221 The Church..had made great progress in digesting those arrogant principles. **1889** *Spectator* 9 Nov. 621/2 The Hapsburgs..have not digested Bosnia completely yet.

intr. **1614** BP. HALL *Recoll. Treat.* 440 Passions must have leasure to digest.

6. To bear without resistance; to brook, endure, put up with; to 'swallow, stomach'.

a. *a* **1553** T. WILSON *Rhet.* (1580) 175 Beeyng greeved with a matter, we saie commonly we cannot digest it. **1588** SHAKS. *L.L.L.* v. ii. 289 It can neuer be, They will digest this harsh indignitie. *a* **1625** ROWLANDS *Terrible Battell* 33 Can you so ill digest to heare your crimes? **1651** N. BACON *Disc. Govt. Eng.* II. xxxix. (1739) 173 The publick danger was such, as might well have digested an extraordinary undertaking. **1798** H. WALPOLE *Remin.* in *Lett.* (1857) I. ix. p. cxl, He..could not digest total dependence on a capricious..grandmother. **1809** W. IRVING *Knickerb.* v. v. (1849) 283 This wanton attack..is too much even for me to digest! [**1837** CARLYLE *Fr. Rev.* II. II. vi. (1848) 119 The forty thousand..have to..digest their spleen, or reabsorb it into the blood.]

β. **1592** WYRLEY *Armorie* 48 Too great abusage, which he not disgested. **1603** KNOLLES *Hist. Turks* (1638) 247 Mahomet could not wel disgest the losse he had to lately receiued. *a* **1661** FULLER *Worthies* I. (1662) 179 His quick and strong Appetite, could disgest any thing but an Injury.

b. To get over the effects of. *arch.*

1576 M. HANMER tr. *Anc. Eccles. Hist.* (1585) 156 Of the phisicians, some not able to digest that wonderfull noysome stinch were slaine. **1580** LYLY *Euphues* (Arb.) 251 In this sort they refreshed themselves 3 or 4 daies, vntil they had digested yͤ seas, and recovered again their healths. **1598** BARCKLEY *Felic. Man* (1631) 377 When hee hath disgested so many evills, and come to bee seven yeeres old. **1647** CLARENDON *Hist. Reb.* VII. (1703) II. 317 He had not yet digested his late deposal from the Lieutenancy of Ireland. **1834** COLERIDGE *Table-t.* 12 Jan., I never can digest the loss of most of Origen's works.

7. To comprehend and assimilate mentally; to obtain mental nourishment from.

a. **1548-9** (Mar.) *Bk. Com. Prayer* Collect 2nd Sund. Advent, Read, marke, learne, and inwardly digeste them. *a* **1592** H. SMITH *Wks.* (1867) II. 81 Record when you are gone, and you shall see the great power of God, what he is able to do for you by one sentence of this book, if ye digest it well. **1651** HOBBES *Leviath.* II. xxvi. 147 Memory to retain, digest and apply. **1732** BERKELEY *Alciphr.* II. §14 This new philosophy seems difficult to digest. **1858** HAWTHORNE *Fr. & It. Jrnls.* I. 265 Having had as many pictures as I could digest. **1866** R. CHAMBERS *Ess.* Ser. I. 149 He likes to digest what he reads. **1879** FROUDE *Cæsar* ix. 94 It might be that they would digest their lesson after all.

β. **1583** GOLDING *Calvin on Deut.* vi. 33 Mee thinkes this is harde, and as for that, I cannot disgest it. **1597** J. PAYNE *Royal Exch.* 43 Hartilie wishinge maryed folkes no less to mark and disgest, then to reade the words of the Apostle. **1647** DIGGES *Unlawf. Taking Arms* § 1. 8 By these generalls throughly disgested, and rightly applyed, we shall be able to rule particular decisions.

†**8.** To mature, or bring to a state of perfection, especially by the action of heat. Also *fig.* *Obs.*

1607 *Schol. Disc. agst. Antichr.* I. iv. 176 There wanteth the heate of the Nurse that doth digest and concockt the milke to make it sweet. **1626** BACON *Sylva* §327 They are ever Temperate Heats that Disgest and Mature. *a* **1652** J. SMITH *Sel. Disc.* i. 11 An inward beauty..which cannot be known but only then when it is digested into life and practice. **1665** *Sir T. Roe's Voy. E. Ind.* 360 They [musk-melons] are better digested there by the heat of the Sun, than these with us. **1700** H. WANLEY in *Pepys' Diary* VI. 233 A love and respect for his person which time..does digest into a habit. *a* **1708** BEVERIDGE *Priv. Th.* I. (1730) 52 God..having digested the Conditions to be performed by us, into Promises to be fulfilled by Himself.

b. *intr.* (for *refl.*).

1726 LEONI *Alberti's Archit.* I. 31 We are..not to make our Bricks of Earth fresh dug, but to dig it in the Autumn, and leave it to digest all Winter.

†**9.** *trans.* To mature (a tumour), to cause to suppurate; also *absol.* to promote healthy suppuration. *Obs.*

1551 TURNER *Herbal* I. (1568) B vij a, Marrysh mallowe soden in wyne..maketh rype or digesteth. **1563** T. GALE *Antidot.* II. 43 It doeth digest and maturate tumours. **1610** MARKHAM *Masterp.* II. clxxiii. 498 The garden rue disgesteth, and mightily comforteth all inflammations. **1612** WOODALL *Surg. Mate* Wks. (1653) 366 The which Medicine doth speedily digest and suppurate a Bubo. **1767** GOOCH *Treat. Wounds* I. 159 The contused parts in a wound must separate and be digested off.

†**b.** *intr.* (for *refl.*) To suppurate. *Obs.*

1713 CHESELDEN *Anat.* IV. i. (1726) 292, I..tied the artery alone..and it digested off in a week's time. **1737** BRACKEN *Farriery Impr.* (1756) I. 185 Try such Things as will bring the Matter to suppurate or digest. **1754-64** SMELLIE *Midwif.* III. 295 The swelling subsided, the lacerated parts digested.

10. *trans.* To prepare by boiling or application of heat; to dissolve by the aid of heat and moisture.

1616 SURFL. & MARKH. *Country Farme* 334 After it hath beene the second time digged and dunged, or marled, you must let it rest and digest his dung and marle. **1727** *Pope's Art of Sinking* 80 Th' almighty chemist..Digests his lightening, and distils his rain. **1791** HAMILTON *Berthollet's Dyeing* II. II. I. ii. 48 Powdered indigo digested in alcohol gave a yellow tincture. **1805** C. HATCHETT in *Phil. Trans.* XCV. 218 Some deal saw dust was digested with the nitric acid until it was completely dissolved. **1838** T. THOMSON *Chem. Org. Bodies* 94 Digest the bark in alcohol, evaporate the alcoholic solution to dryness.

b. *intr.* (for *refl.*) To dissolve in gentle heat.

1578 LYTE *Dodoens* III. lvi. 397 Putting the Scammonie to boyle, or digest in a Quince. **1599** A. M. tr. *Gabelhouer's Bk. Physicke* 206/1 Put then this oyle in a glasse..Close the glasse verye well, and let it ther digeste, as long as pleaseth you. **1652** CULPEPPER *Eng. Phys.* (1809) 382 Let them stand to digest twelve or fourteen days. **1799** G. SMITH *Laboratory* I. 133 Afterwards set it in bal. mariæ to digest for a fortnight. **1895** *Manchester Weekly Times* 26 April *Suppl.* 7/4 Put your orange extract..in some equally warm place, and let it 'digest' for at least six months.

digestant (dɪˈdʒɛstənt). [f. DIGEST *v.* + -ANT[1].] A thing taken to promote digestion.

1875 H. C. WOOD *Therap.* (1879) 607 *Digestants.* In this class are put a few remedies which are used to aid the stomach in dissolving the various articles of food. **1883** *Syd. Soc. Lex., Digestants*..such are pepsin, hydrochloric acid, and lactic acid.

†**digeˈstation.** *rare*[−0]. [f. DIGEST *v.*: see -ATION.] = DIGESTION.

1727 BAILEY, vol. II, *Digestation*, a digesting, ordering or disposing.

†**diˈgestative,** *a.* *rare.* [f. DIGEST: see -IVE.] Having the power to digest; = DIGESTIVE.

1657 TOMLINSON *Renou's Disp.* 92 Made milde and tractable by a digestative heat.

digested (dɪˈdʒɛstɪd, daɪ-), *ppl. a.* [f. DIGEST *v.* + -ED.]

1. Disposed in or reduced to order.

1598 FLORIO, *Digesto*, digested, disgiested..disposed.. ordred. **1622** SPARROW *Bk. Com. Prayer* (1661) 36 David's Psalms which are digested forms of Prayers. **1708** J. CHAMBERLAYNE *St. Gt. Brit.* II. III. x. (1743) 438 The college has..a well digested library. **1790** BEATSON *Nav. & Mil. Mem.* I. 381 A most absurd, ill-digested scheme. **1836** EMERSON *Nat., Prospects* Wks. (Bohn) II. 170 We learn to prefer imperfect theories..which contain glimpses of truth, to digested systems which have no one valuable suggestion.

2. Disposed, conditioned.

1607 TOURNEUR *Rev. Trag.* in Dodsley *O. Pl.* IV. 309 Conjuring me..To seek some strange digested fellow forth Of ill contented nature. **1672** SIR T. BROWNE *Lett. Friend* §27 To live at the rate of the old world..may afford no better digested death than a more moderate period.

3. Of food: That has undergone the process of DIGESTION. Usually in comb. as ***well-digested, half-digested***, etc.

1611 COTGR., *Digeré*, digested, concocted, digested. **1878** MCNAB *Bot.* iv. (1883) 96 The digested matter is.. absorbed.

4. Matured, ripe.

1657 JER. TAYLOR *Disc. Friendship* (Trench), Splendid fires, aromatic spices, rich wines, and well-digested fruits. *a* **1734** WODROW *Analecta* II. 305 The most digested and distinct Master of the Scriptures that ever I met with. **1812** CHALMERS *Let.* in *Life* (1851) I. 302 A more complete and digested acquaintance with the objects of my study. **1861** EMERSON *Soc. & Solit., Old Age* Wks. (Bohn) III. 135 What to the youth is only a guess or a hope, is in the veteran a digested statute.

†**5.** Concocted, condensed. *Obs.*

1669 WORLIDGE *Syst. Agric.* (1681) 292 From which coagulated or digested moisture winds are usually generated.

digestedly (dɪˈdʒɛstɪdlɪ), *adv.* [f. prec. + -LY[2].] In a digested or well-arranged manner.

1608 BP. HALL *Epist.* Ep. Ded., We doe..expresse our selues no whit lesse easily, somewhat more digestedly. **1672** *Mede's Wks.* App. Author's Life 69 (R.) Studiedly and digestedly to give the people the true nature of it. **1687** H. MORE *Answ. Psychop.* (1689) 158, I having writ..so digestedly and coherently..touching this subject.

digester (dɪˈdʒɛstə(r), daɪ-). Also 7 -or. [f. DIGEST *v.* + -ER.] He who or that which digests.

†**1.** That which distributes, disperses, or dissipates (humours). *Obs.*

1578 LYTE *Dodoens* I. lxxiii. 109 All the Scabiouses are.. digesters and diuiders of grosse humors.

2. One who analyses, arranges, and reduces to order, a mass of information; the maker of a digest.

1677 CARY *Chronol.* I. II. I. viii. 66 Varro a learned Digester of Antiquities. **1794** MATHIAS *Purs. Lit.* (1798) 432, I would recommend to..the new Digester of our Laws, not to be too subtle in the process. **1862** MAURICE *Mor. & Met. Philos.* IV. iv. §44. 130 To come into direct contact with facts, instead of receiving them at second hand through digesters and generalizers. **1885** G. W. HEMMING in *Law Q. Rev.* 297 The Digester should..revise every catch-word in the Reports.

3. a. That which digests or promotes the digestion of food; a digestive agent or organ.

1614 W. B. *Philosopher's Banquet* (ed. 2) 83 Galingale..is a Digester of meats. *a* **1698** TEMPLE (J.), Rice is..a great restorer of health, and a great digester. **1731-7** MILLER *Gard. Dict.* (ed. 3) s.v. *Viscum*, The Stomachs of these Birds are too powerful Digesters to suffer any Seeds to pass intire through the Intestines. **1744** BERKELEY *Siris* §97 Its great virtues as a digester and deobstruent.

b. A person or animal that digests its food (well or ill); *fig.* one who digests mentally.

1713 STEELE *Guardian* No. 60 ¶1 The generality of readers must..be allowed to be notable digesters. *Ibid.* No. 142 ¶3 As great princes keep their taster, so I perceive you keep your digester. *c* **1732** ARBUTHNOT (J.), People that are bilious and fat..are great eaters and ill digesters.

4. a. A strong close vessel in which bones or other substances may be subjected to the action of water or other liquid at a temperature and pressure above those of the boiling point, so as to be dissolved.

In its original form called from its inventor, *Papin's digester.*

1681 D. PAPIN (*title*), A New Digester, or Engine for softening Bones. **1682** EVELYN *Diary* 12 Apr., I went..to a supper which was all dressed, both fish and flesh, in Monsieur Papin's digestors, by which the hardest bones of beef itself, and mutton, were made as soft as cheese. **1708** J. KEILL *Anim. Secretion* 122 The Jelly extracted by Papin's Digester out of dry and solid Bones. **1783** PRIESTLEY in *Phil. Trans.* LXXIII. 415 A cast-iron vessel, which I could close at one end, like a digester. **1794-6** E. DARWIN *Zoon.* (1801) II. 412 A close vessel, which is called Papin's digester; in which it is said water may be made red hot. **1885** *Pall Mall G.* 4 May 10/2 The vessel which contained the explosive used at the Admiralty Offices..was what is known as a digester or stock pot, such as is used in kitchens.

b. An apparatus in which the carcases of beasts unfit for food are by the action of heat dissolved into their proximate elements, tallow, gelatine, earthy phosphates, etc.

1874 KNIGHT *Dict. Mech.* I. 702/2. **1892** *Daily News* 26 Oct. 3/5 Animals and carcases should be removed in.. enclosed vans, the animals at once slaughtered..and the carcases destroyed in a digester.

c. An apparatus whereby substances are dissolved by chemical action instead of by heat and pressure.

d. *Papermaking.* An apparatus in which wood, grass, etc., are turned into pulp by the action of hot water, chemicals, etc.

1898 *Sci. Amer.* LXXVIII. 185/3 The digester is filled to the top with chips..and the acid is then piped in. **1906** *Chambers's Jrnl.* Feb. 206/2 These pieces [of wood]..are fed into a 'digester', which in some cases is large enough to produce fifteen tons of pulp at one operation. **1962** F. T. DAY *Introd. to Paper* i. 13 The principle was to boil the wood with soda in digesters.

digestibility (dɪˌdʒɛstɪˈbɪlɪtɪ). [f. DIGESTIBLE + -ITY. Cf. F. *digestibilité.*] The quality of being digestible.

1740 CHEYNE *Regimen* ii. (R.), The digestibility and easy dissolution of it [meat] is obstructed. **1851** *Fraser's Mag.* XLIII. 269 Certain fish were held in repute for their digestibility. **1876** FOSTER *Phys.* II. i. (1879) 277 The digestibility of any food is determined chiefly by mechanical conditions.

digestible (dɪˈdʒɛstɪb(ə)l, daɪ-). Also 5-9 -able. [a. F. *digestible* (14th c. in Hatz.-Darm.), ad. L.

dīgestibilis, f. *dīgest-* ppl. stem of *dīgerĕre* to DIGEST.]

1. Capable of being digested or assimilated.

c **1386** CHAUCER *Prol.* 437 His diete..was of no superfluitee But of greet norissyng and digestible. **1599** H. BUTTES *Dyets drie Dinner* I, Of a lash and yet grosse substance, not very digestible. **1614** W. B. *Philosopher's Banquet* (ed. 2) 30 It is found more..digestable. **1826** *Blackw. Mag.* XIX. 660 They can digest anything digestable. **1842** A. COMBE *Physiol. Digestion* (ed. 4) 300 Albuminous aliments..easily digestible and very nourishing.

fig. **1651** HOBBES *Leviath.* II. xix. 101 The Romans..to make their Government digestible, were wont [etc.].

†**b.** Able to be concocted or matured by heat.

c **1470** HENRY *Wallace* III. 2 In joyows Julii, quhen the flouris suete, Degesteable, engenered throu the heet, Baith erbe and froyte.

†**2.** That causes or promotes digestion (of food).

1651 BIGGS *New Disp.* ¶295 By the vigour of the digestible, esurine, and depascent ferment.

†**3.** To be digested or prepared by the action of heat. *Obs.*

1477 NORTON *Ord. Alch.* v. in Ashm. (1652) 62 Nethles heate of the digestible thinge, Helpeth digestion and her working.

Hence **di'gestibleness**, quality of being digestible; **di'gestibly**, *adv.*, in a digestible form.

1662 H. STUBBE *Ind. Nectar* iii. 30 Its dissolving by the least fire..argues its facile digestibleness. **1879** G. MEREDITH *Egoist* I. Prel. 3 To give us those interminable milepost piles of matter in essence, in chosen samples, digestibly.

†**di'gestic**, *a. Obs. rare.* [irreg. f. DIGEST *v.* + -IC.] = DIGESTIVE.

1797 GODWIN *Enquirer* II. vi. 244 A wise man..would exercise his digestic powers. **1799** E. DU BOIS *Piece of Family Biog.* II. 99 In search of one who made more use of his 'digestic powers'.

‖**digestif** (diʒɛstif). [Fr.] = DIGESTIVE *sb.* I.

1908 *Daily Chron.* 15 Apr. 4/6 My husband thought a cigarette an excellent digestif. **1934** H. MILLER *Tropic of Cancer* 164 She will be obliged..to flop somewhere on the boulevard and sip her *digestif.* **1962** *Guardian* 13 July 8/1 Drambuie..ranks with Benedictine and Cointreau among the world's five top-selling digestifs.

di'gesting, *vbl. sb.* [f. DIGEST *v.* + -ING[1].] The action of the verb DIGEST in various senses.

1540 ELYOT *Image Gov.* (1556) 72 b, The concoctynge and digistyng of that, which the bodie receiveth. **1662** STILLINGFL. *Orig. Sacr.* I. v. §5 Scaliger..hath taken so much pains in digesting of them. **1805** W. SAUNDERS *Min. Waters* 359, I tried to redissolve this substance..by long boiling and digesting. **1823** LAMB *Elia* Ser. II. *Poor Relation*, After the digesting of this affront.

b. *attrib.*

1581 MULCASTER *Positions* xxxii. (1887) 116 Exercise.. maketh the naturall heat strong against digesting time.

di'gesting, *ppl. a.* [f. as prec. + -ING[2].] That digests.

1605 TIMME *Quersit.* I. vii. 32 The flower of salt..is of a sharpe qualitie and much digesting. **1799** G. SMITH *Laboratory* I. 371 Give a digesting fire for three days. **1809** GREGOR in *Phil. Trans.* XCIX. 198 The process of solution is..accelerated by a digesting heat.

Hence **di'gestingly** *adv.*

1885 G. MEREDITH *Diana* III. ii. 48 They rose from table at ten..digestingly refreshed.

digestion (dɪ'dʒɛstjən, daɪ-). Also α. 4–5 **digestioun**, 5 **degestyon**, 5 **dy-**. β. 6–7 (9 *dial.*) **disgestion**. [a. F. *digestion* (13th c. in Hatz.-Darm.), ad. L. *dīgestiōn-em*, digestion, arrangement, n. of action f. *dīgerĕre* (pa. pple. *dīgest-*) to DIGEST.]

1. The physiological process whereby the nutritive part of the food consumed is, in the stomach and intestines, rendered fit to be assimilated by the system.

c **1386** CHAUCER *Sqr.'s T.* 339 The Norice of digestioun the sleepe. *c* **1400** *Lanfranc's Cirurg.* 169 þat þe mete miȝte abide in þe stomak for to make digestion. **1553** T. WILSON *Rhet.* 37 Heavinesse and care hinder digestion. **1590** SPENSER *F.Q.* II. ix. 31 The Kitchin Clerke, that hight Digestion, Did order all th' Achates in seemely wise. **1593** SHAKS. *Rich. II* I. iii. 236 Things sweet to tast, proue in digestion sowre. **1667** MILTON *P.L.* v. 4 His sleep Was Aerie light, from pure digestion bred. **1704** F. FULLER *Med. Gymn.* (1711) 156, I don't believe Digestion is perform'd by Putrefaction. **1834** McMURTRIE *Cuvier's Anim. Kingd.* 279 Insects vary infinitely as to the form of the organs of the mouth, and those of digestion. **1860** EMERSON *Cond. Life, Fate* Wks. (Bohn) II. 312 In certain men, digestion and sex absorb the vital force. **1871** R. ELLIS *Catullus* xxiii, Who can wonder? In all is health, digestion, Pure and vigorous. **1878** *Masque Poets* 47 Is it trouble of conscience or morbid digestion?

b. The analogous process in insectivorous plants.

1875 DARWIN *Insectiv. Pl.* vi. 85 It becomes an interesting inquiry, whether they [Drosera]..have the power of digestion. **1878** McNAB *Bot.* iv. (1883) 96 The insects..are ..covered with a secretion containing an acid, and a substance closely resembling pepsine, and a true process of digestion goes on similar to the digestion in the stomach of an animal.

†**c.** In old Physiology. ***first, second, and third digestion***: see CONCOCTION 1 b. Also *fig. Obs.*

1398 TREVISA *Barth De P.R.* v. xxxix. (1495) 154 The lyuer drawyth in to his holownes of the woos of the fyrst degestyon. **1614** W. B. *Philosopher's Banquet* (ed. 2) 22 The act digestively is finished in the third digestion. **1614** BP. HALL *Recoll. Treat.* 440 To choose the season for counsell.. and that season is, after the first digestion of sorrow. **1658–9** *Burton's Diary* (1828) IV. 207 If there be an error..of the first digestion, it is incurable.

d. *fig.*

c **1592** MARLOWE *Massacre Paris* II. vi. (version in Dyce), Hote enough to worke Thy just degestione with extreamest shame. **1614** RALEIGH *Hist. World* v. ii. §3. 589 If no other state gave the Romans something to trouble their digestion.

e. ***slow, easy, hard of digestion***: slow, easy, hard to be digested. So ***of hard*** (etc.) ***digestion***: cf. 4. Also *fig.*

1533 ELYOT *Cast. Helthe* II. xiii. (1539) 31 b, It is slowe of digestion. **1599** H. BUTTES *Dyets drie Dinner* M viij b, Oyster ..somewhat hard of degestion. **1653** HOLCROFT *Procopius* II. 64 Their laws hard of disgestion, and their commands intollerable. **1699** BURNET *39 Art.* ix. (1700) 116 A Doctrine that seems to be of hard digestion to a great many. *a* **1715** —— *Own Time* (1766) I. 448 These conditions were not of an easy digestion. **1732** ARBUTHNOT *Rules of Diet* 252 Flesh roasted, not so easy of Digestion as boil'd. **1761** HUME *Hist. Eng.* II. xxxi. 200 These points were of hard digestion with the princess. **1838** *Penny Cycl.* X. 343 Mucus..is deemed both nutritious and of easy digestion. **1863–72** WATTS *Dict. Chem.* II. 327 Raw flesh is generally regarded as more difficult of digestion than boiled or roast meat.

2. The power or faculty of digesting food.

1398 TREVISA *Barth. De P.R.* v. xlvi. (1495) 163 In wynter is grete appetyte and strong degestyon. *c* **1430** *A Diatorie* in *Babees Bk.* (1868) 54 Cleer eir & walking makiþ good digestioun. **1531** ELYOT *Gov.* III. xxii, A man hauing due concoction and digestion as is expedient. **1589** NASHE *Anat. Absurd.* 34 Our digestion would be better, if our dishes were fewer. *a* **1710** SOUTH in *Tatler* No. 205 ¶5 Every Morsel to a satisfied Hunger, is only a new Labour to a tired Digestion. **1846** G. E. DAY tr. *Simon's Anim. Chem.* II. 41 Indications of a morbid digestion. **1861** FLO. NIGHTINGALE *Nursing* ii. 27 Weakness of digestion depends upon habits.

3. *fig.* The action of digesting, or obtaining mental nourishment from (books, etc.).

a **1610** HEALEY *Epictetus' Man.* lxix. (1636) 90 Effectes following the due disgestion of verball precepts. *a* **1661** FULLER *Worthies* III. 205 He had a great appetite to learning, and a quick digestion. **1839–40** W. IRVING *Wolfert's R.* (1855) 57 Glencoe supplied me with books, and I devoured them with appetite, if not digestion.

4. The action of putting up with or bearing without resistance; brooking, endurance. ? *Obs.*

1653 H. COGAN tr. *Pinto's Trav.* iv. 9 Having received so bold an answer..found it very rude, and hard of digestion. **1760** STERNE *Serm.* (1784) III. 6 The silent digestion of one wrong provokes a second.

5. *Chem.* †**a.** The operation of maturing or preparing a substance by the action of gentle heat; concoction, maturation, condensation, coagulation; also susceptibility to this operation, and *concr.* the condition resulting from it. *Obs.*

1477 NORTON *Ord. Alch.* v. in Ashm. (1652) 61 Then of divers degrees and of divers digestion, Colours will arise towards perfection. **1563** W. FULKE *Meteors* (1640) 67 Brasse, latine, and such like..differ in digestion: the Copper being purest, is of best digestion. *Ibid.* 68 Iron..also being of too extreame digestion, passing all other metals in hardnes. **1594** PLAT *Jewell-ho.* I. 32 It [clay] should seeme to differ onely in digestion from marle. **1626** BACON *Sylva* §327 We conceive..that a perfect good Concoction, or Disgestion, or Maturation of some Metalls, will produce Gold. **1641** FRENCH *Distill.* i. (1651) 10 *Digestion*, is a concocting, or maturation of crude things by an easie, and gentle heat. **1669** WORLIDGE *Syst. Agric.* (1681) 293 Their digestion or coagulation is more in some than in others. **1677** HALE *Prim. Orig. Man.* IV. ii. 307 The latter [Minerals] seem to be Concretions and Digestions in the Bowels of the Earth.

b. The operation of exposing a substance to the action of a liquid with the aid of heat, for the purpose of extracting the soluble constituents.

1610 B. JONSON *Alch.* II. iii, [I put the ingredients] in a Bolt's-head nipp'd to digestion. **1660** BOYLE *New Exp. Phys. Mech.* xxii. 164 In our Digestions and Distillations. **1757** A. COOPER *Distiller* I. v. (1760) 32 A Vessel for Digestion, called by chemists a pelican or circulatory Vessel. **1807** T. THOMSON *Chem.* (ed. 3) II. 366 The digestion was continued till the solution was complete. **1822** IMISON *Sc. & Art* II. 19 When a solid substance..is left for a certain time in a fluid, and the mixture is kept exposed to a slow degree of heat, the process is called digestion. **1868** ROYLE, etc. *Man. Materia Medica* (ed. 5) 10 Digestion is similar to Maceration, but the action is promoted by a heat from 90° to 100°.

†**6.** *Surg.* The process of maturing an ulcer or wound; disposition to healthy suppuration. *Obs.*

1676 WISEMAN *Chirurg. Treat.* 111, I shewed him that by Digestion the remaining fleshy body..would come away. **1689** MOYLE *Sea Chyrurg.* II. iv. 34 Prepare your fomentation to help on digestion. **1748** HARTLEY *Observ. Man* I. ii. 126 Lacerations are never cured without coming to Digestion. **1830** S. COOPER *Dict. Pract. Surg.* (ed. 6) 374 By the digestion of a wound or ulcer, the old Surgeons meant bringing it into a state, in which it formed healthy pus.

†**7.** *fig.* The process of maturing (plans) by careful consideration and deliberation. *Obs.*

1671 TEMPLE *Ess., Constit. of Empire* Wks. 1731 I. 86 The Digestion of their Counsels is made in a Senate consisting of Forty Counsellors.

†**8.** The action of methodizing and reducing to order. *Obs.*

1553 T. WILSON *Rhet.* 106 Digestion is an ordely placyng of thynges, partyng every matter severally.

†**b.** The result of this process, a digested condition; a methodical arrangement; a DIGEST. *Obs.*

1613 CHAPMAN *Revenge Bussy D'Ambois* v, The chaos of eternal night (To which the whole digestion of the world Is now returning). **1668** HALE *Pref. to Rolle's Abridgm.* 7 Every Student..may easily Form unto himself a general Digestion of the Law. **1754** FARRO (title), Royal Universal British Grammar and Vocabulary, being a digestion of the entire English Language into its proper parts of speech.

digestive (dɪ'dʒɛstɪv, daɪ-), *a.* and *sb.* Also 6–7 **dis-**. [a. F. *digestif -ive* (14th c. in Hatz.-Darm.), ad. L. *dīgestīvus*, f. *dīgest-* ppl. stem of *dīgerĕre* to DIGEST: see -IVE.]

A. *adj.*

1. a. Having the function of digesting food; engaged in or pertaining to digestion.

c **1532** DEWES *Introd. Fr.* in *Palsgr.* 1053 The sayd vegetable [the soul] hath in her four vertues..the atractyve or appetityve, the retentyve, the digestyve, and expulsive. **1610** MARKHAM *Masterp.* I. vi. 16 The vertue digestiue whereby it concocteth and disgesteth. **1725** N. ROBINSON *Th. Physick* 253 To..raise the digestive Powers to their natural Standard. **1837** M. DONOVAN *Dom. Econ.* II. 23 Resting on a couch, until the digestive organs have recovered the fatigue. **1841–71** T. R. JONES *Anim. Kingd.* (ed. 4) 109 The digestive cavity..is exceedingly short.

b. in reference to plants.

1875 DARWIN *Insectiv. Pl.* xiii. 301 Experiments..on the digestive power of Drosera. **1884** BOWER & SCOTT *De Bary's Phaner.* 100 According to this digestive function these organs may be termed *Digestive glands*.

2. a. Promoting or aiding digestion; digestible.

1528 PAYNEL *Salerne's Regim.* Q ij, Through the digestiue heate of the night. **1616** B. JONSON *Epigr.* ci, Digestive cheese, and fruit there sure will be. **1725** BRADLEY *Fam. Dict.* s.v. *May blossom*, As to the medicinal Vertues of this Plant; it..is digestive. **1760–72** tr. *Juan & Ulloa's Voy.* (ed. 3) I. 99 These waters are very light and digestive, and..good to create an appetite. **1863–72** WATTS *Dict. Chem.* II. 327 *Digestive salt*, Syn. with Chloride of Potassium. **1881** *Times* 18 May 6/1 The most digestive and nutritious bread.

b. *spec.* Designating a type of wholemeal biscuit. Also *ellipt.*

1876 *Off. Guide Cunard Steamship Co.* 158 (Advt.), Huntley & Palmers..Digestive Biscuits. **1894** L. HERITAGE *Cassell's New Universal Cookery Book* 1022 *Digestive Biscuits.*—Required: a pound of finely-granulated, or.. wholemeal [flour], half a pound of white flour [etc.]. **1925** ST. JOHN ERVINE *Anthony & Anna* I. 24 Which will you 'ave, sir—the charcoal or the digestive biscuits? **1935** G. BULLETT *Jury* xxiii. 234, I had to open a parcel of grocery to find the right kind of biscuits... Digestives were what she fancied. **1949** N. MITFORD *Love in Cold Climate* II. ii. 194 A few rather broken digestive biscuits. *Ibid.* 197 Weeks since I tasted digestives, my favourite food, too. **1955** *Observer* 19 June 7/5 Biscuits long known as *digestive* are being renamed *sweetmeal*.

3. Pertaining to or promoting chemical digestion.

1651 BIGGS *New Disp.* ¶287 Wanting its digestive ferment. *a* **1691** BOYLE *Hist. Air* (1692) 210 We removed the ..receiver, and put it on the digestive furnace. **1799** DE CRELL in *Phil. Trans.* LXXXIX. 63 Applying only a digestive warmth. **1799** G. SMITH *Laboratory* I. 131 To submit their contents to a digestive heat.

4. Promoting healthy suppuration in a wound or ulcer; as ***digestive ointment***: see B 2.

†**5.** Characterized by bearing without resistance or in silence. *Obs.*

1608 HEYWOOD *Sallust's Jugurth* iii, Adherbal was..no souldier, of a frolicke disposition, disgistive of injuries.

†**6.** That tends to methodize and reduce to order.

1662 DRYDEN *Astræa Redux* 89 To business ripened by digestive thought, His future rule is into method brought.

B. *sb.*

1. A medicine or substance promoting digestion of food.

c **1386** CHAUCER *Nun's Pr. T.* 141 A Day or two ye schul have digestives Of wormes, or ye take your laxatives. **1460–70** *Bk. Quintessence* 14 And so I seie of medicyns comfortatyues, digestyues, laxatyues, restriktyues, and alle oþere. **1612** *Enchyr. Med.* 97 Wee leaue our digestiues..and proceede to other medicines. **1700** DRYDEN *Fables, Cock & Fox* 189 These digestives prepare you for your purge. **1883** in *Syd. Soc. Lex., Digestives.*

2. A substance which promotes healthy suppuration in a wound or ulcer; digestive ointment (*Unguentum terebinthinæ compositum*).

1543 TRAHERON *Vigo's Chirurg.* (1586) 436 In Chirurgerie a digestive is taken for that that prepareth the mattier to mundification. **1582** HESTER *Secr. Phiorav.* II. xi. 91 You shall dresse it with a digestiue vntill it be mundified. **1643** J. STEER tr. *Exp. Chyrurg.* xv. 62, I applyed this following digestive with soft plegets upon the incisions. **1737** BRACKEN *Farriery Impr.* (1757) II. 240 The Wound requires a strong Digestive. **1767** GOOCH *Treat. Wounds* I. 136 Linnen cloth, spread with the common Digestive. **1854–67** C. A. HARRIS *Dict. Med. Terminol., Digestives*, in Surgery, substances which, when applied to a wound or ulcer, promote suppuration.

†**3.** An agent of chemical digestion. *Obs. rare.*

1477 NORTON *Ord. Alch.* v. in Ashm. (1652) 62 But our cheefe Digestiue [*printed* -ure] for our intent, Is virtuall heate of the matter digerent.

di'gestively, *adv.* [f. prec. + -LY[2].] In a digestive manner; in a way that promotes digestion; with regard to digestion.

1614 W. B. *Philosopher's Banquet* (ed. 2) 22 The act digestiuely is finished in the third digestion. **1857** W. COLLINS *Dead Secret* (1861) 34 Digestively considered..

even the fairest and youngest of us is an Apparatus. **1885** *Pall Mall G.* 6 May 4/2 Round the garden, groups pose themselves digestively.

di'gestiveness. [f. as prec. + -NESS.] The quality of being digestive or of aiding digestion.
1727 BAILEY vol. II, *Digestiveness*, digestive Faculty. **1876** L. TOLLEMACHE in *Fortn. Rev.* Mar. 362 May not this superiority.. be due.. to the extreme digestiveness of the St. Moritz air?

† **di'gestly,** *adv. Sc. Obs.* Also **de-**. [f. DIGEST *a.* + -LY[2].] Maturely, deliberately, composedly.
1513 DOUGLAS *Æneis* IX. v. 48 Alethes.. Onto thir wordis digestly maid ansueris. **1536** BELLENDEN *Cron. Scot.* (1821) I. 49 Quhen thir oratouris had sene and degeistlie considerit this regioun. **1544** *Sc. Acts Mary* (1814) 449 (Jam.), My.. lordis of parliament suld avise degestlie quhat is to be done herein. **1606** *Sc. Acts Jas. VI* (1814) 312 (Jam.) For sindrie vtheris sene and proffitable caussis digestlie considerit.

† **di'gestment.** *Obs. rare*[−1]. [f. DIGEST *v.* + -MENT.] The action or process of digesting; methodical disposition or arrangement.
1610 W. FOLKINGHAM *Art of Survey* iv. Concl. 88 Compose in computable digestment all the Tenants with their Tenements and Rents in particular.

digestor, var. form of DIGESTER.

† **di'gestory,** *a.* and *sb. Obs.* [ad. L. *dīgestōri-us*, f. *dīgest-* ppl. stem of *dīgerĕre* to DIGEST: see -ORY.]
A. *adj.* = DIGESTIVE.
1612 WOODALL *Surg. Mate* Wks. (1653) 270 Digestion is simple maturation, whereby things uncocted in artificiall digestory heat.. is digested.
B. *sb.* A vessel or organ of digestion.
1675 EVELYN *Terra* (1729) 43 Of all Waters, that which descends from Heaven we find to be the richest.. as having been already meteorized, and circulated in that great Digestory. **1768–74** TUCKER *Lt. Nat.* (1852) I. 475 The whole human body, together with all its viscera, yea, chylopoietic digestories.

† **di'gesture.** *Obs.* Also 6–7 **dis-**. [f. L. *dīgest-* ppl. stem (see prec.) + -URE: cf. *gesture*.] The process or faculty of digesting.
1. = DIGESTION 1, 2.
1565 J. HALLE *Hist. Expost.* 21 A sanguine man is he that hathe a good disgesture. **1591** HARINGTON *Orl. Fur.* XXXI. lviii. (1634) 254 To make him drink beyond all good disgesture. **1615** LATHAM *Falconry* (1633) 41 At that time of the yeere, old food is more drie and hard of digesture. **1674** R. GODFREY *Inj. & Ab. Physic* 128 Having contracted a Disease through catching Cold and want of Digesture. *a* **1700** G. HARVEY (J.), Meals of easy digesture.
2. The putting up with or brooking of anything unpleasant; = DIGESTION 4.
1566 PAINTER *Pal. Pleas.* II. 146b, The lords.. will thincke it straunge, and receyve the same with ill digesture. **1606** J. RAYNOLDS *Dolarny's Prim.* (1880) 92 He already can The calmie lines with faire digesture brooke.

diggable ('dɪgəb(ə)l), *a.* [f. DIG *v.* + -ABLE.] Capable of being digged.
1552 HULOET, Diggable or which may be digged, *fossilis*. **1847** CRAIG, *Diggable*, that may be digged.

digger ('dɪgə(r)). [f. DIG *v.* + -ER.] One who or that which digs.
1. One who excavates or turns up the earth with a mattock, spade, or other tool; also an animal that turns up the earth. With adverb, as ***digger-up***.
c **1400** *Promp. Parv.* 118/1 Deluar or dyggar, *fossor*. **1585** J. B. tr. *Viret's Sch. Beastes* B vj, The Connies.. are such continuall diggers and scrapers, that they.. cleave a sunder and make hollow the stones and rockes. **1608** CAPT. J. SMITH *Let.* in *Virginia*. (1624) III. 72 Send.. gardiners, fisher men, blacksmiths.. and diggers vp of trees, roots, well provided. **1650** R. STAPYLTON *Strada's Low C. Warres* x. 2 Prince Alexander.. sometimes visiting the Diggers, sometimes the Miners. **1723** *Lond. Gaz.* No. 6188/8 B. P. Gardiner, Digger and Builder. **1751** JOHNSON *Rambler* No. 154 ¶ 11 Treasures are thrown up by the ploughman and the digger. **1895** *Blackw. Mag.* Apr. 623 The digger-up of primeval bones.
2. *spec.* **a.** A miner, especially one who works surface or shallow deposits.
1531–2 *Act 23 Hen. VIII*, c. 8 §1 That no person or persons.. shall labour, dig, or wash any tin in any of the said tin workes, called Streme workes, vnlesse the saide digger, owner or wassher, shall make.. sufficient hatches and ties in the ende of their buddels and cordes [etc.]. **1570** DEE *Math. Pref.* 36 For.. Miners, Diggers for Mettalls.. any man may easily perceaue.. the great aide of Geometrie. *a* **1661** FULLER *Worthies, Wales* (R.), Fresh aire.. whereby the candle in the mine is daily kept burning, and the diggers recruited constantly with a sufficiency of breath. **1661** BOYLE *Style of Script.* Ep. Ded. (1675) 6 As a homely digger may shew a man a rich mine.
b. *esp.* One who digs or searches for gold in a gold-field. Also *attrib.*
1853 VALIANT *Let.* in McCombie *Hist. Victoria* xvi. (1858) 248 It caused the diggers.. to pause in their headlong career. **1856** EMERSON *Eng. Traits, Lit.* Wks. (Bohn) II. 113 Like diggers in California 'prospecting for a placer' that will pay. **1869** R. B. SMYTH *Goldfields Victoria* 609 Digger.. applied formerly to all persons who searched for gold; and now generally restricted to those who seek for gold in the shallow alluviums. **1875** *Spectator* (Melbourne) 19 June 79/2 The rough digger of the primitive era. **1881** H. W. NESFIELD *Chequered Career* vii. 75 Their manner of accosting me was simply their 'digger' style of humour. **1894** C. J. O'REGAN *Voices of Wave & Tree* 10 But that was digger nature.

c. One of a tribe or class of N. American Indians who subsist chiefly on roots dug from the ground.
1837 W. IRVING *Capt. Bonneville* II. 209 Sometimes the Diggers aspire to nobler game, and succeed in entrapping the antelope. **1848** *Blackw. Mag.* LXIV. 132 They came upon a band of miserable Indians, who, from the fact of their subsisting chiefly on roots, are called the Diggers. **1883** B. HARTE *Carquinez Woods* vii. 154 *note*, Diggers, a local name for a peaceful tribe of Indians inhabiting Northern California, who live on roots and herbs.
attrib. **1865** TYLOR *Early Hist. Man.* vii. 185 The miserable 'Digger Indians', of North America. **1875** F. PARKMAN in *N. Amer. Rev.* CXX. 43 The abject 'Digger' hordes of Nevada. **1882** B. HARTE *Flip* v, Ye might do it to please that digger squaw.
d. (*a*) *Eng. Hist.* A section of the Levellers in 1649, who adopted communistic principles as to the land, in accordance with which they began to dig and plant the commons. (*b*) In modern use, a member of a group of hippies who believe in a society where all food and possessions are shared freely and land is cultivated to feed the poor. Also *attrib.*
1649 [*Information*, dated 16 April, in *Clarke Pa.* (Camd. Soc. 1894) II. 211 One Everard and two more.. all living att Cobham, came to St. George's Hill in Surrey, and began to digge on that side the Hill next to Campe Close, and sowed the ground with parsenipps, and carretts, and beans]. *Ibid.* 215 (Dec.) To his Excellency the Lord Fairfax.. the Brotherly Request of those that are called Diggers, sheweth, That whereas we have begun to digg upon the Commons for a livelihood, first, for the righteous law of Creation that gives the earth freely to one as well as another. *Ibid.* 221 [*The Digger's Song*] You noble Diggers all, stand up now, stand up now.. The wast land to maintain, seeing Cavaliers by name, Your digging does disdaine, and persons all defame, Stand up now, Diggers all. **1650** NEEDHAM *Case Commw.* 79 There is a new Faction started up out of ours [Levellers], known by the name of Diggers; who.. have framed a new plea for a Returne of all men *ad Tuguria*, that like the old Parthians.. and other wild Barbarians, we might renounce Townes and Cities, live as Rovers, and enjoy all in common. *a* **1676** WHITELOCKE *Memorials* (1853) III. 17. **1894** C. H. FIRTH in *Clarke Pa.* II. 222 *note*, Three of the Diggers.. were brought before the Court at Kingston for trespass in digging upon St. George's Hill, and infringing the rights of Mr. Drake, the Lord of the Manor.
1967 G. LEGMAN *Fake Revolt* 19 Try to round up votes and get a bearded Digger or mock-saintly Provo elected mayor. **1967** *Economist* 15 July 217/2 A loosely knit group called the Diggers—taking the name from agrarian communists in the seventeenth century who cultivated waste lands to feed the poor—is operating pads for homeless hippies and dispensing free food and clothing, obtained by soliciting contributions from shopkeepers. **1968** *Guardian* 29 Apr. 7/5 The first Digger conference opened at London Anti-university over the weekend. **1969** *Ibid.* 27 Sept. 9/1 A leader of the London Diggers.. describes his group as 'communal hippies, nonviolent basically and nonauthoritarian'.
e. A person who digs for archæological purposes. Cf. DIG *v.* 1 a and 3 a.
1911 T. E. LAWRENCE *Home Lett.* (1954) 149 Thompson is not a digger, so the direction of that part would be my share. **1914** KIPLING *Lett. Travel* (1920) 256 Their dream (the diggers' dream always) is to discover a virgin tomb. **1960** *Times* 22 Feb. 14/1 Woolley will always be remembered as one of the most successful diggers ever engaged in field archaeology.
f. *colloq.* An Australian or New Zealander; *spec.* in the wars of 1914–18 and 1939–45, a soldier from Australia or New Zealand, esp. a private soldier; freq. as a term of address = COBBER *sb.*[2] Also *attrib.* Cf. DIG *sb.*[3]
1917 *Chrons. N.Z.E.F.* 5 Sept. 28/1 He ain't no digger; that's the colonel or the sergeant-major. *Ibid.* 14 Nov. 154/2 Two hefty diggers escorted the little lady to her home. **1917** E. MILLER in *Camps, Tramps & Trenches* (1939) xxiv. 192 A digger officer would have worded the message quite differently. **1918** *Digger* 13 On the wing with the jam, Digger. **1919** [see AUSSIE *sb.* and *a.* 1]. **1919** W. H. DOWNING (*title*) Digger dialects. A collection of slang phrases used by the Australian soldiers on active service. **1923** D. H. LAWRENCE *Kangaroo* v. 98 We're mostly diggers back from the war. **1929** C. C. MARTINDALE *Risen Sun* 14 Where my experience of the Diggers really began was a little club in the Turl, to which hospital cases came. **1940** *War Illustr.* 16 Feb. p. iii/1, They are forming a new Digger Expeditionary Force, but old blokes like me are not wanted. **1941** *Illustr. London News* CXCIX. 534/1 They are a mixed lot, these 'diggers', some from offices, others from factories. **1948** R. FINLAYSON *Tidal Creek* i. 8 Put your bag under the seat, digger. **1963** *Evening Post* (Wellington, N.Z.) 26 Dec., Remembering the old diggers at this festive time of the year.
3. An instrument for digging, a digging tool; also the digging part of a machine. Also in various combs. as ***hop-digger***, ***potato-digger***, etc.
1686 PLOT *Staffordsh.* 353 They weed their Wheat.. with an Iron digger. **1819** G. SAMOUELLE *Entomol. Compend.* 308 The digger is best with an arrow-headed point. **1839** GRAY *Lett.* (1893) 144 He presented me with a beautiful botanical digger of fine polished steel, with a leathern sheath. **1861** S. THOMSON *Wild Fl.* III. (ed. 4) 155 A short 'digger' or hand 'spud'. **1861** *Times* 11 July, As the engine travels slowly forward, the digger cuts and throws up the soil behind.
4. A division of Hymenopterous insects, also called ***digger-wasps***.
1847 CARPENTER *Zool.* §693 The *Crabronidæ, Labridæ, Bembecidæ, Sphegidæ, Scioliдæ, Mutilidæ*.. may be termed from their peculiar habits.. *Fossores* or Diggers; and they are commonly known as *Sand* and *Wood-Wasps*. **1871** E. F. STAVELEY *Brit. Insects* 203 The second division of the predacious stinging Hymenoptera, known as Fossores, or *diggers*, consists of the Sand-wasps and Wood-wasps.

5. *slang.* **a.** A spur. **b.** A finger-nail. **c.** A card of the spade suit; ***big-digger***, the ace of spades (Farmer *Slang*).
1789 G. PARKER *Life's Painter* 173 s.v. (Farmer). **1811** *Lex Balatronicum* s.v. (Farmer). **1859** MATSELL *Vocabulum* s.v. (Farmer). **1881** *N.Y. Slang Dict.* (Farmer), 'I will fix my diggers in your dial-plate and turn it up with red.'
6. *Comb.*, as **digger-pine**, a N. American species of pine, *Pinus sabiniana*; **digger plough**, a plough that breaks down the furrow-slice by means of a projecting wing or continuation of the mould-board; **digger's delight** *Austral.*, a species of speedwell, *Veronica perfoliata*, so called from the supposition that it grows only on auriferous soil; **digger-wasp** (see sense 4).
1935 *Hutchinson's Techn. & Sci. Encycl.* I. 38/2 Modern mould-board ploughs fall generally into one or other of two classes: general purpose ploughs.. and digger ploughs, which leave the soil flat and broken. *Ibid.*, In the general purpose plough the share is a pointed wedge... In the digger plough the share is wider and steeper and has a concave upper surface. **1960** *Farmer & Stockbreeder* 23 Feb. 64/2 Both competitors will use two ploughs—a free digger plough on stubble and a semi-digger on a one-year ley. **1878** W. R. GUILFOYLE *1st Bk. Austral. Bot.* 64 Digger's Delight. .. A pretty, blue-flowering shrub with smooth stem-clasping leaves. **1888** D. MACDONALD *Gum Boughs* 147 Such native flowers as the wild violet, the shepherd's purse, or the blue-flowered 'digger's delight'. **1880** *Libr. Univ. Knowl.* IX. 123 The digger-wasps.. catch locusts.. and bury them in their nests for their newly hatched young.

diggeress ('dɪgərɪs). [f. DIGGER + -ESS.] A female digger; a digger's wife.
1864 ROGERS *New Rush* II. 36 I'm tired of being a diggeress.

digging ('dɪgɪŋ), *vbl. sb.* [f. DIG *v.* + -ING[1].]
1. a. The action of the verb to DIG, in various senses; an instance of this.
1552 HULOET, Dyggynge and deluinge of a ground to bring it eftsones in temper, *repastinatio*. **1651** JER. TAYLOR *Holy Dying* i. §2 (L.) Let us not project long designs, crafty plots, and diggings so deep that the intrigues of a design shall never be unfolded. **1663** GERBIER *Counsel* 25 In the digging of the foundations. **1725** BRADLEY *Fam. Dict.* s.v. *Yew Tree*, This first digging is to be done always in March. **1738** LABELYE *Short Acc. Piers Westm. Br.* 27 After the digging the Pit.. was finished. **1891** *Law Times* XCII. 106/2 He was only paid for his digging.
b. with an adverb.
1573 BARET *Alv.* D. 687 A digging vnder, an undermining, *suffossio*. **1817** COBBETT *Addr. Bristol* Wks. XXXII. 47 A digging and rooting up of all corruptions. **1890** *Daily News* 4 Sept. 6/4 All digging down work should be paid for at the rate of 1d. per hour extra.
2. *fig.* The action of studying hard. *U.S.*
1827–8 *Harvard Reg.* 312, I find my eyes in doleful case, By digging until midnight. **1873** W. MATHEWS *Getting on* xv. 244 Men of genius have seldom revealed to us how much of their fame was due to hard digging.
3. *concr.* The materials dug out.
1559 in Boys *Sandwich* (1792) 737, iij laborers may carry his diggins away. *a* **1626** BACON *Impeachm. Waste* (L.), He shall have the seasonable loppings; so he shall have seasonable diggings of an open mine.
4. a. A place where digging is carried on, an excavation; in *pl.* (sometimes treated as a *sing.*) applied to mines, and especially to the gold-fields of California and Australia. Also with prefixed word, as ***gold-diggings***, ***river-diggings***, ***surface-diggings***, etc. ***dry-*** or ***wet-diggings*** (see quot. 1889).
1538 LELAND *Itin.* I. 13 On the South side of Welleden.. ys a goodly quarre of Stone, wher appere great Diggyns. **1653** BOGAN *Mirth Chr. Life* 122 The earth.. yields a smell wholesome to the digger in the diggings. **1712** J. JAMES tr. *Le Blond's Gardening* 206 The Wall.. of one Foot thick, from the Bottom of the Digging, to the Level of the Ground above. **1769** *De Foe's Tour Gt. Brit.* I. 39 At Norton, near Wulpit, King Henry VIII. was induced to dig for Gold. He was disappointed, but the Diggings are visible at this Day. **1835** C. F. HOFFMAN *Winter in Far West* xxv. (Bartlett) Mr. ——.. has lately struck a lead.. We are now, you observe, among his diggings. **1839** MARRYAT *Diary Amer.* Ser. I. II. 62 The diggings as they term the places where the lead is found.. were about sixteen miles distant. **1849** *Illustr. Lond. News* 17 Nov. 325/1 Letter from the Gold Diggings. **1852** EARP *Gold Col. Australia* 138 The diggings are on a creek called Araluen Creek. **1857** BORTHWICK *California* 120 (Bartlett) The principal diggings near Haugtown were surface diggings, but, with the exception of river diggings, every kind of mining was seen in full force. **1889** FARMER *Americanisms*, *Wet-diggings* and *Dry-diggings* are terms in gold districts, for mines near rivers or on the higher lands as the case may be. **1890** BOLDREWOOD *Miner's Right* vii. 71 It was a goldfield and a diggings in far-away Australia.
b. Archæological excavation, or the site of such an excavation.
1911 T. E. LAWRENCE *Let.* 31 Mar. (1938) 101 Digging results will appear in *The Times*. *Ibid.* 23 May 106 She was really too captious at first, coming straight from the German diggings at Kalaát Shirgat. **1938** D. GARNETT in *Lett. T. E. Lawrence* 40 It was in this bungalow that he lodged his Arab friends.. when he brought them from the Carchemish diggings to visit England.
5. *colloq.* in *pl.* Lodgings, quarters.
1838 J. C. NEAL *Charcoal Sketches* II. 119 (Farmer), I reckon it's about time we should go to our diggings. **1844** DICKENS *Mart. Chuz.* xxi. She won't be taken with a cold chill when she realises what is being done in these diggings? **1882** *Chamb. Jrnl.* 87, I returned to my diggings. **1889** J. K. JEROME *Three men in Boat* 187 We took out the hamper.. and started off to look for diggings.

6. *attrib.* and *Comb.*, as ***digging-machine, -spade, -spur, -stick***; **digging-life**, life at the gold-diggings; **digging-party** (see PARTY *sb.* 7 and 8); **digging plough** = *digger plough* (see DIGGER 6); **digging-stick**, a primitive digging implement consisting of a pointed stick, sometimes weighted by a stone.

1875 A. SMITH *New Hist. Aberdeensh.* II. 1120 The next experiment was with the 'digger'..formed by taking the mouldboard off the plough and putting on the digging breasts. **1859** CORNWALLIS *New World* I. 120 Shafts were sunk, windlasses erected, and the whole paraphernalia of digging life called into requisition. **1874** KNIGHT *Dict. Mech.* I. 702/2 *Digging machine* (Agric.), a spading-machine for loosening and turning the soil. **1853** MRS. C. CLACY *Lady's Visit to Gold Diggings of Australia* iii. 19 But for our digging party entire, which consisted of my brother, four shipmates, and myself, no accommodation could be procured. *Ibid.* 32 Four other of our shipmates had also joined themselves into a digging-party. **1923** KIPLING *Irish Guards in Gt. War* I. 55 Some Garrison gunners threw three bombs at an enemy digging-party. **1891** R. WALLACE *Rural Econ. Austral. & N.Z.* xix. 272 Howards Digging Plough.. turns over the furrow slices most perfectly and breaks what is then left at the surface by means of a projecting wing or continuation of the mould-board. **1719** DE FOE *Crusoe* (1840) II. vi. 125 A digging spade. **1865** LUBBOCK *Preh. Times* 358 The digging-sticks are made of a young mangrove tree. **1947** I. L. IDRIESS *Isles of Despair* xii. 82 Women.. carrying their food baskets and digging sticks. **1959** TINDALE & LINDSAY *Rangatira* ii. 199 The hoe and digging-stick method of cultivating the soil [by the Maoris]. **1960** K. M. KENYON *Archæol. in Holy Land* ii. 49 Cultivation of the ground was probably carried out by digging-sticks, pointed sticks weighted by stones, of which the evidence survives in the form of heavy stones pierced by a hole.

diggish ('dɪgɪʃ), *a. Children's slang.* [f. DIG *v.* 6c + -ISH[1].] Excellent, splendid.

1963 *Daily Mail* 22 Jan. 6/3 Schoolchildren produce their own variations. Mr. Peter Opie..tells me that instead of merely saying they dig something, they describe it as *diggish*.

diggy ('dɪgɪ), *a. colloq.* [f. DIG *sb.*[1] 4b + -Y[1].] Inclined to give sly digs.

1904 *Daily Chron.* 26 Mar. 3/3 General Frey is very 'diggy' against what we should have thought he would have found to be equally fine representatives of our Indian Army—the Sikhs. **1906** *Ibid.* 23 Jan. 3/1 Our official German critics..are always very 'diggy' towards Buller.

†**dighel**, *a.* Forms: 1 **díeȝel, díeȝol, dýȝel**, 3 **diȝel**. [OE. *dieȝel, -ol* (:—OTeut. **daugilo-*), found beside *déaȝol* (:—*daugolo-*), = OHG. *taugal, tougal* (*daugal, dougal*) dark, secret: cf. *tougan, dougan* concealed, secret.] Secret, obscure.

Beowulf 2719 Hie dyȝel lond wariȝeað. *a* **1000** *Be Domes Dæge* (1876) 40 þæt hit ne sy dæȝcuð þæt þæt dihle wæs. *Ibid.* 135 Diȝle ȝeþancas. *a* **1250** *Owl & Night.* 2 Ich was.. In one swiþe diȝele hale. *c* **1275** LAY. 26935 Hii comen in one wode..in one dale deope, diȝele bi-halues [*c* **1205** diȝelen bihælues].

Hence '**dighelliche, digheliche** (also **dihlice, diȝeliche, dieliche**) *adv.*, secretly; '**dighelness** (**diȝelnesse, dihelness**), secrecy; also '**dighenlich** *a.* [cf. OHG. *tougan*], secret; '**dighenliche** *adv.*, secretly.

c **893** ÆLFRED *Oros.* II. i. §5 þurh Godes dieȝelnessa. *Ibid.* VI. xxi, He wearð dieȝellice cristen. *c* **961** ÆTHELWOLD *Rule St. Benet* (1885) 134 Swa dihlice wuniende. *c* **1000** *Ags. Gosp.* Matt. xiii. 35 Ic bodiȝe diȝelnesse. *a* **1200** *Winteney Rule St. Benet* xxvii. (1888) 67 Hiȝ scullan oft dihlice ealde witan..sændan. *c* **1200** *Trin. Coll. Hom.* 191 He secheð forte þat he open fint, and diȝeliche smuhȝð þer inne. *c* **1200** ORMIN 5501 Full wel tunnderrstanndenn Off all þe boc in Godess hus þe deope diȝhellnesse. *c* **1205** LAY. 415 Assaracus hit redde mid diȝenliche runen. *Ibid.* 13539 Forð riht faren we him to, diȝelliche & stille. *a* **1225** *St. Marher.* 16 To understonden so derne þing ant so derf, of godes dihelnesse. *c* **1275** LAY. 6659 Diȝenliche [**1205** duȝeliche] hine bi-witie, and his name deorne.

dighere, obs. form of DYER.

dight (daɪt), *v.* Now *arch.* and *dial.* Forms: 1 **diht-an**, 2–3 **diht-en**, 3–4 **diȝt-e(n**, (4 **dyghte, diȝt, diȝth**, 4–5 **dyht, diȝte**), 4–6 **dighte** (5 **dyte, dyth**, 5–7 **dite**, 6 **dyght**), 4– **dight** (6– *Sc.* **dicht**, 8–9 *north. dial.* **deeght, deet**). Pa. t. 1 **dihte, dihtode**, 2–4 **dihte, diȝte**, 4 **diȝted, -id**, 4–5 **diȝt, dyȝt**, 4– **dight** (6– *Sc.* **dichtit**). Pa. pple. 1 (**ȝe**)**diht, dihted**, 3–4 (**i**)**diht**, 3– **dight**, (7 **dighted**, 6– *Sc.* **dichtit**). [OE. *dihtan*, ad. L. *dictāre* to dictate, compose in language, appoint, prescribe, order, in med.L. to write, compose a speech, letter, etc.: see DICTATE *v.* Parallel forms are OHG. *dihtôn, tihtôn, tictôn, thictôn* to write, compose, MHG. *tihten, dichten*, to write, compose, invent, contrive, mod.G. *dichten* to compose verses or poetry, MLG. *dichten* to compose, institute, contrive, set (oneself), LG. *dichten, digten* to versify, invent, contrive, think out, MDu. *dichten* to compose (in writing), contrive, institute, prepare, mod.Du. *dichten* to invent, compose, versify; also Icel. *dikta* to compose or write in Latin, to write a romance, to romance, lie, Sw. *dikta* to feign, fable, Da. *digte* to make poems (from Ger.). The mutual relations of the OE., OHG., and Norse words are not quite clear; but the difference of formation between OE. *dihtan* :—**dihtjan*, and OHG. *tihtôn* v. :—**dihtôjan*, indicates that they are independent adoptions of the Latin, although the change of *d* to *t* shows that the word is old in German. The Norse word must be of later adoption: if it were old, the expected form would be **détta*.

From the senses of literary dictation and composition in which it was originally used, this verb received in ME. an extraordinary sense-development, so as to be one of the most widely used words in the language. Special representatives of these ME. senses, survive dialectally, *esp.* in the north; the modern literary language knows the pa. pple. *dight*, which after being nearly obsolete in the 18th c., has been largely taken up again by poets and romantic writers of the 19th c. in senses 10, 14. (In MHG. *dichten* had also a much greater development of meaning than in mod.German.)]

I. To dictate, appoint, ordain, order, dispose of, deal with, treat.

†**1.** *trans.* To dictate, give directions to, direct. *Obs.* (Only in OE.)

c **1000** *Ags. Gosp.* Matt. xxviii. 16 Ða ferdon þa endlufun leorning-cnihtas on þone munt, þær se hælynd heom dihte. *c* **1000** ÆLFRIC *Gen.* xvi. 3 Abram þa dyde swa swa him dyhte Sarai. *Ibid.* xxxix. 23 Drihten þær..dihte him hwæt he don sceolde. *c* **1000** —— *On O. Test* (in Sweet *A.S. Reader* 60) Moyses awrat..swa swa him God silf dihte on heora sunderspræce.

†**2.** To appoint, ordain. *Obs.*

c **1000** *Ags. Gosp.* Luke xxii. 29 Ic eow dihte swa min fæder me rice dihte. *a* **1225** *Leg. Kath.* 1606 þe deore drihtin haueð idiht ow ba þe blisfule crune of his icorene. *a* **1300** *Cursor M.* 9369 (Cott.) How þe fader of heuen Dight his dere sun to send. *c* **1330** R. BRUNNE *Chron.* (1810) 127 þat Steuen to dede was dight. **1340** *Ayenb.* 7 He mæde þe worlde an ordaynede [*v.r.* diȝte]. **1340** HAMPOLE *Pr. Consc.* 7795 þe ioyes sere þat God has ordaynd þare and dyght. *c* **1374** CHAUCER *Troylus* IV. 1160 (1188) Ther as þe dom of Mynos wolde it dyghte. *a* **1400** *Pistill of Susan* 267, I am deolfolich dampned, and to deþ diht. *c* **1400** *Apol. Loll.* 60 A iuge is seid for he ditiþ riȝt to þe peple. **14..** *E.E. Misc.* (Warton Club) 12 A dredefulle payne is for me dyȝte. **1558** *Will of Willyson* (Somerset Ho.), Consyderyng y[t] death to euery man is dight. [**1808** SCOTT *Marm.* I. vi, The golden legend bore aright, 'Who checks at me, to death is dight.']

†**3.** To order, keep in order, manage, govern, rule. *Obs.*

c **1205** LAY. 6848 Wel wes þisse londe idiht. *Ibid.* 7220 He makede þane kalender þe dihteð þane moneð & þe ȝer. *Ibid.* 10201 þa setten heo biscopes þan folken to dihten. *c* **1230** *Hali Meid.* 7 Deð hire in to drecchunge to dihten hus & hinen. **1297** R. GLOUC. (1724) 424 Kyng Henry & hys wyf ..So wel dyȝte Engelond, þat yt was wyde ytold. *c* **1400** *St. Alexius* (Laud 622) 28 Religious þat her lijf willen diȝth. ?*a* **1500** *Chester Pl., Balaam & Balak* 397 A Childe..in Bethlem shall be born, That shall be Duke to dight and deale, and rule the folke of Israell. **1522** *World & Child* in Hazl. *Dodsley* I. 274 Christ rose upon the third day..That all shall deem and dight.

†**4.** To deal with, treat, handle, use (in some manner); often to maltreat, abuse. *Obs.*

c **1205** LAY. 11020 Hu he mihte dihten Ælene his dohter. *c* **1275** *Ibid.* 25907 þus he vs diht to-day a soueniht. *a* **1300** *Cursor M.* 21447 (Gött.) Sai me hu þu wile him dight, If þat he be dempt to þe wid right. **1303** R. BRUNNE *Handl. Synne* 724 What mercy mayst þou aske..Whan þou þus my sone hast dyghte? *c* **1400** *Lanfranc's Cirurg.* 320 þouȝ þe fynger ne be but a litil lyme ȝitt þou muste have good kunnyng and good witt for to diȝte it wel. *c* **1450** *Mirour Saluacioun* 1758 Two stronge ȝonge men..Dight Helyodore with thaire whippes til he als dede thare laye. **1513** DOUGLAS *Æneis* VI. viii. 51 How euir wes ony suffirit the so to dycht? **1563** B. GOOGE *Eglogs* (Arb.) 115 Acteon wofull wyght, In what a manner, all to torne, his cruell Dogs him dyght. **1650** B. *Discolliminium* 52, I feare also at length some or other will come and dight us to purpose.

†**b.** *spec.* To have to do with sexually. *Obs.*

c **1386** CHAUCER *Wife's Prol.* 398 Al my walkynge out by nyghte Was for tespye wenches þat he dighte. *Ibid.* 767 Lete hir lecchour dighte hire al the nyght. *c* **1386** —— *Manciple's T.* 208. **1393** LANGL. *P. Pl.* C. II. 27 In hus dronke-nesse a day hus douhtres he [Lot] dighte And lay by hem boþe.

†**5.** To dispose, place, put, remove. *Obs.*

1297 R. GLOUC. (1724) 148 Cuþeþ now ȝoure myȝte, How ȝe mow þis stones best to þe schip dyȝte. *a* **1300** *Cursor M.* 17312 (Cott.) Quy Blame ȝe me..for I a man in graf diȝt, In a toumb þat was myn awen? **1340** *Ayenb.* 210 Alle þoȝtes ulessliche and wordleliche me ssel diȝte uram þe herte þet wyle god bidde. **1393** GOWER *Conf.* III. 270 Whan he was to bedde dight. *c* **1450** *St. Cuthbert* (Surtees) 6612 On þe pament þai it dyght. *Ibid.* 7138 þe thrid in tughall þai þaim dyght. **1535** STEWART *Chron. Scot.* II. 524 The deid corpis in tha flang; And syne kest on the muldis on the clay, The grene erd syne, and dycht the laif away.

†**b.** *fig.* To put into a specified state or condition; *esp.* in ***to dight to death***, to put to death, kill, slay (see also 2). *Obs.*

13.. *E.E. Allit. P.* B. 1266 Diȝten dekenes to deþe, dungen doun clerkkes. *c* **1340** *Cursor M.* 18043 (Trin.) þat dede from deþ to lif he diȝt. **1393** GOWER *Conf.* II. 145 Ha, to what peine she is dight. **1415** *Pol. Poems* (Rolls) II. 125 Thorow hem many on to deth were dyght. **1460** *Lybeaus Disc.* 1719 To dethe they wyll her dyghte. *c* **1470** HENRY *Wallace* IV. 68 Your selff sone syne to dede thai think to dycht. **1579–80** NORTH *Plutarch* (1676) 13 Bold Theseus to cruel death him dight. **1586** J. HOOKER *Girald. Irel.* in *Holinshed* II. 179/2 The earle would haue..dighted the lord gouernour and all the garisons to greater troubles. **1664** *Floddan F.* viii. 78 For unto death till we be dight I promise here to take thy part. **1817** SCOTT *Harold the Dauntless* VI. vi, Still in the posture as to death when dight.

†**c.** With inverted construction: To cause, bring about, inflict (death). *Obs.*

1307 *Elegy Edw. I*, i, A stounde herkneth to my song, Of duel that Deth hath diht us newe. *c* **1350** *Will. Palerne* 151 Hire deth was neiȝ diȝt. *c* **1400** *Destr. Troy* 9558 Myche dole is vs dight to-day. *a* **1450** *Cov. Myst.* 265 On of ȝou is bezy my dethe here to dyth. *c* **1475** *Partenay* 3444 Yff atwixst his handis he hym haue myght, He wold make hym ende, And shameuous deth dight!

II. To compose, construct, make, do.

†**6.** To compose (with words); to set down in writing. *Obs.*

c **1000** ÆLFRIC *Life Oswold* in Sweet *A.S. Reader* (1879) 102 Nu cwæþ se halȝa Beda, ðe ðas boc ȝedihte. *c* **1205** LAY. 3150 He letten writen a writ & wel hit lette dihten. *c* **1275** *Ibid.* 20669 Nis hit in none boke idiht þat euere her were soch fiht. *c* **1425** *Hampole's Psalter* Metr. Pref. 48 Whos wol it write, I rede hym rygth, wryte on warly lyne be lyne, And make no more þen here is dygth. *a* **1440** *Sir Degrev.* 153 A lettre has he dyght.

†**7.** To compose, put together, frame, construct, make. *Obs.*

a **1175** *Cott. Hom.* 233 He alle ȝesceop, and all dihte wið-ute swince. *c* **1200** *Trin. Coll. Hom.* 25 Ure fader in heuene feide þe lemes to ure licame..and swo diȝeliche hit al dihte, þat on elche feinge is hem onsene. *c* **1205** LAY. 23532 Walles heo gunnen rihten, þa ȝæten heo gunnen dihten. *a* **1300** *Cursor M.* 1665 (Cott.), A schippe be-houes þe to dight. *Ibid.* 12388 (Cott.) Plogh and haru cuth he dight. *c* **1340** *Ibid.* 23216 (Trin.) No more..þen peynted fire ..þat on a wal bi mon were diȝt. *c* **1400** MAUNDEV. (1839) vi. 70 The place..is fulle well dyghte of Marble. *c* **1420** *Pallad. on Husb.* I. 509 Nygh thi bestes dight A fire in colde. **1607** *Schol. Disc. agst. Antichr.* I. ii. 72 Hee dight himselfe a triple crowne.

†**b.** To perform, do. *Obs.*

c **1205** LAY. 15513 Fulle þreo nihten heore craftes heo dihten. *c* **1460** *Play Sacram.* 849 Alas y[t] euer thys dede was dyght. **1596** SPENSER *F.Q.* V. ii. 18 Curst the hand which did that vengeance on him dight.

III. To put in order, array, dress, direct, prepare, make ready, or proper.

†**8.** To put or place in order, to set in array, to array; to arrange. *Obs.*

c **1205** LAY. 20563 Howel sculde dihten þritti þusend cnihten. *Ibid.* 27337 þa þas ferde wes al idiht, þa wes hit dailiht. *c* **1330** R. BRUNNE *Chron.* (1810) 2 A hede, þat vs to werre can dight. **1375** BARBOUR *Bruce* II. 565 His men in hy he gert be dycht. ?*a* **1500** *Merline* 1784 in Furniv. *Percy Folio* I. 477 All they can out ryde, & dighten them without fayle to giue Sir Vortiger battayle. [**1821** JOANNA BAILLIE *Met. Leg., Wallace* lxi, Were with their leader dight.]

9. To equip, fit out, furnish (*with* what is needed).

In later use blending with sense 10: which see as to the modern use of the pa. pple. in romantic language.

c **1205** LAY. 15104 Ælc scip he dihte mid þreo hundred cni[h]ten. *a* **1300** *Cursor M.* 24807 (Edin.), Wit tresori his schip was diht. *c* **1330** R. BRUNNE *Chron. Wace* (Rolls) 617 Do dight a schip wiþ sail & ore Ryght as þou a marchaund wore. **1460** CAPGRAVE *Chron.* 33 Nyne hundred cartis dith with hokis of yrun. **1470–85** MALORY *Arthur* II. xv, He entryd in to a chambyr that was merueillously wel dyȝte and rychely. **1555** ABP. PARKER *Ps.* li. 149 Wyth sacrifice of calfe and cow, they shall thyne aulters dyght. **1590** SPENSER *F.Q.* I. iv. 6 The hall..With rich array and costly arras dight. **1805** SCOTT *Last Minstr.* I. vi, Why do these steeds stand ready dight? *Ibid.* v. xxvii, In Sir William's armour dight, Stolen by his Page, while slept the knight.

†**b.** With inverse constr.: To fit (some equipment) *to* or *upon*. (Cf. 10b.) *Obs.* or *arch.*

c **1475** *Rauf Coilȝear* 677 With Dosouris to the duris dicht. **1871** P. H. WADDELL *Ps.* xlv. 3 Dicht yer swurd ontil yer thie.

10. To clothe, dress, array, deck, adorn (*lit.* and *fig.*). †***to dight naked***, to undress, strip.

In this sense the pa. pple. *dight* is used by Sir Walter Scott, and in later poetic and romantic language: it appears to be often taken as an archaic form of *decked*.

c **1200** *Trin. Coll. Hom.* 87 Clensed of fule sinnes, and diht mid loðlesnesse. *a* **1300** *Cursor M.* 24552 (Edin.), þan nicodem..Wit Iosep nam þat cors to diht. *c* **1330** *King of Tars* 848 The soudan dihte him naked anon. *c* **1340** *Cursor M.* 2249 (Fairf.), þai dight ham in þat tide wiþ hors skynnys and camel hide. **1388** WYCLIF *Isa.* xl. 19 A worchere in siluer schal diȝte it with platis of siluer. *a* **1450** *Knt. de la Tour* (1868) 69 The thinge that she dite so her selff with. **1530** PALSGR. 516/1 A foule woman rychly dyght semeth fayre by candell lyght. **1579** SPENSER *Sheph. Cal.* Jan. 22 Thy sommer prowde with Daffadillies dight. **1596** —— *F.Q.* IV. x. 38 Damzels in soft linnen dight. **1600** HOLLAND *Livy* II. vi. 48 Dight [decoratus] in our roiall ensignes and ornaments. **1632** MILTON *L'Allegro* 62 The clouds in thousand liveries dight. **1632** —— *Penseroso* 159 Storied windows richly dight Casting a dim religious light. **1632** MASSINGER & FIELD *Fatal Dowry* IV. i, To see a young, fair, handsome beauty unhandsomely dighted and incongruently accoutred. **1663** BUTLER *Hud.* I. iii. 928 Just so the proud insulting Lass Array'd and dighted Hudibras. **1808** SCOTT *Marm.* VI. Introd. iii, But, O! what maskers richly dight. **1817** WORDSW. *Vernal Ode* i, All the fields with freshest green were dight. *a* **1845** BARHAM *Ingol. Leg., Wedding-day*, There stand the village maids dight in white. **1887** BOWEN *Virg. Æneid* III. 517 Orion, in golden panoply dight.

b. With inverse constr.: To put on (armour, apparel, etc.). (A Spenserian use.)

1590 SPENSER *F.Q.* I. vii. 8 Ere he could his armour on him dight. **1590** —— *Muiopotmos* 91 His shinie wings..he did about him dight. **1591** —— *M. Hubberd* 1279 Tho on his head his dreadfull hat he dight. **1654** GAYTON *Pleas. Notes* II. vi. 59 She straightway dight her robes.

†**c.** To dress (a wound); to attend to as a surgeon or 'leech'. *Obs.*

c 1340 *Cursor M.* 14064 (Fairf.), Ho hir oynement me boȝt & diȝt þar-wiþ my fote & shank. 1464 *Mann. & Househ. Exp.* 246 To Watkyn the Kynggys horseleche, ffor dytynge my masterys horsses iij.s. iiij.d. 1467 *Ibid.* 423 My wyffe payd to a schorgon, fore dytenge of heme wane he was horte, xij.d. c 1500 *Spir. Remedies* in Halliwell *Nugae Poet.* 64 My ..woundys..bene..depe..Her smertyng wylle nat suffre me to slepe, Tylle a leche with dewte have theme dyght. 1533 BELLENDEN *Livy* II. (1822) 136 He deceissit sone eftir that his wound wes dicht.

d. *ironically.* To dirty, befoul. *dial.*

1632 MARMION *Holland's Leaguer* I. ii, Straight we shall fall Into a lake that will foully dight us. 1674 RAY *N.C. Words* 14 To Dight: Cheshire to foule or dirty one. 1869 *Lonsdale Gloss.*, *Deet*, to dirty. 1877 *N.W. Linc. Gloss.* s.v., Thy han's is strange an' dighted up wi' dirt.

†**11.** To make ready, get ready (a person): chiefly *refl.* to make oneself ready, prepare, set, or address oneself (*to do* something). *Obs.*

c 1205 LAY. 12429 Seoððe heo heom dihten to bi-witen þa dich mid cnihten. a 1300 *Cursor M.* 11179 (Cott.), Ioseph dight him for to ga To bethleem. 1375 *Cantic. de Creatione* in *Anglia* I. 303 etc., Eue diȝte here to childyng. c 1400 *Destr. Troy* 8636 The dethe of þat Duke he dight hym to venge. c 1425 *Seven Sag.* (P.) 289 Lat dyght messangers ȝare Aftir hym for to fare. a 1550 *Christis Kirke Gr.* ii, To dans thir damysellis thame dicht. ?1591 C'TESS PEMBROKE *Dolefull Lay Clorinda* 105 in Spenser *Astroph.*, Full many other moe..'Gan dight themselves t' express their inward woe With doleful lays. 1596 SPENSER *F.Q.* VI. ii. 18 He.. straight bids him dight Himself to yeeld his Love.

†**12.** *refl.* To direct *oneself* or one's *way*; to make one's way, repair, go. *Obs.*

a 1300 *Cursor M.* 10551 (Gött.), Quen þis angel away was diht, Tua men þer cam were clad in quiht. c 1330 R. BRUNNE *Chron.* (1810) 113 Siþen [he] dight him to Scotland. c 1386 CHAUCER *Monk's Prol.* 26 And out at dore anon I moot me dighte. 1430 LYDG. *Chron. Troy* IV. xxix, To-warde Troye your way was not dyght. c 1450 *St. Cuthbert* (Surtees) 788 To þe currok þai þaim dyght. 1596 SPENSER *F.Q.* IV. i. 16 They both uprose and to their waies them dight. *Ibid.* V. iv. 43 She fiercely towards him her self gan dight.

†**13.** *trans.* To direct, address, proffer, offer. *Obs. rare.*

a 1300 *Cursor M.* 13990 (Cott.) Ful fair seruis symon him dight, Als was to suilk a lauerding right. 1393 GOWER *Conf.* II. 173 Goddes..To whom ful great honour they dighten. 1568 T. HOWELL *Arb. Amitie* (1879) 46 Hir wylling helpe she dightes.

14. To prepare, make ready for use or for a purpose; **a.** in general sense. (Revived in poetic and romantic use.)

a 1325 *Prose Psalter* Song of Simeon, For myn eȝen seȝen þyn helþe, þe which þou diȝted to-fore þe face of alle folkes. c 1340 *Cursor M.* 13767 (Fairf.), þer-in was angels wont to liȝt and þat ilk water diȝt. c 1400 *Rom. Rose* 4240 A nyght His instrumentis wolde he dight, For to blowe & make sowne. c 1420 *Pallad. on Husb.* I. 1123 Grounden shelles dight With flour of lyme. c 1440 *Promp. Parv.* 123/2 Dyhtyn', *paro, preparo.* 1476 *Plumpton Corr.* 36 As for the cloth of my ladies, Hen. Cloughe putt it to a shereman to dight. 1520 *Lanc. Wills* II. 11 My yarne yt is sponne, to dyght it and make in cloth. 1590 SPENSER *F.Q.* II. xi. 2 Alma..to her guestes doth bounteous banket dight. 1596 DALRYMPLE tr. *Leslie's Hist. Scot.* I. 94 Thay take the hail meklewame of ane slain ox, thay turne and dicht it, thay fill it partlie with water partlie with flesche. 1609 SKENE *Reg. Maj.* 127 And gif they dicht, or prepair the flesh not well, they sall restore the skaith to the awner of the beast. 1613 BEAUM. & FL. *Coxcomb* IV. iii, Have a care you dight things handsomely. 1821 JOANNA BAILLIE *Met. Leg.*, *Elder Tree* xxv, To dight him for earth or heaven. 1871 B. TAYLOR *Faust* (1875) II. v. i. 272 Haste and let the meal be dighted 'Neath the garden's blooming trees. 1887 MORRIS *Odyss.* IV. 768 This Queen of the many wooers dights the wedding for us then.

In specific senses: †**b.** To prepare, make ready (food, a meal); to cook; to prepare or mix (a potion or medicine). *Obs.*

a 1300 *Cursor M.* 24398 (Cott.) þai did him dight a bitter drink,..of gall of aissil graid. c 1320 R. BRUNNE *Medit.* 49 þe soper was dyȝt as y herd sey. c 1400 MAUNDEV. (Roxb.) xiv. 64 For þai hafe lytill wode, þai dight þaire mete with dung of bestez dried at þe sonne. 14.. *Noble Bk. Cookry* (Napier 1882) 96 To dight a pik in sauce. 1459 *Corpus Christi Coll. Contract* in Willis & Clark *Cambridge* (1886) I. 259 His mete to be dyght in the kechyn at there costis. 1483 CAXTON *Gold. Leg.* 68/1 She slewe a paske lambe..and dighted and sette it to fore hym. 1535 COVERDALE *Gen.* xxv. 29 And Jacob dight a meace of meate. —— *1 Esdras* i. 12 As for the thank offeringes & the other, they dight them in kettels & pottes. 1561 HOLLYBUSH *Hom. Apoth.* 20 Chap it smal and dight it lyke a thycke potage. a 1569 KINGESMYLL *Godly Advise* (1580) 2 The fine cooke men dight the rude morsell with some conceite of their cunning. 1721 KELLY *Sc. Prov.* 12 (Jam.) A friend's dinner is soon dight.

c. To repair, put to rights, put in order (what is out of order). Now *dial.*

a 1300 *Cursor M.* 19755 (Cott.) 'Rise', he said, 'þi bedd þou dight'. c 1450 *St. Cuthbert* (Surtees) 2570 With in thre days all hale dyght. 1580 *Vestry Bks.* (Surtees) 121 Item paid to Thomas Sim for dighting the leads, iiij d. [1877 *N.W. Linc. Gloss.*, *Dight up*, to repair, put in order. 'I mun hev these yates an' stowps dighted up afore th' steward comes'.]

d. To polish or burnish up so as to fit for use; to cleanse from rust, or the like. *Obs.* or *dial.*

a 1400 CHAUCER *Rom. Rose* 941 Arowis..shaven wel and dight. c 1500 *Debate Carp. Tools*, Halliwell *Nugae Poet.* 15, I schalle rube, with all my myght, My mayster tolys for to dyght. 1513 DOUGLAS *Æneis* VIII. vii. 133 Ane part polyst, burnyst weill and dycht. 1532-33 *Christ's Coll. Audit-Bk.* in Willis & Clark *Cambridge* (1886) II. 206 Item payd..for dyghtyng the egle and candyllstykkes xd. 1535 COVERDALE *Baruch* vi. 22 Excepte some body dight off their rust, they wil geue no shyne. 1536 BELLENDEN *Cron. Scot.* (1821) I. Proheme p. xii, And dois the saule fra all corruption dicht. a 1605 MONTGOMERIE *Misc. Poems* xli. 34 All curageous knichtis Againis the day dichtis The breist plate that bright is To feght with thair fone. 1674-91 RAY *N.C. Words* 140 To Deeght, *Extergere, mundare.* a 1774 FERGUSSON *Poems* (1789) II. 69 (Jam.), Wi mason's chissel dichted neat. 1825-80 JAMIESON s.v., The act of smoothing a piece of wood by means of a plane is called 'dichting a deal'.

e. To winnow, so as to separate the clean corn from the chaff and other refuse. *Sc.* and *north. dial.*

c 1611 CHAPMAN *Iliad* V. 498 And as, in sacred floors of barns, upon corn-winnowers flies The chaff, driven with an opposite wind, when yellow Ceres dites. 1618 —— *Hesiod* II. 343 To dight the sacred gift of Ceres' hand, In some place windy, on a well-plan'd floor. 1619 *Naworth Househ. Bks.* 91 For threshing and dighting v bushells and a peck of wheat. 1786 BURNS *Addr. Unco Guid*, heading, The cleanest corn that e'er was dight May hae some pyles o' caff in. 1801 JO. HOGG *Poems* 104 (Jam.) That it was lawful, just, an' right Wi' windasses folk's corn to dight. 1808 R. ANDERSON *Cumberld. Ball.* 72 I'll ax his wark, an muck the byres, Or deet, an thresh the cworn. 1816 SCOTT *Old Mort.* vii, A new-fangled machine for dighting the corn frae the chaff. 1878 *Cumbld. Gloss. Deet, deeght*, to winnow or dress corn. *Mod. Sc.* (Roxb.) Dichtin' in the barn wi' the windasses is a dusty job.

f. To wipe clean or dry. *Sc.* and *north Eng. dial.*

1681 COLVIL *Whigs Supplic.* (1751) 120 With his hankerchief he dights off Tears from his eyes. 1724 RAMSAY *Tea-t. Misc.* (1733) I. 8 He dighted his gab, and he pri'd her mou'. 1728 —— *Anacreontic on Love* 21, I..Dighted his face, his handies thow'd. a 1803 *Douglas Trag.* viii. in Child *Ballads* (1882) I. 101/1 She's taen out her handkerchief,.. And aye she dighted her father's bloody wounds. 1816 SCOTT. *Old Mort.* xl, Morton..underwent a rebuke for not 'dighting his shune'. 1830 GALT *Lawrie T.* VII. iii. (1849) 327 She may dight her neb and flee up. 1878 *Cumbld. Gloss.*, *Deet, deeght*, to wipe or make clean. 1892 *Northumbld. Gloss. Mod. Sc.* Dicht the table before you set anything on it. Take a cloth and dicht it up.

†**15.** To 'dress' in husbandry (vines, land, etc.); to cultivate, till, or attend to (plants, crops, etc.).

c 1400 MAUNDEV. (Roxb.) xxii. 103 þe whilk telez þe land and dightez vynes. c 1420 *Pallad. on Husb.* II. 81 Yf the vyne is dight with mannes hond. 1496 *Dives & Paup.* (W. de W.) III. xiv. 149/2 Yf corn or grasse be in the felde & sholde be lorne but it were dyght & gadred, it is lefull in the holy dayes to saue it. 1532 HERVET *Xenophon's Househ.* (1768) 78 The ground that is well tylled and dyght, wyll coste moche more money. 1567 MAPLET *Gr. Forest* 46 It groweth in waterie places and those softlye dighted and banked about.

¶**16.** To lift, raise. (An erroneous use by Spenser.)

1590 SPENSER *F.Q.* I. viii. 18 With which his hideous club aloft he dights.

Hence †**dight, dighted,** *ppl. a. Obs.*

1422 tr. *Secreta Secret.*, *Priv. Priv.* 165 Put þer ynne of þe forsayd dightyd hony thre Rotes. 1535 COVERDALE *Jer.* xxxvii. 21 To be geuen him a cake of bred, and els no dighte meate. 1569 *Wills & Inv. N.C.* (Surtees 1835) 310 Eight dight calffe skinnes vs.

dight, *sb. dial.* In *Sc.* dicht. [f. DIGHT *v.*] A wipe, a rub in order to clean or dry: see DIGHT *v.*

1887 in DONALDSON *Suppl. Jamieson.* 1889 J. M. BARRIE *Window in Thrums* iii, 'For mercy's sake, mother', said Leeby, 'gie yer face a dicht, an' put on a clean mutch'.

b. (See quot.)

1890 *Glouc. Gloss.*, *Dight*, 'a dight of a body', a proud thing: of a woman.

†**dight,** *adv. Obs. rare.* Properly, fitly.

a 1800 *Lord Randal* 66 (Child *Ballads* 1864 II. 25) The birdie sat on the crap o' a tree, And I wat it sang fu' dight.

dighter ('daɪtə(r)). *Obs.* exc. *dial.* [OE. *dihtere*, f. *dihtan* to dictate, etc.: see DIGHT. Corresp. to MHG. *tihtære, tihter*, writer, poet, Ger. *dichter* poet.] One who dights, in various senses of the verb: **a.** A composer, author, director, ruler, preparer; a winnower. **b.** A winnowing machine.

a 1000 *St. Guthlac* Prol. (Goodw. 4) Ic write swa me ða dihteras sædon ðe his lif..cuðon. c 1000 ÆLFRIC *Gloss.* in Wr.-Wülcker 140/21 *Commentator, expositor*, dihtere. 1340 *Ayenb.* 100 Efterward zeþþe þet he ys uader, he is diȝtere and gouernour and purueyour of his mayné. c 1537 *Thersytes* in Hazl. *Dodsley* I. 422 David Doughty, dighter of dates. 1598 FLORIO, *Prestatore*, a prouider, a dighter, a vsurer. c 1611 CHAPMAN *Iliad* V. 499 The chaff..Which all the diters' feet, legs, arms, their heads and shoulders whites. 1805 A. SCOTT *Poems, Dighting of Barley* 69 (Jam.) The floating atoms did appear, To dab the dighters over. 1892 *Northumbld. Gloss.*, *Dighter*, a winnower of corn. Also a winnowing machine.

dighting ('daɪtɪŋ), *vbl. sb.* [f. DIGHT *v.*]

1. The action of the verb DIGHT, in various senses: putting in order, arraying, dressing, preparing, repairing; winnowing (of corn); wiping.

1340 *Ayenb.* 24 þe diȝtinge of his house. *Ibid.* 47 Levedi of uaire diȝtinge. c 1410 LOVE *Bonavent. Mirr.* xv. (Gibbs MS.) 38þere is no bodyly mete so lykynge to me as þat is of hyre dyghtynge. 1450 *Churchw. Acc. Walberswick, Suffolk* (Nichols 1797) 188 For dityng of the belles. 1458 *Churchw. Acc. St. Andrew's, East Cheap* in *Brit. Mag.* XXXI. 249 Item, paied to a laborer for dightyng of the Churchawe, iijd. 1464 *Mann. & Househ. Exp. Eng.* 274 To Wyllyam Hore for dytynge of a gowne of my ladyis, xxiij.d. 1535 COVERDALE *Ezek.* xxi. 11 He hath put his swearde to ye dightinge. 1567 MAPLET *Gr. Forest* Introd., Things..of Natures tempering and dighting. 1611 FLORIO, *Accóncio*, a dighting, a making fit or readie. a 1774 FERGUSSON *Farmer's Ingle* Poems (1845) 35 When..lusty lassies at the dightin tire.

2. *concr.* (*pl.*) †**a.** That with which something is dighted; fittings. *Obs.* **b.** The winnowings or siftings of corn; refuse in general. *dial.*

1598 FLORIO, *Corrédi*, ornaments, equipage..furnitures, or dightings. 1768 ROSS *Helenore* 35 Had my father sought the warld round, Till he the very dightings o't had found. 1808 JAMIESON s.v., 1. Refuse, of whatever kind. 2. The refuse of corn, after sifting, given to horses or cattle.

†'**dightly,** *adv. Obs.* [f. DIGHT *ppl. a.* + -LY[2].] In a well-equipped manner, fitly.

c 1633 T. ADAMS *Pract. Wks.* (1861) I. 27 (D.) Grounds full stocked, houses dightly furnished, purses richly stuffed.

digit ('dɪdʒɪt), *sb.* [ad. L. *digit-us* finger.]

1. One of the five terminal divisions of the hand or foot; a finger or toe. **a.** In ordinary language, a finger. Now only *humorous* or *affected.*

1644 BULWER *Chirol.* A iij b, Where every Digit dictates and doth reach Unto our sense a mouth-excelling speech. 1677 W. HUBBARD *Narrative* Postcr. 10 They had dismembred one hand of all its digits. 1864 SALA in *Daily Tel.* 21 Nov., Why should they spoil their pretty digits with thimble and housewife?

b. *Zool.* and *Comp. Anat.* (The proper term.)

1802 *Med. Jrnl.* VIII. 283 We find among reptiles, all the combinations of digits, from five to one, taken between two pairs of hands or claws. 1854 OWEN *Skeleton* in *Circ. Sc.*, *Organ. Nat.* I. 219 In the marine chelonia the digits of both limbs are elongated. 1870 ROLLESTON *Anim. Life* 17 In the foot the fifth or outer digit is never present. 1881 MIVART *Cat* 285 The special organ of touch is the skin, above all the skin of the muzzle, tongue, and digits.

2. The breadth of a finger used as a measure; a finger's breadth, three-quarters of an inch. Sometimes used as = an inch.

The Roman *digitus* was $\frac{1}{16}$ of the foot (*pes*) = 0·728 of an inch, or 18·5 millimeters.

a 1633 AUSTIN *Medit.* (1635) 108 The Inch (or digit,) the Palme, the Foote..are (all) Measures, which wee carry in our Bodie. 1635 N. CARPENTER *Geog. Del.* I. viii. 195 A cubit contains, according to Heron, a Foot and halfe, or 24 Digits. 1649 G. DANIEL *Trinarch.*, *Hen. V*, ccliv, 'Tis..farre beyond our Skill To measure out by Digits, Harrie's fame. 1669 BOYLE *Contn. New. Exp.* II. (1682) 5 When..the Mercury in the Tube..descends to the height of 29 Digits (I take Digits for Inches throughout all this Tract). 1807 ROBINSON *Archæol. Græca* III. xx. 321 A certain round plate three or four digits (or between two and three inches) thick. 1864 H. SPENCER *Illustr. Univ. Progr.* 161 The Egyptian cubit..was divided into digits, which were finger-breadths.

3. a. *Arith.* Each of the numerals below ten (originally counted on the fingers), expressed in the Arabic notation by one figure; any of the nine, or (including the cipher, 0) ten Arabic figures.

[1398 TREVISA *Barth. De P.R.* XIX. cxxiii. (1495) 923 Eche symple nombre byneth ten is Digitus: and ten is the fyrst Articulus.] c 1425 *Craft Nombrynge* (E.E.T.S.) 3 þere ben thre spices of nombur. Oone is a digit, Anoþer is an Articul, & þe toþer a Composyt. 1542 RECORDE *Gr. Artes* (1575) 53 A Digit is any number vnder 10. 1646 SIR T. BROWNE *Pseud. Ep.* IV. iv. 186 On the left [hand] they accounted their digits and articulate numbers unto an hundred, on the right hand hundreds & thousands. 1674 JEAKE *Arith.* (1696) 5 Integers are..divided into Digits, Articles, and mixt numbers. 1788 PRIESTLEY *Lect. Hist.* V. xxxvi. 264 The nine digits in Arithmetic. 1827 HUTTON *Course Math.* I. 4 The Numbers in Arithmetic are expressed by the..ten digits, or Arabic numeral figures. 1893 SIR R. BALL *Story of Sun* 56 The seven..may be in error by one or even two digits.

attrib. 1613 JACKSON *Creed* I. 91 Three from foure, or one digite number from the next vnto it.

b. Freq. used *attrib.*, esp. of parts and data in mechanical calculators, digital computers, etc., as ***digit counter, pulse,*** etc.

1921 C. D. LAKE *U.S. Pat. 1,372,965* 2/2 If the hole in the card represents the numeral 5, the register wheel will be turned five digit spaces. 1946 *Nature* 12 Oct. 500/2 'Digit trays' for carrying pulse groups representing numerical data from one unit to another. 1948 *Proc. Symposium Large-Scale Digital Calculating Mach.* 34 Numbers are transferred from one unit of the ENIAC to another by digit trunks, which carry eleven lines, one for each digit of the number, and one for the sign of the number. *Ibid.* 271 If we now look at the digit pattern in the register at the beginning of digit time 1, we will find that all the digits will have been advanced by one digit position, excepting digit number 1, which has been deleted. 1955 R. K. RICHARDS *Arith. Operations in Digital Computers* vii. 193 'Digit counter' will be used to describe the individual multistable counting elements. 1959 *Economist* 20 June 1110/2 In the search for higher computer speeds, one obvious approach was to raise the 'digit frequency' or pulse rate of the machine. 1959 C. V. L. SMITH *Electronic Digital Computers* x. 238 Some means is needed to reduce the four levels of *Vs* essentially to two... This is accomplished by a circuit called a 'digit resolver'. 1963 GOULD & ELLIS *Digital Computer Technology* iv. 29 Single logic elements can be made to work at digit rates of say 100 megacycles per second. *Ibid.* vi. 50 It is not uncommon to speak of pulses which represent unit signals as 'digit pulses'. *Ibid.* 51 Such circuits are also of use where a deliberate delay of one digit time is required, and are commonly called digit delays.

4. *Astron.* The twelfth part of the diameter of the sun or moon; used in expressing the magnitude of an eclipse.

1591 NASHE *Prognostication*, Wheras the Sun is darkned but by digits, and that vpon ye south points. 1687 DRYDEN *Hind & P.* II. 609 We..Can calculate how long th' eclipse endur'd, Who interpos'd, what digits were obscur'd. 1706 HEARNE *Collect.* 2 May, Ye Sun..was darkned 10 digits $\frac{1}{2}$. 1854 MOSELEY *Astron.* xlv. (ed. 4) 147 The usual method.. is to divide the whole diameter of the disc into twelve equal parts called digits. **1879** PROCTOR *Rough Ways* (1880) 9 The ring was about a digit in breadth.

†**5.** *Geom.* A degree of a circle, or of angular measure. *Obs. rare.*

1653 GATAKER *Vind. Annot. Jer.* 35 By their Calculation it was but eleven digits, and one fourth, which I conceiv to be fifteen minutes..a digit consisting of sixty minutes.

†**'digit**, *v. Obs. rare.* [f. prec. sb.: cf. L. *digito monstrare* to point out with the finger.] *trans.* To point at with the finger; to point out, indicate.

1627-77 FELTHAM *Resolves* I. xxviii. 48, I shall never care to be digited, with a That is he. **1708** *Brit. Apollo* No. 107. 2/2 A most Pathetic Emblem this, To Digit out the Surest Bliss.

digital ('dɪdʒɪtəl), *a.* and *sb.* [ad. L. *digitālis* of or belonging to the finger, f. *digit-us* a finger, DIGIT. Cf. F. *digital* (1545 in Hatz.-Darm.)]

A. *adj.* **1.** Of or pertaining to a finger, or to the fingers or digits.

1656 BLOUNT *Glossogr.*, *Digital*, pertaining to a finger. **1783** *Anat. Dial.* v. (ed. 2) 285 At the ends of the fingers these digital arteries..unite. **1802-25** SYD. SMITH *Ess.* (ed. Beeton) 77 Here are 160 hours employed in the mere digital process of turning over leaves! **1840** G. ELLIS *Anat.* 410 The digital nerves of the superficial branch of the ulnar are two. **1874** *Athenæum* 30 May, A lady, with an unparalleled degree of digital dexterity.

2. Resembling a digit or finger or the hollow impression made by one: applied in *Anat.* to various parts or organs.

digital cavity, the posterior corner of the lateral ventricle of the brain. ***digital fossa***, a pit-like depression on the thigh-bone, where five muscles are inserted: see quot. 1855. ***digital impressions***: see quot. 1883.

1831 R. KNOX *Cloquet's Anat.* 428 The Digital Cavity or Posterior Horn is entirely lined by medullary substance. **1855** HOLDEN *Hum. Osteol.* (1878) 195 Behind the neck of the femur, and beneath the projecting angle of the trochanter major, is a deep excavation called the digital fossa. **1883** *Syd. Soc. Lex.*, *Digital impressions*, the grooves on the inner surface of the cranial bones which correspond to the convolutions of the brain; so called from their shape.

3. Having digits; hence ***digital-footed***.

1833 SIR C. BELL *Hand* (1834) 98 There are some very rare instances of a horse having digital extremities. **1887** SIR S. FERGUSON *Ogham Inscript.* 148 The digital feet unite these..examples with other symbolisms..Here also are found digital-footed equine figures.

4. Of, pertaining to, or using digits [DIGIT *sb.* 3]; *spec.* applied to a computer which operates on data in the form of digits or similar discrete elements (opp. *analogue computer*).

1938 C. CAMPBELL *U.S. Pat. 2,113,612* 9/1 The emitter.. differs from the other emitters in that it has twelve digital conducting spots. **1945** J. ECKERT et al. *Appl. Math. Panel Rep.* 171.2R (*title*) Description of the ENIAC and comments on electronic digital computing machines. **1946** D. R. HARTREE in *Nature* 12 Oct. 500/2 [Computers] of the other class handle numbers directly in digital form... The American usage is 'analogue' and 'digital' machines. **1947** *Electronic Engin.* XIX. 178 Digital computing apparatus works out problems by methods which are basically the same as those which would be employed if an attempt were made to perform the calculations on paper. **1947** *Math. Tables & Other Aids to Computation* Oct. 359 We are engaged at the RCA Laboratories in the development of a storage tube for the inner memory of electronic digital computers. **1957** *Technology* July 182/2 The digital computer in normal use plays a purely deductive role in that it follows explicit instructions in operating on data that are fed into it. **1958** *Engineering* 28 Mar. 389/2 An in-line display of a digital form, which shows the unknown voltage to four significant figures. **1958** *IBM Jrnl. Res. & Devel.* II. 191/1 Voltage-to-digital conversion is accomplished by connecting a precision potentiometer to the output shaft of a servo-driven converter. **1964** *Times Rev. Industry* Mar. 58/2 A digital clock that presents the hours and minutes in figures. **1968** *Brit. Med. Bull.* XXIV. 189/1 Of the various types of computer which play a useful part in medical practice and research,..the most important..is the electronic digital computer.

5. a. Designating (a) recording in which the original waveform is digitally coded and the information in it represented by the presence or absence of pulses of equal strength, making it less subject to degradation than a conventional analogue signal; of or pertaining to such recording.

1960 *IRE Trans. Electronic Computers* Mar. 11/2 The nature and features of digital recording. **1966** *IEEE Trans. Magnetics* II. 1/1 The performance of thin magnetic tape as a digital storage medium. **1977** *Rolling Stone* 19 May 96/3 The problem with PCM or digital recording in the past has been that the tape medium could not accommodate the millions of pulses per second required when an audio signal is translated into coded pulses. **1978** *Gramophone* June 136/3 It would be a great pity if this opportunity for a 'quantum leap' in audio standards were spoilt by the emergence of several conflicting, incompatible digital discs. **1979** *Financial Rev.* (Sydney) 7 Nov. 28/6 Digital discs are on the market already. **1981** *New Scientist* 6 Aug. 355/2 Digital video recording has been demonstrated with modified analogue machines. **1984** *Sunday Times* 14 Oct. 40/2 The performances could hardly be more authentic, with magnificent playing and an ample resonance in this fine digital recording.

b. ***digital audio tape***, (a length of) magnetic tape on which sound is recorded digitally, analogous to digital recording on compact discs; abbrev. DAT *sb.*

1981 *Business Week* 14 Dec. 122D/1 No less than five totally incompatible prototypes of digital-audio tape decks have been unveiled this fall by as many Japanese companies. **1984** *Electronics Week* 15 Oct. 13/2 Digital audio tape.. probably won't appear as a commercial product before the spring of 1986. **1986** *Electronics* 20 Jan. 20 Onkyo's Birch-Jones does not think that digital audio tape products will have a negative impact on Compact Disc sales. **1986** *Observer* 4 May 25/2 The DAT (digital audio-tape) cassette will record or play-back prerecorded tapes about two-thirds the size of the familiar compact cassette. Maximum playing time will be about two hours, with quality roughly equivalent to compact disc.

B. *sb.* †**1.** = DIGIT *sb.* 3. *Obs.*

c **1430** *Art Nombryng* (E.E.T.S.) 1 Another digitalle is a nombre with-in 10.

2. A finger (*humorous*).

1840 *Fraser's Mag.* XXI. 160 To fling his broad plebeian paws and right cannie digitals around Sir Robert Peel. **1840** *Ibid.* XXII. 397 Hundreds of thousands vanish at the touch of royal digitals. **1858** LYTTON *What will he do* IV. ix, Who wear..paste rings upon unwashed digitals.

3. A key played with the finger in a musical instrument, as a piano or organ.

1878 W. H. STONE *Sci. Basis Music* v. 62 Colin Brown's Natural Fingerboard..The digitals consist of three separate sets..The first, second, fourth, and fifth tones of the scale are played by the white digitals.

digi'talia, *Chem.*: see DIGITALIN.

digitalic (dɪdʒɪ'tælɪk), *a.* [f. DIGITAL-IS + -IC.] Of or pertaining to digitalis; in ***digitalic acid***, an acid obtained from the leaves of the foxglove, crystallizing in white acicular prisms.

1858 HOGG *Veg. Kingd.* cxlv. 566 M. Morin, of Geneva, has also discovered in the leaves [of the Fox-glove] two acids; one fixed, which he calls digitalic acid, the other volatile, and called antirrhinic acid. **1863-72** WATTS *Dict. Chem.* II. 328 Digitalic acid crystallises in needles.

digitaliform (-'tælɪfɔːm), *a. Bot.* [f. L. *digitālis* (see below) + -FORM.] Of the form of the corolla of the fox-glove, 'like campanulate, but longer and irregular'.

1859 C. DRESSER *Rudim. Bot.* 313 Digitaliform..when a corolla which is somewhat campanulate is contracted near the base, and has one oblique limb. **1883** *Syd. Soc. Lex.*, *Digitaliform*, finger- or glove-shaped.

digitalin ('dɪdʒɪtəlɪn). *Chem.* [f. DIGITAL-IS + -IN.] The substance or substances extracted from the leaves of the fox-glove, as its active principle.

Originally supposed to be an alkaloid, and hence named *digitalia*, *digitaline*, but now known not to contain nitrogen. There is reason to think, however, that different bodies are included under the name.

1837 *Penny Cycl.* VIII. 496/1 An extractive substance..to which the name of Digitaline has been given. [*Ibid.* 495 *Digitalia*, a vegetable alkali procured from the..foxglove. **1838** T. THOMSON *Chem. Org. Bodies* 283 Digitalina has not yet been obtained in an isolated state.] **1872** WATTS *Dict. Chem.* VI. 545 The more soluble (so-called German) digitalin is obtained from the seeds, the less soluble or crystallised variety from the leaves of the foxglove. **1875** H. C. WOOD *Therap.* (1879) 134 Crystallizable digitalin occurs in..needle-shaped crystals, and possesses an intense and persistent bitter taste. **1881** *Standard* 30 Dec. 2/5 He asked for five grains of pure digitalin, the active principle of foxglove.

Hence **digitalinic** (-'lɪnɪk) *a.*, in ***digitalinic acid***, 'an acid obtained by boiling insoluble digitalin with soda' (*Syd. Soc. Lex.*).

‖**digitalis** (dɪdʒɪ'teɪlɪs). [mod.L., from L. *digitālis* of or pertaining to the fingers; the plant was so named by Fuchs 1542, in allusion to the German name *Fingerhut*, i.e. thimble.]

1. *Bot.* A genus of plants of the N.O. *Scrophulariaceæ*, including the foxglove (*D. purpurea*).

[**1568** TURNER *Herbal* III. 16 It is named of some in Latine, Digitalis.] **1664** EVELYN *Kal. Hort.* (1729) 200 Sow divers Annuals.. as double Marigold, Digitalis, Delphinium. **1791** E. DARWIN *Bot. Gard.* (1799) II. 108 Assumes bright Digitalis' dress and air.

attrib. **1883** *Syd. Soc. Lex.* s.v. *Digitalis tinctura*, Five parts of pounded digitalis leaves.

2. A medicine prepared from the fox-glove.

1799 *Med. Jrnl.* I. 57 A frequent cause of the failure of digitalis may be attributed to the careless mode of preparing it for use. **1800** *Ibid.* IV. 532 He has taken the tincture of Digitalis.. **1837** *Penny Cycl.* VIII. 496 Digitalis has the power of reducing in a remarkable degree the heart's action.

digitalization (ˌdɪdʒɪtəlaɪ'zeɪʃən). *Med.* [f. DIGITAL(IS 2 + -IZATION.] The administration of digitalis or one of its active constituents to a patient or an animal so that the required physiological changes occur in the body; also, the state of the body resulting from this.

1882 in *Syd. Soc. Lex.* **1919** *Jrnl. Amer. Med. Assoc.* LXXIII. 1823/1 Only after a considerable number of days will a patient on this dosage come to be much below the grade of digitalization at which he started. **1951** [see DIGITALIZE *v.*[1]]. **1961** *Lancet* 9 Sept. 573/2 Prompt return of nausea precluded further digitalisation. **1970** PASSMORE & ROBSON *Compan. Med. Studies* II. viii. 2/1 The patient is then said to be fully digitalized... Thereafter, digitalization is sustained by the maintenance dose.

digitalize ('dɪdʒɪtəlaɪz), *v.*[1] *Med.* [f. prec.: see -IZE.] *trans.* To subject to digitalization; to administer digitalis to. So **'digitalized** *ppl. a.*[1], **'digitalizing** *vbl. sb.*

1927 *Jrnl. Amer. Med. Assoc.* 10 Sept. 884 The general practitioner should not thoughtlessly digitalize his patient unless he has..facilities for determining the exact condition of his heart. **1951** A. GROLLMAN *Pharmacol. & Therap.* xviii. 351 If rapid digitalization is required, a so-called digitalizing dose may be administered at one time. *Ibid.* 353 The full digitalizing dose of digitoxin. **1961** D. M. DUNLOP *Textbk. Med. Treatment* (ed. 8) 565 On an average the total dose required to digitalize a fully grown adult is of the order of 1·5 to 2 g. (20 to 30 gr.) of digitalis powder..over a period of several days. **1970** [see DIGITALIZATION].

digitalize ('dɪdʒɪtəlaɪz), *v.*[2] [f. DIGITAL *a.* 4 + -IZE.] *trans.* = DIGITIZE *v.* 2. So **'digitalized** *ppl. a.*[2]

1962 *Aeroplane* 10 May 25/2 A digitalized radar terminal-area control system. **1965** *Math. in Biol. & Med.* (*Med. Res. Council*) I. 31 They already had a simple program worked out which would deal with digitalized outputs from recorders. **1967** COX & GROSE *Organization & Handling Bibl. Rec. by Computer* II. 45 The film may be the backing store and the picture digitalized for insertion.

digitally ('dɪdʒɪtəlɪ), *adv.* [f. DIGITAL *a.* + -LY[2].]

1. By means of or with respect to the fingers.

1832 *Fraser's Mag.* V. 432 The present paper..is not by the same hand that indited the other. We have had nothing to do, digitally speaking, with either. **1845** FORD *Hand-bk. Spain* 83 The ancient contemptuous 'fig of Spain'..is digitally represented by inserting the head of the thumb between the fore and middle fingers.

2. By means of digits (DIGIT *sb.* 3); in digital form.

1957 N. CHAPIN *Introd. Automatic Computers* ii. 5 In addition to digital computers, there is an important group of computing machines known as analog computers because they operate with a physical analogy of a problem rather than with digitally expressed information about a problem. **1960** *McGraw-Hill Encycl. Sci. & Technol.* IV. 175/2 *Digital computer.* Any device for performing mathematical calculations on numbers represented digitally. **1964** *Data Acquisition & Processing in Biol. & Med.* II. 219 A digitally coded paper tape suitable for direct computer usage. **1970** *Nature* 12 Sept. 1123/2 The outputs of two receivers..were combined, and the detected signal was sampled digitally every 50 ms over a period of 13 m 39 s.

†**'digitary**, *a. Obs.* [f. L. *digit-us* DIGIT: see -ARY.] Of or pertaining to the fingers.

1767 A. CAMPBELL *Lexiph.* (1774) 38 A pruriginous.. eruption of pustules in the digitary interstices.

digitate ('dɪdʒɪtət), *a.* (*sb.*) [ad. L. *digitāt-us* having fingers or toes, f. *digit-us* finger.]

1. *Zool.* Of quadrupeds: Having separate or divided digits or toes.

1661 LOVELL *Hist. Anim. & Min.* Introd., Solipeds and bisulcs usually being greater than the digitate. **1835-6** TODD *Cycl. Anat.* I. 470/2 The characters of the Carnivora as distinct from the rest of the digitate animals.

2. Divided into parts resembling fingers: *spec.* **a.** *Bot.* Of leaves, etc.: Having deep radiating divisions; now usually applied to compound leaves consisting of a number of leaflets all springing from one point, as in the horse-chestnut. (Hence in *Comb.*, as ***digitate-pinnate***.) **b.** *Zool.* Having, or consisting of, finger-like processes or divisions.

1788 J. LEE *Introd. Bot.* III. vi. (ed. 4) 201 The Folioles of which the digitate Leaf consists. **1828** STARK *Elem. Nat. Hist.* II. 373 Wings..cleft or digitate. **1870** HOOKER *Stud. Flora* 423 Spikes digitate, spikelets minute—Cynodon. **1880** GRAY *Struct. Bot.* iii. §4. 101 Palmate or Digitate Leaves.. in which the leaflets all stand on the summit of the petiole.

†**B.** as *sb.* A digitate quadruped (see A. 1). *Obs.*

1661 LOVELL *Hist. Anim. & Min.* Introd., Oviparous digitates, having diverse toes, and bringing forth eggs.

digitate ('dɪdʒɪteɪt), *v.* [f. L. *digit-us* + -ATE[3]: cf. DIGIT *v.*]

†**1.** *trans.* To point at with finger; *fig.* to point out, indicate. *Obs. rare.*

1658 J. ROBINSON *Eudoxa* viii. 46 The supine resting on Water onely by retention of Air..doth digitate a reason.

2. *intr.* To become divided into finger-like parts.

1796 STEDMAN *Surinam* II. xix. 68 These again diverge or digitate in long broad leaves. **1840** G. ELLIS *Anat.* 39 Processes of it..cross or digitate with the white bundles.

3. *trans.* To express with the fingers. (*nonce-use.*)

1823 *New Monthly Mag.* VII. 498 They talk with their fingers and digitate quotations from Shakspeare.

digitated ('dɪdʒɪteɪtɪd), *a.* [f. L. *digitāt-us* DIGITATE *a.* + -ED.]

1. *Zool.* and *Bot.* = DIGITATE *a.*

1646 SIR T. BROWNE *Pseud. Ep.* VI. vi. 298 Animals multifidous, or such as are digitated or have severall divisions in their feete. **1753** CHAMBERS *Cycl. Supp.* s.v. *Leaf, Digitated Leaf*, expresses a compound one, formed of a number of simple foliola, placed regularly on a common petiole. **1839-47** TODD *Cycl. Anat.* III. 95/2 The structure alluded to is a digitated extension of the whole substance of the upper part of the iris. **1840** F. D. BENNETT *Whaling Voy.* II. 146 The bones of the arms coincide with those of digitated quadrupeds. **1845** DARWIN *Voy. Nat.* xviii. (1879) 403 The bread-fruit, conspicuous from its..deeply digitated leaf.

2. Having divisions for the toes.

1882 *Times* 27 Mar. 6 Digitated stockings for pedestrians. **1882** *Standard* 19 Sept. 5/1 Digitated socks.

digitately (ˈdɪdʒɪteɪtlɪ), *adv.* [f. DIGITATE *a.* + -LY².] In a digitate manner.

1846 DANA *Zooph.* (1848) 619 Branches compressed, digitately subdivided. **1882** BAKER in *Jrnl. Bot.* XI. 70 The leaves are simple or digitately trifoliolate.

digitation (dɪdʒɪˈteɪʃən). [f. DIGITATE *v.* or *a.*: see -ATION. Cf. F. *digitation* Cotgr.]

†**1.** A touching, or pointing, with the finger. *Obs.*

1658 PHILLIPS *Digitation*, a pointing with the fingers. **1688** R. HOLME *Armoury* II. 387/1 Digitation..is a bare or simple touching of a thing. **1721–1800** in BAILEY.

2. The condition of being digitate; division into fingers or finger-like processes.

[**1656** BLOUNT *Glossogr.*, *Digitation*, the form of the fingers of both hands joyned together, or the manner of their so joyning. *Cotgr.* **1721–1800** in BAILEY]. **1847** CRAIG, *Digitation*, division into fingers, or finger-like processes, as exhibited by several of the muscles..in their coalescence on the ribs.

3. *concr.* (*Zool.* and *Bot.*) One of a number of finger-like processes or digitate divisions.

1709 BLAIR in *Phil. Trans.* XXVII. 114 Where the Ligaments cease, they become..at their upper extremities half round, and sometimes form'd into Digitations. **1802** BINGLEY *Anim. Biog.* (1813) I. 17 Sometimes, as in the Bats, the digitations of the anterior feet are greatly elongated. **1837** QUAIN *Elem. Anat.* (ed. 4) 350 Its anterior border presents eight or nine fleshy points or digitations. **1856–8** W. CLARKE *Van der Hoeven's Zool.* I. 393 Wings..cloven, with fringed digitations.

digitato- (dɪdʒɪˈteɪtəʊ), comb. form of DIGITATE *a.*; in **digitato-palmate**, *a.*, shaped like a hand with finger-like divisions; **digitato-pinnate**, *a.*, *Bot.* having finger-like divisions bearing pinnate leaflets.

1846 DANA *Zooph.* (1848) 527 Apex often digitato-palmate.

digiti- (ˈdɪdʒɪtɪ), combining form of L. *digitus* finger (see DIGIT *sb.*). **ˈdigitiform** *a.*, finger-like, digitate. **ˌdigitiˈnervate**, **ˌdigitiˈnerved**, **ˌdigitiˈnervous**, *adjs.*, *Bot.*, having the ribs of the leaf radiating from the top of the leaf-stalk. **ˌdigitiˈpartite**, **ˌdigitiˈpinnate** *adjs.* (see quot.).

1846 DANA *Zooph.* (1848) 433 The branchlets above nearly simple, digitiform. **1849–52** TODD *Cycl. Anat.* IV. 1218/1 The mouth..is surrounded by six little digitiform processes. **1866** *Treas. Bot.*, *Digitinerved*, when the ribs of a leaf radiate from the top of the petiole. **1870** BENTLEY *Bot.* 156 When there are more than 5 lobes of a similar character, it is sometimes termed digitipartite. **1883** *Syd. Soc. Lex.*, Digitinervate, Digitinervous. *Ibid.*, *Digitipinnate*, term applied to leaves the petiole of which terminates in secondary petioles bearing leaflets, either pinnate or digitate, forming doubly compound leaves.

digitigrade (ˈdɪdʒɪtɪˌgreɪd). *a.* and *sb. Zool.* [a. F. *digitigrade*, in mod.L. *digitigrada* (Cuvier 1817), f. L. *digit-us* (DIGIT) + *-gradus*, going, walking.]

A. *adj.* Walking on the toes; *spec.* in *Zool.* belonging to the tribe *Digitigrada* of Carnivora (in Cuvier's classification); also said of the feet, or walk, of such an animal. (Opp. to PLANTIGRADE.)

1833 *Penny Cycl.* I. 4 The legs also are completely digitigrade; that is to say, the heel is elevated, and does not come into contact with the surface..Digitigrade animals, which tread only upon the toes..have much longer legs than plantigrade animals. **1839–47** TODD *Cycl. Anat.* III. 450/2 The feathered tribe traverse the surface of the earth as digitigrade bipeds. **1881** MIVART *Cat* 129 The cat's mode of progression is spoken of as digitigrade.

B. *sb.* A digitigrade animal. (Chiefly in *pl.*)

1835 KIRBY *Hab. & Inst. Anim.* II. xvii. 212 Digitigrades ..consist of the feline, canine, and several other tribes. **1845** WHEWELL *Indic. Creator* 41 Some of the orders of quadrupeds, namely the rodents, ruminants, digitigrades.

Hence **ˈdigitiˌgradism**, digitigrade condition.

1887 E. D. COPE *Origin of Fittest* 376 The groove of the astragalus deepens coincidently with the increase of digitigradism.

ˈdigitin. *Chem.* [f. DIGITALIS + -IN: differentiated from *digitalin.*] A crystalline substance obtained from digitalis.

1879 WATTS *Dict. Chem. 3rd Suppl.* 647 A precipate is obtained consisting of digitalin and digitin.

digitize (ˈdɪdʒɪtaɪz), *v.* [f. DIGIT + -IZE.]

1. *trans.* To manipulate or treat in some way with the fingers: to finger; to point at or count with the fingers. *rare.*

a **1704** T. BROWN *Wks.* (1760) II. 211 (D.), None but the devil, besides yourself, could have digitiz'd a pen after so scurrilous a manner. **1730–6** BAILEY (folio), *Digitize*, to point to with the finger. **1823** HONE *Anc. Myst.* 266 The sempstresses, who were very nicely digitising and pleating turnovers.

2. To convert (a continuously variable quantity) into a sequence of digits, generally for use in a digital computer, etc.; to represent in digital form. So **ˈdigitized** *ppl. a.*, **ˈdigitizing** *vbl. sb.*

1953 *Proc. Inst. Radio Engin.* XLI. 1456/2 It is..desirable to digitize the analog input signals as near to the system full scale as possible. **1957** *Electronic Engin.* XXIX. 568/2 Digitizing an analogue quantity makes the basic assumption that it may adequately be represented by a sufficient number of discreet intervals. **1959** *Times Rev. Industry* Aug. 24/3 All analogue quantities generated..are digitized. **1963** *Engineering* 8 Nov. 604/3 After digitising, the information is stored in 10 bit binary form. **1965** *Math. in Biol. & Med.* (*Med. Res. Council*) IV. 166 The slight discrepancy of the digitized wave. **1971** *Sci. Amer.* Feb. 81/3 We shall assume that our slab is a square and that it has been digitized into 64 *x*, *y* values or mesh points.

ˈdigitizer. [f. DIGITIZE *v.* + -ER] **1.** One who points at or counts with the fingers.

1767 G. CANNING *Poems* Pref. 3 Your mere mechanical Digitizers of verses.

2. An instrument that converts continuously variable quantities into digital form, generally for use in a digital computer.

1953 *IRE Trans. Electronic Computers* II. III. 1/1 The digitizer..operates by 'reading' a coded representation of a given shaft position. **1956** *Electronic Engin.* XXVIII. 113/1 There are many ingenious ways of performing the analogue to digital conversion..and the commutator and digitizer types are probably the most useful. **1961** *Flight* LXXIX. 431/2 A digitizer converts the signals into a serial bit stream of binary data for transmission. **1970** *Computers & Humanities* IV. 244 A digitizer was used to measure and record the coordinates of bends in the outline.

digito-, shortened from *digitalis*: the basis of the names of a series of chemical substances derived from digitalis or fox-glove: see quots.

1863–72 WATTS *Dict. Chem.* II. 330 *Digitoleic acid*, a kind of fatty acid contained in the leaves of Digitalis purpurea. **1875** H. G. WOOD *Therap.* (1879) 135 Digitonin is asserted to form the bulk of the soluble digitalin of commerce, and to be the same as saponin, the active principle of soap-bark. **1883** *Syd. Soc. Lex.*, *Digito·genin*, a crystallisable substance, ..obtained by the action of dilute acids on Digitoresin. *Digito·lein*, a fat obtained from digitalis leaves. It is a combination of glycerin with digitoleic acid. *Digito·nin*, a white amorphous substance..is said to form a large part of the soluble digitalis of commerce. *Digito·xin*..is highly poisonous. It forms colourless crystals. *Digitores·in*, obtained, along with glucose and Digitonein, on boiling Digitonin with dilute acids.

digitorium (dɪdʒɪˈtɔərɪəm). [f. DIGIT *sb.* + -ORIUM.] A small portable keyboard used for exercising and strengthening the fingers in piano-playing; a dumb piano.

1876 in STAINER & BARRETT *Dict. Mus. Terms.* **1921** *Times* 15 Jan. 1/3 Wanted, Digitorium.—State size and price.

Digitron (ˈdɪdʒɪtrɒn). *Electr.* Also **digitron.** [f. DIGI(T *sb.* 3 + -TRON.] The proprietary name of a cold-cathode character display tube.

1958 *Trade Marks Jrnl.* 18 June 622/1 *Digitron.* Electric discharge tubes... Ericsson Telephones Limited. **1960** N. MCLOUGHLIN et al. in *Electronic Engin.* Mar. 140/1 A new form of visual indication which has recently been developed is the Digitron, a cold-cathode character display tube. This tube, unlike the Dekatron, is not a counting device but is used to indicate the state of count or of switching position in the associated circuits. **1961** *New Scientist* 10 Aug. 350/1 The digitron..is essentially a neon lamp in which the cathode is formed in the shape of the required character—a number, a letter or a symbol.

†**diˈgladiate**, *v. Obs.* [ad. L. *dīgladiāri* f. *di-*, *dis-* asunder, in different directions + *gladius* a sword: cf. *gladiātor.*] *intr.* To 'cross swords'; to contend, dispute.

a **1656** HALES *Gold. Rem.* (1688) 56 Mutual Pasquils and Satyrs against each others lives, wherein digladiating like Eschines and Demosthenes, they reciprocally lay open each others filthiness to the view and scorn of the world.

digladiation (daɪglædɪˈeɪʃən). Now *rare* or *arch.* Also 7 de-. [noun of action f. L. *dīgladiārī*: see DIGLADIATE.]

1. Fighting or fencing with swords; hand-to-hand fight.

1589 PUTTENHAM *Eng. Poesie* I. xvii. (Arb.) 52 In those great Amphitheatres were exhibited all manner of other shewes..as their fence playes, or digladiations of naked men. **1650** R. STAPYLTON *Strada's Low C. Warres* IX. 44 *margin*, His Digladiations in the night time. **1715** tr. *Pancirollus' Rerum Mem.* II. xx. 393 This manner of Digladiation was very ancient; such was the Skirmish we read of in the poet Horace.

2. *fig.* Strife or bickering of words; wrangling, contention, disputation.

1590 R. BRUCE *Serm.* i. B ij b, Gif they had keeped the Apostles words..all this digladiatioun, strife and contention appearandly had not fallen out. *a* **1619** FOTHERBY *Atheom.* I. v. §3 (1622) 34 Their contentions and digladiations grew to be so notorious, as made them all ridiculous. **1692** J. EDWARDS *Remarkable Texts* 211 A Christian, whose religion forbids all foolish bickerings and digladiations about mean and inconsiderable matters. **1819** MCCRIE *Melville* II. xi. 304 Scholastic wrangling and digladiation. **1879** M. PATTISON *Milton* ix. 107 In these literary digladiations readers are always ready to side with a new writer.

diˈgladiator. *Obs.* or *arch.* [agent-n. f. L. *dīgladiārī*, on analogy of GLADIATOR.] A combatant; one who contends or disputes.

1803 *Monthly Mag.* XVI. 225 Those polemical digladiators, who..divided and convulsed all literary institutions.

diglossia (daɪˈglɒsɪə). *Philol.* [mod.L., ad. F. *diglossie*, f. Gr. δίγλωσσος bilingual + -IA¹.] (See quot. 1964.)

1959 C. A. FERGUSON in *Word* XV. 325 Diglossia. In many speech communities two or more varieties of the same language are used by some speakers under different conditions. *Ibid.*, The term 'diglossia' is introduced here, modeled on the French *diglossie*,..since there seems to be no word in regular use for this in English. **1964** E. PALMER tr. *Martinet's Elem. General Linguistics* v. 139 Linguists have proposed the term 'diglossia' to designate a situation where a community uses..both a more colloquial idiom of less prestige and another of more learned and refined status. **1965** *Language* XLI. 502 The concept of diglossia rests..on the observation that different languages or dialects enjoy varying social and political status within a community.

Also **diˈglossic** *a.*, of, pertaining to, or characterized by diglossia; capable of using two varieties of a language.

1959 C. A. FERGUSON in *Word* XV. 334 A full analysis of standard German and Swiss German might show this not to be true in that diglossic situation in view of the extensive morphophonemics of Swiss. **1968** *Amer. Speech* XLIII. 130 The possibility of an individual being both diglossic and bilingual at the same time is not excluded. **1971** J. SPENCER *Eng. Lang. W. Afr.* 23 For much of the area we are considering there has never existed a diglossic situation, with varieties of Krio and Pidgin competing against the English of the classroom and the written word. **1974** *Florida FL Reporter* XIII. 32/3 Native speakers of non-standard English (NSE) who have acquired standard typically develop a set of diglossic language habits. **1982** J. SLEDD in *Eng. World-Wide* III. II. 246 While claiming that Black English is not inferior, many popularizing linguists act as if it is—and set out to guarantee that as the low language in a diglossic situation, it will remain so.

diglot, diglott (ˈdaɪglɒt), *a.* and *sb.* [ad. Gr. δίγλωττ-ος speaking two languages, f. δι-, δισ- twice + γλῶττα, Attic for γλῶσσα, tongue, language.] Using or containing two languages, bilingual; expressed or written in two languages; also as *sb.* A diglot book or version (cf. *polyglot*). So **diˈglottic**, *a.* (in quot., Speaking two languages); **ˈdiglottism**, the use of two languages, or of words derived from two languages.

1863 in *Smith's Dict. Bible* III. 1557 The conquests of Alexander and of Rome had made men diglottic to an extent which has no parallel in history. **1871** EARLE *Philol. Eng. Tongue* §78 Words run much in couples, the one being English the other French..In the following..there are two of these diglottisms in a single line. 'Trouthe and honour, fredom and curteisye'. **1885** *Rept. Brit. & For. Bible Soc.* App. B 361 The other edition [of the Breton N.T.] is a diglot form with the Revised Ostervald New Testament. **1890** *Academy* 8 Nov. 424/1 Of the Bibles, &c., printed in more than one language..there are 21 English 'di-glotts', 12 French, and 6 German.

diglute, obs. f. DEGLUTE, to swallow.

diglyˈceric, -ˈglyceride, -ˈglycerol, -glyˈcollic, *Chem.*: see DI-² 2 d, and GLYCERIC, etc.

1873 *Fownes' Chem.* (ed. 11) 626 Diglyceric acid has not been actually obtained. *Ibid.* 706 Diglycollic Acid is also called Paramalic Acid. **1881** *Nature* XXIII. 245 Diglycollic acid..obtained by the action of sodium hydrate on diglycollamic acid.

diglyph (ˈdaɪglɪf). *Arch.* [mod. ad. Gr. δίγλυφ-ος doubly indented, f. δι- twice + γλύφειν to carve; cf. F. *diglyphe* (Littré).] An ornament consisting of a projecting face or tablet with two vertical grooves or channels. (Cf. TRIGLYPH.)

1727–51 CHAMBERS *Cycl.*, *Diglyph*, a kind of imperfect triglyph, console, or the like, with only two chanels, or engravings, instead of three. **1823** P. NICHOLSON *Pract. Build.* 584 Diglyph, a tablet with two engravings or channels. **1854** E. DE WARREN tr. *De Saulcy's Round Dead Sea* II. 254 These metopes are divided from each other by triglyphs, which may be called more correctly diglyphs, as they only bear two flutes and two drops.

†**dignation** (dɪgˈneɪʃən). *Obs.* [a. OF. *dignation*, *-acion*, ad. L. *dignātiōn-em*, n. of action f. *dignāre*, *-ārī* to think worthy, deign.]

The action of deeming or treating any one as worthy, the conferring of dignity or honour; favour shown or honour conferred; condescension: chiefly said of the gracious action of a superior.

c **1450** tr. *De Imitatione* III. liv, For þou takist not þis wiþ þin ovne þouȝt..but onely by dignacion of þe most hie grace, & of godly beholdyng. **1526** *Pilgr. Perf.* (W. de W. 1531) 201 b, This werke is the effecte of his hye dignacion, power and goodnes. **1649** JER. TAYLOR *Gt. Exemp.* I. §2. 22 S. Elizabeth..wondering at the dignation and favour done to her. **1659** HAMMOND *On Ps.* viii. Paraphr. 44 The magnifying of God's wonderfull goodnesse..and his dignations to mankind. *a* **1703** BURKITT *On N.T.* Rom. vi. 19 The great dignation and gracious condescension of Christ. **1737** STACKHOUSE *Hist. Bible* (1767) IV. VI. v. 207 A great favour and dignation done her.

†**digne**, *a. Obs.* Also α. 4 **dingne, dyngne**, 5 **dign, dynge**, 5–6 **dygne**, 6 *Sc.* **ding, dyng.** β. 4–5 **deyn(e.** [ME. *digne*, a. F. *digne* (11th c. in Hatz.-Darm.), early ad. L. *dignus* worthy. The form *deyn* might

represent an OF. *dein, inherited form of *dignus*: but cf. DAIN *a.*]

1. Of high worth or desert; worthy, honourable, excellent (in nature, station, or estimation); cf. DIGNITY 1, 2).

1297 R. GLOUC. (1724) 132 þe digne sege ywys..þat at London now ys. 1340 *Ayenb.* 109 þe þri uerste benes of þe pater noster..byeth þe heȝeste and þe dingneste. a1400-50 *Alexander* 882 Darius þe deyne [*Dubl. MS.* digne] Empereure. *Ibid.* 1958, I, sir Dari, þe deyne [*Dubl. MS.* digne] and derfe Emperoure. c1440 *York Myst.* xxviii. 1 Beholde my discipulis þat deyne is and dere. a1450 *Knt. de la Tour* ii. 5 It is an higher and more digne thinge forto praise and thanke God. 1513 DOUGLAS *Æneis* XIII. ix. 67 Of conquerouris and soueran pryncis dyng [*rime* kyng]. 1535 STEWART *Cron. Scot.* II. 367 With diamontis ding, and margretis mony one. 1578 *Ps.* cvi. in *Scot. Poems 16th C.* II. 107 Declair..Thy nobill actes and digne remembrance.

2. Worthy, deserving. Const. *of (to)*, or *inf.*

a1375 *Joseph Arim.* 252 Cum þou hider, Iosaphe; for þou art Iugget clene, And art digne þer-to. c1386 CHAUCER *Pars. T.* ¶715 Hem þat ȝeuen chirches to hem þat ben not digne. c1430 LYDG. *Bochas* IV. ix. (1544) 106 a, To write also hys triumphes digne of glorye. c1450 *Merlin* 583 Ye be full digne to resceyve the ordre of chiualrie. a1555 LYNDESAY *Tragedie* 86 In France..I did Actis ding of Remembrance. 1643 PRYNNE *Open. Gt. Seale* 6 The state of the Church is come unto this, that she is not digne to be governed But of ill Bishops.

3. Befitting, becoming, appropriate, fit. Const. *to, unto, of, for.*

c1385 CHAUCER *L.G.W.* 1738 *Lucretia*, Hyre cuntinaunce is to here herte digne. c1386 —— *Man of Law's T.* 680 O Domegyld, I haue non englisch digne Vnto þy malice and þy tyrannye. c1420 *Pallad. on Husb.* XI. 7 Lande lene, or fatte, or drie, is for it digne. 1504 ATKYNSON tr. *De Imitatione* III. liv, Gyue dygne & moost large graces to the hye goodnes of god. 1549 CHALONER *Erasmus on Folly* K ij a, All the worlde ..offreth me..farre dearer and more digne sacrifices, than theirs are.

4. Having a great opinion of one's own worth; proud, haughty, disdainful; *esp.* in phr. *as digne as ditch-water* (cf. 'stinking with pride'), *as digne as the devil.* Cf. DAIN *a.*

1340-70 *Alisaunder* 313 þe menne of þat marche..were so ding of þeir deede, dedain þat they had þat any gome under God gouern hem sholde. c1386 CHAUCER *Prol.* 517 He [the Parson] was nat to synful man despitous Ne of his speche daungerous ne digne. c1386 —— *Reeve's T.* 44 She was as digne [*Harl. Lansd.* deyne] as water in a dich, as ful of hoker and of bismare. c1394 *P. Pl. Crede* 355 For wiþ þe princes of pride þe prechours dwellen; þei ben digne as þe devel þat droppeþ fro heuene. *Ibid.* 375 þer is more pryue pride in prechours hertes þan þer lefte in Lucyfer er he were lowe fallen; þey ben digne as dich water.

†**'dignely**, *adv.* *Obs.* Also 4 -li, 4-5 -liche, -lyche, 6 -lie. [f. prec. + -LY[2].]

1. Worthily, honourably; befittingly, deservingly, condignly.

c1315 SHOREHAM 32 Thou hest of-served dygnelyche The pyne of helle vere. 1340 *Ayenb.* 20 þet þou nere naȝt digneliche y-diȝt be ssrifþe and by vorþenchinge. c1380 WYCLIF *Serm.* Sel. Wks. II. 62 þei wolen sitte wiþ lordis and ladies at þe mete ful dignely. c1400 *Test. Love* I. (1561) 287 b/1 The name of Goddes dignely ye mow beare. 1513 DOUGLAS *Æneis* II. Prol. 7 Bot sen I follow the poete principall..God grant me grace him dingly to ensew. 1567 DRANT *Horace Epist.* A vj, When mortall man cannot reforme Nor dignely plage the cryme.

2. Haughtily, scornfully.

c1374 CHAUCER *Troylus* II. 975 (1024) Touchynge þi lettre ..I wot thow nylt it digneliche endite.

†**di'gnesse**. *Obs.* [a. AFr. **dignesse*, f. *digne* worthy + *-esse* repr. L. *-itia*: cf. *bassesse, richesse, vilesse*, etc.] Worthiness, dignity; haughtiness.

1399 LANGL. *Rich. Redeles* III. 127 Swiche ffresshe ffoodis beth ffeet in to chambris, And ffor her dignesse en-dauntid of dullisshe nollis.

dignification (ˌdɪgnɪfɪ'keɪʃən). Now *rare.* [ad. med.L. *dignificātiōn-em*, n. of action from *dignificāre*: cf. obs. F. *dignificacion* (Godef.).] The action of dignifying, or fact of being dignified; conferring of dignity.

1577 DEE *Relat. Spir.* I. (1659) 63 In respect of thy dignification.. I say with the[e] Hallelujah. a1612 DONNE *Βιαθανατος* (1644) 57 Humane nature after the first fall, till the restitution and dignification thereof by Christ. 1653 WALTON *Angler* 13 Where a noble and ancient Descent and such merits meet in any man, it is a double dignification of that person. c1781 in Boswell *Johnson* 4 June an. 1781 To demean themselves with..equanimity..upon their.. dignification and exaltation.

dignified ('dɪgnɪfaɪd), *ppl. a.* [f. DIGNIFY + -ED[1].]

1. Invested with dignity; exalted.

1763 J. BROWN *Poetry & Mus.* vi. 100 We shall see the Bard's Character rising again in its dignified State. 1781 COWPER *Charity* 2 Fairest and foremost of the train that wait On man's most dignified and happiest state.

†2. Holding a position of dignity; ranking as a dignitary (esp. ecclesiastical). *Obs.*

1667-8 MARVELL *Corr.* xc. Wks. 1872-5 II. 240 It hath bin ..mov'd to raise 100,000li...upon the dignifyd Clergy. 1712 E. COOKE *Voy. S. Sea* 396 To the Cathedral belong.. five dignify'd Priests, being the Dean, Arch-Deacon, School-Master, Chanter, and Treasurer. 1726 AYLIFFE *Parergon* 6 Abbots are stiled dignify'd Clerks, as having some Dignity in the Church. 1860 MRS. GASKELL *Right at Last* 30 My father was the son of a dignified clergyman.

3. Marked by dignity of manner, style, or appearance; characterized by lofty self-respect without haughtiness; stately, noble, majestic.

a1812 J. S. BUCKMINSTER (Webster, 1828) To the great astonishment of the Jews, the manners of Jesus are familiar, yet dignified. 1840 CARLYLE *Heroes* v. (1891) 147 A Pulpit, environed with all manner of complex dignified appurtenances and furtherances. 1853 J. H. NEWMAN *Hist. Sk.* (1873) II. II. xiii. 299 The general character of the oratory was dignified and graceful. 1855 MACAULAY *Hist. Eng.* IV. 447 His State papers..are models of terse, luminous, and dignified eloquence. 1874 L. STEPHEN *Hours in Library* (1892) I. viii. 291 A man of dignified appearance. 1878 BOSW. SMITH *Carthage* 262 Silence, mournful..but dignified, was observed in the public streets.

'dignifiedly, *adv.* [f. prec. + -LY[2].] In a dignified manner; with dignity or its appearance.

1818 *Chron.* in *Ann. Reg.* 481 The same littleness of mind which made..Boniface dignifiedly incommunicative to all without badges or titles. 1868 BROWNING *Ring & Bk.* III. 391 Whereon did Pietro..sally forth dignifiedly into the square. 1885 *Century Mag.* XXX. 384 Verona is dignifiedly disagreeable.

dignifier ('dɪgnɪfaɪə(r)). [f. DIGNIFY + -ER[1].] One who dignifies; one who confers dignity.

1612 R. SHELDON *Serm. St. Martin's* 50 God the Dignifier, the Sanctifier, and Beautifier of the sacrifice. 1741 RICHARDSON *Pamela* (1742) II. 284 The vilest lowest Taste in his sordid Dignifier.

dignify ('dɪgnɪfaɪ), *v.* [a. OF. *dignefier, dignifier*, ad. med.L. *dignificāre*, f. *dign-us* worthy + *-ficāre*: see -FY.]

1. *trans.* To make worthy or illustrious; to confer dignity or honour upon; to ennoble, honour.

1526 *Pilgr. Perf.* (W. de W. 1531) 210 Illumyned & dignyfyed of Chryst. 1597 SHAKS. *2 Hen. IV*, I. i. 22 Such a Day..Came not, till now, to dignifie the Times Since Cæsars Fortunes. c1600 —— *Sonn.* lxxxiv, He that writes of you, if he can tell That you are you, so dignifies his story. 1667 MILTON *P.L.* IX. 940 Us his prime Creatures, dignifi'd so high, Set over all his Works. 1732 POPE *Hor. Sat.* II. ii. 141 No Turbots dignify my boards. 1824 L. MURRAY *Eng. Gram.* (ed. 5) I. 357 As accent dignifies the syllable on which it is laid, and makes it more distinguished by the ear than the rest. 1877 MRS. OLIPHANT *Makers Flor.* Introd. 16 There arose to dignify the struggle the moral principle which all this time it had wanted.

b. To render majestic or stately.

1749 SMOLLETT *Gil Bl.* XI. v, He would write as well as he speaks, if, in order to dignify his style, he did not affect expressions which render it stiff and obscure. c1790 COWPER *On Milton's P.L.* I. 689 How an act or image, vulgar and ordinary in itself, may be dignified by mere force of diction. 1791 —— *Odyss.* XXIII. 181 Then Pallas..dignified his form With added amplitude.

c. In lighter use: To represent as worthy (by implication, as worthier than it is); to give a high-sounding name or title to.

[1606 SHAKS. *Tr. & Cr.* IV. v. 103 Yet giues he not till iudgment guide his bounty, Nor dignifies an impaire thought with breath. 1665 GLANVILL *Scepsis Sci.* 80 'Tis usual for men to dignifie what they have bestowed pains upon.] 1750 H. WALPOLE *Lett. H. Mann* (1834) II. ccxxii. 374 You will think my letters are absolute jest and story books unless you..dignify them with the title of Walpoliana. 1791-1823 D'ISRAELI *Cur. Lit.* (1839) III. 341 The science of books, for so bibliography is sometimes dignified. *Mod.* A school dignified with the name of a college.

†2. To invest with a dignity or honour; to exalt in rank; to confer a title of honour upon. ? *Obs.*

1563-87 FOXE *A. & M.* (1596) 5/2 Emperors in ancient time haue dignified them in titles. 1660 BLOUNT *Boscobel* II. (1680) 21 The Earl of Southampton..now with much merit dignifyed with the great office of Lord High Treasurer. 1727 W. MATHER *Yng. Man's Comp.* 105 Nor ought Sons of the Nobility to be Dignified..with less than the Title of Honourable, as being their due by Birth-Right.

Hence **'dignifying** *vbl. sb.* and *ppl. a.*

1630 *R. Johnson's Kingd. & Commw.* 101 The Grand-Seignior never nameth us with dignifying titles. 1639 LD. DIGBY, etc. *Lett. conc. Relig.* (1657) 81 Those dignifying circumstances..belong onely to such doctrines [etc.]. *Ibid.* 82 That seal, with those quarterings and dignifyings wherewith you blazon it.

dignitarial (dɪgnɪ'tɛərɪəl), *a.* [f. DIGNITARY + -AL[1].] Of or belonging to a dignitary.

1885 *Ch. Times* 20 Feb. 135/3 The perversity of the dignitarial mind was curiously exemplified.

dignitary ('dɪgnɪtərɪ), *sb.* (*a.*) Also 7 -ory. [f. L. *dignitās* or Eng. DIGNITY + -ARY: cf., for the sense, *prebendary*, for the form, L. *voluntārius* voluntary, from *voluntās*: so F. *dignitaire* sb. (1752 in Trévoux).]

A. *sb.* One invested with a dignity; a personage holding high rank or office, esp. ecclesiastical.

1672-3 MARVELL *Reh. Transp.* I. 282 There was a gentleman of your robe, a Dignitory of Lincoln. a1745 SWIFT (J.), If there be any dignitaries, who preferments are ..not liable to the accusation of the superfluity. 1756-7 tr. *Keysler's Trav.* (1760) I. 15 Princes, bishops, counts, rich dignitaries, abbots. 1815 W. H. IRELAND *Scribbleomania* 248 A very high ecclesiastical dignitary. 1836 IRVING *Astoria* I. 100 The captain..paid a visit to the governor. This dignitary proved to be an old sailor, by the name of John Young. 1851 D. WILSON *Preh. Ann.* (1863) II. IV. ii. 266 It represents three dignitaries, probably priests.

B. *adj.* Of, belonging to, or invested with a dignity (esp. ecclesiastical).

1715 M. DAVIES *Ath. Brit.* I. 163 The most eminent Dignitary Churchmen. 1733 NEAL *Hist. Purit.* II. 148 They complimented the Roman Catholick priests with their dignitary titles.

digni'torial, *a.* [erroneous for DIGNITARIAL.]

1817 T. C. BANKS (*title*), History of the Ancient Noble Family of Marmyun..also their Dignitorial Tenures and the services of London, Oxford, &c.

dignity ('dɪgnɪtɪ). Forms: 3-4 **dignete**, 3-6 **-ite**, 4 **dyng-, dingnete**, 4-5 **dignitee, -ytee**, 4-6 **dy-, dignyte**, 6-7 **dignitie**, 7- **dignity**. [a. OF. *digneté*, F. *dignité* (12th c. in Hatz.-Darm.), ad. L. *dignitāt-em* merit, worth, f. *dignus* worthy: see -ITY. Cf. also DAINTY, a. OF. *deintié*, the inherited form of *dignitātem*.]

1. The quality of being worthy or honourable; worthiness, worth, nobleness, excellence.

a1225 *Ancr. R.* 140 Nis nout eðcene of hwuche dignite heo [the soul] is, ne hu heih is hire cunde. c1230 *Hali Meid.* 5 Of se muche dignete, and swuch wurðschipe. c1393 CHAUCER *Gentilesse* 5 For vn-to vertue longeth dignytee. c1400 MAUNDEV. (Roxb.) vi. 18 A name of grete dignitee and of grete worschepe. 1552 ABP. HAMILTON *Catech.* (1884) 20 Of the preeminens and excellent dignitiee of the *Pater noster.* 1602 SHAKS. *Ham.* I. v. 48 From me, whose loue was of that dignity, That it went hand in hand even with the Vow I made to her in Marriage. 1657 AUSTEN *Fruit Trees* I. 11 The dignity and value of Fruit-trees. 1787 T. JEFFERSON *Writ.* (1859) II. 95, I recollect no work of any dignity which has been lately published. 1795 WORDSW. *Yew-tree Seat*, True dignity abides with him alone Who, in the silent hour of inward thought, Can still suspect, and still revere himself, In lowliness of heart. 1836 SIR H. TAYLOR *Statesman* xv. 107 It is of the essence of real dignity to be self-sustained, and no man's dignity can be asserted without being impaired. 1874 BLACKIE *Self-Cult.* 75 The real dignity of a man lies not in what he *has*, but in what he *is*.

†b. The quality of being worthy of something; desert, merit. *Obs. rare.*

1548 R. HUTTEN *Sum of diuinitie* E 5 a, Fayth leaneth onelye vpon mercy, not of our dygnytye. 1677 GALE *Crt. Gentiles* IV. 154 To suppose that God should fetch the commun rule of his giving or not giving grace, from mans dignitie or indignitie.

2. Honourable or high estate, position, or estimation; honour; degree of estimation, rank.

c1230 *Hali Meid.* 15 Eadie meiden, understond in hu heh dignete þe mihte of meidenhad halt te. 1340 *Ayenb.* 215 þere ssolle þe greate lhordes and þe greate lheuedyes uoryete.. hare dingnete, and hare heȝnesse. 1399 *Rolls Parl.* III. 424/1 Ye renounsed and cessed of the State of Kyng, and of Lordeshipp and of all the Dignite and Wirsshipp that longed therto. c1400 *Rom. Rose* 7682 I..have pouste To shryve folk of most dignyte. 1538 STARKEY *England* I. iv. 139 Gyuyng somewhat to the dygnyte of presthode. 1594 HOOKER *Eccl. Pol.* I. vi. (1611) 12 Stones, though in dignitie of nature inferior to plants. 1611 SHAKS. *Wint. T.* V. i. 183 His Sonne, who ha's (His Dignitie, and Dutie both cast off) Fled from his Father, from his Hopes, and with A Shepheards Daughter. 1711 SWIFT *Lett.* (1767) III. 177, I fear I shall be sometimes forced to stoop beneath my dignity, and send to the ale-house for a dinner. 1751 HARRIS *Hermes* (1841) 119 There is no kind of subject, having its foundation in nature, that is below the dignity of a philosophical inquiry. 1786 HAN. MORE *Florio* 78 Small habits well pursued betimes, May reach the dignity of crimes. 1891 *Law Times* XCII. 124/1 The post of Irish Chancellor has increased rather than diminished in dignity since the Union.

fig. 1541 COPLAND *Guydon's Quest. Chirurg.* H j b, May the herte..sustayne dysease longe? Answere. No, for his great dygnyte. 1656 RIDGLEY *Pract. Physick* 215 Consider the dignity of the part affected, so that the heart must not be tryed by vehement remedies.

b. *collect.* Persons of high estate or rank (cf. *the quality*).

1548 W. PATTEN *Exped. Scotl.* Pref. in Arb. *Garner* III. 73 My Lord's Grace, my Lord of Warwick, the other estates of the Council there, with the rest of the dignity of the army did ..tarry.. at Berwick. 1793 BURKE *Corr.* (1844) IV. 149, I cannot see the dignity of a great kingdom, and, with its dignity, all its virtue, imprisoned or exiled, without great pain.

attrib. 1833 MARRYAT *P. Simple* xxxi, A dignity ball is a ball given by the most consequential of their coloured people [in Barbadoes].

3. An honourable office, rank, or title; a high official or titular position.

c1290 *S. Eng. Leg.* I. 72/54 Bischop him made..seint Edward þe king, And a-feng him in his dignete. c1330 R. BRUNNE *Chron. Wace* (Rolls) 15112 Seint Gregore tok þe dignete, And was pope þrytty ȝer. 1520 *Caxton's Chron. Eng.* ccxxxvi. 258 Tho that were chose to bisshoppes sees and dignytees. 1548 HALL *Chron., Edw. IV*, 208 Edward duke of Yorke, whiche..had untrewly usurped the Croune and Imperial dignitie of this realme. 1659 B. HARRIS *Parival's Iron Age* 123 He procured the Dignity of General to be taken away from the duke of Frithland. 1726 AYLIFFE *Parergon* 98 By a Dignity, we understand that Promotion or Preferment, to which any Jurisdiction is annex'd. 1781 GIBBON *Decl. & F.* III. 231 He..distributed the civil and military dignities among his favourites and followers. 1844 LINGARD *Anglo-Sax. Ch.* (1858) I. i. 18 The dignity of Roman prefect. 1884 *L'pool Mercury* 3 Mar. 5/1 Her Majesty has conferred the dignity of a viscountcy upon Sir Henry B. W. Brand.

b. *transf.* A person holding a high office or position; a dignitary.

c1450 HOLLAND *Howlat* 690 Denys and digniteis. 1598 FLORIO Ep. Ded., That I..may..entertaine so high, if not deities yet dignities. 1611 BIBLE *Jude* 8 These filthy dreamers..speake euill of dignities. 1656 HEYLIN *Surv. France* 93 There is..in this Church a Dean 7 Dignities and

50 Canons. **1667** Milton *P.L.* I. 359 Godlike shapes and forms..Princely Dignities, And Powers that earst in Heaven sat on Thrones. **1865** Kingsley *Herew.* i, Thou art very like to lose thy tongue by talking such ribaldry of dignities.

4. Nobility or befitting elevation of aspect, manner, or style; becoming or fit stateliness, gravity. (Cf. DIGNIFIED 2.)

1667 Milton *P.L.* VIII. 489 Grace was in all her steps.. In every gesture dignitie and love. **1725** Pope *Odyss.* VI. 73 A dignity of dress adorns the Great. **1752** Fielding *Amelia* I. viii, He uttered this..with great majesty, or, as he called it, dignity. **1811** Syd. Smith *Wks.* (1859) I. 205/1 All establishments die of dignity. They are too proud to think themselves ill, and to take a little physic. **1853** J. H. Newman *Hist. Sk.* (1873) II. II. i. 248 He preserved in his domestic arrangements the dignity of a literary and public man. **1854** J. S. C. Abbott *Napoleon* (1855) II. xxx. 557 He opposed the effect of these instructions with such silent dignity as to command general respect. **1878** B. Taylor *Deukalion* II. iv. 77 So much of dignity in ruin lives.

b. *Rhet.*

1828 Webster, *Dignity*, in oratory, one of the three parts of elocution, consisting in the right use of tropes and figures.

5. *Astrol.* A situation of a planet in which its influence is heightened, either by its position in the zodiac, or by its aspects with other planets.

c **1391** Chaucer *Astrol.* Table of Contents, Tables of dignetes of planetes. *Ibid.* II. §4 The lord of the assendent.. whereas he is in his dignite and conforted with frendly aspectys of planetes. **1632** Massinger *City Madam* II. ii, Saturn out of all dignities..and Venus in the south angle elevated above him. **1647** Lilly *Chr. Astrol.* vi. 49 *Almuten*, of any house is that Planet who hath most dignities in the Signe ascending or descending upon the Cusp of any house. **1706** Phillips (ed. Kersey) s.v., In Astrology, Dignities are the Advantages a Planet has upon account of its being in a particular place of the Zodiack, or in such a Station with other Planets, etc. by which means its Influences and Virtue are encreas'd. **1839** Bailey *Festus* (1872) 121 Ye planetary sons of light! Your aspects, dignities, ascendances.

†**6.** The term for a 'company' of canons. *Obs.*

1486 *Bk. St. Albans* F vij a, A Dignyte of chanonys.

†**7.** *Alg.* = POWER. *Obs.*

1715 *Phil. Trans.* XXIX. 211 Mr. Newton introduced.. the Fract, Surd, Negative and Indefinitive Indices of Dignities.

¶**8.** [Erroneous or fantastic rendering of Gr. ἀξίωμα 'honour, worth, dignity', also 'first principle, axiom'.] A self-evident theorem, an axiom.

1646 Sir T. Browne *Pseud. Ep.* I. vii. 25 These Sciences [mathematics], concluding from dignities and principles knowne by themselves, they receive not satisfaction from probable reasons, much lesse from bare and peremptory asseverations.

† **'dignorate**, *v.* *Obs.* *rare*[-0]. [f. L. *dīgnōrāre*, quoted in the same sense from Paul. ex Fest.]

1623 Cockeram, Dignorate, to marke a beast. **1656** Blount *Glossogr.*, *Dignorate*, to mark, as men do beasts, to know them.

† **dig'nosce**, *v.* *Obs.* [ad. L. *dīgnōscĕre* to recognize apart, distinguish, f. *di-*, *dis-*, DI-[1] + *(g)nōscĕre* to know.]

To distinguish, discern. **a.** *trans.*

a **1639** Spottiswood *Hist. Ch. Scot.* IV. (1677) 200 All the Painters and Writers were called for dignoscing the letters and draughts. **1645** *Liberty of Consc.* 16 The true worshippers of God cannot be certainly and infallibly dignosced from the false worshippers. **1671** *True Nonconf.* 391 The consideration..whereupon the right dignoscing of such deeds doth mostly depend, is oftentimes most difficult.

b. *intr.* To discern; to decide.

1641 *Sc. Acts Chas. I* (1870) V. 344 Who shall have pouer to dignose and take cognitione whither the same falles within the said act of pacificatione. **1676** W. Row *Contn. Blair's Autobiog.* xii. (1848) 539 A committee appointed to dignosce upon the supplication.

Hence †**dig'noscible** *a.*, discernible; †**dig'noscitive** *a.*, having the quality of discerning.

1671 *True Nonconf.* 189 As dignoscible by..these characters, as the night is by darkness. **1674** [Z. Cawdrey] *Catholicon* 22 That dignoscitive power..whereby their spiritual sense discerns betwixt good and evil.

† **dig'note**, *v.* *Obs.* *rare*[-1]. [f. L. **dīgnōt* ppl. stem of *dīgnōscere*] = DIGNOSCE.

1657 Tomlinson *Renou's Disp.* Pref., Every Simple.. may be dignoted in its nature and quality.

† **dig'notion.** *Obs.* [n. of action f. *dīgnōt-* ppl. stem of L. *dīgnōscĕre*: see DIGNOSCE and -ION[1].] The action of distinguishing or discerning; a distinguishing mark or sign.

1578 Banister *Hist. Man* I. 10 The dignotion of sauors. **1657** Tomlinson *Renou's Disp.* 42 That this dignotion may be certain. **1658** Sir T. Browne *Pseud. Ep.* V. xxii. 327 Temperamentall dignotions, and conjecture of prevalent humours.

† **'dignous**, *a.* *Obs.* [f. L. *dign-us* worthy + -OUS.] Worthy, honourable.

1630 T. Westcote *Devon.* 170 A dignous family of this diocese. *Ibid.* (1845) 314 The ancient and dignous family of Coffin.

digonal ('dɪgənəl, daɪ'gəʊnəl), *a.* *Cryst.* [f. DI-[2] + Gr. γωνία angle + -AL.] Denoting an axis of two-fold symmetry.

1890 G. H. Williams *Elem. Crystallogr.* (ed. 2) iii. 47 Two other sets of axes are of use in the isometric system. One is the set of intersection-lines between the principal and secondary planes of symmetry... The first..are called the digonal. **1898** *Nature* 27 Jan. 309 Only digonal, trigonal, [tetragonal,] and hexagonal axes [of symmetry] are possible with crystals. **1911** A. E. Tutton *Crystallography* x. 136 A digonal axis..is such that half a complete revolution about it restores the original appearance of the crystal. **1929** H. A. Miers *Mineralogy* (ed. 2) i. 65 The crystals of this class.. possess three digonal axes coinciding with the crystal axes, and no other symmetry.

digoneutic (daɪgəʊ'njuːtɪk), *a.* *Entom.* [f. Gr. δι-, twice + γονεύ-ειν to beget, of which the vbl. adj. would be *γονευτ-ος.]

Producing two broods in a year; double-brooded. Hence **digo'neutism**, the condition of being digoneutic.

1889 S. H. Scudder in *Nature* XXXIX. 319 Capt. Elwes ..fails to make a distinction between the successive seasonal forms of a digoneutic butterfly.

digonous ('dɪgəʊnəs, daɪ-), *a.* *Bot.* [ad. mod.L. *digōn-us*, f. Gr. δι-, twice + -γωνος angled: cf. τρίγωνος three-cornered.] Having two angles.

1788 Jas. Lee *Introd. Bot.* III. iv. (ed. 4) 181 Digonous, Trigonous, Tetragonous..having two, three, four..Angles. **1883** in *Syd. Soc. Lex.*

digoxigenin (dɪdʒɒk'sɪdʒənɪn, dɪdʒɒksɪ'dʒɛnɪn). *Chem.* [f. DIGOX(IN + GENIN.] A hydrolysis product of digoxin, $C_{23}H_{34}O_5$.

1930 Sydney Smith in *Jrnl. Chem. Soc.* 509 Digoxigenin separates from ethyl acetate in stout colourless prisms. **1956** *Nature* 11 Feb. 278/2 A higher dose of digoxigenin is required to produce the same degree of potentiation as digoxin.

digoxin (dɪ'dʒɒksɪn). *Chem.* [f. DIG(ITALIS + T)OXIN.] A crystalline glycoside, $C_{41}H_{64}O_{14}$, obtained from the leaves of the woolly foxglove, *Digitalis lanata*, and used chiefly in the treatment of heart-diseases.

1930 Sydney Smith in *Jrnl. Chem. Soc.* 508 Digoxin, a new digitalis glucoside. *Ibid.*, This new glucoside, which has been named *digoxin*, resembles gitoxin in its sparing solubility in chloroform. **1956** [see prec.]. **1961** *Lancet* 9 Sept. 573/2 He was placed on maintenance digoxin. **1968** J. H. Burn *Lect. Notes Pharmacol.* (ed. 9) 36 Thus digoxin is given by mouth, or it is given intravenously.

† **digradu'ation.** Obs. var. of DEGRADUATION[1]: cf. also DISGRADUATE *v.*

1577 Hanmer *Anc. Eccl. Hist.* (1619) 218 But Eusebius.. wrote unto Alexander that he should revoke the deprivation and digraduation past.

'digram. A proposed synonym of DIGRAPH[1].

1864 in Webster. **1964** *Endeavour* Jan. 15/2 In English ..'TR' is more frequent than 'TU', and Q is always followed by U. Such 'di-gram', and even some 'tri-gram', frequencies have frequently been counted.

digraph[1] ('daɪgrɑːf, -æ-). [f. Gr. δι- twice, DI-[2], + γραφή writing, etc.] A group of two letters expressing a simple sound of speech.

a **1788** T. Sheridan (L.), All improper diphthongs, or, as I have called them, digraphs, are changed into the single vowels which they stand for. **1812** J. C. Hobhouse *Journey Albania* App. 1061 If these combinations of vowels had been distinguished in writing only..their name would have been *digraphs*, and not *dipthongs*. **1873** Earle *Philol. Eng. Tongue* §193 He would therefore recognise the consonantal digraphs *ch, gh..sh, th, wh, ng*, as alphabetic characters. **1877** Sweet *Phonetics* 174 If..we exclude new letters..we are obliged to fall back on digraphs.

digraph[2] ('daɪgrɑːf, -æ-). *Math.* [f. DI(RECTED *ppl. a.* + GRAPH *sb.*[1]] A graph (sense 1) in which each line has a direction associated with it; a finite, non-empty set of elements together with a set of ordered pairs of these elements.

1955 F. Harary in *Trans. Amer. Math. Soc.* LXXVII. 445 Our object is..to count various kinds of generalizations of graphs. These include directed graphs (digraphs), rooted graphs [etc.]. **1965** —— *Structural Models* i. 2 The theory of directed graphs, or more briefly 'digraphs' (a term suggested by G. Pólya). **1973** C. W. Gear *Introd. Computer Sci.* vii. 299 A road map in which every road is one-way would be a digraph. **1976** Bondy & Murty *Graph Theory with Applications* x. 171 Every concept that is valid for graphs automatically applies to digraphs too... However, there are many concepts that involve the notion of orientation, and these apply only to digraphs. **1980** *Sci. Amer.* Mar. 18/2 No matter how the arrowheads are placed on a complete digraph, there will always be a directed path that visits each point just once. Such a path is called a Hamiltonian.

digraphic (daɪ'græfɪk), *a.* [f. DIGRAPH *sb.*[1] + -IC: after Gr. γραφικός, pertaining to writing, graphic.]

1. Pertaining to or of the nature of a digraph.

1873–4 Sweet *Hist. Eng. Sounds* 23 Cases of the arbitrary use of consonants as digraphic modifiers also occur.

2. Written in two different characters or alphabets.

1880 *Scribner's Mag.* June 205 This was a bilingual (or digraphic, as both inscriptions are in the same language), published by De Vogüé. **1895** *Times* 5 Feb. 12/3 The Digraphic Copybook, Longhand and Shorthand.

'digrave, obs. or dial. var. of DIKE-GRAVE.

1721–1800 Bailey, *Digrave, Dike-grave*, an Officer who takes Care of Banks and Ditches.

digress (dɪ'grɛs, daɪ-), *v.* Also 6–7 disgress. [f. L. *dīgress-* ppl. stem of *dīgredī* to go aside, depart, f. *di-*, DIS- 1 + *gradī* to step, walk, go.]

1. *intr.* To go aside or depart from the course or track; to diverge, deviate, swerve.

1552 Huloet, Digresse or go a little out of the pathe, *digredior*. **1582** N. Lichefield tr. *Castanheda Conq. E. Ind.* 65 b, It was not vnpossible but that they might somewhat digresse from their right course. **1603** Dekker *Grissil* (Shaks. Soc.) 22, I must disgress from this bias, and leave you. **1649** *Alcoran* 86 God..punisheth them that digresse from the right path. **1750** Johnson *Rambler* No. 25 ¶11 Frighted from digressing into new tracts of learning. **1825** Lamb *Elia* Ser. II. *Superannuated man*, I find myself in Bond Street..I digress into Soho, to explore a bookstall.

†**b.** *Astron.* Cf. DIGRESSION 3. *Obs.*

1601 Holland *Pliny* I. 12 Shee (Venus) beginnes to digresse in latitude and to diminish her motion from the morn rising: but to be retrograde, and withall to digresse in altitude from the euening station.

†**2.** *fig.* To depart or deviate (*from* a course, mode of action, rule, standard, etc.); to diverge. *Obs.*

1571 Golding *Calvin on Ps.* lxxi. 16 As the other translation agreeth very well, I would not digresse from it. **1592** Shaks. *Rom. & Jul.* III. iii. 127 Thy Noble shape, is but a forme of waxe, Digressing from the Valour of a man. **1603** Holland *Plutarch's Mor.* 25 Digresse good sir from such lewd songs. **1611** Ussher in Gutch *Coll. Cur.* I. 39 The subjects rebelled, and digressed from their allegiance.

†**3.** To diverge from the right path, to transgress. *Obs.*

1541–93 [see DIGRESSING below]. **1640** G. Watts tr. *Bacon's Adv. Learn.* VII. iii. (R.), So man, while he aspired to be like God in knowledge, digressed and fell.

†**b.** *trans.* To transgress. *Obs.*

1592 Wyrley *Armorie* 56 Faire points of honor I would not digresse.

4. *intr.* To deviate from the subject in discourse or writing. (Now the most frequent sense.)

1530 Palsgr. 516/1, I dygresse from my mater and talke of a thyng that nothynge belongeth therunto. **1555** Eden *Decades* 8 To returne to the matter from which we haue digressed. **1597** Morley *Introd. Mus.* 74 Let vs come againe to our example from which wee haue much digressed. **1682** Burnet *Rights Princes* viii. 292, I shall not digress to give any account of these. **1727** Swift *Modest Proposal*, I have too long digressed, and therefore shall return to my subject. **1752** Johnson *Rambler* No. 200 ¶10 While we were conversing upon such subjects..he frequently digressed into directions to the servant. **1813** W. Taylor in *Ann. Rev.* I. 374 Mr. P. digresses on the subject of parliamentary reform. **1869** Farrar *Fam. Speech* iii. (1873) 99, I will not here digress into the interesting question as to the origin of writing.

Hence **di'gressing** *vbl. sb.* and *ppl. a.*, **di'gressingly** *adv.*

1529 More *Comf. agst. Trib.* II. Wks. 1200/1 Were it properly perteining to ye present matter, or sumwhat disgressing therfro. **1541** *Act 33 Hen. VIII*, (Bolton *Stat. Irel.* (1621) 218) Albeit that upon any disloyaltie or digressing contrary to the duety of a subject. **1593** Shaks. *Rich. II*, V. iii. 66 This deadly blot, in thy digressing sonne. **1864** *Q. Rev.* CXVI. 168 The sarcophagus on which appears the incident we have thus digressingly analysed.

† **digress**, *sb.* *Obs.* [ad. L. *dīgress-us* departure, f. ppl. stem of *dīgredī*: see DIGRESS *v.*] = DIGRESSION 2.

1598 Yong *Diana* 76, I thee espie Talking with other Shepherdesses, All is of feastes and brauerie, Who daunceth best, and like digresses. **1655** Fuller *Ch. Hist.* XI. x. §43 Nor let any censure this a digress from my history. **1679** Harby *Key Script.* I. 9, I am driven..here..to a brief Digress.

digresser (dɪ'grɛsə(r), daɪ-). [f. DIGRESS *v.* + -ER[1].] One who digresses.

1654 Baxter (*title*), Reduction of a Digresser or Mr. Baxter's reply to Kendall's Digression. **1824** Scott *St. Ronan's* xiv, Who, though somewhat of a digresser himself, made little allowance for the excursions of others.

digression (dɪ'grɛʃən, daɪ-). Also 5–7 dis-, 5–8 de-. [a. OF. *disgressiun*, *digressiun* (12th c.), mod.F. *digression*, ad. L. *dīgressiōn-em*, n. of action from *dīgredī*: see DIGRESS *v.*]

1. The action of digressing, or turning aside from a path or track; swerving, deviation. (Now somewhat *rare* in *lit.* sense.)

1552 Huloet, Digression, *digressio*. **1670** Cotton *Espernon* I. IV. 144 By this little digression into Gascony, the Duke had an opportunity..to re-inforce himself with some particular Servants of his. **1673** Ray *Journ. Low C.* Rome 379 We made a digression to S. Marino. **1823** J. D. Hunter *Captiv. N. Amer.* 86 This digression up the Kansas was undertaken [etc.].

†**b.** *fig.* Moral deviation or going astray. *Obs.*

1509 Hawes *Past. Pleas.* I. xxi, Nature..More stronger had her operacion Then she had nowe in her digression. **1588** Shaks. *L.L.L.* I. ii. 121, I may example my digression by some mighty president. **1593** —— *Lucr.* 202 Then my digression is so vile, so base, That it will liue engrauen in my face.

†**c.** Deviation from rule. *Obs.*

1615 Crooke *Body of Man* 299 Monsters Aristotle calleth Excursions and Digressions of Nature.

2. Departure or deviation from the subject in discourse or writing; an instance of this. (The earliest and most frequent sense.)

c **1374** Chaucer *Troylus* I. 87 (143) It were a long digression Fro my matere. **1430** Lydg. *Chron. Troy* I. i, I wyll no longer make disgression. **1494** FABYAN *Chron.* IV. lxix. 49, I woll retourne my style to Octauis, from whom I haue made a longe degression. *a* **1535** MORE *De quat. Noviss.* Wks. 99 Which thyng I might proue..sauing that the degression would be ouer long. **1621** *Three Quest. Answ. conc. Fourth Commandm.* 6 But this, by way of disgression. **1675** *Essex Papers* (Camden) I. 206, I begg yr Excellencies pardon for this degression. **1751** JOHNSON *Rambler* No. 147 ⁋7 Without..any power of starting into gay digressions. **1813** SCOTT *Rokeby* I. x, [He] started from the theme, to range In loose digression wild and strange. **1863** MRS. OLIPHANT *Salem Ch.* xiii, Breaking off now and then into a momentary digression.

3. *Astron.* and *Physics.* Deviation from a particular line, or from the mean position; deflexion; e.g. of the sun from the equator, or of an inferior planet from the sun (= ELONGATION 1).

1646 SIR T. BROWNE *Pseud. Ep.* VI. iv. 288 This digression [of the Sun] is not equall, but neare the Æquinoxiall intersections, it is right and greater, near the Solstices, more oblique and lesser. **1705** C. PURSHALL *Mech. Macrocosm* 122 Their Degression, or Departure North, and South, are sometimes Greater, and sometimes Less, than that of the Sun. **1726** tr. *Gregory's Astron.* I. 116 These lesser Bodies may be lessen'd till that digression or those mutual attractions be less than any given ones. **1837** BREWSTER *Magnet.* 215 The needle having arrived at the limit of its western digression. **1847** CRAIG, *Digression*, in Astronomy, the apparent distance of the inferior planets, Mercury and Venus, from the sun.

digressional (dɪˈgrɛʃənəl), *a.* [f. prec. + -AL[1].] Of or pertaining to digression; characterized by digression.

1785 WARTON *Notes on Milton's Juvenile Poems* (T.), Milton has judiciously avoided Fletcher's digressional ornaments. **1787** HEADLEY *On Daniel's Poems* (R.), He seems fearful of supplying its [his subject's] defects by digressional embellishments. **1841** DE QUINCEY *Homer* Wks. VI. 326 He adds a short digressional history of the fortunate shot.

digressionary (dɪˈgrɛʃənərɪ), *a.* [f. as prec. + -ARY.] Of the nature of a digression.

1741 *Betterton's Eng. Stage* 4 A..short digressionary History of the Fate and Fortunes of the most considerable Actresses. **1859** LEVER *Davenport Dunn* i, All this is, however, purely digressionary.

digressive (dɪˈgrɛsɪv, daɪ-), *a.* [ad. L. *dīgressīvus*, f. *dīgress-* ppl. stem of *dīgredī*: see DIGRESS *v.* and -IVE.]

1. Characterized by digressing; diverging from the way or the subject; given to digression; of the nature of, or marked by, digression.

c **1611** CHAPMAN *Iliad* XIV. 105 These digressive things Are such as you may well endure. **1641** 'SMECTYMNUUS' *Vind. Answ.* §2. 30 We will not make digressive excursions into new controversies. **1651** BAXTER *Inf. Bapt.* Apol. 15, I came not to satisfie the people..by digressive discourses.. but to dispute with him. **1745** ELIZA HEYWOOD *Female Spectator* (1748) III. 310 But all this..is digressive of the subject I sat down to write upon. **1783** H. BLAIR *Lect.* 39 (Seagar) Pindar is perpetually digressive and fills up his poems with fables of the gods and heroes. **1874** T. HARDY *Far from Madding Crowd* I. xxvi. 285 That remark seems somewhat digressive.

†2. That turns any one out of his way. *Obs. rare.*

c **1611** CHAPMAN *Iliad* x. Argt., Then with digressive wiles they use their force on Rhesus' life.

Hence **diˈgressively** *adv.*, in a digressive manner; **diˈgressiveness**, the quality of being digressive.

1731–1800 BAILEY, *Digressively*, by way of Digression. **1768** *Woman of Honor* IV. 92 An example, which you will hardly think digressively introduced. **1877** H. A. PAGE *De Quincy* II. XIX. 163 If it is to blame for not a little of his digressiveness, still it imparts to everything he does a bouquet. **1879** FARRAR *St. Paul* II. App. 611 The digressiveness becomes more diffuse.

diguanide (ˈdaɪgwænaɪd). *Chem.* [f. DI-[2] + GUANID(IN)E.] **a.** A colourless crystalline compound, $NH[C(NH)NH_2]_2$, which is a condensation product of two guanidine molecules with the loss of a molecule of ammonia; guanylguanidine.

1910 *Jrnl. Chem. Soc.* XCVIII. I. 896 Diguanide $NH[C(NH_2):NH]_2$, crystallises from absolute alchohol in glistening prisms, m. p. 130°. **1928** G. M. DYSON *Chem. Chemotherapy* v. 95 Several guanidine derivatives..can be considered pharmacologically inactive... Thus, guanyl urea (315)..is inactive and diguanide (316) in the form of its hydrochloride is inactive. **1946** *Nature* 16 Nov. 707/2 The diguanide system..provided structural features similar to those found in the earlier active pyrimidine compound '2666'. **1952** MORTON & HOGGARTH in E. H. Rodd *Chem. Carbon Compounds* IB. xiv. 935 Diguanide itself is a strongly basic substance.

b. Any compound derived from diguanide by replacement of hydrogen atoms by other atoms or groups; also, a diguanidine.

1911 *Jrnl. Chem. Soc.* C. I. 928 Diguanides of the type $NH:C(NHR)\cdot NH\cdot C(NH_2):NH$, where R = aryl, are readily obtained in the form of their hydrochlorides by heating dicyanodiamide with the hydrochlorides of aromatic amines in aqueous solution. **1961** *Lancet* 9 Sept. 563/2 The present compounds are not diguanides like synthalin. **1961** [see next]. **1966** *New Scientist* 24 Nov. 433/1 The longing of diabetics for a hypoglycaemic drug which could be taken orally..was realized ten years ago when the sulphonylureas and diguanides were introduced.

diguanidine (daɪˈgwænɪdɪn, -iːn). *Chem.* [f. DI-[2] + GUANIDINE.] †**a.** = DIGUANIDE a. *Obs.* **b.** Any compound containing two of the radicals $-NH\cdot C(NH)NH_2$, derived from guanidine by the loss of a hydrogen atom.

1879 *Jrnl. Chem. Soc.* XXXVI. 781 It is now found that this substance is a di-acid base, diguanidine, $NH:C(NH_2)\cdot NH\cdot C(NH_2):NH$. *Ibid.*, Diguanidine and its salts are colourless. **1927** *Brit. Pat.* 274,259, An improved process for the production of alkylene diguanidines. **1952** MORTON & HOGGARTH in E. H. Rodd *Chem. Carbon Compounds* IB. xiv. 931 This compound depresses the concentration of blood sugar, a property which is even more marked in certain diguanidines such as 'Synthalin'. **1960** *Brit. Med. Bull.* XVI. 251/1 Diguanidines..may be considered as being made up of two guanidine molecules joined by a chain of methylene groups. **1961** *Lancet* 30 Sept. 776/1 Synthalin with two guanidines joined by a chain of methyl groups is a diguan*idine*. In phenformin the two guanidines coalesce..and it is a diguanide (or biguanide).

‖**digue.** [F. *digue*, in OF. also *dique*, a. Flem. *dijk*, DIKE q.v.] = DIKE. (In reference to Holland, Flanders, or France. Now only used for local colouring.)

1523 LD. BERNERS *Froiss.* 4 b/1 With the fyrste flodde they came before the Digues of Holande [*pr.* Dignes; *hence* GRAFTON *Chron.* II. 210 dignesse]. **1645** *City Alarum* 10 Opposing a Digue to stop the torrent. **1673** TEMPLE *Obs. United Prov.* Wks. 1731 I. 13 In Zealand they absolutely gave over the working at their Digues. **1702** DENNIS *Monument* xvi. 8 Whose stately Tow'rs Are to the Storms of Arbitrary Pow'r, What its Digues are to the Tempestuous Main. **1886** *Athenæum* 22 May 686/1 Girls gossiping on the *digue* of stone which defends the place against the sea.

digust, rare obs. var. of DISGUST.

‖**Digynia** (daɪˈdʒɪnɪə). *Bot.* [mod.L. (Linnæus 1735) f. Gr. δι-, DI-[2] + γυνή woman, wife + abstr. ending -ια, *-ia.*] The second Order in many classes of the Linnæan Sexual System, comprising plants having two pistils.

1762 in HUDSON *Flora Anglica.* **1794** MARTYN *Rousseau's Bot.* x. 99. **1858** CARPENTER *Veg. Phys.* §458 One portion of the class Pentandria, order Digynia, corresponds with the Natural Order Umbelliferae.

Hence **ˈdigyn**, a plant of the order *Digynia*; **diˈgynian, diˈgynious** *adjs.*, belonging to the order *Digynia*; **ˈdigynous** (ˈdaɪdʒɪnəs) *a.*, having two pistils.

1806 J. GALPINE *Brit. Bot.* 390 *Carex* Digynous; spikes filiform. **1828** WEBSTER, *Digyn. Ibid., Digynian.* **1847** CRAIG, *Digynious.* **1850** COMSTOCK *Introd. Bot.* (ed. 21) 470 (*Gloss.*) *Digynous*, having two styles.

dihedral (daɪˈhiːdrəl), *a.* and *sb. Cryst.* Also diedral. [f. next + -AL[1]: cf. F. *dièdre* in same sense.]

A. *adj.* 1. Having or contained by two planes or plane faces. ***dihedral angle***, the inclination of two planes which meet at an edge. ***dihedral summit***, a summit (of a crystal) terminating in a dihedral angle. spec. *Aeronaut.*, designating the inclination, esp. upwards, of a wing or other surface to the horizontal, or the angle to the horizontal so formed; ***dihedral board***, a device used in measuring the dihedral angle of the wings of an aeroplane.

1799 G. SMITH *Laboratory* I. 2 Terminating in dihedral pyramids. **1808** THOMSON in *Phil. Trans.* XCVIII. 69 Oxalate of potash..crystallizes in flat rhomboids.. terminated by dihedral summits. **1826** HENRY *Elem. Chem.* I. 38 Variations of temperature produce a..difference in.. a crystal of carbonate of lime..As the temperature increases, the obtuse dihedral angles diminish..so that its form approaches that of a cube. **1863–72** WATTS *Dict. Chem.* II. 124 [In the rhombic dodecahedron] The dihedral angles formed by the meeting of the faces are all equal to 120°. **1909** *Westm. Gaz.* 11 Mar. 4/1 The problem of automatic transverse stability is solved by giving the aeroplanes a dihedral angle or keels. **1916** H. BARBER *Aeroplane Speaks* iii. 108 Another method of securing the dihedral angle..is by means of the dihedral board. **1917** C. C. TURNER *Aircraft of To-Day* viii. 140 Inherent stability is secured..by a dihedral setting of the wings, i.e. sloping up to right and left from the body. **1960** C. H. GIBBS-SMITH *Aeroplane* I. ix. 38 They had at first rigged it with a dihedral angle, and found it flew badly in gusty winds.

2. *Math.* Of the nature of a dihedron.

1893 HARKNESS & MORLEY *Theory of Functions* 29 A simple dihedral configuration. **1893** FORSYTH *Functions of a Complex Variable* 625 Functions which are unaltered for the dihedral group of substitutions.

B. *sb. Aeronaut.* A dihedral angle or inclination. Also *transf.*

1913 A. E. BERRIMAN *Aviation* iii. 37 The tail plane is invariably set at a lesser effective angle of incidence than the main wings. This arrangement is commonly described as the fore-and-aft dihedral. **1929** W. FAULKNER *Sartoris* v. 364 While in level flight, dihedral would be eliminated for speed. **1935** C. G. BURGE *Complete Bk. Aviation* 581/2 If the planes are inclined upwards towards the wing tips, the dihedral is positive; if downwards, it is negative. **1962** *Times* 25 May 18/5 Michelotti has..lifted the dihedral of the wings [of a car], setting twin headlamps beneath. **1969** J. M. BRUCE *War Planes of First World War* III. 134 This aircraft differed from the first in having no dihedral on the lower wings.

dihedron (daɪˈhiːdrən). *Math.* [mod. f. Gr. δι-, δισ- twice + ἕδρα seat, base: cf. *tetrahedron.*] In the geometrical theory of groups, the portion of two superposed planes bounded by (or contained within) a regular polygon.

According to Klein, the six regular solids are dihedron (*dieder*), tetrahedron, octahedron, cube or hexahedron, ikosahedron, pentagon-dodecahedron.

[**1828** WEBSTER, *Dihedron*, a figure with two sides.] **1888** G. G. MORRICE tr. *F. Klein's Lect. on Ikosahedron* 3 We can denote this latter by considering the portion of the plane limited by the sides of the n-gon to be doubled, as a regular solid—a dihedron, as we will say: only that this solid, contrary to the elementary notion of such, encloses no space.

‖**diˈhelios.** *Astr.* Also **dihelium** (in mod. Dicts. **dihely**). [mod.L. f. Gr. δι- = διά through + ἥλιος sun.] (See quot.)

1727–51 CHAMBERS *Cycl.*, *Dihelios*, in the elliptical astronomy, a name which Kepler gives to that ordinate of the ellipsis, which passes through the focus, wherein the sun is supposed to be placed.

diˈheptyl. *Chem.*: see DI-[2] and HEPTYL.

dihexagonal (ˌdaɪhɛkˈsægənəl), *a. Cryst.* [f. DI-[2] + HEXAGONAL.] Having twelve angles, of which the first, third, fifth,... eleventh, are equal to one another, and the second, fourth, sixth,... twelfth, also equal to one another, but those of the one set not equal to those of the other; as a ***dihexagonal pyramid*** or ***prism***. See also quot. 1864.

1864 WEBSTER, *Dihexagonal*, consisting of two hexagonal parts united; thus, a dihexagonal pyramid is composed of two hexagonal pyramids placed base to base. **1895** STORY-MASKELYNE *Crystallog.* 141 Symmetry of a form dihexagonal. *Ibid.* 277 Two dihexagonal quoins form the vertices of the pyramids, and are composed by edges S and Σ alternating with each other, adjacent edges representing dihedral angles of different magnitude. *Ibid.* 278 The dihexagonal prism or hexagonal diprism.

†**di-hexaˈhedral**, *a. Cryst. Obs.* [f. as next + -AL[1].] Having twice six faces: see quot.

1805–17 R. JAMESON *Char. Min.* (ed. 3) 203 *Di-hexahedral* (di-hexaèdre), when it is a six-sided prism, having three planes on the extremities. [204] Example, Di-hexahedral felspar (feldspath di-hexaèdre), which is a broad six-sided prism, bevelled on the extremities, the bevelling planes set on two opposite lateral edges, and on each of the extremities, one of the angles, formed by the meeting of the bevelling planes with the lateral edges, and on which they are set, truncated.

di-hexaˈhedron. *Cryst.* [f. DI-[2] + HEXAHEDRON.] A six-sided prism with trihedral summits, making twelve faces in all. Also sometimes, a double hexagonal pyramid.

1888 *Amer. Naturalist* XXII. 247 Dihexahedra of quartz and various rare minerals are noted in them [trap dikes in Scotland].

dihoti, var. of DIOTI, wherefore.

†**ˈdihtende.** *Obs. rare*[−1]. [early ME., subst. use of pr. pple. of *dihten*, OE. *dihtan* to rule: see DIGHT.] Ruler, disposer.

c **1200** *Trin. Coll. Hom.* 123 Almihti god . shuppende and wealdende . and dihtende of alle shafte.

dihybrid (daɪˈhaɪbrɪd). *Biol.* [f. DI-[2] + HYBRID *sb.*] A hybrid that is heterozygous with respect to two independent genes. Also *attrib.* So **diˈhybridism.**

1907 R. C. PUNNETT *Mendelism* (ed. 2) 34 Where the original parents differ in two pairs of characters, the case is termed one of dihybridism. *Ibid.* 62 In the dihybrid cases.. the two pairs of characters behaved quite independently, in so far as the process of segregation was concerned. **1918** BABCOCK & CLAUSEN *Genetics Rel. Agric.* v. 86 The F_2 segregates in accordance with normal dihybrid expectations. **1965** BELL & COOMBE tr. *Strasburger's Textbk. Bot.* (new ed.) II. ii. 334 Hybrids heterozygous for two characters are known as dihybrids. **1969** G. W. BURNS *Sci. Genetics* iv. 68 The F_1 individuals in this instance are referred to as dihybrid individuals because they are heterozygous for each of the two pairs of genes.

dihydric (daɪˈhaɪdrɪk), *a. Chem.* [f. DI-[2] + HYDRIC.] Applied to a compound of two atoms of hydrogen with an acid radical; denoting dibasic acids regarded as salts of hydrogen, as ***dihydric sulphate*** = sulphuric acid H_2SO_4.

1876 HARLEY *Mat. Med.* 187 It..is readily soluble in water acidulated with an excess of citric acid, when the acid or magnesic dihydric citrate is formed.

dihydrite (daɪˈhaɪdraɪt). *Min.* [f. Gr. δι-, DI-[2] + ὕδωρ, ὑδρ- water + -ITE.] A variety of pseudomalachite or native phosphate of copper, containing two equivalents of water.

1868 DANA *Min.* 568.

dihydro-, dihydr-. *Chem.* [f. DI-[2] + HYDR(O)-.] Having two atoms of hydrogen in combination. **diˌhydrostreptoˈmycin**, a hydrogenated derivative of streptomycin with similar antibiotic properties.

1873 *Fownes' Chem.* (ed. 11) 334 Dihydro-tetrasodic carbonate may be regarded as a compound of the neutral and acid salts. **1946** *Jrnl. Amer. Chem. Soc.* LXVIII. 1390/2 Streptomycin has been catalytically hydrogenated to dihydrostreptomycin. **1951** A. GROLLMAN *Pharmacol. & Therap.* xxii. 456 Although large doses of dihydrostreptomycin induce the same vestibular disturbances as does streptomycin, it is much less neurotoxic. **1970** PASSMORE & ROBSON *Compan. Med. Studies* II. xx. 31/2 Dihydrostreptomycin..is now rarely used because it is more likely than streptomycin to damage the cochlear nerve and produce deafness.

dihydrobromide, -chloride, -iodide. *Chem.* See DI-[2] and HYDROBROMIDE, etc.

1873 *Fownes' Chem.* (ed. 11) 559 The dihydrobromides and dihydriodides have the same composition as the dibromides of the olefines.

,dihydroxy'acetone. *Chem.* [f. DI-[2] + HYDROXY- + ACETONE.] A colourless crystalline compound, $CH_2OH{\cdot}CO{\cdot}CH_2OH$, isomeric with glyceraldehyde and having strong reducing properties.

1895 *Jrnl. Chem. Soc.* LXVIII. I. 496 Attempts to prepare dihydroxyacetone by the action of nitrous acid on diamidoacetone hydrochloride were not very successful. **1951** I. L. FINAR *Org. Chem.* xviii. 358 Dihydroxyacetone..is not optically active, and hence, by the definition given above, is not a sugar. If..the proviso that a sugar is always optically active is rejected, then dihydroxyacetone will be a ketotriose. **1967** [see GLYCEROSE]. **1969** OTTAWAY & IRVINE tr. *Netter's Theor. Biochem.* xiii. 715 In the mitochondria a very active oxidation of glycerol phosphate takes place. The dihydroxyacetone phosphate which is formed diffuses into the cytoplasm,..and so acts as a transporter of hydrogen to the respiratory chain.

dihy'droxyl, *a. Chem.* See DI-[2] and HYDROXYL.

1875 H. C. WOOD *Therap.* (1879) 72 The dihydroxyle quinia is physiologically inert.

diiamb (daɪaɪ'æmb). *Pros.* Also in L. form **diiambus** (in 8 **dijambus**). [ad. L. *di-iambus*, Gr. διΐαμβος a double iambus, f. δι-, DI-[2] + ἴαμβος iambus.] A metrical foot consisting of two iambs.

1753 CHAMBERS *Cycl. Supp.*, *Dijambus*..is compounded of two iambics, as *sēvēritās*. **1844** BECK & FELTON tr. *Munk's Metres* 10 Feet of six times..⏑–⏑– Diiambus, Diiamb.

di-iodide (daɪ'aɪədaɪd). *Chem.* [f. DI-[2] + IODIDE.] A compound of two atoms of iodine with a dyad element or radical, as mercuric di-iodide, $Hg\ I_2$.

1873 *Fownes' Chem.* (ed. 11) 227 The di-iodide melts at 110°. **1881** *Athenæum* 9 Apr. 496/1 On the co-efficients of Expansion of the Diiodide of Lead (Pb I_2).

di-'iodo-, di-'iod-. *Chem.* [f. DI-[2] + -IOD(O)-.] Having two atoms of iodine replacing two of hydrogen, as ***di-iodomethane*** CH_2I_2. **,diiodo'tyrosine,** an iodine-containing derivative of tyrosine, $C_9H_9NO_3I_2$, which is the precursor of thyroxine in the body and the compound into which iodine is first converted when absorbed by the thyroid gland from the blood.

1869 ROSCOE *Elem. Chem.* 417 Prepared by the action of caustic potash on di-bromo- or di-iodo-salicylic acid. **1877** WATTS *Fownes' Chem.* II. 68 Di-iodomethane..crystallises in colourless shining laminæ of specific gravity 3·34. **1927** *Biochem. Jrnl.* XXI. 170 It is highly probable that thyroxine is formed in nature by the coupling of two molecules of diiodotyrosine with the loss of one side chain. **1949** *Blakiston's New Gould Med. Dict.* 297/2 *Diiodotyrosine*, $C_9H_9O_3NI_2$. A substance found in skeletons of corals, sponges, and other marine organisms. It..has been used in hyperthyroidism. **1964** L. MARTIN *Clinical Endocrinol.* (ed. 4) iii. 122 In goitrous cretins..the thyroid may be unable to trap iodide from the blood, or..to couple molecules of diiodotyrosine to form thyroxine.

di-isopentyl, di-isopropyl. *Chem.* See DI-[2] and ISO-.

diject, obs. erron. form of DEJECT *v.*

dijiridu, var. DIDGERIDOO.

† di'judicant. *Obs. rare.* [ad. L. *dījūdicānt-em*, pr. pple. of *dījūdicāre*: see next.] One who judges, determines, or decides.

1661 GLANVILL *Scepsis Sci.* xxvii. 226 If great Philosophers doubt of many things, which popular dijudicants hold as certain as their Creeds. **1691** WOOD *Ath. Oxon.* II. 496 He..did altogether disapprove the streightness and sloath of elder dijudicants.

dijudicate (daɪ'dʒuːdɪkeɪt), *v.* Now *rare.* [f. L. *dījūdicāt-*, pa. ppl. stem of *dījūdicāre* to judge, determine, f. *dī-* apart (DI-[1]) + *jūdicāre* to judge.] **a.** *intr.* To judge or pass judgement between contending parties or in contested matters; to determine, decide.

1607 WALKINGTON *Opt. Glass* 3 The..touchstone of true wisdome which dijudicates not according to external semblances. **1641** BRATHWAIT *Eng. Intelligencer* 11, It being solely in your powers to dijudicate of his necessity. **1656** in BLOUNT *Glossogr.* **1676** W. HUBBARD *Happiness of People* 5 Dijudicating of the time and season.

b. *trans.* To judge of; to pronounce judgement on, decide formally or authoritatively.

1666 J. SMITH *Old Age* (ed. 2) 41 To dijudicate them as they are in themselves, and to discern them as they differ from all other. **1865** PUSEY *Eirenicon* 32 [tr. *Bossuet*] The matter being dijudicated.

Hence **di'judicating** *vbl. sb.*

a **1656** HALES *Gold. Rem.* 260 (T.) The church of Rome..commends unto us the authority of the church in dijudicating of scriptures.

dijudi'cation. Now *rare.* [ad. L. *dījūdicātiōn-em* deciding, n. of action from *dījūdicāre*: see prec.]

1. The action of judging (between matters); judicial distinction, discernment, discrimination.

1549 GRINDAL *Rem.* (1843) 198 Speaking of the dijudication of the sacraments. **1653** H. MORE *Conject. Cabbal.* (1713) 134 Because Dijudication implies a Duality in the Object, it is called Διάκρισις. **1668** HOWE *Bless. Righteous* (1825) 76 Surely heaven will not render the Soul less capable of dijudication. **1704** J. HARRIS *Lex. Techn.*, *Diacrisis*, is a distinction and dijudication of Diseases and Symptoms. **1835** C. HODGE *Comm. Rom.* xiv. 392 The former..means the faculty of discrimination..dijudication, judgment.

2. The pronouncing of a judgement; authoritative decision.

1615 BYFIELD *Expos. Coloss.* i. 20 Discretion or dijudication of the cause. **1651** J. ROCKET *Christian Subj.* xi. (1658) 123 He likewise assumes to himselfe the power of Dijudication in all causes. **1677** GALE *Crt. Gentiles* IV. 204 Plato adds..the beginning and end of this controversie ought to be brought to the people, but the examen and dijudication to the three chief Magistrates.

† di'judicative, *a.* [f. L. ppl. stem *dījūdicāt-* (see above) + -IVE.] Determinative, decisive.

1659 STANLEY *Hist. Philos.* III. II. 100 To number all things reference have—that is to dijudicative reason.

† di'junge, *v. Obs. rare.* [ad. L. *dījungĕre* to disjoin, f. *dī-* apart (DI-[1]) + *jungĕre* to JOIN.] *trans.* To disjoin, divide, separate.

1768–74 TUCKER *Lt. Nat.* (1852) I. 474 The..line of separation dijunging the province of organism from the rest of the mechanism territory.

dik, obs. form of DIKE.

‖ **dika** ('daɪkə). [W. African name.] In ***dika-bread***, a vegetable substance somewhat resembling cocoa, prepared from the fruit of a West African species of mango-tree (*Mangifera gabonensis*). ***dika-fat, -oil***, the fatty substance of dika-bread.

1859 *Pharmac. Jrnl.* Ser. II. I. 308 Mr. P. L. Simmonds introduced to the notice of the meeting a specimen of Dika bread from Gaboon, on the West Coast of Africa. **1863–72** WATTS *Dict. Chem.* II. 330 The fruit, which is about as large as a swan's egg, contains a white almond having an agreeable taste. These almonds, when coarsely bruised and warm-pressed, form dika-bread, which has a grey colour, with white spots, smells like roasted cocoa and roasted flour..and is greasy to the touch. Dika-bread contains a large quantity of fat. **1888** W. T. BRANNT *Anim. & Veget. Fats* 320 Dika oil, oba oil, or wild mango oil is obtained from..a tree indigenous to the west coast of Africa.

'dikage, dykage. Also 7 dicage, dyckage. [f. DIKE + -AGE.] The work of diking.

1634 (*title*), Boke of Accounts of the Participants of the Dyckage of Haitfield chace (in J. Tuckett *Catal. MSS.* Apr. (1868) 54). **1652** in Stonehouse *Axholme* (1839) 91 The dicage and draynage of the Levell of Hatfield Chase.

‖ **dikamali** (dɪkə'mɑːlɪ). *E. Ind.* Also **decamalee.** [Marāthī *dikāmālī.*] The native name of a resinous gum which exudes from the ends of young shoots of *Gardenia lucida*, a rubiaceous shrub of India.

1858 SIMMONDS *Dict. Trade*, *Decamalee-gum*..obtained from the *Gardenia lucida* of Roxburgh. **1866** *Treas. Bot.*, *Decamalee* or *Dikamali*. **1873** H. DRURY *Useful Plants Ind.* 224 A fragrant resin, known..as *Dikamali* resin is procured from the tree, which is said to be useful in hospitals. **1879** F. POLLOK *Sport. Brit. Burmah* I. 247 Boil the powdered Gallnut in the oil, then add the dikkamalay, and when it is melted, strain.

dikaryon (daɪ'kærɪən). *Biol.* Also **dicaryon.** [a. Fr. *dikaryon* (R. Maire 1912, in *Mycol. Centralblatt* I. 214), f. DI-[2] + Gr. κάρυον nut, taken as = nucleus.] A pair of unfused haploid nuclei of opposite mating type in a cell or spore which divide simultaneously when the cell divides; also, a dikaryotic cell, spore, or mycelium. Hence **dikary'otic** *a.*, containing a dikaryon; composed of dikaryons.

1913 W. B. GROVE *Brit. Rust Fungi* i. 5 The two adjacent nuclei are said to be 'paired', and together they consititute a *synkaryon* or *dikaryon*. **1941** *Bot. Rev.* VII. 393 A dikaryotic hybrid may be defined as a hybrid made up of dikaryotic diploid cells, *i.e.* cells containing a conjugate pair of haploid nuclei. **1947** C. E. SKINNER et al. *Henrici's Molds, Yeasts & Actinomycetes* (ed. 2) i. 9 The mycelium with paired nuclei of opposite 'sex' which divides conjugately is known as the dikaryon or is described as dikaryotic. **1971** *Nature* 30 Apr. 552/2[They] report the successful growth *in vitro* of the corn smut (*Ustilago maydis*) dikaryon. *Ibid.* 552/3 It is the fusion of two of these non-pathogenic haploid cells which gives rise to the pathogenic dikaryotic mycelium.

dikaryophase (daɪ'kærɪəfeɪz). *Biol.* Also **dicaryophase.** [f. prec. + PHASE.] A phase in the life-cycle of a fungus when it contains dikaryotic cells. So **di'karyophyte**, a dikaryotic mycelium.

1916 B. D. JACKSON *Gloss. Bot. Terms* (ed. 3) 110/2 *Dicaryophase*, the stage ending in the production of teleutospores. **1932** *Proc. 6th Int. Congress of Genetics* II. 191 The haploid nuclei..remain associated in the relatively long, parasitic dikaryophase. *Ibid.*, New 'dikaryophytes'..have been found in nature. **1940** *Chambers's Techn. Dict.* 246/1 *Dikaryophase*, that part of the life-history of many Basidiomycetae in which the hyphae are made up of segments, each containing two nuclei.

dik-dik ('dɪkdɪk). Also **dikdik.** [Native name in E. Africa; also in Afrikaans.] Any of several small African antelopes.

[**1870** W. T. BLANFORD *Geol. & Zool. Abyssinia* III. 268 The '*Beni Israel*' or '*Om-dig-dig*', one of the smallest Antelopes known, abounds on the shores of the Red Sea.] **1883** F. L. JAMES *Wild Tribes of Soudan* ix. 76 A *dik-dik*..made its appearance,..uttering the peculiar cry from which it has obtained its name. **1895** *19th Cent.* Sept. 489 Besides lion and rhinoceros there were..Gerenook, Dik-Dik (*Nanotragus Saltii*),..and many kinds of birds. **1906** *Daily Chron.* 23 Mar. 3/3 The dainty little Somali dik-dik. **1920** *Blackw. Mag.* May 660/1 There is nothing to be seen of wild life save occasional tracks of dik-dik. **1928** *Daily Express* 31 July 4 The dikdiks and smaller gazelles. **1970** *East African Standard* 23 Jan. 6/3 There have been bushbuck, dikdik and a porcupine born to inmates of the Orphanage. Another dikdik..has been presented to the Orphanage.

dike, dyke (daɪk), *sb.*[1] Forms: 1–3 díc, 3–5 dik, 4 dick, 4–7 dyk, 4–9 dike, dyke, 6 dyik, dycke, 7 dicke, deeke, 7–9 deek, 8 (*dial.*) dick. [OE. *díc* masc. and (esp. in later use) fem., ditch, trench, cognate with OS., OFris. *dîk* masc., mound, dam, MDu. *dijc* mound, dam, ditch, pool, Du. *dijk* dam; MLG. *dîk*, LG. *dîk*, *diek* dam, MHG. *tîch* pond, fishpond, Ger. *teich* pond, also (from LG.) *deich* embankment; Icel. *dík*, *díki* neut. ditch, fishpond, Sw. *dike* ditch, Da. *dige* dam, embankment, formerly also 'ditch'. The application thus varies between 'ditch, dug out place', and 'mound formed by throwing up the earth', and may include both. The OE. *díc* has given *ditch* as well as *dike*, and the conditions under which the two forms severally have arisen are not clear: cf. LIKE. The spelling *dyke* is very frequent, but not etymological.]

I. † 1. An excavation narrow in proportion to its length, a long and narrow hollow dug out of the ground; a DITCH, trench, or fosse. *Obs.*

Used from ancient times as the boundary of lands or fields, as the fence of an enclosure, as the defence or part of the defences of a camp, castle, town, or other entrenched place. In such excavations water usually gathers or flows: hence sense 2.

847 *Charter* in Sweet *O.E.T.* 434 Ðonne on ðone dic, ðær esne ðone weȝ fordealf. *c* **900** *Bæda's Hist.* I. v. (1890) 32, & hit begyrde and ȝefæstnade mid dice and mid eorð-wealle from sæ to sæ. **1016** *O.E. Chron.* 7 May, And dulfon þa ane mycele dic. *c* **1205** LAY. 15472 þa þe dic wes idoluen, & allunge ideoped, þa bi-gunnen heo wal a þere dic [**1275** a þan dich] ouer al. *a* **1300** *Cursor M.* 9889 (Cott.) A dipe dik [*v.rr.* dick, diche] þar es a-bute [þe castel] Dughtili wroght witven dute. *c* **1330** R. BRUNNE *Chron. Wace* (Rolls) 5829 Til he [Severus] dide make an ouerthwert dik, Bitwyxte to sees a ful gret strik. *c* **1380** WYCLIF *Serm.* Sel. Wks. I. 11 If þe blynde lede þe blynde boþe fallen in þe dyke. *c* **1470** HENRY *Wallace* II. 125 Atour the dike thai ȝeid on athir side, Schott doun the wall. **1535** *Goodly Prymer* Ps. vii. 15 He is fallen into the dyke which he made. **1573** TUSSER *Husb.* To Rdr. (1878) 12 Here we see, Things severall be, And there no dike, But champion like. **1575** CHURCHYARD *Chippes* (1817) 85 The cheef capitaine Manneryng had his deathes wounde, and fell doune in the dike before the gate.

2. a. Such a hollow dug out to hold or conduct water; a DITCH.

Cf. *February fill-dike*: see FEBRUARY 2.

c **893** K. ÆLFRED *Oros.* II. iv. §7 Ymbutan þone weall is se mæsta díc, on þæm is iernende se unȝefoȝlecesta stream. *c* **1400** *Destr. Troy* 1566 With depe dikes and derke doubull of water. **1549** *Compl. Scot.* vi. 38 The fresche deu, quhilk of befor hed maid dikis and dailis verray donc. **1594** PLAT *Jewell-ho.* II. 60 Syr Edward Hobbie..hath stored certeine dikes in the Ile of Sheppey, with sundrie kindes of Sea-fish, into which dikes by sluces, he doth let in..change of sea-water. **1634–5** BRERETON *Trav.* (1844) 43 An invention well deserving to be put in practice in England over all moats or dykes. *a* **1687** C. COTTON *Poet. Wks.* (1765) 108 In Dike lie, Drown'd like a Puppy. **1693** EVELYN *De la Quint. Compl. Gard.* II. 184, I made..some little dikes or water-courses about a foot deep..to receive the mischievous waters. **1697** DRYDEN *Virg. Georg.* I. 441 Whole sheets descend of slucy Rain, The Dykes are fill'd. **1791** *Cottingham Inclos. Act.* 28 Division drains or dikes and ditches. **1821** CLARE *Vill. Minstr.* I. 99 Some rushy dyke to jump, or bank to climb. **1873** G. C. DAVIES *Mount. & Mere* vi. 49 A heron sailed majestically away from a dyke.

b. Extended to any water-course or channel, including those of natural formation. On the Humber, a navigable channel, as *Goole Dike*, *Doncaster Dike*, etc. (A local use.)

1616 SURFL. & MARKH. *Country Farme* 335 The water may haue a descent or falling away into some Brooke, Riuer, or other Dike. **1728** POPE *Dunc.* II. 261 Thames, The King of dykes! **1853** PHILLIPS *Rivers Yorksh.* viii. 216 Dikes..in the low marshy grounds, the ditches, and even canals, becks, and rivers are so called. **1883** *Huddersfield Gloss.*, *Dike*..a watercourse or stream, as Rushfield Dyke, Fenay Bridge Dyke, Denby Dyke, all fast-flowing water. **1888** *Sheffield Gloss.*, *Dike or dyke*, a river or collection of water..The Don or Dun at Wadsley is often called 't' owd dyke.' **1893** *Spectator* 12 Aug. 213 Our sluggish East Anglian rivers, widening into 'broads' and 'dykes'.

c. A water-closet or urinal. *slang.*

1923 MANCHON *Le Slang* 104 *Dike*, les cabinets; *to do a dike*, aller aux lieux, aux *gogues*. **1940** M. MARPLES. *Public*

School Slang 112 Other synonyms [for 'lavatories'] are *rears, lats,*..*dykes* (Oundle, 1920 +), [etc.]. **1960** N. HILLIARD *Maori Girl* 74 But the dyke's in the bathroom. **1965** G. MCINNES *Road to Gundagai* v. 76 The outside (and only) lavatory, known locally as the dyke. **1967** J. CLEARY *Long Pursuit* iii. 82, I learned..to respect her privacy. And I don't mean just when she went to the dike.

3. A small pond or pool. *dial.*

1788 MARSHALL *Yorksh.* Gloss., *Dike*..also a puddle or small pool of water. **1847-78** HALLIWELL, *Dyke*, 2. A small pond. **1877** *Holderness Gloss., Dike*, a ditch; in N[orth Holderness], a pond. **1889** *N.W. Linc. Gloss., Dyke*, a natural lakelet, mere, or pond—as Shawn Dyke formerly on Brumby Common.

†**4.** Any hollow dug in the ground; a pit, cave, or den. *Obs.*

c **1250** *Gen. & Ex.* 281 Twen heuone hil and helle dik. *a* **1340** HAMPOLE *Psalter* ix. 31 He waytes in hidell as leon in his dyke. *Ibid.* cxlviii. 7 Draguns ere..cumand out of þaire diks. **1413** *Pilgr. Sowle* (Caxton 1483) I. xv. 11 He wyl me caste in to helle dyke. *c* **1440** *Promp. Parv.* 121/1 Dyke, *fossa, fovea, antrum.* *c* **1475** *Voc.* in Wr.-Wülcker 799/26-29 *Hec fossa, fovia, cavea, antra*, a dyke.

II. An embankment, wall, causeway.

5. 'A bank formed by throwing the earth out of the ditch' (Bosworth).

The early existence of this sense in Eng. is doubtful: probably all the OE. quotations for which it is assumed in Bosworth-Toller, belong to 1.

1487 *Newminster Cartul.* (1878) 263 An olde casten dike. **1535** COVERDALE *Isa.* xxix. 3, I wil laye sege to the rounde aboute and graue vp dykes agaynst ye. **1595** DALRYMPLE *Leslie's Hist. Scot.* IV. (1895) I. 203 The dyk betuene Abircorne and clyd mouth..be a noble capitane called Grame was..douncastne..fra quhome..it is ȝit called Grames Dyke. **1853** PHILLIPS *Rivers Yorksh.* viii. 215 Earthworks..constructed for defence..Such are the dike at Flamborough [etc.]. **1892** *Northumbld. Gloss.*, There are many earth-works of ancient date which are commonly called *dikes*. One such is known as the *Black-dyke*..there are also several *Grime's* dikes, or Graham's dikes on the Borders.

6. A wall or fence. †**a.** The wall of a city, a fortification. *Obs.*

c **1400** *Destr. Troy* 1533 Sone he raght vpon rowme, rid vp þe dykis, Serchit vp the soile þere þe Citie was. *c* **1400** *Melayne* 125 And sythen þou birne vp house and dyke. **1535** STEWART *Cron. Scot.* (1858) I. 13 Syne forcit it with fowseis mony one, And dowbill dykes that stalwart wer of stone.

b. A low wall or fence of turf or stone serving as a division or enclosure.

Now the regular sense in Scotland. ***dry-stone dyke***, a wall constructed of stones without mortar, as usual on the northern moors; ***fail dyke***, one made of sods or turf cut in squares.

c **1425** WYNTOUN *Cron.* VIII. xxxvii. 112 The mwde wall dykis þai kest all downe. *c* **1470** HENRY *Wallace* III. 133 A maner dyk off stanys thai had maid. **1558** Q. KENNEDIE *Compend. Tractive* in *Wodr. Soc. Misc.* (1844) I. 145 The dyik or closure of the wyne-zard. **1609** *Vestry Bks.* (Surtees) 289 For mending of the church dicke iiijd. **1637-50** ROW *Hist. Kirk* (1842) 434 She..climbed up and got over the dyke in to the yaird. **1774** PENNANT *Tour Scotl. in 1772* 91 It was well defended by four ditches and five dikes. *Ibid.* 182 A great dike of loose stones. **1802** HOME *Hist. Reb.* v, He came to a dry stone dyke that was in his way. **1889** J. M. BARRIE *Window in Thrums* xv, Clods of earth toppled from the garden dyke into the ditch.

c. In some dialects applied to a hedge, or a fence of any kind.

1567-8 *Durham Depos.* (Surtees) 84 That she should teir a cheffe and a neckurcheffe of a dycke. **1878** *Cumbld. Gloss., Dyke, deyke*, a hedge. **1892** *Northumbld. Gloss., Dike, dyke*, a fence..applied alike to a hedge, a ditch, an earthen, or a stone wall when used as a fence. A *dike stower* is a hedge stake.

7. a. A ridge, embankment, long mound, or dam, thrown up to resist the encroachments of the sea, or to prevent low-lying lands from being flooded by seas, rivers, or streams.

Such are the dikes of Holland, and of the English coasts round the Humber and Wash.

[**1531-2** *Act 23 Hen. VIII*, c. 5 §2 The walles, dyches, bankes..and other defenses by the costes of the sea.] **1635-56** COWLEY *Davideis* IV. 904 The main Channel of an high-swoln Flood, In vain by Dikes and broken works withstood. **1642** HOWELL *For. Trav.* (Arb.) 73 Seeing their Dikes and draynings in the Netherlands. **1703** MAUNDRELL *Journ. Jerus.* (1732) 20 A large Dike thirty yards over at top. **1756** NUGENT *Gr. Tour* I. 156 The land here is lower than the waters; for which reason they have the strongest dams or dykes in the whole country. **1766** GIBBON *Decl. & F.* I. xxiv. 705 The camp of Carche was protected by the lofty dykes of the river. **1832** tr. *Sismondi's Ital. Rep.* v. 107 They undertook the immense labour..of making dikes to preserve the plains from the inundation of the rivers.

b. A beavers' dam.

1774 GOLDSM. *Nat. Hist.* (1776) IV. 164 They..are equally industrious in the erection of their lodges, as their dikes.

c. A jetty or pier running into the water. *local.*

1789 BRAND *Newcastle* II. 679 *note*, Query, Why are staiths, in the common language of the keelmen, called dikes? **1825** E. MACKENZIE *Hist. Northumbld.* II. 425 A pier or dike run out at the north entrance at Blyth Harbour.

d. A raised causeway.

1480 CAXTON *Chron. Eng.* xxii. (1482) 21 Two other weyes this belyn made in bossyng thurghout the land that one is callyd fosse and that other fosse dyke. **1774** GOLDSM. *Nat. Hist.* (1862) I. VI. v. 480 This dike, or causey, is sometimes ten, and sometimes twelve feet thick, at the foundation. **1843** PRESCOTT *Mexico* III. viii. (1864) 187 The Spaniards came on the great dike or causeway. **1892** *Northumbld. Gloss.*, Dikes were also frequently trackways.

8. *fig.* A barrier, obstacle, or obstruction.

1770 *Junius Lett.* xxxvi. 171 Gain a decisive victory..or..perish bravely..behind the last dike of the prerogative. **1821** BYRON *Juan* III. xcv, He there builds up a formidable dyke Between his own and others' intellect. **1833** I. TAYLOR *Fanat.* vi. 165 If..the dyke of despotism had not bulged and gaped. **1855** MOTLEY *Dutch Rep.* II. i. (1866) 128 A solid, substantial dyke against the arbitrary power which was for ever chafing and fretting to destroy its barriers.

9. a. *Mining* (*Northumb.*). A fissure in a stratum, filled up with deposited or intrusive rock; a fault.

1789 BRAND *Newcastle* II. 679 Dikes are the largest kind of fissures..a crack..of the solid strata..From the matter..between the two sides of the..dike, it is denominated a clay-dike, stone-dike, etc. **1892** *Northumbld. Gloss., Slip dikes* usually contain fragments of the adjacent strata. When the dike [= fault] interrupts the working of a seam of coal, it is called a down-cast dike if the continuation of the seam lies at a lower level, and an upcast dike, if it is continued at a higher level.

b. Hence, in *Geol.* A mass of mineral matter, usually igneous rock, filling up a fissure in the original strata, and sometimes rising from these like a mound or wall, when they have been worn down by denudation.

1802 PLAYFAIR *Illustr. Hutton. Th.* 67 Whin..exists..in veins (called in Scotland dykes) traversing the strata. **1843** PORTLOCK *Geol.* 114 A trap dike of considerable size..cuts through the chalk. **1845** DARWIN *Voy. Nat.* xii. (1852) 261 Shattered and baked rocks, traversed by innumerable dykes of greenstone. **1865** LIVINGSTONE *Zambesi* ix. 185 A dyke of black basaltic rock crosses the river. **1875** LYELL *Princ. Geol.* I. II. xxv. 628 The inclined strata..are intersected by veins or dikes of compact lava.

c. ***blue dike***: see quot.

1855 DAWSON *Acadian Geol.* iii. 25 Near the edge of the upland, it [the soil] passes into a gray or bluish gray clay called 'blue dike', or, from the circumstance of its containing many vegetable fragments and fibres, 'corky dike'.

10. *attrib.* and *Comb.*, as ***dike-back, -bottom, -delver, -road, -side***; **dike-hopper**, the wheat-ear; **dike-louper** (*Sc.*), a person or animal (e.g. an ox or sheep) that leaps over fences; *fig.* a transgressor of the laws of morality; **dike-phase, -rock, -swarm** (in sense 9 b see quots.); †**dike-row**, a row of trees bordering a field; **dike-seam**, a seam or bed of coal worked nearly on end (*dial.*).

a **1810** TANNAHILL *Barrochan Jean* Poems (1846) 117 Around the peatstacks, and alangst the dyke-backs. *a* **1400-50** *Alexander* 712 Þat doune he drafe to þe depest of the dyke bothom. **1847-78** HALLIWELL, *Dike-cam*, a ditch bank. *North.* **1852** *Meanderings of Mem.* I. 15 Dyke-cloistered Taddington, of cold intense. *Ibid.* I. 57 The dikeside watch when Midnight-feeders stray. **1876** *Whitby Gloss., Diker* or *Dike-delver*, a ditcher; a digger of drains. **1530** LYNDESAY *Test. Papyngo* 992 Now dyke lowparis dois in the kirk resort. **1909** *Q. Jrnl. Geol. Soc.* LXV. 642 In our district..the main dyke-phase intervenes between the uprise of the Cruachan and the Starav Granites. **1954** G. W. HIMUS *Dict. Geol.* 44 *Dyke phase*, the closing episode in a volcanic cycle, characterized by the injection of minor intrusions, especially dykes. **1810** WELLINGTON in Gurw. *Desp.* VII. 72, I request you to have the dyke roads on the island well ascertained and known. **1896** *Science Progress* IV. 476 A..difference of opinion exists as to the propriety of establishing an intermediate division between the plutonic and the volcanic types of struture. Such a division is roughly represented by the 'dyke-rocks' of Rosenbusch. **1903** A. GEIKIE *Text-bk. Geol.* (ed. 4) I. II. II. 197 Professor Rosenbusch [in *Mikrosk. und Physiogr. d. Massingen Gesteine* (ed. 2, 1887) II. 277]..groups the igneous rocks in three great sections: 1st, the deep-seated rocks..; 2nd, dyke-rocks (Gang-gesteine), which may have been injected as dykes and veins at a less distance from the surface (hypabyssal) [etc.]. **1965** G. J. WILLIAMS *Econ. Geol. N.Z.* xi. 167/2 Alkalic dyke-rock material which occurs in the alluvium of New River. **1664** SPELMAN *Gloss.* s.v. *Thenecium*, Arbores crescentes circa agros pro clausura eorum. Volgo dicimus *Dike rowes*. **1909** *Q. Jrnl. Geol. Soc.* LXV. 646 A suggestion as to the relationship of the dyke-swarms to this focus. **1960** L. D. STAMP *Britain's Structure* (ed. 5) ix. 79 Into these cracks molten rock forced its way so that dykes were formed, so numerous that the expression 'dyke swarm' is often used.

dike (daɪk), *sb.*[2] and *v.*[2] *U.S. slang* or *colloq.* [Of obscure origin; perh. a corruption of DECK *v.* 2.] (See quots.)

1851 B. H. HALL *College Words* 100 At the University of Virginia, one who is dressed with more than ordinary elegance is said to be *diked out*. **1871** SCHELE DE VERE *Americanisms* 597 *Dike*, denoting a man in full dress, or merely the dress, is a peculiar American cant term as yet unexplained. To be *out on a dike* is said of persons, mainly young men, who are dressed more carefully than usual, in order to pay visits or to attend a party. **1899** B. W. GREEN *Virginia Folk-Speech* 115 *Dike*, to dress fine. 'You are diked up to-day.' **1902** S. CLAPIN *Dict. Amer.* 159 *Dike*, to attire oneself faultlessly for social purposes. *Diked out*, to be dressed up, with connotation of being in one's best clothes. **1923** M. WATTS *Luther Nichols* 62 All right for you..comin' round here all diked out like Sunday.

dike, dyke (daɪk), *sb.*[3] *slang.* [Of obscure origin.] A lesbian; a masculine woman. Also *attrib.*

1942 BERREY & VAN DEN BARK *Amer. Thes. Slang* §405/3 Masculine woman,..*dike, dyke.* **1959** F. NORMAN *Stand on Me* iii. 37 Nearly everyone is kinkey on dykes for some reason. **1964** E. AMBLER *Kind of Anger* ii. 54 You know about that dike partner of hers? **1965** 'E. MCBAIN' *Doll* (1966) vii. 92 'Was your wife a dyke?' 'No.' 'Are you a homosexual?' 'No.'

dike, dyke (daɪk), *v.*[1] Also 4 (*Sc.*) dik. [f. DIKE *sb.*[1] OE. had *dícian*; but the ME. and modern verb is prob. a new formation.]

1. *intr.* To make a dike, ditch, or excavation; to dig.

[*c* **900** *Bæda's Hist.* I. ix. §3 (1890) 46 Þær Seuerus se casere iu het dician and eorþwall ȝewyrcan.] **1377** LANGL. *P. Pl.* B. v. 552, I dyke and I delue, I do þat treuthe hoteth. *c* **1386** CHAUCER *Prol.* 538 He wolde..dyke and delue, For cristes sake, for euery poure wight. **14..** *Voc.* in Wr.-Wülcker 579/43 *Effodio*, to dyke, or delve. *c* **1440** *Promp. Parv.* 121/1 Dyken, or make a dyke, *fosso.* **1483** CAXTON *Fables of Æsop* 2 b, He sente hym..to dyke and delve in the erthe. *c* **1530** *Ploughman & Paternoster* in *Rel. Ant.* I. 43 He cowde..dyke, hedge, and mylke a cowe. **1573** TUSSER *Husb.* xxiii. (1878) 61 When frost will not suffer to dike and to hedge. **1892** ST. BROOKE *E. Eng. Lit.* ix. 202 Men at work dyking and delving, ploughing and clodding.

†**2.** *trans.* To excavate, dig out (a ditch or hollow).

c **1350** *Will. Palerne* 2233 Þei saie..a semliche quarrere..al holwe newe diked. **1393** LANGL. *P. Pl.* C. XXII. 365 To delue and dike a deop diche.

3. *trans.* To provide with a dike or dikes, in various senses. **a.** To surround with dikes or trenches; to entrench.

c **1330** R. BRUNNE *Chron.* (1810) 272 Now dos Edward dike Berwik brode and long, Als þei bad him pike, and scorned him in þer song. **1375** BARBOUR *Bruce* XVII. 271 [He] ger dik thame so stalwardly. *c* **1400** MAUNDEV. (Roxb.) ix. 35 It es wele walled all aboute and dyked [*fermez entour ad bonz fossez*]. **1513** DOUGLAS *Æneis* VI. iv. 6 Ane dirk, and profound caue..Quhilk wes weill dekkit [*ed.* **1553** dykit] and closit for the nanis With ane foule laik. **1538** LELAND *Itin.* I. 38 A praty Pile or Castelet wel dikid, now usid for a Prison. **1555** WATREMAN *Fardle Facions* Pref. 8 [They]..diked in themselues.

b. To enclose with an earthen or stone wall. *Sc.*

c **1575** BALFOUR *Practicks* (1754) 145 (Jam.) And dike and park the samin surelie and keip thame sikkerlie. **1774** PENNANT *Tour Scotl. in* 1772. 336 A fortress diked round with stone.

c. To defend with a dike or embankment against the sea or river; in quot. 1813 *absol.*

a **1687** PETTY *Pol. Arith.* i. (1691) 14 In the Marshes, Impassible ground Diked and Trenched. **1808** J. BARLOW *Columb.* IV. 592 Quay the calm ports and dike the lawns I lave. **1813** SCOTT *Let. to Miss J. Baillie* 10 Jan. in *Lockhart*, I have been..dyking against the river. **1862** MARSH *Eng. Lang.* 50 The low lands, subject to overflow by the German Ocean..were not diked.

4. To clean out, scour (a ditch or watercourse).

1519 *Presentm. Juries* in *Surtees Misc.* (1890) 31 All watter-sewers..be dykid and scoried. **1562** *Act 5 Eliz.* c. 13 §7 The Heyes, Fences, Dikes or Hedges..shall from Time to Time be diked, scoured, repaired and kept low.

5. To place (flax or hemp) in a dike or water-course to steep.

1799 A. YOUNG *Linc. Agric.* 164 Pull it the beginning of August..Bind and dyke it: leave it in about ten days.

diked, dyked (daɪkt), *ppl. a.* [f. DIKE *sb.*[1] + -ED.] Furnished with a dike or dikes.

1830 *Westm. Rev.* XIII. 173 Dyked marsh owes its formation to a natural phenomenon which appears to have been in operation for ages on the upper shores of the bay of Fundy. **1884** S. E. DAWSON *Handbk. Dom. Canada* 67 The dyked meadow-lands of the Acadians.

'dike-grave. Also 7 -greave, 8- digrave. [a. MDu. *dijcgrave*, mod.Du. *dijkgraaf*, f. *dijk* dike + *graaf* count, earl.] **a.** In Holland, an officer whose function it is to take charge of the dikes or sea-walls. **b.** In England (esp. Lincolnshire), an officer who has charge of the drains, sluices, and sea-banks of a district under the Court of Sewers; = DIKE-REEVE. Now only *dial.* (*di'grave*).

1563 *Court-roll Settrington* in *Yorksh. Archæol. Jrnl.* X. 75 Milo Herkey et Johannes Holden electi sunt in officiis le dyke graues de anno sequente. **1637** *Kirton-in-Lindsey Fine Roll* in *N.W. Linc. Gloss.*, Of Iohn Slater and William Ellys, dikegreaues, for not executing their office, viij[d]. *c* **1645** HOWELL *Lett.* I. i. 5 The chief Dike-Grave here, is one of the greatest Officers of Trust in all the Province. **1672** MARVELL *Poems, Char. Holland* 49 Some small dyke-grave, unperceiv'd, invades The pow'r. **1721** *New Gen. Atlas* 119 The Dykegrave and his Assistants meet to take care of the Dykes, Sluices, Banks, and Channels..in the Rhineland. **1721** BAILEY, *Digrave, Dike-grave*, an Officer who takes care of Banks and Ditches. **1889** *N.W. Linc. Gloss., Dykegrave, Dykereve*, a manorial or parochial officer, whose duty it is to superintend the dykes.

diker, dyker ('daɪkə(r)). Also 5 dikar, dycare. [OE. *dícere, díkere*, f. *díc-ian* to dike, to ditch; in ME. perh. formed anew from DIKE *v.*[1]]

1. A man who constructs or works at dikes. **a.** One who digs ditches or trenches.

c **1000** ÆLFRIC *Gloss.* in Wr.-Wülcker 149/16 *Fossor*, dikere. **1377** LANGL. *P. Pl.* B. VI. 109 Dikeres and delueres digged vp þe balkes. **1496** *Dives & Paup.* (W. de W.) I. xlvi. 872/1 Labourers, deluers and dykers..ben full poore comonly. **1587** FLEMING *Contn. Holinshed* III. 1541/2 They knew not the order of Romneie marsh works..for they were onelie good dikers and hodmen. **1723** THORESBY in *Phil. Trans.* XXXII. 344 When the Labourers or Dikers first discovered..the Jetties..it might be about the Depth of 8 or 10 Foot. **1865** KINGSLEY *Herew.* (1866) II. ix. 153 Their..weapons were found at times by delvers and dykers for centuries after.

b. One who builds enclosure walls (of earth or dry stone). *Sc.*

1497 *Ld. Treas. Acc. Scot.* I. 332 The dikaris of the park of Falkland. **1864** *Cornh. Mag.* Nov. 613 Dry-stone dykers, as well as masons, have twenty-four shillings per week. **1884** J. TAIT in *Un. Presbyterian Mag.* Apr. 156 He was to meat the dykers while bigging the fold dyke.

c. One who constructs embankments.

1481–90 *Howard Househ. Bks.* (Roxb.) 510 Payd to Prynce, the dyker, for the dykyng off ij. rodde in the old parke of a pond ther, viij.*s.*

2. A local name of the hedge-sparrow.

1892 *Northumbld. Gloss.*, *Diker*, a hedge sparrow.

'dike-reeve, dyke-. [f. DIKE *sb.*[1] + REEVE: perhaps an alteration of *dike-grave*, *-greave*, by identifying its final part with the Eng. *reeve*, as in *port-reeve*.] An officer appointed or approved by the Commissioners of Sewers, to take charge of the drains, sluices, and sea-banks of a district of fen or marsh-land in England.

1665 *Act 16 & 17 Charles II*, c. 11 §7 Summes of Money ..by the said Dykereeves and Surveyours of Sewers or any of them expended in and about the takeing, repairing and amending of any such Breach or Breaches, Goole or Gooles, Overflowing or Overflowings of waters. **1726** *Laws of Sewers* 189 The Dyke-Reeves, Officers, or other Inhabitants there may set down the Slough of such Drains. **1848** *Act 12 & 13 Vict.* c. 50 §3 To appoint one or more competent person or persons, being an occupier of sewable lands..to act as dyke-reeve within each of such sub-districts. **1883** *Notice* 19 Oct. (Worle View of Sewers, Weston-super-Mare), Owing to the violence of the Gale on the 17th. a Special View of the Dyke Reeves was held, and your Work..was found to require repairing. **1894** *Minute-bk. Court of Sewers, Wapentake of Manley &c.*, Dec. 17 Being occupiers of not less than ten acres of sewable land in the Messingham District..they are hereby appointed to act as dykereeves within the said district.

†dikesmowler, dyke-. [f. DIKE *sb.*[1]] An obsolete name of the hedge-sparrow.

1611 COTGR., *Mari cocu*, an Hedge-sparrow, Dikesmowler, Dunnecke. [**1847** in HALLIWELL. **1885** in SWAINSON *Prov. Names Brit. Birds.*]

diketone (daɪ'kiːtəʊn). *Chem.* [f. DI-[2] + KETONE.] Any compound in which there are two carbonyl groups, ——CO——, each attached to two carbon atoms.

1896 *Jrnl. Chem. Soc.* LXX. I. 586 By the action of bromine water on quercitol, a diketone, $C_6H_8O_5$, is probably formed. **1946** *Nature* 10 Aug. 205/2 The glycol from butaldehyde gives mostly a keto-alcohol, further oxidation to the diketone being much more difficult. **1967** I. L. FINAR *Org. Chem.* (ed. 5) I. v. 268 Butane-2, 3-dione,.. $CH_3{\cdot}CO{\cdot}CO{\cdot}CH_3$, is the simplest α-diketone.

dike-warden. [f. DIKE *sb.*[1] + WARDEN: cf. *way-warden*.] = DIKE-GRAVE.

1890 SAINTSBURY *Ess.* 253 Seithenyn, the drunken prince and dyke-warden.

dikey ('daɪkɪ), *a. slang.* [f. DIKE *sb.*[3] + -Y[1].] Having the appearance or characteristics of a lesbian.

1964 S. BELLOW *Herzog* 99 Lucas warned me to look out for something dikey. **1966** C. ISRAEL *Hostages* 155 The tall, dikey French woman. **1969** 'J. MORRIS' *Fever Grass* ix. 83 Helen's gone dikey in her old age.

dikh (dɪk). *India.* Also dik(k. [ad. Hind. *diq.*] Trouble, worry, vexation.

1873 W. HEELEY *Lay Mod. Darjeeling* (Y.), And if his locks are white as snow, 'Tis more from dikh than age! **1923** KIPLING *Land & Sea Tales* 243 There has been great *dikh* in this case? *Ibid.* 246 There has been great *dikh-dari* [i.e. trouble-giving].

diking, dyking ('daɪkɪŋ), *vbl. sb.* [OE. *dícung*, f. *díc-ian* to DIKE: see -ING[1].]

1. The action of making a dike; the construction of dikes (in various senses of the sb.).

c **1000** ÆLFRIC *Gloss.* in Wr.-Wülcker 149/15 *Fossio*, dicung. **1377** LANGL. *P. Pl.* B. VI. 250 Eche a wyght wrouȝte or in dykynge or in deluynge. **1486** *Nottingham Rec.* III. 246 For dykyng at the Cheynybrigg Close. **1526** *Customs of Pale* (Dillon 1892) 82 To minishe everie yere j[d] unto the time that his betterings of such dikenge be owte or Run uppe. **1569** *Nottingham Rec.* IV. 135 For dykyng the gret dyke in Westcroft. **1641** BEST *Farm. Bks.* (Surtees) 120 Two dayes ..dykinge aboute it. **1726** *Laws of Sewers* 188 Keep the Rivers thereof with sufficient Dyking, Scouring [etc.]. **1830** N. S. WHEATON *Jrnl.* 464 Much of the land..reclaimed from the marsh by ditching and dykeing. **1865** CARLYLE *Fredk. Gt.* VI. XVI. viii. 223 Upon this Dollart itself there is now to be diking tried. **1884** *Manch. Exam.* 6 Sept. 5/2 The land..wants draining, and dyking.

2. Work consisting of dikes.

1436 *Pol. Poems* (Rolls) II. 153 Defens off herth and dikyng. **1483** *Cath. Angl.* 100/1 A Dikynge, *fossatus.* **1522** *MS. Acc. St. John's Hosp., Canterb.*, Paied for castyng of xxj roddis of dykyng.

3. *Comb.* **diking-boots**, stout boots, reaching up to the thigh, used in ditching; **diking-mitten**, a glove used by a diker.

1820 BEWICK *Mem.* (1882) 13 Equipt with an apron, an old dyking-mitten and a sharpened sickle, to set off among the whin bushes. **1877** *Holderness Gloss.*, *Dikin-beeats*, used for wading in the water and mud when diking.

dikkar, obs. form of DICKER *sb.*[1]

dikkon, Var. DICKEN, DICKIN *int.*

dikkop ('dɪkɔp). *S. Afr.* Also diccop, dickop, dik-kop, dikop. [Afrikaans, f. *dik* thick + *kop* head.]

1. The stone-curlew.

1853 *Edin. New Philos. Jrnl.* LV. 83 The *dickop*..seem to emerge from their daylight concealment. **1858** A. W. DRAYSON *Sporting Scenes* 17 One or two of the bustard tribe are also found here, and are called the *diccop, coran*, and *pouw.* **1873** tr. *J. Verne's Meridiana* xvi. 148 The hunters shot..some '*dikkops*', whose flesh is very delicate eating. **1891** *Daily Graphic* 17 Aug. 5 Eleven snipe, one dikkop, one wild turkey, one blue crane. **1903** E. GLANVILLE *Diamond Seekers* 116 They're playing dik-kop... The dik-kop drops his wing and shams hurt to lead you off. **1939** S. CLOETE *Watch for Dawn* ix. 114 The moonlit nights when dikkops and the kievietjes screamed as they flew to water. **1947** J. STEVENSON-HAMILTON *Wild Life S. Afr.* xxxii. 270 The dikkops or stone curlews.—Two species of these are described in South Africa, the Cape Dikkop (*Burhinus capensis*), and the Water Dikkop (*Burhinus vermiculator*).

2. A form of blue tongue (see BLUE TONGUE 1).

1870 T. BAINES *Diary* 8 Dec. (1946) III. 762 One of whose horses was standing apart, suffering from the 'dikkop' form of horse sickness. **1959** *Cape Times* 28 Jan. 2/3 Dikkop, the dreaded sheep-killing disease, is raging at Murraysburg.

‖**diktat** ('dɪktæt). [a. G. *diktat* DICTATE *sb.*] **a.** A severe settlement or decision, esp. one imposed by a victorious nation upon a defeated nation, a dictated peace; used *spec.* with reference to the Treaty of Versailles of 1919. **b.** A dictate, decree, or command; a categorical assertion.

1933 'A GERMAN DIPLOMAT' *Hitler—Germany & Europe* (Friends of Europe, No. 2) 9 The treaty of Versailles..was not a 'Diktat' which artificially imposed a solution foreign to reality. **1940** *Time* 1 Jan. 47/1 If a Final Treaty is negotiated between victor and vanquished..at least a year after the Preliminary Treaty, or *Diktat*, is imposed. **1940** *Times Weekly* 7 Aug. 9/3 (*headline*) Axis plans for Rumania—popular resistance to 'Diktat'. **1941** *Mind* L. 290 He decreed that sense-data are not to have unnoticed characteristics... This *Diktat* of his would seem to imply that sense-data can have determinable shapes without having determinate ones. **1948** A. J. TOYNBEE *Civilization on Trial* v. 79 The psychological effect of the British *diktat* of A.D. 1842. **1959** *Listener* 22 Jan. 158/2 The Soviet draft was fundamentally different from the Versailles '*diktat*'. **1963** *Times* 27 May 13/4 Naked aggression against any state in Africa which does not accept the diktat of himself and his friends.

†di'lacerate, *ppl. a. Obs.* [ad. L. *dīlacerātus* torn asunder, pa. pple. of *dīlacerāre*: see next.] Rent asunder, torn: used as *pple.* and *adj.*

1602 WARNER *Alb. Eng.* Epit. (1612) 368 England.. dilacerate and infested..by the Danes. **1608** MIDDLETON *Trick to catch Old-one* I. i, What may a stranger expect from thee but *vulnera dilacerata*, as the poet says, dilacerate dealing? **1649** ROBERTS *Clavis Bibl.* 489 His dilacerate members.

dilacerate (dɪ-, daɪ'læsəreɪt), *v.* Also 7 de-. [f. ppl. stem of L. *dīlacerāre* (f. *di-*, *dis-* asunder (DI-[1]) + *lacerāre* to tear, lacerate); also *dēlacerāre*, whence the formerly frequent variant *delacerate*.] trans. To tear asunder, tear in pieces. Also *fig.*

α. **1604** R. CAWDREY *Table Alph.*, *Dilacerate*, to rent in sunder. **1618** *Hist. Perkin Warbeck* in *Select. Harl. Misc.* (1793) 80 You..know how the house of York hath been dilacerated and torn in pieces by the cruel hand of tyrants and home-bred wolves. **1634** SIR T. HERBERT *Trav.* 38 Their eares are extended and dilacerated very much. **1650** *Descr. Future Hist. Europe* Pref. 2 The Church is dilacerated, the Commonwealth disjoynted. **1708** MOTTEUX *Rabelais* IV. lii. (1737) 211 All were dilacerated and spoil'd. **1822** T. TAYLOR *Apuleius* 11 Shall we first dilacerate this man? **1848** J. A. CARLYLE tr. *Dante's Inferno* (1849) 334 See how I dilacerate myself.

β. **1624** T. SCOTT *Vox Cœli* Ded. 5 The Match long since prophetically delacerated. **1647** R. BARON *Cyprian Acad.* 15 Acteons dogs..greedy to delacerate his limbes instead of the innocent beast he persued.

Hence **di'lacerated** *ppl. a.*

1650 A. B. *Mutat. Polemo* To Rdr. 2 My poor dilacerated Countrey. **1668** H. MORE *Div. Dial.* IV. xxxiii. (1713) 385 The dilacerated Empire of Rome.

dilaceration (dɪ-, daɪˌlæsə'reɪʃən). Also 7 de-. [a. F. *dilacération* (1419 in Hatzf.), ad. L. *dīlacerātiōn-em*, n. of action from *dīlacerāre*: see prec.]

1. The action of rending asunder or tearing (parts of the body, etc.); the condition of being torn or rent.

α. **1634** T. JOHNSON tr. *Parey's Chirurg.* XI. i. (1678) 278 Wounds..by Gunshot..are accompanied with contusion, dilaceration, [etc.] **1646** SIR T. BROWNE *Pseud. Ep.* III. xvi. 146 Conceiving a dilaceration of the..belly of the viper. **1732** ARBUTHNOT *Rules of Diet* 396 Dilaceration of the nervous Fibres. **1805** B. MONTAGUE tr. *Bacon's Wisd. Ancients* Wks. (Bohn 1860) 259 The riddles of Sphinx.. have two conditions annexed..dilaceration to those who do not solve them, and empire to those that do. **1838** *New Monthly Mag.* LIV. 403 His right-hand nails..threatened instant dilaceration.

fig. **1545** JOYE *Exp. Dan.* xi. CC ij b, Many dilaceracions & divisions. **1610** HEALEY *St. Aug. Citie of God* 731 His nobles ..after his death making..a dilaceration of his monarchy. **1808** LAMB *Char. Dram. Writ., Ford* Wks. 531/2 This dilaceration of the spirit and exenteration of the inmost mind.

β. **1624** T. SCOTT *Vox Cœli* 58 God himselfe hath.. Confirmed the breach and delaceration of the [Spanish] Match. **1727** BAILEY vol. II, *Delaceration*, a tearing in pieces. **1755** in JOHNSON. **1883** in *Syd. Soc. Lex.*, *Delaceration.*

2. *spec.* In *Dental Surgery*, used 'to describe a condition of tooth resulting from displacement of the calcified portion from the tissues which are instrumental in its production, the development being continued after the normal position of the calcified part has been lost' (*Syd. Soc. Lex.*).

1859 J. TOMES *Dental Surg.* 164 The crown and the fang being joined at an angle, presenting that peculiarity of conformation which has been denominated *dilaceration.* **1878** T. BRYANT *Pract. Surg.* I. 562 Dilaceration is due to a shifting of the forming tooth on its base.

dilactic (daɪ'læktɪk), *a. Chem.* [f. DI-[2] 2 + LACTIC.] In *dilactic acid*, a pale yellow, amorphous, easily fusible substance, formed, along with lactide, by heating lactic acid. Formula $C_6H_{10}O_5{\cdot}2(C_3H_4O){\cdot}O_2H_2$. Its salts are **di'lactates.**

(So called because it contains two equivalents of lactyl, C_3H_4O, the radical of lactic acid.)

1863–72 WATTS *Dict. Chem.* III. 461.

dilambdodont (daɪ'læmdəʊdɒnt), *a. Zool.* [f. Gr. δι-, DI-[2] + λάμβδα the letter lambda, Λ + ὀδοντ- tooth.] Having oblong molar teeth with two Λ- or V-shaped ridges; as is the case with the Insectivorous Mammals of the northern hemisphere, the mole, hedgehog, etc.

dilamination (daɪlæmɪ'neɪʃən). *Bot.* [n. of action from L. *dīlāmināre* to split in two, f. *di-*, *dis-* asunder + *lāmina* thin plate, layer.] Separation into laminæ, or splitting off of a lamina.

1849 BALFOUR *Man. Bot.* 184 A process of dilamination, or chorization. **1875** *Ibid.* (ed. 5) 371 Parts of the flower are often increased by a process of deduplication, unlining, dilamination, or chorization, i.e. the separation of a lamina from organs already formed. **1883** *Syd. Soc. Lex.*, *Dilamination*, the separation into layers of parts originally continuous.

†di'laniate, *v. Obs.* [f. L. *dīlaniāt-* ppl. stem of *dīlaniāre* to tear in pieces, f. *dī-* apart + *laniāre* to tear.] *trans.* To rend or tear in pieces. Hence **di'laniated** *ppl. a.*

1535 W. OVERBURY *Let. to Crumwel* in Strype *Eccl. Mem.* I. xxix. 206 There be many perverse men, which do dilaniate the flock of Christ. **1597** *1st Pt. Return fr. Parnass.* III. i. 965, I have restored thy dylaniated back..to those prittie clothes wherin thou now walkest. **1644** HOWELL *Eng. Tears* in *Harl. Misc.* (Malh.) V. 451 Rather than they would dilaniate the intrails of their own mother, fair Italy..they met halfway. **1653** W. SCLATER *Fun. Serm.* (1654) 8 Being dilaniated, and rent in his body.

†dilani'ation. *Obs.* [n. of action f. prec.: cf. L. *laniātiōn-em* tearing.] The action of tearing or rending in pieces.

1569 J. SANFORD tr. *Agrippa's Van. Artes* 11 b, The dilaniation of Bacchus. *a* **1656** BP. HALL *Wks.* (1837–9) VI. 348 (D.) To challenge and provoke the furious lions to his dilaniation. **1690** *Secr. Hist. Chas. II & Jas. II* 32 The scars of his cruel dilaniations.

†di'lapidate, *ppl. a. Obs.* or *arch.* Also 7 delapidat. [ad. L. *dīlapidāt-us*, pa. pple. of *dīlapidāre*: see next.] = DILAPIDATED. (Chiefly as *pa. pple.*)

1590 [see next 2]. **1638** SIR T. HERBERT *Trav.* (ed. 2) 114 It was taken An. 1622, and by them delapidat and depopulated. **1865** KINGSLEY *Herew.* (1866) I. i. 29 The keep even in Leland's time..somewhat dilapidate.

dilapidate (dɪ'læpɪdeɪt), *v.* Also 7–9 de-. [ad. L. *dīlapidāre* lit. 'to scatter as if throwing stones', to throw away, destroy, f. *di-*, *dis-* asunder + *lapidāre* to throw stones, f. *lapid-em* stone. Taken in Eng. in a more literal sense than was usual in L.]

1. *trans.* To bring (a building) into a state of decay or of partial ruin. Also *fig.*

1570 LEVINS *Manip.* 41/36 To Dilapidate, *dilapidare.* **1634** SIR T. HERBERT *Trav.* 216 A ruined Chappell..built by the Spaniard, and delapidated by the Dutch. **1706** SIBBALD *Hist. Picts* in *Misc. Scot.* I. 111 It has been sadly dilapidated of late, to obtain stones to build a house. **1824** W. IRVING *T. Trav.* I. 14 The whole side was dilapidated, and seemed like the wing of a house shut up. **1854** LOWELL *Jrnl. Italy* Prose Wks. 1890 I. 208 His whole figure suddenly dilapidates itself, assuming a tremble of professional weakness.

2. *fig.* To waste, squander (a benefice or estate).

1590 in Row *Hist. Kirk* (Maitland) 408 All quho have dilapidat benefices..to the preiudice of the Kirk. **1642** FULLER *Holy & Prof. St.* III. vi. 168 Those who by overbuilding their houses have dilapidated their lands. *a* **1711** KEN *Serm.* Wks. (1838) 160 Nothing..more certainly dilapidates their estates..than the surfeits of intemperance. **1844** LINGARD *Anglo-Sax. Ch.* (1858) I. vi. 234 *note*, Having dilapidated the revenues.

absol. **1692** H. WHARTON *Def. Pluralities* 159 (T.) Many pluralists..do neither dilapidate, nor neglect alms.

3. *intr.* To become dilapidated; to fall into ruin, decay, or disrepair.

1712 PRIDEAUX *Direct. Ch.-wardens* (ed. 4) 25 [Charged] with the supervisal..of..the..House, to see that [it] be [not] permitted to dilapidate and fall into decay. **1775** JOHNSON *Journ. West. Isl., Elgin*, The church of Elgin..was

..shamefully suffered to dilapidate by deliberate robbery and frigid indifference. **1858** De Quincey *Pope* Wks. IX. 30 To find one's fortune dilapidating by changes so rapid.

Hence **di'lapidating** *ppl. a.*

1779–81 Johnson *L.P., Dyer*, In the neighbourhood of dilapidating Edifices. **1805** Whitaker *Hist. Craven* 500 How..are our dilapidating churches to be rebuilt? **1854** H. Miller *Sch. & Schm.* (1858) 220 Thirty years..[have] exerted their dilapidating effects on [the obelisks].

dilapidated (dɪˈlæpɪdeɪtɪd), *ppl. a.* [f. prec. + -ED[1].] Fallen into ruin or disrepair; ruined, impaired, broken down. (*lit.* and *fig.*)

a **1806** Bp. Horsley *Serm.* xxxv. (R.), The inconvenience of succeeding to dilapidated houses. **1817** Sir J. Newport in *Parl. Deb.* 1484 The danger was to be apprehended from the dilapidated state of the finances. **1865** Dickens *Mut. Fr.* II. i, A dilapidated old country villa. **1874** Ruskin *Fors Clav.* IV. xxxvii. 2 A large and dilapidated pair of woman's shoes.

dilapidation (dɪˌlæpɪˈdeɪʃən). Also 5–9 de-. [ad. L. *dīlapidātiōn-em* a squandering, n. of action f. *dīlapidāre*: see DILAPIDATE *v.*]

1. The action of dilapidating or expending wastefully; wasteful expenditure, squandering.

c **1460** Fortescue *Abs. & Lim. Mon.* x, Sellynge off a kynges livelod, is propirly callid delapidacion off his crowne. **1604** R. Cawdrey *Table Alph.*, *Dilapidation*, wastefull spending, or suffering to goe to decay. **1682** Burnet *Rights Princes* Pref. 24 Against the Dilapidations of the Revenues of the Church. **1798** Malthus *Popul.* (1878) 427 The dilapidation of the national resources. **1818** Hallam *Mid. Ages* viii. III. (1855) III. 160 The dilapidation which had taken place in the royal demesnes.

2. The action of bringing (a building, etc.) into ruin, decay, or disrepair.

1820 W. Irving *Sketch Bk.* I. 272 Subject to the dilapidations of time and the caprice of fashion. **1886** *Act 49–50 Vict.* c. 29. §1 (3) The crofter shall not..persistently injure the holding by the dilapidation of buildings.

3. *Law.* The action of pulling down, allowing to fall into a state of disrepair, or in any way impairing ecclesiastical property belonging to an incumbency.

c **1425** Wyntoun *Cron.* IX. xx. 116 Ane auld abbote swa put downe For opyn dilapidatioune. **1511** Colet *Serm. to Conuocacion* A vij a, Suynge for tithes, for offrynge, for mortuaries, for delapidations, by the right and title of the churche. *a* **1613** Overbury *Charac.*, *Ordinary Widdow* Wks. (1856) 140 A churchman she dare not venture upon; for she hath heard widowes complain of dilapidations. **1768** Blackstone *Comm.* III. 91 Dilapidations..are a kind of ecclesiastical waste, either voluntary, by pulling down; or permissive, by suffering the chancel, parsonage-house, and other buildings..to decay. **1874** Micklethwaite *Mod. Par. Churches* 237 Experience in the valuation of dilapidations.

b. *loosely.* The sums charged against an incumbent or his representatives to make good such damage incurred during his incumbency.

1553 *Lanc. Wills* (1857) II. 263, I thinke my successors cannot..requyer any dylapidacions ffor Sefton. **1868** Milman *St. Paul's* 317 Considerable sums as dilapidations for the repair of the body of the church.

attrib. **1772** *Ann. Reg.* 145 His Lordship..will lay out the dilapidation sum..in building a house for the see.

4. The action of falling into decay; the condition of being in ruins or in disrepair. (*lit.* and *fig.*)

1638 Sir T. Herbert *Trav.* (ed. 2) 219 The Calyph pittied her delapidations, and..begun to reare her up againe, and builded [etc.]. **1684** Goodman *Winter Evening Confer.* I. (L.), By keeping a strict account of incomes and expences, a man might easily preserve an estate from dilapidation. **1796** Morse *Amer. Geog.* I. 507 The works..are in such a state of delapidation. **1860** Mrs. Harvey *Cruise Claymore* xi. 303 In striking contrast to the wretched delapidation of the Holy Sepulchre. **1861** F. Hall in *Jrnl. Asiat. Soc. Bengal* 14 An edifice now lying in littered dilapidation.

5. The falling of stones or masses of rock from mountains or cliffs by natural agency.

1794 Sullivan *View Nat.* II. 165 In the course of time they shall be exposed from the dilapidations of the mountain. **1816** Keatinge *Trav.* (1817) I. 61 The dilapidation taking place on the east, has caused an opening ..into the heart of the mountain. **1875** Lyell *Princ. Geol.* I. II. xv. 356 The rocks have been suffering from dilapidation.

b. *concr.* A mass or collection of stone which has fallen from a mountain or height; debris.

1816 Keatinge *Trav.* (1817) I. 68 Masses of dilapidation of various sizes. *Ibid.* II. 48 The whole tract is covered with reduced dilapidation, either hornstone, trapp, or basalt.

dilapidator (dɪˈlæpɪdeɪtə(r)). [agent-n., in L. form, from *dīlapidāre*: see DILAPIDATE *v.* and -OR. Cf. F. *dilapidateur* (15th c. in Hatz.-Darm.] One who dilapidates or brings into a ruinous condition; one who allows a building to fall into disrepair.

1692 H. Wharton *Def. Pluralities* 156 (T.) You shall seldom see a non-resident, but he is also a dilapidator. **1697** Bp. of Lincoln *Adv. Clergy* 33 Dilapidators many times die insolvent and so leave the whole Burden of the Repair upon the Successour. **1812** Sir R. Wilson *Priv. Diary* I. 39, I only allowed myself to become a purchaser and not a dilapidator. **1890** *Tablet* 24 May 813 Power to restrain both builders and dilapidators within reasonable limits.

dilapse, var. of DELAPSE *v.*, to slip down.

1816 Keatinge *Trav.* (1817) I. 149 A round hill, one side of which has dilapsed nearly perpendicularly.

dilash, var. of DELASH *v. Obs.*, to let off.

1582–8 *Hist. James VI* (1804) 209 He cawsit dilashe sum cannons in face of the fyre, to terifie the people to approach.

dilatability (daɪˌleɪtəˈbɪlɪtɪ, dɪ-). [f. next: see -ITY.] The quality of being dilatable, capacity of being dilated.

1691 Ray *Creation* I. (1714) 28 We take notice of the wonderful dilatability or extensiveness of the throats..of serpents. **1773** *Phil. Trans.* LXIII. 435 Substances that.. differed in their dilatability. **1826** Henry *Elem. Chem.* I. 138 The law of the dilatability of gases by heat has already been stated. **1875** Croll *Climate & T.* vii. 116 Taking the dilatability of sea water to be the same as that of fresh.

dilatable (daɪˈleɪtəb(ə)l, dɪ-), *a.*[1] [f. DILATE *v.* + -ABLE. Cf. F. *dilatable* (Cotgr. 1611).] Capable of being dilated, widened out, extended, or enlarged; expansible.

1610 Healey *St. Aug. Citie of God* XI. v. (1620) 391 They will neither make God's essence dilatable nor limitable. *a* **1691** Boyle *Hist. Air* i. (1692) 1 That thin..compressible and dilatable Body in which we breath. **1782** A. Monro *Compar. Anat.* (ed. 3) 28 Owls..have the pupil very dilatable. **1851** Herschel *Stud. Nat. Phil.* III. v. 319 Of the several forms of natural bodies, gases and vapours are observed to be most dilatable.

Hence **di'latableness.**

1727 Bailey vol. II., *Dilatableness*, capableness of being widened.

†**dilatable**, *a.*[2] *Obs.*, erroneous f. DELITABLE (also *diletabil*, *dilitable*, etc.).

c **1400** tr. *Secreta Secret.*, *Gov. Lordsh.* 57 A lyf þat may noght be chaungyd, a kyngdome ay lastand dilatable.

dilatancy (daɪˈleɪtənsɪ, dɪ-). [f. next: see -ANCY.] The property of dilating or expanding; *spec.* that of expanding in bulk with change of shape, exhibited by granular masses, and due to the increase of space between their rigid particles when their position is changed.

1885 O. Reynolds in *Proc. Brit. Assoc.* 896 (*title*) On the Dilatancy of Media composed of Rigid Particles in Contact. —— *Ibid.*, A very fundamental property of granular masses. To this property he [O. Reynolds] gave the name of *dilatancy*. It is exhibited in any arrangement of particles where change of bulk is dependent upon change of shape. **1886** *Sat. Rev.* 28 Aug. 295 Owens College had at that time only begun to display its 'dilatancy', if we may make bold to use a term recently applied by one of its professors to a force which he claims to have discovered in the physical world.

dilatant (daɪˈleɪtənt, dɪ-), *a.* and *sb.* [ad. L. *dīlātānt-em* (or a. F. *dilatant*) pr. pple. of L. *dīlātāre* (F. *dilater*) to DILATE: see -ANT.]

A. *adj.* Dilating, expanding; expansive.

1841 *Fraser's Mag.* XXIII. 216 My mind had greatly the advantage of my body; this being small, mean, and unseemly, that capacious, lively, and dilatant. **1885** O. Reynolds in *Proc. Brit. Assoc.* 897 When the dilatant material, such as shot or sand, is bounded by smooth surfaces, the layer of grains adjacent to the surface is in a condition differing from that of the grains within the mass.

B. *sb.* **a.** A substance having the property of dilating or expanding. **b.** A surgical instrument used for dilating, a dilatator.

†'**dilatate**, *v. Obs.* [f. L. *dīlātāt-* ppl. stem of *dīlātāre*: see DILATE *v.*[2]] = DILATE *v.*[2].

1613 Jackson *Creed* II. 259 Such pleasant obiects as might dilatate the heart and spirites.

dilatate (ˈdaɪləteɪt), *ppl. a. Zool.* [ad. L. *dīlātātus*, pa. pple. of *dīlātāre* to DILATE.] Dilated.

1846 Dana *Zooph.* (1845) 134 Sparingly dilatate at each extremity.

dilatation (daɪləˈteɪʃən). [a. OF. *dilatacion*, *-ation* (14th c. in Hatz.-Darm.) = It. *dilatazione*, Sp. *dilatacion*, ad. L. *dīlātātiōn-em*, n. of action f. *dīlātā-re* to DILATE *v.*[2]]

1. a. The action or process of dilating; the condition of being dilated; widening out, expansion, enlargement. (Chiefly in *Physics* and *Physiol.*)

c **1400** *Lanfranc's Cirurg.* 66 And if þat þe blood go out of arterie þou schalt knowe it bi construccion and dilatacion of þe same arterie. **1589** Cogan *Haven Health* ccxliii (1636) 299 By blowing of the winde or dilatation of the ayre. **1660** Boyle *New Exp. Phys. Mech.* i. 28 It appears not that any compression of the Air preceded its spontaneous Dilatation or Expansion of it self. **1685** —— *Effects of Mot.* ix. 108 The dilatation of metals..by Heat. **1732** Arbuthnot *Rules of Diet* 389 There may be a Dropsy..by a Dilatation of the serous Vessels. **1826** Henry *Elem. Chem.* I. 80 The expansion or dilatation of bodies..is an almost universal effect of an increase of temperature. **1849** Mrs. Somerville *Connect. Phys. Sc.* xvii. 156 Alternate condensations and dilatations of the strata. **1871** W. A. Hammond *Dis. Nerv. Syst.* 46 The emotions of shame, of anger, and others, cause the face to become red from dilatation of the blood-vessels.

fig. **1659** Stanley *Hist. Philos.* XIII. (1701) 590/2 Pleasure ..is produced with a kind of dilatation and exaltation of the Soul. **1762** Kames *Elem. Crit.* (1833) 221 We feel a gradual dilatation of mind. **1877** Wraxall *Hugo's Miserables* IV. xlix. 33 There is a dilatation of thought peculiar to the vicinity of a tomb.

b. *concr.* A dilated form, formation, or portion of any structure.

1833 Thirlwall in *Philol. Museum* II. 163 Memnon is only a dilatation of Menon. **1854** Woodward *Mollusca* II. 161 A similar contractile dilatation exists at the end of the foot. **1857** Berkeley *Cryptog. Bot.* §73 The only semblance of a root is a little dilatation of the base. **1861** Hulme tr. *Moquin-Tandon* II. I. 43 This dilatation divides the digestive canal into three parts.

c. dilatation and curettage (or **curetting**) *Gynæcol.*, an operation involving dilatation of the cervix and curettage of the uterus, carried out for diagnostic purposes, to terminate a pregnancy, or to arrest irregular menstrual bleeding.

1906 D. B. Hart in Allbutt et al. *Syst. Gynaecol.* (ed. 2) 70 *Dilatation and curetting.* This is a very important procedure where malignant disease of the mucous membrane of the body is suspected. **1920** H. S. Crossen *Operative Gynecol.* (ed. 2) v. 268 (*caption*) The safe method of securing the necessary fixation of the cervix, for Dilatation and Curettage. **1964** *Jrnl. Obstetrics & Gynaecol.* LXXI. 668/2 Dilatation and curettage has a major place in the diagnostic and therapeutic armamentarium of the obstetrician and gynaecologist.

2. The spreading abroad, extension, expansion (of immaterial or abstract things). *arch.*

1448 *Will of Hen. VI.* in Willis and Clark *Cambridge* (1886) I. 353 Dilatacion, and stablisshement of christen feith. **1610** Bp. Carleton *Jurisd.* 174 For preseruation and dilatation of peace and iustice. **1646** Sir J. Temple *Irish Rebell.* 65 Before I..come to declare the universal dilatation of [the rebellion] throughout the whole kingdom. **1839** Cdl. Wiseman *Cath. & Angl. Ch.* Ess. (1853) II. 232 To the end of the world, room will be left for the dilatation of religion.

3. The action or practice of dilating upon a subject in speech or writing; amplification, enlargement, diffuse treatment.

c **1386** Chaucer *Man of Law's T.* 134 What needeth gretter dilatacioun? *c* **1440** Capgrave *Life St. Kath.* IV. 2278 But this dilatacyon..longeth not to this lyf present. **1605** Bacon *Adv. Learn.* II. vii. §5. 28 God [is] Holy in the description or dilatation of his workes. **1645** Gaule *Cases Consc.* (1646) 4, I resolue against all such dilatations in this Epitome. **1779** Johnson *L.P., Dryden* Wks. II. 428 Little more than a dilatation of the praise given it by Pope. **1873** Lowell *Among my Books* Ser. II. 285, I have spoken of Spenser's fondness for dilatation as respects thoughts and images.

Hence **dila'tational** *a.*, of or pertaining to a dilatation.

1884 Bower & Scott *De Bary's Phaner.* 539 The first dilatational bands of the external cortex. **1895** Story-Maskelyne *Crystallogr.* i. 11 The dilatational changes resulting from variation of temperature in a crystal.

dilatative (daɪˈleɪtətɪv, ˈdaɪləteɪtɪv), *a.* [f. L. *dīlātāt-*, ppl. stem of *dīlātāre* + -IVE.] Of the nature of or tending to dilatation.

1727–51 Chambers *Cycl.* s.v. *Dilatation*, A new impetus is impressed thereon, from the dilatative cause. **1740** Stack in *Phil. Trans.* XLI. 429 Therefore the dilatative Effort of the Layers increases with the Layers in a greater Proportion than these Layers.

dilatator (ˈdaɪləˌteɪtə(r)). [a. L. *dīlātātor*, agent-n. from *dīlātā-re* to DILATE. In F. *dilatateur* (Cotgr. 1611). When treated as Latin, the stress is on the third syllable.] **a.** *Anat.* A muscle which dilates or expands a part; also *attrib.* **b.** *Surgery.* An instrument for dilating or distending an opening. (Also DILATER, and less correctly DILATOR.)

1611 Cotgr., *Dilatateur*, a dilatator, inlarger, widener; extender. **1878** Bell *Gegenbaur's Comp. Anat.* 571 In the Reptilia these are replaced by a constrictor and a dilatator muscle. **1883** *Syd. Soc. Lex.*, *Dilata'tor*, a widener. Applied to certain muscles whose office is to widen or dilate the parts on which they act; also applied to instruments for opening or enlarging the entrances to cavities or passages.

dilatatory (daɪˈleɪtətərɪ). *Surg.* Also in Lat. form -'orium. [ad. F. *dilatatoire* (16th c. in Hatz.-Darm.), ad. med. or mod.L. *dīlātātōrium* (see quot. 1731), f. L. *dīlātāt-*, ppl. stem of *dīlātā-re* to dilate.] An instrument for dilating a part or organ.

1611 Cotgr., *Dilatatoire*, a dilatatorie or inlarger; an Instrument wherewith Chirurgions open those partes that by sicknesse, or other accident, are too much closed. **1656** in Blount *Glossogr.* **1706** Phillips *Dilatatory* or *Dilater*. **1731–1800** Bailey, *Dilatatorium* (with Surgeons) an instrument to open any part, as the mouth, womb or fundament. **1823** Crabb *Techn. Dict.*, *Dilatato'rium* (*Surg.*), a surgical instrument for dilating the mouth; also for pulling barbed irons out of a wound. **1883** *Syd. Soc. Lex.*, *Dilatato'rium.*

†**di'late**, *v.*[1] *Obs.* Also 4 **deleate**, 5 **dylate**, 5–6 **de-**. [a. F. *dilater* to defer, delay, temporize, ad. med.L. *dīlātāre* to defer, delay, put off, protract, freq. of *differre* to DEFER: cf. DILATORY. The sense 'prolong' comes so near 'enlarge', 'expand', or 'set forth at length', in DILATE *v.*[2], that the two verbs were probably not thought of as distinct words.]

1. *trans.* To delay, defer.

1399 *Pol. Poems* (Rolls) II. 14 To ȝive ous pes, which longe hath be deleated. **1485** Caxton *Chas. Gt.* 45 Thou oughtest to dylate the vengeaunce tyll the furour be passed. *c* **1485** *Digby Myst.* II. 497 To delate yt any lenger yt ys not best. **1556** J. Heywood *Spider & F.* lii. 19 Without more time delated. **1574** Hellowes *Gueuara's Fam. Ep.* (1577) 158 Sometimes the sorrowful sutor doth more feele a rough word they speake, then the iustice they dilate. **1581** T. Howell *Deuises* (1879) 213 Some..with delayes the matter will delate. **1620** Shelton *Quix.* II. IV. ix. 120 Why dost thou with these so many untoward breathings delate the making of mine end happy?

2. To extend in time, protract, prolong, lengthen.

1489 CAXTON *Faytes of A.* II. vi. 103 The cas happed that the battaylle was somwhat dylated. **1596** BELL *Surv. Popery* II. II. v. 168 These houres are sometimes dilated. **1658** OSBORN *Adv. Son* (1673) 146 A..way to dilate a remembrance beyond the banks of Forgetfulness.

Hence **di'lated** *ppl. a.*, **di'lating** *vbl. sb.*

1509-10 *Act 1 Hen. VIII*, c. 4, Preamb., Delatyng of so longe tyme. **1556** J. HEYWOOD *Spider & F.* xxxv. 10 Without more delated delaie. *a* **1657** R. LOVEDAY *Lett.* (1663) 165 Your dilated resolutions of seeing London.

dilate (dɪ-, daɪ'leɪt), *v.*[2] Also 6-7 **delate**. [a. F. *dilate-r* (Oresme, 14th c.), ad. L. *dīlātāre* to spread out, amplify, extend, widen, f. *dī-*, *dis-* (DIS- 1) + *lāt-us* broad, wide.]

1. *trans.* To make wider or larger; to increase the width of, widen; to expand, amplify, enlarge.

1528 PAYNEL *Salerne's Regim.* Y b, Lekes delate the matrice. **1555** EDEN *Decades* 261 Al thynges..are dilated by heate. **1579** TWYNE *Phisicke agst. Fort.* II. Ep. Ded. 161 a, I might dilate this discourse with a thousand argumentes. **1646** SIR T. BROWNE *Pseud. Ep.* III. xxi. 162 It is enforced to dilate and hold open the jawes. **1697** POTTER *Antiq. Greece* III. xvi. (1715) 135 The sails were contracted, dilated, or chang'd from one side to another. **1749** SMOLLETT *Regicide* IV. v, While the deep groan Dilates thy lab'ring breast? **1835-6** TODD *Cycl. Anat.* I. 403/2, Haller found..the bladder so dilated that it was capable of containing twenty pounds of water. **1851** HERSCHEL *Stud. Nat. Phil.* II. vii. 193 Heat dilates matter with an irresistible force.

b. *fig.*

c **1450** tr. *De Imitatione* III. liv, Dilate þin herte, & resceyue þis holy inspiracion wiþ all maner desir. **1526** *Pilgr. Perf.* (W. de W. 1531) 275 b, Holy charite..dilateth & spredeth the herte of man or woman. **1625** F. MARKHAM *Bk. Hon.* II. ii. 47 Another sort, who haue dilated and made excellent their bloods, by the great happiness of their fortunate Issues and Noble Matches or Mariages. **1704** HEARNE *Duct. Hist.* (1714) I. 139 The Reader may take Eachard's Roman History as being..proper to dilate the Student's knowledge in Roman Affairs. **1871** FARRAR *Witn. Hist.* v. 193 As we have seen, it [Christianity] dilates our whole being.

c. *refl.*

1539 TAVERNER *Erasm. Prov.* (1552) 60 We be therefore warned that we dylate not our selues beyond our condition and state. **1653** WHARTON *Disc. Comets* Wks. (1683) 149 There at first appeared a small Comet, afterward it mounted and dilated it self on high. **1715** LEONI *Palladio's Archit.* (1742) I. 5 Copper is..very pliable, and dilates it self into very thin Leaves. **1875** JOWETT *Plato* (ed. 2) III. 379 Will he not dilate and elevate himself in the fulness of vain pomp and senseless pride?

†**2.** To spread abroad; to extend, diffuse, or disperse through a wide space or region. *lit.* and *fig. Obs.*

1430 *Instr. Ambass.* in Rymer *Foedera* (1710) X. 725 Christen Feith and beleue had..be dilated through the World. **1520** *Caxton's Chron. Eng.* III. 20 b/1 In al this tyme the Empyre of Rome was not dylated passynge 12 myle. **1548-77** VICARY *Anat.* ii. (1888) 21 This Artere..is more obedient to be delated abrode through al the lunges. **1549** *Compl. Scotl.* Epist. 1 The immortal gloir..is abundantly dilatit athort al cuntreis. **1590** SPENSER *F.Q.* II. xii. 53 Bowes and braunches which did broad dilate Their clasping armes. **1644** EVELYN *Sylva* (1679) 4 The tree being of a kind apt to dilate its roots. **1719** J. T. PHILIPPS tr. *34 Conferences* 348 This Juncture..favourable for dilating the Knowledge of Christ among these Nations.

b. *refl.*

1660 R. COKE *Power & Subj.* 258 The curing of this Gangrene so dilating it self both in Church, Court and State. **1702** ECHARD *Eccl. Hist.* (1710) 246 The joy of which preferment..dilated itself through all the Roman empire.

3. *intr.* (for *refl.*) To become wider or larger; to spread out, widen, enlarge, expand.

1636 G. SANDYS *Paraphr. Ps.* 107 And Naphtali, which borders on Old Jordan, where his stream dilates. **1641** WILKINS *Math. Magick* II. v. (1648) 182 Shall be like the fins of a fish to contract and dilate. **1822** LAMB *Elia* Ser. I. *Praise Chimneysw.*, The nostrils of the young rogues dilated at the savour. **1849** MISS MULOCK *Ogilvies* ii, Her eye dilating and her cheek glowing. **1871** B. STEWART *Heat* §32 When a body increases in temperature it also expands in volume or dilates. **1879** HARLAN *Eyesight* ii. 16 The pupil has the property of contracting and dilating.

b. *fig.* To expand itself; †to have full scope.

1651 N. BACON *Disc. Govt. Eng.* II. xiii. (1739) 73 The Duke of Gloucester was of such noble parts, that they could hardly dilate in any work inferior to the Government of a Kingdom. **1847** H. ROGERS *Ess.* I. v. 260 These flimsy objections dilate into monstrous dimensions. **1863** DRAPER *Intell. Devel. Europe* iii. (1865) 66 A false inference like this soon dilated into a general doctrine.

†**4.** *trans.* To relate, describe, or set forth at length; to enlarge or expatiate upon. *Obs.*

1393 GOWER *Conf.* III. 190 It nedeth nought that I dilate The pris which preised is algate. *c* **1460** CAPGRAVE *Chron.* 1 It plesed me..to gader a schort remembrance of elde stories, that whanne I loke upon hem..I can sone dilate the circumstaunses. *a* **1533** FRITH *Disput. Purgat.* Prol. (1829) 94 Rastell hath enterprised to dilate this matter, and hath divided it into three Dialogues. **1632** LITHGOW *Trav.* viii. 346 Having met with some of their Brethren..and delated to them their deathes. *c* **1790** COWPER *Comm. Milton's P.L.* II. 1024-33 It is..a common thing with poets to touch slightly beforehand, a subject which they mean to dilate in the sequel. **1801** GOUV. MORRIS in Sparks *Life & Writ.* (1832) III. 150, I dare give only hints; it would be presumptuous to dilate them.

5. *intr.* To discourse or write at large; to enlarge, expatiate. Const. †*of* (obs.), *on*, *upon*.

1560 WHITEHORNE *Arte Warre* (1588) 105, I might haue delated more vpon the seruice on horsebacke, and after haue reasoned of the warre on the Sea. **1592** NASHE *P. Penilesse* (ed. 2) 13 a, Experience reproues me for a foole, for delating on so manifest a case. **1609** W. M. *Man in Moone* (1849) 25, I could amply delate of thy sinne, but I know it needlesse. **1689-92** LOCKE *Toleration* III. vii. Wks. 1727 II. 379 The terrible Consequences you dilate on..I leave you for your private use. **1697** COLLIER *Ess. Mor. Subj.* I. (1709) 238 Were it not too sad an Argument to dilate upon. **1786** T. JEFFERSON *Writ.* (1859) II. 33 You were dilating with your new acquaintances. **1820** LAMB *Elia* Ser. I. *South-sea Ho.*, How would he dilate into secret history. **1838** DICKENS *Nich. Nick.* xxvi, She proceeded to dilate upon the perfections of Miss Nickleby. **1861** F. HALL in *Jrnl. Asiat. Soc. Bengal* 146 But it is needless to dilate. **1874** STUBBS *Const. Hist.* (1875) III. xviii. 122 The chancellor..dilated at length on the perjuries of Duke Philip.

†**b.** *refl.* To express oneself at length or diffusely. *Obs. rare.*

1644 DIGBY *Nat. Bodies* II. (1645) 9 Concerning which wee shall not need to dilate our selves any further. **1655** FULLER *Ch. Hist.* IV. i. §6 In process of time, Wicliffe might delate himself in supplemental and additional Opinions. *a* **1672** WOOD *Life* (Oxf. Hist. Soc.) I. 161 Dr. Richard Gardiner..dilating himself on Christ's miracle of turning water into wine.

dilate (daɪ'leɪt), *a. arch.* Also 7 **delate**. [In form, ad. L. *dīlāt-us* carried in different ways, spread abroad, dispersed, published, pa. pple. of *differre*; but in sense, answering to L. *dīlātāt-us*, widened, expanded, and so perh. short for *dilated*.] = DILATED, widely extended or expanded.

1471 RIPLEY *Comp. Alch.* XI. in Ashm. (1652) 182 With mykyll more Lycour dylate. **1603** B. JONSON *Sejanus* I. ii, Instructed With so dilate and absolute a power. **1614** W. B. *Philosopher's Banquet* (ed. 2) 12 A minde so delate and ample. **1677** HALE *Prim. Orig. Man.* II. vii. 187 The Seas possibly more dilate and extended. **1803** W. TAYLOR in *Ann. Rev.* I. 301 Who narrates with dilate diffusion. **1883** FENN *Eli's Childr.* III. III. ii. 180 Her dilate and frightened eyes softened with tears.

†**di'late**, *sb. Obs. rare.* [f. DILATE *v.*[2]] = DILATATION 3.

1595 MARKHAM *Sir R. Grinvile* (Arb.) 58 Thanks hardie Midleton for thy dilate.

dilate, obs. form of DELATE, DELETE.

dilated (daɪ'leɪtɪd), *ppl. a.* [f. DILATE *v.*[2] + -ED[1].] Widened, expanded, distended, diffused, etc.: see the verb.

c **1450** tr. *De Imitatione* III. lvi, þat þou wiþ a dilated herte mowe renne þe way of my commandementes. **1606** SHAKS. *Tr. & Cr.* II. iii. 261 A shore confines Thy spacious and dilated parts. **1651** STANLEY *Poems* 29 In an elms dilated shade. **1667** MILTON *P.L.* IV. 986 Satan allarm'd Collecting all his might dilated stood. **1758** J. S. *Le Dran's Observ. Surg.* (1771) 264 The dilated Urethra was very thin. **1859** TENNYSON *Enid* 1445 Then there flutter'd in, Half-bold, half-frighted, with dilated eyes, A tribe of women. **1865** KINGSLEY *Herew.* x. (1866) 157 His dilated nostril.

†**b.** Enlarged upon. *Obs.*

1599 JAS. I *Βασιλ. Δωρον* (1682) 74 Exercise true wisdome; in discerning wisely betwixt true and false reports; first..and last [considering] the nature and by-past life of the dilated person.

†**c.** *Cryst.* (See quot.) *Obs.*

1805-17 R. JAMESON *Char. Min.* 215 *Dilated*, the name given to a variety of dodecahedral calcareous spar, in which the bases of the extreme pentagons are in some degree enlarged by the inclination of the lateral planes.

d. *Her.* 'Opened or extended. Applied to a Pair of Compasses, Barnacles, etc.' Cussans, 1882.

Hence **di'latedly** *adv.*, in a dilated manner, with dilatation; diffusely.

1627 FELTHAM *Resolves* xxi. (ed. 1) 64 His..aberrations, wherein he hath dilatedly tumbled himselfe.

†**di'latement**. *Obs. rare.* [f. DILATE *v.*[2] + -MENT.] A dilating; a dilated or diffuse passage.

1593 NASHE *Christ's T.* (1613) 86 Euen in this dilatement against Ambition, the diuel seekes to set in a foote of affected applause.

dilater (daɪ'leɪtə(r)). [f. DILATE *v.*[2] + -ER[1]. Now mostly supplanted by the less correctly formed DILATOR[1].] One who or that which dilates.

1605 SHELTON *Commend. Verses* in Verstegan *Dec. Intell.*, Thy labours shew thy will to dignifie The first dilaters of thy famous Nation. **1640** BP. HALL *Chr. Moder.* (ed. Ward) 38/1 Away, then, ye cruel torturers of opinions, dilaters of errors, delators of your brethren.

b. *spec.* A surgical instrument used to dilate a part; = DILATOR *sb.*[1] a.

1634 T. JOHNSON *Parey's Chirurg.* 464 A dilater made for to open the mouth and teeth. **1668** R. L'ESTRANGE *Vis. Quev.* (1708) 28 In the tail of these, came the Surgeons, laden with Pincers..Dilaters, Scissers. **1706** PHILLIPS (ed. Kersey), *Dilatatory*, or *Dilater*, a Surgeon's dilating Instrument, hollow on the inside, to draw barbed Iron, &c. out of a Wound: Also an Instrument with which the Mouth of the Womb may be dilated. **1721-1800** BAILEY, *Dilater*.

c. *Anat.* A muscle which dilates or expands a part; = DILATATOR a, DILATOR *sb.*[1] b.

1683 SNAPE *Anat. Horse* IV. xiv. (1686) 171 Of the Dilaters or those that widen the Chest there are four pair.

dilater, obs. form of DELATOR, accuser.

dilating (daɪ'leɪtɪŋ), *vbl. sb.* [f. DILATE *v.*[2] + -ING[1].] The action of the verb DILATE, in various senses; enlargement, expansion.

1529 MORE *Comf. agst. Trib.* III. Wks. 1213/2 Among other [tokens] the comyng in of the Jewes, and yᵉ dilating of christendome againe. **1532** —— *Confut. Tindale* ibid. 648/2 For now in dylating and declaring of hys conclusion, he addeth one thinge. **1586** J. HOOKER *Girald. Irel.* in *Holinshed* II. 36/1 Doo grant that you for the dilating of Gods church ..doo enter to possesse that land. **1657** J. SMITH *Myst. Rhet.* 114 Paradiastole is a dilating or enlarging of a matter by interpretation. **1703** MAUNDRELL *Journ. Jerus.* (1732) 12 Where the waters by dilating were become shallower. **1791** MAD. D'ARBLAY *Diary* Sept., A few memorandums for my own dilating upon at our meeting.

di'lating, *ppl. a.* [f. DILATE *v.*[2] + -ING[2].] That dilates or expands: see the verb.

1581 T. HOWELL *Deuises* (1879) 192 In my delating brains, a thousand thoughts were fed. **1593** *Tell-Troth's N.Y. Gift* 4 With such a dilatinge narration. **1644** DIGBY *Nat. Bodies* I. (1645) 290 To fill those capacities which the dilating heat hath made. **1805** SOUTHEY *Madoc in W.* iv, Through the broken cloud, Appeared the bright dilating blue of heaven. **1854** BADHAM *Halieut.* 248 A dilating crest which grows red at the nuptial season.

Hence **di'latingly** *adv.*

1891 G. MEREDITH *One of our Conq.* II. vi. 150 The colonel eyed Mrs. Blathenoy dilatingly.

†**di'lation**[1]. *Obs.* Also 5-6 **de-**, **dy-**. [a. OF. *dilacion* (13th c. in Hatz.-Darm.), mod.F. *dilation*, It. *dilazione*, ad. L. *dīlātiōn-em*, n. of action from *differre*, *dīlāt-* to defer, delay, put off: cf. DILATE *v.*[1]] Delay, procrastination, postponement.

14.. LYDG. *Temple of Glas* 877 Beþe not astoneid of no wilfulnes, Ne nouȝt dispeired of þis dilacioun. **1430** —— *Chron. Troy* III. xxv, Without abode or longe delacyon. *Ibid.* IV. xxxiv, I wyll nowe make no dylacyon. **1552** LATIMER *Serm. Lord's Pray.* iv. 31 The Angels..whiche doe the will and pleasure of God without dilation. **1585** PARSONS *Chr. Exerc.* II. v. 350 So the matter by delation came to no effect. **1627** BP. HALL *Heaven vpon Earth* §5 Some desperate debters, whom, after long dilations of payments..we altogether let goe for disability. **1665** J. WEBB *Stone-Heng* (1725) 160 The Dilation that attended the ultimate Appeal.

dilation[2] (daɪ'leɪʃən, dɪ-). [Improperly f. DILATE *v.*[2], which does not contain the verbal suffix *-ate*, but a stem *-late* from L. *lāt-us* broad, so that the etymologically correct formation is *dilatation*. (Cf. *coercion*, *dispution* for *disputation*, etc.).]

1. = DILATATION 1.

1598 FLORIO, *Dilatione*, a dilation, enlarging or ouerspreading. [But **1611** corrects to *Dilatatione* a dilating, *Dilatione* a delaying.] **1603** HOLLAND *Plutarch's Mor.* 76 The dilations of the arteries. **1615** CROOKE *Body of Man* 641 The dilation is the cause of deepe and base voyces. **1796** SOUTHEY *Lett. fr. Spain* (1799) 125 The beauty of its dilation and contraction. **1847** TENNYSON *Princ.* VI. 172 At first her eye with slow dilation roll'd Dry flame. **1870** ROLLESTON *Anim. Life* 27 Transverse dilation of the thorax.

fig. **1647** H. MORE *Poems* 293 The soul..a sure fixation And centrall depth it hath, and free dilation. **1787** J. FRERE in *Microcosm* No. 25 ¶8 The mind perceives a sensible dilation of its faculties. **1823** LAMB *Elia* Ser. II. *Child Angel*, Those natural dilations of the youthful spirit.

†**2.** = DILATATION 2. *Obs.*

a **1631** DONNE in Spurgeon *Treas. Dav.* Ps. xc. 14 A prayer not only of appropriation to ourselves..but of a charitable dilation and extension to others.

3. = DILATATION 3.

1605 BACON *Adv. Learn.* II. vii. §6. 28 In the description or dilation of his works. **1623** COCKERAM II, A Speaking at large, *Dilation*. **1774** WARTON *Hist. Eng. Poetry* III. xxxix. 377 By needless dilations, and the affectations of circumlocution. **1851** AGN. STRICKLAND *Queens Scot.* II. 193 Frivolous terms and dilations cut away.

dilation[3], obs. var. of DELATION, accusation.

dilative (daɪ'leɪtɪv), *a.* [f. DILATE *v.*[2] + -IVE.]

1. Having the property of dilating or expanding (*trans.* and *intr.*) = DILATATIVE.

1634 T. JOHNSON *Parey's Chirurg.* III. i. (1678) 52 The Vital [faculty] is divided into the dilative and contractive faculty of the heart and arteries. **1671** GREW *Anat. Plants* I. ii. §4 A Body Porous, Dilative and Pliable. **1808** COLERIDGE *Lit. Rem.* (1836) II. 408 The..astringent power, comparatively uncounteracted by the dilative. *Ibid.* 411 The dilative force.

†**2.** Serving to diffuse (the food). *Obs.*

1528 PAYNEL *Salerne's Regim.* P, Drinkynge delatiue is moste conuenient after the fyrst digestion regularlye. **1589** COGAN *Haven Health* ccxv. (1636) 233 If any of these three uses of drinke be omitted, the drinke delative may be best spared. **1620** VENNER *Via Recta* (1650) 275 This drinking of Wine or Beer between meales..may well be termed both dilutive and dilative. **1634** H. R. *Salerne's Regim.* 90 Regularly, conuenient drinke dilatiue, or permixtiue, ought to be Wine, Ale, Beere, Perry, or such like.

dilatometer (daɪlə'tɒmɪtə(r)). [f. DILATE *v.*[2] + -(O)METER.] An instrument for determining the dilatation or expansion of a liquid by heat. Hence **dilato'metric** *a.*, relating to a dilatometer.

1882 *Nature* No. 639. 290 The numerous determinations of the expansion of water by heat..Experimenters..have used two methods—the hydrostatic and the dilatometric. **1883** *Syd. Soc. Lex.*, *Alcoholic dilatometer*, an instrument invented by Silvermann to determine the quantity of alcohol in a liquid, founded on the principle that water in passing from 0° C. to 100° C...expands ·0466 of its volume, and alcohol..·1252.

dilatometry (daɪlə'tɒmɪtrɪ). [f. DILATO-(METER + -METRY.] The measurement of expansion by means of a dilatometer.
1929 *Engineering* 13 Sept. 361/1 The very slow rates of heating or cooling, which can be used.. in dilatometry. **1930** *Ibid.* 16 May 654/1 *Dilatometry.* The specimens made for measuring the permeability were also used for measuring the dilatation.

dilator (daɪ'leɪtə(r)), *sb.*[1] [f. DILATE *v.*[2]: an irregular formation, the regular types being DILATER from Eng. *dilate*, and DILATATOR from L. *dīlātāre*.] One who or that which dilates: *spec.* **a.** *Surg.* An instrument used to dilate or distend an opening, passage, or organ; = DILATATOR b, DILATER b.
[**1634–1706**: see DILATER b.] **1688** R. HOLME *Armoury* III. 420/2 The Dilator is an Instrument to open or stretch out a thing to its breadth. **1830** S. COOPER *Dict. Pract. Surg.* (ed. 6) s.v. *Urethra*, With respect to dilators, as they are called.. their use is far from being much approved by the best modern surgeons. **1864** T. HOLMES *Syst. Surg.* (1870) IV. 963 The stricture being now fairly split, the dilator should be rotated.
b. *Anat.* A muscle or nerve which dilates or widens a part; = DILATATOR a, DILATER c. Also *attrib.*
[**1683**: see DILATER c.] *a* **1735** ARBUTHNOT (J.), The dilators of the nose are too strong in cholerick people. **1807** *Med. Jrnl.* XVII. 407 The radiating (or dilator) muscle of the Iris. **1844** J. G. WILKINSON *Swedenborg's Anim. Kingd.* II. i. 3 The muscles of the nose are three pair; two pair of dilator, and one pair of constrictors. **1878** FOSTER *Phys.* II. i. §2. 210 It acts energetically as a dilator-nerve.

†'**dilator, -our,** *a.* and *sb.*[2] *Sc. Obs.* Forms: 5–8 dilatour, 6 delatour, 8 dilator, delator. [a. F. *dilatoire* adj. 'dilatory', formerly also sb. 'delay', ad. L. *dīlātōri-us*, *dīlātōri-um*, dilatory, delaying, f. *dīlāt-* ppl. stem of *differre*: see DEFER *v.*[1], DILATE *v.*[1] For the form of the word cf. *declarator*.]
A. *adj.* (*Sc. Law.*) DILATORY; delaying, causing delay.
1503 *Sc. Acts Jas. IV* (1597) §65 There salbe na exception dilatour admitted against that summounds. *Ibid.* §95 Vpon dilatour or peremptour exception. **1609** SKENE *Reg. Maj.* 104 Gif the partie defendand will not vse any exception or defence dilatour. **1752** J. LOUTHIAN *Form of Process* (ed. 2) 267 All his Defences, both dilator and peremptor, which the Sheriff shall either advise in Court, or allow [etc.].
B. *sb.* (*Sc. Law.*) A delay; a cause of delay, a dilatory plea; = DILATORY *sb.*
1473 *Treaty w. Scotl.* in Rymer *Foedera* (1710) XI. 789 Withoutyn any dilatour or delais. **1583** SEMPILL *Leg. Bp. Andrews Life* 194 *Ballates* (1872) 205 Bot Doctor Patrick still replyed, With trickis and delatouris he denyed. **1717** WODROW *Corr.* (1843) II. 328, I scarce mention the unaccountable dilatours of settling vacancies. **1718** *Ibid.* II. 381 This was reckoned a delator, and opposed. **1752** J. LOUTHIAN *Form of Process* (ed. 2) 97 All these Objections, properly called Dilators, must be first proponed. **1888** RAMSAY *Scotl. in 18th C.* I. ii. 41 He is said to have excelled in what was called proponing dilators.

dilator, obs. form of DELATOR, accuser.

dilatorily ('dɪlətərɪlɪ), *adv.* [f. DILATORY *a.*[1] + -LY[2].] In a dilatory manner; delayingly.
1700 TYRRELL *Hist. Eng.* II. 873 The Prelates answered him dilatorily. **1781** JOHNSON in Boswell *Life* (1848) 665/1, I wrote in my usual way, dilatorily and hastily, unwilling to work, and working with vigour and haste. **1849** LOWELL *Lett.* I. 167, I remain very sincerely (and dilatorily) Your friend.

dilatoriness ('dɪlətərɪnɪs). Forms: see DILATORY. [f. next + -NESS.] The quality of being dilatory; tendency to procrastination or delay.
1642 in Rushw. *Hist. Coll.* III. (1692) I. 610 Lest his Majesty should think it a delatoriness in the Parliament to return an Answer. **1667** WATERHOUSE *Fire Lond.* 95 The sluggards dilatoriness is upon men; and they will sit still a little longer. **1718** *Free-thinker* No. 56. 4 The Holy See proceeded with its usual dilatoriness in that Affair. **1825** SCOTT *Jrnl.* 7 Dec., Letters.. lying on my desk like snakes, hissing at me for my dilatoriness. **1861** M. PATTISON *Ess.* (1889) I. 38 His delay in setting out was due to pure procrastination and dilatoriness.

dilatory ('dɪlətərɪ), *a.*[1] and *sb.* Forms: 6–7 dilatorie, 7– dilatory, (8 *erron.* dilitary). Also 6–7 delatorie, (6 delaterye, deletary), 7 delatory. [ad. L. *dīlātōri-us*, f. *dīlātōr-em* a delayer, agent-n. from *differre*, *dīlāt-* to DEFER, delay: see DILATE *v.*[1] Cf. F. *dilatoire* (13th c. in Hatz.-Darm.).]
A. *adj.*
1. Tending to cause delay; made for the purpose of gaining time or deferring decision or action.
1581 LAMBARDE *Eiren.* IV. xxi. (1588) 622 It was very Dilatorie for the Justices of Peace, to take those Wages, at the handes of the Shirife. **1592** NASHE *P. Penilesse* (ed. 2) 9 a, For his delaterye excuse. **1613** SHAKS. *Hen. VIII*, II. iv. 237, I abhorre This dilatory sloth and tricks of Rome. **1655** FULLER *Ch. Hist.* VIII. ii. §46 Dilatory letters excusing themselves from coming thither. **1671** SHADWELL *Humourists* v. Wks. 1720 I. 202, I will.. make no hesitation or dilatory scruple. **1751** JOHNSON *Rambler* No. 178 ⁋4 By long deliberation and dilatory projects they may both be lost. **1860** MOTLEY *Netherl.* (1868) I. iii. 80 The policy of England continued to be expectant and dilatory.
b. *Law.* ***dilatory plea***, a plea put in for the sake of delay. ***dilatory exception***: see EXCEPTION *sb.* 4 a. ***dilatory defence*** (in Sc. Law): see quot.
[**1292** BRITTON II. xvii. §1 Par excepciouns dilatories.] **1535** *Act 27 Hen. VIII*, c. 14 §5 None essoin.. or other dilatorie ple for the defendant shall be admitted. **1611** RICH *Honest. Age* (1844) 21 They.. do seeke for nothing more then to checke the course of iustice by their delatory pleas. **1678** HICKES in Ellis *Orig. Lett.* Ser. II. IV. 49 At last all the dilatory exceptions being answered, the Jury was impanelled and the witnesses sworn. **1768** BLACKSTONE *Comm.* III. 301 Dilatory pleas are such as tend merely to delay or put off the suit, by questioning the propriety of the remedy, rather than by denying the injury. **1861** W. BELL *Dict. Law Scot.*, *Dilatory Defence* is a plea offered by a defender for eliding the conclusions of the action, without entering on the merits of the cause. **1880** MUIRHEAD *Gaius* IV. §120 Those [Exceptions] are dilatory that are available only for a time, such as that of an agreement not to sue say for five years.
2. Given to or characterized by delay; slow, tardy. **a.** Of persons, their characters, habits, etc.
1604 SHAKS. *Oth.* II. iii. 379 Wit depends on dilatory time. **1711** ADDISON *Spect.* No. 89 ⁋1 Women of dilatory Tempers, who are for spinning out the Time of Courtship. **1742** YOUNG *N. Th.* i. 413 Poor dilatory man. **1781** COWPER *Lett.* 25 Aug., The most dilatory of all people. **1838** THIRLWALL *Greece* III. xix. 106 They are as prompt, as you are dilatory. **1884** PAE *Eustace* 38 You shall have no longer cause to think me dilatory.
b. Of actions.
1648 BOYLE *Seraph. Love* xii. (1700) 64 Being press'd to give an account of such a Dilatory way of proceeding. **1751** JOHNSON *Rambler* No. 144 ⁋11 But between dilatory payment and bankruptcy there is a great distance. **1843** PRESCOTT *Mexico* VI. v. (1864) 369 Cortez was not content to wait patiently the effects of a dilatory blockade. **1879** FROUDE *Caesar* xxii. 386 His political advisers were impatient of these dilatory movements.
B. *sb.* *Law.* A means of procuring delay; a dilatory plea: see A. 1 b.
1563–87 FOXE *A. & M.* (1684) II. 22 Shifting off the matter by subtil dilatories and frivolous cavilling about the law. **1585** ABP. SANDYS *Serm.* (1841) 226 Delatories and shiftings off wear out many a just cause, and beggar many a poor man. **1681** *Trial of S. Colledge* 16 You ought not to have helps to plead dilatories. *a* **1734** NORTH *Lives* (1826) I. 302 Criminals of that sort.. should defend upon plain truth, which they know best, without any dilatories, arts or evasions. **1848** WHARTON *Law Lex.* s.v. *Dilatory Pleas*, No man shall be permitted to plead two dilatories at separate times.

†**di'latory,** *a.*[2] *Obs. rare.* [A bad formation for *dilatatory*, f. DILATE *v.*] Used for dilating, dilative.
1691 MULLINEUX in *Phil. Trans.* XVII. 822 The Chyrurgion.. inserted his Dilatory Instrument.

‖'**dilature.** *Sc. Obs.* [A variant of *dilatour*, DILATOR[2], assimilated in spelling to L. *dīlātūra*, delaying, delay, f. *dīlāt-* ppl. stem of L. *differre*: see DILATE *v.*[1]] = DILATORY *sb.*
1552 LYNDESAY *Monarche* 5766 Throw Delaturis [*v.r.* delatouris] full of dissait, Quhilk mony one gart beg thare mait. **1714** *Let.* in *Lockhart Papers* I. 439 The Court tricked them with dilatures till the.. opportunity was past.

dilavy, var. of DELAVY *a. Obs.*

dilay(e, obs. form of DELAY.

dilce, Sc. form of DULSE.

dildo[1]. Also dildoe. **a.** A word of obscure origin, used in the refrains of ballads.
Also, a name of the penis or phallus, or a figure thereof; *spec.* an artificial penis used for female gratification; the lingam of Hindoo worship; formerly, also, a contemptuous or reviling appellation of a man or lad; and app. applied to a cylindrical or 'sausage' curl.
c **1593** T. NASHE *Choise of Valentines or the Merie Ballad of Nash his Dildo* (1899) 20 Curse Eunuke dilldo, senceless counterfet. **1598** FLORIO *Worlde of Wordes* 261/3 *Pastinaca muranese*, a dildoe of glasse. *Ibid.* 278/2 *Pinco*, a prick, a pillicock, a pintle, a dildoe. **1610** B. JONSON *Alch.* v. iii, Here I find.. The seeling fill'd with poesies of the candle: And Madame, with a Dildo, writ o' the walls. **1611** SHAKS. *Wint. T.* IV. iv. 195 He has the prettiest Loue-songs for Maids.. with such delicate burthens of Dildo's and Fadings. *a* **1627** MIDDLETON *Chaste Maid* I. ii, What, has he got a singing in his head now? Now's out of work he falls to making dildoes. **1638** FORD *Fancies* IV. i, This page a milk-livered dildoe. **1647** *Parl. Ladies* 12 The very sight of this Madam with a Dildoe.. put the House into a great silence. *c* **1650** *Roxb. Ball.* II. 455 She prov'd herself a Duke's daughter, and he but a Squire's son. Sing trang dildo lee. **1656** S. HOLLAND *Zara* (1719) 41 That Gods may view, With a dildo-doe, What we bake, and what we brew. **1659** TORRIANO, *Bacillo* .. a simple gull, a shallow pate, also a dill-doe, or pillie-cock. **1661** R. W. *Conf. Charac.* To Rdr. (1860) 7 O thou faint-hearted dildo. **1688** R. HOLME *Armoury* II. 463/2 A Campaign Wig hath Knots or Bobs (or a Dildo on each side) with a curled Forehead. **1698** FRYER *Acc. E. India* 179 Under the Banyan Tree, an Altar with a Dildo in the middle being erected, they offer Rice. **1785** GROSE *Dict. Vulgar T.* s.v., Dildoes are made of wax, horn, leather, and diverse other substances. **1886** BURTON *Arab. Nts.* X. 239 Of the penis succedaneus,.. which the Latins called phallus and fascinum, the French godemiché and the Italians passatempo and diletto (whence our 'dildo'), every kind abounds. **1952** AUDEN *Nones* 11 The nude young male who lounges Against a rock displaying his dildo. **1965** *New Statesman* 9 Apr. 570/2 Why does it matter so much to them whether lesbians use a dildo or not?
b. *Comb.* **dildo-glass**, a cylindrical glass; ? a test-tube.
c **1625** FLETCHER *Nice Valour* III. i, Whoever lives to see me Dead, gentlemen, shall find me all mummy, Good to fill galipots, and long dildo-glasses.

dildo[2]. [prob. the same word as prec., from its cylindrical form like a 'dildo-glass'.] A tree or shrub of the genus *Cereus* (N.O. *Cactaceæ*). Also ***dildo-tree, dildo-bush, dildo pear tree.***
1672 W. HUGHES *Amer. Physitian* 43 The Tree was long since called by the Spaniards, and by the Negroes that lived there, the Dildoe-Tree; and the English retain the same name still. **1696** *Phil. Trans.* XIX. 296 The Dildoe-tree is the same with the Cereus or Torch-Plant. **1697** DAMPIER *Voy.* I. 81 Barren Islands without any Tree, only some Dildo-bushes growing on them. *Ibid.* 101 The Dildoe-tree is a green prickly shrub, that grows about 10 or 12 foot high, without either Leaf or Fruit. It is as big as a mans Leg, from the root to the top, and it is full of sharp prickles, growing in thick rows. **1700** W. KING *Transactioneer* 11 The Toddy-Tree, the Sower-Sop, the Bonavists, and the Dildoe. **1756** P. BROWNE *Nat. Hist. Jamaica* (1789) 238 The larger erect Indian Fig, or Dildo Pear Tree. **1926** FAWCETT & RENDLE *Flora of Jamaica* V. 279 C[*ereus*] *peruvianus*... Dildo. Dry parts of Jamaica on southern side. **1956** J. HEARNE *Stranger at Gate* xix. 156 It's like getting a dildo thorn out of your foot.

†**di'lect,** *ppl. a. Obs. rare.* [ad. L. *dīlect-us* 'beloved', pa. pple. of *dīligĕre* to esteem highly, to love (see DILIGENT).] Beloved.
1521 J. T. in Bradshaw *St. Werburge* Prol. ii, A virgin resplendent Dilect of our lorde.

dilectacion, obs. form of DELECTATION.

†**dilection** (dɪ'lɛkʃən). *Obs.* Also 5–6 dy-, 6 de-. [a. F. *dilection* (12th c. in Hatz.-Darm.), ad. L. *dīlectiōn-em* love (of God, etc.) (Tertullian, Vulgate), n. of action from *dīligĕre* to select to oneself from others, to esteem highly, hold dear, love; f. *di-, dis-* (DIS- 1) + *legĕre* to gather, cull, choose.]
1. Love, affection: almost always, spiritual or Christian love, or the love of God to man or of man to God; cf. CHARITY 1.
1388 WYCLIF *Rev.* Prol., Ion, the apostil and euangelist of oure Lord Ihesu Crist, chosen and loued, in so gret loue of dileccioun is had. *a* **1420** HOCCLEVE *De Reg. Princ.* 851 Frenship, adieu; farewele, dileccioun. *c* **1485** *Digby Myst.* III. 1323 His desypylles.. to hym had dyleccyon. *c* **1520** *Wyse Chyld & Emp. Adrian* (1860) 15 They were by dyleccion all of one hart and of one wyll. **1623** FAVINE *Theat. Hon.* IX. vi. 399 In token of love and Brotherly dilection. **1683** E. HOOKER *Pref. Ep. Pordage's Mystic Div.* 56 This dilection, love, charitie towards God, and towards His Image, man.
2. The action of choosing, choice (of that on which one's desire or affection is set); *esp.* in *Theol.* = ELECTION 3.
c **1450** HENRYSON *Mor. Fab.* 62 And when the saul Giues consent vnto delection, The wicked thought beginnes for to breird In deadly sinne. **1633** T. ADAMS *Exp. 2 Peter* ii. 12 We are adjured by our election, selection, dilection, to be merciful. **1656** JEANES *Fuln. Christ* 51 Christ is the only begotten son of God, not by dilection, but by eternall generation.
¶**3.** Used by Carlyle to render Ger. *liebden* as a title of honour.
1864 CARLYLE *Fredk. Gt.* (1865) IV. XI. v. 81 These things We expect from your Dilection, as Kurfürst of Brandenburg. **1865** *Ibid.* VII. XVII. iv. (1873) 37 [I] apprise your dilection, though under deepest secrecy.

dilemma (dɪ'lɛmə, daɪ-), *sb.* Also β. 6–7 (after French) dilemme (dylem). [a. L. *dilemma*, a. Gr. δίλημμα double proposition, f. δι-, twice (DI-[2]) + λῆμμα assumption, premiss: see LEMMA.]
1. In *Rhetoric.* A form of argument involving an adversary in the choice of two (or, *loosely*, more) alternatives, either of which is (or appears) equally unfavourable to him. (The alternatives are commonly spoken of as the 'horns' of the dilemma.) Hence in *Logic*, a hypothetical syllogism having a conjunctive or 'conditional' major premiss and a disjunctive minor (or, one premiss conjunctive and the other disjunctive).
Very different views have been taken by different logicians as to what syllogisms are properly dilemmas; several of the arguments commonly so called being considered by some writers to be only ordinary conjunctive syllogisms, constructive or destructive. See FOWLER, *Deductive Logic*, v. §4.
1523 in W. H. Turner *Select. Rec. Oxford* 36 They are.. excommunicated.. wth a dilemma made concerninge the.. Mayor's.. perplexitie. **1551** T. WILSON *Logike* (1580) 34 b, Dilemma, otherwise.. called a horned argument, is when the reason consisteth of repugnant members, so that what so ever you graunt, you fall into the snare. **1622** BACON *Hen. VII*, Wks. (Bohn) 377 A dilemma, that bishop Morton.. used, to raise up the benevolence to higher rates; and some called it his fork, and some his crotch... 'That if they met with any that were sparing, they should tell them, that they must needs have, because they laid up: and if they were spenders, they must needs have, because it was seen in their port and manner of living'. **1638** CHILLINGW. *Relig. Prot.* I. ii. §154 Thus haue we cast off your dilemma, and broken both the hornes of it. **1677** GALE *Crt. Gentiles* II. IV. Proem 11 A Dilemma is an argumentation from two members, whereof both are attended with incommoditie. **1725** WATTS *Logic* III. ii. §6 A Dilemma becomes faulty or ineffectual..

when it may be retorted with equal force upon him who utters it. **1837-8** SIR W. HAMILTON *Logic* xviii. (1866) I. 351 An hypothetico-disjunctive syllogism is called the dilemma or horned syllogism. *Ibid.* 352 If the disjunction..has only two members, the syllogism is then called a dilemma in the strict and proper signification. If..three..members, it is called trilemma, etc. **1842** ABP. THOMSON *Laws Th.* §109 (1860) 203 The Dilemma is a complex argument, partaking both of the conditional and disjunctive. **1887** FOWLER *Deductive Logic* 121 In disputation, the adversary who is refuted by a dilemma is said to be 'fixed on the horns of a dilemma'; he is said to *rebut* the dilemma, if he meet it by another with an opposite conclusion. *Ibid.* 122 It seems less arbitrary and more systematic to define dilemma as 'a syllogism of which one premiss is a conjunctive and the other a disjunctive proposition'.

β. **1587** A. FLEMING *Cont. Holinshed* III. 1307/2 This bishop, hauing heard all these excuses, vsed this dilemme. **1616** LANE *Sq. Tale* (1888) 121, I see his saftie and thine maie not bee, bot as Dylems or Contraries agree.

2. Hence, in popular use: A choice between two (or, *loosely*, several) alternatives, which are or appear equally unfavourable; a position of doubt or perplexity, a 'fix'.

1590 GREENE *Neuer too late* (1600) 19 Every motion was intangled with a dilemma:..the loue of Francesco gaue such fierce assaults to the bulwarke of her affection..the feare of her Fathers displeasure..draue her to meditate thus. **1598** SHAKS. *Merry W.* IV. v. 87 In perplexity, and doubtful dilemma. **1655** FULLER *Ch. Hist.* IV. i. §53 He is reduced to this doleful Dilemma; either voluntarily, by resigning, to depose himself; or violently, by detrusion, to be deposed by others. **1796** MORSE *Amer. Geog.* II. 297 Kosciusko was.. reduced to the unpleasant dilemma of being obliged either to kill the father or give up the daughter. **1841-44** EMERSON *Ess.*, *Experience* Wks. (Bohn) I. 189 In the dilemma of a swimmer among drowning men, who all catch at him. **1888** BRYCE *Amer. Commw.* II. liii. 332 They were..in the dilemma of either violating the Constitution or losing a golden opportunity.

3. *Comb.* as ***dilemma-making***.

1895 *Westm. Gaz.* 16 Apr. 3/3 Dilemma-making is at best a somewhat puerile..form of dialectic.

di'lemma, *v. rare.* [f. prec. sb.]

1. *trans.* To place in a dilemma; *pa. pple.* = in a dilemma or 'fix'.

1656 S. H. *Gold. Law* 44 Both sides are Dilemma'd, and stand postur'd like Lots wife. **1698** FRYER *Acc. E. India & P.* 325 Now we were dilemma'd, not knowing what to wish. *a* **1849** POE *Marginalia* Wks. 1864 III. 485 Like a novel-hero dilemma'd, I made up my mind to be guided by circumstances.

†**2.** *intr.* To be in a dilemma; to hesitate or be in doubt between two alternatives. *Obs. rare.*

1687 R. L'ESTRANGE *Answ. Diss.* 39 He runs away with the Fact, for Granted; Dilemma's upon it, and so leaves the Matter.

dilemmatic (dɪ-, daɪlɛ'mætɪk), *a.* [f. Gr. διλημματ- stem of δίλημμα (see prec.) + -IC.] Of the nature of, or relating to, a dilemma.

1837-8 SIR W. HAMILTON *Logic* xiii. (1860) I. 241 Dilemmatic judgments are those in which a condition is found, both in the subject and in the predicate. *Ibid.* xv. (1860) I. 291 The Hypothetico-disjunctive or Dilemmatic Syllogism. **1867** ATWATER *Elem. Logic* 95 Dilemmatic Judgements involve a combination of the conditional and disjunctive. **1870** JEVONS *Elem. Logic* xix. 168 Dilemmatic arguments are..more often fallacious than not. **1891** WELTON *Manual Logic* IV. v. 447 The peculiar feature of a dilemmatic argument is the choice of alternatives which it thus offers.

†**dile'mmatical**, *a. Obs.* [f. as prec. + -AL[1].] = prec. Hence **dile'mmatically** *adv.*

1659 BAXTER *Key Cath.* xlv. 316 The Jesuites..went Dilemmatically to work, thinking to make sure which way ever things went, to effect their ends. **1661** K. W. *Conf. Charac. Good-old cause* (1860) 60 And bring upon us a dilemmaticall confusion. **1677** GILPIN *Dæmonol.* (1867) 342 These were perplexing, entangling temptations. They were dilemmatical, such as might ensnare, either in the doing or refusal.

di'lemmist. *rare.* [f. DILEMMA + -IST.] One who bases his position upon a dilemma; used as the name of a Buddhist school of philosophy.

1858 *Appleton's Amer. Cycl.* IV. 70/2 [The philosophic school] of the Vaibhâshikas, or dilemmists, who maintain the necessity of immediate contact with the object to be known.

†**di'leriate**, *a. Obs. rare.* [Erron. for *delirate*, ad. L. *dēlīrātus*, or for *deliriate*.] = DELIRIOUS.

1689 MOYLE *Sea Chyrurg.* III. xi. 117 Before the Feaver comes to its height, usually men are dileriate.

dilettant ('dɪlɪtɑːnt, -æ-), *a.* and *sb.* [A partially Anglicized adaptation of next: cf. F. *dilettante*; also *adjutant*, *confidant*, etc.] = next.

A. *adj.*

1851 CARLYLE *Sterling* II. vii. (1872) 160 Sterling returned from Italy filled with..great store of artistic, serious, dilettant and other speculation for the time.

B. *sb.*

1875 HAMERTON *Intell. Life* III. v. 100 If the essence of dilettantism is to be contented with imperfect attainment, I fear that all educated people must be considered dilettants. **1888** *Eng. Illustr. Mag.* Jan. 316 Teach by salutary smarts, These dilettants to understand That Learning is the first of Arts. **1891** F. M. WILSON *Prim. on Browning* 34 Browning draws a sharp line between the dilettant and the artist.

‖**dilettante** (dɪlɪ'tæntɪ, It. dilet'tante). Pl. dilettanti (-tiː), rarely -es. [It. *dilettante* 'a lover of music or painting', f. *dilettare*:—L. *dēlectāre* to delight: see DELECT, etc. So mod.F. *dilettante*, 1878 in *Dict. Acad.*]

1. A lover of the fine arts; originally, one who cultivates them for the love of them rather than professionally, and so = *amateur* as opposed to *professional*; but in later use generally applied more or less depreciatively to one who interests himself in an art or science merely as a pastime and without serious aim or study ('a mere dilettante').

1733-4 ['The Society of Dilettanti' was founded]. **1748** CHESTERF. *Lett.* II. xl, You are likely to hear of it as a *virtuoso*; and if so, I should be glad to profit of it, as an humble *dillettante.* **1769** (*title*), Ionian Antiquities, By the Society of Dilettanti. **1770** FOOTE *Lame Lover* I. i, Frederick is a bit of Macaroni and adores the soft Italian termination in *a*... Yes, a delitanti all over. **1775** MAD. D'ARBLAY *Diary* 21 Nov., A female dilettante of great fame and reputation..as a singer. **1789** BURNEY *Hist. Mus.* III. ii. 161 Personages whose [musical] talents are celebrated whether they are regarded as professors or Diletanti. **1801** W. TAYLOR in *Monthly Mag.* XII. 576 Religious dilettanti, of every sex and age, reinforce the industry of the regular priesthood. **1802** *Edin. Rev.* I. 165 Dilettanti who have pushed themselves into high places in the scientific world. **1826** B'NESS BUNSEN in Hare *Life* II. vii. 265 It would be difficult to find a dilettante who understood the art of managing it [a parlour organ]. **1831** CARLYLE *Sart. Res.* I. x, Thou hitherto art a Dilettante and sandblind Pedant. **1840** MACAULAY *Ess.*, *Clive* (1854) 534/2 The Dilettante sneered at their want of taste. The Maccaroni black-balled them as vulgar fellows. **1879** FROUDE *Cæsar* ii. 17 [The Romans] cared for art as dilettanti; but no schools either of sculpture or painting were formed among themselves. **1886** RUSKIN *Præterita* I. 271 Rogers was a mere dilettante, who felt no difference between landing where Tell leaped ashore, or standing where 'St. Preux has stood'.

†**b.** with *of*: a lover, one who is fond *of*. *Obs.*

1783 HAMILTON in *Phil. Trans.* LXXIII. 189 Those who are professed dilettanti of miracles.

2. *attrib.* **a.** In apposition, as ***dilettante musician***, etc. = amateur.

1774 'J. COLLIER' *Mus. Trav.* (1775) 4 That great Dilettante performer on the harp. **1789** MAD. D'ARBLAY *Lett.* 27 Oct., A Dilettante purchaser may yet be found. **1806-7** J. BERESFORD *Miseries Hum. Life* (1826) xv. iii, You are almost entirely reduced to Dilletanti Musicians. **1816** T. L. PEACOCK *Headlong Hall* iii, Sir Patrick O'Prism, a dilettante painter of high renown. **1821** CRAIG *Lect. Drawing* v. 252 Suited for the dilettante artist. **1871** MORLEY *Voltaire* (1886) 57 The dilettante believer is indeed not a strong spirit, but the weakest.

b. Of, pertaining to, or characteristic of a dilettante (in the shades of meaning the word has passed through).

1753 SMOLLETT *Ct. Fathom* xxxii, He sometimes held forth upon painting, like a member of the Dilettanti club. **1774** 'J. COLLIER' *Mus. Trav.* (1775) 58 He ordered his servant to bring in his Dilettante ring and wig. **1794** MATHIAS *Purs. Lit.* (1798) 386 The dilettante spirit which too frequently prevails in Dr. Warton's comments. **1840** CARLYLE *Heroes* vi. (1891) 198 To us it is no dilettante work, no sleek officiality; it is sheer rough death and earnest. *a* **1847** MRS. SHERWOOD *Lady of Manor* II. xiii. 151, I will have a dilletante play, or concert, or some such thing, got up. **1868** M. PATTISON *Academ. Org.* v. 148 A dilettante fastidiousness, an aimless inertia.

Hence **dile'ttante** *v.*, **dile'ttantize** *v.*, to play the dilettante (also ***to dilettante it***); **dile'ttanting** *ppl. a.*; **dile'ttantedom**, the world of dilettanti; **dile'ttanteship**, the condition of a dilettante.

1835 JAMES *Gipsy* v, In the elegant charlatanism of dilettanteship. **1837** *Blackw. Mag.* XLII. 515 To go on dilettanteing it in the grossness of the moral atmosphere of the Continental cities. **1843** *Tait's Mag.* X. 346 Shooting partridges and dilettantizing at legislation. **1887** *Pall Mall G.* 1 Jan. 5/2 The favourite actress of dilettantedom. **1890** *Spectator* 11 Oct. 495 The Shakespeare temptation remains as strong as ever with the dilettanting world.

dile'ttantish, *a.* Also -teish. [f. prec. + -ISH.] Savouring of the nature or quality of a dilettante.

1871 GEO. ELIOT *Middlem.* xix, You are dilettantish and amateurish. **1881** H. JAMES *Portr. Lady* xxiii, It made people idle and dilettantish, and second-rate; there was nothing tonic in an Italian life. **1893** *Nation* (N.Y.) 16 Feb. 129/3 It presents..a dilettantish 'appreciation' of Dante.

dile'ttantism. Also dile'ttanteism. [f. as prec. + -ISM: so mod.F. *dilettantisme*, adm. by Acad. in 1878.] The practice or method of a dilettante; the quality or character of dilettanti.

1809 HAN. MORE *Cœlebs* I. 119 (Jod.) She..extolled the air with all the phrases, cant and rapture of dilettanteism. **1830** CARLYLE in Froude *Life* (1882) II. 90 The sin of this age is dilettantism: the Whigs and all 'moderate Tories' are dilettanti. **1849** ROBERTSON *Serm.* Ser. I. xii. 182 Virtue no longer means manhood: it is simply dilettantism. **1862** SHIRLEY *Nugæ Crit.* iv. 187 A national society..has no right to indulge in religious dilletanteism. **1873** LOWELL *Among my Bks.* Ser. II. 22 A period, for Italy, of sceptical dilettanteism. **1894** *Times* 23 Feb. 4/4 To prevent their falling into an attitude of indifference or dilettantism.

dile'ttantist, *a.* [f. prec.; see -IST.] Characterized by dilettantism.

1859 *Sat. Rev.* VIII. 226/1 Nothing more than the playthings of dilettantist philanthropy. **1887** *Ibid.* 10 Sept. 345 Difficult branches of science were dealt with in this same dilettantist spirit. **1889** J. M. ROBERTSON *Ess. towards Crit. Meth.* 3 It is become, as it were, parasitic and dilettantist, a pedant habit of tasting and relishing and objecting.

dilex, var. *dillesk*, DULSE.

dilful, obs. form of DOLEFUL *a.*

c **1420** *Anturs of Arth.* xiii, Lo! hou dilful dethe hase thi Dame dyȝte! ? *a* **1500** *Chester Pl.* (1843) I. 69 But that I do this dilfull dede The Lord will not quite me in my nede.

†**dilghe, dilie**, *v. Obs.* Forms: 1 dilȝian, 3 dillȝhenn (*Orm.*), dilie. [OE. *dileȝian*, *dilȝian* = OLG. *diligōn* (MLG. *del(l)igen*, *delgen*, *diligen*, LG. *delgen*, *dilgen*, Du. *delgen*; OHG. *tilōn*, *dīlōn*, *tīligōn*, MHG. *tillen*, *tīligen*, *tilgen*, Ger. *tilgen*; supposed to be ad. L. *dēlēre* to blot out, erase.] *trans.* To destroy, blot out, erase; also *fig.*

c **897** K. ÆLFRED *Gregory's Past.* liv. 82 Swa se writere, ȝif he ne dileȝað ðæt he ær wrat..ðæt bið ðeah undileȝod ðæt he ær wrat. *c* **1200** ORMIN 4083 To ben Fullhtnedd, to dillȝhenn sinne. *Ibid.* 5301 Forr swa to cwennkenn Crisstenndom, And Cristess laȝhess dillȝhenn. **12..** *Hymn of St. Godric* (Ritson), Dilie min sinne, rix in mine mod.

diligat, obs. Sc. form of DELICATE.

diligence[1] ('dɪlɪdʒəns). In 5-6 dily-, dyly-, deli-, delygence, -ens. [a. F. *diligence* (13-14th c. in Hatz.-Darm.), ad. L. *dīligentia*, f. *dīligent-em* DILIGENT: see -ENCE. Cf. Pr. and Sp. *diligencia*, It. *diligenza*.] The quality of being diligent.

1. Constant and earnest effort to accomplish what is undertaken; persistent application and endeavour; industry, assiduity.

c **1374** CHAUCER *Troylus* III. 86 (135) With al my wit and al my deligence. **1393** GOWER *Conf.* II. 37 As for thy diligence, Whiche every mannes conscience By reson shulde reule and kepe. *c* **1425** WYNTOUN *Cron.* VI. iv. 74 To mak defens For hys Land wyth diligens. **1577** B. GOOGE *Heresbach's Husb.* IV. (1586) 190 By the carefull toile and diligence of the Bee. **1644** MILTON *Educ.* Wks. (1847) 98/1 The extraordinary pains and diligence which you have used in this matter. *a* **1718** PENN *Tracts* Wks. 1726 I. 908 Diligence is a discreet and understanding Application of one's self to Business. **1718** *Freethinker* No. 89 ¶9 Manage Business with Regularity and Diligence. **1751** JOHNSON *Rambler* No. 85 ¶1 Many writers..have laid out their diligence upon the consideration of those distempers. **1871** E. F. BURR *Ad Fidem* viii. 130 Patient diligence the only sure key to Divine treasures.

†**b.** Assiduity in service; persistent endeavour to please; officiousness. *Obs.*

1493 *Petronilla* 142 (Pynson) To do servise with humble diligence Unto thy fader. **1500-20** DUNBAR *Poems* lvii. 3 Sum be seruice and diligence. **1591** SHAKS. *1 Hen. VI*, v. iii. 9 This speedy and quicke appearance argues proofe Of your accustom'd diligence to me. **1671** MILTON *P.R.* II. 387 Why shouldst thou, then, obtrude this diligence In vain, where no acceptance it can find? **1674** PLAYFORD *Skill Mus.* I. xi. 41 Which sort of People we should endeavour to please with all diligence.

†**c.** with *a* and *pl.*: an act of diligence; *pl.* labours, exertions, diligent efforts. *Obs.*

1443 HEN. VI in Ellis *Orig. Lett.* Ser. III. I. 79 By whos notable..labours and diligences it hath liked our Lord to shewe us his grete fauour. **1549** COVERDALE, etc. *Erasm. Par. Phil.* II. 9 All them..that with their dilygences helpe forewarde the businesse of the gospell. **1600** E. BLOUNT tr. *Conestaggio* 314 Not suffering his men to discharge one volley..for that it seemed unto him a vaine diligence. **1652** J. WADSWORTH tr. *Sandoval's Civ. Wars Spain* 253 Whilest the Lord High Constable was making all these diligences, the Cardinal stole secretly out of Valladolid.

†**d.** One in whom the quality is personified; a diligent person. (*nonce-use.*)

1610 SHAKS. *Temp.* v. i. 241 *Ar.* Was't well done? *Pr.* Brauely (my diligence); thou shalt be free.

†**e.** Phrases. ***to put diligence***, ***to do one's diligence***, to do one's utmost endeavour, to exert oneself. ***to report one's diligence***, to report what one has done, to report progress. *Obs.* or *arch.*

c **1386** CHAUCER *Melib.* ¶27 Whan thou hast for-goon thy freend, do diligence to gete another freend. *c* **1386** —— *Manciple's T.* 37 And nyght and day did euere his diligence Hir for to plese. **1389** *Eng. Gilds* (1870) 4 þe same maistres & breþeren shul do her diligence trewly to redresse it. **1477** EARL RIVERS (Caxton) *Dictes* 128, I shal put my peyn and dyligence to distroye the. **1481** CAXTON *Myrr.* I. vi. 30 They [kynges] doo their diligence to lerne such clergye & science. **1509** BARCLAY *Shyp of Folys* (1570) 6 Neuer wise man loued ..To haue great riches put ouer great diligence. **1539** CRANMER *2 Tim.* iv. 9 Do thy diligence, that thou mayest come shortly vnto me. **1637-50** ROW *Hist. Kirk* (1842) 208 That they be carefull to correct what they can, and report their diligence to the nixt Assemblie. **1690** W. WALKER *Idiomat. Anglo-Lat.* 143, I will doe my diligence.

†**2.** Speed, dispatch, haste. *Obs.*

1490 CAXTON *Eneydos* xxvi. 95 Yf thou departe not with all diligence thou shalt soone see the see alle couered with vesselles of werre commynge ayenst the. **1548** HALL *Chron.* 37 This phisician dyd not long lynger..but with good diligens repaired to the quene. **1605** SHAKS. *Lear* I. v. 4 If your Dilligence be not speedy, I shall be there afore you. **1632** J. HAYWARD tr. *Biondi's Eromena* 21 Posting on with such diligence that by darke night hee reached [etc.]. **1703** ROWE *Ulyss.* IV. i. 1415 With thy swiftest Diligence return. **1781** GIBBON *Decl. & F.* III. 41 His rival..fled before him with the diligence of fear.

†**b.** A 'company' of messengers. *Obs.*

1486 *Bk. St. Albans* F vj b, A Diligens of Messangeris.

†**3.** Careful attention, heedfulness, caution. ***to do*** or ***have diligence***, to take care, take heed, beware; to take care *of* or *about* a thing, to look after it carefully. *Obs.*

1340 *Ayenb.* 238 þeruore hi ssolle do greate payne and grat diligence wel to loki hare chastete. **1382** WYCLIF *1 Tim.* iii. 5 If ony man kan not gouerne his hous, how schal he haue diligence of the chirche of God. *c* **1400** *Lanfranc's Cirurg.* 141 It is necessarie þat a surgian have more diligence in þe woundis of þe face. **1483** CAXTON *Cato* B v b, Thou oughtest to take dyligence and cure of thy werkes. **1535** COVERDALE *Prov.* iv. 23 Kepe thine hert with all diligence. **1577** B. GOOGE *Heresbach's Husb.* III. (1586) 152 To keepe your Bacon any long time, you must use greate diligence in the salting and drying of it. **1587** MASCAL *Govt. Cattle, Horses* (1627) 100 A horse doth aske a greater diligence to be meated and kept.. then other cattell. **1665** HOOKE *Microgr.* 47 Moscovy-glass.. with care and diligence may be slit into pieces.. exceeding thin. **1795** SOUTHEY *Joan of Arc* VIII, Thou wilt guard them with due diligence, Yet not forgetful of humanity.

†**b.** with *pl. Obs.*

1675 M. CLIFFORD *Hum. Reason* in *Phenix* 1708 II. 530 Those necessary Diligences which are requir'd for so doubtful and dangerous a Passage.

4. *Law.* The attention and care due from a person in a given situation; *spec.* that incumbent upon the parties to a contract.

1622 MALYNES *Anc. Law Merch.* 407 The diligences which are requisite to bee done herein, are.. to be obserued accordingly. **1781** SIR W. JONES *Ess. Bailments* 16. **1848** WHARTON *Law Lex.* s.v., The common law recognizes three degrees of diligence. (1) Common or ordinary.. (2) High or great, which is extraordinary diligence.. (3) Low or slight, which is that which persons of less than common prudence, or indeed of any prudence at all, take of their own concerns. **1875** POSTE *Gaius* 477 The opposite of Negligence is Diligence, vigilance, attention, which, like Negligence, admits of an infinite variety of gradations. *Ibid.* 480 If the interests of the parties are not identical, the Roman law, at least, requires extraordinary diligence.

5. *Sc. Law.* **a.** The process of law by which persons, lands, or effects are attached on execution, or in security for debt. **b.** The warrant issued by a court to enforce the attendance of witnesses, or the production of documents.

1568 in Calderwood *Hist. Kirk* (1843) II. 426 The persons addebted for payment of the same being at the horne, and no further diligence used for obteaning of payment. **1752** J. LOUTHIAN *Form of Process* (ed. 2) 37 Therefore, necessary it is for the Complainers to have our Warrant and Diligence for summoning the said *C.D.* to compear before Our Lords Justice-General. **1754** ERSKINE *Princ. Sc. Law* (1809) 12 In our supreme courts of Session and Exchequer, not only process, but execution of diligence, runs in the name of the Sovereign. **1827** SCOTT *Jrnl.* 13 Oct., Mr. Abud.. has given the most positive orders to take out diligence against me for his debt of 1500*l.* **1858** POLSON *Law & L.* 197 Witnesses are brought into Court upon a *diligence*.

diligence[2] ('dɪlɪdʒəns; Fr. diliʒɑ̃s). [mod.F.: a particular use of *diligence*, DILIGENCE[1] sense 2, also in Ger. and Du.; It. *diligenza*, Sp. *diligencia*.] A public stage-coach. (Now used only in reference to France or other continental countries.)

1742 LADY M. W. MONTAGU *Lett.* (1893) II. 110 Travelled from Paris to Lyons in the diligence. **1756** NUGENT *Gr. Tour* France IV. 19 The Diligence is a kind of stage coach so called from its expedition, and differs from the carosse or ordinary stage-coach, in little else but in moving with greater velocity. It is used chiefly in travelling from Paris to Lyons, and from Paris to Brussels. **1815** M. BIRKBECK *Journ. through France* 17 From Rouen to Louviers we travelled by diligence. **1838** J. L. STEPHENS *Trav. Greece, etc.* 62/1 We mounted a drosky and rode to the office of the diligence, which was situated in the Podolsk, or lower town. **1883** S. C. HALL *Retrospect* II. 207 When travelling.. on the top of a Diligence, Turner sketched, on the back of a letter, Heidelberg.

†**b.** Formerly used also in Great Britain. *Obs.*

1748 SMOLLETT *Rod. Rand.* xi, I shall make my lord very merry with our adventures in the diligence. [Satirically: it was a *wagon*.] **1776** WESLEY *Wks.* (1830) IV. 90, I set out for Bedford in the diligence. **1777** SHERIDAN *Sch. Scand.* I. i, Her guardian caught her just stepping into the York Diligence with her dancing-master. **1780** MAD. D'ARBLAY *Lett.* 9 June, If.. possible to send me a line by the diligence to Brighton. **1782** SIR J. E. SMITH in *Mem.* (1832) I. 55 We went in the diligence to Dumbarton. **1797** *Papers on Reform of Posts* App. ii. 3 The Diligence that sets out from Bath.. on Monday afternoon, will deliver a letter on Tuesday morning. **1849** MACAULAY *Hist. Eng.* I. 379 The interests of large classes had been unfavourably affected by the establishment of the new diligences.

c. Used for the passengers of a 'diligence'. (Cf. COACH *sb.* 1 c.)

1887 RUSKIN *Præterita* II. 400 The hour when the diligence dined.

d. *attrib.*

1861 *Sat. Rev.* 14 Dec. 607 Continuous diligence journey of three days and nights required to reach Madrid. **1866** MISS THACKERAY *Village on Cliff* in *Cornh. Mag.* 527, Catherine.. looked out through the diligence windows at the château.

†'**diligency.** *Obs.* [ad. L. *dīligentia*: see DILIGENCE[1] and -ENCY.] = DILIGENCE[1].

1494 FABYAN *Chron.* VI. clxxviii. 175 He caused the sayd Charlys.. to be norysshed & broughte vp with moost dylygensi. **1556** J. HEYWOOD *Spider & F.* lxxix. 53 Lack of this somers dayes diligentsie, May make me fast two dayes in winter. **1619** W. SCLATER *Exp. 1 Thess.* (1630) 192 Meanes, with more diligency attended. **1672** MRS. ALLEINE *Life Jos. Alleine* vi. (1838) 60 With greater ardency, diligency, and courage.

diligent ('dɪlɪdʒənt), *a.* (*adv.*) Also 5–6 deligent. [a. F. *diligent* (13–14th c. in Hatz.-Darm.), ad. L. *dīligent-em* attentive, assiduous, careful, in origin pr. pple. of *dīligĕre* to value or esteem highly, love, choose, affect, take delight in (doing); cf. Pr. *diligent*, Sp. and It. *diligente*.]

1. Of persons: 'Constant in application, persevering in endeavour, assiduous', industrious; 'not idle, not negligent, not lazy.' J.

1340 *Ayenb.* 32 Uolk.. þet by diligent ine þet hi byeþ yhyealde to done. *c* **1386** CHAUCER *Sompn. T.* 268 Oure covent To pray for yow is ay so diligent. *c* **1430** *Syr Gener.* 1152 Thei wer diligent in here seruice. **1500–20** DUNBAR *Poems* xc. 7 To fast and pray.. We synfull folk sulde be more deligent. **1535** COVERDALE *Prov.* xiii. 4 The soule of the diligent shal haue plenty. **1577** B. GOOGE *Heresbach's Husb.* I. (1586) 14 b, A painefull and diligent Bayliffe. **1583** HOLLYBAND *Campo di Fior* 53 Philopon is diligentest, and honestest of all. **1674** PLAYFORD *Skill Mus.* III. 38 He that will be diligent to know.. the true allowances. **1771** BURKE *Corr.* (1844) I. 351 Though he is not very active in the House, few are more diligent attenders. **1849** MACAULAY *Hist. Eng.* I. 427 Comforts and luxuries.. now unknown.. may be within the reach of every diligent and thrifty working man. **1877** MRS. OLIPHANT *Makers Flor.* ix. 224 He was a diligent student, working day and night.

2. Of actions, etc.: Constantly or steadily applied; prosecuted with activity and perserverance; assiduous.

c **1430** LYDG. *Min. Poems* 89 (Mätz.) Al these thynges, Founde of olde tyme by diligent travaile. ? *a* **1500** *Wycket* (1828) I Not in ydle lyuynge, but in diligente labourynge. **1703** DAMPIER *Voy.* III. Pref. A iv b, Things.. worthy of our Diligentest Search and Inquiry. **1847** LONGF. *Ev.* II, Silent awhile were its treadles, at rest was its diligent shuttle. **1887** BOWEN *Virg. Æneid* I. 455 Artist's cunning, and workman's diligent hand.

†**3.** Attentive, observant, heedful, careful. (Of persons and their actions, etc.) *Obs.*

c **1400** *Lanfranc's Cirurg.* 199 Men moun be delyuerid of manye greet sijknessis if her leche is kunnynge & diligent aboute hem. ? *c* **1460** SIR R. ROS *La Belle Dame sanz Mercy* 112 in *Pol. Rel. & L. Poems* (1866) 55 In his langage not gretely dyligente. **1535** COVERDALE *Job* xlii. 5, I haue geuen diligent eare vnto the. *a* **1552** SOMERSET in Foxe *A. & M.* (1563) 730 b, It maie appere vnto vs mete, more diligenter hede to be taken. **1593** HOOKER *Eccl. Pol.* III. i. (1611) 85 For lacke of diligent obseruing the difference. **1697** DAMPIER *Voy.* I. 73 A very diligent and observing person. **1701** SWIFT *Contests Nobles & Commons* iii, That exact and diligent writer Dionysius Halicarnasseus. **1756** BURKE *Subl. & B.* v. iv, On a very diligent examination of my own mind.. I do not find that.. any such picture is formed.

†**b.** Attentive to others; assiduous in service.

1566 *Wills & Inv. N. C.* (Surtees 1835) 264 All my children to be delegent and obbedient to hir as becummithe them. **1632** J. HAYWARD tr. *Biondi's Eromena* 105 Not like a waiting woman, but like a diligent Squire. **1689** SHADWELL *Bury F.* I. i, He will be diligent and fawning.

†**B.** *adv.* = DILIGENTLY. *Obs.*

1479 *Eng. Gilds* 413 So that.. they may the better, sewrer, and more diligenter, execute.. their said Officez. **1556** LAUDER *Tractate* 228 Quhilk suld be taucht most deligent Be faithfull Pastors. **1590** SPENSER *F.Q.* I. iii. 9 He wayted diligent, With humble service to her will prepard.

†'**diligent,** *v. Obs. rare.* [ad. F. *diligent-er* to execute with diligence (15th c. in Hatz.-Darm.), f. *diligent* DILIGENT.] *trans.* To bestow diligence upon; to work at diligently.

1545 RAYNOLD *Byrth Mankynde* (1634) IV. vi. 197 Be [the earth].. neuer so well diligented and picked, yet alwayes therein will remaine.. seeds of vnlooked for weeds.

diligently ('dɪlɪdʒəntlɪ), *adv.* [f. DILIGENT *a.* + -LY[2].] In a diligent manner; with diligence.

a. With steady application; assiduously, industriously; not idly or lazily; †with dispatch.

1340 *Ayenb.* 208 Huo þet zecþ diligentliche. **1382** WYCLIF *2 Chron.* xix. 11 Takith coumfort and doith diligently, and the Lord schal ben with ȝou in goodis. **1477** EARL RIVERS (Caxton) *Dictes* 128 If he be pouer to laboure dylygentely. **1530** TINDALE *Answ. to More* I. xxvi. Wks. (1573) 287/2 The Jewes studyed the scripture the deligenterly. *c* **1540** BOORDE *The boke for to Lerne* C ij b, They.. serue god the holy dayes.. more dylygentlyer, than to do theyr worke. **1568** GRAFTON *Chron.* II. 822 That all thinges.. shoulde be spedily and diligently done. **1612** T. TAYLOR *Comm. Titus* i. 6 Study to doe thy owne dutie diligently. **1752** JOHNSON *Rambler* No. 207 ¶8 When we have diligently laboured for any purpose. **1870** ANDERSON *Missions Amer. Bd.* III. iv. 53 Applying himself diligently.. to natural and theological science. **1894** J. T. FOWLER *Adamnan* Introd. 70 Columba laboured diligently among the Picts.

†**b.** Attentively, carefully, heedfully. *Obs.*

c **1391** CHAUCER *Astrol.* II. §17 Espie diligently whan this.. sterre passeth any-thing the sowth westward. **1483** CAXTON *Gold. Leg.* 72/1 Beholdyng hym dylygently in the clere lyght. **1559** W. CUNNINGHAM *Cosmogr. Glasse* 139 Marking diligentlye that the Center of the second Circle, be in the line of sighte. **1656** RIDGLEY *Pract. Physick* 87 It must be diligently distinguished from an Imposthume. **1695** LD. PRESTON *Boeth.* v. 226 It hath not yet been diligently and thorowly determined.

†'**diligentness.** *Obs. rare*[−0]. [f. as prec. + -NESS.] The quality of being diligent; diligence, assiduity.

1530 PALSGR. 212/2 Delygentnesse, *diligence*. **1580** BARET *Alv.* Q 15 Diligentnesse, lustinesse, quicknesse, *Impigritas*. **1727** BAILEY vol. II, *Diligentness*, diligence.

dilirious, -ium, obs. erron. ff. DELIRIOUS, -IUM.

dilituric (daɪlɪ'tjʊərɪk), *a. Chem.* [f. DI-[2] 2 + LITH-IC + URIC.] In *dilituric acid*, $C_4H_3(NO_2)N_2O_3$, a substitution product of urea, crystallizing in colourless square prisms and laminæ. Its salts are **dili'turates.**

1872 WATTS *Dict. Chem.* II. 966 Dilituric acid is tribasic... The diliturates have a white or yellow colour, and are remarkably stable.

diliuer(e, obs. forms of DELIVER.

dill (dɪl), *sb.*[1] [OE. *dili, dile,* (*dil*) *dyle* masc. = OLG. *dilli*, MDu. and Du. *dille* f., OHG. *tilli*, MHG. *tille* m. and f., Ger. *dill* m., *dille* f., Dan. *dild*, Sw. *dill*. Ulterior derivation unknown.]

1. An umbelliferous annual plant, *Anethum graveolens*, with yellow flowers, a native of the South of Europe, Egypt, India, South Africa, etc., cultivated in herb gardens in England and other countries, for its carminative fruits or 'seeds'. Also called ANET.

a **700** *Epinal* [& *a* **800** *Erf.*] *Gloss.* 21 *Anetum* dil. *a* **800** *Corpus Gloss.* 159 *Anetum* dili. *c* **1000** *Ags. Gosp.* Matt. xxiii. 23 Wa eow, boceras.. ȝe þe teoðiað mintan and dile and cymyn. *c* **1000** *Sax. Leechd.* II. 20 Wiþ heafod ece ȝenim diles blostman. *a* **1387** *Sinon. Barthol.* (Anecd. Oxon.) 10 *Anetum*, dile *vel* dille. *c* **1420** *Pallad. on Husb.* IV. 167 Nowe sette in places colde, senvey and dyle. **1578** LYTE *Dodoens* II. xc. 270 They sowe Dill in al gardens, amongst wortes, and Pot herbes. **1590** SPENSER *F.Q.* III. ii. 49 Had gathered rew, and savine, and the flowre Of camphora, and calamint, and dill. **1612** DRAYTON *Poly-olb.* xiii. 218 The wonder-working Dill.. Which curious women use in many a nice disease. **1627** DRAYTON *Agincourt, etc., Nymphidia* 127 Therewith her Veruayne and her Dill, That hindreth Witches of their will. **1778** BP. LOWTH *Transl. Isaiah* xxviii. 25 Doth not he then scatter the dill, and cast abroad the cummin? **1794** MARTYN *Rousseau's Bot.* v. 57 Some, as fennel, dill.. have yellow flowers. **1855** SINGLETON *Virgil* I. 11 The bloom of scented dill.

2. Applied locally to other umbelliferous plants; also to some species of vetch; see quots.

c **1680** *Enquiries* 2/2 Do you sow hereabout the GoreVetch.. Dills or Lentils? **1789** W. MARSHALL *Glouc.* Gloss., *Dill*, *ervum hirsutum*, two-seeded tare; which has been cultivated (on the Cotswold Hills) time immemorial, principally for hay. **1847–78** HALLIWELL, *Dill*, hedge parsley. *Var. dial.* **1881** *Leicester Gloss., Dill*, tare; vetch (*Vicia sativa*). **1884** *Cheshire Gloss., Dills*, Vetches. 'Dills and wuts' are often sown to be cut as green meat for horses.

3. *attrib.* and *Comb.*, as ***dill-flower, -fruit, -seed***; †**dill-nut** (*dil-note*), an old name of the Earth-nut, *Bunium* (also, by confusion of 'pig-nut' and 'sow-bread', taken in the herbals as Cyclamen); **dill pickle** orig. *U.S.*, a pickled cucumber, gherkin, etc., flavoured with dill; **dillwater**, a carminative draught prepared from dill; **dill weed**, a name in U.S. for May weed, *Anthemis Cotula*.

a **1450** *Alphita* (Anecd. Oxon.) 134 *Panis porcinus, ciclamen, malum terre*, dilnote *uel* erthenote. *a* **1500** *Laud MS.* 553 in Cockayne *Sax. Leechd.* III. 321 Ciclamum, eorþenote or dillnote or slyte or halywort. þis herbe hath leues ylich to fenel & whyte floures & a small stalk & he groweth in wodes & medes. **1586** W. WEBBE *Eng. Poetrie* (Arb.) 78 And dyll flowres most sweete that sauoureth also. **1641** FRENCH *Distill.* ii. (1651) 49 Adde to them.. of Dill-seed bruised two ounces. **1858** HOGG *Veg. Kingd.* 377 The carminative draught known as Dill water. **1860** *All Year Round* No. 52. 48 The dill-water stands upon the shelf. **1906** 'O. HENRY' *Four Million* (1916) 157 He saw her beginning upon a huge Dill pickle. **1916** H. L. WILSON *Somewhere in Red Gap* v. 217 A big dill pickle, two deviled eggs, and a half of one of these Camelbert [*sic*] cheeses. **1971** J. SANGSTER *Your Friendly Neighbourhood Death Pedlar* ii. 38 She.. pulled out a bottle. 'Dill pickle?'.. She laid one pickle on each plate.

†**dill,** *sb.*[2] *Obs. Rogues' Cant.* [Variant of, or error for, DELL[2].] A girl, wench.

a **1627** MIDDLETON *Spanish Gipsy* IV. i, Who loves not his dill, let him die at the gallows.

dill, *sb.*[3] *Naut.* The space underneath the cabin floor in a wooden fishing vessel, into which the bilge-water drains.

1882 *Standard* 11 Mar. 3/4 The lad was placed in the dill, a place at the bottom of the vessel, full of bilge water.

dill *sb.*[4], obs. form of DOLE, grief, mourning.

c **1420** *Anturs of Arth.* xv, I in dungun, and dill, is done for to duelle. *a* **1765** *Sir Cawline* iv. in Child *Ballads* III. lxi. 58/1 Great dill to him was dight.

dill *sb.*[5], erron. f. *dilse*, DULSE, a sea-weed.

1867 in SMYTH *Sailor's Word-bk.*

dill (dɪl), *sb.*[6] *Austral.* and *N.Z. slang.* Also dil. [app. back-formation from DILLY *a.*[1]] A fool or simpleton; *spec.* one who is duped by a trickster.

1941 BAKER *Dict. Austral. Slang* 23 *Dil*, a simpleton or fool. (2) A trickster's victim. **1949** *Evening News* 16 Feb. 4/6 Sydney has developed its own picturesque slang. They talk of.. 'a dill' (a weak character). **1957** 'N. CULOTTA' *They're a Weird Mob* (1958) i. 13 Well don't stand there like a dill. *Ibid.* ix. 133 Joe said they were a 'lot o' dills'. **1961** P. WHITE *Riders in Chariot* xv. 503, I am the same dill that always stuck around! **1969** *Telegraph* (Brisbane) 28 Aug. 2/7 At the start he felt a bit of a dill in a wig and robes. **1970** *N.Z. Listener* 12 Oct. 12/5 She acted like a dill. She shouldn't have antagonised us.

†**dill,** *a. north. dial. Obs.* Also 4 dil, dille, deille, dylle. [Perh. early form of DULL *a.* q.v.] Sluggish, slow, stupid, dull.

c **1200** ORMIN 3714 Mannkinn þatt wass stunnt & dill, & skilllæs swa summ asse. *a* **1300** *Cursor M.* 17225 (Cott.) Bot i þat es sa dedli dill, Me spedis ai me-self to spill. *Ibid.* 27238 Yong man [is] idel, and ald man dill. **13..** *E.E. Allit. P.* A. 679 Hymself to onsware he is not dylle. **13..** *Gaw. & Gr. Knt.* 1529 3e demen me to dille your dalyaunce to herken. *a* **1400** *Relig. Pieces fr. Thornton MS.* ix (1867) 91 All þe dedes þay couthe doo þat derfe ware and dill. *c* **1440** *York Myst.* xxvii. 149 So wel away! That euer I did þat dede so dill.

† **dill**, *v.*[1] *Obs.* Also 4 **dil, dyle.** [a. ON. *dylja* (pa. t. *duldi, dulði*, pa. pple. *duldr, duliðr*), Sw. *dölja*, Da. *dölge* to conceal, hide, keep close, disguise: cf. ON. *dul* concealment, *dulr* silent, close, *dul*-secret.]

1. *trans.* to conceal, hide, keep secret.

a **1300** *Cursor M.* 202 (Cott.) Iuus wit þer gret vnschill Wend his vprisyng to dill. *Ibid.* 1081 His broiþer ded sua wend he dil, Bot he moght nourquar it hil. *Ibid.* 4271 And ioseph lette he wist it noght; He wist and dild it, als þe wis. *Ibid.* 13031 Naman aght it thol ne dill. [*Fairf.* dyle.] *Ibid.* 21363 Þe right rode þai wend to dil [*Fairf.* dille] Vte of þe cristen men skil.

2. *intr.* To conceal oneself, to hide.

a **1300** *Cursor M.* 9292 (Cott.) Fra him for-soth sal nan cun dil [*v. rr.* stele, wiþdrawe].

dill, *v.*[2] *north. dial.* [Related to DILL *a.*: cf. DULL *v.*; also ON. *dilla* intr. to trill, to lull.] *trans.* To soothe, assuage, lull, quiet down.

c **1450** HENRYSON *Robin & Ma.* v, My dule in dern bot gif thow dill Doutles bot dreid I de. *c* **1460** *Towneley Myst.* xv. 80 (Surtees) 136 My son? alas, for care! who may my doyllys dyll? **1641** R. BAILLIE *Lett. & Jrnls.* (1841) I. 310 The noise of the Queen's Voyage to France is dilled down. **1820** J. STRUTHERS *Brit. Minstrel* II. 80 The word dill means simply to soothe or assuage. **1851** S. JUDD *Margaret* 140 (Bartlett) This medecine. It'll dill fevers, dry up sores.. kill worms. **1855** ROBINSON *Whitby Gloss.*, *Dill*, to ease pain, to lull, as something 'to dill the toothache'. **1875** *Lanc. Gloss.*, *Dill*, to lull or soothe a child.. 'thee dill that chylt an' git it asleep'.

b. *absol.* To benumb, cause dullness.

c **1450** *St. Cuthbert* (Surtees) 4034 With þaim þe seke man fete he hilde For þare þe paralisy first dilde.

† **dill**, *v.*[3] *Obs.* [Origin uncertain.] *trans.* To trim, deck, dress up. (Also *absol.*)

1548 HOOPER *Declar. 10 Commandm.* x. Wks. (Parker Soc.) 377 Other sort.. are a-dilling and burling of their hair a longer time than a godly woman.. is in apparelling of three or four young infants. **1594** WILLOBIE *Arisa* xx. i. (1635) 38 No maruell well, though you haue thriu'd That so can decke, that so can dill. **1616** J. LANE *Cont. Sqr.'s T.* xi. 160 The vanities of thother knightes and ladies; The fickell pompe of dilld-vp whifflinge babies.

‖**Dillenia** (dɪˈliːnɪə). *Bot.* [mod.L. after *Dillenius*, professor of botany at Oxford 1728–1747.] A genus of plants, typical of the N.O. *Dilleniaceæ*, natives of India and the Eastern peninsula, consisting of lofty forest trees with handsome flowers. Hence **dilleniˈaceous** *a.*, of or belonging to the natural order *Dilleniaceæ*. **diˈlleniad**, a member of this natural order.

1753 CHAMBERS *Cycl. Supp.*, *Dillenia*,.. a genus of plants. **1807** J. E. SMITH *Phys. Bot.* 377 Dillenia, with its beautiful blossoms and fruit, serves to immortalize two of the most meritorious among botanists. **1837** *Penny Cycl.* VIII. 497 Dilleniaceous plants are distinguished.. from Magnoliaceæ by their want of stipules. **1866** *Treas. Bot.* I. 408 The species of this genus of dilleniads are handsome lofty trees inhabiting dense forests in India.

† **dilli-ˈdarling.** *Obs. rare.* [First element app. identical with DILLING.] A term of endearment: a darling. So **dilli-ˈminion.**

[These terms translate F. *dorelot* and *bedault*, both of which Cotgr. renders 'dilling'.]

a **1693** URQUHART *Rabelais* III. xiv. 114 As if I had been a.. neat dillidarling Minion, like Adonis. *Ibid.* III. xviii. 146 My dainty Fedle-darling, my gentiel Dilli-minion.

ˈdilligrout. *Obs.* exc. *Hist.* Also **dile-, dille-, dilly-.** [Derivation unknown.

In the recent form of the word, the second element is app. taken as *grout* porridge of coarse meal; but this appears to be only a 17th c. mis-reading of the Anglo-French *del girunt* or *geroun* of unknown meaning. Cf. *Testa de Neville* (Recd.), Debet facere ferculum [quendam] quod vocatur [del] girunt. **1304** *Lib. de Antiq. Leg.* p. lxxix. Ferculum pro domino Rege quod vocatur mees de geroun.]

A kind of pottage, of which a mess was offered to the Kings of England on their coronation-day, by the lord of the manor of Addington in Surrey, being the 'service' by which that manor was held.

(In Domesday the manor is held by Tezelin the King's cook.)

1662 *St. George's Day* (1685) 10 Thomas Leigh Esquire was brought up to the Table with a Mess of Pottage called *Dilegrout*, by reason of his Tenure of the Manor of Addington. **1679** BLOUNT *Anc. Tenures* 1. **1727** *Ceremonies Coronations* 49 Then follows the Mess of Pottage, or Gruel, called *Dillegrout*. **1778** *Eng. Gazetteer* (ed. 2) s.v. *Addington*, The Ld. of this manor, in the R. of Henr. III. held it by this service, viz. to make his Majesty a mess of pottage in an earthen pot in the K's kitchen at his coronation, called Dilligrout. **1880** BURTON *Reign Q. Anne* I. i. 51.

dilling (ˈdɪlɪŋ). *Obs.* exc. *dial.* [Of doubtful etymology: it has been variously conjectured to be connected with DILL *v.*[2], or ON. *dilla* to trill, to lull, or to be a modification of *derling*, DARLING. Further evidence is wanted.] A term of endearment, sometimes equivalent to *darling*, sometimes, the youngest of a family, the last born. In modern dialects applied to the weakling of a litter.

[**1547** SALESBURY *Welsh Dict.*, Dillin Mignyon.] **1584** B. R. *Herodotus* 106 After this there befell unto him another mischiefe that sate as neere his skirtes as the death of his dilling. **1598** FLORIO, *Mignone*, a minion, a fauorit, a dilling, a minikin, a darling. **1607** MARSTON *What you Will* II. i, Sunne, Moone, and seauen Starres make thee the dilling of Fortune. **1611** COTGR., *Besot*, a dilling, or swill-pough; the last, or yongest child one hath. **1612** DRAYTON *Poly-olb.* ii. 26 The youngest and the last.. Saint Hellen's name doth beare, the dilling of her mother. **1617** MINSHEU *Ductor in Ling.*, A *Dilling* or wanton, one borne his father being very old.. he is loved more than the rest. *a* **1639** WHATELY *Prototypes* II. xxvi. (1640) 76 For Joseph and Benjamin.. they were his youngest sons, dillings as we call them. **1674** RAY *S. & E.C. Words* 64 A *Dilling*; a Darling or best-beloved child. **1890** ROBERTSON *Glouc Gloss.*, *Dilling pig* or *dolly pig*, the weakly pig of a litter.

dillisk, -esk, -osk, dills, Irish and Sc. names of DULSE.

dill-nut: see under DILL *sb.*[1]

† **ˈdillue**, *v. Mining. Obs.* Also 8 **dilleugh**, 7–8 erron. **dilve.** [a. Cornish *dyllo* to send forth, emit, let out, liberate, discharge (Williams) = Welsh *dillwng* to let go, liberate. (The final *o* in the Cornish was very close, hence the Eng. spelling *ue*.)] *trans.* To finish the dressing of (tin-ore) by shaking it in a fine sieve in water. Hence **dilluer, dilluing-sieve.**

1671 in *Phil. Trans.* VI. 2110 We.. dilue [*printed* dilve] it (i.e. by putting it into a Canvass Sieve, which holds water, and in a large Tub of water lustily shake it) so that the filth gets over the rim of the Sieve, leaving the Black Tin behind. **1721** BAILEY, *Dilving*, a word used in the dressing Tin Ore. **1778** W. PRYCE *Min. Cornub.* 223 The latter [waste] will run or fly over, and is called dilleughing smalls or pitworks. *Ibid.* 319 *Dillueing.* (*Dilleugh*, To let go, let fly, send away. *Dylyr*, id. Cornish.) A method of washing or finishing the dressing of Tin in very fine hair sieves, called Dillueing sieves, or Dilluers.

dill weed: see under DILL *sb.*[1]

dilly (ˈdɪlɪ), *sb.*[1] [Abbreviation of DILIGENCE[2].]

† **1.** A familiar term for the diligence or public stage-coach of former days. *Obs.*

1786 MACKENZIE *Lounger* No. 54 ¶ 5 A coach with eight insides, besides two boys and their governor in the dilly. **1798** J. W. FRERE *Loves of the Triangles* (*Anti-Jacobin*) 179 So down thy hill, romantic Ashbourn, glides The Derby dilly, carrying *Three* Insides. **1811** E. LYSAGHT *Poems* 39 Some to avoid mad care's approaches Fly off in dillies, or mail-coaches. **1818** MOORE *Fudge Fam. Paris* x. 35 'Beginning gay, desperate, dashing down-hilly; And ending as dull as a six-inside Dilly!' **1894** SIR J. D. ASTLEY *Fifty Years of my Life* I. 93 This always swung at the side of the 'dilly' [*Note, i.e.* diligence].

† **2.** A kind of vehicle, private or plying for hire. *Obs.*

1794 W. FELTON *Carriages* (1801) II. App. 14 The price of a simple Dilly or Chair Box caned or ruled with springs is five guineas. **1833** MARRYAT *P. Simple* (1863) 47 We sallied forth, and.. found all sorts of vehicles ready to take us to the fair. We got into one which they called a dilly. **1840** —— *Poor Jack* xi, Dillies.. plied at the Elephant and Castle.

3. Applied dialectally to various carts, trucks, and other wheeled vehicles, used in agriculture and industrial operations.

1850 *Jrnl. R. Agric. Soc.* XI. II. 727 Crops of vegetables.. which they carry to the Bristol market in their 'dillies' as their light platform carts are called. **1863** MORTON *Cycl. Agric.* Gloss., *Dilly* (West. Eng.), a frame on wheels for carrying teazles and other light matters. **1877** *N.W. Linc. Gloss.*, *Dilly*, a vehicle used for removing manure. **1888** ELWORTHY *W. Somerset Word-bk.* 194 *Dilly*, A cask on wheels for carrying liquids; a water-cart. Also a low four-wheeled truck on which mowing-machines and other implements are drawn. **1892** *Northumbld. Gloss.*, The old engine on the Wylam railway was.. called.. 'the Wylam dilly'. The counter-balance mounted upon two pairs of tramwheels, by means of which the empty tubs in a pit are carried up an incline, is called a dilly.

ˈdilly, *sb.*[2] *colloq.* or *dial.* A call to ducks; hence, a nursery name for a duck (also *dilly-duck*).

.. *Nursery Song* 'Mrs. Bond', John Ostler, go fetch me a duckling or two; Cry, dilly, dilly, dilly, dilly, come and be killed. *a* **1845** HOOD *Drowning Ducks* xiv, The tenants.. Had found the way to *Pick a dilly*. **1880** BLACKMORE *Mary Anerley* I. xviii. 283 The sweetness and culture of tame dilly-ducks. **1888** *Berksh. Gloss.*, *Dill* or *Dilly*, Call for ducks.

ˈdilly, *sb.*[3] A familiar shortening of DAFFODILLY.

1878 BRITTEN & HOLLAND *Plant-n.*, *Dilly*, an abbreviation of daffodilly. *Derby. White Dillies*, i.e. white daffodillies, *Narcissus poeticus. Lanc.*

ˈdilly, *sb.*[4] [Shortened from *Sapodilla*, the name used by Catesby *Nat. Hist. Carolina* II. 87.] In ***wild dilly***, a small sapotaceous tree, *Mimusops Sieberi*, found in the W. Indies and on the Florida keys, and yielding a very hard wood.

1895 SARGENT *Silva N. America* V. 183 Wild Dilly, discovered on the Bahamas by Mark Catesby. Catesby calls it 'Sappodillo Tree'.

dilly (ˈdɪlɪ), *sb.*[5] *slang* (orig. *U.S.*). [f. DILLY *a.*[2]] A delightful, remarkable, or excellent person or thing; freq. ironical.

1935 *Amer. Mercury* June 229/1 Ain't that a *dilly* (or *honey*)! **1950** 'S. RANSOME' *Deadly Miss Ashley* vi. 65 She looked as if she had had a rugged night of it; but she was easily repairable and still a dilly. **1951** R. S. PRATHER *Bodies in Bedlam* vii. 48 In order to get inside you have to pass three guards at three different gates. The first two aren't so tough, but the last one is a dilly if you don't have an appointment. **1958** R. CHANDLER *Playback* xix. 159 You're the most impossible man I ever met. And I've met some dillies. **1968** M. KANE *Walk of Devil* vii. 79 'Did you swing it, Jake?' Berger asked Winthrop... 'It's a dilly,' Winthrop said. **1970** *Daily Colonist* (Victoria, B.C.) 1 Dec. 9/4 The new [oil] well, also in Norwegian waters, looks a dilly.

dilly (ˈdɪlɪ), *a.*[1] *dial.* or *colloq.* (chiefly *Austral.*). [Perh. f. DAFT *a.* + SILLY *a.*] **a.** (See quot. 1873.) **b.** Foolish, stupid, mad.

1873 WILLIAMS & JONES *Gloss. Somersetshire* 11 *Dilly*,.. cranky, queer. **1906** E. DYSON *Fact'ry 'Ands* xvi. 214 Who should come sprintin' upstairs but me nibs, pale's er blessed egg, hair on end—fair dilly. **1908** J. GUNN *We of Never-Never* xiii. 168 Gone clean dilly, I believe. **1915** C. J. DENNIS in *Bulletin* (Sydney) 15 Apr. 43/2 Ther's a Gawd 'Oo's leaning near To watch our dilly little lives down 'ere. **1942** BERREY & VAN DEN BARK *Amer. Thes. Slang* §151/10 Foolish; nonsensical; ridiculous,.. *dilly*.

dilly (ˈdɪlɪ), *a.*[2] *colloq.* [f. the first syllable of DELIGHTFUL *a.* or DELICIOUS *a.* + -Y[6].] Delightful; delicious.

1909 *Punch* 26 May 362/1, I sent out the ordinary cards.. with 'Dancing' in one corner of the card, but in the *other* corner was 'Bare feet'. Wasn't it a dilly idea? **1922** C. E. M. JOAD *Highbrows* iii. 103 Have you heard that new waltz, 'Luscious Love'? It's simply dilly.

ˈdilly-bag. *Australia.* Also simply **dilli, dilly.** [*dilli* native name in Queensland.] **a.** An Australian native-made bag or basket, plaited of rushes or bark. Hence **dillyful**.

1847 LEICHHARDT *Jrnl.* iii. 90 In their 'dillis' (small baskets) were several roots or tubers. *Ibid.* 91 Dillis neatly worked of Koorajone bark. **1885** MRS. C. PRAED *Australian Life* 34, I learned too at the camp to plait dilly-bags. **1889** —— *Romance of Station* 75 A fresh dillyful of live crabs. **1890** BOLDREWOOD *Colonial Reformer* xvii. 210 May-boy came forward dangling a small dilly-bag. **1893** MRS. C. PRAED *Outlaw & Lawmaker* I. 103 The dilly-bag, which had been plaited by the gins, smelled atrociously.

b. *Austral. colloq.* Any small bag in which articles are carried.

1934 *Bulletin* (Sydney) 5 Dec. 48/1 He had seen young Willie leave the farmhouse carrying the tea and a dilly-bag of cakes. **1937** PARTRIDGE *Dict. Slang* 221/1 *Dilly-bag*, a wallet; a civilian haversack... In C. 20, often used by women for a small shopping-bag or for a general-utility purse-bag.

dilly-dally (ˈdɪlɪˈdælɪ), *v.* [A varied reduplication of DALLY *v.*, with the same alternation as in *zig-zag, shilly-shally*, etc., expressing see-saw action.] *intr.* To act with trifling vacillation or indecision; to go on dallying *with* a thing without advancing; to loiter in vacillation, to trifle.

(Prob. in colloquial use as early as 1600: cf. the sb.)

1741 RICHARDSON *Pamela* (1824) I. 100 What you do, sir, do; don't stand dilly-dallying. **1801** MAR. EDGEWORTH *Belinda* (1832) I. xvii. 320, I.. knew she'd dilly dally with Clary till he would turn upon his heel and leave her. **1877** SPURGEON *Serm.* XXIII. 598 Every man.. who dilly-dallies with salvation and runs risks with his soul. **1883** STEVENSON *Treasure Isl.* IV. xvi, There is no time to dilly-dally in our work.

Hence **ˈdilly-ˈdallying** *vbl. sb.* and *ppl. a.*; **ˈdilly-ˈdallier.**

1879 MRS. L. B. WALFORD *Cousins* III. 214 Mind you I'll have no dilly-dallying this time. **1880** WEBB *Goethe's Faust* Prel. for Theatre 14 Don't say you're not in time to show it! The dillydallier ne'er will be. **1881** *Durham Univ. Jrnl.* 17 Dec. 133 Half-hearted, dilly-dallying work.

ˈdilly-ˈdally, *sb.*, *a.*, *adv.* [f. the vb.]

† **A.** *sb.* Dilly-dallying, trifling hesitancy. Also the name of a game. *Obs.*

a **1610** BABINGTON *Comf. Notes, Gen.* xxiv. 57 Such dilly dally is fitter for heathens that know not God, than for sober Christians. **1698** E. WARD *Trip Jamaica* Wks. 1717 II. 156 The chief sports we had on board, to pass the tedious hours, were Hob, Spie the Market, Shove the Slipper, Dilly-Dally.

B. *adj.* (*dial.*). **C.** *adv.* (*nonce-use.*)

1749 FIELDING *Tom Jones* XVIII. xii, If I had suffered her to stand shill I shall I, dilly dally, you might not have had that honour yet awhile. **1888** ELWORTHY *W. Somerset Word-bk.* 194 *Dilly-dally*, undecided; shilly-shally. **1893** Q. [COUCH] *Delectable Duchy* 240 Of all the dilly-dallyin' men I must say, John, you'm the dilly-dalliest.

† **dillydown.** *Obs. rare.* Cf. DILLI-DARLING, DILLING.

c **1460** *Towneley Myst.* (Surtees) 115 A pratty child is he.. A dylly downe, perde, To gar a man laghe.

dillyful: see DILLY-BAG.

dilmond, var. f. DINMONT.

dilnote, obs. f. *dill-nut*: see DILL *sb.*[1] 3.

dilo ('diːləʊ). The Fijian name for the domba, *Calophyllum inophyllum*. Also *attrib.*, as *dilo oil, tree*.
1874 in LINDLEY & MOORE *Treas. Bot.* Suppl. **1879** *Encycl. Brit.* IX. 156/2 The dilo.., the oil from its seeds being much used in the [Fiji] islands.., in the treatment of rheumatism. **1894** B. THOMSON *S. Sea Yarns* 184 His arm was thick and knotted as yon dilo-tree.

dilogical (daɪˈlɒdʒɪkəl), *a.* [f. Gr. δίλογος doubtful, διλογία repetition + -IC + -AL^1, after *logical*.] Having a double meaning; equivocal.
*c***1633** T. ADAMS *Wks.* (1861–2) I. 10 (D.) In such spurious, enigmatical, dilogical terms as the devil gave his oracles.

dilogy ('dɪlədʒɪ, 'daɪlədʒɪ). *Rhet.* [ad. L. *dilogia* ambiguity, a. Gr. διλογία, f. δίλογος, f. δι- twice + -λογος speaking. In mod.F. *dilogie*.]
1. The use of an ambiguous or equivocal expression; the word or expression so used.
1656 BLOUNT *Glossogr.*, *Dilogy*, a doubtful speech, which may signifie or be construed two ways. **1832** J. C. HARE in *Philol. Museum* I. 460 A double meaning or dilogy is the saying only one thing, but having two things in view.
2. Repetition of a word or phrase, in the same context. In recent Dicts.

†**di'loricate**, *v. Obs. rare*$^{-0}$. [f. L. *dīlōrīcāt-*, ppl. stem of *dīlōrīcāre* to tear apart or open (one's dress, etc.), f. *dī-* (*dis-*) apart + *lōrīca* leathern cuirass.]
1623 COCKERAM, *Diloricate*, to rip. **1656** BLOUNT *Glossogr.*, *Diloricate*, to undo, cut or rip a coat that is sewed.

dilruba (dɪlˈruːbə). An Indian musical instrument having a long neck, three or four main strings played with a bow, and several sympathetic strings.
[**1887** *Hindu Mus. & Gayan Samaj* III. 53 List of musical instruments in India... Dilarubâba.] **1921** H. A. POPLEY *Music of India* vii. 107 The *Dilruba* is very much like a sitār, but smaller; and instead of a bowl, it has a belly, covered with sheep-parchment. In shape it is something like the sārangī, and like that instrument it is played with a bow made of horsehair. **1969** R. SHANKAR *My Music* i. 38/1 Several other bowed stringed instruments not as popular as the *sarangi* are the *dilruba*, *esraj*, and *sarinda*.

dilse, Sc. form of DULSE.

†**di'lucid**, *a. Obs.* [ad. L. *dīlūcid-us* clear, bright, f. *dīlūcēre* to be clear, f. *dī-*, *dis-* apart (DIS- 1) + *lūcēre* to shine, be light.]
1. *lit.* Clear to the sight; pure, bright. *rare.*
1650 BULWER *Anthropomet.* vii. (1653) 133 Eares..soft and delicate, aspersed with the dilucid colour of Roses.
2. Clear to the understanding; lucid, plain, manifest.
*a***1640** JACKSON *Creed* x. xiii, His illustrations out of scripture are far more dilucide. **1640** G. WATTS tr. *Bacon's Adv. Learn.* VIII. iii. (R.), An ambiguous, or not so perspicuous and dilucide description of lawes. **1671** *True Nonconf.* 224 A dilucide and th[o]rough knowledge.

†**di'lucidate**, *ppl. a. Obs.* [ad. L. *dīlūcidātus*, pa. pple. of *dīlūcidāre* to make clear, to explain, f. *dīlūcid-us*: see prec.] Made clear or lucid; = prec. Hence †**dilucidateness**.
1651 BIGGS *New Disp.* ¶ 297 Very often more dilucidate in their abstracted part. **1727** BAILEY vol. II, *Dilucidateness*.. clearness, plainness.

†**di'lucidate**, *v. Obs.* Also 6–7 de-. [f. L. *dīlūcidāt-* ppl. stem of *dīlūcidāre*: see prec.] *trans.* To make clear or plain; to elucidate.
1538 *St. Papers Hen. VIII*, I. 576 Such annotacions.. as shall douteles delucidate and cleare the same. **1611** COTGR., *Dilucider*, to cleere, dilucidate, explain, manifest. **1638** SIR T. HERBERT *Trav.* (ed. 2) 95 Till time might delucidate his innocency. **1761** STERNE *Tr. Shandy* III. xxxviii, He has.. examined every part of it dialectically..dilucidating it with all the light which..the collision of his own natural parts could strike. **1764** T. PHILLIPS *Life Reg. Pole* (1767) I. 43 His conscience was interested in having the lawfulness of it dilucidated.
Hence **di'lucidated** *ppl. a.*; **dilucidating** *vbl. sb.*; **dilucidator**.
*a***1660** HAMMOND *Wks.* II. III. 6 (R.) For the dilucidating of obscurities in ancient story. **1689** (*title*), The Dilucidator, or Reflections upon modern transactions, by way of Letters from a person at Amsterdam to his friend in London. **1759** DILWORTH *Pope* 2 A concise and dilucidated account of the life of Pope.

†**diluci'dation**. *Obs.* [ad. L. *dīlūcidātiōn-em*, n. of action from *dīlūcidāre* to DILUCIDATE.] The action of making lucid or clear; a clearing up; explanation, elucidation.
1615 CROOKE *Body of Man* 698 It remaineth that wee proceede vnto the dilucidation of some difficult questions concerning the Eares. **1657** TOMLINSON *Renou's Disp.* 502 It needs no further dilucidation. *a***1661** HOLYDAY *Juvenal* 121 As Marcellus Donatus observed in his Dilucidations of Livie. **1744** WARBURTON *Wks.* (1811) XI. 277 A full dilucidation of my four propositions.

†**dilu'cidity**. *Obs.* [f. DILUCID: see -ITY.] The quality of being dilucid; clearness, lucidity.
1603 HOLLAND *Plutarch's Mor.* 1199 Together with plainnesse, and dilucidity, beliefe was so turned and altered.

†**di'lucidly**, *adv. Obs.* [f. DILUCID + -LY^2.] Lucidly; clearly, plainly.
1638 MEDE *Ep. to Hartlib* Wks. (1672) IV. 869 If I have not expressed myself so dilucidly as I should, I pray help it. **1677** CARY *Chronol.* II. II. Concl. 270 Provided that he..do first Dilucidely answer those Objections.

diludge, obs. var. of DELUGE.

diluent ('dɪl(j)uːənt), *a.* and *sb.* [ad. L. *dīluent-em*, pr. pple. of *dīluĕre* to wash away, dissolve: see DILUTE.] **A.** *adj.*
1. Diluting; serving to attenuate or weaken the consistency of any fluid by the addition of water or the like; *spec.*, in medicine, making thin the fluids of the body.
1731 ARBUTHNOT *On Aliments* v. (R.), There is no real diluent but water; every fluid is diluent as it contains water in it. **1757** JOHNSTONE in *Phil. Trans.* L. 546 To drink plentifully of thin broths, and other soft diluent liquors. **1833** E. FITZGERALD *Lett.* (1889) I. 20 None of the washy, diluent effects of green vegetables. **1884** H. W. BEECHER in *Chr. World Pulpit* XXV. 234 As men mix strong wines with diluent water.
2. That has the property of dissolving; solvent.
1878 MOZLEY *Ess.* II. 379 (*Argt. Design*) A rule much more diluent of all certainty.
B. *sb.*
1. That which dilutes, dissolves, or makes more fluid; a diluting agent; a solvent.
1775 SIR E. BARRY *Observ. Wines* 392 This is the universal diluent. **1827** ABERNETHY *Surg. Wks.* I. 31 The pancreatic juice has been considered as an useful and necessary diluent. **1856** R. A. VAUGHAN *Mystics* (1860) I. 215 A chemist might call the former the sublimate, the latter the diluent, of the Actual. **1878** MOZLEY *Ess.* II. 382 (*Argt. Design*) They are dissolved as soon as they enter this strong diluent.
2. *spec.* A substance which increases the proportion of water in the blood and other bodily fluids.
1721 BAILEY, *Diluents*..medicines serving to thin the blood. **1732** ARBUTHNOT *Rules of Diet* 270 Diluents, as Water, Whey, Tea. **1782** J. C. SMYTH in *Med. Commun.* I. 77 Warm diluents were..all that were necessary for the cure. **1861** FLO. NIGHTINGALE *Nursing* 53 The patient requires diluents for quite other purposes than quenching the thirst. **1875** H. C. WOOD *Therap.* (1879) 588 A diluent is an indifferent substance which is absorbed and in its passage through the body simply dilutes the various fluids of the organism as well as the excretions.

dilute (dɪ-, daɪˈl(j)uːt), *ppl. a.* [ad. L. *dīlūt-us* diluted, weak, thin, pa. pple. f. *dīluĕre* to dissolve, dilute, f. *di-*, *dis-* (DIS- 1) + *luĕre* to wash.]
1. Weakened in consistency or strength by the addition of water or of anything having a like effect; watered down.
1658 PHILLIPS, s.v. *Dilution*, Wine dilute signifieth wine that is mingled with water. *c***1698** LOCKE *Cond. Underst.* §45 A large dose of dilute tea. **1757** A. COOPER *Distiller* I. xvi. (1760) 70 The Wash should be made dilute or thin. **1843** SIR C. SCUDAMORE *Med. Visit Gräfenberg* 22 In the most dilute urine, I found the evidence of saline matter.
b. *spec.* of a chemical substance.
1800 HENRY *Epit. Chem.* (1808) 118 Weigh the dilute acid employed. **1816** ACCUM *Chem. Tests* (1818) 176 Soluble in dilute nitric and acetic acid. **1871** B. STEWART *Heat* §129 One of dilute sulphuric acid.
c. Of a weakened or weaker colour (as in an infusion to which water is added); washed-out.
1665 *Phil. Trans.* I. 106 After a while it [matter]..grows dilute and pale. **1728** PEMBERTON *Newton's Philos.* 346 The yellow which preceded this was at first pretty good, but soon grew dilute. **1796** WITHERING *Brit. Plants* IV. 262 Gills fixed, dilute green..or whitish towards the edges. **1813** PRICHARD *Phys. Hist. Mankind* (1836) I. 221 A much lighter, or more dilute shade. **1860** TYNDALL *Glac.* I. xviii. 128 And permit the sun to shed a ghastly dilute light.
2. *fig.* Weak, enfeebled, poor, paltry. *Obs.* (exc. as directly *fig.* from 1).
1605 BACON *Adv. Learn.* II. xxv. §12. 125 The more you recede from the Scriptures..the more weake and dilute are your positions. *a***1631** DONNE *Serm. Hosea* ii. 19 (1634) 22 How pallid, and faint, and dilute a thing all the honours of this world are. **1664** H. MORE *Myst. Iniq.* 208 It were a dilute business for the Apostle to describe Antichrist onely by the bare denial of Jesus his being the Christ. **1722** WOLLASTON *Relig. Nat.* viii. 166 The relation between the children of these children grows more remote and dilute, and in time wears out. **1814** *Monthly Mag.* XXXVII. 333 Many a work of art distilled to its essential beauties would keep, which putrifies in its dilute state.

dilute (dɪ-, daɪˈl(j)uːt), *v.* [f. L. *dīlūt-* ppl. stem of *dīluĕre*: see prec. Cf. F. *diluer*.]
1. *trans.* To dissolve or make liquid by the addition of water, *esp.* to make thinner or weaker by this means, to water down; to reduce the strength of (a fluid) by admixture.
1664 EVELYN *Kal. Hort.* (1729) 207 Diluting it with a Portion of Water. **1712** BLACKMORE *Creation* VI. (R.), By constant weeping mix their watery store With the chyle's current, and dilute it more. **1791** COWPER *Iliad* IX. 251 Replenish it with wine Diluted less. **1791** HAMILTON *Berthollet's Dyeing* I. I. I. i. 5 Sulphuric acid diluted with a very large quantity of water. **1799** G. SMITH *Laboratory* I. 270 Lay on it muscle-shell gold or silver, diluted with size. **1800** tr. *Lagrange's Chem.* I. 294 Dilute one part of calcined bones in four parts of water. **1830** M. DONOVAN *Dom. Econ.* I. 373 A small quantity of brandy, diluted with much water. **1856** EMERSON *Eng. Traits, Result* Wks. (Bohn) II. 133 In bad seasons, the porridge was diluted. **1867** W. W. SMYTH *Coal & Coal-mining* 223 An adequate amount of ventilation ..to dilute and render harmless noxious gases.
†**b.** *Med.* To treat with diluents. *Obs.*
1740 E. BAYNARD *Health* (ed. 6) 11 They cool, dilute, and quench the thirst. **1768** FOOTE *Devil on 2 Sticks* III. Wks. 1799 II. 275 Full power..to pill..dilute..and poultice, all persons.
2. To weaken the brilliancy of (colour); to make of a faint or washed-out hue.
1665 HOOKE *Microgr.* 69 Saline refracting bodies which do dilute the colour of the one, do deepen that of the other. *Ibid.* 71 There are other Blues, which..will not be diluted by grinding. *a***1727** NEWTON (J.), The chamber was dark, lest these colours should be diluted and weakened by the mixture of any adventitious light. **1794** HOME in *Phil. Trans.* LXXXV. 3 Which by diluting the image formed in the focus ..makes that image appear far less bright.
3. *fig.* To weaken, take away the strength or force of: generally with obvious reference to the literal sense.
*c***1555** HARPSFIELD *Divorce Hen. VIII* (1878) 124 These arguments the adversaries went about to dilute and solve. **1810** SYD. SMITH *Ess., Fem. Educ.* (1869) 199 Can there be any reason why she should be diluted and enfeebled down to a mere culler of simples? **1831** BREWSTER *Newton* (1855) I. x. 225 The second dissertation..in which he dilutes the objections made against the theory. **1852** H. COLERIDGE *North. Worthies* Advt. 16 The Author finds..nothing which he is resolved to Dilute into no meaning. *a***1853** ROBERTSON *Serm.* Ser. III. i. (1872) 2 That unreal religion of excitement which diluted the earnestness of real religion in the enjoyment of listening.
4. *intr.* (for *refl.*) To suffer dilution; to become dissolved; to become attenuated.
1764 REID *Inquiry* vi. §22 Wks. I. 191/1 The colours of the stone and of the cement begin to dilute into one another.

diluted (dɪ-, daɪˈl(j)uːtɪd), *ppl. a.* [f. prec. + -ED.] Weakened by the addition of water or other attenuating admixture, watered down; reduced in strength, colour, or characteristic quality.
1681 tr. *Willis' Rem. Med. Wks.* Vocab., *Diluted*, rinsed or washed. **1783** MASON *Art of Painting* 672 (R.) The social circle, the diluted bowl. **1800** tr. *Lagrange's Chem.* II. 193 Pour diluted nitric acid over sugar. **1837** BABBAGE *Bridgew. Treat.* vii. 90 A denser central nucleus surrounded by a more diluted light. **1847** EMERSON *Poems, Bacchus* Wks. (Bohn) I. 469 We buy diluted wine.
fig. **1831** CARLYLE *Sart. Res.* II. x, Almost like diluted madness. **1837** EMERSON *Addr., Amer. Schol.* Wks. (Bohn) II. 180 The rough, spontaneous conversation of men they [clergymen] do not hear, but only a mincing and diluted speech. **1865** LECKY *Ration.* (1878) I. 259 A diluted and rationalistic Catholicism.

di'lutedly, *adv.* [f. prec. + -LY^2.] In a diluted or weakened manner or form.
*a***1846** WORCESTER cites *Med. Jrnl.* **1870** C. B. CLARKE in *Macm. Mag.* Nov. 50/1 An article..describing the same thing, somewhat dilutedly.

dilutee (daɪljuːˈtiː). [Irreg. f. DILUTE *v.* + -EE^1.] An unskilled or semi-skilled worker who takes a place hitherto occupied by a skilled worker.
1918 *Glasgow Herald* 18 Dec. 7/6 It is being considered whether the dilutee should go and leave the skilled workman at his job, and whether the dilutee should be discharged to provide for the re-entry of the skilled worker who has been to the war. **1921** *Ibid.* 7 Mar. 12 The 50,000 dilutees whom the Government were particularly anxious to force upon the building trade. **1923** G. D. H. COLE *Trade Un. & Munit.* 135 Before any skilled men were taken for the army, all 'dilutees' of military age and fitness should first be removed. **1960** *Guardian* 4 May 18/2 Dilutees were not now needed because there was not enough work..for skilled men.

†**di'lutement**. *Obs. rare*$^{-1}$. [f. DILUTE *v.* + -MENT.] = DILUTION.
1807 SOUTHEY *Rem. H. K. White* (1819) I. 12 As if there were not enough of the leaven of disquietude in our natures, without inoculating it with this dilutement——this *vaccine virus* of envy.

di'luteness. [f. DILUTE *a.* + -NESS.] Dilute quality; fluidity; thinness.
1668 WILKINS *Real Char.* III. xii. (R.), What that diluteness is which..is more ..proper to *F* than *Q*, I understand not. **1817** W. TAYLOR in *Monthly Rev.* LXXXII. 89 His style diffuses a sort of milk and water, which is perspicuous from diluteness, not from transparency. **1834** J. M. GOOD *Study Med.* (ed. 4) IV. 103 The..fluid may be secreted..merely in a state of morbid diluteness.

diluter (dɪ-, daɪˈl(j)uːtə(r)). Also 8 -or. [f. DILUTE *v.* + -ER^1.] A person or thing that dilutes; a diluent.
1718 QUINCY *Compl. Disp.* 233 As a Diluter, it is to be prefer'd. **1737** BRACKEN *Farriery Impr.* (1756) I. 39 A Diluter and Cooler of the Blood. **1746** R. JAMES *Introd. Mouffet's Health's Improv.* 22 These Diluters are either Water itself, or Decoctions of animal or vegetable Substances made with Water. **1863** *Jrnl. R. Agric. Soc.* XXIV. II. 633 Chaff is so valuable a diluter of corn.

diluting (dɪˈl(j)uːtɪŋ), *vbl. sb.* [f. DILUTE *v.* + -ING^1.] The action of the verb DILUTE. (Now chiefly *gerundial*.)
1665 HOOKE *Microgr.* 58 From the composition and dilutings of these two. **1732** ARBUTHNOT *Rules of Diet* 252 Mere diluting dissolves and carries off Salts.

di'luting, *ppl. a.* [-ING^2.] That dilutes.
1732 ARBUTHNOT *Rules of Diet* 276 Diluting things are cooling, as Whey, Water, Milk. **1789** W. BUCHAN *Dom.*

Med. (1790) 159 Drinking plentifully of diluting liquors; as water-gruel, or oatmeal-tea, clear whey, barley-water, balm-tea, apple-tea. **1863** J. HANNAH *Relat. Div. & Hum. Elem. Holy Script.* iii. 85 A diluting exposition. *c* **1865** LETHEBY in *Circ. Sc.* I. 116/1 The *diluting gases* are marsh gas, hydrogen, and carbonic oxide..important constituents of common gas.

dilution (dɪ-, daɪˈl(j)uːʃən). [n. of action f. L. *dīlūt-* ppl. stem of *dīluĕre* to DILUTE: so in mod.F., adm. by Acad. 1878.]

1. The action of diluting; a making thin, fluid, or weaker by the admixture of water or other reducing substance; watering down.

1646 SIR T. BROWNE *Pseud. Ep.* III. xxi. 161 Water.. serving for refrigeration, dilution of solid aliment..in the stomacke. **1656** BLOUNT *Glossogr.*, *Dilution*..a washing, or clensing, a purging or clearing. **1731** ARBUTHNOT *Aliments* v. (R.), Opposite to dilution is coagulation, or thickning. **1878** HUXLEY *Physiogr.* 106 The activity of the oxygen being tempered by dilution with nitrogen.

fig. **1871** MORLEY *Voltaire* (1886) 220 The Protestant dilution of the theological spirit. **1885** SPURGEON *Treas. Dav.* Ps. cxxvi. 3 Strange dilution and defilement of Scriptural language!

2. Dilute condition.

1805 W. SAUNDERS *Min. Waters* 386 Owing to the state of very great dilution in which the earthy salt existed in this solution. **1827** FARADAY *Exp. Res.* No. 41. 226 Equal quantities..in the same state of dilution.

3. A thing in a dilute state, that which is diluted.

1861 EMERSON *Soc. & Solit.*, *Old Age* Wks. (Bohn) III. 131 Tobacco, coffee, alcohol..strychnine, are weak dilutions: the surest poison is time. **1874** L. STEPHEN *Hours in Library* (1892) II. i. 18 A feeble dilution of the most watery kind of popular teaching.

4. The substitution of unskilled or semi-skilled for skilled workers.

1916 *Times* 17 June 7/5 They had no objection to the Admiralty introducing dilution all round, but..they must ask..that the position of the skilled workers would not be unduly harmed. **1919** *Daily Mail Year Bk.* 111/1 True, the dilution of labour includes the employment of a large contingent of unskilled men besides women. **1921** *Ibid.* 60/2 Dilution by taking in unskilled and partially skilled men, and particularly ex-Service men. **1940** *Economist* 24 Feb. 322/1 No decisions have been reached about the scale and conditions of dilution in general, female employment in particular, and retraining. **1964** *Times Rev. Industry* Feb. 71/2 They may..sponsor dilution (more jobs for women at equal pay and quicker apprentice training).

diˈlutionist. [f. prec. + -IST.] In homœopathy, an advocate of the use of attenuated drugs.

A dilutionist is said to be 'high' or 'low' as he prescribes a more or less extreme dilution of medicine.

1892 J. ELLIS *Pers. Exper. Physician* 11 Dr. Gray was a low dilutionist..I called on Dr. Edward Bayard, who was a high dilutionist.

dilutive (dɪ-, daɪˈl(j)uːtɪv), *a. rare.* [f. L. *dīlūt-* ppl. stem of *dīluĕre* to DILUTE: see -IVE.] Having the property of diluting, tending to dilute.

1620 VENNER *Via Recta* viii. 184 They wholly betwixt dinner and supper abstaine from drinke, excepting onely a Dilutiue draught.

‖**dilutum** (dɪ-, daɪˈl(j)uːtəm). *Med.* [L.; = 'that which is diluted', neuter pa. pple. of *dīluĕre* to DILUTE.] A dilution; a solution.

1706 PHILLIPS (ed. Kersey), *Dilutum*, an Infusion. **1750** RUTTY in *Phil. Trans.* LI. 472 Galls added to its dilutum in distilled water turned it of a deep blue. **1753** N. TORRIANO *Gangr. Sore Throat* 98, I then gave him a Dilutum of Cassia. **1883** *Syd. Soc. Lex.*, *Dilutum*, a liquid in which something has been dissolved.

†**diˈluve.** *Obs.* [a. OF. *diluve*, also *de-*, *du-*, *delouve* (Littré), ad. L. *dīluvium*: cf. Pr. *diluvi*, *dulivi*, Sp. and It. *diluvio*. See DELUGE, DILUVIUM, DILUVY.]

c **1386** CHAUCER *Pars. T.* ⁋765 (Harl.) God dreinte all þe world at þe diluve. [So *Petw. & Lansd.*; 3 *MSS.* diluge, *Selden* dilivio.]

diluvial (dɪˈl(j)uːvɪəl), *a.* [ad. L. *dīluviāl-is* of a deluge or flood, f. *dīluvi-um* a washing away of the earth, flood (f. *dīluĕre* to wash in pieces, dissolve): see -AL[1].]

1. Of or belonging to a deluge or flood, *esp.* to the Flood as recorded in Genesis.

1656 BLOUNT *Glossogr.*, *Diluvial*, of or belonging to the Deluge or great Flood. **1831** *Fraser's Mag.* IV. 161 The 'Asiatic style of oratory' with all its tawdry tinsel..its diluvial verbiage. **1865** TYLOR *Early Hist. Man* xi. 322 The formation of diluvial traditions. **1866** J. B. ROSE *Virgil* 167 We have the diluvial theory of the Arkites in respect to many of these mounds, that they are mimic Mount Ararats.

2. *Geol.* **a.** Applied to the theory which explained certain geological phenomena by reference to a general deluge, or to periods of catastrophic action of water.

1816 KEATINGE *Trav.* I. 85 The diluvial wash has worn it into deep valleys. **1823** W. BUCKLAND *Reliq. Diluv.* 2, I have felt myself fully justified in applying the epithet *diluvial* to the results of this great convulsion. **1830** LYELL *Princ. Geol.* I. 31 This doctrine..conceded both that fossil bodies were organic, and that the diluvial theory could not account for them. **1839** MURCHISON *Silur. Syst.* I. xxxix. 536 The earliest theory, usually called the 'diluvial', supposed that these blocks had been forced into their present positions by one or more tremendous inundations, passing over a subsoil which had been dry land. **1859** DARWIN *Orig. Spec.* iv. (1873) 76 Modern geology has almost banished such views as the excavation of a great valley by a single diluvial wave. **1893** HOWORTH *Glacial Nightmare* I. 83 Dr. Buckland, the originator of the term *diluvium*, and the most famous champion of diluvial causes.

b. Of or pertaining to the *diluvium* or drift-formation of early geologists; now generally called the Glacial Drift. ***diluvial clay***, the boulder clay.

(For the connexion of a and b see DILUVIUM.)

1823 W. BUCKLAND *Reliq. Diluv.* 38 The diluvial gravel both of England and Germany. **1842** H. MILLER *O. R. Sandst.* vii. (ed. 2) 142 A deep wooded ravine cut through a thick bed of red diluvial clay. **1851** D. WILSON *Preh. Ann.* (1863) I. i. 27 The closing epoch of Geology, which embraces the diluvial formations. **1853** PHILLIPS *Rivers Yorksh.* 289 Clay, gravel, and sand, with large boulders scattered here and there, which were till lately termed diluvial deposits.

diˈluvialist. *Geol.* [f. prec. + -IST.] One who explains certain geological features by the hypothesis of a universal deluge, or of an extraordinary movement of the waters.

1838 *Penny Cycl.* XI. 129/1 The fanciful diluvialists, who followed in the wake of Woodward. **1851** RICHARDSON *Geol.* ii. 45 The diluvialist, still retaining his floating ice-bergs as the most efficient agents in the transport of drift and erratic blocks to regions distant. **1876** PAGE *Adv. Text-bk. Geol.* vi. 113 Battles of opinion..between Cosmogonists, Diluvialists, and Fossilists. **1887** *Athenæum* 31 Dec. 896/3 Would have delighted the heart of Murchison and the older school of diluvialists.

diluvian (dɪˈl(j)uːvɪən), *a.* Also 8–9 de-. [f. L. *dīluvi-um* flood + -AN: see DILUVIAL.] Of or pertaining to a deluge; *esp.* of the Noachian Flood.

1655 EVELYN *Diary* 28 Aug., From the calculation of coincidence with the diluvian period. **1696** WHISTON *Th. Earth* II. (1722) 202 The Diluvian matter from two Comets' Atmosphere contained in it a great quantity of..stony particles. **1703** T. N. *City & C. Purchaser* Prel. 3 Of the Diluvian Ark, mentioned Gen. 6. **1766** PENNANT *Zool.* (1768) I. 41 Remains which fossilists distinguish by the title of diluvian. **1799** KIRWAN *Geol. Ess.* 87 A shock so violent and universal as that which pervaded the globe during the diluvian revolution. **1823** W. BUCKLAND *Reliq. Diluv.* 39 Scattered by the violence of the diluvian waters. **1862** LYTTON *Str. Story* II. 235 On the surface of uplands undulating like diluvian billows fixed into stone in the midst of their stormy swell.

Hence **diˈluvianism**, a theory which attributes certain phenomena to a universal deluge.

1816 G. S. FABER *Orig. Pagan Idol.* I. 272 The cosmogony of the Virginians seems also to be mingled with diluvianism. **1885** WHITNEY in *Encycl. Brit.* XVIII. 765/2 Linguistic philology has been..created..out of the crude observations and wild deductions of earlier times, as truly as chemistry out of alchemy, or geology out of diluvianism.

†**diˈluviate,** *v. Obs.* In 6 de-. [f. ppl. stem of L. *dīluviāre* to flood, inundate, f. *dīluvium* flood.] *intr.* To flow in a deluge or flood. In quot. said of the deluge of the northern barbarians which overflowed the Roman Empire.

1599 SANDYS *Europæ Spec.* (1632) 187 Those septentrionall inundations..have..wildly deluviated over all the South.

diluviˈation. *rare.* [n. of action f. prec.] The action of a flood, inundation.

1816 KEATINGE *Trav.* (1817) VII. 37 The ravines.. having the appearance of being more the effect of atmospherical diluviation.

diluvie, var. of DILUVY, *Obs.*

diˈluvion. ? *Obs. rare.* [ad. L. *dīluviōn-em* inundation, flood, f. *dīluĕre*: see next and cf. ALLUVION.] = DILUVIUM.

18.. BUCKLAND is cited by Worcester 1846.

‖**diluvium** (dɪˈl(j)uːvɪəm). [a. L. *dīluvium* flood, inundation, deluge, f. *dīluĕre* to wash to pieces, wash away, dissolve by water: see DILUTE.] A term applied to superficial deposits which appear not to have been formed by the ordinary slow operations of water, but to be due to some extraordinary action on a vast scale; such were at first attributed to the Noachian or Universal deluge, whence the name; the chief of these deposits were those of the Northern Drift or Boulder formation at the close of the Tertiary Period, to which the name continued to be applied after the theory of their origin was given up; it is now generally 'applied to all masses apparently the result of powerful aqueous agency'.

1819 J. HODGSON in Raine *Mem.* (1857) I. 265 The cliffs are very white, excepting where they are tarnished by diluvium falling from the tops of the cliffs. **1823** W. BUCKLAND *Reliq. Diluv.* 2 The word *diluvium*..I apply to those extensive and general deposits of superficial loam and gravel, which appear to have been produced by the last great convulsion that has affected our planet. **1832** DE LA BECHE *Geol. Man.* 183 The old transported gravel, or *diluvium* of Prof. Buckland. **1839** MURCHISON *Silur. Syst.* I. xxxvii. 509 'Diluvium' as used by Elie de Beaumont and the modern foreign geologists, means precisely what I term drift. **1849** MRS. SOMERVILLE *Connect. Phys. Sc.* x. 87 Strata containing marine diluvia..must have been formed at the bottom of the ocean. **1862** J. TAYLOR in *Macm. Mag.* Sept. 390 Tusks and teeth in a bed of diluvium..immediately incumbent on stratified beds of lias. **1873** GEIKIE *Gt. Ice Age* xxvii. 369 Ancient alluvium or diluvium overlying moraine-profonde. **1874** LYELL *Students' Geol.* xi. (ed. 3) 145 The term 'diluvium' was for a time the popular name of the boulder formation, because it was referred by many to the deluge of Noah, while others retained the name as expressive of their opinion that a series of diluvial waves raised by hurricanes.. or by earthquakes..had swept over the continents, carrying with them vast masses of mud and heavy stones.

†**diˈluvy.** *Obs.* Forms: 4–5 deluuy(e, diluuy, 4–6 di-, dyluuye, -ie. [ad. L. *dīluvi-um* deluge: see prec. and cf. DILUVE.] = DELUGE *sb.*

a **1325** *Prose Psalter* xlv[i]. 4 Þe deluuy [*mispr.* deluuþ] gladeþ þe hous of heuen, þe almyȝtful halwed Noe and his. **1382** WYCLIF *2 Pet.* ii. 5 Bringynge in the diluuye, or greet flood, to the world of vnpitouse men. *c* **1393** CHAUCER *Scogan* 14 Þu causist þis deluuye of pestelence. *c* **1400** MAUNDEV. (Roxb.) xxiv. 109 Þir three sonnes of Noe after þe diluuy parted amanges þam all þe erthe. **1546** BALE *Eng. Votaries* I. (1550) 9 b, Suche vnspeakable fylthynesse..as brought vpon them the great dyluuye or vnyuersall flod.

dilve: see DILLUE.

dilyte, dilyuer(e, obs. ff. DELIGHT, DELIVER.

dim (dɪm), *a.* and *sb.* Forms: 1– dim; also 3–4 dime, 4 dyme, 4–6 dym, dymme, 5 dimm, 6 dymbe, 6–7 dimme, 7 dimn, dimb. [OE. *dim(m* = OFris. *dim*, ON. *dimm-r*. Cf. OHG. *timbar* (MHG. *timber*, *timmer*, mod.Swiss. dial. *timmer*) 'dim, obscure, dark', which may represent an OTeut. **dim-ro-* and contain the same root. Not known outside Teutonic.]

A. *adj.*

1. a. Of a light, or an illuminated object: Faintly luminous, not clear; somewhat dark, obscure, shadowy, gloomy. The opposite of *bright* or *clear*.

a **1000** *Cædmon's Sat.* 455 (Gr.) Drihten sealde him dimne and deorcne deaþes scuwan. *a* **1000** *Boeth. Metr.* ii. 11 On þis dimme hol. *Ibid.* xii. 16 Sio dimme niht. *c* **1250** *Gen. & Ex.* 286 Euerilc on ðat helden wid him, ðo wurðen mirc, and swart, and dim. **13..** *E.E. Allit. P.* B. 472 Dryf ouer þis dymme water. **1387** TREVISA *Higden* (Rolls) III. 467 Whan þe day is dym and clowdy. **1398** TREVISA *Barth. De P.R.* x. v. (1495) 377 The flamme yeuyth dymme and derke lighte. **1508** FISHER *Wks.* (1876) 68 O dymbe cloude. **1549** *Compl. Scot.* vi. 38 Fayr dyana, the lantern of the nycht, be cam dym ande pail. **1632** MILTON *Penseroso* 160 Storied windows richly dight, Casting a dim religious light. **1732** BERKELEY *Alciphr.* VI. §31 A light, dimmer indeed, or clearer, according to the place. *c* **1750** SHENSTONE *Elegies* iv. 1 Through the dim veil of ev'ning's dusky shade. **1820** SHELLEY *Witch Atl.* xli. 2 Her beauty made The bright world dim. **1860** TYNDALL *Glac.* I. ii. 16 The oftener light is reflected the dimmer it becomes.

b. *fig.* esp. of qualities usually clear or bright.

a **1000** *Cædmon's Gen.* 685 (Gr.) Hio speon hine on ða dimman dæd. *c* **1325** *Metr. Hom.* 111 That..did awai his dedes dim, And mad an hali man of him. *c* **1400** *Rom. Rose* 5353 Love is..whilom dymme, & whilom clere. **1661–98** SOUTH *12 Serm.* III. 287 Man's..Understanding must now be contented with the poor, dimn Light of Faith. **1817–8** SHELLEY *Ros. & Hel.* 692 Public hope grew pale and dim. **1874** MORLEY *Compromise* (1886) 36 The old hopes have grown pale, the old fears dim.

2. a. Not clear to the sight; obscured by an intervening imperfectly transparent medium, by distance, or by blurring of the surface; scarcely visible, indistinct, faint; misty, hazy.

c **1000** *Martyrology* (E.E.T.S.) 46 Seo byrȝen is bewriȝen mid dimmum stanum ond yfellicum. **1632** SANDERSON *Serm.* 436 Dimme and confused and scarce legible. **1651** HOBBES *Leviath.* I. ii. 5 At a great distance of place, that which wee look at appears dimme. **1654** FULLER *Two Serm.* 58 Civilized Pagans..have scowred over the dimme inscription of the Morall Law that it appeared plaine unto them. **1818** SHELLEY *Eugan. Hills* 19 The dim low line before Of a dark and distant shore Still recedes. **1856** STANLEY *Sinai & Pal.* i. (1858) 69 One more glimpse of Egypt dim in the distance.

b. *fig.* Not clear to the mind or understanding; obscure, faint.

c **1350** *Leg. Rood* (1871) 93 Vnto me es þis mater dym. *c* **1440** *Promp. Parv.* 121 Dymme, or harde to vndyrstonde, *misticus*. **1587** FLEMING *Contn. Holinshed* III. 1965/2 Like to be buried in the dimme booke of obliuion. **1821** LAMB *Elia* Ser. I. *Old & New Schoolm.*, I have most dim apprehensions of the four great monarchies. **1836** KINGSLEY *Lett.* (1878) I. 33 There were dim workings of a mighty spirit within. **1871** R. ELLIS *Catullus* lxviii. 52 (50) A memory dim.

3. Of colour: Not bright; dull, faint; dusky or dark; lustreless.

a **1250** *Owl & Night.* 577 Thu art dim, an of fule howe. **1535** COVERD. *Lam.* iv. 1 O, how is the golde become so dymme? **1563** W. FULKE *Meteors* (1640) 36 For the Rayne-bow is more dimme, and of purple colour. **1611** SHAKS. *Wint. T.* IV. iv. 119 Violets dim, But sweeter than the lids of Juno's eyes. **1728** YOUNG *Love Fame* v. (1757) 127 Others, with curious arts, dim charms revive. **1887** STEVENSON *Underwoods* I. iii. 5 All retired and shady spots Where prosper dim forget-me-nots.

4. a. Not seeing clearly, having the eyesight dulled and indistinct.

a **1220** *Bestiary* 60 Siðen his fliȝt is al unstrong, and his eȝen dimme. *a* **1300** *Cursor M.* 3570 (Cott.) Þe freli fax [biginnes] to fal of him, And þe sight to wax well dim. *c* **1422** HOCCLEVE *Learn to Die* 228 Myn yen been al dymme and dirke. **1535** COVERDALE *Eccl.* xii. 2 The sight of the wyndowes shal waxe dymme. **1577** *Test. 12 Patriarchs* (1604) 17 Jacob..somewhat dim for age. **1636** MASSINGER *Gt. Dk. Florence* III. i, I am dim, sir; But he's sharp-sighted. **1766** FORDYCE *Serm. Yng. Wom.* (1767) II. viii. 8 Unheeded by the dim inattentive eye. **1842** TENNYSON *Two Voices* 151 Whose eyes are dim with glorious tears.

b. *fig.* Not clearly apprehending; dull of apprehension. Applied to a person: not 'bright' intellectually; somewhat stupid and dull.

a **1729** J. ROGERS *Serm.* (J.), The understanding is dim, and cannot by its natural light discover spiritual truth. **1731** FIELDING *Grub Str. Op.* Introd., Men's sense is dimmer than their eyes. **1878** B. TAYLOR *Deukalion* I. iv. 33 Teach your dim desire A form whereby to know itself and seek. **1892** STEVENSON & OSBOURNE *Wrecker* xxi. 325 He's a very pleasing creature, rather dim, and dull, and genteel, but really pleasing. **1910** R. BROOKE *Let.* 3 July (1968) 243 They were very dim, and said, couldn't *we* find an advance agent? **1916** M. BEERBOHM in *Cornhill Mag.* June 719 The young writers of that era.. strove earnestly to be distinct in aspect. This man had striven unsuccessfully.. I decided that 'dim' was the *mot juste* for him. **1923** J. TREVELYAN *Life of Mrs. H. Ward* x. 192 Teachers and many 'dim' people of various professions would find her as accessible as her strenuous hours of labour would allow. **1924** 'W. FABIAN' *Sailors' Wives* v. 63 The sexperts, which is a combination of sex and expert: I glued it together myself. Not so dim; yes? **1933** J. C. MASTERMAN *Oxford Tragedy* xv. 229 The dim little research Fellow with clumsy manners and no conversation. **1950** *Listener* 7 Dec. 709/2 Constable and Turner were neglected and the dim and second-rate were crowned with triumphant laurels.

c. Of a thing, situation, etc.: dull, poor, undistinguished. *colloq.*

1958 B. HAMILTON *Too Much Water* xi. 248, I personally had rather a dim war. *Ibid.* xii. 266 A rather dim situation for the M.C.C.

d. Colloq. phr. *to take a dim view*: see VIEW *sb.*

5. *transf.* Of sound, and esp. of the voice: Indistinct, faint.

c **1386** CHAUCER *Knt.'s T.* 1575 He herde a murmurynge Ful lowe and dym. **1398** TREVISA *Barth. De P.R.* v. xxi, (1495) 128 They that haue grete tongues haue dymme voyce. *c* **1450** *St. Cuthbert* (Surtees) 3672 His speche was bathe short and dym. **1795** SOUTHEY *Vis. Maid of Orleans* I. 124 The damp earth gave A dim sound as they pass'd. **1817** SHELLEY *Marianne's Dream* 40 She then did hear The sound as of a dim low clanging.

B. *sb.* **a.** Dimness; obscurity; dusk.

c **1400** *Destr. Troy* 755 The day vp droghe & the dym voidet. *c* **1430** *Hymns Virg.* (1867) 53 He liȝtneþ his folk in dym. **1509** *Parl. Deuylles* xciii, Quod Symeon, 'he lyghtneth his folke in dym Where as derkenes shedeth theyr states'. **1857** HEAVYSEGE *Saul* (1869) 87 To sit were pleasant, in the dim.

b. Dimness of vision.

1726 LAW *Chr. Perfect.* i. 30 Further than the Dim of Eyes of Flesh can carry our Views.

†**C.** *adv.* Dimly, faintly, indistinctly. *Obs.*

1393 GOWER *Conf.* II. 293 He herde a vois, which cried dimme. **1821** SHELLEY *Adonais* liv, That Light.. Which.. Burns bright or dim, as each are mirrors of The fire.

D. *Comb.* **a.** adverbial, as ***dim-brooding, -coloured, -discovered, -gleaming, -grey, -lighted, -lit (-litten), -remembered, -seen, -yellow***, etc. **b.** parasynthetic, as ***dim-browed, -eyed, -lettered, -sheeted***, DIM-SIGHTED.

1837 CARLYLE *Fr. Rev.* I. IV. iv. 166 The whole Future is there, and Destiny *dim-brooding. **1776** MICKLE tr. *Camoens' Lusiad* 43 And night, ascending from the *dim-brow'd east. *c* **1400** MAUNDEV. (Roxb.) xvii. 79 Þai er mare *dymme coloured þan þe cristall. **1746** COLLINS *Ode to Evening* x, Hamlets brown, and *dim-discover'd spires. **1627-47** FELTHAM *Resolves* I. xcvi. 302 The ghessive interpretations of *dim-ey'd man. **1829** CARLYLE *Misc.* (1857) I. 273 The public is a dim-eyed animal. **1840** CLOUGH *Early Poems* v. 11 Through the *dim-lit inter-space. **1870** MORRIS *Earthly Par.* II. III. 9 After the weary tossing of the night And close *dim-litten chamber. **1827** MOIR *Dead Eagle* ii, Down, whirling.. to the *dim-seen plain. **1859** TENNYSON *Enid* 600 Fair head in the *dim-yellow light.

dim, *v.* [f. DIM *a.*: OE. had the compounds *adimmian*, *fordimmian*, ON. the intr. *dimma* to become dim; the simple vb. is found from 13th c.]

1. *intr.* To grow or become dim; to lose brightness or clearness. *lit.* and *fig.*

a **1300** *Christ on Cross* 7 in *E.E.P.* (1862) 20 His fair lere falowiþ and dimmiþ is siȝte. *a* **1300** *Cursor M.* 23695 (Cott.), Mani flurs.. þat neuermar sal dime ne duine. *c* **1400** *Destr. Troy* 9932 The day ouerdrogh, dymmet the skewis. **1607** BREWER *Lingua* I. viii, Suddenly mine eyes began to dim. ?*c* **1710** ? E. WARD *Welsh-monster* 28 My Lady's Beauty, tho' divine, Would dim, without the Muses shine. **1814** BYRON *Lara* I. xii, The lone light Dimm'd in the lamp. **1871** B. TAYLOR *Faust* (1875) II. IV. ii. 250 The near horizon dims.

2. a. *trans.* To make dim, obscure, or dull; to render less clear, or distinct; to becloud (the eyes).

[*c* **888** K. ÆLFRED *Boeth.* xxiv §4 Ðeah heora mod.. sie adimmad.] *a* **1300** *E.E. Psalter* lxviii. 24 Dimmed be þair eghen, þat þai ne se. *c* **1400** *Song Roland* 580 Dew diskid adoun and dymmyd the floures. *c* **1440** *Promp. Parv.* 121 Dymmyn, or make dymme, *obscuro.* **1530** PALSGR. 516/3, I dymme the coloure or beautye of a thyng.. Se howe these torches have dymmed this gylting. **1592** DAVIES *Immort. Soul* XXXI. viii. (1714) 109 As Lightning, or the Sun-beams dim the Sight. **1751** JOHNSON *Rambler* No. 184 ¶1 The writer of essays.. seldom.. dims his eyes with the perusal of antiquated volumes. **1820** W. IRVING *Sketch Bk.* I. 202 The light streamed through windows dimmed with armorial bearings. **1836** LANDOR *Pericles & Asp.* II. 393 The mirror is too close to our eyes, and our own breath dims it.

b. *fig.*

1526 *Pilgr. Perf.* (W. de W. 1531) 35 b, It dymmeth or maketh derke theyr lytell holynesse. **1659** B. HARRIS *Parival's Iron Age* 109 Forced the Conquerours to retreat, and in some sort, dimmed their Triumph. **1840** KINGSLEY *Lett.* (1878) I. 49 My natural feelings of the just and the beautiful have been dimmed by neglect. **1851** D. G. MITCHELL *Fresh Glean.* 275 Its quaint houses.. are dimmed to memory by the fresher recollections of that beautiful river.

c. *to dim out*: to reduce the brightness of (street-lighting, etc.), esp. in time of war; to impose a 'dim-out' on (a city, etc.).

1942 *Amer. Speech* XVII. 204/2 The city was dimmed-out. **1945** *Daily Express* 20 Apr. 1/8 Street lighting need no longer be dimmed out.

†**dim**, *sb. Obs.* Abbreviation of L. *dimidium* half.

1477 *Churchw. Acc. Croscombe* (Somerset Rec. Soc.) 6 Hath in his hands of the Cherche lede one cwt, dim, iiij lb. **1634-5** BRERETON *Trav.* (1844) 22 Adorned with stones a yard and *dim.* high. *Ibid.* 180 A vault or gallery about one yd. or one yd. and *dim.* wide.

dim., dimin. (*Mus.*), abbrev. of DIMINUENDO.

dim, obs. form of DEEM *v.*

dimag'nesic, *a. Chem.*: see DI-² 2 d.

1876 HARLEY *Mat. Med.* 66 Dimagnesic pyro-phosphate.

dimagnetite (daɪ'mægnɪtaɪt). *Min.* [f. DI-² twice + MAGNETITE.] A mineral consisting mainly of ferroso-ferric oxide, occurring in rhombic prisms, regarded by Dana as a pseudomorph of magnetite after lievrite (Watts).

1852 *Amer. Jrnl. Sc.* Ser. II. XIII. 392 Dimagnetite. **1868** DANA *Min.* (1880) 151 Dimagnetite of Shepard.. appears to be a magnetite pseudomorph.

†**di'mane**, *v. Obs.* Also 6 **dimaine, -mayne.** [ad. L. *dīmānā-re* to flow different ways, spread abroad, f. *dī-*, *dis-* apart + *mānāre* to flow.] *intr.* To flow forth *from*; to spring, originate, or derive its origin *from.*

1610 W. FOLKINGHAM *Art of Survey* Ep. Ded. 1 Merits dimayning from the sacred Source of true Nobility. *Ibid.* I. vi. 12 Springs dimayning from thicke sand.. gather mudde. **1642** W. BALL *Caveat for Subjects* 8 Motion and Feeling dimane from the Braine. **1657** HAWKE *Killing is M.* 10 By the Right of Warre, and by the consent of the people, which two Titles dimane also from the Divine providence.

di'manganous, *a. Chem.* See DI-² 2 d.

1881 WATTS *Dict. Chem.* 3rd Suppl. II. 1600 An anhydrous dimanganous phosphate, $Mn_2(PO_4H)_2$.

dimaris ('dɪmərɪs). *Logic.* The mnemonic term designating the third mood of the fourth figure of syllogisms, in which the major premiss is a particular affirmative (*i*), the minor a universal affirmative (*a*), and the conclusion a particular affirmative (*i*). Formerly called *drimatis*, *dimatis.*

The initial *d* indicates that the mood can be reduced to *Darii* by (*m*) transposition of the premisses, and (*s*) simple conversion of the conclusion.

1827 WHATELY *Logic* II. III. §4. **1864** BOWEN *Logic* vii. 200. **1891** WELTON *Logic* I. IV. iii. §137. 403 *Dimaris*, An example is 'Some parallelograms are squares; all squares are regular figures; therefore, some regular figures are parallelograms'.

dimastigate (daɪ'mæstɪgət), *a. Zool.* [f. DI-² twice + Gr. μαστιγ-(μάστιξ) whip + -ATE² 2: cf. L. *mastigātus* whipped.] Having two flagella; biflagellate; applied to those flagellate Infusoria (*Dimastiga*) which have two flagella.

dimatis, earlier form of DIMARIS.

'dimber, *a. Rogues' Cant.* Pretty.

1671 R. HEAD *Eng. Rogue* I. v. (1874) 48 (Farmer). **1692** COLES, *Dimber (canting)* pretty. *a* **1700** B. E. *Dict. Cant. Crew*, *Dimber*, pretty. *Dim[ber]-mort*, a pretty Wench. **1837** DISRAELI *Venetia* I. xiv., ''Tis a dimber cove', whispered one of the younger men to a companion. *Ibid.* Tip me the clank like a dimber mort.

Hence **dimber-damber**, a captain of thieves or vagrants.

1671 R. HEAD *Eng. Rogue* I. v. (1874) 48 (Farmer). **1834** H. AINSWORTH *Rookwood* III. v. (Farmer), Dick Turpin must be one of us. He shall be our Dimber Damber. **1890** *Daily News* 1 Feb. 4/7.

dimble ('dɪmb(ə)l). *Obs.* exc. *dial.* [Of uncertain origin, possibly a deriv. or comb. of DIM, gloom or obscurity being a usual attribute; connexion with DINGLE is also possible. The midland districts (e.g. Leicester, Derby, Warwick, Shropsh.) retain the word, usually in the form *dumble*, occasionally *drumble.*]

A deep and shady dell or hollow, a dingle.

1589 R. ROBINSON *Gold. Mirr.* (Chetham Soc.) 5 Eccho.. That liues in woodes, And rocky ragged tours, and Dales with Dymbles deep. **1612** DRAYTON *Poly-olb.* ii. 27 Satyres that in shades and gloomy dimbles dwell. **1622** *Ibid.* xxviii. (1748) 378 Dimbles hid from day. **1637** B. JONSON *Sad Sheph.* II. vii, Within a gloomy dimble, she doth dwell Downe in a pitt, ore-growne with brakes and briars. **1879** MISS JACKSON *Shropsh. Word-bk.*, *Dumblehole*; also *Drumble*, a rough wooded dip in the ground; a dingle. **1881** *Leicester Gloss.*, *Dimble*, a dingle, dell.

dime (daɪm), *sb.* Forms: 4-5 dyme, (5 des(s)ime, dyeme), 5-6 dysme, 5-9 disme, 6 dism, desme, deeme, deme, 6-9 dime. [a. OF. *disme*, *dime*:—L. *decima* tithe, tenth part, fem. of *decimus* tenth.]

†**1. a.** A tenth part, a tithe paid to the church or to a temporal ruler. *Obs.* or *Hist.*

1377 LANGL. *P. Pl.* B. xv. 526 Take her landes, ȝe lordes, and let hem lyue by dymes. *c* **1380** WYCLIF *Wks.* (1880) 418 þat pariȝschens shulden drawe fro persouns offeringis & dymes. **1399** *Pol. Poems* (Rolls) I. 412 His purvyours toke, withoute preiere at a parliament, a poundage.. and a fifteneth and a dyme eke. *c* **1460** FORTESCUE *Abs. & Lim. Mon.* xii. (1885) 139 Owre commons.. give to thair kynge, at somme tymes quinsimes and dessimes [MS. Digby 145 dismes.] **1494** FABYAN *Chron.* VI. cxlviii. 134 That he myght leuy certayne dymys to wage therwith souldyours. **1502** *Ord. Crysten Men* (W. de W. 1506) II. xvii. 131 He fasted, he payed the demes, he gaue almesse. **1563-87** FOXE *A. & M.* (1684) I. 799/2 The Cardinal sued a Pardon from Rome, to be freed from all Disms, due to the King by the Church of Winchester. **1580** NORTH *Plutarch* (1676) 404 Now Sylla consecrating the dismes of all his goods unto Hercules [etc.]. *a* **1618** RALEIGH *Rem.* 50 In his forty ninth year he had a disme and a fifteenth granted him freely. **1659** HOWELL *Lexicon* Fr. Prov. 27 From all tymes it was ordained to pay dimes or tithes unto the Lord. **1884** L. OLIPHANT *Haifa* (1887) 133 The dime.. has heretofore been the share of the government.

b. *fig.* A 'tithe' of war, a tenth man sacrificed.

1606 SHAKS. *Tr. & Cr.* II. ii. 19 Euery tythe soule 'mongst many thousand dismes, Hath bin as deere as Helen.

2. a. A silver coin of the United States of America, of the value of 10 cents, or $\frac{1}{10}$ of a dollar. *pl.* Money; financial gain; freq. ***the dimes*** (*U.S. colloq.*).

1786 *Ord. Continent. Congress U.S.* 8 Aug., Mills, Cents, Dimes, Dollars. **1809** KENDALL *Trav.* I. xviii. 193 Dimes or tenth parts are mentioned by writers, but never enter into accounts. **1821** T. JEFFERSON *Autobiog.* Writ. 1892 I. 75 The division into dimes, cents and mills is now.. well understood. **1843** *Spirit of Times* 21 Jan. 560/3 Times are hard, and dimes are scarce. **1845** S. F. SMITH *Theatr. Apprenticeship* (1847) 7, I, in search of 'the dimes', acted plays in newly-built theatres. *a* **1861** T. WINTHROP *J. Brent* (1883) xxvi. 233 Count out yer dimes, and I'll fill out a blank bill of sale. **1871** *Harper's Mag.* June 37/2 Among the excursionists there would be.. such as travel to gather ideas rather than dimes. **1872** O. W. HOLMES *Poet Breakf.-t.* xii. (1885) 320 Not bad, my bargain! Price one dime. **1893** *Boston* (Mass.) *Jrnl.* 1 Apr. 6/3 The so-called middle-classes.. the people who are accustomed to count their nickels and dimes as well as their dollars.

b. *attrib.* Costing a dime; as in ***dime novel***, applied especially to a cheap sensational novel: cf. *penny dreadful*, *shilling shocker*; hence ***dime-novelish*** adj., ***dime-novelist.*** **dime-store** *U.S.*, a shop in which the maximum price was originally a dime; also *attrib.* or as *adj.*, *spec.* designating a cheap and inferior article; cf. *five-and-ten (cent store)* (FIVE C. 2).

1859 (*title*) Beadle's dime song book. **1860** (*title*) Beadle's dime book of dreams.. compiled from the most accredited sources for the 'Dime series'. **1861** *Vanity Fair* 26 Jan. 38/2, I invested in the dime editions of startling narratives. **1864** *N. Amer. Rev.* July 304 A Dime Novel is issued each month. **1865** A. H. STEPHENS *Diary* (1910) 424 A little primer-looking sort of a child's book. It was a dime novel. **1879** H. GEORGE *Progr. & Pov.* x. ii. (1881) 443 The boy who reads dime novels wants to be a pirate. **1879** *Amer. Punch* Apr. 40/1 Written to order by the hundred, by a Dime novelist in New York. **1882** *Century Mag.* XXV. 212/1 You are as bad as a dime novel. **1887** *Scribner's Mag.* July 120/1 It was a trifle boyish, and 'dime-novelish'. **1892** *Daily News* 29 Mar. 2/5 The nuisance of 'dime shows' as they are called in America. **1914** R. HERRICK *Clark's Field* 7 The facts are not all dime-novelish, but very human and significant. **1928** WESEEN *Crowell's Dict. Eng. Gram.* 188 *Dime store*, colloquial name for a store that specializes in articles selling for ten cents. *The five and ten* is a variant. **1931** *Kansas City Star* 23 Oct., A dime store in Emporia. **1938** *Newsweek* 31 Jan. 36/1 'Best buy' was a dime-store product, which cost 5 cents a gram. **1942** BERREY & VAN DEN BARK *Amer. Thes. Slang* §21/14 Cheap; paltry,.. *dime-store.*

c. Phr. ***a dime a dozen***, so plentiful as to be almost worthless. Also ***dime-a-dozen*** attrib. phr. *N. Amer. colloq.*

1930 C. TERRETT *Only Saps Work* 188 These are mere dime-a-dozen rackets, compared with the truly big-time stock market swindles. **1948** *Galveston* (Texas) *News* 14 June 7/7 Sunday night at the cocktail party and buffet supper, choice fishing stories were a dime a dozen. **1970** M. PEI *Words in Sheep's Clothing* ii. 12 Coinages of the type of 'power-pak' are a dime a dozen. **1977** I. SHAW *Beggarman, Thief* III. ix. 328 'I thought you were too good looking just to be *nobody*.' 'A dime a dozen,' Wesley said. 'I'm just a seaman at heart.'

†**dime**, *v. Obs. rare.* Also 5 dyme, 7 disme. [a. F. *dîme-r*, OF. *dismer*, *diesmer* = Pr. *desmar*, Sp. *dezmar*, Pg. *dezimar*, It. *decimare*:—L. *decimāre* to take a tithe, (later) to pay tithes, f. *decima*: see prec.] *trans.* **a.** To take a tenth part of, to tithe. **b.** To divide into tenths.

1483 CAXTON *Gold. Leg.* 64 b/2 He shall taske and dyme your corn and sheues. **1610** W. FOLKINGHAM *Art of Survey* II. iv. 52 Disme or deuide each foote of the Rule.. into decimals or Tenths.

Hence †**'dimable** (in 5 dym(e)able) *a.*, tithable.

1489 *Plumpton Corr.* 61 It is not the Kyngs mynd to ses no dymeable land, and we have no suit land, but it is dymable.

dime, obs. form of DIM *a.* and *v.*

dimediate, obs. form of DIMIDIATE.

† **di'mense**, *sb. Obs.* [ad. med.L. *dīmens-um* q.v. below.] A space measured out, an extent.

1632 LITHGOW *Trav.* x. 426 Having compassed all Europe, our Resolution, was to borrow a larger dimmense [1682 dimense] of ground in Affricke.

† **di'mense**, *v. Obs.* [f. L. *dīmens-* ppl. stem of *dīmetīrī* to measure out, f. *dī-*, *dis-* (DIS- 1) + *metīrī* to measure.] *trans.* To measure *out.*

*a*1641 BP. MOUNTAGU *Acts & Mon.* (1642) 217 It sufficeth some, to have things delivered unto them in a generality, which others must have dimensed out unto them .. peece after peece.

dimension (dɪ'mɛnʃən), *sb.* Also 5-6 **dy-**, **-sioun**, **-cion**, **-cyon**, 6-7 **dimention**, 7 **demension**, **-tion**. [a. F. *dimension* (1425 in Hatz.-Darm.), ad. L. *dīmensiōn-em*, n. of action from *dīmetīrī* (ppl. stem *dīmens-*): see prec.]

† **1. a.** The action of measuring, measurement. *Obs.*

1555 EDEN *Decades* 243 Accordynge to the ordinarie accoumpte and dimension which the pylotes and cosmographers doo make. 1589 GREENE *Menaphon* (Arb.) 80 Things infinite, I see, Brooke no dimension. 1656 STANLEY *Hist. Philos.* (1701) 183/2 If a Man pursue it [geometry] not only for Mechanical Dimension, but that he may by the help thereof ascend [etc]. 1793 SMEATON *Edystone L.* §97 Taking such dimensions as would enable me to make an accurate model .. of the rock.

† **b.** *Mus.* The division of a longer note into shorter notes, constituting 'time' or rhythm; *pl.* 'measures', measured strains. *Obs.*

1597 MORLEY *Introd. Mus.* 13 *Phi.* What call they time? *Ma.* The dimension of the Breefe by semibreeues. 1635 BRATHWAIT *Arcad. Pr.* I. 165 Harmonious reports in these Musicall dimensions.

2. a. Measurable or spatial extent of any kind, as length, breadth, thickness, area, volume; measurement, measure, magnitude, size. (Now commonly in plural: cf. *proportions.*) Also *fig.* Magnitude, extent, degree (of an abstract thing).

1529 MORE *Dyaloge* II. Wks. 188/1 Though thei be not cyrcumscribed in place, for lack of bodily dymencion and measuring, yet are .. angels .. diffinitively so placed where thei be for the time. 1596 DAVIES *Orchestra* xcv, Whose quick eyes doe explore The just dimension both of earth and heaven. 1615 J. STEPHENS *Satyr. Ess.* 292 Confounding (like a bad Logician) the forme and the dimention. 1651 HOBBES *Leviath.* III. xxxiv. 208 Whatsoever has dimension, is Body. 1660 BARROW *Euclid* I. xxxv. Schol., The dimension of any Parallelogram is found out by this Theorem. 1663 GERBIER *Counsel* 6 He will never rightly describe the dimensions of solid Bodies .. his Circles will seem Ovals in Breadth, and his Ovals Circles. 1667 MILTON *P.L.* II. 893 A dark Illimitable Ocean without bound, Without dimension, where length, breadth, and highth, And time and place are lost. *a*1745 SWIFT (J.), My gentleman was measuring my walls, and taking the dimensions of the room. 1756 BURKE *Subl. & B.* II. vii, Greatness of dimension is a powerful cause of the sublime. 1772 *Hist. Rochester* 44 All the beams .. ought to be of large dimensions. 1847 EMERSON *Repr. Men, Shaks.* Wks. (Bohn) I. 360 That imagination which dilates the closet he writes in to the world's dimension. 1893 *Law Times* XCV. 104/2 Posts of the dimensions of 3 in. by $2\frac{1}{2}$ in.

fig. 1660 HICKERINGILL *Jamaica* (1661) 51 The Expedition against Hispaniola; .. The Dimensions of this great Preparation vastly exceeding the difficulties. 1676 HALE *Contempl.* I. 106 The Afflictions of his Soul .. were of a higher Dimension in the Garden. 1889 *Pall Mall G.* 17 Oct. 2/3 That passion for athletics which in Oxford has now almost reached the dimensions of a mania.

† **b.** *transf.* Extension in time, duration.

1605 BP. ANDREWES *Serm.* II. 170 The cross .. is *mors prolixa*, a death of dimensions, a death long in dying. 1677 HALE *Prim. Orig. Man.* IV. ii. 308 We have no reason to imagin that the sixth day was of any other dimension than the seventh day.

c. *fig.* Any of the component aspects of a particular situation, etc., esp. one newly discovered; an attribute of, or way of viewing, an abstract entity. Cf. ASPECT 9, 12.

1929 R. S. & H. M. LYND *Middletown* xviii. 263 Like the automobile, the motion picture is more to Middletown than simply a new way of doing an old thing; it has added new dimensions to the city's leisure. 1952 *Times* 1 Aug. 7/3 It is in helping nations to provide the material for their own or for one another's defence, instead of having it provided direct from America, that the value of off-shore purchasing lies. Here, in another dimension, is the principle of 'trade, not aid'. 1956 R. MACAULAY *Towers of Trebizond* xxv. 287 A dimension has been taken out of my life, leaving it flat, not rich and rounded. 1961 A. O. J. COCKSHUT *Imagination of Dickens* xi. 158 The religious dimension, which would have given coherence and deeper meaning to the withered and touching scraps of virtue displayed by Flora and Mrs. Plornish, and even by Mrs. Clennam—a triumph of fairness—this is absent. 1973 P. WHITE *Eye of Storm* vi. 237 This work of ours .. will add another dimension to the art of theatre. 1985 *Times* 24 Jan. 14/4 The effect of 'sub-clinical' nutrient deficiencies too small to cause acute illness is another elusive dimension.

3. *Math.* **a.** *Geom.* A mode of linear measurement, magnitude, or extension, in a particular direction; usually as co-existing with similar measurements or extensions in other directions.

The three dimensions of a body, or of ordinary space, are length, breadth, and thickness (or depth); a surface has only two dimensions (length and breadth); a line only one (length). Here the notion of *measurement* or *magnitude* is commonly lost, and the word denotes merely a particular mode of spatial extension. Modern mathematicians have speculated as to the possibility of more than three dimensions of space.

1413 *Pilgr. Sowle* (Caxton 1483) v. xiv. 107 Ther is no body parfit withouten thre dymensions, that is breede, lengthe, and depnesse. *c*1430 *Art of Nombryng* (E.E.T.S.) 14 A lyne hathe but one dymensioun that is to sey after the lengthe .. a superficialle thynge hathe .2. dimensions, þat is to sey lengthe and brede. 1570 BILLINGSLEY *Euclid* I. def. ii. 1 There pertaine to quantitie three dimensions, length, bredth, and thicknes. 1635 N. CARPENTER *Geog. Del.* II. ii. 14 These two Dimensions are length and breadth, whereof euery plaine figure consists. 1794 SULLIVAN *View Nat.* I. 100 All physical magnitude must have three dimensions, length, breadth, and thickness. 1858 WHEWELL *Hist. Sci. Ideas* II. viii. §§4-5 (L.) Time is conceived as a quantity of one dimension .. Indeed the analogy between time, and space of one dimension, is so close, that the same terms are applied to both ideas. *Ibid.* vi. The eye .. sees length and breadth, but no third dimension. In order to know that there are solids, we must infer as well as see. 1873 CLIFFORD *Pure Sciences* in *Contemp. Rev.* Oct. (1874) 716 Out of space of two dimensions, as we call it, I have made space of three dimensions. 1878 STEWART & TAIT *Unseen Univ.* vii. §220. 221 Suppose our (essentially three-dimensional) matter to be the mere skin or boundary of an Unseen whose matter has four dimensions.

b. *Alg.* Since the product of two, or of three, quantities, each denoting a length (i.e. a magnitude of one dimension), represents an area or a volume (i.e. a magnitude of two, or of three, dimensions), such products themselves are said to be of so many dimensions; and generally, the number of dimensions of a product is the number of the (unknown or variable) quantities contained in it as factors (known or constant quantities being reckoned of no dimensions); any power of a quantity being of the dimensions denoted by its index. (Thus x^3, x^2y, xyz are each of three dimensions.) The dimensions of an expression or equation are those of the term of highest dimensions in it. (The number of dimensions corresponds to the *degree* of a quantity or equation: see DEGREE *sb.* 13.)

1557 RECORDE *Whetst.* Hij, The nomber that doeth amounte thereof (3 × 3 × 3) hath gotten 3. dimensiones, whiche properly belongeth to a bodie, or sound forme. And therfore is it called a Cube, or Cubike nomber. 1690 LEYBOURN *Curs. Math.* 334 Every Power hath so many Dimensions as the Letters wherewith it is written. 1706 W. JONES *Syn. Palmar. Matheseos* 40 The Quantity produc'd by the Multiplication of Two, Three, etc. Quantities, is said to be of Two, Three, etc. Dimensions. 1806 HUTTON *Course Math.* I. 190 To find the Greatest Common Measure of the Terms of a Fraction .. Range the quantities according to the dimensions of some letters. *c*1865 in *Circ. Sc.* I. 476/1 When the .. equations are .. of two dimensions.

c. [a. F. *dimension* (J. B. J. Fourier *Théorie anal. de la Chaleur* (1822) ii. §ix. 154).] The power to which any one of the fundamental quantities or units is raised in the expression defining a derived quantity or unit in terms of them; also (in *pl.*), all the fundamental quantities in such an expression, each raised to its appropriate power, which together show how the unit of the derived quantity depends on the fundamental units; ***method of dimensions***, dimensional analysis.

The 'fundamental quantities' are usually taken to be mass, length, and time, with the addition of one or more other quantities in certain cases (such as electrical and magnetic phenomena).

1864 *Rep. Brit. Assoc. 1863* 132 The value of a force is directly proportional to a length and a mass, but inversely proportional to the square of a time. This is expressed by saying that the dimensions of a force are LM/T^2. 1877 LD. RAYLEIGH *Theory of Sound* I. iii. 47 From the necessity of a complete enumeration of all the quantities on which the required result may depend, the method of dimensions is somewhat dangerous. 1878 A. FREEMAN tr. *Fourier's Anal. Theory of Heat* ii. 128 Every undetermined magnitude or constant has one dimension proper to itself, and .. the terms of one and the same equation could not be compared, if they had not the same exponent of dimension. We have introduced this consideration .. in order to make our definitions more exact, and to serve to verify the analysis. *Ibid.* 129 The dimensions of x, t, v with respect to the unit of time are 0, 1, 0, and those of K, h, c are −1, −1, 0. 1911 *Encycl. Brit.* XXVII. 736/2 Velocity is of +1 dimension in length and −1 dimension in time. 1925 *Phil. Mag.* 6th Ser. L. 32 The dimensions of the viscosity, η, are $ML^{-1}T^{-1}$, of the density, ρ, ML^{-3}, whilst σ/σ' is of no dimensions. *Ibid.* 31 Much information can be obtained concerning F by means of the method of dimensions. 1933 A. W. PORTER (*title*) The method of dimensions. 1960 *McGraw-Hill Encycl. Sci. & Technol.* IV. 197/2 Quantities with the same dimensions can be expressed in the same units. 1964 H. S. HVISTENDAHL *Engin. Units* i. 7 For example, in the case of force, the term 'dimensions' is now generally understood to mean LMT^{-2}, and not merely 1, 1, −2. 1969 L. YOUNG *Syst. Units Electr. & Magn.* i. 7 Area has dimensions of length squared; denoting 'dimensions of' by square brackets, we write $[A] = [L]^2$. 1970 *Nature* 29 Aug. 935/2 In SI units the constant $\mu_0 = 4\pi \times 10^{-7}$ is indispensable in many formulae, if the dimensions are to balance.

† **4.** Measurable form or frame; *pl.* material parts, as of the human body; 'proportions'. *Obs.*

1596 SHAKS. *Merch. V.* III. i. 62 Hath not a Iew hands, organs, dementions, sences, affections, passions? 1601 —— *Twel. N.* I. v. 280, I .. know him noble .. And in dimension, and the shape of nature, A gracious person. 1605 —— *Lear* I. ii. 7 My dimensions are as well compact, My minde as generous, and my shape as true. 1634 W. WOOD *New Eng. Prosp.* I. viii, The Humbird is .. no bigger than a Hornet, yet hath all the dimensions of a Bird, as bill, and wings, with quills, spider-like legges, small clawes. 1667 MILTON *P.L.* I. 793 In thir own dimensions like themselves The great Seraphic Lords and Cherubim In close recess and secret conclave sat.

fig. 1653 A. WILSON *Jas. I* 162 The Younger having all the Dimensions of a Courtier. 1660 WATERHOUSE *Arms & Arm.* 28 Nations, whose polity had all the dimensions of order in it.

5. *Comb.*, as **dimension lines**, straight lines usually having an arrow at each end, indicating the parts or lines to which the figured dimensions refer in a technical drawing; **dimension-lumber**, **-timber**, **-stone**, i.e. that which is cut to specified dimensions or size; **dimension-work**, masonry built of 'dimension-stones'. (Chiefly *U.S.*)

1864 THOREAU *Cape Cod* vii. (1894) 156 Houses built of what is called 'dimension timber', imported from Maine, all ready to be set up. 1874 KNIGHT *Dict. Mech.*, *Dimension Lumber*, lumber sawed to specific sizes to order. 1887 D. A. Low *Machine Drawing* 5 Dimension lines and centre lines are best put in of different colour. 1902 P. MARSHALL *Metal Tools* 18 The marking of dimension lines on metal surfaces is generally done with a steel scriber. 1927 G. E. DRAYCOTT *Technical Drawing* xii. 184 No dimension line should run closer than $\frac{1}{4}''$ to a line to which it is parallel. 1961 BELLIS & SCHMIDT *Archit. Drafting* xiii. 81/2 Use a 2H pencil for extension and dimension lines.

di'mension, *v.* [f. prec. sb.] **1.** *trans.* To measure or space out; to reduce to measurement. *rare.*

1754 H. WALPOLE *Lett.* I. 335 (D.), I propose to break and enliven it by compartments in colours, according to the enclosed sketch, which you must adjust and dimension.

2. *trans.* To mark the dimensions on (a working drawing, diagram, or sketch). Chiefly in *pa. pple.* or *ppl. a.* So **di'mensioning** *vbl. sb.*, the action of marking dimensions; the dimension lines, etc., on a drawing.

1885 *Marine Engineer* 1 Apr. 27/1 Twenty-five large plates of fully dimensioned drawings. 1887 D. A. LOW *Machine Draw.* 5 Many a good drawing has its appearance spoiled through being slovenly dimensioned. 1892 *Ibid.* 99 Rough dimensioned sketches. 1904 *Westm. Gaz.* 28 July 2/1 All parts being carefully illustrated by dimensioned drawings. 1907 *Install. News* Oct. 1/2 Diagrams are more valuable when dimensioned. 1927 G. E. DRAYCOTT *Technical Drawing* xiv. 219 (*heading*) Inking-in and dimensioning drawings. 1966 *McGraw-Hill Encycl. Sci. & Technol.* IV. 611/1 Working types of drawings may differ in styles of dimensioning. 1966 G. K. & H. J. STEGMAN *Archit. Drafting* ix. 211/1 A modular detail requires fewer small fractional dimensions than a detail dimensioned in the regular method.

di'mensionable, *a. nonce-wd.* [f. prec. + -ABLE: cf. *companionable.*] Capable of being measured; having dimensions.

1884 E. A. ABBOTT *Flatland* II. xix. 87 Some yet more spacious Space, some more dimensionable Dimensionality.

dimensional (dɪ'mɛnʃənəl), *a.* [f. DIMENSION *sb.* + -AL[1].]

1. Of or pertaining to dimension or magnitude.

1816 KEATINGE *Trav.* (1817) I. 66 *note*, About the same relative situation and dimensional proportion. 1888 J. T. GULICK in *Linn. Soc. Jrnl.* XX. 234 If structural or dimensional characters are not correlated.

2. *Geom.* Of or relating to (a specified number of) dimensions: see DIMENSION 3 a.

1875 CAYLEY in *Phil. Trans.* CLXV. 675 Coordinates of point in (s + 1)-dimensional space. 1880 *Academy* 30 Oct. 314 Four-dimensional space may be built up with .. ikosatetrahedroids. 1882 MINCHIN *Unipl. Kinemat.* 116 The general, or three dimensional, motion of a rigid body. 1883 *American* VII. 75 We can, I think, conceive of space as being two or even one dimensional.

3. a. Of, pertaining to, or involving dimensions of units or physical quantities.

1888 *Proc. Physical Soc.* X. 49 Prof. S. P. Thompson considered part of the difficulties of dimensional equations arose from the fact that no distinction was made between scalar and vector quantities. 1914 *Physical Rev.* 2nd Ser. IV. 369 The application of dimensional reasoning to mechanical problems is often useful in the interpretation of model experiments. 1964 H. S. HVISTENDAHL *Engin. Units* i. 10 The reason for the apparent ambiguity of the dimensions in such cases, is that our dimensional formulae do not distinguish the relative directions of the lengths combining as some power of L in those formulae.

b. ***dimensional analysis***, a method of mathematical analysis in which physical quantities are expressed in terms of their dimensions (i.e. length, mass, time, etc.) so that conclusions may be drawn regarding their mutual relations; it is based on the fact that quantities added to or equated with each other must have the same dimensions.

1922 P. W. BRIDGMAN *Dimensional Analysis* ii. 17 The purpose of dimensional analysis is to give certain information about the relations which hold between the measurable quantities associated with various phenomena. 1949 O. G. SUTTON *Sci. of Flight* iii. 68 In analysing complex physical phenomena .., mathematicians .. employ a dissection process known as *dimensional analysis.* 1957 *Encycl. Brit.* VI. 387/2 The principal use of dimensional analysis is to deduce from a study of the dimensions of the variables in any physical system certain necessary limitations on the form of any possible relationship between those variables. **1958** J. S. SCOTT *Dict. Civ. Engin.* 105 *Dimensional analysis*, in the model analysis of rivers, ships, ports..and other structures involving the flow of fluids, the use of dynamic similarity to enable the experimenter to see quickly what is the relationship between different variables.

Hence **dimensio'nality**, the condition of having (a particular number of) dimensions; dimensional quality,

1875 CAYLEY in *Phil. Trans.* CLXV. 675 The notion of density is dependent on the dimensionality of the element of volume *d ω*. **1884** E. A. ABBOTT *Flatland* II. xxii. 101 A race of rebels who shall refuse to be confined to limited Dimensionality.

di'mensionalize, *v.* [f. DIMENSIONAL *a.* + -IZE.] *trans.* To consider or describe (an object, a concept) from the point of view of its dimensions in time, space, etc. Hence **di'mensionalized** *ppl. a.*

1966 J. S. BRUNER *Beyond Information Given* (1974) xviii. 323 The subject..was asked, 'Which one is the longest?'.. By offering him dimensionalized verbal labeling as she did, she encouraged symbolic representation by linguistic encoding. **1973** E. S. SHNEIDMAN *Deaths of Man* (1975) xi. 127 There is nothing at all inexorable about our ways of dimensionalizing death. Conceptualizations of death are man-made and mutable; what man can make he can also clarify and change. **1977** R. HOLLAND *Self & Social Context* v. 156 It is possible to study the content of a person's construing, its dimensionality and the structures of the dimensionalized life space. **1983** S. I. OFFENBACH *Concept of Dimension in Research on Children's Learning* 33 Younger children might be able to dimensionalize stimuli whose colours are red and green (or whose shapes are star and triangle), whereas they cannot dimensionalize stimuli that are red and blue (or circle and triangle).

di'mensionally, *adv.* [f. DIMENSIONAL *a.* + -LY[2].] With regard to dimensions; in a dimensional way.

1888 *Proc. Physical Soc.* X. 44 We can transform both dimensionally and numerically by the relation $[K^{-\frac{1}{2}}\mu^{-\frac{1}{2}}] = v[LT^{-1}]$. **1927** I. B. CRANDALL *Theory Vibr. Syst.* ii. 56 Dimensionally, the *r* in this formula merely offsets other linear dimensions in the definition of *μ* and *ρ*. **1957** *New Biol.* XXII. 58 The choice of this dimensionally insignificant object for detailed study. **1969** L. YOUNG *Syst. Units Electr. & Magn.* x. 126 To each constant of proportionality that is treated dimensionally there corresponds a base unit.

†**dimensionate**, *v. Obs. rare.* [f. L. *dīmensiōn-em* DIMENSION + -ATE[3] 7.] *trans.* To give or lay down the dimensions of.

14.. *Harl. MS.* 2261 lf. 217b, In whiche bookes he dimencionate the worlde clerely with his contentes.

dimensioned (dɪ'mɛnʃənd), *ppl. a.* [f. DIMENSION + -ED[2].] †**a.** Having material 'dimension' or extension (cf. DIMENSION *sb.* 2, 4). *Obs.* **b.** Having a particular dimension or measurement. **c.** *Geom.* Having (a specified number of) dimensions: see DIMENSION *sb.* 3 a.

1533 TINDALE *Supper of Lord* in *More's Answ. Poysoned Bk.* Wks. (1557) 1092/1 Inuisible wyth al hys dymencioned body vnder the forme of breade transubstanciated into it. **1725** POPE *Odyss.* XIX. 276 A mantle purple-tinged, and radiant vest, Dimensioned equal to his size. **1882** PROCTOR *Fam. Science Stud.* 15 While a line could be infinitely produced in this singly dimensioned world, the world itself ..would be finite. **1884** E. A. ABBOTT *Flatland* 86 Look down..upon this land of Three Dimensions, and see the inside of every three-dimensioned house.

di'mensionless, *a.* [f. as prec. + -LESS.]

1. a. Without dimension or physical extension. **b.** Of no (appreciable) magnitude; extremely minute. **c.** Without dimensions: see DIMENSION 3 a.

1667 MILTON *P.L.* XI. 17 To Heav'n thir prayers Flew up ..in they pass'd Dimentionless through Heav'nly dores. **1752** WARBURTON *Wks.* (1811) IX. ii. 34 As the Earth is but a point compared to the orb of Saturn, so the orb of Saturn itself grows dimensionless when compared to that vast extent of space which the stellar-solar Systems possess. **1825** COLERIDGE *Aids Refl.* App. C. (1858) I. 394 If we assume the time as excluded, the line vanishes, and we leave space dimensionless. **1890** J. H. STIRLING *Gifford Lect.* viii. 150 With our scales and weights..and measuring-rods, we do but deceive ourselves: what is, is dimensionless: the truth is not in time; space is all too short for a ladder to the Throne.

d. Of a physical quantity or its unit: having no dimensions (DIMENSION *sb.* 3 c); of the nature of a pure number or ratio, and therefore having a value independent of the choice of units for other quantities.

1904 *Proc. Inst. Mech. Engineers* 248, *K* is a dimensionless quantity approximating to unity, and the working formula becomes $V = K\sqrt{(2P/\rho)}$. **1914** *Physical Rev.* 2nd Ser. IV. 345 The coefficients of a complete equation are dimensionless numbers, i.e. if the quantities *Q* are measured by an absolute system of units, the coefficients of the equation do not depend on the sizes of the fundamental units but only on the fixed interrelations of the units which characterize the system and differentiate it from any other absolute system. **1970** *Nature* 28 Nov. 889/2 It would..be incorrect to say: 'the molecular weight of protein X is 25,000 daltons', for the dalton is a unit of mass, and molecular weight is dimensionless.

2. Measureless, immense, boundless, vast.

1813 HOGG in *New Monthly Mag.* (1836) XLVI. 446 Here, in these almost dimensionless regions, nature is seen on a large scale. *a* **1839** GALT *Demon of Destiny* III. (1840) 28 As if man were not but an atom thing In the dimensionless, the Universe.

†**di'mensious**, *a. Obs. rare*[−1]. Also -tious. [f. DIMENSION: see -IOUS. Cf. *pretentious*, *religious*, *suspicious*.] Having (great) dimension or magnitude; spacious, extensive.

1632 LITHGOW *Trav.* x. 507 The generall computation of which dimensious spaces..amounteth to [etc.].

†**di'mensity.** *Obs. rare*[−1]. [f. L. *dīmens-us*, after *immensity*.] Dimension, magnitude.

c **1645** HOWELL *Lett.* (1655) IV. xliv, If of the smallest starrs in sky We know not the dimensity.

dimensive (dɪ'mɛnsɪv), *a.* Now *rare* or *Obs.* [f. L. *dīmens-* ppl. stem (see DIMENSE *v.*) + -IVE.]

†**1.** Having, or related to, physical dimension or extension in space. *Obs.*

1563-87 FOXE *A. & M.* (1596) 210/1 In heauen the existence of his bodie is dimensiue. **1596** BELL *Surv. Popery* III. x. 434 When the unequall dimensiue quantities are placed togither. **1694** R. BURTHOGGE *Reason* 106 Matter is.. the first subject of dimensive spacious Quantity.

†**2.** Serving to measure or trace out the dimensions of something. ? *Obs.*

1592 DAVIES *Immort. Soul* IV. vi. (1714) 35 All Bodies have their measure and their space, But who can draw the Soul's dimensive Lines? **1610** *Histrio-m.* I. 43 The very state of Peace shall seeme to shine In every figure or dimensive lyne.

3. Of or belonging to dimension or magnitude; dimensional. *rare.*

1845 STOCQUELER *Handbk. Brit. India* (1854) 129 A few of the streets in the European town are of great dimensions;.. the Chowringhee Road..is nearly two miles long, and in average width not less than eighty feet..The Dhurrumtollah is nearly equal, in dimensive character, to this.

Hence †**di'mensively** *adv.*, †**di'mensiveness.**

1601 DEACON & WALKER *Spirits & Divels* 55 Neither spirites nor diuels (they being no corporal substances stretched out by Dimensions..) may truely be said to be in a place commensuratiuelie, or dimensiuelie. *Ibid.* 89 It ariseth..from the finitenesse, and dimensiuenesse of the angelicall nature.

‖**di'mensum.** *Obs.* [med.L. *dīmensum* measured quantity, measure, sb. use of pa. pple. of *dīmetīrī* to measure out: see DIMENSE *v.*] A measured portion; a fixed allowance; = DIMENSE *sb.*

1630 B. JONSON *New Inn* III. i, You are to blame to use the poor dumb Christians So cruelly, defraud 'em of their dimensum. Yonder's the colonel's horse..the devil a bit He has got, since he came in yet! **1643** LIGHTFOOT *Glean.* 26 The dimensum of their diet in the Wildernesse.

†**dimensu'ration.** *Obs.* [n. of action f. L. type **dīmensūrāre*, f. *dī-* + *mensūrāre* to measure, after *dīmetīrī*, *dīmensus*, f. *di-* + *metīrī*, *mensus* to measure.] Measuring out or off, measurement.

1593 NORDEN *Spec. Brit., M'sex* I. Prepar. 15 Such an expected geographicall description..doeth require dimensuration betweene euery station. **1677** PLOT *Oxfordsh.* To Rdr. B ij, As true as actual dimensuration..could direct me to put them.

So †**di'mensurable** *a.*, capable of being measured; †**di'mensurated** *ppl. a.*, measured; †**di'mensurator**, an instrument for taking measurements. (All *obs.* and *rare.*)

1660 STANLEY *Hist. Philos.* (1701) 404/1 The point by fluxion makes a Line, the Line..a Superficies, the Superficies..a Body, three ways dimensurable. **1675** OGILBY *Brit.* Pref. 3 Dimensurators or Measuring Instruments. *Ibid.* (1698) 1 Shewing the dimensurated miles and furlongs answerably.

dimer ('daɪmə(r)). *Chem.* [f. DI-[2] + Gr. μέρ-ος share, part (after *polymer*).] A compound related to some other compound by having twice the number of atoms of the various elements in its molecule; usually, a compound the molecule of which is a double molecule formed by the joining together of two identical molecules.

1930 *Jrnl. Amer. Chem. Soc.* LII. 320 From the distillate was isolated a very small amount..of a crystalline solid having the analytical composition of tetramethylene carbonate. Molecular weight determinations indicated that it is a dimer:

$$\overline{\mathrm{COO(CH_2)_4OCOO(CH_2)_4O}}.$$

1951 S. COFFEY tr. *Wibaut's Org. Chem.* vii. 105 If two molecules of the monomer combine, the polymer so formed is called a *dimer*, if three molecules combine, a *trimer*..and so on. **1964** J. W. LINNETT *Electronic Struct. Molecules* iii. 50 Let us consider the dimer of CN, namely cyanogen, C_2N_2. **1965** *New Scientist* 29 Apr. 291/1 An excited molecule can join with a ground-state molecule to form a new double molecule (or dimer).

dimeran ('dɪmərən). *Entom.* [f. mod.L. *dimera*, neuter pl. of *dimerus* (see DIMEROUS) + -AN.] A member of the division *Dimera* of hemipterous insects, having the tarsi two-jointed.

1847 in CRAIG.

dimercaprol (ˌdaɪmə'kæprəl). *Chem.* [Abbrev. of *dimercaptopropanol*; the full form is also used occas.] = B.A.L. (see B III).

1945 *Nature* 24 Nov. 617/1 The new compound 2 : 3 dimercaptopropanol (III) was made. **1947** *Chem. Abstr.* 4570 Antimalarials, dimercaprol, radiotherapy, and rutin are discussed. **1949** H. W. FLOREY et al. *Antibiotics* II. VIII. xxi. 815 Dimercaptopropanol (also known as 'British Anti-Lewisite' (BAL)). **1963** *Brit. Pharmaceutical Codex* 267 Dimercaprol is used in the treatment of acute poisoning by arsenic, mercury, gold, bismuth, thallium and antimony.

di'mercur-, -'mercuro-, -'mercury. *Chem.* [DI-[2] 2.] Used in *comb.* and *attrib.* to express the presence of two equivalents of mercury.

Thus ***dimercura'mmonium*** $Hg_2H_4.N_2$, an ammoniacal mercury base in which half the hydrogen in ammonium is replaced by two atoms of divalent mercury.

1873 *Fownes' Chem.* (ed. 11) 347 A brown precipitate.. consisting of dimercurammonium iodide. **1881** *Nature* XXIV. 467 Dimercury methylene iodide $CH_2(HgI)_2$ is obtained by exposing methylene iodide with an excess of mercury to the action of light.

dimeric (daɪ'mɛrɪk), *a.* [f. Gr. διμερ-ής bipartite + -IC; in sense 2 formed directly on DIMER.]

1. a. *Zool.* Bilateral; having a right and left side. **b.** *Bot.* = DIMEROUS *a.* b.

1897 L. H. BAILEY in *Ann. Rep. Smithsonian Inst.* 455 A comparison of bilateral or dimeric animals with rotate or polymeric animals. **1900** in B. D. JACKSON *Gloss. Bot. Terms* 78 *Dimeric, dimerous*, with two members in each part or circle.

2. *Chem.* That is a DIMER; having a molecular formula in which the numbers of atoms are twice those for some other compounds.

1929 *Jrnl. Amer. Chem. Soc.* LI. 2553 The products of such reactions..have..been assumed to be dimeric (and cyclic) for no other reason than that they were obviously not monomeric. **1938** [see DIMERIZE *v.*]. **1964** J. W. LINNETT *Electronic Struct. Molecules* vii. 107 Dimerization to the tetrazane occurs..because, in the dimeric molecule, each of the nitrogen atoms has a formal charge of zero.

dimerism ('dɪmərɪz(ə)m). [f. mod.L. *dimer-us* + -ISM.] Dimerous condition or constitution; in *Bot.* the arrangement of floral organs two in a whorl: see DIMEROUS *a.*

dimerize ('daɪməraɪz), *v.* [f. DIMER(IC *a.* + -IZE.] **a.** *trans.* To render dimeric; to form a dimer of. **b.** *intr.* To undergo dimerization; to be converted into a dimer. Hence **dimeri'zation**, the process by which two identical molecules join to form a single molecule; the action of forming a dimer; **'dimerized, 'dimerizing** *ppl. adjs.*

a **1855** C. B. MANSFIELD *Theory of Salts* (1865) III. ii. 247 It does not at all follow..that therefore two molecules of the same body, when formed side by side, shall become polymerized or dimerized into a compound of double equivalent weight. **1931** *Chem. Abstr.* XXV. 5139 (*title*) Dimerization of isoprene. **1938** H. GILMAN *Org. Chem.* I. iv. 442 Two types of addition of alkali metals take place. One is a simple 1, 2-addition..and the other has been termed a dimerizing addition... The dimerized addition products show the general reactions of Grignard reagents. **1938** *Jrnl. Chem. Soc.* 288 In the formation of a methylene-dicyclane by dimerisation of an open-chain diene the first step is..the production of an open-chain dimeric structure. **1952** *Chem. Rev.* L. 485 Fluoranthene dimerizes by a free-radical mechanism. **1959** CRAM & HAMMOND *Org. Chem.* xv. 352 Olefins which are heavily substituted with halogen and other electron-attracting substituents dimerize to form cyclobutanes at high temperatures. **1964** J. W. LINNETT *Electronic Struct. Molecules* iii. 45 Why does NO not dimerize to N_2O_2 since it has an odd number of electrons? **1965** *New Scientist* 30 Dec. 921/2 The thioketones..tend to dimerise spontaneously—that is, to form new compounds out of molecular pairs. **1970** *Nature* 28 Nov. 805/2 The bifunctional protein of the double mutant retains the ability to dimerize.

dimerous ('dɪmərəs), *a.* [f. mod.L. *dimer-us* (F. *dimère*), f. Gr. διμερής bipartite (f. δι- twice + μέρος part) + -OUS.] Consisting of two parts or divisions: *spec.* **a.** *Entom.* Having two joints: applied to the tarsus of an insect. **b.** *Bot.* Of a flower: Having two divisions or members in each whorl. (Often written *2-merous.*) Of a leaf: Consisting of two leaflets (*rare*).

1826 KIRBY & SP. *Entomol.* xlvii. (1828) IV. 387 Tarsi mostly trimerous, rarely dimerous. **1845** LINDLEY *Sch. Bot.* viii. (1858) 129 Flowers dimerous. **1869** *Student* II. 12 Polymerous leaves may be dimerous, trimerous, etc. according to their number of meriphylls. **1872** OLIVER *Elem. Bot.* II. 174 Observe the dimerous symmetry of Enchanter's Nightshade (*Circæa*), the parts of the flower being in twos. **1882** VINES *Sachs' Bot.* 646 True tetramerous flowers are allied..to those with dimerous whorls.

dime'tallic, *a. Chem.* [f. DI-[2] 2 d: cf. *diacid*, *dibasic*.] Containing two equivalents of a metal.

1861 ODLING *Manual of Chem.* I. 338 We have monometallic, dimetallic and trimetallic compounds, represented respectively by the formulæ MH_2AsO_4, M_2HAsO_4, and M_3AsO_4. Of dimetallic or neutral, and trimetallic or basic arsenates, those of the alkali-metals are alone soluble in water.

dimeter ('dɪmɪtə(r)). *Prosody.* [a. L. *dimetrus* sb., *dimeter*, *-metrus* adj., a. Gr. δίμετρος of two measures, f. δι- twice + μέτρον measure.] A verse consisting of two measures, i.e. either two feet or four feet.

1589 PUTTENHAM *Eng. Poesie* II. (Arb.) 143 In the *dimeter*, made of two sillables entier. *ēxtrēme dēsīre.* **1625** B. JONSON *Staple of N.* IV. Wks. (Rtldg.) 399/1 When he comes forth With dimeters, and trimeters, tetrameters,

Pentameters, hexameters, catalectics..What is all this, but canting? **1775** TYRWHITT *Ess. Lang. & Versif. Chaucer* III. §7 in *Chaucer's Wks.*, The Octosyllable Metre..was in reality the antient Dimeter Iambic. **1837–39** HALLAM *Hist. Lit.* (1847) I. 30 The line of eight syllables, or dimeter iambic. **1882** GOODWIN *Gk. Gram.* 317 In most kinds of verse, a monometer consists of one foot, a dimeter of two feet.

dimethyl (daɪˈmɛθɪl). *Chem.* [See DI-² 2 and METHYL.]

1. as *sb.* A name of Ethane (C_2H_6), regarded as two molecules of the radical methyl (CH_3).

1873 *Fownes' Chem.* (ed. 11) 568 A colourless gaseous mixture containing ethane or dimethyl. **1877** WATTS *Fownes' Chem.* II. 47 *Ethane.* This compound..may also be regarded as *dimethyl*, or as ethyl hydride.

2. *attrib.* and in *Comb.* denoting an organic compound in which two equivalents of methyl take the place of two of hydrogen, as ***dimethyl ketone*** = Acetone $CO(CH_3)_2$; ***dimethylaniline***, $H_5N(CH_3)_2$, one of the aniline bases; ***dimethyl-benzene*** $C_6H_4(CH_3)_2$; ***dimethyl-ethyl carbinol*** = tertiary pentyl alcohol, $C{\cdot}OH{\cdot}(CH_3)_2{\cdot}(C_2H_5)$; ***dimethylamine***, a colourless gas, $(CH_3)_2NH$, which liquefies at 7° C. and has an ammoniacal odour; ***dimethyl phthalate***, a colourless liquid ester, $C_6H_4(COOCH_3)_2$, used esp. in insect repellents and as a plasticizer.

1852 WATTS tr. *Gmelin's Handbk. Chem.* VII. 319 Dimethylamine..is formed as a hydriodate..by the action of ammonia on iodide of methyl. **1869** ROSCOE *Elem. Chem.* 330 The secondary propyl alcohol or dimethyl carbinol boils at 84°. **1877** WATTS *Fownes' Chem.* II. 428 Dimethyl-benzene or Xylene. **1880** FRISWELL in *Soc. Arts Jrnl.* 444 The dimethyl compound resulting from the use of two molecules of the alcoholic compound. **1910** *Jrnl. Soc. Chem. Ind.* XXIX. 1398/2 Perfectly clear solutions of rosin are obtained by warming it with 30 per cent. of its weight of dimethyl or diethyl phthalate. **1944** KNIPLING & DOVE in *Jrnl. Econ. Ent.* XXXVII. 479/2 Dimethyl phthalate had been found by the Orlando workers to be a good flea repellent. **1946** *Lancet* 13 Apr. 559/2 Dimethyl-phthalate (D.M.P.), a repellant used against the mosquito during the war. **1947** *Thorpe's Dict. Appl. Chem.* (ed. 4) VIII. 7/2 Dimethylamine has been employed as an accelerator in vulcanising rubber, and in the manufacture of detergent soaps. **1947** R. L. WAKEMAN *Chem. Commercial Plastics* xxii. 665 The number of plasticizers which can be used successfully with cellulose acetate is also restricted. Dimethyl and diethyl phthalates..are often used.

Dimetian, var. DEMETIAN *a.* and *sb.*

dimetient (daɪˈmiːʃɪənt), *a.* and *sb.* [ad. L. *dīmetient-em*, pr. pple. of *dīmetīrī* to measure out: see DIMENSE.]

A. *adj.*

†**1.** That measures across through the centre: ***dimetient line*** = DIAMETER. *Obs.*

1601 HOLLAND *Pliny* I. 15 The dimetient line, or diameter, taketh a third part of the circumference, and little lesse than a seuenth part. **1603** —— *Plutarch's Mor.* 1045 That the Diameter or Dimetient line of the earth is triple to that of the moone. **1729** SHELVOCKE *Artillery* IV. 264 The Orifice of the Chamber, whose Dimetient Line is exactly ⅓ of the whole Diameter.

2. *Math.* That expresses the dimension.

1842 DE MORGAN *Diff. & Int. Calculus* 323 Usually x^a is the dimetient function of Algebra; we must come to the consideration of transcendental quantities before we find a function which is not of the same order as x^a, for some value or other of *a*; and then between x^a and x^{a+k} may be found an infinite number of functions, higher in dimension than the first, and lower than the second, however small *k* may be.

†**B.** *sb.* (Short for *dimetient line*). = DIAMETER.

[**1570** BILLINGSLEY *Euclid* VI. xxiv. 172 In euery parallelogramme, the parallelogrammes about the dimeciens are lyke vnto the whole.] **1571** DIGGES *Pantom.* I. Elem. B ij b, A Right line drawne through the Centre vnto the Circumference of both sides, is named his Diameter or Dimetient. **1690** LEYBOURN *Curs. Math.* 328 The Dimetient of a Sphere.

dimetric (daɪˈmɛtrɪk), *a. Crystallography.* [f. Gr. δι-, δίς twice + μέτρον measure + -IC: cf. METRIC.] Applied to a system of crystals having three axes at right angles, the two lateral axes being equal to each other but unequal to the vertical axis; = TETRAGONAL.

1868 DANA *Min.* Introd. 21 The names Monometric, Dimetric, and Trimetric, used in former editions of this work, have been set aside..The names want precision, the hexagonal system being as much *dimetric* as the tetragonal. *Ibid.* 24 Tetragonal System (also called Quadratic, Pyramidal, Monodimetric, Dimetric). **1873** *Fownes' Chem.* (ed. 11) 279 The dimetric are also very symmetrical, about three axes at right angles to each other.

dimication (dɪmɪˈkeɪʃən). Now *rare.* [ad. L. *dīmicātiōn-em*, n. of action f. *dīmicāre* to fight.] Fighting; strife, contention.

1623 COCKERAM, *Dimication*, a battell. **1650** S. CLARKE *Eccl. Hist.* I. (1654) 66 In the dimication which arose about Arius. **1660** FISHER *Rusticks Alarm* Wks. (1679) 229 In thy meer demi-digested demications against them. **1884** *Times* 28 July 6 In such a continual dimication..the defeated impersonations of error will be found fighting as briskly as ever they did to-morrow.

So †**ˈdimicate** *v.*, to fight, contend; **dimicatory** *a.* (*affected* or *humorous*), relating to fighting or fencing.

1657 TOMLINSON *Renou's Disp.* 314 When Snailes are about to dimicate with Serpents. **1892** *Sat. Rev.* 2 Apr. 400/1 For matters dimicatory.

dimiceries, var. DIMISSARIES *Obs.*

dimidiate (dɪˈmɪdɪət, daɪ-), *a.* [ad. L. *dīmidiātus*, pa. pple. of *dīmidiāre* to halve, f. *dīmidium* half, f. *di-, dis-* asunder + *medius* mid, *medium* middle.]

1. Divided into halves; halved, half.

1768–74 TUCKER *Lt. Nat.* (1852) I. 475 The dimidiate platform of your staircase. **1825** LAMB *Elia* Ser. II. *Pop. Fallacies*, He..allows his hero a sort of dimidiate preeminence:—'Bully Dawson kicked by half the town, and half the town kicked by Bully Dawson'. **1847** SIR W. HAMILTON *Let. to A. De Morgan* 43 Dimidiate quantification. **1854** HOOKER *Himal. Jrnls.* I. iii. 61 When the tree is dimidiate, one half the green, the other the red shades of colour.

2. *Bot.* and *Zool.* **a.** Of an organ: Having one part much smaller than the other, so as to appear to be wanting. **b.** Split in two on one side, as the calyptra of some mosses. **c.** *Zool.* Relating to the lateral halves of an organism: applied to hermaphrodites having one side male and the other female.

1830 LINDLEY *Nat. Syst. Bot.* 322 The dimidiate calyptra. **1846** DANA *Zooph.* (1848) 432 *Dimidiate*, a tubular calicle bisected vertically nearly to its base. **1855** OWEN *Comp. Anat.* 18 (L.) Insects, like crustaceans, are occasionally subject to one-sided or dimidiate hermaphroditism. **1863** BERKELEY *Brit. Mosses* Gloss. 312 *Dimidiate*, the same with cucullate. **1880** GRAY *Struct. Bot.* vi. §6. 255 The anther of Gomphrena is completely unilocular by abortion..of the companion cell. Thus losing one half, it is said to be dimidiate, or halved.

3. *Comb.* in botanical terms, as ***dimidiate-cordate***, said of a dimidiate leaf (see 2 a) of which the full-grown part is cordate; so ***dimidiate-oblong***, ***-obovoid***. (Sometimes written *dimidiato-cordate*, etc.)

1866 *Treas. Bot.*, *Dimidiato-cordate*, when the larger half of a dimidiate leaf is cordate. **1870** HOOKER *Stud. Flora* 329 *Euphorbia peplis*..leaves dimidiate-cordate. *Ibid.* 435 *Leersia oryzoides*..Spikelet dimidiate-oblong.

dimidiate (dɪˈmɪdɪeɪt, daɪ-), *v.* [f. ppl. stem of L. *dīmidiāre*: see prec.]

1. *trans.* To divide into halves; to halve; to reduce to the half.

1623 COCKERAM, *Dimediate*, to part into two parts. **1652** W. SCLATER *Civ. Mag.* (1653) 42 Who dimidiate Christ, would have him onely by halfes. **1652** SPARKE *Prim. Devot.* (1663) 321 Dimidiated, as 'twere by forked tongues. **1789** S. PARR *Wks.* (1828) VII. 412, I hope he had a complete service, not mutilated and dimidiated, as it was for poor Johnson at the Abbey.

2. *Her.* To cut in half; to represent only half of (a bearing), *esp.* in one half of a shield party per pale: see DIMIDIATED, DIMIDIATION. Hence **diˈmidiating** *vbl. sb.*

1864 BOUTELL *Heraldry Hist. & Pop.* xiv. §1 (ed. 3) 146 This was styled Impaling by Dimidiation or Dimidiating. **1880** WARREN *Book-plates* xii. 128. **1893** E. HOWLETT in *Reliquary* July 160 The arms of the Cinque Ports, England dimidiating azure three ships' hulls in pale or.

diˈmidiated, *ppl. a.* [f. prec. + -ED.] Halved; divided into halves, or having only one half shown or represented; *spec.* in *Her.* of a bearing or coat of arms. (Cf. DIMIDIATION, DEMI B. 1.)

1572 BOSSEWELL *Armorie* II. 42 Sundrie wayes they [Lions] are borne in armes..Dimidiated, Parted, Couped. **1647** A. ROSS *Myst. Poet.* iv. (1675) 98 In respect of her [the moon's] corniculated, dimidiated, and plenary aspect. **1752** SIR J. HILL *Hist. Anim.* 52 (Jod.) The dytiscus with twenty dimidiated striæ on the extended wings. **1864** BOUTELL *Heraldry Hist. & Pop.* xxxii. (ed. 3) 467 Or, a dimidiated eagle to the sinister sa. **1892** *Proc. Soc. Antiquaries* XIV. 279 The arms of France and Burgundy are shown dimidiated.

dimidiately (dɪˈmɪdɪətlɪ), *adv.* [f. DIMIDIATE *a.* + -LY².] In a dimidiate manner.

1857 T. MOORE *Handbk. Brit. Ferns* (ed. 3) vii. 168 Pinnules obovate, obliquely ovate, or dimidiately subquadrate. **1887** W. PHILLIPS *Brit. Discomycetes* 51 Cup subsessile, externally pruinose, dimidiately elongated, or obliquely contorted.

dimidiation (dɪˌmɪdɪˈeɪʃən, daɪ-). [ad. L. *dīmidiātiōn-em*, n. of action from *dīmidiāre* to halve: see DIMIDIATE *a.*] The action of halving, or condition of being halved; *spec.* in *Her.* the combination or 'marshalling' of two coats of arms by placing side by side the dexter half of one and the sinister half of the other; an early form of *impalement*.

c **1425** *Craft Nombrynge* (E.E.T.S.) 5 þer ben .7...partes of þis craft. The first is called addicion, þe seconde.. subtraccion. The thryd is called duplacion. The 4... dimydicion. **1658** PHILLIPS, *Dimidiation*, a dividing in the midst, a cutting into two halves. **1780** J. EDMONDSON *Heraldry* 179 This method of impaling arms by dimidiation hath been for some time laid aside in England. **1847** PARKER *Gloss. Brit. Her.* 113 *Dimidiation*, the dexter half of the husband's arms being joined to the sinister half of the wife's. **1882** CUSSANS *Handbk. Her.* xii. (ed. 3) 164 Marshalling by Dimidiation was, towards the close of the Fourteenth Century, superseded by Impalement.

dimilance, obs. form of DEMI-LANCE.

diminew, var. DIMINUE *v. Obs.*, to diminish.

Dimini (dɪˈmiːnɪ). Also Dh-. [Gr. Διμήνι.] The name of a locality of north-eastern Greece used *attrib.* to designate a kind of pottery ornamented with spirals, found there by excavation.

1912 WACE & THOMPSON *Prehist. Thess.* 16 Painted pottery, Dhimini ware. **1925** V. G. CHILDE *Dawn Eur. Civiliz.* 69 The invaders [of Eastern Thessaly]..introduced a new pottery, Dimini ware, rather coarser than the older fabric.

diminicion, obs. form of DIMINUTION.

diminish (dɪˈmɪnɪʃ), *v.* Also 5–6 y for *i*, sshe for *sh*; 5–6 **deminish(e**, 6 *Sc.* **dimimiss, dininuse.** [Formed under the joint influence of the earlier DIMINUE, F. *diminuer*, L. *dīminuĕre*, and MINISH, earlier *menusen*, OF. *menuiser*, L. type **minūtiāre* to cut small, having the prefix of the one with the suffix of the other. Ancient L. had *dīminuĕre* to break into small pieces, dash to pieces, and *dēminuĕre* to make smaller, lessen, reduce in size. In late L. and Romanic the *di-* derivative supplanted the *dē-* form; hence the modern derivatives of L. *dēminuĕre* all have *dimin-*]

I. *trans.*

1. To make (or cause to appear) less or smaller; to lessen; to reduce in magnitude or degree. (The opposite of *enlarge, increase, augment, magnify.*)

1417 in Ellis *Orig. Lett.* Ser. II. I. 61 Yf your forces be not here alwayes soe strongly mayntayned & continued without being deminished your Irish enimies..will rise agayne. **1526** *Pilgr. Perf.* (W. de W. 1531) 4 Perauenture it diminysshed theyr payne in hell. **1577** B. GOOGE *Heresbach's Husb.* IV. (1586) 162 It greatly deminisheth the substance of them. **1600** J. PORY tr. *Leo's Africa* II. 169 The whole towne is diminished into one streete. **1612** BRINSLEY *Lud. Lit.* xxiv. (1627) 268 Whatsoever may diminish his estimation and authority. **1641** WILKINS *Math. Magick* I. xii. (1648) 85 The weight must..be diminished in the same proportion. **1790** PALEY *Horæ Paul.* Rom. i. 12 What diminishes very much the suspicion of fraud. **1880** GEIKIE *Phys. Geog.* ii. §8. 53 The ascent of warm air must necessarily diminish atmospheric pressure.

†**b.** To clip, sweat, etc. (coin). *Obs.*

1568 GRAFTON *Chron.* II. 126 There should be no deceyt used by diminishing or clipping yᵉ same. **1698** LUTTRELL *Brief Rel.* (1857) IV. 350 A French man is committed to Newgate for diminishing our coin.

†**2.** To break in pieces, break small. *Obs. rare.* [class. L. *dīminuĕre.*]

1607 TOPSELL *Four-f. Beasts* (1658) 491 In Rhetia..they hold betwixt the fighting of Rams a stick, or bat of Corn-tree, which in a bout or two they utterly diminish and bruise in pieces.

3. To lessen in importance, estimation, or power; to put down, degrade, humiliate; to detract from, disparage, belittle. *arch.* (See also DIMINISHED 2.)

1560 BIBLE (Genev.) *Ezek.* xxix. 15, I wil diminish them, that they shal no more rule the nations. **1666** PEPYS *Diary* 24 June, He do plainly diminish the commanders put in by the Duke, and do lessen the miscarriages of any that have been removed by him. **1667** MILTON *P.L.* VII. 612 While impiously they thought Thee to diminish, and from thee withdraw The number of thy worshippers. **1712** STEELE *Spect.* No. 348 ¶ 2 This impertinent Humour of diminishing every one who is produced in Conversation. **1828** SCOTT *F.M. Perth* viii, You would have accused me of diminishing your honour. **1880** MISS BROUGHTON *Sec. Th.* I. vi, She..passes out, angered, humbled, diminished past compare.

†**4.** To take away (a part) *from* something, so as to make it less; hence *gen.* to take away, subtract, remove. *Obs.*

1504 ATKYNSON tr. *De Imitatione* IV. ix, Take from our hertis..all that may..dimynyshe vs from thy eternall loue. *a* **1533** FRITH *Disput. Purgat.* 181 Neither add any thing nor diminish. **1548** HALL *Chron.*, *Edw. IV*, 217 The..love betwene them, washed awaie and diminished all suspicion. **1576** FLEMING *Panopl. Epist.* 24 Thus much was diminished from the state of the empyre. **1610** SHAKS. *Temp.* III. iii. 64 Your swords..may as well Wound the loud windes..as diminish One dowle that's in my plumbe. **1611** BIBLE *Deut.* iv. 2 Ye shall not adde vnto the word which I command you, neither shall you diminish ought from it. *a* **1627** HAYWARD (J.), Nothing was diminished from the safety of the king by the imprisonment of the duke.

†**b.** *absol.* To abate, subtract. *Obs.*

1662 STILLINGFL. *Orig. Sacr.* II. vii. §6 That we should not add to nor diminish from Gods commands. **1762** GOLDSM. *Cit. W.* cv, Nothing..should be admitted to diminish from the real majesty of the ceremony. **1826** R. H. FROUDE *Rem.* (1838) I. 74 His command..will no more diminish from the sum of our pleasures than [etc.].

†**5.** To deprive (a person) in part, to curtail *of.*

1559 BP. COX in Strype *Ann. Ref.* I. vi. 98 If now then the builders..be diminished of their wages. **1609** BIBLE (Douay) *Ps.* xxxiii. 11 They that seeke after our Lord shal not be diminished of any good. **1762** GOLDSM. *Cit. W.* lii, The whole circle seemed diminished of their former importance.

6. *Arch.* To make (a thing) such that its successive parts in any direction are continuously less and less; to cause to taper or progressively decrease in size, as a tapering column: see DIMINUTION 9.

1624 WOTTON *Archit.* (1672) 22 They [pillars] are all diminished..from one third part of the whole Shaft. **1797** *Monthly Mag.* III. 221 The sides form the arch joints of the bridge, and are diminished, so as to tend towards the centre of the circle.

7. *Mus.* †a. To reduce in loudness, make gradually softer: cf. DIMINUENDO. *Obs.* b. To lessen (an interval) by a semitone: see DIMINISHED 4.

1674 PLAYFORD *Skill Mus.* I. xi. 43 It will work a better effect to Tune the Voice diminishing it, rather than Increasing it.

II. *intr.*

8. To become less or smaller; to lessen, decrease.

1520 *Caxton's Chron. Eng.* II. 11/2 Kyng Goffars people encreased dayly and his dyminished. **1565** EARL BEDFORD in Ellis *Orig. Lett.* Ser. I. II. 215 As their force dimenesshede so dyd her Grace increace. **1700** DRYDEN *Fables* Pref. (Globe) 495 What judgment I had increases rather than diminishes. **1725** POPE *Odyss.* XIV. 284 Crete's ample fields diminish to our eye. **1860** TYNDALL *Glac.* I. ii. 16 The sound ..diminishes in intensity. **1878** HUXLEY *Physiogr.* 78 The air diminished in bulk, while the quicksilver increased in weight.

b. *Arch.* To have its dimensions successively smaller in the same direction; to taper.

1715 LEONI *Palladio's Archit.* (1742) I. 12 In the diminishing of them it must be observ'd, that by how much longer they are, by so much the less they must diminish.

diminishable (dɪˈmɪnɪʃəb(ə)l), *a.* [f. prec. + -ABLE.] Capable of being diminished or lessened.

Hence **di'minishableness**.

1782 KIRWAN in *Phil. Trans.* LXXII. 223 Phlogisticated air, after it has been purified from phlogiston..is again diminishable by phlogistic processes. **1864** *Spectator* 20 Aug. 948/1 A five years' sentence..being thus at best diminishable by.. one year and three weeks. **1875** VEITCH *Lucretius* 33 The absolute diminishableness of the Sum of matter.

diminished (dɪˈmɪnɪʃt), *ppl. a.* [f. as prec. + -ED[1].]

1. a. Made smaller, lessened: see the verb. (†In quot. 1607, Lowered in condition, weakened, wasted, emaciated.) ***diminished return*** (cf. DIMINISHING *ppl. a.* 1 b).

1607 TOPSELL *Four-f. Beasts* (1658) 532 For the encouraging of a feeble and diminished horse Eumelius reporteth the flesh of swine..mingled in wine and given to drink, to be exceeding good. **1742** YOUNG *Nt. Th.* IX. 1715 How swift I mount! Diminish'd Earth recedes. **1817** D. RICARDO *Princ. Pol. Econ.* ii. 61 On the best land, the same produce would still be obtained with the same labour as before, but its value would be enhanced in consequence of the diminished returns obtained by those who employed fresh labour and stock on the less fertile land. **1843** J. R. MCCULLOCH *Princ. Pol. Econ.* (ed. 3) III. vii. 494 The greatest amount of capital and labour may be employed in fashioning raw produce and adapting it to our use, and in transporting it from where it is produced to where it is consumed, without a diminished return. *a* **1850** CALHOUN *Wks.* (1874) VI. 140 Rays of sovereignty..to be reflected back, not in diminished, but increased splendor.

b. ***diminished responsibility***: a state of mental disturbance or abnormality, not classifiable as insanity, but recognized in law as a ground for exempting a person from full liability for criminal behaviour.

1957 *Act 5 & 6 Eliz. II* c. 11 §2 Persons suffering from diminished responsibility. Where a person kills..he shall not be convicted of murder if he was suffering from such abnormality of mind..as substantially impaired his mental responsibility. **1958** *Spectator* 31 Jan. 126/1 Suppose that at his trial Taper should plead diminished responsibility, alleging that Sir Reginald's speeches had driven him.. barmy. **1963** *Times* 6 Feb. 6/2 Found Not Guilty of murdering the girl but Guilty of manslaughter on the grounds of his diminished responsibility.

2. Lowered in importance, estimation, or power (see DIMINISH *v.* 3).

1667 MILTON *P.L.* IV. 35 O thou [sun]..at whose sight all the Starrs Hide their diminisht heads. **1698** CONGREVE *Birth of Muse* 119 She feels..the Shame, Of Honours lost, and her diminish'd Name. **1840** E. E. NAPIER *Scenes & Sports For. Lands* I. p. xxxv, Crest-fallen and dejected..[they] hide.. their diminished heads. **1925** BELLOC *Mr. Petre* i. 22 A diminished man. One who had 'had an accident'. **1932** A. HUXLEY *Brave New World* xii. 204 Bernard had to slink back, diminished, to his rooms. **1960** *Woman's Own* 3 Dec. 18/3 Amy hated..to have him look like that, diminished and remote.

3. *Arch.*, etc. (See quots.)

1726 LEONI *Alberti's Archit.* I. 53/2 The imperfect, or diminish'd Arch..is not a compleat Semi-circle, but a determinate part less. **1823** P. NICHOLSON *Pract. Build.* 584 *Diminished Bar*, in joinery, the bar of a sash that is thinnest on the inner edge. **1876** GWILT *Archit.*, Gloss., *Diminished Column*, a column whereof the upper diameter is less than the lower.

4. *Mus.* a. Of an interval: Less by a chromatic semitone than a perfect, or than a minor, interval of the same name: opp. to *augmented*. ***diminished triad***, a triad containing a diminished (instead of a perfect) fifth. b. ***diminished subject***, a subject repeated in diminution (see DIMINUTION 5 a). c. ***diminished chord***, a chord containing a diminished interval or intervals. d. ***diminished seventh*** (***chord***), a chord in which the interval between the outer notes is a diminished seventh.

1727-51 CHAMBERS *Cycl.*, *Diminished interval*, in music, is ..an interval which is short of its just quantity by a lesser semitone. **1753** *Ibid. Supp.* s.v. *Interval*, A Table of Musical Intervals..Diminished Fourth..Diminished Fifth.. Diminished Seventh. **1839** [see SEVENTH *sb.* 2]. **1855** BROWNING *Toccata of Galuppi's* vii, Those lesser thirds so plaintive, sixths diminished, sigh on sigh. **1880** C. H. H. PARRY in Grove *Dict. Mus.* I. 448 The diminished seventh ..is a semitone less than the ordinary minor seventh. **1920** P. C. BUCK *Unfigured Harmony* (ed. 2) 12 Diminished sevenths are extremely useful, though more liable to be over-used than any other chord. **1926** A. NILES in W. C. Handy *Blues* 16 The device..of ending up the tune on the diminished seventh chord. **1949** L. FEATHER *Inside Be-Bop* II. 71 The diminished chord, for no apparent reason, is used less frequently in bebop than in earlier jazz. **1953** R. VAUGHAN WILLIAMS *Some Thoughts on Beethoven's Choral Symphony* 49 So is the diminished seventh of Bach's *Barabbas* a well-worn device. **1955** G. ABRAHAM in H. van Thal *Fanfare for E. Newman* 14 Equally characteristic of the more mature Wagner is the lightening of the diminished sevenths.., leaving a purely string chord. **1958** C. WILFORD in P. Gammond *Decca Bk. Jazz* ii. 32 The harmonies of ragtime..are made distinctive by very wide use of diminished chords.

di'minisher. *rare.* [f. as prec. + -ER[1].] One who or that which diminishes or lessens.

1601 WEEVER *Mirr. Mart.* A vij, This paynted wether-cocke, Arts diminisher, With cowardize beginneth to empeach me. **1637** CLARKE *Serm.* 241 (L.) The diminisher of regal, but the demolisher of episcopal authority.

di'minishing, *vbl. sb.* [f. as prec. + -ING[1].]

1. The action of the verb DIMINISH; lessening, diminution.

1513 MORE in Grafton *Chron.* (1568) II. 782 Thinges.. redoundyng to the diminishyng of his honor. **1582** R. WIMBLEDON (*title*), A Sermon no less fruitful than famous.. set foorth by the olde copy, without addings or diminishings. **1649** MILTON *Eikon.* x, That their liberties and rights were the impairing and diminishing of his regal power. **1863** GEO. ELIOT *Romola* III. xii, The one end of her life seemed to her to be the diminishing of sorrow.

2. *Arch.* Tapering; = DIMINUTION 9. ? *Obs.*

1563 SHUTE *Archit.* C iij a, How to close and finish the diminishing of the pillors. **1613-39** I. JONES in Leoni *Palladio's Archit.* (1742) II. 46 The diminishing of the Pilasters. **1776** G. SEMPLE *Building in Water* 142 In every Course to make a two Inch set off..will preserve the diminishing of the Pier.

di'minishing, *ppl. a.* [f. as prec. + -ING[2].]

1. That diminishes or lessens: a. That makes less. Spec. ***diminishing glass***, an instrument which causes objects to appear smaller than they appear to the naked eye; ***diminishing mirror***, a convex mirror in which the image is reduced in scale; ***diminishing rod***, that part of the mechanism of a cotton-roving machine which gives the bobbins of roving their conical ends.

1665 HOOKE *Microgr.* 3 [It] may by..some convenient Diminishing-Glasses, be made vanish into a scarce visible Speck. **1816** KEATINGE *Trav.* (1817) II. 210 If they could read through a diminishing glass. **1861** DICKENS *Gt. Expect.* II. xiv. 225 A private sitting-room..fitted up with a diminishing mirror. **1868** C. M. YONGE *Chaplet of Pearls* I. i. 2 They [*sc.* children] looked like a full-grown couple seen through a diminishing-glass. **1890** J. NASMITH *Mod. Cotton Spinning* x. 168 The slide in its reciprocal vertical movement causes, by means of the 'diminishing rod' or 'hangar bar', the upper cradle to oscillate in its centre. **1896** *Daily News* 28 May 2/2 Diminishing and magnifying glasses such as are used by artists.

b. That grows less. Esp. in ***the law of diminishing return(s)***, in Economics, the principle that the expenditure of labour or capital beyond a certain point does not produce a proportionately corresponding return (see quot. 1938); also *transf.*

1793 SMEATON *Edystone L.* Introd. 4 The building is carried up..by diminishing stories, to the height of 115 feet. **1815** E. WEST *Ess. Application of Capital to Land* 12 In the progress of improvement an equal quantity of work extracts from the soil a gradually diminishing return. **1848** MILL *Pol. Econ.* I. xii. §2. 216 The general law of diminishing return from land would have undergone..a temporary supersession. **1883** F. A. WALKER *Pol. Econ.* II. 23 The great comprehensive principle to which we give the name, 'the law of diminishing returns in agriculture'. **1894** *Nature* 26 July 291 The diminishing speed of the earth's rotation. **1930** J. S. HUXLEY *Bird-Watching* iv. 61 From the point of view of..the collector of birds seen and recorded, the law of diminishing returns has set in; only very seldom is he rewarded by the sight or sound of a species new or little known to him. **1938** F. BENHAM *Economics* ix. 130 We may now state the Law of Diminishing Returns. As the proportion of one factor in a combination of factors is increased, after a point, the marginal and average product of that factor will diminish. **1965** *Listener* 24 June 926/1, I, for one, am not prepared to accept that the law of diminishing returns applies to television. I do not believe that what is trivial and bad will drive out what is serious and good. **1970** *Times* 7 Jan. 9/8 The law of diminishing returns has begun to set in: we can't go on forever extending our hearts to shapely matrons.

†2. Disparaging, depreciative. *Obs.*

1675 EVELYN *Mem.* (1857) II. 105 The Lords accused the Commons for their..provoking, and diminishing expressions. **1705** STANHOPE *Paraphr.* III. 501 St. Paul, who..disdains all false and diminishing Reflections.

3. *Arch.*, *Ship-building*, etc. Thinning or tapering off gradually.

1867 SMYTH *Sailor's Word-bk.*, *Diminishing stuff*, in ship-building, the planking wrought under the wales, where it is thinned progressively to the thickness of the bottom plank. **1869** R. W. MEADE *Naval Archit.* 354. **1876** GWILT *Archit.*, Gloss., *Diminishing Rule*, a board cut with a concave edge, so as to ascertain the swell of a column, and to try its curvature. *Diminishing Scale*, a scale of gradation used in finding the different points for drawing the spiral curve of the Ionic volute. **1882** *Worc. Exhib. Catal.* iii. 5 Four diminishing joints.

di'minishingly, *adv.* [f. prec. + -LY[2].]

1. In a diminishing manner or degree; decreasingly.

1827 *Examiner* 262/1 The light..is spread diminishingly over the picture. **1873** *Contemp. Rev.* XXI. 449 Most powerful and varied in man, diminishingly so in the lower animals.

†2. Disparagingly, depreciatively. *Obs.*

1672 *Mede's Wks.*, *Life* 7 Some..were induc'd to speak somewhat diminishingly, and below the worth of his [Mede's] Clavis and Commentary upon the Apocalyps. **1707** NORRIS *Treat. Humility* vi. 289 To lessen and vilify himself, and speak very diminishingly..of his own worth.

di'minishment. Now *rare.* Also 6 de-. [f. DIMINISH *v.* + -MENT. App. obsolete before 1700; used again in 19th c., but not common.] The action or process of diminishing (*trans.* and *intr.*); diminution, lessening, decrease, abatement.

1546 BALE *Eng. Votaries* II. (1550) 94 b, All is to demynyshment of a kynges power. **1561** T. NORTON *Calvin's Inst.* I. xiii. 35 His diuine majestie..the offence of diminishment wherof is an unpardonable crime. **1662** J. CHANDLER *Van Helmont's Oriat.* Pref. to Rdr., A pure, everlasting..Light, which will illustrate all things, without dammage and diminishment. **1837** LOCKHART *Scott* xliv, He received us..with little perceptible diminishment in the sprightliness of his manner. **1893** G. D. LESLIE *Lett. to Marco* xxvi. 171 A diminishment in their numbers.

diminitif, -ive, obs. forms of DIMINUTIVE.

di'minuate, *v. nonce-wd.* [f. L. *dī-*, *dēminuĕre* to lessen + -ATE[3]: cf. next.] *intr.* To use a diminutive word or expression. (Cf. DIMINUENT.)

1883 M. COLLINS *Midnight to Midn.* viii. 174 'You are a little wild.' 'A little! you diminuate!'

†**diminu'ation.** *Obs. rare.* [a. OF. *diminuacion* (1488 in Godef.), f. *diminuer* to DIMINISH.] = DIMINUTION.

1477 EARL RIVERS (Caxton) *Dictes* 28 My tresor..may not be mynisshed for noo thing that I yeue..but thou maist departe with noon of thyn withoute dymynuacion.

†**diminue,** *v. Obs.* Forms: 4 dymynue, 6 -ew, diminew, *Sc.* dimunue. [a. F. *diminue-r* (1308 in Godef. *Suppl.*), ad. L. *dēminu-ĕre* to lessen, DIMINISH. Cf. Pr. *diminuar*, also with other conjugational suffixes, Pr., Sp., and Pg. *diminuir*, Cat. *disminuir*, It. *diminuire*. In all the Romanic langs. the prefix is *di-*, which was also the common med.L. spelling, but ancient L. had *dēminuĕre* to lessen, diminish, *dīminuĕre* to break into small pieces; cf. DIMINISH.] = DIMINISH *v.* (in various senses). In first quot. *intr.* to speak disparagingly; cf. DIMINISH *v.* 3.

1382 WYCLIF *Ezek.* XXXV. 13 3e..han dymynued [*gloss* or spoken yuel] a3eins me [**1388** deprauyd a3ens me, *Vulg.* derogastis]. **1513** DOUGLAS *Æneis* I. Prol. 74 Nor na reproche diminew thi guid name. **1549** *Compl. Scot.* vi. 56 God almychty..mittigatis, augmentis, or dimunueis..the ..operations of the planetis. **1568** SKEYNE *The Pest* (1860) 16 Rather depart riche nor leife pure, or diminew their fortune ony wayis.

‖**diminuendo** (diminuˈɛndo, dɪˌmɪnjʊˈɛndəʊ). *Mus.* [It. *diminuendo* lessening, diminishing, pr. pple. of *diminuire* to diminish: see prec.] A musical direction indicating a gradual decrease in force or loudness of tone (abbrev. *dim.*, *dimin.*); as *sb.* a gradual decrease in force of tone, or a passage where this occurs. Also *transf.* and *fig.* (Opp. to CRESCENDO *sb.*) Also *attrib.* or as *adj.*

1775 'J. COLLIER' *Mus. Trav.* (ed. 3) 65, I stood still some time to observe the *diminuendo* and *crescendo*. **1789-1826** [see CRESCENDO *sb.*]. **1870** MISS BRIDGMAN *Ro. Lynne* II. iii. 70 'Ah!' this from Dicky Blake, diminuendo. **1890** W. JAMES *Princ. Psychol.* II. xviii. 71 Certain violin-players take advantage of this in diminuendo terminations. **1891** *Daily News* 26 Oct. 3/3 A similar trimming..on a smaller scale, edged..the bodice, and was repeated in a further diminuendo round the neck. **1937** A. HUXLEY *Let.* 15 Dec. (1969) 429 Pardon this diminuendo, due to my not noticing that the ribbon had to change its direction! **1955** *Times* 9 May 3/4 There were 'expressive' ritenutos and diminuendos and protracted cadences. *Ibid.* 26 May 11/6 Labour's promise to do away with the 11 plus examination for selective secondary education was another scheme that suffered a *diminuendo*. **1958** A. J. TOYNBEE *East to West* xiii. 38 En route one changes, *diminuendo*, from South Australian broad gauge to Commonwealth standard gauge. **1959** *Encounter* Aug. 34/1 He was looking a bit diminuendo, and smiled rather nervously.

Hence as *v. intr.*, to become quieter or fainter; to grow less.

1901 *Westm. Gaz.* 12 Nov. 2/1 Their booming note crescendoes up the scale with increasing speed and diminuendoes with the slackening of it. **1905** *Daily Chron.*

27 Oct. 6/4 The wail of Niobe diminuendoes in the receding distance. **1962** *Guardian* 19 Oct. 11/7 He began to howl and diminuendoed down to a mutter.

† **di'minuent**, *a.* *Obs. rare.* [ad. L. *dī-*, *dēminuent-em*, pr. pple. of *dī-*, *dēminuĕre* to DIMINISH.] Diminishing; lessening the force of anything.

1608 W. SCLATER *Comm. Malachy* (1650) 38 When the Scripture speaks of spirituall Sacrifices, it useth a Terme diminuent. **1647** SANDERSON *Serm.* II. 221 Such kind of limiting and diminuent terms. **1657** —— *Serm.* Pref. (1681) 16 The Comparative degree (Δεισιδαιμονεστέρους) in such kind of speaking being usually taken for a Diminuent terme.

diminuse, obs. Sc. form of DIMINISH.

† **dimi'nute**, *a.* *Obs.* Also 5-6 de-. [ad. L. *dī-*, *dēminūt-us*, pa. pple. of *dī-*, *dēminuĕre* to DIMINISH.] Diminished, lessened; abated; incomplete, defective.

diminute conversion (Logic), *conversio per accidens*, in which the converse asserts less than the convertend, as in 'All the natives were slaves: Some slaves were natives.'

c **1450** HENRYSON *Fables* Prol. 41 (Jam. Suppl.) Gif that ye find ocht.. Be diminute, or yit superfluous. *c* **1475** *Partenay* 5680 He and his land shold be disherite, Exile and deminute by his dedes smart. **1533** MORE *Apol.* viii. Wks. 861/2 That hee neuer wrote that sermon himselfe, but that some of hys audience.. dydde wryte it dyminute, and mangled for lacke of good remembraunce. **1557** RECORDE *Whetst.* A iv b, If the partes make lesse than the whole nomber.. then is that nomber called Diminute, or Defectiue. As .8. hath these partes .1..2..4. whiche make but .7. **1651-3** JER. TAYLOR *Serm. for Year* I. xxiv. 304 Affix prices made diminute and lessened to such proportions and abatements. **1731** CHANDLER tr. *Limborch's Hist. Inquis.* II. 32 He who confesses an heretical Action or Word, but denies the wicked Intention.. is.. to be delivered over as a diminute, impenitent, and negative Heretick.

b. Diminutive, minute.

1611 SIR A. GORGES (T.), The first seeds of things are little and diminute.

di'minute, *v. rare.* [f. L. *dī-*, *dēminūt-* ppl. stem of *dī-*, *dēminuĕre* to DIMINISH.] *trans.* To lessen; to belittle; = DIMINISH *v.* 3.

1560 ROLLAND *Crt. Venus* III. 905, I imploir..ȝe not deiect the dignitie nor gloir, Spulȝe, nor reif, diminute nor deploir Into na sort thes deifeit Goddes. **1883** J. C. MORISON in *Macm. Mag.* 200 The repugnant task of diminuting our hero has been forced upon us.

† **dimi'nutely**, *adv.* *Obs.* [f. DIMINUTE *a.* + -LY[2].] In a diminished manner or form; incompletely.

1521 *St. Papers Hen. VIII*, I. 79, I never rehersydde Your Graces letters, diminutely, or fully, but by the Kyngis expresse commaundement. **1659** BAXTER *Key Cath.* xx. 95 Sciences diminutely and insufficiently delivered by their authors. **1841** *Fraser's Mag.* XXIV. 25 He could.. make even Old Hal diminutely to sing ['to sing small'].

diminution (dɪmɪ'njuːʃən). Forms: 4-6 **diminucion** (also with *y* for *i*), **diminicion**, 7 **deminution**, 6- **diminution**. [a. AF. *diminucium* (*a* 1300), F. *diminution* = Pr. *diminutio*, Sp. *diminucion*, Pg. *diminuição*, It. *diminuzione*, ad. L. *dīminūtiōn-em* later spelling of *dēminūtiōn-em*, n. of action from *dēminuĕre* to lessen. Classical L. analogies would give the form *deminution*: see DIMINISH, DIMINUE.]

1. a. The action of diminishing or making less; the process of diminishing or becoming less; reduction in magnitude or degree; lessening, decrease.

c **1374** CHAUCER *Troylus* III. 1286 (1335) To encrece or maken dyminucioun Of my langage. **1495** *Act 11 Hen. VII*, c. 2 §6 Dymynucion of punysshment.. shalbe had for women greate with child. **1594** HOOKER *Eccl. Pol.* III. xi. (1611) 120 Change by addition or diminution. **1617** MORYSON *Itin.* II. III. i. 213 The remainder can hardly beare such deminution, as all Armies are subiect vnto. **1682** BURNET *Rights Princes* viii. 315 Rather than consent to the least diminution of that Right. **1691** T. H[ALE] *Acc. New Invent.* p. cvii, Enlargements or Diminutions of Wharfs or Banks. **1712** ADDISON *Spect.* No. 517 ¶1 A copy of his letter, without any alteration or diminution. **1857** WHEWELL *Hist. Induct. Sc.* II. 175 The Diminution of the Obliquity of the Ecliptic.

b. Apparent lessening, as by distance. ? *Obs.*

1611 SHAKS. *Cymb.* I. iii. 18 To looke vpon him, till the diminution Of space, had pointed him sharpe as my Needle. **1667** MILTON *P.L.* VII. 369 From human sight So farr remote, with diminution seen.

† **2. a.** Representation of something as less than it is; extenuation. **b.** as a *Rhet.* figure. *Obs.*

1303 R. BRUNNE *Handl. Synne* 12416 Ȝyt þer ys an enchesun Ys kallede 'dymynucyun', On englys hyt ys to mene To make þy synne lytyl to seme. **1586** A. DAY *Eng. Secretary* II. (1625) 93 Example.. for diminution, might be this.. these I must confesse are injuries to some, but unto me they are trifles. **1659** O. WALKER *Oratory* 75 Gradation is by Oratours most-what observed, and the weightiest word said last: or, in diminutions, the contrary.

† **3.** Lessening of honour or reputation; derogation, depreciation, belittling. *Obs.*

1586 A. DAY *Eng. Secretary* I. (1625) 9 What approbations, diminutions, insinuations. **1599** *Life Sir T. More* in Wordsw. *Eccl. Biog.* (1853) II. 181 Under pardon of those saints.. for I intend not the diminution of their glorious deaths. **1646** FULLER *Wounded Consc.* (1841) 351 A diminution to the majesty of God. **1648** *Eikon Bas.* 49, I shall not much regard the worlds opinion or diminution of me. **1712** STEELE *Spect.* No. 468 ¶4 Thinking nothing a Diminution to me, but what argues a Depravity of my Will. *a* **1734** NORTH *Lives* (1826) II. 176 All that appeared.. of diminution to the reputation.. which his Lordship.. had acquired.

† **4.** Partial deprivation, curtailment, abatement.

1548 HALL *Chron., Hen. V*, 70 b, That we suffre harme or diminicion in person, estate, worship, or goodes. **1661** BRAMHALL *Just Vind.* iv. 78 Untill it came to sentence of death, or diminution of member. **1675** BAXTER *Cath. Theol.* II. I. 20 Had this been any injury or diminution to the rest?

5. *Mus.* **a.** The repetition of a subject (in contrapuntal writing) in notes of half or a quarter the length of the original: opp. to *augmentation.* † **b.** (quot. 1614) The condition of being diminished (of an interval): see DIMINISHED 4 (*obs. rare*).

1597 MORLEY *Introd. Mus.* 24 Diminution is a certaine lessening or decreasing of the essential value of the notes and rests. **1609** DOULAND *Ornith. Microl.* 48 Diminution.. is the varying of Notes of the first quantity.. or it is a certain cutting off of the measure. **1614** T. RAVENSCROFT (*title*), A briefe Discourse of the true but neglected Vse of characterizing the Degrees by their perfection, imperfection and diminution, in measurable Musicke. **1869** OUSELEY *Counterp.* xv. 104 [In] imitation by diminution.. the consequent substitutes notes of smaller value for those proposed by the antecedent.

6. *Her.* With earlier authors: The defacing of part of an escutcheon. By later writers said to be = DIFFERENCE.

1610 GUILLIM *Heraldry* I. viii. (1660) 43 *Diminution* is a blemishing or defacing of some particular point.. of the Escocheon, by reason of the imposition of some stain and colour thereupon. **1787** PORNY *Her.* Gloss., *Diminution*, word sometimes used instead of *Difference*. **1830** ROBSON *Brit. Herald* III. Gloss., *Diminution of Arms*, an expression sometimes used.. instead of *differences*, or, as the French call them, *brisures*.. from the Latin *diminutiones*, lessenings, as showing a family to be less than the chief.

† **7.** *Gram.* The formation of a diminutive word from a primitive. *Obs. rare.*

a **1637** B. JONSON *Eng. Gram.* xi, The common affection of nouns is diminution.. The diminution of substantives hath these four divers terminations: El.. Et.. Ock.. Ing.. Diminution of adjectives is in this one end, *ish*.

8. *Law.* An omission in the record of a case sent up by an inferior court to a superior, in proceedings for reversal of judgement.

[**1610** COKE *Bk. of Entries* 242 a/2 (*marg.*) Le def. alledge diminution en le Here. fac. seisinam. *Ibid.* 251 b/1 (*marg.*) Diminution alledge per le def. en les proclamations. **1626** SIR W. JONES *Reports, Weever v. Fulton* 2 Car. 1 (1675) 140 Car apres in nullo est Erratum plede, neque le Plaintiff neque le Defendant poient alledge diminution, car per le joinder ils allowe recorde.] **1657** GRIMSTON tr. *Croke's Repts.* (1683) II. 597, *Johns v. Bowen*, 18 Jas. I, After the Record certified, the plaintiff in the Writ of Error alledges Diminution for want of an Original, which was certified and entered. **1708** *Termes de la Ley* 248, *Diminution*, is when the Plaintiff or Defendant in a Writ of Error alledges.. that part of the Record remains in the Inferiour Court not certifyed, and prays that it be certifyed by Certiorari. **1848** in WHARTON *Law Lex.*

9. *Arch.* The gradual decrease in diameter of the shaft of a column, etc.; the tapering of a column or other part of a building; also, the amount of this tapering in the whole length.

1706 PHILLIPS (ed. Kersey), *Diminution*.. in Architecture, the lessening of a Pillar by little and little from the Base to the Top. **1726** LEONI *Alberti's Archit.* II. 20/1 The diameter of the lower diminution. **1727-51** CHAMBERS *Cycl.* s.v., The Gothic architects.. observe neither diminution nor swelling; their columns are perfectly cylindrical. **1766** ENTICK *London* IV. 356 [The] turret.. ends with a fine diminution. **1842-76** GWILT *Archit.* III. i. 809 The diminution or tapering form given to a column.. sometimes commences from the foot of the shaft, sometimes from a quarter or one third of its height. *Ibid.* 814 Vitruvius in this order [the Tuscan] forms the columns six diameters high, and makes their diminution one quarter of the diameter.

10. *Cytology.* [a. F. *diminution* (V. Herla 1895, in *Arch. de Biol.* XIII. 485).] The loss or expulsion, during the embryogenesis of certain organisms, of some chromosome material from the nuclei of cells that go to form somatic tissue.

1925 E. B. WILSON *Cell* (ed. 3) iv. 326 In these cases.. the process of diminution is somehow connected with the segregation of germ-cells from somatic cells. **1942** *Nature* 17 Jan. 67/2 In Sorghum we know that the chromosomes which undergo 'diminution' are in fact dispensable not only in parts of the plant but also in parts of the species. **1965** C. D. DARLINGTON *Cytology* II. iii. 658 Coordinated reactions of centromeres, heterochromatin and cytoplasm are no doubt responsible for diminution.

diminutival (dɪˌmɪnjuː'taɪvəl), *a.* (*sb.*) *Gram.* [f. L. *dīminūtīv-us* DIMINUTIVE + -AL[1].] Of, pertaining to, or of the nature of, a diminutive. **b.** as *sb.* A diminutival suffix.

1868 T. H. KEY *Philol. Essays* x. 213 The Latin.. forming contemptuous terms for men, by means of a diminutival suffix. **1871** ROBY *Lat. Gram.* III. vii §862 Adjectives, chiefly diminutival. **1880** EARLE *Philol. Eng. Tongue* (ed. 3) §317 In *-kin*.. a widely prevalent diminutival.

diminutive (dɪ'mɪnjʊtɪv), *a.* and *sb.* Also 4 **diminitif (-yf,** etc.), 6-7 **diminitive**, 6 **demynutyve.** [a. F. *diminutif*, *-ive* (14th c. in Godef. *Suppl.*), ad. L. *dī-*, *dēminūtīv-us*, f. *dī-*, *dēminūtus*, pa. pple. of *dī-*, *dēminuĕre* to lessen. The sb. use is found in Eng. earlier than the adj.]

A. *adj.*

1. *Gram.* Expressing diminution; denoting something little: usually applied to derivatives or affixes expressing something small of the kind denoted by the primitive word. (Opp. to *augmentative.*)

1580 NORTH *Plutarch* (1676) 5 Where they honoured this old woman [Hecale], calling her by a diminutive Name, Hecalena. **1659** O. WALKER *Oratory* 32 Verbal nouns.. some of them being augmentative, some diminutive. **1755** JOHNSON *Pref. to Dict.*, Diminutive adjectives in *-ish*, as *greenish*. **1756** BURKE *Subl. & B.* III. xiii, In most languages the objects of love are spoken of under diminutive epithets. **1876** MASON *Eng. Gram.* §313 The diminutive sense easily passes into that of depreciation, as in *worldling*, *groundling*.

† **2.** Making less or smaller; tending to diminution. *Obs.*

1677 GALE *Crt. Gentiles* IV. 266 God.. cannot fal under any mutation either.. augmentative or diminutive. **1711** SHAFTESB. *Charac.* (1737) III. III. ii. 175 Any thing diminutive either of their inward Freedom or national Liberty.

† **3.** Representing or describing something as less than it is; disparaging, depreciative. *Obs.*

1662 GLANVILL *Lux Orient.* ii. (1682) 9 A diminutive and disparaging apprehension of the infinite.. Goodness of God. **1737** WATERLAND *Eucharist* 443 The Death of Christ.. a federal Rite.. appears to be too low and too diminutive a Name for it. **1791** PAINE *Rights of Man* (ed. 4) 122 A scene so new.. that the name of a Revolution is diminutive of its character, and it rises into a Regeneration of man.

4. Characterized by diminution; hence, of less size or degree than the ordinary; small, little. In later use, generally, a more forcible expression for 'small': = minute, tiny. (Usually in reference to physical size.)

1602 MARSTON *Ant. & Mel.* II. Wks. 1856 I. 19 Balurdo cals for your diminutive attendance. **1605** SHAKS. *Macb.* IV. ii. 10 The poore Wren (the most diminutiue of Birds). **1623** COCKERAM, *Diminutiue*, little. **1641** BRATHWAIT *Eng. Intelligencer* 11, Our Progenitours esteemed diminutive Cottages as Kingdomes. **1712** tr. *Pomet's Hist. Drugs* I. 146 A diminutive Pine, which grows not above the Height of a Man. **1727** SWIFT *Gulliver* I. i. 26, I could not sufficiently wonder at the intrepidity of those diminutive mortals. **1741** GRAY *Let.* Poems (1775) 108 Last post I received a very diminutive letter. **1818** JAS. MILL *Brit. India* II. IV. viii. 283 The summer.. passed in unavailing movements and diminutive attempts. **1851** BRIMLEY *Ess.* 120 (*Wordsw.*) We.. know that children are not diminutive angels. **1870** E. PEACOCK *Ralf Skirl.* III. 24 Small, almost diminutive, in stature.

B. *sb.*

1. *Gram.* A diminutive word or term (see A. 1); a derivative denoting something small of the kind.

1398 TREVISA *Barth. De P.R.* XVII. xcvi. (Tollem. MS.), Of 'Lens, lentis,' comeþ 'Lenticula,' þe diminityf þerof. **1530** PALSGR. 303 Adjectyves whiche be demynutyves in signyfication. **1591** PERCIVALL *Sp. Dict.* B iij, Diminutiues end commonly in *ito, illo.* **1678** CUDWORTH *Intell. Syst.* 264 The word δαιμόνιον.. is not a diminitive.. but an adjective substantiv'd. **1709** STEELE *Tatler* No. 135 ¶1 Cicero.. calls those small Pretenders to Wisdom.. certain Minute Philosophers, using a Diminutive even of the Word Little. **1864** TENNYSON *Aylmer's Field* 539 In babyisms and dear diminutives Scatter'd all over the vocabulary Of such a love. **1894** J. T. FOWLER *Adamnan* Introd. 80 His name, Adamnan, is a diminutive of Adam.

2. *Her.* One of the smaller ordinaries corresponding in form and position to the larger, but of less width.

[**1486** *Bk. St. Albans, Her.* C iv b, This cros [croslet] is not so oft borne in armys by him selfe.. neuer the lees mony tymys hit is borne in dimynutiuys, that is to say in littyll crossis crossit.] **1572** BOSSEWELL *Armorie* II. 32 b, The Barrulet is a Diminutive thereof, and is but the fourth parte of the Barre. **1766** PORNY *Her.* iv. (1787) 60 The Pale.. Its Diminutives are the Pallet, which is the half of the Pale, and the Endorse, which is the fourth part of a Pale. **1882** CUSSANS *Handbk. Her.* iv. 57 The diminutives of the Bend are the Bendlet, or Garter, which is half the width of the Bend; the Cost, or Cotice, which is half the Bendlet; and the Riband, half of the Cost. *Ibid.* 72 All the Ordinaries (but not their diminutives) may be charged.

3. A diminutive thing or person. **a.** A small variety or form *of* something; a 'miniature'. † **b.** Something very small (*obs.*). † **c.** *in diminutive*: on a small scale, in miniature (*obs.*).

1606 SHAKS. *Tr. & Cr.* v. i. 38 How the poore world is pestred with such water-flies, diminutiues of Nature. —— *Ant. & Cl.* IV. xii. 37 Most monster-like be shewne For poor'st Diminitiues, for Dolts. **1627-77** FELTHAM *Resolves* I. xxxiii. 57 All families are but diminutives of a Court. **1658** SIR T. BROWNE *Gard. Cyrus* iii, In what deminutives the plastick principle lodgeth is exemplified in seeds. *a* **1687** COTTON (J.) Sim.. Was then a knave, but in diminutive. **1796** *Mod. Gulliver's Trav.* 46 A reflection.. which I often found myself justified in bringing home to these diminutives. **1842** C. WHITEHEAD *R. Savage* (1845) I. xi. 145 The diminutive tells me he believes he has wronged you. **1853** KANE *Grinnell Exp.* xix. (1856) 150 A stimulus, acting constantly, like the diminutive of a strong cup of coffee.

† **4.** Something that diminishes or lessens; *spec.* in *Med.* A medicine that abates the violence of a disease. *Obs.*

1602 WARNER *Alb. Eng.* x. liv. (1612) 242 If his Fames Diminutiue in any thing we finde. **1621** BURTON *Anat. Mel.* II. v. I. vi, When you have used all good meanes and helpe of alteratives, averters, diminitives.

diminutively (dɪˈmɪnjʊtɪvlɪ), *adv.* [f. prec. + -LY².] In a diminutive manner or degree.

1. In the way of diminution; so as to represent anything as small, or as less than it is: †extenuatingly, disparagingly, depreciatively (*obs.*).

1613 F. ROBARTS *Revenue of Gospel* 125 They will cheerfully..say, It was but fiue pounds..It comes but once a yeare, I hope to recouer it by the grace of God. Thus diminutiuely and hopefully men mention any great charge, suitable to their owne humors. **1663** BAXTER *Divine Life* 175 Thinking diminutively of God's love and mercy. **1788** MAD. D'ARBLAY *Diary* July, I began to think less diminutively of that [room]. **1824** L. MURRAY *Eng. Gram.* (ed. 5) I. 256 When I say, 'There were few men with him'; I speak diminutively, and mean to represent them as inconsiderable: whereas, when I say, 'There were a few men with him'; I evidently intend to make the most of them.

2. In a smaller or minute degree.

1750 tr. *Leonardus's Mirr. Stones* 218 Prassius..has all the Virtues of the Emerald, tho' diminutively.

diˈminutiveness. [f. as prec. + -NESS.] The quality or condition of being diminutive.

1727 BAILEY vol. II., *Diminutiveness*, littleness. **1750–1** *Student* II. 225 (T.) While he stood on tip-toes thrumming his bass-viol, the diminutiveness of his figure was totally eclipsed by the expansion of his instrument. **1830** MISS MITFORD *Village* Ser. IV. (1863) 199 Next to names simple in themselves, those which fall easily into diminutiveness seem to me most desirable..Lizzy, Bessy, Sophy, Fanny—the prettiest of all! **1894** *Daily News* 15 Oct. 6/4 In keeping with the universal neatness and diminutiveness.

diˈminutize, *v. rare.* [f. DIMINUTE *a.* + -IZE.] *trans.* To turn (a word) into a diminutive form.

In recent Dicts.

†**diˈmiss,** *v. Obs.* [f. cl. L. *dīmiss-* ppl. stem of *dīmittĕre* to send away, dismiss: cf. DIMIT, DISMISS, and DIS- *pref.*] = DISMISS *v.*

1543 GRAFTON *Contn. Harding* (1812) 567 Charles did dimisse yᵉ young man. **1546** LANGLEY *Pol. Verg. De Invent.* V. ix. 110 a, When Masse is ended the deacon turning to the people sayeth, Ite missa est, which wordes are borrowed of the rytes of the Paganes, and signifieth that then the companye may be dimissed. **1655** STANLEY *Hist. Philos.* III. (1701) 99/2 Theætetus disputing of Knowledge, he dimist. **1729** SHELVOCKE *Artillery* V. 399 It is shot easily from a large Bow, for if it be violently dimissed, the Fire of it will be extinguished.

†**ˈdimissaries,** *sb. pl. Obs.* Also 5 **dismyssaries,** 6 **dimiceries, demisaris.** [? f. L. *dēmissus*, hanging down, descending + -ARY: cf. *emissary*.] Testicles.

1494 FABYAN *Chron.* VII. 357 Some malicious dysposed persones, in despyte..kut of his hode and his dismyssaries. **1546** BALE *Eng. Votaries* I. (1550) 50 b, Chosen, as stoned horses are..by their outye dimiceries. **1569** T. UNDERDOWN *Ovid agst. Ibis* O iij b, He..cut of his Demisaris. **1577** STANYHURST *Descr. Irel.* in *Holinshed* VI. 68 For default of other stuffe, they pawne..the nailes of their fingers and toes, their dimissaries.

†**dimission** (daɪˈmɪʃən). *Obs.* [ad. L. *dīmissiōn-em*, n. of action from *dīmittĕre* to send away, dismiss, etc.]

1. The action of giving up or relinquishing; resignation, abdication; = DEMISSION² 1.

1494 FABYAN *Chron.* VII. 548, I swere..that I shall neuer repugne to this resygnacion, dymyssyon or yeldynge vp. **1568** Q. ELIZ. *Let.* 8 June in *Love-lett. Mary Q. Scots* App. 31 She..was..compelled to make a dimission of her crown.

2. Conveyance by lease; = DEMISE *sb.* 1.

1495 *Act 11 Hen. VII*, c. 9. §2 All maner of leasses dymyssions made. *Ibid.* c. 33 §17 Any graunte or lesse made by..lettres patentes of dimission.

3. Sending away, dismission, dismissal, discharge.

1530 in Froude *Hist. Eng.* (1856) II. 82 Under sureties.. that he should appear the first day of the next term..and then day by day until his dimission. *a* **1555** BRADFORD in Coverdale *Lett. Mart.* (1564) 307 It is..a deliueraunce from bondage and prison, a dimission from warre. **1633** BP. HALL *Hard Texts* 620 This common dimission of your wives. **1736** LEDIARD *Life Marlborough* I. 106 The King..sent him a Dimission of all his Employs, and forbid him the Court. **1823** SOUTHEY *Hist. Penins. War* I. 44 Whosoever..left the University without a letter of dimission.

dimissorial (dɪmɪˈsɔərɪəl). *Eccl.* [f. as next + -AL¹.] A dimissory letter: see next, sense 2.

1885 *Catholic Dict.* s.v., Abbots may not give dimissorials to seculars.

dimissory (ˈdɪmɪsərɪ), *a.* (*sb.*) Also 7 **dimissary,** 7–8 **demissory.** [ad. L. *dīmissōri-us* (in *litteræ dimissōriæ* a dimissory letter), f. *dīmiss-* ppl. stem of *dīmittĕre* to send away, dismiss: see -ORY. (Also DISMISSORY: cf. DIS- *pref.*)]

†1. Pertaining to dismission or leave-taking; dismissory; valedictory. *Obs.* in *gen.* sense. (In quot. 1650, *fig.* from 2.)

1581 MARBECK *Bk. of Notes* 305 In witnes wherof I giue vnto thee this Bill of diuorcement and dimissorie Epistle, being an instrument of libertie according to yᵉ law of Moses. **1650** BP. PRIDEAUX *Euchol.* (1656) 101 (T.) Old Simeon's craving his letters demissory. *a* **1656** USSHER *Ann.* (1658) 431 The Original of that Petaroth or dimissary Lecture, after which the people were dismissed.

2. *Eccl. dimissory letter* (usually in pl. *letters dimissory*): **a.** In the ancient church, a letter from a bishop dismissing a clergyman from one diocese and recommending him to another. **b.** A letter from a bishop, the superior of a religious order, etc., authorizing the bearer as a candidate for ordination.

1583 STUBBES *Anat. Abus.* II. (1882) 91 If he..haue letters dimissorie from one bishop to another. *a* **1631** DONNE *Ignat. Concl.* (1635) 115 Accompany them with Certificates, and Demissory letters. **1672** CAVE *Prim. Chr.* III. iii. (1673) 310 Letters Dimissory whereby Leave was given to persons going into another Diocese (if ordained) to be admitted and incorporated into the Clergy of that Church. **1708** J. CHAMBERLAYNE *St. Gt. Brit.* I. III. i. (1743) 143 He must have Letters Demissory from the Bishop. **1726** AYLIFFE *Parerg.* 128 A Bishop of another Diocess ought neither to ordain nor admit a Clerk..without letters Dimissory. **1818** C. SIMEON *Let.* in *Mem.* xx. (1847) 497 Letters dimissory for a young man who has distinguished himself. **1819** SOUTHEY in *Q. Rev.* XXII. 73 The abbot was cautioned not to receive a member of any other known monastery without dimissory letters from his superior.

†**B.** *sb.* (*pl.*) = Letters dimissory: see prec. *Obs.*

c **1380** *Antecrist* in Todd 3 *Treat. Wyclif* (1851) 147 Bi tytle and by dymyssories. **1619** BRENT tr. *Sarpi's Counc. Trent* (1676) 462 In respect of the dimisories of Bishops. **1725** tr. *Dupin's Eccl. Hist.* I. v. II. 69 The Dimissories were given to the Laity and Clergy, who went out of one Diocese ..to live in another.

†**diˈmit,** *v. Obs.* [In Branch I, ad. L. *dīmittĕre* to send apart, away, or forth, to dismiss, release, put away, let go, lay down (office), renounce, forsake, f. *dī-*, *dis-* asunder + *mittĕre* to send, let go. A doublet (more etymologically formed) of DISMIT, DISMISS: cf. also DEMIT *v.*², and DIMISS, DEMISE. In Branch II, a variant of DEMIT *v.*¹]

I. 1. *trans.* To send away, let go, dismiss: = DEMIT *v.*² 1.

1548 UDALL, etc. *Erasm. Par. Acts* v. 26 So were they contented upon this punishement to dimitte them. **1563–87** FOXE *A. & M.* (1596) 941/2 Thus Frith..was freely dimitted out of the stockes, and set at libertie. *a* **1639** SPOTTISWOOD *Hist. Ch. Scotl.* II. (1677) 50 The Pope..did ..dimit the Scottish Commissioners..with great promises of favour.

2. To lay aside, give up, resign, abdicate: = DEMIT *v.*² 3.

1563 N. WINȜET *Four Scoir Thre Quest.* xxvii. Wks. 1888 I. 93 Salamon..commanding ws naways to dimit the law of our mother, quhilk is the Kirk. **1637–50** ROW *Hist. Kirk* (1842) 40 That these who haue pluralitie of benefices be compelled to dimitt all except one. **1678** *Trans. Crt. Spain* II. 141 It behoved him instantly to dimit his charge of Inquisitour General.

3. To convey by lease, demise: = DEMIT *v.*² 4.

1495 *Act 11 Hen. VII*, c. 9 That noe persone..haue auctorite..to dymytte or lette to ferme..any londes or tenementis within the lordship. **1541** *Act 33 Hen. VIII*, c. 39 Power and auctoritie..to couenant dimit let or set to ferme..any of the landes. **1609** SKENE *Reg. Maj.* 122 He may dimitt the land destroied and not inhabite, vntill he be of power to big it againe.

4. *intr.* Of a river: To empty itself, debouch.

16.. FOUNTAINHALL in M. P. Brown *Suppl. Decis.* (1826) 293 The public river of Tweed..which dimits in the sea.

II. 5. *trans.* To send, put, or let down, cause to descend, lower: = DEMIT *v.*¹ 1.

1627–77 FELTHAM *Resolves* I. lxix. 105 Like the night.. dimitting unwholesom vapours upon all that rest beneath. **1638** SIR T. HERBERT *Trav.* (ed. 2) 343 When Apollo dimits his perpendicular rayes. **1646** SIR T. BROWNE *Pseud. Ep.* V. xiii. 253 To teach horses to incline, dimit, and bow downe their bodies. **1671** J. WEBSTER *Metallogr.* iv. 75 Doth dimit it down into the centre of the Earth.

b. *fig.* To abase, let down: = DEMIT *v.*¹ 2.

1655 GURNALL *Chr. in Arm.* verse xi. 183/2 He was a man of rare humble spirit, that..could so dimit and humble himself in his adresse to Christ.

dimit, var. DEMIT *sb.*

dimity (ˈdɪmɪtɪ). Forms: 5 **demyt,** 6 **dimite,** 7 **dimmety, dimmity, dimetty,** 8 **demity, dimitty,** 8– **dimity.** [In 15–16th c. *demyt, dimite*, a. It. *dimito* 'a kind of coarse cotton or flanell' (Florio 1598), 'a kind of course linzie-wolzie' (ibid. 1611) = med.L. *dimitum* (12th c. in Du Cange), ad. Gr. δίμιτος of double thread, sb. dimity, f. δι-, δίς twice + μίτος thread of the warp. It is not certain how the final *-y* arose: could it represent It. pl. *dimiti*? Cf. the plural in Du Cange's quot.: 'amita, dimitaque, et trimita', explained to mean fabrics woven with one, two, or three threads respectively. The relation to these of the Persian word *dimyāṭī*, explained as 'a kind of cotton cloth, dimity', which has the form of a derivative of *Dimyāṭ*, Damietta, is not clear.]

A stout cotton fabric, woven with raised stripes or fancy figures; usually employed undyed for beds and bedroom hangings, and sometimes for garments.

1440 in E. Peacock *Eng. Ch. Furniture, Lincolnsh.* 182 A vestment of white demyt for lenten and vigils. **1570** CAMPION in Hakluyt *Voy.* (1599) II. I. 127 We do vse to buy many of their silke quilts, and of their Scamato and Dimite, that the poore people make in that towne [Scio]. **1632** LITHGOW *Trav.* VIII. 358 A hundred Camels loaden with Silkes, Dimmeties, and other Commodities. **1636** DAVENANT *Witts* (1673) 171 A Book wrapt up in Sea-green Dimmity. *c* **1710** C. FIENNES *Diary* (1888) 236 A half bedstead as the new mode, dimity wᵗʰ fine shades of worstead works well made up. **1743** FIELDING *Jon. Wild* I. x, His waistcoat was a white dimity, richly embroidered with yellow silk. **1819** BYRON *Juan* I. xii, Her morning dress was dimity. **1879** E. GARRETT *House by Works* I. 97 Else.. washed the pretty dimities oftener than even Lois thought necessary. **1880** BIRDWOOD *Ind. Arts* II. 76 Fustians, dimities and vermilions from cotton-wool had been made in London and in Manchester from 1641.

b. *attrib.* Made of dimity.

1639 MAYNE *City Match* I. iv, Thy dimity breeches. **1762** *Gentl. Mag.* 204 Put on a dimitty waistcoat. **1856** MISS MULOCK *J. Halifax* 114 Some sort of white dimity gown that she wore. **1861** MRS. CARLYLE *Lett.* III. 79 In our white dimity beds. **1876** MISS BRADDON *J. Haggard's Dau.* I. 108 The dimity window curtains.

dimly (ˈdɪmlɪ), *adv.* In 3 **dimluker** (compar.), 4–5 **dymly.** [repr. OE. type **dimlice*, from *dimlic* adj. dim, obscure: cf. -LY².] In a dim manner; in or with a dim light; obscurely; somewhat darkly; faintly, indistinctly.

a **1225** *Ancr. R.* 210 Heo wolden..iðe deofles seruise dimluker bemen. **13..** *E.E. Allit. P.* C. 375 Dymly bisoȝten, þat þat penaunce plesed him. *a* **1400–50** *Alexander* 718 þan Anec..Dryvez up a dede voyce, and dymly he spekes. **1538** STARKEY *England* II. iii. 206 As Sayn Poule sayth dymely, hyt ys the pedagoge of Chryst. **1667** MILTON *P.L.* v. 157 To us invisible or dimly seen In these thy lowest works. **1712** ADDISON *Spect.* No. 265 ¶9 A Fire burns dimly..in the Light of the Sun. **1858** HAWTHORNE *Fr. & It. Jrnls.* II. 49 The figures looked dimly down like gods out of a mysterious sky. **1871** R. ELLIS *Catullus* lxvi. 49 Perish who earth's hid veins first labour'd dimly to quarry. **1885** *Spectator* 8 Aug. 1041/1 This was dimly felt at the time and has been more distinctly recognised since.

b. *Comb.*, as *dimly-labouring*, *-lit.*

1863 I. WILLIAMS *Baptistery* II. xxiii. (1874) 75 Like the dimly-labouring moon. **1880** OUIDA *Moths* xviii, Dimly-lit chambers.

dimmed (dɪmd), *ppl. a.* [f. DIM *v.* + -ED¹.] Rendered dim.

1590 SPENSER *F.Q.* I. ii. 45 Her eyelids blew And dimmed sight..At last she up gan lift. **1594** *Ord. Prayer* in *Liturg. Serv. Q. Eliz.* (1847) 654 Being..not any clearer enlightened, than by the dimmed glimpse of nature. *a* **1605** MONTGOMERIE *Misc. Poems* xi. 25 Quhen my dimmit sight greu cleir. **1845** DARWIN *Voy. Nat.* ii. (1879) 20 The scene by the dimmed light of the moon was most desolate. **1863** GEO. ELIOT *Romola* I. iii, The somewhat dimmed glory of their original gilding.

Hence **ˈdimmedness.**

1610 BARROUGH *Meth. Physick* VI. ix. (1639) 367 Such as hath not the whitish colour inclining to dimmednesse.

dimmen, *v. rare.* [f. DIM *a.* + -EN⁵.] *intr.* To grow dim. Hence **ˈdimmening** *ppl. a.*

1828–30 W. TAYLOR *Surv. Germ. Poetry* I. 301 Scenery.. on which his dimmening eyes are preparing to close for ever.

dimmer (ˈdɪmə(r)), *sb.* [f. DIM *v.* + -ER¹.] One who or that which dims. *spec.* A device for reducing the brilliance of a light, esp. in a theatre, cinema, etc. Also *fig.* and *attrib.*

1822 *Blackw. Mag.* XI. 594 A dimmer to the daylights. **18..** J. H. NEWMAN *Idea of University*, To remove the original dimmer of the mind's eye. **1905** *Chambers's Jrnl.* 26 Aug. 624/2 What is called a 'dimmer' is in use at some such places [*sc.* theatres] already. **1909** *Cent. Dict.* Suppl., *Dimmer*, in *elect.*, an adjustable reactive coil used for reducing the amount of light of incandescent lamps. **1913** *Work* 14 June 212/1 The resistance of the dimmer coils. **1916** H. L. WILSON *Somewhere in Red Gap* ix. 378 It was a suit that the automobile law in some states would have compelled him to put dimmers on. **1926** H. T. WILKINS *Marvels Mod. Mechanics* 236 Levers on these dials operate the 'dimmers'. **1933** P. GODFREY *Back-Stage* i. 18 The electrician has been busy sliding the stops on his dimmer-board.

dimmer (ˈdɪmə(r)), *v.* [f. DIM *v.* + -ER⁵.] To appear dimly, faintly, or indistinctly.

1873 C. G. LELAND *Egypt. Sketch-Bk.* 22 He..looked over the top-rail at the beautiful Monte Christo, which was dimmering in the distance. **1892** KIPLING *Barrack-r. Ballads* 123 As the shape of a corpse dimmers up through deep water. **1914** —— *Lett. Travel* (1920) 269 Then the river dimmered up like pewter.

dimmety, obs. form of DIMITY.

dimming (ˈdɪmɪŋ), *vbl. sb.* [f. DIM *v.* + -ING¹.] The action of the verb DIM, q.v.

13.. *Coer de L.* 6977 Be the dymmyng off the more, Men myghte see, where Richard fore. *c* **1435** *Torr. Portugal* 512 Yt Drew nere-hande nyght By dymmynge of the Day. **1552** HULOET, Dymminge of the syght, *caligatio*. **1594** SHAKS. *Rich. III*, II. ii. 102 All of vs haue cause To waile the dimming of our shining Starre.

ˈdimming, *ppl. a.* [f. as prec. + -ING².] That dims: see the verb.

1734 R. ERSKINE in R. Palmer *Bk. of Praise* 397 My Lord will break the dimming glass And show His glory face to face. **1816** J. WILSON *City of Plague* II. ii. 183 The driving blast—the dimming rains. **1875** WHITNEY *Life Lang.* iv. 66 The specific quality of which [vowels] is due to a dimming action along the whole mouth.

dimmish (ˈdɪmɪʃ), *a.* [f. DIM *a.* + -ISH.] Somewhat dim.

1683 TRYON *Way to Health* 96 Its flame is not clear..but of a dimmish Brimstone colour. **1724** SWIFT *Stella's Birthday* 42 My eyes are somewhat dimish grown. **1826** *Blackw. Mag.* XX. 899 Our eyes have got rather dimmish. **1884** 'MARK TWAIN' *Huck. Finn* xxxvi. 372 We was a standing there in the dimmish light. **1967** A. LASKI *Seven Other Years* xiii. 183 An amiable but..'dimmish' heavy-weight of fifteen. **1969** J. Drummond *People in Glass House* xvii. 72 She was a sort of goose-girl type... Dimmish. But pretty.

dimmit (ˈdɪmɪt). *s.w. dial.* Also 8 **dimmet.** [f. DIM *a.*] Dusk, twilight.

1746 *Exmoor Scolding* (E.D.S.) 42 In the Desk o' tha Yeaveling, just in tha Dimmet. *Ibid.* Gloss., *Dimmet*..the Dusk of the Evening..the evening twilight. **1859** Capern *Ball. & Songs* 132, I, with my arms, in the dimmit of day, Will snare the bold son of the sea. **1879** G. Macdonald *P. Faber* III. xiv. 237 He likes his little ones to tell their fancies in the dimmits about the nursery fire.

dimmy (ˈdɪmɪ), *a.* [f. DIM *a.* + -Y: cf. *blacky*, *bluey*.] Having dimness; more or less dim.

1430 Lydg. *Chron. Troy* I. vi, The derkenesse of the dymmy night. **1580** Sidney *Arcadia* IV. (1622) 441 You dimmie clouds. **1582** Bentley *Mon. Matrones* 181 Dazeled with the dimmie and darke mists of Sathan. **1594** Carew *Tasso* (1881) 119 The dimmy ayre now cleerer growes. **1855** Singleton *Virgil* I. 98 If she [the moon] shall have clipped The darksome ether with a dimmy horn.

dimn, dimne, obs. ff. DIM *a.* and *v.*

dimness (ˈdɪmnɪs). [OE. *dimnis*, *dymnys*, f. *dim* DIM + -NESS.] The quality of being dim; want of clearness, brightness, or distinctness; dullness of vision or perception, dimsightedness.

*c***825** *Vesp. Psalter* xcvi[i]. 2 Wolcen & dimnis in ymbhwyrfte. *c***1000** *Sax. Leechd.* I. 200 Wiþ eaʒena dymnysse, ʒenim ðysse sylfan wyrte leaf. *a***1300** *E.E. Psalter* xvii. 10 Dimnes under his fete. **1398** Trevisa *Barth. De P.R.* XIII. xx. (1495) 450 Abyssus that is depnesse of water hath of hymself dympnesse and depnesse. **1572** Bossewell *Armorie* II. 67b, The Eagle in age hath darkenes, and dymnes of eyne. **1633** G. Herbert *Temple, Sonne* 8 A sonne ..a fruitfull flame Chasing the fathers dimnesse. **1751** Johnson *Rambler* No. 155 ⁋3 In proof of the dimness of our internal Light. **1775** S. J. Pratt *Liberal Opin.* (1783) IV. 3 Tumbling into the ditch, which my dimness prevented me from seeing. **1863** Geo. Eliot *Romola* I. v, The once splendid patch of carpet..had long been worn to dimness. **1887** Morris *Odyss.* VII. 42 Round about him still She shed that holy dimness.

dimond, obs. form of DIAMOND.

di,monosyˈllabic, *a. nonce-wd.* [see DI-².] Consisting of two monosyllables.

1844 Whewell in Todhunter *Acc. Whewell's Wks.* (1876) II. 322 Dimonosyllabic endings.

dimoric (daɪˈmɒrɪk), *a. Pros.* [f. DI-² + MORA¹ 3 + -IC.] Containing two *moræ*; having the length of two short syllables.

1901 [see TRIMORIC *a.*].

dimorph (ˈdaɪmɔːf). [mod. f. Gr. δίμορφ-ος of two forms: cf. mod.F. *dimorphe* adj.] One of the two forms in which a dimorphous substance exists; as 'aragonite and calcite are dimorphs.'

In recent Dicts.

dimorphemic (daɪmɔːˈfiːmɪk), *a. Linguistics.* [f. DI-² + MORPHEMIC *a.*] Containing, or belonging to, two morphemes.

1936 *English Studies* XVIII. 160 *Glazier* differs further from *glacier* in that it is dimorphemic. **1952** A. Cohen *Phonemes Eng.* iv. 102 The dimorphemic diphthongs [i—ə] and [u—ə] are manifested by the tendency to preserve the length of the first vowel.

dimorphic (daɪˈmɔːfɪk), *a.* [mod. f. Gr. δίμορφ-ος of two forms (f. δι-, δίς twice + μορφή form) + -IC.] Existing or occurring in two distinct forms; exhibiting dimorphism. **a.** *Bot.* Occurring in two distinct forms in the same plant or species, as the submerged and floating leaves in water-plants, disk and ray florets in *Compositæ*, and (*spec.*) flowers or plants having stamens and pistils of different relative lengths. **b.** *Zool.* Of individuals of the same species (or of the same colony of polyps): Occurring in two forms differing in structure, size, markings, etc., according to sex, season, or function. **c.** *Chem.* and *Min.* Occurring in two distinct crystalline forms not derivable from one another.

1859 Darwin *Orig. Spec.* ii. (1878) 36 The two forms of an allied dimorphic species. *c***1865** J. Wylde in *Circ. Sc.* I. 311/2 Some bodies have two different forms, or are dimorphic, under different circumstances. **1870** Hooker *Stud. Flora* 299 Primula..Flowers usually dimorphic, having long styles with anthers deep in the tube or the reverse. *Ibid.* 319 Atriplex patula..sub-sp. hastata..seeds dimorphic, larger brown rough, smaller black smooth. **1878** Bell *Gegenbaur's Comp. Anat.* 123 When the persons of a colony are dimorphic, those which are the more developed are..functionally sexual, while the others are sterile. **1888** Rolleston & Jackson *Anim. Life* 238 The Medusa and Hydroid polype are dimorphic forms..The worker bee is a dimorphic female.

dimorphism (daɪˈmɔːfɪz(ə)m). [mod. f. Gr. δίμορφ-ος of two forms (see prec.) + -ISM.] The condition of being DIMORPHIC. **a.** *Cryst.* The property of assuming two distinct crystalline forms, not derivable from each other.

1832 Johnston *Progr. Chem.* in *Rep. Brit. Assoc.* (1835) 432 The different causes to which, under different circumstances, dimorphism may be traced. **1850** Daubeny *Atom. Th.* iv. (ed. 2) 123 A familiar instance of dimorphism is exhibited in the case of carbonate of lime, which..is found, sometimes in the form of calcareous spar, sometimes in that of arragonite. **1851** Richardson *Geol.* v. 78 Dimorphism is a law which, though previously known, has been confirmed by the discoveries of Mitscherlich.

b. *Biol.* The occurrence of two distinct forms of flowers, leaves, or other parts on the same plant or in the same species; or of two forms distinct in structure, size, colouring, etc. among animals of the same species.

1859 Darwin *Orig. Spec.* ii. (1878) 35 There are..cases of dimorphism and trimorphism, both with animals and plants. Thus..the females of certain..butterflies.. regularly appear under two or even three conspicuously distinct forms. **1875** Bennett & Dyer tr. *Sachs' Bot.* III. vi. 809 Another contrivance for..mutual fertilisation.. Dimorphism (or Hetero-stylism)..In one individual the flowers all have a long style and short filaments, while in another individual all the flowers have a short style and long filaments. **1888** Rolleston & Jackson *Anim. Life* 238 The phrase *sexual dimorphism* is used to denote the differences other than the usual anatomical characters which separate the two sexes..In [Lepidoptera] the individuals of broods appearing at different times of the year often differ from one another..In this case the phrase *seasonal dimorphism* is employed.

c. *Philol.* The existence, in one language, of a word under two different forms, or of two words of the same ultimate derivation (doublets).

1877 F. A. March *Anglo-Sax. Gram.* 28 Where it [bifurcation] is produced by a foreign word coming into English in different ways, it has been called dimorphism: ration, reason.

dimorphite (daɪˈmɔːfaɪt). *Min.* [mod. f. Gr. δίμορφ-ος of two forms + -ITE.] A sulphide of arsenic occurring in very small orange-coloured crystals of two different forms. Also called **diˈmorphine.**

1852 Shepard *Min.* 351 Dimorphine. **1868** Dana *Min.* 28 Dimorphite.

dimorphotheca (daɪ,mɔːfəʊˈθiːkə). *Bot.* [mod.L. (S. Vaillant 1722, in *Hist. et Mémoires Acad. Sci. 1720* 279), f. Gr. δίμορφος DIMORPHOUS *a.* + THECA 2.] A plant of the South African genus of herbs or sub-shrubs so named, of the family Compositæ; the Cape Marigold (see MARIGOLD 1 d).

1861 *Curtis's Bot. Mag.* LXXXVII. 5252 (*heading*) Grassy-leaved Dimorphotheca. **1866** Lindley & Moore *Treas. Bot.* I. 409/1 *Dimorphotheca*, the Cape Marigold. **1890** *Garden* XXXVIII. 180/3 Like many other handsome composites from the Cape, this Dimorphotheca had long ceased to obtain much notice as a garden plant. **1960** *Times* 10 Sept. 9/3 The dimorphothecas have also done well this year.

dimorphous (daɪˈmɔːfəs), *a.* [f. Gr. δίμορφ-ος of two forms + -OUS.] = DIMORPHIC. (Mostly in *Chem.* and *Min.*)

1832 Johnston *Progr. Chem.* in *Rep. Brit. Assoc.* (1835) 432 Sulphur and carbon therefore possess two forms, or they are dimorphous. **1850** Daubeny *Atom. Th.* iv. (ed. 2) 123 Bodies..capable of assuming two distinct crystalline forms..according to the circumstances under which they had been brought into the solid condition..are termed dimorphous. **1869** Mrs. Somerville *Molec. Sc.* I. i. 16 The diamond crystallizes in octohedrons, while graphite.. crystallizes in six-sided plates:..and thus carbon possesses the property of being dimorphous. **1874** Lubbock *Wild Flowers* ii. 35 The majority of species of the genus Primula appear to be dimorphous.

dim-out (ˈdɪmaʊt). [f. phr. *to dim out* (DIM *v.* 2c).] A reduction in the brightness or use of lighting, e.g. as a precaution against air-raids; in a theatre or cinema, the ending of a scene, etc., by a slow rather than fast diminution of lighting; the resulting partial darkness. Also *transf.* and *attrib.* Cf. BLACK-OUT.

1942 *N.Y. Times* 3 May 2E/5 In New York City the dim-out recalled the 'lightless nights' caused by the coal shortage in 1917. **1943** J. Steinbeck *Once there was War* (1959) 3 It is evening, and the first of the dim-out lights come on. **1944** *Times* 9 Nov. 2/3 One of the effects of the reduced gas-pressure at Manchester will be that the dim-out in the city will be more dim. **1947** 'N. Blake' *Minute for Murder* v. 100 Darkness. Damn the dim-out. **1960** Lindsay & Crouse *Sound of Music* 7 Sister Sophia enters below the curtains and crosses the stage, carrying a large ring of keys. Dim Out. **1965** *B.B.C. Handbk.* 11 It would be naïve to suppose the new [television] channel was launched into an entirely friendly world. The black-out of the first night was succeeded by the dim-out of the first few months. **1968** O. Wynd *Sumatra Seven Zero* iv. 54 There didn't appear to be any activity at the hotel entrance, and there was a dim-out down there, as though all the staff had gone to bed.

†**diˈmove,** *v. Obs. rare.* [ad. L. *dīmovē-re* to move away, remove.] *trans.* To remove.

1540 R. Wisdome in Strype *Eccl. Mem.* I. App. cxv. 320 You wil not dimove that evil wel placed. **1788** *Trifler* No. 25 ⁋3. 323 It dimoves every discruciating pain from the stomach.

dimp, *v. rare.* [app. shortened from DIMPLE *v.*] *trans.* To dimple, or mark with dimples.

1821 Clare *Vill. Minstr.* I. 132 Rain-drops how they dimp'd the brook. *Ibid.* II. 123 Ere yet a hailstone pattering comes, Or dimps the pool the rainy squall.

dimple (ˈdɪmp(ə)l), *sb.* Also 5 **dympull.** [Evidenced only from 15th c., and app. not common till late in the 16th: origin uncertain. Its form answers to OHG. *dumphilo*, MHG. *tumpfel*, *tümpfel*, mod.G. *dümpfel*, *tümpel* pool, but connexion is not historically made out. It has also been collated with *dimble*, and conjectured to be a nasalized deriv. of *dip*, or a dim. of *dint* with consonantal change.]

1. A small hollow or dent, permanent or evanescent, formed in the surface of some plump part of the human body, esp. in the cheeks in the act of smiling, and regarded as a pleasing feature.

*c***1400** *Destr. Troy* 3060 Hir chyn full choise was..With a dympull full derne, dayntė to se. **1588** Greene *Pandosto* (1607) 19 Shee hath dimples in her cheekes. **1598** Florio, *Pozzette*, dimples, pits, or little holes in womens cheekes. **1611** Shaks. *Wint. T.* II. iii. 101 The Valley, The pretty dimples of his Chin, and Cheeke. **1632** Milton *L'Allegro* 30 Wreathėd Smiles, Such as hang on Hebe's cheek, And love to live in dimple sleek. **1784** Mad. D'Arblay *Diary* 4 Oct., Three letters in her hand, and three thousand dimples in her cheek and chin! **1813** Byron *Giaour* (Orig. Draft) ii. Wks. (1846) 63/1 *note*, Like dimples upon Ocean's cheek. **1870** Emerson *Soc. & Solit.*, *Dom. Life* Wks. (Bohn) III. 42 Parents, studious of the witchcraft of curls and dimples and broken words.

b. The action of dimpling.

1713 Steele *Guardian* No. 29 ⁋6 The dimple is practised to give a grace to the features, and is frequently made a bait to entangle a gazing lover.

2. *transf.* Any slight surface depression or indentation resembling the preceding, as a dip in the surface of land or a ripple on the water.

1632 Lithgow *Trav.* vi. 278 Whereon (say they) Elias oft slept, and..that the hollow dimples of the stone was onely made by the impression of his body. **1664** Power *Exp. Philos.* I. 3 Not absolute perforations, but onley dimples in their crustaceous Tunica Cornea. **1796** Withering *Brit. Plants* IV. 82 Upper part [of fungus] convex, with or without a dimple in the centre. **1801** Southey *Thalaba* XI. xxxviii, The gentle waters gently part In dimples round the prow. **1815** *Guide to Watering Places* 299 In a dimple of the hill..rises St. Anne's Well. **1892** J. Mather *Poems* 51 In dimples of the mountain lay The panting herd of deer.

3. *Comb.*

1874 Mrs. Whitney *We Girls* ix. 184 Her dimple-cleft and placid chin. **1892** A. Sterry *Lazy Minstr.* 80 Sweet little dimple-cheek—Merrily dancing.

ˈdimple, *v.* [f. prec. sb.]

1. *trans.* To mark with, or as with, dimples.

1602 Marston *Antonio's Rev.* III. iii. Wks. 1856 I. 110, I will laugh, And dimple my thinne cheeke With capring joy. **1697** Dryden *Æneid* vii. 43 With whirlpools dimpl'd. **1796** Southey *Ball. Donica*, No little wave Dimpled the water's edge. **1830** Tennyson *Lilian* 16 The lightning laughters dimple The baby-roses in her cheeks. **1847-8** H. Miller *First Impr.* vi. (1857) 102 Here the surface is dimpled by unreckoned hollows: there fretted by uncounted mounds. **1891** B. Harte *First Fam. Tasajara* xiii, Leaden rain.. dimpling like shot the sluggish pools of the flood.

2. *intr.* To break into dimples or ripples, to form dimples, to ripple.

*a***1700** Dryden (J.), Smiling eddies dimpled on the main. **1735** Pope *Prol. Sat.* 316 As shallow streams run dimpling all the way. **1762** Goldsm. *Cit. W.* cxiv, She is then permitted to dimple and smile, when the dimples and smiles begin to forsake her. **1805** Wordsw. *Prelude* VI. 652 A lordly river..Dimpling along in silent majesty. **1851** Thackeray *Eng. Hum.* II. (1876) 181 Cheeks dimpling with smiles. **1864** Tennyson *Aylmer's F.* 149 Low knolls That dimpling died into each other.

ˈdimpled, *ppl. a.* [f. DIMPLE *sb.* or *v.* + -ED.] Marked with or as with dimples.

*a***1577** Gascoigne *Wks.* (1587) 67 That dimpled chin wherein delight did dwell. **1599** H. Buttes *Dyets drie Dinner* C v b, Choise. Right Quinces: small: dimpled or dawked. **1606** Shaks. *Ant. & Cl.* II. ii. 207 Pretty Dimpled Boys, like smiling Cupids. **1634** Milton *Comus* 119 By dimpled brook and fountain-brim. **1753** Hogarth *Anal. Beauty* x. 65 The taper dimpled [finger] of a fine lady. **1878** B. Taylor *Deukalion* I. iii. 30 Beyond the dark blue, dimpled sea, Lie sands and palms.

ˈdimplement. *rare.* [f. DIMPLE *v.* + -MENT.] The fact or condition of being dimpled; a dimpling.

1856 Mrs. Browning *Aur. Leigh* I. 39 And view the ground's most gentle dimplement. **1862** —— *False Step* iv, Where the smile in its dimplement was.

ˈdimpler. *nonce-wd.* [f. DIMPLE *v.* + -ER¹.] One who 'dimples' or forms dimples.

1713 Steele *Guardian* No. 29 ⁋5 We may range the several kinds of laughers under the following heads: The Dimplers. The Smilers. The Laughers. The Grinners. The Horse-laughers.

ˈdimpling, *vbl. sb.* [f. as prec. + -ING¹.] The action of the verb DIMPLE (usually in *intr.* sense).

1602 Beaumont *Hermaphrodite* Wks. (Rtldg.) II. 700/1 She prais'd the pretty dimpling of his skin. **1771** Goldsm. *Prol. Craddock's Zobeide* 5 While botanists all cold to smiles and dimpling, Forsake the fair, and patiently—go simpling. **1820** W. Irving *Sketch Bk., Spectre Bridegroom* I. 338 A soft dimpling of the cheek.

ˈdimpling, *ppl. a.* [f. as prec. + -ING².] That dimples; that forms or breaks into dimples.

1735 Somerville *Chase* IV. 407 Ev'ry..hollow Rock, that o'er the dimpling Flood Nods pendant. **1795** Mad. D'Arblay *Let.* 18 June, When I look at my dear baby, and see its dimpling smiles. **1824** W. Irving *T. Trav.* I. 295 A trim, well made, tempting girl, with a roguish dimpling face.

1844 FABER *Sir Lancelot* (1857) 7 With..dimpling globes of nuphar netted o'er.

dimply ('dɪmplɪ), *a.* [f. DIMPLE *sb.* + -Y.] Full of or characterized by dimples.

1726–46 THOMSON *Winter* 83 The wanderers of heaven.. flutter round the dimply pool. **1727** PHILIPS *Ode to Miss Pulteney* Dimply damsel, sweetly smiling. *a* **1790** T. WARTON *Triumph of Isis* Poet. Wks. (1802) I. 5 The smooth surface of the dimply flood. **1884** *Illustr. Sydney News* 26 Aug. 15/2 Aunt Flo's face grew dimply.

dimps. *dial.* Also 9– **dampse, dempse, dimpse(s), dimpsey, dimpsie, dumps.** [? deriv. of DIM, or dial. variant of *dumps*, DUMP *sb.*] Dusk, twilight.

1693 R. LYDE (of Topsham, Devon) *Retaking of Ship* in Arb. *Garner* VII. 450, I got no nearer than a mile from the bar, in the dimps [dusk] of the night. **1810** *Monthly Mag.* XXIX. II. 435/1 *Dumps, dimpse, dampse, dimmet*, twilight. D[evonshire]. **1867** W. F. ROCK in W. W. Skeat *Nine Specimens Eng. Dial.* (1896) 47, I thort I glimpsed Jan slinge to tha rebeck i' the dimpse. **1885** F. T. ELWORTHY *Rep. Comm. Devonshire Verbal Provincialisms* 91 Just as the dempse was coming on. **1886** ELWORTHY *W. Somerset Word-bk.*, *Dumps*, twilight; same as *Dimmet*. **1891** R. P. CHOPE *Dial. Hartland* 40 Twaz gittin' dimps avore us stairted. **1892** H. C. O'NEILL *Devonshire Idyls* 25 But 'twas got quite dark all of a minute, and 'twere only in the dimpses when the maid shut her eyes. **1896** G. CHANTER *Witch of Withyford* xii. 149 There be pixies in the dimpsey here. **1925** *Glasgow Herald* 1 Aug. 4 At the 'dimpsie' the colours of the flowers become more etherealised. **1950** L. A. G. STRONG *Which I Never* 161 'Twasn't dark. 'Twasn't more than dimpsey. **1965** in P. Jennings *Living Village* (1968) 95 The Somerset village of Compton Martin..is on the lower north flanks of the Mendips... Local words include..*Dimpsey*: dark, twilit.

Hence **dimpsy** *a. dial.*, dusky, as 'It's getting a bit dimpsy'. (*Devonsh.*)

'dim-,sighted, *a.* Having dim sight (*lit.* and *fig.*).

1561 T. NORTON *Calvin's Inst.* I. 11 b, Olde men..or they whose eyes are dimm sighted. **1679** BEDLOE *Popish Plot* A ij b, They are very dim-sighted that cannot see through such Impostures. **1775** ADAIR *Amer. Ind.* 230 Our dim-sighted politicians. **1840** DICKENS *Barn. Rudge* xxix, Mr. Chester was not the kind of man to be..dim-sighted to Mr. Willet's motives. **1887** *Spectator* 20 Aug. 1116 When the dog gets old and dim-sighted.

Hence **,dim'sightedness.**

1662 HICKERINGILL *Wks.* (1716) I. 278 It may seem cross to us..through our short and dimsightedness. **1822–56** DE QUINCEY *Confess.* (1862) 190 If a veil interposes between the dim-sightedness of man and his future calamities.

‖**dim sum** (dɪm sʌm). Also **deem sim, tim-sam, -sum,** etc. Pl. **sum, sums.** [Cantonese *dím sàm*; cf. Chinese *diǎnxin*.] A savoury Cantonese-style snack; a meal consisting of these. Also *attrib.*

1948 R. W. DANA *Where to eat in N.Y.* 75 Dim sum varies according to the season. **1952** D. Y. H. FENG *Joy of Chinese Cooking* ii. 56 The Chinese word for appetizer is *deem sum*.. which means 'touch the heart'. **1956** B. Y. CHAO *How to cook & eat in Chinese* II. xxi. 242 Then dishes of *tim-sam* (Cantonese for *tien-hsin*), each containing four pieces, are placed before you. **1966** M. GLASER *Underground Gourmet* 125 Dim-Sum is served continually every day. **1967** *New Idea* (Austral.) 25 Feb. 20/2 It was all pretty authentic except for the Australian dim sims that went with Chinese beer. **1977** 'S. LEYS' *Chinese Shadows* (1978) ii. 37 The sacred custom..of spending a good part of the morning eating *tim-sun* (*tien-hsin*) in the teahouses (*ch'a-lou*). **1984** *N.Y. Times* 2 Dec. XI. 33/2 The dim sum—four Cantonese-style dumplings—were juicy, and the ground-pork filling was full of flavor.

†**di'muriate.** *Chem. Obs.* [DI-² 2 a ¶.] The old name for a (supposed) compound of one atom of hydrochloric acid with two of a base.

1838 T. THOMSON *Chem. Org. Bodies* 228 When we dissolve cinchonina in muriatic acid we always obtain a dimuriate..This is obviously 2 atoms of cinchonina to 1 atom of muriatic acid.

dim-wit, dimwit ('dɪmwɪt). *colloq.* (orig. *U.S.*). Also **dim wit.** [f. DIM *a.* + WIT *sb.*] A stupid or slow-witted person.

1922 *Dialect Notes* V. 141 She's the worst dim-wit on campus. **1925** *New Yorker* 20 June 15/2 An archduke, a sort of royal dim wit. **1943** [see *bird brain* s.v. BIRD *sb.* 9]. **1944** *Penguin New Writing* XIX. 71 'What's the matter?' 'Cramp, you dimwit, cramp!' **1956** 'J. WYNDHAM' *Seeds of Time* 217 He had an uncomfortable awareness of how many ways there were for even a dimwit to contrive a fatal accident.

Hence **dim-witted** *a.*, stupid, dull; **dim-wittedness,** the quality of being dim-witted.

1940 E. B. MANN *Troubled Range* (1941) xi. 135 Of all the damn' dim-witted stunts! **1948** 'E. CRISPIN' *Buried for Pleasure* ix. 68 They say he's got 'a madman's cunning', which is their excuse for being too dim-witted to catch him. **1960** *20th Cent.* Oct. 359 Some Northerners..can give an impression of dim-wittedness.

dimyary ('dɪmɪərɪ), *a.* and *sb. Zool.* [f. mod.L. *dimyārius* (*Dimyāria* name of group), f. Gr. δι- twice + μῦ-ς muscle (*lit.* 'mouse'): see -ARY¹.]

A. *adj.* Double-muscled: said of those bivalve molluscs which have two adductor muscles for closing the shell. Also **dimyarian** (dɪmɪ'ɛərɪən) *a.* **B.** *sb.* A dimyary bivalve.

1835 TODD *Cycl. Anat.* I. 712/2 Shells which have belonged to dimyary mollusks. **1854** WOODWARD *Mollusca* (1856) 26 The cytherea and other dimyaries. **1866** TATE *Brit. Mollusks* ii. 18 The freshwater Conchifera are all dimyarian bivalves.

din (dɪn), *sb.*¹ Forms: 1–5 **dyne,** 1–7 **dyn,** 3 **dune** (-y-), 3–7 **dine,** 3– **din** (also 4 **deone, dene,** 5–6 **dynne,** 5–7 **dinne,** 7 **deane, dynn, dinn**). [OE. *dyne* (:—OTeut.**duni-z*), and *dynn*, corresp. to ON. *dynr* din (:— **dunju-z* or **dunjo-z*); f. Germanic root *dun-*: cf. Skr. *dhûni* roaring, a torrent; also ON. *duna* fem. 'rushing or thundering noise' (perh. a later formation from the verb). Elsewhere in WGer. only the derived vb. appears: see DIN *v.*] A loud noise; particularly a continued confused or resonant sound, which stuns or distresses the ear.

a **1000** *Satan* 466 (Gr.) Se dyne becom hlud of heofonum. *a* **1000** *Sal. & Sat.* 324 (Gr.) þæt heo domes dæȝes dyn ȝehyre. *c* **1200** *Trin. Coll. Hom.* 117 þo com a dine of heuene. *c* **1205** LAY. 11574 þer wes swiðe muchel dune þeines þer dremden. *c* **1250** *Gen. & Ex.* 3467 Smoke upreked and munt quaked..Ai was moses one in ðis dine. **1340** HAMPOLE *Pr. Consc.* 7427 Als wode men dose..and makes gret dyn. **1393** LANGL. *P. Pl.* C. XXI. 65 The erthe quook..And dede men for þat deon comen oute of deope graues. *c* **1400** *Destr. Troy* 274 Sone he dressit to his dede & no dyn made. **1535** STEWART *Cron. Scot.* II. 281 To vincust thame with litill sturt or dyn. **1589** R. HARVEY *P. Perc.* (1590) 21 A man may stop his eares to hear their dinne. **1610** SHAKS. *Temp.* I. II. 371 Ile..make thee rore, That beasts shall tremble at thy dyn. **1667** MILTON *P.L.* X. 521 Dreadful was the din Of hissing through the Hall. **1712** STEELE *Spect.* No. 509 ¶2 The din of squallings, oaths, and cries of beggars. **1810** SCOTT *Lady of L.* I. iii, Faint, and more faint, its failing din Returned from cavern, cliff, and linn. **1848** LYTTON *Harold* XI. vi, From the hall..came the din of tumultuous wassail. **1855** MACAULAY *Hist. Eng.* III. 1 All the steeples from the Abbey to the Tower sent forth a joyous din.

b. The subjective impression of a sounding or ringing in the ears.

1651 HOBBES *Leviath.* I. i. 3 Pressing the Eare, produceth a dinne. **1787** COWPER *Let.* 29 Sept., I have a perpetual din in my head and..hear nothing aright.

DIN (dɪn), *sb.*² Also **D.I.N.** [a. Ger., acronym f. the initials of *D*eutsche *I*ndustrie-*N*orm German Industrial Standard, as laid down (from 1917) by the *Deutsches Institut für Normung* German Standards Institution (formerly *Deutscher Normenausschuß* German Standards Committee).] **1.** (Any of) a series of West German technical standards widely used outside West Germany (*esp.* for the description of paper sizes and film-speed ratings, and for electrical specifications); goods, etc., conforming to these standards. Freq. *attrib.*, esp. preceding classification number. Cf. *ASA* s.v. A III, *BSI* s.v. B III.

1932 *Industr. Standardization* III. 205/2 (*caption*) German standard sheet DIN 826 showing make-up of magazine page. **1937** E. J. LABARRE *Dict. Paper* 282/2 In this country [*sc.* Russia] the DIN sizes of the A-series have been adopted as standard sizes. **1938** G. H. SEWELL *Amateur Film-Making* ii. 18 The most general methods of speed notation in use to-day are the H. & D., Scheiner, and DIN (Deutsche Industrie Norm). **1940** F. J. MORTIMER *Wall's Dict. Photogr.* (ed. 15) 573 The figures used to represent speed are on a logarithmic scale, a plate of 18/10 D.I.N. requiring double the exposure of one of speed 21/10 D.I.N. **1965** BERG & MANNHEIM in *Focal Encycl. Photogr.* (ed. 2) II. 1437/1 When DIN speed ratings were..revised in 1961.. the degree sign was..eliminated, so that 15° DIN became 15 DIN. **1972** *Electr. & Electronics Abstr.* LXXV. 471/1 (*heading*) An electronic automatic staircase lighting switch for quick mounting on a DIN support bar. **1973** A. PARRISH *Mech. Engineer's Ref. Bk.* x. 62 The German standards authority published DIN 24255 for water duties and DIN 24256 for chemical duties [of pumps]. **1976** *Which?* Sept. 203/1 We've done signal to noise measurements CCIR weighted this time — a better measure of how annoying the noise is in practice than the DIN weighting. **1983** *New Electronics* 25 Jan. 70/3 The DIN 41612 connector constitutes a universal system utilising only a small number of connector families while meeting the pre-requisites of both user and manufacturer. **1984** *What Video?* Aug. 17/1 The leads supplied (7-pin DIN 3V32 and 5-pin DIN on TV) are not compatible.

2. Special Comb.: **DIN plug, socket,** a type of multipin plug and socket used to connect audio equipment.

1976 *Pract. Electronics* Oct. 819/2 The power for Digiscope comes from external supplies, and this is connected via a four-core cable terminated in a seven-pin DIN plug. **1982** *Listener* 16 Dec. 34/4 A couple of leads with phono plugs at one end and DIN plugs on sockets at the other end. **1975** *Gramophone* Jan. 1421/1 The fifth DIN socket separates the pre-amplifier from the power amplifier.

din, *v.* Pa. t. and pple. **dinned** (dɪnd). Forms: 1 **dynnan, dynian,** 3 **dunen, -ien, denie, dinen,** 4 **denen, dennen, donen,** 4–6 **dyn(n,** 5 **dunnyn,** 4– **din.** [In I., OE. *dynnan, dynian* = OS. *dunian* to give forth a sound, ON. *dynja* (*dundi*) to come rumbling down, to gush, pour, MDu. and NRh. *dunen*, MHG. *tünen* to roar, rumble, thunder, all:—OTeut. **dunjan*, from root of DIN *sb.* ON. had also *duna* to thunder, rumble:—OTeut. **dunôjan*. In II. app. a new formation from the sb.]

I. †**1.** *intr.* (In OE. and ME.) To sound, ring with sound, resound. *Obs.*

Beowulf 1538 (Th.) Siðþæt se hearm-scaða to Heorute ateah, dryht-sele dynede. *c* **1205** LAY. 30410 þa eorðe gon to dunien. *a* **1225** *St. Marher.* (1866) 20 þa þuhte hit as þah a þunre dunede. *a* **1300** *Cursor M.* 1770 (Cott.) þe erth quok and dind again [*v.rr.* dinned, dynet, dened]. *a* **1300** *K. Horn* 592 þe fole schok þe brunie þat al þe curt gan denie. **1375** BARBOUR *Bruce* XVI. 131 To schir colyne sic dusche he gave That he dynnyt on his arsoune. *c* **1430** *Syr Gener.* (Helm. MS.) 1 b, He uncoupled his houndes and blew his horn, Al the forest dynned of that blast. **1513** DOUGLAS *Æneis* XI. i. 89 So lowd thair wofull bewaling habundis, That all the palice dynnis and resoundis.

†**b.** Of persons: To make a loud noise; to roar.

c **1450** *Golagros & Gaw.* vii, Than dynnyt the duergh, in angir and yre, With raris, quhil the rude hall reirdit agane.

II. 2. *trans.* To assail with din or wearying vociferation.

1674 N. FAIRFAX *Bulk & Selv.* To Rdr., Why should the ears of all the neighborhood be dinn'd..with the Cackle? **1786** tr. *Beckford's Vathek* (1868) 85, I want not to have my ears dinned by him and his dotards. **1855** SINGLETON *Virgil* I. 377 With never-ceasing words On this and that side is the hero dinned. **1872** BLACK *Adv. Phaeton* xix. 265 The deafening causeway that had dinned our ears for days past.

3. To make to resound; to utter continuously so as to deafen or weary, to repeat *ad nauseam*; *esp.* in phr. *to din* (something) *into* (some one's) *ears*.

1724 SWIFT *Drapier's Lett.* Wks. 1755 V. II. 32 This hath often been dinned in my ears. **1830** SCOTT *Demonol.* vii. 218 Horrors which were dinned into their ears all day. *a* **1839** PRAED *Poems* (1864) II. 272 My own and other people's cares Are dinned incessant in my ears. **1842** S. LOVER *Handy Andy* i, The head man had been dinning his instructions into him. **1877** BLACK *Green Past.* xxxix. (1878) 315 It was the one word *Gazette* that kept dinning itself into his ears.

4. *intr.* To make a din; to resound; to give forth deafening or distressing noise.

1794 WORDSW. *Guilt & Sorrow* xlvi, The bag-pipe dinning on the midnight moor. **1820** W. IRVING *Sketch Bk.* I. 63 His wife kept continually dinning in his ears about his idleness. **1831** J. WILSON *Unimore* vi. 13 Steep water-falls, for ever musical, Keep dinning on. **1875** JOWETT *Plato* (ed. 2) III. 228, I am perplexed when I hear the voices of Thrasymachus and myriads of others dinning in my ears.

din, dial. form of DUN *a.*

dinah ('daɪnə). *slang.* [Corruption of DONA 2.] A man's sweetheart or favourite woman.

1898 [see TART *sb.* 2]. **1909** J. R. WARE *Passing Eng.* 109/2 *Dinah*, a favourite woman; *e.g.* 'Is Mary your Dinah?'

‖**Dinanderie** (dinɑ̃dəri). [Fr.; f. *Dinant*, formerly *Dinand*, a town of Belgium, on the Meuse, 'wherein copper kettles, etc., are made' (Cotgr. 1611); so F. *dinandier* a copper-smith or brazier.] Kitchen utensils of brass, such as were formerly made at Dinant; extended in recent times to the brass-work of the Levant and India.

1863 KIRK *Chas. Bold* I. viii. 343 Kitchen utensils..which under the name of Dinanderie were known to housewives throughout Europe, being regularly exported not only to France and Germany, but to England, Spain, and other countries.

Dinantian (dɪ'nænʃɪən), *a. Geol.* [ad. F. *dinantien* (A. de Lapparent *Traité de Géol.* (ed. 3, 1893) 11. 819), f. *Dinant*, a town in Belgium + -IAN.] The name of the series of rocks in continental Europe deposited during the Lower Carboniferous period, and of the corresponding geological epoch. Also *absol.*

[**1888** J. PRESTWICH *Geol.* II. i. 8 Belgium..Carboniferous ..Lower..Limestones of Dinant.] **1903** A. GEIKIE *Text-bk. Geol.* (ed. 4) II. VI. II. 1051 The Carboniferous system of the European continent has been grouped by some geologists in three major divisions: 1st, the Lower (Culm, Dinantian), comprising all the Lower Carboniferous rocks up to the Millstone Grit, [etc.]. **1905** *Q. Jrnl. Geol. Soc.* LXI. 264 The designation Dinantian, as including the whole of the Carboniferous Limestone, seems hardly justified by the continuity or clearness of the sequence in the district which has suggested the name. **1959** *Chambers's Encycl.* III. 104/2 The Carboniferous System is well developed throughout Europe where the Dinantian, Namurian, Westphalian and Stephanian are recognized. **1969** T. N. GEORGE in *C.R. 6me Cong. Int. Stratigraphie & Géol. du Carbonifère, 1967* I. 193/1 British Dinantian rocks were deposited under conditions of sustained subsidence. *Ibid.* 197/2 It is still uncertain whether Vaughan's Avonian precisely equates with the earlier-named Dinantian.

‖**dinar** (diː'nɑː(r), 'diːnɑː(r)). Also 7 **dina, dyna, denier,** 8 **denaer,** 9 **denaur, dínár, dīnār.** [Arab. and Pers. *dīnār*, a. late Gr. δηνάριον, a. L. *dēnārius*: see DENARIUS.] **a.** A name given to various oriental coins: applied anciently to a gold coin, corresponding to the Byzantine *denarius auri*, or crown of gold, and to the gold mohr of later times; afterwards to the staple silver coin corresponding to the modern rupee; in modern Persia a very small imaginary coin, of which 10,000 make a tomaun (*c* 1897 = about 7*s.* 6*d.*, but in 1677 = £3. 6*s.* 8*d.*, Yule). Now a standard monetary unit of Iraq, Jordan, Kuwait, Tunisia, etc. (see quots.).

1634 SIR T. HERBERT *Trav.* 41 The usuall Coine..within the Moguls Territories are Pice, Mammoodees, Rowpees, and Dynaes. **1638** *Ibid.* (ed. 2) 38 The Dina is gold worth thirty shillings. **1698** FRYER *Acc. E. India & P.* 407 And 100 Deniers one Mamoody. And 20 Pise one Shahee: Both which are Nominal, not Real. **1753** HANWAY *Trav.* (1762) I. v. lxiv. 292 The toman, bistie, and denaer are imaginary. *Ibid.* 293 We always computed the mildenaer or 1000 denaers, equal to an english crown of 5*s.* *Ibid.* 294 The silversmiths commonly make use of pieces of money instead of weights, especially sisid denaers of 1½ muscal in weight. **1811** P. KELLY *Universal Cambist* I. 346 Persia. Accounts are kept in Tomans of 50 Abassis.. or 10,000 Dinars simple. **1815** ELPHINSTONE *Acc. Caubul* (1842) I. 391 In towns, the common pay of a labourer is one hundred denaurs (about fourpence half-penny) a-day, with food. **1841** —— *Hist. Ind.* II. 67, 2000 dinārs were given to him 'to pay for his washing'. **1850** W. IRVING *Mahomet* xxxiii. (1853) 172 An annual tribute of three thousand dinars or crowns of gold. **1883** C. J. WILLS *Mod. Persia* 63 *note*, The merchant-class, too, use the dinar, an imaginary coin... one thousand dinars make a keran, so one dinar is the $\frac{1}{1000}$ of 9*d.* **1931** W. F. SPALDING *Tate's Money Manual* I. 54 The monetary unit [of Iraq] will be the gold dinar of 1000 fils. **1951** *Statesman's Year-Book* 1211 On 1 July, 1950, Jordan began to issue its own currency, the Jordan dinar, divided into 1,000 fils. **1958** *Economist* 8 Nov. 534/2 A new currency made its bow to the exchange markets this week. It is the Tunisian dinar, based on the French franc... The dinar has been given an equivalent of 1,000 French francs. **1962** *Statesman's Year-Book* 1186 The Kuwait Dinar (at par with the £ sterling) of 1,000 fils, replaced the Indian external Rupee on 1 April 1961. **1970** *Financial Times* 23 Mar. 12/2 The average per capita income [in Algeria] of 910 dinars.

b. [a. Serbian *dinar*, f. L. *dēnārius* DENARIUS.] The monetary unit of Yugoslavia (formerly of Serbia).

1882 *Statesman's Yearbook* 402 The Servian dinar is equal to one franc. **1907** *Macm. Mag.* Sept. 839 In Belgrade.. they gauged my ignorance of the number of nickel *paras* and *piastres* that go to the *dinar*, or franc. **1926** *Survey of Budget 1927–8* (Yugoslavia) 3 The changes in the economic conditions of this country, which were the consequences of the stabilisation of the dinar. **1927** *Economic Jugoslavia* 34 The National Bank.. has paid up capital to the amount of 30 million dinars.

† **dinarchy.** *Obs. rare*$^{-0}$. [a. obs. F. *dinarchie* (Cotgr.), f. *din-* improp. for DI-² (after *bi-*, *bin-*) + Gr. ἀρχή rule.]

1656 BLOUNT *Glossogr.*, *Dinarchy*, the joynt Rule or Government of two Princes. **1721** BAILEY, *Dinarchy*, a Government by two.

Dinaric (dɪˈnærɪk), *a.* [f. *Dinara*, a mountain in Dalmatia + -IC.] Denoting a mountain range which extends in a south-easterly direction along the eastern side of the Adriatic, and a race of people inhabiting the coast of the northern Adriatic, characterized by tall stature, a very short head, dark wavy hair, and straight or aquiline nose. Hence as *sb.*, a member of this race.

1833 *Penny Cycl.* I. 387/1 The Dinaric Alps. **1862** *Chambers's Encycl.* III. 572/1 Dinaric Alps, that branch of the Alpine system which connects the Julian Alps with the western ranges of the Balkan. **1898** *Pop. Sci. Monthly* Oct. 732 The Adriatic or Dinaric race. **1900** DENIKER *Races of Man* ix. 333 Dark, brachycephalic, tall race, called Adriatic or Dinaric, because its purest representatives are met with along the coast of the Northern Adriatic and especially in Bosnia, Dalmatia, and Croatia. **1924** *T. P.'s & Cassell's Weekly* 13 Sept. 658/2 The pyramid-headed man from the Dinaric lands. **1928** C. DAWSON *Age of Gods* xvi. 370 There is.. no evidence for the occurrence of the Dinaric type in the neolithic period. **1939** C. S. COON *Races of Europe* v. 140 This is our first meeting with the Dinaric race. *Ibid.*, The stature was tall, as with modern Dinarics, and the long bones slender. **1944** A. HOLMES *Princ. Physical Geol.* xviii. 397 Farther south the backward thrusts maintain their direction and mark the beginning of the Italian ranges which pass round the head of the Adriatic into the Dinaric Alps.

Dinas (ˈdɪnəs). [f. *Dinas* Rock, in the Vale of Neath, Wales.] Used *attrib.* in **Dinas brick**, fire-brick made from **Dinas clay**, a kind of rock consisting almost entirely of silica.

1875 HUNT & RUDLER *Ure's Dict. Arts* (ed. 7) I. 532 Stone bricks.. are manufactured at Neath, in Glamorganshire... They are usually known as the 'Dinas bricks'. **1879** *Encycl. Brit.* IX. 844/1 Dinas clay, which is really nearly pure silica. **1880** *Ibid.* XIII. 294/2 Dinas brick, which perfectly resists the ordinary steel melting temperatures of coke-fired furnaces.

dinast-: see DYNAST-.

dincum, var. DINKUM *sb.* and *a.*

ˈ**dinder.** *dial.* [app. a modification of *dener*, *dinneere*, early forms of DENIER.] A local term for the *denarii* or small coins found on sites of Roman settlements, *esp.* at Wroxeter in Shropshire.

1778 *Eng. Gazetteer* (ed. 2) s.v. *Roxcester*, Peasants, often plough up coins, called Dinders, that prove its antiquity. **1847–78** HALLIWELL, *Dinders*, small coins of the lower empire found at Wroxeter, Salop. Spelt *dynders* by Kennett. **1859** *All Year Round* No. 3. 55 The dullest ploughboy working here.. picks up denarii, and calls them dinders. **1873** C. W. KING *Early Chr. Numism.* 256 The clay disks, variously impressed, often found amongst Roman remains in this country, popularly called *dinders*.

dindge, var. of DINGE *sb.*¹ and *v.*

din-din (ˈdɪndɪn). *colloq.* Also **din-dins.** [Childish or jocular reduplication of DIN(NER *sb.*] Dinner.

1905 E. M. FORSTER *Where Angels fear to Tread* ii. 47 'Din-din's nearly ready,' said Lilia. **1920** WODEHOUSE *Summer Lightning* xiii. 265 'Come along, Carmody. Din-dins.' Hugo had sunk into a chair. 'I don't want any dinner,' he said, dully. **1957** E. TAYLOR *Angel* v. 220 Must be time for dindins, madam. **1958** F. NORMAN *Bang to Rights* 113 If you get captured with one you'll get a few days no din-din.

dindle (ˈdɪnd(ə)l, ˈdɪn(ə)l), *v.* Chiefly (now only) *Sc.* and *north. dial.* In 5–6 **dyn(d)le**, 9 **dinn'le**, **dinnel**, **dinle**. [Derivation obscure; probably more or less onomatopœic: cf. *dingle*, *tingle*, and *tinkle*; also Du. *tintelen* to ring, and to tickle, to prick or sting lightly, Flem. *tinghelen* to sting as a nettle (Kilian); also F. *tintillant*, tinging, ringing, tingling, *tintoner* to ting often, to glow, tingle, dingle (Cotgr.); in which there is a similar association of the vibration of sound with the thrill of feeling.]

1. *intr.* To tinkle; to ring or make a noise that thrills and causes vibration.

c **1440** *Promp. Parv.* 121/2 Dyndelyn, *tinnio.* **1808** MAYNE *Siller Gun* I. 115 Wi' that, the dinlin drums rebound. **1827** TENNANT *Papistry Storm'd* 5 Dinnelin Deaf Meg and Crookit Mou [two Cannons] Begoud wi' ane terrific blatter At the great steeple's found to batter. **1893** STEVENSON *Catriona* 165 'The voice of him was like a solan's, and dinnle'd in folks' lugs.'

b. *trans.* To thrill or cause to vibrate with sound.

(*to dindle the sky* = to make the welkin ring.)

1513 DOUGLAS *Æneis* X. xiv. 160 Than the Latynis and eyk pepill Troianys The hevynnys dyndlit [**1553** dynlyt] with a schowt at anis. **1845** *Whistlebinkie* (Sc. Songs) Ser. III. (1890) I. 379 A steeple that dinlit the skye Wi' a clinkin' auld timmer-tongued bell.

2. *intr.* To be in a state of vibration from some loud sound, shock, or percussion; to tremble, quiver, reel.

1470–85 MALORY *Arthur* V. viii, He dyd commaunde hys trompettes to blowe the blody sownes, in suche wyse that the ground trembled and dyndled. **1513** DOUGLAS *Æneis* VIII. iv. 126 The brayis dyndlit [**1553** dynlit], and all doun can dusche. **1566** DRANT *Horace* A vij, They made the quaueryng soyle To dindle and to shake again. **1814** SCOTT *Wav.* xliv, 'Garring the very stane and lime wa' dinnle wi' his screeching.' **1871** P. H. WADDELL *Psalm* civ. 32 Wha leuks on the lan', an' it dinnles.

3. *intr.* To tingle, as with cold or pain.

1483 *Cath. Angl.* 100/1 To Dindylle, *condolere.* **1577** STANYHURST in Holinshed *Chron.* (1587) II. 26/1 His fingers began to nibble.. his ears to dindle, his head to dazzle. **1787** GROSE *Provinc. Gloss.*, *Dindle*, to reel or stagger from a blow. **1855** ROBINSON *Whitby Gloss.*, *To Dindle or Dinnle*, the thrill or reaction of a part after a blow or exposure to excessive cold. **1892** *Northumbld. Gloss.*, *Dinnell*, to tingle as from a blow, or in the return of circulation after intense cold. **1893** STEVENSON *Catriona* 173 'Young things wi' the reid life dinnling and stending in their members.'

Hence ˈ**dindling** *vbl. sb.* and *ppl. a.*

1578 LANGHAM *Gard. Health* 234 Eares ache and dindling, put in the juice [of Feuerfew] and stope it in. **1635** D. DICKSON *Pract. Wks.* (1845) I. 87 The dinneling of the rod is yet in the flesh. **1669** W. SIMPSON *Hydrol. Chym.* 90 He could after a while feel it.. run along his arms to his very fingers ends, with a dindling and pricking as it run along. **1808** [see DINDLE *v.* 1.]

dindle (ˈdɪnd(ə)l, ˈdɪn(ə)l), *sb.*¹ *dial.* Also **dinnle.** [f. DINDLE *v.*] A thrill, a tingle.

1818 SCOTT *Hrt. Midl.* xxv, 'At the first dinnle o' the sentence.' **1858** MRS. OLIPHANT *Laird of Norlaw* III. 90 It's something to succeed.. even though you do get a dinnle thereby in some corner of your own heart.

ˈ**dindle**, *sb.*² *dial.* Popular name of various yellow Composite flowers: see quots.

1787 W. MARSHALL *E. Norfolk* Gloss., *Dindles*, common and corn sow-thistles; also the taller hawkweeds. **1878** BRITTEN & HOLLAND *Plant-n.*, Dindle..(2) *Leontodon Taraxacum. Norf. Suff.*

dindle-dandle, *v.* [Reduplicated form of DANDLE *v.*, with change of vowel, expressing alternation.] *trans.* To dandle or toss up and down, or to and fro.

c **1550** COVERDALE *Carrying Christ's Cross* x. (ed. 1) 107 Rem. (Parker Soc. 1846) 263 Whether it be semeli that Chrystes body should be dyndle-danled & vsed, as thei vse it.

dine (daɪn), *v.* [ME. *dine-n*, a. F. *dîne-r*, in OF. *disner* (*digner*, *disgner*) = Pr. *disnar*, (*dirnar*, *dinar*), It. *disinare*, *desinare*, med.L. *disnare* (from OF.). Generally held to be:—late L. type **disjūnare*, for *disjejūnāre* to breakfast, f. *dis-* expressing undoing (DIS- 4) + *jejūnium* fast; the intervening stages being *disj'nar*, *disnar*, *disner*.

In this view *disner* contains the same elements ultimately as F. *déjeuner*, OF. *desjuner* to breakfast, DISJUNE, and owes its greater phonetic reduction (cf. *aider*:—L. *adjūtāre*) to its belonging to an earlier period. The shifting of meaning whereby *disner* ceased to be applied to the first meal of the day, while its form ceased to recall L. *jejūnium* or OF. *jeüner*, would facilitate the subsequent introduction of *desjeüner* with the required form and sense.]

1. a. *intr.* To eat the principal meal of the day, now usually taken at or after mid-day; to take DINNER. Const. *on* or *upon* (what is eaten), *off* (a stock or supply).

1297 R. GLOUC. (1724) 558 [Hii] nolde þanne wende a vot, ar hii dinede þere. *c* **1320** *Seuyn Sag.* (W.) 3830 For my wil es with tham to dine. **1362** LANGL. *P. Pl.* A. Prol. 105 Goode gees and grys, Gowe dyne, gowe! *c* **1430** *Stans Puer* 64 in *Babees Bk.* (1868) 31 And where-so-euere þou be to digne or to suppe, Of gentilnes take salt with þi knyf. **1526–34** TINDALE *John* xxi. 12 Jesus sayde vnto them: come and dyne [WYCLIF, ete 3e; *Rev. Vers.* break your fast]. *a* **1533** LD. BERNERS *Huon* lxii. 217 They rose & herd masse, & dynid. **1590** SPENSER *F.Q.* I. ix. 35 His raw-bone cheekes.. Were shronke into his iawes, as he did never dine. **1603** SHAKS. *Meas. for M.* IV. iii. 159, I am faine to dine and sup with water and bran. **1709** STEELE *Tatler* No. 104 ¶ 1 Jenny sent me Word she would come and dine with me. **1782** COWPER *Gilpin* 195 All the world would stare, If wife should dine at Edmonton, And I should dine at Ware. **1817** BYRON *Beppo* xliii, I also like to dine on becaficas. **1841–4** EMERSON *Ess.*, *Heroism* Wks. (Bohn) I. 106 A great man scarcely knows how he dines [or] how he dresses. **1886** BESANT *Childr. Gibeon* I. x, Malenda dines off cold tea and bread.

b. Phrases. (*a*) ***to dine forth*** or ***out***: to dine away from home (cf. DINER 1 b, DINING *vbl. sb.* 1 b); ***to dine out on***: to be given hospitality at dinner partly or chiefly for the sake of one's conversation or knowledge about (a specific incident or topic, etc.).

1590 SHAKS. *Com. Err.* II. ii 211 If any aske you for your Master, Say he dines forth. **1816** JANE AUSTEN *Emma* II. vii. 120 They will not take the liberty with you; they know you do not dine out. **1835** DICKENS *Let.* (1965) I. 67, I have received an Invitation to dine out to day. **1852** W. S. LANDOR *Let.* 11 Apr. in *N. & Q.* (1968) CCXIII. 414/1, I never dine out, or go into parties in the evening. **1923** W. S. MAUGHAM *Our Betters* III. 170 Don't you remember that killing story about your father's death. You dined out a whole season on it. **1934** N. MARSH *Man lay Dead* xv. 268 In a couple of years you will be dining out on this murder. **1936** A. CHRISTIE *Cards on Table* vii. 66 If I were only to dine in houses where I thoroughly approved of my host I'm afraid I shouldn't dine out very much. **1951** J. C. FENNESSY *Sonnet in Bottle* VII. 245 He does a very good imitation of it —he's dined out on it ever since. **1966** H. YOXALL *Fashion of Life* xi. 109, I dined out for the rest of this African journey on my acquaintance with the Princess's fiancé. **1970** 'D. HALLIDAY' *Dolly & Cookie Bird* v. 66 I've dined out on a few stories about her.

(*b*) ***to dine with Duke Humphrey***: to go dinnerless.

Of this phrase the origin is not altogether clear. In the 17th c. it was associated with Old St. Paul's, London, and said of those who, while others were dining, passed their time walking in that place, or sitting in 'the chair of Duke Humphrey', or 'at Duke Humphrey's table'. According to Stowe, the monument of Sir John Beauchamp there was 'by ignorant people misnamed to be' that of Humphrey Duke of Gloucester, son of Henry IV (who was really buried at St. Albans). Nares says an (adjacent) part of the church was termed *Duke Humphrey's Walk.* (A different origin is however given by Fuller.) The equivalent phrase in Edinburgh appears to have been 'To dine with St. Giles and the Earl of Murray' (who was interred in St. Giles's Church): see quot. 1680, and Irving *Hist. Sc. Poetry* 579.

[**1592** G. HARVEY *Four Lett.* (Nares s.v. *Duke Humphrey*), To seek his dinner in Poules with duke Humphrey. **1599** BP. HALL *Sat.* III. vii. 6 Trow'st thou where he din'd to day? In sooth I saw him sit with Duke Humfray.] **1604** *Penniless Parl. Threadbare Poets* (Farmer), Let me dine twice a week at Duke Humphry's table. [**1633** ROWLEY *Match at Midn.* II. in Hazl. *Dodsley* XIII. 31 Are they none of Duke Humphreys furies? Do you think that they devised this plot in Paul's to get a dinner? **1639** MAYNE *City Match* III. iii. Ibid. XIII. 264 Your penurious father, who was wont To walk his dinner out in Pauls.. Yes, he was there As constant as Duke Humphrey.] **1655** FULLER *Hist. Camb.* (1840) 225 Being.. loath to pin himself on any table uninvited, he was fain to dine with the chair of duke Humphrey.. namely, reading of books in a stationer's shop in Paul's churchyard. *a* **1661** —— *Worthies, London* (198), After the death of Duke Humphrey (when many of his former alms-men were at a losse for a meal's meat,) this proverb did alter its copy; to dine with Duke Humphrey importing to be dinnerless. **1680** FR. SEMPILL *Banishm. Poverty* 87, I din'd with saints and noblemen, Even sweet St. Giles and the Earl of Murray. **1748** SMOLLETT *Rod. Rand.* lv. (Farmer), My mistress and her mother must have dined with Duke Humphrey, had I not exerted myself. **1835** COL. HAWKER *Diary* (1893) II. 88, I was obliged to 'dine with Duke Humphrey', and content myself with a few buns. [**1858** GEN. P. THOMPSON *Audi Alt.* II. lxxviii. 33 To turn them all over to Duke Humphrey's mess.]

† **2.** *trans.* To eat; to have for dinner. *Obs.*

c **1380** *Sir Ferumb.* 1277 3yf ous sum what to dyne. *c* **1386** CHAUCER *Sompn. T.* 129 'Now, maister, quod the wyf, 'What wil ye dine?' **1470–85** MALORY *Arthur* XVI. viii, She prayd hym to take a lytyl morsel to dyne.

3. To furnish or provide (a person) with a dinner; to entertain at dinner; to accommodate for dining purposes.

1399 LANGL. *Rich. Redeles* III. 60 The dewe dame dineth hem.. And ffostrith hem fforthe till they ffle kunne. **1633** ROWLEY *Match at Midn.* II. i. in Hazl. *Dodsley* XIII. 28 As much bread.. as would dine a sparrow. *a* **1714** M. HENRY *Wks.* (1835) II. 674 He often dined the minister that preached. **1815** SCOTT *Guy M.* xxvi, An oaken table massive enough to have dined Johnnie Armstrong and his merry men. **1840** LEVER *H. Lorrequer* i, We.. were dined by the citizens of Cork. **1876** G. MEREDITH *Beauch. Career* II. xi. 197 The way to manage your Englishman.. is to dine him. **1887** *Illustr. Lond. News* 4 June 644 The saloon is capable of dining 118 passengers.

dine (daɪn), *sb. Obs.* exc. *dial.* [f. DINE *v.*] The act of dining; dinner.

c **1400** *Rom. Rose* 6502 They ben so pore.. They myght not oonys yeve me a dyne. **1560** ROLLAND *Crt. Venus* IV. 631 That thay to thair dine suld dres thame haistelie. **1793** BURNS *Auld Lang Syne* iii, We twa hae paidlet i' the burn, Frae mornin sun till dine. ? *a* **1800** *Fair Annie & Sweet Willie* xiii. in Child *Ballads* (1885) III. lxxiii. 194/1 When ye come to Annie's bower, She will be at her dine.

diner (ˈdaɪnə(r)). [f. DINE *v.* + -ER.]

1. a. One who dines; a dinner-guest.

1815 L. HUNT *Feast of Poets* 8 The diners and barmaids all crowded to know him. **1851** MAYNE REID *Scalp Hunt.* ii, After the regular diners had retired. **1881** *Harper's Mag.* LXIII. 218 Dinners are far fewer than formerly, and the diners are chosen rather more exclusively.

b. diner-out: one who is in the habit of dining from home; *esp.* one who cultivates the qualities which make him an eligible guest at dinner-tables.

1807-8 SYD. SMITH *Plymley's Lett.* Wks. 1859 II. 162/1 He is..a diner out of the highest lustre. **1824** BYRON *Juan* XVI. lxxxii, A brilliant diner out, though but a curate. **1856** MRS. BROWNING *Aur. Leigh* IV. Poems 1890 VI. 154 A liberal landlord, graceful diner-out. **1862** *Fraser's Mag.* July 46 He was also a *bon-vivant*, a 'diner-out' and a story-teller, and a man of convivial habits.

2. a. *U.S.* A railway dining car.

1890 *Commercial Gaz.* (Cincinnati) 29 June, One coach, the chaircar, sleeper and diner..overturned. **1894** *Columbus* (Ohio) *Dispatch* 3 Jan., A new dining car which..is the first diner..built by that company.

b. A restaurant, orig. and still occasionally one built to resemble a railway dining-car. *N. Amer.*

1935 *Amer. Mercury* July 311/2 The diner was back from the sidewalk, under a couple of big trees. **1960** *Weekend Mag.* 23 Apr. 42/2 My own test began at a roadside diner.. over coffee. **1965** *New Statesman* 5 Nov. 713/1 These diners are roughly equivalent to our pull-ups and the French *relais routiers* before they were turned into haunts of gastronomic fashion. The first 'diners' were old Pullman dining-cars sold off by railway companies and I was amused to see that the newest ones, specially built, attempt to imitate the dining-cars.

3. Special Comb.: **Diners' Club** orig. *U.S.*, a proprietary name for an international organization providing personal charge cards for its members; also *attrib.*

1952 *N.Y. Times* 6 Jan. II. 19/4 Anyone who can sign his name and pay his bills can charge his way through some of the better hotels, restaurants and night clubs of the country under a new credit card system known as the *Diners Club. **1956** *Official Gaz.* (U.S. Patent Office) 19 June TM135/2 Hamilton Credit Corporation, New York,...now The Diners' Club, Inc....the Diners' Club... For extension of credit to customers who purchase at subscribing retail establishments and making collections from such customers through a central billing system. **1961** A. BUCHWALD *How much is that in Dollars?* (1962) I. 10 There isn't any special evacuation plan for Diners' Club members, is there? **1969** 'R. STARK' *Blackbird* (1970) v. 34 Murray looked at his watch..and began waving his Diners Club card for the check. **1979** F. E. PERRY *Dict. Banking* 58/1 The best known cards in the U.K. are Barclaycard, Access, Diner's Club and American Express... Diner's Club and American Express charge an entrance fee, but allow unlimited credit, to be paid for on receipt of the account.

diner(e, obs. forms of DINNER.

dineric (daɪˈnɛrɪk), *a. Physics.* [f. DI-[2] + Gr. νηρ-ός wet: see -IC.] Of or pertaining to the interface of two liquids.

1905 *Jrnl. Physical Chem.* IX. 546 The exponential formula has been found to describe a large number of dineric equilibria, especially organic liquids, over very wide ranges of concentration. **1915** *Ibid.* XIX. 275 To avoid circumlocution the surface separating two liquid phases will be called a dineric interface.

‖**dinero** (diˈnero). [Sp. *dinero* penny, coin, money:—L. *dēnārius*: cf. DENIER.] **a.** 'A money of account in Alicante, the twelfth part of a sueldo' (Simmonds *Dict. Trade* 1858). **b.** A Peruvian coin, one tenth of the sol, equivalent (*c* 1897) to about 4*d*. English.

1835 P. KELLY *Univ. Cambist* i. 5 Each Sueldo being divided into 12 Dineros. **1868** SEYD *Bullion* 147 The Spanish Assay Mark is..12 dineros of 24 grains..for Silver.

†**dines.** *Obs.* [? a corruption of DIGNESSE.] In phr. ***by God's dines***, by God's dignity or honour: cf. DENTIE.

1599 PORTER *Angry Wom. Abingd.* (Percy Soc.) 81 Giue me good words, or, by God's dines Ile buckle ye for all your birdspit. *Ibid.* 102 Ile fight with the next man I meet..by Gods dines. **1605** *Tryall Chev.* II. i, Gods dynes, I am an Onyon if I had not rather [etc.].

†**diˈnetic,** *a. Obs. rare.* [f. Gr. δινητ-ός whirled round (f. δινέ-ειν to spin round; cf. δῖνος whirling, rotation) + -IC.] Of or belonging to rotation; rotatory.

1668 GLANVILL *Plus Ultra* x. 72 Of the Spots and Dinettick motion of the Sun.

†**diˈnetical,** *a. Obs.* [f. as prec. + -AL[1]] = prec.

1646 SIR T. BROWNE *Pseud. Ep.* VI. v. 294 The Sun..hath also a dineticall motion and rowles upon its owne poles. **1664** POWER *Exp. Philos.* III. 168 This great Argument against the Dinetical Motion of the Earth. **1691** RAY *Creation* (1714) 193 A spherical figure is most commodious for dinetical motion or revolution upon its own Axis.

dinette (ˈdaɪnɛt, daɪˈnɛt). orig. *U.S.* [irreg. f. DINE *v.* + -ETTE.] **a.** A small room, an alcove, or part of a room set aside for meals. **b.** A set of articles of dining furniture, usu. compactly designed. Also *attrib.* **c.** A small restaurant.

1930 *Ladies' Home Jrnl.* Jan. 38/3 Two clumsy, heavy French doors between the living room and the dinette. **1931** *Sears Catal.* Spring 622 (*heading*) Stylish dinette at bigger savings. **1940** S. LEWIS *B. Merriday* ii. 26 Fun, frolic, and 'fried dogs' at Dinty's dinette. 'Where all of Sladesbury's Bohemia hangs out.' **1942** *Archit. Rev.* XCI. 101/3 The usual worker's house [in Canada] has three bedrooms, a living-room, kitchen with 'dinette', bathroom, [etc.]. **1953** W. R. BURNETT *Vanity Row* viii. 63 A little dinette, hidden by a beaverboard partition. **1955** J. CANNAN *Long Shadows* iii. 35 The kitchenette is situated in close proximity to the dinette. **1957** W. H. WHYTE *Organiz. Man* xxiv. 313 A wife was so ashamed of the emptiness of her living room that she smeared the picture window with Bon Ami; not until a dinette set arrived did she wash it off. **1962** *Radio Times* 29 Mar. 28/2 The divans and 'dinette' seats [in a caravan] are upholstered in deep foam rubber. **1970** *Globe & Mail* (Toronto) 26 Sept. 52/3 (Advt.), 20% off! Dinette sets. Has drop-leaf table, two well-padded chairs.

dinful (ˈdɪnfʊl), *a.* [f. DIN *sb.* + -FUL.] Full of din or resonant noise; noisy.

1877 BLACKIE *Wise Men* 31 The trumpet-tongued exploits of dinful war. **1889** A. T. PASK *Eyes Thames* 73 The gong is beaten at quick intervals, but even that dinful sound is not sufficient to keep one awake.

ding (dɪŋ), *v.*[1] *arch.* or *dial.* Also 4-6 dyng(e. *Pa. t. sing.* 4- **dang** (5- *north.*), 3-5 **dong**, 3-4 **dannge**, 4-5 **dange**, 7 **dung**; *pl.* 4-5 **dungen (-yn)**, **dongen**, 5-6 **dong(e**, 6-7 **dung**; also 4-5 **dange**, 4- (5- *north.*) **dang**; 4 (*south.*) **dynged**, 6 **ding'd**, **dingde**, 6-7 **danged**. *Pa. pple.* 3-6 **dungen (-yn, -in)**, 5 **dwngyn**, **doungene**, 4-5 **dongen (-yn, -un)**, 6- *Sc.* **dung** (6-7 **doung**, 6 **donge**); also 6-7 (*south.*) **dingd**, **ding'd**. [Frequent from the end of the 13th c. (in later use chiefly northern), but not recorded in OE. Probably from Norse: cf. Icel. *dengja* to hammer, to whet a scythe, Sw. *dänga* to bang, thump, knock hard, Da *dænge* to bang, beat. In Norse it is a weak verb, and the strong conjugation in Eng., which after 15th c. is Sc. or north. dial., may be on the analogy of *sing*, *fling*, etc.: cf. BRING.]

†**1.** *intr.* (or *absol.*) To deal heavy blows; to knock, hammer, thump. *Obs.* (or ? *north dial.*)

a **1300** *Cursor M.* 19356 (Edin.) Þan wiþ suaipis þai þaim suang, and gremli on þair corsis dange. *c* **1300** *Havelok* 2329 Þe gleymen on þe tabour dinge. **13..** *Coer de L.* 5270 Kyng Richard took his ax ful strong, And on the Sarezyn he dong. **1393** LANGL. *P. Pl.* C. XVII. 179 Noþer peter þe porter · ne paul with his fauchon, That wolde defende me heuene dore · dynge ich neuere so late. **15..** *Merry Jest Mylner Abyngton* 133 in Hazl. *E.P.P.* III. 105 With two staues in the stoure They dange thereon, whyles they myght doure. **1828** SCOTT *F. M. Perth* xix, That Harry Smith's head was as hard as his stithy, and a haill clan of Highlandmen dinging at him?

2. *trans.* To beat, knock, strike with heavy blows; to thrash, flog. ***to ding to death***: to kill by repeated blows. (Now *dial.*, chiefly *Sc.* or *north.*)

c **1300** *Havelok* 215 The king..ofte dede him sore swinge, And wit hondes smerte dinge. *Ibid.* 227 Thanne he hauede ben..ofte dungen. *c* **1325** *Metr. Hom.* (1862) 71 Thai.. dange hym that hys body blede. *c* **1400** *Apol. Loll.* 38 He þat knowiþ his lordis wille, & maad him not redy to do þer after, schal be dongun wiþ mani dingings. *c* **1400** *Destr. Troy* 2135 Dyng hom to deth er any dyn ryse. *c* **1400** *Ywaine & Gaw.* 3167 With his tayl the erth he dang. *a* **1529** SKELTON *Now sing we, &c.* 17 Behold my body, how Jewes it donge with.. scourges strong. **1533** BELLENDEN *Livy* II. (1822) 115 He dang his hors with the spurris. **1549** *Compl. Scot.* xvii. 151 He [the horse] vas put in ane cart to drug and drau, quhar he vas euyl dung & broddit. **1563-7** BUCHANAN *Reform. St. Andros* Wks. (1892) 11 Nor ȝit sal it be leful to the said pedagogis to ding thair disciples. **1647** H. MORE *Song of Soul* II. iii. III. xxv, The rider fiercely dings His horse with iron heel. **1674** RAY *N.C. Words* 14 *To Ding*, to Beat. **1862** HISLOP *Prov. Scot.* 88 He's sairest dung that's paid wi' his ain wand. **1870** RAMSAY *Remin.* v. 146 Let ae deil ding anither. *Mod. Suffolk colloq.* Say that again, and I'll ding you in the head.

†**b.** To crush with a blow, smash. *Obs.*

c **1380** *Sir Ferumb.* 104, [I] wil kuþe on hem my miȝt; & dyngen hem al to douste. **1583** STANYHURST *Æneis* III. (Arb.) 89 Dingd with this squising and massiue burthen of Ætna.

†**c.** To thrust through, pierce (with a violent thrust). *Sc. Obs.*

1536 BELLENDEN *Cron. Scot.* IX. xxix. (Jam.), Scho dang hir self with ane dagger to the hert, and fell doun deid. *Ibid.* xv. ix. (Jam.), He dong hym throw the body with ane swerd afore the alter.

3. *fig.* To 'beat', overcome, surpass, excel.

[**1500-20** DUNBAR *Poems* xxxviii. 9 Dungin is the deidly dragon Lucifer.] **1724** RAMSAY *Tea-t. Misc.* (1733) I. 24 Auld springs wad ding the new. **1814** SCOTT *Wav.* lxvi, It dings Balmawhapple out and out. **1884** *Cheshire Gloss.*, *Ding*, to surpass or get the better of a person. **1893** STEVENSON *Catriona* 188 We'll ding the Campbells yet in their own town. *Mod. Berwickshire Prov.*, Duns dings a'.

4. To knock, dash, or violently drive (a thing) in some direction, e.g. *away*, *down*, *in*, *out*, *off*, *over*, etc. ***to ding down***, to knock down, thrust down, overthrow, demolish; ***to ding out***, to drive out or expel by force.

13.. *E.E. Allit. P.* B. 1266 Diȝten dekenes to deþe, dungen doun clerkkes. *a* **1340** HAMPOLE *Psalter* Cant. 504 He dyngis out þe deuyl fra þe hertis of his seruauntis. *c* **1400** *Apol. Loll.* 71 If I bigge ageyn þe þing þat I ding doun, I mak mesilfe a trespasor. *c* **1425** WYNTOUN *Cron.* VIII. xxvii. 36 Bot þai ware dwngyn welle away. **1513** DOUGLAS *Æneis* x. v. 154 Manfully..to wythstand At the cost syde, and dyng thame of the land. *c* **1565** LINDESAY (Pitscottie) *Chron. Scot.* (1728) 64 His Thigh-Bone was dung in two by a Piece of a misframed Gun. *a* **1572** KNOX *Hist. Ref.* Wks. 1846 I. 204 Thei dang the sclattis of[f] housis. **1593** NASHE *Christ's T.* 31 a, The bespraying of mens braines donge out against them. **1598** MARSTON *Pygmal.* v. 156 Prometheus..Is ding'd to hell. **1601** —— *Pasquil & Kath.* III. 4 Hee dings the pots about. **1610** B. JONSON *Alch.* v. v, *Gur.* Downe with the dore. *Kas.* 'Slight, ding it open. **1613** HAYWARD *Norm. Kings* 20 The Duke brandishing his sword..dung downe his enemies on euery side. **1644** MILTON *Areop.* (Arb.) 57 Ready..to ding the book a coits distance from him. **1645** RUTHERFORD *Lett.* 357 That which seemeth to ding out the bottom of your comforts. **1653** URQUHART *Rabelais* I. xxvii, He..dang in their teeth into their throat. **1663** SPALDING *Troub. Chas. I*, (1829) 24 They masterfully dang up the outer court gates. **1676** ROW *Contn. Blair's Autobiog.* ix. (1848) 145 Rudders being..dung off their hinges. **1686** tr. *Chardin's Trav.* 67 Wind..which if it be violent dings 'em upon the coast. **1785** *Spanish Rivals* 8 Sometimes he dings his own head against a post. **1816** SCOTT *Old Mort.* xxviii, 'You and the whigs hae made a vow to ding King Charles aff the throne.' **1871** C. GIBBON *Lack of Gold* xii, I have been ..trying to ding you out of my head. **1886** HALL CAINE *Son of Hagar* I. i, 'That's the way to ding 'em ouer.'

b. Without extension. (In quots. *neuter passive*, as in 'a loaf that cuts badly'.)

1786 BURNS *A Dream* iv, But Facts are cheels that winna ding, An' downa be disputed. *Mod. Sc. Prov.* Facts are stubborn things; they'll neither ding nor drive [i.e. they can neither be moved by force as inert masses, nor driven like cattle].

†**5.** *intr.* (for *refl.*) To throw oneself with force, precipitate oneself, dash, press, drive. *Obs.*

c **1400** *Sowdone Bab.* 1263 Tho thai dongen faste to-geder While the longe day endured. *c* **1430** *Hymns Virg.* (1867) 122 All they schall to-gedyr drynge, And euerychon to oþer dynge. *c* **1470** HENRY *Wallace* I. 411 On ather side full fast on him thai dange. **1627** DRAYTON *Moon Calf* Poems (1748) 182 They..drive at him as fast as they could ding.

b. To precipitate or throw oneself *down*, fall heavily or violently. ***to ding on***: to keep falling heavily, as rain (but in this use, associated with *beating* on). (Now only *Sc.*)

c **1460** *Towneley Myst.* (Surtees) 141 Greatt dukes downe dynges for his greatt aw, And hym lowtys. **1552** LYNDESAY *Monarche* 1422 Frome the Heuin the rane doun dang Fourty dayis and fourty nychtis. **1602** MARSTON *Antonio's Rev.* IV. iii. Wks. 1856 I. 123 As he headlong topsie turvie dingd downe, He still cri'd 'Mellida!' **1663** SPALDING *Troub. Chas. I* (1829) 44 A great rain, dinging on night and day.

c. To throw oneself violently about, to fling, to bounce. ***to huff and ding***: to bounce and swagger.

1674 RAY *S. & E.C. Words* 64 *To Ding*, to fling. **1680** *New Catch in Roxb. Ball.* V. 249 Jack Presbyter huffs and dings, And dirt on the Church he flings. *a* **1700** B. E. *Dict. Cant. Crew*, *To Huff and Ding*, to Bounce and Swagger. **1706-7** FARQUHAR *Beaux' Strat.* III. iii, I dare not speak in the House, while that Jade Gipsey dings about like a Fury. **1712** ARBUTHNOT *John Bull* II, iii, He huffs and dings at such a rate, because we will not spend the little we have left.

6. In imprecations: = DASH *v.* 11. *dial.*

1822 SCOTT *Nigel* xxvii, 'Deil ding your saul, sirrah, canna ye mak haste.' *a* **1860** *Maj. Jones Courtsh.* (Bartlett), You know it's a dinged long ride from Pineville. **1861** GEO. ELIOT *Silas M.* 85 Ding me if I remember a sample to match her. **1879** TOURGEE *Fool's Err.* (1883) 292 Ding my buttons if she ain't more Southern than any of our own gals. **1883** C. F. SMITH in *Trans. Amer. Philol. Soc.* 47 *Ding* and *dinged*, moderate forms of an oath..peculiar to the South.

7. *Slang* or *Cant*: (see quot.)

1812 J. H. VAUX *Flash Dict.*, *Ding*, to throw, or throw away..To ding a person is to drop his acquaintance totally; also to quit his company, or leave him for the time present.

8. *Arch.* To cover a brick wall-surface with a thin coat of fine mortar, trowelled smooth, and jointed to imitate brickwork, not necessarily following the actual joints.

1893 A. BEAZELEY in *Let.* 21 Nov., An architect, who showed me the letter containing the word *Dinging* told me the verb is in living technical use. **1894** [see below].

Hence ˈ**dinging** *vbl. sb.*

a **1340** HAMPOLE *Psalter* cxxii. 3 Þat he delyuer vs of all temptacioun & dyngynge. **1340** —— *Pr. Consc.* 7010 Dyngyng of develes with hamers glowand. *c* **1400** [see 2]. **1611** COTGR., *Enfonsure*, a beating or dinging. **1894** *Laxton's Price Book* 49 'Dinging (a coat of thick lime-white and the joints afterwards struck with a jointer)'.

ding (dɪŋ), *v.*[2] [Echoic. But in use confounded with DING *v.*[1] and DIN *v.*]

1. *intr.* To sound as metal when heavily struck; to make a heavy ringing sound.

1820 SHELLEY *Œdipus* I. 236 Dinging and singing, From slumber I rung her. **1848** DICKENS *Dombey* ix, Sledge hammers were dinging upon iron all day long. **1871** *Daily News* 20 Jan., The bellow of the bombardment..has been dinging in our ears.

2. *intr.* To speak with wearying reiteration. Cf. DIN *v.*

1582 in Calderwood *Hist. Kirk* (1842-6) III. 658 To ding continuallie in his eares, and to perswade him to thinke his raigne unsure, wanting his mothers benedictioun. **1847-78** HALLIWELL, *Ding*, to taunt; to reprove. **1881** MISS JACKSON *Shropsh. Word-bk.*, s.v., The Missis 'as bin dingin' at me.. about Bessey knittin' the Maister a stockin' in a day. **1882** in *W. Worcestersh. Gl.*

¶ ***to ding into the ears***, 'to drive or force into the ears', appears to unite this with DING *v.*[1] and DIN *v.*

1596 DALRYMPLE tr. *Leslie's Hist. Scot.* IV. (1887) 233 Inculcating and dinging it in the eiris and myndes of all. **1773** GOLDSM. *Stoops to Conq.* II. iii, If I'm to have any good, let it come of itself, not to keep dinging it, dinging it into one so. **1853** THACKERAY in *Four C. Eng. Lett.* 557 To try and ding into the ears of the great, stupid, virtue-proud English ..that there are some folks as good as they in America. **1879** BROWNING *Ned Bratts* 227 What else does Hopeful ding Into the deafest ear except—hope, hope's the thing?

Hence ˈ**dinging** *vbl. sb.* and *ppl. a.*

1820 W. IRVING *Sketch-bk., Boar's Head Tavern* (1887) 139 The din of carts, and the accursed dinging of the dustman's bell.

ding (dɪŋ), *sb.*[1] *dial.* [f. DING *v.*[1]] **1.** The act of dinging: **a.** a knock, a smart slap; **b.** a violent thrust, push, or driving.

a **1825** FORBY *Voc. E. Anglia, Ding*, a smart slap; particularly with the back of the hand. **1876** *Whitby Gloss., Ding*, a blow or thrust; the disturbance of a crowd. 'A ding an' a stour', a commotion and dust.

2. *Surfing.* (See quot. 1962.)

1962 T. MASTERS *Surfing made Easy* 64 *Dings*, dents or holes in surfboard. **1968** W. WARWICK *Surfriding in N.Z.* 17/2 When repairing a ding or damaged area on your board, don't rush. **1970** *Surf* I. x. 33/1 Real ridiculous—we all got dings.

ding, *sb.*[2] and *adv.* The stem of DING *v.*[2], used as an imitation of the ringing sound of a heavy bell, or of metal when struck. Often adverbial or without grammatical construction, esp. when repeated.

1600 SHAKS. *A.Y.L.* v. iii. 21 When Birds do sing, hey ding a ding, ding. **1801** M. G. LEWIS *Tales of Wonder, Grim White Woman* xxiii, 'Ding-a-ding! ding-a-ding!' Hark! hark! in the air how the castle-bells ring! **1808** MAYNE *Siller Gun* IV. 143 Ding, ding, ding, dang, the bells ring in. *a* **1845** HOOD *To Vauxhall* 2 It hardly rains—and hark the bell!—ding-dingle. **1859** CAPERN *Ball. & Songs* 92 Whistling and cooing, Ding, down, delly.

¶ Confounded with DIN *sb.*

1749 J. RAY *Hist. Reb.* (1752) 383 The noisy ding of the great falls of water. **1868** DORAN *Saints & Sin.* I. 114 The Puritan pulpits resounded..with the ding of politics.

†**ding,** *sb.*[3] *Obs.* Also dinge. Some kind of household vessel.

1594 *Inv.* in *Archæol.* XLVIII. 131 Imprimis one great dinge for bread iiij[s]. **1624** *Ibid.* 150 One trunck, one ding, one flagon.

ding, Sc. var. of DIGNE *a. Obs.* worthy.

Dingaan('s) apricot (ˌdɪŋgɑːn(z) ˈeɪprɪkɒt). [f. the name of *Dingaan*, chief of the Zulus from 1829 to 1840.] A name in Natal for the Keiapple.

1853 E. ARMITAGE in *Jas. Chapman's Trav.* (1868) II. 449 The Kei apple, or Dingan's apricot, invaluable for forming thorny fences and yielding a pleasant fruit. **1891** R. RUSSELL *Natal* 31 The Dingaan apricot, or Kaw apple.

ding-a-ling. Also dingaling. [Echoic.]

1. = DING *sb.*[2]

1894 E. L. BANKS *Campaigns Curios.* 77, I was awakened by the ding-a-ling of the front-door bell.

2. One who is crazy or insane (orig. of a prisoner driven mad by confinement); an eccentric or oddball. Also *loosely*, a fool. *N. Amer. slang.*

[**1935** A. J. POLLOCK *Underworld Speaks* 31/1 *Ding-a-ling*, brainless.] **1940** L. L. STANLEY *Men at their Worst* xvi. 142 When a convict tells me another man is a 'dingaling', then I am certain the man is crazy. **1955** *Western Folklore* Apr. 135/1 *Ding-a-ling*, one who is mentally unbalanced. **1967** *New Yorker* 27 May 33/2 Always wearing black tights under her dress and other kinds of kinky gear... This kid is a dangerous ding-a-ling and I don't know why I handle her. **1971** *Time* 12 Apr. 52 A generally staid, middle-class group, the jurors were unprepared for the grueling experience, which was enough to make ding-a-lings out of the most stable personalities. **1978** J. CARROLL *Mortal Friends* v. ii. 512 Hell, Pius—that dingaling—would never of given me my hat. Thank God for Pope John.

3. The penis. *slang.*

1972 [see MASTURBATION]. **1975** R. H. RIMMER *Premar Experiments* (1976) i. 52 My damned ding-a-ling was pointing my bathrobe into a tent, and other than grabbing it and holding it down, there wasn't much I could do. **1980** R. QUIRK in Michaels & Ricks *State of Lang.* 5 This has meant ..despising..the smut of the music hall, Chuck Berry and his 'ding-a-ling', sexual innuendoes conveyed by *it, do, thing.*

‖**Ding an sich, Ding-an-sich** (ˌdɪŋ an ˈzɪç). *Philos.* Also ding an sich. [G.] A thing in itself (see THING *sb.*[1] 14 e). Cf. AN SICH.

1846 G. H. LEWES *Biogr. Hist. Philos.* IV. 169 If we are to believe that *Dinge an sich* exist. **1865** S. H. HODGSON *Time & Space* i. 25 The Ding-an-sich is that which cannot be reached or affected by consciousness. **1872** [see NOUMENALIZE *v.*]. **1897** *Mind* VI. 240 This Reality for us remains little more than a *Ding an Sich.* **1940** AUDEN *Another Time* 69 Do all clerks for instance Pigeon-hole creation, Brokers see the Ding-an-Sich as Real Estate?

dingbat (ˈdɪŋbæt). *slang.* Also ding bat, ding-bat. [? f. DING *v.*[1] + BAT *sb.*[2]]

1. *U.S.* In various uses (see quots.); esp. (*a*) a piece of money; *pl.* money; (*b*) = THINGUMMY (cf. DINGUS); (*c*) a tramp or hobo.

1838 in *Amer. Speech* (1963) XXXVIII. 10 We can take a '*Quaker*' before we start—apply a '*Ding Bat*' [some kind of drink?] at Providence. **1861** in Bartlett *Dict. Amer.* (ed. 4, 1877) 177 It has been found necessary to expend the *dingbats*, to put something more substantial on the 'fly' [= in motion]. **1864** G. A. SALA in *Daily Tel.* 19 Oct., Little John, erst a hog-driver..and recently in trouble for manufacturing bogus 'dingbats'. *Ibid.* 1 Nov., I paid for my Kissingen in five-cent 'dingbat' or 'spondulick'—two of the many names given to the fractional currency. **1877** BARTLETT *Dict. Amer.* (ed. 4) 177 *Dingbat*, a bat of wood that may be thrown (dinged); a piece of money; a cannon-ball; a bullet. **1895** *Dialect Notes* I. 387 *Dingbat.* Mr. Philip Hale, of the *Boston Journal*, has been collecting information.. concerning this word. The following definitions appear:—(1) Balls of dung on buttocks of sheep or cattle. (2) Blow or slap on the buttocks. (3) Flying missile. (4) Squabble of words or pushing. (5) Money. (6) In some of the N.E. schools, the word is student slang for various kinds of muffins or biscuit. (7) Affectionate embrace of mothers hugging and kissing their children. (8) Term of admiration. 'They are regular *ding-bats*' (speaking of girls). **1918** 'A-No. 1' *Mother Delcasse of Hoboes* 44 Stew Bum..Ding Bat.. Fuzzy Tail..the dregs of vagrantdom. **1923** *Frontier* May 10 That blasted 'ding bat' of a Ford, as Stub calls it, just naturally stood on its hind legs..and turned a flip-flop. **1926** J. BLACK *You can't Win* vi. 65 If you was some kind of a rank dingbat you wouldn't have been invited down here. **1931** J. THURBER *Owl in Attic* II. 78 It is sitting on a strange and almost indescribable sort of iron dingbat. **1944** F. BROWN *Angels & Spaceships* (1955) 208 It was his dingbat. I mean, he made it and he thought he knew what it was.

2. a. A foolish or stupid person; someone crazy or insane; also used as a general term of disparagement. Chiefly *U.S.*

[**1911** *Dialect Notes* III. 542 *Dingbatty*, half crazy, imbecile. 'That fellow is dingbatty.'] **1915** *Dialect Notes* IV. 203 *Dingbat*, a fool. 'The boss called Ralph a *dingbat* because he made fun of him.' **1935** N. ERSINE *Underworld & Prison Slang* 32 *Dingbat*, a *screwy* person; a *stircrazy* convict. **1950** H. E. GOLDIN *Dict. Amer. Underworld Lingo* 58/2 *Dingbat*, a fool; a worthless fellow. **1957** 'N. CULOTTA' *They're a Weird Mob* (1958) ii. 29 'Who is ut?' Some ding bat after that job... He sounds a bit crackers to me. **1971** *Newsweek* 29 Nov. 52 A rising tide of..weirdos, dumb Polacks, dingbats, meatheads, and four-eyes. **1978** J. IRVING *World according to Garp* ii. 41 Midge was such a dingbat..that she went to Hawaii for a *vacation* during World War II. **1982** S. B. FLEXNER *Listening to Amer.* 282 By 1940 *dingbat* also meant a stupid person, especially a dumb girl or woman; this meaning was popularized in the 1970s TV situation comedy series *All in the Family*, whose lovable, bumbling, narrow-minded character Archie Bunker called his wife *dingbat.* **1985** *N.Y. Times* 13 Jan. II. 3/2 Miss Sternhagen's mother increases in giddiness, even to wearing what appears to be a feather in her hair. She is, in fact, a certifiable dingbat.

b. *Austral.* and *N.Z.* In pl., esp. in phr. ***to have the dingbats, to be dingbats***, to be mad, stupid, eccentric; also, to be a victim of delirium tremens; ***to give*** (a person) ***the ding-bats***, to inflict a feeling of nervous discomfort.

1918 *Chrons. N.Z.E.F.* 27 Sept. 109/2 'Ave you got the dingbats? **1926** J. DEVANNY *Butcher Shop* x. 96 George, 'e 'ad the dingbats. **1933** L. ACLAND in *Press* (Christchurch) 14 Oct. 15/7 *Dingbats.* Slang, of Australian origin, for delirium tremens. The dingbats, I believe, are really the snakes, weasels, etc., which a sufferer sees. **1937** PARTRIDGE *Dict. Slang* 221/2 *Dingbats*, eccentric; mad, gen. slightly: Australian military. **1943** F. SARGESON in *Penguin New Writing* XVIII. 71, I knew it would give me the dingbats if I just stayed on there waiting. **1945** *Southern Cross* (London) 15 Dec. 4/3 Even old George, used as he was to pink snakes, ding-bats, and spotted elephants, seemed a little surprised. **1949** *Landfall* III. 146 Your mother's dingbats. **1959** G. SLATTER *Gun in Hand* iv. 42 Boozin' again! You'll end up with the dingbats, you will.

3. *Austral.* [Perh. f. DING(O + BAT(MAN[2].] An army batman.

1919 in DOWNING *Digger Dial.* **1940** *Bulletin* (Sydney) 3 Jan. 35/3 There is a vast difference between a dingbat in the British Army and one in the A.I.F.

†**ding-ding.** *Obs.* Also **ding-dong.** An expression of endearment.

1564 BULLEYN *Dial. agst. Pest.* (1888) 91 He goeth a woyng, my dyng, dyng; and if he spedeth, my dearlyng, what getteth he, my swetyng? **1602** WITHALS *Dict.* 61 My ding-ding, my darling. *a* **1611** BEAUM. & FL. *Philaster* v. iv, Let Philaster be deeper in request, my ding dongs, My pairs of dear indentures, kings of clubs.

ding-dong (ˈdɪŋˈdɒŋ), *adv.*, *sb.* and *a.* [Echoic.]

A. *adv.*, or without grammatical construction.

1. An imitation of the sound of a bell.

c **1560** T. RYCHARDES *Misogonus* in Collier *Hist. Dram. Poetry* (1879) II. 376 [In the midst of his play he hears the] 'saunce bell goe ding dong'. **1610** SHAKS. *Temp.* I. ii. 403 Full fadom fiue thy Father lies..Sea-Nimphs hourly ring his knell. (Burthen: ding dong) Harke now I heare them, ding-dong bell. **1675** DRYDEN *Mistaken Husb.* I. ii, The Gold in his Pocket Chimes ding dong. **1844** DICKENS *Christm. Carol* v, Clash, clang, hammer; ding, dong, bell. Bell, dong, ding. *a* **1882** ROSSETTI *Wks.* (1890) II. 343 And bells say ding to bells that answer dong.

2. 'Hammering away' at a subject; in good earnest, with a will.

1672 R. WILD *Poet Licen.* 29 Their learned men will write Ding-dong. **1680** OTWAY *Caius Marius* III. ii, They are at it ding dong. **1719** D'URFEY *Pills* (1872) VI. 361 We rallied the Church militant, And fell to work ding-dong, Sir. **1825** MISS MITFORD in L'Estrange *Life* (1870) II. 207, I shall set to work at the 'Heiress' ding-dong. **1888** ELWORTHY *W. Somerset Word-bk., Ding-dong*, in good earnest, with a will ..We in to it ding-dong, hammer and tongs.

B. *sb.*

1. a. The sound of a bell, a repeated ringing sound; a jingle of rime in verse or song; also a bell or other instrument that makes a ringing sound.

c **1560** T. RYCHARDES *Misogonus* in Collier *Hist. Dram. Poetry* (1879) II. 375 [The old gentleman pulls the points off his own hose to give them as a reward to Cacurgus, who calls them 'ding-dongs', and rejoices that some of them have 'golden noses'.] **1611** COTGR., *Dindan*, the ding-dong, or ringing out of bells. **1709** *Brit. Apollo* II. No. 70. 3/2 Her Sing-Songs..sound as well as Country Ding-Dongs. *a* **1845** HOOD *Pair'd not Match'd* ix, If the bell Would ring her knell, I'd make a gay ding-dong of it. **1854** EMERSON *Lett. & Soc. Aims, Poet. & Imag.* Wks. (Bohn) III. 158 Who would hold the order of the almanac so fast but for the ding-dong, 'Thirty days hath September, etc.'? *Ibid.* 160 They do not longer value rattles and ding-dongs, or barbaric word-jingle.

b. *fig.* Esp. (*a*) a heated argument; a quarrel; 'cut and thrust'; (*b*) a tumultuous party or gathering. *colloq.*

1922 JOYCE *Ulysses* 266 Yes, she was back. To the old dingdong again. **1928** *Manch. Guardian Weekly* 19 Oct. 301/1 Accustomed to cut a good figure in the ding-dong of public argument. **1933** H. BELLOC *Charles I* 351 A ding-dong of assertion and counter-assertion. **1935** G. INGRAM *Cockney Cavalcade* ix. 142 I've been having a ding-dong with my old man. **1936** N. COWARD *Hands across Sea* in *To-Night at 8.30* II. 18 Are you going to Nina's Indian ding-dong? **1956** 'J. WYNDHAM' *Seeds of Time* 84 You can't have a proper ding-dong with those quiet ones. **1961** ASHLEY SMITH *East-Enders* vi. 93 The sons and daughters..coming up for a ding-dong which went on till far into the night.

2. *Horology.* An arrangement for indicating the quarters of the hour by the striking of two bells of different tones. Also *attrib.*

1822 SCOTT *Nigel* i, O! St. Dunstan has caught his eye.. he stands astonished as old Adam and Eve ply their ding-dong. **1860** E. B. DENISON *Clocks & Watches* (1867) 170 When there are more than 2 bells the hammers are worked by a chime barrel, because the chimes are not generally the same thing repeated, as they are with ding dong quarters. *Ibid.* 171 This may be..made to indicate half quarters..at about 50 min. past the hour..the clock would strike 3 ding dongs and one bell more.

3. A term of endearment; = DING-DING, q.v.

C. *adj.* (attrib. use.)

1. Of or pertaining to the sound of bells or the jingle of rime.

ding-dong theory, in Science of Lang., a humorous name for the theory which refers the primitive elements of language to phonetic expression naturally given to a conception as it thrilled for the first time through the brain, the utterance thus called forth being compared to the sound naturally emitted by a sonorous body when struck.

1792 SOUTHEY *Lett.* (1856) I. 9 You complain of the bells at Portslade, dingdong spot. **1820** —— *Devil's Walk* 39 In ding dong chime of sing-song rhyme. **1872** A. J. ELLIS *Presid. Addr. to Philol. Soc.* 10 Take the three principal theories, irreverently termed *Pooh-pooh! Bow-wow!* and *Ding-dong!* *Ibid.* 13 The Ding-dong theory has, so far as I know, received no other name; let us call it *symphonesis.* **1880** D. ASHER tr. *L. Geiger's Hist. Hum. Race* 28 It has in England been called the ding-dong theory.

2. Characterized by a rapid succession or alternation of blows or vigorous strokes; vigorously maintained, downright, desperate. ***ding-dong race***: a neck-and-neck race.

1864 *Daily Tel.* 7 Dec., A ding-dong race ensued for the remainder of the distance. **1870** *Daily News* 7 Dec., Could they hold the place under such a ding-dong pelting? **1879** *Pall Mall Budget* 17 Oct. 22 To read the..story of that ding-dong fighting. **1883** W. E. NORRIS *No New Thing* III. xxxv. 224 If it came to a regular ding-dong tussle between us. **1883** E. PENNELL-ELMHIRST *Cream Leicestersh.* 333 By help of example and ding-dong determination.

3. *dial.* 'Great, startling, extraordinary.'

1887 *S. Cheshire Gloss.* s.v., I've gotten a job..the wages bin nothin' very ding-dong.

D. *Comb.* **ding-dong-ˈdoggedly** *adv.* (*nonce-wd.*), with vigorous and dogged repetition of effort.

1870 DICKENS *Lett.* (1880) II. 439, I have been most perservingly and ding-dong-doggedly at work.

ˈding-ˈdong, *v.* [Echoic: cf. prec. sb.]

1. *intr.* To ring as a bell, or like a bell; also *fig.* in reference to peristent or monotonous repetition.

1659 TORRIANO, *Tintillare*, to jangle, to gingle, to ding-dong, or ring shrill and sharp, as some bells do. **1837** CARLYLE *Fr. Rev.* II. IV. i, But hark..the tocsin begins ding-dong-ing. *a* **1845** BARHAM *Ingol. Leg., Knight & Lady*, First dinner bell rang out its euphonious clang At five..and the last Ding-donged..at half-past. **1890** *Daily News* 2 Jan. 5/3 She rarely takes up a new song..year by year she 'ding-dongs at the same old ditties'. **1891** G. MEREDITH *One of our Conq.* (1892) 136 You could have hammer-nailed and ding-donged to your heart's content.

2. *trans.* To assail with constant repetition of words. **b.** To repeat with mechanical regularity.

1797 T. PARK *Sonnets* 85 Honest Ned Whose jealous wife ding-dongs him. **1854** W. WATERWORTH *Eng. & Rome* 173 Some men..dare to ding dong in our ears the words.

dinge (dɪndʒ), *sb.*[1] Also 7 dindge. [See DINGE *v.*[1]]

A broadish dint or depression on a surface caused by a knock or blow; a slight hollow or indentation.

1611 COTGR., *Bosselure*, a bruise, dindge, or dint, in a peece of plate, or mettall. **1844** BAMFORD *Life of Radical* 42 His hat was napless, with..dinges on the crown. **1862** MRS. RIDDELL *World in Church* xvii. (1865) 189 In my keeping your pride shall not even get a dinge. **1884** *Cheshire Gloss., Dinge*, an indentation. **1894** *Times* 27 Oct. 8/1 The paint only is scratched, and there is not a dent or dinge anywhere else.

dinge (dɪndʒ), *sb.*[2] [f. DINGE *v.*[2], or back-formation from DINGY *a.*] Dinginess.

1846 E. D. BANCROFT *Let.* 2 Nov. (1904) 12, I cannot get accustomed to the London dinge. **1854** THACKERAY *Newcomes* xxxv, A noble dinge, a venerable mouldy splendour. **1860** —— *Round. Papers* (1863) 117 The dinge and wrinkles of their wretched old cotton stockings. **1916** GALSWORTHY *Five Tales* (1918) 249 His mood threw a dinge even over the children. **1968** J. R. ACKERLEY *My Father & Myself* xvi. 182 The dust and dinge of the cluttered house.

dinge (dɪndʒ), *sb.*^{3} *U.S. slang.* Also **dingy.** [f. DINGY *a.*] A derogatory term for a Negro. Also *attrib.* or as *adj.*, esp. with reference to a jazz style developed by Negro musicians. (See also quot. 1942.)

1848 *Ladies' Repository* Oct. 316/1 *Covess dinge*, a negress, sometimes called *dinge blowen*... *Dinge kinch*, a negro child... *Dinge*, a negro man. **1904** in 'No. 1500' *Life in Sing Sing* xiii. 247. **1909** 'O. HENRY' *Roads of Destiny* 134 These dingies will cheat you out of the gold in your teeth if you don't understand their ways. **1933** E. HEMINGWAY *Winner take Nothing* 43 That big dinge took him by surprise.. the big black bastard. **1940** R. CHANDLER *Farewell, my Lovely* i. 9 'A dinge,' he said. 'I just thrown him out.' *Ibid.* 10 'You say this here is a dinge joint?'.. 'I told you it's a coloured joint.' **1942** BERREY & VAN DEN BARK *Amer. Thes. Slang* §32/8 *Dinge*, of negroes, dark or dusky in colour, dingy. *Ibid.* §385/14 Negro,.. *dinge, dingy. Ibid.* §576/2 *Dinge*,.. a negro musician. *Ibid.* §579/1 *Dinge*, 'Negro vibrato' played with a very rapid, violent shake. **1958** V. BELLERBY in P. Gammond *Decca Bk. Jazz* xvii. 205 The 'dinge' piano trill, deriving from the efforts of the early Negro instrumentalists to sing through their instruments, instinctively holding the rich overtones of Negro speech. **1969** A. HUNTER *Gently Coloured* i. 4 A big buck nigger. A dinge. A spade. *Ibid.* 8 A dinge bit. It has to be.

dinge, *v.*^{1} Also 7 dindge. [app. a northern dialect word, of recent appearance in literature; origin uncertain.

Possibly representing an earlier *denge from ON. *dęngja* to hammer, bang, beat: see DING *v.*, and cf. *singe* from OE. *sęngan*:—*sangjan*. But later onomatopœic origin from *dint* seems also possible.]

trans. To make a broadish hollow or depression in the surface of (anything), as by a knock; to dint, bruise, batter.

1611 COTGR., *Bosseler*, to dindge, or bruise, to make a dint in vessell of mettall, or in a peece of plate. **1869** *Lonsdale Gloss.*, *Dinge*, to dint, to bruise, to make a hollow. **1871** *Daily News* 21 Sept., Its brass scabbard is dinged and bent in two or three places. **1888** *Sheffield Gloss.*, *Dinge*, to indent, to bruise. (It rhymes with *hinge*.)

Hence **dinged** (dɪndʒd) *ppl. a.*; **dinged work**, repoussé work in metal.

1874 KNIGHT *Dict. Mech.*, *Dinged-work*, work embossed by blows which depress one surface and raise the other. **1885** FITZPATRICK *Life T. N. Burke* I. 239 A heavy long-tailed coat and a dinged high hat.

dinge, *v.*^{2} *dial.* or *rare colloq.* [Belongs to DINGY *a.*] *trans.* To make dingy.

1823 LAMB *Elia* Ser. II. *Amicus Rediv.*, A suit, originally of a sad brown, but which.. has been dinged into a true professional sable. **1883** *Chamb. Jrnl.* 525 'My cabin is rather dinged' was the apology of the oyster dredger as he ushered me into his yawl. **1891** *Rutland Gloss.*, s.v., It dinges (or ? dingies) my hands sitting in the house.

dinged *ppl. a.*^{1}: see DING *v.*^{1} 6.

dinged (dɪndʒd), *ppl. a.*^{2}: see DINGE *v.*^{1}

dingee. *nonce-wd.* [f. DINGHY: cf. BARGEE.] One of the crew of a dinghy.

1836 E. HOWARD *R. Reefer* xxxiv, I ordered the *dingees* to be piped away.

†**dinger**^{1}. *Obs.* ? = DING *sb.*^{3}

1533 J. KENE in Weaver *Wells Wills* (1890) 40, Ij candelstyks of latyn, vj dyngers of pewter.

dinger^{2} ('dɪŋə(r)). *dial.* and *slang* (orig. and chiefly *U.S.*). [f. DING *v.*^{1} 3.] Something superlative; a 'humdinger'.

1809 *Amer. Mag.* Nov. 1 This land of our dads.. is a dinger at nailing the scads. **1892** *Leeds Merc. Suppl.* 22 Oct. 8/8 *Dinger*, anything of a superlative character, as in size, quality, &c. 'It's a dinger.' **1904** *Topeka* (Kan.) *Daily Capital* 1 June 4 The alfalfa crop this year is going to be a 'dinger'. **1939** STEINBECK *Grapes of Wrath* iv. 37 See how good the corn come along until the dust got up. Been a dinger of a crop.

dinghy ('dɪŋgɪ). Also 9 **dingy, dingee, dinghee, dingey.** [a. Hindī *ḍēngī* or *ḍingī* small boat, wherry-boat, dim. of *ḍēngā, ḍōngā*, a larger boat, sloop, coasting vessel. The spelling with *h* in Eng. is to indicate the hard *g*.]

1. Originally, a native rowing-boat in use upon Indian rivers; of various sizes and shapes, resembling sometimes a canoe, sometimes a wherry. In the West of India applied to a small sailing-boat used on the coast.

[**1794** *Rigging & Seamanship* I. 242 *Dingas* are vessels used at Bombay.. and are navigated sometimes by rowing with paddles. They have one mast.. which rakes much forward. On the mast is hoisted a sail.. resembling a settee-sail.] **1810** T. WILLIAMSON *E. Ind. Vade Mecum* II. 159 (Y.) On these larger pieces of water there are usually canoes, or dingies. **1832** MUNDY *Pen & Pencil Sk. Ind.* II. 148 A little dinghee, or Ganges wherry. **1835** BURNES *Trav. Bokhara* (ed. 2) I. 15 We were met by several 'dingies' full of armed men. **1845** STOCQUELER *Handbk. Brit. India* (1854) 185 Wherries, or dinghees, manned by two rowers and a steersman, are to be found in numbers at all the wharfs. **1851** *Great Exhib. Offic. Cat.* II. 909 The Dingee or Bumboat of Bombay, is a small boat, from 12 to 20 feet in length .. with a raking mast, and a yard the same length as the boat. *Ibid.* 910 Cutch Dingee. These vessels are from 30 to 50 feet in length.. some of them are decked wholly, others only abaft the mizen mast, and a small part forward. **1879** F. POLLOK *Sport Brit. Burmah* I. 19 We set out on our hopeless task in a small dinghy.

2. Hence extended to small rowing-boats (and, subsequently, small motor-driven boats) used elsewhere: *spec.* **a.** 'a small extra boat in men-of-war and merchant ships' (Smyth *Sailor's Word-bk.*); also, the boat or 'tender' of a yacht, steam-launch, or similar craft; **b.** a small pleasure rowing-boat; usually on the Thames, a small light skiff, clinker-built, for one, sometimes two, pair of sculls, and with or without outriggers.

1818 'A. BURTON' *Adv. J. Newcome* iii. 176 The coofs hae stown awa the dingey. **1836** MARRYAT *Midsh. Easy* xi, Jump up here and lower down the dingey. **1845** DARWIN *Voy. Nat.* viii. (1879) 169 Mr. Chaffers took the dingey and went up two or three miles further. **1873** *Daily News* 16 Aug., Credit must.. be given to the scullers for even venturing out in their little dingies in such rough water. **1882** NARES *Seamanship* (ed. 6) 147 A dingy is.. useful for landing the men. **1884** *Illustr. Lond. News* 20 Sept. 268/3 They had but just time to get into the dinghy, a boat 13 ft. long and 4 ft. wide.. in which they drifted nearly a thousand miles across the Atlantic. **1885** *Act 48–9 Vict.* c. 76 §29 The term 'vessel' shall include any.. boat, randan, wherry, skiff, dingey, shallop, punt, canoe, raft, or other craft. **1932** T. E. LAWRENCE *Lett.* (1938) 757 Our two Squadrons both sent us their dinghies, asking us to check the timing and tune them. **1935** *Ibid.* 855 We launched the Dinghy: the quietest and sweetest tick-over of any Dinghy yet! **1957** *Encycl. Brit.* XV. 878/2 (*heading*) The Motor Dinghy. This is an open boat.. driven by an engine installed inside.. or, more usually, by an outboard motor.

c. An inflatable rubber boat, esp. one carried on an aircraft for use in an emergency. In full, ***rubber dinghy***.

1939 *War Illustr.* 14 Oct. 156/2 We alighted and, after signalling the men in the boat, blew up our rubber dinghy and pushed it out with a line to each end. **1942** *Jrnl. R. Aeronaut. Soc.* XLVI. 3 When folded the dinghy forms a cushion.. which is strapped to the seat-type parachute. **1958** *Daily Mail* 15 Aug. 2/7 He radioed: 'Can see wreckage of an aircraft. Two tyres floating in sea. Several inflated dinghies on surface.'

3. *Comb.* **dinghy-man.**

1878 D. KEMP *Yacht & Boat Sailing* (1880) 518 Dinghy-man. The man who has charge of the dinghy of a yacht, whose duty it is to go ashore on errands.

dingily ('dɪndʒɪlɪ), *adv.*^{1} [f. DINGY *a.* + -LY^{2}.] In a dingy manner; with a dirty or dull black appearance.

1826 *Lit. Souvenir* 102 This wainscotting.. looks but dingily. **1830** *Fraser's Mag.* I. 757 Trowsers, dimly and dingily seen through the separation of his swallow-tailed coat. **1837** HAWTHORNE *Twice-told T.* (1851) II. xv. 226 Yonder dingily white remnant of a huge snow-bank.

†**dingily**, *adv.*^{2} *Obs. nonce-wd.* [? f. DING *v.*] ? Forcibly, as one that *dings* a thing down.

a **1555** PHILPOT *Exam. & Writ.* (Parker) 370 These.. do confute so dingily the sentence and saying of Floribell.

dinginess ('dɪndʒɪnɪs). [f. DINGY *a.* + -NESS.] The quality or condition of being dingy; disagreeable want of brightness or freshness of colouring.

1818 in TODD. **1824** W. IRVING *T. Trav.* I. 208 Something in.. the dinginess of my dress.. struck the clerks with reverence. **1867** TROLLOPE *Chron. Barset* II. xlv. 10 A certain dinginess of appearance is respectable. **1888** MISS BRADDON *Fatal Three* I. ii, There was not even a flower-box to redeem the dinginess of the outlook.

dingle ('dɪŋg(ə)l), *sb.* [Of uncertain origin. A single example meaning 'deep hollow, abyss' is known in 13th c.; otherwise, the word appears to have been only in dialectal use till the 17th c., when it began to appear in literature. In the same sense *dimble* is known from the 16th c. *Dimble* and *dingle* might be phonetic doublets: cf. *cramble* and *crangle*.] A deep dell or hollow; now usually applied (app. after Milton) to one that is closely wooded or shaded with trees; but, according to Ray and in mod. Yorkshire dialect, the name of a deep narrow cleft between hills.

a **1240** *Sowles Warde* in *Cott. Hom.* 263 His runes ant his domes þe derne beoð ant deopre þen eni sea dingle [= abyss of the sea: cf. Ps. xxxv. 6 *Vulg.* Judicia tua abyssus multa]. **1630** DRAYTON *Muses Elizium* ii. 29 In Dingles deepe, and Mountains hore.. They cumbated the tusky Boare. **1634** MILTON *Comus* 311, I know each lane, and every alley green, Dingle, or bushy dell of this wild wood. **1636** JAMES *Iter Lanc.* 357 Amongst yᵉ Dingles and yᵉ Apennines. **1674** RAY *N.C. Words* 14 *Dingle*, a small clough or valley between two steep hills. **1757** DYER *Fleece* I. 134 Dingles and dells, by lofty fir embow'r'd. **1796** SOUTHEY *Occas. Pieces* v. Poems II. 226 Seek some sequestered dingle's coolest shade. **1810** SCOTT *Lady of L.* III. i. 12 Both field and forest, dingle, cliff, and dell, And solitary heath, the signal knew. **1876** *Whitby Gloss.*, *Dingle*, a cleft or narrow valley between two hills.

Hence '**dingly** *a.*, abounding in dingles, of the nature of a dingle.

1841 HODGSON *Hist. Northmbld.* II. III. 393/2 Stonecroft burn.. joins the dingly channel of the brook. **1855** *Chamb. Jrnl.* III. 260 Sweet dingly dells and bosky bowers.

dingle ('dɪŋg(ə)l), *v.* [In sense 1 app. dim. of DING *v.*^{2}: cf. *tingle, jingle*. But in the other senses mixed up with *dindle* and *tingle*.]

1. *intr.* To ring as a bell, or glass; to tinkle, jingle. Hence '**dingling** *vbl. sb.*

1827 PRAED *Poems* (1865) II. 220 Thus north and south, and east and west, The chimes of Hymen dingle. **1849** *Knife & Fork* 16 Amid the dingling of glasses.

†**2.** *intr.* To ring or tingle, as the ears with sound.

1573–80 BARET *Alv.* D 750 Dingle or dindle: mine eares ring, or dingle, *tiniunt aures*.

3. *intr.* and *trans.* To tingle (with cold, a blow, etc.).

1854 R. H. PATTERSON *Ess. Hist. & Art* (1862) 18 If its particles happen to be set a-vibrating by a sharp dingling blow. **1877** *N.W. Linc. Gloss.*, *Dingle*, to tingle. 'I've nettled mysen, an' my fingers dingles unberable.' **1886** *S.W. Linc. Gloss.* s.v., My arm begins to dingle and feel queer.

4. *intr.* To vibrate with sound; = DINDLE *v.* 2.

1833 SCOTT *Wav.* xliv, 'Garring the very stane-and-lime wa's dingle wi' his screeching.' [So later edd.; *original ed.*, 1814, had *dinnle*, the Scotch form of DINDLE.]

dingle-bird. [f. DINGLE *v.*^{1}] The bell-bird of Australia, *Myzantha melanophrys*.

1870 WILSON *Austral. Songs* 30 The bell-like chimings of the distant dingle-bird. **1883** HARPUR *Poems* 78, I.. list the tinkling of the dingle-bird.

dingle-dangle ('dɪŋg(ə)l'dæŋg(ə)l), *adv.*, *sb.*^{1}, and *a.* [redupl. f. DANGLE. Cf. Icel. and Sw. *dingla* to dangle, Da. *dingle* to dangle, to bob.]

A. *adv.* In a dangling manner; hanging loosely.

1598 FLORIO, *Spendolone*, dingle-dangle, dangling downe. **1611** COTGR., *Triballer*.. to goe dingle dangle, wig wag. **1785** WARTON *Notes on Milton* (T.), By dingle.. he understands boughs hanging dingle-dangle over the edge of the dell.

B. *sb.* A dangling or swinging to and fro; *concr.* a dangling appendage.

1622 MABBE tr. *Aleman's Guzman D'Alf.* II. 240 With as many Bobs and other Dingle-Dangles hanging at every one of these. **1702** VANBRUGH *False Friend* II. i, He'll be hanged: and then what becomes of thee?.. Why, the honour to a dingle-dangle by him. **1855** CAPT. CHAMIER *Journ. France, etc.* I. xi. 173 Rustic Beauties, who.. adorned their hair with silver skewers and with dingle-dangles.

C. *adj.* Hanging loosely and moving to and fro; swinging, dangling.

a **1693** URQUHART *Rabelais* III. 11 (Jam.) This dingle-dangle wagging of my tub. **1746** *Brit. Mag.* 294 This dingle dangle Figure of Gallantry that capers next.

So '**dingle-'dangle** *v.*, to hang loosely dangling or swinging to and fro.

1632 SHERWOOD, To dingle-dangle, *triballer*. **1708** WILSON, etc. tr. *Petronius Arbiter* 46 Purple Tassels and Fringes dingle dangle about it. **1869** *Lonsdale Gloss.*, *Dingle-dangle*, to dangle loosely.. said of pendulous or swinging objects.

'**dingle-'dangle**, *sb.*^{2} *rare*$^{-1}$. [f. DING-DONG: cf. DINGLE *v.*] A dingling or ringing of metal.

1708 MOTTEUX *Rabelais* v. i. (1737) 2 This dingle dangle with Pans, Kettles, and Basons, the Corybantin Cymbals of Cybele.

So '**dingle-'dongle** *v.* [after DING-DONG].

1859 CAPERN *Bal. & Songs* 41 The dinner-bell, the dinner-bell, That dingle dongles through the dell.

dingne, obs. form of DIGNE *a.*, DINE *v.*

dingo ('dɪŋgəʊ), *sb.* [Native Australian name in an obs. dialect of N.S. Wales.

The nearest name in Ridley *Kamilaroi* is *jūnghō* in the (now probably extinct) language of George's River; in the extinct Turuwul of Botany Bay, the name was *jūgūng*.]

1. The wild, or semi-domesticated dog of Australia, *Canis dingo*.

1789 TENCH *Botany Bay* 83 The only domestic animal they [the Aborigines] have is the dog, which in their language is called *Dingo*. **1790** J. HUNTER *App. White's Voy. N.S. Wales* Wks. 1837 IV. 493 A Dingo, or Dog of New South Wales. **1802** G. BARRINGTON *Hist. N.S. Wales* xi. 430 The Dog or Dingo barks in a way peculiar to itself. **1852** MUNDY *Our Antipodes* vi. 153 The dingo, warragal, or native dog does not hunt in packs. **1868** CARLETON *Austral. Nights* 5 The fierce dingo's hideous eye. **1884** *Illustr. Sydney News* 26 Aug. 5/3 The.. sundowners.. are becoming as rare as the dingoes.

2. *Austral. slang.* A contemptuous term for a person: a cheat, scoundrel, traitor, coward.

1928 'BRENT OF BIN BIN' *Up Country* xvi. 182 The bitch has twice the guts of the old dingo. **1941** K. TENNANT *Battlers* viii. 90 The bagmen are a mob of dingoes. **1948** V. PALMER *Golconda* ix. 67 That old she-dingo.. wants us to believe this boy was loosing hell on them. *Ibid.* xxxi. 261 I'd be a hell of a dingo.. if I didn't help you now.

dingo ('dɪŋgəʊ), *v. Austral. slang.* [f. the sb.] **a.** *intr.* To retreat, back out, act in a cowardly or treacherous manner; *to dingo on* (someone) (see quot. 1941). **b.** *trans.* To back out of; to shirk.

1935 *Bulletin* (Sydney) 29 May p. ii/4, I gave him a rather hot time for the first half; in the second round he 'dingoed', letting us through repeatedly, much to his team-mates' disgust. **1941** BAKER *Dict. Austral. Slang* 23 *To dingo on*, to betray, let down, 'rat on' a person. **1952** J. CLEARY *Sundowners* iii. 186 You ain't dingoing it, are you? You can't toss in the towel now.

†**dingthrift** ('dɪŋθrɪft). *Obs.* [f. DING *v.*^{1} + THRIFT.] A spendthrift, a prodigal.

1567 DRANT *Horace' Sat.* i. (R.), Wilte thou therefore, a drunkard be A ding thrift and a knaue? **1579** E. HAKE *Newes Powles Churchyarde* E ij b, That gallowes should such Dingthrifts recompence. **1624** SANDERSON *Serm.* (1632) 494 The Ding-thrifts proverbe is, Lightly come, lightly goe. **1681** W. ROBERTSON *Phraseol. Gen.* (1693) 1160 The spendthrift or dingthrift had spent that money also.

attrib. **1597–8** BP. HALL *Sat.* IV. v. 59 The ding-thrift heire, his shift-got summe mispent.

2. The name of an obsolete game.

1312 in *Mem. Ripon* II. 72 Will. Pistor de Rypon..fuit inventor..cujusdam ludi pestiferi et a jure reprobati, qui in vulgari dicitur Dyngethryftes. [**1887** *Academy* 3 Sept. 147/3.]

Hence **'dingthrifty** *a.*, prodigal, wasteful.

1655 R. YOUNGE *Agst. Drunkards* 3. What may the many millions of these ding-thrifty dearth-makers consume.

dingus ('dɪŋgəs). *colloq.* Also **dinges, dingis,** [f. Du. *ding* thing; cf. DINGBAT.] A gadget, contraption, 'thingummy'.

1876 *Pioche* (Nev.) *Jrnl.* 23 Sept. 3/1 The latest thing in the way of a soul-warmer that the youths of Pioche have got is a dingis made thusly. **1882** G. W. PECK *Peck's Sunshine* 21 They pull out a dingus and three joints of fish-pole come out. **1898** *Empire* 27 Aug. (Pettman), 'Where d'ye find the animile?' 'Animal, Mr. Pike?' 'The dingus—the gentleman who lumbers round in space.' **1913** PETTMAN *Africanderisms, Dinges*, thing, almost universal in its application, things animate and inanimate in Dutch-speaking districts are all of them *dinges* if the speaker fails to recall their names. **1915** S. LEWIS *Trail of Hawk* xxii. 203 That dingus in front is a whirling motor. **1928** *Blackw. Mag.* Jan. 30/1 Even an oiler, sent in an emergency to start such a homely inadequate dingus, can do no more. **1937** ROBINSON & BROWNE *How to be Perfect Husband* 126 To people who have been married for years this dingus should have a powerful appeal. **1939** 'N. BLAKE' *Smiler with Knife* 19 I'll just stick the whole dingus together again.

dingy ('dɪndʒɪ), *a.* [A recent word of obscure orgin: not recognized by Dr. Johnson. Richardson (1837) says '*Dingy* and *dinginess* are common in speech, but not in writing', and gives only quot. 1790 (sense 2). If Pegge's and Ellis's word be the same (which from the ambiguity of the spelling *ng* is uncertain) it would appear to be a south-eastern dialect word which has slowly made its way into literary use.

It has been conjectured to be a deriv. of *dung*, which is favoured by the explanation of sense 1, given by Pegge, and in other dialect glossaries; but the pronunciation should then have been (dɪŋɪ). Also the early quots. for sense 2 appear to refer solely to *colour*.]

1. *dial.* Dirty.

1736 PEGGE *Kenticisms, Dingy*, dirty. **1749** W. ELLIS *Shepherd's Guide* 351 What we, in Hertfordshire, call tagging a sheep..is cutting..away, with a pair of shears, the dingy wool from the hinder parts. **1888** *Berksh. Gloss., Dingey* ('g' soft), coated with dirt.

2. a. Of a (disagreeably) dark and dull colour or appearance; formerly applied to a naturally blackish or dusky brown colour; but now usually implying a dirty colour or aspect due to smoke, grime, dust, weathering, or to deficiency of daylight and freshness of hue; and so of depreciatory connotation.

1751 R. LLOYD *Progress of Error* xxiii, Black was her [Envy's] chariot, drawn by dragons dire..And land their dingy car on Caledonian plain. **1752** SIR J. HILL. *Hist. Anim.* 56 (Jod.) The smoaky and dingy black are easily distinguishable in it. **1790** G. ELLIS tr. *Athelstan's Ode Victory* 27 in *Spec. Eng. Poetry* (T.), On the dingy sea [mistransl. of OE. *on dinges (dynges, dyniges, dinnes) mere*] Over deep waters, Dublin they seek. **1794** SULLIVAN *View Nat.* II. 374 The dingy vault, in whose profundity we were lost. **1796** *Hull Advertiser* 27 Feb. 2/3 The dingy mother [an African woman] rov'd With eager step, and sought her child. **1826** DISRAELI *Viv. Grey* III. vii, Its plumage of a dingy, yellowish white. **1837–9** HALLAM *Hist. Lit.* I. iii. I. §60. 180 Herds of buffaloes, whose dingy hide..contrasted with the greyish hue of the Tuscan oxen. **1854** HAWTHORNE *Eng. Note-bks.* (1879) I. 358 A dim, dingy morning. **1855** MACAULAY *Hist. Eng.* IV. 603 Wretchedly printed on scraps of dingy paper such as would not now be thought good enough for street ballads. **1866** G. MACDONALD *Ann. Q. Neighb.* xiii. (1878) 268 A great faded room, in which the prevailing colour was a dingy gold. **1877** BLACK *Green Past.* xxxv. (1878) 280 His clothes getting dingier..summer by summer. **1884** *Manch. Exam.* 13 May 5/2 More disagreeable than the dingy weather and unlovely streets without.

b. *fig.* Shabby, shady in reputation. Also, 'drab'; dull.

1855 THACKERAY *Newcomes* II. 319 Doing me the honour to introduce me by name to several dingy acquaintances. **1881** H. JAMES *Portr. Lady* xxi, I know plenty of dingy people; I don't want to know any more. **1920** H. G. WELLS *Outl. Hist.* 201 Narrow and dingy-spirited specialists.

c. As an epithet in the vernacular name of certain butterflies and moths.

1832 J. RENNIE *Butterfl. & Moths* 20 The Dingy Skipper ..appears about the end of May and middle of July. *Ibid.* 69 The Dingy (*M[amestra] furva*). *Ibid.* 142 The Dingy Wave ..appears in June. **1876** *Encycl. Brit.* IV. 596 Plate XXIX, *Hesperia tages* (Dingy Skipper). **1907** R. SOUTH *Moths Brit. Isles* I. 181 The Dingy Footman (*Lithosia griseola*). **1908** *Ibid.* II. 8 The Dingy Shears (*Dyschorista fissipuncta*). *Ibid.* 139 Dingy Mocha (*Ephyra orbicularia*). *Ibid.* 219 [The] Dingy Shell..is in the male..sprinkled and shaded with darker brown. **1955** E. B. FORD *Moths* v. 70 The Dingy Footman, *Eilema griseola* Hb...is usually of a light greyish shade. **1970** HIGGINS & RILEY *Butterflies of Britain & Europe* 331 *Erynnis tages* Dingy Skipper.

3. *Comb.*, as ***dingy-looking*** adj.; frequently qualifying colours, as ***dingy white, yellow,*** etc.

1774 STRANGE in *Phil. Trans.* LXV. 40 Angular lapilli..of a dingy-whitish colour. **1838** T. BEALE *Nat. Hist. Sperm Whale* (1839) 377 A crowd of dingy-looking natives. **1875** W. MCILWRAITH *Guide Wigtownshire* 45 The church is a dingy-looking edifice.

dingy, var. of DINGHY.

dingy, var. DINGE *sb.*[3]

dinic ('dɪnɪk), *a.* and *sb. rare*[−0]. [f. Gr. δῖν-ος a whirling + -IC.]

A. *adj.* Relating to dizziness or vertigo. **B.** *sb.* A medicine used to cure dizziness. Also **'dinical** *a.*, in same sense.

[**1706** PHILLIPS (ed. Kersey), *Dinica*, Medicines against Dizziness.] **1721** BAILEY, *Dinicks*, Medicines against the Vertigo or Dizziness in the Head. **1854–67** C. A. HARRIS *Dict. Med. Terminol., Dinical*, medicines which relieve vertigo. **1883** *Syd. Soc. Lex., Dinic*, of, or belonging to, giddiness. Also, applied to medicines that remove giddiness.

dining ('daɪnɪŋ), *vbl. sb.* [f. DINE *v.* + -ING[1].]

1. a. The action of the verb DINE; a dinner.

? a **1400** *Arthur* 142 þere was Vrweyn þe kynge Of scottes at þat dynynge. **1646** CRASHAW *Poems* 212 Whole days and suns devoured with endless dining. *c* **1815** JANE AUSTEN *Persuas.* (1833) I. viii. 268 This was but the beginning of other dinings and other meetings. **1837** CARLYLE *Fr. Rev.* III. III. iii. (1857) II. 227 Dinings with the Girondins.

attrib. **1806** *Syd. Smith Elem. Sk. Mor. Philos.* (1850) 332 Dining and supping virtues. **1831** CARLYLE *Sart. Res.* I. xi, Dining repartees and other ephemeral trivialities.

b. ***dining-out***: dining out of one's own house.

1846 R. FORD *Gatherings from Spain* viii. 84 There we make our home—far from..distant dining-outs, visits, [etc.]. **1861** WILSON & GEIKIE *Mem. E. Forbes* iii. 83 Occasional dinings out and tea-drinkings are recorded. **1877** TYNDALL in *Daily News* 2 Oct. 2/4 Faraday..formally renounced dining out.

2. *Comb.* with sense 'used for dining', as ***dining alcove, area, -cap, chair, -hall, -parlour, -place, recess***; †**dining-bed**, the couch on which the Romans reclined at table (*obs.*); **dining-car, -carriage, -coach**, a railway carriage fitted up for dining on the journey; **dining-chamber** = DINING-ROOM; **dining-coat** *U.S.*, a dinner jacket; **dining-table**, a table for dining at; *spec.* a rectangular table with legs at the four corners, and capable of enlargement by the insertion of leaves.

1937 'M. HILLIS' *Orchids on Budget* (1938) ix. 147 A large living-room with a *dining-alcove. **1961** 'J. WELCOME' *Beware of Midnight* ix. 102 The dining alcove in the kitchen where we were breakfasting. **1957** 'A. VAIL' *Love me Little* xii. 90 He came into the *dining *area* (I hate words like that). **1581** SAVILE *Tacitus' Hist.* I. lxxxii. (1591) 46 Otho standing vpon his *dining bed..at last..refrained their rage. **1599** NASHE *Lenten Stuffe* (1871) 94 An infant squib of the inns of court, that hath not half greased his *dining-cap, or scarce warmed his lawyer's cushion. **1838** *Amer. Railroad Jrnl.* VII. 328 The introduction of *dining cars. **1839** *Mech. Mag.* 5 Jan. 240 (from *Baltimore American*) All that is wanting now is a dining car. **1892** KIPLING *Lett. Travel* (1920) 80 He knows when the train will..drop the dining-car. **1959** *New Statesman* 7 Nov. 610/2 The unofficial strike by railway dining-car workers in protest against the extension of Pullman car services. *a* **1896** *Mod. Advt.*, First and Third Class *Dining Carriages between London and Glasgow. **1911** *Daily Colonist* (Victoria, B.C.) 27 Apr. 20/6 (Advt.), *Dining Chairs,..with shaped head and three slats in back. **1970** *Country Life* 1 Oct. (Suppl.) 34 (Advt.), [A] set of 8 18th century Walnut Dining Chairs of unusual design. **1597** SHAKS. *2 Hen. IV*, II. i. 153 To pawne both my Plate, and the Tapistry of my *dyning Chambers. *a* **1625** FLETCHER *Nice Valour* II. i, What a great space there is Betwixt Love's dining-chamber, and his garret! **1890** *Times* (weekly ed.) 1 Mar. 1/3 A *dining coach and two passenger coaches were.. forced through the structure. **1907** LADY GROVE *Social Fetich* 152 'Tuxedo', '*dining coats', or 'dinner jackets'. **1667** J. LAUDER *Jrnl.* Oct. (1900) 172 The *dining hall, a large roome with a great many tables. **1815** *View N.Y. State Prison* 12 A corresponding room in the south wing is used as a dining-hall. **1870** 'F. FERN' *Ginger-Snaps* 237 Mrs. Fire-Fly..swept into the dining hall in a train about six yards long. **1700** PEPYS *Let.* 22 Feb. (1926) I. 291 Try whether you can recollect enough of my..*dining parlour. **1761** MRS. FR. SHERIDAN *S. Bidulph* II. 317 She asked..why I had not been shewn into the dining-parlour. **1826** MISS MITFORD *Village* Ser. II. (1863) 348 The dining-parlour..might pass for his only sitting room. **1790–1810** WM. COMBE *Devil on 2 Sticks in Eng.* (1817) VI. 258 A *dining party in high life. **1906** M. H. B. SCOTT *Houses & Gardens* iv. 20 The introduction as an appendage to the hall of a *dining recess. **1959** 'M. HALLIDAY' *Thicker than Water* iv. 40 They would eat in the little dining recess in the kitchen; they seldom used the dining-room when they were on their own. **1594** *Wills & Inv. N.C.* (Surtees 1860) 244 [In] the Haull, Towe *dyninge tables. **1875** W. S. HAYWARD *Love agst. World* 2 He took the seat at the foot of the dining-table. **1892** *Daily News* 19 Mar. 7/4 A man used to make anything, but now he is asked whether he is a dining-table maker, a sideboardmaker, and so on.

dining-room ('daɪnɪŋruːm). **1.** The room in a private house or other principal establishment in which dinner and other principal meals are taken, and which is furnished for this purpose.

1601 HOLLAND *Pliny* II. 481 The fashion came vp at Rome, that our dames had their beds couered all ouer with siluer, yea, and some dining rooms with tables laid with the same. **1661** COWLEY *Prop. Adv. Exp. Philos., College*, A large and pleasant Dining-Room within the Hall for the Professors to eat in. **1681** T. JORDAN *London's Joy* in Heath *Grocers' Comp.* (1869) 547 London's the Dining Room of Christendom. **1708** in *Swift's Wks.* (1755) II. I. 163 She.. shows him into the dining-room. **1856** LEVER *Martins of Cro' M.* 129 The dark-wainscoted dining-room, with its noble fireplace of gigantic dimensions.

2. *attrib.* and *Comb.*

1702 S. SEWALL *Diary* in *Coll. Mass. Hist. Soc.* (1879) 5th Ser. VI. 65 Mr. Nehemiah Walter marries Mr. Sam Sewall and Mrs. Rebekah Dudley, in the Dining Room Chamber about 8. **1771** SMOLLETT *Humph. Cl.* I. 53 Mrs. Tabitha's favourite dog Chowder..set upon him at once, and drove him up stairs to the dining-room door. **1788** GROSE *Dict. Vulgar T.* (ed. 2), *Dining room post*, a mode of stealing in houses that let lodgings, by rogues pretending to be postmen, who send up sham letters to the lodgers, and, whilst waiting in the entry for the postage, go into the first room they see open, and rob it. **1828** H. G. LEWIS *Let.* 14 Oct. in J. Constable *Corr.* (1966) IV. 75 The only convenient place to fix the column, will be within the fence, before the old dining room windows. **1883** *Heal & Son Catal.: Dining Room Furnit.* 181 (*caption*) Dining room and library chairs. **1935** A. J. POLLOCK *Underworld Speaks* 31/2 *Dining room furniture*, the teeth. **1977** *Washington Post* 14 Oct. (Weekend Suppl.) 3/1 From his command post—the dining-room table of a Suitland apartment—Dobson, a mere yeoman in the Coast Guard's office of ocean policy, has altered history.

†**dining-time.** The time at which people dine, dinner-time; the time occupied with dinner.

c **1450** LONELICH *Grail* xii. 391 In the ost it was dyneng tyme, Fore it was ny noon, and passed þe pryme. **1633** FORD *'Tis Pity* v. v, Now there's but a dining-time 'Twixt us and our confusion. **1679** SHADWELL *True Widow* I. Wks. 1720 III. 121 Let's take the air, and while away a dining-time.

dinite ('daɪnaɪt). *Min.* [Named 1852 after Prof. Dini.] A yellowish fossil resin found in the lignite of Lunigiana in Tuscany.

1854 DANA *Min.* 475 Deposits large crystals of the dinite. **1863–72** WATTS *Dict. Chem.* II. 334.

dinitro- (daɪ'naɪtrəʊ-). *Chem.* (Before a vowel dinitr-). [f. DI-[2] + NITRO-.]

1. Having two equivalents of the radical NO_2 taking the place of two atoms of hydrogen, as ***dinitrobenzene*** $C_6H_4(NO_2)_2$, ***dinitrophenol*** $C_6H_4(NO_2)_2O$.

1869 ROSCOE *Elem. Chem.* 409 We also know a solid substance called di-nitro-benzol. **1873** *Fownes' Chem.* (ed. 11) 760 Dinitrobenzene is produced by warming benzene with a mixture of nitric and sulphuric acids. **1892** *Pall Mall G.* 17 Oct. 7/2 Aniline colours which are positively poisonous..are picric acid and its salts..dintro-cresol, and aurantia.

2. dinitro-'cellulose, a substance $C_6H_8(NO_2)_2O_5$, analogous to gun-cotton (*trinitro-cellulose*), produced by the action of a mixture of nitric and sulphuric acids on cotton, whereby two of the hydrogen atoms in the cellulose $C_6H_{10}O_5$ are replaced by NO_2. Also called *soluble pyroxylin*: its solution in ether and alcohol forms COLLODION.

dink (dɪŋk), *a.*[1] *Sc.* and *north. dial.* [Origin unknown.] Finely dressed, decked out; trim.

1508 DUNBAR *Tua Mariit Wem.* 377 Him that dressit me so dink. *? a* **1550** *Freiris of Berwik* 55 (*Dunbar's Poems* (1893) 287) Ane fair blyth wyf he had, of ony ane, Bot scho wes sumthing dynk and dengerous. **1724** RAMSAY *Tea-t. Misc.* (1733) II. 200 As dink as a lady. *a* **1795** BURNS '*My Lady's Gown*', My lady's dink, my lady's drest, The flower and fancy o' the west. **1821** SCOTT *Kenilw.* xxv, The mechanic, in his leather apron, elbowed the dink and dainty dame, his city mistress. **1891** F. O. MORRIS in *Morn. Post* 25 July 3/6 The pied wagtail, running about so nimbly, dink and dainty, over the lawn.

Hence **'dinkly** *adv.*

1788 R. GALLOWAY *Poems* 163 (Jam.) They stand sae dinkly, rank and file. **1871** P. H. WADDELL *Psalm* cxix. 32.

dink, *v. Sc.* [f. DINK *a.*[1]] *trans.* To dress finely, to deck.

1811 A. SCOTT *Poems* 132 (Jam.) In braw leather boots.. I dink me. **1820** SCOTT *Abbot* xx, I am now too old to dink myself as a gallant to grace the bower of dames.

dink (dɪŋk), *sb.*[1] *Austral.* [Origin unknown.] A ride or lift on the bar of a bicycle. Also *v. trans.*, to give (a person) such a lift.

1934 *Bulletin* (Sydney) 5 Sept. 20/2 The fortunate Melbourne schoolkid with a bike..is asked by his cobbers for a 'dink'. **1941** BAKER *Dict. Austral. Slang* 25 *Double-dink*, to carry a second person on the top bar of a bicycle. It is also a noun. Exchangeable terms are 'dink', 'donk', and 'double-bank', both as verbs and nouns. **1948** *Coast to Coast 1947* 135 The lame one who used to let me dink him home on his bicycle.

dink (dɪŋk), *sb.*[2] *U.S.* [Imitative.] A drop-shot in lawn tennis. Also *attrib.* So as *v. intr.* (see quot. 1942).

1939 J. D. BUDGE *On Tennis* 120 Some players resent their opponent's using the drop shot, or the 'dink' shot as they scornfully refer to it. **1942** BERREY & VAN DEN BARK *Amer. Thes. Slang* §717/2 *Dink*, a ball that drops just beyond the net. *Ibid.* §717/3 *Dink*, to barely knock the ball over the net. **1959** *Times* 30 June 3/3 Some delicate touch shots, cross-court and half-court—the dink as the Americans call it. *Ibid.* 1 Sept. 3/3 Drop shots, stop volleys and dinks were conspicuous by their absence. **1969** *New Yorker* 14 June 45/2 Nobody in his right mind, really, would try those little dink shots he tries as often as he does. *Ibid.* 61/2 He will dink. He spins his first serve in more.

dink (dɪŋk), *sb.*[3] *U.S. Mil. slang.* [Origin unknown.] A derogatory or contemptuous term for a Vietnamese person.

1969 *Eugene* (Oregon) *Register-Guard* 3 Dec. 2A/4 He also criticized U.S. military training, which he said permits references to the Vietnamese as 'gooks, dinks, or slopes'. **1970** *Guardian* 30 July 7/5 These are not people... They are dinks and gooks and slant-eyed bastards.

dink, *sb.*[4] and *a.*[2] Abbrev. of DINKUM *sb.* and *a.* *Austral.* (and *N.Z.*) *colloq.*

1906 E. DYSON *Fact'ry 'Ands* viii. 92 'Twasn't fair dink t'go outside ther firm. **1939** W. E. MCKINLAY *Ways & Byways of Singing Kiwi* i. 24 One of the Battalions being known as the 'Square Dinks' and another as the 'Fair Dinks'.

Dinka ('dɪŋkə), *sb.* and *a.* [f. native name *Jieng* people.] **A.** *sb.* A member of a Sudanese people or their language; *collect.*, this people. **B.** *adj.* Of or pertaining to this people.

1861 J. PETHERICK *Egypt, Soudan & Cent. Afr.* xx. 345 The Dinka, an extensive negro tribe, inhabit the eastern interior. *Ibid.* 348 Five Dinka children. *Ibid.* 360 The Djibba speak a different language from the Dinkas. **1873** E. E. FREWER tr. *Schweinfurth's Heart of Africa* II. 501 List of mammalia observed during my travels..with their native names... Dinka: Agohk. Dyoor: Abworro. Bongo: Gumbi. **1900** *Daily News* 27 Feb. 5/7 Four days before reaching Bahr el Jaraf I was attacked by Dinkas. **1926** *Blackw. Mag.* Oct. 561/2 Wol explained in the Dinka dialect the reason and object of my sudden visit. *Ibid.* 562/1 The native Dinka never hurries unless he is being hunted. **1949** E. E. EVANS-PRITCHARD in M. Fortes *Social Structure* 86 The adoption of a Dinka boy. *Ibid.*, Marriages of adopted Dinka into collateral major, and even minor, lineages undoubtedly take place sometimes. **1968** Y. R. CHAO *Language & Symbolic Systems* 99 Dinka and Luo..have almost 1 million speakers each.

dinkel ('dɪŋkəl). [G.] A species of wheat, *Triticum spelta*.

1866 LINDLEY & MOORE *Treas. Bot.* I. 409/2 Dinkel... *Triticum monococcum.* [**1884** tr. *A. de Candolle's Orig. Cultivated Plants* v. 364 European names [for spelt], on the contrary, are numerous... *Spelta* in Saxon, whence the English name, and the French, *épeautre*; *Dinkel* in modern German.] **1921** J. PERCIVAL *Wheat Plant* xxii. 325 Of the wheats with a brittle rachis Common Spelt or Dinkel is the race most extensively grown. *Ibid.* 327 A considerable amount of Dinkel grain is used in South Germany in soups. **1965** R. F. PETERSON *Wheat* i. 14 (*heading*) *Triticum spelta*: spelt or dinkel wheat.

dinki-di, var. DINKY-DI(E *a.*

dinkum ('dɪŋkəm), *sb.* and *a.* *dial.* and *colloq.* (chiefly *Austral.* and *N.Z.*). Also **dincum.** [Origin unknown.] **A.** *sb.* **1.** Work; esp. hard work; a due share of work.

1888 'R. BOLDREWOOD' *Robbery under Arms* v, It took us an hour's hard dinkum to get near the peak. **1891** S. O. ADDY *Suppl. Sheffield Gloss.* 18 'I can stand plenty o' dincum.' This word is used by colliers at Eckington. **1900** WRIGHT *Eng. Dial. Dict.* s.v., You have gotten to do your dinkum, soä you understand. **1941** BAKER *Dict. Austral. Slang.* 23 *Dinkum*, hard work or honest toil.

†**2.** An Australian; spec. an Australian soldier in the war of 1914–18 (see also quot. 1919[2]). *Obs.*

1919 [see AUSSIE *sb.* and *a.* 1]. **1919** DOWNING *Digger Dial.* 19 *Dinkums (the)*, the 2nd Division. Also applied to the New Zealanders.

3. = ***dinkum oil*** (see sense B, and cf. *fair dinkum*).

1916 *Anzac Bk.* 56 A friend met me and asked if I had heard the latest dinkum. **1933** *Bulletin* (Sydney) 22 Feb. 34 First time I have a cert I'll pass the dinkum to you.

B. *adj.* Honest, genuine, real; as *adv.*, honestly. Phr. ***fair*** (or ***square, straight***) ***dinkum***, fair and square, honest; as *advb. phr.*, honestly, genuinely; *interrog.*, really?, is that so? Also ***dinkum oil***, the honest truth, true facts. Cf. *dial.* '*fair dinkum!* fair play' (see quot. 1900).

1894 *Bulletin* (Sydney) 5 May 13/3 'And did yer stouch him back?' 'No.'.. 'Fair dinkum?' 'Yes.' **1895** A. A. GRACE *Maoriland Stories* 105 Well it ain't goin' to be *honest injun*, that's plain; not what I call *square dinkum.* **1900** WRIGHT *Eng. Dial. Dict.* s.v., *Fair dinkum!* fair play! n. Lin[colnshire]. **1906** E. DYSON *Fact'ry 'Ands* vi. 64 'Meanin'?' he pointed to the centre of his breast, and his eyes were round with inquiry. 'Fair dinkum,' telegraphed Linda. **1911** L. STONE *Jonah* I. ix. 106 'I don't run after people I don't want,' said Pinkey, smiling through her tears. 'Fair dinkum?' cried Chook. **1916** *Anzac Bk.* 22/2 'Ere's some er the dinkum coc'nut ice the tart useter make. **1916** C. J. DENNIS *Ginger Mick* 87 That's the dinkum oil frum Ginger Mick. **1919** V. MARSHALL *World of Living Dead* 36 This was the dinkum stuff—straight from one of the heads. **1921** *Spectator* 5 Feb. 169/1 This, as we Australians say, is 'dinkum'. **1922** [see CROSS *v.* 3 b]. **1925** *Spectator* 21 Nov. 930/1 Every 'dinkum Bushman'. **1927** R. REES *Life's what you make It* iii. 177 'What does dinkum mean?' 'You've been in New Zealand for months and months and you don't know what dinkum means? It's good, excellent, superlatively fine, genuine, not faked. That's what dinkum is.' **1927** *Weekly Dispatch* 23 Oct. 2/5 Real dinkum Australians..knew..that wombats can't fly. **1930** A. W. GROOM *Merry Christmas* iii. 21 I'll strike a dinkum business deal with you—fair and square. **1934** *Punch* 24 Oct. 454/3 Indeed I am a bit wounded that you [*sc.* Melbourne] did not invite me to come and open the new century for you. I would have made a dinkum speech for you. **1937** N. MARSH *Vintage Murder* vii. 73 Give you a pain in the neck, dinkum, she would. **1942** C. BARRETT *On Wallaby* iii. 43 Mobs of [goanas], mister. They was twelve foot long. Square dinkum. **1944** F. CLUNE *Red Heart* 42 The Simpson Desert..is the only fair-dinkum desert in Australia. **1944** J. H. FULLARTON *Troop Target* ii. 18 Anyway there's no dinkum oil. Only latrinograms..it may be all hooey. **1957** 'N. SHUTE' *On Beach* iv. 111 He's dinkum, and she's not a bad sort. **1969** *Private Eye* 6 June 14 'Here's fifty pounds down.'.. 'Are you fair dinkum? I can do with the oscar.' **1969** *Sun* (Melbourne) 12 July 58/1 Fair dinkum, North's been waiting so long for its ship to come in, the pier's collapsed.

dinky ('dɪŋkɪ), *a.*[1] and *sb.*[1] *dial.* and *colloq.* (chiefly *Sc.* and *N. Amer.*). Also **dinkey, dinkie.** [f. DINK *a.*] **A.** *adj.* Neat, trim, dainty; small, tiny, trifling.

1788 E. PICKEN *Poems* 230/1 *Dinkie*, neat, handsome. **1858** M. PORTEOUS *Real 'Souter Johnny'*, 29 Ye'll observe yon dinkie pile In your ain cauf-lan'. **1880** MRS. L. PARR *Adam & Eve* xxviii, You must leave me a dinkey little corner to squeeze into by. **1887** *Courier-Journal* (Louisville, Ky.) 1 Feb. 8/4 Jumping on a dinkey train while in motion. **1893** *Columbus* (Ohio) *Dispatch* 8 Apr., The British Artillerymen wore little dinky caps with a yellow band. **1896** ADE *Artie* xvii. 154 I'll come hot-footin' in here with my knee-pants and a dinky coat. **1904** 'O. HENRY' *Cabbages & Kings* x. 169 A train of cars was waitin' for us on a dinky little railroad. **1905** E. PHILLPOTTS *Secret Woman* I. i. 16 You're all angel yourself—all, to the dinky dimple there at the corner of your li'l mouth. **1915** *Punch* 20 Jan. 49, I shall have a couple of the dinkiest little wounded subs to show you. **1917** 'CONTACT' *Airman's Outings* 224 Winkle, the dinky Persian with a penchant for high life, has presented the family with five kittens. **1929** D. COKE *Monkey Tree* xvi, Miss Des Vaux asserted her superiority by saying that it was a 'dinky notion'. **1960** K. M. WELLS *Cruising North Channel* 24 You will need a stove of sorts, something better than the dinky little two-burner alcohol contraption with which so many so-called cruising ships are fitted.

B. *sb.* Any small object or contrivance; *spec.* a small boat (perhaps a corrupt form of DINGHY) or a small locomotive. Chiefly *U.S.* (in spelling *dinkey*).

1849 *Pacific News* (S.F.) 27 Nov. 4/2 Picked up adrift, in San Pablo bay, a small copper Dinkey. **1874** *Kalama* (Wash.) *Beacon* 20 Jan. 4/2 The passenger train from Tacoma..passed the Des Chuttes bridge..an hour or two previous to the 'dinkey'. **1905** *Terms Forestry & Logging*, *Dinkey*, a small logging locomotive. **1905** G. S. WASSON *Green Shay* 195 They'll make out to cast loose their dinky all right. **1948** *Milwaukee Jrnl.* 18 July 6/3 The huffing and puffing steam dinkeys..still see service when traffic is heavy.

dinky, *a.*[2] and *sb.*[2] = DINKUM *a.* and *sb.* *Austral.* (and *N.Z.*) *slang.*

1941 BAKER *Dict. Austral. Slang* 23 *The dinky*, the truth. Also adj., *dinky*, true.

Dinky ('dɪŋkɪ), *sb.*[3] Also **dinky.** [Cf. DINKY *a.*[1] and *sb.*[1]] A proprietary name for a make of toy model motor vehicles, etc., esp. as ***Dinky car, toy.*** (No longer trading.)

1950 *Trade Marks Jrnl.* 5 July 624/2 *Dinky toys*... Toy models. Meccano Limited, 236, Binns Road, Liverpool, 13; Toy Manufacturers. **1957** *Economist* 28 Dec. 1111/2 As they [*sc.* children] often seem to bring back the same toy from each party—most usually, a surplus dinky car. **1966** N. FREELING *King of Rainy Country* 45 That brand new Porsche means about as much to a fellow like this as a Dinky toy. **1977** *Private Eye* 1 Apr. 20/2 (Advt.), Collector wishes to purchase Dinky toys. **1982** *Sunday Times* 13 June 49/4 American foods group General Mills bought Airfix and its Meccano, Great Model Railway and Dinky lines. **1982** *Economist* 3 July 30/3 Much of that ocean is even more dangerous than the South Atlantic: within reach of Russian land-based aircraft (which can carry sea-skimming missiles that make Exocet look like a Dinky toy).

dinky-di(e ('dɪŋkɪ'daɪ), *a.* *Austral.* and *N.Z.* *slang.* Also **dinki-di.** [f. DINKUM *a.*] = DINKUM *a.*

1918 N. CAMPBELL (*title*) The Dinky-di soldier and other jingles. **1928** A. WAUGH *Last Chukka* 84 That was absolutely dinky die, my dear. **1938** P. LAWLOR *House of Templemore* xviii. 194 'Dinky die?' asked Percy Andrews. **1952** J. CLEARY *Sundowners* ii. 104 We're in for a dinky-di storm. **1956** S. HOPE *Diggers' Paradise* 237 No one but dinky-di Aussies need submit a manuscript. **1969** *Australian* 24 May 18/3 Sinister karate chopping Japanese battling with true-blue, dinki-di locals.

dinmont ('dɪnmənt). *Sc.* and *north. dial.* Forms: 5 **dymmond,** 6 **dilmond, dynmonthe,** 9 **dinman, dinment, dimment, dinmond, dynmont,** 6– **dinmont.** [Etymology obscure: the second syllable looks like 'month' as in *towmont* twelvemonth, but the first is unexplained.] The name given in Scotland, and the Border counties of England, to a wether between the first and second shearing.

1424 *Sc. Acts Jas. I* (1814) 4 (Jam.) Item, Gymmer, Dynmont, or Gaitis, ilk ane to xiid. **1494** *Act. Dom. Conc.* 353 (Jam.) Vij^{xx} of gymmeris and dymmondis. **1542** *Wills & Inv. N.C.* (Surtees 1835) 119, I yeue vnto saynt cuthb'te guild a dynmonthe or ellis the price. **1549** *Compl. Scot.* vi. 66 The laif of ther fat flokkis follouit..gylmyrs and dilmondis. **1584** *Vestry Bks.* (Surtees) 18 Item at Shaudforthe a weather, a yowe, a dinmont, and ij lams. **1791–2** *Statist. Acc. Berw.* III. 155 (Jam.) When they are 18 months old, after the first fleece is taken off..they are called dimmotts. **1814** SCOTT *Wav.* xi, Killancureit talked..of top-dressing and bottom-dressing, and year-olds, and gimmers, and dinmonts. **1892** *Northumbld. Gloss.* 236 A lamb is called a hog in autumn, and after the first shearing of the new year, a dinmont if it be a male sheep, and a gimmer if an ewe.

dinna, Sc. for *do not*: see DO *v.*

dinnage, obs. f. DUNNAGE, material used for packing on shipboard.

dinned (dɪnd), *ppl. a.* *rare.* [f. DIN *v.* + -ED[1].] Assailed or disturbed with din: see DIN *v.*

1820 KEATS *Hyperion* II. 128 When other harmonies.. Leave the dinn'd air vibrating silverly.

dinnel(l, Sc. form of DINDLE *v.*

dinner ('dɪnə(r)), *sb.* Forms: 3–6 **diner, dyner,** 4–5 **dinere, dener,** 4–7 **dynere,** 5 **dynnere, dyneer,** 6 **denere, dynar, dynnor, dynner** (*Sc.* **dennar, denner**), 6– **dinner.** [ME. *diner*, a. F. *dîner* (11th c. in Hatz.-Darm.), subst. use of pres. inf. *dîner* to DINE.]

1. a. The chief meal of the day, eaten originally, and still by the majority of people, about the middle of the day (cf. Ger. *Mittagsessen*), but now, by the professional and fashionable classes, usually in the evening; particularly, a formally arranged meal of various courses; a repast given publicly in honour of some one, or to celebrate some event.

1297 R. GLOUC. (1724) 558 Þulke to diners deluol were, alas! *a* **1300** *Cursor M.* 3508 His fader..Oft he fed wit gode dinere. **1393** LANGL. *P. Pl.* C. v. 38 Thei wolde don for a dyner..More þan for oure lordes loue. **1432–50** tr. *Higden* (Rolls) V. 459 Syttenge with Oswaldus the Kynge at dyner [= *in mensa*]. *a* **1450** *Knt. de la Tour* (1868) 26 Whos wiff that obeiethe worst, lete her husbonde paie for the dener. **1553** ASCHAM in *Lett. Lit. Men* (Camden) 14 Dynnor and supper he had me comonlie with him. **1557** W. TOWRSON in Hakluyt *Voy.* (1589) 116, I had the Captaine of the towne to dinner. **1563** WINȜET *Four Scoir Thre Quest.* xviii. Wks. 1888 I. 84 Quhy mak ȝe ȝour communioun afoir dennar, sen our Saluiour institutet His haly sacrament efter suppare? **1581** J. BELL *Haddon's Answ. Osor.* 458 As he sate in the house of Simon at Dyner. **1606** BRYSKETT *Civ. Life* 97 After dinner a man should sit a while, and after supper walk a mile. **1620** VENNER *Via Recta* viii. 173 Our vsuall time for dinner ..is about eleuen of the clocke. **1712** HEARNE *Collect.* (Oxf. Hist. Soc.) III. 372 At eleven Clock this Day, I being then at Dinner in Edmund Hall Buttery. **1718** LADY M. W. MONTAGU, *Let. to C'tess. Mar* 10 Mar., She gave me a dinner of fifty dishes of meat. **1856** EMERSON *Eng. Traits*, Wks. (Bohn) II. 50 In an aristocratical country like England, not the Trial by Jury, but the dinner, is the capital institution.

†**b.** ***to seek his dinner with duke Humphrey***: see DINE *v.* 1 b.

c. In colloq. phr. ***to have had more*** (..) ***than*** (another) ***has had hot dinners***, and varr.: used jocularly to emphasize the subject's wide experience of a particular activity or phenomenon.

1961 H. S. TURNER *Something Extraordinary* iv. 89 The general theory is that they *are* tarts; and one of them—of whom he says 'she's been done more times than I've had hot dinners'—quite possibly is. **1965** J. OSBORNE *Inadmissible Evidence* I. 31 She looks as though she could do with a bit. She's got the galloping cutes all right. Joy. *She's* had more joy sticks than hot dinners. **1976** *Daily Mirror* 17 Mar. 23/3 Mr. Essex has been subjected to more 'East End wonderboy' rubbishings than he has had hot dinners.

2. *attrib.* and *Comb.*, as ***dinner-bag, -basket, -book, -club, -company, -course, -doctrine, -dress, -furniture, -giver, -gong, -gown, -guest, -meal, -money, -napkin, -plate, -pot, -roll, -room, -service, -tea, -ware, -wine; dinner-giving, -like*** adjs.; **dinner-bucket** *U.S.* = *dinner-pail*; **dinner-call** *U.S.*, a formal call upon one's host or hostess after a dinner party; **dinner-card,** (*a*) a card bearing an invitation to dinner (*Obs.*); (*b*) a card bearing a name and indicating a person's place at a dinner-table; **dinner-coat,** a dinner jacket; hence ***dinner-coated*** adj.; **dinner-dance,** a dinner followed by dancing; hence ***dinner-dancing*** vbl. sb.; **dinner-horn** *U.S.*, a horn used to announce dinner on a farm, etc.; **dinner-hour,** the hour at which dinner is taken, the hour or time occupied by dinner; **dinner jacket,** a dress-coat without tails worn in the evening as a less formal alternative to the swallow-tailed coat; hence ***dinner-jacketed*** adj.; **dinner lady,** a woman who works part-time in a school, supervising children during the midday meal and in the playground; **dinner-pail** *U.S.*, a pail in which a workman carries his dinner with him; hence in slang phr. ***to hand, pass,*** or ***turn in one's dinner-pail,*** to die; **dinner-pair,** the pairing of two members of parliament of opposite parties during the dinner-hour: see PAIR; **dinner-party,** a party of guests invited to dinner; the social gathering which they compose; **dinner-set,** a set of plates and other ware of the same pattern for the dinner table; **dinner speech** *U.S.*, an after-dinner speech; so ***dinner-speaking*** vbl. sb.; **dinner-table,** the table at which dinner is eaten, and round which a party of guests sit; **dinner theatre** *U.S.*, a theatre at which the price of a ticket includes a meal followed by the play or show; **dinner-wagon,** a tray with shelves beneath, supported by four legs, usually on castors, so as to be easily moved, for the service of a dining-room.

1885 T. HARDY *Mayor Casterbr.* i, His hoe on his shoulder, and his *dinner-bag suspended from it. **1821–8** D. WORDSWORTH *Tour on Continent* in *Jrnls.* (1941) II. 318 The mother..hastening to her *dinner-basket, chearfully presented me with her whole stock. **1939** F. THOMPSON *Lark Rise* i. 15 The leazer's water-can and dinner-basket. **1854** W. WATERWORTH *Orig. Anglicanism* 134 This contradiction of belief and practice, of prayer-book and *dinner-book, has long been censured. **1901** *Scribner's Mag.* XXIX. 404/2 Billy put on his coat, took his *dinner-bucket. **1895** J. L. WILLIAMS *Princeton Stories* 263 It's two years now, and it's not good form to let a *dinner call go more than two years in Princeton. **1754** *Connoisseur* 2 May 80, I received..a *dinner-card from a friend, with an intimation that I should meet some very agreeable ladies. **1865** DICKENS *Mut. Fr.* II. III. xvii. 152 Mrs. Veneering..sends them every one a dinner-card. **1881** C. C. HARRISON *Woman's Handiwork* II. 125 Designs for dinner cards for Thanksgiving or Christmas. **1905** E. WHARTON *House of Mirth* I. iv. 60 There would be notes and dinner-cards to write. **1907** M. C. HARRIS *Tents of Wickedness* I. iii. 35 His dinner-card lay on the side of the cloth next her, and she.. glanced at it. 'Mr. Paul Fairfax'—so that was his name. **1836–48** B. D. WALSH *Aristoph., Acharnians* II. vi, Involved by *dinner-clubs and debts. **1922** F. SCOTT FITZGERALD *Let.* 31 Jan. (1964) 153 He looks like a sawed-off young tough in his first *dinner-coat. **1929** YEATS *Let.* 2 Mar. (1954) VI. 758 To-night we dine with Ezra—the first *dinner-coated meal since I got here. **1816** JANE AUSTEN *Emma* II. vii. 119 Their love of society..prepared every body for their keeping *dinner-company. **1901** *Lady's Realm* X. 613/1 From one *dinner-dance to the next. **1910** *Westm. Gaz.* 15 Apr. 5/2 A dinner-dance—quite a small affair. *c* **1430** LYDG. in Turner *Dom. Archit.* III. 81 The *dynere coursis eke at euery feste. **1965** *Observer* Suppl. 18 Apr. 46/1 *Dinner-dancing after 11.30. **1649** MILTON *Eikon.* xix. Wks. (1847) 320/1 Far holier and wiser men than parasitic preachers; who, without their *dinner-doctrine, know that neither king, law, civil oaths, or religion, was ever established without the parliament. **1815** *Belle Assemblée* July 274/1 Round dress.. made to answer the double purpose of a morning or *dinner-dress. **1897** M. CORELLI *Ziska* xiii. 262 The Princess herself, attired in a dinner-dress made with quite a modern Parisian elegance. **1956** J. D. CARR *P. Butler for Defence* vi. 62 Helen, in her dark-blue dinner-dress, stood in the doorway. **1865** DICKENS *Mut. Fr.* I. ii, An innocent piece of *dinner-furniture that went upon easy castors. **1864** BURTON *Scot Abr.* I. iii. 109 The one keeps a *dinner-giving house, the other does not. **1838** *Knickerbocker* XII. 227 How startling is the sound of the *dinner-gong! **1922** D. H. LAWRENCE *Aaron's Rod* xiv. 200 He did not notice the dinner-gong, and only the arrival of the chamber-maid..sent him down to the restaurant. **1891** *Truth* 10 Dec. 1240/2 Ecstasies of admiration over a superb *dinner-gown. **1811** L. M. HAWKINS *Countess* I. xiv. 240 Mr. Sydenham, his son, and his charge, were to be *dinner-guests. **1965** F. SARGESON *Memoirs of Peon* vii. 207 It was upon dinner-guest occasions that my gastropodous writhings were dispensed with. **1835** C. GILMAN in *Southern Rose* 5 Sept. 2/1 The business was scarcely settled, when the *dinner-horn sounded. **1849** *Congress. Globe* 10 Jan. App. 80/2 The dinner horn will be heard across broad fields, and will be answered by the keen appetites attendant upon honest labor. **1867** 'T. LACKLAND' *Homespun* III. 290 From that time until the dinner-horn sounds, no tented field..ever furnished a busier..spectacle. **1800** *Spirit Publ. Journals* (1801) IV. 160 You step to a friend's house on business, near his *dinner-hour. **1892** *Pall Mall G.* 5 Apr. 3/2 That period of the evening—from seven to ten—which in parliamentary phrase is called the 'dinner hour'. **1891** M. E. BRADDON *Gerard* III. vii. 208 Jermyn took up the loose pages, folded them carefully, put them in an inner pocket of his *dinner jacket. **1894** *To-day* 17 Mar. 182/1, I see that the so-called 'dinner-jacket' is getting to be the regular wear at the theatres. **1924** GALSWORTHY *White Monkey* I. iv, Full fig, or dinner jacket? **1968** *Listener* 6 June 748/1 The struggle to rescue opera from the dinner-jacket brigade and to present it to ordinary people at reasonable prices. **1911** C. E. W. BEAN '*Dreadnought' of Darling* I. 5 Any other *dinner-jacketed, white-shirted, black-tied visitor in the room. **1936** 'M. INNES' *Death at President's Lodging* (1937) iv. 63 Round the high-table there stood, gowned and for the most part dinner-jacketed, the Fellows. **1967** *Economist* 23 Sept. 1072/3 '*Dinner lady' is a popular part-time job for many women, especially where small children are concerned—and where extra supervision is most needed. **1983** *Daily Tel.* 30 Nov. 8/1 Dinner ladies helping with playground supervision have been jostled and abused while trying to tackle unruly pupils. **1984** *Listener* 22 Mar. 4/2 He hopes that the majority of the dinner ladies will, in the end, accept. **1835** DICKENS *Sk. Boz* (1836) 2nd Ser. 14 Investing part of the day's *dinner-money in the purchase of the stale tarts. **1942** A. P. JEPHCOTT *Girls Growing Up* iii. 47 Ordinary timetable lessons are supplemented by..dinner money collections [etc.]. **1861** DICKENS *Gt. Expect.* xxii, A *dinner-napkin will not go into a tumbler. **1856** M. J. HOLMES *Homestead* VI. i, The little 'tin bucket'..serves the treble purpose of *dinnerpail, washbowl, and drinking cup. **1900** *Nation* LXXI. 323/2 He comes something short of ex-President Harrison's ability to see a 'spiritual significance' in the full dinner-pail. **1904** *N.Y. Even. Post* 19 Feb. 3 Thousands of men with their dinnerpails on their way to work. **1905** A. M. BINSTEAD *Mop Fair* iv. 65 Evelyn Godolphin Mountprospect..passed in his dinner pail. **1922** WODEHOUSE *Clicking of Cuthbert* i. 14 A sliced ball, whizzing in at the open window, had come within an ace of incapacitating Raymond Parsloe Devine... Two inches, indeed, to the right and Raymond must inevitably have handed in his dinner-pail. **1964** —— *Frozen Assets* iii. 49 My godfather..recently turned in his dinner pail and went to reside with the morning stars. **1894** *Westm. Gaz.* 24 Apr. 1/3 He frequently secures a *dinner-pair, and manages to get away from the House..at 6.30. **1815** JANE AUSTEN *Emma* xvi, Out of humour at not being able to come..for forty-eight hours without falling in with a *dinner-party. **1775** P. V. FITHIAN *Jrnl.* (1934) II. 68 Tea..is boild in a common *Dinner-Pot, of ten or fifteen gallons. **1871** MRS. STOWE *Old Town Fireside Stories* v. 168 A gret iron pot as big as your granny's dinner-pot with an iron bale to it. **1833** *Chambers's Jrnl.* II. 32/2 You find Mrs B...flying about the dining-room,..marshalling glasses and *dinner rolls. **1962** *Which?* May 144/1 We made plain dinner rolls, using ½ pint of water to 1 lb flour—a heavy dough. **1845** *Ainsworth's Mag.* VIII. 117 The furniture of the table..reminds one of..a Russian *dinner-service. **1968** *Guardian* 9 July 7/5 Their bargain dinner service..costs £4 5*s*. **1823** in Cobbett *Rur. Rides* (1885) I. 344 The decanters, the glasses, 'the *dinner-set' of crockery-ware. **1910** *Westm. Gaz.* 11 Apr. 8/3 Mr. W. W. Jacobs..said..*Dinner-speaking was a gift which was never put into his stocking. **1852** *Harper's Mag.* VI. 89* That celebrated public *dinner-speech. **1890** *Ibid.* Apr. 799/2 The modern dinner speech is a happy blending of sparkling banter, [etc.]. **1813** *Examiner* 10 May 299/2 A.. greater number of persons than assemble at a *dinner or a tea-table. **1852** MRS. CARLYLE *Lett.* II. 162, I am to have a *dinner-tea with them next Wednesday. **1960** *Cue* 2 July 2 (Advt.), Theatre in-the-round restaurant. Meadowbrook *Dinner Theatre. B'way Musical. Dinner. Dancing. **1973** *Times* 3 July (Houston Suppl.) p. vi/6 The city's only professional theatre, besides the dinner theatres (do you have them over there yet? You get an extra-bland buffet dinner and a dreary second-rate Broadway comedy for one price) is the Alley. **1984** *New Yorker* 18 June 44/1 She is very beautiful. She is always playing countesses at the local dinner theatre. **1862** *Illustr. Catal. Internat. Exhib.* XI. No. 5719, A wainscot sideboard; *dinner wagon, to correspond. **1895** *Catal.*, Dinner wagons, three-shelf, plain turned pillars, on castors, mahogany, oak or walnut. **1895** *Montgomery Ward Catal.* 527/1 Pure white *dinner ware.. with gold decoration. **1905** *Daily Chron.* 2 May 7/1 The kitchen was strewn with smashed dinner-ware. **1961** *Times* 6 June 5/6 The dinner-ware is based on melamine crystal developed by Cyanamid. **1905** *Wine List of T. W. Stapleton & Co.* July, Sherry... Good *Dinner Wine 36/-. **1920** G. SAINTSBURY *Notes on Cellar-Bk.* v. 78 Good Carbonnieux or Olivier..are admirable dinner wines.

dinner ('dɪnə(r)), *v.* [f. DINNER *sb.*]

1. *intr.* To dine, have dinner: also ***dinner it.***

1748 [see DINNERING below]. **1786** BURNS *Lines on Interv. w. Ld. Daer* i, I dinner'd wi' a Lord. **1818** MOORE *Fudge Fam. Paris* viii. 20 Where in temples antique you may breakfast or dinner it.

2. *trans.* To entertain at dinner; to provide dinner for.

1822 *Blackw. Mag.* XI. 481 Hogg would have been dinnered to his death. **1826** *Examiner* 337/1 Before that worthy governor..left the Cape, he was twice dinnered. **1859** CHADWICK *De Foe* vi. 310 Harley dinnered himself into the Speaker's chair. **1885** GRACE STEBBING *Aggravating Sch.-girl* xxxiv, I'll dinner them and I'll supper them, but if they want rooms..they may go elsewhere.

Hence '**dinnering** *vbl. sb.*

1748 RICHARDSON *Clarissa* Wks. 1883 V. 118 To think how I had drawn myself in by my summer-house dinnering. **1837** *Q. Rev.* 142 Few people are there so bored, as at the grand dinnerings of the London season. **1867** CARLYLE *Remin.* II. 143 Liverpool, with its dinnerings..was not his element.

'**dinner-bell.** The bell rung to announce dinner; usually, the ordinary bell of the house, hotel, ship, etc., rung at a fixed time; also, a particular bell used for this purpose.

1682 O. N. *Boileau's Lutrin* IV. 206 For all Agree, no Knell Could more concern them than the Dinner-bell! **1782** *Phil. Trans.* LXXII. 376 Close to the chimney..a dinner-bell hung in a common frame. *a* **1859** L. HUNT *Robin Hood* IV. v, The horn was then their dinner-bell. **1879** F. W. ROBINSON *Coward Consc.* I. viii, The dinner-bell rang for the first time. **1887** *Spectator* 26 Feb. 287/2 The dinner-bell would begin to ring at half-past 5.

dinne'rette. [see -ETTE.] A little dinner; a dinner on a small scale, or for a small party.

1872 M. COLLINS *Pr. Clarice* II. v. 74 He has a luxurious bachelor's first floor in Piccadilly..where he sometimes gives excellent dinnerettes.

'**dinnerless,** *a.* [-LESS.] Without dinner; fasting.

a **1661** FULLER *Worthies, London* (1662) 198 To Dine with Duke Humphrey importing to be dinnerlesse. **1708** *Brit. Apollo* No. 29. 3/1 Such as walk'd Dinnerless the Streets. *c* **1820** S. ROGERS *Italy* (1839) 201 Screwing a smile into his dinnerless face. **1859** TENNYSON *Idylls, Enid* 1083, I left your mowers dinnerless.

dinnerly ('dɪnəlɪ), *a.* and *adv.* [f. DINNER *sb.* + -LY.] **A.** *adj.* Of or pertaining to dinner. **B.** *adv.* In a manner appropriate to dinner.

1614 COPLEY *Wits, Fits, etc.* (N.), A merry recorder of London..met..in the street, going to dinner to the lord maior.. The dinnerly officer was so hasty on his way that he refused to heare him. **1836–48** B. D. WALSH *Aristoph., Acharnians* IV. iv, Did'st hear..How cookishly, how dinnerly He manages his duties?

'**dinner-time.** The usual time of dining; the time occupied by, or allowed for, dinner.

1371 in Britton *Cathedrals, York* (1819) 80 Swa y^t^ yai sall noghte dwell fra yair werk in ye forsayde loge na tyme of ye yer in dyner tyme. **1596** SHAKS. *Merch. V.* I. i. 105 We will leaue you then till dinner time. *a* **1627** MIDDLETON, etc., *Changeling* (N.), Dinner time? thou meanst twelve o'clock. **1710** *Tatler* No. 258 ¶2 We were disturbed all Dinner-Time by the Noise of the Children. **1869** TROLLOPE *He knew, etc.* vi. (1878) 28 Before dinner-time a reconcilation had been effected.

dinnerward, toward dinner: see -WARD.

dinnery ('dɪnərɪ), *a.* [f. DINNER *sb.* + -Y[1].] Characterized by dinner or dinners.

a **1865** MRS. GASKELL *Curious if True* in *Gray Woman, etc.* (1865) 83, I..disliked the dinnery atmosphere of the *salle à manger.* **1889** LOWELL *Lett.* (1894) II. 363 Philadelphia was very dinnery, of course, with lunches and Wister parties thrown in.

dinnick, local var. of DUNNOCK, hedge-sparrow.

dinning ('dɪnɪŋ), *vbl. sb.* [f. DIN *v.* + -ING[1].] The action of the verb DIN; the making of a din or noise of any kind; †wailing, etc.

13.. *Cursor M.* 18630 (Gött.) Was adam bidan in his bale, Thoru dome into þat dinning dale. **1375** BARBOUR *Bruce* XIII. 153 Gret dynnyng ther wes of dyntis As wapnys apon armor styntis. *c* **1400** *Destr. Troy* 9618 With dynnyng & dole for dethe of hor lord. *c* **1489** CAXTON *Blanchardyn* xliii. 162 The stour dynnyng and noyse that their horses made. **1683** E. HOOKER *Pref. Ep. Pordage's Mystic Div.* 15 What shal wee sai then, or think of..Scurrilities, Huffings and Dinnings? **1814** CARY *Dante, Paradise* XIV. 111 The chime Of minstrel music..a pleasant dinning makes. **1859** SMILES *Self-Help* vi. 150 After four years dinning of his project into the ears of the great.

'**dinning,** *ppl. a.* [f. as prec. + -ING[2].] Making a din, disturbing with din or noise.

1813 L. HUNT in *Examiner* 1 Mar. 129/1 The noise of these dinning fetters. **1832** TENNYSON *Eleänore* 131 With dinning sound my ears are rife.

dinnle, dinn'le, mod.Sc. ff. DINDLE *sb.*[1] and *v.*

dinny ('dɪnɪ), *a.* [f. DIN *sb.* + -Y[1].] Resounding with or filled with din.

1768–74 TUCKER *Lt. Nat.* (1852) I. 461 Sometimes my ears are a little dinny.

‖**Dinoceras** (daɪ'nɒsəræs). [mod.L. (Marsh, 1872) f. Gr. δειν-ός fearful, terrible + κέρας horn.] A genus of extinct ungulated quadrupeds (*Dinocerata*) of huge size, and having apparently three pairs of horns. Hence **di'nocerate** *a.*, related to the dinoceras, as *a dinocerate animal.*

1872 MARSH *Amer. Jrnl. Sc. & Art* Ser. III. IV. 344. **1877** LE CONTE *Elem. Geol.* (1879) 506 The brain of the Middle Eocene Dinoceras is only about one eighth the size of a living Rhinoceros of equal bulk. **1886** A. WINCHELL *Walks Geol. Field* 256 The dinoceras was like an elephant in size. It had short legs, and perhaps three pairs of horns,—one on the snout, one on the cheeks, and one on the forehead.

dinoflagellate (daɪnəʊ'flædʒəleɪt). *Zool.* [f. mod.L. *Dinoflagellata* (O. Bütschli 1885, in Bronn *Kl. u. Ordn. Thier-Reichs* I. II. 907), f. Gr. δῖνο-ς whirling, rotation + L. *flagellum*: see FLAGELLATE *sb.*] A member of the subclass Dinoflagellata, which includes protistans having two flagella. Also *attrib.* or as *adj.* (*Cent. Dict.*, 1889).

1901 G. N. CALKINS *Protozoa* 260 The dinoflagellate *Ceratium hirundinella.* **1934** *Discovery* Aug. 218/2 They have the characteristic flagella and horizontal groove of the Dinoflagellates. **1959** *New Biol.* XXIX. 43 A dense growth of phytoplankton, often dinoflagellates such as *Gymnodinium* or *Goniaulax.* **1967** P. A. MEGLITSCH *Invert. Zool.* iii. 42/2 Most of the dinoflagellates are marine although there are a number of fresh-water forms.

dinomic (daɪ'nɒmɪk), *a.* [f. Gr. δι-, (DI-[2]) twice + νομ-ός district + -IC.] Belonging or restricted to two districts or divisions (of the globe).

1863 BALFOUR *Bot.* §1151 A natural family, common to all the divisions [of the globe] is *polynomic*.. If restricted to two or more divisions, the groups are *dinomic*, *trinomic*, etc.

‖**Dinornis** (daɪ'nɔːnɪs). [mod.L. (Owen 1843) f. Gr. δειν-ός fearful, terrible + ὄρνις bird.] A name given by Prof. Owen to a genus of recently extinct birds of great size, the remains of which have been discovered in New Zealand; the moa of the Maori. Hence **dinor'nithic, di'nornithine** *adjs.*, related to, or of the nature of, the dinornis.

1843 *Proc. Zool. Soc.* 14 Feb. 19 A communication from Prof. Owen was read, proposing to substitute the name *Dinornis* for that of *Megalornis*, applied to the Great Bird of New Zealand in his paper read at the previous meeting.. Mr. G. Gray having previously used the term *Megalornis* for a genus of Birds. **1865** BARING-GOULD *Werewolves* 6 Like the dodo or the dinornis, the werewolf may have become extinct in our age. **1875** A. NEWTON in *Encycl. Brit.* III. 729/2 The fragmentary cranium of a large Bird, combining Dinornithic and Struthious characters. **1891** *Athenæum* 14 Nov. 651/2 An extinct dinornithine bird from New Zealand.

dinosaur, ('daɪnəsɔː(r)). Also in Lat. form **dino'saurus, deino-.** [mod.L. *dīnosaurus* (Owen 1841), f. Gr. δειν-ός fearful, terrible + σαῦρ-ος (= σαύρα) lizard.] **1.** A member of an extinct race of Mesozoic Saurian reptiles (group *Dinosauria*, typical genus *Dinosaurus*), some of which were of gigantic size; the remains point to an organism resembling in some respects that of birds, in others that of mammals.

1841 OWEN in *Rep. Brit. Assoc.* 104 A remarkable approach in the present gigantic Dinosaur to the crocodilian structure. **1873** DAWSON *Earth & Man* viii. 202 We have thus brought before us the Dinosaurs—the terrible Saurians —of the Mesozoic age. **1885** C. A. BUCKMASTER *Brit. Alm. Comp.* 193 The group of fossil reptiles known as Dinosaurs has long been remarkable for certain curious resemblances to birds which it presents.

2. *fig.* Someone or something that has not adapted to changing circumstances; also, an object, institution, etc., that is extremely large and unwieldy.

1952 *Manch. Guardian Weekly* 3 Apr. 3/2 This Dinosaur school of Republican strategy. **1959** *New Yorker* 12 Dec. 213/1 We are familiar with the American Academic style in such enterprises, those great dinosaurs with brains the size of a teacup. **1970** 'W. HAGGARD' *Hardliners* vi. 60 The man was a sort of dinosaur, a survival from another age. **1979** *Time* 8 Jan. 63/2 It's now perfectly clear that we can process dinosaur cases if we can persuade judges to seize control from the lawyers and manage those cases. **1982** I. GORDON in *N.Z. Listener* 4 Sept. 84 One of my correspondents, at the age of a mere 30-plus, wonders if he is not already a linguistic dinosaur... He tells me he is hearing, over the air, forms like 'He drunk a couple of beers' and 'The yacht sunk at its moorings'.

dino'saurian, *a.*, *sb.* [f. as prec. + -IAN.]

A. *adj.* Of the nature of, or related to, a dinosaur; belonging to the group *Dinosauria*.

1873 [see DICYNODONTIAN]. **1880** *Libr. Univ. Knowl.* VII, 216 The number of dinosaurian reptiles was very large. **1881** G. MACDONALD *Mary Marston* II. iii. 52 The old-fashioned horror would inevitably raise its deinosaurian head afresh above the slime of his consciousness.

B. *sb.* A member of the *Dinosauria*, a DINOSAUR.

1841 OWEN in *Rep. Brit. Assoc.* 102 Dinosaurians..A distinct tribe or sub-order of Saurian Reptiles, for which I would propose the name of *Dinosauria*. **1859** DARWIN *Orig. Spec.* xi. (1878) 295 The Mastodon and the more ancient Dinosaurians having become extinct. **1881** LUBBOCK in *Nature* No. 618. 403 It seems to be now generally admitted that birds have come down to us through the Dinosaurians.

dinothere, deino- ('daɪnəθɪə(r)). [f. mod.L. *dino'therium* (1829, Kaup, in Oken's *Isis* XXII. 402), f. Gr. δειν-ός fearful, terrible + θηρίον wild beast. Also used in the Lat. form.] A member of a genus of extinct proboscidean quadrupeds of great size, whose remains have been discovered in the miocene formations of Europe and Asia.

1835 KIRBY *Hab. & Inst. Anim.* II. xxiv. 497 One of the most remarkable animals of this Sub-order..on account of its enormous tusks, is named Deinotherium. **1847** ANSTED *Anc. World* xv. 353 A pachydermatous species..showing many curious points of resemblance to the Dinothere. **1880** DAWKINS *Early Man* 143 The deinotheres and mastodons.. were either dragged in by the carnivores, or swept in by the flow of water.

Hence **dino'therian** *a.*

1839–47 TODD *Cycl. Anat.* III. 867/2 Those Mastodons.. manifest the Dinotherian character.

dinoxide, erron. f. (after *binoxide*) for DIOXIDE.

1854 J. SCOFFERN in *Orr's Circ. Sc.* Chem. 495 Black Oxide (Suboxide or Dinoxide) of Mercury.

†**'dinrie.** *Sc. Obs.* [f. DIN *sb.* + -RY.] = DIN.

1563–7 BUCHANAN *Reform. St. Andros* Wks. (1892) 15 Disputing without dinrie or pertinacite in contention.

dinsome ('dɪnsəm), *a. Sc.* [f. DIN *sb.* + -SOME.] Full of din; noisy.

1724 RAMSAY *Tea-t. Misc.* (1733) I. 66 O Katy wiltu gang wi' me And leave this dinsome town awhile. *a* **1774** FERGUSSON *King's Birthd.* Poems (1845) 2 The hills..would echo to thy dinsome rout. **1786** BURNS *Scotch Drink* xi, Till block an' studdie ring an' reel Wi' dinsome clamour. **1876** BLACKIE *Songs Relig. & Life* 112 The stir Of dinsome life.

dint (dɪnt), *sb.* Forms: 1 dynt, 2–4 dunt (-y-), 4–6 dynt(e, 6 dinte, 3– dint. [OE. *dynt*, cogn. with ON. *dyntr*, *dyttr* in same sense; cf. Sw. dial. *dunt*. Not recorded in the other Teut. langs. See also DENT *sb.*¹ and DUNT. Sense 3 is manifestly influenced by *indent* and its family.]

†**1.** A stroke or blow; *esp.* one given with a weapon in fighting, etc.; = DENT *sb.*¹ 1. *Obs.* or blending with 3.

c **897** K. ÆLFRED *Gregory's Past.* xlv. 338 Ac ondræden him ðone dynt swæ neah, ða þe noht to gode ne doð. *c* **950** *Lindisf. Gosp.* John xviii. 22 An..ðara ðegna salde dynt mið honde uutearde ðæm hælende. *c* **1175** *Lamb. Hom.* 153 Þe duntes boð uuel to kepen. *c* **1200** ORM. 4290 Þurrh Adamess gilltes dinnt Wass all mannkinn þurrhwundedd. *a* **1225** *Ancr. R.* 60 Sweordes dunt is adunriht..vor sweord..ȝifð deaðes dunt. *a* **1300** *Cursor M.* 20990 Hefdid he was wit dint o suord. *c* **1320** *Cast. Love* 1161 Such beo þe duntes of batayle. *c* **1475** *Rauf Coilȝear* 514, I sall dyntis deill, quhill ane of vs be deid. **1555** ABP. PARKER *Ps.* lxxxix, Thou hast whole stynt hys weapons dynt. **1697** DRYDEN *Virg. Georg.* III. 576 With dint of Sword, or pointed Spears. **1791** COWPER *Iliad* XVII. 676 From the dint Shield me of dart and spear. **1837** CARLYLE *Fr. Rev.* III. I. i. (1848) 16 The dints and bruises of outward battle.

b. The stroke of thunder; = DENT *sb.*¹ 1 b.

c **1374** CHAUCER *Troylus* v. 1505 How Cappaneus þe proude with þonder dynt was slayn. *c* **1386** —— *Wife's Prol.* 276 With wilde thonder dynt and firy leuene Moote thy welked nekke be to-broke. **1600** FAIRFAX *Tasso* XI. xxxi. 201 Like thunders dint or lightnings new. **1808** SCOTT *Marmion* I. xxiii, The Mount, where Israel heard the law 'Mid thunder-dint, and flashing levin.

2. The dealing of blows; hence, force of attack, assault, or impact (*lit.* and *fig.*); violence, force, attack, impression. Now *rare* exc. as in c.

c **1330** R. BRUNNE *Chron.* (1810) 70 If he wild it wynne with dynt, als duke hardie. **1513** DOUGLAS *Æneis* II. x. 63 The auld waiklie but force or dynt A dart did cast. **1530** LYNDESAY *Test. Papyngo* 355 Quho clymith moist heych moist dynt hes of the wedder. **1579** SPENSER *Sheph. Cal.* Nov. 104 Such pleasaunce now displast by dolors dint. **1601** SHAKS. *Jul. C.* III. ii. 198, I perceiue, you feele The dint of pitty. **1687** DRYDEN *Hind & P.* III. 200 But dint of argument is out of place. **1748** J. MASON *Elocut.* 7 Mechanical Minds ..affected with mere Dint of Sound and Noise. **1770** GOLDSM. *Misc. Wks.* (1837) III. 420 He had gone as far..as the mere dint of parts and application could go. **1845** R. W. HAMILTON *Pop. Educ.* vi. 126 (ed. 2). Their soul gathered all dint and courage.

†**b.** phr. ***by dint of sword***: by attack with weapons of war; by force of arms. *Obs.*

Ranging from the literal sense as in 1, to the vague use in c.

a **1330** *Roland & V.* 10 Alle the londes that were in Spayne, With dint Of swerd wan Charlmain. *c* **1440** *Gesta Rom.* xvii. 330 (Add. MS.) The sones..goten mekell good by dynte of swerd. **1577–87** HOLINSHED *Chron.* III. 1178/1 With the dint of sword The hand of bondage brast. **1602** DEKKER *Satiromastix* Wks. 1873 I. 242 You have put all Poetrie to the dint of sword. **1663** BUTLER *Hud.* I. II. 248 He ..by his Skill No less than Dint of Sword, cou'd kill. **1728** MORGAN *Algiers* II. iv. 262 Even now they [Turks] maintain what they have by mere Dint of Sabre.

c. Hence ***by (the) dint of***: by force of; by means of (with implication of vigour or persistence in the application of the means). (The current idiom.)

[**1597** see DENT *sb.*¹ 3.]

1664 BUTLER *Hud.* II. III. 291 Chace evil spirits away by dint Of Cickle, Horse-shoe, Hollow-flint. **1685** COTTON tr. *Montaigne* (1877) I. 36 Subdued by..dint of valour. **1712** ADDISON *Spect.* No. 411 ¶7 Pleasures of the Fancy..which are worked out by Dint of Thinking. **1764** GOLDSM. *Hist. Eng.* (1772) II. 102 Tallard..had risen by the dint of merit alone. **1771** SMOLLETT *Humph. Cl.* (1815) 159 By dint of cross-examination, I found he was not at all satisfied. **1826** SCOTT *Jrnl.* 25 Dec., By dint of abstinence..I passed a better night. **1871** L. STEPHEN *Playgr. Europe* ii. (1894) 65 Schiller endeavours to give the local colour..by dint of inserting little bits of guide-book information. **1878** BROWNING *La Saisiaz* 29 We..Earned, by dint of failure, triumph.

†**d.** ***under, within*** (etc.) ***the dint of***: exposed to, or within the reach or range of assault of. Cf. DENT *sb.*¹ 2 b. *Obs.*

1577–87 HOLINSHED *Chron.* II. 23/2 Sparing none that came under their dint. **1627–77** FELTHAM *Resolves* II. lvi. 275 He that comes within the dint on't [noysom breath] dies. **1640** A. HARSNET *God's Summ.* 383 We shall be out of the Dint of many a Tentation. *a* **1734** NORTH *Exam.* I. iii. §71 (1740) 175 Standing in the Dint of an Air, that was..sure to blast him.

3. A mark or impression made by a blow or by pressure, in a hard or plastic surface; an indentation; = DENT *sb.*¹ 4. (Also *fig.*)

1590 SPENSER *F.Q.* I. i. 1 Ycladd in mightie armes and silver shielde, Wherein old dints of deepe woundes did remaine. **1612** BRINSLEY *Lud. Lit.* 47 The very little ones.. may make some secret markes..with some little dint with their naile. **1657** AUSTEN *Fruit Trees* I. 46 Make the cut smooth and even..without dints or ridges. **1700** DRYDEN *Fables, Pygmalion* 32 Afraid His hands had made a dint. **1818** BYRON *Mazeppa* 17 Nor dint of hoof, nor print of foot, Lay in the wild luxuriant soil. **1847** S. WILBERFORCE in *Life & Lett.* I. 402 The single opportunity of making..a dint in a character. **1856** MRS. BROWNING *Aur. Leigh* II. 927 Beside her bed Whose pillow had no dint.

dint (dɪnt), *v.* [ME. *dynt-*, *dünt-*, *dint-en*, f. DINT *sb.* Not recorded in OE.; cf. Icel. *dynta* to dent, Sw. dial. *dunta* to strike, shake; and see also DENT *v.* and DUNT.]

†**1.** *trans.* To strike, beat, knock. *Obs.*

a **1300** *Cursor M.* 4302 (Cott.) To bi dint of his mangonele. *c* **1300** *Havelok* 2448 He [*pl.*]..dunten him, so man doth bere, And keste him on a scabbed mere. *a* **1400** *Leg. Rood* (1871) 138 Wiþ sharpe nayles dunted and driue. **1596** SPENSER *F.Q.* VI. x. 31 His wounds worker, that with lovely dart Dinting his brest had bred his restlesse paine. *a* **1649** DRUMM. OF HAWTH. *Poems* Wks. (1711) 50/2 Ye, who with gawdy wings and bodies light Do dint the air.

†**b.** *intr.* or *absol. Obs.*

c **1460** *Towneley Myst.* (Surtees) 234 In alle this warld..Is none so doughety as I, the best, Doughtely dyntand on mule and on stede.

†**2.** *intr.* To make a dint or impression *in* something; = DENT *v.* 4. *Obs. rare.*

1398 TREVISA *Barth. De P.R.* XVII. lxxiv. (1495) 648 Yf the fynger dynteth in therto and finde it neshe. **1590** SPENSER *F.Q.* I. viii. 8 The ydle stroke..So deepely dinted in the driven clay, That three yardes deepe a furrow up did throw.

3. *trans.* To mark or impress with dints; to make a dint or dints in.

1597 BP. HALL *Sat.* I. ix, Let your floor with horned satyrs hoofs Be dinted and defiled every morn. **1639** FULLER *Holy War* IV. i. (1647) 167 This Emperour's heart was.. furrowed, dinted, and hollowed at last. **1812** BYRON *Ch. Har.* I. xlix, Wide scattered hoof-marks dint the wounded ground. **1851** LONGF. *Gold. Leg.* III. (Street in Strasburg), He dints With his impatient hoofs the flints.

b. To impress or drive in with force.

1631 T. POWELL *Tom All Trades* 142 The scars which my unthriftines hath dinted upon their fortunes. **1826** J. WILSON *Noct. Ambr.* Wks. 1855 I. 232 'Dinna dint the pint o' your crutch into my instep, Mr. North.' **1855** TENNYSON *Maud* I. ii, A body was found..Mangled, and flatten'd, and crush'd, and dinted into the ground.

†**4.** To take the sharp edge off; to reduce the acrimony of (corrosive liquids). *Obs.*

1669 W. SIMPSON *Hydrol. Chym.* 27 Those corrosive fretting, pontick, and acid juyces..are I say dinted, softned and sweetned. *Ibid.* 101 The waters of the spaw may..help to dint the acrimony.

Hence **'dinted, 'dinting** *ppl. adjs.*

1566 DRANT *Horace' Sat.* viii. E v b, When he with dyntyng axe is hewed rounde aboute. **1579** *Poor Knt.'s Pallace*, No feare of dinting death. **1596** SPENSER *F.Q.* (J.), They do impress Deep dinted furrows in the batter'd mails. **1697** DRYDEN *Æneid* (J.), Deep dinted wrinkles on her cheeks she draws. **1808** SCOTT *Marm.* VI. xxviii, With dinted shield, and helmet beat. *a* **1881** ROSSETTI *Rose Mary* iii. 142 On either hand There hung a dinted helm and brand.

din't, dint (dɪnt), contracted colloq. form of *didn't, did not* (see DO *v.* 29).

1961 *New Left Rev.* Jan.–Feb. 24/1 He din't see why I shouldn't. **1967** C. DRUMMOND *Death at Furlong Post* iv. 39, I dint expect the pleasure of your cumpny. **1967** 'A. BLAISDELL' *Something Wrong* (1968) xiv. 162 'I thought maybe she'd asked you,' said Sue... 'I get you. But she dint.' *Ibid.*, I dint *know* her. **1968** *Punch* 14 Feb. 227/3 'Course, I 'ad to 'elp her with joining the letters up, din't I?

dintless ('dɪntlɪs), *a.* [f. DINT *sb.* + -LESS.] Without a dint or dints.

1. Not producing a dint or impression.

1558 PHAER *Æneid* II. E iij, On his targat side it hit, where dyntlesse down it hyng. **1647** TRAPP *Comm. 1 Thess.* iii. 4 Darts fore-seen are dintlesse. **1847** BLACKIE in *Blackw. Mag.* LXII. 238 Dintless the missile hail is pour'd.

2. That has, or receives, no dint.

1860 RUSKIN *Mod. Paint.* V. VI. x. §24. 102 Veiling with hushed softness its dintless rocks.

3. *dial.* See quot., and cf. DINT *sb.* 2.

1878 *Cumbld. Gloss.*, *Dintless*, lacking in energy.

†**di'numerate,** *v. Obs. rare*$^{-0}$. [f. ppl. stem of L. *dīnumerāre* to count over one by one, reckon up, f. *dī-*, *dis-* apart, separately + *numerāre* to number.] *trans.* To number one by one.

1721 BAILEY, *Dinumerate*, to Account or Number.

†**di'numerately,** *adv. Obs. rare.* [f. **dinumerate*, ad. L. *dīnumerāt-us* reckoned up, enumerated (see prec.) + -LY².] By separate enumeration; one by one.

1668 H. MORE *Div. Dial.* II. v, I had not dinumerately and articulately mustered up..the particular Arguments.

dinume'ration. [ad. L. *dīnumerātiōn-em*, n. of action from *dīnumerāre*: see DINUMERATE.]

1. 'The act of numbering out one by one' (Ash).

1626 COCKERAM, *Dinumeration*, numbring or reckoning. **1721** in BAILEY. **1755** JOHNSON, *Dinumeration*, the act of numbering out singly.

2. *Rhet.* Enumeration; = APARITHMESIS.

‖**dinus** ('daɪnəs). *Path.* [mod.L., a. Gr. δῖνος whirling, vertigo.] Dizziness, giddiness, vertigo.

1706 PHILLIPS (ed. Kersey), *Dinus*..a giddiness or swimming of the Head, a Disease otherwise call'd *Vertigo*. **1775** in ASH. In mod. Dicts.

diobely (daɪ'əʊbəlɪ). [ad. Gr. διωβελία an allowance of two obols, f. δι- twice + ὀβολ-ός obol.] An allowance of two obols to each citizen during the Athenian festivals.

1849 GROTE *Greece* II. lxii. V. (1862) 421 The disbursement of the Diobely..on occasion of various religious festivals. **1852** *Ibid.* II. lxxv. IX. 526 A portion of the money..was employed in the distribution of two oboli per head, called the diobely, to all present citizens.

diobol (daɪ'əʊbɒl). *Numism.* [ad. Gr. διώβολον, f. δι- (DI-²) twice + ὀβολ-ός OBOL.] A silver coin of ancient Greece equal to two obols.

1887 B. V. HEAD *Hist. Numorum* 36 The well-known type of the Tarentine diobol, Herakles strangling the lion, recurs on diobols of Arpi, Cælia, Rubi, and Teate. *Ibid.*, The currency of Apulia..consisted..of silver diobols and didrachms of Tarentum.

di'ocesal, *a. rare.* [f. DIOCESE + -AL¹.] Of or relating to a diocese.

1880 *Libr. Univ. Knowl.* II. 281 His diocesal functions being afterwards extended over New Hampshire.

diocesan (daɪ'ɒsɪsən), *a.* and *sb.* Also 5–6 dyocesyan(e, 6 diocesain, dyocysen, 7 diocesane, diœcesan. [Formerly *dyocysen*, *diocesain*, a. F. *diocesain* (15th c.), f. *diocise*, *diocese*: see -AN 1, and cf. med.L. *diœcēsānus* (1311 in Du Cange); the regular L. f. *diœcēsis* (DIOCESE) would be *diœcēsiānus*: cf. OF. *dyocesiien* (1332 in Godef. *Suppl.*), and see DIOCESIAN.]

A. *adj.* Of or pertaining to a diocese.

1450–1530 *Myrr. our Ladye* 71 Wythout lycense of the bysshope dyocesan. **1637–50** ROW *Hist. Kirk* (1842) 54 That office of a diocesan Lord Bishop..unprofitable and unlawfull. **1640** BP. HALL *Episc.* Ep. Ded., Either the publike, or my own Diœcesan Occasions. **1712** PRIDEAUX *Direct. Ch.-Wardens* (ed. 4) 104 Their Business..was to attend Diocesan Synods. **1859** JEPHSON & REEVE *Brittany* 279 The old diocesan town of Dol. **1894** *Athenæum* 5 May 572/2 The first bishops of Ireland were not diocesan. Their authority seems to have been concurrent, and only limited by the ocean.

B. *sb.* **1.** He who is in charge of an ecclesiastical diocese; the bishop of a diocese.

c **1440** *Jacob's Well* (E.E.T.S.) 61 Whanne a man..is bodyn com hom to his dyocesan, or to his ordynarye, to takyn his penauns of hym. **1493** *Festivall* (W. de W. 1515) 194 Also ye shall praye..for the bysshop of .N. of our dyocysen. **1552** *Bk. Com. Prayer* Ordering Deacons, He may be admitted by his Diocesan to the ordre of Priesthode. **1689** in Somers *Tracts* II. 278 Whether they are more obliged to their Metropolitan than to their Diocesan. **1765** T. HUTCHINSON *Hist. Mass.* I. iv. 418 They would be no longer subject to any diocesan in England. **1881** W. R. W. STEPHENS *S. Sax. Diocese*, Langton belonged to that class of prelates who were statesmen rather than diocesans.

2. One of the clergy or people of a diocese.

1502 *Ord. Crysten Men* (W. de W. 1506) IV. vii. 187 These bysshoppes, or theyr diocesains, these curates. **1532** MORE *Confut. Tindale* Wks. 398/2 As the..godfather blesseth yᵉ chyld..or the bishop his dyocesane. **1555** WATREMAN *Fardle Facions* II. xii. 283 These [Bishopes] mighte not then gouerne their Clergie, and other their Diocesans, at their owne pleasure. **1728** MORGAN *Algiers* II. v. 317 Titular Prelates..very unlikely ever to visit their Diocesans *in partibus Infidelium*. **1821** LAMB *Elia* Ser. I. *Valentine's day*, Faithful lovers..content to rank themselves humble diocesans of old Bishop Valentine. **1839** LOWELL *Lett.* (1894) I. 50 Latimer..said..that the devil was the faithfullest of bishops.. His diocesans, too, are no whit less zealous.

Hence **di'ocesanist**, an advocate of a diocesan system.

1887 *Ch. Q. Rev.* XXIII. 347 The desire of the Diocesanist leaders.. to introduce.. certain usages.

diocese ('daɪəsɪs, -siːs). Forms: α. 4-6 dio-, dyocise, -cyse, 5-6 -cis, (diecise, dyosys), 6 *Sc.* diosise. β. 5-7 diocesse, 6-7 dioces, 6-9 diocess, (5 diosses, 6 dioses, dyoces, dyesses). γ. 6- diocese (6 diœcese). δ. (*Sc.*) 5-6 dyocye, -cie, 6 diocye, dy-, diosie, diœsie, 6- diocie. ε. 5-6 dio-, dyocesy, -sie, 6 diocœsie. [ME. *diocise*, etc., a. OF. *diocise* (*diozcise*, 13th c. in Hatz.-Darm.), ad. med.L. *diocēsis*, for L. *diœcēsis* a governor's jurisdiction, a district, in later eccl. L. a bishop's jurisdiction, a diocese, a. Gr. διοίκησις, orig. 'housekeeping', hence 'management, administration, government, the province of a (Roman) governor', and in Byz. Gr. 'a bishop's jurisdiction, a diocese', f. διοικέ-ειν to keep house, to manage, administer, govern, f. δι-, δια- through, thoroughly + οἰκέ-ειν to inhabit, occupy, manage. Under Latin influence at the Renascence, the form became in Fr. and Eng. *dioces*; whence, for phonetic reasons, in Fr. *diocèse*, in Eng. *diocesse, diocess*. *Diocess* was the classical English type from the 16th to the end of the 18th c.; it was the only form recognized by Dr. Johnson and the other 18th century lexicographers, and was retained by some (notably by the *Times* newspaper) in the 19th c., in which, however, *diocese* (as in Fr.) has become the established spelling. In Scotch, *diocis(e*, lost the terminal *s* in the singular, and was reduced to *diocie, diocy*. The Gr.-L. word was also independently adapted as *di'ocesy, -ie*: cf. *paralysis*, F. *paralysie, palsy*. (Cf. Pr. *diocesa, diocezi*, Sp. *di'ocesis*, Pg. *diocese*, It. *di'ocesi, -cese*.)]

†1. Administration, dominion, rule. *Sc. Obs.*

1596 Dalrymple tr. *Leslie's Hist. Scot.* x. 272 Barounis and Nobles of the Lenox, and diosie of Ramfrwe [*ditione Ramfroa*]. *Ibid.* x. 317 Monie men of weir cum be sey eislie ..and subiected the toune lychtlie to thair authorietie and diosie, na man resisteng.

2. A district or division of a country under a governor; a province; *esp.* one of the provinces into which the Roman empire was divided after Diocletian and Constantine. *Obs.* exc. *Hist.*

1494 Fabyan *Chron.* vii. 518 The Kyng of Englande, to haue.. the cytie of Lymoges, yᵉ cytie of Caours, wᵗ all the dyocis of yᵉ sayd cyties belongynge. 1525 Ld. Berners *Froiss.* II. clxxxiv. [clxxx.] 556 To enioy styll peasably all that euer they were as then in possessyon of in Acquytayne, and nyne dyoces to be quite delyuered. 1601 Holland *Pliny* I. 98 The diocesse Arsinoetis, in the Lybian coast. 1671 L. Addison *W. Barbary* ii. (T.), Wild boars are no rarity in this diocess, which the Moors hunt and kill in a manly pastime. 1741 Middleton *Cicero* I. vi. 551 Cilicia.. this Province included also Pisidia, Pamphilia, and three Dioceses, as they were called, or Districts of Asia. 1781 Gibbon *Decl. & F.* II. 36 The civil government of the empire was distributed into thirteen great dioceses, each of which equalled the just measure of a powerful kingdom.

3. *Eccl.* The sphere of jurisdiction of a bishop; the district under the pastoral care of a bishop. (The earlier and ordinary sense in English.)

α. c1330 R. Brunne *Chron. Wace* (Rolls) 5773 To a dyocise langed a cite, & ordened paroschens for to be. c1380 Wyclif *Wks.* (1880) 85 ȝif prestis wolen seie here masse & techen þe gospel in a bischopis diocise. c1386 Chaucer *Prol.* 664 In daunger hadde he at his owene gise The yonge girles of the diocise. 1483 *Cath. Angl.* 100/2 A diocis, *diocesis*. a1535 More *Wks.* 231 (R.) He walked about as an apostle of the Deuill.. & had in euery diocyse a dyuerse name. 1538 Starkey *England* I. iv. 127 Wyth-out examynatyon or sentence gyuen in the Dyosys. 1596 Dalrymple tr. *Leslie's Hist. Scot.* x. 449 Sum of the Clergie.. war callit.. of the maist notable, Johone Leslie.. ffirst estemet Juge of the diosise, primat als of the same.

β. 1494 Fabyan *Chron.* vi. ccvi. 218 In the diocesse of Magburgh. *Ibid.* vii. ccxxi. 244 Yᵗ the farther brynke of Humber shuld be the begynnynge of his diosses. 1548 Latimer *Ploughers* (Arb.) 30 The Deuyl.. is the moste dyligent preacher of al other, he is neuer out of his dioces. 1554 *Chron. Gr. Friars* (Camden) 93 Alle the parich churches of the dioses of London. a1600 Hooker *Eccl. Pol.* vii. viii. §3 The local compass of his authority we term a diocess. 1641 Milton *Reform.* I. (1851) 32 For one Bishop now in a Dioces we should then have a Pope in every Parish. 1646 Sir T. Browne *Pseud. Ep.* vi. i. 279 Austin forbad that [*i.e.* the translation] of Jerom to be used in his Diocesse. 1761 Hume *Hist. Eng.* II. xxviii. 135 Fox, bishop of Winchester.. withdrew himself wholly to the care of his diocess. 1782 Priestley *Corrupt. Chr.* I. iv. 384 Serenus ordered.. that they should be removed from.. his diocess. 1867 *Times* 26 Nov., (Leading Art.) A bishop must needs have great influence in his diocess. 1868 R. Arthur Arnold in *Times* 8 Jan., There would be no sufficient plea for the maintenance of a bishop in that diocess.

γ. 1528 More *Dyalogue* I. Wks. 120/2 Any bishop.. within his diocese. 1546 Langley *Pol. Verg. De Invent.* iv. vi. 89 b, Parishes to Curates and Dioceses to Byshoppes. 1614 Selden *Titles Hon.* 301 Vnder the Diocese of Chichester. 1765-9 Blackstone *Comm.* (1793) 477 An arch-deacon hath an ecclesiastical jurisdiction, immediately subordinate to the bishop, throughout the whole of his diocese, or in some particular part of it. 1849 Macaulay *Hist. Eng.* I. 283 Reports were laid before him from all the dioceses of the realm. 1856 Froude *Hist. Eng.* I. iv. 341 The bishops had settled.. that each diocese should make its own arrangements.

δ. c1470 Henry *Wallace* I. 172 Glaskow thai gaif.. To dyocye in Duram to commend. 1535 Stewart *Cron. Scot.* III. 34 Of Eborak all in the dyocie. 1552 Abp. Hamilton *Catech.* (1884) 3 Within our awin Diocye. 1596 Dalrymple tr. *Leslie's Hist. Scot.* x. 266 That tyme in the diœsie of S. Androis was done na kynde of diuine seruice. 1637-50 Row *Hist. Kirk*, Three Presbyteries.. to make up a Provinciall Synode and a Diocie, and everie Provinciall Synod shall appoynt the place of the nixt Synod within that same Diocie. *Sc. Prov.* Ramsay *Remin.* (1870) v. 146 The deil's a busy bishop in his ain diocie.

ε. c1425 Wyntoun *Cron.* vii. ix. 542 In all þe kyrkis halyly Of Abbyrdenys Dyocesy. 1562 Winȝet *Last Blast Trompet* Wks. 1888 I. 43 In euery diocesie and parochin. 1580 *Wills & Inv. N.C.* (Surtees 1835) 428 Wythin the diocœsie of Durham.

b. *transf.* and *fig.*

1616 S. Ward *Coale fr. Altar* (1627) 14 True zeale loues to keepe home, studieth to bee quiet in other mens Dioces. a1631 Donne *Poems* (1650) 99 Haile Bishop Valentine, whose day this is, All the Aire is thy Diocis. a1635 Corbet *Poems* (1807) 18 Their plays had.. A perfect diocess of actors Upon the stage. 1644 Milton *Divorce* (ed. 2) ii. xxi. 75 The causes.. reside so deeply in the.. affections of nature, as is not within the diocese of Law to tamper with. 1822 Lamb *Elia* Ser. i. *Artif. Com. Last Cent.*, I am glad for a season to take an airing beyond the diocese of the strict conscience. 1891 Morley in *Daily News* 10 Dec. 3/2 To go about, as my friend does, through the whole of what I may call his diocese of those northern countries, and breathe out Liberalism.

Hence **'dioceseless** *a.*, without a diocese; †**diocesener**, one who belongs to a diocese; = diocesan *sb.* 2; **dio'cesiarch**, the ruler of a diocese; †**'diocesser** = diocesan *sb.* 1.

1885 R. W. Dixon *Hist Ch. Eng.* III. 175 A dioceseless bishop. a1626 Bacon *Case of Post-nati* Wks. (Ellis & Spedding) VII. 657 They say this unity in the bishop or the rector doth not create any privity between the parishioners or dioceseners, more than if there were several bishops, or several parsons. 1805 W. Taylor in *Monthly Mag.* XX. 512 Diocesan properly means 'belonging to the diocese'. In English this word is applied oddly to the diocesiarch, or chief of the diocese. 1606 Warner *Alb. Eng.* xiv. xci. 370 More than be Conuocations now Diocessers were stout.

†**dio'cesian**, *a.* and *sb. Obs.* [f. L. type *diœcēsiān-us*, f. *diœcēsis*, in OF. *dyocesiien*: see diocesan, which is a less regular formation.] = diocesan *a.* and *sb.*

1686 J. Sergeant *Hist. Monast. Conventions* 49 If the Diocesian refuse to give Ordination. 1715 M. Davies *Athen. Brit.* I. 131 The Clergy .. of his Diocesian City.

diocess, -cise, earlier forms of diocese.

dioch ('daɪɒk). Also **diock**. [? Native name.] An African weaver-bird of the genus *Quelea*.

1889 *Cent. Dict.*, Diock. 1905 G. E. Shelley *Birds Afr.* IV. i. 119 Quelea cardinalis... The Cardinal Dioch inhabits Eastern Africa from 7° S. lat. to 5° N. lat. 1930 G. L. Bates *Handbk. Birds W. Afr.* 495 The Red-headed Dioch is a bird of the Savannah Belt going all the way to Portuguese Guinea. 1964 *New Scientist* 18 June 736/1 The Black-Faced Dioch (*Quelea quelea*), commonly known as the Quelea bird.

†**di-octa'hedral**, *a. Crystal. Obs.* [di-² i + octahedral.] Bounded by twice eight planes; i.e. having the form of an octahedral prism with tetrahedral summits.

1805-17 R. Jameson *Char. Min.* (ed. 3) 204 Di-octahedral topaz.

diode ('daɪəʊd), *a.* and *sb.* [mod.f. Gr. δι-, (di-²) twice, doubly + ὁδός way.] **A.** *adj. lit.* Of two ways: applied by Mr. Preece to a mode of working, which converts a single telegraphic wire into two ways or ducts for signalling messages, without reference to direction; one application of the *multiplex* system of working.

1886 W. H. Preece in *Jrnl. Soc. Teleg. Engineers* XV. 231 A mode [of working] by which two messages are practically sent at the same time will be *diode* working.

B. *sb. Electr.* **a.** A thermionic valve of the simplest kind with just two electrodes, a cathode or 'filament' and an anode or 'plate'. **b.** = *semiconductor diode*: cf. *crystal diode* (see crystal *sb.* 9 d). Also *attrib.* or as *adj.*

1919 W. H. Eccles in *Electrician* 18 Apr. 475/2, I propose to give the name 'diode' to a tube with two electrodes. 1921 —— *Contin. Wave Wireless Telegr.* I. 257 A bulb with two electrodes, namely, anode and cathode, is called a diode tube. *Ibid.* 306 This example shows plainly that two constants are required to define the chief properties of a diode. 1929 J. A. Ratcliffe *Physical Princ. Wireless* ii. 23 The diode usually consists of a straight wire filament which is heated by an electric current. 1943 C. L. Boltz *Basic Radio* x. 154 The diode's only use is as a rectifier. By adding another electrode we can increase the utility of the valve. 1944 *Electronic Engin.* XVI. 408, C charges through a diode valve. 1955 [see crystal *sb.* 9 d]. 1958 *Times Rev. Industry* July 29/1 Impurities in single crystals in connexion with the production of transistors and diodes. 1959 K. Henney *Radio Engin. Handbk.* (ed. 5) ix. 7 Logic circuits using diodes may be considered another class of switching applications. 1970 D. F. Shaw *Introd. Electronics* (ed. 2) xi. 226 The rectifying property of a semi-conductor diode is a consequence of the asymmetrical conduction across the contact between a metal and a semi-conductor.

‖**Diodon** ('daɪədɒn). *Zool.* [mod.L., f. Gr. type *διόδον doubly-toothed (sc. θηρίον animal), f. δι-, (di-²) twice + ὀδούς, ὀδοντ- (in neuter adjs. -οδον) tooth.] A genus of globe-fishes, having the jaws tipped with enamel, forming a tooth-like tubercle in the centre of the beak above and below.

The name has also been improperly given to a genus of South American falcons, and to the cetacean genus Ziphius.

1776 Pennant *Zool.* III. 129 Oblong Diodon.. Sun-fish from Mount's Bay. *Ibid.* 131 Short Diodon.. Sun-fish from Loo. *Ibid.* 132 Globe Diodon. This species is common to Europe and South Carolina. 1840 F. D. Bennett *Whaling Voy.* II. 264 The Round Diodon, or Toad-fish. 1854 Owen in *Circ. Sc., Organ. Nat.* II. 95/2 The.. grinding tubercle of the diodon.

'diodont, *a.* and *sb.* [See prec.] *adj.* Having two teeth: *spec.* of or pertaining to the *Diodontidæ* or family of fishes of which *Diodon* is the typical genus; *sb.* a fish of this family. So **dio'dontoid** *a.* and *sb.*

In modern Dicts.

‖**Diœcia** (daɪ'iːʃɪə). *Bot.* [mod.L. (Linnæus 1735), a. Gr. type *διοικία, abstr. sb. from *δίοικος having two houses, f. δι-, (di-²) twice + οἶκος house. Cf. Monœcia.] The twenty-second class in the Sexual System of Linnæus, comprising plants which have male (staminiferous) and female (pistilliferous) flowers on separate individuals.

1753 Chambers *Cycl. Supp.*, *Dioecia*, in Botany, a class of plants which have the male and female parts.. in different flowers, and.. on different plants of the same species. Among the plants of this class are the willow, mistletoe, hemp, spinach. 1794 Martyn *Rousseau's Bot.* ix. 96.

Hence **di'œcian** *a.* = diœcious.

1828 Webster, *Diecian.*

diœcio- (daɪ'iːʃɪəʊ), comb. f. diœcious, = diœciously; as *diœciodimorphous, diœcio-polygamous*.

1883 *Syd. Soc. Lex.*, *Diœciopolygamous*.. a term applied to those plants of which some individuals bear unisexual and some bisexual flowers.

diœcious (daɪ'iːʃ(ɪ)əs), *a.* [f. Diœcia + -ous.] **1.** *Bot.* Of plants: Having the unisexual male and female flowers on separate plants.

1748-52 Sir J. Hill *Nat. Hist.*, *Plants* 291 (Jodr.) The rhamnus with terminatory spikes and quadrified diœcious flowers. 1789 G. White *Selborne* (1853) 393 Hops are diœcious plants. 1877 Darwin *Forms of Fl.* Introd. 3 A species tending to become diœcious, with the stamens reduced in some individuals and with the pistils in others.

2. *Zool.* Having the two sexes in separate individuals; sexually distinct.

1826 Kirby & Sp. *Entomol.* (1828) IV. xlvii. 394 Certain intestinal worms in which the sexes are diœcious. 1880 Gunther *Fishes* 157 All fishes are diœcious, or of distinct sex. 1882 A. Macfarlane *Consanguinity* 8 Sex in Man is diœcious.

Hence **di'œciously** *adv.*, in a diœcious manner; **di'œciousness**, diœcious state or condition.

1859 Darwin *Orig. Spec.* iv. (1873) 74 Some.. species of holly in North America, are, according to Asa Gray.. more or less diœciously polygamous. 1874 F. A. Kitchener *Year's Bot.* vii. 118 This idea of benefit to the plant in diœciousness. 1877 Darwin *Forms of Fl.* vii. 279 Otherwise every step towards diœciousness would lead towards sterility.

diœcism (daɪ'iːsɪz(ə)m). [ad. mod.L. *diœcismus*, Ger. *diöcismus* (Sachs), f. Gr. *δίοικ-ος (in L. form *diœcus*: see Diœcia) + -ism.] Diœcious condition.

1875 Bennett & Dyer *Sachs' Bot.* 807 This distribution of the sexes, which is generally termed Diœcism, occurs in all classes and orders of the vegetable kingdom.

diœcy (daɪ'iːsɪ). *Biol.* [f. diœc(ism + -y³.] = diœcism.

1944 *Nature* 1 Apr. 392/1 Plants are not mobile, and hence sex separation. or diœcy as it is here called, is not an efficient method of control... Consequently, diœcy is relatively uncommon in plants. 1970 T. Dobzhansky *Genetics Evol. Process* xi. 386 Muller (1925) surmised that this is due to the preponderance of hermaphroditism (monœcy) among plants, and the separation of sexes (diœcy) among animals.

Diogenes (daɪ'ɒdʒɪniːz). The name of a celebrated Greek Cynic philosopher, who according to tradition showed his contempt for the amenities of life by living in a tub: see cynic. Hence **Di'ogenes-crab**, a species of West Indian hermit crab, which chooses an empty shell for its residence. **Di'ogenes-cup**, the cup-like cavity formed in the palm of the hand by arching the fingers, and bending the thumb and little finger toward each other; from a story that the Cynic substituted this for a cup in raising water to his mouth.

1802 Mar. Edgeworth *Moral T.* (1816) I. i. 4 A table covered with a clean table cloth; dishes in nice order.. appeared to our young Diogenes absurd superfluities. 1883 *Syd. Soc. Lex.*, *Diogenes-cup*. 1884 J. Hall *Chr. Home* 176 Exceptional natures, that, Diogenes-like, prefer to be let alone.

Hence **Diogenic** (daɪəʊ'dʒɛnɪk) *a.*, of, pertaining to, or of the nature of Diogenes. So

Dio'genical *a.*; **Dio'genically** *adv.*; **Di'ogenize** *v.*, to render cynical.

1831 CARLYLE *Sart. Res.* II. v, Socratic or rather Diogenic utterances. **1593** NASHE *Christ's T.* (1613) 112 There is vaine-glory..in being Diogenicall and dogged. **1603** DEKKER *Grissil* (Shaks. Soc.) 21 Sweet signior, be not too Diogenical to me. **1719** OZELL tr. *Misson's Trav. Eng.* 154 (D.) To despise riches, not Diogenically, but indolently. **1623** COCKERAM II, One growne Churlish, *Diogeniz'd*.

dioic ('daɪɔɪk), *a.* *rare*–⁰. [ad. F. *dioïque* (Bulliard 1783), or mod.L. *dioicus* (Linnæus 1753), a. Gr. type **δίοικος*: see DIŒCIA.] = DIŒCIOUS. So **di'oicous** *a.*

1883 in *Syd. Soc. Lex.*

diol(e, obs. early ff. DOLE, DOOL, grief.

-dione, *suffix*. *Chem.* [f. DI-² 2 + -ONE.] A suffix used to form the names of compounds containing two carbonyl groups, as in MENADIONE.

dionine ('daɪənɪn). *Pharm.* Also **dionin**. [ad. G. *dionin*, a former proprietary name.] Ethylmorphine hydrochloride, used in the treatment of glaucoma, iritis, etc., and to alleviate coughing.

1899 *Jrnl. Chem. Soc.* LXXVI. I. 724 *Ethylmorphine hydrochloride* or *dionine*..is a white, odourless, finely crystalline powder,..used as an anodyne and narcotic. **1923** J. JOYCE *Let.* 28 Mar. (1966) III. 73 Dr Borsch thinks it is useless to prolong the dionine treatment. **1949** M. A. JENNINGS in H. W. Florey et al. *Antibiotics* II. xxxi. 998 The use of the drugs 'dionin' and pilocarpine also tended to reduce the effective dose. **1963** A. H. DOUTHWAITE *Hale-White's Mat. Med.* (ed. 32) 173 Dionine is ethyl morphine. .. Its action is like that of codeine.

†**'dionise**. *Obs.* Also 5 **diones**, and in L. form **dionysia**. [a. OF. *dionise, dyonise* (13.. in Godef.), ad. med.L. *dionȳsia* (Albertus Magnus), L. *dionȳsias* (Pliny), Gr. *διονῡσιάς*, f. *Διόνῡσος* Bacchus.] A precious stone, of a black colour streaked with red, reckoned, by mediæval writers, a preservative against drunkenness.

[**1398** TREVISA *Barth. De P.R.* XVI. xxxiv. (1495) 563 Dionisius is a blacke stoon or broune spronge wyth red veynes..yf it is groundid and medelyd wyth water it smellyth as wyne, and yet it wythstondyth dronkenshyp.] **1483** *Cath. Angl.* 100/1 Diones, *dionisia*. **1567** MAPLET *Gr. Forest* 6 The Dionise is black, or rather browne, all bestrowed with bloudie strokes or vaines. **1601** CHESTER *Love's Mart.* lxxxvi. (1878) 18 The Adamant, Dionise, and Calcedon. **1688** R. HOLME *Armoury* II. 40/1 The Dionise stone. **1750** tr. *Leonardus' Mirr. Stones* 94 Dionysia. **1855** SMEDLEY *Occult. Sc.* 354 *Dionysia*.

dionym ('daɪənɪm). [ad. Gr. *διώνυμ-ος, -ον* having two names, f. *δι-*, (DI-²) twice + *ὄνομα* name.] A name consisting of two terms (as the names in zoology or botany, the two terms of which denote respectively the genus and species).

18.. COUES is cited by *Cent. Dict.*

dionymal (daɪ'ɒnɪməl), *a.* [f. as prec. + -AL¹.] Of or pertaining to a dionym; = BINOMINAL.

1656 BLOUNT *Glossogr.*, *Dionymal*, that hath two names. **1884** J. A. ALLEN *On Zoöl. Nomen.* in *The Auk* Oct. 352 The binomial (or dionymal) system.

Dionysiac (daɪə'nɪsɪæk), *a.* [ad. L. *Dionȳsiac-us*, a. Gr. *Διονῡσιακός*, f. *Διονῡσια* the feast of *Διόνῡσος* Dionysus or Bacchus. So mod.F. *Dionysiaque* (Acad. 1762).]

A. *adj.* Of or pertaining to Dionysus or Bacchus, or to his worship.

1844 BECK & FELTON tr. *Munk's Met.* 149 Dionysiac and erotic poems. **1860** RUSKIN *Mod. Paint.* V. IX. iv. §4. 236 The new Dionysiac revel. **1865** GROTE *Plato* II. xxiii. 162 The Orphic or Dionysiac religious mysteries. **1871** BROWNING *Balaust.* 37 Ours the great Dionusiac theatre, And tragic triad of immortal fames.

B. *sb. pl.* The Dionysiac festivals or *Dionysia*, celebrated periodically in ancient Greece.

1827–38 HARE *Guesses* (1867) 154 At Athens, Homer, the Dionysiacs and Pericles, by their united influence, fostered them into dramatists.

So **Diony'siacal** *a.*; **Diony'siacally** *adv.*

1858 HOGG *Shelly* II. xi. 373 The goat is a Dionysiacal quadruped, habitually given to scale Parnassus. **1816** T. TAYLOR in *Pamphleteer* VIII. 57 The mundane intellect..is Bacchus..the soul is particularly distributed into generation Dionysiacally.

Dionysian (daɪə'nɪsɪən), *a.* [f. L. *Dionȳsi-us* of or pertaining to Dionysus or Bacchus; also as sb. a personal name + -AN.]

1. Of or pertaining to Dionysus or Bacchus, or the *Dionysia* or festivals held in honour of Dionysus; = DIONYSIAC.

a **1610** HEALEY *Theophrastus* (1636) 13 The Seas after the Dionysian feasts will be more smooth. **1822** T. MITCHELL *Aristoph.* I. p. xxiii, The Dionysian festivals..were the great carnivals of antiquity.

2. Pertaining to or characteristic of the Elder or Younger Dionysius, tyrants of Syracuse, notorious for cruelty.

1607 TOPSELL *Serpents* (1658) 839 Who..would not.. hate..those Dionysian Tyrants in Sicilia? **1879** *Encycl. Brit.* IX. 688/2 He..punished with Dionysian severity the slightest want of respect.

3. Pertaining to the abbot Dionysius the Little, who lived in the sixth century, and is said to have first practised the method of dating events from the birth of Christ of which he fixed the accepted date.

Dionysian period, a period of 532 Julian years, after which the changes of the moon recur on the same days of the year; said to have been introduced by Dionysius for calculating the date of Easter.

1727–52 CHAMBERS *Cycl.* s.v. *Period*, *Victorian Period*, an interval of five hundred and thirty-two Julian years..Some ascribe this period to Dionysius Exiguus; and hence call it the Dionysian Period. **1768** HORSEFALL in *Phil. Trans.* LVIII. 102 Encreased by three dionysian periods, or multiples of 28 and 19. **1876** CHAMBERS *Astron.* 470 The Dionysian Period is obtained by a combination of the Lunar and Solar cycles. **1879** FARRAR *St. Paul* (1883) 11 Our received Dionysian era.

4. Of Dionysius the Areopagite (Acts xvii. 34); *esp.* applied to early ecclesiastical works attributed to him.

1885 *Catholic Dict.* 264/1 Pearson places the composition of the Dionysian writings before 340.

Dionysic (daɪə'nɪsɪk), *a.* [f. L. or Gr. form of *Dionysus* + -IC.] Of Dionysus or Bacchus; Dionysiac.

1831 *Examiner* 501/1 The true Dionysic metre; the predominant metre of Greek theatrical music. **1832** *Ibid.* 453/1 The Dionysic wreath, the symbol of theatric honor. **1882** A. JESSOPP in *19th Cent.* May 728 A survival of the old belief in the Dionysic possession. **1920** D. H. LAWRENCE *Women in Love* xix. 279 But I hate ecstasy, Dionysic or any other.

Diophantine (daɪəʊ'fæntɪn, -aɪn), *a.* *Math.* [f. proper name *Diophant-us* + -INE.] Of or pertaining to Diophantus of Alexandria, a celebrated mathematician, who flourished in the fourth century; *spec.* applied to problems involving indeterminate equations, and to a method of solving these (***Diophantine analysis***) attributed to him.

1700 GREGORY in *Collect.* (Oxf. Hist. Soc.) I. 321 The resolution of the indetermined arithmetical or Diophantine problems. **1811** P. BARLOW (*title*), An Elementary Investigation of the Theory of Numbers, with its application to the indeterminate and diophantine analysis. **1888** *Blackw. Mag.* June 794 She solves a diophantine problem.

diophysite, -ism, improper ff. DIPHYSITE, DYOPHYSITE, etc.

diopside (daɪ'ɒpsaɪd). *Min.* [a. F. *diopside* (Haüy 1801), irreg. f. Gr. *δι-*, (DI-²) twice + *ὄψις* appearance, aspect, but viewed by later authors as a deriv. of Gr. *δίοψις* a view through, f. *δι-*, *δια-* through.] A synonym of PYROXENE; now usually restricted to the transparent varieties.

1808 ALLAN *Names Min.* 26 *Diopside*..a mineral from Mussa in Piémonte. **1868** DANA *Min.* 223 Diopside has been observed as a furnace product. **1879** RUTLEY *Study Rocks* xiii. 264 The diopside has a rough or stepped appearance on the abraded surfaces of sections.

dioptase (daɪ'ɒpteɪs). *Min.* [a. F. *dioptase* (Haüy 1801), irreg. f. Gr. *δι-*, *δια-* through + *ὀπτός* seen, visible: cf. *διόπτης* a looker through.] A translucent silicate of copper, crystallizing in six-sided prisms, called emerald copper ore.

1804 W. NICHOLSON tr. *Fourcroy's Chem.* II. 430 Dioptase is an ore of copper. **1868** DANA *Min.* 402 Dioptase occurs disposed in well defined crystals and amorphous on quartz.

diopter (daɪ'ɒptə(r)). Also in Lat. form **dioptra**. [a. F. *dioptre* (1547 in Hatz.-Darm.), ad. L. *dioptra*, a. Gr. *δίοπτρα* an optical instrument for measuring heights, levelling, etc.; cf. also Gr. *δίοπτρον* spying-glass, f. *δι-*, *δια-* through + stem *ὀπ-* to see + instrumental suffix, *-τρα, -τρον*.]

1. An ancient form of theodolite, or instrument for taking angles.

1613 M. RIDLEY *Magn. Bodies* 112 Make a hole as in a Diopter, that the Sunne may shine in at it. **1641** W. GASCOIGNE in Rigaud *Corr. Sci. Men* (1841) I. 51 Two dioptraes..fitted with glasses, hair, and moveable rims. **1851** OTTÉ tr. *Humboldt's Cosmos* III. 53 Long tubes.. employed by Arabian astronomers..to the extremities of which ocular and object diopters were attached. **1857** WHEWELL *Hist. Induct. Sc.* I. 354 He wrote..a treatise on the Dioptra..an instrument for taking angles.

2. The index-arm of a graduated circle; = ALIDAD.

1594 BLUNDEVIL *Exerc.* IV. xx. (ed. 7) 476 Having set the Diopter of your Astrolabe at that Altitude. **1662** J. DAVIES tr. *Olearius' Voy. Ambass.* 192, I took the Horizon with my Astrolabe, and having put my Dioptra into it, I turn'd my self towards the Sea..and could easily discern it. **1874** KNIGHT *Dict. Mech.* I. 172/1 To measure an angle with the astrolabe, the latter is placed with its center over the vertex of the angle, and turned until the fixed diopters sight in the direction of one side. The movable strip with its diopters is then sighted in the direction of the other side, and the angle contained between the two strips is read off.

†**3.** A surgical speculum. *Obs.*

1706 PHILLIPS (ed. Kersey), *Dioptra*..a Surgeon's Instrument. **1727–51** CHAMBERS *Cycl.*, *Dioptra*, among surgeons, denotes an instrument whereby to dilate the matrix, or anus, and inspect any ulcers therein; called also *speculum matricis*, and *dilatatorium*. **1872** THOMAS *Dis. Women* 37 If therefore, says Paul of Ægina, the ulceration be within reach, it is detected by the dioptra.

4. An instrument for obtaining drawings of the skull by projections.

1878 BARTLEY tr. *Topinard's Anthrop.* II. iii. 269.

5. A unit of measurement for lenses; = DIOPTRIC *sb.* 2.

Usu. spelt DIOPTRE in the U.K.

1890 GOULD *New Med. Dict.* 133/1 *Diopter* or *Dioptric*.

†**di'optic**, *a.* and *sb.* *Obs.* [f. Gr. *δι-*, *δια-* through + *ὀπτικ-ός* of or pertaining to sight or vision, f. root *ὀπ-* to see.]

A. *adj.* = DIOPTRIC. Also **di'optical**.

1656 BLOUNT *Glossogr.*, *The Dioptick Art*, the Perspective Art, or that part of Astronomy, which by Quadrants and hollow instruments pierces the Heavens, and measures the distance, length, bigness, and breadth of the Cœlestial bodies. **1818** TODD, *Dioptical*, and *Dioptick*, so the next words [*dioptrical*, *dioptric*] are now sometimes written.

B. *sb.* **a.** One skilled in DIOPTRICS. **b.** (*pl.*) = DIOPTRICS.

1664 POWER *Exp. Philos.* I. 58 If our Diopticks could attain to that curiosity as to grind us such Glasses, as would present the Effluviums of the Magnet. **1665–6** *Phil. Trans.* I. 56 He intends to give the..demonstration in his Diopticks which he is now writing.

dioptra: see DIOPTER.

†**di'optral**, *a.* *Obs.* [f. L. *dioptra* DIOPTER + -AL¹.] = DIOPTRIC *a.*

1610 W. FOLKINGHAM *Art of Survey* II. ii. 50 Degrees of angular production obserued by some Dioptrall instrument.

dioptre (daɪ'ɒptə(r)). [The usual spelling in Great Britain of DIOPTER in sense 5.] A unit for expressing the power of a lens, equal to the reciprocal of its focal length in metres.

[**1876** *Compte-rendu: Congrès internat. des Sciences médicales 1875* (Brussels) 610 L'unité du système métrique, c'est le mètre: l'unité dioptrique..sera nommée *dioptre*.] **1882** E. NETTLESHIP *Dis. Eye* (ed. 2) i. 15 Some system of numbering is required which shall indicate the refractive power of the lenses used for spectacles... In the *second system*, which is fast displacing the old one, the metrical scale is used; the unit is a weak lens of 1 metre (100 cm.) focal length, and known as a dioptre (D). **1907** *Practitioner* June 820 Patient was myopic to 2·0 dioptres. **1964** S. DUKE-ELDER *Parsons' Dis. Eye* (ed. 14) v. 51 A lens with a focal length of half a metre will be twice as strong as one with a focal length of 1 metre: the refractive power of such a lens is therefore 2 dioptres.

dioptric (daɪ'ɒptrɪk), *a.* and *sb.* [mod. ad. Gr. *διοπτρικ-ός* of or pertaining to the use of the *δίοπτρα* (DIOPTER); in neuter pl. *διοπτρικά* as sb., the science of dioptrics. See -IC, -ICS.]

A. *adj.* †**1.** Of the nature of, or pertaining to, a DIOPTER (sense 1). *Obs.*

1635 N. CARPENTER *Geog. Del.* I. v. 107 Two signes of the Zodiacke diametrally opposite should not be seene by a Dioptricke instrument. **1681** tr. *Willis' Rem. Med. Wks.* Vocab., *Dioptric*, belonging to the perspective, or a mathematical instrument, thorow which they look to take the height of a thing.

2. Serving as a medium for sight; assisting vision (or rendering it possible) by means of refraction (as a lens, the humours of the eye).

1653 H. MORE *Antid. Ath.* II. xii. (1712) 84 To view the Asperities of the Moon through a Dioptrick-glass. **1660** —— *Myst. Godl.* II. iii. 36 None of the external Organs have any Sense at all in them, no more then an Acousticon or a Dioptrick glass. **1858** J. MARTINEAU *Stud. Chr.* 186 A dead mechanism..ready to serve as the dioptric glass, spreading the images of light from the Infinite on the tender and living retina. **1878** T. BRYANT *Pract. Surg.* I. 299 The refraction is said to be normal or abnormal according to the position of the retina with regard to the focus of the dioptric system.

3. Relating to the refraction of light; pertaining to dioptrics (see B. 3); *esp.* (of a telescope, etc.), refractive, refracting. (Opp. to CATOPTRIC.)

dioptric system, in lighthouses, also called *refracting system*: see quot. 1879.

1672 NEWTON in *Phil. Trans.* VII. 5086 For Dioptrique Telescopes..the difficulty consisted not in the Figure of the glass, but in the Difformity of Refractions. **1688** R. HOLME *Armoury* III. 146/2 The..Dioptrick, or broken sight, is rightly seen in a Tub of Water where the Surface is cut. **1753** *Phil. Trans.* XLVIII. 167 Our common telescopes whether dioptric or reflecting. **1871** TYNDALL *Fragm. Sc.* (1879) II. xvi. 436 The light was developed in the focus of a dioptric apparatus. **1879** *Cassell's Techn. Educ.* IV. 75 The Dioptric arrangement is that in which the rays issuing from the flame are collected and refracted in a given direction by a lens placed in front of the light.

†**4.** Capable of being seen through: see quot.

1801 *Farmer's Mag.* II. 48 As to dioptric beehives [i.e provided with glass windows on opposite sides] the best I have seen is of wood. **1860** J. P. KENNEDY *W. Wirt* II. xiii. 220 These few fragments..give us..glimpses into that 'dioptric bee hive', the heart of the writer.

B. *sb.*

1. = DIOPTER 1.

1849 OTTÉ tr. *Humboldt's Cosmos* II. 545 The Alexandrian astronomers..possessed..solstitial armils, and linear dioptrics.

2. A unit for expressing the refractive power of a lens, being the power of a lens whose focal distance is one metre.

1883 *Syd. Soc. Lex.*, One dioptric, which is written 1 D, is a glass of one meter, or 39·37 inches, focal distance. **1887** A. Bruce in *Encycl. Brit.* XXII. 373.

3. *pl.* **dioptrics**: that part of the science of Optics which treats of the refraction of light. (Opp. to CATOPTRICS.)

1644 Digby *Nat. Bodies* I. (1645) 131 The demonstration ..Renatus Des Cartes has excellently set down in his book of Dioptrikes. **1667** *Phil. Trans.* II. 626 The Dioptricks, that consider Rays Refracted. **1718** J. Chamberlayne *Relig. Philos.* (1730) II. xxii. §41 One that is well versed in Dioptricks, and understands the Nature of Vision. **1831** Brewster *Optics* Introd. 3 Light..through transparent bodies is transmitted according to particular laws, the consideration of which constitutes the subject of dioptrics.

di'optrical, *a.* [f. as prec. + -AL[1].]

†**1.** = DIOPTRIC *a.* 1. *Obs.*

1612 Brerewood *Lang. & Relig.* xiii. 134 Of which height ..it is observed in Pliny, that Dicæarchus, by dioptrical instruments, found the hill Pelius..to be. **1656** Blount *Glossogr., Dioptrical,* pertaining to Dioptra.

2. = DIOPTRIC *a.* 2, 3.

1664 Power *Exp. Philos.* Pref. 1 Dioptrical Glasses are but a Modern Invention. **1677** Horneck *Gt. Law Consid.* ii. (1704) 17 Little animals..viewed through Dioptrical glasses. **1769** S. Hardy (*title*), A Translation of Scheffer's Treatise on the Emendation of Dioptrical Telescopes.

3. Of or belonging to dioptrics; skilled in dioptrics.

1664 Power *Exp. Philos.* I. 78 Dioptrical Artists. **1752** Short in *Phil. Trans.* LIX. 507 Of a radius somewhat longer than the focal length you want, for a dioptrical reason. **1800** Young *ibid.* XCI. 27 Dioptrical propositions.

†**4.** = DIOPTRIC *a.* 4. *Obs.*

1759 Sterne *Tr. Shandy* I. xxiii, To have gone softly, as you would to a dioptrical bee-hive, and look'd in.

Hence **di'optrically** *adv.*, by means of refraction.

1732 *Hist. Litteraria* III. 363 To produce very extraordinary Effects..either dioptrically or catoptrically. **1849–52** Todd *Cycl. Anat.* IV. 1441/2 Dioptrically-formed coloured margins. **1883** Carpenter in *Encycl. Brit.* XVI. 266/1 s.v. *Microscope*, Images dioptrically formed of the general outlines and larger details of microscopic objects.

dioptrician (daɪɒp'trɪʃən). *rare.* [f. DIOPTRIC; cf. *optician.*] One skilled in dioptrics.

1670 *Phil. Trans.* V. 2045 An Un-usual kind of Refraction, hitherto un-observed by Dioptricians.

dioptrics: see DIOPTRIC B 3.

diorama (daɪɒ'rɑːmə, -æ-). [mod. (in F. 1822) f. Gr. δι-, δια- through + ὅρᾱμα that which is seen, a sight: cf. διορά-ειν to see through.] **a.** A mode of scenic representation in which a picture, some portions of which are translucent, is viewed through an aperture, the sides of which are continued towards the picture; the light, which is thrown upon the picture from the roof, may be diminished or increased at pleasure, so as to represent the change from sunshine to cloudy weather, etc. The name has also been used to include the building in which dioramic views are exhibited; and in later times has been transferred to exhibitions of dissolving views, etc.

The Diorama, invented by Daguerre and Bouton, was first exhibited in London, 29 Sept. 1823, the building being erected in Regent's Park. It was patented in 1824 by J. Arrowsmith, No. 4899.

1823 *Ann. Reg.* 309* It is called the Diorama, and the idea is borrowed from the panorama. **1824** J. Arrowsmith *Specif. Patent* No. 4899 (*title*) An improved mode of publicly exhibiting pictures..which I denominate a 'diorama'. **1872** Geo. Eliot *Middlem.* liii, The memory has as many moods as the temper, and shifts its scenery like a diorama.

fig. **1876** L. Tollemache in *Fortn. Rev.* Jan. 117 Literature is able..to give a diorama of what it depicts, while art can give only a panorama. **1892** E. Reeves *Homeward Bound* 331 Entering the river Thames, we were delighted with the double diorama of ships and green meadows.

attrib. **1848** Maria Hare in A. J. C. Hare *Mem. Quiet L.* (1874) II. xvi. 310 Like the gradual change of the diorama views from light to dark.

b. A small-scale representation of a scene, etc., in which three-dimensional figures or objects are displayed in front of a painted background, the whole often being contained in a cabinet and viewed through a window or aperture in the front; hence, any small-scale model of a scene, building-project, or the like; also, a miniature set (SET *sb.*[1]) used in Cinematography and Television where a full-sized set or location would be impracticable.

1902 *Westm. Gaz.* 10 June 3/2 The most interesting feature of the Museum..is the diorama gallery, in which are shown about a dozen large tableaux of battles. **1926** *Ann. Report Imperial Inst.* 33 A certain number of 'dioramas' or modelled panoramas have been put in position in various courts. These models are electrically lit and are so placed that the exhibits relating to the particular industry or activity can be grouped around them. **1939** *Illustr. London News* 29 Apr. 715 The 'Perisphere', a huge sphere, 200 ft. in diameter, enclosing a diorama of a city of tomorrow. **1959** W. S. Sharps *Dict. Cinemat.* 90/2 *Diorama*, a small set used in place of a much larger one, usually in order to suggest location or time.

Hence **dio'ramist**, a proprietor or exhibitor of a diorama.

1834 Hood *Tylney Hall* (1840) 246 Here an indignant dioramist raves at a boggling scene-shifter.

dioramic (daɪɒ'ræmɪk), *a.* [f. DIORAMA + -IC. (Gr. analogies would require *dioramatic.*)] Of the nature of, or pertaining to, a diorama.

1831 Brewster *Nat. Magic* iv. (1833) 66 The same picture exhibited under all the imposing accompaniments of a dioramic representation. **1861** Musgrave *By-roads* 251 There is another chapel..where the same dioramic effect has been produced by concealed coloured glass lights. **1881** *Daily Tel.* 27 Dec., Well-managed dioramic effects, depicting a terrible storm with..thunder and lightning.

diorism ('daɪərɪz(ə)m). *rare.* [ad. Gr. διορισμ-ός, distinction, logical division, f. διορίζ-ειν to draw a boundary through, divide, distinguish.] The act of defining; distinction, definition: by H. More used app. as = distinctive sense or application.

1664 H. More *Exp. 7 Churches* 71 To eat things sacrified to Idols is one mode of Idolatry; but, by a Propheticall Diorism, it signifies Idolatry in general. **1860** —— *Apocal. Apoc.* 92 If they were not just four..yet by a Prophetick Diorisme they might be called four. **1685** —— *Illustration* 335 In a Mystical sense, by a Diorism, The Musick may be that at their Idolatrous worship.

†**dio'ristic,** *a. Obs.* [ad. Gr. διοριστικ-ός distinctive; f. as prec.] Serving to define or distinguish; defining.

1675 Collins in Rigaud *Corr. Sci. Men* (1841) I. 216 In this case one of the dioristic limits is lost. **1684** *Phil. Trans.* XIV. 575 A Cardanick Æquation..such as shall have the dioristick limits rational.

†**dio'ristical,** *a. Obs.* [f. as prec. + -AL[1].] = prec. Hence **dio'ristically** *adv.*, by distinctive application: see DIORISM.

1664 H. More *Exp. 7 Churches* 72 Ye are not..free from the Lusts of the flesh (which Vice is here noted by Nicolaitism dioristically, as Idolatry in general before by eating things sacrificed to Idols). **1668** —— *Div. Dial.* v. xl. (1713) 521 The Lake of Fire and Brimstone not symbolical or dioristical, but visible or natural.

diorite ('daɪəraɪt). *Min.* [a. F. *diorite* (Haüy), irreg. f. διορίζ-ειν to distinguish + -ITE.] A variety of GREENSTONE, consisting of hornblende combined with a triclinic feldspar (albite or oligoclase).

1826 W. Phillips *Outl. Mineral. & Geol.* 151 The Diabase, Diorite, and Amphibolite of French authors, seems to include both Greenstone and Hornblende rock. **1858** Geikie *Hist. Boulder* xii. 239 Hornblendic greenstones, or diorites. **1865** Lubbock *Preh. Times* vi. (1869) 182 The axe was preeminently the implement of antiquity. Serpentine and diorite were the principal materials.

attrib. **1877** A. B. Edwards *Up Nile* xxii. 709 The magnificent diorite statue of Shafra, the builder of the Second Pyramid. **1890** *Goldfields Victoria* 17 The stone.. running through a diorite dyke.

dioritic (daɪɒ'rɪtɪk), *a.* [f. DIORITE + -IC.] Of the nature of diorite; containing diorite.

1847 in Craig. **1853** Kane *Grinnell Exp.* vii. (1856) 55 A similar range..on the Atlantic side, evidently a continuation of the same dioritic series. **1862** Dana *Man. Geol.* iii. 78 Dioritic Schist.

‖**diorthosis** (daɪɔː'θəʊsɪs). [mod.L., a. Gr. διόρθωσις, n. of action f. διορθό-ειν to make straight, f. δι-, δια- through, thoroughly + ὀρθός straight, right.] The act of setting straight or in order: **a.** in *Surg.*, the straightening of crooked or fractured limbs. **b.** The recension or revision of a literary work.

1704 in J. Harris *Lex. Techn.* (J.). **1706** Phillips (ed. Kersey), *Diorthosis*, in Surgery, an Operation, whereby crooked or distorted Members are made even, and restor'd to their Original and Regular Shape. **1873** *Brit. Q. Rev.* LVII. 297 The diorthosis (i.e. the setting free from figure and parable, the fulfilment) of the Old Testament in the New. **1874** H. R. Reynolds *John Bapt.* viii. 500 Christ was the diorthosis of the temple.

diorthotic (daɪɔː'θɒtɪk), *a.* [ad. Gr. διορθωτικ-ός corrective: derived as prec.] Of or pertaining to recension of a literary work (see prec. b).

1860 M. Pattison *Ess.* (1889) I. 162 No sooner had Scaliger placed himself by common consent at the head of textual criticism, than he took leave for ever of diorthotic criticism.

dioscoreaceous (daɪɒˌskəʊrɪ'eɪʃəs), *a. Bot.* [f. mod.L. *Dioscoreāceæ*, f. *Dioscorea*, the typical genus, containing the yams.] Of or belonging to the N.O. *Dioscoreaceæ* of Monocotyledons.

dioscorein (daɪɒ'skəʊrɪɪn). [f. *Dioscorea* + -IN.] 'An impure substance made by precipitating the tincture of *Dioscorea villosa* with water' (*Syd. Soc. Lex.* 1883).

Dioscuric (daɪə'skjʊərɪk), *a.* Also dioscuric. [f. Gr. Διόσκουροι, f. Διός, gen. of Ζεύς Zeus + κοῦρ-ος, κόρ-ος boy, son + -IC.] Of, pertaining to, or resembling the legend of the twins Castor and Pollux. Also **Dio'scurian** *a.* Hence **Dioscurism** (daɪ'ɒskjʊərɪz(ə)m).

1903 J. R. Harris *Dioscuri* 42 Let us..examine a third case of twin saints in the Christian calendar, and test it..for Dioscurism. *Ibid.* 47 We naturally enquire..whether there are any Dioscuric features about them. *Ibid.* 61 The popular religion was deeply tinctured with Dioscurism. **1956** E. E. Evans-Pritchard *Nuer Relig.* v. 129 These dioscuric descriptions of twins are common to many peoples.

diose ('daɪəʊz, -s). *Chem.* [f. DI-[2] + -OSE[2].] A generic term, analogous to triose, hexose, etc., for a 'sugar' containing two carbon atoms; the only possible one is glycolaldehyde, CH-O·CH_2OH.

1904 *Jrnl. Phys. Chem.* VIII. 509 Dioses, trioses, tetroses. **1948** W. W. Pigman *Chem. Carbohydrates* i. 17 Carbohydrates are usually classified according to the number of carbon atoms, *e.g.* pentoses, hexitols, heptonic acids. 'Monose', however, has been used as a short term for the preferred term 'monosaccharide', and also as a superfluous synonym for 'formaldehyde'. Similarly, glycolic aldehyde is called a 'diose', whereas the ending '-biose' denotes a disaccharide, as in 'melibiose' and 'gentibiose'.

diosgenin (daɪ'ɒsdʒənɪn). *Chem.* [a. G. *diosgenin* (Tsukamoto & Ueno 1936, in *Jrnl. Pharm. Soc. Japan* (*Trans.*) LVI. 136), f. mod.L. *Dios(corea* (see below) + GENIN.] A crystalline sapogenin, $C_{27}H_{42}O_3$, obtained chiefly from Mexican yams of the genus *Dioscorea* and used in the preparation of steroid hormones such as cortisone.

1937 *Chem. Abstr.* XXXI. 3493 (*heading*) Constitution of diosgenin. **1955** *Sci. Amer.* Jan. 59/3 Several groups sought a route to cortisone from the abundantly available natural sterols, particularly cholesterol, ergosterol and diosgenin. **1966** *New Scientist* 15 Dec. 619/1 Chemists..had revolutionized steroid therapy by synthesizing progesterone from the diosgenin found in the roots of the wild Mexican yam. **1966** E. Palmer *Plains of Camdeboo* xvii. 275 Our Elephant's Foot is *Dioscorea elephantipes* (*Testudinaria elephantipes*), and its genus has recently leaped to fame for certain of its members—among them our Elephant's Foot —contain diosgenin from which cortisone is manufactured.

‖**Diosma** (daɪ'ɒsmə). *Bot.* [mod.L., f. Gr. δῖ-ος divine + ὀσμή odour.] A genus of South African heath-like plants (N.O. *Rutuaceæ*), with strong balsamic odour.

1794 Martyn *Rousseau's Botany* xvi. 209. **1800** J. Abercrombie *Ev. Man his own Gardener* (ed. 16) 251 African heaths..diosmas..will require to be frequently refreshed with moderate waterings. **1866** *Treas. Bot.* 411/1 *Diosma*..cultivated for their white or pinkish flowers.

Hence **di'osmin** (see quot. 1883).

1837 *Penny Cycl.* IX. 5/1 Brandes considers the extractive to be peculiar, and terms it Diosmin. **1883** *Syd. Soc. Lex.*, *Diosmin*, a bitter principle, of brownish yellow colour, soluble in water, obtained from the Diosma crenata.

‖**diosmosis** (daɪɒs'məʊsɪs). Also in anglicized form **'diosmose**. [mod. f. Gr. δι-, δια- through + OSMOSIS: cf. *end-*, *exosmosis*.] The transudation of a fluid through a membrane; = OSMOSIS.

1825 W. Stirling tr. *Landor's Text-bk. Hum. Phys.* I. 393 This exchange of fluids is termed *endosmosis* or *diosmosis*. **1883** *Syd. Soc. Lex.*, *Diosmose*..*Diosmosis*, same as *Osmosis*.

Hence **dio'smotic** *a.*, pertaining to diosmosis; = OSMOTIC.

diosphenol (daɪəs'fiːnəl). *Chem.* [f. DIOS(MA + PHENOL.] A crystalline odoriferous compound, $C_{10}H_{16}O_2$, the main constituent of buchu leaf oil.

1880 F. A. Flückiger in *Pharm. Jrnl.* XI. 219/1 On submitting 35 kilograms of round buchu leaves to distillation (*Barosma betulina*), I obtained 180 grams of essential oil... An oily layer..concretes, and affords a crystallized mass of what we may call *diosphenol*, with allusion to Diosma, the original Linnean name bestowed on the buchu plants. **1934** *Jrnl. Chem. Soc.* I. 240 The very intense absorption of diosphenol is, of course, due to its being an enolised ketone. **1949** E. Guenther *Essential Oils* III. 371 The main constituent of buchu leaf oil is diosphenol (buchu camphor) $C_{10}H_{16}O_2$, a ketophenol.

‖**diota** (daɪ'əʊtə). *Gr.* and *Rom. Antiq.* [L. *diōta*, a. Gr. διώτη two-eared, f. δι-, (DI-[2]) doubly + ὠτ- stem of οὖς ear.] A vessel with two ears or handles.

1857 Birch *Anc. Pottery* (1858) I. 199 The emblems upon them were various, comprising leaves, an eagle, a head of Hercules, diota, and bunch of grapes. **1890** W. Smith *Dict. Gr. & Rom. Antiq.* (ed. 3) I. 640 *Diota*..is generally used as synonymous with amphora, though it may signify any two-handled vessel..A diota of the earliest style.

diothelism, -ite, irreg. ff. DYOTHELISM, etc.

‖**di'oti, dihoti.** *Obs.* [Gr. διότι wherefore, for what reason, for the reason that, f. διά (τοῦτο) ὅτι for the reason that.] A 'wherefore'.

1651 Biggs *New Disp.* Summary 35 The Schools ignorant of the Quiddities and Dihoties of things. **1687** *Pharisee Unmask'd* 6 To satisfie those to whom he hath promised a Demonstration Dioti. **1734** Watts *Reliq. Juv.* (1789) 79 He set forth the analysis of the words in order, shewed the *Hoti* and the *Dioti* (i.e. that it was so, and why it was so).

Diotrephes (daɪˈɒtrɪfiːz). The name of a man mentioned 3 John 9, 10, as loving to have the preeminence in the church; hence used typically of persons to whom this character is attributed. Hence **Diotreˈphesian**, **Dioˈtrephian**, **Dioˈtrephic** *adjs.*, like Diotrephes; **Diˌotreˈphetically** *adv.*, in the manner of Diotrephes; **Diˈotrephist**, an imitator of Diotrephes.

1628 WITHER *Brit. Rememb.* VI. 711 And, some there be, that with Diotrophes, Affect preheminence in these our dayes. **1660** FISHER *Rusticks Alarm* Wks. (1679) 357 A meer Diotrephetically impudent and impositively prating Spirit. *Ibid.* 557 Chief Priests, aspiring Rabbies, Divinity Doctors, proud Diotrepheses. **1674** OWEN *Holy Spirit* (1693) 161 Fuel in it self unto the Proud, Ambitious Minds of Diotrephists. **1829** SOUTHEY *Sir T. More* II. 59 A man may figure as the Diotrephes of a Meeting. **1838** G. S. FABER *An Inquiry* IV. iv. 585 The diotrephic lovers of preëminence. **1845** T. W. COIT *Puritanism* 475 Is there any of the old Diotrephian spirit left? **1862** J. MACFARLANE *Life G. Lawson* iv. 194 Dr. Lawson asked the name of this Diotrephesian female.

dioxan (daɪˈɒksən). *Chem.* Also **dioxane** (-eɪn). [f. DIOXY-, DIOX- + -AN, -ANE.] Any of three liquids, $C_4H_8O_2$, with a molecular structure consisting of a saturated ring of four carbon and two oxygen atoms; *spec.* 1, 4-dioxan, used in large quantities as a solvent. Also, any of the derivatives of these compounds.

1912 *Jrnl. Chem. Soc.* CI. 1803 This compound rapidly loses dioxan. **1946** *Nature* 19 Oct. 553/2 Alginic acid diacetate swells, but does not dissolve, in water,..dioxan and glacial acetic acid at ordinary temperatures. **1947** *New Biol.* III. 124 A solution of Formvar in 1–4 dioxane is commonly used. **1951** A. GROLLMAN *Pharmacol. & Therap.* xii. 230 A number of dioxane derivatives have been.. demonstrated to have an adrenolytic but not a sympatholytic action. **1960** E. H. RODD *Chem. Carbon Compounds* IV. xvi. 1525 The 1:3-dioxans are methylene ethers of l:3-glycols and the 1:2-dioxans, of which little is known, are cyclic peroxides. **1965** PHILLIPS & WILLIAMS *Inorg. Chem.* I. xv. 568 Advantages accrue on going to a solvent such as dioxan or dimethyl-formamide which have very low solvolysis constants.

dioxide (daɪˈɒksaɪd, -sɪd). *Chem.* [f. DI-² 2 + OXIDE.] An oxide formed by the combination of two equivalents of oxygen with one of the metal or metalloid, as Carbon dioxide CO_2, Manganese dioxide MnO_2.

Originally applied to an oxide containing two equivalents of the chlorous element: see DI-² 2 ¶.

1847 in CRAIG. **1854** J. SCOFFERN in *Orr's Circ. Sc.* Chem. 491 Corresponding with the sub or di-oxide of copper. **1869** A. J. JARMAN in *Eng. Mech.* 17 Dec. 330/1 The easiest way to prepare oxygen gas is to heat together in a retort three parts potassic chlorate with one part dioxide of manganese. **1878** HUXLEY *Physiogr.* 80 An invisible gas, known as *carbon dioxide*, or more commonly *carbonic acid*.

dioxin (daɪˈɒksɪn). *Chem.* [f. DIOXY-, DIOX- + -IN¹.] **a.** Any of three unsaturated heterocyclic compounds, two having the formula $C_4H_6O_2$ and the third $C_4H_4O_2$; *spec.* *p*-dioxadiene, $C_4H_4O_2$, a liquid.

1919 *Chem. Abstr.: Decennial Index I–X* 2841/2 Dioxin. **1939** *Jrnl. Amer. Chem. Soc.* LXI. 3020/1 Dioxadiene, although hitherto unknown, has long been listed in chemical abstracts under the name of Dioxin. It is used as the fundamental or parent nucleus for the cataloging of dioxane, dioxene, and their derivatives.

b. Any of numerous derivatives of dioxin; *spec.* = *tetrachlorodibenzo(-p-)dioxin* s.v. TETRA- 2 a.

1970, etc. [see *tetrachlorodibenzoparadioxin* s.v. TETRA- 2 a]. **1970** *New Yorker* 14 Mar. 124/3 Extensive teratogenic, or fetus-deforming, effects were discovered in chick embryos when the dioxin, or a distillate predominantly consisting of it, was present at concentrations of little more than a trillionth of a gram per gram of the egg. **1974** *Sci. Amer.* Apr. 50/1 The committee found no hard evidence of human illness or of congenital malformations attributable to the herbicides, although 2,4,5-T in particular, and its contaminant, dioxin, have been seriously implicated in animal studies. **1976** *Nature* 19 Aug. 637/1 The dioxin TCDD is a contaminant present in 2,4,5-T at levels variously estimated at between 0.07 and 50 p.p.m. **1978**, etc. [see *tetrachlorodibenzoparadioxine* s.v. TETRA- 2 a]. **1980** *Science* 24 Oct. 386/2 The term chlorinated dibenzo-*p*-dioxins, or more simply chlorinated dioxins, refers to 75 compounds or any combination of the 75. **1986** *St. Louis* (Missouri) *Post-Dispatch* 28 May 7A/3 The Illinois court reversed a multi-million-dollar verdict in a suit over a spill of dioxin in Sturgeon, Mo.

diˈoxy-, diox-. *Chem.* [f. DI-² 2 + OXY-(GEN.] A combining element expressing the presence in a compound of two atoms of oxygen; *spec.* the presence in an organic compound of two equivalents of the monad radical hydroxyl (OH) taking the place of two atoms of hydrogen, as ***dioxy-acid***, ***dioxybenzene***, $C_6H_4(OH)_2$ (benzene being C_6H_6).

1877 WATTS *Fownes' Chem.* (ed. 12) II. 541 Two dioxybenzoic acids are obtained by fusing the two disulphobenzoic acids with potassium hydroxide. One of these dioxy-acids forms crystals..not coloured by ferric chloride.

dip (dɪp), *v.* Pa. t. and pple. **dipped, dipt**, pr. pple. **dipping**. Forms: 1 **dypp-an, dipp-an**, 2–6 **dypp-e(n**, 3–5 **duppe(n (y)**, 3–6 **dippe**, 6– **dip**. *Pa. t.* 6 **dypte, dypped**, 6– **dipped** (*Sc.* **dippit**), 7 **dipp'd, dip'd**, 7– **dipt**. *Pa. pple.* 1–6 **dypped**, (5 **deppyd**), 6– **dipped** (*Sc.* **dippit**), 7– **dipt**. [OE. *dyppan* wk. vb. (pa. t. *dypte*, pple. *dypped*:—OTeut. **dupjan*, f. weak grade *dup-* of ablaut series **deup-*, *daup-*, *dup-*, whence the adj. DEEP (:—**deup-oz*). Cf. the cognate DEPE *v.*]

I. Transitive senses.

1. To put down or let down temporarily or partially *in* or *into* a liquid, or the like, or the vessel containing it (usually with the notion of wetting, or of taking up a portion of the liquid, etc.); to immerse; to plunge (but with less implication of force and splashing, the sound of the word expressing a light though decided act).

c **1000** *Ags. Gosp.* Mark xiv. 20 Se ðe his hand on disce mid me dypð. *c* **1000** *Sax. Leechd.* III. 118 Nim þanne hnesce wulle and dupe on ele. **1340** HAMPOLE *Pr. Consc.* 8044 A vesselle dypped alle bidene In water, or in other lycour thyn. **1382** WYCLIF *Luke* xvi. 24 Fadir Abraham..send Lazarus, that he dippe the last part of his fyngur in watir, and kele my tunge. **1535** COVERDALE *John* xiii. 26 It is he vnto whom I dyppe the soppe & geue it. And he dypte in the soppe and gaue it vnto Iudas Iscarioth. **1581** MULCASTER *Positions* xxvii. (1887) 104 The Germains..vsed then to dippe their new borne children into extreme cold water. **1602** SHAKS. *Ham.* IV. vii. 143, I but dipt a knife in it. **1651** HOBBES *Leviath.* III. xxxvi. 224 Clothed in a garment dipt in bloud. **1742** POPE *Dunc.* IV. 163 A Poet the first day he dips his quill. **1801** *Med. Jrnl.* XXI. 82 A piece of loaf bread, dipt in cold water. **1823** LAMB *Elia* Ser. II. *New Year's Coming of Age*, He dipt his fist into the middle of the great custard. **1839** G. BIRD *Nat. Philos.* 144 If a magnet be dipped in iron filings, it will attract, and cause them to adhere to its surface.

absol. **1607** SHAKS. *Timon* III. ii. 73 Who can call him his Friend, That dips in the same dish? **1878** BROWNING *Poets Croisic* 83 Up with quill, Dip and indite!

fig. **1581** PETTIE *Guazzo's Civ. Conv.* II. (1586) 67 For you dip somewhat the Pensill of your Tongue in the fresh and cleere coulour of the Tuscane tongue. **1602** SHAKS. *Ham.* IV. vii. 19 The great loue the generall gender beare him, Who dipping all his Faults in their affection, Would..Conuert his Gyues to Graces. **1818** SHELLEY *Rev. Islam* IX. xii, By.. the name Of thee, and many a tongue which thou hadst dipped in flame.

2. To immerse in baptism; to baptize by immersion (now usually *contemptuous*). In quot. 1602 = CHRISTEN *v.* 3. Also *absol.*

c **975** *Rushw. Gosp.* Matt. iii. 11 Ic eowic depu & dyppe in wættre in hreunisse. *c* **1200** ORMIN 1551 þurrh þatt tatt tu fullhtnesst hemm & unnderr waterr dippesst. *c* **1315** SHOREHAM 11 And wanne hi cristneth ine the founȝt The prestes so thries duppeth, In the honur of the Trinite. *c* **1400** MAUNDEV. (Roxb.) iii. 10 þai make bot ane vnccioun, when þai cristen childer, ne dippes þaim bot anes in þe fount. **1552** *Bk. Com. Prayer, Publ. Baptism* Rubric, Then the Priest shall take the child..and..shall dip it in the water. **1602** MARSTON *Ant. & Mel.* I. Wks. 1856 I. 15 It pleas'd the font to dip me Rossaline. **1639** SALTMARSH *Policy* 73 These whom wee would have members of a Visible Church, we baptize and dip. **1766** WESLEY *Wks.* (1872) III. 248 He and six-and-twenty more have been dipped! **1876** BANCROFT *Hist. U.S.* II. xxx. 262 The confessions..began to be directed against the Anabaptists. Mary Osgood was dipped by the devil.

3. In various technical processes: see also DIPPING *vbl. sb.* I. *spec.* **a.** To immerse in a colouring solution; to dye, imbue. Also with the colouring matter as subject, or with the resulting colour as object. (*poetic*)

1667 MILTON *P.L.* V. 283 Six wings he [a Seraph] wore.. the middle pair..round Skirted his loines and thighes with downie Gold And colours dipt in Heav'n. *Ibid.* XI. 244 Iris had dipt the wooff. **1712–4** POPE *Rape Lock* II. 65 Thin glitt'ring textures of the filmy dew, Dipt in the richest tincture of the skies. **1780** COWPER *Table T.* 703 Fancy that from the bow that spans the sky Brings colours dipped in Heaven. **1887** BOWEN *Virg. Æneid* V. 112 Raiment dipped in the purple.

b. To make (a candle) by repeatedly dipping a wick in melted tallow.

1712 *Act 10 Anne* in *Lond. Gaz.* No. 5031/6 Before he begins to make or dip any Making or Course of Candles. *c* **1865** LETHEBY in *Circ. Sc.* I. 93/2 To dip a number of candles at the same time.

c. *to dip sheep*: To bath them in a poisonous liquor for the purpose of killing the vermin and cleansing the skin.

1840 *Jrnl. Roy. Agric. Soc.* Ser. I. I. 324 A person who travels from farm to farm dipping sheep for the ticks. **1847** *Trans. Highl. & Agric. Soc. Scot.* Ser. III. II. 300 Three men to dip and a boy to drive water, can easily bathe 600 to 800 sheep in a day. **1853** *Catal. R. Agric. Soc. Show* I Such is the importance..of dipping with this composition, that no extensive flock-master ought to be without it.

4. a. To suffuse with moisture; to impregnate by, or as if by, immersion.

1634 MILTON *Comus* 802 A cold shuddering dew Dips me all o'er. **1678** DRYDEN *All for Love* II. i, These poison'd Gifts ..Miriads of bluest Plagues lie underneath 'em, And more than Aconite has dipt the Silk.

†**b.** *fig.* Applied to the use of the liquor in which a toast is drunk. *Obs.*

a **1657** R. LOVEDAY *Lett.* (1663) 36 We dip'd some choice healths..in the best Laurentian Liquor. *Ibid.* 95 Diping your health in the noblest liquor.

c. To penetrate, as by dipping; to dip into. *rare.*

1842 TENNYSON *Morte d'Arthur* 143 But ere he dipt the surface, rose an arm..And caught him [i.e. Excalibur the sword] by the hilt.

5. a. To obtain or take *up* by dipping; to lift out of a body of liquid, etc.: usually with *up*.

to dip snuff (*South. U.S.*): to take snuff by dipping a split or brush-like stick or bit of rattan into it and rubbing it upon the teeth and gums. Also *absol.*

1602 CAREW *Cornwall* 30 b, The shrimps are dipped up in shallow water by the shore side, with little round nets. **1824** MISS MITFORD *Village* Ser. I. (1863) 45 There she stands at the spring, dipping up water for to-morrow. **1848–60** BARTLETT *Dict. Amer.*, *To dip snuff*, a mode of taking tobacco. **1849** *Knickerbocker* XXXIV. 117 The 'gude woman' sat in the corner 'rubbing snuff', or 'dipping'. **1861** L. L. NOBLE *Icebergs* 272 Fresh water may be dipped in winter, from small open spaces in the bay. **1864** J. T. TROWBRIDGE *Cudjo's Cave* xxxiv. 332 For this excellent woman snuffed, 'dipped' and smoked. **1886** *Century Mag.* Feb. 586 Sam Upchurch smoked his pipe, and Peggy dipped snuff, but Dyer declined joining them in using tobacco. **1913** M. W. MORLEY *Carolina Mts.* 169 Nor is snuff taken after the manner of former generations of snuff-takers. Here the people 'dip'.

b. *intr.* or *absol.* To pick pockets. Also *trans.* *slang.*

[**1817** *Sporting Mag.* (Farmer), I have dipped into 150.. pockets and not found a shilling.] **1857** 'DUCANGE ANGLICUS' *Vulgar T.* 6 *Dip*, to pick pockets. **1925** *Brit. Weekly* 12 Mar. 573/2 If you don't want to get 'dipped' [*i.e.*, have your pocket picked], buy..small nuts and put them in your pocket with your cash. There isn't one of the boys can dip you then. **1929** *Detective Fiction Weekly* 2 Mar. 696/1 The first fourteen years I dipped I got grabbed eleven times. **1930** E. WALLACE *White Face* vii. 89 You went over and you dipped him for his clock and pack. **1967** *Listener* 14 Sept. 325/3 Somebody is..going to dip his back pocket.

6. *transf.* **a.** To lower or let down for an instant, as if dipping in a liquid; *spec.* to lower and then raise (a flag) as a naval salute, or (a sail) in tacking.

1776 *Trial of Nundocomar* 43/2 He dipt his seal on the cushion [ink-pad], and sealed the bond. **1859** READE *Love me little* II. iv. 174 'They have not got to dip their sail, as we have, every time we tack'..'I and the boy will dip the lug'.. Now this operation is always a nice one, particularly in these small luggers, where the lug has to be dipped, that is to say, lowered and raised again on the opposite side of the mast. **1882** NARES *Seamanship* (ed. 6) 148 The men who dip the sail should stand on the lee side. **1894** C. N. ROBINSON *Brit. Fleet* 179 To-day, 'dipping the flag' is an act of courtesy; men-of-war do not do it to one another, but if merchant ships 'dip' their ensigns to them they reply in a similar manner.

b. To cause to sink; to lower, depress.

1879 GEO. ELIOT *Coll. Breakf. P.* 418 Duty or social good ..Would dip the scale.

c. *Forestry.* (See quot.)

1877 T. KELLY in *N.Z. Country Jrnl.* I. 244 On the side the tree will most easily fall [the experienced bushman] dips it—that is, he cuts in a deep notch from the circumference towards the centre.

d. To lower (the beams of the headlights of a vehicle). Also *absol.*

1909 KIPLING *Actions & Reactions* 117 'No. 162' lifts to a long-drawn wail of a breeze..and we make Valencia..at a safe 7000 feet, dipping our beam to an incoming Washington packet. **1922** *Motor* 31 Oct. Suppl. p. xxxiv (Advt.), The A-L Anti-Dazzle Focus Headlight Attachment... No 'dipping'. No 'dimming'. **1928** '*Motor*' *Manual* (ed. 27) xi. 152 The type of headlamp which is so arranged that the beam can be dipped, swivelled, or both, at the will of the driver. **1936** *Discovery* Oct. 302/1 One effect of this beneficent discovery will be to render unnecessary the regulations for dipping and extinguishing headlights. **1959** '*Motor*' *Manual* (ed. 36) viii. 218 Do not engage in headlight battles. Always dip when another vehicle approaches. **1965** PRIESTLEY & WISDOM *Good Driving* ii. 20 A dipper switch..enables you to dip the beam. **1969** G. BLACK *Cold Jungle* x. 142 Headlights came at us. Rob dipped.

7. *fig.* **a.** To immerse, involve, implicate (*in* any affair, esp. of an undesirable kind). Chiefly in *pass.* (Cf. DEEP *a.* 19.) *Obs.* exc. as in b.

a **1627** MIDDLETON *Changeling* III. iv, A woman dipp'd in blood, and talk of modesty! **1671–3** SIR C. LYTTELTON in *Hatton Corr.* (1878) 74 Sʳ Steph. Fox is dipt 70,000ˡⁱ deepe in that concerne. **1678** DRYDEN *Kind Keeper* Prol., True Wit has seen its best Days long ago, It ne'er look'd up, since we were dipt in Show. **1700** —— *Fables* Pref. (Globe) 500 He was a little dipped in the rebellion of the Commons. **1775** BURKE *Corr.* (1844) II. 50 Then we shall be thoroughly dipped, and then there will be no way of getting out, but by disgracing England, or enslaving America. **1789** MRS. PIOZZI *Journ. France* I. 139 He was a man deeply dipped in judicial astrology. **1798** H. WALPOLE *Lett.* (1857) I. Remin. iii. p. cix, Having been deeply dipped in the iniquities of the South Sea.

b. To involve in debt or pecuniary liabilities; to mortgage (an estate); to pawn. (*colloq.*)

1640 GLAPTHORNE *Wit in Constable* v, If you scorne to borrow, you may dip Your chaine. **1693** DRYDEN *Persius* VI. 160 Never dip thy Lands. *a* **1700** B. E. *Dict. Cant. Crew* s.v. *Layd-up*..Cloaths..are pawn'd or dipt for..Money. **1817** MAR. EDGEWORTH *Tales & Novels* (Rtldg.) IX. xii. 116 My little Jessica has..played away at a rare rate with my ready money—dipped me confoundedly. **1880** MISS BRADDON *Just as I am* ii, Nobody had ever been able to say that the Courtenay estate was 'dipped'. **1883** —— *Phant. Fort.* xxxv. (1884) 299 The young lady was slightly dipped.

II. Intransitive senses (some for *refl.*; others *absolute* uses).

8. To plunge down a little into water or other liquid and quickly emerge. Const. *in*, *into*, *under*.

1387 TREVISA *Higden* (Rolls) I. 119 A lantern wiþ lyȝt fleteþ and swymmeth aboue, and ȝif þe liȝt is iqueynt, it duppeþ doun and dryncheþ. **1719** DE FOE *Crusoe* (1840) I. iv. 66, I was fain to dip for it into the water. **1820** W. IRVING *Sketch Bk.*, *Voyage* (1887) 24 Her yards would dip into the water; her bow was almost buried beneath the waves. **1843** MACAULAY *Lays Anc. Rome*, *Horat.* vii, Unharmed the water-fowl may dip In the Volsinian mere. **1865** SWINBURNE *Atalanta* 16 Oars Break, and the beaks dip under, drinking death. **1884** W. C. SMITH *Kildrostan* I. i. 239 Slowly the muffled oars dip in the tide.

9. a. To plunge one's hand (or a ladle or the like) into water, etc., or into a vessel, esp. for the purpose of taking something out. **b.** *slang.* To pick pockets. **c.** *to dip* (*deeply,* etc.) *into one's purse, means,* etc.: (*fig.*) to withdraw or expend a considerable sum, to trench upon means.

1697 DRYDEN *Persius* II. 38 Suppose I dipp'd among the worst and Staius chose. **1817** *Sporting Mag.* (Farmer), I have dipped into 150..pockets and not found a shilling. *a* **1847** MRS. SHERWOOD *Lady of Manor* I. viii. 334 In early life he had dipped so deeply into his property as obliged him to leave the country. **1884** *Chr. World* 19 June 453/2 As new schools are built, Mr. Mundella must dip more deeply into the national purse.

10. To fish by letting the bait dip and bob lightly on the water; = DAP *v.* 1, DIB *v.*[2] 3, DIBBLE *v.*[2] 2.

1799 G. SMITH *Laboratory* II. 272 The few which you may..take, by dipping or dapping, will scarcely be eatable. **1875** [see DIPPING *vbl sb.*].

11. *transf.* **a.** To sink or drop down through a small space, or below a particular level, as if dipping into water; to go down, sink, set.

a **1375** *Joseph Arim.* 534 He mette a gome on an hors..He hente vp his hachet and huttes him euene..Wiþ þe deþ in his hals downward he duppes. **1654** WHITLOCK *Zootomia* 312 Use the North Starre of the Ancients, till..that Guide dippeth under the Horizon. **1720** *Lett. fr. Lond. Jrnl.* (1721) 58 Before he had told it all, the Sun dipt in. **1781** COWPER *Hope* 374 Suppose the beam should dip on the wrong side. **1798** COLERIDGE *Anc. Mar.* 111, The Sun's rim dips; the stars rush out. **1853** KANE *Grinnell Exp.* iv. (1856) 31 During the bright twilight interval he [the sun] will dip but a few degrees below the horizon. **1884** BLACK *Jud. Shaks.* ix, The swallows dipping and darting under the boughs.

b. To move the body downwards in obeisance; to drop a curtsy; to 'bob'.

1817 BYRON *Beppo* lxv, To some she curtsies, and to some she dips.

c. To extend a little way downwards or below a surface (without motion); to sink.

1854 RONALDS & RICHARDSON *Chem. Technol.* (ed. 2) I. 292 The short pipes *v* are consequently allowed to project about that much above the level of the plate, while their lower extremities dip into shallow cups which remain filled with liquid. **1878** L. P. MEREDITH *Teeth* 68 Superficial decay [of the tooth] is confined to the enamel covering, or dips but slightly into the dentine. **1887** BOWEN *Virg. Æneid* III. 536 Two turreted precipice blocks Dip, like walls, to the wave.

12. To have a downward inclination; to incline or slope downwards; to be inclined to the horizon: *spec.* of the magnetic needle, and in *Geol.* of strata (see DIP *sb.* 4, 5).

1665 HOOKE *Microgr.* 172 The plain of it lies almost horizontal, but onely the forepart does dip a little, or is somewhat more deprest. **1727-51** CHAMBERS *Cycl.* s.v. *Dipping-needle*, A magnetical needle so hung as that..one end dips, or inclines to the horizon. **1747** HOOSON *Miner's Dict.* G iij, *Dipp* is when the Flat-Beds lies not Levell, but declines some way, and it is by them that we know when the Rock Dipps, unless we be on the Top of it. **1796** WITHERING *Brit. Plants* IV. 251 [Fungi]..Pileus convex..edge dipping down, 1½ to 2 inches over. **1806** *Gazetteer Scotl.* (ed. 2) 70 The strata are in some instances perpendicular to the horizon, and in all dip very much. **1820** SCORESBY *Acc. Arctic Reg.* II. 539 In this hemisphere, the north end of the needle dips, but the contrary in the southern hemisphere, where the south end of the needle dips. **1879** E. GARRETT *House by Works* I. 140 You have no idea how the road dips.

13. To go (more or less) deeply into a subject.

1755 YOUNG *Centaur* ii. Wks. 1757 IV. 134 But I shall not dip so deep in its consequences. **1842** TENNYSON *Locksley H.* 15 Here about the beach I wander'd..When I dipt into the future far as human eye could see.

14. *to dip into* (a book, a subject of study): to enter slightly and briefly into a subject, without becoming absorbed or 'buried' in it; said especially of reading short passages here and there in a book, without continuous perusal.

(Cf. *skim*, to read superficially and slightly but continuously.)

1682 DRYDEN *Relig. Laici* Pref. (Globe) 191 They cannot dip into the Bible, but one text or another will turn up for their purpose. **1686** GOAD *Celest. Bodies* II. i. 123 You cannot dip into a Diary but you will find it. **1760** GRAY *Lett.* Wks. 1884 III. 24, I have not attentively read him, but only dipp'd here and there. **1777** W. DALRYMPLE *Trav. Sp. & Port.* Pref. 4, I have endeavoured to dip a little into the state of government. **1794** SULLIVAN *View Nat.* II, Might not Moses have dipped..in the same source with the authors of the Shaasta? **1877** A. B. EDWARDS *Up Nile* iv. 96 We have of course been dipping into Herodotus.

dip (dɪp), *sb.* [f. DIP *v.*]

1. a. An act of dipping; a plunge or brief immersion in water or other liquid; a bathe; also *transf.* and *fig.*: see various senses of the verb.

1599 MARSTON *Sco. Villanie* I. iv. 189 For ingrain'd Habits, died with often dips, Art not so soone discoloured. **1686** GOAD *Celest. Bodies* I xvi. 101 The Celerity of a Boat is continued by a successive dip of the Oar. **1727-51** CHAMBERS *Cycl.* s.v. *Candle*, A trough to catch the droppings, as the Candles are taken out each dip. **1778** F. BURNEY *Evelina* I. xix. 122, I should advise you to take another dip. **1796** MRS. GLASSE *Cookery* xiv. 248 Have ready ..a pan of clean cold water, just give your pudding one dip in. **1843** JAMES *Forest Days* ii, 'I'll give him a dip in the horse pond'. **1871** J. MILLER *Songs Italy* (1878) 14 There was only the sound of the long oars' dip, As the low moon sailed up the sea. **1874** L. STEPHEN *Hours in Library* (1892) II. ii. 51 He rode sixty miles from his house to have a dip in the sea. **1879** J. J. YOUNG *Ceram. Art* 81 Stone-ware is very seldom glazed by a 'dip'.

b. *a dip in* or *into* (a book): see DIP *v.* 14.

1760 FOOTE *Minor* I. (1767) 25 Come, shall we have a dip in the history of the Four Kings this morning? **1838** JAS. GRANT *Sk. Lond.* 373 A half-hour's 'dip' into some circulating-library book.

c. The act of dipping up liquid, e.g. ink with the pen; the quantity taken up at one act of dipping.

1841 S. WARREN *10,000 a year* III. 10 He took his pen in his right hand with a fresh dip of ink in it. **1889** *Durham Univ. Jrnl.* 196 The same 'dip of ink' is always ready.

d. A curtsy, a 'bob': cf. DIP *v.* 11 b.

1792 WOLCOTT (P. Pindar) *Ode to Burke* Wks. 1812 III. 38 Then the Dame will answer with a dip. **1808** —— *Ep. to Mrs. Clarke* ibid. V. 392 The nods of Monarchs and the dips of Queens.

e. A going down out of sight or below the horizon.

1864 TENNYSON *En. Ard.* 244 Ev'n to the last dip of the vanishing sail She watch'd it.

f. *Naut.* The position of being dipped or lowered (of a sail: see DIP *v.* 6): in phr. *at the dip.*

1886 J. M. CAULFEILD *Seamanship Notes* 6 The church pendant is used at the dip at the mizen truck while working cables. **1893** MARKHAM in *Daily News* 3 July 5/6, I directed my flag lieutenant to keep the signal..at the dip.

g. *Pros.* An unstressed element in a line of alliterative verse. (G. *senkung.*) Cf. LIFT *sb.*[2]

1894 H. SWEET *Anglo-Saxon Reader* (ed. 7) p. lxxxviii, Each verse usually consists of four metrical elements, two lifts and two dips—that is, two strong- and two weak-stress elements. **1961** *Rev. Eng. Stud.* XII. 346 A metrical interpretation which..sets up metrical units ('lifts' and 'dips') which are defined in terms of stress relationships. *Ibid.* 347 Sequences of two unstressed syllables are counted as two 'dips', not one, if the two syllables belong to separate 'breath-groups'.

h. A receptacle from which a prize may be obtained by dipping; also *fig.*; *lucky dip* = LUCKY-BAG 1, or *bran-tub.*

1915 'BARTIMEUS' *Tall Ship* vii. 129 Pennies..to be extracted at great personal risk from an electric dip. **1927** W. E. COLLINSON *Contemp. Eng.* 20 Here one could for a small sum put one's hand into the..lucky dive (dip) and draw out a prize. **1933** J. THORPE *Happy Days* i. 28 Most of the sweet-shops at that time had 'lucky-dips'. **1934** [see BLIGHTY, BLIGHTY *sb.* c]. **1956** 'J. WYNDHAM' *Seeds of Time* 25 A sort of rigid, lucky-dip, take-it-or-leave-it system. **1967** P. MOYES *Murder Fantastical* xv. 219 Everything for the Lucky Dip is *wrapped* because of the bran.

2. Depth or amount of submergence (e.g. of a paddle-wheel) or depression; depth or distance below a particular level; depth of a vessel, etc.

1793 SMEATON *Edystone L.* §97 That ruler would mark upon the upright rod, the dip of the point on which it stood, below the level of the instrument. **1874** KNIGHT *Dict. Mech.*, *Dip*, the depth of submergence of the float of a paddlewheel. **1880** *Act 43-4 Vict.* c. 24 §17 Any attempt.. to deceive him in taking the dip or gauge of any vessel.

3. *Astron.* and *Surveying.* The angular distance of the visible horizon below the horizontal plane through the observer's eye; the apparent depression of the horizon due to the observer's elevation, which has to be allowed for in taking the altitude of a heavenly body.

1774 M. MACKENZIE *Maritime Surv.* I. 18 A Table of the Depression, or Dip, of the Horizon of the Sea. **1820** SCORESBY *Acc. Arctic Reg.* I. 444 The dip of the sea..at 20 feet height of the eye, the error would be 56 miles. **1828** J. H. MOORE *Pract. Navig.* (ed. 20) 154 The dip to be subtracted in the fore observation, and to be added in the back observation. **1875** BEDFORD *Sailor's Pocket-bk.* v. (ed. 2) 181 Measure angle..from maintop; add dip for that height.

4. The downward inclination of the magnetic needle at any particular place; the angle which the direction of the needle makes with the horizon.

1727-51 CHAMBERS *Cycl.* s.v. *Dipping-needle*, The dip..in the year 1576 he found at London to be 71° 50'. But the dip varies. **1820** SCORESBY *Acc. Arctic Reg.* II. 545 The intensity of the magnetic force was the greatest where the dip was the greatest. **1832** *Nat. Philos., Magnetism* iii. §98. 24 (Useful Knowl. Soc.) The dip diminishes as we approach the equator, and increases as we recede from it on either side. *c* **1865** J. WYLDE in *Circ. Sc.* I. 245/2 At the present time, the dip for London is about 67°.

5. a. Downward slope of a surface; *esp.* in *Mining* and *Geol.* the downward slope of a stratum or vein: estimated, as to direction, by the point of the compass towards which the line of greatest slope tends, and as to magnitude, by its angle of inclination to the horizon.

1708 J. C. *Compl. Collier* (1845) 40 There is a Rise, or Ascent, for a Colliery under Ground, and so by Consequence the Contrary Way a Dip or Setling. **1747** W. HOOSON *Miner's Dict.* G iij, The natural Dipp of a Vein is when it runs it self more down into the Rock. **1789** BRAND *Hist. Newcastle* II. 679 The strata..have an inclination or descent, called the dip, to some particular part of the horizon. **1832** DE LA BECHE *Geol. Man.* (ed. 2) 545 The direction of faults and mineral veins, and the dip of strata, are daily becoming of greater importance. **1877** A. H. GREEN *Phys. Geol.* 343 The line of dip is the line of greatest inclination that can be drawn on the surface of a bed. **1891** S. C. SCRIVENER *Fields & Cities* 10 The very sudden lowering of the water-line in the river just around the gap, and the dip of the water quickly and more quickly approaching the gap.

b. *Mining.* Short for *dip-head* (see 11).

1877 *Encycl. Brit.* VI. 69/1 The drawing roads for the coal may be of three different kinds,—(1) levels driven at right angles to the dip,..(2) rise ways, known as jinny roads, jig-brows, or up-brows,..(3) dip or down-brows, requiring engine power. **1883** W. S. GRESLEY *Gloss. Coal-M., Dip*.., a heading or other underground way driven to the deep... It is usual to drive a pair of dips about 10 yards apart every 180 yards or so. **1967** *Gloss. Mining Terms (B.S.I.)* VIII. 11 *Dip*, an underground roadway driven downhill, usually following the inclination of the strata.

6. A hollow or depression to which the surrounding high ground dips or sinks.

1789 W. GILPIN *Wye* 129 Woody hills which form beautiful dips at their intersections. **1834** BECKFORD *Italy* I. 175 We saw groves and villages in the dips of the hills. **1863** GEO. ELIOT *Romola* II. viii, The great dip of ground.. making a gulf between her and the sombre calm of the mountains. **1878** H. M. STANLEY *Dark Cont.* I. xvi. 434 The main column arrived at the centre of the dip in the Uzimba ridge.

7. (Short for *dip-candle.*) A candle made by repeatedly dipping a wick into melted tallow.

1815 W. H. IRELAND *Scribbleomania* 15 Paper..brown sugar to fold, Tea, soap..dip or choice mould. **1829** MARRYAT *F. Mildmay* viii. A purser's dip—*vulgo*, a farthing candle. *c* **1865** LETHEBY in *Circ. Sc.* I 93/2 Two sorts of candles are commonly met with in commerce—namely *dips* and *moulds*. **1887** STEVENSON *Underwoods* I. xxx. 63, I am a kind of farthing dip Unfriendly to the nose and eyes.

8. a. A preparation into which something is dipped, as *bronzing-dip, sheep-dip,* etc. (cf. DIP *v.* 3). Also, a vat or tank in which sheep-dip is used. So *dip yard.*

1871 *Trans. Highl. & Agric. Soc. Scot.* Ser. IV. III. 269 Any other dips I have seen. **1877** *N.W. Linc. Gloss., Dip*, a poisonous liquid in which sheep are dipped to kill fags. **1878** E. S. ELWELL *Boy Colonists* 103 A large dip was built there. **1883** R. HALDANE *Workshop Receipts* Ser. II. 244 The bronzing dip may be prepared by dissolving in 1 gal. hot water ½ lb. each perchloride of iron and perchloride of copper. **1885** *Daily News* 15 Feb. 5/6 Before the arrival of the last convoy there the carbolic acid was exhausted. Sheep dip had to be substituted. **1900** S. E. BLACKE *Flights from Land of Bellbird* i. 16 Then there were visits to the 'dip' beyond, where the sheep were washed. **1922** W. PERRY *Sheep Farming in N.Z.* iii. 20 It is wise to build a dip. **1933** L. G. D. ACLAND in *Press* (Christchurch) 2 Dec. 15/7 *Yards* for dipping [sheep]..are generally called *dip yards.*

b. A grade of turpentine. (See quot 1884, and cf. DIPPING *vbl. sb.* 2 b.)

1856, 1884 [see *virgin-dip* s.v. VIRGIN *a.* 18 b]. **1862** 'E. KIRKE' *Among Pines* 167 I've four barr'ls of 'dip' and tu of 'hard'. **1896** *Pop. Sci. Monthly* Feb. 473 The *dip* or crude turpentine is emptied.

9. a. A sweet sauce for puddings, etc. Also, any sauce or dressing; *spec.* the fat and juice left in the pan after meat has been cooked. (*local Eng.* and *U.S.*)

a **1825** FORBY *Voc. E. Anglia, Dip*, a sauce for dumplings, composed of melted butter, vinegar, and brown sugar. **1846** WORCESTER, *Dip*,..sauce made of fat pork for fish. *U.S.* **1884** *Cheshire Gloss., Dip*, sweet sauce eaten with pudding. If flavoured with brandy it is called *Brandy-dip*. **1894** T. F. ROBLEY *Hist. Bourbon Co., Kansas* 26 Some 'rashers' are cut from the 'flitch' of bacon and the grease tried out; eggs are fried, and 'dip' is made. **1931** 'N. BELL' *Life & Andrew Otway* viii. 345 'Lots of eggs..and loads of what cook used to call dip.'.. 'I shall eat the dip..with a piece of bread. You know, rub it round the plate.' **1960** *Spectator* 10 June 848 Jam-butties one day and bread and dip the next.

b. *pl.* Dough-boys. *Austral. colloq.*

1859 D. BUNCE *Trav. with Leichhardt* 161 Dr. Leichhardt gave the party a quantity of dough-boys, or, as we called them, dips. *Ibid.* 171 Dr. Leichhardt ordered the cook to mix up a lot of flour, and treated us all to a feed of dips.

c. A savoury mixture into which biscuits, etc., are dipped.

1960 J. KIRKWOOD *There must be a Pony!* (1961) viii. 61 We were up to our necks in dips: clam dip, cheese dip, mushroom dip. **1962** L. DEIGHTON *Ipcress File* xxi. 143, I was loaded with anchovy, cheese dip, hard egg and salmon. **1962** *Woman's Own* 1 Dec. 49/2 Have a trolley of savouries and 'dips' ready to wheel in. *Ibid.* 50/2 Use as a dip with crisps or savoury biscuits.

10. *Thieves' slang.* A pickpocket; also pocket-picking. (Cf. DIP *v.* 9 b.)

1859 in MATSELL *Vocab.* 26 (Farmer). **1888** *St. Louis Globe Democrat* (Farmer *Amer.*), A dip touched the Canadian sheriff for his watch and massive chain while he was reading the Riot Act. **1926** J. BLACK *You can't Win* iv. 35 No Missouri dip would take his roll, extract two fifty-dollar bills, and put the rest back in his pocket. **1936** J. CURTIS *Gilt Kid* xxix. 279 'Ginger King,' he said, 'I'm going to nick you for a dip.' **1938** F. D. SHARPE *Sharpe of Flying Squad* i. 13 They have rich, picturesque names, such as ..'Jimmy the Dip'. **1970** *Daily Tel.* 29 Apr. 4/6 New Yorkers who have had their pockets picked or handbags rifled on the city's Underground in recent years learned yesterday that the person responsible was probably a professional 'dip'.

11. a. *Comb.* [In some cases it is the verb-stem rather than the sb.]: **dip-bucket**, a bucket contrived to turn easily and dip into water; **dip-candle**, a candle made by repeatedly dipping a wick in melted tallow, a dipped candle; **dip-circle**, a dipping-needle having a vertical graduated circle for measuring the amount of the dip; **dip compass** = *dipping compass* (see DIPPING-NEEDLE); **dip equator**, the magnetic equator (see EQUATOR 3 b); **dip-head**, a heading driven to the dip in a coal-mine in which the beds have a steep inclination; whence *dip-head* *level*; **dip-needle** = DIPPING-NEEDLE; **dip-net**, a small net with a long handle, used to catch fish by dipping it in the water; **dip pen**, one that has to be dipped in the ink (opp. *fountain-pen*); **dip-pipe**, a valve in the hydraulic main of gas works, etc., arranged to dip into water or tar, or other liquid, and form a seal; a seal-pipe; **dip regulator** (see quot.); **dip-rod**, (*a*) a rod on which candle-wicks are hung to be dipped; (*b*) = *dipstick*; **dip-roller**, a form of roller used in printing-works for taking up ink; **dip-section**, a section showing the dip of the strata; **dip-sector**, a reflecting instrument on the principle of the sextant, used to ascertain the dip of the horizon: see SECTOR; **dip-side**, the side on which the dip or declivity is; **dip-splint**, a kind of friction match; **dip-stick, dipstick**, a rod for measuring the depth of liquid; **dip-switch, dipswitch**, a switch that dips the beams of a vehicle's headlights; **dip-trap**, a drain trap formed by a dip or depression of the pipe in which water stands so as to prevent the upward passage of sewer-gas; **dip-well**, a well whence water is got by dipping.

1829 MARRYAT *F. Mildmay* ii, On it stood a brass candle-stick, with a *dip-candle. **1864** THACKERAY *D. Duval* vii. (1869) 96 The apprentice.. came up.. from the cellar with a string of dip-candles. **1876** DAVIS *Polaris Exp.* ix. 218 One of the snow houses was designed for the *dip-circle. **1881** MAXWELL *Electr. & Magn.* II. 116 A new dip-circle, in which the axis of the needle.. is slung on two filaments of silk or spider's thread, the ends of the filaments being attached to the arms of a delicate balance. **1897** *Strand Mag.* Mar. 344/2 Its [*sc.* the Pole's] variable position was approximately determined by Sir James Clark Ross by help of the *dip compass. **1883** *Encycl. Brit.* XVI. 164/2 The line of no dip is called the magnetic or *dip equator. **1875** URE *Dict. Arts* III. 326 Were the coal-field an entire elliptical basin, the *dip-head levels carried from any point would be elliptical. *Ibid.* III. 328 It is, moreover, proper to make the first set of pillars next the dip-head much stronger. **1881** MAXWELL *Electr. & Magn.* II. 113 The magnetic dip is found by means of the *Dip Needle. **1858** THOREAU *Lett.* (1865) 171 The villagers catching smelts with *dip-nets in the twilight. **1945** B. MACDONALD *Egg & I* (1947) viii. 96 An ink bottle and a *dip pen. **1949** 'N. BLAKE' *Head of Traveller* xi. 172 'What are you looking for?'.. 'My dip pen.' 'Stylo run out?' **1874** KNIGHT *Dict. Mech.* I. 705 The seal-cup is charged with tar, which permits the movable *dip-pipe to be lifted into or out of the main. *a* **1884** KNIGHT *Dict. Mech.* Suppl., **Dip regulator*, a device used in gas works for regulating the seal of the dip-pipes in the hydraulic main, and for drawing off the heavy tar from the bottom of the main without disturbing the seal. **1923** *Man. Seamanship* II. 201 Care should be taken that the correct amount of oil is in the oil pump at the bottom of the base chamber; an oil cock or *dip rod is fitted for this purpose. **1934** *Times* 13 Feb. 10/4 The diprod, coil, Lockheed fluid tank on the dash.. are all handy. *a* **1884** KNIGHT *Dict. Mech.* Suppl., **Dip-roller* (Printing), a roller to dip ink from the fountain. **1884** *Nature* 13 Nov. 33 It is admirably seen in *dip-section on the east and north slopes. **1833** HERSCHEL *Astron.* i. 16 The visible area, as measured by the *dip-sector. **1834** *Mechanic's Mag.* 445. **1853** KANE *Grinnell Exp.* ix. (1856) 67 Minute observations of dip-sectors and repeating-circles. **1875** URE *Dict. Arts* III. 325 Have on the *dip side of the level a small quantity of water.. so as to guide the workmen in driving the level. **1892** *Northumbld. Gloss., Dip-side*, the low side. **1927** *Observer* 4 Dec. 11/4 The near side of the engine [of a new Ford motor vehicle] carries the self-starter and the oil-filler and a *dip-stick gauge only, and has almost a European appearance. **1953** *Word for Word (Whitbread & Co.)* 18/1 *Dipstick*, an instrument used to measure the quantity of wort in the fermenting squares prior to fermentation. **1970** *Motoring Which?* July 92/1 Apart from the awkward dipstick of the 18/85, day-to-day servicing was easy on all three cars. **1952** *San Francisco Chron.* 15 June 13L, American: dimmer switch. British: *dip switch. **1962** *Times* 13 Feb. 3/4 The floor buttons for dipswitch and screen-washers are too small. **1967** E. RUDINGER *Consumer's Car Glossary* (ed. 2) 33 *Dipswitch*, foot-operated button or hand-operated lever with which the driver changes the headlamps from the main beam to the dipped beam. **1883** E. A. PARKES *Pract. Hygiene* x. §2. 367 The common mason's or *dip-trap, and the notorious D trap. **1894** B. FOWLER in *Proc. Geol. Assoc.* XIII. 364 This clay throws out two fine springs, forming *dip-wells, in Hammer village.

b. In various attrib. uses of sense 5.

1839 URE *Dict. Arts* 964 Where the coal-measures are horizontal, and the faults run at a greater angle than 45° to the line of bearing, they are termed dip and rise faults. *Ibid.* 968 The true dip-line of the plane which leads to the outcrop. *Ibid.* 974 On the dip side of the gallery. *Ibid.* 992 The subterraneous fire broke forth with two heavy discharges from the dip-pit. *Ibid.* 994 In the dip-mine a double tram-road is laid. **1877** *Encycl. Brit.* VI. 63/2 Galleries driven at right angles to these [*sc.* the dip head level and lodgment level] are known as 'dip' or 'rise headings', according to their position above or below the pit bottom. **1879** *Ibid.* X. 297/1 A quarry is usually worked to the dip of a rock, hence the strike-joints form clean-cut faces in front of the workmen as they advance. These are known as 'backs', and the dip-joints which traverse them as 'cutters'. *Ibid.* 303/1 Dip-faults will often be observed to deviate considerably from the normal direction of dip. **1882** A. GEIKIE *Text-bk. Geol.* 502 In general they [*sc*. joints of stratified rocks] have two dominant trends, one coincident, on the whole, with the direction in which the strata are inclined from the horizon, and the other running transversely at a right angle or nearly so. The former set is known as dip-joints, because they run with the dip or inclination of the rocks. **1887** P. MCNEILL *Blawearie* 24 The firm.. had turned their whole force of men into the dip-workings, in order to exhaust the coal bordering on the march. **1900** *Geogr. Jrnl.* XV. 220 Its [*sc.* the Arun's] course was determined by the original dip-slope of the Wealden dome. **1957** *Encycl. Brit.* IX. 119/1 The dip-slip is the component of the net-slip measured directly down the dip of the fault plane. **1960** L. D. STAMP *Britain's Struct.* (ed. 5) v. 45 Valleys parallel to the dip of the rocks (dip valleys). **1961** J. CHALLINOR *Dict. Geol.* 61/2 *Dip-slope*, a slope of the ground which is determined.. by the dip of the beds. It is applied particularly to such a slope which ends upwards along the top of an escarpment and which is then opposed to the, usually steeper, scarp slope on the other side. **1965** G. J. WILLIAMS *Econ. Geol. N.Z.* xviii. 309/2 The amount of dip coal is difficult to estimate and it was suggested that 'the amount of workable dip coal is likely to be somewhat greater than the rise coal'. **1967** *Gloss. Mining Terms (B.S.I.)* VIII. 11 *Dip face*, a coal face advancing downhill. *Ibid.*, *Dip workings*, workings lying to the dip of any designated point in a seam.

Dip, dip (dɪp). (Also with full point.) Colloq. abbrev. of DIPLOMA *sb.* 2; so **Dip. AD**, Diploma in Art and Design; **Dip. Ed.**, Diploma in Education; see also DIP. TECH.

1895 W. C. GORE in *Inlander* Nov. 64 *Dip*, diploma. **1963** *Times* 11 May 9/4 Only four of the 29 colleges awarded DipAD recognition will be allowed to offer diploma courses in all four areas of art and design. **1967** M. DRABBLE *Jerusalem the Golden* v. 96, I would be stealing the state's money, wouldn't I? By doing a Dip Ed without meaning to teach? **1969** NAIRN & SINGH-SANDHU in Cockburn & Blackburn *Student Power* 104 The problems of art education in this country centre around the enigmatic initials 'Dip. AD'. This stands for the degree now conferred by authority after four years' attendance at our leading colleges of art: the Diploma in Art and Design. **1971** 'P. HOBSON' *Three Graces* i. 9, I can do my engineering dip. at the Tech.

dipar, obs. form of DIAPER.

dipartite (daɪˈpɑːtaɪt), *a.* [f. DI-[1], L. *dis-* asunder + *partīt-us* divided, f. *partīre* to divide, part. (The L. compound was *dispertītus*.)] Divided into various parts. So **dipartited** *ppl. a.*; **dipar'tition**, division, parting asunder.

1825 *New Monthly Mag.* XIII. 61 Whose form is either dipartited, or disposed in conglomerated magnificence. **1838** G. S. FABER *Hist. Vallenses* III. ix. 399 All men shall pass two ways; the good, to glory; the wicked, to torment. But, if any one shall not believe this dipartition, let him attend to Scripture from the end to the commencement. **1885** RUSKIN *Præterita* I. iii. 83 Upon which I found my claim to the sensible reader's respect for these dipartite writings.

di'paschal, *a.* [f. DI-[2] twice + PASCHAL.] Including two passovers.

a **1840** L. CARPENTER cited in WORCESTER.

dip-bucket, -circle: see DIP *sb.* 11.

dipchick, var. of DABCHICK.

dipe, obs. form of DEEP.

dip-ears (ˈdɪpɪəz). Also **dip-ear**. [f. DIP *v.* + EAR: 'from its graceful movements.' Swainson.] A marine bird, the Little Tern, *Sterna minuta*.

1885 SWAINSON *Prov. Names Brit. Birds* 204 Little Tern (*Sterna minuta*).. Dip ears (Norfolk).

dipeptidase (daɪˈpɛptɪdeɪz, -s). *Biochem.* [a. G. *dipeptidase* (Grassmann & Haag 1927, in *Zeitschr. f. physiol. Chemie* CLXVII. 189), f. DIPEPTIDE + -ASE.] Any enzyme that catalyses the hydrolysis of a dipeptide into its two constituent amino-acids but does not act on tripeptides or higher peptides.

1927 *Brit. Chem. Abstr.* A. 794/1 The dipeptidase hydrolyses all the dipeptides tested, but has no action on various natural proteins. **1939** W. B. YAPP *Introd. Animal Physiol.* i. 29 In the crab *Maia squinado* and in the marine snail *Murex anguliferus*.. the gut contains the same four proteases as are present in vertebrates, namely proteinase, carboxypolypeptidase, aminopolypeptidase, and dipeptidase. **1954** A. WHITE et al. *Princ. Biochem.* xi. 233 Dipeptidases.. specifically act only on certain dipeptides; an example is glycylglycine dipeptidase. **1960** E. L. SMITH in P. D. Boyer et al. *Enzymes* IV. i. 8 *Dipeptidases.* As yet, none of these enzymes have been obtained in homogeneous form.. however, it has been demonstrated that these enzymes do not attack tripeptides.

dipeptide (daɪˈpɛptaɪd). *Chem.* Also †-id. [f. DI-[2] + PEPTIDE.] Any compound composed of two amino-acid residues linked by a peptide bond.

1903 *Jrnl. Chem. Soc.* LXXXIV. I. 694 (*heading*) Derivatives of dipeptides and their behaviour towards pancreas ferments. **1955** *Sci. Amer.* May 37/1 A group of linked amino acids is known as a peptide: two units form a dipeptide, three a tripeptide and so on. **1965** G. W. ANDERSON in Florkin & Stotz *Comprehensive Biochem.* VI. vii. 258 When the term *dipeptide* is used, one ordinarily thinks of a compound formed of *alpha* amino acids which are joined by amide linkage of the carboxyl group of one acid with the amino of another. **1970** *New Scientist* 30 Apr. 217/3 The resulting dipeptide joins successively onto valine, then ornithine, then leucine.

dipetalous (daɪˈpɛtələs), *a.* *Bot.* [f. mod.L. *dipetal-us* (f. Gr. δι- (DI-[2]) twice + πέταλ-ον leaf, PETAL *sb.*) + -OUS.] Having two petals.

1707 SLOANE *Jamaica* I. Pref., Those which are Monopetalous first, those Dipetalous next. **1883** in *Syd. Soc. Lex.*

diphanite (ˈdɪfənaɪt). *Min.* [f. (1846) Gr. δι-, δίς twice, doubly + -φαν-ης showing, appearing + -ITE: 'because it has quite a different aspect according to the direction in which it is looked at'.] A name given by Nordenskiöld to a mineral now regarded as belonging to the species MARGARITE.

Viewed from the side, its prisms are bluish, transparent, and of vitreous lustre; looking down on the base, they are white, opaque, and of nacreous lustre.

1850 DANA *Min.* 292. **1868** *Ibid.* 507 Diphanite is from the Emerald mines of the Ural, with chrysoberyl and phenacite.

diphasic (daɪˈfeɪzɪk), *a.* [f. Gr. δι- (DI-[2]) twice + φάσις appearance, phase + -IC.] Characterized by having two phases: *spec.* (*a*) used of an electric variation of which the period of duration is divided into two stages, one positive and the other negative; (*b*) marked by two phases or stages (e.g. of growth); (*c*) consisting of two phases of matter (solid, liquid, or gas).

1881 BURDON SANDERSON in *Phil. Trans.* CLXXIII. 7 The diphasic character of the variation.. is due to the interference of the opposite electromotive actions of the upper and under cells. **1900** DORLAND *Med. Dict.* 206/1 *Diphasic*, doubly varied; said of electric currents of action in muscle. **1932** J. S. HUXLEY *Probl. Relative Growth* II. v. 70 'Diphasic' mammals or birds such as arctic fox,.. herons, owls, etc. **1936** *Discovery* Sept. 291/2 The diphasic wave that accompanies muscular and nervous activity. **1940** *Chambers's Techn. Dict.* 247/2 *Diphasic*, (of certain Trypanosomes) having a life-cycle which includes a free active stage. **1956** *Nature* 11 Feb. 280/1 Protozoa of this group [*sc.* Trypanosomidæ] being usually cultivated on complex diphasic media.

dip-head: see DIP *sb.* 11.

diphen- in chemical terms: see DI-[2] 2, PHEN-.

diphenhydramine (ˌdaɪfɛnˈhaɪdrəmiːn). *Pharm.* [f. DIPHEN(YL + *hydr-* (perh. from HYDROL) + AMINE.] An antihistamine compound, $(C_6H_5)_2CH{\cdot}O{\cdot}CH_2CH_2N(CH_3)_2$, used in the form of its hydrochloride, a white powder with a bitter taste, in the treatment of allergic disorders. Also *ellipt.* for ***diphenhydramine hydrochloride***.

1947 *Jrnl. Amer. Med. Assoc.* 27 Sept. 225/2 Diphenhydramine hydrachloride... The following dosage form has been accepted:.. Kapseals Benadryl Hydrochloride: 50 mg. **1952** *Brit. Encycl. Med. Practice* (ed. 2) XII. 147 Synthetic antihistamine compounds.. for the treatment of allergic disorders.. include diphenhydramine. **1964** W. G. SMITH *Allergy & Tissue Metabolism* vi. 69 In order to inhibit the activity due to histamine in the samples 2 to 3 mg. of diphenhydramine were added to the bath.

diphenic (daɪˈfiːnɪk), *a.* *Chem.* [f. DI-[2] + PHENIC.] In ***diphenic acid*** $(2C_6H_4.CO.OH)$ obtained by the oxidation of phenanthrene, one of the constituents of coal-tar. Its salts are **diphenates**.

1875 WATTS *Dict. Chem.* VII. 434 Diphenic acid heated with excess of quick lime, is converted, not into diphenyl, but into diphenylene ketone.

diphenol (daɪˈfiːnɒl). *Chem.* [f. DI-[2] + PHENOL (f. as next + -OL in *alcohol*).]

An aromatic alcohol having the composition $(C_6H_4OH)_2$ (that of PHENOL being C_6H_5OH). It has isomeric modifications, crystallizing in colourless rhombic crystals, and in shining needles.

1877 WATTS *Fownes' Chem.* II. 567 Dioxydiphenyl or Diphenol.

diphenyl (daɪˈfɛnɪl). *Chem.* [f. DI-[2] + PHENYL, F. *phényle* (f. φαίνειν to show, bring to light + ὕλη substance: see -YL.] An aromatic hydrocarbon having the formula C_6H C_6H_5, or twice that of the radical PHENYL.

1873 *Fownes' Chem.* (ed. 11) 758. **1877** WATTS *ibid.* (ed. 12) II. 562 Diphenyl crystallizes from alcohol in iridescent nacreous scales.

b. *attrib.* and *Comb.*, as ***diphenyl group***, ***diphenyl ketone***, ***diphenyl-methane***, etc.

di'phenyla,mine, a crystalline substance having a pleasant odour and weakly basic properties, prepared by the dry distillation of rosaniline blue, and used in the preparation of various dye-stuffs; hence *diphenylamine blue* = spirit blue.

1863–72 WATTS *Dict. Chem.* IV. 453 Diphenylamine heated with chloride of benzoyl yields diphenyl-benzamide. **1882** *Athenæum* 25 Mar. 384/3 This colour is the chloride of a base which the author has proved to be diphenyldiamido-triphenylcarbinol. **1884** *Manch. Exam.* 6 Oct. 4/5 The process of manufacture.. of diphenylaminenaphtol, resorcine, or alizarine dyes.

diphonemic (daɪfəʊˈniːmɪk), *a.* *Linguistics.* [f. DI-[2] + PHONEMIC *a.*] Applied to a sound that can be assigned to either of two phonemes. So **di'phoneme**, a sound of this kind.

1950 D. JONES *Phoneme* xx. 99 If a sound is assigned to two phonemes, it may be termed 'di-phonemic'. *Ibid.* 100 The sound might be treated as di-phonemic, i.e. assigned to one phoneme in some words and the other phoneme in other words. **1953** W. J. ENTWISTLE *Aspects of Lang.* iv. 114 There may be diphonemes, i.e. phonemes which belong to two different orders, but these are set at a convenient distance in Hindustani and Japanese. *Ibid.* 115 Perhaps it would be simplest not to admit the existence of diphonemes (i.e. of single phonemes which have two values simultaneously) until more evidence is available. **1957** *Phonetica* I. 103 The existence of di-phonemic /h/ + /j/.

di'phosphate. *Chem.* See DI-[2] 2 and PHOSPHATE *sb.*

1826 HENRY *Elem. Chem.* II. 121 There is also..a diphosphate, consisting of 1 atom of phosphoric acid and 2 atoms of the protoxide. *c* **1865** G. GORE in *Circ. Sc.* I. 220/2 Pyrophosphate of soda is easily formed by heating to redness the common diphosphate of soda.

di,phospho'pyridine 'nucleotide. *Biochem.* [f. DI-[2] + PHOSPHO- + PYRIDINE + NUCLEOTIDE.] One of the names of the co-enzyme nicotinamide-adenine dinucleotide (NAD).

1938 *Biochem. Jrnl.* XXXII. 2235 Reduced coenzyme I (diphosphopyridinenucleotide) is oxidized extremely slowly by methylene blue and other exidation-reduction indicators. **1955** *Sci. Amer.* Jan. 76/3 It turned out that the rickettsiae very definitely used the coenzymes known as DPN (diphosphopyridine nucleotide) and coenzyme A, both of which are essential for many oxidation reactions in animal cells. **1962** T. O. SIPPEL in A. Pirie *Lens Metabolism Rel. Cataract* 368 The oxidized and reduced forms of diphospho-and triphosphopyridine nucleotide were measured flourometrically.

di,phospho'thiamine. *Biochem.* Also -in. [DI-[2] + PHOSPHO- + THIAMINE.] = COCARBOXYLASE.

1939 BARRON & LYMAN in *Jrnl. Biol. Chem.* CXXVII. 144 Lipmann's studies..on the action of diphosphothiamine as a catalyst for the oxidation of pyruvic acid have been confirmed by experiments. **1942** *Ann. Reg. 1941* 344 Important advances in vitamin research included the clarification of the functions of diphosphothiamin in carbohydrate metabolism. **1960** A. E. BENDER *Dict. Nutrition* 32/2 Cocarboxylase is the diphosphate of vitamin B_1, alternatively known as thiamine pyrophosphate or diphosphothiamine.

diphre'latic, *a.* *nonce-wd.* [f. Gr. διφρηλάτ-ης charioteer + -IC.] Relating to the driving of a chariot, chariot-driving. (*humorous* or *affected.*)

1849 DE QUINCEY *Eng. Mail Coach* Wks. IV. 327 Under this eminent man, whom in Greek I cognominated Cyclops diphrélates..I..studied the diphrelatic art.

diphtheria (dɪf'θɪərɪə). *Path.* [ad. F. *diphthérie*, substituted by Bretonneau for his earlier term *diphtherite*: see DIPHTHERITIS.]

An acute and highly infectious disease, characterized by inflammation of a mucous surface, and by an exudation therefrom which results in the formation of a firm pellicle or false membrane. Its chief seat is the mucous membrane of the throat and air passages, but other mucous surfaces are at times attacked, as are also wounds or abrasions of the skin.

1857 GODFREY in *Lancet* Nov. 542 Report on Cases of Diphtheria or malignant sore throat. **1858** *Chron.* in *Ann. Reg.* 1 A disease of a new name has been recognised. From having first been noticed at Boulogne it was called the Boulogne sore throat; it has now received the medical name of Diphtheria. **1858** *Sat. Rev.* VI. 11/2 To save us from cholera, typhus, and diphtheria. **1860** *New Syd. Soc. Year-bk.* 151 Ranking publishes a lecture on diphtheria, in which he describes the disease as one wholly new to this country. **1884** SIR L. PLAYFAIR *Sp. in Parl.* 18 Mar., Diphtheria.. when first imported from France in 1855, we used to call the Boulogne sore throat.

attrib. **1881** *Daily News* 14 Sept. 5/4 The Russian journals publish some terrible details of the diphtheria epidemic in Russia. **1892** *Daily News* 21 Mar. 6/2 The diphtheria handbill which the sanitary authorities have published. **1895** *Brit. Med. Jrnl.* 30 Mar. 721 The girl's throat was.. found to contain the diphtheria bacillus.

Hence **diph'therial, diph'therian** *adjs.*, of or belonging to diphtheria.

1883 *Syd. Soc. Lex., Diphtherial.* **1893** *Brit. Med. Jrnl.* 26 Aug. 487 A detailed report on..the chemical pathology of diphtheria, and on diphtherial palsy. **1884** *Pall Mall G.* 3 July 3/1 Sucking a tube to draw out the 'diphtherian matter' in his child's throat. **1891** G. MEREDITH *One of our Conq.* I. xii. 228 The diphtherian whisper the commonalty hear of the commonalty.

diphtheric (-'ɛrɪk), *a.* [f. DIPHTHERIA + -IC.] = DIPHTHERITIC.

1859 SEMPLE *Mem. Diphtheria* v. 177 The diphtheric virus. **1860** *New Syd. Soc. Year-bk.* 152 Diphtheric affection of the skin. **1887** J. C. MORISON *Service of Man* (1889) 192 The surgeon who sucks diphtheric poison from a dying child's throat and dies himself in consequence.

‖**diphtherite** (French): see DIPHTHERITIS.

diphtheritic (dɪfθə'rɪtɪk), *a.* [mod. f. DIPHTHERITIS; in F. *diphthéritique* (Littré).] Of the nature or character of diphtheria; belonging to or connected with diphtheria.

1847–9 TODD *Cycl. Anat.* IV. 118 The deposits which we include under the title Diphtheritic. **1850** RAMSAY in *Dublin Med. Press* Aug. 137 (title) Diphtheritic Inflammation of the Pharynx and Tonsils. **1884** R. MARRYAT in *19th Cent.* May 845 A woman..suffering from a diphtheritic sore-throat.

b. Affected with or suffering from diphtheria.

1880 *Boston Jrnl. Chem.* Dec. 143 Dr. Day has often prescribed for diphtheritic patients..a gargle composed of ..salt dissolved in..water.

Hence **diphthe'ritically** *adv.*, in the manner of diphtheria.

1886 CRESSWELL in *Sanitarian* (N.Y.) XVII. 202 Likelihood of rendering them diphtheritically infectious.

diphtheritis (dɪfθə'raɪtɪs). *Path.* Also ‖(Fr.) diphtherite. [mod. f. Gr. διφθέρα or διφθερίς skin, hide, piece of leather + -ITIS; the disease being so named on account of the tough membrane developed upon the parts affected.

First used in 1821 in the French form *diphthérite* by Bretonneau of Tours in a paper before the French Academy, published 1826; the word was taken into English and German medical literature, usually as *diphtheritis*, though the Fr. form was occasional in the scanty English notices of the disease before 1857. In 1855, Bretonneau in a new memoir substituted the name *diphthérie*, probably because terms in *-ite*, -ITIS, are properly formed on names of the part affected, as in *bronchitis*, *laryngitis*; in Eng. this was adapted as *diphtheria*, when 'Boulogne sore-throat' became epidemic here in 1857–58; but the adj. *diphtheritic* was generally retained in preference to *diphtheric* used by some. (Contributed by Dr. W. Sykes.)]

= DIPHTHERIA.

[**1826** BRETONNEAU *Traité de la Diphthérite* (Hatz.-Darm.), Qu'il me soit permis de désigner cette phlegmasie par la dénomination de 'diphthérite'. **1839–47** TODD *Cycl. Anat.* III. 116/1 Examples of croup..analogous to the diphtherite of Bretonneau. **1860** *New Syd. Soc. Year-bk.* 151 The great distinctive mark between diphtherite and croup.]

1826 *Lond. Med. Rev.* XXVI. 499 Review of Bretonneau on Diphtheritis. **1840** A. TWEEDIE *Syst. Pract. Med.* IV. 48 This species of angina is characterized by the formation of albuminous pellicles on the surface of the inflamed membrane, whence it was named by M. Bretonneau of Tours 'Diphtheritis'. **1855** A. SMITH in *Dublin Hosp. Gaz.* II. 149 Diphtheritis successfully treated by chlorate of potash. **1858** *Sat. Rev.* VI. 2/1 Diphtheritis has become a name more terrible than the small-pox. **1859** C. WEST *Dis. Infancy & Childhood* (ed. 4) xxv. 381 This other disease, Angina Maligna, Diphtheritis, or more correctly Diphtheria, is no new malady.

diphtheroid ('dɪfθərɔɪd), *a.* and *sb.* [f. as prec. + -OID.] **A.** *adj.* Of the form or appearance of diphtheria.

1861 BUMSTEAD *Ven. Dis.* (1879) 450 Diphtheroid [chancre] of the glans. **1883** *Syd. Soc. Lex., Diphtheroïd*, like a tanned skin, or like Diphtheria, or a diphtheritic product. *Ibid.*, *Diphtheroid ulceration.*

B. *sb.* Any bacillus, esp. of the genus *Corynebacterium*, which resembles the diphtheria bacillus but is not pathogenic.

1908 *Practitioner* Jan. 138 The true diphtheria bacillus, and not one of these diphtheroids. **1949** H. W. FLOREY et al. *Antibiotics* I. v. 221 Diphtheroids, streptococci, and *L. acidophilus* were completely inhibited by that concentration. **1962** *Lancet* 5 May 933/1 The effect could also be elicited by ..a diphtheroid.

diphthong ('dɪfθɒŋ), *sb.* Forms: 5–6 diptong(e, (dypton), 6 **dyphtong, diphthonge, -gue,** 7–9 **dipthong,** 8 **dipthongue,** 6– **diphthong.** [a. F. *diphthongue*, earlier *dyptongue*, ad. L. *diphthong-us*, a. Gr. δίφθογγος, adj. having two sounds, sb. a diphthong, f. δι-, δίς twice, doubly + φθόγγος voice, sound.]

A union of two vowels pronounced in one syllable; the combination of a sonantal with a consonantal vowel.

The latter is usually one of the two vowels *i* and *u*, the extremes of the vowel scale, which pass into the consonants *y*, *w*. When these sounds, called by Melville Bell *glides*, follow the sonantal vowel, the combination is called a 'falling diphthong', as in *out*, *how*, *boil*, *boy*; when they precede, the combination is a 'rising diphthong', as in It. *uovo*, *piano*. It is common in the latter case to consider the first element as the consonant *w* or *y*.

1483 *Cath. Angl.* 100/2 A Diptonge [*MS.* A. Dypton], *diptongus.* **1530** PALSGR. 213/2 Diphthonge, *diphthongue.* *a* **1637** B. JONSON *Eng. Gram.* v, Dipthongs are the complexions, or couplings of Vowells. **1668** WILKINS *Real Char.* 15 *I* and *u* according to our English pronunciation of them, are not properly Vowels, but Diphthongs. **1749** *Power Pros. Numbers* 9 All Dipthongs are naturally long. But in English Numbers they are often short. **1876** C. P. MASON *Eng. Gram.* (ed. 21) §17 When two vowel sounds are uttered without a break between them, we get what is called a vocal or sonant diphthong. **1888** J. WRIGHT *O.H. German Prim.* §10 All the OHG. diphthongs..were falling diphthongs; that is, the stress fell upon the first of the two elements. **1892** SWEET *New Eng. Gram.* 230 If two vowels are uttered with one impulse of stress, so as to form a single syllable, the combination is called a *diphthong*, such as (oi) in *oil*.

b. Often applied to a combination of two vowel characters, more correctly called DIGRAPH[1].

When the two letters represent a simple sound, as *ea*, *ou*, in *head* (hɛd), *soup* (su:p), they have been termed an ***improper diphthong***: properly speaking these are *monophthongs* written by *digraphs*.

1530 PALSGR. 15 This diphthong *ou*..in the frenche tong shalbe sounded lyke as the Italians sounde this vowell *u*. *c* **1620** A. HUME *Brit. Tongue* (1865) 10 We have of this thre diphthonges, tuae with a befoer, ae and ai, and ane with the e befoer, ea. **1668** PRICE in A. J. Ellis *E.E. Pronunc.* I. iii. (Chaucer Soc.) 125 That is an improper dipthong that loseth the sound of one vowel. There are eight improper dipthongs, *ea ee ie eo*, *ea oo ui*, *ou* obscure as in cousin. **1876** C. P. MASON *Eng. Gram.* (ed. 21) §17 When two of the letters called vowels are written together to represent either a sonant diphthong or a simple vowel sound, we get a written diphthong or digraph. *Ibid.* §25 The same letter or diphthong often represents very different vowel sounds.

c. *esp.* In popular use, applied to the ligatures *æ*, *œ* of the Roman alphabet.

As pronounced in later L., and in modern use, these are no longer diphthongs, but monophthongs; the OE. ligatures *æ* and *œ* always represented monophthongs.

1587 HARRISON *England* II. xix. (1877) I. 312 Waldæne with a diphthong. **1631** WEEVER *Anc. Fun. Mon.* To Rdr. Aij, I write the Latine..as I find it..*E* vocall for *E* diphthong, diphthongs being but lately come into use. **1702** ADDISON *Dial. Medals* (1727) 20 We find that Felix is never written with an œ dipthongue. **1756–7** tr. *Keysler's Trav.* (1760) III. 222 The epitaph, in which the dipthong *æ*, according to the custom of those times, is expressed by a single *e*..*Vitam obiit VII Id. Oct. etatis sue ann. I. & L.*

d. *transf.* Applied to a combination of two consonants in one syllable (***consonantal diphthong***), especially to such intimate unions as those of *ch* (tʃ) and *dg* or *j* (dʒ), in *church*, *judge*.

1862 M. HOPKINS *Hawaii* 65 The Hawaiian alphabet..is ..destitute of consonant diphthongs. **1889** PITMAN *Man. Phonogr.* (new ed.) §64 The simple articulations *p*, *b*, *t*, *d*, etc. are often closely united with the liquids *l* and *r*, forming a kind of consonant diphthong..as in *plough*..*try*.

e. *attrib.* = DIPHTHONGAL.

1798 H. BLAIR *Lect.* I. ix (R.), We abound more in vowel and diphthong sounds, than most languages.

'diphthong, *v.* [f. prec. sb.: cf. mod.F. *diphthonguer.*] *trans.* To sound as a diphthong; to make into a diphthong.

1846 WORCESTER cites *Chr. Observ.* **1888** SWEET *Eng. Sounds* 21 Isolative diphthonging or 'vowel-cleaving' mainly affects long vowels. *Ibid.* 277 The characteristic feature of the [living English] vowel-system is its diphthonging of all the earlier long monophthongs. **1894** F. J. CURTIS *Rimes of Chariodus* 50 Arguments for the diphthonging of *ī* in early texts.

diphthongal (dɪf'θɒŋgəl), *a.* [f. DIPHTHONG *sb.* + -AL[1].] Of or belonging to a diphthong; of the nature of a diphthong.

1748 *Phil. Trans.* XLV. 403 That 7 vocal Notes or Vowels ..struck, as one may say, in diphthongal or triphthongal Chords with each other, may well enough account for the Sounds of our Language. **1806** M. SMART in *Monthly Mag.* XXI. 14 So easily does *r* slide into vowel or dipthongal sounds. **1867** A. J. ELLIS *E.E. Pronunc.* I. iii. 116 Ben Jonson ..entirely ignores the diphthongal character of long *i*. **1888** SWEET *Eng. Sounds* 248 A diphthongal pronunciation of the ..words.

Hence **diph'thongally** *adv.*

1846 WORCESTER cites WYLIE. *Mod.* The question whether long *i* was already pronounced diphthongally in 1500.

diphthon'gation. *rare*[−0]. [f. DIPHTHONG *v.*: see -ATION. Cf. mod.F. *diphthongaison.*] = DIPHTHONGIZATION.

In mod. Dicts.

diphthongic (dɪf'θɒŋgɪk), *a.* [f. Gr. δίφθογγ-ον DIPHTHONG *sb.* + -IC.] = DIPHTHONGAL.

1880 SWEET in *President's Addr. Philol. Soc.* 41 The treatment of the diphthongic vowel. **1886** —— in *Academy* 24 Apr. 295/3 The older true diphthongic pronunciation of [Latin] *ae* and *oe* nearly as in English *by* and *boy*.

diphthongize ('dɪfθɒŋgaɪz), *v.* [ad. Gr. διφθογγίζ-ειν to spell with a diphthong: see -IZE.]

1. *trans.* To turn into a diphthong.

1868 G. STEPHENS *Runic Mon.* I. 52 All sorts of broadenings and thinnings of vowels, diphthongizings [etc.]. **1874** SWEET *Eng. Sounds* 56, *ii* and *uu* being diphthongized. **1877–9** *Trans. Philol. Soc.* 458 In German, original long *i* was already diphthongized when the orthography began to settle down into its present form.

2. *intr.* To form a diphthong.

1867 A. J. ELLIS *E. Engl. Pronunc.* I. iii. 196 This second (ɪ) may diphthongise with any preceding vowel.

Hence **,diphthongi'zation**, the changing of a simple vowel into a diphthong.

1874 SWEET *Eng. Sounds* 70 The most prominent feature of our present English is its tendency to diphthongization.

diphthongous (dɪf'θɒŋgəs), *a.* *rare.* [f. as DIPHTHONG + -OUS.] Of the nature of a diphthong; diphthongal.

1833 *Philol. Museum* II. 116 Mere modulations of the vowels, or at most different diphthongous combinations.

diphy-, ad. Gr. διφυ- from διφυ-ής, of double nature or form, double, bipartite; a frequent formative of modern scientific words: as **'diphycerc** *Ichth.* [Gr. κέρκ-ος tail], a diphycercal fish. **diphycercal** (dɪfɪ'sɜːkəl) *a.*, having the tail divided into two equal halves by the caudal spine. **'diphycercy**, diphycercal condition. **'diphyid** *Zool.*, a member of the *Diphyidæ*, a family of Hydrozoa, having a pair of swimming-bells opposite each other on the upper part of the stem. **'diphyodont** *a.*, [Gr. ὀδοντ- tooth], having two distinct sets of teeth; consisting (as teeth) of two sets: as in the deciduous and permanent teeth of mammals; as *sb.* a diphyodont mammal. **diphy'zooid, diphyo-** *Zool.*, a free-swimming organism consisting of a group of zooids detached from a colony of Hydrozoa of the order *Siphonophora*.

1883 *Syd. Soc. Lex.*, **Diphycerc*, a fish with the form of tail called *Diphycercal*. **1870** ROLLESTON *Anim. Life* Introd. 70 A true *diphycercal tail is finally produced in the Acanthopteri. **1871** HUXLEY *Anat. Vert. Anim.* i. 16 The extremity of the spine divides the caudal fin-rays into two nearly equal moieties, an upper and a lower, and the fish is said to be *diphycercal*. **1884** SEDGWICK tr. *Claus' Zool.* I. 250 These groups of individuals may in some *diphyids become free and assume a separate existence as Eudoxia. **1854** OWEN in *Circ. Sc.* (c 1865) II. 100/1 The **diphyodonts*.. generate two sets of teeth. *Ibid.*, The diphyodont mammalia. **1883** FLOWER in *Glasgow Weekly Her.* 14 July 8/1 Teeth.. of the simple homodont and diphyodont type. **1861** J. R. GREENE *Man. Anim. Kingd.*, *Cœlent.* 100 The same naturalist [Huxley] has proposed the distinctive term of '*Diphyozoöids' for those singular detached reproductive portions of adult *Calycophoridæ* which received the name of 'monogastric *Diphydæ*'. **1877** HUXLEY *Anat. Inv. Anim.* iii. §3. 145 As they attain their full development, each set becomes detached, as a free-swimming complex Diphyzooid. In this condition they grow and alter their form and size so much that they were formerly regarded as distinct genera.

diphyletic (daɪfɪˈlɛtɪk), *a. Taxonomy.* [f. DI-² + PHYLETIC *a.*] Having two lines of descent; supposedly derived from two distinct sets of ancestors; also, of or pertaining to a classification of groups of organisms in accordance with the view that they have a diphyletic origin.

1902 *Nature* 25 Sept. 526 The 'Myriapoda', if a natural group, are diphyletic. **1903** *Amer. Nat.* Jan. 74 The diphyletic origin of the birds as represented by the Ratitæ and Carinatæ. **1912** *Rep. Brit. Assoc.* 578 Yet others claim a diphyletic origin for Man from the Apes. **1963** DAVIS & HEYWOOD *Princ. Angiosperm Taxon.* ii. 46 A species (or unit of lower rank) derived by hybridisation between two ancestral species.. is diphyletic by either definition.

diphyllous (daɪˈfɪləs), *a. Bot.* [f. mod.L. *diphyll-us* (f. Gr. δι-, (DI-²) twice + φύλλ-ον leaf) + -OUS.] Having two leaves (or sepals).

1788 JAS. LEE *Introd. Bot.* I. xi. (ed. 4) 25 The Calyx.. In respect to its Parts it is.. *Diphyllous*, of two [leaves] as in *Fumaria*. **1819** *Pantologia*, *Diphyllous*, in botany, a twoleaved calyx: as in papaver and fumaria.

diphyo-: see DIPHY-.

diphysite (ˈdɪfɪsaɪt), *sb.* (*a.*) *Theol.* [f. Gr. δι-, δίς twice, doubly + φύσις nature + -ITE.] One who held the doctrine (ˈ**diphysiˌtism**), of two distinct natures in Christ, a divine and a human, as opposed to the monophysite doctrine: see DYOPHYSITE.

diplanar (daɪˈpleɪnə(r)), *a. Math.* [f. DI-² + PLANAR *a.*] Of or pertaining to two planes.

a **1865** W. R. HAMILTON *Elem. Quaternions* (1866) 113 Any two quaternions (or quotients), which have different planes (intersecting therefore in a right line through the origin), may be said, by contrast, to be Diplanar.

diplanetic (daɪpləˈnɛtɪk), *a. Bot.* [mod. f. Gr. δι- DI-² - twice + πλανητικ-ός disposed to wander, f. πλανητός wandering (see PLANET).] Having two active periods separated by a period of rest: said of the zoospores of certain Fungi of the family *Saprolegnieæ*. So **diˈplanetism**, the condition or property of being diplanetic.

1888 M. M. HARTOG in *Annals of Bot.* 203 *note*, The 'first form' of zoospore.. is ovoid with a pair of flagella from the front.. The 'second form' is uniform with an anterior and posterior flagellum diverging from the hilum. The existence of these two forms constitutes the phenomenon of diplanetism.

† **diplanˈtidian**, *a. Obs.* [f. Gr. διπλό-ος double + ἀντί against, opposite + εἶδος form, image + -IAN.] Applied to a form of telescope proposed by Jeaurat in 1778, giving two images, one direct and the other reversed, the coincidence of which might be used to determine transits.

1807 T. YOUNG *Lect. Nat. Phil. & Mech. Arts* II. 351.

diplarthrous (dɪˈplɑːθrəs), *a. Zool.* [f. Gr. διπλό-ος double + ἄρθρ-ον joint + -OUS.] Having the carpal or tarsal bones doubly articulated, i.e. the several bones of one row alternating with those of the other, as in ungulate mammals: opp. to *taxeopodous*. So **diˈplarthrism**, the condition of being diplarthrous.

1887 E. D. COPE in *Amer. Nat.* XXI. 987 All ungulates in passing from the taxeopodous to the diplarthrous stages, traversed the amblyopodous. *Ibid.* 988 The advance of diplarthrism is in direct ratio to the advance of digitigradism, for the greater the length of the foot, the greater is the elasticity of the leg, and the greater is the torsion.

diplasic (dɪˈplæzɪk, daɪ-), *a. Pros.* [f. Gr. διπλά-σιος twofold, double, f. δι-, δίς twice + -πλασιος -fold.] Double, twofold; having the proportion of two to one, as in ***diplasic ratio***, = Gr. διπλασίων λόγος.

1873 J. HADLEY *Ess.* 98 They may have a ratio of two to one—a *diplasic* ratio, as the ancients called it—as in the trochee. *Ibid.*, The diplasic ratio answers to our common time.

diˈplatinamine. *Chem.*: see DI-² 2 and + PLATINAMINE.

‖ **diple** (ˈdɪpliː). [Gr. διπλῆ, fem. of διπλοῦς double (sc. γραμμή stroke, line).] A marginal mark of this form >, used by the ancient grammarians to indicate various readings, rejected verses, beginning of a new paragraph, etc.

1656 BLOUNT *Glossogr.*, *Diple*, a note or mark in the Margent to signifie that there is somewhat to be amended.

‖ **diplegia** (daɪˈpliːdʒɪə). *Path.* [mod.L., f. Gr. δι-, δίς twice + πληγή stroke.] Paralysis affecting corresponding parts on both sides of the body. Hence **diplegic** (daɪˈplɛdʒɪk) *a.*, relating to diplegia, or to corresponding parts on both sides.

1883 in *Syd. Soc. Lex.*

dipleidoscope (dɪˈplaɪdəskəʊp). [f. Gr. διπλό-ος double + εἶδος form, image + -σκοπος viewing, a watcher.] An instrument consisting of a hollow triangular prism, with two sides silvered and one of glass, used for determining the meridian transit of a heavenly body by the coincidence of the two images formed by single and double reflexion.

1843 E. J. DENT (*title*), A Description of the Dipleidoscope. *Ibid.* (1867) 14 The criterion for determining the position of the Dipleidoscope is, that the two images must coincide, or appear as one, when the chronometer shows, according to the equation table for 1868, 11h. 49m. 12.1s. **1851** *Offic. Catal. Exhib.* I. 414. **1884** F. J. BRITTEN *Watch & Clockm.* 88 The advantages of the dipleidoscope over the ordinary forms of sun dials are: the passage of the sun over the meridian is indicated with greater exactness, and the reflections may be discerned in weather too cloudy to see any shadow on the sun dial.

‖ **dipleura** (daɪˈplʊərə), *sb. pl. Morphol.* [mod.L., neuter pl. of *dipleur-us*, f. Gr. δι-, δίς twice + πλευρά side (of the body).] Organic forms with bilateral symmetry having a single pair of antimeres or corresponding opposite parts. Hence **diˈpleural** *a.*, zygopleural with only two antimeres. **diˈpleuric** *a.*, having right and left sides; exhibiting bilateral symmetry.

1883 P. GEDDES in *Encycl. Brit.* XVI. 844/2 The Zygopleura include forms bilaterally symmetrical in the strictest sense, in which not more than two radial planes, and these at right angles to each other, are present. Haeckel again divides these, according to the number of antimeres, into *Tetrapleura* and *Dipleura*. *Ibid.*, The term bilateral.. must be rigidly restricted.. to the Centropipeda if not indeed to dipleural forms.

dipleurobranchiate (daɪˌplʊərəʊˈbræŋkɪət), *a. Zool.* [f. mod.L. *Dipleurobranchia* (f. Gr. δι- twice + πλευρά side + βράγχια gills) + -ATE².] Having the characters of the *Dipleurobranchia* or *Inferobranchiata*, nudibranchiate gastropods having foliaceous branchiæ situated in a fold on each side of the shell-less body.

dipleurula (daɪˈplʊərjʊlə). [mod.L., dim. of DIPLEURA.] A supposed bilaterally symmetrical ancestor of the echinoderms. Also, a stage in the development of some echinoderms.

1896 H. M. & M. BERNARD tr. *Lang's Text-bk. Compar. Anat.* II. viii. 546 The radiate, but at the same time asymmetrical Echinoderm proceeds ontogenetically from a bilaterally symmetrical larva, the so-called Dipleurula. *Ibid.* 547 (*heading*) Metamorphosis of the Dipleurula Larva. **1900** F. A. BATHER et al. in Lankester *Treat. Zool.* III. viii. 4 Zoologists have imagined a phylogenetic stage, the two-sided or *Dipleurula* stage,.. more or less repeated in the *Dipleurula* larvae of recent Echinoderms. *Ibid.* 5 The simplest larval form among recent Echinoderms,.. known as *Auricularia*,.. differs from the *Dipleurula* in being bent upon its ventral surface. **1902** *Encycl. Brit.* XXVII. 620/1 We reach the conception that this supposed bilateral ancestor (or *Dipleurula*) may have become fixed. **1962** D. NICHOLS *Echinoderms* x. 121 It is not strange that early in life a common plan exists between those forms with larvae, or most of them. This stage has been termed the *dipleurula* ('little two sides'), a word which has unhappily been used to denote also a hypothetical common ancestor to the entire phylum.

diplex (ˈdaɪplɛks), *a.* [An arbitrary alteration of *duplex* after DI-² twice (Preece).] *Telegr.* Characterized by the passing of two messages simultaneously in the same direction.

'Now (1895) properly restricted to the system whereby the transmission of one message is effected by means of a change in strength of current only, irrespective of direction, and that of the other by change of direction of the currents without reference to their strength' (W. H. Preece).

1878 W. H. PREECE in *Post Office Official Techn. Instruct.*, Diplex telegraphy consists in sending two messages in the same direction at the same time. **1879** G. PRESCOTT *Sp. Telephone* 346 Two messages may be sent over a single wire in the same or in opposite directions, and when we do not care to particularize either, we simply allude to them under the more common generic name of duplex transmission, which includes both. When, however, we wish to speak of either method by itself, we use the term diplex for simultaneous transmission in the same direction, and contraplex for that in opposite directions.

diplo- (ˈdɪpləʊ), before a vowel dipl-, combining form of Gr. διπλό-ος, διπλοῦς twofold, double, occasional in ancient Greek, now used in many scientific terms; e.g. **diplaˈcusis** *Path.* [Gr. ἄκουσις hearing], double hearing, the hearing of two notes when only one is produced, due to the hearing of a different tone in each ear, or to the arousing of two tonal sensations in the same ear. ˌ**diplobaˈcillus** (see quot. 1957¹). **diplobacˈteria** *sb. pl.*, bacteria consisting of two cells, or adhering in pairs. **diploˈblastic** *a. Biol.*, having two germinal layers, the hypoblast and epiblast. **diploˈcardiac** *a. Zool.*, having the heart double, i.e. with the right and left halves completely separate, as birds and mammals. **diploˈcephaly**, monstrosity consisting in having two heads. **diploˈconical** *a.*, of the form of a double cone. ˈ**diplodal** *a. Zool.* [Gr. ὁδ-ός way + -AL¹], of sponges, having both canals, prosodal (of entrance) and aphodal (of exit) well developed. ˈ**diplodoxy** *nonce-wd.* (see quot.). **diploˈgangliate** *a.*, having ganglia arranged in pairs; said of a division of animals (*Diplogangliata*) nearly equivalent to Cuvier's Articulata. **diploˈgenesis**, (*a*) the production of double organs or parts instead of single ones; the formation of a double monster; (*b*) the supposed change of germ plasm produced by changes due to environment, bringing about inheritance of acquired characteristics; hence **diplogeˈnetic** *a.*; **diploˈgenic** *a.*, 'producing two substances; partaking of the nature of two bodies' (Craig 1847). ˈ**diplograph** (see quot.); so **diploˈgraphic**, **diploˈgraphical** *a.*, of or pertaining to writing double; also **diˈplography**. **diploˈhaplont** *Biol.*, an organism whose life-cycle embraces a diploid and a haploid phase; so **diplohaˈplontic** *a.* **diploˈneural** *a. Anat.*, supplied by two nerves of separate origin, as a muscle; **diploneuˈrose** *a. Zool.*, belonging to the *Diploneura* (Grant's term for the *Articulata*, as having a double nerve-cord running along the body); **diploˈneurous** *a.*, 'having two nervous systems; also, belonging to the *Diploneura*' (*Syd. Soc. Lex.*). **diplo-peˈristomous** *a. Bot.*, of mosses, having a double peristome, or fringe round the mouth of the capsule. ˈ**diplophase** *Biol.* [a. G. *diplophase*], the phase in the lifecycle of an organism when the nuclei are diploid. **diploˈplacula** *Embryol.*, a PLACULA composed of two layers resulting from transverse fission; hence **diploˈplacular**, **diploˈplaculate** *a.* ˈ**diplopod** *a.* and *sb. Zool.*, belonging to the order *Diplopoda* (= *Cheilognatha*) of Myriapods, having two pairs of limbs on each segment of the body; a member of this order; hence **diˈplopodous** *a.* ˈ**diplopore** *Zool.*, any of the pores that occur in pairs on the surface of the theca of certain cystoids (order Diploporita); also, a thecal canal that ends in one of these pores. **diˈplopterous** *a. Entom.*, belonging to the family *Diploptera* (the true wasps) in Latreille's classification of insects, which have the fore wings folded when at rest. **diplosˈphenal** *a.*, ˈ**diplosphene**, *Anat.* = HYPOSPHENAL, HYPOSPHENE. **diplosponˈdylic** *a. Zool.*, said of a vertebral segment having two centra, or of a vertebral column having twice as many centra as arches, as in fishes and batrachians; hence **diploˈspondylism**, the condition of being diplospondylic. **diˈplostichous** *a.*, arranged in two rows, as the eyes of certain spiders. **diploˈsyntheme** = DISYNTHEME.

1890 BILLINGS *Med. Dict.* 400/2 Diplakousis or Diplacusis. **1895** E. B. TITCHENER tr. *Külpe's Outl. Psychol.* 299 The abnormality (*diplacusis*) may be restricted to a single ear. **1970** J. V. TOBIAS *Found. Mod. Auditory Theory* I. x. 391 One possible explanation for diplacusis is distortion. **1901** *Jrnl. Exper. Med.* V. 213 The occurrence of acid-resisting diplococci or diplo-bacilli. **1908** *Practitioner* Feb. 203 The diplobacillus of Morax-Axenfeld. **1957** M. B. JACOBS et al. *Dict. Microbiol.* 78/2 *Diplobacilli*, bacillus-type bacteria occurring in pairs, as, for example, *Moraxella lacunata*. **1957** *Bergey's Man. Determinative Bacteriol.* (ed. 7) 419 Genus VII. *Moraxella*... Small rod-shaped cells which occur as diplobacilli. **1888** F. P. BILLINGS in *Amer. Nat.* XXII. 123 We may find two apparently mature organisms enclosed in a common capsule.. These diplobacteria may assume a curved or sausage shape. **1854-67** C. A. HARRIS *Dict. Med. Terminol.*, *Diplocardiac*, having a double heart. **1847** CRAIG, *Diplocephalia*. **1883** *Syd. Soc. Lex.*, *Diplocephaly*, in Teratology, the condition of a fœtus having two heads on one body. **1887** W. J. SOLLAS in *Encycl. Brit.* XXII. 415/1 This, which from the marked presence of both prosodal and aphodal canals may be termed the *diplodal* type of the Rhagon canal system, occurs but rarely. **1851** *Fraser's Mag.* XLIII. 289 An orthodoxy with two tails—or a diplo-doxy—to coin a word—which affirms the co-existence of two separate beliefs, while it expresses no dogma as to the truth of either. **1851** RICHARDSON *Geol.* viii. 257 The nervous system is composed of a chain of ganglia disposed in pairs, and united by nervous cords: hence the term diplo-gangliata. **1835-6** TODD *Cycl. Anat.* I. 509/1 That form of monstrosity.. called Diplogenesis. **1878** BARTLEY tr. *Topinard's Anthrop.* v. 162 Diplogenesis, in which the whole body is more or less double. **1896** *Nat. Sci.* Nov. 288 Cope's theory of Diplogenesis. **1876** *Catal. Sci. App. S. Kens.* No. 2052 *Diplograph*. Writing machine for the Blind, by which writing in relief and ordinary writing are performed at the same time. **1823** J. ELMES *Mem. & Life C. Wren* 23 In 1647..he had a patent granted him for seventeen years, for a diplographic instrument for writing with two pens. **1750** C. WREN *Parentalia* 212 He [Wren] invented the art of double writing..by an instrument called the *Diplographical Instrument*. **1758** *Grand Mag. of Mag.* Nov., In 1647, about three years before Mr. Wren publicly produced his diplographical instruments. **1824** *Mech. Mag.* No. 60. 59 Diplography. **1921** *Bot. Abstr.* VI. 251 (*heading*) Genetical phenomena and taxonomy in haplonts and diplohaplonts in the vegetable kingdom. **1938** *Bot. Rev.* IV. 136 Diplohaplonts with unlike alternating generations are common among the Phaeophyceae. *Ibid.* 137 A lifecycle identical with that of the diplohaplontic Phaeophyceae with dissimilar generations has been described for *Stigeoclonium*. **1965** BELL & COMBE tr. *Strasburger's Textbk. Bot.* (new ed.) I. i. 36 In many of the more highly developed algae..the diploid zygote grows first into a multicellular diploid plant, the sporophyte. After the development of numerous diploid spore-mother cells meiosis takes place freely. Thus from the original nuclear fusion..a multitude of haploid cells (gonospores) are produced. These organisms are termed diplohaplonts. **1836-9** TODD *Cycl. Anat.* II. 412/2 Belonging to the diploneurose..divisions of the animal kingdom. **1870** BENTLEY *Bot.* 369 With two rows, they are diploperistomous. **1925** E. B. WILSON *Cell* (ed. 3) 1130 *Diplophase*, that phase of the life-history, particularly in the antithetic alternation of generations, in which the nuclei are haploid, as in the sporophyte. **1965** J. WILKINSON tr. *Langeron's Outl. Mycology* (ed. 2) ix. 374 Meiosis intervenes between the diplophase and the haplophase, fertilization between the haplophase and the diplophase. **1884** A. HYATT in *Proc. Boston Soc. Nat. Hist.* XXIII. 89 In this way the primitive differentiation of the placula into two layers is established in what we have designated the diploplacula. **1864** WEBSTER, *Diplopod* (*Zool.*), one of a group of myriapods. **1883** *Smithsonian Inst. Rep.*, *Zool.* (Cent. Dict.), One of the diplopod myriopods. **1899**, **1962** Diplopore [see *haplopore* s.v. HAPLO-]. **1884** O. C. MARSH *Amer. Jrnl. Sc.* CXXVII. 334 In Ceratosaurus ..These vertebræ show the diplosphenal articulation seen in Megalosaurus. **1888** ROLLESTON & JACKSON *Anim. Life* 525 The lateral eyes in *Scorpionidæ* and all the eyes of *Limulus* are monostichous; the central eyes of the former group and other Arachnids, so far as known, diplostichous.

diplococcus (dɪpləʊˈkɒkəs). *Bacteriol.* Pl. diplococci (-ˈkɒkaɪ, -ˈkɒkiː). [mod.L., f. Gr. διπλό-ος double + κόκκος grain, seed, adopted as a genus name by A. Weichselbaum 1886, in *Wiener med. Jahrb.* LXXXII. 483.] Any coccus that occurs predominantly in pairs, esp. one belonging to the genus of parasitic bacteria so called, which includes the pneumococcus, *D. pneumoniæ*.

1883 MACALISTER tr. *Ziegler's Pathol. Anat.* I. §185 Masses of cocci enclosed in a cylindrical sheath are called ascococci; coupled spherules are diplococci; chains or chaplets of spherules, streptococci; and in like manner he [Billroth] describes diplobacteria and streptobacteria. **1911** M. HERZOG *Text-bk. Disease-producing Microörg.* xxxii. 378 The diplococci show particularly often in the shape of candle-lights, hence the name *Diplococcus lanceolatus*, which means lancet-shaped. **1927** R. A. KELSER *Man. Vet. Bacteriol.* xi. 133 In the affected lung tissue Streptococcus equi commonly appears singly and in pairs. This characteristic led some investigators to consider the organism a diplococcus. **1949** KELLY & HITE *Microbiol.* vi. 68 Whereas the term diplococcus means any paired coccus, the same word begun with a capital letter refers only to the gram-positive paired cocci of the genus *Diplococcus*. **1969** S. T. LYLES *Biol. Microorg.* xx. 438 Another gram-negative diplococcus type is associated with the nervous system and produces meningitis.

Hence **diploˈcoccal** *a.*, of, pertaining to, or caused by a diplococcus; **diploˈcoccoid** *a.*, resembling a diplococcus or diplococci.

1903 *Med. Record* 2 May 705/1 Two cases of diplococcal septicaemia. **1908** *Lancet* 15 Feb. 484/1 A diplococcal infection of the throat. **1950** K. A. BISSET *Cytol. & Life-hist. Bact.* ix. 117 The two-celled structure [of *Neisseria gonorrhœæ*] is concealed by the gram-complex in the gram-positive species, and has been misinterpreted as 'diplococcal' in the gram-negative. **1910** *Practitioner* Apr. 489 The characteristic diplococcoid arrangement of the germs.

diplodocus (dɪˈplɒdəkəs, ˌdɪpləʊˈdəʊkəs). [mod.L. (O. C. Marsh 1878, in *Amer. Jrnl. Sci.* 3rd Ser. XVI. 414), f. Gr. διπλό-ος double + δοκός a beam.] An individual of the extinct genus of gigantic herbivorous dinosaurs of the order Sauropoda, of which remains have been found in the Upper Jurassic of western North America. Also *allusively*.

1884 *Amer. Jrnl. Sci.* 3rd Ser. XXVII. 161 The skull of *Diplodocus* is of moderate size. **1890** *Guide Exhib. Gall. Dept. Geol. & Palæontol. Brit. Mus.* (*N.H.*) II. 9 The *Diplodocus*, an animal intermediate in size between *Atlantosaurus* and *Morosaurus*. **1905** E. R. LANKESTER *Extinct Animals* v. 204 Mr. Andrew Carnegie has presented to the Natural History Museum a complete reconstruction of the skeleton of a closely allied Dinosaur—the Diplodocus —which was excavated in Wyoming. **1905** *Westm. Gaz.* 6 July 2/1 Divo Pietro Aretino, the heroic literary blackguard, the diplodocus of the reptile press. **1927** HALDANE & HUXLEY *Anim. Biol.* xi. 242 Diplodocus (herbivorous, gigantic, and semi-aquatic). **1928** G. B. SHAW *Intell. Woman's Guide Socialism* xlii. 162 Adam Smith's eighteen men are as extinct as the diplodocus. **1962** E. H. COLBERT *Dinosaurs* vi. 111 In the long, attenuated sauropod *Diplodocus*, from western North America, the nostrils are on the very top of the skull.

‖**diploe** (ˈdɪpləʊiː). [mod.L., a Gr. διπλόη doubling, fold, overlapping of the bones of the skull (Hippocrates), f. διπλόος double.]

1. *Anat.* The light porous or cancellated bone-tissue lying between the hard dense inner and outer layers of the bones of the skull.

1696 in PHILLIPS (ed. 5). **1699** *Phil. Trans.* XXI. 139 The Blood Vessels of the *Diploe* might be burst by some accidental blow. **1741** MONRO *Anat Bones* (ed. 3) 68 The Bones of the *Cranium* are composed of two bony Tables, and an intermediate cellular Substance, commonly called their *Diploe*. **1767** GOOCH *Treat. Wounds* I. 307 In some parts of the skull, there is naturally very little *Diplöe*, and in old subjects, scarce any remains. **1878** T. BRYANT *Pract. Surg.* I. 197 An acute inflammation of the diploë of the skull.

2. *Bot.* = DIACHYMA.

1866 *Treas. Bot.*, *Diploe*, that part of the parenchyme of a leaf which intervenes between the two layers of epiderm. **1884** BOWER & SCOTT *De Bary's Phaner.* 406 The space in the lamina of the leaf which is left free by the ribs and vascular bundles, is mainly occupied by parenchyma, which is simply called leaf-parenchyma or in the special case of flat foliage-leaves *Diachyma* or *Diploe* according to Link, *Mesophyll* according to De Candolle.

Hence **diploˈetic** *a.*, bad form for DIPLOIC.

1883 *Syd. Soc. Lex.*, *Diploetic*, of, or belonging to, the Diploe.

diplohedron (dɪpləʊˈhiːdrən). *Cryst.* [f. DIPLO- + Gr. ἕδρα seat, base: cf. *trihedron*.] A crystalline form contained by twenty-four trapezoidal planes with two sides equal; a dyakis-dodecahedron.

1878 LAWRENCE *Cotta's Rocks Class.* 211 The large diplohedrons of quartz are very much rounded off. **1895** STORY-MASKELYNE *Crystallogr.* 216 The terms dyakis-dodecahedron and diplohedron have been employed to convey the idea of the form [twenty-four-trapezohedron] being a doubled or broken-faced pentagon-dodecahedron. *Ibid.* 217 Other diplohedra are met with on crystals of pyrites, and occur also on those of hauerite and cobaltine.

Hence **diploˈhedral** *a.*, of the nature of a diplohedron.

1878 GURNEY *Crystallogr.* 54 A diplohedral form is one in which each normal bears two parallel faces, one at each end. **1895** STORY-MASKELYNE *Crystallogr.* 207 Hemisystematic diplohedral forms; hemi-tesseral diplohedra.

diploic (dɪˈpləʊɪk), *a.* *Anat.* [f. DIPLOE + -IC.] Belonging to the diploe.

1855 HOLDEN *Hum. Osteol.* (1878) 118 We may speak of the frontal, temporal, and occipital diploic veins.

diploicin (dɪˈplɔɪsɪn). *Chem.* [a. G. *diploïcin* (W. Zopf 1904, in *Ann. d. Chem.* CCCXXXVI. 60), f. *Diploicia* (see def.) + -IN[1].] A crystalline depsidone, $C_{16}H_{10}O_5Cl$, isolated from the lichen *Buellia* (= *Diploicia*) *canescens*.

1904 *Jrnl. Chem. Soc.* LXXXVI. I. 1020 *Diploicin* forms sheaves of brown, thick crystals, melts at 225°, is only slightly soluble in alcohol, ether, glacial acetic acid, or benzene, has only a slight tendency to redden litmus paper, and gives no coloration with ferric chloride. **1946** *Nature* 26 Oct. 590/1 Diploicin..according to Burger and associates, possesses tuberculostatic activity *in vitro*. **1949** FLOREY et al. *Antibiotics* I. xiii. 574 Barry..found that when diploicin was treated with aqueous alkali it was converted to a sodium salt of the acid (II) which inhibited the growth of *Myco. smegmatis*..and of *Myco. tuberculosis*...Although it was not determined whether diploicin was actually antibacterial Barry stated that he was using the substance in a 'limited animal protection experiment'. **1967** M. E. HALE *Biol. Lichens* viii. 117 The first successful synthesis of a depsidone, diploicin.

diploid (ˈdɪplɔɪd), *sb.* and *adj.* [f. Gr. διπλό-ος double + εἶδος form.]

A. *sb.* **a.** *Crystal.* A solid belonging to the isometric system, contained within twenty-four trapezoidal planes; = DIPLOHEDRON. **b.** *Biol.* A diploid organism.

B. *adj.* *Biol.* [a. G. *diploid* (E. Strasburger 1905, in *Jahrb. f. wissensch. Bot.* XLII. 62): see -PLOID.]Of a cell or its nucleus: having two homologous sets of chromosomes, one from each parent, each containing the haploid number of chromosomes; also, of or pertaining to diploidy, (of an organism) having somatic cells that are diploid. Hence **ˈdiploidy**, the condition of being diploid; **ˌdiploidiˈzation**; **ˈdiploidize** *v. trans.* (see quot. 1930).

1908 [see HAPLOID *a.*]. **1914** G. N. CALKINS *Biol.* ix. 209 Each has the number of chromosomes characteristic of the species (in modern terminology the diploid number). **1924** E. W. MACBRIDE *Study Heredity* viii. 216 Other examples of such 'tetraploidy' (i.e. doubling the ordinary 'diploid' number of chromosomes) are known to occur amongst the progeny of hybrids between different species. **1928** *Amer. Naturalist* LXII. 57 Stronger evidence for diploidy of biparental males appears when three character differences, all affecting one structure, the wing, are involved. **1930** A. H. R. BULLER in *Nature* 1 Nov. 687/1 The term *diploidisation* has been introduced here for the first time to designate the process by which a haploid cell is converted into a diploid cell or a haploid mycelium into a diploid mycelium by the formation of conjugate nuclei within the cell's or the mycelium's interior. A haploid mycelium of one sex may be said to *diploidise* a haploid mycelium of opposite sex. **1952** *New Biol.* XIII. 31 Most animals and many flowering plants are diploids. **1955** *Sci. Amer.* June 56/3 The body cells of a normal salamander are diploid. **1957** *Encycl. Brit.* XI. 486 Forty-eight is the diploid chromosome number in man... Haploid cells arise from diploid ones by a complex process known as meiosis. **1957** [see HAPLOID *a.*]. **1964** G. H. HAGGIS et. al. *Introd. Molecular Biol.* x. 277 It is possible by exploiting a special phenomenon, known as sexduction, to bring about a stable state of diploidy for a short length of the chromosome. **1968** [see HAPLOID *a.*]. **1971** *Nature* 7 May 49/2 If a diploid spermatozoon fertilizes a normal ovum, the resulting zygote would be triploid.

‖**diploidion** (dɪpləʊˈɪdɪən). *Gr. Antiq.* [Gr. διπλοΐδιον dim. of διπλοΐς: see next.] A form of the chiton or tunic worn by women, having the part above the waist double with the outer fold hanging loose, somewhat like a sleeveless mantle; sometimes applied to this outer fold itself.

1850 LEITCH *Müller's Anc. Art* §340. 405 It was twisted across round the chest, and was there pinned together; it has often also a kind of cape in the manner of the diploïdion.

‖**diplois** (dɪˈpləʊɪs). *Gr. Antiq.* [Gr. διπλοΐς double cloak, f. διπλό-ος double.] = prec.

1887 B. V. HEAD *Hist. Numorum* 177 A woman clothed in a sleeveless talaric chiton with diplois.

diploite (ˈdɪpləʊaɪt). *Min.* [mod. f. Gr. διπλό-ος (DIPLO-) + -ITE.] A variety of Anorthite, also called Latrobite.

1825 *Amer. Jrnl. Sc.* IX. 330 Diploite of Breithaupt. **1832** SHEPARD *Min.* 186 Diploite.

diploma (dɪˈpləʊmə), *sb.* Pl. **-as**, sometimes **-ata**. [a. L. *diplōma* a state letter of recommendation, an official document conferring some favour or privilege, a. Gr. δίπλωμα (-ματ-), (lit. a doubling), a folded paper, a letter of recommendation, later a letter of licence or privilege, f. διπλό-ειν to double, to bend or fold double, f. διπλό-ος double. Cf. F. *diplome* (Aubert 1728).]

1. A state paper, an official document; a charter.

'In modern times, a general term for ancient imperial and ecclesiastical acts and grants, public treaties, deeds of conveyance, letters, wills, and similar instruments, drawn up in forms and marked with peculiarities varying with their dates and countries' (*Encycl. Brit.* s.v.)

c **1645** HOWELL *Lett.* (1650) II. II. 19 The king of Spain.. was forced to publish a diploma wherein he dispens'd with himself (as the Holland story hath it) from payment. **1684** *Scanderbeg Rediv.* vi. 150 To pass a Diploma constituting his Lordship a Count of the Empire. **1845** S. AUSTIN *Ranke's Hist. Ref.* I. 425 They carefully avoided consulting the elector, and kept the diploma of his nomination to themselves. **1851** D. WILSON *Preh. Ann.* (1863) II. IV. i. 196 The curious diploma addressed to Eric..respecting the genealogy of William St. Clair. **1877** *Encycl. Brit.* VII. 254/1 The Merovingian sovereigns authenticated their diplomas by the addition of their signature.

b. An original document as a matter of historical investigation or literary study; *pl.* historical or literary muniments.

[**1697** H. WANLEY *Let. to T. Smith* in *Lett. Eminent Persons* (1813) I. 80 My present design..is more relating to the nature of Letters, than to the Diplomata or Charters themselves.] **1845** DE QUINCEY *Suspiria* Wks. 1890 XIII. 347 If in the vellum palimpsest, lying amongst the other diplomata of human archives or libraries, there is anything fantastic. **1891** H. H. HOWORTH in *Spectator* 12 Dec. 843/1 It [the Old Canon of Scripture]..contained books originally written in Hebrew, in so-called Chaldee, and in Greek..all of them treated as their most sacred diplomata by the early Christians and the early Councils.

2. A document granted by a competent authority conferring some honour, privilege, or licence; *esp.* that given by a university or college, testifying to a degree taken by a person, and conferring upon him the rights and privileges of such degree, as to teach, practise medicine, or the like.

a **1658** CLEVELAND *Gen. Poems, etc.* (1677) 153 You have Ennobled me with your Testimony, and I shall keep your Paper as the Diploma of my Honour. **1682** GREW *Anat. of Plants* Pref. A ij a, The Printer, whose Name was to be inserted therein, not having received his Diploma till that time. **1702** C. MATHER *Magn. Chr.* IV. (1853) II. 26 This university did present their President with a diploma for a doctorate. **1703** MAUNDRELL *Journ. Jerus.* (1732) 110 This morning our Diplomata were presented to us..to certify we had visited all the holy places. **1711** *Lond. Gaz.* No. 4812/4 Pretends to be a Physician, having a Diploma to that effect from the College of Doway. **1772** WESLEY *Jrnl.* 28 Apr., They..presented me with the freedom of the city. The diploma ran thus. **1795** in Sir J. Sinclair *Corr.* (1831) II. 21 My sincere thanks..for the diploma..admitting me a foreign honorary member of the Board of Agriculture. **1841** BORROW *Zincali* I. i. §1. 15 The writ of diploma or privilege of settling near the free and royal towns. **1849** LEWIS *Authority in Matters Opin.* ix. §17. 330 The granting of diplomas by universities or other learned bodies proceeds on the supposition that the public require some assistance to their judgment in the choice of professional services, and that such an official scrutiny into the qualifications of practitioners is a useful security against the imposture or incompetency of mere pretenders to skill. **1863** EMERSON *Misc. Papers, H. D. Thoreau* Wks. (Bohn) III. 333 No college ever offered him a diploma, or a professor's chair.

b. *attrib.*, as *diploma picture* (in chartered academies and societies of art), one given to the society by a member on his election; in the case of the Royal Academy kept in the *Diploma Gallery*.

1861 THORNBURY *Turner* (1862) I. 258 Turner's diploma picture was 'Dolbadern'..full of the grand solemnity of evening. **1883** *Pall Mall G.* 10 Oct. 1/2 The least known public collection of art in London is certainly the Diploma Gallery of the Royal Academy.

¶ **3.** The following mediæval L. senses are also given in dictionaries, but with no claim to English use. **a.** = DIPLOE 1; **b.** A folded cloth; **c.** A double vessel used in chemical operations.

1706 PHILLIPS (ed. Kersey) (a and b). **1823** CRABB *Technol. Dict.* (c), Thus, 'To boil in diploma' is to put the vessel..into a second vessel, to which the fire is applied. **1853** SOYER *Pantropheon* 262 (c).

Hence **di'plomaless** *a.*, without a diploma.

1837 G. WILSON *Let.* in *Life* (1860) II. 82 Diplomaless folks. **1873** H. CURWEN *Hist. Booksellers* 61 A diplomaless doctor.

di'ploma, *v.* [f. prec. sb.] *trans.* To furnish with a diploma. Chiefly in *ppl. a.* **diplomaed** (partly from the sb.: cf. *certificated*).

1831 TRELAWNY *Adv. Younger Son* I. 238 Surgical knowledge, superior to many of the diploma'd butchers. **1843** CARLYLE *Past & Pr.* IV. vii, Doggeries never so diplomaed, bepuffed, gas-lighted, continue doggeries, and must take the fate of such. **1869** W. R. GREG *Lit. & Social Judg.* (ed. 2) 400 They have, as it were, been diploma-ed and laureated to this effect, stamped with the Hall Mark.

diplomacy (dɪˈpləʊməsɪ). [a. F. *diplomatie* (pronounced *-cie*), f. *diplomate, diplomatique*, after *aristocrate, aristocratique, aristocratie*: see DIPLOMATIC and -ACY. So It. *diplomazia*, Sp. *diplomacia*, Ger. and Du. *diplomatie*, all from Fr.]

I. 1. The management of international relations by negotiation; the method by which these relations are adjusted and managed by ambassadors and envoys; the business or art of the diplomatist; skill or address in the conduct of international intercourse and negotiations.

1796 BURKE *Regic. Peace* II. Wks. VIII. 243 *note*, He did what he could to destroy the double diplomacy of France. He had all the secret correspondence burnt. **1797** *Ibid.* III. 348 The only excuse for all our mendicant diplomacy is.. that it has been founded on absolute necessity. **1809** W. IRVING *Knickerb.* IV. xi. (1849) 246 His first thoughts were all for war, his sober second thoughts for diplomacy. **1828** WEBSTER, *Diplomacy*.. the customs, rules and privileges of embassadors, envoys and other representatives of princes and states at foreign courts; forms of negotiation. **1855** MACAULAY *Hist. Eng.* IV. 257 The business for which he was preeminently fitted was diplomacy. **1862** T. C. GRATTAN *Beaten Paths* II. 223 Cardinal Richelieu seems to be..considered the founder of the present system of diplomacy properly so called..I can find no better signification for the word which typifies the pursuit..than double-dealing..it is expressive of concealment, if not of duplicity. **1865** LECKY *Ration.* (1878) II. 271 The appointment of consuls in the Syrian towns..gave the first great impulse to international diplomacy. **1877** *Encycl. Brit.* VII. 251/1 Diplomacy is the art of conducting the intercourse of nations with each other..It is singular that a term of so much practical importance in politics and history should be so recent in its adoption that it is not to be found in Johnson's dictionary. **1880** STUBBS *Med. & Mod. Hist.* x. (1886) 235 As diplomacy was in its beginnings, so it lasted for a long time; the ambassador was the man who was sent to lie abroad for the good of his country.

†**2.** The diplomatic body. [= F. *diplomatie*, 'le personnel des ambassades' (Littré).] *Obs.*

1796 BURKE *Regic. Peace* IV. Wks. IX. 48 The diplomacy ..were quite awestruck with 'the pomp, pride and circumstance' of this majestick Senate. **1806** SOUTHEY *Lett.* (1856) I. 387 If there be no English diplomacy at Lisbon.. away go my hopes in that quarter.

3. Skill or address in the management of relations of any kind; artful management in dealing with others.

1848 W. H. KELLY tr. *L. Blanc's Hist. Ten Y.* I. 339 The aristocracy were already..acquiring control over public affairs by the crafts of diplomacy. **1865** LIVINGSTONE *Zambesi* vi. 147 Masakasa felt confident that he could get it out of these hunters by his diplomacy. *Mod.* The lady thought it better to attain her ends by diplomacy.

II. 4. = DIPLOMATIC *sb.* 3. *rare.*

1870 J. HADLEY *Ess.* vii. (1873) 130 These [forms of letters] would probably give ground for a near guess to one expert in Anglo-Saxon diplomacy.

diplomat (ˈdɪpləʊmæt). Also -ate. [a. F. *diplomate*, a back-formation from *diplomatique*, after *aristocrate, aristocratique*.] One employed or skilled in diplomacy; a diplomatist.

1813 SIR R. WILSON *Diary* I. 312 The diplomates will.. have to rest on their arms until the bayonets have clashed. **1838** LYTTON *Alice* 96 He was the special favourite of the female diplomats. **1870** E. PEACOCK *Ralf Skirl.* III. 204 A parliamentary debater and diplomat in foreign service. **1885** MABEL COLLINS *Prettiest Woman* v, She went everywhere as a *diplomate* and a political spy.

Hence **di'plomatess**, a female diplomat.

1874 GREVILLE *Mem. Geo. IV* (1875) II. xix. 325 This clever, intriguing, agreeable diplomatess. **1890** *Athenæum* 1 Feb. 141/2 The Russian diplomatess of reality and the Russian diplomatess of, say, M. Sardou, have very little in common.

diplomatal (dɪˈpləʊmətəl), *a.* [f. Gr. διπλωματ- DIPLOMA + -AL[1].] Of or pertaining to a diploma.

1889 *Microcosm* (N.Y.) Oct., The diplomatal sheepskin.

diplomate (ˈdɪpləʊmeɪt), *sb.* [f. DIPLOMA *sb.* + -ATE[1].] One who holds a diploma.

1879 *Brit. Med. Jrnl.* 21 May 786/1 The London students and the diplomates of London Corporations.

†**'diplomate**, *v. Obs.* [f. DIPLOMA *sb.* + -ATE[3].] *trans.* To invest with a degree, privilege, or title by diploma.

1660 WOOD *Life* (Oxf. Hist. Soc.) I. 334 The former..was afterwards diplomated. **1683** *Ibid.* III. 56 Th. White, chaplain to the lady Anne..was diplomated D.D. **1738** NEAL *Hist. Purit.* IV. 268 Within..little more than six months the Universities diplomated above one hundred and fifty Doctors of Divinity.

[**diplomatial**: error in Dicts. for DIPLOMATICAL.]

diplomatic (dɪpləʊˈmætɪk), *a.* and *sb.* Also 8–9 -ique, -ick. [ad. mod.L. *diplōmatic-us* (Mabillon, 1681, *De re diplomatica*), f. Gr. διπλωματ-: see DIPLOMA and -IC. In senses 2, 3, a. F. *diplomatique* (1788 in Hatz.-Darm.).

The transition from sense 1 to sense 3 appears to have originated in the titles of the *Codex Juris Gentium Diplomaticus* of Leibnitz 1695, containing original texts of important public documents from the 11th to 15th c., and the *Corps universel diplomatique du Droit des gens* of Dumont, historiographer to the Emperor, 1726, containing the original texts of 'the treaties of Alliance, of Peace, and of Commerce, from the Peace of Munster to 1709'. In these titles (as in the *Codex Diplomaticus Ævi Saxonici* of Kemble), *diplomaticus, diplomatique*, had its original meaning (sense 1 below) as applying to a body or collection of *original official documents*. But as the subject-matter of these particular collections was *international* relations, 'corps diplomatique' appears to have been treated as equivalent to 'corps du droit des gens', and *diplomatique* taken as 'having to do with international relations'. The transition is shown in sense 2, which refers to *documents* connected with international relations, while in the fully developed sense 3 the connexion with documents disappears. This sense became established in English at the time of the French Revolution, and its French origin comes out emphatically in the writings of Burke on French affairs.]

A. *adj.*

1. Of or pertaining to official or original documents, charters, or manuscripts; textual.

diplomatic copy, edition, an exact reproduction of an original.

1711 T. MADOX *Hist. Exchequer* p. ix, The diplomatick or law word *Charta* was not received amongst the Anglo-Saxons. **1780** VON TROIL *Iceland* 295 A diplomatic description was not so much required in that letter, as I had directed my attention more to the contents of the book than its external appearance. **1784** ASTLE *Origin & Progr. of Writing* Introd. 2 Diplomatic science, the knowledge of which will enable us to form a proper judgement of the age and authenticity of manuscripts, charters, records, and other monuments of antiquity. **1812** W. TAYLOR in *Monthly Rev.* LXVII. 71 The historical part of this volume; to which a diplomatic appendix of thirty-three several documents..and a copious index are attached. **1846** TRENCH *Mirac.* (1889) 267 The last clause of the verse..has not the same amount of diplomatic evidence against it. **1861** SCRIVENER *Introd. Crit. N.T.* iii. 376 Designated by Professor Ellicott 'paradiplomatic evidence'..as distinguished from the 'diplomatic' testimony of codices, versions, etc. **1874** H. R. REYNOLDS *John Bapt.* ii. 70 There is..not a shadow of diplomatic doubt thrown over the integrity of the third gospel.

2. Of the nature of official papers connected with international relations.

1780 *Hist. Europe* in *Ann. Reg.* 18/1 These were followed, at due intervals, and according to all the established rules of form, by measured and regular discharge of the diplomatique artillery on all sides [i.e. manifestos and proclamations by the French and Spanish governments].

3. Of, pertaining to, or concerned with the management of international relations; of or belonging to diplomacy. ***diplomatic bag***, one containing the official mail of members of the diplomatic body; cf. BAG *sb.* 7 b; ***diplomatic body, corps*** (F. *corps diplomatique*), the body of ambassadors, envoys, and officials attached to the foreign legations at any seat of government; ***diplomatic immunity***, the exemption from arrest, taxation, searches, etc., granted under international law to diplomatic personnel, their families and staff, when staying in a foreign country; ***diplomatic service***, that branch of the public service which is concerned with foreign legations.

1787 *Hist. Europe* in *Ann. Reg.* 175 Employed there in civil, diplomatique, and mercantile affairs. **1790** BURKE *Fr. Rev.* Wks. V. 32 Members of the diplomatick body. **1791** —— *Th. Fr. Affairs* Wks. VII. 63 The Prussian ministers in foreign courts have talked the most democratic language.. The whole corps diplomatique, with very few exceptions, leans that way. **1796** —— *Regic. Peace* I. Wks. VIII. 114 A pacification such as France (the diplomatick name of the regicide power) would be willing to propose. **1813** N. CARLISLE *Topogr. Dict. Scot.* II. s.v. *Preston Pans*, Sir Robert Murray Keith..well known for his diplomatique talents. **1815** WELLINGTON in Gurw. *Desp.* XII. 310 It would introduce him into the diplomatic line. **1840** CARLYLE *Heroes* iii. (ed. 1858) 244 Petrarch and Boccaccio did diplomatic messages..quite well. **1849** MACAULAY *Hist. Eng.* I. 246 He had passed several years in diplomatic posts abroad. **1860** MOTLEY *Netherl.* (1868) I. i. 18 Diplomatic relations..were not entrusted to the Council. **1868** E. EDWARDS *Raleigh* I. xxv. 587 The English statesman..was not a match for the Spaniard in diplomatic craft. **1877** *Encycl. Brit.* VII. 251/2 The ancient world had its treaties and leagues, but no systematic diplomatic relations. **1889** *John Bull* 2 Mar. 149/2 The members of the Diplomatic Corps. **1911** *Encycl. Brit.* VIII. 299/2 In certain cases..the ex-territoriality of ambassadors implies a fairly extensive criminal jurisdiction; in other cases the dismissal of the servant would deprive him of his diplomatic immunity and bring him under the law of the land. **1936** M. OGDON (*title*) Juridical bases of diplomatic immunity. **1956** *N. & Q.* July 277 These papers were returned to Commander Bulloch via the United States Diplomatic Bag in January of 1895. **1970** R. G. FELTHAM *Diplomatic Handbk.* v. 52 The diplomatic bag is a sealed bag or container clearly marked as such and containing official documents and articles for official use, which a head of mission is entitled to receive and dispatch without it being interfered with. **1971** J. SANGSTER *Your Friendly Neighbourhood Death Pedlar* ii. 43 Do you need traveller's cheques,..a gun permit, diplomatic immunity?

4. Skilled in the art of diplomacy; showing address in negotiations or intercourse of any kind.

1826 DISRAELI *Viv. Grey* IV. iii, Treachery and cowardice, doled out with diplomatic politesse. **1837** HALE *In His Name* x, Gabrielle's busy, active, diplomatic managing of the party. **1862** MAURICE *Mor. & Met. Philos.* IV. viii. §6. 440 Cautious and reserved yet not diplomatic in his intercourse with men. **1877** *Encycl. Brit.* VII. 251/1 Conduct which is wily and subtle, without being directly false or fraudulent, is styled 'diplomatic'.

B. *sb.* **1.** A diplomatic agent; = DIPLOMATIST.

1791 PAINE *Rights of Man* (ed. 4) 93 Dr. Franklin..was not the diplomatic of a Court, but of Man. **1836** MARRYAT *Midsh. Easy* II. ix. 238 It would soon be all in his favour when it was known that he was a diplomatic.

2. The diplomatic art, diplomacy. Also in pl. **diplomatics**, and † in L. form *diplomatica* (*obs.*).

1794 BURKE *App. Pref. Brissot's Addr.* Wks. VII. 343 Cambon, incapable of political calculation, boasting his ignorance in the diplomatick. **1796** *State Papers* in *Ann. Reg.* 198 Truth and justice are the only basis of their diplomatica. **1803** W. TAYLOR in *Ann. Rev.* I. 356 Our ministers are not great in diplomatics.

3. 'The science of diplomas, or of ancient writings, literary and public documents, letters, decrees, charters, codicils, etc., which has for its object to decipher old writings, to ascertain their authenticity, their date, signatures, etc.' (Webster, 1828). Also in *pl.*

[**1681** MABILLON (*title*), De Re Diplomatica.] **1803–19** A. REES *Cycl.* (L.), The science of diplomatics owes its origin to a Jesuit of Antwerp named Papebroch. **1819** *Pantologia* s.v., The celebrated Treatise on the Diplomatic by F. Mabillon. **1838** J. G. DOWLING *Eccl. Hist.* iii. §1. 125 It was written.. when Diplomatic..did not exist as a science. **1846** JOHNSTON tr. *Beckmann's Hist. Inv.* (ed. 4) I. 140 A seal of blue wax, not coloured blue merely on the outer surface, would be as great a rarity in the arts as in diplomatics. **1894** *Oxf. Univ. Gaz.* XXIV. 412/1 Medieval Latin palaeography and diplomatic.

diplo'matical, *a.* (*sb.*) [f. as prec. + -AL[1].]

A. *adj.* **1.** = DIPLOMATIC *a.* 1.

1780 VON TROIL *Iceland* 296 Its diplomatical descriptions would have afforded no information.

2. = DIPLOMATIC *a.* 3.

1823 BYRON *Juan* XIII. xv, It chanced some diplomatical relations Arising out of business, often brought Himself and Juan..Into close contact. **1882–3** SCHAFF *Encycl. Relig. Knowl.* III. 2096 Paul III..employed him frequently in diplomatical negotiations with Francis I and Chas. V.

B. *sb.* (*rare.*)

1. A diplomatic person; a diplomatist.

1830 GALT *Lawrie T.* VI. iii. (1849) 262 He proved himself a clever diplomatical.

2. *pl.* Diplomatic arts or proceedings.

1833 GALT in *Fraser's Mag.* VIII. 654, I had recourse to the usual diplomaticals of womankind.

diplo'matically, *adv.* [f. prec. + -LY[2].]

1. In a diplomatic manner; according to the rules or art of diplomacy; artfully in reference to intercourse; with clever management.

1836 E. HOWARD *R. Reefer* lxii, My lord shook his head.. diplomatically. **1837** CARLYLE *Fr. Rev.* (1848) II. v. ix. 294 Old Besenval diplomatically whispering to him. **1862** SHIRLEY *Nugæ Crit.* ix. 417 Hitherto we had diplomatically and passively resisted the Alliance. **1875** MRS. RANDOLPH *W. Hyacinth* I. 123 She at once knew that her work must be done diplomatically.

2. In reference to, or in the matter of, diplomacy.

1877 *Public Opinion* 7 July 9 The policy of the Hapsburg Monarchy is..both diplomatically and militarily, absolutely free and unfettered.

3. With reference to diplomatics (sense 3); so far as concerns the evidence of original documents.

1885 *Amer. Jrnl. Philol.* VI. 192 The indiction-number.. is diplomatically uncertain, and so of no independent value.

diplomatician (dɪpləʊməˈtɪʃən). *rare.* [f. DIPLOMATIC: see -ICIAN.] = DIPLOMATIST.

1821 W. TAYLOR in *Monthly Rev.* XCIV. 499 With the usual spiteful feeling of a French diplomatician.

diplomatics: see DIPLOMATIC B 2, 3.

di'plomatism. *rare*[−0]. [f. as next + -ISM.] The practice of the diplomat; DIPLOMACY.

1864 in WEBSTER.

diplomatist (dɪˈpləʊmətɪst). [f. DIPLOMAT *sb.*, or stem of *diplomat-ic*, etc. + -IST: cf. F. *philologue*, Eng. *philologist*.] **a.** One engaged in official diplomacy. **b.** One characterized by diplomatic address; a shrewd and crafty person.

1815 MACKINTOSH *Sp. in Ho. Com.* 27 Apr. Wks 1846 III. 317 Long familiarity with the smooth and soft manners of diplomatists. **1826** DISRAELI *Viv. Grey* III. i, Vivian..

dropped the diplomatist altogether, and was explicit enough for a Spartan. **1849** MACAULAY *Hist. Eng.* I. 246 Diplomatists, as a class, have always been more distinguished by their address..than by generous enthusiasm or austere rectitude. **1860** FROUDE *Hist. Eng.* V. 219 So accomplished a diplomatist as Paget could only despise the tricks which he was ordered to practise.

attrib. **1858** CARLYLE *Fredk. Gt.* (1865) II. VII. iv. 282 The Diplomatist world of Berlin is in a fuss.

diplomatize (dɪˈpləʊmətaɪz), *v.* [In I. f. Gr. διπλωματ- DIPLOMA + -IZE; in II. a new formation from *diplomat, -ic, -ist.*]

I. 1. *trans.* To invest with a diploma. Hence **diˈplomatized** *ppl. a.*, diplomaed. *rare.*

1670 *Lex Talionis* 21 As able Physitians as any that Practise, and better than many dyplomatized Doctors. **1834** *Knickerbocker* Aug. 120 Ladies were invited..to prepare themselves for future honors..by becoming Latinized, Græcised, mathematicized, and at length diplomatized.

II. 2. *intr.* To act or serve as a diplomat or diplomatist; to practise diplomacy; to use diplomatic arts; to act with address or astuteness.

1826 DISRAELI *Viv. Grey* III. i, He diplomatised, in order to gain time. **1837** CARLYLE *Fr. Rev.* (1848) II. II. vi. 119 Brave Bouillé mysteriously diplomatising in scheme within scheme. **1850** *Tait's Mag.* XVII. 285/1 He was too impatient to diplomatise. **1875** *Contemp. Rev.* XXV. 798 One who had been campaigning and diplomatizing almost from his childhood.

3. a. *trans.* To treat in the manner of a diplomatist, to act diplomatically towards.

1855 *Fraser's Mag.* LI. 239 His only chance..was to cajole—we mean to diplomatize—his neighbours. **1898** *Daily News* 6 Aug. 7/3 Italian unity is owing in great part to the work of the people with Garibaldi, and Cavour did nothing but diplomatize the movement. **1906** *Daily Chron.* 24 Dec. 4/6 Count Nicholas Ignatieff who may be said to have 'diplomatised' the Russo-Turkish War of 1877.

b. To do *out of* by diplomacy or address.

1885 LOWE *Bismarck* I. viii. 479 Louis Napoleon had not long been diplomatised out of Luxemburg.

Hence **diˈplomatizing** *vbl. sb.* and *ppl. a.*

1855 CARLYLE *Prinzenraub* 106 No more, either of fighting or diplomatizing, needed for him. **1882** *Pall Mall G.* 5 July 2/1 The two Powers were thinking of their own diplomatizings.

diplomatology (dɪpləʊməˈtɒlədʒɪ). [f. Gr. διπλωματ- DIPLOMA + -λογια discourse: see -LOGY.] The science of Diplomatic; the scientific study of original documents.

1880 G. S. HALL in *Nation* (N.Y.) XXX. 347 Many of the young docents, whose specialty is Semitic philology, or Hebrew archæology, or church history, or diplomatology.

†**diˈplome.** *Obs. rare.* [a. F. *diplome*, ad. L. *diplōma.*] An official document issued by authority; = DIPLOMA 1.

1669 GALE *True Idea Jansenism* 22 And thou hast vindicated the truth and vigor of this Bull, by a new *Diplome.*

diploneural, -neurose, etc.: see DIPLO-.

diplont (ˈdɪplɒnt). *Biol.* [a. G. *diplont*, f. DIPLO- + Gr. ὤν, ὀντ- being: see ONTO-.] A sexual organism that is diploid at all stages of its life other than the gamete, which is haploid.

1925 E. B. WILSON *Cell* (ed. 3) vi. 492 From this organism [the haplont] arise the gametes..and by their union is produced the zygote from which arises a diploid, asexual spore-producing diplont (in plants the sporophyte), thus completing the life-cycle. **1943** L. W. SHARP *Fund. Cytol.* xi. 160 *Cladophora glomerata* is also reported to be a diplont, but it differs from *Codium* in having zoöspores. **1951** [see HAPLONT]. **1965** BELL & COOMBE tr. *Strasburger's Textbk. Bot.* (new ed.) I. i. 37 Meiosis can be deferred right up to the formation of gametes. In this case, rare in plants, all the cells other than the gametes are diploid and the organisms are termed diplonts.

Hence **diˈplontic** *a.*

1929 *Hereditas* XIII. 333 Diplontic sterility may be caused by species crosses, special genetic factors and by inbreeding. **1970** *Jrnl. Phycol.* VI. 122 The life cycle of *N*[*octiluca*] *miliaris* appears thus to be of the diplontic type.

‖**diplopia** (dɪˈpləʊpɪə). *Phys.* and *Path.* Also in anglicized form **diplopy**. [mod.L., f. Gr. διπλο- DIPLO- double + -ωπια from ὤψ eye: cf. AMBLYOPIA.] An affection of the eyes, in which objects are seen double. Hence **diplopic** (dɪˈplɒpɪk) *a.*, pertaining to diplopia.

1811 HOOPER *Med. Dict., Diplopia.* **1864** WEBSTER, *Diplopia, Diplopy.* **1875** H. C. WOOD *Therap.* (1879) 242 This dryness..is associated with..dilated pupils, disordered vision, and possibly diplopia. **1878** A. HAMILTON *Nerv. Dis.* 228 Diplopia, amaurosis, and other visual troubles.

diploplacula, -pod, etc.: see DIPLO-.

diplostemonous (dɪpləʊˈstiːmənəs), *a. Bot.* [f. DIPLO- + Gr. στήμων warp, thread, taken as = στῆμα stamen + -OUS.] Having the stamens in two series, or twice as many as the petals. So **diploˈstemony**, the condition of being diplostemonous.

1866 *Treas. Bot., Diplostemonous*, having twice as many stamens as petals. **1880** GRAY *Struct. Bot.* vi. §2. 177 *note.* **1888** HENSLOW *Floral Struct.* 188 If a flower have one whorl of stamens of the same number as the petals it is isostemonous; if two, diplostemonous. **1888** *Athenæum* 14 Jan. 54/3 Investigations..on the diplostemony of the flowers of angiosperms.

‖**diplotegia** (dɪpləʊˈtiːdʒɪə). *Bot.* Also **-ium.** [f. DIPLO- + Gr. τέγος roof, covering.] A dry dehiscent fruit with an adnate calyx.

1866 *Treas. Bot., Diplotegia*, an inferior capsule. **1870** BENTLEY *Bot.* 313 Diplotegia is the only kind of inferior fruit which presents a dry dehiscent pericarp.

diplotene (ˈdɪpləʊtiːn). *Biol.* [ad. Fr. *diplotène* (H. von Winiwarter 1900, in *Archives de Biol.* XVII. I. 70), f. DIPLO- + -TENE.] The fourth stage of the prophase of meiosis (following pachytene), in which the four chromatids of each tetrad begin to separate into two pairs, each pair containing one chromatid from each of the two orginal paired chromosomes. Also *attrib.* or as *adj.*

1925 E. B. WILSON *Cell* (ed. 3) vi. 545 Probably, therefore, the diffuse stage should be regarded as a highly modified diplotene in which the duality of the early diplotene..in some manner persists throughout. **1929** *Jrnl. Genetics* XXI. 5 *Diplotene looping.* As soon as the double threads begin to open to form the loops characteristic of *diplotene*..it appears as though..real association has been taking place only between two chromosomes..for the third chromosome is seen to be lying free. **1931** *Nature* 9 May 711/1 At meiosis, it does not happen until pachytene (possibly at the moment at which the diplotene loops appear). *Ibid.*, This condition is fulfilled by the pairing of chromosome threads when they are still single, and their separation at diplotene when they have at last come to divide. **1951** G. H. BOURNE *Cytol. & Cell Physiol.* (ed. 2) x. 435 After 3 days the oocytes entered the contraction phase, from which most of them had emerged by the 6th day, to pass into the pachytene phase; this was quickly followed by the diplotene. **1965** BELL & COOMBE tr. *Strasburger's Textbk. Bot.* (new ed.) I. i. 34 In diplotene the pairing of the still extended chromosomes, completed in pachytene, is again lost.

‖**Diplozoon** (dɪpləʊˈzəʊɒn). *Zool.* Pl. **-zoa.** [f. DIPLO- + Gr. ζῷον animal.] A genus of trematode worms, parasitic on the gills of fishes; the mature organism is double, consisting of two individuals (*Diporpæ*) fused together in the form of an X.

1835 KIRBY *Hab. & Inst. Anim.* I. 355 One [parasitic worm] first discovered by Dr. Nordmann upon [the gills] of the bream..to which he has given the name of Diplozoon or Double animal. **1859** TODD *Cycl. Anat.* V. 32/1 This animal corresponds..with the half of the Diplozoon. **1888** ROLLESTON & JACKSON *Anim. Life* 650 The cones and suckers fuse completely; in other respects, however, the two Diporpæ which make up a single Diplozoon are independent of one another.

dip-net: see DIP *sb.*

dipneumonous (dɪpˈnjuːmənəs), *a. Zool.* [f. mod.L. *dipneumonus* (f. Gr. δι-, δίς twice + πνεύμων lung) + -OUS.] Having two lungs or respiratory organs; said of the *Dipneumona* or two-lunged fishes, and of the *Dipneumones* or two-lunged spiders; also of Holothurians having a pair of respiratory organs.

dipneustal (dɪpˈnjuːstəl), *a.* [mod.L. *Dipneusta* (f. Gr. δι- twice + πνευστός, πνεῖν to breathe), a name given by some to the dipnoan fishes + -AL[1].] = DIPNOAN.

[**1892** E. R. LANKESTER tr. *Haeckel's Hist. Creation* II. 290 Of the still living Dipneusta, Ceratodus possesses a simple single lung (Monopneumones), whereas Protopterus and Lepidosiren have a pair of lungs (Dipneumones).]

dipnoan (ˈdɪpnəʊən), *a.* and *sb. Zool.* [f. mod.L. *Dipnoi* (see DIPNOOUS) + -AN.]

A. *adj.* Belonging to the *Dipnoi*, a sub-class or order of fishes, having two kinds of respiratory organs, gills and lungs. **B.** *sb.* A fish belonging to this order.

1883 *Athenæum* 7 Apr. 447/1 Prof. Huxley came to the conclusion that..to separate the elasmobranchs, ganoids, and dipnoans into a group, apart from and equivalent to the teleosteans, was inconsistent with the plainest anatomical relations of these fishes. **1886** *Ibid.* 18 Dec. 830/2 A paper on the development..of the ovum in the dipnoan fishes.

dipnoid (ˈdɪpnɔɪd), *a.* and *sb. Zool.* [f. mod.L. *Dipnoi* (see next) + -ID.] = DIPNOAN.

1878 F. DAY *Fishes of India*, 709 Whether the Ganoids and Dipnoids should be included with the *Chondropterygii.* **1880** —— *Fishes Gt. Brit.* Introd. 41 Among the Dipnoids, the air-bladder has a lung-like function..Among the Ganoids there is a divergence from the Dipnoid organization. **1881** GÜNTHER in *Encycl. Brit.* XII. 686/1 The dentition is that of a Dipnoid.

dipnoous (ˈdɪpnəʊəs), *a.* Also erron. **dipnous.** [f. mod.L. *dipno-us* (in pl. *Dipnoi*, an order of Fishes), a. Gr. δίπνο-ος with two breathing apertures, f. δι- twice + πνοή breathing, breath.]

1. *Zool.* Having both gills and lungs, as a dipnoan fish.

1881 GÜNTHER in *Encycl. Brit.* XII. 686/1 The relations of the chimaeras to the Ganoid, and more especially to the Dipnoous type. *Ibid.* 686/2 It is impossible to decide..whether the Fossil should be referred to the Holocephalous or the Dipnoous type.

2. *Path.* Of a wound: 'Having two openings for the entrance of air or other matters' (*Syd. Soc. Lex.* 1883).

1811 HOOPER *Med. Dict., Dipnous*, an epithet for wounds which are perforated quite through, and admit the air at both ends.

dipnosophist, obs. form of DEIPNOSOPHIST.

1581 MULCASTER *Positions* xxxv. (1887) 129 All natural.. dipnosophistes, symposiakes, antiquaries.

dipodic (daɪˈpɒdɪk), *a.* [f. Gr. διποδ- (see DIPODY) + -IC.] Of the nature of a dipody; characterized by dipodies; as 'a dipodic measure'.

In recent Dicts.

ˈdipodous, *a.* [f. Gr. διποδ- (see next) + -OUS.] 'Having two feet' (*Syd. Soc. Lex.* 1883).

dipody (ˈdɪpədɪ). *Pros.* [ad. L. *dipodia* (also in Eng. use), a. Gr. διποδία two-footedness, dipody, f. δίπους, διποδ- two-footed, f. δι-, DI-[2] + πούς, ποδ- foot.] A double foot; two feet constituting a single measure.

1844 BECK & FELTON tr. *Munk's Metres* 16 A series of one foot is called a monopody; of two feet, a dipody. **1859** J. W. DONALDSON *Grk. Gram.* 646 The simplest form of this dactylic dipodia is the Adonius, which finishes off the Sapphic stanza. **1882** GOODWIN *Grk. Gram.* 317 In trochaic, iambic, and anapæstic verses, which are measured by dipodies (i.e. pairs of feet), a monometer consists of one dipody (or two feet), a dimeter of four feet. **1891** *Harper's Mag.* Mar. 576/2 [Folk-songs] in Hungarian music consisting of dipodies, tetrapodies, tripodies, pentapodies, and hexapodies.

dipolar (daɪˈpəʊlə(r)), *a.* [f. DI-[2] + POLAR.] Of or pertaining to two poles; having two poles, esp. poles such that the relations of the body or quantity remain the same when it is turned end for end.

1864 in WEBSTER. **1873** MAXWELL *Electr. & Magn.* §381 II. 7 When a dipolar quantity is turned end for end it remains the same as before. Tensions and pressures in solid bodies, Extensions, Compressions and Distortions, and most of the optical, electrical, and magnetic properties of crystallized bodies are dipolar quantities. **1882** SIR W. THOMSON *Math. & Phys. Papers* I. xlviii. §168. 283 The rotatory property with reference to light discovered by Faraday as induced by magnetization in transparent solids which I shall call dipolar, to distinguish it from such a rotatory property with reference to light as that which is naturally possessed by many transparent liquids and solids, and which may be called an isotropic rotatory property. **1884** TAIT *Light* §298 Along the axis of a crystal of quartz there is dipolar symmetry; along the lines of force in a transparent diamagnetic there is dipolar asymmetry.

diˈpolarize, *v. Optics.* [f. DI-[2] + POLARIZE *v.*] A word used by some instead of DEPOLARIZE (sense a). So **diˈpolarized, diˈpolarizing** *ppl. adjs.*; also **diˈpolarization.** (See quots.)

1837 WHEWELL *Hist. Induct. Sc.* IX. ix. (*heading*), Discovery of the Laws of Phenomena of Dipolarized Light. *Ibid.*, The effect which the mica produced was termed *depolarization*; —not a very happy term, since the effect is not the destruction of the polarization, but the combination of a new polarizing influence with the former. The word *dipolarization*, which has since been proposed, is a much more appropriate expression. *Ibid.* xi. §4 The phenomena of depolarized, or rather, as I have already said, *di*polarized light. *Ibid.* §5 Fresnel explained very completely..the dipolarizing effect of the crystal; and the office of the *analysing plate*, by which certain portions of each of the two rays in the crystal are made to interfere and produce colour. **1864** H. SPENCER *Illustr. Univ. Progr.* 180 Brewster's discoveries respecting double refraction and dipolarization.

dipole (ˈdaɪpəʊl). [f. DI-[2] + POLE *sb.*[2]]

1. A pair of non-coincident equal and opposite electric charges or magnetic poles (usu. but not necessarily close together); an object, esp. a molecule, atomic particle, etc., having such charges or poles; **dipole moment**, the product of the distance between the two charges or poles of a dipole and the magnitude of either of them; the electric or magnetic moment of a dipole.

1912 *Sci. Abstr.* A. XV. 184 Taking the view that in dielectrics the electrons when displaced are urged back by forces proportional to those displacements, and that *dipoles* of constant electric moment are present also, the author [*sc.* Debye] obtains the following expression. **1931** W. M. DEANS tr. *Debye's Dipole Moment & Chem. Struct.* 15 The methods in general use for the determination of dipole moments depend on the measurement of the dielectric constant of the substance in question. **1934** *Nature* 17 Mar. 415/2 The permanent dipole of a molecule in a solution may be regarded as surrounded by an 'atmosphere' of dipoles of opposite sign produced partly by induction in the polarisable solvent molecules and partly by orientation of adjacent permanent dipoles. *Ibid.* 26 May 802/1 Few branches of physical chemistry can show a more rapid development than the study of dipole moments. **1956** *Sci. News* XLI. 51 The electrical properties of organic materials are critically influenced by whether or not they contain permanent molecular dipoles. **1957** *Endeavour* XVI. 188/1 Nuclei with spin quantum numbers greater than one-half usually possess an electric quadrupole moment as well as a magnetic dipole moment. **1965** A. HOLMES *Princ. Physical Geol.* (ed. 2) xxvii. 989 The main part of the magnetic field is..like that of a powerful bar magnet (a 'dipole') placed near the middle of the earth. **1968** R. A. LYTTLETON *Myst. Solar Syst.* iii. 97 The dipole-moment [of Mars] can be at most 1/3000th that of the Earth.

2. *Radio.* An aerial consisting either of two equal metal rods mounted close together in line or of a single rod, with the electrical connection made to the centre of the aerial and with a total length usually about half the wavelength to be transmitted or received; freq. *attrib.* (See also quots. 1947, 1960.)

1929 *Proc. Inst. Radio Engin.* Dec. 2207 (*caption*) Position of the dipole on the airplane... Securely stretched dipoles are most commonly used... Fig. 15 shows the installation of such a dipole antenna. **1930** *Telegr. & Teleph. Jrnl.* XVII. 31/1 These arrays generally consist of a number of dipoles.. arranged in the form of a curtain. **1931** *Jrnl. R. Aeronaut. Soc.* XXXV. 761 The directional properties were investigated with a di-pole receiver. **1943** *Electronic Engin.* XVI. 197 Dipoles of length other than half wavelength. **1947** SIEGERT & PURCELL in L. N. Ridenour *Radar System Engin.* iii. 82 'Window' is the British and most commonly used code name for conducting foil or sheet cut into pieces of such a size that each piece resonates as a dipole at enemy radar frequency. **1955** *Sci. Amer.* Mar. 38/1 A parabolic 'dish', either solid or made of a wire screen, reflects incoming radio waves to a focal point, where a small dipole or rod picks up the energy and converts it into an electric current which is then conveyed by a cable to a sensitive receiver. **1960** *Times* 16 Sept. 6/7 The idea of using a cloud of thin strips of metal foil to reflect radio waves originated during the war... Such a strip is tuned automatically to a wavelength twice the length of the strip—an aerial or reflector of this kind being known as a dipole. **1964** *Ann. Reg. 1963* 185 On 9 May..the U.S. released..some 400 million copper dipoles, or space needles, each about ¾ inch long.

†**di'pondiary**, *a. Obs. rare*$^{-0}$. [f. L. *di-*, *dupondiārius*, f. *di-*, *dupondium*, the sum of two asses.]

1656 BLOUNT *Glossogr.*, *Dipondiary*, that is of two pound weight.

‖**diporpa** (daɪ'pɔːpə). *Zool.* Pl. -æ. [f. Gr. δι-, δίς twice, doubly + πόρπη pin of a buckle.] The solitary immature form of a DIPLOZOON.

1888 ROLLESTON & JACKSON *Anim. Life* 650 The embryo known as Diporpa is at first free-swimming. *Ibid.*, The two Diporpae which make up a single Diplozoon.

dipped, dipt (dɪpt), *ppl. a.* [f. DIP *v.* + -ED[1].]

1. a. Immersed (briefly or partially) in a liquid: see the verb. (In quots. 1646 and 1781, Baptized by immersion.)

1548 UDALL, etc. *Erasm. Par. John* 89 b, He..to whome I shall geue a dipte soppe. **1579** FULKE *Heskins's Parl.* 309 We read not that Christ gaue dipped bread to others, except that disciple only. **1646** R. BAILLIE *Anabaptism* (1647) 30 Churches of anabaptized and dipped Saints. **1781** COWPER *Charity* 609 E'en the dipt and sprinkled live in peace. **1814** BYRON *Corsair* I. xvii, Flash'd the dipt oars. **1876** RUSKIN *Fors Clav.* VI. lxi. 2 All your comfort in such charity is.. Christ's dipped sop.

b. Of candles: Made by dipping (see DIP *v.* 3 b).

1727–51 CHAMBERS *Cycl.* s.v. *Candle*, Tallow Candles are of two kinds; the one dipped, the other moulded. *Ibid.*, Making of dipped Candles. **1833** HT. MARTINEAU *Loom & Lugger* I. ii. 17 That which curled magnificently from the dipped candles on either side.

c. *transf.* Extended or carried below a surface or level.

1925 PENDEREL-BRODHURST & LAYTON *Gloss. Eng. Furniture*, *Dropped or dipped seat*, the seat of a chair having a concave upper surface between the two side rails. **1929** *Evening News* 18 Nov. 10 A wonderfully flared skirt dipped at sides.

d. Of the beams of the headlights of a vehicle: lowered.

1937 *Sunday Times* 10 Jan., Even in London, I always drive with my headlamps in the dipped position, except in extremely well-lighted thoroughfares. **1963** *Times* 28 Feb. 4/5 Birmingham's campaign for dipped headlights has 'sensationally' cut night accidents and casualties in the city. **1969** *Guardian* 23 June 7/5 In town traffic, dipped beams produce appreciable glare.

2. *fig.* Involved in debt; mortgaged (see DIP *v.* 7 b). (*colloq.*)

1676 WYCHERLEY *Pl. Dealer* III. i, Some young Wit, or Spendthrift, that has a good dip'd Seat and Estate in Middlesex. **1708** MOTTEUX *Rabelais* (1737) V. 214 Redeemers of dipt, mortgag'd, and bleeding Copy-holds.

Dippel's oil. [f. The name of the discoverer J. C. *Dippel* (1672–1734), German alchemist.] Bone oil. In full *Dippel's animal oil.*

1819 W. T. BRANDE *Man. Chem.* vii. 429 When horn, hoofs, or bones, are distilled *per se*, a quantity of solid carbonate of ammonia, and of the same substance combined with empyreumatic oil,..are obtained; hence the pharmaceutical preparations called spirit and salt of hartshorn, and Dippel's animal oil. **1904** in GOODCHILD & TWENEY *Technol. & Sci. Dict.* **1938** *Thorpe's Dict. Appl. Chem.* (ed. 4) II. 29/2 'Dippel's oil', sometimes also termed 'bone oil',..is obtained by the destructive distillation of bones in the preparation of bone charcoal. **1966** MILLAR & SPRINGALL *Sidgwick's Org. Chem. Nitrogen* (ed. 3) xxi. 619 Pyrrole..was first isolated in a pure condition by Anderson in 1858 who obtained it from a product of distillation of bone, bone oil or Dippel's oil.

dipper ('dɪpə(r)). [f. DIP *v.* + -ER[1].]

1. One who dips, in various senses; *spec.* **a.** One who immerses something in a fluid; chiefly in technical uses.

1611 COTGR., *Trempeur*, a dipper, wetter, moistener. **1762** DERRICK *Lett.* (1767) II. 51 There are women always ready to present you with a cup of water who call themselves Dippers. **1825** J. NICHOLSON *Operat. Mechanic* 473 By the side of this tub stands the dipper, and a boy, his assistant. **1881** *Guide Worcest. Porcel. Wks.* 8 The action of the Dipper shows the..process in glazing..wares. **1881** BESANT & RICE *Chapl. of Fleet* II. ii. (1883) 130 There was in the room [at Epsom Wells] a dipper, as they call the women who hand the water to those who go to drink it. **1883** *Birm. Daily Post* 11 Oct., Tallow Chandlers.—Wanted immediately, a first-class Dipper.

b. One who 'dips' snuff: see DIP *v.* 5.

1870 W. M. BAKER *New Timothy* 75 (Cent. Dict.) The fair dipper holds in her lap a bottle containing the most pungent Scotch snuff, and in her mouth a short stick of soft wood, the end of which is chewed into a sort of brush.

c. One who 'dips' into a book, etc.: see DIP *v.* 14.

1824 W. IRVING *T. Trav.* I. 326, I became also a lounger in the Bodleian library, and a great dipper into books. **1889** *Temple Bar Mag.* Dec. 553 The dippers are those readers who are only by an euphemism called readers.

d. *Thieves' slang.* A pickpocket. (Farmer 1891.)

1889 in BARRÈRE & LELAND *Dict. Slang.* **1896** A. MORRISON *Child of Jago* xi. 111 Such dippers—such pickpockets—as could dress well. **1968** M. ALLINGHAM *Cargo of Eagles* ii. 34 [The wallet] could have been pinched ..and ditched there... Dippers often do that.

2. One who uses immersion in baptism; *esp.* an Anabaptist or Baptist: *spec.* one of a sect of American Baptists, called also *Dunkers*.

1617 COLLINS *Def. Bp. Ely* I. v. 200 To be dippers and baptisers. **1642** FEATLY (*title*), The Dippers dipt, or the Anabaptists duck'd and plung'd over Head and Ears, at a Disputation in Southwark. **1823** LAMB *Elia* Ser. II. *Amicus Rediv.*, Fie, man, to turn dipper at your years, after so many tracts in favour of sprinkling only. **1887** C. W. SUTTON in *Dict. Nat. Biog.* XI. 5/2 He became a dipper or anabaptist (immersed 6 Nov. 1644).

3. A name given to various birds which dip or dive in water. **a.** The Water Ouzel, *Cinclus aquaticus*; also other species of the genus, as, in N. America, *C. Mexicanus*. **b.** *locally* in England: The Kingfisher. **c.** = DABCHICK 1, DIDAPPER 1. ? *Obs.* **d.** in *U.S.* A species of duck, *Bucephala albeola*, the buffle.

1388 WYCLIF *Lev.* xi. 17 An owle, and dippere [**1382** deuedep, deuedoppe.]. —— *Deut.* xiv. 17 A dippere, a pursirioun, and a reremous..alle in her kynde. **1678** RAY *Willughby's Ornith.* 340 The Didapper, or Dipper, or Dobchick, or small Doucker. **1752** SIR J. HILL *Hist. Anim.* 446 (Jod.), The dobchick..we call it by several names expressive of its diving; the didapper, the dipper, etc. **1833** SELBY in *Proc. Berw. Nat. Club* I. No. 1. 20 The only bird which attracted notice was the dipper (*Cinclus aquaticus*). **1864** THOREAU *Maine W.* iii. 170 A brood of twelve black dippers, half grown, came paddling by. **1881** MISS JACKSON *Shropsh. Word-bk.*, *Dipper*, the King-fisher. **1882** A. HEPBURN in *Proc. Berw. Nat. Club* IX. No. 3. 504 Of the Thrush family, the Dipper or Watercrow frequented all the streams.

4. A genus of gastropod molluscs, *Bulla*.

1776 DA COSTA *Conchol.* 174 (Jod.) The sixth family is the nuces, seu bullæ; commonly called the pewits eggs, or dipping snails, but which I shall henceforward call dippers, or seanuts. **1835** KIRBY *Hab. & Inst. Anim.* I. ix. 276 The dippers (Bulla) which are furnished with a singular organ or gizzard that proves their predaceous or carnivorous habits.

5. a. A utensil for dipping up water, etc.: *spec.* a ladle consisting of a bowl with a long handle. (Chiefly *U.S.*)

1801 MASON *Supp. Johnson*, *Dipper*, a spoon made in a certain form. Being a modern invention, it is not often mentioned in books. **1828** WEBSTER, *Dipper*..2 A vessel used to dip water or other liquor; a ladle. **1855** LONGF. *Hiaw.* XXII. 107 Water brought in birchen dippers. **1858** SIMMONDS *Dict. Trade*, *Dipper*, an utensil for taking up fluids in a brewery. **1864** LOWELL *Fireside Trav.* 155 The little tin dipper was scratched all over. **1885** G. ALLEN *Babylon* xi, Each of whom brought his own dipper, plate, knife, fork. **1891** R. KIPLING *Naulahka* iv, It's like trying to scoop up the ocean with a dipper.

b. The popular name in the United States for the configuration of seven bright stars in Ursa Major (called in Britain 'the Plough', or 'Charles's Wain'). *Little Dipper*: the similar configuration of seven stars in Ursa Minor.

1842 *Lowell* (Mass.) *Offering* II. 234, 236 (Th.), You all know the Dipper? Yes, it is in the Great Bear. The Little Dipper is in Ursa Minor. **1858** THOREAU *Autumn* (1894) 74 Its [comet's] tail is at least as long as the whole of the Great Dipper. **1858** HAWTHORNE *Fr. & It. Jrnls.* II. 111 The constellation of the Dipper..pointing to the North Star. **1890** C. A. YOUNG *Uranography* §5 The familiar Dipper is sloping downward in the north-west.

c. In full *dipper dredge*. A type of dredging boat or machine (see quots.).

1877 *Encycl. Brit.* VII. 465/1 The dipper dredge consists of a barge, with a derrick-crane reaching over the stern, suspending a large wrought-iron bucket which brings up the dredged material. **1879** *Scribner's Monthly* Nov. 55/1 The channel has also been assisted somewhat in its development, by an Osgood dipper dredge. *a* **1884** KNIGHT *Dict. Mech.* Suppl., *Dipper*, a form of dredging machine which has a large ladle on the end of a spar. **1959** *Chambers's Encycl.* IV. 634/2 Such a crude form of dipper dredge is still to be found in China.

6. *Photogr.* An apparatus for immersing negatives in a chemical solution: see quots.

1859 *Photogr. News* 186 *Dipper*, the piece of glass or other substance on which the iodised plate is laid, in order to be dipped into the nitrate of silver bath. **1878** ABNEY *Photogr.* 79 The dipper, employed for carrying the plate into the solution during the operation of sensitising, may be conveniently made of pure silver wire. **1879** *Cassell's Techn. Educ.* III. 65 In this bath must be a dipper for the purpose of raising and lowering the plate during the sensitising process.

7. a. A receptacle for oil, varnish, etc., fastened to a palette.

1859 GULLICK & TIMBS *Paint.* 199 The Dipper is made so that it can be attached to the palette. It serves to contain oil, varnish, or other vehicle used. **1883** *Spectator* 3 Nov. 1413 It blew the medium out of its dipper, and spread it in a shower upon the middle of the picture.

b. = DIP *sb.* 8.

1891 R. WALLACE *Rural Econ. Austral. & N.Z.* xvi. 247 The dipper..consists of a narrow well or trough of masonry. **1956** J. GIBBONS et al. in D. L. Linton *Sheffield* 258 Installation of electricity, sheep pens and dippers.

c. As the name of various mechanical devices or instruments; *big dipper*, see BIG *a.* B. 2.

1925 *Morris Owner's Man.* 28 In the bottom case are fitted the troughs for feeding oil to the connecting-rod big ends through the oil dippers which are fitted to same. **1928** *Daily Express* 28 Sept. 9 It should be made compulsory for all motorists to have dippers affixed to their headlights. **1951** N. BALCHIN *Way through Wood* iii. 46, I suppose he was driving dipped and it was one of those dippers that switches off the offside light. **1963** [see HEADLIGHT].

8. *attrib.* and *Comb.*, as **dipper-bird** (see 3 a); **dipper-clam** (*U.S.*), a bivalve mollusc, *Mactra solidissima*, common on the Atlantic coast of the United States; **dipper-gourd** (*U.S.*), a gourd used as a dipper (sense 5); **dipper switch** = *dip-switch*.

1894 CROCKETT *Raiders* (ed. 3) 260 A man stole off up the waterside, jumping across it in running skips like a dipper bird. **1880** *New Virginians* I. 199 A bucket of spring-water, with a dipper-gourd in it. **1935** *Times* 1 Oct. 8/4 The equipment includes such fittings as self-cancelling traffic indicators..and a foot-operated dipper switch. **1965** PRIESTLEY & WISDOM *Good Driving* ii. 20 A dipper switch.. enables you to dip the beam.

dipperful ('dɪpəfʊl). *U.S.* [f. DIPPER + -FUL.] As much as fills a dipper (see prec. 5).

1874 MRS. WHITNEY *We Girls* vi. 136 We poured some dipperfuls of hot water over them. **1883** E. INGERSOLL in *Harper's Mag.* Jan. 197/2 We were just in time to get a dipperful of the buttermilk.

dipping ('dɪpɪŋ), *vbl. sb.* [f. DIP *v.* + -ING[1].]

1. The action of the verb DIP in various senses.

c **1440** *Promp. Parv.* 121/2 Dyppynge yn lycore, *intinctio.* **1548** CRANMER *Catech.* 215 He knoweth not what baptisme is..nor what the dyppyng in the water doth betoken. **1655** JER. TAYLOR *Unum Necess.* v. §4 (R.) That which is dyed with many dippings is in grain, and can very hardly be washed out. **1667** *Phil. Trans.* II. 434 Nice Observations of the Variations and Dippings of the Needle, in different Places. **1719** J. T. PHILIPPS 34 *Conferences* 218, I ask'd them, how daily Dipping and Plunging did avail them? **1856** EMERSON *Eng. Traits, Lit.* Wks. (Bohn) II. 113 No hope, no sublime augury, cheers the student..but only a casual dipping here and there. **1867** J. KER *Lett.* (1890) 33 From any little dippings of conversation I had among the people. **1870** PUMPELLY *Across Amer. & Asia* i. 1 The woman a very hag, ever following the disgusting habit of dipping—filling the air, and covering her clothes with snuff. **1874** KNIGHT *Dict. Mech.* I. 705/1 *Dipping.* 1 The process of brightening ornamental brass-work..The work is..Dipped in a bath of pure nitrous acid for an instant. **1875** 'STONEHENGE' *Brit. Sports* I. v. vi. §3. 348 The tackle for dipping is much more simple than that employed in whipping. **1882** *Standard* 2 Sept. 6/4 The Prisoner said she had only had a month for 'dipping' (picking pockets). **1883** *Fisheries Exhib. Catal.* 22 Improved Mast to do away with Dipping of Lug.

2. *concr.* **a.** A liquid preparation in which things are dipped for any purpose: a wash for sheep; dubbing for leather (*Sc.*).

1825–80 JAMIESON, *Dipping*, the name given to a composition of boiled oil and grease, used by curriers for softening leather, and making it more fit for resisting dampness. **1888** ELWORTHY *W. Somerset Word-bk.*, *Dipping*, a strong poisonous liquor, for dipping sheep, to kill vermin, and to prevent the scab.

b. A grade of turpentine. (Cf. DIP *sb.* 8 b.) *U.S.*

1832 D. J. BROWNE *Sylva Amer.* 232 The turpentine thus procured is the best, and is called pure dipping.

3. *attrib.* and *Comb.*, chiefly in reference to technical processes, as *dipping-bath*, *-house*, *-ladle*, *-liquid*, *-machine*, *-net*, *-pan*, *-process*, *-room*, *-tank*, *-trough*, *-tub*, *-tube*, *-vat*, *-vessel*, *-works*; also *Naut.* (cf. DIP *v.* 6), as *dipping-line*, *-lug*, *-mark*; also **dipping-frame**, a frame used in dipping tallow candles, and in dyeing; †**dipping-place**, a baptistery; **dipping-shell**, **-snail** = DIPPER 4; **dipping-well**, the receptacle in front of an isobath inkstand; **dipping-wheel** *U.S.*, a wheel consisting of revolving buckets or nets set in a river for catching fish.

1841 *Awards Highl. & Agric. Soc. Scotland*, To Mr. Thomas Bigg, London, for a Sheep *Dipping Apparatus. **1894** *Brit. Jrnl. Photogr.* XLI. 3 Procure a glass vertical *dipping bath with a glass dipper. **1893** *Labour Commission* Gloss., **Dipping House*, the part of the factory in which the operation of dipping..is carried on. *Dipping House Women*, are the women and girls in the potting industry who clean the ware after it has been dipped and become dry. **1867** SMYTH *Sailor's Word-bk.*, **Dipping-ladle*, a metal ladle for taking boiling pitch from the cauldron. **1886** CAULFEILD *Seamanship Notes* 1 Work *dipping-line and hoist sail. *c* **1865** G. GORE in *Circ. Sc.* I. 216/1 He will require several ..pans, one containing nitric acid, another filled with '*dipping' liquid. **1875** BEDFORD *Sailor's Pocket-bk.* vi. (ed. 2) 214 Sling a *dipping lug ⅓ from the foremost yard-arm. **1886** C. SCOTT *Sheep-farming* 145 The material best adapted for making the tub of a *dipping machine is concrete... On a sheep farm the dipping-trough should be always the landlord's property, and a fixture. *c* **1860** H. STUART *Seaman's Catech.* 7 How would you dip a 'lug'? Lower the halyards to the *dipping mark. **1867** SMYTH *Sailor's Word-bk.*, **Dipping-net*, a small net used for taking shad and other fish out of the water. **1874** KNIGHT *Dict. Mech.* I. 705/1 **Dipping-pan* (Stereotyping), a square, cast-iron tray in which the floating-plate and plaster-cast are placed for obtaining a stereo-type cast. **1616** *MS. Acc. St. John's Hosp., Canterb.*, Payd vnto a carpenter for making of a *depping place xvj*d.* **1766** ENTICK *London* IV. 374 In this parish [is] the Ana-baptist dipping-place. **1881** *Guide Worcest. Porcel. Wks.* 27 From the *dipping room the ware is brought to the drying stove. **1711** *Phil. Trans.* XXVII. 352 A sort of *Diping Shell, very common on the Shoars of Jamaica and Barbadoes. **1776** *Dipping-snail [see DIPPER 4]. **1903** *Daily Chron.* 10 Feb. 6/4 The molten spelter, with which the *dipping tanks were filled ready for the day's work. **1853** *Catal. R. Agric. Soc. Show* 1 Sheep Dipping Apparatus.. It consists of a *dipping-tub, a draining-vessel, and an inclined plane. **1883** *Syd. Soc. Lex.*, **Dipping-tube*, a fine glass tube used to collect a small quantity of liquid or some solid matter in a liquid, for examination under the microscope. *a* **1884** KNIGHT *Dict. Mech.* Suppl., **Dipping vat*, the trough containing fine glazing slip in which biscuit ware is dipped to be covered with the material which, baked on, forms glaze. *c* **1865** LETHEBY in *Circ. Sc.* I. 93/2 The tallow is kept in the *dipping-vessel, at a temperature just over the point of solidification. **1889** *Durham Univ. Jrnl.* 196 It.. has a small *dipping-well in which the ink is always at the same height. *a* **1884** KNIGHT *Dict. Mech.* Suppl., **Dipping wheel*, a contrivance used in Southern rivers to meet local demand for fish. It is set in the stream so as to be turned by the current, and has a number of dip-nets which raise the fish and tumble them out at the axis in the manner of the scoop-wheel.

'dipping, *ppl. a.* [f. DIP *v.* + -ING².] That dips, in various senses: see the verb. *spec.* Of the beams of headlights: lowered or capable of being lowered (cf. DIP *v.* 6 d).

1798 COLERIDGE *Anc. Mar.* I. 12 With sloping masts and dipping prow. **1866** MRS. GASKELL *Wives & Dau.* xlvi, With formal dipping curtseys the ladies separated. **1869** JEAN INGELOW *Raven in White Chine* vi, With a crimson hue The dipping sun endowed that silver flood. **1887** STEVENSON *Underwoods* I. iii. 4 My dipping paddle scarcely shakes The berry in the bramble-brakes. **1922** *Motor* 7 Nov. 744/2 (*caption*) Duco dipping headlights. **1957** *Act 5 & 6 Eliz. II* c. 51 §3 No light shown by a vehicle, other than a dipping headlight, shall be moved by swivelling, deflecting or otherwise while the vehicle is in motion.

Hence **dippingly** *adv.*, in a dipping way.

1852 G. W. CURTIS *Lotos-eating* 67 The summer-bird of a traveller who skims up the Hudson dippingly.

'dipping-,needle. [see DIP *v.* 12, DIP *sb.* 4] A magnetic needle mounted so as to be capable of moving in a vertical plane about its centre of gravity, and thus indicating by its dip the direction of the earth's magnetism. So ***dipping-compass***, an instrument consisting of a dipping-needle with a vertical graduated circle for measuring the 'dip' or angle of inclination; = *dip-circle*.

1667 *Phil. Trans.* II. 438 The Dipping-Needle is to be used as frequently as the former Experiment is made. **1713** DERHAM *Phys.-Theol.* v. i, *note* 21 (R.), I have not yet been so happy to procure a tolerable good dipping-needle. **1805** M. FLINDERS in *Phil. Trans.* XCV. 195 Taking the theodolite and dipping-needle, I landed. **1871** TYNDALL *Fragm. Sc.* (1879) I. xiii. 373 Previous to magnetization, a dipping needle.. stands accurately level.

dip-pipe, -rod: see DIP *sb.*

dippy ('dɪpɪ), *a. slang.* [Origin obscure; ? f. DIP *v.*] Mad, insane, crazy. Also const. *about*, *over*, in love (with). Also *absol.*

1903 C. E. MERRIMAN *Lett. from Son* ix. 119 Her desolateness appeared to touch a hidden, sympathetic chord in my nature. Whatever the cause, I was dippy for fair. **1904** ADE *True Bills* 35 It is just as easy to love a girl who has the coin as it is to get dippy over the Honest Working-Girl. **1905** A. M. BINSTEAD *Mop Fair* i. 6, I should be compelled to lament the fact that I had become hopelessly dippy. **1922** J. A. DUNN *Man Trap* xii. 167, I got lost there... Damned fool. No water! Too much sun! Went dippy and threw away everything. **1923** WODEHOUSE *Adv. Sally* x. 121 I'd be just as happy in two rooms and a kitchenette, so long as Fillmore was there. You've no notion how dippy I am about him. **1930** J. B. PRIESTLEY *Angel Pavement* vii. 353 The daughter she talks about seems to be completely dippy. **1938** F. S. ANTHONY *Me & Gus* ii. 11 A chap dippy over a girl. **1967** *Times Rev. Industry* Mar. 29/2 In past days the senile and the slightly dippy were clapped into institutions.

diprionid (daɪ'praɪənɪd), *a.* = DIPRIONIDIAN *a.*

1888 ROLLESTON & JACKSON *Anim. Life* 769 Specimens of diprionid Graptolites.

diprionidian (daɪpraɪəʊ'nɪdɪən), *a. Palæont.* [f. Gr. δι- twice (DI-²) + πρίων a saw.] Having serrations on both sides of the stem: said of graptolites.

1872 NICHOLSON *Palæont.* 82 Two leading types may be distinguished amongst the Graptolites.. 'monoprionidian' and 'diprionidian'.

†dipris'matic, *a. Min. Obs.* [f. DI-² + PRISMATIC.] Doubly prismatic; pertaining to two prismatic systems: see quot.

1821 R. JAMESON *Mineralogy* Introd. 10 Cleavage is said to be *diprismatic*, if its planes have the direction of the faces of a vertical, and at the same time of a horizontal prism.

dipropargyl (daɪprɒ'pɑːdʒɪl). *Chem.* [f. DI-² 2 + PROPARGYL.] A hydrocarbon isomeric with benzene (C_6H_6) having the constitution of a double molecule of the radical Propargyl or Propinyl ($CH \equiv C{\cdot}CH_2$); a mobile, highly refractive liquid, with an intensely pungent odour.

1875 WATTS *Dict. Chem.* VII. 1008 Dipropargyl.. is easily distinguished from benzene by its property of combining with explosive violence with bromine. **1881** *Nature* XXIII. 566 Recent observations on dipropargyl by Henry, the discoverer of this curious compound.

‖**diprotodon** (daɪ'prəʊtədɒn). *Palæont.* [mod.L., f. Gr. δι- twice + πρῶτο-ς first + -οδον, neuter of -οδους, f. ὀδούς tooth.] A genus of huge extinct marsupials, having two incisors in the lower jaw.

1839 *Penny Cycl.* XIV. 469/1 Anterior extremity of the right ramus, lower jaw, of Diprotodon. **1880** NICHOLSON *Zool.* lxix. 670 In size Diprotodon must have many times exceeded the largest of living Kangaroos. **1892** *Pall Mall G.* 30 Sept. 6/3 Remains of the extinct monster diprotodon.

di'protodont, *a.* and *sb.* [f. as prec., with stem ὀδοντ-.]

A. *adj.* Having two incisors in the lower jaw; having the dentition or characteristics of the genus *Diprotodon*. **B.** *sb.* A marsupial of this genus.

1881 *Times* 28 Jan. 3/4 In the nototheres and diprotodonts, progressive movement is performed in the ordinary four-footed fashion of the tapir and rhinoceros.

dipsacaceous (dɪpsə'keɪʃəs), *a. Bot.* [f. mod.L. *Dipsacāce-æ*, f. *Dipsacus*, Gr. δίψακος teasel, f. δίψα thirst, in allusion to the retention of water in the hollows formed by the axils of the connate leaves.] Belonging to the Natural Order *Dipsacaceæ*, containing the teasels and their allies.

Also **dip'saceous,** *a.* (Smart *Suppl.* 1849.)

†'dipsad. *Obs. rare.* [a. F. *dipsade* (Rabelais, 16th c.), ad. L. *dipsad-em*, Gr. διψάδ-α (accus.): see DIPSAS.] = DIPSAS 1.

1607 TOPSELL *Serpents* (1658) 698 [tr. Lucan] And dipsads thirst in midst of water floud.

dipsadine ('dɪpsədaɪn), *a. Zool.* [f. L. *dipsad-* stem of *dipsas* + -INE.] Of or belonging to the family of non-venomous snakes, *Dipsadinæ*, to which belongs the genus *Dipsas* (DIPSAS 2 a).

‖**dipsas** ('dɪpsæs). Pl. **dipsades** ('dɪpsədiːz). Also 5 dypsa, 6 (*Her.*) dipsez, 8 dipsa, dypsas. [L. *dipsas*, Gr. διψάς a serpent whose bite caused great thirst, orig. adj., causing thirst, f. δίψα thirst. Cf. F. *dipsade*, *dipsas*, older *dipse* (13th c. in Hatz.-Darm.).]

1. A serpent whose bite was fabled to produce a raging thirst.

1382 WYCLIF *Deut.* viii. 15 Scorpioun, and dipsas, that is, an eddre that whom he biteth, he maketh thurȝ threste die. **1496** *Dives & Paup.* (W. de W.) v. iii. 198/1 Flaterers be lykened to an adder that is called dypsa. **1572** BOSSEWELL *Armorie* II. 63 A Dipsez verte, charged on the firste quarter. **1609** HOLLAND *Amm. Marcell.* XXII. xv. 213 Of serpents, to wit.. the Dipsades, and the Vipers. **1627** MAY *Lucan* IX. 703 Dipsases in midst of water dry. **1667** MILTON *P.L.* x. 526 Scorpion, and Asp, and Amphisbæna dire, Cerastes hornd, Hydrus, and Ellops drear, And Dipsas. *c* **1750** SHENSTONE *Elegies* xx. 39 Here the dry dipsa writhes his sinuous mail. **1821** SHELLEY *Prometh. Unb.* III. iv. 19 It thirsted As one bit by a dipsas. **1894** F. S. ELLIS *Reynard* 336 A dipsas is a worm accurst, From whose bite follows raging thirst.

2. *Zool.* **a.** A tropical genus of non-venomous serpents. **b.** A genus of fresh-water bivalves of the family *Unionidæ*, or river-mussels.

1841 *Penny Cycl.* XXI. 280 Under the non-venomous [serpents] are arranged the following genera:—*Tortrix*: *Boa* .. *Coluber*.. *Dipsas*. **1843** *Ibid.* XXVI. 5 Mr. J. E. Gray makes the *Unionidæ* the eighth family of his order *Cladopoda*. Genera:—*Anodon*, *Margaritana*, *Dipsas*.

dipsetic (dɪp'sɛtɪk), *a.* and *sb.* [ad. Gr. διψητικ-ός provoking thirst, thirsty, f. διψά-ειν to thirst, δίψα thirst.]

A. *adj.* Producing thirst. **B.** *sb.* A substance or preparation that produces thirst.

1847 in CRAIG. **1883** in *Syd. Soc. Lex.*

dipsey, -sie, -sy, var. of DEEP-SEA (apparently associated with *dip*), *esp.* in ***dipsy-lead, -line***.

1626–1698 [see DEEP SEA]. **1837** MARRYAT *Dog-Fiend* xliii, I may.. as well go down like a dipsey lead. **1860** BARTLETT *Dict. Amer.*, *Dipsy*, a term applied, in some parts of Pennsylvania, to the sinker of a fishing-line. **1867** SMYTH *Sailor's Word-bk.*, *Dipsy*, the float of a fishing-line.

†'dipsian, *a. Obs.* [f. *dipsa* form of DIPSAS, or Gr. δίψι-ος thirsty + -AN.] Of thirst: such as was caused by the bite of the dipsas; raging.

a **1618** SYLVESTER *Du Bartas, Auto-machia* 100 Gold, Gold bewitches mee, and frets accurst My greedy throat with more than Dipsian thirst.

[**dipsin,** app. mispr. for *dipsie*, DIPSEY, deep-sea.

1598 HAKLUYT *Voy.* I. 435 Sound with your dipsin lead, and note diligently what depth you finde.]

dipso, colloq. abbrev. of DIPSOMANIAC *sb.* and *a.*

1880 G. B. SHAW *Let.* 29 Nov. (1965) 36 How long do you suppose an average woman (dipso as described).. would last alive after the inability to retain food or drink set in? **1923** A. HUXLEY *Antic Hay* xiv. 217 Vicious young women. Lesbians, drug-fiends, nymphomaniacs, dipsos—thoroughly vicious, nowadays. **1935** E. WILLIAMS *Night must Fall* 30 Maniacs can't get far without cash.. however dipso or nympho they may be. **1959** J. BRAINE *Vodi* xxv. 269, I didn't mean that you were a dipso... But I've never been out with you when we didn't go into a pub.

‖**dipsomania** (dɪpsəʊ'meɪnɪə). *Path.* [f. Gr. διψο- comb. form of δίψα thirst + μανία madness, MANIA.] A morbid and insatiable craving for alcohol, often of a paroxysmal character. Also applied to persistent drunkenness, and formerly to the delirium produced by excessive drinking.

1843–4 A. S. TAYLOR *Med. Jurispr.* lxvi. 655 *Dipsomania*, drunkenness. This state, which is called in law frenzy, or '*dementia affectata*', is regarded as a temporary form of insanity. **1851–60** in MAYNE *Expos. Lex.* **1862** tr. *Caspar's Handbk. Forensic Med.* (New Syd. Soc.) II. 91[She] had been for many years excessively given to drinking, and in her case it had developed to actual 'dipsomania'. **1866** A. FLINT *Princ. Med.* (1880) 512 Dipsomania is a term sometimes used to denote the peculiar delirium arising from the abuse of alcohol, but it is commonly applied to an uncontrollable desire for alcoholic drinks. **1881** S. ALFORD in *Med. Temp. Jrnl.* XLVII. 163 *Dipsomania*, or inebriety, is a fundamental disease of the nervous system, primarily of a functional character. **1883** *Syd. Soc. Lex.*, *Dipsomania*.. is to be distinguished from ordinary and habitual drunken-ness, in that the craving is paroxysmal, and comes on apparently without the external temptation of what is called good company.

dipso'maniac, *sb.* and *a.* [f. prec. + -AC (after MANIAC).]

A. *sb.* A person affected with dipsomania; one who suffers from an ungovernable craving for drink.

1858 A. S. TAYLOR *Med. Jurispr.* lxx. (ed. 6) 950 The two jurors.. considered that she was a dipsomaniac. **1866** *Lond. Rev.* 13 Oct. 404/2 There are several places where Dipsomaniacs are treated, under the rule and care of religious orders. **1884** MRS. C. PRAED *Zero* ix, A craving for excitement as keen as that of the dipsomaniac for alcohol.

B. *adj.* = next. (In recent Dicts.)

dipsoma'niacal, *a.* [f. as prec. + -AL¹.] Affected with dipsomania.

1865 tr. *Caspar's Handbk. Forensic Med.* (New Syd. Soc.) IV. 267 She had given herself up to drunkenness and had become dipsomaniacal.

dipsopathy (dɪp'sɒpəθɪ). [f. Gr. διψο-, δίψα thirst + πάθεια, f. πάθος suffering (taken after *homœopathy*, *hydropathy*, etc., in sense 'method of cure').] The treatment of disease by abstinence from liquids.

1883 in *Syd. Soc. Lex.*

‖**dip'sosis.** *Med.* [irreg. f. Gr. δίψα thirst + -OSIS: the actual Gr. word was δίψησις.] 'A term for a morbid degree of thirst: nearly synonymous with *Polydipsia*' (Mayne *Expos. Lex.* 1851–60).

1847 in CRAIG.

dipsy, variant of DIPSEY.

dipt, variant of *dipped*, pa. t. and pple. of DIP *v.*

diptani, obs. form of DITTANY.

Dip. Tech., colloq. abbrev. of *Diploma in Technology*. Also, a person who holds this qualification.

1957 *Technology* Oct. 292/3 Recognition of Dip. Tech. courses. **1958** *Times* 19 Sept. 5/6 First Crop of Dip. Techs. .. The names are announced to-day of the first crop of students to be awarded the Diploma in Technology by the National Council for Technological Awards. **1958** *Economist* 15 Nov. 591/2 The universities have.. agreed that the Dip Tech (created in 1956) shall rank as equivalent to first degrees in universities, and this means that Dip Techs should be able to work for higher research degrees in universities if opportunity offers. **1969** R. LAYARD et al. *Impact of Robbins* 73 There were 5,500 students on these courses, if we include those leading to the Diploma in Technology (Dip. Tech.), most of which have now been converted to degree courses.

dipter ('dɪptə(r)). *Entom.* [ad. F. *diptère* (1791 in Hatz.-Darm.), L. *dipter-us*, a. Gr. δίπτερος two-winged, f. δι-, δίς twice + πτερόν wing.] One of the *Diptera*; a two-winged fly.

1828 WEBSTER s.v., The dipters are an order of insects having only two wings, and two poisers, as the fly.

‖**'Diptera,** *sb. pl. Entom.* [mod. L. = Gr. δίπτερα (Aristotle), pl. neuter of δίπτερος two-winged (sc. *insecta* insects, *animalia* animals): see prec.] The two-winged flies, a large order of insects having one pair of membranous wings, with a pair of halteres or poisers representing a posterior pair. Well-known examples are the common house-fly, the gnats, gad-flies, and crane-flies.

1819 *Pantologia, Diptera*, in zoology, an order of the class insecta, characterised by having two wings, under each of which is a clavate poise with its appropriate scale. **1867** F. FRANCIS *Angling* vi. (1880) 196 The other orders in most use by the fly-fishers are..the *Diptera*, or two-winged. **1879** A. W. BENNETT in *Academy* 33 Abundantly visited by insects, especially Diptera.

dipte'raceous, *a. Bot.* [f. mod. Bot. L. *Dipterăceæ*, f. *Dipter-* contracted from *Dipterocarpus* generic name (f. δίπτερ-ος two-winged + καρπός fruit): see -ACEOUS.] Of or belonging to the Natural Order *Dipteraceæ* (*Dipterocarpeæ*): see DIPTEROCARP. So **dipterad**, a plant of this order.

1849 SMART *Suppl.*, *Dipteraceous*, epithet of an order of arborescent exogens, found only in India and the Indian Archipelago, which includes the camphor tree; an order chiefly marked by the enlarged, foliaceous, unequal segments of the calyx investing the fruit. **1866** *Treas. Bot.* I. 415/2 *Dipteraceæ* (*Dipterocarpeæ, Dipterads*), a natural order of thalamifloral dicotyledons or Exogens..containing large trees with resinous juice.

dipteral ('dɪptərəl), *a.* [f. L. *dipter-os* (Vitruv.), a. Gr. δίπτερος (DIPTER) + -AL¹.]

1. *Arch.* Having a double peristyle.

1812 W. WILKINS *Civil Archit. Vitruvius* 37 It was perhaps the intention of the author to represent dipteral temples with a treble portico in that front only through which they were approached. **1846** ELLIS *Elgin Marb.* I. 72 A temple was of the kind called dipteral, when it had two ranges of columns resting on the pavement. **1886** *Century Mag.* Nov. 139/1 A dipteral temple.

2. *Entom.* = DIPTEROUS.

1828 in WEBSTER.

'dipteran, *a.* and *sb. Entom.* [f. as DIPTER, DIPTERA + -AN.]

A. *adj.* = DIPTEROUS. **B.** *sb.* A dipterous insect.

1842 in BRANDE *Dict. Sci., etc.*: and in mod. Dicts.

†**dip'teric**, *a. Arch. Obs. rare.* [a. F. *diptérique* (17th c.), f. Gr. δίπτερ-ος two-winged + -IC.] = DIPTERAL.

1664 EVELYN tr. *Freart's Archit.* 37 It was of the dipteryque figure; that is, inviron'd with a two-fold range of Columns.

dipterist ('dɪptərɪst). [f. DIPTER-A + -IST.] An entomologist who studies the *Diptera*.

1872 O. W. HOLMES *Poet Breakf.-t.* ii. (1885) 48 Competition..between the dipterists and the lepidopterists.

dipterocarp ('dɪptərəʊkɑːp). *Bot.* [ad. mod.L. *Dipterocarp-us*, f. Gr. δίπτερ-ος two-winged + καρπός fruit.] A member of the genus *Dipterocarpus* or Natural Order *Dipterocarpeæ*, comprising East Indian trees characterized by two wings on the summit of the fruit, formed by enlargement of two of the calyx-lobes. Cf. DIPTERACEOUS. So **diptero'carpous** *a.*, belonging to this genus or order.

1876 HARLEY *Mat. Med.* 702 Dipterocarps..Gigantic trees abounding in resinous juice, natives of India. **1885** H. O. FORBES *Nat. Wand. E. Archip.* 135 Various species of coniferous and dipterocarpous trees.

dipte'rology. [f. DIPTERA: see -(O)LOGY.] That branch of entomology which relates to the *Diptera*. Hence ˌ**diptero'logical** *a.*, **dipte'rologist** = DIPTERIST.

1881 *Nature* XXIV. 46 Descriptions of new diptera, and dipterological notes.

‖**'dipteros.** *Arch.* Formerly, also dipteron, and, after Fr., diptere. [a. Gr. δίπτερος (sc. ναός) two-winged (temple).] A temple or building with double peristyle.

1706 PHILLIPS (ed. Kersey), *Dipteron* (in *Archit.*) a Building that has a double Wing or Isle. The Ancients gave that Name to such Temples as were surrounded with two ranges of Pilars..which they call'd Wings. **1727-51** CHAMBERS *Cycl.*, *Diptere*, or *Dipteron.* **1730-6** BAILEY (folio), *Diptere.* **1882** OGILVIE, *Dipteros.*

dipterous ('dɪptərəs), *a.* [f. mod.L. *dipter-us* (see DIPTER) + -OUS.]

1. *Entom.* Two-winged; of, pertaining to, or of the nature of the DIPTERA.

1773 WHITE in *Phil. Trans.* LXIV. 201 They..are greatly ..annoyed by a large dipterous insect. **1802** BINGLEY *Anim. Biog.* (1813) I. 48 Dipterous insects..are those having only two wings, each furnished at its base with a poise or balancer. **1816** KIRBY & SP. *Entomol.* (1843) II. 304 The noisiest wings belong to insects of the dipterous order. **1874** LUBBOCK *Orig. & Met. Ins.* i. 24 Smooth ovate bodies, much resembling ordinary dipterous pupae.

2. *Bot.* Having two wing-like appendages or processes, as certain fruits, seeds, etc.

1851-60 MAYNE *Expos. Lex.*, *Dipterus*..having two wings: dipterous. *Bot.* Applied to a pericarp when it has lateral appendages like wings. **1866** in *Treas. Bot.*

‖**'Dipterus.** *Palæont.* [mod.L., f. Gr.: see DIPTER.] A genus of Palæozoic dipnoous fishes, having two dorsal fins, opposite the ventral and anal respectively. Hence **dip'terian** *a.* and *sb.*, belonging to, or a member of, this genus.

1842 H. MILLER *O.R. Sandst.* (ed. 2) 103 The *Dipterus* or double-wing, of the Lower Old Red Sandstone. **1847** ANSTED *Anc. World* iv. 70 These ancient fishes (Dipterians). **1854** F. C. BAKEWELL *Geol.* 29 Other fishes, of which the dipterus is the type, bear more resemblance to fishes of the present day.

dipterygian (dɪptə'rɪdʒ(ɪ)ən), *a.* (*sb.*) *Ichth.* [f. mod.L. *Dipterygii* (f. δι-, δίς twice + πτερύγι-ον fin) + -AN.] Having two fins: applied to fishes having, or supposed to have, only two fins. Also **dipte'rygious** *a.*

1847 CRAIG, *Dipterygians*, a family of fishes, furnished with two fins only. **1883** in *Syd. Soc. Lex.* [both words].

diptong(e, obs. form of DIPHTHONG.

diptote ('dɪptəʊt), *sb.* and *a. Gram.* Also 7-8 **-tot**, 8 **-toton**. [ad. L. *diptōta* (pl.) nouns that have only two case-endings, a Gr. δίπτωτα, pl. neuter of δίπτωτο-ς with a double case-ending, f. δι-, δίς twice + πτωτός falling (πτῶσις case).]

A. *sb.* A noun having only two cases. **B.** *adj.* Having only two cases.

1612 BRINSLEY *Pos. Parts* (1669) 101 *Q.* What words do you call Diptots? *A.* Such as have but two cases. **1656** BLOUNT *Glossogr.*, *Diptote.* **1751** WESLEY *Wks.* (1872) XIV. 40 Diptots, which have but two cases; as, *Spontis, Sponte.* **1885** tr. *Socin's Arab. Gram.* 56 The triptote are distinguished from the diptote nouns by the nunation being always written over the former.

diptych ('dɪptɪk). Forms: 7 **diptyck**, 7-8 **diptick**, **dyptick**, 7-9 **diptyc**, 8 **dyptic**, 7- **diptych**. [ad. L. *diptycha* (pl.), a late Gr. δίπτυχα pair of writing-tablets, neut. pl. of δίπτυχος double-folded, f. δι-, δίς twice + πτυχή fold. Cf. mod. F. *diptyque*, *c* 1700 in Hatz.-Darm.]

1. Anything folded, so as to have two leaves; *esp.* a two-leaved, hinged tablet of metal, ivory or wood, having its inner surfaces covered with wax, used by the ancients for writing with the stylus.

1622 SPARROW *Bk. Com. Prayer* Pref., Diptychs or Folded Tables. **1731** GALE in *Phil. Trans.* XXXVII. 161 The Diptychs and Triptychs that were covered with Wax, served only for common Occurrences. **1829** J. FLAXMAN *Lect. Sculpt.* iii. 98 The Greeks executed small works of great elegance, as may be seen in the dyptics, or ivory covers, to consular records, or sacred volumes. **1859** GULLICK & TIMBS *Paint.* 306 The diptychs..were among the Romans formed of two little tablets of wood or ivory, folding one over the other like a book.

b. *spec.* (in *pl.*) Applied to the artistically wrought tablets distributed by the consuls, etc. of the later Empire to commemorate their tenure of office; hence transferred to a list of magistrates.

1781 GIBBON *Decl. & F.* II. 27 Their names and portraits, engraved on gilt tablets of ivory, were dispersed over the empire as presents to the provinces..the senate..the people. (*Note*) Montfaucon has represented some of these tablets or dypticks. **1797** *Monthly Mag.* 506 The consular dyptics contain similar cyphers.

2. *Eccl.* (in *pl.*) Tablets on which were recorded the names of those of the orthodox, living and dead, who were commemorated by the early Church at the celebration of the eucharist. Hence, The list or register of such names; the intercessions in the course of which the names were introduced.

1640 HAMMOND *Poor Man's Tithing* Wks. 1684 IV. 5 Enrol their names in the book of life, in those sacred eternal diptycks. **1680** STILLINGFL. *Mischief Separation* (ed. 2) 30 Atticus restored the name of St. Chrysostom to the Diptychs of the Church. **1725** tr. *Dupin's Eccl. Hist. 17th C.* I. v. 64 The Dipticks..have been famous, in the Councils of the East ever since the Council of Chalcedon. **1855** MILMAN *Lat. Chr.* (1864) I. III. iii. 40 The Names of Acacius and all who communicated with him were erased from the diptychs. **1882-3** SCHAFF *Encycl. Relig. Knowl.* I. 643 In the twelfth century the diptychs fell out of use in the Latin Church.

3. An altar-piece or other painting composed of two leaves which close like a book.

1852 MRS. JAMESON *Leg. Madonna* Introd. (1857) 52 A Diptych is an altar-piece composed of two divisions or leaves, which are united by hinges, and close like a book. **1863** BARING-GOULD *Iceland* 158 Svinavatn church contains a curious diptych with mediæval figures.

'diptychous, *a.* [f. as prec. + -OUS.] Double-folded.

1883 in *Syd. Soc. Lex.*

‖**Dipus** ('daɪpəs). *Zool.* [mod.L., ad. Gr. δίπους two-footed.] **a.** The typical genus of the jerboas, a race of rodents which progress like the kangaroo, by leaping with the long hinder legs. **b.** A small marsupial quadruped of Australia, *Chæropus castanotis*.

1799 B. J. BARTON in *Trans. Amer. Soc.* IV. 114 (*title*) Some account of the American Species of Dipus, or Jarboa. **1849** C. STURT *Exp. Centr. Austral.* II. 5 Mr. Browne and I had chased a Dipus into a hollow log, and there secured it. **1859** CORNWALLIS *New World* I. 194 The wallabi, the dipus, the talpero, the wombat.

Dipylon ('dɪpɪlən), *a.* and *sb. Gr. Archæol.* Also **Dipylum**, and with small initial. [L., a. Gr. δίπυλον, neut. of δίπυλος double-gated, f. δι- two + πύλη gate.] **A.** *sb.* A double gateway in which the two gates are placed side by side, *spec.* a gateway in Athens on the north-west side of the city. **B.** *adj.* Denoting or pertaining to the Dipylon of Athens; *spec.* designating a style of Greek pottery belonging to the Geometric period found during excavations near this gate, or a similar Bœotian ware of the same period and of similar style, or to the designs found on such pottery.

1835 *Penny Cycl.* III. 10/1 The direction of the wall from the Ilissus along the south and west sides of the city to the Dipylum is quite clear. **1896** *Daily News* 12 June 5/1 Through the modifications of the Dipylon period..the fashions of Greek ladies were always changing. **1902** *Encycl. Brit.* XXV. 572/2 We engrave an excerpt from a Dipylon vase. *Ibid.* 759/1 The discovery of the Dipylon Gate, the principal entrance of ancient Athens. **1911** W. M. F. PETRIE *Revolutions of Civilisation* iii. 59 The rise of a new art began to dawn in the dipylon vases. **1950** H. L. LORIMER *Homer & Monum.* v. 164 The numerous indications that the Dipylon shield was wielded by a hand-grip dissociate it from the Minoan shield. *Ibid.* 165 The form of the Dipylon shield is simple, produced apparently by taking a hide cut to an oblong shape and stiffening it by a vertical stave down the middle and a horizontal one at top and bottom. **1955** *Archit. Rev.* CXVII. 295 A truncated dipylon gripped between canted buttresses.

dipyre (dɪ'paɪə(r)). *Min.* [mod. (Haüy 1801) ad. L. *dipӯros*, Gr. δίπυρος twice put into the fire, f. δι- twice + πῦρ fire: so called because when heated it exhibits both phosphorescence and fusion.] A silicate of alumina with small proportions of the silicates of soda and lime, occurring in square prisms.

1804 *Fourcroy's Chem.* II. 441 The dipyre. **1807** AIKIN *Dict. Chem. & Min.* s.v. **1868** DANA *Min.* §302 Dipyre occurs in rather coarse crystals, often large or stout, and rarely columnar, in metamorphic rocks.

dipyrenous (daɪpaɪ'riːnəs), *a. Bot.* [f. Gr. δι-, twice + πυρήν fruit-stone + -OUS.] Containing two fruit-stones.

1866 in *Treas. Bot.* **1880** GRAY *Struct. Bot.* vii. §2. 298 The fruits are dipyrenous, tripyrenous, tetrapyrenous, etc., according as they contain 2, 3, or 4 pyrenæ.

diquat ('daɪkwɒt). *Chem.* [f. DI-² + QUAT(ERNARY *a.*)] A quaternary compound with herbicidal properties (see quot. 1960).

1960 *Agric. & Vet. Chem.* I. 197/2 Diquat is one of a group of quaternary dipyridylium salts which possess quite unique properties. *Ibid.*, Diquat is thus a contact herbicide with a very rapid action, two main outlets being as a pre-harvest desiccant and as a contact weedkiller. **1962** *New Scientist* 22 Feb. 441/3 Diquat is quickly absorbed by weeds, killing rapidly on contact with their foliage. **1965** *Economist* 9 Jan. 130/2 A product like the paraquat/diquat 'chemical ploughing' agents (for squares: weedkiller).

Dirac (dɪ'ræk). The name of Paul Adrien Maurice *Dirac* (born 1902), British mathematician and physicist, used *attrib.* to designate phenomena, theories, etc., in *Math.* and *Physics* discovered, described, or postulated by him. Also in FERMI-DIRAC.

1933 HARNWELL & LIVINGOOD *Exp. Atomic Physics* 461 (Index), Dirac-Fermi statistics. **1934** *Physical Rev.* XLVI. 110/1 When the electron is very intimately connected with an attractive center, something happens to its spin which is not adequately described by the Dirac theory. **1935** *Ibid.* XLVIII. 284/2 The interaction of the heavy particles with the electrons (represented, for instance, by the Dirac 'density matrix'). *Ibid.* 435/1 The frequencies of the emitted light are determined by the eigenvalues of the Dirac equation. **1955** W. PAULI *Niels Bohr* 33 The coupling between one Boson field and one Dirac field. *Ibid.* 39 The Dirac equations for spinors are preserved. *Ibid.* 47 A Dirac spinor with four components can be decomposed into two irreducible parts. **1970** G. K. WOODGATE *Elem. Atomic Struct.* iii. 36 The radiation field also is treated as a quantized system (Dirac method).

†**di'radiate**, *v. Obs.* [f. L. *dī-*, *dis-* asunder + RADIATE.] *trans.* To shed abroad in rays.

1651 BIGGS *New Disp.* ⁋85 [To] diradiate their vertues. **1727** BAILEY vol. II, *Diradiated*, spread forth in Beams of Light.

diradiation (daɪreɪdɪ'eɪʃən). [n. of action from prec.]

1. The diffusion of rays from a luminous body.

1706 PHILLIPS (ed. Kersey), *Diradiation*, a spreading abroad of Beams of Light; also a plashing or setting of Vines in form of Sun-beams. **1883** *Syd. Soc. Lex.*, *Diradiation*, the emission of light-rays from a luminous body.

2. *Med.* (See quots.)

1730-6 BAILEY (folio), *Diradiation* (in Medicine) an invigoration of the muscles by the animal spirits. **1823** in CRABB *Technol. Dict.* **1883** *Syd. Soc. Lex.*, *Diradiation*..a synonym for *Hypnotism*.

†**'diral**, *a. Obs. rare.* [f. L. *Dīræ* the Furies, the dire (sisters) + -AL¹.] Of or pertaining to the Furies; dire.

1606 DOD & CLEAVER *Exp. Prov.* xiii.-xiv. (1609) 102 That we expose not our hearts to these dirall and bitter terrors.

†**dira'mation.** *Obs. rare*⁻¹. [f. L. *dī-*, *dis-* asunder + *rām-us* branch + -ATION.] Branching out, ramification.

1778 *Nat. Hist.* in *Ann. Reg.* 109/2 The course and diramations of the vessels in stones.

Dircæan (dəˈsiːən), *a.* [f. L. *Dircæus*, f. *Dirce*, Gr. *Δίρκη* name of a fountain in Bœotia.] Of or belonging to the fountain of Dirce: used of Pindar, called by Horace *Dircæus cygnus* the Dircæan swan; Pindaric, poetic.

1730 YOUNG *Merchant* IV. ii, O thou Dircaean Swan on high. **1884** *Q. Rev.* July 136 The voice of poet and prophet . . blended in a sublime Dircaean strain. **1894** GLADSTONE in *19th Cent.* Sept. 318 Air buoyant and copious enough to carry the Dircaean swan.

dirdum (ˈdɜːdəm). *Sc.* and *north. dial.* Forms: 5 durdan, 6– dirdum, 7–9 -dam, -dom, durdum, 9 durden, durdem, dordum, dyrdum. [Derivation unknown: app. not connected with Sc. *dird* stroke, blow. It has been compared with Gaelic *diardan* anger, surliness, snarling, and with Welsh *dwrdd*, 'sonitus, strepitus' (Davies).]

1. Uproar, tumultuous noise or din.

c **1440** *York Myst.* xxxi. 41 And se þat no durdan be done. *a* **1510** DOUGLAS *King Hart* II. 453 Than rais thair meikle dirdum and deray. **1535** STEWART *Cron. Scot.* (1858) I. 4 Lat be thi dirdum and thi din. **1655** CLARKE *Phraseol.* 170 (Halliw.) An horrible dirdam they made. **1674–91** RAY *Local Words* 129 *Durdom*, noise. **1686** G. STUART *Joco-Ser. Disc.* 70 For aw their Dirdom, and their Dinn, It was but little they did winn. **1802** R. ANDERSON *Cumberld. Ball.*, *Peace* i, Sec a durdem, Nichol says, They've hed in Lunnon town. **1832** W. STEPHENSON *Gateshead Poems* 99 Their dirdum ye may hear each neet, If ye'll but gan to Robbins. **1855** ROBINSON *Whitby Gloss.*, *Durdum*, riotous confusion. 'The street is all in a durdum.' **1869** *Lonsdale Gloss.*, *Durden*, *Durdum*, uproar, hubbub. **1892** *Northumbld. Gloss.*, *Dirdum*, *Durdum*, *Dordum*, noise and excitement, a confusion, a hurly-burly.

2. Outcry; loud reprehension, obloquy, blame.

1709 M. BRUCE *Soul Confirm.* 14 (Jam.) A clash of the Kirk's craft . . a fair dirdim of their synagogue. **1816** SCOTT *Old Mort.* vii, 'This is a waur dirdum than we got frae Mr. Gudyill when ye garr'd me refuse to eat the plum-porridge on Yule-eve.' **1823** MISSES CORBETT *Petticoat Tales* I. 280 (Jam.), 'I gi'ed her such a dirdum the last time I got her sitting in our laundry.' **1824** SCOTT *Redgauntlet* Let. xi, 'We had better lay the haill dirdum on that ill-deedie creature.' **1886** STEVENSON *Kidnapped* xix, If I get the dirdum of this dreadful accident, I'll have to fend for myself.

dire (daɪə(r)), *a.* and *sb.* Also 6–7 dyre. [ad. L. *dīr-us* fearful, awful, portentous, ill-boding.]

A. *adj.* 'Dreadful, dismal, mournful, horrible, terrible, evil in a great degree' (J.).

1567 DRANT *Horace's Epist.* xvi. Fj, With gyues, and fetters Ile tame the under a galow dyre. **1590** SPENSER *F.Q.* I. xi. 40 All was covered with darknesse dire. **1605** SHAKS. *Macb.* II. iii. 63 Strange Schreemes of Death, And Prophecying, with Accents terrible, Of dyre Combustion. **1667** MILTON *P.L.* II. 628 All monstrous, all prodigious things . . Gorgons and Hydra's and Chimera's dire. **1681** *Lond. Gaz.* No. 1649/3 And His Majesty, with advice foresaid, recommends to His Privy Council to see this Act put to dire and vigorous Execution. **1768** BEATTIE *Minstr.* II. ii, To learn the dire effects of time and change. *a* **1774** GOLDSM. *Double Transform.* 75 That dire disease, whose ruthless power Withers the beauty's transient flower. **1784** COWPER *Task* II. 270 Gives his direst foe a friend's embrace. **1853** C. BRONTE *Villette* xxv, Forced by dire necessity. **1868** HELPS *Realmah* xvii. (1876) 462 Ostentation, the direst enemy of comfort.

b. ***dire sisters*** (L. *dīræ sorōres*, *Diræ*): the Furies.

1743 J. DAVIDSON *Æneid* VII. 195 From the Mansion of the dire Sisters.

c. In weakened (now trivial) use, apparent first in ***dire necessity***: terrible, dreadful; awful, 'frightful'; unpleasant, objectionable. *colloq.*

1836 E. B. BROWNING *Lett. to M. R. Mitford* (1983) I. 7 The dire necessity of having every window in the house open to the ceaseless rolling of carriages. **1928** E. O'NEILL *Strange Interlude* VIII. 180, I didn't say anything so dire, did I—merely that Gordon resembles you in character. **1933** G. HEYER *Why Shoot Butler?* ii. 32 'I practically had to accept,' she explained. 'Apparently things are pretty dire since the murder. Basil's got nerves, or something.' **1969** N. COHN *AWopBopaLooBop* (1970) xix. 179 They were small ravers, loud and brash and really a bit dire. **1985** *Times Lit. Suppl.* 16 Aug. 902/1 She finds herself courted . . by the defector from *The Purple Rose*, a dire social comedy.

†**B.** *sb. Obs.*

1. Dire quality or matter, direness.

1660 WOOD *Life* (Oxf. Hist. Soc.) I. 367 Their sermons . . before were verie practicall and commonly full of dire.

2. *pl.* = L. *Diræ*, Furies, dire sisters.

1610 G. FLETCHER *Christ's Tri. over Death* xxi, Arme, arme your selues, sad Dires of my pow'r.

C. *Comb.* (chiefly adverbial or parasynthetic), as ***dire-clinging***, ***-gifted***, ***-lamenting***, ***-looking***, ***-visaged***.

1591 SHAKS. *Two Gent.* III. ii. 82 After your dire-lamenting Elegies, Visit . . your Ladies chamber-window With some sweet Consort. **1633** MILTON *Arcades* 52 The cross dire-looking planet. **1730–46** THOMSON *Autumn* 875 Here the plain harmless native . . to the rocks Dire-clinging, gathers his ovarious food. *a* **1881** ROSSETTI *Rose Mary, 2nd Beryl-Song* 2 Dire-gifted spirits of fire.

direckar, obs. Sc. form of DIRECTOR.

direct (dɪˈrɛkt, daɪ-), *v.* Also 5 de-, 5–6 dy-, 5 derekt, 6 *Sc.* direck. [f. L. *dīrect-* (*dērect-*), ppl. stem of *dīrigĕre* (*dē-*) to straighten, set straight, direct, guide, f. *dī-* apart, asunder, distinctly (or *dē-* down) + *regĕre* to put or keep straight, to rule. It is probable that the ppl. adj. *direct* was first formed immediately from L. *dīrect-us*, and that this originated a verb of the same form: cf. -ATE³ 3. Both the pa. pple. and finite tenses of the verb were used by Chaucer. There is a close parallelism of sense-development between *direct* and *address*, arising out of their etymological affinity: cf. also DRESS *v.*]

A. 1. *trans.* To write (something) directly or specially *to* a person, or for his special perusal; to address. †**a.** To dedicate (a treatise) *to*. *Obs.*

c **1374** CHAUCER *Troylus* v. 1868 O morall Gower, this booke I directe To thee. **1447** BOKENHAM *Seyntys* (Roxb.) Introd. 7 You sone and fadyr to whom I dyrecte This symple tretyhs. **1555** EDEN *Decades* 136 They dyrected and dedicated suche thinges to kynges and princes. **1581** *Satir. Poems Reform.* xliv. 2 To ȝou, ministers, and Prelattis of perdition, This schedul schort I do direct. **1607** TOPSELL *Four-f. Beasts* (1658) 129 The Treatise of English Dogs . . translated by A.F. and directed to that noble Gesner.

†**b.** To write (a letter or message) expressly *to*. [L. *dirigere epistolam*, 4th c., Servius and Jerome; also attributed by Servius to Cicero.] *Obs.*

1397 *Rolls of Parlt.* III. 378/2 As it is . . declared in the same Commission directid to William Rikhill, Justice. **1467** *Mann. & Househ. Exp.* 173, I have reseyved ȝower moste grasyou[s] leter to me dereketed, to be wethe ȝowere hynes . . the nexte morow after Kandelmas day. **1490** CAXTON *Eneydos* xxii. 84 Yf he take the lettre vnto hym whome it is dyrected vnto. **1511–2** *Act 3 Hen. VIII*, c. 23 §5 The Kinges Highnes shall . . direct his lettres missyves to twayn of his honourable Counseillours. **1535** BOORDE *Let.* in *Introd. Knowl.* (1870) Foreward 53 To . . Master Thomas Cromwell be þis byll dyrectyd. **1601** R. PARSONS (*title*), An Apologeticall Epistle: directed to the right honourable Lords . . of her Maiesties Privie Counsell. **1730** GAY in *Swift's Lett.* (1766) II. 115 If you knew how often I talk of you . . you would now and then direct a letter to me.

c. *spec.* In modern usage, To write on the outside of (a letter or the like) the name, designation, and residence of the person to whom it is to be delivered; to write the 'direction' or 'address' on.

(In early examples not separable from b.)

1588 SHAKS. *L.L.L.* IV. ii. 132 But Damosella virgin, Was this directed to you? **1642** *King's Reply* in Rushw. *Hist. Coll.* (1721) V. 63 His Message . . was . . taken . . by the Earl of Essex, and though not to him directed, was by him opened. **1697** *Lond. Gaz.* No. 3334/4 The Box nail'd up and Directed to Mrs. Ann Perriot. **1713** ADDISON *Guardian* No. 123 ⁋3 A letter folded up and directed to a certain nobleman. **1726** SHELVOCKE *Voy. round World* 134 Put them all up together in one packet, and direct them to me. **1855** LD. HOUGHTON in *Life* (1891) I. xi. 527 Lady Ellesmere's letter missed me altogether, although directed as I desired.

absol. **1707** THORESBY in *Lett. Lit. Men* (Camden) 337 If I had sooner known how to direct to you, I had long ago . . written. **1751** BURKE *Corr.* (1844) I. 26 Direct to me at Mr. Hipkis's, Ironmonger in Monmouth. **1775** JOHNSON *Let. to Mrs. Thrale* 6 June, I hope my sweet Queeney will write me a long letter, when . . she knows how to direct to me. **1812** SHELLEY *Let.* 18 June (1964) I. 195 You may direct the Post Off. at Chepstow for if we are gone Eliza will be there. **1835** DICKENS *Let.* 4 July (1965) I. 68 You may direct to me if you please at 18 York Place Fulham Road.

2. a. To address (spoken words) *to* any one; to utter (speech) so that it may directly reach a person. *arch.*

c **1450** tr. *De Imitatione* I. xxiii, þider directe praiers & daily mornynges wiþ teres. **1591** SHAKS. *1 Hen. VI*, v. iii. 179 Words sweetly plac'd, and modest[l]ie directed. **1611** BIBLE *Ps.* v. 3 In the morning will I direct my prayer vnto thee. **1651** HOBBES *Leviath.* II. xxv. 131 To whom the Speech is directed.

†**b.** To impart, communicate expressly, give in charge *to* a person. *Obs.*

a **1400** *Pistill of Susan* 278 He directed þis dom . . To Danyel þe prophete. **1598** BARRET *Theor. Warres* I. i. 1 The straite charges and commands directed from her Maiestie. **1633** BP. HALL *Hard Texts* 324 If God should direct his precepts to a child.

3. To put or keep straight, or in right order.

†**a.** To set or put in right order, to arrange. *Obs.*

1509 HAWES *Past. Pleas.* x. iii, Dysposicion, the true seconde parte Of rethorike, doth evermore dyrecte The maters formde of this noble arte, Gyvyng them place after the aspect.

b. To keep in right order; to regulate, control, govern the actions of.

c **1510** MORE *Picus* Wks. 32 O holy God . . whiche heauen and earth directest all alone. **1548–9** (Mar.) *Bk. Com. Prayer* 132 b (Commun. Coll.) To direct, sanctifye and gouerne, both our heartes and bodies. **1552** ABP. HAMILTON *Catech.* (1884) 29 It [the eye] direckis al the membris of our bodie. **1713** ADDISON *Cato* I. i. 41 He . . cover'd with Numidian Guards, directs A feeble army. **1847** EMERSON *Repr. Men*, *Napoleon* Wks. (Bohn) I. 373 His grand weapon, namely, the millions whom he directed. **1883** FROUDE *Short Stud.* IV. I. i. 1 The mind, or spiritual part of man, ought to direct his body.

c. *absol.*

1611 BIBLE *Eccl.* x. 10 Wisedom is profitable to direct.

4. a. *trans.* To cause (a thing or person) to move or point straight *to* or *towards* a place; to aim (a missile); to make straight (a course or way) *to* any point; to turn (the eyes, attention, mind) straight *to* an object, (a person or thing) *to* an aim, purpose, etc.

1526 *Pilgr. Perf.* (W. de W. 1531) 95 Yᵉ vice yᵗ most maketh man lyke to beestes, & directeth hym from god. **1559** W. CUNNINGHAM *Cosmogr. Glasse* 137 Directe the ruler with hys two sightes unto anye one place. **1576** FLEMING *Panopl. Epist.* 23, I came out of Asia, and directed my saile from Aegina towardes Megara. *Ibid.* 350 But if he failed . . in directing his shafte. **1632** LITHGOW *Trav.* III. 99 Directing his course to rush up on the face of a low Rocke. **1655** STANLEY *Hist. Philos.* Ded., I send this book to you because you first directed me to this design. *c* **1676** LADY CHAWORTH in *12th Rep. Hist. MSS. Comm.* App. v. 31, I . . had the good luck to escape the squibs . . especially directed to the balcone over against me. **1703** MOXON *Mech. Exerc.* 205 Do not direct the cutting Corner of the Chissel inwards. **1711** ADDISON *Spect.* No. 159 ⁋8, I directed my Sight as I was ordered. **1726** *Adv. Capt. R. Boyle* 31 They directed their Steps towards my Confinement. **1790** PALEY *Horæ Paul.* i. 8 A different undertaking . . and directed to a different purpose. **1855** MACAULAY *Hist. Eng.* III. 26 Howe . . directed all his sarcasms . . against the malecontents. **1856** EMERSON *Eng. Traits, Times* Wks. (Bohn) II. 119 But the steadiness of the aim suggests the belief that this fire is directed . . by older engineers. **1860** TYNDALL *Glac.* II. xxiv. 355 To direct attention to an extremely curious fact. **1867** SMILES *Huguenots Eng.* i. (1880) 9 These measures were directed against the printing of religious works generally. **1871** B. STEWART *Heat* §35 These telescopes are directed towards two marks. **1874** GREEN *Short Hist.* vi. §4. 302 The efforts of the French monarchy had been directed to the conquest of Italy. **1875** JOWETT *Plato* (ed. 2) I. 207 Everybody's eyes were directed towards him.

absol. **1639** FULLER *Holy War* v. ix. (1647) 244 Good deeds wᶜʰ direct to happinesse.

b. To inform, instruct, or guide (a person), as to the way; to show (any one) the way.

1607 SHAKS. *Cor.* IV. iv. 7 Direct me, if it be your will, where great Auffidius lies. **1632** J. HAYWARD tr. *Biondi's Eromena* 92, I would faine be so directed as I might . . finde him out. *Mod.* Can you direct me to the nearest railway station?

†**c.** *intr.* for *refl.* To point. *Obs.*

1665 HOOKE *Microgr.* 205 Little white brisles whose points all directed backwards. **1723** CHAMBERS tr. *Le Clerc's Treat. Archit.* I. 64 Care . . taken that . . each Plume direct to its Origin.

5. a. *trans.* To regulate the course of; to guide, conduct, lead; to guide with advice, to advise.

1559 W. CUNNINGHAM *Cosmogr. Glasse* 11 Directe thy Chariot in a meane, clymbe thou not to hye. **1581** PETTIE *Guazzo's Civ. Conv.* II. (1586) 114 b, [He] maketh her the starre by whose aspect he doth direct all his doings. **1585** T. WASHINGTON tr. *Nicholay's Voy.* I. xv. 16 b, Having prepared a frigat to direct us. **1596** SHAKS. *Merch. V.* II. vii. 14 Some God direct my iudgement. **1634** SIR T. HERBERT *Trav.* 5 Sharkes . . are alwayes directed by a little specled fish, called a pilot fish. **1769** *Junius Lett.* xxxv. 162 The choice of your friends has been singularly directed. **1776–81** GIBBON *Decl. & F.* xxvii. (1875) 440/2 The conscience of the credulous prince was directed by saints and bishops. **1856** FROUDE *Hist. Eng.* (1858) I. v. 414 He directed, or attempted to direct, his conduct by the broad rules of what he thought to be just.

b. *Mus.* To conduct (a musical performance).

1880 GROVE *Dict. Mus.* I. 390/1 At the concert which he had to direct (during the series of 1820). **1893** W. P. COURTNEY in *Academy* 13 May 413/1 The music . . was composed and directed by Handel.

c. *trans.* and *intr.* To supervise and control the making of a film or the production of a play, etc.; to guide or train (an actor, etc.) in his performance. orig. *U.S.*

1913 F. W. SARGENT *Technique Photoplay* (ed. 2) xxix. 162 *Director*, one who produces photoplays, directing the preparation and action. **1933** *Punch* 6 Dec. 638/2 Little Robert Lynen . . had he been properly directed would have us all in tears. **1938** W. S. MAUGHAM *Summing Up* 154 The remedy of course is for the author to direct his own play. **1967** *Listener* 12 Jan. 59/1 Ronald Neame has directed efficiently.

6. a. To give authoritative instructions to; to ordain, order, or appoint (a person) *to do* a thing, (a thing) *to be done*.

1598 SHAKS. *Merry W.* IV. ii. 98 I'le first direct my men what they shall doe with the basket. **1611** —— *Cymb.* v. v. 280 A feigned Letter . . which directed him To seeke her on the Mountaines. **1632** LITHGOW *Trav.* x. 457 He made fast the doore . . as he was directed. **1727** DE FOE *Hist. Appar.* iii. (1840) 22 Whether he is ever sent or directed to come. **1747** *Col. Rec. Pennsylv.* V. 101 The Order of the King in Council which was directed to be laid before us. **1752** JOHNSON *Rambler* No. 200 ⁋14 One of the golden precepts of Pythagoras directs, that 'a friend should not be hated for little faults'. **1873** B'NESS BUNSEN in Hare *Life* (1879) I. ii. 59 The seeming arbiter of war . . directed his legions to remove from Boulogne. **1891** *Law Times* XCII. 107/1 Finally the master directed an issue to be tried.

b. *intr.* or *absol.* To give directions; to order, appoint, ordain.

1655 DIGGES *Compl. Ambass.* 6 Her skill and years was now to direct . . not to be directed. **1700** S. L. tr. *Fryke's Voy. E. Ind.* 39 The President is one of the Council, but cannot direct in any thing of moment without the consent of the General. **1764** GOLDSM. *Trav.* 64 Who can direct, when all pretend to know? **1818** JAS. MILL *Brit. India* II. v. v. 520 Cast their anchors as chance or convenience directed. **1888** *Law Times' Rep.* LIX. 165/1 [To] be conveyed to them as tenants in common, or joint tenants, as they should direct.

c. *trans.* To order, appoint, prescribe (a thing to be done or carried out).

1816 KEATINGE *Trav.* (1817) II. 20 On the present occasion, the alcaid . . directed a different arrangement. **1863** H. COX *Instit.* I. vii. 81 The House of Commons had directed an impeachment against Lord Treasurer Danby. **1883** *Law Rep. 11 Q. Bench Div.* 591 [The Judge] was of opinion that the words above mentioned were privileged.. and directed a nonsuit.

†**d.** To prescribe (medically). *Obs.*

1754-64 SMELLIE *Midwif.* III. 77, I directed some Thebaick drops.

e. In a national emergency, etc.: to assign (workers) to a particular industry or employment.

1943 *Hutchinson's Pict. Hist. War* 17 Feb.–11 May 33 The keenness which was so wonderful a feature of the old volunteer Home Guard is no less marked in those who are known as the 'directed men'. **1945** *Yorkshire Post* 29 June, Men and women who were released from the Forces to undertake civilian jobs into which they were directed by the Ministry of Labour. **1946** *Lancet* 5 Jan. 19/2 The charge that the Government was seeking to direct medical labour.

7. *Astrol.* To calculate the arc of direction of (a significator): see DIRECTION 10.

1819 JAS. WILSON *Compl. Dict. Astrol.* s.v. *Directions*, Problem 1st.—To direct the Sun when not more than 2° distant from the cusp of the mid-heaven to any conjunction or aspect..Problem 7th.—To direct a significator with latitude to any conjunction or aspect.

†**B.** Examples of *direct* as pa. pple. = DIRECTED. (Cf. also next.) *Obs.*

c **1386** CHAUCER *Man of Law's T.* 650 Another lettre wroght ful synfully, Vn to the kyng direct of this mateere. *c* **1392** —— *Compl. Venus* 75 Pryncesse, resceyveþe þis complaynt in gree Vn to youre excellent benignytee Dyrect. **1423** JAS. I *Kingis Q.* lxii, The ditee there I maid Direct to hire that was my hertis quene. *c* **1450** tr. *De Imitatione* III. lxiv, To þe are myn eyen dyrecte, my god, fader of mercies. **1503** HAWES *Examp. Virt.* VII. 126 Thrugh whome his subgectes be dyrect. **1512** *Act 4 Hen. VIII*, c. 4 §1 One writte of proclamacion to be direct to the Shirif of the Countie. **1567** *Satir. Poems Reform.* (1890) vi. (*title*), Ane Exhortation derect to my Lord Regent.

direct (dɪˈrɛkt, daɪ-), *a.* and *adv.* Also 4-6 **dy-**, **directe**, 6 **derect**. [prob. a. F. *direct* (13th c. in Godef. *Suppl.*) = Pr. *direct*, It. *diretto*, Sp. *derecho* right, ad. L. *dīrect-us* (*dērectus*), pa. pple. of *dīrigĕre*, *dērigĕre*: see DIRECT *v.* The pa. pple. was used as a simple adj. already in Latin. For the strictly ppl. use in Eng. see after prec. vb.]

A. *adj.*

1. a. In reference to space: Straight; undeviating in course; not circuitous or crooked.

[**1391**: see c.] **1548** HALL *Chron., Hen. IV* 13 The confederates..toke the directe way..toward Windsor. **1559** CUNNINGHAM *Cosmogr. Glasse* 60 The directe distance from Portsmouth to Barwicke, is 330. miles. **1699** DAMPIER *Voy.* II. iii. 10 Being the directest Course they can steer for Barbadoes. **1748** *Relat. Earthq. Lima* 40 The Streets are in a direct Line, and of a convenient Breadth. **1751** JOHNSON *Rambler* No. 142 ¶1 We turned often from the direct road to please ourselves with the view. **1834** MEDWIN *Angler in Wales* II. 90, I soon left the horseroad, and took a direct line over black heathery hills. **1874** MORLEY *Compromise* (1886) 1 To consider in a short and direct way, some of the limits that are set [etc.].

b. Of rays, etc.: Proceeding or coming straight from their source, without reflexion, refraction, or interference of any kind. Of a shot: That travels to the point which it strikes without ricocheting, or touching any intermediate object.

So *direct vision*, vision by unrefracted and unreflected rays; (*direct-vision spectroscope*, one in which direct vision is used); also used *attrib.* to designate (*a*) in *Photogr.*, a type of view-finder in which the subject is viewed directly through a lens or sight; (*b*) in *Television*, a picture that can be viewed without magnification, or the apparatus for receiving such a picture. *direct-draft* (attrib.), applied to a boiler, etc. from which the hot air and smoke pass off in a single direct flue, instead of circuitously to economize the heat. ***direct wave*** or ***ray***, in *Radio*, the wave that passes from a transmitter to a receiver along the surface of the earth or (distinguished from *surface wave*) directly through the intervening air.

1706 PHILLIPS (ed. Kersey), *Direct Vision* is when the Rays of Light come from the Object directly to the Eye. **1839** T. BEALE *Nat. Hist. Sperm Whale* 156 Under the direct rays of a tropical sun. **1849** MRS. SOMERVILLE *Connect. Phys. Sc.* xxvi. 277 Places sheltered from the direct rays of the sun. **1890** *Daily News* 21 Aug. 3/2 The target was examined, when it was found that it was a direct hit..The 1st Midlothian got a direct at first shot. **1706** PHILLIPS (ed. Kersey), *Direct Ray* (in Opticks) is the Ray which is carry'd from a Point of the Visible Object directly to the Eye,through one and the same Medium. **1876** *Catal. Sc. App. S. Kens. Mus.* §1802 The instrument..may be used as a small direct vision spectroscope. **1911** B. E. JONES *Cassell's Cycl. Photogr.* 188 *Direct finder*, or *direct-vision finder*, a finder in which the view or object is inspected direct. **1915** —— *Cinemat. Bk.* iii. 19 A wire-frame direct-vision finder.. is fitted in addition. **1937** *Discovery* Oct. 317/1 The receiver itself is a 23-valve superhet model with a direct vision television picture. **1952** HOWE & DUCLOUX tr. *Kerkhof & Werner's Television* (Photo 36), Television picture with 625 lines, as reproduced by a direct-vision receiver. *Ibid.* 408 *Direct-vision tube*, picture tube intended for direct viewing without magnification. **1919** E. W. STONE *Elem. Radiotelegr.* (1920) ix. 198 A reflected wave from a station cannot arrive at the receiving station as soon as the direct wave which followed its normal path along the surface of the earth. **1943** C. L. BOLTZ *Basic Radio* ix. 142 Always there is a wave travelling along the surface of the earth. This is called the ground ray or direct ray. **1943** F. E. TERMAN *Radio Engineers' Handbk.* x. 674 The ground wave can conveniently be divided into..a surface wave and a space wave. The surface wave travels along the surface of the earth. The space wave is the result of..a direct wave and a ground-reflected wave.

†**c.** phr. ***in direct of***: in a straight line with.

c **1391** CHAUCER *Astrol.* II. §44 Loke where the same planet is wreten in the hede of thy tabele, and than loke what þou findest in directe of the same ȝere of owre lord wyche is passid. *Ibid.*, Wryte þat þou findest in directe of the same planete þat þou worchyst fore.

2. a. Moving, proceeding, or situated at right angles or perpendicularly to a given surface, etc.; not oblique.

1563 W. FULKE *Meteors* (1640) 4 b, In places where the beames are cast indirectly and obliquely, and that where they are not too nigh to the direct beames, nor too far off from them, there is a moderate heate. **1658** DUGDALE in Sir T. Browne *Hydriot.* (1736) 50 Some of them are..Twenty Feet in direct Height from the Level whereon they stand. **1660** F. BROOKE tr. *Le Blanc's Trav.* 322 Ships cannot enter it without a direct wind. **1700** S. L. tr. *Fryke's Voy. into E. I.* 350 We hoisted up Sail all together, with a direct Wind for us at S.E.

b. Of the sphere: Having the pole coinciding with the zenith (*parallel sphere*), or lying on the horizon (*right sphere*); not oblique. Of a sundial: Facing straight to one of the four cardinal points; not declined.

1659 D. PELL *Impr. Sea* To Rdr. D v b, *note*, They are like a direct North Dial, that hath but morning and evening hours on it. **1703** MOXON *Mech. Exerc.* 310 Of Dyal Planes some be Direct, others Decliners, others Oblique. **1727-51** CHAMBERS *Cycl.* s.v. *Dial*, Dials which respect the cardinal points of the horizon, are called direct dials..North Dial or erect direct north Dial, is that described on the surface of the prime vertical looking northward.

c. *Mil.* Applied to a battery, etc. whose fire is perpendicular to the line of works attacked. Also applied to gunnery fire with an elevation not exceeding 15°.

1851 J. S. MACAULAY *Field Fortif.* 8 The defence is called *direct* when the flanking line is perpendicular to the line flanked; when not perpendicular, it is termed *oblique*. **1879** *Man. Artill. Exerc.* I. v. 24 Direct fire at masonry is either for demolition or for breaching.

d. *Mech.* (see quot.).

1879 THOMSON & TAIT *Nat. Phil.* I. I. 102 111 When a body rolls and spins on another body, the trace of either on the other is the curved or straight line along which it is successively touched. If the instantaneous axis is in the normal plane perpendicular to the traces, the rolling is called direct.

e. *Cryst.* Opposed to *oblique*: see quot.

1878 GURNEY *Crystallogr.* 65 Those [rhombohedrons] in which the unequal index is algebraically greater than the equal indices are called direct. **1895** STORY-MASKELYNE *Crystallogr.* 141 and 312.

3. *Astron.* Of the motion of a planet, etc.: Proceeding in the order of the zodiacal signs, in the same direction as the sun in the ecliptic, i.e. from west to east; also said of the body so moving. Opposed to *retrograde*.

c **1391** CHAUCER *Astrol.* II. §35 *heading*, This is the workinge of the conclusioun, to knowe yif that any planete be directe or retrograde. *Ibid.*, Yif so be þat this planete be vp-on the Est side..thanne is he retrograde & yif he be on the west side, than is he directe. **1700** DRYDEN *Fables, Palamon & Arc.* II. 616 Two geomantick figures were displayed..a warrior and a maid, One when direct, and one when retrograde. **1726** tr. *Gregory's Astron.* I. III. 453 After the Planet which is nearer to the Sun, has pass'd the second Station at *d*, it becomes direct again. **1786-7** BONNYCASTLE *Astron.* 419 A planet is said to be direct, when it moves according to the order of the signs. **1837** *Penny Cycl.* IX. 14 The course of these celestial motions is always from west to east, which is the direct course.

4. Of relations of time, order, succession, etc., which can be figured or represented by those of space: Straightforward, uninterrupted, immediate.

a. *gen.*

1494 FABYAN *Chron.* v. lxxvi. 54, I shal..sette theym in suche a direct ordre, that it shalbe apparant to the Reder.

b. Of succession: Proceeding in an unbroken line from father to son, or the converse; lineal, as opposed to *collateral*; as a ***direct heir*** or ***ancestor***.

1548 HALL *Chron., Hen. IV*, 21 b, Edmonde Mortimer.. then next and direct heire of England and of Fraunce. **1600** E. BLOUNT tr. *Conestaggio* 117 The last King of Portugall, in whom ended the direct masculine line. *a* **1661** FULLER *Worthies, Warwicksh.* (1662) 126 Sir James Drax, a direct descendant from the Heirs male. **1727-51** CHAMBERS *Cycl.* s.v. *Direct*, The heirs in a direct line always precede those in the collateral lines.

c. *Logic.* Proceeding from antecedent to consequent, from cause to effect, ect.; uninterrupted, immediate.

1828 WHATELY *Rhetoric* in *Encycl. Metrop.* 258/1 Either Direct or Indirect Reasoning being employed indifferently for Refutation as well as for any other purpose. **1864** BOWEN *Logic* viii. 243 In the other Figures, there are two indifferent Conclusions, neither of which is more direct or immediate than the others. **1891** WELTON *Logic* I. IV. iv. 422 Reduction is direct when the original conclusion is deduced from premises derived from those given. *Ibid.* 426 This indirect process is not reduction in the same sense as the direct method is.

d. *Math.* Following the simple or natural order: opposed to *inverse*: see quots.

1594 BLUNDEVIL *Exerc.* I. xi. (ed. 7) 33 Working by the common or direct Rule of Three. **1727-51** CHAMBERS *Cycl.* s.v. *Direct.* **1806** HUTTON *Course Math.* I. 44 The Rule of Three Direct is that in which more requires more, or less requires less. **1807** *Ibid.* II. 279 The Direct and Inverse Method of Fluxions..the direct method..consists in finding the fluxion of any proposed fluent or flowing quantity; and the inverse method, which consists in finding the fluent of any proposed fluxion. **1839** G. BIRD *Nat. Philos.* 64 In the direct ratio of the arms of the lever.

e. ***direct opposite*** or ***contrary***: that which is in the same straight or vertical line on the opposite side of the centre; that which is absolutely or exactly contrary.

1786 BURKE *W. Hastings* Wks. 1842 II. 173 He had not scrupled to assert the direct contrary of the positions by him maintained. **1875** JOWETT *Plato* (ed. 2) I. 482 Is not this the direct contrary of what was admitted before?

f. *Music.* Opposed to *inverted* (of intervals, etc.), or to *contrary* (of motion).

1828 WEBSTER s.v., In *Music*, a direct interval is that which forms any kind of harmony on the fundamental sound which produces it; as the fifth, major third, and octave. **1864** —— *Direct chord* (*Mus.*), one in which the fundamental tone is the lowest. **1867** MACFARREN *Harmony* ii. 50 The augmented 5th, which stands between the mediant and the leading note in a minor key, is always dissonant, in whatever position it occurs, whether direct or inverted. **1880** GROVE *Dict. Mus.* I. 448 *Direct Motion* is the progression of parts or voices in a similar direction.

5. a. That goes straight to, or bears straight upon, the point, without circumlocution or ambiguity; straightforward.

1530 PALSGR. 387 'To serve you' maketh a dyrecte answere to the questyon. **1535** COVERDALE *Job* xxxviii. 3, I will question the, se thou geue me a dyrecte answere. **1589** PUTTENHAM *Eng. Poesie* III. xix. (Arb.) 238 Which had bene the directer speech and more apert. **1600** SHAKS. *A.Y.L.* v. iv. 90, I durst go no further then the lye circumstantial: nor he durst not giue me the lye direct. **1651** HOBBES *Leviath.* II. xviii. 93 If the Soveraign Power..be not in direct termes renounced. **1759** ROBERTSON *Hist. Scot.* I. IV. 308 No direct evidence had as yet appeared against Bothwell. **1849** MACAULAY *Hist. Eng.* II. 114 They ventured to bring direct charges against the Treasurer. **1888** R. KIPLING *Tales fr. Hills* (1891) 245 This was at once a gross insult and a direct lie.

b. Straightforward in manner or conduct; upright, downright.

1586 A. DAY *Eng. Secretary* I. (1625) 31 Just or unjust, godly or wicked, direct or indirect, worthy or to be dispraised. **1602** SHAKS. *Ham.* II. ii. 298 Be euen and direct with me, whether you were sent for or no. **1604** —— *Oth.* III. iii. 378 Take note, take note, (O World!) To be direct and honest, is not safe. **1646** SIR T. BROWNE *Pseud. Ep.* I. v. 17 Yet was the Idolatry direct and downe-right in the people. **1768** STERNE *Sent. Journ.* (1778) I. 168 (*Pulse*) When my views are direct..I care not if all the world saw me. **1792** A. YOUNG *Trav. France* 279 His conduct in the revolution has been direct and manly. **1871** MORLEY *Voltaire* (1886) 9 If he was bitter, he was still direct. **1894** BARING-GOULD *Kitty Alone* II. 107 She was one of those direct persons who, when they have taken a course, hold to it persistently.

†**c.** Downright, positive, absolute (in character).

1668 PEPYS *Diary* 19 Aug., What should it be but Jane, in a fit of direct raving, which lasted half an hour. **1751** PALTOCK *P. Wilkins* (1784) II. 232 I then perceived they were direct forges.

6. a. Effected or existing without intermediation or intervening agency; immediate.

1596 SHAKS. *Merch. V.* IV. i. 350 That by direct, or indirect attempts He seeke the life of any Citizen. **1601** —— *All's Well* III. vi. 9 In mine owne direct Knowledge, without any malice..he's a most notable Coward. **1805** FOSTER *Ess.* I. ii. 29 Direct companionship with a few. **1820** SCORESBY *Acc. Arctic Reg.* II. 356 The fisher is liable to receive..direct blows from its fins or tail. **1860** RUSKIN *Mod. Paint.* V. IX. i. 202 The directest manifestation of Deity to man is in His own image, that is, in man. **1863** BRIGHT *Sp. America* 30 June, There is no man in England who has a more direct interest in it than I have. **1891** *Law Times* XCI. 425/2 The Reform Act of 1832 placed the representatives of the people in direct touch with their constituencies.

b. Of speech or narration: In the form in which it was uttered; not modified in form by being reported in the third person.

1727-51 CHAMBERS *Cycl.* s.v. *Direct*, A very good historian uses the phrase Direct Speech, or harangue, when he introduces any one speaking, or haranguing of himself. **1879** ROBY *Latin Gram.* II. IV. xxiii. 325 The indicative expresses a fact; or a direct statement of opinion of the writer or speaker. *Ibid.* 333 A direct question (or exclamation) is put in the indicative mood.

c. *Biol.* Of cell division: Effected without the formation of nuclear figures; amitotic.

1888 ROLLESTON & JACKSON *Anim. Life* Introd. 22 The division of the protoplasm is preceded or accompanied by division of the nucleus. The process may be direct or amitotic, the nucleus simply elongating, and being split by a constriction.

d. ***direct action***, (*a*) action which takes effect without intermediate instrumentality.

direct-action or ***direct-acting steam-engine***, one in which the piston-rod or cross-head acts directly upon the crank without the intervention of a working-beam.

direct-acting or ***direct-action pump***: a steam-pump in which the steam-piston and the pump-piston are connected by a straight piston rod, without intervening crank.

[**1842** *Penny Cycl.* XXII. 507/1 [It] effects the direct connection of the piston with the crank. *Ibid.* 507/2 Engines of direct connection.] **1843** *Proc. Inst. Civil Engin.* II. 69 The comparatively recent introduction of direct-action steam-engines on board the steam-vessels of the Royal Navy. **1857** CHAMBERS *Information* I. 396 The best and simplest form of direct-acting engine is that known as the oscillating. **1874** KNIGHT *Dict. Mech.* I. 356/1 (Westinghouse-brake) A small but powerful direct-acting steam-engine..operates the air-pump. *Ibid.* 705 In Napier's direct-action steam-engine, the beam is retained, but only for the purpose of working the pumps. **1878** *Proc.*

Inst. Civil Engin. LIII. 98 (*title*) Direct Acting or Non-Rotative Pumping Engines and Pumps. *Ibid.* 364 The construction of the second direct-action pumping engine on a new system for the Paris waterworks at St. Maur.

(*b*) the exertion of pressure on the community through any action which is directly effective, such as strikes, sabotage, or demonstrations, as distinguished from action through constitutional processes; also *attrib.* Hence ***direct actioner***, ***actionist***, one who engages in direct action.

1912 J. R. MacDonald *Syndicalism* iv. 24 The Programme of Direct Action. **1919** *Times* 28 June 14/3 He had been a direct actionist for 35 years. **1920** S. & B. Webb *Hist. Trade Un.* (ed. 5) 672 The vast majority of Trade Unionists object to Direct Action.. for objects other than those connected with the economic function of the Direct Actionists... Trade Unionists.. are not prepared to disapprove of Direct Action as a reprisal for Direct Action taken by other persons or groups. **1920** *Edin. Rev.* Oct. 361 The root idea of direct action dates back in this country to Chartist days. In practice, direct action almost invariably implies either a sectional strike by a particular group or groups of labour, or a general strike by all groups of labour combined. **1931** S. Jameson *Richer Dust* iv. 86 The men were talking of 'direct action', and not taking much notice of their elected [trade-union] leaders. **1957** *Peace News* 18 Jan. 1/4 We have confined ourselves.. too naïvely to public meetings. There is a kind of direct action which.. can have most profitable results. **1958** *Observer* 7 Dec. 1/3 Members and supporters of the Direct Action Committee Against Nuclear War climbed a barbed-wire fence yesterday and 'invaded' a rocket base being built near Swaffham, Norfolk. **1961** *New Left Rev.* Mar.-Apr. 21/2 People who sneer at intellectuals and direct actioners. **1965** P. Arrowsmith *Jericho* xxvi. 285 Charles sat down on the ground. The other forty direct actionists followed his example. **1970** *Guardian* 4 Apr. 10/4 Why is direct action working where 'constructive', peaceful protest did not?

e. ***direct tax***: one levied immediately upon the persons who are to bear the burden, as opposed to *indirect* taxes levied upon commodities, of which the price is thereby increased, so that the persons on whom the incidence ultimately falls pay indirectly a proportion of taxation included in the price of the article. So ***direct rate***, ***rating***, ***taxation***, etc.

The chief direct taxes in Great Britain are the Income and Property Taxes; local and municipal rates are also examples of direct taxation.

1776 Adam Smith *W.N.* v. ii. (1869) II. 442 There are.. two different circumstances which render the interest of money a much less proper subject of direct taxation than the rent of land. **1801** A. Hamilton *Wks.* (1886) VII. 192 There is, perhaps, no item in the catalogue of our taxes which has been more unpopular than that which is called the direct tax. **1802** M. Cutler in *Life* (1888) II. 65 There are two objects in view—one is to attack the funded debt, and the other, a direct tax upon the people. **1828** Webster s.v., *Direct tax* is a tax assessed on real estate, as houses and lands. **1845** McCulloch *Taxation* Introd. (1852) 1 A Tax is called *direct* when it is immediately taken from property or labour; and *indirect* when it is taken from them by making their owners pay for liberty to use certain articles, or to exercise certain privileges. **1845** Disraeli *Sybil* (1863) 220 The ruinous mystification that metamorphosed direct taxation by the Crown into indirect taxation by the Commons. **1849** Macaulay *Hist. Eng.* I. 287 The discontent excited by direct imposts is.. almost always out of proportion to the quantity of money which they bring into the Exchequer. **1894** *Daily News* 13 Feb. 5/5 Having fabricated a direct-rating test for parish councillors, the House did the same for guardians of the poor.

f. Of or pertaining to the work and expenses actually incurred during production as distinct from subsidiary work and overhead charges, i.e. to prime or initial costs or charges; also, applied to labour employed for the construction of works directly (without the intervention of a contractor).

1898 S. S. Dawson *Accountant's Compendium* 71/1 The prime cost.. is the original or direct cost of same. **1903** *Encycl. Accounting* II. 263 These 'expenses' or charges are broadly divisible into 'direct' and 'indirect'. **1922** J. D. Hackett in *Management Engineering* Feb., Absence, such as is being considered here, applies mainly to direct or 'productive' labor and not to indirect or 'non-productive' employees. **1923** *Ibid.* May, *Direct labor*, work done exclusively in the making of a product, in contradistinction to subsidiary work also necessary for production. **1925** Ryall *Primer of Costing* 49 Direct labour may therefore be defined as—'Labour applied to a works order which can be measured and directly charged to that order or product'. **1930** *Daily Mail* 1 Aug. 7/7 The Office of Works is about to substitute direct labour for the present system of work done by contract.

g. Of a dye: not requiring a mordant; = substantive *a.* 1 c.

1902 *Encycl. Brit.* XXVII. 558/1 Direct Colours.—The characteristic feature of the dyestuffs belonging to this class is that they dye cotton 'direct'. *Ibid.* 558/2 Wool and silk are dyed with the Direct Colours in the same manner as cotton. **1927** Horsfall & Lawrie *Dyeing of Textile Fibres* ix. 225 Deltapurpurine and Diamine Scarlets B and 3B are direct cotton colours in common use. **1966** R. C. Cheetham *Dyeing Fibre Blends* i. 8 The classes of dye in general use can be graded in a descending order of molecular size, ranging from aggregated acid and direct dyes to finely dispersed and levelling acid dyes.

h. *Metallurgy.* Designating a process by which wrought iron is obtained from the ore without the intermediate stage of cast iron.

1875 *Ure's Dict. Arts* (ed. 7) II. 941 Chenot's sponge may be obtained by an 'internal' or 'direct' method, in which the ore is reduced.. by a hot current of carbonic-oxide gas. **1880** *Encycl. Brit.* XIII. 291/1 The 'direct' methods of Clay, Chenot, Yates, Blair, Snelus, Du Puy, Siemens, and others. **1884** W. H. Greenwood *Steel & Iron* xi. 212 The direct processes necessitate the use of purer and richer ores and fuels than the indirect processes. **1925** *Jrnl. Iron & Steel Inst.* CXII. 18 The difficulties that beset the commercial production of iron and steel direct from the ore in other direct processes.

i. ***direct broadcasting by satellite***, television broadcasting in which viewers have special aerials to pick up the signal direct from the satellite used to receive and retransmit it; abbrev. *DBS* s.v. D III. 3; also ***direct broadcast*** or ***broadcasting satellite***.

[**1967** *Economist* 1 July 32/2 What about direct satellite-to-home broadcasting?] **1977** *Aviation Week* 17 Oct. 135/1 European Space Agency is seeking about $260 million.. for development in Western Europe of a direct broadcasting satellite capability. **1980** *Hansard Commons: Written Answers* 13 Mar. 652 Mr. Charles Irving asked.. whether there are any plans to establish direct broadcasting by satellite in the United Kingdom. **1983** *Daily Tel.* 22 Aug. 7/5 The imminent arrival of DBS (Direct Broadcasting by Satellite) has brought a new situation. **1986** *Times* 7 July 4/7 A new type of television, Direct Broadcasting by Satellite (DBS). **1980** *Radio-Electronics* Mar. 12/2 Sony, which makes equipment for the Japanese direct-to-home satellite experiment, is looking at the U.S. and could introduce components or entire systems when direct-broadcasting satellites arrive here. **1981** Direct-broadcast satellite [see *DBS* s.v. D III. 3]. **1983** *Fortune* 18 Apr. 92/2 Until recently interference and atmospheric 'noise' made it impossible for small antennas to receive clear signals from a direct-broadcast satellite.

7. **direct address** *Computing*, an address (address *sb.* 7 c) which specifies the location of data to be used as an operand; cf. *indirect address* s.v. indirect *a.* 2 a; hence **direct addressing** *vbl. sb.*; **direct-arc furnace**, an electric-arc furnace in which the arc is formed between an electrode and the charge in the furnace; **direct-connected** *a.* = next (*a*); **direct-coupled** *a.*, (*a*) coupled without an intermediate transmission device; (*b*) in *Electr.*, applied to two circuits coupled by means of one or more resistors, capacitors, or inductors common to them both; also to an amplifier in which the signal path from one stage to the next contains only a resistor (or no circuit element at all), so that d.c. signals can be amplified; so ***direct coupling***; **direct coupler** (see quot.); **direct current** *Electr.*, a current flowing in one direction only, as distinguished from an alternating current; abbrev. d.c., D.C.; also *attrib.*; **direct-cut** *a.*, designating or pertaining to: (*a*) a record whose groove was cut by a stylus rather than formed by a stamper, or (*b*) a record made from a disc cut by the sound to be recorded (rather than a tape recording of it); **direct dialling** *Teleph.*, the action or process of dialling a long-distance number direct, without the intervention of an operator, by using national and area codes before the local number; the facility to do this; cf. *subscriber trunk dialling* s.v. subscriber 3; hence (as a back-formation) **direct-dial** *v. trans.*; **direct distance dialling** *U.S. Teleph.* = *direct dialling* above; **direct drilling** *Agric.*, the practice of sowing seed by drill into soil which has not been specially cultivated after harvesting the previous crop; **direct grant**, a grant of money paid directly to a school by the government; freq. *attrib.*, esp. in **direct-grant school**, a school that receives a direct grant and in return observes certain conditions regarding the admission of pupils, etc.; also *ellipt.*; **direct injection**, a kind of fuel injection whereby fuel is supplied directly to the combustion chambers or their intakes in an internal combustion engine, without the use of a carburettor; usu. *attrib.*; so ***direct-injected*** adj.; **direct mail**, advertising matter or the like sent through the post to prospective customers; also *attrib.*; **direct method**, a method of teaching a foreign language through conversation, reading, etc., in the language itself without using the pupil's native language and without study of formal rules of grammar; also *attrib.*; **direct-reading** , applied *attrib.* to a measuring instrument calibrated in the actual quantity measured; **direct realism** *Philos.*, the theory that in perception we are directly aware of external or physical objects as they really are; **direct rule**, a system of government in which power and administration are exercised by central government, rather than one in which there is any measure of devolution; *spec.* with reference to N. Ireland; contr. with *indirect rule* s.v. indirect *a.* 2 a; cf. Home Rule; **direct sowing** *Forestry* (see quot. 1891); **direct voice** *Spiritualism*, speech said to emanate directly from a disembodied spirit, without using a medium.

1964 *Honeywell Gloss. Data Processing* 1/2 *Direct address. **1963** *IBM Systems Jrnl.* II. 88 The use of direct addressing is limited to applications where the key set may be freely chosen to conform to the restrictions of the available set of addresses. **1980** C. S. French *Computer Sci.* xxiv. 180 Direct addressing is simple, fast and effective but the number of locations addressable is limited. **1985** *Computerworld* 22 Apr. 76/1 A random-access memory disk .. does not offer the instant gratification of direct address. **1921** J. N. Pring *Electric Furnace* xi. 202 In the *direct-arc furnaces, such as those of Héroult and Girod, a zone of very high temperature is produced in the slag immediately below the electrodes. **1962** *Times* 2 Mar. 15/5 One of the Birlec three-ton direct-arc furnaces. **1901** *Feilden's Mag.* IV. 441/2 A *direct-coupled electrically-driven fan. **1910** G. W. Pierce *Princ. Wireless Telegr.* 96 Direct coupled transmitting and receiving circuits. **1953** F. Langford-Smith *Radio Designer's Handbk.* (ed. 4) xii. 529 A direct-coupled amplifier is one which the plate of one stage is connected to the grid of the next stage directly, or through a biasing battery or equivalent. **1962** Simpson & Richards *Junction Transistors* ix. 214 Another very useful direct-coupled amplifier is the Darlington compound connection. **1916** *Standard Rules Amer. Inst. Electr. Engin.* 97 **Direct coupler*, an apparatus which magnetically joins two circuits having a common conductive portion. **1907** J. Erskine-Murray *Handbk. Wireless Telegr.* ii. 43 This method of connection is now called '*direct coupling', as opposed to inductive coupling by means of a separate primary and secondary. **1910** *Hawkins's Electr. Dict.* 119/1 *Direct coupling*, connecting the shaft of a dynamo armature directly to the shaft which drives it. **1931** Moyer & Wostrel *Radio Handbk.* ii. 87 In direct capacity coupling, the coupling is made closer by reducing the capacity of the common condenser... In indirect capacity coupling, the coupling is made closer by increasing the capacity of the coupling condensers. [**1886** *Jrnl. Soc. Telegr. Engin.* XV. 193, I am glad that people are beginning to use the term 'direct' when they mean a current which does not alternate.] **1889** E. J. Houston *Electr. Words* 165 *Direct current. **1893** D. C. Jackson *Electro-Magn.* I. 92 A current constant in direction, but not necessarily so in value, is often called a Direct Current. **1893** *Jrnl. Soc. Arts* XLI. 623/2 The general merits of alternate-current, as against those of the direct-current systems. **1915** Hawkhead & Dowsett *Techn. Instr. Wireless Telegr.* 83 A direct current may be passed through a known resistance and the amount of heat generated may be measured. **1959** *Chambers's Encycl.* XI. 547/2 The term rectifier is used of any electrical device which can convert an alternating current into a source of direct current. **1962** A. Nisbett *Technique Sound Studio* iv. 87 Cut by the hot-stylus method.. and subjected to no more than medium to low playing weights a microgroove *direct-cut disc can survive very many replays without appreciable signs of wear. **1978** *Gramophone* June 116/1 The recording has a remarkable clarity and absence of distortion, the expected virtues of the direct-cut technique which bypasses the usual tape recording processes. **1968** J. D. MacDonald *Pale Grey for Guilt* (1969) xi. 127, I *direct-dialled my love. **1976** *CB Mag.* June 63/3 An on-board phone lets him direct-dial any place in the world. **1958** *N.Y. Times* 7 June 39/3 The company said that if the trial were successful it would extend to more than 600,000 customers the *direct dialing of person-to-person, collect or credit card calls. **1969** P. Dickinson *Pride of Heroes* 100 We're on direct dialling —shall I get the number for you? **1984** D. Lodge *Small World* i. i. 43 Three things.. have revolutionized academic life in the last twenty years.. jet travel, direct-dialling telephones and the Xerox machine. **1955** *Fortune* Feb. 224 (Advt.), *Direct distance dialing is easy and faster. Just by dialing three more digits than a local call, telephone users in certain towns can already reach as many as 14 million telephones. **1958** *N.Y. Times* 7 June 39/3 To make a call now to San Francisco, customers who have telephones equipped for direct distance dialing merely dial 415 and then the telephone number. **1983** *Summary of World Broadcasts* (B.B.C.) 29 June B/1 Changchun City telecommunication bureau has installed direct distance dialling equipment. **1973** *Times* 8 Jan. 14/6 The latest technical innovation is *direct drilling of root crops. **1983** Biscoe & Dawson in C. R. W. Spedding *Fream's Elem. Agric.* (ed. 16) xxiv. 479 A good tilth often exists after a cereal harvest and, when there has been a good burn, drilling can be performed with no cultivation at all, i.e. direct drilling. **1945** *Guide to Educational System* (Min. Education) 58 **Direct-grant school*, school receiving grant direct from the Ministry of Education (*e.g.* nursery, special or grammar school). **1957** *Economist* 21 Dec. 1030/1 A number of excellent schools known in the jargon as 'direct grant'. *Ibid.*, To qualify for direct grant status, a school must not make a profit. **1958** *Times* 29 July 9/6 The direct-grant grammar school may be given a choice of accepting local authority rule or becoming entirely independent of the public system and public funds. **1970** *Guardian* 9 Apr. 12/3 Obviously the Conservatives will look on the 'direct grants' with tenderness. **1962** *Economist* 17 Mar. 1039/2 By making it reversible, lighter, faster and *direct-injected, the company turned the diesel into a marine engine. **1935** *Jrnl. R. Aeronaut. Soc.* XXXIX. 802 Americans to give serious attention to the *direct-injection engine, thus eliminating the carburettor. **1930** H. Crane *Let.* 29 Dec. (1965) 360 The *direct mail advertising business. **1959** *Times Lit. Suppl.* 23 Jan. 49/1 The work shown covers the realm of the poster, Press, direct mail, showcards, [etc.]. **1962** E. Godfrey *Retail Selling* x. 109 Direct mail advertising of this type can create a big response. *Ibid.* 110 Another useful direct mail prestige advertisement which many shops use is to send a Christmas card to all their regular customers. **1904** S. Bertelsen tr. *Jespersen's How to teach Foreign Lang.* i. 2 The method is by some called the 'new' or 'newer' ;.. the '*direct' comes a little nearer. **1914** W. Owen *Let.* 3 Feb. (1967) 232 The majority of English Teachers have an execrable Accent, and what is worse, no notion of the *Direct Method.* **1917** H. E. Palmer *Scientific Study & Teaching of Lang.* iv. 72 In many cases.. the Direct Method.. resolves itself into the negative precept: there must be no translation. **1885** *Jrnl. Soc. Telegr. Engin.* XIV. 497 Ten years ago hardly anyone had even seen a *direct-reading instrument. **1887** *Ibid.* XVI. 618 An instrument.. which indicates the quantity to be measured without any adjustment on the part of the observer, is a 'direct-reading' instrument. **1956** *Nature* 17 Mar. 513/1 Electronic circuits for a direct-reading spectrograph. **1925** J. E. TURNER *(title)* A theory of *direct realism. **1956** H. H. PRICE in H. D. Lewis *Contemp. Brit. Philos.* 391 These three arguments..do at least refute the 'Direct Realism' of common sense. **1963** W. SELLARS *Sci., Perception & Reality* 61 Direct realism and classical phenomenalism share..the 'phenomenalistic theme'. **1967** *Encycl. Philos.* VII. 78/1 Naive realism is the simplest form of direct realism. **1922** F. D. LUGARD *Dual Mandate in Brit. Tropical Africa* xi. 227 'Tell us what you want done,' they say to their foreign monitors, 'and we will take care that your wishes are carried out, but do not attempt to see to their execution yourself.' This is the whole difference between *direct rule and rule through the native rulers. **1936** *Discovery* Nov. 360/1 Policy may vary from..colonial exploitation to virtual native freedom under the paternal supervision of 'direct rule'. **1964** P. WORSLEY in I. L. Horowitz *New Sociol.* 384 Thus the attributes of bureaucracy under indirect rule differ profoundly from direct-rule situations. **1970** *Guardian* 12 Aug. 1/4 The Prime Minister [of N. Ireland]..said: 'I think if direct rule were imposed, it might provoke a very violent reaction on the part of the Protestant loyalist population.' **1891** W. SCHLICH *Man. Forestry* II. ii. 41 Under '*direct sowing' is understood the formation of a wood by the sowing of seed directly on the area which it is proposed to stock. **1953** H. L. EDLIN *Forester's Handbk.* x. 164 Many trials of direct sowing of various kinds of tree have been carried out in Britain, but no system has come into general use. **1926** A. CONAN DOYLE *Hist. Spiritualism* I. xiv. 330 Again, in reporting upon Mrs. Lord the Commission got the *Direct Voice, and also phosphorescent lights after the medium had been searched. **1946** G. N. M. TYRRELL *Personality of Man* VIII. xxv. 217 The 'direct voice' in which, it is alleged, a deceased person speaks from some isolated point in space. **1967** *Listener* 19 Oct. 488/2 The Society for Psychical Research has a standing offer of £1,000 to any medium who can produce physical phenomena such as materialisation, levitation or direct voice under test conditions.

B. *adv.* = DIRECTLY. **a.** Straight in direction or aspect. **b.** Immediately. **c.** Absolutely, exactly. **d.** *Comb.* with adjs., as ***direct acting*** (see A 6 d), ***direct-dealing***.

c **1450** HENRYSON *Test. Cres.* (R.), Her [Venus'] golden face in oppositioun Of God Phebus direct descending down. ? *a* **1550** *Freiris of Berwik* 342 in *Dunbar's Poems* (1893) 296 And to the eist direct he turnis his face. **1614** ROWLANDS *Fooles Bolt* 14 Saying grace in mentall wise, Holding his Hatt direct before his eyes. **1667** MILTON *P.L.* III. 526 Direct against which op'nd from beneath..A passage down to th' Earth. **1743** CHESTERF. *Lett.* I. xcix. 277 You will observe, they are direct contrary subjects. **1830** *Westminst. Rev.* XII. 292 We do not think that any direct-dealing man..can admire the figure. **1840** MACAULAY *Ess., Ranke* (1854) 556/2 His orders have come down to him..direct from on high. **1868** FREEMAN *Norm. Conq.* (1876) II. App. 669 He fancies that the embassy went direct to Hungary. **1880** *Law Rep.* 29 Ch. Div. 460 This property is held direct from the Crown. **1884** *Ibid.* 9 App. Cases 1 Securities..procurable only from the corporations direct.

direct (dɪˈrɛkt), *sb.* [app. f. DIRECT *v.*]

1. *gen.* A direction.

1615 T. ADAMS *Lycanthropy* 4 'Behold'! is..in Holy Writ, evermore the *avant-courier* of some excellent thing..It is a direct, a reference, a dash of the Holy Ghost's pen.

2. *Mus.* A sign (✓) placed on the stave at the end of a page or line to indicate the position of the following note.

1674 PLAYFORD *Skill Mus.* I. xi. 35 A Direct is usually at the end of a Line, and serves to direct to the place of the first Note on the next Line. **1880** GROVE *Dict. Mus.* I. 448/2 *Direct*, a mark (✓) to be found in music up to the present century..like the catchword at the foot of a page.

†**3.** *in direct of*: see DIRECT *a.* 1 c.

di'rectable, *a.* Also -ible. [f. DIRECT *v.* + -ABLE.] Capable of being directed.

1884 *Pall Mall G.* 25 Aug. 2/1 No argument..would have persuaded..the spectators that I had not guided with singular expertness my directable balloon. **1884** *Commercial Advert.* (N.Y), Once the principle of directible ballooning is discovered.

di'rected, *ppl. a.* [f. DIRECT *v.* + -ED[1].] Aimed, addressed, guided, etc.: see the vb.

1598 FLORIO, *Diretto*..directed or adrest. **1727** *Philip Quarll* 93 The Coach was arriv'd to the directed Place. **1855** MACAULAY *Hist. Eng.* III. 236 The Dartmouth poured on them a well directed broadside. **1891** *Daily News* 6 May 5/6 To create and maintain a large amount of organized and directed activity within the limits of his large diocese.

Hence †**di'rectedly** *adv. Obs.*, directly.

1539 TONSTALL *Serm. Palm Sund.* (1823) 49 We shuld put an other foundation of the churche than Christe, whyche is dyrectedly agaynst saint Paule. *a* **1641** BP. MOUNTAGU *Acts and Mon.* (1642) 277 Directedly intending for his owne advancement.

di'rectedness. [f. DIRECTED *ppl. a.* + -NESS.] The quality of being directed.

1922 J. Y. SIMPSON *Man & Attainm. Immort.* xii. 267 The specificity of action, the directedness, the working out of what looks like purpose. **1929** E. BOWEN *Last Sept.* x. 117 She still had that quality of directedness.

directee (dɪrɛkˈtiː). [f. DIRECT *v.* + -EE.] One who is directed or is under direction.

1928 G. B. SHAW *Intell. Woman's Guide Socialism* lxx. 337 By paying the director more than the directee it creates a difference of class between them. **1938** *Mind* XLVII. 252 Some relation between the director and the directee which is explicitly to be proved absurd.

directer, -ible: see DIRECTOR, -ABLE.

di'recting, *vbl. sb.* [f. DIRECT *v.* + -ING[1].] The action of the verb DIRECT (q.v.); direction (in various senses).

1530 PALSGR. 213/2 Directyng, *adresse.* **1559** CUNNINGHAM *Cosmogr. Glasse* 161 As touchinge the directing of anye shippe. **1632** *Star Chamb. Cases* (Camden) 97 The countenancing of causes and directing of juries. **1751** LABELYE *Westm. Br.* 66 The Directing the Persons concerned therein, was committed to one Person only. **1890** G. B. SHAW *Fabian Ess. Socialism* 119 The 'directing' of companies and the patronizing of nitrogenous Volunteer Colonels.

di'recting, *ppl. a.* [-ING[2].] That directs: see the verb.

1588 J. MELLIS *Briefe Instruct.* G viij, Aboue the directing line. **1670** *Devout Commun.* (1688) 69 Some beams of thy directing consolatory light. **1719** DE FOE *Crusoe* (1840) I. xv. 259 A secret directing Providence. **1889** *Spectator* 19 Oct., That is the true end of arranging work, and it is one which the directing classes do not forget when arranging work for themselves.

b. *spec.* **directing-circle**, a circle made of two hoops, one within the other, to guide sappers in the making of gabions; **directing-plane** (*Persp.*), a plane passing through the point of sight parallel to the plane of the picture; **directing-point** (*Persp.*), the point at which any original line meets the directing plane (Gwilt *Arch.* Gloss. 1876); **directing-post**, a finger-post on a road.

1851 J. S. MACAULAY *Field Fortif.* 66 The directing circle is then laid on a level piece of ground, and seven, eight, or nine pickets are driven at equal distances apart, between the hoops. **1876** Directing plane, point [see DIRECTOR 3 f]. **1876** HARDY *Ethelberta* (1890) 28 Reaching the directingpost where the road branched into two, she paused.

direction (dɪˈrɛkʃən, daɪ-). [a. L. *dīrectiōn-em*, n. of action from *dīrig-ĕre* to DIRECT; cf. F. *direction*, 15th c. in Hatz.-Darm., possibly the immediate source in some senses.]

1. The action or function of directing: **a.** of pointing or aiming anything straight towards a mark; **b.** of putting or keeping in the right way or course; guidance, conduct; **c.** of instructing how to proceed or act aright; authoritative guidance, instruction; **d.** of keeping in right order; management, administration.

1509 HAWES *Past. Pleas.* XXIV. xiii, She [nature] werketh upon all wonderly..In sondry wyse by great dyreccyon. **1568** GRAFTON *Chron.* II. 138 Which thing was shewed unto the kinges counsaile, by whose direction, the matter was committed unto Sir Philip Basset. **1604** SHAKS. *Oth.* II. iii. 128 He is a Souldier, fit to stand by Caesar And giue direction. **1618** RALEIGH in *Four C. Eng. Lett.* 38 Where without any direccion from me, a Spanish village was burnt. **1659** B. HARRIS *Parival's Iron Age* 109 Father Arnout, who was preferred by the Duke of Luynes, to the direction of the [King's] Conscience. **1662** J. DAVIES tr. *Olearius' Voy. Ambass.* 36 The Steeples give a great direction to the Ships that sail that way. **1689–92** LOCKE *Toleration* III. ii. Wks. 1727 II. 324 Their want of Knowledge during their Nonnage, makes them want Direction. *a* **1719** BP. SMALRIDGE (J.), The direction of good works to a good end. **1765** A. DICKSON *Treat. Agric.* (ed. 2) 217 He may use one of his hands when necessary for the direction of the horses. **1801** STRUTT *Sports & Past.* II. i. 60 [No] such precision..in the direction of the arrows. **1828** SCOTT *F.M. Perth* xxxii, Who shall arraign the head by whose direction the act was done? **1856** FROUDE *Hist. Eng.* (1858) I. v. 422 The French prince followed the direction of his wiser instincts. **1863** GEO. ELIOT *Romola* II. ix, She felt the need of direction even in small things.

e. The art, technique, or an instance of directing a play, film, etc. (see DIRECT *v.* 5 c).

1938 C. MORGAN *Flashing Stream* 36 The play was first performed at the Lyric Theatre, London under the direction of Mr. Godfrey Tearle. **1939** W. C. & H. S. PRYOR *Let's go to Movies* 45 *(heading)* Direction. **1949** G. B. SHAW in E. J. West *Shaw on Theatre* (1958) 279 They are not concerned with direction as a fine art; but they cover the mechanical and teachable conditions which are common to all productions. **1959** *Oxf. Mag.* 12 Mar. 338/1 The pace and punch of his direction, camera-work and cutting are far better than anything he ever did in England.

†**2.** Capacity for directing; administrative faculty.

1585 J. B. tr. *Viret's Sch. Beastes* A vij, Because of their industrie..and of that prudence and direction that they have. **1594** SHAKS. *Rich. III*, V. iii. 16 Call for some men of sound direction. **1636** MASSINGER *Bashf. Lover* II. iv, The enemy must say we were not wanting In courage or direction.

3. a. The office of a director; a body of directors; = DIRECTORATE.

1710 STEELE *Tatler* No. 206 ¶2 We met a Fellow who is a Lower Officer where Jack is in the Direction. **1771** SMOLLETT *Humph. Cl.* (1815) 225 A friend..will recommend you to the direction. **1855** THACKERAY *Newcomes* I. 62, I will ask some of the Direction. **1878** F. S. WILLIAMS *Midl. Railw.* 124 Resignation by Mr. Hudson of his position on the direction.

b. *Mus.* The office or function of the conductor of an orchestra or choir: see DIRECT *v.* 5 b.

†**4.** Orderly arrangement or disposition of matters; arranged or ordered course; arrangement, order. Chiefly in ***to take*** or ***set direction***. *Obs.*

1407 *Mann. & Househ. Exp.* 173 Ȝeff ther be any derekesyon take at thes kowensel for the Kinges goenge. **1475** *Plumpton Corr.* 33 He shall see such a derection betwixt his brother Gascoin & you, as shalbe to your harts ease & worship. **1494** FABYAN *Chron.* VII. 491 The whiche variaunce to apese the Kynge toke therein some payne, but no direccion he myghte set therein, so that the saide duke & sir John deperted with wordes of diffiaunce. **1548** HALL *Chron., Hen. VIII*, 14/b, And there remained at the kynges charge, til other direccion was taken for theim.

5. a. with *a* and *pl.*: An instruction how to proceed or act; an order to be carried out, a precept.

1576 FLEMING *Panopl. Epist.* 257, I set downe directions and precepts, how you should order and dispose your studies. **1654** WHITLOCK *Zootomia* 129 He..took little or nothing but by the Doctors directions. **1722** DE FOE *Plague* (1754) 10, I desire this Account may pass with them, rather for a Direction to themselves to act by. **1801** STRUTT *Sports & Past.* Introd. 24 The stage direction then requires the entry of Two men. **1845** H. J. ROSE in *Encycl. Metrop.* II. 897/1 His [Christ's] direction in the case of an offending brother, 'tell it to the Church'..would be unintelligible, if there were no visible Church. **1854** J. S. C. ABBOTT *Napoleon* (1855) II. xxx. 569 His instructions contained the following directions.

b. Instruction how to go to a place.

1596 SPENSER *F.Q.* VI. i. 6 Withouten guyde Or good direction how to enter in. **1749** FIELDING *Tom Jones* XVI. x, Fitzpatrick..was inquiring in the street after his wife, and had just received directions to the door. **1762** GOLDSM. *Cit. W.* ciii, I..beg of you to provide him with proper directions for finding me in London.

6. a. The action of directing or addressing a letter, or the like. †**b.** The dedication or address of a writing (*obs.*). **c.** The superscription or address upon a letter or parcel sent, indicating for whom it is intended, and where it is to be taken; the name of the place at which letters for a particular person are to be delivered; = ADDRESS *sb.* 7. **d.** *U.S. Law.* 'In equity pleading, that part of the bill containing the address to the court' (Cent. Dict.). (Called in England the *address.*)

1524 WOLSEY *Let. to Dacres* 24 Apr. in M.A.E. Wood *Lett. Illustr. Ladies* (1846) I. 315 It was folded in the said paper, without direction to any person, and sealed semblably with a letter of a contrary tenor. **1586** A. DAY *Eng. Secretary* I. (1625) 4 That it [a writing] containe not base..or scurrile matter, unbeseeming a direction so worthy. *Ibid.* I. 16 The directions, which on the outside of every Letter..are always fixed, and commonly are termed by the name of Superscriptions. **1663** CHAS. II, in Cartwright *Madame Henrietta* (1894) 138 A little booke..by the derections you will see where 'tis to be had. **1718** LADY M. W. MONTAGU *Let. to C'tess Mar* 10 Mar., I have received..that short note..in which you..promise me a direction for the place you stay in. **1749** FIELDING *Tom Jones* XIII. ii, The proper direction to him was, *To Dr. Misaubin in the World.* **1786** BURNS *Let. to W. Chalmers* 27 Dec., My direction is—care of Andrew Bruce, merchant, Bridge-street. **1840** CLOUGH *Amours de Voy.* V. vii, Has he not written to you?—he did not know your direction. **1886** *N. & Q.* 7th Ser. II. 425/1 These letters..retain their directions..and bear the postmarks of the period.

†**7.** Disposition, turn of mind. *Obs. rare.*

1642 *Life Dk. Buckhm.* in *Select. Harl. Misc.* (1793) 286 His religious lady, of sweet and noble direction.

†**8.** Direct motion (of a planet): see DIRECT *a.* 3. *Obs. rare.*

1658 PHILLIPS, *Direction*, a Planet is said direct, when it moveth in its natural course according to the direction of the Signs. **1727–51** CHAMBERS *Cycl.*, *Direction*, in astronomy, the motion, and other phænomena, of a planet, when direct. **1790** SIBLY *Astrol.* (1792) I. 147 Direction signifies a planet moving on in its natural course from west to east.

9. a. The particular course or line pursued by any moving body, as defined by the part or region of space, point of the compass, or other fixed or known point, towards which it is directed; the relative point towards which one moves, turns the face, the mind, etc.; the line towards any point or region in its relation to other lines taken as known.

angle of d., *line of d.*: see quots. 1706, 1727.

1665 HOOKE *Microgr.* 100 The undulating pulse is..at right angles with the Ray or Line of direction. **1706** CLARKE *Attrib. God* ix. (R.), The direction of all their [the planets'] progressive motions..from the west to the east. **1706** PHILLIPS (ed. Kersey), *Line of Direction* (in *Mechan.*) is the Line of Motion that any natural body observes according to the Force impressed upon it. **1727–51** CHAMBERS *Cycl.* s.v., *Angle of Direction*, in mechanics, is that comprehended between the lines of direction of two conspiring powers. **1756** C. LUCAS *Ess. Waters* II. 47 The tides..move it in two different directions four times in the natural day. **1756** BURKE *Subl. & B.* III. xv, Their parts never continue long in the same right line. They vary their direction every moment. **1834** MEDWIN *Angler in Wales* II. 103 The trout were darting about in all directions. **1842** GROVE *Corr. Phys. Forces* 70 The direction of this rotation is changed by changing the direction of the magnetic force. **1878** HUXLEY *Physiogr.* 6 These terms—north and south, east and west..indicate definite directions. **1879** THOMSON & TAIT *Nat. Phil.* I. I. §218 The direction of a force is the line in which it acts. If the place of application of a force be regarded as a point, a line through that point, in the direction in which the force tends to move the body, is the direction of the force. *Mod.* Tell me in what direction to look. He has gone in the direction of Warwick. In what direction is Versailles from Paris?

b. *fig.* in reference to a course of action or the like, viewed as motion.

1752 JOHNSON *Rambler* No. 206 ¶3 A Man, actuated at once by different desires, must move in a direction peculiar to himself. *c* **1790** WILLOCK *Voy.* 306 Of late..politics have taken a new direction. **1830** D'ISRAELI *Chas. I*, III. i. 5 Too often the impulse which sprang from a public source, took the direction of a private end. **1874** GREEN *Short Hist.* vi. §4. 308 Efforts..in the direction of educational and religious reform. **1875** JOWETT *Plato* (ed. 2) IV. 519 New directions of enquiry.

10. *Astrol.* (See quots.)

1706 PHILLIPS (ed. Kersey). **1727–51** CHAMBERS *Cycl.*, *Direction*..is a kind of calculus, whereby they pretend to find the time wherein any notable accident shall befal the person whose horoscope is drawn. **1819** JAS. WILSON *Compl. Dict. Astrol.* s.v., Primary directions are arithmetical calculations of the time of events caused by the significator forming conjunctions, or aspects, with the places of promittors. *Ibid.*, The distance of the place of a significator in a nativity from the place he must arrive at before he can form the aspect..is called the arc of direction.

11. *attrib.* and *Comb.*, as ***direction-giver***, ***-paper***; **direction cosines**, the cosines of the angles which a given direction makes with the three axes of coordinates in space; **direction-finder** *Telecommunications*, a receiving device that determines from which direction radio waves come to it; so ***direction-finding***; **direction indicator**, a device on a motor vehicle used to indicate the direction the driver intends to take; = TRAFFICATOR; **direction-post**, a finger-post at the branching of a road, a directing post; **direction-ratio**, the ratio of one of the oblique coordinates of a point to the distance of the point from the origin; **direction-word** = CATCHWORD 1.

1913 *Year-Bk. Wireless Telegr. & Teleph.* 307 Direction-finding from ship-board. *Ibid.* 316 The uses of the direction-finder. **1919** R. STANLEY *Wireless Telegr.* (ed. 2) II. 270 A direction-finding aerial system. **1920** *Discovery* May 131/2 The Marconi direction-finder not only receives wireless signals; it also indicates the direction of the sending station. **1921** L. B. TURNER *Wireless Telegr.* 178 Direction-finding stations on land..are usually grouped in pairs at the ends of a suitable base line, so that the intersection of the two orientations determined gives the position of the source of signal, e.g. a ship or an aeroplane. **1935** *Discovery* June 155/2 The practical problems of direction-finding are closely connected with the vagaries of the waves returned from the ionosphere, and continued success has been attained in the development of direction-finders less subject to the errors produced by these waves. **1946** *Electronic Engin.* XVIII. 20 An automatic V.H.F. direction finder. **1966** M. R. D. FOOT *SOE in France* x. 324 He tried to get in touch with Dowlen; but Dowlen was caught by direction-finders. **1591** SHAKS. *Two Gent.* III. ii. 90 Sweet Protheus, my direction-giuer, Let us into the City presently. **1937** *Times* 13 Apr. p. xxii/4 The makers of direction indicators and fog and anti-dazzle lamps. **1959** *Motor Manual* (ed. 36) vi. 183 Another change since the war has been the progressive displacement of the semaphore-type of direction indicator by flashing light signals. **1769** FRANKLIN *Lett.* Wks. 1887 IV. 233 Enclosed is his direction-paper for opening and fixing it. **1795** K. P. MORITZ *Trav.* 142 Where there are cross-roads, there are direction posts, so that it is hardly possible to lose oneself in walking. **1844** DICKENS *Mart. Chuz.* ii, A direction-post, which is always telling the way to a place. **1861** MILL *Utilit.* ii. 35 To inform a traveller..is not to forbid the use of direction-posts on the way. **1706** PHILLIPS (ed. Kersey), *Direction-word*..a Word set at the bottom of a Page directing or shewing the first word of the next page.

Hence **di'rectionism**, the theory of a directing power underlying the material forces of the universe; **di'rectionless** *a.*, void of aim or direction.

1860 RUSKIN *Mod. Paint.* V. VI. iv. §8 An aspen or elm leaf is thin, tremulous, and directionless, compared with the spear-like setting and firm substance of a rhododendron or laurel leaf. **1873** PATER *Renaissance* viii. 190 The eyes are wide and directionless, not fixing anything with their gaze. **1894** *Month* June 281 He..supposes a power underlying the whole, which he calls 'directionism'; as an antagonistic view to that of mere materialism.

directional (dɪ'rɛkʃənəl), *a.* [f. prec. + -AL[1].]

†**1.** Serving for direction or guidance: see quot. *Obs.*

1612 STURTEVANT *Metallica* (1854) 67 Directional is that moddle which is made only to guide the Artificer in the dimensions of all the parts, as also for to direct them for the kinds of the matter and the stuffe..to make the engin intended.

2. Of or relating to direction in space.

1881 MAXWELL *Electr. & Magn.* II. 168 These directional relations. **1881** SPOTTISWOODE in *Nature* No. 623. 546 There is a dissymmetry at the two ends or 'terminals' of a battery..or other source of electricity, implying a directional character either in that which is transmitted, or in the mode of its transmission.

3. *Alg.* ***directional coefficient*** (of an imaginary quantity), the quotient obtained by dividing the quantity by its modulus.

4. a. Of or pertaining to the direction or guidance of affairs.

1921 *Glasgow Herald* 5 Mar. 6 The responsibility of so improving his directional control of the conditions of working. **1922** *Ibid.* 21 Mar. 7 Their doctrine of one directional authority. **1928** *Daily Express* 26 Sept. 1 All directional and organisation expenses.

b. Of or pertaining to the direction of films, etc.

1949 *Here & Now* (N.Z.) Oct. 29/3 Camera, lighting, directional 'touches' are in their subordinate and proper place. **1962** *Movie* Sept. 25/1 The emotional effect of *Exodus* is the stronger for being free from directional nudges and promptings.

5. *Telecommunications.* Concerned with the record of directions indicated by radio signals received from a vessel, etc. Also, pertaining or relating to apparatus that transmits or receives radio signals, etc., more strongly in or from certain directions than others.

1914 R. STANLEY *Wireless Telegr.* 179 To illustrate the effect of directional aerials at the sender and at the receiver. **1929** *Bell Syst. Techn. Jrnl.* VIII. 313 The use of directional receiving antennas is essential to satisfactory and economic results over such distances as the transatlantic radio path. **1930** *Aberdeen Press & Jrnl.* 26 June 7/1 An occasional directional message from the Cape Race wireless station was the only guidance they could pick up. **1935** *Economist* 30 Nov. 1062/2 Aerial navigation without wireless is to-day almost unthinkable. Night flying has only been made feasible by directional wireless. **1957** *BBC Handbk.* 60 To provide an effective signal in the area served by each programme, highly directional short-wave transmitting aerials are used. *Ibid.* 219 An efficient type of directional aerial. **1962** A. NISBETT *Technique Sound Studio* 255 The microphone is thus intensely directional.

Hence **di'rectionally** *adv.*, with respect to direction.

1879 THOMSON & TAIT *Nat. Phil.* I. I. §107 A fixed ring in space (directionally fixed, that is to say, but having the same translational motion as the earth's centre).

directionality (dɪˌrɛkʃə'nælɪtɪ). [f. DIRECTIONAL *a.* + -ITY.] The state or quality of being directional; maintenance of direction.

1951 PARSONS & SHILS *Gen. Theory of Action* 405 An individual or group shows a consistent directionality in its selections. **1964** *Language* XL. 250 Linguistic relativity implies a one-way directionality. **1967** *Technology Week* 20 Feb. 34/3 Equipped with dipoles, the spacecraft was making cosmic noise measurements with no directionality. **1968** CHOMSKY & HALLE *Sound Pattern Eng.* 386 There is..no reason to assume that the restriction has directionality, i.e., should be formalized to operate from left to right.

†**di'rectitude.** *Obs.* Humorous blunder, used apparently for *wrong* or *discredit*.

1607 SHAKS. *Cor.* IV. v. 222 Which Friends sir, durst not ..shew themselues..his Friends, whilest he's in Directitude.

directive (dɪ'rɛktɪv, daɪ-), *a.* (*sb.*) [ad. med.L. *dīrectīv-us*, f. *dīrect-* ppl. stem of *dīrigĕre* to direct: see -IVE. In F. *directif*, *-ive* (13–14th c.), Sp. and Pg. *directivo*, It. *direttivo* ' having or giving direction vnto, directiue' (Florio 1598).]

A. *adj.* **1. a.** Having the quality or function of directing, authoritatively guiding, or ruling: see DIRECT *v.*

1594 HOOKER *Eccl. Pol.* I. viii. (1611) 18 A law therefore generally taken, is a directiue rule vnto goodnesse of operation. **1614** RALEIGH *Hist. World* II. 245 To the power Directive they ought to be subject. **1659** PEARSON *Creed* (1839) 414 The..directive conscience tells us what we are to do, and the subsequent or reflexive conscience warns us what we are to receive. **1712** BERKELEY *Passive Obed.* §7 Laws being rules directive of our actions. **1729** SAVAGE *Wanderer* v. 656 No friendly stars directive beams display. **1853** M. KELLY tr. *Gosselin's Power Pope* II. 364 The directive power of the Church. **1861** MILL *Utilit.* ii. 16 Utility or Happiness, considered as the directive rule of human conduct.

†**b.** *Law.* = DIRECTORY *a.* b. *Obs.*

1610 BP. CARLETON *Jurisd.* 166 His meaning is by lawes directiue..that Princes haue no coactiue power ouer the Clergie but onely power directiue. *a* **1649** WINTHROP *New Eng.* (1826) II. 205 There is a threefold power of magistratical authority, viz. legislative, judicial, and consultative or directive of the public affairs of the country. **1698** R. FERGUSON *View Eccles.* 30 He fulfilled the Directive Part of the Law..he likewise underwent the Penalty of it.

2. Having the quality, function, or power of directing motion; causing something to take a particular direction in space.

(Used especially of the force by which a magnet takes a north and south direction.)

1625 N. CARPENTER *Geog. Del.* I. iii. (1635) 44 The vertue Directiue, by which a needle touched with the Magnet, directs and conformes it selfe North and South. **1667** *Phil. Trans.* II. 437 The Verticity or Directive faculty of the Loadstone. **1794** S. WILLIAMS *Vermont* 377 The directive power of the magnet. **1842–3** GROVE *Corr. Phys. Forces* 65 It is..directive, not motive, altering the direction of other forces, but not..initiating them. **1881** MAXWELL *Electr. & Magn.* II. 70 The directive action of the earth's magnetism on the compass needle.

†**3.** Subject to direction. *Obs. rare.*

1606 SHAKS. *Tr. & Cr.* I. iii. 356 Limbes are his instruments, In no lesse working, then are Swords and Bowes Directive by the Limbes.

B. *sb.* †(*a*) That which directs. *Obs.* (*b*) *spec.* a general instruction how to proceed or act.

1642 ROGERS *Naaman* To Rdr. §2 That directive of minde, and freedome of pure will that kept him. **1654** Z. COKE *Logick* (1657) 35 Spirituall Vertue..is..the common directive of all other vertues.

1902 *Encyl. Brit.* XXXIII. 647/1 The ecclesiastical régime..arrogates to itself the right of interfering by means of 'Directives' with the political life of nations. **1910** *Ibid.* II. 603/2 A few simple orders called 'directives' sufficed to set armies in motion with a definite purpose before them. **1941** *Economist* 15 Feb. 209/2 The actual handling of news items [by the B.B.C.] is subject to 'directives' or advice from Government departments. **1941** *Manch. Guardian Weekly* 14 Mar. 214/4 You would think it enough to call an order a direction. No, he [*sc.* the Civil Servant] has to make it 'a directive'. **1961** B. FERGUSSON *Watery Maze* ii. 52 A 'Directive' in Service parlance is a form of order, setting out one's terms of reference, defining one's responsibilities, and showing the extent and limitations of one's authority. **1971** *N.Y. Rev. Bks.* 22 Apr. 34/1 This authorization of September 1970 made official a practice which long preceded the issuance of the directive.

Hence **di'rectively** *adv.*, in a directive manner, so as to direct or guide; **di'rectiveness**, the quality of being directive.

1642 MILTON *Observ. his Majesty's late Answ. & Expresses* 44 Those..that allow humane Laws to obleage Kings more then directively. **1653** BAXTER *Chr. Concord* 79 If a Presbyter may not Govern directively, then he may not Teach. **1710** NORRIS *Chr. Prud.* ii. 74 Prudence..actually directs and conducts men in the management of themselves ..and this actual Directiveness is of the very essence of Prudence. **1858** BUSHNELL *Serm. New Life* 374 God will co-work..directively in all the great struggles of believing souls.

directivity (dɪrɛk'tɪvɪtɪ, daɪ-). [f. DIRECTIVE *a.* + -ITY.] **1.** The quality or state of being directed by a vital force or power as distinguished from the physical forces, *spec.* as a theory of evolution.

1903 *Daily Chron.* Apr., That directivity which could not be explained without the power of the Deity behind it. **1907** *Hibbert Jrnl.* Oct. 150 Sheep, oxen, horses, and even geese may be feeding in the same grass-land. In each case the molecular compounds of the grass are identical, but they find themselves ultimately disposed in very different arrangements in the different animals. This can only be possible under the influence of directivity, but 'directing' differently in each creature.

2. The property or degree of being directional (see DIRECTIONAL *a.* 5). Also *attrib.*

1928 *Jrnl. Inst. Electr. Engin.* LXVI. II. 955 General considerations of the directivity of beam systems. **1930** *Techn. News Bull., U.S. Bureau of Standards* Dec. 117/2 Directivity of reception or transmission, or both, will inform the pilot of the direction of danger. **1935** *Proc. Inst. Radio Engin.* XXIII. 357 Experiments with directivity steering for fading reduction. *Ibid.*, It has been noticed in the past that fading was affected by the directivity of the receiving antenna.

directly (dɪ'rɛktlɪ), *adv.* [f. DIRECT *a.* + -LY[2].] In a direct manner or way.

1. a. In a straight line of motion; with undeviating course; straight.

1513 MORE in Grafton *Chron.* (1568) II. 800 The king with Queene Anne his wife, came downe out of the white Hall..and went directly to the kinges Benche. **1601** SHAKS. *Jul. C.* IV. i. 32 A Creature that I teach to fight, To winde, to stop, to run directly on. **1658** SIR T. BROWNE *Hydriot.* (1736) 52 Cutting thro' one of them either directly or cross-wise. **1678** BUNYAN *Pilgrim's Prog.* I. 3 Keep that light in your eye, and go up directly thereto. **1790** PALEY *Horæ Paul.* Rom. i. 9 To proceed from Achaia directly by sea to Syria. **1820** SCORESBY *Acc. Arctic Reg.* I. 304 [It] advanced directly towards us with a velocity of about three knots.

b. *fig.* Straightforwardly; pointedly; simply; plainly; †correctly, rightly (*obs.*).

1509 HAWES *Past. Pleas.* V. ii, [Grammar] doth us tech.. In all good ordre to speke directly. **1513** MORE in Grafton *Chron.* (1568) II. 786 He would that point should be lesse.. handled, not even fully playne and directly, but touched a slope craftily. **1568** *Ibid.* II. 1339 He might firste aske a question before he aunswered directly to the poynte. **1660** F. BROOKE tr. *Le Blanc's Trav.* 249 Not being able to discern directly what likenesse they were of. **1711** STEELE *Spect.* No. 136 ¶3, I never directly defame, but I do what is as bad. **1791** BURKE *Corr.* (1844) III. 274, I asked him his opinion directly, and without management.

c. *Math.* Opposed to *inversely*.

1743 W. EMERSON *Doctrine Fluxions* III. vii. 274 The Times of describing any Spaces uniformly are as the Spaces directly, and the Velocities reciprocally. **1796** HUTTON *Math. Dict.* I. 384/2 Quantities are said to be directly proportional, when the proportion is according to the order of the terms. **1799** CT. RUMFORD in *Phil. Trans.* LXXXIX. 191 The time taken up..is..as the capacity of the body to receive and retain heat, *directly*, and as its conducting power, *inversely*. **1864** BOWEN *Logic* xii. 413 The theory of gravitation, or the doctrine that every body attracts every other body with a force which is directly as its mass and inversely as the square of its distance.

2. At right angles to a surface; perpendicularly; vertically; not obliquely.

1559 W. CUNNINGHAM *Cosmogr. Glasse* 29 Take a quadrant..and set it directly upright. **1563** W. FULKE *Meteors* (1640) 4 b, In place where the Sunnes beames strike directly against the earth..the heate is so great, that [etc.]. **1665** HOOKE *Microgr.* 130 This does shoot or propend directly downwards. **1698** FRYER *Acc. E. India & P.* 186 Nearer the Equator the Sun and Stars ascend and descend more directly, but the farther from the Equator the more obliquely. **1745** P. THOMAS *Jrnl. Anson's Voy.* 243 They use a Pencil, held..not obliquely, as our Painters, but directly, as if the Paper were to be prick'd. *Mod.* The wind is blowing directly on shore.

3. *Astron.* In the order of the signs, from west to east. See DIRECT *a.* 3.

1509 HAWES *Past. Pleas.* XXII. vi, The bodies above to have their moving In the xii. signes..Some rethrogarde, and some dyrectly.

4. Completely, absolutely, entirely, exactly, precisely, just.

Esp. in ***directly contrary*** (see DIRECT *a.* 4 e); thence extended to other relations.

c **1400** *Apol. Loll.* 4 If he..leuiþ to wirke, and doþ contrarily directly. **1455** *Rolls of Parlt.* V. 280 Entendyng to drawe directly togidres with you. **1583** STUBBES *Anat. Abus.* II. (1882) 88 It is most directly against the word of God. **1601** SHAKS. *Twel. N.* III. iv. 73 This concurres directly with the Letter. **1665** HOOKE *Microgr.* 192, I found one described and Figur'd directly like that which I had by me. **1696** tr. *Du Mont's Voy. Levant* 219 It stands directly in the middle of the City, between the Old and New Town. **1720** SWIFT *Mod. Education* Wks. 1755 II. II. 31 In better times it was directly otherwise. **1768** BOSWELL *Corscia* (ed. 2) 356 He was directly such a venerable hermit as we read of in the old romances. **1863** MARY HOWITT *F. Bremer's Greece* II. ii. 20 The wind..is directly contrary. **1891** SIR R. V. WILLIAMS in *Law Times' Rep.* LXV. 608/2, I find no decision directly in point on this question.

5. Without the intervention of a medium or agent; immediately; by a direct process or mode.

1526 *Pilgr. Perf.* (W. de W. 1531) 165 Immediatly or mediatly, that is to say, without meane, or by some meane, directly or indirectly. *a* **1533** FRITH *Wks.* 147 (R.) Now of this maior or first proposition thus vnderstand, doth the conclusion folowe directly. **1651** HOBBES *Leviath.* II. xxviii. 163 Corporall Punishment is that, which is inflicted on the body directly..such as are stripes or wounds. **1816** KEATINGE *Trav.* (1817) I. 58 When the needful does not come directly out of their own pockets. **1860** TYNDALL *Glac.* II. v. 251 The sun cannot get directly at the deeper portions of the snow. **1870** MAX MÜLLER *Sc. Relig.* (1873) 137 A universal primeval language revealed directly by God to man.

6. a. Immediately (in time); straightway; at once.

1602 SHAKS. *Ham.* III. ii. 219 And who in want a hollow friend doth try, Directly seasons him his enemy. **1743** BULKELEY & CUMMINS *Voy. S. Seas* 18 Sent the Barge ashore..to see if the Place was inhabited, and to return aboard directly. **1848** C. BRONTE *J. Eyre* xxvii, He sat down: but he did not get leave to speak directly. **1881** BLADES *Caxton* (1882) 230 It was probably put to press directly after if not during the translation. *Mod.* I will come directly. Directly after this, he was taken away.

b. *colloq.* as *conj.* As soon as, the moment after. (Elliptical for *directly that, as,* or *when.*)

1795 *Montford Castle* I. 88 Directly you refused [his] assistance, a judgement overtook you. **1827** R. H. FROUDE *Remains* (1838) I. 68, I quite forget all my scepticism directly I fancy myself the object of their perception. **1837** J. H. NEWMAN *Proph. Office Ch.* 2 But it admits of criticism, and will become suspected, directly it is accused. **1837** R. B. EDE *Pract. Chem.* 74 Iodine and phosphorus combine directly they come into contact. **1857** BUCKLE *Civiliz.* I. xii. 677 The celebrated work of De Lolme on the English constitution was suppressed..directly it appeared.

c. Shortly; very soon; in a little while. *dial.* and *U.S.*

1851 H. MELVILLE *Moby Dick* I. iii. 20 Supper?—you want supper? Supper'll be ready directly! **1882** 'MARK TWAIN' *Stolen White Elephant* xvi. 268 When you say you will do a thing 'directly', you mean 'immediately'; in the American language—generally speaking—the word signifies 'after a little'. **1891** R. P. CHOPE *Dial. of Hartland, Devonshire* 40 *Drackly* or *dreckly*, directly; in the dialect this does not mean immediately, but shortly. 'I'll kom drackly; I mus' finish ot I'm 'bout fust.' **1936** M. MITCHELL *Gone with Wind* xlvi. 824 Scarlett..leaned over the banisters. 'I'll be down terrectly, Rhett,' she called.

directness (dɪˈrɛktnɪs). [f. DIRECT *a.* + -NESS.] The state or quality of being direct (*lit.* and *fig.*); straightness, straightforwardness, plainness.

1598 FLORIO, *Diritezza*, directnes, straightnes. *c* **1614** CORNWALLIS in Gutch *Coll. Cur.* I. 141 So would he use much sincerity and directness in the answer. **1668** TEMPLE *To Lord Keeper* 12 Feb. (Seager), Our alliance, if it be pursued with the same directness it has been contracted. **1793** BURKE *Corr.* (1844) IV. 201 Our politics want directness and simplicity. **1816** KEATINGE *Trav.* (1817) II. 48 The directness of the courses of the rivers. **1852** LD. COCKBURN *Mem.* ii. (1874) 100 His clear abrupt style imparted a dramatic directness and vivacity to the scene. **1860** TYNDALL *Glac.* I. xiv. 96 An eagle could not swoop upon its prey with more directness of aim. **1874** GREEN *Short Hist.* vii. §1. 344 His denunciations of wrong had a prophetic directness and fire.

directo-e'xecutive, *a. nonce-comb.* That combines directive with executive functions.

1864 H. SPENCER *Illustr. Univ. Progr.* 419 The directo-executive system of a society (its legislative and defensive appliances).

Directoire (dɪˈrɛktwɑː(r)), *sb.* and *a.* [Fr.; see DIRECTORY *sb.* 6.] **A.** *sb.* = DIRECTORY *sb.* 6.

1795 *Amer. State Papers, For. Relat.* (1832) I. 378 (Stanford) It is probable that this act of the minister proceeds from himself, and not from the directoire. **1886** *Athenæum* 27 Mar. 432/1 The thanks of all playgoers are due to Mrs. Langtry for dressing the character of Pauline in the costume of the *Directoire.* **1937** J. LAVER *Taste & Fashion* vii. 96 In France the Directoire and the Empire introduced a whole new class of speculators and adventurers.

B. *adj.* (Also with small initial.) **1.** Of, pertaining to, or resembling a style of dress prevalent at the time of the French Directory, characterized by its extravagance of design and its imitation of Greek and Roman costume. Also ellipt. as *sb.*, a hat of this style.

Spec. ***Directoire knickers***, a fashion name (see quot. 1968).

1878 *Cassell's Family Mag.* 756 The Directoire..very nearly obscures the face. **1880** [see REDINGOTE]. **1888** [see EMPIRE *sb.* 8]. **1896** *Godey's Mag.* Feb. 214/2 An immense *directoire* bow of ribbon or chiffon. **1904** *Daily Chron.* 18 June 8/2 Such hats, with their picturesque brims, are known as Directoires. **1908** *Ibid.* 16 June 4/5 Worth has made a feature of Directoire gowns for Ascot. **1911** *Alfred Weeks's Sales Catal.*, Stockinette Directoire Knickers, slightly soiled, were 3/11, Reduced to 1/6½d. **1938** E. BOWEN *Death of Heart* I. iv. 75 Eddie's letter..she slipped up inside her woollen directoire knickers. It stayed just inside the elastic band, under one knee. **1951** E. PAUL *Springtime in Paris* xiv. 260 The Carthaginian Queen, as a soloist, was permitted to wear a 'Directoire' gown. **1968** J. IRONSIDE *Fashion Alphabet* 68 Directoire knickers..are straight knickers to the knee, with elastic at waist and knee.

2. Of, pertaining to, or resembling a style of furniture or objets d'art prevalent at the time of the French Directory.

1942 *Burlington Mag.* Nov. 286/2 Members of the Royal Family have contributed several unique French 18th century snuff-boxes,..the Duke and Duchess of Gloucester a directoire example chased and enamelled. **1955** A. WEST *Heritage* ii. 57 The pleasant directoire chairs and tables, which gracefully paid their frivolous tributes to the arts of Greece and Rome. **1962** *House & Garden* Dec. 63/1 An enormous bamboo Directoire bed. **1963** *Ibid.* Feb. 76/4 Directoire is the name given to the style of works of art produced in the last five years of the eighteenth century.

director (dɪˈrɛktə(r)). Also 5-7 -our, 6-9 -er (6 *Sc.* **direkkare, direckar**). [a. AF. *directour* = F. *directeur*, ad. L. **dīrector*, agent-n. from *dīrigĕre* to direct.]

1. a. One who or that which directs, rules, or guides; a guide, a conductor; 'one that has authority over others; a superintendent; one that has the general management of a design or work' (J.).

director-general, a chief or supreme director, having under him directors or managers of departments.

1477 CAXTON in *Earl Rivers' Dictes* 145 Erle of Ryuyers.. Defendour and directour of the siege apostolique. **1552** ABP. HAMILTON *Catech.* (1884) 47 To be ledar, techar and direckar of the same kirk. **1581** MARBECK *Bk. Notes* 741 They use hir [the moon] as the directer of their festiuall daies. **1594** HOOKER *Eccl. Pol.* I. (1676) 74 It cannot be but Nature hath some Directer of infinite knowledge to guide her. **1614** RALEIGH *Hist. World* II. 225 The North Starre is the most fixed directour of the Seaman to his desired Port. **1660** R. COKE *Power & Subj.* 77 The husband is the director and ruler of his wife. **1746–7** HERVEY *Medit.* (1818) 78 Whatever thou doest, consult them as thy directors. **1839** *Penny Cycl.* XV. 467/1 In 1769 Mozart was appointed director of the archbishop of Salzburg's concerts. **1876** BANCROFT *Hist. U.S.* V. xvi. 526 He was created director-general of the finances. **1880** GROVE *Dict. Mus.* I. 412/2 The theatre was turned permanently into an opera-house.. The director was Mr. Frederick Beale. **1890** W. A. WALLACE *Only a Sister* 86 Stable-master and director-in-general of everything. **1891** S. C. SCRIVENER *Our Fields & Cities* 135 It is a better knowledge of the effect produced by inevitable 'weather' that the director of cultivation requires.

b. *spec.* A member of a board appointed to direct or manage the affairs of a commercial corporation or company.

1632 (*title*), A remonstrance of the directors of the Netherlands East India Company..touching the bloudy proceedings against the English Merchants..at Amboyna. **1673** *Phil. Trans.* VIII. 6113 He..is still one of the chief of the Court of Committees, which a foreigner would call Directors. **1697** *Lond. Gaz.* No. 3303/3 (Bank of Eng.), A General Court will be held for the Election of Twenty four Directors. **1711** ADDISON *Spect.* No. 3 ¶1, I looked into the great Hall where the Bank is kept, and was not a little pleased to see the Directors, Secretaries, and Clerks. **1732** POPE *Ep. Bathurst* 117 What made Directors cheat in South-sea year? **1758** JOHNSON *Idler* No. 29 ¶6, I was hired in the family of an East India director. **1825** SCOTT *Diary* 13 Dec. in *Lockhart*, Went to the yearly court of the Edinburgh Assurance Company, to which I am one of those graceful and useless appendages called Directors extraordinary. **1876** BESANT & RICE *Gold. Butterfly* vii, Gabriel Cassilis was a director of many companies.

c. *spec.* A member of the French Directory of 1795–9: see DIRECTORY *sb.* 6.

1798 CANNING *Elegy* xiii. in *Anti-Jacobin* (1852) 134 The French Directors Have thought the point so knotty. **1837** *Penny Cycl.* IX. 15/1 The executive power was entrusted to five directors.. The directors had the management of the military force, of the finances, and of the home and foreign departments.

d. *Eccl.* (chiefly in *R.C. Ch.*) An ecclesiastic holding the position of spiritual adviser to some particular person or society.

1669 WOODHEAD *St. Teresa* I. xiii. 80 He will have great need of a Directour, if he can meet with an experienced one. **1690** DRYDEN *Don Sebastian* II. i, He prates as if kings had not consciences, And none required directors but the crowd. **1697** JOS. WOODWARD *Relig. Soc.* ix. (1701) 133 That an orthodox and pious Minister should be chosen by each Society, as the Director and visitor of it. **1748** SMOLLETT *Rod. Rand.* iv, The parson of the parish, who was one of the executors, and had acted as ghostly director to the old man. **1849** MACAULAY *Hist. Eng.* II. 648 Tillotson..as a spiritual director, had, at that time, immense authority. **1877** *Daily News* 25 Oct. 5/7 A director is not the same as a confessor.. A confessor hears avowals of sin, a director is consulted in 'cases of conscience'.

†**e.** *Mus.* = DIRECT *sb.* 2. *Obs.*

1597 MORLEY *Introd. Mus.* 20 It is called an *Index* or *director*: for looke in what place it standeth, in that place doth the first note of the next verse stand. **1667** C. SIMPSON *Compend. Musick* 22 This mark √ is set to direct us where the first Note of the next five Lines doth stand, and is therefore called a *Directer*.

f. A small letter inserted by the scribe for the direction of the illuminator in the space left for an illuminated initial.

1881 BLADES *Caxton* (1882) 230 Space is left at the beginning of the chapters with a director, for the insertion of 2 to 5-line initials.

g. One who directs a film or play, etc. (see DIRECT *v.* 5 c). orig. *U.S.*

1911 *Moving Picture World* 22 July 108/2 The director explains to the players the action of a..scene. **1914** R. GRAU *Theatre of Science* 362 The world-famous director, D. W. Griffith. **1915** E. A. DENCH *Making Movies* i. 1 Good actors, authors and photographers are indispensable, but unless they are guided by a talented director, results will be disappointing. **1933** *Punch* 30 Aug. 234/2 Mr. Herbert Wilcox, its [*sc.* the film's] director, has skilfully overcome the difficulties of adaptation. **1938** W. S. MAUGHAM *Summing Up* 107 The director shouts 'curtain up'. *Ibid.*, I use the American word director rather than the English one, producer, because I think it better describes what should be the function of the person in question. **1944** *Sunday Times* 16 Jan. 2/6 In the meantime I pity the poor director, as we are beginning to call the producer. **1963** [see DIRECTORIAL *a.* 1 b].

†**2.** The dedicator of a book or the like. *Obs.*

1553 *Douglas' Æneis* (1710) 481 Here The Direkkare and Translatare of this Buke direkkis it.

3. a. One who or that which causes something to take a particular direction.

1646 SIR T. BROWNE *Pseud. Ep.* II. ii. 62 [The] Needle.. will not hang parallel, but decline at the north extreme, and at that part will first salute its Director.

†**b.** One who aims a missile. *Obs. rare.*

1632 LITHGOW. *Trav.* VII. 300 The best director may mistake his ayme.

c. *Surg.* A hollow or grooved instrument for directing the course of a knife or scissors in making an incision.

1667 R. LOWER in *Phil. Trans.* II. 544 Take it [the Incision-knife] out, and put in a Director, or a small Quill made like it. **1767** GOOCH *Treat. Wounds* I. 383 Carefully introduce a very small director, to avoid injuring the intestines. **1851–60** MAYNE *Expos. Lex.*, *Director*..grooved instrument for guiding a bistoury, etc., in certain operations.

d. 'A metallic rod in a non-conducting handle connected with one pole of a galvanic battery, for the purpose of transmitting the current to a part of the body.' *Syd. Soc. Lex.* 1883.

1795 CAVALLO *Electr.* II. (ed. 4) 122 Each of these instruments, justly called directors, consists of a knobbed brass wire. **1816** J. SMITH *Panorama Sc. & Art* II. 267 The other extremities of the wires must be fastened to the wires of the instruments YZ, which are called directors. **1846** JOYCE *Sci. Dial.* xv. 394 (*Electricity*).

e. An apparatus for directing a torpedo.

1889 C. SLEEMAN *Torpedoes & Torp. Warf.* (ed. 2) 252 The Torpedo director..consists of a brass circular casting ..faced out and graduated.

f. *Perspective.* (See quots.)

1876 GWILT *Archit.* Gloss., *Director of an Original Line*, the straight line passing through the directing point and the eye of a spectator. *Director of the Eye*, the intersection of the plane with the directing plane perpendicular to the original plane and that of the picture, and hence also perpendicular to the directing and vanishing planes.

g. *Geom.* = *director circle*: see below and cf. DIRECTRIX 2 b.

1852 GASKIN *Geom. Constr. Conic Sect.* Pref. 6 There are several remarkable properties of this locus, which, as far as the author is aware, have not been hitherto noticed, and he has found it convenient to denominate it the 'director' of the conic section, which in the case of the parabola coincides with the directrix.

4. *attrib.* and *Comb.* **director-circle** (of a conic), the locus of intersection of tangents at right angles to each other; so also ***director-sphere*** (of a surface of the second degree); **director-plane**, a fixed plane used in describing a surface, analogous to the line called a DIRECTRIX; **director-tube** (= sense 3 e).

Director-circle is also sometimes used to denote the circle described about a focus of an ellipse or hyperbola with radius = major axis. See TAYLOR *Anc. & Mod. Geom. of Conics* (1881) 90. (H. T. Gerrans.)

1864 WEBSTER, *Directer plane.* **1867** R. TOWNSEND in *Quart. Jrnl. Math.* VIII. 11 For the paraboloid..the director sphere opens out into a plane. *Ibid.* The director plane of the paraboloid. **1876** *Catal. Sci. App. S. Kens.* §99 The director planes..of these conoïds are at right angles to one another. **1882** *Daily News* 8 June 5/8 Equation to the Director Circle of a Conic, [by] Professor Wolstenholme. **1887** *Pall Mall G.* 25 Mar. 5/1 Director tube..is the telescopic apparatus through which aim is taken at the enemy's vessel, and by means of which the torpedo is fired.

di'rector, *v. nonce-wd.* [f. prec. sb.] *trans.* To manage as a director.

1892 *Pall Mall G.* 5 May 2/1 Another typical mine..the Langlaagte, which is directored by Mr. G. B——.

directoral (dɪˈrɛktərəl), *a. rare.* [f. as prec. + -AL[1].] Of, pertaining to, or of the nature of a director; directive, directory.

1874 GLADSTONE in *Daily News* 10 July 2/5 The business of law is to prevent and to punish crime, and directoral laws are comparatively rare. Directoral statutes, telling 20,000 clergymen what to do every day of their lives, and how their congregations are to be led..must of necessity be exceptional.

directorate (dɪˈrɛktərət). [mod. f. DIRECTOR: see -ATE[1]. Cf. F. *directorat*, 17th c. in Hatz.-Darm.] **a.** The office of a director, or of a body of directors; management by directors. **b.** *concr.* A board of directors.

1837 CARLYLE *Fr. Rev.* III. VII. viii. (1872) 272 Directorates, Consulates, Emperorships..Succeed this business in due series. **1858** *Sat. Rev.* V. 31/1 The Directorates of the East India Company and of the Bank of England are the Garter and the Bath of Commerce. **1861** SMILES *Engineers* II. 203 Under the joint directorate of the East and West India Dock Company. **1881** *Athenæum* 30 Apr. 601/3 The Musical Union..under the directorate of M. Lasserre. **1887** *Times* 2 Sept. 8 The successful efforts made..by the directorate of the Royal Gardens at Kew.

directoress: see DIRECTRESS.

directorial (dɪ-, daɪrɛk'tɔərɪəl), *a.* [f. L. *dīrectōri-us* (f. **dīrectōr-em* DIRECTOR) + -AL[1].]

1. a. Of, pertaining to, or of the nature of a director, or of direction or authoritative guidance.

1770 W. GUTHRIE *Geogr. Gram., Germ.* (T.), The emperour's power in the collective body, or the diet, is not directorial, but executive. **1839** G. S. FABER *Husenbeth's Professed Refut.* 37 *note*, Directorial books..with which I conclude Mr. Husenbeth, as a zealous Romish Priest, to be not altogether unacquainted.

b. *spec.* Of or pertaining to directors or the direction of films, etc.

1921 *Moving Picture Stories* 5 Aug. 26/3 Lloyd Ingraham is taking a month's vacation at the estate of David Kirkland, his directorial colleague. **1937** *Times* 25 Oct. 12/3 The directorial work was done by Mr. Clarence Brown. **1963** *Listener* 28 Feb. 392/3 BBC television has recently been.. holding on to the directorial talent it has itself developed and at the same time luring in the best directors from independent television.

2. Of or pertaining to a body of directors; *spec.* belonging to the French Directory (see DIRECTORY *sb.* 6).

1797 BURKE *Regic. Peace* III. Wks. VIII. 342 This object was to be weighed against the directorial conquests. **1804** *Ann. Rev.* II. 93/2 The national institute was established under the directorial government. **1818** JAS. MILL *Brit. India* II. v. ix. 706 Copies of all proceedings of Directorial and Proprietary Courts. **1862** LD. BROUGHAM *Brit. Const.* v. 69 The Directorial Constitution of 1795 gave one elector for every two hundred of the Primary Assembly. **1886** *Law Times* LXXX. 150/2 He brought..charges of misfeasance in their directorial duties against the two directors.

Hence **direc'torially** *adv.*, in a directorial manner; according to the principles of the French Directory.

1839 *Fraser's Mag.* XIX. 127 He lived..with kings, monarchically;..with the nobility, aristocratically;..with the convention, conventionally; with the directory directorially.

†**direc'torian,** *a. Obs. rare*$^{-1}$. [f. as prec. + -AN.] Pertaining to or of the nature of a directory: see DIRECTORY *sb.* 2 a.

1661 R. L'ESTRANGE *Relapsed Apostate* Introd. Biij b, Your New Liturgy it self, is down-right Directorian.

†**di'rectorize,** *v. Obs. rare.* [f. DIRECTOR + -IZE.] *trans.* To bring under the authority of a directory (see DIRECTORY *sb.* 2 a).

1651 RANDOLPH, etc. *Hey for Honesty* II. v, There would be no Presbyters to directorise you. **1659** GAUDEN *Tears of Ch.* 609 Undertaking to Directorize, to Unliturgize, to Catechize, and to Disciplinize their Brethren.

di'rectorship. [f. DIRECTOR + -SHIP.] The office or position of a director, guiding.

1720 A. HILL *Let. to G. Sewel* 3 Sept. Wks. 1753 I. 9 Yourself have much the fairest pretence to the directorship. **1795** WASHINGTON *Lett.* Writ. 1892 XIII. 106 The directorship of the mint. **1885** *Manch. Exam.* 12 Aug. 5/4 It is difficult to associate the idea of a railway directorship with the authorship of melodious verse.

directory (dɪ'rɛktərɪ), *a.* [ad. L. *dīrectōri-us* that directs, directive, f. **dīrectōr-em* DIRECTOR: see -ORY. Cf. obs. F. *directoire* (Cotgr.).] Serving or tending to direct; directive, guiding.

a **1450** LYDG. *Secrees* 593 Rewle directorye, set up in a somme. **1611** COTGR., *Directoire*, directorie, directiue, directing. **1613** M. RIDLEY *Magn. Bodies* 62 The iron barres ..being..placed North and South, do receive a polar vertue, and directory faculty. **1645** TOMBES *Anthropol.* 11 The power of Pastors..being..not in a compulsory, but a directory way. **1647** N. BACON *Disc. Gov. Eng.* I. xxiv. (1739) 41 Neither was the..Sheriff's work in that Court, other than directory or declaratory; for the Free-men were Judges of the fact. **1733** CHEYNE *Eng. Malady* I. Introd. (1734) 4 Having no necessary Connection with what is Directory or Practical. **1838-9** HALLAM *Hist. Lit.* III. IV. III. §7. 134 In the directory business of the confessional.

b. *spec.* Applied to that part of the law which directs what is to be done, esp. to 'a statute or part of a statute which operates merely as advice or direction to the person who is to do something pointed out, leaving the act or omission not destructive of the legality of what is done in disregard of the direction'.

1692 WASHINGTON tr. *Milton's Def. Pop.* v. (1851) 160 That Princes were not bound by any Laws, neither Coercive, nor Directory. **1765-9** BLACKSTONE *Comm.* (T.), Every law may be said to consist of several parts: one declaratory..another directory. **1884** *Law Times* 11 Oct. 383/2 There was no necessity..to comply with the directory provisions of the Act as to delivery of copies in England. **1886** *Law Times* LXXX. 241/1 The section is directory only, and a mortgage is not rendered invalid merely by reason of non-registration.

†**c.** *directory needle*, a magnetic needle. *Obs.*

1613 M. RIDLEY *Magn. Bodies* Pref. 2 A Directory-needle, or a little flie Magneticall in the boxe, fastened at the bottome in his convenient distance. *a* **1646** J. GREGORY *Terrestrial Globe* Posth. (1650) 281 This Needle..directing towards the North and South, the Mariners..call their Directorie-Needle. **1664** POWER *Exp. Philos.* III. 156 A well polished Stick of hard Wax (immediately after frication) will almost as vigorously move the Directory Needle, as the Loadstone it self.

directory (dɪ'rɛktərɪ), *sb.* [ad. med. or mod.L. *dīrectōrium*, subst. use of neuter of *dīrectōri-us*: see prec. and -ORY. Cf. F. *directoire*, 15th c. in Godef. *Suppl.*, It. *direttorio* a directorie (Florio).]

1. Something that serves to direct; a guide; *esp.* a book of rules or directions.

1543 J. HARRISON *Man of Synne* title-p., An alphabetycall dyrectorye or Table also in the ende therof. *c* **1550** (*title*), The Directory of Conscience, a profytable Treatyse to such that be tymorous..in Conscyence. **1621** MOLLE *Camerar. Liv. Libr.* IV. xx. 312 Sometimes a light occasion serueth as a directorie for the execution of most weighty things. **1675** TEONGE *Diary* (1825) 7 Wee..hast toward the Downes; looking for our dyrectory, the Foreland light. **1691-8** NORRIS *Pract. Disc.* 76 At a time when God had not given any express Directory for the Manners of Men. **1775** *Phil. Trans.* LXV. 184 The compilers of those popular directories. **1796** MORSE *Amer. Geog.* II. 454 The Rhodian law was the directory of the Romans in maritime affairs. **1878** J. P. HOPPS *Princ. Relig.* vii. 24 We might have preferred a written directory, or a visible teacher.

2. *Eccl.* A book containing directions for the order of public or private worship; *spec.* **a.** The set of rules for public worship compiled in 1644 by the Westminster Assembly, ratified by Parliament and adopted by the Scottish General Assembly in 1645.

1640 A. HENDERSON in C. G. M'Crie *Worship Presbyt. Scotl.* (1892) 194 [Expressing the wish that there were] one Directory for all the parts of the public worship of God. **1641** MILTON *Animadv.* xi. (1847) 93/1 Perhaps there may be usefully set forth by the Church a common directory of publick prayer. **1645** (*title*), The Directory for the Publick Worship of God; agreed upon by the Assembly of Divines at Westminster, with the assistance of Commissioners from the Church of Scotland. **1736** NEAL *Hist. Purit.* III. 157 The Parliament..imposed a fine upon those ministers that should read any other form than that contained in the Directory. **1827** HALLAM *Const. Hist.* (1876) II. x. 172 The English commissioners..demanded the complete establishment of a presbyterian polity, and the substitution of what was called the directory for the Anglican liturgy. **1892** C. G. M'CRIE *Worship Presbyt. Scotl.* 194 The word Directory exactly describes the nature and contents of a Presbyterian as distinguished from a liturgical Service-book.

fig. **1663** BUTLER *Hud.* I. iii. 1193 When Butchers were the only Clerks, Elders and Presbyters of Kirks, Whose Directory was to kill, And some believe it is so still.

b. *R.C. Ch.* A manual containing directions for the repetition of the daily offices; an ordinal.

1759 (*title*) The Laity's Directory (*Cath. Dict.*). **1837** (*title*) The Catholic Directory (*ibid.*). **1867** (*title*) Catholic Directory and Ordo for Ireland. **1885** *Catholic Dict.* 265/2 The *Catholic Directory*..familiar to English Catholics.. contains besides the Ordo a list of Clergy, Churches, etc.

3. a. A book containing one or more alphabetical lists of the inhabitants of any locality, with their addresses and occupations; also a similar compilation dealing with the members of a particular profession, trade, or association, as a *Clerical* or *Medical Directory*, etc.

1732 J. BROWN (*title*) The Directory, or List of Principal Traders in London. **1778** (*title*) Whitehead's Newcastle Directory, for 1778. **1838** GRAY *Lett.* (1893) 71 Returning to the hotel I consulted the city directory. **1888** A. K. GREEN *Behind Closed Doors* vi, Gryce..searched for an address in the directory.

b. = *telephone directory* (s.v. TELEPHONE *sb.*); freq. *attrib.*, as **directory enquiries**, the section of the telephone-exchange which supplies callers with information about telephone numbers, etc.

1908 *Daily Chron.* 21 Sept. 4/6 Daily reports of all new and changed names for the Directory are forwarded to this department. *Ibid.*, The latest Directory information. **1922** JOYCE *Ulysses* 697 Vulcanite automatic telephone receiver with adjacent directory. **1946** 'S. RUSSELL' *To Bed with Grand Music* v. 68 She hunted through telephone directories, questioned directory-enquiries. **1966** 'S. WOODS' *Enter Certain Murderers* ix. 157 Will you do something for me..? Get on to Directory Inquiries.

†**4.** Direction, ordering, control. *Obs. rare.*

1647 N. BACON *Disc. Govt. Eng.* I. xxxvii. (1739) 56 This manner of trial..and that of Ordeale [were] under the directory of the Clergy. *Ibid.* I. xlvii. (1739) 81 Present as Assistants in directory of judgment.

†**5.** *Surg.* = DIRECTOR 3 c. *Obs.*

1691 MULLINEUX in *Phil. Trans.* XVII. 822 By help of a Directory and Forceps..he brought away the Stone. **1754-64** SMELLIE *Midwif.* II. 18 This opening was enlarged upon a directory.

6. *Fr. Hist.* [transl. F. *Directoire.*] The executive body in France during part of the revolutionary period (Oct. 1795–Nov. 1799), consisting of five members called directors (*directeurs*).

[**1795**: see DIRECTOIRE.] **1796** WASHINGTON *Lett.* Writ. 1892 XIII. 273, I little expected..that a private letter of mine..would have found a place in the bureau of the French Directory. **1796** BURKE *Regic. Peace* I. Wks. VIII. 202 It is said by the directory..that we of the people are tumultuous for peace. **1796** —— *Corr.* (1844) IV. 397 Shall you and I find fault with the proceedings of France, and be totally indifferent to the proceedings of directories at home? **1810** T. JEFFERSON *Writ.* (1830) IV. 143 This does, in fact, transform the executive into a directory. **1867** G. F. CHAMBERS *Astron.* (1876) 66 General Buonaparte..when the Directory was about to give him a fête, was very much surprised.

7. A body of directors; = DIRECTORATE b.

1803 W. TAYLOR in *Ann. Rev.* I. 407 Within the proprietary, we had almost said within the directory of the company, persons are now found [etc.]. **1883** *Harper's Mag.* July 926/2 The principal working members of the directory.

directress (dɪ'rɛktrɪs). Also 6-7 -esse, 8 directoress. [f. DIRECTOR + -ESS.] A female who directs; †a governess. Also *fig.*

1580 SIDNEY *Arcadia* (1622) 336 Directresse of my destinie. **1647** R. STAPYLTON *Juvenal* 236 We stile him happy too, that..life for his directresse takes. **1737** JOHNSON *Irene* III. i, Reason! the hoary dotard's dull directress. **1741** RICHARDSON *Pamela* II. 64 You shall be the Directress of your own Pleasures, and your own Time. **1801** MISS C. SMITH *Solitary Wanderer* I. 240 Her cunning directress had foreseen that I should endeavour to obtain that proof of her regard. **1848** THACKERAY *Bk. Snobs* vi, She..is a directress of many meritorious charitable institutions. **1884** *Law Times* 4 Oct. 369/1 The mother..obtained a conditional order for a *habeas corpus* addressed to the directress of the home.

di'rectrice. [a. F. *directrice* (ad. med. or mod.L. *dīrectrix, dīrectrīc-em*), fem. of *directeur* DIRECTOR.] = prec.

1631 BRATHWAIT *Eng. Gentlew.* (1641) 323 Where vertue is not directrice. *c* **1730** BURT *Lett. N. Scotl.* (1818) I. 193 The directrice or governess who is a woman of quality. **1960** *Guardian* 25 July 4/3 The terrible Mlle Renée..who is the directrice of his salons. **1963** *N. & Q.* Mar. 112/1 Ibsen Club.—Founded November, 1909..with Miss Catherine Lewis as Directrice and Producer. **1969** *Daily Tel.* 13 Sept. 5/2 Madame Eve was also the training directrice of her attractive sales force.

directrix (dɪ'rɛktrɪks). Pl. -ices. [a. med. or mod.L. *dīrectrix*, fem. of **dīrector* DIRECTOR.]

1. = DIRECTRESS.

1622 H. SYDENHAM *Serm. Sol. Occ.* II. (1637) 112 As if the same pen had beene as well the directrix of the languages, as the truth. **1656** *Artif. Handsom.* (1662) 31 The Regent and directrix of the whole bodies culture, motion, and welfare. **1678** CUDWORTH *Intell. Syst.* I. iii. §37. 164 The several parts ..acting alone..without any common directrix. **1843** H. ROGERS *Ess.* (1860) III. 40 An unfailing directrix in all difficulties. **1892** J. RICKABY *Aquinas Ethicus* I. 224 Reason is the directrix of human acts.

2. *Geom.* †**a.** = DIRIGENT *sb.* 3; (see quot. 1753). *Obs.* **b.** A fixed line used in describing a curve or surface; *spec.* the straight line the distance from which of any point on a conic bears a constant ratio to the distance of the same point from the focus.

1702 RALPHSON *Math. Dict.*, Directrix of the Conchoid. *Ibid.* App., The two Conchoids, whereof the line CD will be the common Asymptote, which is also called the Directrix. **1753** CHAMBERS *Cycl. Supp.*, *Directrix*, in geometry, the line of motion, along which the describing line, or surface, is carried in the Genesis of any plane or solid figure. **1758** *Monthly Rev.* 403 A certain circle on the same surface, which is, as it were, the conical directrix. **1807** HUTTON *Course Math.* II. 117 If, through the point G, the line GH be drawn perpendicular to the axis, it is called the directrix of the parabola. **1840** LARDNER *Geom.* xx. 269 Lines drawn perpendicular to the transverse axis, through the points D,D', are called *directrices* of the ellipse.

3. *directrix of electrodynamic action* (of a given circuit): the magnetic force due to the circuit.

1881 MAXWELL *Electr. & Magn.* II. 157 Their resultant is called by Ampère the directrix of the electrodynamic action. *Ibid.* 158 We shall henceforth speak of the directrix as the magnetic force due to the circuit.

†**di'recture.** *Obs. rare*$^{-1}$. [ad. L. *dīrectūra* (in Vitr. a making straight or levelling), f. *dīrect-* ppl. stem of L. *dīrigĕre* to DIRECT.] The action of directing; direction.

a **1677** MANTON *Disc. Peace* Wks. 1871 V. ii. 167 Led by the fair directure and fair invitation of God's providence.

direful ('daɪəfʊl), *a.* [f. DIRE *a.* (or *sb.*) + -FUL.] Fraught with dire effects; dreadful, terrible.

1583 STUBBES *Anat. Abus.* I. (1879) 70 Except these women weare minded to..folowe their direfull wayes in this cursed kind of..Pride. **1590** SPENSER *F.Q.* I. xi. 55 Whenas the direfull feend She saw not stirre..She nigher drew. **1604** SHAKS. *Oth.* v. i. 38 'Tis some mischance, the voyce is very direfull. **1634** MILTON *Comus* 357 The direful grasp Of savage hunger, or of savage heat. **1715-20** POPE *Iliad* I. 1 Achilles' wrath, to Greece the direful spring Of woes unnumber'd. **1781** GIBBON *Decl. & F.* II. xlii. 561 Their sincerity was attested by direful imprecations. **1825** J. NICHOLSON *Operat. Mechanic* 477 The direful effects of using lead in the manufacture of pottery. **1850** MERIVALE *Rom. Emp.* (1865) II. xi. 8 Prodigies of direful import.

Hence **'direfully** *adv.*, dreadfully, terribly; **'direfulness**, dreadfulness, terribleness.

a **1656** USSHER *Ann.* (1658) 244 Curtius..describes..the direfullnesse of the tempest. **1756** J. WARTON *Ess. Pope* (T.), The direfulness of this pestilence is..emphatically set forth in these few words. **1775** ASH, *Direfully* (..not much used). **1845-6** TRENCH *Huls. Lect.* Ser. II. iv. 196 These convictions ..men were too direfully earnest in carrying..out. **1848** THACKERAY *Van. Fair* lxii, He passed the night direfully sick in his carriage.

direge, obs. form of DIRGE.

direkkare, obs. Sc. form of DIRECTOR.

direly ('daɪəlɪ), *adv.* [f. DIRE *a.* + -LY[2].] In a dire manner; dreadfully; in a way that bodes calamity.

1610 G. FLETCHER *Christ's Vict.* III, Screech-owls direly chant. **1630** DRAYTON *David & Goliah* (L.), And of his death he direly had forethought. **1633** P. FLETCHER *Purple Isl.* XII. xxxix, Direly he blasphemes. **1824** CAMPBELL *Theodric* 131 A check in frantic war's unfinished game, Yet dearly bought, and direly welcome, came. **1848** THACKERAY *Van. Fair* xxiv, Some great catastrophe..was likely direly to affect Master G.

†**di'rempt**, *ppl. a. Obs.* [ad. L. *dirempt-us*, pa. pple. of *dirimĕre* to separate, divide, f. *dir-*, DIS-1 apart + *emĕre* to take.] Distinct, divided, separate.

1561 STOW *Eng. Chron.* Aij, (N.), Bodotria and Glota have sundry passages into the sea, and are clearly dirempt one from the other.

di'rempt, *v.* [f. L. *dirempt-* ppl. stem of *dirimĕre*: see prec.] *trans.* To separate, divide; to break off. Also **di'rempted** *ppl. a.*

1586 J. HOOKER *Girald. Irel.* in Holinshed *Chron.* II. 52/1 That if either part refused to stand to his arbitrement, the definitive strife might be dirempted by sentance. **1657** TOMLINSON *Renou's Disp.* 287 Leaves like Fig leaves dirempted into three angles. **1885** W. JAMES *Meaning of Truth* (1909) i. 5 Does not the word 'content' suggest that the feeling has already dirempted itself as an act from its content as an object? **1900** —— *Let.* 10 June in R. B. Perry *Tht. & Char. W.J.* (1935) I. 647 Once as streams of individual thinking, once as physical permanents, without the *immediately real* ever having been either of these dirempted things.

diremption (dɪ'rɛm(p)ʃən). Now *rare.* [ad. L. *diremptiōn-em*, n. of action f. *dirimĕre* to separate, divide.] **a.** A forcible separation or severance.

1623 COCKERAM, *Diremption*, a separation. **1678** HOBBES *Decam.* iii. 25 They cannot be parted except the Air or other matter can enter and fill the space made by their diremption. **1874** C. E. APPLETON in *Life & Lit. Relics* (1881) 159 The diremption of the two kinds of development may be possible to the individual. **1876** *Contemp. Rev.* XXVII. 960 The successive stages..on the way through self-diremption to the return unto self.

b. *spec.* Forcible separation of man and wife.

1649 BP. HALL *Cases Consc.* (1650) 331 The displeasure of the Canon law against such marriages is so high flowne, that no lesse can take it off then an utter diremption of them. *a* **1653** GOUGE *Comm. Heb.* xiii. 4 Marriage..ought not to be dissolved, but by diremption, which is, by severing man and wife by death.

c. *Bot.* An abnormal separation or displacement of leaves.

1869 M. T. MASTERS *Veget. Teratol.* 87 The term 'diremption' has sometimes been applied to cases where leaves are thus apparently dragged out of position. **1900** B. D. JACKSON *Gloss. Bot. Terms*, *Diremption*, the occasional separation or displacement of leaves.

direness ('daɪənɪs). [f. DIRE *a.* + -NESS.] The quality of being dire or of dreadful operation.

1605 SHAKS. *Macb.* v. v. 14, I haue supt full with horrors; Direnesse, familiar to my slaughterous thoughts, Cannot once start me. **1610** HEALEY *St. Aug. Citie of God* 356 Trismegistus and Capella averre the direnesse of his [Mercury's] name. **1833** M. SCOTT *Tom Cringle* xvii. (1859) 458 Direness of this kind cannot daunt me.

direnȝe *v.*, obs. form of DERAIGN, to decide.

†**di'reption**. *Obs.* [ad. L. *dīreptiōn-em*, n. of action f. *dīripĕre* to tear asunder, lay waste, snatch away, f. *dī-*, *dis-* asunder + *rapĕre* to snatch, tear away; cf. 16th c. F. *direption* (Godef.).]

1. The sacking or pillaging of a town, etc.

1528 GARDINER in Pocock *Rec. Ref.* I. I. 118 Such as before dwelt in Rome, and in the direption lost their substance. **1536** BELLENDEN *Cron. Scot.* (1821) I. 181 Calphurnius, nochtwithstanding thir direptionis, went forthwart with his army. **1611** SPEED *Hist. Gt. Brit.* VII. i. 191 The whole Country by these continuall direptions, was vtterly depriued of the staffe of food. **1660** GAUDEN *Brownrig* 203 The arrears..due to him before the direption and depraedation. **1828** G. S. FABER *Sacr. Cal. Prophecy* (1844) III. 133 The direption and spoliation of the Empire.

2. The action of snatching away or dragging apart violently.

1483 CAXTON *Gold. Leg.* 76/2 For we haue not obeyed thy comandementis, therfore we ben betaken in to dyrepcion, captyuyte, deth. **1550** BALE *Apol.* 21 A bonde indispensable by autorite of the churche, and a dyrepcion or sackynge of matrimony. **1623** COCKERAM, *Direption*, a violent taking away. **1650** ASHMOLE *Chym. Collect.*, *Arcanum* (ed. 3) 238/2 Of the conflict of the Eagle and the Lion..the more Eagles, the shorter the Battaile, and the direption of the Lyon will more readily follow. *a* **1693** URQUHART *Rabelais* III. xlviii. 393 Direption, tearing and rending asunder of their Joynts.

†**direp'titious**, *a. Obs.*$^{-0}$ [f. L. *dīrept-us*, pa. pple. of *dīripĕre* (see DIREPTION) + -ITIOUS (after *surreptitious*).] Characterized by direption, plundering, or pillaging. Hence †**direp'titiously** *adv.*, by way of pillaging or plundering.

1532 R. BOWYER in Strype *Eccl. Mem.* I. xvii. 135 The grants surreptitiously and direptitiously obtained.

diresioun, obs. form of DERISION.

dirge (dɜːdʒ), *sb.* Forms: α. 3–7 (8–9 *Hist.*) dirige, (4–6 dir-, dyr-, der-, -ige(e, -yge, -ege, -egi, -egy, 6–7 dirigie). β. 6 *Sc.* dergie, (6– 8 dregy, dredgy, drudgy), 7 dirgie, 7–8 dirgee. γ. 4 derge, 5 derche, dorge, 5–6 dyrge, 6– dirge. [Originally *dirige*, the first word of the Latin antiphon *Dirige, Domine, Deus meus, in conspectu tuo viam meam* 'Direct, O Lord, my God, my way in thy sight', taken from Psalm v. 8.]

1. In the Latin rite: The first word of the antiphon at Matins in the Office of the Dead, used as a name for that service; sometimes extended to include the Evensong (*Placebo*), or, according to Rock, also the Mass (*Requiem*).

a **1225** *Ancr. R.* 22 Efter euesong anonriht siggeð ower Placebo eueriche niht hwon ȝe beoð eise; bute ȝif hit beo holiniht vor þe feste of nie lescuns þet kumeð amorwen, biuore Cumplie, oðer efter Uhtsong, siggeð Dirige, mit þreo psalmes, and mit þreo lescuns eueriche niht sunderliche..et Placebo ȝe muwen sitten vort Magnificat, and also et Dirige. *c* **1320** *Sir Beues* 2902 Beues is ded in bataile þar fore..Hit is Beues dirige! **1350** *Eng. Gilds* (1870) 35 He ssal sende forthe þe bedel to alle þe breþeren and þe systeren, þat þey bien at the derge of þe body. **1408** *E.E. Wills* (1882) 15 Brede & Ale to Spende atte my dyryge. *c* **1420** *Chron. Vilod.* 2170 He continuede algate..In doyng of masse, of derche, & of almys-dede. **1494** in *Eng. Gilds* (1870) 191 When any Broder or Suster of this Gilde is decessed oute off this worlde..yᵉ Steward of this Gilde shall doo Rynge for hym, and do to say a Placebo and dirige, wᵗ a masse on yᵉ morowe of Requiem. **1537** WRIOTHESLEY *Chron.* (1875) I. 71 Allso a solempne dirige songen in everye parishe churche in London. **1539** BP. HILSEY *Manual of Prayers* in *Three Primers Hen. VIII* 407 Of those old Jewish customs hath there crept into the church a custom to have a certain suffrages for the dead, called Dirige, of Dirige, the first anthem hereof; but by whom or when these suffrages were made, we have no sure evidence. *Ibid.* 408 For this only cause have I also set forth in this Primer a Dirige; of the which the three first lessons are of the miseries of mans life; the middle of the funeral of the dead corpse; and the last three are of the last resurrection. **1591** SPENSER *M. Hubberd* 453 They whilome used..to say..Their Diriges, their Trentals, and their shrifts. **1642** ROGERS *Naaman* 165 Give moneyes and yearly gifts to a Priest to read Masse or Dirigies for the weale of his soule after his decease. *a* **1654** SELDEN *Table-T.* (Arb.) 88 The Priest said Dirgies, and twenty Dirgies at fourpence a piece comes to a Noble. **1711** *C.-M. Lett. to Curat* 7 This Primer consisted of the very same parts that the Popish Primer does, viz. of Mattins..Dirige..and such other Ecclesiastical Jargon. **1846–7** MASKELL *Mon. Rit.* II. 111 *note*, The Office of the Dead (or Dirge), consisted of two parts: the Evensong or Vespers: and the Matins. **1849** ROCK *Ch. of Fathers* II. 503 As the first anthem at matins commenced with *Dirige*..the whole of the morning's service, including the Mass, came to be designated a *Dirige* or Dirge. **1875** J. T. FOWLER in *Ripon Ch. Acts* (Surtees) 83 *note*, The 'Vigiliæ Mortuorum'..consisting of Vespers, called 'Placebo'..and Matins, called 'Dirige', from its first antiphon, 'Dirige Domine', etc.

2. *transf.* A song sung at the burial of, or in commemoration of, the dead; a song of mourning or lament. Also *fig.*

1500–20 DUNBAR *Dregy* 111 Heir endis Dunbaris Dergy to the King, bydand to lang in Stirling. **1593** SHAKS. *Lucr.* 1612 And now this pale swan in her watery nest Begins the sad dirge of her certain ending. **1638** SIR T. HERBERT *Trav.* (ed. 2) 228 Most memorable battels; as when Crassus lost his life, Valerian and others, occasioning those dirgees of the Roman Poets. **1655** FULLER *Ch. Hist.* VI. 297 Musick, which in some sort sung her own Dirige..at the dissolution of Abbies. **1713** POPE in *Guardian* No. 40 In another of his pastorals, a shepherd utters a dirge not much inferior to the former. **1814** SCOTT *Ld. of Isles* II. i, Let mirth and music sound the dirge of Care! **1819** SHELLEY *Ode West Wind* ii. 9 Thou dirge Of the dying year. **1832** HT. MARTINEAU *Ireland* iv. 65 The waves..renewed their dirge with every human life that they swept away. **1887** BOWEN *Virg. Æneid* VI. 220 Dirge at an end, the departed is placed in the funeral bed.

3. A funeral feast or carouse; cf. *dirge-ale* in 4; quot. 1408 in 1. (*Sc.*)

c **1730** BURT *Lett. N. Scotl.* (1754) I. 268–9 (Jam.) Wine is filled about as fast as it can go round; till there is hardly a sober person among them..This last homage they call the Drudgy [*read* Dredgy], but I suppose they mean the Dirge, that is, a service performed for a dead person. ? *a* **1750** in Herd *Collect. Sc. Songs* (1776) II. 30 (Jam.) But he was first hame at his ain ingle-side, And he helped to drink his ain dirgie.

4. *attrib.* and *Comb.*, as ***dirge-man***, ***-mass***, ***-note***, ***-priest***; ***dirge-like*** adj.; also **dirge-ale**, an ale-drinking at a funeral (cf. quot. 1408 in 1); **dirge-groat**, **-money**, money paid for singing the dirge.

1587 HARRISON *England* II. i. (1877) I. 32 The superfluous numbers of..church-ales, helpe-ales, and soule-ales, called also *dirge-ales..are well diminished. **1564** BECON *Displaying Popish Mass* Prayers, etc. (1844) 258 Have ye not well deserved your *dirige-groat and your dinner? **1721** STRYPE *Eccl. Mem.* III. xii. 114 The priests did not seldom quarrel with their parishioners for..dirge-groats and such like: for that was the usual reward for singing mass for a soul. **1561** BP. PARKHURST *Injunctions*, Whether they vse to sing any number of psalmes, *dirige lyke at the buryall of the dead? **1827** KEBLE *Chr. Year* Restoration iii, One dirge-like note Of orphanhood and loss. **1862** LYTTON *Str. Story* II. 91 Other dogs in the distant village..bayed in a dirge-like chorus. **1824** J. SYMMONS *Æschylus' Agamemnon* 99 Why for Loxias woe, woe, woe? He has no *dirgemen. **1563–87** FOXE *A. & M.* (1684) III. 544 To say a *Dirge Mass after the old custom, for the Funeral of King Edward. **1564** *Brief Examinat.* ******, You can be content *Dirige money be conuerted to preachynges. *a* **1835** MRS. HEMANS *Swan & Skylark* Poems (1875) 553 The *dirge-note and the song of festival. **154.** *Def. Priests' Marriage* 24 (Strype *Mem.* I. lii. 393) Mass-priests, *dirige-priests, chantry-priests, sacrificing-priests.

dirge, *v. rare.* [f. prec. sb.] **a.** *trans.* To sing a dirge over, commit with a dirge.

a **1845** HOOD *Loss Pegasus* ii, Dirged by Sea Nymphs to his briny grave! —— *She is far fr. Land* 62 Waves over-surging her, Syrens a-dirgeing her.

b. To sing as a dirge.

1895 *Punch* 5 Oct. 162/2 They might all dirge in chorus the old duet of 'Again we come to thee, Savoy'.

c. *intr.* To utter a dirge.

1907 C. E. MULFORD *Bar-20* xxi. 206 Shortly afterward the mournful cry of a whip-poor-will dirged out on the early morning air. **1921** *Chambers's Jrnl.* 211/2 The dead tops of the Gwynfrwyn trees were swaying and dirging dismally.

dirge(e, var. DURZEE.

dirgee, var. of DURZEE, *Anglo-Ind.*, tailor.

dirgeful ('dɜːdʒfʊl), *a.* [f. DIRGE + -FUL.] Mournful, full of lamentation, moaning, wailing.

1787 BURNS *To Miss Cruikshank*, Thou, amid the dirgeful sound, Shed thy dying honours round. **1794** COLERIDGE *Chatterton*, Soothed sadly by the dirgeful wind. *a* **1851** MOIR *Poems, To a wounded Ptarmigan* x, While the dirgeful night-breeze only Sings.

†**dirgy** ('dɜːdʒɪ), *a. rare*$^{-1}$. [f. DIRGE *sb.* + -Y.] Of the nature of a dirge.

1830 W. TAYLOR *German Poetry* II. 47 How glumly sownes yon dirgy song! [*affected archaism.*]

‖**di'rhem**, **dirham**. Also **derham**. [Arab. *dirham*, *dirhim*, ad. L. *drachma*, Gr. δραχμή: see DRACHM. Formerly in It. *diremo*.] An Arabian measure of weight, originally two-thirds of an Attic drachma (44·4 grains troy), now used with varying weight from Morocco to Abyssinia, Turkey, and Persia; in Egypt (1895) = 47·661 troy grains. Also a small silver coin of the same weight, used under the caliphs, and (1895) in Morocco, where its value was less than 4*d.* English.

1788 GIBBON *Decl. & F.* lii. V. 397 *note*, Elmacin..compared the weight of the best or common gold dinar, to the drachm or dirhem of Egypt. **1850** W. IRVING *Mahomet* xxxix. (1853) 199 Omar Ibn Al Hareth declares that Mahomet, at his death, did not leave a golden dinar nor a silver dirhem. **1872** E. W. ROBERTSON *Hist. Ess.* 3 In Turkey, Syria, Egypt, Barbary and Arabia, the Dirhem, as a standard of weight, continues at the present day to be divided into 16 killos, or carats, and 64 grains. *Ibid.* 48 *note*, The drachma of Constantinople..the original of the Egyptian dirhem. **1885** BURTON *Arab. Nts.* (1887) III. 36, I now adjudge him the sum of ten thousand dirhams. **1970** *New Yorker* 29 Aug. 48/2 There were ten dirhams in her pocket. **1971** *Ashmolean Mus. Rep. of Visitors 1970* 43 The purchase of a group of silver dirhams of the 'Arab-Sasanian' type.

dirhombohedron (daɪrɒmbəʊ'hiːdrən). *Cryst.* (See quot., and DI- *pref.*^{2} 1.)

1878 GURNEY *Crystallogr.* 66 The dirhombohedron is a double six-sided pyramid, whose faces are similar isosceles triangles.

†**di'ribitory**. *Obs.* [ad. L. *diribitōrium*, f. *diribēre* to distribute, f. *dir-*, *dis-* asunder + *habēre* to hold.] (See quot.)

1656 BLOUNT *Glossogr.*, *Diribitory*, a place wherein Souldiers are numbered, mustered, and receive their pay; A place where the Romans gave their voyces.

dirige ('dɪrɪdʒiː), obs. and historical f. DIRGE.

†**dirigent** ('dɪrɪdʒənt), *a.* and *sb. Obs.* [ad. L. *dīrigent-em*, pr. pple. of *dīrigĕre* to DIRECT.]

A. *adj.* **1.** That directs, directing, directive.

1617 COLLINS *Def. Bp. Ely* II. ix. 359 Imperant only, not elicient; dirigent, not exequent, as your School-men loue to speak.

2. *Pharm.* Formerly applied to certain ingredients in prescriptions which were held to guide the action of the rest.

1851–60 in MAYNE *Expos. Lex.*

3. *Geom.* (See quot.)

1704 J. HARRIS *Lex. Techn.* (J.), The dirigent line in geometry is that along which the line describent is carried in the generation of any figure.

B. *sb.* **1.** = DIRECTOR 1.

1756 T. AMORY *Life Buncle* (1770) I. xiii. 45 You will be the guide and dirigent of all my notions and my days.

2. *Pharm.* A dirigent ingredient: cf. A. 2.

1854–67 C. A. HARRIS *Dict. Med. Terminol.* 217 *Dirigent*, that constituent in a prescription which directs the action of the associated substances.

3. *Geom.* A dirigent line: see A. 3.

1706 PHILLIPS (ed. Kersey), *Dirigent*, the Line of Motion along which, the Describent Line or Surface is carry'd in the Genesis or Production of any plain or solid Figure. **1796** in HUTTON *Math. Dict.*

dirigibility (ˌdɪrɪdʒɪ'bɪlɪtɪ). [f. DIRIGIBLE *a.*: see -ILITY.] The quality of being dirigible; controllability.

1875 *Q. Rev.* CXXXIX. 137 One most important use of dirigibility would be in facilitating the descent, and in avoiding the many dangers to which the aeronaut, in his present helpless position, is so often exposed. **1902** *Westm. Gaz.* 25 Mar. 9/2 Proving the dirigibility of the aerostat. **1903** *Ibid.* 16 Nov. 7/3 Wireless dirigibility experiments. **1908** *B'ham Inst. Mag.* Jan. 254 The problem of..perfect dirigibility of dynamic flying machines.

dirigible ('dɪrɪdʒɪb(ə)l), *a.* and *sb.* Also 7 derigible, 9 dirigeable. [ad. L. type **dīrigibil-is*, f. *dīrigĕre* to DIRECT. Cf. mod.F. *dirigeable*.]

A. *adj.* Capable of being directed or guided.

1581 LAMBARDE *Eiren.* I. x. (1588) 62 It would avayle greatly to the furtherance of the Service, if the *Dedimus potestatem* to giue these Oaths were dirigible to the Iustices (and none other). **1649** BP. REYNOLDS *Hosea* vii. 119 The proper conclusions deducible from these principles, and derigible unto those ends. **1688** NORRIS *Theory Love* II. i. 63 Why love as Dirigible is made the subject of Morality rather than understanding. **1833** SIR W. HAMILTON *Discuss.* (1852) 137 Intellectual operations.. in so far as they were dirigible, or the subject of laws. **1881** *Sat. Rev.* LI. 110/1 For eighteen years.. no attempt was made to render balloons dirigible. **1884** *Cassell's Fam. Mag.* 764 The balloon was dirigeable. **1887** *St. Jas'. Gaz.* 23 Sept. 5 A greater speed than has yet been attained by any other dirigible torpedo.

B. *sb.* A dirigible balloon or airship. Also *transf.* (Cf. Fr. *dirigeable* sb.)

1885 *Sci. Amer.* 26 Dec. 405/1 He has devised two systems of dirigible balloons... The first of these, the independent dirigible, is of much the greater importance. **1907** *Daily Chron.* 26 July 5/6 He had been up in a captive balloon, but never before in a dirigible. **1910** *Daily Mail* 6 June 8/1 Night-flying dirigibles. **1927** *Glasgow Herald* 28 Apr. 15 A new dictionary of air terms has been compiled... So far as England is concerned, the word 'dirigible' will disappear and only 'airship' remain. **1953** [see AQUALUNG].

‖**dirigisme** (diriʒizm). Also **dirigism.** [Fr. *dirigisme*, f. *diriger* to direct.] The policy of state direction and control in economic and social matters. Also *transf.* Hence **dirigiste, dirigistic** *adjs.*

1951 *Archivum Linguisticum* III. 220 Linguistic *dirigisme*, standards of correctness in a constantly evolving language. **1952** V. A. DEMANT *Religion & Decline of Capitalism* iv. 94 These are but a few of the reasons for the increasing *dirigisme* of economic life on the part of the state. **1957** *Times* 26 Feb. 4/3 Their [Sinn Fein] programme is a strange amalgam of bombast, Chauvinism, and dirigism. **1957** *Economist* 12 Oct. 16/2 The French hope that the new community will pursue a 'dirigiste', or at least a Keynesian policy regulating and guiding investment on a European scale, and ensuring that the Germans do not upset the whole scheme by deflating too much. **1959** *Times Rev. Industry* Dec. 75/3 A 'manifest crisis'.. accompanied by dirigistic measures such as restrictions on production. **1967** *New Scientist* 9 Nov. 329/1 He warned his listeners against 'too much dirigism', reminding them of the USSR where crude political interference had forced men into politically neutral fields. **1971** HALSEY & TROW *Brit. Academics* iv. 88 The liberal critique.. fears.. that 'dirigism' will supplant university autonomy.

dirigo-motor (ˌdɪrɪgəʊˈməʊtə(r)), *a. Physiol.* [irreg. f. L. *dīrig-* stem of *dīrigĕre* to DIRECT + MOTOR.] That both produces and directs muscular motion.

1855 H. SPENCER *Princ. Psychol.* (1872) I. I. iii. 49 Each efferent nerve is a dirigo-motor agent.

diriment (ˈdɪrɪmənt), *a.* [ad. L. *diriment-em*, pr. pple. of *dirimĕre* to separate, interrupt, frustrate: see DIREMPT. Cf. F. *dirimant* that nullifies (a marriage).] That renders absolutely void; nullifying; chiefly in ***diriment impediment***, one that renders marriage null and void from the beginning.

1848 J. WATERWORTH *Council of Trent* (1888) p. ccxxv, The Church having authority to establish.. new essential and diriment impediments of matrimony. **1875** *Contemp. Rev.* XXVI. 423 There is another diriment impediment which has lately attracted more than ordinary attention. **1888** *Ch. Times* 2 Mar. 179 In England.. marriages, not hindered by a diriment impediment, are valid wherever solemnised.

† **ˈdirity.** *Obs. rare.* [ad. L. *dīritās*, f. *dīrus* fell, DIRE.] Direness, dreadfulness.

c **1586** HOOKER *Serm. Pride* v. Wks. III. 794 So unappeasable is the rigour and dirity of his corrective justice. **1623** COCKERAM, *Diritie*, crueltie, fiercenesse. **1656** in BLOUNT *Glossogr.* **1721–1800** in BAILEY.

dirk (dɜːk), *sb.* Forms: 7 **dork,** 7–9 **durk,** (7 **durke**), 8– **dirk.** [Origin unknown. Found in 1602 spelt *dork*, then common from second half of 17th c. as *durk*; the spelling *dirk* was adopted without authority in Johnson's Dict. 1755, app. from the falling together of *ir*, *ur*, in Eng. pronunciation; cf. *Burmah*, *Birmah*, *dirt*, *durt*, etc. Although early quots. and Johnson's explanation suggest that the name was Gaelic, there is no such word in that language, where the weapon is called *biodag*. O'Reilly's *duirc* is merely the 18th c. English word spelt Irish-fashion.

The suggestion has been offered that the word may be the Da. *Dirk*, familiar form of the personal name *Diederik*, which name, in Ger. *dietrich*, LG. *dierker* (Bremen Wb.), Da. *dirik*, *dirk*, Sw. *dyrk*, is actually given to a pick-lock; but besides the difficulty that *dirk* is not the original form of the English word, no such sense as 'dagger' belongs to the continental word. If of continental origin, the earliest form *dork* might possibly be a soldier's or sailor's corruption of Du., Da., Sw. *dolk*, Ger. *dolch*, dagger.]

1. A kind of dagger or poniard: *spec.* **a.** The dagger of a Highlander. †**b.** 'A small sword or dagger formerly worn by junior naval officers on duty.' Smyth *Sailor's Word-bk.* (*Obs.*).

1602 *Form of ancient trial by battel* in Nicholson and Burn's *Hist. Westmoreland* (1777) I. 596 *note*, Two Scotch daggers or dorks at their girdles. ?**16..** *Robin Hood & Beggar* II. 90 (Ritson) 1795 I. 106 A drawen durk to his breast. **1680** G. HICKES *Spirit of Popery* 36 Armed men, who ..fell upon them with Swords and Durkes. **1681** COLVIL *Whigs Supplic.* (1695) 4 Some had Halbards, some had Durks, Some had crooked swords like Turks. **1724** RAMSAY *Tea-t. Misc.* (1733) I. 7 With durk and pistol by his side. *a* **1740** T. TICKELL *Imit. Prophecy Nereus* 29 The shield, the pistol, durk, and dagger. **1746** *Rep. Cond. Sir J. Cope* 184 Some few of their Men.. arm'd only with Durk, Sword, and Pistol. **1755** JOHNSON, *Dirk*, a kind of Dagger used in the Highlands of Scotland. **1786** BURNS *Earnest Cry & Prayer* xvii, Her tartan petticoat she'll kilt, An' durk an' pistol at her belt, She'll tak the streets. **1794** —— *Let. to J. Johnson* ? Feb. Wks. 1857 IV. 58, I have got a Highland dirk, for which I have great veneration, as it once was the dirk of Lord Balmerino. **1806** *Gazetteer Scotl.* Introd. 15 The Highland durk is certainly an imitation of the Roman short dagger. **1822** J. FLINT *Lett. Amer.* 113 The dirk has a pointed blade, four or five inches long, with a small handle. It is worn within the vest, by which it is completely concealed. **1830** SCOTT *Demonol.* x. 396 We saw the dirk and broadsword of Rorio Mhor. **1833** MARRYAT *P. Simple* iv, I.. wrote another [letter] asking for a remittance to purchase my dirk and cocked hat. **1839–40** W. IRVING *Wolfert's R.* (1855) 193, I pocketed the purse.. put a dirk in my bosom, girt a couple of pistols round my waist. **1881** JOWETT *Thucyd.* I. 162 The highland Thracians.. are independent and carry dirks.

2. *Comb.*, as ***dirk-hilt, -knife***; ***dirk-like*** adj.; **dirk-hand,** the hand that grasps the dirk; **dirk-knife,** a large clasp-knife with a dirk-shaped blade.

1835 C. F. HOFFMAN *Winter in West* I. 212, I.. gave the game the *coup de grace* with a dirk-knife which I had about me. **1837** LOCKHART *Scott* xli. (1839) V. 340 Its bottom is of glass, that he who quaffed might keep his eye the while upon the dirk hand of his companion. **1843** 'R. CARLTON' *New Purchase* I. xx. 189 Tom [was] talking and laughing away like a fellow whittling poplar with a dirk knife! **1851** D. WILSON *Preh. Ann.* (1863) II. IV. vi. 347 Ivory dirk-hilts elegantly turned and wrought by the hand.

dirk (dɜːk), *v.* [f. prec. sb.] *trans.* To stab with a dirk.

a **1689** W. CLELAND *Poems* (1697) 13 For a misobliging word She'll durk her neighbour o'er the board. *Ibid.* 15 Had it not been for the Life-guard She would have durkt him. **1808** J. BARLOW *Columb.* VII. 356 They.. Wrench off the bayonet and dirk the foe. **1822** SCOTT *Nigel* iii, 'I thought of the Ruthvens that were dirked in their ain house.' **1840** R. H. DANA *Bef. Mast* xxvii. 88 With a fair prospect of being stripped and dirked.

dirk(e, -ness, obs. ff. DARK, -NESS.

dirl, *v. Sc.* and *north. dial.* [Allied to Sc. *thirl* to pierce, to THRILL, and to DRILL. It is not a simple phonetic development of *thirl*, since *th* does not become *d* in the north; but it seems to be due to some onomatopœic modification.]

1. *trans.* To pierce, to thrill; to cause to vibrate, cause a thrilling sensation in by a sharp blow.

1513 [see DIRLING *vbl. sb.* below]. **1568** *Bannatyne MS.* in Sibbald *Chron. Scot. Poetry* (1802) III. 236 (Jam.) Young Pirance.. Was dirlit with lufe of fair Meridiane. **1826** T. WILSON *Pitman's Pay* (1872) 8 (Northumb. Gloss.) Thy tongue.. dirls my lug like wor smith's hammer. **1837** LOWELL *Lett.* (1894) I. 23 But she, alas! my heartstrings dirls. **1871** P. H. WADDELL *Psalms* 4 Horns o' the siller.. dirlin the lug an' wauk'nin the heart. **1892** *Northumbld. Gloss.* s.v., To 'dirl the elbow' is to strike the sensitive bone of that part—the 'funny bone', as it is called.

2. *intr.* To vibrate as when pierced or sharply struck, or in response to sound; to have a thrilling sensation, to tingle.

1715 RAMSAY *Christ's Kirk* II. 7 Meg Wallet wi' her pinky een Gart Lawrie's heart-strings dirle. **1790** BURNS *Tam o' Shanter* 124 He screw'd the pipes and gart them skirl, Till roof and rafters a' did dirl. *a* **1835** HOGG *Ringan & May* 38 Though.. the merle gar all the greenwood dirl. **1869** *Lonsdale Gloss., Dirl*, to tingle, or thrill with pain, the sensation being the result of a blow or other violence. **1884** *Nugæ Eccles.* I. 26 When I smash the table till it dirls.

b. To produce a vibrating sound; to ring.

1823 GALT *R. Gilhaize* I. 131 (Jam.) Twisting a rope of straw round his horse's feet, that they might not dirl or make a din on the stones. **1892** *Northumbld. Gloss., Dirl*, to produce a deafening or a painful vibration. 'Hear hoo the win's dorlin'.

Hence **ˈdirling** *vbl. sb.*

1513 DOUGLAS *Æneis* XII. vii. 97 The pane vanyst als clene ..as thocht it had bene Bot a dyrling or a litill stond. **1810** CROMEK *Nithsdale Song* App. 334 (Jam.) [The Brownie] keeping the servants awake at nights with the noisy dirling of its elfin flail.

dirl, *sb. Sc.* and *north. dial.* [f. DIRL *v.*] A thrill or vibration, with or without sound; a thrilling effect or sensation; a tremulous sound.

1785 BURNS *Death & Doctor Hornbook* xvi, It just play'd dirl on the bane, But did nae mair. **1818** SCOTT *Hrt. Midl.* xvii, 'A'body has a conscience.. I think mine's as weel out o' the gate as maist folk's are; and yet it's just like the noop of my elbow, it whiles gets a bit dirl on a corner.' **1837** CARLYLE *Fr. Rev.* II. VI. iii. (1848) 330 Successive simultaneous *dirl* of thirty-thousand muskets shouldered. **1862** HISLOP *Prov. Scot.* 18 An elbuck dirl will lang play thirl. **1878** *Cumbld. Gloss., Dirl*, a tremulous sound.

dirndl (ˈdɜːnd(ə)l). [G. dial., dim. of *dirne* girl; cf. G. *dirndlkleid* peasant dress.] A style of woman's dress imitating Alpine peasant costume with bodice and full skirt; also **dirndl skirt,** a full skirt with a tight waistband.

1937 M. HILLIS *Orchids on Budget* iii. 43 And an evening frock cut like a dirndl is amusing only if you don't have to wear it too often. **1938** *Times* 1 June 19/2 Nor must the ever popular dirndl be left out of the cotton catalogue. **1947** N. CARDUS *Autobiogr.* 272 Painted dames sporting the Tyrolean dirndl. **1957** J. BRAINE *Room at Top* xxiv. 193 She was wearing a blue dirndl skirt and a white blouse. **1968** *Times Lit. Suppl.* 3 Oct. 1131/2 Austria was 'in' and English country house guests frolicked in dirndls.

dirt (dɜːt), *sb.* Forms: 4–5 **drit, dryt, dritt(e, dryte,** (4 **dryit**), 5 **drytt,** 5–6 **dyrt(e,** 5–7 **durt,** 5– **dirt.** [By metathesis from ME. *drit*, not known in OE. and prob. a. ON. *drit* neuter, excrement (mod. Icel. *dritr* masc., Norw. *dritt*); cf. also MDu. *drete*, Du. *dreet*, Fl. *drits*, *drets* excrement: see DRITE *v.*]

1. Ordure; = EXCREMENT 2 b.

a **1300** *Cokaygne* 179 in *E.E.P.* (1862) 161 Seue ȝere in swine-is dritte He mot wade. **1387** TREVISA *Higden* (Rolls) V. 295 (Mätz.) Ureyne and dritte. **1388** WYCLIF *Phil.* iii. 8 All thingis.. Y deme as drit, [**1382** toordis] that Y wynne Crist. **1398** TREVISA *Barth. De P.R.* XVIII. v. (1495) 752 The lambe hath blacke dyrte. *c* **1440** *Promp. Parv.* 132/2 Dryte.. doonge, *merda*, *stercus*. *c* **1460** *Towneley Myst.* (Surtees) 194 The dwillys durt in thi berd, Vyle fals tratur! **1561** HOLLYBUSH *Hom. Apoth.* 13 b, Take whyte dogges dyrte thre unces. **1642** FULLER *Holy & Prof. St.* v. xii. 406 Some count a Jesting lie.. like the dirt of oysters, which.. never stains. **1830** MARRYAT *King's Own* xxvi, It's the natur of cats always to make a dirt in the same place.

2. a. Unclean matter, such as soils any object by adhering to it; filth; *esp.* the wet mud or mire of the ground, consisting of earth and waste matter mingled with water.

a **1300** *Sarmun* vii. in *E.E.P.* (1862) 2 Þi felle wiþ-oute nis bot a sakke ipudrid ful wiþ drit and ding. *a* **1300** *Ten Commandm.* 21 ibid. 16 Þe ful dritte of grunde. **14..** *Sir Beues* 1196 (MS. M.) He.. tredith hym vnder his fete In the dirte amyddus the strete. **1577** B. GOOGE *Heresbach's Husb.* III. (1586) 151 b, The Swine.. delighteth.. to wallow in the durt. **1596** SHAKS. *Tam. Shr.* IV. i. 80 How she waded through the durt to plucke him off me. **1611** BIBLE *Isa.* lvii. 20 The troubled sea.. whose waters cast vp myre and dirt. **1661** PEPYS *Diary* 29 May, The spoiling of my clothes and velvet coat with dirt. **1669** PENN *No Cross* ii. §10 Poor Mortals! But living Dirt; made of what they tread on. **1684** BUNYAN *Pilgr.* II. 64 The Dirt will sink to the bottom, and the Water come out by itself more clear. **1782** COWPER *Gilpin* 189 Let me scrape the dirt away That hangs upon your face. **1852** MRS. STOWE *Uncle Tom's C.* xi. 95 Now comes my master.. and grinds me down into the very dirt! **1878** HUXLEY *Physiogr.* 131 The muddy matter in these streams is merely the dirt washed from the roofs of the houses and the stones of the street. *Mod.* Dirt is only matter in the wrong place.

b. *fig.* As the type of anything worthless: cf. the phrase *filthy lucre*.

1357 *Lay Folks Catech.* (Lamb. MS.) 771 Þey sellyn sowlys to satanas for a lytyl worldly dryt. *c* **1380** WYCLIF *Wks.* (1880) 68 Bischopis, munkis & chanons sillen.. trewe prechynge for a litil stynkyng muk or drit. *c* **1679** R. DUKE *To Dryden on Tr. & Cr.* (R.), You found it dirt, but you have made it gold. **1720** DE FOE *Capt. Singleton* xix. (1840) 329 The wealth.. was all like dirt under my feet. **1734** POPE *Ess. Man* IV. 279 Is yellow dirt the passion of thy life? **1753** A. MURPHY *Gray's-Inn Jrnl.* No. 42 ⁋1 Ever since.. Convenience stamped an imaginary Value upon yellow Dirt.

c. A scornful name for *land* (as a possession).

1602 SHAKS. *Ham.* V. ii. 90 'Tis a Chowgh; but as I say spacious in the possession of dirt. **1616** BEAUM. & FL. *Scornful Lady* I. ii, Your brother's house is big enough; and to say truth, he has too much land: hang it, dirt!

d. Applied abusively to persons.

c **1300** *Havelok* 682 Go hom swithe, fule, drit, cherl. **1658** CLEVELAND *Rustick Rampant* Wks. (1687) 457 That Dirt of a Captain.. had butchered the English Patriarch. **1871** C. GIBBON *Lack of Gold* iv, Are you to turn your back on them like the dirt they are? **1894** HALL CAINE *Manxman* II. xi. 88 I hate the nasty dirts.

e. A mean action, remark, etc. *U.S.*, *Austral.*, and *N.Z. slang.*

1893 S. CRANE *Maggie* (1896) iii. 20, I got dis can fer dat ole woman, an' it 'ud be dirt teh swipe it. **1916** C. J. DENNIS *Songs of Sentimental Bloke* 34 A bloke 'ud be a dawg to kid a skirt Like 'er. An' me well knowin' she was square. It 'ud be dirt! **1947** 'A. P. GASKELL' *Big Game* 31 That was dirt, kicking mine [*sc.* my balloon] over the fence.

f. Scurrilous information or gossip; scandal. Also *attrib.*

1926 HEMINGWAY *Sun also Rises* ii. 9 'Do you know any dirt?' I asked. 'No.' 'None of your exalted connections getting divorces?' **1934** E. WAUGH *Handful of Dust* ii. 82 Good morning, darling, what's the dirt today? **1958** [see ANGLE *sb.*[2] 1 c]. **1959** P. MOYES *Dead Men don't Ski* iv. 41 'Come on, spill the dirt. What were they saying?'.. 'I always thought you didn't listen to gossip.' **1964** WODEHOUSE *Frozen Assets* v. 87 He doesn't think much of you... He thinks you fall short in the way of dishing the dirt.

3. a. Mud; soil, earth, mould; brick-earth. *colloq.*

1698 FRYER *Acc. E. India & P.* 26 A Fort or Blockade (if it merit to be called so) made of Dirt. **1709** STEELE *Tatler* No. 49 ⁋10 As Infants ride on Sticks, build Houses in Dirt. **1795** WINDHAM *Sp. Parl.* 27 May (1812) I. 270 Children, who had surrounded a twig with a quantity of dirt, would think that they had planted a tree. **1823** P. NICHOLSON *Pract. Build.* 344 Place Bricks, being made of clay, with a mixture of dirt and other coarse materials.. are.. weaker and more brittle. **1841** CATLIN *N. Amer. Ind.* (1844) I. x. 77 Throwing up the dirt from each excavation in a little pile. **1889** FARMER *Dict. Amer.* 202/2 The gardener fills his flower-pots with dirt.

b. *Mining, quarrying*, etc. Useless material, rubbish; the vegetable soil comprising a DIRT-BED.

1799 KIRWAN *Geol. Ess.* 308, 3 feet of coal, under which is a bad sort, called dirt, and again, 2 feet of coal. **1881** J. W. URQUHART *Electro-typing* v. 130 The common qualities [of copper] give off a great deal of foreign matter known as 'dirt'. **1884** *Chesh. Gloss., Dirts*, salt-making term. Cinders and ashes left after fuel is consumed. **1885** *Lyell's Elem. Geol.* 290 A stratum called by quarrymen 'the dirt', or 'black dirt', was evidently an ancient vegetable soil.

c. The material from which a metallic ore or other valuable substance is separated; esp. the alluvial deposit from which gold is separated by washing; = WASHDIRT.

1857 BORTHWICK *California* 120 (Bartlett), In California, 'dirt' is the universal word to signify the substance dug; earth, clay, gravel, or loose slate. The miners talk of rich dirt and poor dirt, and of stripping off so many feet of 'top dirt' before getting to 'pay-dirt', the latter meaning dirt with so much gold in it that it will pay to dig it up and wash it. **1890** BOLDREWOOD *Miner's Right* xiv. 142 We were clean worked out..before many of our neighbours at Greenstone Gully were half done with their dirt.

4. a. The quality or state of being dirty or foul; dirtiness, foulness, uncleanness in action or speech.

1774 GOLDSM. *Nat. Hist.* (1776) I. 328 The sloth and dirt of the inhabitants. **1789** MRS. PIOZZI *Journ. France* I. 144 Literature and dirt had long been intimately acquainted. **1857** C. G. GORDON *Lett.* III. 141 The Turkish steamer.. was in a beastly state of dirt. **1872** E. PEACOCK *Mabel Heron* I. ii. 16 The dirt, darkness, and savagery of the town.

b. Meanness, sordidness.

1625 FLETCHER *Noble Gent.* III. i, Our dunghill breeding and our durt. **1746** MELMOTH *Pliny* VII. xxix (R.), Honours, which are thus sometimes thrown away upon dirt and infamy; which such a rascal..had the assurance both to accept and to refuse.

5. a. *dial.* 'Dirty' weather.

1836 MARRYAT *Three Cutt.* iii, Shall we have dirt? **1870** *Whitby Gloss., Dirt*, a weather term for rain or snow. 'We're likely to have some dirt.'

b. *Mining.* Inflammable gas which constitutes 'foulness' in a mine; = FIRE-DAMP.

1831 *Examiner* 765/1 We examined if there was any dirt (inflammable air). **1851** GREENWELL *Coal-trade Terms Northumb. & Durh.* 23. **1892** *Northumbld. Gloss., Dirt*..is also used to express foul-air or firedamp in a pit.

6. Phrases. †**a.** *to fall to dirt*: to fall to the ground, to come to nothing; so *to be all in the dirt, to lay all in the dirt*, and the like. *Obs.*

1546 *St. Papers Hen. VIII*, XI. 181 To the which we will in no wise agree, but wil rather laye all in the durt. **1657** *North's Plutarch, Add. Lives* (1676) 28 Here Saladin was handsomely beat to dirt. **1658** BRAMHALL *Consecr. Bps.* vi. 148 Mr. Mason squeesed the poore Fable to durt. **1667** PEPYS *Diary* 19 Feb., Our discourse of peace is all in the dirt. **1670** MARVELL *Corr.* cxli. Wks. 1872-5 II. 315 We heard them 'pro formâ', but all falls to dirt.

b. *to cast, throw, or fling dirt*: to asperse any one with scurrilous or abusive language.

1642 SIR E. DERING *Sp. on Relig.* i Cast what dirt thou wilt, none will sticke on me. *c* **1645** HOWELL *Lett.* (1650) II. 62 Any sterquilinious raskall is licenc'd to throw dirt in the faces of soveraign princes in open printed language. **1655** FULLER *Ch. Hist.* IX. vii. 19 The best of men..are more carefull to wash their own faces, then busie to throw durt on others. **1678** B. R. *Letter Pop. Friends* 7 'Tis a blessed Line in Matchiavel—If durt enough be thrown, some will stick. **1706** E. WARD *Hud. Rediv.* I. II. 11 Fling dirt enough, and some will stick. **1738** POPE *Epil. Sat.* II. 145 To me they meant no hurt, But 'twas my Guest at whom they threw the dirt.

c. *to eat dirt*: to submit to degrading treatment; also (*U.S.*) humiliating confession or retractation. *Proverb.* 'Every man must eat a peck of dirt before he dies': see PECK.

1857 KINGSLEY *Two Y. Ago* II. v. 200 You have wonderfully changed your tone. Who was to eat any amount of dirt, if he could but save his influence thereby? **1859** FARRAR *J. Home* ix, Lord Fitzurse..made up for the dirt which they had been eating by the splendour of his entertainment. **1885** *Mag. Amer. Hist.* Feb. 199/2 'To eat dirt' is to retract or 'eat humble pie'. **1890** *Sat. Rev.* 18 Oct. 462/2 In times of revolution a good many pecks of dirt have to be eaten. **1891** FARMER *Slang* s.v. *Dirt, To eat dirt*,..to retract. **1903** CLAPIN *Dict. Amer., Eat dirt*, to retract, to be penitent, the Yankee equiv. of 'to eat one's words'.

d. *to cut dirt*: to take one's departure, be off. *U.S. slang.*

1829 *Negro Song* (Farmer s.v. *Cut*), He cut dirt and run. **1843-5** HALIBURTON *Sam Slick in Eng.* (Bartlett), The way the cow cut dirt. **1853** *Western Scenes* (Farmer), Now you cut dirt, and don't let me see you here again.

e. *to do dirt (to)*, to harm or injure maliciously. (Cf. DIRTY *a.* 2 d.) *slang* (orig. *U.S.*).

1893 S. CRANE *Maggie* (1896) xiv. 111 Yer doin' me dirt, Nell! I never taut ye'd do me dirt. **1893** M. A. OWEN *Voodoo Tales* 274 Ef I tek ter doin' dirt, den Ise willin' ter be jacky-me-lantuhn—an' sarve me right, too! **1913** E. C. BENTLEY *Trent's Last Case* vi. 137 They have been known to dynamite a man..who had done them dirt. **1926** J. BLACK *You can't Win* v. 57 You are the only human being I've met..that hasn't tried to do me some kind of dirt. **1929** D. H. LAWRENCE *Sex, Lit. & Censorship* (1955) 203 The so-called 'humour' is just a trick of doing dirt on sex. **1951** N. BALCHIN *Way through Wood* iv. 63 She doesn't do you dirt with characters like Bule—not serious dirt. **1951** J. C. FENNESSY *Sonnet in Bottle* VII. i. 245 It was doing dirt to one of their own people. **1956** E. POUND tr. *Sophocles' Women of Trachis* 22, I'm telling you: do dirt to others but..Don't weasel to me. **1959** 'W. HAGGARD' *Venetian Blind* vi. 84 Dotties could do you dirt; they could remark..in public, that..you were living with the curate.

7. *attrib.* and *Comb.* **a.** *attrib.*, 'of or for dirt', as ***dirt-band, -box, -car, -cart, -cone, -floor, -heap, -pellet, -roof*** (also ***-roofed*** adj.) *U.S.*, ***-spot, -streak***, etc.

1860 TYNDALL *Glac.* I. xi. 68, I could see..the looped *dirt-bands of the glacier. **1889** G. F. WRIGHT *Ice Age N. Amer.* 19 Neither moulins nor regular dirt-bands are present. **1884** *Health Exhib. Catal.* 55/2 Man-hole Cover for sewers, with elm blocks and fixed *Dirt Boxes. **1870** EMERSON *Soc. & Solit.* vi. 120 The railroad *dirt-cars are good excavators. **1860** BARTLETT *Dict. Amer.* 122 The '*dirt-cart', or cart which removes street sweepings, would, in London, be called a 'dust-cart'. **1860** TYNDALL *Glac.* I. ii. 18 Here are also '*dirt-cones' of the largest size. **1858** P. CARTWRIGHT *Autobiog.* xxx. 471 We walked on *dirt floors for carpets, sat on benches for chairs. **1862** BUNYAN *Holy War* Advt. to Rdr., John such *dirt-heap never was. **1709** SWIFT *T. Tub* Apol., Do they think such a building is to be battered with *dirt-pellets? **1881** *Rep. Indian Affairs* (U.S.) 121 Carpenter shop,..log, *dirt roof. **1910** *Outlook* 2 July 483 A log cabin of two rooms, with a dirt roof. **1873** J. H. BEADLE *Undevel. West* xxxiv. 734 To his joy he came upon a *dirt-roofed log-house. **1856** KANE *Arct. Expl.* II. xi. 113 Coming nearer, you see that the *dirt-spots are perforations of the snow. **1864** LOWELL *Fireside Trav.* 47 Cleanness, incapable of moral dirt spot. **1860** TYNDALL *Glac.* II. viii. 267 The only trace of the moraines is a broad *dirt-streak.

b. instrumental, as ***dirt-besmeared, -born, -grimed, -incrusted, -rotten, -smirched, -soaked*** adjs.

1606 SHAKS. *Tr. & Cr.* V. i. 23 Dirt-rotten livers, wheezing lungs. **1754** J. SHEBBEARE *Matrimony* (1766) I. 70 It is the Devil to have to do with such dirt-born Fellows. **1838** DICKENS *O. Twist* l. Dirt-besmeared walls. **1886** J. K. JEROME *Idle Thoughts* (1889) 74 Little dirt-grimed brats, trying to play in the noisy courts.

c. objective, as DIRT-EATER, -EATING, ***-flinging, -loving, -thrower***; (sense 3 c) ***dirt-washer, -washing***.

1819 *Metropolis* II. 133 The very last of dirt-throwers thereof [of the Canongate]. **1824** *Westm. Rev.* II. 467 This is done by assumption and dirt-flinging. *Ibid.*, Le Clerc divides the..Dirt-flinging argument into sixteen species. **1869** S. BOWLES *Our New West* ix. 179 The dirt-washers swept eagerly over the rich surface deposits. *Ibid.*, The old and simple dirt washing for gold was resumed.

d. Special combs.: **dirt bike**, a type of motorcycle designed for riding on unmade roads or tracks, esp. in motorcycle scrambling; cf. *trail bike* s.v. TRAIL *sb.*[1] 17; hence **dirtbiker**; **dirt-board** (see quot.); **dirt farmer** *U.S.*, a practical farmer; one who farms his own land; so ***dirt-farming***; **dirt-fast** *a.*, stuck fast in the dirt; **dirt-fear, -ed** *a.*, **dirt-gabard** (see quots.); **dirt-line**, a layer of dirt and debris accumulated on the surface of a glacier and imprisoned by the seasonal layer of snow; **dirt money** = *dirty money* (see DIRTY *a.* 6 b); **dirt-poor** *a.* (orig. *U.S.*), extremely poor; **dirt road** (chiefly *N. Amer.*), an unmade road, having merely the natural surface; **dirt-roller**, a roller in a cotton-spinning machine for removing dirt; **dirt-scraper**, a road-scraper; also a grading-shovel used in grading or levelling up ground; **dirt track**, an unpaved track or course; spec. (*a*) made of cinders and brick-dust for motor-cycle racing; (*b*) composed of soil, esp. as distinguished from turf, for flat-racing; **dirt-weed** (see quots.). Also DIRT-BED, -CHEAP, etc.

1970 *Pop. Mechanics* Oct. 138 The *dirt-bike boom has bred all-new machines designed just for running in the rough. **1975** *New Yorker* 17 Feb. 16/3 He can do headers, glass packs, fuel injectors, funny cars, dirt bikes and snowmobiles. **1986** P. THEROUX *O-Zone* xli. 464 His dirt bike was beautiful, with chrome brush guards. **1983** *Out of Town* Dec. 40/2 Last year's show attracted more than 12,000 enthusiasts, almost half the number of active *dirtbikers in the country... There's plenty to tempt you for the beginning of the new dirtbike season at Easter. **1924** H. CROY *R.F.D. No. 3* 148, A real *dirt farmer, not..one of them city dudes. **1932** E. WILSON *Devil take Hindmost* xvi. 170 He himself has been a dirt farmer, not a white-collar farmer! **1955** *Sci. News Let.* 23 July 50/2 It appears that all visiting experts are high officials in Russian agriculture, not one being a 'dirt farmer'. **1874** KNIGHT *Dict. Mech.*, *Dirt-board [in carriage], a board for warding off earth from the axle-arm. A cutto-plate. **1920** *Boston Even. Transcript* 2 Oct. IV. 1/1 Doing its multiple duty of making *dirt-farming a fine art. **1508** KENNEDIE *Flyting w. Dunbar* 33 *Dirtfast dearch. **1767** MESTON *Poems* 131 (Jam.) He trembl'd, and, which was a token Of a *dirt-fear, look'd dun as docken. **1722** W. HAMILTON *Wallace* x. 250 (Jam.) The Bishop of St. Andrews..Who would not Wallace' coming there abide, Was so *dirt-fear'd, even for all Scotland wide. **1867** SMYTH *Sailor's Word-bk.*, *Dirt-gabard, a large ballast-lighter. **1894** J. GEIKIE *Gt. Ice Age* (ed. 3) 30 The beds of snow..being usually marked off by a '*dirt-line' or crust formed of a mixture of dust, small grit, and occasional remains of insects. **1949** 'M. INNES' *Journeying Boy* x. 119 *Dirt money ..the extra pay dockers and people get for doing something thoroughly nasty. **1937** *Time* 26 Apr. 41/1 Nearly blind and *dirt-poor, Inventor Dave Mallory (Karloff) devises a burglar alarm worked by electric eyes. **1971** D. O'CONNOR *Eye of Eagle* xix. 128 They were dirt-poor; they could not bribe people. **1852** MRS. STOWE *Uncle Tom's C.* vii. 62 Der's two roads to de river—de *dirt road and de pike. **1931** G. T. CLARK *Leland Stanford* iv. 85 Traveling by horse-drawn stage..over rough and dusty dirt roads. **1959** A. FULLERTON *Yellow Ford* v. 40, I heard the noise of the car and a moment later saw it come bumping up the dirt road. **1959** N. LOFTS *Heaven in your Hand* 109 The dirt road became a cobbled street. **1969** E. W. MORSE *Fur Trade Canoe Routes* II. v. 58 This little channel, still evident, leads from Bell Lake to the present dirt road. **1902** *Encycl. Brit.* XXIX. 335/2 Practically all flat racing in the United States is held on '*dirt-tracks', *i.e.*, courses with soil specially prepared for racing, instead of turf courses. **1924** MASEFIELD *Sard Harker* I. 63 The road was not macadam but dirt-track, with soft going, after the first mile. **1928** *Daily Tel.* 20 Mar. 14/2 Motor-cycle racing on 'dirt tracks', a form of sport very popular in Australia. **1928** *Times* 2 July 6/7 Dirt Track Racing. **1949** KOESTLER *Promise & Fulfilment* xv. 168 A tiny two-seater training plane..which performed perilous hops from an improvised dirt-track runway in Jerusalem to Tel Aviv and back. **1961** W. VAUGHAN-THOMAS *Anzio* viii. 162 One column struck south-east down the dirt track that led towards the Spaccasassi Creek. *a* **1825** FORBY *Voc. E. Anglia*, *Dirt-weed, *Chenopodium viride*, an expressive name for what generally grows on dunghills or other heaps of dirt. **1884** MILLER *Plant-n.* 38/2 Dirt-weed, or Dirty Dick, *Chenopodium album.*

dirt, *v.* Also 6-7 durt. [f. DIRT *sb.* See also the earlier strong vb. DRITE.] *trans.* To make dirty or foul; to defile or pollute with dirt; to dirty, to soil.

a **1587** FOXE *A. & M.* (1596) 1581 Riding in his long gowne downe to the horse heels..dirted vp to the horse bellie. **1611** BARRY *Ram-Alley* I. ii, How light he treads For dirting his silk stockings! **1660** FULLER *Mixt Contempl.* (1663) 89 For fear to dirt the soles of their shoes. **1727** *Th. Var. Subjects* in Swift's Wks. 1755 II. I. 226 Ill company is like a dog, who dirts those most whom he loves best. **1826** LAMB *Lett.* (1888) II. 149 Don't thumb and dirt the books. **1833** J. H. NEWMAN *Lett.* (1891) I. 386 Sitting down on the ashes..which are so dry as not to dirt.

Hence **'dirting** *vbl. sb.*

1591 PERCIVALL *Sp. Dict., Enlodadura*, durting, fouling with durt, *lutamentum*.

dirt-bed. *Geol.* A stratum consisting of ancient vegetable mould; *spec.* A bed of dark bituminous earth containing the stumps of trees, occurring in the lower Purbeck series of the Isle of Portland, and overlying the Portland oolite.

1824 T. WEBSTER in *Geol. Trans.* (1829) II. 42 A bed about one foot thick, consisting of a dark-brown substance, and containing much earthy lignite; this bed is very remarkable and extends all through the north end of the Isle of Portland ..It is called by the quarrymen the *Dirtbed.* **1836** BUCKLAND *Geol.* xviii. §3. (1858) 457 A single stump rooted in the dirt-bed in the Isle of Portland. **1851** RICHARDSON *Geol.* (1855) 397 A mass of bituminous earth, called the 'dirt-bed', which is an ancient vegatable soil, containing numerous trunks of fossil trees, standing erect at a height of from one to three feet, with their summits jagged.

dirt-bird. A local name of the skua, *Stercorarius crepidatus*, called also Dirty Allan; also of the green woodpecker, *Gecinus viridis.*

1847-78 HALLIW., *Dirt-bird*, the woodpecker. *North.* **1885** SWAINSON *Prov. Names Brit. Birds* 100 Green Woodpecker..The constant iteration of its cry before rain (which brings out the insects on which it feeds) gives it the names Rain bird..Dirt bird, Storm cock. *Ibid.* 210 Richardson's Skua (*Stercorarius crepidatus*)..from the vulgar opinion that the gulls are *muting*, when, in reality, they are only disgorging fish newly caught. Dirt bird (Dundrum Bay)..Dirty allan or aulin..Dung bird. **1886** W. BROCKIE *Leg. & Superst. Durham* 136 Several species of small birds are confounded under the..title of 'dirt birds', because they sing on the approach of rain.

dirt-cheap ('dɜːt,tʃiːp), *a.* (*adv.*) [See CHEAP *a.* 6.] As cheap as dirt; exceedingly cheap. Hence **dirt-'cheapness**.

1821 *Blackw. Mag.* VIII. 616 Dirt-cheap, indeed, it was, as well it might. **1849** DICKENS *Dav. Copp.* xxii, Five bob.. and dirt-cheap. **1883** *Pall Mall G.* 26 Oct. 5/1 It appears likely that November will bring an alteration in that dirt-cheapness of money of which brokers and bankers now complain. **1886** H. F. LESTER *Under two Fig Trees* 102 I'll do it cheap, that I will,..dirt cheap. **1891** T. HARDY *Tess* i, I was no more than the commonest, dirt-cheapest feller in the parish.

'dirt-dauber.

†**1.** One who daubs or plasters with dirt or mud; a maker of cob-walls; also, a term of abuse. *Obs.*

c **1515** *Cock Lorell's B.* (Percy Soc.) 5 Here is..partycke peuysshe a conynge dyrte dauber, Worshypfull wardayn of slouens In. **1563-87** FOXE *A. & M.* (1596) 532/1 A man would thinke him some dirtdaubers sonne. **1630** J. TAYLOR (Water P.) *Jacke-a-Lent* Wks. I. 115/2 Vntyling houses..to ..the profit of Plaisterers, and Dirtdawbers, the game of Glasiers, Joyners, Carpenters, Tylers and Bricklayers. **1647** TRAPP *Comm. Epistles* 472 These are the devils dirt-dawbers, that teach such doctrine.

2. A species of sand-wasp; = DAUBER 4.

1844 GOSSE in *Zoologist* II. 582 These were the nests of dirt-daubers.

'dirt-eater. One who eats dirt: see next. *spec.* one of a class of 'poor whites' in some parts of the southern United States; = *clay-eater* (CLAY *sb.* 9).

1802 BEDDOES *Hygëia* VIII. 70 The dirt-eaters of the West-Indies. **1840** C. F. HOFFMAN *Greyslaer* III. xii. 223 Even Bettys, little fastidious as he was, recoiled from the fare which these 'Dirt Eaters', as the Indians called them, placed before him. **1866** *Ret. Agric. Soc. Maine* 46 It rests with you ..whether you will take rank with the poor whites, the dirt-eaters of the South, or with the best classes of the north. **1940** R. O. CUMMINGS *American & his Food* 87 Distinguished from other southerners by hookworm disease were dirt-eaters scattered in sand barrens and pine woods from South Carolina to Mississippi.

dirt-eating ('dɜːtiːtɪŋ), *vbl. sb.*

1. The eating of some kinds of earth or clay as food, practised by some primitive peoples, as the Ottomaks of South America and some Arctic tribes.

2. A disorder of the nutritive functions characterized by a morbid craving to eat earth or dirt.

1817 *Edin. Rev.* XXVIII. 359 The accounts..of the Stomach-evil, sometimes called Dirt-eating. **1828** *Life Planter Jamaica* (ed. 2) 97 For some time past she had been addicted to dirt-eating (eating earth)..a disease, which.. terminates in dropsy and death. **1834** *W. Ind. Sk. Book* II. 49 The singular propensity to dirt-eating, a disease which has acquired from the French the name of *mal d'estomac*.

† **'dirten**, *a. Obs.* exc. *dial.* [In early use, for *dritten*, pa. pple. of DRITE *v.*; in later use f. DIRT *sb.* + -EN[4]: cf. *earthen*.]

1. Dirtied, defiled with excrement or filth.

1508 KENNEDIE *Flyting w. Dunbar* 25 Dirtin Dumbar, quhome on blawes thow thy boist? **1508** DUNBAR *Flyting w. Kennedie* 248 Rottin crok, dirtin dok, cry cok, or I sall quell the. **1536** BELLENDEN *Cron. Scot.* XVI. xix. (Jam.) Thairfor this jurnay wes callit the dirtin raid.

2. *dial.* Made of dirt.

1847–78 HALLIWELL, *Dirten*, made of dirt. *West.*

dirten Allan: see DIRTY ALLAN.

dirtily ('dɜːtɪlɪ), *adv.* [f. DIRTY *a.* + -LY[2].]

1. In a dirty manner; foully, filthily.

1598 FLORIO, *Sporcamente*, filthily, foully..durtily. *a* **1613** OVERBURY *A Wife* (1638) 90 He lookes like his Land, as heavily and durtily. **1777** W. DALRYMPLE *Trav. Sp. & Port.* xiii, We put up at a Fonda..where we are dirtily lodged. **1789** MRS. PIOZZI *Journ. France* I. 10 The hounds were always dirtily and ill kept.

2. In a manner that stains morality or honour; dishonourably, despicably, sordidly.

a **1631** DONNE *Elegie* xii. (R.), Such gold as that, wherewithal Almighty chymics.. Are dirtily and desperately gull'd. **1661** R. L'ESTRANGE *Interest Mistaken* 133 How dirtily..the Presbyterian crew treated his Majesty. **1709** MRS. CENTLIVRE *Gamester* v, 'Tis dirtily done of you..to kick a man for nothing. **1796** T. JEFFERSON in Sparks *Corr. Amer. Rev.* (1853) IV. 484 An intriguer, dirtily employed in sifting the conversations of my table.

dirtiness ('dɜːtɪnɪs). [f. DIRTY *a.* + -NESS.]

1. a. The quality or state of being dirty; foulness, filthiness.

1561 STOW *Eng. Chron.* Romans, an. 386 (R.) Paris, which ..was called Lutecia, because of the mudde and dirtinesse of the place wherein it standeth. **1617** MARKHAM *Caval.* v. 17 There will come much filth and durtinesse from the horse. **1776** ADAM SMITH *W.N.* I. x. (1869) I. 105 The wages of labour vary with..the cleanliness or dirtiness..of the employment. **1885** *Law Times* 30 May 74/2 To throw up a contract..on the..ground of the dirtiness of the house.

b. The quality or state of an atomic or nuclear weapon having considerable radioactive fall-out. (Cf. DIRTY *a.* 1 g.) *colloq.*

1956 *Life* 29 Oct. 44/2 To have any meaning, the ban would not be limited to the *size* of bombs..but to the amount of radioactivity they would be allowed to generate —their 'dirtiness'. **1961** *Guardian* 25 Oct. 2/5 Asked if the explosion..was of a 'dirty' bomb, he replied..'The question of "dirtiness" does not bear a direct relation to yield.' **1961** *Daily Tel.* 31 Oct. 22/5 Fall-out from last week's test is expected to reach Britain tomorrow. It may give an indication of the 'dirtiness' or otherwise of Russia's latest hydrogen weapons.

2. Uncleanness of language; sordidness of action.

1649 FULLER *Just Man's Fun.* 22 Let not the dimness of our eyes be esteemed the durtiness of his actions. *a* **1677** BARROW *Serm.* Wks. 1716 I. 137 Degenerate wantonness and dirtiness of speech. **1742** H. WALPOLE *Lett. H. Mann* (1834) I. 106 You know I am above such dirtiness. **1856** F. E. PAGET *Owlet Owlst.* 74 The darkness and the dirtiness of the money-loving mind.

dirtless ('dɜːtlɪs), *a.* (*adv.*). [f. DIRT *sb.* + -LESS.] Void of dirt.

a **1618** SYLVESTER *Mayden's Blush* 577 The Wayes so dustlesse, and so dirtlesse faire. *a* **1745** SWIFT (F. Hall). **1892** *Pall Mall G.* 21 Mar. 3/1 With a smile at the almost dirtless room.

dirt-pie. Mud or wet earth formed by children into a shape like a pie; a mud-pie.

a **1641** SUCKLING (J.), That which has newly left off making of dirt-pies, and is but preparing itself for a green-sickness. **1695** CONGREVE *Love for L.* IV. xiii, And for the young Woman..I thought it more fitting for her to learn her Sampler, and make Dirt-Pies, than to look after a Husband. *a* **1734** NORTH *Exam.* III. vi. §64 (1740) 470 Their Towns.. gave Way like Dirt Pyes before his Army. **1793** BURKE *Policy of Allies* Wks. VII. 159 Busy in the confection of the dirt-pyes of their imaginary constitutions. **1854** THACKERAY *J. Leech's Pict.* (1869) 333 Poor little ragged Polly making dirt-pies in the gutter.

dirty ('dɜːtɪ), *a.* Also 6–7 durtie, durty. [f. DIRT *sb.* + -Y[1].]

I. 1. a. Characterized by the presence of dirt; soiled with dirt; foul, unclean, sullied.

15.. *Chester Pl.* (E.E.T.S.) 143 Dryve downe the dyrty arses, all by deene. **1530** PALSGR. 310/1 Dyrty with myers, *boueux*. **1576** FLEMING *Panopl. Epist.* 405 You..in stormy weather, and durtie wayes..come tripping to mee in your silcken sleppers. **1590** SHAKS. *Mids. N.* II. i. 75 Heere the maiden sleeping sound, On the danke and durty ground. **1630** *R. Johnson's Kingd. & Commw.* 133 A beastly Towne and durtie streets. **1684** BUNYAN *Pilgr.* II. 64 Now 'tis Dirty with the feet of some that are not desirous that Pilgrims here should quench their Thirst. **1709** STEELE *Tatler* No. 35 ¶1 Taking Snuff, and looking dirty about the Mouth by Way of Ornament. **1838** DICKENS *Nich. Nick.* iii, Her apartment was larger and something dirtier. **1840** —— *Old C. Shop* iii, His hands..were very dirty.

b. Of the nature of dirt; mixed with dirt.

a **1533** FRITH *Wks.* 136 (R.) To decline from the dignitie of diuinitie into the dirtie dregges of vayne sophistrye. **1590** SPENSER *F.Q.* II. vi. 41 All his armour sprinckled was with blood, And soyld with durtie gore. **1621** BURTON *Anat. Mel.* I. ii. III. x. (1651) 106 Taking up some of the durty slime. **1842** ABDY *Water Cure* (1843) 80 Covered with a dirty purulent mass. **1894** *Labour Commission* Gloss. s.v. *Coal, Dirty coal*, pure coal mixed with stones, shale and other refuse.

c. That makes dirty; that soils or befouls.

1774 GOLDSM. *Nat. Hist.* (1776) VIII. 138 They partake of the same dirty drudgery with the rest. **1893** J. PULSFORD *Loyalty to Christ* II. 381 Whoever does hard work, or dirty work, as to the Lord, under the disguise of his soiled hands and garments, is putting on nobility.

d. ***dirty half-hundred***: applied to the 50th foot (1st Battalion Royal West Kent), from the fact that, during the Peninsular war, the men wiped their faces with their black facings. ***dirty shirts***: the 101st foot (1st Battalion Munster Fusiliers), from the fact that they fought in their shirt-sleeves at Delhi in 1857. (Farmer.)

1841 LEVER *C. O'Malley* xciv. (Farmer), A kind of neutral tint between green and yellow, like nothing I know of except the facings of the 'Dirty half-hundred'. **1887** *Daily News* 11 July (ibid.), As the old Bengal European Regiment..they had won their honourable sobriquet of the dirty shirts. **1892** *Ibid.* 20 July 3/1 One who fought with the old 'Dirty Shirts' in the Sutlej campaign.

e. Phr. ***the dirty end*** (***of the stick***), the difficult or unpleasant part (in a situation). (See also STICK *sb.*[1] 15 e.)

1924 'SAPPER' *Third Round* vi. 167 I've been had for a mug. Somehow or other they've handed us the dirty end. **1930** J. DOS PASSOS *42nd Parallel* v. 71, I guess I always get the dirty end of the stick, all right. **1936** WODEHOUSE *Laughing Gas* v. 62, I mean what's downtrodden and oppressed and gets the dirty end of the stick all the time. That's me. **1957** *Listener* 31 Oct. 681/2 The Indians [in Malaya]..may be given the dirty end of the stick.

f. *transf. colloq.* Not streamlined; opp. CLEAN *a.* 13 c; spec. (*a*) of untidy or imperfect oarsmanship; (*b*) of the lines of an aircraft, used esp. of one with its landing gear unretracted.

1925 'IAN HAY' *Paid with Thanks* xvi. 213 Stroke,..you have still got a dirty finish. **1932** *Flight* 23 Sept. 891/1 One would imagine that what with the external wing bracing struts joining their lower ends to the hull on the chine, and with a planing bottom showing no flare or reversed curvature towards the chine, the boat would be extremely 'dirty' at certain running speeds. **1959** *Times* 13 Mar. 18/1 They went up quickly, in spite of some dirty bladework. **1962** *Flight Internat.* 1 Mar. 330/1 Stalling speeds clean and fully 'dirty' are almost 30 kt apart.

g. Of a nuclear weapon: having considerable radioactive fall-out. *colloq.*

1956 *Life* 29 Oct. 44/1 The H-bomb..is a relatively 'clean' bomb unless it is made 'dirty' (more radioactive) by using the tremendous heat of fusion to set off another fission process. **1958** *Observer* 13 Apr. 13/3 Those tests which are really hazardous to health—the tests of large 'dirty' H-bombs—cannot be held undetected. **1958** *New Statesman* 9 Aug. 162/3 He had to..admit that the US is now deliberately withdrawing A-bombs from its stockpile in order to make them 'dirtier'. They are then known as 'salted'.

2. a. Morally unclean or impure; 'smutty'. Spec. ***dirty book***, a pornographic book; so ***dirty bookshop***; ***dirty joke***, ***story***, a 'smutty' joke or story; ***dirty weekend***, a sexually illicit weekend.

1599 SANDYS *Europæ Spec.* (1632) 20 No such blaspheming nor dyrtie speaking as before. **1637** B. JONSON *Sad Sheph.* II. i, Foul limmer, dritty lown! **1768** STERNE *Sent. Journ.* (1778) II. 111 (*Case Consc.*) Then I shall let him see I know he is a dirty fellow. **1783** BLAIR *Rhet.* (1812) I. xv. 350 Disagreeable, mean, vulgar, or dirty ideas. **1850** E. FITZGERALD *Lett.* (1889) I. 206, I took it up by mistake for one of Swift's dirty volumes. **1912** R. BROOKE *Let.* 7 Aug. (1968) 392, I shall..repeat poetry to you; you will repeat dirty stories to me. **1913** —— *Let.* 22 May (1968) 461 We must do some show together..where poetry & music &.. satire and suffering & dirty jokes & triumphal processions shall be..mixed together. **1916** W. S. MAUGHAM *Writer's Notebk.* (1949) 107 When at last he became more communicative it was..to show one a collection of dirty postcards. **1940** G. MARX *Let.* 16 Dec. (1967) 189 A master comic, not a dirty line or joke in the entire two and a half hours. **1944** 'G. ORWELL' *Crit. Essays* (1946) 125 The dirty post cards that used to be sold in Mediterranean seaport towns. **1959** J. BRAINE *Vodi* xxiv. 250 Each had some kind of talent, even if it were only for billiards or dirty jokes. **1960** *Guardian* 2 Nov. 11/2 For Lawrence to be confined always to dirty-book shops would be perhaps the greatest irony in literary history. **1963** P. MOYES *Murder à la Mode* xii. 208 You and Veronica were going off for what, in my day, used to be called a dirty week-end. **1965** K. GILES *Some Beasts No More* iv. 74 He was probably a messenger boy from the dirty book trade. **1969** D. BARRON *Man who was There* i. 21 An angry German at the Karachi customs who was being accused of smuggling dirty books into the country. **1969** R. QUEST *Cerberus Murders* xvii. 93, I get reasonably well paid —enough to enable me to..have a dirty weekend in Scarborough now and again. **1970** B. SPOCK *Decent & Indecent* 51 Fear of sexual impotence is its most obvious aspect; this is an important ingredient of a large proportion of all jokes and dirty stories.

b. That stains the honour of the persons engaged; dishonourably sordid, base, mean, or corrupt; despicable. Colloq. phr. ***dirty work at the crossroads***.

1670 COTTON *Espernon* II. v. 219 Branded with the durtiest and most hateful of all Crimes. **1674** *Essex Papers* (Camden) 253 To me he called it a dirty trick. *a* **1764** PULTENEY in Beatson *Nav. & Mil. Mem.* (1790) I. 26 Some Ministers..cannot do their dirty work without them. **1859** KINGSLEY *Misc.* (1860) I. 39, I have done a base and dirty deed, and have been punished for it. **1888** BRYCE *Amer. Commw.* II. lvii. 399 These two classes do the..dirty work of politics. **1914** WODEHOUSE *Man Upstairs* 269 A conviction began to steal over him that in some way he was being played with, that some game was afoot which he did not understand, that—in a word—there was dirty work at the cross-roads. **1915** 'IAN HAY' *First Hundred Thou.* xvi. 221 That..usually means dirty work at the cross-roads at no very distant period. **1927** R. KNOX *Three Taps* v. 47 No question of accident..or of dirty work at the cross-roads? These rich men have enemies, don't they? **1960** A. CHRISTIE *Adv. of Christmas Pudding* 184 Good for you, old boy. Some dirty work at the crossroads—eh?

c. Earned by base or despicable means.

1742 YOUNG *Nt. Th.* IV. 353 Shall praise..Earn dirty bread by washing Æthiops fair? **1784** COWPER *Task* III. 808 Fish up his dirty and dependent bread From pools and ditches of the commonwealth. **1805** *Naval Chron.* XIV. 17 Nor is there one single penny of *dirty money*.

d. Also *absol.* in phrase ***to do the dirty***: to play a dirty trick.

1914 *Daily Express* 13 Nov. 514 The Germans have been 'doing the dirty' on us by donning khaki and kilts to approach our trenches. **1915** D. O. BARNETT *Lett.* 157, I hope our friends the 133rd will..do the dirty on their Prussian friends. **1929** J. B. PRIESTLEY *Good Comp.* III. v. 607 Anyhow they did the dirty on yer. **1930** R. H. MOTTRAM *Europa's Beast* xii. 282 If you've been doing the dirty on my friends. **1942** G. KERSH *Nine Lives Bill Nelson* iii. 15 It took me to do the dirty on him.

3. An epithet of disgust or aversion: repulsive, hateful, abominable, despicable.

1611 SHAKS. *Cymb.* III. vi. 55 Those Who worship durty Gods. **1618** BP. HALL *Serm.* v. 111 To scorn this base and ..dirty god of this world, and to aspire unto the true riches. **1712** ADDISON *Spect.* No. 451 ¶4 Every dirty Scribbler is countenanced by great Names. **1730** GAY in *Swift's Lett.* (1766) II. 111, I am determined to write to you, though those dirty fellows of the post-office do read my letters. **1819** BYRON *Juan* I. cli, 'Twas for his dirty fee, And not from any love to you.

4. Of the weather: Foul, muddy; at sea, wet and squally, bad.

1660 JER. TAYLOR *Duct. Dubit.* II. 168 (L.) When this snow is dissolved, a great deal of dirty weather will follow. **1745** P. THOMAS *Jrnl. Anson's Voy.* 102 As soon as we came out to Sea, we had the same squally dirty Weather as before we came in. **1836** MARRYAT *Midsh. Easy* xix, It begins to look very dirty to windward. **1845** STOCQUELER *Handbk. Brit. India* (1854) 404 Distinguished by the popular term of dirty spring, or mud season. **1890** W. E. NORRIS *Misadventure* viii, He became aware that dirty weather was setting in.

fig. **1883** STEVENSON *Treas. Isl.* IV. xxi, If they can..fire in upon us through our own ports, things would begin to look dirty.

5. a. Of colour: Tinged with what destroys purity or clearness; inclining to black, brown, or dark grey.

1665 HOOKE *Microgr.* 74 The fouler the tincture be, the more dirty will the Red appear. *a* **1704** LOCKE (J.), Pound an almond, and the clear white colour will be altered into a dirty one. **1823** J. F. COOPER *Pioneer* xviii, The clouds were dense and dirty.

b. Prefixed, as a qualification, to adjectives of colour. (Usually hyphened with the adj. when the latter is used attributively.)

1694 SCOT in *Acc. Serv. Late Voy.* II. (1711) 99 Both of them are of a dirty white, but the Eggs have black specks. **1796** WITHERING *Brit. Plants* IV. 235 Pileus dusky greyish hue with a cast of dirty olive. **1836** MACGILLIVRAY tr. *Humboldt's Trav.* xxii. 309 The colour of the troubled waters upon it was of a dirty gray. *c* **1865** LETHEBY in *Circ. Sc.* I. 97/2 The spermaceti solidifies as a dirty-brown crystalline mass.

c. Of jazz music: having a slurred or rasping tone.

1927 *Étude* May 339 (*title*) More hot and dirty breaks. **1952** B. ULANOV *Hist. Jazz* (1958) x. 111 The brass smears and 'dirty' reed inflections then much favored by jazz musicians. **1955** L. FEATHER *Encycl. Jazz* vii. 277 His plaintive tone and style, sometimes called 'dirty' and often employing 'growl' effects. **1963** *Listener* 7 Feb. 264/2 The lady..had the 'dirty' tone and tough attack, while the man played straight and smooth.

6. *Comb.* **a.** parasynthetic, as ***dirty-coloured***, ***-faced***, ***-handed***, ***-minded***, ***-shirted***, ***-shoed***, ***-souled***. So ***dirty-face***, a dirty-faced person; ***dirty-mindedness***. Also ***dirty-looking*** adj.

1705 *Lond. Gaz.* No. 4132/4 Wears a light dirty-coloured Coat. **1658** COKAINE *Trappolin* v. iii, Goodman dirty-face, why did not you keep me these in prison till I bid you let them out? **1817** W. TUCKER *Family Dyer & Scourer* i. 7 A kind of dirty looking green. **1920** D. H. LAWRENCE *Lost Girl* xiv. 325 There was a strange mountain town, dirty-looking. **1887** *Pall Mall G.* 20 Aug. 7/1 It is not the weak but the dirty-minded Christians who see evil in ballet dancing. **1915** F. M. HUEFFER *Good Soldier* III. iv. 183 The sorts of dirty-mindedness that counsel in that sort of case can impute. **1935** 'G. ORWELL' *Clergyman's Daughter* v. 289 Just generalised suspicion. A sort of instinctive rustic dirty-mindedness. **1823** in Cobbett *Rur. Rides* (1885) I. 34 The house too neat for a dirty-shoed carter to be allowed to come into. **1663** KILLIGREW *Parson's Wed.* in Dodsl. *O. Pl.* (1780) XI. 392 She looks like a dirty-soul'd bawd.

b. Special comb.: **dirty Dick**, **dirty John**, popular names of species of *Chenopodium*; **dirty dog** *slang*, a despicable or untrustworthy person; also with implication of lasciviousness; **dirty-filling** (see quot.); **dirty look** *colloq.*, a scowl, sour expression; **dirty money** (see quot. 1897); **dirty old man** *slang phr.*, used with the implication of lasciviousness; **dirty protest**, a form of protest by prisoners (esp. those demanding political as opp. to criminal status in N. Irel.), in which they refuse to wash and deliberately foul their cells; cf. *on the blanket* s.v. BLANKET *sb.* 3; **dirty tricks** orig. *U.S.*, covert intelligence operations, esp. those carried out by the Central Intelligence Agency (the plans division of which was nicknamed the 'department of dirty tricks'); now also applied to any underhand political activity designed to discredit an opponent; freq. *attrib.*; cf. sense 2 b above; hence **dirty-trickery, dirty-trickster**; **dirty word**, (*a*) a vulgar or 'smutty' word; (*b*) a word made disreputable by what are regarded as its discreditable associations;) see also DIRTY ALLAN.

1878 BRITTEN & HOLLAND *Plant-n.*, Dirty Dick, *Chenopodium album. Chesh.* From its growth on dunghills.—Dirty John, *Chenopodium Vulvaria. W. Chesh.* **1928** S. VINES *Humours Unreconciled* xv. 204 Who's been calling me a dirty dog, I should like to know. **1959** I. & P. OPIE *Lore & Lang. Schoolch.* x. 189 Less specifically he [*sc.* the tell-tale] is a..'dirty dog',..'spoil sport'. **1964** J. PORTER *Dover One* ix. 107 'Bit of a dirty dog, our Gordon Pilley,' said Sergeant MacGregor with a smirk. **1894** *Labour Commission* Gloss., *Dirty Filling*, loading the hutches or tubs with an excess of dirt in proportion to the quantity of coal. **1928** J. P. MCEVOY *Showgirl* xi. 164, I sneaked a peep across the room and caught Jimmy giving me a dirty look. **1933** *Punch* 19 Apr. 444/1 It is therefore customary..to incline the head in the direction of the culprit, composing the features to an expression of great hatefulness but of even greater contempt. The correct adjustment of that expression constitutes the Dirty Look. **1934** WODEHOUSE *Right Ho, Jeeves* xi. 137 Deprived of Anatole's services, all he was likely to give the wife of his b. was a dirty look. **1897** S. & B. WEBB *Industr. Democr.* I. 313 When any class of work involves special unpleasantness or injury to clothing, 'black money' or 'dirty money' is sometimes stipulated for. **1960** *Sunday Express* 14 Aug. 1/1, 1,100 dockers..are claiming 'dirty money' for handling a cargo of red oxide. **1932** R. LEHMANN *Invit. Waltz* III. xiv. 240 Mum thinks he's harmless... In fact she was quite umbrageous with me when I called him a dirty old man. **1942** T. RATTIGAN *Flare Path* II. ii. 137 You don't think I waited up for you, do you? Keeping the women company, that's all. *Teddy.* Then you're a dirty old man. **1957** 'R. GORDON' *Doctor in Love* i. 10 I'm going to stay a bachelor. Changing imperceptibly from gay young to dirty old. **1971** D. CLARK *Sick to Death* i. 9 A man of my age on the look out for a lovely young lass puts me into the dirty-old-man class. **1979** *Daily Tel.* 12 Nov. 1/1 There were fears..that the next step by the Albany protesters could be Ulster-style 'dirty protests' in which cells are deliberately fouled with excreta. **1980** *Christian Science Monitor* (Midwestern ed.) 4 Dec. 6/3 They had earlier been part of the 'dirty protest', which since 1978 has found some prisoners deliberately fouling their cells with human waste. **1986** Dirty protest [see *H-block* s.v. H 2.] **1963** J. JOESTEN *They call it Intelligence* v. 47 In the 'Department of Dirty Tricks',..our Intelligencers behave like babes in the wood. **1967** *Time* 24 Feb. 16/3 Deputy to the chief of the plans division, the so-called 'dirty tricks' department. **1973** *Newsweek* 28 May 38/3 *Newsweek* has also learned that at least two other Nixon dirty-tricksters were imitating Segretti's tactics around that time. **1974** *Ibid.* 18 Mar. 26/2 Before the week was out, Mr. Nixon did a radio speech previewing his campaign-reform package, including proposed ceilings on individual gifts..shorter national campaigns and prohibitions against dirty-trickery. **1976** *Economist* 16 Oct. 56/2 As for Watergate, Mr Weicker's record—and his strong stand against dirty tricks—should help him with many voters. **1984** *Listener* 30 Aug. 34/1 They were some of the earliest exponents of dirty tricks and destabilisation. **1842** LOVER *Handy Andy* xiv. 126 'Don't say popery,' cried the cook; 'it's a dirty word! Say Roman Catholic when you speak of the faith.' **1925** *New Yorker* 19 Sept. 6, I shall insert into the second act of each play one of the three remaining Dirty Words that haven't yet been pronounced on the stage. **1937** E. ST. VINCENT MILLAY *Conv. Midnight* i. 36 Charity is a dirty word, it's gone to bed Too often with philanthropists, it's *effutata*. **1957** D. KARP *Leave me Alone* xx. 298 To young people compromise is a dirty word. **1959** *Listener* 25 June 1094/1 Since then 'liberalism' has become a dirty word in Indonesia.

II. Used adverbially as an intensive: very, exceedingly. *slang.*

1920 GALSWORTHY *Foundations* I. i, 'E wants to syve 'is dirty great 'ouse. **1943** BAKER *Dict. Austral. Slang* (ed. 3) 26 *Dirty big*, used adjectively as an equivalent of 'bloody'. **1944** J. H. FULLARTON *Troop Target* ix. 67, I was lying flat on my back when a great dirty black Junkers dropped a big one. **1945** J. HENDERSON *Gunner Inglorious* xvi. 134 I'm going to grow a dirty big fig-tree outside my home. **1958** F. NORMAN *Bang to Rights* III. 124 There was one chap who had a dodgey foot, and he had to wear a dirty great boot and because of this they called him the Boot. **1970** D. M. DAVIN *Not Here, Not Now* IV. v. 311 The buggers are in now. They've got a dirty big majority already. **1971** D. CLARK *Sick to Death* iii. 65 Time for a dirty great pint.

ˈdirty, *v.* [f. prec.]

1. a. *trans.* To make dirty or unclean; to defile or pollute with dirt; to soil. Also *fig.* (sometimes const. *up*).

1591 GREENE *Disc. Coosnage* (1592) 22 They durty their hose and shoos vpon purpose. **1672–3** MARVELL *Reh. Transp.* I. 212 The passage..being so dirtyed with the Nonconformists thumbs. **1762** DERRICK *Lett.* (1767) II. 61 It would be dirtying paper to send you any such productions. **1845** DARWIN *Voy. Nat.* i. (1879) 5 The dust falls in such quantities as to dirty everything on board.

fig. *a* **1661** FULLER *Worthies, London* (R.), He rather soyled his fingers, then dirtied his hands in the matter of the Holy Maid of Kent. **1835** R. H. FROUDE *Rem.* (1838) I. 395 Innocent as such phrases are in themselves, they have been dirtied. **1846** LANDOR *Imag. Conv.* II. 200 Mostly they dirty those they fawn on. **1953** W. P. MCGIVERN *Big Heat* iii. 32 It might occur to her to blackmail you..with the threat of dirtying up your husband's name. **1959** 'P. QUENTIN' *Shadow of Guilt* v. 46 She, too, would be dirtied up by scandal. **1964** WODEHOUSE *Frozen Assets* i. 25 He's writing a novel... He keeps clutching his brow and muttering 'This damned thing needs dirtying up.'.. If it isn't the sort of stuff small boys scribble on fences, nobody will look at it.

b. To contaminate with radioactive matter (cf. DIRTY *a.* 1 g).

1955 *Sci. News Let.* 26 Mar. 197/2 Great bangs that dirty the planet's atmosphere with radioactive debris, signaling atomic advances, may be used sparingly, hiding progress to competitive nations.

2. *intr.* To become dirty or soiled.

1864 MRS. CARLYLE *Lett.* III. 231 Dark blue morocco.. which won't dirty in a hurry.

Hence **ˈdirtying** *vbl. sb.*

1674 N. FAIRFAX *Bulk & Selv.* 23 A foolish blasphemy or dirtying of God.

dirty Allan. Also 9 **dirten-, -allen, -aulin.** A species of skua, *Stercorarius crepidatus*, which obtains its food chiefly by pursuing gulls and other sea-birds, and forcing them to disgorge their prey, which it then catches up; = DIRT-BIRD.

1771 PENNANT *Tour Scotl. in 1769*, 78 (Jam. s.v. *Aulin*), An Arctic Gull flew near the boat. This is the species that persecutes and pursues the lesser kinds, till they mute through fear, when it catches their excrement ere they reach the water: the boatmen, on that account, styled it the dirty Aulin. **1806** NEILL *Tour Orkn. & Shetl.* 201 (Jam. s.v. *Scouti-aulin*) This bird is sometimes simply called the Allan; sometimes the Dirten-allan. **1821** A. FISHER *Jrnl.* 18 Commonly called by our Greenland seamen the boatswain, and sometimes dirty Allen, a name somewhat analogous to that by which it is characterized by the Danes. **1844** *Zoologist* II. 515 Richardson's skua, 'Dirten Allen.' **1885** [see DIRT-BIRD].

ˈdirtyish, *a.* [f. DIRTY *a.* + -ISH.] Somewhat dirty.

1825 HONE *Every-day Bk.* I. 1189 Her hair was of a dirtyish flaxen hue. **1840** *Tait's Mag.* VII. 127 Dirtyish yellow gloves. **1877** BESANT & RICE *Son of Vulc.* Prol. 17 Forty dirtyish five-pound notes.

dirump, obs. var. of DISRUMP *v.*

†**diˈruncinate**, *v. Obs. rare*$^{-0}$. [app. f. L. *dī-*, *dis-* apart + *Runcīna* goddess of weeding.]

1623 COCKERAM, *Diruncinate*, to weed.

†**diˈrupt**, *ppl. a. Obs. rare.* [ad. L. *dīrupt-us*, pa. pple. f. *dīrumpĕre* to burst or break asunder. See also DISRUPT.] Rent asunder, burst open.

1531–2 *Act 23 Hen. VIII*, c. 5 §2 The walles..by rage of the sea..be so dirupte, lacerate, and broken.

†**diˈrupt**, *v. Obs. rare.* [f. L. *dīrupt-*, ppl. stem of *dīrumpĕre*.] *trans.* To break asunder.

1548 HALL *Chron., Edw. IV* (1809) 341 Atropos.. dirupted and brake the threde of his naturall life the 9th daie of Aprill.

†**diˈruption.** *Obs. rare.* [ad. L. *dīruptiōn-em*, n. of action f. *dīrumpĕre*: see prec.] Breaking or rending asunder; disruption.

1656 BLOUNT *Glossogr.*, *Diruption*, a bursting, or breaking asunder. **1680** H. MORE *Apocal. Apoc.* 233 As if that Division had been a diruption caused by that Earthquake.

†**dirutor.** *Obs. rare*$^{-0}$. [f. L. *dīruĕre*.]

1656 BLOUNT *Gl.*, *Dirutor*, he that destroys or puls down.

dirvesh, var. of DERVISH.

dirworthe, var. of DEARWORTH *a. Obs.*

diryge, obs. form of DIRGE.

dirzie, var. DURZEE.

dis (dɪs). *v. Printer's slang.* Also **diss.** Colloq. abbrev. of DISTRIBUTE *v.* 5. Hence **dis** *sb.*, type ready for distribution.

1889 BARRÈRE & LELAND *Dict. Slang*, *Diss* (printers), abbreviation for distribution, *i.e.*, printed off type—to be returned to its respective cases, and re-composed. **1899** J. SOUTHWARD *Mod. Printing* II. 168 It is not necessary for an operator to read the matter to be 'dis'd'. *Ibid.* 169 The type being ordinary 'dis', and in no way assorted. **1903** 'No. 7' *25 Yrs. in 17 Prisons* x. 96 There was 'pie' to the left of us, 'pie' to the right of us..and what had only taken a week to 'set up' took nearly a month to 'dis'. *Ibid.* xii. 115 For the first week or two I was put upon 'dissing'. **1970** *Brit. Printer* Aug. 69/1 Type is not dissed and some fairly elaborate machines are needed to cast refills for the cases.

dis (dɪs), *a.* Colloq. abbrev. of DISCONNECTED *ppl. a.* Hence, broken, not working (see also quot. 1925). Also as vb.

1925 FRASER & GIBBONS *Soldier & Sailor Words* 106 *Gone dis*, a colloquialism for mentally weak. The term comes from a telegraph or telephone signaller's phrase meaning disconnected. **1931** T. R. G. LYELL *Slang* 219 The poor old chap's brain's going dis. **1932** 'R. STRANGER' *Outl. Wireless* iii. 151 If the circuit is broken at any point, electron current ceases to flow, and we say that the circuit is 'dis'. **1932** *Telegr. & Teleph. Jrnl.* July 218/2 Her mistress had just gone out intending to report her line 'dis.' via a call office. **1937** *Wireless World* 26 Feb. 215/3 There's no warning whistle to tell him [*sc.* the wireless listener] the speaker is 'dissed'. **1969** P. DICKINSON *Pride of Heroes* 124 You've heard about me dissing my wirelesses? **1971** —— *Sleep & his Brother* v. 122 That dismal little switchboard in her room went dis... I found a hairpin which she'd dropped across the terminals.

dis., abbreviation of DISCOUNT; †also of L. *disputābilis* proper for disputation (see quot.)

1574 M. STOKYS in Peacock *Stat. Cambridge* (1841) App. A. p. xiv, One of the Bedels must..proclayme thorder of their standynge..upon the Dis Dayes.. Yf it be Dys, then.. from one of the Clocke untyll fyve.

dis- (ME. also **dys-**) *prefix*, of L. origin. [L. *dis-* was related to *bis*, orig. **dvis* = Gr. δις twice, from *duo*, δύο two, the primary meaning being 'two-ways, in twain'.] In L., *dis-* was retained in full before *c, p, q, s, t*, sometimes before *g, h, j*, and usually before the vowels, where, however, it sometimes became *dir-* (as in *dirībēre* = *dis* + *habēre*, *dirimēre* = *dis* + *emēre*); before *f*, it was assimilated, as *dif-* (as in *dif-ferre, dif-fūsus*); before the other consonants, it was reduced to *dī-* (DI-[1]). In late L. the full *dis-* was often restored instead of *dī-* (cf. Eng. *dismiss, disrupt*); and the prefix itself became of more frequent use by being substituted in many words for L. *dē-*: see DE- *pref.* I. 6. The regular Romanic form of *dis-* (*dif-*) was *des-* (*def-*) as in OIt., Sp., Pg., Pr., OFr. In F. *s* (*f*) before a consonant became mute, and was finally dropped in writing, giving mod.F. *dé-*. In OF. words of learned origin adopted from L., the L. *dis-* was usually retained; and under the influence of these, *dis-* was often substituted for, or used alongside of, *des-* in the inherited words, e.g. *descorder, discorder.* The early OF. words in English exhibit the prefix in these forms; *des-* prevailing in the popular words, *dis-* (*dys-*) in those of learned origin. But before the close of the ME. period, the latinized form *dis-* (*dys-*) was uniformly substituted, and *des-* became entirely obsolete, or was retained only in a few words in which its nature was not distinctly recognized, as DESCANT. All words taken from L. in the modern period have *dis-*.

Hence, in English, *dis-* appears (1) as the English and French representative of L. *dis-* in words adopted from L.; (2) as the English representative of OF. *des-* (mod.F. *dé-, dés-*), the inherited form of L. *dis-*; (3) as the representative of late L. *dis-*, Romanic *des-*, substituted for L. *dē-*; (4) as a living prefix, arising from the analysis of these, and extended to other words without respect to their origin.

In Latin, compounds in *dis-* were frequently the opposites of those in *com-, con-*; e.g. *concolor* of the same colour, *discolor* of different colours; *concordia* concord, *discordia* discord; *conjunctio* joining together, *disjunctio* separation; *compendium* profit, *dispendium* loss; *consentīre* to agree in feeling, *dissentīre* to disagree in opinion, etc. In cl.L. *dis-* was rarely prefixed to another prefix, though *disconducĕre* to be unprofitable, is used by Plautus, and *disconvenīre* to disagree, by Horace; but in late L. and Romanic, compounds in *discon-*, expressing the separation of elements of which *com-, con-* expressed the junction, became very numerous; many words of this type have come down through Fr. into English, where others have been formed after them: cf. *discoherent, discomfit, discomfort, discommend, discompose, discompound, disconnect, disconsolate, discontent, discontinue.*

In some words beginning with *dis-*, the prefix is *di-*, the *s* being the initial of the radical (e.g. *di-sperse, di-stinguish*). But by identity of phonetic change, *dis-* here also became *des-* (sometimes reduced to *de-*) in OF., whence also *des-* in ME. as *desperse, destincte*; at the Renascence these were rectified to *dis-*.

The following are the chief senses of *dis-* in Latin and English:

I. As an etymological element. In the senses:

1. 'In twain, in different directions, apart, asunder,' hence 'abroad, away'; as *discernĕre* to discern, *discutĕre* discuss, *dīlapidāre* dilapidate, *dīmittĕre* dismiss, *dīrumpĕre* disrupt, *dissentīre* dissent, *distendĕre* distend, *dīvidĕre* divide.

2. 'Between, so as to separate or distinguish'; as *dījūdicāre* to dijudicate, *dīligĕre* choose with a preference, love.

3. 'Separately, singly, one by one'; as *dīnumerāre* to dinumerate, *disputāre* dispute.

4. With privative sense, implying removal, aversion, negation, reversal of action (cf. DE- I. 6), as *discalceātus* unshod, *diffibulāre* to unclasp, *disjungĕre* disjoin, *displicēre* displease, *dissociāre* dissociate, *dissuādēre*, dissuade.

5. With verbs having already a sense of division, solution, separation, or undoing, the addition of *dis-* was naturally intensive, 'away, out and out, utterly, exceedingly', as in *disperīre* to perish utterly, *dispudēre* to be utterly ashamed, *distædēre* to be utterly wearied or disgusted; hence it became an intensive in some other verbs, as *dīlaudāre* to praise exceedingly, *discupĕre* to desire vehemently, *dissuavīrī* to kiss ardently. In the same way, English has several verbs in which *dis-* adds intensity to words having already a sense of undoing, as in *disalter*, *disaltern*, *disannul*.

II. As a living prefix, with privative force.

(Extended from 4, and like F. *des-*, *dé-*, used with verbs, substantives, and adjectives, without regard to their origin.

1659 O. Walker *Oratory* 31 Some Prepositions there are, which may be prefixed at pleasure, as, *un*, *dis*, *re*.)

6. Forming compound verbs (with their derivative sbs., adjs., etc.) having the sense of undoing or reversing the action or effect of the simple verb.

Usually formed by the addition of *dis-* to an existing verb; sometimes, however, formed from a sb. or adj. by prefixing *dis-* and adding a verbal suffix, *-ize*, *-ate*, *-fy*, etc.

Most of these formations, including all the more important and permanent, are treated in their alphabetical places as Main words, e.g. DISAFFIRM, DISESTABLISH, DISOWN. Of others, chiefly nonce-words, examples are, ***disanagrammatize***, ***disangularize***, ***disasinate***, ***disasinize*** (to deprive of asinine nature), ***disByronize***, ***discompound***, ***disdeify***, ***disdenominationalize***, ***disdub***, ***disexcommunicate***, ***dishellenize***, ***dislegitimate***, ***dispantheonize***, ***dispapalize***, ***dispericra-niate***, ***disrestore***.

1610 Donne *Pseudo-Martyr* §54. 150 In the wordes of him..who cals himself Clarus Bonarscius but is unmask'd and *Disanagrammatized by his fellow who calls him Carolus Scribanus. *c* **1820** G. S. Faber *Eight Dissert.* (1845) II. 14 The more flowing character, thus ultimately rounded off or *disangularized, is..denominated Rabbinical Hebrew. **1660** Howell *Parly of Beasts* 28 Doth he [that asse] desire to be *disasinated and become man again? **1868** Lowell *Witchcraft* Prose Wks. 1890 II. 361 Two witches who kept an inn made an ass of a young actor..But one day making his escape..he..was *disasinized to the extent of recovering his original shape. **1878** *Scribner's Mag.* XV. 45/2 Europe was getting sadly *dis-Byronized. **1627–47** Feltham *Resolves* I. xvi. 53 The Papists pourtray Him [God] as an old man and by this means *disdeifie Him. **1870** *Q. Rev.* Jan. 292 The existing system [of education] might be *dis-denominationalized to the utmost extent compatible with the maintenance of..energy in the conduct of the schools. **1566** Drant *Horace Sat.* v. D, I nowe can dubbe a protestant, and eke *disdubbe agayne. **1647** *Power of Keys* iv. 105 [It] signifies receiving men into the Church, *disexcommunicating. **1852** Grote *Greece* II. lxxvi. X. 21 During most part of the Peloponnesian war, Cyprus became sensibly *dishellenised. **1864** Carlyle *Fredk. Gt.* IV. 258 Legitimated in 1673..dislegitimated again. **1801** *Paris as it was* II. xlviii. 137 Marat..was..*pantheonized*, that is, interred in the Pantheon. When..reason began to resume her empire, he was *dispantheonized. **1616** M. A. De Dominis *Motives* 78 A Spectacle..dangerous for Romanists to behold, lest it should presently *dispapalize them. **1803** Lamb *Let. to Mr. Manning* (1888) I. 204 Liquor and company..have quite *dispericraniated me, as one may say. **1874** Micklethwaite *Mod. Par. Churches* 224 Old churches which have been restored must be **dis*-restored.

7. With substantives, forming verbs (with their ppl. adjs., etc.) in the senses: **a.** To strip of, free or rid of, to bereave or deprive of the possession of (the thing expressed by the sb. element). Examples: ***discharacter***, ***discrested***, ***disennui***, ***diseye***, ***disfoliaged***, ***disgeneral***, ***disgig***, ***disheaven***, ***dislaurel***, ***dislipped***, ***disnosed***, ***disnumber***, ***disperiwig***, ***dispowder***, ***disring***, ***distrouser***, ***diswench***. See also DISCLOUD, DISEDGE, DISFROCK, DISHORN, DISPEOPLE, DISQUANTITY, DISWORTH, etc.

1563–87 Foxe *A. & M.* (1596) 131/2 If he did well in so dispreesting and *discharactering Formosus for such privat offenses. **1887** Swinburne *Locrine* III. ii. 66 Discrowned, disrobed, *discrested. **1829** *Young Lady's Bk.* 363 Many persons..have..run all over the world, to *disennui themselves. **1719** London & Wise *Compl. Gard.* 192 We search about the Foot of the Artichoak, and separate or slip off the Suckers or Off-slips..and that is called slipping or *diseying. **1885** *Science* Apr. V. 352 The *disfoliaged forest. **1890** *Star* 26 Nov. 2/7 If Parnell retires, Ireland is enfeebled, and *disgeneraled. **1837** Carlyle *Misc. Ess.* (1872) V. 156 Gigmanity *disgigged, one of the saddest predicaments of man! **1889** *Daily News* 6 Dec. 3/1 The effort of 'gig-manity' to escape 'disgigging'. **1877** Patmore *Unknown Eros* (1890) 16 Yet not for this do thou *disheavened be. **1836** E. Howard *R. Reefer* lvi, To the assistance of the almost *dislipped master's-mate. **1881** Duffield *Don Quix.* III. xxvi. 189 Showing me here a *disnosed Melisendra. **1892** *Pall Mall G.* 1 Sept. 2/3 Stating that the coming Congress of Orientalists is *disnumbered. **1865** Carlyle *Fredk. Gt.* IX. vii, She was much heated and *dispowdered (*dépoudrée*). **1836** T. Hook *G. Gurney* I. iii. 106, I had forgotten to *dis-ring my finger. **1603** Florio *Montaigne* II. xxxvii. (1893) 508 Mine [attacks of stone] doe strangely *dis-wench me.

b. To deprive of the character, rank, or title of; as ***disanimal***, ***disarchbishop***, ***disboy*** (***-ment***), ***discommittee***, ***disconventicle***, ***diselder***, ***disminion***, ***disminister***, ***disprince***, ***disquixot***, ***dis-Turk***. See also DISBISHOP, DISBROTHER, DISCHURCH, DISMAN, etc.

1864 *Times* 10 Oct. 7/4 The boy has been so far *disanimaled that his reasoning powers have been roused into full vitality. **1875** Tennyson *Q. Mary* IV. ii, We had to *disarchbishop and unlord And make you simple Cranmer once again. **1649** *Discommittee [see DISJUSTICE]. **1683** O. U. *Parish Ch. no Conventicles* 34 Their little Variations about Modes..will not be of validity to conventicle or *disconventicle Parochial Churches. **1655** Fuller *Ch. Hist.* VIII. xvi. §12 Preferring rather..to un-Pastor and *dis-Elder themselves. **1599** Chapman *Hum. Dayes M.* Dram. Wks. 1873 I. 73 Neuer was minion so *disminioned. **1743** H. Walpole *Lett. H. Mann* (1833) I. 280 (D.) Can you think.. him [Lord Orford] so totally *disministered as to leave all thoughts of what he has been? **1847** Tennyson *Princess* v. 29 For I was drenched with ooze, and torn with briers..And all one rag, *disprinced from head to heel. **1832** J. P. Kennedy *Swallow B.* v, The most *disquixotted cavalier that ever hung up his shield. **1891** G. Meredith *One of our Conq.* II. iii. 54 To *dis-Turk themselves.

c. To turn out, put out, expel, or dislodge from the place or receptacle implied (cf. DE- II. 2 b); as ***discastle***, ***dischest***, ***discoach***, ***disroost***. See also DISBAR, DISBENCH, DISBOSOM, DISCRADLE, etc.

1876 G. Meredith *Beauch. Career* I. ii. 24 The answer often unseated, and once *discastled, them. **1579** J. Jones *Preserv. Bodie & Soule* I. xxiv. 45 Apt to out breathe, and to *dischest the moistures, humors and iuyces of the body. **1629** Shirley *Grateful Servant* II. i, Madam, here is Prince Lodwick Newly *discoached. **1702** C. Mather *Magn. Christi* VII. App. (1852) 600 To disturb and *disroost these mischievous rooks.

d. To undo or spoil: as DISCOMPLEXION.

8. With adjectives, forming verbs in the sense of: To undo or reverse the quality expressed by the adjective; as DISABLE, ***disabsolute***, ***disgood***, ***disnew***.

1640 Quarles *Enchirid.* To Rdr., The variableness of those Men *disabsolutes all Rules, and limits all Examples. **1647** Ward *Simp. Cobler* 15 A dislocation, which so farre *disgoods the Ordinance, I feare it altogether unhallows it.

9. With a substantive, forming a new substantive expressing the opposite, or denoting the lack or absence, of (the thing in question). Such are: ***disaffectation***, ***disagglomeration***, ***discare***, ***discharity***, ***discircumspection***, ***disconcord***, ***disgenius***, ***dishealth***, ***disindivisibility***, ***disinvagination***. Cf. also DISEASE, DISHONOUR, etc.

1887 *Pall Mall G.* 1 Aug. 12/1 A prince of plain speaking and *disaffectation. **1870** *Contemp. Rev.* XVI. 53 My remarks upon decentralization and *disagglomeration. **1649** J. H. *Motion to Parl. Adv. Learn.* 16 A grosse neglect, and ugly *dis-care of the Publick. *a* **1868** Ld. Brougham in Hinsdale *Garfield & Educ.* (1882) II. 203 The parent of all evil..all discharity, all self-seeking. **1671** J. Davies *Sibylls* I. vi. 12 We meet with many instances of *dis-circumspection, weakness, and an excessive credulity. *a* **1631** Donne *Serm. John* v. 22 (1634) 10 Take the earth..in this concord, or this *disconcord. **1657** Reeve *God's Plea* 20 If he look not the better to it, this Genius will be *disgenius to him. **1887** *Scot. Congregationalist* Oct. 136 Though suffering from *dishealth, he was attentive to the sick. **1799** *Spirit Pub. Jrnls.* (1800) III. 39 This indivisibility of yours turns out downright *disindivisibility.

10. Prefixed to adjectives, with negative force; as DISHONEST, ***disalike***, ***disanswerable***, ***dispenal***.

1563–87 Foxe *A. & M.* (1596) 328/1 They are not cleane contrary, but *disalike. **1600** Hakluyt *Voy.* (1810) III. 13 Nothing *disanswerable to expectation. **1604** *Supplic. Masse Priests* §2 Through the benefite of the *dispenall use or toleration of their Religion.

¶ In Florio's Italian-Engl. Dictionary (esp. in ed. 1611), a large number of words in *dis-* are coined to render It. words in *dis-*, *s-*. Besides those elsewhere dealt with, the following occur:

Disabound, *disabondare*; disapostled, *disapostolato*; disbolden, *sbaldanzire*; discourtiered, *discortegianato*; discrupper, *sgroppare*; diseclips, *diseclissare*; disfury, *disfuriare*; disgianted, *disgigantito*; disgreaten, *disgrandire*; disharnish, *smagliare*; dishumble, *dishumiliare*; disimplaster, *disimpiastrare*; disinpouerish, *dispouerish*, *spouerire*; dislanguish, *dislanguidire*; disobstinate, *disostinare*; dispearle, *disperlare*; dispoeted, *spoetato*; dispupill, *spupillare*; dispurpose sb., *disproposito*; disruded, *disuillanito*; disuermillion, *disuermigliare*; disuigor, *disuigorire*; diswhiten, *sbiancare*; diswoman'd, *sfeminato*.

disa ('daɪsə). *Bot.* [mod.L. (P. J. Bergius *Descr. Plant. ex Capite Bonæ Spei* (1767) 348), of obscure origin.] A tropical African terrestrial orchid of the genus so named, with dark green leaves.

1844 *Curtis's Bot. Mag.* LXX. 4091 (*heading*) Horned-flowered Disa. **1890** Watson & Bean *Orchids* xxx. 235 A position in a house which suits cool Odontoglossums will be found agreeable to Disas. **1930** T. W. Briscoe *Orchids for Amateurs* vi. 109 The Disas are terrestrial, with more or less tuberous roots. **1951** L. G. Green *Grow Lovely, growing Old* vi. 63 Disas and proteas lasted longer too, and cost less than garden flowers. **1966** E. A. C. L. E. Schelpe *Introd. S. Afr. Orchids* 9 Only a few of the Disas would be recognised as orchids by the non-botanist.

disability (dɪsə'bɪlɪtɪ). [f. DISABLE *a.*, after *able*, *ability*.]

1. Want of ability (to discharge any office or function); inability, incapacity, impotence. **b.** An instance of this. (Now *rare* in *gen.* sense.)

1580 Lupton *Sivqila* 139 His disabilitie to performe his promise. **1772–84** Cook *Voy.* (1790) VI. 2038 Their whole frame trembling and paralytic, attended with a disability of raising their heads. **1856** Lever *Martins of Cro'M.* 205 A disability to contest the prizes of life even with such as Mr. Massingbred. **1870** Anderson *Missions Amer. Bd.* IV. xxxix. 364 Crippled by the disability of its oldest native helper.

b. **1645** Milton *Colaster.* Wks. (1847) 223/1 Disabilities to perform what was covenanted. **1768–74** Tucker *Lt. Nat.* II. xxi. (R.), Bringing on the inconveniences, disabilities, pains and mental disorders spoken of. **1824** *Westm. Rev.* II. 194 The author labours under many disabilities for making a good book.

c. Pecuniary inability or want of means.

1624 Jas. I *Sp.* in A. Wilson *Life* (1653) 267 My disabilities are increased by the Charge of my Sonnes journey into Spain. **1648** Boyle *Seraph. Love* (1660) 23. **1701** J. Law *Counc. Trade* (1751) 72 It [Taxing] leaves a dissability equal, and in proportion to its weight. **1857** Ruskin *Pol. Econ. Art* 18 What would you say to the lord of an estate who complained to you of his poverty and disabilities?

2. Incapacity in the eye of the law, or created by the law; a restriction framed to prevent any person or class of persons from sharing in duties or privileges which would otherwise be open to them; legal disqualification.

1641 *Termes de la Ley* 118 b, Disabilitie is when a man.. by any..cause is disabled or made incapable to doe, to inherit, or to take..advantage of a thing which otherwise he might have had or done. **1765–9** Blackstone *Comm.* (1793) 554 The next legal disability is want of age. *a* **1832** Mackintosh *France in 1815* Wks. 1846 III. 193 Of all the lessons of history, there is none more evident in itself..than that persecutions, disabilities, exclusions—all systematic wrong to great bodies of citizens,—are sooner or later punished. **1832** Ht. Martineau *Ireland* 117 The law has at length emancipated us from our civil disabilities. **1849** Macaulay *Hist. Eng.* II. 11 His eagerness to remove the disabilities under which the professors of his religion lay.

† **dis'able**, *a.* *Obs.* [DIS- 10.] Unable; incapable; impotent.

14.. *Certain Balades, Lenuoy* (R.), Consider that my conning is disable To write to you. **1598** Drayton *Heroic. Ep.*, *Rich. II. to Isabel*, As my disable and unworthy Hand Never had Power, belonging to command. **1615** Markham *Eng. Housew.* Pref., This imperfect offer may come to you weak and disable. **1649** Jer. Taylor *Gt. Exemp.* II. Add. §12. 98 To forgive debts to disable persons, to pay debts for them.

disable (dɪs'eɪb(ə)l), *v.* Also 5 **dysable**, 6–7 **dishable**. [f. DIS- 8 + ABLE *a.*]

1. *trans.* To render unable or incapable; to deprive of ability, physical or mental, to incapacitate. Const. *from*, formerly *to*, *for*, or with *inf.*

1548 Gest *Pr. Masse* 89 Lesse hys fyrst offering..be dishabled to the ful contentation of syn. **1574** J. Dee in *Lett. Lit. Men* (Camden) 34 My father was dishabled for leaving unto me due mayntenance. *a* **1602** W. Perkins *Cases Consc.* (1619) 328 Immoderate excesse, whereby we are vtterly disabled from these..duties. *a* **1627** W. Sclater *Romans IV* (1650) 127 We are wilfully disabled to performance. **1772–84** Cook *Voy.* (1790) IV. 1534 Incumbered by many garments..which must disable them to exert their strength in the day of battle. **1848** Hampden *Bampt. Lect.* Introd. (ed. 3) 20 Men..are disabled from understanding what they have been taught to condemn. **1885** Ld. Selborne in *Law Rep.* 28 Ch. Div. 361 The Plaintiff..by selling the property ..disables himself from doing that which by his pleadings he offers to do.

b. *spec.* To render (a man, animal, ship, etc.) incapable of action or use by physical injury or bodily infirmity; to cripple.

1491 Caxton *Vitas Patr.* (W. de W. 1495) II. 204 b/1, I am all dysabled of my membres. **1583** Stanyhurst *Aeneis* II. (Arb.) 63 Thee Gods thee cittye dishable. *a* **1600** Shaks. *Sonn.* lxvi, Strength by limping sway disabled. **1606** G. W[oodcocke] tr. *Hist. Ivstine* 576 His continual sicknes.. was like to dishable the gouernment and sway of so high a place. **1712** Hearne *Collect* (Oxf. Hist. Soc.) III. 296 My writeing hand hath been disabled by a sprain. **1745** P. Thomas *Jrnl. Anson's Voy.* 283 A Wound in his Breast by a Musket-ball..disabled him at present. *c* **1790** Willock *Voy.* 56 We were struck by a sea, which totally disabled us. **1893** *Weekly Notes* 85/2 A member being permanently disabled by an accident.

†**c.** To injure, impair, or render less able *in* some capacity; to deprive of the use *of* (some faculty, power, or possession). Const. *in*, *of*. *Obs.*

1604 Jas. I *Counterbl.* (Arb.) 110 How you are by this custome disabled in your goods. **1622** Malynes *Anc. Law-Merch.* 435 All things that depriue or disable the debtor in any of these, do weaken and lessen his meanes. **1660** F. Brooke tr. *Le Blanc's Trav.* 292 He..disabled them of sixteen thousand good horses.

2. *spec.* To incapacitate legally; to pronounce legally incapable; to hinder or restrain (any person or class of persons) from performing acts or enjoying rights which would otherwise be open to them; to disqualify.

1485 in *Paston Lett.* No. 883. III. 316 Piers, Bisshop of Exeter..with other dyvers his rebelles and traytours disabled and atteynted by the..High Court of Parlement. **1524** in *Vicary's Anatomie* (1888) App. iii. 156 Doctour

Bentley & doctour Yakesley.. examyners Admytted to hable or disable suche as practise phisik & Surgery in London. **1612** DAVIES *Why Ireland, etc.* (1747) 105 The Irish were disabled to bring any action at the Common Lawe. **1632** *Star Chamb. Cases* (Camden) 111 Mr Tuke the elder was fyned 100li for this contempt, and to be imprisoned and disabled in their testimony for ever. **1637** *Decree Star Chamb.* §19 in *Milton's Areop.* (Arb.) 18 Vpon paine of being for euer disabled of the vse of a Presse or printing-house. **1678** LUTTRELL *Brief Rel.* (1857) I. 4 An act.. disabling papists from sitting in either house of parliament. **1700** *Ibid.* IV. 673 Papists, by the Act of Settlement, are disabled to inherit the crown. **1862** LD. BROUGHAM *Brit. Const.* xvii. 274 Statutory provisions disabling the Judges from sitting in the House of Commons.

3. To pronounce incapable; hence, to disparage, depreciate, detract from, belittle; *refl.* to depreciate one's own competence or fitness for an appointment or honour (chiefly as a conventional tribute to modesty). *arch.* or *Obs.*

a **1529** SKELTON *Replyc.* 26 Our glorious lady to disable And heinously on her to bable. *c* **1555** HARPSFIELD *Divorce Hen. VIII* (1878) 92 That.. presume so far to disable.. disgrace and infame this marriage. **1600** SHAKS. *A.Y.L.* IV. i. 34 Farewell Monsieur Traueller:.. disable all the benefits of your owne Countrie: be out of loue with your natuitie. **1619** *Crt. & Times Jas I* (1849) II. 142 He disabled himself divers ways, but specially, that he thought himself unworthy to sit in that place. **1709** STRYPE *Ann. Ref.* I. xxvi. 294 When Sir Edward Rogers.. had recommended him to the house to be their speaker, and Williams [the speaker recommended] had disabled himself, Cecil.. required him to take the place. **1763** [see DISABLING *ppl. a.*]

†**4.** To make or pronounce of no force or validity.

1552 HULOET, Disable, or refuse, or reiect, *ocquinisco.* **1584** R. SCOT *Discov. Witchcr.* II. iii. 18 The depositions of manie women at one instant are disabled as insufficient in lawe. **1598** HAKLUYT *Voy.* I. 221 (R.) Neither meane I to auouch.. ne to disable or confute those thinges which.. have beene reported. **1665** GLANVILL *Scepsis Sci.* 53 Some few of whose charges against Aristotle our Author indeavours to defeat and disable. **1693** *Apol. Clergy Scot.* 25 The Council may stop and disable the Laws.

dis'able, *sb.* [f. prec. vb.] The act of disabling; disablement.

1827 SIR J. BARRINGTON *Pers. Sk.* II. 16 A disarm is considered the same as a disable.

disabled (dɪs'eɪb(ə)ld), *ppl. a.* [f. DISABLE *v.* + -ED[1].] Rendered incapable of action or use, *esp.* by physical injury; incapacitated: see the verb.

1633 G. HERBERT *Temple, Crosse* iii, I am in all a weak disabled thing. **1695** LOND. GAZ. No. 3142/2 He saw off the Durces a disabled Ship. **1725** POPE *Odyss.* III. 381 Shatter'd vessels, and disabled oars. **1837** HT. MARTINEAU *Soc. Amer.* III. 190 The families of intemperate or disabled men.

disablement (dɪs'eɪb(ə)lmənt). [f. as prec. + -MENT.]

1. The action of disabling; the fact or condition of being disabled.

1684 PH. HENRY *Diaries & Lett.* (1882) 322, I heard of ye Death of Mr. Jo. Tho... after several yeares disablement. *c* **1716** SOUTH *Serm.* V. iv. 182 (T.) This is only an interruption of the acts, rather than any disablement of the [intellectual judging] faculty. **1806** W. TAYLOR in *Ann. Rev.* IV. 230 This practice brings on diseases of the foot and ankles, and disablement for military service. **1853** GROTE *Greece* II. lxxxv. XI. 249 Encouraged by the evident disablement of their enemies. **1884** *Law Times* 27 Sept. 356/1 Compulsory assurance.. against sickness and disablement.

2. The imposition of a legal disability.

1485 *Act 1 Hen. VII* in *Materials Hist. Hen. VII* (Rolls) I. 120 Actes of attainder, forfeiture, and disablement. **1503-4** *Act 19 Hen. VII*, c. 35 §2 The seid acte of Atteyndre .. or eny other thinges to the disabilment of the seid Gilbert and of his heirez. *a* **1626** BACON *Observ. Libel in 1592* (T.), The penalty.. was.. disablement to take any promotion, or to exercise any charge. **1680** BAXTER *Answ. Stillingfl.* iv. 26 By Imprisonment, Banishment, or Death, or such Disablement.

3. *attrib.*

1898 *Westm. Gaz.* 23 June 9/1 A crushing liability for death and disablement claims. **1898** *Daily News* 25 June 6/6 The first 26 weeks' disablement pay. **1920** *Act 10 Geo. V.* c. 10 §2 The rate of disablement benefit. **1961** *Lancet* 2 Sept. 539/2 A disablement resettlement officer (D.R.O.) from the local labour exchange attends the weekly assessment conference.

†**dis'ableness.** *Obs.* [f. DISABLE *a.* + -NESS.]

1. Inability, incapacity.

1614 MARKHAM *Cheap Husb.* (1623) 65 A disablenesse to bow downe his necke. **1665** WITHER *Lord's Prayer* 122 A natural disableness to do any good.

2. The state of being disabled or injured.

1666 PEPYS *Diary* 4 July, Many of our ships coming in with very small disableness.

disabler (dɪs'eɪblə(r)). [f. DISABLE *v.* + -ER[1].] One who or that which disables. (By Puttenham used for the figure *meiosis* in rhetoric, expressing disparagement: cf. DISABLE *v.* 3.)

1589 PUTTENHAM *Eng. Poesie* III. xvii. (Arb.) 195 Such speach is by the figure Meiosis or the disabler spoken of hereafter in the place of sententious figures. *Ibid.* III. xix. 227 We call him the Disabler or figure of Extenuation.

disabling (dɪs'eɪblɪŋ), *vbl. sb.* [f. as prec. + -ING[1].] The action of the verb DISABLE, q.v.

1495 *Act 11 Hen. VII*, c. 30 Preamb., The said atteyndre and dishabling of the said Gervys. **1555** ABP. PARKER *Ps.* lxix. 188 They did it cast, to my disabelyng. **1658-9** *Burton's Diary* (1828) III. 248, I was against utter disabling in the other case, because I would not have you meddle with after Parliaments.

dis'abling, *ppl. a.* [f. as prec. + -ING[2].] That disables: see the verb.

1756 *Monitor* I. xxxii. 293 Must that fire.. be smothered by disabling clauses in statutes? **1763** HARDWICKE in Ld. Campbell *Chancellors* (1857) VI. cxxxvii. 288, I made all the dutiful, grateful, but disabling speeches that became me. **1832** LEWIS *Use & Ab. Pol. Terms* xv. 142 The absence of a disabling law. **1856** MRS. BROWNING *Aur. Leigh* II. 501 The creaking of the door.. Which let upon you such disabling news.

†**disa'bridge**, *v. Obs. rare.* [DIS- 6.] *trans.* To undo the abridgement of; to lengthen out.

1592 SYLVESTER *Du Bartas, Tri. Faith* III. xi, Hee, whose life the Lord did dis-abbridge.. The most religious matchless Ezechias.

disabusal (dɪsə'bju:zəl). [f. DISABUSE *v.* + -AL[1]; after *abusal.*] The action of disabusing; = DISABUSE *sb.*

1876 MRS. WHITNEY *Sights & Ins.* II. iii. 364 Whatever.. she risked in her own disabusal by taking a course that should make all plain.

†**disa'buse**, *sb. Obs.* [f. DIS- 9 + ABUSE *sb.*, under influence of DISABUSE *v.*] The act of disabusing, or fact of being disabused.

1620 SHELTON *Quix.* IV. xxxiii. 253 I am aggrieved that this Disabuse hath happened so late unto me. **1700** ASTRY tr. *Saavedra-Faxardo* I. 339 Disabuse is the Son of Truth.

disabuse (dɪsə'bju:z), *v.* [f. DIS- 6 + ABUSE *v.*]

1. *trans.* To free from abuse, error, or mistake (see ABUSE *v.* 4 b, *sb.* 2); to relieve from fallacy or deception; to undeceive.

1611 COTGR., *Desabuser*, to disabuse, to rid from abuses. **1653** WALTON *Angler* 6, I hope in time to disabuse you and make the contrary appear evidently. **1669** GALE *Crt. Gentiles* I. Introd. 7 To.. disabuse our minds from those false Images. **1732** POPE *Ess. Man* II. 14 [Man] still by himself abus'd, or dis-abus'd. **1856** FROUDE *Hist. Eng.* (1858) I. ii. 136 It remained for Clement VII to disabuse men of their alarms. **1872** MINTO *Eng. Prose Lit.* Introd. 24 To disabuse their minds of the idea that the one is wrong, the other right.

2. As an intensive of *abuse*: To mar, spoil, misuse. *Sc.*

1825-80 in JAMIESON.

Hence **disa'bused** *ppl. a.*

1611 COTGR., *Desabusé*.. disabused; unblinded; deliuered of errors, rid from abuses. **1649** JER. TAYLOR *Gt. Exemp.* xii. §20 Wise and disabused persons.

†**disac'cept**, *v. Obs. rare.* [f. DIS- 6 + ACCEPT *v.*] *trans.* To refuse acceptance to, not to accept; to decline.

1647 N. BACON *Disc. Govt. Eng.* I. xlvii. (1739) 77 It had formerly made many fair proffers of service to this Island, but it was disaccepted.

†**disac'ceptable**, *a. Obs. rare.* [f. DIS- 10.] Not acceptable, unacceptable.

1687 SETTLE *Refl. Dryden* 63 Yet I hope my instructions.. may not be wholly disacceptable.

†**disac'ceptance.** *Obs.* [f. DISACCEPT *v.*, after *acceptance.*] Refusal to accept, non-acceptance.

1642 O. SEDGWICKE *Eng. Preserv.* 36 Particular and exclusive actings.. serve onely to the disacceptance of the workes. *a* **1652** J. SMITH *Sel. Disc.* vii. 351 God's acceptance or disacceptance of things is.. proportionable to his judgment. **1720** S. SEWALL *Diary* 23 July (1882) III. 258 Gave the Govr. £500 only.. He sent it back with a Note expressing his Disacceptance.

disaccharide (daɪ'sækəraɪd). *Chem.* Also †-id. [f. DI-[2] 2 + SACCHARIDE.] Any sugar that consists of two monosaccharide residues linked together.

1892 [see BIOSE]. **1905** E. F. ARMSTRONG in *Proc. R. Soc.* B. LXXVI. 592 The enzymes which are capable of inducing the hydrolysis of disaccharides or bioses. **1938** *Thorpe's Dict. Appl. Chem.* (ed. 4) II. 298/1 The formulæ of the disaccharides have undergone revision on the basis of the accepted pyranose formula for glucose. **1954** *Ibid.* XI. 176/1 Disaccharides.. can be split by acid hydrolysis or enzymes into their constituent hexose monosaccharides. **1970** R. W. MCGILVERY *Biochem.* xxvi. 634 The infant living on the milk produced by his mother's mammary glands generates approximately 60 per cent of his ATP by oxidizing the fat in the milk and 40 per cent by oxidizing the disaccharide, lactose.

disaccommodate (dɪsə'kɒmədeɪt), *v.* ? *Obs.* [f. DIS- 6 + ACCOMMODATE *v.*] *trans.* To put to inconvenience, to incommode; the reverse of to ACCOMMODATE.

1611 COTGR., *Desaccommoder*, to disaccommodate. **1640** J. ROUS *Diary* (Camden) 96 It may not only disaccommodate, but occasion the hurte.. of many of his Majesties subjects. **1767** WARBURTON *Lett.* (1809) 394, I hope this will not disaccommodate you. **1826** SOUTHEY in *Q. Rev.* XXXIV. 330 The neck and the hands.. were disaccommodated with a haircloth tippet and haircloth gloves.

disaccommodation (dɪsə,kɒmə'deɪʃən). ? *Obs.* [n. of action f. prec.: cf. ACCOMMODATION and DIS- 9.] The action of disaccommodating or condition of being disaccommodated; want of accommodation; unsuitableness; disagreement.

1619 NAUNTON in *Fortesc. Papers* 95 The Venetians' disaccommodations with the Pope. **1660** BLOUNT *Boscobel* 37 John.. acquainted Mr. Whitgreave.. that His Majesty was return'd to Boscobel, and the disaccommodation he had there. **1662** PETTY *Taxes* 23 Too great a confinement.. and withall a disaccommodation in the time of the work. **1677** HALE *Prim. Orig. Man.* II. ix. 217 According to the accommodation or disaccommodation of them [the places] to such Calamities. *Ibid.* IV. v. 332 The least disproportion or disaccommodation of one to the other would spoil the whole Work.

†**disa'ccompany**, *v. Obs. rare.* [f. DIS- 6 + ACCOMPANY *v.*] *trans.* To cease to accompany or frequent; to deprive of one's company. Hence †**disa'ccompanied** *ppl. a.*, deprived of company; unaccompanied; unfrequented; companionless.

1598 FLORIO, *Sconuersare*, to disaccompanie, to vnfrequent. *Sconuersatione*, a disaccompanying, an vnfrequenting. **1618** DANIEL *Coll. Hist. Eng.* (1621) 20 To come disaccompanied was for neither [life nor honour]. **1631** *Celestina* XXI. 201 Tell me what hast thou done with my daughter? where hast thou bestow'd her? who shall accompany my disaccompanied habitation?

disaccord (dɪsə'kɔ:d), *sb.* [f. DIS- 9 + ACCORD *sb.*; after *disaccord* vb.: cf. F. *désaccord.*] The reverse of accord or harmony; disagreement, variance.

1809 SOUTHEY *Lett.* (1856) II. 132 Upon the ground of his disaccord with their principles of politics. **1871** FARRAR *Witn. Hist.* ii. 62 It was in flagrant disaccord with the ideal of the Society in the bosom of which it rose. **1889** *Sat. Rev.* 19 Oct. 436/2 There is no disaccord between what he is at the outset and what he becomes.

disaccord (dɪsə'kɔ:d), *v.* [ME. *disacorde-n*, a. OF. *desa(c)corder*, f. *des-*, DIS- 4 + *a(c)corder* to ACCORD, after *desa(c)cord* sb. (12th c. in Hatz.-Darm.).] *intr.* To be out of accord or harmony; to be at discord, to disagree; to refuse assent.

c **1400** *Test. Love* III. (R.), Trewly presence and predestinacion in nothing disacorden. *c* **1400** tr. *Secreta Secret., Gov. Lordsh.* 101 And if it disacorde to þy demynge, þanne it ys to þe to loke whether it be helpand and profytable. *Ibid.* 51 Opyn þinge ys þat qualytes er to be despysed whenne þey disacord fro þeir mein. **1561** T. NORTON *Calvin's Inst.* IV. 111 From which also not muche disaccordeth the other place of the Apostle aboue alleged. **1596** SPENSER *F.Q.* VI. iii. 7 A noble Lord.. sought her to affy To a great pere; but she did disaccord, Ne could her liking to his love apply. **1805** *Monthly Mag.* XX. 147 This disaccords with the precise date. **1874** MIVART *Contemp. Evol.* (1876) 210 An action.. which disaccords with the action of blind chance.

disa'ccordance. *rare.* [f. DISACCORD *v.*, after *accordance*: cf. OF. *desacordance.*]

Disagreement: = DISACCORD *sb.*

1862 T. A. TROLLOPE *Marietta* II. viii. 127 A line of action so wholly in disaccordance with Tuscan ideas. **1891** E. & D. GERARD *Sensitive Plant* III. III. xi. 76 Had her own feelings been all along in disaccordance to her mother's verdict?

disa'ccordant (dɪsə'kɔ:dənt), *a. rare.* [a. F. *désaccordant*, AF. *disaccordant* (14th c. in Godef.), pr. pple. of *désaccorder* to DISACCORD.] Not agreeing, not in accord.

1494 FABYAN *Chron.* V. c. 75 It is disacordaunt vnto other wryters. **1839** BAILEY *Festus* xix. (1848) 206 Built up an idol of all elements Most disaccordant.

†**disa'ccount**, *v. Obs. rare.* [f. DIS- 6, 7 + ACCOUNT *v.* or *sb.*] *trans.* To strike out of an account or reckoning.

1640 EARL CORK in *Sir R. Boyle's Diary* Ser. I. (1886) V. 160 That 150li is by him to be repaid and disaccownted.

disaccustom (dɪsə'kʌstəm), *v.* In 5 dysac-. [a. OF. *desacoustumer, desacostumer* (12-13th c.), mod.F. *désaccoutumer*, f. *des-*, DIS- 4 + *acostumer, accoutumer* to ACCUSTOM.]

1. *trans.* To render (a thing) no longer customary; to disuse, break off (a habit or practice). *arch.*

1484 CAXTON *Curiall* 3 He shal dine.. and.. soupe in suche facon that he shal dysacustome hys time and hys maner of lyuyng. **1594** CONSTABLE *Diana* VIII. iv, And I though disaccustoming my Muse.. May one day raise my stile as others use. **1610** DONNE *Pseudo-Martyr* 45 Those stiles, which Christian humilitie hath made them dis-accustome and leave off. **1814** CARY *Dante, Paradise* XVI. 11 With greeting such as Rome was first to bear, But since hath disaccustom'd.

2. To render (a person) unaccustomed or unused to something (to which he was previously accustomed); to cause to lose a habit. Const. *to*, †*from.*

1530 PALSGR. 517/1 For one that is disacustumed, it is a great payne to be brought in good order. **1636** E. DACRES tr. *Machiavel's Disc. Livy* I. xvii. 90 Sufficient, to disaccustome them to the ill, and accustome them throughly to the good. **1686** F. SPENCE tr. *Varillas' Ho. Medicis* 306 The people might be disaccustom'd from exercising them. **1836** SIR W. HAMILTON *Discuss.* (1852) 271 Such application insensibly disaccustomed us to the use of our reason. **1881** H. JAMES *Portr. Lady* xxxii, Disaccustomed to living with an invalid.

Hence **disa'ccustomed** *ppl. a.*; **disa'ccustomedness**; also †**disa'ccustomance** (*obs.*), disuse.

1502 *Ord. Crysten Men* (W. de W. 1506) IV. xxii. 299 Moeuynge the helpe of god hym to dyscustome, unto the whiche dysacustomaunce be not many comyn in the espace of .xx. or .xxx. yeres. **1580** SIDNEY *Arcadia* IV. (1622) 412 Some long disaccustomed paines. **1632** SHERWOOD, Disaccustomednesse, *desaccoustumance*. **1825** SOUTHEY *Tale Paraguay* III. 46 How strangely to her disaccustom'd ear Came even the accents of her native tongue!

disacidify (dɪsəˈsɪdɪfaɪ), *v. rare.* [DIS- 6.] *trans.* To do away with the acidity of.
1864 in WEBSTER. **1883** in *Syd. Soc. Lex.*

† **disack'nowledge**, *sb. Obs.* [f. next: cf. ACKNOWLEDGE *sb.*] The act of dis-acknowledging; non-acknowledgement.
1603 FLORIO *Montaigne* III. ix. (1632) 536 The most ordinary assurance I take of my people, is a kinde of disacknowledge or neglect.

disacknowledge (dɪsækˈnɒlɪdʒ), *v.* [f. DIS- 6 + ACKNOWLEDGE *v.*] *trans.* To refuse to acknowledge; to renounce, disown.
1598 FLORIO, *Sconóscere*, to disacknowledge. *Sconosciuto*, disacknowledged, forgotten. **1613** MARKHAM *Eng. Husbandman* I. II. xiv. (1635) 187 These violent opinions I altogether disacknowledge. **1692** SOUTH *12 Serm.* (1697) I. 108 By words and oral expressions verbally to deny, and disacknowledge it. **1836** MARRYAT *Japhet* lxxiv, I disinherit, I disacknowledge you. **1859** TROLLOPE *Bertrams* II. v. 75 You are not the man to disacknowledge the burden.
Hence **disack'nowledging** *vbl. sb.*; also **disack'nowledger**, one who disacknowledges; **disack'nowledgement**, the fact of dis-acknowledging.
1650 B. *Discolliminium* 8 No..conscientious Subject ought to obey such a Power..with an acknowledgement of its Authority, or without a disacknowledgement of it. *a* **1660** HAMMOND *Wks.* II. II. 135 (R.) A disacknowledging or rejecting the due government. **1661** BP. SANDERSON *Episc.* (1673) 55 A disacknowledgment of the Kings Authority and Supremacy Ecclesiastical. **1665** J. SERGEANT *Sure-footing* 101 Disacknowledgers of Tradition.

disa'cquaint, *v.* ? *Obs.* [f. DIS- 6 + ACQUAINT *v.*] *trans.* To make no longer acquainted; to estrange; to render unfamiliar (quot. 1567). Hence **disa'cquainted** *ppl. a.*
1548 UDALL, etc. *Erasm. Par. Luke* xvi. 16 Ye must now disacquaint and estraunge yourselfes from the sour old wine of Moses lawe. **1567** DRANT *Horace' Epist.* vi. Dj, Seeke how to chase that griefe awaye to make it disaquainted. **1635** QUARLES *Emblems* I. viii. (1718) 33 When disacquainted sense becomes a stranger, And takes no knowledge of an old disease. **1677** HALE *Contempl.* II. 89 This kind of dealing.. will in a little time dis-acquaint the Soul with them, and make the Soul and them strangers one to another.

disacquaintance (dɪsəˈkweɪntəns). ? *Obs.* [f. prec., after *acquaintance*: cf. DIS- 9.] The state of being disacquainted; want of acquaintance; unfamiliarity.
1589 PUTTENHAM *English Poesie* III. ix. (Arb.) 169 The straungenesse..proceedes but of noueltie and disaquaintance with our eares. **1672** BAXTER in *Life J. Alleine* (1838) I. 3 Men's strangeness and disacquaintance with those that are good. **1830** LAMB *Let. to Gilman* Wks. (1865) 165 The innocent taste of which [milk-porridge] I am anxious to renew after half a century's disacquaintance.

disacrone: see next.

disacryl (dɪsˈækrɪl). *Chem.* [f. DIS- (implying disintegration or dissolution) + ACRYL.] A white flocculent substance into which acrolein changes when kept for some time. Called also *disacrone*. Also *attrib.*, as *disacryl resin*, a resinous matter similarly formed.
1863–72 WATTS *Dict. Chem.* II. 336 Acrolein when kept.. changes sometimes..into a resinous matter, disacryl resin. Disacryl is a white, tasteless, inodorous powder which becomes strongly electrical by friction.

† **disa'dapt**, *v. Obs. rare*$^{-0}$. [f. DIS- 6 + ADAPT *v.*] *trans.* To render unfit. Hence **disa'dapted** *ppl. a.*, **disa'dapting** *vbl. sb.*
1611 COTGR., *Desagencer*, to disadapt, disadiust. *Ibid.*, *Desagencé*, disadapted, disadiusted. *Ibid.*, *Desagencement*, a disadapting, disadiusting.

† **disa'djust**, *v. Obs. rare.* [f. DIS- 6 + ADJUST *v.*] *trans.* To undo the adjustment of; to unsettle, disturb. Hence **disa'djusted** *ppl. a.*, **disa'djusting** *vbl. sb.*
1611 COTGR. [see prec.] **1746–7** HERVEY *Medit.*, *On Night* II. (1748) 50 When the Thoughts are once disadjusted, why are they not always in Confusion?

† **disad'monish**, *v. Obs. rare.* [f. DIS- 6 + ADMONISH *v.*] *trans.* To dissuade, to disadvise.
1611 COTGR., *Desadmonesté*, disadmonished, or dissuaded. **1847–78** in HALLIWELL.

† **disa'dorn**, *v. Obs. rare.* [f. DIS- 6 + ADORN *v.*] *trans.* To deprive of adornment; to disfigure.
1598 FLORIO, *Disbrauare*, to disadorne or spoile of brauerie. **1621** G. SANDYS *Ovid's Met.* IX. (1626) 176 My brow..[he] disadornes: By breaking one of my ingaged hornes. *a* **1729** CONGREVE *Homer's Hymn Venus* (T.), She saw grey hairs begin to spread, Deform his beard, and disadorn his head.

† **disad'vance**, *v. Obs.* [ME. *disavaunce*, a. OF. *desavancer* to repel, push back, hinder (14th c. in Godef.), f. *des-*, DIS- 4 + *avancer* to ADVANCE (q.v. for non-etymological change of *a-* to *ad-*).]
1. *trans.* To check the advance of, hinder from advancing, drive back, cause to retreat.
1374 CHAUCER *Troylus* II. 462 (511) Right for to speken of an ordenaunce, How we þe Grekes myghte disauaunce. *c* **1450** *Merlin* 658 To disavaunce the Emperour, and by-reve hym the wey to Oston. **1659** D. PELL *Impr. Sea* 131 The more they sail southward, the more they advance the Antartick, and disadvance the Artick [pole].
b. To draw back; to lower (anything put forward).
1596 SPENSER *F.Q.* IV. iii. 8 That forced him his shield to disadvaunce. *Ibid.* IV. iv. 7 Which th' other seeing gan his course relent, And vaunted speare eftsoones to disadvaunce. **1611** SPEED *Hist. Gt. Brit.* IX. vii. (1632) 533 Hee displayed his Ensignes, till for the French Kings loue he was content to dis-aduance them.
2. *fig.* To hinder from advancement, progress, or promotion; to throw back; to cast into a lower conditon or position.
a **1420** HOCCLEVE *De Reg. Princ.* 1358 He slipirly stant whom that thow [Fortune] enhauncest, For sodeynly thow hym disavauncest. *c* **1450** *Merlin* 250 Men..hadden grete drede that for the faute of her prowesse that holy cherche and cristin feith were disavaunced. **1530** PALSGR. 517/2, I disavaunce, I disalowe or hynder, *je desaunce*. **1566** PAINTER *Pal. Pleas.* (1890) II. 102 The daughters..be disauaunced and abased.
3. *intr.* To cease to advance, stop short.
1610 G. FLETCHER *Christ's Vict.* II. iii, But when they saw their Lords bright cognizance Shine in his face, soon did they disadvance, And some unto him kneel, and some about him dance.
Hence **disad'vancing** *vbl. sb.*, retrogression.
1659 D. PELL *Impr. Sea* 13 Their [the stars'] advancings and disadvancings.

disadvantage (dɪsædˈvɑːntɪdʒ, -æ-), *sb.* Also 4–6 des-, 5 dys-. [ME. *des-*, *disavauntage*, a. F. *désavantage* (13th c. in Hatz.-Darm.), f. *des-*, DIS- 4 + *avantage* ADVANTAGE.]
1. Absence or deprivation of advantage; an unfavourable condition or circumstance.
1530 PALSGR. 213/2 Disavauntage, *desauantaige*. **1597** SHAKS. *2 Hen. IV*, II. iii. 36 Him did you leaue vn-seconded by you, To looke vpon the hideous God of Warre, In disaduantage. **1607** —— *Cor.* I. vi. 49 Martius we have at disaduantage fought And did retyre to win our purpose. **1639** FULLER *Holy War* IV. xii. (1840) 199 Never could the Christian religion be showed to Pagans..on more disadvantages. **1751** JOHNSON *Rambler* No. 180 ⁋3 Every condition has its disadvantages. **1782** COWPER *Let.* 7 Mar., You must have seen her to a disadvantage. **1837** DISRAELI *Venetia* II. ii, Her regret of the many disadvantages under which he laboured. **1881** JOWETT *Thucyd.* I. 85 A noble nature should not be revenged by taking at a disadvantage one as good as himself.
2. Detriment, loss, or injury to interest; diminution of or prejudice to credit or reputation.
c **1380** WYCLIF *Sel. Wks.* III. 351 Whoso synneþ for avantage of himsilf, his synne makiþ disavauntage of þat þat he weneþ turne to good. **1387** TREVISA *Higden* (Rolls) II. 161 childern leueþ Freynsch & construeþ & lurneþ an Englysch, & habbeþ þer-by avauntage in on syde, & desauauntage yn anoþer. **1488–9** *Act 4 Hen. VII*, c. 22 Your seid liegemen.. susteyn and bere grete losses hinderaunce and disavauntage. **1618** NAUNTON in *Fortesc. Papers* 68 They speake there all they can to the disadvantage of our nation. **1667** MILTON *P.L.* VI. 431 Some disadvantage we endur'd and paine, Till now not known. **1711** STEELE *Spect.* No. 136 ⁋3, I..never speak Things to any Man's Disadvantage. **1755** JOHNSON s.v. He sold to disadvantage. **18..** BANCROFT (Webster 1864) They would throw a construction on his conduct to his disadvantage before the public. *Mod.* Having to realize on a falling market we had to sell to disadvantage.

disad'vantage, *v.* [f. prec. sb.: cf. ADVANTAGE *v.*, and F. *désavantage-r* (1507 in Hatz.-Darm.), f. *désavantage* sb.] *trans.* To cause disadvantage to; to place in an unfavourable position; to affect unfavourably.
c **1534** tr. *Pol. Verg. Eng. Hist.* (Camden) I. 262 Canulus ..knew that the pollicie of his adversarie wolde muche disadvayntage him. **1579–80** NORTH *Plutarch* (1676) 951 He ..made their lands waste, to disadvantage their enemies by so much the more. **1647** WARD *Simp. Cobler* 73 Sun and wind cannot disadvantage you. **1731** FIELDING *Let. Writers* III. vi, You will be disadvantaged by the discovery. **1871** BROWNING *Balaust.* 414 Yet faltering too..As somehow disadvantaged, should they strive.
Hence **disad'vantaged** *ppl. a.* (*absol.*, esp. in *sociol.*), **disad'vantaging** *vbl. sb.*
1611 COTGR., *Desavantagé*, disaduantaged. **1646** SALTMARSH *Smoke in Temple* 2 To the advantaging or disadvantaging the cause. **1648** BOYLE *Seraph. Love* x. (1700) 58 Their..disadvantaged Beauty is made the Compliment and Hyperbole of that Quality. **1879** H. SPENCER *Data of Ethics* xi. §69. 188 The uniform principle has been that the ill-adapted, disadvantaged in the struggle for existence, shall bear the consequent evils. **1934** H. G. WELLS *Exper. Autobiogr.* II. viii. 572 This mannered ungraciousness towards disadvantaged people. **1949** R. K. MERTON *Social Theory* (1951) i. 76 Social mobility for the otherwise disadvantaged. **1962** *Amer. Speech* XXXVII. 18 A large mass of bottom-income, unskilled, manual, and service workers, including what our sociologist colleagues call the 'disadvantaged'. **1966** *Sat. Rev.* 16 Apr. 100/1 Schools in economically disadvantaged neighbourhoods. *Ibid.* 104/1 It's the familiar story of the disadvantaged child. **1967** *Boston Globe* 20 May 2/2 He said urban school teachers generally hold 'negative and fearful attitudes toward the disadvantaged and disordered youngsters in their schools'. **1970** *New Yorker* 26 Sept. 108/2 A revolt by the disadvantaged aimed at those holding power.

† **disad'vantageable**, *a. Obs.* [f. as prec., after *advantageable*: cf. DIS- 10.]
Attended by disadvantage; disadvantageous, prejudicial.
1597–8 BACON *Ess.*, *Expense* (Arb.) 54 Hastie selling is commonly as disaduantageable as interest. **1613** F. ROBARTES *Revenue Gospel* 116 It is very disaduantageable to the glorie of God and saluation of men. **1631** BP. WEBBE *Quietn.* 127 A disaduantageble peace is to be preferred before a just war.
Hence † **disad'vantageably** *adv. Obs.*, in a disadvantageous manner, to the disadvantage or prejudice (of any one).
1627 *Lisander & Cal.* x. 222 Hee had..spoken so disadvantagably of her.

disadvantageous (dɪsˌædvənˈteɪdʒəs), *a.* Also 7–8 -ious. [f. DIS- 10 + ADVANTAGEOUS, perh. after F. *désavantageux* (15–16th c. in Hatz.-Darm.).] Attended with or occasioning disadvantage; unfavourable, prejudicial.
1603 HOLLAND *Plutarch's Mor.* 168 To enter into some disadvantageous promise. **1608** T. MORTON *Pream. Encounter* 70 Intolerably disaduantagious vnto the Romish part. **1670** MILTON *Hist. Eng.* VI. *Harold* (1847) 560/2 The English were in a streight disadvantageous place. **1749** FIELDING *Tom Jones* III. ii, We are obliged to bring our hero on the stage in a much more disadvantageous manner than we could wish. **1861** EMERSON *Soc. & Solit.*, *Old Age* Wks. (Bohn) III. 131 The creed of the street is, Old Age is not disgraceful, but immensely disadvantageous. **1874** GREEN *Short Hist.* ix. §8. 684 To consent to a disadvantageous peace.
b. Tending to the disadvantage or discredit of the person or thing in question; unfavourable; derogatory, depreciative, disparaging. ? *Obs.*
1663 COWLEY *Ode Restoration* viii, Seen..in that ill disadvantageous Light, With which misfortune strives t'abuse our sight. **1709** SWIFT *T. Tub* Apol., Fixes..a disadvantageous Character upon those who never deserved it. *a* **1776** HUME *Ess. Princ. Govt.* (R.), Whatever disadvantageous sentiments we may entertain of mankind. **1807** G. CHALMERS *Caledonia* I. I. ii. 69 Herodian concurs with Dio in his disadvantageous representation of the civilisation..among the Caledonian clans.

disadvan'tageously, *adv.* [f. prec. + -LY².] In a disadvantageous manner; with disadvantage; to the disadvantage of the person or thing in question; unfavourably, prejudicially.
1611 COTGR., *Desadventageusement*, disaduantagiously. **1631** *Star Chamb. Cases* (Camden) 20 It hath fallen out to be heard disadvantagiously for some. **1696** tr. *Du Mont's Voy. Levant* 353 You have spoken disadvantageously of the Government before a Guardian. *a* **1797** H. WALPOLE *Mem. Geo. II*, (1847) II. ii. 49 The question was opened disadvantageously for the court. **1862** S. LUCAS *Secularia* 47 That national indifference to social philosophy, in which we compare so disadvantageously with the first nations of the continent.

disadvan'tageousness. [f. as prec. + -NESS.] The quality of being disadvantageous; unfavourableness.
1727 in BAILEY vol. II. **1782** TYERS *Rhaps. on Pope* 5 (T.) This disadvantageousness of figure he converted..into a perpetual spur to..deliver himself from scorn.

† **disad'venture.** *Obs.* [ME. *disaventure*, a. OF. *desaventure*, *desadventure* (in Godef.), f. *des-*, DIS- 4 + *aventure* ADVENTURE *sb.*] Misadventure, mischance, mishap, misfortune.
c **1374** CHAUCER *Troylus* II. 366 (415) If I, thurgh my disaventure, Had lovid other hym or Achilles. *c* **1470** HARDING *Chron.* II. ii, With streames to and fro, And tempestes greate, and sore disauenture. **1577** FENTON *Gold. Epist.* 214 It is accounted more to disaduenture than to sinne. **1590** SPENSER *F.Q.* I. i. 45 For never knight, that dared warlike deed, More luckless disadventures did amate. **1638** SIR T. HERBERT *Trav.* (ed. 2) 275 Barames a noble Persian by hap escaped, but not a second disadventure.

† **disad'venturous**, *a. Obs.* Also 6 disadventrous, disaventrous. [f. prec., after ADVENTUROUS: cf. obs. F. *desaventureux* (in Cotgr. 1611).] Unfortunate, disastrous.
1590 SPENSER *F.Q.* I. ix. 11 And who most trustes in arme of fleshly might..Doth soonest fall in disaventrous fight. **1591** —— *M. Hubberd* 100 For to wexe olde at home in idlenesse, Is disaduentrous, and quite fortunelesse. **1596** —— *F.Q.* IV. viii. 51 An hard mishap and disaventrous case Him chaunst. **1702** ROWE *Tamerl.* I. i. 283 The Merit of his Virtue hardly match'd With disadventurous Chance.

† **disad'vest**, *v. Obs. rare*$^{-0}$. [a. OF. *desadvestir*, f. *des-*, DIS- 4 + *advestir* to ADVEST.]
1611 COTGR., *Desadvestir*, to disseise, disaduest, dispossesse, disinherite.
Hence † **disad'vesture**.
1611 COTGR., *Desadvest*, a disseisin, dispossession, disaduesture, disinheriting.

disad'vise *v.* [f. DIS- 6 + ADVISE.]
1. *trans.* To give advice against (an action or course); to advise that (it) should not be done.
1636 LD. WENTWORTH *Let.* in Carte *Ormonde* (1735) 14, I must in any case disadvise it, till you hear further from me. **1653** HOLCROFT *Procopius* IV. 149 Thorisin demanded herein the opinion of the principall Gepædes, who plainely disadvised it. **1749** FIELDING *Tom Jones* IV. iv, I should disadvise the bringing any such action. **1798** W. TAYLOR in

Robberds *Mem.* I. 216 Every one of his friends has disadvised the measure. **1882** C. EDWARDES tr. *Leopardi's Ess. & Dial* 166, I do not fail..to disadvise the search after that cold and miserable truth.

2. To advise (a person) against an action or course; to dehort *from.*

1687 BOYLE *Martyrd. Theodora* iv. (1703) 55 An apostle, who, though not unfavourable to the Marriage state, disadvises those women that are free, from entering into it. **1855** TROLLOPE *Warden* xviii, I am sure he disadvised you from it.

†**disad'vised,** *ppl. a. Obs.* [f. DIS- 10 + ADVISED, after OF. *desavisé.*] Imprudent, ill-advised, inconsiderate.

15.. in *Q. Eliz. Acad.* (1869) 73 In whatsoeuer you doe, be neyther hasty nor disaduised.

†**disa'ffect,** *sb. Obs. rare*[-1]. [f. DIS- 9 + AFFECT *sb.* after AFFECT *v.*[2]] = DISAFFECTION 3.

1683 SALMON *Doron Med.* II. 391 Convulsions, Gouts, Cholick and other Disaffects coming from frigidity.

†**disaffect,** *a. Obs. rare.* [f. DIS- 10 + AFFECT *ppl. a.*: prob. viewed as short for *disaffected.*] = DISAFFECTED 1.

1682 *Lond. Gaz.* No. 1694/3 Levying War upon..the Arbitrary Orders of a Disaffect..part of Parliament.

disaffect (dɪsəˈfɛkt), *v.*[1] [f. DIS- 6 + AFFECT *v.*[1] Cf. mod.F. *désaffecter* (19th c.)]

1. *trans.* To lack affection for; to dislike, regard with aversion, be unfriendly to. *Obs.* or *arch.*

1621 BP. H. KING *Serm.*, To Rdr., I haue not yet so doted on their part, or dis-affected my owne. **1626** SHIRLEY *Brothers* I. i, Unless you disaffect His person. **1708** SHAFTESBURY *Inquiry Virtue* i. 2 The heart must rightly and soundly affect what is just and right, and disaffect what is contrary. **1755** YOUNG *Centaur* i. Wks. (1757) IV. 124 How comes it to pass, that men of parts should so much disaffect the Scriptures? **1890** *Wesl. Meth. Mag.* Jan. 47 I you disaffect a Vestry or a Class-room, set apart your drawing-room once a week.

2. To estrange or alienate the affection of; to make unfriendly or less friendly; *spec.* to discontent or dissatisfy, as subjects with the government; to make disloyal. (Mostly in *passive*: see DISAFFECTED 1.)

1641 *Remonstr. Commons* in Rushw. *Hist. Coll.* III. (1692) I. 439 To disaffect the King to Parliaments by Slanders and false Imputations. **1680** LUTTRELL *Brief Rel.* (1857) I. 36 Many libells are thrown about to disaffect the king and his people. **1792** G. WASHINGTON *Let.* Writ. 1891 XII. 172 We have fresh..representations..of their endeavoring to disaffect the four southern tribes of Indians towards this country. **1893** *Chamb. Jrnl.* 21 Jan. 46/1 You..began to raise Cain by disaffecting the other workmen. **1893** MARIE CORELLI *Barabbas* iv. (1894) 28 A pestilence in this man's shape doth walk abroad to desolate and disaffect the province.

†**disa'ffect,** *v.*[2] *Obs.* [f. DIS- 6 + AFFECT *v.*[2]] *trans.* To affect in an evil manner; to disorder, derange, disease.

1625 DONNE *Serm.* xx. 192 The more it works upon good Men, the more it disaffects the Bad. *a* **1656** USSHER *Ann.* VI. (1658) 773 That disease was like none of ours; the head was disaffected, and that being dried, killed many. *a* **1660** HAMMOND *Serm.* xxiii. (T.), It disaffects the bowels, entangles and distorts the entrails. **1688** BOYLE *Final Causes Nat. Things* iv. 200 If the eyelids, which are subject to more than one distemper, be considerably disaffected.

disaffected (dɪsəˈfɛktɪd), *ppl. a.* [f. DISAFFECT *v.*[1], [2] + -ED[1].] **I.** Pa. pple. of DISAFFECT *v.*[1]

1. Evilly affected; estranged in affection or allegiance, unfriendly, hostile; almost always *spec.* Unfriendly to the government or to constituted authority, disloyal.

1632 *St. Trials, H. Sherfield* (R.), But in as much as he is accused of infidelity..to Almighty God..and to be disaffected to the king. **1678** HICKES in Ellis *Orig. Lett.* Ser. II. IV. 51 The Court was full of disaffected villains. **1711** ADDISON *Spect.* No. 131 ¶7, I pass among some for a disaffected Person. **1809** *Morning Post* 13 July, The disaffected crowded to the standard of these traitors. **1823** SCOTT *Peveril* i, Major Bridgenorth was considered..as a disaffected person to the Commonwealth. **1849** COBDEN *Speeches* 42 A measure which will tend to make the people contented and happy citizens, instead of being miserable, dejected, and disaffected.

2. Disliked, regarded with aversion. *rare.*

1649 BP. HALL *Cases Consc.* (T.), To cast her against her mind upon a disaffected match.

II. Pa. pple. of DISAFFECT *v.*[2]

†**3.** Affected with disease, disordered. *Obs.*

1664 BUTLER *Hud.* II. ii. 505 As if a man should be dissected, To find what part is disaffected. **1665** GLANVILL *Scepsis Sci.* x. (R.), And if our disaffected palates resent nought but bitterness from our choicest viands.

Hence **disa'ffectedly** *adv.*, **disa'ffectedness.**

1709 STRYPE *Ann. Ref.* I. xlviii. 522 Out of private hatred and disaffectedness. **1730–6** BAILEY (folio), *Disaffectedly*, disatisfiedly. **1793** J. WILLIAMS *Calm Exam.* 59 They look disaffectedly and with scorn at the present rulers.

disaffection (dɪsəˈfɛkʃən). [f. DIS- 9 + AFFECTION; or n. of action f. DISAFFECT *v.*[1] and [2], after *affection.*]

1. Absence or alienation of affection or kindly feeling; dislike, hostility: see AFFECTION 6.

1640 SANDERSON *Serm.* II. 145 Chastening is..far from being any argument of the father's dis-affection. **1643** MILTON *Divorce* II. vii. (1851) 78 Not to root up our naturall affections and disaffections. **1655** FULLER *Ch. Hist.* x. iii. §6 His disaffection to the discipline established in England. **1706–7** FARQUHAR *Beaux Strat.* III. iii, What Evidence can prove the unaccountable Disaffections of Wedlock? **1879** STEVENSON *Trav. Cevennes* 87 Modestine..seemed to have a disaffection for monasteries.

2. *spec.* Political alienation or discontent; a spirit of disloyalty to the government or existing authority: see DISAFFECTED 1.

1605 B. JONSON *Volpone* II. i, Nor any dis-affection to the state Where I was bred. **1683** *Brit. Spec.* 218 To take away all Occasions of Disaffection to the Anointed of the Lord. **1697** DAMPIER *Voy.* I. 371 The whole Crew were at this time under a general disaffection, and full of very different Projects. **1751** JOHNSON *Rambler* No. 204 ¶2 Thou hast reconciled disaffection, thou hast suppressed rebellion. **1808** SYD. SMITH *Wks.* (1867) I. 115 A very probable cause of disaffection in the troops. **1874** GREEN *Short Hist.* 556 The popular disaffection told even on the Council of State.

†**3.** The condition of being evilly affected physically; physical disorder or indisposition. *Obs.*

1654 GAYTON *Pleas. Notes* III. xi. 144 Forc'd to fly to Physick, for cure of the disaffection. **1676** WISEMAN (J.), The disease took its original merely from the disaffection of the part, and not from the peccancy of the humours. **1688** BOYLE *Final Causes Nat. Things, Vitiated Sight* 260 This woman..had a disaffection of sight very uncommon. **1741** *Compl. Fam.-Piece* I. i. 78 If the Patient be subject to..any Swelling, Heat, or Disaffection in the Eyelids.

†**disa'ffectionate,** *a. Obs. rare.* [f. DIS- 10 + AFFECTIONATE *a.*]

1. Wanting in affection: unloving.

1796 HAYLEY *Life of Milton* (T.), A beautiful but disaffectionate and disobedient wife.

2. Characterized by disaffection; disloyal.

1636 SIR H. BLOUNT *Voy. Levant* (1650) 99 (T.) They..were found dampably corrupt, and disaffectionate to the Turkish affairs.

†**disa'ffiance,** *sb. Obs. rare*[-1]. [DIS- 9.] Want of affiance, trust, or confidence; distrust.

1631 *Celestina* II. 34 Not caring..how thou puttest a disaffiance in my affection.

†**disa'ffiance,** *v. Obs. rare*[-1]. [f. DIS- 6 + AFFIANCE *v.*] *trans.* To put out of affiance, trust, or confidence.

1631 *Celestina* x. 117 Already disaffianced in his hope, for want of a good and faire answer, hee hath set both his eyes and his heart upon the love and person of another.

disaffiliate (dɪsəˈfɪlɪeɪt), *v.* [f. DIS- 6 + AFFILIATE *v.*]

1. *trans.* To undo the affiliation of, to detach (that which is affiliated): the reverse of to AFFILIATE.

1870 C. J. SMITH *Syn. & Antonyms, Affiliate*, Disannex, Disaffiliate. **1892** *Graphic* 21 May 598/3 Eleven branch associations have 'disaffiliated' themselves in consequence of the dispute over the suffrage guestion.

2. *intr.* To cancel an affiliation; to detach oneself *from* an organization.

1947 *N.Y. Times* 13 Dec. 1/3 The scrap of white paper..bore this laconic message in Mr. Lewis' characteristically bold handwriting in blue pencil: Green AFL. We disaffiliate. Lewis. **1977** *Economist* 29 Jan. 23/2 One union, the electricians', even threatened to disaffiliate from the party if no action were taken on the Underhill report. **1980** *N.Y. Times* 4 Dec. B5/3 The Milwaukee union leader said his local had not moved to disaffiliate. **1982** *Financial Times* 8 Sept. 10/8 After the shock decision by TUC unions..to disaffiliate from the patronage of the Transport and General Workers' Union, left-wing delegates suffered a new blow yesterday.

disaffiliation (ˌdɪsəfɪlɪˈeɪʃən). [f. DISAFFILIATE *v.*: see -TION.] The action of disaffiliating.

1926 *Amer. Review of Reviews* Nov. 473 The British Labor party confirms disaffiliation with the Communists. **1927** *Glasgow Herald* 9 Mar. 11 The ground upon which disaffiliation is urged. **1927** *Observer* 10 July 14/6 The announcement of the disaffiliation of the Union of Post Office Workers. **1955** *Times* 9 July 11/7 The defendant union were unwilling to expel him and were only concerned to do so by virtue of the award and the sanction (of disaffiliation) hanging over their heads. **1969** *Listener* 16 Jan. 87/1 The various modes of disaffiliation that have been adopted by the post-Hiroshima young.

disaffirm (dɪsəˈfɜːm), *v.* [f. DIS- 6 + AFFIRM *v.*] *trans.* To contradict, deny, negative: the contrary of to AFFIRM 4.

1548 GEST *Pr. Masse* 97 Disaffyrmynge the masse sacryfyce to bee propiciatorye. **1615** DAVIES *Reports Cases* Pref. (T.), Neither doth Glanvil or Bracton disaffirm the antiquity of the reports of the law. **1816** SIR R. DALLAS in Taunton *Rep.* VI. 529 The suggestion that this was a voluntary payment, is disaffirmed by the averment of compulsion.

b. *Law.* To annul or reverse (some former decision, etc.); to repudiate (a settlement or agreement): the contrary of AFFIRM 1, 2, CONFIRM.

1531 *Dial. Laws Eng.* I. xxvi. (1638) 46 Therefore..the said Statute neither affirmeth nor disaffirmeth the title. **1634** EARL STRAFFORD *Lett. & Disp.* (1739) I. 298 Leaving the other..in the State they now are, either affirmed or disaffirmed. **1883** *N.Y. Tribune* XLIII. 5 The Supreme Court of the United States has disaffirmed the view of the Post Office Department and affirmed that of the Company. **1890** SIR A. KEKEWICH in *Law Times' Rep.* LXIII. 682/1 She could disaffirm the settlement on attaining twenty-one.

disaffirmance (dɪsəˈfɜːməns). [f. DISAFFIRM *v.*, after *affirm, affirmance.*] The action of disaffirming; negation; annulment, repudiation.

1610 BACON in Howell *St. Trials* (1816) II. 399/1 If it had been a disaffirmance by law they must have gone down in solido. **1643** PRYNNE *Open. Gt. Seal* 24 Done in affirmance, onely, not disaffirmance of it, as Lawyers speake. **1677** HALE *Prim. Orig. Man.* I. iv. 102 As much a Demonstration in disaffirmance of any thing that is affirmed as can possibly be. **1818** COLEBROOKE *Oblig. & Contracts* I. 36 A suit..in disaffirmance of it [an illegal contract]..is consonant to the policy of the law. **1868** BENJAMIN *On Sales* (1884) 404 The vendor has done some act to disaffirm the transaction..Before the disaffirmance the vendee has transferred the..interest.

disaffirmation (dɪsæfəˈmeɪʃən). [f. DISAFFIRM *v.*, after *affirm, -ation.*] The action of disaffirming; denial, negation; repudiation.

1842 in BRANDE *Dict. Science, etc.* **1875** MAINE *Hist. Inst.* vii. 205 The disaffirmation of the legality of Tanistry. **1893** *Weekly Notes* 49/2 Notwithstanding her disaffirmation of her settlement when she attained twenty-one.

disa'ffirmative, *a.* [f. as prec., after *affirmative.*] Characterized by disaffirming; tending to disaffirm; negative.

a **1832** in BENTHAM (F. Hall).

disa'fford, *v. Obs. rare*[-1]. [DIS- 6.] *trans.* To refuse to afford; to prevent from obtaining.

1597 DANIEL *Civ. Wars* VIII. lviii, Let not my being a Lancastrian bred, Without mine own Election, disafford Me Right, or make my Cause disfigured.

disafforest (dɪsəˈfɒrɪst), *v.* [ad. med. (Anglo-) L. *disafforestāre* (in *Charter of Forests* 13th c.), f. DIS- 4 + *afforestāre* to AFFOREST. Cf. the synonymous DE-AFFOREST, DEFOREST, DISFOREST.]

1. *trans.* To free from the operation of the forest laws; to reduce from the legal state of forest to that of ordinary land.

[**1225** *Charta Forestæ an.* 9 *Hen. III*, c. 3 (Spelman s.v. *Afforestare*) Omnes bosci qui fuerunt afforestati per Richardum avunculum nostrum..statim Disafforestentur.] **1598** STOW *Surv.* xli. (1603) 424 The Forest of Midlesex, and the Warren of Stanes were disaforested. **1598** MANWOOD *Lawes Forest* xvi. §9 (1615) 116/2 By the Charter, all new forests were generally to bee disafforested. **1677** N. COX *Gentlem. Recr.* I. (ed. 2) 24 *Afforest*, is to turn Land into Forest. *Disafforest*, is to turn Land from being Forest to other uses. **1725** *Lond. Gaz.* No. 6350/3 The whole inclosed with a Pale, and disaforested. **1888** BLACK *Adv. House-boat* 71, I don't know when the district was disafforested; but in Shakespeare's own time they hunted red-deer in these Warwickshire woods.

fig. a **1631** DONNE *Poems, To Sir Herbert* (1650) 157 How happy is he, which hath due place assign'd To his beasts; and disaforested his mind.

absol. **1638** SIR R. COTTON *Abstr. Rec. Tower* 14 [Edward I] disafforested in most Counties of England.

2. To strip or clear of forests or trees. *rare.*

1842 DE QUINCEY in *Blackw. Mag.* LII. 126 From the wreck of her woods by means of incendiary armies, Greece is, for a season, disafforested.

Hence **disa'fforested** *ppl. a.*; **disa'fforesting** *vbl. sb.* and *ppl. a.*; also **disa'fforestment.**

1857 TOULMIN SMITH *Parish* 469 For the disafforesting of the royal forests and chases. **1875** BUCKLAND *Log-bk.* 240 This was before the miserable cheese-paring policy of disafforesting, when the red-deer were still to be seen in the forest glades. **1882** *Standard* 14 Mar., A Commissioner under the Hainault Disafforesting Commission. **1889** *Blackw. Mag.* CXLVI. 661/1 The great disafforestment proceeds apace.

disafforestation (dɪsəfɒrɪˈsteɪʃən). [n. of action f. med.L. *disafforestāre* to DISAFFOREST.] **a.** The action of disafforesting; exemption from forest laws. **b.** Destruction of forests or woods.

1598 MANWOOD *Lawes Forest* xvi. §9 (1615) 116/2 All those, that were put out of the Forest by the disafforestation. **1888** *Athenæum* 10 Mar. 302/3 The gradual obsolescence of our forest law and the steady progress of disafforestation. **1888** *Times* 4 Oct. 9/5 The rapid progress of disafforestation will be understood, and it is certain that the natural growth cannot keep pace with it.

†**disa'ffright,** *v. Obs. rare.* [DIS- 6.] *trans.* To free from fright or alarm; to reassure.

1676 HOBBES *Iliad* IV. 216 His own Commanders first to disaffright.

†**disa'ffy,** *v. Obs. rare.* [In 16th c. *desafie*, a. OF. *desafie-r* to distrust, f. *des-*, L. *dis-* (DIS- 4) + *afier* to trust: see AFFY *v.*] *trans.* To put out of relations of affiance: DEFY *v.*[1] 1.

1546 *St. Papers Hen. VIII*, XI. 239 He fledde like a traytour..and being for the same desafied by Julyan, doth maynteyn his acte and him silf to be honest, and to fight in that quarrell with the said Julyan.

†**dis'age.** *Obs. rare.* [ad. It. *disagio* dis-ease, trouble, want, f. *dis-*, DIS- 4 + *agio* leisure, ease; cf. AGIO, ADAGIO.] Hardship, trouble.

1665 J. WEBB *Stone-Heng* (1725) 156 [They] were thick-skin'd Fellows, and could patiently undergo such and greater Disages.

†**dis'aggravate,** *v. Obs. rare.* [DIS- 6.] *trans.* To release from a burden or charge: see AGGRAVATE *v.* 3.

1598 FLORIO *Disgrauio*, a discharge, a disagrauating.

dis'aggregate, *v.* [f. DIS- 6 + AGGREGATE *v.* Cf. F. *désagréger*, Sp. *desagregar*.]

1. *trans.* To separate (an aggregated mass) into its component particles.

1828 in WEBSTER. **1858** G. P. SCROPE *Geol. Centr. France* (ed. 2) 47 Its parts are then disaggregated. **1876** tr. *Schützenberger's Ferment.* 172 The cellular tissue is either partly or completely disaggregated.

2. *intr.* (for *refl.*) To separate from an aggregate.

1881 MORGAN *Contrib. Amer. Ethnol.* 87 As soon as they had disaggregated.

disaggregation (dɪsægrɪ'geɪʃən). [n. of action f. prec. vb.: cf. mod.F. *désagrégation* (1878 in *Dict. Acad.*).]

1. The separation of the component particles of an aggregated mass or structure; disintegration.

1828 in WEBSTER. **1858** *Sat. Rev.* 20 Nov. 501/1 A million of entire skeletons..bound together by the fine powder resulting from the disaggregation of their fellows and of other calcareous organisms. **1865** ESQUIROS *Cornwall* 41 Deposits formed by the disaggregation of the primitive rocks. **1879** G. PRESCOTT *Sp. Telephone* 436 Neither disaggregation nor sparks. **1881** *Nature* XXIV. 67 An electric disaggregation of the electrode.

2. *transf.* in various non-physical senses.

1831 BENTHAM *Wks.* (1838–43) XI. 73 Power of aggregation; power of disaggregation. **1881** MORGAN *Contrib. Amer. Ethnol.* 87 A further consequence of this disaggregation was..the necessity for an official building. **1890** *Times* 11 Jan. 5/1 Centralization would disappear..to make way for a disaggregation as troublesome for the Monarchy of Portugal as for the French Republic.

disagree (dɪsə'griː), *v.* [ad. F. *désagréer* (12th c. in Hatz.-Darm.), f. *des-* (DIS- 4) + *agréer* to AGREE. See also DISGREE.]

1. *intr.* To differ, to be unlike; not to AGREE, correspond, accord, or harmonize. Const. *with*, †*to*, †*from*.

1494 FABYAN *Chron.* IV. lxvi. 45 That sayinge disagreeth to the wrytynge of Eutropius. **1579** LYLY *Euphues* (Arb.) 191 [He] sorroweth to see thy behaviour so far to disagree from thy birth. **1637** GILLESPIE *Eng. Pop. Cerem.* IV. iii. 8 Those things we call morally good, which agree to right reason: those morally evill, which disagree from right reason. **1655** STANLEY *Hist. Philos.* III. (1701) 86/1 Which [account] disagrees not with the other. **1685** STILLINGFL. *Orig. Brit.* i. 4 A Tradition..disagreeing to the Scripture. **1725** WATTS *Logic* II. iv. §2 We have neither a very clear Conception in our selves of the two Ideas contained in the Words, nor how they agree or disagree. **1874** A. B. DAVIDSON *Hebr. Gram.* §48 The other numerals are nouns, and disagree in gender with the words which they enumerate. **1884** tr. *Lotze's Logic* iv. 235 Particular circumstances which agree or disagree with given facts.

2. To differ in opinion; to dissent.

1559 in Strype *Ann. Ref.* I. App. xi. 35 If any..disagreed from his forefathers, he is..to be judged suspected. **1662** STILLINGFL. *Orig. Sacr.* I. i. §20 Those who disagree from that former Computation, place it yet lower. **1732** POPE *Ep. Bathurst* 1 Who shall decide when Doctors disagree? **1874** MORLEY *Compromise* (1886) 181 The sincere beliefs and conscientiously performed rites of those..from whose religion he disagrees. **1883** FROUDE *Short. Stud.* IV. II. ii. 187 He could not place himself in the position of persons who disagreed with him. **1891** *Spectator* 13 June 823/1 Men who hoped against hope that the jury would disagree.

3. To refuse to accord or agree (to any proposal, etc.); to dissent. Const. *to*, *with*; †*from*. Indirect passive, *to be disagreed to*.

1495 *Act 11 Hen. VII*, c. 36 Preamb., If the..Duke..disagree to the seid acte. **1574** tr. *Littleton's Tenures* 52 a, If the parcener..hathe yssue and dyeth, the issue maye disagree to the particion. **1589** WARNER *Alb. Eng.* VI. xxx. (1612) 155 Mine is to loue, but hers to disagree. **1818** CRUISE *Digest* (ed. 2) IV. 495 In such cases the grantee may, by deed only, disagree, and disclaim the estate. **1825** T. JEFFERSON *Autobiog.* Wks. 1859 I. 31 The Delaware counties had bound up their delegates to disagree to this article. **1869** GLADSTONE *Sp. in Parlt.* (*Daily News* 16 July), I shall move to disagree to that clause..I beg now to move that the House disagree with the Lords' amendment..of the preamble of the Irish Church Bill. *Ibid.*, The Lords' amendment was then disagreed to. **1869** *Daily News* 27 July, The Lower House has disagreed from the amendment.

4. To be at variance, to dispute or quarrel.

1548 HALL *Chron. Hen. IV*, 29 b, Takyng a corporall othe ..never after to disagre or renewe any displeasure. **1667** MILTON *P.L.* II. 497 Devil with Devil damn'd Firm concord holds, men onely disagree Of Creatures rational. **1758** S. HAYWARD *Serm.* xvii. 531 Children of the same family ought not to disagree. **1835** LYTTON *Rienzi* II. i, Come, we must not again disagree.

5. Of food, climate, etc.: To conflict in physical operation or effect; to be unsuitable. Const. *with*.

1563 etc., [see DISAGREEING *ppl. a.* 4.] **1768** tr. *Cornaro's Disc.* 15 To try, whether those, which pleased my palate, agreed or disagreed with my stomach. *Ibid.* 45 Fruit, fish, and other things of that kind disagree with me. **1813** MARTIN in *Med.-Chirurg. Trans.* IV. 47 Increasing one drop every day until it might begin to disagree with the stomach. **1820** SHELLEY *Œdipus* II. ii. 28 So plain a dish Could scarcely disagree. **1827** SCOTT *Napoleon* xlvi, Ascribed to his health's disagreeing with the air of that capital. **1865** MRS. CARLYLE *Lett.* III. 288 It couldn't have been sound, that champagne ..or it wouldn't have so disagreed with me. *Mod.* The confinement and close application to work disagrees with him.

†disa'gree, *sb.* *Obs. rare*⁻¹. [f. prec. vb.] Disagreement.

1589 GREENE *Tullies Love* (1609) D iv b, It may bee that the destinies have appointed their disagree.

disagreeability (dɪsə,griːə'bɪlɪtɪ). [f. next + -ITY: cf. *agreeability*.] The quality or condition of being disagreeable; unpleasantness.

1788 MAD. D'ARBLAY *Diary* IV. IV. 188 These only formed its disagreeability. **1790** *Ibid.* V. IV. 163 Difficulties and disagreeabilities in carrying on a week's intercourse. **1852** *Fraser's Mag.* XLVI. 248 He will be exposed to many 'disagreeabilities' from the police. **1889** MRS. RANDOLPH *New Eve* II. ix. 62 Ill-health meant ill-temper, discomfort, disagreeability of all sorts.

disagreeable (dɪsə'griːəb(ə)l), *a.* (*sb.*) Also 5 dys-. [a. F. *désagréable* (13th c. in Hatz.-Darm.), f. *dés-* (DIS- 4) + *agréable* AGREEABLE.]

A. *adj.* **†1.** Not in agreement; characterized by difference or incongruity; disagreeing, discordant, at variance. Const. *to*, *with*. *Obs.*

c **1400** *Rom. Rose* 4717 It [love] is Carybdis perillous Disagreeable and gracious, It is discordaunce that can accord, And accordaunce to discord. **1494** FABYAN *Chron.* VII. ccxxxiv. 270 But..I se the mater dysagreable to other wryters, and also thynke that moche therof is fayned. **1538** COVERDALE *Ded. to N.T.*, It was disagreeable to my former translation in English. **1563** GOLDING *Cæsar* Pref. (1565) 1 Cæsar in hys descryption of Gallia..may seeme dysagreable wyth other authors. **1651** HOBBES *Leviath.* I. xv. 79 What is conformable or disagreeable to Reason, in the actions of common life. **1725** BAILEY *Erasm. Colloq.* 407 Compare their Lives and nothing can be more disagreeable. **1759** JOHNSON *Rasselas* xxviii. (1787) 78 The obstinate contests of disagreeable virtues. **1766** F. BLACKBURNE *Confessional* 262 In determining what is the proper sense and extent of the Articles, and what shall be judged agreeable or disagreeable to them.

2. Not in accordance with one's taste or liking; exciting displeasure or disgust; unpleasing, unpleasant, offensive.

1698 FRYER *Acc. E. India & P.* 254 Yet he found it disagreeable, because the Nights now were as intensely Cold, as the Days were Hot. **1705** BOSMAN *Guinea* 230 This is such a horrible ugly Creature, that I don't believe any thing besides so very disagreeable is to be found. **1754** E. DARWIN *Let. to Dr. Okes* in Dallas *Life* (1879), Yesterday's post brought me the disagreeable news of my father's departure out of this sinful world. **1794** S. WILLIAMS *Vermont* 90 This animal is without any ill scent, or disagreeable effluvia. **1838** JAMES *Robber* iv, Your society is any thing but disagreeable to me. **1841–44** EMERSON *Ess.*, *Prudence* Wks. (Bohn) I. 100 In regard to disagreeable.. things, prudence does not consist in evasion..but in courage.

3. a. Of persons: Of unpleasant temper or humour; actively unamiable; offensive.

It ranges from an active sense, of which the person in question is the subject, as in quot. 1474, to a subjective one of which the person in question is the object, both being often present.

[**1474** CAXTON *Chesse* (1481) D viij b, Not plesyd but disagreable whan they haue receyued the yefte.] **1710–11** SWIFT *Lett.* (1767) III. 109, I dined to-day with my mistress Butler, who grows very disagreeable. **1825** J. NEAL *Bro. Jonathan* II. 323 A very disagreeable man was here. **1875** W. S. HAYWARD *Love Agst. World* 11 My cousin is dreadfully disagreeable.

b. Uncomfortable, in an unpleasant position.

1827 J. F. COOPER *Prairie* xii, We are disagreeable about his camping on the prairie, instead of coming in to his own bed. **1836** *Knickerbocker* VIII. 151 Had I not become accustomed to such dangers, I should have felt very disagreeable. **1844** *P. Parley's Ann.* V. 180 The King felt quite disagreeable. The Russians might drop in upon him very unceremoniously.

B. as *sb.* (Cf. AGREEABLE 6.) **†a.** A disagreeable person. *Obs.*

1829 MRS. SOUTHEY *Church Yards* II. 242 Whatever some superior-minded disagreeables may say to the contrary.

b. A disagreeable thing or experience; *esp.* in *pl.*

1781 COWPER *Let.* 4 Feb., Some disagreeables and awkwardnesses would probably have attended your interview. **1797** HOLCROFT tr. *Stolberg's Trav.* (ed. 2) II. xlii. 64 The Greek artists are..careful to keep the disagreeable out of sight. **1804** W. IRVING *Life & Lett.* (1864) I. iv. 78, I am seasoned..to the disagreeables from my Canada journey of last summer. **1849** C. BRONTE *Shirley* ix. 127 When the disagreeables of life—its work and privations were in question.

disagreeableness (dɪsə'griːəb(ə)lnɪs). [f. prec. + -NESS.] The quality of being disagreeable.

†1. Want of agreement; discordancy, incongruity. *Obs.*

1571 GOLDING *Calvin on Ps.* lxix. 18 This disagreeableness of the wicked is easly washt away. **1686** HORNECK *Crucif. Jesus* xxiv. 828 Remove and conquer that disagreeableness, that is betwixt my nature, and thy harmony. **1712** ADDISON *Spect.* No. 413 ¶1 We know neither the Nature of an Idea, nor the Substance of a human Soul, which might help us to discover the Conformity or Disagreeableness of the one to the other. **1716** ATTERBURY *Serm.* (1734) I. 215 Its disagreeableness to the eternal rules of right reason.

2. Unpleasantness; also, an unpleasant feature.

1648 W. MOUNTAGUE *Devout Essays* I. xvii. §1 Many who have figured Solitude..have sought to sweeten all they could the disagreeableness. **1709** STEELE *Tatler* No. 84 ¶5, I found the Disagreeableness of giving Advice without being asked it. **1748** RICHARDSON *Clarissa* (1811) I. xvi. 109 Look upon that man—see but the disagreeableness of his person. **1833** *Fraser's Mag.* VII. 4 With all its manifold disagreeablenesses (to coin a word), it must be grappled with boldly. **1861** SWINHOE *N. China Camp.* 9 There was just that amount of disagreeableness that usually occurs among Englishmen who are strangers to one another.

disa'greeablism. *nonce-wd.* [see -ISM.]

1887 BESANT *Fifty Years Ago* in *Graphic* Jubilee No. 20 June 2/3 Together with discontent, chartism, republicanism, atheism—in fact all the disagreeablisms.

disagreeably (dɪsə'griːəblɪ), *adv.* [f. DISAGREEABLE + -LY².] In a disagreeable manner or degree; unpleasantly; offensively.

1730–6 BAILEY (folio), *Disagreeably*, unpleasantly. **1766** GRAY in *Corr. w. N. Nicholls* (1843) 61, I passed..all June in Kent not disagreeably. **1838** DICKENS *Nich. Nick.* xxix, You may find yourself very disagreeably deceived. **1847** EMERSON *Repr. Men, Swedenborg* Wks. (Bohn) I. 333 Swedenborg is disagreeably wise..and repels.

†disa'greeance. *Obs.* [f. DISAGREE *v.*, after AGREEANCE: cf. also OF. *desagreance* (Godef.).] = DISAGREEMENT.

1548 UDALL, etc. *Erasm. Par. Acts* viii. 36 There is no disagreaunce where is faith. **1589** *Late Voy. Sp. & Port.* (1881) 98 Our disagreeance with them, will impeach the trade of our Merchants. **1597** *Sc. Acts Jas. VI* (1814) 158 (Jam.) They sall..report the groundis and caussis of their disagreiance to his maiestie.

disa'greed, *ppl. a.* [f. DISAGREE *v.* + -ED¹.] The reverse of AGREED; not in agreement; at variance.

1598 FLORIO, *Scordato*, forgotten, put out of tune, vnstrung, disagreed. **1658** BAXTER *Saving Faith* Ded. A ij, Well worth his labor to prove us disagreed. **1875** JOWETT *Plato* (ed. 2) IV. 42 The partisans of utility are disagreed among themselves.

disagreeing (dɪsə'griːɪŋ), *vbl. sb.* [f. as prec. + -ING¹.] The action of the verb to DISAGREE; disagreement.

1548 UDALL, etc. *Erasm. Par. Luke* 94 a, There ought to bee no discorde ne disagreyng emong theim in their preachyng. **1567** R. MULCASTER *Fortescue's De Laud. Leg.* (1572) 103 b, To be troubled with so many disagreeings. **1647** JER. TAYLOR *Lib. Proph.* xvii. 219 Such complying with the disagreeings of a sort of men, is the total overthrow of all Discipline. *Mod.* Their disagreeing was happily prevented.

disagreeing, *ppl. a.* [f. as prec. + -ING².] That disagrees.

†1. Out of harmony or agreement; discordant, incongruous; diverse. *Obs.*

1551 T. WILSON *Logike* (1580) 39 The places..declare.. what be incidente, what be disagreeyng from the matter. **1561** T. HOBY tr. *Castiglione's Courtyer* (1577) E vij b, Oratours..vnlike and disagreeing..to their predecessours & folowers. **1593** Q. ELIZ. tr. *Boethius* (E.E.T.S.) 105 Me thinkes it a crosse mater and in it self disagreing, that God all knowes, and yet ther should be a free will. **1656** W. D. tr. *Comenius' Gate Lat. Unl.* §559 Many Islands, replenished with disagreeing nations and tongues. **1690** LOCKE *Govt.* I. ii. §7 A Figure..very disagreeing with what..Children imagine of their Parents.

2. Differing in opinion; dissentient.

1552 HULOET, Disagreeynge, *dissentaneus*. **1625** K. LONG tr. *Barclay's Argenis* I. xx. 63 The nobles about them, in agreeing silence covered their disagreeing thoughts. **1677** HALE *Prim. Orig. Man.* II. xii. 244 Finding the Philosophers and Wise Men so uncertain and disagreeing. **1856** MRS. CARLYLE *Lett.* II. 271 A half-perplexed, half-amused, and wholly disagreeing expression.

3. At variance, quarrelling.

1621 BURTON *Anat. Mel.* III. i. II. ii. (1651) 421 Hard-hearted parents, disobedient children, disagreeing brothers. **1732** BERKELEY *Alciphr.* v. §19 The most contentious, quarrelsome, disagreeing crew, that ever appeared.

4. Of incompatible or prejudicial operation; unsuitable.

1563 HYLL *Art Garden.* (1593) 90 The Greek writers think the Basil so disagreing and contrary to women, that if [etc.]. **1683** TRYON *Way to Health* 483 The eating of this.. Food becomes offensive to them, and disagreeing. **1794** WOLCOTT (P. Pindar) *Rowl. for Oliver* Wks. II. 41 This was a puzzling, disagreeing question, Grating like arsenic on his host's digestion.

Hence **†disa'greeingly** *adv.* *Obs.*

1591 PERCIVALL *Sp. Dict.*, *Desacordamente*, disagreeingly.

disagreement (dɪsə'griːmənt). [f. DISAGREE *v.* + -MENT, after *agreement*. Cf. F. *désagrément* (*desagreement*, Oudinot, 1642) anything disagreeable, or not to one's liking.]

1. Want of agreement or harmony; difference; discordancy, diversity, discrepancy.

1576 FLEMING *Panopl. Epist.* 284 As well their words as their deedes bee at disagreement. **1699** BENTLEY *Phal* 154 There's a seeming disagreement between Diodorus and Herodotus. **1737** WHISTON *Josephus, Antiq.* Diss. ii, The apparent disagreement of any command to the moral attributes of God. *a* **1847** MRS. SHERWOOD *Lady of Manor* I. vii. 267 Sin is a disagreement or nonconformity of the will of any creature with the will of God. **1864** BOWEN *Logic* v. 105 The Judgement, *quadrupeds are not rational*, determines the relation of disagreement between the two Terms.

2. Refusal to agree or assent.

1495 *Act 11 Hen. VII*, c. 36 §1 Any disagreement or disassent by the seid Duches..notwithstandyng. **1642** PERKINS *Prof. Bk.* i. §43. 19 The disagreement of the husband ought to be shewed.

3. Difference of opinion; dissent.

1576 FLEMING *Panopl. Epist.* 83, I agaiNe with you was not at disagreement. **1613** JACKSON *Creed* I. 445 *note*, His disagreement from some of his owne profession. **1658** T. WALL *Charac. Enemies Ch.* 7 Disagreement in matters of faith causeth enmity. **1868** F. EDWARDS *Raleigh* I. xvii. 348

Men of very different natures, apart from their utter disagreement in religion.

4. Quarrel, dissension, variance, strife.

1589 FLEMING *Virg. Georg.* II. 34 Disagreement vexing brethren faithles and vntrustie. **1626** MEADE in Ellis *Orig. Lett.* Ser. I. III. 223 There hath been some Disagreement at Court between their Majesties, by reason of the French Ambassador. **1770** *Junius Lett.* xxxviii. 190 Is it..for your interest..to live in a perpetual disagreement with your people? **1858** FROUDE *Hist. Eng.* III. xii. 10 The occasion of their disagreement being removed, he desired to return to the old terms of amity.

5. Unsuitableness (of food, climate, etc.) to the constitution.

1702 C. MATHER *Magn. Chr.* I. ii. (1853) I. 48 The probable disagreement of so torrid a climate unto English bodies.

6. An unpleasantness, a disagreeable condition. [F. *désagrément.*] *rare.*

1778 GATES in Sparks *Corr. Amer. Rev.* (1853) II. 532 You would have avoided many disagreements, had it pleased you to have accepted that offer.

disagreer (dɪsə'griːə(r)). *rare.* [f. DISAGREE *v.* + -ER[1].] One who disagrees: a dissenter.

a **1660** HAMMOND *Wks.* II. I. 605 (R.) To awe disagreers in all matters of faith.

disagyse, obs. Sc. f. DISGUISE.

†**dis'ailment.** *Obs. rare.* [see DIS- 5.] Ailment, indisposition.

1657 REEVE *God's Plea* 256 Without the least disaylment or distemper.

disa'larm, *v. rare.* [DIS- 6 or 7 a + ALARM.] *trans.* To free or relieve from alarm.

1617 SIR F. BURDETT in *Parl. Deb.* 1693 Who had taken.. care that not a syllable should be inserted that could tend to disalarm the country.

disalike: see DIS- 10

†**disa'llegiance.** *Obs. rare.* [f. DIS- 9 + ALLEGIANCE.] Contravention of allegiance.

1641 LAUD *Wks.* (1857) VI. 216 Consider a little with what insolency, and perhaps disallegiance, this Lord and his roundhead crew would use their Kings.

†**disa'lliege,** *v. Obs. rare.* [f. DIS- 6 + **alliege*, deduced from ALLEGIANCE, under the influence of LIEGE: cf. prec.] *trans.* To withdraw or alienate from allegiance.

1648 MILTON *Observ. Art. Peace* Wks. (1847) 263/2 By a pernicious and hostile peace, to disalliege a whole feudary kingdom from the antient dominion of England.

disallow (dɪsə'laʊ), *v.* Forms: 4-5 **desalowe,** 4-6 **dis-,** 6 **dysalowe, dissalow,** 6- **disallow.** [a. OF. *desaloue-r, disalower* to blame, etc. (in Godef.), f. *des-,* DIS- 4 + *alouer* ALLOW. In med. (Anglo) L. *disallocāre*: see Du Cange.] To refuse to ALLOW (in various senses).

†**1.** *trans.* To refuse to laud, praise, or commend; to discommend, to blame. See ALLOW I. 1.

1393 GOWER *Conf.* I. 83 This vice of Inobedience..he des-alloweþ. *c* **1430** *Pilgr. Lyf Manhode* IV. xxix. (1869) 191 Nouht þat I wole blame it ne despeise it ne disalowe it. **1510** BARCLAY *Mirr. Gd. Manners* (1570) G j, Both is like errour which wise men disalowe. **1573** G. HARVEY *Letter-bk.* (Camden) 7, I praefer Tulli before Caesar in writing Latin; do I therefore disable or disalow Caesar? **1612** T. TAYLOR *Comm. Titus* iii. 1 According to their care herein haue they been commended or disallowed in the Scriptures. **1656** COWLEY *Prologue to Guardian,* Who says the Times do Learning disallow? 'Tis false; 'twas never Honour'd so as Now.

2. To refuse to approve or sanction; to disapprove of: see ALLOW I. 2. *arch.*

1494 FABYAN *Chron.* VII. 616 Whiche conclucion was after disalowyd. **1540** *Act 32 Hen. VIII,* c. 46 The auditors general..shal haue auctority to examin thaccomptes..and to allowe and disalow all that shal be reasonable. **1552** *Bury Wills* (1850) 141 Furthermore I denull, disalow, and sett att nothing all former wills and testaments which I have made. **1673** RAY *Journ. Low C.* Glaris 436 Though they..do take liberty to..use..sports and exercises upon the Lords day, yet most of their ministers disallow it. *a* **1745** SWIFT (J.), It was known that the most eminent of those who professed his own principles, publickly disallowed his proceedings. **1892** *Pall Mall G.* 7 Sept. 6/2 The auditor also disallowed the refreshments the committee had, which..amounted to 9*s.* 6½*d.* each.

†**b.** *intr.* with *of.* To refuse approval of. *Obs.*

1576 FLEMING *Panopl. Epist.* 44, I..might in no wise disallow of his doings: for he was very circumspect..in his master's businesse. **1649** MILTON *Eikon.* xiv. (1851) 448 He returnes againe to disallow of that Reformation which the Covnant vowes. **1681** CHETHAM *Angler's Vade-m.* xxviii. §3 (1689) 164 Others disallow thereof.

†**3.** To refuse to accept with approval; to reject, disown. *Obs.*

1377 LANGL. *P. Pl.* B. XIV. 130 For þei [the rich] han her hyre here . an heuene as it were..And whan he deyeth, ben disalowed. **1413** *Pilgr. Sowle* (Caxton) I. xiii. (1859) 9 Sithen that he come to yeres of discrecyon, this laboure he hath in dede disalowid. **1526-34** TINDALE 1 *Pet.* ii. 4 A livynge stone disalowed of men, but chosen of god and precious. **1660** STANLEY *Hist. Philos.* IX. (1701) 435/1 [tr. *Archytas*] The fates of young and old together croud, No head is disallow'd By merciless Proserpina.

†**b.** *intr.* with *of.* *Obs.*

1576 FLEMING *Panopl. Epist.* 422 Wee ought not..to disalowe of what soever is appointed us by Gods good providence. **1595** SHAKS. *John* I. i. 16 What followes if we disallow of this?

4. To refuse to accept as reasonable, true, or valid; to refuse to admit (intellectually). See ALLOW II. 4.

c **1399** *Pol. Poems* (Rolls) II. 11 Every child is holden for to bowe Unto the modir..Or elles he mot reson desalowe. **1583** *Exec. for Treason* (1675) 37 Who with common reason can disallow that her Majesty used her principal Authority? **1692** RAY *Dissol. World* III. v. §3. 135 This whole Hypothesis [of Des Cartes] I do utterly disallow and reject. **1778** MISS BURNEY *Evelina* Ded. (1784) 10 His influence is universally disallowed. **1841** MYERS *Cath. Th.* III. §40. 145 By disallowing any human element..we are deprived at once of much feeling of sympathy with the writers of the Bible.

5. To refuse to acknowledge or grant (some claim, right, or privilege), or to accede to (some request or suggestion); to reject.

a **1555** LATIMER *Serm. & Rem.* (1845) 11, I must not suffer the devil to have the victory over me..I must disallow his instinctions and suggestions. **1698** FRYER *Acc. E. India & P.* 275 Use Christian Liberty in respect of Matrimony, it being disallowed none but the Vortobeeds. **1786** T. JEFFERSON *Writ.* (1859) II. 1 To discuss the propriety of his charges, and to allow or disallow them as you pleased. **1841** JAMES *Brigand* xxii, Your claim upon her hand is already disallowed.

6. To refuse to allow or permit; to forbid the use of, to prohibit.

1563 *Homilies* II. *Agst. Excess Apparel* (1859) 308 The abuses thereof, which he forbiddeth and disalloweth. **1568** *Form Submission Papists* in Strype *Ann. Ref.* I. lii. 549 Nor willingly suffer any such..to offend, whom I may reasonably let, or disallow. *a* **1600** HOOKER (J.), God doth in converts, being married, allow continuance with infidels, and yet disallow that the faithful, when they are free, should enter into bonds of wedlock with such. **1621** BURTON *Anat. Mel.* I. ii. II. iv, He utterly disallowes all hote Bathes in melancholy. *a* **1654** SELDEN *Table-T.* (Arb.) 30 If he disallows a book it must not be brought into the Kingdom. **1713** BENTLEY *Freethinking* xi. (R.), They disallow'd self defence, second marriages, and usury. **1831** COLERIDGE *Table-t.* 27 Oct., Advocates, men whose duty it ought to be to know what the law allows and disallows. **1854** LOWELL *Camb. Thirty Y. Ago* Prose Wks. 1890 I. 96 The great collar disallowing any independent, rotation of the head..he used to turn his whole person.

b. Const. with *infin.*, or †*from* and *vbl. sb.*

1746 W. HORSLEY *Fool* (1748) II. 54 If a poor Barber shall be disallowed from taking Money. **1868** BROWNING *Ring & Bk.* VI. 38, I being disallowed to interfere, Meddle, or make in a matter none of mine. **1887** *Pall Mall G.* 23 June 12/1 A law of the trade which disallowed an employer to take more than one apprentice at a time.

Hence **disa'llowed** *ppl. a.*, **disa'llowing** *vbl. sb.* and *ppl. a.*

1377 LANGL. *P. Pl.* B. XIV. 139 Nouȝt to fonge bifore . for drede of disalowynge. *c* **1555** HARPSFIELD *Divorce Hen. VIII* (Camden) 195 The public judgment of certain universities for the disproving and disallowing of his first marriage. **1637** GILLESPIE *Eng. Pop. Cerem.* II. ix. 53 To practise the Ceremonies, with a doubting and dissalowing conscience. **1818** JAS. MILL *Brit. India* III. ii. 79 The objection..was founded upon a disallowed assumption. **1884** *Pall Mall G.* 12 Feb. 11/2 If the House went on voting disallowing motions for ever, Mr. Bradlaugh would still be one ahead.

†**disa'llowable,** *a. Obs.* [f. DISALLOW + -ABLE.] Not to be allowed or permitted; not to be approved or sanctioned.

1494 FABYAN *Chron.* VII. 417 With these and many other disalowable condicions he was exercysed, which tourned hym to great dishonoure. **1576** FLEMING *Panopl. Epist.* 280 What judge you of the words which I uttered: were they approvable, or were they disalowable? **1678** R. L'ESTRANGE *Seneca's Mor.* (1702) 474 Our Passions are nothing else but certain Disallowable Motions of the Mind. **1716** BP. SMALRIDGE *1st Charge* 21 Which though not wholly unlawful, nor in the laity disallowable, yet in the clergy are of evil fame.

Hence †**disa'llowableness,** the quality of being disallowable.

1727 in BAILEY, vol. II.

disallowance (dɪsə'laʊəns). [f. DISALLOW + -ANCE.] The action of disallowing; refusal to sanction, admit, or permit; disapproval, rejection, prohibition.

1565 in *Parker's Corr.* (1853) 267 We have consulted how to proceed, whereby we may have your allowance or disallowance. **1585-7** T. ROGERS 39 *Art.* (1607) 206 *note,* The approbation or disallowance of a general assembly.. should be a matter and cause spiritual. **1631** GOUGE *God's Arrows* iii. §14. 211 Centurions..are commended..without any reproofe or dis-allowance of their warlike profession. **1733** NEAL *Hist. Purit.* II. 559 They declare their disallowance of all seditious libels. **1846** GROTE *Greece* I. xxi. II. 180 This disallowance of the historical personality of Homer. **1883** A. H. DE COLYAR in *Rep. Co. Crt. Cases* Pref. 11 *note,* The Rules of the Supreme Court..come into operation on the 24th October next, subject to disallowance by Parliament.

†**b.** *Mus.* Something disallowed or forbidden by rule; an irregularity. *Obs.*

1597 MORLEY *Introd. Mus.* 16 The..allowances and disallowances in the composition of foure parts. **1674** PLAYFORD *Skill Mus.* III. 37 The last disallowance..is when the upper part stands, and the lower part falls from a lesser third to a fifth. **1789** BURNEY *Hist. Mus.* III. viii. 527 An excellent composition might now be produced merely from ancient disallowances. **1854** J. W. MOORE *Compl. Cycl. Music, Disallowance,* A term applied to any anomalous formation, or succession of chords. Two succeeding eighths, or two consecutive perfect fifths, in the same direction, constitute a *disallowance.*

disa'llower. [f. DISALLOW + -ER[1].] One who disallows, or refuses to sanction.

1672 H. MORE *Brief Reply* 74 Himself was an Opposer and disallower of that fond and Idolatrous Superstition.

disallowment (dɪsə'laʊmənt). *rare.* [f. as prec. + -MENT.] The action or fact of disallowing.

1884 J. H. MCCARTHY *Eng. under Gladstone* xiv. 290 The disallowment roused a strong display of public feeling in all the Australian colonies.

disally (dɪsə'laɪ), *v. rare.* [f. DIS- 6 + ALLY *v.*] *trans.* To free from alliance or union.

1671 MILTON *Samson* 1022 Nor both so loosely disallied Their nuptials. **1864** SWINBURNE *Atalanta* 301 Disallied From breath or blood corruptible.

†**dis'alter,** *v. Obs. rare*$^{-1}$. [f. DIS- 5 + ALTER *v.*] *trans.* To alter or change for the worse.

1579 FENTON *Guicciard.* VII. (1599) 281 No other thing had disaltered the people, but the pride of the gentlemen.

†**disal'tern,** *v. Obs. rare.* [f. DIS 5 + L. *alternāre* to change from one thing to another.] *trans.* To alter or change for the worse: cf. prec.

1635 QUARLES *Embl.* III. iv, O wilt thou disaltern The rest thou gav'st?

disamay, obs. var. of DISMAY.

disambiguate (dɪsæm'bɪgjuːeɪt), *v.* [f. DIS- 8 + AMBIGU(OUS *a.* + -ATE[3].] *trans.* To remove ambiguity from.

1963 *Language* XXXIX. 175 A speaker can disambiguate parts of a sentence in terms of other parts. **1967** *Ibid.* XLIII. 619 When necessary, the Greek spelling is disambiguated by an appended phonetic transcription.

disambiguation (ˌdɪsæmbɪgjuː'eɪʃən). [f. as prec. + -ATION.] Removal of ambiguity; also, the result of such removal.

1827 G. BENTHAM *Outl. Logic* 88 Disambiguation—where it is to fix the sense of an *ambiguous* term. This operation has been termed *distinction* by some Logicians. *a* **1832** J. BENTHAM *Logic* in *Wks.* (1843) VIII. 249/1 Disambiguation is distinction applied to words. **1967** R. H. ROBINS *Short Hist. Linguistics* vi. 138 Limitation of a word's field of reference or its disambiguation as the result of specific collocations. **1968** *Proc. Arist. Soc.* Suppl. XLII. 135 We already know the correct syntactical or semantical disambiguation of his utterance. **1970** *Language* XLVI. 100 Pairs of sentences can easily be found in which disambiguation rests upon comma intonation alone.

disamenity (dɪsə'mɛnɪtɪ, -'iːnɪtɪ). [f. DIS- 9.] A disadvantage or drawback (of a locality, etc.). Freq. in *pl.*

1924 *Glasgow Herald* 19 Apr. 4 The disamenities of warm countries in the summer time. *Ibid.* 29 Nov. 4 The disamenities attendant on the growth of civilisation. **1938** *Rep. Brit. Assoc. Advancem. Sci. 1937* 383 The increased social expenditure and disamenities of social life (such as road congestion, housing shortage, loss of open spaces) in expanding areas. **1965** *Listener* 13 May 711/1 The political disamenity, dislocation, and social disturbance suffered both by the inhabitants and the immigrants. **1970** *New Scientist* 13 Aug. 342/2 Two other rapidly growing sources of disamenity..are air travel and tourism.

disamis ('dɪsəmɪs). *Logic.* The mnemonic term (introduced by Petrus Hispanus, *c* 1250) designating the second mood of the third figure of syllogisms, in which the major premiss is a particular affirmative (*i*), the minor a universal affirmative (*a*), and the conclusion a particular affirmative (*i*).

The initial letter *d* shows that the mood can be reduced to *Darii,* by simple conversion of the major, transposition of the premisses, and simple conversion of the conclusion, as indicated by the letters *s, m, s,* following the three vowels.

1551 T. WILSON *Logike* (1580) 30 The third figure..This argument is reduced to Darii..*Di.* Mercie onely forgiveth synnes. *sa.* All mercie is purchased by faithe; *mis.* Therfore by faith onely forgivenes is obteined. **1624** DE LAWNE tr. *Du Moulin's Logick* 144. **1891** WELTON *Logic* I. IV. iii. §136 *Disamis*..As example we may give: 'Some pronouns in English are inflected; all such pronouns are words of English origin; therefore, some words of English origin are inflected'. *Ibid.*, As an *I* proposition can be simply converted, it is a matter of very small moment whether an argument is expressed in *Disamis* or in *Datisi.*

disanagrammatize: see DIS- 6.

†**disa'nalogal,** *a. Obs.* [DIS- 10.] = next.

1676-7 HALE *Contempl.* II. *Works of God* (R.), That knowledge, which we have in ourselves, which is utterly unsuitable and disanalogal to that knowledge, which is in God.

disanalogous (dɪsə'næləgəs), *a.* [DIS- 10.] Having no analogy.

1816 KEATINGE *Trav.* (1817) II. 174 The words..have their ordinary denominations in an idiom totally disanalogous to what they have with us.

disa'nalogy. *rare.* [DIS- 9.] Want of analogy; a condition the reverse of analogous.

1610 W. FOLKINGHAM *Art of Survey* Pref. Verse 15 For Dis-analogies strange, strained, rude, Nor Deuiations curious-ill-scande. **1641** CAPT. A. MERVIN in Rushw. *Hist. Coll.* III. (1692) I. 218 Where first I observe the disanalogy. **1948** M. BLACK *Lang. & Philos.* (1949) i. 10 Risk is always involved in neglecting the disanalogy between the things compared. **1959** P. F. STRAWSON *Individuals* v. 171 These analogies and disanalogies. **1966** J. J. KATZ *Philos. Lang.* iii. 35 There is a certain disanalogy here.

disanchor (dɪ'sæŋkə(r)), *v.* Also 5–7 dis-, dysa(u)ncre, 6–7 disan(c)kar, -er. [a. OF. *desancre-r*, f. *des-*, DIS- 4 + *ancrer* to ANCHOR, f. *ancre* ANCHOR *sb.*[1]]

1. *trans.* To loosen (a ship) from its anchorage; to weigh the anchor of.

c **1477** CAXTON *Jason* 56 Thene the good patrone.. disancred the noble shippe and went again to the see. **1481** —— *Godfrey* 189 They shold disancre theyr shippes and flee. **1600** HOLLAND *Livy* XXXI. vii. 776 After he is disankered once..& under saile from Corinth. **1609** HEYWOOD *Brit. Troy* V. xxxix. 116 Sixe Gallies they Disanker from the Isle.

fig. *a* **1871** CARLYLE in *J. W. Carlyle's Lett.* (1883) II. 346 *note*, Miserable feature of London life, needing to be disanchored every year, to be made comparatively a nomadic, quasi-Calmuck life.

2. *intr.* To weigh anchor: said of a ship or its crew.

a **1470** TIPTOFT *Cæsar* iii. (1530) 3 He dysauncred & departed about thre of the clocke. *c* **1477** CAXTON *Jason* 38 She went to the ship that sholde disancre for to go to Athenes. **1595** DRAKE *Voy.* (Hakluyt Soc.) 9 The enemie labored to cause us to disankar. *a* **1656** USSHER *Ann.* (1658) 644 [They] were commanded..to disanchor, and to depart from those places. **18..** SOUTHEY (F. Hall).

Hence **dis'anchoring** *vbl. sb.*

1851 CARLYLE *Sterling* II. vi. (1872) 138 We need not dwell at too much length on the foreign journeys, disanchorings, and nomadic vicissitudes of household, which occupy his few remaining years.

†**disan'gelical**, *a.* *Obs.* [DIS- 10.] Not angelical; the reverse of angelical.

a **1687** H. MOPE in Norris *Theory of Love* (1688) 191 It were a thing Disangelical, if I may so speak, and undivine. **1736** H. COVENTRY *Philemon to Hyd.* II. (T.), The opinion of that learned casuist..who accounts for the shame attending these pleasures of the sixth sense, as he is pleased to call them, from their disangelical nature.

disangularize, *v.*: see DIS- 6.

disanimal, *v.*: see DIS- 7 b.

†**dis'animate**, *a.* *Obs. rare.* [f. DIS- 10 + ANIMATE *a.*] Deprived of life; inanimate.

1681 P. RYCAUT *Critick* 228 They saw..many disanimate Bodies.

disanimate (dɪs'ænɪmeɪt), *v.* [f. DIS- 6 + ANIMATE *v.*, prob. after F. *désanimer* (15–16th c. in Godef. *Suppl.*).]

1. *trans.* To deprive of life, render lifeless.

1646 SIR T. BROWNE *Pseud. Ep.* IV. vii. 196 In carcasses warme and bodies newly disanimated. **1678** CUDWORTH *Intell Syst.* 38 That Soul and Life that is now fled and gone, from a lifeless Carcase, is only a loss to that particular Body or Compages of Matter, which by means thereof is now disanimated. **1833** [see DISANIMATED below].

2. To deprive of spirit, courage, or vigour; to discourage, dispirit, dishearten.

1583 STUBBES *Anat. Abus.* II. (1882) 39 [They] also rather animate, than disanimate them to perseuere in their wickednes. **1591** SHAKS. *1 Hen. VI*, III. i. 183. **1638** SIR T. HERBERT *Trav.* (ed. 2) 183 Yet the sublime height did not disanimate us. **1702** C. MATHER *Magn. Chr.* VII. App. (1852) 604 The garrisons were so disanimated at these disasters. **1791–1814** [see DISANIMATING below].

Hence **dis'animated** *ppl. a.*; **dis'animating** *vbl. sb.* and *ppl. a.*

1624 CAPT. SMITH *Virginia* III. xii. 94 After the expence of fifteene yeares more..grow they disanimated. **1677** LD. ORRERY *Art of War* 199 May it not be a greater Disanimating of the Soldiery? **1791** E. DARWIN *Bot. Gard.* I. 87 To..stay Despair's disanimating sigh. **1814** SOUTHEY *Roderick* XVIII. 83 From whence disanimating fear had driven The former primate. **1833** LAMB *Elia* Ser. II. *Product. Mod. Art*, [The Dryad] linked to her own connatural tree, co-twisting with its limbs her own till both seemed either—these animated branches; those disanimated members.

dis,ani'mation. [n. of action f. DISANIMATE *v.*] The action of disanimating: **a.** Privation of life. **b.** Discouragement, disheartening.

1646 SIR T. BROWNE *Pseud. Ep.* III. x. 128 Affections which depend on life, and depart upon disanimation. *Ibid.* III. xxv. 178 A Glow-worme will afford a faint light, almost a dayes space when many will conceive it dead; but this is a mistake in the compute of death, and terme of disanimation. **1828** WEBSTER, *Disanimation*, the act of discouraging; depression of spirits.

disannex (dɪsə'nɛks), *v.* Also 5 disanex. [a. OF. *desannexe-r* (1475 in Godef.): see DIS- 1 and ANNEX.] *trans.* To separate (that which is annexed); to disjoin, disunite.

1495 *Act 11 Hen. VII*, c. 34 Preamb., The same.. Hereditamentes shuld be..separat severed and disanexed from the Duchie of Cornwall. **1628** COKE *On Litt.* 190 b, The feoffor cannot disannex the advowson from the manor, without deed. **1719** T. GORDON *Cordial for Low Spirits* I. 270 [It] became part of the English Dominions..and could not be disannexed but by Act of Parliament. **1869** *Echo* 9 Mar., The object of the Bill was to disannex from the Provostship of the College [Oriel] a canonry of Rochester and a valuable rectory, which now formed part of the endowment.

Hence **disa'nnexing** *vbl. sb.*

1831 COLERIDGE *Table-t.* 17 Dec., The disannexing and independence of Ireland.

disannexation (dɪsænɪk'seɪʃən). [f. DISANNEX, after *annexation*.] The action of disannexing; separation (of something annexed).

1884 *Q. Rev.* July 148 *note*, The idea of the disannexation of the Transkei has been abandoned. **1885** LADY HERBERT tr. *Lagrange's Dupanloup* II. 130 Ceaseless fears of annexation and disannexation.

disannul (dɪsə'nʌl), *v.* Also 5–6 **dys-**, 5–8 **-anull.** [f. DIS- 5 + ANNUL *v.* Cf. the parallel forms DISNULL, DENULL.]

1. *trans.* To cancel and do away with; to make null and void, bring to nothing, abolish, annul.

1494 FABYAN *Chron.* VII. 347 He laboured that he myght do dysanull yᵉ former ordenaunces and statutes, and to cause them to be broken. **1526** TINDALE *Matt.* v. 17 Ye shall not thinke that I am come to disanull the lawe. **1535** COVERDALE *Job* xl. 3 Wilt thou disanulle my judgment? **1590** SHAKS. *Com. Err.* I. i. 145 Our Lawes..Which Princes, would they, may not disanull. **1634** CANNE *Necess. Separ.* (1849) 52 The whole action is disannulled and made void. **1691** RAY *Creation* I. (1704) 44 They endeavour to evacuate and disannul our great Argument. **1745** in *Col. Rec. Pennsylv.* IV. 775 To disanull the Engagements and destroy the Amity subsisting between them. **1849** MISS MULOCK *Ogilvies* xiv, A solemn troth-plight, which..no earthly power ought ever to disannul.

†**2.** To deprive by the annulment of one's title; *fig.* to do out *of*. Const. *from*, *of*. *Obs.*

1556 *Chron. Gr. Friars* (Camden) 79 Soo by that they be dyschargyd and dyssanullyd from alle maner of inherrytans of the imperialle crowne. **1604** T. M. *Black Bk.* B iv b, Are we disanuld of our first sleepe, and cheated of our dreames and fantasies? **1613** *Answ. Uncasing Machivil's Instr.* E ij, That will..disanul thee of thy quiet rest.

Hence **disa'nnulling** *vbl. sb.*; also **disa'nnuller**, one who disannuls; **disa'nnulment**, the fact of disannulling.

1586 T. B. *La Primaud. Fr. Acad.* I. 337 The disanulling of all gold and silver coine, and the appointing of yron monie onely to be currant. **1600** E. BLOUNT tr. *Conestaggio* 65 If any thing were done by them that was absolutely good, it was the disannulling of the impost of salt. **1611** COTGR., *Nullité*, a nullitie, annihilation, disannulment. *a* **1625** FLETCHER *Woman's Prize* II. v, In which business Two of the disanullers lost their night-caps. **1755** JOHNSON, *Disannulment.* **1792** G. WASHINGTON *Let.* Writ. 1891 XII. 157 The right of disannulling is reserved to the government. **1818** COLEBROOKE *Treat. Obligations* I. 101 He is debarred from..insisting on the delay as a disannulment of it. **1882** *Standard* 23 Dec. 1/2, I agree to the disannulment of our engagement on certain conditions.

disanoint (dɪsə'nɔɪnt), *v.* [f. DIS- 6 + ANOINT.] *trans.* To undo the anointing or consecration of. Hence **disa'nointed**, **disa'nointing** *ppl. adjs.*

1648 MILTON *Tenure Kings* (1649) 2 They have..bandied and borne armes against their King, devested him, disanointed him. **1820** KEATS *Hyperion* II. 98 For Fate Had pour'd a mortal oil upon his head, A disanointing poison. **1867** TRENCH *Shipwrecks Faith* 47 There is something unutterably pathetic in that yearning of the disanointed King [Saul]. **1871** SWINBURNE *Songs bef. Sunrise, Halt bef. Rome* 175 His blessings, as other men's curses Disanoint where they consecrate Kings.

disanswerable *a.*: see DIS- 10.

†**disa'pparel**, *v.* *Obs.* [f. DIS- 6 + APPAREL *v.*: perhaps after F. *désappareiller* (11th c. in Littré) cf. Sp *desaparejar* to unharness, unrig, Pg. *desaparelhar* to unrig, unmast.] *trans.* To deprive of apparel; to disrobe, undress. Also *fig.*

1580 SIDNEY *Arcadia* III. 336 Zelmane disapparelling herself. **1627–77** FELTHAM *Resolves* I. lxxxiv. 128 The Cup is the betrayer of the mind, and does disapparel the soul. *a* **1649** DRUMM. OF HAWTH. *Cypress Grove* Wks. (1711) 119 Every day we rise and lie down, apparel and disapparel our selves, weary our bodies and refresh them. **1652** BENLOWES *Theoph.* XIII. c. 249 Thus entertain we death, as friend To disapparel us for Glories endlesse end.

b. *intr.* for *refl.* Cf. *undress.*

1655 H. VAUGHAN *Silex Scint.* I. (1858) 51 I'le disapparell, and to buy But one half glaunce most gladly dye.

†**disappa'rition.** *Obs. rare.* [f. DIS- 9 + APPARITION; after *disappear.*] = DISAPPEARANCE.

1790 HERSCHEL in *Phil. Trans.* LXXX. 479 Its disapparition in general, and in my telescopes its faintness when turned edgeways, are in no manner favourable to this idea. **1796** W. TAYLOR in Robberds *Mem.* I. 97 The still disapparition of the tumult and bustle.

disappear (dɪsə'pɪə(r)), *v.* Forms: 6 **disapere**, 7 **disappeer**, **-appeare**, 7– **disappear.** [f. DIS- 6 + APPEAR *v.*, after F. *disparaître*, *disparaiss-*, of which the earlier direct reprs. were DISPARISH and DISPEAR, q.v.

(In Palsgr., but app. not in common use before 17th c. Not in Shaks., nor in Bible of 1611.)]

1. a. *intr.* To cease to appear or be visible; to vanish from sight. The reverse of APPEAR. Also with advb. expressions introduced by prepositions.

1530 PALSGR. 517/1 The vysion disapered incontynent. **1623** COCKERAM, *Disappeare*, to vanish out of sight. **1647** CLARENDON *Hist. Reb.* I. (1843) 17/2 There appeared to him, on the side of his bed, a man..after this discourse he disappeared. **1665** SIR T. HERBERT *Trav.* (1677) 388 When the Sun is deprest and disappearing. **1667** MILTON *P.L.* VIII. 478 She disappeerd, and left me dark, I wak'd To find her, or for ever to deplore Her loss. *a* **1704** LOCKE (J.), The pictures drawn in our minds are laid in fading colours, and, if not sometimes refreshed, vanish and disappear. **1726** *Adv. Capt. R. Boyle* 271 The Cloud upon my Wife's Face began to disappear by degrees. **1837** E. HOWARD *Old Commodore* I. iv. 111 Richard Stubbs..disappeared down the Jacob's ladder. **1842** LEVER *J. Hinton* lii, A mounted party.. entering one of the gates of the city, disappeared from our sight. **1860** TYNDALL *Glac.* I. xxvii. 212, I saw the leader sink and suddenly disappear. **1881** MRS. RIDDELL *Senior Partner* xxii, The boy disappeared into the retirement of the back room. **1888** MRS. H. WARD *R. Elsmere* v, Almost every year he disappeared to France. *Ibid.* x, Rose caught a gray dress disappearing up the little stairs. **1922** JOYCE *Ulysses* 427 He disappears into Olhousen's the pork butcher's.

b. Of a line or thing extended in space, which ends by gradually ceasing to be distinguishable, or 'dies away' by blending with something else; to be traceable no farther.

1753 HOGARTH *Anal. Beauty* 9 Its opposite thread is lost, and disappears on the other. **1860** TYNDALL *Glac.* I. ix. 63 A moraine..disappearing at the summit of the cascade. *Mod.* (*Entomol.*) A species of moth with a particular line disappearing at the subcostal vein.

2. a. To cease to be present, to depart; to pass from existence, pass away, be lost.

1665 HOOKE *Microgr.* 98 If..the surface has been long expos'd..these small caverns are fill'd with dust, and disappear. **1784** COWPER *Task* III. 814 As duly as the swallows disappear. **1874** MORLEY *Compromise* (1886) 235 A species of plant or animal disappears in face of a better adapted species. **1884** GUSTAFSON *Found. Death* i. (ed. 3) 13 The works of the few writers of antiquity who ventured to treat of these mysteries..have tracelessly disappeared.

b. of things immaterial.

a **1700** DRYDEN (J.), When the night and winter disappear, The purple morning rising with the year, Salutes the Spring. **1809–10** COLERIDGE *Friend* (1865) 38 Effects will not, indeed, immediately disappear with their causes. **1862** H. SPENCER *First Princ.* . iv. §26 (1875) 91 Our conception of the Relative itself disappears, if our conception of the Absolute is a pure negation. **1893** *Weekly Notes* 83/2 The distinction between meritorious and non-meritorious creditors had disappeared.

3. *trans.* To cause to disappear.

1897 *Chem. News* 19 Mar. 143 We progressively disappear the faces of the dodecahedron. **1949** *Amer. Speech* XXIV. 41 The magician may speak of disappearing or vanishing a card.

disappearance (dɪsə'pɪərəns). [f. DISAPPEAR *v.* + -ANCE, after *appearance.*] The action of disappearing; passing away from sight or observation; vanishing.

1712 ADDISON *Spect.* No. 317 ¶2 Not likely to be remembred a Moment after their Disappearance. **1794** S. WILLIAMS *Vermont* 115 The usual times of the appearance and disappearance of these birds. **1847** EMERSON *Repr. Men, Montaigne* Wks. (Bohn) I. 352 Let a man learn..to bear the disappearance of things he was wont to reverence, without losing his reverence. **1856** STANLEY *Sinai & Pal.* viii. (1858) 328 The sudden appearances and disappearances, which baffled all the zeal of his enemies. **1871** MORLEY *Voltaire* (1886) 351 The final disappearance of many ideas which foster anti-social tendencies.

disappearer (dɪsə'pɪərə(r)). [f. DISAPPEAR + -ER[1].] One who disappears or vanishes.

1882 *N.Y. Tribune* 14 June, Prickly comfrey, which..was going to do such great things for our agriculture, seems to have joined the mysterious disappearers. **1889** *Daily News* 8 Oct. 5/1 The learned Feithius, who 'chanced to pop his head into a fuller's shop' and never came out again, was a model of a disappearer.

disa'ppearing, *vbl. sb.* [f. as prec. + -ING[1].] **a.** The action of the verb to DISAPPEAR.

1611 COTGR., *Disparoissance*, a disappearing, or vanishing out of sight. **1662** S. P. *Acc. Latitude Men* in *Phenix* II. 514 The appearing of new Stars and disappearing of old. **1726** *Adv. Capt. R. Boyle* 285 All the Discourse was of Don Roderigo's sudden disappearing. **1807** T. THOMSON *Chem.* II. 115 It is impossible..to account for the disappearing of the two gases, or the appearance of the water, without admitting that this liquid is actually composed of oxygen and hydrogen.

b. In colloq. phr. *to do a* (or *the*) *disappearing act* (or *trick*), to disappear suddenly or without warning; to vanish, as if by magic. Chiefly of persons. Cf. *vanishing act*, *trick* s.v. VANISHING *vbl. sb.* 3. orig. *U.S.*

1913 E. D. BIGGERS *Seven Keys to Baldpate* x. 193 'Got the news, Magee?' asked the haberdasher. 'Peters has done a disappearing act.' **1934** R. KNOX *Still Dead* xxii. 266, I think we are now going to hear how it was that the unfortunate young man's body came to do the disappearing trick. **1940** F. GRUBER *Laughing Fox* xvi. 223 When suspects who're supposed to stick around do a disappearing act. **1961** J. WEBB *One for my Dame* (dust-jacket), Carla was a beautiful redhead... Rick thought they could play a swinging scene together. Then she did a disappearing act. **1978** F. NORMAN *Dead Butler Caper* v. 34, I was doing a bit of straight forward divorce snooping for some chick when all of a sudden her high-born lover does a disappearing act. **1983** *Financial Times* 8 Jan. 9/1 A year which started with the Laker empire going into a tailspin and ended with the Magic Bus doing a disappearing trick.

disa'ppearing, *ppl. a.* [f. as prec. + -ING[2].] That disappears or passes out of sight.

1886 *Daily News* 9 Nov. 2/7 The defendant..performed the trick with his daughter as the disappearing lady. **1887** *Fortn. Rev.* Nov. (*Brit. Army*), We are behindhand..in disappearing guns, in cupolas and shields, and in submarine mining. **1891** *Daily News* 7 Oct. 5/3 Witnessing target practice with the so-called disappearing gun..The gun is hoisted for firing, and immediately upon the discharge falls back into position.

† **disa'ppendancy, -ency.** *Obs. rare*$^{-1}$. [f. DIS- 9 + APPENDANCY.] *Law.* The condition or quality of being disappendant; an instance of this.

1760 BURN *Eccles. Law* (1767) I. 6 (Jod.) A disappendency may be also temporary.

† **disa'ppendant, -ent,** *a. Obs.* [f. DIS- 10 + APPENDANT.] *Law.* The opposite of APPENDANT; detached from being an appendancy.

1642 PERKINS *Prof. Bk.* v. §436. 188 If the Baylywick or faire be disappendant in fee from the Manour. **1760** BURN *Eccles. Law* (1767) I. 7 (Jod.) The advowson is made disappendent.

disappoint (dɪsə'pɔɪnt), *v.* Also 5–6 disapoynte, 6 disapoincte, -apoint, -apoynt, -appoynte, dys-. [ad. F. *désappointer* (14th c. in Hatz.-Darm.), f. *des-* (DIS- 4) + *appointer* to APPOINT. See also DISPOINT.]

1. *trans.* To undo the appointment of; to deprive of an appointment, office, or possession; to dispossess, deprive. *Obs.* (exc. as *nonce-wd.*)

[**1489** see DISPOINT.] **1586** T. B. *La Primaud. Fr. Acad.* I. 582 A monarch..hath power..to appoint or to disappoint the greatest officers. **1824** BYRON *Juan* XVI. lxxv, He would keep it Till duly disappointed or dismiss'd. **1869** SPURGEON *Treas. Dav.* Ps. xi. 6 God's Anointed is appointed, and shall not be disappointed.

2. a. To frustrate the expectation or desire of (a person); to defeat, balk, or deceive in fulfilment of desire. Const. †*of, in, with.* Also *absol.*, to cause disappointment.

1494 FABYAN *Chron.* VII. ccxxxiv. 270 He, contrary his promyse, dyd disapoynte them, and nothynge ayded them. **1555** WATREMAN *Fardle Facions* Ded. 4 Neuer disapointed of honourable successe. **1697** POTTER *Antiq. Greece* II. ii. (1715) 183 [They] were miserably disappointed of their expectations. **1749** FIELDING *Tom Jones* x. iii, Disappointed in the woman whom..he had mistaken for his wife. **1821** SHELLEY *Prometh. Unb.* III. iv. 128, I..first was disappointed not to see Such mighty change as I had felt within Expressed in outward things. **1839** T. BEALE *Nat. Hist. Sperm Whale* 204, I was much disappointed with its appearance. **1842** LEVER *J. Hinton* ix, The Duke has disappointed so often, that he is sure to go now. **1881** MRS. RIDDELL *Senior Partner* xxxii, I shall look out for you at Waterloo at a quarter to five, and trust you will not disappoint. *c* **1897** *Mod.* I should be sorry to disappoint you. If they rely on him, he will be sure to disappoint them. **1927** *Daily Tel.* 3 May 16 Innuendo [*sc.* a racehorse] has disappointed in the past when fancied. **1966** *Listener* 13 Oct. 549/3 Ormandy's CBS album of the Berlioz *Requiem*.., of which I had high hopes, disappoints.

†**b.** To defeat (*of* action, effort, etc.). *Obs.*

1582 N. LICHEFIELD tr. *Castanheda's Conq. E. Ind.* lxv. 132 Howbeit to disappoint them of their suttle dealing. **1587** GOLDING *De Mornay* x. (1617) 149 The Adamant or Lodestone..is disappointed of his force by Garlicke.

†**3.** To break off (what has been appointed or fixed); to fail to keep or comply with (an engagement); to fail to fulfil an appointment with (a person). Cf. APPOINT *v.* 3. *Obs.*

1530 PALSGR. 517/1, I disapoynte, I breake a poyntement with a person. **1542** HENRY VIII *Declar. Scots* 193 The.. metyng was not onely disappoynted, but..an inuasion made ..into our realme. **1581** *York Bakers' Guild* §39 in *Archæol. Rev.* (1888) May, If any jurneyman..dothe promise anie maister to come and helpe him to bake at tyme appointed, and..go to an other to worke, and disapoint the maister. **1633** BP. HALL *Hard Texts, N.T.* 363 So as to put off and disappoint the day which he had set.

4. a. To undo or frustrate anything appointed or determined; to defeat the realization or fulfilment of (plans, purposes, intentions); to balk, foil, thwart (anticipations, hopes, etc.).

1579 TOMSON *Calvin's Serm. Tim.* 99/2 Not y^t any mortall men can disappoint that which God hath established from heauen. **1611** BIBLE *Prov.* xv. 22 Without counsell, purposes are disappointed. **1689** C. HATTON in *H. Corr.* (1878) II. 133 Y^t fatall resolution..hath disapointed ye delivery of y^r letter. **1715–20** POPE *Iliad* VII. 304 The wary Trojan shrinks, and, bending low Beneath his buckler, disappoints the blow. **1718** LADY M. W. MONTAGU *Let. to Lady Rich* 16 Mar., I can answer without disappointing your expectations. **1818** CRUISE *Digest* (ed. 2) II. 433 On purpose that the testator's intention should be wholly frustrated, and that the tenant for life should be under a temptation to disappoint the will. **1832** HT. MARTINEAU *Homes Abroad* ix, The junction of penal with voluntary emigration tends..to disappoint the purposes of the one, and to extinguish the benefits of the other. **1855** MACAULAY *Hist. Eng.* III. 165 This ambitious hope Louvois was bent on disappointing. **1873** F. HALL in *Scribner's Mag.* VI. 466/2 Nor is this expectation frequently disappointed.

†**b.** To undo, destroy, overthrow. *Obs.*

1611 COTGR., *Desbraquer*, to vnplant, or dismount artillerie; to wry, or disappoint the leuell thereof. **1633** BP. HALL *Hard Texts* 311 All those curious and wealthy Trades of them who worke in fine flaxe..Shall be utterly undone and disappointed. **1709** STEELE *Tatler* No. 135 ¶1 They endeavour to disappoint the good works of the most learned ..of men. **1712** tr. *Pomet's Hist. Drugs* I. 26 Disappointing all the ill Effects of the Viperine poison.

†**5.** To appoint, equip, or accoutre improperly. Cf. APPOINT 15. *Obs.*

1587 GOLDING *De Mornay* i. 7 In painting thy Pictures thou doest not so disapoint thy selfe.

† **disa'ppoint,** *sb. Obs. rare.* [f. prec. vb.] The act of disappointing; disappointment.

1642 ROGERS *Naaman* 267 The more desirable the object, the greater the disappoint. *a* **1656** BP. HALL *Soliliquies* 45 There is nothing more troublesome in human Society than the disappoint of trust and failing of friends.

† **disa'ppointable,** *a. Obs. rare*$^{-0}$. [f. DISAPPOINT *v.* + -ABLE.] Liable to be deprived of office, etc.

1611 COTGR., *Destituable*, destituable, disappointable.

disa'ppointed, *ppl. a.* [f. as prec. + -ED^1.]

1. Having one's anticipations frustrated; foiled, thwarted.

1552 HULOET, Disapoynted, *frustratus.* **1744** R. LIDDELL *Let. to Lady Denbigh* 10 May in *8th Rep. Hist. MSS. Comm.*, The disappointed people who were invited have lost their dance. **1781** GIBBON *Decl. & F.* II. 107 The disappointed monarch..was thrice repulsed with loss and ignominy. **1861** GEO. ELIOT *Silas M.* 10 The anguish of disappointed faith.

†**2.** Improperly appointed, equipped, or fitted out; unfurnished, unprepared. *Obs.*

1602 SHAKS. *Ham.* I. v. 77 Cut off euen in the Blossomes of my Sinne, Vnhouzzled, disappointed, vnnaneld. *a* **1659** CLEVELAND *Sing-song* xxxv, The Bridegroom in at last did rustle, All *disappointed* in the Bustle, The Maidens had shav'd his Breeches.

Hence **disa'ppointedly** *adv.*, in a disappointed manner.

1880 MRS. BURNETT *Louisiana* 12, I would rather have 'Louise', she said, disappointedly.

disa'ppointer. [f. as prec. + -ER^1.] One who or that which disappoints.

1812 LEIGH HUNT in *Examiner* 14 Dec. 786/2 He is not the disappointer of hopes. **1820** *Ibid.* No. 616. 66/1 Royal disappointers and promise-breakers.

disa'ppointing, *vbl. sb.* [f. as prec. + -ING^1.] The action of the vb. DISAPPOINT; disappointment.

1580 HOLLYBAND *Treas. Fr. Tong, Destitution & Delaissement*, destituting or disappointing. **1643** MILTON *Divorce* iii. (1851) 26 The disappointing of an impetuous nerve.

disa'ppointing, *ppl. a.* [f. as prec. + -ING^2.] That disappoints; that belies hope or expectation.

1530 PALSGR. 310/1 Disapoyntyng, *frustratif.* **1836** KEBLE in *Lyra Apost.* (1849) 199 Vain disappointing dream! **1884** *Fortn. Rev.* June 812 The sons of Jacob were..a disappointing set of young men.

Hence **disa'ppointingly** *adv.*, in a disappointing manner. **disa'ppointingness,** disappointing quality.

1870 *Pall Mall G.* 25 Aug. 5/1 [Apparatus] disappointingly useless. **1874** L. STEPHEN *Hours in Library* (1892) I. x. 371 The light verses and essays..are disappointingly weak. **1887** CHEYNE *Job & Solomon* vi, The main point for us to emphasise is the disappointingness of the events of the epilogue regarded as the final outcome of Job's spiritual discipline.

disappointment (dɪsə'pɔɪntmənt). [f. DISAPPOINT *v.* + -MENT: cf. F. *désappointement* (14–15th c. in Hatz.-Darm.); also DISPOINTMENT.]

1. The fact of disappointing; the frustration or non-fulfilment of expectation, intention, or desire.

1614 RALEIGH *Hist. World* IV. v §11 (R.) Such disappointment of expectation doth much abate the courage of men in fight. **1690** NORRIS *Beatitudes* (1692) I. 25 Not that which the World understands by Disappointment, the not compassing what you design'd..but the not enjoying what you have compassed, the Disappointment of Fruition. **1700** TYRRELL *Hist. Eng.* II. 1107 Penalties..for the disappointment of the Lord by his Ward's marrying himself without his consent. **1794** S. WILLIAMS *Vermont* 139 All the prospects of success and disappointment. **1860** TYNDALL *Glac.* II. ix. 271 Severe labour and frequent disappointment had taught observers the true conditions of success.

b. with *a.* and *pl.* An instance of this.

1614 BP. HALL *Recoll. Treat.* 935 Lest..he..should want means of speedy thanksgiving for so gratious a disappointment; beholde a Ram stands ready for the sacrifice.

1752 JOHNSON *Rambler* No. 196 ¶4 Hope will predominate in every mind, till it has been suppressed by frequent disappointments. **1866** GEO. ELIOT *F. Holt* (1868) 23 She saw clearly that the meeting with the son had been a disappointment in some way.

2. The state or condition of being disappointed, with its resulting feeling of dejection.

1756 BURKE *Subl. & B.* I. v, If pleasure be abruptly broken off, there ensues an uneasy sense called disappointment. **1822** LAMB *Elia* Ser. II. *Detached Th. on Bks.*, Newspapers always excite curiosity. No one ever lays one down without a feeling of disappointment. **1856** FROUDE *Hist. Eng.* (1858) I. ii. 118 The disappointment was intense in proportion to the interests which were at issue.

3. *ellipt.* A cause of disappointment; a thing or person that disappoints.

1765 COWPER *Lett.* 1 Aug., One who has been a disappointment and a vexation to them ever since he has been of consequence enough to be either. **1843** MISS MITFORD in L'Estrange *Life* III. x. 177 Bath is a disappointment—monotonous, bald, poor, and dead.

disappreciate (dɪsə'priːʃɪeɪt), *v.* [f. DIS- 6 + APPRECIATE.] *trans.* To regard with the reverse of appreciation; to undervalue.

1828 in WEBSTER; whence in mod. Dicts.

So **disappreci'ation,** the reverse of appreciation.

disapprobation (dɪsæprəʊ'beɪʃən). [f. DIS- 9 + APPROBATION, after *disapprove*: so mod.F. *désapprobation* (18th c. in Hatz.-Darm.).] The action or fact of disapproving; the feeling or utterance of moral condemnation; disapproval.

1647 CLARENDON *Hist. Reb.* v. (1843) 217/2 Which implied a disapprobation, at least, if not a contempt of their carriage towards him. **1693** *Lond. Gaz.* No. 2843/1 The Pope has declared..his Dis-approbation of his Imperial Majesties having Erected a Ninth Electorate. **1792** *Anecd. W. Pitt* I. xx. 323 His Majesty betrayed some signs of disapprobation. **1831** SCOTT *Cast. Dang.* vii, A murmur of disapprobation ran through the warriors present. **1887** R. GARNETT *Carlyle* iv, 'Sartor', the publisher acquainted him, 'excites universal disapprobation'.

disapprobative (dɪs'æprəbeɪtɪv), *a.* [f. DIS- 10 + APPROBATIVE; after *disapprove, disapprobation.*] Characterized by or expressing disapprobation; disapprobatory.

1824 J. GILCHRIST *Etym. Interpr.* 83 They are all approbative or disapprobative. **1873** MISS BROUGHTON *Nancy* II. 102 Now I look at him with a disgustful and disapprobative eye.

disapprobatory (dɪs'æprəbeɪtərɪ), *a.* [f. DIS- 10 + APPROBATORY: cf. prec.] Characterized by disapproving; conveying or implying disapproval.

1828 WEBSTER, *Disapprobatory*, containing disapprobation; tending to disapprove. **1867** CARLYLE *Remin.* (1881) II. App. 322 Eminent men..had stood pointedly silent, dubitative, disapprobatory. **1877** FLORA L. SHAW *Castle Blair* (1882) 38 Mr. Plunkett looked as though he felt somehow vaguely disapprobatory.

disappropriate (dɪsə'prəʊprɪət), *ppl. a.* [ad. med. or mod.L. *disapprōpriāt-us*, f. DIS- 4 + *apprōpriātus* APPROPRIATE. In F. *désapproprié.*] Deprived of appropriation; severed from connexion with a religious corporation.

1613 SIR H. FINCH *Law* (1636) 14 A Church appropriated to a spiritual corporation, becommeth disappropriate, if the corporation be dissolued. **1765** BLACKSTONE *Comm.* I. 386 If the corporation which has the appropriation is dissolved, the parsonage becomes disappropriate at common law.

disappropriate (dɪsæ'prəʊprɪeɪt), *v.* [f. ppl. stem of med. or mod.L. *disapprōpriāre*, f. DIS- 4 + *apprōpriāre* to APPROPRIATE: in F. *désapproprier*, (17th c. in Hatz.-Darm.).]

1. *trans.* To dissolve the appropriation of; to take away from that to which it has been appropriated. See APPROPRIATE *a.* 1.

1656 *Burton's Diary* (1828) I. 299 A Bill for the disappropriating of the Rectory appropriate to Preston. **1765** BLACKSTONE *Comm.* I. 386 At the dissolution of monasteries..the appropriations of the several parsonages, which belonged to those respective religious houses..would have been by the rules of the common law disappropriated. **1798** BENTHAM *Let. to Pole Carew* 16 Aug. Wks. (1838–1843) X. 325 If the portion of revenue at present appropriated.. was to be disappropriated.

†**2.** To render (a thing) no longer the private property or possession of any one. *Obs. rare*$^{-1}$.

1645 MILTON *Tetrach.* (1851) 186 To assist nature in disappropriating that evil which by continuing proper becomes destructive.

disappropri'ation. [n. of action, f. prec.: cf. F. *désappropriation* (17th c.).] The action of rendering disappropriate.

1727–51 CHAMBERS *Cycl.* s.v. *Appropriation*, To dissolve an appropriation, it is enough to present a clerk to the bishop, and he to institute and induct him: for that once done, the benefice returns to its former nature. This is called disappropriation. **1964** *Listener* 19 Nov. 797/2 This demands an act of *disappropriation*, a disowning of the self, ..and the substitution of the passive, perfectly detached will centred on God.

disapprovable (dɪsə'pruːvəb(ə)l), *a.* [f. DISAPPROVE *v.*, after APPROVABLE.] To be disapproved of; worthy of disapproval.

1657 TOMLINSON *Renou's Disp.* 554 That manner wherein the Cassia is so long cocted, is disapproveable. **1875** M'COSH *Scott. Philos.* xii. 101 Distinguishing good and approvable actions from bad and disapprovable ones.

disapproval (dɪsə'pruːvəl). [f. DISAPPROVE *v.*, after APPROVAL.] The action or fact of disapproving; moral condemnation of what is considered wrong; disapprobation.

1662 GLANVILL *Lux Orient.* iv. (R.), There being not a word let fall from them in disapproval of that opinion. **1818** TODD, *Disapproval*, a word, like *approval* not common, but which has been used, I think, in modern times, for *disapprobation.* **1856** FROUDE *Hist. Eng.* I. 173 The disapproval with which good men regard acts of sin. **1874** GREEN *Short Hist.* vi. §6. 336 His silent disapproval was more telling than the opposition of obscurer foes.

disapprove (dɪsə'pruːv), *v.* [prob. a. OF. **desaprove-r*, mod.F. *désapprouve-r* to disapprove, f. *des-*, DIS- 4 + *aprover, approuver* to APPROVE. Our earliest quot. however is earlier than the first recorded in Hatz.-Darm. (1535).]

†**1.** *trans.* To prove to be untrue or wrong; to DISPROVE. *Obs.*

1481 CAXTON *Tully's Friendship, Orat. G. Flaminius* F j a, The vulgar oppynyon.. I holde it ful easy to disapprove syth it is so full of errours. **1540** COVERDALE *Confut. Standish* Wks. II. 378 Sundry places of scripture, the circumstances whereof doth utterly disapprove your doctrine. **1607** TOPSELL *Serpents* (1658) 723 Such like vanities have the ancient Heathens.. firmly believed, till.. experience disapproved their inventions. **1760–72** tr. *Juan & Ulloa's Voy.* (ed. 3) I. Pref. 9 Things not thoroughly proved, or absolutely disapproved; but which are reserved for further examination. **1793** MRS. PARSONS *Mem. Mrs. Menville* IV. 15 My conduct shall disapprove her malicious conjectures.

2. The reverse of to APPROVE: to regard with disfavour or moral condemnation; to feel or express disapprobation of.

1647 COWLEY *Mistress, Love gone over*, iii, Fate does disapprove Th' Ambition of thy Love. **1651** HOBBES *Leviath.* III. xlii. 280 Some approved, others disapproved the Interpretation of St. Paul. **1713** STEELE *Englishman* No. 31. 197 Why must I hear what I disapprove, because others see what they approve? **1833** HT. MARTINEAU *Brooke Farm* i, I disapprove the object of such a meeting. **1856** MRS. BROWNING *Aur. Leigh* II. 960 Henceforth none Could disapprove me.

absol. **1717** POPE *Eloisa* 259 Nature stands check'd; Religion disapproves. **1849** MACAULAY *Hist. Eng.* II. 97 Rochester, disapproving and murmuring, consented to serve.

3. *intr.* with *of* (†rarely *to*). = 2. Also with *indirect passive.*

1726 SHELVOCKE *Voy. round World* (1757) 113 This.. was not disapproved of by some of my people who eat of it. **1745** WESLEY *Answ. Ch.* 4, I wholly disapprove of all these Positions. **1799** SICKELMORE *Agnes & L.* I. 182 Don Sebastian enquired to what.. the Count de Tourville could disapprove. **1828** SCOTT *F.M. Perth* xxxiv, The leader disapproved of this arrangement. **1875** JOWETT *Plato* (ed. 2) V. 181 Modern jurists would disapprove of the redress of injustice being purchased only at an increasing risk.

Hence **disaˈpproved** *ppl. a.*, **disaˈpproving** *vbl. sb.* and *ppl. a.*; **disaˈpprovingly** *adv.*, in a disapproving manner; also †**disaˈpprovement**, disapproval; **disaˈpprover**, one who disapproves.

1648 J. GOODWIN *Right & Might* 11 A disapprovement of the factious carriage of things. **1653** MILTON *Hirelings* Wks. (1851) 375 Wrung out of mens Purses to maintain a disapprov'd Ministry against thir Conscience. **1654–5** LD. HATTON in *Nicholas Papers* (Camden) II. 165, I find my selfe exceedingly out in the approving or disapproving of persons. **1661** BOYLE *Style of Script* Ep. Ded. (1675) 8 Not incompetent judges.. have been pleased to give these papers no disapproving character. **1794** *Hist.* in *Ann. Reg.* 107 Every disapprover of their politics and religious tenets. **1820** FOSTER *Ess. Evils Pop. Ignorance* 178 The disapprovers of the designs for educating the people. **1832** *Examiner* 646/1, I have spoken disapprovingly of the method. **1860** ELLICOTT *Life our Lord* v. 229 *note*, The opinion.. is noticed, not disapprovingly, by Lightfoot. **1866** GEO. ELIOT *F. Holt* (1868) 26 There was unkind triumph or disapproving pity in the glances of greeting neighbours.

disaproned (dɪsˈeɪprənd), *ppl. a.* [f. **disapron* vb.: see DIS- 7 a.] Divested or devoid of an apron.

1831 CARLYLE *Sart. Res.* II. iii, I entered the main street of the place, and saw.. the aproned or disaproned Burghers moving in to breakfast.

disˈapt, *v. Obs. rare.* [f. DIS- 6 + APT *v.*] *trans.* To render unfit.

1611 COTGR., *Disadjusté*.. disapted. *Disadjuster*, to disadiust.. disapt. *a* **1618** SYLVESTER *Tobacco Battered* 619 Yet doth the custome Disnerve the bodie, and disapt the minde.

†**disˈapten,** *v. Obs. rare.* [see -EN[5].] = prec.

a **1655** VINES *Lord's Supper* (1677) 36 Such sins as carnalize the heart, and disapten us for spiritual fruition.

disar, obs. form of DICER.

disarchbishop: see DIS- 7 b.

disard, obs. or archaic form of DIZZARD.

disare, var. DISOUR, *Obs.*

†**disaˈrithmetic,** *v. nonce-wd.* [DIS- 7.]

1606 WARNER *Alb. Eng.* XVI. ci. 400 Minerva suffreth violence when Phao makes her faire, May such be disarithmetickt, his Creatures that are.

disarm (dɪsˈɑːm), *v.* Also 5 des-, dys-. [In 15th c. *desarm* (*e*, a. F. *désarmer* (11th c. in Hatz-Darm.), f. *des-*, DIS- 4 + *armer* to ARM.]

1. *trans.* To deprive of arms, to take the arms or weapons from. Const. *of.*

1481 CAXTON *Godfrey* (E.E.T.S.) 224 The Turkes.. toke thise .xij. men by force, and desarmed them. **1618** ROWLANDS *Night Raven* 33 All those he after ten a clocke did finde, He should disarme of weapons they did beare. **1667** MILTON *P.L.* III. 253 Death.. shall.. stoop Inglorious, of his mortal sting disarm'd. **1765–9** BLACKSTONE *Comm.* (1793) 328 A proclamation for disarming papists. **1828** SCOTT *F.M. Perth* xxxii, The new comers had.. entered the Castle, and were in the act of disarming the small garrison. **1849** MACAULAY *Hist. Eng.* II. 139 A royal order came from Whitehall for disarming the population.

b. To force his weapon from the hand of (an opponent) in fighting or fencing.

1530 PALSGR. 517/1 He was desarmed at the first course. **1548** HALL *Chron., Hen. VIII*, 82 b, The kyng of England with few strokes disarmed his counter partie. **1610** SHAKS. *Temp.* I. ii. 472 Come, from thy ward.. I can heere disarme thee with this sticke, And make thy weapon drop. **1700** S.L. tr. *Fryke's Voy. E. Ind.* 160, I made another pass at him, and fortunately run him into the Shoulder, and disarm'd him. **1833** *Regul. Instr. Cavalry* I. 123 He may be disarmed by the 'Left Parry'.

c. To divest of armour; to strip the defensive armour off (a man or horse). *arch.*

c **1489** CAXTON *Sonnes of Aymon* iii. 91 They.. made hym come in, and dysarmed hym, and dyde to hym grete honoure. **1548** HALL *Chron., Hen. VIII*, an. 2 (R.) These justes fynished.. the kynge was disarmed, and at time conuenient he and the quene heard euen song. **1611** COTGR., *Desbarder*, to vnbarbe or disarme a horse of seruice. **1841** JAMES *Brigand* ii, The page.. came up to disarm his lord.

d. *refl.* To put off one's armour and divest oneself of arms.

1481 CAXTON *Godfrey* (E.E.T.S.) 275 Thenne departed the barons, and disarmed them and toke of theyr harnoys in theyr hostellys. *c* **1489** —— *Sonne of Aymon* viii. 198 They dysarmed theym selfe, and ete right well. **1632** J. HAYWARD tr. *Biondi's Eromena* 28 The Prince disarm'd and uncloath'd himselfe. **1700** TYRRELL *Hist. Eng.* II. 920 Earl Richard.. disarmed himself.

2. *intr.* (for *refl.*) = 1 d.

1598 BARRET *Theor. Warres* II. i. 22 The Ensigne-bearer is not to disarme vntil the gates of the Fort.. be first shut. **1602** MARSTON *Ant. & Mel.* III. Wks. 1856 I. 31 Sweet lord, abandon passion, and disarme. **1626** C. POTTER tr. *Sarpi's Quarrels Pius V*, 433 Order was also giuen.. to the Count de Fuentes that he should disarme.

3. *trans.* To deprive of munitions of war or means of defence, to dismantle (a city, ship, etc.). (Also **b.** *intr.* for *refl.*)

1602 WARNER *Alb. Eng.* Epit. (1612) 355 The Romaines .. still to hold this Land theirs, had disarmed it of munition. **1611** COTGR., *Desmonter vne navire*, to disarme a ship, to despoile her of all her munition, and furniture. **1685** *Lond. Gaz.* No. 2081/1 Orders have been sent to the Galleys.. to return hither, that they may be disarmed and laid up. **1726** CAVALLIER *Mem.* I. 40 We disarm'd and burn'd some Churches, for fear the Enemy should put Garrisons in them. *Ibid.* II. 125, I disarmed Brujiere and some other Villages near Holy-Ghosts-Bridge.

b. **1694** *Lond. Gaz.* No. 3027/1 All the Ships were Disarming.

c. To deprive (an animal) of its natural organs of attack or defence, as horns, claws, teeth; to divest anything of that with which it is armed.

1607 TOPSELL *Four-f. Beasts* (1658) 34 Heliogabalus.. suddenly, in the night, would put in among them bears, wolves, lyons, and leopards, muzled and disarmed. *Ibid.* 98 They lose their horns in March.. When the head of this beast is disarmed, there issueth blood from the skull. **1687** DRYDEN *Hind & P.* I. 300 Their jaws disabl'd, and their claws disarm'd. *a* **1800** COWPER *Iliad* (ed. 2) XVI. (R.) Hector, drawing nigh To Ajax, of its brazen point disarm'd His ashen beam. **1820** W. IRVING *Sketch Bk.* I. 47 Have the courage to appear poor, and you disarm poverty of its sharpest sting.

4. To reduce (an army, navy, etc.) to the customary peace footing. Usually *absol.* or *intr.* (for *refl.*).

1727–51 CHAMBERS *Cycl.* s.v. *Disarming*, On the conclusion of a peace, it is usual for both sides to disarm. **1801** NELSON 4 Apr. in Nicolas *Disp.* (1845) IV. 334 He knew the offer of Great Britain, either to join us, or disarm. 'I pray, Lord Nelson, what do you call disarming?'.. 'I considered it as not having on foot any force beyond the customary establishment.' **1868** *Spectator* 14 Nov. 1332 The old difficulty that a drilled nation cannot disarm, that disarmament in a country like Prussia is a mere phrase, is still unaffected. **1886** *Manch. Exam.* 13 Jan. 4/7 Greece.. will not disarm, but will go to war if her demands are not agreed to.

5. *fig.* To deprive of power to injure or terrify; to divest of aversion, suspicion, hostility, or the like; to render harmless, divest of its formidable character. Const. *of* († rarely *from*).

c **1374** CHAUCER *Boeth.* I. metr. iv. 13 So schalt þou desarmen þe ire of þilke vnmyȝty tyraunt. *c* **1600** SHAKS. *Sonn.* cliv. 8 The general of hot desire Was sleeping by a virgin hand disarm'd. **1649** MILTON *Eikon.* iv. Wks. (1847) 285/2 His design was.. to disarm all, especially of a wise fear and suspicion. *a* **1704** T. BROWN *Upon a Yng. Lady* Wks. 1730 I. 67 A tongue that every heart disarms. **1776** GIBBON *Decl. & F.* I. vii. 136 Conscious security disarms the cruelty of the monarch. **1788** LADY HAWKE *Julia de G.* I. 230 Disarmed from the slightest remains of envy, Julia returned to the company. **1841–44** EMERSON *Ess. Manners* Wks. (Bohn) I. 213 Society loves.. the air of drowsy strength, which disarms criticism. **1871** MACDUFF *Mem. Patmos* vi. 75 What could disarm that amphitheatre and these blazing faggots of their horrors? **1894** J. T. FOWLER *Adamnan* Introd. 70 His hostility was soon disarmed, and his conversion effected.

absol. *a* **1719** ADDISON *Rosamond* I. i, No fear shall alarm, No pity disarm.

†**6.** *transf.* To take off as armour. *Obs. rare.*

c **1613** ROWLANDS *Paire Spy-Knaves* 6 Disarme this heauy burden from my backe.

†**b.** *Magnetism.* To take away the armature. See ARMATURE 6. *Obs.*

1730 SAVERY in *Phil. Trans.* XXXVI. 325, I took off the Armour and bound it to that which was newly touched, and therewith retouched that which I had disarmed.

7. *Manège.* (See quot.) [F. *désarmer un cheval, les lèvres d'un cheval.*]

1727 BAILEY vol. II. s.v. *Disarm*, To disarm the Lips of a Horse, is to keep them subject, and out from above the Bars, when they are so large as to cover the Bars, and prevent the Pressure or *Appui* of the Mouth, by bearing up the Bit, and so hindring the Horse from feeling the Effects of it upon the Bars.

Hence **disˈarming** *ppl. a.*

1839 T. BEALE *Nat. Hist. Sperm Whale* 302 Beckoned us to approach with winning and disarming smiles.

disˈarm, *sb.* [f. prec.] The act of disarming (an opponent): *esp.* in *Fencing.*

1809 ROLAND *Fencing* 9 The crossing of the blade signifies a kind of disarm, performed by a jirk from the wrist. **1827** BARRINGTON *Pers. Sk.* II. 16 A disarm is considered the same as a disable. **1833** *Regul. Instr. Cavalry* I. 149 The 'Second Point'.. should be given with great caution, the wrist being then so liable to the disarm.

disarmament (dɪsˈɑːməmənt). [f. DISARM *v.*, after *armament*; cf. F. *désarmement* (1594 in Hatz.-Darm.), f. *désarmer*, to which the corresponding Eng. type would be *disarmment.*] The action of disarming; *esp.* the reduction of an army or navy to the customary peace footing.

1795 BURKE *Corr.* IV. 327 If the disarmament had been common to all descriptions of disorderly persons, the measure would have been excellent. **1861** *Lond. Rev.* 20 Apr. 434/2 They propose the disarmament of the country. **1862** HELPS *Organiz. Daily Life* 54 What Europe really needed was a congress that should dare to speak boldly to ambitious monarchs respecting the vital subject of disarmament. **1889** B. F. WESTCOTT *Let. in Guardian* 6 Apr., Such a disarmament would secure the lasting and honourable peace which the leaders of Europe.. desire.

disˈarmature. *rare.* [f. DISARM *v.*, after ARMATURE.] The action of disarming; divestiture of armour or means of defence.

18.. SIR W. HAMILTON (O.), On the universities, which have illegally dropt philosophy and its training from their course of discipline, will lie the responsibility of this singular and dangerous disarmature.

disarme: see DISARMY.

disarmed (dɪsˈɑːmd), *ppl. a.* [f. DISARM + -ED[1].]

1. Deprived of arms; unarmed; without arms or weapons; divested of means of attack or defence.

1594 SPENSER *Amoretti* xii, I then disarmed did remaine. **1598** B. JONSON *Ev. Man in Hum.* IV. v, I hold it good polity not to go disarmed. **1628** HOBBES *Thucyd.* (1822) 141 The Plateans.. aimed their arrows and darts at their more disarmed parts. **1678** PHILLIPS (ed. 4) *Disarmed*, (among Hunters) Deers are said to be when the Horns are faln. **1821** JOANNA BAILLIE *Met. Leg., Wallace* xciii, As sleeping and disarmed he lay.

2. *Her.* (See quot.)

1830 ROBSON *Brit. Herald* III. Gloss., *Disarmed*.. is said of an animal or bird of prey, without claws, teeth, or beak. **1882** CUSSANS *Handbk. Her.* 128.

disarmer (dɪsˈɑːmə(r)). [f. DISARM + -ER[1].]

a. One who disarms.

a **1660** HAMMOND *Wks.* II. 62 (T.) So much learning and abilities, as this disarmer is believed to have. **1820** *Examiner* No. 612. 2/1 The disarmers.. of the country which enabled them to disarm it. **1827** BARRINGTON *Pers. Sk.* II. 16 The disarmer may break his adversary's sword.

b. An advocate of disarmament. So ***nuclear disarmer*** (see NUCLEAR *a.*).

1906 *Westm. Gaz.* 30 July 7/1 England is so richly provided with naval equipment that she can easily afford to masquerade as a 'disarmer'. **1960** *Guardian* 21 Sept. 8/5 One can be a pacifist and a unilateral disarmer, prepared to accept the consequences for oneself and one's country.

disarming (dɪsˈɑːmɪŋ), *vbl. sb.* [f. DISARM + -ING[1].] The action of the verb DISARM.

1548 HALL *Chron., Hen. VIII*, 81 b, The two kynges set their countre parties to disarmyng. **1611** COTGR., *Desarmement*, a disarming, a depriuing of Armes. *a* **1660** HAMMOND *Wks.* II. 63 (T.) For the disarming of schism. **1848** W. H. KELLY tr. *L. Blanc's Hist. Ten Y.* II. 37 In the departments de La Sarthe, de La Mayenne.. some disarmings were effected without violence.

attrib. **1753** *Stewart's Trial* 273 The part of the country where the pannel lives, fell under the *disarming Act.* **1894** *Daily News* 29 June 5/2 This mode of protection [paint] was unknown to the Highlanders, when they hid their weapons, after the Disarming Act.

disarmingly (dɪsˈɑːmɪŋlɪ), *adv.* [f. DISARMING *ppl. a.* + -LY[2].] In a disarming manner; so as to disarm opponents (usu. *fig.*).

1901 'L. MALET' *R. Calmady* VI. iv. 525 An expression of disarmingly innocent penitence. **1905** *Daily Chron.* 11 Mar. 7/2 Hascombe smiled disarmingly. **1920** *Blackw. Mag.* Dec. 714/2 A name.. which she.. disarmingly admitted there was small prospect of her ever otherwise being able to change. **1928** *Daily Tel.* 21 Aug. 8/5 He is a business man himself, speaking in terms which are disarmingly straightforward.

†**disˈarmy.** *Obs. rare.* (Also 9 **disarme.**) [a. obs. F. *désarmée* action of disarming, f. *désarmer* to disarm (:—Romanic type *desarmata*: see ARMY).] A disarming.

1548 HALL *Chron., Hen. VIII*, 78 b, The herauldes cried the disarmy [ed. 1809 disarme].

disarrange (dɪsəˈreɪndʒ), *v.* [f. DIS- 6 + ARRANGE; cf. F. *désarranger* (17th c. in Littré).] *trans.* To undo the arrangement of; to put into a state of disorder.

1744 AKENSIDE *Pleas. Imag.* III. 519 (Seager) Quick disgust From things deform'd or disarrang'd. **1764** GRAINGER *Sugar Cane* I. 189 The glebe.. Will journey, forc'd off by the mining rain; And.. disarrange Thy neighbours' vale. **1834** HT. MARTINEAU *Farrers* ii. 35 She.. would not let his chamber be disarranged just at present. **1892** *Speaker* 8 Oct. 427/1 Sudden.. fluctuations in the standard of value undoubtedly disarrange trade.

Hence **disa'rranged** *ppl. a.*, **disa'rranging** *vbl. sb.*; **disa'rranger**, one who disarranges.

1827 CH. WORDSWORTH *Chas. I*, etc. 19 A lamentably miscalculating and dis-arranged understanding. **1862** F. HALL *Hindu Philos. Syst.* 40 The arranging and disarranging of the multitudinous constituents of the world. **1885** *Athenæum* 14 Nov. 645/2 The name of the arranger —or rather disarranger—was not given in the programme.

disarrangement (dɪsə'reɪndʒmənt). [f. prec. + -MENT, after *arrangement.*] The fact or process of disarranging or putting out of order; the condition of being disarranged; disorder.

c **1730** A. BAXTER *Enq. Nat. Soul* (1737) II. 137 (T.) How .. is it possible that the mere disarrangement of the parts of matter should perform this? **1790** BURKE *Army Estimates* Wks. V. 10 The whole of the arrangement, or rather disarrangement of their military. **1837** CARLYLE *Fr. Rev.* III. II. i. (1857) II. 180 They are the Heart and presiding centre of a France fallen wholly into maddest disarrangement. **1885** *Manch. Exam.* 18 Feb. 3/2 The various organic diseases and functional disarrangements.

disarray (dɪsə'reɪ), *sb.* Forms: 4-7 **disaray(e**, 5 **dysaray**, 6 **disarey**, 6- **disarray**. [Probably a. OF. **desarei* (14th c. *desarroy* in Littré, mod.F. *désarroi*), vbl. sb. from *desareer*, *desarroyer*: see next. The earlier OF. synonym was *desrei*, *desrai*, *derai*, whence Eng. *desray*, DERAY, DISRAY, of which *disarray* may be regarded as a modification.]

1. The condition of being out of array or regular order; disorder, confusion; = DERAY *sb.* 1, 1 c.

c **1386** CHAUCER *Pars. T.* ⁋853 (*Elles.*) As the woman hath the maistrie she maketh to muche desray [*MSS. Camb.* disray, *Harl.*, *Petw.*, *Lansd.*, *Selden* disaray(e)]. *c* **1477** CAXTON *Jason* 31 b, They tourned their back and put hem to flyght and disaraye. *c* **1489** —— *Sonnes of Aymon* xv. 354, I wolde not for noo good that rowlande & olivere.. sholde fynde vs in dysaray. **1530** PALSGR. 214/1 Disarey, out of order, *desaroy*. **1580** C'TESS PEMBROKE *Ps.* lxviii. 1 His very face shall cast On all his haters flight and disarray. **1664** PEPYS *Diary* 27 Mar., So much is this city subject to be put into a disarray upon very small occasions. **1715-20** POPE *Iliad* XIV. 19 Dire disarray! the tumult of the fight. **1835** J. P. KENNEDY *Horse Shoe R.* xviii. (1860) 216 Their.. weapons lay around in disarray. **1882** SHORTHOUSE *J. Inglesant* II. 181 The wild confused crowd of leaping and struggling figures, in a strange and ghastly disarray.

transf. **1818** MILMAN *Samor* 32 As clouds.. Gather their blackening disarray to burst Upon some mountain turret.

2. Imperfect or improper attire; disorderly undress. *arch.*

1590 SPENSER *F.Q.* II. iv. 4 A wicked Hag.. In ragged robes and filthy disaray. **1814** SOUTHEY *Roderick* xxv. 215 He who in that disarray Doth.. bestride the noble steed. **1857** HAWTHORNE *Scarlet Lett.* iii, Clad in a strange disarray of civilized and savage costume.

disarray (dɪsə'reɪ), *v.* Also 5-7 **disaray**. [f. DIS- 6 + ARRAY *v.*: perh. immediately after OF. *desareer*, *-eier* (*-oyer*) to put into disorder (in Godef.), f. *des-*, DIS- 4 + *areyer* to ARRAY. Cf. prec. sb. and the synonymous DISRAY.]

1. *trans.* To throw out of array or order, to put into disorder or confusion; to rout, disorder, disorganize. (Chiefly of military array.)

c **1470** HENRY *Wallace* IX. 856 All dysarayit the ost was, and agast. **1513** DOUGLAS *Æneis* XIII. vi. 32 The cite, quhilk was disarayt and schent. **1600** HOLLAND *Livy* II. lxiii. 86 At the first skirmish the enemies were disaraied [*fusi*]. **1641** MILTON *Animadv.* (1851) 223 To rout, and disaray the wise and well-coucht order of Saint Pauls owne words. **1650** EARL MONM. tr. *Senault's Man bec. Guilty* 205 They rob Gardens without disaraying them. **1660** HICKERINGILL *Jamaica* (1661) 68 The small Remnant left in Iamaica.. will be able to disaray the Spaniards in Hispaniola or Cuba. **1713** C'TESS WINCHELSEA *Misc. Poems* 244 You Winds! Whilst not the Earth alone, you disarray. *a* **1848** R. W. HAMILTON *Rew. & Punishm.* v. (1853) 222 What disarrays like death?

†**b.** *intr.* (for *refl.*) To fall out of array or order, to become disordered. *Obs.*

1523 LD. BERNERS *Froiss.* I. ccxxv. 297 If any of our batayls breke, or disaray by any adueuture, drawe thyder and confort them.

2. *trans.* To strip or spoil of personal array, raiment, or attire; to disrobe.

1483 *Cath. Angl.* 100/2 To Disaray [*v.r.* Disray or disgise], *exornare*. **1590** SPENSER *F.Q.* I. viii. 46 That witch they disaraid, And robd of roiall robes. **1611** COTGR., *Deshabiller*, to disarray, vncloth. **1715** ROWE *Jane Gray* v. i, Help to disarray And fit me for the Block. **1814** MRS. J. WEST *Alicia de L.* III. 226 Attendant damsels to prepare the bath, to help to disarray her.

b. *intr.* for *refl.*

1678 BUTLER *Hud.* III. i. 250 I'd hardly time to lay My weapons by, and disarray.

c. *trans.* To despoil, strip *of* any adjunct.

1579 SPENSER *Sheph. Cal.* Feb. 105 A goodly Oake.. With armes full strong.. But of their leaves they were disarayde. **1610** G. FLETCHER *Christ's Vict.* in Farr *S.P. Jas. I* (1848) 34 As when a vapour from a moory slough.. Doth heaven's bright face of his rayes disarray. **1820** SHELLEY *Liberty* xix, My song, its pinions disarrayed of might, Drooped. **1852** M. ARNOLD *Poems, Empedocles on Etna* 11, Ere quite the being of man, ere quite the world Be disarray'd of their divinity.

Hence **disa'rraying** *vbl. sb.*

1611 COTGR., *Desarrengement*, an vnranking, disordering, disarraying.

disarrayed (dɪsə'reɪd), *ppl. a.* [f. DISARRAY *v.* + -ED[1].]

1. Out of array; disordered, in disorder.

1611 SPEED *Hist. Gt. Brit.* VI. xlviii. §16. 170 Following the disarraied flight of the Persians. **1742** YOUNG *Nt. Th.* v. 826 His disarray'd oblation he devours. **1827** T. DOUBLEDAY *Sea-Cave* 11 Some sea-born maid.. with her green tresses disarrayed. **1864** PUSEY *Lect. Daniel* ix. 563 Mists, which hurry along.. like hosts disarrayed.

2. Divested of personal array or attire, stripped.

1611 COTGR., *Descoeffé*.. whose head is disarrayed or vncouered. **1725** POPE *Odyss.* XVII. 98 Then dis-array'd, the shining bath they sought. **1859** TENNYSON *Idylls, Enid* 516 She.. found, Half disarray'd as to her rest, the girl.

†**disa'rrayment.** *Obs. rare.* [f. DISARRAY *v.* + -MENT: after *arrayment.*] The fact of disarraying or deranging; the condition of being disarrayed; disorder, derangement.

1627-77 FELTHAM *Resolves* II. liii. 269 Inward Enemies, our vices, our weaknesses, and our own disarayments.

†**disa'rrest,** *v. Obs.* [ad. OF. *desarrester* to release from arrest (14th c. in Godef.), f. *des-*, DIS- 4 + *arrester* to ARREST.] *trans.* To set free from arrest; to reverse the arrest of.

1528 HACKET *Let. to Wolsey* (MS. Cott. Galba B. ix. 54 b), That sche schowld cawse to dysarest the forsayd Korn. **1643** PRYNNE *Doom Coward.* 9 The King.. wills that he shall be disarrested, and suffered to goe at large.

disarticulate (dɪsɑː'tɪkjʊleɪt), *v.* [f. DIS- 6 + ARTICULATE *v.*]

1. *trans.* To undo the articulation of, to disjoint; to separate joint from joint.

1840 G. V. ELLIS *Anat.* 278 Disarticulate, entirely, the odontoid process. **1854** OWEN *Skel. & Teeth* in *Orr's Circ. Sc., Organ. Nat.* I. 175 The entire segment, here disarticulated.. is called the 'occipital vertebra'. **1892** *Pall Mall G.* 27 Sept. 2/1 From time immemorial the plan has been adopted of filling the bony case with peas and then causing them to swell with water whenever a skull was required to be 'disarticulated'.

2. *intr.* (for *refl.*) To become disjointed; to separate at the joints.

1830 LINDLEY *Nat. Syst. Bot.* 334 In some of these the joints disarticulate, and appear to be capable of reproduction. **1835** —— *Introd. Bot.* (1868) I. 261 The leaflets.. spontaneously disarticulate. **1892** *Natural Science* Mar. 57 Stems.. which ultimately disarticulated and left the surface marked by scars.

Hence **disar'ticulated** *ppl. a.*; also **disar'ticulator**, he who or that which disarticulates.

1861 HULME tr. *Moquin-Tandon* II. VII. xi. 378 The disarticulated stems. *Ibid.* II. VII. xiii. 401 The cucurbitins are disarticulated zoonites. **1877** DAWSON *Orig. World* xiv. 302 Disarticulated remnants of human skeletons.

disarticulation (dɪsɑːˌtɪkju'leɪʃən). [n. of action from prec.: after *articulation.*] The action of disarticulating; separation at the joint; disjointed condition.

1830 R. KNOX *Béclard's Anat.* Introd. 23 Béclard invented or improved several modes of.. disarticulation of the metatarsal bones. **1830** LINDLEY *Nat. Syst. Bot.* 251 In Orchideæ.. a complete disarticulation of the stem and leaves takes place.

†**dis'artuate,** *v. Obs. rare.* [f. DIS- 6 + ARTUATE.] *trans.* To disjoint.

1660 SHARROCK *Vegetables* 145 If any man please to disartuate the whole [Horse-tail] they will finde the frame exquisite enough to deserve a better esteem.

disasinate, disasinize *v.*: see DIS- 6.

disassemble (dɪsə'sɛmb(ə)l), *v.* [f. DIS- 6 + ASSEMBLE *v.*] †**a.** *trans.* To separate, scatter, disperse. *Obs. rare*—[0].

1611 COTGR., *Desassembler*, to disassemble, disioyne, disunite.

b. To take to pieces, to take apart. (The opposite of ASSEMBLE *v.*[1] 2 b.) So **disa'ssembly**, the act or process of disassembling.

1922 *Short Stories* Feb. 41/2 This generating plant was partly disassembled. **1930** *Sci. Amer.* Nov. 389 The entire 50-foot line can be assembled or disassembled in six minutes. **1954** *New Biol.* XVI. 36 The assembly and disassembly of protein molecules in tissue fluids has been shown.. to be continually taking place. **1958** *Times Lit. Suppl.* 11 Apr. 192/1 The reconstruction of disassembled paintings. **1958** *New Scientist* 1 May 31/1 (*diagram*) Disassembly cell. **1967** KARCH & BUBER *Offset Processes* x. 462 Remove the screws from the bars and disassemble.

†**disa'ssent,** *v. Obs.* Also 5 **dis-, dysasent**. [ad. OF. *desassent-ir* (13-14th c. in Godef.), f *des-*, DIS- 4 + *assentir* ASSENT *v.*] *intr.* To refuse assent *to*, withhold assent *from*; to disagree.

c **1400** *Destr. Troy* 9369 All the most of þo mighty.. Dyssassent to the dede, demyt hit for noght. **1533** BELLENDEN *Livy* I. (1822) 82 Servius nouthir assentit nor yit dissentit to thair mariage. **1620** W. SCOT *Apol. Narr.* (1846) 104 He disassented from all the proceedings. *a* **1635** NAUNTON *Fragm. Reg.* (Arb.) 16, I dissent from the common received opinion. **1641** *Protests Lords* I. 6 We whose names are underwritten did dissent. **1643** PRYNNE *Sov. Power Parl.* IV. 18 It is obligatory and legall, though the King himselfe consent not, or disassent thereto. **1692** WAGSTAFFE *Vind. Carol.* vi. 60 If he may dis-assent, it is a sufficient Proof of this Negative Voice.

Hence †**disa'ssenter**, one who disassents; †**disa'ssenting** *vbl. sb.* and *ppl. a.*, dissentient.

1634 *St. Trials, Lord Balmerino* (R.), The names of the disassenters. **1635** PERSON *Varieties* I. xi. 45 In this point also I finde them variable and disassenting. **1643** PRYNNE *Sov. Power Parl.* II. 66 Such a disassenting Voyce.. is inconsistent with the very office, duty of the King.

†**disa'ssent,** *sb. Obs.* [f. prec., after ASSENT *sb.*] Refusal of assent; dissent, disagreement.

1495 *Act 11 Hen. VII*, c. 36. §1 Any disagreement or disassent by the said Duches.. notwithstandyng. **1548** HALL *Chron.*, *Hen. VII* an. 7 (R.) Whether he departed without the French kynges consent or disassent, he.. returned agayn to the Lady Margaret. *a* **1639** SPOTTISWOOD *Hist. Ch. Scot.* IV. (1677) 189 Fearing that her disassent might work some delay. **1643** PRYNNE *Sov. Power Parl.* I. (ed. 2) 34 Notwithstanding his owne personall disassent.

†**disa'ssertor.** *Obs. rare.* [agent-n. from **disassert*, f. DIS- 6.] One who contradicts an assertion or asserts the contrary.

1651 J. GOODWIN *Red. Redeemed* iv. §38. 69 Imputations .. which the Dis-assertors of it have charged upon it.

†**disassi'duity.** *Obs.* [f. DIS- 9 + ASSIDUITY.] Want of assiduity; failure to be assiduous in attentions, etc.; slackness.

1613 WOTTON in *Reliq. Wotton.* (1672) 412 Some argue.. that disassiduity in a Favorite is a degree of Declination. *a* **1639** —— *Parall. Essex & Buckingh.* ibid. (1651) 25 Knowing that upon every little absence or disassiduity, he should be subject to take cold at his back. *a* **1635** NAUNTON *Fragm. Reg.* (Arb.) 46 He came in, and went out, and through disassiduity, drew the Curtain between himself and the light of her grace.

†**disa'ssiege,** *v. Obs. rare*—[1]. [a F. *désassiéger* (15th c. in Godef.) 'to raise a siege, to deliuer from a siege' (Cotgr.), f. *des-*, DIS- 4 + *assiéger*: see ASSIEGE, BESIEGE.] *trans.* To free from the state of siege; to raise the siege of.

1630 M. GODWYN tr. *Bp. Hereford's Ann. Eng.* II. 232 John Lord Russell entring the City.. disassieged it.

disassimilation (dɪsəˌsɪmɪ'leɪʃən). [f. DIS- 9 + ASSIMILATION.] The process which reverses assimilation; in *Physiol.* the transformation of assimilated substances into less complex and waste substances; catabolism.

1880 *Libr. Univ. Knowl.* X. 751 Appropriation of new material, and the disassimilation, or elimination of old. **1883** *Glasg. Weekly Her.* 5 May 8/1 Coffee always causes an increased excretion and an augmented disassimilation. **1883** *Syd. Soc. Lex.*, *Disassimilation*, the downward metabolism of the body, by which its components form lower planes of chemical compounds whilst force of one kind or another is disengaged. **1889** BURDON SANDERSON *Addr. to Brit. Assoc.* in *Nature* 26 Sept. 525/1 The words.. 'anabolism', which.. means winding up, and 'catabolism', running down, are the creation of Dr. Gaskell. Prof. Hering's equivalents for these are ' assimilation', which.. means storage of oxygen and oxidizable material, and 'disassimilation', discharge of these in the altered form of carbon dioxide and water.

So **disa'ssimilate** *v.*, to transform by catabolism.

In mod. Dicts. (1894).

disa'ssimilative, *a.* [f. DIS- 10 + ASSIMILATIVE.] Of or pertaining to disassimilation.

1880 *Libr. Univ. Knowl.* IX. 91 Dr. Flint has demonstrated that cholesterine is a disassimilative product of nervous function.

†**disa'ssist,** *v. Obs. rare.* [f. DIS- 6 + ASSIST.] *trans.* To do the reverse of assisting; to hinder, obstruct.

1669 WOODHEAD *St. Teresa* I. 2 My Brothers also were such, as in nothing dis-assisted me from serving God. *Ibid.* I. xiv. (1671) 85 The other.. Faculties.. assist the Will; although now and then it happen that they disassist it.

disassociate (dɪsə'səʊʃɪeɪt), *v.* [f. DIS- 6 + ASSOCIATE, after F. *désassocier* (16th c. in Littré), f. *des-*, DIS- 4 + *associer* to associate.] *trans.* To free or detach from association; to dissociate, sever. Const. *from* (*with*).

1603 FLORIO *Montaigne* (1613) 630 As if our minde had not other houres enough to doe hir businesse, without disassociating hirselfe from the body. ? **1650** *Don Bellianis* 70 So said the Princesse Aurora, that never would disassociate her knights. **1850** L. HUNT *Autobiog.* vii. (1860) 146, I can never disassociate the feeling from their persons. **1859** C. BARKER *Associative Princ.* i. 5 They were at no time disassociated with useful labour.

Hence **disa'ssociated** *ppl. a.*

1611 in COTGR. **1881** P. BROOKS *Candle of Lord* 183 Disassociated and apparently contradictory ideas.

disassociation (dɪsəˌsəʊsɪ'eɪʃən). [n. of action f. prec. vb.: cf. ASSOCIATION.] **a.** The action of disassociating, or the condition of being disassociated; dissociation.

1873 B. STEWART *Conserv. Energy* iv. §159 At very high temperatures it is possible that most compounds are decomposed, and the temperature at which this takes place, for any compound, has been termed its *temperature of disassociation*. **1890** *Cornh. Mag.* Sept. 252 A sensible, mild youth, of whom you cannot think in disassociation from his spectacles.

b. = DISSOCIATION 3.

1934 H. C. Warren *Dict. Psychol.* 82/1 *Dissociation*,.. redundant syn. *disassociation.* **1936** W. Temple *Church & Teaching* ii. 30 Psychology..is suffering badly from what it has itself taught us to call the disassociation of personality.

† **disa'ssure**, *v. Obs. rare*⁻⁰. [f. dis- 6 + assure]. *trans.* To deprive of assurance or security.

1611 Cotgr., *Disassurer*, to disassure; to put in feare, or bring into doubt, one that was well resolued.

disaster (dɪ'zɑːstə(r), -æ-), *sb.* Also 7 **dys-**. [ad. F. *désastre* (1564 in Hatz.-Darm.) 'a disaster, misfortune, calamitie, misadventure, hard chance'; f. *des-*, dis- 4 + *astre* 'a starre, a Planet; also destinie, fate, fortune, hap' (Cotgr.), ad. L. *astrum*, Gr. ἄστρον star; after It. *disastro* 'disastre, mischance, ill lucke' (Florio). Cf. Pr., Sp., Pg. *desastre*, also Pr. *benastre* good fortune, *malastre* ill fortune, and Eng. *ill-starred*.]

† **1.** An unfavourable aspect of a star or planet; 'an obnoxious planet'. *Obs.*

1602 Shaks. *Ham.* I. i. 118 Stars with trains of fire and dews of blood, Disasters in the sun; and the moist star, Upon whose influence Neptunes empire stands, Was sick almost to dooms-day with eclipse. **1635** Quarles *Embl.*, *Hieroglyph* vii, What dire disaster bred This change, that thus she veils her golden head?

2. a. Anything that befalls of ruinous or distressing nature; a sudden or great misfortune, mishap, or misadventure; a calamity. Usually with *a* and *pl.*, but also without *a*, as 'a record of disaster'.

'*Disaster* is etymologically a mishap due to a baleful stellar aspect' (Whitney *Life Lang.* vi. (1875) 99).

1591 Horsey *Trav.* (Hakluyt Soc.) 253 Let those soulls suffer that ar the occasioners of thy disaster and myne. **1598** Florio, *Disastro*, disastre, mischance, ill lucke. **1601** Shaks. *All's Well* III. vi. 55 It was a disaster of warre that Cæsar him selfe could not haue preuented. **1605** —— *Lear* I. ii. 131 We make guilty of our disasters the Sun, the Moone, and Starres. **1659** B. Harris *Parival's Iron Age* 100 Fate, it seems, would needs involve them in the same disasters. **1770** Goldsm. *Des. Vill.* 200 Well had the boding tremblers learn'd to trace The day's disasters in his morning's face. **1849** Macaulay *Hist. Eng.* I. 84 Faithlessness was the chief cause of his disasters, and is the chief stain on his memory. **1874** Morley *Compromise* (1886) 27 Such a system must inevitably bring disaster.

† **b.** A bodily affliction or disorder. *Obs. rare.*

1684 F. Rogers *Let.* in *Sir H. Slingsby's Diary* (1836) 377, I am very ill of a disaster upon my stomach, yᵗ I cannot ride.

3. *attrib.*, as **disaster area**, an area in which a major disaster has occurred; also *fig*; **disaster movie**, a film of which the plot centres around a catastrophe or major accident, esp. one involving many people; also, ***disaster film***.

1960 *Times* 14 Sept. 8/1 President Eisenhower designated sections of the state [of Florida] a major *disaster area. **1969** M. Drabble *Waterfall* 244, I was merely a disaster area, a landscape given to such upheavals. **1970** *Guardian* 25 Nov. 2/1 Pakistani officials..described the difficulties they had experienced in bringing aid to the disaster area. **1975** *Times* 7 Feb. 7/6 *The Taking of Pelham 1 2 3*..has..a touch of the current '*disaster film' cycle. **1976** *Times* 10 Jan. 7/1 My 12-year-old daughter..has loved every *disaster movie since *The Poseidon Adventure.* **1986** *Christian Science Monitor* 15 July 30, I began to see that what appeared to be an evacuation scene from a disaster movie was actually a quite efficient operation.

† **di'saster**, *a. Obs.* [Either an attrib. use of the sb., or repr. obs. F. *desastré* (Cotgr.) disastrous, f. *desastre* disaster. The simple word is not used as an adj. in any Romanic lang.] = disastrous.

1590 Greene *Never too late* (1600) 23 No disaster fortune could driue her to make shipwrack of her fixed affection. *Ibid.* 28 Saturne conspiring with all balefull signes, calculated the houre of thy birth full of disaster accidents. **1600** *Look about you* xxix. in Hazl. *Dodsley* VII. 481 Let this be to me a disaster day. **1603** Knolles *Hist. Turks* (1638) 167 Whom disaster fortune..hath inforced to wander here and there.

† **di'saster**, *v. Obs.* [f. disaster *sb.* No corresp. vb. is found in the Romanic langs., though French had in 16th c. the ppl. adj. *desastré*: see disaster *a.*] *trans.* To bring disaster or misfortune upon; to strike with calamity; to ruin, afflict, injure seriously, endamage.

(Todd's sense 'To blast by the stroke of an unfavourable star', repeated in later Dicts., seems to be unsupported; his quotation is of a *ppl. a.* in sense 'ill-starred,' 'hapless'.)

1580 [see disastered]. **1606** Shaks. *Ant. & Cl.* II. vii. 16 The holes where eyes should bee, which pittifully disaster the cheeks. **1607** Topsell *Four-f. Beasts* (1658) 158 Neither was there ever any more easie way to disaster these monster-seeming souldiers [elephants in battle] then by casting of stones. **1689** Moyle *Sea Chyrurg.* II. xiii. 61 The Cable running out, a Kink therein happened to disaster a Man's Leg. **1778** M. Cutler in *Life, etc.* (1888) I. 70 The French fleet was so disastered they could by no means afford us any assistance. **1784** *Ibid.* 107 This occasioned the thermometer's being more slightly secured..and..it was so disastered as to lose almost all the mercury. **1812** W. Tennant *Anster F.* III. lvi, Some were cuff'd and much disaster'd found.

Hence † **di'sastered**, stricken with disaster; ill-starred, hapless. *Obs.*

1580 Sidney *Arcadia* II. (1613) 163 Ah, chastest bed of mine..how canst thou now receiue this desastred changeling? **1598** Barret *Theor. Warres* v. i. 170 At his disastred iourney made into Barbary. **1726–46** Thomson *Winter* 279 In his own loose revolving fields, the swain Disastered stands.

† **di'sasterly**, *adv. Obs.* [f. disaster *a.* + -ly².] In a disastrous or ill-starred manner.

1593 Nashe *Christ's T.* (1613) 93 What Gentleman hath been cast away at Sea, or disasterly souldiouriz'd it by Land. **1598** Drayton *Heroic. Ep.* (1748) 131 Nor let the envy of invenom'd tongues..Thy noble breast disasterly possess. **1654** Vilvain *Epit. Ess.* IV. 46 Who died disasterly in New Forest.

disastrous (dɪ'zɑːstrəs, -æ-), *a.* Also 6–7 **des-**, 7 **dysastrous, disasterous.** [a. F. *désastreux, -euse* (16th c. in Hatz.-Darm.), f. *désastre*: cf. It. *disastroso* 'vnfortunate, vnluckie' (Florio 1598). See disaster *sb.* and -ous.]

† **1.** Stricken with or subject to disasters; ill-starred, ill-fated; unfortunate, unlucky. *Obs.*

1586 B. Young tr. *Guazzo's Civ. Conv.* IV. 184 If she aford mee but one sparkle of hope and favour, she doth it to no other ende, but to make mee more desastrous. **1602** Marston *Ant. & Mel.* Induct. Wks. 1856 I. 2 He prov'd alwaies desastrous in love. **1603** *Adv. Don Sebastian* in *Harl. Misc.* (Malh.) II. 368 The unfortunate accidents this disasterous king hath sustained. *c* **1750** Shenstone *Poems, Economy* iii. 43 Ah disastrous wight! In evil hour and rashly dost thou trust The fraudful couch! **1790** Beatson *Nav. & Mil. Mem.* I. 225 The various calamities that befel this disastrous fleet.

2. Foreboding disaster, of evil omen, unpropitious, ill-boding. *arch.*

1603 Holland *Plutarch's Mor.* 1292 Reputing the third of these intercalar daies to be desasterous and dismall. **1648** Gage *West. Ind.* xii. (1655) 47 At whose birth could not but be some dysastrous aspect of the Planets. **1667** Milton *P.L.* I. 597 As when the Sun..from behind the Moon In dim Eclips disastrous twilight sheds On half the Nations. *a* **1849** Mangan *Poems* (1859) 42 By the bell's disastrous tongue.

3. Of the nature of a disaster; fraught or attended with disaster; calamitous.

1603 R. Johnson *Kingd. & Commw.* (1630) 573 A faction no lesse disasterous to the State of Persia, than the warre of Turkie. **1608** D. T. *Ess. Pol. & Mor.* 76 b, The very first allarum of any sinister, and disastrous accident. **1684** *Contempl. State Man* I. ii. (1699) 18 All human greatness..must end, and perhaps in a disasterous and unhappy conclusion. **1769** Robertson *Chas. V*, V. III. 344 Events more disastrous to France. **1794** Sullivan *View Nat.* I. 225 The Samyal wind..so disastrous in its effects. **1874** Green *Short Hist.* v. §1. 217 We have followed the attack on Scotland to its disastrous close. **1875** Lyell *Princ. Geol.* II. III. xlvii. 549 Heavy rains followed by disastrous floods.

Hence **di'sastrousness.** *rare.*

1727 Bailey vol. II, *Disastrousness*, unluckiness, unfortunateness.

di'sastrously, *adv.* [f. prec. + -ly².] In a disastrous manner; calamitously, ruinously.

1603 Drayton *Bar. Wars* v. (R.), Whilst things were thus disast'rously decreed. **1678** Butler *Hud.* III. i. 62 To answer, with his Vessel, all That might disastrously befall. **1794** Sullivan *View Nat.* V. 187 The almost universal darkness, which licentious desolation..disastrously introduced into the world. **1869** Freeman *Norm. Conq.* (1876) III. xii. 180 The great invasion of Normandy, which ended so disastrously for the French.

disattach (dɪsə'tætʃ), *v.* [f. dis- 6 + attach *v.*] *trans.* To undo what is attached; = detach 1.

1851 Cdl. Wiseman *Actions N.T.* Ess. 1853 I. 586 To disattach importance from all that relates to her.

disa'ttachment. [dis- 9.] = detachment 4 b.

1860 T. T. Carter *Imit. our Lord* (1861) 19 Chastening our being into disattachment and heavenly-mindedness.

disattaint (dɪsə'teɪnt), *v.* [dis- 6.] *trans.* To free from attainder: see attaint *v.* 6.

1865 Carlyle *Fredk. Gt.* IX. xx. vii. 149 Earl Marischal ..has been..pardoned, disattainted, permitted to inherit.

† **disa'ttention.** *Obs.* [f. dis- 9 + attention.] Active inattention; neglect.

1624 Bp. Mountagu *Gagg* i. 3 Slownesse of heart: that is ..disattention unto those things. **1693** W. Freke *Sel. Ess.* xxv. 147 Carelessness and Disattention..are the Daughters of Folly. **1757** *Herald* x. ¶9 Disattention to duty.

† **disa'ttire**, *v. Obs.* [f. dis- 6 + attire *v.*] *trans.* To divest of attire; disrobe.

a **1598** Spenser cited by Webster (1864). **1611** Cotgr. *Descoeffer*..to disarray, disattire, vnhood, vncouer, the head. **1677** Holyoke *Dict.*, Disattire, *divestio.*

disattune (dɪsə'tjuːn), *v.* [f. dis- 6 + attune.] *trans.* To put out of tune or harmony.

1853 Lytton *My Novel* XI. xvi. (D.), Thus ever bringing before the mind of the harassed debtor images at war with love and with the poetry of life, he disattuned it, so to speak, for the reception of Nora's letters.

† **disaug'ment**, *v. Obs.* [dis- 6.] *trans.* To reverse the augmentation of; to diminish.

1611 Cotgr., *Desaugmenter*, to disaugment, wane, diminish. **1635** Quarles *Embl.* v. xiii, That everlasting treasure which hope deprives not, fortune disaugments not.

† **disau'thentic**, *a. Obs.* [dis- 10 + authentic.] The reverse of authentic; not authoritative (see authentic 1).

1591 G. Fletcher *Russe Commw.* (Hakl. Soc.) 126 Certeine bookes..of Moses..which they say are al made disauthentique, and put out of use by the comming of Christ. **1619** Purchas *Microcosmus* lxix. 691 They..account disauthentike the foure last Bookes of Moses.

disau'thenticate, *v.* [dis- 6.] *trans.* To prove or pronounce non-authentic.

1895 A. W. Benn in *Academy* 1 June 457/2 Among passages disauthenticated, or at least pronounced doubtful.

† **dis'authorize**, *v. Obs.* [f. dis- 6 + authorize.] *trans.* To strip of authority; to make or treat as of no authority.

1548 Gest *Pr. Masse* 90 Then is yᵉ once sacrifice of Christ utterly to be abandoned and disauthorized. **1563** Man *Musculus' Commonpl.* 153 a, Thei judged it best to disauthorise them [the scriptures of the Old Testament]. **1615** Wadsworth in Bedell *Lett.* (1624) 8 As if their new censure were sufficient to disaucthorize the others auncient sentences. **1689** *Def. Liberty agst. Tyrants* 142 The general Assembly..may..even dis-authorize and depose a King.

disa'vail, *v.* ? *Obs.* [f. dis- 6 + avail *v.*]

† **1.** *intr.* To be the reverse of advantageous; to be prejudicial or harmful. *Obs.*

1430 Lydg. *Chron. Troy* v. xxxvi, They..toke nought that might disauayle Unto that lande but it were vitayle. **1549** Chaloner *Erasm. on Folly* I iij a, The same not seeldome disavaileth to the..pleasure of the lyfe.

2. *trans.* To disadvantage, injure, harm.

1471 Marg. Paston in *P. Lett.* No. 681 III. 24 Lete hym helpe me now, or elles it shall dysawayll hym better than the trebyll the money. *a* **1529** Skelton *Col. Cloute* 1106 Hyndering and dysavaylyng Holy Churche, our Mother. **1530** Palsgr. 517/1, I disavayle one, I hynder his avauntage ..he hath disavayled me more than an hundred pounde. **1754** Richardson *Grandison* (1781) II. iv. 52 'I am an Englishman, gentlemen', said I..judging..that plea would not disavail me.

† **disa'vail**, *sb. Obs.* [f. prec. vb., after avail *sb.*] Disadvantage, harm, loss.

c **1430** Lydg. *Bochas* I. xix. (1558) 33 a Hys wyfe of frowarde doublenes, Which euer wrought to his disauayle. **1603** J. Davies *Microcosmos* Wks. (1876) 11 If subjects' peace and glorie be the King's, And their disgrace and strife his disavaile.

disavaunce, disaventure, obs. forms of disadvance, disadventure.

† **disa'vouch**, *v. Obs.* [f. dis- 6 + avouch *v.* In med.L. *disadvocāre.*] = disavow.

1597 Daniel *Civ. Wars* IV. xxvi, They flatly disavouch To yeld him more obedience. **1637** R. Humphrey tr. *St. Ambrose* Pref., Numa Pompilius ceremonies were disavouched by Quintus Petilius. **1679** Kid in G. Hickes *Spir. Popery* 7 Disowning and dissavouching that which sometime we judged our honour to testifie for and avouch.

disavow (dɪsə'vaʊ), *v.* Also 4 **des-**, 5 **dys-**. [a. F. *désavouer* (13th c. in Hatz.-Darm.), f. *des-*, dis- 4 + *avouer* avow *v.*¹ In med.L. *disavouāre, disadvocāre.*]

1. *trans.* To refuse to avow, own, or acknowledge; to disclaim knowledge of, responsibility for, or approbation of; to disown, repudiate.

1393 Langl. *P. Pl.* C. IV. 322 Boþe kyng and kayser and þe coroned pope May desauowe þat þey dude. *c* **1489** Caxton *Sonnes of Aymon* v. 134 Our fader hath dysavowed vs for the love of hym. **1596** Spenser *F.Q.* VI. v. 37 Weary ..Of warres delight..The name of knighthood he did disavow. **1659** B. Harris *Parival's Iron Age* 285 One of his Masters drew profit from it, and the other disavowed it. **1748** Chesterf. *Lett.* (1792) II. clxxii. 137 Comte Pertingue ..far from disavowing, confirms all that Mr. Harte has said. **1787** T. Jefferson *Writ.* (1859) II. 212 The Emperor disavowed the concessions which had been made by his governors. **1855** Macaulay *Hist. Eng.* III. 327 Melfort never disavowed these papers. **1874** Green *Short Hist.* vi. §6. 328 The plan was simply that the King should disavow the Papal jurisdiction.

† **2.** To refuse to admit or acknowledge as true or valid; to deny. *Obs.*

1611 Cotgr., *Nier*, to denie, disaduow; say nay, gainsay. **1629** Gaule *Pract. The.* 86 One disauowes him begotten of God; another, borne of Mary. **1634** Ford *P. Warbeck* IV. ii, Yet can they never..disavow my blood Plantagenet's. **1660** F. Brooke tr. *Le Blanc's Trav.* 387 Complaining I had sold her a broken stone, which I disavowed.

† **3.** To refuse to accept or entertain; to decline.

1629 Chapman *Juvenal* v. 167 An oil, for whose strength Romans disavow To bathe with Boccharis. **1640** Fuller *Joseph's Coat* iii. (1867) 135 They..disavow to have any further dealing with worldly contentments. **1660** F. Brooke tr. *Le Blanc's Trav.* 364 The Mexicans disavow all peace with their neighbouring enemies..that they may be stored with prisoners of war for sacrifice.

Hence **disa'vowed** *ppl. a.*, **disa'vowing** *vbl. sb.* and *ppl. a.*; also **disa'vowable** *a.*, liable to be disavowed; **disa'vowedly** (-ɪdlɪ) *adv.*, in a disavowed manner; **disa'vower**, one that disavows (Ash 1775).

1611 Cotgr., *Niement*, a denying, disaduowing, or gainsaying. **1651–3** Jer. Taylor *Serm. for Year* I. iv. 43 No publick or imaginative disavowings..can be sufficient. **1698** R. Ferguson *View Eccles.* 7 As that great and learned man Mr. Baxter..disavowedly, and with an openess natural to him, doth express himself. **1889** *Sat. Rev.* 28 Sept. 345/2 The disavowable, but not yet disavowed, agents of Russia.

disavowal (dɪsə'vaʊəl). [f. disavow *v.* after avowal.] The action of disavowing or refusing to acknowledge; repudiation, denial.

1748 Richardson *Clarissa* (J.), An earnest disavowal of fear, often proceeds from fear. **1828** D'Israeli *Chas. I*, I. v. 114 The disavowal of the acts of a minister threw everything back. **1868** E. Edwards *Raleigh* I. ii. 30 An official disavowal followed in due course.

† **disa'vowance.** *Obs. rare.* [f. DISAVOW *v.*, after AVOWANCE and OF. *desavouance* (14th c. in Godef.).] = DISAVOWAL.

a **1716** SOUTH *Serm.* VI. i. (R.) The very corner-stone of the English Reformation was laid in an utter denial and disavowance of this point [the papal supremacy].

† **disa'vower**[1]. *Obs. rare.* [f. DISAVOW *v.* + -ER *suffix*[4]: corresp. to F. *desavouer*, infinitive used subst.] Disavowing, disavowal.

1648 FAIRFAX, etc. *Remonstrance* 33 This..we can take to intend no lesse then a plaine dissavouer of this Treaty.

disa'vower[2]: see after DISAVOW *v.*

† **disa'vowment.** *Obs. rare.* [f. DISAVOW *v.* + -MENT: perh. repr. OF. *desavouement* (14th c. in Godef.)] = DISAVOWAL.

1637 WOTTON *Let. to Regius Professor* in *Reliq. Wotton.* (1672) Fiva, His Holiness..will not press you to any disavowment thereof.

† **disa'vowry.** *Obs.* [f. DISAVOW *v.*, after AVOWRY and OF. *desavouerie, desavowry* (in Godef.).] The action of disavowing; disavowal.

1588 J. H[ARVEY] *Discoursive Probl.* 65 Concerning the generall disauory, and discredit of such speciall matters. *a* **1641** BP. MOUNTAGU *Acts & Mon.* (1642) 498 He disclaymeth it utterly in that disavowry; My Kingdome is not of this world. **1650** B. *Discolliminium* 9 Christ..thought such a Disavowry..a sufficient salvo for his act.

disazo- (dɪs'æzəʊ). *Chem.* [f. Gr. δίς twice + AZO-.] A combining form used in organic chemistry to denote the presence in the molecule of a compound of two azo groups. Also used *attrib.* as *disazo.*

1886 E. F. SMITH tr. *von Richter's Chem. Carbon Compounds* 465 Such compounds can also be obtained by a second introduction of two molecules of a diazo-compound into phenols.., and are called disazo-derivatives. **1891** ROSCOE & SCHORLEMMER *Treat. Chem.* (ed. 2) III. III. 353 Disazobenzene..is obtained from the corresponding amidodisazobenzene..by diazotizing and boiling with alcohol. **1913** BLOXAM & LEWIS *Chem.* (ed. 10) 719 Disazo-dyestuffs..contain the ·N:N· group twice, and are of three kinds. **1930** E. FYLEMAN tr. *Curtis's Artificial Org. Pigments* i. 6 In the patent literature a number of disazo-dyestuffs are also mentioned, but none of these have attained any importance. **1966** MILLAR & SPRINGALL *Sidgwick's Org. Chem. Nitrogen* (ed. 3) xvii. 588 The azo dyes form the largest class of organic dyes... Monoazo, disazo, trisazo, and polyazo dyes are distinguished.

disbalance (dɪs'bæləns), *v.* [f. DIS- 6 + BALANCE *v.*] *trans.* To disturb the balance or equilibrium of, to put out of balance. Hence **dis'balanced, dis'balancing** *ppl. adjs.*, **dis'balancement**, disturbance of equilibrium.

1853 LYNCH *Self-Improv.* v. 111 Some are shy..there is a decomposing, disbalancing force in them. **1866** ALGER *Solit. Nat. & Man* IV. 252 To..enlarge existing disbalancements, and intensify the discords already experienced. **1885** *Sat. Rev.* 7 Feb. 170/2 The disbalanced mind of this particular woman.

† **dis'balass,** *v. Obs.* [f. DIS- 6 + *balass*, 16th c. form of BALLAST *v.*] *trans.* To free from ballast or burden; to disburden.

1576 NEWTON *Lemnie's Complex.* (1633) 170 Man.. having disburdened and disbalassed himselfe of his provocative superfluous Sperme to fetch his breath the better. **1592** G. HARVEY *New Letter* 14 But now you must lend me patience untill I have disbalased my mind.

disband (dɪs'bænd), *v.* [ad. 16th c. F. *desbander*, mod.F. *débander*; in military sense after It. *sbandare* (cf. Sp., Pg. *disbandar*), f. It. *banda*, F. *bande*, BAND *sb.*[3].

In the sense 'to unbind, loosen, let loose, unbend a bow', etc. *desbander* (also *desbender*) goes back to 12th c. in OF.: cf. DISBEND.]

I. *trans.* **1.** To break up (a band or company); to dissolve and dismiss from service (a military or other force).

1591 GARRARD *Art Warre* 156 And afterwards disband them in such a place. **1649** BP. GUTHRIE *Mem.* (1702) 45 The Marquiss of Huntley..disbanded his Forces. **1701** DE FOE *True-born Eng.* I. 148 No Parliament his Army cou'd disband. **1771** *Junius Lett.* lxii. 322 You talk of disbanding the army with wonderful ease and indifference. **1868** *Pall Mall G.* 23 July 5 The 1st East York Artillery Volunteers.. has been disbanded on account of insubordinate conduct. **1878** BOSW. SMITH *Carthage* 72 When Agathocles died, his mercenary troops were disbanded.

† **b.** To dismiss, discharge, or expel from a band or company. *Obs.*

1626 J. YATES *Ibis ad Caesarem* ii. 6 You haue fathered vpon mee that bastard, which your selfe disbands. **1666** LD. ORRERY *State Letters* (1743) II. 54 To take notice of my securing and disbanding Langley. **1667** FLAVEL *Saint Indeed* (1754) 124 Thou art disbanded by death, and called off the field. **1699** DAMPIER *Voy.* II. I. 71 After 30 years service a Soldier may petition to be disbanded.

c. *refl.* (= 4.)

1603 KNOLLES *Hist. Turks* (J.), They disbanded themselves, and returned every man to his own dwelling. **1614** SYLVESTER *Bethulia's Rescue* v. 20 Each, as him listeth, dares him now dis-band. **1651** tr. *Hist. Don Fenise* 275 Leon disbanded himselfe upon the instant. **1659** B. HARRIS *Parival's Iron Age* 77 *marg.*, His Army disbands it self. **1855** MACAULAY *Hist. Eng.* III. 252 They paid..so much respect to William's authority as to disband themselves when his proclamation was published.

† **2.** To let loose, turn off or out, dismiss from union or association, send away. *Obs.*

1604 EARL STIRLING *Aurora* iv. (R.), What savage bull disbanded from his stall, Of wrath a signe more inhumane could make? **1625** BP. MOUNTAGU *App. Cæsar* II. ii. 114 M. Mountagu..hath disbanded them from their shelter. **1643** MILTON *Divorce* vii. (1851) 37 And therfore by all the united force of the Decalogue she [the wife] ought to be disbanded, unlesse we must set marriage above God and charity. **1715** tr. *Pancirollus' Rerum Mem.* I. II. x. 90 They disband all Trouble and Anxiety from the pensive Mind. **1790** J. B. MORDON *West India Islands* 108 Her husband..took the.. little ones into his own protection, and disbanded their vile mother.

† **3.** To break up the constitution of, dissolve, disintegrate. *Obs.*

1695 WOODWARD *Nat. Hist. Earth* III. ii. (1723) 176 That a Quantity of Water sufficient to make such a Deluge was created..and, when the Business was done, all disbanded again and annihilated. **1793** W. ROBERTS *Looker-on* lxvi. (1794) III. 31 The very elements of civilization have been destroyed in a moment, and society itself disbanded.

II. *intr.* (for *refl.*)

4. To break up as a body of soldiers, to cease to be a band or company; to break rank, fall into disorder, disperse; to leave military service.

1598 BARRET *Theor. Warres* II. i. 28 Shewing them..how to disband, and how to fal into troupes. *a* **1608** SIR F. VERE *Comm.* 8, I commanded our men not to disband, but pursue them. **1611** SPEED *Hist. Gt. Brit.* VI. xiv. §12. 92 The rest disbanded, turned their backes, and fled toward the desert. **1724** DE FOE *Mem. Cavalier* (1840) 200 They began to disband, and run every way. **1835** ALISON *Hist. Europe* (1849–50) III. xiii. §30. 26 The troops..openly threatened to disband. **1855** MACAULAY *Hist. Eng.* III. 268 Feversham had ordered all the royal army to disband.

† **5.** To break up into its constituent parts, dissolve; to separate, retire from association. *Obs.*

1633 G. HERBERT *Temple, Assurance* vi, When both rocks and all things shall disband. **1649** JER. TAYLOR *Gt. Exemp.* II. viii. 81 He makes a confident resolution..though the purpose disbands upon the next temptation. **1697** COLLIER *Ess. Mor. Subj.* I. (1709) 117 They [Men of Honour] should throw up their Fortune; and Disband from Society.

Hence **dis'banded** *ppl. a.*, turned loose out of their ranks; disordered; scattered or dispersed; dismissed; **dis'banding** *vbl. sb.* and *ppl. a.*

1611 COTGR., *Desbandade*, a disbanding; a cassing of whole troups, or companies of souldiours. —— *Desbandé*, disbanded. **1625** MARKHAM *Souldier's Accid.* 15 The Sergeants are..to leade loose and disbanded fyles of Shot in Skirmish. **1641** *Nicholas Papers* (Camden) 18 Letters.. touchinge the disbandinge of the Scottishe Armie. **1679–88** *Secr. Serv. Money Chas. II & Jas. II* (Camden) 36 To.. 2,159[li] 13[s] 9[d]..paid..for the disbanding tax for the county of Leicest[r]. **1689** LUTTRELL *Brief Rel.* (1857) I. 547 The house of commons had the late disbanded judges before them. **1712** ARBUTHNOT *John Bull* III. iii, A poor disbanded officer. *a* **1859** MACAULAY *Hist. Eng.* xxiv. V. 170 He admitted it to be necessary for him to give his assent to the disbanding bill. **1874** GREEN *Short Hist.* viii. §6. 524 The disbanded soldiers of the army..spread over the country.

disbandment (dɪs'bændmənt). [f. prec. + -MENT: cf. F. *débandement* (1701 in Hatz.-Darm.)] The action or fact of disbanding or dispersing; dismissal from corporate existence.

1720 *Lond. Gaz.* No. 5875/2 Full Pay allowed..for doing Duty after Disbandment. **1768–74** TUCKER *Lt. Nat.* (1852) II. 182 The very recent disbandment of that body-guard of popery the Jesuits. **1837** CARLYLE *Fr. Rev.* II. II. iii. (1848) 97 The august Assembly..dare nowise resolve, with Mirabeau, on an instantaneous disbandment and extinction. **1864** *Daily Tel.* 3 Sept., The disbandment of the Basingstoke Rifles.

† **dis'bandon,** *v. Obs. rare.* [By-form of DISBAND *v.* after BANDON.] = DISBAND.

1640–1 *Kirkcudbr. War-Comm. Min. Bk.* (1855) 48 Thair sogers are disbandoning for want of manteanment. **1641** EARL MONMOUTH tr. *Biondi's Civill Warres* I. 74 The King writ unto him to disbandon his forces.

† **dis'bank,** *v. Obs. rare.* [f. DIS- 7 c + BANK *sb.*[1]] *intr.* (for *refl.*) To pass over its banks or borders; to overflow, to debord.

1660 F. BROOKE tr. *Le Blanc's Trav.* 218 The River Zuama, which disbanks as Nile do's.

† **dis'bar,** *v.*[1] *Obs.* [f. DIS- 1 + BAR *v.*: cf. OF. *desbarrer*, mod.F. *débarrer* to unbar: see DEBAR.] *trans.* To exclude, shut out, prevent, stop; = DEBAR *v.*

1565 GOLDING *Ovid's Met.* x. (1593) 255 Then Neptunes impe her swiftnesse to disbarre, Trolld downe a tone-side of the way one apple of the three. **1571** —— *Calvin on Ps.* To Rdr. 10 Too the intent all vaunting myght bee disbarred the further of. **1598** BARRET *Theor Warres* IV. iv. 114 To disbarre all odds and inconueniences.

disbar (dɪs'bɑː(r)), *v.*[2] [f. DIS- 7 + BAR *sb.*[1]]

1. *trans.* To expel from the bar; to deprive of the status and privileges of a barrister.

1633 R. VERNEY in *Verney Papers* (1853) 157 He is to be degraded in the universitie, disbarred at the innes of court. **1828** *Edin. Rev.* XLVIII. 495 In his Utopia such practisers ..would be disbarred. **1848** WHARTON *Law Lex.*, *Disbarring*, expelling a barrister from the bar, a power vested in the benchers of the four inns of court, subject to an appeal to fifteen Judges. **1871** *Daily News* 15 Apr. 2 In the event of a barrister being disbarred..the Judges may revise and reverse the decrees of the benchers.

† **2.** To deprive of bars or that which bars. *Obs.*

1636 N. WALLINGTON in *Ann. Dubrensia* (1877) 33 When all forts are disbarr'd Of Battlements, of Gunnes, and Bulwarkes marr'd.

dis'barbarize, *v. rare.* [f. DIS- 6 + BARBARIZE.] **a.** *trans.* To free from barbarism; = DEBARBARIZE. **b.** *intr.* (for *refl.*) To cease to be barbarous; to lay aside barbarism.

1803 W. TAYLOR in *Ann. Rev.* I. 362 A new proof that benevolence alone disbarbarizes the savage. **1805** *Ibid.* III. 322 The slave-coast began from that period to disbarbarize.

† **disbark** (dɪs'bɑːk), *v.*[1] *Obs.* Also 6–7 **-barke**, 7–8 **-barque.** [ad. F. *desbarquer* (1564 in Hatz.-Darm.), mod.F. *débarquer*, f. *des-*, DIS- 4 + *barque* BARK *sb.*[2]: cf. It. *sbarcare.*] = DEBARK *v.*[1], DISEMBARK. **a.** *trans.*

1552 *Act 5–6 Edw. VI*, c. 14 §12 If he..there do disbark, unlade and sell the same. **1632** LITHGOW *Trav.* v. 187 That in the night, they should have entred the Haven, disbarke their men, and scale the walles. **1709** *Royal Proclam.* 20 Oct. in *Lond. Gaz.* No. 4605/1 [To] be..carried..to the Port.. and there to disbarque and sell the same. **1725** POPE *Odyss.* XI. 22 We..Disbark the sheep, an offering to the gods.

b. *intr.* (for *refl.*)

1585 T. WASHINGTON tr. *Nicholay's Voy.* II. vii. 37b, From Constantinople into Italy, where I disbarked to go to Rome. **1692** HACKE *Collect. Orig. Voy.* (1699) IV. 16 Being now got to Leghorn..I there disbarqued. **1842** MANNING *Unity of Church* I. iv. 107 We read that he 'disbarking from the ship with great joy, hastened to see St. Polycarp'.

Hence **dis'barking** *vbl. sb.*

1598 FLORIO, *Sbarcamento*, an vnshipping, a disbarking, a landing. **1625** J. GLANVILL *Voy. to Cadiz* 33 [To] finde a landing place fitted for our disbarkeing.

dis'bark, *v.*[2] Also 6–7 **-barke**, 7 **-barque.** [f. DIS- 7 a + BARK *sb.*[1]: cf. DEBARK *v.*[2]] *trans.* To divest of the bark, strip the bark off (a tree), decorticate; = DEBARK *v.*[2]

1578 FLORIO *1st Fruites* 86 The forreyne knyfe doothe disbarke it. **1657** AUSTEN *Fruit Trees* I. 102 If we disbarke a bough or branch where sap is up. **1797–1803** FOSTER in *Life & Corr.* (1846) I. 176 Oaks cut down, disbarked and embrowned by time. **1812** *Sporting Mag.* XXXIX. 192 Disbarking those whose tops they [rabbits] cannot reach.

b. To strip off (bark).

1659 *Gate Lang. Unl.* x. §109 *marg.*, The hard rinde (outward bark which may be disbarked) is without.

Hence **dis'barked** *ppl. a.*, divested of bark; **dis'barking** *vbl. sb.*, decortication.

1601 HOLLAND *Pliny* I. 541 Neither doth the tree Adrachne find any hurt or offence by disbarking. **1657** AUSTEN *Fruit Trees* I. 137 This bough may be cut off below the disbarked place. **1725** BRADLEY *Fam. Dict.* s.v. *Tree*, The pricking and disbarking of the Roots.

disbarment (dɪs'bɑːmənt). [f. DISBAR *v.*[2] + -MENT.] The action of disbarring a barrister.

1862 *Sat. Rev.* XIII. 639/2 Appealing..against the Benchers' sentence of disbarment. **1874** *Daily News* 5 Dec., As he means to appeal against their order of disbenchment, he should include in that appeal their order for disbarment.

† **dis'base,** *v. Obs. rare.* [f. DIS- 5 + BASE *v.*[1]: cf. ABASE, DEBASE.] *trans.* = DEBASE.

a **1592** GREENE *Alphonsus* Dram. Wks. II. 56 First I will die in the thickest of the foe Before I will disbase mine honour so. **1601** B. JONSON *Poetaster* II. i, Before I disbased [*v.r.* disbast] myself, from my hood and my farthingal to these bum-rowls and your whale-bone bodice.

dis'beautify, *v. rare.* [DIS- 6.] *trans.* To undo the beautifying of, deprive of beauty.

1577 STANYHURST *Descr. Irel.* in *Holinshed* VI. 5 The women have an harsh and brode kind of pronuntiation.. which dooth disbeautifie their English above measure.

† **disbe'come,** *v. Obs.* [f. DIS- 6 + BECOME *v.* III.] *trans.* To misbecome; to be unbefitting for or unworthy of. Hence **disbe'coming** *ppl. a.*, unbecoming, unbefitting.

1632 MASSINGER & FIELD *Fatal Dowry* v. ii, [Lest] your compassion..Move you to anything that may disbecome The place on which you sit. *a* **1639** W. WHATELY *Prototypes* II. xxix. (1640) 163 No calling..can so much disbecome a man, or reproach and abase him..then this of having no calling. *Ibid.* II. xxxiv. (1640) 174 This forgetfulnesse..is a most disbecomming vice.

disbelief (dɪsbɪ'liːf). [f. DIS- 9 + BELIEF.] The action or an act of disbelieving; mental rejection of a statement or assertion; positive unbelief.

1672 WILKINS *Nat. Relig.* I. iii. (R.), Those who will pretend such kind of grounds for their disbelief of any thing. *a* **1694** TILLOTSON (J.), Our belief or disbelief of a thing does not alter the nature of the thing. **1696** WHISTON *Th. Earth* III. (1722) 277, I have, I think, just reasons for my Disbelief. **1791** MRS. RADCLIFFE *Rom. Forest* vii, Your good sense, Adeline, I think, will teach you the merit of disbelief. **1865** LECKY *Rationalism* I. i. 12 A disbelief in ghosts and witches was one of the most prominent characteristics of scepticism in the seventeenth century. **1874** CARPENTER *Ment. Phys.* II. xx. (1879) 699 [They] will drift away into either vague unbelief or absolute disbelief.

disbelieve (dɪsbɪ'liːv), *v.* [f. DIS- 6 + BELIEVE *v.*]

1. *trans.* Not to believe or credit; to refuse credence to: **a.** a statement or (alleged) fact: To reject the truth or reality of. (With simple obj. or obj. clause.)

1644 [see DISBELIEVING below]. **1678** CUDWORTH *Intell. Syst.* 18 (R.) There have been doubtless in all ages such as have disbelieved the existence of any thing but what was sensible. **1712** *Spect.* No. 527 ¶2 People will be as slow and unwilling in disbelieving scandal, as they are quick and forward in believing it. **1795** SOUTHEY *Joan of Arc* I. 77 That misgiving which precedes belief In what was disbelieved and scoff'd at late For folly. **1864** J. H. NEWMAN *Apologia* 162 Did Henry VIII..disbelieve Purgatory? **1874** CARPENTER *Ment. Phys.* I. ix. §2 (1879) 395 It does not rest with any man to determine what he shall believe or what he shall disbelieve. **1878** BROWNING *La Saisiaz* 68 He disbelieves In the heart of him that edict which for truth his head receives.

b. a person in making a statement.

1699 BENTLEY *Phal.* 273 Plutarch disbelieved Phanias. **1826** HALLAM in *Edin. Rev.* XLIV. 2 There would be no historical certainty remaining, if it were possible to disbelieve such a contemporary witness as Sir Thomas More.

2. *absol.* or *intr.*

1755 YOUNG *Centaur* i. Wks. 1757 IV. 106 Eve doubted, and then eat..most of Eve's daughters first taste, and then disbelieve. **1795** SOUTHEY *Joan of Arc* III. 188, I feel it is not possible to hear and disbelieve. **1818–60** WHATELY *Commonpl. Bk.* (1864) 48 It is very evident that the opposite to credulity is scepticism, and that to disbelieve is to believe.

3. *intr.* with *in*: Not to believe in; to have no faith in: cf. BELIEVE 1, 3.

1834 *W. Ind. Sketch-bk.* I. 172 He disbelieves in the glowing changes of colour in the dying dolphin. **1856** MRS. BROWNING *Aur. Leigh* v. 739, I disbelieve in Christian pagans, much As you in women-fishes. **1869** FREEMAN *Norm. Conq.* (1876) III. xii. 222, I do not altogether disbelieve in the story.

Hence **disbe'lieving** *vbl. sb.* and *ppl. a.*; **disbe'lievingly** *adv.*, in a disbelieving manner; with disbelief.

1644 HAMMOND *Pract. Catech.* (J.), The disbelieving of an eternal truth of God's. **1893** *Chicago Advance* 22 June, Hester shook her head disbelievingly, but Daisy rattled on.

disbe'liever. [f. prec. + -ER[1].] One who disbelieves or refuses belief; an unbeliever.

1648 W. MOUNTAGUE *Devout Ess.* I. viii. §2 (R.) The incredulous and disbelievers of the facility of this medium. *a* **1748** WATTS (J.), An humble soul is frighted into sentiments, because a man of great name pronounces heresy upon the contrary sentiments, and casts the disbeliever out of the church. **1799** SOUTHEY *Lett.* (1856) I. 64, I am not a disbeliever in these things, but that story is not among the credible ones. **1818** WHEWELL in *Todhunter's Acct.* (1876) II. 26 He attacks *dis*believers, but has very little to say to mere *un*believers.

disbench (dɪs'bɛntʃ), *v.* [f. DIS- 7 c + BENCH *sb.*]

† **1.** *trans.* To remove or displace from a bench or seat; to unseat. *Obs.*

1607 SHAKS. *Cor.* II. ii. 75 Sir, I hope my words dis-bench'd you not?

2. to deprive of the status of a bencher; to strike off the name of (a person) from the roll of the senior members of the Inns of Court.

1874 *Observer* 2 Aug., After a long deliberation they decided to disbench Dr. Kenealy..It was further intimated that if the publication of the *Englishman* was continued..as heretofore, the Benchers might have to consider the necessity of disbarring him.

Hence **dis'benchment**, the fact or process of disbenching (sense 2).

1874 [see DISBARMENT].

† **dis'bend,** *v. Obs.* [f. DIS- 6 + BEND *v.*: cf. OF. *desbender*, var. of *desbander* in same sense.] *trans.* To unbend (*e.g.* a bow), relax, let loose.

1607 EARL STIRLING *Jul. Cæsar* III. ii. Chor., As libertie a courage doth impart, So bondage doth disbend, els breake the heart. **1632** LITHGOW *Trav.* x. 488, I Organize the Truth, you Allegate the Sense, Disbending cominous defects, in your absurd pretence.

disbenefit (stress variable). [DIS- 9.] Loss or absence of benefit; a disadvantage or drawback, esp. one which counterbalances a benefit.

1968 *Saturday Rev.* (U.S.) 2 Mar. 51/3 The argument [about supersonic transport]..should be about the benefits to the thousands and the disbenefits to the millions. **1971** *Nature* 30 Apr. 541/1 There is even..a sophisticated attempt to measure in pounds sterling what is called the 'disbenefit' to people living near the alternative sites for the third airport. **1975** *Physics Bull.* Jan. 20/3 Science and engineering have brought disbenefits to our societies and raised very difficult problems. **1982** *Times* 29 Oct. 13/3 If a third child was wantonly produced the family suffered by what are now being called disbenefits: the advantages going to the virtuous were reversed. **1984** *Oxf. Univ. Gaz.* Suppl. 16 Feb. 504/2 They are frequently given the disbenefit of the doubt and assumed to have II(2)s, on the ground that if they had II(1)s they would have said so.

Also (*rare*) as *v. trans.*, to cause disbenefit to, to affect unfavourably.

1978 *Jrnl. R. Soc. Arts* CXXVI. 430/1 To the extent that the bus services concerned become slower or more irregular as a result, the larger number of people on the buses will be disbenefited.

† **dis'bind,** *v. Obs. rare.* [DIS- 6.] *trans.* To unbind, to loose.

a **1638** MEDE *Disc. Matt.* vi. 9 (1672) I. 12 How dare we dis-bind or loose our selves from the tye of that way of agnizing and honouring God?

dis'bishop, *v. nonce-wd.* [f. DIS- 7 b.] *trans.* To deprive of episcopal office or dignity.

1585 ABP. SANDYS *Serm.* (1841) 43 He is easily dealt withal if he be disbishopped.

† **dis'blame,** *v. Obs.* [a. OF. *desblasmer*, *-blâmer*, f. *des-* (DIS- 4) + *blasmer* to BLAME.] *trans.* To free from blame, acquit, exculpate. Hence **dis'blaming** *vbl. sb.*, exculpation.

c **1374** CHAUCER *Troylus* II. Prol. 17, I..pray yow mekely, Disblameth me yf ony word be lame, For as myn auctor seyde so sey I. **1631** *Celestina* VI. 75 Thou hadst come to disblame and excuse thy doings. **1638** BAKER tr. *Balzac's Lett.* III. (1654) 79 But to disblame both of us, I beseech you hereafter to have more care of my modesty. **1656** FINETT *For. Ambass.* 240 (T.) His humble request but of one quarter of an hour's audience for his disblaming.

dis'block, *v. rare.* [f. DIS- 7 c + BLOCK *sb.* 4 c, d.] *trans.* To remove (something) from the block (or head) on which it is placed.

1665 J. WILSON *Projectors* I. Dram. Wks. (1874) 224 Do you not observe, sir, how hard he wrings his brows, to the manifest hazard of disblocking his periwig?

dis'bloom, *v.* [f. DIS- 7 a + BLOOM *sb.*] *trans.* To deprive of bloom. Hence **dis'bloomed** *ppl. a.*

1884 STEVENSON *Old Mortality* in *Longm. Mag.* IV. 76 A faint flavour of the gardener hung about them [the grave-diggers], but sophisticated and disbloomed.

† **dis'board,** *v. Obs. rare.* Also 7 disbord. [a. OF. *desborder* (mod. F. *déborder*) (in various senses), f. *des-* (DIS- 1) + *bord*, BOARD.]

1. *intr.* = DISEMBARK.

1615 CHAPMAN *Odyss.* XIV. 486 They streightly bound me, and did all disbord To shore to supper, in contentious rout.

2. To pass outside or over the border or edge. Cf. DEBORD *v.* 2.

1725 BRADLEY *Fam. Dict.* s.v. *Shoeing*, If the Foot be very narrow let the Shoe disboard without the Hoof.

disbody (dɪs'bɒdɪ), *v.* [f. DIS- 7 + BODY *sb.*] *trans.* = DISEMBODY. Hence **dis'bodied** *ppl. a.*, disembodied.

1646 J. HALL *Poems* 38 Come, Julia, come! let's once disbody what Strait matter ties to this and not to that. **1662** GLANVILL *Lux Orient.* 143 (T.) They conceive that the disbodied souls shall return..and be joined againe to bodies of purified and duly prepared air. **1734** WATTS *Reliq. Juv.* (1789) 9 Ten thousand tongues Of hymning seraphs and disbodied saints. **1870** LOWELL *Cathedral* Poet. Wks. (1879) 448 We cannot make each meal a sacrament, Nor with our tailors be disbodied souls.

† **dis'bogue,** *v. Obs. rare.* [f. DIS- 6 + stem of EM-BOGUE, perh. after Sp. *desbocar* = *desembocar* to disembogue, f. *des-* = DIS- 1 + *boca* mouth: the corresp. Fr. is *déboucher*: see DEBOUCH.] *intr.* = DISEMBOGUE.

1600 HAKLUYT *Voy.* (1810) III. 302 The current of the Bay of Mexico, disbogging betweene the Cape of Florida and Havana. **1628** HOBBES *Thucyd.* (1822) 25 Near unto it disbogueth into the sea the lake Acherusia.

disbo'scation. [ad. med.L. *disboscātiōn-em* (Du Cange), f. DIS- 4 + med.L. *boscus*, *boscum* wood.] The clearing away of woods; the conversion of wooded land into arable or pasture.

1726 *Dict. Rust.* (ed. 3), *Disbo[s]cation*, a turning of Wood-ground into Arable or Pasture. Hence **1727** in BRADLEY *Fam. Dict.*; **1764** in BAILEY (folio, ed. Scott); **1775** in ASH; and in mod. Dicts.

disbosom (dɪs'bʊzəm), *v.* [DIS- 7 c.] *trans.* To disburden one's bosom of; to unbosom; to confess. Hence **dis'bosoming** *vbl. sb.*

1844 BROWNING *Colombe's Birthday* I. Poems 1887 II. 185 This prompt disbosoming of love. **1868** —— *Ring & Bk.* III. 614 Home went Violante and disbosomed all.

† **dis'bound,** *v.*[1] *Obs. rare.* [f. DIS- 1 + BOUND *v.*[1]] *trans.* To separate by boundaries.

1621 AINSWORTH *Annot. Pentat.* Lev. xxi. 24 Separated, in Greeke disparted (or disbounded) you from all the nations.

dis'bound, *v.*[2] [f. DIS- 7 c + BOUND *sb.*[1]] *intr.* To extend beyond its bounds. (Cf. DISBANK, DISBOARD 2.)

1843 E. JONES *Poems, Sens. & Event* 39 The company multiplies, the space disbounds.

disbourgeon, obs. form of DISBURGEON.

disbowel (dɪs'baʊɪl), *v.* In 5 dysbowalyn. [f. DIS- 7 a + BOWEL *sb.*] *trans.* To take out the bowels of, eviscerate; = DISEMBOWEL. *lit.* and *fig.*

c **1440** *Promp. Parv.* 122 Dysbowalyn, *eviscero, exentero.* **1591** SPENSER *Ruins of Rome* 383 A great Oke..halfe disbowel'd lies aboue the ground. **1708** WILSON, etc. tr. *Petronius Arbiter* 75 The Cook that had forgotten to disbowel the Hog. **1711** LUTTRELL *Brief Rel.* (1857) VI. 704 His body has been disbowelled, and put into pickle.

b. To take out (bowels or viscera).

1591 R. W. *Tancred & Gismunda* v. i. in Hazl. *Dodsley* VII. 83 Thus was Earl Palurin Strangled unto the death, yea, after death His heart and blood disbowell'd from his breast.

Hence **dis'bowelled** *ppl. a.*, **dis'bowelling** *vbl. sb.*

c **1440** *Promp. Parv.* 122 Dysbowalynge, *evisceracio.* **1680** *Lond. Gaz.* No. 1508/4 A most Curious and Excellent way of Preserving Dead Bodies, from Putrefaction..without Disbowelling, seer-cloathing, mangling or Cutting any part thereof. *a* **1719** ADDISON tr. *Horace* Wks. (1758) 146 Nor the disbowell'd earth explore In search of the forbidden ore. **1871** ROSSETTI *Poems, Burden of Nineveh* ii, 'Twas bull, 'twas mitred Minotaur, A dead disbowelled mystery.

disbrain (dɪs'breɪn), *v.* [f. DIS- 7 a + BRAIN *sb.*] *trans.* To deprive of the brain; to dash out the brains of; to remove the brain from. Hence **disbrained** *ppl. a.*

1631 *Celestina* XX. 196 What cruelty were it in me, he dying disbrained, that I should live pained all the daies of my life? **1884** *Nature* XXX. 260 If the cerebrum were removed..disbrained and decapitated animals manifested much stronger reflex movements.

disbranch (dɪs'brɑːnʃ, -æ-), *v.* [f. DIS- 7 a + BRANCH *sb.*: cf. OF. *desbrancher*, *-chir* (in Godef.), f. *des-* (DIS- 4) + *brancher*, f. *branche* BRANCH *sb.*]

1. *trans.* To cut or break off the branches of; to deprive or strip of branches.

1575 *Art of Planting* 15 If the trees be great..ye must disbranch them afore ye set them agayne. **1600** SURFLET *Countrie Farme* III. xlvi. 517 It is best to disbranch and prune trees when the sap beginneth to rise vp into them. **1719** LONDON & WISE *Compl. Gard.* IX. i. 279 Peas that are disbranched, bear a more plentiful Crop than others. **1889** G. G. A. MURRAY *Gobi or Shamo* xiv. 228 The fury of the explosion had uprooted and disbranched the..trees.

2. To cut or break off, as a branch; to sever.

1605 SHAKS. *Lear* IV. ii. 34 She that herself will sliver and disbranch From her material sap, perforce must wither And come to deadly use. **1611** SPEED *Hist. Gt. Brit.* IX. viii. §28 (R.) That duke-dome..disbranched from France since the year eight hundred eighty-fiue, was againe rent away. **1796** LAMB *Let.* Wks. (1840) 14, I conjecture it is 'disbranched' from one of your embryo hymns. **1865** SWINBURNE *Atalanta* 126 All this flower of life Disbranched and desecrated miserably.

† **3.** *intr.* To branch off, spring *out of*. *rare.*

1622 PEACHAM *Compl. Gent.* 162 Cavendish: out of which familie disbranched that famous Travailer, Master Thomas Cavendish.

Hence **dis'branched** *ppl. a.*, **dis'branching** *vbl. sb.*

1616 SURFL. & MARKH. *Country Farme* 401 This disbranching must be done in the decrease of the Moone. **1843** *Zoologist* I. 305 An old disbranched fir.

† **dis'brother,** *v. Obs. nonce-wd.* [DIS- 7 b.] *trans.* To undo the brotherhood of; to make no longer brothers.

1622 MABBE tr. *Aleman's Guzman d'Alf.* I. (1623) 75 Nothing did difference them, but their Religion, whereof..they never argued, that they might not dis-brother themselues.

† **dis'buckle,** *v. Obs. rare.* [DIS- 6.] *trans.* To undo the buckling of, to unbuckle, draw apart.

1562 PHAER *Æneid* IX, Armes disbukling seuerall wayes [diversaque brachia ducens].

disbud (dɪs'bʌd), *v.* [f. DIS- 7 a + BUD *sb.*] *trans.* To remove the buds of; to deprive of (superfluous) buds.

1727 BRADLEY *Fam. Dict.* s.v. *Disbudding*, Peaches, Apricocks, etc. are..disbudded, that the remaining Branches may be the better preserv'd. **1861** DELAMER *Fl. Gard.* 167 Disbud dog-rose stocks, leaving only those buds to shoot, on which you intend to insert your bud. **1882** *Garden* 14 Jan. 28/2 To prevent our Cherries and Plums from being entirely disbudded we are obliged to use a considerable amount of powder and shot every year.

Hence **dis'budding** *vbl. sb.*; **dis'budder**, one who disbuds.

1725 BRADLEY *Fam. Dict.* s.v. *Peach*, The disbudding or nipping..consists in taking away the useless Branches, and such as are found to be irregularly scituated. **1765** EARL OF HADDINGTON *Forest-trees* 9 Such disbuddings and prunings as I have advised. **1888** WOOD *Farmer's Friends & Foes* 47 The bullfinch..acting the part of a pruner and disbudder.

disburden, -burthen (dɪs'bɜːd(ə)n, -'bɜːð(ə)n), *v.* [f. DIS- 7 + BURDEN, BURTHEN *sb.*]

1. *trans.* To remove a burden from (the bearer); to relieve of a burden. *lit.* and *fig.*

1531–2 *Act 23 Hen. VIII*, c. 20. §3 The Kynges Highnes ..coveting to disborden this realme of the seid great exaccions and intollerable charges of annates. **1576** FLEMING *Panopl. Epist.* 40, I am disburthened and eased of many cares and troubles. **1681** DRYDEN *Sp. Friar* IV. i, You know, she disburthened her conscience this morning to you. **1734** tr. *Rollin's Anc. Hist.* (1827) II. III. 155 To ease and disburden the hive of its superfluous inhabitants. **1863** GEO. ELIOT *Romola* I. xvii, The need she felt to disburden her mind.

refl. **1612** *Proc. Virginia* 47 in *Capt. Smith's Wks.* (Arb.) 125 The Ship having disburdened her selfe of 70 persons.. set forward. **1821** A. FISHER *Jrnl.* 19 Gulls are not the only birds that disburden themselves of their prey when pursued. **1840** DICKENS *Old C. Shop* lii, Having now disburdened himself of his great surprise, the schoolmaster sat down.

2. *trans.* To get rid of (a burden); to discharge, unload.

a **1586** SIDNEY (J.), Though by my thoughts I've plunged Into my life's bondage, I yet may disburden a passion. **1662** J. DAVIES tr. *Olearius' Voy. Ambass.* 31 Obliging strangers to disburthen in the City all the Merchandises which pass through it. **1713** ADDISON *Cato* I. vi, Lucia, disburden all thy cares on me. **1801** SOUTHEY *Thalaba* V. iii, A desert Pelican..Her load of water had disburthen'd there. **1828** *Life Planter Jamaica* (ed. 2) 149 Obtaining an excuse for disburdening his wrath upon her.

b. *refl.* To discharge or empty itself; to fall as a river. Also *fig.*

1600 J. PORY tr. *Leo's Africa* II. 333 This small river.. disburdeneth it selfe into the sea not farre from the citie. **1647** STAPYLTON *Juvenal* 231 The port of Hostia, where Tiber disburdens it self into the Tyrrhene sea. **1761** HUME

Hist. Eng. I. iii. 65 A new generation of men..who could no longer disburden themselves on Normandy.

3. *intr.* (for *refl.*) To unload, to discharge its load.

1667 MILTON *P.L.* v. 319 Where Nature multiplies Her fertil growth, and by disburd'ning grows More fruitful. *c* **1820** S. ROGERS *Italy, St. Mark's Place* 217 The prison-boat, that boat with many oars..Disburdening in the Canal Orfano, That drowning-place.

dis'burdened, -'burthened, *ppl. a.* [f. prec. + -ED[1].] Freed from burden.

1598 FLORIO, *Scarico*, free, quit, discharged, disburthened. **1615** J. STEPHENS *Satyr. Ess.* 133 Verses proceed from a disburthend braine. **1772** FLETCHER *Logica Genev.* 11 The disburdened clouds begin to break. **1832** G. DOWNES *Lett. Cont. Countries* I. 506 Two or three disburthened vehicles. **1856** BRYANT *Poems, Ages* xxv, With glad embrace The fair disburdened lands welcome a nobler race.

dis'burdening, -'burthening, *vbl. sb.* [f. as prec. + -ING[1].]

1. A freeing from burden; discharge; unloading.

1581 in W. H. Turner *Select. Rec. Oxford* 415 Towardes the disburdening of the ffee farme. **1644** MILTON *Areop.* (Arb.) 61 This is not..the disburdning of a particular fancie. **1709** STRYPE *Ann. Ref.* I. ii. 55 For the disburthening of their consciences.

†**2.** That which is discharged; a discharge. *Obs.*

1686 *Æthiopian Adv. Heliodorus* 7 (Jod.) A valley, that receives the inundations and disburdenings of Nilus.

dis'burdening, *ppl. a.* [f. as prec. + -ING[2].] That disburdens.

1836 THIRLWALL *Greece* II. xi. 34 Solon..met the reasonable expectations..by his disburdening ordinance.

dis'burdenment, -'burthenment. [f. DISBURDEN *v.* + -MENT.] The act or process of disburdening; the fact of being disburdened.

1818 BENTHAM *Ch.-Eng.* Pref. 35 Whether any such disburthenment shall be attempted. **1859** GEO. ELIOT *A. Bede* xi, He had never yet confessed his secret to Adam, but now he felt a delicious sense of disburthenment.

†**dis'burgeon,** *v. Obs. rare.* Also 7 **-gen.** [f. DIS- 7 a + BURGEON *sb.*] *trans.* = DISBUD. Hence **dis'burgeoning** *vbl. sb.*

1601 HOLLAND *Pliny* I. 533 For disburgening of vines, and clensing them of their superfluous leaues. *Ibid.* 538 Not ..to disburgen or deffoile altogether such trees.

disbursable (dɪsˈbɜːsəb(ə)l), *a.* [f. DISBURSE *v.* + -ABLE.] Capable of being disbursed.

1885 G. MEREDITH *Diana* I. xiv. 291 Anecdotes also are portable..they can be carried home, they are disbursable at other tables.

†**dis'bursage.** *Obs. rare.* [f. as prec. + -AGE.] The act of disbursing; disbursement; expenditure.

1721 STRYPE *Eccl. Mem.* II. xxix. 490 An account..of the payment, and disbursage and discharge of the same.

disbursal (dɪsˈbɜːsəl). [f. DISBURSE *v.* + -AL.] The act of disbursing, disbursement.

1589 in *Rep. Hist. MSS. Comm., Var. Coll.* (1904) III. 49 Divers disbursalles..as for some bookes. **1895** *Manchester Guardian* 30 Sept. 6/8 Accommodation..upstairs for the disbursal and reception of goods. **1898** in *Westm. Gaz.* 9 Mar. 2/3 All moneys received shall be duly acknowledged, and their disbursal shall be controlled by the Mansion House committee.

disbursatory (dɪsˈbɜːsətərɪ), *a.* [f. L. type **disbursāre*: see next, and -ORY.] Characterized by or given to disbursing.

1863 MRS. C. CLARKE *Shaks. Char.* vi. 161 Fenton, the least capable of the three suitors to be disbursatory.

disburse (dɪsˈbɜːs), *v.* Also 6 -bourse, -bource, -bursse. [orig. *disbourse*, a. OF. *desbourser* (13th c. in Hatz.-Darm.), mod.F. *débourser*, in same senses, f. *des-*, DIS- 4 + *bourse* purse. Afterwards assimilated to L. *bursa*, as if repr. a L. **disbursāre*. Cf. DEBURSE, DISPURSE.]

1. a. *trans.* To pay out or expend (money); to pay or defray (costs, expenses).

1530 PALSGR. 517/2, I have disboursed for hym above a hundred pounde. **1590** SHAKS. *Com. Err.* IV. i. 38 Take the Chaine, and bid my wife Disburse the summe, on the receipt thereof. **1591** HORSEY *Trav.* (Hakluyt Soc.) 220, I disburst to him and them 300 dollers. **1647** N. BACON *Disc. Govt.* II. vii. (1739) 42 Importation does bring in more profit than Exportation disburseth. **1701** DE FOE *Trueborn Eng.* Introd. 33 Who Fifty Millions Sterling have disburs'd. **1776** *Trial of Nundocomar* 16/2 Whatever contingent expenses you may find it necessary to disburse in Calcutta. *a* **1859** MACAULAY *Hist. Eng.* V. 251 They had disbursed money largely, and had disbursed it with the certainty that they should never be re-imbursed unless the outlay proved beneficial to the public.

†**b.** To defray (a charge). *Obs.*

1548 HALL *Chron., Hen. IV*, 31 To disbource and pay al the costes and charges. **1594** PLAT *Jewell-ho.* III. 30 Disbursing the charge both of the Beere, and the ingredients. **1611** CORYAT *Crudities* 377 Rupertus Duke of Alemanny disbursed the greatest charge thereof.

c. To pay for or on account of (anything). *rare.*

1860 *Merc. Marine Mag.* VII. 73 Commission on cash advanced to disburse the ship, 5 per cent.

d. *absol.* To make disbursement. Also *fig.*

1615 J. STEPHENS *Satyr. Ess.* 12 Each alike constraines The hunger-bitten Client to disburse. **1636** DAVENANT *Wits* IV. ii, Sir..you must disburse, For gold is a restorative. **1789** *Loiterer* 21 Mar. 6 Any intention to defraud, or any inability to disburse. **1920** E. POUND *Umbra* 111 Disburse Can she, and wake Such firm delights.

†**2.** *fig.* and *transf.* To spend, give out or away.

1593 SHAKS. *Lucr.* 1203 And all my Fame that liues disbursed be To those that liue and thinke no shame of me. **1621** QUARLES *Argalus & P.* (1678) 52 In a whispering language, he disburs'd His various thoughts. **1642** FULLER *Holy & Prof. St.* II. xix. [b] 126 He had rather disburse his life at the present. **1671** GREW *Anat. Plants* I. i. §40. (1682) 8 The said Sap being disbursed back into all the seminal Root.

Hence **dis'bursed** *ppl. a.*; **dis'bursing** *vbl. sb.* and *ppl. a.*

1564 GOLDING *Justine* 35 (R.) He demanded to haue the disbursing of the mony himselfe. **1611** COTGR., *Desboursé*, disbursed, laid out of a purse. **1615** G. SANDYS *Trav.* I. 61 His incomes are great, his disbursings little. **1858** *Merc. Marine Mag.* V. 173 These are deposited..in charge of the ..disbursing agent.

†**dis'burse,** *sb. Obs.* [f. prec. vb.: cf. OF. *desbours* (16th c. in Littré).] = DISBURSEMENT. *to be in disburse*, to be out of pocket.

1608 MACHIN *Dumb Knight* v. ii, Come, there is Some odd disburse, some bribe, some gratulance Which make you lock up leisure. **1682** SCARLETT *Exchanges* 186 Lest on the one hand he be in disburse, on the other, in cash for his Principal. **1716** S. SEWALL *Diary* 8 Feb. (1882) III. 73 [He] offers to be his Quota towards this Disburse. **1742** *De Foe's Tour Gt. Brit.* I. 288 The annual Rent..would abundantly pay the Publick for the first Disburses. **1782** ELPHINSTON tr. *Martial* II. lxiii. 117 Of wealth in love luxuriant the disburse!

disbursement (dɪsˈbɜːsmənt). [f. DISBURSE *v.* + -MENT: cf. F. *desboursement* (16th c. in Hatz.-Darm.), now *déb-*.]

1. The action or fact of disbursing.

1596 SPENSER *State Irel.* Wks. (Globe) 651/1 The Queenes treasure in soe greate occasions of disbursementes ..is not allwayes soe..plentifull, as it can spare soe greate a somme togither. **1665** HOOKE *Microgr.* Pref. Gb, His chearful Disbursment for the replanting of Ireland. **1756–7** *Keysler's Trav.* (1760) I. 245 Upon any..extraordinary disbursement, the cause of the difference in the account must be carefully entered. **1849** GROTE *Greece* II. lxii. (1862) V. 421 And that deficit was never so complete as to stop the disbursement of the Diobely.

2. That which has been disbursed; money paid out; expenditure.

1607 *Vestry Bks.* (Surtees) 148 This is the whole disbursement for this yeare 1607. **1818** JAS. MILL *Brit. India* II. IV. ix. 294 The surplus of receipts above disbursements. **1847** GROTE *Greece* II. xxviii. (1862) III. 52 The visitors, whose disbursements went to enrich the inhabitants of Kirrha.

disburser (dɪsˈbɜːsə(r)). [f. DISBURSE *v.* + -ER[1].] One who disburses. Also *fig.*

1611 SPEED *Hist. Gt. Brit.* IX. xxiv. 297 The sparing of money by the grand disbursers. **1660** W. SECKER *Nonsuch Prof.* 409 Faith is the great receiver, and love is the great disburser. **1746** *Gen. Assembly Rec.* (1838) 86 Mr. Dalrymple was appointed receiver and disburser of said money. **1881** *Times* 2 May 11/3 The military disbursers knew they had drawn more than the audit testified to.

disburthen: see DISBURDEN.

disbury (dɪsˈbɛrɪ), *v. rare.* [f. DIS- 6 + BURY *v.*] *trans.* To release from a buried condition; to disentomb, disinter. Hence **disburied** *ppl. a.*

1835 LYTTON *Rienzi* II. iii, Disburied secrets. **1862** —— *Str. Story* II. 238 The quartz was shattered by the stroke, and left disburied its glittering treasure.

disbutton (dɪsˈbʌt(ə)n), *v. rare.* [f. DIS- 6 or 7 a + BUTTON *sb.* or *v.*] *trans.* **a.** To deprive of buttons. **b.** To undo the buttons of, to unbutton.

1883 G. H. BOUGHTON in *Harper's Mag.* Apr. 700/2 His eldest son..was disrobed and disbuttoned. **1887** *Twin Soul* I. vii. 58 As the Spartan boys kept their foxes under their waistcoats, defying the world to disbutton them.

dis-Byronize: see DIS- 6.

disc, disk (dɪsk). [ad. L. *disc-us*, a. Gr. δίσκος quoit, dish, disc: cf. F. *disque*, (1556).

The earlier and better spelling is *disk*, but *disc* is now the more usual form in British English, except in sense 2 g, where *disk* is commoner as a result of US influence.]

1. The DISCUS or quoit used in ancient Greek and Roman athletic exercises; the game played with this. *Obs.* exc. *Hist.* (Cf. DISH *sb.* II.)

1715–20 POPE *Iliad* II. 941 In empty air their sportive jav'lins throw, Or whirl the disk. **1727–51** CHAMBERS *Cycl.*, *Disc* or *Disk*, *Discus*, in antiquity, a kind of round quoit.. about a foot over, used by the antients in their exercises. **1728** NEWTON *Chronol. Amended* 36 The Disc was one of the five games called the Quinquertium. **1791** COWPER *Iliad* II. 948 His soldiers hurled the disk or bent the bow. **1835** THIRLWALL *Greece* I. viii. 329 He could run, leap, wrestle, hurl the disk. **1876** DOWDEN *Poems* 67 In manage of the steed Or shooting the swift disc.

2. a. A thin circular plate of any material.

1803 *Med. Jrnl.* X. 26 Volta constructed a pile made up of disks of different metals with layers of cloth interposed. **1827** FARADAY *Chem. Manip.* xxiii. 568 Clipping fragments of plate glass into circular discs. **1865** LUBBOCK *Preh. Times* vi. (1878) 283 A small oval disk of white sandstone. **1872** RUSKIN *Eagle's N.* §224 The shield [is] a disk of leather, iron fronted. **1881** GREENER *Gun* 198 Allowing the breech-ends to rise clear of the discs.

†**b.** Used *poet.* of a shield.

1791 COWPER *Iliad* XI. 528 Ulysses' oval disk he smote. Through his bright disk the stormy weapon flew.

c. *spec.* In ancient armour, a plate of metal used to protect the body at certain joints of the armour; a roundel.

d. A phonograph or gramophone record. Also *attrib.* and *Comb.*

1888 *Leisure Hour* 209/1 A disc about eleven inches in diameter can, it is said, contain four minutes' talk. **1907** *Sound Wave & Talking Machine Record* Dec. 60/2 The world today always associates Edison's phonograph with a cylinder apparatus, but the first phonograph we look at in this patent is a disc (he called it a disk) machine. **1919** A. SEYMOUR *Good-bye-ee!*, A gramaphone [*sic*] record with the picture of a foxterrier on the disc. **1929** *Sunday Dispatch* 20 Jan. 16 A fine disc by his orchestra. **1941** *B.B.C. Gloss. Broadc. Terms* 9 *Disc recording.* (1) Process of registering sound by electro-mechanical means in the form of lateral corrugations in a spiral groove on a disc coated with, or composed of, plastic material. (2) (Also *Disc.*) Disc on which sound has been so recorded. (3) (By extension.) Programme material so recorded. **1951** *Ann. Reg. 1950* 386 A whole classical symphony could be recorded on the two sides of a 12-inch disc without any break in the course of the movements. **1958** *Listener* 18 Dec. 1049/2 The puerile pop singer who becomes the demi-god of the frenzied disc-addicts. **1962** *Melody Maker* 7 July 4 His discs have sold in millions all over the globe... He doesn't make hit discs today. **1962** A. NISBETT *Technique Sound Studio* vii. 134 *Disc editing.* Discs are edited by dubbing (i.e. copying), and extensive professional equipment is required. **1968** *Listener* 27 June 845/3 The only complete opera-in-English available on disc in this country.

e. Short for ***identity disc*** (see IDENTITY).

a **1918** W. OWEN *Poems* (1931) 104 Let my inscription be this soldier's disc.

f. In full ***parking disc.*** A device used in *disc parking*.

1960 *Economist* 9 Apr. 193/3 A parking disc is a device a driver himself displays on his vehicle to show the time he arrived or the time he ought to leave a parking area, or both times. **1970** *Oxford Mail* 13 July 6 Whilst there is adequate warning, on entry into the city, that disc parking is operative it does seem ridiculous that an ample supply of discs is not readily available from garages, stores and traffic wardens.

g. *Computing.* A rotatable disc used to store data in digitally coded form, e.g. in a magnetic coating or optically. Cf. ***compact disc*** s.v. COMPACT *ppl. a.*[1] II. 1 c, ***floppy disc*** s.v. FLOPPY *a.* 2, ***hard disc*** s.v. HARD *a.* 22 c, ***optical disc*** s.v. OPTICAL *a.* 6.

See the note to the etymology for the spelling of *disc* in this sense.

1947 *Math. Tables & Other Aids Computation* II. 229 The program of the Symposium was as follows:.. 4. 'Magnetic and phosphor coated disks' by Dr. B. L. Moore. **1952** *Electr. Engin.* Aug. 745/1 The new 'memory' stores data in the form of magnetic pulses on both sides of thin metal disks. *Ibid.* 745/2 When the heads are in position, the disk is rotated past them while information, in the form of coded magnetic pulses, is recorded or read out. **1956** *Proc. 9th Western Joint Computer Conf.* 42/1 The information is stored, magnetically, on 50 rotating disks. **1964** T. W. MCRAE *Impact of Computers on Accounting* i. 8 This machine stored its records on the 'juke-box' principle, that is 48 disks were stored one above the other and an arm moving up and down the side of the file was able to interrogate any disk record within about half a second. **1964**, etc. [see MAGNETIC *a.* 1]. **1969** *Jrnl. Assoc. Computing Machinery* XVI. 617 A multi-head disk is a disk with two or more recording heads, each of which is capable of independent movement. **1982** *What's New in Computing* Nov. 12/4 Back up for the discs is provided on a tape streamer, tape cartridge or floppy. **1983** *Computers & Electronics* Mar. 48 Most people who buy a moderately priced computer..will use cassette storage rather than disks. **1985** P. LAURIE *Databases* i. 34 Instead of the 20 milliseconds one expects of a medium sized Winchester, a laser disk may well take some 100–200 ms to write a record. **1986** *Times* 20 May 30 Data is registered as changes in the reflectivity of the disc's surface; these are picked up from a low-power laser beam.

3. Anything resembling a circular plate.

a **1711** GREW (J.), The crystal of the eye, which in a fish is a ball, in any land animal is a disk or bowl. **1860** MAURY *Phys. Geog. Sea* iv. §265 About the Arctic disc, therefore, there should be a whirl. **1865** GROTE *Plato* II. xxiii. 169 Whether the earth was a disk or a sphere. **1872** C. KING *Mountain. Sierra Nev.* xi. 236 The whole great disc of world outspread. **1878** HUXLEY *Physiogr.* xvi. 267 Multitudes of very minute saucer-shaped disks.

4. a. *spec.* The (apparently flat) surface or 'face' of the sun, the moon, or a planet, as it appears to the eye.

1664 *Phil. Trans.* I. 3 He hath..at length seen them emerge out of his Disk. **1714** DERHAM *Astro-Theol.* v. iv. (1726) 130 Jupiter..hath manifestly..his Belts and Spots, darker than the rest of his Disk. **1769** W. HIRST in *Phil. Trans. Abr.* XII. 639 (*title*) Of several Phenomena observed during the Ingress of Venus into the Solar Disc. **1797** GODWIN *Enquirer* II. xi. 364 The spots discoverable in the disk of the sun. **1834** MRS. SOMERVILLE *Connect. Phys. Sc.* iv. (1849) 34 The eclipses [of the satellites] take place close to the disc of Jupiter. **1893** SIR R. BALL *Story of Sun* 39 Mars at the time..shows a large and brilliant disk.

b. *transf.* Any round luminous (or coloured) flat surface; the surface of a flame or the like.

1758 REID tr. *Macquer's Chym.* I. 315 The surface of the Lead appearing..bright and shining like a luminous disc. **1855** LONGF. *Hiaw.* VIII. 101 [The sun-fish] Slowly rising through the water, Lifting his great disc of whiteness [*v. v.* disk refulgent]. *c* **1860** FARADAY *Forces Nat.* 180 (*Electric Light*) If you look at the disc of light thrown by the apparatus. **1878** HUXLEY *Physiogr.* xxi. 359 It presents the appearance of a luminous disc. **1881** *Daily Tel.* 28 Jan., So long as the position of the disk which he is legally obliged to affix somewhere upon the vessel's side is left to the discretion of the owner.

5. *Bot.* A round and flattened part in a plant. *spec.* **a.** A collection of tubular florets in the flower-head of *Compositæ*, forming either the whole head (as in the tansy), or the central part of it, as distinguished from the *ray* (as in the daisy). **b.** An enlargement of the torus or receptacle of a flower, below or around the pistil. (In these senses always spelt *disk*.) **c.** A disc-shaped marking or 'bordered pit' in the wood-cells of Gymnosperms, etc. **d.** One of the disc-shaped adhesive bodies formed on the tendrils of the Virginia creeper and other plants. **e.** The flat surface of a leaf, etc., as distinguished from the margin. **f.** The disc-shaped hymenium of a discomycetous fungus; = DISCOCARP (b).

[**1706** PHILLIPS (ed. Kersey), Among Herbalists, *Discus*.. the middle, plain, and flat part of some Flowers; because its Figure resembles the ancient *Discus*.] **1727** BAILEY vol. II., *Disk*, with Florists, is a Body of Florets collected together, and forming as it were a plain Surface. **1794** MARTYN *Rousseau's Bot.* vi. 65 In the radiate flowers the disk is often of one colour and the ray of another. **1807** J. E. SMITH *Phys. Bot.* 454 *Polygamia frustranea*, florets of the disk.. perfect or united; those of the margin neuter, or destitute of pistils as well as of stamens. **1830** LINDLEY *Nat. Syst. Bot.* Introd. 29 Immediately between the stamens and the ovarium is sometimes found a fleshy ring or fleshy glands called a Disk, and supposed.. to represent an inner row of imperfectly developed stamens. **1870** HOOKER *Stud. Flora* 347 Coniferæ .. wood-cells studded with disks. **1872** OLIVER *Elem. Bot.* II. 195 In Daisy.. the inner florets are much smaller, regular, tubular, and yellow, constituting the disk. **1875** DARWIN *Insectiv. Pl.* x. 246 The four leaves.. with their tentacles pointing.. to the two little masses of the phosphate on their discs. **1875** BENNETT & DYER tr. *Sachs' Bot.* III. iv. 781 Some tendrils, strikingly those of the Virginian creeper and *Bignonia capreolata*, have the.. power of developing broad discs at the end of their branches.. which attach themselves like cupping glasses to rough surfaces.

6. *Zool.* A roundish flattened part or structure in an animal body. *spec.* **a.** In the animals formerly grouped as *Radiata* (Echinoderms, Cœlenterates, etc.): The central rounded and flattened part containing the oral opening and usually surrounded by rays, tentacles, or arms: from its resemblance to the disc and rays of a composite flower. **b.** The set of feathers surrounding the eye of an owl. **c.** The part of a bivalve shell between the margin and the umbo. **d.** The most elevated portion of the thorax or elytra of an insect; the central portion of the wing. **e.** The flat locomotive organ or 'foot' of a gastropod.

1761 GAERTNER in *Phil. Trans.* LII. 82 Out of the top part, or the disk of the polype, grow the feelers. **1834** McMURTRIE *Cuv. Anim. Kingd.* 272 Some of them.. expand into a disk comparable to that of a flower or of an Actinia. **1847** CARPENTER *Zool.* §1015 In the Ophiuræ we find a more distinct central disk.. it is furnished with arms. *Ibid.* §1013 In others the disk seems almost absent, the animal being, as it were, all rays. **1855** GOSSE *Marine Zool.* I. 41 *Acalepha.* Body in form of a circular disk, more or less convex and umbrella-like.. moving by alternate contractions and expansions of the disk: *Discophora* [Sea-blubbers, etc.] *Ibid.* 63 *Comatula.* When adult, free, stemless, with simple thread-like jointed appendages around the dorsal disk. **1861** J. R. GREENE *Man. Anim. Kingd., Cœlent.* 132 The expanded *Actinia*.. attaching itself by one of its flattened ends, known as the ' base,' a mouth being placed in the centre of the 'disc,' or opposite extremity. **1866** TATE *Brit. Mollusks* iii. 46 The foot is a broad flat expanded disk. **1888** ROLLESTON & JACKSON *Anim. Life* 707 The mouth in the *Phylactolaemata*.. lies in the centre of a disc, or lophophore, either circular or horse-shoe shaped, along the edges of which are arranged.. a row of tentacles.

7. *Anat.* Applied to various round flat structures: *spec.* **a.** The mass of fibrous cartilage lying between the bodies of adjacent vertebræ; ***slipped disc*** (see SLIPPED *ppl. a.*). **b.** The flattened corpuscles of the blood (***blood-discs***). **c.** One of the flat circular bodies formed by the transverse cleavage of a muscular fibre; called specifically *Bowman's discs*. **d.** ***optic disc***: the round or oval spot where the optic nerve enters the eyeball. ***choked disc***, a diseased condition of this, in which.. the retinal veins are distended and tortuous (*Syd. Soc. Lex.*).

1845 TODD & BOWMAN *Phys. Anat.* I. 60 Certain particles, the blood-discs, which float in it in great numbers. **1848** CARPENTER *Anim. Phys.* 35 In the blood of all the higher animals, we also find a vast number of minute discs, sometimes round, sometimes oval. **1859** TODD *Cycl. Anat.* V. 41/1 Minute embryoes, scarcely longer than the blood discs of the frog. **1870** ROLLESTON *Anim. Life* Introd. 43 All the other vertebræ have their centra articulated together by fibro-cartilaginous discs. *Ibid.* 5 The crocodiles [have] interarticular fibrocartilaginous discs. **1883** *Syd. Soc. Lex.* s.v., *Intermediate disks*, the membrane of Krause, separating muscle fibre into compartments. **1887** *Ibid.*, *Intervertebral discs*, lenticular elastic masses interposed between, and of the same shape as, the bodies of two adjacent vertebræ through the spinal column.

8. *attrib.* and *Comb.* **a.** Of or belonging to a disc, as ***disc-bud***, ***-budding*** (see 6 a), ***-floret***, ***-flower*** (see 5 a), ***-lobe***. **b.** Consisting, or having the form, of a disc, as ***disc brake*** (hence ***-braked*** adj.), ***-brooch***, ***-crank***, ***-micrometer***. **c.** Characterized by or furnished with a disc or discs, as ***disc-coupling***, ***-cutter***, ***-electrometer***, ***-fan***, ***-signal***, ***-telegraph***; also in the names of agricultural machines (orig. *U.S.*), as ***disc-cultivator***, ***drill***, ***-harrow***, (hence as *v. trans.*), ***plough***. **d.** objective and obj. genitive, as ***disc-bearing*** adj., ***-worship***. **e.** parasynthetic, as ***disc-shaped*** adj.; also instrumental and similative, as ***disc-adjusting***, ***-capped***, ***-like*** adjs. **f.** Special combs. **disc area** *Aeronaut.* (see quots.); **disc-armature**, an armature wound so that its coils lie in the form of a disc; **disc-barrow**, a flat circular barrow or tumulus; **disc-clutch**, a form of friction-clutch in which one revolving disc acts upon another; **disc controller** *Computing*, a device or system that controls the transfer of data to and from discs; **disc drive** *Computing*, a mechanism for rotating a disc; now *spec.* a storage device with one or more read/write heads and means for rotating a disc or disc pack; cf. *tape drive* s.v. TAPE *sb.*[1] 4; **disc-dynamo**, a dynamo furnished with a disc-armature; **disc electrode** (see quot. *a* 1884); **disc-engine**, **-steam-engine**, a type of rotary engine in which the steam acts upon a revolving or oscillating disc; **disc-jockey** orig. *U.S. slang*, a person who selects and introduces gramophone records for transmission on radio or television; abbrev. D.J., DEE-JAY; also as *v. intr.*; hence **disc-jockeying** *vbl. sb.*; **disc loading** *Aeronaut.* (see quots.); **disc operating system**, an operating system for a computer that uses discs; abbrev. *DOS* s.v. D III. 3; **disc-owl**, the barn-owl: so called from the completeness of the facial disc (see 6 b); **disc pack** *Computing*, a storage device consisting of an assembly of rigid magnetic discs mounted on a central spindle and with a removable protective cover; **disc parking**, a parking scheme for vehicles whereby each must display a disc on which is shown the time when the vehicle was parked; **disc storage** *Computing*, storage of data on a disc or discs; **disc system**, a computer system in which storage is on discs rather than tape, etc.; **disc-valve**, a valve formed by a circular disc with rotatory or reciprocating motion; **disc-wheel**, a kind of worm-wheel in which the spur-gear is driven by a spiral thread in the face of the disc.

1898 *Cycling* 54 *Disc-adjusting bearings. **1919** H. SHAW *Text-Bk. Aeronaut.* xi. 146 The propeller during rotation marks out a circular area which is known as the '*disc area'. **1962** *Gloss. Aeronaut. Terms* (*B.S.I.*) v. 16 *Disk area*, the area of the circle described by the tips of the blades. **1895** A. J. EVANS in *Folk-lore* Mar. 15 Like the *disk-barrows it is surrounded by a ditch and bank. **1870** BENTLEY *Bot.* 39 *Disc-bearing Woody Tissue is composed of those wood cells called Disc-bearing Wood-cells. **1904** M. MACLEAN *Mod. Electr. Pract.* IV. 241 Electric *disc brake.—This is a brake that is not very largely in use [on trams] in this country. **1928** *Flight* 20 Dec. 1325/2 The multiple disc brake offers unlimited possibilities for having large braking surfaces. **1950** *Autocar* 15 Dec. 1257 At the moment the disc brake, like most innovations, is more expensive than the system which it seems to supplant. **1964** J. GRIFFITHS *Your Car* x. 105 *Disc Brakes.* These are a comparatively recent development on popular cars... The modern type was developed on racing cars, but it originated with the brakes used for the landing wheels on large aircraft. **1959** G. FREEMAN *Jack would be Gentleman* x. 221 Prosser with his *disc-braked car is able to leave his braking that little bit longer. **1937** *Burlington Mag.* Feb. 99/1 The first Kentish jewelled *disc-brooches. **1958** D. WHITELOCK *Changing Currents in Anglo-Saxon Studies* 21 Mr. Bruce-Mitford's article on the late Saxon disc-brooches. **1846** DANA *Zooph.* iv. §54 The *disk-buds, like the lateral, probably proceed from one of the same lamellæ. *Ibid.* iv. §53 In *disk-budding, a new mouth opens in the disk. **1928** *Daily Express* 17 Aug. 2/7 The system of milk distribution by means of *disc-capped bottles. **1906** *Daily Chron.* 14 Nov. 9/3 The enormously increased popularity of the multiple *disc or 'plate' clutches. **1909** *Westm. Gaz.* 11 Feb. 4/2 A multiple disc-clutch. **1970** *AFIPS Conf. Proc.* XXXVII. 564/1 A *disk controller can be blocked for a limited number of contiguous cycles. **1978** *Pract. Computing* July–Aug. 55/3 A typical hardware configuration.. will comprise a processor containing two Intel 8080s and a bit-sliced disc controller, 20K Bytes of memory, [etc.]. **1985** *Personal Computer World* Feb. 183 (Advt.), Incorporating Xebec performance-proven disk controllers. **1888** *Lockwood's Dict. Mech. Engin.*, **Disc crank*, or *crank disc*, or *crank plate*, a crank of circular outline in which the metal is so disposed that the varying motion of the connecting-rod is suitably balanced. **1894** *Irrigation Age* Jan. 34/1, I have found one of the best tools that we have yet used to be the *disc cultivator. **1835** URE *Philos. Manuf.* 198 A toothed pinion.. gives each *disc-cutter a quick rotatory motion on its centre. **1897** *Sears, Roebuck Catal.* 159/3 The *disc drill when polished will cut through sod and trash. **1907** L. H. BAILEY *Cycl. Amer. Agric.* I. 207 The disc drill is also used very extensively in many sections of the country. **1952** *Electr. Engin.* Aug. 747/1 In the small machine, the *disk drive is somewhat different. [**1963**: see *disc pack* below.] **1968** *Dataweek* 24 Jan. 1/1 Direct Access Storage disk drives can also be added—at least two and not more than eight drives—connected as a subsystem to the central processor. **1971** *New Scientist* 18 Mar. 614/2 Enhancements to the little System 3 computer were.. announced, including.. double-fast Dolphin disc-drives. **1983** *Computerworld* 1 Aug. 6 An Apple Computer, Inc. Apple II+ computer with 48K bytes of memory, two diskdrives and an Apple language system. *a* **1884** KNIGHT *Dict. Mech.* Suppl., **Disk electrode*,.. an electrode for telegraphic instruments in which the connection is secured by the contact of the peripheries of two disks. **1884** F. KROHN tr. *Glaser de Cew's Magn. & Dyn.-electr. Mach.* 104 A kind of voltaic battery in which only one metal was employed, the disk-electrodes of which were rendered active by polarisation. **1876** *Catal. Sci. App. S. Kens.* §1422 Attracted *Disc Electrometer, with double micrometer screw. **1833** *Mechanics Mag.* XVIII. 242 One of these half oscillatory, half revolving *disc engines. **1855** *Ibid.* LXIII. 266 In 1849 disc engines.. were employed with great success in the printing office of the *Times*. **1903** *Westm. Gaz.* 9 Dec. 8/2 The air.. is drawn out by a *disc-fan. **1872** OLIVER *Elem. Bot.* II. 195 In Daisy, and many other plants with ray and *disk florets. **1870** HOOKER *Stud. Flora* 185 Asteroideæ.. *Disk-flowers 2-sexual. *a* **1884** KNIGHT *Dict. Mech.* Suppl., **Disk harrow* , a harrow.. carrying a number of sharp-edged and concave disks. **1891** R. WALLACE *Rural Econ. Austral. & N.Z.* xix. 270 The Disc-Harrow.. with its saucer-shaped discs strung on two axle-shafts. *Ibid.* xxii. 309 After the land has been disc-harrowed. **1907** L. H. BAILEY *Cycl. Amer. Agric.* I. 385 The revolving disc harrow or plow, with its concave discs moving obliquely through the soil. **1948** *British Birds* XLI. 29 This area of waste ground had been disc harrowed a few days before. **1960** *Farmer & Stockbreeder* 15 Mar. 98/1 A more recent development is the powered disc-harrow. **1941** *Variety* 13 Aug. 36/3 Gilbert is a *disc-jockey who sings with his records. *Ibid.* 51 (*headline*) Art Green disc-jockeys from Manhattan Beach. **1942** *Time* 6 July 67/1 Some stations merely hired 'disk-jockeys' to ride herd on swing records, in the traditional milk-man's matinee style. **1955** *Times* 22 July 9/4 We will do well to try to emulate the disc-jockeys and to put into our voices the warm, gay humanity which they lavish on Mrs. Soup and Mrs. Gravel. **1971** *N.Y. Times* (Entertainment section) 9 May 17/4 All the other disk jockeys had names like Brown and Green. **1941** *Variety* 13 Aug. 36/3 (*headline*) *Disc-jockeying in Fifth Avenue window. **1955** N. FITZGERALD *House is Falling* x. 164 I've had to take a spot of disc-jockeying on commercial programmes to make ends meet. **1893** J. TUCKEY tr. *Hatschek's Amphioxus* 137 A *disc-like thickening of the hypoblast. **1956** *Nature* 11 Feb. 277/2 Red cells retain their disk-like form. **1934** *Jrnl. R. Aeronaut. Soc.* XXXVIII. 508 (W/A) is the air column loading in lbs. per square foot of cross-section of the downwardly displaced column of air. In conformity with helical propeller practice this may be referred to as the *disc loading. **1962** *Gloss. Aeronaut. Terms* (*B.S.I.*) v. 16 *Disk loading*, the thrust of the rotor divided by the disk area. **1870** HOOKER *Stud. Flora* 159 Cicuta.. *Disk-lobes depressed, entire. **1783** HERSCHEL in *Phil. Trans. Abr.* XV. 325 (*heading*) A Description of the Dark and Lucid *Disc and Periphery Micrometers. **1802** —— in *Phil. Trans.* XCII. 214 To remove the disk-micrometer. **1967** *Data Processing Mag.* Jan. 28/2 IBM split BOS into three distinct operating systems... The three new levels of operating systems were designated: *Disk Operating System (DOS) for users of the 16k-byte (minimum) disk-oriented systems; [etc.]. **1967** *Data-Processing* Nov./Dec. 287 An advanced disc operating system developed by English Electric Computers for use with the System 4-50 computer. **1980** R. ZAKS *CP/M Handbk. with MP/M* v. 185 One of the primary functions of any disk operating system (DOS) is to provide effective and convenient management of disk-based files. **1963** *AFIPS Conf. Proc.* XXIV. 327 (*heading*) A new high density recording system: the IBM 1311 Disk Storage Drive with interchangeable *disk packs. **1967** D. G. HAYS *Introd. Computational Linguistics* iii. 44 When information is moved to external storage but is intended for later use in the computer, only magnetic tape or a disc pack is truly suitable. **1971** *Science* Jan. 28 How many magnetic drums or disc-packs are needed to hold 10^{12} bits? **1985** *Inmac Catal.* Spring/Summer 21/1 Dust and impact are the two major problems you face when transporting data — both can cause dropouts on tapes, disk packs and cartridges. **1960** *Daily Tel.* 2 Apr. 1/1 Provision of *disc parking on the lines of the system used in Paris. **1970** Disc parking [see sense 2 f above]. **1881** *U.S. Patent 9603*, Disk plow. **1907** Disc plow [see *disc harrow* above]. **1940** *Chambers's Techn. Dict.* 251/2 *Disc plough*, a plough which cuts a furrow slice by means of a sharp-edged steel disc, of saucer-like shape, set obliquely to the ground surface. **1836–9** TODD *Cycl. Anat.* II. 414/1 A *disc-shaped capsule. **1856** *Engineer* 535/1 (Railway signals) The disc, a form in very general use. *Ibid.* 535/2 *Disc signals. **1889** G. FINDLAY *Eng. Railway* 69 The disc signal is used to indicate to a driver whose train is in a goods siding, when he may pass on to the main line. **1951** J. A. WEIDENHAMMER (*title*) Rabinow selective multiple magnetic *disk storage device. (IBM Technical Rep.) **1957** *Proc. 11th Western Joint Computer Conf.* 44/1 The 60-word block of core storage serves as a static buffer for information transferred between the computer and tape, between computer and disk storage or between tape and disk storage under computer control. *Ibid.*, Each disk storage unit has a capacity for six million numeric digits. **1984** C. S. PARKER *Understanding Computers* iii. 71 Disk storage was also introduced during the second generation, although its full potential was not realized until a generation later. **1966** *Computer Jrnl.* IX. 242/1 Protection of a *disk system requires that no user be able to modify the system, purposely or inadvertently, thus preserving the integrity of the software. **1978** *Pract. Computing* July–Aug. 33/2 The disc system is complete with controller, and disc operating system. **1984** J. HILTON *Choosing & using your Home Computer* 11/1 You will also require a means of saving programs for future use. A cassette recorder or disk system are typical methods. **1874** KNIGHT *Dict. Mech.* I. 708/2 **Disk-telegraph*, one in which the letters and figures are arranged around a circular plate and are brought consecutively to an opening, or otherwise specifically indicated. **1876** ROUTLEDGE *Discov.* 7 The position.. assumed by the apparatus when the engine is in motion, the *disc-valve being partly open. **1883** V. STUART *Egypt* 365 Some Egyptologists assert that Amunoph III already had adopted *disk-worship from his Semitic wife.

disc (dɪsk), *v.* Chiefly *U.S.* and *N.Z.* Also **disk**. [f. the sb.] To cultivate with a disc cultivator or disc harrow. So 'discing *vbl. sb.*; *discing machine* (see quot. *a* 1884).

a 1884 KNIGHT *Dict. Mech.* Suppl., *Disking machine*,..a steam-cultivating implement to be drawn by an engine over sod or plowed sod. **1917** *Nat. Weather & Crop Bull.* Mar. 4/2 Cutting corn-stalks, disking, and plowing have commenced. **1945** B. MACDONALD *Egg & I* (1946) iii. 45 When the garden..had been ploughed, disked, harrowed and dragged. **1950** *N.Z. Jrnl. Agric.* Mar. 227/1 The soil should be disced and worked down to a fine tilth. *Ibid.* 314/1 Stalks should be ploughed or disced in..after the tobacco harvest. **1952** M. H. HOLCROFT *Dance of Seasons* x. 75 After the ploughing came the discing, a confused and bumpy distribution of clods which marred the beauty of the furrows. **1960** *Farmer & Stockbreeder* 15 Mar. 107/3 The amount of discing needed varies of course with the seasons.

† **dis'cabinet**, *v. Obs. rare.* [f. DIS- 7 + CABINET *sb.*] *trans.* To divulge or disclose, as the secrets of a cabinet.

1658 MILTON (*title*), The Cabinet-Council, containing the chief Arts of Empire, and Mysteries of State, discabineted in Political and Polemical Aphorisms, grounded on Authority and Experience..By the ever renown'd Knight Sir Walter Raleigh.

discage (dɪs'keɪdʒ), *v.* [f. DIS- 7 c + CAGE *sb.*] *trans.* To release or let out as from a cage; to uncage.

1649 G. DANIEL *Trinarch., Hen. V*, ccxxvii, Trampling the Mud of mixed Brains discag'd From double fence. **1872** TENNYSON *Gareth & Lynette* 19 Until she let me fly discaged to sweep In ever-highering eagle-circles up To the great Sun of Glory.

discal ('dɪskəl), *a.* [f. L. *disc-us* DISC + -AL[1].] Of, pertaining to, or of the nature of, a disc; discoid.

1848 R. HILL in Gosse *Nat. in Jamaica* (1851) 345 The exceedingly discal character of the extremity. **1883** in *Syd. Soc. Lex.*

discalceate (dɪ'skælsɪeɪt), *ppl. a.* and *sb.* [ad. L. *discalceāt-us* unshod, barefooted: see next.]

A. *ppl. a.* Unshod, barefooted; *spec.* applied to certain orders of friars and nuns.

1658 J. BURBURY *Hist. Christine, Q. Swedland* 103 The.. present of 25 great bottles of wine, which the Queen caus'd to be given to the Carmelite discalceat Nuns. *a* **1667** JER. TAYLOR *Reverence due to Altar* (1848) 51 Justin Martyr.. saith that the Gentiles when they came to worship were commanded..to be discalceate. **1715** M. DAVIES *Athen. Brit.* I. Pref. 37 Unless..some of the discalceat Mercenary Troops..stay behind. **1861** NEALE *Notes on Dalmatia, etc.* 180 Originally written by a Discalceate Carmelite.

B. *sb.* A barefooted friar or nun.

1669 WOODHEAD *St. Teresa* II. xvii. 118 Ten Covents of Discalceates. **1706** tr. *Dupin's Eccl. Hist. 16th C.* II. IV. xi. 449 From the Carmelites came the Congregation of those whom they call Discalceates.

† **dis'calceate**, *v. Obs. rare*[−0]. [f. *discalceāt-* ppl. stem of L. *discalceāre* to pull off the shoes, f. DIS-[4] + *calceāre* to shoe, *calceus* a shoe.]

1623 COCKERAM, *Discalceate*, to put off ones Shoes. **1656** in BLOUNT *Glossogr.*

dis'calceated, *ppl. a.* [f. as prec. + -ED[1].] = DISCALCEATE *ppl. a.*

1639 W. SCLATER *Worthy Commun. Rew.* 15 In those hotter climates [they] went discalceated, and without shoes. **1655** FULLER *Ch. Hist.* VI. vii. 364 The discalceated Nunnes of the Order of S. Clare. **1762** tr. *Busching's Syst. Geog.* V. 145 The Lutheran churches and convents here are the church of the discalceated. **1856** R. A. VAUGHAN *Mystics* (1860) II. 120 But thirteen 'fervent virgins' shall dwell there, discalceated (that is, sandalled, not shod).

† **discal'ceation**. *Obs.* [n. of action from L. *discalceāre*: see DISCALCEATE *v.*] The action of taking off the shoes, *esp.* in token of reverence.

a **1638** MEDE *Reverence God's Ho.* Wks. (1672) II. 347 An allusion..to that Rite of Discalceation used by the Jews and other Nations of the Orient at their coming into Sacred places. **1669** GALE *Crt. Gentiles* I. II. ix. 138 The Pythagorean mode of discalceation, or putting off the shoes, at entrance into the Temple.

discalced (dɪ'skælst), *ppl. a.* [as if from a vb. **discalce*, repr. L. *discalceā-re* + -ED. Cf. DISCHAUCE.] = DISCALCEATE *ppl. a.*

1631 WEEVER *Anc. Fun. Mon.* 139 They are called Carmes discalced, or bare footed Friers. **1700** RYCAUT *Hist. Turks* III. 264 The King..walked in Procession..to the Church of the Franciscans discalced. **1867** LADY HERBERT *Cradle L.* ix. 233 Carmel is the head-quarters of the Discalced Carmelites. **1885** *Catholic Dict.* 265 The Carmelite reform both of men and women, instituted by St. Teresa, is also discalced. The discalced Augustinians (Hermits) were founded by Father Thomas of Jesus, a Portuguese.

† **di'scale**, *v. Obs.* [f. *di-* = DIS- 7 a + SCALE *sb.*] *trans.* To deprive of the shell or scales.

1655 MOUFET & BENNET *Health's Improv.* (1746) 271 Each of them [crevisses and shrimps] must be discaled, and clean picked with much pidling. **1661** LOVELL *Hist. Anim. & Min.* 192 To be sodden in milk till they be tender, being first discaled, and the long gut pulled out.

† **dis'calendar**, *v. Obs.* Also 7 diskal-. [f. DIS- 7 c + CALENDAR *sb.*] *trans.* To erase or remove from the calendar.

1593 NASHE *Christ's T.* (1613) 40 The feast of Tabernacles, the feast of sweet Bread, and the feast of Weekes, shall quite bee discalendred. **1667** WATERHOUSE *Fire Lond.* 84 Which Sept...let it be Discalendred, and not be numbered amongst the Twelve.

disca,leno'hedron. *Cryst.* [f. DI-[2] + SCALENOHEDRON.] (See quot.)

1878 GURNEY *Crystallogr.* 63 A double twelve-sided pyramid, the faces of which are symmetrically arranged with respect to each of the seven planes of the hexagonal type of symmetry..is called the discalenohedron.

† **discame'ration.** *Obs. rare*[−1]. [n. of action from L. type **discamerāre*, f. DIS- 6 + L. *camera* chamber.] = DISINCAMERATION.

1670 G. H. *Hist. Cardinals* II. III. 200 Clement the ninth was never to be perswaded to the discameration of Castro.

† **discamp** (dɪ'skæmp), *v. Mil. Obs.* [ad. It. *scampare*, with substitution of the full form of the prefix *dis-* for *s-*: cf. DECAMP.]

1. *intr.* To raise or break up a camp; to depart from a place of encampment; to decamp. Also *fig.*

1579 FENTON *Guicciard.* (1618) 213 After which accident ..they discamped secretly in the night to go to Quiercy. **1652** URQUHART *Jewel* Wks. (1834) 211 Fidelity, fortitude, and vigilancie, must needs discamp, if Mammona give the word. *a* **1693** —— *Rabelais* III. xxxvii. 311 He was about discamping.

2. *trans.* a. To remove or abandon (a camp). b. To force (any one) from a camp, force to abandon a camp.

1574 HELLOWES *Gueuara's Fam. Ep.* (1577) 272, I command you to leaue your armour, to discamp your camp. **1606** HOLLAND *Sueton.* 25 No enemie put he ever to flight, but he discamped him and draue him out of the field. **1658** J. COLES tr. *Cleopatra* vii. 140 He discamped his Army, and marched to meet Ariamenes.

Hence **di'scamping** *vbl. sb.*

1579 FENTON *Guicciard.* II. (1599) 84 The King departed with his army before day, without sound of trumpets, to couer his discamping as much as he could. **1611** COTGR., *Descampement*, a discamping.

† **dis'candy**, *v. Obs. rare.* (Also 7 erron. discander.) [f. DIS- 6 + CANDY *v.*] *intr.* To melt or dissolve out of a candied or solid condition.

1606 SHAKS. *Ant. & Cl.* III. xiii. 165 By the discandering of this pelletted storme. *Ibid.* IV. xii. 22 The hearts..to whom I gaue Their wishes, do dis-Candie, melt their sweets On blossoming Cæsar.

† **dis'canon**, *v. Obs. rare.* [f. DIS- 7 c + CANON *sb.*] *trans.* To exclude from the canon.

1608 *2nd Pt. Def. Reasons Refusal Subscription* 218 He acknowledgeth arguments more forcible..to discanon those bookes.

dis'canonize, *v.* [f. DIS- 6 + CANONIZE.]

† 1. *trans.* To exclude from the canon. *Obs.*

1605 SUTCLIFFE *Briefe Exam.* xviii. 87 We discanonize no book of canonicall scriptures. **1638** CHILLINGW. *Relig. Prot.* I. ii. §38. 67 Divers books must be discanoniz'd. **1660** FISHER *Rustick's Alarm* Wks. (1679) 289 Dis-Canonizing all others save such as are in your Bibles, called Canonical.

2. To undo the canonization of.

1797 W. TAYLOR in *Monthly Rev.* XXIV. 521 They are discanonizing the heroes of religion, and raising altars to the apostles of philosophy.

Hence **discanoni'zation**.

1811 SHELLEY in Dowden *Life* (1887) I. 151 The discanonisation of this saint of theirs is impossible.

discant, variant of DESCANT.

discapacitate (dɪskə'pæsɪteɪt), *v. rare.* [f. DIS- 6 + CAPACITATE.] *trans.* To deprive of capacity, to incapacitate.

1660 Z. CROFTON *Fastening Peter's Fetters* 38 Circumstances attending themselves, and discapacitating them unto the Act. **1825** LAMB *Biog. Mem. Liston* Misc. Wks. (1871) 406 An unavoidable infirmity absolutely discapacitated him for tragedy.

† **discapi'tation.** *Obs. rare.* [n. of action from Rom. *descapitare*, OF. *descapiter*, for L. *dēcapitāre*: see DE- I. 6.] = DECAPITATION.

1787 W. MARSHALL *Norfolk* II. 332 Whether it be a universal faculty belonging to flies..to live in a state of discapitation.

discard (dɪ'skɑːd), *v.* [f. DIS- 7 c + CARD *sb.*; cf. OF. *descarter* (see DECARD); Sp., Pg. *descartar* (Minsheu 1599), It. *scartare* (for **discartare*) 'to discard at cards' (Florio 1598).] *trans.*

1. *Cards.* To throw out or reject (a card) from the hand. Also *absol.*

In whist, etc., applied to the action of playing a card from one of the two remaining suits when not able to follow the lead and not trumping.

1591 FLORIO *2nd Fruites* 69 Let vs agree of our game..goe to, discarde. **1680** COTTON *Gamester* in Singer *Hist. Cards* 265 By discarding the eights, nines, and tens, there will remain thirteen cards. **1744** HOYLE *Piquet* 49 After he has discarded he cannot alter his discard. **1816** SINGER *Hist. Cards* 238 The player..discards three inferior cards. **1862** CAVENDISH *Whist* (1879) 93 You weaken a suit by discarding from it. **1870** HARDY & WARE *Mod. Hoyle, Whist* 8.

2. To cast off, cast aside, reject, abandon, give up.

1598 FLORIO, *Dare nelle scartate*..to fall among ill companie, as a man would say among such as are discarded from others. **1603** HOLLAND *Plutarch's Mor.* 1206, I was very much angry and offended that I was so discarded and left out. **1662** J. DAVIES tr. *Olearius' Voy. Ambass.* 81 Sentiments of shame and honesty..are quite discarded by the Muscovites. **1727** SWIFT *Let. on Eng. Tongue* Wks. 1755 II. I. 191 Many gross improprieties, which however authorised by practice..ought to be discarded. **1764** REID *Inquiry* ii. §6. 109 They discarded all secondary qualities of bodies. **1802** MAR. EDGEWORTH *Moral T.* (1816) I. x. 87 He had displeased his friends, and had been discarded in disgrace. **1856** SIR B. BRODIE *Psychol. Inq.* I. i. 25 We have ..discarded our faith in astrology and witches. **1878** HUXLEY *Physiogr.* 200 It is generally so warm that the miners are glad to discard most of their clothing.

† b. To cast or force away (*from* another). *rare.*

1596 SPENSER *F.Q.* V. v. 8 He that helpe [i.e. her shield] from her against her will discarded.

† c. To divest, rid, or free (any one) *of*; also *refl. Obs. rare.*

1656 S. HOLLAND *Zara* (1719) 73 The more peaceful Souls [are] discarded of their Anxieties. **1732** *Gentleman Instructed* (ed. 10) 293 (D.), I only discard myself of those things that are noxious. *Ibid.* 492 (D.) The old man's avarice discarded him of all the sentiments of a parent.

3. To dismiss from employment, service, or office; to cashier, discharge.

a **1586** SIDNEY (J.), These men..were discarded by that unworthy prince, as not worthy the holding. **1688** LUTTRELL *Brief Rel.* (1857) I. 472 A soldier haveing spoken base words..was whipt, and the next day..dis-carded. **1712** SWIFT *Jrnl. to Stella* 9 Jan., My man..is a sad dog; and the minute I come to Ireland I will discard him. **1858** BUCKLE *Civiliz.* (1873) II. viii. 573 Having discarded the able advisers of his father, he conferred the highest posts upon men as narrow and incompetent as himself.

† b. With double object: To dismiss or banish (a person) from (a place). *Obs.*

1650 W. BROUGH *Sacr. Princ.* (1659) 66 Lest I be disgraced and discarded Thy Palace and Presence for ever. **1670** WALTON *Lives* I. 48 A Person of Nobility..was at this very time discarded the Court, and justly committed to prison.

di'scard, *sb.* [f. prec. vb.]

1. *Cards.* a. The act of discarding or rejecting a card from the hand. b. The card so rejected.

1744 [see DISCARD *v.* 1.] **1778** C. JONES *Hoyle's Games Impr., Piquet* 119 In order to capot the Elder-hand, you are to make a deep Discard, such as the Queen, Ten, and Eight of a Suit. **1876** A. CAMPBELL-WALKER *Correct Card* Gloss., *Discard*, the card you play when you cannot follow suit, and do not trump it. **1878** H. H. GIBBS *Ombre* 22 Having placed his discard on the pool dish, he takes from the Stock a number equal to his discard. **1885** PROCTOR *Whist* viii. 92 Your original discard indicates your shortest suit if trump strength is not declared against you.

c. *gen.* The fact of being discarded; dismissal. Also, the act of dismissing or abandoning.

1782 L. L. DALRYMPLE *Jrnl.* 12 Oct. in E. V. Mason *Jrnl. Young Lady Virginia* (1871) 29 Nancy had an admirer lately. .. He got his discard yesterday. **1906** *Daily Chron.* 29 Sept. 5/4 'The Chief's' sudden discard of South Africa and adoption of Protection under the name of Tariff Reform.

2. a. That which is discarded, an offcast.

1892 STEVENSON *Across the Plains* 297 In the brothel the discard of society. **1926** *Jrnl. Iron & Steel Inst.* CXIII. 76 The charts show the results of the analyses..throughout the section of the ingot, after the removal of the top and bottom end discards. **1943** E. H. THOMPSON *A.L.A. Gloss. Library Terms* 47/2 *Discard*, a book officially withdrawn from a library collection because it is unfit for further use or is no longer needed. **1949** R. T. ROLFE *Dict. Metallogr.* (ed. 2) 62 *Crop, crop end or discard*, the end (or ends) of an ingot cut off and discarded, as containing the central pipe or other defects. **1955** W. W. DENLINGER *Complete Boston* II. 65 The litter should be looked over carefully for possible defectives and discards. **1967** *Times Rev. Industry* Aug. 36/1 Using the discard of coal preparation plants to make lightweight concrete or building blocks.

b. Fig. phr. *(in)to the discard*: into oblivion or disuse.

1905 *Smart Set* Oct. 14/1 I'm much obliged to the lady; but she goes to the discard, too. **1927** H. E. FOSDICK *Pilgr. Palestine* 260 One surely does not mean to sweep into the discard as spiritually futile the elaborate symbolism of Eastern worship. **1944** J. S. HUXLEY *Living in Revol.* ii. 27 The old concept of economic man has gone into the discard.

discarded (dɪ'skɑːdɪd), *ppl. a.* [f. DISCARD *v.* + -ED[1].]

1. *Cards.* Thrown out from the hand.

a **1631** DONNE *Serm.* xxxviii. 377 We have seen in our age Kings discarded and..the discarded Cards taken in againe and win the Game. **1816** SINGER *Hist. Cards* 239 The dealer for whom the discarded cards count.

2. Cast off, rejected; dismissed from employment, discharged.

1595 SHAKS. *John* V. iv. 12 Welcome home againe discarded faith. **1718** *Freethinker* No. 76 ¶ 2 A discarded Servant has it in his power to dishonour his Master or Mistress. **1849** MACAULAY *Hist. Eng.* II. 13 The wisdom and virtue of the discarded statesman. **1875** JOWETT *Plato* I. 69 We have again fallen into the old discarded error.

discarder (dɪ'skɑːdə(r)). [f. as prec. + -ER[1].] One who discards or rejects.

1880 BURTON *Q. Anne* II. x. 158 That eccentric discarder of conventionalities.

† **di'scardinate**, *v. Obs.* [f. DIS- 6 + L. *cardinem* hinge + -ATE[3]: cf. L. *cardināt-us* hinged.] *trans.* To unhinge.

1652 BENLOWES *Theoph.* V. xviii, Canst Motion fix? count Sands?..Discardinate The Sphears?

discarding (dɪ'skɑːdɪŋ), *vbl. sb.* [f. DISCARD *v.* + -ING[1].] The action of the verb DISCARD.

1. *Cards.* The rejection or throwing out of a card from the hand. Also *attrib.*

1593 PEELE *Chron. Edw. I* (1829) I. 129 Since the King hath put us among the discarding cards, and as it were turned us with deuces and treys out of the deck. 1594 CAREW *Huarte's Exam. Wits* viii. (1596) 112 To know..the skill of discarding. 1778 C. JONES *Hoyle's Games Impr., Piquet* 119 By which Manner of discarding, you have a Probability of scoring fifteen Points for your Quint in Diamonds.

2. Rejection, abandonment; dismissal from employment, discharge. In quot. 1840 *concr.* That which is discarded.

1660 T. M. *Hist. Independ.* IV. 55 A hot-spur zealot.. whose ambition made old Nol lay him aside as dangerous, and that dishonourable discarding created him a desperate Enemy to the Cromwelian..name. 1663 J. SPENCER *Prodigies* (1665) 306 The discarding of that rash Principle. 1840 BROWNING *Sordello* VI. 444 Then subject..to thy cruce the world's discardings.

di'scardment. *rare.* [f. DISCARD *v.* + -MENT.] The action of discarding; rejection, abandonment.

1844 *N. Brit. Rev.* I. 395 Their discardment by the Hindus as religious authorities.

†**di'scardure.** *Obs. rare.* [f. DISCARD *v.* + -URE.] = prec.

1780 HAYTER *Hume's Dial* II. 38 In what shape does it constitute a plea for the entire discardure of religion?

discare: see DIS- 9.

discarg, -carge, obs. var. DISCHARGE.

†**di'scarnate**, *a.* [ad. late L. type *discarnāt-us (for L. *dē-carnāt-us*: see DE- I. 6), f. DIS- 4 + *carn-em* flesh, *carnāt-us* fleshy; cf. It. *(di)scarnato*, Sp. *descarnado*, OF. *descarné*, mod.F. *décharné*.]

†1. Stripped of flesh. *Obs. rare.*

1661 GLANVILL *Van. Dogm.* 143 A memory, like a sepulchre, furnished with a load of broken and discarnate bones.

2. Divested of the flesh or the body, disembodied.

1895 *Westm. Gaz.* 5 Nov. 2/3 Any *à priori* belief in a discarnate existence of one's personality. *a* 1901 MYERS *Hum. Pers.* (1903) II. 274 We cannot simply admit the existence of discarnate spirits as inert or subsidiary phenomena. 1901 J. H. HYSLOP in *Proc. Soc. Psychical Research* XVI. 216 We ought to expect *a priori* that a discarnate memory should be defective in its communications from a transcendental world. 1920 *Public Opinion* 9 July 34/3 It is rash to claim that a given phenomenon..must..be due to discarnate influences. 1922 E. PHILLPOTTS *Grey Room* iv. 106 This death-dealing ghost, or discarnate but conscious being.

So †**di'scarnated** *ppl. a.*, deprived of 'flesh' or bodily form, disembodied: the reverse of *incarnated*; *Obs.* **discar'nation**, disembodiment.

1728 EARBERY tr. *Burnet's St. Dead* I. 66 Jesus went thro' all, for he went to the Region of Humane Souls, and being discarnated, he was a living rational Soul, like to a humane one. 1901 *Contemp. Rev.* Aug. 221 The discarnation of personality in death.

†**dis'carve**, *v. Obs. rare.* [f. DIS- 1 + CARVE.] To dissect.

1541 R. COPLAND *Guydon's Quest. Chirurg.*, Procede in dyscaruynge almoste vnto yleon where as the gut begynneth that hyght Collon.

discase (dɪs'keɪs), *v. arch.* [f. DIS- 7 a + CASE *sb.*] *trans.* To remove the case or covering of; to uncase, unsheathe, undress. Also *intr.* (=*refl.*)

Hence **dis'cased** *ppl. a.*

1596 BELL *Surv. Popery* I. III. ii. 97 Fell upon his discased sword. 1610 SHAKS. *Temp.* v. i. 85 Fetch me the Hat, and Rapier in my Cell, I will dicase me, and my selfe present As I was sometime Millaine. 1825 LAMB *Reflect. Pillory*, Discase not, I pray you. 1882 B. NICHOLSON in *New Shaks. Soc. Trans.* (1880–2) 343 Having discased himself of his doublet and vest.

†**dis'cask**, *v. Obs. rare.* [f. DIS- 7 c + CASK.] *trans.* To take out of the cask.

1615 G. SANDYS *Trav.* 239 No Tunny is suffered to be sold at Venice, vnlesse first discaskt, and searcht to the bottome.

discaste (dɪs'kɑːst, -æ-), *v. nonce-wd.* [f. DIS- 7 c + CASTE.] *trans.* To cause to lose caste.

1881 *Sat. Rev.* No. 1323. 318 With the deliberate and formal purpose of discasting idolators.

discastle: see DIS- 7 c.

di'scatter, *v. Obs.* Also 4 deskater, 5 descater, 8 dis-scatter. [In ME. *de-scater*, f. F. *de-, des-* (DE- 6, DIS- 1) + SCATTER; the prefix being subsequently conformed to L. *dis-, di-*.] *trans.* To scatter abroad, disperse. Hence **discattered** *ppl. a.*

c 1325 *Poem Times Edw. II*, 315 in *Pol. Songs* (Camden) 337 Hit is so diskatered bothe hider and thidere. 1496 *Dives & Paup.* (W. de W.) v. viii. 206 Woo be to the shepeherdes that thus descateren..the flocke. 1597 DANIEL *Civ. Wars* VI. lxxvi, The broken remnants of discattered [*ed.* 1717 dis-scattered] power. 1613–8 DANIEL *Coll. Hist. Eng.* (1626) 32 Petty revolts made by discattered troupes. 1635 BRATHWAIT *Arcad. Pr.* II. 43, I begunne to recollect my discatered senses.

disceas(e, -cees, etc., obs. ff. DECEASE, DISEASE.

disceat, -ceipte, -ceit, obs. ff. DECEIT.

disceaue, -ceiue, etc., obs. ff. DECEIVE, etc.

†**di'scede**, *v. Obs.* [ad. L. *discēd-ĕre* to separate, depart, f. DIS- 1 + *cēdĕre* to go.] *intr.* To depart, deviate. (Usually *fig.*) Hence **di'sceding** *vbl. sb.*

1650 BULWER *Anthropomet.* 247 They who onely discede from this exact rule. 1665 HOOKE *Microgr.* 30 One part of the said Cork would approach and make toward the stick, whereas another would discede and fly away. *Ibid.* 36 This Disceding of the heat in glass drops by the..cooling Irradiations.

discede, obs. (bad) form of DECIDE.

discence, discend, etc., obs. ff. DESCENCE, DESCEND, etc.

discension, -tion, obs. ff. DESCENSION, DISSENSION.

discent, obs. var. of DESCEND.

1612 W. PARKES *Curtaine-Dr.* (1876) 14 If any vice arise from the Court..it immediately discents to the Cittie. 1659 MACALLO *Can. Physick* 37 The wandering discenting pains.

discent, obs. form of DESCENT, DISSENT.

discept (dɪ'sɛpt), *v. rare.* [ad. L. *discept-āre* to contend, debate, decide, determine, f. *dis-* (DIS- 2, 3) + *captāre* to try to catch, catch at, strive after, etc.] *intr.* To dispute, debate; to express disagreement or difference of opinion, to 'differ'.

1652 GAULE *Magastrom.* 27 It is God that thus discepts with you. 1818 T. L. PEACOCK *Nightmare Abbey* xi. 150 Permit me to discept. 1855 BROWNING *Master Hugues of Saxe-Gotha* xiv, One dissertates, he is candid; Two must discept,—has distinguished; Three helps the couple, if ever yet man did. 1868 —— *Ring & Bk.* x. 1350, I try it with my reason, nor discept From any point I probe and pronounce sound.

discept, obs. form of DECEIT.

disceptation (dɪsɛp'teɪʃən). *arch.* Also 4–7 decept-, 6 dyscept-, 6–7 descept-, 7- dissept-, 4–6 -acio(u)n. [a. F. *disceptation* (14th c. in Godef.), ad. L. *disceptātiōn-em*, n. of action f. *disceptāre*: see DISCEPT.] Disputation, debate, discussion.

1382 WYCLIF *Rom.* xiv. 1 Take ȝe a syk man in bileue, not in deceptaciouns [*Gloss.* or dispeticiouns] of thouȝtis. 1529 MORE *Dyaloge* III. Wks. 203/1 Our formar dysceptacion and reasonyng, had betwene vs before his departyng. 1602 FULBECKE *Pandectes* 15 The Emperour..did cause a.. generall assemblie of estates to be held for the disceptation, and deciding of this doubt. 1670 WALTON *Lives* Wks. 1793 I. 65 These unhappy disceptations between Hooker and Travers. 1755 MAGENS *Insurances* II. 565 Such Controversy shall be decided by the Arbitration of good and honest Men ..who shall decide the Affair in such Manner as that no Damage may happen to the Owner during the Time of Disceptation. 1833 SIR W. HAMILTON *Discuss.* (1852) 118 Their subtlety in philosophical disceptations.

†**discep'tatious**, *a. Obs. rare.* [f. prec.: see -OUS.] Disputatious; controversial.

1682 D'URFEY *Butler's Ghost* 99 Buzzing Whimseys warm'd the Addle Part of his disceptatious Noddle.

†**discep'tator.** *Obs. rare.* [a. L. *disceptātor*, agent-n. f. *disceptāre* to debate, DISCEPT.] A disputer, debater, controversialist.

1623 COCKERAM, *Disceptator*, a Iudge in a matter. 1656 BLOUNT *Glossogr.*, *Disceptator*..also he that argues or disputes. 1675 J. SMITH *Chr. Relig. Appeal* I. 29 The inquisitive disceptators of this Age..who with their altercation and Ergo's had turned out of their Creed the Amen of their Progenitors.

†**discepta'torial**, *a. Obs. rare.* [f. L. type *disceptātōri-us (f. *disceptātor*: see prec.) + -AL¹.] Pertaining to disputation or controversy.

1810 BENTHAM *Packing* (1821) 141 What with ratiocinatory, or at least disceptatorial cunctation.

†**di'sception.** *Obs. rare.* Erroneous form of DISCEPTATION.

1492 *Act. Dom. Conc.* 298 (Jam.) For the discepcione of the Kingis leigis be aulde summondis.

disceptre, var. of DIS-SCEPTRE *v.*

†**di'scerebrate**, *v. Obs.* [f. DIS- 6 + L. *cerebr-um* brain + -ATE³. Cf. *decerebrize*.] *trans.* To deprive of the brain; to disbrain.

1654 GAYTON *Pleas. Notes* III. viii. 121 For the discerebrating of his Knights head.

discern (dɪ'zɜːn, now usu. dɪ'sɜːn), *v.* Also 4 disserne, 4–7 discerne, 5–6 des-, dyscerne, 6 dysserne. See also DECERN. [a. F. *discerner*, in OF. also *disserner* (13th c. in Hatz.-Darm.), ad. L. *discern-ĕre* to separate, distinguish, determine, f. DIS- 1 + *cernĕre* to separate. In early times sometimes confused with DECERN, which in OF. also appears as *descerner*.]

†1. *trans.* To separate (things, or one thing *from* another) as distinct; to distinguish and divide.

c 1430 LYDG. *Min. Poems* (1840) 87 (Mätz.) Pictagoras.. Fonde first out .y., a figure to discerne Theyre lyff here short, and lyff that is eterne. 1533 MORE *Answ. Poysoned Bk.* Wks. 1050/2 Our sauiour would not discerne & deuide fayth from the woorke, but sayth that the faith it selfe was the woorke of god. 1549 COVERDALE *Erasm. Par. 1 John* 48 It is not the sacramentes that discerne the children of God from the children of the devyll; but the puritie of lyfe, and charitie. 1614 R. TAILOR *Hog hath lost Pearl* IV. in Hazl. *Dodsley* XI. 481 That precious gem of reason, by which solely We are discern'd from rude and brutish beasts. 1645 USSHER *Body Div.* 39 That so he might be discerned from all things created. For nothing is like unto God.

2. To recognize as distinct; to distinguish or separate mentally (one thing *from* another); to perceive the difference between (things). *arch.*

1483 CAXTON *G. de la Tour* H iv, By the knowyng of it they shalle..discerne the good fro the euyll. 1551 T. WILSON *Logike* (1580) 20 b, To discerne the truthe from that whiche is false. 1579 FULKE *Heskins' Parl.* 363 If we discern the two testaments, the promises are not the same. 1611 BIBLE *2 Sam.* xiv. 17 As an Angel of God, so is my lord the king to discerne good and bad. 1727–38 GAY *Fables* I. x, Can he discern the different natures? 1834 J. H. NEWMAN *Paroch. Serm.* I. xvii. 257 Like men who have lost the faculty of discerning colours. 1837–9 HALLAM *Hist. Lit.* IV. iv. IV. §38. 172 We discern good from evil by the understanding. 1886 RUSKIN *Præterita* I. vi. 199 Not having yet the taste to discern good Gothic from bad.

3. *intr.* To perceive or recognize the difference or distinction; to make a distinction; to distinguish or discriminate *between*. *arch.*

13.. *E.E. Allit. P.* C. 513 Wymmen..þat..Bitwene þe stele and þe stayre disserne noȝt cunen. *c* 1400 MAUNDEV. (Roxb.) xxii. 103 Þai..can discerne betwix gude and euill. 1535 COVERDALE *Ezek.* xxii. 26 They put no dyfference betwene the holy and vnholy, nether discerne betwene the clene and vnclene. 1651 HOBBES *Leviath.* II. xix. 97 One that cannot discerne between Good and Evill. 1711 ADDISON *Spect.* No. 255. ¶5 Some Men cannot discern between a noble and a mean Action. 1841 MYERS *Cath. Th.* III. §5. 18 The spiritual mind..discerns and separates between the things which differ in excellence.

4. *trans.* To distinguish (one thing or fact) by the intellect; to recognize or perceive distinctly. (With simple obj., or clause expressing a proposition.)

13.. *Cursor M.* 15066 (Gött.) Cum nu forth vr sauueour, we haue discernd [3 *MSS.* desired] þe, þu es right king of israel, qua sum þe soth can se. *c* 1386 CHAUCER *Knt.'s T.* 2145 Than may men wel by this ordre discerne, That thilke moevere stabul is and eterne. 1529 MORE *Dyaloge* I. Wks. 164/2 If..ye coude not make your audience to discerne the truthe. 1641 WILKINS *Math. Magick* I. vi. (1648) 41 Hence also may wee discerne the reason why [etc.]. 1667 MILTON *P.L.* I. 326 His swift pursuers from Heav'n Gates discern Th' advantage. 1679 L. ADDISON *First State of Mahumedism* 126 If we look into the condition of Christianity..at the time ..we shall discern it miserably shaken and convuls'd. 1736 BUTLER *Anal.* I. v. 124 We do not discern how food and sleep contribute to the growth of the body. 1850 TENNYSON *In Mem.* lxviii, I wake, and I discern the truth. 1861 M. PATTISON *Ess.* I. 33 Incapable of discerning where their true interest lay.

b. *intr.* or *absol.*

c 1374 CHAUCER *Troylus* III. Prol. 9 (Harl.) In heuene and helle and erthe and salte se Is felt þi myght If þat I wol descerne. 1581 MULCASTER *Positions* iii. 9 Which skill to discern so narrowly..is not in all. 1728 YOUNG *Love Fame* iv. (1757) 110 Compton, born o'er senates to preside, Deep to discern, and widely to survey.

c. *intr.* To have cognizance, to judge *of*.

a 1622 BACON *Hen. VII*, Wks. (1860) 353 This court of Star-chamber..discerneth..of forces, frauds, crimes various of stellionate, and the inchoations..towards crimes capital..not actually committed. 1633 BP. HALL *Hard Texts, N.T.* 135 Is there nobody, thinkest thou, that can discerne of truth, but thou and thy followers? *a* 1649 WINTHROP *New Eng.* (1853) I. 380 The magistrates.. discerned of the offence clothed with all these circumstances.

5. *trans.* To distinguish (an object) with the eyes; to see or perceive by express effort of the powers of vision; to 'make out' by looking, descry, behold.

c 1386 CHAUCER *Knt.'s T.* 1131 Wyndowe..was ther noon, Thurgh which men myghten any light discerne. 1548 HALL *Chron., Rich. III*, 50 A bekon wᵗ a greate lanterne.. which maie be sene and discerned a great space of. 1653 H. COGAN tr. *Pinto's Trav.* v. 12 The smoak was..so thick, as we could hardly discern one another. 1732 BERKELEY *Alciphr.* I. §10 The best eyes are necessary to discern the minutest objects. 1842 TENNYSON *Lord of Burleigh* 42 Till a gateway she discerns With armorial bearings stately. 1860 TYNDALL *Glac.* II. xvii. 317 We could discern no trace of rupture [in the ice].

†b. *intr.* or *absol. Obs. rare.*

c 1384 CHAUCER *H. Fame* II. 401 (*Fairf. & Bodl.* MSS.) Or elles was the aire so thikke That y ne myght[e] not discerne [*Caxt.* that I myght it not decerne]. *a* 1649 WINTHROP *New Eng.* (1853) II. 72 It was frozen also to sea so far as one could well discern. *Ibid.* II. 81 There was such a precipice as they could scarce discern to the bottom.

c. *trans.* To distinguish or perceive distinctly by other senses. *rare.*

1578 BANISTER *Hist. Man* v. 71 Sundry portions of sinewes..scattered onely to discerne annoyaunce at any tyme offred. 1863 GEO. ELIOT *Romola* I. x, His ear discerned a distressed childish voice crying.

¶6. Formerly sometimes used for DECERN.

1494 FABYAN *Chron.* VII. 549 We..pronounce, dyscerne and declare, the same kynge Rycharde..to be..vnable.. and vnworthy to the rule and gouernaunce of the foresayd realmys. 1533 COVERDALE *Lord's Supper* Wks. (Parker Soc.) I. 449 It pertaineth not to every private person to judge and discern, who ought to be admitted. 1563 FOXE *A. & M.* 770 b, We do..discerne, deme, and iudge the same to be committed to yᵉ..custodye of such person or persons as his maiesty shall apoynte. 1596 DALRYMPLE tr. *Leslie's Hist. Scot.* I. 66 That, quhilke Ptolomie discernet to be among the hindmost Iles of Schytland.

discern (dɪˈzɜːn), *sb. rare*⁻¹. [f. DISCERN *v.*] The act of discerning; discernment, perception.
1830 W. PHILLIPS *Mt. Sinai* II. 582 Afront was stationed, facile of discern, An orb immiscible of mist profound.

discernable, var. of DISCERNIBLE.

†**di'scernance.** *Obs.* [f. DISCERN *v.* + -ANCE: perh. from a French original.]
1. Distinction, difference.
1592 NASHE *P. Penilesse* (ed. 2) 36b, Those bodies..are distinguisht by no difference of sex, because they are simple; and the discernance of sex belongs to bodies compound.
2. Discernment, discrimination, judgement.
1612 tr. *Benvenuto's Passenger* (N.), He..manifesteth, that either he hath but a blinde discernance, or that in wisedome he is inferiour to a woman.

di'scernant. *rare.* [a. F. *discernant*, pr. pple. of *discerner* to DISCERN.] One who discerns or discriminates.
1822 SOUTHEY in *Q. Rev.* XXVIII. 35 These persons were called the discernants.

discerner (dɪˈzɜːnə(r), -s-). [f. DISCERN *v.* + -ER[1].] One who or that which discerns, discriminates, or perceives: see the verb.
1526 *Pilgr. Perf.* (W. de W. 1531) 274 To be vynteners, discerners, and tasters of the same. **1539** CRANMER *Heb.* iv. 12 The worde of God..is a discerner of the thoughtes and of the intentes of the herte. **1613** SHAKS. *Hen. VIII*, I. i. 32 'Twas said they saw but one, and no Discerner Durst wagge his Tongue in censure. **1712** STEELE *Spect.* No. 515 ¶2, I am too nice a Discerner to laugh at any, but whom most other People think fine Fellows. **1875** JOWETT *Plato* (ed. 2) I. 292 Discerners of characters..who would have known our future great men.

discernible (dɪˈzɜːnɪb(ə)l, -s-), *a.* Also 6–8 discernable, (7 discerneable, decerneable). [orig. a. F. *discernable*, f. *discerner*; after middle of 17th c. conformed to the L. form *discernibilis*, f. *discernĕre* to DISCERN: see -BLE.]
1. Capable of being discerned; perceptible: **a.** by the sight: Visible, that can be descried.
1561 T. NORTON *Calvin's Inst.* I. Pref., If the godly hadde then sought any discernable forme with their eies. **1597** HOOKER *Tract. & Serm.* in *Eccl. Pol.* v. lxvii. (1617) 363 When I behold with mine eyes some small scarce discernable Graine or Seed. **1652–62** HEYLIN *Cosmogr.* II. (1682) 112 The Cathedral easily discernable by Mariners as they sail along. **1748** *Anson's Voy.* I. v. 43 It is scarce discernible at the distance of ten leagues. **1866** GEO. ELIOT *F. Holt* ii, There was the slightest possible quiver discernible across Jermyn's face.
b. by other senses. *rare.*
1665 HOOKE *Microgr.* 212 Nor did it cause the least discernable pain. **1684–5** BOYLE *Min. Waters* 83, I did not find..the Purging Springs..to have any discernible Acidity. **1794** G. ADAMS *Nat. & Exp. Philos.* II. xiii. 67 A discernible weight. **1866** GEO. ELIOT *F. Holt* xxx, The buzz and tread and the fitfully discernible voices.
c. by the understanding.
1620 SANDERSON *Serm.* I. 142 Hypocrisie is spun of a fine thred, and is not easily discernable, without very diligent examination. **1660** JER. TAYLOR *Duct. Dubit.* I. v. rule iv. §1 When we are in a perceiued, discernible state of danger. **1754** EDWARDS *Freed. Will* I. iv. (ed. 4) 32 That discernible and obvious course of events. **1863** E. V. NEALE *Anal. Th. & Nat.* 181 Under all their differences there would be discernible a principle of unity.
†**2.** Distinguishable (*from* something else). *Obs.* (Cf. DISCERN *v.* 2.)
1601 R. JOHNSON *Kingd. & Commw.* (1603) 2 If..any man affirme that true Judgement cannot be severed from true valour, yet ordinarily the one doth appeere more discernable from the other in divers subjects. **1670** WALTON *Lives* III. 220 He never [laboured]..to get glory to himself; but glory only to God: which intention, he would often say, was as discernable in a Preacher, as a Natural from an Artificial beauty.
†**3.** *actively.* Capable of discerning. *Obs. rare.*
1603 DANIEL *Panegyric to King* lxvii, God..Hath..framed thy heart Discernable of all apparencies.
Hence **di'scernibleness**, the quality of being discernible.
1727 BAILEY vol. II, *Discernibleness*, visibleness. **1881** J. CAIRNS *Unbelief 18th C.* vi. 270 The concession he makes as to the discernibleness of Creation. **1890** J. H. STIRLING *Gifford Lect.* ix. 160 Discernibleness involves negation. We should not know what warmth is, were there no cold.

discernibly (dɪˈzɜːnɪblɪ, -s-), *adv.* Also 7 -ably. [f. prec. + -LY[2].] In a discernible manner or degree; perceptibly.
1643 T. GOODWIN *Trial Christian's Growth* 67 Christians doe not grow discernably till after some space. **1669** W. SIMPSON *Hydrol. Chym.* 364 Its taste is more discernably nitrous. **1736** BUTLER *Anal.* I. iii. Wks. 1874 I. 48 Whether ..a righteous government be not discernibly planned out. **1766** LEE in *Phil. Trans.* LVI. 103 The filtered liquors were not discernibly different in colour and taste. **1839** FOSTER in *Life & Corr.* (1846) II. 368 Revealed discernibly through the solemn mystery.

discerning (dɪˈzɜːnɪŋ, -s-), *vbl. sb.* [f. DISCERN *v.* + -ING[1].] The action of the verb DISCERN (q.v.); distinction, discrimination; intellectual perception, discernment.
1509 HAWES *Past. Pleas.* XXIV. I, By the inwarde wyttes to have decernynge. **1526** *Pilgr. Perf.* (W. de W. 1531) 123b, The discernynge of true reuelacyons..from false illusyons. **1644** MILTON *Judgm. Bucer* Wks. 1738 I. 275 If it be in man's discerning to sever Providence from Chance. **1711** STEELE *Spect.* No. 149 ¶4 If they are Men of discerning, they can observe the Motives of your Heart. **1822** T. MITCHELL *Aristoph.* I. 85 It asks not his nicer discerning To observe [etc.].

discerning, *ppl. a.* [f. as prec. + -ING[2].] That discerns (see the verb); distinguishing, discriminating, perceiving; *esp.* (of persons or their minds, etc.) Having or showing discernment; quick in intellectual perception; penetrating.
1608 D. T. *Ess. Pol. & Mor.* 49b, Directed..by a better discerning wisdom. **1680–3** SOAME & DRYDEN tr. *Boileau's Art of Poetry* III. 801 A glance, a touch, discovers to the wise; But every man has not discerning eyes. **1711** ADDISON *Spect.* No. 261 ¶9 Before Marriage we cannot be too inquisitive and discerning in the Faults of the Person beloved. **1781** COWPER *Conversation* 373 True modesty is a discerning grace, And only blushes in the proper place. **1840** MACAULAY *Ess., Clive* (1854) 531/2 Every discerning and impartial judge will admit, that there was really nothing in common.
†**b.** Separating, dividing: cf. DISCERN *v.* I. *Obs.*
1660 JER. TAYLOR *Worthy Commun.* ii. §1. 119 Are we improved by the purification of the discerning flames?

di'scerningly, *adv.* [f. prec. + -LY[2].] In a discerning manner; with discernment.
1634 M. SANDYS *Prudence* 74 (T.) Memory discerningly and distinctly reverts unto things. **1717** GARTH *Pref. Ovid* (1810) 419 These two errours Ovid has most discerningly avoided. **1850** KINGSLEY *Alt. Locke* Pref. (1879) 99 That they may judge discerningly and charitably of their fellow-men. **1866** GEO ELIOT *F. Holt* v, Here his large eyes looked discerningly through the spectacles.

discernment (dɪˈzɜːnmənt, -s-). [f. DISCERN *v.* + -MENT. Cf. F. *discernement* (17th c. in Hatz.-Darm.).]
1. a. The act of discerning or perceiving by the intellect; intellectual perception or apprehension.
168. in Somers *Tracts* II. 340 Leading me to a right Discernment of the present Condition into which we are now brought. **1729** BUTLER *Serm.* Wks. 1874 II. 174 Reason tends to and rests in the discernment of truth. **1875** JOWETT *Plato* (ed. 2) IV. 277 The savage..has a quicker discernment of the track than the civilized man. **1882** FARRAR *Early Chr.* II. 536 A power of critical discernment.
b. The faculty of discerning; discrimination, judgement; keenness of intellectual perception; penetration, insight.
1586 [see DECERNMENT, s.v. DECERN]. **1646** SIR T. BROWNE *Pseud. Ep.* I. iii. 9 Things invisible, but unto intellectuall discernments. **1781** GIBBON *Decl. & F.* II. xlvi. 726 His discernment was expressed in the choice of this important post. **1875** MANNING *Mission H. Ghost* vii. 177 The eye of the soul acquires a discernment whereby some can instantly read the characters of others.
†**2.** The act of distinguishing; a distinction. *Obs.* (Cf. DISCERN *v.* 2.)
1586 A. DAY *Eng. Secretary* II. (1625) 107 But that touching the difference of counsels, or tender of his life, should make a discernement. **1648** W. MOUNTAGUE *Devout Ess.* I. x. §4 (R.) It is not practicable, to frame rules for the discernment between due praises and flatteries.
3. Perception by the senses; distinguishing by sight, distinct vision. ? *Obs.* (Cf. DISCERN *v.* 5.)
1727 *Philip Quarll* 6 Being come within reach of plain Discernment.

discerp (dɪˈsɜːp), *v.* Now *rare.* Pa. t. and pple. discerped, discerpt. [ad. L. *discerp-ĕre* to tear in pieces, f. DIS- 1 + *carpĕre* to pick, pluck, etc. Cf. EXCERP. The pa. pple. *discerpt* rests, partly at least, on the L. pa. pple. *discerpt-us.*]
1. *trans.* To pluck or tear asunder, pull to pieces; *fig.* to divide forcibly into parts or fragments, to dismember.
1482 *Monk of Evesham* (Arb.) 51 The cruelle..wodnes of wykyd spirytys the whiche al to bete me discerpte me..and al to brend me. **1567** MAPLET *Gr. Forest* 28 Being once so discerped [they] can neuer after neither in applying their owne parts togither, neither yet in fastning..them to any body..reuiue and quicken againe. **1668** H. MORE *Div. Dial.* IV. xxxiii. (1713) 385 This Horn..is the Roman Empire discerped into so many Kingdoms. **1682** —— *Annot. Glanvill's Lux O.* 182 It is no derogation to his Omnipotence that he cannot discerp a Spirit once created.
2. To pluck or tear off, sever (*from* a whole).
1655 H. MORE *Antid. Ath.* (1662) 173, There is no means ..to discerp or separate any one ray of this Orbe, and keep it apart by it self. **1778** APTHORPE *Preval. Chr.* 311 His principle was, that the human soul, discerped from the soul of the universe, after death was re-fused into the parent-substance. **1845** T. COOPER *Purgatory Suicides* (1877) 115 The Soul Lived consciously discerpt from her clay shrine. **1869** BARING-GOULD *Origin Belief* (1878) I. xii. 247 Infinite space may have parts in it discerped, and the interval subdivided.

†**di'scerpible,** *a. Obs.* [ad. L. type **discerpibilis*, f. *discerpĕre*: see prec., and cf. *discernible*. Later supplanted by *discerptible*.]
= DISCERPTIBLE.
1655 H. MORE *Antid. Ath.* (1662) 150 One part is not separable or discerpible from another, but the intire Substance..is indivisible. **1661** GLANVILL *Van. Dogm.* 51 What is most dense and least porous, will be most coherent and least discerpible. **1720** *Bibliotheca Biblica* I. 435 A Vapour, or a Fluid Discerpible Substance.
Hence †**discerpi'bility,** †**di'scerpibleness** = DISCERPTIBILITY.
1682 H. MORE *Annot. Glanvill's Lux O.* 220 In Fire, no doubt the Discerpibility is yet harder. **1722** WOLLASTON *Relig. Nat.* v. 74 A natural discerpibility and susceptivity of various shapes. **1727** BAILEY vol. II, *Discerpibleness*, capableness or aptness to be pulled in Pieces.

discerpt, pa. pple. of DISCERP *v.*, q.v.

†**discerpted,** *ppl. a. Obs.* [f. L. *discerpt-us*, pa. pple. of *discerpĕre* to DISCERP + -ED[1] 2. Cf. *excerpt* vb.] Plucked or torn asunder, divided, separated.
1607 J. KING *Serm.* Nov. 4 Manie a thousand discerpted limme. **1631** J. BURGES *Answ. Rejoined* 203 A few discerpted parcells. **1633** P. ADAMS *Exp. 2 Peter* ii. 7 Dead corpses and discerpted limbs.

discerptible (dɪˈsɜːptɪb(ə)l), *a.* [f. L. *discerpt-* ppl. stem of *discerp-ĕre*: see -BLE.] Capable of being plucked asunder, or divided into parts or pieces; divisible.
1736 BUTLER *Anal.* I. i. 16 Upon supposition that they are compounded and so discerptible. **1837** J. MCCULLOCH *Attributes of God* (1843) III. 514 Not only extensible but discerptible. **1867** *Contemp. Rev.* V. 226 The soul is discerptible, and perishes with the body.
Hence **discerpti'bility,** divisibility; **di'scerptibleness** (Ash, 1775).
1755 JOHNSON, *Discerptibility*, liableness to be destroyed by disunion of parts. **1837** MCCULLOCH *Attributes of God* (1843) II. 466 Without any apparent regard to hardness, rigidity, weight, toughness, flexibility, softness, discerptibility. **1867** *Contemp. Rev.* V. 228 The attempt is made to prove the perishable quality of the soul by its discerptibility.

discerption (dɪˈsɜːpʃən). Now *rare.* [ad. L. *discerptiōn-em* (in Vulgate), n. of action from *discerp-ĕre*: see DISCERP.]
1. The action of pulling to pieces, dilaceration; *fig.* division into parts or fragments.
1647 BP. HALL *Peacemaker* (T.), Hence are churches, congregations, families, persons, torn asunder..so as the whole earth is strewed over with the woful monuments of our discerptions. **1741** COVENTRY *Phil. to Hyd.* iv. (T.) The discerpsion of Osiris's body into fourteen parts by his relentless adversary. **1844** LINGARD *Anglo-Sax. Ch.* (1858) II. xiv. 306 The discerption of his members. **1868** GLADSTONE *Juv. Mundi* ix. (1869) 373 Heracles suffers a strange discerption of individuality; for his eidolon or shade moves and speaks here, while 'he himself is at the banquet of the immortals'.
2. The action of tearing off, severance (of a part *from* a whole); *concr.* a portion torn off or severed.
1688 in Somers *Tracts* II. 242 Even the Propagation of Light is by Discerption; some Effluvia or Emanations of the enlightening Candle passing into that which is lightened. **1768–74** TUCKER *Lt. Nat.* (1852) I. 402 The discerption of souls from thence [the mundane soul] to inhabit human bodies. *Ibid.* II. 291 Supposing it could be proved, that [brutes]..are discerptions too from the general fund of spiritual substance. **1822** T. TAYLOR *Apuleius* 37 If he.. does not..restore the dead body entire, he is compelled to repair the whole of whatever has been bitten and taken from it, with discerptions from his own face.

di'scerptive, *a. rare.* [f. L. *discerpt-* ppl. stem of *discerp-ĕre* + -IVE.] Having the quality of dividing or separating; tending to pull to pieces.
18.. OGILVIE cites *N.B. Rev.*

di'scert, obs. form of DESERT *sb.*[1]
c **1330** R. BRUNNE *Chron.* (1810) 316, I herd neuer telle, for what maner discert.

discese, -cess(e, etc., obs. ff. DECEASE, DISEASE, DISSEISE.

†**discess.** *Obs. rare.* [ad. L. *discess-us* departure, f. *discēdĕre*: see DISCEDE.] Departure.
c **1380** WYCLIF *Wks.* (1880) 299 Aftir myn discess wolues of raueyn shal come [quoting *Acts* xx. 29].

†**discession.** *Obs.* Also 7 dissession. [ad. L. *discessiōn-em*, n. of action from L. *discēdĕre*: see prec.] Departure; secession; separation.
1521 FISHER *Wks.* (1876) 337 Before the comynge of antichryst there shall be a notable discession and departyng from the fayth of the chirche. **1611** SPEED *Hist. Gt. Brit.* IX. ix. §20 So vniuersall an oppression, as might cause a generall dissession from the Church of Rome. **1612–15** BP. HALL *Contempl., N.T.* IV. xv, Their slinking away (one by one) may seem to carry a shew of deliberate and voluntary discession. **1662** HOBBES *Seven Prob.* Wks. 1845 VII. 19 As you pull, the wax grows..more and more slender; there being a perpetual parting or discession of the outermost parts.

discette, var. DISKETTE.

disceue, -eyue, -eyt(e, obs. ff. DECEIVE, -CEIT.

†**di'sceyvous,** *a. Obs. rare.* [ad. OF. *deceveux* (Godefroy), in AF. **decevous*, f. *decevoir* to DECEIVE: see -OUS.] Deceptive, deceitful.
1422 tr. *Secreta Secret., Priv. Priv.* (E.E.T.S.) 217 Suche a man is lechelorus and disceyuous.

†**dis'chain,** *v. Obs.* [ad. 16th c. F. *deschainer* (mod.F. *déchaîner*), f. *des-*, DIS- 4 + *chaîner* to chain.] *trans.* To set free as from a chain; to unchain, unloose. Hence **dischained** *ppl. a.*
1598 SYLVESTER *Mathieu's Trophies Hen. IV France*, To W. Cecil 8 Henry's Death through Hell's dis-chained Rage.

1603 HOLLAND *Plutarch's Mor.* 51 Their owne irregular lusts and unordinate appetites, which now he (as it were) dischainid and let loose.

†**dis'channel**, *v. Obs.* [f. DIS- 7 c + CHANNEL *sb.*] *trans.* To turn (a stream) out of its channel; *refl.* and *intr.* to quit its channel; to discharge itself (into the sea, etc.).

1607 A. BREWER *Lingua* III. v. in Hazl. *Dodsley* IX. 394 The river Alpheus at that time pursuing his beloved Arethusa dischannelled himself of his former course. **1652–62** HEYLIN *Cosmogr.* III. (1673) 4/1 Cataractes, dischannelling into the Mediterranean. *Ibid.* III. (1682) 165 Mixt with those streams they are dischannelled in the Caspian Sea.

discharacter *v.*: see DIS- 7.

discharge (dɪs'tʃɑːdʒ), *v.* Forms: 4–6 descharge, (4–7 discarge, 5–6 dyscharge, 6 dis-, dyschardge, *Sc.* dischairge, 6–7 discharg, 7 discarg), 4– discharge. [a. OF. *descharge-r*, (mod.F. *décharger*) in 12th c. *deschargier*, ONF. *deskargier* = Pr. and Sp. *descargar*, It. (*di*)*scarcare*, *-caricare*, in med.L. *des-*, *discargāre* (12th c. in Du Cange):—late L. type **discarricāre*, f. DIS- 4 + *carricāre* to load, to CHARGE.]

I. To free, rid, or relieve *a thing* (or *person*) from that with which it is charged.

1. a. *trans.* To unload (a ship, etc.) from that with which it is charged or loaded; to rid of a charge or load; to disburden. (Also *absol.*, and *intr.* for *refl.*)

1382 WYCLIF *Acts* xxvii. 38 And thei..discargeden [*v.rr.* dischargeden, -chargiden] the schipp, castinge whete in to the see. **1481** CAXTON *Godfrey* 260 The maronners of Gene receyued them moche honorably..and discharged theyr shippes. **1513** MORE in Grafton *Chron.* (1568) II. 765 No man unoccupied, some lading..some discharging, some commyng for more. **1570–6** LAMBARDE *Peramb. Kent* (1826) 167 At the first, ships were accustomed to discarge at Lymne. **1601** HOLLAND *Pliny* I. 193 Himselfe saw at Puteoli, a certain ship discharged of Elephants embarked therein. **1712** W. ROGERS *Voy.* 20 We..discharg'd the Bark, and parted the small Cargo between our two Ships. **1891** *Law Times* XCI. 78/2 A strike took place amongst the men employed to discharge the vessel.

b. To disburden (a weapon, as a bow or gun) by letting fly the missile with which it is charged or loaded; to fire off (a fire-arm). Also *absol.*

1555 EDEN *Decades* 159 The gouernoure discharged aboute .xx. pieces of ordinaunce ageynste them. **1644** NYE *Gunnery* (1670) 39 He should know how to charge and discharge Gunner like. **1745** WESLEY *Answ. Ch.* 32 To discharge your Spleen and Malice! Say, Your Muskets and Blunderbusses. **1872** YEATS *Techn. Hist. Comm.* 334 When his piece was discharged, he had to defend himself with his sword.

c. *intr.* (for *refl.*) Of a fire-arm: To go off.

c **1580** J. HOOKER *Life Sir P. Carew* in *Archæol.* XXVIII. 139 The matche gave fier, and the pece dyschardged. **1582** N. LICHEFIELD tr. *Castanheda's Conq. E. Ind.* lxxi. 144 b, Some of the Ordinaunce of the fleete beganne to discharge. **1899** *Daily News* 12 June 3/4 Kennerley was not aware that the firearm was loaded, and it discharged in his face.

d. *Electr.* (*trans.*) To rid of an electric charge; to withdraw electricity from. (Also *intr.* for *refl.*)

1748 FRANKLIN *Lett.* Wks. 1840 V. 199 The bottle being thereby discharged, the man would be charged. **1794** G. ADAMS *Nat. & Exp. Philos.* IV. xlvii. 295 It [a Leyden phial] will be discharged of its fire with a loud snap. **1836–9** TODD *Cycl. Anat.* II. 83/1 The torpedo sometimes bears great irritation..without discharging. **1869** T. GRAHAM in *Sci. Opinion* 10 Feb. 270/3 On charging and discharging portions of the same palladium wire repeatedly, the curious retraction was found to continue.

e. *transf.* and *fig.* To rid, clear (*of*); to deprive (*of*). Now *rare.*

13.. *K. Alis.* 3868 Y am of Perce deschargid, Of Mede, and of Assyre aquyted. **1393** GOWER *Conf.* I. 13 þei [the clergy] wolde hemself descharge Of pouerte and become grete. **1480** CAXTON *Chron. Eng.* ccxliii. (1482) 285 Quene Isabell was dyscharged of al hir dower, and sente oute of Englond. **1520** in W. H. Turner *Select. Rec. Oxford* 26 The same person..shalbe dischargied of his ffraunches. **1600** J. PORY tr. *Leo's Africa* II. 157 He is bound..to discharge the citie of all leprous persons. **1658** EVELYN *Fr. Gard.* (1675) 92 You need only discharge them of the dead wood. **1712** J. JAMES tr. *Le Blond's Gardening* 188 At that Time the Earth being wholly discharged of its Moisture, is very dry. **1736** BAILEY *Househ. Dict.* 355 Discharge the fish of its scales and entrails. **1862** F. HALL *Hindu Philos. Syst.* 103 The assertion ..that whatever has misery for a quality can never be discharged of it.

f. *refl.* To disburden oneself by utterance; to give vent to words, feelings, etc. ? *Obs.*

1523 SKELTON *Garl. Laurel* 1353, I wyll myself discharge To lettered men at large. **1713** STEELE *Guardian* No. 29 ¶26 We now and then discharge ourselves in a symphony of laughter. **1752** FIELDING *Amelia* v. i, The colonel.. discharged himself of two or three articles of news.

2. *fig.* **a.** To relieve *of* (an obligation or charge); to exonerate; to exempt, let off, release *from.*

to discharge a bankrupt: to release him from further legal liability for debts contracted before his bankruptcy.

c **1330** R. BRUNNE *Chron.* (1810) 313 Discharged wille þei be of þe grete oth þei suore. *a* **1450** *Knt. de la Tour* (1868) 56 She might have saide, 'Aske myn husbonde that questyon and not me', and thus she might have discharged her of her ansuere. **1513** MORE in Grafton *Chron.* (1568) II. 771 Neither king nor Pope can geve any place such a privilege that it shall discharge a man of his debtes beyng able to pay. **1599** SHAKS. *Much Ado* v. i. 328, I discharge thee of thy prisoner, and I thanke thee. **1607** *Schol. Disc. agst. Antichr.* I. iii. 126 Doth not the Lawe discarg from a vowe that which hath a superfluous member. **1714** *Fr. Bk. of Rates* 11 We have established the Imposition of 50 Sols per Ton, on the Freight of all Strangers Ships, at the same time discharging those of our own Subjects. **1784** *Form Bankrupt's Certif.* in Tomlins *Law Dict.* s.v., We..testify and declare our consent..that the said John Thomas..be discharged from his debts in pursuance of the same act. **1786** J. BACON *Liber Regis* Pref., An Account of the Valuations of all the Ecclesiastical Benefices in England and Wales, which are now charged with the Payment of First Fruits and Tenths, or were lately discharged from any Payment to those Revenues, on account of the Smallness of their Income. **1858** *Sat. Rev.* VI. 448/1 We are not discharged of our duties towards our female readers by any coyness on their part. **1863** H. COX *Instit.* I. viii. 95 Some boroughs were discharged by the sheriffs from sending members.

†**b.** *refl.* To relieve oneself of an obligation by fulfilling it. ***to discharge oneself of***: to acquit oneself of, perform, fulfil (a duty or obligation) = sense 11; to pay (a debt) = sense 10. *Obs.*

1586 HOLINSHED *Chron.* II. 447 Such magistrates..as neither are comburgesses nor apt to discharge themselves of such offices. **1659** B. HARRIS *Parival's Iron Age* 252 To discharge themselves of a part of their debts. **1705** ADDISON *Italy* 94 Yet 'tis observ'd of 'em, that they discharge themselves with a great deal of Dexterity in such Embassies ..as are laid on 'em.

3. a. *trans.* To relieve of a charge or office; (more usually) to dismiss from office, service, or employment; to cashier. Constr. *from*, †*of*; prep. rarely omitted.

1476 in *York Myst.* Introd. 37 All..insufficiant personnes ..to discharge, ammove, and avoide. **1548** HALL *Chron.*, *Hen. VI*, 135 b, The duke of Yorke was discharged of the office of Regent. **1599** HARSNET *Agst. Darell* 94 About a Moneth or five weekes after he was Discharged of M. Brakenburies Service. **1664** EVELYN *Mem.* (1857) III. 144 Being..discovered to be a rampant Socinian, he was discharged of employment. **1738** *Comm. Sense* (1739) II. 203 Enemies..insisted I should be forthwith discharged his Service. **1836** MARRYAT *Midsh. Easy* xxiii, He wanted to leave the service; he hoped that Captain Wilson would discharge him and send him home. **1884** PAE *Eustace* 67 You are an idle, drunken vagabond, and I'll have you discharged.

†**b.** *refl.* To disburden or relieve oneself *of* an office or employment by quitting or renouncing it.

c **1400** *Destr. Troy* 8939 Now is tyme in this tru..To discharge me as cheftain. **1483** CAXTON *G. de la Tour* N iv, Syre I rendre and dyscharge me of your offyce.

†**4.** *trans.* To clear of a charge or accusation; to exculpate, acquit. *Obs.*

c **1500** *Lancelot* 3227 Bot, if god will, I sal me son discharg. Say to sir kay I sal not ber the charg, He sal no mater have me to rapref. **1552** HULOET, Discharge..*extra culpam ponere.* **1638** *Penit. Conf.* vii. (1657) 132 We may well doubt if every Sir John's absolution discharge us before god. **1661** BRAMHALL *Just Vind.* ix. 245 But it is not enough to charge the Church of Rome, unless we can discharge our selves, and acquit our own Church of the guilt of Schisme. **1742** FIELDING *J. Andrews* I. xvi, The constable hath not been discharged of suspicion on this account.

5. a. To dismiss (a prisoner in charge of the officers of the law, or one charged with an offence); to release from custody, liberate.

1556 *Chron. Gr. Friars* (Camden) 82 The duke of Norfoke ..and the byshoppe of Wyssiter had their pardone, and ware dyschargyd. **1699** in *Col. Rec. Pennsylv.* I. 549 Requesting to be discharged from his confinement. **1771** *Junius Lett.* xliv. 239 The..magistrate..declares the warrant illegal and discharges the prisoner. **1797** *Monthly Mag.* III. 550 The sheriff may then discharge the defendant. **1887** *Times* 26 Aug. 10/2 Mr. d'Eyncourt discharged a man accused of picking pockets.

b. To dismiss, send away, let go. (Cf. also 3.) (†Also with *indirect obj.* by omission of *from.*)

1586 A. DAY *Eng. Secretary* II. (1625) 20 Whom your selfe knew an houre before our conference, to have bin discharged our company. **1600** E. BLOUNT tr. *Conestaggio* 120 They woulde not discharge the souldiers. **1652** WADSWORTH tr. *Sandoval's Civil Wars Sp.* 333 Requiring the Commissioners forthwith to discharge him the Citie. **1807** *Med. Jrnl.* XVII. 316 At the end of which time..the girl was a second time discharged cured. **1893** *Law Times* XCV. 249/2 The jury, having informed the court that they had no presentment to make, were discharged.

6. To charge or command not to do something (cf. CHARGE *v.* 14); to prohibit, forbid. Also with the action as obj. *Obs.* exc. *dial.* (Chiefly *Sc.*)

1570 LEVINS *Manip.* 31 To discharge, *inhibere, absoluere.* **1596** DALRYMPLE tr. *Leslie's Hist. Scot.* VIII. 89 This parleament..discharges al man the futball, and al sik games. **1632** LITHGOW *Trav.* IX. 389 The Cardinall..discharged him to say Masse for a yeare. **1693** *Col. Rec. Pennsylv.* I. 368 And discharge all others from Transporting Anie persons over the Skuillkill. **1707** *Act. agst. Innov. Worship* 21 Apr. (Jam.), The General Assembly..doth hereby discharge the practice of all such innovations. **1716** *Wodrow Corr.* (1843) II. 120 The ministers..were discharged to pray for King George even in their families. [**1881** *Leicestersh. Gloss.*, s.v., A dischaa'ged 'im of ivver comin' agen o' the graound. **1889** *N.W. Linc. Gloss.* s.v., I discharge you fra iver speäkin' to oor 'Melia ony moore.]

7. *Arch.* **a.** To relieve (some part) of superincumbent weight or pressure by distributing this over adjacent parts. (Also **b.** with the weight as obj.)

1667 PRIMATT *City & C. Build.* 82 One Lintal to discharge the two windows and Balcony-door. **1703** MOXON *Mech. Exerc.* 138 Put a Girder between, to Discharge the Length of the Joysts. **1715** LEONI *Palladio's Archit.* (1742) I. 51 The arched ceilings..are made of cane, to discharge the Walls. **1788** [see DISCHARGING *ppl. a.*]. **1879** *Cassell's Techn. Educ.* III. 195/2 The arch..not only supports the wall above, but 'discharges' the weight over the walls on each side.

II. To remove, throw off, clear away *a charge.*

8. To remove (that with which anything is charged); to clear out, send out or forth, emit. *spec.* **a.** To take out, clear away, empty out, unload from a vessel, etc. (Also predicated of the vessel: cf. c below.)

1479 in *Eng. Gilds* (1870) 425 All smalwodde to be discharged at the Bak. **1582** N. LICHEFIELD tr. *Castanheda's Conq. E. Ind.* xlii. 96 That ther were setled a Factorie, to discharge the Merchandize the which were appointed for that place. **1699** DAMPIER *Voy.* II. I. 4 The Ships as usually take in water..yet they do as frequently discharge it again at some of these Islands, and take in better. **1720** *Col. Rec. Pennsylv.* III. 112 Preventing Sickly Vessels from discharging their goods or passengers. **1840** R. H. DANA *Bef. Mast* xx. 59 They came to anchor, moored ship, and commenced discharging hides and tallow. *Ibid.* xxii. 67 Having discharged her cargo and taken in ballast, she prepared to get under weigh. **1840** THACKERAY *Paris Sk.-bk.* (1869) 1 The two coaches draw near, and from thence.. trunks, children..and an affectionate wife are discharged on the quay.

b. To send forth, let fly (a missile, a blow, etc.); to fire off (a shot).

c **1500** *Melusine* lxii. 369 He..wold haue take the swerd to haue descharged it vpon the serpent. **1604** SHAKS. *Oth.* II. i 57 They do discharge their Shot of Courtesie. **1669** STURMY *Mariner's Mag.* v. 75 Of the..Motion or Course of a Shot discharged out of any Piece of Ordnance. **1725** POPE *Odyss.* XXII. 276 Let each at once discharge the deadly dart. **1771** GOLDSMITH *Hist. Eng.* I. 196 A Norman knight.. discharged at his head two..furious strokes of a sabre. **1817** WOLFE *Burial Sir J. More* i, Not a soldier discharged his farewell shot O'er the grave where our hero we buried. *c* **1850** *Arab. Nts.* (Rtldg.) 466 The king, my father, discharged an arrow, which pierced his breast.

absol. **1481** CAXTON *Godfrey* 147 Oure meyne discarged [i.e. arrows] on them. **1684** *Scanderbeg Rediv.* vi. 144 The Turks having Discharged, again retired. **1734** tr. *Rollin's Anc. Hist.* IV. VIII. xiv. 94 Archers who discharged perpetually upon them. *a* **1774** GOLDSM. *Hist. Greece* I. 297.

c. To give vent to, allow to escape or pass out; to send or pour forth, emit; *fig.* to give utterance or expression to.

1600 E. BLOUNT tr. *Conestaggio* 299 There they discharged their choler. **1605** SHAKS. *Macb.* v. i. 81 Infected minds To their deafe pillowes will discharge their Secrets. **1676** WISEMAN *Surgery* (J.), The matter being suppurated, I opened an inflamed tubercle..and discharged a well-concocted matter. **1711** SHAFTESB. *Charac.* (1737) I. 73 'Tis the only manner in which the poor cramp'd Wretches can discharge a free Thought. **1833** *Act 3–4 Will. IV*, c. 46 §114 The same [pipes] shall not discharge the water..upon the foot pavements. **1845** M. PATTISON *Ess.* (1889) I. 11 The shoals of the frivolous and dissipated which this country annually discharges upon the Continent.

d. *refl.* To find vent, escape; *esp.* of a river, to empty itself, disembogue (also *intr.*).

1600 J. PORY tr. *Leo's Africa* II. 333 This small river.. dischargeth it selfe into the Mediterran sea. **1794** S. WILLIAMS *Vermont* 30 Twenty five run westerly and discharge themselves into Lake Champlain. **1816** KEATINGE *Trav.* (1817) II. 42 A deep and rapid river, which discharges at Larache. **1820** SCORESBY *Acc. Arctic Reg.* I. 338 The chimney..through which the smoke discharges itself.

†**9. a.** *trans.* To remove (anything of the nature of a charge, obligation, etc.); to get rid of, do away with, abolish. *Obs.*

1523 FITZHERB. *Surv.* 12 b, Mater in writyng may nat be discharged by..bare wordes. **1626** BACON *Sylva* §236 All this dischargeth not the wonder. **1654** tr. *Scudery's Curia Pol.* 173, I resolved to remove and discharge the Office of the Major of the Pallace. **1732** NEAL *Hist. Purit.* I. 234 The Earl of Murray..convened a Parliament..in which the Pope's authority was again discharged. **1741** RICHARDSON *Pamela* (1742) IV. 34 If it be the natural Duty of a Mother, it is a Divine Duty; and how can a Husband have Power to discharge a Divine Duty? **1778** BP. LOWTH *Transl. Isaiah* Prelim. Diss. (ed. 12) 44 We can hardly expect..more.. than to be able..to discharge and eliminate the errors that have been gathering..for about a thousand years past.

b. *Law.* To put an end to the obligation of, cancel, annul (an order of a court).

1798 DALLAS *Amer. Law Rep.* II. 33 Therefore adjudge that the order of the court be discharged. **1808** *Parl. Deb.* 1409 Other..business..might render it improper to discharge the order: the call might be postponed for a few days without being discharged. **1885** *Law Times* LXXIX. 175/1 The order..was entirely wrong, and must be discharged with costs.

c. *Arch.* To get rid of (a weight): see 7 b.

10. a. To clear off, or acquit oneself of (an obligation) by fulfilment or performance; to pay (a debt, vow, etc.).

1525 LD. BERNERS *Froiss.* II. ccxxiv. [ccxx.] 701 His entent was not to departe thens tyll euery thynge was payed and discharge[d]. **1542** UDALL in *Lett Lit. Men* (Camden) 2 Only of an honest purpose to discharge my debtes. **1590** SHAKS. *Com. Err.* IV. i. 13, I will discharge my bond. **1606** —— *Ant. & Cl.* IV. xvi. 28 Death of one person can be paide but once, And that she ha's discharg'd. **1725** POPE *Odyss.* I. 329 Soon may your sire discharge the vengeance due. **1767** BLACKSTONE *Comm.* II. 141 If I am bound to pay money on any certain day, I discharge the obligation if I pay it before twelve o'clock at night. **1827** HALLAM *Const. Hist.* (1876) I. vi. 337 By no means sufficient to defray his expenses, far less to discharge his debts. **1885** *Law Times* LXXIX. 172/1 If forbearance were shown, the defaulting solicitor would be able to discharge his liabilities.

†**b.** To pay or settle for. *Obs.*

1593 NASHE *Four Lett. Confut.* 6 That thou mayst haue money to goe home to Trinitie Hall to discharge thy commons. **1646** EVELYN *Mem.* (1857) I. 239 The next morning..discharging our lodgings, we agreed for a coach to carry us. **1729** Swift *Libel on Delany* Wks. 1755 IV. I. 95 Crazy Congreve scarce cou'd spare A shilling to discharge his chair. **1815** W. H. Ireland *Scribbleomania* 156 She literally was without a shilling to discharge the vehicle which had conveyed her to the metropolis. **1842** C. Whitehead *R. Savage* (1845) II. iv. 218 I had discharged my lodging that morning. *Ibid.* III. xi. 446 That insult shall be discharged at the same time with the other debts.

†**c.** To pay, settle with (a creditor). *Obs.*

a **1560** Amy Robsart *Let.* in *Westm. Gaz.* 21 Apr. (1894) 4/1 To make this gowne of vellet whiche I sende you..and I will se you dyscharged for all. **1596** Shaks. *Merch. V.* iii. ii. 276 If he had The present money to discharge the Jew, He would not take it. **1698** Fryer *Acc. E. India & P.* 392 The Husbandman..reaps the Fruit of his Labour, provided he take care to discharge his Landlord.

†**d.** To clear oneself of, account for, give account of. *Obs. rare.*

1596 Spenser *F.Q.* vii. xii. 17 He bade her Cease to molest the Moone to walke at large Or come before high Jove her dooings to discharge.

†**e.** To transfer the responsibility for (something) by charging it *on* some one else (cf. charge *v.* 16). *Obs. rare.*

1651 Hobbes *Leviath.* ii. xxvii. 292 Part of the fault may be discharged on the punisher. **1697** Dryden *Æneid* xii. (R.), 'Tis not a crime t' attempt what I decree, Or if it were, discharge the crime on me.

11. To acquit oneself of, fulfil, execute, perform (a charge, office, duty, trust, function, etc.).

1548 Latimer *Ploughers* (Arb.) 21 A soore word for them that are neglygent in dyschargeinge theyr office. **1590** Shaks. *Mids. N.* v. i. 206 Thus haue I Wall, my part discharged so. *a* **1661** Fuller *Worthies* (1840) II. 214 He was high-sheriff of this county, 1635, discharging the place with great honour. **1719** in Perry *Hist. Coll. Am. Col. Ch.* I. 216 Let me..exhort you to discharge a good conscience in this matter. **1755** Johnson *Let. to Langton* 6 May in *Boswell*, When the duty that calls me to Lichfield is discharged, my inclination will call me to Langton. *a* **1853** Robertson *Serm.* Ser. iii. vii. 92 They appointed one of their number..to discharge those offices for them.

12. a. *Dyeing*, etc. To remove (the dye or colour with which it has been charged) *from* a textile fabric, etc. **b.** To print (a fabric) with a pattern by discharging parts of the ground colour.

1727 Pope, etc. *Art of Sinking* 91 Take off the gloss, or quite discharge the colour. **1764** Churchill *Poems, Ep. to Hogarth*, Wash the Ethiop white, Discharge the leopard's spots. **1802** Mar. Edgeworth *Moral T.* (1816) I. xix. 150 The colours had been discharged by some acid. **1836** *Penny Cycl.* VI. 155/1 The second style of calico-printing consists in giving a general dye to the cloth, and discharging portions of the ground, which has the effect of producing a number of white or variously coloured figures upon it. **1875** *Ure's Dict. Arts* I. 288, That is, 224 handkerchiefs are discharged every ten minutes.

c. *intr.* Of ink, dye, etc.: To be washed out; to 'run' when wetted.

1883 R. Haldane *Workshop Receipts* Ser. ii. 336/2 The ink..dries quickly, and may even be varnished without discharging.

discharge (dɪs'tʃɑːdʒ, 'dɪs-), *sb.* [f. prec. vb.: cf. OF. *descharge* (13–14th c. in Hatz.-Darm.), mod.F. *décharge*, f. *des-*, *décharger*.]

1. The act of freeing from or removing a charge or load; disburdenment, unloading (*of* a vessel, etc.); clearing away, removal (*of* a cargo, etc.).

1580 Hollyband *Treas. Fr. Tong, Passe-porte*, a bill of discharge for any marchandise. **1626** Bacon *Sylva* §92 Marke well the Discharge of that Cloude; And you shall see it euer breake vp, first in the Skirts, and last in the middest. **1891** *Law Times* XCII. 78/2 The discharge of her cargo began on the 14th Nov.

2. The act of discharging a weapon or missile; the act of firing off a fire-arm, letting fly an arrow, etc. Also *fig.*

1596 Shaks. *1 Hen. IV*, i. i. 57 By discharge of their Artillerie. **1653** H. Cogan tr. *Pinto's Trav.* xxii. 79 Without any noise or discharge of Ordnance. **1785** Sarah Fielding *Ophelia* I. xiv, I had stood her discharge of nonsense. **1831** J. W. Croker in *Croker Papers* (1884) 8 Feb., I am as convinced..as I am that the discharge of my gun will follow the pulling the trigger. **1844** H. H. Wilson *Brit. India* III. 76 The howitzers were then brought up, and after a few discharges, the work was taken in flank.

3. a. The act of sending out or pouring forth; emission, ejection; the rate or amount of emission.

1600 Shaks. *A.Y.L.* ii. i. 37 The wretched annimall heau'd forth such groanes That their discharge did stretch his leatherne coat Almost to bursting. **1695** Woodward *Nat. Hist. Earth* iii. (1723) 161 Wherever there are any extraordinary Discharges of this [subterraneous] Fire, there also are the neighbouring Springs hotter than ordinary. **1783** Pott *Chirurg. Wks.* I. 309 The discharge of this mucus. **1823** J. Badcock *Dom. Amusem.* 180 And give a more easy issue or discharge to the water. **1880** Haughton *Phys. Geog.* iii. 141 This gives a discharge of water to the southward, equal to 32·28 cubic miles per hour.

b. *Electr.* The emission or transference of electricity which takes place between two bodies positively and negatively charged, when placed in contact or sufficiently near each other. Applied *attrib.* to a tube or an electric lamp containing a gas or metal vapour in which an electric discharge can be produced between two electrodes. Cf. *gas-discharge.*

1794 G. Adams *Nat. & Exp. Philos.* IV. xlvii. 295 The person who holds the discharger feels nothing from the discharge. **1836–9** Todd *Cycl. Anat.* II. 82/2 The shock caused by an electrical fish is said to be produced by a discharge of its electricity. **1863–72** Watts *Dict. Chem.* II. 388 The recombination of the opposite electricities which constitutes discharge may..be either continuous or sudden. **1894** *Times* 19 Apr. 13/6 Three modes of electric discharge—the glow discharge, the spark discharge, and the arc discharge. **1898** *Phil. Mag.* 5th Ser. XLVI. 296 Hertz made the rays travel between two parallel plates of metal placed inside the discharge-tube. **1935** *Discovery* Apr. 111/2 The latest drifting signs make use of small electric discharge tubes instead of filament lamps. **1936** *Nature* 14 Nov. 836/1 The new discharge bulb lamps are already in use on the Continent... In appearance they are like the ordinary 'pearl' lamp but they have no filament. They contain a small quartz mercury vapour discharge lamp..and they are corrected for colour. **1936** *Discovery* Dec. 365/2 The methods of determining with accuracy the masses of swift charged atoms and molecules produced in the discharge tube. **1959** *Listener* 12 Mar. 454/1 About 1930, the discharge lamp emerged as a competitor of the tungsten filament lamp for street lighting.

c. *concr.* That which is emitted or poured forth; *esp.* matter issuing from a wound or running sore.

1727 P. Hardisway in *Phil. Trans.* (1727) VII. 216 (*title*) A Purulent Discharge. **1804** Abernethy *Surg. Obs.* 223, I directed that this discharge should be pressed out..and a poultice applied. **1862** Marg. Goodman *Exper. Eng. Sister of Mercy* 103 The discharge was so offensive as to nauseate him and prevent him taking nourishment.

d. The place where something is discharged; e.g. the mouth of a river (cf. discharge *v.* 8 d); an opening for discharging something.

1798 Pennant *Hindoostan* II. 110 The water contained in them [rivers] is increased by dams made across their discharges. **1808** Pike *Sources Mississ.* iii. App. 6 From its sources to its discharge into the head of the gulf of California. **1828** Scott *F.M. Perth* (ed. 1) xxix, On the meadow at the Ballough, that is, the discharge of the lake into the river.

4. a. The act of freeing from obligation, liability, or restraint; release, exoneration, exemption.

discharge of a bankrupt: release from further legal liability for debts contracted before his bankruptcy.

c **1460** Fortescue *Abs. & Lim. Mon.* ix, Wich encrease, any subget desirith ffor his owne discharge off þat he beyrith to the sustenance off his prince. **1532** More *Confut. Tindale* Wks. 518/2 Of whiche commaundement in scripture we see no discharge. **1559** Abp. Hethe in Strype *Ann. Ref.* I. ii. App. vi. 11 Thus muche I have here said..for the dyscharge of my conscience. **1683** *Brit. Spec.* 155 After that Honorius had by Letters of Discharge quitted the Britains of the Roman Jurisdiction. **1705** *Act 4 Anne* c. 17 That a bankrupt trader..should be entitled to his discharge from all further liability for the debts theretofore contracted. **1818** Cruise *Digest* (ed. 2) III. 66 Neither will any prescription *de non decimando* avail in total discharge of tithes, unless it relates to such abbey lands. **1835** *Penny Cycl.* III. 401/1 *Bankrupt Law Sc.*, The bankrupt..may apply to the Court of Session for a *discharge*..A discharge..frees the debtor from all debts previous to the date of the first deliverance on the petition for sequestration, except debts due to the crown. **1895** *Times* (Weekly Ed.) 558/2 [Bankruptcy Court] Although he did not treat the debtor as immaculate, he thought the order of discharge might be granted subject to the minimum suspension laid down by the Act—namely, two years.

b. Exoneration from accusation or blame; exculpation, acquittal, excuse.

1526 *Pilgr. Perf.* (W. de W. 1531) 160 b, It is not sufficyent to my discharge. *a* **1557** Mrs. M. Basset tr. *More's Treat. Passion* Wks. 1373/2 Wold that..haue serued theym for theire dyscharge? **1656** Earl Monm. *Adv. Fr. Parnass.* 328 He published in his own discharge, those his unfortunate relations. *a* **1716** South (J.), Not condemning..which word imports properly an acquittance or discharge of a man upon some precedent accusation. **1836** J. Gilbert *Chr. Atonem.* i. (1852) 20 His receiving a discharge from guilt.

c. Dismissal from service, employment, or office.

1548 Hall *Chron., Hen. VI*, 139 b, He..nothyng more coveted and desired then libertie and discharge. **1590** Greene *Mourn. Garm.* (1616) 36 The Seruingmen..brookt their discharge with patience. **1611** Bible *Eccl.* viii. 8 There is no discharge in that warre. **1755** Magens *Insurances* II. 111 If the Master..give the Mate his Discharge. **1844** *Regul. & Ord. Army* 195 In the cases of Soldiers who obtain their Discharge by Purchase, no charge is allowed by the Public for their passage from abroad.

d. Release from custody, liberation.

c **1590** C'tess Pembroke *Ps.* lxvi. vii, I cried to him, my cry procured My free discharge from all my bandes. **1671** Milton *Samson* 1573 Death, who sets all free, Hath paid his ransom now and full discharge. **1771** Mackenzie *Man Feel.* xi. (1803) 88 You will receive..a sum more than sufficient for your husband's discharge. *Mod.* The magistrate ordered the discharge of the prisoner as the evidence did not warrant his committal for trial.

e. *concr.* Something that frees from obligation; *esp.* a document conveying release from obligation; a receipt for the payment of money due, an acquittance; a certificate of freedom from liability.

1495 *Act 11 Hen. VII*, c. 54 §5 The Kingis lettres under his pryve seale..shalbe sufficient discharge for the..payment thereof. **1523** Fitzherb. *Surv.* 12 b, Than must the tenaunt shewe a discharge by suffycient writyng, and nat by wordes, or elles to paye the same. **1640–1** *Kirkcudbr. War Comm. Min. Bk.* (1855) 91 To call for a sight of the said discharges and tak coppies thairof. **1719** De Foe *Crusoe* I. xix. (1840) 341, I sent for a notary, and caused him to draw up a general release or discharge for the four hundred and seventy moidores. **1792** Mrs. C. Smith *Desmond* III. 53 He [the steward] is very honest..and I have given him his discharges. **1866** Crump *Banking* v. 107 An alteration made by the drawer..without the consent or knowledge of the acceptor, is considered a full discharge to the acceptor. **1895** *Times* (Weekly Ed.) 16 Aug. 652/2 Sending up parchment discharge and other documentary evidence of the..good conduct of the deceased.

5. The act of clearing off a pecuniary liability; payment.

1611 Shaks. *Cymb.* v. iv. 173 Oh the charity of a penny Cord..you haue no true Debitor, and Creditor but it: of what's past, is, and to come, the discharge. **1688** *Pennsylv. Archives* I. 104 Help us wth some money ffor the Discharge of the Great Expence wee are at. **1809** Jefferson *Writ.* (1830) IV. 136 The discharge of the debt, therefore, is vital to the destinies of our government. **1888** Bryce *Amer. Commw.* II. xliii. 140 Providing for the discharge of existing liabilities.

6. Fulfilment, performance, execution (*of* an obligation, duty, function, etc.).

1610 Shaks. *Temp.* ii. i. 254 An act Whereof what's past is Prologue; what to come In yours and my discharge. **1622** R. Hawkins *Voy. S. Sea*, I know the Spaniard too too well and the manner of his proceedings in discharge of promises. **1675** Traherne *Chr. Ethics* xxx. 478 The discharge of our duty. **1829** Southey *Sir T. More* I. iii, Such tribute..rendered, in discharge Of grateful duty. **1845** Stephen *Laws Eng.* (1874) II. 627 The discharge of the office is, in general, compulsory upon the party chosen. **1883** *Law Reports 11 Q. Bench Div.* 596 *note*, In discharge of his functions as advocate.

7. †**a.** The act of sending away; dismissal. *Obs.* **b.** *Law.* Dismissal or reversal of an order of a court.

1677 Gilpin *Demonol.* (1867) 430 Positive discharges, like that of Christ in the same case, 'Get thee hence, Satan'. **1892** Sir N. Lindley in *Law Times Rep.* LXVII. 150/1 The discharge of the order..ought not to be granted except upon the terms of bringing the money into court.

8. *Arch.* The relieving some part of a building of superincumbent weight; *concr.* a contrivance for effecting this. (Cf. discharge *v.* 7.)

1703 Moxon *Mech. Exerc.* 159 A Brick-wall or a Post trim'd up to a piece of Timber over charg'd for its Bearing, is a Discharge to that Bearing. **1823** P. Nicholson *Pract. Build.* 222 *Discharge*, a post trimmed up under a beam, or part of a building which is weak.

9. a. *Dyeing*, etc. The act or process of removing the colour with which a textile fabric is charged. **b.** *concr.* A composition or mixture used for this purpose. (Cf. discharge *v.* 12.)

1836 *Penny Cycl.* VI. 155/1 *Calico-printing*, Discharges are of two kinds: the simple, and the compound or mordanted. *Ibid.* 155/2 Compound discharges not only remove the mordant from the ground..but introduce a new mordant on the discharged points. **1854** J. Scoffern in *Orr's Circ. Sc.* Chem. 422 Some varieties of calico-printing by the process of discharge. **1874** W. Crookes *Pract. Handbk. Dyeing* 317 By the word discharge is designated any compound or mixture which has the property of bleaching, or taking away, the colour already communicated to a fabric.

10. *attrib.* and *Comb.*

1836 *Penny Cycl.* VI. 155/1 The goods..are..impressed with the discharge paste by means of the engraved block or cylinder. *Ibid.* 155/2 Mordanted goods..intended for the discharge process. **1864** *Daily Tel.* 26 July, The discharge culverts, through which the sewage is poured into the river, are visible only at the time of low-water. **1874** Knight *Dict. Mech.*, *Discharge-valve*, in marine engines, a valve covering the top of the air-pump, opening when pressed from beneath. **1891** R. Kipling *City Dreadf. Nt.* 26 His statements tally with the discharge-certificate of the United States.

dischargeable (dɪs'tʃɑːdʒəb(ə)l), *a.* [f. discharge *v.* + -able.] Capable of being discharged: in quot., liable to be paid for (see discharge *v.* 10 b).

1781 T. Jefferson *Lett.* Writ. 1893 II. 514 And we will give you moreover 150 lbs. of Tobacco a Day each dischargeable in current money at the rate affixed by the grand Jury. **1897** *Daily News* 20 July 5/6 The notes are dischargeable on August 1st, 1900.

discharged (dɪs'tʃɑːdʒd), *ppl. a.* [f. as prec. + -ed[1].] Freed from a charge, load, obligation, etc.; exonerated, released, dismissed, emitted, etc.

Discharged Living, (in *Ch. of Engl.*) a benefice that is exempt from the payment of First-fruits, its value having been returned in the *Liber Regis* of K. Henry VIII as less than £10. Cf. discharge *v.* 2, quot. 1786.

1398 Trevisa *Barth. De P.R.* xii. Introd. (Tollem. MS.), Fowles of praye, þat ben dischargid of weyȝte of flesche, and fleþ most hyȝe. **1483** *Cath. Angl.* 100 Discharged, *exoneratus.* **1631** May tr. *Barclay's Mirr. Mindes* ii. 36 Of such men..the labour..is precious, as filling their discharged mindes with a new strength. **1719** De Foe *Crusoe* (1840) I. xvi. 280 Laying down the discharged pieces. **1758** *M.P.'s Let. on R. Navy* 35 *Dead* and *discharged* Tickets ..are paid at the Navy-Office, without being chequed. **1786** J. Bacon *Liber Regis* 1253 Livings discharged. **1836** [see discharge *sb.* 9]. **1849** R. Garnett in *Proc. Philol. Soc.* IV. 179 In the same degree that a magnetized steel bar differs from an ordinary one, or a charged Leyden jar from a discharged one. **1859** *Autobiog. Beggar Boy* 3 My mother's marriage with a discharged soldier. **1891** *Kelly's P.O. Direct. Bucks* 364/2 Datchet, the living is a discharged vicarage, net yearly value £306.

dischargee (dɪstʃɑːˈdʒiː). [f. DISCHARGE *v.* + -EE.] A person who has been discharged.

1894 *Scottish Rev.* July 58 Government finds place for its deserving dischargees in its public service. **1952** *N.Y. Times* 28 Sept. 23 Dischargees without combat service.

discharger (dɪsˈtʃɑːdʒə(r)). [f. DISCHARGE *v.* + -ER[1]. Cf. F. *deschargeur* (13th c.).]

1. One who discharges (in various senses; see the verb).

1533 ELYOT *Cast. Helthe* xii. (R.), Deth is the discharger of al griefes and myseries. **1585** ABP. SANDYS *Serm.* (1841) 230 A sure discharger of his debts to the uttermost. **1646** SIR T. BROWNE *Pseud. Ep.* II. v. 89 By Borax and Butter mixed in a due proportion; which, sayeth he, will so goe off as scarce to be heard by the discharger. **1875** *Ure's Dict. Arts* I. 288 The discharger..admits the liquor, the air, and the water. **1892** *Labour Commission Gloss.*, *Dischargers*, men in the chemical industry engaged in loading and unloading waggons.

2. An instrument or appliance for discharging. *spec.* **a.** An apparatus for producing a discharge of electricity.

1794 [see DISCHARGE *sb.* 3 b]. **1832** *Nat. Philos.*, *Electr.* ix. §136. 37 (Useful Knowl. Soc.) In order to direct the charge with more certainty..an apparatus, called the *Universal Discharger*, was contrived by Mr. Henley. *c* **1865** J. WYLDE in *Circ. Sc.* I. 179/1 An instrument, called a discharger.. which consists of two brass knobs, fixed to a bent wire.

b. *Dyeing.* = DISCHARGE *sb.* 9 b.

In mod. Dicts.

discharging (dɪsˈtʃɑːdʒɪŋ), *vbl. sb.* [f. as prec. + -ING[1].] The action of the verb DISCHARGE in various senses. (Now chiefly *gerundial.*)

a **1483** *Liber Niger* in *Househ. Ord.* 29 Bycause of newe charging and discharging of servants, officers, etc. **1538** *Bury Wills* (Camden) 135 In dyschargyng of my concyence. **1666** PEPYS *Diary* 16 Oct., Orders..about discharging of ships. **1762** GOLDSM. *Cit. W.* lxxxiv. ¶6 Bequeathed..to the discharging his debts. **1832** MARSHALL (*title*) On the Enlisting, the Discharging, and the Pensioning of Soldiers. **1890** *Pall Mall G.* 24 Nov. 6/3 The proposals..by the large shipowners to undertake their own discharging.

dis'charging, *ppl. a.* [f. as prec. + -ING[2].] That discharges: see the verb.

discharging arch (*Arch.*): an arch built in the substance of a wall, which relieves a part below it (as a lintel, etc.) from the superincumbent weight; cf. DISCHARGE *v.* 7 and *sb.* 8; similarly ***discharging strut***, etc. ***discharging rod*** (*Electr.*) = DISCHARGER 2 a.

c **1788** *Langley's Builder's Compl. Assist.* (ed. 4) 152 If.. there be discharging Struts framed into the Beams and Prick Posts..they will discharge the principal Rafters from the greatest Part of the whole Weight. **1797** *Monthly Mag.* III. 301 The spirit becomes sooner condensed, before it reaches the discharging cock. **1812** J. SMYTH *Pract. of Customs* (1821) p. viii, Copious instructions for the discharging Officers. **1812-6** J. SMITH *Panorama Sc. & Art* II. 137 The condenser and the discharging-pump communicate by means of a horizontal pipe containing a valve opening towards the pump. **1819** P. NICHOLSON *Arch. Dict.*, *Discharging Arches*, rough brick or stone arches, built over the wooden lintels of apertures. **1819** *Pantologia* s.v. *Electrical Battery*, Care should be taken not to touch the wires..before the discharging rod be repeatedly applied to its sides. **1856** KANE *Arct. Expl.* I. xii. 135 An icy wall, which constantly threw off its discharging bergs. **1858** *Archit. Publ. Soc. Dict. Discharging piece, strut, etc.*, a piece of timber so placed as to discharge any weight, in framing or shoring, upon a better point of support. **1875** *Ure's Dict. Arts.* I. 288 The bleaching or discharging liquor.

dis'charity *sb.*: see DIS- 9.

discharm (dɪsˈtʃɑːm), *v.* [ad. OF. *descharmer*, *décharmer* to free from enchantment (15th c. in Littré), f. *des-*, DIS- 4 + *charmer* to CHARM.] *intr.* and *trans.* To undo a charm; to free from the influence of a charm or enchantment.

1480 CAXTON *Ovid's Met.* XIV. vii, The more she discharmed, the more we gate our forme humayne. **1634** HEYWOOD *Witches Lanc.* v. Wks. 1874 IV. 255 So they are discharm'd. **18..** LOWELL *To W. L. Garrison* v, That thunder's swell Rocked Europe, and discharmed the triple crown.

dischase (dɪsˈtʃeɪs), *v.* [f. DIS- 7 b + CHASE *sb.*[1] 3.] *trans.* To reduce from the legal status and condition of a chase to that of ordinary land.

1725-6 *Act 12 Geo. I*, c. 4 (Jod.) An act for dischasing and disfranchising the chase of Alrewas Hay.

†**dis'chauce,** *v. Obs. rare.* [ad. OF. *deschaucer*, *-chaucier*, *-chalcier* (12th c. in Littré), mod.F. *déchausser*:—L. *discalceāre*, f. DIS- 4 + *calceāre* to shoe, *calceus* a shoe: cf. DISCALCEATE, -CALCED, also CHAUSSES.] *trans.* To divest of shoes, or of hose.

c **1400** *Beryn* 471 And þerfor, love, dischauce yewe nat till þis chek be do.

dischayte, obs. erratic form of DECEIT.

?*a* **1400** *Morte Arth.* 3790 Sekerly assembles thare one sevenschore knyghtes, Sodaynly in dischayte by tha salte strandes.

†**dis'cheer,** *v. Obs. rare*[−1]. [DIS- 6.] *trans.* To put out of cheer; to distress, dishearten.

1587 TURBERV. *Trag. T.* (1837) 99 An other thing there was, that most discheerde Her kinsfolkes then in place.

dischest: see DIS- 7.

dischevel, etc., obs. form of DISHEVEL, etc.

†**dis'chisel,** *v. Obs.* [f. DIS- 6 + CHISEL *v.*] *trans.* To undo the chiselling of. Hence †**dischiselling (dischesiling)** *vbl. sb.*

1652 J. HALL *Height of Eloquence* p. xxv, That was meerly a dischesiling of the general design.

dischone, obs. Sc. form of DISJUNE *sb.* and *v.*

dischort, obs. f. DISHORT *Sc.*, injury, mischief.

†**dis'church,** *v. Obs.* [f. DIS- 7 + CHURCH *sb.*]

1. *trans.* To deprive (a church) of its character; to cause to be no longer a church; to unchurch.

1629 BP. HALL *Reconciler* 11 This heresie..makes Rome justly odious and execrable..but cannot utterly dischurch it. *a* **1656** —— *Rem. Wks.* (1660) 408 These are enough to deforme any Church, not enough to dis-church it. **1656** S. WINTER *Serm.* 37 That Church shall never be dischurched.

2. To exclude or expel (persons) from the church.

1651 C. CARTWRIGHT *Cert. Relig.* I. 113 All dis-union of people is not enough to dis-church them.

Hence **dis'churching** *vbl. sb.* and *ppl. a.*

1680 ALLEN *Peace & Unity* 51 They were not under the dischurching cause of as many of the Jews as were dischurched. **1695** J. ST. N. *Widow's Mite* 11 The Apostacy ..for which the Judgment of Dischurching came upon them.

†**di'scide,** *v. Obs.* [ad. L. *discīd-ĕre* (rare) to cut in pieces, f. DIS- 1 + *cædĕre to cut.*] *trans.* To cut asunder or in pieces; to cut off or away. *lit.* and *fig.*

1494 FABYAN *Chron.* VII. 406 No parte of bounte from hym was discided. **1596** SPENSER *F.Q.* IV. i. 27 Her lying tongue was in two parts divided..And as her tongue so was her hart discided. **1599** A. M. tr. *Gabelhouer's Bk. Physicke* 16/1 Discide from this roote the little eares and iagges. **1679** PRANCE *Addit. Narr. Pop. Plot* 34 The distinction of *errante clave*..doth at least cut, if not discide that Knot.

discide, obs. form of DECIDE.

disciferous (dɪˈsɪfərəs), *a. Bot.* [f. L. *disc-us*, *disci-*, DISC + -FEROUS.] Bearing a disc or discs.

1883 in *Syd. Soc. Lex.*

discifloral (dɪsɪˈflɔərəl), *a. Bot.* [f. L. *discus*, *disci-* DISC + *-flōrus* flowering, flowered + -AL[1]: cf. *floral.*] Having flowers with the receptacle enlarged into a conspicuous disc surrounding the ovary: *spec.* applied to a series of orders of polypetalous exogens (*Disciflorӕ* in *Eng. Bot.*, ed. 3, 1863) having this character, including *Rutaceӕ*, etc.

1873 HOOKER in *Le Maout & Decaisne's Syst. Bot.* (App.) 998 Series II. Discifloral—Sepals distinct or connate, free or adnate to the ovary—*Disk usually conspicuous*, as a ring or cushion, or spread over the base of the calyx-tube, or confluent with the base of the ovary.

disciform (ˈdɪsɪfɔːm), *a.* [f. L. *discus* (see prec.) + -FORM.] Having the form of a disk; disk-shaped, discoidal.

1830 LINDLEY *Nat. Syst. Bot.* 134 Stamens..inserted round the base of the stalk of the calyx, which is sometimes disciform. **1874** COOKE *Fungi* 167 The one is a cylinder as long as it is broad, the other is disciform. **1875** BLAKE *Zool.* 200 The Torpedoes have the body covered with naked unarmed skin, disciform, and rounded.

discigerous (dɪˈsɪdʒərəs), *a. Bot.* [f. as prec. + -GEROUS.] Bearing a disk or disks.

1872 NICHOLSON *Palӕont.* 489 Porous, discigerous, or pseudo-scalariform tissue. **1877** LE CONTE *Elem. Geol.* v. 347 Known to be conifers by the exogenous structure of the trunk, together with the discigerous tissue of the wood.

di'scinct, *a. rare.* [ad. L. *discinctus*, pa. pple. of *discingĕre* to ungird.] Ungirt (*lit.* & *fig.*).

1647 TRAPP *Comm. Luke* xii. 35 A loose, discinct, and diffluent mind is unfit to serve God. **1656** BLOUNT *Glossogr.*, *Discinct*, ungirded, dissolute, negligent. **1846** LANDOR *Wks.* (1868) I. 85/2 In the country I walk and wander about discinct.

So †**di'scincture,** ungirding (*obs.*).

1610 GUILLIM *Heraldry* (1660) II. vi. 67 The depriving of the Belt..tearmed, the discincture or ungirding.

†**di'scind,** *v. Obs.* [ad. L. *dīscind-ĕre* to tear or cleave asunder, divide, f. *dī-* DI-[1] + *scindĕre* to tear, rend.] *trans.* To tear asunder, cleave, sever, divide, separate.

1640 REYNOLDS *Passions* xxxii. 393 Neither can any Seed be discinded or issue out from the soule. **1650** HOWELL *Lett.* II. Introd. Poem 2, Credentiall letters..golden Links that do enchain Whole Nations, though discinded by the Main. *a* **1691** BOYLE (J.), Concretions so soft, that we could easily discind them betwixt our fingers.

discipher, obs. form of DECIPHER *v.*

disciple (dɪˈsaɪp(ə)l), *sb.* Forms: 1-4 discipul, 2-3 diciple, 3-4 deciple, -cipil, -cyple, desciple, -pil, 4 desiple, disiple, dissiple, -pil, 4-6 discipil(l, 5 dycyple, dysciple, -cyple, -cypull, dyssyple, -sypull, 6 discyple, 3- disciple. [In OE. *discipul*, ad. L. *discipul-us* learner, pupil, f. *discĕre* to learn. In early ME. *di-*, *deciple*, a. OF. *deciple*, semi-popular ad. L. *discipul-us*. Both in OF. and ME., *deciple* was gradually conformed to the L. spelling as *disciple*; ME. had occasional variants in *-il*, *-yl*, *-ul*.]

1. One who follows or attends upon another for the purpose of learning from him; a pupil or scholar.

It has not been at any period in English the ordinary term for *scholar* or *pupil*, as *discipulus* was in Latin; but has come into use through the New Testament versions, being applied chiefly to the Twelve Disciples of Jesus Christ, and used in similar Scriptural applications or later extensions of them. Hence the sense-development in Eng. is not that of Latin, where the order of sub-senses was d, c, a, b.

a. One of the personal followers of Jesus Christ during his life; esp. one of the Twelve.

Rare in OE. the word in *Ags. Gospels* being *leorningcniht*, in *Lindisf. Gl.* usually *ðeᵹn*.

c **950** *Lindisf. Gosp.* Matt. xxvii. 57 Summ monn..ðe discipul wæs ðæs hælendes. *c* **1200** *Trin. Coll. Hom.* 101 Ure louerd stod among his diciples. *a* **1225** *Ancr. R.* 106 He biheold hu his deore deciples fluen alle vrom him. *c* **1380** *Sir Ferumb.* 5733 Suþþe sente þe holy gost To ys decyples he louede most. **1382** WYCLIF *John* xix. 38 Ioseph of Armathi ..was a disciple of Ihesu, forsothe priuey, for the drede of Iewis. **1538** STARKEY *England* I. ii. 40 Al Chrystys dyscypullys and apostyllys were sympul and pore. **1611** BIBLE *Luke* x. (*heading*), Christ sendeth out, at once, seuenty disciples to worke miracles. **1667** MILTON *P.L.* XII. 438 His Disciples, Men who in his Life Still follow'd him. **1850** ROBERTSON *Serm.* I. xvi. 242 One disciple who had dipped in the same dish..deceived and betrayed him.

b. Also applied in the N.T. to the early Christians generally; hence, in religious use, *absol.* a professed follower of Christ, a Christian or believer. (Hence sense 3.)

c **1380** WYCLIF *De Dot. Eccl.* ii. Sel. Wks. III. 433 Crist seiþ þat noo man may be his discipul but ȝif he renunce alle siche þingis. **1388** —— *Acts* xi. 26 The disciplis weren namyd first at Antioche cristen men. **1526-34** TINDALE *Acts* xx. 7 The disciples came to geder for to breake breed. **1607** HIERON *Wks.* I. 384 If a true disciple, a true Christian; if but a formall disciple, surely but a hollow Christian. **1853** ROBERTSON *Serm.* II. xix. 244 To the true disciple a miracle only *manifests* the Power and Love which are silently at work everywhere. **1890** J. HUNTER *Devot. Services, Dedic. Serv.*, You are gathered here..to take upon yourselves the obligations of Christ's disciples.

c. A personal follower or pupil of any religious or (in more recent use) other teacher or master. (This passes almost imperceptibly into sense 2.)

(Rare in OE.: see a.)

c **900** *Bæda's Hist.* v. ix. (1891) 410 An ðara broðra, se wæs iu on Breotene Bosles discipul and þeᵹn. *a* **1300** *Cursor M.* 21199 (Cott.) Lucas was..disciple o paule ai foluand fer. **1382** WYCLIF *Isa.* viii. 16 Marke the lawe in my disciples. —— *Matt.* xxii. 16 Thanne Pharisees..senden to hym her disciples, with Erodyanys. —— *Luke* vii. 19 And John clepide to gidere tweyne of his disciples, and sente to Ihesu. **1393** GOWER *Conf.* III. 374 (MS. Harl. 3490) And grete well Chaucer, whan ye mete, As my disciple and my poete. **1756** NUGENT *Gr. Tour* France IV. 90 The cieling..is painted in fresco, by Francesco Romanelli, a disciple of Peter of Cortona. **1838** THIRLWALL *Greece* II. 137 His fellow-citizen, friend, and disciple, the courageous and unfortunate Zeno.

d. *generally.* A scholar or pupil. (Now *arch.*, *rhet.*, *affected*, or *jocular*, or with conscious reference to c.)

1489 CAXTON *Faytes of A.* I. x. 29 Al thinges seme dyfficyle to the dysciple or scoler. **1563-7** BUCHANAN *Reform. St. Andros* Wks. (1892) 11 Nor ȝit sal it be leful to the said pedagogis to ding thair disciples. **1758** JORTIN *Life Erasmus* I. 321 Lord Mountjoy, who was formerly my disciple, gives me a yearly pension of an hundred crowns. *Mod.* I am afraid you may not find him a very apt disciple.

2. One who follows, or is influenced by, the doctrine or example of another; one who belongs to the 'school' of any leader of thought. [An extension of 1 c, or *fig.* from 1 a.]

a **1300** *Cursor M.* 16636 (Cott.) Þai spitted on his luueli face, þaa disciplis of hell. **1375** BARBOUR *Bruce* IV. 18 A discipill of Judas, Maknab, a fals tratour. **1594** HOOKER *Eccl. Pol.* IV. vii. (1611) 139 To become disciples vnto the most hatefull sort that liue. **1613** SHAKS. *Hen. VIII*, v. iii. 112 This man, whose honesty the Diuell And his Disciples onely enuy at. **1711** ADDISON *Spect.* No. 163 ¶4, I am one of your Disciples, and endeavour to live up to your Rules. **1849** JAMES *Woodman* xxx, All who are disciples of St. Hubert, prepare your horses. **1868** G. DUFF *Pol. Surv.* 75 M. Pierre Lafitte and his English disciples. **1893** *Chr. World* 16 Nov. 885/3 An advanced Theist, of the school of the late Professor Green, of whom he was a pupil and is a disciple.

3. *pl.* The name of a denomination of Christians, a branch of the Baptists, which originated in the early part of the 19th c. and is chiefly found in the United States; called also Campbellites. [A specific application of 1 b; the name was suggested by Alex. Campbell of Lexington, Kentucky, in 1832.]

1834 J. M. PECK *Gaz. Illinois* 203 A new sect [was] recently organized by a union of 'Reformed Baptists' and 'Christians' who call themselves 'Disciples'. **1835** J. MARTIN *Gaz. Virginia* 76 The precise distinction between the regular Baptist and the Reformers, called the disciples of Christ, not being in all cases drawn. **1858-60** GARDNER *Faiths World* I. 718/1 The principles of the Disciples have found their way into England and Wales..and the census of 1851 contains a return of three congregations or churches calling themselves by the name of the Disciples of Christ. **1867** *Even. Standard* 19 Nov., A new sect is attracting some attention in this city. Its members give themselves the name of 'the Disciples'. They profess a religion most primitive and simple. **1881** W. M. THAYER *Log-Cab. to White Ho.* ii, Abram Garfield..united with a comparatively new sect, called Disciples, though Campbellites was a name by which they were sometimes known.

4. *Comb.*

1641 MILTON *Reform.* II. Wks. (1847) 17 Honoured as a father and physician to the soul, with a sonlike and disciple-like reverence. **1823** BENTHAM *Not Paul* 392 Apparatus employed by him in his trade of disciple-catcher.

di'sciple, *v.* Now *rare* or *arch.* [f. prec. sb.: in sense 3 in earlier use in the form DISPLE; cf. '*disciple*, as stressed by Spenser.]

†1. *trans.* To teach, train, educate. *Obs.*

1596 SPENCER *F.Q.* IV. Introd. i, Fraile youth is oft to follie led.. That better were in vertues discipled. **1601** SHAKS. *All's Well* I. ii. 28 He did looke farre Into the seruice of the time, and was Discipled of the brauest. **1662** HICKERINGILL *Wks.* (1716) I. 303 Every hypocrite can afford to disciple himself thereunto. **1681** W. NICHOLSON *Exp. Catech.* 183 To disciple, or enter into a School to be taught.

2. To make a disciple of; to convert to the doctrine of another. Now *rare* or *arch.*

1647 SALTMARSH *Sparkl. Glory* (1847) 26, I Disciple those Nations, and Baptize them with the Holy Ghost in your ministration. **1651** BAXTER *Inf. Bapt.* 29 When the parents are by teaching made Disciples, the Children are thereby Discipled also. *a* **1711** KEN *Hymns Evang.* Poet. Wks. 1721 I. 179 Go out with Zeal, Disciple all Mankind. **1862** NEALE *Hymns East. Ch.* 36 That every race beneath the skies They should disciple and baptize.

†3. To subject to discipline; to chastise, correct, punish. *Obs.*

1492, **1563**, etc. [see DISPLE]. **1607** WALKINGTON *Opt. Glass* 3 Let us so disciple our selves that each one may throughly know himselfe. **1622** DRAYTON *Poly-olb.* xxiv. (1748) 356 Alban.. who, strongly discipled In Christian patience, learnt his tortures to appease. **1651** N. BACON *Disc. Govt. Eng.* lxix. 289 He was discipled with rods three times.

Hence **di'scipling** *vbl. sb.* and *ppl. a.*

a **1617** HIERON *Wks.* II. 482, I must marshall Christs Disciples into two ranks: the first I may call for this once discipling Disciples; that is, such as haue a calling to call others vnto Christ; plainely, Ministers. *a* **1638** MEDE *Disc. Rev.* iii. 19 Wks. (1672) I. 296 Such a correction as.. we use to call a discipling, a punishment of discipline. **1697** COLLIER *Ess. Mor. Subj.* I. (1709) 161 None but Mr. Hobs, and some few of his Discipling. **1713** BEVERIDGE *Priv. Th.* I. (1730) 65 Discipling, or bringing the Nations over to the Profession of the Christian Religion. **1812** SOUTHEY *Omniana* I. 2 Such penances, such fasting, such discipling.

†**di'sciplehood.** *Obs.* [f. DISCIPLE *sb.* + -HOOD. OE. had *discipulhád.*] The condition or state of a disciple; = next.

[*c* **900** *Bæda's Hist.* IV. xxviii. [xxvii]. (1891) 362 Ðisses discipulhada Cuðbyrht wæs eadmodlice underþeoded.] *a* **1400** *Gloss.* in *Rel. Ant.* I. 6 *Discipulatus*, a discipylhod. *c* **1449** PECOCK *Repr.* 295 Euydence that Crist here clepid this ȝong man into Apostilhode or vnto Disciplehode. **1697** *State of Philadelph. Soc.* 7 Great and glorious Ends, worthy of a true Disciplehood of Jesus Christ.

di'scipleship. [f. DISCIPLE *sb.* + -SHIP.] 'The state or function of a disciple, or follower of a master' (J.).

1549 LATIMER *6th Serm. Edw. VI*, (Arb.) 177 [He] dyd it not onely to allure them to hys discipleshippe, but also for our commoditye. **1607** HIERON *Wks.* I. 384 Such as is a mans disciple-ship, such is his christianity. **1710** NORRIS *Chr. Prud.* viii. 355 Wisdom.. invites us to come into her Discipleship. **1832** CARLYLE in *Fraser's Mag.* V. 383 The old reverent feeling of Discipleship.. had passed utterly away. **1889** SWINBURNE *Study B. Jonson* 98 No Lydgate or Lytton was ever more obsequious in his discipleship.

†**di'scipless.** *Obs.* [f. DISCIPLE *sb.* + -ESS.] A female disciple.

1382 WYCLIF *Acts* ix. 36 In Ioppe was sum disciplisse, bi name Tabyta. *c* **1410** LOVE *Bonavent. Mirr.* xliv. (Gibbs MS. 95) Mawdeleyne þe trewe louede dyscyplesse. **1548** UDALL, etc. *Erasm. Par. Luke* viii. 88 b, Joanna yᵉ wife of Chusa.. became a disciplesse vnto Christ. **1611** SPEED *Hist. Gt. Brit.* VII. xxxi. (1632) 376 She was afterwards recommended to a Disciplesse of the said Lady.

disciplinable ('dɪsɪplɪnəb(ə)l), *a.* [ad. L. *disciplīnābil-is* to be learnt by teaching, f. *disciplīnāre* to instruct: see DISCIPLINE *v.* and -BLE. Cf. F. *disciplinable*, 15th c. in Hatz.-Darm.]

1. Amenable to discipline or teaching; capable of being instructed; docile.

1542 UDALL *Erasm. Apoph.* 196 b, Of Elephantes, how disciplinable and of how greate prudence, docilitee and.. capacitee and aptitude thei are. **1559** ABP. PARKER *Corr.* 63 If ye see ought in my quire worth reformation ye know I am disciplinable. **1639** MARCOMBES in *Lismore Papers* Ser. II. (1888) IV. 101 Your hopefull sons.. are very noble, vertuous, discret and disciplinable. **1840** MILL *Diss. & Disc.* (1859) II. 146 Instead of the most disciplinable one of the most intractable races among mankind. **1889** *Temple Bar Mag.* Nov. 406 Lads.. who were disciplinable to take a special line.

†2. Of or pertaining to instruction; disciplinary.

1644 DIGBY *Nat. Bodies* II. ix. (1645) 84 Those Philosophers, who in a disciplinable way search into nature. **1677** HALE *Prim. Orig. Man.* 311 Animals.. are advanceable by Industry and disciplinable Acts to a great perfection.

3. Subject or liable to discipline or correction.

1870 ANDERSON *Missions Amer. Bd.* II. xix. 155 [They] had maintained their standing as Christians, and avoided all disciplinable offences.

Hence **disciplinableness**, the quality of being amenable to discipline; docility.

1677 HALE *Prim. Orig. Man.* I. i. 16 We find in Animals.. something of Sagacity, Providence, Disciplinableness.

disciplinal ('dɪsɪplɪnəl, dɪsɪ'plaɪnəl), *a.* [ad. med.L. *disciplīnāl-is* (Du Cange), f. *disciplīna* DISCIPLINE: see -AL¹.]

†1. = DISCIPLINABLE 1. *Obs.*

a **1628** PRESTON *New Covt.* (1634) 144 Those two [seeing and hearing] are the only disciplinal senses we have.

2. Of, belonging to, or of the nature of discipline.

1853 E. J. SHEPHERD *3rd Let. to Dr. Maitland* 9 By strong expositions of disciplinal views. **1855** BRIMLEY *Ess.* 16 (*Tennyson*) Pain that serves no disciplinal aim. **1863** M. PATTISON *Serm.* (1885) 88 The.. struggle of the disciplinal system of education against the doctrinal. **1881** FITCH *Lect. Teaching* iv. 107 One of the hardest of the disciplinal problems of a boarding-school is the regulation of the employments of Sunday. *Ibid.* ix. 256 All study of language is in itself disciplinal.

'disciplinant. [a. Sp. *disciplinantes* (pl.), or It. *disciplinanti* (pl.) 'a religious order of such as will scourge themselues' (Florio 1598), sbst. use of pr. pple. of med.L. *disciplināre* to chastise, correct, beat with rods (Du Cange).]

One who subjects himself to a course of discipline; *spec.* a member of a religious order in Spain, who publicly scourged themselves by way of discipline.

1620 SHELTON *Quix.* IV. xxv. II. 277 Presently he 'spy'd, descending from a certain Height, several Men apparell'd in white, like Disciplinants. **1718** MOTTEUX *Quix.* (1733) II. 297 The Disciplinants lifting up their Hoods and grasping fast their Whips, as the Priests did their Tapers. **1766** SMOLLETT *Trav.* 242 The very disciplinants, who scourge themselves in the Holy-Week, are generally peasants or parties hired for the purpose. **1881** DUFFIELD *Don Quix.* III. lxxi. 699, I have no mind to catch cold, which is the danger run by all new disciplinants.

Disciplinarian (ˌdɪsɪplɪ'nɛərɪən), *a.* and *sb.* [f. as DISCIPLINARY + -AN.]

A. *adj.* 1. *Ch. Hist.* Of or pertaining to the Disciplinarians (see B. 1); Presbyterian.

1593 ABP. BANCROFT *Surv. Discipline* iii. 56 Those Disciplinarian practises. *Ibid.* xix. 215 The Papistes.. and our disciplinarian men. **1598** *Conspir. Pretended Ref.* 98 Doe not many of the Disciplinarian veine despise and condemne all helpes of good Artes? **1654** H. L'ESTRANGE *Chas. I* (1655) 157 The hole Parliament (whereof some members began now to incline to the Disciplinarian Sect). **1889** A. H. DRYSDALE *Hist. Presbyter. Eng.* II. iv. 223 The Disciplinarian or Presbyterian party was extinct.

2. Of or pertaining to discipline; disciplinary.

1640 SIR E. DERING *Sp. on Relig.* 18 Dec. vi. 22 The other three are disciplinarian in the present way of Novellisme. **1678** OWEN *Mind of God* viii. 215 The Second sort of means I call Disciplinarian. **1751** JOHNSON *Rambler* No. 141 ¶5 My tutor.. after a few months began to relax the muscles of disciplinarian moroseness. **1876** MOZLEY *Univ. Serm.* iv. 89 The self-made trial is a poor disciplinarian weapon.

B. *sb.*

1. *Ch. Hist.* A name applied to the Puritans of the Elizabethan age, who aimed at establishing the Genevan or Presbyterian ecclesiastical polity or 'discipline' in England: see DISCIPLINE 6 b.

1585-7 T. ROGERS *39 Art.* (1607) 331 The erroneous and evil minds.. Of the late schismatics, namely.. The Disciplinarians or Puritans among ourselves. **1639** SANDERSON *Serm.* II. 33 All sectaries pretend to scripture; papists, anabaptists, disciplinarians. **1673** R. LEIGH *Transp. Reh.* 98 Bishop Bramhall speaking of the Scotch Disciplinarians. **1886** J. H. BLUNT *Dict. Sects* 125 At one time the Disciplinarians had so much expectation of carrying out their plans as openly to express their conviction that Parker would be the last archbishop of Canterbury.

2. One who enforces discipline (in an army, school, family, etc.).

1639 FULLER *Holy War* IV. xii. (1647) 189 He, being a strict Disciplinarian, would punish their vitious manners. **1705** HEARNE *Collect.* 7 Dec., He was like to prove a good Disciplinarian. **1742** FIELDING *J. Andrews* III. v, Because one man scourges twenty or thirty boys more in a morning than another, is he therefore a better disciplinarian? **1835** ALISON *Hist. Europe* (1854) IV. xxii. 20 A severe.. disciplinarian.. he yet secured the affections of.. his.. men. **1882** B. M. CROKER *Proper Pride* I. ii. 18 A strict disciplinarian, and a most excellent teacher.

3. An upholder or advocate of strict discipline.

1746 WESLEY *Princ. Methodist* 32 Nor did the strictest Disciplinarian scruple suffering me to exercise those Powers wherever I came. **1859** MILL *Liberty* i. 29 A despotism of society over the individual, surpassing anything contemplated in the political ideal of the most rigid disciplinarian among the ancient philosophers.

Hence **discipli'narianism**, the principles and practice of a disciplinarian.

1872 SYD. MOSTYN *Perplexity* II. iii. 56 The house was full of the suggestions of disciplinarianism.

'disciplinarily, *adv. rare.* [f. next + -LY².] In the way of discipline.

1706 A. SHIELDS *Inquiry Ch. Communion* (1747) 26 No church would censure disciplinarily all guilty of epidemick backslidings.

disciplinary ('dɪsɪplɪnərɪ), *a.* (*sb.*). [ad. med.L. *disciplīnāri-us*, f. *disciplīna* DISCIPLINE: see -ARY¹. Cf. It. *disciplinario* (1598 Florio) and F. *disciplinaire* (1611 Cotgr.).]

1. Relating to ecclesiastical discipline. †b. *spec.* in 16–17th c. = DISCIPLINARIAN *a.* 1.

1593 ABP. BANCROFT *Surv. Discipline* xviii. 198 Of the disagreement about the new disciplinarie Deacons. *Ibid.* xix. 226 Amongest the Disciplinary brotherhoode. **1640** R. BAILLIE *Canterb. Self-Convict.* 89 This to him.. is doctrinall Puritanisme, much worse than disciplinary. **1641** T. EDWARDS *Reasons agst. Independ.* Ep. Ded. 2 The chiefe question is about the.. discipline of the Church, and our Controversie may fitly be tearmed the Disciplinary Controversie. **1702** C. MATHER *Magn. Chr.* I. v. (1853) I. 76 A few disciplinary points which are confessed indifferent by the greatest zealots for them. **1719** J. T. PHILIPPS tr. 34 *Confer.* 349 There is no disciplinary Institution observed among these Christians.

2. Of, pertaining to, or of the nature of discipline; promoting discipline or orderly observance of rules.

1598 FLORIO, *Disciplinario*, disciplinarie, pertaining to discipline or correction. *a* **1612** DONNE *Βιαθανατος* (1644) 27 A man which undertook an austere and disciplinary taming of his body by fasts or corrections. **1825** COLERIDGE *Aids Refl.* (1848) I. 303 That watchful and disciplinary love and loving-kindness, which.. Christ himself had enjoined. **1865** *Sat. Rev.* 2 Sept. 298/2 The internal disciplinary regulations of the celebrated seminary of Bonn savour a little of barbarism. **1866** *Law Times' Rep.* LIII. 665/1 All these restrictions are merely disciplinary, and do not affect the tenancy.

b. Of a person: Given to enforcing discipline.

a **1601** BACON *Lett. to Earl of Essex* (T.), It may make you in your commandments rather to be gracious than disciplinary.

3. Pertaining to the acquirement of learning or mental training.

1644 MILTON *Educ.* Wks. 1738 I. 139 The Studies wherin our noble and our gentle Youth ought to bestow their time in a disciplinary way from twelve to one and twenty. **1864** BOWEN *Logic* ii. 39 Encumbered it with a mass of disciplinary precepts. **1869** J. MARTINEAU *Ess.* II. 27 An excellent disciplinary instrument for the formation of character.

†4. Acquired by learning. *Obs. rare.*

1647 TRAPP *Comm. Phil.* iii. 10 A naturall man may have a disciplinary knowledge of Christ, that is, by hear-say, as a blinde man hath of colours, not an intuitive. **1658** BAXTER *Saving Faith* vi. 36 Temporary Believers may have more then this meer Disciplinary knowledge. *Ibid.* 37 He saith that one sort of knowledge is Disciplinary.. and the other is Intuitive.

†B. *sb.* = DISCIPLINARIAN *sb.* 1. *Obs. rare.*

1585-7 ROGERS *39 Art.* (1607) 271 Such adversaries in our time be the.. Disciplinaries (usually termed Puritans).

†**'disciplinate**, *v. Obs.* [f. L. *disciplīnāt-* ppl. stem of *disciplīnāre* to DISCIPLINE.] *trans.* To subject to instruction or discipline; to discipline. Hence **'disciplinated** *ppl. a.*, **-ating** *vbl. sb.*

a **1586** SIDNEY *Wanstead Play* Arcadia, etc. (1613) 571 A Pedagogue, one not a little versed in the disciplinating of the iuuentall frie. *a* **1624** BP. M. SMITH *Serm.* (1632) 125 She is faine to teach them, and disciplinate them. **1633** AMES *Agst. Cerem.* II. 203 As if those of our disciplinating were so conceyted. **1647** WARD *Simple Cob.* 43, I have.. seen.. such Epidemicall and lethall formality in other disciplinated Churches.

†**discipli'nation.** *Obs. rare*⁻¹. [ad. med.L. *disciplīnātiōn-em*, n. of action from *disciplīnāre*: see prec.] Subjection to discipline.

1673 F. KIRKMAN *Unlucky Citizen* 280 These were they that had passed under his Disciplination.

'discipliˌnative, *a. rare.* [f. L. ppl. stem *disciplīnāt-*: see -ATIVE.] = next.

1792 T. TAYLOR *Comm. Proclus* I. 82 Disciplinative science. **1855** SMEDLEY *Occult Sciences* 8 The good they contain is not *disciplinative* but *mystic.*

disciplinatory ('dɪsɪplɪˌneɪtərɪ, -'plaɪnətərɪ), *a.* [ad. med.L. *disciplīnātōri-us* (Du Cange): see prec. and -ORY.] Tending to promote discipline.

1851 I. TAYLOR *Wesley* (1852) 255 His abhorrence of laxities.. led him to adopt a complicated disciplinatory system. **1853** LYNCH *Self-Improv.* iii. 62 There are.. Elementary and Disciplinatory books. **1865** *Spectator* 28 Jan. 102/2 Education is not merely disciplinatory nor useful, but should combine both objects.

discipline ('dɪsɪplɪn), *sb.* Also 4 dici-, 4–6 disci-, discy-, 4–7 dissi-, dyssy-, dyssi-, 5 dyscy-, -pline, -plyne. [a. F. *discipline* (OF. also *dece-*, *dese-*, *desce-*, 11th c. in Hatz.-Darm.), ad. L. *disciplīna* instruction of disciples, tuition, for *discipulīna*, f. *discipulus* pupil, DISCIPLE.

Etymologically, *discipline*, as pertaining to the disciple or scholar, is antithetical to *doctrine*, the property of the doctor or teacher; hence, in the history of the words, *doctrine* is more concerned with abstract theory, and *discipline* with practice or exercise.]

†1. a. Instruction imparted to disciples or scholars; teaching; learning; education, schooling. *Obs.*

1382 WYCLIF *Prov.* iii. 4 Thou shalt finde grace, and good discipline [**1388** teching] befor God and men. *c* **1510** BARCLAY *Mirr. Gd. Manners* (1570) F vj, If thou haue in greke had all thy discipline, To dispute in latin what needeth thee to seeke. **1548** HALL *Chron., Edw. IV*, 223 b, He firste holpe his awne young scholers, to attein to discipline, and for them he founded a solempne schoole at Eton. **1606** SHAKS. *Tr. & Cr.* II. iii. 31 Heauen blesse thee from a Tutor, and Discipline come not neere thee! **1615** *Stow's Annals*

(1631) 307/2 Apt to all offices of worthinesse, if in his childhood hee had not wanted discipline.

b. A particular course of instruction to disciples.

Discipline of the Secret (a translation of modern L. *disciplina arcāni*, used by Tentzel and Schelstrate 1683–5): a term of post-Reformation controversy, applied to modes of procedure held to have been observed in the early Church in gradually teaching the mysteries of the Christian faith to neophytes, and in concealing them from the uninitiated. **1620–55** I. JONES *Stone-Heng* (1725) 9 They communicated nothing, but to those of their own Society, taking special Order..their Discipline might not be divulged. **1833** ROCK *Hierurgia* II. 1 §3 *note*, The Discipline of the Secret. **1885** *Catholic Dict.* 266 *Discipline of the Secret* ..a convenient name for the custom which prevailed in the early Church of concealing from heathen and catechumens the more sacred and mysterious doctrines and rites of.. religion.

2. A branch of instruction or education; a department of learning or knowledge; a science or art in its educational aspect.

c **1386** CHAUCER *Can. Yeom. Prol.* & *T.* 700 Assaye in myn absence This disciplyne and this crafty science. **1500–20** DUNBAR *Poems* lxv. 4 To speik of science, craft, or sapience ..Off euerie study, lair, or discipline. **1549** COVERDALE, etc. *Erasm. Par. Eph.* II. 2 Being singularely learned in humayne disciplines, ye haue excelled other sortes of men euer vnto this day. **1597** MORLEY *Introd. Mus.* 184 Ye tearmeth he musick a perfect knowledge of al sciences and disciplines. **1654** Z. COKE *Logick* (1657) 2 Objective disciplines be.. principally four. 1 Theologie. 2 Jurisprudence. 3 Medicine. 4 Philosophy. **1685** BOYLE *Enq. Notion Nat.* 375 Acquainted with Physico-Mathematical Disciplines, such as Opticks, Astronomy, Hydrostaticks, and Mechanicks. **1741** MIDDLETON *Cicero* I. vi. 454 Skill'd in all the Tuscan discipline of interpreting portentous events. **1844** EMERSON *Lect. New Eng. Ref.* Wks. (Bohn) I. 266 The culture of the mind in those disciplines to which we give the name of education. **1864** BURTON *Scot Abr.* II. i. 48 Professors of arts and disciplines at Paris. **1878** BELL *Gegenbaur's Comp. Anat.* 1 The department of Science which has organic nature for its investigations, breaks up into two great divisions, Botany and Zoology..The two disciplines together form the science of living nature. **1942** *Spectator* 27 Feb. 204/1 The distribution of academic disciplines in which they [*sc.* candidates for the Foreign Office] had specialised. **1958** G. J. WARNOCK *Eng. Philos. since 1900* xiii. 172 It is only quite recently that the subject-matter, or rather the tasks, of philosophy have come to be clearly distinguished from those of other disciplines. **1962** *Lancet* 13 Jan. 113/1 Sir Leonard Parsons..had been the first to draw into the paediatrics of his time other disciplines such as biochemistry and immunology.

3. a. Instruction having for its aim to form the pupil to proper conduct and action; the training of scholars or subordinates to proper and orderly action by instructing and exercising them in the same; mental and moral training; also used *fig.* of the training effect of experience, adversity, etc.

1434 MISYN *Mending of Life* 112 Qwhat is disciplyne bot settyng of maners or correctynge?..be disciplyne we ar taght rightwysnes, & of ill correctyd. **1607** BACON *Ess., Marriage & Single L.* (Arb.) 268 Certainely wife and children are a kind of discipline of humanity. **1697** DRYDEN *Virg. Georg.* III. 323 The pamper'd Colt will Discipline disdain. **1713** STEELE *Englishman* No. 7. 46 Clowns under the Discipline of the Dancing-Master. **1736** BUTLER *Anal.* I. v. Wks. 1874 I. 85 The present life was intended to be a state of discipline for a future one. **1741** MIDDLETON *Cicero* I. VI. 461 Caelius..was a young Gentleman..trained under the discipline of Cicero himself. **1849** MACAULAY *Hist. Eng.* II. 240 A mind on which all the discipline of experience and adversity had been exhausted in vain. **1857** RUSKIN *Pol. Econ. Art* i. (1868) 23 The notion of Discipline and Interference lies at the root of all human progress or power. **1862** SIR B. BRODIE *Psychol. Inq.* II. v. 177 No part of early education is more important than the discipline of the imagination. **1892** WESTCOTT *Gospel of Life* 270 Every sorrow and pain is an element of discipline.

b. *spec.* Training in the practice of arms and military evolutions; drill. Formerly, more widely: Training or skill in military affairs generally; military skill and experience; the art of war. (Cf. sense 2.)

1489 CAXTON *Faytes of A.* I. i. 3 Rules, techyngs and dyscyplyne of armes. **1555** EDEN *Decades* 21 A man not ignorant in the disciplyne of warre. **1602** WARNER *Alb. Eng.* IX. xlvi. (1612) 216 Martialists in Discipline and ordering their war. **1659** B. HARRIS *Parival's Iron Age* 41 School of war..where all the Martiall Spirits resorted, to learn Discipline, and to put it in practice. **1775** R. H. LEE in Sparks *Corr. Amer. Rev.* (1853) I. 52 Without discipline armies are fit only for the contempt and slaughter of their enemies. **1776** GIBBON *Decl. & F.* I. 297 It was the rigid attention of Aurelian, even to the minutest articles of discipline, which bestowed such uninterrupted success on his arms.

†**c.** A course of training. *Obs.*

1577 B. GOOGE *Heresbach's Husb.* III. (1586) 153 The knowledge of keeping cattell hath a discipline, wherein a man must from his very Childhood be brought up. **1664** EVELYN *Kal. Hort.* (1729) 188 By such an Oeconomy and Discipline, as our Industrious Gardiner may himself be continualy improving. **1683** *Brit. Spec.* 40 To those..who ..underwent the Severities of a long and tedious Discipline.

4. The orderly conduct and action which result from training; a trained condition.

1509 FISHER *Fun. Serm. C'tess. Richmond* Wks. (1876) 290 The comparyson of them two may be made..In noblenesse of Persone, in discyplyne of theyr bodyes. **1551** T. WILSON *Logike* (1580) 15 b, The politicall lawe doeth cause an outward discipline to be observed, even of the wicked. **1611** BIBLE *Transl. Pref.* 1 Seeking to reduce their Countreymen to good order and discipline. **1728** NEWTON *Chronol. Amended* iv. 312 He..reduced the irregular and undisciplined forces of the Medes into discipline and order. **1781** GIBBON *Decl. & F.* III. liii. 287 The discipline of a soldier is formed by exercise rather than by study. **1827** POLLOK *Course T.* IV, Sound-headed men, Of proper discipline and excellent mind.

5. a. The order maintained and observed among pupils, or other persons under control or command, such as soldiers, sailors, the inmates of a religious house, a prison, etc.

[*c* **1450** tr. *De Imitatione* I. xxv, Fervent & devoute breþren & wel manered & under discipline.] **1667** PEPYS *Diary* 1 Apr. (Wheatley, 1895, VI. 249) [Sir] W. Coventry is wholly resolved to bring him to punishment; for, 'bear with this', says he, 'and no discipline shall ever be expected.' **1697** DRYDEN *Virg. Georg.* II. 509 Let crooked Steel invade The lawless Troops, which discipline disclaim. **1813** WELLINGTON in Gurw. *Desp.* X. 539 The fact is, that, if discipline means obedience to orders, as well as military instruction, we have but little of it in the army. **1827–38** HARE *Guesses* Ser. II. (1873) 494 Discipline..should exercise its influence without appearing to do so. **1836** MARRYAT *Midsh. Easy* xiii, If I do not punish him, I allow a flagrant and open violation of discipline to pass uncensured. **1849** MACAULAY *Hist. Eng.* I. 424 The discipline of workshops, of schools, of private families..was infinitely harsher. **1889** *Times* 9 Mar. 16/1, I recently heard a learned limb of the law..confound prison punishment with prison discipline, forgetting that the former is merely a means of enforcing the latter.

b. A system or method for the maintenance of order; a system of rules for conduct.

1659 B. HARRIS *Parival's Iron Age* 40 The Mutiners governed themselves in form of a Republick, observing a most exact discipline. **1726** SHELVOCKE *Voy. round World* (1757) 227 Having regulated themselves according to the discipline of Jamaica. **1861** M. PATTISON *Ess.* (1889) I. 47 The inmates..were submitted to an almost monastic discipline.

6. a. *Eccles.* The system or method by which order is maintained in a church, and control exercised over the conduct of its members; the procedure whereby this is carried out; the exercise of the power of censure, admonition, excommunication, or other penal measures, by a Christian Church.

1549 *Bk. Comm. Prayer, Commination*, In the primitive church there was a godly discipline, that, at the beginning of Lent, such persons as were notorious sinners were put to open penance. **1561** T. NORTON *Calvin's Inst.* (1578) IV. xii. 2 The first foundation of discipline is, that priuate monitions should haue place. **1574** tr. *Marlorat's Apocalips* 18 Our meeting vpon that day rather than vpon any other, is onely for orders sake, and for a certeine discipline in the Churche. **1621** *First Book of Discipline* (1721) IX. i. 568 The order of Ecclesiastical Discipline, which stands in reproving and correcting of the Faults which the Civill Sword either doth neglect, or may not punish. **1858–60** GARDNER *Faiths World* I. 479/1 The ancient discipline of the church, while it excluded offenders from spiritual privileges, left all their natural or civil rights unaffected.

b. Hence, generally, the system by which the practice of a church, as distinguished from its doctrine, is regulated. *spec.*, in *Eng. Ch. Hist.*, The ecclesiastical polity of the Puritan or Presbyterian party (thence styled DISCIPLINARIANS) in the 16th and 17th c.

Books of Discipline: the name of two documents, adopted in 1561 and 1581 respectively, constituting the original standards of the polity and government of the Reformed Church of Scotland, and also dealing with schools, universities, and other matters.

1574 [W. TRAVERS (*title*) Ecclesiasticæ Disciplinæ et Anglicanæ Ecclesiæ ab illa aberrationis..explicatio.] —— T. CARTWRIGHT [transl. of prec.] (*title*) A full and plain Declaration of Ecclesiastical Discipline owt of the Word off God, and of the declining of the Churche of England from the same. **1588** W. TRAVERS (*title*) A Defence of the ecclesiastical discipline ordayned of God to be used in his Church, agaynst a reply of Maister Bridges. **1593** ABP. BANCROFT (*title*) A Survay of the Pretended Holy Discipline. *Ibid.* v. 70 (*heading*) The pretended Antiquitie of the Consistorian Discipline. **1594** HOOKER *Eccl. Pol.* (1888) I. 126 The wonderful zeal and fervour wherewith ye have withstood the received order of this Church..to join..for the furtherance of that which ye term the *Lord's Discipline*. *Ibid.* 127 Let it be lawful for me to rip up to the very bottom how and by whom your Discipline was planted. *Ibid.* 138 That which Calvin did for establishment of his discipline, seemeth more commendable than that which he taught for the countenancing of it when established. **1610** B. JONSON *Alch.* III. i, This heat of his may turn into a zeal, And stand up for the beauteous discipline Against the menstruous cloth and rag of Rome. **1642** CHAS. I, *Roy. Protestations* 4 New doctrines and disciplines. **1643** MILTON (*title*) The Doctrine and Discipline of Divorce restored..from the Bondage of Canon Law. **1676** W. HUBBARD *Happiness of People* 35 Wee in New England that profess the doctrine of Calvin, yet practise the discipline of them called Independant, or Congregational Churches. **1792** BURKE *Let. to Sir H. Langrishe* Wks. 1842 I. 547 Three religions.. each of which has its confession of faith and its settled discipline. **1874** GREEN *Short Hist.* viii. §5. 509 The Presbyterian organization remained untouched in doctrine or discipline. **1885** *Catholic Dict.* 265 Usually, discipline in its ecclesiastical sense signifies the laws which bind the subjects of the Church in their conduct, as distinct from dogmas or articles of faith, which affect their belief.

c **1566** KNOX *Hist. Ref. Scot.* (1848) II. 181 (anno 1561) The Preacheris vehementlie exhorted us to establische *The Buke of Discipline*, by ane Act and publict Law. **1621** CALDERWOOD *Hist. Kirk* (1843) II. 50 At the same conventioun [1561], the Booke of Discipline was subscribed by a great part of the nobilitie. *Ibid.* 51 To establishe a more perfyte discipline, which was done twentie yeeres after..as we sall see in the Second Booke of Discipline. **1621** (*title, 1st printed ed.*) The First and Second Booke of Discipline, together with some Acts of the Generall Assemblies. **1860** J. LEE *Hist. Ch. Scot.* I. 151 The first head of the original Book of Discipline treats of Doctrine..The second head relates to Sacraments..The fourth head related to Ministers and their lawful election.

7. a. Correction; chastisement; punishment inflicted by way of correction and training; in religious use, the mortification of the flesh by penance; also, in more general sense, a beating or other infliction (humorously) assumed to be salutary to the recipient. (In its monastic use, the earliest English sense.)

a **1225** *Ancr. R.* 138 Auh ancre schal..temien ful wel hire fleschs..mid heuie swinke, mid herde disciplines. **1340** *Ayenb.* 236 Hit be-houeþ þet uless beate and wesse be dissiplines and be hardnesses. **1382** WYCLIF *Prov.* iii. 11 The discipline of the Lord, my sone, ne caste thou awey. **1482** *Monk of Evesham* (Arb.) 22 Alle that were there wyth grete contricion of herte toke discyplynys of roddys. **1509** FISHER *Fun. Serm. C'tess Richmond* Wks. (1876) 293 The blessyd Martha is praysed in chastysynge her Body by crysten dyscyplyne. **1620** SHELTON *Quix.* IV. xxv. II. 277 They did institute Rogations, Processions, and Disciplines throughout all that Country. **1686** J. SERGEANT *Hist. Monast. Convent.* 34 If any be found unchast, she receives three Disciplines or Scourgings. *c* **1790** WILLOCK *Voy.* 36 With a rope's-end..he continued this discipline till he rendered me incapable of moving. **1811** *Sporting Mag.* XXXVII. 133 [She] came in for her share of the discipline which her husband was undergoing. **1888** BERNARD *Fr. World to Cloister* v. 113 The corporal austerities which are known as 'the discipline'.

b. *transf.* Hence applied to the instrument of chastisement: A whip or scourge; esp. one used for religious penance.

1622 PEACHAM *Compl. Gent.* 120 By Chastity standeth Pennance having driven away with her discipline Winged Love. **1630** WADSWORTH *Pilgr.* iii. 20 Approaching his bed side with two good disciplines in their hands, the ends of some stucke with wyery prickes, they did..raze his skinne. **1707** J. STEVENS *Quevedo's Com. Wks.* (1709) Rij, The Whipsters..laid aside their Disciplines. **1825** SCOTT *Talism.* iv, On the floor lay a discipline, or penitential scourge. **1848** J. H. NEWMAN *Loss & Gain* III. x. 376 In the cell..hangs an iron discipline or scourge, studded with nails.

†**8.** Treatment for some special purpose, e.g. medical regimen. *Obs. rare.*

1754 MRS. E. MONTAGU in *Four C. Eng. Lett.* 280 He has been under discipline for his eyes, but his spirits and vivacity are not abated. **1816** JANE AUSTEN *Let.* 9 July (1952) 457 Her illness must have been a very serious one indeed... Tell your Father I..most sincerely join in the hope of her being..much the better for her present Discipline.

9. *attrib.* as in **discipline-master**, a master in a school employed not to teach, but to keep order among the pupils.

1892 *Pall Mall G.* 2 Nov. 6/3 A discipline master, who was running with the hounds, plunged in to catch the 'hares'. **1895** *Daily News* 3 Apr. 8/3 Deceased was employed as discipline master..at..the Police Orphanage.

'discipline, *v.* [a. F. *discipliner* (12th c. in Hatz.-Darm.) or med.L. *disciplīnāre*, f. L. *disciplīna* DISCIPLINE *sb.*]

1. *trans.* To subject to discipline; in earlier use, to instruct, educate, train; in later use, more especially, to train to habits of order and subordination; to bring under control.

1382 [see DISCIPLINED below]. **1589** PUTTENHAM *Eng. Poesie* I. xii. (Arb.) 44 With vs Christians, who be better disciplined, and do acknowledge but one God. **1638** BAKER tr. *Balzac's Lett.* II. (1654) 97 When some Discipline themselves, others run to debauches of all kindes. **1641** HINDE *J. Bruen* Ep. to Rdr., I would send such to be disciplined by Erasmus. **1695** BLACKMORE *Pr. Arth.* I. 591, I form'd and disciplin'd their untaught Hate. **1711** ADDISON *Spect.* No. 160 ¶4 Great natural Genius's that were never disciplined and broken by Rules of Art. **1795** SOUTHEY *Joan of Arc* IX. 145 Heaven by sorrow disciplines The froward heart. **1871** R. W. DALE *Ten Commandm.* viii. 206 The whole organisation of the world is intended to discipline our moral nature. **1888** BURGON *Lives 12 Gd. Men* II. x. 242 He had been disciplined in the school of adversity.

b. *spec.* To train in military exercises and prompt action in obedience to command; to drill.

1598 BARRET *Theor. Warres* I. i. 7 Warres well conducted and disciplined. **1606** SHAKS. *Tr. & Cr.* II. iii. 255 He that disciplin'd thy armes to fight. **1692** LUTTRELL *Brief Rel.* (1857) II. 629 Orders were come from England..to discipline the militia. **1792** *Anecd. W. Pitt* I. v. 138 A farmer ..may be a good soldier if you take care to have him properly disciplined. **1855** MACAULAY *Hist. Eng.* IV. 79 He addressed himself vigorously to the task of disciplining these strange soldiers. **1861** *Even. Star* 4 Oct., The Western men take longer to discipline into soldiers than the citizens of New England.

c. To subject to ecclesiastical discipline; 'to execute the laws of the church on offenders, with a view to bring them to repentance and reformation of life' (Webster).

1828 in WEBSTER. [**1870** cf. DISCIPLINABLE 3.] **18..** H. W. BEECHER *Plymouth Pulpit* Ser. VI. II. 134 (Funk & Wagn.) He whose orthodoxy inspires bitterness should be disciplined.

2. To inflict penitential discipline upon; to scourge or flog by way of penance or mortification of the flesh; hence, by extension, to chastise, thrash, punish.

c **1300** *Beket* 2384 Of Ech Monek of the hous: he let him discipline, With a 3urd. **1482** *Monk of Evesham* (Arb.) 31 Y made a signe to hym, to discypline me in lyke wyse ageyne as he dyd afore. **1483** CAXTON *Gold. Leg.* 432 b/2 He chastysed his body by abstynence of mete & drynke &.. dyscyplyned it..with chaynes of yron right ofte wyth his owne handes. **1607** SHAKS. *Cor.* II. i. 139 Ha's he disciplin'd Auffidius soundly? **1647** N. BACON *Disc. Govt. Eng.* I. lxix. (1739) 181 First he was disciplin'd with rods three times. **1740** GRAY *Let.* Poems (1775) 83 Half a dozen wretched creatures..are in a side-chapel disciplining themselves with scourges full of iron prickles. **1786** tr. *Beckford's Vathek* (1868) 103 Having well disciplined their asses with nettles behind. **1865** T. F. KNOX tr. *Life of Henry Suso* 65 He used to..go into the choir in front of the Blessed Sacrament and there discipline himself.

†**b.** *intr.* (for *refl.*). To chastise oneself. *Obs.*

a **1300** *E.E.P.* (1862) 154 Wiþ seint benetis scurge lome ȝe disciplineþ.

†**3.** *trans.* To deal with or treat of in an orderly manner. *Obs. rare.*

1658 EVELYN *Fr. Gard.* (1675) 261 Your fruit, your herbs, and your pulses are disciplin'd in the two former treatises.

Hence **'disciplined** *ppl. a.*; **'disciplining** *vbl. sb.* and *ppl. a.*

1382 WYCLIF *Jas.* iii. 13 Who is wijse, and disciplined [**1388** tauȝt] among ȝou? *c* **1400** *Test. Love* (R.) After a good disciplining with a yerde, they kepe right well doctrine of their schole. **1641** MILTON *Ch. Govt.* i. (1851) 99 They are left to their own disciplining at home. **1645** EVELYN *Mem.* (1857) I. 191 Amongst other things, they shew St. Catharine's disciplining cell. **1668** PEPYS *Diary* 20 Dec., How the Spaniards are the best disciplined foot in the world. **1669** WOODHEAD *St. Teresa* II. xxvi. 161 Her penances, and disciplinings were numerous. **1781** GIBBON *Decl. & F.* III. 165 Alaric was a Christian and a soldier, the leader of a disciplined army. **1862** H. SPENCER *First Princ.* II. iv. §53 (1875) 175 A developed and disciplined intelligence.

'discipliner. [f. DISCIPLINE *sb.* or *v.* + -ER[1].] One who disciplines or subjects to discipline; an adherent of a system of discipline.

1611 SPEED *Hist. Gt. Brit.* IX. xv. (1632) 784 The King incensed against these discontented disciplinersc **1644** MILTON *Areop.* (Arb.) 42 Had an Angel bin his discipliner. **1656** DUCHESS OF NEWCASTLE *Life* (1886) 280 Two of my three brothers were excellent soldiers, and martial discipliners. **1731** MRS. PENDARVES in *Mrs. Delany's Life & Corr.* 312 The gout or rheumatism you have never provoked —it would be hard indeed if you should suffer by those severe discipliners. **1895** *19th Cent.* Aug. 251 Any monk lying abed later than four without excuse was sent to the discipliner for birching.

discipling, *vbl. sb.* and *ppl. a.*: see DISCIPLE *v.*

†**'disciplinize,** *v. Obs. rare.* [f. DISCIPLINE *sb.* + -IZE.] *trans.* To bring under discipline; spec. under the Presbyterian ecclesiastical discipline.

1659 GAUDEN *Tears of Ch.* 609 These were to do the Journey-work of Presbytery..undertaking to Directorize, to Unliturgize, to Catechize, and to Disciplinize their Brethren.

†**discipli'zation.** = *discipling*: see DISCIPLE *v.*

1657–83 EVELYN *Hist. Relig.* (1850) II. 55 The unprofitableness and weakness of the former disciplization.

discipular (dɪ'sɪpjʊlə(r)), *a.* [f. L. *discipul-us* DISCIPLE + -AR[1].] Of, belonging to, or of the nature of, a disciple.

1859 *Sat. Rev.* 13 Aug. 198/1 Mr. Mansel's..discipular spirit marks him out to carry onward the new Scottish Philosophy. **1862** F. HALL *Hindu Philos. Syst.* 181 By S'ankara and by all his discipular successors. **1873** MORLEY *Rousseau* II. xi. 93 His discipular patience when his master told him that his verses were poor.

di'scipulate. *rare.* [f. as prec. + -ATE[1].] The state of a disciple; discipleship, pupilage.

1842 *Tait's Mag.* IX. 681 During the period of his discipulate.

di'scipulize, *v. rare.* [f. as prec. + -IZE.] *trans.* = DISCIPLE *v.* 2.

1863 *Kitto's Cycl. Bibl. Lit.* (ed. 3) I. 293/2 When we come to ask, what is implied in discipleship? in what relation does baptism stand to the discipulising of nations?

discission (dɪ'sɪʃən). Also 7 discition, discision. [ad. L. *dīscissiōn-em*, n. of action f. *dīscindĕre* to cleave, cut asunder: see DISCIND. But the 17th c. spelling *discision* appears to come from L. *dis-* and *cædere, -cīdere* to cut, ppl. stem *-cīs-*: see DISCIDE, and cf. *excision, incision.*] A cleaving, rending, or cutting asunder; now only in *Surg.*: An incision into a tumour or cataract: see DECISION 4.

1647 H. MORE *Song of Soul* II. iii. III. xlviii, So gentle Venus..Casts ope that azur curtain by a swift discission. **1661** G. RUST *Origen* in *Phœnix* I. 37 As painful as the violent discision of very Life would be could it be forcibly torn in pieces. **1684** tr. *Bonet's Merc. Compit.* XVII. 590 You must slant your Knife and endeavour discision with an oblique Hand. **1883** *Syd. Soc. Lex., Discission*, a cutting into: especially an incision into or laceration of the capsule of the lens in the operation for the removal of cataract.

discition, obs. form of DECISION.

1633 PRYNNE *Histrio-Mastix* II. iv. 92 (R.) Declining their owne particular discitions to avoid all partiality.

disclaim (dɪs'kleɪm), *v.* [a. AF. *des-, disclamer* (accented stem *desclaime*), f. *des-*, DIS- 4 + *clamer* to CLAIM; in med.(Anglo)L. *disclāmāre.*]

1. *intr. Law.* To renounce, relinquish, or repudiate a legal claim; to make a formal disclaimer. Const. † *in* the thing disclaimed, †*out of* or *from* the claim of the other party.

Originally said in reference to the renunciation of the claim of feudal lordship or tenancy by the lord or tenant respectively.

[**1302** *Year-books Edw. I* an. 30–31. 83 (Godefroy) Si le tenaunt portat sun bref 'de homagio recipiendo' seriez vus rescuz a desclamer en sun homage. **1304** *Ibid.* 119 En plee qe chiet par voye de destresse le tenaunt poet desclamer. **1409** *Act 9 Hen. IV*, c. 4 Ordines est et establies que nul home larron n'autre felon en Gales ouvertement conus ne soit soeffert par disclaimer hors del seignourie ou la felonie fust faict et qe tielx manere de disclaime soit de tout oustes. [*Pulton's transl.* It is ordained and stablished, that no Thiefe nor Felon in Wales, openly knowne, be suffered to disclaime out of the Seigniorie where the felony was done, and that such maner of disclaiming be vtterly put out.] [*a* **1481** LITTLETON *Tenures* (ed. Houard) 145 Si l'seignior que est vouché ne avoit resceivé pas homage del tenant ne d'ascun de ses auncesters, le seignior (s'il voit) poit disclamer en le seigniory, et issint ouste le tenant de son garranty.] **1574** tr. *Littleton's Tenures* 32 a, The lorde..may disclaime in the lordship, and so put his tenaunte of his warranty. **1597** SKENE *De Verb. Sign.* (s.v. *Disclamation*) *Disclamare* is to disclaime, disavow or deny, as to deny an vther to be his superiour; as quhen the superiour affirmis the landes to be halden of him, and the vassall denies the samin. **1628** COKE *On Litt.* 102 a, The lord may disclaime..which signifieth utterly to renounce the seignory. **1647** N. BACON *Disc. Govt. Eng.* I. lxii. (1739) 125 If the Lord fail, he loses his Tenure, and the Tenant might thenceforth disclaim, and hold over for ever. **1651** *Ibid.* II. xiii. (1739) 71 He that hath both Right and Power, and will not seize, disclaims. **1809** TOMLINS *Law Dict.* s.v. *Disclaimer*, Such person as cannot lose the thing perpetually in which he disclaims, shall not be permitted to disclaim. **1818** CRUISE *Digest* (ed. 2) IV. 494 The law adjudges the frank tenement in B. till he disagrees or disclaims. **1848** WHARTON *Law Lex.* 182 He cannot so disclaim after he has proved the will of his own testator.

†**2.** *intr. transf.* **a.** To renounce or disavow all part *in*; = sense 4. *Obs.*

1560 A. L. tr. *Calvin's Foure Serm. Songe Ezech.* iv, As if God would reject them, and utterly disclaime in them. **1581** MULCASTER *Positions* xxxix. (1887) 195 Dysclayming in that which vertue auaunceth not. **1605** SHAKS. *Lear* II. ii. 59 You cowardly Rascall, nature disclaimes in thee. **1637** B. JONSON *Sad Sheph.* I. ii, The sourer sort Of shepherds now disclaim in all such sport.

†**b.** To proclaim one's renunciation of, or dissent *from. Obs.*

1604 R. PARSONS *3rd Part Three Convers. Eng.* 360 He disclaymed from the Bohemians or Hussits and their opinions. **1605** *Answ. Discov. Romish Doctr.* 39 They not wholy disclaime from the Kinges Authority. **1624** LD. WILLIAMS in *Fortesc. Papers* 203 He disclayminge from all fees and proffitts of the place. **1632** J. HAYWARD tr. *Biondi's Eromena* 125 Catascopo disclaimed from having ever named me.

fig. **1644** DIGBY *Nat. Bodies* II. (1645) 67 These two conditions..doe openly disclaime from quantity and from matter.

3. *trans. Law.* To renounce a legal claim to; to repudiate a connexion with or concern in.

[Arising by omission of the preposition in sense 1: with quot. 1607, cf. **1534** FITZHERBERT *La Nouv. Nat. Brevium* (1567) 197 b, Sil ne disclaime en le sank; *transl.* **1652** If he do not disclaim in the blood.]

1595 SHAKS. *K. John* I. i. 247, I am not Sir Roberts sonne, I haue disclaim'd Sir Robert, and my land, Legitimation, name, and all is gone. **1607** COWELL *Interpr.* s.v. *Disclaimer*, If a man deny himselfe to be of the blood or kindred of another in his plee, he is said to disclaime his blood. *Ibid.* If a man arraigned of felonie do disclaime goods, being cleared he leeseth them. **1651** W. G. tr. *Cowel's Inst.* 48 Nor can an Infant disclaim that Guardian who prosecutes an action for him as being next of Kinn. **1670** [see DISCLAIMER 1 b]. **1754** [see DISCLAMATION 1]. **1768** BLACKSTONE *Comm.* III. 249 Upon this the bishop and the clerk usually disclaim all title. **1818** CRUISE *Digest* (ed. 2) I. 123 Tenant for life may also forfeit his estate by disclaiming to hold of his lord. **1848** WHARTON *Law Lex.* 182 A devisee in fee may, by deed, without manner of record, disclaim the estate devised. *Ibid.* An executor may, before probate, disclaim the executorship.

b. To relinquish a part of (a patent) by a disclaimer.

1835 LD. BROUGHAM 3 June, in *Hansard* ser. 3. XXVIII. 474 The parts disclaimed should not detrimentally affect the other parts of the invention. **1888** R. GRIFFIN *Patent Cases decided* 12 Application..to disclaim the 8th claim.

4. To disavow any claim to or connexion with; to renounce or reject as not belonging to oneself; to disown formally or emphatically.

1593 SHAKS. *Rich. II*, I. i. 70 There I throw my gage, Disclaiming heere the kindred of a King, And lay aside my high bloods Royalty. **1636** HEYWOOD *Challenge* II. Wks. 1874 V. 21 Sir, shee's yours, Or I disclaime her ever. **1647** CLARENDON *Hist. Reb.* II. (1843) 47/2 A short protestation.. in which all men should..disclaim and renounce the having any intelligence, or holding any correspondence with the rebels. **1704** POPE *Spring* 87 Tell me but this, and I'll disclaim the prize. **1791–1823** D'ISRAELI *Cur. Lit., Liter. Forgeries*, The real author..obliged him afterwards to disclaim the work in print. **1875** JOWETT *Plato* (ed. 2) IV. 224 Socrates disclaims the character of a professional eristic. **1895** GLADSTONE *Let.* 8 Aug. in *Daily News* 12 Aug. 5/4, I entirely disclaim the hatred and hostility to Turks, or any race of men, which you ascribe to me.

†**b.** (with complement.) To refuse to acknowledge (any one, or oneself) to be (so and so). *Obs.*

1597 T. BEARD *Theat. Gods Judgem.* (1612) 220 [He]..also disclaimed him from being his father. *Ibid.* 524 Disclaiming him to be her son. **1602** WARNER *Alb. Eng.* XI. lxvii. (1612) 288 That Helen may disclaime her selfe for Helen in her glas. **1670** WALTON *Lives* II. 133 To perswade him..to disclaim himself a Member of the Church of England.

5. To refuse to admit (something claimed by another); to reject the claims or authority of, to renounce.

1659 B. HARRIS *Parival's Iron Age* 28 They likewise disclaimed the Authority of the Pope. **1769** ROBERTSON *Chas. V*, V. III. 130 It was lawful for the people to disclaim him as their sovereign. **1781** GIBBON *Decl. & F.* II. xliii. 585 The troops..disclaimed the command of their superiors. **1841** ELPHINSTONE *Hist. India* I. 203 They agree with the Báudhas..in disclaiming the divine authority of the Védas.

†**b.** To refuse (a thing claimed). *Obs. rare.*

1647 N. BACON *Disc. Govt. Eng.* I. lix. (1739) 114 These then are the rights that the King claimed, and the Clergy disclaimed at the first. **1725** POPE *Odyss.* VIII. 39 Let none to strangers honours due disclaim.

†**c.** To decline or refuse (*to do* something). *Obs.*

1586 A. DAY *Eng. Secretary* I. (1625) 63 Yet disclaime you to be married, you will heare of no suters. **1589** WARNER *Alb. Eng.* Prose Addit. (1612) 340, I that will not liue to heare it so, heartily disclaime to haue it so. **1805** *Miniature* No. 32 ¶13 The errors of the schoolboy will become the errors of the man, if he disclaims to adopt my practice.

†**6.** To denounce the claims or pretensions of; to cry out upon. *Obs.*

1590 J. EGERTON in *Confer.* 32, I shalbe readye to disclayme you wheresoeuer I come, not only for men voyde of pietie, but euen of ciuile honestie also. **1659** B. HARRIS *Parival's Iron Age* 63 The Arminians [were] reviled, and disclaimed, as no better then half Traytors, by the very dregs of the people.

†**b.** *intr.* ***disclaim against***: to cry out against, DECLAIM against. *Obs.*

1615 J. STEPHENS *Satyr. Ess.* 202 Hee is not..ashamed to quarrell, first with his Patron, and openly disclaim against the poor value of his Benefice. **1706** J. SERGEANT *Chapter of William* (1853) 81 That he resolutely oppose it, and disclaim against it, in the chapter's name. **1749** FIELDING *Tom Jones* XI. i, Which bears an exact analogy to the vice here disclaimed against.

7. *trans. Her.* To declare not to be entitled to bear arms; to 'make infamous by proclamation' (those who used arms without any right, or assumed without authority the title of Esquire or Gentleman) as formerly done by the heralds at their visitations. (Said also of the persons, in sense 4.)

1634 *Visitation of Bucks* (in Rylands, *Disclaimers* (1888, ix.) Robᵗ. Wilmott, Chadderton, for usurping the Title of Gent, notwithstanding having been disclaimed in the Visitation made 1611. —— *Visitation of Worcestersh.* (ibid.), Edmd. Brothby..to be spared from disclaiming in regard of his being a souldier and of deserts. —— *Visit. Hereford* (ibid. viii.), John Phillips of Ledbury to be disclaimed at our next sizes because he was not disclaimed at our being in the country, being respyted then for proofe. **1888** J. P. RYLANDS *Disclaimers at the Heralds' Visitations* viii, The practice seems to have been for the visiting Herald to induce the persons summoned to disclaim under their hands if they would..and if they declined, or did not attend..they were disclaimed at the Assizes.

Hence **disclaimed** *ppl. a.*, **disclaiming** *vbl. sb.* and *ppl. a.*

1602 SHAKS. *Ham.* V. ii. 252 Let my disclaiming from a purpos'd euill, Free me so farre in your most generous thoughts. **1607** HIERON *Wks.* I. 268 In all those which thinke and hope to bee saued, there must bee a disclaiming, a renouncing, an vtter forsaking of those sinnes. **1659** B. HARRIS *Parival's Iron Age* 60 A Disciple of that so much disclaimed Italian. **1802** MRS. RADCLIFFE *Poet. Wks.* (1833) II. 271 The Baron..bowed with a disclaiming gesture. **1885** BRIDGES *Nero* III. iv. 16/2 Thou wert right in that, Wrong now returning on disclaimed ambition. **1892** *Rep. Patent Cases* IX. 83 The language of this disclaiming clause.

†**disclaim,** *sb. Obs.* [a. AF. *disclaime*, f. *disclamer*: see prec. vb.] An act of disclaiming; formal renunciation or repudiation of a claim.

[**1409** see DISCLAIM *v.* 1]. **1475** *Bk. Noblesse* 35 And so the said king Lowes relese was..a disclayme frome the kinges of Fraunce for ever. **1611** SPEED *Hist. Gt. Brit.* VII. i. §2. 190 The associates of Britaine were now returned with vtter disclaime of further assistance. **1662** *Jesuits' Reasons* (1675) 128 You..make your disclaim of these..Opinions. **1674** A. G. *Quest. conc. Oath of Alleg.* 29 The disclaim of His indirect Authority over Kings. **1786** *Francis the Philanthropist* III. 85 A blush, not of disclaim, spread her cheek.

disclaimant. [f. DISCLAIM *v.*, after *claimant.*] One who disclaims (a part of a patent): cf. DISCLAIM *v.* 3 b.

1892 *Rules of Practice U.S. Patent Off.* 52 To which the disclaimant does not choose to claim title.

disclaimer[1] (dɪs'kleɪmə(r)). [a. AF. *disclaimer* inf. used sbst.: see -ER[4].] An act or action of disclaiming.

1. *Law.* The action of disclaiming in reference to the feudal relationship, *esp.* on the part of the vassal or tenant; repudiation of a legal claim.

1579 *Termes de la Ley* 68 b, If the tenant say that hee disclaymeth to hold of him, this is called a disclaimer, and if yᵉ Lord thereupon bring a writ of right, sur disclaimer, and it be found against the tenaunt, hee shall lose the land. **1618** PULTON *Stat.* (1632) 269, 9 Hen. IV, c. 4 (*title*) Disclaimer in felony in Wales shall be vtterly excluded and put out. **1650** B. *Discolliminium* 9 Christ..seems to judge it necessary to make a cautelous Disclaimer of the Power that requir'd it. **1767** BLACKSTONE *Comm.* II. 275 Equivalent..to an illegal alienation by the particular tenant, is the civil crime of disclaimer, as where a tenant, who holds of any lord, neglects to render him the due services, and, upon an action brought to recover them, disclaims to hold of his lord.

b. An act of renouncing or relinquishing a legal claim; a formal refusal to accept an estate, trust, duty, etc.: see DISCLAIM *v.* 3.

[**1573** STAUNDFORD *Les Plees del Coron* III. 186 Icy par cel disclaimer: il perdra les biens.. as queux il disclaima]. **1670** BLOUNT *Law Dict.* s.v., In Chancery, if a Defendant by his Answer Disclaim the having any interest in the thing in question, this is also called a Disclaimer. **1809** TOMLINS *Law Dict.* s.v., There is a deed of disclaimer of executorship of a will, etc., where an executor refuses, and throws up the same. **1876** DIGBY *Real Prop.* x. § I. 371 In all other cases the proper mode of refusing to accept a conveyance or devise of land.. is an execution by an alienee of full capacity of a deed of disclaimer.

c. *Patent Law.* An alteration by which a specification is amended in such a manner as to relinquish a portion of the invention, when in danger of being invalidated on account of the comprehensiveness of the claim. Formerly (up to 1883), an instrument executed by a patentee abandoning a part of his claim of invention.

1835 *Act 5 & 6 Will. IV*, c. 83 [He] may enter a disclaimer of any part of his specification. **1879** *Cassell's Techn. Educ.* IV. 102/2 (Patents) A means by which a grantee may abandon portions of the title,.. this process is called a disclaimer. **1883** *Act 46 & 47 Vict.* Chap. 57 (*Patents Act*) §18 Amend his specification.. by way of disclaimer, correction, or explanation. **1892** *Rules of Practice U.S. Patent Off.* 77 Such disclaimer shall be in writing.

2. *generally.* A disavowal of claims or pretensions; a renunciation, denial, or rejection.

1790 BURKE *Fr. Rev.* Wks. V. 164, I think the honour of our nation to be somewhat concerned in the disclaimer of the proceedings of this society. **1825** COLERIDGE *Aids Refl.* (1848) I. 109 If after these disclaimers I shall without proof be charged by any with renewing or favouring the errors. **1862** MRS. GASKELL *C. Bronte* 228 It conveys a peremptory disclaimer of the report that the writer was engaged to be married to her father's curate. **1868** G. DUFF *Pol. Surv.* 42 Our emphatic disclaimer of fellow feeling with the Cretan insurgents.

3. *Her.* A proclamation or announcement made by English heralds, during their regular visitations, of persons having no right to armorial bearings, or to the title of Esquire or Gentleman, especially of such as were found usurping these without right.

1854 SIR T. PHILLIPS (*title*) Heralds' Visitation Disclaimers. **1888** J. P. RYLANDS *Disclaimers at the Heralds' Visitations* x, He notes the press-mark of each MS. in the College of Arms, from which he copied the list of disclaimers.

disclaimer[2]. [f. DISCLAIM *v.* + -ER[1].] One who disclaims.

1702 ECHARD *Eccl. Hist.* (1710) 176 The multitude might have abandoned him as a disclaimer of his own sovereignty. **1754** RICHARDSON *Grandison* (1781) IV. v. 43 Girls, writing of themselves on these occasions, must be disclaimers, you know.

disclamation (dɪsklə'meɪʃən). [n. of action from med.L. *disclāmāre* to DISCLAIM.]

1. *Sc. Law.* The action of disclaiming on the part of a tenant, etc.: see DISCLAIM *v.* 1, and cf. DISCLAIMER[1] 1.

1592 *Sc. Acts Jas. VI* (1814) 604 (Jam.) With all richt.. be ressone of ward, nonentries.. purprusionis, disclamatiounis, bastardrie [etc.]. **1754** ERSKINE *Princ. Sc. Law* (1809) 176 Disclamation is that casualty whereby a vassal forfeits his whole feu to his superior, if he disowns or disclaims him without ground, as to any part of it. **1861** W. BELL *Dict. Law Scotl.* 290 Disclamation signifies a vassal's disavowal.. of a person as a superior, whether the person so disclaimed be the superior or not.

2. Renunciation, repudiation, disclaimer.

1610 BP. HALL *Apol. Brownists* §7 To speake as if before her late disclamation of Poperie.. shee [Ch. of Engl.] had not beene. **1649** —— *Cases Consc.* 403 Let.. servants.. count their (infidell) masters worthy of all honour; not worthy therefore of desertion and disclamation. **1772** *Scots Mag.* 457 Mr. Wallace's disclamation of a late publication. **1814** SCOTT *Wav.* vi, The bibliopolist greeted him, notwithstanding every disclamation, by the title of Doctor. **1892** STEVENSON & OSBOURNE *Wrecker* xvii. 275, I cannot tell with what sort of disclamation I sought to reply.

disclamatory (dɪs'klæmətərɪ), *a. rare.* [f. as prec. + -ORY.] Of the nature of, or tending to disclamation: having the character of disclaiming.

1853 READE *Chr. Johnstone* ii. 30 'My Lord, my Lord!' remonstrated Saunders, with a shocked and most disclamatory tone.

† **dis'clander**, *sb. Obs.* Forms: 4-6 des-, dys-, discla(u)nder, -dre, -dir, -dyr, 5 disclandar, disklander, deslaundre, 5-6 disla(u)nder, -dre, dyssclaunder. [a. AF. **desclandre*, *disclaunder* (15th c.) deriv. of OF. *escla-ndre*, earlier *escandre*, *escandle*, *escandele*:—L. *scandalum*: see ESCLANDRE; cf. SCANDAL and SLANDER. The prefix *des-* in Anglo-Fr. was prob. due to some analogy, or to confusion of *des-* and *es-*.]

1. Malicious speech bringing opprobrium upon any one; slander.

c **1300** *Beket* 2073 Thu missaist foule thine owe louerd.. Ho miȝte suffri such desclandre, bot he nome wrecche? **1471** *Arriv. Edw. IV* (Camden) 21 The false, faynyd fables, and disclandars, that.. were wont to be seditiously sowne and blowne abowt all the land. **1548** HALL *Chron., Hen. VI*, 99 b, He declareth you a true man to hym.. the saied dislaunder and noysyng notwithstandyng. **1562** in *Stow's Surv.* (1754) II. v. xxi. 411/2 If their offences be great.. offending his master by theft or dislander or such like, then to command him to Newgate.

2. Reproach or reprobation called forth by what is considered shameful or wrong; public disgrace or opprobrium; scandal.

1362 LANGL. *P. Pl.* A. v. 75, I haue.. Ablamed him behynde his bak to bringe him in disclaundre. *c* **1374** CHAUCER *Troylus* IV. 536 (564) For yf I wolde it openly distourbe, It most ben disclaundre to here name. **1402** HOCCLEVE *Letter of Cupid* 70 No worshippe may he thus to him conquere, but grete disclander vnto him and here! **1432-50** tr. *Higden* (Rolls) V. 143 The disclaunder of your ylle disposicion scholde not be knowen amonge your enmyes. **1462** J. PASTON in *Paston Lett.* No. 439. II. 89 To deliver seison accordynge to the same feffement, to the gret disclaundre of the seid Sir John and all his. **1531-2** *Act 23 Hen. VIII*, c. 1 [They] suffre them to make their purgacions ..to the greatte disclaunder of suche as pursue suche misdoers.

† **dis'clander**, *v. Obs.* Forms: see prec. [ME. *desclandre*, f. prec. sb., perh. through an AF. **desclandre-r* for OF. *esclandrer* to slander.]

1. *trans.* To speak evil of, so as to expose to opprobrium; to slander.

c **1290** *Beket* 1246 in *S. Eng. Leg.* I. 142 Þe bischopes comen bi-fore And desclandreden seint thomas, þat he was fals and for-suore. *c* **1380** WYCLIF *Wks.* (1880) 138 Þes proude.. possessioners disclaundren trewe prechours. **14..** *E.E. Misc.* (Warton Club) 63 Awyse the welle who syttys the by, Lest he wylle report thi talle, And dyssclaundre the after to gret and smalle. **1530** PALSGR. 513/2, I desclaunder, I hurte or hynder ones good name by reporte.

2. To bring into public disgrace or opprobrium; to bring scandal upon.

c **1385** CHAUCER *L.G.W.* 1031 *Dido*, We that weryn in prosperite Been now disclanderyd. *c* **1430** LYDG. *Min. Poems* (Percy Soc.) 143 Now as ye seen, for disobedience Disclaundrid is perpetually my name. *a* **1483** *Liber Niger* in *Househ. Ord.* (1790) 70 That the owner be not hurte, nor this famous courte disclaunderyd by any outerage of cravinge or crakyng.

† **dis'clanderer.** *Obs.* [f. prec. + -ER[1].] A slanderer.

1493 *Festivall* (W. de W. 1515) 70 b, To stone hym to deth as for a dyssclaunderer.

† **dis'clanderous,** *a. Obs.* [f. DISCLANDER *sb.* + -OUS.] Slanderous.

1494 FABYAN *Chron.* IV. lxv. 44 In this whyle, by styrynge of disclaunderous & deuylysshe persones, a grudge was arreryd attweene the kynge and a Duke of his lande. *Ibid.* VII. ccxxviii. 258 Of this duke Wyllyam some desclaunderous wordes are lefte in memory.

disclare, obs. var. of DECLARE [cf. OF. *desclairier*].

1375 BARBOUR *Bruce* I. 75 He suld that arbytre disclar, Off thir twa that I tauld off ar.

disclass (dɪs'klɑːs, -æ-), *v.* [f. DIS- 7 c + CLASS *sb.*] *trans.* = DECLASS; to remove or cut off from one's class. Hence **dis'classed** *ppl. a.*

1890 *Times* 31 Jan. 9/1 Worked by a Union largely composed of the broken-down, disclassed waifs and strays who gravitate to the dock-gates in search of casual employment. **1916** G. B. SHAW *Pygmalion* 196 Her father.. formerly a dustman, and now fantastically disclassed, had become extremely popular in the smartest society. **1934** —— *Prefaces* 626/2 The baron's cadet.. cannot avail himself of the public elementary and secondary schools because such a step would disclass the man of family.

disclassify (dɪs'klæsɪfaɪ), *v.* [f. DIS- 6 + CLASSIFY.] *trans.* To undo the classification of.

a **1866** J. GROTE *Exam. Utilit. Philos.* xx. (1870) 336 The process of levelling, disclassifying, making everybody like everybody else.

discless ('dɪsklɪs), *a.* Also **diskless.** [f. DISC + -LESS.] Without a disc; not showing a disc.

1846 PATTERSON *Zool.* 50 It is now badly represented in my cabinet by an armless disc and a discless arm. **1871** tr. *Schellen's Spectr. Anal.* 338 In the largest instruments the stars remain discless.

dis'climax. *Ecol.* [f. DIS- 9 + CLIMAX *sb.* 4 b.] (See quots.)

1936 F. E. CLEMENTS in *Jrnl. Ecol.* XXIV. 265 Disclimax. .. The most frequent examples of this community result from the modification or replacement of the true climax, either as a whole or in part, or from a change in the direction of succession. *Ibid.* 266 Selective cutting not infrequently initiates disclimaxes, as may likewise the similar action of other agents such as fire or epidemic disease. **1938** WEAVER & CLEMENTS *Plant Ecol.* (ed. 2) iii. 86 Disturbance climaxes or *disclimaxes* are nearly always the result of disturbance by man or domesticated animals. **1962** H. HANSON *Dict. Ecol.* 110 *Disclimax*, an enduring climax community altered by disturbance by man or domesticated livestock, e.g., a grassland which has replaced a deciduous forest.

† **dis'cloak,** *v. Obs.* Also 7 **discloke.** [f. DIS- 6 or 7 a + CLOAK.] *trans.* To take off the cloak of; to unrobe.

1599 B. JONSON *Cynthia's Rev.* III. v, Now goe in, discloke yourselfe. **1616** —— *Devil an Ass* I. vi, If you interrupt me, Sir, I shall discloak you. **1627-77** FELTHAM *Resolves* I. l. (R.), That feins what was not, and discloaks a soul.

† **dis'clog,** *v. Obs.* [f. DIS- 6 + CLOG *v.*] *trans.* To free from that which clogs; to unclog.

1611 CORYAT *Crudities* 234 They shall make a restitution of all their ill gotten goods, and so disclogge their soules and consciences.

disloister (dɪs'klɔɪstə(r)), *v.* [f. DIS- 6 or 7 c + CLOISTER.] *trans.* To turn or let out of a cloister; to release or remove from seclusion.

1660 HOWELL *Parly of Beasts* 134 They [nuns] fell a murmuring.. and to think too often on man with inordinat desires to be discloysterd. **1881** PALGRAVE *Visions Eng.* 282 A girl by lustful war and shame Discloistered from her home.

disclosal (dɪs'kləʊzəl). *rare.* [f. DISCLOSE *v.* + -AL[1].] The act of disclosing, disclosure.

1795 COLERIDGE *Conciones ad Populum* 37 In the disclosal of Opinion, it is our duty to consider the character of those, to whom we address ourselves.

† **dis'close,** *sb. Obs.* [f. DISCLOSE *v.*: cf. CLOSE *sb.*[2]] The act of disclosing; = DISCLOSURE (in various senses).

1548 GEST *Pr. Masse* 73 Wolde God.. such a person.. had openly publyshed the worthy disclose and disprove of the unsufferable abhomination of the popyshe private pryvye masse. **1602** SHAKS. *Ham.* III. i. 174 There's something in his soule, O're which his Melancholly sits on brood, And, I do doubt the hatch, and the disclose Will be some danger. **1622** WITHER *Mistr. Philar.* Wks. (1633) 623 They [those lips] are like in their discloses To the mornings dewie roses. **1625** W. B. *True School War* 42 It is an Embryo that.. waites the good houre for the disclose and deliuery. **1742** YOUNG *Nt. Th.* ix. 1576 Glasses.. Haue they not led us deep in the disclose Of fine-spun nature.

† **dis'close,** *ppl. a. Obs.* Also 4 **desclos.** [a. OF. *desclos*, pa. ppl. of *desclore* to disclose :—Romanic (and med.L.) *disclaus-us*, pa. pple. of *disclaudĕre*: see DISCLOSE *v.*] Disclosed; unclosed; let out. In quots., used as *pa. pple.*

1393 GOWER *Conf.* I. 285 For drede it shulde be disclose And come unto her faders ere. *Ibid.* II. 354 A maiden, which was.. kept so clos, That selden was, whan she desclos Goth with her moder for to play.

disclose (dɪs'kləʊz), *v.* [ME. *des-*, *dis-closen*, a. OF. *desclos-* pres. stem (pres. subj. *desclose*) of *desclore*, *-clorre* to unclose, open, free = Pr. *desclaure*:—Romanic (and med.L.) *disclaudĕre*, f. DIS- 4 + L. *claudĕre* to close, shut.]

† **1.** *trans.* To open up (that which is closed or shut); to unclose, unfold; to unfasten. *Obs.*

a **1400-50** *Alexander* 3632 Þire Olifantis.. disclosid þai þe chaviles. *c* **1420** *Pallad. on Husb.* II. 331 Almoundes me may make.. her shelles to disclose. **1577** B. GOOGE *Heresbach's Husb.* II. (1586) 67 b, It [a rosebud] discloseth it selfe and spreadeth abroad. **1596** SPENSER *F.Q.* IV. v. 16 Full oft about her wast she it enclos'd, And it as oft was from about her wast disclos'd. **1596** B. GRIFFIN *Fidessa* (1876) 31 Armes still imbrace and neuer be disclosed. *c* **1600** SHAKS. *Sonn.* liv, The perfumed tincture of the Roses.. When Sommers breath their masked buds discloses.

† **b.** To hatch (an egg). Cf. 3 b. *Obs.*

a **1626** BACON (J.), It is reported by the ancients, that the ostrich layeth her eggs under the sand, where the heat of the sun discloseth them.

2. *intr.* (for *refl.*) To unclose or unfold itself by the falling asunder of parts; to open.

1591 GARRARD *Art Warre* 101 Which upon occasion disclosing again may let out the shot. **1706** PHILLIPS (ed. Kersey), *To Disclose*.. to bud, blow, or put out Leaves. **1626** T. H. *Caussin's Holy Crt.* 166 If the hen brood not her eggs, she hath no desire to make them disclose. **1727-46** THOMSON *Summer* 1138 Over head a sheet Of livid flame discloses wide, then shuts And opens wider.

3. *trans.* To uncover (anything covered up from view); to remove a cover from and expose to view (anything material).

1393 GOWER *Conf.* II. 262 As she, that was with thaire enclosed And might of no man be desclosed. **1530** PALSGR. 518/1, I disclose, I uncover a thing that is hydde.. This treasure shall never be disclosed for me. **1611** BIBLE *Isa.* xxvi. 21 The earth also shall disclose her blood, and shall no more couer her slain. **1696** TATE & BRADY *Ps.* cvi. 9 The parting Deep disclos'd her Sand. **1795** SOUTHEY *Joan of Arc* x. 197 The open helm Disclosed that eye. **1832** TENNYSON *Œnone* 65 He smiled, and opening out his milk-white palm Disclosed a fruit of pure Hesperian gold. **1838** LYTTON *Leila* I. iv, Her full rich lips disclosed teeth, that might have shamed the pearl.

b. To uncover or set free (a young bird, etc.) from the egg; to hatch; also *fig.* to 'hatch' (mischief). Rarely, to exclude or lay (eggs).

1486 *Bk. St. Albans* A ij a, Now to speke of hawkys. first thay been Egges. and afterwarde thy bene disclosed hawkys. **1602** SHAKS. *Ham.* V. i. 310 Anon as patient as the female Doue, When that her golden Cuplet are disclos'd. **1602** WARNER *Alb. Eng.* x. lv. (1612) 245 Papists heere, forren and Land-leapt Foes, Did mischiefes that imported more our practiz'd State disclose. **1653** H. COGAN tr. *Pinto's Trav.* xxx. 122 They leave the eggs there till they think the young ones are disclosed. **1697** DRYDEN *Virg. Georg.* III. 633 Snakes, familiar, to the Hearth succeed, Disclose their Eggs, and near the Chimney breed. **1707** *Curios. in Husb. & Gard.* 322 Forcing Eggs to disclose their Young by the artificial Heat of an Oven. **1816-26** KIRBY & SP. *Entomol.* (1843) II. 18 As soon as one of these young caterpillars is disclosed from the egg it begins to feed.

† **4.** To open up to one's own knowledge, to discover. *Obs.*

c **1450** *Crt. of Love* 112 Many a thousand other bright of face: But what they were, I coud not well disclose. **1599** SANDYS *Europæ Spec.* (1632) 168 He was disclosed and ceased [= seized] on by his Master. *c* **1611** CHAPMAN *Iliad* XXI. 467 Old Priam in his sacred tow'r stood, and the flight disclos'd On his forc'd people, all in rout.

5. To open up to the knowledge of others; to make openly known, reveal, declare (secrets, purposes, beliefs, etc.).

1393 GOWER *Conf.* II. 277, I dare min herte well disclose. **1509** HAWES *Past. Pleas.* XXIX. (Percy Soc.) 142 They are not all disposed So for to do as ye have here disclosed. **1551** T. WILSON *Logike* (1580) 77 b, If you will promise me to kepe that close, whiche I shall disclose unto you. **1561** T. NORTON *Calvin's Inst.* I. 22 The faithful should not admit him [God] to be any other than such as he had disclosed himself by his word. **1601** SHAKS. *Jul. C.* II. i. 298 Tell me your Counsels, I will not disclose 'em. **1697** DRYDEN *Virg. Georg.* IV. 6 Their Arms, their Arts, their Manners I disclose. **1712-4** POPE *Rape Lock* II. 9 Her lively looks a sprightly mind disclose. **1726** *Adv. Capt. R. Boyle* 44 As for disclosing the Secret, it is what I never can do. **1874** GREEN *Short Hist.* iii. §2. 121 The great league which John had so long matured at last disclosed itself. *Ibid.* vii. §7. 413 The strange civilization of Mexico and Peru disclosed by Cortez and Pizarro. **1876** MOZLEY *Univ. Serm.* iii. 64 The modest light of faith discloses a real future life.

†**b.** *intr.* (for *refl.*) To show itself, to come to light. *Obs.*

1494 FABYAN *Chron.* VII. 349 The displeasure atwene the Kynge & his barons began to appere and disclose. **1627-77** FELTHAM *Resolves* I. xii. 18 Vices..which I can see, when they do disclose in them. **1746-7** [see DISCLOSING *ppl. a.*].

Hence **dis'closed** *ppl. a.* (*a*) In senses of the vb.

1486 [see DISCLOSE *v.* 3 b]. **1605** BACON *Adv. Learn.* II. xvii. §5. 62 Another diuersitie of Methode there is..and that is Enigmaticall and Disclosed. **1891** *Echo* 7 Dec. 2/7 The defendant..pleaded that he was only an agent for a disclosed principal.

(*b*) *Her.*: see quots.

1864 BOUTELL *Heraldry Hist. & Pop.* x. 64 The expanded wings..of all birds that are not Birds of Prey, are disclosed. **1882** CUSSANS *Her.* vi. 91 The most common attitude in which the Eagle appears in Heraldry, is Displayed. This term is peculiar to Birds of Prey; when other Birds (such as the Dove) are represented with their wings expanded..they are said to be Disclosed.

discloser (dɪs'kləʊzə(r)). [f. prec. + -ER[1].] One who or that which discloses or reveals.

1569 J. SANFORD tr. *Agrippa's Van. Artes* 138 b, In all dishonestie that men shall commytte I will that thou be their judge and discloser. **1608-11** BP. HALL *Medit. & Vows* II. §39, I will not long after..secrets, least I should procure doubt to my selfe, and zealous feare to the discloser. **1650** SIR T. BROWNE *Pseud. Ep.* III. xxvii. (1658) 226 That occular Philosopher, and singular discloser of truth, Dr. Harvey. **1894** *Columbus* (Ohio) *Dispatch* 13 Oct. 9/4 The policeman's mace is a veritable mind discloser.

disclosing (dɪs'kləʊzɪŋ), *vbl. sb.* [f. as prec. + -ING[1].] The action of the verb DISCLOSE: **a.** Opening up, revelation, bringing to light; disclosure. **b.** Hatching. Also *attrib.*

1494 FABYAN *Chron.* VII. ccxxii. 245 The forenamed .ii. erles were warned of disclosynge of this matyer. **1543** BALE (*title*), Yet a course at the Romyshe Foxe. A dysclosynge or openynge of the manne of synne. **1586** J. HOOKER *Girald. Irel.* in *Holinshed* II. 21/1 The king..being in loue with the falcon, did yearelie at the breeding and disclosing time send thither for them. **1605** BACON *Adv. Learn.* II. v. §3. 22 Being of so excellent use for the disclosing of nature. **1626** —— *Sylva* §759 The Distance..betweene the Egge Layed and the Disclosing or Hatching.

¶ *predicatively* for 'in or a disclosing' = 'in process of disclosure', 'a-hatching': thus simulating a neuter-passive use of the verb. See A *prep.*[1] 12.

1737 LILLO *Fatal Curiosity* III. 44 Heard you that? What prodigy of horror is disclosing? To render murther venial.

dis'closing, *ppl. a.* [f. as prec. + -ING[2].] That discloses or opens up: see the verb.

1730-46 THOMSON *Autumn* 1358 Through the disclosing deep Light my blind way. **1746-7** HERVEY *Medit.* (1818) 147 Like these disclosing gems under the powerful eye of day. **1892** *Pall Mall G.* 27 Apr. 1/2 The forcible and disclosing coincidence to which we referred at the outset.

disclosure (dɪs'kləʊʒ(j)ʊə(r)). [f. DISCLOSE *v.* + -URE, after CLOSURE.]

1. The action of disclosing or opening up to view; revelation; discovery, exposure; an instance of this.

a **1598** in Hakluyt *Voy.* I. 271 (R.) Whereas by the voyage of our subjects..towards the discouerie and disclosure of vnknown places. *a* **1626** BACON (J.), She was, upon a sudden mutability and disclosure of the king's mind, severely handled. **1665** BOYLE *Occas. Refl* §3 (R.) An unseasonable disclosure of flashes of wit. **1802** PALEY *Nat. Theol.* xxvii. (1819) 479 We may well leave to Revelation the disclosure of many particulars which our researches cannot reach. **1844** THIRLWALL *Greece* VIII. lxiii. 215 A public disclosure of his motives. **1874** GREEN *Short Hist.* viii. §1. 448 The disclosure of the stores of Greek literature had wrought the revolution of the Renascence.

b. The hatching of young from the egg; the liberation of an insect from the pupa state.

1640 BP. HALL *Chr. Moder.* (Ward) 9/1 I have observed that the small and scarce sensible seed which it [the silkworm] casts comes not to life and disclosure until the mulberry..yields her leaf. **1826** KIRBY & SP. *Entomol.* III. xxxii. 345 Immediately after the disclosure of the insect from the pupa.

†**2.** The opening of a river into sea or lake; the embouchure or mouth. *Obs. rare.*

1660 F. BROOKE tr. *Le Blanc's Trav.* 328 The disclosure of this River frames a square harbour.

3. That which is disclosed; a revelation.

1825 J. NEAL *Bro. Jonathan* III. 246 Preparing him for the disclosure. **1855** PRESCOTT *Philip II*, I. III. iii. 354 Put to the rack..to draw from him disclosures to the prejudice of Egmont. **1878** BROWNING *La Saisiaz* 6 Earth's most exquisite disclosure heaven's own God in evidence.

†**dis'clothe,** *v. Obs.* [f. DIS- 6 + CLOTHE *v.*] *trans.* To strip of clothing, unclothe, undress.

1563-87 FOXE *A. & M.* (1684) III. 570 Being dis-cloathed to their Shirts. **1596** R. L[INCHE] *Diella* (1877) 69 Hee.. straight disclothes him of his long-worne weed.

discloud (dɪs'klaʊd), *v.* [f. DIS- 7 a + CLOUD *sb.*] *trans.* To free or clear from clouds; to free from gloom or obscurity; to reveal, disclose.

1600 TOURNEUR *Transf. Metam.* Author to Bk., For 'tis the haire of crime To shunne the breath that doth discloude it [= its] sinne. **1615** J. STEPHENS *Satyr. Ess.* 50 To discloud Your vertues lost in the confused crowd Of headstrong rumor. **1642** FULLER *Holy & Prof. St.* Pref. §6 That God would be pleased to discloud these gloomy dayes with the beames of his mercie. **1650** —— *Pisgah* To Rdr., Are these gloomy days already disclouded?

Hence **dis'clouded** *ppl. a.*

1615 J. STEPHENS *Satyr. Ess.* 133 A rejoycing heart, an apprehensive head, and a disclouded fancy. **1889** *Univ. Rev.* Sept. 41 My lord Shone in his harness for a passing while An orb disclouded.

†**dis'clout,** *v. Obs. rare*[-1]. [f. DIS- 7 a + CLOUT *sb.*] *trans.* To take out of a clout.

1597-8 BP. HALL *Sat.* II. iii. 34 Tho must he buy his vainer hope with price, Disclout his crownes, and thank him for advice.

†**dis'clown,** *v. Obs. rare*[-0]. [f. DIS- 7 b + CLOWN *sb.*] *trans.* To divest of the character or condition of a clown.

1659 TORRIANO, *Splebiáto*, disclouned, become from a base plebeian to be a Gentleman.

†**dis'clude,** *v. Obs.* [In form a. L. *disclūd-ĕre* to shut up apart or separately; but in sense conformed to DISCLOSE.] *trans.* To disclose.

c **1420** *Pallad. on Husb.* VI. 84 Then his magnitude By brekyng of this potte me may disclude.

†**dis'clusion.** *Obs. rare.* [In form ad. L. *disclūsiōn-em*, n. of action from *disclūdĕre* to separate by shutting up apart; but in H. More app. influenced in sense by DISCLOSE *v.*] 'Emission'. (So J., but the sense is obscure.)

1656 BLOUNT *Glossogr.*, *Disclusion*, a shutting out, a separation. **1659** H. MORE *Immort. Soul* (1662) 73 The composition of them and disclusion and various disposal of them. **1668** —— *Div. Dial.* II. v. (1713) 99 That the continued Shadow of the Earth should be broken by sudden miraculous eruptions or disclusions of light.

disco ('dɪskəʊ). **1. a.** Colloq. abbrev. (orig. *U.S.*) of DISCOTHÈQUE. Also, the equipment for playing records at a discothèque.

1964 *Playboy* Sept. 55/3 Los Angeles has emerged with the biggest and brassiest of the discos. **1970** R. GARRETT *Run Down* i. 29 I've watched the smut bookshops, the neon palaces, the gambling dens, the discos. **1972** *Oxf. Mail* 7 Jan. 2 (Advt.), Velvet Sound's Disco for hire.

b. *ellipt.* for *disco music.*

1975 *N.Y. Times* 12 July 27/4 The hustle..is danced to 'disco', a black-based rhythm and blues characterized by a strong, rhythmic bass guitar, that in itself is achieving wide popularity. **1979** *Guardian* 16 June 10/2 Disco..[is] the most commercially successful new movement in pop music. **1980** *Oxford Times* 4 Jan. 15/2 The music..is tedious disco produced by Pete Bellotte... The disco beat hardly varies from number to number.

2. a. *attrib.* and *Comb.*, as *disco-beat, -dancer, -dancing, sound*, etc.

1965 *N.Y. Times* 8 Apr. 46/1 A couple of scantily clad girls swiveled and undulated to the disco-beat. **1968** *Sunday Times* 14 July 49 She is essentially a 3-minute discogirl, but her finale gave her a new dimension. **1970** *Times* 17 June 27 Rivals Watneys have had a great success with their Birds Nest disco-pubs. **1974** *New Statesman* 31 May 759/2 At the disco-dance in the evening, nonetheless, people said: 'Aren't you frightened, surrounded by a mass of queers?' **1975** *Forbes* (N.Y.) 1 Aug. 35/3 (*caption*) Disco dancers. **1975** *Time* (Canada ed.) 25 Aug. 49/2 Though New York City's blacks and Puerto Ricans have been doing the Hustle for years, its current vogue among people of all colors and ages has coincided with the explosion of 'disco' sound—rhythm and blues with a strong Latin beat. **1977** *Fanfare* (Toronto) 19 Oct. 3/3 Nevertheless, club owners have not been slow to cash in on disco fever. **1978** *Financial Rev.* (Sydney) 8 Sept. 2/1 Today, his weekly income is $1,200—and that's excluding profits from his disco dancers, [etc.]. **1978** *N.Y. Times Mag.* 17 Dec. 124 Mr. Nagy, however, does not disco-dance. 'I feel I have two left legs when it comes to that,' he says. **1978** *Chatelaine* Dec. 68/2 A bright exciting silk disco dress printed with exotic flowers. It's slashed to the waist and wraps the body on the bias. **1982** *Money* Jan. 47/1 However, a decade of rapid inflation sent the market gyrating like a frenzied disco dancer. **1984** S. TOWNSEND *Growing Pains A. Mole* 54, I dropped a hint by looking knowingly at her figure in its lycra body stocking and miniskirt but then the roller disco started and she sped off to do wild disco dancing on her skates.

b. Special Combs.: **disco-funk,** a style of popular music which combines the heavy beat of disco music with the qualities of funk (FUNK *sb.*[2] 2); also **disco-funky** *a.*; **discomania,** addiction to or obsession with discothèques, disco music, or disco-dancing; hence **discomaniac; disco music,** a style of popular music frequently played in discothèques, which is characterized by a heavy bass beat.

1977 *Sounds* 1 Jan. 17 And the Lord gave unto Moses the gift of *Disco Funk, and Moses gave it unto the people, who saw that it was good. **1984** *Oxford Times* 6 Jan. 12/3 Relaxed disco-funk from the British singer who started with Hi-Tension and then had a couple of solo hits. **1976** *Sounds* 11 Dec. 28/6 You know the sort of thing, smacking disco-funky rhythm tracks draped with vast sheets of strings. **1977** *Time* 27 June 56/1 *Discomania is the latest passion of faddish, fickle American city dwellers. **1986** *N.Y. Times* 25 May 22/4 Another recent New York production has been compared to discomania. **1977** *Telegraph* (Brisbane) 2 Nov. 42/3 His co-star, Karen Gorney, is in fact a discomaniac. **1976** *Globe & Mail* (Toronto) 11 Sept. 29/5 *Disco music, like clothes, may be desperately draining the past; the music is nowhere, but the listeners are in Nirvana. **1986** *Christian Science Monitor* 2 June 13/3 Children..chased their friends through a bamboo maze to the sound of Hong Kong disco music.

Hence as *v. intr.*, to dance at a discothèque or in the manner of disco-dancing.

1979 *N.Y. Post* 12 Jan. 18 It was a hot night the following spring and she was at Studio 54 and she was discoing with a kid who looked like Bruce Jenner. **1985** *N.Y. Times* 10 Nov. 11NJ 37/4 If not for her headache and his back, they probably would have discoed till dawn on this romantic weekend.

disco- (dɪskəʊ), combining form of Gr. δίσκος quoit, DISC, occurring in numerous scientific terms; as **disco'blastic** *a. Embryol.* [Gr. βλαστός germ], (of an ovum), having discoidal segmentation of the formative yolk (*Syd. Soc. Lex.*): **disco'morula,** *Embryol.*, the morula or 'mulberry-mass' resulting from the partial and discoidal segmentation of the formative yolk of a meroblastic egg: it develops from earlier stages called **discomo'nerula** and **disco'cytula,** and proceeds to develop into the forms called **disco'blastula** and **disco'gastrula** : see quots. and CYTULA, etc. **'discocarp** *Bot.* [ad. mod.L. *discocarpium*, f. Gr. καρπός fruit], (*a*) a fruit consisting of a number of achenes within a hollow receptacle, as in the rose; (*b*) the disc-like hymenium or fructification of discomycetous fungi and gymnocarpous lichens; hence **disco'carpous** *a.*, relating to, or having, a discocarp. **disco'cephalous** *a. Zool.* [Gr. κεφαλή head], belonging to the suborder *Discocephali* of fishes, having a sucking-disc on the head. **disco'dactyl(e, disco'dactylous** *adjs. Zool.* [Gr. δάκτυλος finger], having toes dilated at the end so as to form a disc, as a tree-frog. **disco'glossid** *a.* and *sb. Zool.* [Gr. γλῶσσα tongue], belonging to, or a member of, the family *Discoglossidæ* of toad-like batrachians; also **discoglossoid** *a.* **discohe'xaster** *Zool.*, in sponges, a six-rayed spicule (HEXASTER) with the rays ending in discs. **discome'dusan** *a.* and *sb. Zool.*, belonging to, or a member of, the order *Discomedusæ* of acalephs or jelly-fishes, having an umbrellar disc; also **discome'dusoid** *a.* **discomy'cetous** *a. Bot.*, belonging to the order *Discomycetes* of Fungi, having a disc-shaped hymenium or *discocarp.* **discopla'cental, discoplacen'talian** *adjs. Zool.*, belonging to the section *Discoplacentalia* of mammals, having a disc-shaped placenta. **'discoplasm,** see quot. 1913. ‖**disco'podium** *Bot.*, 'the foot or stalk on which some kinds of discs are elevated' (*Treas. Bot.* 1866). **di'scopodous** *a. Zool.*, having the foot shaped as a disc; belonging to the section *Discopoda* of Gastropods. **disco'stomatous** *a. Zool.* [Gr. στόμα mouth], pertaining to or belonging to the class *Discostomata* of *Protozoa* (in Saville Kent's system), containing the sponges and collar-bearing monads. **'discotriæne,** see quot. 1888.

1883 *Syd. Soc. Lex*, *Discoblastula, Häckel's term for the small fluid-containing cavity lying between the discomorula and the nutritive yolk of a meroblastic ovum. *Ibid.*, **Discocarp*, a collection of fruits in a hollow receptacle, as in the rose. [**1866** *Treas. Bot.*, *Discocarpium.*] **1887** GARNSEY & BALFOUR tr. *De Bary's Fungi* v. 198 Of gymnocarpous and *discocarpous forms. **1883** *Syd. Soc. Lex.*, **Discogastrula*, Häckel's term for that form of gastrula which develops from a disc situated on a mass of food yolk, as in Ganoid fishes. **1888** *Athenæum* 3 Mar. 279/2 Evidence of the pelobatoid rather than the *discoglossid affinities of the..genus. **1883** *Syd. Soc. Lex.*, **Discomorula*, Häckel's term for the disc of cells which, during the segmentation of the impregnated meroblastic ovum, covers the nutritive vitellus as with a hood. **1879** tr. *Haeckel's Evol. Man* II. xix. 168 All other *Discoplacental Animals. **1881** *Standard* 23 June 5/2 The *discoplacentalian mammals. **1900** W. MYERS tr. *Ehrlich & Lazarus's Histol. Blood* 51 The *discoplasm loses its power of retaining the hæmoglobin, and gives it up to the blood plasma in ever increasing quantity. **1913** DORLAND *Med. Dict.* (ed. 7), *Discoplasm*, the structural part of a red blood-corpuscle. **1888** SOLLAS in *Challenger Rep.* XXV. p. lvii, Varieties of the Triæne... **Discotriæne*... The cladome is a disc in which separate cladi are not distinguishable; and the axial rods representing them extend but a short distance from the cladal origin. *Ibid.*, The discotriæne combines in itself the characters of the desma and the ordinary spicule.

dis'coach, *v.*: see DIS- 7 c.

† **disco'agulate**, *v. Obs.* [f. DIS- 6 + COAGULATE *v.*] *trans.* To undo the coagulation of; to dissolve.

1683 PETTUS *Fleta Min.* II. 5 This Salt.. having a nature to discoagulate Metals.

† **dis'coast**, *v. Obs.* Also 7 discost. [f. DIS- 6 + COAST *v.*]

1. *intr.* To withdraw from the coast or side.

1598 STOW *Ann., Q. Eliz.* an. 1588 (R.) The Spanish nauie for six days space.. coasting and discoasting from England to the coast of Fraunce, and from thence to England, and thence to Fraunce agayne.

2. *fig.* To withdraw, depart: the opposite of COAST *v.* 8, to approach.

a **1677** BARROW *Serm.* (1683) I. xx. 280 Do we not sometimes grievously reproach them.. for discosting from our practice? *Ibid.* II. xxiii. 341 Never willingly to discost from truth and equity.

Hence † **dis'coasted** *ppl. a.*, withdrawn from contiguity, removed, distant. (= F. *éloigné.*) *Obs.*

1610 G. FLETCHER *Christ's Vict.* IV. 119 As far as heaven and earth discoasted lie. **1622** H. SYDENHAM *Serm. Sol. Occ.* II. (1637) 67 His will.. as farre discoasted from tyranny, as injustice. **1625** LISLE *Du Bartas* 119 It is discoasted further from the plain of Sennaar. *a* **1677** BARROW *Serm.* (1683) II. xvi. 232 To settle himself in, or to draw others to, a full persuasion.. discosted from truth.

discoblastic, -blastula: see DISCO-.

'discobole. *Zool.* [a. mod.F. *discobole* (Cuvier), in pl. *discoboles*, ad. mod.L. *discoboli* (pl. of DISCOBOLUS: see below).] A fish of the group *Discoboli*, in Günther's system, a family of *Acanthopterygii gobiiformes*, having the ventral fins formed into a disc or sucker.

discobolic (dɪskəʊ'bɒlɪk), *a. rare.* [f. L. *discobol-us* (see next) + -IC.] Pertaining to a discobolus or quoit-thrower; quoit-throwing.

1822 T. L. PEACOCK *Maid Marian* v. 202 His discobolic exploit proved the climax of his rage.

‖ **discobolus** (dɪ'skɒbələs). *Class. Antiq.* Also erron. **-bulus.** [L., a. Gr. δισκοβόλος discus-thrower, f. δίσκος disc, discus + -βολ ος -throwing, -thrower, f. ablaut-grade of βάλλειν to throw.] A thrower of the DISCUS; an ancient statue representing a man in the act of throwing the discus.

1727 ARBUTHNOT & POPE *Martin. Scriblerus* I. vi, The Discoboli.. were naked to the middle only. **1851** J. GIBSON in Eastlake *Life* (1857) 185 (Stanf.) In the same room is the Discobulus of Myron, in the act of throwing his discus. **1877** WRAXELL *Hugo's 'Miserables'* II. cxxx. 28 Vejanus the discobolus lives again in the rope-dancer Forioso.

discocarp, discocephalous, etc.: see DISCO-.

† **dis'cognisance.** *Obs. rare*[−1]. [a. OF. *descognesance, -oissance* ignorance (13th c. in Godef.), f. *des-*, DIS- 4 + *cognoissance* knowledge, COGNIZANCE.] Non-recognition.

c **1477** CAXTON *Jason* 33 b, Put not ye your [*error for* the] herte in discognysaunce by the whiche your noble royaume is put in pees [*Fr.* ne mettez le cueur en descognoissance].

discography (dɪ'skɒgrəfɪ). [f. DISC *sb.* 2 d + -OGRAPHY. Cf. Fr. *discographie.*] A catalogue raisonné of gramophone records; a list of the recordings of a single composer or performer; also, the study of recordings. Hence **disco'graphical** *a.*, pertaining or relating to discography; **di'scographer**, one skilled in discography.

1933 *Repository* (Canton), The March number of *The Gramophone*.. contains an up-to-date discography. **1935** *Melody Maker* 14 Dec. 8/3, I have seen all kinds of discology, discography, and long lists of records. **1936** R. D. DARRELL *Gramophone Shop Encycl. Recorded Music* p. vii, A presentation of each composer's discography work by work, with complete recorded versions of each composition in its original form. **1941** *Jazz Information* Nov. 22/1 Important as these items are to discographers, they were merely sidelines with James P. **1946** *Jazz Mag.* III. I. 3/2 Eric S. Tonks' new complete Jazz discography is to be released in sections. *Ibid.* 12/1 It seems.. obvious.. without even hearing the records but just glancing through the discographical details, that these records hardly represent a short 'History of Jazz'. **1946** R. VENABLES in A. McCarthy *PL Yearbk. Jazz* 140 Those to whom discography appears a needlessly involved science. **1952** [see DISCOPHILE]. **1955** R. BLESH *Shining Trumpets* (ed. 3) xiv. 323 The assembling of discographical information and biographical material in America. **1957** *Times Lit. Suppl.* 29 Nov. 714/3 Its scholarship is the 'discography' (a curious discipline analogous to bibliography). **1966** *Guardian* 8 Mar. 12/6 Leonard Petts.. has spent some time compiling a discography of Sir Winston Churchill for the British Institute of Recorded Sound... [Churchill] must have left his words behind in odd corners not yet found by the discographers.

discohere (dɪskəʊ'hɪə(r)), *v.* [DIS- 6.] **1.** *Electr.* = DECOHERE *v.*

1899 *Standard* 8 May, The current causes a small hammer to strike the coherer and to cause the filings to discohere, so that the circuit may be completed and broken at will.

2. *fig.* To cease to cohere.

1954 W. FAULKNER *Fable* (1955) 31 [The malleable mass] has relinquished, dis-cohered.. flowing.. back to its own base anonymity.

† **disco'herent**, *a. Obs.* [f. DIS- 10 + COHERENT.] Without coherence; incoherent, incongruous. So † **disco'herence** *Obs.*, want of coherence or agreement; incoherence, incongruity.

a **1600** HOOKER *Serm.* iii. Wks. 1845 II. 730 An opinion of discoherence.. between the justice of God and the state of men in this world. **1675** J. SMITH *Chr. Relig. Appeal* I. 32 They.. made the parts so incongruous, discoherent, inconsequent, nay, contradictory to one another.

discohexaster: see DISCO-.

discoid ('dɪskɔɪd), *a.* and *sb.* [ad. L. *discoīdēs*, a. Gr. δισκοειδής quoit-shaped, f. δίσκος DISCUS, quoit + -ειδης -form. In mod.F. *discoïde.*]

A. *adj.*

1. Of the form of a quoit or disc, disc-shaped; (more or less) flat and circular; in *Conchol.*, used of spiral shells of which the whorls lie in one plane.

1830 LINDLEY *Nat. Syst. Bot.* 101 Stigmas.. discoid and 4-lobed. **1849** MURCHISON *Siluria* ix. 197 Discoid and angular univalves. **1854** JONES & SIEV. *Pathol. Anat.* (1874) 7 The red corpuscles are round discoid bodies, with two concave surfaces.

2. *Bot.* Of composite flowers: Having or consisting of, a disc only, with no ray, as in Tansy.

1794 MARTYN *Rousseau's Bot.* x. 102 Ray called them discoid flowers [*Discoideæ*]. **1857** HENFREY *Bot.* §131 Some capitula are wholly discoid, such as those of Groundsel, of Thistles, etc. **1870** HOOKER *Stud. Flora* 184 Flowers all tubular (head discoid).

B. *sb.* A body resembling a disc in shape. **b.** *Conchol.* See quot. 1846 and cf. A. 1.

1828 WEBSTER, *Discoid*, something in form of a discus or disk. **1846** WORCESTER, *Discoid* (Conch.), a univalve shell of which the whorls are disposed vertically on the same plane so as to form a disk.

discoidal (dɪ'skɔɪdəl), *a.* [f. as prec. + -AL[1].] = DISCOID.

discoidal segmentation of an ovum (*Embryol.*): segmentation producing or resulting in a disc-shaped mass of cells.

1706 [see DISCOUS]. **1819** G. SAMOUELLE *Entomol. Compend.* 148 Elytra.. with some impressed discoidal punctures. **1854** WOODWARD *Mollusca* iv. (1856) 41 The discoidal planorbis sometimes becomes perforated by the removal of its inner whirls. **1869** HUXLEY *Phys.* iii. 67 By adding dense and weak solutions alternately, the [blood] corpuscles may be made to become successively spheroidal and discoidal.

discolith ('dɪskəʊlɪθ). *Biol.* [f. DISCO- + -LITH.] A kind of coccolith of the form of a flattened disc. (Cf. CYATHOLITH.)

1875 CARPENTER *Microsc. & Rev.* §367 Two distinct types are recognizable among the Coccoliths, which Prof. Huxley has designated respectively *discoliths* and *cyatholiths.* **1883** J. H. WRIGHT *Sci. Dogmatism* 8 This jelly [Bathybius].. forming deposits thirty feet thick, with.. imbedded granules, coccoliths, discoliths [etc.]. **1883** *Syd. Soc. Lex.*, *Discolith*, flattened or concavo-convex circular coccoliths found in the ooze brought up in deep-sea dredgings.

discolor ('dɪskʌlə(r), -kɒlə(r)), *a. Nat. Hist.* [a. L. *discolor, discolōr-us* not the same colour, variegated, f. *dis-*, DIS- 1 + *color* COLOUR; the opposite of *concolor*. Cf. F. *discolore* in same sense.]

a. Of different colours; having one part of one colour and another of another. **b.** Of a different colour from some other (adjacent) part or organ.

1866 in *Treas. Bot.* **1883** in *Syd. Soc. Lex.*

discolor, *v.*: see DISCOLOUR.

discolorate (dɪs'kʌlər-, -'kɒlərət), *a.* [ad. med.L. *discolōrāt-us*, pa. pple. of *discolōrāre* (Du Cange) to DISCOLOUR; cf. OF. *descoloré* (Godef.).] Discoloured; of different colours.

In recent Dicts.

discolorate (dɪs'kʌləreɪt), *v. rare.* Also 7 discolourate. [f. med.L. *discolōrāt-*, ppl. stem f. *discolōrāre*: see prec.] *trans.* = DISCOLOUR *v.* 1.

1651 BIGGS *New Disp.* ¶234 [It] doth variously affect and perturb the bloud, and discolorate it. **1655** FULLER *Ch. Hist.* III. vi. §31 The Clergie complained, that.. the least mixture of Civil concernment in Religious matters so discolourated the Christian candor and purity thereof, that [etc.]. **1871** R. ELLIS *Catullus* xi. 7 Fields the rich Nile discolorates, a seven-fold River abounding.

discoloration, discolouration (dɪskʌlər-, -kɒlə'reɪʃən). [n. of action f. DISCOLORATE *v.*: cf. OF. *discoloracion* (1495 in Godef.).] The action of discolouring, or condition of being discoloured; alteration or loss of colour; discolourment.

1642 H. MORE *Immort. Soul* III. ii. 36 Pure light without discolouration. **1763** W. LEWIS *Commerc. Phil. Techn.* 38 There is no other metallic body, so little susceptible of tarnish or discoloration. *c* **1870** J. G. MURPHY *Comm. Lev.* xiii. 49 The sources of discoloration or decay in woven or leather fabrics. **1892** STEVENSON *Across the Plains* 44 With none of the litter and discoloration of human life.

b. *concr.* A discoloured formation, marking, or patch; a stain.

1684 BOYLE *Porousn. Anim. & Solid Bod.* iii. 17 Black and blew Discolorations of the skin, that happen upon some.. contusions. **1842** PRICHARD *Nat. Hist. Man* 89 Brown discolorations are often found. **1860** MAURY *Phys. Geog. Sea* xviii. §747 These discolourations are no doubt caused by organisms of the sea.

discolori'zation. *rare.* [f. **discolorize* (f. DIS- 6 + COLORIZE) + -ATION: cf. *colorization.*] = DISCOLORATION, DISCOLOURMENT.

1851 CARLYLE *Sterling* I. iii. (1871) 17 The shadow of the archway, the discolorisations of time on all the walls. **1893** *Daily News* 21 Feb. 3/3 The discolourization and close texture which was characteristic of the bread.

discolorous (dɪs'kʌlərəs, -'kɒlərəs), *a.* [f. L. *discolor, discolōr-us* (see above) + -OUS.] = DISCOLOR *a.*

1882 *Encycl. Brit.* XIV. 554 (Lichens) Usually they [apothecia] are discolorous, and may be black, brown, yellowish, or also less frequently rose-coloured, rusty-red, orange-reddish, saffron, or of various intermediate shades.

discolour, discolor (dɪs'kʌlə(r)), *v.* [In senses 1, 2, ad. OF. *descolorer, -coulourer*, in 11th c. *desculurer* = Pr. and Sp. *descolorar*, It. and med.L. *discolorare*, Romanic deriv. f. *des-, dis-* (DIS- 4) + L. *colōrāre* to colour, taking the place of L. *dēcolōrāre*: see DE- *pref.* I. 6, and cf. DECOLOUR *v.* In sense 3, from L. *discolor* adj.: see DISCOLOR.]

1. *trans.* To alter the proper or natural colour of; *esp.* to make of a duller, less pleasing, dingy, or unnatural colour; to spoil the colour of, stain, tarnish. (Sometimes *spec.* To deprive of colour, render pale or faded.)

c **1380** *Sir Ferumb.* 1079 Ac ys Fysage al discolourid was, for is blod was gon away. **1382** WYCLIF *Song Sol.* i. 5 Wileth not beholden, that I be broun, for discoloured me hath the sunne. **1484** CAXTON *Chivalry* 6 By the penaunce that he dayly made he was moche discolourd and lene. **1599** SHAKS. *Hen. V*, III. vi. 171 If we be hindred, We shall your tawnie ground with your red blood Discolour. **1647** CLARENDON *Contempl. Ps.* Tracts (1727) 466 Herbs, which.. the first frost nips and discolours. **1794** SULLIVAN *View Nat.* I. 220 The sulphurous acid in the mephitic waters, which have the property of discolouring silver. **1842-5** BROWNING *The Glove* Wks. 1889 V. 42 Does the mark yet discolour my cheek? **1880** GEIKIE *Phys. Geog.* iv. 289 After heavy rain even the clearest brook has its water discoloured by the earth it is carrying down.

b. *fig.*

1599 MARSTON *Sco. Villanie* I. iv. 189 Ingrain'd Habits, died with often dips, Are not so soone discoloured. **1626** T. H[AWKINS] *Caussin's Holy Crt.* 53 Friuolous employments .. discolour the lustre, and honour of your name. *a* **1748** WATTS (J.), Lest some beloved notion.. so prevail over your mind as to discolour all your ideas. **1881** STEVENSON *Virg. Puerisque* 16 Some whimsy in the brain.. which discoloured all experience to its own shade.

2. *intr.* (for *refl.*) To become discoloured or pale; to lose or change colour. (Also *fig.*)

[**1555-1598** See below, DISCOLOURING.] **1641** J. SHUTE *Sarah & Hagar* (1649) 29 Those.. that, having had good education and great estates left, discolour from the one and dissipate the other. **1654** WHITLOCK *Zootomia* 187 Such like Imputations, seemingly black and dark, will discolour into Encomiums. **1883** *Hardwick's Photogr. Chem.* (ed. Taylor) 287 This Nitrate of Silver must.. be very pure, else the developer will soon discolour.

† **3.** *trans.* To render of different colours; to adorn with various colours, to variegate. (Cf. DISCOLOURED 3.) *Obs.*

1656 BLOUNT *Glossogr.*, *Discolor*.. to make of divers colours. **1665** SIR T. HERBERT *Trav.* (1677) 129 High Towers.. leaded in some part, in other part discoloured with gold and blue.

† **b.** To render different in colour. *Obs. rare.*

a **1661** FULLER *Worthies* (1840) III. 88 Thereby it is discoloured from ox-beef that the buyer be not deceived.

Hence **dis'colouring** *vbl. sb.* and *ppl. a.*

1555 EDEN *Decades* 310 These colours.. from whyte they go to yelowe by discolouryngе to browne and redde. **1598** FLORIO, *Scoloramento*, a discolouring, a growing pale or sallowe. *a* **1657** LOVELACE *Poems* (1864) 161 Not that you feared the discolo'ring cold Might alchymize their silver into gold. **1670** J. SMITH *Eng. Improv. Reviv'd* 197 It.. clears the.. skin from spots and discolourings. **1741** MONRO *Anat.* (ed. 3) 291 Swelling, Discolouring, or other Mark of Bruise. **1875** tr. *Vogel's Chem. Light* i. 3 This discolouring effect of light has been long turned to practical use in the bleaching of linen.

dis'colour, dis'color, *sb.* Now *rare.* [f. DIS- 9 + COLOUR *sb.*, after DISCOLOUR *v.*] The state of being discoloured; loss or change of colour; discoloration, stain.

1398 TREVISA *Barth. De P.R.* XIX. viii. (1495) 868 Soden palenesse and dyscolour is a token of drede. **1664** EVELYN *Sylva* (1776) 459 The jaundice in trees known by the Discolour of the leaves and buds. **1812** *Examiner* 7 Sept. 563/2 The blue tinge of mildew.. will only tip with a slight discolour a part of the kernels. **1847** BUSHNELL *Chr. Nurt.* iv. (1861) 102 No moral discolor.

discoloured, -ored (dɪs'kʌləd), *ppl. a.* [f. DISCOLOUR *v.* + -ED[1].]

1. Altered from the proper or natural colour; deprived of colour, pale; changed to a duller, dingier, or unnatural colour; stained, tarnished. (Also *fig.*)

1393 GOWER *Conf.* III. 339 The discoloured pale hewe Is now become a ruddy cheke. **1422** tr. *Secreta Secret., Priv. Priv.* (E.E.T.S.) 234 Who-so hath the visage litill and streyte, yelowe and discolourid, he is ful malicious. **1593** SHAKS. *Lucr.* 708 With lank and lean discolour'd cheek. **1732** POPE *Ep. Cobham* 34 All Manners take a tincture from our own; Or come discolour'd thro' our Passions shown. **1840** F. D. BENNETT *Whaling Voy.* II. 112 The green, or discoloured, water which marks the extent of D'Agulhas Bank.

b. *Her.* (See quot.)

1610 GUILLIM *Heraldry* III. xii. (1611) 123 Foure footed beasts, whether they be borne proper, or discoloured (that is to say varying from their naturall colour).

†**2.** Without colours, divested of colours. *Obs. nonce-use.*

1599 B. JONSON *Cynthia's Rev.* v. ii, *Amo.* And you have still in your hat the former colours. *Mer.* You lie, sir, I have none: I have pulled them out. I meant to play discoloured.

†**3.** Variously coloured; of different colours; variegated, particoloured. [from L. *discolor*, *discolōrus*.] *Obs.*

1471 RIPLEY *Comp. Alch.* III. viii. in Ashm. (1652) 141 Wyth Flowers dyscoloryd bewtyosely to syght. **1595** SPENSER *Epithal.* 51 Diapred lyke the discolored mead. *a* **1597** PEELE *David & Bethsabe* (1599) 8 May that sweet plain.. Be still enamell'd with discolour'd flowers. **1660** F. BROOKE tr. *Le Blanc's Trav.* 307 Beautifyed with columns of discolour'd marble.

b. Differently coloured, the one from the other.

1651 CLEVELAND *Poems* 25 Who askt the Banes 'twixt these discolour'd Mates?

Hence **dis'colouredness**, the quality of being discoloured.

1674 R. GODFREY *Inj. & Ab. Physic* 77 Losing that discolouredness which appeared in the Fever.

discolourment (dɪs'kʌləmənt). [f. DISCOLOUR *v.* + -MENT.] The act of discolouring, or fact of being discoloured; discoloration.

1810 BENTHAM *Packing* (1821) 176 A picture which cannot be charged with hostile distortion or discolourment. **1839** J. R. DANLEY *Introd. Beaum. & Fl. Wks.* I. 25 They had not his imagination to throw its splendid discolourment over all realities. **1859** TENNENT *Ceylon* II. IX. v. 490 Accidents.. involving the damage of the coffee by sea-water, or its discolourment by damp.

discom'bine, *v. rare.* [DIS- 6.] *trans.* To undo the combination of, to disjoin, disunite. (In quot. *intr.* for *refl.* To become disunited.)

1888 A. S. WILSON *Lyric of Hopeless Love* III. 9 The parts can never discombine One essence which contain.

discombobulate (dɪskəm'bɒbjʊleɪt), *v. U.S. joc.* Also **discomboberate** and other variants. [Prob. jocular alteration of *discompose* or *discomfit*.] *trans.* To disturb, upset, disconcert. So **discom'bobulated** *ppl. a.*; **discombobu'lation**, upset, embarrassment.

1834 *Sun* (N.Y.) 21 Mar. 2/3 May be some of you don't get discombobracated. **1838** J. C. NEAL *Charcoal Sk.* 14 While you tear the one, you'll discombobberate the nerves of the other. **1839** *Spirit of Times* 16 Mar. 24/2 Finally, Richmond was obliged to trundle him, neck and heels, to the earth, to the utter discombobulation of his wig. **1926** R. FROST *Let.* 11 Feb. (1964) 178, I put my own discombobulation first to lead up unnoticably to yours. **1943** *Sat. Rev. Lit.* 23 Jan. 9/1 President Roosevelt's sarcastic reply, when asked as to the wisdom of raising an army too large to be supplied from the home-front, in terms of 'discombobulating the domestic economy'. **1957** M. MILLAR *Soft Talkers* ii. 21 It seems as though we were getting all discombobulated for nothing. **1962** R. P. BLACKMUR in E. Hubler et al. *Riddle of Shakespeare's Sonnets* 138 The hues attract, draw, *steal* men's eyes, but penetrate, discombobolate, *amaze* the souls or psyches of women. **1970** 'E. QUEEN' *Last Woman* I. 17, I don't want you people to be in any way discombobulated.

discomedusan: see DISCO-.

†**discomfect**, *ppl. a.*, latinized by-form of DISCOMFIT, discomfited.

a **1529** SKELTON *Agst. Scottes* 84 That late were discomfect with battle marciall.

discomferd, obs. pa. pple. of DISCOMFORT *v.*

dis'comfis, -fish, *v. Sc.* Forms: *Pa. pple.* and *pa. t.* 5 discumfyst, 6 -fist, -feist, -comfeist, -fest, -confeist, 9 discomfisht. [A by-form of DISCOMFIT *v.*, a. OF. *desconfis-* present stem of *desconfire* (pr. pple. *desconfisant*, pr. subj. *-confise*). In early use chiefly in pa. pple. and pa. t. *discumfist* (cf. F. pret. *il desconfist*); modern present tense *discomfish*, also SCOMFISH.] = DISCOMFIT *v.*

c **1470** HENRY *Wallace* I. 429 Ane that has discumfyst ws all. **1536** BELLENDEN *Cron. Scot.* (1821) I. p. xxvii, Discumfist be thair ennimes. **1549** *Compl. Scot.* ix. 77 Gedeon, vitht thre hundretht men, discumfeist ane hundretht and tuenty thousant. **1553** *Douglas' Æneis* x. xiv. 24 Ane man was brocht to ground And discomfest [MS. discumfyt] wyth sa grislie ane wound. **1570** *Tragedie* 264 in *Satir. Poems Reform.* (1890) 90 Bot we the Langsyde hill befoir thame wan, And.. disconfeist thame. **1825–80** JAMIESON, *Discomfisht*, overcome. **1894** *Liberal* 1 Dec. 72/1 Ye're a puir feckless fushionless discomfisht body.

discomfit (dɪs'kʌmfɪt), *v.* Forms: *Pa. pple.* 3 deskumfit, 4 desconfit, -cumfit(e, -coumfit, -confet, 4–6 discumfit, -fyt, -comfit, -fyt, -confit(e, dyscumfyt, 5 -dis, dyscounfite, -comfyd, -fid. *Pres.* 4 discounfit, dyscumfyte, 4–6 disconfit(e, -fyte, discomfite, -fyte, 5 dyscowmfytyn, 5–6 dyscomfyt, 5– discomfit (6 -feit). [ME. *desconfit, -cumfit,* etc., a. OF. *desconfit, -cunfit, -cumfit* (:—L. type **disconfectus*), pa. pple. of *desconfire*, mod.F. *déconfire* to discomfit:—late pop.L. *disconficĕre* (Du Cange), f. *dis-* + L. *conficĕre* to put together, frame, make ready, accomplish, complete, finish; also, to finish up, destroy, consume; f. *con-* together + *facĕre* to do, put. In Romanic, *conficĕre, confectāre*, retained the constructive sense, as in F. *confire*, Sp. *confeitar*, while *disconficĕre*, from DIS- 4, has that of 'destroy, undo' (so Pr. *desconfir*, It. *disconfiggere*). The OF. *desconfit* was first taken into Eng. in its proper sense as a participle, and used to form a passive voice, as 'he was *desconfit*', i.e. completely undone; whence it was subsequently taken as the stem of a verb, *desconfit-en*. The pa. pple. (and pa. t.) continued to be *disconfit* (also *-confid*) till end of 15th, and occasionally till end of 16th c., but *discomfited* from the verb is found from 15th. For the Sc. form, see prec.]

1. *trans.* To undo in battle; to defeat or overthrow completely; to beat, to rout.

a **1225** *Ancr. R.* 250 Þeo ne muwen beon deskumfit ne ouer-kumen, o none wise. *a* **1300** *Cursor M.* 7799 (Cott.) Þai er discumfit [*Gött.* scumphited] wit Þair fas, Saul es slan and ionathas. **1303** R. BRUNNE *Handl. Synne* 4986 Þey ordeynede hem.. Aȝens Þe Phylystynes for to go, And hem dyscumfyte and slo. *c* **1330** —— *Chron. Wace* (Rolls) 1003 Schamely.. ar we desconfit! *a* **1375** *Joseph Arim.* 61 And Þei discounfitede him han and scaÞet ful ofte. **1393** LANGL. *P. Pl.* C. I. 108 Þei were disconfit in bataille. *c* **1400** MAUNDEV. (Roxb.) xiii. 55 Gedeon and ccc. men with him discoumfit three kynges. *c* **1440** *Promp. Parv.* 122/1 Dyscowmfytyn, *confuto, supero, vinco.* *c* **1450** *St. Cuthbert* (Surtees) 5900 Þai wer all discomfyd. **1548** HALL *Chron., Edw. IV*, 204 b, Hys men.. which wer in maner disconfit, and redy to flye. **1587** *Mirr. Mag., Brennus* viii, In the ende I was discomfit there. **1596** SHAKS. *1 Hen. IV*, III. ii. 114 Thrice hath this Hotspur Mars in swathing Clothes.. Discomfited great Dowglas. **1678** WANLEY *Wond. Lit. World* v. i. §78. 466/2 He went after to the Holy Land, where he discomfited the Turks in three great Battels. **1792** *Anecd. W. Pitt* I. 305 Her [France's] arms had been discomfited in every quarter. **1852** MISS YONGE *Cameos* II. ii. 20 'Come, and we shall discomfit them!'

fig. **1651** BIGGS *New Disp.* ¶281 Farre lesse able.. to discomfit, overcome, and expell diseases.

2. *gen.* **a.** To defeat or overthrow the plans or purposes of; to thwart, foil. **b.** To throw into perplexity, confusion, or dejection; to cast down utterly; to disconcert.

1375 BARBOUR *Bruce* III. 197 And fra the hart be discumfit, The body is nocht worth a myt. *c* **1400** *Ywaine & Gaw.* 1349 A sari man than was Sir Kay.. Al descumfite he lay on grownde. **1530** PALSGR. 518/1, I discomfyte, I put one out of comforte.. *je desconfys.* **1596** SHAKS. *Tam. Shr.* II. i. 164 Wel go with me, and be not so discomfited. **1639** FULLER *Holy War* I. xvii. (1647) 26 Many secretly stole away, whereat the rest were no whit discomfited. **1660** SHARROCK *Vegetables* 149 Not impeded by those wants that usually discomfit private persons in such enquiries. **1848** DICKENS *Dombey* i, Dombey was quite discomfited by the question. **1872** BLACK *Adv. Phaeton* ix. 132 Bell, conscious of past backslidings, seemed rather discomfited.

†**c.** To frustrate or defeat *of*. *Obs. rare.*

1548 HALL *Chron., Hen. VI* (1809) 155 The Capitain discomfited of al releve and succour rendered the fortresse.

Hence **dis'comfited** *ppl. a.*; **dis'comfiting** *vbl. sb.*, discomfiture.

c **1386** CHAUCER *Knt.'s T.* 1861 Ne ther was holden no disconfitynge But as a Justes or a turneiynge. **1535** COVERDALE *1 Macc.* iv. 35 Lysias seynge the discomfetynge of his men and the manlynesse of the Iewes. **1603** KNOLLES *Hist. Turks* (1638) 170 The rest of his discomfited army flying headlong back again to Constantinople. **1877** MRS. OLIPHANT *Makers Flor.* 255 The shamed and discomfited ambassadors.. went hastily away.

†**dis'comfit**, *sb. Obs.* [f. DISCOMFIT *v.*] The act of discomfiting, or fact of being discomfited; undoing, defeat, rout, discomfiture.

1422 tr. *Secreta Secret., Priv. Priv.* (E.E.T.S.) 216 The Sterrys makyth many mewyngys in the coragis of mene, and of that comyth.. victories, and dyscomfites. *c* **1425** *Engl. Conq. Irel.* (E.E.T.S.) 30 The other weneden that they departed yn dyscomfyte. **1593** SHAKS. *2 Hen. VI*, v. ii. 86 Vncureable discomfite Reignes in the hearts of all. **1671** MILTON *Samson* 469 Dagon must stoop, and shall e're long receive Such a discomfit, as shall quite despoil him Of all these boasted Trophies won on me. **1834** MEDWIN *Angler in Wales* II. 314 'Twere slight to boast The foul discomfit of that felon-host.

discomfit, obs. pa. pple. of DISCOMFIT *v.* See in the verb.

dis'comfiter. Also 6 *Sc.* discomfatour. [In early use a. OF. *desconfitour* (in Godef.); in later, f. DISCOMFIT *v.* + -ER[1].] One who or that which discomfits.

1528 LYNDESAY *Dreme* 569 The Martyris war as nobyll stalwart Knychtis,—Discomfatouris of creuell battellis thre, The flesche, the warld, the feind. **1820** MILMAN *Fall Jerusalem* (1821) 89 What birth So meet and fitting for the great Discomfiter? **1886** *Sat. Rev.* 24 Apr. 571/1 The discomfiter of Mr. Chamberlain.

discomfiture (dɪs'kʌmfɪtjʊə(r)). Forms: 4 desconfiture, 5 -comfiture, 4– dis-. See also the shortened SCOMFITURE. [a. OF. *desconfiture* rout, defeat (12th c. in Hatz.-Darm.), F. *déconfiture*, = Pr. *descofitura*, OIt. *sconfittura*, med.L. *disconfectūra*, f. *disconficĕre* to rout, overthrow (Du Cange): see DISCOMFIT and -URE.] The action of discomfiting, or fact of being discomfited.

1. Complete defeat in battle, overthrow, rout.

c **1330** R. BRUNNE *Chron. Wace* (Rolls) 14212 Moddred ne myghte in bataille dure But euere was at desconfiture. *c* **1400** MAUNDEV. (Roxb.) xiii. 56 When he come fra Þe descomfiture of his enmys. **1489** CAXTON *Faytes of A.* I. viii. 20 After the desconfiture Hanybal dyde doo serche the felde. **1560** ROLLAND *Crt. Venus* II. 234 Of Italie siclik disconfeitour. **1591** SHAKS. *1 Hen. VI*, I. i. 59 Sad tidings bring I.. Of losse, of slaughter, and discomfiture. **1777** ROBERTSON *Hist. Amer.* (1778) II. v. 84 A few days after the discomfiture of Narvaez, a courier arrived. **1849** MACAULAY *Hist. Eng.* I. 561 What army commanded by a debating club ever escaped discomfiture and disgrace?

2. *gen.* **a.** Defeat, overthrow, or frustration of plans or hopes; utter disappointment. **b.** Complete disconcertment or putting to confusion.

c **1374** CHAUCER *Anel. & Arc.* 326 For in the worlde nys Creature Wakynge in moore discomfiture Þane I. **1513** BRADSHAW *St. Werburge* I. 2140 Yet after all heuynesse, penaunce, and dysconfyture, She reioysed in soule. **1675** *Art Contentm.* x. v. 231 That accursed thing which has caused our discomfeiture. **1828** *Life Planter Jamaica* 79 To rely upon promises.. would end in regret and discomfiture. **1885** DUNCKLEY in *Manch. Exam.* 23 Mar. 6/1 A ripple of laughter follows the discomfiture of his questioner.

†**3.** Physical damage or injury. *Obs. rare.*

1599 H. BUTTES *Dyets drie Dinner* A a iij b, If thy lungs have tane discomfiture By slie assault of Rume.

discomfort (dɪs'kʌmfət), *sb.* Forms: see COMFORT. [ME. *disconfort*, a. OF. *desconfort* (12th c. in Littré), mod.F. *déconfort*, vbl. sb. from *desconforter* to DISCOMFORT. Cf. also DIS- 9.]

†**1.** Undoing or loss of courage; discouragement, disheartening. *Obs.*

1375 BARBOUR *Bruce* XI. 488 Oftsiss of ane vord may riss Discomfort and tynsall with-all. *c* **1470** HENRY *Wallace* x. 168 The tothir Scottis.. For disconford to leiff the feild was boun. **1496** *Dives & Paup.* (W. de W.) VI. xviii. 264/1 More dyscomforte it is to an oost yf they see theyr chefteyne flee ..and more comfort to the enmyes. **1512** *Act 4 Hen. VIII*, c. 20 §2 To the great discomforte and fere of your true officers. **1551** CROWLEY *Pleas. & Payne* 81 Wyth spytefull wordis of disconforte.

†**2.** Absence or deprivation of comfort or gladness; desolation, distress, grief, sorrow, annoyance. *Obs.* (exc. as in 3).

1382 WYCLIF *Matt.* xxiv. 15 The abhomynacioun of discomfort, that is seid of Danyel, the prophete. **1413** *Pilgr. Sowle* Caxton (1483) I. iii. 4 This grysely ghoost also bygan to cryen, wherof I was ful gretely annoyed and in ful hyghe discomfort. **1529** MORE *Comf. agst. Trib.* I. Wks. 1144/1 So is the discomfort of that persone desperate, that desyreth not his owne coumforte. **1577** B. GOOGE *Heresbach's Husb.* III. (1586) 150 For swine.. eate not onely their owne, but yoong children.. to the pittiful discomfort of the parent. **1606** SHAKS. *Ant. & Cl.* IV. iii. 34 What meane you (Sir) To giue them this discomfort? Looke they weepe. *a* **1716** SOUTH (J.), In solitude there is not only discomfort but weakness also. **1847** LONGF. *Ev.* II. i. 68 Thus did that poor soul wander in want and in cheerless discomfort.

†**b.** with *pl.* Something that causes distress; a trouble, grief. *Obs.* or *arch.* (exc. as in 3 b).

c **1386** CHAUCER *Frankl. T.* 168 Here freendes sawe that it was no disport To romen by the see but disconfort. **1536** WRIOTHESLEY *Chron.* (1875) I. 33 Which was a great discompfort to all this realme. **1562** I. S. (*title*), Truth tried: very comfortable to the faithful, but a discomfort to the enemies of God. **1859** TENNYSON *Elaine* 1066 This discomfort he hath done the house.

3. Now in weakened sense: The condition of being uncomfortable; uneasiness (of mind or body): cf. COMFORT *sb.* 6, COMFORTABLE *a.* 7, 10.

1841 LANE *Arab. Nts.* I. 85, I will cure thee without any discomfort to thy person. **1842** A. COMBE *Physiol. Digestion* (ed. 4) 205 The great discomfort which attends the subsequent indigestion of a heavy dinner. **1855** MACAULAY *Hist. Eng.* III. 255 The Scots.. began to find that independence had its discomfort as well as its dignity. **1862** SIR B. BRODIE *Psychol. Inq.* III. iv. 126 The excitement produced by the cigar is followed by a feeling of discomfort.

b. with *pl.* Something that makes one uncomfortable; an inconvenience, hardship. (Cf. COMFORT *sb.* 7.)

1841 JAMES *Brigand* i, The inconveniences and discomforts which those beautiful days of the south sometimes bring. **1849** MACAULAY *Hist. Eng.* II. 485 The troops who had gone on shore had many discomforts to endure. **1885** E. GARRETT *At Any Cost* i. 19 Mrs. Sinclair was one of those who instinctively avoid all avoidable discomforts.

¶ Formerly, like the vb., confused with DISCOMFIT *sb.*

1589 PUTTENHAM *Eng. Poesie* I. xxiv. (Arb.) 62 Ouerthrowes and discomforts in battell.

discomfort (dɪs'kʌmfət), *v.* Also 4–6 dys-, -con-: see COMFORT. [ME. *discomfort, desconfort*, a.

OF. *desconfort-er* (12th c. in Littré), mod.F. *déconforter*, f. *des-*, DIS- 4 + *conforter* COMFORT *v.*; cf. It. *disconfortare*.]

†**1.** *trans.* To deprive of courage or strength of mind; to discourage, dishearten, dismay. *Obs.*

c **1330** R. BRUNNE *Chron.* (1810) 70 Discomfort no þing þe, so faire happe neuer þou fond. *c* **1340** *Cursor M.* 15543 (Fairf.) Loke ȝe ȝu disconfort [*earlier texts* mismay] noȝt. **1503-4** *Act 19 Hen. VII*, c. 28 Preamb., The seid sueters.. were..disconforted & in dispayre of expedicion of ther suetes. **1606** SHAKS. *Tr. & Cr.* v. x. 10 My Lord, you doe discomfort all the Hoste. *a* **1677** MANTON *True Circumcision* Wks. 1871 II. 39 The mind..which is naturally discomforted and weakened..is mightely revived and encouraged with these glad tidings. **1706** PHILLIPS (ed. Kersey), *Discomfort*..to afflict, cast down, or put out of Heart.

†**2.** To deprive of comfort or gladness; to distress, grieve, sadden; to render disconsolate or sorrowful. *Obs.* or *arch.* (exc. as in 3).

1413 *Pilgr. Sowle* (Caxton 1483) I. iii. 4 The syght of some thynges that I sawe gladyd moche my herte and the syght of somme other thynges dyscomfortyd me hugely. *c* **1489** CAXTON *Sonnes of Aymon* xxviii. 590 Ye doo not well for to make soo grete sorowe, nor to discomforte yourself so moche as ye doo. *a* **1533** LD. BERNERS *Huon* xlvii. 159 She was ryght sorowfull and sore dyscomfortyd. **1698** NORRIS *Pract. Disc.* IV. 109 Is not every Man concern'd to provide that neither the Desire of Life may imbitter his Death, nor the Fear of Death discomfort his Life? **1845** T. W. COIT *Puritanism* 386 The man who went to discomfort Abp. Laud in his imprisonment. **1882** ROSSETTI *Ball. & Sonn., Rose Mary*, Long it was ere she raised her head And rose up all discomforted.

†**b.** *intr.* (for *refl.*) To distress oneself, grieve. *Obs. rare.*

1554-9 in *Songs & Ball., Philip & Mary* (1860) 3 O why shold we be..sad? Or for to dyscomfort what thyng shold us compell?

3. Now in weakened sense: To make uncomfortable or uneasy (mentally or physically).

1856 RUSKIN *Mod. Paint.* IV. v. xix. §27 He is careless.. nor feels discomforted, though his walls should be full of fissures like the rocks. **1859** THACKERAY *Virgin.* (1879) I. 296 Mr. Wolfe looked very much discomforted. **1893** Q. [COUCH] *Delectable Duchy* 37 The Registrar..was discomforted by a pair of tight boots. *Mod.* Does the want of the cushion discomfort you?

¶ Formerly often confused with or used for DISCOMFIT *v.*, q.v.

1382 WYCLIF *Matt.* xii. 25 Eche kyngdam departid aȝeins hym self, shal be desolat, or discounfortid. **1483** CAXTON *G. de la Tour* L iij, He allone discomforted and ouercame thre thousand persones. **1596** J. NORDEN *Progr. Pietie* (1847) 102 When the wicked shall fall and be utterly discomforted. **1603** KNOLLES *Hist. Turks* (1638) 288 The Turks discomforted with the inuincible courage of these old soldiers..betooke themselues to flight. **1628** *Crt. & Times Chas. I* (1848) I. 410 The news..almost discomforted our hopes.

Hence **dis'comforted** *ppl. a.*, **dis'comforting** *vbl. sb.* and *ppl. a.*; **dis'comfortedly, dis'comfortingly** *advs.*

1297 R. GLOUC. (1724) 212 þo þe Romeyns were wyþ out chef, dyscomforted hii were. **1375** BARBOUR *Bruce* III. 193 For throw mekill disconforting Men fallis off into disparyng. *c* **1400** *Melayne* 240 The Sarazen slewe oure cristyn knyghte, It was dyscomforthynge. **1556** *Aurelio & Isab.* (1608) L ij, The bitter teares of the disconfortede Quene. **1787** *William of Normandy* I. 114 Amid the unavailing sorrows of a now discomforted people. **1857** SIR F. PALGRAVE *Norm. & Eng.* II. 418 A most discomforting knowledge of the consequences which had ensued. **1873** MISS BROUGHTON *Nancy* III. 64, I snubbedly and discomfortedly put them in my own breast. **1891** G. MEREDITH *One of our Conq.* II. i. 13 Involuntarily, discomfortingly.

discomfortable (dɪsˈkʌmfətəb(ə)l), *a.* [a. OF. *desconfortable* (in Godef.), f. *desconforter*: see DISCOMFORT *v.* and COMFORTABLE.]

1. Causing discouragement, distress, grief, or annoyance; destroying, or tending to destroy, comfort or happiness. *Obs.* or *arch.* (exc. as in 2).

1413 *Pilgr. Sowle* (Caxton 1483) IV. xx. 68 Nothyng agreable . hit is to me but ful discomfortable. **1535** COVERDALE *Ecclus.* xviii. 15 Speake no discomfortable wordes. *a* **1572** KNOX *Hist. Ref.* Wks. (1846) I. 375 We hard nothing of him bot threatning and disconfortable wordis. **1593** SHAKS. *Rich. II*, III. ii. 36 Discomfortable cousin! knowest thou not, [etc.]. **1600** HAKLUYT *Voy.* (1810) III. 349 As ioyfull to me, as discomfortable to them. **1655** DIGGES *Compl. Ambass.* 374 She said she would write a few words to you..which I prayed her might not be discomfortable. **1846** TRENCH *Mirac.* xxiii. (1862) 345 He breaks the silence..but it is with an answer more discomfortable than was even the silence itself. **1891** *Sat. Rev.* 14 Nov. 543/1 Lord Salisbury's perhaps discomfortable remarks.

†**b.** Marked by absence of comfort or happiness; comfortless, miserable. *Obs.*

1529 MORE *Comf. agst. Trib.* II. Wks. 1180/1 The nyght is, of the nature self, dyscomfortable & ful of feare. **1586** BRIGHT *Melanch.* xvii. 103 The body thus possessed with the discomfortable darknes of melancholie. **1622** DONNE *Serm.* cxix. V. 117 Though it be the discomfortablest thing in the world, not to have known Christ.

2. Wanting in material comfort or convenience; causing physical discomfort or uneasiness; positively uncomfortable, comfortless.

1607 DEKKER *Northw. Hoe* I. Wks. 1873 III. 17 Lodge me in some discomfortable vault Where neither Sun nor Moone may touch my sight. **1614** RALEIGH *Hist. World* II. 224 Neither could Moses forget the length of the way through those discomfortable Desarts. **1854** HAWTHORNE *Eng. Note Bks.* (1883) II. 208 Of all discomfortable places, I am inclined to reckon Aldershot Camp the most so. **1888** STEVENSON in *Scribner's Mag.* Feb. 254 Pacing to and fro in his discomfortable house.

3. Characterized by, or in a state of, discomfort or uneasiness; uncomfortable, uneasy.

1844 KINGLAKE *Eothen* (1847) 157, I never saw..in the most horridly stuffy ball room such a discomfortable collection of human beings.

†**4.** Not to be comforted; disconsolate, inconsolable. *Obs. rare.*

1535 COVERDALE *Tobit* x. 4 She wepte with discomfortable teares. [WYCL., vnremediable teris.]

Hence **dis'comfortableness; dis'comfortably** *adv.*

1580 SIDNEY *Arcadia* (1622) 317 A death where the maner could bee no comfort to the discomfortablenesse of the matter. **1585** ABP. SANDYS *Serm.* (1841) 369 Weary of the discomfortableness of the night. **1619** W. SCLATER *Exp. 1 Thess.* (1630) 435 Thy conscience must..inferre the conclusion discomfortably. **1653** J. BAMPFEILD in *Nicholas Papers* (Camden) II. 29 [They] speake very discomfortably of it. **1873** MISS BROUGHTON *Nancy* III. 105 'How can I tell?' reply I, discomfortably.

dis'comforter. [f. DISCOMFORT *v.* + -ER[1]. Cf. OF. *desconforteur.*] One who discomforts, discourages, or distresses.

1628 EARLE *Microcosm., Plodding Student* (Arb.) 72 Hee is a great discomforter of young Students. **1653** BOGAN *Mirth Chr. Life* 80 Thus will Christians comfort themselves, let their discomforters say what they will.

†**dis'comforture.** *Obs. rare.* [f. DISCOMFORT *v.*: cf. *discomfiture.*] Discomfort, distress.

1559 *Primer* in *Priv. Prayers* (1851) 92 My heart is almost like to brast, so great is my discomforture.

discommend (dɪskəˈmɛnd), *v.* [f. DIS- 6 + COMMEND: cf. OF. *descommander* (13th c. in Hatz.-Darm.).]

1. *trans.* To find fault with, express disapprobation of: the opposite of COMMEND (sense 3).

1494 FABYAN *Chron.* VI. clvi. 145 In hym was no thynge to be dyscommendyd, but that he helde his doughter so longe vnmaryed. **1509** BARCLAY *Shyp Folys* (1570) 122, I shall.. Lawde iust and good, and the euill discommende. **1557** NORTH tr. *Gueuara's Diall of Princes* 90 a/2, I do discommend, that the women should goe gadding a broade in visitacion. *a* **1639** W. WHATELEY *Prototypes* I. iv. (1640) 31 The Lord bids men goe and learne of the Pismire, and discommends idlenesse. **1676** SHADWELL *Virtuoso* IV, I cannot abide the sight of her since she discommended thee, my dear. **1860** PATMORE *Faithful for ever* I. 49 Who else shall discommend her choice?

absol. **1632** BROME *Novella* III. Wks. 1873 I. 136 It is the chapmans rule to discommend. **1737** STACKHOUSE *Hist. Bible* (1767) IV. VII. iv. 519 The author neither commends nor discommends.

2. To speak of dissuasively; the opposite of RECOMMEND (cf. COMMEND 2).

1533 ELYOT *Cast. Helthe* II. vii. 23 The juyce of oranges eaten with Sugar in a hotte fever is not to be dyscommended. **1621** BURTON *Anat. Mel.* I. ii. II. i, Savanarola discommends Goats flesh. **1879** MACFARREN *Counterp.* (ed. 2) iii. 7 Their use..is discommended to students.

3. To cause (anything) to be unfavourably viewed or received. ? *Obs.*

1579 LYLY *Euphues* (Arb.) 131 The manners of the childe at the first are to be looked to that nothing discommend the minde. *a* **1659** BOGAN in Spurgeon *Treas. Dav.* Ps. xxiii. 1 Only private defects discommend a thing.

Hence **disco'mmended** *ppl. a.*; **disco'mmending** *vbl. sb.* and *ppl. a.*; also **disco'mmender**, one who discommends.

1544 BALE *Chron. Sir J. Oldcastell* in *Harl. Misc.* (Malh.) I. 249 Wyth no small discommendings of some princes. **1586** A. DAY *Eng. Secretary* I. (1625) 128 To the intent hee may..be instructed in the vilenesse and discommended parts of the same. **1611** COTGR., *Vitupereur*, a dispraiser, discommender. **1678** DRYDEN *All for Love* Pref., No part of a poem is worth our discommending, where the whole is insipid. **1702** S. PARKER tr. *De Finibus* 192 Having something in them Discommending and Unacceptable. **1755** JOHNSON, *Discommender*, one that discommends; a dispraiser.

discommendable (dɪskəˈmɛndəb(ə)l), *a.* [f. prec. + -ABLE.]

1. To be discommended; worthy of censure.

1527 ANDREW *Brunswyke's Distyll. Waters* Prol., It is not dyscomendable for a man of more base lernynge to put to his helping hande. **1583** STUBBES *Anat. Abuses* I. To Rdr. p. xii, It is an exercise altogether discommendable and vnlawfull. **1650** BULWER *Anthropomet.* 201 Splendid apparel, counterfeit crisped haire is more discommendable then the nakednesse of these Barbarians. **1711** W. KING tr. *Naude's Ref. Politics* ii. 62 An act very discommendable and shameful. **1737** STACKHOUSE *Hist. Bible* (1767) IV. VII. iv. 517 The motives..are not discommendable. **1833** LAMB *Elia* Ser. II. *Poor Rel.*, In a vein of no discommendable vanity.

†**2.** Not to be recommended; to be represented dissuasively. *Obs.*

1533 ELYOT *Cast. Helthe* II. xiii. (1539) 31 b, To them, whiche use moche exercise, it is not discommendable. **1655** MOUFET & BENNET *Health's Improv.* (1746) 329 Rice is.. discommendable only in that it is over-binding. **1684** tr. *Bonet's Merc. Compit.* xviii. 644 The eating of Flesh is not discommendable, especially of Animals.

Hence †**disco'mmendableness;** †**disco'mmendably** *adv. Obs.*

1656 W. D. tr. *Comenius' Gate Lat. Unl.* §663 Those that do discommendably, reprove, rebuke, slight them. **1727** BAILEY vol. II, *Discommendableness*, undeservingness of commendation.

discommendation (dɪsˈkɒmənˈdeɪʃən). [n. of action from DISCOMMEND *v.*] The action of discommending; dispraise.

1573 ABP. PARKER *Corr.* 427 In whose discommendation ..your honour once did write to me. **1599** BRETON *Scholler & Souldiour* 25 Oh good Sir! speake not so in Discommendation of a Scholler. **1754** RICHARDSON *Grandison* (1781) VI. lvi. 374, I had much rather have been in the company..than grubbing pens in my closet and all to get nothing but discommendation. **1837** CARLYLE *Mirabeau* Misc. Ess. (1888) V. 232 Let him come, under what discommendation he might, into any circle of men.

b. (with *a* and *pl.*) A special instance of this.

1580 LUPTON *Sivqila* 98 Truely the crab is a discommendation to the Peare tree that bare it. **1677** GILPIN *Dæmonol.* (1867) 117 That rebuke, 'Mary hath chosen the better part,' is only a comparative discommendation. **1841** L. HUNT *Seer* ii. (1864) 55 [We] hereby present the critics.. with our hearty discommendations.

†**disco'mmission,** *v. Obs.* [f. DIS- 7 + COMMISSION *sb.*] *trans.* To deprive of a commission.

1622 *Crt. & Times Jas. I* (1849) II. 287 All justices are like to be discommissioned shortly, and a new choice made. **1641** LAUD *Hist. Acc. Chancellorship* 142 (L.), I shall.. proceed to discommission your printer and suppress his press. **1659** MILTON *Rupt. Commw.* Wks. (1851) 401 For discommissioning nine great Officers in the Army.

discommittee: see DIS- 7.

†**di'scommodable,** *a. Obs. rare*[−1]. [f. F. *discommoder* to inconvenience, DISCOMMODATE + -ABLE.] Disagreeable, annoying.

1579 TWYNE *Phisicke agst. Fort.* I. xxii. 29 a, The smel of womens oyntmentes is more discommodable then the odour of flowres.

†**di'scommodate,** *v. Obs.* [f. DIS- 6 + COMMODATE *v.*, after obs. F. *discommod-er* (Cotgr.).] *trans.* To put to inconvenience; to disturb, trouble; = next. Hence †**di'scommodated** *ppl. a.*

1610 *Crt. & Times Jas. I* (1849) I. 119 After the sending away her stuff, which..will much discommodate her. **1620** WOTTON in *Reliq. Wotton.* (1672) 533 None..shall.. discommodate, pillage..or trouble one another. *c* **1645** HOWELL *Lett.* I. II. xv, These Wars did so drain and discommodate the King of Spain. **1649** CROMWELL *Let.* 13 Aug. (Carlyle), Sir, I desire you not to discommodate yourself because of the money due to me.

discommode (dɪskəˈməʊd), *v.* [f. DIS- 6 + COMMODE *v.*, after obs. F. *discommoder*; see prec.] *trans.* To put to inconvenience or trouble; to incommode, inconvenience.

1721 BAILEY, *Discommode*, to incommode. **1753** L. M. tr. *Du Boscq's Accomplish'd Woman* II. 127 For fear of discommoding his curls. **1818** SCOTT *Hrt. Midl.* l, It could not discommode you to receive any of his Grace's visiters or mine. **1830** GALT *Lawrie T.* III. i. (1849) 84 Finding herself and the younger children discommoded in the boat. **1885** CHILD *Ballads* III. lxxviii. 235/2 The hero comes out of his mound..to tell her how she discommodes him..every [tear] drop pierces, cold and bloody, to his breast.

Hence **disco'mmoded** *ppl. a.*, inconvenienced.

1828 in WEBSTER. **1880** *Daily Tel.* 30 Apr., Half-smothered ejaculations of discommoded men.

†**disco'mmodiate,** *v. Obs. rare.* [f. DIS- 6 + COMMODIATE, used by the same author.] = prec.

1654 EARL MONM. tr. *Bentivoglio's Warrs of Flanders* 59 To have fought the Enemy by discommodiating them.

disco'mmodious, *a.* [f. DIS- 10 + COMMODIOUS.] **a.** Causing trouble or inconvenience; inconvenient; disadvantageous, troublesome.

1540 *Act 32 Hen. VIII*, c. 44 The..distaunce of the towne from the parishe churches..is veraie discommodious. **1577** B. GOOGE *Heresbach's Husb.* IV. (1586) 179 b, The fixed, or standing Hives, bee discommodious, as which you can neither sell, nor remoove. **1601** R. JOHNSON *Kingd. & Commw.* (1603) 141 So discommodious is gluttonie to the proceedings of the Christians. **1645** MILTON *Tetrach.* (1851) 154 A mariage..totally discommodious, distastfull, dishonest and pernicious to him. **1668** WILKINS *Real Char.* 29. **1897** *Blackw. Mag.* Nov. 593/2 [A fashion] discommodious for warm weather. **1928** *Ibid.* Feb. 160/2 Confound and blister that blasted German and all his damned discommodious works.

b. as *sb.* = Discommodious quality. *rare.*

1583 B. GOOGE *Let.* in *N. & Q.* Ser. III. III. 242, I can verry well away with the dyscomodious off the contrey.

†**disco'mmodiously,** *adv.* [f. prec. + -LY[2].] Inconveniently.

1633 T. JAMES *Voy.* 69 They had laine very discommodiously all the winter. **1638** MAYNE *Lucan* (1664) 81 Having..discommodiously washt.

†**disco'mmodiousness.** *Obs.* [f. as prec. + -NESS.] Discommodious quality; unsuitability, inconvenience; a disadvantage.

1580 NORTH *Plutarch* (1676) 24 The discommodiousness of the place, where was neither ground..to fly, nor yet any space for any long chace. **1637** SANDERSON *Serm.* II. 90 We ..begin to find those discommodiousnesses and incumbrances which before we never thought of. **1675** OGILBY *Brit.* 186 The Discommodiousness of the Harbor is a great Occasion of its not being well-frequented.

discommodity (dɪskəˈmɒdɪtɪ). [f. DIS- 9 + COMMODITY.]

1. The quality of being discommodious; unsuitableness, inconvenience, disadvantageousness.

1513 MORE *Rich. III* in Grafton *Chron.* (1568) II. 798 He had declared the discommoditie of discord, and the commoditie of concord. **1577** B. GOOGE *Heresbach's Husb.* III. (1586) 147 b, Of the discommoditie of Essex Cheese, our ..John Haywood..meerily writeth. **1603** KNOLLES *Hist. Turkes* (1621) 1335 Nassuf excused himself..by reason of the discommoditie of his health. *a* **1718** PENN *Tracts* Wks. 1726 I. 688 The Reason of the Alteration of the Law, ought to be the Discommodity of continuing it. **1829** LAMB *Lett.* (1888) 224 You go about, in rain or fine, at all hours, without discommodity.

2. (with *a* and *pl.*) A disadvantage, inconvenience, trouble.

1531 ELYOT *Gov.* II. vi, These discommodities do happen by implacable wrath. **1652–62** HEYLIN *Cosmogr.* II. (1682) 138 Patiently enduring all Discommodities of Cold, Rain, and Hunger. **1662** PETTY *Taxes* 35 It would be a great discommodity to the Prince to take more then he needs. **1690** W. WALKER *Idiomat. Anglo-Lat.* 476, I have thought of all the discommodities that may come unto me.

b. *concr.*

1879 JEVONS *Pol. Econ.* iii. (1888) 58 As the noun *commodities* has been used..as a concrete term, so we may now convert *discommodity* into a concrete term, and speak of *discommodities* as substances or things which possess the quality of causing inconvenience or harm.

discommon (dɪsˈkɒmən), *v.* [f. DIS- 7, 8 + COMMON *sb.* and *a.*: cf. also COMMON *v.*]

†**1.** *trans.* To cut off from the membership of a community; *spec.* **a.** to deprive of citizenship, disfranchise; **b.** to exclude from church fellowship, excommunicate. *Obs.*

1478 in *Eng. Gilds* (1870) 303 In opyn Court, the Mayer and baylleffes..declared the said persones nott discomened nor disfraunchesid. **1588** BP. ANDREWES *Ninety-six Sermons* (1843) V. 41 Every man doeth what in him lieth to discommon communities. *a* **1600** HOOKER *Eccl. Pol.* VIII. Wks. 1845 II. 491 What though a man being severed by excommunication from the Church, be not thereby deprived of freedom in the city; nor being there discommoned, is thereby forthwith..excluded from the Church? **1650–3** tr. *Hales' Dissert. de Pace* in *Phenix* (1708) II. 382 We also ought to know the causes why we discommon any of the Citizens in that..Commonwealth. *a* **1655** VINES *Lord's Supp.* (1677) 230 Ground to discommon, or dis-franchize a reputed member.

c. *fig.* To exclude, banish.

1586 *Praise of Mus.* 77 By a commission onely of Sic volumus, Sic iubemus, to discommon that which is the principall [music].

2. In the Universities of Oxford and Cambridge: To deprive (a tradesman) of the privilege of dealing with the undergraduates.

1530 in W. H. Turner *Select. Rec. Oxford* 80 The hedds of the Unyversite..dyscoumenyd hym, and commaunded all the mansebylls, cooks, and all others of the Unyversite that they shulde nother bye nor sell wᵗ hym. **1655** FULLER *Ch. Hist.* III. vi. §39 A civil penalty (equivalent to the Universities discommoning a Townsman in Cambridg). **1762** *Gentl. Mag.* 91 An action depending in the vice-chancellor's court at Oxford against a tradesman of that place was determined, when the defendant was publickly discommoned. **1864** J. H. NEWMAN *Apol.* 173, I had been posted up by the marshal on the buttery hatch of every College of my University, after the manner of discommoned pastry-cooks.

b. To deprive of commons; = DISCOMMONS 1.

1825 C. M. WESTMACOTT *Eng. Spy* I. 167, I was instantly expelled college, discommoned.

3. a. To deprive of the right of common; to exclude from pasturing on a common: see COMMON *sb.*[1] 5, 6. Also *fig.* **b.** To deprive of the character of a common; to inclose (common land).

1597–8 BP. HALL *Sat.* V. iii. 72 Whiles thou discommonest thy neighbour's kine, And warn'st that none feed in thy field. **1828** WEBSTER, *Dis-common*, to appropriate common land; to separate and inclose common. *Cowel.* **1865** LOWELL *New Eng. Two C. Ago* Prose Wks. 1890 II. 76 To develop the latent possibilities of English law and English character, by clearing away the fences by which the abuse of the one was gradually discommoning the other from the broad fields of natural right.

dis'commonize, *v.* [f. DIS- 6 + COMMONIZE *v.* (or COMMON *sb.* + -IZE).] = DISCOMMON 2.

1886 H. V. BARNETT in *Home Chimes* 150 Slippy's discommonized, and the proctors are down on the Three Crows. **1893** *Westm. Gaz.* 5 Apr. 7/2 The boat-builder who lends out a boat to an undergraduate who prevails on him to omit his name from the list might, if detected, be for ever discommonised.

discommons (dɪsˈkɒmənz), *v.* [f. DIS- 7 a + COMMONS *sb. pl.*, 3, 4.] Hence **dis'commonsed** *ppl. a.*, **dis'commonsing** *vbl. sb.*

1. *trans.* To deprive of commons in a college.

1856 F. E. PAGET *Owlet Owlst.* 112 The world that could be ruled by being discommonsed, imposed, rusticated, expelled, lay at his mercy. **1881** SAINTSBURY *Dryden* i. 6 On July 19th, 1652..he was discommonsed and gated for a fortnight for disobedience and contumacy. **1881** *Pall Mall Budget* 4 Nov. 20 Like a great school where a lecture, an imposition, a discommonsing, a gentle personal castigation, or..expulsion were the only punishments in use. **1894** ASTLEY *50 Years' Sport* I. 34, I was discommonsed for keeping a dog contrary to the statutes.

2. = DISCOMMON 2.

1852 BRISTED *5 Years in Eng. Univ.* (ed. 2) 81 *note*, The owners [of lodging-houses] being solemnly bound to report all their lodgers who stay out at night, under pain of being 'discommonsed'. **1861** HUGHES *Tom Brown at Oxf.* i. (1889) 6 To keep all discommonsed tradesmen..and bad characters generally, out of the college.

†**dis'commonwealth**, *v. nonce-wd.* [DIS- 7 c.] *trans.* To cut off from the commonwealth or state. Hence †**discommonwealthing** *vbl. sb.*

1647 WARD *Simp. Cobler* 47 The divell himselfe..as he is a creature, hee fears decreation, as an Angell dehominations; as a Prince dis-commonwealthings.

discommune (dɪsˈkɒmjuːn), *v.* [f. DIS- 6 + COMMUNE *v.*, or DIS- 7 a + COMMUNE *sb.*] Hence **dis'communed** *ppl. a.*, **dis'communing** *vbl. sb.*

†**1.** *trans.* To cut off or exclude from communion, fellowship, or association. *Obs.*

1590 D. ANDROES in Greenwood *Collect. Sclaund. Art.* E ij, The other was a ciuile discommuning. **1618** HALES *Gold. Rem.* (1688) 424 By suspending, discommuning, by expelling them from their Churches, etc. **1647** FULLER *Good Th. in Worse T.* (1841) 130 Must I be discommuned from my husband's devotion? **1659** GAUDEN *Tears of Ch.* 409 When they have disputed, and discommuned, and unchurched, and unchristened one another.

2. = DISCOMMON *v.* 2.

1677 WOOD *Life* (Oxf. Hist. Soc.) II. 383 Brickland, a discommuned cobler. **1691** —— *Ath. Oxon.* II. 507 He..did expel the said Dobson, and discommune for ever the Bookseller called Edward Thorne. **1710** HEARNE *Collect.* (Oxf. Hist. Soc.) III. 98 Mr. Ryley was one of the Persons discommun'd, which he attributes chiefly to Dr. Sacheverell. **1852** *Queen's Bench Rep.* XVIII. 650 The said Vice Chancellor and certain Heads of Colleges.. pronounced the plaintiff to be discommuned until the end of next term.

†**disco'mmunion**. *Obs.* [DIS- 9: cf. prec.] Exclusion from communion or fellowship.

1590 T. SPERIN in *Confer.* II. 20 The Bishop his excommunication is but a Ciuile discommunion. **1660** GAUDEN *Brounrig* 163 Dough-baked Protestants, that are afraid to own their discommunion and distance from the Church politick, or Court of Rome.

discommunity (dɪskəˈmjuːnɪtɪ). *rare*⁻¹. [f. DIS- 9 + COMMUNITY.] Absence of community; the quality of not having something in common.

1859 DARWIN *Orig. Spec.* (1888) II. xiv. 253 Dissimilarity of embryonic development does not prove discommunity of descent.

discomonerula, discomorula: see DISCO-.

†**dis'companied**, *ppl. a. Obs. rare.* [pa. pple. of **discompany* vb., ad. OF. *descompaignier*, f. *des-*, DIS- 4 + *compaignier* to COMPANY.] Destitute of company, unaccompanied.

1599 B. JONSON *Cynthia's Rev.* III. v, If shee bee alone, now, and discompanied. **1613–18** DANIEL *Coll. Hist. Eng.* (1626) 13 [His] step-mother..murthered him, comming to her house, estrayed, in hunting, and discompanied.

discom'panion, *v. rare.* [f. DIS- 7 a.] *trans.* To deprive of companionship.

1883 G. MACDONALD *Donal Grant* I. xxiv. 254 A youth, fresh from college and suddenly discompanioned at home.

†**discompensate**, *v. nonce-wd.* [f. DIS- 6 + COMPENSATE *v.*] *trans.* To do the reverse of compensating; to counterbalance in the way of loss instead of gain.

1704 F. FULLER *Med. Gymn.* (1718) 21 It will not suffice to discompensate the Benefit.

†**discom'plexion**, *v. Obs. rare.* [f. DIS- 7 d.] *trans.* To spoil the complexion or aspect of; to render unsightly, disfigure, deface.

1635 SHIRLEY *Coronat.* I. i, His band may be disordered.. his rich cloaths be discomplexioned With bloud. *Ibid.* IV. iii, Can a sorrow enter but upon thy garment, Or discomplexion thy attire?

discom'pliance. *rare*⁻¹. [f. DIS- 9 + COMPLIANCE.] Refusal to comply, non-compliance.

1664 PEPYS *Diary* 23 July, A compliance will discommend me to Mr. Coventry, and a discompliance to my Lord Chancellor.

discompose (dɪskəmˈpəʊz), *v.* [f. DIS- 6 + COMPOSE *v.* The Caxton instance, in sense 1, stands alone in time, and prob. represents an OF. **descomposer* = F. *décomposer*.]

1. *trans.* To destroy or disturb the composure or calmness of; to ruffle, agitate, disquiet: **a.** (persons, or their minds, feelings, etc.).

1483 CAXTON *Cato* I iij b, Thou oughtest not to wepe ne to discompose the when thow losest the rychesses and temporalle goodes of thys world. **1645** BP. HALL *Remed. Discontents* 6 Prosperity may discompose us, as vvel as an adverse condition. **1665** GLANVILL *Scepsis Sci.* 168 Every opposition of our espous'd opinions..discomposeth the minds serenity. **1732** POPE *Ess. Man* I. 168 Better for Us, perhaps, it might appear, That never passion discompos'd the mind. **1765** WALPOLE *Cas. Otranto* iv. (1798) 65 Discompose not yourself for the glosing of a peasant's son. **1876** T. HARDY *Ethelberta* xlvii, Sol's bitter chiding had been the first thing to discompose her fortitude.

b. (things, as the sea, the air).

1646 J. HALL *Poems* 65 That breath of thine can onely raise New stormes and discompose the Seas. **1661** COWLEY *Disc. Govt. O. Cromwell* Wks. 1710 II. 626 No Wind..the Air to discompose. **1793** SMEATON *Edystone L.* §300 Not a breath of wind discomposed the surface of the water.

2. To disturb the order or arrangement of; to throw into confusion; to disarrange, disorder, unsettle. Now *rare* or *Obs.*

1611 FLORIO, *Discomporre*, to vnframe, to discompose. **1649** CROMWELL *Let.* 19 July, Sir, discompose not your thoughts or estate for what you are to pay me. **1667** MILTON *P.L.* v. 10 So much the more His [Adam's] wonder was to find, unwak'ned Eve With Tresses discompos'd, and glowing Cheek As through unquiet rest. **1747** GOULD *Eng. Ants* 104 This Species [of red ants] is..the most daring and venemous, as Experience will teach any that presume to discompose their Settlements. **1816** KEATINGE *Trav.* (1817) II. 2 Our whole body was discomposed and dispersed in an instant. **1875** JOWETT *Plato* (ed. 2) V. 357 These minutiæ alter and discompose the characters of the citizens.

†**b.** To upset or disorder the health of; *pa. pple.* indisposed, out of health. *Obs.*

1694 LUTTRELL *Brief Rel.* (1857) III. 404 The lord keeper on Sunday last fell backwards in his chamber and came with his head to the ground, which much discomposes him. **1708** HEARNE *Collect.* 16 Oct., Is much discomposed with a cold. **1712** W. ROGERS *Voy.* (1718) 213 Being discomposed I was not with them.

†**3.** To displace, discard. *Obs.*

1622 BACON *Hen. VII*, 242 (R.) Hee neeuer put downe, or discomposed counsellor, or neare seruant, saue onely Stanley, the Lord Chamberlaine. **1640** FULLER *Joseph's Coat* iii. (1867) 133 It is recorded in the honour of our King Henry the Seventh, that he never discomposed favourite.

discomposed (dɪskəmˈpəʊzd, *poet.* -zɪd), *ppl. a.* [f. prec. + -ED[1].] Disordered, disturbed, agitated, disquieted: see the verb.

1625–8 tr. *Camden's Hist. Eliz.* IV. (1688) 615 His unsettled and discomposed Countenance. **1626** T. H[AWKINS] *Caussin's Holy Crt.* 121 It is an absolute folly of a discomposed iudgement. **1670** DRYDEN *1st Pt. Conq. Granada* II. i, I met Almanzor coming back from Court, But with a discompos'd and speedy Pace. **1828** SCOTT *F.M. Perth* xxxv, With a discomposed aspect and faltering voice.

Hence **discom'posedly** *adv.*; **discom'posedness**, disturbedness, disquietude.

1627 DONNE *Serm.* xxii. 218 Thir inordinatenesse thir discomposednesse and fluctuation of passion. **1655–62** GURNALL *Chr. in Arm.* (1669) 356/2 David behaved himself discomposedly. **1677** HALE *Contempl.* II. Afflictions (R.), Sickness..is a time of distemper and discomposedness. **1881** MRS. C. PRAED *Policy & P.* II. 33 She rose discomposedly.

discomposing (dɪskəmˈpəʊzɪŋ), *ppl. a.* [f. as prec. + -ING[2].] That discomposes.

1694 BOYLE *Excell. Theol.* II. v. 220 A man that is not in love with a fair lady..may have as true and perfect, though not as discomposing an idea of her face. **1741** RICHARDSON *Pamela* II. 385, I hope I have not one discomposing thing to say. **1893** CROCKETT *Stickit Minister* 92 A tall girl..took the dominie round the neck in a discomposing manner.

Hence **discom'posingly** *adv.*, in a way that discomposes or disturbs.

1891 G. MEREDITH *One of our Conq.* III. xii. 247 Perfectly satisfactory, yet discomposingly violent appeals.

†**discompo'sition**. *Obs.* [n. of action from DISCOMPOSE, after COMPOSITION.] The condition of being discomposed; disorder, discomposure.

1624 DONNE *Devotions* 8 (T.) O perplexed discomposition, O riddling distemper, O miserable condition of man! **1656** FINETT *For. Ambass.* 63 He was.. brought to the presence of his Majesty without discomposition of countenance.

†**discom'posture**. *Obs.* [ad. Sp. *descompostura* disorder (Minsheu 1599), f. *descomponer* to discompose. Cf. *composture*.] = next.

1622 MABBE tr. *Aleman's Guzman D'Alf.* I. 76 Daraxa never gaue way by any dis-composture or vnjointed behaviour, or any other occasion whatsoever. **1626** BACON *Sylva* §836 This is wrought..by the disordination and discomposture of the Tangible Parts.

discomposure (dɪskəmˈpəʊʒ(j)ʊə(r)). [f. DISCOMPOSE, after COMPOSURE.] The fact or condition of being discomposed.

1. Disorder, confusion, derangement. ? *Obs.*

1641 MILTON *Animadv.* (1851) 223 The Prelates..which way soever they turne them, put all things into a foule discomposure. **1677** HALE *Prim. Orig. Man.* IV. vii. 348 The Wonder and Miracle is ten times greater in the state of things as they now stand, than it would be in such a discomposure of Nature. **1756** BULLOCK in *Phil. Trans.* XLIX. 402 Several pieces of minerals were dropped from the sides and roof, but all the shafts remained intire, without the least discomposure.

†**b.** Derangement of health, indisposition. *Obs.*

1665 BOYLE *Occas. Refl.* II. i. (1845) 98 You left me free from any other discomposure than that which your leaving me is wont to give me. **1669** W. SIMPSON *Hydrol. Chym.* 275 In cases of uterine discomposures. **1734** WATTS *Reliq. Juv.* (1789) 110 Latrissa is often indisposed..Last Friday she was seized with her usual discomposures.

†**c.** The condition of being taken to pieces; dismemberment. *Obs.*

1660 W. SECKER *Nonsuch Prof.* 73 We see more in the discomposure of a Watch then when its wheels are set together.

2. Disturbance of mind or feelings; agitation, perturbation. (Cf. COMPOSURE, sense 10.)

1647 CLARENDON *Hist. Reb.* I. (1843) 13/1 And he continued in this melancholic and discomposure of mind many days. **1690** NORRIS *Beatitudes* (1692) 66 Without any the least shew of Impatience or Discomposure of Spirit. **1741** RICHARDSON *Pamela* (1742) IV. 205 Did I betray any Impatience of Speech or Action, any Discomposure? **1828** SCOTT *F.M. Perth* vi, His face was pale, his eyes red; and there was an air of discomposure about his whole person. **1849** MACAULAY *Hist. Eng.* I. 471 A series of sermons was preached there by Popish divines, to the great discomposure of zealous churchmen.

†**3.** Want of harmony; disagreement, dissension. *Obs. rare.*

1661 BOYLE *Style of Script.* (1675) 73 How exquisite a symmetry.. Omniscience doth.. discover in the Scripture's method, in spite of those seeming discomposures that now puzzle me. **1673** WOOD *Life* (Oxf. Hist. Soc.) II. 271, I was not there.. because of the present discomposures between the scholars and townsmen.

discompt, obs. form of DISCOUNT.

†**discompu'tation.** *Obs.*$^{-0}$ [DIS- 9.] An erroneous reckoning.

1611 FLORIO, *Scomputo*, a discomputation.

discomycetous: see DISCO-.

†**discon'ceit**, *v. Obs.* [f. DIS- 7 a + CONCEIT *sb.*] *trans.* To deprive of the conception or notion; to put (any one) out of the conceit (*of* something).

1640 J. DYKE *Worthy Commun.* 61 An over good conceit of a mans owne condition and estate.. disconceits a man of the necessity of Christ.

Hence †**discon'ceited** *ppl. a.*; †**dis-con'ceitedness**, the being out of conceit with something.

1659 D. PELL *Impr. Sea* 114 An ill affectedness, and disconceitedness, both towards good people, and all godly and religious exercises.

†**dis'concert**, *sb. Obs. rare.* [f. DIS- 9 + CONCERT *sb.*: cf. It. *sconcerto*, for *disconcerto*, Sp. *desconcierto*, mod.F. *déconcert.*] Want of concert or concerted action; disunion, disagreement in action.

1668 TEMPLE *Let. to Ld. Arlington* Wks. 1731 II. 113 Avoid all Pretexts.. of France's breaking the Business.. which I knew they would be strongly tempted to.. by our Disconcert for their Defence. **1673** —— *Observ. Netherl.* Pref. (Seager), The remainders of their state are.. kept alive by neglect or disconcert of their enemies. **1839** POE *Masque Red Death* Wks. 1864 I. 341 The waltzers perforce ceased their evolutions; and there was a brief disconcert of the whole gay company.

disconcert (dɪskən'sɜːt), *v.* [a. obs. F. *disconcerter* (1611 Cotgr., *disconcerté*, 'disordered, confused; set awry'), mod.F. *déconcerter*, f. *dis-*, *dé-*, DIS- 4 + *concerter* to CONCERT: cf. It. *disconcertare* 'to vntune' (Florio), Sp. *desconcertár* 'to disagree, to break a match, to set at variance' (Minsheu).]

1. a. *trans.* To put out of concert or harmonious action; to throw into confusion, disarrange, derange, spoil, frustrate; now *esp.* to disarrange or upset measures or plans concerted.

1687 A. LOVELL tr. *Bergerac's Com. Hist.* II. 134 The best Harmony of the four Qualities may be dissolved.. and the loveliest Proportion of Organs disconcerted. **1704** SWIFT *T. Tub* xi. 128 Which a drop of film can wholly disconcert. **1769** ROBERTSON *Chas. V*, V. II. 293 But an unforeseen accident disconcerted all his measures. **1818** JAS. MILL *Brit. India* II. IV. iv. 154 One of the four divisions.. fell behind its time, and disconcerted the operations of the remainder. **1849** MACAULAY *Hist. Eng.* I. 151 This scheme was.. completely disconcerted by the course which the civil war took.

†**b.** To disturb or displace in material position. *Obs. rare.*

1747 *Gentl. Mag.* 102 His shatter'd leg being cut off, the bandage was disconcerted by the ship's motion.

2. To disturb the complacency of self-possession of; to confuse, ruffle, 'put out'. Also *absol.*

1716 COLLIER tr. *Panegyrick* 59 'Tis part of the Devil's business to disconcert our Mind, to ruffle our Humour, and blow us up to Rage and Passion. **1752** JOHNSON *Rambler* No. 188 ¶10 He never.. disconcerts a puny satirist with unexpected sarcasms. **1856** MRS. BROWNING *Aur. Leigh* III. 606 He would not disconcert or throw me out. **1875** JOWETT *Plato* (ed. 2) I. 482 Are you at all disconcerted, Cebes, at our friend's objection? **1908** *Smart Set* Sept. 47 She was conscious of a baffling reserve, a poise that disconcerted.

Hence **discon'certing** *ppl. a.*, that disturbs self-possession or complacency.

1807 BARRETT *All the Talents* (ed. 9) 41 A hundred disconcerting measures mov'd. **1891** R. KIPLING *City Dreadf. Nt.* 61 A stolid and disconcerting company is this ring of eyed monsters. **1892** *Athenæum* 2 Apr. 434/2 Curious and disconcerting problems relating to human nature.

disconcerted (dɪskən'sɜːtɪd), *ppl. a.* [f. prec. + -ED^1.] Disturbed from self-possession; put to confusion; ruffled; 'put out'. Hence **discon'certedly** *adv.*; **discon'certedness**, the state of being put out.

1723 BLACKMORE *Hist. Conspiracy* B ij a, The Government was more disconcerted and embroil'd. **1752** A. MURPHY in *Gray's-Inn Jrnl.* No. 6 ¶8 Florio has an uneasy disconcerted Temper. **1752** MISS TALBOT *Lett.* (1809) II. 80 It is very foolish to look disconcerted in the way I have seen you do.. Whence is this disconcertedness? **1847** DICKENS *Haunted Man* (C.D. ed.) 210 Mr. Williams, standing behind the table, and rummaging disconcertedly among the objects upon it. **1878** BROWNING *Poets Croisic* Epil. 8 Our singer For his truant string Feels with disconcerted finger.

disconcertingly (dɪskən'sɜːtɪŋlɪ), *adv.* [f. DISCONCERTING *ppl. a.* + -LY^2.] In a disconcerting manner.

1898 *Westm. Gaz.* 5 Apr. 2/2 The Japs have found it disconcertingly expensive. **1900** H. G. WELLS *Love & Mr. Lewisham* xi, He regarded Lewisham critically and disconcertingly over gilt glasses. **1906** GALSWORTHY *Man of Property* I. i, He had sherry-coloured eyes, disconcertingly inattentive at times.

disconcertion (dɪskən'sɜːʃən). [irreg. f. DISCONCERT *v.*; after etymological formations like *insert*, *insertion.*] The action of disconcerting, or the condition of being disconcerted; confusion.

('*Disconcertion* has the authority of Mr. Curran' R.)

[Not in J. or Todd.] **1794** *St. Trials, Hamilton Rowan* (R.), If I could entertain a hope of finding refuge for the disconcertion of my mind in the perfect composure of yours. **1816** J. SCOTT *Vis. Paris* (ed. 5) 31 No embarrassment is discoverable; neither disconcertion nor anger takes place. **1881** *Mem. G. Thomson* xii. 176 To his still greater disconcertion [he] was asked to make a speech.

disconcertment (dɪskən'sɜːtmənt). [f. DISCONCERT *v.* + -MENT; perh. after F. *déconcertement.*] The action of disconcerting; the fact or condition of being disconcerted.

1866 HOWELLS *Venet. Life* vii. 89 House-hunting, under the circumstances, becomes an office of constant surprise and disconcertment to the stranger. **1881** J. HAWTHORNE *Fort. Fool* I. vii, His disconcertment.. seemed to show that there was more in the matter than had been suspected. **1890** *Temple Bar Mag.* May 2 His disconcertment is written.. on his features.

†**discon'clude**, *v. Obs.*$^{-0}$ [DIS- 6.]

1611 FLORIO, *Disconchiudere*, to disconclude.

disconcord: see DIS- 9.

†**disconde'scend**, *v. Obs.* [f. DIS- 6 + CONDESCEND *v.*] *intr.* To withdraw from condescension, consent, or compliance.

1579 FENTON *Guicciard.* I. (1599) 5 The king.. satisfied him in the effect, but not in the manner, plainely declaring to Lodowyke that he did not discondescend from the first plot and resolution for the ambassadors.

†**discon'duce**, *v. Obs.* [f. DIS- 6 + CONDUCE *v.*] *intr.* To be non-conducive *to*. Hence **discon'ducing** *ppl. a.*, non-conducive.

16.. DONNE *Serm.* xli. 408 Of things that conduce or disconduce to his glory. **1626** *Ibid.* lxxvii. 782 It were impertinent.. and disconducing to our owne end to vex.. the Pope.

†**discon'ducive**, *a. Obs. rare.* [f. DIS- 10 + CONDUCIVE, after prec. vb.] Not conducive.

1819 SEAGER *Suppl. Johnson*, *Disconducive*, disadvantageous, obstructive, impeding, that makes against.

disconfeis, -fis, -feit, -fet, etc.: see DISCOM-.

†**discon'fide**, *v. Obs. rare.* [f. DIS- 6 + CONFIDE *v.*] *intr.* To do the reverse of confiding; to put no confidence or trust *in*.

1669 WOODHEAD *St. Teresa* I. viii. 50 Placing all my confidence in his Divine Majesty, and totally disconfiding in myself.

†**dis'confidence.** *Obs. rare.* [f. DIS- 9 + CONFIDENCE *sb.*, after prec. vb.] The opposite of confidence; distrust.

1621 BP. MOUNTAGU *Diatribæ* 156 Iosephus doth not confidently say it: shew me any such confidence or disconfidence in Iosephus, and I yeeld vnto all the Iewes. **1799** tr. *Diderot's Nat. Son* II. 35 As I expected this timidity, or rather disconfidence, I had brought with me all your letters [etc.].

†**dis'confident**, *a. Obs. rare*$^{-0}$. Wanting in confidence. Hence †**dis'confidently** *adv.*, without confidence.

1666 J. SERGEANT *Let. of Thanks* 74 To speak disconfidently and condescendingly.

disconfirm (dɪskən'fɜːm), *v.* [DIS- 6.] *trans.* (To tend) to show the falsity or invalidity of (a hypothesis, etc.); to count against. (Opp. CONFIRM *v.*) Hence **discon'firming** *ppl. a.*

1936 R. CARNAP in *Philos. Sci.* III. 425 We may, if we wish, call a sentence disconfirmed in a certain degree if its negation is confirmed in that degree. **1943** *Jrnl. Symbolic Logic* VIII. 122 Certain observation sentences confirm or disconfirm a hypothesis... The concepts of confirmation, disconfirmation, and neutrality.. have just been loosely characterized. **1945** *Mind* LIV. 2 A statement is called testable in principle, if it is possible to describe the kind of data which would confirm or disconfirm it. *Ibid.*, Judgments as to the confirming or disconfirming character of experiential data obtained in the test of a hypothesis are often made. **1949** A. PAP *Elem. Anal. Philos.* xiii. 336 A statement is meaningful if and only if one can describe evidence which would confirm it and evidence which would disconfirm it. **1968** P. M. POSTAL *Aspects Phonol. Theory* viii. 161 All such assertions are, however, easily disconfirmed.

disconfirmation (dɪˌskɒnfə'meɪʃən). [DIS- 9.] The process or result of disconfirming.

1937 O. NEURATH in *Philos. Sci.* IV. 276, I.. proposed that we employ the terms 'confirmation' and 'disconfirmation'. **1943** [see DISCONFIRM *v.*]. **1945** *Mind* LIV. 2 The concepts of confirmation and disconfirmation.. are.. more comprehensive than those of conclusive verification and falsification. **1965** *Language* XLI. 261 Critics of transformational theory take these experimental results as disconfirmation.

disconfiture, obs. form of DISCOMFITURE.

disconford, obs. form of DISCOMFORT.

discon'form, *a. Sc.* [f. DIS- 10 + CONFORM *a.*, after L. *dis-similis*, etc.] Not conformable. In *Sc. Law* the opposite of CONFORM *a.*

1609 SKENE *Reg. Maj.* 120 The forme and proving of exception be witnes, is divers, and disconforme to the maner of the probation of the libell. **1890** *Scott. Leader* 29 Jan. 4 That they were 'disconform' to the spirit of the Improvement Act. **1891** *Law Times* XCII. 188/2 It was seen conclusively that the wheat was disconform to sample.

†**discon'form**, *v. Obs.* [f. DIS- 6 + CONFORM *v.*] *intr.* To do the opposite of conforming; to disagree or differ in practice. Const. *to*, *from*.

a **1670** HACKET *Abp. Williams* I. (1692) 212 (D.) That they do it only out of crossness to disconform to your practise. **1678** NORRIS *Coll. Misc.* (1699) 86 Thy Pardon my sweet Saint I implore, My soul ne're disconform'd from thine before.

discon'formable, *a.* [f. DIS- 10 + CONFORMABLE.]

†**1.** The reverse of conformable; unconformable; disagreeing. Const. *from*, *to*. *Obs.*

1603 JAS. I in *Contn. Stow's Chron.* (1615) 842/1 As long as they are disconformable in religion from vs, they cannot be but halfe my Subiects. **1710** NORRIS *Chr. Prud.* vi. 232 Always disconformable to himself, doing what he would not, and not doing what he would and should. **1823** BENTHAM *Not Paul* 329 By means disconformable to the uniform course of nature.

2. *Geol.* Containing or constituting a disconformity.

1905 A. W. GRABAU in *Science* 27 Oct. 534/2 We need a term to express the relation where two formations thus conform in their bedding but comprise between them a time break of greater or less magnitude. To speak of such strata as unconformable, without qualifying the term,.. suggests that the older strata have suffered folding and erosion before the deposition of the later... We might speak of such formations as *disconformable*. **1925** N. E. ODELL in E. F. Norton *Fight for Everest: 1924* 295 The true nature of this important junction it is difficult to tell, but it has the appearance of being a disconformable one. **1970** *Nature* 12 Sept. 1127/1 The glacial beds.. are disconformable on Aztec siltstone.

disconformity (dɪskən'fɔːmɪtɪ). [f. DIS- 9 + CONFORMITY: cf. Sp. *desconformidad* disagreement; also DISCONFORM *a.*]

1. The opposite of conformity or practical agreement; nonconformity.

1602 SEGAR *Hon. Mil. & Civ.* III. xliv. 178 The Cardinals.. were seuenteene, whose disconformitie continued the seat voyd almost three yeeres. *a* **1639** SPOTTISWOOD *Hist. Ch. Scotl.* I. (1677) 13 He thus excuses his disconformity with Rome in the keeping of Easter. *a* **1680** J. CORBET *Free Actions* II. xvi. (1683) 24 [It] hath necessarily, in the manner of it, a disconformity to Gods Law. **1793** *Trial Fyshe Palmer* 16 As to the disconformity in the copy of the Indictment. **1818** JAS. MILL *Brit. India* I. II. v. 186 Practices.. forced into a disconformity with their ancient institutions. **1843** MILL *Logic* I. vi. § 1 Conformity or disconformity to usage or convention.

2. *Geol.* An unconformity between two parallel, approximately horizontal sets of strata, the lower set having undergone erosion but not deformation before the upper set was deposited.

1906 A. W. GRABAU in *Bull. Geol. Soc. Amer.* XVII. 569 Generally this kind of overlap implies some erosion of the underlying concordant formations, thus producing a disconformity. **1925** W. J. MILLER *Introd. Physical Geol.* vi. 137 If.. two sets of beds separated by an erosion surface have their stratification surfaces practically parallel, there is a more or less deceptive unconformity called a disconformity. **1965** G. J. WILLIAMS *Econ. Geol. N.Z.* i. 3/1 The limestones were followed in many areas by disconformities on which greensand accumulated.

disconfort, -fyte, obs. ff. DISCOMFORT, -FIT.

discon'gruity. ? *Obs.* [f. DIS- 9 + CONGRUITY.] The quality of being 'discongruous'; absence of congruity; disagreement, inconsistency; incongruity.

1624 BP. MOUNTAGU *Gagg* 42 Upon Erasmus' bare word who savoured some discongruity of style. **1625** —— *App. Cæsar* II. vi. 163 That much discongruity betwixt Him and us. **1677** HALE *Prim. Orig. Man.* I. vi. 118 The intrinsecal discongruity of the one to the other. **1728** EARBERY tr. *Burnet's St. Dead* I. 80 The Soul forms its absolute Judgment upon them in itself, by a Congruity and Discongruity with its own Nature. *a* **1806** BP. WORSLEY *Serm.* II. 117 Internal perceptions of moral fitnesses and discongruities.

† **dis'congruous**, *a. Obs. rare*⁻¹. [f. DIS- 10 + CONGRUOUS.] Wanting in congruity; incongruous; disagreeing.

1678 CUDWORTH *Intell. Syst.* I. v. 673 Discongruous forms.

disconjure, *v. rare.* [f. DIS- 6 + CONJURE *v.*] *trans.* † **a.** ? To disenchant. *Obs.* **b.** To deprive of the power of conjuring.

1651 HOWELL *Venice* 191 Ravenous Birds such as these are, who stand about me now, to disconjure me with their hideous noise. **1837** CARLYLE *Fr. Rev.* I. v. i, Necker [returns] to the Œil-de-Bœuf, with the character of a disconjured conjuror there,—fit only for dismissal.

disconnect (dɪskə'nɛkt), *v.* [f. DIS- 6 + CONNECT *v.*]

1. *trans.* To sever the connexion of or between; to disjoin, disunite, separate. Const. *with, from.*

1770 BURKE *Pres. Discont.* 50 It is not easy to foresee, what effect would be, of disconnecting with Parliament the greatest part of those who hold civil employments. **1792** —— *Let. to Sir H. Langrishe* Wks. VI. 317 The Episcopal Church of England, before the Reformation, connected with the See of Rome, since then, disconnected and protesting against some of her doctrines, and against the whole of her authority. **1840** HOOD *Up Rhine* 224 It was impossible to disconnect him with old clothes and oranges. **1854** G. B. RICHARDSON *Univ. Code* v. 7591 Disconnect your screw propeller. **1892** *Law Times' Rep.* LXVII. 210/1 To disconnect the drains of the defendants from the sewer.

2. To separate into disconnected or detached parts. *Obs.* exc. in *pa. pple.*: see DISCONNECTED 2.

1790 BURKE *Fr. Rev.* (R.), Thus the commonwealth itself would..crumble away, be disconnected into the dust and powder of individuality. **1810** WELLINGTON in Gurw. *Desp.* V. 611 They shall not induce me to disconnect my army.

disco'nnect, *ppl. a. rare*⁻¹. [short for next: cf. CONNECT *ppl. a.*] = DISCONNECTED.

1839 BAILEY *Festus* xx. (1848) 254 In shadowy glimpses, disconnect The story, flowerlike, closes thus its leaves.

disconnected (dɪskə'nɛktɪd), *ppl. a.* [f. DISCONNECT *v.* + -ED¹: but in sense usually privative of CONNECTED.]

1. Having no connexion (*with* something else, or with each other); detached (*from*); unconnected, separate.

1783 BLAIR *Lect. Rhet.* xv. (Seager), An allegory..may be allowed to stand more disconnected with the literal meaning. **1799** HAN. MORE *Fem. Educ.* (ed. 4) I. 177 The chronology being reduced to disconnected dates, instead of presenting an unbroken series. **1831** *Westm. Rev.* XIV. 51 An inland sea, totally disconnected from the ocean. **1865** *Sat. Rev.* 12 Aug. 205/2 One [paper] wholly disconnected with the county. **1879** D. M. WALLACE *Australas.* ii. 19 The elevations consisting more frequently of low disconnected hills.

b. Without family connexions; not well-connected.

1848 C. BRONTË *J. Eyre* xvi, A Governess, disconnected, poor, and plain.

2. Destitute of connexion between its parts; incoherent. (Also *transf.* of a speaker or writer.)

1870 *Daily News* 10 Oct., The plot is complicated and disconnected. **1870** LOWELL *Study Wind.* (1886) 157 He [a lecturer] was disconnected.

Hence **disco'nnectedly** *adv.*, in a disconnected manner; **disco'nnectedness**, the quality of being disconnected.

1864 *Athenæum* No. 1920. 215/3 Accomplished disconnectedly during growth. **1874** *Daily News* 26 June 2/1 A roar of 'Divide!' arose, which completely drowned his voice and lent an appearance of disconnectedness to the general tenour of his remarks. **1881** S. COLVIN *Landor* v. 100 It was thus an essential habit of Landor's mind..to think in fragments and disconnectedly. **1885** *Athenæum* 23 May 660/3 The style reminds us throughout of that of Miss Thackeray..by reason of its occasional disconnectedness.

disconnecter, -or (dɪskə'nɛktə(r)). [f. DISCONNECT *v.* + -ER¹.] One who or that which disconnects; an apparatus or device for disconnecting.

1884 *Health Exhib. Catal.* 59/1 Sewer Disconnectors.

disco'nnective, *a.* [f. DISCONNECT *v.*, after *connective.*] Having the function of disconnecting; disjunctive. Hence **disco'nnectiveness.**

1824 J. GILCHRIST *Etym. Interpr.* 104 *Either*..and *Neither*..are disconnective. **1870** C. J. SMITH *Syn. & Antonyms* *Aberration*, Syn..Desultoriness, Disconnectiveness, Inconsecutiveness.

disconnexion, -nection (dɪskə'nɛkʃən). [f. DIS- 9 + CONNEXION, after DISCONNECT *v.*]

1. The action of disconnecting (*rare*); the fact or condition of being disconnected or unconnected; undoing of connexion; separation, detachment, disunion. (Const. *from, between.*)

1735 FRANKLIN *True Happiness* Wks. 1887 I. 423 We shall soon see the disconnexion between that and true, solid happiness. **1769** BURKE *Pres. St. Nat.* Wks. II. 193 A spirit of disconnexion, of distrust, and of treachery among public men. **1846** TRENCH *Mirac.* xxix. (1862) 416 The power was most truly his own, not indeed in disconnexion from the Father. **1875** OUSELEY *Harmony* iv. 61 An awkward harmonic disconnection between the 6th and 7th of the Scale. **1894** *Times* 23 July 6/6 [It] involves the complete disconnexion of one part of the machinery before the other can be brought into working order. **1895** PARKES *Health* 60 By disconnection [of drains] is meant that the waste-pipe should discharge by an open end in the outer air.

2. Want of connexion between the component parts; disconnectedness.

1815 W. TAYLOR in *Monthly Rev.* 454 The Iliad has too much of the disconnection which offends in the Orlando.

† **dis'conscient**, *a. Obs.* [f. DIS- 10 + CONSCIENT.] Devoid of conscience, unconscientious.

1640 LD. J. DIGBY *Sp. in Ho. Com.* 9 Nov. (1641) 8 Seeking to remove from our Soveraigne such unjust Judges, such pernitious Counsellours, and such disconscient Divines.

dis'consecrate, *v. rare*⁻⁰. [f. DIS- 6 + CONSECRATE *v.*: cf. DECONSECRATE.] *trans.* To deprive of consecration, to desecrate.

1864 in WEBSTER.

† **discon'sent**, *v. Obs.* [ad. OF. *desconsentir* to be at variance with (Godef.), f. *des-*, DIS- 4 + *consentir* to agree, accord, CONSENT.] *intr.* To refuse consent; not to consent; to disagree, dissent. Const. *with, from.*

1530 TINDALE *Answ. More* Wks. 307 A man must immediately loue God and his commaundementes, and therefore disagree and disconsent vnto the fleshe, and be at bate therewith. **1549** COVERDALE *Erasm. Par. Rom.* Prol. ††iv, For the law declareth that our hertes are bounde and that we cannot disconsent from him. **1641** MILTON *Prel. Episc.* 18 If..the tradition of the Church were now grown so ridiculous, and disconsenting from the Doctrine of the Apostles.

† **discon'sent**, *sb. Obs.* [f. prec. vb., after CONSENT *sb.*] Negation of consent. *by his disconsent*: without his consent.

1651 N. BACON *Disc. Govt. Eng.* II. viii. (1739) 52 All which was done in the presence of the King, and by his disconsent, as may appear by his discontent thereat.

disconsider (dɪskən'sɪdə(r)), *v. rare.* [f. DIS- 6 + CONSIDER *v.*] *trans.* To lower in consideration, bring into disrepute: cf. CONSIDER 9.

1887 STEVENSON *Misadv. J. Nicholson* i. 3 It was the sort of exploit that disconsidered a young man for good with the more serious classes. **1889** —— *Master of B.* iii. 53 The man was now disconsidered and as good as deposed.

So **disconside'ration**, the action of disconsidering, or fact of being disconsidered; disrepute.

1880 T. W. ALLIES *Life's Decision* 238 Its poverty and worldly disconsideration. **1885** STEVENSON *Dynamiter* 190, I have now arrived at such a pitch of disconsideration that..I do not know a soul that I can face.

† **dis'consolacy.** *Obs.* [f. DISCONSOLATE *a.*: see -ACY.] The state or condition of being disconsolate; disconsolateness.

1653 WATERHOUSE *Apol. Learning* 148 (L.) My repair shall be to God..in all spiritual doubts and disconsolacies. *a* **1677** BARROW *Exp. Creed* (T.), Penury, baseness, disconsolacy.

[**disconsolancy.** Explained as: disconsolateness. Error for DISCONSOLACY.

[**1818** TODD Addenda, *Disconsolacy*, disconsolateness (quoting Barrow *On the Creed*, Penury, baseness, disconsolacy).] Entered in **1846** WORCESTER as *Disconsolancy* (citing *Barrow*); hence in some later Dicts.

From this has been derived an erron. **disconsolance** (1849 in CRAIG, and some later Dicts.).]

disconsolate (dɪs'kɒnsələt), *a.* (*sb.*). [a. med.L. *disconsōlāt-us* comfortless (Du Cange), f. *dis-*, DIS- 4 + L. *consōlātus*: see CONSOLATE *ppl. a.* Cf. 16th c. F. *desconsolé*, It. *sconsolato*, Sp. *desconsolado.*]

1. Destitute of consolation or comfort; unhappy, comfortless; inconsolable, forlorn.

1429 *Pol. Poems* (Rolls) II. 145 Rewe on the poore and folk desconsolate. **1494** FABYAN *Chron.* v. cxl. 127 Thou mother to wretchis and other disconsolate. **1594** SPENSER *Amoretti* lxxxviii, So I alone, now left disconsolate, Mourne to my selfe the absence of my love. **1663** PEPYS *Diary* 19 Oct., The King..is most fondly disconsolate for her, and weeps by her. *a* **1704** T. BROWN *Two Oxf. Scholars* Wks. 1730 I. 7 A poor disconsolate widow. **1709** STEELE *Tatler* No. 23 ¶2 The Disconsolate soon pitched upon a very agreeable Successor. **1863** LONGF. *Wayside Inn* I. *Falc. Ser Fed.* xix, She..passed out at the gate With footstep slow and soul disconsolate. **1864** TENNYSON *En. Ard.* 678 On the nigh-naked tree the robin piped Disconsolate.

2. Of places or things: Causing or manifesting discomfort; dismal, cheerless, gloomy.

c **1374** CHAUCER *Troylus* v. 542 O paleys desolat!.. O paleys empti and disconsolat! **1655–62** GURNALL *Chr. in Arm.* (1669) 256/2 When the Christians affairs are most disconsolate, he may soon meet with a happy change. **1691** RAY *Creation* (1714) 66 The disconsolate Darkness of our Winter Nights. **1720** DE FOE *Capt. Singleton* ix. (1840) 156 It was..a desolate, disconsolate wilderness. **1855** MACAULAY *Hist. Eng.* III. 665 The island..to French courtiers was a disconsolate place of banishment.

B. as *sb.* A disconsolate person.

1781 S. J. PRATT *Emma Corbett* III. 14 Raymond, our poor disconsolate, the mutual joy of our hearts.

† **dis'consolate**, *v. Obs.* [f. prec. adj.: cf. CONSOLATE *v.*] *trans.* To make disconsolate or comfortless; to deprive of consolation. Also *refl.*

1530 PALSGR. 518/1, I disconsolate, I bring out of comfort, *je desconsolate.* This terme is nat yet comenly used. Who hath thus disconsolated hym: *qui la ainsi desconsolatê?* **1601** YARINGTON *Two Lament. Traj.* II. iii. in Bullen *O. Pl.* IV, Ah, do not so disconsolate your selfe. **1642** SIR T. STAFFORD in *Lismore Papers* Ser. II. (1888) V. 84 We are..disconsolated when report brings vs the contrarie.

Hence **dis'consolated** *ppl. a.*, rendered or become disconsolate; **dis'consolating** *ppl. a.*

a **1665** J. GOODWIN *Filled w. Spirit* (1867) 68 Everything that is of a discouraging and disconsolating nature in or from the world. **1695** TRYON *Dreams & Vis.* vi. 64 What a disconsolated..Condition would this be to the soul. *a* **1768** STERNE *Serm.* III. xxv. (R.), A poor disconsolated drooping creature.

disconsolately (dɪs'kɒnsələtlɪ), *adv.* [f. DISCONSOLATE *a.* + -LY².] In a disconsolate manner; without comfort or consolation.

1648 JOS. BEAUMONT *Psyche* XIX. lxxix. (R.), Psyche here observ'd a serious maid..Upon the ground disconsolately laid. *a* **1717** PARNELL *Elysium* (R.), There at a solemn tide, the beauties slain..Through gloomy light..In orgies, all disconsolately rove. **1830** J. G. STRUTT *Sylva Brit.* 98 Formal rows of Pollard Willows standing disconsolately by the sides of ditches. **1875** FARRAR *Seekers* I. vi. 75 Peer about disconsolately amid insulting smiles.

dis'consolateness. [f. as prec. + -NESS.] The quality or state of being disconsolate or destitute of consolation.

c **1620** DONNE *Serm.* cxli. (1848) V. 532 In the night of disconsolateness, no comfort. **1633** T. ADAMS *Exp. 2 Peter* iii. 10 Some shadows of dimness and clouds of disconsolateness have shed themselves upon our souls. **1754** RICHARDSON *Grandison* (1781) I. iv. 15 He bowed to the very ground, with such an air of disconsolateness! **1862** GOULBURN *Pers. Relig.* 185 The disconsolateness of the dreary twilight, as the breeze springs with the daybreak.

disconsolation (dɪs'kɒnsə'leɪʃən). [f. DIS- 9 + CONSOLATION, after *disconsolate.* Cf. It. *sconsolatione* (Florio).] The condition of being disconsolate; want of consolation, disconsolateness.

1593 NASHE *Christ's T.* (1613) 51 Tuning his owne priuate disconsolations to the darke gloomy aire. **1612–15** BP. HALL *Contempl. O.T.* XIV. v, The earth yeelded him nothing but matter of disconsolation and heavinesse. **1755** CARTE *Hist. Eng.* IV. 210 Their doors being shut close..in a time of mourning and disconsolation. **1840** DICKENS *Old C. Shop* (C.D. ed.) 85 They have had their disconsolation pasted up.

† **discon'solatory**, *a. Obs.* [f. DIS- 10 + CONSOLATORY; after *disconsolate.*] The reverse of consolatory; tending to make or leave disconsolate.

1654 WARREN *Unbelievers* 67 Our doctrine is no way disconsolatory to the soules of any. **1659** D. PELL *Impr. Sea* To Rdr. D iv b, A restless, unquiet, and disconsolatory Sea.

† **dis'consonancy.** *Obs.* [f. next: cf. *consonancy.*] The quality of being disconsonant; want of consonancy or harmony; incongruity.

1664 FALKLAND *Marriage Night* II. i. in Hazl. *Dodsley* XV. 125 Madam, there's disconsonancy in the name, methinks. **1680** R. L'ESTRANGE *Tully's Offices* (1681) 72 In Musical Instruments, let them be never so little out of Tune, a skilful Ear presently takes Cheque at it: and that's the Case in the least disconsonancy of Life.

† **dis'consonant**, *a. Obs.* [f. DIS- 10 + CONSONANT *a.*] The reverse of consonant; out of agreement or harmony; discordant.

1630 J. TAYLOR (Water P.) *Elegy Bp. Andrewes* Wks. II. 332/1 He shew'd them..How far from truth they were disconsonant. **1634** —— *Gt. Eater Kent* 7 Men, being compounded and composed all of one mould and mettle, are different and disconsonant in estates, conditions, and qualities. **1674** HICKMAN *Quinquart. Hist.* (ed. 2) 72 Either disconsonant to Scripture, or injurious to God. **1767** MRS. S. PENNINGTON *Lett.* III. 163 A certain arrangement of really disconsonant sounds. **1806** *Med. Jrnl.* XV. 407 A train of operations, disconsonant to general experience.

† **discon'sort**, *v. Obs.* [f. DIS- 6 + CONSORT *v.* I.] *trans.* To be out of harmony or at variance with. Hence **discon'sorted** *pa. pple.*, out of harmony, at variance.

1604 T. WRIGHT *Passions* I. ix. 36 Passions disconsorting nature [are] punished with payne. *Ibid.* IV. ii. 125 If mens words or actions be disconsorted, doubtlesse the soule cannot be well disposed.

discontent (dɪskən'tɛnt), *sb.*¹ [f. DIS- 9 + CONTENT *sb.*, after the vb. and adj.: cf. It. *scontento* for *discontento* discontentment (Florio 1598).]

1. The state or condition of being discontented; want of content; dissatisfaction of mind: the opposite of *content* or *contentment.*

1591 SPENSER *M. Hubberd* 898 To wast long nights in pensive discontent. **1594** SHAKS. *Rich. III*, I. i. 1 Now is the Winter of our Discontent Made glorious Summer by this Son of Yorke. **1647** CLARENDON *Hist. Reb.* I. (1843) 31/2 The country full of pride, mutiny, and discontent. **1720** GAY *Poems* (1745) I. 54 Lose not in sullen discontent your peace. **1839** CARLYLE *Chartism* i. (1858) 4 What means the bitter discontent of the Working Classes? **1860** TYNDALL *Glac.* I. i. 2 That feeling of intellectual discontent which..is very useful as a stimulant.

†**b.** Formerly sometimes in stronger sense: Displeasure, vexation. *Obs.*
1605 BACON *Adv. Learn.* I. vii. §4 (1873) 54 Some inward discontent at the ingratitude of the times. **1678** WANLEY *Wond. Lit. World* v. i. §81. 466/2 The Romanes abused his servants, whereupon he departed Rome in great discontent.
c. (with *pl.*) A feeling of discontent or dissatisfaction.
1588 SHAKS. *Tit. A.* I. i. 443 Dissemble all your griefes and discontents. **1659** RUSHW. *Hist. Coll.* I. 662 The discontents of the common people..were heightened against the powerful men at Court. *a* **1745** SWIFT *Wks.* (1841) II. 37 It would..either prevent or silence all discontents. **1845** M^{c}CULLOCH *Taxation* III. i. (1852) 430/1 The means of traducing the new government, of inflaming popular discontents.
†**2.** *transf.* A cause or occasion of discontent or dissatisfaction; a grievance. (Usually in *pl.*) *Obs.*
1605 BACON *Adv. Learn.* I. vii. §9 (1873) 58 The good administration of justice..and the moderation of discontents. **1620** ROWLANDS *Night Raven* 25 An ill Liuer is my discontent.

discon'tent, *a.* and *sb.*[2] [f. DIS- 10 + CONTENT *a.*: cf. obs. F. *descontent* (Godef.), It. *discontento* (Florio).] **A.** *adj.*
1. Not content; unquiet in mind through having one's desires unsatisfied or thwarted; dissatisfied, discontented. Const. *with*, *to* with *inf.*
1500–20 *Dunbar's Poems* (1893) 312 He that wantis ane of thir thre, Ane luvar glaid may neuir be, Bot ay in sum thing discontent. *a* **1555** LATIMER *Serm. & Rem.* (1845) 237 Ever giving thanks to their Lord God..discontent with nothing that he doth. **1651** JER. TAYLOR *Holy Living* (1727) 119 He ..is discontent and troubled when he fails. **1724** RAMSAY *Tea t. Misc.* (1733) I. 68 Tho' ilka ane be discontent, Awa' wi' her I'll gae. **1845** M. PATTISON *Ess.* (1889) I. 25 He.. withdrew disconcerted and discontent. **1863** KINGLAKE *Crimea* II. 418 Moving slowly, and as though discontent with its fate, the column began to fall back.
†**2.** In stronger sense: Displeased, vexed. *Obs.*
1494 FABYAN *Chron.* I. v. 12 Lotrinus enamowryd hym selfe vpon a fayre wenche named Estrilde..wherwith his wyfe..beynge sore discontent, excyted her fader and frendes to make warre vpon..her husbande. *a* **1533** FRITH *Another Bk. agst. Rastell* (1829) 219 Be not discontent with me if I ask you one question. **1655** STANLEY *Hist. Philos.* I. (1701) 53/1 Discontent That such grave Men should on the stage be brought.
B. *sb.*[2] A discontented person or member of a body, a malcontent. Now *rare*.
1596 SHAKS. *1 Hen. IV*, v. i. 76 Fickle Changelings, and poore Discontents. **1653** DOROTHY OSBORNE *Lett. to Temple* (1888) 169 You would not have been taken for a discontent. **1695** TEMPLE *Introd. Hist. Eng.* (Seager) Having overthrown his brother and his army of strangers or discontents. **1872** FREEMAN *Gen. Sketch* xiii. §2 (1874) 238 There had all along been religious discontents among particular men. **1887** SIR W. HARCOURT in *Scott. Leader* 23 Nov. 5 What would he say to them?.. They are only Celts and Irish Papists, vulgar discontents, people who would like to have some voice in the management of their own affairs.

discon'tent, *v.* [f. DIS- 6 + CONTENT *v.*: cf. obs. F. *descontent-er, -tant-er* (16th c. in Godef.).]
1. *trans.* To deprive of contentment; to make unquiet in mind by failing or refusing to satisfy desire; to dissatisfy. (Now chiefly in pa. pple.: see DISCONTENTED.)
1549 COVERDALE, etc. *Erasm. Par. 1 Cor.* xii. 13 Thou.. that..discontenteste thy selfe, because of the counterfaycte glorye of hym, of whom thou haste receyued baptisme. **1591** UNTON *Corr.* (Roxb.) 100 The French manner of incamping dothe discontente me moste. **1623** HEXHAM *Tongue-Combat* 22 All these pressures were vpon purpose cast vpon the people to discontent them. **1666** PEPYS *Diary* (1879) VI. 21 So fearful I am of discontenting my wife. **1794** G. WASHINGTON *Lett.* Writ. 1891 XII. 451 Attempts to discontent the public mind. **1887** *Pall Mall G.* 23 Mar. 4/1 The Ameer..is discontenting his troops by paying them in provisions instead of in cash.
†**2.** In stronger sense: To displease, vex. *Obs.* or *arch.* (See also DISCONTENTED 2.)
1494 [see DISCONTENTED 2]. **1530** PALSGR. 518/1, I discontent, I displease, *je mescontente.* I have served you well all my lyfe, and never discontented you by my good wyll. **1632** J. HAYWARD tr. *Biondi's Eromena* 118 Which as much contented the people, as it madded and discontented my husband. **1878** SIMPSON *Sch. Shaks.* I. 75 The Queen used to beat Secretary Cecil about the ears when he discontented her.

†**disconten'tation.** *Obs.* [f. DISCONTENT *v.*, after CONTENTATION.]
1. Dissatisfaction; displeasure; = DISCONTENT *sb.*[1], DISCONTENTMENT.
1528–9 HENRY VIII in Fiddes *Wolsey* II. (1726) 145 Being informed, to our no little marvell and discontentation [etc.]. **1580** SIDNEY *Arcadia* II. (1622) 215 Rather then my ease discontentation Should breed to her, let me for aye deiected be From any ioy, which might her griefe occasion. **1611** SPEED *Hist. Gt. Brit.* IX. xii. (1632) 687 To the high discontentation..of the English Subiects. **1759** ROBERTSON *Hist. Scot.* II. App. x. 155 For the discontentation they have of the queen's majesty.
2. *transf.* Something that causes discontent; a grievance; = DISCONTENT *sb.*[1] 2.
1585 PARSONS *Chr. Exerc.* II. iii. 291 Who can number the hurtes and discontentations, that dailie insue vppon vs, from our neighbours?

discon'tented, *ppl. a.* [f. prec. *v.* + -ED[1].]
1. Deprived or devoid of contentment; dissatisfied, unquiet in mind; marked by or showing discontent; = DISCONTENT *a.* 1.
1548 HALL *Chron., Hen. V*, (an. 5) 55 b, Surely there was no creature whiche with that war was either discontented or displeased. **1595** SHAKS. *John* v. i. 8 Our discontented Counties doe reuolt. **1672** *Essex Papers* (Camden) 10 Ther are Thousands of Discontented People in Ireland who may be apt to Rise. **1725** POPE *Odyss.* XI. 329 Sullen and sow'r with discontented mien. **1783** WATSON *Philip III*, II. (1839) 89 The troops, discontented with his treatment of them.. refused to obey. **1855** MACAULAY *Hist. Eng.* IV. 519 The discontented gentry of Cheshire and Lancashire.
†**2.** Displeased, vexed. *Obs.*
1494 FABYAN *Chron.* v. lxxvi. 55 With which answere the Romaynes beynge sore discontented, made newe warre vpon ye sayd Sicambris. **1568** GRAFTON *Chron.* II. 142 For the which presumption the king was grievously discontented against the Citie. **1656** STANLEY *Hist. Philos.* v. (1701) 169/1 Plato discontented hereat..[said] he could not stay, Dion being used so ignominiously.

discon'tentedly, *adv.* [f. prec. + -LY[2].] In a discontented manner; with discontent.
1588 THOMAS *Lat. Dict.* (1606), *Molestè*, grievously, discontentedly, painefully. **1599** *Broughton's Lett.* 47 Vnlesse they bee..discontentedly malicious, or schismatically factious. **1647** TRAPP *Comm. Rom.* vii. 24 We must discontentedly be contented to be exercised with sin while we are here. **1838** DICKENS *Nich. Nick.* xvi, 'They may begin, my dear', replied the collector discontentedly.

discon'tentedness. [f. as prec. + -NESS.] The quality or condition of being discontented; discontent, dissatisfaction.
1597 DANIEL *Civ. Wars* VIII. iii, For those high purposes He had conceived in discontentedness. **1653** MANTON *Exp. James* iii. 14 Envy..is Discontentedness at another man's good and prosperous estate. **1764** *Mem. G. Psalmanazar* 100 What added still more to my discontentedness was, that [etc.]. **1881** MASSON *Carlyle* in *Macm. Mag.* XLV. 150 A soul..whose cardinal peculiarity should be despondency, discontentedness, and sense of pain.

†**discon,ten'tee.** *Obs. rare*$^{-1}$. [f. DISCONTENT *v.* or *a.* + -EE.] A discontented person; a malcontent.
a **1734** NORTH *Exam.* (1740) 55 The Priests..traded much in Conventicles, and among the Discontentees.

discon'tentful, *a. arch.* [f. DISCONTENT *sb.* + -FUL.] Full of discontent; fraught with or expressing discontent.
1615 *Trade's Incr.* in *Harl. Misc.* (Malh.) III. 314 All the more discontentful. **1622** W. WHATELEY *God's Husb.* II. 118 At last..the smallest imperfections are more discontentfull, and breed more anguish, then at first the greatest did. *a* **1677** BARROW *Serm.* (1686) III. xxiv. 277 Discontentfull murmurings.

discon'tenting, *vbl. sb.* [f. DISCONTENT *v.* + -ING[1].] The action of the verb DISCONTENT. (In quot. 1633, the cherishing or exhibition of discontent: cf. next, sense 2.)
1494 FABYAN *Chron.* VI. clix. 149 Withoute consent or knowlege of..Lewes, and some deale to the discontentyng of his mynde. **1593** T. WATSON *Tears of Fancie* v. Poems (Arb.) 181 Then Cupid..Vnto his mother vowd my discontenting. **1633** P. FLETCHER *Elisa* II. xi. Poet. Misc. 120 Religion blames impatient discontenting.

discon'tenting, *ppl. a.* [f. as prec. + -ING[2].]
1. That discontents; causing discontent; †displeasing, unpleasant (*obs.*); dissatisfying.
1586 A. DAY *Eng. Secretary* II. (1625) 25 That..which in the end..will be to you most discontenting. **1645** MILTON *Colast.* Wks. (1851) 368 How unpleasing and discontenting the society of body must needs be between those whose mindes cannot bee sociable. **1825** CARLYLE *Schiller* II. (1845) 55 Literature is apt to form a dangerous and discontenting occupation.
†**2.** Feeling or showing discontent. *Obs.*
1605 *Play Stucley* 2050 in Simpson *Sch. Shaks.* (1878) I. 240 Leave such discontenting speech. **1611** SHAKS. *Wint. T.* IV. iv. 543 And with my best endeauours..Your discontenting Father striue to qualifie. **1613** F. ROBARTS *Reven. Gospel* 115 That..not one sower looke, not one discontenting gesture be observed.

†**discon'tentive,** *a. Obs.* [f. DISCONTENT *v.* + -IVE; after CONTENTIVE.] **a.** Feeling or showing discontent; inclined to discontent. **b.** Causing or tending to discontent; unsatisfactory.
1607 BRETON *Murmerer*, To conceive one discontentive thought of his Majestie. **1618** BOLTON *Florus* IV. ii. 286 The fight was..doubtfull for a long time, and discontentive. **1627–47** FELTHAM *Resolves* II. xcviii. 444 Pride is ever discontentive.

discon'tentment. [f. DISCONTENT *v.* (or *a.*) + -MENT, after CONTENTMENT. Cf. obs. F. *descontentement* (1553 in Godef.).]
1. The action or fact of discontenting (*rare*); the fact or condition of being discontented; dissatisfaction; = DISCONTENT *sb.*[1] 1.
1579 FENTON *Guicciard.* (1618) 325 It seemed his discontentment proceeded chiefly of feare. **1580** *Proscr. agst. Pr. Orange* in *Phenix* (1721) I. 433 There did..appear some Discontentment of our said Subjects. **1601** HOLLAND *Pliny* II. 457 Seeing what trouble and discontentment was risen hereupon throughout the city. **1645** BP. HALL *Remed. Discontents* 71 Discontentment is a mixture of anger, and of grief. **1720** STRYPE *Stow's Surv.* (1754) II. v. xi. 294/2 Finding a general Exclamation and Discontentment against patents of privilege. **1825** CARLYLE *Schiller* I. (1845) 12 His discontentment devoured him internally.
†**b.** Displeasure, vexation; = DISCONTENT *sb.*[1] 1 b. *Obs.*
1588 R. PARKE tr. *Mendoza's Hist. China* 242 The newe baptised..wept bitterly, with discontentment to see how [etc.]. **1600** HOLLAND *Livy* XXXVIII. liii. 1017 With words of indignation, testifying his discontentment for this course and manner of proceeding. *a* **1639** W. WHATELEY *Prototypes* I. xvi. (1640) 159 So transported with discontentment against a parent for some sharpenesse, as even to hate him. **1659** B. HARRIS *Parival's Iron Age* 221 This War..expired ..1648 to the..great discontentment of the French, who had much reason to be angry at [the peace].
c. with *pl.* A feeling or instance of discontentment or dissatisfaction; = DISCONTENT *sb.*[1] 1 c.
1594 HOOKER *Eccl. Pol.* I. iv, No shadow of matter for teares, discontentments, griefes, and vncomfortable passions. *a* **1649** DRUMM. OF HAWTH. *Hist. Scot.* (1655) 46 He nourished discontentments in all parts. **1724** T. RICHERS *Hist. R. Geneal. Spain* 156 The Discontentments which.. subsisted between Berengaria and the House of Lara.
†**2.** *transf.* A cause or occasion of discontentment; a grievance; = DISCONTENT *sb.*[1] 2. *Obs.*
1586 A. DAY *Eng. Secretary* II. (1625) 37 Thinke you not that I have already received discontentment enough? **1627–36** FELTHAM *Resolves* I. ii. 5 The best way to perish discontentments, is either not to see them, or convert them to a dimpling mirth.

†**discon'tigue,** *a. Sc. Obs.* [f. DIS- 10 + CONTIGUE.] = DISCONTIGUOUS.
1538 in Balfour *Practicks* (1754) 175 (Jam.) Landis lyand discontigue fra uther landis. **1609** SKENE *Reg. Maj.* Forme of Proces 125 Gif the lands lyes within sundrie Schirefdomes..or gif they ly in any ane of them, discontigue.

disconti'guity. [f. DIS- 9 + CONTIGUITY.] The quality of being discontiguous; discontinuity or isolation of parts.
1676 H. MORE *Remarks* 60 A Discontinuity or Discontiguity of matter. *Ibid.* 140 Not because there is any more fear then of discontiguity or a vacuum.

discon'tiguous, *a. Sc.* [f. DIS- 10 + CONTIGUOUS.] Not contiguous, not in contact; consisting of parts not in contact.
1792 *Statist. Acc. Scot.* VI. 222 Tarland is one of the most disjoined and discontiguous parishes in Scotland. **1793** J. MILL *Diary* (1889) 163 Parcelled out in discontiguous plots. **1861** W. BELL *Dict. Law Scot.* s.v. *Dispensation*, Where heritable subjects lay locally discontiguous..a clause of dispensation was sometimes inserted. *Mod.* Cromarty is the typical example of a discontiguous shire.

discon'tinuable, *a. rare*$^{-0}$. [f. DISCONTINUE *v.* + -ABLE.] Capable of being discontinued.
1846 in WORCESTER.

†**discon'tinual,** *a. Obs.* Also 5 **dys-, -tyn-, -elle.** [f. DIS- 10 + CONTINUAL.]
1. = DISCONTINUOUS.
1398 TREVISA *Barth. De P.R.* VII. xxxvi. (1495) 251 The cause and the solucion of all rootyd feuers is knowe in generall whether thei ben contynuall or dyscontynuall. *c* **1430** *Art Nombryng* (E.E.T.S.) 13 Of progressioun one is naturelle or contynuelle, þat oþer broken and discontynuelle. **1611** FLORIO, *Discontinuo*, discontinuall.
b. *Math.* Said of *proportion*: = DISCONTINUED.
1557 RECORDE *Whetst.* C ij b, When I saie thus: as 5. is to 15. so 6. is to 18. Here is a triple proportion, but not continualle..And therefore it is called a proportion discontinualle. **1570** BILLINGSLEY *Euclid* v. def. vii. 131 Proportionalitie, is of two sortes; the one is continuall, the other is discontinuall. **1706** in PHILLIPS (ed. Kersey).

discontinuance (dɪskən'tɪnjuːəns). Also 4–5 **dys-, -tyn-,** 4–6 **-aunce.** [a. AF. *discontinuance*, f. F. *discontinuer* to DISCONTINUE: see -ANCE.]
1. The action of discontinuing or breaking off; interruption (temporary or permanent) of continuance; cessation; intermission.
1398 TREVISA *Barth. De P.R.* VIII. xxviii. (1495) 341 Shynynge comyth of lyght wythout mynisshynge of lyght and..wythout dyscontynuaunce therof. **1489** CAXTON *Faytes of A.* I. viii. 20 The romayns in lyke wyse..lefte on a tyme thexcercyte of armes, whiche by theyr discontynuaunce they were by hanybal..desconfyted. **1598** BARRET *Theor. Warres* III. i. 31 My fiue or six yeares discontinuance from action. **1603** HOLLAND *Plutarch's Mor.* 651 And not suffer the auncient custome..by use and discontinuance to be utterly neglected. **1726** LEONI *Alberti's Archit.* II. 105/1 At the distance of every hundred foot the line is broken off by a kind of transverse step, which makes a discontinuance in the layer. **1809** WELLINGTON in Gurw. *Desp.* IV. 455 The cause of the discontinuance of the works at Lisbon. **1875** *Lyell's Princ. Geol.* II. III. xl. 402 A large proportion of them would perish with the discontinuance of agriculture. **1886** WILLIS & CLARK *Cambridge* II. 307 The discontinuance of an external stringcourse.
†**b.** Solution of continuity, want of cohesion of parts; disruption. *Obs.*
1626 BACON *Sylva* §24 If there bee no Remedy, then they [stillicides of water] cast themselues into round Drops; Which is the Figure that saueth the Body most from Discontinuance.
†**c.** *Math.* Of proportion: The condition of being discontinued or not continued. *Obs.*
1570 BILLINGSLEY *Euclid* v. def. vii. 131 By reason of the discontinuaunce of the proportions in this proportionalitie.

†**2.** A (temporary) ceasing to dwell or be present in a place; absence. *Obs.*

1604 R. CAWDREY *Table Alph., Discontinuance*, absence. **1633** HEYWOOD *Eng. Trav.* III. Wks. 1874 IV. 59 Hee writes mee heere, That at my discontinuance hee's much grieu'd. *a* **1635** NAUNTON *Fragm. Reg.* (Arb.) 42 They quote him for a person..of too often recesses, and discontinuance from the Queens presence. **1677** S. HERNE *Domus Carthusiana* 188 Their time of discontinuance is usually excepted in the Certificate.

†**3.** *Law.* In the old law of real property: An interruption or breaking off of a right of possession, or right of entry, consequent upon a wrongful alienation by the tenant in possession for a larger estate than he was entitled to. *Obs.*

This could regularly happen only in the case of a feoffment to a stranger by a tenant in tail in possession. The heir in tail had then no right to enter upon the land and turn out the intruder, but had to resort to the expensive course of asserting his title by process of law (SIR F. POLLOCK *Land Laws* (ed. 2) 80).

[**1304** *Year-bk. 32–3 Edw. I.* 255 (Godef.) L'estatut ne fet mye mencioun de continuaunce ne de discontinuaunce.] **1494** *Act 11 Hen. VII*, c. 20 All such Recoveries, Discontinuances, Alienations..be utterly void. **1574** tr. *Littleton's Tenures* 115a. **1598** KITCHIN *Courts Leet* (1675) 308 A Grant without Livery doth not make a discontinuance. **1768** BLACKSTONE *Comm.* III. 171 The injury of discontinuance. **1892** H. W. CHALLIS *Law Real Prop.* (ed. 2) 79 A discontinuance..was the result of certain assurances which, by the common law, had a tortious operation, whereby, under certain circumstances, one person might wrongfully destroy the estate of another; or rather, interrupt and break off the right of possession, or right of entry, subsisting under that estate, without any assent or *laches* on the other's part..The word *discontinuance* properly denotes this *turning of an estate to a right of action.*

4. *Law.* The interruption of a suit, or its dismissal, by reason of the plaintiff's omission of formalities necessary to keep it pending.

1540 *Act 32 Hen. VIII*, c. 30. §1 Any miscontinuance or discontinuance or misconueiyng of process. **1607–72** COWELL s.v., The effect of Discontinuance of Plea or Process, when the instant is lost, and may not be regained, but by a new Writ to begin the Suit a fresh. **1613** SIR H. FINCH *Law* (1636) 431 If the Plaintife do nothing, it is called a discontinuance: if any errour bee in the continuing, as by awarding a *Capias* where a distresse should bee, it is called a miscontinuance. **1638** SANDERSON *Serm.* II. 102 The devil ..is an unwearied sollicitor, and will not lose his claim by discontinuance. **1884** *Law Times Rep.* 10 May 322/1 What the plaintiff has done amounts to a discontinuance of his original action.

†**discon'tinuate**, *ppl. a. Obs.* [ad. med.L. *discontinuāt-us*, pa. pple. of *discontinuāre* to DISCONTINUE: see -ATE.] Discontinued, discontinuous. So **discon'tinuated** *ppl. a.*

1625 N. CARPENTER *Geog. Del.* I. ii. (1635) 24 Continuate and diuisible things cannot bee made out of such things as are meerely discontinuate and indiuisible. **1641** WILKINS *Mercury* vi. (1707) 26 Placing [the words]..in four Lines, and after any discontinuate Order. **1666** G. HARVEY *Morb. Angl.* viii. 70 A Disease of discontinuated Unity.

discontinuation (dɪskɒnˌtɪnjuːˈeɪʃən). [a. F. *discontinuation* (14th c. in Littré), ad. med.L. *discontinuātiōn-em*, n. of action f. *discontinuāre* to DISCONTINUE: cf. CONTINUATION.] **1.** The action of discontinuing. **a.** = DISCONTINUANCE 1.

1611 COTGR., *Discontinuation*, a discontinuation or discontinuing. **1649** *Alcoran* 185 The righteous shall enjoy eternally the delight of Paradise without discontinuation. **1736** ENTICK *Proposals Chaucer's Wks.* 1 Gentlemen need not fear to be imposed upon by a Discontinuation of this Work. **1862** T. A. TROLLOPE *Marietta* I. ii. 25 The discontinuation of the houses. **1880** *Contemp. Rev.* July 164 No one ever dreams of the discontinuation of the race.

b. Solution of continuity; = DISCONTINUANCE 1 b.

a **1727** NEWTON (J.), Upon any discontinuation of parts, made either by bubbles or by shaking the glass, the whole mercury falls.

2. *concr.* A breach or interruption of continuity.

1728 MORGAN *Algiers* I. vi. 188 Pumps [shoes] in very bad order at the Sides, with some discontinuations in the Upper Leathers.

†**3.** = DISCONTINUANCE 3. *Obs.* (? error).

1721 BAILEY, *Discontinuation* [of Possession].

discontinue (dɪskənˈtɪnjuː), *v.* Also 5–6 **-tyn-**, **-ew**. [a. F. *discontinue-r* (14th c. in Littré), ad. med.L. *discontinuā-re*, f. DIS- 4 + *continuāre* to CONTINUE.]

I. *trans.*

1. To cause to cease; to cease from (an action or habit); to break off, put a stop to, give up.

1479 in *Eng. Gilds* (1870) 414 King Edwarde the thirdde ..exemptid the saide maires, and discontynewed theym, to feche their saide charges at the castell yate of the foresaide Constable. **1553** *Act 1 Mary* 3rd Sess. c. 7. §1 Many good Clothiers..have been enforced to leave off and clearly discontinue their Cloth-making. **1633** EARL MANCH. *Al Mondo* (1636) 95 It doth not disanull, but discontinue life. **1692** LUTTRELL *Brief Rel.* (1857) II. 589 The queen hath been pleased to order that the monthly fast should for the present be discontinued. **1726** *Adv. Capt. R. Boyle* 140 [He] begg'd that he would discontinue his Visits. **1796** MORSE *Amer. Geog.* II. 33 They never discontinue their work on account of the darkness. **1893** *Law Times* XCV. 5/2 Persons who had been customers discontinued their custom.

b. *ellipt.* To cease to take or receive, give or pay; to give up, leave off.

Mod. I shall discontinue the newspaper at the end of the year. He has discontinued his subscription to the Society.

†**2.** To cease to frequent, occupy, or inhabit.

14.. *Mann. & Househ. Exp.* 555 Mowe I be ryte well.. loged here, ȝete I wol nat desskontenew that kontery, bote some tyme ther and some tyme here as schal plese me beste. **1596** SHAKS. *Merch. V.* III. iv. 75 Men shall sweare I haue discontinued schoole Aboue a twelue moneth. **1599** —— *Much Ado* V. i. 192, I must discontinue your companie. **1645** EVELYN *Mem.* (1857) I. 166 A great city..now discontinued and demolished by the frequent earthquakes.

3. *Law.* **a.** To dismiss or abandon (a suit, etc.).

1487 *Act 3 Hen. VII*, c. 10 Yf..the seid writte of errour be discontynued in defaute of the partie. **1589** *Act 31 Eliz.* c. 1. **1607–72** COWELL s.v. *Discontinuance*, To be discontinued, and to be put *sine die*, is all one, and nothing else but to be dismissed finally the Court. **1704** LUTTRELL *Brief Rel.* (1857) V. 501 Yesterday the lords adjourned..having first discontinued the writt of error brought by Dr. Watson..he having not assign'd errors in due time. **1848** WHARTON *Law Lex.* s.v. *Discontinuance*, A rule to discontinue is obtained by a plaintiff when he finds that he has misconceived his action. **1891** *Law Times* XC 473/1 After delivery of defence the plaintiff discontinued his action.

†**b.** To alien land in such a manner as operates to the 'discontinuance' of the heir in tail. *Obs.*

1495 *Act 11 Hen. VII*, c. 60 Preamb., The seid John Mayne in his lyf discontinued dyvers londes and tenementis whiche were intailed to him and to his Auncestres. **1574** tr. *Littleton's Tenures* 32 b, The continuance of the tenancye in the tenaunte and in his bloode by the alyenacion is discontinued. *a* **1626** BACON *Max. & Uses Com. Law* ix. (1636) 37 If tenant in taile discontinue, and the discontinuee make a lease for life. **1818** CRUISE *Digest* (ed. 2) V. 255 A fine is one of those assurances by which an estate tail may be discontinued.

†**4.** To break the continuity of; to interrupt, disrupt, sunder. *Obs.*

1529 MORE *Comf. agst. Trib.* I. Wks. 1154/1 A man hathe greate cause of feare and heauines that continueth alway stil in welth, discontinued wyth no tribulacion. **1660** BOYLE *New Exp. Phys. Mech.* xxxvii. 310 By heating a lump of Crystal..and quenching it in..Water, it would be discontinu'd by..a multitude of Cracks. **1673** RAY *Journ. Low C.* 149 This bank of Earth..is discontinued by seven.. breaks or apertures..by which the Lagune communicate with the gulf. **1678** CUDWORTH *Intell. Syst.* 814 Solid bodies ..being once discontinued, are not easily consolidated together again. **1727–51** CHAMBERS *Cycl.* s.v. *Disease*, The bones, and flesh..may be..discontinued by fractures, and contusions.

II. *intrans.*

5. To cease to continue; to cease, stop.

1555 EDEN *Decades* 33 Leaste theyre handes shulde discontinewe from sheadinge of bludde. **1568–9** *Act 11 Eliz.* (in Bolton *Stat. Irel.* (1621) 318) The O Neyles and other of the Irishrie..tooke opportunitie to withdraw from their duetie of allegeance..and so discontinued uncontrolled untill the foure and thirtieth yeare of..King Henry the eight. **1580** BARET *Alv.* D 792 To discontinue a while from labour.

†**b.** To be cut off or severed *from*; to cease to reside; to be absent. *Obs.*

1611 BIBLE *Jer.* xvii. 4 And thou, euen thyselfe, shalt discontinue from thine heritage that I gaue thee. **1677** S. HERNE *Domus Carthusiana* 188 They have liberty..to discontinue two months in a year.

†**6.** To cease to be continuous; to become disrupted. *Obs.*

1626 BACON *Sylva* §24 Stillicides of Water..will Draw themselues into a small thread, because they will not discontinue.

discontinued (dɪskənˈtɪnjuːd), *ppl. a.* [f. prec. vb. + -ED[1].] Broken off, interrupted, stopped; made not continuous in time or space.

discontinued proportion: see quot. 1827, and cf. CONTINUED 4 a.

1561 T. NORTON *Calvin's Inst.* I. 16 He deceiued silly men, and hath oft tymes vsed discontinued phrases, that vnder such visor he might hide his deceites. **1599** HAKLUYT *Voy.* II. I. 137 (R.) By renewing of the foresayd discontinued trade. **1624** N. DE LAUNE tr. *Du Moulin's Logick* 13 Number may be counted by it selfe..but continued quantitie cannot be measured but by the helpe of the discontinued quantity. **1728** PEMBERTON *Newton's Philos.* 155 This is the case of discontinued fluids. **1748** RICHARDSON *Clarissa* (1811) VII. 302 I'll see if the air, and a discontinued attention will help me. **1827** HUTTON *Course Math.* I. 113 When the difference or ratio of the consequent of one couplet, and the antecedent of the next couplet, is not the same as the common difference or ratio of the couplets, the proportion is discontinued. So 4, 2, 8, 6, are in discontinued arithmetical proportion.

Hence **discon'tinuedness**, the quality of being discontinued; interruptedness.

1727 in BAILEY vol. II.

discontinuee (dɪskənˌtɪnjuːˈiː). In 6 **-tinue**. [f. DISCONTINUE *v.* + -EE: corresp. in form to F. *discontinué* pa. pple.] One to whom an estate is aliened to the 'discontinuance' of the heir in tail.

1574 tr. *Littleton's Tenures* 121 a, If the tenaunte in the taile discontinue the taile, and after he disseiseth his discontinue. *a* **1626** BACON *Max. & Uses Com. Law* ix. (1636) 35 The Feme takes another husband, who takes a feoffement from the discontinuee to him and his wife. **1642** PERKINS *Prof. Bk.* v. §397. 171 If the issue in taile doth disseise the discontinuee of his Father of the land entailed. **1818** CRUISE *Digest* V. 186 He afterwards disseised the discontinuee.

discon'tinuer. [f. DISCONTINUE *v.* + -ER[1].] One who discontinues. †**b.** *esp.* One who discontinues his residence or attendance; an absentee.

a **1613** OVERBURY *Characters, Puritane* Wks. (1856) 80 He ever prayes against non residents, but is himselfe the greatest discontinuer, for he never keepes near his text. **1639** in *Laud's Rem.* II. 174 (T.) The new statutes at Oxford permit none but those who..reside there to take degrees.. so that many discontinuers cannot in so short a time proceed as formerly. **1655** FULLER *Ch. Hist.* II. iii. §16 He was no.. Discontinuer from his Convent, for a long time. **1655** —— *Hist. Camb.* 166 M. Bernard, a Discontinuer, and Lecturer of S. Sepulchers in London.

discon'tinuing, *vbl. sb.* [f. as prec. + -ING[1].] The action of the verb DISCONTINUE; cessation, interruption.

1611 COTGR., *Discontinuation*, a discontinuation, or discontinuing. **1653** H. COGAN tr. *Pinto's Trav.* lvii. (1663) 224 All these pilgrims, which..are all the year long without discontinuing. *a* **1715** BURNET *Own Times* (R.), There were so many discontinuings, and so many new undertakings.

†**discon'tinuingly**, *adv. Obs. rare.* [f. *discontinuing* pr. pple. + -LY[2].] In a discontinuing manner; without continuance.

1611 COTGR., *Discontinuément*, discontinuingly, intermissiuely, by stops, with interruptions.

discontinuity (dɪsˌkɒntɪˈnjuːɪtɪ). [f. med.L. type **discontinuitās*, f. *discontinu-us*: see next and -ITY. Cf. F. *discontinuité* (1775 in Hatz.-Darm.).]

1. a. The quality or state of being discontinuous; want or failure of continuity or uninterrupted sequence; interrupted condition.

1570 DEE *Math. Pref.* 35 They will not be extended, to discontinuitie. **1626** BACON *Sylva* §846 The Second is the Stronger or Weaker Appetite, in Bodies, to Continuitie, and to flie Discontinuitie. **1733** CHEYNE *Eng. Malady* I. x. §4 (1734) 97 Nature seems only to have provided proper Juices to fill up the Discontinuity [in wounds]. **1874** L. STEPHEN *Hours in Library* (1892) I. ix. 329 He passes from one conception to the other without the smallest consciousness of any discontinuity. **1893** J. PULSFORD *Loyalty to Christ* II. 377 We are at the foot of the ladder, and they at the top; but they know there is no discontinuity between lowest and highest.

b. with *a* and *pl.* A break or gap in a structure.

1794 SULLIVAN *View Nat.* II. 413 The spots may also be ..temporary holes, or discontinuities in the luminous meteor. **1835** R. H. FROUDE *Rem.* (1838) I. 408, I see such jumps and discontinuities as make me despair of ever being intelligible.

c. *spec.* in *Math.* said of a function or its variation: see DISCONTINUOUS.

2. *attrib.*, as **discontinuity layer**, a layer of water in a lake or the sea in which the temperature changes rapidly with depth from that of the water above it to that of the water below; a thermocline separating an epilimnion from a hypolimnion.

1911 E. M. WEDDERBURN in *Trans. R. Soc. Edin.* XLVII. 625 Attention has been drawn to the very rapid temperature changes which are found at the discontinuity layer. **1931** *Discovery* June 199/2 In general the presence of the 'discontinuity layer' tends to prevent the free mixing of the layers [of water in the sea]. **1942** P. M. JENKIN in *Jrnl. Animal Ecol.* XI. 252 The term 'Discontinuity Layer' is revived to cover the layer of very variable thickness in which there is a sufficient temperature gradient to impede mixing of the epilimnion with the cool hypolimnion below. **1964** *Oceanogr. & Marine Biol.* II. 125 At depths of hundreds of metres, perhaps below the discontinuity layer, there is a decline to 20–35% of surface mass.

discon'tinuˌor. *Law.* [f. DISCONTINUE *v.* + -OR.] The tenant in tail whose alienation of an estate has caused a discontinuance.

1768 BLACKSTONE *Comm.* III. 178 The law will not suppose the discontinuor to have aliened the estate without power so to do, and therefore leaves the heir in tail to his action at law, and permits not his entry to be lawful.

discontinuous (dɪskənˈtɪnjuːəs), *a.* [f. med.L. *discontinu-us* (in F. *discontinu*), f. DIS- 4 + *continuus*: see CONTINUOUS.] (Not in Johnson.)

†**1.** Producing discontinuity; breaking continuity between parts; gaping. *Obs.*

1667 MILTON *P.L.* VI. 329 So sore The griding sword with discontinuous wound Pass'd through him. **1703** J. PHILIPS *Splendid Shilling* (T.), A horrid chasm, disclos'd with orifice Wide, discontinuous.

2. Not continuous in space or time; characterized by want of continuity; having interstices or breaks; interrupted, intermittent.

1718 ROWE tr. *Lucan* III. 755 (Seager) Towers, engines, all come thundering to the ground: Wide spread the discontinuous ruins lie. **1750** tr. *Leonardus' Mirr. Stones* 32 In which case the stones would be discontinuous and appear like little stones. **1832** *Nat. Philos., Electro-Magnet.* xi. §176 (Useful Knowl. Soc.) When the conductors are imperfect, the currents are discontinuous. **1880** A. R. WALLACE *Isl. Life* 13 This is one of the best cases..of the discontinuous distribution of a species. **1883** SIR J. W. CHITTY in *Law Rep.* 26 Ch. Div. 442 A right of way..is a discontinuous easement, because a man is not always walking in and out of his front door.

3. Math. *discontinuous function*: one that varies discontinuously, and whose differential coefficient may therefore become infinite: opp. to *continuous function* (see CONTINUOUS 3).

1837 BABBAGE *Bridgew. Treat.* iii. 59 *note*, Every law so imagined might be interrupted by any discontinuous function. **1845** CAYLEY *Inverse Elliptic Funct.*, Analytically discontinuous. **1881** MAXWELL *Electr. & Magn.* I. 8 The first derivatives of a continuous function may be discontinuous. **1885** WATSON & BURBURY *Math. Th. Electr. & Magn.* I. 50 If ρ, the density of matter, be finite in any portion of space, the first differential coefficients of *V* cannot be discontinuous in that portion of space.

discon'tinuously, *adv.* [f. prec. + -LY².] In a discontinuous manner; without continuity.

1836 DE MORGAN *Diff. & Integr. Calculus* 626 Those [series] which can become divergent, or as near divergency as we please, never are discontinuously connected with different functions; that is, never represent one function for a value of *x* between one pair of limits, and another for values between another pair. **1874** LEWES *Probl. Life & Mind* I. 177 All the phenomena constituting the external reality to us are presented discontinuously. **1881** SPOTTISWOODE in *Nature* No. 624. 570 The effect of this is to discharge the electricity discontinuously.

discon'tinuousness. [f. as prec. + -NESS.] A discontinuous condition; want of continuity.

1865 GROTE *Plato* I. ii. 97 The advocates of absolute plurality and discontinuousness. **1883** H. DRUMMOND *Nat. Law in Spir. W.* (ed. 2) 43 Is not this another instance of the discontinuousness of Law?

discon'venience, *sb. Obs.* exc. *dial.* [ad. L. *disconvenientia* (Tertullian *c* 200), f. *disconvenientem*: see DISCONVENIENT and -ENCE. Cf. F. *disconvenance*, Pr. and Sp. *dis-, desconveniencia*.]

†**1.** Want of agreement or correspondence; incongruity, inconsistency. (The opposite of CONVENIENCE *sb.* 1.) *Obs.*

c **1430** LYDG. *Min. Poems* (1844) 82 Where mesure faileth is disconuenience. *a* **1619** FOTHERBY *Atheom.* II. iii. §2 (1622) 213 A necessary disconuenience, where any thing is allowed to bee cause of it selfe. **1656** HOBBES *Liberty, etc.* (1841) 87 Fear ariseth many times out of natural antipathies, but in these disconveniences of nature deliberation hath no place at all. **1660** R. COKE *Justice Vind.* 39 The dictate of right reason, shewing to any action, from its convenience or disconvenience with Rational nature, that there is in it a Moral turpitude or a Moral necessity.

†**2.** Unfitness, unsuitableness, impropriety. (The opposite of CONVENIENCE *sb.* 4.) *Obs.*

14.. LYDG. *Secrees* 953 Ther is a maneer disconvenience In Re publica is hoolde vicious, A kyng to pleyne vpon Indigence, Outhir in desirs to been Avaricious. **1598** FLORIO *Sconuenenolezza*, disconuenience, vnseemelines.

3. Inconvenience, incommodity, disadvantage; (with *pl.*) something inconvenient, an inconvenience. (The opposite of CONVENIENCE *sb.* 5-7.) *Obs.* exc. *dial.*

1553 GRIMALDE *Cicero's Offices* Pref. to Rdr., To such sortes of annoyaunce and disconuenience light and moderation is brought by morall doctrine. **1566** PAINTER *Pal. Pleas.* I. 183 What tormentes be in love, what travailes in pursute.. what disconveniences. **1615** J. STEPHENS *Satyr. Ess.* 202 Hee..lookes to the disconveniences, not the commodity, hee getts by possession. **1645** QUARLES *Sol. Recant.* II. 65 What harm, what disconvenience lies In being foole? what vantage to be wise? **1825-80** JAMIESON, *Disconvenience*, inconvenience. *Aberd.*

discon'venience, *v. dial.* [f. prec.: cf. CONVENIENCE *v.*] *trans.* To put to inconvenience; to inconvenience.

1825-80 JAMIESON, *Disconvenience*, to put to inconvenience. [*Aberd.*] **1894** CROCKETT *Raiders* xviii. 159 Sand had no cloak..yet he did not appear in the least disconvenienced.

†**discon'veniency.** *Obs.* [f. L. *disconvenientia*: see DISCONVENIENCE and -ENCY.] The quality of being disconvenient; = DISCONVENIENCE *sb.*

1621 BP. MOUNTAGU *Diatribæ* 42 The disconueniency or inconueniency of the duty commanded. **1640** BP. REYNOLDS *Passions* 39 The natural conveniency or disconveniency which it beareth to the faculty. **1650** T. VAUGHAN *Anima Magica* 7 None but God..foresaw the Conveniencies and Disconveniencies of his Creatures.

discon'venient, *a. Obs.* exc. *dial.* [ad. L. *disconvenient-em*, pr. pple. of *disconvenīre* to disagree, be inharmonious or inconsistent, f. DIS- 4 + *convenīre* to agree, suit: see CONVENIENT.]

†**1.** Not in accordance (*with*), not consonant (*to*), incongruous; unsuitable, inappropriate. (The opposite of CONVENIENT 1-4.) *Obs.*

1398 TREVISA *Barth. De P.R.* IX. xv. (1495) 356 That tyme is moost dysconuenyent and vnacordynge to medycyne. **1526** *Pilgr. Perf.* (W. de W. 1531) 49 To chose that is conuenyent for our nature, and to eschewe & flee all that is disconuenient to the same. **1660** R. COKE *Justice Vind.* 39 Actions convenient or disconvenient with Rational nature.

2. Inconvenient, disadvantageous. (The opposite of CONVENIENT 6.) *Obs.* exc. *dial.*

c **1450** tr. *De Imitatione* III. liv, Suche þinges as semeþ to the disconuenient & lest profitable. **1538** STARKEY *England* I. iv. 140 Such pryuylege at the fyrst begynnyng of the Church..were veray expedyent..no les then they be now dysconuenyent. **1632** J. HAYWARD tr. *Biondi's Eromena* 132 To continue as I am, is for many respects disconvenient unto me. **1825-80** JAMIESON, *Disconvenient*, inconvenient. [*Aberd.*]

disconventicle: see DIS- 7b.

discophile ('dɪskəʊfaɪl). Also discophil. [f. DISC *sb.* 2d + -PHIL, -PHILE.] An enthusiast for and collector of gramophone records.

1940 *Commonweal* 14 June 174 Many discophiles might have preferred one of the less hackneyed earlier symphonies. **1952** *Times Lit. Suppl.* 15 Aug. 534/2 The little world of discography and the discophil has been expanding internationally and for some years has needed a comprehensive encyclopedia of..the electric recordings of ..classical music. **1959** *Sunday Times* 17 May 20/8 While learned liturgists still thresh out the relationship between the Ambrosian and Gregorian Chant, humbler discophiles may now make their own comparisons at home. **1962** *Times Lit. Suppl.* 12 Jan. 20/4 The discophile's cult of the vocal record.

discophoran (dɪ'skɒfərən), *a.* and *sb. Zool.* [f. mod.L. *Discophora*, pl. neut. of *discophorus*, a. Gr. διακοφόρος bearing the discus (f. δίσκος discus, + -φορος bearing), taken in sense 'bearing a disk'.]

A. *adj.* **1.** Belonging to the subclass *Discophora* of Hydrozoa, comprising the jelly-fishes. **2.** Belonging to the order *Discophora* of suctorial worms, synonymous with *Hirudinea* or leeches.

B. *sb.* One of the *Discophora* (in either sense). Also **discophore** ('dɪskəʊfɔə(r)).

1878 BELL *Gegenbaur's Comp. Anat.* 98 Forms..closely allied to the larvæ of the Discophora.

discophorous (dɪ'skɒfərəs), *a. Zool.* [f. mod.L. *discophor-us* (a. Gr. διακοφόρος: see prec.).]

1. Having an umbrellar disc, as a jelly-fish: see prec. A. 1. **2.** Having a sucking-disc, as a leech: see prec. A. 2. **3.** Of or pertaining to the *Discophora*.

1879 G. ALLEN *Col. Sense* iii. 28 The..conjectural limit of discophorous vision.

discoplacental, etc.: see DISCO-.

discord ('dɪskɔːd), *sb.* Also 3-4 **des-**, 4-5 **dys-**. [ME. *des-, discord*, a. OF. *descord, descort* (12th c.), *discord, -cort* (14-15th c.), vbl. sb. f. *descorder*: see DISCORD *v.* (OF. had also *des-, discorde* (ad. L. *discordia*), whence perh. ME. spelling *discorde*.]

1. Absence of concord or harmony (between persons); disagreement of opinions and aims; variance, dissension, strife.

apple of discord: see APPLE *sb.* 5.

1297 R. GLOUC. (1724) 196 Vor July Cesar yt nom vorst ..þoru descord & contek, þat bytuene or elderne vas þo. *a* **1300** *Cursor M.* 22223 (Cott.) Bot if dissenciun bi-tide, ..þat es..discord and strijf. **1340** *Ayenb.* 43 Þe zenne of ham þet zaweþ discord. *c* **1400** MAUNDEV. (1839) v. 38 Thei weren at gret Discord, for to make a Soudan. **1535** COVERDALE *Prov.* xv. 18 An angrie man stirreth vp strife, but he yᵗ is pacient stilleth discorde. **1591** SHAKS. *1 Hen. VI*, v. v. 63 For what is wedlocke forced? but a Hell, An Age of discord and continuall strife. **1632** LITHGOW *Trav.* VIII. 354 These two Barones were at great discord, about the love of a young Noble woman. **1779-81** JOHNSON *L.P.*, *Fenton*, Men who at that time of discord and debate consulted conscience..more than interest. **1859** KINGSLEY *Misc.* (1860) I. 13 Trying to sow discord between man and man, class and class.

b. *personified.*

1667 MILTON *P.L.* x. 707 Discord first, Daughter of Sin, among th' irrational, Death introduced. **1784** COWPER *Task* IV. 482 Fell Discord, arbitress of such debate. **1832** TENNYSON *Love Thou thy Land* 68 Regard gradation, lest the Soul Of Discord race the rising wind.

2. Want of agreement or harmony (between things); diversity, difference.

1387 TREVISA *Higden* (Rolls) IV. 35 (Mätz.) Þis seventy.. translated þe lawe wiþoute discorde of wordes oþer of menynge. **1520** *Caxton's Chron. Eng.* IV. 37/1 For the dyscorde of the paschal tyme he called a counsell in Alexander. **1590** SHAKS. *Mids. N.* v. i. 60 Merry and tragicall..How shall wee finde the concord of this discord? **1608-11** BP. HALL *Medit. & Vowes* II. §49 Nothing makes so strong and mortall hostility, as discord in religions. **1732** POPE *Ess. Man* I. 291 All Nature is but Art, unknown to thee ..All Discord, Harmony not understood. *a* **1806** BP. HORSLEY *Serm.* III. xxxix. (R.), The discordance of these errors is mistaken for a discord of the truths on which they are severally grafted. **1882-3** SCHAFF *Encycl. Relig. Knowl.* II. 1041/1 The relations of the Church to the government of Baden..were entirely at discord with his own views.

3. *Mus.* (The opposite of CONCORD.) **a.** Disagreement or want of harmony between two or more musical notes sounded together; dissonance. **b.** A combination of two or more notes not in harmony with each other; a chord which by itself is unpleasing or unsatisfactory to the ear, and requires to be 'resolved' or followed by some other chord. **c.** The interval between two notes forming a discord; any interval except the unison, octave, perfect fifth and fourth, major and minor thirds, and major and minor sixths (and the octaves of these). **d.** A single note which is dissonant with another, or with the other notes of a chord.

c **1440** *Promp. Parv.* 122/1 Dyscorde yn songe, *dissonancia*. **1579** E. K. in *Spenser's Sheph. Cal.* Ep. Ded. §1 Oftentimes a dischorde in Musick maketh a comely concordaunce. **1600** SHAKS. *A.Y.L.* II. vii. 6 If he, compact of iarres, grow Musicall, We shortly shall haue discord in the Spheares. **1609** DOULAND *Ornith. Microl.* 79 A Discord..is the mixture of diuers sounds, naturally offending the eares. **1674** PLAYFORD *Skill Mus.* III. 1 The Discords are, a Second, Fourth, and Seventh, with their Eighths. **1691-8** NORRIS *Pract. Disc.* 229 As in Musick, what is Discord in particular and separately considered, will be Harmony upon the whole. **1795** MASON *Ch. Mus.* i. 55 An adept..might give his scientific hearers supreme pleasure by his skilful manner of resolving his discords. **1864** BROWNING *Abt Vogler* xi, Why rushed the discords in but that harmony should be prized? **1875** OUSELEY *Harmony* viii. 95 The chord in which the dissonance is heard is called a Discord. **1881** MACFARREN *Counterp.* i. 2 A discord is a chord that is unsatisfactory in itself, or it is a note foreign to the prevailing harmony.

fig. **1650** B. *Discolliminium* 46 My harmonious Pulse beats nothing but melodious Discords, to the tune of the Crosse and the Harpe. **1878** J. P. HOPPS *Jesus* viii. 30 He had silenced the discords of passion in his own breast.

4. Disagreement or want of harmony between sounds; a mingling or clashing of sounds, a confused noise; a harsh or unpleasing sound. (Often with allusion to the musical sense: see prec.)

1590 SHAKS. *Mids. N.* IV. i. 123, I neuer heard So musicall a discord, such sweet thunder. **1602** MARSTON *Ant. & Mel.* v. Wks. 1856 I. 67 There remaines no discord that can sound Harsh accents to the eare of our accord. **1667** MILTON *P.L.* VI. 209 Arms on Armour clashing bray'd Horrible discord, and the madding Wheeles Of brazen Chariots rag'd. **1791** MRS. RADCLIFFE *Rom. Forest* v, The bravura of La Motte whose notes sounded discord to his ears. **1835** LYTTON *Rienzi* I. iv, The very sight, the very voice of a Colonna, was a blight to his eye and a discord to his ear.

5. *Comb.*, as ***discord-wasted*** adj.

1813 SHELLEY *Q. Mab* IV. 79 The discord-wasted land.

†**'discord,** *a. rare.* [a. F. *discord*, in 1304 *discors* (Godef.), ad. L. *discors, discord-em* discordant, at variance: see next.] Discordant.

a **1425** *Chaucer's Pars. T.* ⁋744 [MSS. Lansd., Petw., Selden] Vnmesurable & discorde [*other MSS.* desordeynee, disordeyned] couetise. **1509** HAWES *Past. Pleas.* XVI. xiii, For musike doth sette in all unyte The discorde thynges whiche are variable. **1606** G. W[OODCOCKE] tr. *Hist. Ivstine* Ep. Ded., In Musicke, manie discord notes and manie tunes make one consent.

discord (dɪ'skɔːd), *v.*¹ Also 4-6 **dys-**. [a. OF. *des-, discorde-r* (13th c. in Littré), ad. L. *discordāre* to be a variance, f. *discors, discord-* adj. discordant, f. DIS- + *cor, cord-* heart: cf. *concord*.]

1. *intr.* Of persons: To disagree, 'differ'; to be at variance, to quarrel; also, to dissent *from*.

a **1300** *Cursor M.* 23640 (Cott.) Þe gode..wit alkin thing sal þire acorde, þe wicked..wit alkin scaft þai sal discord. *a* **1340** HAMPOLE *Psalter* cxix. 6 With þaim þat discordis fra þe charite of halikyrke i held anhede. *c* **1400** *Lanfranc's Cirurg.* 72 Þer ben manye men þat discorden of dietynge of men þat ben woundid. **1494** FABYAN *Chron.* I. xxv. 18 Here discordyth myn Auctour with some other wryters. **1535** STEWART *Cron. Scot.* II. 275 How the Lordis of Scotland discordit at the Huntis. **1677** GALE *Crt. Gentiles* II. IV. 404 The human wil cannot discord from the Divine. **1848** THACKERAY *Van. Fair* xlv, They discorded with her. **1867** CARLYLE in *Remin.* (1881) II. 124 We discorded commonly on two points.

2. Of things (chiefly): To be different (*from*), discordant or inconsistent (*with*).

1388 WYCLIF *Rom.* Jerome's Prol., He wolde shewen the newe to not discorden fro the olde testament. *c* **1450** *Mirour Saluacioun* 1227 Thire two last preceptes semes to discorde in nothing. **1494** FABYAN *Chron.* I. lxxv. (R.), Thyse two nacions discorde in maners, but nat in clothing and in fayth. **1608** HIERON *Def. Ministers' Reasons Refus. Subscription* II. 166 Not because it accordeth or discordeth with the original. **1818** JAS. MILL *Brit. India* II. v. v. 484 The party, the views of which were apt to discord with those of the leading members of the government.

b. Of sounds: To be discordant or dissonant; to jar, clash.

a **1340** HAMPOLE *Psalter* cl. 4 Acorde, as of sere voicys, noght discordand, is swete sange. *c* **1440** *Promp. Parv.* 122/1 Dyscordyn yn sounde, or syngynge, *dissono, deliro*. **1530** BARET *Alv.* D 801 To Discord, or disagree in tune. **1626** BACON *Sylva* §227 But Sounds do disturb and alter one the other..Sometimes the one jarring or discording with the other and making a confusion.

†**3.** *trans.* To make discordant. *Obs. rare.*

1599 SANDYS *Europæ Spec.* (1632) 42 They adventure not to play upon that string..for fear of discording all the rest of their harmonie. *a* **1627** [see DISCORDED].

†**dis'cord,** *v.*² *Obs. Farriery.* [f. DIS- 7a + CORD *sb.*¹] *trans.* To replace (the intestine) of an incorded or ruptured horse. So **dis'cording** *vbl. sb.*, the relieving of hernia in this way.

1607 TOPSELL *Four-f. Beasts* (1658) 307 Having so discorded, that is to say, returned the gut into his right place. *Ibid.*, Forget not the next day after his discording to unloosen the list, and to take it away..and at the three weeks end..it were not amisse to geld the stone on that side away, so shall he never be encorded again on that side.

†**discordable,** *a. Obs.* [ME. *discor'dable*, a. OF. *des-, discordable*, ad. L. *discordābil-is* disagreeing, discordant, f. *discordāre*: see DISCORD *v.* and -BLE.] Characterized by discord, discordant.

c **1374** CHAUCER *Troylus* III. 1704 (1753), Elements, that been so discordable. **1393** GOWER *Conf.* II. 225 It is nought discordable Unto my word, but accordable. **1549** *Compl. Scotl.* xi. 100 The samnetes herd the tua discordabil consellis of herenius.

discordance (dɪˈskɔːdəns). [a. OF. *des-, discordance* = It. *scordanza* for *discordanza* (Florio), L. type **discordāntia*, f. *discordāre*: see DISCORD *v.* and -ANCE.]

1. The fact of being discordant; disagreement, want of concord.

1340 *Ayenb.* 259 Vor of þe discordance of þe herte comþ þe discordance of þe bodie. *c* **1386** CHAUCER *Pars. T.* ¶201 After the diverse discordances of oure wikkednesses. **1483** CAXTON *Gold. Leg.* 427 b/2 Thys holy saynt Yues laboured euer to pease alle dyscordaunce and stryf. **1494** FABYAN *Chron.* I. VI. ccxiii. (R.), In this sayinge appereth some discordaunce with other writers. *a* **1619** FOTHERBY *Atheom.* II. xii. §1 (1622) 329 The whole concordance of the world consists in discordances. **1656** HOBBES *Liberty, etc.* (R.), The discordance between the action and the law. **1819** MACKINTOSH *Sp. in Ho. Com.* 2 Mar. Wks. 1846 III. 374 This rapidly increasing discordance between the letter and the practice of the Criminal Law, arose in the best times of our history. **1864** J. H. NEWMAN *Apol.* 106 They were in discordance with each other, from the first, in their estimate of the means, [etc.].

2. Discord of sounds; harsh or dissonant noise.

c **1400** *Rom. Rose* 4251 In floites made he discordaunce. **1483** *Cath. Angl.* 101/1 A Discordance..*desonancia.* **1801** SOUTHEY *Thalaba* XII. viii, Cries, Which rung in wild discordance round the rock. **1878** BESANT & RICE *Celia's Arb.* xviii. (1887) 132 The curious mixture of discordances which rose to the organ-loft.

discordancy (dɪˈskɔːdənsɪ). [ad. L. type **discordāntia*: see prec. and -ANCY.]

1. The condition or quality of being discordant.

1608 D. T. *Ess. Pol. & Mor.* 94 Where there is a difference therefore in Religion, there is alwaies lightly a discordancie in affection. **1780** BURKE *Sp. at Bristol* Wks. III. 357 In such a discordancy of sentiments, it is better to look to the nature of things than to the humours of men. **1815** JANE AUSTEN *Emma* I. xii. 83 Our discordancies must always arise from my being in the wrong. **1855** BROWNING *Ferishtah* (1884) 128 How reconcile discordancy.

2. = DISCORDANCE 2.

1607 WALKINGTON *Opt. Glasse* v. 33 The body is like an instrument of musicke, that when it hath a discordancy in the strings, is wont to jarre. **1796** STEDMAN *Surinam* II. xvi. 4 Absolutely deafened by discordancy and noise.

discordant (dɪˈskɔːdənt), *a.* (*sb.*) [ME. *des-, dis-, dyscordant*, a. OF. *des-, discordant*, pr. pple. of *descorder*: see DISCORD *v.* and -ANT.]

1. Not in accord, not harmoniously connected or related; at variance; disagreeing, differing; incongruous. Const. *to, from, with.*

[**1292** BRITTON I. Prol. (1865) 2 En taunt qe lour usages ne soynt mie descordauntz a dreiture.] *c* **1374** CHAUCER *Troylus* II. 988 (1037) No discordaunt þing y-fere, As þus, to vsen termes of Physik. *a* **1420** HOCCLEVE *De Reg. Princ.* 96 As discordant as day is to the nyght. **1550** BALE *Apology* 75 (R.) So long as he is so dyscordaunte to hymself. **1651** HOBBES *Leviath.* II. xxvi. 140 The reasons and resolutions are, and must remain discordant. **1677** HALE *Prim. Orig. Man.* I. ii. 57 If discordant from it, the sentence of Condemnation [follows]. **1781** COWPER *Retirement* 173 Discordant motives in one centre meet. **1868** E. EDWARDS *Raleigh* I. iv. 52 The current accounts are in some points curiously discordant; yet far less discordant than are the portraits. **1868** GLADSTONE *Juv. Mundi* i. (1870) 16 Testimony..in no case discordant with that of the Iliad.

b. Living in discord, disagreeing, quarrelsome.

1547 J. HARRISON *Exhort. Scottes* H iij, I..accuse..myne awne rebellious, discordant and graceles children. **1597** SHAKS. *2 Hen. IV*, Induct. 19 The blunt monster with vncounted heads, The still discordant, wauering multitude. **1776** JOHNSON *Let. to Boswell* 21 Dec., When once a discordant family has felt the pleasure of peace, they will not willingly lose it. **1803** WELLESLEY in Owen *Desp.* 328 He united that discordant and turbulent race in the common cause.

2. Of sound: Inharmonious, dissonant, jarring.

c **1400** *Rom. Rose* 4247 Discordaunt ever fro armonye, And distoned from melodie. **1701** CONGREVE *Hymn to Harmony* vi, War, with discordant notes and jarring noise The harmony of peace destroys. **1762** KAMES *Elem. Crit.* ii. §6 (1833) 68 Two sounds that refuse incorporation or mixture, are said to be discordant. **1784** COWPER *Task* VI. 787 No passion touches a discordant string, But all is harmony and love. **1871** L. STEPHEN *Playgr. Eur.* (1894) vii. 156 Some discordant shrieks from our guides made the summer night hideous.

†**B.** *sb.* in *pl.* Discordant things, attributes, or propositions. *Obs.*

c **1400** *Test. Love* II. (1542) 319 a/2 By these accordaunces, discordantes ben ioyned. **1551** T. WILSON *Logike* (1580) 52 Contraries, are suche discordauntes, as can not be, at one and the same tyme, in one substaunce. *Ibid.* 52 b, Note further, that all discordauntes are not contrary, accordyng to their..common accidentes, but accordyng to their proper difference.

Hence **diˈscordantness**, discordant quality.

1727 BAILEY vol. II, *Discordantness*, disagreeableness.

discordantly (dɪˈskɔːdəntlɪ), *adv.* [f. prec. + -LY[2]] In a discordant manner; inharmoniously, incongruously.

1663 BOYLE *Colours* Wks. I. 741 (R.) If they be discordantly tuned..being struck together they make but a harsh and troublesome noise. **1843** CARLYLE *Past & Pr.* I. i. (1845) 6 Human faces gloom discordantly, disloyally on one another. **1876** MOZLEY *Univ. Serm.* i. (1877) 15 The most discordantly opposite characters have yet exhibited a common element in this inspiration of a great hatred.

†**diˈscorded,** *ppl. a. Obs.* [f. DISCORD *v.* + -ED[1].] Set at variance; fallen out.

a **1627** MIDDLETON *Anything for Quiet Life* v. *ad fin.*, Discorded friends aton'd, men and their wives.

†**diˈscorder.** *Obs.* Also 5 -our. [a. AF. *discordour*, OF. *discordeor*, f. *des-, discorder* to DISCORD: see -ER[1].] A quarreller; a maker of discord.

c **1400** tr. *Secreta Secret., Gov. Lordsh.* (E.E.T.S.) 115 A full ffače withouten bolnyng, bytokyns a stryuer, a dyscordour. *a* **1628** F. GREVILLE *Sidney* (1652) 111 Tributes to their common Idol Discorder.

diˈscordful, *a. rare.* [f. DISCORD *sb.* (earlier *diˈscord*) + -FUL.] Full of discord; quarrelsome.

1596 SPENSER *F.Q.* IV. ii. 30 Unmindfull both of that discordfull crew. *Ibid.* IV. iv. 3 Blandamour full of vainglorious spright, And rather stird by his discordfull dame. **1867** G. MACDONALD *Poems* 167 Why should I discordful things Weave into cadence ordered right?

discording (dɪˈskɔːdɪŋ), *vbl. sb.* [f. DISCORD *v.* + -ING[1].] Disagreeing, disagreement, discordance.

1297 R. GLOUC. (1724) 255 Bytuene hem nas non dyscordyng. **1483** *Cath. Angl.* 101/1 A Discordynge of voces, *diaphonia.* **1593** BILSON *Govt. Christ's Ch.* 96 The false report of their discording everywhere spread by these deceivers.

discording (dɪˈskɔːdɪŋ), *ppl. a.* [f. as prec. + -ING[2].] Disagreeing, discordant.

c **1374** CHAUCER *Boeth.* III. Pr. ii. 68 Dyuerse sentences and discordyng. **1398** TREVISA *Barth. De P.R.* v. xxiii. (1495) 131 A dyscordyng voyce..trowbleth the acorde of many voyces. *c* **1400** MAUNDEV. (Roxb.) iv. 11 þe land of Grece es þe next cuntree þat variez and es discordand in faith and letters fra vs and oure faith. **1596** DALRYMPLE tr. *Leslie's Hist. Scot.* I. 68 Nathing..discordeng wᵗ the truth of the historie. **1633** STRUTHER *True Happiness* 128 Yet they have but a discording concord. **1706** DE FOE *Jure Div.* XI. 247 Discording Parties can no Pleasure bring, No Safety to the People, or the King. **1808** SCOTT *Marm.* III. Introd. viii, Whose doom discording neighbours sought.

†**ˈdiscordous,** *a. Obs.* [f. L. *discors, discord-* adj. (or Eng. DISCORD *sb.*) + -OUS. Cf. med.L. *discordiosus*, OF. *descordieus*, of which the Eng. repr. would be *discordious.*] Characterized by or full of discord; of the nature of discord; discordant.

1597–8 BP. HALL *Sat.* III. i. 42 And men grue greedie, discordous, and nice. **1612–15** —— *Contempl., O.T.* XIII. v, The harsh and discordous notes. **1633** —— *Hard Texts* 555 I heare and abhorre the discordous noise of your sins.

†**diˈscoriate,** *ppl. a. Obs. rare.* [ad. med.L. *discoriāt-us*, pa. pple. of *discoriāre* to flay, skin, scourge (in Du Cange), f. L. *dis-* (DIS- 4) + *corium* skin, hide: cf. earlier L. *dēcoriāre* to skin, and see DE- *pref.* 6.] Flayed.

1483 CAXTON *Gold. Leg.* 271 b/1 He was of them discoryate and flayn quyck, and deyde not.

discorporate (dɪsˈkɔːpərət), *ppl. a. rare.* [f. DIS- 10 + CORPORATE *a.*: perh. ad. med. (Anglo) L. *discorporātus* dissolved, 'corpus discorporatum dissolutum declaramus' Rymer XV. 244/1.]

†**1.** Deprived of corporate character and privileges; made no longer a corporation; disincorporated. *Obs.*

1682 *Enq. Elect. Sheriffs* 45 The City was never to this day discorporate. **1688** *Lond. Gaz.* No. 2391/1 Such of the said Corporations..are not Discorporate or Dissolved.

2. Not corporate; not united into a corporation; dissociated. (*nonce-use.*)

1833 CARLYLE *Diderot* in *Misc. Ess.* (1888) V. 11 Corporations of all sorts have perished from corpulence); and now instead of the seven corporate selfish spirits, we have the four and twenty millions of discorporate selfish.

discorporate (dɪsˈkɔːpəreɪt), *v. rare.* [f. DIS- 6 + CORPORATE *v.*: perh. immed. repr. a med.L. **discorporāre*: cf. prec.]

1. *trans.* To deprive of corporate character; to dissolve (a corporate body).

1683 T. HUNT *Def. Charter Lond.* 40 A Corporation or Society of men may discorporate and dissolve themselves.

2. To separate from a corporate body; to dissociate, disconnect.

1891 *Edin. Rev.* Oct. 309 Grattan..predicted..that a priesthood unconnected with the English Government would lead to a Catholic laity discorporated from the people of England.

†**discorreˈspondency.** *Obs.* [f. DIS- 9; cf. next.] Want of correspondence.

a **1641** BP. MOUNTAGU *Acts & Mon.* (1642) 420 Those words..make very much dis-correspondency *inter* parts which doe hang handsomely enough together.

†**discorreˈspondent,** *a. Obs. rare*[−1]. [f. DIS- 10.] Lacking correspondence or congruity; not answering one to another.

1654 W. MOUNTAGUE *Devout Ess.* II. vii. §3 (R.) It would be discorrespondent in respect of God.

†**disˈcorsive,** *a. Med. Obs.* [f. DIS- 10 + CORSIVE.] Not 'corsive', corrosive, or escharotic.

1662 R. MATHEW *Unl. Alch.* §99. 163 It is altogether discorsive, and not contractive, and therefore safe and profitable for Women that have Cankers in their breasts.

†**diˈscose,** *a. Obs. rare.* [ad. mod.L. *discōs-us*, f. *discus* DISC: see -OSE.] Characterized by a disc.

1686 *Phil. Trans.* XVI. 285 These haue radiated, discose, and flat Flowers.

discost, var. of DISCOAST *v. Obs.*

†**discostate** (dɪsˈkɒstət), *a. Bot. Obs.* [f. DIS- 1 + L. *costāt-us* ribbed, COSTATE, f. *costa* a rib.] Of leaves: Having radiately divergent ribs.

1849 BALFOUR *Man. Bot.* 72 Discostate [*later edd.* Divergent].

discostomatous: see DISCO-.

discothèque, -theque (ˈdɪskətɛk). [a. Fr. *discothèque*, after BIBLIOTHÈQUE. Cf. DISC *sb.* 2 d.] A club, etc., where recorded music is played for dancing.

[**1951** SACKVILLE-WEST & SHAWE-TAYLOR *Record Guide* 32 On the analogy of 'bibliothèque', the French have taken to using the very attractive 'discothèque' for 'record library'; it is a pity that this formation is impossible in English.] **1954** *New Yorker* 25 Sept. 107 The St.-Germain-des-Prés *discothèque* night clubs..where phonograph *disques* are played for dancing. **1960** *Atlantic Monthly* Sept. 46/1 We go after dinner, to a Left Bank *discothèque. Ibid.* 46/2 Since this is a *discothèque*, jazz is blaring from the walls and record sleeves are scattered about. **1964** *TV Guide* (U.S.) 12–18 Dec. 19/1 A discotheque is a small, intimate night club that plays recorded music for dancing—and discotheque dresses make dancing the frug, the monkey, and the Watusi a delight because they move with the beat. **1965** F. RAPHAEL *Darling* xxii. 105 They danced in smoky *discothèques.* **1970** *Morning Star* 6 Jan. 3 Mr. Moon, his wife and two friends had attended the opening of a discotheque at the Red Lion public house on Sunday.

discoum-, -counfite, etc., obs. ff. DISCOMFIT.

†**diˈscounsel,** *v. Obs.* In 5 discounseylle. [ad. OF. *descon-, descunseillier* = It. *disconsigliare*: prob. common Romanic, f. *des-, dis-* (DIS- 4) + L. *consiliāre* to COUNSEL.]

1. *trans.* To counsel (a person) against some undertaking or course of action; to give advice dissuading *from*; = DISADVISE 2. (Also with double object, quot. 1477.)

c **1477** CAXTON *Jason* 96 b, [The king] cam to Jason..and moche dis-counceylled him thenterprise of colchas. **1483** —— *Gold. Leg.* 117 b/1 Ye discounseylle your frendes fro the euerlastyng lyf. *a* **1557** MRS. M. BASSET tr. *More's Treat. Passion* Wks. 1392/1 He dyscounsayled hym to take thys death vppon hym. **1600** HOLLAND *Livy* XXXVI. xxxiv. 938 He..would have discounselled and skared them..from foolish and furious dessignes.

absol. **1559** *Homilies* I. *Adultery* II. (1859) 122 Holy Scripture disswadeth (or discounselleth) from doing that filthy sinne.

2. To give counsel against (an action or undertaking); = DISADVISE 1.

1599 SANDYS *Europæ Spec.* (1632) 108 They..not onely inhibite..the reading of Protestant Bookes..but discounsell also all joyning with them in any service of God. *a* **1631** DONNE *Serm.* cii. (1848) IV. 361 Joab..did yet dissuade and discounsel this numbering of the people.

†**diˈscounselled,** *ppl. a. Obs.* In 5 **descounceylled.** [after OF. *desconseillié* discouraged, left without comfort, disconsolate, pa. pple. of *desconseillier*: see prec.] Without resource or support, desolate, disconsolate.

[**1292** BRITTON III. v. §1 Soen heritage, qe fust endormi et desconselé [*v.r.* descounseillee, *tr.* unsupported]. *Ibid.* IV. iii. §4 Si la eglise demoerge desconseilé [unprovided] outre vi meys. *Ibid.* §10 Cum ele fust tout voide et desconselé.] **1480** CAXTON *Ovid's Met.* XIII. ix, Now I am..fallen in orphanyte of parents & of my lorde, and am poure & desherytid, exilled & descounceylled.

discount (ˈdɪskaʊnt), *sb.* Also 7 **discompt.** [a. 16th c. F. *descompte*, earlier *desconte*, mod.F. *décompte*, vbl. sb. f. *descompter* to DISCOUNT.

The French *descompte, décompte* has not the technical sense of *discount*, which is expressed by *escompte*, with vb. *escompter*, adapted from It. *sconto, scontare.* The earlier sense of *discount* in Eng. was app. as in French, the technical sense being later, taken perhaps from Italian *sconto*, though attached to the existing word.]

†**1. a.** An abatement or deduction from the amount, or from the gross reckoning or value of anything. *Obs.* (exc. as in 2).

1622 *Eng. Commissioners to Jas. I*, in *Fortesc. Papers* 189 The discount of the pepper brought into Hollande. **1669–70** MARVELL *Corr.* cxxxix. Wks. 1872–5 II. 306 In discount of the third yeare to be layd at the Custome House, to supply what falls short. **1727–51** CHAMBERS *Cycl.*, *Discount*, is also used with less propriety for the tare, or waste of any commodity, sum, etc. There are 12 shillings discount in this bag. The cag of oil sent me from Spain leaks; there are fifty pints discount. **1798** BAY *Amer. Law Rep.* (1809) I. 16 Against plaintiff's bill, defendant filed a discount for the loss of rent by plaintiff's delay. *Ibid.* 117 Permitted to offer [their claim] in discount against plaintiff's demand.

b. *fig.* (partly from 2.)

1753 A. MURPHY *Gray's-Inn Jrnl.* No. 56 ¶9 The Peevishness of these my Creditors is a great Discount upon my Happiness. **1794** MISS GUNNING *Packet* III. 38 Present fears are a heavy discount on future expectations. **1859** F.

HALL *Vâsavadattâ* 54 The partiality for Bauddhas..must, very likely, be received with liberal discount.

2. *Commerce.* **a.** A deduction (usually at a certain rate per cent.) made for payment before it is due, or for prompt payment, of a bill or account; a deduction for cash payment from the price of an article usually sold on credit; any deduction or abatement from the nominal value or price.

1690 LEYBOURN *Curs. Math.* 110 For discompt or rebate of money, this is the Proportion. **1702** *Burlesque R. L'Estrange's Vis. Quev.* 269 Here's ready Money: Speak, what Discount? **1837** *Penny Cycl.* IX. 18/1 The name of discount is also applied to certain trade allowances upon the nominal prices of goods. *Ibid.*, The rates of discount in [a list now before us] vary from 5 to 40 per cent. upon the nominal prices of the different articles. **1862** BURTON *Bk. Hunter* (1863) 252 Draw all the profits without discount or percentage. *Mod.* A retail bookseller who gives twopence in the shilling discount. A discount of 5 per cent. is offered for payment of this account before the end of the month.

b. The deduction made from the amount of a bill of exchange or promissory note, by one who gives value for it before it is due, this deduction being calculated at a defined rate per cent. for the time the document has to run; practically, the interest charged by a banker or bill-discounter for advancing the value of a bill before it is due.

This is the common form in which banks and discount-houses advance money to persons engaged in commerce; the banker or discounter having thus purchased the bill at a discount keeps it till maturity, when he realizes the full amount. In practice, discount is calculated as the interest on the amount of the bill for the time it has to run; this is more than what arithmeticians call the *true discount*, which is reckoned as interest on the *present worth* (*i.e.* that sum which if invested at the given rate for the given time would amount to the face value).

1683 R. CLAVEL (*title*), Tables for the Forbearance and Discompt of Money. **1732** DE FOE *Eng. Tradesman* I. Pref. 11 The dismal consequences of usury, high discount, and paying interest for money. **1859** BARN. SMITH *Arith. & Algebra* (ed. 6) 491 We may define the Discount of a sum of money to be the interest of the Present Worth of that sum, calculated from the present time to the time when the sum would be properly payable. **1863** FAWCETT *Pol. Econ.* III. vi. (1876) 361 The value of money is said to be represented by the Bank-rate of discount. **1881** J. BROOK-SMITH *Arith.* (ed. 6) 323 With bankers and bill-discounters, discount is the *interest* of the sum specified, whereas, properly speaking, it is the interest of the present worth of that sum. And as the present worth of a sum due at a future time is less than the sum itself, the *true* discount is less than the banker's or *mercantile* discount; and therefore the banker obtains a small advantage.

3. The act of discounting a bill or note; with *pl.*, a single transaction of this nature.

1839-40 W. IRVING *Wolfert's R.* (1855) 119 To establish a bank of deposit, discount, and circulation. **1846** MCCULLOCH *Acc. Brit. Empire* (1854) II. 43 The Scotch banks make their advances partly by discount of bills, and partly by what are termed cash accounts, or cash credits. **1866** CRUMP *Banking* iii. 78 Shall you require either loans or discounts, and to what amount? **1878** JEVONS *Prim. Pol. Econ.* 114 The most common and proper way in which a banker gives credit and employs his funds is in the discount of bills.

4. ***at a discount***: at less than the nominal or usual value; below par; *fig.* in low esteem, reduced in estimation or regard, depreciated. (Opp. to *at a* PREMIUM.)

1701 *Lond. Gaz.* No. 3710/3 Their Bills go at 50 per Cent. Discount. **1833** HT. MARTINEAU *Berkeley the Banker* I. vi. 120 When its notes were at a discount. **1848** MILL *Pol. Econ.* III. xx. §2 (1876) 372 The price of bills would fall below par; a bill for 100*l.* might be bought for somewhat less than 100*l.*, and bills would be said to be at a discount. **1861** GOSCHEN *For. Exch.* 5 Though one system of coinage were adopted for all countries, claims on foreign countries would nevertheless vary in price, and would still be either at a premium or at a discount.

fig. **1832** GEN. P. THOMPSON *Exerc.* (1842) II. 237 'Conservative' principles are at a discount throughout the world. **1842** MARRYAT *Percival Keene* xxi, We should be at a pretty discount with the red-coats. **1856** READE *Never too late* lxxxv, Servants are at a great premium, masters at a discount, in the colony.

5. *Billiards.* An allowance made by a superior to an inferior player of a deduction of one or more counts from his score for every count made by the latter. (*U.S.*)

6. *attrib.* and *Comb.* (chiefly in sense 2b), as **discount-broker**, one whose business is to cash or procure the cashing of notes or bills of exchange at a discount; also ***discount accommodation, business, house, market***; (in sense 4) applied *attrib.* to a shop that sells goods below the normal retail price; also ***discount selling, trading***.

1863 FAWCETT *Pol. Econ.* II. v. (1876) 163 Applying to a banker or discount-broker for loans. *Ibid.* III. ix. (1876) 415 The English discount-houses collect all the bills which are drawn upon France. **1866** CRUMP *Banking* ix. 190 The directors..contracted the discount accommodation to the public. **1876** *World* V. No. 117. 5 At to-day's rates there cannot possibly be any appreciable profit in discount business. **1889** *Spectator* 31 Aug. 268/2 Harper's, which discount booksellers sell at 9*d.* a copy. **1891** G. CLARE *Money-market Primer* xii. 135 The very important part performed in the economy of the discount-market by the middleman, through whom..nearly the whole of the better class of business is transacted. **1922** W. F. SPALDING *London Money Market* vii. 106 The discount market is one of the most important sections of the London Money Market. **1933** B. ELLINGER *This Money Business* iii. 20 The Discount Market in London has been in existence for about seventy years. **1949** *Consumer Rep.* Aug. 343/2 Buying..nationally-advertised goods from discount houses at savings up to 20%. **1958** *Oxf. Mail* 16 July 6/5 Service in discount shops [in the U.S.] is poor. **1960** *Guardian* 10 June 7/2 All forms of discount trading are violently denounced by trade associations. *Ibid.* 7/3 A London supermarket firm..is to build a..discount store in Manchester. **1962** *Listener* 13 Dec. 994/2 The discount house, which sells all these things by self-service at very low prices, has grown phenomenally in recent years in the United States, but there are still only half a dozen or so in this country. **1964** *Times Rev. Industry* Apr. 72/3 One supermarket chain in California..has switched over entirely to discount selling, including leasing departments in discount stores. **1970** *Times* 23 Sept. 14/6 Strictly speaking a Discount Store is an enormous single storey self-service store..which sells a huge range of goods ..at below normal retail prices.

discount (dɪˈskaʊnt, ˈdɪskaʊnt), *v.*[1] Also 7 discompt. [a. OF. *desconter* (13th c. in Littré), *descompter* (14th c.), mod.F. *décompter* = Sp. *descontar* (Minsheu 1599), It. *discontare, scontare* 'to vnreckon, to abate in reckoning' (Florio 1598), med.L. *discomputāre* (1293 in Du Cange), a late L. or Com. Romanic formation from *dis-*, DIS- 4 + *computāre* to COUNT, COMPUTE.]

†**1.** *trans.* To reckon as an abatement or deduction from a sum due or to be accounted for. *Obs.*

1629 SIR R. CHAMBERS *Petit.* in Rushw. *Hist. Coll.* (1659) I. 679 The other moity to be discompted upon such Goods as the Petitioner shall make entries of by Exportation or Importation in the Custom-house, London, until his debt with the interest be fully satisfied and paid. **1645** *Parl. Hist., Chas. I*, an. 1645 (R.) That all provisions, or other necessaries, provided by your care, be so ordered, that account may be made what is taken; and that the said provisions may be discounted upon the pay of the said army. **1696** LUTTRELL *Brief Rel.* (1857) IV. 93 The Turky merchants have offered to advance a considerable summe to the king, provided it may be discounted out of the customes of their fleet. **1726** R. NEWTON in *Reminiscences* (Oxf. Hist. Soc.) 64 Decrements..so call'd as so much did..*decrescere*, or was discounted from a Scholar's Endowment.

†**b.** To abate, to deduct. *Obs.*

1652 NEEDHAM tr. *Selden's Mare Cl.* 266 By dis-counting 38 years from the year 1051, that year 1012, is sufficiently manifest. **1664** BUTLER *Hud.* II. III. 1105 All which [plunder] the Conq'rer did discompt, To pay for curing of his Rump. *a* **1715** BURNET *Own Time* II. 327 They made such exceptions to those of the other side, that they discounted as many voices as gave them the majority. **1828** WEBSTER s.v., Merchants discount five or six per cent., for prompt or for advanced payment.

†**c.** ***to discount interest***: to deduct 'interest' (now called *discount*) on receiving the amount of a bill or note before it is due: see sense 3. *Obs.*

1684 *Lond. Gaz.* No. 1945/4 Because it may be some conveniency..to have present Money, if they please to discount Interest, they may have it at the Office. **1701** *Ibid.* No. 3708/4 The whole Loss being to be paid by the Undertakers within 60 days.., or sooner upon discounting the Interest.

†**d.** To reduce the amount of (a debt) by a set-off. *Obs.*

1713 SWIFT *To Earl Oxford* III Wks. 1758 III. II. 46 Parvisol discounts arrears By bills for taxes and repairs.

†**2.** *intr.* ***to discount for***: to provide a set-off for; to meet, satisfy. *Obs.*

1647 in Rushw. *Hist. Coll.* IV. II. 1025 Public monies which..Mr. Thornton had no ways satisfied or discounted for before his death. **1687** R. L'ESTRANGE *Hist. Times* I. 159 Discounting..for what we have Receiv'd from the Westminster-Insurance Offices. **1690** DRYDEN *Don Sebastian* III. i, My prayers and penance shall discount for these, And beg of heaven to charge the bill on me.

3. *trans.* To give or receive the 'present worth' of (a bill of exchange or promissory note) before it is due. **a.** To pay the value beforehand, with a deduction equivalent to the interest at a certain percentage for the time which it has still to run. **b.** Of the holder: To obtain cash for (a bill or note), with such deduction, before it is due. (See DISCOUNT *sb.* 2b.)

1694 *Lond. Gaz.* No. 3008/4 Foreign Bills of Exchange will be Discounted after the Rate of Four and half per Cent. per Annum. **1732** DE FOE *Eng. Tradesman* I. Suppl. ii. 389 The seller had a supply by discounting the bills. **1777** SHERIDAN *Sch. Scand.* III. ii, Have you been able to get me that..bill discounted? **1848** MILL *Pol. Econ.* III. xi. §4 A bill of exchange, when merely discounted..does not perform the functions..of money, but is itself bought and sold for money. **1854** H. MILLER *Sch. & Schm.* xxiii. (1860) 251/1, I was fortunate enough not to discount for him a single bad bill. **1878** JEVONS *Prim. Pol. Econ.* 114 A banker will.. discount such a bill, that is, buy it up for the sum due, after subtracting interest..for the length of time the bill has to run.

4. *fig.* In various senses derived from the foregoing: **a.** To leave out of account; to disregard, omit. **b.** To deduct or detract from, to lessen. **c.** To part with a future good for some present consideration. **d.** To settle or account for beforehand. And now *esp.*: **e.** To make a deduction in estimating the worth of (a statement, etc.); to make allowance for exaggeration in. **f.** To take (an event, etc.) into account beforehand, thus lessening its effect or interest when it takes place.

1702 S. PARKER *Cicero's De Finibus* 237 To relinquish himself, to discount his Body, and take up with a Summum Bonum Uncommensurate to the Whole of his Person. **1716** M. DAVIES *Athen. Brit.* III. *Critic. Hist.* 26 The Jacobits unaccountable Schism has been thoroughly discounted by our learned Dr. Turner. **1768** *Woman of Honor* I. 165 In this light..how much would [they] have to discount of their boasts of having had a number of women as worthless as themselves? **1836-7** SIR W. HAMILTON *Metaph.* xl. (1859) II. 402 Of the three opinions (I discount Brown's), under this head, one supposes [etc.]. **1851** J. H. NEWMAN *Cath. in Eng.* 329 Absolution for a week! then it seems, she has discounted, if I may so speak, her prospective confessions, and may lie, thieve, drink, and swear for a whole seven days with a clear conscience. **1855** BRIMLEY *Ess., Poetry & Crit.* 185 Discounting immortality for pottage. **1858** *Sat. Rev.* V. 660/1 Making its own little profit by cleverly discounting a part of the great conception. **1860** *Ibid.* IX. 825/1 His father discounted and exhausted the policy of perfidious concession. **1873** H. SPENCER *Stud. Sociol.* v. 112 We..have to estimate [the] worth [of evidence] when it has been discounted in many ways. **1876** E. MELLOR *Priesth.* iv. 172 To discount from the teaching of Christ the words 'eat' and 'drink', as modal terms..is to relinquish the literal interpretation. **1880** *Daily News* 23 Sept., Acquaintance from books with the place to be visited 'discounts' the enjoyment of the visit. **1882** BITHELL *Counting-house Dict.* s.v., To *discount* news or intelligence, a cant phrase much used in City circles, is to anticipate or expect such intelligence, and then act as though it had already arrived. **1883** C. J. WILLS *Mod. Persia* 315 After a time one learns to mentally discount the statements made by the natives. *a* **1884** M. PATTISON *Mem.* (1885) 214 Nor had his [Newman's] perversion, so long looked for, and therefore mentally discounted, at all fallen upon me like a blow.

5. *Billiards.* To allow discount to, as to *discount* an inferior player. (*U.S.*)

Hence **di'scounted** *ppl. a.*, **di'scounting** *vbl. sb.* and *ppl. a.*

1682 SCARLETT *Exchanges* 6 Discounted Exchange, is, when the Drawer and the Remitter is one and the same Person. **1732** DE FOE *Eng. Tradesman* I. Suppl. ii. 391 Discounting of bills is certain death to the tradesman. **1861** GOSCHEN *For. Exch.* 41 The discounting establishments at home. **1884** *Manch. Exam.* 22 May 5/1 Fraudulent discounting of worthless accommodation bills. **1964** *Times Rev. Industry* Feb. 98/2 The principles of discounted cash flow and sinking fund accounting.

†**discount**, *v.*[2] *Obs. rare.* [f. DIS- 1 + COUNT *v.*] *trans.* To count or reckon separately or in separate series.

1655 FULLER *Ch. Hist.* Index, Know that the discounting of Sheets (to expedite the work at severall Presses) hath occasioned in the Fifth book after page 200. compleated, to go back again to page (153) surrounded in this fashion, to prevent confusion. **1662** J. FULLER 'To the Reader' in Fuller *Worthies*, The discounting of Sheets (to expedite the Work at severall Presses) hath occasioned the often mistake of the Folio's. [Cf. **1653** GAUDEN *Hieraspistes* 320 Reader, The Reason why the Folios of this Book do not follow is because the Copy (for Expedition) was divided to two Printers.]

discountable (dɪˈskaʊntəb(ə)l), *a.* [f. DISCOUNT *v.*[1] + -ABLE.] That may be discounted; in quot. 1800, within which a bill may be discounted.

1800 T. JEFFERSON *Writ.* (1859) IV. 420 Within the discountable period. **1802** H. THORNTON in Mill *Pol. Econ.* III. xi. §4 Each is a discountable article.

discountenance (dɪˈskaʊntɪnəns), *v.* [ad. obs. F. *descontenancer* (16th c. in Littré, and in Cotgr.), to abash, put out of countenance, mod.F. *décontenancer*, f. *des-*, DIS- 4 + *contenancer* to COUNTENANCE. In some of the English senses, it is used as if f. DIS- 7 + COUNTENANCE *sb.* Cf. DEFACE in some of its senses.]

†**1.** *trans.* To put another countenance on, to mask. *Obs. rare.*

1587 GOLDING *De Mornay* xii. 171 His own ambition, which was peraduenture discountenanced to the common people, but could not be counterfetted before God, who seeth the very bottome of our hearts.

2. To put out of countenance, put to shame, disconcert, discourage, abash. (Chiefly in *pa. pple.*)

1580 SIDNEY *Arcadia* (1613) 69 Thinking it want of education which made him so discountenanced with vnwonted presence. **1599** B. JONSON *Cynthia's Rev.* III. i, Sir, let not this dis-countenance, or dis-gallant you a whit. **1671** MILTON *P.R.* II. 218 How would one look from his majestic brow..Discountenance her despised. **1690** *The Gt. Scanderbeg* 89 He was no more discountenanced then, than if he had been at the head of his Army. **1707** NORRIS *Treat. Humility* ix. 359 How is my pride further discountenanced, when I see thee my Lord..chusing to unite thyself..with flesh and blood. **1862** CARLYLE *Fredk. Gt.* (1865) III. VIII. vi. 55 He appeared much discountenanced at this last part of my narrative.

3. To withdraw one's countenance from, set the countenance against; to show disapprobation of; to discourage, disfavour:

a. a person.

1591 SPENSER *Tears Muses* 340 We silly Maides, whom they..with reprochfull scorne discountenaunce. **1631** GOUGE *God's Arrows* i. §45. 76 Discouraging and discountenancing the upright. **1656** H. MORE *Enthus. Tri.* 23 Such Mock-prophets and false Messiases as these will be discountenanced and hissed off of the stage. **1807** W. H. IRELAND *Mod. Ship of Fools* 251 *note*, He..discountenanced him from that hour. **18..** *Proclamation at Quarter Sessions*, That all Persons of Honour, or in Place of Authority, will..

to their utmost contribute to the discountenancing Persons of dissolute and immoral Lives.

b. an act, practice, or the like.

1589 FLEMING *Georg. Virg.* Ded., Ripe to deface and discountenance, but rawe to correct or imitate the commendable trauels of well affected Students. **1646** P. BULKELEY *Gospel Covt.* III. 256 Profanenesse is discountenanced by all. **1709** STEELE *Tatler* No. 39 ¶10 Duels are neither quite discountenanc'd, nor much in vogue. **1766** BURKE *Wks.* II. 5 The late administration.. discountenanced..the dangerous and unconstitutional practise of removing military officers for their votes in Parliament. **1872** YEATS *Growth Comm.* 343 The traffic was discountenanced.

Hence **di'scountenanced** *ppl. a.*, **-ing** *vbl. sb.*

1597 BP. J. KING *Jonas* (1618) 76 Discountenancings, disturbings, dispossessings of them. **1612** BRINSLEY *Lud. Lit.* xxvii. (1627) 276 By the incouragement and commendation of vertue, and discountenancing of vice. **1643** MILTON *Divorce* Introd. (1851) 4 The sole advocate of a discount'nanc't truth. **1667** LOCKE *Ess. Toleration* in Fox Bourne *Locke* (1876) I. iv. 189 The discountenancing of popery amongst us. **1675** *Art Contentm.* IV. ix. 198 The most discountenanc'd child oft makes better proof than the dearling. **1749** W. DODWELL *Free Answer* 97 To prevent their preaching a discountenanced Doctrine.

discountenance (dɪ'skaʊntɪnəns), *sb. arch.* [partly ad. OF. *descontenance* (14th c. in Littré), partly an Eng. formation from DIS- 9 + COUNTENANCE *sb.*, after the vb.]

1. The act or fact of discountenancing; unfavourable aspect, disfavour or disapprobation shown.

1580 NORTH *Plutarch* (1595) 829 He thought that the estimation of Cato was altogether the discountenance of his [own] power and greatnesse. **1642** JER. TAYLOR *Episc.* (1647) 338 All discountenance and disgrace done to the Clergy reflect upon Christ. **1673** *Essex Papers* (Camden) I. 151 The countenance given to the subscribers and discountenance to the refusers. **1779–81** JOHNSON *L.P., Milton* Wks. II. 176 His great works were performed under discountenance. **1812** SHELLEY *Proposals* Pr. Wks. 1888 I. 272 The discountenance which Government will show to such an association. **1862** LD. BROUGHAM *Brit. Const.* i. 4 Discountenance of warlike policy.

b. with *a* and *pl.*

a **1628** F. GREVILLE *Sidney* (1652) 19 Any man..might.. see how to set a good countenance upon all the discountenances of adversitie. **1749** FIELDING *Tom Jones* XVIII. iii, Whether it be that the one way of cheating is a discountenance or reflection upon the other, or [etc.].

†**2.** The fact or state of being put out of countenance; discomposure of face; abashment. *Obs.*

a **1628** F. GREVILLE *Sidney* vii. (1652) 86 The discountenance, and depression which appeared in Sir Francis. **1656** FINETT *For. Ambass.* 39 Much to their discountenance and discontent.

di'scountenancer. [f. DISCOUNTENANCE *v.* + -ER[1].] One who discountenances, or discourages with cold looks or disfavour.

1622 BACON *Hen. VII* (J.), A great taxer of his people and discountenancer of his nobility. **1702** *Addr. fr. Maryland* in *Lond. Gaz.* No. 3853/1 A Discountenancer of Immorality and an Encourager of Virtue. **1721** WODROW *Hist. Suff. Ch. Scot.* (1828) I. Introd. 10 A discountenancer of ministers.

discounter (dɪ'skaʊntə(r)). [f. DISCOUNT *v.*[1] + -ER[1].]

1. One who discounts a bill or note; i.e. either the person who, before it is due, pays the amount with deduction of discount, or the person who obtains cash for it in this way: see DISCOUNT *v.* 3.

1732 DE FOE *Eng. Tradesman* I. Suppl. ii. 391 These discounters of bills are sometimes bit. **1791** BURKE *Let. Member Nat. Assembly* Wks. VI. 17 The whole gang of usurers, pedlars, and itinerant Jew-discounters. **1848** MILL *Pol. Econ.* III. xi. §4 A bill of exchange..discounted, and kept in the portfolio of the discounter until it falls due. **1861** GOSCHEN *For. Exch.* 38 The purchaser of the bills in this case takes the place of the discounter of accommodation paper. **1883** E. PAXTON HOOD *Scot. Char.* iii. 59 'Oh, you need not hesitate about him, Mr. Carrick [the banker]', said the proposed discounter. **1884** J. BACON in *Law Rep.* 26 Ch. Div. 134 The discounter, whether of a bill, or bond, or any other security, becomes the owner.

2. One who is involved in discount trading.

1921 A. WALL *Analytical Credits* v. 246 It is essential for him to be known in the trade as a discounter. **1964** *Economist* 1 Feb. 411/1 The discounters—a terribly misleading word for retail traders who take only a modest profit. **1964** *Times Rev. Industry* Apr. 72/3 Retailers of other merchandise, such as shoes, jewellery, [etc.]..have also sought to cut their losses by leasing departments from discounters.

dis'countess, *v. rare.* [DIS- 7b.] *trans.* To deprive of the rank or dignity of countess.

1630 B. JONSON *New Inn* IV. iii, Though I am discountess'd, I am not yet dis-countenanced. **1874** TROLLOPE *Lady Anna* v, Let them bring that Italian countess over if they dared! He'd countess her and discountess her too!

discouple (dɪs'kʌp(ə)l), *v.* [a. OF. *descupler* (12th c. in Hatz.-Darm.), *descoupler* (Cotgr.) to separate, uncouple, f. *des-*, DIS- 4 + *coupler* to COUPLE.] *trans.* To separate or disunite what is coupled, to uncouple.

c **1489** CAXTON *Sonnes of Aymon* ix. 241 Now are dyscoupled the four sones of Aymon, for I have slayne Richarde. **1549** HOOPER *Declar. Ten Commandm.* x. Wks. (Parker Soc.) 384 Neither doth the magistrate dissolve that God hath bound, nor discouple that God coupled. **1883** W. S. DUGDALE tr. *Dante's Purgatorio* xxv. 280 Ascending the steps whose narrowness discouples those who mount.

b. *intr.* for *refl.*

1599 T. M[OUFET] *Silkwormes* 66 When they die after discoupling.

discour, -coure, obs. ff. DISCOVER *v.*

†**di'scourage,** *sb. Obs.* [f. DIS- 9 + COURAGE *sb.*: or f. DISCOURAGE *v.*] Want or failure of courage; the state of discouragement.

c **1500** *Three King's Sons* 105 Their enemyes were in suche discourage that thei durst not wele be seen at no scarmyssh. **1548** UDALL, etc. *Erasm. Par. Matt.* v. (R.), Many..be brought in discourage of themselves, by the reason of pouertie..or by aduersitie. **1586** BRIGHT *Melanch.* xxxiii. 184 They are faint-hearted, and full of discourage. **1611** SPEED *Theat. Gt. Brit.* ix. (1614) 17/1 Causing their king Canute with discourage to retire.

discourage (dɪ'skʌrɪdʒ), *v.* Also 5–6 dis-, dyscorage (6 dischorage). [ad. OF. *descoragier*, later *descourager*, mod.F. *décourager*; f. *des-*, DIS- 4 + *corage*, COURAGE *sb.*]

1. *trans.* To deprive of courage, confidence, or moral energy; to lessen the courage of; to dishearten, dispirit. The opposite of *encourage*.

1481 CAXTON *Godfrey* cxxxii. 196 How therle of chartres discoraged themperour of Constantinople that he shold not goo and socoure our peple. **1535** COVERDALE *Jer.* xxxviii. 4 Thus he discorageth the hondes of the soudyers yt be in this cite, and the hondes of all the people. **1611** BIBLE *Transl. Pref.* 2 His Royall heart was not daunted or discouraged. **1684** BUNYAN *Pilgr.* II. 21, I think no Slow of Despond would discourage me. **1725** DE FOE *Voy. round World* (1840) 253 He would be very far from discouraging me. **1855** MACAULAY *Hist. Eng.* III. 232 No trick, no lie, which was thought likely to discourage the starving garrison was spared.

absol. **1789** ANNA SEWARD *Lett.* (1811) II. 226 Difficulty rather stimulates than discourages.

b. with *complement*: To deter (by discouragement) †*to do* something (*obs.*); *from* (†*for*) an act.

1529 MORE *Suppl. Soulys* Wks. 337/1 Not for yt we wold discourage you to dispose well your goodes when ye dye. **1529** *Supplic. to King* (E.E.T.S.) 36 This they doo to dyscorage all men from the studye of Gods Worde. **1598** R. BERNARD tr. *Terence* (1607) 337 The poet..was nowe almost discouraged for taking any more paines. *a* **1682** SIR T. BROWNE *Tracts* (1684) 191 It discouraged from all Navigation about it. *a* **1698** TEMPLE (J.), Unless you..discourage them to stay with you by using them ill. **1699** DAMPIER *Voy.* II. I. 89 The Seamen are discouraged from fishing for them by the King. **1756** C. LUCAS *Ess. Waters* II. 3 We shall be discouraged from the laborious..task.

†**c.** *transf.* and *fig. Obs.*

a **1529** SKELTON *Replyc.* 355 For to disparage And to discorage The fame matrycula̅te Of poetes laureate. **1577** B. GOOGE *Heresbach's Husb.* II. (1586) 87 You shall sometime have one branch more gallant then his fellowes, which if you cutte not away, you discourage all the rest. **1657** in *Burton's Diary* (1828) II. 150 Though the face of public worship of late be discouraged.

2. *transf.* To lessen or repress courage for (an action or project); to discountenance, express disapproval of, 'throw cold water on'.

1641 WILKINS *Math. Magick* II. xv. (1648) 292, I would be loath to discourage the enquiry of any ingenuous artificer. *a* **1649** *Eikon Bas.* xii. (1824) 106, I might neither Incourage the rebels insolence, nor discourage the Protestants loyalty and patience. **1699** DAMPIER *Voy.* II. I. 85 Thro their oppression..trading is discouraged. **1735** BERKELEY *Querist* §42 Idleness should of all things be discouraged. **1809** SYD. SMITH *Wks.* (1867) I. 173 A set of lectures upon political economy would be discouraged in Oxford. **1872** YEATS *Growth Comm.* 56 Laws were made to discourage usury.

†**3.** *intr.* (for *refl.*) To lose courage or confidence. *Obs.*

1553 BALE *Vocacyon* in *Harl. Misc.* (1808–12) VI. 464 (D.) Because that poore Churche shulde not utterly discourage, in her extreme adversitees. **1574** HELLOWES *Gueuara's Fam. Ep.* (1577) 33 Scipio considering the Numantines to increase in pride, and the Romanes to discourage.

discourageable (dɪ'skʌrɪdʒəb(ə)l), *a. rare.* [f. DISCOURAGE *v.* + -ABLE.] Capable of being discouraged or disheartened; to be discouraged.

1612–15 BP. HALL *Contempl., N.T.* IV. xxvi, O loue to unthankfull souls! not discourageable by the most hatefull indignities.

di'scouraged, *ppl. a.* [f. as prec. + -ED[1].] Deprived of courage or confidence, disheartened.

1548 UDALL, etc. *Erasm. Par. Matt.* xix. (R.), He wente awaye with a discouraged and heauye mynde. **1667** FLAVEL *Saint Indeed* (1754) 44 Discouraged souls, how many do you reckon the Lord for? **1847** TENNYSON *Princ.* III. 137, I grew discouraged, Sir. **1888** *Pall Mall G.* 8 June 4/1 Seductive terms about fettered industry, discouraged capital, and the undue taxation of the necessaries of life.

discouragement (dɪ'skʌrɪdʒmənt). [ad. OF. *descouragement*, *descoragement* (12th c. in Hatz.-Darm.), mod.F. *découragement*, f. *descoragier*, *descourager* to DISCOURAGE: cf. ENCOURAGEMENT.]

1. The action or fact of discouraging.

1600 HAKLUYT *Voy.* III. 131 (R.) To the great discouragement and hinderance of the same marchants and fishermen. *a* **1797** H. WALPOLE *Geo. II* (1847) I. iv. 89 His severity to and discouragement of that pest of society, Attorneys. **1880** C. R. MARKHAM *Peruv. Bark* XII. 414 From that time there was nothing but discouragement and obstruction. *Mod.* The discouragement of rash and premature attempts.

2. The fact or state of being discouraged; want of spirit or confidence; depression of spirit with regard to action or effort. (The more usual sense.)

1561 T. NORTON *Calvin's Inst.* III. ii. (1634) 261 The feeling..turneth onely to terrour and discouragement. *a* **1600** HOOKER *Disc. Justif.* Wks. 1617 II. 53 That repining discouragement of heart, which tempteth God. **1612** BRINSLEY *Lud. Lit.* iii. (1627) 20 About which I have taken no small griefe and discouragement. **1844** THIRLWALL *Greece* VIII. 157 He represents it as having caused so much discouragement at Sparta, that [etc.]. **1860** FROUDE *Hist. Eng.* V. 30 [It] showed how great was the discouragement into which the loss of Beton had thrown them. **1878** LECKY *Eng. in 18th C.* II. v. 50 Poverty and discouragement became more general than ever.

3. That which discourages; a disheartening or deterrent influence.

1612 WOODALL *Surg. Mate* Pref. Wks. (1653) 9 Notwithstanding all such discouragements..he proceeded on with courage. **1720** SWIFT *Mod. Educ.*, The books read at school and colleges are full of..discouragements from vice. **1725** DE FOE *Voy. round World* (1840) 319 Their first discouragement was, the country was all open with very little wood. **1868** E. EDWARDS *Raleigh* I. viii. 123 Strong discouragements which had often chilled the glowing anticipations.

discourager (dɪ'skʌrɪdʒə(r)). [f. DISCOURAGE *v.* + -ER[1].] One who or that which discourages or disheartens; one who discountenances or 'throws cold water' upon efforts.

1631 GOUGE *God's Arrows* i. §46. 80 None [are] greater discouragers of the upright. **1710** MACCLESFIELD in Ld. Campbell *Chancellors* (1857) VI. cxxi. 10 Discouragers of those who preach virtue and piety. **1849** LEWIS *Influence Author. Opin.* ix. (L.), The promoter of truth and the discourager of error. **1884** G. P. LATHROP *True* i. 5 Antiquity is a great discourager of the sympathies.

di'scouraging, *vbl. sb.* [f. as prec. + -ING[1].] The action of the verb DISCOURAGE; discouragement. (Now chiefly gerundial.)

1545 *Primer Hen. VIII*, in *3 Primers* (1848) 519 In all trouble and adversity to be quiet..without discouraging and desperation. **1578** T. N. tr. *Conq. W. India* 318 The overthrow [was] a great discouraging of the enemie. **1603** KNOLLES *Hist. Turks* (1638) 35 To the great discouraging of all other Christian Princes.

di'scouraging, *ppl. a.* [f. as prec. + -ING[2].] That discourages or causes discouragement; disheartening.

1678 BUNYAN *Pilgr.* I. 77 Over that Valley hangs the discouraging Clouds of confusion. **1715** DE FOE *Fam. Instruct.* I. iii, With many discouraging thoughts for the event. **1849** GROTE *Greece* II. lviii. (1862) V. 158 The answer returned was discouraging. **1876** T. HARDY *Ethelberta* (1890) 185 Despite her discouraging words, he still went on.

Hence **di'scouragingly** *adv.*, in a discouraging manner; †**di'scouragingness.**

1690 J. MACKENZIE *Siege London-Derry* 21/2 Collonel Lundy..spoke so discouragingly to many of them concerning the indefensibleness of the place. **1727** BAILEY vol. II, *Discouragingness*, discouragement. **1882** ANNIE THOMAS *Allerton Towers* II. viii. 151 Treating her confidences coldly, not to say, discouragingly.

†**discoursative, -itive,** *a. Obs. rare.* [f. DISCOURSE: see -ATIVE.] **a.** Pertaining to discourse or conversation. **b.** Of or belonging to 'discourse' or reason, rational.

1600 C. SUTTON *Disce Mori* ii. (1838) 23 As if it were only some arbitrable matter or discoursitive. **1610** MARKHAM *Masterp.* I. vii. 17 Horses discerne by meanes of the vertue Imaginatiue, Discoursatiue, and Memoratiue.

discourse (dɪ'skɔəs, 'dɪs-), *sb.* Also 4–5 discours, discors. [a. F. *discours*, ad. L. *discurs-us* 'running to and fro, conversation, discourse' (after *cours*:—L. *cursus*): cf. It. *discorso*, Sp. *discurso*. L. *discurs-us* is f. *discurs-*, ppl. stem of *discurrĕre*: see next.]

†**1.** Onward course; process or succession of time, events, actions, etc.; = COURSE. *Obs.*

1540–1 ELYOT *Image Gov.* (1549) 134 The naturall discourse of the sunne. **1548** UDALL, etc. *Erasm. Par. 1 Pet.* i. (R.), But when ye day shal come, & the discourse of things turned vp side down, they shall be tormented, and you shal reioyce. **1565** JEWEL *Def. Apol.* (1611) 91 It is most euident by the whole discourse of the Text. **1577** HELLOWES *Gueuara's Chron.* 65 The riuer Tygris in the discourse of his currant maketh an Ilande. **1588** GREENE *Pandosto* (1607) 18 This tragicall discourse of Fortune so daunted them, as they went like shadowes. **1612** SHELTON *Quix.* I. II. v. 89 The Knights-errant..did..suffer much Woe and Misery in the Discourse of their Lives.

b. In the following the meaning is perhaps 'course of arms or combat' (cf. COURSE *sb.* 5); though other explanations have been proposed.

1596 SPENSER *F.Q.* VI. viii. 14 The villaine..Himself addrest unto this new debate, And with his club him all about so blist That he which way to turne him scarcely wist: Sometimes aloft he layd, sometimes alow, Now here, now there, and oft him neare he mist..At last the caytive, after long discourse, When all his strokes he saw avoyded quite, Resolved in one t'assemble all his force. **1611** BEAUMONT & FL. *King & No King* II. i, Good captain Bessus, tell us the discourse [viz. of single combat] Betwixt Tigranes and our king, and how We got the victory.

†**2.** 'The act of the understanding, by which it passes from premises to consequences' (J.); reasoning, thought, ratiocination; the faculty of reasoning, reason, rationality. *Obs.* or *arch.*

c **1374** CHAUCER *Boeth.* v. Pr. iv. 165 It [intelligence] byholdeþ alle þinges so as I shal seye by a strok of þouȝt formely wiþ oute discours or collacioun. **1413** *Pilgr. Sowle* (Caxton 1483) IV. xxviii. 75 He knoweth all thynge, therfore there is nought ferther to seken by discours. **1604** EDMONDS *Observ. Cæsar's Comm.* 39 The soule of man is endued with a power of discourse, whereby it concludeth either according to the certainetie of reason, or the learning of experience. *a* **1618** RALEIGH *Rem.* (1644) 131 The Dog..we see is plentifully furnished with inward discourse. **1672** WILKINS *Nat. Relig.* 56 The discerning of that connexion or dependance which there is betwixt several propositions.. which is called ratiocination, or discourse. **1788** WESLEY *Wks.* (1872) VI. 353 Discourse, strictly speaking, is the motion or progress of the mind from one judgment to another. **1864** BOWEN *Logic* vii. 177 Discourse (*discursus*, *διάνοια*) indicates the operation of comparison.

†**b.** Phr. ***discourse of reason***: process or faculty of reasoning. *Obs.* or *arch.*

1413 *Pilgr. Sowle* (Caxton 1483) IV. xxviii. 74 The soule seketh by discors of reson the skyles and the causes of the wonderful beaute of creatures. **1553** EDEN *Treat. Newe Ind.* (Arb.) 9 As could hardely be comprehended by the discourse of reason. **1602** SHAKS. *Ham.* I. ii. 150 A beast that wants discourse of Reason. **1675** SOUTH *Serm. Ingratitude* (1715) 455 By the Discourses of Reason, or the Discoveries of Faith. **1836–7** SIR W. HAMILTON *Metaph.* App. I. 415 No one with the ordinary discourse of reason could commit an error in regard to them.

3. Communication of thought by speech; 'mutual intercourse of language' (J.); talk, conversation. *arch.*

1559 W. CUNNINGHAM *Cosmogr. Glasse* 112 But what make I discourse in these things to you, whiche knowe them muche better then I. **1594** SHAKS. *Rich. III*, v. iii. 99 Ample enterchange of sweet Discourse. **1597–8** BACON *Ess.*, *Discourse* (Arb.) 14 Some in their discourse, desire rather commendation of wit..then of iudgement. **1667** MILTON *P.L.* VIII. 211 Sweeter thy discourse is to my eare Then Fruits of Palm-tree. **1713** SWIFT *Frenzy J. Dennis*, I..laid hold of that opportunity of entering into discourse with him. **1726** *Adv. Capt. R. Boyle* 306, I finding she did not much care for talking upon that Subject, chang'd the Discourse. **1863** LONGF. *Wayside Inn* II. Prel. vii, Meanwhile the Student held discourse With the Musician.

†**b.** The faculty of conversing; conversational power. *Obs.*

1590 SHAKS. *Com. Err.* III. i. 109, I know a wench of excellent discourse, Prettie and wittie. **1606** —— *Tr. & Cr.* I. ii. 275 Is not birth, beauty, good shape, discourse..and so forth..the Spice, and salt that seasons a man? **1641** EVELYN *Mem.* (1857) I. 1 His wisdom was great, and his judgement most acute: of solid discourse, affable, humble.

c. (with *a* and *pl.*) A talk, a conversation. *arch.*

1632 LITHGOW *Trav.* VI. 286 In the midst of my Discourses, I told his Highnesse..the Guardians request. **1644** MILTON *Educ.* Wks. (1847) 98/1 The satisfaction which you profess to have received from those incidental discourses. **1715** DE FOE *Fam. Instruct.* I. viii, I have had a long discourse with my father. **1727** SWIFT *Gulliver* III. ii. 183 They neither can speak nor attend to the discourses of others. **1887** BOWEN *Virg. Æneid* I. 748 Dido the while with many discourses lengthens the night.

†**d.** A common talk, report, rumour. *Obs.*

1692 R. L'ESTRANGE *Josephus' Antiq.* II. ix. (1733) 43 There went a Discourse about that made their malice against them still more implacable. *a* **1715** BURNET *Own Time* (1823) I. 287 Many discourses were set about upon this occasion.

†**4.** Narration; a narrative, tale, account. *Obs.*

1572 SIR T. SMITH in Ellis *Orig. Lett.* Ser. II. III. 21 This is hitherto a brief discourse of that which hath passed sith my lord Admiralls commyng to Paris. **1575** (*title*), A brief Discours off the Troubles..abowte the Booke off Common Prayer and Ceremonies. **1632** LITHGOW *Trav.* v. 237 Troubling me..to show them the rare Discourses of my long two yeares survey of Turkey. **1647** MAY *Hist. Parl.* II. i. 545 Out of whose faithfull relation of that Rebellion..I have partly collected my discourse of it.

5. A spoken or written treatment of a subject, in which it is handled or discussed at length; a dissertation, treatise, homily, sermon, or the like. (Now the prevailing sense.)

1581 PETTIE *Guazzo's Civ. Conv.* I. 18 b, Referring to yᵉ long discourses which yᵉ divines make of it. **1596** HARINGTON *Metam. Ajax* (1814) 15 The discourse ensuing is divided into three parts. **1644** MILTON *Areop.* (Arb.) 47 The acute and distinct Arminius was perverted meerly by the perusing of a namelesse discours writt'n at Delf. **1711** ADDISON *Spect.* No. 106 ¶7 Authors who have published Discourses of Practical Divinity. **1764** REID *Inquiry* iii. 116 Dr. N. Grew read a discourse before the Royal Society in 1675. **1803** *Med. Jrnl.* IX. 84 The volume opens with a short preliminary Discourse on the education and duties of a Surgeon. **1849** MACAULAY *Hist. Eng.* II. 176 In the pulpit the effect of his discourses, which were delivered without any note, was heightened by a noble figure.

†**6. a.** Familiar intercourse, familiarity. **b.** Familiarity with a subject; conversancy (*in*). *Obs.*

1602 SHAKS. *Ham.* III. i. 108 If you be honest, and fair, your Honesty should admit no discourse to your Beautie. **1604** E. G. *D'Acosta's Hist. Indies* I. v. 17 The Portugals.. a Nation that hath more discourse in the Arte of Navigation then any other.

7. *Comb.*

1628 EARLE *Microcosm., Scepticke in Relig.* (Arb.) 67 He is strangely vnfix't, and a new man euery day, as his last discourse-books Meditations transport him.

8. Special Comb.: **discourse analysis** *Linguistics*, a method of analysing the structure of texts or utterances longer than one sentence, taking into account both their linguistic content and their sociolinguistic context; analysis performed using this method.

1952 Z. S. HARRIS in *Language* XVIII. 1 (*title*) *Discourse analysis. *Ibid.*, One can approach discourse analysis from two types of problem, which turn out to be related. **1957** —— in *Discourse Analysis Reprints* (1963) 7 Discourse analysis is a method of seeking in any connected discrete linear material..which contains more than one elementary sentence, some global structure characterizing the whole discourse. **1964** K. L. PIKE in *Oceanic Linguistics* III. 5 (*title*) Discourse analysis and tagmeme matrices. **1969** W. A. COOK *Introd. Tagmemic Analysis* ii. 40 Discourse analysis, however, has been little developed. **1983** BROWN & YULE *Discourse Analysis* i. 26 'Doing discourse analysis' certainly involves 'doing syntax and semantics', but it primarily consists of 'doing pragmatics'.

discourse (dɪˈskɔəs), *v.* [f. DISCOURSE *sb.*; prob. influenced by F. *discourir* 'to discourse of' Cotgr., ad. L. *discurrĕre* to run to and fro, discourse, f. DIS- 1 + *currĕre* to run: cf. F. *courir* to run, secondary form of OF. *courre*:—L. *currĕre*. OF. had also the more literal senses 'to run to and fro, to traverse'.]

†**1.** *intr.* To run, move, or travel over a space, region, etc.; *transf.* to 'run out', extend. *Obs. rare.*

a **1547** SURREY *Aeneid* IV. 475 With silence [silent] looke discoursing over al. **1555** EDEN *Decades* 213 A greate parte of lande..discoursynge towarde the West.

†**2.** *intr.* 'To pass from premises to conclusions' (J.); to reason. (Also with obj. clause.) *Obs.* (Cf. DISCOURSE *sb.* 2.)

1592 DAVIES *Immort. Soul* I. (R.), Nor can herself discourse or judge of ought, But what the sense collects, and home doth bring; And yet the pow'rs of her discoursing thought, From these collections is a diverse thing. *a* **1652** J. SMITH *Sel. Disc.* iv. 105 A mind, i.e. something within us that thinks, apprehends, reasons, and discourses. **1660** JER. TAYLOR *Duct. Dubit.* I. ii. rule iii. §5 If in philosophy we discourse that the true God, being a Spirit without shape or figure, cannot be represented by an image. *a* **1700** DRYDEN *Ovid's Met.* xv. (R.), Those very elements..translated grow, have sense or can discourse.

†**b.** *trans.* To turn over in the mind, think over. *Obs.*

1581 PETTIE *Guazzo's Civ. Conv.* I. (1586) 19 He discoursed many things in his minde. *c* **1611** CHAPMAN *Iliad.* II. 2 He discourst, how best he might approue His vow made for Achilles grace.

3. *intr.* To hold discourse, to speak with another or others, talk, converse; to discuss a matter, confer. (Cf. DISCOURSE *sb.* 3.)

1559 [see DISCOURSING *vbl. sb.*]. **1590** SHAKS. *Mids. N.* v. i. 152 For all the rest, Let Lyon, Moone-shine, Wall, and Louers twaine, At large discourse. **1601** —— *Jul. C.* III. i. 295 Thou shalt discourse To yong Octavius, of the state of things. **1660** *Trial Regic.* 154 We would sit up discoursing about these unhappy wars. **1677** C. HATTON in *Hatton Corr.* (1878) 152 Several persouns are discoursed of to succeed him. **1695–6** R. FISHER in Blackmore *Hist. Conspir.* (1723) 75 It was discoursed..about seizing on the King in Kensington House. **1726** *Adv. Capt. R. Boyle* 204 And he in return, instructed me in the Portugueze Language: so that in a short time we could discourse in either. **1801** SOUTHEY *Thalaba* II. xxxvi, Now his tongue discoursed of regions far remote. **1875** JOWETT *Plato* (ed. 2) I. 89 I am quite willing to discourse with Socrates in his own manner.

fig. **1592** SHAKS. *Rom. & Jul.* II. ii. 13 She speakes, yet she sayes nothing, what of that? Her eye discourses, I will answere it. **1607** BEAUM. & FL. *Woman-Hater* III. i, I'll promise peace, and fold mine arms up; let but mine eye discourse. **1644** [see DISCOURSING *ppl. a.* 2].

b. *trans.* (with *compl.*) To pass (time) *away* in discourse or talk; to bring (a person) by discourse *into* (some state).

1611 SHAKS. *Cymb.* III. iii. 38 How..shall we discourse The freezing houres away? **1672** EACHARD *Hobbs' State Nat.* 106, I always found it an endless thing to reason and discourse people into any soundness of mind. **1820** HAZLITT *Lect. Dram. Lit.* 137 Seated round [they] discourse the silent hours away.

4. *intr.* To speak or write at length on a subject; to utter or pen a discourse. (Cf. DISCOURSE *sb.* 5.)

1564 [implied in DISCOURSER]. **1628** PRYNNE *Cens. Cozens* 23 They haue discoursed of these seuen sinnes. **1632** LITHGOW *Trav.* VI. 239 Josephus..largely discourseth of many hundred thousands famished..within this multipotent City. *a* **1704** LOCKE (J.), The general maxims we are discoursing of are not known to children, ideots, and a greater part of mankind. **1750** LARDNER *Wks.* (1838) III. 38 Mr. Wolff has discoursed largely of this matter. *a* **1862** BUCKLE *Civiliz.* (1869) III. iv. 203 If he discoursed for two hours without intermission, he was valued as a zealous pastor.

5. *trans.* To go through in speech; to treat of in speech or writing; to talk over, discuss; to talk of, converse about; to tell, narrate, relate. *arch.*

1563–87 FOXE *A. & M.* (1684) III. 357 We have discoursed the Story of Mr. Robert Glover. **1591** SHAKS. *1 Hen. VI*, I. iv. 26 How wert thou handled, being Prisoner? .. Discourse I prethee on this Turrets top. *a* **1592** MARLOWE & NASHE *Dido* II. Wks. (Rtldg.) 256/2 To discourse at large, And truly too, how Troy was overcome. *a* **1652** J. SMITH *Sel. Disc.* IX. iii. (1821) 422 Having discoursed the nobleness of religion in its original and nature; we come now to consider the excellency of religion in its properties. **1654** WHITLOCK *Zootomia* 388 Alcibiades cut of his Dogs Taile..that so the talkative people might lesse discourse his other Actions. **1716** COLLIER tr. *Greg. Nazianzen* 57, I need not discourse, that Passion, Rancour, and Malice, are not allow'd a Christian. **1727** SWIFT *Gulliver* II. viii. 170 Discoursing this matter with the sailors while I was asleep. **1822** B. CORNWALL *Dram. Scenes, Tartarus*, Moans, beside Its waters rising, discourse tales of sin.

fig. **1591** GREENE *Maiden's Dreame* xxix, His open hands discours'd his inward grace.

†**b.** To utter, say; to speak or write formally. (With the utterance or thing said as object.) *Obs.*

1604 SHAKS. *Oth.* II. iii. 282 Drunke? And speake Parrat? .. And discourse Fustian with ones owne shadow? **1654** WHITLOCK *Zootomia* 446 Who it may be can discourse nothing but slander, or censure. **1744** HARRIS *Three Treat.* III. I. (1765) 108 The Joy..in recollecting what we have discoursed on these Subjects.

c. To utter, give forth (musical sounds).

(Chiefly as a reminiscence of the Shakspere passage.)

1602 SHAKS. *Ham.* III. ii. 374 Giue it breath with your mouth, and it will discourse most excellent Musicke. **1837** CARLYLE *Fr. Rev.* III. III. ix. (1872) 135 The tocsins discourse stern music. **1881** *Scribner's Mag.* XXI. 267/2 The Ridgemont brass band was discoursing familiar strains. **1882** BESANT *Revolt of Man* xi. (1883) 263 On the Green the band was discoursing sweet music.

†**6.** *trans.* To speak or converse with (a person), to talk to; to discuss a matter with, confer with; to speak to, address, harangue. *Obs.* or *arch.*

(Very common down to 1750).

1677 A. YARRANTON *Eng. Improv.* 25 All the People..will discourse their Parliament Men in these things hinted at. **1689–92** LOCKE *Toleration* III. ii. Wks. 1727 II. 330 A Friend whom I discoursed on this Point. *a* **1695** WOOD *Life* (O.H.S.) III. 408 He overtook me on horse back..and discours'd me aloud. **1702** ECHARD *Eccl. Hist.* (1710) 226 While Peter thus discoursed the people. **1763** FRANKLIN *Let.* Wks. 1887 III. 229 That I might..have more convenient opportunities of discoursing them on our publick affairs. **1866** WHITTIER *Marg. Smith's Jrnl.* Prose Wks. 1889 I. 21 Sir Thomas discoursed us in his lively way.

†**diˈscourseless**, *a.* *Obs.* [f. DISCOURSE *sb.* + -LESS.] Void of reasoning power; unreasoning.

1620 SHELTON *Quix.* II. vi. 69 To attempt things whence rather harm may after result unto us then good, is the part of rash and discourseless brains.

discourser (dɪˈskɔəsə(r)). Also 6 -our, 7 -or. [f. DISCOURSE *v.* + -ER¹.] One who discourses; a speaker, talker, narrator, preacher, orator; the writer of a discourse or dissertation.

1564 *Brief. Exam.* **iij b, There are much paynes bestowed of these discoursours. **1579** J. STUBBES *Gaping Gulf* A vj b, These discoursers that vse the word of God with as little conscience as they doe Machiavel. **1600** O. E. *Reply Libel* I. vii. 166 An idle discourser, that mooueth questions, that bee not to purpose. **1630** *R. Johnson's Kingd. & Commw.* 300 Some few particulars..worthy a much more ample discourse, and a..better informed discourser. **1713** BENTLEY *Freethinking* 65 (R.) Our discourser here has quoted nine verses out of it. **1768–74** TUCKER *Lt. Nat.* (1852) II. 415 It behoves the discourser upon religious matters to consider [etc.]. **1884** CHURCH *Bacon* iii. 62 Perhaps she distrusted in business and state affairs so brilliant a discourser.

diˈscoursing, *vbl. sb.* [f. DISCOURSE *v.* + -ING¹.] The action of the verb DISCOURSE, q.v.; talking, conversation; discussion.

1559 BP. SCOT in Strype *Ann. Ref.* I. App. x. 33 Let the prestes..meet together..for the discoursinge therof. **1667** BP. S. PARKER *Cens. Platon. Phil.* 37 Plato's discoursings about practicall matters are exceeding handsome and pertinent. **1683** HACKE *Collect. Voy.* (1699) I. 7 We concluded the discoursing of Women at Sea was very unlucky, and occasioned the Storm. **1894** *Athenæum* 17 Mar. 339/1 To listen to the discoursing of an accomplished man of letters..is always a pleasure.

diˈscoursing, *ppl. a.* [f. as prec. + -ING².] That discourses; see the verb.

†**1.** Passing from premisses to consequences, reasoning; reasonable, rational. *Obs.*

1592 DAVIES *Immort. Soul* II. xi. (1714) 29 Brutes do want that quick discoursing Pow'r, Which doth in us the erring Sense correct. **1638** K. DIGBY *Let. conc. Relig.* ii. (1651) 14 The Fathers works..will fairly inform a rational and discoursing man of the true state of them. **1642** R. CARPENTER *Experience* II. v. 156 Motives..sufficient to induce a discoursing man to forsake the Jesuits.

†**b.** Passing rapidly from one thought to another; busily thinking. *Obs.*

a **1568** ASCHAM *Scholem.* I. (Arb.) 78 A factious hart, a discoursing head, a mynde to medle in all mens matters. **1625** BACON *Ess., Truth* (Arb.) 499 And though the Sects of Philosophers of that Kinde be gone, yet there remaine certaine discoursing Wits. **1638** FORD *Lady's Trial* III. iii, We..Frame strange conceits in our discoursing brains.

2. Talking, holding discourse; delivering a discourse.

a **1568** ASCHAM *Scholem.* (Arb.) 76 A busie head, a discoursing tong, and a factious harte. **1644** BULWER (*title*), Chirologia: or the Naturall Language of the Hand. Composed of the Speaking Motions, and Discoursing Gestures thereof. **1891** *Daily News* 2 Oct. 5/6 Mrs. Theodore Fry..and Miss Orme, were the discoursing ladies.

†**diˈscoursist.** *Obs.* [f. DISCOURSE *v.* + -IST.] One who reasons or draws conclusions.

1622 MABBE tr. *Aleman's Guzman d'Alf.* II. 205 Thereby every good Discoursist might come to the knowledge of the fault, and repent himselfe thereof.

discoursitive: see DISCOURSATIVE.

† **di'scoursive**, *a.* *Obs.* [f. DISCOURSE *v.* + -IVE: cf. *discursive*, which follows Latin analogies.]

1. Of or pertaining to 'discourse' or reason; having the power of reasoning; rational.

1594 CAREW *Huarte's Exam. Wits* (1616) 60 Vnderstood of the faculties or reasonable wits, which are discoursiue and actiue. **1645** RUTHERFORD *Tryal & Tri. Faith* (1845) 286 The prime faculty, reason, the discoursive power. **1649** DAVENANT *Love & Honour* I. Dram. Wks. 1873 III. 109 The brute herd..though they want Discoursive soul, are less inhuman far than he. **1678** *Lively Orac.* II. §62. 261 He must be suppos'd..to have given men discoursive faculties.

b. Proceeding by reasoning, argumentative.

1588 J. HARVEY (*title*), Discoursive Probleme concerning Prophesies. **1592** NASHE *P. Penilesse* (ed. 2) 22a, Hee fell into a discoursive consideration, what this world was. *a* **1652** J. SMITH *Sel. Disc.* iv. 94 All such actions..we know, without any great store of discoursive inquiry, to attribute to their own proper causes. **1753** L. M. tr. *Du Boscq's Accomplish'd Woman* I. 221 Fortune gives kingdoms, but art no more than discoursive knowledge and science.

2. Passing from one thing to another, discursive.

1592 DAVIES *Immort. Soul* VIII. xi. (1714) 52 His sight is not discoursive, by degrees; But seeing the whole, each single Part doth see. **1613** W. BROWNE *Sheph. Pipe* vii. (R.) Thou..In thy discoursive thought, dost range as farre.

3. Disposed or ready to discourse or converse; talkative; conversable, communicative.

1605 DANIEL *Philotas* Poems (1717) 321 See how these vain Discoursive Bookmen talk. **1642** HOWELL *For. Trav.* (Arb.) 30 The one Discoursive and Sociable, the other Reserved and Thoughtfull. **1669** WOOD *Life* (Oxf. H.S.) II. 169 He found him a complaisant man, very free and discoursive.

b. Of the nature of discourse or dialogue; conversational.

a **1592** MARLOWE & NASHE *Dido* I. (Rtldg.) 254/2 But thou art gone, and leav'st me here alone, To dull the air with my discoursive moan. *c* **1645** HOWELL *Lett.* (1650) III. ix. 17 You promised a further expression of your self by way of a Discoursive Letter what you thought of Copernicus opinion. **1668** DRYDEN *Ess. Dram. Poesy* in Arb. *Garner* III. 567 For the Epic way is euery where interlaced with Dialogue or Discoursive Scenes. **1716** M. DAVIES *Athen. Brit.* III. *Crit. Hist.* 111 The Editioning of..Ancient Authors, without any..long discoursive Comments, or long-winded Sententions-Notes.

† **di'scoursively**, *adv.* *Obs.* [f. prec. + -LY².] In a 'discoursive' way: **a.** Rationally; **b.** Conversationally; **c.** By way of a discourse or set speech.

1588 J. HARVEY *Disc. Probl.* 7 To proceede tentatiuely, and discoursiuely, as the foresaid schoolemen vse to call it. **1593** R. HARVEY *Philad.* 7 You are very bookishly and literally wise, not reasonably and discoursively. **1642** HOWELL *For. Trav.* (Arb.) 39 He hath made an introduction into the Spanish tongue..so that..he may easily come to speake it discoursively. **1656** CROMWELL *Sp.* 17 Sept., Not discoursively, in the oratoric way; but to let you see the matter of fact..how the state of your affairs stands.

† **di'scoursiveness.** *Obs.* [f. as prec. + -NESS.] The quality of being 'discoursive'.

1627-77 FELTHAM *Resolves* II. xliv. 245 The discoursiueness of Reason.

† **dis'court**, *v.* *Obs.* [f. DIS- 7b + COURT *sb.* 6.] *trans.* To dismiss or expel from court; to deprive of court favour; = DECOURT.

1585 WOTTON *Let. to Walsingham* 1 June in Tytler *Hist. Scot.* (1864) IV. 99/2 Whether he might not be better discourted by way of justice. **1611** SPEED *Hist. Gt. Brit.* VI. xlv. 155 Jehu..commanded all his officers to offer sacrifice to the Idoll-Gods, pretending to dis-court all such as refused. **1676** W. ROW *Contn. Blair's Autobiog.* xii. (1848) 436 Middleton was like to be discourted. **1721-2** WODROW *Hist. Suff. Ch. Scot.* I. v. (1828) 384 The chancellor threatened to disgrace and discourt him.

discourteous (dɪs'kɔətjəs, -'kɜːtjəs), *a.* [f. DIS- 10 + COURTEOUS *a.*; prob. after F. *discourtois* (Cotgr.), earlier *des-*, or It. *discortese* (Florio 1598).] Void of or lacking in courtesy; rude, uncivil.

1578 T. N. tr. *Conq. W. India* 7 Cortez..used discourteous words unto him in the presence of many. **1590** GREENE *Orl. Fur* Wks. (Rtldg.) 98/1 Discourteous women, natures fairest ill. **1690** CROWNE *Eng. Frier* v. 44 Ladies are discourteous to themselves who take liberties discretion will not allow. **1814** SOUTHEY *Roderick* XVI, That e'er of old in forest of romance 'Gainst knights and ladies waged discourteous war. **1877** RITA *Vivienne* III. vii, Pardon me that in a moment of just indignation I have seemed discourteous.

dis'courteously, *adv.* [f. prec. + -LY².] In a discourteous manner; with incivility.

1584 C. ROBINSON *Handf. Delites* (Spencer Soc.) 19 Alas my love, ye do me wrong, to cast me off discurteously. **1647** TRAPP *Comm. Matt.* v. 44 Abraham rescueth his nephew Lot, that had dealt so discourteously with him. **1845** LD. CAMPBELL *Chancellors* (1857) VI. cxxiii. 74 Peter, though so discourteously treated in this controversy, did not flinch. **1870** DISRAELI *Lothair* xlvi, Lord St. Aldegonde..moved discourteously among them.

dis'courteousness. *rare.* [f. as prec. + -NESS.] Rudeness, incivility.

1727 in BAILEY vol. II. **1866** [see DISCOURTESY].

discourtesy (dɪs'kɔətɛsɪ, -'kɜː-). [f. DIS- 9 + COURTESY, after F. *discourtoisie* (Cotgr.), earlier *des-* (15th c. in Hatz.-Darm.); cf. It. *discortesia* (Florio), Sp. *descortesia* (Minsheu).] The opposite of courtesy; rude or uncivil behaviour; incivility; an instance of this.

1555 EDEN *Decades* 252 Mee thynke it shulde seeme a great discurtesie if I shuld not shewe yowe all that I knowe. **1599** SANDYS *Europæ Spec.* (1632) 154 Some jealousies and discurtesies passed lately betweene them and the Pope. **1611** SHAKS. *Cymb.* II. iii. 101, I pray you spare me, 'faith I shall vnfold equall discourtesie to your best kindnesse. **1670** EACHARD *Cont. Clergy* 16 Such pretended favours and kindnesses, as these, are the most right down discourtesies in the world. **1849** MACAULAY *Hist. Eng.* II. 78 Ample apologies were therefore made for the discourtesy. **1859** TENNYSON *Idylls, Elaine* 968, I pray you, use some rough discourtesy To blunt or break her passion. **1866** MRS. STOWE *Lit. Foxes* 100 (*heading*) Discourteousness..I think one of the greatest destroyers of domestic peace is Discourtesy.

† **dis'courtship.** *Obs. rare.* [f. DIS- 9 + COURTSHIP 1 b.] = DISCOURTESY.

1599 B. JONSON *Cynthia's Rev.* v. ii, Monsieur, we must not so much betray ourselves to discourtship, as to suffer you to be longer unsaluted.

† **'discous**, *a.* *Obs.* [ad. mod.L. *discōsus* f. *discus* DISC: see -OUS.] Having a disc or discs; discoid.

1706 PHILLIPS (ed. Kersey), *Discous* or *Discoidal Flowers* ..whose *Flosculi* or little Leaves, are set together so close, thick, and even, as to make the surface of the Flower plain and flat like a Dish. **1727** BAILEY vol. II. *Discous* Flower.. is that which has a Disk without any Rays, as in Tansy, etc. **1794** MARTYN *Rousseau's Bot.* xxvi. 384 Discoid, or as some call them discous flowers.

† **di'scovenable**, *a.* *Obs.* [a. OF. *descovenable*, *-convenable*, unsuitable, unbefitting, inconvenient, f. *des-*, DIS- 4 + *co(n)venable*: see CONVENABLE, COVENABLE.] Unsuitable, unbefitting, inappropriate.

[**1292** BRITTON I. xxix. §5 Si la condicioun soit inpossible ou descovenable.] **1474** CAXTON *Chesse* II. v. D viij b, The peple of rome..no thynge shamefast to demaunde thynges discouenable. **1484** —— *Chivalry* 18 A discouenable thyng it shold be that a man that wold lerne to sewe shold lerne to sewe of a carpenter.

† **dis'covenant**, *v.* *Obs.* [f. DIS- 6 + COVENANT *v.* 1, or DIS- 7a + COVENANT *sb.*] *trans.* To dissolve covenant with; to exclude from a covenant. Hence **dis'covenanted** *ppl. a.*

1650 TRAPP *Comm. Pentat.* II. 101 God will own them no longer; they are now dis-covenanted. **1667** FLAVEL *Saint Indeed* (1754) 34 If he had..discovenanted my soul, I had reason to be cast down. **1702** C. MATHER *Magn. Chr.* v. App. (1852) 292 They were once in covenant and never since discovenanted. **1861** LYTTON & FANE *Tannhäuser* 97 No more..rebuild The rainbow of discovenanted Hope.

dis'covenanter. *rare*⁻¹. [f. DIS- 9 + COVENANTER 2.] One who refused to sign or adhere to the (Scottish) Covenants; cf. COVENANT sb. 9.

1827 AIKMAN *Hist. Scot.* IV. VIII. 186 The secret malignants and discovenanters.

discover (dɪ'skʌvə(r)), *v.* Forms: α. 4- **discover**; also 4 **deschuver**, **discovir**, 4-5 **dys-**, 4-7 **discouer**, 5 **-cuuer**, **-couyr**, **-couuer**. β. 4 **diskyuer**, 5 **dis-**, **dyskeuer**. γ. 4 **descure**, 4-6 **discour(e**, **-cure**, 5 **-cuyre**, 5-6 **-kure**, 6 **-cuir**. δ. 5-6 **dis-**, **dyskere**. [a. OF. *descovr-ir*, *descouvr-ir* = Pr. and Sp. *descubrir*, It. *discovrire* (later *-coprire*), ad. med.L. *discooperīre*, late L. or Romanic f. DIS- 4 + L. *cooperire* to COVER. The OF. stressed form *descuevre*, *-queuvre*, gave the Eng. variant, *diskever* (still *dial.*), and the vocalizing of *v* between vowels, gave the reduced *discour*, *-cure*, and *diskere*.]

† **1.** *trans.* To remove the covering (clothing, roof, lid, etc.) from (anything); to bare, uncover; *esp.* to uncover (the head), to unroof (a building). *Obs.*

1382 WYCLIF *Lev.* xxi. 10 His heed he shal not discouer, his clothis he shal not kitt. **14..** LYDG. *Temple of Glas* 916 Who þat wil..Fulli be cured..He most..Discure his wound, & shew it to his lech. *c* **1449** PECOCK *Repr.* II. x. 206 The principal Crucifix of the chirche schal be Discovered and schewid baar and nakid to alle the peple of the Processioun. **1483** CAXTON *Gold. Leg.* 362/2 She..said to her sustres that they sholde discouere their hedes. **1520** WHITINTON *Vulg.* (1527) 40 Let hym also..set his cuppe surely before his superyour, discouer it and couer it agayne with curtesy made. **1571** GRINDAL *Articles* 50 Whether any man hath pulled downe or discouered any Church, chauncell, or chappell. **1627** *Lisander & Cal.* v. 80 At the end of his sermon having discovered his head. **1628** COKE *On Litt.* I. 53 If the house be discouered by tempest, the tenant must in conuenient time repaire it.

† **2.** To remove, withdraw (anything serving as a cover); to cause to cease to be a covering. *Obs.*

1535 STEWART *Cron. Scot.* II. 139 At the last the cloud ane lytill we Discouerit wes, that tha micht better se. **1611** BIBLE *Jer.* xiii. 22 For the greatnesse of thine iniquitie are thy skirts discouered. **1618** CHAPMAN *Hesiod* I. 161 When the woman the unwieldy lid Had once discover'd, all the miseries hid.. dispersed and flew About the world.

3. a. To disclose or expose to view (anything covered up, hidden, or previously unseen), to reveal, show. Now *rare.*

c **1450** LONELICH *Grail* lv. 175 Thanne browhte Aleyn this holy vessel anon..& there it discouerede & schewed it þe kyng. **1535** COVERDALE *Isa.* xxvi. 21 He wil discouer the bloude that she hath deuoured. **1613** *Voy. Guiana* in *Harl. Misc.* (Malh.) III. 182 A goodly river, discovering a gallant Country. **1660** HICKERINGILL *Jamaica* (1661) 39 Columbus, to whose happy search, the West-Indies first discovered it self. **1689** —— *Modest Inq.* v. 35 Which Wrinckles I had rather Masque over and cover, than discover. **1716** LADY M. W. MONTAGU *Let. to Pope* 14 Sept., The stage was built over a..canal, and, at the beginning of the second act, divided into two parts discovering the water. **1797** MRS. RADCLIFFE *Italian* xxxii, This discovered to Schedoni the various figures assembled in his dusky chamber. *a* **1861** CLOUGH *Ess. Class. Metres, Actaeon* 13 She..Swift her divine shoulders discovering. **1882** STEVENSON *New Arab. Nts.* (1884) 121 The nurseryman..readily discovered his hoard. *fig.* **1892** NEWMAN SMYTH *Chr. Ethics* I. iii. 188 This mode of thinking discovers a cosmical moral significance in the incarnation.

† **b.** To afford a view of, to show. *Obs.*

1600 E. BLOUNT tr. *Conestaggio* 212 Upon the hils, which discover the enimies lodging and their trenches. **1638** SIR T. HERBERT *Trav.* (ed. 2) 73 'Tis wall'd about, and to the N.N.W. discovers a lake or fish-pond five miles over. **1667** MILTON *P.L.* I. 64 From those flames No light, but rather darkness visible Serv'd only to discover sights of woe. *c* **1710** C. FIENNES *Diary* (1888) 112 An advanced piece of ground above all the rest..discovers the Country a great Circuit round.

c. *to discover check* (*Chess*): to remove a piece or pawn which stands between a checking piece and the king, and so to put the latter in check.

[**1614** A. SAUL *Chess* viii, The Mate by discovery, the most industrious Mate of all.] **1816** *Stratagems of Chess* (1817) 11 Place the queen, bishop or castle behind a pawn or a piece in such a manner as upon playing that pawn or piece you discover a check upon your adversary's king. **1847** STAUNTON *Chess Pl. Handbk.* 20 When the King is directly attacked by the Piece played, it is a simple check; but when the Piece moved does not itself give check, but unmasks another which does, it is called a discovered check. *Ibid.* 28 A striking though simple instance of the power of a discovered check. *Ibid.* 29 White must play his Rook to K.Kt.'s sixth square, discovering check with the Bishop. **1870** HARDY & WARE *Mod. Hoyle, Chess* 42 Double Check is when check is discovered..the King being also attacked by the piece moved.

4. To divulge, reveal, disclose to knowledge (anything secret or unknown); to make known. *arch.*

a. With *simple object.*

a **1300** *Cursor M.* 28293 (Cott.) Priuetis o fremyd and frende I haue discouerd als vn-hende. *c* **1350** *Will. Palerne* 3192 þis dede schal i neuer deschuuer. *c* **1386** CHAUCER *Can. Yeom. Prol. & T.* 143 Thou sclaundrest me..And eek discouerest that thou sholdest hyde. *c* **1470** HARDING *Chron.* II. i, The youngest suster the mater all discured To her husbande. ? *c* **1475** *Sqr. lowe Degre* 868 Anone he made hym swere His counsayl he should never diskere. **1592** SHAKS. *Rom. & Jul.* III. i. 147 O Noble Prince, I can discouer all The vnluckie Mannage of this fatall brall. **1662** J. DAVIES tr. *Mandelslo's Trav.* 5 They contain some secrets which Time will discover. **1712** W. ROGERS *Voy.* 9 [I] now thought it fit to discover to our Crew whither we were bound. **1751** JOHNSON *Rambler* No. 97 ¶14 He honestly discovers the state of his fortune.

b. With *subord. cl.*

1599 SHAKS. *Much Ado* I. ii. 12 The Prince discouered to Claudio that hee loued my niece your daughter. **1845** J. H. NEWMAN *Lett.* (1891) II. 460 Continually do I pray that He would discover to me if I am under a delusion.

† **c.** *absol.* *Obs.*

14.. LYDG. *Temple of Glas* 629 Lich him þat..knoweþ not, to whom forto discure. **1659** *Burton's Diary* (1828) IV. 302 All means were used to make him discover, but he.. would not confess.

† **5.** To reconnoitre. Also *absol.* *Obs.*

1375 BARBOUR *Bruce* XIV. 268 Furth till discouir, thair way thai ta. *c* **1475** *Rauf Coilȝear* 798 Derflie ouir Daillis, discouerand the doun, Gif ony douchtie that day for Iornayis was dicht. **1513** DOUGLAS *Æneis* IX. iii. 196 Of the nycht wach the cure We geif Mesapus, the ȝettis to discure. **1592** UNTON *Corr.* (Roxb.) 330 The king this day goeth to the warr to discover. **1600** E. BLOUNT tr. *Conestaggio* 211 He issued foorth..with his whole army, onely with an intent to discover.

6. To reveal the identity of (a person); hence, to betray. *arch.*

c **1320** *Sir Beues* 74 Maseger, do me surte, þat þow nelt nouȝt discure me To no wiȝt! *c* **1386** CHAUCER *Merch. T.* 698 Mercy, and that ye nat discouere me. **1465** *Paston Lett.* No. 527 II. 234 A told me..in noo wyse that ye dyskure not Master Stevyn. **1599** *Warn. Faire Wom.* II. 524 Whither shal I fly? The very bushes wil dis-cover me. **1632** J. HAYWARD tr. *Biondi's Eromena* 71 When hee asked who hee was, the Marquesse durst not discover him (so strictly was he tied by promise to conceale him). **1726** *Adv. Capt. R. Boyle* 264 She at last discover'd herself to me: She was Daughter-in-law to [etc.]. **1865** KINGSLEY *Herew.* xix, He was on the point of discovering himself to them.

† **7. a.** To manifest, exhibit, display (an attribute, quality, feeling, etc.). *Obs.*

c **1430** *Pilgr. Lyf Manhode* I. cxxv. (1869) 66 It is michel more woorth..þan to diskeuere his iustice, and to say, bihold mi swerde whiche i haue vnshethed you. **1576** FLEMING *Panopl. Epist.* 338 M. Clemens, to whome S. T. Moore hathe discovered a fewe sparckles of his benevolence towardes mee. **1589** GREENE *Menaphon* (Arb.) 33, I haue not ..store of plate to discover anie wealth. **1615** J. STEPHENS *Satyr. Ess.* 213 He will enter into a Taverne..onely to discover his gold lace and scarlet. **1682** BUNYAN *Holy War* (Cassell) 141 With what agility..did these military men discover their skill in feats of war. **1771** SIR J. REYNOLDS *Disc.* IV. (1876) 347 He takes as much pains to discover, as the greater artist does to conceal, the marks of his subordinate assiduity.

b. *esp.* To manifest by action; to display (unconsciously or unintentionally); to exhibit, betray, allow to be seen or perceived. *arch.*

c **1460** *La Belle Dame* 403 in *Pol. Rel. & L. Poems* (1866) 65 If youre grace to me be Discouerte, Thanne be your meane soon shulde I be relevyd. **1556** *Aurelio & Isab.* (1608) I. vii, Then yowre regard discoverethe..the desire of yowre harte. **1600** E. BLOUNT tr. *Conestaggio* 117 The more he mounted, the more he discovered his incapacitie. **1658** SIR T. BROWNE *Hydriot.* ii. (1736) 29 The remaining Bones discovered his Proportions. **1739** LABELYE *Short Acc. Piers Westm. Bridge* 59 The Timber..discover'd a strong Smell of Turpentine upon the first Stroke of a Plane. **1836–7** SIR W. HAMILTON *Metaph.* (1877) I. xviii. 341 She had never discovered a talent for poetry or music. **1887** *Times* 27 Aug. 11/3 He was bitten by a pet fox which subsequently discovered symptoms of rabies.

c. With *subord. clause.*

1596 SPENSER *State Irel.* Wks. (Globe) 640/1 The which name doth discover them to be also auncient English. **1622** J. MEADE in Ellis *Orig. Lett.* Ser. I. III. 126 How could that discover they were for Spaine? **1713** POPE *Guardian* No. 4 ¶2 A lofty gentleman Whose air and gait discovered when he had published a new book. **1802–3** tr. *Pallas' Trav.* (1812) I. 425 All the Nagais still discover by their features, that they are of Mongolian origin. **1856** EMERSON *Eng. Traits, First Visit* Wks. (Bohn) II. 7 Rousseau's Confessions had discovered to him [Carlyle] that he was not a dunce.

8. To obtain sight or knowledge of (something previously unknown) for the first time; to come to the knowledge of; to find out.

a. With *simple object.*

1555 EDEN *Decades* 2 Colonus..in this fyrst nauigation discouered vj Ilandes. **1585** T. WASHINGTON tr. *Nicholay's Voy.* I. v. 4 Wee discovered at the Seas two Foystes which came even towardes the place where we were. **1670** MAYNWARING *Physician's Repos.* 90 This alkalisate property was first discovered by preparation and tryals. **1783** H. BLAIR *Lect. Rhet.* x. (Seager), We invent things that are new; we discover what was before hidden. Galileo invented the telescope; Harvey discovered the circulation of the blood. **1840** *Penny Cycl.* XVI. 176 Banks's Islands..were discovered by Captain Bligh in 1789. **1860** TYNDALL *Glac.* II. xvii. 317 The sounds continued without our being able to discover their source.

b. With *subord. clause* or *inf. phrase.*

1556 *Aurelio & Isab.* (1608) Biij, Your love shal be discovered to be false. **1676** LISTER in *Ray's Corr.* (1848) 125, I am glad you have discovered those authors to be plagiaries. **1727** SWIFT *Gulliver* II. viii. 169 He sent out his long-boat to discover what I was. **1868** LOCKYER *Elem. Astron.* vi. (1879) 228 Dr. Wollaston in..1802 discovered that there were dark lines crossing the spectrum in different places. **1892** SIR H. E. LOPES in *Law Times' Rep.* LXVII. 150/2 The defendant Burton says he discovered that he had made a mistake.

c. To catch sight of; to sight, descry, espy. *arch.*

1576–90 N. T. (L. Tomson) *Acts* xxi. 3 And when we had discouered Cyprus, we left it on the left hand. **1585** T. WASHINGTON tr. *Nicholay's Voy.* I. xi. 13 In the evening we discovered the citie of Gigeri. **1660** F. BROOKE tr. *Le Blanc's Trav.* 23 From the top of the hill you discover Aden, standing in a large plain. **1726** *Adv. Capt. R. Boyle* 373 November 3, we discover'd England, whose Chalky Cliffs gave us all a vast Delight. **1817** SHELLEY *Rev. Islam* VII. xl. 5 Day was almost over, When through the fading light I could discover A ship approaching.

d. *spec.* To bring to public notice, make famous or fashionable.

1908 *Busy Man's Mag.* Sept. 114/2 It is interesting just here to note that while editor of the Westminster, Mr. Macdonald 'discovered' Ralph Connor (Rev. Dr. Gordon), the celebrated Canadian novelist. **1926** M. BARING *Daphne Adeane* i. 3 She was merged in the ranks of the unnoticed, till she was suddenly 'discovered'. **1932** *Times Lit. Suppl.* 8 Sept. 625/3 In a very short time she had producers..vying with each other for the honour of 'discovering' her. **1963** J. FLEMING *Death of Sardine* iii. 41 One day, when Trigoso Praia, or Plage, was 'discovered' the road might be an important promenade.

†**9.** To bring into fuller knowledge; to explore (a country, district, etc.). *Obs.*

1582 N. LICHEFIELD tr. *Castanheda's Conq. E. Ind.* lxxv. 154 In commission to go & discover the red Sea with the Countreyes adiacent. **1670** NARBOROUGH *Jrnl.* in *Acc. Sev. Late Voy.* I. (1711) 43, I sent in my Boat to discover the Harbour, and see if the Pink was there. **1778** *Eng. Gazetteer* (ed. 2) s.v. *Tingmouth*, The Danes landed here in 970, to discover the country previous to their invasion of it. **1850** PRESCOTT *Peru* II. 192 He was empowered to discover and occupy the country for the distance of two hundred leagues.

†**10. a.** *intr.* To make discoveries, to explore. *Obs.*

1582 N. LICHEFIELD tr. *Castanheda's Conq. E. Ind.* iv. 10 b, Vpon Christmas daye, they had discouered along the Coast, three score and tenne leagues to the Eastward. **1685** R. BURTON *Eng. Emp. Amer.* ii. 39 Capt. Henry Hudson in 1607 discovered farther North toward the Pole than perhaps any before him. **1821** SOUTHEY *Exped. of Orsua* 129 We set out from Peru for the river Maranham, to discover and settle there.

†**b.** To have or obtain a view: to look; to see.

1599 HAKLUYT *Voy.* II. I. 234 Standing at the one gate you may discouer to the other. **1647** SALTMARSH *Spark. Glory* (1847) 141 They that have discovered up into free-grace or the mystery of salvation. **1653** HOLCROFT *Procopius* I. 20 From a hil discovering round, they saw a dust, and soon after a great troop of Vandals. **1667** LD. DIGBY *Elvira* II. vii, There's nobody in the street, it is so light One may discover a mile. **1709** POPE *Ess. Crit.* 647 He steer'd securely, and discover'd far, Led by the light of the Mæonian star.

†**11.** *trans.* and *intr.* To distinguish, discern. *Obs.*

1620 E. BLOUNT *Horae Subsec.* 453 This kind of Flatterie ..is so closely intermixed with friendship, that it can hardly be discouered from it. **1650** W. BROUGH *Sacr. Princ.* (1659) 551 Discover better betwixt the Spirit of God and the World. **1655** MRQ. WORCESTER *Cent. Inv.* vi, Far as Eye can discover black from white. **1796** MRS. E. PARSONS *Myst. Warning* III. 59 A semblance of honour I had not the penetration to discover from a reality.

Hence **di'scovering** *vbl. sb.* and *ppl. a.*

c **1350** *Will. Palerne* 1044, I drede me of descuuering, for ȝe haue dwelled long. **1375** BARBOUR *Bruce* I. 242 Thus contrar thingis euir-mar, Discoweryngis off the tothir ar. *c* **1477** CAXTON *Jason* 37 The mouth whiche is instrument of the dischargyng and discouering of hertes. **1555** EDEN *Decades* 311 The fyrste discoueryng of the Weste Indies. **1583** GOLDING *Calvin on Deut.* lviii. 349 To the end they might not vse any odde shiftes to keepe their naughtinesse from discouering. *a* **1631** DONNE in *Cornh. Mag.* May (1865) 618 All will spy in thy face A blushing, womanly, discovering grace. **1663** GERBIER *Counsel* 19 The middle Transome would be opposite to a mans eye, hindersome to the free discovering of the Countrey. **1668** CLARENDON *Contemp. Ps.*, Tracts (1727) 668 Who love such discovering words [etc.]. **1695** WOODWARD *Nat. Hist. Earth* IV. (1723) 244 Rivers and Rains also, are instrumental to the Discovering of Amber.

discovera'bility. [f. next: see -ITY.] The quality of being discoverable; capability of being found out.

1840 CARLYLE *Heroes* i. (1872) 4 Belief that there is a Greatest Man; that he is discoverable..the 'discoverability' is the only error here. **1867** *Sabbath on Rock* ii. 42 To set up absolute discoverability as *the* test of a moral law.

discoverable (dɪˈskʌvərəb(ə)l), *a.* [f. DISCOVER *v.* + -ABLE.] Capable of being discovered or found out; discernible, perceptible, ascertainable.

1572 in *Sir F. Drake revived* (1628) 24 Some fit place.. where we might safely leave our Ship at Anchor, not discouerable by the enemy. **1628** EARLE *Microcosm., A weake Man* (Arb.) 59 One discouerable in all sillinesses to all men but himselfe. **1736** BUTLER *Anal.* II. i. Wks. 1874 I. 154 Containing an account of a dispensation of things not discoverable by reason. **1751** JOHNSON *Rambler* No. 183 ¶8 Its effects..are everywhere discoverable. **1856** FROUDE *Hist. Eng.* II. x. 413 The report..is no longer extant. Bonner was directed by Queen Mary to destroy all discoverable copies of it. **1873** M. ARNOLD *Lit. & Dogma* (1876) 284 Provoking it by every means discoverable.

di'scoverably, *adv.* [f. prec. + -LY².] So as to be discovered; perceptibly.

1646 SIR T. BROWNE *Pseud. Ep.* II. iv. 79 Saltes [attract] ..but weakely..nor very discoverably by any frication. **1843** CARLYLE *Past & Pr.* II. iii. (1845) 69 The river Lark, though not very discoverably, still runs or stagnates in that country.

†**di'scoverance.** *Obs. rare*⁻¹. [f. DISCOVER *v.* + -ANCE: cf. obs. F. *descouvrance* (16th c. in Godef.).] The action of discovering; discovery.

1664 POWER *Exp. Philos.* I. 33, I have another advantageous way of discoverance of them to the bare eye also.

discovered (dɪˈskʌvəd), *ppl. a.* [f. DISCOVER *v.* + -ED¹.]

†**1.** Uncovered; bare; having the head bare.

1484 CAXTON *Chivalry* 88 That daye that he seeth the hede of his wyf or ony other bare and discourd. **1579** FENTON *Guicciard.* (1618) 99 The campe of the Florentines ..being pitched in a place so open and discouered. **1594** BLUNDEVIL *Exerc.* III. II. iv. (ed. 7) 378 Leaving other parts of the earth drie, and discovered. *a* **1638** MEDE *Wks.* (1672) 61 Having their faces discovered, their hair dishevelled. **1644** R. BAILLIE *Lett. & Jrnls.* (1841) II. 149 In preaching he [Mr. Nye] thinks the minister should be covered and the people discovered. **1692** J. M. *Zingis* 147 Seeing his Head discover'd, he knew him to be the Prince of Brema.

2. Made manifest; found out, revealed, divulged.

1581 J. BELL *Haddon's Answ. Osor.* 173 Whatsoever is decreed either by his covered or discovered will. **1603** KNOLLES *Hist. Turks* (1638) 91 Which companies..came neer to the town unseen or discouered. **1670** CLARENDON *Ess.* Tracts (1727) 133 Upon the most discovered and notorious transgressions. **1718** MOTTEUX *Quix.* (1892) II. xxxvi. 278 The whole length of the discovered world. **1864** PUSEY *Lett. Daniel* ix. 542 His discovered error.

b. *discovered check* (*Chess*): see DISCOVER *v.* 3 c.

Hence †**di'scoveredly** *adv.*, openly, manifestly.

1659 TORRIANO, *Alla-scopérta*, openly, discoveredly, in view of all.

discoverer (dɪˈskʌvərə(r)). Forms: 4 discurer, 5 des- dys- discoverour, dyscowerer, -cuerer, -curer, discurrour, -owr, -cowrrour, 6 (*Sc.*) discuriour, 6– discoverer. [ad. OF. *descouvreur, -eor* (13th c. in Hatz.-Darm.). mod.F. *découvreur*, f. *descouvrir* to DISCOVER = It. *discopritore*. Sp. *descubridor*; repr. late L. type **discooperitōr-em*.]

†**1.** One who makes known, discloses, or reveals (a secret); an informer. *Obs.*

a **1300** *Cursor M.* 27469 (Cott.) Þe tent if he tell o þis man o scrift es he discurer þan. *c* **1440** *Promp. Parv.* 122/1 Dyscurer, or dyscowerer of cownselle (*v.r.* discuerer), *arbitrer.* **1586** A. DAY *Eng. Secretary* II. (1625) 122 Wine saith Ovid, is the discoverer of secrets. **1691–8** NORRIS *Pract. Disc.* (1707) IV. 155 Jesus Christ is the first Discoverer of the other world. **1692** LUTTRELL *Brief Rel.* (1857) II. 606 The authors are searched for, and great rewards offered to the discoverers. **1710** PALMER *Proverbs* 198 There is somewhat of a universal abhorrence in men's minds to a discoverer. **1778** *Phil. Surv. S. Irel.* 251 I'll turn discoverer, and in spite of you..I shall become heir.

†**2.** One sent out to reconnoitre; a scout, spy, explorer. *Obs.*

1375 BARBOUR *Bruce* IX. 244 The discurrouris saw thame cumande With baneris to the vynd vafand. **1513** DOUGLAS *Æneis* I. viii. 124 And with discuriouris keip the coist on raw. **1577** B. GOOGE *Heresbach's Husb.* IV. (1586) 175 b, They [bees] send abroad their discoverers to finde out more foode. **1597** SHAKS. *2 Hen. IV*, IV. i. 3 Here..send discouerers forth, To know the numbers of our Enemies. **1625** BP. MOUNTAGU *Appeal Cæsar* xxxvii. 320 A field of Thistles seemed once a battell of Pikes unto some Discoverers of the Duke of Burgundy.

3. One who discovers or finds out that which was previously unknown.

1600 HAKLUYT *Voy.* III. 20 (R.) This frier..was the greatest discouerer by sea, that hath bene in our age. **1602** WARNER *Alb. Eng.* XI. lxii. (1612) 271 Caboto (whose Cosmographie and selfe-proofe brake the Ise To most our late discouerers). **1718** PRIOR *Knowledge* 319 Foreign isles which our discoverers find. **1855** MACAULAY *Hist. Eng.* IV. 691 He was not..the first great discoverer whom princes and statesmen had regarded as a dreamer.

†**4.** (?) An umpire between two combatants in a tournament. *Obs.*

Cf. 1440 in 1.

1460 *Lybeaus Disc.* 925 Taborus and trompours, Herawdes goode descoverours, Har strokes gon descrye. **1548** HALL *Chron., Hen. IV*, (an. 1) 12 Not onely..to see.. their manly feates..but also to be the discoverer and indifferente judge..of their courageous actes.

†**di'scoverment.** *Obs. rare*⁻¹. [f. DISCOVER *v.* -MENT: cf. OF. *descouvrement* mod.F. *découvrement*, Sp. *descubrimiénto*.]

= DISCOVERY.

1600 FAIRFAX *Tasso* XV. xxxix. 274 The time..prefixt for this discouerment.

di'scovert, *a.* and *sb.* [a. OF. *descovert, -couvert*, pa. pple. of *descouvrir* (also used subst.), mod.F. *découvert* = med.L. *discoopertus*, pa. pple. of *discooperīre* to DISCOVER.]

A. *adj.*

†**1.** Uncovered, exposed, unprotected. *Obs.*

c **1380** *Sir Ferumb.* 738 As he huld is scheld vp so, discouert was al ys side. **1491** CAXTON *Vitas Patr.* (W. de W. 1495) I. xlviii. 94/2 Seenge the caue broken and dyscouuerte. *a* **1500** *Chaucer's Dreme* 6 Flora..with hire mantel hole coverte That winter made had discoverte. **1525** LD. BERNERS *Froiss.* II. clvii. [cliii.] 429 The quenes lytter was richely apparelled and discouert.

2. *Law.* Of an unmarried woman or a widow: Not covert, not under the cover, authority, or protection of a husband; cf. COVERT *a.* 4.

1729 G. JACOB *Law Dict.* (1736), *Discovert* is used in the law for a woman unmarried or widow, one not within the bands of matrimony. **1883** *Law Rep.* 23 Ch. Div. 715 The wife's..interest cannot come into existence until she is discovert. **1886** *Law Times* LXXXI. 171/2 The married lady had not disposed of the income when discovert.

†**B.** *sb.* An uncovered or exposed state. ***in*** or ***at discovert***, in an uncovered condition; off one's guard. [OF. *à descovert.*] *Obs.*

[**1292** BRITTON III. xv. §3 En presence de bones gentz tut a descovert.] **13..** *K. Alis.* (Laud MS.) 7407 (W. 7418) Ac Alisaunder was sone hym by And smoot hym in þe discouerte Wiþ þe strooke al to þe herte. *c* **1386** CHAUCER *Pars. T.* ¶640 Þe deueles may..scheten at hym at discouert by temptacion on euery syde. *c* **1450** *Merlin* 331 Nascien.. smote the kynge Rion so harde at discouert vpon the lifte side that he bar hym to the erthe. **1590** T. LODGE *Euphues' Gold. Leg.* in Halliw. *Shaks.* VI. 15 Love..taking her at discovert stroke her so deepe, as she felt herselfe growing passing passionate. *a* **1592** GREENE *Arbasto* viii, Cupid.. seeing her now at discovert, drew home to the head.

discoverture (dɪˈskʌvətjʊə(r)). *Law.* [f. DISCOVERT *a.* 2 after *coverture.* Cf. OF. *descouverture* discovery (15th c. in Godef.).] The state or condition of being discovert, or not under coverture: cf. COVERTURE 9.

1818 CRUISE *Digest* (ed. 2) III. 502 Within ten years next after his and their full age, discoverture, coming of sound mind..or coming into this realm. **1884** *Law Times Rep.* LI. 157/1 During..the minority and discoverture of any female.

discovery (dɪˈskʌvərɪ). Also 6–7 -rie. [f. DISCOVER *v.*, app. after the analogy of *recover, recovery*. But the latter represents OF. *recovrée, recuvrée, recouvrée*, Romanic n. of action from pa. pple. feminine, L. type *recuperāta*. The corresp. sb. from *descovrir*, viz. *descoverte*, mod.F. *découverte*, It. *discoperta*, L. type **discooperta*, was not taken in English in this sense: in early times *discovering* was used; subsequently we find *discoverance, discoverment*; *discovery* was established in the latter half of the 16th c., and is frequent in Shakspere. Cf. *deliver-y*, also *battery, flattery*, which associate themselves with *batter, flatter*, though not actually derived from these.]

†**1.** The action of uncovering or fact of becoming uncovered; opening (of a bud, etc.). *Obs.*

1658 SIR T. BROWNE *Gard. Cyrus* iii, Seeds themselves in their rudimentall discoveries, appear in foliaceous surcles.

2. The action of disclosing or divulging (anything secret or unknown); revelation, disclosure, setting forth, explanation. Now *rare*.

1586 A. DAY *Eng. Secretary* II. (1625) 101 In the discovery whereof my minde is..to deliver what is my owne opinion. **1601** HOLLAND *Pliny* I. 219 How significant is their discouerie of the beast vnto the hunter. **1614** [see DISCOVER 3 c]. **1662** J. DAVIES tr. *Olearius' Voy. Ambass.* 285 Certain Dutch Merchants, cloath'd in Persian habits..they made no discovery of themselves. **1678** DRYDEN *Kind Keeper* II. i, Come, make a free discovery which of 'em your Poetry is to Charm. **1737** *Col. Rec. Pennsylv.* IV. 276 Resolved..to make a Discovery of the whole affair. **1766** BLACKSTONE *Comm.* II. xxxi. 482 The bankrupt, upon this examination, is bound upon pain of death to make a full discovery of all his estate and effects, as well in expectancy as possession. **1828** SCOTT *F.M. Perth* xxv, She would then meet him, determined to make a full discovery of her sentiments.

b. *Law.* Disclosure by a party to an action, at the instance of the other party, of facts or documents necessary to maintain his own title.

1715 *Act 2 Geo. I* in *Lond. Gaz.* (1716) No. 5455/2 The Person suing..shall be entitled..to demand a Discovery of all Incumbrances..any way affecting the same. **1768** BLACKSTONE *Comm.* III. xxvii. 437 From the..compulsive discovery upon oath, the courts of equity have acquired a jurisdiction over almost all matters of fraud. **1848** WHARTON *Law Lex.* s.v., A bill of discovery, emphatically so called, is a bill for the discovery of facts resting in the knowledge of the defendant, or of deeds, or writings, or other things, in his custody or power. **1863** H. COX *Instit.* II. iv. 405 In the superior courts of common law..either party to a cause has a right..to obtain discovery of documents in his opponent's possession relating to the matter in dispute. **1883** *Law Times* 20 Oct. 411/1, I obtained discovery, and the result was that an authority, signed by the defendant, who had forgotten all about it, was disclosed.

†**c.** The action of displaying or manifesting (any quality); manifestation. *Obs.*

1576 FLEMING *Panopl. Epist.* 57 That they..should not only in the discoverie of their skill make him glorious, but themselves also. **1692** DRYDEN *St. Euremont's Ess.* 42 It was then the Romans..made a discovery of their Magnificence. **1759** JOHNSON *Rasselas* xvi, His companions..could make no discovery of their ignorance or surprise.

d. The unravelling or unfolding of the plot of a play, poem, etc.

1727-51 CHAMBERS *Cycl.*, *Discovery*, in dramatic poetry, a manner of unravelling a plot, or fable..wherein, by some unforeseen accident, a discovery is made of the name, fortune, quality, and other circumstances, of a principal person, which were before unknown. **1870** L'ESTRANGE *Miss Mitford* I. iv. 108 The dénouement of 'Marmion' and that of 'The Lay of the Last Minstrel' both turn on the same discovery.

3. The finding out or bringing to light of that which was previously unknown; making known: also with *a* and *pl.*, an instance of this.

1553 in Hakluyt *Voy.* (1589) 265 The voyage intended for the discouerie of Cathay and diuers other regions, dominions, islands, and places unknown. **1601** SHAKS. *All's Well* III. vi. 99 He will steale himselfe into a mans fauour, and for a weeke escape a great deale of discoueries, but when you finde him out, you haue him euer after. **1653** H. COGAN tr. *Pinto's Trav.* xx. 71 Attired after the Chinese fashion, for fear of discovery. **1676** RAY *Corr.* (1848) 126 Those discoveries and new inventions are not granted even to such men..unless [etc.]. **1748** *Anson's Voy.* II. x. 232 The discovery of new countries and of new branches of commerce. **1794** PALEY *Evid.* II. ii. (1817) 67 Morality..does not admit of discovery, properly so called. **1846** LANDOR *Imag. Conv.* II. 1 Shew me..a discoverer who has not suffered for his discovery..whether a Columbus or a Galileo. **1846** GROTE *Greece* I. xviii. (1862) II. 458 The voyage was one of discovery. **1894** *Whitaker's Almanac* 594/2 Ferrier's discovery of cerebral localization.

†**b.** Exploration, investigation, reconnoitring, reconnaissance. *Obs.*

1605 SHAKS. *Lear* V. i. 53 The Enemys in view..Heere is the guesse of their true strength and Forces, By diligent discouerie. **1669** N. MORTON *New Eng. Mem.* 17 About thirty of them went out on this second Discovery..but upon the more exact discovery thereof, they found it to be no Harbour for Ships, but onely for Boats. **1719** DE FOE *Crusoe* (1840) I. vi. 115 I had a great desire to make a more perfect discovery of the island. **1774** GOLDSM. *Grecian Hist.* II. 275 He was therefore commanded to make some further discoveries.

†**c.** The getting a view (of anything); descrying, viewing; view. *Obs.*

1613 PURCHAS *Pilgrimage* VII. xi. 592 In the first place presents it selfe to our Discoverie that Sea. **1616** SURFL. & MARKH. *Country Farme*, The hills, which are commonly called the views or discoveries of parkes. **1650** FULLER *Pisgah* II. v. ii. 144 He could not at that distance have taken a discovery of them.

d. *U.S. Mining.* 'The first finding of the mineral deposit in place upon a mining claim' (Raymond).

1812 BRACKENRIDGE *Views Louisiana* (1814) 147 What is called a discovery, by those engaged in working the mines, is, when any one happens upon an extensive body of ore. **1881** RAYMOND *Mining Gloss.* s.v., A discovery is necessary before the location can be held by a valid title. The opening in which it is made is called *discovery-shaft, discovery-tunnel*, etc.

†**4.** Information, indication, or evidence that brings anything to light. *Obs.*

1648 CROMWELL *Let.* 17 June in *Carlyle*, We have plain discoveries that Sir Trevor Williams..was very deep in the plot of betraying Chepstow. **1699** BENTLEY *Phal.* 356 By this we may have some Discovery of Nossis's Age. **1705** STANHOPE *Paraphr.* I. 273 Marks which were thought sufficient Discoveries of their being dictated by the same Spirit.

5. a. That wherein the discovery consists; the matter or thing which is discovered, found out, revealed, or brought to light. (In quot. 1657, property discovered to be held without title.)

1632 MARMION *Holland's Leaguer* V. v, I'll open but one leaf..And you shall see the whole discovery. **1657** *Burton's Diary* (1828) II. 102 A Bill for settling of Worcester House ..upon Margaret, Countess of Worcester..and some discoveries in lieu of the arrears of her fifths. *a* **1682** SIR T. BROWNE *Tracts* (1684) 210 The Friers..brought back into Europe the discovery of Silk and Silk Worms. **1780** COWPER *Table t.* 752 Then spread the rich discovery, and invite Mankind to share in the divine delight. **1837** *Penny Cycl.* VII. 419/2 No indication that the mariner's compass was a recent discovery.

b. Someone whose talents are recognized and made known for the first time.

1930 *Daily Tel.* 1 Dec. 21/1 McRosty, who was last year's 'discovery', obtaining his Blue at the first time of asking, is a scratch player of sturdy build. **1955** *Times* 19 May 4/1 He called his discoveries 'new and unknown artists'. **1986** *Guardian* 1 Feb. 13/8 Juliette Binoche was the discovery of the 1985 Cannes Film Festival.

6. *attrib.* and *Comb.* **discovery-claim** (*Mining*), the portion of mining-ground to which the discoverer of a mineral deposit has a claim; the extra 'claim' to which a discoverer is entitled: see 3 d; **discovery method** *Educ.* (orig. *U.S.*), a method of instruction in which pupils are encouraged to acquire knowledge actively by their own investigations, rather than passively by listening and reading; cf. HEURISTIC *a.* b; **discovery well**, the first successful oil well in a newly explored area.

[**1960** *Math. Teacher* Mar. 169/2 There is proposed in this study a student experience-discovery method. **1960** J. S. BRUNER in *Ibid.* Dec. 611/2 Probably we do violence to the subtlety of such technique by labelling it simply the 'method of discovery'.] **1961** *Nat. Assoc. Sec. School Principals Bull.* Dec. 19 A second aspect of the Progressive Education movement relevant to the evolution of the discovery method was the child-centered approach to instruction. **1975** *Language for Life* (Dept. Educ. & Sci.) xxvi. 558, I would question the notion..that a child can learn by talking and writing as certainly as he can by listening and reading, for it appears to me that in its context it is being used as an attempt to promote the merits of 'discovery methods'. **1779** SHERIDAN *Critic* III. i, One of the finest discovery-scenes I ever saw. **1840** F. D. BENNETT *Whaling Voy.* I. 44 The British discovery-sloop Swallow. *Ibid.* 228 To enforce the restitution of property stolen from the discovery-ships. **1820** SCORESBY *Acc. Arctic Reg.* II. 99 One or two discovery vessels were generally attached to every whale-fishing expedition sent out. **1912** *Econ. Geol.* VII. 370 A test well near the discovery well at Spindle Top entered gypsum at 1,200 feet, salt rock at 1,650 feet and stopped at 1,900 feet from the surface. **1948** *Time* 19 Jan. 87/2 The discovery well was pouring out 55 barrels a day, the maximum under Texas regulations. **1977** R. E. MEGILL *Introd. Risk Analysis* xiv. 160 Fields smaller than the cutoff size are non-commercial and their discovery wells are classed as dry holes.

†**dis'cradle**, *v. Obs. rare.* [f. DIS- 7 c + CRADLE *sb.*] *trans.* To turn out of a cradle. *intr.* (for *refl.*) To emerge from the cradle.

1634 FORD *P. Warbeck* I. iii, We know all, Clifford, fully since this meteor, This airy apparition first discradled From Tournay into Portugal.

discrase, -crasite, etc.: see DYSCRASE, etc.

discreace, -crease, obs. var. DECREASE.

discreate (dɪskriː'eɪt), *v.* [f. DIS- 6 + CREATE *v.*] *trans.* To uncreate, annihilate, reduce to nothing or to chaos (anything created).

1570 DEE *Math. Pref.* 4 There and then, that particular thyng shalbe Discreated. **1591** SYLVESTER *Du Bartas* I. ii. 318 Both vniting..appeas'd the brall, Which doubtless else had discreated all. *c* **1845** CLOUGH *Early Poems*, Ἐπὶ Λάτμῳ 40 Self-created, discreated, Recreated, ever fresh, Ever young! **1870** SWINBURNE *Ode Proclam. Fr. Rep.*, Thou hast set thine hand to unmake and discreate.

Hence **discre'ated** *ppl. a.*; also **discre'ation**, the action of uncreating; the undoing of creation.

1627-77 FELTHAM *Resolves* II. lxxvii. 324 The latter is a double Creation, or at least a Dis-creation, and Creation too. *a* **1628** F. GREVILLE *Sidney* x. (1652) 130 The dark Prince, that sole author of dis-creation and disorder. **1879** G. MACDONALD *Sir Gibbie* III. vii. 108 The strange, eerie, silent waste, crowded with the chaos of dis-created homes.

discredence (dɪs'kriːdəns). *rare.* [f. DIS- 9 + CREDENCE; cf. OF. *dis-*, *descredence* distrust.]

†**1.** Discredit, ill repute. *Obs.*

1591 *Troub. Raigne K. John* (1611) 53 We all are vndone, And brought to discredence.

2. Disbelief.

1626 W. SCLATER *Exp. 2 Thess.* (1629) 171 Discredence of such truths doth not preiudice any in his saluation. **1813** T. BUSBY *Lucretius* III. Comm. xxxvi, A total discredence of the soul's mortality. **1849** *Tait's Mag.* XVI. 753 The denial would imply discredence of the faith.

†**dis'credible**, *a. Obs.* [f. DIS- 10 + CREDIBLE.]

1. Not to be believed, unworthy of belief.

1580 LUPTON *Sivqila* 139 Giving men warning..not to deale with such a discredible person.

2. Reflecting discredit; discreditable.

1594 *Death of Usurie* 39 The discredible account hath beene made of Vsurers in most ages. **1652** URQUHART *Jewel* Wks. (1834) 179 [They] have in the mindes of forraigners engraven a discredible opinion of that nation.

discredit (dɪs'krɛdɪt), *sb.* [f. DIS- 9 + CREDIT *sb.*, after DISCREDIT *v.*; cf. Sp. *descredito* (Minsheu 1599), It. *discredito*, F. *discrédit* (1719 in Littré).]

1. Loss or want of credit; impaired reputation; disrepute, reproach; an instance of this.

1565 *Act 8 Eliz.* c. 7. §1 The Slander and Discredit of the said Commodities in Foreign Parts, where..they are grown out of Estimation and Credit. **1576** FLEMING *Panopl. Epist.* 290 Penning infamous libels to the discredit of his freende. **1591** GREENE *Disc. Coosnage* (1592) 9 Either driuen to run away, or to liue in discredite for euer. **1605** BACON *Adv. Learn.* I. i. §1. 3 Learning..I thinke good to deliuer..from the discredites and disgraces which it hath receiued. **1749** FIELDING *Tom Jones*, Both religion and virtue have received more real discredit from hypocrites, than..infidels could ever cast upon them. **1791** BOSWELL *Johnson* Advt., A failure would have been to my discredit. **1875** JOWETT *Plato* (ed. 2) I. 342 Such conduct brings discredit on the name of Athens.

2. Loss or want of belief or confidence; disbelief, distrust.

1647 N. BACON *Disc. Govt. Eng.* I. xl. (1739) 63 The Saxons were utter enemies to Perjury; they punished it with eternal discredit of testimony. **1863** GEO. ELIOT *Romola* III. xxxix, There were obvious facts that at once threw discredit on the printed document. **1868** *Morn. Star* 25 Feb., The answers..had the effect of throwing discredit upon his previous evidence.

b. *Comm.* Loss or want of commercial credit.

1740 W. DOUGLASS *Discourse* 30 Insensibility of Discredit, does naturally follow long Credit. **1779** FRANKLIN *Lett.* Wks. (1889) VI. 355 Any measure attending the discredit of the bills. **1861** GOSCHEN *For. Exch.* 105 The influence of credit or discredit will not be forgotten. **1885** *Pall Mall G.* 13 Apr. 5/1 The course of the discount market depends upon credit or discredit, as the case may be.

discredit (dɪs'krɛdɪt), *v.* [f. DIS- 6 + CREDIT *v.*: prob. after F. *discrédit-er* (16th c. in Littré), or It. *discreditare*.]

1. *trans.* To refuse to credit, give no credit to; to disbelieve.

1559 BP. SCOT in Strype *Ann. Ref.* I. App. vii. 17 If they returne to the truthe agayne, their testimonies in the truthe be not to be discredetid. ? **1656** BRAMHALL *Replic.* ii. 100 To discredit any one of these lesser truths..is as much as to deny the truth of God. **1815** W. H. IRELAND *Scribbleomania* 201 A statement which there is no reason to discredit. **1871** ALABASTER *Wheel of Law* 251, I see no particular reason to discredit the Ceylonese tradition.

2. To show to be unworthy of belief; to take away the credibility of; to destroy confidence in.

1561 T. NORTON *Calvin's Inst.* I. viii. 19 Now let these dogges deny [it]..or let them discredit the historie. **1570-6** LAMBARDE *Peramb. Kent* (1826) 69 If he shall seeke to discredit the whole worke. ? **1656** BRAMHALL *Replic.* v. 206, I spake..this..to discredit that supposititious treatise. **1703** MAUNDRELL *Journ. Jerus.* (1721) 97 The behaviour of the Rabble without very much discredited the Miracle. **1866** J. MARTINEAU *Ess.* I. 161 The idea is..discredited by modern science.

3. To injure the credit or reputation of; to bring into discredit, disrepute, or loss of esteem.

1579 G. HARVEY *Letter-bk.* (Camden) 60 Doist thou not verelye suppose I shalbe utterlye discredditid and quite disgracid for ever? **1579** LYLY *Euphues* (Arb.) 191 He obscureth the parents he came off, and discrediteth his owne estate. **1659** B. HARRIS *Parival's Iron Age* 63 Many retired themselves from this Party, which for a time was much discredited. **1769** ROBERTSON *Chas. V*, V. v. 400 In order to recover the reputation of his arms, discredited by so many losses. **1868** FREEMAN *Norm. Conq.* (1876) II. App. 636 Henry is said to have been discredited for the death of Thomas.

†**b.** To injure the commercial credit of. *Obs.*

1622 [see DISCREDITED]. **1732** DE FOE *Eng. Tradesman* ii. 25 The clothier is discourag'd, and for want of his money discredited.

Hence **dis'crediting** *vbl. sb.* and *ppl. a.*

1571 *St. Trials, Duke Norfolk* (R.), It is not for my Lord of Norfolk to stand so much upon the discrediting the witnesses. **1589** COOPER *Admon.* 21 Which they looke to bring to passe, by the discrediting of the Bishops. **1770** J. CLUBBE *Physiognomy* 73 Any discrediting circumstances. **1892** *Athenæum* 6 Feb. 173/1 The utter and final discrediting of the Government.

discreditable (dɪs'krɛdɪtəb(ə)l), *a.* [f. DIS- 10 + CREDITABLE: after DISCREDIT *sb.* and *v.*] The reverse of CREDITABLE; such as to bring discredit; injurious to reputation; disreputable, disgraceful.

1640 R. BAILLIE *Lett. & Jrnls.* (1841) I. 250 Eishu [eschew] that discreditable stroke. **1738** WARBURTON *Div. Legat.* III. iv. Wks. 1811 III. 132 He contends..for God's having a human form: No discreditable notion, at that time in the Church. **1776** ADAM SMITH *W.N.* I. v. (1869) I. 46 They would be precluded..from this discreditable method. **1849** MACAULAY *Hist. Eng.* II. 151 Employing in self-defence artifices as discreditable as those which had been used against him. **1856** FROUDE *Hist. Eng.* (1858) I. iv. 290 A discreditable effort to fasten upon him a charge of high treason.

Hence **discredita'bility**, the quality of being discreditable, disreputableness; **dis'creditably** *adv.*, in a discreditable manner, disreputably.

1837-9 HALLAM *Hist. Lit.* vi. II. §32 Many names, which might have ranked not discreditably by the side of these tragedians. **1888** A. J. BALFOUR in *Daily News* 17 May 6/3 The meanness and the discreditability of such a proceeding. **1891** *Law Times* XCI. 1/2 Work in both Chancery and Divorce is discreditably in arrear.

dis'credited, *ppl. a.* [f. DISCREDIT *v.* + -ED.] Brought into discredit or disrepute; that has lost credit.

1611 COTGR., *Deshonoré*, dishonoured, discredited, disgraced. **1622** MALYNES *Anc. Law-Merch.* 113 If the Factor do sell another mans commoditie to a man discredited..and it falleth out that this man breaketh [etc.]. **1674** BOYLE *Excell. Theol.* II. v. 203 Obsolete errours are sometimes revived as well as discredited Truths. **1790** BURKE *Fr. Rev.* Wks. V. 88 The discredited paper securities of impoverished fraud. **1887** *Spectator* 29 Oct. 1456 Natural theology, he says, has become a discredited science.

†**dis'creditor.** *Obs. rare.* [f. DISCREDIT *v.* + -OR: cf. *creditor.*] One who discredits or destroys confidence in anything.

1654 W. MOUNTAGUE *Devout Ess.* II. iii. §3 (R.) This course, which the wise man reproaches in the licencious discreditors of future accounts.

discreet (dɪ'skriːt), *a.* (*adv.* and *sb.*). Forms: 4-6 discret, 4-7 discrete, 6-7 discreete, 5- discreet, (5 discrett, dyscrete, 5-6 *Sc.* discreit, 6 disscrete). [ME. *discret*, *discrete*, a. F. *discret*, *-ète* (12th c. in Littré), 'qui se conduit avec discernement', ad.L. *discrētus*, in late L. and Rom. sense: cf. It. and Sp. *discreto* 'discreet, wise, wary, considerate, circumspect' (Florio), 'discreet, wise to perceive' (Minsheu). A doublet of DISCRETE, differentiated in sense and spelling.

In cl. Lat., *discrēt-us* had only the sense 'separate, distinct', as pa. pple. of *discernĕre*, whence the corresponding mod.F. sense of *discret*, and Eng. DISCRETE. The late L. sense, which alone came down in popular use in Romanic, seems to have been deduced from the cognate sb. *discrētiōn-em*, originally the action of separating, distinguishing, or discerning, and then the faculty of discernment; hence the adjective may have taken the sense 'possessed of discernment'.

In Eng., *discrete* was the prevalent spelling in all senses until late in the 16th c., when on the analogy of native or early-adopted words in *ee* from ME. close *ē*, as *feet*, *sweet*, *beet*), the spelling *discreet* (occasional from 1400) became established in the popular sense, leaving *discrete* for the scholastic and technical sense in which the kinship to L. *discrētus* is more obvious: see DISCRETE. Shakspere (1st Folio) has always *discreet*.]

A. *adj.*

1. Showing discernment or judgement in the guidance of one's own speech and action; judicious, prudent, circumspect, cautious; often *esp.* that can be silent when speech would be inconvenient. **a.** Of persons.

1340 [implied in DISCREETLY]. *c* **1386** CHAUCER *Doctor's T.* 48 (Ellesm.) Discreet she was in answeryng alway [so *Heng.*; *Harl.* & *Corp.* discret, 3 *MSS.* discrete]. **1388** WYCLIF *Ecclus.* xxxi. 19 Vse thou as a discreet and temperat man these thingis. *c* **1440** *Gesta Rom.* i. 4 The clerke..is a discrete confessour. **1500-20** DUNBAR *Poems* lxxxii. 66 Gar ȝour merchandis be discreit, That na extortiounes be. **1534** TINDALE *Titus* ii. 5 To be discrete [so CRANMER & *Geneva*; **1611** discreet], chast, huswyfly. **1569** J. ROGERS *Gl. Godly Love* 180 A wife ought to be discret. **1579** LYLY *Euphues* (Arb.) 145 To be silent and discreete in companye..is most requisite for a young man. **1598** FLORIO, *Discreto*, discreet. **1644** MILTON *Jdgm. Bucer* (1851) 332 We must ever beware, lest..we make our selvs wiser and discreeter then God. **1660** F. BROOKE tr. *Le Blanc's Trav.* 251 His wife being very reserv'd and discreet in her husbands presence, but in his absence more free and jolly. **1733** POPE *Hor. Sat.* II. i. 69 Satire's my weapon, but I'm too discreet To run a muck, and tilt at all I meet. **1832** W. IRVING *Alhambra* II. 111 You are a discreet man, and I make no doubt can keep a secret: but you have a wife. **1839** THIRLWALL *Greece.* VI. 33 A well-meaning and zealous officer, but not very discreet or scrupulous.

b. Of speech, action, and the like.

c **1374** CHAUCER *Troylus* III. 894 (943) So wyrcheth now in so discret a wyse, That I honour may haue and he plesaunce. **1393** LANGL. *P. Pl.* C. VI. 84 Preyers of a parfyt man and penaunce discret. **1483** CAXTON *Gold. Leg.* 217/1 She aroos up with a glad visage a dyscrete tongue and wel spekyng. **1533** ELYOT *Cast. Helthe* II. xix. (1539) 346 There is neyther meate nor drynke, in the use wherof ought to be a more discrete moderation, than in wyne. **1601** SHAKS. *Twel. N.* IV. iii. 19 A smooth, discreet, and stable bearing. **1608** BP. HALL *Char. Virtues & V.* 47 Not by flattery, but by discreet secrecie. **1667** MILTON *P.L.* VIII. 550 What she wills to do or say Seems wisest, virtuousest, discreetest, best. **1791** COWPER *Iliad* XIII. 562 At length as his discreeter course, he chose To seek Æneas. **1883** WILLS *Mod. Persia* 48 We maintained a discreet silence.

2. In *Sc.* applied more to behaviour towards others; hence, well-spoken, well-behaved, civil, polite, courteous; 'not rude, not doing anything inconsistent with delicacy towards a female' (Jam.).

[**1727-46** THOMSON *Summer* 1370 Dear youth!..By fortune too much favoured, but by love, Alas! not favoured less, be still as now Discreet.] **1782** SIR J. SINCLAIR *Observ. Scot. Dial.* 100 (Jam.) He is a very discreet (civil) man, it is true, but his brother has more discretion (civility). **1812** A. FULLER *Let.* in *Life C. Anderson* vii. (1854) 198 You are what your countrymen call 'a discreet man'. **18..** *Blackw. Mag.* (O.), I canna say I think it vera discreet o' you to keep pushing in before me in that way. **1860** RAMSAY *Remin.* Ser. I. (ed. 7) 105 *Discreet*..civil, kind, attentive.

†**3.** Rare 16th c. spelling of DISCRETE, q.v.

†**B.** as *adv.* = DISCREETLY. *Obs.*

1586 A. DAY *Eng. Secretary* II. (1625) 101 Best advised, discreetest governed, and worthiest.

†**C.** *sb.* A discreet person; a sage counsellor; a confidential adviser: applied to ecclesiastics; cf. DISCRETION 8. *Obs.*

1528 ROY *Rede me* (Arb.) 90 Wardens, discretes, and ministers, And wother offices of prelacy. **1533** MORE *Apol.* xxii. Wks. 882/2 A great some remaining after al the spirituall folke sufficiently prouided for, then had it bene good that he hadde yet farther deuysed, how it would please him that his discretes should order the remanaunt.

†**di'screetfully**, *adv. Obs.* = next.

1737 L. CLARKE *Hist. Bible* (1740) I. VI. 279 Hushai answered him discreetfully enough.

discreetly (dɪ'skriːtlɪ), *adv.* [f. DISCREET + -LY[2].] In a discreet manner; with discretion; prudently; with self-regarding prudence.

c **1340** HAMPOLE *Prose Tr.* 25 Wysely and discretely thei departed hir levynge in two. *c* **1380** WYCLIF *Sel. Wks.* III. 170 Crist askes two þinges of þin almes, þat þou do it in hys name, and also discretly. **1494** FABYAN *Chron.* I. vi. 12 Hauynge possession of the sayd Ile, Wele and discretly she ruled it. **1526-34** TINDALE *Mark* xii. 34 Iesus sawe that he answered discretly. **1596** SHAKS. *Tam. Shr.* I. i. 247 Vse your manners discreetly in all kinds of companies. **1664** EVELYN *Kal. Hort.* (1729) 201 Flowers of that class should be discreetly prun'd, where they mat too thick. **1775** JOHNSON *Tax. no Tyr.* 79, I could wish it more discreetly uttered. **1871** MORLEY *Voltaire* (1886) 7 He never counted truth a treasure to be discreetly hidden in a napkin. **1891** E. PEACOCK *N. Brendon* I. 32 Ellen remained discreetly silent.

discreetness (dɪ'skriːtnɪs). [f. as prec. + -NESS.] The quality of being discreet; discretion.

1530 PALSGR. 214/1 Discretenesse, *discretion.* **1647** H. MORE *Song of Soul* II. iii. III. lviii. (R.) Patience, discreetnesse, and benignitie..These be the lovely playmates of pure veritie. **1863** KINGLAKE *Crimea* II. 150 They had relied upon the mature judgment and the supposed discreetness of Lord Raglan. **1865** LEWES in *Fortn. Rev.* II. 699 We detect..the sensitive discreetness of the style.

†**di'screeve**, *v. Obs. rare.* App. a form of DESCRIVE, in its erroneous use (¶4) for *descry*, and so = To disclose, discover.

a **1765** *Ballad*, '*Sir Cawline*' iii. in Child *Ballads* (1885) III. No. 61. 58/1 Nothing durst hee say To discreeue his councell to noe man. —— '*Christopher White*' ii. *Ibid.* IV. No. 108. 439/1 Loth I was her councell to discreene [?-eeue].

discrepance ('dɪskrɪpəns, dɪ'skrɛpəns). [a. OF. *discrepance* (Godef.), ad. L. *discrepāntia* discordance, dissimilarity, f. *discrepāre* not to harmonize, to differ: see DISCREPANT.]

1. The fact of being discrepant; want of agreement or harmony; disagreement, difference.

c **1425** WYNTOUN *Cron.* II. x. 45, I fynd sic discrepance That I am noucht of sufficiance For to gare þame all accorde. **1460** CAPGRAVE *Chron.* 54 There was no discrepauns in sentens, ne variauns in wordes. **1563-87** FOXE *A. & M.* (1596) 3/1 We..will search out what discrepance is between them. **1640** R. BAILLIE *Canterb. Self-convict.* Postscr. 14 Betwixt us and our Prince there is no discrepance. **1804** *Edin. Rev.* V. 66 The only instance of discrepance we have remarked. **1881** *Nature* XXIV. 387 The authors are unable to discover the cause of this discrepance.

†**2.** Distinction, difference. *Obs.*

1531 ELYOT *Gov.* II. iii, Ther hath bene euer a discrepance in vesture of youthe and age. *a* **1555** LATIMER *Serm. & Rem.* (1845) 337 There is a great discrepance between certain knowledge and clear knowledge. **1572** BOSSEWELL *Armorie* 10 Almightie God..euen in the heauens hathe made a discrepance of his heauenly Spirites, giuinge them seuerall names, as Ensignes of honour. *c* **1611** CHAPMAN *Iliad* XI. 442 The discrepance He made in death betwixt the hosts.

†**3.** Variation, change (of action). *Obs. rare.*

c **1560** A. SCOTT *Poems* (E.E.T.S.) 35 Continewance in Cupeidis dance, Bot discrepance, withowt remeid.

discrepancy (dɪ'skrɛpənsɪ, 'dɪskrɪpənsɪ). [f. as prec. + -ANCY.] The quality of being discrepant; want of agreement; variance, difference, disagreement.

1623 COCKERAM, *Discrepancie*, disagreeing, difference. **1625** BP. MOUNTAGU *App. Cæsar* 147 There is..discrepancie of opinion among Divines both old and new. **1748** J. GEDDES *Composition of Antients* 13 Who again is not offended with discrepancy and discord? **1837** WHEWELL *Hist. Induct. Sc.* (1857) II. 186 Their discrepancy as to quantity was considerable. **1868** FREEMAN *Norm. Conq.* (1876) II. App. 617 There is little or no discrepancy as to the facts.

b. with *a* and *pl.* An instance of this; a difference, an inconsistency.

1627-77 FELTHAM *Resolves* II. xlvii. (R.) It would be evinced from these two seeming discrepancies. **1794** PALEY *Evid.* I. ix. §6. (1817) 249 Eusebius..wrote expressly upon the discrepancies observable in the Gospels. **1855** H. SPENCER *Princ. Psychol.* (1872) I. IV. ii. 410 Discrepancies between thoughts and facts. **1875** JOWETT *Plato* (ed. 2) IV. 515 Some discrepancies may be observed between the mythology of the Politicus and the Timaeus.

discrepant ('dɪskrɪpənt, dɪ'skrɛpənt), *a.* and *sb.* Also 6 discripant, discrepante. [ad. L. *discrepānt-em*, pr. pple. of *discrepāre* to differ, lit. to sound discordantly, f. DIS- 1 + *crepāre* to make a noise, creak.] A. *adj.*

1. Exhibiting difference, dissimilarity or want of harmony; different, discordant, inharmonious, inconsistent. Const. *from*, †*to*.

1524 *St. Papers Hen. VIII*, IV. 100 It were ferre discrepant from the Kinges honour to have the treaty of peax with Scotland concluded..by Lieutenauntes. **1531** ELYOT *Gov.* I. xxv, Wherin he is moste discrepant from brute beastes. *c* **1555** HARPSFIELD *Divorce Hen. VIII* (1878) 236 This marriage..was much more discrepant to the said laws. **1678** CUDWORTH *Intell. Syst.* 478 The Vulgar Theology of the Pagans..was oftentimes very discrepant from the Natural and True Theology. *a* **1734** NORTH *Exam.* III. vii. §49 (1740) 539 The King's Notions and his were very discrepant. **1846** GROTE *Greece* I. xviii. II. 11 A desire..to blend together..two discrepant legends. **1866** ROGERS *Agric. & Prices* I. xiii. 196 Since the price is so discrepant from that in the neighbourhood of Oxford.

†**2.** Apart or separate in space. *Obs. rare.*

1592 R. D. *Hypnerotomachia* 49 b The Tilastrelles were discrepant fowre paces one from another. *a* **1649** DRUMM. OF HAWTH. *Poems* Wks. (1711) 13/1 Further discrepant than heaven and ground. **1818** KEATS *Endym.* III. 343 Sea-mew's plaintive cry Plaining discrepant between sea and sky.

†**B.** *sb.* One who disagrees; a dissentient. *Obs.*

1647 JER. TAYLOR *Lib. Proph.* vii. 141 None could have triumph'd so openly over all discrepants as this. *Ibid.* xvi. 216 If you persecute hereticks or discrepants, they unite themselves as to a common defence.

Hence **discrepantly** *adv.*, with discrepancy; in contrary ways.

1603 FLORIO *Montaigne* III. ix. (1632) 562, I am..precisely vowed..to speake confusedly, to speak discrepantly.

discrepate ('dɪskrɪpeɪt), *v. rare.* [f. L. *discrepāt-*, ppl. stem of *discrepāre* to differ: see prec.]

†**1.** *intr.* To differ, be discrepant. *Obs. rare.*

1623 in COCKERAM [*printed* Discrepitate]. **1657** TOMLINSON *Renou's Disp.* 331 Some make three varieties..which seem solely to discrepate in magnitude.

2. a. *trans.* To distinguish. **b.** *intr.* To discriminate or make a distinction.

1846 L. HUNT *Stories Ital. Poets* in Longf. *Dante* (Rtldg.) 472 To discrepate Samson from Hercules. **1894** G. R. MATHER *Two great Scotsmen* 2 It would be akin to sacrilege for us to discrepate between the two brothers.

discrepation (dɪskrɪ'peɪʃən). *rare.* [n. of action f. prec.] †**a.** Difference. *Obs.* **b.** Discrimination.

1616 R. C. *Times Whistle, etc.* (1871) 151 Twixt his first coming and his latter one There will be found much discrepation. **1847** L. HUNT *Men, Women, & B.* II. i. 4 Pope's own discrepation of immorality from debauchery.

discrese, -cresse, obs. var. DECREASE.

discrested: see DIS- 7 a.

discrete (dɪ'skriːt), *a.* (*sb.*) Also 6 discreet. [ad. L. *discrēt-us* 'separate, distinct', pa. pple. of *discernĕre* to separate, divide, DISCERN: cf. later sense of F. *discret*, *discrète* 'divided, separate'.

In the sense of cl. L. *discrētus*, *discrete* was used by Trevisa (translating from L.), but app. was not in general use till late in 16th c. But in another sense, 'discerning, prudent' (derived through French), *discret*, *discrete* was well-known in popular use from the 14th c.; this, even in late ME., was occasionally spelt *discreet*, which spelling was appropriated to it about the time that *discrete* in the L. sense began to be common; so that thenceforth *discrete* and *discreet* were differentiated in spelling as well as in meaning: see DISCREET. Before this, while *discrete* was the prevalent form for the later *discreet*, it is only rarely (see 1 β below) that *discreet* appears for the present *discrete*.]

A. *adj.*

1. a. Separate, detached from others, individually distinct. Opposed to *continuous*.

1398 TREVISA *Barth. De P.R.* XIX. cxvi. (1495) 919 One is the begynnynge of alle thynges that is contynual and dyscrete. **1570** DEE *Math. Pref.* 13 Of distinct and discrete Vnits. **1594** BLUNDEVIL *Exerc.* III. I. xxxi. (ed. 7) 339 Of which Arkes some are called continuall, and some discrete or divided. *Ibid.*, That Arke is called discrete or broken, which doth not take his beginning from the first point of Aries. **1634** PEACHAM *Gentl. Exerc.* III. 137 Raine or water..being divided by the cold ayre, in the falling downe, into discreet parts. **1775** HARRIS *Philos. Arrangem.* (1841) 308 The motion of all animals..by being alternate, is of the discrete kind. **1851** NICHOL *Archit. Heav.* 47 Any telescope capable of resolving these various masses into discrete stars. **1883** A. BARRATT *Phys. Metempiric* 59 To hold together, and keep discrete, simultaneous phenomena.

†*β.* spelt *discreet.*

1590 SPENSER *F.Q.* II. xii. 71 The waters fall with difference discreet, Now soft, now loud, unto the wind did call.

†**b.** *Music.* Applied to tones separated by fixed or obvious steps or intervals of pitch, as the notes of a piano; also to a movement of the voice from one pitch to another, as distinguished from a concrete movement or slide. Cf. CONCRETE 1 b.

1864 WEBSTER cites RUSH.

c. *Pathol.* Separate, not coalescent or confluent: applied to stains, spots, or pustules, when scattered separately from each other over a surface, as in ***discrete small-pox*** [F. *variole discrète*].

1854-67 C. A. HARRIS *Dict. Med. Terminol.* 218. **1882** CARPENTER in *19th Cent.* Apr. 531 The discrete, 'distinct', or 'benign' form being by no means a severe disease, even among the unvaccinated. **1893** *Daily News* 4 Mar. 5/4 A woman..whose children had been removed for discrete small-pox.

d. *Logic.* Individually distinct, but not different in kind.

1837-8 SIR W. HAMILTON *Logic* xi. (1866) I. 209 In so far as Conspecies are considered to be different but not contradictory, they are properly called Discrete or Disjunct

Notions. *Ibid.* xii.(1860) I. 224 Notions co-ordinated in the quantity or whole of extension..are only relatively different (or diverse); and in logical language are properly called *Disjunct* or *Discrete Notions.* **1864** Bowen *Logic* iv. 66.

e. ***discrete degrees***: applied by Swedenborg to the various degrees or levels of spiritual existence, conceived as so distinct and separate from each other, as to render it impossible for any subject to pass out of that one for which he is constituted.

1788 tr. *Swedenborg's Wisd. Angels* III. §236 In every Man from his Birth there are three Degrees of Altitude, or discrete Degrees, one above or within another. **1856** Grindon *Life* (1863) 319 Where things are differentiated by a discrete degree, the commencement of the new one is..on a distinct and higher level.

2. a. Consisting of distinct or individual parts; discontinuous.

discrete quantity, quantity composed of distinct units, as the rational numbers; number. Distinguished from *continuous quantity* = magnitude.

1570 Billingsley *Euclid* II. i. 62 Two contrary kynds of quantity, quantity discrete or number, and quantity continual or magnitude. **1687** H. More *Answ. Psychop.* (1689) 123 Inseperability, continued Amplitude, belongs to Spirits as well as discrete Quantity. **1785** Reid *Int. Powers* III. iii. 311 Duration and extension are not discrete, but continued quantity. *Ibid.* 342 Number is called discrete quantity, because it is compounded of units. **1837–9** Hallam *Hist. Lit.* II. viii. II. 322 *note*, They were dealing with continuous or geometrical, not merely with descrete or arithmetical quantity. **1876** H. Spencer *Princ. Sociol.* (1877) I. 475 The parts of an animal form a concrete whole; but the parts of a society form a whole that is discrete. **1893** Forsyth *Th. Functions* 584 If there be no infinitesimal substitution, then the group is said to be *discontinuous*, or *discrete*. **1893** Harkness & Morley *Th. Functions* 50 To Hankel we owe the idea of a discrete mass of points.

b. Belonging to, pertaining to, or dealing with, distinct or disconnected parts.

discrete proportion = discontinued proportion.

1660 R. Coke *Justice Vind.* 23 All Geometrical proportion is either discrete, or continued. Discrete is, when the *similitudo rationum* is only between the 1. and the 2. and the 3. and 4. term. **1706** Phillips (ed. Kersey), *Discrete* or *Disjunct Proportion.* **1856** Dove *Logic Chr. Faith* 422 *note*, Scepticism is discrete and proceeds in detail.

†**3.** *Gram.* & *Logic.* Of conjunctions: adversative. Of propositions: discretive. Applied also to the two members of such a proposition, separated by the adversative conjunction. *Obs.*

1628 T. Spencer *Logick* 237 That Axiome is discrete, that hath a discrete Coniunction for the band thereof. *Ibid.* 239 The coniunction which tyes the parts together, is called discrete: and in this place it imports no more but a thing that keepes two asunder, for the present. *a* **1638** Mede *Apost. latter Times* i. Wks. 1672 III. 623 The Words..of my Text [Nevertheless, the Spirit, etc. *1 Tim.* iv. 1] depend upon the last of the former Chapter, as the second part of a Discrete proposition. **1654** Z. Coke *Logick* (1657) 119 A discrete sentence, is, which hath a discrete conjunction; as, *although, yet, notwithstanding*, etc. **1664** H. More *Myst. Iniq.* Apol. 538[It will] run in this form of a Discrete Axiome, I will have you wait on me at such a meeting, though your cloaths be old or out of the mode.

4. *Metaph.* Not concrete; detached from the material, abstract.

1854 *Fraser's Mag.* L. 343 The mental march from concrete or real notions to discrete or abstract truths. **1862** H. Spencer *First Princ.* (1870) 27 This formation of symbolic Conceptions, which inevitably arises as we pass from small and concrete objects, to large and to discrete ones.

B. *sb.* A separate part.

1890 J. H. Stirling *Gifford Lect.* xviii. 353 Break it up into an endless number of points..an endless number of discretes. **1967** *Electronics* 6 Mar. 116 Integrated circuits will be turning up routinely in new products throughout 1967. The big switch from discretes is on.

discrete, early form of discreet.

†**di'screte**, *v. Obs.* [f. L. *discrēt-* ppl. stem of *discernĕre* to separate: see discern.] *trans.* To divide into discrete or distinct parts; to separate distinctly, dissever.

1646 Sir T. Browne *Pseud. Ep.* II. i. 55 The reason thereof is its continuity, as..its body is left imporous and not discreted by atomicall terminations. **1656** Blount *Glossogr.*, *Discreted*, severed, parted, discerned. **1857–8** Sears *Athan.* vii. 316 This essential dualism discretes for ever the two worlds of spirit and matter.

discretely (dɪˈskriːtlɪ), *adv. rare.* [f. discrete *a.* + -ly².] In a discrete manner; separately.

1706 Phillips (ed. Kersey), s.v. *Discrete proportion*, These Numbers are proportional; but 'tis only discretely [*mispr.* directly] or disjunctly. **1727–51** Chambers *Cycl.* s.v. *Discrete.* **1872** Proctor *Ess. Astron.* xxvii. 338 The same telescope shows the stars projected discretely on a perfectly black background.

discreteness (dɪˈskriːtnɪs). [f. as prec. + -ness.] The quality of being discrete: **a.** Discontinuity. **b.** The consisting of many individual parts.

1862 H. Spencer *First Princ.* I. ii. §9 (1875) 29 When the size, complexity, or discreteness of the object conceived becomes very great, only a small portion of its attributes can be thought of at once. **1877** E. Caird *Philos. Kant* II. xvii. 605 We bring together the two moments of unity and diversity..continuity and discreteness. **1893** P. S. Moxon in Barrow *World's Parl. Relig.* I. 467 The whole significance of man's existence lies ultimately in its discreteness—in the evolution and persistence of the self-conscious ego.

discretion (dɪˈskrɛʃən). Forms: 4–6 discrecion, 4– discretion; also 4 discrescioun, dyscrecyun, -ioun, 4–5 discression(e, 4–6 -cretioune, 5 dis-, dyscrecioun, -yone, -youn, -crescion, -cressioun, -cretyown, 6 discrecyon, -tione, -creation, dyscreccion, -cretion. [a. OF. *des- discrecion* distinction, discernment (It. *discrezione*, Sp. *discrecion*) ad. L. *discrētiōn-em* separation, distinction, and later, discernment, n. of action from *discernĕre* (ppl. stem *discrēt-*) to separate, divide, discern.]

I. [From ancient Latin sense of *discrētio*.]

1. The action of separating or distinguishing, or condition of being distinguished or disjunct; separation, disjunction, distinction.

This is perhaps the meaning in quot. 1340; otherwise this sense is found only since end of 16th c.: cf. discrete.

[*c* **1340** Hampole *Prose Tr.* 12 Thynkynge of heuen with discrecyone of all mene dedes.] **1590** R. Bruce *Sermons*, Without discretion of His substance fra His graces. **1607** Topsell *Serpents* (1658) 747 It is some question among the learned, whether there be any discretion of sex. **1614** Jackson *Creed* III. 197 The same rule..might..serue for certaine discretion of true Prophets from false. **1677** Gale *Crt. Gentiles* II. IV. 82 Al the notions of Virtue or Sanctitie ..import Discretion, Separation, Singularitie, Preeminence. **1890** J. H. Stirling *Gifford Lect.* xviii. 351 Time and space are a concrete, of which the one is the discretion and the other the continuity. **1892** E. Caird *Ess. Lit. & Philos.* II. 522 Mind is a pure self-determined unity ..which has no discretion of parts or capacity of division or determination from without.

II. [In late Latin sense of *discrētio*.]

†**2.** The action of discerning or judging; judgement; decision, discrimination. *Obs.* (exc. as passing into 4, or the phrases in 5.)

c **1374** Chaucer *Boeth.* III. pr. x. 93 Take now þus þe discressioun [*Camb. MS.* descression] of þis questioun, quod she. *c* **1400** *Lanfranc's Cirurg.* 283 Sumtyme a man mai not ȝeue a discrecioun of blood fro urine. *c* **1460** Fortescue *Abs. & Lim. Mon.* xx, Considryng that they lak it bi the discrecioun of þe kynges counseil. **1463** *Bury Wills* (Camden) 16 By the discrecion of my executours. **1547–8** *Ordre of Commvnion* 17 Twoo peces, at the least, or more by the discrecion of the minister. **1568** Mary Q. Scots in Ellis *Orig. Lett.* Ser. I. II. 253 Y refer all to your discretion. **1842** C. Whitehead *R. Savage* (1845) I. viii. 90 She put it to Myte's discretion whether he would continue to harbour a young knave.

†**3.** The faculty of discerning; discernment. *Obs.*

1380 *Lay Folks Catech.* (Lamb. MS.) 620 Ofte þou hast brokyn godys hestys sytthe þou haddyst dyscrecioun of good and euyl. **1382** Wyclif *1 Cor.* xii. 10 To another [is ȝouun] discressioun, or verrey knowynge, of spiritis. **1526** *Pilgr. Perf.* (W. de W. 1531) 123 b, The gyfte..called discrecyon, or discernynge of spirytes is but in fewe persones. **1563** J. Davidson *Confut. Kennedy* in *Wodr. Soc. Misc.* (1844) I. 253 Discretione betwix the rycht understanding of thaim fra the wrang. **1651** Hobbes *Leviath.* I. viii. 33 The Discretion of times, places, and persons necessary to a good Fancy.

4. Liberty or power of deciding, or of acting according to one's own judgement or as one thinks fit; uncontrolled power of disposal.

1399 *Rolls of Parlt.* III. 451/2 Mercy and grace of the Kyng as it longes to hym..in his owene discretion. **1432** *Paston Lett.* No. 18 I. 32 Where he shal have eny persone in his discrecion suspect of mysgovernance. **1581** Pettie *Guazzo's Civ. Conv.* III. (1586) 153 Not to put himselfe to the discretion of his servants, for the ordering of his house. **1693** *Mem. Cnt. Teckely* III. 73 If Transilvania were left to the Discretion of the Turks [etc.]. **1724** Swift *Drapier's Lett.*, *Let. to Harding* 4 Aug., He leaves it to our discretion. **1780** Burke *Econ. Reform* Wks. III. 334 If a discretion, wholly arbitrary, can be exercised over the civil list revenue ..the plan of reformation will still be left very imperfect. **1812–16** J. Smith *Panorama Sc. & Art* I. 386 This practice ..leaves to the discretion of the workman the determination of the very matter in which he is most apt to err. **1849** Macaulay *Hist. Eng.* I. 185 As to the form of worship, a large discretion was left to the clergy. **1874** Morley *Compromise* (1886) 182 We may all write what we please, because it is in the discretion of the rest of the world whether they will hearken or not.

b. *Law.* The power of a court of justice, or person acting in a judicial capacity, to decide, within the limits allowed by positive rules of law, as to the punishment to be awarded or remedy to be applied, or in civil causes how the costs shall be borne, and generally to regulate matters of procedure and administration.

In English-speaking countries a criminal judge dealing with offences not capital has generally a considerable discretion as to the punishment.

[**1292** Britton I. xvi. §7 Et si autrefoix de mauvesté soint atteyntz, adunc soit en la descrecioun des justices de juger les a la mort, ou de fere couper le autre oraille.] **1467** *Ordin. Worcester* in *Eng. Gilds* (1870) 379 Vppon the peyne of xxs. or more, after the discression of the Bailey and Aldermen of the seid cite. *a* **1626** Bacon *Max. & Uses Com. Law* (1636) 21 The judges may set a fine upon him at their pleasure and discretions. **1890** Ld. Esher in *Law Times Rep.* LXIII. 734/2 The judge..should not treat it as a matter within his discretion whether he will order the witness to answer or not. **1891** *Law Rep.* Weekly Notes 72/2 That the costs of references..should be in the discretion of the arbitrators. **1892** Sir. E. E. Kay in *Law Times Rep.* LXVII. 151/2 It is a matter of discretion whether the judge should give that leave to defend, and if he does, what terms he will impose.

5. Phrases. **a.** ***at the discretion of***, according to the discernment or judgement of, according as (he) thinks fit or pleases; ***at discretion***, at one's own sense of fitness, mere good pleasure, or choice; as one thinks fit, chooses, or pleases. **b.** ***to surrender, yield***, etc., ***at discretion***, formerly ***to the enemy's discretion, on, upon discretion***, i.e. to be disposed of as he thinks fit; at his disposal, at his mercy; unconditionally.

1577 Hanmer *Anc. Eccl. Hist.* (1619) 389 Distribute them at thy discretion among the poore. **1630** *R. Johnson's Kingd. & Commw.* 525 Their office is to place and displace Churchmen at discretion. **1700** S. L. tr. *Fryke's Voy. E. Ind.* 218 One Vessel of Beer..free for any body to go to, and Drink at Discretion. *Ibid.* 294 This I leave the Reader to believe at Discretion. **1706** Phillips (ed. Kersey) s.v., To Live at Discretion (a Military Phrase) to have free Quarters. **1724** De Foe *Mem. Cavalier* (1840) 189 We reckoned ourselves in an enemy's country, and had lived a little at large, or at discretion, as it is called abroad. **1834** *W. Ind. Sketch Bk.* II. 4 Admitting at discretion as much light and air as may be agreeable. **1863** Fr. A. Kemble *Resid. in Georgia* 43 Power to inflict three dozen lashes at his own discretion.

1548 Hall *Chron., Hen. VI*, 85 All the garrison yelded them symply to his mercy and discrecion. **1628** Hobbes *Thucyd.* (1822) 110 Conceiving that they might have gotten the city to discretion. **1632** Massinger *Maid of Hon.* II. i. (Rtldg.) 191/1 He..exacts..the goods and lives Of all within the walls, and of all sexes, To be at his discretion. **1632** J. Hayward tr. *Biondi's Eromena* 151 [This] gave occasion to such as remained to yeeld themselves to the enemies discretion. **1659** B. Harris *Parival's Iron Age* 224 General Wranghel..took..Paderborn at discretion. **1684** *Lond. Gaz.* No. 1953/3 They write from Duseldorp..that Buda was Surrendred on discretion. **1691** Luttrell *Brief Rel.* (1857) II. 272 The garison surrendring upon discretion. **1702** *Lond. Gaz.* No. 3830/2 All the Country..will lie at our Discretion. **1732** *Gentl. Instr.* 154 (D.) If she stays to receive the attack, she is in danger of being at discretion. **1758** Jortin *Erasm.* I. 592 Roterdam was some days at the discretion of these rioters. **1878** Bosw. Smith *Carthage* 83 The inhabitants surrendered at discretion, but they had to undergo all the horrors of a place taken by storm.

III. [Cf. discreet.]

6. Ability to discern or distinguish what is right, befitting, or advisable, esp. as regards one's own conduct or action; the quality of being discreet; discernment; prudence, sagacity, circumspection, sound judgement.

1303 R. Brunne *Handl. Synne* 10162 Dyscrecyun a ryȝt wyt ys, On boþe partys ryȝtly to ges. **1340** *Ayenb.* 155 Hit be-houeþ hyealde riȝtuolnesse and discrecion. *c* **1477** Caxton *Jason* 4 b, Thou art not yet poureyed of discrecion for to gouerne thy Royaume. **1548** Hall *Chron., Hen. VI*, 97 b, Eche of them, shal as farfurth as their connynges and discrecions suffisen, truly..advise the kyng. **1596** Shaks. *1 Hen. IV*, v. iv. 121 The better part of Valour is Discretion. **1597–8** Bacon *Ess.*, *Discourse* (Arb.) 20 Discretion of Speech is more than Eloquence. **1682** Glanius *Voy. Bengala* 149 This King..derided his discretion. **1720** Swift *Fates of Clergymen*, Discretion, a species of lower prudence. **1796** Jane Austen *Sense & Sens.* (1849) 53 Do you not now begin to doubt the discretion of your own conduct? **1849** Ruskin *Sev. Lamps* iv. §21. 110 That portion of temper and discretion which are necessary to the contemplation of beauty.

b. ***age of, years of, discretion***: the time of life at which a person is presumed to be capable of exercising discretion or prudence; in *Eng. Law* the age of fourteen.

1395 *E.E. Wills* 5 If Thomas here sone forsayd dyeth or he haue age of discrecioun. **1447** Bokenham *Seyntys* (Roxb.) 47 Whan she to ȝeris of dyscrescyon Was comyn aftyr ther lawes guyse..Wedded she was. **1545** Brinklow *Compl.* v. (1874) 18 The partyes neuer fauor the one the other after thei come to discrecyon. **1574** tr. *Littleton's Tenures* 23 a, The age of discretion is saide the age of xiiii. yeares. **1605** Rowlands *Hell's Broke Loose* 24 Wee'le have no Babes to be Baptized, Vntill they come to yeeres of ripe discretion. **1773** Goldsm. *Stoops to Conq.* I. i, He's not come to years of discretion yet. **1848** Wharton *Law Dict.* 21/1 A male..at fourteen is at years of discretion, so far at least that he may enter into a binding marriage.

7. *Sc.* Propriety of behaviour, esp. of female conduct, as opposed to lightness or coquetry; civility, courtesy to a guest, etc. (Jam.)

1782 [see discreet *a.* 2].

†**8.** An honorary title formerly frequently applied to bishops, and sometimes to noblemen (Du Cange). Cf. *your worship, your honour.*

1426 *Surtees Misc.* (1890) 10 If it lyke vn to your wirshipfull and wyse discrecion. **1523** Ld. Berners *Froiss.* I. ccccix. 712 Right dear and puissaunt lordes: to your right noble discressyons, please it you to known, that we haue receyued right amiably the letters to vs sent. *a* **1555** Latimer *Serm. & Rem.* (1845) 296 Your discretion, therefore, will take this matter into consideration.

†**b.** A fanciful term for a 'company' of priests.

1486 *Bk. St. Albans* F vij a, A Discrecion of Prestis.

†**di'scretionable**, *a. Obs. rare.* [f. prec. + -able.] Subject to or decided by discretion.

1799 G. Smith *Laboratory* II. 437 Take a discretionable quantity of garlic.

discretional (dɪˈskrɛʃənəl), *a.* [as prec. + -al¹.]

1. Of or pertaining to discretion; discretionary.

1657 *Burton's Diary* (1828) II. 168 There is a difference of opinion about those writs. Some will have them but discretional. **1683** Hickes *Case Inf. Bapt.* 79 The Gospel indulging a discretional Latitude in both Cases. *a* **1715** Burnet *Own Time* (1766) I. 258 Without leaving any discretional power with the king. **1770–4** A. Hunter *Georg. Ess.* (1803) I. 431 The discretional use of the plough, roller, and harrows. *a* **1859** De Quincey *Wks.* XIV. 176 Conversation suffers from the want of some discretional power, lodged in an individual for controlling its movements.

†**2.** Surrendered at discretion. *Obs.*

1777 J. WILKINSON in Sparks *Corr. Amer. Rev.* (1853) II. 14 We have made, during the Campaign, upwards of two thousand discretional prisoners.

†**3.** Characterized by discretion; discreet. *Obs.*

1785 MRS. A. M. BENNETT *Juvenile Indiscretions* (1786) IV. 148 Not yet arrived at that discretional time of life.

di'scretionally, *adv.* [f. prec. + -LY².] In a manner or degree decided by discretion; at discretion.

1754 RICHARDSON *Grandison* (1781) VI. xviii. 87, I always mean to include my dear Lady L... Any-body else, but discretionally. **1766** ENTICK *London* I. 437 The wealthier sort of people were assessed discretionally by the commissioners. **1837** DE QUINCEY *Revolt of Tartars* Wks. 1862 IV. 118 Setting aside discretionally whatsoever should arise to disturb his plots.

di'scretionarily, *adv.* [f. next + -LY².] In a discretionary way; at discretion.

1683 *Vind. Case Green-Wax-Fines* 3 Officers may discretionarily tax, or add to the Suitors Costs. **1794** NELSON in Nicolas *Disp.* (1845) I. 436, I will discretionarily order them a little wine as an encouragement.

discretionary (dɪ'skrɛʃənərɪ), *a.* [f. DISCRETION + -ARY: cf. F. *discrétionnaire.*]

1. Pertaining to discretion; left to or exercised at discretion; limited or restrained only by discretion or judgement.

1698 ATTERBURY *Disc. Lady Cutts* 24 Amongst all her discretionary Rules, the chief was to seem to have none. **1726** AYLIFFE *Parergon* (J.), It is discretionary in the bishop to admit him to that order at what time he thinks fit. **1741** H. WALPOLE *Lett. H. Mann* (1834) I. xii. 34 He had discretionary powers to act as he should judge proper. **1827** HALLAM *Const. Hist.* (1876) I. v. 234 The privy council in general arrogated to itself a power of discretionary imprisonment. **1863** H. COX *Instit* I. vii. 71 The reference to the House of Lords is entirely discretionary in the Crown. **1960** *Life* 1 Feb. 53/1, 34 million families.. control most of the $84 billion 'discretionary income' (money left after necessary expenditures) in the country. **1961** *Times* 10 June 11/4 American sociologists have invented the term 'discretionary time' to cover the hours left over from eating, sleeping, and earning a living. **1965** HALL & HOWES *Church in Social Work* 285 In mid-1958 boys earned an average of £5 12s. and girls £5 6s., about £3 of which was available for discretionary spending.

†**2.** Characterized by discretion; discreet. *Obs.*

1712 STEELE *Spect.* No. 402. ¶2, I am never alone with my Mother, but she tells me Stories of the discretionary Part of the World. **1753** L. M. tr. *Du Boscq's Accomplish'd Woman* I. 28 All.. unprofitable without a discretionary Silence.

¶**3.** as *adv.* At discretion.

1751 ELIZA HEYWOOD *Betsy Thoughtless* III. 63 A small fortune, and that to be paid discretionary.

discretive (dɪ'skriːtɪv), *a.* and *sb.* [ad. L. *discrētīv-us* serving to distinguish (Priscian), f. *discrēt-* ppl. stem of *discernĕre* to distinguish, divide, DISCERN. Cf. OF. *discretif* (15th c. in Godef.).]

A. *adj.* **1.** = DISJUNCTIVE. **a.** *Gram.* and *Logic.*

discretive conjunction, proposition: see quots.; ***discretive distinction,*** a distinction expressing a difference in kind, as 'not a plant, but an animal'. Cf. DISCRETE *a.* 3.

1588 FRAUNCE *Lawiers Log.* II. v. 93 In absolute copulative and discretive axiomes, there is no ὑπόθεσις, no condition at all. *a* **1602** W. PERKINS *Cases Consc.* (1619) 240 The latter is coupled to the former by a discretiue coniunction. **1690** LOCKE *Hum. Und.* III. vii. 5 *But* is a Particle,.. and he that says it is a discretive Conjunction,.. thinks he has sufficiently explain'd it. **1753** S. SHUCKFORD *Creation & Fall Man* 43 It is not here a discretive Particle, disjoining and distinguishing two Parts of one Period; but it is illative. **1819** G. S. FABER *Dispensations* (1823) II. 389 The word *only*, as I have just observed, is no doubt discretive. **1891** WELTON *Logic* I. II. i. 192 *Discretive Propositions*, where two affirmative propositions are connected by an adversative conjunction.

b. *generally.*

1660 STANLEY *Hist. Philos.* IX. (1701) 432/2 He held that there are four Elements, Fire, Air, Water, Earth; and two principal powers, Amity and Discord; one unitive, the other discretive. **1836** I. TAYLOR *Phys. Th. Another Life* (1857) 59 Mind allied to matter.. thus lives.. by its own discretive act.

†**2.** Serving to distinguish or discriminate; distinctive; discriminative; diacritic. *Obs.*

1601 DEACON & WALKER *Spirits & Divels* To Rdr. 8 Not hauing vpon them some discretiue stampe or discerning censure. *a* **1631** DONNE *Serm. Gen.* i. 26 (1634) 33, I have a power to judge; a judiciarie, a discretive power, a power to discern between a naturall accident and a judgement of God. **1669** GALE *Crt. Gentiles* I. I. x. 51 A name is an instructive and discretive instrument of the essence. **1803** W. TAYLOR in *Monthly Mag.* XIV. 487 Such sub-division is neither discretive nor exhaustive. **1819** G. S. FABER *Dispensations* (1823) II. 388, *note*, Grounds on which the Socinians assume the title of *rational Christians* as a specifically discretive appellation.

†**B.** *sb.* **1.** A disjunctive conjunction or proposition. *Obs.*

1612 BRINSLEY *Pos. Parts* (1669) 48 Discretives, by which the parts are lightly Severed. **1650** R. HOLLINGWORTH *Exerc. Usurped Powers* 19 Joyning them together with the copulative (*and*) and not using the discretive (*or*). **1654** Z. COKE *Logick* (1657). 119 To the truth of a discretive is required the truth of both parts. **1725** WATTS *Logic* II. ii. §6 All compound propositions, except copulatives and discretives, are properly denied or contradicted when the negation affects their conjunctive particles.

†**2.** A discriminative phrase or concept. *Obs.*

1660 Z. CROFTON *St. Peters Bonds abide* 2 His universal discretive, 'All Episcopacy'.

di'scretively, *adv.* [f. prec. + -LY².] In a discretive manner; disjunctively; distinctively.

a **1638** MEDE *Daniel's Weeks* Wks. (1672) III. 701 The particle [*ki*] (Nehem. xiii. 6) seems not to be taken rationally for (*Quia*), but discretively for [*ki 'im*] (*Sed*, But). *a* **1654** BP. J. RICHARDSON *Observ. O. Test.* 237 (T.) The plural number being used discretively to note out and design one of many. **1836–7** SIR W. HAMILTON *Metaph.* xxxvii. (1870) II. 338 Reasoning is either from the whole to its parts; or from all the parts, discretively, to the whole they constitute collectively.

di'scretiveness. [f. as prec. + -NESS.] The quality or power of discriminating or discerning.

1844 G. S. FABER *Eight Diss. Mighty Deliv.* (1845) II. 344 Even in a common writer of ordinary discretiveness.

discretization (dɪˌskriːtaɪ'zeɪʃən, ˌdɪs-). [f. DISCRETE *a.* + -IZATION.] **a.** The process of making discrete; in *Math.*, (a) representation by, or approximation by means of, a discrete quantity or quantities. **b.** The state of being discrete. **c.** *attrib.*, as ***discretization error.***

1960 FORSYTHE & WASOW *Finite-Difference Methods for Partial Differential Equations* i. 54 *Discretization error* is a more descriptive designation for the quantity *v*, and we shall use it. *Ibid.* iii. 176 This process we call discretization, and in its general form it assumes nothing about whether the members of the set *S* are points, arcs.., or other entities. **1968** H. M. LIEBERSTEIN *Course Numerical Analysis* iv. 70 Ways of obtaining error bounds.. from good approximations of discretizations. **1971** *Nature* 13 Aug. 506/3 The second part of the book.. starts by examining a sample of thirty-one galaxies for evidence of discretization. **1972** *Science* 13 Oct. 157/1 Chief among these is truncation (discretization) error, caused by the coarseness of the grid. **1976** *Physics Bull.* Mar. 117/2 Note that at this point we have introduced a discretization of the time. **1979** Y. OVCHINNIKOV et al. in W. H. Banks *Adv. in Printing Sci. Technol.* viii. 120 Discretization and quantization of signals. **1980** [see DISCRETIZE *v.* below]. **1983** *Computerworld* 28 Nov. 96/5 The Differential Systems Simulator,.. containing spatial discretization routines for initial-value ordinary and partial differential equations. **1984** *Mech. Engin.* CVI. 88/1 This paper presents a quantitative assessment of mass discretization by utilizing exact analytical solution to the discrete problem of beam and bar vibrations.

Hence **di'scretize** *v. trans.*, to subject to discretization, to render discrete; **di'scretized** *ppl. a.*

1968 H. M. LIEBERSTEIN *Course Numerical Analysis* ix. 158 Partitioning (0, *l*) and (0, *T*) with equal meshes *h* and *k*, we discretize the problem by asking for values of *u* on the discrete set indicated. **1976** *Biometrika* LXIII. 444 The linear programming dual to problem I.. or, rather, the dual to the discretized version (7·1) and (7·3), is as follows. **1980** *Topic* (Imperial College, London) June 4/1 This work led to a more general study of duality concepts in discretized structural mechanics. **1980** R. BARTELS et al. tr. *Stoer & Bulirsch's Introd. Numerical Analysis* i. 1 Many approximating problems *P* are obtained by 'discretizing' the original problem *P*: definite integrals are approximated by finite sums, differential quotients by difference quotients, etc. In such cases, the approximation error is often referred to as discretization error.

†**di'scribe,** *v. Obs. nonce-wd.* [f. L. *di-, dis-* (DIS- 6) + *scrībĕre* to write, after *proscribe*, etc.: it does not in sense represent L. *discrībĕre* to apportion (by writing).] *trans.* To undo by a writing.

1647 WARD *Simp. Cobler* (1843) 59 If a King.. will circumscribe himself at Oxford, and proscribe or discribe his Parliament at Westminster.

discrier, obs. form of DESCRIER.

1580 SIDNEY *Arcadia* III. Wks. (1724) II. 792 The poor Shepherds.. who were the first discriers of these matters.

discriminability (dɪˌskrɪmɪnə'bɪlɪtɪ). [f. DISCRIMINABLE *a.* + -ILITY.]

1. The quality of being discriminable.

1901 E. B. TITCHENER *Exper. Psychol.* I. ii. 189 Clearness implies a maximal discriminability or separability from other processes. **1954** BROWN & LENNEBERG in Saporta & Bastian *Psycholinguistics* (1961) 489/2 A total of six numbers will express.. the discriminability of that color. **1965** *Times Lit. Suppl.* 25 Nov. 1082/2 Tarski's doubts about the effective discriminability of a class of logical truths. **1970** *Jrnl. Gen. Psychol.* Jan. 81 It was also predicted that increasing the discriminability of the items by incorporating an additional attribute into each item would enhance performance.

2. The capacity to discriminate; discriminative power.

1931 *Brit. Jrnl. Psychol.* XXII. 38 The ability.. to set up different responses to *A* and *A'*.. falls short of the limits of temporary discriminability.

di'scriminable, *a.* [f. L. *discrīminā-re* to DISCRIMINATE + -BLE.] Capable of being discriminated.

1730–6 in BAILEY (folio). **1813** W. TAYLOR *Eng. Synon.* (1856) vii, *Understanding* and *intellect* are tending to.. discriminable meaning. **1946** *Mind* LV. 131 Feelings.. are discriminable elements. **1964** GOULD & KOLB *Dict. Social Sci.* 447/2 A great deal of human behaviour.. cannot be directly associated with any specific, discriminable organismic states. **1970** *Jrnl. Gen. Psychol.* Jan. 85 The middle of the list is least discriminable.

discriminal (dɪ'skrɪmɪnəl), *a. rare.* [ad. L. *discrīmināl-is* serving to divide or separate, f. *discrīmen* division, distinction: see -AL¹.] Of the nature of a distinction or division.

discriminal line in *Palmistry*: see quot.

1842 BRANDE *Dict. Sc. etc.* 224 [*Chiromancy*] The lines on the palm of the hand are divided into principal and inferior; the former are five: the line of life.. the dragon's tail, or discriminal line, between the hand and the arm.

†**di'scriminance.** *Obs. rare*⁻¹. [f. as next: see -ANCE.] = DISCRIMINATION.

1647 H. MORE *Song of Soul* II. ii. II. xxiv, They together blended are That nought we see with right discriminance.

di'scriminancy. *rare.* [f. next: see -ANCY.] The quality of being discriminant; faculty of discriminating.

a **1846** *Penny Mag.* is cited by WORCESTER.

discriminant (dɪ'skrɪmɪnənt), *a.* and *sb.* [ad. L. *discrīminānt-em*, pr. pple. of *discrīmināre* to DISCRIMINATE: see -ANT¹.]

A. *adj.* **1.** Discriminating; showing discrimination or discernment.

1836 *Fraser's Mag.* XIV. 411 Taylor's notes are not all so discriminant as this. **1866** J. H. NEWMAN *Gerontius* (1874) 334 With a sense so apprehensive and discriminant.

2. *Math.* Implying equal roots or a node (cf. B). ***discriminant relation,*** a one-fold relation between parameters determining a nodal point.

3. ***discriminant function,*** in *Statistics*, a function (usually linear) of a set of variables which is used to allocate items to any of several classes with minimum probability of misclassification, each variable taking one value for each item.

1936 R. A. FISHER in *Ann. Eugenics* VII. 179 Discriminant functions. When two or more populations have been measured in several characters, $x_1, \ldots, x_s$, special interest attaches to certain linear functions of the measurements by which the populations are best discriminated. **1948** *New Biol.* IV. 43 The technique of discriminant functions is a means of finding the best combination of two or more measurable attributes for the distinction of two sub-classes of a population. **1962** *Lancet* 15 Dec. 1238/2 To combine the information on prognosis derived from each of these compounds a simple combination of their values, known as a discriminant function, was calculated previously.

B. *sb. Math.* **1.** The eliminant of the *n* first derived functions of a homogeneous function of *n* variables.

Introduced in 1852 by Sylvester for *determinant*, which is still found occasionally (H. T. Gerrans).

1852 SYLVESTER in *Camb. & Dubl. Math. Jrnl.* VI. 52. **1876** SALMON *Mod. Higher Alg.* (ed. 3) §109 The discriminant is equal to the product of the squares of all the differences of the differences of any two roots of the equation.

2. That which enables one to discriminate; a discriminating feature; *spec.* a discriminant function.

1920 *Expositor* May 338 The formula ought not to be used as a discriminant between one Gospel and another. **1958** *New Scientist* 16 Oct. 1083/2, I should like to suggest the word 'determinant' or possibly 'discriminant' [for the factors responsible for variance]. **1962** *Lancet* 15 Dec. 1236/1 The discriminant has now been calculated for the normal women in this series. *Ibid.* 1239/2 Over half the patients.. have negative discriminants.

discrimi'nantal, *a. Math.* [f. prec. + -AL¹.] Relating to a discriminant.

discriminantal index of a singular point of a curve, the number of intersections of the polar of an arbitrary point with the curve at the given point. ***total discriminantal index*** of a curve, the sum of the discriminantal indices of all its singular points.

1875 SMITH *Higher Singularities Plane Curves* in *Proc. Lond. Math. Soc.* VI. 154.

discriminate (dɪ'skrɪmɪnət), *a.* [ad. L. *discrīmināt-us* divided, separated, distinguished, pa. pple. of *discrīmināre*: see next.]

1. Distinct, distinguished, discriminated. *arch.*

1626 BACON *Sylva* §875 It is certaine that Oysters and Cockles, and Mussles.. haue no discriminate Sex. **1805** W. TAYLOR in *Monthly Mag.* XIX. 657 The characters of the savages are well-drawn; they are more discriminate and various than those of the Europeans. **1887** E. JOHNSON *Antiqua Mater* 69 A Hellenistic ecclesiastical as discriminate from a synagogal literature and life.

2. Marked by discrimination or discernment; making careful or exact distinctions: opp. to *indiscriminate.*

1798 MALTHUS *Popul.* (1817) III. 289 The best.. mode in which occasional and discriminate assistance can be given. *Ibid.* (1878) 479 Much may be done by discriminate charity. **1834** FOSTER in *Life & Corr.* (1846) II. 250 Discriminate perception. **1895** *Westm. Gaz.* 20 Mar. 2/1 The discriminate ascetic is the true hedonist.

Hence **di'scriminately** *adv.*, with discrimination; **di'scriminateness**, the quality of having discrimination.

1727 BAILEY vol. II, *Discriminateness*, distinguishingness. **1779–81** JOHNSON *L.P.*, *Shenstone*, His conception of an Elegy he has in his Preface very judiciously and discriminately explained. **1884** *Bookseller* Sept. 909/2 Discriminately he purchased everything that came in his way.

discriminate (dɪ'skrɪmɪneɪt), *v.* [f. L. *discrīmināt-* ppl. stem of *discrīmināre* to divide, separate, distinguish, f. *discrīmen, -crīmin-* division, distinction, f. stem of *discernĕre* to distinguish, DISCERN. (Cf. CRIME.)]

1. *trans.* To make or constitute a difference in or between; to distinguish, differentiate.

1628 PRYNNE *Love-lockes* 26 Who poll one side of their heads—of purpose to discriminate themselues from others. **1666** BOYLE *Orig. Formes & Qual.*, Such slight differences as those that discriminate these Bodies. **1774** WARTON *Hist. Eng. Poetry* (1775) I. Diss. I. 65 No peculiarity..more strongly discriminates the manners of the Greeks and Romans from those of modern times. *a* **1871** GROTE *Eth. Fragm.* iii. (1876) 59 Capacities which discriminate one individual from another.

2. To distinguish with the mind or intellect; to perceive, observe, or note the difference in or between.

1665 HOOKE *Microgr.* 66 The surfaces..being so neer together, that the eye cannot discriminate them from one. *a* **1677** BARROW *Wks.* (1687) I. xx. 283 We take upon us..to discriminate the goats from the sheep. **1836** J. GILBERT *Chr. Atonem.* v. (1852) 139 It is in the nature of the reward sought ..that we discriminate a mean from a noble transaction. **1891** F. HALL in *Nation* (N.Y.) LII. 244/1 How is one..to discriminate the teachings of Dr. Trench's reviser from those of Dr. Trench himself?

3. a. *intr.* or *absol.* To make a distinction; to perceive or note the difference (*between* things); to exercise discernment. *spec.* To exercise racial discrimination (cf. DISCRIMINATION 1 c).

1774 J. BRYANT *Mythol.* II. 523 The purport of the term, which discriminates, may not be easy to be deciphered. **1857** BUCKLE *Civiliz.* I. vii. 321 It is by reason, and not by faith, that we must discriminate in religious matters. **1866** A. JOHNSON *Speech* 27 Mar. in H. S. Commager *Documents Amer. Hist.* (1935) II. 16/2 Congress can repeal all State laws discriminating between whites and blacks in the subjects covered by this bill. **1876** GREEN *Stray Stud.* 26 He would discriminate between temporary and chronic distress. **1936** *New Statesman* 8 Aug. 190/2 When discriminating racially, popular opinion lays emphasis on the Negro's colour.

b. *to discriminate against*: to make an adverse distinction with regard to; to distinguish unfavourably from others. With *indirect pass.*

1880 MARK TWAIN (Clemens) *Tramp Abr.* II. 153, I did not propose to be discriminated against on account of my nationality. **1885** *Pall Mall G.* 24 Feb. 8/1 The action of the German Government in discriminating against certain imports from the United States. **1886** *Ibid.* 19 July 3/2 If the police, as the Socialists declare, discriminate against them on account of their opinions. **1899** B. T. WASHINGTON *Fut. Amer. Negro* vi. 130 We find the Negro forgetting his own wrongs, forgetting the laws and customs that discriminate against him in his own country. **1968** *Listener* 3 Oct. 427/2 If you move around for ever with the expectation of being discriminated against, the chances are you won't ever be disappointed.

Hence **di'scriminated** *ppl. a.*, distinguished from others; perceived as distinct.

1783 J. YOUNG *Crit. Gray's Elegy* (1810) 49 The discriminated catalogue of the dead. **1848** R. I. WILBERFORCE *Incarnation* v. (1852) 137 The two titles [Father, and Son] imply a real co-existence of discriminated Persons.

di'scriminating, *ppl. a.* [f. prec. + -ING[2].]

1. That discriminates (sense 1); distinguishing, making or constituting a distinction, or affording a ground for distinction.

1647 TRAPP *Comm. Epistles* 102 In these shedding and discriminating times. *a* **1677** HALE *True Relig.* III. (1684) 38 Each Party espousing some odd Discriminating Habits. **1797** M. BAILLIE *Morb. Anat.* (1807) 81 The discriminating mark of this disease. **1838** TUPPER *Prov. Philos., Gifts* 228 A discriminating test Separating honesty from falsehood.

2. That discriminates (sense 2); that perceives or notes distinctions with accuracy; possessing discrimination or discernment.

1792 MARY WOLLSTONECR. *Rights Wom.* iii. 102 The discriminating outline of a caricature. **1794** SULLIVAN *View Nat.* I. 17 A sound and discriminating judgment. **1849** MACAULAY *Hist. Eng.* I. 172 No man observed the varieties of character with a more discriminating eye.

3. *discriminating duty* or *rate*: one that varies in amount according to the country or place whence the merchandise is imported or carried, or according to the persons rated; a differential duty or rate.

1845–52 McCULLOCH *Taxation* II. v. 218 The 7 & 8 Victoria..reduced the duty on foreign sugar..leaving a discriminating duty of 10*s.* 6*d.* a cwt. in favour of our own sugars. **1870** *Daily News* 16 Apr., Is it not absurd to revive a distinguishing rate, preferential and discriminating, in favour of one class of dealers and against another?

4. *Math.* *discriminating circle*, in the Theory of Functions with essential singularities, the circle on which all the singularities of another connected function lie. [= Ger. *Grenzkreis.*] *discriminating cubic*, a cubic equation whose roots are the reciprocal of the principal radii vectores of a quadric surface referred to its centre.

1874 SALMON *Geom. three Dimensions* (ed. 3) 58 If two roots of the discriminating cubic vanish, the equation.. represents a cylinder whose base is a parabola. **1893** FORSYTH *Th. Functions* vi. §71. 111 To divide the plane of the modified variable ζ into two portions..The boundary.. is a circle of finite radius, called the *discriminating circle* of the function..All the singularities (and the branch-points, if any) lie on the discriminating circle.

Hence **di'scriminatingly** *adv.*, in a discriminating way, with discrimination.

1855 BAIN *Senses & Int.* III. i. §65 The ear must be discriminatingly sensitive to pitch, and to the harmonies and discords of different pitches. **1856** KINGSLEY *Misc., Froude's Hist. Eng.* II. 47 It is written as history should be, discriminatingly, patiently, and yet lovingly and genially.

discrimination (dɪskrɪmɪ'neɪʃən). [ad. L. *discrīminātiōn-em*, n. of action from *discrīmināre* to DISCRIMINATE.]

1. a. The action of discriminating; the perceiving, noting, or making a distinction or difference between things; a distinction (made with the mind, or in action). Also with *against.*

1648 *Eikon Bas.* xxvii. (1824) 265 Take heed of abetting any factions, of applying to any publique discriminations in matters of religion, contrary to what is, in your judgement, and the Church well setled. **1678** PHILLIPS, *Discrimination* a putting a difference between one thing and another. In Rhetorick it is the same figure with *Paradiastole.* **1705** STANHOPE *Paraphr.* I. 24 A perfect Discrimination shall then be made between the Good and Bad. **1864** BOWEN *Logic* i. 4 A conscious discrimination of those respects in which it is similar to others from those in which it is unlike them. **1889** *Spectator* 9 Nov., Life is a constant series of discriminations between what it is well to attempt and what it is not well to attempt. **1949** *Times* 10 Sept. 5/6 Any sort of discrimination against the trade of any country or countries. .. Discrimination always tends to be practised against exports from 'hard-currency countries'. **1951** J. R. WINTON *Dict. Econ. Terms* 28 As the result of the world dollar shortage..discrimination has been widely practised.. against the U.S.A.

b. *passively.* The fact or condition of being discriminated or distinguished. ? *Obs.*

a **1699** STILLINGFL. (J.), There is a reverence to be showed them on account of their discrimination from other places, and separation for sacred uses. **1791–1823** DISRAELI *Cur. Lit., Mast. Ceremon.*, Precedence, and other honorary discriminations, establish the useful distinctions of ranks.

c. *spec.* The making of distinctions prejudicial to people of a different race or colour from oneself; racial discrimination.

1866 A. JOHNSON *Speech* 27 Mar. in H. S. Commager *Documents Amer. Hist.* (1935) II. 16/2 Thus a perfect equality of the white and colored races is attempted to be fixed by Federal law in every State of the Union over the vast field of State jurisdiction covered by these enumerated rights. In no one of these can any State ever exercise any power of discrimination between the different races. **1899** B. T. WASHINGTON *Fut. Amer. Negro* vi. 148 Let the very best educational opportunities be provided for both races; and add to this an election law that shall be incapable of unjust discrimination. **1906** *Ann. Amer. Acad. Pol. & Soc. Sci.* XXVII. III. 550 So long as the North treats the negro workman with blighting discrimination it is left little moral ground for complaint against the South where a like spirit assumes a different form of manifestation. **1955** *Ann. Reg. 1954* 135 Direct talks between South Africa..and India and Pakistan..on the..dispute over alleged discrimination against Indians in the Union. **1971** *Times* 9 Mar. 14/7 Mr. Maudling could still say that 'it [*sc.* the Immigration Bill] is not a matter of discrimination, unless you're looking for discrimination'.

d. *Psychol.* In a learning situation, the identification of a stimulus and the choice of an appropriate response. Freq. *attrib.*

1890 W. JAMES *Princ. Psychol.* I. iii. 94 The reaction may be withheld until the signal has consciously awakened a distinct idea (Wundt's discrimination-time, association-time) and then performed. **1894** CREIGHTON & TITCHENER tr. *Wundt's Hum. & Anim. Psychol.* 279 By subtracting the previously determined simple time from this longer time we get a discrimination-time. **1898** E. B. TITCHENER *Primer Psychol.* 260 In the discrimination reaction, he [*sc.* the subject] moves when he has apperceived some one or two or more familiar stimuli. **1948** E. R. HILGARD *Theories of Learning* v. 130 Skinner believes that his arrangement for obtaining discrimination is superior to that usually used. *Ibid.*, The discrimination experiment is always complicated by an additional fact of importance. **1953** C. E. OSGOOD *Method & Theory Exper. Psychol.* III. viii. 352 What is it in behavior that enters to check this overboard generalization of response? The process is called *discrimination.* **1963** J. H. FLAVELL *Developmental Psychol. J. Piaget* ii. 56 Discrimination is the complement of generalization, as students of learning have long known. **1967** NEIMARK & ESTES *Stimulus Sampling Theory* iv. 430 The classification of discrimination theories..is based upon the number of elementary processes invoked. *Ibid.* 431 Any comprehensive account of learning must provide an adequate account of stimulus generalization and discrimination. **1970** L. ELKINGTON tr. *Le Ny's Learning & Memory* 57 The maze is a more complex discrimination situation in which there are possible alternative responses. *Ibid.* 58 In both types of situation (discrimination apparatus and maze), the reaction..is a partially new reaction.

2. Something that discriminates or distinguishes; a distinction, difference (existing in or between things); a distinguishing mark or characteristic. Now *rare* or *Obs.*

1646 SIR T. BROWNE *Pseud. Ep.* III. xxiii. 166 [These] are discriminations very materiall, and plainly declare, that under the same name Authors describe not the same animall. **1759** JOHNSON *Rasselas* xxviii. (1787) 79 Where we see..the whole at once, we readily note the discriminations. **1807** G. CHALMERS *Caledonia* I. I. i. 2 To that event the various tribes owe their discrimination and their origin.

3. The faculty of discriminating; the power of observing differences accurately, or of making exact distinctions; discernment.

1814 SCOTT *Wav.* xxiii, His character was touched with yet more discrimination by Flora. **1838** DICKENS *Nich. Nick.* xviii, It does..credit to your discrimination that you should have found such a very excellent young woman. **1866** GEO. ELIOT *F. Holt* II. xvi. 15 It was essential..that his waistcoat should imply much discrimination.

†**4.** = RECRIMINATION. *Obs. rare.*

a **1670** HACKET *Abp. Williams* I. (1692) 16 (D.), Reproaches and all sorts of unkind discriminations. **1684** BAXTER in *Hale's True Relig.* Introd. Ab, Schisms and Factions, and Personal Animosities, discriminations, Censoriousness.

Hence **discrimi'national** *a.*, of or pertaining to discrimination; in *Palmistry* = DISCRIMINAL.

1879 R. A. CAMPBELL *Philosophic Chiromancy* 167 The *Wrist Lines*, also known as the Rascette and Discriminational lines, separate the hand from the arm by a single, double, or triple transcursion at the wrist.

discriminative (dɪ'skrɪmɪnətɪv), *a.* [f. L. ppl. stem *discrīmināt-*: see -IVE.] Tending to discriminate; characterized by discriminating.

1. Serving to discriminate or distinguish; constituting a distinction; distinctive, distinguishing.

a **1677** HALE *True Relig.* I. (1684) 11 This is made the discriminative Mark of a True Christian. **1779–81** JOHNSON *L.P., Dryden* Wks. II. 414 The discriminative excellence of Homer is elevation and comprehension of thought. **1848** JOHNSTON in *Proc. Berw. Nat. Club* II. No. 6. 307, I must impose upon ours a name and discriminative mark.

2. Having the quality or character of observing or making distinctions with accuracy; marked by or showing discrimination; discerning. (Of persons, their faculties, actions, utterances, etc.)

a **1638** MEDE *Disc. Matt.* vi. 9 Wks. (1672) I. 8 After the same manner were the Holy Oyntment and the Holy Perfume or Incense to be sanctified by a discriminative, singular, appropriate usance of them. **1653** H. MORE *Antid. Ath.* II. ix. (1712) 66 Discriminative Providence, that knew afore the nature and course of all things. **1805** FOSTER *Ess.* IV. i. 101 A more discriminative censure. **1865** MILL *Exam. Hamilton* 222 Mr. Bain recognises two..modes of discriminative sensibility in the muscular sense.

b. *transf.* (Of, or in reference to, things.)

1826 SOUTHEY in *Q. Rev.* XXXIV. 317 Bombs and rockets are not discriminative. **1881** *Eng. Mechanic* 27 May 277/3 The..well-known discriminative power possessed by bichromatised gelatine of absorbing printers' ink in accordance with the action of the light upon it.

c. = DISCRIMINATING *ppl. a.* 3; differential.

1872 YEATS *Growth Comm.* 132 [They] sealed their ports against fresh comers by heavy discriminative duties.

Hence **di'scriminatively** *adv.*, in a discriminative manner, with discrimination.

a **1638** MEDE *Disc. Matt.* vi. 9 Wks. (1672) I. 14 When the same are worthily and discriminatively used. **1797–1803** FOSTER in *Life & Corr.* (1846) I. 206 Some one said that women remarked characters more discriminatively. **1862** F. HALL *Hindu Philos. Syst.* 45 Certitude is the distinguishing property of intellect..and to cognize discriminatively, that of mind.

di'scriminator. [a. L. *discrīminātor* (Tertull.), agent-n. from *discrīmināre* to DISCRIMINATE.]

1. One who or that which discriminates.

1828 COLEBROOKE in *Trans. R. Asiat. Soc.* (1830) II. 183 He [the judge] discriminates, and is, consequently, the discriminator (*vivēca*). **1961** *Lancet* 12 Aug. 360/1 The high number of poor discriminators is an indication that most of them can be omitted in future and other questions substituted. **1963** *Amer. Speech* XXXVIII. 72 Plosives, fricatives, and affricatives are best discriminators between speakers with adequate and inadequate velopharyngeal closure.

2. *Electr.* **a.** (See quot.)

1931 S. R. ROGET *Dict. Electr. Terms* (ed. 2) 89/2 *Discriminator*, an instrument used with an earlier system of charging of an electric supply which automatically switches over to a different meter when a predetermined maximum demand has been exceeded.

b. Any circuit the output of which depends on how some property of the input departs from a fixed level or value; *esp.* one that converts a frequency-modulated signal to an amplitude-modulated one by modulating the output amplitude according to the deviation of the input frequency from a fixed (carrier) frequency.

1935 *Proc. Inst. Radio Engineers* XXIII. 1126 An automatic frequency control system will consist of two distinct units; a frequency discriminator or frequency sensitive detector that generates a bias varying with changes of the intermediate-frequency signal carrier frequency, and a control unit that is acted upon by this bias. **1947** *Nature* 4 Jan 16/1 In order to render a frequency-modulated signal audible, the receiver uses a device known as a 'discriminator', which in effect converts it into an amplitude-modulated signal, which may then be detected by any of the usual methods. **1962** SIMPSON & RICHARDS *Junction Transistors* xviii. 462 The most common type of frequency-modulation detector, the discriminator, was developed originally for vacuum-tube receivers. **1962** F. J. M. FARLEY *Elem. Pulse Circuits* (ed. 2) i. 19 This circuit is an example of a discriminator, that is, a circuit which transmits only the upper portion of a pulse. In common with other discriminator circuits..it may be used..to select signals of amplitude greater than a predetermined threshold value.

di'scriminatory, *a.* [f. L. type **discrīminātōrius*, f. *discrīminātor*: see prec. and -ORY.] = DISCRIMINATIVE.

1828 W. FIELD *Mem. Dr. Parr* II. 414 Proofs of a pure taste and a discriminatory judgment. **1892** *Columbus* (Ohio) *Dispatch* 1 Mar., The Government still hoped for discriminatory rights with Great Britain. **1954** P. MASON *Essay on Racial Tension* x. 88 The way was made easier by discriminatory devices which were defensible as in the interests of the African. **1965** *Times* 7 Apr. 12/3 The fact that companies will have to pay on their gains at the higher corporation tax level..was thought to be discriminatory. **1971** *Guardian* 8 Mar. 6/4 Asians..have not forgotten the similar 'discriminatory' Immigrants Act of 1968.

di'scriminoid. *Math.* [f. after DISCRIMINANT: see -OID.] A function of which the vanishing expresses the equality of all the integrating factors of a differential equation. Hence **discrimi'noidal** *a.*

1879 SIR J. COCKLE in *Proc. Lond. Math. Soc.* X. 111 It will be found convenient to give a name to the functions □ and □₂. Let us call them discriminoids. *Ibid.*, This first species of discriminoidal solution.

†**di'scriminous,** *a. Obs. rare.* [ad. late L. *discrīminōs-us* decisive, critical, f. *discrīmen*: see DISCRIMINATE *v.* and -OUS.] Critical, hazardous.

1666 G. HARVEY *Morb. Angl.* (J.), Any kind of spitting of blood imports a very discriminous state. *Ibid.* xvii. 195 Consumptives, though their case appears not with so discriminous an aspect. **1727** BAILEY vol. II, *Discriminous*, full of Jeopardy.

Hence **di'scriminousness.**

1731 in BAILEY vol. II.

discription, discrive, obs. ff. DESCRIPTION, DESCRIVE.

discrown (dɪs'kraʊn), *v.* [f. DIS- 6 + CROWN *v.* or DIS- 7 + CROWN *sb.*: cf. OF. *descoroner* (12th c. in Hatz.-Darm.); also DECROWN.] *trans.* To deprive of a crown, take the crown from; *spec.* to deprive of royal dignity, to depose; *transf.* and *fig.* to deprive of supremacy, dignity, or adornment.

1586 WARNER *Alb. Eng.* III. xvi. (R.) The one restored.. The other..Dis-crowned. **1612-5** BP. HALL *Contempl., N.T.* IV. xxxi, He discrownes not the body, who crowns the soule. **1803** W. TAYLOR in *Monthly Mag.* XIV. 54 On the shorn hair discrown'd of bridal flow'rs, Weeping lies scorn'd and trampled Liberty. **1863** KINGLAKE *Crimea* (1876) I. xiv. 301 To crown or discrown its Monarchs. **1871** MORLEY *Voltaire* (1886) 13 Discrowning sovereign reason, to be the serving drudge of superstition or social usage.

Hence **dis'crowned** *ppl. a.*, deprived of the crown; **dis'crowning** *vbl. sb.*

1837 CARLYLE *Fr. Rev.* (1871) III. IV. vii. 167 A worn discrowned Widow. **1866** *Pall Mall G.* No. 510. 966/1 The successive contemporary discrownings. **1878** BOSW. SMITH *Carthage* 353 The discrowned queen of the seas.

†**di'scruciament.** *Obs. rare.* [f. L. *discruciā-re* to torture + -MENT; cf. *excruciament* (also in Nashe). (L. had *cruciāmentum* from *cruciāre.*)] Torment, torture.

1593 NASHE *Christ's T.* (1613) 181 What then is it, to liue in threescore times more grinding discruciament of dying? **1623** COCKERAM II, Endlesse Paine, *discrutiament.*

†**dis'cruciate,** *v. Obs.* [f. *discruciāt-*, ppl. stem of L. *discruciāre*, f. DIS- 5 + *cruciāre* to torture, rack, torment, f. *crux, cruc-em* CROSS.]

1. *trans.* To torment, torture, excruciate.

1600 ABP. ABBOT *Exp. Jonah* 484 The conscience of the transgressing sinner..doth use to discruciate the person affected. **1633** BP. HALL *Hard Texts* 253 To discruciate and rack his thoughts with an insatiable desire of what he hath not. **1660** SHARROCK *Vegetables* 149, I mean that we puzzle not ourselves over-much nor discruciate our spirits to resolve what are the causes.

2. *nonce-use.* To puzzle out, unravel, solve (a 'crux' or riddle: cf. CRUX 3).

a **1745** SWIFT *To Sheridan* Wks. 1745 VIII. 206 Pray discruciate what follows.

Hence †**dis'cruciating** *ppl. a.*, tormenting; also †**discruci'ation**, torture, torment, anguish.

1631 R. H. *Arraignm. Whole Creature* xi. §2. 100 They produce anxiety, griefe, vexation, anguish, discrutiation and discontent. **1666** BP. OF NORWICH *Serm. in Westm. Abb.* 7 Nov. 30 Discruciating Fears..impatient Hopes. **1788** *Trifler* xxv. 323 It dimoves every discruciating pain from the stomach.

†**discru'tator.** *Obs. rare*⁻¹. [f. *di-*, DIS- 5 + SCRUTATOR.] ? A caviller or searcher for objections.

a **1626** W. SCLATER *Serm. Exper.* (1638) 109 It signifies the Discrutatour, or Disputer, against the promise.

discry(e, -cryghe, obs. ff. DESCRY *v.*¹ and ².

†**discu'bation.** *Obs. rare*⁻¹. [ad. assumed L. type **discubātio*, n. of action f. **discubāre*, f. *dis-* (DIS-) + *cubāre* to recline. The actual L. word was *discubitio* from *discumbĕre*; but the parallel forms *cubātio, accubātio*, occur in L.: cf. CUBATION, ACCUBATION.] Reclining at meals.

1635-56 COWLEY *Davideis* I. Notes §52 What was the fashion in Samuel's time, is not certain; it is probable enough..that Discubation was then in practice.

†**di'scubitory,** *a. Obs. rare*⁻¹. [ad. L. type **discubitōri-us*, f. *discubit-*, ppl. stem of *discumbĕre* see DISCUMB and -ORY.] Adapted for reclining.

1646 SIR T. BROWNE *Pseud. Ep.* V. vi. 241 Custome by degrees changed their cubiculary beds into discubitory.

†**di'scubiture.** *Obs. rare.* [ad. L. type **discubitūra*, f. *discubit-*, ppl. stem of *discumbĕre*: see prec. and -URE.] The posture of reclining.

a **1655** VINES *Lord's Supp.* (1677) 113 The gesture, which was discubiture or lying on couch-beds. *Ibid.* 154.

†**di'sculp,** *v. Obs. rare*⁻¹. [ad. med.L. *disculpā-re* (Du Cange), f. DIS- 4 + *culpāre* to blame, *culpa* fault.] *trans.* = DISCULPATE.

1738 WARBURTON *Div. Legat.* I. 294 He himself disculps them.

disculpate (dɪ'skʌlpeɪt), *v.* [f. *disculpāt-* ppl. stem of med.L. *disculpāre*: see prec.] *trans.* To clear from blame or accusation; to exculpate.

1693 W. BATES *Serm.* vii. 249 [Satan's] prevailing Temptations do not disculpate Sinners that yield to them. *a* **1734** NORTH *Lives* I. 40 Being faithful and just, with the testimony of things to disculpate him. **1768** H. WALPOLE *Hist. Doubts* 122 The authors of the Chronicle of Croyland ..charge him directly with none of the crimes, since imputed to him, and disculpate him of others. **1880** VERN. LEE *Stud. Italy* IV. iv. 173 The hero accused of regicide.. and unable to disculpate himself. **1888** H. C. LEA *Hist. Inquisition* I. 43 *note*, Disculpating himself to Eugenius IV from an accusation of doubting the papal power.

disculpation (dɪskʌl'peɪʃən). [n. of action from med.L. *disculpāre* to DISCULPATE.] The action of clearing from blame; exculpation.

1760-97 H. WALPOLE *Mem. Geo. II* (1847) III. x. 252 This disculpation under the hand of a Secretary of State was remarkable. **1770** BURKE *Pres. Discont.* Wks. 1837 I. 150 A plan of apology and disculpation. **1891** W. M. ROSSETTI *Shelley's Adonais* 9 *note*, Arguments..tending to Harriet's disculpation.

di'sculpatory, *a. rare*⁻⁰. [f. *disculpāt-* ppl. stem of med.L. *disculpāre*: see prec. and -ORY.] Tending to disculpate.

1847 in CRAIG: and in later Dicts.

†**di'scumb,** *v. Obs. rare.* [ad. L. *discumb-ĕre* to lie down, recline, f. DIS- 1 + *-cumbĕre* to lie down: cf. CUMBENT.] *intr.* To recline (at table). Hence **di'scumbing** *vbl. sb.* and *ppl. a.*

1683 J. EVANS *Kneeling at Sacrament* I. 21 At the beginning of the Paschal Feast the Jews did put themselves into this Discumbing or Leaning posture..while they Eat and Drank the two first Cups of Wine. **1684** *Vind. Case Indiff. Things* 38 The posture of discumbing. **1699** T. BENNET *Dissenters' Pleas* (1711) 170 Some convenient posture, such as kneeling, sitting, discumbing, standing.

†**di'scumbence.** *Obs. rare.*⁻⁰. [f. as next + -ENCE.] = next.

1656 in BLOUNT *Glossogr.*

†**di'scumbency.** *Obs.* [f. DISCUMBENT, after L. type **discumbentia*: see -ENCY.] Discumbent condition; the reclining posture at meals.

1646 SIR T. BROWNE *Pseud. Ep.* V. vi. 243 This discumbency at meales was in use in the days of our Saviour. **1682-3** *Case Indiff. Things* 11 The Jews..did eat in the posture of discumbency. **1737** STACKHOUSE *Hist. Bible, N.T.* (1765) II. VIII. iv. 149 *note*, They used this posture of discumbency and especially at the pascal supper.

†**discumbent,** *a.* and *sb. Obs.* Also 6 discom-. [ad. L. *discumbent-em*, pr. pple. of *discumbĕre*: see DISCUMB.] **A.** *adj.* Reclining.

1715 I. MATHER *Several Serm.* III. 95 The Jews..sat at their Tables in a discumbent posture. **1756** C. LUCAS *Ess. Waters* I. 197 Bathing is best administered in a discumbent posture.

B. *sb.*

1. One who reclines at table; a guest at a feast.

1562 BULLEYN *Use Sickmen* 73 b, He cast doune al the meate from the borde, fallyng out with all the discombentes. **1614** T. ADAMS *Devil's Banquet* 135 A beastiall Banket; wherein either man is the Symposiast, and the Deuill the discumbent; or Sathan the Feastmaker, and man the Guest.

2. One confined to bed by sickness; = DECUMBENT *sb.*

1765 GALE in *Phil. Trans.* LV. 193 A.D. 1721 The discumbents were 5,989, whereof 844 died. *Ibid.* 194 The discumbents were estimated at 4,000, whereof about 500 died.

discumber (dɪs'kʌmbə(r)), *v.* [f. DIS- 6 + CUMBER *v.* Cf. OF. *descombrer*, mod.F. *décombrer.*]

1. *trans.* To relieve; to disencumber.

1725 POPE *Odyss.* V. 474 The chief..His limbs discumbers of the clinging vest. **1806** J. GRAHAME *Birds Scot.* 17 Her young, Soon as discumbered of the fragile shell Run lively round their dam. **1873** HELPS *Anim. & M.* vi. (1875) 149 Discumbering our minds of what we have crammed up for the occasion.

¶**2.** To put away or get rid of, as an encumbrance. (But in the quot. app. a misreading.)

.. *Chaucer's Pars. T.* ⁋816 (ed. Tyrwhitt) The vengeance of avoutrie is awarded to the peine of helle, but if so be that it be discombered by penitence. [*Early MSS. and edd.* destourbed, disturberid, distroubled.]

†**di'scumbitory,** *a. Obs. rare*⁻¹. A non-etymological by-form of DISCUBITORY, influenced by the L. present stem *discumb-*.

1715 tr. *Pancirollus' Rerum Mem.* I. IV. x. 186 Those discumbitory Couches, upon which they loll'd when at their Repast.

†**di'scumbiture.** *Obs. rare.* A non-etymological by-form of DISCUBITURE: see prec.

1684 *Vind. Case Indiff. Things* 39 It was required that discumbiture should be used in all Religious Feasts. **1696** J. EDWARDS *Demonstr. Exist. God* II. 82 This is a soft bed of itself, and makes discumbiture a delightful posture.

†**di'scumbrance.** [DIS- 5.] = CUMBRANCE.

c **1450** *Merlin* 511 At foure cours thei haue hem perced thourgh with-oute eny other discombraunce.

discumfit, discumfort, obs. ff. DISCOMFIT, DISCOMFORT.

†**di'scur, di'scurre,** *v. Obs.* [ad. L. *discurr-ĕre* to run to and fro, f. DIS- 1 + *currĕre* to run.]

1. *intr.* To run about.

c **1550** *Disc. Common Weal. Eng.* (1893) 25 We be not so agill and light as..birdes of the ayere be, that we might discurre from one place to an other.

2. *trans.* To run over or through.

1586 B. YOUNG *Guazzo's Civ. Conv.* IV. 206 b, Mans minde..in moment of a time it discurres all things. **1598** —— *Diana* Pref., The delight..in discurring most of those townes and places in it with a pleasant recordation of my pen.

discure, obs. form of DISCOVER *v.*

†**dis'cured,** *ppl. a. Obs.* [f. DIS- 7 a + CURE *sb.*¹ 4.] Without cure of souls: see CURE *sb.*¹ 4.

1604 TOOKER *Fabrique Ch.* 92, I..maintaine it more lawfull..to hold two Benefices with cure of soules then two discured or impropriated livings.

†**dis'current,** *a.*¹ *Obs. rare.* [f. DIS- 10 + CURRENT *a.*] Not current or in circulation.

1599 SANDYS *Europæ Spec.* (1632) 122 To make discurrent ..those very books..in such wise as not to suffer them to be commonly salable. *Ibid.* 129 Whose bookes being discurrent in all Catholike Countries.

†**di'scurrent,** *a.*² *Obs. rare.* [ad. L. *discurrent-em*, pr. pple. of *discurr-ĕre*: see DISCUR *v.*] Running hither and thither.

1656 BLOUNT *Glossogr.*, *Discurrent*, that wanders or runs hither and thither. **1710** M. HENRY *Comm., Dan.* xii. 4 (1848) 992 They shall 'run to and fro' to inquire out copies of it..discurrent, they shall discourse of it.

discurrour, obs. form of DISCOVERER.

†**discur'sation.** *Obs.* [ad. L. *discursātiōn-em*, n. of action f. *discursāre*, freq. of *discurrĕre*: see DISCUR.]

1. A running hither and thither, or from place to place.

1652 GAULE *Magastrom.* 55 Making long discursations, to learn strange tongues.

2. A passing from one subject to another.

1647 TRAPP *Comm. Matt.* vi. 6 That being sequestered from company, we may..be the freer from..discursation and wandering of mind.

di'scursative, *a. rare.* [f. L. *discursāt-* ppl. stem of *discursāre*: see prec. and -IVE.] Passing from one object of thought to another; discursive. Hence **di'scursativeness.**

1819 P. MORRIS in *Blackw. Mag.* VI. 311 The Discursative Sentiment, draws off the imitative principle, and transfers it from one object to another, so as to keep it revolving. *Ibid.*, That sort of Discursativeness which relates to space. *Ibid.*, The curiosity generated from Discursativeness has a spring of motion within itself.

†**di'scurse.** *Obs.* [ad. L. *discurs-us* a running to and fro or away, f. *discurs-*, ppl. stem of *discurrĕre*: see next.] Onward course; = DISCOURSE *sb.* 1.

1555 H. PENDILTON in Bonner *Homilies* 35 By contynuall discurse of tyme euery one hath deliuered the fayth.

discursion (dɪ'skɜːʃən). *rare.* Also 6 discorsioun. [ad. L. *discursiōn-em*, n. of action from *discurrĕre* to run to and fro: see DISCUR.]

†**1.** The action of running or moving to and fro.

1535 STEWART *Cron. Scot.* III. 404 Richt grit displesour he had euerie da Of the discorsioun maid be Inglismen. **1684** tr. *Bonet's Merc. Compit.* XVIII. 618 Volatils are most needful, for greater penetration and quicker discursion.

2. *fig.* The action of passing from the subject under consideration; digression.

1851 BRIMLEY *Ess., Wordsw.* 169 The name recalls us from our discursion to speak of one whom, [etc.].

3. The action of passing from premisses to conclusions; reasoning; = DISCOURSE *sb.* 2.

1603 HOLLAND *Plutarch's Mor.* 132 Turning the discursion of his judgement from things abroad, to those which are within himselfe. **1650** HOBBES *Human Nature* iv. 31 The succession of conceptions in the Minde..may be orderly..and this is discourse of the Minde. But because the word Discourse is commonly taken for the coherence and consequence of words, I will, to avoid equivocation, call it discursion. **1817** COLERIDGE *Biog. Lit.* I. x. 160 Discourse here..does not mean what we now call discoursing; but the discursion of the mind. **1846** O. BROWNSON *Wks.* V. 506 An act of intuition or of discursion as well as of faith..involves it.

† **di'scursist.** *Obs. rare*⁻¹. [f. L. *discursus*, in sense 'discourse' + -IST.] One who practises discoursing, a disputer.

1671 L. ADDISON *West Barbary* Pref. (T.), Great discursists were apt to intrigue affairs, dispute the Prince's resolution, and stir up the people.

discursive (dɪ'skɜːsɪv), *a.* (*sb.*) [f. L. *discurs-* ppl. stem of *discurrĕre* (see DISCURSION) + -IVE.]

1. Running hither and thither; passing irregularly from one locality to another. *rare* in *lit.* sense.

1626 BACON *Sylva* §745 Whatsoeuer moueth Attention.. stilleth the Naturall and discursiue Motion of the Spirits. **1834** *West Ind. Sketch Bk.* II. 240 Misgivings, that Our road ..might prove somewhat more discursive. *Ibid.* 282 The regularity of the streets..prevented the breezes being so discursive as..among the unconnected dwellings.

2. *fig.* Passing rapidly or irregularly from one subject to another; rambling, digressive; extending over or dealing with a wide range of subjects.

1599 MARSTON *Sco. Villanie* III. xi. 231 Boundlesse discursiue apprehension Giving it wings. **1665** HOOKE *Microgr.* Pref. G., Men are generally rather taken with the plausible and discursive, then the real and the solid part of Philosophy. **1791** BOSWELL *Johnson* an. 1774 (1816) II. 296 Such a discursive Exercise of his mind. **1827** CARLYLE *Richter* Misc. Ess. 1872 I. 8 The name Novelist..would ill describe so vast and discursive a genius. **1850** TENNYSON *In Mem.* cix, Heart-affluence in discursive talk From household fountains never dry. **1867** FREEMAN *Norm. Conq.* (1876) I. iv. 149 A most vivid, though very discursive and garrulous, history of the time.

3. Passing from premisses to conclusions; proceeding by reasoning or argument; ratiocinative. (Cf. DISCOURSE *v.* 2.) Often opp. to *intuitive*.

1608 D. T. *Ess. Pol. & Mor.* 117 Ignorance..depriveth Reason of her discursive facultie. *a* **1652** J. SMITH *Sel. Disc.* v. 137 We cannot attain to science but by a discursive deduction of one thing from another. **1667** MILTON *P.L.* v. 488 Whence the soule Reason receives, and reason is her being, Discursive, or Intuitive; discourse Is oftest yours, the latter most is ours. **1817** COLERIDGE *Biog. Lit.* I. x. 161 Philosophy has hitherto been *discursive*: while Geometry is always and essentially *intuitive*. **1836–7** SIR W. HAMILTON *Metaph.* (1877) II. xx. 14 The Elaborative or Discursive Faculty..has only one operation, it only compares. **1874** L. STEPHEN *Hours in Library* (1892) II. i. 15 Johnson..is always a man of intuitions rather than of discursive intellect.

† **B.** as *sb.* A subject of 'discourse' or reasoning (as distinguished from a subject of perception). *Obs. rare.*

1677 HALE *Prim. Orig. Man.* IV. viii, 364 Sometimes..the very *subjectum discursus* is imperceptible to Sense..such are also the discursives of moral good and evil, just, unjust, which are no more perceptible to Sense than Colour is to the Ear.

discursively (dɪ'skɜːsɪvlɪ), *adv.* [f. prec. + -LY².] In a discursive manner.

1. By passing from premisses to conclusions; by 'discourse of reason' (cf. DISCOURSE *sb.* 2): opp. to *intuitively*.

1677 HALE *Prim. Orig. Man.* I. i. 22 Whereby we do discursively, and by way of ratiocination, deduce one thing from another. **1816** COLERIDGE *Biog. Lit., etc.* (1882) 360 In each article of faith embraced on conviction, the mind determines, first, intuitively on its logical possibility; secondly, discursively on its analogy to doctrines already believed. **1828** DE QUINCEY *Rhetoric* Wks. XI. 42 All reasoning is carried on discursively; that is, *discurrendo*,—by running about to the right and the left, laying the separate notices together, and thence mediately deriving some third apprehension.

2. In a rambling manner, digressively.

1829 I. TAYLOR *Enthus.* viii. 183 An intelligent Christian ..who should peruse discursively the ecclesiastical writers. **1846** POE *Halluk* Wks. 1864 III. 61 [He] has read a great deal, although very discursively. **1876** BANCROFT *Hist. U.S.* VI. lv. 437 He [George III] spoke discursively of his shattered health, his agitation of mind.

di'scursiveness. [f. as prec. + -NESS.] The quality of being discursive: **a.** of reasoning from premisses to conclusions; **b.** of passing from one subject to another.

a **1677** BARROW *Serm.* Wks. 1686 III. xxii. 252 The exercise of our mind in rational discursiveness, about things, in quest of truth. **1829** I. TAYLOR *Enthus.* iv. (1867) 72 That discursiveness of inventive faculties which is a principal source of heresy. **1857** LEVER *Fort. Glencore* xxiii. (1873) 159 Discursiveness is the mother of failure. **1885** *Manch. Exam.* 12 Aug. 5/1 There was nothing to limit the discursiveness of anyone who had a taste for original research.

discursivity (dɪskɜː'sɪvɪtɪ). *Philos.* [f. DISCURSIVE *a.* + -ITY.] = DISCURSIVENESS.

1940 *Mind* XLIX. 447 Kant..never completely abandoned his view of the discursivity of the human intelligence. **1946** *Ibid.* LV. 52 Kant..never suggests that the possession of such [*a priori*] concepts can be used as evidence against its [*sc.* the understanding's] thoroughgoing discursivity.

discursory (dɪ'skɜːsərɪ), *a. rare.* Also 6 discoursory. [f. L. *discurs-* (see above) + -ORY.]

† **1.** Of the nature of 'discourse' or reasoning; argumentative. *Obs.*

1581 MULCASTER *Positions* vii. (1887) 50 A number of such like discoursory argumentes. **1614** BP. HALL *Recoll. Treat.* Ded. A ij b, Here shall your Maiestie finde..speculation interchanged with experience, positiue theologie with polemicall, textuall with discursorie, popular with scholasticall.

2. Of the nature of a digression, discursive.

1881 RUSKIN *Love's Meinie* I. iii. 126 If there be motive for discursory remark.

† **dis'curtain,** *v. Obs.* [f. DIS- 6 or 7 a + CURTAIN *v.* or *sb.*] *trans.* To draw aside the curtain from; to unveil.

1616 J. LANE *Contn. Sqr.'s T.* (1887) 41 Phebus, discurtaininge his murninge face. **1653** BRATHWAIT *Arcad. Pr.*, Ded., One, who discurtains the vices of that time. **1659** *Lady Alimony* I. ii. in Hazl. *Dodsley* XIV. 280 Your acrimonious spirit will discurtain our changeable taffeta ladies.

‖ **discus** ('dɪskəs). [L. *discus* quoit, plate, a. Gr. δίσκος quoit.]

1. *Gr.* and *Rom. Antiq.* A disc of metal or heavy material used in ancient Grecian and Roman athletic exercises; a quoit. Also, *ellipt.*, the game of hurling the discus.

1656 COWLEY *Pindaric Odes, Praise Pindar* iii. *note*, The chief Exercises there were Running, Leaping, Wrestling, the Discus, which was the casting of a great round Stone, or Ball, made of Iron or Brass. **1725** POPE *Odyss.* VIII. 137 From Elatreus' strong arm the Discus flies. **1892** P. GARDNER *Chap. Grk. Hist.* ix. 295 The discus..weighed about twelve pounds. It was round and flat, and a skilful athlete..would sometimes hurl it more than a hundred feet. *Ibid.*, These three competitions—leaping, throwing the spear, and hurling the discus—were the chief and essential parts of the pentathlic contest.

b. In other ancient senses: (see quots.)

1706 PHILLIPS (ed. Kersey), *Discus*, a Dish or Platter for Meat..Also a round Consecrated Shield made to represent a Memorable Deed of some Hero of Antiquity, and hung up in a Temple of the Gods. *Ibid.*, *Discus* or *Descus* (in old Records), a Desk or Reading-shelf in a Church. **1849** LONGF. *Kavanagh* xxx, The untoward winds will blow the discus of the gods against my forehead. **1850** LEITCH *Müller's Anc. Art* §232 Isis, human, with cow horns and a discus between them.

† **2.** = DISC in its various technical senses.

1664 EVELYN *Mem.* 24 Oct. (1857) I. 406 Observing the discus of the sun for the passing of Mercury that day before it. **1665** *Phil. Trans.* I. No. 6. 105 The inclination of the discus of the Cometical Body. **1706** PHILLIPS (ed. Kersey), Among Herbalists, *Discus* is taken to signifie the middle, plain, and flat part of some Flowers; because its figure resembles the ancient Discus.

discuss (dɪ'skʌs), *v.* Forms: 4–7 **discusse**, (4–5 **discuse**, 5–6 **dyscus(se**, 6 **diskousse**, *pa. pple.* **discust**, 7 **discus**), 7– **discuss**. [f. L. *discuss-* ppl. stem of *discut-ĕre* to dash or shake to pieces, agitate, disperse, dispel, drive away; in late L. and Romanic to discuss, investigate: see DISCUTE. App. the L. pa. pple. *discussus* was first Englished as *discussed* (in Hampole *c* 1340, also Anglo Fr. *discussé*, 1352, in *Statutes of the Realm* I. 328), and *discuss* thence taken as the verb.]

† **1.** *trans.* To drive away, dispel, disperse, scatter. *lit.* and *fig. Obs.*

c **1374** CHAUCER *Boeth.* I. metr. iii. 9 When þat nyȝt was discussed and chased awey, derknesses forleften me. **1532** MORE *Confut. Tindale* Wks. 401/2 They wil clerely dissipate and discusse the myst. **1651** J. F[REAKE] *Agrippa's Occ. Philos.* 17 The Northern Wind, fierce and roaring, and discussing clouds.

† **b.** To shake off; also to set free, loosen. *Obs.*

a **1541** WYATT *Poet. Wks.* (1861) 201 To loose, and to discuss The sons of death out from their deadly bond. **1590** SPENSER *F.Q.* III. i. 48 All regard of shame she had discust, And meet respect of honor putt to flight.

† **c.** To put off, remove (dress). *Obs. rare.*

1640 GLAPTHORNE *Hollander* IV. Wks. (1874) I. 138 Now Cosen Sconce, you must discusse your doublet.

2. *Med.* To dissipate, dispel, or disperse (humours, tumours or obstructions). *arch.*

1533 ELYOT *Cast. Helthe* IV. i. (1539) 77 a, To rubbe them agayne with some oyle, that dothe open the poores, and dyscusse the vapours. **1597** GERARDE *Herbal* I. xx. (1633) 28 To discusse hard swellings in womens brests. **1684** tr. *Bonet's Merc. Compit.* III. 103 Of all edibles Garlick discusses wind most. **1751** JOHNSON *Rambler* No. 130 ¶5 A pomade..of virtue to discuss pimples. **1804** ABERNETHY *Surg. Obs.* 35 Three diseased lymphatic glands..resisted the attempts which had been made to discuss them.

b. *intr.* (for *refl.*) To disperse, pass away.

1758 J. S. *Le Dran's Observ. Surg.* (1771) 228 If the Erysipelas does not discuss, the Membrane falls into Putrefaction.

† **3.** *trans.* To examine or investigate (a matter); to try (as a judge). *Obs.*

1340 HAMPOLE *Pr. Consc.* 2415 We may noght fle, Until al our lyf examynd be, And alle our dedys, bathe gude and ille, Be discussed, after Goddes wille. *Ibid.* 6247 Crist, at his last commyng, Sal in dome sitte and discusse alle thyng. *c* **1400** *Lanfranc's Cirurg.* 141, I bileue, if..he wole wisely discussen alle þe opynyons of auctouris, þat he schal seen [etc.]. *c* **1450** tr. *De Imitatione* I. xiv, In demyng oþir men, a man laboriþ in veyn..but in demying & discussyng a man self, euere he laboriþ fruytuously. **1535** *Act 27 Hen. VIII*, c. 27 Anie matter or cause depending or to be discussed in the same courte. **1555** EDEN *Decades* 13 They haue onely discussed that superficiall parte of the earth which lyeth betwene the Ilandes of Gades and the ryuer of Ganges. **1613** SIR H. FINCH *Law* (1636) 479 A *Supersedeas* to stay execution till the error be discussed.

† **4.** To settle or decide (as a judge). *Obs.*

c **1381** CHAUCER *Parl. Foules* 624 Sith it may not here discussed be Who loveth her best. **1486** *Henry VII at York* in *Surtees Misc.* (1890) 55 To discuse up in conscience ich judiciall cace. **1551** ROBINSON tr *More's Utop.* (Arb.) 22, As an vmpier or a Iudge, with my sentence finallye to discusse. **1587** GOLDING *De Mornay* vii. 88 This vaine disputing whether of them was the first; which question the holy scripture will discusse in one word Yea, and nature it selfe also will discusse it. **1600** J. PORY tr. *Leo's Africa* II. 123 Which etymologie seemeth to me not improbable..But.. we leave that to be discussed by others. **1771** SMOLLETT *Humph. Cl.* (1797) VII. 192, I make no doubt but that in a day or two this troublesome business may be discussed.

† **b.** *absol.* To decide (*of*). *Obs.*

1514 BARCLAY *Cyt. & Uplondyshm.* (Percy Soc.) 32 Why sholde thyng mortall of endeles thyng dyscus. **1628** GAULE *Pract. Th.* (1629) 50 Pryingly to sift out, and peremptorily to discusse of the inscrutable Nature and Being of Christ.

† **5.** To make known, declare, pronounce. *Obs.*

(The history and place of this sense are not clear.)

1389 in *Eng. Gilds* (1870) 726 No brother no sister ne shalle discuse þe counseil of þis fraternite to no straungere. **1480** *Miracle Plays* (ed. Pollard 1890) 63 Lord thi rythwysnesse here dyscus. **1520** *Caxton's Chron. Eng.* III. 19/2 [Daniel] dyscussed the dreames of the kynge. **1598** SHAKS. *Merry W.* I. iii. 104, I will discusse the humour of this Loue to Ford. **1599** —— *Hen. V*, IV. iv. 5 Art thou a Gentleman? What is thy Name? discusse. *Ibid.* 30 Discusse the same in French vnto him. **1632** LITHGOW *Trav.* IX. 379 Time discussing you A miracle of Mettall.

6. To investigate or examine by argument; to sift the considerations for and against; to debate. (Now the ordinary sense.)

c **1450** [see DISCUSSING *vbl. sb.*]. **1530** RASTELL *Bk. Purgat.* III. vii. 2 Wherby man knowith the good from the evell, dyscussyng the thynge by argumentes. **1553** T. WILSON *Rhet.* (1580) 1 Rhetorique is an arte to set forthe..any cause, called in contention, that maie through reason largely be discussed. **1662** STILLINGFL. *Orig. Sacr.* I. ii. §3 Who that Jerombaal was, is much discussed among learned men. **1720** GAY *Poems* (1745) I. 238 We've business To discuss, a point of law. **1753** L. M. tr. *Du Boscq's Accompl. Wom.* II. 157 *note*, See the discourse..wherein it is discussed, whether brutes have the use of reason. **1777** PRIESTLEY *Philos. Necess.* x. 118 Mr. Hume..discusses the question.. with great clearness. **1847** TENNYSON *Princ.* II. 422 They, the while, Discuss'd a doubt and tost it to and fro. **1849** MACAULAY *Hist. Eng.* I. 598 Several schemes were proposed and discussed.

b. *absol.* To hold discussion; to debate.

1587 TURBERV. *Trag. T.* (1837) 42 Amongst themselves the feasters gan discusse And diversly debate from young to old. **1628** T. SPENCER *Logick* 311 A Method whereby wee come to know how to discusse.

7. *trans.* To sift or investigate (material). *rare.*

1802 PALEY *Nat. Theol.* xii. (1824) 483/2 These serrated or dentated bills..form a filtre. The ducks by means of them discuss the mud; examining with great accuracy the puddle.

8. To investigate or try the quality of (food or drink); to consume, make away with. (*Somewhat humorous.*)

1815 SCOTT *Guy M.* xxii, A tall, stout, country-looking man..busy discussing huge slices of cold boiled beef. **1836** MARRYAT *Midsh. Easy* i. 5 They allowed him to discuss the question, while they discussed his port wine. **1861** THORNBURY *Turner* II. 264 Turner was always to be seen between ten and eleven at the Athenæum, discussing his half-pint of sherry. **1884** LD. MALMESBURY *Mem. Ex-min.* II. 281 The time was passed in discussing a substantial luncheon.

9. *Civil Law.* To 'do diligence' (DILIGENCE 5 a) or exhaust legal proceedings against (a debtor), esp. against the person primarily liable (or his property), before proceeding against the property of a person secondarily liable.

Used with local peculiarities of application in Scotland, Lower Canada, and Louisiana, also as rendering Fr. *discuter* in analogous sense. See DISCUSSION 5.

1681–93 STAIR *Inst. Law Scot.* I. xvii. §5 Cautioners cannot be pursued till the principal debitor be discust. *Ibid.* III. v. §17 Heirs of Blood..and also Executors must be discussed before Heirs of Provision or Tailzie. **1766** W. GORDON *Gen. Counting-ho.* 340 The accepter being discussed, the bill must recoil upon the drawer. **1848** WHARTON *Law Lex.* s.v. *Discussion*, The obligation contracted by the surety with creditor is, that the latter shall not proceed against him until he has first discussed the principal debtor, if he is solvent. **1861** W. BELL *Dict. Law Scot.* 291 Where a special heir is burdened with a debt, the creditor must discuss that heir before he can insist against that heir-at-law..By discussing an heir is meant, charging him to enter; and if he do not renounce the succession, obtaining decree against him, and raising diligence both against his person and his estate, whether belonging to himself or derived from his ancestor, as in the case of the discussion of a cautioner. **18..** *Civil Code of Quebec* Art. 1942 The creditor is not bound to discuss the principal debtor unless the surety demands it when he is first sued. [See also DISCUSSION 5.]

Hence **di'scussed** *ppl. a.*

1598 FLORIO, *Discusso*, discussed, searched. **1892** *Pall Mall G.* 22 June 3/1 The only other discussed matter.

† **di'scuss,** *sb. Obs.* [app. f. DISCUSS *v.*; but cf. L. *discussus* dashing, agitating, f. ppl. stem of *discutĕre*: see DISCUSS *v.*] = DISCUSSION. **a.** Decision (of a judge), settlement. **b.** Examination, investigation. **c.** Debate; in quot. *fig.*

a. 1556 J. HEYWOOD *Spider & F.* lxv. 19 By his discus, Streight to blisse go they, streight to bale go wee. *Ibid.* Concl. 26 That they and we by goddes mercifull discus, May ..Liue and loue together. **1616** *Burgh Rec. Aberdeen* 5 Mar. (Jam. Supp.), To attend vpone the said actioun, vntil the finall end and discus thairof.

b. 1586 HOLINSHED *Chron. Scot.* II. 386/2 To refer my selfe to the discusse and consideration of his demands. **1609** SIR E. HOBY *Let. to Mr. T. H.* 6 In this my discusse..I will ..confine my selfe within this list. **1650** T. VAUGHAN

Anthrop. Theom. 7 These are *Magnalia Dei & Naturae*, and require not our Discusse so much as our Reverence.
c. **1655** H. VAUGHAN *Silex Scint.* I. *Storm* (1858) 57 When his waters billow thus, Dark storms and wind Incite them to that fierce discusse.

discussable, var. of DISCUSSIBLE.

di'scussal. *rare.* [f. DISCUSS *v.* + -AL[1].] = DISCUSSION.
1828 *Life Planter Jamaica* (ed. 2) 124 This discussal of a one-day's wonder.

discussant (dɪ'skʌsənt). orig. *U.S.* [f. DISCUSS *v.* + -ANT[1].] One who discusses, esp. one who takes part in a set discussion.
1927 *Jrnl. Amer. Med. Assoc.* 4 June 1818 The discussants were Drs. Sydney Kuh and Francis Gerty. **1966** D. G. HAYS *Readings in Automatic Language Processing* i. 2 To take the case of group discussions, how can.. authority be predicted from what the discussants have said to one another in the course of a few hours of conversation? **1967** *Listener* 6 Apr. 469/1 Besides the speakers there were ten discussants who did not contribute papers of their own. **1970** *Language* XLVI. 688 Travel stipends were granted to 'discussants' whose function was to belabor controversial points of each paper after summary oral presentation.

discusser (dɪ'skʌsə(r)). [f. as DISCUSS *v.* + -ER[1].] He who or that which discusses, in various senses. †**a.** One who settles or decides questions (*obs.*). **b.** One who engages in discussion or debate. †**c.** A medicine that disperses humours, etc. (*obs.*).
a. 1596 DALRYMPLE tr. *Leslie's Hist. Scot.* I. VI. 337 Quha was cheife discusser in controuersies, quhom thay call grett Justice of Jngland. **1597** HOOKER *Eccl. Pol.* VIII. vi. §12 That thereof God himself was *inventor, disceptator, lator*, the deviser, the discusser, the deliverer.
b. 1611 COTGR., *Discuteur*, a discusser, examiner, debater. **1689** *Answ. Desertion Discussed* in *11th Collect. Papers Present Juncture of Affairs* 6 Thus the Discusser rambles out of one Untruth into another. **1691** WOOD *Ath. Oxon.* I. 349 A discusser of controversies against Bellarmine. **1893** *Chicago Advance* 23 Nov., [The biblical preacher] is not a discusser, whose office is to break to pieces and sift for better construction and consolidation.
c. 1612 WOODALL *Surg. Mate* Wks. (1653) 29 This Minium-plaster is a good discusser of hot humors. **1656** RIDGLEY *Pract. Physick* 31 First give astringent Syrups, then add discussers.

discussible (dɪ'skʌsɪb(ə)l), *a.* Also 7 **-able**. [f. L. *discuss-*: see DISCUSS *v.* + -BLE.] Capable of being discussed. †**a.** *Med.* That can be dispersed, as a humour. **b.** That can be debated or examined by argument.
1662 J. CHANDLER *Van Helmont's Oriat.* 330 To consume water, and the more light discussible things, into vapours. **1862** MILL *Logic* (ed. 5) II. 18 *note*, To have rendered so bold a suggestion.. admissible and discussible even as a conjecture. **1889** J. M. ROBERTSON *Ess. Crit. Method* 71 It is discussible under three aspects.

discussient, obs. by-form of DISCUTIENT.

di'scussing, *vbl. sb.* [f. DISCUSS *v.* + -ING[1].] The action of the verb DISCUSS; = DISCUSSION (in various senses).
c **1450** *R. Gloucester's Chron.* (1724) 483/2 *note* (MS. Coll. Arms) Among righte welle lettred men.. he hathe busy discussyng of questions. *c* **1555** *Fisher's Life* in *Wks.* (E.E.T.S.) II. 139 To have referred the hearing and discussing of his crime to his metropolitan. **1611** COTGR., *Liquidation*.. a discussing, or examination. **1681-93** STAIR *Inst. Law Scot.* III. v. §17 Heirs.. have the benefit of an order of discussing. **1726** AYLIFFE *Paregon* 192 To commit the Discussing of Causes privately to certain Persons learn'd in the Laws.

di'scussing, *ppl. a.* [f. as prec. + -ING[2].] That discusses; in various senses of the vb.; *spec.* of medicine. That disperses humours, tumours, etc.
1607 TOPSELL *Four-f. Beasts* (1658) 437 There is such a dispersing and discussing nature in Wine, that it dissolveth all.. hard things in the bodies of Beasts. **1632** BRUEL *Phys. Pract.* 276 These discussing medicines shalbe vsed. **1707** FLOYER *Physic. Pulse-Watch* 279 Hot discussing Unctions.

discussion (dɪ'skʌʃən). Also 4 discucion. [a. OF. *discussion, discucion* (12th c. in Littré), ad. L. *discussiōn-em* shaking, examination, discussion, n. of action from *discutĕre*: see DISCUTE, DISCUSS.]
†**1.** Examination, investigation, trial (by a judge) judicial decision. *Obs.*
a **1340** HAMPOLE *Psalter* I. 1 Here fordos he discussion of syn, for he grauntes the dede. **1340** —— *Pr. Consc.* 2582 When þe devels and þe angels Has desputed our lif.. And discucion made, als fals to be. *c* **1440** *Jacob's Well* xv. 98 Seynt Gregorie seyth, þat doom is a dyscussyoun of þe cause. **1526** *Pilgr. Perf.* (W. de W. 1531) 60 b, Make dayly discussyon of thy conscyence.
2. a. Examination or investigation (*of* a matter) by arguments for and against; 'the ventilation of a question' (J.).
a **1556** CRANMER *Wks.* (Parker Soc.) I. 61 Where you seem to be offended with the discussion of this matter, what hurt .. can gold catch in the fire, or truth with discussing? **1558** BP. WATSON *Sev. Sacram.* viii. 44 The subtlenesse of mans wyt.. is to bee reiected from the iudgement and discussion of this holy mystery. **1647** H. MORE *Philos. Poems, Democritus Platonissans* Pref. 190 Discussion is no prejudice but an honour to the truth. **1771** *Junius Lett.* lix. 310, I do not mean to renew the discussion of such opinions. **1874** GREEN *Short Hist.* viii. §2. 477 He [James].. forbade any further discussion of State policy. **1891** LD. HERSCHELL in *Law Times, Rep.* LXV. 567/1 Much learning was expended in the discussion of the point.
b. Argument or debate with a view to elicit truth or establish a point; a disquisition in which a subject is treated from different sides.
1789 BELSHAM *Ess.* II. xl. 519 Passionate dogmatists, the avowed enemies of discussion. **1790** BURKE *Fr. Rev.* Pref. 3 The Author began a second and more full discussion on the subject. **1856** FROUDE *Hist. Eng.* (1858) I. iii. 205 In the House of Commons.. there was in theory unrestricted liberty of discussion. **1875** JOWETT *Plato* (ed. 2) IV. 14 This discussion is one of the least satisfactory in the dialogues of Plato.
3. Investigation of the quality of an article of food, etc. by consumption of it. *humorous* and *colloq.*
1853 C. BRONTË *Villette* I. vi. 89 The small dainty messes Miss Marchmont's cook used to send up.. to the discussion of which we could not bring half an appetite between us! **1862** SALA *Seven Sons* I. iii. 49 [He] has.. five minutes for the discussion of his beloved cheroot. **1864** D. G. MITCHELL *Sev. Stor.* 54 We fell presently to discussion of the mutton. **1870** E. PEACOCK *Ralf Skirl.* II. 143 The discussion of a bottle of port in Mr. Rudd's back parlour.
†**4.** *Med.* The dissipation or dispersal of humours, the resolution of tumours, etc.
1620 VENNER *Via Recta* Introd. 3 Discussion of vaporous superfluities. **1656** H. MORE *Enthus. Tri.* 26 Evident from the suddain and easy discussion of the fit. **1753** N. TORRIANO *Gangr. Sore Throat* 35 The Parents earnestly desiring the Discussion of it, I was constrained to put upon the Tumour.. Diabotanum. **1758** J. S. *Le Dran's Observ. Surg.* (1771) 330 The Termination of the Erysipelas was not only by Discussion, or Resolution, but also by Suppuration.
5. *Civil Law.* The exhaustion of legal proceedings against a debtor, esp. against a person primarily liable for a debt or payment, before proceeding against a person secondarily liable.
A term of Roman Law, whence of the old law of France, and of the Code Napoléon; thence of the codes of Quebec, and Louisiana; also of the law of Scotland, where the 'discussion of heirs' is a specific feature.
benefit of discussion: the right of a person liable to pay a certain sum in case of the failure of the person primarily liable, to require legal proceedings to be exhausted against the latter before demand is made upon himself. ***discussion of heirs*** (*Sc. Law*), the proceeding against heirs for debts due by the deceased, in a determined order, with use of diligence against the first, before proceeding against the second, and so on.
1681-93 STAIR *Inst. Laws Scot.* III. v. §20 To sist process against such Heirs as have the benefite of Discussion. **1751-3** A. M'DOUALL *Inst. Law Scot.* I. xxiii. 30 One who becomes bound either to cause the debtor to pay or pay the debt himself.. has not the benefit of discussion. **1848** WHARTON *Law Lex.* 184/2 By the Roman law sureties were .. liable only after the creditor had sought payment from the principal debtor, and he was unable to pay. This was called the benefit or right of discussion. **1861** W. BELL *Dict. Law Scot.* 290/2 *Discussion.* This is a technical term in the law of Scotland, and may be applied either to the discussion of a principal debtor, or to the discussion of heirs. *Ibid.* The privilege of discussion is now taken away by the Act 19 and 20 Vict., c. 60, §8, 1856, unless expressly stipulated for in the instrument of caution. *Ibid.* 291 *Discussion of heirs*.. The following is the legal order in which the heirs must be discussed:—*1st* The heir of line.. *2d* the heir of conquest.. *3d* the heir-male.. *4th* heirs of tailzie and provision by simple destination, where they represent the debtor; and *lastly* Heirs under marriage-contracts, where they are not themselves creditors. **18..** *Civil Code of Quebec* Art. 1941 The surety is liable only upon the default of the debtor, who must previously be discussed, unless the surety has renounced the benefit of discussion. **18..** *Law of Louisiana* Arts. 3014-17 (old Nos.), 3045-8 (new Nos.).
6. *Comb.*, as ***discussion-circle, group, -meeting, programme.***
1937 C. DAY LEWIS *Starting Point* III. iii. 269 When the Neale clan gets together, it's just one devastating discussion-circle from morning to night. **1921** H. J. LASKI *Let.* 31 July (1953) I. 356 A discussion group to thresh out the problems of governmental re-organisation. **1940** GRAVES & HODGE *Long Week-End* xxii. 387 The B.B.C.. appointed Education Officers.. whose duty it was to organize 'Discussion Groups'. **1853** LYNCH *Self-Improv.* iv. 97 The young man.. may get and give much good in discussion-meetings. **1958** *New Statesman* 15 Mar. 332/3 One radio feature which is not yet practicable on TV is the BBC's monthly international discussion-programme, *Radio Link.*

di'scussional, *a.* [f. prec. + -AL[1].] Of the nature of or pertaining to discussion.
1848 *Fraser's Mag.* XXXVIII. 341 In this whole array of discussional ostentation.

di'scussionist. [f. as prec. + -IST.] One who advocates or practises discussion or debate.
1867 *Ch. & State Rev.* 30 Mar. 292 The discussionists cannot resist the temptation.. to air their vocabulary. **1879** *Cassell's Techn. Educ.* I. 152 In religious sects and theological discussionists.

discussive (dɪ'skʌsɪv), *a.* and *sb.* [f. L. *discuss-* ppl. stem of *discutĕre* to DISCUSS + -IVE.]
A. *adj.* †**1.** *Med.* = DISCUTIENT *a. Obs.*
1580 *Well of W. Hill, Aberdeen* A iij, [The water] being laxatiue, attenuatiue.. and discussiue. **1628** VENNER *Tobacco* (1650) 407 Its faculty being both discussive and expulsive. **1727** BRADLEY *Fam. Dict.* s.v. *Burdock*, It.. is discussive and bitter to the taste.
†**2.** Having the quality of settling (a matter in dispute); decisive. *Obs.*
1604 T. WRIGHT *Passions* v. iv. 18 Things.. not discussive for questions or disputes. **1644** *Presbytery Display'd* (1668) 20 [They] have *vocem deliberativam, vocem decisivam*, have a debating, discussive voice.
3. Pertaining to discussion or debate. *arch.*
1644 MILTON *Jdgm. Bucer* (1851) 304 Ready, in a fair and christianly discussive way, to debate and sift this matter. **1698** J. COCKBURN *Bourignianism Detected* i. 16 Those Rational discussive Faculties which help others to the knowledge of Truth. **1816** KEATINGE *Trav.* (1817) I. 125 Judiciously curtailed of some.. verbose discussive scenes.
†**B.** *sb. Med.* A dissipating or resolving agent; a discutient. *Obs.*
1612 *Enchir. Med.* 92 Beware of immoderate discussiues. **1671** SALMON *Syn. Med.* III. xvi. 364 Discussives are such as generally disperse the matter, and so dissolve it insensibly.
Hence †**di'scussively** *adv.* †**di'scussiveness.**
1613 M. RIDLEY *Magn. Bodies* 6 These being artificially and discussively fastened to this Loadstone. **1727** BAILEY vol. II, *Discussiveness*, dissolving or dispersing quality.

†**di'scussment.** *Obs. rare.* [f. DISCUSS *v.* + -MENT.] = DISCUSSION.
1559 ABP. PARKER *Corr.* 94 We beseech your Majesty.. to refer the discussment and deciding of them to a synod of your bishops and other godly learned men. **1651** CARTWRIGHT *Cert. Relig.* I. 57 Requisite for the Churches understanding, and by.. her consultations and discussments.

di'scussory, *a. rare*[−0]. [f. L. *discuss-* (see DISCUSSIVE) + -ORY.] Discutient.
1823 CRABB *Technol. Dict.*, *Discutient* or *Discussory medicines*, those which dissolve impacted matter.

†**di'scussure.** *Obs. rare*[−1]. [f. L. *discuss-* (see DISCUSSIVE) + -URE.] = DISCUSSION.
1610 W. FOLKINGHAM *Art of Survey* I. ii. 2 The Matter comprises the Elementarie composition and constitution of Possessions: and in discussure thereof, the Materiall parte is most conuersant.

†**dis'custom,** *sb. Obs. rare*[−1]. [f. DIS- 9 + CUSTOM *sb.*: prob. after DISCUSTOM *v.*] Discontinuance of a custom; disuse.
1603 FLORIO *Montaigne* III. xii. (1632) 611 Better.. than for ever through discustome.. lose the commerce and conversation of common life.

†**dis'custom,** *v. Obs.* [ad. OF. *descostumer, -coustumer* to lose the habit or custom of, f. *des-*, DIS- 4 + *costumer* to render customary, etc.: see CUSTOM *v.*] *trans.* To render unaccustomed; to cause to discontinue a custom or habit; = DISACCUSTOM. Hence **dis'customed** *ppl. a.*
1502 *Ord. Crysten Men* (W. de W. 1506) IV. xxii. 299 Moeuynge the helpe of god hym to dyscustome. **1598** SYLVESTER *Du Bartas* II. ii. I. (1641) 113/1 If now no more my sacred rimes distill With Art-lesse ease from my discustom'd quill. **1677** E. PLEDGER in Spurgeon *Treas. Dav.* Ps. xxx. 7 Discustom ourselves to the exercise of faith.

di'scutable, *a. rare.* [a. mod.F. *discutable*, f. *discuter*, ad. L. *discutĕre* to DISCUSS: cf. next.] Capable of being discussed; DISCUSSIBLE.
1893 *Sat. Rev.* 11 Feb. 150/1 Many insoluble or discutable points.

'discutant. *rare.* [a. F. *discutant*, pr. pple. of *discuter* to discuss, used subst.: see -ANT[1].] One who discusses.
1871 H. B. FORMAN *Living Poets* 166 The contrast between the half-frank discutant and the unctuous but immoral dignitary discussed.

†**di'scute,** *v. Obs.* [a. F. *discute-r* (14th c. in Hatz.-Darm.), ad. L. *discutĕre* to dash or shake asunder, in late L. to discuss, investigate, f. DIS- 1 + *quatĕre* (in comb. *-cutĕre*) to shake, strike with a shock. Now displaced by DISCUSS.] *trans.* To discuss; to investigate, examine.
1483 CAXTON *Cato* A viij, Euery juge ought to discute and examyne the caas of bothe partyes in suche manere that he may do equite and justyce. **1484** —— *Fables of Alfonce* (1889) 9 The cause to be discuted or pleted before the Juge.
b. *intr.* with *of.*
a **1521** *Helyas* in Thoms *Prose Rom.* (1858) III. 53 To discute of a mater.
Hence **di'scuting** *vbl. sb.*, discussing.
1483 CAXTON *Gold. Leg.* 431 b/1 O dylygente dyscutyng of causes and maters he rendred or yelded juste jugemente.

discutient (dɪ'skjuːʃɪənt). *a.* and *sb. Med.* Also 7 **discussient**. [ad. L. *discutient-em*, pr. pple. of *discutĕre*: see DISCUTE.]
A. *adj.* Having the quality of 'discussing' or dissipating morbid matter; resolvent.
1612 WOODALL *Surg. Mate* Wks. (1653) 311 A discutient Cataplasme. **1740** AYLETT in *Phil. Trans.* XLIII. 10 An hot, discutient, and restringent Fomentation. **1876** BARTHOLOW *Mat. Med.* (1879) 411 Preparations of conium were much used for a supposed discutient or resolvent action.. in certain kinds of tumors.
B. *sb.* A discutient medicine or preparation.
1655 CULPEPPER *Riverius* I. xv. 54 When the matter is somwhat thin.. use not strong discussients and dissolvers. **1718** QUINCY *Compl. Disp.* 109 It enters.. into many Fomentations, as a good Discutient. **1830** LINDLEY *Nat. Syst. Bot.* 30 Employed externally as a discutient.

disdain (dɪs'deɪn), *sb.* Forms: *α.* 3-5 dedeyn(e, 4 dedeigne, -eyng, -ayn, 5 dedein. *β.* 4-5 desdeyn, -dayn. *γ.* 4 disdein(e, 4-5 -deyn(e, 4-6 -deigne, 4-7 -dayn(e, 5 dysdane, -dene, -dayne, *Sc.*

disdenȝe, -**dene**, 6–7 **disdaine**, 6– **disdain**. Cf. SDEIGN. [ME. *dedeyn*, *desdeyn*, a. OF. *desdeign*, *-daign*, *-daing*, *-dain*, AF. *dedeigne* (Langtoft Chron. II. 430), mod.F. *dedain* = Pr. *desdaing*, *-denh*, Cat. *desdeny*, Sp. *desdeño*, It. *disdegno* (*sdegno*), Romanic deriv. of *des-*, *disdegnare* to disdain: see next.]

1. The feeling entertained towards that which one thinks unworthy of notice or beneath one's dignity; scorn, contempt.

α. *c* **1290** *S. Eng. Leg.* I. 414/387 He hadde gret de-deyn smale þeþes to do. *a* **1300** *Cursor M.* 11309 (Cott.) O pouert na dedeigne [*later MSS.* disdeyn, -dayne], had he. *a* **1340** HAMPOLE *Psalter* xxviii. 6 Þai ere kald vnycorns for pride & dedeyne. *c* **1450** MYRC 1159 Hast [þow] had any dedeyn Of oþer synfulle þat þou hast seyn?

γ. **1393** GOWER *Conf.* I. 121 He, which love had in disdeigne. **1540–1** ELYOT *Image Gov.* Pref. (1556) 3 Although disdeigne and envie dooe cause them to speake it. **1599** SHAKS. *Much Ado* III. i. 51 Disdaine and Scorne ride sparkling in her eyes, Mis-prizing what they looke on. **1667** MILTON *P.L.* I. 98 That fixt mind And high disdain, from sence of injur'd merit. **1749** FIELDING *Tom Jones* XI. vii, As I received no answer..my disdain would not suffer me to continue my application. **1824** L. MURRAY *Eng. Gram.* (ed. 5) I. 440 Haughtiness is founded on the high opinion we entertain of ourselves; disdain, on the low opinion we have of others. **1855** MILMAN *Lat. Chr.* (1864) V. IX. viii. 401 They were called in disdain the Puritans, an appellation which perhaps they did not disdain. **1875** F. HALL in *Lippincott's Mag.* XV. 342/1, I..had conceived a disdain of feathered things, bustards excepted.

†**b.** with *pl.* An instance or exhibition of this.

a **1631** DONNE *Dial. w. Sir H. Wotton* (T.), So her disdains can ne'er offend. **1632** SIR T. HAWKINS tr. *Mathieu's Vnhappy Prosp.* 152 My disdaines have served my purposes.

†**2.** Indignation; anger or vexation arising from offended dignity; dudgeon. *to have d.*: to be indignant, take offence. *to have in d.*, *to have d. of*: to be indignant or offended at. *Obs.*

α. **1297** R. GLOUC. (1724) 193 Of þyn vnryȝt ychabbe gret dedeyn. *a* **1340** HAMPOLE *Psalter* xxxvi. 1 *Noli emulari in malignantibus*..Will not haf dedeyn in ill willand. *Ibid.* lxxxiv. 3 *Auertisti ab ira indignacionis tue*..þou turnyd fra þe wreth of þi dedeyn. *c* **1380** WYCLIF *Serm.* Sel. Wks. II. 70 Þis eldere sone hadde dedeyn, and wolde not come in. *a* **1400–50** *Alexander* 3155 He dedeyne [*Dubl. MS.* disdayne] hade, þat þai ware comen doun of kyngis, and be no cause ellis.

β. *c* **1386** CHAUCER *Frankl. Prol.* 28 (Ellesm. MS.), I prey yow haueth me nat in desdeyn [*v.r.* disdeyne] Though to this man I speke a word or two. *a* **1450** *Knt. de la Tour* (1868) 17 The king saide, 'y chese the yongest of the .iij. doughters ..' of the whiche the eldest and the secounde had gret meruaile and desdeyn. **1481** CAXTON *Myrr.* II. vi. 72 Of grete desdayn he suffreth to be slayn and dye.

γ. *c* **1386** CHAUCER *Prol.* 789 (Sloane MS.) But take it nought I praie ȝow in disdeigne [*v.rr.* disdeyne, disdayn, desdeyn]. **1393** GOWER *Conf.* II. 345 But Phebus, which hath great disdein Of that his maiden was forlein. **1513** DOUGLAS *Æneis* VII. xiii. 160 Than Jupiter..Haifand disdene ony mortall suld be Rasit to lyf. **1600** E. BLOUNT tr. *Conestaggio* 299 The defeat of the Armie..caused.. throughout the Realme a great griefe and disdaine. **1606** SHAKS. *Tr. & Cr.* I. ii. 35 The disdain and shame whereof, hath euer since kept Hector fasting and waking. **1659** B. HARRIS *Parival's Iron Age* 229 Having conceived some disdain against his Master. *a* **1677** BARROW *Serm.* Wks. 1716 I. 62 The great person..took the neglect in huge disdain.

†**b.** *fig.* Of a wound: Angriness, inflamed condition. *Obs. rare.* (Cf. *proud flesh.*)

c **1400** *Lanfranc's Cirurg.* 102 Whanne þilke wounde was sowdid þe pannicle þat was not weel heelid hadde a dedein & was cause of gendrynge of a crampe.

†**3.** Loathing, aversion, dislike. *Obs.*

[**1370–80** in *O.E. Misc.* 228 And hedden of mony metes de-deyn.] **1655** CULPEPPER *Riverius* I. vii. 30 These are the forerunners of an Epilepsy; disdain of meat [etc.].

†**b.** *transf.* The quality which excites aversion; loathsomeness. (Cf. DAIN *sb.* 3.) *Obs.*

1590 SPENSER *F.Q.* I. i. 14 Most lothsom, filthie, foule, and full of vile disdaine.

disdain (dɪsˈdeɪn), *v.* Forms: α. 4 **dedeyngne**, 4–5 **dedeyne**, 5 **dedene**; β. 4 **desdaine**, **-deigne**, 6 **-dayne**. γ. 5 **disdeyne**, **-daigne**, (**disdeynt**), 5–6 **dys-**, 5–7 **disdayne**, 6 **disdeine**, **-dane**, 6–7 **-daine**, **-deigne**, 6– **disdain**. Cf. also SDEIGN *v.* [ME., a. OF. *desdeignier*, *-deigner* (3rd s. pres. *-deigne*), in later F. *dédaigner*, = Pr. *desdegnar*, Cat. *desdenyar*, Sp. *dedeñar*, Pg. *desdenhar*, It. *disdegnare* (*sdegnare*); a Common Romanic vb. representing, with *des-* for L. *dē-* (see DE- 6), L. *dēdignāre* (collateral form of *dēdignārī*) to reject as unworthy, disdain. f. DE- 6 + *dignāre*, *-ārī* to think or treat as worthy; cf. DEIGN.]

1. *trans.* To think unworthy of oneself, or of one's notice; to regard or treat with contempt; to despise, scorn. **a.** with *simple obj.*

α and β. *c* **1386** CHAUCER *Clerk's T.* 42 (Ellesm. MS.) Lat youre eres nat my voys desdeyne [*other MSS.* disdeyne]. **1483** *Cath. Angl.* 93/1 To Desden (Deden *A.*), *dedignari, detrahere, detractare*; *vbi.* to disspise.

γ. *c* **1386** [see α and β]. **1509** HAWES *Past. Pleas.* XVI. lvii, I fere to sore I shal disdayned be. **1573** G. HARVEY *Letter-bk.* (Camden) 4 He laid against me..that I did disdain everi mans cumpani. **1613** PURCHAS *Pilgrimage* V. xvii. 459 Whose proud top would disdaine climing. **1754** EDWARDS *Freed. Will* IV. iv. 217 Some seem to disdain the Distinction that we make between natural and moral Necessity. **1821** SHELLEY *Prometh. Unb.* I. 52 If they disdained not such a prostrate slave. **1858** LYTTON *What will he do?* I. x, I disdain your sneer.

b. with *inf.* or *gerund.* To think it beneath one, to scorn (*to do* or *doing* something).

α. *c* **1380** *Sir Ferumb.* 2179 Ys herte was so gret, þat he dedeynede to clepe, 'oundo'; bot ran to wiþ is fet.

β. **1393** GOWER *Conf.* III. 227 If..a king..Desdaineth for to done hem grace.

γ. **1489** CAXTON *Faytes of A.* I. xv. 43 They dysdayne to obeye to theyre capytayne. *a* **1533** LD. BERNERS *Huon* xxiv. 70 They dysdayne to speke to me. **1611** BIBLE *Transl. Pref.* 11 Neither did we disdaine to reuise that which we had done. **1769** GOLDSM. *Roman Hist.* (1786) I. 397 This..was the title the Roman general disdained granting him. **1786** W. THOMSON *Watson's Philip III* (1839) 357 [They] disdained to follow this example of submission. **1868** E. EDWARDS *Raleigh* I. xx. 455 Grey..had disdained to beg his life.

c. To think (a thing) unworthy of (something). (Cf. DEIGN *v.* 2.)

1646 J. HALL *Horæ Vac.* 23 Nature disdeigned it a Roome.

d. To think (anything) unworthy *of.*

1591 SPENSER *Ruins of Time* Ded., God hath disdeigned the world of that most noble Spirit.

†**2.** To be indignant, angry, or offended at. *Obs.*

1494 FABYAN *Chron.* II. xlviii. 32 The kynge disdeynynge this demeanure of Andragius, after dyuers monycions.. gatheryd his knyghtes and made warre vpon Andragius. **1632** LITHGOW *Trav.* Prol. B, To shun Ingratitude, which I disdaine as Hell. **1633** T. STAFFORD *Pac. Hib.* vi. (1821) 84 His answer was much disdained. **1695** LD. PRESTON *Boeth.* III. 106 Hence..we often so much disdain their being conferr'd upon undeserving Men.

b. with subord. clause: To be indignant *that.*

1548 HALL *Chron., Rich. III*, 45 The kyng of Scottes disdeignynge that the stronge castell of Dumbarre should remayne in thenglish mennes handes. **1587** TURBERV. *Trag. T.* (1837) 128 Who highly did disdaine That such..abuse his honour should distaine. **1602** MARSTON *Ant. & Mel.* II. Wks. 1856 I. 27, I have nineteene mistresses alreadie, and I not much disdeigne that thou shold'st make up the ful score. **1796** W. TAYLOR in *Monthly Mag.* I. 14 Disdaining that the enemies of Christ should abound in wealth.

†**3.** *intr.* To be moved with indignation, be indignant, take offence. Const. *at* (rarely *against, of, on*). *Obs.*

α. **1382** WYCLIF *Job* xxxii. 3 But aȝen the thre frendis of hym he dedeynede, forthi that thei hadden not founde a resounable answere. —— *Matt.* xxi. 15 The princis of prestis and scribis..dedeyneden, and seiden to hym, Heerist thou what these seyen? *a* **1400** *Relig. Pieces fr. Thornton MS.* 90 Þat deuyls lymme, dedeyned at þi dede.

γ. **14..** *Epiph.* in *Tundale's Vis.* 108 Of whos cumyng though thou dysdeyne Hyt may not pleynly help. **1526** TINDALE *Matt.* xx. 24 They disdayned at the two brethren. —— *John* vii. 23 Disdayne ye at me, because I made a man every whit whoale? *c* **1563** CAVENDISH *Ld. Seymour* iv., in *Wolsey*, etc. (1825) II. 105 To disdayn ayenst natures newe estate. **1636** B. JONSON *Discov.* ad fin., Ajax, deprived of Achilles' armour..disdains; and growing impatient of the injury, rageth, and runs mad. **1634** SIR T. HERBERT *Trav.* 150 Cheese and Butter is among them, but such as squemish English stomacks will disdaine at.

†**4.** *trans.* To move to indignation or scorn; to offend, anger, displease. *Obs.*

a **1470** TIPTOFT *Caesar* x. (1530) 12 Induciomarus was sore displeased and dysdayned at thys doynge. **1627** *Vox Piscis* A v b, It shall nothing disdaine you; for it is no new thing, but even that which you have continually looked for. **1650** HOWELL *Giraffi's Rev. Naples* 18 The people..being much disdain'd that the Vice-Roy had scap'd. **1790–1817** COMBE *Devil upon Two Sticks in Lond.* I. 251 Fashionable amusements delight him not, and even elegant vice disdains him.

†**b.** impers. *it disdains me*: it moves my indignation, offends me.

c **1440** *York Myst.* v. 11 Me thoght þat he The kynde of vs tane myght, And þer-at dideyned me.

dis'dainable, *a. rare.* [a. OF. *desdaignable*: see prec. and -ABLE.] Worthy of disdain.

1611 COTGR., *Desdaignable*, disdainable, contemptible. **1895** *Daily News* 9 Sept. 4/7 That tenth of a second of allowance was..not disdained..Yet to one not to the manner born of racing it might have certainly seemed 'disdainable'.

disdained (dɪsˈdeɪnd), *ppl. a.* [f. DISDAIN.]

1. Treated with disdain; despised, scorned.

1598 YONG *Diana* 6 The disdained Shepherd. **1670** MILTON *Hist. Eng.* II. Wks. (1851) 54 A new and disdained sight.

†**2.** Characterized by disdain; disdainful, scornful. *Obs. rare.*

1596 SHAKS. *1 Hen. IV*, I. iii. 183 Reuenge the geering and disdain'd contempt Of this proud King.

†**dis'dainedly**, *adv. Obs. rare.* [f. prec. + -LY[2].] Scornfully, disdainfully.

1535 COVERDALE *1 Sam.* xvii. 10, I haue spoken diszdanedly vnto the hoost of Israel. —— *Ps.* xxx. 18 Which cruelly, diszdanedly & despitefully speake agaynst the rightuous.

dis'dainer. [f. DISDAIN *v.* + -ER[1].] One who disdains; a scorner, despiser.

1580 HOLLYBAND *Treas. Fr. Tong*, *Mespriseur*, a disdayner, a despiser. **1587** GOLDING *De Mornay* ii. 22 To make his greatest disdainers..confesse his arte. *c* **1630** *Trag. Rich. II.* (1870) 49 The tooe, a disdayner or spurner.

disdainful (dɪsˈdeɪnfʊl), *a.* [f. DISDAIN *sb.* + -FUL.]

1. Full of or showing disdain; scornful, contemptuous, proudly disregardful.

a **1542** WYATT *Wauering Louer* in *Tottell's Misc.* (Arb.) 35 Vnder disdainfull brow. **1600** SHAKS. *A.Y.L.* III. iv. 53 The proud disdainfull Shepherdesse That was his Mistresse. **1663** COWLEY *Ode Restoration* xii, Cast a disdainful look behind. **1750** GRAY *Elegy* viii, Nor [let] Grandeur hear with a disdainful smile The short and simple annals of the poor. **1849** MACAULAY *Hist. Eng.* I. 122 They..marched against the most renowned battalions of Europe with disdainful confidence.

b. Const. *inf.* or *of.*

1580 LYLY *Euphues* (Arb.) 446 They are..not disdainfulle to conferre. **1613** SHAKS. *Hen. VIII*, II. iv. 123 Stubborne to Iustice..Disdainfull to be tride by 't. **1746** MORELL *Oratorio 'Judas Maccabæus'*, Disdainful of danger, we'll rush on the foe. **1874** GREEN *Short Hist.* viii. §5. 505 An administrator, disdainful of private ends.

†**2.** Indignant, displeased; inimical. *Obs. rare.*

1548 HALL *Chron., Rich. III*, 45b, The malicious attemptes and disdeynfull invencions of his envious adversaries. **1550** COVERDALE *Spir. Perle* xii. Wks. (Parker Soc.) I. 133 Vexed in his mind and disdainful that he is not so..fortunate as other be.

†**3.** That is the object of indignation, hateful; that is the object of disdain. *Obs.*

a **1547** SURREY *Æneid* II. 850 For I my yeres disdainfull to the Gods [*invisus divis*] Have lingred fourth. **1586** MARLOWE *1st Pt. Tamburl.* IV. ii, Villain..Fall prostrate on the low disdainful earth.

disdainfully (dɪsˈdeɪnfʊlɪ), *adv.* [f. prec. + -LY[2].] In a disdainful manner; with disdain; scornfully, contemptuously; †with indignation.

a **1533** LD. BERNERS *Gold. Bk. M. Aurel.* xiii. (R.), Enemies, that disdeinfully wold put theim vnder. **1548** HALL *Chron., Hen. VI*, 159 This proude byll, was both of the kyng, and his counsaill, disdainfully taken. **1606** SHAKS. *Tr. & Cr.* III. iii. 53 Either greete him not, Or else disdainfully. **1749** FIELDING *Tom Jones* XVII. ii, You would not have so disdainfully called him fellow. **1838** DICKENS *Nich. Nick.* xix, He smiled disdainfully and pointed to the door.

dis'dainfulness. [f. as prec. + -NESS.] The quality of being disdainful.

1548 UDALL, etc. *Erasm. Par. Luke* vii. 37 (R.) With howe great stately disdeignfulnesse, and straunge countenance the Pharisiacall sort vsed to turne awai their faces from sinners. **1641** 'SMECTYMNUUS' *Vind. Answ.* xv. 184 The extreame disdainfulnesse that breaths in every page and line. **1719** D'URFEY *Pills* IV. 113 Her Disdainfulness my Heart hath Cloven. **1856** R. A. VAUGHAN *Mystics* (1860) II. VIII. viii. 287 *note*, Should she leave her sting in the flower, if its juices are not to her taste, as man doth in his disdainfulness?

dis'daining, *vbl. sb.* [f. DISDAIN *v.* + -ING[1].] The action of the verb DISDAIN; the expression of disdain or scorn.

1556 *Aurelio & Isab.* (1608) B vj, That the sodain disdaining rendred him rigorouser. *a* **1631** DONNE *Dial. w. Sir H. Wotton* (T.), Say her disdainings justly must be grac'd With name of chast. **1633** P. FLETCHER *Purple Isl.* x. 19 In thy place is stept Disdaining vile, And Flatterie, base sonne of Need and Shame. **1722** ELIZA HAYWOOD *Brit. Recluse* 131 Her very Countenance discover'd the secret Disdainings of her Soul.

dis'daining, *ppl. a.* [f. as prec. + -ING[2].] That disdains; disdainful, scornful.

Hence **dis'dainingly** *adv.*

c **1485** *Digby Myst.* IV. 1352 To be scornyd most dedenynglye. **1519** HORMAN *Vulg.* 116 He goeth statly, and disdaynyngly. **1611** SPEED *Hist. Gt. Brit.* IX. iii. (1632) 462 The Noble Helias disdainingly storming.

†**dis'dainish**, *a. Obs.* [f. DISDAIN *sb.* + -ISH.] Inclined to be disdainful or scornful.

Hence **dis'dainishly** *adv.*

1540 HYRDE tr. *Vives' Instr. Chr. Wom.* I. xii. (R.), Nor set her countenance..disdainishly.

†**dis'dainous**, *a. Obs.* Forms: α. 4 **dedeignous**, **dedeynous**; β. 5 **desdeynous**; γ. 5–6 **dys-**, **disdeinous**, **-deynous**, **-daynous**, 6 **dysdegnous**, **-danus**, **disdainous**. [a. OF. *desdeignos*, *-eus*, *-eux* (12th c. in Hatz.-Darm.), = Pr. *desdenhos*, Sp. *desdeñoso*, It. *disdegnoso* (*sdegnoso*), a Com. Romanic adj. f. *disdegno* DISDAIN *sb.*: see -OUS.]

1. Full of or showing disdain; disdainful, scornful; proud, haughty.

c **1374** CHAUCER *Troylus* II. 1168 (1217) (MS. Gg. 4. 27), Sche..gan hire herte onfetere Out of disdaynis [*v.rr.* disdainys, dis-, desdaynes, disdaynous, dis-, desdayns] prisoun. **1377** LANGL. *P. Pl.* B. VIII. 83 Who-so..is nouȝt dronkenlew ne dedeignous, dowel hym folweth. *c* **1400** *Rom. Rose* 7412 His looking was not disdeinous, Ne proud, but meeke, and ful pesible. **1413** *Pilgr. Sowle* (Caxton) II. xlv. (1859) 51 Prowde men, and desdeynous, that settyn att nought al other men. **1533** *Star Chamb. Proc.* in *Proc. Soc. Antiq.* (1869) 321 With a hye and a dysdanus countynans. **1556** *Aurelio & Isab.* (1608) G iv, It pleasethe you more to be towardes hus disdaingieux. *a* **1563** CAVENDISH *L'auctor G.C.* iii, in *Wolsey*, etc. (1825) II. 140 Ther disdaynous dispyghts and onnaturall debates.

2. Full of indignation; indignant.

c **1430** *Pilgr. Lyf Manhode* II. civ. (1869) 114 Myn herte so disdeynows therof j haue, that litel lakketh it ne bresteth on tweyne. **1531** ELYOT *Gov.* II. xii. (1883) 150 They..began to murmure, and to cast a disdaynous and greuous loke upon Gysippus.

†**dis'dainously**, *adv. Obs.* [f. prec. + -LY[2].] Disdainfully, scornfully, haughtily.

1494 FABYAN *Chron.* VII. 563 He was dysdeynously answeryd. **1568** GRAFTON *Chron.* II. 113 The Magistrates.. did likewise vilipend and disdeynously mocke all that the Pope had there commaunded.

disdar, var. of DIZDAR (Pers.), warden of a fort.

† **dis'dare**, *v. Obs. rare*⁻¹. [f. DIS- 6 or 7a + DARE.] *trans.* To strip of daring, cow, quell.

1612 SYLVESTER tr. *Mathieu's Henry the Great* 450 Whose awfull frowne Dis-dared Vice.

† **disde'ceive**, *v. Obs.* [DIS- 6.] *trans.* To deliver from deception; to undeceive.

1622 MABBE tr. *Aleman's Guzman d'Alf.* I. 8 His owne miserie doth dis-deceiue him. *Ibid.* I. 77 He that truely loves is deceiv'd with that which ought to dis-deceive him. **1647** FARINGDON *Serm.* ii. 38 Goe to my palace in Silo and there learn to disdeceive yourselves. **1649** EARL MONM. tr. *Senault's Use of Passions* (1671) 295 Christian Religion.. hath not been able to dis-deceive all Infidels.

† **dis'deify**, *v. Obs. rare*⁻¹. [f. DIS- 6 + DEIFY.] *trans.* To deprive of deity: cf. DISGODDED *ppl. a.*.

1627–77 FELTHAM *Resolves* I. xvi. 27 The Papists portray him as an old Man; and by this means, dis-deifie him.

disdein(e, -deigne, -dene, -denȝe, deyn(e, obs. ff. DISDAIN.

disdenominationalize: see DIS- 6.

disde'serve, *v. nonce-wd.* [DIS- 6] *trans.* To do the reverse of deserving; to deserve to lose; = DEMERIT *v.* 3.

1668 LD. ORRERY *State Lett.* (1743) II. 347 Which though I cannot hope to merit, yet I am sure I will never disdeserve.

† **disde'sire**, *v. nonce-wd.* [DIS- 6.] *trans.* To do the reverse of desiring; to desire to be without.

1651 N. BACON *Disc. Govt. Eng.* II. xxxiv, They..lived to dis-desire and unwish their former choice, by late repentance.

† **disde'termine**, *v. nonce-wd.* [DIS- 6.] *trans.* To undo that which is determined, to annul.

1651 N. BACON *Disc. Govt. Eng.* II. xl. (1739) 176 Why that which is once by the Representative of the People determined..should be dis-determined by one or a few.

‖ **disdiaclasis** (dɪsdaɪ'æklǝsɪs). *Optics.* [mod.L., irreg. f. Gr. δίς twice (in comb. regularly δι-, DI-²) + διάκλασις: see DIACLASIS.] Double refraction (*Syd. Soc. Lex.* 1883).

disdiaclast (dɪs'daɪǝklæst). [ad. mod.L. *disdiaclast-us* adj. (see next.)] 'A term applied by Brücke to dark particles forming, by their apposition on the same plane, the doubly-refracting disc, band, or layer of striated muscular tissue' (*Syd. Soc. Lex.*).

1867 J. MARSHALL *Outlines Physiol.* I. 51 The dark portions have been described as crystalline, and as being composed of minute doubly-refracting particles, named *disdiaclasts.* **1876** QUAIN *Elem. Anat.* (ed. 8) II. 114 The doubly refracting parts of a muscular fibre have been conceived by Brücke to be made up of an aggregation of minute doubly refracting particles, termed by him disdiaclasts. **1877** ROSENTHAL *Muscles & Nerves* 102 At these points the disdiaclasts are probably arranged regularly and in large groups.

disdia'clastic, *a. rare.* [f. mod.L. *disdiaclast-us* doubly refracting (irreg. f. Gr. δίς twice + *διακλαστός, vbl. adj. of διακλάειν to break in two) + -IC.] Doubly refracting: applied to crystals; also, of the nature of disdiaclasts.

[**1665** E. BARTHOLINE (*title*) Experimenta Crystali Islandici disdiaclasti]. **1670** *Phil. Trans.* V. 2044 From this peculiar and notable propriety of the double Refraction in this Island-stone, we have not scrupled to call it Dis-diaclastick.

† **disdia'pason.** *Mus. Obs.* [a. L. *disdiapāsōn*, a. Gr. δίς διὰ πασῶν 'twice through all (the chords)', a double octave in music: see DIAPASON.] The interval of a double octave; a fifteenth; (in quot. 1760) the compass or range of notes included within the same.

1609 DOULAND *Ornith. Microl.* 21 Disdiapason, is an Interuall by a Fifteenth, occasioned..by a quadruple proportion. **1651** J. F[REAKE] *Agrippa's Occ. Philos.* 259 Sol obtains the melody of the octave voice viz. Diapason; in like manner by fifteen Tones, a Disdiapason. **1760** *Phil. Trans.* LI. 702 The lyre..took in the compass of a disdiapason, or double octave. **1774** BURNEY *Hist. Mus.* (1789) I. i. 3 It was the opinion of the ancients that this disdiapason or double octave was the greatest interval which could be received in melody.

† **dis'diet.** *Obs. rare.* [f. DIS- 9 + DIET *sb.*] Improper or irregular diet or regimen of food.

1576 NEWTON *Lemnie's Complex.* (1633) 81 Old age is.. not well able to beare out even the least disdyet that may bee. **1619** DENISON *Heav. Banq.* (1631) 268 If the patient afterwards distemper himselfe by disdyed.

† **dis'dignify**, *v. Obs. rare.* [DIS- 6.] *trans.* To deprive of dignity; to dishonour.

1625 JACKSON *Creed* v. xxix. 286 They no way honour but ..disdignifie him in such solemnities.

† **dis'domage.** *Obs. rare*⁻¹. [a. OF. *desdommage* (in Godef.) a sum paid to indemnify, f. *des-*, DIS- 4 + *dommage* DAMAGE.] Indemnification.

1502 *Ord. Crysten Men* (W. de W. 1506) IV. xxi. 227 By reason of dysdomage, as yf..the lenner were in domage without fyccyon.

† **dis'doubt**, *v. Obs. rare.* [DIS- 5.] *trans.* To have adverse doubts about; to distrust, mistrust, MISDOUBT.

a **1656** BP. HALL *Soliloquies* 55 The stamp is too well known to be disdoubted.

disdub: see DIS- 6.

† **dise, dyse**, decapitated form of *adise, addis*, ADZE, the initial *a* being mistaken for the indefinite article.

a **1400** *Gloss.* in *Rel. Ant.* I. 8/1 *Ascia*, a dyse. *c* **1460** J. RUSSELL *Bk. Nurture* 112 Haue a gymlet, & a dise.

dise, obs. form of DICE; see DIE *sb.*¹

disease (dɪ'zi:z), *sb.* Forms: 4 deses, deisese, disseease, dishese, 4–5 disese, -sese, desese, dysese, 5 disess, -cese, -ees(e, -seese, -easse, desesse, -eas, -eyce, dyses, -esse, -hese, -sese, -ase, -easse, -eze, -zese, -eysse, 5–6 dysease, -sease, *Sc.* diseis, 6 desease, disseyse, dysseasse, *Sc.* dises, 5– disease. [ME. *di-, desese*, a. AF. *disease, desaese* (Stat. Rich. II), OF. *desaise, -ayse* (14th c. in Godef.), f. *des-*, DIS- 4 + *aise* EASE *sb.*]

1. a. Absence of ease; uneasiness, discomfort; inconvenience, annoyance; disquiet, disturbance; trouble. (For long *Obs.* but revived in modern use with the spelling *dis-ease.*)

In later use, generally with distinct reference to the etym. elements of the word: cf. DISEASE *v.* 1.

c **1330** R. BRUNNE *Chron.* (1810) 166 Go and mak his pes, or he do þe more stoure, And þou to þi deses may haf þe frute and floure. **1388** WYCLIF *John* xvi. 33 In the world ȝe schulen haue disese. *c* **1410** LOVE *Bonavent. Mirr.* xxvii, His disciples were in the see in grete disese. *c* **1450** *Merlin* 54 Thei shull haue grete dissese for lakke of water. *a* **1547** SURREY in *Tottell's Misc.* (Arb.) 22 Till thou know my hole disseyse my hart can haue no rest. **1615** CHAPMAN *Odyss.* IV. 1088 Doth sleep thus seize Thy powers, affected with so much dis-ease? **1623** LISLE *Ælfric on O. & N. Test.* Ded. xxiii, Some grudge of old disease, Which will enforce us fortifie our townes.

1909 *Daily Chron.* 17 May 3/1 Perhaps he..kept dark the apprehensions of his artist soul, communicated his ease not his dis-ease. **1922** A. S. M. HUTCHINSON *This Freedom* II. x. 166 They were in a curious dis-ease whose occasion was not to be defined. **1925** —— *One Increasing Purpose* III. xiv, She had a curious dis-ease in meeting socially doctors whom also she met professionally. **1960** *Encounter* Mar. 78/1 The fear and dis-ease which underlie the more obvious nostalgia.

† **b.** A cause of discomfort or distress; a trouble, an annoyance, a grievance. *Obs.*

c **1386** CHAUCER *Nun's Pr. Prol.* 5 It is a greet disese, Where as men han been in greet welthe and ese, To heeren of hire sodeyn fal. **1443** *Paston Lett.* No. 36 I. 49 Sende me a letter as hastely as ȝe may, yf wrytyn be non dysesse to yow. *a* **1667** JER. TAYLOR *Serm.* xxv. §5 Wks. 1847–54 IV. 641 The disemployed is a disease, and like a long sleepless night to himself, and a load to his country. **1712** PRIDEAUX *Direct. Ch.-wardens* (ed. 4) 59 [It] is only for their own ease, and that must not be made a dis-ease to the rest of the Parish.

† **c.** Molestation. *to do disease to*, to molest.

c **1400** MAUNDEV. (Roxb.) xxi. 98 Nedders and oþer venymous bestez of þat cuntree duse na diseese to na straungers ne pilgrimes. *c* **1440** *Gesta Rom.* II. xxvi. (1838) 353 The Emperour comaundede, that no man shulde dispoile the ymages..ne to hem do no disease. **1493** *Festivall* (W. de W. 1515) 71 To praye for his enemys and them that..dyde him dysease.

2. A condition of the body, or of some part or organ of the body, in which its functions are disturbed or deranged; a morbid physical condition; 'a departure from the state of health, especially when caused by structural change' (*Syd. Soc. Lex.*). Also applied to a disordered condition in plants.

(A gradual restriction of sense 1, in early use only contextual: cf. the similar use of 'trouble' in dialects.)

a. *gen.* The condition of being (more or less seriously) out of health; illness, sickness.

1393 GOWER *Conf.* III. 35 He was full of such disese, That he may nought the deth escape. *a* **1400–50** *Alexander* 2549 He was fallen in a feuire..þai..said ilkane to othire: Be þis disese to ser Darie and his dukis knawen, He sall vs..surely encounbre. **1555** EDEN *Decades* Pref. to Rdr. (Arb.) 53 Least thy disease become vncurable. **1727–46** THOMSON *Summer* 1035 The dire power of pestilent disease. **1788** GIBBON *Decl. & F.* I. (1846) V. 10 The legions of Augustus melted away in disease and lassitude. **1875** H. C. WOOD *Therap.* (1879) 21 Disease often fortifies the system against the action of remedies. **1879** E. GARRETT *House by Works* II. 42 Suppressing disease instead of curing it.

b. An individual case or instance of such a condition; an illness, ailment, malady, disorder.

1526 *Pilgr. Perf.* (W. de W. 1531) 38 Cured many diseases or syckenesses. **1552** LATIMER *Serm. & Rem.* (1845) II. 67 [The burial ground being within the city] be the occasion of much sickness and diseases. **1602** SHAKS. *Ham.* IV. iii. 9 Diseases, desperate growne, By desperate appliance are releeued. **1671** MILTON *Samson* 618 My griefs..pain me As a lingering disease. **1765** A. DICKSON *Treat. Agric.* viii. (ed. 2) 83 The diseases of plants we may possibly do something to prevent, but we can do little to remove. **1847** EMERSON *Repr. Men, Montaigne* Wks. (Bohn) I. 343 To entertain you with the records of his disease.

c. Any one of the various kinds of such conditions; a species of disorder or ailment, exhibiting special symptoms or affecting a special organ.

Often with defining words, indicating its nature, or derived from the name of a person who has suffered from it, or of the physician who first diagnosed it: e.g. ***Addison's disease***, a structural disease of the suprarenal capsules, resulting in anæmia and loss of strength, and commonly characterized by a brownish-olive discoloration of the skin (see BRONZED 4); first described by Thomas Addison (1793–1860). ***bad disease, foul disease***, names for syphilis (*Syd. Soc. Lex.*). BLUE *disease*, BRIGHT'S DISEASE, FISH-SKIN *disease*, FOOT-AND-MOUTH DISEASE, FRENCH *disease*, POTATO *disease*, etc.: see these words.

1460–70 *Bk. Quintessence* 18 Oure quinte essence auri et perelarum heelith þese disesis. **1555** EDEN *Decades* 230 The disease of saynt Iob whiche wee caule the frenche poxe. **1651** HOBBES *Leviath.* II. xxix. 173 A Disease, which resembleth the Pleurisie. **1725** N. ST. ANDRÉ in *Lond. Gaz.* No. 6349/1 The..Woman had the Foul Disease. **1727–51** CHAMBERS *Cycl.*, *Diseases of plants*..Mildew, a kind of epidemical disease. **1799** *Med. Jrnl.* II. 183 The diseases of human teeth and bones. **1836** *Penny Cycl.* VI. 93/2 Cabbages are subject to a peculiar disease..called clubbing. **1885** *Law Times* LXXIX. 161/2 The mare was suffering from no catching disease.

3. *fig.* A deranged, depraved, or morbid condition (of mind or disposition, of the affairs of a community, etc.); an evil affection or tendency.

1509 HAWES *Past. Pleas.* XVI. xlviii, A, a! said Counseyle, doubte ye never a dele, But your disease I shal by wysdome hele. **1597** SHAKS. *2 Hen. IV*, I. ii. 138 It is the disease of not Listning, the malady of not Marking, that I am troubled withall. **1607** ROWLANDS *Famous Hist.* 57 Ambitious pride hath been my youths disease. *a* **1661** FULLER *Worthies, Warwicksh.*, Bad Latin was a catching disease in that age. **1785** FRANKLIN *Lett.* Wks. 1840 VI. 526 The common causes of the smoking of chimneys..the principles on which both the disease and the remedy depend. **1844** EMERSON *Lect., New Eng. Ref.* Wks. (Bohn) I. 266 The disease with which the human mind now labours is want of faith.

4. *Comb.*, as ***disease-germ, -maker; disease-causing, -producing, -resisting, -spreading***, etc., adjs.

1865 TYLOR *Early Hist. Man.* vi. 128 In the New Hebrides, there was a colony of disease-makers. **1883** *Chamb. Jrnl.* 27 What is known..in regard to the nature of disease-germs. **1886** *Athenæum* 7 Aug. 178/1 The coffee tree is the patient, the fungus..is the disease-causing agent. **1890** *Daily News* 22 Oct. 5/4 The disease-resisting potatoes. **1906** *Westm. Gaz.* 27 Aug. 5/1 The invasion of the body by disease-producing organisms. **1941** J. S. HUXLEY *Uniqueness of Man* III. v. 98 Disease-producing bacteria.

disease (dɪ'zi:z), *v.* Forms: 4–5 dissese, 4–6 disese, 5 disees(e, -esse, -sease, -sase, dysese, -esse, -sese, -sesse, desese, dessayse, deshese, *Sc.* discese, 5–6 dys-, desease, 6 desesse, 7 diseaase, 5– disease. [a. AF. **diseaser, -eeser, -aeser*, for OF. *desaaisier* to deprive of ease, f. *desaise* sb., after *aaisier, aiser* to EASE.]

† **1.** *trans.* To deprive of ease, make uneasy; to put to discomfort or inconvenience; to trouble, annoy, incommode, molest. *Obs.*

c **1340** HAMPOLE *Prose Tr.* 41 Ouþer for to put þe fra thi mete or thi slepe..or for to disesse any oþer mane vnskilfully. **1393** GOWER *Conf.* II. 8 In parte he was right inly glad And eke in parte he was disesed. *a* **1420** HOCCLEVE *De Reg. Princ.* 754 It ruethe me, yf I have you disesede. **1526** TINDALE *Mark* v. 35 Thy doughter is deed: why deseasest thou the master eny further? **1554** KNOX *Godly Let.* A viij, He wold not disease hymself to heare a sermon. **1638** CHILLINGW. *Relig. Prot.* I. iv. §19. 200 That I should disease myself or my Reader with a punctual examination of it, may seem superfluous. **1697** CONGREVE *Mourn. Bride* III. iv, What racking cares dis-ease a monarch's bed.

† **b.** To disturb (from quiet, rest, or sleep). *Obs.*

c **1374** CHAUCER *Troylus* III. 1419 (1468) And sufferyst hire [þe dawyng] to sone vp..ryse ffor to disese loueris in þis wyse. **1482** *Monk of Evesham* (Arb.) 34 Sum what troubulde and disesyd by the noyse of the couent when they went oute of the chirche. **1568** *Jacob & Esau* I. i. in Hazl. *Dodsley* II. 191 We disease our tent and neighbours all With rising over early. *c* **1611** CHAPMAN *Iliad* x. 45 Brother, hie thee to thy ships, and Idomen dis-ease, With warlike Ajax. **1653** T. BAILEY *Fisher* xxii. 202 He was loath to disease him of his rest.

2. To bring into a morbid or unhealthy condition; to cause illness, sickness, or disease in, to infect with disease. Usually in pa. pple. DISEASED, q.v.

1467 [see DISEASED]. **1496** *Dives & Paup.* (W. de W.) IX. vi. 354 He hurte his fote and dyseased all his bodye. **1577** B. GOOGE *Heresbach's Husb.* IV. (1586) 191 Little children diseased with the dry cough. **1888** J. ELLIS *New Christianity* iv. 116 No other poison..so perverts, diseases, pollutes and degrades a man..as does alcohol.

fig. *a* **1637** B. JONSON *Eng. Gram.* Pref., We free our Language..from the opinion of Rudeness, and Barbarism, wherewith it is mistaken to be diseas'd. *c* **1680** HICKERINGILL *Hist. Whiggism* Wks. 1716 I. 143 Evil Ministers Disease the Common-wealth. **1865** LECKY *Ration.* (1878) II. 375 Those ghastly notions..which.. diseased the imaginations..of men.

Hence **di'seasing** *vbl. sb.* and *ppl. a.* (in sense 1 (*Obs.*) and sense 2).

1558 FORREST *Grysilde Sec.* (1875) 101 She was remoued, to more diseasinge, To a towne Cowemoulton. **1615** T. ADAMS *Blacke Devill* 30 A diseasing displeasing change to be banished into a mountainous desert. **1628** WITHER *Brit. Rememb.* III. 147 In those diseasings, I more joy received. **1915** W. MEYNELL *Aunt Sarah & War* vii. 68 There's no disgraceful and diseasing drunkenness, but only this divine inebriation.

disease, obs. form of DECEASE.

diseased (dɪ'ziːzd), *ppl. a.* [f. prec. + -ED[1].] Affected with disease; in a disordered bodily condition. Now usually of the bodily organs or fluids: In an unhealthy or disordered state, infected.

1467 *Mann. & Househ. Exp.* 173, I hame deshesed in schweche weyse that I may nate ryde norre wel goo. **1540** *Act 32 Hen. VIII*, c. 42 §4 Diseasid personnes..infected with the pestilence. **1611** BIBLE *John* vi. 2 His miracles which hee did on them that were diseased. **1801** *Med. Jrnl.* V. 113 The diseased heels of horses. **1842** TENNYSON *Voyage* x, His eyes were dim: But ours he swore were all diseased. **1846** G. E. DAY tr. *Simon's Anim. Chem.* II. 68 The most striking changes in the diseased milk are the diminution of the solid constituents..and the extraordinary increase of the salts.

absol. **1542-3** *Act 34-5 Hen. VIII*, c. 8 §1 Surgions.. mindinge..nothing the profit or ease of the diseased or pacient. **1667** MILTON *P.L.* XI. 480 A Lazar-house it seemd, wherein were laid Numbers of all diseas'd.

b. Characterized by disease; †subject to disease (quot. 1651); pertaining to or symptomatic of disease; morbid, unhealthy.

1574 HYLL *Conject. Weather* i, Then shall follow a diseased yeare. **1651** tr. *Bacon's Life & Death* 9 The Sheep is a diseased Creature; And rarely lives to his full age. **1707** FLOYER *Physic. Pulse-Watch* ii. 188 Diseas'd Pulses either exceed, or are deficient in respect of the natural Pulse in Number..Strength, Celerity. **1797** M. BAILLIE *Morb. Anat.* (1807) p. vii, When a person has become well acquainted with diseased appearances.

c. *fig.* In a disordered or depraved condition (of mind, of affairs, etc.); pertaining to such a condition, morbid.

1608 T. JAMES *Apol. Wyclif* 69 The faultes of the diseased Cleargie. **1611** SHAKS. *Wint. T.* I. ii. 297 Good my Lord, be cur'd Of this diseas'd Opinion. **1835** LYTTON *Rienzi* I. vi, The times are..diseased. *a* **1859** MACAULAY *Hist. Eng.* (1861) V. 104 The divines whose business was to sooth his not less diseased mind.

Hence **di'seasedly** *adv.*, **di'seasedness**.

1614 T. ADAMS *Devil's Banquet* 157 All men [catch] their diseasedness by falling from their Christ. **1672** BAXTER in *Life J. Alleine* (1838) I. 8 He laid not out his zeal diseasedly. **1684** T. BURNET *Th. Earth* II. 184 That state of indigency, and misery, and diseasedness, which we languish under at present. **1829** SOUTHEY in *Q. Rev.* XLI. 294 A nervous system already diseasedly susceptible.

di'seaseful, *a.* [f. DISEASE *sb.* + -FUL.]

†**1.** Fraught with discomfort, trouble, or annoyance; troublesome. *Obs.*

1388 WYCLIF *Gen.* xxxix. 10 The womman was diseseful to the 3ong waxynge man. —— *Judg.* xiv. 17 Sche was diseseful to hym. *a* **1626** BACON *Charge at Sess. of Verge* (T.) It is both disgraceful to the king, and diseaseful to the people, if the ways near about be not fair and good.

2. Full of or affected with disease; morbid, diseased. Now *rare*.

1596 SPENSER *State Irel.* (Globe) 646/2 His languishing sowle being disquieted by his diseaseful bodye. **1624** DONNE *Devot.* (ed. 2) 261 This great hospital, this sick, this diseaseful world. **1889** TENNYSON *Happy* ix, This coarse diseaseful creature [a leper].

b. Causing or tending to disease, unwholesome.

1605 TIMME *Quersit.* I. xviii. 97 By the taking away of the diseasefull impurities. **1762** J. WARTON *Poems, Enthusiast* 82 Diseaseful dainties, riot and excess.

Hence †**di'seasefulness**, discomfort, uneasiness.

1580 SIDNEY *Arcadia* III. (1622) 300 The same consideration made them attend all diseasefulnesse.

di'seaseless, *a. rare.* [f. DISEASE *sb.* + -LESS.] Free from disease.

1653 W. JENKYN *Fun. Serm.* (1654) 44 A strong, hayl, vigorous, diseaselesse old age.

†**di'seasely**, *a. Obs.* [f. DISEASE *sb.* + -LY[1].] Affected with disease or sickness.

c **1400** *Test. Love* III. in *Chaucer's Wks.* (1542) 326 a/2 A disesely habitacion letteth ye witte many thynges, & namely in sorowe.

di'seasement. [f. DISEASE *v.* + -MENT.]

†**1.** The action of depriving, or condition of being deprived, of ease; uneasiness, discomfort. *Obs.*

a **1617** BAYNE *On Eph.* (1658) 24 Men will content themselves with sorry lodgings and pass by little diseasements. **1664** H. MORE *Myst. Iniq.* xvi. 172 With his back resting on that bar, to his unspeakable diseasement. **1668** —— *Div. Dial.* v. xiv. (1713) 456 The State of Vice and Sin is a state of Diseasement and Unnaturalness.

2. The condition of being affected with disease; ailment. *nonce-use.*

1826 LAMB *Lett.* (1888) II. 149 You'll be lost in a maze of remedies for a labyrinth of diseasements.

†**di'seasify**, *v. Obs. rare.* [f. DISEASY *a.* + -FY.] To cause disease. Hence **di'seasifying** *ppl. a.*

1662 J. CHANDLER *Van Helmont's Oriat.* 181 In an Erisipelas..the vitall Spirit being incensed, and as it were provoked to anger by the diseasifying cause, waxeth exceeding hot. *Ibid.* 238.

†**di'seasy**, *a. Obs.* [prob. a. AF. *disaisé, -eesé* = OF. *desaaisié*, pa. pple of *desaaisier* to DISEASE: but possibly an English formation from *disease*, after *easy*.]

1. Marked by or causing discomfort or trouble; annoying, troublesome.

1387 TREVISA *Higden* (Rolls) VII. 111 Canute wente unto Denmark, ledynge Englisshe men wiþ hym a3enst þe Wandales, þat war disesy [*infestos*] unto hym. *c* **1440** *Gesta Rom.* viii. 22 (Harl. MS.), Strait and disesy is þe wey þat ledith to life. **1483** *Cath. Angl.* 97/1 Desesy, *nocuus*.

2. Affected with, pertaining to, or producing disease; diseased, unhealthy, morbid.

c **1450** LONELICH *Grail* liv. 19 Al deseysy & ful syk he wente. **1603** HOLLAND *Plutarch's Mor.* I. III. 238 (L.) Like diseasy, sharp choler. **1674** R. GODFREY *Inj. & Ab. Physic* 93 Nature who before was weak, and admitted the Diseasy Fæx, will again expell it.

Hence †**di'seasiness** *Obs.*, morbid quality or elements.

1674 R. GODFREY *Inj. & Ab. Physic* 126 Upon sight of a full Close-stool and imagining all diseasiness in it.

diseconomy, dis-economy (dɪsɪ'kɒnəmɪ). *Econ.* [DIS- 9.] The opposite of economy; an absence of economy; *spec.* an increase in costs arising when a business organization exceeds an 'optimum size'.

1937 *Economica* IV. 441 This fall may be caused by..large scale dis-economies. **1954** *Encounter* Dec. 30/1 Orthodox 20th century economists..have postulated certain 'dis-economies' of large-scale operation which ensure that a firm has an optimum size, growth beyond which again reduces its efficiency. **1960** *Times Rev. Industry* Apr. 31/1 Advantages of mass production have saddled us with the 'diseconomies' ..of mass storage. **1969** *Daily Tel.* 17 Nov. 18/6 Early loss of recently-trained people to overseas employment..may have its dis-economies in a narrowly national sense.

†**di'sect**, *v. Obs.* [irreg. f. DI-[1] + L. *sect-* ppl. stem of *secāre* to cut: cf. *dissect.*] *trans.* To cut asunder, to separate by cutting.

1674 JEAKE *Arith.* (1696) 22 As if in the former Example, 8 should be disected into 2.2.2.2. *Ibid.* 41 Expressed..by two termes..disected as it were the one from the other.

disedge (dɪs'ɛdʒ), *v.* [f. DIS- 7a + EDGE *sb.*] *trans.* To take the edge off; to deprive of its sharpness; to blunt, dull. Hence **dis'edged** *ppl. a.*

1611 SHAKS. *Cymb.* III. iv. 96 When thou shalt be disedg'd by her, That now thou tyrest on. **1647** WARD *Simp. Cobler* 77, I hold him prudent, that in these fastidious times, will helpe disedged appetites with convenient condiments. **1859** TENNYSON *Idylls, Enid* 1038 Served a little to disedge The sharpness of that pain.

disedification (dɪs,ɛdɪfɪ'keɪʃən). [n. of action from DISEDIFY: cf. *edify, edification.*] The action of disedifying; the reverse of edification; the weakening of faith or devotion.

1664 H. MORE *Myst. Iniq.* xvii. 62 The dedicating of an unknown Tongue to their Publick Prayers..to the great disedification of the People. **1836** CDL. WISEMAN *Lect. Cath. Ch.* (1847) II. 74 The scandal and disedification committed before the Church. **1872** *Contemp. Rev.* XX. 725 That unhappy system of concealing truths which are supposed to tend to disedification.

disedify (dɪs'ɛdɪfaɪ), *v.* [f. DIS- 6 + EDIFY.] *trans.* To do the reverse of edifying; to shock or weaken the piety or religious sense of.

1526 *Pilgr. Perf.* (W. de W. 1531) 58 Let euery thynge that is done or spoken euer edyfye the, & no thynge to disedyfye the. *a* **1684** LEIGHTON *Comm. 1 Pet.* v. 5 Were it not for disedifying his brethren he would rather disguise and hide not only other things by humility but even humility itself. **1844** C. E. A. *Yng. Communicants* (1848) 21 The party of visitors..were much surprised and disedifed by this scene in a convent school.

Hence **dis'edifying** *ppl. a.*, that disedifies, or weakens faith or devotion.

1844 LINGARD *Anglo-Sax. Ch.* (1858) I. iii. 97 [A] person of light or disedifying deportment. **1874** PUSEY *Lent. Serm.* 285 Gloominess is very disedifying, disennobling, paralysing. **1894** J. T. FOWLER *Adamnan* Pref. 11 Colgan has summarized it, omitting 'disedifying' passages.

diseducate (dɪs'ɛdjuːkeɪt), *v.* [f. DIS- 6 + EDUCATE.] *trans.* To undo or pervert the education of.

1886 LOWELL *Gray* Lit. Ess. (1891) 14 Educated at Eton and diseducated, as he [Gray] seemed to think, at Cambridge. **1887** *Q. Rev.* Oct. 274 The change of institutions educates or diseducates men to think.

disees(e, diseis, obs. ff. DECEASE, DISEASE.

†**dise'ffect**, *v. Obs. rare*[−1]. [f. DIS- 6 or 7 + EFFECT *v.* or *sb.*] *trans.* To divest of an effect.

1613 TOURNEUR *Death Pr. Henrie* 28 Nothing had the might To diseffect his actions of delight; No, nor his sufferings.

diselder, *v.*: see DIS- 7b.

diselectrify (dɪsɪ'lɛktrɪfaɪ), *v.* [f. DIS- 6 + ELECTRIFY *v.*] *trans.* To undo the electrified condition of; to render non-electric.

1876 SIR W. THOMSON *Pop. Lect.* (1889) I. 437 Moist cotton thread will gradually diselectrify it. **1881** *Philad. Rec.* No. 3473. 6 A Method of diselectrifying dry wool..and alpaca.

Hence **dise,lectrifi'cation**, the action or process of diselectrifying.

1895 *Athenæum* 30 Mar. 412/1 Royal Society..The following papers were read..'The Diselectrification of Air', by Lord Kelvin and Messrs. M. McClean and A. Galt.

†**dis-'element**, *v. Obs.* [f. DIS- 7c + ELEMENT.] *trans.* To put (anything) out of its element; to remove from its proper sphere of activity.

1612 W. PARKES *Curtaine-Dr.* (1876) 56 It cannot indure to lie naked no more then the fish dis-elemented on the shore. **1654** WHITLOCK *Zootomia* 449 How doth this fifth Element [i.e. detraction] dis-element all the other foure? **1727** *Philip Quarll* (1754) 184 A vast Number of which had, by the Wind, been dis-elemented.

diselenide (daɪ'sɛlɪnaɪd), etc., *Chem.*: see DI-[2] 2 and SELENIDE, etc.

1877 WATTS *Dict. Chem.* V. 822 The diselenide or stannic selenide, Sn Se_2. **1881** *Ibid.* VIII. 1787 A quantity of acid sufficient for the formation of a diselenite. **1884** HUMPIDGE tr. *Kolbe's Inorg. Chem.* 179 Diselenium dichloride, Se_2Cl_2, is prepared in precisely the same manner as disulphur dichloride, which it closely resembles.

disem-: see DISEN-.

disem'balm, *v. rare*[−1]. [DIS- 6.] *trans.* To undo the embalming of.

1858 O. W. HOLMES *Aut. Breakf.-t.* (1883) 53 The disembalming and unbandaging of..literary mummies.

disem'bargo, *v.* [f. DIS- 7c + EMBARGO.] *trans.* To release from embargo.

1877 *Times* 15 Mar. 5/6 General Urquiza..successfully besieged..Buenos Ayres, and then disembargoed Rosa's property.

disembark (dɪsɪm'bɑːk), *v.* Also 6-7 -em-, -imbarque. [a. F. *désembarque-r* (1564 in Hatz.-Darm.), or ad. It. *disimbarcare*, or Sp. *desembarcár*; f. *des-*, DIS- 4 + the Common Rom. vb. *imbarcare, embarcar*, F. *embarquer* to EMBARK. Cf. DEBARK.]

1. *trans.* To put ashore from a ship; to land.

1582 N. LICHEFIELD tr. *Castanheda's Conq. E. Ind.* ii. 7b, When ours were disimbarked and landed. **1591** SHAKS. *Two Gent.* II. iv. 187, I must vnto the Road, to dis-embarque Some necessaries. **1653** H. COGAN tr. *Pinto's Trav.* xvi. 55, I will not counsel you to disimbarque your goods on land. **1838** *Murray's Hand Bk. N. Germ.* 293 To allow steam-boats to..embark and disembark their passengers at once.

trans. **1852** R. S. SURTEES *Sponge's Sp. Tour* (1893) 76 Away went the train; and the..railway staff..returned to disembark the horses.

†**b.** *refl.* = 2. *Obs.*

1582 N. LICHEFIELD tr. *Castanheda's Conq. E. Ind.* 79 Untill..y^e Captaine generall did disimbarke himselfe a lande. **1653** H. COGAN tr. *Pinto's Trav.* viii. 24 Until our arrival at Malaca, where dis-imbarquing my self, the first thing I did was to go to the Fortress.

2. *intr.* To go on shore from a ship; to land.

1582 N. LICHEFIELD tr. *Castanheda's Conq. E. Ind.* ii. 6b, The Generall being disimbarked and come to land. **1600** E. BLOUNT tr. *Conestaggio* 28 Yet did he stay eight daies in the Port, and never disimbarked. **1659** B. HARRIS *Parival's Iron Age* 323 The Commander had leisure to disimbark and enter the Town. **1791** COWPER *Odyss.* III. 15 The Ithacans Push'd right ashore, and..disembark'd. **1859** TENNYSON *Merlin & V.* 200 Touching Breton Sands, they disembark'd.

Hence **disem'barking** *vbl. sb.*

1611 COTGR., *Desembarquement*, a disembarking. **1632** J. HAYWARD tr. *Biondi's Eromena* 144 He ranne hastily to the shore to hinder their disembarking. **1653** H. COGAN tr. *Pinto's Trav.* ix. 27 To impeach the Enemies dis-imbarquing.

attrib. **1895** *Daily News* 9 Feb. 8/4 Special Continental embarking and disembarking water stations.

disembar'kation. [f. DISEMBARK *v.*, after *embark, -ation.*] The action of disembarking.

a **1776** GOLDSM. *Nat. Hist.* (1790) III. xxviii. (Jod.) No proper measures were yet consulted for their disembarkation. **1808** *Convent. Evac. Portugal* §20 in Napier *Penins. War* (1828) I. App. p. xliii, On the disembarkation of the French troops in their own country. **1855** MACAULAY *Hist. Eng.* III. 651 Tourville determined to try what effect would be produced by a disembarkation.

†**disem'barkment.** *Obs.* [a. F. *désembarquement* (1564 in Hatz.-Darm.), f. *désembarquer* to DISEMBARK: see -MENT.] = prec.

1598 BARRET *Theor. Warres* v. i. 122 The disembarkment should haue beene betwixt the city and..Castle. **1659** B. HARRIS *Parival's Iron Age* 97 The English Fleet made a descent or disembarkment in the Isle of Ree in..July 1627.

disembarrass (dɪsɪm'bærəs), *v.* [f. DIS- 6 + EMBARRASS *v.*: prob. after F. *désembarrasse-r* 'to vnpester, disintangle, rid from intricateness, or troubles' (Cotgr.). Cf. also DEBARRASS.] *trans.* To free from embarrassment, encumbrance, complication, or intricacy; to rid; to relieve: cf. EMBARRASS.

1726 BERKELEY *Let. to Prior* 6 Feb., I hope..that you will have disembarrassed yourself of all sort of business that may detain you here. **1727** BRADLEY *Fam. Dict.* s.v. *Corn*, They steep the Corn..for three Days, that it may swell up, and that the Germes may open, dilate, and be disembarrassed. **1751** SMOLLETT *Per. Pic.* (1779) II. lxiii. 207 Assistance..in disembarrassing him from the disagreeable consequences of his fear. **1820** SCOTT *Abbot* i, When he had disembarrassed the little plaything [a boat] from the flags in which it was entangled. **1877** E. R. CONDER *Bas. Faith* ii. 63 We may at once disembarrass ourselves of those formidable terms—'absolute' and 'unconditioned'.

b. To disentangle (one thing *from* another).

1742 WARBURTON *Comm. Pope's Ess. Man* II. 197 Though it be difficult to distinguish genuine virtue from spurious.. yet they may be disembarrased. **1864** J. G. NICHOLS in *Herald & Genealogist* II. 458 One of the earliest results..is to disembarrass the biography of Serlo..from that of another monk of the same name.

Hence **disem'barrassed** *ppl. a.*, unhampered.

1741 BETTERTON [OLDYS] *Eng. Stage* vi. 109 By pronouncing it trippingly on the Tongue, he means a clear and disembarrass'd Pronunciation.

disem'barrassment. [f. DISEMBARRASS *v.* + -MENT, after *embarrass, -ment.*] The action of disembarrassing or fact of being disembarrassed; freedom from embarrassment.

1818 in TODD. **1821** COLERIDGE *Lett. Convers. etc.* I. xv. 163 The pleasure I anticipate from disembarrassment. **1862** MERIVALE *Rom. Emp.* (1871) V. xli. 78 The disembarrassment of the limbs, the elasticity of the circulation.

disembattle (dɪsɪm'bæt(ə)l), *v. rare.* [f. DIS- 6 + EMBATTLE *v.*[1]] *trans.* To deprive of battlements, make no longer embattled. Hence **disem'battled** *ppl. a.*

1875 H. JAMES *Transatlantic Sketches* 9 It is the gentlest and least offensive of ramparts..without a frown or menace in all its disembattled stretch.

†**disembay** (dɪsɪm'beɪ), *v. Obs.* [f. DIS- 6 + EMBAY *v.*] *trans.* To bring out of a bay.

1651 SHERBURNE *Poems, Forsaken Lydia* (T.), The fair inamorata who from far Had spy'd the ship..now quite disembay'd, Her cables coiled, and her anchors weigh'd.

disembed (dɪsɪm'bɛd), *v.* [f. DIS- 6 + EMBED *v.*] *trans.* To liberate (something embedded).

1885 *Leeds Mercury* 10 Dec. 4/4 A train is snowed up near Fraserburgh, and there was no hope last evening of being able to disembed it. **1893** *Daily News* 16 Dec. 5/3 There were 200,000 blocks of stone to be disembedded.

disembellish (dɪsɪm'bɛlɪʃ), *v.* [f. DIS- 6 + EMBELLISH; app. after F. *désembelliss-* extended stem of *désembellir* (Cotgr.).] *trans.* To deprive of embellishment or adornment.

1611 COTGR., *Desembellir*, to disimbellish, disfigure. **1624** QUARLES *Sion's Sonn.* i. 5 What if Afflictions doe disembellish My naturall glorie? **1831** CARLYLE *Sart. Res.* I. x. (1858) 41 Weep not that the reign of wonder is done, and God's world all disembellished and prosaic. **1875** BROWNING *Aristoph. Apol.* 131 Embellish fact? This bard may disembellish yet improve!

disem'bitter, *v. rare*[−1]. [DIS- 6.] *trans.* To undo the embittering of, to free from bitterness.

1622 [See DISSWEETEN]. **1716** ADDISON *Freeholder* (J.) Such innocent amusements as may disembitter the minds of men.

disemble, obs. form of DISSEMBLE.

disembo'cation. *rare*[−1]. [f. Sp. *desembocár* to DISEMBOGUE: see -ATION.] The action of disemboguing.

1846 FORD *Gatherings fr. Spain* iii. 24 The..water..is carried off at once in violent floods, rather than in a gentle gradual disembocation.

disembodied (dɪsɪm'bɒdɪd), *ppl. a.* [f. DISEMBODY + -ED[1].]

1. Divested (as a spirit) of a body; freed from that in which it has been embodied.

1742 YOUNG *Nt. Th.* III. 452 The disembody'd power. **1796** MORSE *Amer. Geog.* I. 135 The disembodied spirit does not enter dancing into the Elysian fields. **1835** THIRLWALL *Greece* I. vi. 197 Orion..chasing the disembodied beasts, which he had killed on the mountains, over the asphode meadow. **1872** LONGF. *Michael Angelo* II. ii. 10 Sudden as inspirations, are the whispers Of disembodied spirits.

2. Discharged from military incorporation.

1882 PEBODY *Eng. Journalism* xxiii. 180 He owned the..uniform he wore to be that of the late disembodied 'militia'.

disembodiment (dɪsɪm'bɒdɪmənt). [f. next + -MENT.] The action of disembodying: **a.** Separation (of a spirit) from the body. **b.** Disbanding (of a body of soldiers).

1860 tr. *Tieck's Old Man of Mountain* (L.), A rapid and noisy disembodiment of souls and spirits now followed. **1871** *Daily News* 7 Sept., The militia as a whole have much to learn..but..they will learn much before the time comes for their disembodiment. **1884** *Ch. Times* 29 Aug. 631 Disembodiment is a death out of manhood.

disembody (dɪsɪm'bɒdɪ), *v.* [f. DIS- 6 + EMBODY.]

1. *trans.* To separate (a soul) from the body; to deliver or free (anything) from the form in which it is embodied.

1714 ADDISON *Spect.* No. 571 ¶9 Our souls, when they are disembodied..will..be always sensible of the divine presence. **1873** SYMONDS *Grk. Poets* x. 339 Disembodying the sentiments which were incarnated in simple images. **1877** SPARROW *Serm.* xiv. 186 So attuned was his [Enoch's] soul to heavenly things..that it was not thought fit to disembody it.

2. To discharge from military embodiment, as in the case of the militia at the close of each annual period of training.

1762 *Act 2 Geo. III*, c. 20 (T.) If the same [corps] shall be embodied, then, within two months after, it shall be disembodied, and returned to the respective counties. **1769** *Lloyd's Evening Post* 27–30 Oct. 413/3 On Friday the Hertfordshire Militia were disembodied at St. Alban's.

disembogue (dɪsɪm'bəʊg), *v.* Forms: 6 desemboque, 6–7 disem-, -imboque, 7 disem-, disim-, -boke, -boake, -boge, dissemboque, 7–8 disimbogue, dissembogue, 6– disembogue. [In 6 *disemboque*, ad. Sp. *desemboc-ar* 'to come out of the mouth of a river or hauen' (Minsheu 1599): f. *des-*, DIS- 4 + *embocar* 'to runne as the sea into a creeke or narrow riuer' (ibid.); f. *en* in + *boca* mouth: cf. F. *emboucher*, and see EMBOGUE.]

†**1.** *intr.* To come out of the mouth of a river, strait, etc. into the open sea. *Obs.*

1595 MAYNARDE *Drake's Voy.* (Hakl. Soc.) 20 Sir Thomas Baskervile..talked with such as hee hearde intended to quite companie before they were disemboged. **1596** RALEIGH *Discov. Gviana* 18 He was inforced to desembogue at the mouth of the said Amazones. **1613** *Voy. Guiana* in *Harl. Misc.* (Malh.) III. 203 We disembogued through the broken islands on the north side of Anguilla. **1633** T. STAFFORD *Pac. Hib.* viii. (1821) 318 Neither could they disimboge from thence without an Easterly winde.

†**b.** *trans.* with the strait, etc. as object. *Obs.*

1622 R. HAWKINS *Voy. S. Sea* (1847) 117 Another channell, by which a man may disemboake the straite. *Ibid.* 128 We set sayle once againe, in hope to disemboke the straite; but..before we came to the mouth of it, the wind changed.

2. *intr.* Of a river, lake, etc.: To flow out at the mouth; to discharge or empty itself; to flow *into.*

1598 HAKLUYT *Voy.* I. 104 The riuer of Volga..issueth from the North part of Bulgaria..and..disimboqueth into a certain lake. **1661** EVELYN *Fumifugium* Misc. Writ. (1805) II. 233 As far as any fresh waters are found disemboguing into the Thames. **1774** GOLDSM. *Nat. Hist.* (1862) I. xiv. 75 The Danube disembogues into the Euxine by seven mouths. **1871** BROWNING *Hervé Riel* vi, 'Twixt the offing here and Grève where the river disembogues.

3. *fig.* and *transf.* To come forth as from a river's mouth, to emerge; to discharge itself as a river.

1619 FLETCHER *M. Thomas* III. i, Those damn'd souls must disembogue again. **1670** *Moral State Eng.* 134 With that one of the Company disembogued. **1823** DE QUINCEY *Lett. Educ.* iii. (1860) 49 The presses of Europe are still disemboguing into the ocean of literature. **1868** G. DUFF *Pol. Surv.* 222 Hungry as wolves, swift and sudden as a torrent from the mountains, they disembogued.

4. *trans.* Of a river, lake, etc.: To discharge or pour forth (its waters) at the mouth; *refl.* to discharge or empty itself.

1610 HOLLAND *Camden's Brit.* II. 10 [The Tweed] passeth under Berwick..and so disembogeth it selfe into the Sea. **1686** PLOT *Staffordsh.* 64 The immense quantities of water that are disembogued into the Sea by all the Rivers. **1715–20** POPE *Iliad* XVII. 311 Where some swoln river disembogues his waves. **1829** SOUTHEY *Inscriptions* xlv, Where wild Parana disembogues A sea-like stream. **1840** DE QUINCEY *Essenes* Wks. X. 272 A great river..disemboguing itself into main ocean.

b. *fig.* and *transf.* To discharge, pour forth; to empty by pouring forth the contents.

a **1635** NAUNTON *Fragm. Reg.* (Arb.) 13 She was..of a most Noble and Royall extract by Her Father..for on that side there was disimbogued into her veines..the very abstract of all the greatest houses in Christendome. **1687** DRYDEN *Hind & P.* II. 562 Whom, when their home-bred honesty is lost, We disembogue on some far Indian coast. **1765** FALCONER *Demagogue* 401 Methinks I hear the bellowing demagogue Dumb-sounding declamations disembogue. **1837** CARLYLE *Fr. Rev.* I. v. ii, Paris disembogues itself..to witness, with grim looks, the *Séance Royale*.

absol. **1742** YOUNG *Nt. Th.* III. 220 Volcano's bellow ere they disembogue.

†**c.** To dislodge by force, to drive out. *Obs.*

1625 FLETCHER & SHIRLEY *Nt. Walker* v, If I get in adoors, not the power o' th' countrey..shall disembogue me. **1632** MASSINGER *Maid of Hon.* II. ii, Conduct me to The lady of the mansion, or my poniard Shall disembogue thy soul. *Syl.* O terrible! disembogue!

Hence **disem'bogued** *ppl. a.*, furnished with ready outlet.

1669 *Address hopeful Yng. Gentry Eng.* 91 Wit..needs [not] to call a Deity down upon the stage, to make its way open and disembogued.

†**disem'bogue**, *sb. Obs.* [f. the vb.] The place where a river disembogues; the mouth.

1626 CAPT. SMITH *Accid. Yng. Seamen* 18 [Tearmes for the Sea] Disimboage, a gulph, the froth of the sea. **1689** G. HARVEY *Curing Dis. by Expect.* xii. 79 Hammersmith-water ..being too near the disimbogue of the Thames.

disem'boguement. [f. as prec. + -MENT.] The action or place of disemboguing.

a **1828** MEASE cited in Webster. **1851** S. JUDD *Margaret* II. ii. (1871) 198 Neither rock nor night, inundation or ultimate disemboguement, disturbed my little joyous babble. **1862** BORROW *Wild Wales* III. 286 Aber..is the disemboguement, and wherever a place commences with Aber, there..does a river flow into the sea, or a brook..into a river.

disem'boguing, *vbl. sb.* [f. as prec. + -ING[1].] The action of the verb DISEMBOGUE; the place where a river, etc. disembogues.

1605 CAMDEN *Rem.* (1637) 312 At the disemboging, or inlet thereof. *a* **1642** SIR W. MONSON *Naval Tracts* I. (1704) 191/2 Their disimboguing in the Indies. **1698** FROGER *Voy.* Pref. A iv, Reforming the Charts..of the disemboguings of the Isles of Antilles. **1799** W. TOOKE *View Russian Emp.* I. 160 From its origin to its disemboguing into the Oby. **1856** MISS MULOCK *J. Halifax* 399 In its disemboguing of its contents.

disem'boguing, *ppl. a.* [f. as prec. + -ING[2].] That disembogues or discharges its waters.

1725 POPE *Odyss.* IV. 480 The deep roar of disemboguing Nile. **1728** —— *Dunc.* II. 259 To where Fleet-ditch with disemboguing streams, Rolls the large tribute of dead dogs to Thames.

†**disem'bogure.** *Obs. rare.* [f. as prec. + -URE.] The place where a river, etc. disembogues.

1653 HOLCROFT *Procopius* IV. 122 The Natives call this disembogure, Tanais, which reaches from Mæotis to the Euxine.

disem'bosom, *v.* [f. DIS- 6 + EMBOSOM.] *trans.* To cast out or separate from the bosom; to disclose, reveal. (Cf. DISBOSOM.)

1742 YOUNG *Nt. Th.* IX. 2350 He..Who, disembosom'd from the Father, bows The heav'n of heav'ns, to kiss the distant earth! **1878** BROWNING *La Saisiaz* 21 Throb of heart, beneath which..Treasure oft was disembosomed.

b. *refl.* and *intr.* To disclose what is in one's bosom, unburden oneself.

1767 *Babler* I. 226 Miss Lambton..thought it best to disembosom herself entirely, and thus went on. **1858** *Sat. Rev.* VI. 73/1 The irresistable desire to disembosom oneself had its way. **1884** STEVENSON in *Longm. Mag.* IV. 80 What manner of man this was to whom we disembosomed.

Hence **disem'bosoming** *vbl. sb.*

1836 F. MAHONEY *Rel. Father Prout* (1859) 75 In the disembosomings of feeling and the perennial flow of soul.

disem'bowel, *v.* [f. DIS- 6 + EMBOWEL *v.* (in sense 3); but in sense 1 app. only an intensive of DISBOWEL.]

1. *trans.* To remove the bowels or entrails of; to eviscerate; also, to rip up so as to cause the bowels to protrude.

1613–8 DANIEL *Coll. Hist. Eng.* (1626) 124 The Kings Physition disimbowelled his body. **1772–84** COOK *Voy.* VI. III. i. (R.) Soon after their death, they are disembowelled, by drawing the intestines and other viscera out. **1872** BAKER *Nile Tribut.* x. 159 The infuriated animal disembowelled him before his son's eyes. **1875** J. CURTIS *Hist. Eng.* 148 While yet alive, he was..disembowelled and quartered.

b. *transf.* and *fig.*

1603 [see DISEMBOWELLING below]. **1742** YOUNG *Nt. Th.* VI. 797 Earth's disembowel'd! measur'd are the Skies! **1870** SPURGEON *Treas. Dav.* Ps. l. 17 They disembowel texts of their plain meanings.

2. To take out of the bowels. (Cf. EMBOWEL *v.* 3.)

1703 J. PHILIPS *Splendid Shilling* 78 So her disembowell'd web Arachne in a hall or kitchen spreads, Obvious to vagrant flies.

Hence **disem'bowelled** *ppl. a.*, **disem'bowelling** *vbl. sb.* and *ppl. a.*; also **disem'bowelment**, the act of disembowelling.

1603 FLORIO *Montaigne* I. xxv. (1632) 83 High swelling and heaven-disimbowelling words. **1727–46** THOMSON *Summer* 778 Cataracts that sweep From disembowelled Earth the virgin gold. **1746** W. HORSLEY *Fool* (1748) I. 77 No. 11 ¶1 The Ripping up and Disembowelling of the dead Bodies. **1826** SCOTT *Woodst.* xxix, The disembowelling of the deer. **1875** *Contemp. Rev.* XXV. 262 The city is for ever undergoing disembowelment.

disem'bower, *v.* [f. DIS- 6 + EMBOWER.] *trans.* To remove or set free from a bower.

1856 BRYANT *Poems, Ages* xxxii, Streams numberless, that many a fountain feeds, Shine, disembowered.

†**disem'brace**, *v. Obs.* [f. DIS- 6 + EMBRACE *v.*] *trans.* **a.** To refrain or withdraw from embracing. **b.** To undo embracing or the embraces of anything. Hence **disem'bracing** *ppl. a.*; also **disem'bracement**, the act of disembracing.

1638 MAYNE *Lucian* (1664) 187 They bedust one another, to hinder dis-imbracements..and by drying his body, to strengthen his hold on his adversary. **1641** J. SHERMAN *Grk. in Temple* 21 The teacher of the Gentiles instructeth us Christians not to disembrace goodness in any, nor truth in any. **1775** S. J. PRATT *Liberal Opin.* (1783) I. 192 Torn away by the disembracing grasp of death.

†**disem'brangle**, *v. Obs.* [f. DIS- 6 + EMBRANGLE.] *trans.* To free from embranglement or complication; to disentangle.

1726 BERKELEY *Let. to Prior* 19 July Wks. 1871 IV. 130 The difficulty of disembrangling our affairs with Partinton. *Ibid.* 12 Nov. 137 For God's sake disembrangle these matters, that I may once be at ease to mind my other affairs.

disem'broil, *v.* [f. DIS- 6 + EMBROIL; cf. Sp. *desembrollar* (Minsheu); also 16th c. F. *desbrouiller.*] *trans.* To free from embroilment or confusion; to extricate from confusion or perplexity, to disentangle.

1611 FLORIO *Disbrogliare*, to disimbroile. **1622** MABBE tr. *Aleman's Guzman d'Alf.* II. 137 To disimbroyle our selues of this troublesome businesse. **1681** *Char. Illustr. Court-Favourite* 16 The knowledg of things past..That Light which disembroils the intrigues of the Court. **1741** WARBURTON *Div. Legat.* II. 142 To disembroil a Subject that seems to have perplexed even Antiquity. **1830** MACKINTOSH *Eth. Philos.* Wks. 1846 I. 72 It is little wonderful that Cumberland should not have disembroiled this ancient and established confusion. **1868** BROWNING *Ring & Bk.* VI. 22 Let him but decently disembroil himself, Scramble from out the scrape.

†**disem'brute**, *v. Obs.* [DIS- 6.] *trans.* To deliver from an embruted or brutalized condition; to debrutalize.

1767 H. BROOKE *Fool of Qual.* (1859) I. 71 (D.) Of a numerous people he [Peter the Great] disembruted every one except himself.

disem'burden, -'burthen, *v.* [See DISEN-, DISEM-, and BURDEN *v.*] = DISBURDEN. Hence **disem'burdening** *vbl. sb.*

1790–1810 COMBE *Devil upon Two Sticks* (1817) VI. 282 Of all its affairs he has disemburthened himself. **1855** BROWNING *Fra Lippo Lippi*, Never was such prompt disemburdening. **1884** *Law Times* 27 Sept. 361/1 The local courts should be disemburdened of non-contentious business.

disemic (daɪ'siːmɪk), *a.* [f. L. *disēmus* disyllabic, a. Gr. δίσημος of doubtful quantity (f. δι- (DI-[2]) twice + σῆμα a sign) + -IC.] In *Gr.* and *L. Prosody*: Of the value of two moræ or units of time (cf. TRISEMIC).

In recent Dicts.

†**disem'pare**, *v. Obs. rare.* [a. OF. *desempare-r*, f. *des-*, DIS- 4 + *emparer* to possess, get possession of.] *trans.* To dispossess.

c **1500** *Melusine* xxix. 215 My brother..thou wylt so dysempare & putte out fro his royaume.

disempassioned, var. DISIMPASSIONED.

†**disem'pester**, *v. Obs.* Also **disim-**. [f. DIS- 6 + EMPESTER *v.*] *trans.* To rid of that which pesters or plagues.

1613 DANIEL *Coll. Hist. Eng.* 104 To unburthen his charge, and dis-impester his Court. **1654** TRAPP *Comm. Neh.* ii. 4 That the Church might be disempestered of Arians.

†**dis'empire**, *v. Obs. rare.* [f. DIS- 7 c + EMPIRE.] *trans.* To deprive of the imperial power.

1611 SPEED *Hist. Gt. Brit.* IX. viii. (1632) 576 Otho, whom this very Pope..had both..aduanced, and..dis-empyred.

disemploy (dɪsɪm'plɔɪ), *v. rare.* Also 7 **-imploy**. [f. DIS- 6 + EMPLOY *v.*] *trans.* To cease to employ, dismiss from, or throw out of, employment.

1618 BOLTON *Florus* IV. ii. 266 The Senate consulted to disemploy Caesar. **1642** JER. TAYLOR *Episc.* (R.), If personal defailance be thought reasonable to disimploy the whole calling, then neither clergy nor laity should ever serve a prince. **1886** O. LODGE *Inaug. Addr.* in *L'pool Univ. Coll. Mag.* 139 Their fellows employing them or disemploying them as it suits their convenience.

Hence **disem'ployed** *ppl. a.*, not employed, out of employment, unemployed.

1651 JER. TAYLOR *Holy Living* (1727) 13 Sins and irregularities..which usually creep upon idle, disemployed and curious persons. **1669** WOODHEAD *St. Teresa* I. xviii. 109 No one of them is so dis-employed as..to be able to attend to anything else. **1807** W. TAYLOR in *Ann. Rev.* V. 187 The disemployed, the unnecessary, the superfluous poor. **1893** *Columbus* (Ohio) *Disp.* 22 Mar., There is very little disemployed labor in the country.

disem'ployment. *rare.* [f. prec. + -MENT.] Absence or withdrawal of employment.

1651 JER. TAYLOR *Holy Living* i. §1. (1727) 8 In this glut of leasure and disemployment. **1893** *Columbus* (Ohio) *Disp.* 7 Aug., This action is leading to some disemployment of labor at eastern works.

disem'power, *v. rare.* [f. DIS- 6 + EMPOWER.] *trans.* To divest or deprive of power conferred.

1813 T. BUSBY *Lucretius* III. *Comm.* xii, If..he can confuse the brain and disempower the understanding. **1858** BUSHNELL *Nat. & Supernat.* iii. (1864) 68 He is disabled, disempowered, reduced in tone.

disemprison, var. DISIMPRISON.

disen-, disem-. Verbs in *dis-* are sometimes in sense negative or privative of those in *em-*, *en-*: e.g. *en-franchise*, *dis-franchise*; generally, however, verbs in *em-* or *en-* have *dis-* prefixed, as in *dis-embarrass*, *dis-engage*, *dis-entwine*. In not a few cases, both forms occur; e.g. *disbowel* = *disembowel*, *disfranchise* = *disenfranchise*. Forms in *disem-* and *disen-* are found even where no verbs in *em-* or *en-* appear, as in *disemburden*, *disenhallow*, *disenravel*.

disenable (dɪsɪ'neɪb(ə)l), *v.* Also 6–7 **-inable**. [f. DIS- 6 + ENABLE.] *trans.* To render unable or incapable; to disable: the reverse of *enable*.

1604 T. WRIGHT *Passions* VI. 346 By sinnes we are.. wounded in nature, disenabled to goodnes, and incited to ilnes. **1608** HIERON *Defence* II. 197 Bellarmin, by rejecting their testimonies in parte, disinableth them in the whole. **1651** *Fuller's Abel Rediv.*, *Bradford* 188 The Palsie..for eight yeers together disinabled him from riding. **1690** *Secr. Hist. Chas. II & Jas. II*, 110 A Bill to disinable him to inherit the Imperial Crown of the Realm. **1811** LAMB *Edax on Appetite*, I am constitutionally disenabled from that vice. **1873** LOWELL *Among my Bks.* Ser. II. 220 [This] makes all the personages puppets and disenables them for being characters.

absol. **1642** FULLER *Holy & Prof. St.* I. xv. 48 Neither doth an apprenticeship extinguish native, nor disinable to acquisitive Gentry. **1658–9** *Burton's Diary* (1828) III. 434 By the Act of Oblivion they are pardoned, but it is your law in being that does disenable.

Hence **dise'nabled** *ppl. a.*, **dise'nabling** *vbl. sb.*; also **dise'nablement**, the action of disenabling or fact of being disenabled.

1611 SPEED *Hist. Gt. Brit.* IX. xvi. 57 By his deserued death, and the disenablement of his sonnes. **1613** JACKSON *Creed* I. III. xi. [xxviii.] § 1. 175 For disinabling of this Nation from effecting what he feared. **1641** MILTON *Reform.* I. (1851) 8 To set their hands to the disinabling and defeating ..of Princesse Mary. **1663** *Depos. Cast. York* (Surtees) 113 She..was soe infirme and disenabled, that [etc.].

dise'nact, *v. rare.* [f. DIS- 6 + ENACT.] *trans.* To annul that which is enacted; to repeal. Hence **dise'nactment**, the repeal of an enactment.

1651 N. BACON *Disc. Govt. Eng.* II. xxiv. (1739) 110 And did build and pull down, enact and disenact. **1859** SMILES *Self-help* 2 The chief reforms of the last fifty years have consisted mainly in abolitions and disenactments.

dise'namour, *v.* [f. DIS- 6 + ENAMOUR: cf. F. *désenamour-er* (16th c. in Hatz-Darm.) and It. *disinnamorare*.] *trans.* To free from being enamoured; to put out of conceit. Hence †**dise'namoured** *ppl. a.*

1598 FLORIO, *Snamorarsi*, to disinamour, to fall in dislike. *Snamoratosi*, disinamored, falne in dislike. **1620** SHELTON *Quix.* IV. xviii. 144 He makes Don Quixote disenamour'd of Dulcinea del Toboso.

†**disen'cage**, *v. Obs.* in 7 **disin-**. [DIS- 6.] *trans.* To liberate as from a cage; to DISCAGE.

1654 GAYTON *Pleas. Notes* IV. xxii. 274 The Don is disincaged.

†**disen'camp**, *v. Obs.* [f. DIS- 6 + ENCAMP.] *intr.* To move one's camp; to DECAMP.

1652 COKAINE tr. *Calprenede's Cassandra* I. 40 Seeing the Army disencampt. **1658** J. WEBB tr. *Calprenede's Cleopatra* VIII. ii. 142 Then giving order for the march, she disencamped, the next morning, towards Dacia.

disen'chain, *v. rare.* [f. DIS- 6 + ENCHAIN: cf. F. *désenchaîner* (16th c. in Littré).] *trans.* To set free from chains or restraint; to reverse the process of enchaining. Hence **disen'chained** *ppl. a.*

a **1849** POE *Eiros & Charmion* Wks. (1888) 145 Why need I paint, Charmion, the now disenchained frenzy of mankind? **1856** MASSON *Ess.*, *Th. Poetry* 419 Idealizations of what might be..not copied from nature, but imagined and full fashioned by the soul of man, and thence disenchained into nature.

disenchant (dɪsɪn'tʃɑːnt, -æ-), *v.* Also 7–8 **disin-**. [ad. F. *désenchanter* (13th c. in Hatz.-Darm.), f. *des-*, DIS- 4 + *enchanter* to ENCHANT; cf. It. *disincantare*, Sp. *desencantar*.] *trans.* To set free from enchantment, magic spell, or illusion.

a **1586** SIDNEY (J.), Alas! let your own brain disenchant you. **1659** *Gentl. Calling* Pref. 4 Reason and Religion will yield you countercharms, able to disinchant you. **1691** DRYDEN *K. Arthur* IV. Wks. 1884 VIII. 187 A noble stroke or two Ends all the charms, and disenchants the grove. **1759** GOLDSM. *Bee* 13 Oct. *Happiness* No reading or study had contributed to disenchant the fairy-land around him. *c* **1850** *Arab. Nts.* (Rtldg.) 612 Go and solicit the young enchantress, who has caused this metamorphosis, to disenchant her. **1874** GREEN *Short Hist.* viii. § 2. 478 He had disenchanted his people of their blind faith in the Crown.

disen'chanted, *ppl. a.* [f. prec. + -ED[1].] Freed from enchantment or illusion.

1611 COTGR., *Desenchanté*, disinchaunted. **1682** DRYDEN *Medall* 180 Nor are thy disinchanted Burghers few. **1742** YOUNG *Nt. Th.* I. 346 The disinchanted earth Lost all her lustre. **1838** DICKENS *Nich. Nick.* xxx, A crest-fallen, dispirited, disenchanted man.

disen'chanter. [f. as prec. + -ER[1].] One who removes enchantment.

1654 GAYTON *Pleas. Notes* III. viii. 119 Disinchanters of Negromancers, disrobers of gypsies. **1831** [see DISENCHANTRESS]. **1862** MRS. OLIPHANT *Mortimers* I. 253 Harry..gazed with open eyes and mouth at the disenchanter.

disen'chanting, *vbl. sb.* [f. as prec. + -ING[1].] Deliverance from enchantment.

1620 SHELTON *Quix.* III. xxxv. 252 He may..do all that is fitting for her Disenchanting. **1718** MOTTEUX *Quix.* (1892) II. xxxv. 268 May you and your disenchanting go to the devil.

disen'chanting, *ppl. a.* [f. as prec. + -ING[2].] That disenchants. Hence **disen'chantingly** *adv.*

1755 YOUNG *Centaur* vi. 221 At the touch of my disenchanting pen. **1866** NONA BELLAIRS *Wayside Fl.* vi. 69 History comes with its disenchanting wand. **1886** R. DOWLING *Fatal Bonds* I. xi. 219 He was disenchantingly opaque.

disen'chantment. [f. DISENCHANT *v.* + -MENT, after *enchantment*: cf. F. *désenchantement* (17th c. in Hatz.-Darm.).] The action of disenchanting or fact of being disenchanted.

1620 SHELTON *Quix.* IV. xxii. (R.), All concluded in the promise..of the disenchantment. **1675** (*title*), O Brazile, or the inchanted Island; being a Relation of a late Discovery of the Dis-inchantment of an Island in the North of Ireland. **1794** MATHIAS *Purs. Lit.* (1798) 118 All the conjurers.. might assist at the disinchantment. **1876** GEO. ELIOT *Dan. Der.* III. xxvi, This general disenchantment with the world ..only intensified her sense of forlornness.

disen'chantress. [f. DISENCHANTER + -ESS.] A female disenchanter.

1831 CARLYLE *Sart. Res.* II. v, Neither Disenchanter nor Disenchantress..can abide by Feeling alone.

disen'charm, *v. rare.* Also 7 **-in-**. [f. DIS- 6 + ENCHARM.] *trans.* To deliver from a charm.

1651 JER. TAYLOR *Serm. for Year* II. i. 9 The fear of a Sin had disincharmed him. **1884** BROWNING *Ferishtah* 143 A chill wind disencharms All the late enchantment!

†**disen'cloister**, *v. Obs. rare*$^{-1}$. [f. DIS- 6 + ENCLOISTER *v.*] *trans.* To set free from cloistered confinement and seclusion.

1652 BENLOWES *Theoph.* IV. lxxxvii, Let her still Enjoy her discloystred fill In these high Extasies.

†**disen'close**, *v. Obs. rare.* Also 7 **-inclose**. [f. DIS- 6 + ENCLOSE *v.*] *trans.* To throw open (that which is enclosed); to do away with the enclosure of. Hence **disen'closed** *ppl. a.*

1611 COTGR., *Desclorre*, to disparke, vnclose; disinclose, pull downe hedges or inclosures. **1669** WOODHEAD *St. Teresa* I. vii. 33 Neither is this Monastery also of the most open and dis-enclosed.

†**disen'courage**, *v. Obs.* [f. DIS- 6 + ENCOURAGE. Cf. DISCOURAGE.] *trans.* To deprive of encouragement; to DISCOURAGE.

1626 in Rushw. *Hist. Coll.* (1659) I. 371 To disencourage all opposers. **1710** STEELE *Tatler* No. 26 ¶6 Yet that must not disencourage you. **1800** MAD. D'ARBLAY *Diary & Lett.* (1846) VI. 243 The world has acknowledged you my offspring, and I will disencourage you no more. **1803** *Ibid.* 325.

Hence †**disen'couraging**, *ppl. a.*; also †**disen'courager** *Obs.*

1716 M. DAVIES *Athen. Brit.* II. To Rdr. 14 As great.. Disencouragers as our Bibliopolists prove to learned Poverty. *a* **1806** C. J. FOX *Hist. James II* (1808) 27 The most completely disencouraging example that history affords.

†**disen'couragement**. *Obs.* Also 7 **-in-**. [f. prec.; cf. *encouragement*.]

Lack or withdrawal of encouragement; disheartenment, discouragement.

1598 BARRET *Theor. Warres* III. ii. 71 The effect whereof shall breede..disencouragement, and weakening to the enemy. **1632** J. HAYWARD tr. *Biondi's Eromena* 56 Neither should her present humor give you [a suitor] any cause of disincouragement. **1668** ETHEREDGE *She wou'd if she cou'd* I. i. Wks. (1723) 90 The utter decay and disencouragement of Trade and Industry. **1715** M. DAVIES *Athen. Brit.* I. Pref. 68 Under a temptation of a total Disencouragement.

disencrease: see DISINCREASE.

disencumber (dɪsɪn'kʌmbə(r)), *v.* Also 7 **-in-**. [ad. F. *désencombrer*, earlier *desencombre* (12–13th c. in Hatz.-Darm.): see DIS- 4 and ENCUMBER.] *trans.* To relieve or free from encumbrances.

1598 BARRET *Theor. Warres* V. ii. 130 The space..behind the terraplene..shall..be made plaine and disencombred. **1667** MILTON *P.L.* v. 700 Ere dim Night had disincumberd Heav'n. **1751** JOHNSON *Rambler* No. 147 ¶8 Most expeditiously disencumbered from my villatick bashfulness. **1814** WORDSW. *Excursion* IX. 71 On that superior height Who sits, is disencumbered from the press Of near obstructions. **1888** BURGON *Lives 12 Gd. Men* I. iv. 397 The beautiful pillars were disencumbered of the monuments which..encrusted and disfigured them.

disen'cumbered, *ppl. a.* [f. prec. + -ED[1].] Freed from encumbrance.

1611 COTGR., *Descombré*, disincombred, vnpestered. **1681** DRYDEN *Abs. & Achit.* 850 Free from Earth, thy disencumbred Soul Mounts up. **1705** ADDISON *Italy* 76 The Church of St. Justina..is the most handsom, luminous, disencumber'd Building in the Inside that I have ever seen. **1781** COWPER *Retirement* 394 Four handsome bays, That whirl away from business and debate The disencumbered Atlas of the State. **1824** L. MURRAY *Eng. Gram.* (ed. 5) I. 449 That the more important..words may possess the last place, quite disencumbered.

disen'cumberment. *rare.* [f. as prec. + -MENT: cf. F. *désencombrement* (Littré).] The action of disencumbering or fact of being disencumbered.

In recent Dicts.

†**disen'cumbrance**. *Obs.* [f. as prec. + -ANCE, after *encumbrance*.] Deliverance or freedom from encumbrance.

1712 STEELE *Spect.* No. 264 ¶1 Out of mere Choice, and an elegant Desire of Ease and Disincumbrance. **1776** ADAM SMITH *W. N.* v. ii. (1869) II. 455 The waste, and not the disencumbrance, of the estate was the common effect of a long minority. **1793** W. ROBERTS *Looker-on* (1794) II. No. 60. 406 An indecorous ease, and a selfish disincumbrance.

disend, obs. form of DESCEND.

†**disen'damage**, *v. Obs. rare.* [DIS- 6.] *trans.* To relieve from loss or damage.

1655 JENNINGS *Elise* 69 Promising that he would disendamage him of all his pretended wrongs.

disendow (dɪsɪnˈdaʊ), *v.* [f. DIS- 6 + ENDOW.] *trans.* To deprive or strip of endowments.
1861 F. HALL in *Jrnl. Asiat. Soc. Bengal* 4 Descendants who were not entirely disendowed of power. **1868** *Pall Mall G.* 18 Feb., One cannot understand why the Protestant rector should vanish from the land the moment the [Irish] Church is disendowed. **1883** LABOUCHERE in *Fortn. Rev.*, The Established Church will at once be disestablished and disendowed.

Hence **disenˈdowed** *ppl. a.*, **disenˈdowing** *vbl. sb.* and *ppl. a.*; also **disenˈdower**, one who disendows; **disenˈdowment**, the action or fact of disendowing. (All chiefly used in reference to ecclesiastical endowments.)
1864 WEBSTER, *Disendowment.* **1867** BREWER in *Times* 10 Apr. 8 The House of Commons has pledged itself to the disestablishment and disendowment of the Irish Church. **1869** *Daily Tel.* 5 July, The great disestablisher and disendower. **1874** *Eclectic* Sept. 319 The secularized and disendowed priests of a once popular religion. **1874** MORLEY *Compromise* (1886) 99 The disendowment of the national church. **1888** *Pall Mall G.* 9 Apr. 2/2 Used to hearing disestablishers accused of a new Crucifixion and disendowers identified with Judas.

disener, var. of DECENER, *Obs.*
1489 CAXTON *Faytes of A.* II. xxx. 141 Eueryche shal haue undre hym a dyzener of carpenters and a dyzener of helpers and also thre diseners of laborers.

†**disenfiˈlade**, *v.* *Obs. rare.* [f. DIS- 6 + ENFILADE *v.*] *trans.* (See quot.)
1706 *Accomplished Officer* v. 39 Care ought to be taken, that all the Parts of the Covered Way be Disenfiladed. Which is done either by Nature, or by Traverses of all those Parts of the Country which might command them. *Ibid.* 40 To Disenfilade signify's so to dispose the Ground or a Work, as that it may not be seen or discovered by the Enemy, and battered in a straight line.

disenˈfranchise, *v.* [f. DIS- 6 + ENFRANCHISE *v.* II.]
1. *trans.* To deprive of civil or electoral privileges; to DISFRANCHISE.
1664 BUTLER *Hud.* II. ii. 708 And they, in mortal Battel vanquish'd, Are of their Charter dis-enfranchis'd. **1739** H. BROOKE *Gustavus Vasa* (Jod.), That nature..Shall disenfranchise all her lordly race. **1893** LYDIA H. DICKINSON in Barrows *Parl. Relig.* I. 507 There could..be no legal act disenfranchising woman, since she was never legally enfranchised.
†**2.** [f. DIS- 5, or error.] To set free, liberate, enfranchise. *Obs. rare.*
1626 T. H. *Caussin's Holy Crt.* 153 A cruell Tyranny, from whence she may with a litle courage disinfranchize herselfe. **1654** LD. ORRERY *Parthenissa* (1676) 360, I resolv'd my self not a little disenfranchis'd from that obligation.

Hence **disenˈfranchising** *ppl. a.* and *vbl. sb.*; also †**disenˈfranchisement** *Obs.*
1721 BAILEY, *Disenfranchisement*, a being disfranchised. **1865** *Morn. Star* 9 May, This..is not an enfranchising, but a disenfranchising measure.

disengage (dɪsɪnˈgeɪdʒ), *v.* Also 7–8 disingage. [f. DIS- 6 + ENGAGE *v.*; prob. after F. *désengager* (1462 in Hatz.-Darm.).]
†**1.** *trans.* To free from engagement, pledge, contract, or obligation. *Obs.* exc. as *pa. pple.*
1611 COTGR., *Desengager*, to disingage, vngage, redeeme. **1622** MABBE tr. *Aleman's Guzman d'Alf.* II.** ij a, Moneys wherewithall to pay my debts, & to disingage my word. **1648** MILTON *Tenure Kings* (1650) 10 If the king prov'd unfaithful the people would be disingag'd. **1754** RICHARDSON *Grandison* (1781) II. xxix. 278 To be a single woman all my life, if he would not disengage me of my rash, my foolish promise. **1837** [see DISENGAGED].
2. To loosen from that which holds fast, adheres, or entangles; to detach, liberate, free.
1662 J. DAVIES tr. *Olearius' Voy. Ambass.* 34 Two great Ships..between which we were so intangled, that we could not in three hours disengage our selves. **1678** *Lond. Gaz.* No. 1317/4 Sieur Ollier was mortally wounded, and taken, but afterwards disengaged again. **1771** OLIVIER *Fencing Familiarized* (1780) 60, I make an appel and disengage the point of my sword as if my design were to thrust carte over the arm. **1834** MEDWIN *Angler in Wales* I. 74, I had.. previously wound the rope..round my arm: the consequence was, that I could not disengage my wrist. **1878** HUXLEY *Physiogr.* 109 It slowly decomposes the water, combining with its hydrogen and disengaging its oxygen.
b. *fig.*
1603 FLORIO *Montaigne* III. ii. (1632) 456 It is a pleasure unto mee, to bee..disingaged from their contentions. *a* **1618** SYLVESTER *Job Triumphant* I. 390 Hee will..from the sword of war thee dis-ingage. **1634** HABINGTON *Castara* (Arb.) 64 My sacke will disingage All humane thoughts. **1659** B. HARRIS *Parival's Iron Age* 39 Henry the fourth endeavoured to disingage him from the service of the Arch-Duke. **1711** ADDISON *Spect.* No. 63 ¶1 It is very hard for the Mind to disengage it self from a Subject in which it has been long employed. *a* **1871** GROTE *Eth. Fragm.* iv. (1876) 77 To disengage great principles from capricious adjuncts.
c. To loosen a bond or that which binds.
1780 COWPER *Doves* 10 Our mutual bond of faith and truth No time shall disengage. **1856** BRYANT *Old Man's Funeral* vii, Softly to disengage the vital cord.
3. *intr.* (for *refl.*) To free oneself, get loose.
1646 J. HALL *Poems* I. 38 Wee'l disingage, our bloodlesse form shall fly Beyond the reach of Earth. **1697** COLLIER *Ess. Mor. Subj.* II. (1709) 98 In conversing with Books we may chuse our Company, and disengage without Ceremony or Exception. **1832** *Regul. Instr. Cavalry* III. 80 The left Troop ..must disengage..before it can move.
4. *intr.* *Fencing.* To reverse the relative position of the blades by smartly passing the point to the opposite side of the opponent's sword.
1684 R. H. *School Recreat.* 71 When you are on your Guard, and within your Adversary's Sword, disengage and make your Feint without. **1771** OLIVIER *Fencing Famil.* (1780) 38 If you perceive your adversary force your blade, I would always have you disengage, keeping the point strait to his body. **1809** ROLAND *Fencing* 83 To disengage is simply to pass your blade on the other side of your adversary's (it is no matter whether within or over the arm) and to thrust.

Hence **disenˈgaging** *vbl. sb.* and *ppl. a.* ***disengaging gear, machinery***: see ENGAGING *ppl. a.* 3.
1684 R. H. *School Recreat.* 59 Caveating or Disengaging. Here you must..slip your Adversaries Sword, when you perceive him about to bind or secure yours. **1831** *Boy's Own Bk.* 77 Disengaging is performed by dexterously shifting the point of your foil from one side of your adversary's blade to the other; that is, from carte to tierce, or *vice versa.* **1874** KNIGHT *Dict. Mech.*, *Disengaging-gear*, contrivances by which machines are thrown out of connection with their motor, by disconnecting the wheels, chains or bands which drive them.

disenˈgage, *sb.* *Fencing.* [f. prec. vb.] The act of disengaging or reversing the relative position of the blades, so as to free one's own for a thrust. So ***counter-disengage***.
1771 OLIVIER *Fencing Famil.* (1780) 132 Begin trying your adversary with appels, beatings, disengages, and extensions, in order to embarrass him. *Ibid.* 87 The counter-disengage of carte over the arm. **1879** *Encycl. Brit.* IX. 71 (*Fencing*) Cut and disengage, if made inside of the arm, is parried by quarte, or the counter of tierce; if outside, by tierce or counter in quarte. **1889** [see COUNTER-DISENGAGE, *sb.*].

disengaged (dɪsɪnˈgeɪdʒd), *ppl. a.* [f. as prec. + -ED[1]; but often used as f. DIS- 10 + ENGAGED.]
a. Set free from engagement, ties, or prepossession; free from obligatory connexion; detached; not engaged; untrammelled, unoccupied, at liberty. *spec.* in *Theatr. colloq.* Unemployed.
1621 SIR G. CALVERT in *Fortesc. Papers* 155 So long as the Prince Palatine shall keepe himself disengaged from medling in them. **1651** HOBBES *Govt. & Soc.* iii. §24. 51 The Law of Nature therefore commands the Judge to be dis-engag'd. **1676** W. HUBBARD *Happiness of People* 53 Such proceedings..doe but embolden disengaged standers by to complain of both. **1712** STEELE *Spect.* No. 318 ¶1 This Lady is of a free and disengaged Behaviour. **1771** OLIVIER *Fencing Famil.* (1780) 38 Seize the time, and give him a disengaged thrust in carte over the arm. **1794** SULLIVAN *View Nat.* I. 250 The other acids are only in a disengaged state, found in waters accidentally. **1837** DICKENS *Pickw.* ii, Are you disengaged this evening? **1933** P. GODFREY *Back-Stage* v. 70 It takes many years before the superseded actors and actresses will admit to themselves that the professional terms 'at liberty' and 'disengaged' are no longer applicable to them in a temporary sense.
b. Uncommitted; opp. ENGAGED *ppl. a.* 4.
1958 *Oxf. Mag.* 6 Mar. 340/2 Oppressed by the facile and disengaged conformism of the present age. **1960** *20th Cent.* Apr. 303 The accent to-day is on the personal, the disengaged, the apolitical and the *status quo*.

disenˈgagedness. [f. prec. + -NESS.] The quality of being disengaged; freedom from ties, engagement, obligation, or prepossession.
1685 tr. *Gracian's Courtier's Orac.* 195 To speak clearly.. shews not onely a disengagedness, but also a vivacity of wit. **1754** EDWARDS *Freed. Will.* II. xiii. 133 The more the Soul has of this Disengagedness in its acting, the more Liberty. **1849** J. HAMILTON *Let.* in *Life* viii. (1870) 353, I have a singular sensation of disengagedness. **1887** E. GURNEY *Tertium Quid* I. 250 The application of it requires disengagedness and common-sense.

disengagement (dɪsɪnˈgeɪdʒmənt). [f. DISENGAGE *v.* + -MENT, after *engagement*; cf. F. *désengagement* (15th c.)] **a.** The action of disengaging or fact of being disengaged *from* (anything).
1650 EARL MONM. tr. *Senault's Man become Guilty* 378 They call poverty a dis-ingagement from uselesse things. **1699** H. CHANDLER *Bigotry* (1709) 6 Their Believing in Christ was no Disingagement from Judaism. **1716** JER. COLLIER tr. *Nazianzen's Panegyrick* Pref., A noble Disengagement from the World. **1887** R. GARNETT in Lowell *Study Wind.* Introd. 12 He has not that disengagement from all traditional and conventional influences..which characterises younger men.
b. The physical, *esp.* chemical, separation or setting free (*of* anything).
1791 W. NICHOLSON tr. *Chaptal's Elem. Chem.* (1800) III. 113 The disengagement of a considerable quantity of nitrous gas. **1842** DE QUINCEY in *Blackw. Mag.* LII. 138 The restoration and disengagement of the public buildings surmounting the city. **1881** *Nature* XXIII. 616 The gaseous acids are absorbed..with disengagement of heat.
c. Freedom from engagement, prepossession, occupation, or ties; detachment; freedom or ease of manner or behaviour.
1701 STEELE *Funeral* III. i. (1702) 38 Oh, Madam! your Air!..The Negligence, the Disengagement of your Manner. **1710** *Brit. Apollo* III. No. 77. 3/1 Thus you by Disingagement Conquer more, Than all your Sex by Servile Laws before. **1750** JOHNSON *Rambler* No. 14 ¶4 A man proposes his schemes of life in a state of abstraction and disengagement. **1768** *Woman of Honor* II. 182, I appeared with all the freedom and dis-ingagement of a simple spectator. **1866** FERRIER *Grk. Philos.* I. x. 241 This mental disengagement..and liberation.
d. The dissolution of an engagement to be married.
1796 JANE AUSTEN *Sense & Sens.* xxix, She might wound Marianne still deeper by treating their disengagement..as an escape from..evils. **1895** *Westm. Gaz.* 7 Feb. 8/1 'Disengagement' is a pleasing euphemism for a gentle form of 'breach of promise'.
e. *Fencing.* (See DISENGAGE *v.* 4.)
1771 OLIVIER *Fencing Famil.* (1780) 38 Of the Disengagement. **1809** ROLAND *Fencing* 65 The side on which it was usual to parry the disengagement. **1889** W. H. POLLOCK, etc., *Fencing* (Badm. Libr.) ii. 48 Simple attacks are..four: the straight thrust, the disengagement, the coupé, and the counter-disengagement.
f. A withdrawal of military forces; a renunciation of military or political influence in a particular area.
1957 *Economist* 28 Dec. 1113/2 Even if..the sun shines brightly on the hopes of disengagement and..the troops can be pulled back from their forward positions, [etc.]. **1958** *Spectator* 14 Feb. 192/3 A policy of disengagement in Central Europe. **1958** *Observer* 23 Feb. 5/3 Topic No. 1.. was 'Disengagement', by which was meant some plan whereby Russian and American troops would withdraw from the 1945 armistice line in Europe. **1966** SCHWARZ & HADIK *Strategic Terminology* 66 *Disengagement*, design for diminishing international tensions by creating a neutral or demilitarized zone between the armed forces of two antagonistic powers or groups of states.

disenˈgirdle, *v. rare.* [DIS- 6.] *trans.* To undo the engirdling of; to release from a girdle.
1871 SWINBURNE *Songs bef. Sunrise* Prel. 99 And disengirdled and discrowned The limbs and locks that vine leaves bound.

†**disenˈgorge**, *v. Obs. rare.* [DIS- 6.] *trans.* To discharge (as a river); = DISGORGE 2.
1610 HOLLAND *Camden's Brit.* I. 239 At length he disengorgeth himselfe unto the Severn-sea.

disenˈgulf, -ˈgulph, *v. rare.* [DIS- 6.] *trans.* To cast up what has been engulfed.
1839–44 TUPPER *Prov. Philos.* (1852) 386 The maelström [shall] disengulph its spoil.

disenhallow (dɪsɪnˈhæləʊ), *v. rare.* [See DISEN- and HALLOW *v.*] *trans.* To deprive of hallowed character.
1847 LYTTON *Lucretia* 69 The love is disenhallowed.

disenherison, disenherit, etc.: see DISIN-.

disenˈmesh, *v. rare.* [DIS- 6.] *trans.* To free from meshes or enmeshment; to disentangle.
1868 BROWNING *Ring & Bk.* XII. 565 Convulsive effort to disperse the films And disenmesh the fame o' the martyr.

diseˈnnoble, *v.* [f. DIS- 6 + ENNOBLE.] *trans.* To deprive of nobleness; to render ignoble: the reverse of to *ennoble*.
1645 *Mod. Answ. Prynne's Reply* 20 It dis-ennobles mens spirits. **1713** ADDISON *Guardian* No. 137 ¶2 An unworthy behaviour degrades and disennobles a man in the eye of the world. **1842** FABER *Styrian Lake* 335 The disennobling of our lives.

†**diseˈnorm**, *v. Obs. rare.* [f. DIS- 6 or 8 + ENORM *v.* or *a.*] *trans.* To free from irregularity; to make conformable to a norm or standard.
1644 QUARLES *Sheph. Orac.* viii, To prevent Confused babling, and to disenorm Prepost'rous service.

disenˈravel, *v. rare.* [See DISEN-, and RAVEL *v.*] *trans.* To unravel, disentangle.
1881 BLACKIE *Lay Serm.* i. 64 A tissue which no mortal skill can disenravel.

†**disenˈrich**, *v. Obs. rare.* [DIS- 6.] *trans.* To deprive of riches; to impoverish.
1647 TRAPP *Comm. 2 Cor.* viii. 9 He that was heir of all things..disinriched and disrobed himself of all.

†**disenˈrol**, *v. Obs. rare.* In 7 disinroule. [f. DIS- 6 + ENROL: cf. obs. F. *desenrouller.*] *trans.* To remove from a roll or list.
a **1631** DONNE *Let. to C'tess. of Bedford* in *Poems* (1650) 164 He cannot (that's, he will not) dis-inroule Your name.

disensanity: see DISINSANITY.

disenˈshroud, *v. rare.* [DIS- 6.] *trans.* To set free from a shroud or enshrouded state.
1835 W. A. BUTLER in *Blackw. Mag.* XXXVII. 857 When that misty vale Evanid, disenshrouding field and grove, Left us. *Mod.* The disenshrouded statue.

disenˈslave, *v.* Also 7 disin-. [DIS- 6.] *trans.* To set free from enslavement; to liberate from slavery. Hence **disenˈslaved** *ppl. a.*
1649 *Petit.* in J. Harrington *Def. Rights Univ. Oxford* (1690) 1 Your worthy intentions to disinslave the free born People of this Nation from all manner of Arbitrary..Power. **1660** H. MORE *Myst. Godl.* VI. xi. 244 To disenslave him from the bondage of Satan. **1681** P. RYCAUT *Critick* 242 To walk as free and disinslaved as the King of it. *a* **1716** SOUTH *Serm.* (1737) III. viii (R.). They expected such an one as should disenslave them from the Roman yoke.

disentail (dɪsɪnˈteɪl), *v.* Also 7 disin-. [f. DIS- 6 + ENTAIL *v.*[2]] Hence **disenˈtailing** *ppl. a.*
1. *trans.* (*Law.*) To free from entail; to break the entail of (an estate); see ENTAIL *sb.*[2]
1848 WHARTON *Law Lex.* 645/2 The disentailing deed must be enrolled. **1858** LD. ST. LEONARDS *Handy Bk. Prop.*

Law xvii. 129 [A] disentailing assurance. **1861** W. Bell *Dict. Law Scot.* 807/1 An heir born after that date [Aug. 1848] is entitled to disentail the estate under the authority of the Court. *Ibid.*, The exercise of the power to disentail. **1885** Sir N. Lindley in *Law Times Rep.* LIII. 609/2 He intended to disentail everything which he took under the will of his ancestor. *Mod.* Part of the estate has been disentailed.

†**2.** To divest, dispossess, deprive *of*.
1641 Milton *Ch. Govt.* II. iii. (1851) 158 With much more reason undoubtedly ought the censure of the Church be quite devested and disintal'd of all jurisdiction whatsoever.

†**b.** To free oneself from, get rid of. *Obs.*
1667 *Decay Chr. Piety* viii. ¶26 To disintail those two most inestimable blessings, of a pure religion and outward peace, which our immediate progenitors left us.

disen'tail. *sb.* [f. prec. vb.] The act of disentailing or breaking an entail.
1861 W. Bell *Dict. Law Scot.* 807/2 An heir..is not entitled to give consent to a disentail, in opposition to the creditors in such debts. **1868** *Act 31–2 Vict.* c. 101 §112 The execution of a deed of disentail. **1884** *Weekly Notes* 22 Nov. 210/2 The power of sale in the will was destroyed by the disentail.

disen'tailment. [f. as prec. + -ment.] = prec.
1848 Wharton *Law Lex.* 647/2 Thus much as to the disentailment of freehold. **1886** *Law Rep.* 31 Ch. Div. 254 In effecting the disentailment and resettling of this estate.

disentangle (dɪsɪn'tæŋg(ə)l), *v.* Also 7–8 **disin-**. [f. dis- 6 + entangle.]
1. *trans.* To free (anything) from that in or with which it is entangled; to disengage, extricate. Const. *from*, formerly sometimes *of*. **a.** *lit.*
1598 Florio *Ital. Dict.*, *Strigare* to disintangle, to rid. *a***1691** Boyle (J.), Though in concretions particles so entangle one another..yet they do incessantly strive to disentangle themselves, and get away. **1784** Cowper *Task* III. 145 They disentangle from the puzzled skein..The threads of..shrewd design. **1847** J. Wilson *Chr. North* (1857) II. 21 To disentangle our line from the water-lilies. **1860** Tyndall *Glac.* I. xix. 135 Two hours had been spent in the effort to disentangle ourselves from the crags.

b. *fig.* To set free from intellectual, moral, or practical complications; to extricate from difficulties or hindrances.
1611 Cotgr., *Desembarrasser*, to vnpester, disintangle. **1632** J. Hayward tr. *Biondi's Eromena* 116 The Princesse now disentangled of publike affaires, and desirous to know who shee was [etc.]. **1709** Berkeley *Th. Vision* §92 To disentangle our minds from..prejudices. **1769** Robertson *Chas. V*, III. XII. 370 The Emperor disentangled himself..from all the affairs of this world. **1874** Green *Short Hist.* vi. §6. 325 To..disentangle a few fragmentary facts from the mass of fable.

2. To bring (anything) out of a tangled state; to unravel, untwist.
1805 Southey *Madoc in Azt.* vi, Disentangling The passive reptile's folds. **1826** Scott *Diary* 10 Feb. in *Lockhart*, One puzzles the skein in order to excite curiosity and then cannot disentangle it. **1856** Kane *Arct. Expl.* I. xx. 252 Patience to disentangle the knots of my harness.
fig. **1660** Marvell *Corr.* xiii. Wks. 1872–5 II. 40, I shall..inform myselfe here how that annexion stands, and the readiest way of disintangling it. **1751** Johnson *Rambler* No. 169 ¶13 He must..disentangle his method, and alter his arrangement. **1871** Freeman *Hist. Ess.* Ser. I. i. 31 We can disentangle the several elements of which it is made up.

3. *intr.* (for *refl.*) To become disentangled; to disentangle oneself (quot. 1676).
1607 *Ford's Madrigal*, '*Since first I saw your face*', My heart is fast, And cannot disentangle. **1676** Marvell *Mr. Smirke* K iv, Betaking themselves to this Spiritual Warfare, they ought to disintangle from the World. **1726** *Adv. Capt. R. Boyle* 24 My Foot disentangled, and I fell plum into the Sea. **1742** Young *Nt. Th.* II. 455 Thoughts disintangle passing o'er the lip. *Mod.* This skein won't disentangle.

Hence **disen'tangled** *ppl. a.*, **-ing** *vbl. sb.*
1611 Cotgr., *Desmeslement*, vnpestering, disintricating, disintangling. **1633** G. Herbert *Temple, Reprisall* ii, A disentangled state and free. **1675** Traherne *Chr. Ethics* ii. 14 Our thoughts and affections must be always disentangled.

disen'tanglement. [f. prec. + -ment, after *entanglement*.] The fact of disentangling, or state of being disentangled.
1751 Johnson *Rambler* No. 110 ¶10 The disentanglement of actions complicated with innumerable circumstances. **1774** Warton *Hist. Eng. Poetry* (1840) III. xliv. 127 In the disentanglement of this distressful tale. **1856** Froude *Hist. Eng.* I. 228 Such process of disentanglement ..though easy for posterity, is always impossible to living actors in the drama of life.

disen'tangler. *rare.* One who disentangles.
1885 *Manch. Exam.* 13 Apr. 3/1 Mr. Buchanan's work of disentangler is conducted with a good deal of spirit.

†**dis'enter,** *v. Law. Obs.* [f. dis- 6 + enter *v.* 2.] *trans.* To eject, oust, dispossess.
1629 *MS. Acc. St. John's Hosp., Canterb.*, For his charges when he went into Thanett to disenter Sampson from our lands and to take possession. **1631** *Ibid.*, [We] went to Hoath to disenter Baker.

disenter, -erre, obs. ff. disinter *v.*

†**disente'ration.** *Obs. rare.* [n. of action f. **disenterate* vb., f. dis- 7 + Gr. ἔντερα bowels.] Evacuation of the bowels.
1654 Gayton *Pleas. Notes* III. viii. 123 For doing the work of Nature (I meane not that of Disenteration) but of laughing.

disen'thral, -all, *v.* Also 7 **disin-**. [f. dis- 6 + enthral.] *trans.* To set free from enthralment or bondage; to liberate from thraldom.
*a***1643** G. Sandys (J.), God my soul shall disenthral. **1653** Milton *Ps.* iv. 4 In straits and in distress Thou didst me disenthrall And set at large. **1689** *Def. Liberty agst. Tyrants* 149 In seeking freedom from Tyranny, he..was the principal Instrument to dis-inthrall them. **1843** J. Martineau *Chr. Life* (1867) 331 Reverence which disenthrals the mind from lower passions.

Hence **disen'thralled** *ppl. a.*
1848 R. I. Wilberforce *Incarnation* xiii. (1852) 363 Only through union with our disenthralled representative.

disen'thraldom. *rare.* [irreg. f. prec. + -dom, after *thraldom*.] = next.
1823 *New Monthly Mag.* VII. 529 The advocates of disenthraldom from the classic school.

disen'thralment. [f. disenthral + -ment.] The action of freeing, or fact of being freed, from enthralment; emancipation from thraldom.
1825 Ld. Cockburn *Mem.* 262 The disenthralment of those who had liberated themselves. **1870** Lowell *Study Wind.* 54 Enjoying that delicious sense of disenthralment from the actual which..twilight brings.

disenthrone (dɪsɪn'θrəʊn), *v.* Also 7 **disin-**. [f. dis- 6 + enthrone.] *trans.* To put down from a throne; to depose from royal or supreme dignity or authority; to dethrone.
1608 Heywood *Lucrece* I. ii. Wks. 1874 V. 171, I charge thee, Tarquin, disinthrone thy selfe. **1667** Milton *P.L.* II. 229 Either to disinthrone the King of Heav'n We warr..or to regain Our own right lost. **1855** Milman *Lat. Chr.* (1864) IX. XIV. x. 346 The proposal of a new translation of the Scriptures..disenthroned the Vulgate from its absolute exclusive authority.

Hence **disen'throning** *vbl. sb.*; **disen'thronement**, dethroning.
1648 Milton *Observ. Art. Peace* (1851) 559 Which act of any King against the Consent of his Parlament..might of it self strongly conduce to the disinthrowning him. **1848** Hampden *Bampt. Lect.* (ed. 3) 157 The disenthroning of Providence. **1894** Asquith *Sp. at Newburgh* 24 Oct., To seek for the disenthronement of religious privilege.

disentitle (dɪsɪn'taɪt(ə)l), *v.* Also 7 **disin-**. [f. dis- 6 + entitle.] *trans.* To deprive of title or right (*to* something): the reverse of to *entitle*.
1654 Jer. Taylor *Real Pres.* 131 All that eat are not made Christ's body, and all that eat not are not disintitled to the resurrection. *a***1716** South *Serm.* VIII. v. (R.) Every ordinary offence does not disentitle a son to the love of his father. **1856** Froude *Hist. Eng.* I. 99 He..would have pleaded the sacred right of inheritance, refusing utterly the imaginary law which disentitled him.

disentomb (dɪsɪn'tuːm), *v.* [f. dis- 6 + entomb.] *trans.* To take out of the tomb; (*transf.* and *fig.*) to take (anything) out of that in which it is buried or hidden away; to disinter, unearth.
1611 Florio, *Disepelire*, to vnburie, disintombe. **1626** T. H. *Caussin's Holy Crt.* 370 A mad vanity of Nobility of race, which causeth many to dig out, and disentombe their Grand-Sires, as it were, from the ashes of old Troy. **1839** De Quincey *Recoll. Lakes* Wks. 1862 II. 96 Worlds of fine thinking lie buried in that vast abyss, never to be disentombed. **1877** A. B. Edwards *Up Nile* xxi. 659 A mummy..which we saw disentombed. **1880** McCarthy *Own Times* IV. 527 Mr. Freeman..disentombed a great part of the early history of England.

Hence **disentombed** (-'tuːmd), *ppl. a.*; **disentombment** ('tuːmmənt), the act of disentombing.
1859 Smiles *Self-Help* iii. 55 The disentombment of the Nineveh marbles. **1871** Fraser *Life & Lett. Berkeley* iii. 78 The disentombed remains of Herculaneum.

†**disen'trail,** *v. Obs.* [f. dis- 7 a + entrail *sb.*[1] (in early use *en'trail*).] *trans.* To draw forth from the entrails or inward parts. Hence †**disen'trailed** *ppl. a.*
1596 Spenser *F.Q.* IV. iii. 28 The disentrayled blood Adowne their sides like litle rivers stremed. *Ibid.* IV. vi. 16 Heaping huge strokes..As if he thought her soule to disentrayle. **1692** J. Salter *Triumphs Jesus* 22 As if they designed to dis-entrail His very Soul.

disen'trainment. *rare.* [f. dis- 6 + entrain *v.*[2] + -ment.] The action of discharging (troops) from a railway train; detraining.
1881 *Globe* 18 Apr. 5 The disentrainment was superintended by Lieut.-Colonel Knight.

disen'trammel, *v.* [f. dis- 6 + entrammel.] *trans.* To free from its trammels, or from an entrammelled state.
1866 *Pall Mall G.* 22 Jan. 1 Before the Federal Power had been disentrammelled from the civil war. **1878** Swinburne *Poems & Ball.* Ser. II. 11 Any soul..Disrobed and disentrammelled.

disen'trance, *v.* [f. dis- 6 + entrance *v.*] *trans.* To bring out of or arouse from a trance, or from an entranced state.
1663 Butler *Hud.* I. iii. 717 Ralpho by this time disentranc'd, Upon his Bum himself advanc'd. **1809** Coleridge *Friend* (1866) 351 This trifling incident startled and disentranced me. **1855** Browning *Any Wife to Any Husband* xv, Love so, then, if thou wilt! Give all thou canst Away to the new faces—disentranced..obdurate no more.

Hence **disen'trancement**.
In recent Dicts.

†**disen'traverse,** *v. Obs. rare.* [f. dis- 5 + **entraverse* vb., repr. F. *entraverser* to place *en travers* or athwart: cf. entraverse *adv.*] *trans.* To wrest (meaning).
1610 W. Folkingham *Art of Survey* I. viii. 18 Plinie disentrauerses the meaning of *Pulla* to imply a blackish, gentle, mellow, and tender soyle.

disentrayle, obs. form of disentrail *v.*

disen'treat, *v. Obs. rare*$^{-0}$. [f. dis- 6 + entreat.] *trans.* To deprecate, entreat not to have.
1611 Cotgr., *Desprier*, to vnpray, disintreat.

†**disen'trust,** *v. Obs. rare.* [dis- 6.] *trans.* To deprive (a person) of a trust; the opposite of *entrust*.
1648 J. Goodwin *Right & Might* 13 There is the same liberty in a Pupill, or person in his minority, to dis-entrust his Guardian, how lawfully soever chosen, upon suspicion of male-administration, or unfaithfulnesse.

disen'twine, *v.* [f. dis- 6 + entwine.]
1. *trans.* To free from being entwined; to untwine, untwist, disentangle (*lit.* and *fig.*).
1814 Byron *Corsair* I. xiv, My very love to thee is hate to them, So closely mingling here, that disentwined, I cease to love thee when I love mankind. **1821** Shelley *Prometh. Unb.* II. iii. 48 The wind..disentwines my hair. **1877** Owen *Wellesley's Desp.* p. xl, In disentwining the co-ordinate and conflicting claims of native Princes.

2. *intr.* (for *refl.*) To become disentwined.
1875 *Sunday Mag.* June 580 Thoughts..intertwine and disentwine, but the problem remains.

disen'velop, -e, *v.* Also 7–8 **disin-**. [f. dis- 6 or 7 + envelop *v.* or envelope *sb.*] *trans.* To free from that in which it is enveloped; to unfold, develop.
1632 J. Hayward tr. *Biondi's Eromena* 108 Maligne stars ..which being in some sort intricated with the fixed..are never more disinveloped. *Ibid.* 162 He was not likely to be soone disenveloped out of the passions of his fatherly affection. **1655–73** H. More *App. Anted.* b6b, Disenveloping what pretended strength of Argument there may be. **1741** Warburton *Div. Legat.* II. 574 When the prophets..have explained the spiritual meaning of his [Moses'] law and disinveloped his sense.

disen'venom, *v. rare.* [f. dis- 6 + envenom.] *trans.* To undo the process of envenoming; to deprive of its venom.
*a***1711** Ken *Christophil* Poet. Wks. 1721 I. 45 By meekness disenvenoming their spite. —— *Hymns Evang.* ibid. I. 177 Conquer'd Death..By Jesus disenvenom'd is your Sting.

disen'viron, *v. rare.* [dis- 6.] *trans.* To deprive of or set free from its environment.
1875 L. Morris *Evensong* xii, Self-centred and self-contained, disenvironed and isolate.

†**disen'wrap,** *v. Obs. rare.* In 7 **disin-**. [f. dis- 6 + enwrap *v.*] *trans.* To free from that in which it is enwrapped; to unwrap.
1611 Florio, *Disiluppare*, to disinwrap. **1622** Mabbe tr. *Aleman's Guzman d'Alf.* II. 222, I went about to dis-inwrap her hands of her mantle, that I might come to touch them.

disepalous (daɪ'sɛpələs), *a. Bot.* [f. Gr. δι- (di-[2]) twice + mod.L. *sepal-um* sepal + -ous.] Having or consisting of two sepals.
1841 *Penny Cycl.* XXI. 248/1 If there are two sepals, the calyx is disepalous. **1870** Bentley *Bot.* 216 Disepalous for a calyx composed of two distinct sepals.

†**dis'equal,** *a. Obs.* [f. dis- 10 + equal *a.*: cf. OF. *desegal*, *-gual* unequal (in Godef.), also L. *dispar*.] Unequal.
1622 Mabbe tr. *Aleman's Guzman d'Alf.* I. To Rdr., My minde still beating vpon the Barbarisme and dis-equall number of those ignorant Dolts.

†**dise'quality.** *Obs.* [f. disequal, after *equality*: cf. OF. *desegaulte*, *desigalité* inequality (in Godef.).] Inequality, disparity.
1602 Segar *Hon. Mil. & Civ.* III. v. 117 Euery small disequality ought not to make difference chiefly where God is Judge. **1632** J. Hayward tr. *Biondi's Eromena* 110 The disequalitie of yeares (she being at least by six yeares his elder). **1655** Cromwell *Sp.* 22 Jan., If there be a disproportion or disequality as to power.

dis'equalize, *v. rare*$^{-0}$. [f. dis- 6 + equalize.] *trans.* To render unequal. Hence **dis'equalizer**, one who or that which renders unequal.
1847 Lytton *Lucretia* I. Epil., The mechanic—poor slave of the capitalist—poor agent and victim of the arch disequaliser, Civilisation.

disequi'librium. [f. DIS- 9 + EQUILIBRIUM.] **a.** Absence or destruction of equilibrium. So **disequi'librate, dise'quilibrize** *vbs.*, to destroy the equilibrium of, to throw out of balance; **disequili'bration.**

1840 *Aeolus* 12 A finely poised lever, to which the weight of a fly is enough to occasion a disequilibrium. **1882** ELWES tr. *Capello & Ivens' Benguella to Yacca* II. i. 7 The effect of this dis-equilibrium of nature. **1889** *Blackw. Mag.* CXLVI. 742/2 They are disequilibrised. **1891** J. M. GUYAN *Educ. & Heredity* Pref. 23 The disequilibrated are forever lost to humanity. **1891** *Monist* I. 627 A disequilibration of their organism.

b. *spec.* in *Econ.*

1923 J. M. KEYNES *Tract Monetary Reform* iv. 160 When the disequilibrium was purely seasonal, this was an unqualified advantage. *Ibid.* 161 The post-war method is a most rapid and powerful corrective of real disequilibria in the balance of international payments. **1948** G. CROWTHER *Outl. Money* (ed. 2) x. 352 Any excess of Saving over Investment produces disequilibrium—a shortage of purchasing power to buy the products of industry, falling prices and unemployment. **1963** *Economist* 5 Oct. 57/1 The kind of balance of payments disequilibria that might occur.

dise'quip, *v. rare.* [DIS- 6.] *trans.* To divest (any one) of his equipment; *intr.* (for *refl.*) to doff one's equipment.

1831 FR. A. KEMBLE *Jrnl.* in *Rec. Girlhood* (1878) III. 23 [He] arrived just as we had disequipped.

diserde, obs. var. DIZZARD.

diserit, -yt: see DISHERIT.

†**di'sert,** *a. Obs.* [ad. L. *disert-us* skilful in speaking, fluent, var. of *dissertus*, pa. pple. of *dissĕrĕre* to discuss, discourse, f. *dis-*, DIS- 1 or 2 + *serĕre* to interweave, connect, compose.] Able or fluent in speech; well-spoken, eloquent.

c **1425** *Found. St. Bartholomew's* 24 Blessynge the myght and the wysdome of God, the whiche openyth the dumme moweth, and the tongis of infantis maketh opyne and diserte. **1647** WARD *Simp. Cobler* 52 Disert Statesmen. **1675** SHERBURNE *Manilius* Pref., This most Disert Poet.

disert, obs. var. of DESERT *sb.*[2]

†**di'sertitude.** *Obs. rare*$^{-0}$. [ad. late L. *disertitūd-o* eloquence, f. *disert-us* DISERT.]

1656 BLOUNT *Glossogr.*, *Disertitude*, eloquence.

†**di'sertly,** *adv. Obs.* [f. DISERT + -LY[2].] Ably, clearly, eloquently, in plain terms.

1447 BOKENHAM *Seyntys* (Roxb.) 188 By many an argumente She þer dyserthly shewyd hyr entente. **1603** HOLLAND *Plutarch's Mor.* 1306 Heraclitus directly and disertly nameth warre, the Father, King, and Lord of all the world. **1650** BULWER *Anthropomet.* i. 13 They speak a language disertly, briefly, and properly accented. **1798** *Europ. Mag.* in *Spirit Publ. Jrnls.* (1799) II. 322 What hath been already so disertly and irrefragably urged by that learned man.

dises(e, obs. ff. DECEASE, DISEASE.

disespeir, etc.: see DESESPEIR, etc.

†**dise'spouse,** *v. Obs. rare.* [f. DIS- 6 + ESPOUSE *v.*] *trans.* To undo the espousal or betrothal of.

1667 MILTON *P.L.* IX. 17 Not less but more Heroic then the..rage Of Turnus for Lavinia disespous'd.

disestablish (dɪsɪ'stæblɪʃ), *v.* [f. DIS- 6 + ESTABLISH *v.*] *trans.* To deprive of the character of being established; to annul the establishment of. **a.** *gen.* To undo the position of anything instituted, settled, or fixed by authority or general acceptance; to depose.

1598 FLORIO *Disconfermare*, to vnconfirme, to disestablish. **1794** W. TAYLOR in *Monthly Rev.* XIV. 248 Labouring to disestablish those Platonic opinions. **1886** *Pall Mall G.* 16 June 1/1 He has disestablished Money-bags as the arbiter of elections.

b. *spec.* To deprive (a church) of especial State connexion and support; to remove from the position of being the national or state church: cf. ESTABLISH *v.* 7.

1838 GLADSTONE *State in Rel. Ch.* (1839) 113 If religion be injured by the national establishment of the church, it must forthwith and at whatever hazard be disestablished. **1868** BRIGHT *Sp. Ireland* 1 Apr., You may be asked to disestablish their Church. **1874** MORLEY *Compromise* (1886) 116 The designs imputed to the newly reformed parliament of disestablishing the Anglican Church.

Hence **dise'stablished** (-'æblɪʃt), **dise'stablishing** *ppl. adjs.*

1869 *Daily News* 2 July, The disestablished Bishops [of the Irish Church]. **1891** *Spectator* 17 Jan., He should take the wind out of the sails of the disestablishing party.

dise'stablisher. [f. prec. vb. + -ER[1].] One who disestablishes; an advocate of (Church) disestablishment.

1869 *Daily News* 2 July, The disestablishers of the Irish Church. **1885** *Sat. Rev.* 19 Sept. 371 Mr. Chamberlain poses before the Glaswegians as a disestablisher.

dise'stablishment. [f. as prec. + -MENT.] The act of disestablishing. **a.** *gen.*

1806 W. TAYLOR in *Ann. Rev.* IV. 264 From the establishment of Christianity under Constantine, to the beginnings of its disestablishment under Pope Leo X. **1887** *Pall Mall G.* 10 Feb. 6/1 The position of the railways would justify the disestablishment of a railway guarantee fund.

b. *spec.* The withdrawal of especial State patronage and control from a church.

1860 *Sat. Rev.* IX. 305/1 When the disestablishment grows nearer, the Church will cease to be recruited from the ranks of intelligence and education. **1883** *Manch. Exam.* 24 Oct. 5/1 They believe that religion, and justice, and citizenship would gain by Disestablishment.

Hence **dise,stablishmen'tarian,** an adherent of disestablishment (also *attrib.* or *adj.*).

1885 *Times* 4 Dec. 3/4, I have just recorded my vote against the disestablishmentarian. **1885** *Guardian* 2 Dec. 1815/1 The 480 Disestablishmentarian candidates have considerably dwindled through explanations and rejections.

disesteem (dɪsɪ'stiːm), *sb.* [f. DIS- 9 + ESTEEM *sb.*: cf. next, and obs. F. *desestime* (Godef.), It. *disestimo* (Florio).] The action of disesteeming, or position of being disesteemed; want of esteem; low estimation or regard.

1603 FLORIO *Montaigne* (1634) 66 The Turkes, a nation equally instructed to the esteeme of armes, and disesteeme of letters. **1670** MILTON *Hist. Eng.* I. Wks. (1851) 1 Disesteem and contempt of the public affairs. **1697** DRYDEN *Virg. Past.* Pref. (1721) I. 76 Pastorals are fallen into Disesteem. **1754** EDWARDS *Freed. Will* IV. i. 195 Their Worthiness of Esteem or Disesteem, Praise or Dispraise. **1810** BENTHAM *Packing* (1821) 91 Whatever tends to bring a man in power into 'disesteem'. **1884** PENNINGTON *Wiclif* ii. 32 The prevailing disesteem in which the Scriptures were held.

dise'steem, *v.* [f. DIS- 6 + ESTEEM *v.*: perh. after F. *désestimer* (16th c.), It. *disestimare.*]

1. *trans.* To regard with the reverse of esteem; to hold in low estimation, regard lightly, think little (or nothing) of, slight, despise.

1594 DANIEL *Cleopatra* Ded., Ourselves, whose error ever is Strange notes to like, and disesteem our own. **1629** LYNDE *Via tuta* 195 The authority of Prelates would bee disesteemed. **1735** WESLEY *Wks.* (1872) XIV. 208 Nor will he at all disesteem the precious pearl, for the meanness of the shell. **1868** HELPS *Realmah* (1876) 262 Thinking that he had somehow or other offended Ellesmere, or was greatly disesteemed by him.

†**b.** To take away the estimation of. *Obs. rare.*

a **1637** B. JONSON *Underwoods, Ep. to J. Selden* 40 What fables have you vex'd, what truth redeem'd,..opinions disesteem'd, Impostures branded.

†**c.** *intr.* with *of*: To think little of, despise: = sense 1. *Obs. rare.*

1659 D. PELL *Impr. Sea* 432 They that are apt to reject, and disesteem of all Scriptural counsel. **1675** BROOKS *Gold. Key* Wks. 1867 V. 338 The reason why they so much disesteemed of Christ.

†**2.** with *subord. clause*: Not to think or suppose; to think or believe otherwise than. (Cf. ESTEEM *v.* 5 c.) *Obs. rare.*

1677 HALE *Prim. Orig. Man.* I. iii. 89 We have just reason to deny and disesteem this imaginary Eternity can belong at least to the sublunary World.

Hence **dise'steemed** *ppl. a.*, **-ing** *vbl. sb.*

1605 BACON *Adv. Learn.* I. iii. §3 (1873) 20 The disesteeming of those employments wherein youth is conversant. **1618** *Hist. P. Warbeck* in *Select. Harl. Misc.* (1793) 80 Heroick commiseration of a disesteemed prince. **1669** WOODHEAD *St. Teresa* I. xxxiv. 242 The undervaluing and disesteeming of all things in this life. **1860** ELLICOTT *Life Our Lord* ii. 47 A rude and lone village..Nazareth the disesteemed.

dise'steemer. [f. prec. + -ER[1].] One who disesteems; a despiser.

1611 COTGR., *Mespriseur*, a disesteemer, contemner. **1650** BAXTER *Saints' R.* I. iv. (1662) 37, I the unworthy Disesteemer of thy Blood, and slighter of thy Love! **1674** BOYLE *Excell. Theol.* II. v. 231 It would extremely trouble me to see you a disesteemer of those Divine things.

Hence †**dise'steemeress,** a female disesteemer.

1611 COTGR., *Despriseresse*, a disesteemeresse, despiseresse.

†**disestimation** (dɪs,ɛstɪ'meɪʃən). *Obs.* [f. DIS- 9 + ESTIMATION, after *disesteem*: cf. Sp. *desestimacion*, It. *disestimazione*, *-atione* (Florio).]

The action of disesteeming; the condition of being disesteemed; disrepute; = DISESTEEM *sb.*

1619 DENISON *Heav. Banq.* 166 Frequent receiuing may cause a disestimation of the Sacrament. **1626** T. H. *Caussin's Holy Crt.* 37 To rayse vice..and put vertue in disestimation. **1677** GILPIN *Demonol.* (1867) 221 Contempt or disestimation.

‖**diseuse** (dizøz). [Fr., fem. = talker.] A female artiste who specializes in monologue.

1896 *Cosmopolitan* XX. 444 She is only a concert-hall singer (or diseuse, to use a newly-coined and specific title). **1903** *Daily Chron.* 20 June 8/2 Mme. Anna Thibaud, the celebrated *diseuse.* **1927** M. BARING *Tinker's Leave* xxv. 274 Bielor played songs, and Zurova, a well known *diseuse* sang. **1955** *Times* 7 June 2/5 The subtle, cunning art of the *diseuse*, and her invisible company of supporting players.

†**dis'exercise,** *v. Obs. rare.* [DIS- 6.] *trans.* To put out of exercise, cease to exercise.

1644 MILTON *Areop.* (Arb.) 34 It will be primely to the discouragement of all learning, and the stop of Truth..by the disexercising and blunting our abilities.

†**dis'fair,** *v. Obs. rare.* [f. DIS- 8 + FAIR *a.*] *trans.* To deprive of fairness or beauty.

1627-47 FELTHAM *Resolves* I. xxxvi. 118 Even the body is disfaired.

disfaith (dɪs'feɪθ). [f. DIS- 9 + FAITH.] **a.** Want of faith; distrust, disbelief. **b.** Unfaithfulness.

1870 KINGSLEY in *Life & Lett.* (1878) II. 340 Having a firm dis-faith in most English commentators. **1881** *Man's Mistake* III. viii. 127 Her righteous anger against what she believed to be dis-faith on Keith Moriston's part.

†**dis'faithful,** *a. Obs. rare*$^{-0}$. [DIS- 10.] Unfaithful, faithless, false.

1530 PALSGR. 305/2 Begyleful, disfaythfull, *cautelleux.*

disfame (dɪs'feɪm), *sb. rare.* [f. DIS- 9 + FAME. In early use a. OF. *des-*, *disfame*, var. of *def-*, *diffame*: see DIFFAME, DEFAME.] The opposite of fame; disrepute, reproach; defamation.

c **1460** *Play Sacram.* 791 Now þu hast put me from duresse & dysfame. **1620** WILKINSON *Coroners & Sherifes* 11 If three men go together to make a disfame. **1859** TENNYSON *Merlin* 463 And what is Fame in life but half-disfame, And counter-changed with darkness?

†**dis'fame,** *v. Obs.* [a. OF. *des-*, *disfamer*, var. of *def-*, *diffamer*: see DEFAME.] *trans.* To deprive of fame or honour; to bring into reproach or disrepute; to defame.

a **1533** LD. BERNERS *Gold. Bk. M. Aurel.* (1546) Ll vij b, Great peril it is for the honourable, to be with theim that be disfamed. **1550** J. COKE *Eng. & Fr. Heralds* §1 (1877) 55 Perceyvynge the frenche heralde..in all thynges disfamying this most noble realme.

†**dis'fancy,** *v. Obs. rare.* [f. DIS- 6 + FANCY.] *trans.* The reverse of to *fancy*; to regard with disfavour; to dislike.

1657 HAMMOND *Pastor's Motto* Wks. 1684 IV. 545 Orthodox and heretical..are titles, that every man will apply as he lists, the one to himself and his adherents, the other to all others that he disfancies.

disfashion (dɪs'fæʃən), *v.* [f. DIS- 6 + FASHION *v.*: cf. obs. F. *desfaçonner* to beat down, destroy, (14th c. in Godef.).] *trans.* To mar or undo the fashion or shape of, to disfigure. (See FASHION *v.*)

a **1535** MORE *Wks.* 99 (R.) Glotony..disfigureth the face..disfashioneth the body. *a* **1628** F. GREVILLE *Treat. Warres* lii. Poems (1633) 81 Their wealth, strength, glory growing from those hearts, Which, to their ends, they ruine and disfashion. **1881** CHR. ROSSETTI *Pageant, etc.* 156 Shame Itself may be a glory and a grace, Refashioning the sin-disfashioned face. **1885** MACKAIL *Aeneid* 146 Shapes of wolves..whom with her potent herbs the deadly divine Circe had disfashioned.

disfavour, -or (dɪs'feɪvə(r)), *sb.* [f. DIS- 9 + FAVOUR *sb.*, prob. after obs. F. *desfaveur* 'disfauor; want or losse of fauour' (Cotgr.); cf. It. *disfavore* 'a disfauour' (Florio), Sp. *desfavor.*]

1. The reverse or opposite of favour; unfavourable regard, dislike, discountenance, disapproval.

a **1533** LD. BERNERS *Gold. Bk. M. Aurel.* xix. (R.) Ye women..with a littel disfauour ye recouer great hatred. **1535** COVERDALE *Prov.* xix. 12 The kynges disfauoure is like yᵉ roaringe of a Lyon. **1611** SPEED *Hist. Gt. Brit.* VIII. vi. §12. 395 Robert Gemeticensis..spread the Curtaine of disfauour betwixt Goodwin and the King. **1665** WITHER *Lord's Prayer* 27 Not knowing how to please one of their faigned gods without incurring the disfavour of another. **1787** BENTHAM *Def. Usury* Wks. 1843 III. 17 The disfavour which attends the cause of the money-lender in his competition with the borrower. **1863** LONGF. *Wayside Inn* II. *Theol. T.* viii, At the gate the poor were waiting..Grown familiar with disfavor. **1868** M. PATTISON *Academ. Org.* v. 169 The name of 'professor' will never lose its disfavour until..associated among us with the dignity of a life devoted to science.

†**2.** An act or expression of dislike or ill will: the opposite of a favour. *Obs.*

1556 *Aurelio & Isab.* (1608) B, A thousand disfavours and a thousande woes. **1598** YONG *Diana* 277 When I..had so many disfauours of ingratefull Diana. *a* **1631** DONNE *Serm.* lxxxiv. VI. 403, I never needed my mistresses frowns and disfavours to make her favours acceptable to me. **1647** CLARENDON *Hist. Reb.* I. (1843) 20/2 He might dispense favours and disfavours according to his own election.

3. The condition of being unfavourably regarded. Hence *to be* (*live*, etc.) *in disfavour*, *to bring, come, fall*, etc. *into disfavour.*

1581 PETTIE *Guazzo's Civ. Conv.* II. (1586) 53 Devising how to bring some Officer into the disfavour of his Prince. **1600** HOLLAND *Livy* XXVI. xl. 615 Hee was in disgrace and disfavour with Hanno. *a* **1661** FULLER *Worthies* (1840) III. 281 This earl lost the love of king Charles, living many years in his dis-favour. **1669** PEPYS *Diary* 7 Apr., Mr. Eden, who was in his mistress's disfavour ever since the other night that he come in thither fuddled. **1849** LEWIS *Author. in Matters Opin.* vi. §11 (L.) The disfavour into which it [the government] may have fallen. **1858** CARLYLE *Fredk. Gt.* (1865) I. III. xix. 259 The poor young Prince..had fallen into open disfavour.

4. *in (the) disfavour of*, *to the disfavour of*: to the disadvantage of, so as to be unfavourable to.

1590 SWINBURNE *Testaments* 125 The disposition is thereby void: and that in disfauour of the testator. **1600** E. BLOUNT tr. *Conestaggio* 99 He was not bounde to obey, if it were in his disfavour. **1710** STEELE *Tatler* No. 211 ¶3 Acquaintance has been lost through a general Prepossession in his Disfavour. **1838** DICKENS *Nich. Nick.* xxxiv, The first comparisons were drawn between us, always in my disfavour. **1858** FROUDE *Hist. Eng.* III. 208 That actions of doubtful bearing should be construed to their disfavour.

†**5.** Want of beauty; ill-favouredness, disfigurement. *Obs.* [Cf. DISFAVOUR *v.* 2, FAVOUR *sb.* 9.]

1706 PHILLIPS (ed. Kersey), *Disfavour*..Disfigurement. Hence in BAILEY. **1755** JOHNSON, *Disfavour*..3. Want of beauty. *Dict.*

dis'favour, -or, *v.* [f. DIS- 6 + FAVOUR *v.*: cf. the sb.; also It. *disfavorire.*]

1. *trans.* To regard or treat with the reverse of favour or good will; to discountenance; to treat with disapprobation.

1570 BUCHANAN *Admonitioun* Wks. (1892) 27 Ye King having..persavit his unfaythfull dealing evir disfauourit him. **1583** T. WATSON *Centurie of Loue* xxxvi. (Arb.) 72 The heau'ns them selues disfauour mine intent. **1669** CLARENDON *Ess.* Tracts (1727) 97 Persons who are like to disfavour our pretences. *a* **1745** SWIFT (J.), Might not those of..nearer access to her majesty receive her own commands, and be countenanced or disfavoured according as they obey? **1881** *Times* 13 July 6/3 The railway company favours a town by giving preferential low rates, while the trade of another town is disfavoured by having higher rates. **1895** *Edin. Rev.* Jan. 130 He disfavoured controversy.

†**b.** To dislike. *Obs.* or *dial.*

1599 SANDYS *Europæ Spec.* (1632) 175 Who it is thought doth disfavour them as much as his Father doted on them. **1740** DYCHE & PARDON, *Disfavour*, to dislike, to take a pique at, or bear a grudge to a person.

†**2.** To mar the countenance or appearance of; to disfigure; to render ill-favoured. *Obs.*

1535 COVERDALE *Ecclus.* xiv. 6 There is no thinge worse, then whan one disfauoureth himself. **1601** HOLLAND *Pliny* II. 168 It scoureth away freckles and such flecks as disfauor the face. **1607** TOPSELL *Four-f. Beasts* (1658) 159 Their whole visages so disfigured and disfavoured in a moment that their neerest friends..cannot know them.

Hence **dis'favoured** *ppl. a.*

1611 COTGR., *Desfavorisé*, disfauoured, out of fauour with. **1865** *Athenæum* 23 Dec. 889/3 The unfavoured, or rather disfavoured, study of Sanscrit.

†**dis'favourable,** *a.* *Obs.* [f. DIS- 10 + FAVOURABLE, after *disfavour*. Cf. It. *disfavorevole.*] Unfavourable; adverse.

1561 STOW *Rich. II* an. 1377 (R.) And manie other valient personages, who being entred the sea tasted fortune disfauourable.

Hence †**dis'favourably** *adv.*, *Obs.*, with disfavour; unfavourably, adversely.

1654 W. MOUNTAGUE *Devout Ess.* II. iv. §4 (R.) These occurences, which look so aversely to our reasons, and so disfavourably to our nature. **1806** J. PYTCHES in *Monthly Mag.* XXI. 386 Should it be disfavourably received, I shall support my disappointment with becoming resignation.

dis'favourer. *rare.* [f. DISFAVOUR *v.* + -ER[1].] One who disfavours.

a **1626** BACON (J.), Had it not been for four great disfavourers of that voyage, the enterprize had succeeded.

dis'favourite, *sb. rare.* [f. DIS- 9 + FAVOURITE: cf. It. *disfavorito.*] One who is the opposite of a favourite; one regarded with disfavour.

1611 SPEED *Hist. Gt. Brit.* IX. viii. (1632) 555 Kings brooke not to be braued by Subjects, nor is it wisedome for dis-fauourites to doe it. **1884** *Daily News* 30 Oct. 5/1 He has his likes and dislikes, his favourites and his disfavourites (if we may use the word).

So †**dis'favourite** *v. Obs. trans.*, to depose from the position of a favourite, cast out of favour.

1624 BP. MOUNTAGU *Invoc. Saints* 9 Aman that great Minion of the Persian Monarch, was disfavourited in a moment.

disfeat, obs. var. DEFEAT.

disfeature (dɪs'fiːtjʊə(r)), *v.* [f. DIS- 7 a or d + FEATURE *sb.* Cf. the parallel DEFEATURE, and OF. *deffaiturer.*] *trans.* To mar the features of; to disfigure, deface. Hence **dis'featured, dis'featuring** *ppl. adjs.*; **dis'featurement.**

1659 *Lady Alimony* II. ii. in Hazl. *Dodsley* XIV. 291 For fear she should disfeature the comeliness of her body. **1813** COLERIDGE *Remorse* III. ii, The goodly face of Nature Hath one disfeaturing stain the less upon it. **1871** PALGRAVE *Lyr. Poems* 34 Through the steets they ran with flying hair, Disfeatured in their grief. **1879** J. TODHUNTER *Alcestis* 57 The prey of pale disfeaturing death. **1884** H. S. HOLLAND *Good Friday Addr.* 77 The horror..of disfeaturement, of defilement, of impotence, to one Who was Himself Life. **1886** SIR F. H. DOYLE *Remin.* 275, I should be sorry to hear that it [that country] had been entirely disfeatured.

dis'fellowship, *sb.* [f. DIS- 9 + FELLOWSHIP *sb.*] Want of or exclusion from fellowship.

1608 S. HIERON *Defence* III. 7 Kneeling at the Lords feast is a cariage of abasement and inferiority, and such as importeth disfellowship with him. **1619** DENISON *Heav. Banq.* (1631) 323. **1882** A. MAHAN *Autobiog.* xi. 242 The spirit of exclusion and disfellowship.

dis'fellowship, *v.* [DIS- 7 c.] *trans.* To exclude from fellowship (chiefly, religious communion); to excommunicate. (Now *U.S.*)

1831 *Troy* (N.Y.) *Watchman* 3 Sept. (Th.), They were disfellowshipped by the association. **1849** *Mormon Regul.* in *Frontier* (Iowa) *Guard.* 28 Nov. (Bartlett), No person that has been disfellowshipped, or excommunicated from the church, will be allowed [etc.]. **1882** A. MAHAN *Autobiog.* ix. 170 In all directions we were openly disfellowshipped. **1882-3** SCHAFF *Encycl. Relig. Knowl.* I. 836 [Benj. Randall] was called to account for holding to an unlimited atonement and the freedom of the will, and was disfellowshipped. **1889** J. M. WHITON in *Chr. World Pulpit* XXXVI. 139 On the strength of a few sentences..the Calvinists of the last century disfellowshipped the Wesleyans.

dis'fen, *v.* [f. DIS- 7 b + FEN *sb.*] *trans.* To deprive of the character of a fen; to make no longer fen-land.

1881 E. W. GOSSE in *Encycl. Brit.* XII. 62/1 The high fens, of which the greater part have been 'disfenned' or stripped of peat, are found in Groningen, Friesland.

†**dis'fertile,** *v.* *Obs.* [f. DIS- 8 + FERTILE *a.*] *trans.* To deprive of fertility; to make barren.

1605 SYLVESTER *Du Bartas* II. iii. I. *Abraham* 1347 A broad standing Pool..whose infectious breath Corrupts the Ayr, and Earth dis-fertileth.

dis'fever, *v.* [f. DIS- 7 a + FEVER *sb.*] *trans.* To free from fever; to calm.

1880 G. MEREDITH *Trag. Com.* xiv. (1892) 206 He stood.. disfevered by the limpid liquid tumult, inspirited by the glancing volumes of a force that knows no abatement.

†**dis'figurate,** *a.* *Obs.* In 4 **-at.** [ad. med.L. *dis-*, *diffigūrātus* (or It. *disfigurato*), pa. pple. of *disfigurāre*: see DISFIGURE *v.*] Disfigured, deformed, misshapen.

c **1381** CHAUCER *Parl. Foules* 222 Disfigurat [MS. Cambr. Ff. I. 6 (14..) disfygured] was she, I nyl nat lye.

disfiguration (dɪsfɪgjʊə'reɪʃən). [n. of action from DISFIGURE: see -ATION. Cf. DEFIGURATION and OF. *desfiguration.*] = DISFIGUREMENT.

1653 GAUDEN *Hierasp.* 237 We shall easily see the face of the holy Ministry..restored, without any Disfiguration or Essentiall change. *a* **1713** SHAFTESB. *Miscell.* II. iii. (Seager) Prostrations, disfigurations, wry faces, beggarly tones. **1800** *Med. Jrnl.* III. 101, I have seen no disfiguration of the skin from this variety of cow-pock. **1881** JEFFERIES *Wood Magic* II. vii. 195 The prince, full of ambition..submitted to these disfigurations.

dis'figurative, *a.* *rare.* [f. DISFIGURE *v.* + -ATIVE.] Having a disfiguring tendency.

1823 *Examiner* 452/2 You perceive in his left eye a very strong disfigurative cast.

disfigure (dɪs'fɪgjʊə(r), -gə(r)), *v.* Also 5 **dysfyger, -fygure, -fegoure,** 5–6 **disfygure, dysfigure,** 6 **disfygour, desfigure.** [ad. OF. *desfigurer* (mod.F. *dé-*) = Pr. and Sp. *desfigurar*, It. *disfigurare*, med.L. *diffigurare* in Laws of Lombards (Du Cange), a Common Romanic vb. f. L. *dis-* + *figūra* figure, *figūrāre* to figure. See also DEFIGURE.]

1. *trans.* To mar the figure or appearance of, destroy the beauty of; to deform, deface.

c **1374** CHAUCER *Troylus* II. 174 (223) What lyst yow þus your self to disfigure. *c* **1386** —— *Pard. Prol. & T.* 223 O dronke man, disfigured is thy face. *a* **1450** *Knt. de la Tour* (1868) 25 She had her nose croked, the whiche shent and dysfigured her visage. **1526-34** TINDALE *Matt.* vi. 16 They desfigure their faces, that they myght be sene of men how they faste. **1590** SHAKS. *Com. Err.* v. i. 183 To scorch your face, and to disfigure you. **1667** MILTON *P.L.* XI. 521 Disfiguring not Gods likeness, but thir own. **1794** SULLIVAN *View Nat.* I. 195 The least smoke would disfigure the rich landscape. **1889** FROUDE *Chiefs of Dunboy* v. 55 His face.. had been disfigured by a sabre cut.

b. *fig.* To mar or destroy the beauty or natural form of (something immaterial).

1799 S. TURNER *Anglo-Sax.* (1836) I. III. iii. 168 The authentic actions of Arthur have been so disfigured by the additions of minstrels. **1849** MACAULAY *Hist. Engl.* II. 111 Their diction was disfigured by foreign idioms. **1867** FREEMAN *Norm. Conq.* (1876) I. vi. 433 Occasional acts of both craft and violence disfigure the whole of his career.

†**c.** To misrepresent injuriously. *Obs.*

a **1643** J. SHUTE *Judgem. & Mercy* (1645) 145 How ever some detracters dis-figured him to his Prince, he never spake of him without reverence.

†**2.** To alter the figure or appearance of; to disguise. *Obs.*

? *c* **1370** *K. Robt. Cicyle* in Halliw. *Nugæ Poet.* 55 No man myght hym not knowe, He was so dysfygerde in a throwe. *c* **1385** CHAUCER *L.G.W.* 2046 *Ariadne*, And me so wel disfigure..That..ther shal no man me knowe. *c* **1450** *Merlin* 74 May this be true, that oo man may hym-self thus disfigure? **1594** BLUNDEVIL *Exerc.* VIII. (ed. 7) 757 The crookednesse of the Meridians, which..do so much disfigure..the true shape of the Regions, as they can scant be known. **1665** HOOKE *Microgr.* 217 The Sun and Moon neer the Horizon, are disfigur'd. **1713** ADDISON *Cato* IV. ii, Disfigur'd in a vile Numidian dress, and for a worthless woman.

†**3.** The technical expression for: To carve (a peacock). *Obs.*

c **1470** in *Hors, Shepe & G.* etc. (Caxton 1479, Roxb. repr.) 33 A crane displayd A pecok disfigured A curlew unioynted. **1513** *Bk. Keruing* A j in *Babees Bk.* 265 Disfigure that pecocke. **1706** PHILLIPS (ed. Kersey), Disfigure that Peacock, i.e. Cut it up, a Term us'd in Carving at Table.

†**4.** *intr.* To lose its figure, become misshapen.

a **1618** SYLVESTER *Quadrains of Pibrac* xxxix, The right Cube's Figure..Whose quadrat flatnesse never doth disfigure.

Hence **dis'figuring** *vbl. sb.* and *ppl. a.*

1526 *Pilgr. Perf.* (W. de W. 1531) 271 Without ony great disfyguryng of the body. *a* **1631** DONNE in *Select.* (1840) 161 In our fastings, there are disfigurings. **1648** BOYLE *Seraph. Love* (1660) 3 By indistinct or disfiguring considerations. **1775** HAN. MORE *Let.* in W. Roberts *Mem.* (1834) I. 52 Small-pox..cannot be a more disfiguring disease than the present mode of dressing. **1895** *Athenæum* 27 Apr. 532/3 The most disfiguring blemish is the way in which names are rendered.

†**disfigure,** *sb.* *Obs.* [f. prec. vb.] Disfigurement.

c **1386** CHAUCER *Wife's T.* 104 He [Midas] preyde hire that to no creature She sholde tellen of his disfigure. **1590** *Humble Motion with Submission* 25 No small disfigure vnto Christs church. **1697** R. PEIRCE *Bath Mem.* I. vii. 181 It was no small Disfigure to him.

disfigured (dɪs'fɪgjʊəd, -gəd), *ppl. a.* [f. DISFIGURE *v.* + -ED[1].] Defaced, disguised, etc.; see the vb. Hence **dis'figuredness.**

14.. [see DISFIGURATE]. **1565-73** COOPER *Thesaurus* s.v. *Prauitas*, Notable deformities in disfigured partes of the body. *Ibid.* Deformitie and disfigurednesse or crookednesse. **1598** FLORIO, *Sfigurato*, formelesse, shapelesse, disfigured. **1825** SOUTHEY *Tale of Paraguay* II. 27 Strangely disfigured truths.

dis'figurement. [f. DISFIGURE *v.* + -MENT: cf. OF. *deffigureement*, later *défigurement* (Cotgr.).]

1. The action of disfiguring; the fact or condition of being disfigured; defacement, deformity.

1634 MILTON *Comus* 74 And they..Not once perceive their foul disfigurement. **1756-7** tr. *Keysler's Trav.* (1760) II. 49 The Carmelite church is not cieled, the rafters..being quite uncovered; but this disfigurement is abundantly compensated by the beauty and splendor of it in other parts. **1807-26** S. COOPER *First Lines Surg.* 359 The disease creates both great irritation and disfigurement. **1879** M. ARNOLD *Irish Cath.* Mixed Ess. 115 Their vain disfigurements of the Christian Religion.

2. Something that disfigures (by its presence or addition); a deformity, defacement, blemish.

1641 MILTON *Ch. Govt.* vi. (1851) 129 The scaffolding.. would be but a troublesome disfigurement, so soone as the building was finisht. **1752** HUME *Ess.* xx. (R.), Pointed similes, and epigrammatic turns, especially when they recur too frequently, are a disfigurement rather than any embellishment of discourse. **1856** STANLEY *Sinai & Pal.* iii. (1858) 179 This mass of rock must always have been an essential feature or a strange disfigurement of the Temple area. **1874** MICKLETHWAITE *Mod. Par. Churches* 175 A dial is not necessarily a disfigurement to a tower.

dis'figurer. [f. as prec. + -ER[1].] One who or that which disfigures.

1775 HAN. MORE *Let.* in W. Roberts *Mem.* (1834) I. 51, I have just escaped from one of the most fashionable disfigurers, and, though I charged him to dress me with the greatest simplicity, I absolutely blush at myself. **1823** W. TAYLOR in *Monthly Rev.* CII. 542 Some disfigurer of history. **1873** M. ARNOLD *Lit. & Dogma* (1876) 120 A defacer and disfigurer of moral treasures which were once in better keeping.

disfiguringly (dɪs'fɪgjʊərɪŋlɪ, -'fɪgər-), *adv.* [f. DISFIGURING *ppl. a.* + -LY[2].] In a disfiguring manner; so as to disfigure.

1911 MRS. H. WARD *Case of R. Meynell* i, Certain lines on the forehead..showed themselves disfiguringly. **1923** S. BARING-GOULD *Early Remin.* ii. 23 Telegraph stations planted..most disfiguringly, on the summit of church towers.

†**dis'finger,** *v.* *Obs.* [f. DIS- 7 c + FINGER *sb.*] *trans.* To let out of the fingers; to part with.

a **1652** BROME *Covent Gard.* III. Wks. 1873 II. 36 Never to look for money again, once disfinger'd.

†**dis'fit,** *v.* *Obs.* [f. DIS- 6 or 8 + FIT *v.* or *a.*] *trans.* To render unfit; to unfit.

1669 PH. HENRY *Diaries & Lett.* (1882) 218 His Age disfitting him for service. *a* **1714** M. HENRY *Wks.* (1835) I. 107 It disfits you for communion with God. *Ibid.* I. 400 By their intemperance..[they] disfit themselves for the service of God.

dis'flesh, *v.* [f. DIS- 7 a + FLESH *sb.*] *trans.* **a.** To deprive of flesh. **b.** To free from the flesh, disembody.

1620 SHELTON *Quix.* IV. xxv. 201 The best is not to run, that the lean strain not himself..nor the fat man disflesh himself. **1865** SWINBURNE *Atalanta* 17 As one on earth disfleshed and disallied From breath or blood corruptible.

†**dis'flourish,** *v.* *Obs.* [f. DIS- 6 + FLOURISH *v.*] *intr.* To wither, fade away.

1640 O. SEDGWICKE *Christs Counsell* 10 His hand may shrivell and disflourish.

dis'flower, *v.* [f. DIS- 7 a + FLOWER *sb.* Cf. *deflower.*] *trans.* **a.** To deprive or strip of flowers. **b.** To ruin or destroy as a flower. Hence **dis'flowered** *ppl. a.*

1606 SYLVESTER *Du Bartas* II. iv. II. *Trophies* 1238 Our dis-flowred Trees, our Fields Hail-torn. *a* **1618** —— *Selfe-civil-War* 165 A fruitless Fruit, a dry dis-flowered Flower. **1892** *Idler* Feb. 20 What tree..Of its beauty then dis-flowered.

disfoliaged: see DIS- 7 a.

disforest (dɪs'fɒrɪst), *v.* Also 7 **disforrest.** [ad. OF. *desforester*, f. *des-* = DIS- 4 + FOREST. Cf. the synonymous DEFOREST, DE-AFFOREST,

DISAFFOREST, med.L. *deafforestare*, *dis-afforestare*.]

1. *trans.* = DISAFFOREST I.

1502 ARNOLDE *Chron.* (1811) 208 Yf any wood other than yᵉ lordis wood..be aforestid, to yᵉ hurte of hym of whom yᵉ wood were, it shalbe disforestid. **1542-3** *Act 34-5 Hen. VIII*, c. 21 Disparked, disforested or destroied. **1611** SPEED *Hist. Gt. Brit.* IX. xix. 60 [He] disforrested the great Field of Wichwood, which King Edward his Brother had inclosed for his game. **1726** AYLIFFE *Parergon* 217 (L.) The Archbishop of Dublin was fined three hundred marks for disforesting a forest belonging to his archbishoprick. **1860** TROLLOPE *Framley P.* i. 17 The forest will be disforested.

b. *fig.*

1624 BP. HALL *Peace-maker* Wks. (1625) 537 The great King of Heauen will disforest that peece of the World which hee calls his Church, and put it to tillage. **1829** SOUTHEY *Sir T. More* II. 338 My old haunts as a book-hunter in the metropolis were disforested, to make room for the improvements between Westminster and Oxford Road.

2. To clear of forests or trees.

a **1668** DAVENANT *Anglesey* Wks. (1673) 288 Or did her voyce..Make all the Trees dance after her, And so your Woods disforrested? **1796** MORSE *Amer. Geog.* II. 180 The destroying axe..accompanied the sword..till the island became almost disforested. **1876** R. F. BURTON *Gorilla L.* II. 275 These bush-burnings have..disforested the land.

Hence **dis'foresting** *vbl. sb.*; **disfore'station.**

1613-8 DANIEL *Coll. Hist. Eng.* (1626) 167 The allowance of what disforrestation had heeretofore beene made was earnestly vrged. **1862** *Q. Rev.* Apr. 289 Before the disforesting of Cranborne Chace. **1870** H. MACMILLAN *Bible Teach.* iv. 70 Palestine has become a parched and sterile land, on account of the disforesting of its mountains.

† **dis'form,** *a. Obs.* [Variant of DIFFORM *a.*] Not in conformity: the opposite of CONFORM *a.*

1656 *Artif. Handsom.* 171 The..rule of all humane actions..is the mind and end of the doer, either conforme or disforme to the holy revealed will of God.

¶ In this and the following words *disf-* (*diff*) is probably sometimes a misprint for *diff-*.

disform (dɪs'fɔːm), *v. rare.* [f. DIS- + FORM *v.*: cf. the earlier parallel formations DIFFORM, DEFORM, of Romanic origin.]

† **1.** *trans.* To mar the form, character, or condition of; to deform, disfigure, deface. *Obs.*

1527 *Lydgate's Bochas* VII. (1554) 171 b, We be disfourmed [*MS. Harl.* 1766, lf. 175 *b*, dyfformyd] in certeyn. **1557** PAYNEL *Barclay's Jugurth* 11 b, Now disformed by miserable calamite, poore and needy. **1623** tr. *Favine's Theat. Hon.* III. ii. 334 Disformed by abuse and Simonie. **1658** A. FOX *Wurtz' Surg.* III. xviii. 279 The blister..maketh still the wound disformed, so that it groweth brown.

2. To change or alter the form of, put out of shape. **b.** *intr.* (for *refl.*) To lose or alter its form or arrangement. *rare.*

1868 GLADSTONE *Juv. Mundi* viii. (1870) 304 They seem to form, disform, and re-form before us, like the squares of coloured glass in the kaleidoscope. **1890** *Sat. Rev.* 15 Mar. 326/1 A..verb ἐκτυπόω, to diform or disform, and a.. substantive, ἐκτύπωμα, disformation or alteration.

† **dis'formate,** *a. Obs. rare.* [ad. med.L. *disformāt-us*, pa. pple. of *disformāre* (for cl. L. *dēformāre*): cf. It. *disformare*, OF. *desformé* deformed.] Deformed, disfigured.

1491 CAXTON *Vitas Patr.* (W. de W. 1495) II. 219 a/2 It is better for me to walke..bare hede and all dysformate.

disfor'mation. *rare.* [n. of action from DISFORM *v.* 2.] Alteration of shape, deformation.

1890 [see DISFORM *v.* 2].

† **dis'formed,** *ppl. a. Obs. rare.* [f. DISFORM *v.*, or OF. *desformé* + -ED.] **a.** Deformed, misshapen. **b.** Of different form: = DIFFORMED.

1591 PERCIVALL *Sp. Dict.*, *Disforme*, disformed [Minsheu (1623) deformed], disagreeing in shape, *Deformis*. **1644** DIGBY *Nat. Bodies* (1645) I. 405 Another childe..borne disformed, in such sort as Divels are painted.

† **dis'formity.** *Obs. rare.* [Variant of DIFFORMITY: cf. DISFORM.] **a.** = DEFORMITY (quot. 1494). **b.** Want of conformity: = DIFFORMITY.

1494 FABYAN *Chron.* VI. clix. 149 [They] chase rather to dye than to lyue in pryson with yᵗ dysformyte. **1600** F. WALKER *Sp. Mandeville* 21 b, The bones of Orestes..being measured, were 7 cubits long..and yet this is no great disformity in respect of that which followeth.

† **dis'fortune.** *Obs. rare.* [ad. OF. *desfortune*, f. *des-*, DIS- 4 + *fortune* FORTUNE.] Adverse fortune, misfortune.

a **1529** SKELTON *Bk. 3 Foles*, These enuious neuer laughe but..at the disfortune of some body. **1556** *Aurelio & Isab.* (1608) N iv, Wyse men unto their ennemys oughte to keape their disfortunes closse. **1592** BACON *Confer. Pleasure* (1870) 5 A..griefe wᶜʰ ariseth..of..yᵉ accesse of a disfortune.

† **dis'frame,** *v. Obs.* [f. DIS- 6 + FRAME *v.*] *trans.* To destroy the frame, form, or system of; to undo the framing of, put out of order, derange.

c **1629** LAYTON *Syons Plea* Ep. Ded., Our disframed and distempered State, from Head to Foote is all but one sore. **1644** QUARLES *Barnabas & B.* 314, I, the work of thine own hands, but wholly disframed by mine own corruptions.

disfranchise (dɪs'frɑːntʃaɪz, -æ-, -ɪz), *v.* Also 5-6 disfraun-. [f. DIS- 6 + FRANCHISE *v.*: probably representing an AF. *des-*, *disfranchir*, *-franchiser*, f. *des-*, DIS- 4 + *franchir*, *franchiss-*, and *franchiser*. Cf. the synonymous DISENFRANCHISE.

For pronunciation see note to ENFRANCHISE.]

trans. To deprive of the rights and privileges of a free citizen of a borough, city, or country, or of some franchise previously enjoyed.

1467 in *Eng. Gilds* (1870) 375 How a citezen shalle be disfraunchised. **1535** in W. H. Turner *Select Rec. Oxford* (1880) 132 He..shalbe dysfranchesed opynly at Carfox. **1542** *Fabyan's Chron.* VII. 695 In yᵉ sayd mayrs tyme, Sir Wylliam Fitz-William [was] disfraunchysed, because he wolde not be shyryfe. **1638** in Picton *L'pool Munic. Rec.* (1883) I. 126 Hath..beene disfranchised of his freedome of the same towne. **1673** BAXTER *Let.* in *Answ. Dodwell* 86 An Emperor might..depose all the Bishops by dis-franchizing the Cities. **1765** BLACKSTONE *Comm.* I. 484 Any particular member may be disfranchised, or lose his place in the corporation, by acting contrary to the laws of the society, or the laws of the land. **1870** RUSKIN *Lect. Art* i. 29 They are no more to consider themselves therefore disfranchised from their native land than the sailors of her fleets do.

b. *esp.* To deprive (a place, etc.) of the right of returning parliamentary or other representatives; to deprive (persons) of the right of voting in parliamentary, municipal, or other elections.

1702 LUTTRELL *Brief Rel.* (1857) V. 241 The commons ordered a bill to be brought in to disfranchize that borrough. **1772** *Junius Lett.* lxix. 361, I question the power..of the legislature to disfranchise a number of boroughs. **1841** SPALDING *Italy & It. Isl.* III. 55 This system boldly shook off democracy; for the citizens at large were disfranchised. **1862** LD. BROUGHAM *Brit. Const.* viii. 100 The decayed burghs were disfranchised, and their members given to the counties. **1876** BANCROFT *Hist. U.S.* I. xx. 548 The elective franchise was restored to the freemen whom the previous assembly had disfranchised.

c. *transf.* and *fig.* To deprive of or exclude from anything viewed as a privilege or right.

1581 J. BELL *Haddon's Answ. Osor.* 498 We are not so mynded..as to seeke to disfraunchise you of your froward, malapert sawcinesse. **1585-7** T. ROGERS *39 Art.* (1607) 311 A prince contemning the censures of the church, is to be disfranchised out of the church. **1738** WARBURTON *Div. Legat.* I. xliv. Ded., Disfranchized of the Rights you have so wantonly and wickedly abused. **1846** GROTE *Greece* I. xvi. I. 567 Oracles which had once been inspired became after a time forsaken and disfranchised.

Hence **dis'franchised** *ppl. a.*, **dis'franchising** *vbl. sb.* and *ppl. a.*

1467 in *Eng. Gilds* (1870) 378 Vppon peyne of euerych of them of disfraunchesynge. **1646** J. HALL *Horæ Vac.* 13 Wise men are timerous in the disfranchising of their judgement. **1772** *Junius Lett.* lxix. 361 The disfranchising of boroughs.. I consider as equivalent to robbing the parties of their freehold. **1865** *Cornh. Mag.* Aug. 166 The disfranchised agent challenged his disfranchiser. **1870** *Daily News* 28 Dec., The disfranchising effect of the cumulative vote.

disfranchisement (dɪs'frɑːntʃɪzmənt, -æ-). [f. prec. + -MENT: cf. the parallel *franchisement*, *af-*, *en-franchisement*.] The action of disfranchising or fact of being disfranchised; deprivation of the privileges of a free citizen, especially of that of voting at the election of members of the legislature.

1623 COCKERAM, *Disfranchisement*, a taking away of ones freedome. **1647** WARD *Simp. Cobler* 50 Such usurpations are the..disfranchisements of Freedome. **1766** SIR J. BURROW *Reports* I. 525 (Jod.) In Yates's case it is said there must be a custom, or a statute to warrant disfranchisement. **1825** SYD. SMITH *Sp.* Wks. 1859 II. 211/2 These very same politicians are now looking in an agony of terror at the disfranchisement of Corporations containing twenty or thirty persons, sold to their representatives. **1877** MRS. OLIPHANT *Makers Flor.* ii. 33 The revenge taken..was no less than the complete disfranchisement of the Florentine nobility.

dis'franchiser. [f. DISFRANCHISE *v.* + -ER¹.] One who or that which disfranchises.

1861 *Working Men's Coll. Mag.* III. 46 Improvidence and intemperance..are the wholesale disfranchisers of the great 'unrepresented' class. **1865** [see DISFRANCHISED].

† **dis'frange,** *v. Obs. rare.* [irreg. f. DIS- I + L. *frang-ĕre* to break. (The L. compound was *diffringere*.)] *trans.* To break in pieces.

1778 APTHORPE *Preval. Chr.* 254 Broken columns and disfranged marbles.

† **dis'frank,** *v. Obs. rare.* [f. DIS- 7 c + FRANK *sb.* pig-sty, boar-stall.] *trans.* 'To set free from the *frank*, or place in which an animal was confined for feeding' (Nares).

1638 *Hist. Albino & Bellama* 131 (N.) Intending to disfrank an ore-growne boare.

† **dis'fraught,** *v. Obs. rare.* [f. DIS- 7 a + FRAUGHT *sb.* cargo, load.] *trans.* To unload.

1599 NASHE *Lenten Stuffe* (1871) 158 Having disfraughted and unloaded his luggage.

† **disfre'quent,** *v. Obs.* [f. DIS- 6 + FREQUENT *v.*] *trans.* To cease to frequent or attend.

1646 GAULE *Cases Consc.* 82 Noted for long dis-frequenting and neglecting the Church. **1666** G. ALSOP *Maryland* (1869) 41 The Hogs..do disfrequent home more than the rest of Creatures that are look'd upon as tame.

Hence † **disfre'quenter**, one who disuses.

1646 *Kingdomes Weekly Intelligencer* 16 Mar. 453 The Disfrequenters of the Gowne shall put it on againe.

† **dis'friar,** *v. Obs.* [f. DIS- 7 b + FRIAR.] *trans.* To deprive of the order of a friar; *refl.* to divest oneself of friar's orders.

1599 SANDYS *Europæ Spec.* (1632) 22 Over great severitie would cause a great number to disfrier themselves. **1639** FULLER *Holy War* V. vi. (1647) 238 Many did quickly unnunne and disfriar themselves.

† **dis'friendship.** *Obs.* [f. DIS- 9 + FRIENDSHIP.] The opposite of friendship; unfriendliness, enmity, disaffection.

1493 *Sc. Acts Jas. IV* (1597) §40 Swa that it make na mair trouble nor dis-freindship amangst the Kings lieges. **1579** FENTON *Guicciard.* III. 107 They pretended to haue no disfriendship with him. **1652** EARL MONM. tr. *Bentivoglio's Histor. Rel.* 41 They have no occasion of friendship or disfriendship with the King of Polonia.

dis'frock, *v.* [f. DIS- + FROCK *sb.*: cf. OF. *des-*, *deffroquer*, and DEFROCK.] *trans.* To deprive of the clerical garb, and hence of the clerical character; to unfrock. Hence **dis'frocked** *ppl. a.*

1837 CARLYLE *Fr. Rev.* III. I. i. (1872) 4 Disfrocked Chabot adjures Heaven that at least we may 'have done with Kings'. **1856** FROUDE *Hist. Eng.* II. 29 The continent was covered with disfrocked monks. **1879** H. JAMES *American* 309 If the abbé is disfrocked for his share in it.

disful'fil, *v. nonce-wd.* [DIS- 6.] *trans.* To do the opposite of fulfilling; not to fulfil. Hence **disful'filment.**

1818 BENTHAM *Church of Eng.* 456 Should it [prophecy] be disfulfilled, then [etc.]. **1823** —— *Not Paul* 285 His prophecy would have been disfulfilled; but..his purposes would have been fulfilled. *Ibid.*, The disfulfilment would indeed take place.

† **dis'fulȝe,** *v. Sc. Obs.* [a. OF. *desfueille-r*, *deff-*, mod.F. *défeuiller*, f. *des-*, DIS- + *feuille* leaf.] *trans.* To strip of leaves: = DEFOIL *v.*¹, DEFOLIATE *v.*

c **1375** BARBOUR *Troy-bk.* II. 1652 And had þe treis dispulȝeit Of þare faire flouris and disfulȝeit.

'disfunction, dis'functional *a.*, varr. DYSFUNCTION, DYSFUNCTIONAL *a.*

1927 [see ŒSTROGEN]. **1951** PARSONS & SHILS *Gen. Theory of Action* 35 Functional in one content but disfunctional in another. **1952** KOESTLER *Arrow in Blue* xviii. 169 Yet, as far as I know, I have never had any glandular disfunction. **1959** P. RIEFF *Freud* viii. 290 Freud thought only reason could resolve this pull between social functions and disfunctions. **1969** *Indian Mus. Jrnl.* V. 72 The disfunction in the phylum expressed in social interactions resultant from man's neurosis.

dis'furnish, *v.* [ad. OF. *desfourniss-*, extended stem of *desfournir*, also *deff-*, *défournir*, f. *des-*, DIS- 4 + *fournir* to FURNISH.] *trans.* To deprive or divest of that wherewith it is furnished; to strip of furniture or belongings; to render destitute (*of*).

1531 ELYOT *Gov.* II. vii. (1883) 75 Whan the emperour shuld be disfurnisshed of seruauntes. **1577** FENTON *Gold. Epist.* 183 He hath disfurnished them of their principal weapons. **1591** SHAKS. *Two Gent.* IV. i. 14 My riches, are these poore habiliments, Of which, if you should here disfurnish me, You take the sum and substance that I haue. **1649** ROBERTS *Clavis Bibl.* 249 Disfurnishing the Temple of utensils. **1732** NEAL *Hist. Purit.* I. 222 The risk the University would run of being disfurnished of students. **1748** RICHARDSON *Clarissa* Wks. 1883 VIII. 432 Her closet, her chamber, her cabinet, given up to me to disfurnish. **1887** LOWELL *Democr.* 203 The Indians showed a far greater natural predisposition for disfurnishing the outside of other people's heads than for furnishing the insides of their own.

Hence **dis'furnished** *ppl. a.*, **dis'furnishing** *vbl. sb.*

a **1577** GASCOIGNE *Wks.* (1587) 204 Though his absence were unto hir a disfurnishing of eloquence. **1670** COTTON *Espernon* I. II. 46 To succour a weak, and disfurnish'd Prince, against an armed and prevailing Subject. **1799** SOUTHEY *Lett.* (1856) I. 73, I seize a leisure minute, and a disfurnished room..to write to you. **1857** H. MILLER *Test. Rocks* vii. 270 The disfurnished earth was peopled anew.

dis'furnishment. [f. prec. + -MENT.] The action of disfurnishing, or fact of being disfurnished.

1603 BRETON *Dign. or Ind. Man* 202 For his Disfurnishment of Defence, his Defenders are provided. **1613-18** DANIEL *Coll. Hist. Eng.* (1626) 28 [He] withdrawes all cattle and prouisions..for their owne store, and disfurnishment of the enemie. **1820** LAMB *Elia* Ser. I. *Two Races of Men*, Thus, furnished by the very act of disfurnishment; getting rid of the cumbersome luggage of riches.

† **dis'furniture.** *Obs.* [f. DIS- 9 + FURNITURE.] The act of disfurnishing; removal, deprivation; disfurnishment.

1565 *Act 8 Eliz.* c. 11 §1 The Disfurniture of Service to be done to the Queen's Majesty. **1654** W. MOUNTAGUE *Devout Ess.* II. viii. §3 (R.) We may..with much ease bear the disfurniture of such transitory moveables.

† **dis'gage,** *v. Obs.* [a. 16th c. F. *desgager* 'to vngage, disingage' (Cotgr.), OF. *desguagier*, mod.F. *dégager*, f. *des-*, DIS- 4 + *gager* to engage,

pledge, wager.] *trans.* To release from pledge or pawn; to set free, disengage.

1594 KYD *Cornelia* III. in Hazl. *Dodsley* V. 209 But when our soul the body hath disgag'd, It seeks the common passage of the dead. **1603** HOLLAND *Plutarch's Mor.* 232 (R.) Those who had lever lay to gage and pawn their goods.. then to sell up all and disgage themselves at once.

† **dis'gallant,** *v. Obs. rare.* [f. DIS- 8 + GALLANT *a.*] *trans.* To strip or deprive of gallantry or courage; to discourage, dispirit.

1599 B. JONSON *Cynthia's Rev.* III. i, Sir, let not this discountenance or dis-gallant you a whit. **1640** GLAPTHORNE *Ladies Privil.* I. Wks. (1874) II. 97, I would not have.. the least Pimple in her countenance discompos'd, it does Disgallant a whole beauty.

† **disgaol** (dɪs'dʒeɪl), *v. Obs. rare.* [f. DIS- 7 b + GAOL *sb.*] *trans.* To divest of the character or nature of a gaol.

1647 DIGGES *Unlawf. Taking Arms* §4. 160 He will contribute His utmost endeavours, that His owne Castles.. may be disgaoled.

† **dis'garbage,** *v. Obs. rare.* [f. DIS- 7 a + GARBAGE.] *trans.* To deprive of the entrails; to disembowel. Hence † **dis'garbaging** *vbl. sb.*

1612 tr. *Benvenuto's Passenger* (N.), In winter time they are excellent, so they be fat and quickely roasted, without disgarbaging of them.

† **dis'garboil,** *v. Obs.* [f. DIS- 5 + GARBOIL taken in sense 'disbowel', perh. through confusion with *garbage*: cf. prec.] *trans.* To disbowel.

1566 PAINTER *Pal. Pleas.* (1575) II. Pref., Aristotimvs disgarboyleth the intralles of Tiranny. **1599** *Broughton's Lett.* iii. 13 Which sacrifice you could neuer yet offer.. till you.. disgarboyle your selfe of those corrupt affections.

disgarland (dɪs'gɑːlənd), *v.* [f. DIS- 7 a + GARLAND *sb.*] *trans.* To divest of a garland or garlands. Hence **dis'garlanding** *vbl. sb.*

1616 DRUMM. OF HAWTH. *Poems* Wks. (1711) 12 O Pan.. Forsake thy pipe, a scepter take to thee, Thy locks disgarland, thou black Jove shall be. **1879** G. MEREDITH *Egoist* II. 315 Good progress was made to the disgarlanding of themselves thus far.

disgarnish (dɪs'gɑːnɪʃ), *v.* [a. OF. *desgarniss-* extended stem of *desgarnir*, *-guarnir* (11th c. in Hatz.-Darm.), mod.F. *dégarnir*, f. *des-*, DES- 4 + *garnir* to GARNISH.]

trans. To deprive of that which garnishes or furnishes; to strip of garnishment, disfurnish, despoil.

c **1450** *Merlin* 291 Thei wolde not disgarnyssh the londe of peple. **1481** CAXTON *Myrr.* III. xxi. 181 Synne.. is voyde and disgarnysshed of all goodnes. **1530** PALSGR. 519/1 This house is disgarnysshed, me thynke, now he is gone. **1598** BARRET *Theor. Warres* v. i. 148 Whosoeuer is found disgarnished of his Armes. **1649** DRUMM. OF HAWTH. *Hist. Jas. I*, Wks. (1711) 2 If it should fall forth.. that this prince by usurpers and rebels were disgarnished of his own crown. **1653** H. COGAN tr. *Pinto's Trav.* lx. (1663) 247 The Scaffold was disgarnished of all the richest pieces about it. **1831** SIR W. NAPIER *Penins. War* XI. viii. (Rtldg.) II. 125 The front.. was.. disgarnished of troops. **1868** HOLME LEE *B. Godfrey* xxvi. 137 The small sleeping-closets.. had been disgarnished.

Hence **dis'garnished** *ppl. a.*; **-ing** *vbl. sb.*

1483 CAXTON *G. de la Tour* A j, They ben yonge and litil and dysgarnysshed of all wytte and reson. **1523** LD. BERNERS *Froiss.* I. ccclxxvi. 626 Whan they were come to this passage.. they founde it nat disgarnished. **1812** *Edin. Rev.* XX. 249 For the disgarnishing of idolatrous houses.

dis'garrison, *v. Obs.* or *arch.* [f. DIS- 7 a + GARRISON *sb.*] *trans.* To deprive of a garrison.

1594 J. DICKENSON *Arisbas* (1878) 42 The.. discouerers of my desire, disgarisond my thoughts of wonted fancies. **1647** SIR T. FAIRFAX *Let.* in *12th Rep. Hist. MSS. Comm.* App. v. 3, I have thought fit to give order to Major Markham to remove the forces from Belvoir and to disgarrison the place. **1691** WOOD *Ath. Oxon.* II. 298 When Winchester Castle was disgarrison'd, it was given to him. **1879** *Q. Rev.* No. 295. 171 Next year the castle was disgarrisoned.

disgavel (dɪs'gævəl), *v. Law.* [f. DIS- 7 a + *gavel* (GAVELKIND) sb.] *trans.* To relieve or exempt from the tenure of gavelkind. Hence **dis'gavelling** *vbl. sb.* and *ppl. a.*

1683 SIDERFIN *Rep.* I. 137 Les primer Statutes de Disgaveling come Wiats Stat. 15 H. 8. **1741** T. ROBINSON *Gavelkind* i. 6 Before the Time of the disgavelling Statute. **1767** BLACKSTONE *Comm.* II. 85 By statute 31 Hen. VIII. c. 3. for disgavelling the lands of divers lords and gentlemen in the county of Kent, they are directed to be descendible for the future like other lands, which were never holden by service of socage. **1875** BLACKMORE *Alice Lorraine* I. xv. 151 The land had been disgavelled. **1881** *19th Cent.* Aug. 298 Notwithstanding the disgavelling of many estates.. the area subject to the operation of the law is still large.

disgeneral, disgenius: see DIS- 7 a, 9.

disge'neric, *a.* [DIS- 10.] Of different genera: the opposite of *congeneric*.

In recent Dicts.

† **dis'gentilize,** *v. Obs. rare.* [f. DIS- 6 + GENTILIZE.] *trans.* To deprive of gentle rank.

1621 *Court & T. Jas. I* (1849) II. 242 Some say he shall.. be quite disknighted and disgentilised for ever.

disgest, -gestion: see DIGEST, DIGESTION.

† **dis'ghibelline,** *v. Obs. nonce-wd.* [DIS- 7 b.] *trans.* To distinguish, as a Guelph from a Ghibelline.

1672 MARVELL *Reh. Transp.* I. 299 In their conversation they thought fit to take some more license the better to dis-Ghibeline themselves from the Puritans.

disgig *v.*: see DIS- 7 a.

† **dis'gird,** *v. Obs.* [f. DIS- 6 + GIRD *v.*] *trans.* To strip of that which girds; to ungird.

1610 HOLLAND *Camden's Brit.* I. 780 Afterwards disgirded of his militarie Belt.

disgise, etc., obs. form of DISGUISE, etc.

† **dis'glorify,** *v. Obs. rare.* [f. DIS- 6 + GLORIFY *v.*] *trans.* To deprive of glory; to treat with dishonour.

1577 DEE *Relat. Spir.* I. (1659) 64 Angels.. in state disglorified and drent in confusion. **1671** MILTON *Samson* 442 Disglorified, blasphem'd and had in scorn.

† **dis'glory.** *Obs.* [f. DIS- 9 + GLORY *sb.*] The opposite of glory: dishonour.

1547-64 BAULDWIN *Mor. Philos.* (Palfr.) II. ii, What greater ground of disglory? What greater occasion of dishonour? **1577** NORTHBROOKE *Dicing* (1843) 20 How can you say that you are gathered togither in Christes name, when you doe all things to the disglorie thereof.

† **dis'glose,** *v. Obs. rare.* [f. DIS- 5 + *glose*, GLOZE *v.*] To beguile or deceive thoroughly.

1565 *Darius* (1860) 23 Surely my eyes do dysglose If yonder I do not see hym commynge.

† **dis'gloss,** *v. Obs. rare.* [f. DIS- 7 a + GLOSS *sb.*] *trans.* To deprive of gloss or sheen.

1562 PHAER *Æneid.* IX. D d j, Stones with bumpes his plates disglosse.

dis'glut, *v. rare.* [f. DIS- 6 + GLUT *v.*] *trans.* To empty of its contents.

1800 HURDIS *Fav. Village* 100 The sportsman's tube, disglutted o'er the lake, Pours a long echo.

dis'glutinate, *v. rare.* [f. DIS- 6 + GLUTINATE *v.*] *trans.* To unglue, DEGLUTINATE.

1870 C. J. SMITH *Syn. & Antonyms*, Agglutinate, *Antonym*.. Resolve, Disglutinate.

dis'godded, *ppl. a. rare.* [f. DIS- 7 + GOD + -ED.] Deprived of godhead or divinity; ungodlike.

1877 BLACKIE *Wise Men* 36 Leaving For the bright smile that warms the face o' the world A bald, disgodded, lightless, loveless grey!

disgolf, obs. form of DISGULF *v.*

disgood: see DIS- 8.

[**disgore,** spurious word in Ash, etc.: see DISGORGE 3.]

disgorge (dɪs'gɔːdʒ), *v.* [ad. OF. *desgorger* (mod.F. *dégorger*, whence DEGORGE), f. *des-*, DIS- 4 + *gorge* throat, GORGE: cf. It. *(di)sgorgare*.]

1. *trans.* To eject or throw out from, or as from, the gorge or throat; to vomit forth (what has been swallowed).

c **1477** CAXTON *Jason* 75 The which thre bestes so dredefull disgorged and caste out fyre of their throtes. **1601** HOLLAND *Pliny* I. 307 [Rats] swallow.. them whole downe the gullet, and afterwards straine and struggle.. vntill they disgorge again the feathers and bones that were in their bellies. **1677** OTWAY *Cheats of Scapin* II. i, How easily a Miser swallows a load, and how difficultly he disgorges a grain. **1774** GOLDSM. *Nat. Hist.* (1776) VII. 311 The leech.. disgorges the blood it has swallowed, and it is then kept for repeated application. **1873** MISS THACKERAY *Old Kensington* ii, Jonah's whale swallowed and disgorged him night after night.

b. *fig.* To discharge as if from a mouth; to empty forth; *esp.* to give up what has been wrongfully appropriated.

a **1529** SKELTON *Trouth & Information* (R.) But woo to suche informers.. That.. Disgorgith theyr veneme. **1587** TURBERV. *Trag. T.* (1837) 228 Disgorge thy care, abandon feare. **1606** SHAKS. *Tr. & Cr.* Prol. 12 The deepe-drawing Barke do there disgorge Their warlike frautage. **1776** GIBBON *Decl. & F.* I. iv. 84 The dens of the amphitheatre disgorged at once a hundred lions. **1808** WELLINGTON in Gurw. *Desp.* IV. 121 Some mode.. to make the French Generals disgorge the church plate which they have stolen. **1855** PRESCOTT *Philip II*, I. II. iii. 173 It was.. time that the prisons should disgorge their superfluous victims. **1882** J. TAYLOR *Sc. Covenanters* (Cassell) 153 The grandson.. was compelled to disgorge the property of which the General had plundered the Covenanters.

c. *absol.*

1608 ARMIN *Nest Ninn.* 7 The World, ready to disgorge at so homely a present. **1638** SIR T. HERBERT *Trav.* (ed. 2) 223 After I had disgorg'd abundantly, I fell into a sound sleepe. **1667** MILTON *P.L.* XII. 158 The river Nile.. disgorging at seaven mouthes Into the Sea. **1794** SULLIVAN *View Nat.* II. Y iij, Caverns full of water.. disgorging upon the earth. **1868** MILMAN *St. Paul's* 351 At the Restoration he was forced to disgorge.

2. *trans.* To discharge or empty (the stomach, mouth, breast, etc.).

c **1592** MARLOWE *Massacre Paris* III. ii, Then come, proud Guise, and here disgorge thy breast. **1597** SHAKS. *2 Hen. IV*, I. iii. 97 So, so, (thou common Dogge) did'st thou disgorge Thy glutton-bosome of the Royall Richard. **1637** HEYWOOD *Dial.* I. Wks. 1874 VI. 100 Their stomacks some disgorg'd. **1861** HULME tr. *Moquin-Tandon* II. III. iv. 146 It was the custom to throw away all leeches which had been used; they are now disgorged, and preserved for a future occasion.

b. *refl.* To empty or discharge oneself.

1607 J. KING *Serm.* 27 Nov., They.. want but meanes and matter wherein to disgordg themselues. *c* **1645** HOWELL *Lett.* (1650) I. 9 The sea.. meeting.. rivers that descend from Germany to disgorge themselves into him. **1679** *Establ. Test* 24 If the Spirit moves, he can disgorge himself against the Priests of Baal, the Hirelings. **1712** ADDISON *Spect.* No. 309 ¶15 The four Rivers which disgorge themselves into the Sea of Fire. **1868** HAWTHORNE *Amer. Note-bks.* (1879) I. 231 Several vessels were disgorging themselves.

† **3.** *Farriery.* To dissipate an engorgement or congestion [cf. F. *dégorger* in same sense]. *Obs.*

1727 BAILEY vol. II., *Disgorge* [with Farriers] is to discuss or disperse an Inflammation or swelling. **1737** [see DEGORGE]. **1753** CHAMBERS *Cycl. Suppl.* s.v., If a horse's legs are gorged or swelled, we say he must be walked out to disgorge them. [**1775** ASH mispr. *Disgore*; whence in some mod. Dicts.]

Hence **dis'gorged** *ppl. a.*, **dis'gorging** *vbl. sb.*

1611 COTGR., *Desgorgé*, disgorged. *Desgorgement*, a disgorging. **1632** LITHGOW *Trav.* VI. 255 Woefull accidents, and superabounding disgorgings [floods]. **1681** N. RESBURY *Fun. Serm.* 9 As he had been a mighty devourer of Books, so his very disgorgings.. had generally more relish than the first cookery. **1822** T. L. PEACOCK *Maid Marian* xiv, The reluctant disgorgings of fat abbots and usurers.

disgorgement (dɪs'gɔːdʒmənt). [f. prec. vb. + -MENT: cf. OF. *desgorgement* (1548 in Hatz.-Darm.).] The action of disgorging; a discharging as from the throat or stomach.

c **1477** CAXTON *Jason* 115 b, The cloth of golde shone by the disgorgements of the water. **1632** LITHGOW *Trav.* I. 13 This River of Tyber.. made muster of his extravagant disgorgements. *a* **1656** BP. HALL *Rem. Wks.* (1660) 162 The.. presses are openly defiled with the most loathsome disgorgements of their wicked blasphemies. **1788** CLARKSON *Impol. Slave Tr.* 55 There is a continual disgorgement of seamen from these vessels into the islands. **1837** *Blackw. Mag.* XLI. 146 The disgorgement of past plunder.

disgorger (dɪs'gɔːdʒə(r)). [f. as prec. + -ER[1].] One who or that which disgorges. *spec.* A device for extracting a gorged hook from the throat of a fish.

1867 F. FRANCIS *Angling* iv. (1880) 129 A disgorger.. is a piece of metal or bone with a notch at the end. **1875** 'STONEHENGE' *Brit. Sports* I. v. iii. §10. 337 Attempting, by means of the disgorger, to remove them while he is alive. **1883** *Fisheries Exhib. Catal.* 62.

† **dis'gospel,** *v. Obs. nonce-wd.* [f. DIS- 7 a + GOSPEL *sb.*] *trans.* To deprive of the gospel or of gospel character; to oust the gospel from practical life. Hence † **dis'gospelling** *ppl. a.*

1642 MILTON *Apol. Smect.* xii. Wks. 1738 I. 133 Who possess huge Benefices for lazy Performances, great Promotions only for the execution of a cruel disgospelling Jurisdiction.

dis'gospelize, *v. rare.* [DIS- 6.] *trans.* To deprive of or exclude from the gospel.

1888 S. G. OSBORNE in *Times* 6 Oct. 12/3 That tens of thousands.. are living disgospelized, so born and reared as to be of a race the gospel.. teachings cannot touch.

† **dis'gout,** *v. Obs. rare.* [f. DIS- 7 a + GOUT *sb.*] *trans.* To free or relieve from gout.

1611 FLORIO *Sgottare*.. also to disgout. **1748** RICHARDSON *Clarissa* Wks. 1883 VII. 286 Lord M... turning round and round.. his but just disgouted thumb.

dis'govern, *v. nonce-wd.* [DIS- 6.] *trans.* To leave ungoverned; to refrain from governing.

1878 H. WRIGHT *Mental Trav.* 78 The object of statesmanship at Nomunniburgh is not to govern but to disgovern as much as possible.

disgown (dɪs'gaʊn), *v.* [f. DIS- 7 a + GOWN *sb.*: cf. *disrobe*.] **a.** *trans.* To strip or deprive (any one) of his gown, *spec.* of a university or clerical gown, and thus of the degree or office which it symbolizes. **b.** *intr.* (for *refl.*) To throw off or relinquish one's gown.

a **1734** NORTH *Exam.* (1740) 222 (D.) He disgowned and put on a sword. **1887** *Globe* 1 Oct. 2/4 [He] had been a clergyman, but had been disgowned for malpractices.

disgrace (dɪs'greɪs), *sb.* [a. F. *disgrâce* 'a disgrace, an ill-fortune, defeature, mishap; also vncomelinesse, deformitie, etc.' (Cotgr.), ad. It. *disgrazia* 'a disgrace, a mishap, a misfortune' (Florio), f. DIS- 4 + *grazia* GRACE; cf. Sp. *desgracia* 'disgrace, misfortune, unpleasantness', med.L. *disgrātia* (15th c. in Du Cange).]

1. The disfavour of one in a powerful or exalted position, with the withdrawal of honour, degradation, dishonour, or contumely, which accompanies it: †**a.** as exhibited by the personage who inflicts it (*obs.*); **b.** as incurred or experienced by the victim: the state of being out of favour and honour.

a. **1581** PETTIE *Guazzo's Civ. Conv.* I. (1586) 28 b, Shee went about to bring into the disgrace of the Dutches all the Ladies of the Court. **1600** E. BLOUNT tr. *Conestaggio* 12 Ambition and feare of the Kings disgrace were of such force, that the Nobles.. durst not open their mouthes.

b. 1586 A. Day *Eng. Secretary* (1625) I. 142 The disgrace that quickly you shall sustaine. 1605 Shaks. *Macb.* III. vi. 23, I heare Macduffe liues in disgrace. 1659 B. Harris *Parival's Iron Age* 267 The Spaniards offered him [Card. Mazarin] all kindness of favour in his disgrace. 1849 Macaulay *Hist. Eng.* II. 160 The King..had determined that the disgrace of the Hydes should be complete. *Mod.* The minister was living in retirement, being in disgrace at Court.

†c. A disfavour; a dishonour; an affront. *Obs.*

a 1586 Sidney (J.), To such bondage he was..tied by her whose disgraces to him were graced by her excellence. 1586 B. Young *Guazzo's Civ. Conv.* IV. 206 b, With my unluckie sport I have gotten your disgraces. *a* 1626 Bacon (Webster 1864), The interchange continually of favours and disgraces. 1651 Hobbes *Govt. & Soc.* xv. §18. 257 If it command somewhat to be.. done, which is not a disgrace to God directly, but from whence by reasoning disgracefull consequences may be derived. 1739 Cibber *Apol.* (1756) I. 296 Several little disgraces were put upon them.

†2. The disfavour of Fortune (as a disposer of human affairs); adverse fortune, misfortune. *Obs.*

1590 Greene *Neuer too late* (1600) 2 Midst the riches of his face, Griefe deciphred high disgrace. 1600 E. Blount tr. *Conestaggio* 15 Sent his ambassadors to the said King, letting him understand of his disgrace. 1653 H. Cogan tr. *Pinto's Trav.* i. 1 No disgrace of Fortune ought to esloign us ..from the duty which we are bound to render unto God. 1697 Dryden *Virg. Georg.* IV. 143 That other looks like Nature in Disgrace.

†b. A misfortune. *Obs.*

1622 R. Hawkins *Voy. S. Sea* (1847) 173 With these disgraces upon them and the hand of God helping..us. 1627 *Lisander & Cal.* IV. 74, I shall alwaies bless my disgraces which have wrought mee this felicity. 1748 Smollett *Rod. Rand.* (1780) I. 187 Notwithstanding the disgraces which had fallen to her share, she had not been so unlucky as many others.

3. Dishonour in general or public estimation; ignominy, shame.

1593 Shaks. *Rich. II*, I. i. 133, I slew him not; but (to mine owne disgrace) Neglected my sworne duty in that case. 1639 S. Du Verger tr. *Camus' Admir. Events* 54 If ever he saw him approach his wife, he would..resist force by force ..to drive disgrace from his house. 1728 Pope *Dunc.* II. 175 A second effort brought but new disgrace. 1856 Froude *Hist. Eng.* (1858) II. xi. 467 The disgrace which the queen's conduct had brought upon her family. 1863 Geo. Eliot *Romola* II. xxiii, Tito shrank with shuddering dread from disgrace.

†4. The expression of dishonour and reprobation; opprobrium, reproach, disparagement; an expression or term of reprobation. *Obs.* or *arch.*

1586 A. Day *Eng. Secretary* II. (1625) 86 When..a word is either in praise or disgrace..repeated. 1608 Bp. Hall *Char. Vertues & V.* 102 If hee list not to give a verbal disgrace, yet hee shakes his head and smiles. 1617 —— *Recoll. Treat.* 977 Every vice hath a title, and every vertue a disgrace. 1660 *Trial Regic.* 174 You spake..against the King by way of disgrace against him and his family. 1676 Hobbes *Iliad* III. 33 Then Hector him with words of great disgrace Reproved. [1855 Tennyson *Maud* II. i. 14 He.. Heap'd on her terms of disgrace.]

5. An occasion or cause of shame or dishonour; that which brings into dishonour.

1590 Spenser *F.Q.* I. i. 31 To all knighthood it is foule disgrace, That such a cursed creature lives so long a space. 1597 Shaks. *2 Hen. IV*, II. ii. 15 What a disgrace is it to me, to remember thy name? *c* 1710 Baynard (J.), And is it not a foul disgrace, To lose the boltsprit of thy face? 1856 Emerson *Eng. Traits, Wealth* Wks. (Bohn) II. 69, I found the two disgraces..are, first, disloyalty to Church and State, and, second, to be born poor, or to come to poverty. 1875 Jowett *Plato* (ed. 2) V. 178 Is not the knowledge of words without ideas a disgrace to a man of sense?

†6. Marring of the grace of anything; disfigurement. *Obs.*

1581 Pettie *Guazzo's Civ. Conv.* III. (1586) 126 To take away some wart, moale, spot, or such like disgrace comming by chaunce. 1598 *St. John's Coll. Agreem.* in Willis & Clark *Cambridge* (1886) II. 251 The Chimneys..shalbe taken dowen and Raysed in some other Convenient place without disgrace of the new court.

7. Want of grace. †a. of person: ill-favouredness (*obs.*); b. of mind: ungracious condition or character. *rare.*

1596 Spenser *F.Q.* v. xii. 28 Their garments..Being all rag'd and tatter'd, their disgraces Did much the more augment. 1861 T. Winthrop *Cecil Dreeme* v. (1876) 75 Even a coat may be one of the outward signs by which we betray the grace or disgrace that is in us.

disgrace (dɪsˈgreɪs), *v.* [a. F. *disgracier* (1552 in Hatz.-Darm.), ad. It. *disgraziare*, f. *disgrazia* (see prec.). So Sp. *desgraciar.*]

†1. *trans.* To undo or mar the grace of; to deprive of (outward) grace; to disfigure. *Obs.*

1549–62 Sternhold & H. *Ps.* ciii. 16 Like the flower.. Whose glosse and beauty stormy winds do utterly disgrace. 1551 Robinson tr. *More's Utop.* 14 Rude and vnlearned speche defaceth and disgraceth a very good matter. 1555 Watreman *Fardle Facions* I. v. 69 The woman had her nose cut of, wherwith..the whole beautie of her face was disgraced. 1577 B. Googe *Heresbach's Husb.* II. (1586) 115 b, His paunch shal the lesse appeer, which both disgraceth him and burdneth him. 1709 Pope *Ess. Crit.* 24 The slightest sketch..Is by ill-colouring but the more disgrac'd. 1781 Cowper *Convers.* 51 Withered stumps disgrace the sylvan scene.

†2. To put to shame, put out of countenance by eclipsing. *Obs.*

1589 Greene *Menaphon* (Arb.) 35 Flora seeing her face, bids al her glorious flowers close themselues, as being by her beautie disgraced. 1591 Nashe *Pref. to Sidney's Astr. & Stella*, In thee..the Lesbian Sappho with her lyric harpe is disgraced.

†b. To put out of countenance, abash, dismay.

1607 Topsell *Four-f. Beasts* (1658) 160 Casting.. burning torches into the face of the elephant; by which the huge beast is not a little disgraced and terrified.

3. To put out of grace or favour; to treat with disfavour, and hence with dishonour; to dismiss from (royal, etc.) favour and honour.

1593 Nashe *4 Lett. Confut.* 43 Followers, whose dutifull seruice must not bee disgrac'd with a bitter repulse in anie suite. 1600 E. Blount tr. *Conestaggio* 62 Although he were without lands, and disgraced by Henry, yet being favoured by the people, he supposed that Henry dying, he shoulde.. be crowned. 1617 Bp. Hall *Recoll. Treat.* 133 How easie is it for such a man, whiles the world disgraces him, at once to scorne and pitty it. 1711 Pope *Temp. Fame* 294 Some she disgrac'd, and some with honours crown'd. 1745 P. Thomas *Jrnl. Anson's Voy.* 216 His Subjects..whom he either disgraces or honours. 1855 Macaulay *Hist. Eng.* III. 268 Queensberry was disgraced for refusing to betray the interests of the Protestant religion.

†4. To bring into disfavour (*with* any one), or into the bad graces of any one. *Obs.*

1594 Shaks. *Rich. III*, I. iii. 79 Our Brother is imprison'd by your means, My selfe disgrac'd, and the Nobilitie Held in comtempt. 1600 E. Blount tr. *Conestaggio* 35 Which his enimies tooke as an occasion to disgrace him with the King.

†5. To cast shame or discredit upon; to bring (intentionally) into disgrace. *Obs.*

1573 G. Harvey *Letter-bk.* (Camden) 6 How sociablely he hath delt bi me..to disgrace and slaunder me in the toun. 1599 Shaks. *Much Ado* III. ii. 130 As I wooed for thee to obtaine her, I will joyne with thee to disgrace her. *a* 1715 Burnet (J.), Men's passions will carry them far in misrepresenting an opinion which they have a mind to disgrace.

†b. To put to shame. *Obs.*

1594 Hooker *Eccl. Pol.* III. viii. (1611) 97 They never vse reason so willingly as to disgrace reason. 1595 T. Edwards *Cephalus & Procris* (1878) 45 For he that sorrow hath possest, at last In telling of his tale is quite disgra'st.

†6. To speak of dishonouringly; to reprobate, disparage, revile, vilify, speak slightingly of. *Obs.*

1589 Puttenham *Eng. Poesie* I. xix. (Arb.) 57 Such.. would peraduenture reproue and disgrace euery Romance, or short historicall ditty. *c* 1611 Chapman *Iliad* I. 24 The general..viciously disgrac'd With violent terms the priest. 1612 Drayton *Poly-olb.* vi. Notes 93 A Patriot, and so true, that it to death him greeues To heare his Wales disgrac't. 1671 Baxter *Holiness Design Chr.* lxiv. 19 They all agree to cry down sin in the general and to disgrace it. 1720 *Lett. fr. London Jrnl.* (1721) 46 Again he disgraces the Ale.

7. To bring (as an incidental consequence) shame, dishonour, or discredit upon; to be a disgrace or shame to; to reflect dishonour upon.

[1580 Sidney *Arcadia* (1622) 236 Leauing only Mopsa behind, who disgraced weeping with her countenance.] 1593 Shaks. *Lucr.* 718 Against himself he sounds this doom, That through the length of times he stands disgraced. 1600 —— *A.Y.L.* II. iv. 4, I could finde in my heart to disgrace my mans apparell, and to cry like a woman. 1608 D. T. *Ess. Pol. & Mor.* 116 b, Often..such as became a meaner part well, have failed in a greater, and disgraced it. 1752 Johnson *Rambler* No. 196 ¶7 Of his children..some may disgrace him by their follies. 1784 Cowper *Tiroc.* 531 Such vicious habits as disgrace his name. 1849 Macaulay *Hist. Eng.* I. 187 The atrocities which had disgraced the insurrection of Ulster. 1868 J. H. Blunt *Ref. Ch. Eng.* I. 479 The most cruel act against heretics that disgraced our Statute Book.

Hence **disˈgraced** *ppl. a.*, **disˈgracing** *vbl. sb.* and *ppl. a.*

1582 N. Lichefield tr. *Castanheda's Conq. E. Ind.* xvii. 45 He thought the same a disgracing vnto him. 1591 Shaks. *Two Gent.* v. iv. 123 Your Grace is welcome to a man disgrac'd. 1592 R. D. *Hypnerotomachia* 94 They would.. fling the same [flowers] in the faces of their pursuing lovers ..maintaining their fained dis-gracings. *a* 1679 Hobbes *Rhet.* II. ii. (1681) 47 Contumely, is the disgracing of another for his own pastime. 1802 Mrs. Jane West *Inf. Father* III. 145 The poor..disgraced Selborne. 1807 Sir R. Wilson *Jrnl.* 12 July in *Life* (1862) II. viii. 309 As Buonaparte passed ..he gave the right-hand file one of his disgracing crosses.

disgraceful (dɪsˈgreɪsfʊl), *a.* [f. prec. sb. + -ful: cf. *graceful.*]

†1. Void of grace, unbecoming, unpleasing: the opposite of *graceful. Obs.*

1591 Shaks. *1 Hen. VI*, I. i. 86 Away with these disgracefull wayling Robes! 1615 G. Sandys *Trav.* 67 A certaine blacke powder..which by the not disgracefull staining of the lids, doth better set forth the whitenesse of the eye. 1702 *Eng. Theophrast.* 180 Whatever is counterfeit grows nauseous and disgraceful, even with those things, which when natural are most graceful and charming.

2. Full of, or fraught with, disgrace; that brings disgrace upon the agent; shameful, dishonourable, disreputable.

1597 Daniel *Civ. Wars* v. lxiv, Stained with black disgraceful crimes. *a* 1744 Pope (J.), To retire behind their chariots was as little disgraceful then, as it is now to alight from one's horse in a battle. 1794 Southey *Botany-Bay Ecl.* iii, The poor soldier..goes In disgraceful retreat through a country of foes. 1874 Green *Short Hist.* iv. §3. 185 The disgraceful submission of their leaders. 1892 Sir A. Kekewich in *Law Times' Rep.* 140/1, I do think it is disgraceful for directors to..issue such a prospectus.

3. Inflicting disgrace, disgracing, degrading, opprobrious, contumelious. a. Of actions.

1640 Bp. Hall *Rem. Wks.* (1660) 39 Our speculative skill is wont to be upbraided to us, in a disgracefull comparison of our unanswerable practise. 1651 [see disgrace *sb.* 1 c]. 1764 Foote *Patron* III. Wks. 1799 I. 358 Such disgraceful, such contemptible treatment! 1836 H. Coleridge *North. Worthies* (1852) I. 49 It does not appear that Sir Samuel.. ever submitted to this disgraceful punishment.

†b. Of words. *Obs.*

1608–11 Bp. Hall *Medit. & Vowes* I. §52 In the revenge of a disgracefull word against themselves. 1611 Cotgr. s.v. *Vilenie, Laide Vilenie,* slaunderous, reproachfull, disgracefull, defamatorie tearmes. 1613 Sir F. Cottington in Ellis *Orig. Lett.* Ser. I. III. 109 If any of base qualyty shall use disgracefull wordes unto a Jintleman, he is..sent to the gallies. 1774 Sir J. Reynolds *Disc.* VI. (1876) 383 These terrific and disgraceful epithets with which the poor imitators are so often loaded.

disgracefully (dɪsˈgreɪsfəlɪ), *adv.* [f. prec. + -ly[2].] In a disgraceful manner, with disgrace; shamefully, ignominiously. †Formerly also, With opprobrium, opprobriously, contumeliously.

1604 Hieron *Wks.* I. 478 Some of whom to my griefe I haue heard speake very disgracefully, some very scornefully. *a* 1661 Fuller *Worthies* (1840) III. 11 The scholars of Oxford took up the body of the wife of Peter Martyr, who formerly had been disgracefully buried in a dunghill. 1781 Cowper *Expost.* 663 His [name] that seraphs tremble at, is hung Disgracefully on every trifler's tongue. 1893 J. Strong *New Era* xvi. 357 Its progress is painfully and disgracefully slow. *Mod.* The work has been disgracefully scamped.

disˈgracefulness. [f. as prec. + -ness.] The quality or condition of being disgraceful; shamefulness, ignominy.

1581 Sidney *Apol. Poetrie* (Arb.) 61 These men..by their owne disgracefulnes, disgrace the most graceful Poesie. 1841 Lane *Arab. Nts.* III. 486, I knew..that there was no disgracefulness in him..the turpitude and disgracefulness were in my sister. 1880 *Daily News* 9 Jan. 5/2 Barbarous as hanging is, its disgracefulness and horror possibly act as deterrent influences.

†**disˈgracement.** *Obs.* [f. disgrace *v.* + -ment.] The action of disgracing; also, *concr.* that which causes disgrace.

1561 T. Norton *Calvin's Inst.* I. 1 Synce we haue ben spoyled of the diuine apparell, our shameful nakedness discloseth an infinite heape of filthy disgracementes. 1581 J. Bell *Haddon's Answ. Osor.* 454 Defacinges and disgracements of Religion. 1647 H. More *Poems* 169 That disgracement of Philosophie..this Theorie Might take 't away.

disgracer (dɪsˈgreɪsə(r)). [f. as prec. + -er[1].] One who or that which disgraces; one that exposes to shame or causes ignominy; †an opprobrious reviler (*obs.*).

1570 Dee *Math. Pref.* 46 The..continuall disgracer of Gods Veritie. 1589 Nashe *Almond for Parrat* 15 a, He began to..shew himselfe openly a studious disgracer of antiquitie. 1660 R. Coke *Power & Subj.* 267 A Reproacher or disgracer of his Majesties Government. 1732 Swift *Exam. Abuses Dublin*, I have given good advice to those infamous disgracers of their sex. 1789 Mrs. Piozzi *Journ. France* I. 382 Who..were such disgracers of human nature.

‖**disgracia, -grazia.** [Sp. *desgracia* (-graθja) disgrace, misfortune, unpleasantness, It. *disgrazia* (-gratsja), formerly *disgratia.*] An unpleasant accident, misfortune.

1739 Cibber *Apol.* (1756) I. 114 When it has been his ill fortune to meet with a disgraccia. 1845 Ld. Campbell *Chancellors* (1857) IV. lxxxix. 174 This disgrazia happened from meeting a line of brewer's drays at Charing Cross.

†**disˈgraciately,** *adv. Obs. rare*[−1]. [as if f. *disgraciate adj., ad. It. *disgraziato*, in Florio *disgratiato* 'graceless'.] Ill-favouredly, unhappily, unpleasingly.

a 1734 North *Exam.* I. i. §28 All this he would most disgraciately obtrude by his quaint Touch of 'confirming all'.

disgracious (dɪsˈgreɪʃəs), *a.* Also 6–7 -tious. [a. F. *disgracieux* (1518 in Hatz.-Darm.), f. dis- 4 + *gracieux*, perh. after It. *disgrazioso* 'graceless, full of disgrace', (Florio): cf. gracious.]

1. Ungracious, unfavourable, unkind. ? *Obs.*

1598 J. Dickenson *Greene in Conc.* (1878) 144 Deigne rather to quicken them by a gracious regard, then to kill them by a disgratious repulse. 1603 Breton *Dign. or Ind. Men* 207 What indignities are these to prove the disgratious Nature of Man? 1837 *New Monthly Mag.* XLIX. 343 Any one of the disgracious cavillers.

†2. Out of favour; in disfavour; disliked. *Obs.*

1594 Shaks. *Rich. III*, III. vii. 112 I doe suspect I haue done some offence, That seemes disgracious in the Cities eye. *Ibid.* IV. iv. 177 If I be so disgracious in your eye, Let me march on, and not offend you, Madam. 1611 Speed *Hist. Gt. Brit.* IX. xvi. (1632) 849 As for these causes he was in highest grace with the King, so hee was the more disgracious or hated of the people.

†3. Disgraceful, shameful. *Obs.*

1615 *Trades Incr.* in *Harl. Misc.* (Malh.) III. 308 The lazy and disgracious merchandise of our coasters.

4. Without grace of manner; uncomely; unbecoming.

1870 Morier *Rep. Land Tenure* in *Parl. Papers* CLXIII. 202, I heard general complaints..of their [the women's] disgracious attempts to follow the fashions.

†**disˈgraciously,** *adv. Obs.* [f. prec. + -ly[2].] In a disgracious manner; with disgrace or indignity; without grace, ungraciously.

1618 *Hist. P. Warbeck* in *Select. Harl. Misc.* (1793) 95 He read it in publick, and that so disgraciously [etc.]. 1619

Time's Storehouse ii. 182 (L.) All..were eyther at last disgraciously killed, or else receyved some great overthrow.

†**dis'gracive,** *a. Obs. rare.* [irreg. f. DISGRACE *v.* + -IVE: cf. *coercive.*] Conveying or tending to disgrace or reproach; disgraceful, shameful.

1602 BOYS *Wks.* 412 The Syrian *raca*, which is a disgracive term. **1627** FELTHAM *Resolves* I. xxvii. 47 They are unwisely ashamed of an ignorance, which is not disgraciue. *Ibid.* I. lxxviii. 120 He that will question euery disgraciue word, which he hears is spoken of him, shall haue much trouble.

disgradation (dɪsgrə'deɪʃən). ? *Obs.* [n. of action f. DISGRADE *v.*] Punitive deprivation of rank, degree, or dignity; = DEGRADATION[1] I.

1727-51 CHAMBERS *Cycl., Degradation*, in our law-books called disgradation, and deposition. [Not in *Termes de la Ley*, Cowell, Blount, who have *disgrade*, but not *disgradation.*] **1861** W. BELL *Dict. Law Scot.* 291/2 Disgradation, Deposition, or Degradation; the stripping a person for ever of a dignity or degree of honour.

disgrade (dɪs'greɪd), *v.* Also 5-6 **dysgrade, dis-, dysgrate,** 6 **desgrade.** [ad. OF. *desgrader*, by-form of *degrader*, ad. late L. *dēgradāre*, Pr. *degradar, desgradar*: for frequent Romanic interchange of *de-, des-*, see DE- I. 6.] *trans.* To depose formally, as a punitive measure, from honourable rank, degree, or dignity; = DEGRADE *v.* 2.

*c***1430** LYDG. *Bochas* VIII. i. (1554) 177b, Fortune list him to disgrade Among his knightes. **1569** NEWTON *Cicero's Olde Age* 28b, Sore against my will was it, when I deposed and dysgraded L. Flaminius of his senatourship. **1611** SPEED *Hist. Gt. Brit.* IX xvii. (1632) 869 He was first solemnly disgraded, his guilt spurs cut from his heeles by the Master-Cooke. **1880** DIXON *Windsor* III. vii. 67 Voted that the late duke be disgraded from his dignity as a knight. **1888** *Circular to Senate by Coll. of Med. Durham Univ.*, Supposing the Durham University to possess already the power to disgrade its Graduates.

b. To deprive of ecclesiastical status; = DEGRADE *v.* 2b.

*c***1380** WYCLIF *Wks.* (1880) 246 Ony symple mon..schal be enprisoned, disgratid or brent. **1460** CAPGRAVE *Chron.* 112 Formosus..was disgraded be Jon the Pope fro all the ordres of the Cherch onto lay astat. **1586** *Exam. H. Barrowe, etc.* in *Harl. Misc.* (Malh.) II. 28 *Q.* Are yow a Minister? *A.* No, I was one after your orders. *Q.* Who disgraded yow? *A.* I disgraded my self through Gods mercy by repentance. **1641** PRYNNE *Antip.* 98 They did not disgrade and deprive from holy Orders such Malefactors.

Hence **dis'graded** *ppl. a.*, **dis'grading** *vbl. sb.*

1531-2 *Act 23 Hen. VIII*, c. 1 A certificat under his seale testifiynge the said disgradinge. **1546** BALE *Eng. Votaries* II. Liv (T. s.v. *Degrade*), He once yet againe departed the realme with his disgraded abbots. **1602** SEGAR *Hon. Mil. & Civ.* II. iv. 55 The King of Armes and other Heralds cast the warme water vpon the disgraded Knights face..saying Henceforth thou shalt be called by thy right name, Traitour. **1641** *Termes de la Ley* (1708) 257 By the Canon Law there are two kinds of Disgradings; the one summary, by word only, and the other solemn, by Devesting the party disgraded from..the Ensigns of his Order or Degree.

†**dis'gradement.** *Obs. rare*$^{-1}$. [f. prec. + -MENT.] = DISGRADATION; DEGRADATION[1] I.

1538 FITZHERB. *Just. Peas* 107b, With certifycat therof under his seall testifyenge the sayde dysgradement.

†**dis'grader.** *Obs. rare*$^{-1}$. [f. as prec. + -ER[1].] One who degrades from a position of honour.

*a***1603** T. CARTWRIGHT *Confut. Rhem. N.T.* Pref. (1618) 17 Disgracers and disgraders of the Scripture haue taught men to say, that the copies are corrupted.

†**dis'graduate,** *v. Obs.* [f. DIS- 7b + GRADUATE *sb.*] *trans.* To depose from a degree or dignity, deprive of rank or privilege; = DISGRADE, DEGRADUATE.

1528 TINDALE *Obed. Chr. Man* 73b, Yf they be of mine anointed, and beare my marke, disgresse them (I wold saye, disgraduate them). **1550** NICOLLS *Thucyd.* 135 (R.) The saide Lacedemonions did desgraduate and declaire those to be deffamed and dishonoured, that were takene by the Athenyans in the Islande.

†**dis'gree,** *v. Obs. rare.* [a. OF. *desgre-er* (Froissart) to disagree, f. *des-*, DIS- 4 + *gréer* to agree: see GREE *v.*] *intr.* To be out of agreement or harmony; to DISAGREE.

1530 PALSGR. 519/1, I disgre, I agre a mysse, as syngars do, or one note with an other..These synggyng men disgree.

†**dis'greement.** *Obs. rare.* [f. prec. + -MENT.] Discord, DISAGREEMENT.

1503 HAWES *Examp. Virt.* vii. 148 Without disgrement or contradiccyon.

disgregate ('dɪsgrɪgeɪt), *v.* [f. L. *disgregāt-*, ppl. stem of *disgregāre* to separate, f. DIS- 1 + *greg-em* (*grex*) flock, *gregāre* to collect (in a flock).] Hence '**disgregated** *ppl. a.*

†**1.** *trans.* To separate, sunder, sever (*from*).

1593 NASHE *Christ's T.* 64b, It pleased our louing crucified Lord..to disgregate his gifts from the ordinarie meanes.

2. To separate into individual parts, disintegrate.

1603 HOLLAND *Plutarch's Mor.* 630 (R.) Heat doth loosen, disgregate, scatter, and dissolve all thick things. **1660** STANLEY *Hist. Philos.* IX. (1701) 422/1 Heat seems to consist of rare parts, and disgregates bodies. **1726** MONRO *Anat. Nerves* (1741) 4 The Dura Mater is closely wrapt round them, to collect their disgregated Fibres.

†**3.** According to obsolete theories of vision: To scatter or make divergent (the visual rays); hence, to dazzle, confuse, or dim (the sight). *Obs.*

*a***1631** DONNE *Serm.* xcvi. IV. 245 The beames of their eyes were scattered and disgregated..so as that they could not confidently discern him. *c***1645** HOWELL *Lett.* II. li, Her sight is presently dazled and disgregated with the refulgency. *Ibid.* I. VI. lv, Black doth congregat, unite and fortifie the sight; the other doth disgregat, scatter and enfeeble it.

disgregation (dɪsgrɪ'geɪʃən). [n. of action f. prec.: see -ATION.] Separation of individuals from a company, or of component parts from a whole mass; disintegration, dispersal; *spec.* in *Chem.* separation of the molecules of a substance by heat or other agency.

1611 FLORIO *Disgregatione*, a scattering, a disgregation. *a***1626** BP. ANDREWES in Southey *Com.-pl. Bk.* Ser. I. (1850) 354 Without it [concord] a *gregation* it may be, but no *congregation*. The *con* is gone; a *disgregation* rather. **1653** MANTON *Exp. James.* v. 9 In troubles there are not so many scatterings and disgregations in Christ's flock. **1684** tr. *Bonet's Merc. Compit.* XIX. 763 These Diseases do presuppose a Disgregation of Humours. **1865** GROTE *Plato* I. i. 56 The partial disgregation of the chaotic mass.

disgress, -ion, obs. ff. DIGRESS, -ION.

†**dis'gress,** *v. Obs. rare*$^{-1}$. [? f. DIS- 7a + L. *gressus* step, taken as = *gradus* step, degree, position; and hence a synonym of DISGRADE. (Or possibly an early corrupt form of DISGRACE *v.*)]

1528 [see DISGRADUATE].

†**disgross** (dɪs'grəʊs), *v. Obs.* [ad. 16th c. F. *desgrossir, desgrosser* 'to lessen, make small, fine, or less grosse, to polish, refine' (Cotgr. 1611), mod.F. *dégrossir*, f. *des-*, DIS- 4 + *gros, grosse* thick, big, GROSS.] *trans.* To make finer or less gross; *spec.* applied to the initial reduction in thickness of metal bars that are to be made into wire.

1611 FLORIO *Disgrossamento*, a refining, a disgrossing. **1636** *Patent Rolls* 7 May, Fyning, refyning, disgrossing..of all gold and silver. **1662** PETTY *Taxes* 85 If bullion be wrought into plate and utensils, or disgrost into wire or lace. **1687** M. TAUBMAN *Lendon's Tri.* 6 In another apartment is ..Disgrossing, Flatting and Drawing of Gold..Wyre. **1823** HONE *Anc. Myst.* 250.

b. *fig.* (unless misread for *disqwss*, DISCUSS).

1546 *St. Papers Hen. VIII*, XI. 330 The matters..beyng not before disgrossed and brought to a conclusion.

†**dis'grubble,** *v. Obs. rare.* [f. DIS- 5 + **grubble*, perh. for *grumble.*] = DISGRUNTLE.

1689 C. HATTON 16 Apr. in *H. Corr.* (1878) II. 131 Sr R^{t} Atkins is soe disgrubbl'd not to be Ch. J. of y^{e} Com. Pleases y^{t} he sath he will not have his brothers scimm milke.

disgruntle (dɪs'grʌnt(ə)l), *v.* [f. DIS- 5 + GRUNTLE *v.* freq. of GRUNT]. *trans.* To put into sulky dissatisfaction or ill-humour; to chagrin, disgust. Chiefly in *pa. pple.*

1682 H. CAVE *Hist. Popery* IV. 79 Hodge was a little disgruntled at that Inscription. *a***1683** SIR P. WARWICK *Mem. Chas. I* (1701) 226 [He] would not be sent unto her house..which the Lady was much disgruntled at. **1726** AMHERST *Terræ Fil.* xlviii. 256 M'Phelim finds his prince a little disgruntled. **1862** C. THORNTON *Conyers Lea* xii. 224 The fair Tabitha retired to her room somewhat disgruntled. **1884** *Lisbon* (Dakota) *Star* 18 July, [He] is very much disgruntled at Cleveland's nomination.

Hence **dis'gruntled** *ppl. a.*; also **dis'gruntlement,** moody discontent.

1847-78 HALLIW., *Disgruntled*, discomposed. *Glouc.* **1889** *Voice* (N.Y.) 12 Sept., Partisans in all stages of disgruntlement were wandering aimlessly about. **1891** BRYCE in *Contemp. Rev.* Jan., A melancholy or gloomy or —to use an expressive American term—a 'disgruntled' temper.

disguisal (dɪs'gaɪzəl). *rare.* [f. DISGUISE *v.* + -AL[1].] The action of disguising.

1652 COTTERELL tr. *Cassandra* III. 208 To open his heart to her without any disguisal. **1834** *Tait's Mag.* I. 488 The covering invented for their disguisal.

disguise (dɪs'gaɪz), *v.* Forms: 4 **degise,** (**-gyse, desgyze**), 4-5 **des-, disgise, -gyse, dysguyse,** 5-6 **disguyse,** 5-7 **desguise,** 5- **disguise,** (6 **disgease,** 6-7 **disguize**; *Sc.* 6 **dis(s)agyse, dissagyiss**). [ME. *desgise-n, degise-n*, etc., a. OF. *desguisier, deguisier* (11th c. in Littré), later *desguiser*, mod.F. *déguiser*, = Pr. *desguisar*, f. *des-, de-* (DE- I. 6) + Romanic (It., Sp., Pg., Pr.) *guisa*, F. *guise* (11th c.), a. OHG. *wîsa* manner, mode, appearance (cf. WISE *sb.*): the primary sense was thus 'to put out of one's usual guise, manner, or mode (of dress, etc.).']

†**1.** *trans.* To alter the guise or fashion of dress and appearance of (any one); *esp.* to dress in a fashion different from what has been customary or considered appropriate to position, etc.; to dress up fantastically or ostentatiously; to deck out. *Obs.*

*c***1325** *Poem Times Edw. II*, 255 in *Pol. Songs* (Camden) 335 Nu ben theih so degysed and diverseliche i-diht, Unnethe may men knowe a gleman from a kniht. **1362** LANGL. *P. Pl.* A. Prol. 24 In Cuntinaunce of cloþinge queinteliche de-gyset. *c***1400** *Rom. Rose* 2250 He that loveth trewely Shulde..hym disgysen in queyntyse. **1480** CAXTON *Chron. Eng.* ccxix. 209 Mortimer disgised him with wonder riche clothes out of al maner reson both of shapyng and of weryng. **1539** T. CHAPMAN in *Chron. Gr. Friars* (Camden) p. xv, The perfeccion of Christian livyng dothe not consiste in dome ceremonyes..disgeasing our selffes aftyr straunge fassions. **1563** *Hom.* II. *Exc. Appar.* (1859) 312 Many men care not what they spend in disguising themselves, ever.. inventing new fashions.

†**2.** To make different in manner, mode, or dress (*from* others). *Obs.*

1340 *Ayenb.* 97 Hi is zoþliche newe and desgised uram oþre laȝes. *c***1430** LYDG. *Min. Poems* 90 (Mätz.) Amonges wymmen he spanne, In theyre habyte disguysed from a man. **1555** WATREMAN *Fardle Facions* II. iv. 143 Thei ware disguised fro ye commune maner of other.

†**3.** To transform; to alter in appearance (*from* the proper or natural manner, shape, etc.); to disfigure. *Obs.*

1393 GOWER *Conf.* I. 16 þei scholden noght..The Papacie so desguise vpon diuerse eleccion. **1535** COVERDALE *Ecclus.* xii. 18 Whyle he maketh many wordes, he shall dysguyse his countenaunce. ? *a***1550** *Dunbar's Poems, Freiris Berwick* 474 Bot gif it wer on sic a maner wyiss Him to translait or ellis dissagyiss Fra his awin kynd in-to ane vder stait. **1579** TOMSON *Calvin's Serm. Tim.* 49/2 He [Saint Paul] reproveth his enimies which disguised the lawe of God. **1593** SHAKS. *Lucr.* 1452 Her cheeks with chaps and wrinkles were disguised; Of what she was no semblance did remain. **1697** DRYDEN *Æneid* (J.), They saw the faces, which too well they knew, Though then disguised in death.

4. To change the guise, or dress and personal appearance, of (any one) so as to conceal identity; to conceal the identity of by dressing *as* some one or *in* a particular garb. (Now the leading sense.)

*c***1350** *Will. Palerne* 1677, & ȝef ȝe were disgised & diȝt on any wise..ȝe wold be aspied. **1393** GOWER *Conf.* II. 227 She cast in her wit..Hou she him mighte so desguise That no man shuld his body know. **1535** STEWART *Cron. Scot.* III. 207 Robert the Bruce wnder the levis grene..Oft disagysit in ane sempill weid. **1555** EDEN *Decades* 176 They come disguised in an other habite. **1603** KNOLLES *Hist. Turks* (1638) 63 Disguised in the habit of a Turk. **1720** GAY *Poems* (1745) II. 167 The shepherd's garb the woman shall disguise. *c***1850** *Arab. Nts.* (Rtldg.) 297 She disguised him in woman's clothes. **1882** FREEMAN *Amer. Lect.* v. 153 A friend disguised in the garb of an enemy. *Mod.* He attempted to escape disguised as a monk.

b. *refl.*

1340 *Ayenb.* 158 Ine hou uele wyzen he [þe dyeuel] him desgyzeþ. *c***1374** CHAUCER *Troylus* v. 1570 (1577) Yn purpos gret, Hym self lyk a Pylgrym to degyse. **1535** COVERDALE *1 Kings* xiv. 2 Disguise the, so that no man perceaue that thou art Ieroboams wyfe. **1535** LYNDESAY *Satyre* 721 Wee man turne our claithis..And dis-agyse vs, that na man ken vs. **1611** BIBLE *1 Kings* xx. 38 The prophet..disguised himselfe with ashes vpon his face. **1847** MRS. A. KERR *Hist. Servia* xvi. 299 The wife of Milosch was obliged to disguise herself in the dress of a Servian female peasant.

5. To alter the appearance of (anything) so as to mislead or deceive as to it; to exhibit in a false light; to colour; to misrepresent.

1398 TREVISA *Barth. de P.R.* XVII. vi. (Tollem. MS.), This Aloe Caballinum is disgised [*sophisticatur*] with pouder of safron and vynegre, yf it is ten siþes plungid þerin, and dryed. **1623** LD. HERBERT in Ellis *Orig. Lett.* Ser. I. III. 166 To palliate and disguise those thinges which it concernes them to knowe. **1669** GALE *Crt. Gentiles* I. I. ii. 11 Plato's custome to desguise the Traditions he received from the Jews. **1732** LEDIARD *Sethos* II. VII. 127 Some merchants endeavour to disguise and put off a bad commodity. **1855** MACAULAY *Hist. Eng.* IV. 254 To speak the truth, that was to say, substantial truth, a little disguised and coloured.

6. To conceal or cloak the real state or character of (anything) by a counterfeit show or appearance.

1599 SHAKS. *Hen. V*, III. i. 8 Then imitate the action of the Tyger..Disguise fair Nature with hard-fauour'd Rage. **1681** DRYDEN *Abs. & Achit.* 740 This moving Court, that caught the Peoples Eyes, And seem'd but Pomp, did other Ends disguise. **1726** *Adv. Capt. R. Boyle* 104, I think to disguise our Thoughts is an Art better lost, than learnt. **1853** SIR H. DOUGLAS *Milit. Bridges* (ed. 3) 203 A feint to disguise the real intention. **1856** EMERSON *Eng. Traits, Race* Wks. (Bohn) II. 32 The horse finds out who is afraid of it, and does not disguise its opinion.

7. To conceal or hide (a material thing) by any superficial coating or operation.

1591 SYLVESTER *Du Bartas* I. ii. 165 Yet think not, that this Too-too-Much remises Ought into nought; it but the Form disguises In hundred fashions. **1738** WESLEY *Hymns*, '*All Praise to Him*' ii, The deepest shades no more disguise Than the full Blaze of Day. **1791** HAMILTON *Berthollet's Dyeing* I. I. I. iv. 66 The colouring particles..are there disguised by an alkali. **1820** SCORESBY *Acc. Arctic Reg.* I. 116 An insulated cliff..being nearly perpendicular, is never disguised with snow.

b. To conceal the identity of under a different name or title.

1639 S. DU VERGER tr. *Camus' Admir. Events* 50 Whom we will disguise under the name of Anaclete. **1806** SURR *Winter in Lond.* (ed. 3) I. 69 The new title..did not disguise the old friend.

8. *Electr.* To conceal the presence of by neutralization; to dissimulate. (Usually in *passive.*)

1839 G. BIRD *Nat. Philos.* §278 When two insulated conducting bodies are differently electrified, and approached towards each other, so as to be within the influence of their mutual attraction..no signs of electricity are communicated by either to a pith ball electrometer connected with them.. The electric fluids are thus said to become disguised, or paralysed, by their mutual attractive action. *Ibid.* §288 On turning the machine, the positive electricity accumulating in the inside of the battery becomes disguised by the inducting action of the outside coating.

9. To intoxicate (with liquor). *arch.* (pa. pple. still in *slang* use: see DISGUISED 6).

1562 J. HEYWOOD *Prov. & Epigr.* (1867) 184 Three cuppes full at once shall oft dysgyse thee. **1618** DELONEY *Gentle Craft* (1648) H iv b, We will get him out to the tavern and there cause him to be disguised, that he shall neither be able to stand nor go. **1712** tr. *Pomet's Hist. Drugs* I. 138 It may so stupifie and disguise them, that they may be the more easily master'd. **1806–7** J. BERESFORD *Miseries Hum. Life* (1826) xx. 250 Sure, fuddling a trade is Not lovely in Ladies, Since it thus can disguise a Soft sylph like Eliza.

†**10.** *intr.* To dissemble. *Obs.*

1580 SIDNEY *Arcadia* (1622) 97 Zelmane.. disguise not with me in words, as I know thou doest in apparell. **1586** A. DAY *Eng. Secretary* II. (1625) 24 But if I should.. tell you.. you might thinke I did not then disguize with you.

disguise (dɪsˈgaɪz), *sb.* Also 4 **degise, -yse,** 7 **disguize.** [f. DISGUISE *v.*]

†**1.** Alteration of the fashion of dress from that which has been usual; new or strange fashion (esp. of an ostentatious kind). *Obs.*

1340 HAMPOLE *Pr. Consc.* 1518 In pompe and pride and vanite, In selcouthe maners and sere degyse þat now es used of many wyse. *Ibid.* 1524 For swilk degises and suilk maners .. Byfor þis tyme ne has noght ben. **1594** LODGE *Wounds Civ. War* in Hazl. *Dodsley* VII. 143 Prisoners of divers nations and sundry disguises.

2. a. Altered fashion of dress and personal appearance intended to conceal the wearer's identity; the state of being thus transformed in appearance for concealment's sake.

13.. *Coer de L.* 962 The kyng hym [a baroun] tolde.. Hou he founde hym [Rychard] in disguise. **1605** SHAKS. *Lear* v. iii. 220 The banish'd Kent; who, in disguise, Follow'd his enemy king, and did him service. **1659** B. HARRIS *Parival's Iron Age* 214 In this extremity he left that City in disguise. **1726** *Adv. Capt. R. Boyle* 125 His manner of going to the Appointment was in Disguise. **1758** JOHNSON *Idler* No. 29 ¶6 They concluded me a gentlewoman in disguise. *a* **1839** PRAED *Poems* (1864) I. 8 'Twas a Fairy in disguise.

b. *fig.* A disguised condition or form. See also BLESSING *vbl. sb.* 4 c.

1709 *Celebr. Beauties* 10 in *Poet. Miscell.* (Tonson) VI. 514 Praise undeserv'd is Scandal in Disguise. **1742** YOUNG *Nt. Th.* VII. 52 His grief is but his grandeur in disguise. **1751** JOHNSON *Rambler* No. 184 ¶12 None can tell whether the good that he pursues is not evil in disguise. *Mod.* A blessing in disguise.

3. a. 'A dress contrived to conceal the person that wears it' (J.); a garb assumed in order to deceive.

1596 SPENSER *F.Q.* v. vii. 21 Magnificke Virgin, that in queint disguise Of British armes dost maske thy royall blood. **1596** SHAKS. *1 Hen. IV*, II. ii. 78 Ned, where are our disguises? **1667** E. CHAMBERLAYNE *St. Gr. Brit.* I. (1684) 120 In 1648 [the Duke] was.. conveyed in a Disguise or Habit of a girl beyond sea. **1849** JAMES *Woodman* xiii, Now I bring you your disguise. **1875** JOWETT *Plato* (ed. 2) I. 395 You were wrapped in a goatskin or some other disguise.

b. *transf.* and *fig.*

1655 STANLEY *Hist. Philos.* I. (1701) 1/2 Their glory being intercepted.. by some later disguise of alteration or addition. *a* **1674** CLARENDON *Surv. Leviath.* (1676) 193 Without any other clothing or disguise of words. **1789** BELSHAM *Ess.* II. xxxiv. 248 This high-sounding language is merely the splendid disguise of ignorance. **1876** MOZLEY *Univ. Serm.* iv. 82 The passion obliged to act under a disguise becomes different in its nature from the open one.

4. Any artificial manner assumed for deception; a false appearance, a counterfeit semblance or show; deception.

1632 J. HAYWARD tr. *Biondi's Eromena* 36 The Pilot (all disguise laid aside) said unto him. *a* **1655** VINES *Lord's Supp.* (1677) 155 Naked of all humane disguizes. **1781** COWPER *Charity* 558 No works shall find acceptance, in that day When all disguises shall be rent away That square not truly with the Scripture plan. **1838** THIRLWALL *Greece* V. xliii. 273 Philomelus now threw off all disguise. **1865** G. MEREDITH *Rhoda Fleming* vi, Perfect candour can do more for us than a dark disguise.

5. The act or practice of disguising; concealment of the reality under a specious appearance.

1603 SHAKS. *Meas. for M.* III. ii. 294 So disguise shall by th' disguised Pay with falshood false exacting. **1647** CLARENDON *Hist. Reb.* VI. (1843) 373/2 Nor could he have been led into it.. by any open.. temptation, but by a thousand disguises and cozenages. *a* **1720** POPE *Chorus Youths & Virgins* 38 Hence false tears, deceits, disguises. **1746** WESLEY *Princ. Methodist* 9 With regard to Subtlety, Evasion, and Disguise. **1834** MEDWIN *Angler in Wales* I. 252 Thou friend.. to whom I communicate without disguise the inmost secrets of my breast. **1876** MOZLEY *Univ. Serm.* ii. 32 The heathen defied the law within him. There was no disguise in Paganism.

†**6.** A masque; = DISGUISING 3. *Obs.*

1622 B. JONSON *Masque of Augurs* Wks. (Rtldg.) 630/2 Disguise was the old English word for a Masque. **1622** BACON *Hen. VII*, 245 Masques (which they then called Disguises). *c* **1630** MILTON *Passion* iii, O what a mask was there, what a disguise.

7. 'Disorder by drink' (Johnson).

1606 SHAKS. *Ant. & Cl.* II. vii. 131 Strong Enobarbe Is weaker then the Wine, and mine owne tongue Spleet's what it speakes: the wilde disguise hath almost Antickt vs all. **1622** B. JONSON *Masque of Augurs* Wks. (Rtldg.) 630/1 Disguise! what mean you by that? do you think that his majesty sits here to expect drunkards?

8. *Electr.* See DISGUISE *v.* 8.

1839 G. BIRD *Nat. Phil.* §286 In accordance with the conditions of the induction and disguise of electricity, it is obvious that an insulated jar cannot be charged.

disguised (dɪsˈgaɪzd), *ppl. a.* [f. DISGUISE *v.* + -ED[1].]

†**1.** Changed from the usual or natural guise or fashion: **a.** disfigured; **b.** altered in fashion of dress for the sake of modish display. *Obs.*

1393 GOWER *Conf.* III. 260 They sigh her clothes all disguised.. Her haire hangend unkempt about. *c* **1430** *Pilgr. Lyf Manhode* IV. ii. (1869) 175 þilke beste was disgised so vileliche, and so foule figured. **1563** *Homilies* II. *Excess of Apparel* (1859) 312 The haughty stomacks of the daughters of England are so maintained with divers disguised sorts of costly apparell, that [etc.]. **1589** PEELE *Tale Troy* 27 Where ladies troop'd in rich disguised attire.

†**2.** Of dress, etc.: Altered in fashion or assumed for the sake of concealing the identity of the wearer or bearer. *Obs.*

1413 *Pilgr. Sowle* (Caxton 1483) III. ii. 51 These haue ben feyned Religyous ypocrites with theyr desguysed clothes. *a* **1533** LD. BERNERS *Huon* ix. 23 Charlot had a dysgysyd shylde bycause he wolde not be knowen. **1548** HALL *Chron., Hen. VI.* an. 28. 161 Mistrustyng the sequele of yͤ matter, [he] departed secretly in habite disguysed, into Sussex. **1608** D. T. *Ess. Pol. & Mor.* 98 Wine.. doth.. unbare us of that disguis'd, and personated habit, under the which we are accustomed to marche. **1660** BLOUNT *Boscobel* 51 Procur'd him a pass from the Rebel commanders in a disguised name.

3. Of persons, etc.: Dressed in a strange or assumed garb, or having the appearance otherwise changed, for the sake of concealing identity.

1393 GOWER *Conf.* III. 62 And he disguised fledde away By ship. **1599** MARSTON *Sco. Villanie* I. ii. 175 Disguised Gods.. in pesants shape Prest to commit some execrable rape. **1639** T. BRUGIS tr. *Camus' Moral Relat.* 346 Finding no safety in high Germany.. we came downe disguised into this inferiour Germany. **1843** PRESCOTT *Mexico* (1850) I. 332 He.. lay in ambush, directing the disguised Spaniards .. to make signals. **1874** MORLEY *Compromise* (1886) 180 The congregation in the old story were untouched by the disguised devil's eloquence.. it lacked unction.

4. Of a thing, etc.: Altered in outward form so as to appear other than it is.

1590 SPENSER *F.Q.* III. ii. 4 What inquest made her dissemble her disguised kind? **1632** LITHGOW *Trav.* III. 119 We may easily be deceived, by disguised and pretended reasons. **1862** H. SPENCER *First Princ.* I. v. §33 (1875) 120 Convinced as he is that all punishment.. is but a disguised beneficence. **1878** BROWNING *La Saisiaz* 30 Hindrance proved but help disguised.

†**5.** Concealed or hidden so as not to appear.

1594 MARLOWE & NASHE *Dido* I. i. Here in this bush disguised will I stand. **1677** MRS. BEHN *Rover* III. i, Oh! he lay disguized.

6. Intoxicated; drunk, tipsy. *arch. slang.*

1607 DELONEY *Strange Hist.* (1841) 14 The saylors and the shipmen all, through foule excesse of wine, Were so disguisde that at the sea they shewd themselves like swine. **1622** MASSINGER & DEKKER *Virg. Mart.* III. iii, *Har.* I am a prince disguised. *Hir.* Disguised? How? drunk? **1667** DRYDEN *Wild Gallant* I. i, I was a little disguised, as they say .. Well, in short, I was drunk. **1754** CHESTERF. *World* Wks. 1892 V. 293, I never saw him disguised with liquor in my life. **1821** SCOTT *Kenilw.* xxix, What if they see me a little disguised? Wherefore should any man be sober to-night? **1883** W. C. RUSSELL *Jack's Courtship* in *Longm. Mag.* III. 18 A woman, disguised in liquor, with a bonnet on her back. **1884** BESANT *Childr. Gibeon* II. xxi, He was not 'disguised', his speech was clear.

Hence **disˈguisedly** *adv.*, in a disguised manner, in disguise; **disˈguisedness**, disguised state.

1612 BP. HALL *Imprese of God* II. in *Recoll. Treat.* (1614) 674 But alas, the painted faces, and mannishnesse, and monstrous disguisednesse of the one sexe. **1631** WEEVER *Anc. Fun. Mon.* 24 Hee.. fled disguisedly by sea for his owne safety. **1633** PRYNNE *Histrio-Mastix* II. II. ii. (R.) The strange disguisednesse of theatricall attires. **1683** J. BARNARD *Life of Heylin* 172 (L.) He.. studied schism, and faction, by his own example, and his pen disguisedly.

disguiseless (dɪsˈgaɪzlɪs), *a.* [f. DISGUISE *sb.* + -LESS.] Without disguise, undisguised.

1850 BROWNING *Xmas Eve & Easter Day* 232 Naked and disguiseless stayed, And unevadable, the fact. **1878** *Fraser's Mag.* XVII. 427 Nature stood revealed before him, disguiseless, not 'sophisticated'.

disˈguisement. [f. DISGUISE *v.* + -MENT; cf. OF. *desguisement*, mod.F. *dég-*, a disguising, that which serves to disguise.]

1. The fact of disguising, or of being disguised.

1583 GOLDING *Calvin on Deut.* cxi. 684 That they might not be put out of countenance by any faire disguisement. **1632** LITHGOW *Trav.* III. 82 To lend.. an old gowne, and a blacke vaile for his disguisement. **1683** PORDAGE *Myst. Div.* 130 Blessed are they who through all these wiles and disguisements can find him. **1845** *Blackw. Mag.* LVII. 732 No disguisement of natural form is attempted. **1885** *Times* 13 Apr. 4/2 Such disguisement was always a direct infraction of international and military law.

2. That which disguises, or whereby disguising is effected; a disguise; a garb that conceals the wearer's identity.

1580 SIDNEY *Arcadia* (1622) 53 Assuring myselfe, that vnder that disguisement, I should find oportunitie to reueale myselfe to the owner of my heart. **1590** SPENSER *F.Q.* III. vii. 14 What mister wight.. That in so straunge disguizement there did maske. **1801** STRUTT *Sports & Past.* III. iii. 171 Minstrels and persons in disguisements. **1823** LAMB *Elia* (1860) 26 In this disguisement he was brought into the hall. **1861** T. A. TROLLOPE *La Beata* II. xvii. 186 To don a black disguisement, and put our own hands to the work of mercy.

3. *pl.* Additions or accessories that alter the appearance; adornments, bedizenments.

1638 BAKER tr. *Balzac's Lett.* III. (1654) 105 It hath paintings and disguisements, to alter the purity of all worldly things. **1768–74** TUCKER *Lt. Nat.* (1852) II. 153 Stripped of all the disguisements, and foreign mixtures cast upon them. **1867** D. G. MITCHELL *Rur. Stud.* 199 If the charming but costly disguisements of a park cannot be ventured upon at once.

disguiser (dɪsˈgaɪzə(r)). [f. DISGUISE *v.* + -ER[1].] One who disguises. **a.** One who dresses himself up in order to act in a pageant; a masker or mummer, a GUISER.

1481–90 *Howard Househ. Bks.* (Roxb.) 517 Payd.. [for] stuff for dysgysers on Saynt Stevens day.. xvj.d. **1494** FABYAN *Chron.* VII. 558 Fyre was put to the vesturis of the disguysers. **1545** HALL *Chron., Hen. VIII*, an. 10 (R.) Yͤ disguysers dissended from yͭ rock, & daunced a great space.

b. One who or that which changes appearances, and makes things appear other than they are.

1586 T. B. *La Primaud. Fr. Acad.* I. 628 He must use great prudence to discerne flatterers and disguisers of matters. **1603** SHAKS. *Meas. for M.* IV. ii. 186 Oh, death's a great disguiser. **1729** POPE *To Swift* 11 Aug., [He] is quite the reverse to you, unless you are a very dextrous disguiser. **1890** *Temple Bar Mag.* Jan. 22 The two main disguisers and disfigurers of humanity.

†**disˈguisily,** *adv. Obs.* [f. DISGUISY *a.* + -LY[2].] Strangely, extraordinarily.

c **1325** *Orfeo & H.* 322 in D. Laing *Sel. Rem.* (1822), An hundred tours ther were about, Degiselich and bataild stout. *c* **1350** *Will. Palerne* 485 Desparaged were i disgisili ȝif i dede in þis wise. *c* **1430** *Pilgr. Lyf Manhode* I. lxxiv. (1869) 43 To the mille he was born, and disgisyliche grounden.

†**disˈguisiness.** *Obs.* Also **de-.** [f. as prec. + -NESS.] Strangeness of guise or fashion.

c **1386** CHAUCER *Pars. T.* ¶340 Precious clothyng is cowpable.. for his softenesse, and for his strangenesse and degisynesse [*v.r.* disgisinesse]. *c* **1400** *Beryn* 2523 And mervellid much in Geffrey of his disgiseness.

disguising (dɪsˈgaɪzɪŋ), *vbl. sb.* [f. DISGUISE *v.* + -ING[1].]

1. The action of the verb DISGUISE. †**a.** Change of fashion of clothes; strange or fantastic dressing.

1395 *Lollard Conclus.* Art. xii. in J. Lewis *Life Wyclif* (1820) 342 Duodecima Conclusio, quod multitudo artium in nostro regno nutrit multum peccatum in *waste*, curiositate, et inter *disguising*. *c* **1400** *Jacob's Well* 79 ȝif dysgysing, or excesse of clothys.. be þerin.. þanne is þat desyre of praysing & delyȝt in þe clothys & rycches dedly synne. *a* **1450** *Knt. de la Tour* (1868) 62 Noyis flode.. stroied the world for the pride and the disguysinge that was amonge women. **1480** CAXTON *Chron. Eng.* ccxxvi. (1482) 233 They .. chaunged hem euery yere dyuerse shappes and disguysyng of clothyng.

b. The assumption of a disguise.

1591 SHAKS. *Two Gent.* II. vi. 37 Ile giue her father notice Of their disguising and pretended flight.

c. The giving of a false appearance or representation; concealing.

1586 A. DAY *Eng. Secretary* II. (1625) 13 His going to N. to be but a meere disguising his intent. **1587** GOLDING *De Mornay* xxii. (1617) 359 Disguisings of the truth.

2. *concr.* †**a.** Strange or new-fangled dress. *Obs.*

c **1386** CHAUCER *Pars. T.* ¶351 The wrecched swollen membres that they shewe thurgh the degisynge in departynge of hire hoses in whit and reed. *c* **1485** *Digby Myst.* v. 150 These do signyfie Your disgysyng And your Araye.

b. Dress or covering worn to conceal identity.

1485 *Act 1 Hen. VII*, c. 7 The said Mis-doers, by reason of their painted Faces, Visors, and other Disguisings could not be known. **1581** LAMBARDE *Eiren.* IV. iv. (1588) 419.

†**3.** A mask, or masquerade; an acting by 'disguisers' or guisers. *Obs.*

1481–90 *Howard Househ. Bks.* (Roxb.) 389 All suche stoffe .. that he bowgt for the Dysgysing. **1530** TINDALE *Pract. Prelates* Wks. (Parker Soc.) II. 339 The Frenchmen.. of late days made a play, or a disguising at Paris, in which the emperor danced with the pope. **1532–3** *Act 24 Hen. VIII*, c. 13 Iustes, tourneis.. or other marcial feates or disguisings. **1577–87** HOLINSHED *Chron.* III. 893/2 This Christmasse was a goodlie disguising plaied at Graies In. **1688** R. HOLME *Armoury* III. 77/2 King Cassibelane.. gave.. many Disguisings, Plays, Minstrelsie and sports. **1801** STRUTT *Sports & Past.* III. ii. 145 Magnificent pageants and disguisings.

†**4.** An alleged appellation for a 'company' of tailors. *Obs.*

1486 *Bk. St. Albans* F vj b, A Disgysyng of Taylours.

disˈguising, *ppl. a.* [-ING[2].] That disguises.

1561 T. NORTON *Calvin's Inst.* IV. v. (1634) 534 *margin*, The disguising ceremonies which the Church of Rome useth in making of her Priests. **1741** tr. *D'Argens' Chinese Lett.* xxxiii. 250 The European Women besmear their Faces with White and Red, and upon that disguising Paint they stick abundance of little Plaisters of black Taffata.

†**disˈguisy,** *a. Obs.* Forms: 4 **deguise,** (**disgisi, -gesye**), 4–5 **degyse,** 5 **disgyse, -gisee, -guisee, -gisy.** [a. OF. *desguisié, déguisié, -sé*, pa. pple. of *de(s)guisier* to DISGUISE.] Disguised, altered from familiar guise, mode, or appearance.

1. Wearing a disguise; disguised; masked.

c **1330** R. BRUNNE *Chron.* (1810) 298 þe Scottis sent ouer þe se A boye of þer rascaile, quaynt & deguise. *c* **1350** *Will. Palerne* 1610 Also daunces disgisi redi diȝt were.

2. Of changed fashion; of strange guise; new-fashioned, new-fangled; monstrous; wrought, made, or ornamented in a novel or strange fashion.

a **1340** HAMPOLE *Psalter* cxlvi. 11, þaire degyse atyre, & þaire licherous berynge. *c* **1386** CHAUCER *Pars. T.* ¶343 The cost of embrowdynge, the degise endentynge..or bendynge. *c* **1430** LYDG. *Bochas* VI. xii. (1554) 159 a, There is none other nacion Touching aray, that is so disguisee In wast of cloth and superfluite. *c* **1430** *Pilgr. Lyf Manhode* I. cxliv. (1869) 74 To roste a smal hastelet or to make a steike or sum oother disgisee thing.

3. Strange, unfamiliar, extraordinary.

c **1330** R. BRUNNE *Chron. Wace* (Rolls) 14787 To telle hit here hit ys no nede; Hit were a degyse þyng. *c* **1350** *Will. Palerne* 2715 So long þei caired..ouer dales & dounes & disgesye weyes. *c* **1430** *Pilgr. Lyf Manhode* (1869) 74 Whi it is of swich facioun. It is a thing disgisy to me.

4. Feigned, done to deceive.

1375 BARBOUR *Bruce* XIX. 459 Ȝone fleying is right degyse. Thair armyt men behynd I se. *c* **1430** *Pilgr. Lyf Manhode* II. xxii. (1869) 84 Turnynge the gospel al up so doun bi disgisy woordes and lyinge.

dis'gulf, -'gulph, *v.* Also 7 disgolf. [f. DIS- 7 c + GULF, or from radical part of *engulf.*] *trans.* To send forth or discharge as from a gulf.

1635 PERSON *Varieties* I. 24 The perpetuall and constant running and disgolfing of Rivers, brookes and springs from the earth into it [the sea]. **1839** BAILEY *Festus* iv. (1852) 44 Canst thou not disgulph for me..of all thy sea-gods one?

disgust (dɪsˈgʌst), *sb.* [ad. 16th c. F. *desgoust* (Paré), mod.F. *dégoût*; or ad. It. *disgusto* 'distaste' (Florio), f. DIS- 4 + *gusto* taste: cf. DISGUST *v.* This and all the cognate words appear after 1600. They are not used by Shakspere.]

1. Strong distaste or disrelish for food in general, or for any particular kind or dish of food; sickening physical disinclination to partake of food, drink, medicine, etc.; nausea, loathing.

1611 COTGR., *Desappetit*..a queasinesse, or disgust of stomacke. **1682** GLANIUS *Voy. Bengala* 43 This mishap was attended by a disgust to the Leaves which we heretofore found so good. **1799** J. ROBERTSON *Agric. Perth* 326 The Highlanders in general had a disgust at this kind of food. **1803** *Med. Jrnl.* X. 497 The nausea and disgust excited from the exhibition of this medicine. **1837** HT. MARTINEAU *Soc. Amer.* III. 61 The conflict between our appetites and the disgust of the food was ridiculous. **1885** CLODD *Myths & Dr.* I. vi. 106 To this day the [hare]..is an object of disgust in certain parts of Russia.

2. Strong repugnance, aversion, or repulsion excited by that which is loathsome or offensive, as a foul smell, disagreeable person or action, disappointed ambition, etc.; profound instinctive dislike or dissatisfaction.

1611 COTGR., *Desaimer*..to fall into dislike, or disgust of. **1632** J. HAYWARD tr. *Biondi's Eromena* 26 It behooved him to make much of his wife, with no lesse art, than disgust [knowing her false]. **1759** ROBERTSON *Hist. Scot.* II. *Diss. Murder K. Henry* II, Du Croc..represents her disgust at Darnley to be extreme. **1789** T. JEFFERSON *Writ.* (1859) II. 574 His dress, in so gay a style, gives general disgust against him. **1796** R. BAGE *Hermsprong* lx, Unable to conquer her disgust to Sir Philip. **1801** MRS. CHAR. SMITH *Lett. Solit. Wand.* II. 158 In her..disgust towards her conductor. **1822** HAZLITT *Table-t.* Ser. II. vii. (1869) 156 The object of your abstract hatred and implacable disgust. **1845** S. AUSTIN *Ranke's Hist. Ref.* III. 33 He soon retreated in disgust across the Alps.

b. with *a* and *pl.*

1598 FLORIO, *Disparére*, a disopinion..a disgust or vnkindnes. **1659** B. HARRIS *Parival's Iron Age* 64 He left behind him, an immortal disgust, amongst..the Hugenot party. **1751** SMOLLETT *Per. Pic.* (1779) III. lxxxi. 213 A couple so situated would be apt to imbibe mutual disgusts. **1865** BUSHNELL *Vicar. Sacr.* iii. (1868) 77 His griefs, disgusts, and wounded sensibilities.

†c. An expression of disgust. *Obs. rare.*

a **1634** RANDOLPH *Amyntas* Poems (1668) 214 Will I be Archi-Flamen, where the gods Are so remiss? Let wolves approach their shrines, [etc.]..Such disgusts at last Awaken'd Ceres.

†3. An outbreak of mutual displeasure and ill-feeling; a difference, a quarrel. *Obs.*

1628 DIGBY *Voy. Medit.* (1868) 41 Being aduertised of a disgust betweene Captaine Stradling, my Rereadmirall, and Mr. Herris a gentleman of my shippe. **1665** SIR T. HERBERT *Trav.* (1677) 166 Some disgusts happen'd 'twixt Rustan and his Brother. **1761** HUME *Hist. Eng.* II. xxix. 158 Some disgusts also had previously taken place between Charles and Henry.

4. That which causes strong dislike or repugnance; an annoyance, vexation. ? *Obs.*

1654 W. MOUNTAGUE *Devout Ess.* II. x. §5 (R.), When the presenting of the benefit is joined with the presence of the disgust. **1658** SLINGSBY *Diary* (1836) 210 Custome and continuance has sweetned those disgusts. **1761-2** HUME *Hist. Eng.* (1806) III. xliii. 525 Some disgusts which she had received from the States. **1807-8** SYD. SMITH *Plymley's Lett.* Wks. 1859 II. 152/2 Nor can I conceive a greater disgust to a Monarch..than to see such a question as that of Catholic Emancipation argued [etc.].

disgust (dɪsˈgʌst), *v.* [ad. F. *desgouster* (in R. Estienne 1539) 'to distast, loath, dislike, abhorre' (Cotgr. 1611), or ad. It. *disgustare* 'to distaste' (Florio), f. *des-*, DIS- 4 + F. *gouster* (mod.F. *goûter*), It. and L. *gustāre* to taste. (The F. word was itself prob. from It.).]

†1. *trans.* To have a strong distaste for or repugnance to; to loathe, disrelish, dislike, regard with aversion or displeasure. **a.** *lit.* of food. *Obs.*

1659 T. PECKE *Parnassi Puerp.* II. 177 That you may disgust nothing you should eat: Let Hunger give the Hogoo to your Meat. **1669** W. SIMPSON *Hydrol. Chym.* 165 It is not very palatable, which makes some disgust it. **1752** *Scotland's Glory* 27 Our Siloah's streams disgusting For English leeks and onions they And fleshpots still were lusting.

†**b.** generally. *Obs.*

1601 *Imp. Consid. Sec. Priests* (1675) 64 There is no King .. disgusting the See of Rome..that would have endured us. **1611** COTGR., s.v. *Odeur, Il ne l'a pas en bonne odeur*, he disgusts him..he hath no good conceit of him. **1654** H. L'ESTRANGE *Chas. I* (1655) 110 His Majesty..disgusting Parliaments, was enforced to call in the aid of his Prerogative. *a* **1716** SOUTH *Serm.* (1744) X. 282 Had he not known, that I disgusted it, it had never been spoke or done by him. **1873** L. TROUBRIDGE *Life amongst Troubridges* (1966) 46 He is the music master and oh how I do loathe and disgust him and his lesson.

2. To excite physical nausea and loathing in (a person); to offend the taste or smell of.

1650 W. BROUGH *Sacr. Princ.* (1659) 226 The remedy.. disgusts the palate. **1750** JOHNSON *Rambler* No. 78 ¶1 The palate is reconciled by degrees to dishes which at first disgusted it. *Mod.* The smell of soap-works always disgusts me.

3. **a.** To offend the sensibilities of; to excite aversion, repungnance, or sickening displeasure in (a person).

1659 B. HARRIS *Parival's Iron Age* 89 King James..by the negotiations with Spain..had disgusted many of the Reformed Religion. *Ibid.* 273 The Pope was disgusted at the disobedience of the Christians. **1717** ABP. KING in Ellis *Orig. Lett.* Ser. II. IV. 316 Found him engaged in a practice that disgusted and shamed all his friends. **1841** ELPHINSTONE *Hist. Ind.* II. 557 Prince Azim had disgusted many of his principal officers by his arrogance. **1863** MRS. OLIPHANT *Sal. Ch.* xix. 328 He was disgusted with Phoebe for bringing the message, and disgusted with Beecher for looking pleased to receive it.

b. *absol.* To be very distasteful.

1756 BURKE *Subl. & B.* III. v, Want of the usual proportions in men and other animals is sure to disgust. **1763** J. BROWN *Poetry & Mus.* v. 75 The Music and Dance of the Americans..at first disgusts.

4. With *from, of, against*: To raise or excite such aversion in (a person) as dissuades or deters him from a proposed or intended purpose.

1700 S. L. tr. *Fryke's Voy. E. Ind.* 127 The very seeing of her disgusted me from Matrimony. **1781** JUSTAMOND *Priv. Life Lewis XV*, II. 133 The Monarch was ever soon disgusted of gratifications that were merely sensual. **1788** T. JEFFERSON *Writ.* (1859) II. 512 To disgust Mr. Neckar.. against their new fishery, by letting him foresee its expense. **1879** ATCHERLEY *Boerland* 156, I put an expansive ball right on his snout..which..thoroughly disgusted him of attacking us.

†**dis'gustable,** *a. Obs. rare.* [f. DISGUST *v.* + -ABLE.] Capable of exciting disgust; disgusting.

1787 *Minor* 29 A-propos, Mr. O'Nial, this house is like yourself—in many things disgustable.

disgustant (dɪsˈgʌstənt), *a.* and *sb.* [f. DISGUST *v.* + -ANT: in F. *dégoutant.*] **a.** *adj.* Disgusting *rare*$^{-0}$. **b.** *sb.* Something that excites disgust.

1866 *Macm. Mag.* May 62 A deterrent and a disgustant.

disgusted (dɪsˈgʌstɪd), *ppl. a.* [f. DISGUST *v.* + -ED.] †**a.** Distasteful, strongly disliked (*obs.*). **b.** Feeling disgust or aversion; chagrined.

1668 SOUTH *Serm.* xxvii. (1843) 467 Fear..makes him unable to assert a disgusted truth. **1704** HEARNE *Duct. Hist.* (1714) I. 162 Wilson a disgusted Man wrote the Life of K. James. *c* **1790** WILLOCK *Voy.* 11 He retired sullen and disgusted. **1819** *Metropolis* II. 189 [He] staggers from his intemperate banquet, and reels to a disgusted wife.

Hence **dis'gustedly** *adv.*, with disgust or repulsion.

1864 *Louie's last term* (N.Y.) 85 She..put her lips to the glass, turned up her nose very disgustedly. **1881** MISS BRADDON *Asph.* III. 98 Shrugging his shoulders disgustedly.

dis'guster. *rare.* [f. as prec. + -ER[1].]

†1. One who strongly dislikes; cf. DISGUST *v.* 1.

1681 J. COLLINS *Pref. to Glanvill's Sadducismus*, The truth of this story lying so uneasie in the minds of the disgusters of such things.

2. He who or that which excites distaste or aversion.

disgustful (dɪsˈgʌstfʊl), *a.* [f. DISGUST *sb.* + -FUL. Very common in 17-18th c.]

1. Causing literal disgust; offensive to the taste or other sense; disagreeable, sickening, nauseous.

a **1616** BEAUM. & FL. *Bonduca* I. ii, The British waters are grown dull and muddy, The fruit disgustful. **1657** TOMLINSON *Renou's Disp.* 169 All kinds of cordialls save those that are disgustful. **1727** SWIFT *Gulliver* IV. vi, A medicine equally annoying and disgustful to the bowels. **1814** CARY *Dante's Inf.* III. 63 Blood, that mix'd with tears ..by disgustful worms was gather'd there. **1888** LOWELL *Prose Wks.* (1890) VI. 199 These flesh-flies..plant there the eggs of their disgustful and infectious progeny.

2. Distasteful, displeasing; causing dislike, dissatisfaction, or displeasure; offensive. *arch.*

1611 SPEED *Hist. Gt. Brit.* VI. xxi. §6. 108, I grieue; that my life and..Gouernment..should seem so disgustfull vnto any. **1659** C. NOBLE *Mod. Answ. Immod. Q.* 8 If any Prince were disgustfull..asperse and calumniate him. **1748** J. MASON *Elocut.* 15 This unnatural Tone in reading..is always disgustful to Persons of Delicacy. **1774** *Hist. Europe* in *Ann. Reg.* 76/1 A trial by juries was strange and disgustful to them. *a* **1849** POE *Mrs. Browning* Wks. (1864) III. 424 A disgustful gulf of utter incongruity.

3. With stronger implication: Causing disgust or strong aversion; sickeningly repugnant or shocking to the moral sensibilities; repulsive, disgusting.

1678 GALE *Crt. Gentiles* III. 121 It seemeth so disgustful to many, if it be said, that God wils and produceth the act.. of parricide. **1791** BURKE *Let. Member Nat. Ass.* Wks. VI. 34 The spawn of his disgustful amours. **1821** *New Monthly Mag.* II. 385 A tragedy..which exceeds in horror the disgustful atrocities of Titus Andronicus. **1852** HAWTHORNE *Blithedale Rom.* III. ix. 164 Inexpressibly miserable is this familiarity with objects that have been from the first disgustful.

4. Full of disgust; associated with, or characterized by, disgust.

[**1782** V. KNOX *Ess.* (1819) I. xxxvii. 200 It ceases to produce its natural effect, and terminates in disgustful satiety.] **1841** LYTTON *Nt. & Morn.* (1851) 244 He turned with hard and disgustful contempt from pleasure. **1866** STEVENSON *Dr. Jekyll* ix. (ed. 2) 99 This person..had.. struck in me what I can only describe as a disgustful curiosity.

Hence **dis'gustfully** *adv.*, **dis'gustfulness.**

1731 BAILEY (ed. 5), *Disgustfully*, distastefully, unpleasantly. **1782** V. KNOX *Ess.* (1819) III. cxlv. 131 Tristram Shandy is in many places disgustfully obscure. **1832** *Fraser's Mag.* V. 149 This does away with much of the disgustfulness of death. **1863** HAWTHORNE *Our Old Home, About Warwick* (1879) 101 To shrink more disgustfully than ever before from the idea of being buried at all.

dis'gusting, *vbl. sb.* [see -ING[1].] The action of the verb DISGUST. (Now only gerundial.)

1669 WOODHEAD *St. Teresa* II. xxxv. 256 With the extream disgusting of their kindred.

disgusting (dɪsˈgʌstɪŋ), *ppl. a.* [f. DISGUST *v.* + -ING[2].] That disgusts (see the verb); distasteful, sickening, repulsive.

1754 P. H. *Hiberniad* ii. 20 Particular Detail..would become dry, and disgusting to the Stranger's Palate. **1839** KEIGHTLEY *Hist. Eng.* II. 39 The disgusting language of the indictment. **1843** PRESCOTT *Mexico* (1850) I. 302 Their disgusting cannibal repasts.

dis'gustingly, *adv.* [f. prec. + -LY[2].] In a disgusting manner, so as to cause disgust; *colloq.* offensively, aggravatingly, annoyingly.

1758 L. TEMPLE *Sketches* (ed. 2) 16 Neither..flat on the one hand, nor disgustingly stiff on the other. **1804** *Ann. Rev.* II. 52/2 Calcutta is described as disgustingly filthy. *a* **1856** MASSON *Ess.* iii. 75 He stands before them disgustingly unabashed. **1864** *Daily Tel.* 1 June, With these disgustingly long days, the night never would come on. **1892** JESSOPP *Stud. Recluse* vi. (1893) 198 The Younger Pliny..was disgustingly rich.

dis'gustingness. [f. as prec. + -NESS.] The quality of being disgusting; an instance of this.

1851 *Fraser's Mag.* XLIII. 175 The same defect, carried out into sheer disgustingness. **1880** R. S. WATSON *Vis. Wazan* ix. 165 Every disgustingness..lies there bare and open to the day.

†**dis'gustion.** *Obs. rare.* [irreg. f. DISGUST *v.*: see -ION[1].] = DISGUST *sb.*

1659 D. PELL *Impr. Sea* Ded. C viij, Let not the irreligion of those places..breed in you..a disgustion unto the pure.. Religion. *Ibid.* 556 Homer brings in brave Ulysses in great despair, and disgustion of a drowning death.

†**dis'gustive,** *a. Obs. rare*$^{-1}$. [f. DISGUST *v.* + -IVE.] That tends or is fitted to disgust.

1740 A. HILL *Let.* in Mrs. Barbauld *Life Richardson* (1804) I. 45 A heavy disgustive insipidness.

dish (dɪʃ), *sb.* Forms: 1 disc, (3 dischs, diss), 3-5 disch, -e, 4 (dise, dych, diȝsch), dissch, -e, 4-5 dyssh, -e, 4-6 disshe, dishe, 5-6 dyssche, dysch, dysche, 6 diszshe, 3- dish. [OE. *disc* plate, bowl, platter, = OHG. *tisc* plate (MHG. and Ger. *tisch* table), OS. *disk* table, MDu. and Du. *disch* table, ON. *diskr* plate (? from OE.); WGer. **disk(s)*, a. L. *disc-us* quoit, dish (in Vulgate), DISC. The OE. (like OHG. and ON.) represents a Latin sense of the word, while the sense 'table' found in MHG. and other later dialects corresponds to a later Romanic sense, exemplified by It. *desco*, F. *deis, dais* (DESK, DAIS).]

I. 1. **a.** A broad shallow vessel, with flat bottom, concave sides, and nearly level rim, made of earthenware, glass, metal, or wood, and used chiefly to hold food at meals. Now, on the one hand often restricted to those of oval, square, or irregular shape, as distinguished from the circular *plate*, and on the other extended to all open vessels used to contain food at table, as tureens, vegetable dishes, etc.

a **700** *Epinal Gloss.* 786 (O.E.T.), *Patena*, disc. *a* **800** *Corpus Gloss.* 852 *Ferculum*, disc. *c* **950** *Lindisf. Gosp.* Matt. xiv. 8 Sel me..in disc heafud iohannes. *c* **1000** *Ags. Gosp.* Matt. xxvi. 23 Se þe be-dypð on disce mid me hys hand. *a* **1225** *Ancr. R.* 344 Ibroken disch. *c* **1290** *S. Eng. Leg.* I. 46/23 Ane Dischs of seluer he nam also. *a* **1300** *Cursor M.* 13159 (Cott.) Ask him..His heued to giue þe in a diss. *c* **1300** *Havelok* 919 Ful wel kan ich dishes swilen. *c* **1380** Wyclif *Wks.* (1880) 434 Diȝschis & coupis of siluer. *c* **1420** *Liber Cocorum* (1862) 32 In a dysshe thy gose thou close. **1535** Coverdale *Judg.* v. 25 She..broughte forthe butter in a lordly diszshe. **1587** Mascall *Govt. Cattle* (1627) 270 The common saying is, the hog is neuer good but when he is in the dish. **1662** J. Davies tr. *Olearius' Voy. Ambass.* 198 The Wooden dishes that are all over Persia. **1710** Steele *Tatler* No. 245 ¶2 A small Cabinet..in which were..half a Dozen of Portugal Dishes. **1829** Southey *Pilgr. Compostella* ii, They both slipt about in the gravy Before they got out of the dish. **1881** Wheatley & Delamotte *Art Wk. Earthenware* iv. 49 Palissy..took the greatest pains in the moulding of the fishes..which he placed upon these curious dishes.

b. A hollow vessel of wood or metal, used for drinking, and also *esp.* as a beggar's receptacle for alms; a cup; cf. alms-dish, clack-, clap-dish.

1381 [see alms-dish]. [*c* **1394** J. Malverne *Contn. Higden* (Rolls) IX. App. 79 Quoddam jocale argenteum et deauratum formatum ad modum navis, vocatur discus eleemosynarum.] **1488** *Will of Pywale* (Somerset Ho.), A new treen dyssh wt a pynte of ale therin. **1532** [see clapper *sb.*[1] 2]. **1593** Shaks. *Rich. II*, iii. iii. 150 I'll give..My figur'd Goblets, for a Dish of Wood. **1605** *Tryall Chev.* i. iii. in Bullen *O. Pl.* III. 278, I know him as well as the Begger knowes his dish. **1634** Milton *Comus* 391 Who would rob a hermit of..his beads, or maple dish? **1781** Cowper *Truth* 80 Books, beads, and maple dish, his meagre stock.

†**c.** *transf.* Applied to an acorn-cup. *Obs.*

1599 A. M. tr. *Gabelhouer's Bk. Physicke* 172/1 Drie the little akorne dishes..and contunde them smalle.

†**d.** Phrases. *to cast, lay, throw* (something) *in one's dish*: to reproach or taunt him with it. *to have a hand in the dish*: to meddle, interfere. *to have a foot in the dish* (? like a pig in the trough): to gain a footing, have a share (cf. to have a finger in the pie). *Obs.*

1551 T. Wilson *Logike* (1580) 62 b, When wee charge hym with a like fault, and laye some greater matter in his dishe. **1596** Nashe *Saffron Walden* 67 Hee casts the begger in my dish at euerie third sillable. **1611** Cotgr. s.v. *Aliboron*, A..busie-body; one that hath his hand in euery dish. **1615** Swetnam *Arraignm. Women* (1880) p. xviii, Hir dowrie will be often cast in thy dish if shee doe bring wealth with her. **1682** Bunyan *Holy War* 233 We have already also a foot in their dish, for our Diabolonian friends are laid in their bosoms. **1710** Steele *Tatler* No. 164 ¶5 Some..have been so disingenuous, as to throw Maud the Milk-Maid into my Dish. **1722** Sewel *Hist. Quakers* (1795) I. 8 Under the bloody reign of Queen Mary, this was laid in his dish.

2. a. The food ready for eating served on or contained in a dish; a distinct article or variety of food. *transf.* and *fig.*: *spec.*, an attractive person, esp. a woman (now only in informal use).

1526 *Pilgr. Perf.* (W. de W. 1531) 17 b, The moost hye deyntyes or delicate dysshes. **1601** Shaks. *Jul. C.* ii. i. 173 Let's carue him, as a Dish fit for the Gods. **1611** —— *Wint. T.* iv. iii. 8 For a quart of Ale is a dish for a King. **1655** Moufet & Bennet *Health's Improv.* (1746) 190 Cambletes King of Lydia, having eaten of his own Wife, said, he was sorry to have been ignorant so long of so good a Dish. **1675** Hobbes *Odyssey* (1677) 296 To beasts and fowls is he Somewhere..become a dish. **1750** Johnson *Rambler* No. 78 ¶1 The palate is reconciled by degrees to dishes which at first disgusted it. **1849** Macaulay *Hist. Eng.* I. 321 The ladies..retired as soon as the dishes had been devoured. **1853** Soyer *Pantroph.* 73 You will obtain a most delicate dish by boiling the cucumbers with brains.

transf. and *fig.* **1599** Shakes. *Much Ado* ii. i. 283 Heeres a dish I loue not, I cannot indure this Lady tongue. **1606** —— *Ant. & Cl.* ii. vi. 134 He will to his Egyptian dish againe. *Ibid.* v. ii. 275, I know, that a woman is a dish for the Gods, if the diuell dresse her not. **1647** N. Bacon *Disc. Govt. Eng.* i. xiv, The Theme of Marriage was the best Dish in all their Entertainment. **1929** D. Hammett *Dain Curse* (1930) xix. 217 He turned his half-wit's grin on me and said: 'What a swell dish you are.' **1938** J. Curtis *They drive by Night* xxiii. 263 So you're Queenie, are you? And a nice little dish you are. **1945** P. Cheyney *I'll say she Does!* v. 141 She's a swell dish—a lovely piece of frail that one. **1955** Priestley & Hawkes *Journey down Rainbow* 84 The purple band..marched on to the field, accompanied by drum-majorettes—every one a dish, as they say. **1958** A. Wilson *Middle Age of Mrs. Eliot* 68 That man I've been talking to is rather a dish, but I'm sure he's a bottom-pincher. **1959** H. Hobson *Mission House Murder* ix. 65, I got pictures of this dame, she's a swell dish.

b. *by-dish, side-dish*: see by- 3 a, side. *made dish*: a fancy dish of various ingredients, depending for its success on the cook's skill. *standing dish*: one that appears each day or at every meal. (Also used *fig.*)

1621 Burton *Anat. Mel.* i. ii. ii. i. 43 Artificial made dishes, of which our Cooks afford us a great variety. **1654** Whitlock *Zootomia* 146 Meer Quelquechoses, made dishes of no nourishing. **1876** W. H. Pollock in *Contemp. Rev.* June 56 The mysteries had ceased to be the standing dish of theatrical entertainment.

c. Slang phr. *one's dish*: something exactly suited to one's tastes, requirements, abilities, etc.; one's 'cup of tea'. orig. *U.S.*

1918 H. C. Witwer *From Baseball to Boches* 106 They [*sc.* grenades] ought to of been my dish, seein' what a notorious pitcher I was. **1947** Auden *Age of Anxiety* (1948) v. 114 Did you lose your nerve And cloud your conscience because I wasn't Your dish really? **1955** *Bull. Atomic Sci.* Feb. 42/2 Thus they are armed to predict the future, but this, I fear, is not my dish. **1957** Wodehouse *Over Seventy* iii. 42 My output was not everybody's dish.

3. As a term of quantity more or less indefinite. **a.** As much or as many as will fill or make a dish when cooked. **b.** A dishful, a bowlful or cupful.

1596 Shaks. *Merch. V.* ii. ii. 144, I haue here a dish of Doues that I would bestow vpon your worship. **1597** —— *2 Hen. IV*, ii. iv. 5 The Prince once set a Dish of Apple-Iohns before him. **1699** Dampier *Voy.* II. iii. 175 The Boat returned with a good dish of Fish. **1873** Tristram *Moab* xiv. 254 Trotter..secured a good dish of fish in the pools.

b. 1596 Shaks. *1 Hen. IV*, ii. iii. 35 Such a dish of skim'd Milk. **1662** J. Davies tr. *Olearius' Voy. Ambass.* 171 He had taken off two or three Dishes of Aquavitæ. **1679** *Trials of Green, Berry*, etc. 65, I will go to the Coffee-house, and drink a Dish of Coffee. **1711** Addison *Spect.* No. 57 ¶4 She scalded her Fingers, and spilt a Dish of Tea upon her Petticoat. **1795** *Jemima* II. 10 Having finished his dish of chocolate. **1824** Byron *Juan* xvi. xxx, He sate him pensive o'er a dish of tea. **1855** Macaulay *Hist. Eng.* IV. 688 More than one seat in Parliament..had been bought and sold over a dish of coffee at Garraway's. **1862** *Sat. Rev.* XIII. 526/2 The cook anticipates many a cosy dish of tea with friends.

c. *fig.*

1606 Shaks. *Tr. & Cr.* v. i. 10 Thou full dish of Foole. **1608** —— *Per.* iv. vi. 160 My dish of chastity. **1708** Motteux *Rabelais* v. vii. (1737) 24 Roger..had a Dish of Chat with her. **1753** Gray *Lett.* Wks. 1884 II. 241 To entertain you with a dish of very choice erudition. **1820** Lady Granville *Lett.* (1894) I. 183 This new dish of Continental troubles. **1836** *Backwoods Canada* 183 For the sake of a dish of gossip.

4. *transf.* **a.** A shallow concave vessel or receptacle of any kind. See also chafing-dish.

1633 G. Herbert *Temple, Justice* ii, The dishes of thy ballance. **1702** W. J. *Bruyn's Voy. Levant* xxxii. 126 The Ropes which were round the Capstan pulled it out of its Dish. *c* **1865** J. Wylde in *Circ. Sc.* I. 305/2 Evaporating dishes are employed.

b. A microwave reflector or aerial with a concave surface.

1948 *Gloss. Terms Waveguide Technique* (*B.S.I.*) 11 *Dish*, a reflector the surface of which is part of a sphere or of a paraboloid of revolution. **1956** *Electronic Engin.* XXVIII. 539 The actual radiator consists of a 30ft diameter dish. **1957** *Ann. Reg. 1956* 333 The great radio-telescope at Jodrell Bank in Cheshire, with its 250-ft. reflecting 'dish'. **1960** [see antenna 5]. **1965** *New Scientist* 8 July 87/1 The new telescope employs three 60-ft parabaloidal [*sic*] reflectors or 'dishes'. **1967** *Ibid.* 18 May 390/3 The present metal aerial dish weighs 100 lb; but there are plans to use a coated dish of carbon fibre material.

5. A dish-like concavity; e.g. on one side of a wheel (see quots.); a depression in a field, etc. More commonly, the condition of wheels having such concavity; the amount of such concavity.

1810 T. Williamson *Agric. Mech.* 95 The dish given to wheels. **1812–6** J. Smith *Panorama Sc. & Art* I. 372 Wheels are commonly made with what is called a dish, that is, the spokes are inserted not at right angles, but with an inclination towards the axis of the nave or centre-piece; so that..the wheel appears dished or hollow. **1837** W. B. Adams *Carriages* 98 Some wheels..get more dish than others. **1844** H. Stephens *Bk. Farm* III. 1154 The third or front wheel may be found without dish. **1846** Worcester, *Dish*..a hollow in a field. **1888** *Encycl. Brit.* XI. 311/1 The dish is considerable, amounting to 2 inches in the 5-foot wheel. **1891** *Fur, Fin & Feather* Mar. 167 The left hind wheel of his wagon is out of dish.

6. As a specific quantity in various industries: †**a.** An obsolete measure for corn. Cf. toll-dish.

1419 Corn-dish [see corn sb.[1] 11.]. **1774** T. West *Antiq. Furness* (1805) 85, I will provide them mills for their foreign grain at the rate of the twenty first dish.

b. *Tin-mining.* A gallon of ore ready for the smelter. **c.** *Lead-mining.* A rectangular box used for measuring the lead ore; by Act 14 and 15 Vict. c. 94 §3 fixed to contain fifteen pints of water; *brazen-dish*: see brazen *a.* 4. **d.** Also, the proportion of tin or lead ore paid as royalty to the mine landlord, etc.

1531 *Dial. Laws Eng.* ii. lv. (1638) 173 If a man take a Tinne work, and give the Lord the tenth dish. **1602** Carew *Cornwall* 13 b, They measure their blacke Tynne by the..Dish..which containeth..a gallon. **1631** Brazen dish [see brazen *a.* 4]. **1653** Manlove *Lead Mines* 53 But first the finder his two meers must free With oar there found, for the Barghmaster's fee Which is one dish for one meer of the ground. *Ibid.* 75 The thirteenth dish of oar within their mine, To th' Lord for Lot, they pay at measuring time. **1667** Primatt *City & C. Build.* 7 A Horse load..is nine dishes..weighing about Four hundred and Fifty pound. **1681** Houghton *Compl. Miner* Gloss. (E.D.S.), *Dish*, a trough made of wood, about 28 inches long, 4 inches deep, and six inches wide; by which all miners measure their ore. **1884** R. Hunt *Brit. Mining* 83 Mining for tin and copper was carried on, in 1770..Permission was..obtained from the lord of the soil, and an acknowledgment 'dish', or 'dues'—was paid to him..commonly one-sixth, one-seventh, one-eighth, or even to one-twelfth, or less.

e. *Diamond* and *Gold-mining*: see quots.

1890 *Goldfields Victoria* 17, I have obtained good dish prospects after crudely crushing up the quartz. **1893** *Scott. Leader* 19 May 7 About 120 'dishes' go to a 'load'..it is an astonishing 'prospect' (4 carats [of diamonds] obtained from 6 dishes).

II. [immed. from L. *discus*.]

†**7.** A quoit; quoit-playing. *Obs.*

1382 Wyclif *2 Macc.* iv. 14 They hastiden for to be maad felawis of wrastlyng..and of oost, or cumpanye of dishe, or pleyinge with ledun dishe [**1388** in ocupacions of a disch, ether pleiyng with a ledun disch; Vulg. *disci*; Coverdale, to put at yᵉ stone; **1611** the game of Discus]. **1552** Huloet, Dyshe caster, or who that throweth a dyshe, *discobolus*.

III. [f. dish *v.*] **8.** *slang.* The act of 'dishing': see dish *v.* 7.

1891 Sir W. Harcourt *Sp.* 30 July, The last reliance of the Tory in an extremity is a policy of 'dish' as it is called.

IV. *Comb.* **9. a.** attrib. as *dish-rack*; **b.** objective, as *dish-bearer*, *-designer*, *-turner*, *-washing*.

c **1440** *Promp. Parv.* 122/1 Dysshe berer at mete, *discoferus*. **1842** S. Lover *Handy Andy* v, A long procession of dish-bearers. **1884** Tennyson *Becket* 5 A dish-designer, and most amorous Of..Gascon wine. **1889** R. Cooke *Steadfast* i. 16 The song of the kettle as it piped away on the shortened hook, where it kept hot for dish washing. **1894** H. Speight *Nidderdale* 384 Whitesmiths, dish-turners. **1891** *Anthony's Photogr. Bulletin* IV. 336 Dish-washing..includes all that is required, with regard to cleanliness, in amateur photography. **1897** *Outing* (U.S.) XXX. 124/2 A dish-washing machine. **1963** *Which?* 6 Feb. 46/1 Dishwashing machines are comparatively rare.

c. Consisting, or having the form, of a dish; dish-shaped.

a **1823** D. Wordsworth *Second Tour Scotl.* in *Jrnls.* (1941) II. 344 Porters in white hats with dish-crowns close to the head. **1874** S. J. Thearle *Naval Archit.: Wood & Iron Shipbuilding* 72 The hollow or dish keel is a variety of the flat keel system. **1893** *Kennel Gaz.* Aug. 214 Jess III is spoilt by her dish face. **1960** *Times* 2 Jan. 9/1 The working springer tends to be smaller, lower slung, often with a dish face. **1962** *Listener* 19 July 112/1 A dish aerial at Goonhilly Down. **1968** *Times* 20 Dec. 6/8 A special dish telescope 20ft. in diameter.

10. Special comb.: †**dish-bench, -bink** (*north. dial.*), **-board**, a rest for dishes, a dresser, a plate-rack; †**dish-caster** (see 7 above); **dish-cover**, a cover of ware or metal placed over hot food; **dish-cradle, -cratch** (*dial.*; in Nares *-catch*), a plate-rack; **dish-cross, -rim, -ring** (see quots. 1908, 1931); **dish-crowned** *a.*, having a crown shaped like a dish; **dish-faced** *a.* (of dogs and horses) 'having the nose higher at the tip than the stop' (Stables *Friend Dog* vii. 50); (*dial.* of persons) having a round flattish face, like a reversed plate; †**dish-headed** *a.*, an epithet of monks; **dish-heater**, 'a warming closet attached to a stove or exposed in front of a fire to heat dishes' (Knight *Dict. Mech.*); **dish-lift**, = dumb-waiter 2; †**dish-meat**, food cooked in a dish, as e.g. a pie; **dish-monger**, one who deals in, or has much to do with, dishes (of food); **dish-mop** orig. *U.S.*, a small mop used for washing dishes, etc.; †**dish-mustard**, Turner's name for *Thlaspi arvense*; **dish-pan** *U.S.*, a pan in which dishes, etc., are washed; hence **dish-pan hands**, an inflamed or sore condition of the hands caused by washing-up or by the use of cleaning materials in housework; **dish-plate**, *Min.* (see quot.) **dish-rag, -towel** = dish-cloth; chiefly *U.S.* also *transf.*, the dishcloth gourd; **dish-spring**, a spring shaped like a dish; **dish-trough** = dish *sb.* 6 c. Also dish-cloth, -clout, -wash, -water, etc.

1483 *Cath. Angl.* 100/2 *Dische benke, *scutellarium*. **1535** *Richmond. Wills* (Surtees) 12 A cobbord with a dys-bynk. **1877** F. K. Robinson *Whitby Gloss.*, *Dish-bink*, a kitchen rack for the plates. **1523** Fitzherb. *Husb.* §146 Swepe thy hous, dresse vp thy *dysshborde. **1562** *Richmond. Wills* (Surtees) 152 My counter and dishebourd. **1831** *Society* I. 144 The *dish-covers are slowly raised. **1691** Ray *N.C. Words* 133 *Dish-Cradle or Credle, a wooden Utensil for wooden Dishes. ?**16..** *Comical Dial. betw. 2 Country Lovers* (N.), My *dish-c[r]atch, cupboards, boards, and bed. **1785** *Daily Universal Register* 1 Jan. 3/2 *Dish crosses with lamps, 14 oz. to 20 oz. each. **1908** B. Wyllie *Sheffield Plate* 75 'Dish-crosses' or 'spiders'..served two purposes: either to keep a hot dish from marking the polished tables..or to support a spiritlamp which kept the contents of the dish above hot. **1908** H. N. Veitch *Sheffield Plate* 136 These dish-crosses..are suitable for both round and oval dishes. **1600** Rowlands *Let. Humours Blood* vii. 13 *Dish-crown'd Hat. **1737** Bracken *Farriery Impr.* (1757) II. 12 The *Dish-faced, or Roman Nosed Horse. **1825–80** Jamieson, *Dish-faced*, flat-faced; applied both to man and beast. **1869** *Lonsdale Gloss.*, *Dish-faced*, hollow-faced. **1581** J. Bell *Haddon's Answ. Osor.* 489 b, Those *dish-headed dranes of that shavelyng and Cowled rowte. **1859** Sala *Twice round Clock* 81 With every modern convenience and improvement: with bath-rooms..*dish-lifts, [etc.] **1920** *Contemp. Rev.* June 890 He walked to the dish-lift and listened intently. [*c* **1440** *Promp. Parv.* 122/1 *Dysshe mete, *discibarium*.] **1513** Bradshaw *St. Werburge* i. 2558 Delycate dysshe meates were put out of her presence. **1589** R. Harvey *Pl. Perc.* (1590) 3 Let me alone, for my actiuity, at the dish meat. **1688** R. Holme *Armoury* iii. 316/1 All sorts of Bread and Dishmeats are taken out of the Oven. **1607** Walkington *Opt. Glass* 8 *Dish-mongers..running into excesse of riot. **1897** *Sears, Roebuck Catal.* 98/1 This *dish mop is made of cotton and is securely fastened to handle. **1913** E. H. Porter *Pollyanna* v. 47 Nancy, hurrying with her belated work, jabbed her dish-mop into the milk pitcher. **1955** E. Coxhead *Figure in Mist* viii. 229 She picked up a dish-mop and began to scour a..saucepan. **1548** Turner *Names of Herbes* 78 Named in englishe *dyshmustard, or triacle Mustard..because the seede is lyke mustard seede in colour and in tast, and the vessel that conteyneth the seede is lyke a disshe. **1872** *Newton Kansan* 5 Sept. 4/5 Put your corn, while hot, in a *dish-pan. **1942** W. Faulkner *Go Down, Moses* 176 Ash began to beat on the bottom of the dish-pan with a heavy spoon to call them to breakfast. **1944** B. Hutchison *Hollow Men* xiii. 187 'And me'—she chuckled at this—'sunk without trace in domesticity, teaching school, dish-pan hands [etc.].' **1892** HESLOP *Northumbld. Gloss.*, **Dish-plates*, in mining, plates or rails dished to receive the fore wheels of a tub, to faciliate the teeming. **1839** *Southern Lit. Messenger* V. 329/2 When he landed he lay there as limber as a *dish-rag. **1872** 'MARK TWAIN' *Roughing It* 44 It really pretended to be tea, but there was too much dish-rag and sand in it. **1890** *Cent. Dict.* s.v. *sponge-gourd*, Vegetable sponge or dish-rag. **1904** *N.Y. Tribune* 22 May, A novel enterprise, that of raising dishrags, is being exploited by a number of Southern California horticulturists. **1939** DYLAN THOMAS *Map of Love* 21 The horrid Woe drip from the dish-rag hands. **1774** in B. Wyllie *Sheffield Plate* (1908) 71 *Dish-rims. **1908** B. WYLLIE *Ibid.* pl. lxxi, Revolving Dish Stand for round or oval dish. Possibly this is what was meant by a 'dish-rim'. **1931** E. WENHAM *Domestic Silver* v. 75 [Dish-crosses] represent to the English what the misunderstood *dish-rings mean to the Irish, namely, a stand on which to place a hot dish to prevent it from marking the table. **1825** J. NICHOLSON *Operat. Mechanic* 34 CC is a *dish-spring, secured in its place by the pin. **1869** MRS. STOWE *Oldtown Folks* 275 Aunt Lois.. found her *dish-towel freezing in her hand. **1883** *Harper's Mag.* Feb. 365/2 Mr. Ayer removed her dish-towel from its nail. **1747** HOOSON *Miner's Dict.* s.v. *Barmaster*, [The] Barmaster looks after keeping the *Dishtrough.

dish (dɪʃ), *v.*[1] [f. DISH *sb.*]

1. *trans.* To put (food) into a dish, and set it ready for a meal. Also with *up* (†*forth*, *out*).

1586 J. HOOKER *Girald. Irel.* in *Holinshed* II. 81 The thin fare that heere is disht before him. **1598** *Epulario* B iij, Dish the meat, and lay this sauce vpon it. **1652** N. CULVERWELL *Lt. Nat.* 150 (L.) They dish out ambrosia for them. *c* **1685** in *Dk. Buckhm.'s Wks.* (1705) II. 48 She.. neatly dish'd it up with Egg-sauce. **1769** MRS. RADCLIFFE *Eng. Housekpr.* (1778) 189 When your dinner or supper is dished. **1833** MARRYAT *P. Simple* i, Jemima, dish up! **1879** SALA *Paris herself again* (1880) I. xvii. 261 Grilled bones.. dished up for you before bedtime. **1930** BROPHY & PARTRIDGE *Songs & Slang of Brit. Soldier* 116 Cooked food was 'dished out' by the orderly men of the day. **1958** HAYWARD & HARARI tr. *Pasternak's Dr. Zhivago* I. v. 133 Food was dished out and the used plates stacked in the hand-worked service-lift.

2. *fig.* To present (attractively) for acceptance; to serve up. Also with *up* (†*forth*, *out*). In modern use, with *out*: to distribute; to give or hand *out* (often with the pejorative implication of a lack of care or discrimination). So ***to dish it out*** (U.S. colloq.): to deal out punishment; to fight hard.

1611 SHAKS. *Wint. T.* III. ii. 73 For Conspiracie, I know not how it tastes, though it be dish'd For me to try how. **1641** MILTON *Animadv.* (1851) 237 Lest, thinking to offer him as a present to God, they dish him out for the Devill. **1658** GURNALL *Chr. in Arm.* verse 15 ii. §4 (1669) 121/2 The heavenly viands disht forth in the Gospel. **1756** WASHINGTON *Let.* Wks. (1889) I. 265 Their success.. dished up with a good deal of French policy, will encourage the Indians.. to fall upon our inhabitants. **1858** DORAN *Crt. Fools* 70 This story.. has been dished up in a hundred different ways. **1934** *Black Mask Mag.* Oct. 13/1 You take [money] away fast enough, but you don't like to dish it out. **1939** I. BAIRD *Waste Heritage* vi. 82 Gabby could take it and he could dish it out. **1939** *War Illustr.* 21 Oct. p. ii/1 The drivel that is dished out between news bulletins. **1955** A. HUXLEY *Genius & Goddess* 36 Tripe and hogwash dished out by the moulders of public opinion. **1959** *Camb. Rev.* 2 May 471/2 They dish out the gestetnered flysheet which does duty for it, free of charge. **1966** B. KIMENYE *Kalasanda Revisited* 11 Offices.. which dish out highly-coloured literature extolling the wonders of their country.

3. *nonce-uses.* **a.** *to dish about*: to pass round in a dish, to drink in turns from a dish or bowl. **b.** To receive (liquid) as in a dish.

1719 D'URFEY *Pills* (1872) III. 311 Then dish about the Mother's Health. **1847** H. MELVILLE *Omoo* xvi. 59 The Julia reared up on her stern.. and when she settled again forward, fairly dished a tremendous sea.

4. To fashion like a dish; to make concave like a dish or its sides; to hollow *out*; *spec.* to set the spokes of a (carriage-wheel) at such an inclination to the nave that the wheel is concave on one side (purposely or as the result of an accident).

1805 *Agric. Surv. E. Lothian* 74 (Jam.), Formerly the wheel was much dished, from a mistaken principle. **1823** P. NICHOLSON *Pract. Build.* 584 Dish-out, to form coves by means of ribs, or wooden vaults for plastering upon. **1868** *Jrnl. R. Agric. Soc.* Ser. II. IV. II. 262 The yards are dished out in the centre to the depth of five feet. **1886** A. W. GREELY *Arct. Serv.* I. xxvii. 370 Seven hours' travelling over very rough ground 'dished' a wheel, and lunch was taken while repairs were being made. **1887** *Sporting Life* 20 July 7/2 To facilitate turning the sharp ends, the eastern and western ends [of a bicycle-track] were 'dished'.

5. *intr.* To be or become concave; to 'cave in'.

1669 [see DISHING *ppl. a.*]. **1886** A. W. GREELY *Arct. Serv.* I. xxvii. 387 We had much trouble with our wagon, the wheel dishing frequently.

6. *intr.* Of a horse; To move the fore-feet in his trot not straight forward but with a circular or scooping motion.

1846 R. FORD *Gath. Spain* vii. 69 The Andalucian horse.. is given to *dishing* with the feet. **1863** [see DISHING *ppl. a.*] **1869** FITZWYGRAM *Horses & Stables* §931 The more prominent defects.. are rolling, dishing, cutting, and stumbling. **1895** *Letter fr. Corresp.* I think the best description of a horse that dishes, would be a horse that 'winds his forefoot'.

7. *trans. slang.* To 'do for', defeat completely, ruin; to cheat, circumvent. [From the notion of food being *done*, and *dished*.]

1798 *Monthly Mag.* (Farmer), Done up, dish'd. **1811** E. NARES *Thinks I to Myself* (1816) I. 208 (D.) He was completely dished—he could never have appeared again. **1819** *Abeillard & Heloisa* 10 A consummation greatly wish'd By nymphs who have been foully dish'd. **1826** SCOTT *Jrnl.* 31 July, It was five ere we got home, so there was a day dished. **1830** DISRAELI *Let.* 27 Aug. (1887) 32 He dished Prince Pignatelli at billiards. **1835** R. H. FROUDE *Rem.* (1838) I. 419 You are now taking fresh ground, without owning.. that on our first basis I dished you. *a* **1847** MRS. SHERWOOD *Lady of Manor* V. xxix. 103 If Fitzhenry can't raise the sum, he will be dished, and that in a few hours. **1869** *Latest News* 29 Aug. 8 The Conservative leader would be glad again to perform the operation of 'dishing the Whigs'. **1880** DISRAELI *Endym.* xl, I believe it [the House of Commons] to be completely used up. Reform has dished it.

dish, *v.*[2] *Sc.* [variant of DUSH *v.*] *trans.* To push violently, thrust.

1821 GALT *Sir A. Wylie* I. 70 (Jam.) They hae horns on their head to dish the like o' me.

dishabilitate (dɪshəˈbɪlɪteɪt), *v.* [f. DIS- 6 + HABILITATE: cf. OF. *deshabiliter* to disqualify, depose.] *trans.* **a.** *Sc. Law.* To incapacitate, disqualify. **b.** (*nonce-use.*) To render impotent.

1662–81 STAIR in M. P. Brown *Suppl. Decis.* (1826) II. 243 (Jam.) The Earl his father being forefault, and his posterity dishabilitated to bruik estate or dignity in Scotland. **1871** R. ELLIS *Catullus* lxiii. 17 Ye, who.. could in utter hate to lewdness your sex dishabilitate.

Hence **dishabiliˈtation**, disqualification; imposing of a legal disability.

16.. *Sc. Acts Chas. I*, (1814) V. 55 (Jam.) All prior acts of dishabilitatioun. **1861** W. BELL *Dict. Law Scot.*, *Dishabilitation* is a term sometimes used by our older law authorities, and signifies the corruption of blood consequent upon a conviction for treason.

dishabille (dɪsəˈbiːl, -ˈbɪl). Forms: α. 7 dishabillie, -billié, 7–8 dishabillee, 8 dishabilie, -habilly, -abilly, deshabilé, 7–9 déshabillé. β. 7–9 deshabille, déshabile, 8 deshabil. γ. 7– dishabille, 8 dishabile, (9 *dial.* disabil). [ad. F. *déshabillé* (in 1642 *desabillé*, Hatz.-Darm.) undress, subst. use of pa. pple. of *déshabiller* to undress, f. *des-*, DIS- 4 + *habiller* to dress, etc. The final *-é* of the French word (or its equivalent) has been occasional in English since the 17th c., but it was soon changed to *e* mute, and the prefix generally (like OF. *des-*) altered to *dis-*.]

1. The state of being partly undressed, or dressed in a negligent or careless style; undress. Usually in phr. ***in dishabille*** (= Fr. *en déshabillé*).

α. **1705** FARQUHAR *Twin-Rivals* v. iv, I found you a little in the *déshabillé*. **1709** MRS. MANLEY *New Atal.* (ed. 2) I. 38 (Stanf.) Favour'd by his Disabilly all tempting. **1711** STEELE *Spect.* No. 49 ¶3 The Pleasures of their *Deshabilé*. **1711** *Brit. Apollo* III. No. 144. 3/1 The Ladies.. Appear'd in such a Dishabilie there. **1796** G. M. WOODWARD *Eccentric Excurs.* (1807) 26 His lady made a thousand apologies for being catched in such a dishabilly. **1885** *Athenæum* 7 Nov. 601/1 The shortcomings of English costume pale before the *déshabillé* of the Dutch colonial ladies.

β. **1708** MRS. CENTLIVRE *Busie Body* I. i, What would she give now to be in this deshabille in the open air? **1713** SWIFT *Cadenus & Vanessa* 367 (1726) 96 A party next of glitt'ring Dames.. Came early, out of pure Good-will, To see the Girl in Deshabille. **1773** SHERIDAN in *Sheridaniana* 70 In studious deshabille behold her sit. **1861** T. A. TROLLOPE *La Beata* I. vi. 125 The easy, confidential intercourse of her déshabille in the boudoir.

γ. **1684** tr. *Plutarch's Mor.* Pref. (L.), To surprise his mistress in dishabille. **1763–5** CHURCHILL *Journey* Poems II. 5 Nor would I have the Sisters of the hill Behold their Bard in such a Dishabille. **1799** SOUTHEY *Nondescripts* iv, Were it fair To judge a lady in her dishabille? **1874** BURNAND *My time* ii. 13 Standing.. in his shirt-sleeves, for which dishabille he had apologized to us.

2. *concr.* A garment worn in undress; a dress or costume of a negligent style.

1673 WYCHERLEY *Gentl. Dancing-master* v. i, Contented.. instead of variety of new gowns and rich petticoats, with her dishabillie, or flame-colour gown called Indian. **1690** CROWNE *Eng. Friar* v. Dram. Wks. 1874 IV. 111 They only come in dishabilles to visit me, and did not expect your Lordship. **1713** GAY *Guardian* No. 149 ¶6 We have a kind of sketch of dress.. which, as the invention was foreign, is called a Dishabille; every thing is thrown on with a loose and careless air. **1789** MAD. D'ARBLAY *Diary* 21 Aug., She does not become a déshabille. *a* **1847** MRS. SHERWOOD *Lady of Manor* V. xxxi. 224 A neat undress, or dishabille, is much admired in England. **1868** *Gloss. Sussex Words* in Hurst *Horsham*, I'm sorry, ma'am, you see me in such a dirty disabil.

3. *transf.* and *fig.*

1712 POPE *Let.* 5 Dec. Wks. 1737 V. 188 Thoughts just warm from the brain, without any polishing or dress, the very dishabille of the understanding. **1753** FOOTE *Eng. in Paris.* I. Wks. 1799 I. 35 What has been the matter, Squire? Your face seems a little in deshabille. *a* **1817** T. DWIGHT *Trav.* (1821) II. 142 Where nature.. is now naked and deformed, she will suddenly exchange the dishabille; and be ornamented.. with her richest attire. **1825** MISS MITFORD in L'Estrange *Life* II. x. 212 [Pepys] sets down his thoughts in a most becoming dishabille. **1830** GALT *Laurie T.* IV. viii. (1849) 171 The house was in dishabille.

†**B.** as *adj.* [repr. F. *déshabillé* pa. pple.] In undress, negligently dressed. *Obs.*

1691 *Islington Wells* 4 (Stanf.) Three Ladies Drest *Dishabillee*. **1694** N. H. *Ladies Dict.* 14/1 (Stanf.) He is *Deshabille*, that is in a careless Dress.

†**disˈhabit,** *v. Obs. rare.* [f. DIS- 6 + HABIT *v.*: cf. F. *déshabiter* 'to disinhabitate, or depriue of inhabitants' (Cotgr.).] *trans.* To remove from its habitation or place of abode; to dislodge.

1595 SHAKS. *John* II. i. 220 Those sleeping stones.. from their fixed beds of lime Had bin dishabited.

†**disˈhabitable,** *a. Obs. rare.* [f. DIS- 10 + HABITABLE.] Uninhabitable.

1642 LD. FALKLAND *Let. Earl Cumberland* 5 Those false reports.. make London dishabitable.

†**disˈhabited,** *ppl. a.*[1] *Obs.* [f. F. *déshabité* 'disinhabited, without inhabitants' (Cotgr.) + -ED.] Uninhabited; deserted of inhabitants (quot. 1602).

1577 EDEN & WILLES *Hist. Trav.* 232 b, Imaginyng.. the hot Zone, to be altogeather dishabited for heat. **1582** HAKLUYT *Voy.* A, The 17 of Januarie.. we departed from the dishabited rocke. **1602** CAREW *Cornwall* 67 a, The dishabited towns afford them rooting.

†**disˈhabited,** *ppl. a.*[2] [f. DIS- 10 + HABITED.] ? Improperly habited or dressed.

1648 S. KEM in *4th Rep. Hist. MSS. Comm.* 275/1, I have certaine information that Sir Thos. Lunsford is gon up in an ould thredbare coate disshabited.

dishaˈbituate, *v.* [f. DIS- 6 + HABITUATE *v.*, prob. after F. *déshabituer* in same sense.] *trans.* To render unaccustomed, to disaccustom: the reverse of *habituate*.

1868 BROWNING *Ring & Bk.* IX. 1276 To dishabituate By sip and sip, this drainer to the dregs O' the draught of conversation. **1881** *Contemp. Rev.* Nov. 700 That talk and not action has been alone permitted to the clergy as a body has dishabituated them for the conduct of affairs.

dishable, obs. form of DISABLE *v.*

dishadow, var. of DISSHADOW *v.*

†**disˈhair,** *v. Obs.* [f. DIS- 7 a + HAIR *sb.*] *trans.* To deprive of hair, remove the hair from.

1631 *Celestina* VI. 78 They pill, and dis-haire their eyebrowes with nippers.

dishallow (dɪsˈhæləʊ), *v.* [f. DIS- 6 + HALLOW *v.*] *trans.* To undo the hallowing of; to destroy or violate the sacredness of; to profane. Hence **disˈhallowing** *vbl. sb.*, profanation.

1552 LATIMER *Serm. in Lincoln* i. 70 God hateth the dishallowing of the Sabboth. **16..** T. ADAMS *Wks.* (1861–2) II. 289 (D.) Nor can the unholiness of the priest dishallow the altar. **1647** TRAPP *Comm. Matt.* xxvi. 63 To pollute and dishallow.. that 'glorious and fearful name of God'. **1833** LAMB *Lett.* (1888) II. 288 If curses are not dis-hallowed by descending so low! **1869** TENNYSON *Pelleas & E.* 437 Ye, that so dishallow the holy sleep, Your sleep is death.

dishalluciˈnation. [DIS- 9: cf. *disillusion*.] A freeing from hallucination; disillusion.

1881 R. BUCHANAN *Child of Nature* viii, He received.. a good deal of rough treatment and sorry dishallucination. **1889** *Univ. Rev.* Mar. 356 Returning.. under dishallucination, we perceive that he does not really know so much.

†**disˈharbour,** *v. Obs.* [f. DIS- 6 or 7 + HARBOUR *v.* or *sb.*] *trans.* To drive out of its 'harbour' or place of shelter; to send adrift.

1566 DRANT *Wail. Hierim.* K vj, All reste disharboured from my soule. *a* **1612** DONNE *Βιαθανατος* (1644) 108 He [Josephus] says, our Soule is.. committed in trust to us, and we may not neglect or disharbour it.

disharmonic (dɪshɑːˈmɒnɪk), *a.* [DIS- 10.] Not harmonic; without harmony; anharmonic.

1887 H. WALLACH in *Anthrop. Inst. Jrnl.* XVII. 160 The head is disharmonic. The skull is sub-dolichocephalous, very broad, the forehead low, and the prognathism never much accentuated.

†**disharˈmonical,** *a. Obs.* [f. DIS- + HARMONICAL, after *disharmony*.] = prec.

1688 NORRIS *Theory Love* II. i. 88 Some.. strokes upon it [a musical instrument] will.. be harmonical, and other some .. disharmonical. *Ibid.* (1694) 74 The same Strokes, that were before disharmonical, may be now harmonical.

disharmonious (dɪshɑːˈməʊnɪəs), *a.* [f. DIS- 10 + HARMONIOUS; after *disharmony*.]

1. Not in harmony or agreement; marked by want of harmony.

1659 H. MORE *Immort. Soul* (1662) 148 [It] may.. prove painful to the Soul, and dis-harmonious to her touch. **1661** GLANVILL *Van. Dogm.* iv. 39 The musician's soul would be the most disharmonious. **1683** TRYON *Way to Health*, Thus there is caused an unequal disharmonious Life. **1754** J. HILDROP *Misc. Wks.* I. 38 Disharmonious, disorderly Motions of the Fluids and Animal Spirits. **1876** FARRAR *Marlb. Serm.* xxxv. 355 Let me warn you against the fatal delusion that such a dual, such a divided, such a disharmonious life as this, is enough for God.

2. Of sounds: Unharmonious, discordant.

1683 TRYON *Way to Health* 461 The dis-harmonious noise of Drunken Healths and Roaring Huzza's. **1864** CARLYLE *Fredk. Gt.* (1865) IV. XI. iii. 56 Dispute which rose *crescendo* in disharmonious duet.

Hence **disharˈmoniously** *adv.*, in a disharmonious manner, discordantly.

1664 H. MORE *Myst. Iniq.* To Rdr., Whose very title sounds so harshly and disharmoniously. **1865** CARLYLE *Fredk. Gt.* XV. xiii. (1873) VI. 97 This.. victorious campaign .. with which all Europe is disharmoniously ringing.

disharmonize (dɪsˈhɑːmənaɪz), *v.* [f. DIS- + HARMONIZE; after *disharmony*. Cf. mod.F. *désharmoniser*, neologism in Littré, 1874.]

1. *trans.* To put out of harmony, destroy the harmony of; to make unharmonious or discordant.

1801 J. CAREY in *Monthly Mag.* XI. 314 Instances in which the harmony of ancient versification is thus disharmonized by the application of modern accent. **1824** LAMB *Elia* Ser. II. *Blakesmoor in H-shire*, A trait of affectation, or worse, vain-glory.. disharmonizing the place and the occasion. **1843** PUSEY *Holy Eucharist* 10 Our nature jarring still, disharmonized, obscured, deformed. **1858** SEARS *Athan.* III. x. 335 Cleared of disharmonizing elements.

2. *intr.* To be out of harmony; not to harmonize.

1863 B. TAYLOR *H. Thurston* III. 22 A trifle of affectation in her manner did not disharmonize with such a face; it was natural to her.

disharmony (dɪsˈhɑːmənɪ). [f. DIS- 9 + HARMONY; prob. formed after *discord.* Cf. mod.F. *désharmonie*, neologism in Littré, 1874, also corresponding words in other mod. langs.]

1. Want of harmony or agreement, discordance.

*a***1602** W. PERKINS *Cases Consc.* (1619) 6 The want or absence of harmony, which we call disharmony. **1665** GLANVILL *Scepsis Sci.* xiii. 76 Reason and Faith are at perfect Unisons, the disharmony is in the Phancy. **1765** LAW *Behmen's Myst. Magnum* liii. (1772) 324 Of the Properties in their Disharmony, Inequality, and Discord. **1864** CARLYLE *Fredk. Gt.* (1865) IV. XI. ii. 33 Disharmony of mind and tongue. **1879** FARRAR *St. Paul* II. 226 That sense of guilt which is the feeling of disharmony with God.

b. with *a* and *pl.* Something discordant.

1833 LAMB *Elia* (1860) 364 If it ever obtrudes itself as a disharmony, are we inclined to laugh? **1884** *Ch. Times* 25 Apr. 331/4 The manifold disharmonies of Church and State in England.

2. Want of harmony between sounds; discord, dissonance.

*a***1655** VINES *Lord's Supp.* (1677) 10 A string over-stretched makes a jar and disharmony. **1675** R. BURTHOGGE *Causa Dei* 398 No harmony or Dis-harmony in sounds. **1860** TRENCH *Serm. Westm. Abb.* xxiv. 279 Harsh discords and disharmonies.. make themselves heard.

†**diˈshatter,** *v. Obs. rare*⁻¹. [f. *di-* for DIS- 1 + SHATTER.] *trans.* To shatter completely.

1615 DANIEL *Hymen's Tri.* II. iv, I rather will Rend it in Pieces, and dishatter all Into a Chaos.

†**disˈhaunt,** *v. Obs.* (Chiefly *Sc.*) Also 7-8 **dishant.** [ad. OF. *deshanter* (Cotgr.), f. DIS- 4 + *hanter* to HAUNT.] *trans.* To cease to haunt, frequent, or resort to; to absent oneself from.

1584 HUDSON *Du Bartas' Judith* IV. 125 (D.) She dishaunted the resort Of such as were suspect of light report. **1637-50** ROW *Hist. Kirk* (1842) 48 The nobilitie and barons ..now did dishaunt them. **1659** in W. McDowall *Hist. Dumfries* xxxii. (1873) 371 Capt. Ed. Maxwell delate for dishaunting the ordinances. **1808-80** JAMIESON, *Dishaunt*.. is still occasionally used. *Aberd.*

Hence †**disˈhaunting** *vbl. sb.*; †**disˈhaunter,** one who 'dishaunts'. *Obs.*

*a***1651** CALDERWOOD *Hist. Kirk* (1842-6) III. 375 The dishaunting and intermissioun of the exercise. **1665** in Cramond *Ann. Banff* II. 46 Several dishaunters of ordinances ordained to be summoned.

dish-cloth.

1. A cloth used in the kitchen or scullery for washing dishes, etc.

1828 in WEBSTER. **1869** *Lonsdale Gloss.* 25/1 Dish-clout, a dish-cloth. **1887** R. BUCHANAN *Heir of Linne* i, A sort of banner, composed of an old towel or dish-cloth.

2. dishcloth gourd, the gourd or the plant of any of the species of *Luffa*, esp. L. *cylindrica*, of which the spongy inner portion of the fruit may be used as a cloth.

1900 L. H. BAILEY *Cycl. Amer. Hort.* II. 948/2 *Luffa*... Dishcloth Gourd. Vegetable Sponge... *L. cylindrica*... The commonest Dishcloth Gourd. **1963** J. ORGAN *Gourds* vii. 93 British seedsmen on the whole restrict themselves to *L. cylindrica* which is usually listed as *Luffa*, Dishcloth gourd, or Vegetable Sponge.

dish-clout. *arch.* or *dial.* A 'clout' or cloth used for washing dishes, etc.; = prec. ***in the wringing of a dish-clout***: speedily, immediately.

1530 PALSGR. 214/1 Disshecloute, *souillon.* **1577** FENTON *Gold. Epist.* 90 As the saying is, washe their face with faire water, and drie it ouer with a dishcloute. **1677** HORNECK *Gt. Law Consid.* iii. (1704) 68 He that makes a rich carpet, doth not intend it for dish-clouts. **1782** MAD. D'ARBLAY *Diary* 28 Dec., What a slut Mrs. Ord must think me, to put a dish-clout in my pocket! **1821** SCOTT *Kenilw.* ix, Breakfast shall be on the board in the wringing of a dish-clout. **1824** W. IRVING *T. Trav.* II. 36 And have known Hamlet to stalk solemnly on to deliver his soliloquy, with a dishclout pinned to his skirts. **1877** E. PEACOCK *N.W. Linc. Gloss.* 86/1 'Go thee ways or I'll pin th' dishclout to thee tail' is not unfrequently said to men and boys who interfere in the kitchen.

b. taken as a type of limpness and weakness.

1692 TRYON *Good House-w.* i. (ed. 2) 7 You are now weak as Water, and have no more Spirits than a Dish-clout. **1863** MRS. CARLYLE *Lett.* III. 170, I was on foot again—but weak as a dishclout.

c. used in contemptuous comparison or allusion.

*a***1529** SKELTON *Poems agst. Garnesche* 36, A bawdy dyshe-clowte, That bryngyth the worlde abowte. **1592** SHAKS. *Rom. & Jul.* III. v. 221 Romeos a dish-clout to him. **1636** MASSINGER *Bashf. Lover* v. i, I am gazing on this gorgeous house; our cote's a dishclout to it.

d. *transf.*

1615 CROOKE *Body of Man* 97 The Latines [call the caul] *Mappaventris*, the dish-clout or map of the Belly, because it licketh vp the superfluities thereof. **1785** GROSE *Dict. Vulg. Tongue* s.v., To make a napkin of one's dish-clout, to marry one's cook. **1822** SCOTT *Fam. Lett.* 25 June, It was hard he should be made the dish-clout to wipe up the stains of such a man.

e. *attrib.*

1589 NASHE *Almond for Parrat* 11 b, More.. then his dish-clout discipline will sette vp in seauen yeeres. **1755** H. WALPOLE *Let. Geo. Montagu* 20 Dec., That old rag of a dish-clout ministry, Harry Furnese, is to be the other lord.

Hence **dish-clout** *v. trans.*, to wash with a dish-clout.

1861 MAYHEW *Lond. Labour* III. 363 (Hoppe) They are expected.. to dish-clout the whole of the panels [of a cab].

†**disˈheart,** *v. Obs.* Also 7 **dishart.** [f. DIS- 7 a + HEART *sb.*] = DISHEARTEN.

1603 J. DAVIES *Microcosmos* (1876) 42 (D.) When, therefore, divine justice sinne wil scurge, He doth dishart their harts in whom it raignes. **1612** T. TAYLOR *Comm. Titus* i. 13 The which would vtterly disheart them. *a***1616** BEAUM. & FL. *Bonduca* I. i, *Car.* Have not I seen the Britains — *Bond.* What? *Car.* Dishearted.

dishearten (dɪsˈhɑːt(ə)n), *v.* Also 7 **dishartеn.** [f. DIS- 6 + HEARTEN, or from prec. + -EN⁵, after *hearten.*] *trans.* To deprive of 'heart' or courage; to discourage, dispirit, make despondent.

1599 SHAKS. *Hen. V*, IV. i. 117 No man should possesse him with any appearance of feare; lest hee, by shewing it, should dis-hearten his Army. **1606** WARNER *Alb. Eng.* XIV. xc. 365 Their former losse dishartned them so much. **1796** MORSE *Amer. Geog.* I. 120 A great part.. disheartened by the severity of the winter, returned to England. **1838** THIRLWALL *Greece* IV. 115 Lysander exerted his utmost efforts to thwart, discredit, and dishearten his successor.

†**b.** with complement: To discourage *from* doing something (also with *to* and *inf.*). *Obs.*

1634 SIR T. HERBERT *Trav.* 121 The Turkes got the greatest losse, and were disheartned to proceed further. **1642** FULLER *Holy & Prof. St.* II. xvi. 109 They are disheartened from doing their best. **1684** BUNYAN *Pilgr.* II. (1862) 235 She urged what she could to dishearten me to it. **1697** DAMPIER *Voy.* I. 27 Disheartned them from that design.

†**c.** with an action or the like as object: cf. DISCOURAGE 2. *Obs.*

1658 *Whole Duty Man* Pref. 4 Where this is wanting, it disheartens our care. **1668** CLARENDON *Vind.* Tracts (1727) 64 An uncertainty which must dishearten any industry.

disˈheartened, *ppl. a.* [f. prec. + -ED¹.] Discouraged, dispirited: see the verb.

1724 DE FOE *Mem. Cavalier* (1840) 210 We were a disheartened army. **1849** MACAULAY *Hist. Eng.* I. 517 The Whigs were a small and a disheartened minority.

Hence **disˈheartenedness,** dispirited condition.

*a***1679** T. GOODWIN *Wks.* II. I. 170 (R.) A disheartenedness and dejection of mind. **1863** DICEY *Federal St.* II. 273, I heard no cry of despair or disheartenedness.

disˈheartener. [f. DISHEARTEN + -ER¹.] One who disheartens.

1645 *City Alarum* 9 A disheartner of Gods people.

disˈheartening, *vbl. sb.* [f. as prec. + -ING¹.] The action of vb. DISHEARTEN; discouragement.

1619 W. SCLATER *Exp. I. Thess.* (1630) 309 Hierome thought labour a dis-heartning to the Tempter. **1654** WHITLOCK *Zootomia* Pref. A vj, Or else he may lye open to such disheartnings, as become not.. these undertakings.

disˈheartening, *ppl. a.* [f. as prec. + -ING².] That disheartens; discouraging, dispiriting.

1654 *Nicholas Papers* (Camden) II. 101 As serviceable to the Rebells..and as dishartning to honest men. **1748** *Anson's Voy.* I. x. 107 Under these disheartning circumstances. **1860** FROUDE *Hist. Eng.* V. 235 Friends brought in disheartening news.

Hence **disˈhearteningly** *adv.*

1742 BAILEY, *Dishearteningly*, by way of Discouragement. **1882** HALL CAINE *Recoll. D. G. Rossetti* 98 Dishearteningly unpropitious weather.

disˈheartenment. [f. DISHEARTEN + -MENT.] The act of disheartening, or fact of being disheartened; discouragement.

1830 CARLYLE *Misc.* (1857) II. 143 No disheartenment availed with him. **1876** FARRAR *Marlb. Serm.* xxxix. 393 Among the disheartenments of labour and the strife of tongues. **1886** MRS. A. HUNT *That Other Person* III. 211 A sigh of complete fatigue and disheartenment.

dished (dɪʃt), *ppl. a.* [f. DISH *v.*¹ + -ED.] **a.** Put in a dish. **b.** Shaped like a dish; made slightly concave. **c.** *slang*: see DISH *v.* 7.

1586 T. B. *La Primaud. Fr. Acad.* I. (1589) 195 Raddish rosted in the ashes.. was all the dished he had to his supper. **1650** BULWER *Anthropomet.* 241 They use Disht wheat with milk. **1737** BRACKEN *Farriery Imp.* (1757) II. 37 The Soles ..a little hollow or dish'd. **1812-6** J. SMITH *Panorama Sc. & Art* I. 372 Dished wheels have many excellencies. **1878** *Trans. Ill. Dept. Agric.* XIV. 210 The head was short and fine, with a dished face and rather thin jowls. **1908** *Animal Managem.* 21 The face.. 'stag-faced' or 'dished'. **1958** *Daily Mail* 19 Aug. 4/8 The least we can do.. is to adopt 'dished' steering wheels on all cars. **1962** *Which?* (Car Suppl.) Jan. 4/2 *Dished*, when used for a steering wheel, means that the centre hub is lower than the rim.

†**disˈhedge,** *v. Obs. nonce-wd.* [f. DIS- 7 a + HEDGE *sb.*] *trans.* To deprive of its hedge.

*c***1586** C'TESS. PEMBROKE *Ps.* lxxx. iv, Why hast thou now thy self dishedg'd this vine?

†**disˈheir,** *v. Obs. rare.* [f. DIS- 7 b + HEIR.]

1. *trans.* To deprive of or turn out of one's inheritance; to disinherit.

[**1492** *Act. Dom. Conc.* 262 (Jam.) In distitutioun and dishering of the said Gelis [perh. error for *disherising*].] **1607** TOURNEUR *Rev. Trag.* I. iii, Sword.. Thou shalt dis-heire him; it shall be thine honor.

2. To deprive of an heir.

1687 DRYDEN *Hind & P.* III. 705 To hew th' imperial Cedar down, Defraud Succession, and dis-heir the Crown.

[**dishele** (Halliw.), error for *dishese*, DISEASE.]

dishelm (dɪsˈhɛlm), *v.*¹ [f. DIS- 7 a + HELM helmet, after OF. *desheaulmer, -healmer*, in same sense.] *trans.* To deprive or disarm of one's helmet. *intr.* for *refl.* To take off one's helmet.

*c***1477** CAXTON *Jason* 25 b, Incontinent as.. Jason hadde.. smyton doun the geant to the erthe.. he dishelmed. **1525** LD. BERNERS *Froiss.* II. clxviii. [clxiv.] 469 Sir Raynold dishelmed the Englisshe knyght. **1615** CHAPMAN *Odyss.* XIV. 383 Jove made me yield, Dishelm my head. **1847** TENNYSON *Princess* VI. 85 When she saw me lying stark, Dishelm'd and mute.

dishelm (dɪsˈhɛlm), *v.*² [f. DIS- 7 a + HELM.] *trans.* To deprive of the helm or rudder.

*a***1849** H. COLERIDGE *Poems* (1850) II. 155 Fear that dishelms The vessel of the soul. **1861** LYTTON & FANE *Tannhäuser* 75 To float, dishelm'd, a wreck upon the waves.

dishelv'd: see DISHEVELLED.

dishenerite, -yt, obs. f. *disenherit*, DISINHERIT.

disher (ˈdɪʃə(r)). [f. DISH *sb.* and *v.* + -ER¹: cf. *saddler.*]

†**1.** A maker or seller of dishes. *Obs.*

1304 in Riley *Mem. London* (1868) 54 John le Disshere. **1362** LANGL. *P. Pl.* A. v. 166 A Ropere, a Redyng-kyng, and Rose þe disschere. [**1377** B. v. 323 Rose þe dissheres; *v.r.* dyssheres douȝter. **1393** C. VII. 372 disshere]. *a***1500** *Voc.* in Wr.-Wülcker 572 *Cipharius*, a cuppere, or a dysshere. **1892** O. HESLOP *Northumbld. Gloss.* 238 *Disher*, a turner of wooden bowls or dishes. Within the memory of some still living (1886) there was a disher working at Mitford. (Obs.)

2. One who dishes or serves up food. ? *Obs.*

1598 FLORIO, *Imbanditore*, a gentleman sewer, a disher or dresser vp of meates.

3. One who 'dishes': see DISH *v.* 7.

1892 *Pall Mall G.* 21 June 1/3 By the indignation which the dirty trick will excite.. the disher will thus in the end be dished.

†**disˈherbage,** *v. Obs.* [f. DIS- 7 a + HERBAGE *sb.*] *trans.* To deprive or strip of herbage.

1542 UDALL *Erasm. Apoph.* 216 b, These wordes, λειποβοτανεῖν ἐποίησε, that is, 'hath brought this climate to clene *disherbageing*', smellen all of the inkehorne.

disˈherent, *a. nonce-wd.* [f. DIS- 4 + radical part of *co-herent.*] The opposite of *coherent*; incoherent; incongruous.

1890 J. H. STIRLING *Philos. & Theol.* iii. 49 It is the Τὸ ἀντίξουν συμφέρον, the coherent disherent, attributed to Heraclitus by Aristotle.

†ˈ**disheress.** *Obs. rare.* [f. DISHER *sb.* + -ESS.] A woman who makes or sells dishes.

*a***1300** *Hundred Rolls* in Bardsley *Eng. Surnames* (1873) 349 Margaret la Disheress [ed. 2, 1875, p. 393 le Disheresse]. **1377** [see DISHER 1].

disherid, -ied, obs. pa. pple. and pa. t. of DISHERIT *v.*

disherison (dɪsˈhɛrɪzən), *sb.* Forms: α. 3-4 **desertison, -tesoun, diserteisoun,** 4-5 **disheriteson, -itison, -etison, -yteson, desheryteson.** β. 5- **disherison.** [orig. *disheriteson*, a. OF. *des(h)eriteisun, -eison*, n. of action from *des(h)eriter* to DISHERIT. (The full L. type was **dishērēditātiōn-em*: the syllable *ed* was dropped in OF., the *t* before *s* in English.)] The action of depriving of, or cutting off from, an inheritance; disinheritance.

*c***1290** *Beket* 1836 in *S. Eng. Leg.* I. 159 Þat it.. were.. with on-riȝte and a-ȝein lawe In desertison of mine churche to costome i-drawe. *c***1330** R. BRUNNE *Chron.* (1810) 214 To him and his heyres grete disheriteson. **1340** *Ayenb.* 48 Desertesoun of eyr and ualse mariages. **1399** *Rolls of Parlt.* III. 451/2 Forfaitures of heritages, and disheretisons. **1491** *Act 7 Hen. VII*, c. 18 The utter disheriteson of your seid Suppliant. **1495** *Act 11 Hen. VII*, c. 35. §9 To the hurte prejudice nor disherison of the seid George or of his heires. **1523** *Act 14-15 Hen. VIII*, c. 13 The saide hauen is.. likely to be lost for euer, to the kynges disherison, and hurte of the common welth. **1607** COWELL *Interpr.* s.v. *Contra formam collationis*, The Abbot.. hath made a feofment.. to the disherison of the house or church. **1750** CARTE *Hist. Eng.* II. 291 Pardoning them all as to life, limb, imprisonment and disherison. **1844** WILLIAMS *Real Prop.* (1879) 67 To prevent improvident alienations..of landed estates, by..dying persons, to the disherison of their lawful heirs.

† **dis'herison**, *v. Obs. rare*⁻¹. [f. prec. sb.] *trans.* To disinherit.

1654 GAYTON *Pleas. Notes* IV. 212 To defraud rav'nous this expectant of his hopes, and to disherison his malignant issue.

† **dis'heriss**, *v. Obs.* (Chiefly *Sc.*) Forms: 4 **dysherys**, 6 **disheris, -heireis, -hæriss, 7 disheriss, disherize.** [14–16th c. Sc. *disheriss*, as if f. extended stem of an OF. **disherir* to disheir, which may have been used in AF. The corresponding E. form would be *disherish*; the form in -IZE is due to confusion of verbal suffix: cf. *advertise, amortize.*] = next.

1375 BARBOUR *Bruce* II. 101 Ȝe se How Inglis men, throw thar powste, Dysherysys me off my land. **1500–20** DUNBAR *Poems* lxvi. 38 The temporall stait to gryp and gather, The sone disheris wald the father. **1536** BELLENDEN *Cron. Scot.* (1821) I. p. lxiv, This was Edward..disherist of the crown of Ingland. **1609** SKENE *Reg. Maj.* 41 Quhen ane man..does anie thing..for the quhilk he is disherissed: his heretage vses to returne, as escheit to his over-lord. **1611** SPEED *Hist. Gr. Brit.* IX. v. §25 These..thus disherized, ought of right.. giue first assault on their vnrighteous oppressor.

† **disherit** (dɪs'hɛrɪt), *v. Obs.* Forms: 3–4 **deserit(e, -yte, -et, 4 desherit(e, dysheriete, 4–5 diserit(e, -yt, dyserit, 4–7 disherite, 5–6 dis-, dysherit, -yt(e, -et(t, -eit, 4–8 disherit.** [ME. a. OF. *desheriter, deseriter, -ereter, -ireter*, etc., mod.F. *déshériter* = Pr. *des(h)eretar*, Sp. *desheredar*, Pg. *desherdar*, It. *diseredare*, med.L. *disheritāre, deheritāre* (Du Cange):—Rom. *desheretāre*, for L. **de-, *dishērēditāre*, f. DE- 6, DIS- 4 + *hērēditāre* to inherit, f. *hērēditās* heirship, inheritance. The pa. pple. and sometimes the pa. t. had also the shortened form *disherit*, with the variants *disherid, -ied, desered, desirit*: see examples at end of the article.]

1. *trans.* To deprive or dispossess of an inheritance; to disinherit.

c **1290** *S. Eng. Leg.* I. 74/107 Alle oþure weren deseritede. *c* **1385** CHAUCER *L.G.W.* 1065 *Dido*, That euere swich a noble man as he [Eneas] Schal ben diserityd in swich degre. *c* **1465** *Eng. Chron.* (Camden) 16 Thow has thaym slayne vnrightfulli, and disherited thair heiris. **1538** STARKEY *England* II. ii. 196 Hyt were not mete that the father schold dysheryte hys chyld. **1634** SIR T. HERBERT *Trav.* Table 230 [He] rebels against his Father, is disherited by his Fathers will. **1700** DRYDEN *Fables, Pal. & Arc.* III. 968 The dryads and the woodland train Disherited ran howling o'er the plain.

b. Const. *of* (rarely *from*).

c **1330** R. BRUNNE *Chron. Wace* (Rolls) 5394 He scholde.. Deserite Wyder of ylka del. *c* **1386** CHAUCER *Melib.* ¶869 To desherite hem of al þat euere they han. **1523** FITZHERB. *Surv.* Prol., Disheryted of theyr possessyons. **1570** T. NORTON tr. *Nowel's Catech.* (1853) 193 Like children disherited from their father's goods. **1652–62** HEYLIN *Cosmogr.* II. (1682) 5 Disherited of their Fathers kingdom. **1795** SOUTHEY *Joan of Arc* I. 172 The great and honourable men Have seized the earth, and of the heritage Which God ..to all had given, Disherited their brethren!

2. *fig.* To deprive, dispossess; to banish from its rightful domain (quot. 1579¹).

c **1400** MAUNDEV. (Roxb.) xxxii. 145 Ay to þis tyme we bene in peess, of þe whilk þou will now dispoile vs and disherit vs. **1579** E. K. *Ded. to Spenser's Sheph. Cal.*, This Poet..hath labored to restore, as to their rightfull heritage, such good and naturall English wordes, as have beene long time out of use, and almost cleane disherited. **1579** LYLY *Euphues* (Arb.) 192 Thou art an heyre to fayre lyuing, that is nothing, if thou be disherited of learning. **1795** COLERIDGE *Juvenile Poems* (1864) 62 Made blind by lusts, disherited of soul.

Hence **dis'herited** *ppl. a.*, **dis'heriting** *vbl. sb.*

1388 in *Wyclif's Sel. Wks.* III. 471 A pleynt of disherytyng of his riȝt and possessions. *c* **1450** *St. Cuthbert* (Surtees) 5522 Of þair diserytyng to sees [= cease]. **1613–8** DANIEL *Coll. Hist. Eng.* (1626) 154 The dis-herited returne answer to the Legat. **1655** FULLER *Ch. Hist.* III. vii. §2 The premisses tend..to the disheriting of the Crown of England.

¶ Examples of pa. pple. and pa. t. *disherit*, etc.

c **1314** *Guy Warw.* (A.) 6164 Thurch felonie mi fader he slough, Mi brother he desirit with wough. *c* **1375** *Lay Folks Mass Bk.* (MS. B.) 379 Pore, exilde, deserit. *c* **1375** *XI Pains of Hell* 39 in *O.E. Misc.* 211 Þese..deseredyn treu ayrs vnryȝtfully. **1460** CAPGRAVE *Chron.* 289 Many men were disherid of her londis. **1523** FITZHERB. *Surv.* Prol., Theyr heyres shuld nat be disheryt. *a* **1533** LD. BERNERS *Huon* lx. 210 He hath dysheryt me.

† **dis'heritance.** *Obs.* [a. OF. *des(h)eritance*, f. *desheriter*: see prec. and -ANCE.] The act of disinheriting; disinheritance.

c **1450** LONELICH *Grail* xxix. 85 It was cawse of here disheritaunce. **1531** *Dial. on Laws Eng.* II. i. (1638) 61 The alienation is to his disheritance, and therefore it is a forfeiture of his estate. **1660** R. COKE *Power & Subj.* 195 Infinite losses and disheritances are like to ensue to the founders of the said houses..and their heirs.

† **dis'herite.** *Obs.* In 4 **deserite, -yte.** [perh. a. OF. *des(h)erité* disherited, pa. pple. used subst.] A disinherited person.

1297 R. GLOUC. (1724) 452 Hii sette deserytes in þe myddel ost þo, þat þe kyng adde bynome her lond. *Ibid.* 563 Þe kniȝtes were deserites in þe lond aboute wide.

dis'heritment. *rare.* [f. DISHERIT *v.* + -MENT: in OF. *desheritement.*] The act of disinheriting; = DISHERITANCE.

1881 *Scribner's Mag.* XXII. 757 [He] dared to hand to the Tsar..his protest against the act of disheritment.

† **dis'heritor.** *Obs. rare.* [f. DISHERIT *v.* + -OR for AF. *-our.*] One who disinherits.

1607–72 COWELL *Interpr.*, *Disheritor*, one that disinheriteth, or puts another out of his Inheritance, 3 E. 1 cap. 39.

disherize, var. of DISHERISS, *Obs.*

dishero (dɪs'hɪərəʊ), *v.* [f. DIS- 7 b.] *trans.* To deprive of the character of a hero.

1838 CARLYLE *Misc.* (1872) VI. 30 A hypothesis..that Mr. Lockhart at heart has a dislike to Scott, and has done his best in an underhand, treacherous manner, to dishero him.

dishese, obs. form of DISEASE.

† **di'shevel**, *a. Obs.* In 4–5 **discheuel(e, disshevele, dysshyuell,** 5 **dishiuill,** (*Sc.*) **dyschowyll.** [Variant of DISHEVELY, a. OF. *deschevelé*, with final *é* mute in Eng. Cf. ASSIGN *sb.*]

1. Without coif or head-dress; hence, with the hair unconfined and flung about in disorder. Sometimes app. in wider sense: Undressed, in dishabille.

c **1381** CHAUCER *Parl. Foules* 235 In kyrtelles al discheuel [*v.rr.* dysshyuell, discheuele, disshevld, disshevelel, dischieflee] went þei þer. *c* **1385** —— *L.G.W.* 1720 *Lucretia*, This noble wif sat by hire beddys side Discheuele [*v.r.* disshevely] for no maleyce she ne thoughte. *c* **1470** HENRY *Wallace* XI. 1014 Eftyr mydnycht in handis thai haiff him tane, Dyschowyll on sleipe.

2. Of hair: = DISHEVELLED 2.

c **1450** *Crt. of Love* 139 And all her haire it shone as gold so fine Dishiuill crispe down hanging at her backe A yard in length.

dishevel (dɪ'ʃɛvəl), *v.* [perh. a. 16th c. *descheveler* (Cotgr.), mod. *décheveler*; but prob. chiefly a back-formation from DISHEVELLED.]

1. *trans.* To loosen and throw about in disorder (hair and the like); to let (the hair) down.

1598 FLORIO, *Dischiomare*, to disheuell, to touze ones haire. **1611** COTGR., *Descheveler*, to discheuell; to pull the haire about the eares. **1618** *Barnevelt's Apol.* D iij, The Peacock when he's viewd disheuels his faire traine. **1648** JOS. BEAUMONT *Psyche* II. ix, They..dishevel May Round Tellus's springing face. **1800** MRS. HERVEY *Mourtray Fam.* I. 201 He had been at court in the morning; but though he had changed his clothes, he had omitted to dishevel his hair. **1826** *Blackw. Mag.* XX. 397 She now dishevels..the unsinged beauty of her flowing tresses.

† **2.** *intr.* (for *refl.*) Of hair: To hang loose or in disorder. *Obs.*

1638 SIR T. HERBERT *Trav.* (ed. 2) 230 Their haire curling, dishevells oft times about their shoulders. *Ibid.* 355.

Hence **di'shevelling** *vbl. sb.*

a **1656** BP. HALL *Rem. Wks.* (1660) 244 The..wanton fashion of the womans dissheveling her hair. **1786** MAD. D'ARBLAY *Diary* 17 July, Just as I was in the midst of my hair dishevelling, I was summoned.

dishevelled, -eled (dɪ'ʃɛvəld), *ppl. a.* Forms: 5–7 **discheveled,** 5 **dishevilled, dyssheuelled,** 6 **disheuld, discheaueled,** 7 **-evell'd, disheveld, -eviled, euelled,** 7– **dishevelled.** [f. OF. *deschevelé* mod.F. *déchevelé* (see DISHEVELY *a.*) + -ED.]

† **1.** = DISHEVEL *a. Obs.*

c **1450** *Merlin* 453 She was discheueled and hadde the feirest heed that eny woman myght haue. *Ibid.* 646 An olde woman discheueled, and all to-rente hir heir. **1494** *Househ. Ord.* 123 Her [the Queen's] head must bee dishevilled with a riche sircle on her head. **1591** SIDNEY *Ast. & Stella* ciii, She, so disheuld blusht. **1653** H. COGAN *Diod. Sic.* 151 Growing distracted with griefe..she went up and downe.. all discheveled with her haire about her eares.

b. In vaguer sense: With disarranged or disordered dress; untidy.

1612 DRAYTON *Poly-olb.* xiii. 215 With thy disheveld nymphs attyr'd in youthfull greene. **1749** FIELDING *Tom Jones* IX. iii, The dishevelled fair hastily following. **1862** TROLLOPE *Orley F.* lxxiii, Her whole appearance was haggard and dishevelled.

2. Of the hair: Unconfined by head-gear, hanging loose, flung about in disorder; unkempt.

1583 STANYHURST *Aeneis* I. (Arb.) 28 Doune to the wynd tracing trayld her discheaueled hearlocks. **1638** *Penit. Conf.* iii. (1657) 22 Our hair dischiveld, not platted nor crisped. **1718** PRIOR *Pleasure* 567 With flowing sorrow, and dishevell'd hair. **1813** SCOTT *Trierm.* III. xxxviii, Still her dark locks dishevell'd flow From net of pearl o'er breast of snow. **1887** BOWEN *Virg. Æneid* III. 593 Foul rags and a beard dishevelled he wore.

3. *transf.* Disordered, ruffled, disorderly, untidy.

1647 WARD *Simp. Cobler* 32 When States dishevl'd [*printed* dishelv'd] are, and Lawes untwist. **1712–14** POPE *Rape Lock* v. 130 The heav'ns bespangling with dishevell'd light. **1858** *Sat. Rev.* V. 388/1 In vehement diction, but dishevelled grammar. **1882** BLACK *Shandon Bells* xviii, The dishevelled mass of music that she never would keep in order. **1883** H. DRUMMOND *Nat. Law in Spir. W.* (ed. 2) 294 Religion is no dishevelled mass of aspiration, prayer, and faith. **1886** STEVENSON *Pr. Otto* II. ii. 87 A certain lady of a dishevelled reputation.

† **b.** In good sense: Unconstrained, free, easy.

a **1639** WOTTON in *Reliq.* (1685) 482 One of the genialest pieces that I have read..of the same unaffected and discheveled kind.

Hence **di'shevelledness.**

1889 T. GIFT *Not for Night-time* 165 Smiling to myself at my dishevelledness.

dishevelment (dɪ'ʃɛvəlmənt). [f. DISHEVEL *v.* + -MENT.] The action of dishevelling; dishevelled condition.

1837 CARLYLE *Fr. Rev.* II. I. xi. (1872) 50 Their Hebe eyes brighter with enthusiasm, and long hair in beautiful dishevelment. **1880** MISS BROUGHTON *Sec. Th.* II. III. vii. 236 His tone..has made her hotly conscious of her dishevelment.

† **di'shevely, -elee,** *ppl. a.* Also 4–5 **dischieflee,** 5 **discheuelee.** [a. OF. *deschevelé* pa. pple., f. *des-*, DIS- + OF. *chevel, cheveu* hair, = med.L. *dis-, dēcapillātus* stripped of hair, shaven, Sp. *descabellado* 'bald, hauing no haire left on his head': cf. It. *(di)scapigliare* 'to desheuell, to disorder..ones head or haires'. In another form of this word, the *-é* of OF. pa. pple., became mute in ME.: see DISHEVEL *a.*] = DISHEVEL *a.* 1.

a **1430** *Chaucer's Canterb. T. Prol.* 683 (Ellesm. MS.) Discheuelee [*other MSS.* discheuele] saue his cappe he rood al bare. **14..** *Chaucer's L.G.W.* 1315 *Dido* (Fairf. MS.) She falleth him to foote and swowneth there Disshevely with hire bryght gelte here. *c* **1450** *Merlin* 298 She was all discheuelee in her heer. *c* **1470** HARDING *Chron.* CLXXVIII. ii, In chaumbre preuy At discouert descheuely also in all, As seruyng was to estate virginall.

dishful ('dɪʃfʊl). Also 4 **dissuol.** [f. DISH *sb.* + -FUL.] As much as a dish will contain.

c **1320** *Seuyn Sag.* (W.) 1918 Thre dissch-fol of blod he let me blede. **1340** *Ayenb.* 120 Yef me yefþ..ane poure manne ane dissuol of pesen. **1577** B. GOOGE *Heresbach's Husb.* III. (1586) 136 b, Geve to every one a little dishefull of rennet crudes. **1641** BEST *Farm. Bks.* (Surtees) 105 They make account that fower mowter dishfulls is a pecke. **1719** DE FOE *Crusoe* II. vii. (1840) II. 170 A..dishfull of water.

dishing ('dɪʃɪŋ), *vbl. sb.* [f. DISH *v.*¹ + -ING¹.]

a. The action of the verb DISH.

1679 DRYDEN *Troilus & Cr.* I. ii, The dishing, the setting on the table. **1691** WOOD *Ath. Oxon.* I. 160 (L.) In the dishing out of whose Odcombian banquet, he had a considerable hand. *c* **1806** D. WORDSWORTH *Tour Scotl.* in *Jrnls.* (1941) I. 281 We grew impatient for our dinner..but we had to wait at least another half hour before the ceremony of dishing up was completed. **1858** R. S. SURTEES *Ask Mamma* xxxii, Nor do their anxieties end with the dishing-up of the dinner. **1919** W. LANG *Sea-Lawyer's Log* iii. 29 The Duty Watch are busily engaged in the Barrack Room washing and drying their table utensils (a process known in the Service as 'dishing up'). **1955** *Times* 4 May 13/5 The dishing out of Constitutions which did not satisfy the aspirations of these African peoples.

b. Oblique position of the spokes of a wheel, making its outer face concave.

1797 A. CUMMING in *Commun. Bd. Agric.* II. 366 Dishing (or the oblique position of the spokes) added much to the strength and stiffness of wheels. **1880** L. WALLACE *Ben-Hur* 209 The spokes were sections of ivory tusks, set in with the natural curve outward, to perfect the dishing.

'dishing, *ppl. a.* [-ING².] That 'dishes'; *spec.* forming a concave or dish-like surface; see DISH *v.* 4, 5, 6, 7.

1669 WORLIDGE *Syst. Agric.* (1681) 232 They make them [Spokes] concave or dishing..to secure the Wheel from breaking in a fall. **1707** MORTIMER *Husb.* (J.), For the form of the wheels, some make them more dishing..that is, more concave, by setting off the spokes and fellies more outwards. **1863** *Jrnl. R. Agric. Soc.* XXIV. II. 94 Curby or cow hocks [of a horse] with dishing speedy cutting, or slouching action [see CUT *sb.*² 7]. **1895** H. D. TRAILL in *Fortn. Rev.* Sept. 364 Urged..by Conservatives of the 'dishing' school [cf. quot. 1869 in DISH *v.* 7].

† **di'shiver,** *v. Obs.* [f. DIS- 5 + SHIVER *v.*] *trans.* and *intr.* To shiver to pieces. Hence **di'shivered** *ppl. a.*

1562 PHAER *Æneid* IX. Cc iij, Shields dishiuring crack. **1598** YONG *Diana* 290 His tender trembling flesh I will dishiuer. **1624** BP. MOUNTAGU *Treat. Invoc. Saints* 6 The dishivered splinters runne into my hands. **1650** W. SCLATER (son) *Ep. Ded. to W. Sclater's Rom. IV*, As Dagon..falls.. dishivered into dust and ashes.

dishlet ('dɪʃlɪt), **dishling** ('dɪʃlɪŋ). [f. DISH *sb.* + -LET, -LING.] A tiny dish (of food).

1811 LAMB *Edax on Appetite*, A sliver of ham..a slip of invisible brawn..with a power of such dishlings. **1884** *Daily News* 23 Sept. 2/1 It is a very agreeable miniature feed. The dishlets are nine in number.

dishoard (dɪs'hɔːd), *v.* [DIS- 6.] *trans.* To release or bring out of a hoard. So **dis'hoarding** *vbl. sb.*

1926 D. H. ROBERTSON *Banking Policy* v. 48 Automatic Stinting which in each case exactly cancelled the intended Dis-lacking involved in the process of Spontaneous Dishoarding. **1933** —— in *Economic Jrnl.* XLIII. 401 The converse operations to Saving, Lacking and Hoarding may be called Dissaving, Dislacking and Dishoarding. Hoarding (Dishoarding) may be alternatively defined as acting in such a way as to decrease (increase) the velocity of circulation of money against output. **1955** *Ann. Reg. 1954* 258 More food was available in the towns, partly as a result of 'dishoarding' by peasants more ready to surrender their produce as consumer goods became more plentiful. **1963** *Times* 11 Feb. 6/7 Now that industry is 'dishoarding' labour.

†**dis'holy**, *a. Obs. rare.* [f. DIS- 10 + HOLY.] The reverse of holy; unholy, iniquitous.

1593 BELL *Motives Romish Faith* (1605) 16 Cast into the said Romish disholy inquisition. **1596** —— *Surv. Popery* I. I. x. 34 Our disholy fathers the late bishops of Rome.

dishome (dɪs'həʊm), *v.* [f. DIS- 7c + HOME *sb.*] *trans.* To deprive of, or eject from, a home. Hence **dis'homed** *ppl. a.*

1880 *Contemp. Rev.* 179 We have sunk into..being the only dishomed nation. **1882** F. W. H. MYERS *Renewal Youth* 229 Thy soul dishomed shall..be forlorn. **1882** *Daily Tel.* 7 Nov. (Cassell) Poor families being incontinently dishomed to give space for magnificent roadways. **1893** W. T. STEAD in *Rev. of Rev.* 15 Sept. 318/1 To create substitutes for the home for the benefit of the dishomed.

dishonest (dɪs'ɒnɪst), *a.* [ad. OF. *deshoneste* (13th c. in Hatz.-Darm.), mod.F. *déshonnête*; = Pr. *deshonest*, Sp. *deshonesto*, It. *disonesto*, a Romanic formation for L. *dehonestus*, f. *honestus* honourable, HONEST: see DE- 6, DIS- 4.]

†**1.** Entailing dishonour or disgrace; dishonourable, discreditable, misbecoming, shameful, ignominious. *Obs.*

c **1386** CHAUCER *Clerk's T.* 820 Ye koude nat doon so dishoneste a thyng, That thilke wombe, in which youre children leye, Scholde..Be seyn al bare. **1483** CAXTON *Cato* A vij, The galowes and..dyshonest dethe. **1483** —— *G. de la Tour* D viij, The pryde of men..that counterfeted them self of newe and dishonest rayment. **1586** T. B. *La Primaud. Fr. Acad.* I. 12 If we account it a shamefull thing to be ignorant of those things..the not knowing of our selves is much more dishonest. **1702** ROWE *Tamerl.* III. i. 1115 Thou didst an Act dishonest to thy Race. **1710** POPE *Windsor For.* 326 Inglorious triumphs and dishonest scars. **1760** HOME *Siege Aquileia* 11, Some fierce barbarian now insults the dead; Adding dishonest wounds.

†**2.** Unchaste, lewd, filthy. *Obs.*

c **1440** *Jacob's Well* 159 þe leccherous louyth to be in dyshonest cumpanye. **1494** FABYAN *Chron.* VI. cci. 209 This duke, with Gunnore..lyued longe whyle a dishonest lyfe, and contrary to the lawys of the Churche. **1599** SHAKS. *Hen. V*, I. ii. 50 Holding in disdaine the German Women, For some dishonest manners of their life. **1630** WADSWORTH *Pilgr.* vii. 73 Accused him for being dishonest with his owne Neece. **1734** WATTS *Reliq. Juv.* Pref. (1789) 7 Their own dishonest and impure ideas.

†**3.** Unseemly to the sight; ugly, hideous. *Obs.* (Connected with sense 1 by quot. 1585.)

[**1585** T. WASHINGTON tr. *Nicholay's Voy.* III. xx. 108 To cover the dishonest partes of the body.] **1650** BULWER *Anthropomet.* vii. (1653) 129 The Face..appeares very filthy and dishonest. **1697** DRYDEN *Æneid* VI. (R.) Dishonest [tr. *inhonesto*] with lop'd arms, the youth appears. **1725** POPE *Odyss.* x. 462 Enormous beasts dishonest to the eye.

4. Of actions, etc.: Discreditable as being at variance with straightforward or honourable dealing, underhand; now, fraudulent, thievish, knavish.

[**1552** HULOET, Dishonest matter, or any thynge cloked with fayre wordes, *subturpis*.] **1611** BIBLE *Ezek.* xxii. 27 To get dishonest gaine. **1647** COWLEY *Mistress, Counsel* vi, The act I must confess was wise, As a dishonest act could be. **1736** BUTLER *Anal.* I. iv. Wks. 1874 I. 80 Dishonest artifices ..are got into business of all kinds. **1840** MACAULAY *Ess., Ranke* (1851) II. 127 A most dishonest and inaccurate French version.

5. Of persons: Wanting in honesty, probity, or integrity; disposed to cheat or defraud; thievish.

1751–73 JORTIN *Eccl. Hist.* I. (1846) 123 Imposed upon themselves by dishonest brethren. **1793** HOLCROFT tr. *Lavater's Physiogn.* xxxvi. 185 No man is so good as not..to be liable to become dishonest. **1859** KINGSLEY *Good News of God* xxi. (1878) 171 You may be false and dishonest, saith the Lord, but I am honest and true.

†**dis'honest**, *v. Obs.* [ad. OF. *deshonester* (14th c. in Godef.) = Sp. *deshonestar*, It. *disonestare* :— a Romanic formation on *dishonest-us* (see prec.), for L. *dehonestāre*.]

1. *trans.* To bring dishonour, disgrace, or discredit upon; to dishonour; to stain with ignominy.

1382 WYCLIF *Prov.* xxv. 8 Whan thou has dishonestid [Vulg. *dehonestaveris*] thi frend. **1509** FISHER *Fun. Serm. C'tess Richmond* Wks. (1876) 291 To eschewe euery thynge that myght dyshonest ony noble woman. **1526** TINDALE *1 Cor.* xi. 5 Every woman that prayeth or prophesieth bare hedded, dishonesteth her heede. **1606** *Wily Beguiled* in Hazl. *Dodsley* IX. 258, I hope you will not seek to dishonest me. *a* **1670** HACKET *Abp. Williams* I. (1692) 44 He did not dishonest himself for it with any indignity.

2. To impute disgrace or dishonour to (a person); to defame, calumniate.

c **1534** tr. *Pol. Verg. Eng. Hist.* (Camden) I. 251 Hee slaunderuslie dishonested them. **1583** GOLDING *Calvin on Deut.* xxxix. 230 If a man call one a theefe..hee will not abide to bee so dishonested before the worlde. **1615** T. ADAMS *Blacke Devill* 20 He may tho' not disquiet yet dishonest the soule of man.

3. To violate the honour or chastity of; to defile.

1563–87 FOXE *A. & M.* (1684) I. 762/2 If we do see a King to..rob and spoil his Subjects, deflour Virgins, dishonest Matrons. **1565–73** COOPER *Thesaurus, Collutulo*..to dishonest or defile. *a* **1652** BROME *New Acad.* I. Wks. 1873 II. 18 I'll defie the devil to dishonest her. **1922** JOYCE *Ulysses* 383 He would ever dishonest a woman whoso she were..if it so fortuned him to be delivered of his spleen of lustihead.

4. To render unseemly or ugly; to deform.

1581 J. BELL *Haddon's Answ. Osor.* 10 b, Your selfe do disfigure your owne whelpe, you dishoneste your owne creature. **1637** R. HUMPHREY tr. *St. Ambrose* II. 33 Hee.. doth dishonest the grace of his vpper shape.

Hence **dis'honesting** *vbl. sb.*

1530 PALSGR. 214/1 Dishonestyng, *auilement*. **1565–73** COOPER *Thesaurus, Generis dehonestamentum*, the dishonesting of his stocke.

dis'honestly, *adv.* [f. DISHONEST *a.* + -LY².]

†**1.** With dishonour, disgrace, or ignominy; dishonourably, shamefully. *Obs.*

c **1430** LYDG. *Floure of Curtesye* (R.), Dishonestly to speake of any wight She deadly hateth. **15..** *Doctr. Gd. Servauntes* in *Poet. Tracts* (Percy Soc.) 10 Whan that thou arte thus departed Without his loue dyshonestely. **1549** *Compl. Scot.* xi. 93 He gart hang, cruelly and dishonestly.. sexten scoir of the maist nobillis. **1643** PRYNNE *Sov. Power Parl.* App. 58 Who had been shaven a Monke, or dishonestly bald.

†**2.** Unchastely, not in honourable matrimony.

1560 BIBLE (Genev.) *Ecclus.* xxii. 4 Shee that liueth dishonestly is her fathers heauinesse. **1665** SIR T. HERBERT *Trav.* (1677) 71 He dishonestly courts..his Fathers Wife. **1685** EVELYN *Mem.* (1857) II. 238 Monmouth..having lived dishonestly with the Lady Henrietta Wentworth for two years.

3. In a dishonest manner, fraudulently; so as to cheat or deceive.

1590 SHAKS. *Com. Err.* v. i. 3 He had the Chaine of me, Though most dishonestly he doth denie it. **1855** MACAULAY *Hist. Eng.* III. 586 Clarendon, who had refused the oaths, and Ailesbury, who had dishonestly taken them.

dis'honestness. *rare*⁻⁰. [f. as prec. + -NESS.] = next.

1727 in BAILEY vol. II.

dishonesty (dɪs'ɒnɪstɪ). Also 4–5 des-, dishonestee. [a. OF. *desho(n)nesté* (13th c. in Littré, in mod.F. *déshonnêteté*) = Pr. *dezonestat*, It. *disonestà*, a Romanic formation on *dishonest-us* DISHONEST, after L. *honestāt-em* honourableness, HONESTY.] The quality of being dishonest.

†**1.** Dishonour, disgrace, discredit, shame; (with *pl.*) a dishonourable or disgraceful action. *Obs.*

c **1386** CHAUCER *Pars. T.* ¶759 Shame, that eschueth alle deshonestee. *c* **1400** *Destr. Troy* 528 Ne deme no dishonesty in your derfe hert. **1535** COVERDALE *Ecclus.* iii. 13 Where the father is without honoure, it is the dishonesty of the sonne. *a* **1542** WYATT *Compl. Loue* (R.), From thousand dishonesties have I him drawen. **1582** N. T. (Rhem.) *2 Cor.* iv. 2 We renounce the secrete [**1611** hidden] things of dishonestie [WYCL. *Geneva, R.V.* shame, TINDALE, etc. unhonestie.] **1596** DALRYMPLE tr. *Leslie's Hist. Scot.* VIII. 86 To venture he may haue honour; to ly hidd as he la, dishonestie.

†**2.** Unchastity, lewdness. *Obs.*

1535 COVERDALE *Ecclus.* xxii. 4 Shee that commeth to dishonesty, bringeth hir father in heuynes. **1553** S. CABOT *Ordinances* in Hakluyt *Voy.* (1589) 261 No woman to be tempted..to incontinencie or dishonestie. **1630** WADSWORTH *Pilgr.* vii. 73 Accused..of dishonesty with another mans wife. **1639** S. DU VERGER tr. *Camus' Admir. Events* 110 A right temple of Cyprus where the sacrifices were only dishonesties.

†**3.** Shameful or foul appearance, ugliness, deformity. *Obs.*

c **1400** MAUNDEV. (Roxb.) xviii. 82 þare may a man see mykill dishonestee [F. *meinte leide figure*]. **1485** CAXTON *Chas. Gt.* 91 Ye may not see them by cause of the fylthe and dyshoneste of the place. **1535** COVERDALE *Ezek.* xvi. 8 Then spred I my clothes ouer the, to couer thy dishonestie [**1611** nakednesse].

4. The reverse of honesty; lack of probity or integrity; disposition to deceive, defraud, or steal; thievishness; theft, fraud. Also, a dishonest or fraudulent act.

1599 SHAKS. *Much Ado* II. ii. 9 So couertly, that no dishonesty shall appeare in me. **1616** SURFL. & MARKH. *Country Farme* 320 Others are of opinion, that stolne Bees thriue best, but..I neuer knew profit in dishonestie. **1751–73** JORTIN *Eccl. Hist.* (R.), A forger..will avoid.. minute detail, in which he must perpetually expose his ignorance and dishonesty. **1804** SOUTHEY *Lett.* (1856) I. 280, I have caught out Barros in so many dishonesties. **1878** JEVONS *Prim. Pol. Econ.* 59 Nothing is more difficult than for a person convicted of dishonesty to find desirable employment.

dishonorary (dɪs'ɒnərərɪ), *a. rare.* [f. DIS- 10.] Bringing dishounour, tending to disgrace.

1828 WEBSTER cites HOLMES.

†**dis'honorate**, *a. Obs. rare*⁻¹. [f. DISHONOUR *sb.* + -ATE².] = DISHONOURED.

1601 *Death Robert of Huntington* IV. ii. in Hazl. *Dodsley* VIII. 297 Such honour ever proves dishonourate.

dishonour, -honor (dɪs'ɒnə(r)), *sb.* Forms: 4 **des(h)onour, des-, dishonur, -oure,** (4–5 **dyshoner, dyssehonour,** 5 **disonowre,** 5–6 **dyshonowre, -oure,** 6 **-our**), 4– **dishonour,** 6– **dishonor.** [a. OF. *deshonor, -ur, des(h)enor* (11–12th c. in Littré), mod.F. *déshonneur* = Pr., Sp. *deshonor*, It. *disonore*; a Romanic formation f. L. *dis-*, DIS- 4b + *honōrem* HONOUR. In this word, and its derivatives, the spelling *dishonor* is usual in U.S.]

1. The reverse of honour; the withholding of the tokens of esteem, respect, or reverence due to any one; the condition in which these are withheld or the contrary shown; a state of shame or disgrace; ignominy, indignity. ***to do (a) dishonour to***: to treat with indignity, to dishonour, violate the honour of; ***to the dishonour of***, so as to bring into dishonour.

a **1300** *Cursor M.* 4412 (Gött.) Joseph souht on me in boure Forto do me dis-honoure. *Ibid.* 23644 (Gött.) þe wicked..of all sal þai haue dishonur. *c* **1380** *Sir Ferumb.* 563 þys day he falleþ in deshonour. *a* **1533** LD. BERNERS *Huon* lxvii. 231 Suffre none yll to be done to that good lady..nor no dyshonour. **1548** HALL *Chron., Hen. VI*, 167 Many slaunderous woordes to the quenes dishonor. **1553** *Short Catech.* 26 b, He came downe from hiest honour to deepest dishonoure, even the dishonour..of the crosse. **1601** SHAKS. *All's Well* III. vi. 59 Some dishonor wee had in the losse of that drum. **1611** BIBLE *Ps.* lxix. 19 My shame and my dishonor. **1653** H. COGAN tr. *Pinto's Trav.* xii. 38 He would rather dye..then live in dishonor. **1718** LADY M. W. MONTAGU *Let. to C'tess of Bristol* 10 Apr., They have invented lies to the dishonour of their enemies. **1769** *Junius Lett.* xii. 53 They cannot retreat without dishonour. **1821** BYRON *Mar. Fal.* I. ii. 64 Wouldst thou..Harp on the deep dishonour of our house? **1870** BRYANT *Iliad* I. VI. 192 Never bring Dishonor on the stock from which I sprang.

b. with *a* and *pl.*: An instance of this, an infliction of disgrace; a piece of ignominious treatment, an indignity, an insult.

c **1320** *Seuyn Sag.* (W.) 482 Who had the done this desonour? **1422** tr. *Secreta Secret., Priv. Priv.* (E.E.T.S.) 154 Thre dyshonoures in the same day he moste suffyre. **1673** *Lady's Call.* Pref. 2 Women, who could hardly have descended to such dishonours.

2. A cause or source of shame, a disgrace.

1553 EDEN *Treat. Newe Ind.* (Arb.) 34 They toke it for a dishonour, to..forsake theyr Captayne. **1561** T. NORTON *Calvin's Inst.* I. 22 b, Images..displease [God] as certaine dishonors of his maiestie. **1755** YOUNG *Centaur* i. Wks. (1757) 115 Who think it no dishonour to their understandings to credit their Creator. **1842** TENNYSON *Two Voices* 255 His little daughter, whose sweet face He kissed..Becomes dishonour to her race.

3. *Commerce.* Refusal or failure to 'honour' or pay (a bill of exchange, etc.).

1834 J. CHITTY *Law Contracts* (ed. 2) 597 The creditor.. upon dishonour of the instrument brings an action. **1866** CRUMP *Banking* v. 112 Notice of dishonour should be given to each indorser. **1885** *Law Times* 6 June 94/1 The payee of a cheque cannot bring an action for its dishonour against the banker on whom it is drawn.

dishonour, -or (dɪs'ɒnə(r)), *v.* Forms as in *sb.* [a. OF. *deshonnore-r, desonurer* (12th c. in Littré; mod.F. *déshonorer*) = Pr. *desonorar*, Sp. *deshonrar*, It. *disonorare*:—late L. *dishonōrāre* (in Du Cange), f. *dis-*, DIS- 4 + *honōrāre* to HONOUR.] The opposite or reverse of to HONOUR.

1. *trans.* To deprive of honour; to treat with dishonour or indignity; to violate the honour, respect, or recognition of position due to any one.

1388 WYCLIF *Ecclus.* x. 23 This seed schal be disonourid, that passith the comaundementis of the Lord. **1411** *Rolls of Parlt.* III. 650/1 Hym to harme and dishonure. *c* **1450** *Crt. of Love* 1252 Love shal be contrarye To his availe, and him eke dishonoure. **1526–34** TINDALE *John* viii. 49, I honour my father, and ye have dishonoured me. **1651** HOBBES *Leviath.* I. x. 42 To Value a man..at a low rate, is to Dishonour him. **1871** R. ELLIS *Catullus* lxiv. 404 [She] fear'd not unholy the blessed dead to dishonour.

2. To violate the honour or chastity of; to defile.

1393 GOWER *Conf.* II. 322 Which sigh her suster pale and fade And specheles and deshonoured. *a* **1533** LD. BERNERS *Huon* clix. 614 To the entente to haue dyshonored her & to haue had her to his wyfe. **1841** ELPHINSTONE *Hist. Ind.* I. 510 She exclaimed that she was now unworthy of his notice, having been dishonoured by Cásim.

3. To bring dishonour or disgrace upon, by one's conduct, etc.; to disgrace.

1568 TILNEY *Disc. Mariage* B iv b, He was faine to please, and content her, least she should dishonour him. **1593** SHAKS. *Rich. II*, IV. i. 21 Shall I so much dishonor my faire Starres, On equall termes to giue him chasticement? **1725** DE FOE *Voy. round World* (1840) 76 Friendly usage..which we had not in the least dishonoured. **1727** —— *Syst. Magic* I. i. (1840) 14 To find he had dishonoured, by his example, the doctrine of sobriety. **1848** W. H. KELLY tr. *L. Blanc's Hist. Ten Y.* II. 217 America..dishonours herself by tolerating slavery. **1854** RUSKIN *Lect. Archit.* iii. 170 The water is not dishonoured by that thirst of the diseased, nor is nature dishonoured by the love of the unworthy.

†**4.** To strip *of* what is an honour. *Obs.*

1654 GAYTON *Pleas. Notes* IV. ii. 180 As if you should.. dishonour a cock of his spurrs. *a* **1700** DRYDEN tr. *Ovid's Met.* xv. (T.), His scalp..dishonour'd quite of hair.

5. *Commerce.* To refuse or fail to accept or pay (a bill of exchange, etc.); to make default in meeting (a promissory note).

1811 P. KELLY *Univ. Cambist* II. 285 *Dishonour*, a term used when the acceptance or payment of bills of exchange, etc., is refused. **1837** LOCKHART *Scott* lxvii. (1839) VIII. 226 He found..that Hurst & Co. had dishonoured a bill of Constable's. **1887** STEVENSON *Underwoods* I. xxiv. 51 Nor leave Thy debts dishonoured. **1894** BARING-GOULD *Kitty Alone* II. 97 The man to whom he had given the bill that was dishonoured.

Hence **dis'honouring** *vbl. sb.* and *ppl. a.*

1525 LD. BERNERS *Froiss.* II. xcii. [lxxxviii.] 278 To come ..on payne of dishonourynge. **1564** *Brief Exam.* A iv, Horrible..sacriledges and dishonorynges of God. **1843** LYTTON *Last Bar.* IV. vi, I had deemed it dishonouring in a noble nature to countenance insult to a noble enemy in his absence. **1875** POSTE *Gaius* I. Comm. (ed. 2) 68 Any dishonouring outrage.

dishonourable, -honorable (dɪsˈɒnərəb(ə)l), *a.* [app. orig. f. DISHONOUR *v.* + -ABLE; but in some uses regarded as f. DIS- 10 + HONOURABLE. Cf. F. *déshonorable* (14th c. in Godef.).]

1. Entailing dishonour; involving disgrace and shame; ignominious, base.

1533–4 *Act 25 Hen. VIII*, c. 22 §1 The continuance.. whereof..were..dishonorable to the hole realme. **1601** SHAKS. *Jul. C.* I. ii. 138 And peepe about To finde our selues dishonourable Graves. **1651** HOBBES *Leviath.* I. x. 44 Craft, Shifting, neglect of Equity, is Dishonourable. **1749** FIELDING *Tom Jones* XIV. v, The words *dishonourable birth* are nonsense..unless the word *dishonourable* be applied to the parents. **1846** GREENER *Sc. Gunnery* 345 More disgraceful, more dishonourable conduct, has never characterized the British service.

†**b.** Without moral implication: Mean, paltry. *Obs. rare.*

1699 BENTLEY *Phal.* Pref. 66 If the Room be too mean, and too little for the Books;..if the Access to it be dishonourable; is the Library-keeper to answer for 't?

2. Of persons: †**a.** To be regarded with dishonour, disesteemed (*obs. rare*). **b.** Devoid or negligent of honour; meriting shame and reproach; unprincipled, base, despicable.

1611 BIBLE *Ecclus.* x. 31 He that is honoured in pouertie, how much more in riches, and he that is dishonourable in riches, how much more in pouertie? **1749** [see sense 1]. **1864** TENNYSON *Aylmer's F.* 292 Ungenerous, dishonourable, base..trusted as he was. *Mod.* A dishonourable opponent at cards.

Hence **disˈhonourableness**, dishonourable quality, dishonour; **disˈhonourably** *adv.*, in a dishonourable manner, with dishonour; discreditably, basely.

1590 C. S. *Right Relig.* 29 Who (most dishonourably to Christ) acknowledge the Pope the head therof. **1651** HOBBES *Leviath.* II. xxi. 112 They are not esteemed to do it unjustly, but dishonourably. **1727** BAILEY vol. II, *Dishonourableness*, dishonourable quality. **1769** *Junius Lett.* iv, Your own Manilla ransom most dishonourably given up. **1776** ADAM SMITH *W.N.* I. x. (1869) I. 105 The honourableness or dishonourableness of the employment. *a* **1797** H. WALPOLE *Mem. Geo. II* (1847) II. x. 343 The injustice and dishonourableness of retracting what he had authorized Keppel to say.

dishonoured, -ored (dɪsˈɒnəd), *ppl. a.* [f. DISHONOUR *v.* + -ED.] **a.** Treated with dishonour. **b.** Violated, defiled. **c.** Stained with dishonour, disgraced. †**d.** Dishonourable, dishonouring (*obs.*). **e.** Of a bill of exchange: see DISHONOUR *v.* 5.

1603 SHAKS. *Meas. for M.* IV. iv. 34 Receiuing a dishonor'd life. **1605** —— *Lear* I. i. 231 No vnchaste action, or dishonoured step. *c* **1611** CHAPMAN *Iliad* IV. Argt. 82 He ..Gives Menelaus a dishonour'd wound. **1784** COWPER *Task* VI. 821 God..would else In his dishonoured works himself endure Dishonour. **1837** CARLYLE *Fr. Rev.* I. III. i. (*title*) Dishonoured Bills. **1856** KANE *Arct. Expl.* I. xv. 182 Carrying the dishonored vehicle with us. **1881** S. COLVIN *Landor* iii. 62 His dishonoured daughter.

dishonourer, -orer (dɪsˈɒnərə(r)). [f. DISHONOUR *v.* + -ER[1].] One who dishonours.

1671 MILTON *Samson* 861 An irreligious Dishonourer of Dagon. **1787** A. HILDITCH *Rosa de Montmorien* II. 152 The injured Morton recognized his base dishonourer. *c* **1870** J. G. MURPHY *Comm. Lev.* xx. 1–9 Introd., Dishonorers of parents.

b. One who violates female honour; a defiler.

1755 JOHNSON, *Dishonourer*..a violator of chastity. **1881** S. COLVIN *Landor* iii. 62 In order to chastise her [his daughter's] dishonourer.

†**disˈhonourless, -orless,** *a. Obs. rare*$^{-1}$. [-LESS.] Free from dishonour.

1595 CHAPMAN *Ovid's Banq. Sence* (1639) 32 Unwronged and all dishonorlesse.

dishorn (dɪsˈhɔːn), *v.* [DIS- 7a.] *trans.* To deprive of horns, cut off the horns of.

1598 SHAKS. *Merry W.* IV. iv. 63 We'll..dis-horne the spirit, And mocke him home to Windsor. **1603** FLORIO *Montaigne* (1632) 436 A chiefe Gossip of his had a Goate dishorned. **1884** *Law Times* 21 June 139/1 The question was with respect to dishorning cattle, or cutting off their horns quite close to the skull. **1890** *Daily News* 17 Feb. 5/6 A convert to dishorning..Now he dishorns his Guernsey cows.

dishorse (dɪsˈhɔːs), *v.* [DIS- 7c.] *trans.* To unhorse, dismount.

1859 TENNYSON *Idylls, Enid* 563 Then each, dishors'd and drawing, lash'd at each. **1885** —— *Balin & Bal.* Wks. (1894) 375/1 He..dishorsed himself and rose again.

dishort (dɪˈʃɔːt), *sb. Sc.* Also 6 **dischort,** 9 **disshort.** [Origin unknown.]

1. Injury, mischief; anything prejudicial.

1535 STEWART *Cron. Scot.* II. 555 And how hir father did him sic dischort. **1585** JAS. I *Ess. Poesie* (Arb.) 47 But cause they did her such dishort. **1811** W. AITON *Agric. Ayrshire* Gloss. 691 *Dishort*, a mischief.

2. 'A disappointment (*Aberd.*)'; also 'Deficiency, as a disshort in the weight' (Jamieson).

†**dishort** (dɪsˈhɔːt), *v. Obs. rare.* [f. L. *dis-*, DIS- 4a + *hort-ārī* to EXHORT; cf. L. *dēhortārī* to DEHORT.] *trans.* To use exhortation to dissuade.

1549 CHALONER *Erasm. on Folly* M ij b, They dishort us from sinne. **1561** T. NORTON *Calvin's Inst.* III. 320 Paul himselfe in another place dishorteth vs from carefulnesse.

dishouse (dɪsˈhaʊz), *v.* Also 7 **dishowse.** [f. DIS- 6 or 7 + HOUSE *v.* or *sb.*]

1. *trans.* To oust or expel from a house; also, to deprive of a habitation. Chiefly in **disˈhoused** *ppl. a.* (also *absol.*), **disˈhousing** *vbl. sb.*

c **1586** C'TESS PEMBROKE *Ps.* LVIII. iii, Make them melt as the dishowsed snaile. **1648** J. GOODWIN *Right and Might* 12 The Members of Parliament dishous'd by the Army. **1865** MASSON *Rec. Brit. Philos.* ii. 60 The dishoused population of spirits. **1892** *Pall Mall G.* 21 Jan. 3/2 Providing cheap railway accommodation for the dishoused workers. **1900** *Daily News* 4 Jan. 3/1 The evil of dishousing altogether would be substituted for the evil of living in places unfit for habitation. *Ibid.* 8 Jan. 7/1 Such considerations as the fate of the dishoused. **1901** *Westm. Gaz.* 5 Sept. 2/3 To secure sites for the dishoused. **1902** *Ibid.* 13 Dec. 5/1 The dishousing of the inhabitants of the slums. **1921** *Contemp. Rev.* Oct. 451 Large closing orders are out of the question because of the dishousing they would occasion.

2. To clear (ground) of houses.

1640 SOMNER *Antiq. Canterb.* 191, I suppose those houses taken downe..the same ground being so dishoused and laid open. **1891** *Chicago Advance* 5 Mar., To 'dishouse' all the disease-breeding section..and reconstruct its streets.

†**diˈshrivelled,** *ppl. a. Obs. rare.* [f. DIS- 5 + SHRIVEL *v.*] Shrivelled up.

1771 *Muse in Miniature* 49 Thro' languid nature's cold dishrivell'd veins.

†**disˈhuman,** *v. Obs. rare.* [DIS- 8.] = DISHUMANIZE *v.*

1657 REEVE *God's Plea* 245 Oh look with shame..upon this wofull evirating or dis-humaning your selves.

disˈhuman, *a. nonce-wd.* [DIS- 10.] Unhuman.

1920 D. H. LAWRENCE *Lost Girl* vi. 94 Whether she would ever be able to take to his strange and dishuman element, who knows?

disˌhumaniˈzation. *nonce-wd.* [f. DISHUMANIZE *v.* + -ATION.] The act or process of dishumanizing.

1909 H. JAMES *Novels & Tales* XVII. Pref., London was a terrible place to die in; doubtless not so much..by conscious cruelty or perversity as under the awful doom of general dishumanisation.

disˈhumanize, *v.* [DIS- 6.] *trans.* To deprive of human character or attributes; = DEHUMANIZE.

1861 LYTTON & FANE *Tannhäuser* 105 In a desert isle Dwelling till half dishumaniz'd. **1878** B. TAYLOR *Deukalion* II. ii, Visions born of brains Dishumanized.

dishume (dɪsˈhjuːm), *v. rare.* [f. DIS- 7c + L. *humus* earth: after *inhume.*] *trans.* To unearth, disinhume, exhume.

1854 SYD. DOBELL *Balder* xxv. 181 Of what colossal frame Do I..Dishume the giant limb from my rent heart?

†**disˈhumour,** *sb. Obs.* [DIS- 9.] Ill-humour.

1712 STEELE *Spect.* No. 424 ¶6 Any thing that betrays Inattention or Dishumour. *Ibid.* No. 479 ¶1 Subject to dishumour, age, sickness, impatience. **1795** *Jemima* I. 67 Oppression excites disgust; injustice, resentment; ill will, dishumour; pride, contempt.

†**disˈhumour,** *v. Obs.* [DIS- 7d.] *trans.* To put out of humour, vex, 'aggravate'.

1599 B. JONSON *Ev. Man out of Hum.* v. iii, Here were a couple unexpectedly dishumour'd. **1680** *Religion of Dutch* ii. 15 [They] have, by their disputes, distracted and dishumour'd all the Province of Holland.

ˈdish-wash. [see WASH *sb.*] The greasy water in which dishes have been washed. **b.** As a term of contempt.

1592 NASHE *P. Penilesse* (Shaks. Soc.) 65 He..hath his penance assignde him, to carouse himselfe drunke with dish-wash and vineger. **1598** FLORIO, *Stipa*..dish-wash giuen to swyne and hogs. **1737** BRACKEN *Farriery Impr.* (1757) II. 164 What I mean by warm water is not the warm Dish wash so much in use amongst the Vulgar.

b. 1599 NASHE *Lenten Stuffe* in *Harl. Misc.* (1808–12) VI. 180 (D.) Their fathers..were scullions, dish-wash, and durty draffe. *c* **1640** J. SMYTH *Lives Berkeleys* (1883) II. 372 Opprobrious words, of Coward, Cotquene, Milksopp, dishwash, and the like.

ˈdish-washer.

1. One who washes plates and dishes; a scullion or scullery-maid.

a **1529** SKELTON *Poems agst. Garnesche* 26 Ye war a kechyn page A dyshe washer. **1587** HARRISON *England* III. xi. (1878) II. 73 Everie dishwasher refused to looke in other than silver glasses for the attiring of his head. **1872** TENNYSON *Lynette* 750 Dish-washer and broach-turner, loon!—to me Thou smellest all of kitchen as before.

2. An apparatus for washing dishes. orig. *U.S.*

1867 *Rep. Comm. Patents 1865* (*U.S. Pat. Off.*) I. 538 [The] dish-washer..consists of two disks placed one above another [etc.]. **1889** *Kansas Times & Star* 9 July, The patent new dish washer washes a bushel of dishes in a few minutes. **1921** *Daily Colonist* (Victoria, B.C.) 9 Apr. 2/6 (Advt.), Lessen the labors of your wife. Electric washing machines, electric dish washers, [etc.]. **1956** 'N. SHUTE' *Beyond Black Stump* 21 A new dishwasher stood where the old one had stood. **1958** *Woman's Own* 5 Mar. 11/4 Laundry goes straight into the washing machine and no one will dread the washing up with the electric dish washer. **1971** *Which?* Mar. 69/1 Refrigerators have a simpler mechanism than automatics or dishwashers.

3. A popular name of the pied or water wagtail (*Motacilla alba*); also of the Grinder or Restless Flycatcher of Australia (*Seisura inquieta*).

1575 TURBERV. *Faulconrie* 137 The Wagtayles or dish-washer as we terme them. **1730–6** BAILEY (folio), *Dish washer*, a water-wag-tail, a bird. **1832** SLANEY *Outl. smaller Brit. Birds* 65 (Pied Wagtail) Often called by the common people the dish-washer, or washerwoman. **1884** J. COLBORNE *Hicks Pasha* 265, I was surprised to meet my little friend the water wagtail, the dish-washer, where there was not a drop of water to wag his tail at.

ˈdish-washings, *sb. pl.* [see WASHING *vbl. sb.*] **a.** = DISH-WASH. **b.** Turner's name for a species of the plant horsetail (*Equisetum hyemale*), also called *polishing rushes.*

1538 TURNER *Libellus*, Dysshwasshynges; fortassis hujus herbæ ad fricandos discos et patinas aliquis fit usus. **1771** SMOLLETT *Humph. Cl.* III. 30 Sept., Bread soaked in dish-washings.

ˈdish-water. The greasy water in which dishes have been washed. Also *attrib.*

1484 CAXTON *Fables of Æsop* v. xiii, Dysshe water and alle other fylthe. **1587** HARRISON *England* II. xx. (1878) I. 331 The verie dishwater is not without some use amongest our finest plants. **1607** TOPSELL *Four-f. Beasts* (1658) 318 Wash them with a little beef broath or dish water. **1719** D'URFEY *Pills* III. 7 Arabian Tea, Is Dish-water stuff to a dish of new Whey. **1884** *Harper's Mag.* June 22/1 Sally shook the dish-water off her fingers.

transf. and *fig.* **1858** O. W. HOLMES *Aut. Breakf.-t.* (1883) 224 Flash phraseology..is..the dish-water from the washings of English dandyism. **1887** *Sanitary Era* (N.Y.) 15 Nov., Rainwater, after all, is nature's dishwater, from washing the great bowl of the atmosphere.

¶ = DISH-WASHER 3 (for which it is app. only an error). *Obs.*

1674 JOSSELYN *Voy. New Eng.* 100 The Troculus, Wagtail, or Dish-water. **1706** PHILLIPS (ed. Kersey), *Dish-Water* [1715 KERSEY, *Dish-Washer*], a Bird otherwise call'd *Wag-tail.*

ˈdish-ˌwatery, *a.* [See -Y[1].] Resembling dish-water. Also *fig.*

1890 *Columbus* (Ohio) *Dispatch* 13 Feb., The review [of a political quarrel] would be in its tenor dishwatery. **1910** W. JAMES *Mem. & Studies* (1911) xi. 284 Mawkish and dish-watery. **1928** *Sunday Express* 8 Jan. 9/4 Then came the soup. Great greasy tins of a dish-watery liquid.

dishy (ˈdɪʃɪ), *a. slang.* [f. DISH *sb.* 2a + -Y[1].] Very attractive.

1961 *Sunday Tel.* 19 Mar. 9/1 He encountered the dishy St. Tropezienne on his holiday plane. **1961** *Sunday Express* 10 Dec. 19 The manufacturer..dreamed up that dishy little number you're mad for. **1964** J. GARDNER *Liquidator* iii. 50 'Mm, is *that* him?' said the girl, all velvet. 'He's dishy.' **1966** G. N. LEECH *Eng. in Advertising* xxii. 198 The dreamiest, dishiest dress fabrics ever. **1970** *Evening Standard* 17 Mar. 35 (Advt.), I like Peter... And his dishy new sports car.

dishybilly. Joc. corruption of DISHABILLE 1.

1922 JOYCE *Ulysses* 418 See her in her dishybilly. Peels off a credit.

disiccation, -ative, obs. ff. DESICCATION, etc.

†**disiˈdæmony, des-, disiˈdemony.** *Obs.* [ad. Gr. δεισιδαιμονία fear of the gods, superstition.] 'A superstition, also a worshipping God out of fear and not from love' Bailey (folio) 1730–6.

disiˈdentify, *v. nonce-wd.* [DIS- 6.] *trans.* To undo or veil the identity of.

1845 *Blackw. Mag.* LVIII. 374 Gotham is England herself, poetically disidentified by a very transparent disguise.

disiˈllude, *v. rare.* [f. DIS- 6 + ILLUDE: prob. after *disillusion.*] *trans.* To free from illusion; to undeceive, disillusion.

1860 RUSSELL *Diary India* II. 98, I am obliged to disillude many of my visitors. **1892** A. LANG in *Illustr. Lond. News* 16 July 83/1, I confess to feeling uncomfortable and 'disilluded' when I am thus taken behind the scenes. **1894** G. B. SHAW *Let.* 23 Apr. (1965) 427 Sergius in the play,.. when disilluded, declares that life is a farce.

disiˈlluminate, *v. rare.* [DIS- 6.] *trans.* To deprive of light or illumination; to darken.

1865 SWINBURNE *Atalanta* 14 All the fates..burn me blind, and disilluminate My sense of seeing.

disillusion (dɪsɪˈl(j)uːʒən), *sb.* [f. DIS- 5 and 9 + ILLUSION *sb.* Cf. mod.F. *désillusion.*]

†**I.** [DIS- 5.] **1.** Illusion, delusion. *Obs.*

1598 YONG *Diana* 139 What slights, what disillusions.. Haue risen of such sorrowes? **1603** H. CROSSE *Vertues Commw.* (1878) 57 Such fallacies, and disillusions, are incident to a base and seruile condition.

II. [DIS- 9.] **2.** The action of freeing or becoming freed from illusion; the condition of being freed from illusion; disenchantment.

1851 MRS. BROWNING *Casa Guidi Windows* p. vii, The discrepancy between..faith and dis-illusion, between hope and fact. **1854** LONGF. *Epimetheus* vi, Disenchantment! Dis-illusion! Must each noble aspiration Come at last to this conclusion? **1865** *Lond. Rev.* 30 Dec. 712/1 Amidst the disappointments and the disillusions which followed the.. revolutions of 1848. **1877** DOWDEN *Shaks. Prim.* v. 53 It is the comedy of disillusion.

disi'llusion, *v.* [f. prec. sb.; cf. mod.F. *désillusionner*.] *trans.* To free from illusion; to disenchant, undeceive, disillusionize.

1864 *Reader* 1 Oct. 417 Captain Burton..disillusioned many be stating that the plain on which it stands was by no means unlike some parts of central equatorial Africa. **1876** W. C. RUSSELL *Is he the Man?* III. 193 His voice disillusioned me in a second.

Hence **disi'llusioned** *ppl. a.*; **disi'llusioning** *vbl. sb.* and *ppl. a.*; also **disi'llusioner**, **disi'llusionist**, a disillusioning agent.

1855 SMEDLEY *H. Coverdale* xx. 127 Alice..took her revenge upon that disillusioning..lady's maid. **1866** *Lond. Rev.* 724/1 The notion of this coach is commendable, and is a protest against the increase of dis-illusioning. The world, however, will not go back for our fancy, and we must fain keep up with it. **1871** MORLEY *Crit. Misc.* Ser. I. 273 The disillusioned France of '99. **1881** SYMONDS *Shelley* ii. 31 A disillusioned world is inclined to look with languid approbation on benevolence. **1889** *Voice* (N.Y.) 14 Mar., The ballot in woman's hand will prove a disillusionist; she will then be judged as a man. **1892** *Graphic* 9 July 38/3 Marriage is the great disillusioner.

disi'llusionary, *a.* [f. prec. sb., after *illusionary*.] Of, pertaining to, or of the nature of disillusion.

1879 ANNIE THOMAS *London Season* II. 161 Miss Bertram is almost moved from her disillusionary purpose.

disi'llusionize, *v.* [f. DISILLUSION *sb.* + -IZE.] *trans.* = DISILLUSION *v.*

1861 WHYTE MELVILLE *Good for Nothing* I. 236 It was.. disillusionizing him..of the romance in which he had chosen to wrap himself up. **1890** *Times* 27 Jan. 5/2 A free discussion of Social Democracy would do more to.. disillusionize its votaries than all the police repression in the world.

Hence **disi'llusionizing** *vbl. sb.* and *ppl. a.*; **disi'llusionizer**, one who disillusionizes.

1864 *Sat. Rev.* 10 Dec. 708/2 There is something disillusionizing in the sumptuous returns of a successful poem or novel. **1869** *Echo* 7 Sept., A somewhat similar disillusionising is taking place in the United States with respect to President Grant. **1881** *Public Opinion* (N.Y.) 2 Apr. 559 The latest literary disillusioniser. **1890** *Pictorial World* 4 Sept. 293/3 The wife is not always so loyal to the disillusioniser.

disi'llusionment. [f. DISILLUSION *v.* + -MENT: cf. mod.F. *désillusionnement*.] The action of disillusioning, or fact of being disillusioned.

1856 *Leisure Hour* V. 712/2 The first few days in Rome.. must be a disappointment—a sort of disillusionment, if we may coin that term. **1886** *Century Mag.* XXXII. 939 Therein was the beginning of disillusionments. **1891** FARRAR *Darkness & Dawn* II. 327 We have seen..the terrible disillusionment and suicides of Gallio and of Seneca.

disi'llusive, *a.* [f. DISILLUDE, after *illusive*.] Tending to disillusion.

1878 T. HARDY *Return of Native* II. III. i. 74 A long line of disillusive centuries has permanently displaced the Hellenic idea of life.

disi'magine, *v.* [DIS- 6.] *trans.* To banish from the imagination; to imagine not to be.

1647 H. MORE *Song of Soul* To Rdr. B iij a, Exercised Wits that have so writhen and wrested their phansies that they can imagine or disimagine any thing. **1668** —— *Div. Dial.* I. xxviii. (1713) 59 This Extensum we cannot dis-imagine,.. but it is whether we will or no. **1867** EMERSON *Lett. & Soc. Aims, Progr. Cult.* Wks. (Bohn) III. 231 Truth..whose existence we cannot disimagine.

disimbark, disimbogue, etc.: see DISEM-.

disimbroil, obs. var. of DISEMBROIL, *v.*

disi'mmure, *v.* [DIS- 6.] *trans.* To set free from confining walls; to release from imprisonment or confinement; to liberate.

1611 COTGR., *Desemmuré*, disimmured, taken out of a wall wherein it was inclosed. **1878** B. TAYLOR *Deukalion* II. v. 91 Thou shalt dis-immure Her slaves, and give them their abolished sex. **1886** WILLIS & CLARK *Cambridge* II. 127 The ..piers of the nave..were..sufficiently disimmured by pulling down the rubble on each side of them.

disimpale (dɪsɪm'peɪl), *v.* [DIS- 6.] *trans.* To unfix from something pointed. Also *fig.*

1904 E. F. BENSON *Challoners* iv. 73 The leg was caught only by the skin, and holding the animal in one hand he gently disimpaled it, where the iron teeth had clutched it. **1930** W. DE LA MARE *Desert Islands* 185 Though the tale-teller may well keep his reader on the sharpest of tenterhooks, he is bound to disimpale him in the end.

†**disim'park**, *v. Obs.* [DIS- 6.] *trans.* To turn out of a park, to free from the enclosure of a park. Hence **disimparking** *vbl. sb.*

1609 DEKKER *Gvll's Horne-bk.* 81 The spending Englishman who, to maintain a paltry warren of unprofitable conies, disimparks the stately swift-footed wild deer. **1675** J. SMITH *Chr. Relig. Appeal* II. 109 (L.) The disimparking of that nation, and turning it into the wild and common of the world. **1711–14** *Spectator* cited in Webster 1828.

disim'passioned, *ppl. a.* Also disem-. [DIS- 10.] Freed or free from passion; dispassionate.

1861 M. W. FREER *Henry IV*, I. I. ii. 98 The debates.. were generally practical and disimpassioned. **1876** BROWNING *Numpholeptos* 23 That pale soft sweet disempassioned moon. **1889** TENNYSON *Demeter & Persephone* ii, Those imperial, disimpassioned eyes Awed even me at first.

†**disim'pawn**, *v. Obs.* [DIS- 6.] *trans.* To take out of pawn; to redeem (what is in pawn).

1631 *Celestina* xv. 162 Thrice have I freed thee from the gallowes; foure times haue I disimpawnd thee.

†**disim'peach**, *v. Obs. rare.* [ad. obs. F. *desempescher* (Cotgr.), f. *des-*, DIS- 4 + *empescher* to IMPEACH.] *trans.* To free from impeachment.

1611 COTGR., *Desempescher*, to disimpeach, disincomber, cleere. **1657** R. CARPENTER *Astrology proved harmless* 36 The wise man will dis-impeach him, who boldly saith [etc.].

disimperialism (dɪsɪm'pɪərɪəlɪz(ə)m). [DIS- 9.] The reversal of imperialism; the acquisition of independence by former imperial territories.

1959 J. STRACHEY *End of Empire* xiv. 214 The steady march of a voluntary, or at least largely non-violent, process of dis-imperialism. **1962** *Economist* 6 Jan. 14/2 Rhodesia, where Britain faces its most painful test of disimperialism.

disimpester, obs. var. of DISEMPESTER.

†**dis'implicate**, *v. Obs.* [DIS- 6.] *trans.* To free from implication or entanglement; to disinvolve. Hence **dis'implicated** *ppl. a.*, disinvolved, explicit.

1660 tr. *Amyraldus' Treat. conc. Relig.* III. vii. 442 Much more is it impossible for a man to disimplicate himself from sin. **1753** S. SHUCKFORD *Creation & Fall of Man* 56 He had a clear and disimplicated Perception of the Manner in which Eve was taken out of him.

disim'prison, *v.* Also 9 disem-. [f. DIS- 6 + IMPRISON: cf. F. *désemprisonner* (in Cotgr.).] *trans.* To release from imprisonment or confinement; to set at liberty. Also *fig.*

1611 COTGR. *Desprisonner*, to vnprison, or disimprison. **1664** POWER *Exp. Philos.* I. 61 They can hardly be separated, and dis-imprisoned as the now in Minerals. **1671** GREW *Anat. Plants* I. i. §44 (1682) 9 The now effoliated Lobes..being once dis-imprisoned from their Coats..must needs very considerably amplifie themselves. **1845** R. W. HAMILTON *Pop. Educ.* vi. (ed. 2) 134 The keys which shall unlock the word of life to hundreds of millions and disimprison those hundreds of millions themselves. **1858** CARLYLE *Fredk. Gt.* I. I. i. 21 'All History is an imprisoned Epic'..says Sauerteig there. I wish he had disimprisoned it in this instance!

Hence **disim'prisoned** *ppl. a.*, **disim'prisoning** *vbl. sb.* and *ppl. a.*; also **disim'prisonment**, the action of disimprisoning.

1611 COTGR., *Desemprisonné*, disimprisoned..delivered out of prison. **1656** EARL MONM. *Advt. fr. Parnass.* 193 After the disimprisonment of the commendador. **1659** TORRIANO, *Discarceratura*, a disimprisoning. **1777** TOPLADY in R. Palmer *Bk. of Praise* 427 There shall my disimprison'd soul Behold Him and adore. **1837** CARLYLE *Fr. Rev.* (1872) I. VI. i. 184 The open violent Rebellion and Victory of disimprisoned Anarchy against corrupt worn-out Authority. **1878** BROWNING *Poets Croisic* 101 How can the youthful châtelaine but pant For disemprisonment?

†**disim'propriate**, *v. Obs.* [DIS- 6.] *trans.* To undo the impropriation of; to divert what is impropriated.

a **1626** BACON *Max. & Uses Com. Law* ix. (1636) 41 It shall not be disimpropriated to the benefit of the heire.

disim'prove, *v.* [DIS- 6.] **a.** *trans.* To do the reverse of improving; to render worse in quality.

1642 JER. TAYLOR *Episc.* Ep. Ded., No need to disimprove the Royal Banks to pay thanks to Bishops. **1651** —— *Serm. for Year* I. iv. 49 Those unprofitable and hurtful branches which..disimprove the fruit. *a* **1717** PARNELL *Deborah* (Seager), Thus direful was deform'd the country round; Unpeopled towns, and disimprov'd the ground. **1827** LADY MORGAN *O'Briens & O'Flahertys* IV. 352 Something changed, but not disimproved. **1890** *Gentl. Mag.* Feb. 161 Though he raised the tone of the essay, he disimproved its form, as the masterly hand of Addison left it.

b. *intr.* To grow worse, deteriorate.

1846 in WORCESTER, whence in later Dicts. **1904** JOYCE *Let.* 28 Dec. (1966) II. 75 My voice has disimproved greatly for want of practice and from too much smoking.

Hence **disim'proving** *ppl. a.*

1813 COLERIDGE *Remorse* Epil., Dire disimproving disadvantages.

disim'provement. [f. prec. after IMPROVEMENT.] The action of disimproving; the reverse of improvement; a change for the worse.

1649 JER. TAYLOR *Gt. Exemp.* v. §33 It hath also especial influence in the disimprovement of temptations. **1678** NORRIS *Coll. Misc.* (1699) 193 The final issue..would be, an utter neglect and disimprovement of the earth. **1723** SWIFT *Power of Bishops* Wks. 1761 III. 254 Four parts in five of the plantations for thirty years past have been real disimprovements. **1873** HELPS in *Macm. Mag.* Feb. 306 There has been much disimprovement in the matters I have referred to since their first tenure of office.

disinable, disinamour, etc.: see DISEN-.

†**disincame'ration**. *Obs.* [ad. F. *désincamération* (1664 in Littré): see DIS- 4, 6 and INCAMERATION.] The revocation or annulment of an incameration, or annexation of a territory to the domain of the Roman Camera; also called *discameration*.

1668 *Lond. Gaz.* No. 281/1 The Moneys which the Duke [of Parma] was obliged to have formerly paid for the Disincameration of one half of that Dutchy. **1670** G. H. *Hist. Cardinals* II. III. 198 In the business of the disincameration of Castro.

†**disincan'tation**. *Obs. rare.* [DIS- 9.] The undoing of an incantation or enchantment.

1652 BENLOWES *Theoph.* XI. 193 The Vanitie of the World. Canto XI, The Disincantation.

disin'carcerate, *v.* [DIS- 6.] *trans.* = DISIMPRISON. Hence **disincarce'ration**.

1665 G. HARVEY *Advice agst. Plague* 6 To melt and open the surface of the Earth, for to disincarcerate the said venene bodies. **1831** BENTHAM *Wks.* (1838–43) XI. 62 In what way his imprisonment terminated, whether by death or by disincarceration. **1868** G. MACDONALD *Seaboard Parish* II. vi. 103 The disincarcerated spirit.

disin'carnate, *a.* [DIS- 10.] Divested of the flesh; disembodied: the opposite of *incarnate* adj.

1881 PALGRAVE *Death in Forest* in *Vision of Eng.* (1889) 34 The Soul disincarnate.

disin'carnate, *v.* [DIS- 6.] *trans.* To divest of flesh or a material body: the opposite of *incarnate* vb.

1880 *Contemp. Rev.* Feb. 199 The body which Christ had after His resurrection..being as it were re-incarnated at one time and dis-incarnated at another.

disincentive (dɪsɪn'sɛntɪv). [DIS- 9.] A source of discouragement, esp. to economic progress or development. Also as *adj.*

1946 *Daily Tel.* 2 Nov. 4/2 In view of the urgency of the need for maximum production any disincentive is a serious consideration. **1954** *Times* 18 Mar. 9/2 It is admitted also that P.A.Y.E. presents the disincentive effects of taxation in the promptest possible manner. **1957** *Technology* July 168/1 Taxation, Mr. Thorneycroft maintained, was undoubtedly a disincentive. **1963** *Higher Educ.* xiv. 212 in *Parl. Papers 1962–3* (Cmnd. 2154) XI. 639 We think it probable that it [*sc.* the financing of students by loans] would have undesirable disincentive effects. **1964** *New Society* 27 Feb. 8/3 Commuting is not a disincentive for some of the men to take active part in local organizations.

disinchant, obs. var. of DISENCHANT.

disin'clinable, *a.* [f. DIS- 10 + INCLINABLE.] Having a disinclination; disinclined, indisposed.

1769 GOLDSM. *Roman Hist.* (1786) I. 245 The senate were ..no way disinclinable to a peace.

disinclination (dɪsɪnklɪ'neɪʃən). [f. DIS- 9 + INCLINATION.] Want of inclination or liking (usually implying an inclination towards the opposite); slight dislike or aversion; indisposition, unwillingness.

1647 CLARENDON *Hist. Reb.* III. (1843) 75/1 [He] spent his time abroad..where he improved his disinclination to the church. **1697** JER. COLLIER *Ess. Mor. Subj.* II. (1709) 164 This Humour, unless prevented, will slide into Indifferency and Disinclination. **1749** FIELDING *Tom Jones* VI. v, So strong a disinclination as I have at present to this person. **1767** *Babler* No. 67 ¶6 An absolute disinclination for their company. **1788** PRIESTLEY *Lect. Hist.* lx. (R.) The same taste for expensive living will naturally spread to the lower ranks ..and produce a general disinclination to matrimony. **1813** J. C. HOBHOUSE *Jour. Albania* 1122 A disinclination from having recourse to unjust extremities. **1856** EMERSON *Eng. Traits, First Visit* Wks. (Bohn) II. 7 He had the natural disinclination of every nimble spirit to bruise itself against walls.

disincline (dɪsɪn'klaɪn), *v.* [f. DIS- 6 + INCLINE *v.*] *trans.* To deprive of inclination; to make indisposed, averse, or unwilling.

1647 CLARENDON *Hist. Reb.* IV. (1843) 115/2 It served..to disincline them from any reverence or affection to the queen. **1736** BOLINGBROKE *Patriot.* (1749) 242, I know that they disinclined men from the succession. **1804** CASTLEREAGH in Owen *Wellesley's Desp.* 252 The jealousy which even then disinclined the Peishwa to place himself in our hands. **1846** D. KING *Lord's Supper* iv. 106 He disinclines us for sin. **1878** BAYNE *Purit. Rev.* ii. 33 Other considerations..might well disincline him to a warlike expedition.

absol. **1790** HAN. MORE *Relig. Fash. World* (1791) 13 It is not perplexed argument or intricate metaphysics, which can now disincline from Christianity.

b. *intr.* To be indisposed or unwilling; to incline not (*to do* something).

1885 G. MEREDITH *Diana* I. i. 19 She..believed, as men disincline to do, that they grow.

disinclined (dɪsɪn'klaɪnd), *ppl. a.* [f. DIS- 10 + INCLINED.] Having a disinclination or slight aversion; not inclined; averse, indisposed.

1647 CLARENDON *Hist. Reb.* VI. (1843) 297/1 Wherever they found any person of quality inclined to the king, or but disinclined to them, they immediately seized upon his person. **1719** YOUNG *Revenge* II. i, Alvarez pleads indeed, That Leonora's heart is disinclined. **1748** RICHARDSON *Clarissa* (1811) III. xxix. 174, I should not be disinclined to go to London, did I know anybody there. **1797** MRS. RADCLIFFE *Italian* i, He maintained that if she was not disinclined towards him, some sign of approbation would appear. **1856** FROUDE *Hist. Eng.* I. 149 The old aristocracy ..were disinclined by constitution and sympathy from sweeping measures. **1858** CARLYLE *Fredk. Gt.* (1865) I. II. iii. 59 The Wends were highly disinclined to conversion. **1888** F. HUME *Mad. Midas* I. v, [He] felt disinclined for any more sleep.

disinclose: see DISENCLOSE.

disincomber, obs. var. of DISENCUMBER.

†**disin'commodate**, *v.* *Obs.* Erroneous mixture of *discommodate* and *incommodate*.
1635 J. HAYWARD tr. *Biondi's Banish'd Virgin* 22 For feare of disincommodating themselves. 1922 JOYCE *Ulysses* 451, I don't think you need over excessively disincommodate yourself in that regard.

†**disin'corporate**, *ppl. a.* *Obs.* Also 7 **disen-**. [f. DIS- 10 + INCORPORATE *a.*: see next.] Disunited or separated from a body, corporation, or society.
1605 BACON *Adv. Learn.* II. xxv. §9 (1871) 258 Aliens and disincorporate from the Church of God. 1681 R. L'ESTRANGE *Casuist Uncas'd* 78 Ten Millions of men, are but as so many Individuals, when disencorporate, and Lopp'd off from the Body.

disincorporate (dɪsɪn'kɔːpəreɪt), *v.* [f. DIS- 6 + INCORPORATE *v.*: cf. F. *désincorporer* (1690 in Hatz.-Darm.).]
1. *trans.* To undo the incorporation of, to dissolve (a corporation).
1697 COLLIER *Ess. Mor. Subj.* I. (1703) 223 To remove the Magistracy, or disincorporate the State. 1754–62 HUME *Hist. Eng.* IV. 191 (Seager) His Majesty had disincorporated some idle monks. 1893 *Min. Nat. Conf. Council* (1892) 271 The same law disincorporated the Mormon Church.
2. To separate from a corporation or body.
1701 COLLIER *M. Aurel.* (1726) 168 He that is selfish.. disincorporates himself from mankind.
Hence **disincorpo'ration**, the action of disincorporating, or depriving of the rights and privileges of a corporation.
1772 T. WARTON *Life Sir T. Pope* 41 (T.) [He] ranked the king's disincorporation of the monks with his rejection of the see of Rome.. as a matter of an external nature.

†**disin'crease**, *sb.* *Obs.* In 5 **disen-**. [f. DIS- 9 + INCREASE *sb.*] The reverse of increase; decrease, diminution.
1430 LYDG. *Chron. Troy* III. xxvii, In preiudice of his worthynesse And disencrease of his hygh prowesse. *c* 1430 —— *Thebes* II. (R.), The tydings that thou hast brought Shal vnto him be disencrease. *c* 1450 —— *Compl. Loveres Lyfe* 202 Wythout addicyoun, Or disencrese, owther mor or lesse.

†**disin'crease**, *v.* *Obs.* In 5 **disencrese**. [f. DIS- 6 + INCREASE *v.*] To decrease, diminish (*intr.* and *trans.*; in quot. 1430, = DIMINISH 5, to rob, deprive).
c 1374 CHAUCER *Boeth.* v. pr. vi. 173 It faileþ and falleþ in to moeuynge fro þe simplicite of [the] presence of god, and disencresiþ to þe infinite quantite of future and of preterit. *c* 1430 *Pilgr. Lyf Manhode* III. xxiv. (1869) 149 Thei withdrawen and disencresen grace dieu of the tresore of hire rialtee.

disin'crustant. [f. DIS- 10 + L. *incrustānt-em*, pr. pple. of *incrustāre* to INCRUST: see -ANT[1].] Something that removes or prevents incrustation.
1878 *Ure's Dict. Arts* IV. 1012 Zinc as a Disincrustant in Steam Boilers.

disincumber: see DISENCUMBER.

disindi'vidualize, *v.* [DIS- 6.] *trans.* To divest of individuality.
1839 J. STERLING *Ess. & Tales* (1848) I. 327 Self is thus.. dis-individualized, unisolated, rather universalized and idealized. 1870 EMERSON *Soc. & Solit.*, *Art* Wks. (Bohn) III. 19 The artist who is to produce a work which is to be admired.. by all men.. must disindividualize himself, and be a man of no party.

disinfect (dɪsɪn'fɛkt), *v.* [f. DIS- 6 + INFECT *v.*: perh. ad. F. *désinfecter* (1556 in Hatz.-Darm.).]
†**1.** *trans.* To rid (a person or place) of an infection or infectious disease. *Obs. rare.*
1598 FLORIO, *Smorbare*, to disinfect, to cure, to heale. 1722 *Lond. Gaz.* No. 6025/2 La Canourgue and Banassac were disinfecting, none had newly fallen sick there.
2. To cleanse (a room, clothes, etc.) from infection; to destroy the germs of disease in.
1658 R. WHITE tr. *Digby's late Disc.* 63 They use to make great fires, where there is houshold-stuffe of men that died of the Pestilence, to dis-infect [1664 disinfect] them. *Ibid.* 64. 1828 WEBSTER, *Disinfect*, to cleanse from infection; to purify from contagious matter. 1844 *Pharmac. Jrnl.* III. 396 The best mode of disinfecting the clothes of scarlatina patients. 1875 *Ure's Dict. Arts* II. 36 Stenhouse has employed charcoal for disinfecting the air.
absol. 1875 *Ure's Dict. Arts* II. 37 Water disinfects partly by preventing effluvia from arising from bodies.
Hence **disin'fected** *ppl. a.*, **disin'fecting** *vbl. sb.* and *ppl. a.*
1837 *Penny Cycl.* VII. 109/1 As a disinfecting agent.. it [chlorine] is unrivalled. 1853 STONEHENGE *Greyhound* iii. (L.) The walls should be well washed with chloride of lime, or.. disinfecting fluid. 1890 B. A. WHITELEGGE *Hygiene & Public Health* xi. 241 One of these rooms should be strictly reserved for infected and the other for disinfected goods. 1894 *Times* 30 Sept. 3/3 A thorough system of disinfection by disinfecting officers.

disin'fectant, *a.* and *sb.* [ad. F. *désinfectant* (1816 in Hatz.-Darm.), pres. pple. of *désinfecter* to DISINFECT.]
A. *adj.* Having the property of disinfecting.
1875 *Ure's Dict. Arts* III. 1192 The disinfectant liquor of Sir W. Burnett is chloride of zinc.
B. *sb.* Something having this property; an agent used for disinfecting or destroying the germs of infectious disease.
1837 *Penny Cycl.* VII. 107/2 The hypochlorite of lime, usually called chloride of lime.. is a compound of great importance, both in the arts, and as a disinfectant.
fig. 1862 T. WINTHROP *Cecil Dreeme* vi. (Cent.) The moral atmosphere, too, of this honest, cheerful, simple home scene acted as a moral disinfectant.

disin'fecter. [f. DISINFECT *v.* + -ER[1].] He who or that which disinfects.
1845 *Jrnl. R. Agric. Soc.* VI. II. 547 It is a disinfecter of putrid matter.

disinfection (dɪsɪn'fɛkʃən). [n. of action from DISINFECT *v.*: cf. F. *désinfection* (1630 in Hatz.-Darm.).] The action of disinfecting or purifying from infection; destruction of the germs of infectious diseases.
1803 *Duncan's Ann. Med.* II. II. 35 On the influence of Oxygen in the process of disinfection. 1838 *Penny Cycl.* XII. 470/1 The most important and valuable method of disinfection is ventilation. 1890 B. A. WHITELEGGE *Hygiene & Public Health* xi. 234 Disinfection by heat is the simplest and most thorough of all methods.

disin'fector. [f. DISINFECT *v.* + -OR, after L. *infector*, etc.] = DISINFECTER; *spec.* a device for diffusing a disinfectant in the air.
1832 LD. CAMPBELL *Let.* Aug. in *Life* (1881) III. 15 In court we are almost overpowered by fumigations and aspersions.. A druggist has made a little fortune by selling what he denominates disinfectors. 1874 in KNIGHT *Dict. Mech.*

disinfest (dɪsɪn'fɛst), *v.* [DIS- 6.] *trans.* To rid (a person, building, etc.) of infesting insects, vermin, etc. So ˌ**disinfe'station**, the process of disinfesting.
1920 *Lancet* 2 Oct. 681/1 (*heading*) Disinfection and disinfestation in the field. *Ibid.* 681/2 The term 'disinfestation' or 'to disinfest' was employed during the war to differentiate the two processes. 1936 *Discovery* Apr. 116 Hydrogen cyanide, or HCN, is the material most generally used nowadays for disinfestation. *Ibid.* 116/2 The task of thoroughly disinfesting slum property. 1942 *Times* 21 Sept. 5/3 Typhus, which is louse-borne,.. was overcome by active measures of disinfestation. 1959 *Times* 7 Dec. (Agric. Suppl.) p. vi/4 The use of radiation.. could be usefully applied for the disinfestation of products handled in bulk. 1966 *Listener* 10 Mar. 352/1 The irradiation method has great economic potential in.. the disinfestation of dried and smoked fish, the disinfestation of dried fruits, [etc.]. 1970 H. BRAUN *Parish Churches* xix. 225 Disinfestation is nowadays possible, but requires a desperate amount of scraping away of ruined timber before the beetle can be reached and destroyed.

disinfeu'dation. [DIS- 9.] The reversal of infeudation; liberation from feudal tenure.
1881 *Academy* 7 May 336 Some new light upon the disinfeudation of advowsons.

disin'flame, *v. rare.* [DIS- 6.] *trans.* To make no longer inflamed; to deprive of ardour.
c 1611 CHAPMAN *Iliad* XII. 400 O Lycians, why are your hot spirits so quickly disinflam'd?

disin'flation. [DIS- 9.]
1. The reversal of inflation, e.g. of a balloon. Cf. DEFLATION.
1880 *Daily News* 22 Oct. 6/5 The grapnel having held fast in muddy ground, the disinflation process was executed.. before the arrival of the lads, who were very serviceable to us for rolling the balloon.
2. The reversal of a state of monetary inflation; the return to a state of equilibrium from an inflationary state; a policy to check or reduce inflation. So **disin'flationary** *a.*
1947 *Economist* 22 Mar. 424/1 One test.. of a dis-inflationary or at least a non-inflationary policy would be one which stopped the creation of additional money. 1948 G. CROWTHER *Outl. Money* (ed. 2) iii. 108 In the course of the year 1947.. it was necessary to find a word to describe a retreat from inflation which did not go so far as deflation; 'disinflation' was invented to serve the purpose. 1955 *Times* 27 Aug. 7/5 This might make sense if we had heavy unemployment and a favourable trade balance, but it can hardly be expected to make an effective contribution to disinflation. 1957 *Ibid.* 17 Dec. 14/3 A high Bank rate.. although disinflationary in intent, will lose much of its effectiveness if it is not backed by price stability.

diˌsinfor'mation. Also **dis-information**. [f. DIS- + INFORMATION; perh. ad. Russ. *dezinformatsiya* (1949, in S. I. Ozhegov *Slovar' russkogo yazy̆ka*, allegedly ad. Fr., although F. *désinformation* is not recorded until 1954 (Quemada, *Matériaux* (1971) II. 53); cf. MISINFORMATION.] **a.** The dissemination of deliberately false information, esp. when supplied by a government or its agent to a foreign power or to the media, with the intention of influencing the policies or opinions of those who receive it; false information so supplied. Cf. *black propaganda* s.v. BLACK *a.* 19 a; PROPAGANDA 3.
1955 *Times* 3 June 6/1 The elimination of every form of propaganda and disinformation, as well as of other forms of conduct which create distrust or in any other way impede the establishment of an atmosphere conducive to constructive international cooperation and to the peaceful coexistence of nations. 1967 *Observer* 10 Dec. 4/4 This works hand in hand with 'disinformation', designed to make people believe that Soviet society and Soviet policies are not what they are. 1971 *Courier-Mail* (Brisbane) 9 Aug. 4/10 A former Czechoslovak spy and Government official has given a Senate panel a glimpse into 'black propaganda'—the art of disinformation. 1975 *New Republic* 30 June 8/1 One technique of the Central Intelligence Agency.. is dis-information... The Agency has expensive facilities for producing fake documents and other means for misleading foreigners. 1977 'J. LE CARRÉ' *Honourable Schoolboy* i. 35 Only those at the inmost point saw things differently. To them, old Craw's article was a discreet masterpiece of disinformation. 1984 *Daily Tel.* 9 Oct. 9/2 It is Sir James' position that.. the Soviets made a conscious decision to seek to discredit the West German politician.. and mounted a campaign of defamation, disinformation and provocation against him.
b. *attrib.*
1967 *Sunday Mail Mag.* (Brisbane) 26 Nov. 3/4 The CIA claims the disinformation department [of the KGB] was established in 1959. 1975 *Economist* 9 Aug. 36/2 Alternatively, the episode could be a 'disinformation' exercise, designed to draw attention to the methods of Chile's security services. 1977 *Washington Post* 6 Mar. A14/4 The US embassy said today that it was 'a classical disinformation piece laced with slander and innuendo and as such unworthy of further comment at this time'. 1979 *Daily Tel.* 23 July 5/4 Disinformation campaigns to deceive Western opinion. 1983 *Listener* 1 Sept. 24/1 He surveyed the range of surveillance and disinformation technology which modern technology has placed in the hands of governments.
Hence (as a back-formation) **disin'form** *v. trans.*, to supply with false information.
1978 *Guardian Weekly* 30 July 13 Advocates of the change say.. that foreign intelligence services today are increasingly using so-called influencing agents for subverting, deceiving and disinforming French public opinion. 1980 DE BORCHGRAVE & MOSS *The Spike* 85 He had proved a willing collaborator in their efforts to disinform the American press.

disingage, -ment, obs. ff. DISENGAGE, -MENT.

disin'genious, etc., freq. error in 17th c. for DISINGENUOUS, etc.
1655 GURNALL *Chr. in Arm.* i. §1 (1669) 62/2 One is against love, and so dis-ingenious. 1674 *Govt. Tongue* iii. §6. 110 The disingeniousness of embracing a profession to which their own hearts have an inward reluctance. 1678 *Yng. Man's Call.* 161 If duty may be disingeniously put off now. 1707 FLOYER *Physic. Pulse-Watch* 11 'Tis Disingenious to pretend to know by the Pulse that which cannot be discover'd by it.

disingenuity (ˌdɪsɪndʒɪ'njuːɪtɪ). [f. next, after *ingenuous, ingenuity.*] = DISINGENUOUSNESS (which is now more usual).
1647 TRAPP *Comm. Pentat.* (1650) I. 302 Unthankfulness and dis-ingenuity. 1653 MANTON *Exp. Jas.* iii. 17 Uncharitable deductions.. forced by the disingenuity of the adversary. 1690 LOCKE *Hum. Und.* IV. viii. (1695) 350 The disingenuity of one, who will go from the definition of his own Terms. 1769 ROBERTSON *Chas. V*, III. VII. 1 The Emperor's disingenuity in violating his repeated promises. 1835 SIR W. HAMILTON *Discuss.* (1852) 184 Mr. Stewart is far more lenient than Dr. Wallis' disingenuity merited.
b. A piece of unfair treatment or underhand dealing.
1680 H. DODWELL *Disc. Sanchoniathon's Hist.* (1691) 114 For the Practice of such disingenuities. 1804 SOUTHEY in *Ann. Rev.* II. 18 In one instance he has been guilty of a worse disingenuity.

disingenuous (dɪsɪn'dʒɛnjuːəs), *a.* [DIS- 10.] The opposite of *ingenuous*; lacking in candour or frankness, insincere, morally fraudulent. (Said of persons and their actions.)
1655 [see DISINGENIOUS]. 1657 *Burtons's Diary* (1828) II. 291 It will be disingenuous to think that his Highness and the Council should be under an oath, and your members free. 1673 *Lady's Call.* I. v. ¶3. 32 Of such disingenuous addresses, 'tis easy to read the event. 1718 *Freethinker* No. 67. ¶9 A Disingenuous Speaker is most effectually refuted without Passion. 1827 HALLAM *Const. Hist.* (1876) I. ii. 98 Cranmer.. had recourse to the disingenuous shift of a protest. 1875 HELPS *Ess.*, *Advice* 46 It is a disingenuous thing to ask for advice, when you mean assistance.
Hence **disin'genuously** *adv.*, in a disingenuous manner, not openly or candidly, meanly, unfairly.
1661 H. NEWCOME *Diary* (1849) 26 So disingenuously.. I have carryed toward my God. 1678 [see DISINGENIOUS]. 1748 RICHARDSON *Clarissa* (1811) I. xxxix. 289 Although I had most disingenuously declared otherwise to my mother. 1836 J. GILBERT *Chr. Atonem.* viii. (1852) 232 We should deem it to be disingenuously evasive.

disin'genuousness. [f. prec. + -NESS.] The quality of being disingenuous; want of candour and frankness; disposition to secure advantage by means not morally defensible; insincerity, unfairness.
1674 [see DISINGENIOUS, etc.]. 1815 JANE AUSTEN *Emma* III. v. 298 Disingenuousness and double-dealing seemed to meet him on every turn. 1849 MACAULAY *Hist. Eng.* II. 274 Those statutes.. could not without the grossest disingenuousness be so strained. 1881 STANLEY *Chr. Instit.* viii. 167 A singular example either of the disingenuousness or of the negligence with which the Prayerbook was reconstructed.

†**disin'habit**, *ppl. a.* Short for DISINHABITED.
1530 PALSGR. 519/2 This countraye is utterly disinhabyt, *ce pays est entierement depoulé.*

† **disin'habit**, *v. Obs.* [f. DIS- 6 + INHABIT *v.*] *trans.* To rid or deprive of inhabitants; to dispeople.

1530 PALSGR. 519/2, I disinhabyte a countrey, I make it barayne of dwellynge people. **1582** N. LICHEFIELD tr. *Castanheda's Conq. E. Ind.* liv. 117 The Citie beeing thus disinhabited. **1607** TOPSELL *Serpents* (1658) 601 Some places have been disinhabited, and dispeopled by Serpents. **1818** TODD s.v. *Dishabit*, In modern times we sometimes use *disinhabit* for it.

b. *refl.* To remove one's dwelling.

1679 G. R. tr. *Boyatuau's Theat. World* III. 220 Caused the People to dis-inhabit themselves.

Hence †**disin'habited** *ppl. a.*, uninhabited, without inhabitants.

1600 HAKLUYT *Voyages* III. 374 (R.) Nothing but exceeding rough mountaines..vtterly disinhabited and voyd of people. **1622** MABBE tr. *Aleman's Guzman d'Alf.* I. 157 Hee..dwels in places vn-peopled and dis-inhabitted. **1632** LITHGOW *Trav.* VIII. 374 Wee were long or night involved in a dis-inhabited Country. **1684** *Bucaniers Amer.* I. (ed. 2) 5 That part of this Island..is totally dis-inhabited.

† **disin'habitable**, *a. Obs.* [DIS- 10.] Uninhabitable.

1660 F. BROOKE tr. *Le Blanc's Trav.* 342 There was reason to believe these parts disinhabitable. **1660** N. INGELO *Bentivolio & Urania* (1682) I. 74 Will you make this place disinhabitable to ingenuity?

† **disin'habitate**, *v. Obs. rare*$^{-0}$. [DIS- 6.]

1611 COTGR., *Deshabiter*, to disinhabitate, or depriue of inhabitants.

disinherison (dɪsɪn'hɛrɪzən). Also disen-. [f. DIS- 9 + INHERISON: cf. *disherison.*] The action of disinheriting, or fact of being disinherited; disinheritance: = DISHERISON.

1543-4 *Act 35 Hen. VIII*, c. 1 The peril slaunder or dishinherison of any the issues and heires of the kinges maiestie. **1622** BACON *Hen. VII* Wks. (Bohn) 310 It tended directly to the disinherison of the line of York. **1643** PRYNNE *Sov. Power Parl.* II. (ed. 2) 69 The great mischiefs and disinherisons that the people of the Realme of England have heretofore suffered. **1765** BLACKSTONE *Comm.* I. 448 There are fourteen such reasons..which may justify such disinherison. **1862** SALA *Ship Chandler* iii. 53 Commanding him under pain of disinherison..to unite himself to the bride he..had chosen for him.

disinherit (dɪsɪn'hɛrɪt), *v.* Also 6 disen-, dishenerite. [f. DIS- 6 + INHERIT *v.*] *trans.* To deprive or dispossess of an inheritance; 'to cut off from an hereditary right' (J.); to prevent (a person) from coming into possession of a property or right which in the ordinary course would devolve upon him as heir.

c **1450** *Merlin* 452 We hadde leuer be disinherited and chased oute of the londe. *c* **1532** DEWES *Introd. Fr.* in *Palsgr.* 1040 The sonne him shal disenherite. **1548** HALL *Chron., Hen. V* an. 2 (1809) 60 Shamefully to dishenerite ourselfe and the Croune of our Realme. **1577-87** HOLINSHED *Chron.* III. 820/2 Yet had he sent his people to inuade the said dukes countrie..to destroie and dishinherit the said duke. **1653** H. COGAN tr. *Pinto's Trav.* xxvii. 103 A very rich Woman, that had disinherited her kindred, and left her estate to the Pagod. **1718** LADY M. W. MONTAGU *Let. to C'tess Bristol* (1887) I. 240 A child thus adopted cannot be disinherited. **1860** HOOK *Lives Abps.* (1869) I. 363 He was disinherited and turned out of his father's house.

†**b.** Const. *of. Obs.*

1548 HALL *Chron., Hen. VII* an. 4 (1809) 444 Nor yet Entended to disheneryt the yonge Duke Phillippe of his Graundfathers inheritaunce. **1621** *State Trials, Abp. Abbot* (R.) Some right of hunting, which the Archbishop was to disinherit his church of. *a* **1716** SOUTH (J.) Of how fair a portion Adam disinherited his whole posterity!

c. *fig.*

1634 MILTON *Comus* 334 And thou, fair moon..Stoop thy pale visage through an amber cloud, And disinherit Chaos, that reigns here. **1742** YOUNG *Nt. Th.* I. 246 God's image disinherited of day, Here, plung'd in mines, forgets a sun was made. **1840** MRS. BROWNING *Drama of Exile* Wks. 1889 I. 35 Earth, methinks, Will disinherit thy philosophy.

Hence **disin'herited** *ppl. a.*, **disin'heriting** *vbl. sb.* and *ppl. a.*

1583 *Exec. for Treason* (1675) 42 The disinheriting of all the Nobility. **1635** EARL STRAFFORD *Lett.* (1739) I. 471 Those disinherited Princes of the Palatinate. **1777** SHERIDAN *Sch. Scand.* IV. i, An unforgiving eye, and a confounded disinheriting countenance! **1868** FREEMAN *Norm. Conq.* (1876) II. x. 486 A disinherited and dispossessed chieftain still looked on the land as his own.

disin'heritable, *a.* [f. prec. + -ABLE.] Liable to be disinherited.

1646 FULLER *Wounded Consc.* (1841) 291 Heirs of Heaven they are, but disinheritable for their misdemeanour.

disin'heritance. [f. DISINHERIT *v.*, after *inheritance.*] The fact of disinheriting, or of being disinherited; dispossession from an inheritance.

1540 *Act 32 Hen. VIII*, c. 9 §1 Vexation, troubles, wrongs and disinheritance hath followed. **1660** R. COKE *Justice Vind.* 36 To the dispossession and disinheritance of another. **1789** *Trifler* No. 39. 506 He was enjoined..upon pain of disinheritance. **1843** W. H. MILL *Observ. Crit. Gosp.* II. ii. §3. 257 By a direct sentence of disinheritance.

† **disin'heritate**, *v. Obs. rare.* [f. DISINHERIT + -ATE³, on analogy of words from Latin ppl. stem: see -ATE² and ³. Cf. It. *disereditare* = *diseredare* to disinherit.] = DISINHERIT.

Hence **disin'heritated** *ppl. a.*; also **disinheri'tation** = DISINHERITANCE.

1654 COKAINE *Dianea* III. 172 A Princesse disinherited implores your aide. **1835** *Chamb. Jrnl.* 16 May 121 Threatened with disinheritation.

disinhibition (dɪsɪnhɪ'bɪʃən). [DIS- 9.] (See quot. 1927.)

1927 G. V. ANREP tr. *Pavlov's Conditioned Reflexes* iv. 67 We are now afforded some justification for regarding disinhibition, as we did a short while ago, as being the 'inhibition of an inhibition'. **1937** *Brit. Jrnl. Psychol.* July 29 Such disinhibition, as Pavlov calls it, has been found associated with the various types of cessation or diminution of activity we have studied. **1964** J. Z. YOUNG *Model of Brain* xvii. 284 Such a mechanism recalls the suggestion that enzymes exist in an inhibited form and that demand brings them into action by disinhibition.

disinhume (dɪsɪn'hjuːm), *v.* Also disen-. [DIS- 6.] *trans.* To unbury, unearth, exhume.

1821 WORDSW. *Eccl. Sonn.*, *Wicliffe*, The Church is seized with sudden fear, And at her call is Wicliffe disinhumed. **1833** *Fraser's Mag.* VIII. 637 The disinhuming of the primitive history of mankind. **1881** *Cornh. Mag.* Sept. 331 A golden drinking-horn disenhumed in the old England of our ancestors by the Baltic Shore.

† **disin'sanity.** *Obs. rare.* In 7 disen-. [irreg. f. *dis-* (used otiosely or ? intensively; cf. DIS- 5) + INSANITY.] Insanity, madness.

a **1625** BEAUM. & FL. *Two Noble K.* III. v, What tediosity and disensanity Is here among ye!

disinsectize (dɪsɪn'sɛktaɪz), *v.* [f. DIS- 6 + INSECT *sb.*: see -IZE.] *trans.* To remove insects from, esp. from an aircraft. Hence ˌ**disinsecti'zation**, **disin'sectizing** *vbl. sb.*, the removal of insects.

1937 *Times* 11 Nov. 11/6 Further study of disinsectizing agents [for aircraft] was decided on. **1947** *Shell Aviation News* CXII. 8/1 The International Sanitary Convention of Aerial Navigation 1933 and 1934..lays down aircraft disinsectization procedure. **1959** *Times* 9 Nov. 9/4 No completely satisfactory method of disinsectizing aircraft while in flight can be recommended. *Ibid.*, The two prongs of defence are vaccination and disinsectization of aircraft.

disinslave, obs. form of DISENSLAVE.

disinsu'lation. [DIS- 9.] Doing away with insulation; the rendering no longer an island.

1882 *Daily Tel.* No. 8306. 5/3 The dis-insulation of England may or may not be a national calamity.

disinsure, disintail, etc.: see DISEN-.

dis'integrable, *a.* [f. DISINTEGRATE: see -ABLE.] Capable of being disintegrated.

1796 KIRWAN *Elem. Min.* (ed. 2) I. 93 Argillo-calcites. 1st Class. Readily disintegrable by exposure to the atmosphere. **1864** H. SPENCER *Induct. Biol.* §118 (L.) The formations [of land] being disintegrable in different degrees.

dis'integrant, *a.* and *sb.* [f. as prec. + -ANT¹.] **A.** *adj.* Disintegrating, or becoming disintegrated. **B.** *sb.* Something that disintegrates; a disintegrating agent.

1855 H. SPENCER *Princ. Psychol.* (1872) I. I. iv. 75 A direct disintegrant of the tissues. **1866** *Pall Mall G.* 10 Nov. 4 Post-classical and disintegrant Greek.

disintegrate (dɪs'ɪntɪgreɪt), *v.* [f. DIS- 6 + INTEGRATE *v.*]

1. a. *trans.* To separate into its component parts or particles; to reduce to fragments, break up, destroy the cohesion or integrity of (as by mechanical or atmospheric action). Also *fig.*

1796 KIRWAN *Elem. Min.* (ed. 2) I. 99 Marlites..are not disintegrated by exposure to the atmosphere. **1860** TYNDALL *Glac.* I. vii. 49 The adjacent rocks..were disintegrated. **1864** *Daily Tel.* 20 Sept., Most valuable for the purpose of blasting or disintegrating rocks. **1874** HELPS *Soc. Press.* xxii. 333 Bricks..entirely disintegrated by the corrosive influence of the London atmosphere.

fig. **1837** HALLAM *Hist. Lit.* ii. III. §13 A fanatical anarchy, disintegrating every thing like a church. **1860** FROUDE *Hist. Eng.* V. 121 The grazing farms were disintegrated. The cottages of the peasants had again their own grounds attached to them. **1876** GLADSTONE *Homeric Synchr.* 7 Learning and ingenuity..expended in a hundred efforts..to disintegrate the Homeric Poems. **1879** G. MEREDITH *Egoist* vii. (1889) 57 We cannot modify our class distinctions without risk of disintegrating the social structure.

b. To separate or break off as particles or fragments *from* the whole mass or body.

1873 TRISTRAM *Moab* iii. 40 The detached blocks, which have been disintegrated from the mass. **1876** BREWER *Eng. Studies* ii. (1881) 57 'Their personal adventures'..cannot be disintegrated from the general body of our history without blurring its lineaments.

c. To cause (a substance or an atom or nucleus) to undergo disintegration.

1920 RUTHERFORD in *Proc. R. Soc.* A. XCVII. 394 Possibly the actual energy required to disintegrate the atom is small compared with the energy of the α-particle. *Ibid.* 395 No evidence has been obtained to show that helium can be disintegrated by the swift α-particles. **1932** COCKCROFT & WALTON in *Ibid.* A. CXXXVII. 229 We describe experiments which show that protons having energies above 150,000 volts are capable of disintegrating a considerable number of elements. **1942** J. D. STRANATHAN *Particles* v. 183 With these energetic particles it has become a relatively easy matter to disintegrate almost any atom.

2. a. *intr.* (for *refl.*) To become disintegrated, to break up.

18.. R. JAMESON (L.), On exposure to the weather it [chalk marl] rapidly disintegrates. **1851** RICHARDSON *Geol.* ix. 349 The absorption of oxygen and carbonic acid from the air causes rocks..to disintegrate. **1856** FROUDE *Hist. Eng.* I. 336 The Church itself was fast disintegrating.

b. Of a nucleus or particle, or a radioactive substance: to undergo disintegration (see DISINTEGRATION sense a, below); to decay (see DECAY *v.* 2c).

1904 F. SODDY *Radio-Activity* viii. 122 In the case of the disintegrating atoms the cause of the disintegration is at present unknown. It proceeds at a definite rate, a fixed fraction of the total atoms disintegrating in the unit of time, without hindrance or acceleration by any agency known... The internal energy of the chemical atom becomes for the first time knowable when it disintegrates. **1926** R. W. LAWSON tr. *Hevesy & Paneth's Man. Radioactivity* i. 4 We now define a substance as being radioactive when the atoms of which it is composed disintegrate spontaneously. **1942** *Ann. Reg. 1941* 351 Those mesons born practically at rest disintegrate in the stratosphere into electrons. **1962** H. D. BUSH *Atomic & Nuclear Physics* iv. 73 Which nuclei disintegrate in a particular time interval is a matter of chance. **1963** S. TOLANSKY *Introd. Atomic Physics* (ed. 5) xix. 321 Yukawa..postulated that the meson can spontaneously disintegrate, being in this sense radioactive.

dis'integrate, *a. rare.* [f. DIS- 10 + INTEGRATE *a.*, after prec.] Disintegrated.

1875 G. MACDONALD *Malcolm* III. x. 147 The disintegrate returns to resting and capable form.

dis'integrated, *ppl. a.* [f. DISINTEGRATE *v.* + -ED¹.] Reduced to fragments, broken up; broken off as fragments: see the verb.

1796 KIRWAN *Elem. Min.* (ed. 2) I. 321 The felspar, both in granites and porphyries, is frequently found..in a decomposed or disintegrated state. **1854** J. SCOFFERN in *Orr's Circ. Sc.* Chem. 7 Disintegrated particles. **1869** PHILLIPS *Vesuv.* v. 146 This volcanic dust is disintegrated lava. **1879** CHURCH *Spenser* 62 The wreck and clashing of disintegrated customs.

dis'integrating, *ppl. a.* [f. as prec. + -ING².]

1. That disintegrates (*trans.*); reducing or tending to reduce to fragments; destroying cohesion or integrity.

1831 BREWSTER *Nat. Magic* xii. (1833) 298 The disintegrating and solvent powers of chemical agents. **1868** G. DUFF *Pol. Surv.* 220 Those disintegrating forces which have worked so powerfully in breaking up more than one of the States.

2. That disintegrates (*intr.*); breaking up, going to pieces.

1872 C. KING *Mountain. Sierra Nev.* x. 217 A disintegrating race. **1877** ROBERTS *Handbk. Med.* (ed. 3) I. 124 Disintegrating red corpuscles are sometimes seen.

disinte'gration. [n. of action f. DISINTEGRATE *v.*: see -ATION.] The action or process of disintegrating, or the condition of being disintegrated; reduction to component particles, breaking up; destruction of cohesion or integrity.

a. *lit.*; *spec.* in *Geol.*, the wearing down of rocks by rain, frost, and other atmospheric influences; in *Nuclear Physics*, a process which a nucleus may undergo, spontaneously or under bombardment, in which it either emits one or more particles and becomes a different nuclide or else splits up into two or more smaller nuclei; also, the decay of an elementary particle; an instance of such a process. Also freq. *attrib.*

1796 KIRWAN *Elem. Min.* (ed. 2) I. 96 By exposure to the air and moisture, it..chips and falls to pieces. This disintegration is remarkable, for it does not proceed solely from the absorption of water. **1808** HENRY *Epit. Chem.* (ed. 5) 357 The disintegration of stones, consisting chiefly of alumine, is not easily effected by means of potash. **1834** THOMSON in *Proc. Berw. Nat. Club* I. No. 2. 42 The disintegration of the clay-slate rocks. **1860** MAURY *Phys. Geog.* i. 20 The wire wrapping of the Atlantic cable has been found in a state almost of complete disintegration. **1863** A. C. RAMSAY *Phys. Geog.* iii. (1878) 34 The constant atmospheric disintegration of cliffs. **1874** CARPENTER *Ment. Phys.* I. ii. §31 (1879) 30 When a Muscle is called into contraction, there is a certain disintegration or 'waste' of its tissue. **1903** RUTHERFORD & SODDY in *Phil. Mag.* V. 446 The first stage in the disintegration of thorium is not directly into the emanation. *Ibid.* 583 Radioactive change can only be of the nature of an atomic disintegration. **1904** F. SODDY *Radio-Activity* viii. 121 The disintegration theory [of radioactivity] regards the property as due to a fixed proportion of the total number of atoms which are undergoing disintegration. *Ibid.* xii. 172 Consider the case of a disintegration series in which there is a parent element, A, disintegrating at an excessively slow rate. **1914** H. G. WELLS *World set Free* i. §1, He set up atomic disintegration in a minute particle of bismuth. **1932** COCKCROFT & WALTON in *Proc. R. Soc.* A. CXXXVII. 229 (*heading*) The disintegration of elements by high velocity protons. **1933** *Discovery* June 179/2 This third hydrogen has been produced artificially in the Cavendish Laboratories in Cambridge, England, and at Princeton by the nuclear disintegration process. **1942** *Ann. Reg. 1941* 351 Fermi's theory of β-ray disintegration. **1942** STRANATHAN *Particles* viii. 348 Most atoms emit a γ-ray photon and pass to their normal energy states long before they undergo a subsequent nuclear disintegration. **1945** *Electronic Engin.* Sept. 668/1 The enormous energy which may in certain circumstances be obtained from a chain of atomic disintegrations. **1946** *Nature* 14 Sept. 373/3 The disintegration-rate..correctly specifies the strength of a radioactive source. **1949** *Nucleonics* Dec. 49 The curie shall be defined as that quantity of any radioactive species (radioisotope) undergoing exactly 3·700 × 10^{10} disintegrations per second. **1954** H. SEMAT *Introd. Atomic & Nuclear Physics* (ed. 3) xi. 362 A more accurate determination of the half-life of the radioactive disintegration of the neutron.

b. *fig.*

1849 HT. MARTINEAU in *Four C. Eng. Lett.* 545 If the principles of social liberty should demand the disintegration of nations. **1865** MERIVALE *Rom. Emp.* VIII. lxviii. 355 The decay of moral principles which hastened the disintegration of Roman society. **1868** GLADSTONE *Juv. Mundi* i. (1870) 19 There are passages of ancient writers which tend to the disintegration of Homer.

c. *attrib.* and *Comb.*, as ***disintegration-scheme***, ***-theory***; **disintegration constant**, a measure of the rate of disintegration of a radioactive substance.

1865 W. KAY *Crisis Hupfeld.* 59 The principles on which the Disintegration-theory rests. **1926** R. W. LAWSON tr. *Hevesy & Paneth's Man. Radioactivity* iii. 33 The half-value thickness is related to the absorption coefficient in the same way as the half-value period to the disintegration constant. **1962** H. D. BUSH *Atomic & Nuclear Physics* iv. 75 Measurement of the change of activity with time enables the disintegration constant to be found.

Hence **disinte'grationist**, an advocate of disintegration.

1884 DUNCKLEY in *Manch. Exam.* 1 Dec. 6/1 Mr. Forster seems to them to be the great disintegrationist of our time. **1889** *Spectator* 3 Aug., Their own disintegration is a Nemesis upon the disintegrationists.

dis'integrative, *a.* [f. as prec.: see -ATIVE.] Having the quality of disintegrating; tending to disintegrate.

1869 *Contemp. Rev.* XII. 164 Tenets..essentially disintegrative of union. **1876** A. M. FAIRBAIRN *Strauss* II. in *Contemp. Rev.* June 135 Ancient heresies were elaborative, modern disintegrative of dogma.

dis'integratively, *adv.* [f. DISINTEGRATIVE + -LY[2].] In a disintegrative manner, in a way that causes disintegration.

1874 *Rep. Med. Off. P.C.* 6 in *Parl. Papers* (C. 1068) XXXI. 355 A force..acting disintegratively upon organic matter.

dis'integrator. [agent-n. f. DISINTEGRATE *v.*: see -OR.]

1. One who or that which disintegrates.

1844 *N. Brit. Rev.* I. 114 Collectors of authorities and disintegrators of *débris.* **1863** A. C. RAMSAY *Phys. Geog.* i. (1878) 4 Frost is..a powerful disintegrator.

b. *spec.* Applied to machines or appliances for reducing substances to small fragments or to powder.

1874 KNIGHT *Dict. Mech.*, *Disintegrator.* 1. A machine for grinding or pulverizing bones, guano, etc., for manure. 2. A mill in which grain is broken into a fine dust by beaters projecting from the faces of parallel metallic disks revolving in contrary directions. **1890** *Daily News* 26 June 6/1 Amongst the popular instruments is one called the Devil Disintegrator..It grinds everything to powder, and..is largely used in reducing..bones and oyster shells..into a fine mixture that makes an admirable chicken food.

2. = DISINTEGRATIONIST.

1865 W. KAY *Crisis Hupfeld.* 26 The opponents of the Disintegrators.

dis'inte,gratory, *a.* [f. as prec. + -ORY.] Producing or tending to disintegration.

1878 LEWES in *Pop. Sc. Monthly* XIII. 419 Criticism has taken its place among the disintegratory agencies.

disin'tegrity. [DIS- 9.] Want of integrity or entireness; unsound or disintegrated condition.

1785 BENTHAM *Wks.* (1838–43) X. 145 The multitude of the audience multiplies for disintegrity the chances of detection. **1861** WILLIS in *Ecclesiologist* XXII. 91 Nothing short of such a system could have prevented the falling in of Chichester Tower; it was in a state of disintegrity which nothing could arrest.

dis'integrous, *a. rare.* [f. DIS- 10 + L. *integer* entire + -OUS: after *disintegrate*, etc.] Characterized by disintegration or want of cohesion.

1885 *Sci. Amer.* (N.Y.) 8 Aug. 80 Such a disintegrous material as iron could not be spread into layering leaves like gold.

disin'tensify, *v.* [DIS- 6.] *trans.* To deprive of its intensity; to make less intense.

1884 BROWNING *Ferishtah* 119 Black's soul of black Beyond white's power to disintensify.

disinter (dɪsɪn'tɜː(r)), *v.* Also 7 disen-, -terre. [ad. F. *désenterrer* (15th c. in Littré), f. *des-* DIS- 4 + *enterrer* to INTER.]

1. *trans.* To take (something) out of the earth in which it is buried; to take (a corpse, etc.) out of the grave; to unbury, exhume.

1611 COTGR., *Dessevelir*, to disinterre, vnburie. **1627** MAY *Lucan* IX. (R.) Isis (their Goddesse now) I'le disinterre. **1646** SIR T. BROWNE *Pseud. Ep.* VII. xix. 384 To disenterre the bodies of the deceased. **1658** EVELYN *Fr. Gard.* (1675) 96 Dis-interre the greatest roots. **1867** PEARSON *Hist. Eng.* I. 2 The short shallow skulls which are even now disinterred in old barrows.

2. *transf.* and *fig.* To take out as if from a tomb; to bring out of concealment, 'unearth'.

1711 ADDISON *Spect.* No. 215 ¶2 The Philosopher, the Saint, or the Hero..very often lie..concealed in a Plebeian, which a proper Education might have dis-interred. **1818** SCOTT *Hrt. Midl.* i, The two ladies who had been disinterred out of the fallen vehicle.

† disinteress, *v. Obs.* Pa. pple. -essed, -est. [ad. F. *désintéresser* 'to discharge, or saue harmelesse; to rid from all interest in' (Cotgr.), f. *des-* DIS- 4 + *intéresser* to INTEREST.] = DISINTEREST *v.* Hence **dis-interessing** *vbl. sb.*

1622 BACON *Hen. VII*, 55 The higher Bond that tyeth him ..doth dis-interesse him of these Obligations. **1642** R. CARPENTER *Experience* III. iv. 14 Why is every man disinteressed from a lawfull calling? **1642** JER. TAYLOR *Episc.* (1647) 249 To be deposed, or disinterest in the allegeance of subjects. **1646** SALTMARSH *Some Drops* i. 3 We all see how hazardous it is to disinteresse any in the Civill part. *a* **1655** VINES *Lord's Supp.* (1677) 342 The dis-interessing of self-love..is very rare.

† disinteressed, *ppl. a. Obs.* Also des-, disinterest. [f. prec. + -ED[1], or f. DIS- 10 + INTERESSED.]

1. = DISINTERESTED 1.

1603 FLORIO *Montaigne* III. ii. (1632) 456 It is a pleasure unto mee, to bee disinteressed of other mens affayres, and disingaged from their contentions. **1638** CHILLINGW. *Relig. Prot.* I. iii. §81. 179 We that are disinteressed persons. **1648** BOYLE *Seraph. Love* vi. (1700) 48 Such disinteressed and resign'd Habitudes. **1692** DRYDEN *St. Euremont's Ess.* 351 Let us act the disinteressed.

2. = DISINTERESTED 2.

1610 DONNE *Pseudo-martyr.* xii. 358 The Pope..more disinteressed then the neighbour Princes. **1649** JER. TAYLOR *Gt. Exemp.* I. 72 The prudence of a wise and disinterest person. **1696** MARY ASTELL *Proposal to Ladies* 137 The most refin'd and disinteress'd Benevolence. **1700** TYRRELL *Hist. Eng.* II. 1098 This Writer being a Layman is more disinteressed.

Hence **† disinteressedly** *adv.*; **† disinteressedness**, **† disinterestness**, disinterestedness.

1648 BOYLE *Seraph. Love* xiii. (1700) 66 The.. Disinterestness of his Love to us. **1707** *Refl. Ridic.* 253 Disinteressedness and Generosity. **1718** J. T. PHILIPPS tr. *Thirty-four Confer.* 351 Men disinteress'dly holy.

† disinte'ressment. *Obs.* [a. F. *désintéressement* (1657 in Hatz.-Darm.).] Disinterestedness, impartiality.

1662 J. BARGRAVE *Pope Alex. VII* (1867) 110 Let him read them both with an equal disinteressment. **1718** PRIOR *Poems* Postcr. to Pref., He [the Earl of Dorset] has managed some of the greatest charges of the kingdom, with known ability; and laid them down with entire disinteressment.

disinterest, *sb.* [f. DIS- 9 + INTEREST *sb.*]

1. That which is contrary to interest or advantage; disadvantage, prejudice, injury; something against the interest *of* or disadvantageous *to* (a person or thing concerned). Now *rare.*

1662 GLANVILL *Lux Orient.* Pref. (1682) 7 'Tis a great disinterest to so..unusual a Doctrine as this, to be but partially handled. **1678** NORRIS *Coll. Misc.* (1699) 294 Whatever..tends to the Disinterest of the Public, is Evil. **1744** HARRIS *Three Treat.* (1841) 105 You have seen many a wise head shake, in pronouncing that sad truth, How we are governed all by interest. And what do they think should govern us else? Our loss, our damage, our disinterest? **1876** RUSKIN *Fors Clav.* VI. lxviii. 253 All gain, increase, interest ..to the lender of capital, is loss, decrease, and dis-interest to the borrower of capital.

2. Disinterestedness, impartiality.

1658 J. WEBB tr. *Calprenede's Cleopatra* VIII. i. 34 Perswaded of my disinterest in the affaires of Coriolanus. **1718** OZELL *Tournefort's Voy.* I. p. xviii, Physick, which he practised with the most perfect disinterest. **1799** W. TAYLOR in *Monthly Rev.* XXIX. 102 A catching spirit of disinterest and benevolence. **1805** —— in *Monthly Mag.* XX. 40 The taste of Lessing awarded them, if not with equity, with disinterest. **1896** *Sat. Rev.* Suppl. Christmas 4/2 We here see Morris working, with entire disinterest, at his work, and caring above all things for fine workmanship. **1905** *Globe* 19 Sept., The American Press..reproached Japan with her want of disinterest.

3. Absence of interest, unconcern. (Cf. DISINTERESTED *ppl. a.*)

1889 MRS. RANDOLPH *New Eve* I. i. 29 [An expression] of intense disinterest in all earthly things. **1900** *Pilot* 1 Sept. 283/1 The general reader may, without confessing to a heart of stone, feel a certain disinterest in weather and Mrs. Bouveries, however nice and however ill. **1904** *Sat. Rev.* 9 Jan. 34 The whole election was a model of quiet disinterest. **1940** *Economist* 19 Oct. 480/2 Peace may bring back the old disinterest and the old candour in mutual criticism which springs perhaps from friendship but does nothing to advance it. **1962** *Guardian* 9 Apr. 6/3 The days of service disinterest are over. The RAF has begun to think seriously ..about the future of space. **1965** M. MORSE *Unattached* i. 17 The general reaction..was a mixture of curiosity, disinterest, fear, and embarrassment.

dis'interest, *v.* Now *rare.* [f. DIS- 6 + INTEREST *v.*: see DISINTERESS, which this vb. has superseded.]

1. *trans.* To rid or divest of interest or concern; to detach from the interest or party of.

1612 BACON *Charge touching Duels*, When he shall see the law and rule of state disinterest him of a vain and unnecessary hazard. **1675** tr. *Camden's Hist. Eliz.* 539 An advantageous Peace had been offered to him by the Pope's Nuncio..if he would disinterest himself from the Queen. **1692** BEVERLEY *Disc. Dr. Crisp* 15 His present Enmity does not disinterest him in a Right to come, if he would; But it hinders his being willing to come. **1895** *Pall Mall G.* 1 Feb. 2/1 Politics in France are disgusting, and that is why the people have disinterested themselves entirely from taking part in them.

2. To free from self-interest, to render disinterested.

1681 R. L'ESTRANGE *Apol. Prot.* II. 29 That every man dis-interesting himself, may candidly endeavour the retriving of the Truth.

disinterest, var. of DISINTERESSED *ppl. a.*

dis'interested, *ppl. a.* [f. prec. vb. + -ED[1]; or f. DIS- 10 + INTERESTED.]

1. Without interest or concern; not interested, unconcerned. (Often regarded as a loose use.)

a **1612** DONNE *Βιαθανατος* (1644) 99 Cases, wherein the party is dis-interested. **1684** *Contempl. State of Man* I. x (1699) 113 How dis-interested are they in all Worldly matters, since they fling their Wealth and Riches into the Sea. **1767** *Junius Lett.* iii. 18 A careless disinterested spirit is no part of his character. **1928** in C. F. S. Gamble *N. Sea Air Station* xiii. 222 Being disinterested with the rest of the proceedings, I opened the file and began to read the theory of Wave Transmission. **1928** *Daily Express* 21 June 11/4 She is listless and disinterested. **1928** *Sunday Dispatch* 8 July 15/2 The English public is disinterested in its theatre. **1946** 'S. RUSSELL' *To Bed with Grand Music* vii. 95 She was disinterested rather than credulous. **1960** I. BENNETT *Delinquent & Neurotic Children* viii. 299 Parents disinterested and failed to cooperate. **1960** *Guardian* 2 Mar. 7/2, I am always annoyed when anybody refers to me as a religious poet. Could a poet be disinterested in religion? **1970** *Daily Tel.* (Colour Suppl.) 15 May 20/4 Oxford, after three successive defeats, are almost entirely disinterested in the Boat Race.

2. Not influenced by interest; impartial, unbiased, unprejudiced; now always, Unbiased by personal interest; free from self-seeking. (Of persons, or their dispositions, actions, etc.)

1659 O. WALKER *Oratory* 115 The soul..sits now as the most disinterested Arbiter, and impartial judge of her own works, that she can be. **1705** STANHOPE *Paraphr.* III. 435 So should the Love to our Neighbour be..Not mercenary and designing, but disinterested and hearty. **1726** *Adv. Capt. R. Boyle* 273 Any disinterested Person would make the same Judgement; your Passion has blinded yours. **1800** MRS. HERVEY *Mourtray Fam.* II. 82, I fairly own I was not disinterested in wishing you here. **1865** LIVINGSTONE *Zambesi* xxii. 446 His disinterested kindness to us..can never be forgotten.

dis'interestedly, *adv.* [f. prec. + -LY[2].] **1.** In a disinterested manner; impartially; without regard to self-interest; unselfishly.

1711 SHAFTESB. *Charac.* (1737) I. 42 He, who is ever said to do good the most disinterestedly. **1807** SOUTHEY *Lett.* (1856) II. 20 He knows the Arts well, and loves them disinterestedly. **1830** FOSTER in *Life & Corr.* (1846) II. 161 Devotedly and disinterestedly faithful. **1875** HAMERTON *Intell. Life* II. iii. 64 How difficult it is to think out such a problem disinterestedly.

2. Without interest or concern; unconcernedly.

1941 *Penguin New Writing* IX. 9 We lean over the stern, smoking, spitting, staring disinterestedly at the creaming green of the wake. **1955** A. ROSS *Australia 55* 37 Girls, who chain-smoke or read disinterestedly.

dis'interestedness. [f. as prec. + -NESS.] The quality of being disinterested; impartiality; freedom from self-interest or selfish bias.

a **1682** SIR T. BROWNE (J.), These expressions of selfishness and disinterestedness have been used in a very loose and indeterminate manner. **1709** J. JOHNSON in *Ballard MSS.* (Bodl. Libr.) XV. 46 What I most admire him for is Disinterestedness. **1752** JOHNSON *Rambler* No. 196 ¶8 This..gives firmness and constancy, fidelity and disinterestedness. **1866** LIDDON *Bampt. Lect.* iv. (1875) 195 This disinterestedness, this devotion to the real interest of humankind. **1875** JOWETT *Plato* III. 79 He can assume the disguise of virtue or disinterestedness without having them.

dis'interesting, *ppl. a.* [f. DIS- 10 + INTERESTING *ppl. a.*, or f. DISINTEREST *v.* + -ING[2].] Uninteresting; causing lack of interest.

1737 WARBURTON *Let. to Birch* in Boswell *Johnson* (1887) I. 29 A dull, heavy succession of long quotations of disinteresting passages. **1800** W. TAYLOR in *Monthly Mag.* X. 319 The attempt..produces on all the Disciples a similar disinteresting effect. **18..** *The Studio* III. 130 (Cent.) He rarely paints a disinteresting subject.

disinterestness, var. DISINTERESSEDNESS. *Obs.*

disin'terment. [f. DISINTER *v.* + -MENT.]

1. The action of disinterring; exhumation.

1790 P. NEVE (*title*) A Narrative of the Disinterment of Milton's Coffin. **1867** FREEMAN *Norm. Conq.* (1876) I. App. 788 The disinterment of Harold's body. **1872** YEATS *Growth Comm.* 60 The disinterment of Pompeii and Herculaneum.

2. *concr.* The material result or product of disinterring; something disinterred.

1825 W. TAYLOR in *Monthly Rev.* CVI. 526 Among the most curious disinterments are vases for heating water. **1841** D'ISRAELI *Amen. Lit.*, *R. Crowley* II. 150 Our most skilful delver into dramatic history, amidst his curious masses of disinterments, has brought up this proclamation.

disinter'twine, *v.* [DIS- 6.] *trans.* To bring out of an intertwined condition; to untwist.

1861 LYTTON & FANE *Tannhäuser* 32 The carven architrave, Whereon the intricate..design Of leaf and stem disintertwined itself. **1867** GILDERSLEEVE *Ess. & Stud.* (1890) 198 Such intricate compounds as 'disintertwined'.

disinthrall, disinthrone: see DISEN-.

disintomb, obs. var. of DISENTOMB *v.*

disin'tone, *v. rare.* [f. DIS- 6 + INTONE *v.*] *trans.* To deprive of 'tone', weaken, enfeeble.
1892 *Voice* (N.Y.) 14 July, Every brain habitually stimulated by alcohol is more or less disintoned.

disin'toxicate, *v.* [DIS- 6.] *trans.* To free from intoxication; to restore to soberness. Also *fig.* Hence **disintoxi'cation**, removal of the effects of intoxication.
1685 J. CHAMBERLAYNE *Coffee Tea & Choc.* 40 It disintoxicates those that are fuddled. **1927** *Scots Observer* 20 Aug. 9/5 'Spiritual life,' says Mr. Santayana, 'is not a worship of values whether found in things or hypostatised into supernatural powers. It is the exact opposite; it is *disintoxication* from their influence.' **1930** *Advt.*, Natural mineral water of Contrexéville. Diuretic and for disintoxication. **1935** *Mind* XLIV. 94 The lesson of that tragedy is acceptance of life, not through intoxication and excess, but through disintoxication, submission, conciliation, self-limitation. **1936** *Scrutiny* IV. iv. 381 The next stanza is the only one in the poem to be completely disintoxicated and disenchanted. **1963** AUDEN *Dyer's Hand* 27 In so far as poetry, or any other of the arts, can be said to have an ulterior purpose, it is, by telling the truth, to disenchant and disintoxicate.

disintreat: see DISENTREAT.

dis'intricate, *v.* [f. DIS- 6 + INTRICATE *v.*] *trans.* To free from intricacy or complication; to disentangle, unravel, extricate.
1598 FLORIO, *Districare*, to free..to disintricate, to vntangle. **1611** COTGR., *Desmeslement*..a loossing..vnpestering, disintricating. **1660** tr. *Amyraldus' Treat. conc. Relig.* III. iv. 371 The knowledge of the true God..disintricated from the confusion of so many false Deities. **1830** SIR W. HAMILTON *Discuss.* (1852) 45 To disintricate the question, by relieving it of these two errors.

†**disi'nure**, *v. Obs.* [f. DIS- 6 + INURE *v.*] *trans.* To deprive of use or practice; to disaccustom.
1613 JACKSON *Creed* I. 59 God..dis-inuring his chosen Israel from his wonted call. **1644** MILTON *Areop.* (Arb.) 65 We are hinder'd and dis-inur'd by this cours of licencing towards the true knowledge of what we seem to know.

†**disinva'lidity.** *Obs.* [irreg. f. *dis-*, otiose or intensive (cf. DIS- 5) + INVALIDITY.] Invalidity.
1625 BP. MOUNTAGU *App. Cæsar* II. iv. 136, I do call those Some mens doctrines..Private Opinions: and so well may I doe, in respect of the disinvalidity and disproportion of them.

†**disinveigle**, *v. Obs. rare.* [DIS- 6.] *trans.* To free from inveiglement.
1635 J. HAYWARD tr. *Biondi's Banish'd Virg.* 50 Nor had he..beene yet disinveagled so soone as he was..but for the Princesse..who..shew'd him the false carde dealt him.

disinvelope: see DISENVELOP.

disin'vent, *v. nonce-wd.* [DIS- 6.] *trans.* To undo the invention of.
1868 HELPS *Realmah* xiv. (1876) 371, I would disinvent telegraphic communication. *Ibid.* 376 and 386.

disin'vest, *v.* [DIS- 6: cf. mod.F. *désinvestir*.] **1.** *trans.* To deprive of that with which one is invested; to strip, divest (*lit.* and *fig.*).
1630 WADSWORTH *Pilgr.* iii. 12 They made me disinvest my selfe of such prophane garments I had. *a* **1631** DRAYTON *Wks.* I. 270 (Jod.) Having seen His disinvesting and disastrous chance. **1645** W. BALL *Sphere Govt.* 13 By reposing or granting such Trust, they doe not disinvest themselves of their right naturall. **1882** A. AUSTIN in *Contemp. Rev.* Jan. 129 Not..that language has of itself any spell to disinvest man, who employs it, of that dust of the ground which enters so largely into his composition.
2. *intr. Econ.* To reduce or dispose of one's investment (in a place, company, etc.) Const. *from*, *in*, or *absol.*
1961 in WEBSTER. **1975** *Economist* 2 Aug. 4/3 His only remaining realistic course..would seem to be to disinvest — namely to curtail and actually reduce the size and profitability of his company. **1984** *Daily Tel.* 17 Oct. 19/1 He strongly urged foreign businesses to disinvest from South Africa. **1987** *Church Times* 27 Mar. 14/2 Their aims are to put pressure on the Church Commissioners to disinvest in South Africa.
So **disin'vestiture, disin'vesture**, the action of disinvesting or state of being disinvested.
1616 *Court & T. Jas. I* (1849) I. 430 They rather think of his disinvesture of his robe, and after to be questioned in the Star Chamber. **1846** WORCESTER cites *West. Rev.* for *Disinvestiture.*

disinvestment (dɪsɪn'vɛstmənt). *Econ.* [DIS- 9.] The consumption, realization, or reduction of investment; a diminution of capital goods.
1938 J. M. KEYNES in *Times* 7 Oct. 10/1 The balance-of-trade position and the net disinvestment in this country's foreign assets..also needs particular attention. **1940** *Economist* 7 Dec. 704/2 The inflow of the metal [gold] provided a vehicle for disinvestment and was a positively deflationary force. **1948** G. CROWTHER *Outl. Money* (ed. 2) v. 160 In the early part of a depression the gradual liquidation of these stocks [of raw materials] is an important cause of 'dis-Investment'. When it is finished..one reason for the decline in Investment is removed. **1971** *Sunday Express* (Johannesburg) 28 Mar. 15/4 Also noticeable was some disinvestment by institutions.

disin'vigorate, *v. rare.* [DIS- 6.] *trans.* To deprive of vigour, to enervate: the opposite of *invigorate.*
1844 SYD. SMITH *Let.* in *Mem.* (1855) II. 518 This soft, and warm, and disinvigorating climate.

†**disinvi'tation.** *Obs.* [f. DIS- 9 + INVITATION.] The opposite of an invitation; an invitation not to do something.
1654 LD. ORRERY *Parthenissa* (1676) 502 Why do you..give me so great a dis-invitation to obey you?

†**disin'vite**, *v. Obs.* [DIS- 6.] *trans.* To do the opposite of inviting; to retract or cancel an invitation to. Hence **disin'viting** *ppl. a.*
1580 SIDNEY *Arcadia* III. 329 Casting a sideward look on Zelmane, [he] made an imperious sign with a threatening allurement (a dis-inviting inviting of her) to follow. **1656** FINETT *For. Ambass.* 143 (T.) I was upon his highness's intimation sent to disinvite them. **1665** J. SERGEANT *Sure-footing* 27 Which would..disinvite to a pursuit.

‖**disinvoltura** (disinvol'tura). [It., f. *disinvolto* unembarrassed, f. *disinvolgere* to unwind (*volgere* to wrap).] Self-assurance; lack of constraint.
c **1847** F. A. KEMBLE *Records of Later Life* (1882) III. 322 Acted to the life by a woman, who moves with more complete *disinvoltura* in her men's clothes than most men do. **1899** M. BEERBOHM in *Sat. Rev.* 6 May 555/1 When they [*sc.* the English] are drunk, they do, indeed, talk, and do attain even a certain degree of *disinvoltura.* **1947** A. EINSTEIN *Mus. Romantic Era* xvi. 265 Bellini..with his elegant insouciance, with his melancholic *disinvoltura* of intellectual and physical customs.

disin'volve, *v.* [f. DIS- 6 + INVOLVE *v.*] *trans.* To free from an involved condition; to unfold; to disentangle.
1611 FLORIO, *Disinuolto*, disintangled, disinuolued. **1632** SIR T. HAWKINS tr. *Mathieu's Vnhappy Prosperitie* 9 Other inquisitions..from which the most innocent hardly could dis-involve themselves. **1647** *Power of Keys* ii. 12 False illations..which will all vanish..and the truth be dis-involved. **1742** YOUNG *Nt. Th.* IX. 260 To dis-involve the moral world, and give To nature's renovation brighter charms.

disinwrap, obs. var. of DISENWRAP *v.*

disione, var. of DISJUNE *v. Obs.*

dis'jasked, -et, -it, *ppl. a. Sc.* [According to Jamieson 'a corruption of *dejected*': cf. DISJECTED.] Broken down, dilapidated; decayed. *lit.* and *fig.* Also in *comb.*
1816 SCOTT *Old Mort.* xli, 'Tak the first broken disjasked-looking road.' **1822** GALT *Steamboat* 261 (Jam.) In a very disjaskit state, being both sore in lith and limb, and worn out in my mind. **1830** —— *Laurie T.* VII. viii. (1849) 336 Miss Beeny, not having been in bed all night, was in a most disjasket state.

disject (dɪs'dʒɛkt), *v.* [f. L. *disject-*, ppl. stem of *disjicĕre* to throw asunder, scatter, disperse, f. *dis-*, DIS- 1 + *jacĕre* to throw: cf. also L. *disjectāre* freq.] *trans.* To cast or break asunder; to scatter, disperse. Hence **dis'jected** *ppl. a.* separated by force, dismembered.
1581 MARBECK *Bk. of Notes* 159 A Church most rightlie instituted, which was afterward mise[ra]blie disiected and seperated. **1647** TRAPP *Comm. Jas.* i. 1 The Jews at this day are a disjected and despised people. —— *Rev.* xvi. 19 By the earth-quake disjected and dissipated. **1879** SIR G. G. SCOTT *Lect. Archit.* II. 322 My lecture..the last of my long but disjected series. **1893** *Law Times* XCV. 54/1 That branch of the Profession elects to remain disjected, a profession of units without common interests, without cohesion. **1894** G. ALLEN in *Westm. Gaz.* 22 May 1/3 To tear his present critic limb from limb..and then to dance a stately..carmagnole over the disjected members.

‖**disjecta membra.** *Lat. phr.* An alteration of Horace's *disjecti membra poetæ* 'limbs of a dismembered poet', used = Scattered remains.
1722 POPE *Lett.* (1737) 250 (Stanf.) You call'd 'em an Horatian cento and then I recollected the *disjecti membra poetae.* **1754** H. WALPOLE *Lett.* (1857) II. 411 (Stanf.) Shake those words all together, and see if they can be anything but the *disjecta membra* of Pitt. **1872** C. KING *Mountain. Sierra Nev.* ix. 186 The *savant* to whose tender mercies these *disjecta membra* have been committed.

disjection (dɪs'dʒɛkʃən). [ad. L. *disjectiōnem*, n. of action f. *disjicĕre*, to DISJECT: see -TION.] The action of throwing asunder; the fact or condition of being scattered; forcible dispersion, rout.
1735 J. ATKINS *Voy. Guinea* 148 Then like a Cannon in proportion to these, the disjection is with more or less Violence, producing Thunder. *a* **1806** BP. HORSLEY *Biblical Crit.* IV. 395 (L.) The sudden disjection of Pharaoh's host. **1837** CARLYLE *Fr. Rev.* II. iii. vii. These days of convulsion and disjection.

disjeune, var. DISJUNE, *Sc.*, breakfast.

disjoin (dɪs'dʒɔɪn), *v.* Also 5 des-. [ME. *des-*, *disioyne*, a. OF. *desjoign-*, pres. stem of *desjoindre*, mod.F. *déjoindre* = Pr. *desjonher*, It. *disgiugnere*:—L. *disjungĕre*, f. DIS- 4 + *jungĕre* to JOIN.]
1. *trans.* To undo the joining of; to put or keep asunder; to disunite, separate, sunder, part, sever: **a.** persons, places, things, actions, etc.
1483 CAXTON *Gold. Leg.* 257/4 We wold haue disioyned yow and haue drowned yow. **1484** —— *Curiall* 1, I am there where the places and affayres desioyne vs. **1514** BARCLAY *Cyt. & Uplondyshm.* (Percy Soc.) p. xxxii, The smell and tasting partly conjoyned be, And part disjoyned. **1601** R. JOHNSON *Kingd. & Commw.* (1603) 212 Deserts and..mountaines disjoyning the provinces. **1612** WOODALL *Surg. Mate* Wks. (1653) 149 The first Intention..is performed by restoring the bones disjoyned. *c* **1694** PRIOR *Celia to Damon* 114 Shall neither time, nor age our souls disjoin? **1864** A. MCKAY *Hist. Kilmarnock* 134 The two parishes were disjoined in 1642.
absol. **1594** T. B. *La Primaud. Fr. Acad.* II. 283 It is the nature of this enemy of mankind to scatter, to disioyne and separat. *a* **1683** OLDHAM *Wks. & Rem.* (1686) 122 That cruel word for ever must disjoyn, Nor can I hope, but thus, to have him mine.
b. one thing, person, action, etc. (*from* another).
1525 LD. BERNERS *Froiss.* II. cc. (R.) They sayde, they wolde not disioyne nor disceuer them from the crowne. **1581** SAVILE *Tacitus' Hist.* II. lviii. (1591) 87 Spaine being disioyned from it [Africa] by a narrow strayte. **1601** SHAKS. *Jul. C.* II. i. 18 Th' abuse of Greatnesse, is, when it disioynes Remorse from Power. **1741** MIDDLETON *Cicero* I. iv. 271 Our knights are now almost disjoined again from the Senate. **1865** M. ARNOLD *Ess. Crit.* ii. (1875) 77 [He] never disjoins banter itself from politeness.
†**2.** To separate into parts or sections; to disjoint.
1579 FULKE *Heskins' Parl.* 367 Although M. Heskins hath disioyned this place..I haue set it down..entire. **1598** FLORIO, *Slombare*..to disioyne as a butcher doth a sheepe. **1612** BRINSLEY *Pos. Parts* (1669) 134 Latine phrases which cannot fitly be disjoyned are to be taken together.
3. To sunder, dissolve, break up (a state or condition of union); to undo, unfasten (a knot or tie).
1633 MARMION *Fine Companion* I. v, Knots of compliment, which the least occasion disjoins. **1643** MILTON *Divorce* viii. (1851) 42 That mariage therfore God himself dis-joyns. **1695** BLACKMORE *Pr. Arth.* II. 70 Their short Embraces some rude Shocks disjoyn. **1738** GLOVER *Leonidas* v. 617 All with headlong pace..Disjoin their order.
†**4.** *fig.* To put out of joint, unhinge. *Obs. rare.*
a **1633** LENNARD tr. *Charron's Wisd.* I. xvi. §2 (1670) 62 Gallus Vibius..so dislodged and dis-joyned his own judgment, that he could never settle it again.
5. *intr.* (for *refl.*) To separate or sever oneself from a state of union or attachment; to part, become separate: **a.** said of two or more.
1622 CALLIS *Stat. Sewers* (1647) 167 If one of them die, that Action shall survive, for though they were joynt in the personalty, yet they disjoyned in the realty. **1699** GARTH *Dispens.* III. (1706) 42 So Lines that from their Parallel decline, More they advance, the more they still dis-join. *a* **1713** ELLWOOD *Autobiog.* (1765) 268 They, hopeless now..disjoined, and one of them fled the country.
b. said of one thing parting *from* another.
1592 SHAKS. *Ven. & Ad.* 541 Till breathlesse he disioynd, and backward drew. **1635** SWAN *Spec. M.* (1670) 90 Being of clammy nature, it disjoyneth not, but sticketh fast.
Hence **dis'joining** *vbl. sb.* and *ppl. a.*
1530 PALSGR. 214/2 Disjoynyng, *disjunction.* **1615** G. SANDYS *Trav.* 21 Two not farre disioyning vallies. *a* **1643** W. CARTWRIGHT *Lady Errant* IV. iv, This disjoyning Of bodies only is to knit your hearts. **1741** A. MONRO *Anat.* (ed. 3) 192 They may..yield to a disjoining Force. **1794** SULLIVAN *View Nat.* I. 26 The meeting or disjoining of natures.

disjoin, obs. f. DISJUNE, *Sc.*, breakfast.

dis'joined, *ppl. a.* [f. prec. + -ED[1].] Disunited, separated, parted, etc.: see prec. vb.
1594 SOUTHWELL *M. Magd. Fun. Teares* 88 These disjoyned ghests. *a* **1626** BACON *Max. & Uses Com. Law* Pref. (1636) 4 This delivering of knowledge in distinct and disjoyned Aphorismes. **1790** PENNANT *London* (R.) Windmill-street consists of disjoined houses.
Hence †**dis'joinedly** *adv. Obs.*, separately, disjunctly.
1571 DIGGES *Pantom.* I. xx. Fivb, If magnitudes disioynedly or seperatly be proportionall, conioynedly or compounded, they shall also bee proportionall. **1628** T. SPENCER *Logick* 245 Perpetuall life, and death at last, are attributed to Saul..neither of them distinctly, but both disjoynedly.

dis'joiner. *rare.* [f. as prec. + -ER[1].] One who or that which disjoins.
1654 Z. COKE *Logick* (1657) 10 This disjunction of parts must be such a disjoyner which mensurates the whole.

†**dis'joint**, *sb. Obs.* [a. OF. *desjointe*, *disjointe* separation, division, rupture (Godef.):—L. type **disjuncta*, fem. sb. from *disjunctus* pa. pple., analogous to sbs. in *-ata*, *-ada*, *-ade*, F. *-ée*: see -ADE. This takes the place in part of L. *disjunctio.*] A disjointed or out-of-joint condition; a position of perplexity or difficulty; a dilemma, 'fix'.
c **1374** CHAUCER *Troylus* III. 447 (496) What wyght þat stont in swych disioynte. **1430** LYDG. *Chron. Troy* I. v, And thus amiddes of either of these twaine Of loue and shame euen so vpon the poynt Medea stode as tho in great disioynt. **1494** FABYAN *Chron.* VII. 309 The which [warre], at that tyme, was in suche disjoynte, that he cowde not brynge it to any frame. **1553** *Douglas' Æneis* XII. xiii. 30 Thou mycht

quhil now haue cachit at disioynt [MS. **1513** disiunct] The sylly Troianis baith be se and land.

dis'joint, *ppl. a.* [a. OF. *desjoint* (:— L. *disjunct-us*), pa. pple. of *desjoindre* to DISJOIN.]

†**1.** *Obs.* Disjointed, out of joint; disconnected.

c **1420** *Pallad. on Husb.* VIII. 164 That sensis spille or pointe disjoynt be therynne Is not my wille. **1602** SHAKS. *Ham.* I. ii. 20 Thinking by our late deere Brothers death, Our State to be disioynt, and out of Frame. *a* **1717** PARNELL *David* (Seager), My bones.. Disjoint with anguish.

†**2.** *Obs.* In a dilemma, in a difficult position. (Cf. DISJOINT *sb.*)

c **1500** *Lancelot* 2907 For well ȝhe se the perell, how disio[i]nt The adwentur now stondith one the point Boith of my lord his honore, and his lond.

†**3.** *Obs.* Disjoined, separated; separate.

1589 IVE *Fortif.* 37 Because of it [= its] disioint standing from the wall which causeth sharpnes. **1649** MILTON *Eikon.* iv. (1851) 359 Carrying on a disjoynt and privat interest of his own. **1660** H. MORE *Myst. Godliness* 31 The disjoint and independent particles of Matter.

b. quasi-*adv.* Apart, asunder.

c **1430** *Pilgr. Lyf Manhode* II. cxlviii. (1869) 135 The sawe is cleped Hayne [hatred]; bi which disioynct is ysawed the onhede of bretherhede.

4. Of two or more sets of elements: having no elements in common.

1937 *Trans. Amer. Math. Soc.* XLI. 397 Two disjoint closed sets. **1941** BIRKHOFF & MACLANE *Survey Mod. Algebra* vi. 141 Any product of disjoint cycles represents a permutation. **1968** P. M. POSTAL *Aspects Phonol. Theory* i. 7 No doubt most linguists would immediately argue that these sets are disjoint. **1972** *Computer Jrnl.* XV. 229/2 The alphabets 1, 2, 3, and 4 are mutually disjoint. **1978** *Language* LIV. 188 *HDCU* is of potential interest not only to those who are uneasy about their linguistic credentials.., but also to students of language — not to imply that these two sets are disjoint.

disjoint (dɪsˈdʒɔɪnt), *v.* Also 6–7 -ioinct. [orig. f. DISJOINT *ppl. a.* (cf. -ATE³); but in some uses treated as f. JOINT *sb.*]

1. *trans.* To put out of joint; to disturb, destroy the due connexion and orderly arrangement of; to dislocate, wrench, dismember. (Cf. DISJOINT *a.* 1.)

c **1420** *Pallad. on Husb.* I. 873 Thi wortes that the wermes not disyoint [*destruant*]. **1541** R. COPLAND *Guydon's Quest. Chirurg.*, Vpon the rybbes & lyke bones for to reduce and retourne them in to theyr places, whan they are broken or dysioynted. **1605** CAMDEN *Rem.* (1637) 72 Giles, is miserably disjoynted from Ægidius, as Gillet from Ægidia, by the French. **1648** SANDERSON *Serm.* II. 226 If our spirits ..be shattered and dis-joynted, through distrust in God. **1860** PUSEY *Min. Proph.* 347 Selfishness..disjoints the whole frame of society. *a* **1862** BUCKLE *Civiliz.* (1869) III. v. 377 The framework of affairs would be disjointed.

†**b.** *fig.* To distract. *Obs.*

1628 EARLE *Microcosm., Meere Formall Man* (Arb.) 30 He is not disiointed with other Meditations.

c. *fig.* To throw the parts (of anything) out of orderly connexion; to dislocate.

1638 CHILLINGW. *Relig. Prot.* I. vi. §44. 364 Your discourse upon this point, you have..disjoynted, and given us the grounds of it in the begining of the Chapter, and the superstructure..in the end. **1770** GIBBON *Misc. Wks.* (1814) IV. 504 It is..disagreeable..to observe a lyric writer of taste ..disjointing the order of his ideas. **1834** H. N. COLERIDGE *Grk. Poets* (ed. 2) 55 Their collocation having been disjointed by time.

2. To disjoin, disunite.

1583 STANYHURST *Aeneis* III. (Arb.) 83 The sea..rusht in ..Italye disioyncting with short streicts from Sicil Island. **1601** BP. W. BARLOW *Defence* 126 The elect members of Christ can never be disjointed from him. **1650** FULLER *Pisgah* II. vii. 164 Except..some part of Asher lay southward at distance, dis-jointed from the main body of that Tribe. **1759** *Hist.* in *Ann. Reg.* 32/2 According as it is possessed by the English or the French, [it] connects or disjoints the colonies of Canada and Louisiana. **1775** T. JEFFERSON *Let.* Writ. 1892 I. 484 Great Britain, disjointed from her colonies. **1851** ROBERTSON *Serm.* Ser. III. xi. 134 Unite these all and then you have the Reformation.. Disjoint them and then you have some miserable sect.

3. To separate joint from joint; to take in pieces at the joints.

1587 HARMAR *Beza's Serm.* 384 (T.) As for his coach..he would not only have it to be unharnissed as I said..but also unpinned, disjointed, and pulled asunder. **1649** LOVELACE *Poems* (1864) 44 Like watches by unskilfull men Disjoynted, and set ill againe. **1832** LYTTON *Eugene A.* I. ix, The corporal began to disjoint his rod.

absol. **1712** STEELE *Spect.* No. 473 A good Carver..cuts up, disjoints, and uncases with incomparable Dexterity.

4. *intr.* (for *refl.*) To be disjointed; to suffer dislocation; to go out of joint; to come in pieces.

1605 SHAKS. *Macb.* III. ii. 16 Let the frame of things disioynt. **1888** *Harper's Mag.* Apr. 741 A hundred cottages overturn..quiver, disjoint. **1890** CONSTANCE SMITH *Riddle L. Haviland* I. II. ix. 303 Neither will the great scheme of things disjoint, because your lover has left you.

Hence **dis'jointing** *vbl. sb.*

1598 FLORIO, *Disgiontione*, a disioining, a disiointing. **1612** WOODALL *Surg. Mate* Wks. (1653) 149 The disjoynting of the bones. *a* **1715** BURNET *Own Time* (1823) I. 546 Those unhappy jealousies, which began a disjointing between the king and his people. **1794** SULLIVAN *View Nat.* II. 90 Even strong towers are made to vibrate several inches, without any disjointing of the mortar.

dis'jointed, *ppl. a.* [f. prec. + -ED¹.]

1. Separated joint from joint; disjoined, separated; disconnected.

a **1643** G. SANDYS *Job* 45 (T.) Be..their disjointed bones to powder ground. **1684** *Contempl. State of Man* I. vi. (1699) 69 Consider..the disjoynted disposition of the Bones. **1700** DRYDEN *Fables, Ceyx & Alcyone* 27, I saw a-drift disjointed planks. **1726** LEONI *Alberti's Archit.* I. 12/1 Disjoynted and unfinished Members. **1767** BLACKSTONE *Comm.* II. 379 That the construction be made upon the entire deed, and not merely upon disjointed parts of it. **1840** F. D. BENNETT *Whaling Voy.* II. 191 Some of these [casks] are kept in a disjointed state..ready to be put together. **1887** HALL CAINE *Deemster* xxxvii. 247 A little disjointed gipsy encampment of mud-built tents.

2. Consisting of separated or ill-connected parts; disconnected.

1652–62 HEYLIN *Cosmogr.* III. (1682) 96 A dis-joynted People, not under any setled form of Government. **1769** ROBERTSON *Chas. V.* III. x. 258 He felt already..that he was the head of a disjointed body. **1838** THIRLWALL *Greece* II. 188 The huge frame of the Persian empire was disjointed and unwieldy.

3. Of words or a discourse: Without proper connexion or sequence; disconnected; incoherent.

a **1586** SIDNEY (J.), The constancy of your wit was not wont to bring forth such disjointed speeches. **1614** JACKSON *Creed* III. [v] 30 Vpon such broken disiointed surmises. **1817** EARL OF DUDLEY *Lett.* 3 June (1840) 169 His argument ..seems loose and disjointed. **1843** LEVER *J. Hinton* xiii, Our conversation dropped into broken disjointed sentences.

Hence **dis'jointedly** *adv.*, **dis'jointedness**.

1654 LD. ORRERY *Parthenissa* (1676) 505 The disorders and disjointedness of his discourse. **1749** *Phil. Trans.* XLVI. 134 You remark in all their Actions..a Disjointedness. **1871** RUSKIN *Fors Clav.* xi. 19, I must pass, disjointedly, to matters, which, in a written letter, would have been put in a postscript. **1872** MARK TWAIN (Clemens) *Innoc. Abr.* xii. 85 We talked disjointedly.

dis'jointly, *adv.* [f. DISJOINT *a.* + -LY².]

1. Separately, asunder, apart; disjunctly: opp. to *conjointly*.

1634 M. SANDYS *Prudence* 6 (T.) When they are perfect, then are they joined; but, disjointly, no way can they be perfect. **1880** MUIRHEAD *Gaius* II. §199 If the same thing be legated by vindication to two or more persons, whether conjointly or disjointly, they take each a share.

2. Disjointedly, disconnectedly. *rare.*

1621 HAKEWILL *King Davids Vow* A ij a, Discourses which were delivered disiointly and by peece-meale. **1892** *Argosy* Jan. 10 'Let it come out—she can't shoot me,' disjointly muttered Mr. Arthur.

dis'jointure. [f. DISJOINT *v.* + -URE, after *jointure*. Cf. OF. *desjointure* (in Godef.).] The state of being disjointed; disconnexion, separation.

1757 CONWAY *Lett.* in *Fraser's Mag.* (1850) XLI. 424 There is more disjointure to our affairs..than any coalition of our ministers can retrieve. **1879** TOURGEE *Fool's Err.* xix. 104 The disjointure of opinion between them and the Yankee schoolmarms was all because the latter wanted to measure them by Northern ideas of these virtues.

disjone, -joon, obs. ff. DISJUNE, *Sc.*, breakfast.

†**dis'journ**, *v. Obs. rare.* [f. DIS- 1 + stem of *adjourn.*] *trans.* To put off from the day appointed.

1642 SIR W. BRERETON in *13th Rep. Hist. MSS. Comm.* App. i. 51 If this meeting had not been unhappily disjourned and disappointed by some of the Deputy Lieutenants. *Ibid.* 52 Whereof the rest were by some of them disjourned.

†**dis'judge**, *v. Obs.* [f. DIS- 7 b + JUDGE.] To deprive of or remove from the office of judge.

1649 [see DISJUSTICE]. **1658** *State Trials, Dr. J. Hewet* (R.) All the rest of the Judges..were..impeached of high-treason, disjudg'd and put to fines and ransoms.

[disjudication. Error for DIJUDICATION.

[**1664** BOYLE *On Colours ii. 20 The Dijudications we make of Colours.*] **1755** JOHNSON, *Disjudication*, judgment; determination; perhaps only mistaken for *dijudication. Boyle on Colours.* Hence in **1864** WEBSTER (citing Boyle), and some later Dicts.]

†**'disjugate**, *v. Obs. rare*⁻⁰.

1656 BLOUNT *Glossogr.*, *Disjugate*, to disjoyn, part, sever.

†**dis'junct**, *Sc.* Latinized form of DISJOINT *sb.*

1513 DOUGLAS *Æneis* XII. xiii. 30 [see DISJOINT *sb.*].

disjunct (dɪsˈdʒʌŋkt), *a.* and *sb.* [ad. L. *disjunct-us*, pa. pple. of *disjungĕre* to disjoin. Cf. DISJOINT *a.*]

A. *adj.* **1. a.** Disjoined, disconnected, separated, separate, distinct; †distant. (Now *rare* exc. in technical senses: see also below.)

1599 NASHE *Lenten Stuffe* (1871) 15 From the city of Norwich..it is sixteen miles disjunct. **1662** GLANVILL *Lux Orient.* vii. (R.) The divine.. freedome consists not in his acting by meer arbitrarious will, as disjunct from his other attributes. **1688** R. HOLME *Armoury* III. 356/2 The Side Rest is a Rest disjunct from the Lathe. **1774** M. MACKENZIE *Maritime Surv.* p. xvi, A Disjunct Survey is, when the Harbours, Bays, or Islands..are each surveyed separately in a geometrical Manner. **1817** N. DRAKE *Shaks.* I. 56, 3 quatrains with 2 verses of immediate, interposed between 2 verses of disjunct rhime, and a terminating couplet. **1890** J. H. STIRLING *Philos. & Theol.* iv. 60 That congeries of externalities, mere disjunct atoms.

b. *Entom.* Having the head, thorax, and abdomen separated by deep incisions.

†**2.** *Math.* (Opp. to CONJUNCT *a.* 5): = DISCONTINUOUS.

disjunct proportion: a proportion in which the second and third terms have not the same ratio (or difference) as the first and second, or the third and fourth. *Obs.*

1594 BLUNDEVIL *Exerc.* I. xviii. 42 Disiunct proportion Geometricall..is when there is not like proportion betwixt the second and the third, that is betwixt the first and the second, or betwixt the third and the fourth, as 3, 6, 4, 8. **1597** MORLEY *Introd. Mus.* Annot. **1706** [see DISCRETE 2 b].

3. *Mus.* (Opp. to CONJUNCT *a.* 6.)

d. tetrachords, tetrachords separated by an interval of a tone. *d. motion*, motion by intervals exceeding a degree of the scale.

1694 W. HOLDER *Harmony* (1731) 97 Tetrachords..were either Conjunct, when they began the Second Tetrachord at the Fourth Chord..Or else the two Tetrachords were disjunct, the second taking its beginning at the Fifth Chord, there being always a Tone Major between the Fourth and Fifth Chords. **1774** BURNEY *Hist. Mus.* (1789) I. i. 54 When the modulation passed from a conjunct to a disjunct tetrachord. **1879** ROCKSTRO in Grove *Dict. Mus.* II. 88 He [Biordi] has used the diminished fourth in disjunct motion.

4. *Logic*, etc. †**a.** = DISJUNCTIVE *a.* 2. *Obs.* **b.** = DISCRETE *a.* 1 d. **c.** Applied to the several alternative members of a disjunctive proposition.

1608–11 BP. HALL *Epist.* II. iii, Gregory the Third, writing to the Bishops of Bauaria, gives this disjunct charge: 'Let none keepe an harlot or a concubine; but either let him liue chastely, or marry a wife.' **1628** T. SPENCER *Logick* 300 A compound Syllogisme is then disiunct, when the proposition thereof is a disiunct axiome. **1656** STANLEY *Hist. Philos.* VIII. (1701) 312/1 A disjunct axiom is that which is disjoyned, by a disjunctive conjunction; as, either it is day, or it is night. **1837–8** SIR W. HAMILTON *Logic* xii. (1860) I. 224 Notions co-ordinated in the quantity or whole of extension..are only relatively different (or diverse); and in logical language, are properly called *Disjunct* or *Discrete Notions*, (*notiones disjunctæ, discretæ*). **1864** BOWEN *Logic* vii. 218 The Subsumption is a Disjunctive of which these several Antecedents are the Disjunct Members.

B. *sb. Logic.* One of the components in a disjunctive proposition; also, a disjunctive proposition (see quot. 1948 and DISJUNCTIVE *a.* 2).

1921 W. E. JOHNSON *Logic* I. iii. 30 In the disjunctive function 'Not-both *p* and *q*', *p* and *q* are disjuncts. **1922** —— *Ibid.* II. x. 211 We shall take..the implicants and disjuncts to stand for particular propositions. **1948** H. REICHENBACH *Elem. Symbolic Logic* v. 194 We can regard the corresponding combination '*F* v *G*' as one class, which is the disjunct of the classes '*F*' and '*G*'. **1954** I. M. COPI *Symbolic Logic* ii. 12 The two statements so combined are called disjuncts (or alternatives). **1962** W. & M. KNEALE *Devel. Logic* iii. 160 A disjunctive proposition..was said to involve a complete opposition..of its disjuncts.

†**dis'juncted**, *ppl. a. Obs.* [f. as prec. + -ED.] Disjoined, disconnected.

a **1650** MAY *Satir. Puppy* (1657) 40 Farewell Poetry; thou trim Composer of disjuncted Sense.

disjunction (dɪsˈdʒʌŋkʃən). [a. OF. *disjunction* (13th c. in Godef.), or ad. L. *disjunctiōn-em* separation, n. of action f. *disjungĕre* to DISJOIN.]

1. The action of disjoining or condition of being disjoined; separation, disconnexion, disunion. (The opposite of CONJUNCTION 1.)

disjunction certificate, one given to a church member when he leaves to join another church. (Scotland.)

c **1400** *Lanfranc's Cirurg.* 322 Þe firste boon of þe necke.. disiunccioun of þat boon wole sle a man anoon. *c* **1430** LYDG. *Bochas* v. xiv. (1554) 132 a, To make a disiunction Betwene these landes. **1580** SIDNEY *Arcadia* IV. (1590) 430 When they made the greevous disjunction of their long combination. **1653** H. MORE *App. Antid.* (1662) 184 Death being..a disjunction of the Soul from the Body. **1798** *Hist.* in *Ann. Reg.* 51 A total disjunction..between the respective concerns of the church and the state. **1852** DANA *Crust.* II. 1124 The frequent disiunction and remoteness of the two superior [eyes]. **1864** A. MCKAY *Hist. Kilmarnock* 131 After the disjunction of the new parish.

2. *Logic*, etc. The relation of the several terms of a disjunctive proposition; hence, a disjunctive proposition or statement; an alternative.

1588 FRAUNCE *Lawiers Log.* II. vii. 95 b, If the disjunction or separation bee true absolutely..without any thirde thing put betweene, then the whole axiome is true and necessary. **1630** RANDOLPH *Aristippus* Wks. (1875) 7 *Hippathi, hippathi, aut disce, aut discede incontinenter*—a very good disjunction. **1653** H. MORE *Antid. Ath.* I. iv. (1712) 15 If you make choice of the other Member of the Disjunction. **1794** PALEY *Evid.* I. iii. (1817) 56, I am entitled to contend that one side or other of the following disjunction is true. **1864** BOWEN *Logic* vii. 219 The nature of a Disjunction is, that any one of the Disjunct Members exists, or is posited, only by the non-existence, or sublation, of all the others.

Hence **dis'junctionist**, one who leaves a church in order to form a new congregation.

1872 J. S. JEANS *Western Worthies* 135 Dr. Buchanan should accompany the disjunctionists to the new church.

disjunctive (dɪsˈdʒʌŋktɪv), *a.* and *sb.* [ad. L. *disjunctīvus*, f. *disjunct-us* DISJUNCT, DISJOINT: see -IVE. Cf. F. *disjonctif* (*desjointif* in 13th c.).]

A. *adj.*

1. Having the property of disjoining or disconnecting; characterized by or involving disjunction or separation.

1570 LEVINS *Manip.* 153/31 Disiunctiue, *disiunctiuus.* **1698** NORRIS *Pract. Disc.* (1707) IV. 83 Since the original Law did not admit of a Mediator, as not being Disjunctive. **1796** KIRWAN *Elem. Min.* (ed. 2) I. 371 The disjunctive characters..in the description of the original species. **1813** J. THOMSON *Lect. Inflam.* 367, 3dly, In the separation of dead or mortified parts from those which retain their vitality

..to distinguish this from the other modes of morbid absorption, it might be termed the disjunctive.

b. Opposed to joining or uniting.

a **1711** GREW (J.), Such principles, whose atoms are of that disjunctive nature, as not to be united in a sufficient number to make a visible mass.

2. *Logic*, etc. Involving a choice between two (or more) things or statements; alternative.

disjunctive proposition, a proposition in which it is asserted that one or other of two (or more) statements is true. ***disjunctive syllogism***, a syllogism in which the major premiss is disjunctive, and the inference depends on the alternation of its terms: sometimes loosely extended to any syllogism containing a disjunctive premiss.

1584 FENNER *Def. Ministers* (1587) 39 This section beginneth with a disiunctive Sillogisme. *a* **1628** PRESTON *New Covt.* (1630) 542 A disiunctive proposition is true..if either part be true. **1725** WATTS *Logic* III. ii. §5 A disjunctive syllogism is when the major proposition is disjunctive: as, the earth moves in a circle or an ellipsis; but it does not move in a circle; therefore it moves in an ellipsis. **1847** GROTE *Greece* II. lii. (1862) IV. 445 His promise was disjunctive—that they should be either so brought home, or slain. **1887** FOWLER *Deductive Logic* III. v. 113 If [two propositions or sets of propositions] be dissociated, so that the truth of one depends on the falsity of the other, and the falsity of one on the truth of the other, the complex proposition may be called Disjunctive. *Ibid.* 116 A Disjunctive Syllogism is a syllogism of which the major premiss is a disjunctive, and the minor a simple proposition, the latter affirming or denying one of the alternatives stated in the former. **1891** WELTON *Logic* II. i. 209, 210 *margin*, Logicians differ as to whether or not the disjunctive form necessitates the mutual exclusiveness of the alternative predicates..When the alternatives are not incompatible they are not exclusive. Exclusion is not, therefore, due to the disjunctive form of proposition.

3. *Gram.* Applied to conjunctions that express an alternative or imply some kind of adversative relation between the clauses which they grammatically connect.

With the earlier grammarians the division of Conjunctions into *Copulative* and *Disjunctive* was made a main one. It is, however, of grammatical importance (see quot. 1824) only in the *Coordinative* Conjunctions, of which *and* is Copulative, while the Alternative *or, nor*, and the Adversative *but, yet*, are Disjunctive. Of the *Subordinative* Conjunctions, the Causal *lest*, the Hypothetical *unless*, and the Concessive *although*, are also disjunctive in sense; but in their grammatical use these do not differ from the Copulative *that, if, because, as, since*.

1628 T. SPENCER *Logick* 244 That axiome is disiunct, whose band is a disiunctive Coniunction. **1751** HARRIS *Hermes* Wks. (1841) 189 Now we come to the disjunctive conjunctions, a species of words which bear this contradictory name, because, while they disjoin the sense, they conjoin the sentences. **1776** CAMPBELL *Philos. Rhet.* II. III. v. §1 Both the last mentioned orders [*Adversative* and *Exceptive* Conjunctions] are comprehended under the general name *disjunctive*. **1824** L. MURRAY *Eng. Gram.* (ed. 5) I. 229 The conjunction disjunctive has an effect contrary to that of the conjunction copulative; for as the verb, noun, or pronoun, is referred to the preceding terms taken separately, it must be in the singular number: as, 'Ignorance or negligence has caused this mistake'.

b. In French Grammar, sometimes applied to the *indirect nominative* (and objective) case of the personal pronouns (*moi, toi, lui, eux*) as distinguished from the direct nominative (*je, tu, il, ils*), called in this nomenclature *conjunctive*.

4. *Math.* (See quot.)

1853 SYLVESTER in *Phil. Trans.* CXLIII. I. 544 A disjunctive equation is a relation between two sets of quantities such that each one of either set is equal according to some unspecified order of connexion with one of the other set.

B. *sb.*

1. a. *Logic.* A disjunctive proposition: See A. 2. Hence generally, **b.** A statement or condition of affairs involving a choice between two or more statements or courses; an alternative. **c.** Phr. ***in the disjunctive***: in an alternative form or sense; disjunctively. (Cf. AF. *en disjointe, par disjointe*, Britton II. 354, 358.)

1533 MORE *Debell. Salem* Wks. 943/1 To the verity of a disiunctiue, it suffiseth any one part to be tru. **1569** ABP. PARKER *Corr.* (1853) 352 The words of the Injunction (which were once a disjunctive, but by the printer made a copulative [*or* being changed to *and*]). **1614** BACON *To the King* 7 Feb. (R.), Your Majesty..very wisely put in a disjunctive, that the judges should deliver an opinion privately, either to my Lord Chancellor, or to ourselves. **1725** WATTS *Logic* II. ii. §6 The Truth of Disjunctives depends on the necessary and immediate Opposition of the Parts. **1818** CRUISE *Digest* (ed. 2) VI. 105 The clause was to be construed in the disjunctive; viz. either by will, codicil, &c., or by writing signed before three witnesses. **1864** BOWEN *Logic* v. 131 Disjunctives are reduced..to as many Categoricals as there are disjunct members of the Predicate. Thus,—*A* is either *B* or *C* =

{All those *A* which are not *B* are *C*, and
{All those *A* which are not *C* are *B*

2. *Gram.* A disjunctive conjunction: see A. 3.

1530 PALSGR. 148 Some [conjunctions] be disjunctives. **1574** tr. *Littleton's Tenures* 138 b, In such woordes where the heire demaundeth the heritage or mariage of his mother, this worde ['or'] is a disjunctive. **1751** HARRIS *Hermes* II. ii. Wks. (1841) 187 The conjunction *or*, though it join the sentences, yet, as to their respective meanings, is a perfect disjunctive. **1824** L. MURRAY *Eng. Gram.* (ed. 5) I. 229 When a disjunctive occurs between a singular noun.. and a plural one, the verb is made to agree with the plural noun..as, 'Neither poverty nor riches were injurious to him'.

†**3.** One who favours disjunction; a separatist.

1602 WARNER *Alb. Eng.* XII. lxxii. (1612) 299 Disiunctiues, who..lesse loue their Prince than Pope.

†**4.** *pl.* Disjoined or disconnected things. *Obs.*

1627–77 FELTHAM *Resolves* II. iv. 167 God himself is Truth; and never meant to make the Heart and Tongue disjunctives.

dis'junctively, *adv.* [f. prec. + -LY[2].] In a disjunctive manner or sense; separately; alternatively; adversatively; not in combination.

1590 SWINBURNE *Testaments* 182 Although the executors bee appointed alternatiuely, or disiunctiuely..both the persons are to bee admitted executors. **1624** FISHER in F. White *Reply to Fisher* 494 Except you eate and drinke, is to be vnderstood disiunctiuely, Except you eate the flesh or drinke the bloud. **1768–74** TUCKER *Lt. Nat.* (1852) I. 65, I cannot answer the question so generally proposed, but must give my opinion disjunctively. **1824** L. MURRAY *Eng. Gram.* (ed. 5) I. 227 When singular pronouns..are disjunctively connected, the verb must agree with that person which is placed nearest to it: as, 'I or thou art to blame'. **1891** WELTON *Logic* IV. v. 447 [In a Dilemma] the major [premise] contains a plurality either of antecedents or of consequents, which are either disjunctively affirmed, or disjunctively denied, in the minor.

†**dis'junctly**, *adv.* [f. DISJUNCT *a.* + -LY[2].] Disconnectedly, separately, as disjoined. *Obs.*

1649 ROBERTS *Clavis Bibl.* Introd. iii. 52 Christ speaks.. of bearing witnesse to himself disjunctly and solely without the Father. **1650** BAXTER *Saints' R.* I. ii. §3 If considered dis-junctly by themselves. **1706** [see DISCRETELY].

dis'juncture. [ad. med.L. *disjunctūra*, f. *disjungĕre, disjunct-*: cf. OF. *desjointure, -joincture* (Godef.), and JUNCTURE.]

1. The fact of disjoining or condition of being disjoined; disjunction; separation, breach.

c **1400** *Lanfranc's Cirurg.* 63 þanne brynge togidere þe brynkis [in a wound] eiþer þe disiuncture. **1611** FLORIO *Discontinuita*, a disiuncture. **1639** WOTTON in *Reliq.* 477 (R.) The departure of my..dear neice, your long, and I dare say, your stil beloved consort..as well appeareth by your many tender expressions of that disjuncture. *a* **1679** T. GOODWIN *Wks.* II. IV. 347 (R.) Those bruises, disjunctures, or brokenness of bones.

2. *fig.* A juncture or condition of affairs involving disunion; a perplexed or disjointed state of things. (Cf. DISJOINT *sb.*)

1683 CAVE *Ecclesiastici* 225 Basil..was at a loss, how to behave himself in this dis-juncture of Affairs. **1830** *Examiner* 260/2 At this juncture, or rather disjuncture, the contested demesnes are purchased. **1865** CARLYLE *Fredk. Gt.* VIII. XIX. viii. 268 Friedrich..foresaw, in case of such disjunctures in Italy, good likelihood of quarrel there.

disjune (dɪs'dʒuːn), *sb.* Chiefly *Sc.*, *arch.* Forms: 5–7 **disione, 6 desiune, disjoin, -joyn, dischone, 7 disjoon, 6–9 disjune, 9 disjeune.** [a. OF. *desjun, -jeün* (mod.F. dial. *déjun*), f. *desjuner, -jeüner* (mod.F. *déjeûner*) to break fast, breakfast, f. *des-, dé-* (DE- I. 6) + *jeün*:— L. *jējūnus* fasting.]

The first meal of the day; breakfast.

1491 *St. Giles Charters* (1859) p. xx, And than to pas to their disione. **1549** *Compl. Scot.* vi. 43 Eftir there disiune, tha began to talk of grit myrrynes. *c* **1565** LINDESAY (Pitscottie) *Chron. Scot.* (1728) 140 That he might go to his bed the sooner, and have his disjoin ready by four hours. **1589** [see DEJEUNE]. **1599** NASHE *Lenten Stuffe* in *Harl. Misc.* (1808–12) VI. 168 (D.) For a disjune or morning breakfast. **1600** in A. Bisset *Ess. Hist. Truth* v. (1871) 203 This deponer desired Maister Alexander to dischone with him. **1603** *Philotus* xx, And bid your page in haist prepair, For your disjone sum daintie fair. **1706** in Watson *Collect.* I. 54 I trow ye cry for your disjoon. **1816** SCOTT *O. Mort.* iii, King Charles, when he took his disjune at Tillietudlem. **1827** TENNANT *Papistry Storm'd* 51 Tak' your disjeunes afore you gang! **1847** DE QUINCEY *Wks.* (1863) XIII. 110.

†**dis'june**, *v. Sc. Obs.* [a. OF. *desjuner*: see prec. sb.] *intr.* To breakfast.

1536 BELLENDEN *Cron. Scot.* (1821) I. p. lv, Thay disjunit airly in the morning.

†**dis'jungible**, *a. Obs.* [f. L. *disjung-ĕre* to DISJOIN + -IBLE.] Capable of being disjoined or separated.

1676 H. MORE *Remarks* 70 More easily disjungible than Air it self.

†**disjust**, *v. Obs. rare*[−0]. = DISADJUST.

1611 COTGR., *Desruner*, to disorder, disiust, peruert.

†**dis'justice**, *v. Obs.* [f. DIS- 7 b + JUSTICE.] To deprive of the office of Justice of the Peace.

1603 in *14th Rep. Hist. MSS. Comm.* App. viii. 79 To disjustice..Mr. Edw. Dynnys. **1621** *Crt. & Times Jas. I* (1849) II. 233 He is disjusticed, and made incapable of holding any office hereafter. **1649** PRYNNE *Vind. Liberty Engl.* 10 To dis-judge, dis-justice or dis-committee their fellow Judges, Justices and Committee-men.

disked (dɪskt), *a. rare.* [f. DISC, DISK *sb.* + -ED[2].] Having or showing a disc. (Chiefly in comb.).

1864 LOWELL *Fireside Trav.* 85 Spectacles..rising full-disked upon the beholder like..two moons at once.

†**dis'ken**, *v. Obs. rare.* [f. DIS- 6 + KEN *v.*] *trans.* ? To withdraw from notice. In quot. *refl.*

c **1400** *Beryn* 20 The Pardonere beheld the besynes, howe statis wer I-servid, Diskennyng hym al pryuely, & a syde swervid.

diskere, obs. form of DISCOVER *v.*

diskette (dɪ'skɛt). *Computing.* Also **discette.** [f. DISC, DISK *sb.* + -ETTE.] = *floppy disc* s.v. FLOPPY *a.* 2. Also *attrib.*, as ***diskette drive*** (cf. *disc drive* s.v. DISC *sb.* 8 f).

1973 *Digital Design* Oct. 40/1 IBM recently announced the 3740 'diskette' data system for the system/370 line. **1976** *New Scientist* 4 Nov. 281 (Advt.), Including 10 to 90 megabyte discs, diskettes, and our new 30 and 60 cps terminal printers. **1978** *Nature* 19 Oct. p. xvi/1 A microcomputer peripheral bus which supports up to 64 kilobytes of RAM and EPROM memory, diskette drives, [etc.]. **1979** J. E. ROWLEY *Mechanised In-House Information Syst.* I. 67 With diskettes it is possible to have a VDU terminal attached to the processor. **1982** *Which Computer?* June 43/3 TI has come up with a paired minifloppy disc unit, that carries 1.2MB of data on double-sided, double-density diskettes. **1984** *Times* 22 May 28/5 ASI UK Ltd offer an inter-active discette, for in-house self-taught use.

†**dis'kindness.** *Obs.* [DIS- 9.]

1. Unkindness, unfriendliness.

1596 DALRYMPLE tr. *Leslie's Hist. Scot.* (1885) I. 92 Gif ony discorde or diskyndnes had fallin amang thame. **1709** E. WARD tr. *Cervantes* 121 His Diskindness soon chang'd into a perfect Hatred. **1768–74** TUCKER *Lt. Nat.* (1852) II. 651 An effect of diskindness.

2. An unkind act, an ill turn: usually in phr. ***to do*** (a person) ***a diskindness***. (Frequent in 18th c.)

1678 NORRIS *Coll. Misc.* (1699) 189 To do another man a diskindness merely because he has done me one, serves to no good Purpose. **1727** W. MATHER *Yng. Man's Comp.* 70 Remember to requite, at least to own Kindnesses, lest thy Ingratitude prove a considerable Diskindness. **1768–74** TUCKER *Lt. Nat.* (1852) I. 2 He that pulls down his neighbour's house does him a diskindness, however inconvenient soever it were.

†**dis'kingdom**, *v. Obs. nonce-wd.* [DIS- 7 c.] *trans.* To expel from or deprive of the kingdom.

1602 WARNER *Alb. Eng.* XII. lxxii. (1612) 298 Lastly ciuil Strife, and Scots diskingdom'd them [Picts] from hence.

diskless: see DISCLESS.

†**dis'knight**, *v. Obs. rare.* [f. DIS- 6 + KNIGHT *v.*] *trans.* To degrade from knighthood.

1621 [see DISGENTILIZE].

†**dis'know**, *v. Obs. nonce-wd.* [DIS- 6.] *trans.* To fail to know or acknowledge.

1605 SYLVESTER *Du Bartas* II. iii. III. *Lawe* 851 And when He shall (to light thy Sin-full load) Put Manhood on, disknowe him not for God.

†**dis'knowledge**, *v. Obs. nonce-wd.* [DIS- 7 c.] *trans.* To put out of knowledge, make unrecognizable.

1576 NEWTON *Lemnie's Complex.* (1633) 148 All his beauty..was..so faded..his face so incredibly disknowledged.

diskure, obs. form of DISCOVER *v.*

dis'lace, *v. rare.* [DIS- 7 a.] *trans.* To strip or deprive of lace.

a **1734** NORTH *Lives* III. 213, I have..found him very busy in picking out the stitches of a dislaced petticoat.

†**dis'lade**, *v. Obs. rare.* Also 7 *Sc.* **disladin.** [DIS- 6.] *trans.* To unlade, unload.

1609 HEYWOOD *Britaines Troy* v. Argt. 107 Ægeons fulfraught gallies are dis-laded. **1625–49** *Sc. Acts Chas. I* (1814) V. 580 (Jam.) With power..als to laidin and disladin the saidis merchandice and guidis.

†**dis'lady**, *v. Obs. rare.* [DIS- 7 b. Cf. obs. F. *desdamer* in same sense.] *trans.* To deprive of the title or rank of lady.

1630 B. JONSON *New Inn* IV. iii, Nay, it shall out, since you have called me wife, And openly dis-ladied me.

†**dis'land**, *v. Obs. rare.* [DIS- 7 a.] *trans.* To deprive of land, or of a landed estate.

1632 QUARLES *Div. Fancies* IV. xvii, To ruine Wife, or to dis-land an Heir.

dislander, dislaunder, var. DISCLANDER *Obs.*

†**di'slaughter**, *v. Obs. rare.* [f. *di-* for *dis-* (see DIS- 5) + SLAUGHTER *v.*] *trans.* To slaughter.

1661 *Sir A. Haslerig's Last Will & Test.* 3 Our dislaughtered Complices, who lately sacrificed their active lives with undaunted valour to the hands of the common Executioner.

dislavy, var. form of DELAVY *a. Obs.*

dis'lawyer, *v. rare.* [DIS- 7 b.] *trans.* To deprive of the name or standing of a lawyer.

a **1734** NORTH *Lives* (1826) II. 164 Vilifications plenty.. He was neither courtier nor lawyer; which his Lordship hearing, he smiled, saying, 'That they might well make him a whoremaster, when they had dislawyered him.'

dis'leaf, dis'leave, *v.* [f. DIS- 7 a + LEAF.] *trans.* To strip of leaves. Hence **dis'leaved** *ppl. a.*, **dis'leafing** *vbl. sb.*

1598 SYLVESTER *Du Bartas* II. ii. I. *Arke* 3 If now the Laurel..be dis-leau'd and vaded. **1655** HARTLIB *Ref. Silk-worm* 27 They will now be found in the Woods on the dis-leaved trees. **1830** *Fraser's Mag.* I. 36 A disleafing which, as in the vine, ripens and incites the grapes. **1840** CARLYLE *Heroes* i. (1872) 19 Its boughs, with their buddings and disleafings. **1854** LOWELL *Cambridge* 30 *Y. Ago* Prose Wks.

1890 I. 89 The canker-worm that annually disleaved her elms.

†**dis'league**, *v. Obs. rare.* [f. DIS- 6 or 7 + LEAGUE *v.* or *sb.*] *trans.* To dissolve or break off a league of.

1632 LITHGOW *Trav.* VI. 240 When fortune would change friendship, she disleagueth conditionall amity, with.. ingratitude.

†**dis'leal**, *a. Obs. rare.* [ad. It. *disleale* = OF. and Pr. *desleial.* Cf. LEAL] Disloyal.

1590 SPENSER *F.Q.* II. v. 5 Disleall Knight, whose coward corage chose To wreake it selfe on beast all innocent.

dis'levelment. [f. DIS- 6 + LEVEL *v.* + -MENT.] The condition of not being levelled; deviation from the level.

1883 *Nature* XXVII. 225 During the measurement of a base line..the rods are not..accurately levelled, and a correction has to be made for dislevelment.

dis'license, *v. rare.* [DIS- 6 or 7 a.] *trans.* To deprive of a license.

1885 *Manch. Exam.* 30 Oct. 4/7 The Museum Inn..and ..the West Australian..were dislicensed at Brewster Sessions.

dis'likable, *a.* [f. DISLIKE *v.* + -ABLE.] Capable of being disliked; exciting dislike.

1843 CARLYLE *Past & Pr.* III. iv. (1872) 133 One dislikes to see a man and poet reduced to proclaim on the streets such tidings: but on the whole..that is not the most dislikable. *a* **1887** MRS. NORTON in L. Fagan *Life Sir A. Panizzi* I. 322 A receipt for blotting out all dislikable qualities. **1886** R. A. KING *Shadowed Life* II. x. 185 About as likeable or dislikeable as a machine-made American clock.

dislike (dɪs'laɪk), *sb.* [f. DISLIKE *v.*]

†**1.** Displeasure, disapproval (as directed to some object). (Passing gradually into the mod. sense 2.) ***to be in dislike with,*** to be displeased with; so ***to come*** or ***grow into dislike with.*** *Obs.*

1577 LD. BUCKHURST in Ellis *Orig. Lett.* Ser. I. II. 272 To hazard therby..her Ma. [Majesty's] dislike. **1586** J. HOOKER *Girald. Irel.* in *Holinshed* II. 16/1 The king being in some dislike with the earle, and not fauourablie allowing his successe..lingered to giue anie answer. **1630** WADSWORTH *Pilgr.* v. 46 This my father hearing, grew into dislike with the Iesuites. **1703** PENN in *Pa. Hist. Soc. Mem.* IX. 264 A letter from the government, in dislike of such proceedings. **1742** YOUNG *Nt. Th.* IV. 26 Should any..give his thought Full range, on just dislike's unbounded field.

2. The contrary feeling to liking or affection for an object; distaste, aversion, repugnance. (Cf. DISLIKE *v.* 3.)

1597 HOOKER *Eccl. Pol.* v. lxv. (1617) II. 342 As the vsuall ..Ceremonies of common life are in request, or dislike, according to that they import. **1644** DIGBY *Nat. Bodies* II. (1645) 139 [It] is attended with annoy & with dislike. **1711** STEELE *Spect.* No. 76 ¶4 Where Men speak Affection in the strongest Terms, and Dislike in the faintest. **1772** PRIESTLEY *Inst. Relig.* (1782) I. 56 All vices make men subject to.. dislike. **1858** LYTTON *What will he do?* I. xvi, We need not show dislike too coarsely. **1878** JEVONS *Prim. Pol. Econ.* 9 Now there is a kind of ignorant dislike and impatience of political economy.

b. With *a* and *pl.* A particular aversion.

1614 BP. HALL *Recoll. Treat.* 465 Away with these weake dislikes. **1674** N. COX *Gentl. Recreat.* II. (1677) 175 She [the hawk] is apt to take a dislike, and will never afterwards receive it willingly. **1885** *Manch. Exam.* 14 May 5/1 All that the Chancellor said about his likes, his dislikes..carefully reported.

†**3.** Disagreement, discord. *Obs.*

1596 SHAKS. *1 Hen. IV*, v. i. 26, I do protest, I haue not sought the day of this dislike. **1606** —— *Tr. & Cr.* II. iii. 236 My Lord, you feede too much on this dislike. *a* **1632** FAIRFAX (J.), A murmur rose that showed dislike among the Christian peers.

†**dis'like,** *a. Obs.* [f. DIS- 10 + LIKE *a.* Cf. L. *dis-similis.*] Unlike, dissimilar, not alike.

1596 BP. ANDREWES *Serm.* II. 82 Two states..there be after death..disjoined in place, dislike in condition. **1596** J. NORDEN *Progr. Pietie* (1847) 174 It is so dislike that wedding-garment. **1603** HOLLAND *Plutarch's Mor.* 1255 Aristotle..said that the body of harmony is composed of parts dislike, and accordant verily one with another. **1644** DIGBY *Nat. Bodies* II. (1645) 4 That which wee call *a like thing* is not the *same*; for in every part it is dislike.

dislike (dɪs'laɪk), *v.* Also 6 **-lyke.** [f. DIS- 6 + LIKE *v.*] The opposite of LIKE *v.* (q.v.) in its various uses: cf. also MISLIKE.

†**1.** *trans.* (Only in 3rd pers.) To displease, annoy, offend. *Obs.*

1579 LYLY *Euphues* (Arb.) 91 If the sacred bands of amitye did..dislike thee, why diddest thou praise them? **1581** PETTIE *Guazzo's Civ. Conv.* II. (1586) 77, I see not how those thinges can dislike you, which commonly like all men. **1604** SHAKS. *Oth.* II. iii. 49 Ile do't, but it dislikes me. *a* **1619** DANIEL *Sonn.* liv. (R.), Like as the lute delights, or else dislikes, As is his heart that plays upon the same. **1667** PEPYS *Diary* (1877) V. 240 Sir W. Pen's going to sea do dislike the Parliament mightily. **1672** *Mede's Wks.* Life 31 To do that which may displease or dislike others. **1769** S. PATERSON *Another Trav.* II. 208 If the thing dislikes you, use it accordingly. **1814** SOUTHEY *Roderick* xxv, He drew forth The scymitar..its unaccustom'd shape Disliked him.

†**2.** *intr.* To be displeased, offended, or dissatisfied (*with*); to disapprove (*of*). *Obs.*

c **1555** HARPSFIELD *Divorce Hen. VIII* (1878) 301 God.. disliked with the divorce, and liked well of the marriage with Queen Katherine. **1570-6** LAMBARDE *Peramb. Kent* (1826) 149 King John disliked much of the choice. **1612** BRINSLEY *Lud. Lit.* 18, I cannot iustly dislike of any thing which you haue sayd herein. **1677** HALE *Contempl.* II. 211 If you dislike with your success, come no more among them.

3. *trans.* Not to like; to regard with aversion; to have an objection to; to disrelish. (The opposite of LIKE *v.* in its current sense; and so less strong than *hate*, which is the opposite of *love.*)

1594 HOOKER *Eccl. Pol.* IV. iv. (1611) 135 [They] presume all such bad as it pleaseth themselues to dislike. **1596** SHAKS. *Merch. V.* I. ii. 26, I may neither choose whom I would, nor refuse whom I dislike. **1698** FRYER *Acc. E. India & P.* 174 A Warlike and Troublesome Nation, apt to dislike Government, Proud and Brave. **1775** BURKE *Corr.* (1844) II. 18 There are many things amongst most of them, which I rather *dislike* than dare to *condemn.* **1849** MACAULAY *Hist. Eng.* I. 177 He disliked the Puritans indeed, but in him dislike was a languid feeling, very little resembling the energetic hatred which burned in the heart of Laud. **1873** BLACK *Pr. Thule* (1874) 36 He disliked losing a few shillings at billiards, but he did not mind losing a few pounds.

†**b.** To show or express aversion to. *Obs.*

1603 SHAKS. *Meas. for M.* I. ii. 18, I neuer heard any Souldier dislike it. **1641** MILTON *Reform.* II. (1851) 61 Neer their death..they plainely dislik'd and condemn'd the Ceremonies..as foolish and detestable. **1667** —— *P.L.* I. 102 Innumerable force of Spirits arm'd That durst dislike his reign.

Hence **dis'liked** *ppl. a.*

1632 SHERWOOD, Disliked, *desgousté.* **1892** MᶜCRIE *Worship Presbyt. Scot.* 162 A popularly disliked episcopacy.

†**dis'likeful,** *a. Obs.* [f. DISLIKE *sb.* + -FUL.] **a.** Unpleasant, distasteful. **b.** Characterized by dislike or aversion.

1596 SPENSER *F.Q.* IV. ix. 40 Now were it not..to you Dislikefull paine so sad a taske to take. **1596** —— *State Irel.* Wks. 675/2 To bring them to be one people, and to putt away the dislikefull conceit both of the one, and the other.

dis'likelihood. *rare.* [DIS- 9.] Unlikelihood, improbability.

1823 SCOTT *Peveril* xxvii, But consider..the dislikelihood of her pleasing.

†**dis'liken,** *v. Obs.* [f. DISLIKE *a.* + -EN⁵, after *like, liken*: cf. L. *dissimilāre*, F. *dissembler.*] *trans.* To make unlike; to dissemble, disguise.

1611 SHAKS. *Wint. T.* IV. iv. 666 Muffle your face; Dismantle you, and (as you can) disliken The truth of your owne seeming, that you may..to Ship-boord Get vndescry'd.

†**dis'likeness.** *Obs.* [f. DISLIKE *a.* + -NESS, or f. DIS- 9 + LIKENESS.] Unlikeness, dissimilarity.

1623 WODROEPHE *Fr. & Eng. Gram.* 492 (T.) There is a great dislikeness between these things. **1633** AMES *Agst. Cerem.* II. 480 Likenesse of intention..is such as admitteth much dislikenesse. **1690** LOCKE *Hum. Und.* IV. iv. §5 That which is not design'd to represent any thing but it self, can never..mislead us from the true Apprehension of any thing, by its Dislikeness to it.

dis'liker. [f. DISLIKE *v.* + -ER¹.] One who dislikes or disapproves.

1586 HOOKER *Answ. Travers' Supplic.* Wks. 1617 II. 18 It were hard if..[they] make themselues to be thought dislikers of the present state and proceedings. **1653** H. MORE *Conject. Cabbal.* 244 (T.) An unreconcileable disliker of their vices. **1705** HICKERINGILL *Priest-cr.* II. viii. 81 There would not have been any Dissenters, or Dislikers of a Moderate Church of England. **1832-4** DE QUINCEY *Cæsars* Wks. X. 151 He is a general disliker of us and of our doings.

dis'liking, *vbl. sb.* [f. DISLIKE *v.* + -ING¹.] The action of the verb DISLIKE: aversion, disapproval; dislike; the contrary of *liking.*

c **1540** in *Fisher's Wks.* (E.E.T.S.) II, Not for any displeasure or dislykinge of the queens person or age. **1579** LYLY *Euphues* (Arb.) 130 Whereby they noted the great dislyking they had of their fulsome feeding. **1588** *Marprel. Epist.* (Arb.) 24 The good quiet people..at length grew in disliking with their pastor. **1632** LITHGOW *Trav.* x. 481 To their great disliking, I was released. **1659** C. NOBLE *Mod. Answ. to Immod. Queries* 2 The Author..cannot at all palliate his dislikings with moderate and beseeming words. **1748** RICHARDSON *Clarissa* (1811) III. xxxvi. 210 Our likings and dislikings..are seldom governed by prudence. **1851** RUSKIN *Stones Ven.* I. ii. §12 If a man is cold in his likings and dislikings..you can make nothing of him.

dis'liking, *ppl. a.* [f. as prec. + -ING².] That dislikes: see the verb.

†**1.** Displeasing, disagreeable, distasteful. *Obs.*

1596 J. NORDEN *Progr. Pietie* (1847) 62 That I may carefully perform what thou likest, howsoever disliking it be unto me. **1636** in Picton *L'pool Munic. Rec.* I. 211 They were..altogether dislikeinge to the whole Corporacion.

2. Feeling, or showing, dislike or aversion.

1592 SHAKS. *Ven. & Ad.* 182 Adonis..with a heavy, dark, disliking eye, His louring brows o'erwhelming his fair sight. **1649** BP. HALL *Cases Consc.* 389 Divorces..to be arbitrarily given by the disliking husband, to his displeasing and unquiet wife. **1654** WHITLOCK *Zootomia* 460 Nothing sooner striketh Detraction dumbe, than a contemning and disliking Deafnesse. **1795** COLERIDGE *Juvenile Poems* (1864) 53 Chilled friendship's dark disliking eye.

dislimb (dɪs'lɪm), *v.* [DIS- 7 a.] *trans.* To cut off the limbs of; to tear limb from limb; to dismember. Hence **dislimbed** (dɪs'lɪmd) *ppl. a.*

1662 H. MORE *Philos. Writ.* Gen. Pref. 19 Not..unlike the raising from the dead the dislimb'd Hippolytus. **1855** SINGLETON *Virgil* I. 386 His body..Could I not have dislimbed, and o'er the waves Have scattered it? **1860** ADLER *Fauriel's Prov. Poetry* xii. 265 The shoulder of a calf..which he dislimbed with the most admirable dexterity.

dislimn (dɪs'lɪm), *v.* [f. DIS- 6 + LIMN *v.*]

1. *trans.* To obliterate the outlines of (anything limned); to efface, blot out.

1606 SHAKS. *Ant. & Cl.* IV. xiv. 10 Sometime we see a clowd that's Dragonish, A vapour sometime, like a Beare, or Lyon..That which is now a Horse, euen with a thoght The Racke dislimes, and makes it indistinct As water is in water. **1826** DE QUINCEY in *Blackw. Mag.* XX. 738 The flash..of colourable truth, being as frail as the resemblances in clouds, would, like them, unmould and 'dislimn' itself (to use a Shakespearian word). **1851** TRENCH *Poems* 92 Till the faint currents of the upper air Dislimn it. **1864** C. J. BLACK in *Lyra Messianica* No. 225 *Behold the Man*, Time cannot change the eternal fact, Dislimn the abiding vision.

2. *intr.* (for *refl.*) To become effaced, to vanish.

1832-4 DE QUINCEY *Cæsars* Wks. 1862 IX. 108 The nocturnal pageant has dislimned and vanished. **1867** *Contemp. Rev.* IV. 116 The primitive vision dislimns, decomposes, and vanishes away.

dislink (dɪs'lɪŋk), *v.* [f. DIS- 6 + LINK *v.*] *trans.* To unlink, uncouple, disconnect, disjoin, separate (things that are linked). *lit.* and *fig.*

1610 HEALEY *St. Aug. Citie of God* 312 Being dislinked from the love of other beauties. **1621** QUARLES *Argalus & P.* (1678) 74 Death..Hath now..Dissolv'd your vows, dislink'd that sacred chain, Which ti'd your souls. **1847** TENNYSON *Princess* Prol. 70 There a group of girls In circle waited, whom the electric shock Dislink'd with shrieks and laughter. **1861** G. MEREDITH *Evan Harrington* III. iii. 59 [She] dislinked herself from William's arm.

†**dislive** (dɪs'laɪv), *v. Obs.* [app. f. DIS- 7 a or c + LIFE.] *trans.* To deprive of life; to put out of life, to kill.

1598 TOFTE *Alba* (1880) 17 Now that Alba mine is parted, Who hath me left disliude and quite vnharted. **1610** —— *Honour's Acad.* III. 87 He seekes the means to be dislivde. **1615** CHAPMAN *Odyss.* XXII. 355 Telemachus dislived Amphimedon. **1631** —— *Caesar & Pompey* III. G iv b, She not destroyes it When she disliues it.

†**dis'liven,** *v. Obs.* [f. DIS- 6 + *-liven* in ENLIVEN.] *trans.* To do the opposite of *to enliven*; to dispirit.

1630 I. CRAVEN *Serm.* (1631) 46 The Trumpet.. disliueneth the heart of a cowardly souldier.

disload (dɪs'ləʊd), *v.* Also 7 *Sc.* **disloaden.** [f. DIS- 6 + LOAD *v.*] *trans.* and *intr.* To unload, disburden. Hence **dis'loading** *vbl. sb.*

1568 C. WATSON *Polyb.* 70 b, Preparing there to disloade and deliver the victualls. **1625-49** *Sc. Acts Chas. I.* (1814) V. 630 (Jam.) That no ship..aucht to disloadin..vntill the tyme they come to the said burcht. **1831** CARLYLE in Froude *Life* (1882) II. 163 Dust, toil, cotton bags, hampers, repairing ships, disloading stones. **1882** —— in *Century Mag.* XXIV. 21 Their long dangerous loading and disloading.

dislocable ('dɪsləkəb(ə)l), *a. rare.* [f. med.L. *dislocāre* to DISLOCATE: see -BLE.] Capable of being, or liable to be, dislocated or displaced; displaceable. Hence **ˌdisloca'bility.**

1827 BENTHAM *Const. Code.* II. viii. §9 Dislocable is this functionary..by that authority, for the giving execution and effect to whose will he has been located. He is dislocable by the Legislature. *Ibid.* II. viii. §6 Inferior, in respect of his dislocability,—he is superior even to the whole Legislature.

'dislocate, *ppl. a. Obs.* or *arch.* [ad. med.L. *dislocāt-us*, pa. pple. of *dislocāre*: see next.] Dislocated. (Chiefly as ***pa. pple.***)

c **1400** *Lanfranc's Cirurg.* 62 Whanne..þe boon..is to broke atwo & dislocate—þat is to seie out of ioynte. *Ibid.* 63 þe boonys þat weren broken ouþer dislocate [*v.r.* dislocat]. **1814** SOUTHEY *Roderick* XXII, Where the cement of authority Is wanting, all things there are dislocate. **1826** J. WILSON *Noct. Ambr.* Wks. 1855 I. 179 Lying in the middle of the road, his neck dislocate. **1846** in WORCESTER.

dislocate ('dɪsləkeɪt), *v.* [f. *dislocāt-* ppl. stem of med.L. *dislocāre* to put out of place, f. DIS- 1 + L. *locāre* to place, *locus* place: cf. It. *dislocare*, Pg. *deslocar*, Fr. *disloquer.* In Eng. as pa. pple. long before its use as a finite verb: see prec.]

1. *trans.* To put out of place; to shift from its proper (or former) place; to displace. Now *rare.*

1623 COCKERAM, *Dislocate*, to vnplace. **1655** FULLER *Ch. Hist.* III. v. §55 We will conclude this Section with this.. submission of the Dean and Chapter of St. Asaph, sent to the King..though dislocated, and some yeares set back in the date thereof. **1724** A. COLLINS *Gr. Chr. Relig.* 102 He alters some passages and changes the places of others which he supposes dislocated. **1859** HOLLAND *Gold F.* xxiii. 264 A plant may be dislocated from an old, and removed to a new bed. **1879** G. MEREDITH *Egoist* xxxiii. (1889) 323 No sooner was he comfortably established than she wished to dislocate him.

2. To put out of proper position in relation to contiguous parts (without removal to a distance).

1660 BOYLE *New Exp. Phys. Mech.* xv. 103 The Sunbeams..were in their passage..Dislocated and Scattered. **1665** HOOKE *Microgr.* 133 This Clock comes to be broken.. so that several parts of it being dislocated, are impeded. **1695** WOODWARD *Nat. Hist. Earth* II. (1723) 91 They [the Strata] were dislocated. **1755** *Phil. Trans.* XLIX. 441 Some chimnies, though not thrown down, are dislocated..and partly turn'd round. **1869** PHILLIPS *Vesuv.* vii. 197 A great fault dislocating the strata.

b. *spec.* To displace (a bone) from its proper position in the joint; to put out of joint; to 'put out' (a joint or limb). (Rarely with the person as object.) In early use more widely: see quots. 1605, 1668, and cf. DISLOCATION 1 b.

1605 SHAKS. *Lear* IV. ii. 65 These hands..are apt enough to dislocate and tear Thy flesh and bones. **1658** ROWLAND *Moufet's Theat. Ins.* 912 The pain of a joynt that is dislocated. **1668** CULPEPPER & COLE *Barthol. Anat.* IV. iii. 338 Its use is, like a cord to bind together the parts of the body..that they may not be dislocated. **1752** JOHNSON *Rambler* No. 199 ¶3, I have twice dislocated my limbs..in essaying to fly. **1763** FRANKLIN *Lett.* Wks. 1887 III. 244, I write in pain with an arm lately dislocated. **1838** THIRLWALL *Greece* II. xiv. 192 Darius had dislocated a foot in hunting. **1845** CAMPBELL *Lives of Chancellors* (1857) II. xxxv. 120 Anne was still much dislocated by the rack.

3. *fig.* To put (affairs, etc.) 'out of joint'; to throw into confusion or disorder, upset, disarrange, derange, disconcert.

c **1645** HOWELL *Lett.* (1892) II. 658 These sad confusions ..have so unhing'd..tumbled and dislocated all things. *a* **1661** FULLER *Worthies, Barkshire* I. (1662) 85 Since our Civil Wars hath lately dislocated all relations. **1719** DE FOE *Crusoe* (1840) II. i. 7, I was..desolate and dislocated in the world by the loss of her. **1825** T. JEFFERSON *Autobiog.* Wks. 1859 I. 73 He contrived to dislocate all their military plans. **1877** E. R. CONDER *Bas. Faith* ii. 61 In the violent strain put upon his mind, its balance is dislocated. **1889** *Spectator* 9 Nov., That will dislocate the trade of the port.

Hence **ˈdislocating** *ppl. a.*

1863 KINGLAKE *Crimea* I. 484 This perturbing and dislocating course of action.

ˈdislocated, *ppl. a.* [f. prec. + -ED[1].] Displaced; put out of position; out of joint; disarranged; having the continuity broken and the parts displaced, as a line or stratum: see the verb.

1605 CHAPMAN *All Fools* III. i, The incision is not deep nor the orifice exorbitant, the pericranion is not dislocated. **1659** *Vulg. Errors Censured* 35 It was he that..cured Diodorus of ..his dislocated member [shoulder out of joint]. **1793** J. BERESFORD in *Looker-on* (1794) III. No. 85. 360 Parts..not already occupied by the dislocated Frederick. **1830** LINDLEY *Nat. Syst. Bot.* 295 A kind of dislocated calyx. **1854** HOOKER *Himal. Jrnls.* I. xi. 253 Much-crumpled and dislocated gneiss. **1874** STUBBS *Const. Hist.* I. iv. 61 The dislocated state of Britain seems..to have made way for the conquerors.

Hence **ˈdislocatedly** *adv.*; **dislocatedness**, the condition of being displaced.

1827 BENTHAM *Const. Code.* II. vi. §30 From the situation of Member of the Legislative Assembly, causes of dislocatedness are these—1. Resignation..5. Mental derangement. **1883** *American* VI. 377 [They] intrude dislocatedly into Mr. Riley's landscapes.

dislocaˈtee. *nonce-wd.* [f. DISLOCATE *v.* + -EE.] One who is dislocated or displaced.

1827 BENTHAM *Const. Code* II. ix §18. 294/1 Dislocation is ..removal from an official situation, without consent of the dislocatee, and without his being located in any other.

dislocation (dɪsləʊˈkeɪʃən). [a. OF. *dislocation* (14th c. in Littré), or ad. med.L. *dislocātiōn-em*, n. of action f. *dislocāre* to DISLOCATE.] The action of dislocating, or condition of being dislocated.

1. a. Displacement; removal from its proper (or former) place or location.

1604 R. CAWDREY *Table Alph.*, *Dislocation*, setting out of right place. **1614** RALEIGH *Hist. World* II. 216 Which preventeth such dislocation of the Moneths. **1646** *Unhappy Game at Scotch & Eng.* 14 The dislocation of the Kings person by his personall will all this while from the two Houses of Parliament. **1846** GROTE *Greece* I. xiv. (1862) II. 388 Those violent dislocations of inhabitants. **1886** WILLIS & CLARK *Cambr.* III. 463 There has been much dislocation of the glass [in the windows of Jesus College Library].

b. *spec.* Displacement of a bone from its natural position in the joint; luxation. (Formerly, more widely, displacement of any bodily part or organ.)

c **1400** *Lanfranc's Cirurg.* 303 It is sett vpon þe region of þe wombe for fallinge of þe maris, þat is clepid dislocacioun of þe maris. *Ibid.* 322 Dislocacioun of þe rigboonys is a greuous sijknes. **1541** R. COPLAND *Guydon's Quest. Chirurg.*, Demaunde. Yf all the members may regenerate after theyr perdicion, & knytte agayne after theyr dislocacion? **1659** *Vulg. Errors Censured* 35 His Shoulder-bone suffering a dislocation. **1707** *Lond. Gaz.* No. 4362/4 Lost..a..Greyhound Bitch..a Dislocation in her Neck, which causes a Bone to stand up. **1842** ABDY *Water Cure* i. (1843) 1 A slight pain, which I could no otherwise describe than as the sensation of a slight dislocation.

c. *Geol.* A displacement in a stratum or series of strata caused by a fracture, with upheaval or subsidence of one or both parts; a fault.

1695 WOODWARD *Nat. Hist. Earth* II. (1723) 91 This Disruption, and Dislocation of the Strata. **1849** MURCHISON *Siluria* iii. 53 The black schists..are there insulated by a powerful dislocation. **1880** CARPENTER in *19th Cent.* No. 38. 598 Earthquake phenomena involving extensive dislocations of the crust.

d. *Mil.* The distribution of the several corps composing an army to a number of garrisons, camps, etc.

1808 WELLINGTON in Gurw. *Desp.* IV. 33 His Majesty has ..been pleased to command that the following should be the outline of the dislocation of the troops. **1842** ALISON *Hist. Europe* (1849–50) XII. lxxxii. 258 A very considerable dislocation of the forces which had combated at Leipsic immediately took place. **1883** *Manch. Exam.* 19 Dec. 4/6 The dislocation of Russian troops on the Austrian frontier had begun to assume..significant proportions.

e. *Crystallography.* A displacement of the lattice structure of a crystal.

1934 G. I. TAYLOR in *Proc. R. Soc.* A. July 368 The block after the unit slip, or 'dislocation' as we may call it, has passed through from left to right. *Ibid.*, The passage of a positive dislocation across a crystal from left to right produces the same effect as the passage of a negative one from right to left. **1955** *Sci. Amer.* July 81/1 We think of a dislocation as a line running through a crystal (although it is really a region of small but finite cross section). Around such a line is a region of energy higher than in the rest of the crystal. **1958** *Van Nostrand's Sci. Encycl.* (ed. 3) 526/2 Dislocations are important in determining the mechanical and electrical properties of solids, and play an important part in solid state physics. **1969** *New Scientist* 15 May (Feature Section) 6/2 The crystal merely provides a kind of 'space' in which various well-defined families of defect 'particles' exist. The most notable of these elementary defects are vacancies..; interstitials..; and dislocations.

2. *fig.* Displacement of parts or elements; disarrangement (of something immaterial); a confused or disordered state.

1659 O. WALKER *Oratory* 51 Causing a harsh superfluity, or else forcing a dislocation of the words. **1778** BP. LOWTH *Transl. Isaiah* Notes (ed. 12) 203 This whole passage.. healed of the dislocation which it suffers by the absurd division of the chapters. **1860** PUSEY *Min. Proph.* 290 The utter dislocation of society. **1862** MERIVALE *Rom. Emp.* (1865) IV. xxxiii. 91 A dislocation of all social principles.

3. *attrib.*, as ***dislocation forceps***.

1885 in *Syd. Soc. Lex.*

Hence **dislo'cationally** *adv.*, by way of dislocation or displacement.

1827 BENTHAM *Const. Code* II. viii. §5 The omission is.. an anti-constitutional offence..and, punitionally..as well as dislocationally, every offender is responsible.

ˈdislocative, *a. rare.* [f. med.L. *dislocāt-* ppl. stem of *dislocāre* to DISLOCATE + -IVE.] Serving to dislocate or remove from its place. Also *ellipt.* as *sb.* = displacing power.

1827 BENTHAM *Const. Code* II. v. §2 *Dislocative function*: exercised by dislocating, out of the situation in question, the functionary therein located. *Ibid.* II. vi. §30 Dislocation, by his constituents, in virtue of their incidental dislocative.

ˈdislocator (ˈdɪsləʊkeɪtə(r)). [agent-n. in L. form f. DISLOCATE *v.*: see -OR.] One who dislocates.

1818 SIR A. COOPER *Surg. Ess.* I. *Dislocations* (ed. 3) 16 One of those people called bone-setters (but who ought rather to be called dislocators).

dislocatory (ˈdɪsləʊkeɪtərɪ), *a.* [f. L. *dislocāt-* ppl. stem of *dislocāre*: see -ORY.] Having the effect of dislocating; producing dislocation.

1870 E. L. GARBETT in *Eng. Mech.* 11 Mar. 625/1 A frozen pond..roughened by dislocatory cracks. **1881** E. WARREN *Laughing Eyes* (1890) 64 The mistress..had no notion of dislocatory attitudes on damp grass.

dislock (dɪsˈlɒk), *v. Obs.* or *Sc.* Also 7 **disloke.** [In form *disloke* app. ad. F. *disloquer* (1549 in Hatz.-Darm.), ad. med.L. *dislocāre* to DISLOCATE; in form *dislock*, app. associated with LOCK *v.*] = DISLOCATE *v.*

1609 J. DAVIES *Holy Roode* (1876) 20 (D.) His bones and joints..With rackings quite disloked and distracted. **1830** GALT *Laurie T.* III. v. 100 Many a joint-dislocking jolt.

dislodge (dɪsˈlɒdʒ), *v.* Also 5 disloggen, 5–6 des-, disloge, des-, dyslodge, 6 *Sc.* disluge. [a. OF *desloger*, *-logier* to leave or to cause to leave a lodging-place, f. *des-*, DIS- 4 + *loger* to LODGE.]

1. *trans.* To remove or turn out of a place of lodgement; to displace. **a.** *generally.*

a **1500** *Chaucer's Dreme* 2125 Whan every thought and every sorrow Dislodged was out of mine herte. **1579** SPENSER *Sheph. Cal.* Dec. 32 How often haue I scaled the craggie Oke All to dislodge the Rauen of her neste. **1641** BP. HALL *Rem. Wks.* (1660) 71 Rivers changed, Seas dislodged, Earth opening. **1645** —— *Remedy Discontents* 151, I must be dislodged of my former habitation. **1791** 'G. GAMBADO' *Ann. Horsem.* vi. (1809) 93 [A horse] kicking..at such a rate, as to dislodge the Bagman that bestrides him. **1831** J. W. CROKER in *Croker Papers* 1 Mar., It would be madness to dislodge the present Ministry. **1871** L. STEPHEN *Playgr. Europe* v. (1894) 127 Every stone we dislodged went bounding rapidly down the side of the slope.

†**b.** *Mil.* To shift the position of (a force); *refl.* to shift one's quarters. *Obs.*

c **1477** CAXTON *Jason* 27 b, He hadde not entencion for to disloge him ne to reyse his siege. **1568** GRAFTON *Chron.* II. 240 At night, the French King dislodged his armie, and departed. **1607** SHAKS. *Cor.* v. iv. 44 The Volcians are dislodg'd and Marcius gone. **1670** DRYDEN *1st Pt. Conq. Granada* III. i, The Christians are dislodg'd; what Foe is near?

c. *Mil.* To drive (a foe) out of his position.

c **1450** LONELICH *Grail* xliv. 435 Hem to disloggen in this plas, It were best thorwh goddis gras. **1659** B. HARRIS *Parival's Iron Age* 155 The Spanish Army drew towards him, to dislodge him from thence. **1783** WATSON *Philip III* (1839) 23 Judging it necessary..to dislodge the Spaniards from their fortifications. **1839** THIRLWALL *Greece* VI. 169 He had dislodged the barbarians from the position which they had taken up..and made himself master of the pass.

d. *Hunting.* To drive (a beast) out of its lair.

1610 GUILLIM *Heraldry* III. xiv. (1660) 166 You shall say Dislodge the Buck. **1634** SIR T. HERBERT *Trav.* 56 The two and twentieth day we dislodged a wilde Bore. **1827** WORDSW. *Go back to Antique Ages*, While, to dislodge his game, cities are sacked. [**1876** SMILES *Sc. Natur.* vi. 96 A badger endeavoured to dislodge him, showing his teeth.]

2. *intr.* (for *refl.*) To go away from one's lodging or abode; to quit the place where one is lodged; to remove. **a.** *gen.* Of persons and things.

1520 *St. Papers Hen. VIII*, VI. 56 The daunces.. continued..unto thre of the clocke in the mornyng: whiche ..made the Ladyes more unmete to dislodge at the daye appoynctyd. **1528** LYNDESAY *Dreme* 969 In the lawland I come..And purposit thare to mak my residence; Bot singulare proffect gart me soune disluge. **1653** H. COGAN tr. *Pinto's Trav.* lxi. 249 Proclaimed, that all persons..should upon pain of death dislodge speedily out of the Island. **1668** HOWE *Bless. Righteous* (1825) 309 Your souls will dislodge from this earthly tabernacle. **1761** HUME *Hist. Eng.* II. xxvii. 130 Many of the inhabitants of Paris began to dislodge. **1882** MARIO *Garibaldi* in *Macm. Mag.* XLVI. 247 Dislodge immediately from the convent.

†**b.** *Mil.* To leave a place of encampment. *Obs.*

c **1489** CAXTON *Sonnes of Aymon* xx. 446 He commaunded that his oste shold dyslodge. *c* **1500** *Melusine* xxvi. 277 The next day..after the masse herd, desloged the vanward. **1591** GARRARD *Art Warre* 168 In the morning when they dislodge, and at night when they encampe. **1667** MILTON *P.L.* v. 669 He [Satan] resolv'd With all his Legions to dislodge. **1761–2** HUME *Hist. Eng.* (1806) IV. lvi. 309 Dislodging from Thame and Aylesbury..he thought it proper to retreat nearer London.

†**c.** *Hunting.* Of a beast of the chase: To leave its resting-place. *Obs.*

1674 N. COX *Gent. Recreat.* i. (1677) 71 If they [harts] chance once to vent the Hunts-man or the Hound, they will instantly dislodge.

Hence **disˈlodged** *ppl. a.*, **disˈlodging** *vbl. sb.* and *ppl. a.*

1523 LD. BERNERS *Froiss.* I. ccxi. 254 Whan the frenchemen..sawe the dyslodgynge of the Englysshe oost. **1602** MARSTON *Antonio's Rev.* III. iii. Wks. 1856 I. 111 His dislodg'd soule is fled. **1641** EARL STRAFFORD *Let. to Chas. I*, 4 May in Rushw. *Hist. Coll.* (1692) III. I. 251, I forgive all the World, with Calmness and Meekness of infinite Contentment to my dislodging Soul. **1737** L. CLARKE *Hist. Bible* II. (1740) 151 This was the order of their incamping. The manner of their dislodging was thus. **1832** G. DOWNES *Lett. Cont. Countries* I. 84 Among the dislodged was an elderly female..who bitterly deplored her lot.

†**disˈlodge,** *sb. Obs.* [f. prec.] The fact of being dislodged; dislodgement.

1587 TURBERV. *Ventrous Lover, &c.* (R.) Show how long dislodge hath bred Our cruell cutting smart.

dislodgement, -lodgment (dɪsˈlɒdʒmənt). [f. DISLODGE *v.* + -MENT; cf. F. *délogement*, older *des-*.] The act of dislodging; removal of anything from the place where it is lodged; displacement.

1728 MORGAN *Algiers* II. iv. 267 He told them, their Dislodgement was resolved on. **1737** L. CLARKE *Hist. Bible* II, They continued thereabout, making..eighteen several Removes or Dislodgments, and at last they returned to Kadesh Barnea. **1864** in WEBSTER. **1870** *Echo* 11 Nov., The chance dislodgement of a party of Prussians by a band of Franc-tireurs. **1876** BARTHOLOW *Mat. Med.* (1879) 457 [Sulphate of Copper] also occasionally used in croup, to effect the dislodgment of the false membrane.

dislogistic, erron. f. DYSLOGISTIC.

†**disˈloign,** *v. Obs.* [a. Of. *desloignier* to remove or withdraw to a distance, f. *des-*, DIS- 1 + *loin* far: cf. *éloigner*.] Exemplified in pa. pple. **disˈloigned** [= OF. *desloignié*], removed to a distance; distant, remote, far off.

1596 SPENSER *F.Q.* IV. x. 24 Low looking dales, disloignd from common gaze.

disloke: see DISLOCK.

disˈlove, *sb. Obs.* or *nonce-wd.* [DIS- 9.] The reverse or undoing of love; unfriendliness, hatred.

a **1533** LD. BERNERS *Gold. Bk. M. Aurel.* (1546) Oo ij, Disloue in thee, causeth the hope doubtfull in me. **1562** *Child Marriages* 11 Then dislove fell betwene them. **1823** W. TAYLOR *Sayer's Wks.* I. p. lxxviii, Agitated by various loves and dis-loves.

disˈlove, *v. Obs.* exc. *arch.* [DIS- 6.] *trans.* Not to love; to withdraw one's love from.

1568 NORTH *Gueuara's Diall Pr.* IV. iv. 116 b, I care not if all Greece hate and dysloue mee. **1582** *Ibid.* IV. xii. 409 b, Dispraised, defamed, disloued, and ill thought of of all. **1632** J. HAYWARD tr. *Biondi's Eromena* 180 Which he so loved, as for it he disloved everything else. **1922** JOYCE *Ulysses* 50 The foot that beat the ground in tripudium, foot I dislove.

disloyal (dɪsˈlɔɪəl), *a.* (*sb.*) [a. OF. *desloial*, f. *des-*, DIS- 4 + *loial* LOYAL. Cf. also DISLEAL.] Not loyal; false to one's allegiance or obligations; unfaithful, faithless, perfidious, treacherous.

a. Unfaithful to the obligations of friendship or honour, to the marriage tie, etc. (Common in early use: now somewhat *rare.*)

c **1477** CAXTON *Jason* 53 Certes fayr sire Jason ansuerede the disloyal and untrue Peleus [etc.]. **1581** PETTIE tr. *Guazzo's Civ. Conv.* I. (1586) 26 b, The Greekes though singuler in learning and eloquence, yet are they disloiall and faithlesse. **1590** SPENSER *F.Q.* II. vii. 22 Disloyall Treason, and hart-burning Hate. **1593** SHAKS. *Rich. II*, v. ii. 105

Thou do'st suspect That I haue bene disloyall to thy bed. **1639** S. Du Verger tr. *Camus' Admir. Events* 51 The demeanure of his disloyall wife. **1844** Mrs. Browning *Flower in Let.* iv, Without a thought disloyal.

b. Untrue to one's allegiance; wanting in loyalty to the government or to constituted authority.

1585 Abp. Sandys *Serm.* (1841) 200 Absolon rebelled.. but God quickly paid him that which was due to his rebellious and disloyal attempts. **1634** Prynne *Documents agst. Prynne* (Camden) 48 Executed by your Lordship as seditious and disloyall. **1667** Milton *P.L.* iii. 204 Man disobeying, Disloyal breaks his fealtie, and sinns Against the high Supremacie of Heav'n. **1673** [R. Leigh] *Transp. Reh.* 146 His malicious and disloyal reflections on the late Kings Reign. **1711** Hearne *Collect.* (Oxf. Hist. Soc.) III. 222 Disloyal Whiggs dispatch and goe, And visit Noll and Will below! **1837** J. H. Newman *Par. Serm.* (1839) I. xv. 225 Disloyal to the authority of God.

† **B.** *sb.* A disloyal person; a traitor, rebel. *Obs.*

1611 Speed *Hist. Gr. Brit.* ix. xxii. (1632) 1112 The battell of the disloyals. **1651** tr. *De las Coveras' Hist. Don Fenise* 302, I desired to see this disloyall yet once. *Ibid.* 303.

Hence **dis'loyalist**, a person disloyal or disaffected to the government.

1863 in *Boston Sunday Her.* 24 May 1/3. **1870** *Congress. Globe* 7 July 5310/3 The county of Monroe [in Missouri] was the place where disloyalists fleeing from other counties took shelter all the time. **1885** *Pall Mall G.* 10 June 10/1 Two organized bands of disloyalists indulged in hostile manifestations. **1886** J. Cook in *Advance* (Boston) 18 Feb. 99 As dangerous in his character of a disloyalist as that of a polygamist.

dis'loyally, *adv.* [f. disloyal *a.* + -ly².] In a disloyal manner, with disloyalty; with violation of one's allegiance or obligations; unfaithfully.

?**1417** in Ellis *Orig. Lett. Illustr. Eng. Hist.* (1827) 2nd Ser. I. 58 And after that disloyally rose up agayne in warres. **1552** Huloet, Disloyallye, *perfide.* **1578** *Chr. Prayers* in *Priv. Prayers* (1851) 464 Setting.. subjects disloyally to rebel against their princes. **1654** tr. *Scudery's Curia Pol.* 2 Had they all disloyally revolted. **1884** Freeman in *Manch. Guardian* 22 Sept. 5/6 The body which thus disloyally, almost rebelliously, flouted the crown.

† **dis'loyalness.** *Obs. rare.* [-ness.] = next.

1586 Ferne *Blaz. Gentrie* 138 A disloyalnesse of heart. **1727** Bailey vol. II, *Disloyalness*, disloyalty.

disloyalty (dɪs'lɔɪəltɪ). Also 5 des-, disloyalte, 6–7 -tie. [ad. OF. *desloyaute, desloyaulte*, earlier *desloialteit* (mod.F. *déloyauté*), f. *desloyal*, disloyal: cf. *loyal, loyalty*.] The quality of being disloyal; unfaithfulness, falseness.

1481 Caxton *Godfrey* 167 Whan the disloyalte and falsenes of mahomet ran thurgh thoryent. **1483** —— *G. de la Tour* E viij b, He slewe his broder Amon that suche desloyalte and untrouth had done to his Suster. **1548** Hall *Chron., Edw. IV* (an. 15) 237 b, Your moste renoumed name, by suche a desloialtie, and untruthe against promise, to be both blotted and stained. **1599** Shaks. *Much Ado* ii. i. 49 There shall appeare such seeming truths of Heroes disloyaltie, that iealousie shall be cal'd assurance. **1712** Addison *Spect.* No. 397 ¶5 This Princess was then under Prosecution for Disloyalty to the King's Bed. **1874** Morley *Compromise* (1886) 90 The infidelity to truth, the disloyalty to one's own intelligence.

b. Now *esp.* Violation of allegiance or duty to one's sovereign, state, or government.

1600 E. Blount tr. *Conestaggio* 195 Some.. charged him with disloyaltie, saying that he would not fight, having beene corrupted. **1647** N. Bacon *Disc. Govt. Eng.* i. lvii. (1739) 106 Although Richard the First forgot this man's disloyalty, yet God remembered it. **1821** Southey *Vision Judgem.* v, Discontent and disloyalty, like the teeth of the dragon, He had sown on the winds. **1844** H. H. Wilson *Brit. India* II. 385 Several of the Sipahis.. suffered the penalty of their disloyalty.

c. with *pl.* A disloyal act or proceeding.

1659 B. Harris *Parival's Iron Age* 216 The Earle of Holland, repenting himself of his great disloyalties, began [etc.]. **1697** C. Leslie *Snake in Grass* (ed. 2) 369 To upbraid the Presbyterians.. with their former Disloyalties.

dis'lune, *v. nonce-wd.* [f. dis- 4 + L. *lūna* the moon.] *trans.* To cure of lunacy.

1881 A. J. Duffield *Don Quixote* III. lxiv. 641 He wondered if Rozinante would remain humpbacked or not, or his master dislocated: it had been no small fortune had he been disluned. [Sp. *deslocado*, f. *loco* mad, 'cracked'.]

† **dis'lustre**, *sb. Obs.* [dis- 9.] Loss or deprivation of lustre; something that dims lustre.

1656 Finett *For. Ambass.* 151 To exclude the Venetian, that he might not by his Presence be a dis-lustre to him in his march. **1667** Waterhouse *Fire Lond.* 139 Do not glory in her ruines, trample not upon her dislustre.

dislustre (dɪs'lʌstə(r)), *v.* [dis- 7 a.]

1. *trans.* To deprive of lustre or brightness; to dim, sully. Hence **dis'lustred** *ppl. a.*

1638 Baker tr. *Balzac's Lett.* (1654) II. 25 To dislustre so pure a matter with the impression of so black a vapour. **1654** W. Mountague *Devout Ess.* ii. vi. §3 (R.) All those glittering passions.. get their lustre in the absence of that intellectual light, which as soon as it appears, deads and dislustres them. **1667** Digby *Elvira* v. iv, Whose character would it not dislustre? **1868** Lowell *Willows* ii, Her [May's] budding breasts and wan dislustered front.

2. *intr.* To lose its lustre.

1890 R. Bridges *Shorter Poems* iv. 15 When their bloom Dislustres.

dismade, -maid, -maiede, obs. ff. dismayed.

† **dis'magn**, *v. Obs. nonce-wd.* [f. dis- 8 + L. *magn-us* great.] *trans.* To deprive of greatness.

1657 Reeve *God's Plea* 207 It doth grieve me to see how great things are deampled and dismagned amongst you.

† **dis'maiden**, *v. Obs. rare.* [dis- 7 b.] *trans.* To deprive of maidenhood; to devirginate.

1603 Florio *Montaigne* iii. xiii. (1632) 629 At the dismaydening of their wives.

dis'mail, *v. arch.* [a. OF. *desmaille-r*, f. *des-*, dis- 4 + *maille* mail, armour; cf. It. *dismagliare*, obs. Sp. *desmallar.*] *trans.* To divest of mail or armour; to break or strip the mail off.

c **1450** *Merlin* 207 Thei perced haubrekes, and dismailed, and many ther were throwen to grounde. **1485** Caxton *Chas. Gt.* 69 Hys helme was desmaylled & broken. **1590** Spenser *F.Q.* ii. vi. 29 Their mightie strokes their haberjeons dismayld. **1848** J. A. Carlyle tr. *Dante's Inferno* 353 O thou.. who with thy fingers dismailest thyself.

dismain (dɪs'meɪn), *v.* [dis- 8.] *trans.* To deprive of the legal status of being a main road.

1886 *Kent Herald* 21 Oct. 2/1 That the Local Government Board be asked to hold an enquiry with a view to dismain a road. **1893** *Bristol Times* 15 Apr. 7/5 The proposal to dismain a portion of the main road situated at Berkeley.

dismal ('dɪzməl), *sb.*¹ and *sb.*² and *a.* Forms: 4–7 dismall, 4–5 dis(e)male, 5 dysmal, -mel, -mol, 6 diesmoll, dismold(e, 6–7 *Sc.* dismail, 6– dismal. [Mentioned in 1256 as the English or Anglo-French name for Fr. *les mals jours*: whence it appears to be OF. *dis mal* = L. *dies mali* evil days, unlucky days. It was thus originally a substantive of collective meaning; when 'day' was added, making 'dismal days', (cf. '*summer days*,' '*winter days*'), its attributive use passed into an adjective, and, its original application being obscured, it was finally before 1600 extended from *day, days*, to be a general attribute. See Note at end of this article.]

A. *sb.*¹ (The original use.)

† **1.** The *dies mali*, evil, unlucky or unpropitious days, of the mediæval calendar, called also *dies Ægyptiaci*, 'Egipcian daies' (see Egyptian 1 b); hence, by extension, Evil days (generally), days of disaster, gloom, or depression, the days of old age.

The *dies mali* were Jan. 1, 25; Feb. 4, 26; March 1, 28; April 10, 20; May 3, 25; June 10, 16; July 13, 22; Aug. 1, 30; Sept. 3, 21; Oct. 3, 22; Nov. 5, 28; Dec. 7, 22. They are said to have been called 'Egyptian days' because first discovered or computed by Egyptian astrologers; though some mediæval writers connected them with the plagues of ancient Egypt (cf. the Chaucer quot. **1369**, where the word appears to be treated as OF. *dis mal*, ten evils, or plagues, *plagæ*; see Prof. Skeat's note, *Chaucer* I. 493); some, still more fancifully, associated them with the gloom of 'Egyptian' darkness.

[**1256** see *Note* below.] *c* **1300** *Langtoft's Chron.* (Rolls II. 258), Cambr. MS. Gg. I. i. (*c* **1310**), (Satirical Verses on Baliol) Begkot an bride, Rede him at ride In the dismale [*rime* liale]. *c* **1369** Chaucer *Dethe Blaunche* 1206, I trowe hyt was in the dismalle, That was the .x. woundes of Egipte. *a* **1400** *Pystyll of Susan* 305 þou hast I be presedent, þe peple to steere, þou dotest now on þin olde tos in þe dismale [*v. rr.* in þin olde days, in þin elde]. *c* **1400** *Apol. Loll.* 93 A waytiþ not þeis Egipcian daies, þat we call dysmal.

B. *adj.* [orig. attributive use of A.]

† **1.** Of days: Of or belonging to the *dies mali*; unlucky, unpropitious. *Obs.*

c **1400** *Beryn* 650 So trewly for the Pardonere, it was a dismol day. *c* **1420** Lydg. *Story Thebes* iii. (1561) 370 a/1 Her disemale daies and her fatal houres. **1548** Cranmer *Catech.* B vj b, Other.. thinke that when the Sonne, Moone, or any other planetes is in this or yᵗ signe, it is an vnlucky thing to enterprise this or that, and vpon such dismolde daies (as they call them) they will begin no new enterprise. **1552** Huloet, Dismall dayes, *atri dies, dies Ægiptiaci.* **1560** Bp. J. Pilkington *Exp. Aggeus* i. B viij b, Why shall we then be bolde to call them euyll, infortunate, and dysmall days?.. Why shal they not prosper on those dayes, as well as on other? **1576** Fleming *Panopl. Epist.* 24 If she had now escaped her dismall daye: yet, doubtlesse.. within a fewe yeares her life would have ended. **1590** Spenser *F.Q.* ii. vii. 26 An ugly feend, more fowle than dismall day. **1608** Bp. Hall *Char. Virtues & V.* 88 (*Superstitions*) If his journey began.. on the dismall day; or if he stumbled at the threshold. **1618** Bolton *Florus* 12 Hee.. distinguisht the yeere into twelue months, and markt out which dayes were luckie, and which were dismall. [**1738** Birch *Life Milton* M.'s Wks. 1738 I. 75 Before that dismal 30th of January that his Majesty's Life was taken away.]

† **2.** Of other things: Boding or bringing misfortune and disaster; unlucky, sinister, malign, fatal.

1588 Greene *Perimedes* 9 Seest thou not a dismall influence, to inflict a dispairing chaos of confused mishaps. **1593** Shaks. *3 Hen. VI*, ii. vi. 58 Now death shall stop his dismall threatning sound, And his ill-boading tongue, no more shall speake. *Ibid.* iii. ii. 41 A Rauens Note, Whose dismall tune bereft my Vitall powres. **1632** J. Hayward tr. *Biondi's Eromena* 139 Such like love.. could not prove to her otherwise than dismall and unluckie. [**1664** Dryden *Rival Ladies* v. iii, It was that dismal Night Which tore my Anchor up.]

3. Of the nature of misfortune or disaster; disastrous, calamitous. (Now *rare*, and associated with sense 5.)

1592 Shaks. *Rom. & Jul.* iv. iii. 19 My dismall Sceane, I needs must act alone. **1599** T. M[oufet] *Silkwormes* 37 A little dismall fire whole townes hath burnd, A little winde doth spread that dismall fire. **1638** Sir T. Herbert *Trav.* (ed. 2) 188 Many dismall showres of Darts and stones. **1655** Stanley *Hist. Philos.* Biog. (1701) 13 Epilepsies, Convulsions and other Dismal and Affrighting Distempers. **1712** Addison *Spect.* No. 418 ¶6 Torments, Wounds, Deaths, and the like dismal Accidents. **1777** Watson *Philip II* (1793) II. xii. 91 Involved in this dismal catastrophe. **1856** Mrs. Browning *Aur. Leigh* v. 433 If this then be success, 't is dismaller Than any failures.

4. Causing dismay; terrible, dreadful, dire. Now in weakened sense (associated with 5): Causing gloom or dejection, depressing, wretched, miserable.

1588 Shaks. *Tit. A.* iii. i. 262 Be this dismall sight The closing vp of our most wretched eyes. **1605** —— *Macb.* v. v. 12 My Fell of haire Would at a dismall Treatise rowze, and stirre As life were in't. **1686** Horneck *Crucif. Jesus* ii. 24 The Devil appeared unto him in a.. most dismal shape. **1728** Pope *Dunc.* iii. 269 Dire is the conflict, dismal is the din. **1770** Goldsm. *Des. Vill.* 204 Full well the busy whisper circling round Conveyed the dismal tidings when he frowned. **1820** W. Irving *Sketch Bk.* I. 15 The sight of this wreck.. gave rise to many dismal anecdotes. **1875** Jowett *Plato* (ed. 2) V. 460 These things when spoken to a multitude.. take up a dismal length of time.

5. a. Of a character or aspect that causes gloom and depression; depressingly dark, sombre, gloomy, dreary, or cheerless.

Dismal Science, Carlyle's nickname for Political Economy. ***Great Dismal Swamp*** (U.S.): see C. 5.

1617 Minsheu *Ductor, Dismall*.. It signifieth also *Darke.* **1631** Gouge *God's Arrows* i. §23. 30 On a sudden was that faire skie turned into a sulphurious and most dismall skie. **1634** Sir T. Herbert *Trav.* 146 Blacke is not knowne among them, they say tis dismall and a signe of hell and sorrowe. **1696** tr. *Du Mont's Voy. Levant* 48 The Ghastliness of the Prospect is heighten'd by the Pine-Trees, that cast a dismal Shade. **1793** Smeaton *Edystone L.* §311 It looked very dismal and threatening all the time. **1849** Carlyle *Nigger Question*, Misc. Ess. (1872) VII. 84 The Social Science—not a 'gay science', but a rueful,—which finds the secret of this Universe in 'supply and demand'.. what we might call, by way of eminence, the *dismal science.* **1850** —— *Latter-d. Pamph.* iv. (1872) 119 Good monitions, as to several things, do lie in this Professor of the dismal science. **1873** Black *Pr. Thule* i, What a wild and dismal country was this which lay.. all around him! **1882** *Garden* 28 Jan. 54/2 The fogs in London this week have been about at their dismallest.

fig. **1871** Morley *Voltaire* (1886) 246 Doctrines which had naturally sprung up in the dismal age when the Catholic system acquired substance and shape.

b. Of sounds: Dreary, cheerless, woeful. (In late use chiefly *subjective*, as in 6.)

1593 [see 2]. *a* **1700** B. E. *Dict. Cant. Crew, Dismal ditty*, a Psalm at the Gallows. **1703** Dampier *Voy.* III. 131 Whales.. blowing and making a very dismal noise. **1719** De Foe *Crusoe* (1840) I. xix. 350 The dismallest howlings of wolves. **1794** Mrs. Radcliffe *Myst. Udolpho* i, Afar in the woods they raise a dismal shout. *a* **1839** Praed *Poems* (1864) I. 139 And heard her singing a lively song, In a very dismal tone. **1874** Micklethwaite *Mod. Par. Churches* 80 The dismal groans of the harmonium. **1894** Blackmore *Perlycross* 56 A dismal wail of anguish.

6. Of a character or aspect denoting gloom or depression; (subjectively) gloomy or miserable.

1705 Bosman *Guinea* 403 You may be surpriz'd that these poor Wretches should wear Hats, Perukes, &c. which they do in a very particular dismal manner. *a* **1715** Burnet *Own Time* (1766) I. 329 Wrote dismal letters to Court. **1766** Goldsm. *Vic. W.* vii, The only dismal figure in a group of merry faces. **1771** *Junius Lett.* lxvii. 330, I think you should suffer your dismal Countenance to clear up. **1837** W. Irving *Capt. Bonneville* II. 14 Gathering the mangled bodies of the slain.. the warriors returned, in dismal procession, to the village.

quasi-*adv.* **1757** Mrs. E. Griffith *Lett. betw. Henry & Frances* (1767) I. 64, I fear it was a dismal penned piece.

7. ***Dismal Desmond***: a toy dog with drooping ears; also *transf.*, a gloomy person; ***Dismal Jimmy*** (colloq.): a gloomy person.

1926–7 *Army & Navy Stores Catal.* 891/3 Dismal Desmond. An amusing, lovable puppy. **1934** A. Christie *Parker Pyne Investigates* 66 The gentleman selling Dismal Desmonds does not know what to make of it. **1938** E. Bowen *Death of Heart* ii. iii. 219 A Dismal Desmond dog sat on the bed. **1939** 'M. Innes' *Stop Press* ii. vii. 319 A blob of a nose, a mottled snout, a lachrymose eye, a.. drooping ear —the creature is called a Dismal Desmond and is known in every nursery. **1941** A. Christie *N or M?* i. 5, I wasn't conscious of looking a Dismal Desmond. **1968** 'R. Raine' *Night of Hawk* x. 52 Larry's a character and a half. Don't let the dismal Desmond look fool you. **1927** *Melody Maker* Sept. 931/2 We are not prophets nor dismal Jimmies. **1940** H. G. Wells *All Aboard for Ararat* iii. 92 It's up in all the offices now; the Dismal Jimmy stuff is barred.

C. *sb.*² [Elliptical or absolute use of B.]

† **1.** A dismal person. **a.** The devil. **b.** A funeral mute. *Obs.*

?*a* **1500** *Priests of Peblis* in Pinkerton *Scot. Poems Repr.* I. 17 (Jam.) Never bot by the dysmel, or the devil. **1570** Levin *Manip.* 13/20 Yᵉ dismall, deuill, *diabolus.* **1708** *Reply Swift's Bickerstaff detected* Wks. 1755 II. i. 165 Away.. into your flannel gear.. here is a whole pack of dismals coming to you with their black equipage.

† **2.** 'The designation of a mental disease, most probably, melancholy' (Jam.), hypochondria. *Obs.*

a **1605** Montgomerie *Flyting w. Polwart* 315 The doit and the dismall, indifferentlie delt.

† **3.** *pl.* Mourning garments. *Obs.*

1748 Richardson *Clarissa* (1811) VII. 171 How she would have adorned the weeds!.. Such pretty employment in her dismals. **1778** Foote *Trip Calais* iii. Wks. 1799 II. 363 As my lady is deck'd out in her dismals, perhaps she may take a fancy to faint.

4. *pl.* **a.** Low spirits, the dumps, the 'blues'. **1762** FOOTE *Lyar* II. Wks. 1799 I. 298 He..seems entirely wrapt up in the dismals. **1777** J. Q. ADAMS in *Fam. Lett.* (1876) 265 The spleen, the vapors, the dismals, the horrors seem to have seized our whole State. *a* **1834** LAMB *Final Mem.* v. To Mrs. Haslitt 232 When we are in the dismals there is now no hope from any quarter whatever. **1836** MARRYAT *Midsh. Easy* xxxiii, He has frightened that poor old woman into the dismals. **1893** EDNA LYALL *To Right the Wrong* I. 44 What business have you to indulge in a fit of the dismals on this gala-day?

b. *pl.* Expressions of gloom or despondency. **1774** J. Q. ADAMS *Fam. Lett.* (1876) 16 Their mutual reproaches, their declamations..their triumphs and defiances, their dismals and prophecies, are all delusion.

c. *pl.* Depressing circumstances, miseries. **1829** *Sporting Mag.* XXIV. 107 Quitting the dismals, I must relate an amusing anecdote. **1865** *Reader* 25 Feb. 221/3 She harps upon the petty annoyances of her dreary poverty, and on other dismals of life.

5. A local name of dreary tracts of swampy land on the eastern sea-board of the United States, *esp.* in North Carolina. **1763** G. WASHINGTON *Writ.* (1889) II. 198, 5 miles from the aforesaid mills, near to which the Dismal runs. **1812** H. WILLIAMS *Hist. N. Carolina* II. 180 Such are the Dismals, so called, and the other great swamps that are numerous in the flat country. **1856** OLMSTED *Slave States* 149 The 'Great Dismal Swamp', with the smaller 'Dismals'..of the same character, along the North Carolina Coast.

D. *Comb.*, as ***dismal-dreaming***. **1599** SHAKS. *Pass. Pilgr.* 200 And drives away dark dismal-dreaming night.

[*Note.* As to the identity of *dismal* with OF. (= AF.) *dis mal*:—L. *dies mali*, see Professor Skeat in *Trans. Philol. Soc.* 1888, p. 2. Already in 1617, Minsheu (whose own memory doubtless recalled the time when *dismal* was used only to qualify days) derived it from 'L. *dies malus*, en euill and vnhappie time'. Early corroborative evidence comes from OF. and Icelandic sources. (1) The Anglo-French *Art de Kalender* of Rauf de Linham, 1256 (MSS. at Glasgow, Oxford, Cambridge; extracts printed by M. Paul Meyer in his official *Rapport* on *Documents Manuscrits de l'ancienne littérature de la France*, Paris 1871, pp. 127–9), has a passage of sixty lines on the *Dies mali*, beginning 'Ore dirrai des jours denietz, Que vous dismal (*Bodley MS.* dismol) appelletz' [Now shall I tell of the forbidden days, Which you call *dismal*], and further on 'Dismal les appelent plusours, Ceo est a dire les mals jours' [*Dismal* several call them, That is to say the evil days]. Here *dismal* is given as the equivalent of 'mals jours', evil days.

(2) A short Icelandic treatise in a Copenhagen MS. (Arna-Magnæan 350, written 1363, lf. 148*a*), begins 'Her greinir um dismala daga. Tueir ero þeir dagar i huerium manadi er at bokmali kallaz dies mali..enn þat þydiz illir dagar' [Here tells of the dismal days. There are two days in every month that in the book-language (Latin) are called *dies mali*, and that is interpreted 'evil days']. The word *dismal* is not Norse, and must have been learned from England before 1363. In *dismala daga*, it is probably an adj. accus. pl., but may be a sb. gen. pl., 'days of the dismals'. Both the AF. and the Icelandic treatises give a list of the *dis mal* or *dies mali*, identical with that given by various mediæval writers, and computable by the mnemonic distich given by Du Cange s.v. *Dies Ægyptiaci*: see sense 1 above.]

† **'dismal**, *v.* *Obs. nonce-wd.* [f. prec. adj.] *intr.* To feel dismal or melancholy. **1780** MAD. D'ARBLAY *Diary* (1842) I. 344 Miss L. sung various old elegies..O! how I dismalled in hearing them.

dismality (dɪz'mælɪtɪ). [f. DISMAL *a.* + -ITY.] Dismal quality or state; an instance of this. **1714** MANDEVILLE *Fab. Bees* (1725) I. 291 A beggar..assists his cant with a doleful tone and a study'd dismality of gestures. **1779** MAD. D'ARBLAY *Diary, Let. Susan Burney* 25 Aug., After ten we took a comfortable walk, which made up for our late dismalities. **1867** MISS BRADDON *Birds of Prey* v. iii, The desert of Sahara is somewhat dismal..but in its dismality there is at least a flavour of romance. **1890** H. M. STANLEY *Sp.* in *Lit. World* 11 July 33/2 The dismalities of the march from the Albert Nyanza to the East Coast.

'dismalize, *v.* [See -IZE.] *trans.* To make or render dismal. Hence **'dismalized** *ppl. a.* **1734** LADY M. W. MONTAGU *Let. to Duchess of Portland* (1809) I. 19 Dismal faces, which by my art I dismalized ten times more. **1885** MASSON *Carlyle* i. 26 A dull and dismalised blur of the facts.

'dismally, *adv.* [f. DISMAL *a.* + -LY[2].] In a dismal manner; dreadfully; gloomily, dolorously. *a* **1660** HAMMOND *Rev.* ix. (R.), A lion gaping or yawning from his prey, and the blood of it about his mouth, looks very dismally. **1670** EACHARD *Cont. Clergy* 95 If he be either notoriously ignorant or dismally poor. **1709** STEELE *Tatler* No. 38 ¶6, I dismally dread the Multiplication of these Mortals under..a settled Peace. **1794** WORDSW. *Guilt & Sorrow* xlii, Dismally tolled that night the city clock! **1840** DICKENS *Barn. Rudge* i, The wind howled dismally among the bare branches of the trees. **1874** MORLEY *Compromise* (1886) 114 Their doctrine was dismally insufficient, and sometimes..directly vicious.

'dismalness. [f. as prec. + -NESS.] The quality of being dismal; depressing dreariness or gloom; dolefulness. **1620** SHELTON *Quix.* III. xxxiv. 245 The Night came on..not so light and calm..but a certain Dismalness it had. **1653** GATAKER *Vind. Annot. Jer.* 42 All the dismalnes..should be over, as soon as the interruption of those radiant rayes were remooved. **1832** *Examiner* 65/1 He is like to the raven in..the dismalness of his croak. **1879** BLACK *Macleod of D.* xv, The dismalness of being alone here..eats more and more into my heart.

disman (dɪs'mæn), *v.* [f. DIS- 7 + MAN *sb.*]

†**1.** *trans.* To undo as a man; to deprive of what constitutes the man. *Obs.* **1627–47** FELTHAM *Resolves* I. xlvii. 149 Man by death is absolutely divided and disman'd. **1633** EARL MANCH. *Al Mondo* (1636) 162 There is no spectacle..more terrible, than to behold a dying man, to stand by, and see a man dismanned. **1651** N. BACON *Disc. Govt. Eng.* II. i. (1739) 6 All is faint in that man that hath once dismanned himself.

2. To deprive (a country, etc.) of men. **1863** KINGLAKE *Crimea* I. xiv. 293 This is why I have chosen to say that France was dismanned.

† **dis'manacle**, *v.* *Obs. rare.* [DIS- 7 a.] *trans.* To free from manacles or shackles. **1627–47** FELTHAM *Resolves* 311 Till it [the soul] be dismanacled of the clogging flesh. *a* **1641** BP. MOUNTAGU *Acts & Mon.* (1642) 39 Such Caitifes as..are dismanacled, unshackled, raised up.

† **dis'mand, -'maund**, *v.* *Obs.* [ad. Sp. *desmandar* to countermand, refl. *desmandarse* to disband, stray from the flock, obs. It. *dismandarsi* 'in Grison is taken when a horse doth flie or depart out of the ring or compasse where he is ridden' (Florio), f. *des-*, DIS- 4 + *mandar*, L. *mandāre* to command.] *refl.* To disband, to go off duty. **1598** BARRET *Theor. Warres* IV. i. 98 Vpon small occasions doe they dismande themselues. *Ibid.* 103 Not to suffer any souldier..to dismaunde himselfe..vntill the whole Regiment be all entred.

† **dis'mangle**, *v.* *Obs. rare.* [DIS- 5.] *trans.* To cut in pieces; = MANGLE. Hence † **dis'mangling** *ppl. a.* **1659** D. PELL *Impr. Sea* 392 Ships..in which lye murdering Guns, mortal engines, and dismangling bullets. *Ibid.* 611 Decks be-decked with all sorts of dismangling bullets.

dismantle (dɪs'mænt(ə)l), *v.* [ad. obs. F. *desmanteller* 'to take a mans cloake off his backe; also, to dismantle, raze, or beat downe the walls of a fortresse' (Cotgr. 1611), mod.F. *démanteler*, f. *des-* DIS- 4 + *manteler* to cloak, MANTLE.]

†**1.** *trans.* To divest of a mantle or cloak; to uncloak. *lit.* and *fig.* Also **b.** *intr.* (for *refl.*) *Obs.* **1605** BACON *Adv. Learn.* II. xxiii. §32 He must take heed he shew not himselfe dismantelled and exposed to scorne and iniury. **1611** SHAKS. *Wint. T.* IV. iv. 666 Muffle your face, Dis-mantle you, and..disliken The truth of your own seeming. **1623** COCKERAM, *Dismantle*, to vncloath one. **1691** NORRIS *Pract. Disc.* 57 When the warm influence of a like-perswaded Princes Favour, invites him to come abroad and dismantle his Secrecies.

b. **1638** SIR T. HERBERT *Trav.* (ed. 2) 33 A delicious streame..refreshes the fields, forcing Flora to dismantle.

2. To divest or strip *of* (any clothing, covering, protection, or the like). **1602** SHAKS. *Ham.* III. ii. 293 This Realme dismantled was of Ioue himselfe. **1654** H. L'ESTRANGE *Chas. I* (1655) 55 Authority, whereof if Soveraignty be once dismantled, once stript, she is soon trampled upon. **1674** N. COX *Gentl. Recreat.* II. (1677) 166 Pluming, is after the Hawk hath seized her Prey, and dismantles it of the Feathers. **1784** COWPER *Task* VI. 178 All this uniform uncoloured scene Shall be dismantled of its fleecy load. **1821** COMBE *Wife* III. 161 The chin dismantled of its beard. **1879** F. POLLOK *Sport Brit. Burmah* II. 73 Houses..dismantled of their roofs.

†**3.** To strip off or remove (that which covers). **1605** SHAKS. *Lear* I. i. 220 To dismantle So many folds of fauour. **1647** WARD *Simp. Cobler* (1843) 26 Such exotic garbes, as..dismantles their native lustre.

4. To strip (any thing) of the necessary equipment, furniture, or apparatus, to unfurnish; *esp.* to strip (a fortress) of its defences and equipments; to strip (a vessel) of its sails, rigging, etc., to unrig. **1601** HOLLAND *Pliny* I. 136 The Persians caused this Hypparenum to be dismantled. **1639** FULLER *Holy War* III. iv. (1647) 114 Saladine..dismantled all his cities in the Holy land. **1772** *Ann. Reg.* 237/2 The Favorite frigate shall be dismantled, by putting her rudder on shore. **1778** *Eng. Gazetteer* (ed. 2) s.v. *Leicester*, Before the castle was dismantled, it was a prodigious building. **1794** SULLIVAN *View Nat.* II. 198 When Greece was dismantled by the Romans. **1843** PRESCOTT *Mexico* (1850) I. 226 One of those tempests..fell with terrible force on the little navy..dismantling some of the ships. **1891** T. W. REID *Life Ld. Houghton* I. x. 449 Engaged..in dismantling the rooms..which had been for so many years his home in London. *fig.* **1792** W. ROBERTS *Looker-on* (1794) I. 431. No. 30 Calculated..to dismantle the mind and scatter its materials of knowledge.

5. To render (fortifications, or the like) useless for their purpose; to pull down, take to pieces, destroy, raze. **1579** FENTON *Guicciard.* IV. 153 The Florentins..bound them selues..to dismantle euen to the earth, the bastillion which had so much molested the Siennoys. **1581** MULCASTER *Positions* vi. (1887) 42 Vntill such time, as nature shall dismantle, and pull it [the body] downe her selfe. **1653** H. COGAN tr. *Pinto's Trav.* xxxviii. 153 Causing all the walls of it to be dismantelled, he razed the place quite to the ground. **1672** COMBER *Comp. Temple* I. §3 (R.) Sin..defaceth its beauty, dismantles its strength, and brings down its highest and noblest faculties. **1853** SIR H. DOUGLAS *Milit. Bridges* (ed. 3) 371 The gun was dismounted..the carriage dismantled and conveyed piecemeal to the opposite shore.

Hence **dis'mantling** *vbl. sb.*; **dis'mantler**, one who dismantles or strips. **1611** COTGR., *Desmantellement*, a dismantling. **1649** MILTON *Eikon.* xxi. Wks. (1847) 323/1 For the dismantling of his letters he wishes 'they may be covered with the cloak of confusion'. **1747** GOULD *Eng. Ants* 77 The dismantling of the Nymphs is also an additional Task in reference to the Workers. **1758** *Monthly Rev.* 534 The dismantlers of our woods and groves. **1889** *Athenæum* 2 Nov. 596/2 The utterly wanton dismantling of the Guesten Hall [at Worcester].

dis'mantled, *ppl. a.* [f. prec. + -ED[1].] Deprived of clothing, equipment, or fortifications. **1600** E. BLOUNT tr. *Conestaggio* 309 The citie of Angra and all other places being dismantled and weake, they had no other defence then the landing. *a* **1800** COWPER *Iliad* (ed. 2) XII. 486 The dismantled wall. **1868** FREEMAN *Norm. Conq.* (1876) II. viii. 207 He repaired and garrisoned the dismantled fortress. **1879** FARRAR *St. Paul* (1883) 244 The driven dismantled hulk.

dis'mantlement. [f. as prec. + -MENT: cf. mod.F. *démantèlement*, older *desmantellement.*] The act or process of dismantling. **1870** *Daily News* 22 Dec., The fortifications on the horse-shoe *enceinte*..are now also undergoing a vigorous process of dismantlement. **1876** SYMONDS *Grk. Poets* Ser. II. ix. 332 Then came the dismantlement of Athens by Lysander. **1882** *Standard* 14 July, The ultimatum then gave the choice of dismantlement or bombardment.

dis'marble, *v.* [DIS- 7.] *trans.* To free from marble, divest of marble-like appearance. **1830** W. TAYLOR *Hist. Surv. Germ. Poetry* II. 397 Dismarbled, free, he stalks around. **1855** M. ARNOLD *Poems, Youth & Calm* 3 There's nothing can dismarble now The smoothness of that limpid brow.

† **dis'march**, *v.* *Obs.* [ad. 16th c. F. *desmarch-er* 'to step, or goe, backe..to retire..loose ground' (Cotgr.), f. *des-* DIS- 4 + *marcher* to MARCH.] *intr.* To march or fall back, to retreat; to march off, retire. Hence † **dis'marching** *vbl. sb.* **1596** *Life Scanderbeg* 225 He [Scanderbeg] dismarched therefore with as great secrecy as possible. **1600** HOLLAND *Livy* II. lxiii. 86 The enemies..dismarched away [*abeunt*] as speedely as they could. **1623** BINGHAM *Xenophon* 115 To dismarch from an enemy, was euer held dishonourable by a man of valour. **1635** BARRIFFE *Mil. Discipl.* lxxxii. (1643) 234 Of dismarching, or firing in the Reere.

† **dis'march**, *sb.* *Obs. rare.* [ad. 16th c. F. *desmarche*, f. *desmarcher*: see prec.] A retreat. **1600** HOLLAND *Livy* XXV. xxxiii. 574 The enemie..traced him hard at heeles in his dismarch [*abeuntium*].

dis'mark, *v. rare.* [ad. obs. F. *desmarquer* (now *démarquer*) 'to take away the marke from'.] *trans.* To deprive of (distinguishing) marks. **1632** *Thomas of Reading* in Thoms *Prose Rom.* (1858) I. 146 Then before the horse should go from thence, he would dismarke him. **1894** *Blackw. Mag.* Dec. 850/1 Before the horse left this, the man dismarked him, cropped his ears, etc.

dis'market, *v.* [DIS- 7 b.] *trans.* To deprive of the legal character and privileges of a market. **1878** *Daily News* 13 Dec., The Court proposed to dismarket the two existing Leadenhall markets, and had..applied to Parliament for the requisite powers.

† **dis'marry**, *v.* *Obs. rare.* [ad. 16th c. F. *desmarier* 'to diuorce, vnwed, or vnmarrie' (Cotgr.), f. *des-*, DIS- 4 + *marier* to MARRY.] *trans.* To annul the marriage of. **1525** LD. BERNERS *Froiss.* II. cxc. [clxxxvi.] 583 He was dismaryed, and maryed agayne to another gentylwoman.

† **dis'marshall**, *v.* *Obs. rare.* [DIS- 6.] *trans.* To derange, disorder, throw into confusion. **1630** DRUMM. OF HAWTH. *Flowers Sion* 31 What was dismarshalled late..Is now most perfect seen.

† **dis'mask**, *v.* *Obs.* [ad. obs. F. *desmasquer* 'to vnmaske, discouer, pull, or take off his maske' (Cotgr.), f. *des-*, DIS- 4 + *masque* MASK.] *trans.* To divest of a mask or covering; to unmask. **1588** SHAKS. *L.L.L.* v. ii. 296 Faire Ladies maskt, are Roses in their bud: Dismaskt..Are Angels vailing clouds, or Roses blowne. **1599** SANDYS *Europæ Spec.* (1632) 184 Their plausible pretences being now dismasked. **1633** T. STAFFORD *Pac. Hib.* i. (1821) 1 To dismaske themselves of that cloake of subjection which before they pretended. **1651** WALTON in *Reliq. Wotton* (1672) 213 The Marquess..thought best to dismask his Beard.

dismast (dɪs'mɑːst, -'mæst), *v.* [f. DIS- 7 a + MAST *sb.*; cf. F. *démâter*, obs. *desmaster* (1680 in Hatz.-Darm.).] *trans.* To deprive (a ship) of masts; to break down the masts of. **1747** *Gentl. Mag.* XVII. 486 She fired single guns at us, in order to dismast us. **1748** *Anson's Voy.* II. v. 172. **1823** LINGARD *Hist. Eng.* VI. 17 His ship was quickly dismasted by the superior fire of his adversary. **1843** PRESCOTT *Mexico* (1850) I. 200 A furious storm..dismasted his ship.

Hence **dis'masted** *ppl. a.*; also **dis'mastment** [cf. F. *démâtement*], † **dis'masture**, the action of dismasting a ship. **1762** FALCONER *Shipwr.* II. 749 The hull dismasted there awhile may ride. **1781** ARBUTHNOT in *Westm. Mag.* IX. 265 My letter..will have acquainted their Lordships with the..dismasture of the Bedford, in a gale of wind. **1828** WEBSTER refers to MARSHALL for Dismastment. **1868** MORRIS *Earthly Par.* I. 98 Leaky, dismasted, a most helpless prey To winds and waves.

dis'match, *v. rare.* [DIS- 6.] *trans.* Not to match or suit. Hence **dis'matchment**.

1591 SYLVESTER *Du Bartas* I. v. 907 Blush not (my book) nor think it thee dismatches, To beare about vpon thy paper-Tables, Flies, Butterflies, [etc.]. **1847** MRS. GORE *Castles in the Air* iv. (Hoppe), The dismatchment of the furniture.

†**dis'maw**, *v. Obs. rare.* [DIS- 7 c.] *trans.* To empty out from the maw.

1620 SHELTON *Quix.* IV. vii. 50 You may dismaw all that you have in your troubled heart and grieved entrails.

dismay (dɪs'meɪ), *sb.* [f. DISMAY *v.* Cf. Sp. *desmayo* a swoon, dismay, Pg. *desmaio* a fainting fit, It. *smago* (Körting, 2960), from the corresp. vbs.]

Utter loss of moral courage or resolution in prospect of danger or difficulty; faintness of heart from terror or from feeling of inability to cope with peril or calamity.

1590 SPENSER *F.Q.* II. xi. 41 Awhile he stood in this astonishment, Yet would he not for all his great dismay Give over to effect his first intent. **1596** SHAKS. *Merch. V.* III. ii. 61 With much more dismay I view the fight, then thou that mak'st the fray. **1667** MILTON *P.L.* II. 422 Each In other's count'nance red his own dismay. **1740** PITT *Æneid* VIII. (R.), Ev'n hell's grim porter shook with dire dismay. **1791** COWPER *Iliad* XII. 54 He no dismay Conceives or terror in his noble heart. **1836** W. IRVING *Astoria* III. 56 Our unfortunate travellers, contemplated their situation..in perfect dismay. **1838** THIRLWALL *Greece* V. xl. 144 An eclipse of the sun spread universal dismay at Thebes. **1863** GEO. ELIOT *Romola* I. xii, [She] lifted..her hands in mute dismay.

†**b.** Dismaying influence or operation. *Obs.*

1594 SPENSER *Amoretti* lxxxvii, I wander as in darkenesse of the night, Affrayd of every dangers least dismay. **1596** —— *F.Q.* V. ii. 50 Like as a ship, whom cruell tempest drives Upon a rocke with horrible dismay.

dismay (dɪs'meɪ), *v.*[1] Forms: 3-4 **demay(e**, 4 **demayȝe, desmai**, 4-5 **dismaye, dysmay**, 4- **dismay**, (4-6 **dismaie**, 5 **desmaye, dis- dysamay**). [Appears to represent an OF. or AF. type **desmaier*, *démaier* (Palsgr. has a pa. pple. *dismayé*) = Sp. *desmayar* 'to dismay, to discourage..to swoune' (Minsheu), Pg. *desmaiar*, It. *smagare* 'to trouble, to vexe, to annoy' (Florio), Romanic type **dismagāre*, f. *dis-*, DIS- 4 + *-mag-*, app. ad. OHG. *magan* to be powerful or able (see MAY *v*); cf. AMAY, ESMAY, representing the ordinary OF. form *esmaier*:— **exmagāre*.]

1. *trans.* To deprive of moral courage at the prospect of peril or trouble; to appal or paralyze with fear or the feeling of being undone; utterly to discourage, daunt, or dishearten. *refl.* †To be filled with dismay; to lose courage entirely.

1297 R. GLOUC. (1724) 156 He wende forþ, and soȝte out here fon, Some heo fonde ligge slepe, heo demayde hem anon. **13..** *Guy Warw.* (A.) 1645 Nowe goþ Gij sore desmaid, His woundes him han iuel afreyd. *c* **1340** *Gaw. & Gr. Knt.* 470 Dere dame, to day demay yow neuer. *c* **1350** *Will. Palerne* 3800 þouȝh þere be mani mo þan ȝe, dismaie ȝe nouȝt þerfore. **1413** *Pilgr. Sowle* (Caxton 1483) IV. xxxviii. 64 He helde hym self abasshed, and desmayed. *c* **1430** LYDG. *Chron. Troy* V. xxxvi, In herte for loue disamayde. **1577** B. GOOGE *Heresbach's Husb.* III. (1586) 154 That both with his barking he may discover, and with his sight dismay the Theefe. **1615** J. STEPHENS *Satyr Ess.* A viii, Let not this dismay Thee. **1781** GIBBON *Decl. & F.* II. xlvi. 730 The enemies were dispersed and dismayed. **1857** LONGF. *Gold. Leg.* I. *Chamber in Castle Vantsberg*, I heard..Of your maladies..Which neither astonished nor dismayed me.

†**2.** To defeat or rout by sudden onslaught. *Obs.*

[Cf. **1297** in 1.] **1596** SPENSER *F.Q.* V. ii. 8 He..there assaies His foe confused..That horse and man he equally dismaies. *Ibid.* VI. x. 13 When the bold Centaures made that bloudy fray With the fierce Lapithes which did them dismay.

†**3.** *intr.* To become utterly discouraged or faint-hearted. *Obs.*

a **1375** *Joseph Arim.* 31 Whon Ioseph herde þer-of, he bad hem not demayȝen. **1509** HAWES *Past. Pleas.* XXXIV. v, Be of good chere, and for nothyng dismaye. **1578** T. N. tr. *Cong. W. India* 227 For all those bragges Cortez dismaide not. **1591** SHAKS. *1 Hen. VI*, III. iii. 1 Dismay not (Princes) at this accident. **1596** J. NORDEN (*title*), A Christian.. Incouragement vnto all English Subiects not to dismaie at the Spanish Threats.

†**dis'may**, *v.*[2] *Obs. nonce-wd.* [f. DIS- 7 a + MAY *sb.*] *trans.* To strip of May-blossom.

1610 G. FLETCHER *Christ's Vict.* (1888) 99 And may, dismayed, Thy coronet must be.

†**dismayd**, *ppl. a.* (In Spenser.) Explained by editors, for **dismade*, i.e. *mis-made*, mis-shapen.

1590 SPENSER *F.Q.* II. xi. 11 Whose hideous shapes were like to feendes of hell, Some like to houndes, some like to Apes, dismayd.

dismayed (dɪs'meɪd), *ppl. a.* Also 4 **desmaid**, 6 **dismade**, 6-8 **-mai(e)d**. [f. DISMAY *v.*[1] + -ED[1].] Overwhelmed with fear, etc.; appalled.

1513 MORE in Grafton *Chron.* (1568) II. 765 The Queene ..sate alone alowe..all desolate, and dismayed. **1561** HOLLYBUSH *Hom. Apoth.* 22 a, Then is he holye dismade and heavy. **1624** CAPT. SMITH *Virginia* V. 196 Newes was brought the Gouernor by a dismaied Messenger. **1743** J. DAVIDSON *Æneid* VIII. 238 Then first our men beheld Cacus dismaid. **1849** MACAULAY *Hist. Eng.* I. 218 His ardent and unconquerable spirit..soon roused the courage of his dismayed countrymen.

dis'mayedness. [f. prec. + -NESS.] Dismayed state or condition; utter dispiritedness.

1571 GOLDING *Calvin on Ps.* xxii. 2 Hereupon came that dissmaydnesse and dread, which compelled him too crave release of death. **1603** HOLLAND *Plutarch's Mor.* 163 That shame and dismaiednesse which maketh us that we dare not looke a man in the face. *a* **1649** WINTHROP *New Eng.* (1853) I. 12 There appeared no fear or dismayedness amoung them. **1701** W. WOTTON *Hist. Rome* i. 19 Never discovering perplexity, dismayedness..or distrust.

dis'mayer. [f. DISMAY *v.* + -ER[1].] One who dismays or appals.

1594 SOUTHWELL *M. Magd. Fun. Teares* 26 What gained shee by their comming, but..two dismayers of her hope? *a* **1622** AINSWORTH *Annot. Ps.* liv. 5 (1639) 83 Daunting tyrants, terrible dismayers, as Saul and his retinue.

dis'mayful, *a.* [f. DISMAY *sb.* + -FUL.] Full of or fraught with dismay; appalling.

c **1586** C'TESS PEMBROKE *Ps.* CV. ix. For cheerefull lightes dismayfull lightnings shine. **1596** SPENSER *F.Q.* V. xi. 26 Much dismay'd with that dismayfull sight. **1628** R. HOBART *Edw. II*, cix, In that sad dismaifull houre of dying. **1876** G. MACDONALD *T. Wingfield* vi, That thought of all most dismayful.

Hence **dis'mayfully** *adv.*, in dismay.

1596 SPENSER *F.Q.* V. viii. 38 From which like mazed deare dismayfully they flew.

†**dis'maying**, *vbl. sb. Obs.* [f. DISMAY *v.* + -ING[1].] The action of the vb. DISMAY; daunting; dismay.

13.. *K. Alis.* 2801 Men myghte ther y-seo hondis wrynge ..Sway, and gret dismayng. **1571** GOLDING *Calvin on Ps.* xlvi. 3 There is no cause of dismaying in yᵉ faythfull. **1611** BIBLE *Jer.* xlviii. 39 So shall Moab be a derision, and a dismaying to all them about him. **1666** PEPYS *Diary* 4 July, It was pure dismaying and fear which made them all run upon the 'Galloper'.

dis'maying, *ppl. a.* [-ING[2].] That dismays.

1653 GATAKER *Vind. Annot. Jer.* 96 They fil mens heds with dismaying fears. **1816** SCOTT *Bl. Dwarf* ii, They presented themselves with a readiness which he felt to be somewhat dismaying. **1817** SHELLEY *Rev. Islam* II. xix, To tread life's dismaying wilderness Without one smile to cheer.

Hence **dis'mayingly** *adv.*

1731 BAILEY, *Dismayingly*, dishearteningly. **1911** M. & J. FINDLATER *Penny Monypenny* III. iv. 316 It was now dismayingly hot. **1926** *Chambers's Jrnl.* 337/2 She would have found it dismayingly difficult to conduct the most juvenile class.

dismayl(e, obs. form of DISMAIL *v.*

†**dis'mayment.** *Obs.* [f. DISMAY *v.* + -MENT.] = DISMAY *sb.*, dismaying.

1600 F. WALKER *Sp. Mandeville* 66 b, He..bad him be of good courage, and shake off that dismaiment. *a* **1640** W. FENNER *Sacr. Faithfull* (1648) 39 A base dismayment of spirit below or beneath the strength that is in a man. **1642** ROGERS *Naaman* 45 Naaman heere had his dismaiments.

disme (daɪm), var. of DIME *sb.* and *v.* The *sb.*, besides its historical use in the senses 'tenth' and 'tithe', is used, in the earliest Eng. book on the subject, for 'Decimal arithmetic', also *attrib.* or as *adj.* = 'decimal'.

1608 A. NORTON (*title*) Disme: The Art of Tenths, or Decimall Arithmeticke..invented by Simon Stevin. *Ibid.* C j b, Disme is a kind of Arithmeticke, invented by the tenth progression..by which also all accounts..are dispatched by whole numbers, without fractions or broken numbers. *Ibid.* C ij b, The numbers of the second and third Definitions before-going [·364, ·3759] are generally called Disme numbers. *Ibid.*, There are 3 orders of Disme numbers giuen.

†**dis'meanor**, *v. Obs.* [f. DIS- 7 + *meanour* in DEMEANOUR: cf. MISMEANOUR.] To misbehave, misconduct (oneself).

1598 BARRET *Theor. Warres* IV. i. 102 Taking..care..the souldiers dismeanour not themselues.

†**dis'measurable**, *a. Obs.* Also **des-**. [a. OF. *desmesurable* (in Godef.), f. *des-*, DIS- 4 + *mesurable* MEASURABLE.] Beyond measure, immoderate, excessive. Hence **dis'measurably** *adv.*, immoderately, excessively.

1474 CAXTON *Chesse* III. vii. H viij, I make them liue in misery that I see lyue dismeasurably. *c* **1477** —— *Jason* 16 To whom he gaf so demesurable a stroke in the middes of his shelde that he perced hit. *Ibid.* 31 To the knight..he gaf a strook so dismesurably that he clefte his hede.

†**dis'measure**, *a. Obs. rare.* In 5 **dysmesure**. [app. a. OF. *desmesuré*, pa. pple. of *desmesurer*: see next.] = DISMEASURED.

c **1400** tr. *Secreta Secret., Gov. Lordsh.* 102 þay shalle hate þe as dysmesure.

†**dis'measure**, *v. Obs.* [ad. OF. *desmesurer* (Godef.) to go to excess or beyond measure, f. *des-*, DIS- 4 + *mesurer* to MEASURE. Cf. Sp. *desmesurar* 'to be vnmeasurable, to be vnruly' (Minsheu).] *refl.* To show want of moderation in one's conduct.

1598 BARRET *Theor. Warres* II. i. 19 It is his part to apprehend the offenders, yet in such sort, that he dismeasure himselfe with none, but execute the same with great moderation.

†**dis'measured**, *a. Obs.* Also **des-, dys-**. [f. DIS- + MEASURED, repr. OF. *desmesuré*.]

1. Unmeasured; out of measure; immoderate, excessive; going beyond bounds, unrestrained.

1483 CAXTON *Gold. Leg.* 123/3, I..wende to haue saued the and thou art desmesured in worldly loue and flesshly. *a* **1533** LD. BERNERS *Gold. Bk. M. Aurel.* (1546) B ij, I wyll not that my penne bee so dismeasured to reproue so muche the aunciente men. **1585** T. WASHINGTON tr. *Nicholay's Voy.* II. ix. 43 Sapho..in a fury and rage of a love dismeasured, she cast her selfe..into the Sea.

b. Excessive in size, immense.

1584 B. R. *Herodotus* 10 b, A wyld bore strangely dismeasured and overgrowne.

2. Wrongly measured; in false measure.

1574 HELLOWES *Gueuara's Fam. Ep.* 50 To them he giueth all things variable, dismeasured, and by false weight.

3. as *adv.* Immoderately.

1485 CAXTON *Chas. Gt.* 64 O Paynym, dysmesured al day thou vauntest the.

†**dis'meddle**, *v. Obs. rare.* [ad. ONF. *desmedler*, OF. *desmesler*, *-meller* 'to loosse, open ..disintangle' (Cotgr.), mod.F. *démêler*, f. *des-*, DIS- 4 + *medler*, *mesler*, *mêler* to mingle, mix.] *trans.* To unfasten, loosen, disentangle.

1480 CAXTON *Ovid's Met.* XIV. xiii, She opened her breste ..and dysmedlid her blonke heeris.

dismember (dɪs'mɛmbə(r)), *v.* Forms: 4-6 **dis-, dysmembre**, 5 **desmembre**, 5- **dismember**; also 3-6 **demembre**: see DEMEMBER. [a. OF. *desmembre-r* (11th c. in Hatz.-Darm.), mod.F. *démembrer* = Pr., Sp., and It. *desmembrar*, It. *di*)*smembrare*, med.L. *dismembrāre* and *dēmembrāre*, f. DIS- 4, DE- 6 + *membrum* limb.]

1. *trans.* To deprive of limbs or members; to cut off the limbs or members of; to tear or divide limb from limb. (In quot. 1697, to castrate.)

1297 R. GLOUC. (1724) 559 Most reuþe it was ido, þat sir Simon þe olde man demembred was so. *c* **1380** *Sir Ferumb.* 1159 þat we ne scholde to deþe gon, be hangid & to-drawe, Ouþer be demembrid euerechoun. *c* **1400** *Destr. Troy* 3488 Dyssmembrit as marters, & murtheret to dethe. **1540-1** ELYOT *Image Gov.* 46 Ye woulde with your owne handes dismembre hym & plucke him in pieces. *a* **1618** RALEIGH *Mahomet* 42 Seeing Ataulpho entering..dismembred of nose and ears. **1697** POTTER *Antiq. Greece* II. iii. (1715) 204 Some were so rigid Observers of the rules of chastity that.. they dismember'd themselves. **1725** POPE *Odyss.* III. 322 Fowls obscene dismember'd his remains. **1855** MACAULAY *Hist. Eng.* IV. 286 To be torn with redhot pincers, smeared with melted lead, and dismembered by four horses.

b. *transf.*

1705 STANHOPE *Paraphr.* III. 624 A never yet repaired dismembring of this Tree. **1726** SHELVOCKE *Voy. round World* (1757) 257 Palm-cabbage is..the head of this tree, which being cut off, and dismembered of its great spreading leaves, [etc.]. **1830** J. G. STRUTT *Sylva Brit.* 93 Its branches are so tough as to withstand the fury of gales that would dismember most other trees. **1839** MURCHISON *Silur. Syst.* I. xxxi. 424 Their eruption dismembered the strata.

†**c.** To carve: said in reference to herons and some other birds. *Obs.*

1513 *Bk. Keruynge* in *Babees Bk.* 265 Termes of a Kerver ..Dysmembre that heron. **1514** BARCLAY *Cyt. & Uplondyshm.* (Percy Soc.) p. xliv, The Kerver..his Knife in his hande Dismembring a crane, or somewhat deynteous. **1804** FARLEY *Lond. Art Cookery* (ed. 10) 293 To dismember a Hern. Cut off the legs, lace the breast down the sides. **1885** *Illustr. Lond. News* 10 Oct. 362/3.

2. *fig.* To divide into parts or sections, so as to destroy integrity; to cut up, cut to pieces, mangle, mutilate: in recent use chiefly, To divide and partition (a country or empire).

1303 R. BRUNNE *Handl. Synne* 665 To swere grete oþys.. As we folys do..Dysmembre Iesu alle þat we may. *c* **1330** —— *Chron.* (1810) 313 þe coroune forto saue Dismembred not a dele. **1494** FABYAN *Chron.* VI. cxlvii. 133 So dyd this Charlis dismembre and cut or breke the enemyes of Fraunce throughe his hyghe prowesse. **1585** ABP. SANDYS *Serm.* (1841) 246 Such doctrines as do either poison the church with heresy, or dismember and rent it asunder with schism. **1624** N. DE LAWNE tr. *Du Moulin's Logick* 123 He..must dismember the said question into two parts. **1734** tr. *Rollin's Anc. Hist.* (1827) I. 168 His dominions were dismembered. **1840** CARLYLE *Heroes* iii. (1872) 106 Italy..poor Italy lies dismembered, scattered asunder, not appearing in any protocol or treaty as a unity at all. **1874** GREEN *Short Hist.* ii. §2. 65 Mercia had been dismembered to provide another earldom for his son.

†**3.** To cut off, sever from the body (a limb or member). (In quot. 1616, To mangle or mutilate.)

1580 [see DISMEMBERED *ppl. a.* 2]. **1601** HOLLAND *Pliny* II. 423 When any part of the body is cut off or dismembred. **1616** SURFL. & MARKH. *Country Farme* 126 The slitting of a horses nosthrils..by dismembring the organ or instrument whereby he draweth vp the aire, doth breed in him a greater difficultie of breathing. **1675** TRAHERNE *Chr. Ethics* xx. 319 A hand, or foot dismembred from the body. **1694** tr. *Milton's Lett. State* Feb. an. 1655 Wks. (1851) 339 The wresting of the Kingdom of Poland from Papal Subjection, as it were a Horn dismembred from the Head of the Beast.

†**b.** *fig.* and *transf.* To cut off, separate, sever, from the main body: chiefly in reference to a country or region. ? *Obs.*

1580 NORTH *Plutarch* (1676) 922 To dismember the other Towns of Boeotia from the city of Thebes. **1776** GIBBON *Decl. & F.* I. xiii. 271 Britain was thus dismembered from the empire. **1802** R. BROOKES *Gazetteer* (ed. 12) s.v. *Polotsk*, Part of a palatinate of Lithuania, dismembered from Poland by the treaty of partition in 1772. *c* **1815** JANE AUSTEN *Persuas.* II. ii, Having dismembered himself from the paternal tree.

4. [f. DIS- 7 b + MEMBER.] To cut off from membership.

1649 PRYNNE *Vind. Liberty Eng.* 10 The House of Commons.. having no more Authority to dis-member their fellow-members, then any Judges..have to dis-judge.. their fellow Judges. **1683** T. HUNT *Def. Charter Lond.* 42 Leave to go out of that Society, and dismember themselves. *a* **1734** NORTH *Lives* I. 175 The parliament met, and..the new members were attacked..and were soon dismembered by vote of the house. **1884** S. S. SEAL in *Solicitors' Jrnl.* 8 Nov. 30/2 Becoming a defaulter..would have involved his being dismembered from the Exchange.

Hence **dis'membering** *ppl. a.*

1861 J. G. SHEPPARD *Fall Rome* I. 59 Long before the dismembering deed of Constantine.

dis'membered, *ppl. a.* [f. prec. + -ED[1].]

1. Deprived of members or limbs; divided limb from limb; cut or broken in pieces; mangled, mutilated. **a.** *lit.*

1552 HULOET, Dismembred or lackynge some lymmes. *a* **1656** BP. HALL *Occas. Medit.* (1851) 152 We have seen mountebanks, to swallow dismembered toads. **1752** FOOTE *Taste* II. (ed. 4) 25 Let me embrace the dear, dismember'd Bust! **1827** POLLOK *Course T.* VIII, Old vases and dismembered idols.

b. *transf.* and *fig.* (In quot. 1578 of leaves: Divided, cut.)

1578 LYTE *Dodoens* V. xlviii. 612 The leaves be almost lyke the leaves of Coriander, but dismembered and parted into smaller jagges or frengis. **1603** KNOLLES *Hist. Turks* (1621) 85 This dismembered empire, now in the hands of many. **1862** S. LUCAS *Secularia* 5 Dubious fragments of a dismembered truth.

c. *Her.* Of a charge representing an animal: Depicted without limbs or members; or, with the members separate from the body as if just cut off.

1572 BOSSEWELL *Armorie* II. 42 Howe many and sundrie wayes they [Lions] are borne in armes, as..Couped, Dismembred, Vulned. **1727–51** CHAMBERS *Cycl.*, *Dismembered*, in heraldry, is applied to birds that have neither feet nor legs; as also to lions, and other animals, whose members are separated. **1882** CUSSANS *Her.* vi. 90 A Lion rampant dismembered is borne by the Maitland Family.

†**2.** Cut off or severed, as a limb or member; severed from the main body. *Obs.*

1580 NORTH *Plutarch* (1676) 729 When these poor dismembred members were brought to Rome, Antonius.. commanded his head and his hands should..be set up over the pulpit. **1666** BOYLE *Orig. Formes & Qual.*, The dismembred part of the Plant may retain the texture of its more stable parts. **1820** W. IRVING *Sketch Bk.* I. 57 They are a dismembered branch of the great Appalachian family.

dis'memberer. Also 5 de-. [f. as prec. + -ER[1].] One who or that which dismembers. (In Puttenham, the rhetorical figure DIALYSIS.)

1491 [see DEMEMBRER]. **1589** PUTTENHAM *Eng. Poesie* III. xix. (Arb.) 230 *margin*, Dialisis, or the Dismembrer..A maner of speach not vnlike the dilemma of the Logicians. **1865** W. KAY *Crisis Hupfeldiana 17 note*, So much even the Dismemberers are compelled to allow. **1870** *Daily News* 27 Sept., When..the famous 'dismemberer' Frederick II, obtained impunity for his rape of Western Poland.

dis'membering, *vbl. sb.* [f. as prec. + -ING[1].]

1. The action of the verb DISMEMBER; dismemberment.

c **1386** CHAUCER *Pars. T.* ⁋ 517 For cristes sake ne swereth nat so synfully in dismembrynge of Crist, by soule, herte, bones, and body. **1563–87** FOXE *A. & M.* (1596) 157/2 That no bishop nor..clergie should be at the judgement of anie mans death or dismembring. **1612** WOODALL *Surg. Mate* Wks. (1653) 2 In dismembring of the legge or arme below the knee or elbow. **1677** *Govt. Venice* 75 The dismembring of Bressia..from the Dutchy of Milan. **1816** KEATINGE *Trav.* (1817) I. 244 Shooting, beheading, maiming, and dismembering, all are executed as the monarch awards upon the spot.

†**2.** *concr.* A division into members; a separate member or part. *Obs. rare.*

1603 FLORIO *Montaigne* III. x. (1632) 570 Of so many dismembrings [Fr. *membres*] that Sufficiency hath, patience sufficeth us.

3. *attrib.*

1612 WOODALL *Surg. Mate* Wks (1653) 5 The dismembring saw. **1715** KERSEY, *Dismembring-knife*, a Surgeon's Instrument to cut off a Limb, etc.

dis'memberment. [f. DISMEMBER *v.* + -MENT: cf. OF. *desmembrement*, mod.F. *dé-*.]

1. The act of depriving of members or limbs, or of dividing limb from limb.

1816 KIRBY & SP. *Entomol.* (1843) I. 45 The.. dismemberments and lingering deaths that insects often suffer. **1816** KEATINGE *Trav.* (1817) I. 245 Thus dismemberment is now the usual punishment for crimes, whereby death is supposed to be earned.

2. *transf.* and *fig.* Division of a whole into parts or sections, so as to destroy its integrity; cutting to pieces, partition (e.g. of a country or empire).

a **1751** BOLINGBROKE *The Occasional Writer* No. 11 (R.) To prevent the dismemberment of their monarchy. **1772** *Ann. Reg.* 2 The present violent dismemberment and partition of Poland. **1849** COBDEN *Speeches* 69 Now, don't give faith to the idea..that self-government for the colonies is the same thing as dismemberment of the empire. **1866** FELTON *Anc. & Mod. Gr.* I. vii. 111 Modern criticism has ..attempted the same process of dismemberment as with the Iliad.

b. Separation from the main body. *rare.*

1838 PRESCOTT *Ferd. & Is.* (1846) I. ii, Aversion..to the dismemberment of their country from the Aragonese monarchy. *Ibid.* I. v. 233 Isabella..would not consent to the dismemberment of a single inch of the Castilian territory.

c. quasi-*concr.* A detached part formed by separation from the main body.

1830 LINDLEY *Nat. Syst. Bot.* 98 This order approaches more near to Urticeæ and Cupuliferæ than either Plataneæ or Salicineæ, which may be considered dismemberments of it. **1873** MIVART *Elem. Anat.* iv. 169 An extra bone which exists in many vertebrates..is most probably a dismemberment of the scaphoid.

3. Expulsion or cutting off from membership.

1658–9 *Burton's Diary* (1828) III. 262 Reports from the Committee of Privileges and Dismemberment.

'dismembrate, *v. rare.* [f. ppl. stem of med.L. *dismembrāre* to DISMEMBER.] *trans.* To disintegrate or dismember; *spec.* so as to separate the flour from the bran after grinding.

1877 *Specif. Patent* No. 4099 (Pieper), The design of a machine by which the products obtained from roller mills may be finally reduced or 'dismembrated'.

†**dismem'bration.** *Obs.* [ad. med.L. *dismembrātiōn-em*, n. of action f. *dismembrāre*: see -ATION. Cf. OF. *demanbration* (1366 in Godef.), and DEMEMBRATION.]

= DISMEMBERMENT.

1597 [see DEMEMBRATION]. **1653** GATAKER *Vind. Annot. Jer.* 175 A very maimed and mangled dismembration and deartuation, rather then division and distribution of it. **1822** SCOTT *Nigel* xxx, Prosecuted on the lesser offence..*usque ad mutilationem*, even to dismemberation.

'dismembrator. [agent-n. f. med.L. *dismembrāre* to DISMEMBER.] Something that dismembrates or disintegrates; *spec.* an apparatus for separating flour from bran, after crushing in a roller mill.

1877 *Specif. Patent* No. 4099 (Pieper) A dismembrator for flour mills. **1881** *Times* 18 May 6/1 To divide and scatter the crushed meal..the meal passes through a dismembrator, consisting of discs armed with pins or pegs, one rapidly rotating disc driving the stuff between the pins upon [another] stationary [disc].

†**dis'merit,** *v. Obs.* [f. DIS- 6 or 7 a + MERIT *v.* or *sb.*: cf. DEMERIT *v.* 2–4.]

1. a. *trans.* To deprive of merit, take away the merit of; = DEMERIT *v.* 2. **b.** *intr.* To lose merit, incur blame; cf. DEMERIT *v.* 4.

1484 CAXTON *Fables of Æsop* II. xix, An almesse that is done for vayne glorye is not merited but dismeryted. **1622** MABBE tr. *Aleman's Guzman d'Alf.* II. 76 Neither my service dis-merited with My Lord, nor their friendship fayled me at my need.

2. *trans.* To fail to merit; = DEMERIT *v.* 3.

1622 MABBE tr. *Aleman's Guzman d'Alf.* I. 58 Since they have dis-merited this [blessing] by disobedience. **1629** —— tr. *Fonseca's Dev. Contempl.* 409 Our Sauior would therby giue her occasion to confesse her fault, and not to dismerit the mercie that was offered vnto her.

†**dis'mettled,** *ppl. a. Obs. rare.* [DIS- 7 a.] Deprived or devoid of mettle; spiritless.

1650 LLEWELLYN *Pref. Verses J. Gregory's Posthuma*, Graie Customs which our dead dismettled sloth Gave up.

†**dis'might,** *v. Obs. rare.* [DIS- 7 a.] *trans.* To deprive of might, render powerless.

c **1586** C'TESS PEMBROKE *Ps.* lxxi. vii, Make them fall disgraced, shamed, All dissmighted, all diffamed.

†**dis'mingle,** *v. Obs. rare.* [DIS- 6.] *trans.* To extricate, disentangle (= F. *démêler*).

1669 GALE *True Idea Jansenisme* 90 Things being thus dismingled and differenced.

disminion, disminister, *vbs.*: see DIS- 7 b.

dismiss (dɪs'mɪs), *v.* Pa. t. and pple. **dismissed**; in 5–7 **dismyste, -mist.** [app. f. L. *dīmiss-* ppl. stem of *dīmittĕre* to send away (see DIMIT) with the prefix altered to DIS- after the already existing DISMIT, OF. *desmetre*. It appears to occur first in the pa. pple. *dismissed*, used by Caxton (see sense 3) to render the OF. pa. pple. *desmis* (= L. *dīmissus*), and it is probable that this was the way by which *dismiss* became at length the accepted Eng. repr. of L. *dīmittĕre* in all its senses. It was preceded in use by DISMIT, and had to contend in 16–17th c. with the etymologically more regular forms DIMIT, DIMISS, as well as DEMIT *v.*[2] (from F. *démettre*).]

1. a. *trans.* To send away in various directions, disperse, dissolve (a gathering of people, etc.); to disband (an army, etc.).

1582 N.T. (Rhem.) *Acts* xix. 41 He dismissed the assemblie. **1596** SHAKS. *Merch. V.* IV. i. 104, I may dismisse this Court. **1653** H. COGAN tr. *Pinto's Trav.* vi. 16 Relying on this Treaty of Peace he dismist his Army. **1673** RAY *Journ. Low C.* Venice 181 After this..the Council is dismist. **1784** COWPER *Tiroc.* 624 Dismiss their cares when they dismiss their flock. **1819** SHELLEY *Cenci* I. iii. 93 For God's sake Let me dismiss the guests!

b. *intr.* (for *refl.*) To disperse from ordered assembly; to break ranks by word of command.

1809 A. ADAM in Scott *Fam. Lett.* (1894) I. 155 He.. added faintly, 'But it grows dark, very dark, the boys may dismiss'. **1837** CARLYLE *Fr. Rev.* VII. ix. (1872) I. 240 Finally the National Assembly is harangued..and dismisses for this night. **1859** GEN. P. THOMPSON *Audi Alt.* II. xcviii. 86 A ministry, which..scatters the boasted counsellors, like a battalion on the word 'Dis-miss'.

2. a. *trans.* To send away (a person); to give permission to go; to bid depart.

1548 HALL *Chron., Edw. IV.* (an. 10) 214 b, So with fayre wordes..he dismissed the messengers. **1593** SHAKS. *3 Hen. VI*, III. ii. 78 Please you dismisse me, eyther with I, or no. **1667** MILTON *P.L.*, VII. 108 We can..dismiss thee ere the Morning shine. **1725** DE FOE *Voy. round World* (1840) 50 To dismiss my visitor. **1847** TENNYSON *Princ.* IV. 341 Your oath is broken: we dismiss you: go.

b. *transf.* To send forth (a thing); to let go; to give issue or egress to.

1601 SHAKS. *Jul. C.* I. iii. 97 Life being wearie of these worldly Barres, Neuer lacks power to dismisse it selfe. **1670** COTTON *Espernon* I. III. 116 In a moment he vomited out a life, that ought not to have been dismist, till after the horror of a thousand torments. **1768** HAWKESWORTH tr. *Télémaque* xv. (1784) 144/2 As a slinger whirls a stone that he would dismiss with all his strength. **1854** OWEN in *Circ. Sc.* (*c* 1865) II. 65/2 They dismiss the great optic nerves by a notch.

3. a. To send away or remove from office, employment, or position; to discharge, discard, expel. Const. *from*, †*of*, and *double obj.*

c **1477** CAXTON *Jason* 80 Zethephius dismissed of his office ..attemprid his corage..so well..that [etc.]. **1481** in *Eng. Gilds* (1870) 313 To be thysmyste from the forsayde fraternyte. **1579** LYLY *Euphues* (Arb.) 194, I meane shortly to sue to the Empresse to be dismissed of the court. **1692** LUTTRELL *Brief Rel.* (1857) II. 369 Yesterday Sir John Lowther was dismist the treasury. *a* **1700** DRYDEN *To Ld. Clifford* (L.), He soon dismiss'd himself from state affairs. **1719** DE FOE *Crusoe* (1840) II. iv. 72 They dismissed them the society. **1874** GREEN *Short Hist.* viii. §2. 477 The King dismissed those of his ministers who still opposed a Spanish policy.

b. To discharge from service (a hired vehicle, etc.).

1600 E. BLOUNT tr. *Conestaggio* 299 Yet did they not dismisse their hired ships. **1836** MARRYAT *Japhet* lxxi. 137, I dismissed the coach.

c. *Cricket.* To put (a batsman or side) out (usu. *for* a score).

1875 *Field* 22 May 501 Ten runs later Mr Longman was dismissed, and sundry changes were made in the bowling. **1892** *Times* 22 July 7 Afterwards Gunn saw the rest of his side dismissed, and took out his bat for a faultless 98. **1912** A. BRAZIL *New Girl at St. Chad's* vii. 111 The St. Hilary side was dismissed for sixty-seven. **1933** D. L. SAYERS *Murder must Advertise* xviii. 306 The Brotherhoods were dismissed for 155, and the Pym Eleven gathered themselves together from the four corners of the field.

†**4.** To deprive or disappoint *of* or *from* some advantage. Cf. 10 a. *Obs.*

c **1489** CAXTON *Sonnes of Aymon* xx. 445 He was dysmyssed of his purpose. **1590** WEBBE *Trav.* (Arb.) 22 The Turke..might, if he would, dismisse them cleane from hauing any water at all. **1632** LITHGOW *Trav.* III. 104 The Galleys..durst not enter the harbour..The Florentines being dismissed of their Galleys, grew discouraged.

5. a. To release or discharge from confinement.

[*Dysmysse* in Halliwell's ed. of *Coventry Myst.* (1841) 315 is an alteration of the MS. *dymysse*.]

1651 N. BACON *Disc. Govt. Eng.* II. lxvi. 227 Persons taken and imprisoned upon excommunication are ordinarily dismist without satisfaction to the Prelate. **1709** STRYPE *Ann. Ref.* I. i. 38 So to dismiss them, and set them at liberty. **1783** J. C. SMYTH in *Med. Commun.* I 146 She..was dismissed the hospital, perfectly cured.

b. *transf.* and *fig.*

1591 SYLVESTER *Du Bartas* I. i. (1641) 7/2 Blushing Aurora had yet scarce dismist Mount Libanus from the Nights gloomy Mist. **1839** DE QUINCEY *Recoll. Lakes* Wks. 1862 II. 29 Sometimes a fall from the summit of awful precipices has dismissed them from the anguish of perplexity..by dismissing them at once from life.

6. To discard, reject; *esp.* (as Latin *dīmittĕre*) to put away, repudiate (a wife). Also *absol.*

1610 SHAKS. *Temp.* IV. i. 67 Broome-groues; Whose shadow the dismissed Batchelor loues. **1614** BP. HALL *Recoll. Treat.* 473 Whether the wronged husband..should retaine, or dismisse; dismissing, whether he may marry. **1625** BURGES *Pers. Tithes* 34 God..hath dismissed Leui, and repealed that Law of Tithes. **1649** BP. HALL *Cases Consc.* 393 Breach of wedlock..for which only had they dismissed their wives. **1834** S. GOBAT *Abyssinia* 346 When, therefore, a man has dismissed his third wife.

7. To put away, lay aside, divest oneself of, get rid of. (Now *rare* with regard to things material.)

1675 HOBBES *Odyssey* (1677) 162 [Gods] can their form dismiss, And, when they will, put on a new disguise. **1683** MRS. BEHN *Young King* V. i. 53 Dismiss her fetters, and if she please Let her have Garments suitable to her sex. *a* **1700** DRYDEN *Ovid's Met.* I. (R.) The crafty God His wings dismiss'd, but still retain'd his rod. **1772** JOHNSON *Lett. to Mrs. Thrale* 9 Nov., This will soon dismiss all incumbrances; and when no interest is paid, you will begin annually to lay up. **1851** RUSKIN *Stones Ven.* (1874) I. xxviii. 325 That the architrave shall entirely dismiss its three meagre lines.

8. a. To put away from the mind, leave out of consideration, cease to entertain (ideas, emotions, etc.).

1592 SHAKS. *Ven. & Ad.* 425 Dismiss your vows, your feigned tears. **1667** MILTON *P.L.* II. 282 Dismissing quite All thoughts of Warr. **1697** DRYDEN *Virg. Past.* vii. 10 He, smiling, said, Dismiss your Fear. **1784** COWPER *Task* VI. 442 Man may dismiss compassion from his heart, But God will never. **1884** *Manch. Exam.* 17 June 5/1 We may dismiss any apprehension that the political affairs of Egypt will be taken in charge.

†**b.** To allow to pass out of mind; to forgive; to forgo. *Obs.*

1603 SHAKS. *Meas. for M.* II. ii. 102 Those..which a dismis'd offence would after gaule. **1786** WESLEY *Wks.* (1872) IV. 345 The Elders of his Church..would dismiss my promise.

9. To pass from the consideration or the literary treatment of (a subject), to have done with, bring to an end; hence to treat of summarily.

1698 FRYER *Acc. E. Ind. & P.* 47 Before we dismiss this Discourse, it may be noted [etc.]. **1709** BERKELEY *Th. Vision* §40 Before we dismiss this subject. **1711** ADDISON *Spect.* No. 110 ¶7, I shall dismiss this Paper with a Story out of Josephus. **1873** TRISTRAM *Moab* v 70 Both De Saulcy and Lynch have dismissed Kerak very shortly.

10. *Law.* †**a.** *refl.* (with *of* or *inf.*) To relieve or free oneself from (a legal burden); to deprive or exclude oneself from (a legal advantage). *Obs.*

1562 in Strype *Ann. Ref.* I. xxxi. 356 Thereby to be dismissed of all action of debt or trespass. **1574** tr. *Littleton's Tenures* 53 b, Shee hathe utterlye dismissed her selfe to have anye parte of the tenementes. *a* **1626** BACON *Max. & Uses Com. Law* xvii. (1636) 64 The Court may dismisse themselves of discussing the matter by examination. **1642** PERKINS *Prof. Bk.* v. §448. 193 The husband doth presently dismisse himselfe of the possession.

b. To send out of court, refuse further hearing to, reject (a claim or action).

1607 SHAKS. *Cor.* II. i. 85 You..dismisse the Controuersie bleeding. **1713** SWIFT *Cadenus & Vanessa* Wks. 1755 III. II. 5 Therefore he humbly would insist, The bill might be with costs dismist. **1818** CRUISE *Digest* (ed. 2) VI. 352 The appeal should be dismissed and the decree affirmed. **1891** *Law Times* XCII. 93/2 The plaintiff's action was dismissed with costs.

Hence **dismissed** (dɪsˈmɪst) *ppl. a.*, **disˈmissing** *vbl. sb.*

1603-10 [see 8 b, 6, above]. **1611** COTGR., *Manumission*, a manumission, or dismissing. **1627** [see DISMISSION 2 b]. **1824** L. MURRAY *Eng. Gram.* (ed. 5) I. 266 'What is the reason of this person's dismissing of his servant so hastily?'

†**disˈmiss,** *sb. Obs.* [f. prec. vb.] An act of dismissing, a dismissal; also, a document embodying a dismissal.

1589 RALEIGH *Let.* in *N. & Q.* Ser. III. IV. 3 Order from the Queen for a dismis of their cavelacions. **1618** L. PARSONS in *Lismore Papers* (1887) Ser. II. II. 154, I send away this bearer..with his dissmiss hereinclosed. **1645** MILTON *Tetrach.* Wks. 1738 I. 265 Provided that the dismiss was not without reasonable conditions to the Wife. **1678** *Massacre Irel.* 2 The Priests gave the People a dismiss at Mass. **1705** DE FOE *Review* 17 Feb. in Arb. *Garner* VII. 624 At the dismiss of their work.

dismissal (dɪsˈmɪsəl). [f. DISMISS *v.* + -AL[1]; cf. *committal*, *refusal*, *upheaval*. A recent word equivalent to, and now tending to displace the more regular DISMISSION.] = DISMISSION, q.v. for detail of senses.

Not in JOHNSON or ASH.

1818 TODD, *Dismissal*, a word of recent use for *dismission*. **1825** JAMIESON, *Dismissal*, Mr. Todd has introduced this as 'a word of recent usage for dismission'. But it is of long standing in Scotland.

a **1806** BP. HORSLEY *Serm.* xxxviii. (1826) 468 'Send her away', that is, grant her petition, and give her her dismissal. **1816** SCOTT *Old Mort.* v, Never conceived the possibility of such a thing as dismissal. **1842-3** GROVE *Corr. Phys Forces* 3 (L.) Requesting..dismissal from the minds of my readers of preconceived views. **1849** MACAULAY *Hist. Eng.* II. 13 His dismissal produced a great sensation. **1885** *Weekly Notes* 28 Mar. 67/1 Notwithstanding the dismissal of the action. **1889** J. M. DUNCAN *Lect. Dis. Women* xvi. 120 This patient has returned since dismissal [from hospital].

attrib. **1891** *Pall Mall G.* 5 Mar. 6/1 The matron's exercise of her dismissal powers.

dismissible (dɪsˈmɪsɪb(ə)l), *a.* Also **-able.** [f. DISMISS *v.*, on analogy of *permissible*: see -BLE.] Liable to be dismissed or discharged.

1824 *Examiner* 422/2 A motion..for the dismissal of the Recorder—if he be dismissable. **1863** *Sat. Rev.* 370 A King dismissible on proof of legal crime. **1876** GRANT *Burgh Sch. Scotl.* II. xii. 322 The teachers..are appointed and dismissible by the rector.

disˈmissing, *ppl. a.* [f. as prec. + -ING[2].] That dismisses. Hence **disˈmissingly** *adv.*, with a tendency to dismiss.

1802 *Spirit Pub. Jrnls.* (1803) VI. 133 He received his dismissing fee of five guineas. **1880** G. MEREDITH *Trag. Com.* xvii. (1892) 236 She..very bluntly and dismissingly felt now that his madness was at its climax.

dismission (dɪsˈmɪʃən). [n. of action from DISMISS *v.*, corresponding to L. *dīmissiōn-em* and OF. *desmission* 'dismissing, forgoing, resignation', etc. (Cotgr.), mod.F. *démission* renunciation. See the doublets DIMISSION and DEMISSION[2].] The action of dismissing; the fact of being dismissed. Now largely replaced in all senses by the equivalent DISMISSAL, q.v.

1. The formal dispersion, or sending away in various directions, of an assemblage of persons; disbanding of troops.

a **1646** J. GREGORY *De Æris et Epochis* in *Posthuma* (1650) 139 The Indictions began at the verie dismission of the Nicene Council. **1659** B. HARRIS *Parival's Iron Age* 252 To content themselves with that dismission of the new Troops, which was already made. **1711** *Lond. Gaz.* No. 4840/2 The Diet..had this Day a final Dismission. **1798** WELLESLEY in Owen *Desp.* 56 The dismission of the French corps raised at Mauritius would discourage other adventurers of that nation. **1825** *Sporting Mag.* XVI. 406 Watching their twelve o'clock dismission from school.

2. The sending away of a person; permission to go, leave to depart; often in earlier use, formal leave-taking.

1608 BP. HALL *Char. Virtues & V.*, *Busie-Bodie* 81 Hee runnes to them..and after many thanks and dismissions is hardly intreated silence. **1614** RALEIGH *Hist. World* II. 250 After this dismission of Hobab, Israel began to march towards the Desarts. **1660** F. BROOKE tr. *Le Blanc's Trav.* 190 The King..in presence of all the Court, gives him a dismission. **1703** MAUNDRELL *Journ. Jerus.* (1721) 31 To give a civil dismission to the visitants. **1791** COWPER *Odyss.* xv. 19 From brave Menelaus ask Dismission hence.

b. A sending away from, or ushering out of, life.

1627 DONNE *Serm.* xxviii. 282 There falls..a Dismission, a dismissing out of this world. **1685** N. MATHER in C. Mather *Magn. Chr.* (1853) II. 168 Dissolution..is but a dismission of the spirit into its happiness. **1734** WATTS *Reliq. Juv.* (1789) 126 Give me a glorious dismission into that intellectual and blissful world. **1795** GIBBON *Autobiog.* 92 The final dismission of the hero through the ivory gate.

3. Deprivation of office, dignity, or position; discharge from service.

1547 WRIOTHESLEY *Chron.* (1875) I. 187 Synce the dismission of my Lord Wriothesley, late Chauncelor. **1670** MILTON *Hist. Eng.* II. Wks. (1851) 76 He was fain at length to seek a dismission from his charge. **1754** RICHARDSON *Grandison* (1781) VII. vi. 27 The power, madam, of change or dismission thro' the house, is entirely yours. **1816** SCOTT *Old Mort.* ii, Pains, penalties, and threats of dismission were denounced in vain. **1849** MACAULAY *Hist. Eng.* I. 431 To be punished by dismission from the public service.

b. The written or spoken form of words in which such discharge is couched.

1606 SHAKS. *Ant. & Cl.* I. i. 26 Your dismission Is come from Cæsar, therefore heare it Anthony. **1679** CROWNE *Ambit. Statesm.* I. 1 A soft dismission stuft with downy words. **1786** MAD. D'ARBLAY *Diary* 8 Aug., The general form of the dismission..is in these words.

4. Release from confinement; setting free, liberation, discharge.

1609 BIBLE (Douay) *Lev.* xvi. 10 That, whose lotte was to be the goate of dismission. **1642** ROGERS *Naaman* 319 The Jew..slave..at his dismission was to have a gratuity paid him. **1709** STRYPE *Ann. Ref.* I. i. 38 *marg.*, Order for dismission of prisoners in the Queen's bench.

attrib. **1777** HOWARD *Prisons Eng.* (1780) 244 The dismission fee of each prisoner discharged out of custody.

5. Rejection, discarding; *esp.* repudiation or putting away of a wife.

1611 SHAKS. *Cymb.* II. iii. 57 You in all obey her, Saue when command to your dismission tends. **1643** MILTON *Divorce* iv. Wks. (1851) 30 Thence this wise and pious Law of dismission tooke beginning. **1645** —— *Colast.* ibid. 353 If hee dismiss her with a beneficent and peacefull dismission.

6. Putting aside from consideration; expulsion from the mind.

1742 YOUNG *Nt. Th.* v. 295 Friends counsel quick dismission of our grief. **1779-81** JOHNSON *L.P.*, *Pope* Wks. IV. 107 The rectitude of Dryden's mind was sufficiently shewn by the dismission of his poetical prejudices. **1830** HERSCHEL *Stud. Nat. Phil.* §70 To demand of him an instant and peremptory dismission of all his former opinions.

dismissive (dɪsˈmɪsɪv), *a.* [f. DISMISS *v.* + -IVE.]

a. Of the nature of, or characterized by, dismissal; tending to dismiss; valedictory.

1645 MILTON *Tetrach.* Wks. (1851) 221 The law of Moses ..only requires the dismissive writing without other caution. **1683** O. U. *Parish Ch. no Conventicles* 32 The *Ite missa*, or dismissive Blessing. **1888** A. S. WILSON *Lyric Hopeless Love* 131 The loves peruse the leaf To find no revelancy there Dismissive of unsolved despair.

b. Tending to dismiss from consideration as insignificant; characterized by rejection, contemptuous.

1930 *Observer* 22 June 7 What gives length to his shot is the concentration of force on each moment of impact, and a similar dismissive violence is achieved when the final couplet of the Byronic mode adds witty rhyme to witty sense. **1966** *Listener* 27 Oct. 631/1 The visual rhetoric towards the end of the film—people drinking, listening to music, holidaying—was banal and dismissive, an unrelated flourish suggesting abstract happiness. **1974** J. I. M. STEWART *Gaudy* xi. 201 He produced a graciously dismissive inclination of the head. **1982** *Encounter* Apr. 42 Their dicta Relegated to dismissive footnotes.

Hence **disˈmissively** *adv.*

1922 W. J. LOCKE *Tale of Triona* vii. 70 'He has written a book on Russia,' replied Olivia dryly. 'I'm fed up with Russia,' said Lydia dismissively. **1968** S. HILL *Gentleman & Ladies* I. iv. 42 'Some personal bits and pieces,' he said dismissively, 'all shares in property..jointly to be shared between my sisters.' **1972** T. STOPPARD *Jumpers* I. 18 She flaps a hand dismissively at the *jumpers*. **1985** A. T. ELLIS *Unexplained Laughter* 107 'I have a great deal to do,' she said in a dismissively grown-up voice.

†**disˈmissment.** *Obs.* [f. as prec. + -MENT.] = DISMISSION, DISMISSAL.

1591 HORSEY *Trav.* (Hakl. Soc.) 204 Glad of so peaceable a dismistment. **1650** T. BAYLY *Herba Parietis* 20 Maximanus asked..what she meant by that strange picture ..adding, moreover, the dismisment of the artist.

dismissory (dɪsˈmɪsərɪ), *a.* (*sb.*) [f. DISMISS *v.*: see DIMISSORY.] Of or pertaining to dismission or leave-taking; parting, valedictory; = DIMISSORY 1, 2.

1647 TRAPP *Comm. Matt.* xxvi. 30 This [Psalm] they began to sing after that dismissory cup. **1664** H. MORE *Myst. Iniq.* 104 Ordained without Letters dismissory.

†**B.** *sb.* (*pl.*) = DIMISSORY *sb.*

1716 M. DAVIES *Athen. Brit.* III. *Crit. Hist.* 87 Dismissories or Certificats of the Orthodox Ethicks of the Bearer.

†**diˈsmit,** *v. Obs.* Also 4 **dismette,** 4-5 **dis-, dysmytte.** [app. a latinized adaptation, through *dismette*, of OF. *desmetre*, repr. a late pop. L. type *dismittĕre* instead of cl. L. *dīmittĕre* (cf. DIMIT).]

1. *trans.* To send away, dismiss; to let go, release; = DIMIT *v.* 1.

1382 WYCLIF *Acts* iii. 13 Whom ʒe..denyeden bifore the face of Pilate, him demynge for to be dismyttid [Vulg. *dimitti*] or left. *Ibid.* xvii. 10 Bretheren dismittiden Poul and Silas in to Beroan.

2. *refl.* To divest or deprive oneself of; to surrender, relinquish. Cf. DISMISS *v.* 10 a.

13.. *Minor Poems fr. Vernon MS.* 536 As longe as þou mayʒt holde in honde, Dismette þe nouʒt of þi londe [Fr. *Taunt cum poyez aleyne trere, Ne vus demettez de vostre tere*]. **1394** *Recognizance* in *Collect. Top. & Gen.* (1836) III. 257 We hadde ous fulliche dismettyd of the same londis. *c* **1440** *Partonope* 7372 Gaudyn and Aupatryse Have dyssmyttyde him clene of the pryse. **1496** *Dives & Paup.* (W. de W.) IV. iv. 164/1, I wolde not counseyll theym fully to dysmytten them of her good.

dismoded (dɪsˈməʊdɪd), *a.* Anglicization of DÉMODÉ *a.*

1898 *Blackw. Mag.* Nov. 693/2 A tune dismoded, common. **1907** *Ibid.* Sept. 428 His ambition was the ambition now wholly dismoded, to make scholars and gentlemen. **1917** *Daily Mail* 25 Aug. 2/4 The works of Frith, Leighton, and other dismoded veterans. **1922** *Blackw. Mag.* June 806/1 The men of genius who are its peculiar glory seem dismoded to the anarchs who write in hopeless competition with them.

†**disˈmortgage,** *v. Obs. rare.* [DIS- 7 a.] *trans.* To free from mortgage, disencumber.

1640 HOWELL *Dodona's G.* (1645) 52 He dismorgag'd the Crown demeans.

dismount (dɪsˈmaʊnt), *v.* [f. DIS- 6 + MOUNT *v.*: perh. after OF. *desmonter* (12-13th c. in Hatz-Darm.), mod.F. *démonter* = It. *dismontare*, Sp. *desmontar*, med.L. *dismontāre* (Du Cange). Cf. also obs. doublet DEMOUNT, from 15th c. French.]

I. *intransitive.*

1. To come down from a height; to descend.

1579 SPENSER *Sheph. Cal.* May 315 The bright Sunne gynneth to dismount. **1589** GREENE *Menaphon* (Arb.) 60 Cupide [had] dismounted from his mothers lappe, left his bow, and quiuer at random. **1677** CROWNE *Destr. Jerusalem* I. Song, Dram. Wks. 1873 II. 242 Day is dismounted on the watery plain. **1725** POPE *Odyss.* xx. 76 If dismounted from the rapid cloud, Me with his whelming wave let Ocean shrowd!

2. To get down, alight (*from* a horse or other animal; also, formerly, *from* a vehicle).

[**1533** BELLENDEN *Livy* III. (1822) 295 Incontinent the horsmen of twa legionis..demountit haistilie fra thare hors.] **1588** SHAKS. *Tit. A.* v. ii. 54, I will dismount, and by the Waggon wheele, Trot like a Seruile footeman. **1598** BARRET *Theor. Warres* IV. i. 102 Neither yet in the day of battell ought he to dismount. **1605** *Play Stucley* in Simpson *Sch. Shaks.* (1878) I. 251 Dismount thee Muly from thy chariot wheels. **1697** DRYDEN *Virg. Georg.* Ded. (1721) I. 189 He..dismounted from the Saddle. **1705** *Lond. Gaz.* No. 4151/3 Their Dragoons dismounted. **1788** GIBBON *Decl. & F.* l. (1846) V. 16 He instantly dismounted to present the pilgrim with his camel. **1832** W. IRVING *Alhambra* II. 174 Every horseman was obliged to dismount at the gate.

fig. **1817** KEATS *Lett.* Wks. 1889 III. 95, I am in a fair way now to come to a conclusion..I shall be glad to dismount for a month or two.

b. *spec.* of a stallion.

1674 N. COX *Gentl. Recreat.* v. (1686) 17 Cold water to throw on the Mare's Shape, immediately on the dismounting of the Horse.

II. *transitive.*

3. To come down from (a height or elevated place); to descend. *Obs.* (exc. as associated with next.)

1589 *Gold. Mirr.* (1851) 10 Dismounting thus the hill, I did retyre. **1620** QUARLES *Jonah* in Farr *S.P. Jas. I* (1848) 131 He straight dismounts his throne. **1658** R. FRANCK *North. Mem.* (1821) 33 It's only dismounting our apartments to mount our horses. **1844** [see DISMOUNTING below].

4. To get off, alight from (a horse, etc.).

c **1620** Z. BOYD *Zion's Flowers* (1855) 30 Dismount your.. steeds. **1638** SIR T. HERBERT *Trav.* (ed. 2) 96 Hee is made to dismount his Elephant. **1859** REEVE *Brittany* 236 A peasant has just dismounted his white horse.

5. (*causal*) To throw down from a horse, etc.; to unseat, unhorse.

1599 SHAKS. *Hen. V*, III. vii. 84 Your Horse..would trot as well, were some of your bragges dismounted. **1633** P. FLETCHER *Purple Isl.* XI. xx, The Martial Virgins spear.. dismounts her foe on dustie plain. **1667** MILTON *P.L.* VII. 19 Least from this flying Steed unrein'd.. Dismounted, on th' Aleian Field I fall. **1838** LYTTON *Leila* II. ii, Several of his knights were dismounted.

b. To deprive of horses; the opposite of *mount* = to supply with horses.

1866 W. WATSON *Youatt's Horse* vi. (1872) 122 Diseases that used to dismount whole troops.

6. To remove (a thing) from that on which it has been mounted; *esp.* to take or throw down (a gun or cannon) from its carriage or other support, either deliberately for tactical purposes, or by hostile missiles.

1544 *Exped. Scotl.* B iij/1 One of our peices, with shotte out of the sayde castel, was stroken and dismounted. **1585** T. WASHINGTON tr. *Nicholay's Voy.* I. xix. 22 They burst one of their best peeces, and dismounted foure other. **1625** MARKHAM *Soldier's Accid.* 26 Dismount your Musquet, and carrie it with the Rest. **1659** D. PELL *Impr. Sea* 542 Trees are rent up by the roots, and out-housing dismounted. **1707** *Lond. Gaz.* No. 4359/2 One of our Ships..had dismounted Two of their Batteries. **1845** S. AUSTIN *Ranke's Hist. Ref.* II. 345 Part of their cannon..they dismounted and placed on mules. **1879** *Cassell's Techn. Educ.* IV. 46/1 A whole drawer-full of mounted shells may, by bad handling, be dismounted from their tablet at one shock.

7. To take (a thing) out of that in which it is set or enclosed; to remove (a gem, etc.) from its setting or 'mount'; to take (mechanism) from its framework, take to pieces. †*dismount thy tuck* (Shaks.): draw thy rapier from its sheath.

1601 SHAKS. *Twel. N.* III. iv. 244. **1683** BURNET tr. *More's Utopia* (1685) 98 Nor will Men buy it [a precious stone] unless it be dismounted and taken out of the Gold. **1859** *Musketry Instr.* 13 When the lock is dismounted.

8. To set, put, or bring down from an elevated position; to lower. ? *Obs.* (In 1597 *fig.* from 6.)

1597 SHAKS. *Lover's Compl.* 281 His watrie eies he did dismount, Whose sightes till then were leaueled on my face. **1633** G. HERBERT *Temple, Man* iv, His eyes dismount the highest starre. **1665** SIR T. HERBERT *Trav.* (1677) 66 The Doolaes were no sooner dismounted, but that thereout issued the Amazones. **1742** YOUNG *Nt. Th.* VII. 1192 Sorceries of Sense..Dismount her [the soul] from her native Wing.

†**9.** *fig.* (largely from 5): **a.** To bring down from lofty position or high estimation; to cast down, lower, debase. *Obs.*

1608 DAY *Law Trickes* v. (1881) 81 Now Daughter make thee fit To combat and dismount her actiue wit. **1654** WHITLOCK *Zootomia* 447 The positive Detractor.. dismounts the most merited Reputation with some But. *a* **1718** PENN *Maxims* Wks. 1726 I. 824 Drunkenness..spoils Health, dismounts the Mind, and unmans Men.

†**b.** To reduce to an inferior position, degrade, depose (a person). *Obs.*

1607–12 BACON *Ess., Superstition* (Arb.) 342 But Superesticion dismountes all this [Sense, Philosophy, Piety, etc.] and erecteth an absolute Tyranny, in the minde of Men. **1651** N. BACON *Disc. Govt. Eng.* II. xiii. (1739) 69 Dukes were dismounted without conviction. *a* **1677** BARROW *Serm.* (1687) I. xxv. 344, Did not Samuel exercise such a charity, when..injuriously dismounted from his authority?

†**10.** To reduce to a plain; to level. *Obs. rare*⁻¹.

1563 SACKVILLE *Induct. to Mirr. Mag.*, Xerxes.. Dismounted hills, and made the vales uprear.

Hence **dis'mounting** *vbl. sb.* and *ppl. a.*

1560 WHITEHORNE *Ord. Souldiours* (1588) 36 To saue the saide artillerie from dismounting. **1654** WHITLOCK *Zootomia* 446 Cold Praise..or Interruption of it, with a Dismounting But. **1677** GILPIN *Demonol.* (1867) 272 Intended for the dismounting of the confidence of the wicked. **1844** DISRAELI *Coningsby* I. i. (L.), The number of stairs..the time their mountings and dismountings must have absorbed. **1870** *Daily News* 11 Nov., The dismounting of the heavy battery on the bank of the Rhine..commenced yesterday.

dis'mount, *sb.* [f. prec. vb.] An act or method of dismounting.

1654 GAYTON *Pleas. Notes* III. viii. 123 A Tournament, [led] to an Over-turne; that, to a Dismount. **1886** *Cyclist* 6 Oct. 1325/1 The pedal dismount is the best for this form of bicycle. **1888** *Chicago Advance* 5 July, Frequent dismounts [from bicycle] in connection with a hot pace, are fatiguing.

dismountable (dɪsˈmaʊntəb(ə)l), *a.* [f. DISMOUNT *v.* + -ABLE.] Capable of being dismounted. Of a gun or cannon: capable of being removed from its carriage for transport.

1711 *Fingall MSS.* in *10th Rep. Hist. MSS. Comm.* (1885) App. v. 168 The garrison had a battery..which..was not dismountable, by reason of its lowness. **1900** *Engineering Mag.* XIX. 789/2 A gun made dismountable, that it may be easily carried by men or animals. **1903** *Westm. Gaz.* 17 Nov. 9/1 The gun is provided with..dismountable shields. **1960** *Farmer & Stockbreeder* 12 Jan. 81/3 About 50 black-and-white steers are early weaned in these home-made dismountable pens along one side of the dry cows' shed.

dis'mounted, *ppl. a.* [f. DISMOUNT *v.* + -ED¹.]

a. Off one's horse; not on horseback. **b.** Of a cannon: Dislodged from its carriage.

1610 GUILLIM *Heraldry* IV. xiv. (1611) 225 He beareth argent, a culuering dismounted. **1724** DE FOE *Mem. Cavalier* (1840) 232 Our dismounted men..lined the edge of the wood. **1765** *Univ. Mag.* XXXVII. 85/1 The barrel of a dismounted gun. **1886** *Manch. Exam.* 19 Jan. 5/6 A dismounted party of the same regiment.

† **di'smove**, *v. Obs.* In 5 dis-, dys-meve, -moeue. [ad. OF. *desmoveir*, *desmo(u)voir* (14th c. in Godef.), mod.F. *démouvoir*, ad. L. *dismovēre*, variant (and Romanic form) of *dīmovēre*, f. *dis-*, DIS- 1 + *movēre* to move. For the vowel change (*-meve*) see MOVE.] *trans.* To move away, remove.

1480 CAXTON *Ovid's Metam.* XV. ix, To dismeve away her sorowe. **1491** —— *Vitas Patr.* (W. de W. 1495) II. 234 a/2 The montayne of Syon..whiche shall be neuer dismoeued. **1611** FLORIO, *Scomouere*, to dismooue, to disorder.

dis'murdered, -'murderized, *ppl. adjs. nonce-wds.* [DIS- 7b.] Divested of the character of murder; pronounced to be not murder.

1817 BENTHAM *Parl. Reform* Introd. 140 *note*, The commission of legally dismurdered murders. *Ibid.*, The perpetration of the dismurderized murders.

dismutase (ˈdɪsmjuːteɪz). *Biochem.* [f. DISMUT(ATION + -ASE.] Any enzyme that catalyses a dismutation reaction. Chiefly in *Comb.*, esp. **superoxide dismutase** (catalysing the dismutation of superoxide ions into oxygen).

1937 [see ENOL]. **1968** MCCORD & FRIDOVICH in *Jrnl. Biol. Chem.* CCXLIII. 5759/2 This..establishes that the bovine erythrocyte dismutase is distinct from carbonic anhydrase. *Ibid.*, This particular dismutase activity could be of importance to living cells. **1969** *Ibid.* CCXLIV. 6049 (*heading*) Superoxide dismutase. **1975** *Nature* 7 Aug. 510/1 Research on superoxide dismutase has suggested that this enzyme may also have controlled oxygen toxicity in ancient living tissue. **1983** *Oxf. Textbk. Med.* I. VI. 66/1 Once an electron is successfully attached to an oxygen molecule it becomes a highly corrosive superoxide ion... Superoxide dismutase and various peroxidases have evolved to protect most cells from the effects of the spontaneous superoxide ion formation that occurs.

dismutation (dɪsmjuːˈteɪʃən). *Chem.* and *Biochem.* [DIS-.] Disproportionation: usually, disproportionation involving the simultaneous oxidation and reduction of a compound in a biological context.

1926 *Chem. Abstr.* XX. 929 The great biological significance of dismutation instead of simple oxidation is emphasised. **1938** *Nature* 4 June 992/1 The principle of the hydrogen shift (dismutation), which governs the mechanism of alcoholic fermentation, has been carefully studied. **1954** *New Biol.* XVI. 65 The semiquinones probably disappear by dismutation into quinone and quinol. **1970** R. W. MCGILVERY *Biochem.* xiv. 270 Reactions such as this in which the oxidation of half of the substrate is counterbalanced by reduction of the other half are called dismutations.

Hence (as a back-formation) **di'smute** *v. intr.*, to undergo dismutation.

1947 *Science News* V. 91 In neutral or slightly acid soils, tervalent manganese..dismutes forming manganese dioxide and bivalent manganese. **1957** G. E. HUTCHINSON *Treat. Limnol.* I. xv. 802 This material dismutes, the reaction being equivalent to $Mn_2O_3 \rightarrow MnO_2 + MnO$.

dismyssaries, var. DIMISSARIES, *Obs.*

† **dis'mystery**, *v. Obs. rare.* [DIS- 7a or b.] *trans.* To divest of mystery.

1649 BLITHE *Eng. Improv. Impr.* 45 No man..hath published any thing..to dismystery the same [draining].

disna, *Sc.* = does not; see DO *v.*

† **dis'natural**, *a. Obs.* [ad. OF. *desnaturel* (in Godef.), f. *des-*, DIS- 4 + *naturel* NATURAL *a.*] Contrary to nature, unnatural.

[**1292** BRITTON I. xxxii. §22 Si tiels clers..soint a eus desnaturels]. *c* **1430** LYDG. *Bochas* I. i. (1544) 2b, To beholde a thing disnaturall. *c* **1477** CAXTON *Jason* 10 Ryght myserable and right disnaturall enuie. **1677** GALE *Crt. Gentiles* II. IV. 223 Atheisme is a proposition so disnatural, monstrose and difficult to be establisht.

Hence †**dis'naturalness**, unnatural behaviour.

1430 LYDG. *Chron. Troy* I. vii, Iason..Receyued hath *penan tallionis* Of the goddes for his disnaturelnesse.

† **dis'natural**, *v. Obs.* [in a. f. prec. adj.; in b. f. DIS- 8 + NATURAL *a.*: cf. next.] **a.** *trans.* or *intr.* To make or become unnatural; to brutalize. **b.** *trans.* = DENATURALIZE 2, DISNATURALIZE.

1549 *Compl. Scotl.* viii. 73 Al pepil ar disnaturalit fra there gude nature..ȝe ar mair disnaturellit nor is brutal beystis. **1588** R. PARKE tr. *Mendoza's Hist. China* 70 Vpon paine to bee disnaturalled of the countrie.

dis'naturalize, *v.* [f. DIS- 6 + NATURALIZE; cf. Sp. *desnaturalizar* 'to banish, to outlaw' (Minsheu 1599).] = DENATURALIZE *v.* 1, 2. Hence **dis,naturalization** = DENATURALI'ZATION.

a **1704** LOCKE *Hist. Navigation* 490 (Seager) Magellan.. renounced his country, disnaturalizing himself as the custom then was. **1837** SOUTHEY *Doctor* CXV. IV. 127 [If] this well-known name [Job]..were disnaturalized and put out of use. **1874** LD. STANLEY *Magellan's 1st Voy.* p. xi, The custom..of disnaturalization, in accordance with which, any noble who felt aggrieved, formally renounced his fealty to the sovereign.

disnature (dɪsˈneɪtjʊə(r)), *v.* [ad. OF. *desnaturer* to change in nature, or change the nature of (Godef.), 'to make vnnaturall' (Cotgr.), It. *disnaturare*. See DIS- 4 and NATURE.]

†**1.** *intr.* To get into, or be in, an unnatural or disordered condition; to be unhealthy. *Obs.*

1481 CAXTON *Myrr.* I. xii. 37 So..trauaylleth phisyque to brynge Nature to poynt that disnatureth in mannes body whan ony maladye or sekenes encombreth hit.

2. *trans.* To render unnatural; to deprive of natural quality, character, appearance, etc. Hence **dis'natured** *ppl. a.*

c **1450** *Merlin* 425 Ymage repaired and disnatured fro kynde, holde thy pees. **1603** FLORIO *Montaigne* (1632) 493 There are many..who think to honour their nature, by disnaturing themselues. **1753** CHURCHILL *Gotham* III. 18 Can the stern mother..From her disnatur'd breast tear her young child? **1841** D'ISRAELI *Amen. Lit.* (1867) 307 A sister disnatured of all kin, hastening to be the voluntary accuser of her father. **1877** BLACKIE *Wise Men* 161 The disnatured skin Showed livid, flecked with crimson.

† **disne'glect**, *v. Obs. rare.* [f. DIS- 5 + NEGLECT *v.*] *trans.* To neglect.

1800 *True Briton* in *Spirit Pub. Jrnls.* (1801) IV. 50 Disneglecting his duty, out of nothing but a piece of pride!

disner, disnier, var. DECENER, *Obs.*

† **dis'nerve**, *v. Obs. rare.* [DIS- 7a + NERVE *sb.*: cf. obs. F. *desnerver* (Cotgr.).] *trans.* To deprive of nerve or vigour; to weaken, relax.

a **1618** SYLVESTER *Mem. Mortality* lxxxvi, All Idelness disnatures Wit, dis-nerves it. *Ibid.* [see DISAPT].

disnest (dɪsˈnɛst), *v. rare.* [DIS- 7c.] *trans.* To dislodge from, or as from, a nest; also, to void (as a nest) *of* its occupants.

1596 *Life Scanderbeg* 41 To chastise the garrison of the Turkes, and to chase and disnest them out of their holde. *a* **1700** DRYDEN *Life of Lucian* (1711) 43 To disnest Heaven of so many immoral and debauch'd Deities.

† **dis'nestle**, *v. Obs. rare.* [f. DIS- 6 + NESTLE. Cf. *unnestle*.] *trans.* To turn out of a nest.

1626 T. H. *Caussin's Holy Crt.* 221 Birds are disnestled from the kingdome which nature hath allowed them.

Disneyesque (ˌdɪznɪˈɛsk), *a.* [f. the name of Walter Elias *Disney* (1901–66), American cartoonist + -ESQUE.] Having the characteristics or resembling the style of an animated cartoon made by Walt Disney or his company. So **'Disneyland**, the name of a large amusement park near Los Angeles, devised by Walt Disney, applied *transf.* to any fantastic or fanciful land or place; a never-never land.

1939 AUDEN & ISHERWOOD *Journey to War* ii. 63 Lady Precious Stream utters some piercing, Disneyesque sounds. **1956** A. HUXLEY *Adonis & Alphabet* 170 The Mother of the greeting cards inhabits a delicious Disneyland, where everything is syrup and Technicolor, cuteness and schmalz. **1961** *Guardian* 3 Nov. 8/3 There are moments when the animal kingdom threatens to turn into Disneyland. **1963** P. H. JOHNSON *Night & Silence* xxxiii. 237 Already all over America these pretty, Disneyesque buildings proliferated.

disniche (dɪsˈnɪtʃ), *v.* [f. DIS- 7c + NICHE.] *trans.* To remove from its niche.

1889 *Jrnl. Educ.* 1 June 280/1, He could dis-niche, so to speak, whom he pleased.

† **dis'noble**, *a. Obs. rare.* [DIS- 10.] Ignoble, mean, petty.

1609 HOLLAND *Amm. Marcell* XXVIII. i. 326 A disnoble [*ignobilem*] advocat and defender of causes.

† **dis'noble**, *v. Obs.* [f. DIS- 8 + NOBLE *a.*: cf. obs. F. *desnoblir* to disgrace, vilify (Godef.).] *trans.* To deprive of nobility or grandeur; to DISENNOBLE.

1622 H. SYDENHAM *Serm. Sol. Occ.* II. (1637) 30 The chiefest complement of greatnesse is the retinue, take away her equipage you disnoble it. **1638** O. SEDGWICKE *Serm.* (1639) 36 O Watch, that it doth not dis-noble and staine its excellency by a sordid league..with sinfull lusts.

† **dis'nominate**, *v. Obs. rare.* [DIS- 6.] *trans.* To take away the name from.

1683 CAVE *Ecclesiastici* 223 Reducing it unto the rank of a Village, disnominating it, and not suffering it to bear the name of Caesar.

disnosed, disnumber: see DIS- 7a.

† **dis'null**, *v. Obs. rare.* In 6 dys-. [f. DIS- 5 + L. *null-us* none, null: cf. ANNUL. A variant of DENULL, DISANNUL.] *trans.* To bring to nothing, do away with, destroy.

1509 HAWES *Past. Pleas.* VIII. (1845) 31 To dysnull vyce and the vycious to blame. *Ibid.* XLIV. 216 Dysnullynge the sectes of false idolatry.

† **dis'nun**, *v. Obs. rare*⁻⁰. [f. DIS- 7b + NUN; cf. *disfriar*.] *trans.* To deprive of nun's orders; to unnun.

1611 FLORIO, *Dismonacare*, to vnfrier. Also to disnunne.

disobedience (dɪsəʊˈbiːdɪəns). Also 5 dys-, -aunce. [a. OF. *desobedience* (in Godef.); cf. It. *disubbidienza*, Sp. *desobediencia*: a Romanic formation for L. *inobēdientia*, f. DIS- 4 + L. *obēdientia* OBEDIENCE.]

The fact or condition of being disobedient; the withholding of obedience; neglect or refusal to obey; violation of a command by omitting to conform to it, or of a prohibition by acting in defiance of it; an instance of this.

?*a* **1400** *Arthur* 230 To vnderfang oure ordynaunce; For þy dysobediaunce. *c* **1430** LYDG. *Min. Poems* 143 (Mätz.) For disobedience Disclaundrid is perpetually my name. **1509** HAWES *Past. Pleas.* XLIV. xiv, Adam..And Eve..the worlde dampned..By disobedience. **1607** SHAKS. *Cor.* III. i. 117, I say they norisht disobedience. **1644** BP. HALL *Rem. Wks.* (1660) 107 Our wilfull disobediences. **1776** GIBBON *Decl. & F.* i. (1846) I. 11 It was impossible for cowardice or disobedience to escape the severest punishment. **1875** JOWETT *Plato* V. 412 He who obeys the law will never know the fatal consequences of disobedience.

b. *transf.* Non-compliance with a law of nature, an influence, or the like.

a **1729** BLACKMORE (J.), If planetary orbs the sun obey, Why should the moon disown his sovereign sway?..This disobedience of the moon, etc.

† **diso'bediency.** *Obs.* [f. L. *disobēdientia*: see prec. and -ENCY.] The quality of being disobedient.

1597 DANIEL *Civ. Wars* VII. lviii, The out-let Will of Disobediency. **1614** R. TAILOR *Hog hath lost his Pearl* III. in Hazl. *Dodsley* XI. 464 In punishing my disobediency. **1710** STRYPE *Life Grindall*, anno 1580 (R.), You might..have corrected the disobediency of such.

disobedient (dɪsəʊˈbiːdɪənt), *a.* and *sb.* Also 5 dys-, 6 dishob-. [a. OF. *desobedient* (in Godef.); cf. It. *disubbidiente* (Florio), Sp. *desobediente*; a Romanic formation, for L. *inobēdient-em*, f. DIS- 4 + L. *obēdient-em* OBEDIENT.]

A. *adj.* Withholding obedience; refusing or failing to obey; neglectful or not observant of authoritative command; guilty of breach of prescribed duty; refractory, rebellious.

14.. *Why I can't be a Nun* 272 in *E.E.P.* (1862) 145 A-nother lady..That hyȝt dame dysobedyent..set nowȝt by her priores. **1535** COVERDALE *Ps.* cv. 7 Oure fathers..were dishobedient at the see. **1549** CHEKE *Hurt Sedit.* (1641) 15 How is the king obeyed, whose wisest be withstanded, the disobedientest obeyed. **1667** MILTON *P.L.* VI. 687 Michael and his Powers went forth to tame These disobedient. **1819** SHELLEY *Cenci* III. i. 316 Such was God's scourge for disobedient sons. **1828** SCOTT *F.M. Perth* xxxiv, These are not loving subjects, but disobedient rebels.

b. *transf.* Unyielding, intractable, stubborn.

1588 J. READ *Compend. Method* 101 Growing nigh to the manner of a cancer, and disobedient to any medicine. *a* **1802** E. DARWIN (Webster, 1828), Medicines..rendering peculiar parts of the system disobedient to stimuli. **1843** CARLYLE *Past & Pr.* III. x. (1872) 165 Disobedient Cotton fibre, which will not..consent to cover bare backs.

†**B.** *sb.* A disobedient or refractory person.

1548 *Act. 2-3 Edw. VI*, c. 23. §2 Inflicting all such Pains upon the Disobedients. *a* **1670** SPALDING *Troub. Chas. I.* (1829) 70 Refusers to subscribe the covenant..and other disobedients.

† **disobe'dientiary,** (*a.* and) *sb. nonce-wd.* [f. prec. adj. + -ARY.] = prec. sb.

1537 LATIMER *Serm. & Rem.* (1845) 389 Pseudo-prophets ..sly, wily, disobedientiaries to all good orders.

diso'bediently, *adv.* [f. DISOBEDIENT + -LY².] In a disobedient manner; with disregard of commands.

1548 *Privy Council Acts* (1890) II. 209 Arrogantly and disobediently..contrary to an expresse commandement. **1594** HOOKER *Eccl. Pol.* II. ii. (1611) 57 The least thing done disobediently towardes God. *Mod.* These boys have behaved most disobediently.

† **diso'beisance.** *Obs.* Also 4 des-, 5-6 -aunce. [a. OF. *desobeïssance* (13th c. in Hatz.-Darm.), mod.F. *désobé-*, f. *désobéissant*: see next and -ANCE.] = DISOBEDIENCE.

1393 GOWER *Conf.* I. 86 Now.. To telle my desobeissance. **1413** *Pilgr. Sowle* (Caxton 1483) III. x. 57 Adam was..dampned..for disobeisaunce to the hest of god. **1548** GEST *Pr. Masse* 93 Canceled owte of the masse boke, as heresye to God and disobeysaunce to the King.

† **diso'beisant,** *a.* and *sb. Obs.* [a. OF. *desobeïssant* (13th c. in Littré; mod. *désobéissant*), pr. pple. of *désobéir* to DISOBEY.]

A. *adj.* Not submissive, DISOBEDIENT. **B.** *sb.* A rebel.

c **1381** CHAUCER *Parl. Foules* 429 If that I to hyre be founde vntrewe, Dishobeysaunt or wilful necligent. *c* **1430** LYDG. *Min. Poems* (Percy Soc.) 143 Disobeisaunt my tithes for to paye. **1525** LD. BERNERS *Froiss.* II. xliv. 148 To punysshe them that be dysobeysaunt to the kynge of Castell. **1542-3** *Act 34 Hen. VIII* (in Bolton *Stat. Irel.* (1621) 241) In such..perill of invasion by the disobeysants, Irishrie.

disobey (dɪsəʊˈbeɪ), *v.* Also 4 des-, 4-6 dys-; 5 dyshobeye. [a. F. *désobéir* (13th c. in Hatz.-Darm.) = Pr. *desobedir*, It. *disubbidire* :—Romanic *dis-*, *desobēdīre*, for late L. *inobēdīre*, f. DIS- 4 + L. *obēdīre* to OBEY.]

1. *intr.* To be disobedient; not to obey.

This is the original use as in Fr., but most late instances are perhaps absolute uses of the transitive sense 2.

1393 GOWER *Conf.* I. 86 þerof woll I desobeie. **1539** TONSTALL *Serm. Palm Sund.* (1823) 26 Pride..makethe hym that disobeyeth to contemne to obey. **1667** MILTON *P.L.* III. 203 Man disobeying, Disloyal breaks his fealtie. **1727-38** GAY *Fables* I. xx. 24 His bosom burn'd to disobey. **1781** COWPER *Hope* 315 If..some headstrong hardy lout Would disobey. **1886** RUSKIN *Præterita* I. 424 The wish to disobey is already disobedience.

†**b.** Const. *to, unto* [= F. *désobéir à* or *dative*].

14.. *Circumcision* in *Tundale's Vis.* 88 Eyretykes that falsly dysobey To holy chyrche. *a* **1450** *Knt. de la Tour* (1868) 59 She..disobeyed to God and felle in his yre. **1502** *Ord. Crysten Men* (W. de W. 1506) I. ii. 12 Whan Adam & eue..dysobeyed unto god. **1525** LD. BERNERS *Froiss.* II. xxxiii. 97 Moche of his people disobeyed to serue hym. **1526** *Pilgr. Perf.* (W. de W. 1531) 35 We..disobey to theyr commaundementes.

2. *trans.* [The object represents an earlier dative: cf. F. *il me désobéit*, he disobeys (to) me.] To refuse or neglect to obey (any one); to neglect wilfully, transgress, or violate, the commands or orders of (a person in authority, a law, etc.); to refuse submission to.

1393 GOWER *Conf.* I. 338 Her owne liege..That hem forsoke and disobeide. *Ibid.* III. 50 Ther might nothing hem disobey. *a* **1450** *Knt. de la Tour* (1868) 60 He toke and ete thereof, for he wolde not disobeie her. **1470-85** MALORY *Arthur* XVI. xi, It were wel done..that ye dishobeye not the auysyon. **1512** *Act 4 Hen. VIII*, c. 20. §2 Mysgoverned persons disobeyeng your lawes. *c* **1532** DEWES *Introd. Fr.* in *Palsgr.* 1048 Nat be wyllyng to disobey you. **1632** J. HAYWARD tr. *Biondi's Eromena* 59 Seeing no meanes of disobeying the winds, they gave their violence way. **1667** MILTON *P.L.* v. 611 Him who disobeyes Me disobeyes. **1797** MRS. RADCLIFFE *Italian* ii, Where is the principle which shall teach you to disobey a father? **1875** JOWETT *Plato* (ed. 2) V. 79 The chief magistrate..will punish those who disobey God and the law.

Hence **diso'beying** *vbl. sb.* and *ppl. a.*

1649 JER. TAYLOR *Gt. Exemp.* I. ii. 73 Every disobeying person that payes the penalty.

disobeyal (dɪsəʊˈbeɪəl). *rare.* [f. prec. + -AL¹.] An act of disobeying.

1889 *Daily News* 31 July 3/4 Certain financial arrangements followed a disobeyal of the order of the Court.

† **diso'beyant,** *a. Obs.* [irreg. f. DISOBEY *v.* + ANT, in place of the normal DISOBEISANT.] = DISOBEDIENT.

1422 tr. *Secreta Secret., Priv. Priv.* (E.E.T.S.) 122 Some of the Pepyl ther weryn agaynys hym and disobeiaunt.

disobeyer (dɪsəʊˈbeɪə(r)). [f. DISOBEY *v.* + -ER¹.] One who disobeys; a recusant, a rebel.

1513-75 *Diurn. Occurrents* (Bannatyne Club) 69 Vnder the payne of burnying of disobeyaris vpoun the cheik. **1653** A. WILSON *Jas. I.* 11 A strickt Proclamation threatens the disobeyers. **1875** KINGLAKE *Crimea* (1877) V. i. 365 A wilful disobeyer of orders.

disoblegiant, obs. var. DESOBLIGEANT.

† **disobli'gation.** *Obs.* [f. DIS- 9 + OBLIGATION; after *disoblige*.]

1. Freedom or release from obligation.

1616 BRENT tr. *Sarpi's Hist. Council Trent* (1676) 631 The place doth not prove a dispensation, that is, a disobligation from the Law. **1660** JER. TAYLOR *Duct. Dubit.* II. 411 (L.) The conscience is restored to liberty and disobligation. **1770** *Monthly Rev.* 363 The disobligation..being cancelled.. leaves the obligation without abatement.

2. A disobliging action; an act that either negligently or purposely thwarts a person's convenience or wishes; a piece of inconsiderate treatment; a slight, affront, insult.

1647 CLARENDON *Hist. Reb.* IV. §127 By the disobligations his family had undergone from the duke of Buckingham. **1654** H. L'ESTRANGE *Chas. I* (1655) 132 Noy..wheel'd about..and made amends with his future service, for his former dis-obligations. **1739** CIBBER *Apol.* (1756) I. 295 Mrs. Oldfield receiv'd it rather as a favour than a disobligation. **1788** *Hist.* in *Ann. Reg.* 61 Russia had.. heaped disobligation upon disobligation, in her transactions with Great Britain.

3. The fact or feeling of being disobliged.

1645 F. THORPE in *Hull Lett.* (1886) 120 To sowe seedes of discention and disobligation betwixt the two nations. **1713** STEELE *Englishman* No. 1. 9, I..shall never give a Vote out of Peevishness or personal Disobligation. **1754** RICHARDSON *Grandison* (1781) III. ix. 66 Your Lordship's good resolutions..must be built on a better foundation than occasional disgust or disobligation.

b. An instance of this feeling; a grudge.

a **1754** FIELDING *Journ. Lisbon* I. x, Besides his disloyalty ..I have private disobligations to him.

† **dis'obligatory,** *a.* [DIS- 10.] **a.** Not obligatory or binding. **b.** Releasing from obligation.

a **1649** DRUMM. OF HAWTH. *Queries of State* Wks. (1711) 177 All oaths unlawful..being..null and disobligatory. *a* **1649** CHAS. I *Let. to Henderson* Wks. 165 You much mistake in alleaging that the two Houses of Parliament can have this disobligatory power.

disoblige (dɪsəˈblaɪdʒ), *v.* [ad. F. *désobliger* (1307 in Godef. *Suppl.*) = Sp. *desobligar*, It. *disobbligare*:—Romanic **disobligāre*, f. DIS- 4 + L. *obligāre* to OBLIGE.]

†**1.** *trans.* To set free from obligation; to release from duty or engagement. Const. *of, from. Obs.*

1603 FLORIO *Montaigne* III. ix. (1632) 545, I love so much to disoblige and discharge myselfe. *a* **1649** DRUMM. OF HAWTH. *Hist. Jas. V*, Wks. (1711) 79 To disoblige themselves of their greatest duty. **1678** CUDWORTH *Intell. Syst.* 895 They..would be altogether Disobliged, and Consequently, might Justly break any Laws.

absol. **1643** MILTON *Divorce* v. (1851) 74 A particular law absolving and disobliging from a more general command.

†**b.** To disengage, detach. *Obs.*

1647 W. STRONG *Trust & Acc. Steward* 14 Prodigality of the publique purse will ever disoblige the people to their Rulers. **1689** TEMPLE *Misc.* I. 85 (Seager) The failing of his design was thought to have something disobliged him from France; upon whose assistance he reckoned.

2. To refuse or neglect to oblige; not to consult or comply with the convenience or wishes of (a person); hence, to put a slight upon, affront, offend.

1632 J. HAYWARD tr. *Biondi's Eromena* To Rdr. A iv, Loth to disoblige so many deserving and noble personages. **1647** CLARENDON *Hist. Reb.* II. (1843) 46/1 Colonel Lesley.. being lately disobliged (as they called it) by the King, that is, denied somewhat he had a mind to have. **1729** FRANKLIN *Ess.* Wks. 1840 II. 25, I know not how to disoblige her so much as to tell her I should be glad to have less of her company. **1787** S. C. COX *P. Williams' Rep.* I. Notes 681 His daughter Mabell had disobliged him by turning Roman Catholick. **1855** MACAULAY *Hist. Eng.* III. 338 Impossible to pay marked court to one without disobliging the rest.

transf. **1698** COLLIER *Answ. Congreve* (1730) 195 As to the Smut [=indecency], I have endeavoured not to disoblige the Paper with any of it.

absol. **1697** DAMPIER *Voy.* I. 500 For fear of disobliging by our refusal. **1741** RICHARDSON *Pamela* II. 25, I would not disoblige on purpose.

†**b.** To render disobliging. *Obs. rare.*

1716 COLLIER tr. *A Panegyrick* 78 Anxiety and Discontent is apt to spoil Peoples Tempers, and disoblige their Behaviour.

3. In more concrete sense: To inconvenience, incommode, annoy. *Obs.* or *dial.*

1668 [see DISOBLIGING *ppl. a.*]. **1685** TRAVESTIN *Siege Newheusel* 13 The besieged..began to fire upon us..by which they somewhat disobliged our Battery. **1697** COLLIER *Ess. Mor. Subj.* II. (1709) 1 I'm afraid I may disoblige your Business. **1726** SHELVOCKE *Voy. round World* 387 They disobliged us very much by the stench of their dung. **1851** S. JUDD *Margaret* II. i. (1881) 198, I..hope my presence, Madam, will not disoblige you.

Hence **diso'bliged** *ppl. a.*, slighted, affronted.

1673 *Lady's Call.* I. iii. ¶22 Let therefore the disoblig'd not look back upon the injury. **1724** A. COLLINS *Gr. Chr. Relig.* 186 Joiada..and other disoblig'd Refugee Jews. **1814** SCOTT *Wav.* xxxii, His father a disobliged and discontented courtier.

disobligeant, obs. var. DESOBLIGEANT.

diso'bligement. [f. DISOBLIGE *v.* + -MENT.]

†**1.** Release from obligation; = DISOBLIGATION I.

1648 MILTON *Tenure Kings* (1650) 36 If I make a covnant with a man who prove afterward a monster to me, I should conceave a disobligement. **1677** GILPIN *Demonol.* (1867) 107 God delayed to answer them, which they looked upon as a disobligement from duty.

†**2.** A slight; = DISOBLIGATION 2. *Obs.*

1635 J. HAYWARD tr. *Biondi's Banish'd Virgin* 185 Disobligements received and requited. **1672** *Lond. Gaz.* No. 712/4 Some disobligements that Ambassador had lately received there.

3. The action of disobliging or fact of being disobliged.

18.. in H. Adams *Alb. Gallatin* 450 (Cent.) To the great disobligement of some of his strong political friends.

diso'bliger. *rare.* [f. as prec. + -ER¹.] One who disobliges.

1648 W. MOUNTAGUE *Devout Ess.* I. xv. §4 (R.) Loving our enemies, and benefiting our disobligers. **1730** SWIFT *Vind. Ld. Carteret*, Disobligers of England.

diso'bliging, *vbl. sb.* [f. as prec. + -ING¹.] The action of the verb DISOBLIGE.

1692 *Vindication* Pref. A ij b, The disobliging of Wicked Men. **1726-31** TINDAL *Rapin's Hist. Eng.* XVII. II. 59 By this wise Conduct she avoided the disobliging of Men.

diso'bliging, *ppl. a.* [f. as prec. + -ING².] That disobliges; disinclined to gratify the wishes or meet the convenience of another; unaccommodating; also, †inconvenient, annoying (*obs.*).

1652 COKAINE tr. *Calprenède's Cassandra* III. 207 In the least disobliging terms. **1665** SIR T. HERBERT *Trav.* (1677) 238 A Prince of that tyrannical and dis-obliging nature. **1668** DAVENANT *Rivals* 4 To preserve your knees From such a disobliging posture. **1703** DE FOE *Power Body of People*, Misc. 164 Their Proceedings..have been Disobliging to the Nation. **1853** MRS. CARLYLE *Lett.* II. 239, I must..get our disobliging neighbours turned out.

Hence **diso'bligingly** *adv.*; **diso'bligingness**, unwillingness to oblige; want of readiness to accommodate another.

1654 LD. ORRERY *Parthen.* (1676) 596 The disobligingness..of this performance. **1667** G. DIGBY *Elvira* 7 Whose action..hath shown So disobligingly, his rash judgement of me. **1858** MRS. CARLYLE *Lett.* II. 382 Women..whose disobligingness had been the cause of my flurry. **1868** HELPS *Realmah* xvii, Disobligingness..is but too common everywhere.

† **disob'servant,** *a. Obs. rare.* [DIS- 10.] Not observant; disobedient.

1672 W. DE BRITAINE *Dutch Usurp.* 25 A great part of the people became disobservant to the Laws.

† **disob'stetricate**, *v.* *Obs. nonce-wd.* [DIS- 6.] *trans.* To reverse the office of a midwife concerning; to retard or hinder from child-birth.

1652 URQUHART *Jewel* Wks. (1834) 210 With parturiencie for greater births, if a malevolent time disobstetricate not their enixibility.

disob'struct, *v.* ? *Obs.* [DIS- 6.] *trans.* To free from obstruction; = DEOBSTRUCT.

1611 FLORIO, *Disopilare*, to open or vnstop, to disobstruct. **1664** POWER *Exp. Philos.* I. 68 The Optick Nerve being.. disobstructed and relaxed. **1738** A. STUART in *Phil. Trans.* XL. 8 Applications..intended to..discuss stagnating animal fluids, or disobstruct the vessels.

† **dis'occident**, *v.* *Obs. nonce-wd.* [DIS- 8: cf. DISORIENT.] *trans.* To throw out of his reckoning as to the west; to confuse as to the points of the compass.

1672–3 MARVELL *Reh. Transp.* I. 53 Perhaps some roguing Boy that managed the Puppets turned the City wrong, and so disoccidented our Geographer.

disoccu'pation. [f. DIS- 9 + OCCUPATION; cf. F. *désoccupation* (17th c. in Hatz.-Darm.).] Lack of occupation, unoccupied condition.

1834 SOUTHEY *Corr. w. C. Bowles* (1881) 299 There is no interval of disoccupation. **1889** HOWELLS *Hazard New Fort.* 105 A life of luxurious disoccupation.

disoccupy (dɪs'ɒkjʊpaɪ), *v.* [f. DIS- 6 + OCCUPY *v.*, prob. after F. *désoccuper*, Sp. *desocupar*, It. *disoccupare*.] *trans.* To cease to occupy, vacate.

1872 *Daily News* 1 Apr. 3/2 [Let. fr. Madrid] The hall vacated..was merely disoccupied in order that [etc.]. **1882** tr. *Rep. Congr. Chili* in *Chr. World* (N.Y.) Feb. (1883) 50 The refusal of Mr. Gandarillas to disoccupy his post.

disodic (daɪ'səʊdɪk), **disodio'hydric**, etc., *Chem.*: see DI- *pref.*[2] 2.

1873 *Fownes' Chem.* (ed. 11) 340 Disodiohydric Phosphate, or Disodic Orthophosphate, is prepared by precipitating the acid calcium phosphate obtained in decomposing bone-ash with sulphuric acid.

disodour (dɪs'əʊdə(r)). *nonce-wd.* [DIS- 9.] Ill odour; evil repute.

1882 *Society* 11 Nov. 7/2 He..died in the disodour of being..[a] most extortionate old hunks.

† **dis'office**, *sb.* *Obs.* [DIS- 9.] An evil office, an ill turn, a disservice.

1624 *Brief Inform. Affairs Palatinate* 56 It shall be an vnkindnesse and dis-office in his deportment.

† **dis'office**, *v.* *Obs.* [DIS- 7 c.] *trans.* To deprive of or depose from office.

1627 *Crt. & Times Chas. I* (1848) I. 241 The other lords ..which are refusers, are disofficed. **1658** J. R. *Chr. Subj.* vii. 100 To dis-authorize and dis-office a Magistrate. *a* **1670** HACKET *Abp. Williams* II. (1692) 200 All that refuse it must be sequestred, imprisoned, disofficed.

† **di-so'lution.** *Chem. Obs.* [DI-[2] 2 ¶.] A solution of a sub- or proto-salt (e.g. of mercury).

1854 J. SCOFFERN in *Orr's Circ. Sc.* Chem. 501 The action of dry hydrochloric acid on di-solutions of mercury.

disomatous (daɪ'səʊmətəs), *a.* [f. Gr. δισώματ-ος double-bodied (f. δι-, DI-[2] + σῶμα, σωματ-body) + -OUS.] Having two bodies, double-bodied.

1857 DUNGLISON *Med. Dict.* s.v. *Disomus*, A Monster with two bodies..is said to be disomatous.

disome ('daɪsəʊm). *Biol.* [f. DI-[2] + -SOME[4].] Any pair of homologous chromosomes. Hence **di'somic** *a.*, relating to or characterized by a disome; usu. (of a haplont), having one extra chromosome which is homologous with a chromosome of the normal haploid set; also as *sb.*, a disomic organism, etc.

1921 A. F. BLAKESLEE in *Amer. Naturalist* LV. 259 The homologous chromosomes therefore form tetrasomes, to use a new term, instead of disomes as in normals or trisomes as in triploid plants. *Ibid.*, The following terms are suggested to designate sets with numbers of chromosomes from 1 to 12: monosome, disome, trisome, [etc.]. **1924** —— in *Proc. Nat. Acad. Sci.* X. 114 The ratios actually found resemble those in disomic rather than in trisomic inheritance. **1946** *Nature* 21 Sept. 418/1 Genetical tests based on the difference between tetrasomic and disomic ratios. **1954** *Genetics* XXXIX. 339 PWT strains, whether originating as disomics or as heterocaryotic ascospores, might be expected to have a wild phenotype. **1965** FINCHAM & DAY *Fungal Genetics* (ed. 2) v. 120 Although aneuploidy in the nuclei of vegetative mycelium of Neurospora has not been shown to occur.., the occurrence of n + 1 (or disomic) ascospores is well established.

† **diso'pinion.** *Obs.* [f. DIS- 9 + OPINION.]

1. Adverse or mean opinion (*of*); disesteem.

1625 SIR J. ELIOT in Gardiner *Hist. Eng.* (1875) I. vi. 225 The general disopinion..which it would work to him. **1640** BP. REYNOLDS *Passions* xxxix. 501 According to the Disopinion & slender Conceipt which they have of their own Abilities. **1647** MAY *Hist. Parl.* II. iv. 67 A disopinion and dislike of the Parliament. **1705** SIR E. WALKER *Hist. Disc.* 219 He was in some disopinion with the king.

2. Difference of opinion; dissent. *rare.*

1598 FLORIO, *Disparère*, a disopinion, a diuersitie in conceit. **1640** BP. REYNOLDS *Passions* iv, Assenting and dissenting thoughts, belief and disopinion.

Hence † **diso'pinioned** *a.* *Obs.*, thought little of, held in disrepute.

1622 H. SYDENHAM *Serm. Sol. Occ.* II. (1637) 137 A disopinioned undervalued man.

† **dis'oppilate**, *v.* *Med. Obs.* [f. DIS- 6 + OPPILATE: cf. F. *désopiler* (16th c. in Hatz.-Darm.), It. *disoppilare*, obs. Sp. *desopilar*; also DEOPPILATE.] *trans.* To free from obstruction; *absol.* to remove obstructions; = DEOPPILATE.

1577 FRAMPTON *Ioyfull Newes* II. (1596) 54 Being vsed it [Sassafras] dooth disopilate, and make a good colour in the face. **1601** HOLLAND *Pliny* XX. vi. II. 43 Hippocrates..is of opinion, that it will disopilate the neck of the Matrice. **1652** WADSWORTH *Chocolate* 8 It hath also parts of Sulphur and of Quicksilver, which doth open, and disopilate.

disorb (dɪs'ɔːb), *v.* [f. DIS- 7 a, c + ORB *sb.*]

1. *trans.* To remove from its orb or sphere.

1606 SHAKS. *Tr. & Cr.* II. ii. 45 Like a Starre disorb'd. **1800** W. TAYLOR in *Monthly Mag.* VIII. 601 To turn aside the planet..and to disorb its approaching culmination.

2. To deprive of the orb as a symbol of sovereignty.

1863 W. LANCASTER *Praeterita* 54 Until the tale of years disorb my hand. **1887** SWINBURNE *Locrine* III. ii. 66 Discrowned, disorbed, discrested.

dis'orchard, *v. rare.* [DIS- 7 a, b: cf. *disforest.*] *trans.* To change from the condition of an orchard; to divest (land) of orchards.

1796 W. MARSHALL *W. England* I. 216 Land.. encumbered with orchard trees..and which ought..to be disorcharded. **1869** *Pall Mall G.* 24 Sept. 3 Disorcharding must of necessity be a gradual process, and, meanwhile, how is the farmer..to pay the higher rent which the landlord usually expects for his orchard land?

† **dis'ordain**, *v.* *Obs.* Forms: 3 desordeine, 3–5 -deyne, 4–5 disordeyne, 5 -hordeyne. [a. OF. *desorden-er* to disorder, degrade (11th c.), mod.F. *désordonner* = Sp. *desordenar*, It. *disordinare*, a Romanic formation from DIS- 4 + L. *ordināre* to order, ORDAIN. Cf. DEORDINATE.]

1. *trans.* To deprive of or degrade from orders.

1297 R. GLOUC. (1724) 473 ȝuf eni clerc..were itake, & vor felon iproued..That me solde him uerst desordeini. *c* **1300** *Beket* 378 That he scholde the preost take, And desordeyni him of his ordre.

2. To disorder, derange.

1398 TREVISA *Barth. De P.R.* VII. li. (1495) 265 Diaria comyth..of humours whyche renne..fro the hede to the guttes, and disordeynyth them.

† **dis'ordained**, *ppl. a.* *Obs.* Also 6 -ordened, -ined. [f. DISORDAIN *v.* + -ED, but, in sense 2, app. ad. OF. *desordené*: see next.]

1. Disordered, irregular, out of order.

c **1430** *Pilgr. Lyf Manhode* I. cxix. (1869) 62 Bi his disordeyned smellinge.

2. Unrestrained, immoderate: = DISORDINATE I.

a **1425** *Chaucer's Pars. T.* ⁋744 [MSS. Harl. & Camb.] Glotenye is vnresonable and desordeyned [*other MSS.* desordeyne(e, discorde] coueytise to ete and to drynke. **1556** *Aurelio & Isab.* (1608) B iij, After that these two knightes had longe ynough strained together..came in so disordined wordes [*desordonnees parolles*], that taking their..swordes [etc.]. *Ibid.* E vij, Holde backe yowre disordenede answere.

† **di'sordeine, di'sordeny**, *a.* (*sb.*) *Obs.* Forms; 4 des-, disordene, 4–5 des-, dis-, dys-, -ordeynee, -ordenee, -ordeine, -eyne, -eigne, 5 -ordeyne, -ordeny. [a. OF. *desordené* (mod. *désordonné*), pa. pple. of *desordener*: see DISORDAIN and DISORDINATE. The final *é* of OF. appears to have had a double fortune, becoming on the one side mute as in ASSIGN, AVOWE, on the other developing into *-ee*, *-ie*, *-y* as in ASSIGNEE, CITY: cf. *dishevel*, *dishevely*.]

Inordinate, immoderate, excessive; disorderly, irregular. (Cf. DISORDINATE I.)

1340 *Ayenb.* 34 Auarice is disordene loue. *c* **1386** CHAUCER *Pars. T.* ⁋841 Alle the desordeynee [*v.rr.* dysordenee, disordeynet, -deine, -deyne, desordeigne] moewynges that comen of flesshly talentes. *c* **1430** *Pilgr. Lyf Manhode* I. cxxiii. (1869) 65 Whan þou seest þe wille encline to dede disordeynee. *c* **1450** [see B.]. *c* **1475** *Partenay* 2768 All disording [? disordiny] is she All-way.

B. *sb.* Disorder, an irregularity.

c **1450** *St. Cuthbert* (Surtees) 2079, 2083 What disordeny he þare kende, He was besy it to amende..Disordenys when he reproued, Disordeny monkes, þat þaim loued, Of his spekyng were noȝt payed.

Hence † **di'sordeinely** *adv.* *Obs.*, inordinately, immoderately.

1340 *Ayenb.* 55 Hit ne is no zenne uor to ethe þe guode metes ak ethe his [= but to eat them] to uerliche oþer disordeneliche. **1413** *Pilgr. Sowle* (Caxton 1483) III. x. 57 A good thynge desordeynly desyred ageynst goddes wylle.

disorder (dɪs'ɔːdə(r)), *sb.* [f. DIS- 9 + ORDER *sb.*: prob. after F. *desordre* (Palsgr. 1530). Cf. also DISORDER *v.* (which is known earlier).]

1. Absence or undoing of order or regular arrangement; confusion; confused state or condition.

1530 PALSGR. 214/1 Disorder of a thyng, *desbavlx, desordre, desordonnance.* **1555** EDEN *Decades* Pref. to Rdr. (Arb.) 53 Disorder of the partes is a deformitie to the hole. **1651** HOBBES *Leviath.* II. xxx. 176 Common-wealths, imperfect, and apt to relapse into disorder. **1653** H. COGAN tr. *Pinto's Trav.* xxxix. 154 In this order, or rather disorder, we arrived at the Castle. **1667** MILTON *P.L.* III. 713 Light shon, and order from disorder sprung. **1712** W. ROGERS *Voy.* 3 Our Ships out of trim, and every thing in disorder. *a* **1839** PRAED *Poems* (1864) I. 189 The tangled boughs.. Were twined in picturesque disorder. **1875** JOWETT *Plato* (ed. 2) V. 93 Disorder in a state is the source of all evil, and order of all good.

† **b.** Violation of recognized order, irregularity.

1709 POPE *Ess. Crit.* 152 Thus Pegasus, a nearer way to take, May boldly deviate from the common track; From vulgar bounds with brave disorder part, And snatch a grace beyond the reach of art.

2. (with *a* and *pl.*) An instance of want of order or breach of rule; an irregularity.

1574 WHITGIFT *Def. Aunsw.* iii. Wks. (1851) I. 363 If you say that it were a disorder that all should lay on their hands, I grant you. **1582** HESTER *Secr. Phiorav.* I. i. 1 These disorders which are thus committed. **1687** T. BROWN *Saints in Uproar* Wks. 1730 I. 83, I am resolved to..reform these disorders. **1828** SIR W. NAPIER *Penins. War* IV. vi. I. 528 Inexperience was the..principal cause of the disorders which attended the retreat.

concr. **1717** FREZIER *Voy. S. Sea* 263 The Decoration of the Altars..crowded and bad..a man cannot but lament the immense Sums they spend on those gilt Disorders.

† **b.** *spec.* An irregularity of conduct; a disorderly act or practice; a misdemeanour. *Obs.*

1581 PETTIE *Guazzo's Civ. Conv.* To Rdr. (1586) A vij, The disorders of those travailers abroade, are the chiefe cause. **1601** SHAKS. *Twel. N.* II. iii. 105 My Lady bad me tell you, that though she harbors you as her kinsman, she's nothing ally'd to your disorders. *a* **1715** BURNET *Own Time* (1823) I. 457 The king had another mistress..she fell into many scandalous disorders. **1772** S. DENNE *Hist. Rochester* 165 To remedy the disorders of those committed to his charge.

3. Disturbance, commotion, tumult; *esp.* a breach of public order, riot, mutiny, outrage.

1532 BECON *Pomander of Prayer* Prayers, etc. (1844) 80 To send the spirit of love and concord among us, that, without any disorder or debate, every one of us may be content with our calling. **1628** MEAD in Ellis *Orig. Lett.* Ser. I. III. 265 To prevent all disorder the train-bands kept a guard on both sides of the way. **1761** HUME *Hist. Eng.* III. lx. 295 Many disorders in England it behoved him previously to compose. **1834** *West Ind. Sketch Bk.* I. 303 A never ceasing surf.. when the wind blows strong..it breaks with terrific disorder on the coast.

† **4.** Disturbance or agitation of mind, discomposure. *Obs.*

1595 SHAKS. *John* III. iv. 102, I will not keepe this forme vpon my head, When there is such disorder in my witte. **1680** BURNET *Rochester* (1692) 20 He remembering his dream fell into some disorder..and said..he was to die before morning. **1765** H. WALPOLE *Otranto* i. (1798) 27 His voice faltered, and he asked with disorder, 'What is in the great chamber?' **1838** LYTTON *Leila* I. vi, The old man found Boabdil in great disorder and excitement.

5. A disturbance of the bodily (or mental) functions; an ailment, disease. (Usually a weaker term than DISEASE, and not implying structural change.)

a **1704** LOCKE (J.), Sometimes occasioned by disorder in the body, or sometimes by thoughts in the mind. **1725** N. ROBINSON *Th. Physick* iii. 108 A Fever is the first Disorder that affects the Blood and Vessels. **1781** COWPER *Lett.* 18 Mar., A slight disorder in my eye. **1860** B'NESS BUNSEN in Hare *Life* (1879) II. iv. 261 A new and troublesome stage of his chronic disorder. **1883** *Syd. Soc. Lex.*, *Disorder*..a term frequently used in medicine to imply functional disturbance, in opposition to manifest structural change.

disorder (dɪs'ɔːdə(r)), *v.* [app. a modification of earlier *desordene*, *disordeine* vb., OF. *desordener*, after ORDER vb. (Palsgr. has a F. *désordrer* beside *désordonner*, but the latter (OF. *desordener*) was the proper F. form.) (*Disorder* sb. is app. later.)]

1. *trans.* To put out of order; to destroy the regular arrangement of; to throw into disorder or confusion; to disarrange, derange, upset.

1477 EARL RIVERS (Caxton) *Dictes* 70 Workis doon by lesingis is for to disordre good thinges. **1581** FULKE in *Confer.* III. (1584) P ij b, You would obscure the sense by disordering the wordes. **1659** B. HARRIS *Parival's Iron Age* 308 The Polanders..attempted sundry waies to break and disorder the Swedish army. **1667** MILTON *P.L.* x. 914 With ..tresses all disorderd. **1783** BURKE *Rep. Affairs Ind.* Wks. 1842 II. 1 Your committee hold it expedient to collect..the circumstances, by which that government appears to them to be most essentially disordered. **1887** BOWEN *Virg. Æneid* VI. 49 Loose and disordered her fair hair flew.

† **b.** *intr.* (for *refl.*) To become disordered; to fall into confusion. *Obs.*

1523 LD. BERNERS *Froiss.* I. clxii. 198 The batayle of the marshals began to dysorder, by reason of the shot of the archers. **1647** MAY *Hist. Parl.* III. v. 86 The Earle made.. Gull's Horse to retreat and disorder at this first charge.

† **2.** *trans.* To make morally irregular; to vitiate, corrupt; to mar, spoil. *Obs.*

1576 FLEMING *Panopl. Epist.* 401 Many times by reading such tryfles..the manners of younge learners are disordered. **1585** T. WASHINGTON tr. *Nicholay's Voy.* IV. xxxiv. 156 b, A life disordered, corrupted, and ful of al villany.

† **b.** *refl.* To violate moral order or rule; to break loose from restraint, behave in an unruly or riotous manner; to transgress the bounds of

moderation, go to excess. *Obs.* (Cf. DISORDERLY *a.* 2, DISORDINATE 1.)

1579 TOMSON *Calvin's Serm. Tim.* 53/2 Those persons, which disorder themselues, and beecome wild colts, and can abide no law nor bridle. **1613** *Manch. Crt. Leet Rec.* (1885) II. 279 A common Drunckard, and disorders himselffe verie often in quarrelinge and brawlinge. *a* **1654** SELDEN *Table-T.* (Arb.) 44 That he should not disorder himself neither with eating nor drinking, but eat very little of Supper.

†**3.** *trans.* To disturb the mind or feelings of; to agitate, discompose, disconcert. *Obs.*

1575 J. STILL *Gamm. Gurton* v. ii. in Hazl. *Dodsley* III. 236 Dame Chat, master doctor upon you here complaineth, That you and your maids should him much disorder. **1679** BURNET *Hist. Ref.* I. 459 This he uttered with a stern countenance, at which Lambert being a little disordered [etc.]. **1719** DE FOE *Crusoe* (1840) II. i. 4, I looked very earnestly at her; so that it a little disordered her. **1819** SHELLEY *Cenci* II. i. 77 He said, he looked, he did;—nothing at all Beyond his wont, yet it disordered me.

†**b.** To confuse or discompose *the countenance.*

1676 DRYDEN *Aurengz.* III. i. 1518 Disorder not my Face into a Frown. **1791** MRS. INCHBALD *Simp. Story* IV. xii. 150 With an angry voice and with his countenance disordered. **1795** SOUTHEY *Joan of Arc* IV. 461 The youth's cheek A rapid blush disorder'd.

4. To derange the functions of; to put out of health; to 'upset' (a person or animal, or an organ or part of the body, or the mind).

1526 *Pilgr. Perf.* (W. de W. 1531) 263 b, By reason of.. some humour, whiche disordereth the body. **1694** *Acc. Sev. Late Voy.* II. (1711) 80 If you should eat their Fat, it would ..disorder the Stomach very much. **1697** DAMPIER *Voy.* I. 229 They [cochineal insects] take wing..but the heat of the Sun so disorders them, that they presently fall down dead. **1733-4** BERKELEY *Let. to Prior* 17 Mar., The east wind.. never fails to disorder my head. **1735** WESLEY *Wks.* (1872) I. 18 The sea has not disordered me at all. **1853** LD. HOUGHTON in *Life* (1891) I. xi. 490 That doctrine..seems capable of quite disordering the minds of men who adopt it. *Mod.* This climate is apt to disorder the liver.

transf. **1826** *Q. Rev.* XXXIV. 456 It is not full of such disgraceful vice and meanness as the Confessions of Rousseau, but it is as much disordered by vanity as they are by susceptibility.

†**5.** To deprive of, or degrade from, holy orders; = DISORDAIN 1. *Obs.*

1563-87 FOXE *A. & M.* (1596) 131/2 If this Pope Iohn did not erre in his disordering Formosus. **1681** DRYDEN *Sp. Friar* v. ii, *Alph.* I shall do it by proxy, friar; your bishop's my friend, and is too honest to let such as you infect a cloister. *Gom.* Ay, do, father-in-law, let him be stripped of his habit, and disordered.

6. [f. DIS- 6 + ORDER *v.*] To reverse an order for; to countermand.

1643 PRYNNE *Sov. Power Parl.* III. 122 The first word [ἀντιτασσομενος] signifies properly disordered, counter-ordered, or ordered against. **1852** SMEDLEY *L. Arundel* xxvi, Charley Leicester, who dis-ordered the post-horses and postponed his journey to Constantinople.

Hence **dis'ordering** *vbl. sb.* and *ppl. a.*

1523 LD. BERNERS *Froiss.* I. xviii. 19 The next day..all the oste..avaunced, without disorderyng. **1559** *Primer* in *Priv. Prayers* (1851) 105 That we fall not into disordering of ourselves by anger. **1603** KNOLLES *Hist. Turks* (1638) 39 [The] arrowes fell as thick..as if it had bin a perpetual.. showre of haile, to the great disordering and dismaying of the whole armie. **1744** *Ess. Acting* 17 Like one not quite awak't from some disordering Dream.

†**dis'orderable,** *a. Obs. rare*⁻⁰. [f. prec. + -ABLE.] Capable of being put in disorder.

1611 COTGR., *Desemparable*..disorderable.

dis'ordered, *ppl. a.* [f. as prec. + -ED¹.]

1. Put out of order, thrown into confusion; disarranged, confused, irregular.

1571 DIGGES *Pantom.* III. xiv. S ij b, To measure exactly the solide content of any small body, how disordred or irregular so euer it be. **1603** KNOLLES *Hist. Turks* (1638) 39 Baldwin..seeking to restore his disordered companies, and to stay the furie of the enemie. **1635** EARL STRAFFORD *Lett. & Disp.* (1739) I. 394 Pardon my disordered Writing. **1805** SOUTHEY *Madoc in Azt.* xix, They..with disorder'd speed ..Ran to the city gates. **1838** THIRLWALL *Greece* IV. xxix. 79 Thrasybulus suddenly turned upon the enemy..and.. attacked their victorious but disordered centre.

†**b.** Not according to order or rule, irregular.

1561 T. NORTON *Calvin's Inst.* I. 25 b, After once that such disordered counterfaiting of God well liked them, they neuer ended, till..they imagined yᵉ God did shew forth his power in images. **1592-3** *Act 35 Eliz.* c. I. §5 Frequenting disordered and unlawful Conventicles and Assemblies. **1635** PAGITT *Christianogr.* 171 There were fifty of those Popes irregular, disordered and Apostaticall.

†**2.** Morally irregular, vitiated, corrupt; disorderly, unruly, riotous; = DISORDINATE 1. *Obs.*

1548 HALL *Chron., Rich. III* (an. 3) 44 b, The disordered affection whiche this kynde kynseman shewed to his blood. **1579** in W. H. Turner *Select. Rec. Oxford* 407 A number of disordered persons of the Universitie. **1585** ABP. SANDYS *Serm.* (1841) 381 Our own rebellious and disordered desires. **1605** SHAKS. *Lear* I. iv. 263 Men so disorder'd, so debosh'd, and bold. **1630** *Crt. & Times Chas. I* (1848) II. 63 His wife hath..been committed to the same prison for her disordered tongue. **1667** MILTON *P.L.* VI. 696 Warr..hath ..to disorder'd rage let loose the reines. **1743** BULKELEY & CUMMINS *Voy. S. Seas* 84 The People very much disorder'd in Liquor, and very quarrelsome.

†**3.** Discomposed, agitated. *Obs.*

1711 ADDISON *Spect.* No. 42 ¶1 It is..a very odd Spectacle, to see a Queen venting her passion in a disordered Motion. **1800** MRS. HERVEY *Mourtray Fam.* III. 18 She found him pacing the room, with a disordered air.

4. Affected with bodily or mental disorder; out of health; deranged; morbid.

a **1731** ATTERBURY *Job* xxii. 21 (Seager) Notwithstanding that we feel our souls disordered and restless..yet we are strangely backward to lay hold of this method of cure. **1777** PRIESTLEY *Matt. & Spir.* (1782) I. xviii. 212 A disordered mind [is] in many cases, the evident effect of a disordered body. **1830** HERSCHEL *Stud. Nat. Phil.* §82 In some cases of disordered nerves, we have sensations without objects. **1856** SIR B. BRODIE *Psychol. Inq.* I. iii. 92 Mental derangement is in numerous instances preceded by a disordered state of the general health.

Hence **dis'orderedly** *adv.*; **dis'orderedness.**

1571 GOLDING *Calvin on Ps.* xi. 8 Lest the disorderednesse of al things may empair his faith. **1574** tr. *Marlorat's Apocalips* 35 The Nicolaits which liue disorderedly haue for their founder, Nicolas one of the seuen..deacons. *a* **1610** KNOLLES (J.), By that disorderedness of the soldiers a great advantage was offered unto the enemy. **1611** COTGR., *Escorcher les anguilles par la queuë*, to doe things disorderedly, awkwardly, the wrong way.

dis'orderer. *rare*⁻⁰. [f. as prec. + -ER¹.] One who disorders.

1598 FLORIO, *Scorrettore*, a spoiler, a marrer of anie thing, a disordrer.

dis'orderliness. [f. next + -NESS.] The quality or condition of being disorderly.

1584 WHITGIFT *Let. to Burghley*, Not..out of respect of his disorderliness, in the manner of the communion..but also of his negligence in reading. **1678** CUDWORTH *Intell. Syst.* 873 God is not the President..of Irregular..Lust or Appetite, and of loose Erratick Disorderliness. **1748** RICHARDSON *Clarissa* (1811) VIII. 331 Disordering more her native disorderliness. **1885** *L'pool Daily Post* 9 June 4/3 The Speaker pointed out the disorderliness of the proceedings.

disorderly (dɪsˈɔːdəlɪ), *a.* and *sb.* [f. DISORDER *sb.* + -LY¹; after *orderly.*]

A. *adj.* **1.** Characterized by disorder, or absence of order or regular arrangement; in a state of disorder; not orderly; confused, irregular, untidy.

1632 J. HAYWARD tr. *Biondi's Eromena* 59 The winds so outrageously unstable..they were constrained to rome up and downe, with an order so disorderly, that [etc.]. **1655** STANLEY *Hist. Philos.* III. (1701) 112/2 Æschylus, saith he, is of all Poets..the harshest, most disorderly. **1712** BERKELEY *Passive Obed.* §28 A disorderly and confused chaos. **1725** N. ROBINSON *Th. Physick* viii. 175 A disorderly, weak, low Pulse. **1850** PRESCOTT *Peru* I. 302 The disorderly state of Peru was such as to demand the immediate interposition of government. **1855** MACAULAY *Hist. Eng.* IV. 79 A mob of people as naked, as dirty, and as disorderly as the beggars.. on the Continent.

2. a. Opposed to or violating moral order, constituted authority, or recognized rule or method; not submissive to rule, lawless; unruly; tumultuous, riotous. (Of persons, or their actions, etc.)

1585 ABP. SANDYS *Serm.* (1841) 383 To behold the disorderly dealings of the wicked. **1658** A. FOX *Wurtz' Surg.* III. iii. 224 A patient causeth pains to himself with disorderly eating and drinking. *c* **1680** BEVERIDGE *Serm.* (1729) I. 24 Whatsoever disorderly or unworthy persons are admitted to holy orders. **1681-6** J. SCOTT *Chr. Life* (1747) III. 310 To confirm the Weak, and admonish the Disorderly. **1700** S. L. tr *Fryke's Voy. E. Ind.* 217 They [Seamen] ever grow more disorderly and ungovernable as they come nearer home. **1817** *Parl. Deb.* 346 The Speaker submitted..that..if it was a personal charge against an individual member of the House, it was certainly disorderly. **1845** STEPHEN *Comm. Laws Eng.* VI. vii. §14 (1895) IV. 221 If the drunkenness be accompanied with riotous or disorderly behavior.. imprisonment for any term not exceeding one month, with or without hard labour, may be imposed. **1879** *Cassell's Techn. Educ.* III. 163 Disorderly conduct is always severely punished. **1891** *Law Times* XC. 412/1 [He] appeared to be under the influence of drink, and was behaving in a most disorderly manner. *Mod.* He was charged with being drunk and disorderly.

b. *spec.* in *Law.* Violating public order or morality; constituting a nuisance; *esp.* in ***disorderly house*** (see quot. 1877); ***disorderly person,*** one guilty of one of a number of offences against public order as defined by various Acts of Parliament, esp. 5 Geo. IV, c. 83. §3.

1744 *Act 17 Geo. II*, c. 5. §1 They who threaten to run away and leave their wives or children to the parish; or unlawfully return to a parish from whence they have been legally removed; or, not having wherewith to maintain themselves, live idle, and refuse to work for the usual wages; and all persons going from door to door, or placing themselves in streets, etc., to beg in the parishes where they dwell, shall be deemed Idle and Disorderly Persons. **1809** TOMLINS *Law Dict.*, *Disorderly houses*, see *Bawdy Houses*; *Riots*; *Theatres*. **1817** *Parl. Deb.* 435 Be it enacted, that every house, room or place, which shall be opened or used as a place of meeting for the purpose of reading books, pamphlets, newspapers, or other publications..shall be deemed a disorderly house or place, unless the same shall have been previously licensed. **1824** *Act 5 Geo. IV*, c. 83. §3. ....every petty chapman or pedlar wandering abroad and trading, without being duly licensed or authorized by law.. ..[etc. etc.] shall be deemed an idle and disorderly person within the true intent and meaning of this act. **1877** J. F. STEPHEN *Digest Crim. Law* (1883) 122 The following houses are disorderly houses, that is to say: common bawdy houses, common gaming houses, common betting houses, disorderly places of entertainment. **1887** *Times* 30 Sept. 8/3 The charge of keeping..a disorderly house.

†**3.** Affected with disorder or disturbance of the bodily functions; diseased, morbid. *Obs.*

1655 CULPEPPER *Riverius* IV. vii. 121 A thin watery Humor or Choller which abounds in the blood, and makes it more disorderly.

4. Attended with mental agitation or discomposure. *rare.*

1871 R. ELLIS *Catullus* lxv. 24 She in tell-tale cheeks glows a disorderly shame.

B. *sb.* A disorderly person.

1852 G. C. MUNDY *Our Antipodes* III. ii. 80 A brace of disorderlies in handcuffs. **1855** *Illustr. Lond. News* 21 July 74/1 One of the drunk and disorderlies. **1905** *Daily Chron.* 9 Oct. 5/3 The Pope was obliged to threaten the disorderlies with expulsion from the Vatican.

dis'orderly, *adv.* [f. as prec. + -LY².] In a disorderly manner.

1. Without order or regular arrangement; confusedly, irregularly; in disorder or confusion.

a **1577** GASCOIGNE *Devise of a Masque, etc.* (R.) On other side the Turkes..Disorderly did spread their force. **1586** *Exam. H. Barrow, etc.* in *Harl. Misc.* (Malh.) II. 17 Suggestions against me, disorderly framed according to the malitious humour of mine accuser. **1632** J. HAYWARD tr. *Biondi's Eromena* 37 With their heire hanging disorderly about their eares. **1745** P. THOMAS *Jrnl. Anson's Voy.* 182 The Husbandmen at first sow it [rice] disorderly, like other Corn. **1847** TENNYSON *Princess* IV. 152 'To horse' Said Ida; 'home! to horse!' and fled..Disorderly the women.

2. Not according to order or rule; in a lawless or unruly way; tumultuously, riotously.

1564 *Brief Exam.* *iij, Their amendement who haue disorderlye behaued them selues. **1581** LAMBARDE *Eiren.* II. v. (1588) 185 An unlawfull Assemblie, is the companie of three or mo persons, disorderly comming together..to commit an vnlawfull acte. **1611** BIBLE *2 Thess.* iii. 6 That ye withdraw your selues from euery brother that walketh disorderly. **1689** LUTTRELL *Brief Rel.* (1857) I. 528 The Polish letters bring, that the dyet..was lately broken up very disorderly. **1843** J. H. NEWMAN *Miracles* 58 They could use them disorderly.

3. With mental agitation or discomposure. *rare.*

1811 W. R SPENCER *Poems* 211 Disorderly she own'd her glorious passion.

†**dis'orderous,** *a. Obs.* [f. DISORDER *sb.* + -OUS.] = DISORDERLY *a.* Hence †**dis'orderously** *adv.*, †**dis'orderousness.**

1579 TOMSON *Calvin's Serm. Tim.* 115/1 They whiche liue disorderously, and giue euill example to the rest. *Ibid.* 119/2 If there be any disorderous or disolute person. *Ibid.* 143/1 If they see any dronkardes, if they see any whoredome, and such like disorderousnesse. **1581** J. BELL *Haddon's Answ. Osor.* 215 b, One onely disorderous order of people. *Ibid.* 323 The disorderous abuses of all your religion. **1652** J. WADSWORTH tr. *Sandoval's Civil Wars Sp.* 164 Risen in such Commotious and Disordrous manner.

†**dis'ordinance.** *Obs.* Forms: 4-5 dis-, dys-, -orden-, -ordin-, -ordyn-aunce, 5-6 -ordonaunce. [a. OF. *desordenance*, later *-on(n)ance*, f. *desordener* (now *-ordonner*) to DISORDAIN: see -ANCE.] Disorder, confusion, irregularity.

c **1374** CHAUCER *Boeth.* v. pr. i. 150 What place myȝt[e] ben left..to folie and to disordinaunce syn þat god ledip.. alle þinges by ordre? **1481** CAXTON *Tully's Friendship, Orat. G. Flaminius* E iv, They have sette it in grete trouble and disordinaunce. **1489** —— *Faytes of A.* I. xvi. 48 Noo thyng is mor preiudicyable in a bataille than dysordonaunce. **1502** *Ord. Crysten Men* (W. de W. 1506) IV. xiii. 205 Yf he haue not other disordonaunce.

†**dis'ordinate,** *a. Obs.* Forms: α. 4-7 disordinat, 5 dys-, disordynate, disordenate, 6- disordinate. β. 5-6 des-, dys-, 6 disordon(n)ate. [Latinized form of OF. *desordené* (= Sp. *desordenado*, It. *disordinato*), pa. pple. of *desordener* to DISORDAIN. Cf. the synonym DEORDINATE from med.L. **deordināre*, and see DE- I. 6.]

1. Not conformed to moral order, or to what is right, befitting, or reasonable; transgressing the bounds of moderation or propriety; unrestrained, immoderate, inordinate. (Cf. DISORDERLY *a.* 2.)

c **1386** CHAUCER *Pars. T.* ¶348 The horrible disordinat scantnesse of clothing. **1483** CAXTON *Gold. Leg.* 34/2 For this cause putteth gylbert the necglygence of prelates emonge the thyngys dysordynate. **1502** *Ord. Crysten Men* (W. de W. 1506) I. vii. 75 [The soul] falleth by affeccion in loue dysordonate in to powder & asshes of thynges erthely. **1577** NORTHBROOKE *Dicing* (1843) 171 They daunce with disordinate gestures..to dishonest verses. **1579** TWYNE *Phisicke agst. Fort.* II. xlviii. 223 b, Although the lyfe of man in many other thinges be disordinate and out of course. **1660** F. BROOKE tr. *Le Blanc's Trav.* 117 Winter begins in May, because of the disordinate raines which fall from that Moneth to the end of August. *a* **1693** URQUHART *Rabelais* III. xxxii. 271 Disordinate Passions and Perturbations of the Mind.

b. of persons.

1483 CAXTON *Cato* A ij, By whiche they be the more disordynate and obstynate in their Iniquite. **1574** HELLOWES *Gueuara's Fam. Ep.* 4 A Prince..disordinate in eating, and not sober in drinking, is termed but vicious. **1670** MILTON *Hist. Eng.* III. (1851) 99 They..unfitted..the People, now grown worse and more disordinat, to receave..any Liberty. **1671** —— *Samson* 701 With sickness and disease thou bow'st them down..Though not disordinate, yet causeless suffering The punishment of dissolute days.

2. Devoid of order, confused, irregular; = DISORDERLY *a.* 1. (Only in De Quincey.)

1822-56 De Quincey *Confess.* Wks. V. 146 This private Oswestry library wore something of the same wild tumultuary aspect, fantastic and disordinate. **1840** —— *Style* Wks. XI. 182 Artifices peculiarly adapted to the powers of the Latin language, and yet..careless and disordinate.

Hence † **dis'ordinateness**, *Obs.*

1657 *Divine Lover* 113 When shall disordinatenesse be blotted out of thee?

† **dis'ordinately**, *adv. Obs.* [f. prec. + -ly².]

1. Not according to order, propriety, or moderation; irregularly; inordinately, excessively.

1474 Caxton *Chesse* i. i. A iv, To displese..god by synne & the peple by lyuyng disordonatly. *Ibid.* iii. iii. F ij b, They deceyve the symple men & drawen them to the courtes disordenately. **1491** —— *Vitas Patr.* (W. de W. 1495) i. xlvii. 83 a/1 They that louen dysordynatly the honoures of thys worlde. **1548** Hall *Chron., Hen. V.* (an. 2) 35 b, The temporall landes devoutely geven, and disordinatly spent by religious and other spirituall persones. **1624** *Gag for Pope* 7 The king would take into his hands the lands disordinately consumed by the Clergy.

2. Without order or arrangement, confusedly, irregularly.

1830 De Quincey *Kant in Misc. Ess.* Wks. (1890) VIII. 92 No matter how clumsily, disordinately, ungracefully. **1854** —— *Autobiog.* Wks. II. 18 The..library..has been so disordinately collected.

† **disordination** (dɪsɔːdɪ'neɪʃən). [n. of action and condition from disordain *v.*, disordinate *a.*: see -ation.] Disarrangement, putting out of order; disordered condition; = deordination.

1626 Bacon *Sylva* §836 This is wrought by Emission..of the Natiue Spirits; And also by the Disordination and Discomposture of the Tangible Parts. **1684** T. Burnet *Th. Earth* i. 156 How comes this disturbance and disordination in nature? **1896** *Pop. Sci. Monthly* Feb. 521, I would propose the term *disordination*, the etymological opposite of coordination. **1897** *Educ. Rev.* XIII. 52 The phenomena of hypnotic disordination or disruption of consciousness.

disordined: see disordained 2.

disording: see disordeine *a. Obs.*

disordonat, -aunce: see disordinate, -ance.

disorganic (dɪsɔː'gænɪk), *a.* [dis- 10.] Not organic; without organic or organized constitution.

1840 Carlyle *Heroes* v. (1872) 156 This anomaly of a disorganic Literary Class. **1843** —— *Past & Pr.* iv. vi. (1872) 247 This disorganic..hell-ridden world.

dis,organi'zation. [ad. F. *désorganisation* (1764 in Hatz.-Darm.), n. of action f. *désorganiser*: see next. This family of words appears to have entered English at the French Revolution.]

The action of disorganizing, or condition of being disorganized; loss or absence of organization.

1794 W. Burke tr. *Addr. M. Brissot* in *Burke's Wks.* (1808) VII. 329 The anarchy of the administration of Paché, which has completely disorganized the supply of our armies; which by that disorganization reduced the army of Dumourier to stop in the middle of its conquests. **1809** Wellington in Gurw. *Desp.* IV. 458 He found the Portuguese army..in such a state of disorganization, that [etc.]. **1833** Ht. Martineau *Loom & Lugger* ii. v. 80 The total disorganization of society. **1845** Budd *Dis. Liver* 383 Disorganization or atrophy of the lobular substance of the liver. **1884** *Manch. Exam.* 10 Dec. 5/2 Half measures..are fruitful only of disorganization and discontent.

disorganize (dɪs'ɔːgənaɪz), *v.* [ad. F. *désorganiser* (1764 in Hatz.-Darm.), f. *des-*, dis- 4 + *organiser* to organize.] *trans.* To destroy the organization or systematic arrangement of; to break up the organic connexion of; to throw into confusion or disorder.

1793 Burke *Conduct Minority* Wks. 1842 I. 618 Their ever memorable decree of the 15th of December, 1792, for disorganizing every country in Europe, into which they should..set their foot. **1802** A. Hamilton *Wks.* (1886) VII. 324 This will give him fair play to disorganize New England, if so disposed. **1812** Collinson *Treat. Law Idiots & Lunaticks* I. 68 (Jod.), You can not enter into the mind to know by what means it is disorganized, but you find it disorganized. **1849** Macaulay *Hist. Eng.* I. 478 The Whigs ..though defeated, disheartened, and disorganized, did not yield without an effort.

dis'organized, *ppl. a.* [f. prec. + -ed¹.]

Deprived or destitute of organization; having lost, or being without, organic connexion or systematic arrangement; thrown into confusion, disordered.

1812 [see disorganize]. **1840** Macaulay *Ess. Clive* (1854) 529/1 A succession of revolutions; a disorganized administration. **1868** Ruskin *Pol. Econ. Art* Add. 199 A vast and disorganized mob, scrambling each for what he can get. **1879** Harlan *Eyesight* v. 53 The operation for the removal of a disorganized eye is not a serious one.

dis'organizer. [f. as prec. + -er¹.] One who or that which disorganizes.

1795 Helen M. Williams *Lett. on France* II. 131 (Jod.) [They] discredit the cause of liberty..by treating as atheists, that is to say, as universal disorganizers, its partisans and friends. **1835** *New Monthly Mag.* XLV. 301 If he had lived in the French revolution he should have been a great disorganiser. **1894** D. G. Thompson in *Forum* (U.S.) Jan. 592 That greatest disorganizer of society..war.

dis'organizing, *ppl. a.* [f. as prec. + -ing².]

That disorganizes; causing disorganization.

1796 C. Burney *Metastasio* III. 254 Her unprincipled, philosophical, and disorganizing successor. **1799** W. Taylor in *Monthly Rev.* XXVIII. 525 French principles have been called disorganizing. **1800** J. Bowles *Polit. & Moral State Soc.* 160 *note*, The disorganizing and licentious principles of the French Revolution. **1895** *Century Mag.* Aug. 549/1 They weaken the body by..violent, depressing, and disorganizing emotions.

dis'orient, *v.* [ad. F. *désorienter* to turn from an eastward position, cause to lose one's bearings, embarrass, f. *des-* dis- 4 + *orienter* to orient.]

trans. To turn from the east; to cause to 'lose one's bearings'; to put out, disconcert, embarrass. Hence, **disoriented, disorienting,** *ppl. adjs.*

1655 J. Jennings *Elise* 48 'Twas Philippin who was disoriented, but more Isabella. **1740** Warburton *Div. Legat.* v. (R.), I doubt then the learned professor was a little disoriented when he called the promises in Ezekiel and in the Revelations the same. **1835** Syd. Smith *Memoir, etc.* (1855) II. 356, I hope you will disorient yourself soon. The departure of the wise men from the East seems to have been on a more extensive scale than is generally supposed. **1931** A. L. Rowse *Politics & Younger Generation* 21 Others.. emerged from it [*sc.* the war] shaken and disoriented. **1950** M. Lowry *Let.* Jan. (1967) 189, I was trading on your.. disorienting yourself from your own orbit. **1951** R. M. Williams *Amer. Society* (1952) xiv. 535 Individuals are pulled this way and that..until the person is literally disoriented. **1957** J. Kerouac *On the Road* (1958) 274 Where disoriented people have to go to be near a specific elsewhere. **1964** A. W. Gouldner in I. L. Horowitz *New Sociol.* 203 A disorienting normlessness.

disorientate (dɪs'ɔərɪənteɪt), *v.* [dis- 6.]

a. *trans.* To turn from an eastward position; *pa. pple.* not facing due east.

1704 J. Harris *Lex. Techn.*, cited in Johnson. **1730-6** Bailey (folio), *Disorientated* (spoken of a sun-dial), turn'd away from the east, or some of the cardinal points. **1850** *Ecclesiologist* XI. 79 S. John the Evangelist [Guernsey] is a district church, built in 1836. It is disorientated. **1853** *Ibid.* XIV. 361 It has a chancel..strangely disorientated towards the south.

b. *fig.*

1727-51 Chambers *Cycl.* s.v., The word is most frequently used..for the disconcerting, or putting a man out of his way, or element. Speak of law to a physician, or of physic to a lawyer, and they will both be disorientated. **1928** F. Brett Young *My Brother Jonathan* 582 His freedom disorientated him. **1965** *Nursing Times* 5 Feb. 184/1 She was confused and disorientated (unaware of time, place or person).

Hence **dis'orientated** *ppl. a.*

1959 *Times Lit. Suppl.* 16 Oct. 598/2 A somewhat disorientated person, who suddenly discovers that an affair has been taking place in the neighbourhood between a strange blonde girl and someone who has apparently assumed his own identity. **1960** *Times* 23 May 16/2 The talented yet disorientated adolescent.

disorien'tation. [n. of action f. prec. vb.]

1. The condition of being disorientated; deviation from the eastward position.

1860 *Ecclesiologist* XXI. 400 A Roman Catholic church at Wrexham, which, by its intentional disorientation, looks very awkward by the side of..the new church of S. Mark.

2. The condition of having lost one's bearings; uncertainty as to direction. Also, a confused mental state, often due to disease, in which appreciation of one's spatial position, personal identity, and relations, or of the passage of time, is disturbed.

1882 W. James in *Amer. Ann. Deaf & Dumb* Apr. (1883) 109 [One lost in woods or forgetting in the dark the position of his bed] knows the altogether peculiar discomfort and anxiety of such 'disorientation' in the horizontal plane. **1902** A. R. Defendorf tr. *Kraepelin's Clin. Psychiatry* 15 Disorientation..is possibly a special form of a moderate clouding of consciousness. **1957** *Times* 4 Oct. 11/6 Exposure to noise levels of about 150 decibels may result in disorientation, nausea and vomiting. **1962** Henderson & Gillespie *Text-bk. Psychiatry* (ed. 9) vi. 107 Simple inattention..may cause partial disorientation.

† **dis'ornament,** *v. Obs. rare* [dis- 6 or 7 a.] *trans.* To deprive of ornament.

1593 Nashe *Christ's T.* (1613) 58 The disornamenting of this mother of Cities. **1648** E. Sparke in J. Shute *Sarah & H.* (1649) Ep. Ded., The very Executioner of all Ingenuity, which it..rifles and disornaments.

disosit, obs. Sc. f. disused.

† **'disour.** *Obs.* (exc. *Hist.*) Forms: 4 disur, disour, dyssour, 4-6 dysour, 5 dysowre, 6 disor, dyser, dyzar, disare, dissar, (9 *Hist.* dissour, disour). [a. OF. *disour, -eor, -or, -eur*, agent-n. from *dire, dis-ant* to say. Cf. Pr. *dizedor*, Sp. *decidor*, It. *dicitore*, repr. a Romanic type **dīcitōrem*, from L. *dīcĕre* to say, tell. See also dizzard.] A (professional) story-teller; a reciter of 'gestes'; a jester.

a **1300** *Cursor M.* 27932 (Cott.) Speche o disur, rimes vnright, gest of Jogolur. *c* **1330** R. Brunne *Chron. Wace* (Rolls) Prol. 75, I mad nought for no disours..Bot for þe luf of symple menne, þat strange Inglis canne not kenne. **1362** Langl. *P. Pl.* A. vii. 50 Hold not þou with harlotes, here not heore tales..For þei ben þe deueles disours, I do þe to vndurstonde. **1377** *Ibid.* B. xiii. 172 'It is but a dido', quod þis doctour, 'a dysoures tale'. **1496** *Dives & Paup.* (W. de W.) ix. vi. 355/2 This mynstrall is the worlde whiche playeth with folke of this worlde as a mynstrall as a Jogulour and as a dysour. **1530** Palsgr. 214/1 Dissar, a scoffer, *saigefol.* **1532** More *Confut. Tindale* Wks. 374/1 He playeth the deuils disor euen in this point. **1801** Strutt *Sports & Past.* iii. iii. 162 The conteurs and the jestours, who are also called dissours, and seggers..were literally tale-tellers. **1890** *Q. Rev.* Oct. 439 Disours, jongleurs, gleemen.

disown (dɪs'əʊn), *v.* [f. dis- 6 + own *v.*: cf. *disclaim.*

(In some recent dictionaries, this and the simple *own* have each been improperly split up into two verbs, sense 3 being erroneously assumed to be derived from OE. *unnan* to grant, with which it has no connexion: see own *v.*)]

† **1.** *trans.* To cease to own, to relinquish one's possession of; to give up, part with, renounce.

c **1620** H. Anderson *Bidding World Farewell* in Farr *S.P. Jas. I* (1848) 304 The houre is set wherein they must disown The royal pomp, the treasure, and the throne.

2. To refuse to acknowledge as one's own, or as connected with oneself; not to own; to renounce, repudiate, disclaim.

1649 *St. Trials, Col. J. Lilburn* (R.) You say it is impossible for you..without advice of counsel to own or disown books. **1659** D. Pell *Impr. Sea* 415 That Christ will disown, and reject many that have strong hopes..of their Salvation. **1726** *Adv. Capt. R. Boyle* 130 The king..had not the least Regard to his Word, and even disown'd a Letter he had written to..the King of France. **1777** Franklin *Lett.* Wks. (1889) VI. 117, I see..that Mr. Deane is disowned in some of his agreements with officers. **1832** Ht. Martineau *Homes Abroad* i. 4 He had for some time disowned them as sons. **1856** Froude *Hist. Eng.* (1858) I. ii. 116 The prince.. was..required to disown..the obligations contracted in his name.

b. To refuse to acknowledge the authority of (a government, etc.) over oneself; to renounce allegiance to.

1693 Luttrell *Brief Rel.* (1857) III. 89 Sir George Downing, who disowned this government at the beginning of the revolution..has taken the oaths. **1726** *Adv. Capt. R. Boyle* 127 Their Mufti..disowns the Emperor's Authority. **1855** Macaulay *Hist. Eng.* III. 705 As soon as James was restored, it would be a duty to disown and withstand him. The present duty was to disown and withstand his son in law.

c. In the Society of Friends: To disclaim as a fellow-member; to expel from membership.

1727 *Minutes of Yearly Meeting of Soc. Friends* 26 Mar. (J. Phillips, 1783), Any person denied by a Monthly Meeting is adjudged as disowned by Friends and to stand and remain in that state, till by his repentance..he is reconciled to Friends, or reinstated in membership among them. **1783-1883** *Book of Discipline of Soc. Friends* 204 Which Meeting is to receive his acknowledgment or to disown him, as in its judgment the case shall require. **1806** [see disownment].

† **3.** To refuse to acknowledge or admit (anything imputed, claimed, or asserted); to deny. *Obs.*

1666 Pepys *Diary* 24 June, He do not disowne but that the dividing of the fleet..was a good resolution. **1701** De Foe *True-born Eng.* Pref., Nor do I disown..that I could be glad to see it rectified. **1710** *Lond. Gaz.* No. 4752/2 The Court no longer disown his..Majesty's Arrival. **1726** Leoni *Alberti's Archit.* I. 26/1 We cannot disown that it has one Fault.

Hence **dis'owned** *ppl. a.*, **dis'owning** *vbl. sb.*

1654 Ld. Orrery *Parthen.* (1676) 675 A disowning of their Quarrel by the Gods. **1707** Norris *Treat. Humility* iii. 119 A constructive disowning, and vertual denial of our having received what we have from God. **1813** Mar. Edgeworth *Patron.* II. xxiv. 70 Lord Oldborough had never, after the disowning of Buckhurst, mentioned his name. **1829** Lytton (*title*), The Disowned.

† **dis'ownable,** *a. Obs.* [f. prec. + -able.]

Liable to be disowned; *spec.* rendering one liable to be disowned (sense 2 c).

Schaff *Encycl. Relig. Knowl.* (1882-3) III. 197 From 1696 to 1776 the society nearly every year declared 'the importing, purchase, or sale of slaves' by its members to be a 'disownable offence'.

disowner (dɪs'əʊnə(r)). [f. disown *v.*] One who disowns.

1895 J. Smith *Perm. Mess. Exodus* ix. 126 The disowners of God.

dis'ownment. [f. as disown *v.* + -ment.] The act of disowning, renunciation; *spec.* repudiation from membership in the Society of Friends.

1806 Clarkson *Port. Quaker.* I. Discipline i. §11. 195 He is then publicly excluded from membership, or, as it is called, Disowned. This is done by a distinct document, called a Testimony of Disownment. **1883** *Book of Discipline of Soc. Friends* 203 The Monthly Meeting should, after due consideration, issue a testimony of disownment against such person. **1893** *Columbus* (Ohio) *Disp.* 14 Sept., The disownment and desertion [of Burns] by Jean Armour.

† **dis'oxidate,** *v. Chem. Obs.* [dis- 6.] *trans.* To reduce from the state of an oxide: = deoxidate.

Hence **dis'oxidating** *ppl. a.*; also **disoxi'dation** = DEOXIDATION.

1801 CHENEVIX in *Phil. Trans.* XCI. 240 A very small mixture of any disoxidating substance. **1802** SMITHSON *Ibid.* XCIII. 26 The disoxidation of the zinc calx. **1817** COLERIDGE *Biog. Lit. etc.* 403 A handicraftsman from a laboratory, who had just succeeded in disoxydating an earth.

†**dis'oxygenate,** *v. Chem. Obs.* [DIS- 6.] *trans.* To deprive of oxygen: = DEOXYGENATE. Hence **dis'oxygenated** *ppl. a.*; also **disoxyge'nation** = DEOXYGENATION.

1800 HENRY *Epit. Chem.* (1808) 137 The sulphur is not entirely disoxygenated. *Ibid.* 177 The affinity of this acid for its base is weakened by dis-oxygenation. **1822** IMISON *Sc. & Art* II. 199 Indigo will not combine with the cloth except in its disoxygenated or green state. **1831** BREWSTER *Optics* x. 91 Two sets of invisible rays in the solar spectrum, one on the red side which favours oxygenation, and the other on the violet side which favours disoxygenation.

†**di'space,** *v. Obs.* [A Spenserian formation of doubtful derivation. Perh. f. DIS- 1 + PACE *v.*; or else f. L. *di-*, DI-[1] + *spatiārī*, It. *spaziare* to walk.] *intr.* and *refl.* To walk or move about.

1588 SPENSER *Virgil's Gnat* 295 Thus wise long time he did himselfe dispace There round about. **1591** —— *Muiopot.* 250 But when he spide the joyous Butterflie In this faire plot dispacing too and fro. **1610** G. FLETCHER *Christ's Tri. after Death* (R.), [The Saints] in this lower field dispacing wide, Through windy thoughts, that would their sails misguide.

†**dis'pack,** *v. Obs. rare.* [f. DIS- 6 + PACK *v.*: cf. OF. *despacquer* to unpack (1496 in Godef.).] *trans.* To unpack, to open out.

1591 SYLVESTER *Du Bartas* I. i. 518 When God the mingled lump dispackt, From fiery element did light extract.

dis'pageant, *v. rare.* [DIS- 7 b.] *trans.* To strip of pageantry or brilliant display.

1861 LYTTON & FANE *Tannhäuser* 74 The mighty Hall Dumb, dismally dispageanted.

†**dis'paint,** *v. Obs. rare.* [f. DIS- 1 + PAINT *v.*: cf. *depaint*.] *trans.* To paint diversely.

1590 SPENSER *F.Q.* II. ix. 50 His chamber was dispainted all within With sondry colours.

†**dis'pair,** *v.*[1] *Obs.* [f. DIS- 6 + PAIR *v.*] *trans.* To undo the pairing of, separate from being a pair.

1598 SYLVESTER *Du Bartas* II. ii. III. *Colonies* 41 The grissell Turtles (seldome seen alone) Dis-payer'd and parted, wander one by one. *c* **1611** BEAUM. & FL. *Triumph of Love* vii, I have..dispaired two doves, Made 'em sit mourning. **1748** RICHARDSON *Clarissa* (1811) IV. x. 60 Engagements where the minds are unpaired—*dispaired* in my case, may I say.

†**dispair(e,** *v.*[2] *Obs.* [var. of DEPAIR, a. OF. *despeirer, depeirer* to spoil. Cf. also DISPAYRE *sb.*] *intr.* To spoil, become injured, 'go bad'.

1573 TUSSER *Husb.* lvii. (1878) 136 Kell dried [hops] will abide foule weather or faire, where drieng and lieng in loft doo dispaire.

dispair(e, obs. form of DESPAIR.

†**dis'palate,** *v. Obs. rare.* [f. DIS- 6 + PALATE *v.*] *trans.* To make or find unpalatable, disrelish.

1630 BRATHWAIT *Eng. Gentlem.* (1641) 75 His Vocation, which perchance by our nicer and more curious gallants.. will be distasted and dispalated.

†**dis'pale,** *v. Obs. rare.* [DIS- 7 a.] *trans.* To deprive of its pale or enclosing fence.

1658 J. JONES *Ovid's Ibis* 51 An adulterous wife is Acteons park dispal'd.

†**di'spand,** *v. Obs.* [ad. L. *dispand-ĕre*, f. DIS- 1 + *pandĕre* to spread, stretch.] *trans.* To spread abroad, to expand.

1656 BLOUNT *Glossogr.*, *Dispand* (*dispando*), to stretch out or spread abroad. **1657** TOMLINSON *Renou's Disp.* Ded., The rayes of your Learning being dispanded. **1669** WORLIDGE *Syst. Agric.* (1681) 56 This Seed.. being cast into its proper Matrix or Menstruum.. doth dispand its self, and increase into the form and matter by Nature designed. **1692–1732** COLES, *Expand*, dispand, display.

†**dis'pannel,** *v. Obs. rare.* [f. DIS- 6 + PANNEL *v.*] *trans.* To deprive of a 'pannel' or saddle-cloth.

1654 GAYTON *Pleas. Notes* IV. xx. 267 Behind dispannell'd Sancho rode.

†**di'spansion.** *Obs. rare*[−0]. [n. of action from DISPAND.] = EXPANSION.

1658 PHILLIPS, *Dispansion*, a spreading both wayes. **1755** JOHNSON, *Dispansion*, the act of displaying; the act of spreading; diffusion; dilatation.

dispansive (dɪ'spænsɪv), *a.* [f. L. *dispans-*, ppl. stem of *dispandĕre* to DISPAND: see -IVE.] (See quot.)

1883 *Syd. Soc. Lex.*, *Dispansive*, term applied to a system of lenses which has a negative focal distance. Used in opposition to a system of lenses with positive focal distance, which is termed *collective*.

dispantheonize, dis'papalize: see DIS- 6.

†**'dispar,** *a. Obs. rare.* [ad. L. *dispar*, f. DIS- 4 + *par* equal.] Unequal, unlike.

1587 *Misfort. Arthur* IV. ii. in Hazl. *Dodsley* IV. 323 Dispar minds and inward moods unlike.

dispar(e, obs. form of DESPAIR.

†**'disparable,** *a. Obs. rare.* [f. L. *dispar* unequal, or f. L. *dispar-āre* to separate, divide; perhaps after COMPARABLE.] Unlike.

1413 *Pilgr. Sowle* (Caxton) I. iii. (1859) 4 Dyuerse and disparayble, bothe in theyr persounes, and.. occupacyons.

†**dis'paradise,** *v. Obs. rare.* [DIS- 7 c.] *trans.* To turn out of paradise. Also *fig.*

1593 NASHE *Christ's T.* (1613) 78 Thou that ere this hast disparradiz'd our first Parent Adam. **1623** COCKERAM, *Disparadized*, falne from happinesse to miserie.

†**di'sparage,** *sb. Obs.* Also 4–5 des-, disperage. [ME. *despa'rage, dispe'rage*, a. OF. *desparage* unworthy marriage (Godef.), f. as next.]

1. Inequality of rank in marriage; an unequal match; disgrace resulting from marriage with one of inferior rank.

c **1315** SHOREHAM 54 Ne may hem falle after thys lyf Non on-worth desperage. *c* **1386** CHAUCER *Clerk's T.* 852 Hym wolde thynke it were a disparage To his estaat so lowe for talighte. **1574** tr. *Littleton's Tenures* 23 b, No desparage shalbee but where he that hath the warde marieth him within the age of xiiij yeare. **1596** SPENSER *F.Q.* IV. viii. 50 Her friends.. Dissuaded her from such a disparage.

2. Ill-matchedness; incongruity.

c **1430** *Hymns Virg.* (1867) 74 Pride in age Doiþ disperage.

3. Disparagement, dishonour.

a **1592** H. SMITH *Wks.* (1867) II. 481 If I forbear.. I blush, I fear His despite and my disparage. **1615** HEYWOOD *Foure Prentises* I. Wks. 1874 II. 169, I hold it no disparage to my birth, Though I be borne an Earle, to haue the skill And the full knowledge of the Mercers Trade.

disparage (dɪ'spærɪdʒ), *v.* Also 4 des-, 5 dys-; 5 dysparych, 7 disparadge, -parrage, -parge. [a. OF. *desparagier, desperager* to match or cause to marry unequally; later 'to offer vnto, or impose on a man vnfit, or vnworthie conditions' (Cotgr.), f. *des-*, DIS- 4 + *parage* equality of rank.]

†**1.** *trans.* To match unequally; to degrade or dishonour by marrying to one of inferior rank. *Obs.*

[**1292** BRITTON III. iii. §4 Et si acune de juvene age soit marié a tiel ou ele est desparagé. *transl.* If any female heir of tender years be married where she is disparaged.] *c* **1350** *Will. Palerne* 485, I nel leie mi loue so low.. Desparaged were i disgisili ȝif i dede in þis wise. **1480** CAXTON *Chron. Eng.* ccxvii. 204 Moch was this fayr damysel dysparaged sith that she was maryed ayenst al the comune assent of England. **1611** COTGR., *Apparagé*, a maid thats maried vnto her equall, or, thats not disparaged. **1779–81** JOHNSON *L.P.*, *Pope* Wks. IV. 113 History relates that she was about to disparage herself by a marriage with an inferior.

2. To bring discredit or reproach upon; to dishonour, discredit; to lower in credit or esteem.

c **1386** CHAUCER *Reeve's T.* 351 Who dorste be so boold to disparage My doghter that is come of swich lynage? *a* **1400** *Pistill of Susan* 253 Heo keuered vp on hir kneos, and cussed his hand: For I am dampned, I ne dar disparage þi mouþ. **1486** *Bk. St. Albans* B ij b, Then is the hawke disparagid for all that yere. **1612** BP. HALL *Recoll. Treat.* (1614) 657 The place oft-times disparages; As, to put the Arke of God into a Cart, or to set it by Dagon. **1691** HARTCLIFFE *Virtues* 406 Men disparage Religion who profess it, and do not guide their Actions according to its Doctrines. **1754** FOOTE *Knights* I. Wks. 1799 I. 69 If you tell father he'll knock my brains out, for he says I'll disparage the family. **1854** BREWSTER *More Worlds* Pref. 6 A view.. calculated to disparage the science of astronomy.

†**3. a.** To lower in position or dignity; to degrade. **b.** To lower in one's own estimation; to cast down. *Obs.*

1496 *Dives & Paup.* (W. de W.) VI. xv. 258/1 Cryste.. anentysshed hymself and dysparyched hymselfe in to the lykenesse of a seruaunt. **1548** HALL *Chron., Hen. VI* (an. 28) 160 Lest they shoulde.. declare his base byrthe, and lowsy lynage, desparagyng him from his usurped surname of Mortymer. **1590** SPENSER *F.Q.* II. x. 2 How shall fraile pen, with fear disparaged, Conceive such soveraine glory and great bountyhed? **1614** H. GREENWOOD *Jayle Delivery* 471 They that are troubled and amazed at their sinnes, let them not be disparaged. **1704–5** POPE *Let. to Wycherley* 25 Jan., I am disparaged and disheartened by your commendations. **1716** ADDISON *Drummer* I. i, I'll not disparage myself to be a Servant in a House that is haunted.

4. To speak of or treat slightingly; to treat as something lower than it is; to undervalue; to vilify.

1536 CRANMER in *Four C. Eng. Lett.* 14 They should not esteem any part of your grace's honour to be touched thereby, but her honour only to be clearly disparaged. **1599** SHAKS. *Much Ado* III. ii. 131, I will disparage her no farther, till you are my witnesses. *a* **1656** BP. HALL *Rem. Wks.* (1660) 161 One dares question, yea disparage the sacred Scriptures of God. **1660** HICKERINGILL *Jamaica* (1661) 20 The Composition of.. Chocoletta is now so vulgar, that I will not disparage my Reader by doubting his acquaintance in so known a Recipe. **1715** BURNET *Own Time* (1766) II. 48 Took it ill of me that I should disparage the kings evidence. **1837–9** HALLAM *Hist. Lit.* IV. vi. IV. §16. 267 It is a very narrow criticism which disparages Racine out of idolatry of Shakspeare. **1859** MILL *Liberty* ii. (1865) 26/1 It is the fashion of the present time to disparage negative logic.

Hence **di'sparaged** *ppl. a.*

1611 COTGR., *Desparagé*, disparaged. **1802** BEDDOES *Hygëia* v. 22 Would not the disparaged milk afford wholesome aliment? **1885** GLADSTONE *Sp. Ho. Com.* 23 Feb., A disparaged Government and a doubtful House of Commons.

di'sparageable, *a.* [f. DISPARAGE *v.* + -ABLE.]

†**1.** Tending to disparage or bring disgrace upon; lowering, disgraceful. *Obs.*

1617 COLLINS *Def. Bp. Ely* II. vii. 276 Can there be any thing more disparageable to a poore suiter then this? **1635** N. R. *Camden's Hist. Eliz.* I. 53 They disdained this marriage.. as.. disparageable and most unworthy of the blood Royal. **1643** *Oath Pacif.* 21 Much lesse let it be held.. desparagable to the King to hearken to his Parliament.

2. To be disparaged.

1648 J. GOODWIN *Right & Might* 37 The action of the Army is not disparageable by any possibility or likelyhood of evill, that it may bring upon the Kingdome afterwards.

disparagement (dɪ'spærɪdʒmənt). Also 6 disparge-, -perge-, -parrage-, -paradgment. [a. OF. *desparagement*, f. *desparager* DISPARAGE.]

†**1.** Marriage to one of inferior rank; the disgrace or dishonour involved in such a misalliance. *Obs.* exc. *Hist.*

1523 FITZHERB. *Surv.* xii. 23 If he be vnmaryed, than his maryage to gyue or sell to whome he wyll without disparagement. **1570–6** LAMBARDE *Peramb. Kent* (1826) 455. *a* **1577** SIR T. SMITH *Commw. Eng.* III. v. (R.) Couenable marriage without dispergement. **1590** SPENSER *F.Q.* III. viii. 12 He.. thought that match a fowle disparagement. **1651** [see DISPARITY 1]. **1850** MERIVALE *Rom. Emp.* I. ii. 52 Some houses lost their patrician status by marriages of disparagement.

transf. & *fig.* **1585** ABP. SANDYS *Serm.* (1841) 325 In marriage therefore it behoveth us to be careful, that they whom we choose be of the household of God, professing one true religion with us; the disparagement wherein is the cause of all dissention.

2. Lowering of value, honour, or estimation; dishonour, indignity, disgrace, discredit; that which causes or brings loss of dignity, etc.

1486 *Act 3 Hen. VII*, c. 2 Women.. been.. defoiled to the.. Disparagements of the said Women. **1590** SHAKS. *Com. Err.* I. i. 149 Passed sentence may not be recal'd But to our honours great disparagement. **1598** —— *Merry W.* I. i. 31 If Sir John Falstaffe haue committed disparagements vnto you. **1605** BACON *Adv. Learn.* I. viii. §3. 43 To haue commandement ouer Gally-slaues is a disparagement, rather than an honour. **1644** MILTON *Jdgm. Bucer* (1851) 303 In that Doctoral Chair, where once the learnedest of England thought it no disparagement to sit at his feet. **1676** COLES *Eng. Dict.* To Rdr., 'Tis no Disparagement to understand the Canting Terms: It may chance to save your Throat from being cut, or (at least) your Pocket from being pick'd. **1764** REID *Inquiry* ii. §6. 108 No disparagement is meant to the understandings of the authors. **1837–9** HALLAM *Hist. Lit.* (1847) I. xi. §2. 85 Nor is this any disparagement to their ability. **1869** *Pall Mall G.* 11 Oct. 2 These appointments.. have brought all the lesser dignities into disparagement.

3. The action of speaking of in a slighting or depreciatory way; depreciation, detraction, under-valuing.

1591 GREENE *Art Conny Catch.* II. (1592) 13 [He] dare not lift his plumes in disparagement of my credit. *a* **1665** J. GOODWIN *Filled w. the Spirit* (1867) 87 That proverb of disparagement, A fool and his money are soon parted. **1699** BENTLEY *Phal.* Pref. 82 A Disparagement from men of no knowledge in the things they pretend to judge is the least of Disparagements. **1761–2** HUME *Hist. Eng.* (1806) III. xlvii. 705 He had expressed himself with great disparagement of the common law of England. **1859** LEWIN *Invas. Brit.* 61 A strong bias towards the glorification of the writer and the disparagement of the Britons. **1876** MOZLEY *Univ. Serm.* v. (1877) 106 We may observe in the New Testament an absence of all disparagement of the military life.

di'sparager. [f. DISPARAGE *v.* + -ER[1].] One who disparages or discredits; one who speaks slightingly of, or belittles; a detractor.

1611 COTGR., *Vitupereur*, a dispraiser, discommender; disparager, disgracer. **1640** BP. HALL *Episc.* II. xix. 198 It can be no great comfort or credit to the disparagers of Episcopacy. *a* **1715** HICKES *Let. to Nelson* in *Life Bp. Bull* 518 (T.) Despisers and disparagers of the ancient fathers. **1822** LAMB *Elia* Ser. I. *Mod. Gallantry*, The idolator of his female mistress—the disparager and despiser of his no less female aunt. **1848** MILL *Pol. Econ.* II. vii. §2 (1876) 173 The disparagers of peasant properties.

di'sparaging, *vbl. sb.* [f. as prec. + -ING[1].] The action of the vb. DISPARAGE; disparagement.

1574 tr. *Littleton's Tenures* 22 b, A convenient mariage wythout disperagyng. **1654** WHITLOCK *Zootomia* 446 Disparagings of mens Moralls, Naturalls, Fortunes, Pedigree.

di'sparaging, *ppl. a.* [f. as prec. + -ING[2].] That disparages; that speaks of or treats slightingly, that brings reproach or discredit.

1645 MILTON *Tetrach.* (1851) 199 What can be more opposite and disparaging to the cov'nant of love? *a* **1665** J. GOODWIN *Filled w. the Spirit* (1867) 395 If we take the word 'legal' in any disparaging sense. **1771** FOOTE *Maid of B.* III. Wks. 1799 II. 235 As to yourself (I don't speak in a disparaging way), your friends are low folks, and your fortune just nothing at all. **1861** W. BELL *Dict. Law Scot.* s.v. *Disparagement*, If the superior required the heir to make an unsuitable or disparaging marriage, he or she might legally refuse. **1888** F. HUME *Mad. Midas* I. Prol., With a disparaging shrug of the shoulders.

di'sparagingly, *adv.* [f. prec. + -LY².] In a disparaging manner; slightingly.

1707 NORRIS *Treat. Humility* i. 28 We are not to think disparagingly of that excellent nature God has given us. **1834** *Blackw. Mag.* XXXV. 486 The 'dirty acres', as Sir Lucius..disparagingly calls them. **1875** JOWETT *Plato* (ed. 2) I. 351 Not that I mean to speak disparagingly of any one who is a student of natural philosophy.

†**dis'paragon**, *v. Obs. rare.* [f. DIS- 6 + PARAGON *v.*] *trans.* To disparage.

1610 G. FLETCHER *Christ's Tri. after Death* xxv, Lickt with soft and supple blandishment, Or spoken to disparagon his praise.

†**di'sparail**, *a. Obs. rare.* [a. OF. *desparail, -eil* different (14th c. in Godef.) f. *des-*, DIS- 4 + *pareil* equal.] Different, diverse.

1413 *Pilgr. Sowle* (Caxton 1483, repr. 1859) 60 Two ymages huge, of disparayl fourme.

disparate ('dɪspərət), *a.* and *sb.* [orig. ad. L. *disparāt-us* separated, divided, pa. pple. of *disparāre*, f. DIS- 1 + *parāre* to make ready, prepare, provide, contrive, etc.; but in use, app. often associated with L. *dispar* unequal, unlike, different.]

A. *adj.*

1. Essentially different or diverse in kind; dissimilar, unlike, distinct. In *Logic*, used of things or concepts having no obvious common ground or genus in which they are correlated. Hence distinguished from *contrary*, since contrary things are at least correlated in pairs, e.g. *good* and *bad*. Also distinguished from *disjunct*, since disjunct concepts may all be reduced to a common kind.

Disparātus appears first in Cicero *De Inv. Rhet.* 28. 42, applied to the mere separation expressed by *sapere*, *non sapere*, or A is not B, as against the opposition of *hot* and *cold*, *life* and *death*; it is used by Boethius, *De Syll. Hyp.* (ed. Bas.) 608, to denote things which are only different, without any conflict of contrariety (tantum diversa, nulla contrarietate pugnantia). It reappears in 14–15th c. with the school of Occam, e.g. in Rud. Strodus and Paulus Venetus, and is retained in modern transformations of the scholastic logic. According to Ueberweg *Logic* §53, disparate conceptions are those which do not fall within the extent of the same higher, or at least of the same next higher conception. (Prof. W. Wallace.)

1608 BP. J. KING *Serm.* 5 Nov. 5 Two disperate species and sorts of men. **1633** AMES *Agst. Cerem.* II. 243 Can men give manifold disparate senses to one and the same Ceremonies? **1642** FULLER *Holy & Prof. St.* IV. vii. 273 Not onely disparate, but even opposite terms. **1684** T. BURNET *Th. Earth* I. 302 As remote in their nature..as any two disparate things we can propose or conceive; number and colour. **1748** HARTLEY *Observ. Man* I. iii. 296 The Terms must be disparate, opposite, or the same. **1781** BENTHAM *Wks.* (1843) X. 92 A personage of a nature very disparate to the former. **1837-8** SIR W. HAMILTON *Logic* xii. (1860) I. 224 Notions co-ordinated in the whole of comprehension, are, in respect of the discriminating characters, different without any similarity. They are thus, *pro tanto*, absolutely different; and, accordingly, in propriety are called *Disparate Notions*, (*notiones disparatæ*). On the other hand, notions co-ordinated in the quantity or whole of extension..are only relatively different (or diverse); and, in logical language, are properly called *Disjunct* or *Discrete Notions*. **1865** GROTE *Plato* I. vi. 249 Other creeds, disparate or discordant. **1883** F. HARRISON in *Pall Mall G.* 3 Nov. 1/2 The questions are so utterly disparate as not to be reducible to the same argument.

b. (See quot.)

1867 L. H. ATWATER *Elem. Logic* ii. §11. 69 Any one of given Co-ordinate Species, is called, in relation to any one part of a higher or lower Co-ordinate Division under the Summum Genus, Disparate. Thus..lion, as compared to fish, Shetland pony, or bull-dog, is Disparate.

c. (See quot.)

1883 *Syd. Soc. Lex.*, *Disparate points*, two points upon the two retinæ which, when a ray of light falls upon them, do not produce similar impressions. Used by Fachner in opposition to corresponding points.

2. Unequal, on a disparity.

1764 T. PHILLIPS *Life Pole* (1767) I. 6 Which at very disparate years united these two persons. *a* **1834** LAMB *Misc. Wks.* (1871) 449 Between ages so very disparate. **1879** FARRAR *St. Paul* I. 416 Paul proceeds to narrate the acknowledgment of the Three that his authority was in no sense disparate with theirs.

B. *sb.* Chiefly *pl.* Disparate things, words, or concepts; things so unlike that they cannot be compared with each other.

1586 BRIGHT *Melanch.* xii. 59 Contrarie faculties or such as we call desparates in logicke. **1588** FRAUNCE *Lawiers Log.* I. x. 47 Disparates are sundry opposites whereof one is equally and in like manner opposed unto many. **1623** COCKERAM, *Disparates*, words which are differing one from another, but not contrarie, as heat and cold are contraries, but heat and moisture disparates. **1654** JER. TAYLOR *Real Pres.* 109 It is the style of both the Testaments to speak in signs and representments, where one disparate speaks of another; as it does here: the body of Christ, of the bread. **1682** R. BURTHOGGE *An Arg.* (1684) 154 Disparates are distinct, and are not opposites. **1722** WOLLASTON *Relig. Nat.* v. 71 If they are supposed to be only different, not opposite, then if they differ as *disparates*, there must be some *genus* above them. **1849** GROTE *Greece* II. lxviii. (1862) VI. 180 Blending together disparates or inconsistencies.

†'**disparated**, *ppl. a. Obs.* = DISPARATE.

1624 BP. MOUNTAGU *Gagg* 307 Questions..of different natures, of unequall extents, of divers and disparated approbation.

'**disparately**, *adv.* [f. DISPARATE + -LY².] In a disparate manner; separately, without relation to each other.

1881 G. S. HALL *German Culture, Laura Bridgman* 251 After the retina is destroyed..the eyeballs gradually lose the power of moving together, but move disparately.

'**disparateness.** [f. as prec. + -NESS.] The condition or quality of being disparate; dissimilarity of nature or character; absence of relation.

1659 FULLER *App. Injur. Innoc.* (1840) 567 Such foreign Canons, though not against but only besides our Common Law, and containing no repugnancy but disparateness to the laws of our land. **1825** COLERIDGE in *Rem.* (1836) II. 349 By contrasting it with, at least by shewing its disparateness from the Mosaic. **1873** M. ARNOLD *Lit. & Dogma* (1876) 179 Needing only to be carefully studied side by side with this for its disparateness to become apparent.

†**dispa'ration.** *Obs.* [ad. L. *disparātiōn-em* separation: cf. DISPARATE.] The condition of being disparate; the opposition of disparates.

1654 Z. COKE *Logick* (1657) 96 Disparation is an opposition of specialls..by opposite differences; as a man and a beast are disparates, or dissevered. **1656** JEANES *Fuln. Christ* 154 The second argument from the comparison of the extreames of this union..is taken from their disparation.

disparcle, var. of DISPARKLE *v. Obs.*

†'**disparence.** *Obs. rare* [f. as next: see -ENCE.] Disappearance.

1617 COLLINS *Def. Bp. Ely* II. x. 447 A miraculous annihilation, or disparence at least, of the water in the font.

†'**disparent**, *a.*¹ *Obs. rare.* [f. L. type **disparēnt-em* pr. pple. of **disparēre* (It. *disparere*, OF. *disparoir*), f. DIS- 4 + *parēre* to appear. Cf. obs. F. *disparent*.] Disappearing.

1617 COLLINS *Def. Bp. Ely* II. vii. 258 Now when they pray to him in Nyssen, as entire and present..who was mangled and disparent, is there no Rhetorique in this?

†'**disparent**, *a.*² *Obs. rare.* [? f. L. *dispar* unequal, unlike, dissimilar, with ending of *different*; or ? f. DIS- in sense 'diversely' + L. *parēre* to appear.] Unlike, diverse; of various appearance.

c **1611** CHAPMAN *Iliad* II. Comm. (1857) 59 This..deformed mixture of his parts..to follow the true life of nature, being often or always expressed so disparent in her creatures.

disparge, -ment, obs. f. DISPARAGE, -MENT.

†**dispa'rility.** *Obs. rare*⁻⁰. [ad. L. *disparilitās*, f. *disparil-is* = *dispar* unlike.] = DISPARITY.

1656 BLOUNT *Glossogr.*, *Disparility* (*disparilitas*) inequality, unlikeness, difference.

†**di'sparish**, *v.*¹ *Obs.* Also 5 -ys, dysperysh. [f. F. *disparaiss-*, present stem of *disparaître* to disappear: perh. from an OF. by-form **disparir*, *disparissr-*: cf. APPARISH to appear.] *intr.* To disappear.

c **1425** *Found. St. Bartholomew's* 6 In these wordes the visioun disparyschydde. *Ibid.* 41 Thus she seyed, And..sodanly dysperyshid. **1435** MISYN *Fire of Love* 100 All aduersite vanyschis & all oþer desyres aperis not, bot þa ar stillyd and disparischyd. *c* **1450** *St. Cuthbert* (Surtees) 4504 Cuthbert away disparysid. *a* **1632** T. TAYLOR *God's Judgem.* I. xv. Summary (1642) 439 These men or rather Angels..then disparished and were never more seen.

disparish (dɪs'pærɪʃ), *v.*² [DIS- 7.] *trans.* a. To oust from one's parish. b. To cause to be no longer a parish, deprive of the status of a parish.

1593 ABP. BANCROFT *Survey H. Discipline* 5 That all the parishes in England (they say) must be first disparished, and all the people of the land first sanctified. **1667** WATERHOUSE *Fire Lond.* 40 Has not God dis-parished and scattered them, Priest from people? **1864** *Realm* 8 June 5 The Lutheran Chapel..occupies the site of 'Trinity Church', disparished after the great fire.

†**di'sparison.** *Obs.* [ad. L. *disparātiōn-em* (see DISPARATION), after *com-parison*.]

1. = DISPARITY.

1609 BP. W. BARLOW *Answ. Nameless Cath.* 304 There should bee a great disparison betweene them.

2. Depreciatory comparison.

1609 BP. W. BARLOW *Answ. Nameless Cath.* 94 Vttered without enuious comparison, or malitious disparison of others. **1617** COLLINS *Def. Bp. Ely* I. i. 96 Which is euident by the comparison, or disparison rather, of earthly Kings there vsed. **1647** TRAPP *Comm. Matt.* xix. 19 They stand upon their comparisons—I am as good as thou; nay, upon their disparisons, 'I am not as this publican'.

dispa'rition. Also 7 *erron.* -ation. [a. F. *disparition* disappearance (Amyot, 16th c.), f. OF. *disparoir*, after *apparition*. Cf. *disparence*, *disparent*.] Disappearance.

1594 BP. J. KING *On Jonas* (1618) 376 A disparition of it for a time, as if it were not. **1603** HOLLAND *Plutarch's Mor.* 1358 Deaths, destructions and disparitions. **1654** Z. COKE *Logick* (1657) 202 That disparition and vanishing away, which Ubiquitaries feign of his Body. **1773** *Phil. Trans.* LXIII. 207 To consider the debilitation of the light, in this degree, as actual disparition. **1922** JOYCE *Ulysses* 689 The disparition of three final stars, the diffusion of daybreak. **1940** V. WOOLF *Writer's Diary* (1953) 336 This disparition of an echo.

disparity (dɪ'spærɪtɪ). [ad. F. *disparité* (16th c. in Littré) = It. *disparità*, Sp. *disparidad*, after L. type **disparitās*, f. DIS- 4 + *paritās* PARITY.]

1. The quality or state of being of unequal rank, condition, circumstances, etc.; inequality or dissimilarity in respect of age, amount, number, or quality; want of parity or equality.

1597 HOOKER *Eccl. Pol.* v. xlvii. §3 Between Elihu and the rest of Job's familiars, the greatest disparity was but in years. **1610** C. HAMPTON *Serm.* 23, I am bound to obey both powers, but with disparitie. **1651** G. W. tr. *Cowel's Inst.* 21 A wife..fit for him without disparity or Disparagement. **1697** COLLIER *Ess. Mor. Subj.* II. (1703) 59 Disparity in age seems a greater obstacle to an intimate friendship than inequality of fortune. **1773** GOLDSM. *Stoops to Conq.* v, The disparity of education and fortune. **1828** SCOTT *F.M. Perth* xxxiv, Willing and desirous of fighting upon the spot, without regard to the disparity of numbers. **1856** FROUDE *Hist. Eng.* (1858) I. i. 20 No disparity of force made Englishmen shrink from enemies.

b. with *pl.* An instance of this.

1682 SIR T. BROWNE *Chr. Mor.* I. §27 There may be no such vast Chasm or Gulph between disparities as common Measures determine. **1877** H. A. PAGE *De Quincey* II. xix. 163 This keen sense of the ludicrous and the salient disparities of life.

2. The quality of being unlike or different; unlikeness, dissimilarity, difference, incongruity. Also with *pl.* An instance or particular form of this.

c **1555** HARPSFIELD *Divorce Hen. VIII* (1878) 75 There is a great disparity and odds between them. **1580** NORTH *Plutarch* (1676) 993 Who could more eloquently..note the disparities and differences [of men than Plutarch]? **1646** SIR T. BROWNE *Pseud. Ep.* VI. i. 276 In which computes there are manifest disparities. **1674** tr. *Scheffer's Lapland* xv. 77 You may see what a disparity there is between these dialects. **1775** ADAIR *Amer. Ind.* 214 There is not the least disparity between the ancient North-American method of manufacturing, and that of the South Americans. **1875** *Lyell's Princ. Geol.* II. III. xxxiv. 250 We find a striking disparity between individuals..descended from a common stock.

dispark (dɪs'pɑːk), *v.* [f. DIS- 7 b + PARK *sb.* Cf. 16th c. F. *desparquer* (Littré), mod.F. *déparquer*, also *depark* (DE- *pref.* II. 2).] *trans.* To divest of the character of a park; to throw open (park-land), or convert (it) to other uses. Hence **dis'parking** *vbl. sb.*

[**1538** LELAND *Itin.* I. 21 The Frith Park sometyme a mighty large thyng, now partely deparked.] **1542-3** *Act 34-5 Hen. VIII*, c. 21 [If] house or houses, parke, chase or forest, happen to be fallen downe, disparked, disforested or destroied. **1593** SHAKS. *Rich. II*, III. i. 23 You haue fed vpon my Seignories, Dis-park'd my Parkes, and fell'd my Forrest Woods. **1664** J. TAYLOR *Confirmation* §4 This device..disparks the inclosures, and lays all in common. **1778** *Eng. Gazetteer* (ed. 2) s.v. *Yardley*, The manor-house stands in an ancient park, now disparked. **1826** SCOTT *Woodst.* vi, The disparking and destroying of the royal residences of England. **1851** KINGSLEY *Yeast* ix, Many a shindy have I had here before the chase was disparked.

b. *transf.* and *fig.* (In quot. 1633 = DISIMPARK, as deer).

1633 G. HERBERT *Temple, Forerunners* i, Must they have my brain? must they dispark Those sparkling notions, which therein were bred? **1638** SIR T. HERBERT *Trav.* 92 He thereupon disparks his Seralio, and flyes thence..with Assaph-chawns daughter only in his company. **1651-3** JER. TAYLOR *Serm. for Year* I. xvi. 204 The little undecencies and riflings of our souls, the first openings and disparkings of our vertue. *Ibid.* (1678) 220.

†**di'sparkle, -'parcle**, *v.*¹ *Obs.* Also 5 des-, dysperele, 5-6 -parcle, -perkle. [app. a corrupted form of the earlier DISPARPLE, by association with *spark*, *sparkle* (in ME. *sperclen*, *sperkle*, *sparklen*). (No trace of the corruption appears in French.)]

1. *trans.* To scatter abroad, drive apart, disperse; = DISPARPLE 1.

c **1449** PECOCK *Repr.* III. vii. 318 Alle..weren disperclid abrode. *c* **1450** tr. *De Imitatione* I. iii, A pure, simple & a stable spirit is not disparcled [*v.r.* disparpled] in many werkes. *c* **1491** *Chast. Goddes Chyld.* xxv. 69 Riches maye lityll and lityll multeplie but sodenli they ben dysperklid. **1548** RECORDE *Urin. Physick* ix. (1651) 73 There appear..disparkled abroad in the urine..divers kinds of motes. **1601** HOLLAND *Pliny* II. 45 It disparcleth the mist and dimnesse that troubleth the eie-sight. **1611** SPEED *Hist. Gt. Brit.* IX. xix. (1632) 943 His Fleet was disparkled. *a* **1634** R. CLERKE *Serm.* (1637) 471 (L.) Their spawn [is] disparkled over all lands.

b. *intr.* (for *refl.*) To disperse, scatter themselves abroad; = DISPARPLE 2.

1553 BRENDE *Q. Curtius* E iv, Then al hys men for fear disparcled, flynge by such wayes as were open for them. **1583** STUBBES *Anat. Abus.* I. (1879) 78 Not suffering his radiations to disparcle abrode.

2. *trans.* To divide, portion out.
1538 LELAND *Itin.* I. 93 A Gentilman..whos Landes be now disparkelid by Heires General to divers Men. **1661** DUGDALE *Monasticon* II. 136 In processe the landes of the Oilleys wer disparkelyd.

Hence **di'sparkled** *ppl. a.*, **di'sparkling** *ppl. a.*
1529 MORE *Dyaloge* II. Wks. 182/2 Not a company and congregation but a dispercled noumber of only good men. **1611** SPEED *Hist. Gt. Brit.* IX. viii. §30 Hee resolued to recollect his disparkeled troupes.

†**di'sparkle**, *v.*[2] *Obs. rare.* [f. *di-* = DIS- 1 + SPARKLE *v.*] *intr.* To sparkle forth.
1648 HERRICK *Nuptiall Song* iv, Let thy torch Display the bridegroom in the porch, In his desires More towering, more disparkling then thy fires.

†**di'sparple**, *v. Obs.* Forms: 4 **desparple**, **-perple**, 4–7 **disparple** (4–5 **disparpoil(l**, **-parble**, 5 **dys-**, **disperpil**, **-parbel**, **-perble**, **-perbyl**, 5–6 **disperple**, 6 **-pearple**, 7 **-purple**). See also DISPARKLE, DEPERPEYL. [a. Of. *desparpelier*, *-peillier*, *-pillier*, closely akin to It. *sparpagliare*, Sp. *desparpajar*, f. Rom. *des-* (DIS-) + **parpaliāre*, f. **parpilio*, **parpalio* (It. *parpaglione*, Pr. *parpalho* butterfly; cf. Cat. *papalló*), app. a changed form of L. *papilio*, *-ōnem*. The same verbal root in its variant forms appears in OF. *es-parpillier*, mod.F. *éparpiller*, Cat. *es-parpillar*, Pr. *es-parpalhar*: cf. mod.Pr *esfarfalhá*, f. *farfalla* butterfly. In OF. the *-ill-* belonged orig. to the atonic, the *-eill-* to the tonic forms, but these were subseq. confused.]

1. *trans.* To scatter abroad, disperse, drive in different directions; also, to sprinkle.
a **1325** *Prose Psalter* xliii[i]. 3 þyn honde desparplist þe folk, and þou settest hem. **1382** WYCLIF *Mark* xiv. 27, I schal smyte the schepherde, and the scheep of the floc schulen be disparplid. **1460** CAPGRAVE *Chron.* 1 Thoo [exposiciones] that were disparplied in many sundry bokis, my labour was to bring hem into o body. **1472** SIR J. PASTON in *Paston Lett.* No. 692. III. 39 All hys meny ar dysparblyd, every man hys weye. **1483** CAXTON *Gold. Leg.* 56 b/1 Thenne the chyldren were dysperplyd for to gadre chaf. **1613** HEYWOOD *Silver Age* III. Wks. 1874 III. 144 Their hot, fiery brains Are now disparpled by Alcides' club. **1615** CHAPMAN *Odyss.* x. 473 Odorous water was Disperpled lightly on my head and neck.

b. To divide. **c.** To throw into confusion.
1382 WYCLIF *Mark* iii. 25 If an hous be disparpoilid on it silf, thilke hous may not stonde. *a* **1400** *Prymer* (1891) 73 He schal desparple the weyes of synfulmen. **1541** PAYNEL *Catiline* xix. 35 Discorde alone disparpeleth and turneth up sette downe thynges stronge and myghty.

2. *intr.* (for *refl.*) To disperse, move or fly asunder, scatter themselves.
c **1400** MAUNDEV. (1839) Prol. 4 A Flock of Scheep withouten a schepperde..which departeth and desparpleth. *c* **1450** *Merlin* 196 Noon durste hym a-bide, but disparbled a-brode fro hym as from a wode lyon in rage. **1584** HUDSON *Du Bartas' Judith* IV. 339 (D.) Her wav'ring hair disparpling flew apart In seemly shed.

Hence **di'sparpled** *ppl. a.*; **di'sparpling** *vbl. sb.*
1494 FABYAN *Chron.* VI. clxxvi. 173 This disparblynge of the cristen hoost. **1652** URQUHART *Jewel* Wks. (1834) 229 Their transported, disparpled, and sublimated fancies. **1678** PHILLIPS, *Disparpled* or *Disperpled*, loosly scattered, or shooting it self into divers parts; a term used in Heraldry.

disparse, obs. form of DISPERSE.

dispart (dɪ'spɑːt), *sb.* [Derivation uncertain. There appears to be no related name in any other language. An obvious suggestion is that the appellation was derived from DISPART *v.*[1], 'from the mode of ascertaining the dispart, by *disparting* (dividing in two) the difference between the two diameters'. But it is to be observed that the term with its own verb (DISPART *v.*[2]) appears earlier than any known occurrence of DISPART *v.*[1], and that the particular sense 'divide into parts' is not known to us before 1629.]

1. The difference between the semi-diameter of a gun at the base ring and at the swell of the muzzle, which must be allowed for in taking aim.
1588 LUCAR *Appendix to Tartaglia's Colloq.* 4 Every Gunner before he shootes must trulie disparte his Peece, or give allowance for the disparte. **1644** NYE *Gunnery* I. (1647) 42 How to make the true Dispart of any Piece of Ordnance ..subtract the greater Diameter out of the lesser, and take the just half of the difference, and that is the true Dispart, in inches and parts of an inch. *Ibid.* (1670) 45 So much higher as the mark is (which you made at the Base-Ring) then the Mussel-Ring, so much is the true Dispart. **1659** TORRIANO, *Tirare fuora del vivo*, to shoot at random, or without and beyond the dispart (as our Gunners term it). **1859** F. A. GRIFFITHS *Artil. Man.* (1862) 50 *The Angle of dispart* is the number of degrees the axis of the bore would point above the object aimed at, when laid by the surface of the gun. **1867** SMYTH *Sailor's Word-bk., Dispart, or Throw of the Shot*.. An allowance for the dispart is..necessary in determining the commencement of the graduations on the tangent scale, by which the required elevation is given to the gun.

2. *concr.* A sight-mark placed on the muzzle of a gun, to make the line of sight parallel to the axis of the bore.
1578 W. BOURNE *Invent. or Deuises* xxxi. 24 You must giue your leuell iustly vppon the thicker side of the peece, that is to say, the mettall of the breech of the peece, and the dispart, and the marke, to bee all three vppon one right line by the sight of your eye. **1611** FLORIO, *Tirare di punteria*..The disparte is when a piece of wax or sticke is set vpon the mouth of the piece in an euen line with the cornish of the breech. **1669** STURMY *Mariner's Mag.* v. 78 Cause the Piece to be mounted higher or lower, untill you bring the Bead, the top of the Dispert, and the Mark all in one Line. **1692** *Capt. Smith's Seaman's Gram.* II. vi. 95 *Dispart*..is a piece of a small stick or Wyre, set perpendicularly upon the Muzzle-Ring of any Gun, of such length that the top of it may be equal (in height) to the upper part of the Base Ring. **1753** CHAMBERS *Cycl. Supp.* s.v., Take the two diameters of the base-ring, and of the place where the *Dispart* is to stand, and divide the difference..into two equal parts, one of which will be the length of the *Dispart*, which is set on the gun with wax or pitch, or fastened there with a piece of twine or marlin. **1836** MARRYAT *Midsh. Easy* xviii, Gunnery, sir, is a science—we have our own disparts and our lines of sight —our windage, and our parabolas, and projectile forces. **1861** W. H. RUSSELL in *Times* 10 July 5/4 There are no disparts, tangents, or elevating screws to the guns; the officer was obliged to lay it by the eye with a plain chock of wood.

3. *attrib.* **dispart patch**, a notched piece of metal on the muzzle in place of the dispart in sense 2; **dispart-sight** (see quots.).
1867 SMYTH *Sailor's Word-bk.*, *Dispart-sight*, a gun-sight fixed on the top of the second reinforce-ring—about the middle of the piece—for point-blank or horizontal firing, to eliminate the difference of the diameters between the breech and the mouth of the cannon. **1884** F. C. MORGAN *Artill. Mat.* 21 The muzzle sight is recessed into the dispart patch on the muzzle, and is used in conjunction with the hind sight for angles of elevation over 5°, when the centre fore sight becomes fouled by the muzzle. *Ibid.* 28 A fore or dispart sight screwed on in rear of the trunnions.

dispart (dɪ'spɑːt), *v.*[1] [In Spenser, app. ad. It. *dispartire* to divide, separate, part, repr. L. *dispartīre*, *-pertīre* to distribute, divide, f. DIS- 1 + *partīre* to part, share, divide. By others perh. referred directly to the L. vb., or viewed as an Eng. formation from DIS- 1 and PART *v.* It appears to have taken the place of the corresponding senses of DEPART (1–5).]

1. *trans.* To part asunder, to cleave.
1590 SPENSER *F.Q.* I. x. 53 That..man of God, That blood-red billowes, like a walled front, On either side disparted with his rod. **1611** SPEED *Hist. Gt. Brit.* IX. viii. (1632) 556 A sudden gust dis-parting the Fleet. **1641** MILTON *Ch. Govt.* vi. (1851) 128 As often as any great schisme disparts the Church. **1725** POPE *Odyss.* XIV. 482 Expert the destin'd victim to dis-part. **1738** WESLEY *Psalms* CXIV. ii, The Sea..fled, Disparted by the wondrous Rod. **1780** *Hist. Eur.* in *Ann. Reg.* 16/2 A state, already weakened ..and now disparted by defection. **1814** CARY *Dante's Inf.* VI. 17 He..flays them, and their limbs Piecemeal disparts. **1850** MRS. BROWNING *Crowned and Buried* xiv, Disparting the lithe boughs.

2. To separate, sever; to dissolve (a union).
1633 P. FLETCHER *Purple Isl.* IV. xi, Which like a balk.. Disparts the terms of anger, and of loving. **1708** J. PHILIPS *Cyder* II. 54 A strainer to dispart The husky, terrene Dregs from purer Must. **1814** SOUTHEY *Roderick* XVIII. 260 Till death dispart the union. **1851** TRENCH *Poems* 150 To dispart All holiest ties. **1868** BROWNING *Ring & Bk.* x. 1242 I find the truth, dispart the shine from shade.

3. To divide into parts or shares; to distribute.
1629 MAXWELL tr. *Herodian* (1635) 223 The Imperiall Palace..being disparted betwixt them, there would be roome enough for each. **1649** ROBERTS *Clavis Bibl.* 3 The Old Testament..is disparted by the Holy Ghost himself into two general heads. **1718** PRIOR *Solomon* I. 288 And equal Share Of Day and Night, disparted thro' the Year. **1855** SINGLETON *Virgil* I. 83 And evenly to light and shades doth now Dispart the globe.

4. *intr.* To part asunder, fly apart, and open up.
1633 P. FLETCHER *Purple Isl.* XII. lvii, The broken heav'ns dispart with fearful noise. **1727–46** THOMSON *Summer* 709 The flood disparts: behold!.. Behemoth rears his head. **1811** SHELLEY *St. Irvyne* x, Suddenly..the mist in one place seemed to dispart, and through it, to roll clouds of deepest crimson. **1863** KINGLAKE *Crimea* II. 150 Between the fleets thus disparting, the..flotilla of transports passed.

b. To part and proceed in different directions.
1804 J. GRAHAME *Sabbath* 149 The upland moors, where rivers, there but brooks, Dispart to different seas.

†**5.** *dispart with*: to part with. *rare.* (*pseudo-archaism.*)
1820 SCOTT *Abbot* iv, He will enjoy five merks by the year, and the professor's cast-off suit, which he disparts with biennially.

Hence **di'sparting** *vbl. sb.* and *ppl. a.*
1611 FLORIO, *Dispartimento*, a disparting. **1649** ROBERTS *Clavis Bibl.* 93 The disparting or cutting off of Jordans Stream before the Ark. **1728–46** THOMSON *Spring* 309 The deep-cleft disparting orb, that arch'd The central waters round. **1865** GEIKIE *Scen. & Geol. Scot.* ii. 37 Water.. expands, and..exerts a vast disparting force on the rocks in which it is confined. **1890** W. C. RUSSELL *My Shipmate Louise* I. xii. 261 The rush and disparting of the maddened clouds.

di'spart, *v.*[2] Also 7 **dispert** and *erron.* **disport**. [f. DISPART *sb.*]

1. *trans.* To measure or estimate the dispart in (a piece of ordnance); to make allowance for this in taking aim.
1587 W. BOURNE *Art Shooting* iv. 17 The disparting of your peece is but to bryng the mouth of your peece before, to be as high as is the tayle behind. **1588** [see DISPART *sb.* 1]. **1627** CAPT. SMITH *Seaman's Gram.* xiv. 65 To dispert a Peece is to finde a difference betwixt the thicknesse of the metall at her mouth and britch or carnouse. **1644** NYE *Gunnery* (1670) 40 And one chief thing, in the last place, to know very well how to dispart his Peece, be it either true bored, or not true bored.

2. To set a mark on the muzzle-ring, so as to obtain a sight-line parallel to the axis.
1669 STURMY *Mariner's Mag.* v. 79 To Shoot at a Sight seen in the Night, Dispert your Piece with a lighted and flaming Wax-Candle, or with a lighted piece of Match. **1731** J. GRAY *Gunnery* 68 You need only dispart your piece by fixing notched sticks..on its muzzle. **1753** CHAMBERS *Cycl. Supp.* s.v., *Dispart*, in gunnery, is used for the setting a mark on the muzzle-ring of a piece of ordnance, so that a sight-line taken upon the top of the base-ring..by the mark..may be parallel to the axis of the concave cylinder. **1853** STOCQUELER *Milit. Encycl.*

Hence **di'sparting** *vbl. sb.*
1587 [see above, sense 1]. **1611** FLORIO, *Tirare gioia per gioia*, to shoote leuell..without helpe of disparting. **1692** *Capt. Smith's Seaman's Gram.* II. x. 105 These ways.. prescribed for Disparting of a Piece.

†**dispar'tation.** *Obs. rare.* [app. n. of action from DISPART *v.*[1]; but the etymological form would be *dispartition.*] A division, a partition.
1624 MASSINGER *Renegado* II. vi, Why, look you, sir, there are so many lobbies, out-offices, and dispartations here.

di'sparted, *ppl. a.* [f. DISPART *v.*[1] + -ED[1].] Parted or cloven asunder, divided, separated.
1633 T. ADAMS *Exp. 2 Peter* ii. 18 Such a fire as he sent down in disparted tongues..at pentecost. **1667** MILTON *P.L.* x. 416 On either side Disparted Chaos over built exclaimd. **1700** PRIOR *Carmen Seculare* 86 Disparted Britain mourn'd their doubtful Sway. **1800–24** CAMPBELL *Poems, Portrait Female Child* 29 Thy brow, with its disparted locks. **1894** *Fallen Angels* xxvii. 151 Two animals..as far disparted, say, as a horse and a goose.

di'spartment. *rare.* [f. DISPART *v.*[1] + -MENT; cf. It. *dispartimento*, obs. F. *despartement*: see DEPARTMENT I.] A parting asunder; *concr.* a parting, cleft, or opening caused by separation.
1671 GREW *Anat. Plants* I. iv. §3. (1682) 29 Since the Lignous Body is..frequently disparted; through these Dispartments, the said interiour Portions..actually shoot. **1869** BLACKMORE *Lorna D.* (1889) 408 Many troubles, changes, and dispartments.

dis'passion, *sb.* [f. DIS- 9 + PASSION *sb.*] Freedom from passion; dispassionateness; †apathy.
1692 J. EDWARDS *Farther Enq. Rem. Texts O. & N.T.* 249 Those hard and flinty philosophers, who talk'd of an utter dispassion. *a* **1698** TEMPLE *Gardening* (R.), What is called by the Stoics apathy or dispassion; by the Sceptics indisturbance; by the Molinists quietism..seems all to mean but great tranquillity of mind. **1785** SIR C. WILKINS in Jas. Mill *Brit. India* (1818) I. II. vi. 233 Who constantly placeth his confidence in dispassion. **1892** MISS L. T. SMITH in *Academy* 13 Aug. 123/1 The peculiarity of his stand-point gives a calm dispassion to his statements.

†**dis'passion**, *v. Obs.* [f. DIS- 7 a + PASSION *sb.* Cf. mod.F. *dépassioner* (in 16th c. F. 'to put into a passion').] *trans.* To free from passion. Chiefly in *ppl. a.* **dis'passioned**.
? **1608** DONNE *Serm.* cvii. IV. 463 Sober and discreet and dispassioned and disinterested men. *a* **1612** —— *Βιαθανατος* (1648) 193 It became Moses to be reposed and dispassioned ..in his Conversation with God. **1668** CLARENDON *Life* I. (1843) 926/2 In all those controversies, he had so dispassioned a consideration..and so profound a charity in his conscience, that [etc.]. **1746** CAWTHORNE *Equality Hum. Cond.* 131 Ease and joy, dispassion'd reason owns, As often visits cottages as thrones.

dispassionate (dɪ'spæʃənət), *a.* [f. DIS- 10 + PASSIONATE *a.* Cf. It. *disappassionato*, Sp. *desapasionado.*] Free from the influence of passion or strong emotion; calm, composed, cool; impartial. Said of persons, their faculties, and actions.
1594 PARSONS *Confer. Success* II. ix. 218 So themselues do confesse. I meane the wise and dis-passionate among them. **1646** J. HALL *Horae Vac.* 58 Mens judgements have more time to grow dispassionate and disintangled. **1780** COWPER *Progr. Err.* 453 A critic on the sacred book should be Candid and learned, dispassionate and free. **1874** GREEN *Short Hist.* vi. §4. 300 A dispassionate fairness towards older faiths. **1877** E. R. CONDER *Bas. Faith* iii. 102 They account it the prime duty of a dispassionate inquirer.

¶ Used as = 'passionate' (16th c. F. *depassioné*: see DISPASSION *v.*).
1635 BRATHWAIT *Arcad. Pr.* 114 Fixing his ferret eyes in a furious and dispassionate manner.

†**dis'passionate**, *v. Obs. rare.* [f. DIS- 6.] *trans.* To free from passion. Hence †**dis'passionated** *ppl. a.*
1647 MAYNE *Answ. Cheynel* 27 (T.) As all dispassionated men may judge. **1658** WALTON *Life Donne* (ed. 2) 21 These ..had so dispassionated [**1640** dispassioned] Sir George, that..he also could not but see..merit in his new son.

dis'passionately, *adv.* [f. DISPASSIONATE *a.* + -LY[2].] In a dispassionate or calm manner.
1717 KILLINBECK *Serm.* 191 (T.) As if she had only dispassionately reasoned the case with him. **1753** HANWAY *Trav.* (1762) II. I. xi. 59 To speak dispassionately of the conduct of the Dutch. **1806** A. KNOX *Rem.* I. 29 These passages ought to be dispassionately investigated. *a* **1853** ROBERTSON *Lect.* (1858) 270, I ask the meeting to listen to me dispassionately.

¶ Used as = 'passionately': cf. DISPASSIONATE ¶.
1658 SLINGSBY *Diary* (1836) 201, I found no billows dispassionately acting to endanger the passage of my late surcharged vessel..All appeared to me as in a calm sea.

di'spassionateness. [f. as prec. + -NESS.] A dispassionate condition or quality.

1842 J. H. NEWMAN *Par. Serm.* (ed. 2) V. v. 74 St. Paul makes it a part of a Christian character to have a reputation for..dispassionateness. **1886** *Athenæum* 24 Apr. 551/1 A dispassionateness and a sense of humour quite rare in her sex.

dispassioned: see DISPASSION *v.*

dispatch, despatch (dɪ'spætʃ), *v.* Also 6 dispach(e, dyspach(e, -patch; 8–9 despatch. [Found early in 16th c.: ad. It. *dispacciare* 'to dispatch, to hasten, to speed, to rid away any worke' (Florio), or Sp. *despachar* to expedite, 'to dispatch, to rid out of the way' (Minsheu). The radical is the same as in It. *impacciare* to entangle, hinder, stop, prevent, Sp., Pg. *empachar* to impede, embarrass. Not related to F. *dépêcher*, which gave the Engl. *depesshe*, DEPEACH, common in 15–16th c., rare after 1600, and app. superseded by *dispatch* before 1650. The uniform English spelling from the first introduction of the word to the early part of the 19th c. was with *dis-*; but in Johnson's Dictionary the word was somehow entered under *des-* (although Johnson himself always wrote *dispatch*, which is also the spelling of all the authors cited by him); though this has, since *c* 1820, introduced diversity into current usage, *dispatch* is to be preferred, as at once historical, and in accordance with English analogy; for even if this word had begun in ME. with a form in *des-* from OF. (which it did not), it would regularly have been spelt *dis-* by 1500: see DES-, DIS-, prefixes.

The notions of *impede, expedite*, are expressed by different roots in the northern and southern Romanic langs. The radical of F. *empêcher, dépêcher* (Eng. IMPEACH, DEPEACH), OF. *empeechier, despeechier*, is taken to be a L. *-*pedicāre* (extended form of *im-, ex-pedīre*, or deriv. of *pedica* 'fetter, gin'); cf. *prêcher*, PREACH, OF. *preechier*:—L. *prædicāre*. This also occurs in Pr. *empedegar*. But Sp. *empachar, despachar*, Pr. *empaitar*, point to a L. type -*pactāre* (f. *pactus*, 'fastened, fixed, fast', pa. pple. of *pangĕre*). The radical of It. *im-, dis-pacciare*, Pr. *empachar* (with which perh. are to be taken dial. OF. *empachier, ampauchier, dapauchier*: see Godef.), have been referred to a cognate L. type -*pactiāre* (cf., for the phonology, It. *tracciare, docciare, succiare*:—**tractiāre*, **ductiāre*, **sūctiāre*). Thus, these words are quite distinct from F. *empêcher, dépêcher*, in 16th c. also *despecher*, which gave Eng. *impeach*, and *depeach*, also *despeche*, in Caxton *depesshe*, Sc. *depesche*. *Dispatch*, therefore, could not be of French origin. The date of our first quot., 1517, is early for a word from Italian, and still more so for a word from Spanish; but the active intercourse with the Papal Court and with Spain at that date may have facilitated the introduction of *dispatch* as a diplomatic word. Tunstall, our first authority for *dispach(e*, was Commissioner to Spain in 1516 and 1517.]

I. *trans.* * *To dismiss or dispose of promptly.*

1. To send off post-haste or with expedition or promptitude (a messenger, message, etc., having an express destination). The word regularly used for the sending of official messengers, and messages, of couriers, troops, mails, telegrams, parcels, express trains, packet-boats, etc.

1517 BP. TUNSTALL *Let. to Hen. VIII* in Ellis *Orig. Lett.* Ser. I. I. 134 We..dispached that poste..reservyng thys to be written by my selff at laysor. **1585** T. WASHINGTON tr. *Nicholay's Voy.* III. viii. 82 If..the great Lord hath to send and dispatch in hast any matter into any places. **1600** E. BLOUNT tr. *Conestaggio* 21 He..dispatched fower coronels throughout his Realme of Portugall, to levie twelve thousand foote. **1624** DAVENPORT *City Night-Cap* III. i, Embassadors were dispatch'd to Bergamo. **1751** JOHNSON *Rambler* No. 153 ⁋3, I was in my eighteenth year dispatched to the university. **1766** GOLDSM. *Vic. W.* ix, Moses was..dispatched to borrow a couple of chairs. **1840** *Penny Cycl.* XVIII. 459/2 The number of chargeable letters dispatched by the General Post. **1875** F. HALL in *Lippincott's Mag.* XVI. 749/1 The palanquin, as being portable and easy to handle, was dispatched first, its contents included.

β. **1832** LANDER *Exped. to Niger* I. vii. 259 They had been despatched..from Soccatoo to collect the accustomed tribute. **1874** GREEN *Short Hist.* vi. §5. 319 Commissioners were despatched into every county for the purpose of assessment. **1886** *Postal Guide* 210 When the mails are despatched at longer intervals than a week.

fig. **1655** H. VAUGHAN *Silex Scint.* I. (1858) 23, I turn'd me round, and to each shade Dispatch'd an Eye. **1781** COWPER *Conv.* 437 The mind, dispatched upon her busy toil, Should range where Providence has blest the soil.

†**b.** *refl.* To get away quickly: = sense 8. *rare.*

1632 J. HAYWARD tr. *Biondi's Eromena* 180 Though he were desirous to dispatch himselfe thence, yet waited he with all patience.

†**2.** To send away (from one's presence or employment); to dismiss, discharge. *Obs.*

a **1533** LD. BERNERS *Gold. Bk. M. Aurel.* (1546) L vj, As an ydell vacabunde man they dyspatched and sent hym awaie. **1632** LITHGOW *Trav.* IX. 380, I dispatched my Dragoman, and the other Barbarian hireling, with a greater consideration then my..conditions allowed me. **1662** *Grim, Collier of Croydon* III. in *Ant. Brit. Drama* III. 312 To give her warning to dispatch her knaves.

3. To dismiss (a person) after attending to him or his business; to settle the business of and send away; to get rid of. Now *rare.*

1530 PALSGR. 520/1, I have dispatched these four felowes quickly, *jay despeché ces quattre galans vistement.* **1551** in Furnivall *Ballads from MSS.* I. 421 Remembre poore shewters who dothe susteyne wronge; speake and dispatche them, they tarrye to longe. *a* **1625** BOYS *Wks.* (1630) 382 And I can say this of other suitors, if ten be dispatched ninety be despited. **1670** G. H. *Hist. Cardinals* II. III. 198 Dispatching all that came to him with great satisfaction. **1726** *Adv. Capt. R. Boyle* 171 Nor would I suffer another to enter my Ship, till the former was dispatch'd.

β. **1874** MORLEY *Compromise* (1886) 132 Finally we may be despatched with a eulogy of caution and a censure of too great heat after certainty.

4. To get rid of or dispose of (any one) by putting to death; to make away with, kill.

1530 *Proper Dyaloge* (Arb.) 146 Duke Humfray By them of his lyfe was abreuiate. Sythe that tyme I could recken mo Whom they caused to be dispatched so. **1568** GRAFTON *Chron.* II. 1329 He drowned himselfe..the river beyng so shallow that he was faine to lye grovelyng before he could dispatch himselfe. **1580** NORTH *Plutarch* 112 (R.) He drank ..poyson, which dispatcheth a man in 24 hours. **1607** SHAKS. *Cor.* III. i. 286 We are peremptory to dispatch This Viporous Traitor. **1611** BIBLE *Ezek.* xxiii. 47 The companie shall..dispatch [**1885** *R.V.* despatch] them with their swords. **1678** (ed. 2) BUNYAN *Pilgr.* I. (1847) 140 Show them the Bones and Skulls of those that thou hast already dispatch'd. **1726** *Adv. Capt. R. Boyle* 68 If he had made any Resistance, I should certainly have dispatch'd him. **1819** SHELLEY *Cyclops* 446 You think by some measure to dispatch him. **1859** THACKERAY *Virgin.* xxi. 162 Heroes are not dispatched with such hurry and violence unless there is a cogent reason for making away with them.

β. **1848** MRS. JAMESON *Sacr. & Leg. Art* (1850) 419 And then after many torments despatched with a dagger. **1879** FROUDE *Cæsar* xviii. 304 Clodius was dragged out bleeding, and was despatched.

b. (with complement.) ***to dispatch out of life, out of the way, the world,*** etc. ? *Obs.*

1580 BARET *Alv.* D. 884 To dispatch one out of life, *de medio aliquem tollere.* **1697** POTTER *Antiq. Greece* I. iv. (1715) 17 [He] was quickly dispatch'd out of the way, and no enquiry made after the Murderers. *a* **1745** SWIFT *Hist. Stephen* in *Lett.* (1768) IV. 313 To remove the chief impediment by dispatching his rival out of the world. **1796** MORSE *Amer. Geog.* I. 100 To desire that they would be more expeditious in dispatching her out of her misery.

†**c.** ***to dispatch the life of.*** *Obs.*

1586 MARLOWE *1st Pt. Tamburl.* v. ii, The Turk and his great Empresse..Have desperately despatch'd their slavish lives. **1605** SHAKS. *Lear* IV. v. 12 Edmund, I thinke is gone In pitty of his misery, to dispatch His [Glouster's] nighted life. **1632** J. HAYWARD tr. *Biondi's Eromena* 61 Which if it had hit, where he levelled, dispatched had beene the life of Tolmido.

5. To dispose or rid oneself promptly of (a piece of business, etc.); to get done, get through, accomplish, settle, finish off, conclude, execute promptly or speedily.

a **1533** LD. BERNERS *Huon* ci. 330 Dyspatch the mater and reuenge me. **1547** BOORDE *Introd. Knowl.* 145 He had many matters of state to dyspache. **1551** ROBINSON tr. *More's Utop.* II. (Arb.) 74 The worke beyng diuided into so greate a numbre of workemen, was with excedinge maruelous spede dyspatched. **1659** B. HARRIS *Parival's Iron Age* 202 He was so..unlike to live, that his Christening was dispatcht in hast. **1667** PEPYS *Diary* (1879) IV. 239 To my office, where dispatched some business. **1751** JOHNSON *Rambler* No. 161 ⁋4, I..soon dispatched a bargain on the usual terms. **1776** —— *Let. to Mrs. Thrale* 6 May, We dispatched our journey very peacably. **1782** PRIESTLEY *Corrupt. Chr.* II. IX. 152 Dominic easily dispatched this task in six days. **1856** FROUDE *Hist. Eng.* (1858) I. iii. 219 Causes lingering before his commissaries were summarily dispatched at a higher tribunal. **1895** F. HALL *Two Trifles* 27, I must dispatch my errand and be off.

β. **1817** MOORE *Lalla R.* (1824) 126 *Veiled Proph.*, The matter is easily despatched. **1884** CHURCH *Bacon* ix. 218 Two of the great divisions of knowledge..are despatched in comparatively short chapters.

b. To 'dispose of' or 'make away with' (food, a meal) promptly or quickly; to eat up, consume, devour. *colloq.*

1711 ADDISON *Spect.* No. 7 ⁋1, I dispatched my Dinner as soon as I could. **1833** HT. MARTINEAU *Brooke F.* ix. 112 The roast beef and plum-puddings had been dispatched.

β. **1826** SCOTT *Woodst.* v, I saw two rascallions engaged in ..despatching a huge venison pasty. **1837** DISRAELI *Venetia* I. xv, The brother magistrates despatched their rumpsteak.

†**c.** *trans.* To produce or 'turn out' promptly or quickly. *Obs.*

c **1710** C. FIENNES *Diary* (1888) 101 There are also paper mills wch dispatches paper at a quick rate. **1711** STEELE *Tatler* IV. Pref. ⁋2 The great Ease with which he is able to dispatch the most entertaining Pieces of this Nature.

†**6.** To remove, dispel, do away with; to dispose of, get rid of. *Obs.*

1568 GRAFTON *Chron.* II. 395 Dispatching some by death, and other by banishment. **1578** LYTE *Dodoens* III. xlvi. 382 It dissolveth and dispatcheth congeled blood. **1600** HOLLAND *Livy* XXII. vi. 435 The heat of the sunne had broken and dispatched the mist. **1726** *Adv. Capt. R. Boyle* 221 To dispatch all fear of Resistance, I can assure you there are but two more Servants in the House.

†**b.** To 'get rid of' (goods); to dispose of (by sale). *Obs.*

1592 GREENE *Disput.* 17 The Paynters coulde not dispatche and make away theyr Vermiglion, if tallowe faced whoores vsde it not for their cheekes. **1632** LITHGOW *Trav.* VIII. 355 Rings..valued to a hundred Chickens of Malta, eight shillings the peece, which I dispatched for lesser.

†**c.** To put out of the way, stow away. *rare.*

1567 R. EDWARDS *Damon & P.* in Hazl. *Dodsley* IV. 39 Such a crafty spy I have caught..Snap the tipstaff..Brought him to the court, and in the porter's lodge dispatched him.

** *To rid* (*a person*) *of something.*

†**7.** *trans.* To rid (a person, etc. *of, from*, some encumbrance or hindrance); to deliver, free, relieve.

1530 PALSGR. 520/1 We shall dispatche us of hym well ynoughe. *c* **1534** tr. *Pol. Verg. Eng. Hist.* (Camden) I. 161 The thinge which shoulde cleanlie dispatche him of all languor and sorrow. **1548** UDALL, etc. *Erasmus Par.* Pref. 18 Whan I had cleane dispatched myself of this great charge and taske. **1549** COVERDALE, etc. *Erasm. Par. 1 Tim.* vi. 17 Thinges so incertain that yf casualtie take them not awaye, yet at lest death despatcheth vs from them. **1561** DAUS tr. *Bullinger on Apoc.* (1573) 315 Dispatch vs from euils, graunt us the good thinges promised. **1562** TURNER *Baths* 6 b, Some are dispatched of their diseases here in sixe dayes. **1580** BARET *Alv.* D 884 To dispatch himself out of a businesse..To dispatch and ridde out of trouble. **1594** PLAT *Jewell-ho.* III. 57 You shall soone dispatch your barnes..of al these wastfull birds. *a* **1641** BP. MOUNTAGU *Acts & Mon.* (1642) 295 Antipater being dispatched of these two competitors, had an easier course to run.

†**b.** To deprive, bereave. *Obs.* (Cf. 4.)

1602 SHAKS. *Ham.* I. v. 75 Thus was I, sleeping, by a Brothers hand, Of Life, of Crowne, and Queene at once dispatcht. **1606** G. W[OODCOCKE] tr. *Ivstine's Hist.* 94 a, Aristotimus was dispatched both of life and rule.

II. *intransitive.*

†**8.** (for *refl.* 1 b.) To start promptly for a place, get away quickly, make haste to go, hasten away.

1587 TURBERV. *Trag. T.* (1837) 101 Howe he mought.. Dispatche and goe unto the place. **1597** SHAKS. *2 Hen. IV*, IV. iii. 82 And now dispatch we toward the Court. **1670** EACHARD *Cont. Clergy* 52 Dispatch forthwith for Peru and Jamaica. **1712** W. ROGERS *Voy.* 400 That we might dispatch for the Cape of Good Hope, as fast as possible.

9. To make haste (*to do something*), hasten, be quick. *Obs.* or *arch.*

1581 PETTIE *Guazzo's Civ. Conv.* I. (1586) 24 b, Dispatch I pray you to shew me. **1591** FLORIO *2nd Fruites* 5 Dispatch and giue me a shirt. **1692** R. L'ESTRANGE *Josephus' Antiq.* IV. i. (1733) 78/1 Why do we not dispatch then and take possession? **1712** ARBUTHNOT *John Bull* III. iii, Thou hast so many 'If's' and 'And's'! Prithee, dispatch. **1753** FOOTE *Eng. in Paris* I. Wks. 1799 I. 37 Hold your jaw and dispatch. **1828** SCOTT *F.M. Perth* viii, Butler Gilbert, dispatch, thou knave. **1833** L. RITCHIE *Wand. by Loire* 146 'Come—despatch!' said the imperial sponsor; and the ceremony was hurried through.

†**10.** (*absol.* from 5). To conclude or settle a business; to get through, have done (*with*). *Obs.*

1603 SHAKS. *Meas. for M.* III. i. 279 At that place call vpon me, and dispatch with Angelo, that it may be quickly. **1666** BOYLE *Orig. Formes & Qual.* (1667) 51 And thus (to dispatch) by the bruising of Fruit, the Texture is commonly so chang'd, that [etc.].

⁋ *Dispatch* is used by Gabriel Harvey for the pa. pple.

1573 G. HARVEY *Letter-bk.* (Camden) 22, I hope mi long lingering matter is ere now quietly dispatch. **1577** *Ibid.* 58 Ar the[y] so soone dispatche in deede?

Hence **di'spatched** *ppl. a.* (whence †**di'spatchedly** *adv.*); **di'spatching** *vbl. sb.* and *ppl. a.*

1552 HULOET, Dispatched, *expeditus, perfectus.* *a* **1564** BECON *Acts Christ & Antichr.* Prayers, etc. (1844) 531 Unto the dispatching of their torments, if they be in purgatory. **1611** FLORIO, *Spacciatamente*, dispatchedly, out of hand, with riddance or much speed. **1615** W. HULL *Mirr. Maiestie* 78 Not to a dispatching, easy, honourable kind of death, but to the lingring, painefull, ignominious death of the Crosse. **1633** *Costlie Whore* IV. iii. in Bullen *O. Pl.* IV, A cup of poyson Stuft with dispatching Simples. **16..** *Cabbala*, Marq. Ynoiosa to Lord Conway (R.), I have differed the dispatching of a currier. **1893** *Star* 25 Feb. 4/3 The port is at the dispatching point of the Cheshire salt trade.

dispatch, despatch (dɪ'spætʃ), *sb.* Also 7 dispache. [f. DISPATCH *v.*, or perh. immediately ad. It. *dispaccio* (also *spaccio*) 'a dispatch, a hastning, a riddance; also a pleeke or packet of letters' (Florio) = Sp., Pg. *despacho*, Romanic deriv. f. the vb. stem: see prec. Cf. relation of DEPEACH *sb.* and *v.*]

I. The act of dispatching.

1. The sending off (of a messenger, letter, etc.) on an errand or to a particular destination.

1600 E. BLOUNT tr. *Conestaggio* 280 Blaming him to have beene too slacke in the dispatch of the Armie. **1667** PEPYS *Diary* 10 June, So to Woolwich to give order for the dispatch of a ship I have taken under my care to see dispatched. **1805** T. LINDLEY *Voy. Brazil* (1808) 74 He deferred the dispatch of my note. **1840** *Penny Cycl.* XVIII. 457/1 The operations of the Post-office belonging to the dispatch of letters. **1856** FROUDE *Hist. Eng.* (1858) I. i. 70 The despatch of a French embassy to England. **1886** *Postal Guide* No. 119 title-p., Dates of Dispatch of Mails, etc. *Ibid.* 210 Dates of Despatch of Colonial and Foreign Mails.

†**2.** Official dismissal or leave to go, given to an ambassador after completion of his errand; congé. *Obs.*

1571 *St. Trials, Duke Norfolk* (R.), After the dispatch of Rodolph, in Lent last, as he had made show before, that he intended to go over sea, and was all this while practising about this treason. **1603** KNOLLES *Hist. Turks* (1638) 161 To heare Embassadors from forrein Princes, and to giue them their dispatch. **1605** SHAKS. *Lear* II. i. 127 The seuerall Messengers From hence attend dispatch. **1698** FRYER *Acc. E. India & P.* 124, I easily condescended, thinking to procure my Dispatch with more speed.

†**3.** Dismissal (of a suitor, etc.) after settlement of business; attention to or settlement of the business (of a person); see DISPATCH *v.* 3. *Obs.*

1550 CROWLEY *Last Trumpet* 936 If thou be a mans atturney..Let him not waite and spende money, If his dispatch do lie in the.

4. Making away with by putting to death; killing; death by violence.

happy dispatch, a humorous name for the Japanese form of suicide called HARA-KIRI.

1576 FLEMING *Panopl. Epist.* 315 Except I had followed you..the sorrowes..had quite overwhelmed me, and wrought my remedilesse dispatch. **1591** *Troub. Raigne K. John* (1611) 59 Tormentor come away, Make my dispatch the Tyrants feasting day. **1653** H. COGAN tr. *Pinto's Trav.* xv. 51 So furious and bloody a fight, that in less than a quarter of an hour we made a clean dispatch of them all. **1697** BP. PATRICK *Comm. Exod.* xii. 6 There were about two hours and a half for the Dispatch of all the Lambs. **1859** *Times* 26 Mar. 9/2 The Japanese are..taught..the science, mystery, or accomplishment of 'Happy Dispatch'.

5. a. The getting (of business, etc.) out of hand; settlement, accomplishment; (prompt or speedy) execution. ***quick dispatch***: prompt or speedy settlement of an affair; hence, in former use, promptitude in settling an affair, speed, expedition (= sense 6).

1581 PETTIE *Guazzo's Civ. Conv.* II. (1586) 101 b Neither that he be lesse liberall of justice, or quick in dispatch towards them [the poore], than towards the rich. **1601** SHAKS. *All's Well* III. ii. 56 After some dispatch in hand at Court, Thither we bend againe. **1601** CORNWALLYES *Ess.* II. xlvi. (1631) 270 The miles which you must overcome before the dispatch of your journey. **1602** *How Man may chuse a good Wife* III. ii. in *Old Eng. Drama* (1824) 53 About it with what quick dispatch thou can'st. **1651** BAXTER *Inf. Bapt.* 214, I offered you—To Dispute publikely, only for quick dispatch. **1781** GIBBON *Decl. & F.* II. 75 In the dispatch of business, his diligence was indefatigable. **1833** HT. MARTINEAU *Manch. Strike* vii. 73 Three members of the Committee sit daily for the dispatch of common business. **1863** H. COX *Instit.* I. vi. 41 If it be intended that Parliament should meet for *dispatch of business*. **1885** *Act 48–49 Vict.* c. 60. §10 Notwithstanding any vacancy..the Council shall be competent to proceed to the dispatch of business.

β. **1837** CARLYLE *Fr. Rev.* I. III. i, In him is..only clerklike 'despatch of business' according to routine. **1860** MOTLEY *Netherl.* (1868) I. iii. 75 To his credit and dexterity they attribute the despatch of most things.

†**b.** 'Conduct, management' (J.). *Obs. rare.*

1605 SHAKS. *Macb.* I. v. 69 You shall put This Nights great Businesse into my dispatch.

6. a. Prompt settlement or speedy accomplishment of an affair (= *quick dispatch* in 5). Also as a personal quality: Promptitude in dealing with affairs. **b.** Speed, expedition, haste, rapid progress.

a. 1607–12 BACON *Ess., Dispatch* (Arb.) 242 Measure not dispatch by the tymes of sitting, but by the advauncement of the busines. *a* **1680** BUTLER *Rem.* (1759) II. 71 Dispatch is no mean Virtue in a Statesman. **1712** ADDISON *Spect.* No. 469 ¶4 The Dispatch of a good Office is very often as beneficial to the Solicitor as the good Office itself.

b. 1573 TUSSER *Husb.* lxxxv. (1878) 174 Due season is best ..Dispatch hath no fellow, make short and away. **1582** N. LICHEFIELD tr. *Castanheda's Conq. E. Ind.* xxxviii. 91 b, The dispatch he made for the lading of our ships. **1636** DAVENANT *Witts* v. i, This is a time of great dispatch and haste. **1722** WOLLASTON *Relig. Nat.* ix. 206 The business he has to do grows urgent upon him, and calls for dispatch. **1793** SMEATON *Edystone L.* §132 We also made good dispatch with the cutting of the rock. **1865** CARLYLE *Fredk. Gt.* VIII. XVIII. xiv. 84 All turns on dispatch; loiter a little, and Friedrich himself will be here again!

β. **1832** HT. MARTINEAU *Demerara* i. 8 Covering them [the roots] with so much despatch.

†**7.** The act of getting rid (of something), by sale, etc.; riddance, clearance, disposal; the act of putting away hastily. *Obs.*

1605 SHAKS. *Lear* I. ii. 33 *Glou.* What Paper were you reading? *Bast.* Nothing my Lord. *Glou.* No? what needed then that terrible dispatch of it into your Pocket? **1653** H. COGAN tr. *Pinto's Trav.* xiii. 41 In less than eight days he cleared his Warehouse..Now having made a full dispatch of all [etc.].

II. Concrete and transferred senses.

8. A written message sent off promptly or speedily; *spec.* an official communication relating to public affairs, usually conveyed by a special messenger.

1582 N. LICHEFIELD tr. *Castanheda's Conq. E. Ind.* xx. 52 b, Nicholas Coello hauing receiued this dispatch, did forthwith depart, and that in hast. **1585** T. WASHINGTON tr. *Nicholay's Voy.* IV. xxi. 136 Messengers which carry y[e] ordinary dispatches from Raguse to Constantinople. **1660** F. BROOKE tr. *Le Blanc's Trav.* 309 Visier, keeper of the seale, who before he can seale any dispatch, must acquaint the grand Senior. **1782** *Gentl. Mag.* LII. 147 Captain Henry Edwin late of his Majesty's ship Russel, arrived here with dispatches from Rear Admiral Sir Samuel Hood. **1803** WELLESLEY *Let. to Wellington* 23 Dec. in Thornton *Hist. India* (1842) III. xviii. 358 *note*, I received this morning your dispatch of the 30th of November. **1809** WELLINGTON in Gurw. *Desp.* IV. 292 Excepting upon very important occasions I write my dispatches without making a draft. **1844** H. H. WILSON *Brit. India* I. 223 Sir John Malcolm.. announced his arrival to the court, sending his dispatches by one of his officers. **1847** TENNYSON *Princess* IV. 360 Delivering seal'd dispatches which the Head took half-amazed.

β. **1641** *Nicholas Papers* (Camden) 59, I have alsoe made an other despacth to the lords of the privie counsel by his Majesties command. **1838** THIRLWALL *Greece* IV. xxix. 87 They were called away by a despatch from the fleet at Cardia. **1865** LIVINGSTONE *Zambesi* vi. 135 The loss of the mail-bags, containing Government despatches and our friends' letters for the past year.

9. An agency or organization for the expeditious transmission of goods, etc.; a conveyance or vessel by which goods, parcels, or letters are dispatched.

1694 *Lond. Gaz.* No. 2964/1 Died..Don Jean de Angulo, Secretary of the Universal Dispatch. **1703** *Ibid.* No. 3924/4 The Reprisal Dispatch, Jacob Green late Master, from New-England. **1861** [see 12]. *Mod.* The Merchants' Despatch; it was sent by despatch. (*Cent. Dict.*).

†**10.** A body of persons (officially) sent to a particular destination. *Obs.*

1713 WARDER *True Amazons* 69 Dispatches of Guards are sent from the first Disturbance given.

11. *slang.* (*pl.*) A kind of false dice: = DISPATCHER 2.

1812 J. H. VAUX *Flash Dict., Dispatches*, false dice used by gamblers, so contrived as always to throw a nick. **1856** *Times* 27 Nov. 9/2 There are dice called 'despatches'..A 'despatch' has two sides, double fours, double fives, and double sixes.

III. 12. *attrib.* and *Comb.*, as ***dispatch-bearing, -carrier, -writer, -writing***; **dispatch-boat, -box, dispatch cock** (see quots.); **dispatch money** (see quot. 1923); **dispatch note**, a memorandum required to be made in addition to the customs declaration for foreign parcel post; **dispatch-rider**, one who rides on horseback, bicycle, or motor-cycle to carry dispatches; so **dispatch-riding; dispatch-tube** (see quots.); **dispatch-vessel** = *dispatch-boat.*

1841 LEVER *C. O'Malley* xci. 443 In the mere details of note-writing or despatch-bearing. **1794** *Deb. Congress U.S.* 20 Mar. (1849) 1482 The President..[shall] be authorized to employ, as despatch-boats, such of the revenue cutters of the United States, as the public exigencies may require. **1874** KNIGHT *Dict. Mech., Dispatch-boat*, a name given to a swift vessel, formerly a fast sailer, now a small steamboat, used in dispatch duty. **1864** WEBSTER, *Dispatch-box*, a box for carrying dispatches; a box for papers and other conveniences of a gentleman when travelling. **1889** *Repent. P. Wentworth* III. 267 Some papers he had just extracted from his despatch-box. **1905** *Daily Chron.* 1 Aug. 3/1 A dispatch-carrier for the Foreign Office. **1785** GROSE *Dict. Vulg. Tongue, Spatch cock*, abbreviation of a dispatch cock, an Irish dish upon any sudden occasion. **1834** *West Ind. Sketch-bk.* I. 299 These..dispatch cocks..are simply fowls cut down the back and expanded to the purposes of a grill.. they afford an agreeable relief to an appetite that demands haste to be gratified—whence the name. **1712** ADDISON *Spect.* No. 469 ¶5 Gratifications, Tokens of Thankfulness, Dispatch Money, and the like specious Terms, are the Pretences under which Corruption..shelters itself. **1878** *Law Jrnl. Rep.* Q.B. XLVII. 513/1 If the Court shall be of opinion that..despatch-money.. is to be paid per working day of twelve hours. **1923** DE HART & BUCKNILL *Maclachlan's Merchant Shipping* (ed. 6) 428 Despatch money is a term which designates a payment which the Shipowner agrees to make for time saved out of the lay-days. **1892** *Post Office Guide* Oct. 383 Parcels for Foreign Countries must..be accompanied by a Despatch Note. **1968** *Ibid.* 113 Despatch notes can be obtained beforehand from any post office which accepts parcels for abroad. **1899** *Daily News* 18 Oct. 7/2 A report brought from the north by dispatch riders, via Vryburg. **1951** *Oxf. Jun. Encycl.* IV. 267/2 The army dispatch-rider..proves invaluable for messages which cannot be sent by any other method. **1907** *Daily Chron.* 10 Jan. 9/5 An interesting dispatch-riding test from Newcastle and London to Manchester. **1861** *Engineer* XII. 51/3 (*title*) The Pneumatic Despatch. *Ibid.*, The loads, in the pneumatic despatch tubes do not much exceed half-a-ton, unless the despatch carriages are coupled in trains of two or more. **1874** KNIGHT *Dict. Mech.* s.v. *Atmospheric Railway*, A late act of Congress (1872) appropriates $15,000 for a pneumatic dispatch-tube between the Capitol and the Government Printing-Office, Washington. *Ibid., Dispatch-tube*, a tube in which letters or parcels are transported by a current of air. **1809** *Deb. Congress U.S.* 21 Feb. (1853) 432 There may be time for the despatch vessel to go to France and return. **1889** *Sat. Rev.* 26 Jan. 104/1 Despatch-writing had not yet become part of the art of war.

di'spatchable, *a. rare.* [f. DISPATCH *v.* + -ABLE.] Capable of being dispatched.

1821 *Blackw. Mag.* IX. 305 Thou wilt find it no very easy or dispatchable matter.

dispatcher (dɪˈspætʃə(r)). [f. as prec. + -ER[1].]

1. One who or that which dispatches, in various senses: see the verb. *spec.* (*a*) *N. Amer.* = *train-dispatcher* (see TRAIN *sb.*[1] 22 b); (*b*) (see quot. 1954).

1547–64 BAULDWIN *Mor. Philos.* (Palfr.) v. vi, To the godly, death is the most happy messenger and quick dispatcher of all such displeasures. **1549** BALE *Pref. Leland's Itin.* B iv: (T.), Avaryce was the other dyspatcher, whych hath made an ende both of our lybraryes and bokes without respect. **1563–87** FOXE *A. & M.* (1631) III. XI. 551/2 *marg.*, D. Story..the chiefe dispatcher of all Gods saints that suffered in Queene Maries time. **1611** COTGR., *Dataire*, the dater, or dispatcher of the Popes Bulls. **1755** MAGENS *Insurances* II. 212 Likewise the Dispatcher of Averages. **1878** A. PINKERTON *Strikers* xviii. 219 The conductor.. promptly passed the dreaded word to the dispatcher. **1884** A. WAINWRIGHT in *Harper's Mag.* July 272/2 The dispatcher, as the electrician is technically called, puts his finger upon a fourth key. **1886** *Pall Mall G.* 31 Aug. 3/2 The despatcher of a telegram. **1931** H. F. PRINGLE *Th. Roosevelt* II. xii. 441 Orders were telephoned to the chief dispatcher of the Pennsylvania Railroad in New Jersey. A special train was to be made up. **1949** F. MACLEAN *Eastern Approaches* II. viii. 299 The dispatcher beckoned to us and Vivian and I.. made fast the static lines to the special hooks on the inside of the fuselage. **1954** A. W. FIELDING *Hide & Seek* 227 The 'plane's despatcher—the sergeant responsible for launching the personnel and containers out of the body of the machine.

2. *slang.* (*pl.*) A kind of false dice: see quots.

1798 *Sporting Mag.* XI. 85 How long it was since his conscience had permitted him to use dispatchers; these, he said, were loaded dice. **1894** MASKELYNE *Sharps & Flats* 237 Of unfair dice..there are those whose faces do not bear the correct number of pips, and which are known as 'dispatchers'. *Ibid.* 238 A high dispatcher cannot throw less than two, whilst a low one cannot throw higher than three.

di'spatchful, *a. Obs.* or *arch.* [f. DISPATCH *sb.* + -FUL.]

†**1.** Having the quality of dispatching or making away with expeditiously. *Obs.*

1608 MIDDLETON *Trick to Catch Old One* II. ii. D ij, Ile.. Fall like a secret and dispatchfull plague On your secured comforts. **1680** H. MORE *Apocal. Apoc.* 83 Their teeth.. were very dispatchfull of their prey.

2. Full of or characterized by dispatch; speedy, expeditious, quick, hasty. *Obs.* or *arch.*

1642 FULLER *Answ. to Ferne* 3 Those dispatchfull and urgent times. **1667** MILTON *P.L.* v. 331 So saying, with dispatchful looks in haste She turns, on hospitable thoughts intent. **1683** tr. *Erasmus' Moriæ Enc.*, While the dispatchful fool shall rush bluntly on. **1768–74** TUCKER *Lt. Nat.* (1852) II. 592 There is a wide difference between leading a regular life, and living by rule; the one is pleasant, easy, smooth, and dispatchful; the other..toilsome, stiff, and generally wasteful both of time and strength. **1814** H. BUSK *Fugitive Pieces* 230 If despatchful haste thy journey need. **1829** LYTTON *Disowned* 19 The most dispatchful solicitude.

†**b.** quasi *adv.* Speedily, quickly, in haste. *Obs.*

1725 POPE *Odyss.* III. 534 Let one, dispatchful, bid some swain to lead A well-fed bullock from the grassy mead. **1791** COWPER *Iliad* XXIII. 148 Their keen-edged axes to the towering oaks Dispatchful they applied.

†**di'spatchment.** *Obs.* [f. DISPATCH *v.* + -MENT.] The act of dispatching, dispatch (in various senses): prompt execution or settlement; getting rid of, sending away, dismissal; making away with, killing.

1529 *St. Trials, Wolsey*, For want of dispatchment of matters. **1538** M. THROGMORTON *Let. Cromwell* (MS. in *St. Pap. Hen. VIII*, XII. II. No. 552 Recd. Off.) Att Pares..y requeryd off hyme [Pole] my dyspachement [copy in *MS. Cott. Cleop.* E. 6,386 despachement] accordyng to hys promes to me at Rome. **1546** BALE *Eng. Votaries* II. (1550) 110 b, He..confessed that he had sent..false letters and poysons to the dyspachement of hys enemyes. **1570** ABP. PARKER *Corr.* 363 To procure the dispatchment of this offensive court.

dispathy, obs. form of DYSPATHY.

†**dis'patron**, *v. Obs.* [DIS- 7 a.] *trans.* To deprive of a patron or of patronage.

1615 SYLVESTER *Du Bartas, Job Triumphant* II. 62 Townes of late By him dispatroned and depopulate. *c* **1620** Z. BOYD *Zion's Flowers* (1855) 89 By thee dispatron'd..Who could a comforte once afford to me?

dispauper (dɪsˈpɔːpə(r)), *v. Law.* [DIS- 7 b.] *trans.* To decide a person to be no longer a pauper; to deprive of the privileges of a pauper; to disqualify from suing *in formâ pauperis*, that is, without payment of fees.

1631 *Star Chamb. Cases* (Camden) 72 Therfore the Court would dismisse the cause or dispauper the pl[ain]t[iff], for that by his confession he hath 11[li] per annum. **1656** BLOUNT *Glossogr., Dispauper* is a word most used in the Court of Chancery, as when one is admitted to sue *in forma pauperis*, if that privilege be taken from him, he is said to be *Dispaupered.* **1816** J. PHILLIMORE *Rep.* I. 185 (L.) If a party has a current income, though no permanent property, he must be dispaupered. **1885** *Law Times* 7 Mar. 340/1 The plaintiff had, by the fact of his having recovered..more than £5, become dispaupered.

dispauperize (dɪsˈpɔːpəraɪz), *v.* [f. DIS- 6 + PAUPERIZE.] *trans.* **a.** To release or free from the state of pauperism. Also *fig.* **b.** To free (a community or locality) from paupers.

1833 *New Monthly Mag.* XXXVII. 283 What chance do you see of dispauperizing any of the paupers? **1848** MILL *Pol. Econ.* v. xi. §13 (1876) 585 Many highly pauperized districts..have been dispauperized by adopting strict rules of poor-law administration. **1874** *Contemp. Rev.* XXIV. 965 The boy was thoroughly dispauperized in spirit.

Hence **dis'pauperized** *ppl. a.*; **-i'zation.**

1834 *1st Rep. Poor Law Comm.* (1885) 163 The principle of relief..found so efficient in the dispauperized parishes. **1876** PRETYMAN (*title*), Dispauperization, a popular Treatise on Poor-Law Evils and their Remedies.

dispayr(e, obs. form of DESPAIR.

†**di'spayre**, *sb. Obs.* Also dys-, -peir, -peyre. [f. DISPAIR *v.*[2], var. of DEPAIR, to spoil, injure, or suffer injury.] Impaired condition, disrepair.

1467 in *Eng. Gilds* (1870) 397 That it may be remedyed and holpen when that it ys [in] ruyn, or in dispeyre, or before. **1537–8** *Will of J. Sponer* (Somerset Ho.), All the wyndows..that be in dyspeir.

dispeace (dɪsˈpiːs). [f. DIS- 9 + PEACE *sb.* Orig. Scotch, in which it is in familiar use.] The absence or reverse of peace or quietness; uneasiness (of mind); dissension, enmity.

1825 JAMIESON, *Dispeace*, disquiet, dissension. **1851** RUSKIN *Stones Ven.* III. iv. §36. 197 The London of the nineteenth century may yet become as Venice without her despotism, and as Florence without her dispeace. **1856** ——

Mod. Paint. III. IV. xviii. Concl. 338 Two men, cast on a desert island, could not thrive in dispeace. **1867** S. Cox *Quest Chief Good* 123 This very contrast..breeds no dispeace or anger in the heart. **1873** Burton *Hist. Scot.* VI. lxxi. 219 Scotland had elements of dispeace. **1881** Geikie in *Nature* XXIII. 224 The rumours of renewed dispeace among the nations.

Hence **dis'peaceful** *a.*

1892 R. Wallace in *Scott. Leader* 29 Jan. 6 A messenger of that dispeaceful divinity [the goddess of strife].

† **di'spear**, *v. Obs.* [f. dis- 6 + stem of *appear*, *com-pear*; see also the aphetic pear. Cf. OF. *disparoir* (16th c. in Godef.) or It. *disparere* 'to disappeere' (Florio). Mod.Fr. has in the present stem *disparaître, disparaiss-*: cf. disparish *v.*[1] and disappear.] *intr.* To disappear.

1600 Fairfax *Tasso* VII. xliv. 125 All those stars on heau'ns blew face that shone..dispeared were and gone. **1627** Bp. Hall *Gt. Impostor* Wks. 501 This great impostor ..dispeareth and is gone. **1647** H. More *Song of Soul* I. I. li, But he looks on to whom nought doth dispear.

dispeche: var. of despeche, depeach *v. Obs.*, to send away, dispatch. Also **dispechement**, = dispatchment.

1538 M. Throgmorton *Let.*, copy in *MS. Cott. Cleopatra* E. 6, lf. 386, And from thens also to have been dispeched [orig. in *St. Pap. Hen. VIII*, XII. II. No. 552, dyspachyd]. *Ibid.*, And herupon delayed my dispechement ..To come further concernyng my dispechement [original, *in both cases*, dyspachement].

dispect, var. of despect, *Obs.*

† **di'speed**, *v. Obs.* [app. ad. obs. It. *dispedire*, (*spedire*) to dispatch (Florio), f. dis- 1; a parallel form to L. *ex-pedīre, im-pedīre* (expede, impede). But, as the spelling shows, associated in Eng. use with speed: cf. also the parallel form despeed.]

trans. To dispatch, to send off. **b.** *refl.* To get away quickly.

1603 Knolles *Hist. Turks* (L.), To that end he dispeeded an embassadour to Poland. The man returned..and was againe dispeeded. **1624** in *Calend. St. Papers, E. Indies* 16 Aug. (1878) 365 The Dutch have dispeeded sundry ships towards the west. **1630** Lord *Banians* 79 [He] dispeeded his Bramane Madewnauger, and his Pardon, to Delee. **1814** Southey *Roderick* XV. 273 Himself from that most painful interview Dispeeding, he withdrew.

c. To dispatch or finish promptly; to expedite.

1626 Gataker *Spanish Invasion* 16 Iulian..sent one Alypius..furnished with much treasure for the dispeeding of the worke.

dispeir(e, obs. form of despair.

dispel (dɪ'spɛl), *v.* [ad. L. *dispell-ĕre* to drive asunder, scatter, f. dis- 1 + *pellĕre* to drive.]

1. *trans.* To drive away in different directions or in scattered order; to disperse by force, dissipate (e.g. clouds, darkness, doubts, fears, etc.)

a **1631** Donne in *Select.* (1842) 141 More clouds than they could..dispel and scatter. **1662** J. Davies tr. *Olearius' Voy. Ambass.* 210 Lamps..enough to dispell the greatest darknesse. **1667** Milton *P.L.* I. 530 He..gently rais'd Their fainted courage, and dispel'd their fears. **1781** Gibbon *Decl. & F.* III. 63 His apprehensions were soon dispelled. **1883** Froude *Short Stud.* IV. I. viii. 90 He dispelled the illusions of Lewis. **1887** Bowen *Virg. Æneid* I. 199 Ills more dire ye have suffered; and these too Heaven will dispel.

2. *intr.* (for *refl.*) To become dissipated or scattered, as a cloud or the like.

1643 *Kingdomes Wkly. Intellig.* No. 7. 55 [He] still hangs as a cloud over Plimmouth, but it dispells every day. **1799** Campbell *Pleas. Hope* II. 263 Melt, and dispel, ye spectre-doubts. **1840** *Blackw. Mag.* XLVIII. 270 Conventions..in constant succession bubble up, form, and dispel.

Hence **di'spelling** *ppl. a.*, *esp.* in comb., as *care-dispelling*, that dispels care; **di'spellent** (also *-ant*), a dispelling agent; **di'speller**, he who or that which dispels.

1717 Frezier *Voy. S. Sea* 77 It is an admirable dispeller of certain Tumors. **1836** F. Mahoney *Rel. Father Prout, Watergrasshill Carousal* (1859) 78 A dispeller of sorrow. **1869** *Pall Mall G.* 18 Aug. 10 The change of scene..will often act as a good dispellant.

dispence, var. of dispense.

† **di'spend**, *v. Obs.* or *arch.* Also 4–6 des-, dys-. Pa. t. and pple. **dispended, dispent**. [ME. *des-, dispend-en*, a. OF. *despend-re* (mod.F. *dépendre*) = Pr. *despendre*, Sp. *despender*, It. *dispendere*:—late L. *dispendĕre* to weigh out, pay out, dispense, f. dis- 1 + *pendĕre* to weigh. Cf. expend, spend.]

1. *trans.* To pay away, expend, spend: **a.** money, wealth.

c **1330** R. Brunne *Chron.* (1810) 290 Þe kyng sent..For bisshoppes..& oþer þat þei found, þat ilk ȝere mot dispende of londes twenty pound. *c* **1386** Chaucer *Reeve's T.* 63 For hooly chirches good moot been despended On hooly chirches blood that is descended. **1491** Caxton *Vitas Patr.* (W. de W. 1495) I. xxvii. 45 a/1 She had dyspended alle her hauour to leches for to recouure her syghte. **1599** B. Jonson *Ev. Man out of Hum.* II. iii, A poore elder brother of mine, sir, a yeoman, may dispend some seven or eight hundred a yeere. **1642** *Declar. Lords & Com.* 20 June 6 Those summes shall be dispended as the former have been. *c* **1680** Hickeringill *Hist. Whiggism* Wks. 1716 I. 28 All [the money] was dispended.

absol. **1340** *Ayenb.* 53 Ich wylle þet þou ete and drinke and ..despendi. **1629** Gaule *Holy Madn.* 348 When he must needs despend, he..kisses euery Peece he parts from.

b. other things.

a **1300** *Cursor M.* 13410 (Cott.) Þe god drinc suld þou first despend. **1411** *Rolls of Parlt.* III. 650/2 Schal do brynge.. two fatte Oxen..to be dispended on a dyner. **14..** Hoccleve *Compl. Virgin* 244 And hath his blood despent in greet foysoun. **1582** N. Lichefield tr. *Castanheda's Conq. E. Ind.* xlii. 98 a, They were the bolder to dispend amongst them their shot, with the which there were many very sore hurt. **1627** Feltham *Resolves* I. lxix. Wks. (1677) 105 Every Man will be busie in dispending that quality, which is predominant in him. *a* **1745** Swift *Wks.* (1841) II. 69 They insist, that the army dispend as many oaths yearly as will produce £100,000 nett. **1868** Kinglake *Crimea* (1877) IV. xiii. 317 An isolated bastion dispending its strength.

c. *to dispend land*: to have an income from land, to possess land.

1523 Fitzherb. *Surv.* xii. (1539) 27 In some case he shall dispende and have more landes. **1613** Sir H. Finch *Law* (1636) 405 Where that clause needs not, the Iurors must dispend some land of freehold out of ancient demesne within the Countie where the issue is to be tried.

2. To spend, consume, employ, occupy (time).

1340 Hampole *Pr. Consc.* 2435 Thou here dispended thi tym wrang. *c* **1386** Chaucer *Monk's T.* 320 How she in vertu myghte hir lyf dispende [*Harl. erron.* despent]. *c* **1422** Hoccleve *Learn to Die* 239 My dayes I despente in vanitee. **1582** N. Lichefield tr. *Castanheda's Conq. E. Ind.* lxix. 142 b, That vpon them the Caruells might dispend their times. **1582** Bentley *Mon. Matrones* 122 The time of my life euill dispent.

3. *pass.* To be brought to an end or finished up; to be exhausted or spent; to come to an end.

1393 Gower *Conf.* I. 5 Whan the prologe is so despended. **1452** *Will of S. Fyncham* in Blyth's *Fincham* (1863) 154 Til hese issue male be dispended. **1470** Harding *Chron.* IX. i, Anchises dyed and was dispent. **1520** *Caxton's Chron. Eng.* I. 9/2 The vytayles were dispended and fayled.

4. To spend to no purpose; to waste, squander.

1303 R. Brunne *Handl. Synne* 1198 A clerk that folylyche dyspendyth þe godys þat hys fadyr hym ȝyveth. *c* **1385** Chaucer *L.G.W.* 2491 *Phyllis*, Me liste not..Despenden [*v.r.* dispenden] on hym a pennefull of ynke. **1483** Caxton *Cato* B v b, To thende that thou dyspende hyt not folysshly.

5. To distribute, dispense (*esp.* in early use, in charity to the poor).

c **1375** *Cato Major* III. x. in *Anglia* VII, Freliche dispende, þer neod is, euer among. *c* **1400** *Apol. Loll.* 112 If þis be ȝeuen or despendid to þe pore. **1483** Caxton *Gold. Leg.* 275/1 To gyue to the poure peple and dispende it among the nedy. **1517** *Test. Ebor.* (Surt.) V. 88 Dispendyd and dalt at my buryall..xls. **1633** P. Fletcher *Purple Isl.* III. vi, The purple fountain..By thousand rivers through the Is e dispent. **1652** Benlowes *Theoph.* XII. xlix. 225 When Sols Influence descends..And richer Showres, then fell on Danaes lap dispends. *a* **1656** Hales *Gold. Rem.* (1688) 267 To make them..profitable unto us, by charitably dispending them.

6. To dispense *with*, do without. *rare.*

1614 T. Adams *Devil's Banquet* 61 If a present punishment be suspended, the future shall neuer be dispended with.

† **di'spender**. *Obs.* Also 4–5 des-, **dispendour**. [ME. a. OF. *despendour* agent-n. from *despendre*: see prec.] One that expends; a dispenser; an almoner; a steward; = dispensator.

1340 *Ayenb.* 190 He..het his desspendoure þet he him yeaue uyftene pond of gold. Þe spendere..ne yeaf bote uyf. **1382** Wyclif *Tit.* i. 7 It bihoueth a bischop for to be withoute crime, as dispendour of God. **1382** —— *1 Pet.* iv. 10 As goode dispenderes of the..grace of God. *c* **1386** Chaucer *Melib.* ¶687 The gretter richesses that a man hath, the mo despendours he hath. *c* **1430** *Pilgr. Lyf Manhode* III. xvii. (1869) 144 Thilke is executrice, and dispendere of the residue of the testat. **1450–1530** *Myrr. our Ladye* 114 Marye ..that arte..moste ware dyspender..fede the hungry wyth thy benygne prouydence. **1611** Florio, *Dispensatore*..also a dispender.

† **di'spending**, *vbl. sb. Obs.* [f. dispend *v.* + -ing[1].] The action of dispend *v.*; expenditure.

c **1340** Hampole *Prose Tr.* 25 Thes holy mene lefte not witterly..the dispendynge of worldely goodis. **1563** *Homilies* II. *Almsdeeds* III. (1859) 395 There is a kind of dispending that shall never diminish the stock. **1603** Florio *Montaigne* III. ix. (1632) 537 Their dispending and ..artificiall liberalities.

b. Money to defray expenses.

1375 Barbour *Bruce* VIII. 509 He..gaf thame dispending And send thame hame.

c. Dispensation; stewardship.

1388 Wyclif *1 Cor.* ix. 17 Dispending [**1382**, *Geneva*, and **1611** dispensation; *R.V.* stewardship] is bitakun to me.

dispendious (dɪ'spɛndɪəs), *a.* [ad. L. *dispendiōs-us* hurtful, prejudicial, f. dispendium. Cf. mod.F. *dispendieux* expensive (Littré).]

† **1.** Causing loss or injury; hurtful, injurious.

1557 Pole in Strype *Eccl. Mem.* III. App. lxxx. 276 [It] being thought..that for the necessity of money that is to be demanded in the parliament, and otherwise cannot be provided, the prorogation of that should be much dispendious.

2. Costly, expensive; lavish, extravagant.

1727 Bailey vol. II, *Dispendious*, sumptuous, costly. **1861** Beresf. Hope *Eng. Cathedr. 19th C.* ii. 59 A somewhat dispendious use of material may in the end be true economy. **1864** *Ecclesiologist* XXV. 86 What is the good..of this.. dispendious use of materials?

Hence **di'spendiously** *adv.*, at great expense.

1874 T. G. Bowles *Flotsam & Jetsam* 9 Nov. (1883) 116 A green apple which he had dispendiously bought.

di'spenditure. *rare.* [f. dispend, after expenditure.] = expenditure.

1857 Sir F. Palgrave *Norm. & Eng.* II. 506 His exuberant dispenditure speedily received a check.

‖ **di'spendium**. *Obs.* [L. = cost, expense; also, loss, damage; f. *dispendĕre* to dispend: a parallel form to compendium. Cf. It. *dispendio* expense.] Loss, waste; expenditure, expense.

1648 *Petit. Eastern Ass.* 18 Is not Belt-money the dispendium of our possessions? *a* **1661** Fuller *Worthies* I. (1662) 356 This Gentleman in his Title page ingeniously wisheth that his Compendium might not prove a Dispendium to the Reader thereof. **1699** J. Woodward in *Phil. Trans.* XXI. 207 The less they [Plants] are in Bulk, the smaller the Quantity of the Fluid Mass in which they are set is drawn off; the Dispendium of it..being pretty nearly proportioned to the Bulk of the Plant. **1727** S. Switzer *Pract. Gardiner* I. v. 42 The dispendium or expense of water was the less by ½.

dispensa'bility. [f. next + -ity.] The quality of being dispensable. **a.** Capability of being dispensed or made the subject of ecclesiastical dispensation. **b.** Capability of being dispensed with or done without.

a. 1650 R. Hollingworth *Exerc. Usurped Powers* 43 Quoting a Doctor of the Papacy for the dispensabilitie of an oath. **1837–9** Hallam *Hist. Lit.* iv. III. §23 [They] deny.. the dispensability of the decalogue in any part. **1881** Stubbs *Med. & Mod. Hist.* xii. (1886) 284 The theologians disputed as to the dispensability of a marriage with a brother's widow.

b. 1883 Miss Broughton *Belinda* III. III. ix. 81 Weighing the dispensability or indispensability as a travelling companion of each [book].

dispensable (dɪ'spɛnsəb(ə)l), *a.* [ad. med.L. *dispensābil-is*, f. *dispensāre* to dispense: see -ble. Cf. F. *dispensable* (16th c. in Littré).]

1. *Eccl.* Subject to dispensation. **a.** Capable of being permitted in special circumstances, though against the canons; capable of being remitted or condoned, though an offence or sin.

1533 More *Let. to Cromwell* Wks. 1425/1 Sodenly his highnes..shewed me that..his mariage was..in such wise against the lawe of nature, that it coulde in no wyse by the churche be dispensable. **1536** *Act 28 Hen. VIII*, c. 7 §5 The maryage..was..ayenst the lawes of almighty god, and not dispensable by any humayne auctoritie. **1562** Fills in Strype *Ann.* I. xxxiii. 371 Horrible sins are dispensable for money. *a* **1709** Atkyns *Parl. & Pol. Tracts* (1734) 296 The Distinction of *Mala Prohibita*, into such as are dispensable, and such as are not dispensable.

b. Capable of being dispensed with or declared non-obligatory in a special case, as a law, canon, oath, etc.

a **1612** Donne *Βιαθανατος* (1644) 106 If it [the Law] be dispensable in some cases beneficiall to a man. **1679** Burnet *Hist. Ref.* I. I. ii. 152 He was then of opinion that the law in Leviticus was dispensable. **1690** Stillingfl. *Charge to Clergy* (T.), The question..is, whether the church's benefit may not..make the canons against non-residence as dispensable as those against translations. **1837–9** Hallam *Hist. Lit.* iv. III. §23 Durand seems to have thought the fifth commandment (our sixth) more dispensable than the rest. **1890** *Pall Mall G.* 15 Feb. 2/2 Celibate friars with 'dispensable vows' are henceforth to be one of the recognized agencies of the Church of England.

2. Allowable, excusable, pardonable. *arch.* or *Obs.*

1589 Puttenham *Eng. Poesie* III. xxiv. (Arb.) 286 It came not of vanitie but of a fatherly affection, ioying in the sport and company of his little children, in which respect..it was dispenceable in him and not indecent. *a* **1684** Leighton *Comm. 1 Pet.* iii. 8 In his saddest times, when he might seem most dispensable to forget other things. **1704** Swift *T. Tub* vi. (Seager), If straining a point were at all dispensable.

3. That can be dispensed with or done without; unessential, omissible; unimportant.

1649 Jer. Taylor *Gt. Exemp.* III. xvi. 54 Things, which indeed are pious, and religious, but dispensable, voluntary and commutable. **1653** H. More *Conject. Cabbal.* Pref. A vij (T.), Speculative and dispensable truths a man..ought rather to propound..sceptically to the world. **1842** Blackie in *Tait's Mag.* IX. 749 Books..are yet only of secondary use ..and can never render the hearing ear, and the speaking tongue dispensable. **1867** Swinburne *Ess. & Stud.* (1875) 118 Not a tone of colour..is misplaced or dispensable.

4. Capable of being dispensed or administered.

1680 *St. Trials, Col. Andrewe* (R.), If they be laws, they must be..dispensable by the ordinary courts of the land.

Hence **di'spensableness** = dispensability.

1654 Hammond *Fundamentals* xii. §2 (R.) Of Dispensableness of Oaths.

dispensary (dɪ'spɛnsərɪ). [f. L. type *dispensārium, dispensārius* (*liber*): cf. med.L. *dispensārius* (1290 in Fleta = *dispensator* dispenser), and F. *dispensaire* 'a Dispensatorie, or Booke, that teacheth how to make all Phisicall compositions' (Cotgr. 1611); f. *dispens-* ppl. stem of L. *dispend-ĕre* to dispense: see -ARY.]

1. A place, room, or shop, in which medicines are dispensed; an apothecary's shop. *spec.* A charitable institution, where medicines are dispensed and medical advice given gratis, or for a small charge (***charitable*** or ***public dispensary***).

1699 GARTH *Dispens.* Pref. (R.), The dispensary being an apartment in the college, set up for the relief of the sick poor. **1702** (*title*), The necessity and usefulness of the Dispensaries lately set up by the College of Physicians in London, for the use of the sick poor. **1789** MRS. PIOZZI *Journ. France* I. 199 [Venice treacle] can never be got genuine except here, at the original Dispensary. **1806** SURR *Winter in Lond.* I. 58 In the discharge of his duty as physician to a dispensary. **1869** LECKY *Europ. Mor.* II. iv. 86 A Merchant..founded.. a gratuitous dispensary for the monks. **1874** C. GEIKIE *Life in Woods* xvii. 291 He gave me some stuff from a dispensary.

†**2.** *transf.* A collection of the drugs or preparations mentioned in the pharmacopœia or to be found in an apothecary's shop. *Obs.*

1710 STEELE *Tatler* No. 248 ¶3 Natural Gaiety and Spirit ..surpass all the false Ornaments..that can be put on by applying the whole Dispensary of a Toilet. **1768-74** TUCKER *Lt. Nat.* (1852) I. 676 Nor yet does it suffice that we have a complete dispensary of remedies without knowing how to apply them.

†**3.** A book containing formulæ and directions for the making up of medicines; a pharmacopœia; = DISPENSATORY *sb.* 1. *Obs.* or *arch.*

1721 BAILEY, *Dispensary*, a Treatise of Medicines. **1725** BRADLEY *Fam. Dict.* s.v. *Syrup*, You have..a Description.. of it in all Dispensaries.

'dispensate, *v. rare.* [f. L. *dispensāt-*, ppl. stem of *dispensāre*; cf. *compensate.*] = DISPENSE.

1701 BEVERLEY *Glory of Grace* 5 That all is so Dispensated, and Oeconomized in, from, and by the Beloved. **1822** W. IRVING *Braceb. Hall* (1845) 144 Conceptions of widely dispensated happiness.

dispensation (dɪspɛn'seɪʃən). Also 4-6 dys-; -acioun. [a. F. *dispensation* (12th c. in Hatz.-Darm.), or ad. L. *dispensātiōn-em* distribution of money or property, management, stewardship, regulation, economy, from *dispensāre* to DISPENSE.]

I. The action of dealing out or distributing.

1. The action of dispensing or dealing out; distribution or administration to others; expenditure, spending, or disbursement (of money); economical use or disposal (of anything).

1387 TREVISA *Higden* (Rolls) III. 469 (Mätz.) Everych schulde make good for his owne partie, and ȝeve us special helpe and subsidie by his owne dispensacioun. **1649** SELDEN *Laws of Eng.* I. ii. (1739) 2 The dispensation of this grace unto all men. **1695** WOODWARD *Nat. Hist. Earth* I. (1723) 52 A Dispensation of Water promiscuously and indifferently to all Parts of the Earth. *a* **1704** T. BROWN *Praise Wealth* Wks. 1730 I. 86 Blind in the dispensation of all our favours. **1841** D'ISRAELI *Amen. Lit.* (1867) 618 Elizabeth, a queen well known for her penurious dispensations. **1861** TULLOCH *Eng. Purit.* i. 26 Changes in the dispensation of the Lord's Supper. **1878** LECKY *Eng. in 18th C.* II. viii. 439 The dispensation of bribes, places, and pensions.

†**2.** *Anat.* The distribution of blood, the nerves, etc., from some centre. *Obs.*

1668 CULPEPPER & COLE *Barthol. Anat.* I. i. 301 But the Principle of Dispensation from whence the Veins arise, is the Liver, and not the Heart. *Ibid.* III. i. 322 The Beginning of the dispensation of Nerves, or the part whence the Nerves immediately arise, is the *Medulla oblongata.* **1759** tr. *Duhamel's Husb.* II. ii. (1762) 182 This dispensation of the nutritive juices.

3. The process of dispensing medicines or medical prescriptions; 'the making up of medicines in accordance with prescription, and the delivery of them to the patient' (*Syd. Soc. Lex.* 1883).

1646 SIR T. BROWNE *Pseud. Ep.* v. iii. 237 In the due dispensation of medicines desumed from this animall. **1779-81** JOHNSON *L.P., Garth*, The Physicians procured some apothecaries to undertake the dispensation.

II. The action of administering, ordering, or managing; the system by which things are administered.

[This group of senses originates in the L. use of *dispensātio* to render Gr. οἰκονομία in N.T. and patristic writers. The latter is used in 1 Cor. ix. 17, Eph. iii. 2, Col. i. 25 for the 'office of an administrator' (see sense 4 below); but in Eph. i. 10, iii. 9, for 'a method or system of administration' (specifically that which involved the Incarnation). From this latter arose various theological uses: (1) Tertullian (*Adv. Praxean* ii, iii, iv.) uses *dispensatio* = οἰκονομία to denote the Trinity as an administrative arrangement, i.e. a system of distribution and apportionment of functions designed by the Father for administrative purposes. This is known as an *œconomical* as distinguished from an *essential* Trinity: in the latter the personal distinctions are regarded as matters of nature and necessity, in the former of will. (See the distinction between DISPENSATIVE, DISPENSATORY, and *essential.*) (2) It was applied to the Incarnation (*dispensatio assumpti corporis, d. susceptæ carnis*, or simply *dispensatio*) as the basis or organ of the redemptive system under which mankind now live (August. *Serm.* 264 §5). (3) The evangelical system is termed *dispensatio gratiæ* in opposition to the Law or system of works (August. *Ep.* 82 §20), while the method of salvation by means of the Incarnation is *dispensatio salutis nostræ* (August. *Serm.* 237 §1). Hence, in the Latin version of Irenæus, Christ is called *dispensator paternæ gratiæ* (iv. 20. 7). (4) *Dispensatio* was applied to the divine purpose or decree which established the system, and determined its mode of action (Tertull. *Adv. Marc.* vi. 18, Hilar. Pict. *De Trin.* ix. 66, xi. 13); also, by Hilary, to the Passion, as the supreme mystery of Redemption.]

4. The orderly administration of things committed to one's charge; the function or office of administrator or steward; stewardship. *arch.*

1382 WYCLIF *1 Cor.* ix. 17 Forsoth if I willinge do this thing, I haue mede; sothly if aȝens my wil, dispensacioun is bitake to me. **1482** *Monk of Evesham* (Arb.) 98 They shulde geue acomtys of her dispensacyon that haue resceyued benefytys and ryches of the chyrche. **1548** LATIMER *Ploughers* (Arb.) 34, I haue taken at my fathers hande the dispensation of redemynge mankynde. **1647** *Bury Wills* (Camden) 197 According to the will of him whose steward I am, and to whom I must give an accompt of the dispensacion of that which he hath committed vnto me. **1691** NORRIS *Pract. Disc.* 36 A Wise Dispensation of the Fading and Unrighteous Mammon. **1860** TRENCH *Serm. Westm. Abb.* xxxii. 366 A man..may forget or abuse his stewardship in the dispensation of one talent as effectually as in the dispensation of ten.

5. Ordering, management; *esp.* the divine administration or conduct of the world; the ordering or arrangement of events by divine providence.

c **1374** CHAUCER *Boeth.* IV. pr. vi. 108 (Camb. MS.) Thanne the wyse dispensacioun of god sparith hym. **1382** WYCLIF *Col.* i. 25, I poul am made mynystre bi dispensacioun of god. **1398** TREVISA *Barth. De P.R.* (1495) VI. xviii. 204 The dyspensacion of goddis word settyth some men to fore other. **1513** BRADSHAW *St. Werburge* I. 3463 Whiche danes by sufferaunce and dispensacion Of almyghty god for synne and iniquite Punysshed vnpiteously all this region. **1526** *Pilgr. Perf.* (W. de W. 1531) 27 Bothe body and soule, with the hole dispensacion and ordrynge of our lyfe & wyll. **1643-7** *Westm. Confess. Faith* viii. §8 (1877) Overcoming all their enemies by his almighty power and wisdom, in such manner and ways as are most consonant to his wonderful and unsearchable dispensation. **1665** SIR T. HERBERT *Trav.* (1677) 260 Albeit in his dispensation..his strokes are..with an equal hand afflicting the innocent with the nocent. **1671** MILTON *Samson* 61, I must not quarrel with the will Of highest dispensation.

b. An arrangement or provision of Providence or of Nature.

1665 HOOKE *Microgr.* 177 So infinitely wise and provident do we find all the Dispensations in Nature. **1754** SHERLOCK *Disc.* i. (1759) I. 39 The Gospel is a Dispensation of Providence in regard to Mankind. **1816** KEATINGE *Trav.* (1817) I. 18 With the immutable decree that man should labour, comes the benevolent dispensation that he need not want. **1861** MILL *Utilit.* v. 76 Attached to it by a special dispensation of nature.

c. A special dealing of Providence with a community, family, or person, dispensing blessing, affliction, or other event; the event or lot thus dealt out; as ***a mysterious*** or ***merciful dispensation.***

a **1652** ROGERS (J.), Neither are God's methods or intentions different in his dispensations to each private man. **1704** NELSON *Fest. & Fasts* ii. (1739) 29 The Dispensations of God's Providence towards Men..are very promiscuous. **1823** SCOTT *Peveril* xxix, A humbling dispensation on the house of Peveril. **1837** DICKENS *Pickw.* ii, Mysterious dispensations of Providence. **1848** RUSKIN *Mod. Paint.* II. III. I. xiv. §10. 111 Different dispensations of trial and of trust, of sorrow and support. **1895** CROCKETT *Glistering Beaches* in *Bogmyrtle* 154 In the north..everything is either a judgement or a dispensation, according to whether it happens to your neighbour or yourself.

6. *Theol.* A religious order or system, conceived as divinely instituted, or as a stage in a progressive revelation, expressly adapted to the needs of a particular nation or period of time, as the ***patriarchal, Mosaic*** (or ***Jewish***) ***dispensation,*** the ***Christian dispensation***; also, the age or period during which such system has prevailed; = ECONOMY 5 b.

An extension of the patristic use of the word as applied to the evangelical system based on the Incarnation (see note under II above); the patriarchal and Mosaic 'dispensations' being conceived as prophetic of the Christian, all being one in substance though differing in form. This use became common in the theology of the 17th c.

1643-7 *Westm. Confess. Faith* vii. §6 (1877) There are not therefore two covenants of grace, differing in substance, but one and the same under various dispensations. *a* **1652** J. SMITH *Sel. Disc. Div.* 297 The Jewish notion is this, that the law delivered to them on Mount Sinai was a sufficient dispensation from God. **1675** W. CAVE (*title*), Antiquitates Apostolicæ..to which is added An Introductory Discourse concerning the three Great Dispensations of the Church, Patriarchal, Mosaical, and Evangelical. **1706** PHILLIPS (ed. Kersey) s.v., In Divinity, *God's high Dispensation*, is the giving of the Levitical Law to the Jews, the Gospel to the Gentiles, the Sending his Son for the Redemption of Mankind. **1732** BERKELEY *Serm. to Soc. Prop. Gospel* Wks. III. 246 The Christian dispensation is a dispensation of grace and favour. **1772** PRIESTLEY *Inst. Relig.* (1782) II. 124 Christianity is the last dispensation. **1838** GLADSTONE *State in Rel. Ch.* vii. (L.), [They] declared..that the preaching of the Reformers was a kind of renewed commencement of the gospel dispensation. **1877** W. BRUCE *Comm. Rev.* v, As the Israelitish dispensation was abolished by the First Coming of Christ, the Christian dispensation is abolished by His Second Coming.

†**7.** The ordering or arrangement of anything in a particular way; *concr.* An arrangement, a system. *Obs.*

1633 BP. HALL *Hard Texts, N.T.* 135 By my owne voluntary dispensation. **1662** H. MORE *Philos Writ.* Pref. Gen. 10, I never found my mind low or abject enough to sink into sense or conceit of that Dispensation [superstition], experimentally to find what is at the bottom thereof. **1668** — *Div. Dial.* IV. iv. (1713) 295 He that lives in this dispensation of life. **1691** NORRIS *Pract. Disc.* 191 The great uses and advantages of such a Heavenly dispensation of Life.

III. The action of dispensing with some requirement; med.L. *dispensātio.* (See DISPENSE II.)

8. *Eccl.* An arrangement made by the administrator of the laws or canons of the church, granting, in special circumstances or in a particular case, a relaxation of the penalty incurred by a breach of the law, or exempting from the obligation to comply with its requirements, or from some sacred obligation, as an oath, etc.; the granting of licence by a pope, archbishop, or bishop, to a person, to do what is forbidden, or omit what is enjoined, by ecclesiastical law or by any solemn obligation; the licence so given.

c **1380** *Antecrist* in Todd 3 *Treat. Wyclif* 139 þei sellen it for mony, al þat þei maye; as pardons, indulgencis, & oþre dispensaciouns. **1382** WYCLIF *Sel. Wks.* III. 162 Dispensacioun wiþ þis lawe winnes miche money. *Ibid.* 511 Monks and chanouns forsaken þe reules of Benet and Austyn, and taken wiþouten eny dispensacioun þe reule of freres. *c* **1386** CHAUCER *Clerk's T.* 690 That he hath leue his firste wyf to lete As by the popes dispensacion. **1480** CAXTON *Chron. Eng.* ccxxx. 243 Sir Iohan..wedded dame blaunche duk henryes doughter of lancastre cosyn to the same Iohan by dispensacion of the pope. *c* **1555** HARPSFIELD *Divorce Hen. VIII* (1878) 129 A dispensation is but a gracious releasing to some certain person or persons of the common written law. **1588** SHAKS. *L.L.L.* II. i. 87 Then seeke a dispensation for his oath. **1655** FULLER *Ch. Hist.* IX. iii. §30 Richard Cheyney, Bishop of Bristol, holding Glocester therewith in dispensation. **1696** tr. *Du Mont's Voy. Levant* 37 The Profits accruing from the Dispensation of eating Eggs, Milk, Flesh, etc. **1769** BLACKSTONE *Comm.* IV. 114 To sue to Rome for any licence or dispensation, or to obey any process from thence, are made liable to the pains of *praemunire.* **1856** FROUDE *Hist. Eng.* I. 143 The original bull of dispensation which had been granted by Julius II for the marriage of Henry and Catherine. **1873** DIXON *Two Queens* I. I. viii. 56 A dispensation would be needed; but a dispensation could be got from Rome.

b. *transf.* and *fig.*

1664 BUTLER *Hud.* II. ii. 103 That Saints may claim a Dispensation To swear and forswear on occasion. **1673** DRYDEN *Assignation* V. iv, 'Tis a crime past dispensation. **1682** *Enq. Elect. Sheriffs* 11 As if they had a dispensation to speak what they please. **1726** *Adv. Capt. R. Boyle* 44 He had a Dispensation from the Mufty to drink Wine.

9. *Law.* The relaxation or suspension of a law of the realm in a particular case; the exercise of the dispensatory power claimed by Charles II and James II.

1607 TOPSELL *Hist. Four-f. Beasts* (1658) 452 The first that gave dispensation against those laws was Cneius Aufidius. **1667** PEPYS *Diary* 9 Jan., A way of preventing the King's dispensation with Acts. **1686** LUTTRELL *Brief Rel.* (1857) I. 382 Ten [judges] were clear of opinion that the dispensation in the case in question was good. **1689-92** LOCKE *Toleration* i. Wks. 1727 II. 250 The private Judgment of any Person concerning a Law enacted..for the publick Good, does not take away the Obligation of that Law, nor deserve a Dispensation. **1730-6** BAILEY (folio), *Dispensation* by *non obstante.* If any statute tends to restrain some Prerogative incident to the person of the King, as to the right of pardoning, etc., which are inseparable from the King, by a clause of *non obstante*, he may dispense with it; this was disannulled by Stat. 1. W. & M. *a* **1832** MACKINTOSH *Rev. of 1688* Wks. 1846 II. 194 The King answered..that the royal power of dispensation had been solemnly determined to be a sufficient warrant for such acts. **1863** H. COX *Instit.* I. v. 24 It was declared that..no dispensation with any statute should be valid unless such statute allows it.

b. ***clause of dispensation*** (Sc. Law): see quot.

1861 W. BELL *Dict. Law Scot.*, Where heritable subjects lay locally discontiguous..a clause of dispensation was sometimes inserted, specifying a particular place at which it should be sufficient to take infeftment for the whole lands, and other subjects, however discontiguous or dissimilar, and dispensing with any other subjects than earth and stone. The Crown alone could competently grant such a dispensation.

10. *transf.* Exemption, release from any obligation, fate, etc.; remission. *arch.* or *Obs.*

1653 H. COGAN tr. *Pinto's Trav.* lxviii. 275 The richest.. resolved to get a dispensation from this voyage by the means of a great sum of money. **1676** HALE *Contempl.* I. 96 After this third application for a deliverance from this terrible Cup of the wrath of God, and yet no dispensation obtained, he returns to..the three Disciples. *a* **1711** KEN *Serm.* Wks. (1838) 161 Daniel never made business a dispensation from God's service. **1752** JOHNSON *Rambler* No. 200 ¶5 Our intimacy was regarded by me as a dispensation from ceremonial visits. **1771** tr. *Viaud's Shipwreck* 132 The present circumstances..appeared to be a sufficient dispensation from attending..to any other consideration.

11. The action of dispensing *with* anything; a setting aside, disregarding; a doing away with, doing without. [Cf. sense 8, quot. 1382.]

1593 SHAKS. *Lucr.* 248 And [he] with good thoughts makes dispensation Urging the worser sense for vantage still. **1612-15** BP. HALL *Contempl., O.T.* XIV. i, Those temptations..which are raised from arbitrary and private respects, admit of an easie dispensation. **1848** SIR J. PARKE in *Exchequer Rep.* II. 723 Going to the counting-house during business hours, and finding no one there to receive the notice was equivalent to dispensation of notice. **1855**

MILMAN *Lat. Chr.* (1864) V. IX. vii. 359 The dispensation with appeal in certain cases only confirmed [it] in all others.

dispen'sational, *a.* [f. prec. + -AL[1].] Of or pertaining to dispensation, or to a dispensation.
1874 H. R. REYNOLDS *John Bapt.* v. iii. 351 He had certain national and dispensational offices to fill. **1876** *Spectator* 25 Nov. 1478/1 The Day of Pentecost, when the dispensational gifts of the Spirit were bestowed. **1888** *Bibliotheca Sacra* Apr. 237 Not a few..have believed that the limits of certain dispensational periods were revealed in Scripture.

di'spensative, *a.* (*sb.*) [ad. L. *dispensātīv-us*, f. *dispensā-re* to DISPENSE: see -ATIVE. Cf. F. *dispensatif, -ive* (14th c. in Littré).]
†**1.** Administrative, official; pertaining to the office of an administrator or steward. *Obs.*
1528 ROY *Rede me* (Arb.) 58 Though he have here soche prerogative, In all poyntes that be dispensative, To performe it by commyssion. **1633** AMES *Agst. Cerem.* II. 307 Not only in the name of the wholle societie, which in suche cases hath some dispensative superioritie over particular members, but allso by Commission from God. **1637** R. HUMPHREY tr. *St. Ambrose* I. 21 People are drawne away from the office of dispensative mercy. **1656** JEANES *Fuln. Christ* 34 There agreeth unto Christ a twofold power of Authority, essential, and official. 1. Essential or natural, which belongs unto him as God..2. Official, dispensative, or donative, delegated unto him as Mediatour, and head of his Church.
2. Dispensing, giving dispensation; = DISPENSATORY *a.* 2.
1621 HAKEWILL *David's Vow* vii. 270 Onely the dispensative power of the Lawgiver himself can possibly make it lawfull. **1687** *Pol. Ballads* (1860) I. 256 Knaves [that] would set up a Dispensative power, To pull down the Test unto which we have swore. **1738** NEAL *Hist. Purit.* IV. 230 Dr. Barwick..proposed that his Majesty should grant his commission to the Bishops of each province..to elect and consecrate fit persons for the vacant sees, with such dispensative clauses as should be found necessary.

di'spensatively, *adv.* [f. prec. + -LY[2].] In a dispensative way; by dispensation.
1572 FORREST *Theophilus* 542 in *Anglia* VII, Some saye it was doone dispensatively. *a* **1639** WOTTON in *Reliq.* 328 (R.), I can now hold my place canonically, which I held before but dispensatively. **1646** SALTMARSH *Smoke in Temple* 62 Is not their whole power defended to be entirely, essentially, dispensatively in the Presbytery. *a* **1656** BP. HALL *Serm. Canticles* IX. (R.), The state [is] absolutely monarchical in Christ, dispensatively monarchical in respect of particular churches; forasmuch as that power, which is inherent in the Church, is dispensed and executed by some prime ministers.

'dispen,sator. Now *rare.* Also 4 -owr, 4–6 -our, 6 -er, *Sc.* -ure. [a. AF. *dispensatour* = OF. *dispensateur, -tur* (12th c. in Littré), ad L. *dispensātōrem*, agent-n. from *dispensāre* to DISPENSE. Orig. stressed on final, which would have given mod. Eng. *di'spensator*; but conformation to L. gave *dispen'sator*, exemplified in 17th c. and in Johnson, Walker, Craig 1847; Smart 1849 has *'dispen,sator*.]
One who dispenses; a dispenser; a distributor.
1489 CAXTON *Faytes of A.* I. xiii. 35 Gode hede wold be taken that the dyspensatours and vitaillers of the oost be not theuys. **1491** —— *Vitas Patr.* (W. de W. 1495) II. 253 b/2 As a gode & trewe dyspensatour & dystrybutour to the poore people of the goodes of thy fader. **1549** *Compl. Scot.* xix. 158 God hes ordand the to be ane dispensatour of his gyftis amang the ignorant pepil. **1582** HESTER *Secr. Phiorav.* I. xlviii. 59 The Liuer beeyng dispensator bothe of the good and bad qualities of the humours. **1654** tr. *Scudery's Curia Pol.* 180 The ancient Romans (who were such equal dispensators of Glory). *a* **1859** L. HUNT *Shewe Faire seeming* v. Wks. (1860) 178 Much the stage he lov'd, and wise theatre, Counting it as a church, in which the page Of vertuous verse found the sole dispensator.
†**b.** A steward who administers the goods, etc. of another. *Obs.*
1382 WYCLIF *Gen.* xliii. 16 He comaundide to the dispensatowr [**1388** dispendere] of his hows, seiynge, Lede yn the men hoom. *c* **1449** PECOCK *Repr.* III. xix. 409 The richessis of chirchis ben patrimonies of poor men..the mynystris..ben dispensatouris ther of. **1553** BECON *Reliques of Rome* (1563) 155 The chamberlaynes and dispensatoures or stewardes of the mysteryes of God. **1621–51** BURTON *Anat. Mel.* III. iv. II. iii, Out of that treasure of indulgences and merits of which the pope is dispensator, he may have free pardon and plenary remission of all his sins. **1656** BLOUNT *Glossogr.*, *Dispensator*, a Steward, or Officer that laies out money for an houshold. **1698** NORRIS *Pract. Disc.* IV. 341 They are but Stewards and Dispensatours in respect of God. [**1876** FREEMAN *Norm. Conq.* V. xxii. 25 Azor the 'dispensator' had received his land again from King William.]
†**c.** An almoner. *Obs.*
1600 J. PORY tr. *Leo's Africa* II. 222 The kings dispensator or almoner.
d. An administrator.
c **1630** DRUMM. OF HAWTH. *Poems* 31/1 The sun in triumph rides..Time's dispensator, fair life-giving source. **1688** LADY RUSSELL *Lett.* II. lxxix. 4 May the great Dispensator of all these wonderful events dispose our hearts and minds. **1802** *Hatred* III. 95 Providence, the supreme dispensator of events.
Hence ,**dispen'satorship**.
1637 R. HUMPHREY *St. Ambrose* II. 36 [He] that beareth rule in some office, as in the office of the ministery, all dispensatorship.

dispensa'torial, *a. rare.* [f. as DISPENSATORY *a.* + -AL[1].] Administrative.
1776 BENTHAM *Fragm. Govt.* iii. §5 Wks. 1843 I. 278 By dispensatorial power I mean as well that which is exercised by the Board of Treasury, as..the War Office, Admiralty Board.

di'spensatorily, *adv.* [f. DISPENSATORY *a.* + -LY[2].] By dispensation; dispensatively.
a **1641** BP. R. MOUNTAGU *Acts & Mon.* (1642) 159 Prophecy is not all of one and the same assise, either originally..or dispensatorily. *a* **1679** T. GOODWIN *Wks.* I. I. 439 (R.) He is the God of all grace dispensatorily, or by way of performance and execution, and gracious dispensations of all sorts.

di'spensatory, *sb.* [ad. Med. or mod.L. *dispensātōrium, dispensātōrius* (*liber*), absol. use of *dispensātōrius* adj.: see next and -ORY.]
1. A book in which are described the composition, method of preparation, and use of medicinal substances; a pharmacopœia.
1566 SECURIS *Detection Abuses Physick* D vj, Ye poticarie mought not be without the dispensatories of Valerius Cordus, of Fuchsius. **1696** tr. *Du Mont's Voy. Levant* A viij b, Wherto is added a Chirurgical Dispensatory; shewing the Manner how to prepare all such Medicines. **1799** *Med. Jrnl.* II. 91 A cerate, which nearly resembles the unguentum tripharmacum of the old Dispensatory. **1811** A. T. THOMSON (*title*), The London Dispensatory, a Practical Synopsis of Materia Medica, Pharmacy, and Therapeutics. **1879** STILLE & MARSCH (*title*), The National Dispensatory.
attrib. **1716** M. DAVIES *Athen. Brit.* II. 352 Of all our Dispensatory Medicines, there's not one better.
b. *fig.*
a **1626** BP. ANDREWES *Serm.* x. *Holy Ghost* (1661) 462 In all Christ's dispensatory, there is not a medicine for such a heart. **1667** *Decay Chr. Piety* vii. ¶1 [They] defame the Gospel as the dispensatory, and Christ as the physician, and likewise ruine themselves as the patients. **1697** COLLIER *Immor. Stage* i. (1698) 5 One of the Fathers calls Poetry, *Vinum Dæmonum* an intoxicating Draught, made up by the Devils Dispensatory. **1741** WARBURTON *Div. Legat.* II. 44. **1773** BERRIDGE *Chr. World Unmasked* (1812) 27 To hear what my dispensatory says concerning will and prayer.
†**2.** A place where medicines are made up; = DISPENSARY 1. *Obs.*
1597 GERARDE *Herbal* XXXV. XXV. §1. 35 Apothecaries shop or dispensatorie. *a* **1626** BACON *New Atl.* (1650) 29 Dispensatories, or Shops of Medicines. **1644** EVELYN *Diary* 8 Nov., Father Kircher..leading us into their refectory, dispensatory, laboratory, gardens, etc. **1673** *Lady's Call.* I. §3 ¶14. 23 Not only opening their purses, but dispensatories too, providing medicines for such as..want that sort of relief. **1742** RICHARDSON *Pamela* I. 352 [He] praised me that I don't carry my Charity to Extremes, and make his House a Dispensatory. **1799** tr. *Diderot's Nat. Son* II. 196 He had given me a key of the dispensatory, that I might myself take what I wanted.
†**3.** *fig.* A repertory or collection of medicines.
1654 *Triana* in *Fuller's Cause & Cure* (1867) 207 Sickness carrieth with it its own dispensatory for such incivilities. **1707** *Curios. in Husb. & Gard.* 108 If but one half of them were true, we should find in this single Tree an intire Dispensatory; and the Leaves, the Wood, and the Juice of Ash, would be sufficient to furnish an Apothecary's Shop. **1748** G. JEFFREYS in *Duncombe's Lett.* (1773) II. 196 The whole moral dispensatory affords no remedy so universal and efficacious.
4. *gen.* A place whence anything is dispensed or dealt out.
1653 *Consid. Dissolv. Crt. Chancery* 5 The Magazine, store-house, and dispensatory of all Writts remedial. **1752** A. MURPHY *Gray's Inn Jrnl.* No. 17 This place is the grand Dispensatory of Life and Death.

di'spensatory, *a.* [ad. L. *dispensātōr-ius* (Jerome), f. *dispensātor*: see DISPENSATOR and -ORY.]
†**1.** Of or pertaining to a dispensator, administrator, or steward, or to administration; = DISPENSATIVE 1. *Obs.*
The 17th c. theologians contrasted *dispensatory* or *dispensative* power, which is exercised by virtue of office, with *essential* or *inherent* power.
1635 RAINBOW *Serm.* 8 (T.) The dispenser [is] the Son of Man: the author of the dispensatory power, God the Father. **1649** ROBERTS *Clavis Bibl.* iii. 54 Christs Kingdome may be considered in divers respects, viz. As it is Essentiall..As Oeconomical, Dispensatory or Mediatory. **1671** FLAVEL *Fount. Life* xiii. 38 The Divinity of Christ..which was obscured in this Temporary Dispensatory kingdom. *a* **1679** T. GOODWIN *Wks.* I. I. 439 (R.) There is a dispensatory Kingdom (as Divines use to call it), as he [Christ] is considered as Mediator between God and his church: which Kingdom is not his natural due, but it was given him and given him by choice.
2. That gives dispensations; having the power or habit of dispensing with laws or rules.
1647 TRAPP *Comm. Jas.* ii. 10 A dispensatory conscience keeps not any Commandment. **1650** —— *Comm. Gen.* vii. 5, *Exod.* x. 26. **1675** BROOKS *Gold. Key* Wks. 1867 V. 36.

di'spensatress. [f. DISPENSATOR + -ESS.] = next.
In recent Dicts.

dispen'satrix. [a. L. *dispensātrix*, fem. of *dispensātor* DISPENSATOR.] A female dispenser.
a **1864** FABER tr. *De Montfort's Devotion to Virgin*, He has chosen her to be the dispensatrix of all He possesses. **1865** PUSEY *Eiren.* 258 De Montfort speaks of 'the free-thinkers of these [his] times'; who did not believe that the Holy Trinity has made the Blessed Virgin the dispensatrix of all which they possess and will to bestow upon man.

di'spense, *sb.*[1] Forms: 4–5 (7) despens(e, 4–8 dispense, 4–7 dis-, 5 6 dyspence. [In I., a. OF. *despense* act of spending, ad. late L. *dispensa*, sb. from pa. pple. of *dispendĕre* to DISPEND; prob. blending with OF. *despens*:—L. *dispensum* that which is expended. In II. prob. an Eng. deriv. of the vb. in the cognate sense.]
I. †**1.** *Obs.* **a.** The act of spending, expenditure.
c **1320** *Seuyn Sag.* (W.) 330 Your travail and your despens. **1340** *Ayenb.* 21 Huanne he deþ to moche despense oþer of his oȝen oþer of oþre manne. *c* **1386** CHAUCER *Prol.* 441 He was but esy in dispence. *c* **1400** *Rom. Rose* 1141 Alle his purpos..Was for to make gret dispense. *a* **1533** LD. BERNERS *Huon* lxxxix. 283 Huon gaue hym..money for his dyspence. **1613** *William I* in *Harl. Misc.* (Malh.) III. 154 With great dispence, both of their estates and blood. **1664** PEPYS *Diary* (1879) III. 41 [They] are not sufficient to supply our dispense if a warr comes.
b. *pl.* Expenses, charges, costs.
c **1380** WYCLIF *Serm.* Sel. Wks. I. 20 Costlewe housis and greet dispensis. **1416** *Comp. Subs.* in *Rel. Ant.* I. 232 The somme..in clere, without colectours dispencis. *c* **1460** FORTESCUE *Abs. & Lim. Mon.* v. (1885) 119 Thai most serue hym..at thair owne dispenses. **1718** BYROM *Jrnl. & Lit. Rem.* (1854) I. I. 36 With these and other dispenses..I am just as I was before I drew upon you last.
c. Means of meeting expenditure, money to spend or use; means of support; supplies.
1382 WYCLIF *1 Chron.* xxii. 5 Beforn his death he made redy alle the dispensis. *c* **1430** *Hymns Virg.* 63 Wraþþe haþ no Conscience, He makiþ ech man oþeris foo; þer-with he getiþ his dispence. *a* **1510** DOUGLAS *King Hart* II. 443 Thai wantit thame dispence, Ewill purvayit folk. **1652** F. KIRKMAN *Clerio & Lozia* 123 Which might furnish me with so many amorous dispences as these..beauties make by their so long sojourn at my heart.
†**2.** The act of dispensing or bestowing liberally. *Obs.*
1590 SPENSER *F.Q.* II. xii. 42 Whatever..Is sweete..Was poured forth with plentifull dispence. **1596** —— *F.Q.* V. xi. 45 Dealing his dreadfull blowes with large dispence.
3. †**a.** A place where provisions are kept; a store-room, pantry, or cellar; = SPENCE. [Fr. *despence*, a larder, storehouse, gardemanger (Cotgr.)] *Obs.*
1622 MABBE tr. *Aleman's Guzman d'Alf.* I. 237 He went to the Dispense for wine. *Ibid.* II. 348 In a little Dispense, or Pantrie. *Ibid.* II. 351.
b. In full ***dispense bar.*** A bar in a club or hotel for the use of staff.
1934 'C. L. ANTHONY' *Touch Wood* I. 27 A bar! They called it the dispense bar. **1961** *Daily Tel.* 7 Apr. 25 At the club..no intoxicating drinks were to be supplied after 2 a.m., when the bar and dispense were closed.
II. †**4.** = DISPENSATION 8. *Obs.*
1490 CAXTON *Eneydos* xii. 46 [Elysse] leuynge by dyspense abstractyue her first vowes of chastyte promysed. **1578** *Gude & G. Ball.*, *Huntis vp* 153 That cruell beist, he neuer ceist..Under dispens to get our penneis Our saulis to deuoir. **1631** HEYWOOD *2nd Pt. Fair Maid of W.* v. Wks. 1874 II. 411 My honesty, faith, and religion, are all ingag'd; there's no dispence for them. **1667** MILTON *P.L.* III. 492 Indulgences, Dispenses, Pardons, Bulls. **1777** W. DALRYMPLE *Trav. Sp. & Port.* cxi, It is necessary for every knight who [marries] to get a dispense for his vow.

† **di'spense**, *sb.*[2] *Obs.* [deriv. of L. *dēpendĕre* (see DEPEND *v.* 7) with *dis-* for *de-* (cf. DE- I. 6), perh. of AFr. origin Godef. has OF. *despens* for *depens*, and the same change of prefix is found in other OF. derivatives of *dépendre*.] A state of uncertainty; an undetermined condition; SUSPENSE.
1562 in W. H. TURNER *Select. Rec. Oxford* 294 Mr. Tilcocke..shall stand in dispence for his submyssion for his offence untyll the ffeast of Christmas. **1583** RICH *Phylotus & Emelia* (1835) 23 If there be any thyng that hanges in dispence betweene vs. **1647–8** COTTERELL *Davila's Hist. Fr.* (1678) 33 The absense of the Princes held the King and all his Ministers in great dispense.

dispense (dɪ'spɛns), *v.* Also 4–6 des-, 5–6 dys-; 5–8 dispence. [ME. a. OF. *de-, dispenser* (13th c. in Hatz.-Darm.) = Pr., Sp. *despensar*, It. *dispensare*, ad. L. *dispensāre* (freq. of *dispendĕre* to DISPEND: cf. *pensāre* to weigh out); in class. L. to distribute by weight, to weigh out, disburse; to administer as steward, to dispose, arrange; in med.L. to arrange or deal administratively with a person in reference to the requirements of an ecclesiastical canon or law.]
I. from L. *dispensāre* in classical senses.
1. *trans.* To mete out, deal out, distribute; to bestow in portions or from a general stock.
c **1374** CHAUCER *Boeth.* v. pr. vi. 139 (Camb. MS.) Despensynge and ordeynynge Meedes to goode men, and torment to wykked men. *c* **1420** *Pallad. on Husb.* I. 172 Abundaunt wyne the north wynde wol dispence To vynes sette agayne his influence. **1526** *Pilgr. Perf.* (W. de W. 1531) 28 b, Some we must vse, dispence and expende, and truly distribute. **1599** H. BUTTES *Dyets drie Dinner* A a ij, I assume the Carvers office: and..dispense to every of my Guests according to the Season, his Age and Constitution. **1647** CLARENDON *Hist. Reb.* I. (1843) 20/2 He might dispense favours and disfavours according to his own election. **1667** MILTON *P.L.* IV. 157 Now gentle gales..

dispense Native perfumes. **1715** LEONI *Palladio's Archit.* (1742) II. 99 Those Pipes which dispens'd the Heat. **1781** COWPER *Convers.* 1 Though Nature weigh our talents, and dispense To every man his modicum of sense. **1849** MACAULAY *Hist. Eng.* II. 81 Several commissioners..had been appointed to dispense the public alms.

†**b.** To spend (time, talents): both in the sense of expending profitably and of wasting. *Obs.*

c **1624** CHAPMAN *Batrachom.* 13 Who with his wreake dispenst No point of Tyme. **1638** ROUSE *Heav. Univ.* x. (1702) 147 As every man hath received the Gift so let him exercise and dispense it. **1649** G. DANIEL *Trinarch., Rich. II*, cccxxviii, Affliction Is the best Mistresse to dispence our Time.

2. To administer (*e.g.* a sacrament, justice, etc.).

1398 TREVISA *Barth. De P.R.* II. ii (1495) 30 An angel dispensyth thynges that ben abowte vs. **1401** *Pol. Poems* (Rolls) II. 46 The sacrament that we han to dispensen off penaunce to the peple. **1588** A. KING tr. *Canisius' Catech.* 65 It is nocht ye office of euerie man..to consecrat, dispens, and minister ye sacraments. **1616** R. C. *Times' Whistle* IV. 1517 You, which should true equity dispense. *a* **1656** BP. HALL *Serm. Canticles* IX. (R.), That power..is dispensed and executed by some prime ministers. **1678** CUDWORTH *Intell. Syst.* 110 Shall we say..that this whole Universe is dispensed ond ordered, by a mere Irrational..and Fortuitous Principle? **1894** *Law Times* 387/2 Sir Richard Malins..dispensed a home-brewed equity of his own.

b. *absol.*

c **1374** CHAUCER *Boeth.* IV. pr. vi. 109 (Camb. MS.) In the which thing I trowe þat god dispensith. *a* **1633** AUSTIN *Medit.* 106 Lest hee should not dispense, and governe well.

3. *Med.* To make up (medicine) according to a prescribed formula; to put up (a prescription).

1533 ELYOT *Cast. Helthe* (1541) A iij, Some [physitions] were not diligent inough in beholdynge their drouges or ingredience at all tymes dispensid and tried. **1612** WOODALL *Surg. Mate* Wks. (1653) 310, I dispence and administer all [drugs] by Haber-de-pois. **1768–74** TUCKER *Lt. Nat.* (1852) I. 586 That..the apothecary dispense his recipes properly. **1780** COWPER *Progr. Err.* 594 Swallow the two grand nostrums they dispense—That Scripture lies, and blasphemy is sense. **1883** *Syd. Soc. Lex.*, s.v. *Dispensary*, The place where medicines are prepared and given out, or dispensed.

II. from med.L. *dispensāre* in eccles. use.

[In later med.L. (by 1200 or earlier) *dispensāre* was used absol. or intrans. (= *agere dispensatorie* or *dispensative*), in the sense 'to make an arrangement in the character of a steward (οἰκονόμος), administrator, or manager, to deal administratively,' especially in reference to the practical application of a law or rule to a particular case; first, apparently, in the way of relaxing a punishment or penance, which, according to strict law, had been already incurred, but in the particular case ought to be remitted for special reasons; thence, in the remission of a punishment not yet incurred, which amounted in fact to a licence to break the legal rule; and thus, in the general sense of granting relaxation, exemption, indulgence, etc. The chief constructions were *dispensare in tali casu, circa jus, circa aliquem* or *aliquid*, and esp. *cum aliquo* (*ut possit*), etc. (to dispense in such a case, in reference to a certain law, or a certain person or matter, with a person that he may do something, etc.). (Prof. F. W. Maitland, LL.D.)

These intrans. uses passed into English, esp. *dispense with*, which became a combined verbal phrase, with indirect passive, *to be dispensed with*, and has had a wide development of sense: see branch III. By elision of the preposition or other processes, the verb has also become trans. in the sense 'to grant dispensation to, for, or from.' Transitive senses are found also in French from 15th c.]

4. *intr.* To deal dispensatorily, to use dispensatory power; to grant dispensation or relaxation of the strict letter of the law *in* a special case; to make a special arrangement (*with* any one) whereby the penalty of a law is remitted in his case. **a.** simply, or with *in.* (Orig. in reference to ecclesiastical law; said also of a king's dispensing power.)

c **1440** *Promp. Parv.* 122/2 Dyspenson, be auctoryte, of penawnce, *dispenso*. *c* **1555** HARPSFIELD *Divorce Hen. VIII* (1878) 40 When he dispenseth he sheweth the case whereon he dispenseth to be contained under the meaning of the law. **1563** WINȜET *Four Scoir Thre Quest.* lxxx. Wks. 1888 I. 128 Quhat pouer haif ȝe to dispence mair in the ane nor in the wthir? **1688** SIR E. HERBERT *Hales' Case* 29 There is the same Disability in the Case of Sheriffs, and yet resolved that the King can Dispense in that Case. **1810–16** C. O'CONOR *Columbanus ad Hibernos* vii. 62 It asserted..that the Pope could not dispense in the allegiance due by Catholics to their Sovereigns. **1833** R. H. FROUDE *Rem.* (1838) I. 307 In case he could not dispense..at any rate the acts of one Council might be rescinded by another.

†**b.** with clause, expressing purpose or end. *Obs.*

c **1555** HARPSFIELD *Divorce Hen. VIII* (1878) 133 He cannot dispense that a man should keep a concubine, or that a king having a barren wife may marry again. **1639** FULLER *Holy War* IV. xxv. (1647) 212 The Pope would not dispense that Princes should hold pluralitie of temporall Dominions.

c. with *with.* The earliest construction exemplified (in Wyclif *c* 1380), and also the most important: see *dispense with*, III below.

†**d.** with *against.* To relax a law or its penalty in opposition to (some authority); to give dispensation, indulgence, or permission, in opposition to (some law). *Obs.*

c **1555** HARPSFIELD *Divorce Hen. VIII* (1878) 133 Of set purpose spoken to intimate that the Pope cannot dispense against that chapter. *Ibid.* 146 He saith the Pope may dispense against the Apostles' order, as in bigamie, yet not against God's own law. **1561** DAUS tr. *Bullinger on Apoc.* (1573) 185 b, Yea the same gloser..sayth: The Pope if he will, may dispence agaynst the Councell. For he is more than the Councell.

†**5.** *trans.* To relax the law in reference to (some thing or person). **a.** To remit or permit (a thing which is forbidden by the strict letter of the law); to remit or relax the penalty for (an offence); to condone. *Obs.*

1393 GOWER *Conf.* I. 365 His sinne was dispensed With golde, wherof it was compensed. *c* **1540** in *Fisher's Wks.* (E.E.T.S.) II. p. xlii, In this Bull the maryage with Prince Henrie was dispenced, for that the ladie was before maryed to his brother prince Arthur. **1566** *Pasquine in a Traunce* 108 The Pope, dispensing all things for money. **1591** *Troub. Raigne K. John* (1611) 48 Our holy father hath dispenst his sinnes.

†**b.** To permit (a person) to do something contrary to the general law; to permit by dispensation. *Obs.*

1511–2 *Act 3 Hen. VIII*, c. 1. Preamble, No person shuld carie..out of this Realme..Bullion..but suche persons as be desspensed within the Statute. **1605** CAMDEN *Rem.* (1637) 127 Hugh..was dispensed by the Pope to marrie.

†**c.** *absol.* To permit, allow, give dispensation.

1646 SIR T. BROWNE *Pseud. Ep.* To Rdr. A iij a, Would Truth dispense, we could be content with Plato, that knowledge were but Remembrance.

6. *trans.* To dissolve, relax, or release by dispensation. †**a.** To relax or dissolve the obligation of (a vow, oath, or the like) by ecclesiastical authority. *Obs.*

1532 MORE *Confut. Tindale* Wks. 619/2 The churche hathe synce..dispensed and vndone the bonde. **1632** MASSINGER *City Madam* v. iii, Thy holy vow dispensed. **1640** BRATHWAIT *Two Lanc. Lovers* 235 Those vowes..could not so easily be dispenced.

b. To give (a person) dispensation *from* something; to release *from* (†*of*) an obligation; to exempt, excuse.

1627 *Lisander & Cal.* IV. 58 Beleeving that hee was dispensed of his promise. **1639** T. BRUGIS tr. *Camus' Moral Relat.* 345 [He] entreated his Highnes to dispense him from swearing that hee should no more love Goland. **1653** H. COGAN tr. *Pinto's Trav.* xxxi. 122 The Subject I now treat of dispences me to speak of all. **1697** DRYDEN *Virg. Past.* Pref. (1721) I. 91 Extraordinary Genius's have a sort of Prerogative, which may dispense them from Laws, binding to Subject-Wits. **1744** JOHNSON *L.P.*, *Savage* Wks. III. 366 He appeared to think himself..dispensed from all necessity of providing for himself. *a* **1822** SHELLEY *Ess. &c.* (1852) I. 226 This materialism..allows its disciples to talk, and dispenses them from thinking. **1851** J. H. NEWMAN *Cath. Eng.* 173 Who was to dispense them from their oath?

absol. **1768** *Woman of Honor* II. 50 That dispenses from all panegiric.

†**7.** To do without, to forgo; = *dispense with*: see 14. *Obs.*

c **1420** *Pallad. on Husb.* VI. 235 As he as swyfte to be yit I dispence. **1580** SIDNEY *Arcadia* (1674) 122 (D.) Images of battels and fortifications being then delivered to their memory, which after, their stronger judgements might dispence. **1647** N. BACON *Disc. Govt. Eng.* I. lix. (1739) 110 His right of investiture of the Mitred Clergy he dispensed.

†**8.** *intr.* To make amends or compensation *for. Obs. rare.* (Cf. 1393 in 5 a.)

1590 SPENSER *F.Q.* I. iii. 30 One loving howre For many yeares of sorrow can dispence.

III. dispense with.

[Orig. the chief construction of the intrans. sense 4, = med.L. *dispensare cum* (see note under II); which has become a verbal combination, with indirect passive *to be dispensed with*, and extensive development of sense.]

* *to dispense with a person.*

†**9.** To arrange administratively with (a person), so as to grant him relaxation or remission of penalty incurred by breach of law, or special exemption or release from a law or obligation; to let off from doing something; to exempt, excuse. *refl.* To excuse oneself, refrain or abstain *from.*

c **1380** WYCLIF *Wks.* (1880) 390 Her-to þai ben bounden.. And þer may no man dispense with hem of þat boonde. **1460** CAPGRAVE *Chron.* 109 Whan his fader was ded, the Pope dispensid with him [a monk] and made him wedde the doutir of Charles. **1494** FABYAN *Chron.* VII. 299 To gether money..he had lycence of pope Innocent..to dispence with such as hym lykyd..for takynge vpon them the crosse. **1549** LATIMER *2nd Serm. bef. Edw. VI* (Arb.) 57 God had dispensed wyth theym to haue manye wyues. **1606** HOLLAND *Sueton.* 104 He dispensed with a gentleman of Rome for his oath..never to divorce his wife, and gave him leave to put her away. **1705** ADDISON *Italy* 251, I could not dispense with my self from making a little Voyage. **1728** T. SHERIDAN *Persius* Ded. (1739) 6, I hope I shall be dispensed with, for studying Easiness of Style, rather than Elegance. **1775** in *Mad. D'Arblay's Early Diary* (1889) II. 52, I cannot dispense with myself from giving you..my whole sentiments.

†**b.** *transf.* To make an arrangement or compound with, for an offence, etc. *Obs. rare.*

1568 GRAFTON *Chron.* II. 117 These Gualo reserved to his awne auchtoritie, and in the ende for great summes of money [he] dispensed with them. **1593** SHAKS. *2 Hen. VI*, v. i. 181 Canst thou dispense with heauen for such an oath? **1659** B. HARRIS *Parival's Iron Age* 126 They [were] dispensed with for a Garrison, and the Forfeit of an hundred and fifty thousand Rix-dollars.

** *to dispense with a rule, obligation, requirement*, etc.

10. To deal administratively with (a law or rule, ecclesiastical or civil) so as to relax or remit its penalty or obligation in a special case; to give special exemption or relief from.

c **1380** WYCLIF *Sel. Wks.* III. 511 þe pope may dispence wiþ þe reule of ech privat secte or religioun..but he may not dispense wiþ Cristis reule ȝoven to apostlis. **1401** *Pol. Poems* (Rolls) II. 35 When ye prayed him to dispense with the hardnesse of your order. **1500–20** DUNBAR *Fenȝeit Freir* 54 He had dispensit with matynnis channoun. **1538** STARKEY *England* I. iv. 103 Thys ys a grete faute..any one man to have such authoryte to dyspense wyth the commyn lawys. *a* **1626** BACON *Max. & Uses Com. Law* v. (1636) 26 Necessity dispenseth with the direct letter of a statute law. **1818** CRUISE *Digest* (ed. 2) V. 12 Either House of Parliament might dispense with their own orders, whenever they thought fit. **1827** HALLAM *Const. Hist.* (1876) III. xiv. 61 It was agreed..that the king could not dispense with the common law. **1862** LD. BROUGHAM *Brit. Const.* xvi. 247 The right of the King to dispense with penal statutes.

11. To relax the obligation of (a vow, oath, promise, or the like); to dissolve, in a special case, the binding force of (an oath, etc.).

1530 TINDALE *Pract. Prelates*, *Deuorcement* H vij b, If this maryage be of God the pope can not dispence with it. **1593** NASHE *Christ's T.* 15 b, His humour was pacified, his oth was dispenst with. *a* **1618** RALEIGH (J.), How few kingdoms are there, wherein, by dispensing with oaths, absolving subjects from allegiance..the popes have not wrought innumerable mischiefs. **1692** WASHINGTON tr. *Milton's Def. Pop.* iv. (1851) 126 There needs no Pope to dispense with the Peoples Oath. **1868** FREEMAN *Norm. Conq.* (1876) II. vii. 117 The king's vow of pilgrimage was dispensed with. **1883** FROUDE in *Contemp. Rev.* XLIV. 13 A safe-conduct had not saved Huss, and Popes could dispense with promises.

†**12.** To set aside the obligation, observance, or practice of (any duty, etc.); to disregard. *Obs.*

1559 *Mirr. Mag.*, *Warwick* vi, With his fayth he past not to dispence. **1598** SHAKS. *Merry W.* II. i. 47 Hang the trifle (woman) take the honour: what is it? dispence with trifles: what is it? **1607** in Ellis *Orig. Lett.* Ser. I. III. 85 To resume that duty which I have so long dispensed with. **1659** B. HARRIS *Parival's Iron Age* 125 It seems that..men may dispense with their faith or word given, even upon meer doubts. **1748** RICHARDSON *Clarissa* (1811) VII. 310, I never knew her dispense with her word, but once.

13. To do away with (a requirement, need, or necessity); to render unnecessary or superfluous.

1576 FLEMING *Panopl. Epist.* 255 [A Translation] short also, and not tedious, which dispenseth with all maner of cares and businesse. **1625** BACON *Ess.*, *Ambition* (Arb.) 225 The Vse of their Seruice dispensed with the rest. **1729** BUTLER *Serm.* Wks. 1874 II. 111 Guilt or injury..does not dispense with or supersede the duty of love and good-will. **1875** F. HALL in *Lippincott's Mag.* XV. 341/1 Familiar facts dispense with all need to draw on the imagination. **1892** *Law Times* XCIV. 104/1 The possession given on the marriage day..dispensed with the necessity of a writing.

14. To excuse or put up with the absence or want of (a thing or person); to forgo, do without. (The opposite of 16.)

1607 SHAKS. *Timon* III. ii. 93 Men must learne now with pitty to dispence. **1643** SIR T. BROWNE *Relig. Med.* I. §3 At the sight of a Crosse or Crucifix I can dispense with my hat, but scarse with the thought or memory of my Saviour. **1742** RICHARDSON *Pamela* III. 325 Won't you, Sir, dispense with me, on this Occasion? **1840** DICKENS *Barn. Rudge* xii, Let us dispense with compliments. **1856** FROUDE *Hist. Eng.* (1858) I. i. 68 No genius can dispense with experience. **1874** GREEN *Short. Hist.* ii. §8. 105 Resources which enabled him to dispense with the military support of his tenants.

*** *to dispense with a breach of law, fault, offence, objectionable matter*, etc.

†**15.** To deal with (a breach of law) so as to condone it; to grant a dispensation for (something illegal or irregular); to permit, allow, or condone by dispensation; to excuse, pardon. *Obs.*

1540–54 CROKE *Ps.* (Percy Soc.) 8 Vppon me then thou wolt take ruthe, And with my faults clerely dispense. **1548** HALL *Chron.*, *Hen. VIII* (an. 1) 2 The whiche mariage was dispensed with by Pope July, at the request of her father. *c* **1555** HARPSFIELD *Divorce Hen. VIII* (1878) 134 In such kind of marriages with which it hath not been wont to be dispensed, the children cannot prosper. **1603** SHAKS. *Meas. for M.* III. i. 135 Nature dispenses with the deede so farre, That it becomes a vertue. **1651** *Life Father Sarpi* (1676) 45 The Reader will be pleased to dispense with this little digression. **1716** ADDISON *Freeholder* No. 43 (Seager) His religion dispenses with the violation of the most sacred engagements.

†**16.** To deal with indulgently; to manage with; to do with, put up with. *Obs.* (The exact opposite of 14: see quot. 1796.)

1580 SIDNEY *Arcadia* v. (1590) 451, I would and could dispence with these difficulties. **1660** WOOD *Life* (Oxf. Hist. Soc.) I. 366 Though they lately hated a square cap, yet now they could dispense with one. **1665** SIR T. HERBERT *Trav.* (1677) 158 Yea, [they] can dispense with Hogs flesh and account it a dainty. **1703** MOXON *Mech. Exerc.* 130 Some Trades require a deeper, others may dispence with a shallower Shop. **1755** COLMAN & THORNTON in *Connoisseur* No. 91 ¶5 My pantry is stored with more provisions than we can dispense with. **1796** PEGGE *Anonym.* (1809) 460, I can dispense with it, i.e. I can do with it; and, I can dispense with it, i.e. I can do without it.

†**di'spenseless**, *a. Obs. rare.* [See -LESS.] Not subject to dispensation.

1721 CIBBER *Perolla* 11, Dispenseless Oaths.

dispenser (dɪ'spɛnsə(r)). Forms: 3–7 despencer, 4–5 despenser, 4–6 dispensour, 5–6 dyspenser, 6– dispenser. [ME. *dispensour*, a. AF. *des-*, *dispensour* = OF. *despenseor*, *-eur*:—L. *dispensātōr-em*, agent-n. from *dispensāre* to dispense. This has fallen together with AF. &

ME. *despencer, -ser*, = OF. *des- dispensier*, = It. *dispensiere*, Sp. *despensero*, Pg. *-iero* = med.L. *dispensārius*, f. late L. *dispensa*: see DISPENSE *sb.* and -ER² 2.]

1. One who dispenses, deals out, bestows, or administers.

1526 *Pilgr. Perf.* (W. de W. 1531) 33 They may be founde the faythfull dyspensers of the sayd graces. **1592** in *Edin. Rev.* No. 323. 70 The most ordinary carriers and dispensers of the infection of the plague. **1653** MANTON *Exp. James* v. 2–3 God gaue us wealth, not that we should be hoarders, but dispensers. **1774** GOLDSM. *Nat. Hist.* (1776) I. 336 The air ..as a kind dispenser of light and warmth. **1855** MACAULAY *Hist. Eng.* III. 554 A dispenser of bribes. **1868** FREEMAN *Norm. Conq.* (1876) II. vii. 67 The dispensers of church patronage.

2. One who manages or administers. a. A steward of a household. *arch.*

[**1297** R. GLOUC. (1724) 559 Sir Hue þe Despencer, þe noble justice.] *c* **1380** WYCLIF *Serm.* Sel. Wks. II. 229 Men axe þat a man be found trewe amongis dispensours of an house. *c* **1400** MAUNDEV. (1839) xi. 123 Helizeus..þat was þorn. & despenser of Abraham before þat Ysaac was born. **1580** FULKE *Agst. Allen* 112 (T.) Christ's embassadours, ministers, and dispensers. **1605** CAMDEN *Rem.* (1637) 246 Turstane the kings steward, or Le Despencer, as they then called him. **1626** L. OWEN *Rvnning Register* 3 The vnder-Officers of the Colledge, as the Despencer, Cooke, Butler, Baker [etc.]. **1867** FREEMAN *Norm. Conq.* (1876) I. vi. 512 Eadric his dispenser. **1880** MUIRHEAD *Gaius* I. §122 Those slaves who had charge of their owner's money were called dispensers.

b. An administrator of the law, of authority, etc.

1654 *State Case Commw.* 24 Where law is dispensed there should..be a ready passage to redress against the dispensers. **1825** COLERIDGE *Aids Refl.* (1848) I. 111 The dispenser of his particular decrees. **1875** KINGLAKE *Crimea* (1877) V. i. 14 Never did he convince the dispensers of military authority. **1884** *Law Times* 1 Mar. 314/2 The stern majesty of the law of which he is the dispenser.

3. a. One who makes up medical prescriptions and serves out medicines.

1858 SIMMONDS *Dict. Trade*, *Dispenser*, one who distributes or administers; usually applied to medicines. **1861** WYNTER *Soc. Bees* 455 A dispenser who could not stop in the room with an unstoppered bottle of ipecachuana. **1885** *Pall Mall G.* 31 Dec. 5/1 The old saying that 'chemists and dispensers make eleven pence three farthings profit out of every shilling they earn'.

b. Also, one who dispenses a commodity.

1881 W. CARLETON *Lightning-rod Dispenser* 3 This railroad smash reminds me..Of a lightning-rod dispenser that came down on me one day. **1925** *Daily Tel.* 13 May 20 Soda water dispenser required, to supervise six fountains.

4. One who dispenses *with*, or gives a dispensation to (a person or thing).

1604 *Constit. & Canons Eccles.* §118 Such dalliers and dispensers with their own consciences and oaths.

5. A container that dispenses an appropriate measure of a commodity (usu. with defining word).

1947 STEINBECK *Wayward Bus* 104 He passed the sugar dispenser politely to her. **1950** *Brit. Pat.* 694,333, This invention comprises a new and improved dispenser or magazine. **1958** *Woman* 31 May 5 (Advt.), She went shopping for a household dispenser. **1959** *Engineering* 27 Feb. 267/1 Ice-cream dispensers have been installed in a number of factories. **1960** *Woman* 2 Jan. 43/3 Metal detergent dispenser. **1970** *New Scientist* 30 Apr. 244/1 Looking forward to hitting Duboys City (population 300) with its longed-for coke dispenser and comfort station.

Hence **di'spensership**, the office of a dispenser (of medicine).

1891 *Lancet* 3 Oct., Dispensership (out-door) wanted by young man.

† di'spensible, *a.* *Obs.* [repr. L. type **dispensibilis*, f. ppl. stem of *dispendĕre*: see DISPEND.] = DISPENSABLE 1, 2.

1661 *Petit. for Peace* 5 Things dispensible, and.. unnecessary. **1688** SIR E. HERBERT *Hales' Case* 22 If any Penal Laws were..less Dispensible than others. **1689** W. ATWOOD *Ld. Herbert's Acc. Examined* 51 He makes all things not forbid by God's Law to be dispensible by the King. **1766** AMORY *Buncle* (1770) IV. 19 Every rule is dispensible, and must give way when it defeats the end for which it was appointed.

Hence † **di'spensibly** *adv.*

1711 *Peace in Divinity* 15 There is a keeping them [the Commandments] perfectly and indispensably, which is the Condition of the Law; and a keeping them sincerely and dispensibly, with the Relaxation of that Severity, thro' Faith in Christ, which is the Condition of the Gospel.

di'spensil, var. of DEPENCIL *v.* *Obs.*

1631 WEEVER *Anc. Fun. Mon.* 123 Sentences of Scripture appointed to be painted or dispensild in euery Church.

di'spensing, *vbl. sb.* [f. DISPENSE *v.* + -ING¹.] The action of the verb DISPENSE, in various senses: dealing out, distribution, bestowal; administration, management; dispensation; the making up of medicine according to prescription.

c **1380** WYCLIF *Wks.* (1880) 67 As ȝif it were not leful to do profit to mennus soulis wiþ-out dispensynge of anticrist. **1548** UDALL, etc. *Erasm. Par. Luke* xvi. (R.), My Lorde.. taketh awai from me the power and office any longer to have the dispensing of his goodes. **1608** HIERON *Wks.* I. 748/2 The faithfull dispensing of Thy truth. **1643** MILTON *Divorce* II. v. (1851) 75 It is a fond perswasion..that dispencing is a favour. **1688** SIR E. HERBERT *Hales' Case* 20 Acknowledging this power of Dispensing to be in the King. **1724** SWIFT *Reasons agst. Exam. Drugs* Wks. 1755 III. I. 126 The power..lodged in the censors of the college of physicians to restrain any of his majesty's subjects from dispensing. **1727** POPE *Th. on Var. Subj.* in *Swift's Wks.* (1755) II. I. 225 The choice of ladies..in the dispensing of their favours. **1856** F. E. PAGET *Owlet Owlst.* 106 Is not.. Sparrowgrass too liberal in her own dispensings?

b. *attrib.* **dispensing power**, the power of dispensing with or suspending the laws of church or state in special cases.

1621 LD. WILLIAMS in *Fortesc. Papers* 166 This dispensing power were more fitly placed in his Highnes. **1731** SWIFT *Presbyt. Plea Merit* Wks. (1761) III. 275 The King..encouraged by his Presbyterian friends, went on with his dispensing power. **1856** FROUDE *Hist. Eng.* (1858) I. ii. 135 The dispensing power of the popes was not formally limited. **1874** GREEN *Short Hist.* ix. §3. 622 His bill to vest a dispensing power in the Crown had been defeated.

di'spensing, *ppl. a.* [f. as prec. + -ING².] That dispenses: see the verb.

1642 ROGERS *Naaman* 554 The swarme of Pharisees and dispensing hypocrites. **1816** J. SCOTT *Vis. Paris* (ed. 5) 168 That they should come down..from the hands of a dispensing despotism. *Mod.* Take the recipe to a dispensing chemist.

Hence **di'spensingly** *adv.*, in a dispensing manner; distributively.

a **1641** BP. MOUNTAGU *Acts & Mon.* (1642) 117 God is rich in all things towards man, and..cannot but dispensingly under one word sometime imply diverse things.

† di'spension. *Obs.* [n. of action from DISPEND: cf. OF. *despension* expense (Godef.).]

1. Spending; expenditure.

1630 LENNARD tr. *Charron's Wisd.* I. xxi. §1 (1670) 75 Their dispensions themselves..have a scent of Covetousness. **1684** N. S. *Crit. Enq. Edit. Bible* xxv. 231 With what noyse, bustle, and dispension the diversities of Bibles came accompanied into England.

2. Suspension of a law; dispensation.

1483 *Cron. Eng.* (1510) X v b/1 Iohn..wedded dame Blaunche..by dyspencyon of the pope. **1502** ARNOLDE *Chron.* (1811) 82 To sue to y kynges grace for a dispencion of the acte of parlement late made to the contrarie.

† di'spensive, *a.* *Obs.* [f. L. *dispens-* ppl. stem of *dispendĕre* (see DISPEND) + -IVE.]

1. Characterized by or given to dispensing, spending, or distributing.

1627–47 FELTHAM *Resolves* I. liii. 167 To strow about the wealth and means, and to feed that dispensive humour. **1677** CROWNE *Destr. Jerus.* III. i, Dram. Wks. 1873 II. 270 This tempest comes from Heaven's dispensive hand.

2. Subject to dispensation.

1590 MARLOWE *2nd Pt. Tamburl.* II. i, 'Tis superstition To stand so strictly on dispensive faith.

3. = DISPENSATIVE, DISPENSATORY.

1828 *Westm. Rev.* IX. 7 In 1671 the king began to assume his dispensive power.

dispent, pa. t. and pple. of DISPEND.

dispeople (dɪsˈpiːp(ə)l), *v.* [ad. OF. *despeupler*, mod.F. *dépeupler* (1364 in Hatzf.) = Sp. *despoblar*, Pr. *despovoar*, It. *dis-*, *dipopolare*, Romanic formation from *des-*, L. *dis-*, DIS- 4 + *populus* people, parallel to L. *dēpopulāre* (used in med.L. in same sense): cf. DEPOPULATE. In sense 3 f. DIS- 7 b + PEOPLE *sb.*]

1. *trans.* To deprive wholly or partially of people or inhabitants; = DEPOPULATE 2.

1490 CAXTON *Eneydos* xviii. 69 My cytee shalle be dispeopled. **1562** PHAER *Æneid* VIII. X ij b, And voyde of tilmen wide dispeoplyng spoyle the shyres. **1649** BLITHE *Eng. Improv. Impr.* xiii. (1653) 93 Some cruell Lord..could ..dispeople a whole parish, and send many soules a gooding. **1709** tr. *Baltus' Answ. Hist. Oracles* 114 Cities [were seen] to dispeople themselves every Year—to obey these Impostors. **1855** MILMAN *Lat. Chr.* VI. 250 They thought it but compliance with the Divine command to dispeople the land of the Philistines, the Edomites, and the Moabites.

absol. **1602** WARNER *Alb. Eng.* Epit. (1612) 368 Without pittie pyllaging and dispeopling by sea and shore. **1859** R. F. BURTON *Centr. Afr.* in *Jrnl. Geogr. Soc.* XXIX. 352 Their only ambition is to dispeople and destroy.

b. *transf.* and *fig.* To deprive of animated inhabitants, tenants, or constituents.

1632 RANDOLPH *Jealous Lovers* II. ii. Wks. (1875) 92 We will dispeople all the elements To please our palates. **1704** POPE *Windsor For.* 47 And Kings..Who claim'd the skies, dispeopled air and floods. **1777** *Gamblers* 8 The groaning wood dispeopled of its trees. **1890** *Daily News* 29 Sept. 4/8 The whole [fish] breed is ruined, and the water dispeopled.

† 2. To exterminate (people). *Obs.*

1596 J. NORDEN *Progr. Pietie* (1847) 97 To cut us off and to dispeople us. **1643** *Oath Pacif.* 10 Ireland hath seene more than two hundred thousand Families of Brittish Protestants dispeopled and massacred.

† 3. [DIS- 7 b.] To cast out or cut off from being a people. *Obs.*

1633 P. FLETCHER *Purple Isl.* VI. vii, When no rebellious crimes That God-like nation yet dispeopled. **1643** BURROUGHES *Exp. Hosea* iv. (1652) 67 The people of God.. when they are dispeopled they are cast off from this their privilege. **1687** *Reason of Toleration* 17 Traps and Snares to dis-People the Nation.

Hence **dis'peopled** *ppl. a.*, deprived of people or inhabitants, depopulated, uninhabited.

1577 FRAMPTON *Joyfull Newes* II. (1596) 41 Any desert or dispeopled countrie. **1611** SPEED *Hist. Gt. Brit.* IX. viii. (1632) 561 The King was left very dispeopled. **1740** C. PITT *Æneid* V. (R.), Endless crowds..From all the wide dispeopled country round. **1844** THIRLWALL *Greece* VIII. lxii. 187 The dispeopled city was placed..at the disposal of Argos.

dis'peopler. [f. prec. vb. + -ER¹.] One who or that which dispeoples; a depopulator.

1616 BRETON *Good & Badde* 2 Hee is a Dispeopler of his Kingdome. **1711** GAY *Rural Sports* I. (R.), Nor troll for pikes, dispeoplers of the lake. **1767** W. L. LEWIS *Statius' Thebaid* IX. 264 The stern Dispeopler of the Plains.

dis'peopling, *vbl. sb.* [f. as prec. + -ING¹.] Depopulation; extermination of people.

1529 MORE *Suppl. Soulys* Wks. 311/1 The dispepling of hys realme. **1688** BURNET *Lett. conc. Italy* 4 How such a dispeopling, and such a poverty could befall a Nation.

‖ **di'speple, de'speple**, *v.* *Obs. rare.* [a. AF. **despeuple-r*, *-puepler*, OF. *despeupleer*, *-puepleer*, f. *des-*, DIS- 1 + OF. *peupleer*, *puepleer*, later *peuplier* to make public, publish, f. *peuple* people.] *trans.* To publish, promulgate publicly.

1297 R. GLOUC. (1724) 517 (l. 10649) þere þis gode lawes hii despeplede al aboute. *Ibid.* 568 (11966) þere it was despepled, þe edit ywis, þat was þe ban of Kenigwurþe.

dispepsy, obs. var. of DYSPEPSY.

'disper. *Winchester Coll. slang.* Also **dispar**. A portion of food.

1841 HOWITT *Visits Remark. Places* (1882) 201 The scholars [at Winchester] give the name of *dispers* to their breakfasts, suppers and lunchions. **1847–78** HALLIWELL, *Dispar*..a commons or share. *North.* **1870** MANSFIELD *Sch.-Life Winchester Coll.* 84 (Farmer s.v. *Cat's Head*) [The dinner] was divided into portions (Dispars); there were..six of these to a shoulder, and eight to a leg of mutton. **1891** WRENCH *Winchester Word-bk.*, Dispers are thus divided:—Fat flab, Fleshy, Cat's head, Long disper, Middle cut, Rack, Cut.

disperance, -ate, etc. obs. ff. DESPERANCE, etc.

dispercle, obs. form of DISPARKLE.

† disper'dition. *Obs.* [ad. L. *disperditiōn-em* n. of action from *disperdĕre* to destroy, spoil, ruin, f. DIS- 5 + *perdĕre* to destroy. Cf. OF. *desperdition* (mod.F. *dép-*), Sp. *desperdicion.*]

1623 COCKERAM, *Disperdition*, an vndoing.

† di'sperge, *v.* *Obs.* [ad. L. *disperg-ĕre* to scatter, disperse, f. *dī-*, DI-¹ = DIS- 1 + *spargĕre* to strew; cf. OF. *disperger.*] = DISPERSE *v.*

1530 *Compend. Treat.* (1863) 59 Tobye saithe, chap. xiii, that God disperged [*Tobit* xiii. 4 *Vulg.*, Dispersit vos inter gentes. **1611** hath scattered]. **1657** TOMLINSON *Renou's Disp.* 436 Bubbles and lumps which by touching are disperged.

dispergement, obs. form of DISPARAGEMENT.

† di'sperish, -'persh, *v.* *Obs.* [ad. OF. *desperir*, *desperiss-*, ad. L. *disperīre*, f. DIS- 5 + *perīre* to perish.] *intr.* To perish utterly.

1382 WYCLIF *Judith* vi. 3 Al Irael with thee shal dispershen in perdicioun [**1388** shal perische dyuerseli with thee in perdicioun]. —— *Wisd.* xvi. 29 The hope of the vnkinde as cold ijs shal flowen, and dispershen [*Vulg.* disperiet] as watir ouer voide. —— *Lam.* v. 18 For the mount of Sion, for it disperisht.

dispermatous (daɪˈspɜːmətəs), *a.* *Bot.* [f. DI-² twice + Gr. σπέρμα(τ- seed + -OUS.] Having two seeds; dispermous.

1851–60 MAYNE *Expos. Lex.* s.v. *Dispermatus*, Having two seeds; two-seeded: dispermatous.

di'spermous, *a.* *Bot.* [f. as prec.] = prec.

[**1727** BAILEY vol. II, *Dispermos* (with Botanists) is us'd of Plants, which bear two seeds after each Flower.] **1760** JAS. LEE *Introd. Bot.* II. xxxiii. 171 *Rhamnus*, with a dispermous Fruit. **1819** *Pantologia*, *Dispermous*..containing two seeds only, as in umbellate and stellate plants.

dispermy (ˈdaɪspɜːmɪ). *Biol.* [f. DI-² + Gr. σπέρμα seed + -Y³.] The entrance of two spermatozoa into a single egg. Hence **di'spermic** *a.*

1896 E. B. WILSON *Cell* 335 Dispermy. **1905** *Rep. Brit. Assoc.* 432 Dispermic eggs. **1956** *Nature* 3 Mar. 429/1 The egg was presumably dispermic. *Ibid.*, This evidence supports the postulate of dispermy. **1965** *New Scientist* 1 Apr. 35/2 The condition known to biologists as dispermy, in which two sperms fertilise one egg.

† di'spern, *v.* *Obs. rare.* [ad. rare L. *dispernĕre*, f. DI-¹ = DIS- 1 + *spernĕre* to remove, reject, spurn.] *trans.* To drive away, dispel.

1500–20 DUNBAR *Poems* lxxxv. 7 Our tern inferne for to dispern Helpe rialest rosyne.

disperple, var. form of DISPARPLE *v.* *Obs.*

di'spersable, *a. rare.* [f. DISPERSE *v.* + -ABLE.] Capable of being dispersed.

1827 *Examiner* 353/1 The Collective Wisdom would be dispersable (if we may be allowed the coinage) by a very easy process.

dispersal (dɪˈspɜːsəl). [f. DISPERSE *v.* + -AL[1].]

a. The action of dispersing; = DISPERSION.

1821 *Examiner* 15/1 Dispersal of the Dublin meeting by military force. **1833** *New Monthly Mag.* XXXVIII. 160 The phantoms..vanish, and we rejoice in their dispersal. **1863** BATES *Nat. Amazon* i. (1864) 17 Of vast importance to the dispersal and consequent prosperity of the species. **1895** C. DIXON in *Fortn. Rev.* Apr. 640 Next to the question of the Origin of Species, there is..that of their Geographical Dispersal over the globe.

b. *concr.* in *Aeronaut.* One of several stations, situated at scattered points round an airfield, in which aircraft are parked in order to minimize losses from air attack. Also *attrib.*

1940 *Flight* 7 Nov. c/1 The machine is shown at its dispersal point on the aerodrome, where, when not in use, it rests in order to minimise the effect of any attack on the aerodrome. **1942** T. RATTIGAN *Flare Path* 111, She only saw it [*sc.* an aircraft] from the road, sir. It's still out at dispersal. **1943** *Daily Tel.* 24 June 6 At Maupertuis airfield bombs burst in the dispersal area. **1943** P. BRENNAN et al. *Spitfires over Malta* iii. 61 Sitting in dispersal, we discussed the Huns' new tactics. **1944** 'N. SHUTE' *Pastoral* i. 2 Taxiing to dispersal and handing over to the ground crew took a bit of time. **1966** J. BEEDLE *43 Squadron* xiii. 147 The last of the four Hurricanes was ready to taxi back to dispersal.

dispersant (dɪˈspɜːsənt). [f. DISPERSE *v.* + -ANT[1].] An agent which causes a substance to form a dispersion in the surrounding medium, or which helps to maintain an existing state of dispersion; a dispersing agent.

1944 C. W. GEORGI in *Petroleum Refiner* Dec. 504/1 To complete the petroleum dictionary, it seems desirable to coin..Dispersant—An agent for imparting dispersing powers or properties. A dispersing agent or medium (noun). **1948** *Oil & Gas Jrnl.* 8 Jan. 58/1 Dispersants are defined as additives which prevent the flocculation or coagulation of colloidal particles. **1968** *New Scientist* 5 Dec. 560/1 A demonstration CL-215 has been fitted with a boom under each wing for the spraying of a 'dispersant' on oil slicks. **1971** *Sunday Times* (Johannesburg) (Business Section) 28 Mar. 15/3 (Advt.), Governments can today be supplied with oil slick dispersants which will minimize toxic hazards.

†**di'sperse**, *ppl. a. Obs.* Also 4–6 dispers. [a. OF. *dispers, -pars* (in Godef.), ad. L. *dispers-us*, pa. pple.: see next.] Dispersed, scattered about.

1393 GOWER *Conf.* II. 177 Thus was dispers in sondry wise The misbeleve. *Ibid.* II. 185 They liven oute of goddes grace, Dispers in alle londes oute. **1501** DOUGLAS *Pal. Hon.* I. 346 In that desert dispers in sonder skatterit.

disperse (dɪˈspɜːs), *v.* Forms: 5 dysparse, 6 disparse, -pearse, 7 -pearce, -pierce, 6– disperse. [a. F. *disperse-r* (15th c.), f. *dispers*, ad. L. *dispers-us*, pa. pple. of *dispergĕre* to scatter, f. DI-[1], DIS- 1 + *spargĕre* to sprinkle, strew.]

1. a. *trans.* To cause to separate in different directions; to throw or drive about in all directions, to scatter; to rout.

1450–1530 *Myrr. our Ladye* 161 He hathe dysparsed the prowde in the wylle of thy harte..An hooste that ys dysparsed ys not myghty to fyghte, right so the prowde fendes are dysparsed by the passyon of oure lorde Iesu cryste. **1503–4** *Act 19 Hen. VII*, c. 34. Preamb., They were rencountered, vaynquesshed, dispersed. **1581** MARBECK *Bk. of Notes* 287 It must needes be Philip the Deacon, that was disparsed with the rest, & came to Samaria. **1654** tr. *Scudery's Curia Pol.* 82 Such a Fire as cannot be extinguisht, is better to be dispersed. *Ibid.* 102 The Victors are so tryumphant, and the subdued Enemies so afflicted and dispierced. **1758** A. REID tr. *Macquer's Chem.* I. 51 The precipitate..exposed to a certain degree of heat, is instantly dispersed into the air, with a most violent explosion. **1799** WORDSWORTH *Lucy Gray* vii, Her feet disperse the powdery snow, That rises up like smoke. **1887** *Spectator* 16 Apr. 532/1 Reform meetings were dispersed by charges of Dragoons.

b. *intr.* To be driven or fly asunder.

1665 HOOKE *Microgr.* 33 These [Rupert's drops] dispersed every way so violently, that some of them pierced my skin.

2. a. *trans.* To send off or cause to go in different directions; to send to, or station apart at, various points. *spec.* to scatter or station (ships, aircraft, etc.) at separate points in order to minimize losses from air attack. Also *intr.* Esp. in *pa. pple.*: see DISPERSED.

1529 MORE *Comf. agst. Trib.* III. Wks. 1212/1 He taketh the whole people awai, disparsing them for slaues among many sundry countreys. **1591** *Hon. Act. E. Glemham*, Dispearsing sundrye Sentronels, for watche, farre from the Campe, diuers wayes. **1614** RALEIGH *Hist. World* II. v. §9. 308 Those they saved, and disperst [**1634** dispierc't] them among the children of Israel to serve them. **1698** FRYER *Acc. E. India & P.* 125 Made me range for Game, and disperse my Servants for Provant. **1744** HARRIS *Three Treat.* III. I. (1765) 153 That a Portion of every thing may be dispersed throughout all. **1872** YEATS *Techn. Hist. Comm.* 55 They are now dispersed throughout the museums of Europe. **1941** *Manchester Guardian* 24 Apr. 8/3 We took the decision to disperse plant over the countryside..and dispersal has been carried out on a very daring basis. **1944** *Return to Attack* (Army Board, N.Z.) 12/2 During the day vehicles were 'dispersed' 150 to 200 yards apart which meant that no attractive target was presented to enemy aircraft. **1948** *Daily Tel.* 9 Dec. 6 The fleet is well dispersed... The dropping of the 'atomic bomb' flash will provide a searching test of the ability of the fleet to disperse in the face of that all-powerful weapon.

b. *refl.* To spread in scattered order.

1593 SHAKS. *2 Hen. VI*, v. i. 45 Souldiers, I thanke you all: disperse your selues. **1684** *Contempl. State of Man* I. x. (1699) 116 Locusts..shall disperse themselves over the Face of the whole Earth. **1796** MORSE *Amer. Geog.* I. 281 About twenty families..dispersed themselves in various parts of Pennsylvania. **1886** A. WINCHELL *Walks & Talks Geol. Field* 286 These primitive Mongoloids..had dispersed themselves over America.

c. *intr.* (for *refl.*) To separate, go different ways.

a **1672** WOOD *Life* (Oxf. Hist. Soc.) I. 385 Sir Thomas.. desired them to disperse, and not to accompany him. **1718** *Freethinker* No. 68. ¶1 The gay Assemblies meet, and disperse, with the Parliament. **1856** KANE *Arct. Expl.* I. xvi. 190, I gave orders to abandon the sledge, and disperse in search of foot-marks. **1874** MICKLETHWAITE *Mod. Par. Churches* 217 The congregation is dispersing. **1874** GREEN *Short Hist.* v. §4. 246 The mass of the insurgents dispersed quietly to their homes.

†**3.** *trans.* To separate into parts; to part, divide, dispart. *Obs.*

1548 HALL *Chron., Rich. III*, (an. 3) 39 Thynkynge yt not ..beneficiall to disparse and devyde his greate armye into small branches. **1556** J. HEYWOOD *Spider & F.* lx. 33 The flieing ant..dispersth his nature, in two natures throwne.. A creper with spiders, and a flier with flise. **1600** J. PORY tr. *Leo's Africa* I. 2 Europe is of a more..manifolde shape, being in sundry places dispersed and restrained by the sea.

4. a. To distribute from a main source or centre.

1555 EDEN *Decades* 326 The veynes of bludde are disparsed in the bodies of lyuing beastes. **1594** T. B. *La Primaud. Fr. Acad.* II. 361 Conduites whereby the water is brought thither and dispersed in all places thereof. *a* **1626** BACON (J.), In the gate vein which disperseth that blood. **1664** POWER *Exp. Philos.* I. 5 Wings..with black thick ribs or fibers, dispers'd and branch'd through them.

b. To distribute, put into circulation (books, coins, articles of commerce); to give currency to.

1555 EDEN *Decades* 51 Which is nowe printed and dispersed throwghowte Christendome. *Ibid.* 176 The double ducades whiche yowre maiestie haue caused to bee coyned, and are disparsed throughowte the hole worlde. **1600** J. PORY tr. *Leo's Africa* I. 54 The cloth whereof is dispersed along the coast of Africa. **1693** *Col. Rec. Pennsylv.* I. 386 Wee of the Jurie doe find Charles Butler guiltie of dispersing bad monie. **1709** STRYPE *Ann. Ref.* I. xi. 136 A paper of questions that was..privately dispersed. **1838–9** *Act 2–3 Vict.* c. 12. §2 in *Oxf. & Camb. Enactm.* 177 [Any] paper or book..meant to be published or dispersed.

†**5.** To make known abroad; to publish. *Obs.*

1548 HALL *Chron., Hen. V*, (an. 3) 49 Your strength and vertue shalbe spred and dispersed through the whole world. **1612** tr. *Benvenuto's Passenger*, To Rdr. A iij, By their owne diuulged and dispersed ignominie. **1624** B. JONSON *Masques, Neptune's Triumph* (Stage-direction at beg.), The poet entering on the stage, to disperse the argument, is called to by the Master-Cook.

6. a. To spread abroad or about; to diffuse, disseminate.

1576 FLEMING *Panopl. Epist.* 308 If happly other diseases disperse their infecting properties. **1641** SIR E. NICHOLAS in *N. Papers* (Camden) 37 The sicknes and small pox is very much dispersed in Westminster and London. **1715** DESAGULIERS *Fires Impr.* 4 To disperse the Heat so uniformly. **1782** BURNEY *Hist. Mus.* (1789) II. i. 10 A practice..thence dispersed into all parts of the Christian world. **1818** JAS. MILL *Brit. India* III. ii. 69 Complaints were now industriously raised and dispersed.

†**b.** *refl.*

1592 SHAKS. *Rom. & Jul.* v. i. 61 Let me haue A dram of poyson..As will disperse it selfe through all the veines. **1665** HOOKE *Microgr.* 16 Water put into wine..or the like, does immediately..disperse it self all over them.

†**c.** *intr.* (for *refl.*) To extend, be diffused.

1591 SYLVESTER *Du Bartas* I. vii. 256 Th' Almighties care doth diuersely disperse Ore all the parts of all this Vniuerse.

7. a. *trans.* To dissipate; to remove, dispel, cause to disappear (vapours, humours, trouble, etc.).

1563 W. FULKE *Meteors* (1640) 24 b, If the Exhalation [thunder]..doe not at the first disperse it [the cloud], it maketh a..fearefull rumbling. **1590** SPENSER *F.Q.* I. ix. 48 All his manly powres it did disperse, As he were charmed with inchaunted rimes. **1590** SHAKS. *Com. Err.* I. i. 90 At length the sonne..Disperst those vapours that offended vs. **1726** SHELVOCKE *Voy. round World* (1757) 133, I said all that I could..to disperse the melancholy which was fixed in every countenance. **1760–72** tr. *Juan & Ulloa's Voy.* (ed. 3) I. 342 When a tempest appeared brooding in the air, the tolling of the bell dispersed it. **1804** ABERNETHY *Surg. Obs.* 61 [The tumour] increased, notwithstanding applications that were employed to disperse it.

b. *intr.* To become dissipated.

1591 SHAKS. *1 Hen. VI*, I. ii. 135 Glory is like a Circle in the Water, Which neuer ceaseth to enlarge it selfe, Till by broad spreading, it disperse to naught. **1816** KEATINGE *Trav.* (1817) II. 100 At length the thick cloud of dust dispersed. **1887** BOWEN *Virg. Eclog.* VIII. 14 Hardly..had the night's chill shadow dispersed.

8. *trans. Optics.* Of a refractive medium: To open out or scatter (rays of light): see DISPERSION 4.

[**1627** DRAYTON *Agincourt, etc.* 197 In a burning Glasse.. that colour doth dispierce the light, and stands vntainted.] **1654** WHITLOCK *Zootomia* 220 The Rayes that dispersed will scarce warme, collected may burne. **1665** HOOKE *Microgr.* 69 By reason of..its Globular Figure, the Rays that pass through it will be dispers'd. **1812–16** J. SMITH *Panorama Sc. & Art* I. 503 Concave lenses disperse the rays of light. **1868** LOCKYER *Elem. Astron.* vi. §36 (1879) 211 Different media..disperse or open out the light to a greater or less extent.

9. *Chem.* The verb-stem is used *attrib.* in **disperse phase, system** (see quots.). Hence **di'spersoid** = *disperse system.*

1915 E. W. WASHBURN *Princ. Physical Chem.* xxv. 361 If we imagine any phase within a given system to be gradually broken up into smaller and smaller particles, then as the size of these particles gradually decreases the surface of contact between this phase and its neighbors will correspondingly increase and the effects of forces of the nature of surface tension..will gradually become more apparent, and these surface forces will eventually begin to be an important factor in determining the fugacities of the molecular species composing the system. Whenever this situation exists to an appreciable extent..we have what is called a disperse system or a dispersoid. **1927** CROCKER & MATTHEWS *Theoret. & Exper. Physical Chem.* 273 *Disperse phase*, the discontinuous constituent of a colloidal solution corresponding to the solute in true solution. *Disperse system*, any colloidal solution. A two-phase system with greatly developed surfaces. **1934** S. C. BLACKTIN *Dust* vi. 136 Dusts ..will here be regarded as belonging to that section of the colloidal state named aerosols, and consisting of solid disperse phase in gaseous dispersion medium. **1939** *Thorpe's Dict. Appl. Chem.* (ed. 4) III. 292/1 In general the amount of solid substance dispersed or peptised varies with the amount of solid phase present, reaching a maximum for medium quantities. This relationship was termed..the.. solid-phase rule, but..disperse-phase rule is a more suitable name. **1966** *McGraw-Hill Encycl. Sci. & Technol.* IX. 585/2 Condensed dispersoids and fine mechanical dispersoids generally tend to flocculate or agglomerate.

dispersed (dɪˈspɜːst, *poet.* -sɪd), *ppl. a.* [f. prec. + -ED[1].] **a.** Scattered or spread about; driven asunder; diffused.

1526 *Pilgr. Perf.* (W. de W. 1531) 167 The mynde y[t] is dispersed in the waueryng consideracion of many thynges at that time whan it sholde be specially occupyed about one thyng. **1535** COVERDALE *Isa.* xi. 12 He shal..gather together ye dispersed of Israel. *a* **1592** GREENE *Looking Glasse* Wks. (Rtldg.) 142 Come, mournful dames, lay off your broider'd locks, And on your shoulders spread dispersèd hairs. **1605** BACON *Adv. Learn.* II. ii. §9. 13 Many worthy personages that deserue better than dispersed report. **1765** H. WALPOLE *Otranto* iii. (1798) 62 The new proof of..valour, recalled her dispersed spirits. **1855** MACAULAY *Hist. Eng.* IV. 272 Before William..had brought together his dispersed forces.

b. with reference mainly to situation.

a **1547** SURREY *Æneid* II. (R.), The watchmen lay disperst to take their rest. **1553** T. WILSON *Rhet.* (1580) 176 You shall praie for all menne, dispersed throughout the face of the yearth. **1697** DAMPIER *Voy.* I. 140 With a few small Rivers dispers'd up and down. **1756** C. LUCAS *Ess. Waters* I. 150 Both..are plentifully dispersed throughout the creation. **1862** LD. BROUGHAM *Brit. Const.* v. 73 A country of which the population is very unequally dispersed.

c. ***dispersed phase, system***, = *disperse phase, system* (see prec.).

1915 E. W. WASHBURN *Princ. Physical Chem.* xxv. 361 The degree of dispersion of a dispersed phase is usually defined as the ratio of its surface to its volume. **1923** W. CLAYTON *Theory Emulsions* 1 That liquid which is broken up into globules is termed the dispersed phase. **1924** [see DISPERSION 7]. **1939** *Thorpe's Dict. Appl. Chem.* (ed. 4) III. 279/1 Such dispersed systems can be classified into..(*a*) mechanical suspensions, (*b*) colloidal solutions, (*c*) molecular solutions.

dispersedly (dɪˈspɜːsɪdlɪ), *adv.* [-LY[2].] In a dispersed or scattered manner; here and there.

1561 EDEN *Arte Nauig.* Pref., Whiche perhappes fewe haue done otherwyse then disparsedly here and there. **1597–8** *Act 39 Eliz.* c. 25. §1 The same Vyllages..ly dispersedly. **1663** COWLEY *Greatness* Verses & Ess. (1669) 125 The other many inconveniences of grandeur I have spoken of disperstly in severall Chapters. **1727** BRADLEY *Fam. Dict.* s.v. *Apple*, It's a Tree that may be planted dispersedly about your Ground. **1847** HARDY in *Proc. Berw. Nat. Club* II. No. 5. 251 Disk convex..dispersedly punctulate. **1870** LOWELL *Chaucer* Pr. Wks. 1890 III. 325 Their incidents enter dispersedly, as the old stage directions used to say.

di'spersedness. [f. as prec. + -NESS.] The condition or state of being dispersed or scattered; scattered condition or position.

1571 GOLDING *Calvin on Ps.* xiii. 1 They referre to their present dispersednesse. **1652–62** HEYLIN *Cosmogr.* IV. (1682) 50 The dispersedness of the Towns and habitations. **1727** in BAILEY vol. II; and in later Dicts. **1897** *Atlantic Monthly* LXXX. 544 It..gives added cohesion to a great institution whose topographical dispersedness is surpassed only by its enormous enrollment. **1917** A. S. PRINGLE-PATTISON *Idea of God* xiii. 250 The finite facts in their dispersedness and mutability seem to be unable to stand alone.

†**di'sperseness.** *Obs.* [f. DISPERSE *a.* + -NESS.] = DISPERSEDNESS.

1612 BREREWOOD *Lang. & Relig.* x. 88 A libbards skin, the distance of whose spots represent the dispersness of habitations or towns in Africk.

disperser (dɪˈspɜːsə(r)). [f. DISPERSE *v.* + -ER[1].] One who or that which disperses.

1580 HOLLYBAND *Treas. Fr. Tong*, *Dissipateur*, a disperser or scatterer abroad. **1588** in Fuller *Ch. Hist.* IX. vii. §27 The dispersers of the several Libels. **1611** BIBLE *Nahum* ii. 1 He that dasheth in pieces [*margin*, the disperser *or* hammer]. **1722** DE FOE *Plague* (Rtldg.) 39 To suppress the Printing of such Books..and to frighten the dispersers of them. **1867** MILL *Inaug. Addr.* 27 Logic is the great disperser of hazy and confused thinking. **1876** S. A. WYLLIE in *Encycl. Brit.* IV. 269/1 (Brewing) Kiln-drying, An iron or stone plate, 4 or

5 feet square, called the disperser, is placed over each fire to disperse the heat.

di'spersing, *vbl. sb.* [f. as prec. + -ING[1].] The action of the vb. DISPERSE: dispersion.

1604 HIERON *Wks.* I. 523 There must be a disposing and a dispersing of the seed with the hand. **1607** TOPSELL *Four-f. Beasts* (1658) 104 The powder of the bones burned, is an antidote against the falling evill, and the dispersing of the milt. **1670** MILTON *Hist. Eng.* I. (1851) 3 After the Flood, and the dispersing of Nations. **1859** MASSON *Milton* I. 679 This meeting and dispersing cannot go on for ever!

dispersion (dɪˈspɜːʃən). Also 5 -cioune, 6 -tion. [a. F. *dispersion* (*disparcion* 13th c. in Hatz.-Darm.), or ad. L. *dispersiōn-em* scattering, n. of action f. *dispergĕre*: see DISPERSE *v.*]

1. The action of dispersing or scattering abroad; the condition or state of being dispersed; scattering, distribution, circulation.

Early applied to the scattering of the Jews among the Gentiles after the Babylonian Captivity; whence sense 5.

c **1450** *Mirour Saluacioun* 3635 The Jewes y[t] tyme hadde bene thorgh the werlde in dispersionne. **1555** EDEN *Decades* 266 In the fyrst dispertion of nations. **1656** BEN ISRAEL *Vind. Judæorum* in *Phenix* (1708) II. 423, I conceiv'd that our universal Dispersion was a necessary Circumstance to be fulfil'd. **1786** BURKE *W. Hastings* Wks. 1842 II. 180 The dispersion and exile of the reigning family. **1793** *Trial Fyshe Palmer* 22 The alleged dispersion of a seditious writing. **1882** VINES *Sachs' Bot.* 929 The specialities of organisation which effect the dispersion of their seeds.

fig. *c* **1450** tr. *De Imitatione* I. xx, What comeþ þerof but grucching of conscience & dispersion of herte?

2. The action of diffusing or spreading; diffusion.

1664 POWER *Exp. Philos.* I. 29 That all Vegetables have a constant perspiration, the continual dispersion of their odour makes out. **1794** SULLIVAN *View Nat.* II. 36 When the natural dispersion of heat is disturbed..then a sensible heat is produced. **1874** HARTWIG *Aerial W.* ii. 21 By this means is also gradually effected the dispersion of all gases.

3. *Med.* 'The removal of inflammation, suppuration, or other morbid processes, from a part, and restoration to health' (*Syd. Soc. Lex.*); dissipation.

1753 CHAMBERS *Cycl. Supp.* s.v., This is commonly term'd in surgery the resolution or dispersion of tumors. *Ibid.*, Remedies for the dispersion of inflammations. **1789** W. BUCHAN *Dom. Med.* (1790) 573 An inflammation..must terminate either by dispersion, suppuration, or gangrene.

4. *Optics.* The divergence or spreading of the different-coloured rays of a beam of composite light when refracted by a prism or lens, or when diffracted, so as to produce a spectrum: *esp.* in reference to the amount of this divergence.

1727-51 CHAMBERS *Cycl.*, Point of Dispersion, is a point from which refracted rays begin to diverge. **1794** G. ADAMS *Nat. & Exp. Philos.* II. xxii. 447 This diffusion or dispersion of the rays is greater. **1833** N. ARNOTT *Physics* (ed. 5) II. 199 The quality of..bending a beam, or of refraction, and that of dividing it into coloured beams, or of dispersion, are distinct. **1871** tr. *Schellen's Spectr. Anal.* §18. 63 The decomposition of white light into its colored rays is called dispersion. **1881** N. LOCKYER in *Nature* No. 617. 399 [The lines] are..visible when considerable dispersion is employed.

5. ***the Dispersion***: The Jews dispersed among the Gentiles after the Babylonian Captivity; the scattered communities of Jews in general, or the communities in some single country, as ***the Egyptian Dispersion***; = DIASPORA.

1382 WYCLIF *1 Pet.* i. 1 To the chosen gestis of dispersioun [*gloss*, or scateringe abroad]. *c* **1450** *St. Cuthbert* (Surtees) 3781 Of ysrael þe dispercioune he gadird samen fra strete and toune. **1582** N. T. (Rhem.) *John* vii. 35 Wil he goe into the dispersion of the Gentiles, and teach the Gentiles? **1641** EVELYN *Mem.* (1857) I. 30 Transported..to all the desolate ports and havens throughout the world, wherever the dispersion was, to convey their brethren and tribes to the Holy City. **1880** J. E. CARPENTER tr. *Ewald's Hist. Israel* V. 4 The 'Coasts of the Sea'..are now (as in the eighth century) mentioned as a residence of the Dispersion. **1893** SMITH & FULLER *Dict. Bible* s.v., The African Dispersion..preserved their veneration for the 'holy city'.

6. ***law of dispersion***: The 'Law of Error' as regards distance from the mark without reference to the direction of error. So *dispersion* = the degree of scatter of values in a set of observations.

1876 *Catal. Sci. App. S. Kens. Mus.* §48 Testing how far the relative numbers in the several classes accord with the results of the Law of Error or Dispersion. *Ibid.* §49 The well-known bell-shaped curve, by which the law of error or of dispersion is mathematically expressed. **1897** *Jrnl. R. Statist. Soc.* LX. 865 Notice that no term measuring the dispersion of weights enters in the formula; but that the approximation was made on the assumption that the weights were equal. **1930** *Engineering* 13 June 756/1 The observations were characterised by a large dispersion, which was attributed to the numerous factors involved. **1963** B. FOZARD *Instrum. Nucl. Reactors* vii. 70 A commonly used measure of the dispersion or scatter of a number of observed values about the central values is the standard deviation σ.

7. *Physical Chem.* A type of intimate mixture in which one substance is present in a large number of separate small regions distributed throughout another, continuous, substance; examples are emulsions (one liquid in another) and aerosols (a solid or a liquid in a gas); also, the state of being so distributed. Also *attrib.*, as **dispersion medium**; a substance that may contain another substance 'dispersed' in it.

1915 [see DISPERSED *ppl. a.* c]. **1919** E. HENDRICK *Chem. Everyday Life* 74 Soap is a colloid, and when we get a little of it in a great deal of water we have it in dispersion. **1924** A. FINDLAY *Physical Chem.* 173 A colloidal sol..consists of finely divided particles (the dispersed phase) distributed throughout a dispersion medium. **1927** CROCKER & MATTHEWS *Theoret. & Exper. Physical Chem.* 274 *Dispersion medium*, the continuous phase in a colloidal solution, corresponding to the solvent in true solution. **1944** *Petroleum Refiner* Dec. 504/2 The property of maintaining insoluble matter (sludges and contaminants) in dispersion in the oil so that they will not settle out. **1957** *Encycl. Brit.* VI. 25/2 A foam is a gaseous dispersion (usually of air) in a liquid continuum. *Ibid.*, Pastes are concentrated dispersions of fine solid particles in a liquid continuum. **1958** *Times Rev. Industry* May 69/1 The main dispersion mill..will turn out 500 gallons of emulsion paint in an hour.

8. *attrib.* **dispersion hardening** *Metall.*, a process of ageing produced by heating at high temperatures.

1891 *Times* 28 Sept. 13/6 By an appropriate choice of dispersion lenses. **1932** *Metallurgist* VIII. 110/1 The hardening depends on the degree of dispersion of the particles, and it is accordingly sometimes known as dispersion hardening. **1934** H. O'NEILL *Hardness of Metals* vi. 195 'Dispersion hardening' and 'precipitation hardening' are good labels to employ for the phenomenon in general.

dispersive (dɪˈspɜːsɪv), *a.* [f. L. type *dispersīv-us*, ppl. stem of *dispergĕre* to disperse: see -IVE. Cf. F. *dispersif, -ive.*]

Having the character or quality of dispersing; serving or tending to disperse.

1627-77 FELTHAM *Resolves* I. liii. 84 A fond popularity bewitches the soul, to strow about the wealth, and means; and, to feed that dispersive humor, all ways shall be trodden. **1737** M. GREEN *Spleen* 730 Nor wanting the dispersive bowl Of cloudy weather in the soul. **1800** HERSCHEL in *Phil. Trans.* XC. 443 The dispersive power of different mediums with respect to heat. **1874** MORLEY *Compromise* (1886) 133 Thought has become dispersive and the centrifugal forces of the human mind..have..become dominant.

b. *Optics.* Of a refractive medium: Having the quality of causing the different-coloured rays of light to diverge: see DISPERSION 4.

1802 WOLLASTON in *Phil. Trans.* XCII. 373 The dispersive power of fluor spar is the least of any substance yet examined. **1831** BREWSTER *Optics* viii. §66 Flint glass is said to have a greater dispersive power than crown glass, because..it separates the extreme rays of the spectrum..farther from the mean ray. **1893** SIR R. BALL *Story of Sun* 113 The dispersive apparatus of the spectroscope.

Hence **di'spersively** *adv.*, in a dispersive manner, by dispersion; **di'spersiveness**, the quality of being dispersive.

1841 ALFORD in *Life* (1873) 133 An indolence and dispersiveness about my efforts. **1878** MORLEY *Diderot* ii. 18 The characteristic of his activity is dispersiveness.

dispersivity (dɪspɜːˈsɪvɪtɪ). [f. DISPERSIVE *a.* + -ITY.] **a.** The degree to which the refractive index of a substance varies with the wavelength of the light refracted; a numerical measure of the rate of change of refractive index with wavelength. **b.** The degree to which one substance is dispersed in another, e.g. in a colloid.

1913 J. B. COHEN *Org. Chem. Adv. Students* II. iv. 296 The difference between the specific refractivities for light of widely different wave length is called the specific dispersive power or dispersivity. **1947** *Nature* 25 Jan. 114/1 Christiansen filters consist essentially of a powdered solid immersed in a liquid of similar refractive index but different dispersivity. **1984** *Oil & Gas Jrnl.* 30 July 175 The way to study the 'dispersivity' of these clays is with a combination of the filtration time method and the zeta potential technique.

†**di'sperson**, *v. Obs. Sc.* and *north.* [ad. med.L. *dispersōnāre* var. of *dēpersōnāre* to deprive any one of his *persōna* or dignity, f. DIS- 4 + *persōnāre* to dignify, *persōna* person, dignity. Cf. MISPERSON.] *trans.* To treat with indignity, insult.

a **1400-50** *Alexander* 746 For spyte he spittis in his face, Dispises him despetously, dispersons [*Dubl. MS.* revylez] him foule. **1489** *Burgh Recds. Aberdeen* (1844) I. 416 William Porter was convikit..for the strublance of the said bailȝe in the execucione of his office, and in dispersoning of him. **1579-80** *Burgh Recds. Glasgow* (1876) I. 77 George Herbertson is fund and decernit..in the wrong for incurring and dispersoning of George Elphinstone.

dis'personalize, *v.* [DIS- 6.] *trans.* To divest of personality, to depersonalize.

1866 LOWELL *Biglow P.* Introd. Poet. Wks. (1879) 251 He would have enabled me to dispersonalize [Poems 1890, II. 209 depersonalize] myself into a vicarious egotism. **1886** MAUDSLEY *Nat. Causes* 302 Man is only qualified to be immortal when, being dispersonalized, extinct as a self, it is all one whatever the event.

dispersonate (dɪsˈpɜːsəneɪt), *v.* [f. DIS- 6 + L. *persōna* mask, person + -ATE[3].]

†**1.** *trans.* To divest of an assumed character, to unmask. *Obs.*

1624 BOLTON *Nero* 233 To behold any person, according to the truth of his qualities, distinctly, and dispersonated.

2. To divest of one's personality.

1702 S. PARKER tr. *Cicero's De Finibus* 304 'Till a Man has got a way of Dispersonating himself, he cannot avoid hankering after those Things which will turn to Advantage and good account. **1827-38** HARE *Guesses* (1859) 96 We multiply, we dispersonate ourselves: we turn ourselves outside in. We are ready to become *he, she, it, they*, anything rather than *I*.

dispersonify (dɪspəˈsɒnɪfaɪ), *v.* [DIS- 6.] *trans.* To undo the personification of; to represent or regard as impersonal.

1846 GROTE *Greece* I. xvi. I. 467 Anaxagoras and other astronomers incurred the charge of blasphemy for dispersonifying Hêlios. **1855** SELSS *German Liter.* (1864) 182 Others, on the contrary, dispersonified the Divinity.

Hence **disper,sonifi'cation**, the action of dispersonifying.

1873 H. SPENCER *Stud. Sociol.* xvi. (1874) 392 The dispersonification of Hêlios.

disper'suade, *v.* *nonce-wd.* [DIS- 6.] = DISSUADE *v.* 3.

1952 AUDEN *Nones* 17 Nothing..can..dispersuade the Furies.

†**disper'suasion**. *Obs. nonce-wd.* [DIS- 9.] Want of persuasion or feeling of certainty.

1648 SANDERSON *Serm.* (1653) 23 Many a good soul..could never yet..be so well persuaded of the sincerity of his own repentance..as to think that God would..accept it. The censure were very hard..to call such his dis-perswasion by the name of despair.

di'spesh, Sc. var. of DESPECHE, *Obs.*, to dispatch, send away.

1578 in *Scot. Poems 16th C.* II. 159.

†**di'spester**, *v.* *Obs.* [ad. obs. F. *despestrer* 'to vnpester, disintangle' (Cotgr.): see DIS- 4 and PESTER *v.*[1]] *trans.* To rid of that which pesters.

1600 HOLLAND *Livy* XLII. lxvi. 1155 Hardly and with much adoe were they dispestered and rid of this confused and disordered companie of captives.

dispetal (dɪsˈpɛtəl), *v.* [DIS- 7 a.] *trans.* To deprive or strip of petals.

1863 W. LANCASTER *Praeterita* 74 Though the garland rose hereafter hung Dishonoured and dispetalled. **1880** MISS BROUGHTON *Sec. Th.* II. III. vi. 223 The splashed and dispetalled geraniums. **1887** STEVENSON *Underwoods* I. xxxv. 69 When the truant gull Skims the green level of the lawn, his wing Dispetals roses.

dispeticioun, -ison, var. DISPUTISOUN *Obs.*

dispeyr(e, obs. form of DESPAIR, DISPAYRE.

disphenoid (daɪˈsfiːnɔɪd). *Cryst.* [DI-[2] 1.] A solid figure contained by eight isosceles triangles.

1895 STORY-MASKELYNE *Crystallogr.* vii. §211. 256 The faces of the disphenoid being symmetrical in pairs.

dispice, obs. form of DESPISE.

†**di'spicience**. *Obs. rare.* [app. for *dispicions* pl. of next: cf. *accidence*. But it may represent a L. type **dispicientia*; see -ENCE.] Discussion, disputation.

1530 TINDALE *Answ. More* [I. xxv.] 59b, But if our sheperdes had bene as wel willynge to fede as to shere, we had neded no soch dispicience, ner they to haue burnt so many. **1532** MORE *Confut. Tindale* 264 (Quotes Tindale's words).

[**1623** COCKERAM, *Dispitience*, aduisement, diligence. **1656** BLOUNT *Glossogr.*, *Dispicience* (*dispicientia*), circumspection, advisement, diligent consideration.]

†**di'spicion**. *Obs.* Also 6 **des-, dyspycion**. [The form suggests derivation from L. *dispicĕre* 'to look through, investigate, make an examination, consider', the formation being on the analogy of *suspicion*; but the sense suggests association with DISPUTISOUN, disputation, some forms of which, as *dispitesoun, dispeticioun*, might be reduced to *dispit'soun, dispicion*.] Discussion, disputation.

c **1510** MORE *Picus* Wks. 3/2 He taried at Rome an whole yere, in al which time his enuiours neuer durst openly with open dispicions attempt him. **1526** TINDALE *N.T.* Prol., Lest we..fall from meke lernynge into ydle despicions. —— *Acts* xxviii. 29 The Iewes departed from hym and had grete despicions [COVERD. a greate disputacion, CRANMER greate despycions], amonge them selves. **1529** MORE *Dyaloge* IV. Wks. 262/1 He reherseth a certain dispycion had with an heretique. **1530** in Strype *Eccl. Mem.* I. xvii. 132 Not minding to fall in contentions or dispytions [disputations, perhaps, (Str.)] with your highness. **1533** MORE *Answ. Poysoned Bk.* Wks. 1039/2, I shal in this dispicion betwene hym and me, be content for this ones..to cal him mayster Masker. **1553** BALE *Vocacyon* in *Harl. Misc.* (Malh.) I. 331 As great dyspycyons were among the Jewes at Rome concerning Paule.

dispiece (dɪˈspiːs), *v.* Also 5 **des-**. [ad. OF. *despiece-r*, mod.F. *dépiécer* (14th c. in Hatz.-Darm.), f. *des-*, DIS-[1] + *piece*, PIECE.] *trans.* To divide into pieces; to cut or tear to pieces.

c **1477** CAXTON *Jason* 103 The body he dispieced by membres. **1480** —— *Ovid's Met.* XIII. vii, He murdryd the chylde..and despieced in pieces & caste hym into the see.

1885 G. MEREDITH *Diana* II. iv. 102 It lay dispieced like a pulled rug.

dispierce, obs. var. of DISPERSE *v.*

dispight, -iȝt, obs. forms of DESPITE.

† **di'spill**, *v. Obs.* [f. *di-* = DIS- 1 + SPILL *v.*] *trans.* To spill, shed.

1522 *World & Child* in Hazl. *Dodsley* I. 251 For I have boldly blood full piteously dispilled.

dispireme (daɪ'spaɪəriːm). *Cytology.* Also **-em.** [f. DI-[2] + SPIREME.] (See quot. 1896.)

1890 W. TURNER *Cell Theory* 31 In the..dispirem stage, the chromatin threads thicken and shorten. **1896** E. B. WILSON *Cell* 336 *Dispireme*.., that stage of mitosis in which each daughter-nucleus has given rise to a spireme.

dispirit (dɪ'spɪrɪt), *v.* Formerly also **disspirit.** [DIS- 7 a.] To deprive of spirit.

† **1.** *trans.* To deprive of essential quality, vigour, or force; to weaken to deprive of animation; to deprive (liquor) of its spirit, to render flat. *Obs.*

1647 MAY *Hist. Parl.* I. vii. 73 They woulde vaporate and dis-spirit the power and vigour of Religion. **1660** SHARROCK *Vegetables* 139 The fruit, by the loss of the natural seed, would be very much dispirited. **1685** BOYLE *Salub. Air* 40 If the Bottles were not kept well-stopt, they [corpuscles] would in a short time vanish, and leave the Liquor dispirited. **1697** COLLIER *Ess. Mor. Subj.* II. (1709) 38 He that has dispirited himself by a Debauch. **1713** C'TESS WINCHELSEA *Misc. Poems* 9 Trail all your pikes, dispirit every drum, Ye silent, ye dejected Men of War.

2. To lower the spirits of; to make despondent, discourage, dishearten, depress.

1647 [see DISPIRITED]. **1732** GAY in *Swift's Lett.* (1766) II. 151, I find myself dispirited, for want of having some pursuit. **1759** ROBERTSON *Hist. Scot.* I. v. 382 A blow so fatal and unexpected dispirited the party. **1790–1811** COMBE *Devil upon 2 Sticks in Eng.* (1817) VI. 292 To dispirit the sufferer from future exertions. **1868** FREEMAN *Norm. Conq.* (1876) II. viii. 260 One side was cheered and the other dispirited by an unlooked-for incident.

† **3.** To extract and transfuse the 'spirit' or essence of. *Obs. rare.*

1642 FULLER *Holy & Prof. St.* III. xviii. 200 Proportion an houres meditation to an houres reading of a staple authour. This makes a man master of his learning, and dispirits the book into the Scholar.

dispirited (dɪ'spɪrɪtɪd), *ppl. a.* [f. prec. + -ED[1].]

† **1.** Deprived of its essential quality or vigour; destitute of spirit or animation, spiritless. *Obs.*

a **1660** HAMMOND *Wks.* IV. Pref. (R.), Religious offices.. degenerating into heartless dispirited recitations. *a* **1700** B. E. *Dict. Cant. Crew, Pall'd*, Flat, Dispirited, or Dead Drink. **1737** BRACKEN *Farriery Impr.* (1757) II. 111 The Blood becomes so viscid, poor, and dispirited. **1758** WHITWORTH *Acc. Russia* 5 The Laplanders and Samoiedes being too heavy and dispirited.

2. Cast into or characterized by low spirits; discouraged, disheartened, dejected.

1647 TRAPP *Comm. 1 Thess.* v. 14 The dispirited, faint-hearted, sick and sinking. **1717** POPE *Let. to Blount* 27 Nov., My Mother is in that dispirited State of Resignation. **1741** MIDDLETON *Cicero* II. xi. 437 A few unarmed, dispirited men. **1852** MRS. STOWE *Uncle Tom's C.* xxxii. 290 He turned back and caught a glance at the dispirited faces behind him.

Hence **di'spiritedly** *adv.*; **di'spiritedness.**

1654 tr. *Scudery's Curia Pol.* 175 A defatigation and dispiritedness will accompany that oppression. **1673** H. STUBBE *Vind. Dutch War* 4 The decay of Trade, the dispiritedness of the English. **1733** CHEYNE *Eng. Malady* II. ix. §3 (1734) 208 Opiates..when their Force is worn off.. leave a Lowness, Dispiritedness, and Anxiety. **1864** WEBSTER, *Dispiritedly.* **1889** *Temple Bar Mag.* Feb. 186, 'I do not know'..said the lad dispiritedly.

di'spiriting, *ppl. a.* [f. as prec. + -ING[2].] That dispirits; disheartening, depressing.

1733 CHEYNE *Eng. Malady* II. ix. §1 (1734) 206 The Symptoms may be so dispiriting and painful. **1799–1805** S. TURNER *Anglo-Sax.* I. IV. vi. 315 That dispiriting belief, which men on the eve of great conflicts sometimes experience, that he should not survive it. **1872** MISS BRADDON *To Bitter End* xvii, Even though London-bridge terminus was a somewhat dirty and dispiriting place to arrive at.

Hence **di'spiritingly** *adv.*

1882 H. C. MERIVALE *Faucit of B.* I. I. iv. 67 Little enough of their influence, however, seemed to fall dispiritingly upon Daisy and Guy.

di'spiritment. [f. DISPIRIT *v.* + -MENT.] The state of being dispirited; disheartenment; depression of spirits.

1827 CARLYLE *Germ. Romance* IV. *W. Meister* 250 A spirit of dispiritment. **1830** —— *Richter* Misc. (1872) III. 25 Some with their modesty and quiet endurance combining a sickly dispiritment. **1830** —— in Froude *Life* (1882) II. 116, I look ..forward to a life of poverty, toil and dispiritment. **1843** —— *Past & Pr.* III. xiii. 295 You honestly..quit a most muddy confused coil..of sorrows, dispiritments and contradictions. **1866** LOWELL *Lessing* Pr. Wks. 1890 II. 207 What he wrote under the dispiritment of failure.

† **dispiritu'ality.** *nonce-word. Obs. rare.* [DIS- 9.] An unspiritual or worldly act.

1684 H. MORE *Answer* 24 If they do not repent of these immoralities or Dispiritualities, if I may so speak.

† **di'spiritude.** *Obs.* [f. DISPIRIT, after *solicitude*, *decrepitude*, etc.] Dispirited condition.

1797 W. TAYLOR in *Monthly Rev.* XXII. 512 Considering how general was the dispiritude of his troops. **1814** —— *Monthly Mag.* XXXVII. 30 Infidels have complained that the Christian religion..drives men into dispiritude.

dispise, obs. form of DESPISE.

dispit, -ite, -itt, obs. forms of DESPITE.

dispiteous (dɪ'spɪtiːəs), *a.* [A revival or continuation of the 16th c. *dispiteous*, variant of DESPITEOUS (q.v. for earlier instances), related to *despite*; but in later use analysed as f. DIS- 10 + PITEOUS.] Pitiless, merciless.

1803 W. S. ROSE *Amadis* 82 The felon wreck'd dispiteous wrong and shame. **1818** TODD, *Dispiteous*, malicious, furious. **1845** *Blackw. Mag.* LVII. 638 This dispiteous and abominable tyrant. **1863** MRS. C. CLARKE *Shaks. Char.* xiv. 357 The wages he receives are as dispiteous, for he is devoured by a beast. **1865** SWINBURNE *Poems & Ball.*, *Phædra* 81 The most dispiteous out of all the gods.

Hence **di'spiteously** *adv.*; **di'spiteousness.**

1818 TODD, *Dispiteously*, maliciously, without pity. **1861** ROSSETTI *Ital. Poets, Mazzeo di Ricco* 57 Certes, it was of Love's dispiteousness That I must set my life On thee.

dispitesoun, var. DISPUTISOUN, disputation.

dispitous, -uous, -ly: see DESPITOUS.

displace (dɪs'pleɪs), *v.* [ad. OF. *desplacer* (15th c. in Hatz.-Darm.), mod.F. *déplacer* to displace, f. *des-*, DIS- 1, 4 + *place* sb., *placer* to place.]

1. *trans.* To remove or shift from its place; to put out of the proper or usual place. (†In quot. 1551, To transpose.)

1551 T. WILSON *Logicke* (1580) 28 By conuersion of the Propositions, and by displacyng the same, settyng one in an others steede. **1553** —— *Rhet.* (1580) 203 The whiche wordes beyng altered or displaced, the figure straight dooeth lose his name. **1577** B. GOOGE *Heresbach's Husb.* IV. (1586) 187b, Cut away part of the Coames..which you must do with a very sharpe knife, for feare of displacing the rest of the Coames. **1611** SHAKS. *Cymb.* IV. ii. 122 [He] swore..heel'd [= he'd]..Displace our heads, where (thanks the Gods) they grow, And set them on Luds-Towne. **1781** COWPER *Expostulation* 258 Thy diadem displaced, thy sceptre gone. **1837** WHEWELL *Hist. Induct. Sc.* (1857) I. 151 [The moon] may be displaced by this cause to the amount of twice her own breadth.

† **b.** *fig.* To remove, banish. *Obs.*

1580 SIDNEY *Ps.* XXXIX. vi, Ah! yet from me lett thy plagues be displac'd. **1596** SPENSER *Hymne Heavenly Love* 264 All other loves..Thou must renounce and utterly displace. **1605** SHAKS. *Macb.* III. iv. 109. **1675** HOBBES *Odyss.* VIII. 64 When their thirst and hunger was displac'd.

2. To remove from a position, dignity, or office.

1553 T. WILSON *Rhet.* (1580) 68 When God striketh the mightie.. and displaceth those that were highly placed. **1563–87** FOXE *A. & M.* (1596) 6/1 King Solomon displaced Abiathar the high preest. **1687** in *Magd. Coll. & James II* (Oxf. Hist. Soc.) 98 To place, or displace, Members of Colleges. **1709** STEELE *Tatler* No. 84 ¶4 With a Design to displace them, in case I find their Titles defective. **1849** MACAULAY *Hist. Eng.* II. 556 Enjoining him..to displace all the Popish officers who held commands under him. **1853** STOCQUELER *Milit. Encycl.*, Officers are sometimes displaced from a particular regiment in consequence of misconduct, but they are at liberty to serve in any other corps.

3. To oust (something) from its place and occupy it instead: **a.** to put something else in the place of; **b.** to take the place of, supplant, 'replace'.

a. [**1667** MILTON *P.L.* I. 473 Gods Altar to disparage and displace For one of Syrian mode.] **1844** H. H. WILSON *Brit. India* III. 458 To displace by regular garrisons the troops of the Thakurs. **1853** SIR H. DOUGLAS *Milit. Bridges* 41 The desideratum is, to displace as much water, with as little weight of vessel as possible.

b. [**1634** MILTON *Comus* 560 A soft and solemn-breathing sound..stole upon the air, that even Silence..wished she might Deny her nature, and be never more, Still to be so displaced.] **1774** GOLDSM. *Nat. Hist.* (1776) I. 188 A cork, a ship, a buoy, each buries itself a bed on the surface of the water; this bed may be considered as so much water displaced. **1831** LARDNER *Hydrost.* viii. 157 A body when it floats in a liquid, displaces a quantity of the liquid equal to its own weight. **1889** A. R. WALLACE *Darwinism* 29 In three years..this weed..absolutely displaced every other plant on the ground.

displaceable (dɪs'pleɪsəb(ə)l), *a.* [f. prec. + -ABLE.] Capable of being, or liable to be, displaced.

1676 BOYLE in *Phil. Trans.* XI. 806 Its parts were..easily displaceable by the subtile permeating matter. **1810** BENTHAM *Packing* (1821) 43 A Board..paid, placed, and displaceable by the servants of the crown. **1879** J. M. DUNCAN *Lect. Dis. Women* i. (1889) 3 It may be mobile or floating, or it may be merely displaceable.

Hence **displacea'bility.**

1882 *Nature* XXVI. 592 The classification of surfaces according to the displaceability of their geodetic triangles.

displaced (dɪs'pleɪst), *ppl. a.* [f. as prec. + -ED[1].] **a.** Removed from its place; put out of place; deposed: see the verb.

1571 GOLDING *Calvin on Ps.* Ep. Ded. 6 There be..many displaced words. **1823** ELLIS *Mem. Gordon* 18 To retain the head of the bone in its displaced situation. **1839** G. BIRD *Nat. Philos.* 90 Archimedes..discovered that a body, when immersed in a fluid, loses a portion of its weight equal to that of the displaced fluid. **1841** ELPHINSTONE *Hist. Ind.* II. 15 No mention was made of the displaced vizir.

b. ***displaced person***, one removed from his home country by military or political pressure, esp. a non-German compelled to work in Germany in the 1939–45 war, and thereafter homeless. Abbrev. D.P.

1944 *Sat. Even. Post* 22 July 14/1 The Refugees..or, as they term these people here..the Displaced Persons. **1945** *Broadcaster* (U.S.) June 7 The real difficulty was and is the care of the slave laborers, men, women and children the Germans had imported from all over Europe to do their work for them. These we call Displaced Persons and for brevity refer to them as DP's. **1946** *Ann. Reg. 1945* 64 The huge number of 'displaced persons' who were still wandering about. **1961** L. MUMFORD *City in History* vi. 198 The very migrations of prisoners, slaves, refugees, displaced persons, all widened the bonds of human association.

displacement (dɪs'pleɪsmənt). [f. DISPLACE *v.* + -MENT: cf. OF. *desplacement*, mod.F. *déplacement*, perh. the immediate source of sense 1.] The act of displacing or fact of being displaced.

1. Removal from an office or dignity; deposition. (The earliest sense, but somewhat *rare.*)

1611 SPEED *Hist. Gt. Brit.* IX. xvi. §44 His displacement from the Regency of France. **1797** W. TAYLOR in *Monthly Rev.* XXIII. 570 Without the least intention of carrying their schemes farther than the displacement of their adversaries. **1857** TOULM. SMITH *Parish* 91 Election, displacement, and fresh election depend on the Parish only.

2. a. Removal of a thing from its place; putting out of place; shifting, dislocation.

1803 W. TAYLOR in *Ann. Rev.* I. 320 Change of air, removal, displacement, seem to be efficient remedies. **1840** A. TWEEDIE *Pract. Med.* III. 380 When the displacement is very considerable, the functions of the heart may be much embarrassed. **1863** KINGLAKE *Crimea* (1876) I. xv. 354 Occasioned by some accidental displacement of words. **1880** HAUGHTON *Phys. Geog.* ii. 46 *note*, A vertical displacement of the strata.

b. *Physics.* The amount by which anything is displaced; the difference or geometrical relation between the initial position of a body and its position at some subsequent instant.

1837 WHEWELL *Hist. Induct. Sc.* (1857) I. 150 The displacement of the sun by parallax is so small that [etc.]. **1879** THOMSON & TAIT *Nat. Phil.* I. I. §90 We may consider the whole motion as made up of successive elementary displacements.

c. *Thermometry.* (See quot.)

1871 B. STEWART *Heat* §22 It is found that thermometers are liable to an alteration of their zero points, especially when the bulb has been filled not long before graduation.. This displacement may in the course of years amount to about 1° C.

d. *Electr.* (See quots.)

1873 J. C. MAXWELL *Electr. & Magn.* I. i. 60 The electric polarization of an elementary portion of a dielectric is a forced state into which the medium is thrown by the action of electromotive force, and which disappears when that force is removed. We may conceive it to consist in what we may call an electrical displacement, produced by the electromotive force. **1885** WATSON & BURBURY *Electr. & Magn.* I. §258. **1895** SILVANUS THOMPSON *Electr. & Magn.* §57 *Displacement.* Whenever electric forces act on a dielectric, tending to drive electricity in at one side and out at the other..the quantity of electricity which has apparently been transferred..was called by Maxwell 'the displacement'. *Ibid.* §516 Experiment proves that displacement-currents, while they last, set up magnetic fields around them; just as connexion-currents and conduction-currents do.

e. displacement law, any of three laws in *Physics*: (i) that the wavelength at which a black body radiates most energy is inversely proportional to its absolute temperature; (ii) (see quot. 1922); (iii) that when an atom emits an alpha particle its atomic number decreases by two, and when it emits a beta particle its atomic number increases by one.

1904 T. PRESTON *Theory of Heat* (ed. 2) vi. 600 This important equation expresses the fact that if radiation of a particular wave-length corresponding to a definite temperature is adiabatically altered to another wave-length, then the temperature changes in the inverse ratio. This is known as Wien's displacement law. **1922** *Encycl. Brit.* XXXII. 561/1 Perhaps the most comprehensive connexion of spectra with the periodic table is established by the 'displacement law' of Kossel and Sommerfeld... The displacement law states that, when an element is ionized, the enhanced series take on the same type of complexity as the arc series produced by the element to the left (*i.e.* in the preceding group) in the periodic table. **1926** R. W. LAWSON tr. *Hevesy & Paneth's Man. Radioactivity* xiii. 114 In this way we obtain the following 'displacement law': The emission of α particles by an element results in the production of an element situated two places lower down in the natural sequence of the elements, whereas when the disintegrating element emits β-rays, an element is produced which is situated one place higher in the system. **1927** RUTHERFORD in *Proc. Physical Soc.* XXXIX. 360 This generalisation, known as the Displacement Law, first put forward in general form by Russell, Fajans and Soddy, gives us at once the nuclear charge and mass of each element in the radioactive series, and thus fixes the ordinary physical and chemical properties of each radioactive element, as well as its atomic weight. **1968** M. S. LIVINGSTON *Particle Physics* ii. 16 Soddy and others established the displacement law.

f. *Psychol.* The substitution of one idea or impulse for another, as in dreams, obsessions, etc.; the unconscious transfer of intense feelings or emotions to something of greater or less consequence; also = SUBLIMATION 5 c.

1913 A. A. BRILL tr. *Freud's Interpr. Dreams* vi. 286 The result of this displacement is that the dream content no longer resembles the core of the dream thoughts at all. *Ibid.* vi. 402 The dream activity makes use of the displacement of psychic intensities up to the transvaluation of all psychic values. **1955** H. C. ABRAHAM tr. *K. Abraham's Clin. Papers* III. vii. 189 We should be straining the facts if we attempted to make an artificial separation between displacement and secondary elaboration. **1962** HENDERSON & GILLESPIE *Text-bk. Psychiatry* (ed. 9) vii. 128 Displacement consists in the transfer of the emotional setting of one idea to some other apparently insignificant idea. **1964** GOULD & KOLB *Dict. Social Sci.* 204/1 'Fiddling' with objects such as pencils is a masturbation substitute or displacement. *Ibid.* 204/2 In social psychology the concept *displacement* has been used with respect to the hostility expressed toward minority groups.

g. Applied *attrib.* to an activity or behaviour pattern occurring outside its normal context and arising from a conflict of impulses (see quots.).

1947 E. A. ARMSTRONG *Bird Display & Behaviour* ii. 36 Toying with odds and ends may be regarded as.. providing emotional outlets. They are 'displacement' or substitute activities, common enough in human life. *Ibid.* viii. 106 'Displacement' activities will be regarded as a special type within the larger class of false activities. **1951** N. TINBERGEN *Stud. Instinct* v. 114 It is a striking fact that displacement activities often occur in a situation in which the fighting drive and the drive to escape are both activated. *Ibid.* 116 Herring gulls and many other birds.. feed their mates during courtship; it is not at all improbable that this.. is displacement feeding. *Ibid.* 117 If male sticklebacks are forced to nest very closely together, they will show nearly continuous displacement digging. *Ibid.* viii. 210 In man learned patterns, like lighting a cigarette, handling keys or handkerchief, &c., often act as displacement activities. **1957** *New Scientist* 26 Sept. 42 Displacement activities usually result from a conflict between two strongly activated but antagonistic drives, or from strong motivation, usually sexual, in the absence of the necessary stimulus required for the release of the consummatory act. **1962** *Listener* 2 Aug. 169/1 Many such irrelevant actions are known in animals. Dr Tinbergen has called them 'displacement activities'. They are seen in conflict situations, where an animal's automatic behaviour mechanisms cannot work smoothly in its current environment. *Ibid.* 169/2 Human displacement activities are not easily catalogued.

3. a. Removal of a thing by substitution of something else in its place; 'replacement'.

1868 GLADSTONE *Juv. Mundi* iii. (1869) 100 There must have been a great displacement of the Pelasgic vocabulary. **1880** *Libr. Univ. Knowl.* IX. 297 The displacement of human labor through.. machinery.

b. *Hydrostatics.* The displacing of a liquid by a body immersed in or floating on it; the amount or weight of fluid so displaced by a floating body, e.g. a ship. ***centre of displacement***: see CENTRE *sb.* 16.

1802–19 REES *Cycl.* s.v. *Shipbuilding* (L.), To ascertain the centre of displacement, or centre of gravity, of the immersed part of a ship's bottom. **1833** MARRYAT *P. Simple* xiii, He was always talking about centres of gravity, displacement of fluid, and Lord knows what. **1869** SIR E. J. REED *Our Iron-Clad Ships* iv. 71 The dimensions and outside form of a ship determine her displacement. **1876** W. H. G. KINGSTON *Brit. Navy* 535 Her total length is 320 feet.. with a displacement of 11,407 tons. **1935** C. G. BURGE *Complete Bk. Aviation* 263/1 *Displacement*, the mass of air displaced by the gas in an aerostat.

c. *Pharm.* The process of obtaining an extract of a substance by pouring over it successive quantities of a menstruum until all the soluble matters are extracted: = PERCOLATION.

1883 *Syd. Soc. Lex.*, *Displacement*.. In Pharmacy, the term is used in the same sense as *Percolation*.. *D. apparatus*, a means of obtaining extracts, whether aqueous or alcoholic. The body is pulverised, and then partially exhausted with a liquid, which is replaced by an additional quantity of the same, or of another liquid.

d. *Bot.* Abnormality in the position or form of a leaf or organ.

1869 M. T. MASTERS *Veget. Teratol.* 89 Instances of displacement of leaves arising from suppression.

† **dis'placence.** *Obs.* [ad. med.L. *displacēntia*, f. DIS- 4 + *placēntia* pleasantness: cf. OF. *desplaisance*, mod.F. *dép-*, It. *dispiacenza*. The cl.L. word was *displicēntia*, whence DISPLICENCE.] = next: the reverse of *complacence*.

c **1450** *Mirour Saluacioun* 1432 With displacens of all synne and hertly contrycionne. **1668** WILKINS *Real Char.* 229 Displacence, Sorrow, Grief, Discomfort. **1682** SIR T. BROWNE *Chr. Mor.* III. §5 Rake not up envious displacences at things successful unto others.

displacency (dɪs'pleɪsənsɪ). Now *rare* or *Obs.* [f. as prec.: see -ENCY. See also DISPLICENCY.]

The fact or condition of being displeased with something; displeasure, dissatisfaction, dislike. (The reverse of *complacency*.)

a **1652** J. SMITH *Sel. Disc.* x. iii. 503 Their hatred of the devil is commonly nothing else but an inward displacency of nature against something entitled by the devil's name. **1654** WARREN *Unbelievers* 205 His divine displacency against their sins. **1771** WESLEY *Wks.* (1872) VI. 18 Feeling a displacency at every offence against God. **1859** I. TAYLOR *Logic in Theol.* 59 The infant has made himself the object of complacency or of displacency, according to his original dispositions, or his individual character.

displacent (dɪs'pleɪsənt), *a.* *rare.* [f. DISPLACENCE, after *complacent*: cf. OF. *desplaisant*, DISPLEASANT.] Feeling or marked by displeasure: the reverse of *complacent*.

1859 I. TAYLOR *Logic in Theol.* 62 These emotions.. becoming either complacent or displacent.

dis'placer. [f. DISPLACE + -ER[1].]

1. One who or that which displaces.

1588 J. UDALL *Demonstr. Discip.* (Arb.) 73 If the ministers that bee vsually displaced, be called of God.. if it cause the displacers to be esteemed enemies to the Gospell. **1607** *Schol. Disc. agst. Antichr.* II. v. 10 Establishers of that which is good, and displacers of that which is evill.

2. *Pharm.* An apparatus for obtaining an extract by DISPLACEMENT (3 c); a percolator.

1883 *Syd. Soc. Lex.*, *Displacer*, a synonym of *Percolator*.

dis'placing, *vbl. sb.* [f. DISPLACE + -ING[1].] The action of the verb DISPLACE; removal from its place; deposition.

1551 T. WILSON *Logike* (1567) 65 a, In the diuidyng, and displacing of the same. **1583** STUBBES *Anat. Abus.* II. (1882) 84 Authoritie for his displacing, and placing of another that is more able. **1626** in Rushw. *Hist. Coll.* (1659) I. 403 More such displacings and alterations have by his means happened. **1654** LD. ORRERY *Parthen.* (1676) 310 Phanasders displacing gave him the invitation to invade us.

attrib. **1894** *Westm. Gaz.* 30 May 2/1 That displacing process which sounds so easy in political economy. In life, when you are squeezed out of one employment.. you do not find it so simple to slide into another groove.

dis'placing, *ppl. a.* [f. as prec. + -ING[2].] That displaces: see the verb.

1862 F. HALL *Hindu Philos. Syst.* 87 *note*, That one such quality may displace another, their theory is, that the displacing quality must remain with the quality displaced during the last moment of the subsistence of the latter. **1867** FREEMAN *Norm. Conq.* (1876) I. i. 2 Some knowledge of the condition of the displaced nation is necessary to understand the position of the displacing nation.

displant (dɪs'plɑːnt, -plænt), *v.* [ad. OF. *desplanter* = Sp. *desplantar*, It. *dispiantare* :—Romanic **displantāre*, for L. *dēplantāre*, f. DE- I. 6, DIS- + *plantāre* to plant.]

1. *trans.* To take up or remove (a plant) from the ground; to uproot.

1491 CAXTON *Vitas Patr.* (W. de W. 1495) II. 256 a/1 A tree whiche is ofte dysplaunted & transported from one grounde to an other may bere no fruyte. **1635** R. BOLTON *Comf. Affl. Consc.* xv. 79 A strong and mightie Oake.. which no storme or tempest can displant or overthrow. **1725** BRADLEY *Fam. Dict.* s.v. *Saffron Crocus*, After these Bulbs are displanted the Gardiner must be sure to keep them.. Three Weeks without replanting them. **1800** *Trans. Soc. Encourag. Arts* XVIII. 99 When the hops are displanted.

†**2.** To remove (a person) from his settled position; to dislodge (people) from their settlements or country; *spec.* to undo the settlement or establishment of (a 'plantation' or colony). *Obs.*

1592 SHAKS. *Rom. & Jul.* III. iii. 59 Displant a Towne, reuerse a Princes Doome. **1596** SPENSER *State Irel.* Wks. (Globe) 615/1 One of the occasions by which all those countryes, which.. had bene planted with English, were shortly displanted and lost. **1605** HIERON *Short Dial.* 49 Almost 300 preachers are already eyther displanted, inhibited, or under.. censure. **1615** G. SANDYS *Trav.* 39 The.. Greeks had planted certaine Colonies thereabout, and displanted the barbarous. **1650** J. MUSGRAVE *Grievances of North. Co.* 27 All Israel.. were displanted, and carried away into captivity. **1660** F. BROOKE tr. *Le Blanc's Trav.* 370 A Colony.. in Dariana, displanted for the unsoundnesse of the ayre.

†**3.** *fig.* **a.** To root up, eradicate; **b.** to supplant.

1603 H. CROSSE *Vertues Commw.* (1878) 98 Others.. displant all good order established. **1612** T. TAYLOR *Comm. Titus* i. 6 He must.. displant vices, and plant the contrarie vertues. **1624** MASSINGER *Renegado* III. i, Some other hath displanted me, With her dishonour. *a* **1638** MEDE *Apost. Lat. Times* (1641) 83 Three of these.. should the Anti-christian horne depresse and displant, to advance himselfe.

Hence **dis'planting** *vbl. sb.* and *ppl. a.*

1604 SHAKS. *Oth.* II. i. 283 By the displanting of Cassio. **1616** H. GOSNOLD in *Lismore Papers* (1887) Ser. II. II. 20 The stock which I am tyed to purchase vnder paine of displanting. **1725** BRADLEY *Fam. Dict.* s.v. *Tulip*, Take a Gardiners displanting Groove, and thrust it into the Ground. **1727** BAILEY vol. II, *Displanting Scoop*, an Instrument to take up Plants with Earth about them.

† **displan'tation.** *Obs.* [f. prec. after PLANTATION.] The action or fact of displanting; the removal of a plantation or colony.

1614 RALEIGH *Hist. World* I. 46 The Edenites in Thelassar.. whose displantation Senacherib vaunted of. *Ibid.* v. ii. §8. 603 The Boij.. feared the like displantation.

† **dis'plat,** *v.* *Obs.* [DIS- 6 or 7 a.] *trans.* To do out of its plats or plaits, to unplait.

1627 HAKEWELL *Apol.* (1630) 412 Which of these would not rather choose that the state.. should be in combustion then his haire should be displatted?

display (dɪ'spleɪ), *v.* Forms: 5 desplay, dysplay, 6 displeigh. *β.* 5–6 des-, dysploy. [a. OF. *despleier* (*-plier*, *-ployer*), = Pr. *desplegar*, *-pleiar*, Sp. *desplegar*, It. *dispiegare*:—L. *displicāre* to scatter, disperse, (in late and med.L.) to unfold. See also the doublet DEPLOY, and aphetic SPLAY.

In OF. *displicare* became orig. in inf. *desplier*; in tonic forms as 3 sing. pres. *desplei-e*; whence by subseq. confusion of tonic and atonic forms *despleier*, later *desploier*, *desployer*: examples of all these French varieties exist in Eng. in *ply*, *ploy*, *apply*, *comply*, *imply*, *deploy*, *employ*; the forms in *-ploy* being from Central OF., or later F.]

1. a. *trans.* To unfold, expand, spread out; to unfurl (a banner, sail). Now *Obs.* exc. as influenced by sense 3, and understood as 'to unfold to view' (a banner or the like).

[**1292** BRITTON II. xxii. §4 Si la disseisine fust fete a banere desplaé, ou as chevaus covertz.] *c* **1330** R. BRUNNE *Chron.* (1810) 2 Ine.. displayed his banere, & went to þe bataile. *c* **1430** LYDG. *Min. Poems.* (Percy Soc.) 6 Ther yssed oute empresses thre, Theire here displayed. *c* **1460** *Emare* 97 The cloth was displayed sone. **1490** CAXTON *Eneydos* xxvii. 96 To sprede and dysploye the sayles. *c* **1500** *Melusine* xxi. 131 And made hys banere to be dysployed abrode. **1582** N. LICHEFIELD tr. *Castanheda's Conq. E. Ind.* xxxvi. 88 There was displaide a flagge in the top of the Factorie. **1590** SPENSER *F.Q.* III. ii. 47 The old-woman carefully displayd The clothes about her round with busy ayd. **1621** G. SANDYS *Ovid's Met.* IV. (1626) 86 With Dores display'd, the golden Palace shines. **1656** EARL MONM. *Advt. fr. Parnass.* 259 [He] displaid his sails to a prosperous west wind. **1692** BENTLEY *Boyle Lect.* 208 Elastick.. particles, that have a continual tendency and endeavour to expand and display themselves. **1728** POPE *Dunc.* III. 71 See.. her sable flag display'd. **1894** C. N. ROBINSON *Brit. Fleet* 97 A flag was to be displayed on the discovery of a supposed enemy at sea.

intr. (for *refl.*). **1572** R. H. tr. *Lavaterus' Ghostes & Spir.* (1596) 81 When.. their ensignes will not displaie abroade but fold about the stander-bearers heads.

†**b.** *Mil.* To spread out (troops) so as to form a more extended line; = DEPLOY *v.* 2. *Obs.*

1581 SAVILE *Agric.* (1622) 198 Agricola.. fearing lest hee should bee assailed on the front and flankes both at one instant, displayed his army in length. **1581** —— *Tacitus' Hist.* IV. xxxv. (1591) 196 Fought with troupes displayed out thinnely in length. **1610** HOLLAND *Camden's Brit.* I. 151 The Englishmen.. display their ranks and.. press hard upon their enemies. **1823** CRABB *Technol. Dict.*, To display (*Mil.*) in French *déployer*, to extend the front of a column.

2. a. To lay or place (a man or animal) with the limbs extended; to extend (a limb, wing, etc.) *spec.* in *Her.*: see DISPLAYED 2.

c **1320** R. BRUNNE *Medit.* 640 Toward þe cros hys bak he layde, And hys real armes oute he dysplayde. **1486** *Bk. St. Albans* B viij a, Display the wynge esely and holde it betwene the ij partes of the loofe. **1539** HILSEY *Primer* in *Three Primers* (1848) 328 O Lord which hast displayed thine hands and feet, and all thy body on a cross for our sins. **1591** SPENSER *Virg. Gnat* 240 Sleep oppressed him, Displaid on ground. *Ibid.* 336 Thou.. Thy careles limbs in loose sleep dost display.

†**b.** *Carving.* The technical term for: To carve (a crane). *Obs.*

c **1470** in *Hors, Shepe & G.* etc. (Caxton 1479, Roxb. repr.) 33 A crane displayed, a pecok disfigured. **1513** *Bk. Keruynge* in *Babees Bk.* 267 Dysplaye that crane. Take a crane, and vnfolde his legges, and cut of his wynges by the Ioyntes. **1804** FARLEY *Lond. Art Cookery* (ed. 10) 293.

absol. **1711–14** *Spectator* (J.), He carves, displays, and cuts up to a wonder.

3. a. To open up or expose to view, exhibit to the eyes, show.

13.. *Gaw. & Gr. Knt.* 955 Hir brest & hir bryȝt þrote bare displayed Schon shyrer þen snawe. *c* **1430** LYDG. *Min. Poems* (1840) 161 (Mätz.) Displaieth hir crown geyn Phebus bemys brihte. **1591** SHAKS. *1 Hen. VI*, I. ii. 77, I.. to Sunnes parching heat display'd my cheekes. **1695** WOODWARD *Nat. Hist. Earth* IV. (1723) 244 By this means.. the Grain-Gold, upon all the Gold Coast.. is display'd. **1767** SIR W. JONES *Seven Fount.* Poems (1777) 46 Th' alluring stream, That through the grove display'd a silver gleam. **1861** M. PATTISON *Ess.* (1889) I. 45 Round the apartment.. was displayed in close array the silver and pewter plate. **1864** BOUTELL *Heraldry Hist. & Pop.* xix. 301 More recently the Royal Banner has always displayed the Arms of England.

b. *Printing.* To make more prominent (a word, line, etc.) by using larger type, wider spacing, etc.

1888 [see DISPLAY *sb.* 5].

4. To unfold or exhibit to other senses, to observation generally, or to the mind. †**a.** To give utterance to, pour forth, utter. *Obs.*

1580 SIDNEY *Ps.* XXVII. vii, Heare, Lord, when I my voice display. **1638** SIR T. HERBERT *Trav.* (ed. 2) 210 A thousand warbling Notes thy throat displayes.

b. To exhibit, make manifest, cause to be observed or perceived.

1575 LANEHAM *Let.* (1871) 12 At last the Altitonant displeaz me hiz mayn poour. **1635** QUARLES *Embl.* II. i. (1718) 66 Thy busie hands address Their labour to display. **1660** BOYLE *New Exp. Phys. Mech.* xvii. 115 The.. Air.. sufficing.. to display a considerable pressure upon the surface of the Mercury. **1762** SIR W. JONES *Arcadia* Poems (1777) 107 The curling eglantines display'd.. an aromatick shade. **1874** GREEN *Short Hist.* vii. §7. 415 The new English drama.. was beginning to display its wonderful powers. **1885** *Manch. Exam.* 16 June 4/7 The same insubordination was displayed still more offensively.

5. a. *esp.* To exhibit ostentatiously; to show off, make a show of.

1628 EARLE *Microcosm.*, *Bold forward Man* (Arb.) 47 These few good parts hee has, hee is no niggard in displaying. **1659** B. HARRIS *Parival's Iron Age* 126 Many great Divines were fain to display their eloquence. **1709** POPE *Ess. on Criticism* 329 The sparks with awkward vanity display What the fine gentleman wore yesterday. **1729** BUTLER *Serm.* Wks. 1874 II. 47 Their business in coming into company..[is] to display themselves. **1750** Johnson *Rambler* No. 27 ¶8 That part of his discourse in which he most endeavoured to display his imagination.

†**b.** *intr.* (for *refl.*) To make a great show or display; to act in an ostentatious manner. *Obs.*

1605 Shaks. *Lear* II. iv. 41 The fellow which..Displaid so saucily against your Highnesse.

c. *Ornith. intr.* To engage in or use display (see display *sb.* 2 b).

1902 *Zoologist* 4th Ser. VI. 197 The displaying bird crouched, upon which the pairing took place. **1936** *Nature* 27 June 1057/2 Birds of many species pair before they display and often pair for life. **1953** Bannerman *Birds Brit. Isles* II. 188 A male coal tit displaying to an apparently disinterested female with her back turned to the ardent suitor. *Ibid.* 292 To watch a male gold-crest displaying to the lady of his choice.

6. *trans.* To disclose, reveal, or show, unintentionally or incidentally; to allow to be seen or perceived, to betray.

1602 Marston *Ant. & Mel.* III. Wks. 1856 I. 32 If you are but seene, Your armes display you; therefore put them off. **1632** J. Hayward tr. *Biondi's Eromena* 171 He began to display..some token of suspition. **1796** H. Hunter tr. *St. Pierre's Stud. Nat.* (1799) II. 568 All the variety of colours which flowers display. **1853** J. H. Newman *Hist. Sk.* (1873) II. I. iii. 146 A grand entertainment, which displayed both the barbarism and the magnificence of the Asiatic. **1875** Jowett *Plato* (ed. 2) I. 104 Having displayed your ignorance of the nature of courage.

†**7.** To set forth in representation or narrative; to depict, describe, exhibit; to set forth at large, expound; to unfold (a tale). *Obs.* or *arch.*

1726–31 Tindal *Rapin's Hist. Eng.* (1743) II. XVII. 156 To display in a few words the Elogy of this illustrious queen. **1750** Johnson *Rambler* No. 79 ¶8 The princes were once displaying their felicity, and each boasting the advantages of his own dominions. **1766** Pennant *Zool.* (1768) I. Pref. 2 The admirable Linnæus has displayed them [arguments] at large in an oration. **1802** Mar. Edgeworth *Moral T.* (1816) I. 200 Zealous to display every proof of the king's greatness of mind. **1808** Scott *Marm.* IV. ii, He..did his tale display.

†**8.** *Med.* To disperse, dissipate. *Obs.* [Cf. L. *displicare*, Varro.]

1607 Topsell *Four-f. Beasts* (1658) 84 The fat of this beast is reserved by some for heating, softening, and displaying tumours in the flesh. *Ibid.* 504 The use of this by reason it is very hot, is to display Ulcers and tumors in wounds.

¶**9.** To discover, get sight of, descry. [In Spenser and his imitators; as if 'to unfold to one's own view'.] *Obs.*

1590 Spenser *F.Q.* II. xii. 76 They..did at last display That wanton Lady, with her lover. *c* **1611** Chapman *Iliad* XI. 74 He..from his seat took pleasure to display The city so adorn'd with tow'rs. **1615** —— *Odyss.* v. 350 He might display The shady hills of the Phaeacian shore.

di'splay, *sb.* [f. prec. vb.]

1. a. The act of displaying or unfolding to view or to notice; exhibition, manifestation.

a **1680** Glanvill (J.), A glorious display of the highest form of created excellencies. **1752** Johnson *Rambler* No. 205 ¶5 At this display of riches every eye immediately sparkled. **1767** *Junius Lett.* xxv. 116 You were not quite indifferent to the display of your literary qualifications. **1823** Rutter *Fonthill* 8 A too sudden display of the colossal dimensions..of the Abbey. **1853** J. H. Newman *Hist. Sk.* (1873) II. I. i. 4 The display of horsetails at the gate of the Palace is the Ottoman signal of war. **1858** Froude *Hist. Eng.* III. xiv. 193 An occasion for the display of his powers.

†**b.** The act of setting forth descriptively; a description. *Obs.*

1583 Stubbes (*title*) The Second part of the Anatomie of Abuses, containing The display of Corruptions, with a perfect description of such imperfections. **1610** Guillim (*title*) Display of Heraldry. **1706** Phillips (ed. Kersey), *Display*, a particular Explication. *a* **1714** Sharp *Serm.* I. v. (R.), For the more lively display of him..it will be fit that we represent him a little more particular under those several respects and capacities, in which his uprightness is principally seen and expressed.

c. The presentation of radar echoes or signals on the screen of a cathode-ray tube; a visual presentation of data from a computer, whether by means of a cathode-ray tube or some other device; also, a device or system used for this. = *visual display* s.v. visual *a.* 6 e. Also *attrib.*

1945 *Electronic Engin.* XVII. 684 If the target is out of sight the Radar display panel is used. *Ibid.* 716 Photographs of the cathode-ray tube face showing..the main display. **1946** *Ibid.* XVIII. 265 The I.F. rather than the video is fed from the main console to the display units. **1947** L. J. Haworth in L. N. Ridenour *Radar System Engin.* vi. 173 Target range is displayed as a horizontal coordinate and the display is expanded in the vertical dimension. *Ibid.*, The signals from a given target are correlated in the two displays on the basis of range and azimuth position. **1958** *Listener* 30 Oct. 691/1 New radar sets of much higher power, on which the display was sometimes covered with small echoes. **1960** R. S. Ledley *Digital Computer & Control Engin.* xxii. 756 Another scheme is to use an electroluminescent surface... Wires buried in the surface can be controlled by the computer to generate voltages, and hence light, as desired for picture displays. **1962** Huskey & Korn *Computer Handbk.* XVIII. 21 The most common device which functions as a symbol display is the number wheel used in the odometer of an automobile. **1967** *Technology Week* 20 Feb. 22/1 A vigorous developmental effort is in progress..to discover whether future command and control display systems for manned space flight should use all-digital techniques. **1969** *Times* 21 Jan. 5/8 The computer replies with an automatic display of the patient's answer.

2. a. An exhibition, a show; a proceeding or occasion consisting in the exhibiting of something.

1665 Glanvill *Scepsis Sci.* IV. Pref. (R.), Some grains must be allow'd to a rhetorical display, which will not bear the rigour of a critical survey. **1789** Cowper *Queen's Visit Lond.* 10 (17 March) 'Twas hard to tell of streets or squares Which formed the chief display. **1831** Brewster *Nat. Magic* i. (1833) 6 The optical display which hallowed their ancient temples. **1845** *Florist's Jrnl.* 278 The display of dahlias..was most excellent. **1883** Gladstone in *Glasgow Weekly Her.* 9 June 1/7 Constant parades and military displays with bands and flags. **1886** A. Winchell *Walks Geol. Field* 210 Some of our most splendid meteoric displays.

b. *Ornith.* A specialized pattern of behaviour used by birds as a visual means of communication, often in conjunction with characteristic calls. Also *attrib.*

1901 *Zoologist* 4th Ser. V. 344 Whether it was a conscious display or not..the birds could not have adopted an attitude or a position in relation to one another better adapted to show off the beauties of their plumage. **1914** *Proc. Zool. Soc.* 524 The Display Ceremonies..seem so very like the Displays of solitary courtship. **1933** *Brit. Birds* XXVII. 34, I had an opportunity of seeing the display of the male. **1937** *Ibid.* XXX. 274 It seems that 'display-building' (that is, building regarded as a manifestation of sexual excitement) is shown by the Great Crested Grebe. **1938** *Ibid.* XXXII. 86 The display flight was similar to that of related species. **1949** *Ibid.* XLII. 120 He immediately adopted the display attitude, exposing the throat at very close quarters and not attempting to turn round. **1953** Bannerman *Birds Brit. Isles* I. 23 A description of the spring display of the hooded crow has been given by the Misses Baxter and Rintoul, who watched a bird jumping a little distance into the air and then re-alighting at the same place to repeat the performance. *Ibid.*, The aerial display by a pair of birds also included 'corkscrew' or 'figure-of-eight' flights. **1964** A. L. Thomson *New Dict. Birds* 203/2 When two or more incompatible tendencies are present, various types of ambivalent behaviour may occur..and some instances of this have been specialised in evolution for a communicatory function and thus may be designated as displays.

3. Show, ostentation.

1816 Byron *Parisina* xvii, He died, as erring man should die, Without display, without parade. **1838** Emerson *Nature, Lit. Ethics* Wks. (Bohn) II. 214 Fatal to the man of letters, fatal to man, is the lust of display. **1870** —— *Soc. & Solit., Domestic Life* Ibid. III. 45 A house kept to the end of display is impossible to all but a few women.

4. *Printing.* The selection and arrangement of types so as to call attention to important parts of the subject matter: used in regard to title-pages and advertisements.

1824 J. Johnson *Typographia* II. 588 An alteration in the method of display and a new mode in the arrangement of the matter, became now very general.

5. a. *attrib.* and *Comb.*, as (sense 4) *display-ad* (colloq.), *-face*, *-heading*; **display-case**, a case (see case *sb.*[2] 7 a) in which items are displayed for inspection; also **display cabinet**; **display hand**, (*a*) one who sets up display-type; (*b*) a pyrotechnist employed chiefly to assist in firework displays; **display-letter, -type**, a letter or type used for displaying printed matter; cf. 4 above; **display lighting**, lighting used to illuminate objects, buildings, etc., on display; **display-stand**, a stand, rack, shelf, etc. for displaying goods; **display window** orig. *U.S.*, a large shop-window in which merchandise is displayed; **display-work** (see quot.).

1919 Mencken *Amer. Lang.* v. 160 Want-ad, display-ad. **1930** A. Bennett *Imperial Palace* xxxvi. 250 Display-ads of the kind you're putting now in London dailies. **1933** *Connoisseur* Nov. 348/2 Two Chippendale display cabinets in the Chinese taste. **1965** M. Spark *Mandelbaum Gate* iii. 73 The crib-figures..were spread about on the glass top of a display cabinet. **1950** 'N. Shute' *Town like Alice* 328 A glass counter and display-case full of women's things. **1948** H. Missingham *Student's Guide Commerc. Art* II. 80 Display faces..comprise the larger sizes of letters used for newspaper headlines, titlepages, and headings or displayed advertisements. **1896** *Daily News* 1 Dec. 12/7 (Advt.), Compositor.—— First-class Jobbing and Display Hand seeks situation. **1921** *Dict. Occup. Terms* (1927) §148 *Display hand*..; *pyrotechnist*: assists at firework display, lighting fuses [etc.]. **1907** 'Mark Twain' in *N. Amer. Rev.* Jan. 4 According to the display-heading—'Rich Woman Fell Down Cellar'. **1919** B. Sherbow *Making Type Work* 35 Too Many Capital Letters in a Display Heading Confuse the Eye. **1855** W. B. Wood *Recoll. of Stage* xxiii. 452 Proclaiming the name of the star in display letters a foot or a yard long. **1950** *Ann. Reg. 1949* 465 Restrictions were still imposed on shop-window, advertisement, and display lighting. **1863** *Boston Herald* 15 Mar. 4/1 Printers and editors may look out for late sights and display type. **1967** Karch & Buber *Offset Processes* 536 *Display type*, the largest and specially designed type faces used to attract attention. **1934** Webster, Display window. **1945** Steinbeck *Cannery Row* xi. 47 The final climax came with the front of Holman's bootery broken out and the party trying on shoes in the display window. **1964** C. Buchanan *Traffic in Towns* 67 Conventional shopping streets with display windows facing pavements. **1888** Jacobi *Printer's Voc.* 32 *Display work*, Type displayed, such as titles, headings, and jobbing work, is thus termed to distinguish it from ordinary solid composition.

b. *Mus.* Designating a piece of music that specially displays the performer's skill or virtuosity.

1959 *Listener* 9 July 76/3 This is a display piece; it shows off an orchestra's virtuosity. *Ibid.* 17 Dec. 1093/2 Hindemith's thirty-four-year-old Concerto for Orchestra, a rollicking piece of display music. **1961** *Ibid.* 9 Nov. 789/3 The big coloratura aria of Zerbinetta..unhappily revives the most regrettable features of the old display aria.

di'splayable, *a. rare.* [f. as prec. + -able.] Capable of being displayed.

1864 Carlyle *Fredk. Gt.* (1865) IV. XII. xi. 265 Belleisle displayed, so far as displayable, his magnificent Diplomatic Ware.

displayed (dɪ'spleɪd), *ppl. a.* Also 4–6 des-, dys-, -plaied(e, -playit, -plaid, -pleyd. [-ed[1].]

1. Unfolded, unfurled, spread open to view.

c **1425** Wyntoun *Cron.* VIII. xxxix. 32 A Rade of were He made wyth displayid Banere. **1603** Knolles *Hist. Turkes* (1638) 297 The displaied ensignes. **1625** K. Long tr. *Barclay's Argenis* III. iii. 155 Opening now their displayed Pedigrees. **1649** Milton *Eikon.* Wks. 1738 I. 365 Fought against him with display'd Banners in the Field.

b. Expanded, as wings, leaves, etc.

1578 Lyte *Dodoens* III. xvii. 339 The leaves are lyke desplayed winges. **1648** Boyle *Seraph. Love* (1660) 44 The Coy delusive Plant..shrinks in its displayed leaves.

†**c.** Lying supine with the limbs extended.

a **1400** *Octouian* 1516 Well many Sarsyns..ley dyspleyd. *c* **1485** *Digby Myst.* IV. 313 This displaied body. **1591** [see display *v.* 2]. **1647** Cleveland *Poems, Smectymnuus* 90.

2. *Her.* Having the wings expanded: said of a bird of prey used as a bearing. Also ***with wings displayed***: see quot. 1882.

c **1400** *Sowdone Bab.* 190 An Egle of goolde abrode displayed. *a* **1490** Botoner *Itin.* (1778) 164 Ung egle displayed de argent. **1572** Bossewell *Armorie* II. 60 b, The fielde is of the Topaze, a Basiliske displayed, Emeraude, cristed, Saphire. **1766** Porny *Heraldry* (1787) 170 Three Eaglets displayed, points of their wings pendent, Or. **1830** Robson *Brit. Herald* III. Gloss., *Displayed recursant*, or *tergiant*, the wings crossing each other; sometimes termed *backward displayed, the wings crossing. Displayed foreshortened*, eagles, etc. thus borne, are depicted flying straight forward towards you, so as no part but the roundness of the head and body is seen, with the pinion of the wings extended. **1882** Cussans *Her.* vi. 91 The Heraldic student must bear in mind the difference between *An Eagle displayed* and *An Eagle with wings displayed*; when the latter term is employed, the Bird is supposed to be perched.

b. By Puttenham (1589) *Eng. Poesie* II. xi[i]. (Arb.) 106 applied to geometrical figures arranged in pairs somewhat as wings, e.g. the Tricquet displayed [= two triangles joined at their apices]; the egge displayed, the Rondel displayed [= an oval or a circle bisected, and the halves joined at their convex margins].

Hence †**di'splayedly** *adv. Obs.*

1611 Florio, *Spiegatamente*, openly, displaiedly.

di'splayer. [f. as prec. + -er[1].] One who or that which displays; an exhibitor.

1611 Florio, *Spiegatore*, a displayer, an vnfolder. **1627–77** Feltham *Resolves* I. lxxxvi. (L.), Nothing that has sense but is better for this displayer [charity]. **1654** Gayton *Pleas. Notes* (T.), The displayer of his high frontiers. **1815** W. H. Ireland *Scribbleomania* 217 Each pestle's displayer, Who, living by drugs, proves humanity's slayer. **1840** Browning *Sordello* v. (1889) 235 Some displayer, still More potent than the last, of human will.

di'splaying, *vbl. sb.* [f. as prec. + -ing[1].] The action of the verb display; unfolding, disclosing, revelation, exposure.

1556 Huggarde (*title*), The Displaying of the Protestantes, and sondry their Practices. **1611** Cotgr., *Despliement*, an unfoulding; displaying. **1677** J. Webster (*title*), The Displaying of Supposed Witchcraft. **1878** T. Sinclair *Mount* 4 Whatever value these partial displayings may have.

di'splayment. [f. as prec. + -ment.] = prec.

1801 Strutt *Sports & Past.* IV. iii. 326 The displayment of vulgar pastimes.

†**'disple,** *v. Obs.* Also 6 dyspel. [App. a popular formation from discipline *sb.* 7, or *v.* 2.

If derived from *discipline* vb., the final *-in(e* might be confounded with the infinitive suffix *-en*, *-yn*, and disappear along with it. But it is, on the whole, more probable that *discipl-ine* sb. was associated with vbl. sbs. in *-ing*, and so converted into *discipl-ing*, *dissplying*, *dyspelyng*, as in the earliest instances quoted. Thence a verb to *disple* would naturally be deduced. The verb disciple is of later date.]

trans. To subject to discipline, bodily correction, penance, or punishment; *esp.* as a religious practice. Also **'displing** *vbl. sb.* and *ppl. a.*

1492 in Brand *Pop. Antiq., Ash Wedn.* (1870) I. 56 For dissplying rods, ij[d]. **1533** More *Apol.* xxvii. Wks. 893/2 As lothe..as the Ladye was to come..to dyspelyng, that wepte..that the prieste had..with the dyspelyng rodde beaten her hard vppon her lylye white handes. **1563–87** Foxe *A. & M.* (1596) 1339/2 Euery of them had a Taper in his hand, and a rod, wherewith the Preacher did disple them. **1581** Marbeck *Bk. of Notes* 586 The displing of the froward childe. **1590** Spenser *F.Q.* I. x. 27 Bitter Penaunce, with an yron whip, Was wont him once to disple every day. **1605** B. Jonson *Volpone* IV. ii, Who here is fled for liberty of conscience..Her will I disc'ple. **1607** R. C. tr. *Estienne's World of Wonders* 169 Displing friers. **1641** *Vind. Smectymnuus* iii. 49 The Reverend Fathers will have multitudes of disobedient sons to disple.

†**dis'pleasance.** *Obs.* Forms: see displeasant. [a. OF. *desplaisance* (13th c. in Hatz.-Darm.), mod.F. *déplaisance*, f. *desplaisant*: see next and -ance. Cf. also displacence, displicence. Still stressed on final *c* 1530 by Skelton.] The fact of being displeased; displeasure, dissatisfaction,

discontent, annoyance, vexation; a cause or instance of this, a grievance, trouble.

c **1340** HAMPOLE *Prose Tr.* 11 Wordes of myssawe ne vnhoneste ne of displesance. *c* **1386** CHAUCER *Pard. Prol. & T.* 92 Thus quyte I folk, that doon vs displesances. *c* **1430** LYDG. *Min. Poems* (Percy Soc.) 48 So it be noon dysplesaunce to your pay. **1483** *Cath. Angl.* 98/1 A Desplesance; *grauamen, aggrauamen.* **1485** CAXTON *Chas. Gt.* 82 He was in grete desplaysaunce. **1509** BARCLAY *Shyp Folys* (1570) 126 Justice ought to be wayed..Not rigorously for wrath or displeasaunce. **1590** SPENSER *F.Q.* II. x. 28 Whose simple answere..him to displeasaunce moov'd. [**1886** J. PAYNE *Decameron* I. 29 Albeit the husbandmen die there..the displeasance is there the less.]

† **dis'pleasant**, *a. Obs.* Forms: 4-5 des-, 4-7 dis-, 5-6 dys-, 4-6 -ples-, 5 -pleys-, -plays-, 5-7 -pleas-, 4-7 -ant, 5-6 -aunt. [a. OF. *desplaisant*, ppl. adj. of *desplaire* to DISPLEASE.]

1. That displeases or causes displeasure or annoyance; displeasing; unpleasant; disagreeable.

1481 CAXTON *Myrr.* III. viii. 147 One is colde, rayny, and more desplaysant than thother. *c* **1510** BARCLAY *Mirr. Gd. Manners* (1570) G iv, Clense thy bedchamber from all displeasant sent. **1556** J. HEYWOOD *Spider & F.* ii. 64 Loue causeth friendes to hide displeasant trowth. **1609** BIBLE (Douay) *1 Sam.* xviii. 8 Saul was exceeding angrie, and this word was displeasant in his eies. **1668** *Palp. Evid. Witchcr.* 101 That morning it left a sulfurous smell behind it very displeasant and offensive.

b. Const. *to, unto.*

c **1386** CHAUCER *Pars. T.* ¶623 Thanne is this synne moost displesant to Crist. *a* **1450** *Knt. de la Tour* (1868) 149 Pride, whiche is the synne most displesaunt vnto God. *a* **1533** LD. BERNERS *Gold. Bk. M. Aurel.* (1546) S ij b, If your deathe be displeasant to them. **1665** GLANVILL *Scepsis Sci.* xiv. 91 What to one is a most grateful odour, to another is noxious and displeasant.

2. Displeased, angry, grieved.

1485 CAXTON *Chas. Gt.* 62 So desplaysaunt ne sory was he neuer as I shal make hym for the. **1525** *St. Papers Hen. VIII*, VI. 516 Sens that day that we founde the Chancellour so displesaunt for the letters sent. **1530** PALSGR. 310/2 Displeasant for synne, *contrit.* **1599** HAKLUYT *Voy.* II. I. 131 It was not they yt ought to shew one displeasant looke or countenance there against; but to take it patiently. **1709** STRYPE *Ann. Ref.* I. vii. 105 They looked with a very angry and displeasant eye upon them.

† **dis'pleasant**, *v. Obs. rare.* [f. prec. adj.] To render displeasant; to disquiet, vex.

Hence **dis'pleasanting** *vbl. sb.*, vexing, disquieting.

1628 FELTHAM *Resolves* II. xxii. 74 Lamentations that haue no better fruit, then the displeasanting of the soule, that ownes them.

† **dis'pleasantly**, *adv.* [f. as prec. + -LY[2].]

1. Unpleasantly, disagreeably; offensively.

1607 TOPSELL *Four-f. Beasts* (1658) 429 Before it is ripe, it smelleth displeasantly.

2. In a displeased or offended manner.

1540-1 ELYOT *Image Gov.* (1556) 139 b, I speake not displeasantly. **1662** J. CHANDLER *Van Helmont's Oriat.* Pref. to Rdr., I do humbly beseech you all..not displeasantly to receive my ready poor labour. **1721** STRYPE *Eccl. Mem.* I. xii. 103 He thought the Emperor should take it more displeasantly, than if his Holiness had declared himself.

† **dis'pleasantness.** *Obs.* [f. as prec. + -NESS.] The quality of being displeasing or unpleasant, unpleasantness; also, the condition of being displeased, displeasure.

1553 BRENDE *Q. Curtius* III. 29 (R.) When Philip had read the letter, hee shewed more tokens of displeasauntnes than of feare. **1582** W. CICILL in Bentley *Mon. Matrones, Q. Catherine's Lament.* Pref., This good Ladie thought no..displeasantnesse to submit hirselfe to the schoole of the crosse. **1665** J. WEBB *Stone-Heng* (1725) 42 They present..a certain kind of Displeasantness to the Eye.

displease (dɪs'pliːz), *v.* Forms: 4-5 desplese, (displess); 4-6 dis-, dysplese, displece, -pleis, 5 dysplayse, 5-6 dyspleasе, 5- displease. [a. OF. *desplais-*, pres. stem of *desplaisir, desplaire* (pres. subj. *-place, -plaise*), in AF. *desplere, desplese*, refashioned repr. of L. *displicēre*, Rom. **displacēre*: cf. It. *dispia'cere*, Sp. *desplacer*, Pr. *desplacer*: see PLEASE. The 16th c. *ea* represented an AF. and ME. open *ê* from OF. *ai.*]

1. *intr.* To be displeasing, disagreeable, or offensive; to cause displeasure, dissatisfaction, or dislike.

(This is app. the original use, as in Fr. and L.; but in later Eng. it passes into an absolute use of the transitive sense 2.)

13.. *E.E. Allit. P.* C. 1 Patience is a point, þaȝ hit displese ofte. **1414** BRAMPTON *Penit. Ps.* xlv. 17 He may sone dysplese and greve. **1484** CAXTON *Chivalry* 98, I wold demaunde a question yf I shold not displease. **1626** BACON *Sylva* (J.), Foul sights do rather displease, in that they excite the memory of foul things. **1705** POPE *Spring* 83 Ev'n spring displeases, when she shines not here. **1856** EMERSON *Eng. Traits, Manners* Wks. (Bohn) II. 46 They dare to displease.

† b. const. *to. Obs.* [= F. *déplaire à*, or with *dative*; L. *displicēre* with *dat.*]

c **1374** CHAUCER *Boeth.* I. pr. iii. 6 (Camb. MS.) To displese to wikkede men. *c* **1380** WYCLIF *Serm.* Sel. Wks. I. 196 þis displesiþ to sinful men. **1413** *Pilgr. Sowle* (Caxton 1483) III. viii. 55 For somtyme theyr lewd lyf displesid to them seluen. *c* **1425** WYNTOUN *Cron.* VI. xvi. 29 That til hyr fadyr dysplesyd noucht. **1483** CAXTON *G. de la Tour* D vij b, Thexcusations of Eue displeasid moche to god.

2. *trans.* [The object represents an earlier dative: cf. Fr. *cela me deplaît, cela deplaît à Dieu.*] To be displeasing or disagreeable to; to excite the displeasure, dissatisfaction, or aversion of; to offend, annoy, vex, make angry.

13.. *E.E. Allit. P.* B. 1136 þenne þou dryȝtyn dyspleses with dedes ful sore. **1393** GOWER *Conf.* III. 253 If it shulde him nought displese. *c* **1400** MAUNDEV. (Roxb.) vi. 20 If þai speke any thing þat displesez þe sowdan. *c* **1400** *Apol. Loll.* 83 To do synne, & displece God, & deserue peyn. *c* **1440** *Gesta Rom.* (1838) II. xxxviii. 399 It displeasethe me mekelle, that ever I come hedir. **1474** CAXTON *Chesse* 4 He put them al to deth that displesid him. **1529** *Supplic. to King* 53 Afrayed to speake the trewethe, lest they shulde dysplease men. **1596** SHAKS. *Tam. Shr.* I. i. 76 Let it not displease thee good Bianca, For I will loue thee nere the lesse my girle. **1596** —— *1 Hen. IV*, I. iii. 122 You shall heare in such a kinde from me As will displease ye. **1611** BIBLE *Jonah* iv. 1 Bvt it displeased Ionah exceedingly, and he was very angry. **1624** CAPT. SMITH *Virginia* IV. 112 This answer..much displeased him. **1700** S. L. tr. *Fryke's Voy. E. Ind.* 335 When I considered her..as to her Fortune, I must confess she did not altogether displease me. **1734** ARBUTHNOT in *Swift's Lett.* (1766) II. 205 The world, in the main, displeaseth me. **1841** W. SPALDING *Italy & It. Isl.* III. 150 The picture..is one which displeases taste. **1875** JOWETT *Plato* (ed. 2) III. 223, I will not oppose you, lest I should displease the company.

fig. **1590** SHAKS. *Mids. N.* III. ii. 54 Ile beleeue as soone..that the Moone May through the Center creepe, and so displease Her brothers noonetide. **1603** —— *Meas. for M.* IV. i. 13 My mirth it much displeas'd, but pleas'd my woe. **1611** BEAUM. & FL. *Maid's Trag.* IV. i, *E.* Come, you will make me blush. *Mel.* I would, Evadne; I shall displease my ends else.

† b. *refl.* and *intr.* = be displeased: see c. *Obs.*

13.. *E.E. Allit.* P. A. 422 'Blysful', quoth I, 'may þis be trwe, Dysplesez not if I speke errour'. **1377** LANGL. *P. Pl.* B. XIII. 135 'At ȝowre preyere', quod pacyence þo, 'so no man displese hym'. *a* **1450** *Knt. de la Tour* (1868) 160 Madame, displese you not thoughe this lady..goo before. *c* **1470** HENRY *Wallace* XI. 269 Ye suld displese you nocht.

c. *to be displeased*: to be dissatisfied, or moved to disapprobation or dislike; to be vexed; to be full of displeasure or indignation. (Expressing state rather than action: cf. DISPLEASED *ppl. a.*) Const. *with, at,* †*of,* †*against*; also with *infin.*, or *clause.*

c **1386** CHAUCER *Can. Yeom. Prol. & T.* 457 Beeth no thyng displesed, I yow preye. **1393** GOWER *Conf.* III. 173 They pray him..That he will saie no contraire, Wherof the king may be displesed. *c* **1489** CAXTON *Sonnes of Aymon* xxi. 464 My cosin, be not dysplaysed of that I shall telle you. *a* **1533** LD. BERNERS *Huon* lxv. 222 Make as though ye were dyspleasyd with hym. **1548** HALL *Chron., Edw. IV*, (an. 14) 232 b, [He] was sore displeased to se hys master made a jesting stocke. **1563** WINȜET *Four Scoir Thre Quest.* Wks. 1888 I. 133 Ȝe are..displesit that We embrase nocht..ȝour new interpretationis. **1593** SHAKS. *2 Hen. VI*, I. i. 155 There's reason he should be displeas'd at it. **1611** BIBLE *Hab.* iii. 8 Was the Lord displeased against the riuers? **1638** SIR T. HERBERT *Trav.* (ed. 2) 133 Cynthia also lookt pale, as displeasd with so much knavery. **1745** P. THOMAS *Jrnl. Anson's Voy.* 16 We should not have been displeased..to have met them with our whole Force. **1829** D'ISRAELI in *Croker Papers* (1884) 28 Jan., So many were displeased at themselves.

displeased (dɪs'pliːzd), *ppl. a.* [f. prec. + ED.] The reverse of pleased; vexed, angry, annoyed.

1581 MULCASTER *Positions* xxix. (1887) 109 The thinges, which do please the displeased infantes. **1609** *Shaks. Tr. & Cr.* (Qo. 1) Epistle ¶ ij, The most displeased with Playes, are pleasd with his Commedies. **1659** *Gentl. Calling* (1696) 116 The Heathens had Incantations to recal their displeased Deities. **1840** J. W. BOWDEN *Gregory VII*, I. 174 Too wary to put himself into the power of his displeased sovereign.

¶ For *to be displeased*, with its constructions, see DISPLEASE *v.* 2 c.

displeasedly (-'iːzɪdlɪ), *adv.* [f. prec. + -LY[2].] In a displeased or vexed manner; with displeasure.

c **1611** CHAPMAN *Iliad* xv. 97 Thus took she place displeasedly. **1826** SCOTT *Woodst.* xxxv, 'Have I not said it?' answered Cromwell, displeasedly. **1856** *Titan Mag.* July 10/1 He muttered the last words displeasedly.

† **dis'pleasedness.** *Obs.* [f. as prec. + -NESS.] Displeased state or condition, discontent.

1561 T. NORTON *Calvin's Inst.* III. 197 To do penance..is..to vtter a displeasednesse when god is angry with vs. **1680** BAXTER *Cath. Commun.* iii. (1684) 21 It is not Pleasedness with the evil; therefore it is Displeasedness. *a* **1716** SOUTH *Serm.* viii. 150 (T.) What a confusion and displeasedness covers the whole soul!

dis'pleaser. *rare.* [f. DISPLEASE + -ER[1].] One who displeases.

1641 MILTON *Ch. Govt.* II. (1851) 140 It must..be a hatefull thing to be the displeaser, and molester of thousands.

dis'pleasing, *vbl. sb.* [f. as prec. + -ING[1].] The action of the verb DISPLEASE; offending.

1387 TREVISA *Higden* (Rolls) II. 411 Priamus..hadde anon in mynde..þe displesynge [Higden *contemptus*] of his messager Antenor. **1530** PALSGR. 214/1 Displeasyng, *remors, offention.* **1580** BARET *Alv.* D 904 Without any displeasing of the tast. **1750** JOHNSON *Rambler* No. 26 ¶14 A servile fear of displeasing.

dis'pleasing, *ppl. a.* [f. as prec. + -ING[2].] Causing displeasure, giving offence, disagreeable.

1401 *Pol. Poems* (Rolls) II. 17 It is..displeasing to God, and harme to oure soules. **1552** ABP. HAMILTON *Catech.* (1884) 30 Displesand and nocht acceptable to God. **1597** SHAKS. *2 Hen. IV*, Epil. 10 A displeasing Play. **1643** MILTON *Divorce* II. viii. (1851) 80 By reason of some displeasing natural quality or unfitnes in her. **1779** MAD. D'ARBLAY *Diary* Oct., A rich counsellor..but, to me, a displeasing man. **1845** M. PATTISON *Ess.* (1889) I. 16 [The marriage] was also..highly displeasing to his father Chilperic.

Hence **dis'pleasingly** *adv.*; **dis'pleasingness.**

a **1652** J. SMITH *Sel. Disc.* viii. 394 Nothing that might..carry in it any semblance of displeasingness. **1690** LOCKE *Hum. Und.* II. xxi. (1695) 149 'Tis a mistake to think, that Men cannot change the Displeasingness or indifferency, that is in actions, into pleasure. **1731** BAILEY, *Displeasingly*, offensively. **1753** HOGARTH *Anal. Beauty* xi. 128 Although the form..should be ever so confused or displeasingly shaped to the eye! **1841** W. PALMER *6th Let. to Wiseman* 28 A virtual displeasingness in this life. **1843** LYTTON *Last Bar.* I. v, Associated displeasingly with recollections of pain.

dis'pleasurable, *a. rare.* [f. DISPLEASURE *sb.* + -ABLE, after *pleasurable.*] The reverse of pleasurable; unpleasant, disagreeable. Hence **dis'pleasurably** *adv.*

1660 HEXHAM, *Ongeriesticken*, Incommodiously, Displeasurably. **1879** H. SPENCER *Data Ethics* xiv. 245 The required modes of activity must remain for innumerable generations in some degree displeasurable. *Ibid.* 246 A displeasurable tax on the energies.

displeasure (dɪs'plɛʒ(j)ʊə(r)), *sb.* Forms: α. 5 des-, dis-, dysplaisir, -playsir, -yr(e. β. dis-, dysplaysure, -pleysure, 5-6 dyspleasur(e, 6 displesour, -pleis-, -pleas-, displeasur, -or, 6- displeasure. [In type α, a. OF. *desplaisir* (13th c. in Hatz.-Darm.), mod.F. *déplaisir*, subst. use of OF. infin. *desplaisir* to DISPLEASE: cf. Pr. *desplazer*, Sp. *desplacer*, It. *dispiacere*, in subst. use. In type β, conformed to PLEASURE, which see for the relation between *plaisir, pleasure.*]

1. The fact or condition of being displeased or offended; a feeling varying according to its intensity from dissatisfaction or disapproval to anger and indignation provoked by a person or action.

α. **1484** CAXTON *Chivalry* 81 Yre and dysplaysyre gyuen passion and payn to the body and to the sowle.

β. **1495** *Act 11 Hen. VII*, c. 57 Pream., All that that he hath doon to the displeasure of your Highnes. **1535** COVERDALE *Nahum* i. 2 The Lorde..reserueth displeasure for his aduersaries. *c* **1550** CHEKE *Matt.* iii. 7 Who hath counceld to yow, to flie from ye displeasur to come? **1601** SHAKS. *All's Well* II. v. 38, I know not how I haue deserued to run into my Lords displeasure. **1769** *Junius Lett.* xv. 64 The royal displeasure has been signified. **1828** SCOTT *F.M. Perth* xvii, 'Thou art severe'..said the Duke of Rothsay, with an air of displeasure. **1856** FROUDE *Hist. Eng.* (1858) I. ii. 116 An indication of the displeasure of Heaven.

† b. phr. *to take (a) displeasure*: to take offence, take umbrage; to be displeased. *Obs.*

c **1489** CAXTON *Blanchardyn* xxvi. 96 She brought thene in remembraunce how swetly he had kyssed her, wherof she had take so grete a dyspleasure. **1513** BRADSHAW *St. Werburge* I. 1863, No man was greued nor toke dyspleasure At this sayd mayden. **1610** SHAKS. *Temp.* IV. i. 202 Do you heare Monster: If I should Take a displeasure against you: Looke you. **1633** BP. HALL *Hard Texts* 536, I began to take displeasure against them for their wickednesse.

† 2. The opposite of pleasure; discomfort, uneasiness, unhappiness; grief, sorrow, trouble. *Obs.*

α. *c* **1477** CAXTON *Jason* 70 Appollo..considering the right grete displaisir in which they hadde ben,..opened all the entrees. **1485** —— *Paris & V.* 22, I shall deye..for the grete desplaysyr that I have contynuelly in my herte.

β. **14..** *Compl. Mary Magd.* 272 They have him conveyed to my displeasure, For here is lafte but naked sepulture. *c* **1489** CAXTON *Blanchardyn* xxxiv. 129 My sayd lady is in grete displaysure, & ceaseth not nyght nor day to wysshe hym wyth her. **1513** BRADSHAW *St. Werburge* I. 11 Men..Oppressed with pouerte, langour and dyspleasure. **1632** LITHGOW *Trav.* II. 66 He disappointed died for displeasure in his returne. **1630** LENNARD tr. *Charron's Wisd.* (1658) 24 The humane receiveth from his body pleasure and displeasure, sorrow and delight. *a* **1704** LOCKE (J.), When good is proposed, its absence carries displeasure or pain with it. **1875** W. K. CLIFFORD *Lect.* (1879) II. 126 A feeling..as distinct..as the feeling of pleasure in a sweet taste or of displeasure at a toothache.

† b. with *a* and *pl.* An instance of this. *Obs.* Cf. 1 †b.

c **1510** BARCLAY *Mirr. Gd. Manners* (1570) C j, Hauing for one pleasure displeasures eight or nine. **1542** BOORDE *Dyetary* viii. (1870) 246 It doth ingendre the crampe, the gowte & other displeasures. **1681-6** J. SCOTT *Chr. Life* (1747) III. 338 A mutual Sense and feeling of each others Pleasures and Displeasures.

3. That which causes or occasions offence or trouble; injury, harm; a wrong, an offence. *arch.*

α. **1470-85** MALORY *Arthur* IX. xix, I dyd to hym no displeasyre. **1481** CAXTON *Myrr.* III. xiii. 162 Thus auenged he hym on her for the displaysir that she had don to hym.

β. **1494** FABYAN *Chron.* VI. clxi. 154 Ye great daunger that he was in agaynste God for the dyspleasurys doon to hym. **1534** in W. H. Turner *Select. Rec. Oxford* 124 They myght ..doe displeasure and execute theire malice upon the inhabitants. **1577** HANMER *Anc. Eccl. Hist.* (1619) 364 He was..incensed, and promised to worke them a displeasure. **1590** SHAKS. *Com. Err.* IV. iv. 119 Hast thou delight to see a wretched man Do outrage and displeasure to himselfe? **1662** J. BARGRAVE *Pope Alex. VII* (1867) 36 Antonio was still a thorn in his side, doing him all the displeasures he could. **1866** HOWELLS *Venet. Life* 19 To do you a service and not a displeasure.

†**4.** A state of unpleasant or unfriendly relations; a disagreement, 'difference'. *Obs.*

1550 J. COKE *Eng. & Fr. Heralds* (1877) §72. 81 Wyllyam Conquerour..upon certayne dyspleasures betwene hym and the french kyng, passed..into Fraunce. **1568** GRAFTON *Chron.* II. 138 A displeasure and variance began to growe betwene the Constable of the Tower, and the Citizens of London. **1570-6** LAMBARDE *Peramb. Kent.* (1826) 215 During the displeasure betweene him and Earle Godwin.

dis'pleasure, *v. arch.* [f. prec. sb.] *trans.* To cause displeasure to; to annoy; to displease.

1540-1 ELYOT *Image Gov.* 109 Hated be he of goddes and of men that would you displeasure. **1563** *Homilies* II. *Of Almsdeeds* I. (1859) 387 He..is both able to pleasure and displeasure us. **1625** BACON *Ess., Ambition* (Arb.) 227 When the Way of Pleasuring and Displeasuring, lieth by the Favourite. **1829** SOUTHEY *O. Newman* vi, Not for worlds Would I do aught that might displeasure thee. **1849** WHITTIER *Marg. Smith's Jrnl.* Prose Wks. 1889 I. 25 Our young gentleman, not willing to displeaure a man so esteemed as Mr. Richardson.

†**b.** *transf. Obs.*

1570 DEE *Math. Pref.* 24 Elementall bodies, are altered.. and displeasured, by the Influentiall working of the Sunne.

dis'pleasurement. *rare.* [f. prec. + -MENT.] Displeasure.

1882 SYMONDS *Animi Figura* 134 He Quailed 'neath his Maker's just displeasurement.

†**dis'pleited**, *pa. pple. Obs.* [f. DIS- 6 + *pleit*, PLAIT, PLEAT *v.* + -ED.] Not marked with pleats or folds; free from folds.

1619 LUSHINGTON *Repetition-Serm.* in *Phenix* (1708) II. 484 The Kerchief so wrapt and displeited, as tho yet it had not been us'd; and yet so laid aside, as tho he would have come again.

di'splendour, *v. nonce-wd.* [f. *di-* = DIS- 7a + SPLENDOUR.] *trans.* To deprive of splendour.

1854 SYD. DOBELL *Balder* xxiv. 165 Sole wandering, like an unasserted god—Displendoured, undeclared, but not unknown.

displenish (dɪ'splɛnɪʃ), *v. Sc.* [f. DIS- 6 + PLENISH *v.* to furnish: cf. DEPLENISH.] *trans.* To deprive of furniture or supplies of any kind; to divest of (farm) stock; to disfurnish.

1639 R. BAILLIE *Lett.* (1775) I. xi. 166 Albeit we had got these two years a great store of arms..yet we were..sore displenished before. **1873** GEIKIE *Gt. Ice Age* i. 1 Large areas of forest-land had been displenished.

Hence **di'splenishing** *vbl. sb.*; also **di'splenish** *sb.*, **di'splenishment**, the action of displenishing.

displenish(ing) sale (*Sc.*), a sale of farm stock and utensils at the expiry of a lease.

1863 *Montrose Standard* 14 Aug. 1 Displenish sale of growing corn. **1864** *N. Brit. Advertiser* 21 May, Displenishing Sale..at Orbost, Isle of Skye..Cattle, Stock, and Household Furniture. **1893** C. A. MOLLYSON *Parish of Fordoun* v. 107 An important displenish sale.

displeyer, obs. form of DICE-PLAYER.

†**displicable**, *a. Obs.* [ad. med.L. *displicibilis* displeasing (Du Cange), f. L. *displicēre* to DISPLEASE, with Eng. suffix -ABLE.] Displeasing.

1471 RIPLEY *Comp. Alch.* Pref. in Ashm. (1652) 121 That never my lyvying be to thee dysplycable.

†'**displicence.** *Obs.* [ad. L. *displicentia* displeasure, f. *displicēre* to DISPLEASE. Cf. the earlier DISPLACENCE.]

Displeasure, dissatisfaction.

1605 BELL *Motives conc. Romish Faith* 102 Durand saieth, the faulte is remitted in purgatorie, for the displicence of venials, which the soules haue in that place. **1648** W. MOUNTAGUE *Devout Ess.* I. ii. §2 (R.), Put on a serious displicence..that they may not incurre this menace of Christ, 'Woe be unto you that laugh now'. **1680** BAXTER *Cath. Commun.* (1684) 16 Complacence is the first act of the will upon God as Good..Displicence is its contrary, and its object is Evil as Evil. **1736** H. COVENTRY *Philem. to Hyd.* (T.), Devotion towards heaven, and a general displicence and peevishness towards every thing besides.

displicency ('dɪsplɪsənsɪ). [f. as prec. + -ENCY.] The fact or condition of being displeased or dissatisfied; = DISPLACENCY. ***self-displicency***: the condition of being dissatisfied with oneself.

1640 BP. REYNOLDS *Passions* xxxi. 320 A selfe-displicency and severity towards our owne Errours. **1680** BAXTER *Cath. Commun.* (1684) 20 Aquinas, Scotus, Ockam, Durandus.. commonly ascribed Displicency, as well as Complacence to God. **1745** J. MASON *Self-Knowl.* I. xvi. (1853) 119 Complacency and Displicency in reference to the Objects of the Mind. **1816** BP. J. JEBB *Let.* in *Life* lii. 523 It is not without self-displicency, and self-accusation, that I look upon..your letter. **1886** J. WARD in *Encycl. Brit.* XX. 70/2 (*Psychology*) The like holds where self-complacency or displicency rests on a sense of personal worth or on the honour or affection of others.

'**displiment.** *nonce-wd.* [from *compliment*: cf. DIS- 9.] An uncomplimentary speech.

1868 HELPS *Realmah* xvii, It was a high compliment: delicately veiled..All my displiments (if I may coin a word for the occasion) are (when unmasked) highly complimentary.

displing, *vbl. sb.* and *ppl. a.*: see DISPLE.

†**di'splode**, *v. Obs.* [ad. L. *displōd-ĕre* to burst asunder, f. DIS- 1 + *plaudĕre* to clap.] **a.** *trans.* To drive out or discharge with explosive violence. **b.** *intr.* To burst with a noise; to explode. Hence **di'sploded, di'sploding** *ppl. adjs.*

1667 MILTON *P.L.* VI. 605 Rankt..In posture to displode thir second tire Of Thunder. **1704** SWIFT *T. Tub* viii. (1709) 97 Fetching it..in certain bladders, and disploding it among the sectaries in all nations. **1708** J. PHILIPS *Cyder* I. 13 More dismal than the loud disploded Roar Of brazen Enginry. **1742** YOUNG *Nt. Th.* VI. 488 Like rubbish from disploding engines thrown, Our magazines of hoarded trifles fly. **1812** F. JEFFREY in *Edin. Rev.* Nov. 332 The pent-up vapours disploded with the force of an earthquake.

†**di'splosion.** *Obs.* [n. of action f. L. *displōdĕre*, *displōs-* to DISPLODE; cf. EXPLOSION.] The action of disploding; explosive discharge.

1656 BLOUNT *Glossogr.*, *Displosion*, a breaking asunder as a bladder. **1666** G. HARVEY *Morb. Angl.* iv. 32 That impetuous displosion of blood to a great distance. **1715-20** POPE *Iliad* XVI. 904 *note* (Seager) After the displosion of their diabolical enginry. **1742** YOUNG *Nt. Th.* IX. 793 As when whole magazines, at once, are fir'd..The vast displosion dissipates the clouds. **1790** H. BOYD *Ruins of Athens*, With horrible displosion doom'd to shake The thrones of Elam.

†**di'splosive**, *a. Obs.* [f. as prec. + -IVE; cf. EXPLOSIVE.] That pertains to displosion or explosive discharge; eruptive.

1711 DERHAM in *Phil. Trans.* XXVII. 276 Smoaking, Displosive..Matter, that causeth a new Eruption.

†**dis'plot**, *v. Obs.* [DIS- 6 or 7.] **a.** *intr.* To undo a plot or plan. **b.** *trans.* To disarrange.

1600 ABP. ABBOT *Exp. Jonah* 592 Which of these had not much leifer that all the state should be troubled, than his haire be displotted. **1683** CHALKHILL *Thealma & Cl.* 29 Still his working brain Plots and displots, thinks and unthinks again.

displume (dɪs'pluːm), *v.* [f. DIS- 7a + PLUME *sb.*; but in Caxton prob. ad. obs. F. *desplumer* 'to plume or deprive of feathers' (Cotgr.).]

†**1.** *trans.* Of birds: To cast (their feathers); to moult. *Obs.*

1480 CAXTON *Ovid's Met.* XI. i, Lyke as the fowles dysplume theyr fethers and the trees theyr levys.

2. To strip of plumes; = DEPLUME 1.

1623 tr. *Favine's Theat. Hon.* II. i. 63 Desirous to displume the great Romanic Eagle. **1871** SWINBURNE *Songs bef. Sunrise*, Wastes where the wind's wings break Displumed by daylong ache And anguish of blind snows.

b. *transf.* and *fig.* = DEPLUME 2.

1606 SYLVESTER *Du Bartas* II. iv. I. *Trophies* 1347 Humblenes may flaring Pride displume. **1614** JACKSON *Creed* III. To Rdr. A vj a, Academicall wits might displume them of these figge-tree leaues and manifest their nakednes to the world. **1856** R. A. VAUGHAN *Mystics* (1860) II. x. ii. 196 Fénélon, so pitiably displumed of all his shining virtues.

Hence **dis'plumed** *ppl. a.*

1660 F. BROOKE tr. *Le Blanc's Trav.* 250 Abundance of tame ducks, and a number of displumed geese. **1814** W. TAYLOR in *Monthly Mag.* XXXVIII. 440 A helmet displumed overshades his gray hair. **1827** SOUTHEY in *Q. Rev.* XXXV. 139 His companion..reported the vanquished and displumed condor to be still alive. **1883** STEVENSON *Silverado Sq.* (1886) 5 The displumed hills stood clear against the sky.

dispnœa: see DYSPNŒA.

dispoil(e, obs. form of DESPOIL.

†**di'spoint**, *v.*[1] *Obs.* Also 5 des-, 5-6 dis-, dyspoynt. [a. OF. *despointier*, *-pointer* (14th c. in Godef.), f. *des-*, DIS- 4 + *-pointier* in *apointier* to APPOINT; cf. obs. It. *dispontare*, *dispuntare* to disappoint (Florio).]

1. *trans.* To dismiss (from an appointment), discard; to deprive *of*. [OF. *despointer de.*]

1483 CAXTON *Gold. Leg.* 171 b/1 Flaccus seyng hymself dyspoynted and mocked torned hymself. **1489** —— *Faytes of A.* III. v. 175 Thoo that faille theyre lorde in thys behalffe ought to be dyspoynted of the landes that they soo holde.

2. To disappoint, balk. Const. *of.*

1494 FABYAN *Chron.* V. ciii. 78 Cramyrus was thus dispoynted of the ayde of Conobalde. **1530** PALSGR. 521/1, I dispoynt, or hynder him of his purpose, or I breake a poyntement with a person. **1534** MORE *Treat. Passion* Wks. 1313/1 Who so for goddes sake is contente to lacke an howse, shall not be dyspoynted when they shoulde nede it. **1535** COVERDALE *Ps.* xvi[i]. 13 Vp Lorde, dispoynte him & cast him downe. **1565** GOLDING *Ovid's Met.* XI. (1567) 136 a, But Phebus streyght preuenting yᵉ same thing, Dispoynts the Serpent of his bit, and turnes him into stone.

dis'point, *v.*[2] *rare.* [f. DIS- 7a + POINT *sb.* Cf. obs. It. *dispuntare*, mod. *spuntare*, Sp. *despuntar* to take off the point.] To deprive of the point.

? **1611** SYLVESTER *Du Bartas* II. iv. IV. *Decay* 905 His hooks dispointed disappoint his haste.

†**di'spointment.** *Obs. rare.* In 5 des-. [a. OF. *despointement* (15th c. in Godef.): see DISPOINT *v.*[1] and -MENT.] Deprivation of or dismissal from appointment or office.

1484 CAXTON *Curiall* 5 They..that ben hyest enhaunsed ben after theyr despoyntement as a spectacle of enuye.

dispoliate, -ation, var. ff. DESPOLIATE, etc.

dispo'llute, *v. rare.* [DIS- 6.] *trans.* To free from pollution.

1862 *Sat. Rev.* XIV. 537/2 The Thames—to use their own recondite word—is not 'dispolluted'. **1868** *Standard* 21 Mar. 5/1 To combine the whole drainage system of London, so as to dispollute the Thames.

dispond: see DESPOND.

dispondee (daɪ'spɒndiː). *Pros.* [ad. L. *dispondēus*, Gr. διςπόνδειος, f. DI-[2] + σπονδεῖος SPONDEE. (Also used in L. form.)] A double spondee.

1706 PHILLIPS (ed. Kersey), *Dispondæus* (in *Grammar*), a double Spondee, a Foot in Greek or Latin Verse consisting of Four long Sylables; as ōrātōrēs. **1740** DYCHE & PARDON, *Dispondee*, in Latin Poetry, a foot consisting of four long syllables, or two spondees. **1870** LOWELL *Study Wind.* (1886) 241 One has no patience with the dispondæuses, the pæon primuses.

Hence **dispon'daic** *a.*, of or pertaining to a dispondee: cf. SPONDAIC.

In recent Dicts.

dispone (dɪ'spəʊn), *v.* Chiefly *Sc. Obs.* exc. in legal sense 4. Also 5 des-, dyspone, dispoyn, 6 disponde. [ad. L. *dispōnĕre* to set in different places, place here and there, arrange, dispose, f. DIS- 1 + *pōnĕre* to place: cf. rare OF. *disponer* (Godef.). *Dispoyn* and *disponde* were dialectal variants, the latter possibly from OF. *despondre*. The Latin verb exists in It. as *disponere*, *disporre*, in Sp. *disponer*, Pg. *despor*, and survived in OF. *despondre*. The latter was supplanted by *desposer*, *disposer*, as shown under DISPOSE. *Disponer* was a learned adaptation of *disponĕre*.]

†**1.** *trans.* To set in order, arrange, dispose. *Obs.*

c **1374** CHAUCER *Troylus* IV. 936 (964) God seth euery þing ..And hem desponeth, þourgh his ordenaunce. **1375** BARBOUR *Bruce* XI. 29 God..disponis at his liking, Efter his ordinanss, all thyng. **1533** GAU *Richt Vay* (1888) 90 Lat vsz thank thy godlie wil quhilk disponis althing to our guid. **1558-68** WARDE tr. *Alexis' Secr.* 101 b, Putte it, and dispone it, in a panne or scillet, upon sifted ashes. **1588** A. KING tr. *Canisius' Catech.* 107 Yᵉ clerks..to assist yᵉ priests..to dispone yᵉ people resorting to yᵉ haly mysteries.

†**2.** To dispose physically or mentally *to* or *for* (something); to incline. *Obs.*

c **1425** WYNTOUN *Cron.* IX. xxvii. 328 As he dysponit hym for that. *a* **1510** DOUGLAS *K. Hart* II. 58 Than ȝouthheid said..dispone ȝow with me ryde. **1553** Q. KENNEDY *Compend. Tract.* in *Wodrow Soc. Misc.* (1844) 144 The Spirite of God, disponand every gude Christin man to be the mair able to keip the law of God. **1613** M. RIDLEY *Magn. Bodies* 12 The Magneticall Inclinatory-needle..is conformed and disponed unto the Axis of the Earth.

†**3.** To dispose of, give away, distribute. *Obs.*

(In the form *dispond* there is perh. confusion with *dispend.*)

1429 *Wills & Inv. N.C.* (Surtees 1835) 80 All yees goodes and parcelles aforesaid I wyll my son doo and dispoyn as he wol answer afore god. *c* **1500** *Lancelot* 1774 His gudis al for to dispone also In his seruice. **1545** *Wills & Inv. N.C.* (1835) 113 Qwhom I mayke my Executoure to dispone and ordane all thynges for the healthe of my soulle. **1580** *Ibid.* 432 My goodes I will that it be disponded Amongeste yowe thre.

†**b.** To expend, lay out (*upon* some object).

1570 BP. OF ROSS in Robertson *Hist. Scotl.* App. 67 The sums you writ for, to be disponit upon the furnishing of the Castle of Edinburgh.

4. *Sc. Law.* To make over, convey, assign, grant, officially or in legal form.

a **1555** LYNDESAY *Tragedy* 348 Imprudent Prencis.. Quhilk doith dispone all office spirituall. **1560** in Tytler *Hist. Scot.* (1864) III. 397 The duke's grace..is already disponing to sundry men certain rowmes in these north parts. **1639** MRQ. HAMILTON *Explan. Meaning Oath* 16 All bishopricks vaicking..shall be only disponed to actuall preachers and ministers in the kirk. **1721** *Wodrow Corr.* (1843) II. 577 The person who disponed the ground not being able to make his right to it good. **1832** AUSTIN *Jurispr.* (1879) II. li. 864 It is of the essence of property that the person presently entitled may dispone the property. **1861** W. BELL *Dict. Law Scot.* 292 The disponer or maker of the deed 'sells and dispones', or where the deed is gratuitous, 'gives, grants, and dispones', the subject of the deed to the receiver, who is technically called the disponee.

†**5.** *intr.* or *absol.* To order matters, arrange, make disposition or arrangement. *Obs.*

c **1500** *Lancelot* 1590 This maister saith, 'How lykith god dispone!' **1508** DUNBAR *Poems* iv. 98 Sen for the deid remeid is non, Best is that we for dede [*i.e.* death] dispone. **1500-20** *Ibid.* xxxvi. 13 Quhill thow hes space se thow dispone.. Thyne awin gud spend quhill thow hes space. *a* **1605**

MONTGOMERIE *Misc. Poems* xxxiv. 36 All lyes into ȝour will, As ȝe list to dispone.

†**6.** *intr.* with *of* (*on, upon*): To dispose of, deal with. *Obs.*

a. *c* **1374** CHAUCER *Troylus* v. 300 Of my moeble þow dispone Right as þe semeth best is for to done. **1535** STEWART *Cron. Scot.* III. 14 Of his tua sisteris first he wald dispone. *c* **1565** LINDESAY (Pitscottie) *Chron. Scot.* (1768) 120 (Jam.) No casualty could fall to the King in Scotland but was disponed of by the advice of Cochran.

b. **1546** *Sc. Acts Mary* (1814) 474 (Jam.) It is vncertane how thai will dispone vpoun him, and quether thai will let him to liberte or nocht. **1639** J. CORBET *Ungirding Scott. Arm.* 16 Yow spair not.. to.. dispone upon the Kings forts and castles, as you think good. **1818** SCOTT *Br. Lamm.* v, The Laird of Bucklaw's fine to be disponed upon. **1820** —— *Monast.* xxxiii, To dispone upon the goods.

Hence **di'sponed** *ppl. a.*, assinged, conveyed, made over; **di'sponing** *vbl. sb.*, disposing.

1564 J. RASTELL *Confut. Jewell's Serm.* 114 b, The makyng or disponing of any creature. **1823** BROWN *Hist. Brit. Churhes* I. iii. 72 These or higher superiors might seize on said disponed houses or lands for themselves.

disponee (dɪˌspəʊˈniː). *Sc. Law.* [f. prec. + -EE.] The person to whom property is conveyed.

1746–7 *Act 20 Geo. II.* c. 50. §12 A procuratory of resignation in favour of such purchaser or disponee. **1773** ERSKINE *Inst. Law Scotl.* II. vii. §3 (Jam.) Such right, after it is acquired by the disponer himself, ought not to hurt the disponee. **1863** PATERSON *Hist. Ayr* II. 771 He purchased the regality of Failfoord from the disponees of Sir Thomas Wallace Dunlop.

disponent (dɪˈspəʊnənt), *a.* [ad. L. *dispōnentem*, pr. pple. of *dispōnĕre*: see DISPONE.] Disposing; inclining in a certain direction, or towards a particular end.

1613 M. RIDLEY *Magn. Bodies* 36 The disponent vertue of the Magneticall globe of the Earth. **1635** SWAN *Spec. M.* vi. §2 (1643) 197 The sunne is a disponent, though not a productive cause of this saltnesse [of the sea]. **1846** SIR W. HAMILTON *Diss.* in *Reid's Wks.* 771 Its exciting, disponent.. cause.

disponer (dɪˈspəʊnə(r)). *Sc.* [f. DISPONE *v.*]

†**1.** One who disposes or arranges. *Obs.*

1553 Q. KENNEDY *Compend. Tract.* in *Wodrow Soc. Misc.* (1844) 151 The procuraris, disponaris and upsteraris of sick monsterus farssis.

2. The person who conveys or makes over property.

a **1662** D. DICKSON *Pract. Writ.* (1845) I. 229 The disponer of the inheritance. **1773** [see DISPONEE]. **1814** SCOTT *Wav.* x, He possessed himself of the estate.. to the prejudice of the disponer's own flesh and blood. **1868** *Act 31–32 Vict.* c. 101. §8 All unrecorded conveyances to which the disponer has right.

disponge, var. form of DISPUNGE.

disponible (dɪˈspəʊnɪb(ə)l); freq. as Fr. (dispɔnibl), *a.* (and *sb.*) [f. L. *dispōn-ĕre* to DISPONE + -BLE; Cf. F. *disponible.*] Capable of being disponed or assigned. Also *absol.* as *sb.*

1899 G. MEREDITH *Let.* 31 May (1970) III. 1328 You are more disponible and should decide to come to your friend. **1908** H. JAMES *Novels & Tales* III. p. vii, He [*sc.* Turgenev] saw them, in that fashion, as *disponibles*, saw them subject to the chances, the complications of existence. *Ibid.* V. p. xviii, That extremely *disponible* figure of Christina Light whom I had ten years before found left on my hands at the conclusion of 'Roderick Hudson'. **1912** CONRAD *'Twixt Land & Sea* (1914) I. 11 He gave me the names of all the disponible ships with their tonnage and the names of their commanders. **1961** R. C. KNIGHT tr. *Bonnard's Gr. Civ.* III. i. 17 Euripides is open to every interest of mankind... [He] is always disponible... He does not know how to forget his feelings and efface their expression, when any situation touches him too deeply. **1965** *Punch* 24 Mar. 447/3 One's picture of the higher civil servant—adroit, informed, *disponible*, never in the way or out of it.

So **disponi'bility**, capability of being disponed; condition of being at one's disposal.

1862 *Times* 6 Feb. 8/2 We are glad to have a Government in disponibility as well as one actually at work.

dispope (dɪsˈpəʊp), *v.* [DIS- 7 b. Cf. med.L. *dispāpāre.*] *trans.* To deprive of the popedom.

1622 H. SYDENHAM *Serm. Sol. Occ.* (1637) 298 Whilst they endeavour to dis-pope her they would un-bishop all Christendom. **1855** MILMAN *Lat. Chr.* III. 266 Albert was chosen Pope and 'dispoped' in the same day (Muratori says *dispapato*). **1877** TENNYSON *Harold* III. i. 70, I had my Canterbury pallium From one whom they dispoped.

dis'popularize, *v. rare.* [DIS- 6; cf. F. *dépopulariser.*] *trans.* To deprive of popularity.

1803 W. TAYLOR in *Ann. Rev.* I. 301 A secret disposition.. to thwart and dispopularize these ministers.

†**dis'populate**, *v. Obs. rare.* [DIS- 6.] = DEPOPULATE.

1588 R. PARKE tr. *Mendoza's Hist. China* 198 Leauing it [the Cittie] beaten downe and dispopulated.

†**dispopu'losity.** *Obs. rare.* [DIS- 9.] Unpopulous condition.

1632 LITHGOW *Trav.* IV. 166 There is another reason of the dispopulosity of these parts.

disport (dɪˈspɔət), *sb. arch.* Also 4–5 des-, 5 dys-. [a. AF. *disport*, OF. *desport*, commonly *deport* 'disport, sport, pastime, recreation, pleasure' (Cotgr.), f. *desporter*: see next. For sense 5, cf. DEPORT *sb.*]

1. Diversion from serious duties; relaxation, recreation; entertainment, amusement. *arch.*

1303 R. BRUNNE *Handl. Synne* 4110 And come to hym on hys dysport To make Florens gode cumfort. **1375** BARBOUR *Bruce* III. 586 Wes nane that euir disport mycht have Fra steryng, and fra rowyng. *c* **1386** CHAUCER *Man of Law's T.* 45 To Rome for to wende, Were it for chapmanhode or for disport. —— *Merch. T.* 680 Dooth hym disport, he is a gentil man. *c* **1400** MAUNDEV. (1839) xxii. 242 He takeþ his desport passing be the contree. **1483** CAXTON *Gold. Leg.* 433 b/1 Prayed.. that she myght haue.. hir suster wyth hir for hir dysporte, comforte and companye. **1502** *Priv. Purse Exp. Eliz. of York* (1830) 84 Item to the Quenes grace.. for hure disporte at cardes this Crismas.. C s. **1603** KNOLLES *Hist. Turks* (1621) 30 One day for his disport, hunting of the wild boare. **1728** POPE *Dunc.* II. Argt., The Goddess is first pleased for her disport to propose games to the Booksellers. **1820** SCOTT *Ivanhoe* xvii, I would find myself both disport and plenty out of the King's deer. **1881** ROSSETTI *Ball. & Sonn.* 117 The King and all his Court Were met.. for solace and disport.

2. Anything which affords diversion and entertainment; a pastime, game, sport. *arch.*

c **1380** *Sir Ferumb.* 2217 Tel me furst by þy lay; wat doþ ȝour men of fraunce; Of hure disport & ek hure play. *c* **1400** MAUNDEV. (1839) iii. 17 A fair place for justynges or for other Pleyes and desportes. **1576** FLEMING *Caius' Eng. Dogs* ii. in Arb. *Garner* III. 246 Dogs serving the disport of Fowling. **1604** SHAKS. *Oth.* I. iii. 272 That my Disports corrupt, and taint my businesse. **1654** GATAKER *Disc. Apol.* 20 Libertie, for some Disports that might be used on the Sabbath. **1690** E. GEE *Jesuit's Mem.* 126 Some honest kind of Disports. **1861** *Our Eng. Home* 21 The display of those pageants and disports which enlivened the repast.

†**3.** Merriment, mirth, fun. *Obs.*

c **1386** CHAUCER *Prol.* 138 Sikerly she was of greet desport, And ful plesaunt, and amyable of port. **1659** HEYLIN *Animadv.* in *Fuller's Appeal* (1840) 321 It was.. a matter of no mean disport amongst the people for a long time after. **1720** GAY *Poems* (1745) I. 117 They.. in disport surround the drunken wight. **1801** STRUTT *Sports & Past.* III. vi. 220 To the great amusement and disport of the polite spectators.

†**4.** The making sport *of. Obs. rare.*

1667 WATERHOUSE *Fire Lond.* 159 King Sesostrio.. caused four captive Kings to draw his Coach.. he prided his inconstant Fortune, in the desport of their Vassalage.

†**5.** Bearing, carriage, deportment. *Obs. rare.*

1761 STERNE *Tr. Shandy* IV. xxii, I carried myself.. in such fanciful guise of careless disport, that right sore am I ashamed now.

disport (dɪˈspɔət), *v.* Forms: 4–5 desporte, 5–6 dys-, 5– dis-. [a. AF. *desporter* (Bozon), OF. *desporter, depporter*, usually *deporter*, to divert, amuse, please (Godef.); *refl.* 'to cease, forbeare, leaue off, giue ouer: also to disport, play, recreate himselfe, passe away the time' (Cotgr.); f. *des-*, DIS- 1 + *porter*:—L. *portāre* to carry, bear. For the sense 'divert, amuse', cf. the similar development of F. *divertir, déduire*, the notion being that of turning, leading, or carrying away the attention from serious or sad occupations.]

†**1.** *trans.* To divert (from sadness, ennui, or the like); to amuse, to entertain. *Obs.*

c **1374** CHAUCER *Troylus* IV. 696 (724) þey gonnen here comforten.. And with here tales wenden here disporten. **1393** GOWER *Conf.* I. 75 Tho was þis wofull wif conforted Be alle weies and desported. *c* **1430** LYDG. *Min. Poems* 15 Pip[in]s, quinces, blaunderelle to disport, And the pomecedre corageos to recomfort. **1638** SIR T. HERBERT *Trav.* (ed. 2) 275 Hee forces Barames to weare womens apparell, and with a Distaffe in's hand to disport the insulting multitude. **1665** *Ibid.* (1677) 12 Well I remember that all the way we sail'd.. we were disported by Whales.

2. *refl.* ***to disport oneself***: to cheer, divert, amuse, or enjoy oneself; to occupy oneself pleasurably; now *esp.* to play wantonly, frolic, gambol, sport; to display oneself sportively.

c **1385** CHAUCER *L.G.W.* 1441 *Hipsiph. & Medea* (Camb. MS.), To saylyn to that lond hym to disporte. *c* **1400** MAUNDEV. (Roxb.) xxxiv. 154 þare in will he sitt.. for to disporte him and take þe aer. **1530** PALSGR. 521/1 Go disporte you with them, they be good felowes. **1593** SHAKS. *3 Hen. VI*, IV. v. 8 He hath.. attended with weake guard, Come hunting this way to disport himselfe. *a* **1649** DRUMM. OF HAWTH. *Hist. Jas. V.* Wks. (1711) 104 Whilst he disported himself at the court of France. **1742** WARBURTON *Comm. Pope's Ess. Man* Wks. 1811 XI. 142 After having disported himself at will, in the flowery paths of fancy. **1879** BEERBOHM *Patagonia* 9 Seabirds were disporting themselves in the water. **1887** BOWEN *Virg. Eclog.* VI. 2 My Muse in Sicilian measure was well Pleased to disport her.

3. *intr.* (for *refl.*) = prec.

1480 CAXTON *Chron. Eng.* ccxliii. (1482) 287 The emperour.. come in to englond to kyng Henry with hym to speke and to disporte. **1591** SPENSER *Daphn.* 118, I her caught disporting on the greene. **1600** J. PORY tr. *Leo's Africa* II. 157 Every man runs to the taverne to disport.. and to bee drunken. **1712–14** POPE *Rape Lock* II. 66 Where light disports in ever-mingling dyes. **1809** CAMPBELL *Gertr. Wyom.* I. iii, The flamingo.. disporting like a meteor on the lakes. **1847** J. WILSON *Chr. North* (1857) II. 21 See the cubs disporting at the mouth of the briery aperture.

†**4.** ? To deport oneself. *Obs. rare.*

c **1450** LONELICH *Grail* xxxvi. 281 At themperours table Iset he was, and there disported hym al that day As a man that In letargye lay.

†**5.** *trans.* ? To divert, or turn away. *Obs. rare.*

1450 *Paston Lett.* No. 122. I. 163 The day of oier and termyner shall holde at Norwich on Moneday next comyng, and by that cause my Lord of Oxenford shall be disported of his comyng to the Parlement.

†**disportation.** *Obs. rare.* [f. DIS- 1 + L. *portāre* to carry; see -ATION.] The action of carrying away or in different directions.

1622 MALYNES *Anc. Law-Merch.* 413 Merchants cannot enter into consideration of the quantitie of forreine commodities imported at deere rates, and the natiue commodities at lesser rates exported,.. by the disportation whereof, commeth an euident ouerballancing of commodities.

†**di'sporter.** *Obs.* [f. DISPORT *v.* + -ER[1].] One who makes sport or jests; a jester, juggler.

1432–50 tr. *Higden* (Rolls) IV. 31 Bledgarec.. callede god of disporters [Higden *deus joculatorum*].

Hence †**di'sporteress**, *Obs.*, a female jester.

c **1430** *Pilgr. Lyf Manhode* IV. xxxvi. (1869) 194, I thouhte she was a jowgleresse and a disporteresse to folk.

di'sporting, *vbl. sb.* [f. DISPORT *v.* + -ING[1].] The action of the verb DISPORT; diversion, amusement; sportive action, gambolling.

1561 T. HOBY tr. *Castiglione's Courtyer* I. B, Their accustomed trade of disportinge and ordinary recreations. **1593** T. WATSON *Tears of Fancie* xxvi. Poems (Arb.) 191 It pleasd my Mistris once to take the aire Amid the vale of loue for her disporting. **1809** W. IRVING *Knickerb.* II. iv. (1849) 102, I must fain resign all poetic disportings of the fancy. **1887** L. OLIPHANT *Episodes* 149 The clumsy disportings of a baby elephant.

[**disporting** (R., from Prynne), misprint of *dispoiling*, DESPOILING in Act 1 Hen. VII. c. 6.]

di'sportive, *a. rare.* [f. DISPORT *v.* + -IVE; cf. *sportive.*] Inclined to disport; sportive. Hence **di'sportively** *adv.*, in sport.

1773 J. ROSS *Fratricide* I. 739 (MS.) Abel to him calls The sons of Cain disportive from his side. **1793** J. WILLIAMS *Auth. Mem. Warren Hastings* 48 Nero disportively made Innocence and Merit bleed. **1810** *Morning Herald* 30 Apr., Tinting the cheeks of their royal brethren, disportively, as they passed. **1813** T. BUSBY *Lucretius* II. 353 The fleecy breed.. on the joyous grass disportive feed.

di'sportment. [f. as prec. + -MENT.] Diversion, amusement; = DISPORT *sb.*

1660 H. MORE *Myst. Godl.* 81 With their obscene gestures and meretricious disportments. *Ibid.* 150 The enjoyment of those disportments and pleasures. **1894** *National Observer* 13 Jan. 221/1 The old-style novelist plunged into a Bohemia of love and debt and disportment.

disposa'bility. [f. next + -ITY.] The quality of being disposable; ability to be disposed of.

1830 *Examiner* 67/1 The disposibility of the person by Government has obviously been the only point considered. **1833** *Fraser's Mag.* VII. 655 What can bring back the command and disposability of back-rents, while the present national debt remains. **1858** J. MARTINEAU *Stud. Chr.* 352 The ultimate security—on whose disposability in the last resort.. the very existence of Society depends.

disposable (dɪsˈpəʊzəb(ə)l), *a.* Also 7 disposible, 8–9 disposeable. [f. DISPOSE *v.* + -ABLE.]

1. Capable of being disposed or inclined; inclinable (*to* something). *rare.*

1652 GAULE *Magastrom.* 113 That the pupill be naturally inclined to the art, or easily disposible thereto. **1880** [implied in DISPOSABLENESS: see below].

2. a. Capable of being disposed of; that may be got rid of, made over, or dealt with in some way; capable of being put to some use, available; at (some one's) disposal.

1643 PRYNNE *Treachery & Disloyalty, etc.* v. 85 (R.) Most of the great officers.. are hereditary, and not disposable by the king. *a* **1679** T. GOODWIN *Wks.* II. IV. 124 (R.) His own mercy and grace.. the riches thereof are disposable no way but to the use and benefit of creatures. **1796** BURKE *Regic. Peace* II. Wks. VIII. 252 The great riches.. easily afforded a disposeable surplus. **1812** WELLINGTON *Disp.* 26 Oct. in *Examiner* 23 Nov. 740/2 A very large proportion.. would be disposable for service. **1856** MASSON *Ess., Story of 1770*, 233 They were more disposable as literary ware. **1886** *Law Rep.* 31 Ch. Div. 276 There must be some disposable property under the settlement.

b. ***disposable income*** (see quots.).

1948 in *Amer. Speech* (1951) XXVI. 292/2 'Disposable income', then, represents the money actually available for consuming power, for savings and for investments. **1950** T. H. MARSHALL *Citizenship & Social Class* 49 Those whose disposable income and capital do not exceed £420 and £500 respectively. 'Disposable' means the balance after considerable deductions have been allowed for dependants, rent, ownership of house and tools, and so forth. **1971** *Daily Tel.* 23 July 17 Savings have been running at 9¼ p.c. of total personal disposable income.

3. Applied to an article designed to be thrown away after one use. Hence *absol.* as *sb.*

1943 L. E. HOLT *Care & Feeding of Children* (ed. 16) I. 5 The disposable paper diapers are a great convenience and involve relatively little expense. **1951** A. A. WOODMAN *Sunday Express Baby Bk.* iii. 34/1 There are several brands of disposable napkins. **1960** *Which?* Apr. 81/2 It [*sc.* a vacuum cleaner].. could only be used with disposable dust bags. **1965** *Nursing Times* 5 Feb. 181/2 Wall cupboards for the storage of disposables had also been installed. **1965** *Sunday Times* (Colour Suppl.) 25 July 8/1 A lot of ward equipment is disposable now—things like catheters or blood drips.. Bed pans and bottles are made of papier maché, to be disposable. **1970** *Guardian* 9 Apr. 11/2 Visitors to the Design Centre's exhibition of disposables..have been getting..steamed up about its implied refuse problems.

Hence **di'sposableness**.

1880 H. MACMILLAN in *Sund. Mag.* Mar. 173 A disposableness of mind which fits us to take part in any duty.

disposal (dɪ'spəʊzəl). [f. DISPOSE *v.* + -AL[1] 5.] The act or faculty of disposing, in various senses.

†**1.** The action of arranging, ordering, or regulating by right of power or possession; control, direction, management; *esp.* Divine control of the course of events; ordinance, appointment, dispensation; = DISPOSITION 3. *Obs.*

1648 MILTON *Tenure Kings* (1650) 3 God, out of his providence and high disposal. **1671** —— *Samson* 210 Tax not divine disposal. **1696** WHISTON *Th. Earth* (1722) 8 An unusual and miraculous disposal of things. **1710** M. HENRY *Comm. Eccl.* iii. 14 God changeth his disposals and yet is unchangeable in his Counsels.

2. The action of disposing of, putting away, getting rid of, settling, or definitely dealing with.

1648 GAGE *West Ind.* xiv. 93 A Letter which he had writ ..concerning the disposall of our persons. **1688** *Col. Rec. Pennsylv.* I. 235 Touching yᵉ Great Seals's Disposall in his absence. **1731** GAY *Let. to Swift* 11 Apr. in *Swift's Lett.* (1766) II. 125 Directions about the disposal of your money. **1869** E. A. PARKES *Pract. Hygiene* (ed. 3) 505 The disposal of the dead is always a question of difficulty. **1885** *Law Times* LXXX. 138/1 To devote about a week..at the end of each sitting to the disposal of these actions.

3. The action of bestowing, giving or making over; bestowal, assignment.

1660 F. BROOKE tr. *Le Blanc's Trav.* 265 To his second Son he had given the Seniory..with other subsequent disposals. **1727** POPE *Th. Var. Subj.* in *Swift's Wks.* (1755) II. I. 229 To use his credit in the disposal of an employment to a person..fittest for it. **1783** BURKE *Sp. E. India Bill* Wks. IV. 120 The disposal by parliament of any office derived from the authority of the crown.

b. Alienation, making over, or parting with, by sale or the like.

1697 DAMPIER *Voy.* I. 503 To sell some commodities, that he had not yet disposed of..He chose rather to leave the disposal of them to some Merchant there. **1845** STEPHEN *Laws Eng.* (1874) II. 44 The right of disposal is suspended. *a* **1855** MISS MITFORD in L'Estrange *Life* (1870) I. v. 118, I am happy that the speedy disposal of the pictures will enable you..to settle this unpleasant affair.

4. Power or right to dispose of, make use of, or deal with as one pleases; control, command, management: usually in phr. ***at* (*in*) *one's disposal*.**

1630 WADSWORTH *Pilgr.* viii. 82 My Father being dead, and I at my owne disposall. **1667** BP. S. PARKER *Censure Platon. Philos.* 7 Though the biggest portions of our felicity be at our own disposals. *a* **1698** TEMPLE *Ess., Diff. Cond. Life* Wks. 1731 I. 308 A Man in Publick Affairs, is like one at Sea; never in his own Disposal, but in that of Winds and Tides. **1711** STEELE *Spect.* No. 154 ¶3 A very pretty young Lady, in her own Disposal. **1767** BLACKSTONE *Comm.* II. 216 The lords, who had the disposal of these female heiresses in marriage. **1856** FROUDE *Hist. Eng.* (1858) I. i. 84 Sufficient funds having been..placed at the disposal of the Government.

5. Arrangement, placing in a particular order: = DISPOSITION 1.

1828 WEBSTER s.v. *Disposal*, This object was effected by the disposal of the troops in two lines. **1842** *Fraser's Mag.* XXVI. 472 The admirable disposal of the drapery. **1890** A. GISSING *Village Hampden* I. viii. 190 A very tasteful disposal about the granary of flowers..and evergreens.

dispose (dɪ'spəʊz), *v.* Also (5 dispoose, dispoyse); 5-6 dys-, 6-7 des-. [a. OF. *dispose-r*, rarely *desp-* (12-13th c. in Hatzf.), f. L. *dis-*, DIS- 1 + *poser* to place, lay down (see POSE, REPOSE); substituted for L. *dispōnĕre* (which came down in OF. as *despondre*: see DISPONE), by form-association with inflexions and derivatives of the latter, as *dispos*, *disposition*, etc. Cf. COMPOSE, DEPOSE.]

I. Transitive senses.

1. To place (things) at proper distances apart and in proper positions with regard to each other, to place suitably, adjust; to place or arrange in a particular order.

1387 TREVISA *Higden* (Rolls) I. 109 (Mätz.) Þe citee..is disposed þat þe water þat falleþ dounward..no fen makeþ and renneþ into cisternes. *c* **1391** CHAUCER *Astrol.* I. §21 The sterres..ben disposed in signis of bestes, or shape like bestes. **1548** HALL *Chron., Hen. VI* (an. 3) 87b, Or the Frenchmen had either desposed their garrison, or appoynted their lodgynges. **1576** FLEMING *Panopl. Epist.* 257 Directions and precepts, how you should order and dispose your studies. **1590** SPENSER *F.Q.* II. viii. 26 Words, well dispost, [*rimes* ghost, bost, most] Have secrete powre t' appease inflamed rage. **1628** SIR J. BEAUMONT *Bosworth F.* 659 This done, these valiant Knights dispose their Blades. **1628** T. SPENCER *Logick* 248 Precepts, which teach vs, to dispose arguments in a Syllogisme. **1695** WOODWARD *Nat. Hist. Earth* Pref., The said Terrestrial Matter is disposed into Strata or Layers. **1712** ADDISON *Spect.* No. 412 ¶7 The different Colours of a Picture, when they are well disposed, set off one another. **1777** W. DALRYMPLE *Trav. Sp. & Port.* xxvi, The town is situated on a rising ground and handsomely disposed. **1790** PALEY *Horæ Paul.* i. 7, I have disposed several instances of agreement under separate numbers. **1885** *Athenæum* 23 May 669/1 Verdurous masses of foliage and sward disposed with great simplicity and breadth.

b. To put into the proper or suitable place; to put away, stow away, deposit; to put (a number of things) each into the proper place, distribute. Now *rare*.

c **1420** *Pallad. on Husb.* VI. 206 The xxxth day x pounde hony dispose In it wel scommed first, and use it soo. **1574** tr. *Marlorat's Apocalips* 7 Seuerall Churches, which are disposed in euery towne & village, according as mans necessitie requireth. **1606** SHAKS. *Tr. & Cr.* IV. v. 116 His blowes are wel dispos'd there, Aiax. **1662** J. DAVIES tr. *Mandelslo's Trav.* 183 The Gold and Silver is lock'd up in Chests, and dispos'd into the Towers of the Castle. *Ibid.* 256 No man but hath at least two wives, but dispos'd into several huts. **1685** LUTTRELL *Brief Rel.* (1857) I. 356 His majesties standing forces..are disposed into severall parts of this Kingdom. **1725** POPE *Odyss.* XIII. 87 The chearful mates Safe in the hollow deck dispose the cates. **1834** MEDWIN *Angler in Wales* II. 258 A dying lamp was disposed in a niche of the wall.

†**c.** *gen.* To dispose of, deal with in any way.

1590 MARLOWE *2nd Pt. Tamburl.* IV. i, Then bring those Turkish harlots to my tent, And I'll dispose them as it likes me best.

†**d.** To place in a particular employment, situation or condition; to assign, appoint. *Obs.*

1579 LYLY *Euphues* (Arb.) 132 A gentleman that hath honest and discreet seruants dysposeth them to the encrease of his segnioryes, one he appointeth stewarde of his courtes, an other ouerseer of his landes. **1662** J. DAVIES tr. *Mandelslo's Trav.* 190 All the handsome young Damosels.. to be dispos'd into his Ladies service. **1697** DRYDEN *Virg. Georg.* III. 768 Ye Gods, to better Fate good Men dispose.

†**2.** To regulate or govern in an orderly way; to order, control, direct, manage, command. *Obs.*

1398 TREVISA *Barth. De P.R.* II. xviii. (1495) 42 Angels.. haue vnder theym the ordres of men, and ordeyne and dyspose theym. *c* **1430** LYDG. *Min. Poems* (1840) 149 (Mätz.) That Christ Jesus dispoose so the ballaunce, That Petris ship be with no tempest drownyd. **1530** PALSGR. 521/1, I wyll dispose this mater as I shall thynke best. **1581** SAVILE *Tacitus' Hist.* I. lxxvii. (1591) 43 Otho..disposed the affaires of the Empire. **1618** CHAPMAN *Hesiod's Georg.* I. 211 [They] were such great fools at that age [a hundred years] that they Could not themselves dispose a family. **1667** MILTON *P.L.* I. 246 Be it so, since hee Who now is Sovran can dispose and bid What shall be right. **1677** HALE *Prim. Orig. Man.* I. i. 34 A Regent Principle,..which may govern and dispose it as the Soul of Man doth his Body.

†**3.** To assign or deliver authoritatively. *Obs.*

1382 WYCLIF *Luke* xxii. 29 And I dispose to ȝou, as my fadir hath disposid to me, a rewme. **1548** UDALL, etc. *Erasm. Par. Matt.* i. 21 And I will dispose a newe testament to the house of Judas.

†**4.** To bestow, make over, hand over; to deal out, dispense, distribute; = *dispose of* (sense 8). *Obs.*

c **1430** LYDG. *Min. Poems* (1840) 20 (Mätz.) The wiche gyfte they goodly han disposed. **1463** *Bury Wills* (1850) 38 If only come ovir to dispose it in dedys of charite and almesse. **1530** PALSGR. 521/1, I dispose goodes to dyvers folkes, *je distribue*. **1623** WHITBOURNE *Newfoundland* 89 Hauing disposed away such fish and traine oyle as they take there in the Summer time unto merchants. **1679-88** *Secr. Serv. Money Chas. II & Jas. II* (Camden) 81 To the Bp. of London, to be by him disposed to the poor distressed inhabitants of the city..in respect of the extreme hard weather. **1681** R. SHELDON *Let.* in Wood *Life* (1848) 250 Her father hauing sent her two or three [copies] to dispose amongst her friends. **1710** HARLEY in Ellis *Orig. Lett.* Ser. II. IV. 263 The places will be speedily disposed, and the chiefest will fall to the share of the Duchess of Somerset. **1818** CRUISE *Digest* (ed. 2) IV. 243 The enjoyment during life, and the power of disposing to whatever person and in whatever manner she pleased.

5. To put into the proper frame or condition for some action or result; to make fit or ready; to fit, prepare (*to do*, or *to* or *for* something); *refl.* to prepare oneself, get ready, make preparation. *arch.*

c **1375** in *Rel. Ant.* I. 41 It techeth thee how thou schalt dispose the to the almaner of goode lyvynge. *c* **1386** CHAUCER *Friar's T.* 361 Disposeth ay youre hertes to withstonde The feend. *c* **1489** CAXTON *Blanchardyn* li. 196 Blanchardyn.. dysposed him self for to retourne ayen toward Tormaday. **1538** STARKEY *England* II. i. 161 Certayn remedys..wych.. schal meruelousely dyspose the partys also to receyue cure and remedy. **1576** FLEMING *Panopl. Epist.* 62 Therefore will we dispose our selves to suffer. **1629** A. BAKER in Ellis *Orig. Lett.* Ser. II. III. 257 That the prolonging of your daies maie be a meane to dispose you for the better departure, when it shall please God to call you. **1697** DRYDEN *Virg. Georg.* IV. 214 He knew For Fruit the grafted Pear-tree to dispose. **1815** W. TAYLOR in *Monthly Rev.* LXXVII. 513 Those missionaries who are disposing themselves to visit the Syrian churches. **1819** BYRON *Proph. Dante* II. 43 All things are disposing for thy doom.

†**b.** To make suitable, adapt, suit. *Obs.*

1602 MARSTON *Ant. & Mel.* Induct. Wks. 1856 I. 3, I but dispose my speach to the habit of my part. **1736** BUTLER *Anal.* II. Conclusion 410 Assistance, which nature enables, and disposes and appoints them to afford.

c. To bring into a particular physical or mental condition: in *pa. pple.*; see DISPOSED 2, 3.

6. To put into a favourable mood for (something); to give a tendency or inclination to; to incline, make prone (*to* something, or *to do* something).

a. To incline the mind or heart of; *pa. pple.* inclined: see DISPOSED 4. Also *absol.*

c **1340** [see DISPOSED 4]. *c* **1430** *Stans Puer 4* in *Babees Bk.* 27 Dispose þou þee aftir my doctryne To all nortur þi corage to encline. **1509** *Pater noster, Ave, & Creed* (W. de W.) A ij, A ryght profytable treatyse..to dyspose men to be vertuously occupyed in theyr myndes & prayers. **1653** MILTON *Hirelings* Wks. 1738 I. 562 Wherof I promis'd then to speak further, when I should find God disposing me, and opportunity inviting. **1735** BERKELEY *Def. Free-think. in Math.* §7 Wks. 1871 III. 305 Not that I imagine geometry disposeth men to infidelity. **1781** GIBBON *Decl. & F.* III. 51 The respectful attachment of the emperor for the orthodox clergy, had disposed him to love and admire the character of Ambrose. **1853** J. H. NEWMAN *Hist. Sk.* (1873) II. I. i. 29 Circumstances which could not favourably dispose the Hun to new overtures.

b. To impart a physical tendency or inclination to; *pa. pple.* inclined, liable: see DISPOSED 5. Also *absol.*

c **1380** [see DISPOSED 5]. *c* **1430** LYDG. *Min. Poems* (1840) 197 (Mätz.) Satourn disposith to malencolye. **1599** H. BUTTES *Dyets drie Dinner* F viij, In olde time they ate Lettuse after supper..to dispose them selves to sleepe. *a* **1682** SIR T. BROWNE *Tracts* (1684) 45 The great Mists and Dews..might dispose the Corn unto corruption. **1732** ARBUTHNOT *Rules of Diet* 291 Such a state disposeth the Humours of the Body to Heat. **1823** J. BADCOCK *Dom. Amusem.* 18 Smoke dissolves the gelatine, and disposes the meat to rancidity.

II. Intransitive senses.

7. To make arrangements; to determine or control the course of affairs or events; to ordain, appoint.

Esp. in proverb ***Man proposes, (but) God disposes*** [tr. 'Homo proponit, sed Deus disponit,' A Kempis *De Imitatione* I. xix.].

1382 WYCLIF *Acts* vii. 44 The tabernacle of witnessing was with oure fadris in desert, as God disposide to hem. **1388** —— *Rev.* Prol., Therfor God the Fadir..disposid with the Sone and the Hooli Goost to schewen hem, that me dredde hem the lesse. *a* **1400-50** *Alexander* 279 Hym..that shall best dispoyse for þe publyke wele. *c* **1450** tr. *De Imitatione* I. xix, Ffor man purposiþ & god disposiþ. *c* **1500** *Melusine* xxxvi. 265 As the wyse man saith, 'the fole proposeth & god dyspotheth'. **1548** HALL *Chron., Hen. V,* (an. 8) 70 To dispose for the nedes of the foresaied realme. **1634** SANDERSON *Serm.* II. 302 We have a proverb..'man purposeth, but God disposeth'. **1718** PRIOR *Power* 842 'Tis God who must dispose, and man sustain.

†**b.** To settle matters, make terms. *Obs.*

1606 SHAKS. *Ant. & Cl.* IV. xiv. 123 For when she saw.. you did suspect She had dispos'd with Cæsar, and that your rage Would not be purg'd, she sent you word she was dead.

8. dispose of (with indirect passive *to be disposed of*): †**a.** To make a disposition, ordering, or arrangement of; to do what one will with; to order, control, regulate, manage: = sense 2. *spec.* in *Astrol.* (see quot. 1819). *Obs.*

1566 GASCOIGNE, etc. *Jocasta* III. ii. in Child *Four Plays* (1848) 209 You may of me, as of your selfe dispose. **1582** N. LICHEFIELD tr. *Castanheda's Conq. E. Ind.* lxxiii. 151 From this time forward you may dispose of your selues, and do what you shall think best. **1599** SHAKS. *Hen. V,* III. iii. 49 Enter our Gates, dispose of vs and ours, For we no longer are defensible. **1648** *Bury Wills* (Camd.) 200 Not time to dispose of theire affaires. **1692** DRYDEN *St. Euremont's Ess.* 349 By this, Mistresses dispose of their Old Lovers to their Fancy, and Wives of their Old Husbands. **1819** J. WILSON *Compl. Dict. Astrol.* s.v., A planet disposes of any other which is in its house: thus, if ♄ were in ♐ he would be disposed of by ♃. In horary questions, it is a sign that the thing or person signified by the planet so disposed of, is in the power or interest of the planet (or those whom it signifies) that disposes of it.

b. To put or get (anything) off one's hands; to put away, stow away, put into a settled state or position; to deal with (a thing) definitely; to get rid of; to get done with, settle, finish. In recent use sometimes *spec.* to do away with, 'settle', or demolish (a claim, argument, opponent, etc.); also *humorously*, to make away with, consume (food).

1610 SHAKS. *Temp.* I. ii. 225 Of the Kings ship, The Marriners, say how thou hast disposd. **1632** J. HAYWARD tr. *Biondi's Eromena* 32 The King was..laid in his bed, so would the Ladies have likewise disposed of the Queene. **1666** PEPYS *Diary* 16 Aug., It was so pleasing a sight to see my papers disposed of. **1773** GOLDSM. *Stoops to Conq.* I, I'm disposing of the husband before I have secured the lover. **1841** JAMES *Brigand* xxvi, Bernard de Rohan must be met and disposed of at the sword's point. **1863** A. J. HORWOOD *Yearbks. 30-31 Edw. I* Pref. 10 The very words of the Judges in disposing of the cases are set down. **1867** FREEMAN *Norm. Conq.* (1876) I. iv. 253 Several daughters, who were of course well disposed of in marriage. **1873** TRISTRAM *Moab* x. 175 The discovery..seems to dispose of the claims of these Dhra's as to be Biblical sites. **1879** F. W. ROBINSON *Coward Consc.* II. vii, Tom disposed rapidly of two glasses of sherry and the..sandwiches. **1885** SIR R. BAGGALLAY in *Law Rep. 14 Q. Bench Div.* 879 The observations made by the Master of the Rolls sufficiently dispose of that contention. **1885** *Manch. Exam.* 10 July 5/1 The Northern team, batting first, were disposed of for 192.

c. To make over or part with by way of sale or bargain, sell.

1676 *Deed Trin. Coll.* in Willis & Clark *Cambridge* (1886) II. 521 It shalbe lawfull for..him..to dispose of the said two Chambers..to any other beside his kindred. **1704** MRS. RAY in *Lett. Lit. Men* (Camden) 207, I do intend to dispose of Mr. Ray's books. **1774** FOOTE *Cozeners* II. Wks. 1799 II. 173, I am to be disposed of by private contract. **1843** BORROW *Bible in Spain* 273 A large edition of the New Testament had been almost entirely disposed of in the very centre of Spain. **1891** *Law Times* XC. 283/1 The plaintiff was..in possession of two diamond rings which he wished to dispose of.

†**d.** To make fit or ready: = sense 5. *Obs.*

1655 FULLER *Waltham Abby* 13 He..acquainted him with his dying condition, to dispose of his soul for another world.

† **9. dispose upon** or **on**: to dispose of (see prec. b and c). *Sc. Obs.*

1632 LITHGOW *Trav.* IV. 166 The lands they..dispose upon to valerous Souldiers. **1639** DRUMM. OF HAWTH. *Answ. to Obj.* Wks. (1711) 214 To give up the person of their prince, to be disposed on as a stranger nation shall think convenient. **1640-1** *Kirkcudbr. War-Comm. Min. Bk.* (1855) 67 To use and dispose upon the tymber. **1778** W. ROBERTSONE *Let.* in J. Russell *Haigs* xii. (1881) 374 This visit will give you an opportunity to dispose upon oxen; if you have not already done it.

† **10. dispose with**: to dispose of (see 8 c). *Obs.*

1653 H. COGAN tr. *Pinto's Trav.* IV. 8 For his particular he had no power to dispose with any part of the booty.

di'spose, *sb. Obs.* or *arch.* [f. DISPOSE *v.*] The action or fact of disposing: in various senses.

† 1. Arrangement, order; = DISPOSITION 1. *Obs.*

1603 HOLLAND *Plutarch's Mor.* 646 He observed in all points a singular order and dispose.

† 2. The action of ordering; ordinance, appointment; direction, management: = DISPOSAL 1. *Obs.*

1611 SPEED *Hist. Gt. Brit.* VII. xxxi. §2 (R.), Such is the dispose of the sole disposer of empires, that they have their risings, their fuls, and their fals. **1671** MILTON *Samson* 1746 Oft we doubt What the unsearchable dispose Of Highest Wisdom brings about.

† 3. Power or right to dispose of something, or deal with it at one's will; control: = DISPOSAL 4. Esp. in phr. *at* (*in*, etc.) *one's dispose* (very common 1600–1730). *Obs.*

1590 SHAKS. *Com. Err.* I. i. 21 His goods confiscate to the Dukes dispose. **1594** MARLOWE & NASHE *Dido* v. ii, Ye gods, that..order all things at your high dispose. **1610** HOLLAND *Camden's Brit.* I. 325 He was under the dispose of the Generall of the Footemen. **1628** T. SPENCER *Logick* 219 Man is at Gods dispose, and all the other Creatures are at Gods, and mans. **1631** WEEVER *Anc. Fun. Mon.* 115 Left to the dispose and pleasure of the King. **1690** DRYDEN *Don Sebastian* v. Wks. 1883 VII. 450 His life's in my dispose. **1725** POPE *Odyss.* IV. 733 To Fate's supreme dispose the dead resign. **1741** RICHARDSON *Pamela* II. 209 Then you'll have some time at your own Dispose.

† 4. The action of bestowing, making over, or dealing out; bestowal, distribution: cf. DISPOSE *v.* 4, DISPOSAL 3. *Obs.*

1591 GREENE *Maiden's Dreame* Wks. 1881–3 XIV. 310 No man went emptie from his frank dispose, He was a purse bearer vnto the poore. **1606** HOLLAND *Sueton.* 261 What he thoght of the last dispose of the Provinces. **1673** MARVELL in *Collect. Poems* 249 Neglecting to call for any Account of the Dispose of the said Treasury.

† 5. Mental constitution or inclination; frame of mind; = DISPOSITION 6. *Obs.*

1606 SHAKS. *Tr. & Cr.* II. iii. 174 He.. carries on the streame of his dispose..In will peculiar, and in selfe admission. **1609** ROWLANDS *Knaue of Clubbes* 15 Meeting with one iust of his owne dispose, With him he plotted to escape his foes. **1628** LAUD *Wks.* (1847) I. 173 'Peace' stands for a quiet and calm dispose of the hearts of men.

b. External manner; air; pose. *rare.*

1601 ? MARSTON *Pasquil & Kath.* II. 105 More Musick's in thy name, and sweet dispose, Then in Apollos Lyre, or Orpheus Close. **1604** SHAKS. *Oth.* I. iii. 403 He hath a person, and a smooth dispose, To be suspected. **1875** BROWNING *Inn Album* 21 At the haught highbred bearing and dispose.

disposed (dɪ'spəʊzd), *ppl. a.* [f. vb. + -ED[1].]

1. Arranged, appointed, prepared, suitably placed, or situated, etc.: see DISPOSE *v.* 1, 5.

14.. LYDG. *Secrees* 423 Your dispoosyd fate. **1526** *Pilgr. Perf.* (W. de W. 1531) 73 In a prepared or disposed soule he maketh yᵉ fyrst beame of loue to shyne. **1658** BAXTER *Saving Faith* vi. 40 Adams soul was created in a Disposed or prepared Body. **1663** J. SPENCER *Prodigies* (1665) 73 The figure and glory of the Sun drawn by its own beams upon a disposed cloud. **1867** SMYTH *Sailor's Word-bk.*, *Disposed Quarters*, the distribution when the camp is marked about a place besieged.

† 2. a. In a (specified) physical, *esp.* bodily, condition; in a (good or bad) state of health; conditioned. b. Having a (particular) bodily constitution; constituted. c. *absol.* In good health or condition; not *indisposed*. *Obs.*

c **1386** CHAUCER *Manciple's Prol.* 33 Thy breeth ful soure stynketh, That sheweth wel thou art nat wel disposed. *c* **1400** *Lanfranc's Cirurg.* 222 It wole make a man yuel disposid & feuerous. **1470–85** MALORY *Arthur* VII. xxvi, He is as fair an handed man and wel disposed as ony is lyuynge. *c* **1477** CAXTON *Jason* 54 b, The weder was softe and wel disposed. **1488** —— *Chast. Goddes Chyld.* 21 Dyuerse men fallen in to dyuerse feuers after he is dysposed. **1577** FENTON *Gold. Epist.* 234 Whiche made hir bodie disposed, and hir minde liuely. **1590** SIR J. SMYTH *Disc. Weapons* in *Lett. Lit. Men* (Camden) 51 Thousands of the lustiest and dispost sort of English people. **1662** NEWCOME *Diary* (Chetham Soc.) 39, I was somewᵗ aguishly disposed all this day. **1694** *Acc. Sev. Late Voy.* II. (1711) 35 When the Air is so disposed, as the Stars do..look bigger..it is a great Prognostication.

3. Having a (particular) mental constitution, disposition, or turn of mind. † b. *absol.* Well disposed, having a favourable disposition (quot. 1577).

c **1430** LYDG. *Hors, Shepe & G.* 207 Alle folke be nat [lyke] of condicionis, Nor lyke disposyde in wylle, thought, and deede. **1481** CAXTON *Myrr.* III. xiii. 165 Neuer shal the euyl disposed man saye well of that he cannot wel vnderstonde. **1564** *Godly Admon. Decrees Council Trent* title-p., Wrytten for..godlye disposed persons sakes. **1577** FENTON *Gold. Epist.* 242 The one disposed, the other frowarde. **1593** SHAKS. *2 Hen. VI*, III. i. 76 Seemes he a Doue? His feathers are but borrow'd, For hee's disposed as the hatefull Rauen. **1639** LD. DIGBY *Lett. conc. Relig.* iv. 85 A man so disposed as..to leap at once from England to Rome. **1709** STEELE *Tatler* No. 78 ¶ 13, I require all sober disposed persons to avoid meeting the said Lunatick. **1863** FR. A. KEMBLE *Resid. in Georgia* 24 He is remarkably good-tempered and well disposed.

4. Inclined, in the mood, in the mind (*to do* something, *to* or *for* something). Also with adverb, in a (particular) mental condition or mood; *well* or *ill disposed*: favourably or unfavourably inclined (*to*, *towards*, † *for*). See DISPOSE *v.* 6 a.

c **1340** HAMPOLE *Prose Tr.* ix. 24 Othir gosteli occupacions after that thei fele hem disposed. *c* **1386** CHAUCER *Clerk's T.* 651 To tempte his wyf, as he was first disposed. *c* **1430** LYDG. *Min. Poems* (1840) 159 (Mätz.) Som man of herte disposed to pryde. *c* **1489** CAXTON *Sonnes of Aymon* xxii. 476, I am dysposed for to doo the worste that I can agenste hym. **1552** *Bk. Com. Prayer* Pref., That suche as be disposed maye come to heare gods worde. **1596** SHAKS. *1 Hen. IV*, IV. i. 38 To see how Fortune is dispos'd to vs. **1659** B. HARRIS *Parival's Iron Age* 288 Who would have believed, that many should needs be well disposed for the King of Scots? **1712** ADDISON *Spect.* No. 542 ¶ 4, I should be more severe upon myself than the public is disposed to be. **1828** D'ISRAELI *Chas. I*, I. v. 103 The French Cabinet was strongly disposed for a Spanish war. **1892** GARDINER *Stud. Hist. Eng.* 17 He was more disposed to defend the Empire than to extend it.

† b. *ellipt.* Inclined to merriment; in a jocund mood. *Obs.*

1588 SHAKS. *L.L.L.* II. i. 250 Come to our Pauillion, Boyet is disposde. **1593** PEELE *Chron. Edw. I*, 125, I pray let go; Ye are dispos'd I think. *a* **1616** BEAUM. & FL. *Custom Countrey* I. i, You are dispos'd.

5. Having a physical inclination or tendency (*to* something, or *to do* something); inclined, liable, subject. See DISPOSE *v.* 6 b.

c **1380** WYCLIF *Sel. Wks.* III. 68 þe see..is moore, and neer hevene, and moore disposid to take liȝt. **1398** TREVISA *Barth. De P.R.* XIX. xlvi. (1495) 889 Saltnesse..makyth [flesshe] the lesse disposyd to corrupcion. **1541** R. COPLAND *Guydon's Quest. Chirurg.*, To what diseases is yᵉ bladder disposed?.. It is dysposed to opylacyons. **1758** A. REID tr. *Macquer's Chem.* I. 12 All similar substances have an Affinity with each other, and are consequently disposed to unite. **1886** A. WINCHELL *Walks & Talks Geol. Field* 196 [Strata] buffish in colour, and disposed to crumble to pieces.

Hence **di'sposedly**, *adv. rare* (in later instances echoing quot. 1610, = with lofty dignity).

c **1610** SIR J. MELVIL *Mem.* (1735) 100, I said, the Quen dancit not sa hich and disposedly as she did. **1904** R. J. FARRER *Garden of Asia* 187 Go-betweens conduct the negotiations, high and disposedly as Queen Elizabeth. **1907** J. H. MᶜCARTHY *Needles & Pins* viii, The company.. marched up the aisle very disposedly. **1924** WODEHOUSE *Leave it to Psmith* ix. §5. 195 Through the belt of rhododendrons..a portly form..made itself visible, moving high and disposedly in the direction of the back premises.

disposedness (dɪ'spəʊzɪdnɪs). [f. DISPOSED *ppl. a.* + -NESS.] The quality or state of being disposed; inclination, disposition.

1583 GOLDING *Calvin on Deut.* lxix. 423 Lo here..the signe yᵗ we be wel disposed beforehand, and this disposednes is as a white vnwritten paper. **1625** BP. MOUNTAGU *App. Cæsar* I. vii. 66 Their owne disposednesse to evill. *a* **1691** BOYLE *Wks.* II. 236 (R.) Want of leisure, and sometimes of disposedness to write. **1710** NORRIS *Chr. Prud.* v. 222 Disposedness to imbrace Christianity. **1876** GEO. ELIOT *Dan. Der.* IV. xxx, His passion for her..had left a certain dull disposedness which..had prompted in him a vacillating notion of marrying her.

† **dispo'see.** *rare.* [f. DISPOSE *v.* + -EE.] One to whom something is 'disposed' or made over.

1826 BENTHAM in *Westm. Rev.* VI. 464 For a correlative to it [*disposer*], an obvious term is *disposee*.

† **di'sposement.** *Obs.* [f. DISPOSE *v.* + -MENT.] The action of disposing; disposition, disposal.

1583 STUBBES *Anat. Abus.* II. (1882) 56 As though they.. had the world and the disposement thereof in their own hands. *a* **1679** T. GOODWIN *Wks.* II. IV. 54 (R.) This order and disposement of these two several sentences. *Ibid.* 156 Above all such extrinsical contrivances and disposements.

disposer (dɪ'spəʊzə(r)). [f. as prec. + -ER[1].]

One who or that which disposes, in various senses.

1. One who arranges or sets in order.

1624 WOTTON *Archit.* Pref. (J. s.v. *Gatherer*), I am but a gatherer and disposer of other mens stuff. **1677** GALE *Crt. Gentiles* II. IV. Proem. 12 The mind of man..is the orderer and disposer both of notions and things. *a* **1693** URQUHART *Rabelais* III. xxxiii. 278 Disposers of cooling Shades, Composers of green Arbours.

2. One who regulates or governs; a controller, manager, director, ruler: see DISPOSE *v.* 2, 7.

c **1586** C'TESS PEMBROKE *Ps.* LXXXII. vi, Of all the earth king, judge, disposer be. **1667** MILTON *P.L.* IV. 635 My Author and Disposer, what thou bidst Unargu'd I obey; so God ordains. **1708** *Brit. Apollo* No. 66. 1/2 The intentions of our Allwise Disposer. **1772** PRIESTLEY *Inst. Relig.* (1782) II. 173 The..sovereign disposer of all things. **1875** JOWETT *Plato* (ed. 2) I. 476 Mind was the disposer and cause of all.

3. One who distributes or dispenses; a dispenser: see DISPOSE *v.* 4.

1526 *Pilgr. Perf.* (W. de W. 1531) 40 Se that thou be founde a true meke and faythfull disposer of the treasure of thy lorde god. **1526** TINDALE *1 Cor.* iv. 1 Ministers of Christ and disposers of the secretes of God. *a* **1672** GRAUNT *Bill of Mortality* (J.), The magistrate is both the beggar and the disposer of what is got by begging. **1802** LD. ELDON in *Vesey's Rep.* VII. 74 When money is given to a charity, without expressing what Charity, there the King is the disposer of the Charity.

4. One who or that which disposes or inclines to something: see DISPOSE *v.* 6.

1864 VAMBERY *Trav. Centr. Asia* 2 The coolness of the night in Persia is a great disposer to slumber.

5. One who disposes of something: see *vb.* 8.

1606 SHAKS. *Tr. & Cr.* III. i. 95 With my disposer Cressida. **1690** LOCKE *Govt.* II. vi. (Rtldg.) 75 Free disposers of themselves and fortunes. **1706** PRIOR *Ode to Queen* 113 The master sword, disposer of thy pow'r. **1893** *Westm. Gaz.* 11 Mar. 9/2 If the disposer be satisfied with the price offered the transaction is settled.

Hence **di'sposeress**, a female disposer.

1648 HERRICK *Hesper.*, *Beucolick* (1869) 260 And Lallage ..shall be disposeresse of the prize.

di'sposing, *vbl. sb.* [f. DISPOSE *v.* + -ING[1].] The action of the verb DISPOSE.

1. Arrangement, suitable or orderly placing; see DISPOSE *v.* 1. (In quot. 1630, 'get-up', attire.)

c **1440** HYLTON *Scala Perf.* (W. de W. 1494) II. xxvii, After diuers disposynges of men and after sundry states..are dyuers exercises in worchyng. **1570** GOLDING tr. *Chytræus* (*title*), Postill, or Orderly disposing of Certeyne Epistles usually read in the Church. **1630** *R. Johnson's Kingd. & Commw.* 91 Come, and behold the beauty of our Ladies, and their disposing at a night of solemnity. **1712** J. JAMES tr. *Le Blond's Gardening* 117 Figures and Fountains.. whose Diversity, as well in the disposing, as in what they consist of, yields a very agreeable Prospect to the Eye.

2. Ordering, control, management, disposal.

1406 *E.E. Wills* (1882) 13 Seruauntys, at the Dysposyng of Thomas Roos. **1530** PALSGR. 214/1 Disposyng, *administration.* **1611** BIBLE *Prov.* xvi. 33 The lot is cast into the lap, but the whole disposing thereof is of the Lord. **1647** R. GENTILIS tr. *Malvezzi's Chiefe Events* 203 Those..shall be at the Dutchesses disposing. **1656** *Artif. Handsom.* 50 *margin*, An heart unsatisfied with Gods works and disposings.

3. Bestowal, dispensing, expenditure.

1638 DK. HAMILTON in *H. Papers* (Camden) 57 The intentiounes uhich your Maᵗⁱᵉ might..haue had for the desposing of thatt place. **1676** *Deed Trin. Coll.* in Willis & Clark *Cambridge* (1886) II. 520 The free disposeing of the said two Chambers..to such person..as hee shall appoint. **1751** LABELYE *Westm. Br.* 67 Frugality in the disposing of publick Money.

4. The action of making ready or inclined; preparation; disposition, inclination: see *vb.* 5, 6.

c **1380** WYCLIF *Serm.* Sel. Wks. II. 175 Yit disposyng dwelliþ in hem to make hem þenke amys. **14..** LYDG. *Secrees* 1206 Phebus causith dysposyng to gladness. **1611** BIBLE *Prov.* xvi. 1 The preparations [*marg.* disposings] of the heart..are from the Lord.

di'sposing, *ppl. a.* [f. as prec. + -ING[2].] That disposes, in various senses: see the verb.

of (in) disposing mind or ***memory***: so sound in mind and memory as to be capable of making a will.

1627–77 FELTHAM *Resolves* I. x. 15 Surely God that made disposing Nature, knows her better, than imperfect man. **1648** *Bury Wills* (Camden) 200 In full vnderstanding and memory, and of a disposeing and testamentary mind. **1649** *Ibid.* 220, I Mary Chapman..being in disposeing memorie. **1797** BURKE *Will* in *Wks.* (1842) I. 38, I, Edmund Burke.. being of sound and disposing mind, do make my last will and testament. **1803** CHENEVIX in *Phil. Trans.* XCIII. 304 Disposing affinity, and assimilation.

Hence **di'sposingly** *adv.*, in a disposing way.

1625 BP. MOUNTAGU *Appeale to Cæsar* I. ix. 64 Christians doe hold and beleeve it too, [*Deum ire per omnes*] but disposingly, etc. in his providence.

† **di'sposit,** *v. Obs. rare.* [f. L. *disposit-* ppl. stem of *dispōnĕre* to dispose: perh. immediately after *disposition*.] *trans.* To dispose, incline.

1661 GLANVILL *Scepsis Sci.* xiv. (1665) 81 Some constitutions are genially disposited to this mental seriousness.

† **di'spositate,** *v. Obs. rare.* [erron. form for DEPOSITATE, through confusion with DISPOSE *v.*] *trans.* To deposit.

1650 HOWELL *Giraffi's Rev. Naples* I. 44 Two boxes full of Gold..were taken and dispositated upon account in the Kings bank.

disposition (dɪspə'zɪʃ(ə)n). [a. F. *disposition*, OF. also *-icion* (12th c. in Littré), ad. L. *disposition-em*, n. of action from *dispōnĕre* to DISPONE. Not derivationally related to DISPOSE, but associated with it from an early period in OFr., by contact of form, and adoption of *-poser* as virtual representative of L. *-pōnĕre*: cf. COMPOSITION.]

I. The action or faculty of disposing, the condition of being disposed.

1. a. The action of setting in order, or condition of being set in order; arrangement, order; relative position of the parts or elements of a whole.

1563 W. FULKE *Meteors* (1640) 24 It comes of the divers disposition of the clouds. **1597** MORLEY *Introd. Mus.* Annot., In the natural disposition of numbers thus, 1, 2, 3, 4, 5. **1695** WOODWARD *Nat. Hist. Earth* III. i. (1723) 156 The Disposition of the Strata. **1713** SWIFT *Frenzy of J. Denny* Wks. 1755 III. I. 139, I then took a particular survey of.. the furniture and disposition of his apartment. **1756** BURKE

Subl. & B. II. xii, Stonehenge, neither for disposition nor ornament, has anything admirable. **1827** STEUART *Planter's G.* (1828) 15 Single Trees and Bushes, in groups and open dispositions. **1865** GEIKIE *Scen. & Geol. Scot.* vi. 122 Looking at the disposition of the Highland glens and straths.

†**b.** Relative position; situation (of one thing). *Obs.*

1541 R. COPLAND *Guydon's Quest. Chirurg.*, Where is the dysposicion of the yerde? **1712** J. JAMES tr. *Le Blond's Gardening* 99 That..the Tracing-Pin be constantly held in the same Disposition, without varying its Point. **1750** tr. *Leonardus' Mirr. Stones* 102 *Effestis*..being opposed to the Sun, kindles Fire in Matter put in a Disposition for it.

c. *Rhet.* and *Logic.* The due arrangement of the parts of an argument or discussion.

1509 HAWES *Past. Pleas.* x. i, The second parte of crafty Rethoryke Maye well be called Disposicion. **1553** T. WILSON *Rhet.* (1567) 82 a, Inuencion helpeth to finde matter, and Disposicion serueth to place argumentes. **1628** T. SPENCER *Logick* 13. **1788** HOWARD *Roy. Cycl.* II. 715 *Disposition*, in Logic, is that operation of the mind, whereby we put the ideas, operations, and arguments, which we have formed concerning our subject, into such an order as is fittest to gain the clearest knowledge of it, to retain it longest, and to explain it to others in the best manner; the effect of this is called *method*.

d. *Arch.*, etc. The due arrangement of the several parts of a building, *esp.* in reference to the general design: see quots.

1624 WOTTON *Archit.* (1672) 14, I may now proceed to the Disposition thereof [i.e. of the matter], which must form the Work. **1706** PHILLIPS (ed. Kersey), *Disposition*..in Architecture, is the just placing of all the several Parts of a Building, according to their proper Order. *c* **1850** *Rudim. Navig.* (Weale) 115 *Disposition*; a draught or drawing representing the several timbers that compose the frame of the ship, so that they may be properly disposed with respect to the ports, &c. **1876** GWILT *Encycl. Archit.* Gloss., *Disposition*, one of the essentials of architecture. It is the arrangement of the whole design by means of ichnography (plan), orthography (section and elevation), and scenography (perspective view). **1886** WILLIS & CLARK *Cambridge* III. 247 The general inclosure within walls, the disposition into courts..all have their analogies..in the monastic buildings.

e. *Mil.* See 2 b.

2. a. Arrangement (of affairs, measures, etc.), esp. for the accomplishment of a purpose; plan, preparation; condition or complexion of affairs.

1382 WYCLIF *Prov.* xxiv. 6 For with disposicioun me goth in to bataile; and helthe shal ben wher ben many counseilis. **1604** SHAKS. *Oth.* I. iii. 237, I craue fit disposition for my Wife..With such Accomodation and besort As leuels with her breeding. **1712** BUDGELL *Spect.* No. 404 ¶1 In the Dispositions of Society, the civil Oeconomy is formed in a Chain as well as the natural. **1736** BUTLER *Anal.* Introd. Wks. 1874, I. 8 To judge what particular disposition of things would be most..assistant to virtue. **1814** tr. *Klaproth's Trav.* 3 My dispositions for the journey would soon have been completed. **1871** MORLEY *Voltaire* (1886) 317 To observe..those secret dispositions of events which prepared the way for great changes.

b. *Mil.* The arrangement of troops in preparation for a military operation: (*a*) (from sense 1) their actual arrangement in the field; (*b*) (from sense 2) their distribution, allocation, destination, etc.; *pl.* military preparations or measures.

1600 E. BLOUNT tr. *Conestaggio* 37 Having viewed the ill disposition of the Campe. **1734** tr. *Rollin's Anc. Hist.* (1827) II. IV. 257 The Persian troops had been used to engage 24 men in depth, but Cyrus thought fit to change that disposition. **1776** GIBBON *Decl. & F.* I. xxiv. 684 The military dispositions of Julian were skilfully contrived. **1799** STUART in Owen *Wellesley's Desp.* 116, I have made a disposition to defend my position. **1849** MACAULAY *Hist. Eng.* I. 605 Having observed the disposition of the royal forces. **1878** BOSW. SMITH *Carthage* 242 Fabius made all his dispositions to repel the attempt to force a passage.

c. *Naut.* (See quot.)

1867 SMYTH *Sailor's Word-bk.*, *Disposition*, the arrangement of a ship's company for watches, quarters, reefing, furling, and other duties.

3. Ordering, control, management; direction, appointment; administration, dispensation; = DISPOSAL 1. (Cf. DISPOSE *v.* 2, 7.) *arch.*

c **1374** CHAUCER *Troylus* II. 477 (526) O god þat at þi disposicioun Ledest þe fyn by luste purueyaunce Of euery wyght. **1382** WYCLIF *2 Chron.* xxiii. 18 Forsothe Joiada sette prouostis in the hous of the Lord..after the disposicyoun [1388 by the ordynaunce] of Dauid. **1520** *Caxton's Chron. Eng.* v. 56 b/2 To submytte hym to the dyposycyon of God. **1530** PALSGR. 214/1 Disposytion, *disposition, gouvernement, ordre*. **1582** N. T. (Rhem.) *Acts* vii. 53 Who receiued the Law by the disposition of [so **1611**: R.V. as it was ordained by (*marg. or*, as the ordinance of)] Angels, and haue not kept it. **1661** BRAMHALL *Just Vind.* ii. 6 Which things by the just disposition of Almighty God, fell out according to the..desires of these holy persons. **1719** DE FOE *Crusoe* (1840) II. xii. 262 This seemed to me to be a disposition of Providence. **1841** MYERS *Cath. Th.* III. §14. 53 Inexpressibly thankful to receive this Law by the disposition of Angels.

4. a. The action of disposing of, putting away, getting rid of, making over, etc. (see DISPOSE *v.* 8); bestowal; *spec.* in *Law*, the action of disponing; bestowal or conveyance by deed or will.

1393 GOWER *Conf.* I. 269 She [i.e. Nature] preferreth no degree As in the disposicion Of bodely complexion. *c* **1532** DEWES *Introd. Fr.* in *Palsgr.* 1065 Touchyng the disposicion of is goodnes [*ses biens*] after his deth. **1577–87** HOLINSHED *Scot. Chron.* (1805) II. 340 The disposition of officis vacand. **1712** STEELE *Spect.* No. 497 ¶2 The wanton disposition of the favours of the powerful. **1795** WYTHE *Decis. Virginia* 5 His wife could make no disposition of the personal estate. **1861** W. BELL *Dict. Law Scot.* 292 A disposition is an unilateral deed of alienation, by which a right to property, either heritable or moveable, is conveyed. **1884** SIR J. BACON in *Law Rep.* 27 Ch. Div. 47 The point which is said to remain for disposition when the case is heard.

b. Power of disposing of; disposal, control: *esp.* in phrase ***at*** (***in***, etc.) ***one's disposition*** (= DISPOSAL 4).

c **1374** CHAUCER *Troylus* v. 2 Aprochen gan the fatal destyne That loues hath in disposicioun. **1406** *E.E. Wills* (1882) 13 At the dysposicion of myn Executours. **1529** CDL. WOLSEY in Ellis *Orig. Lett.* Ser. I. II. 12 Yf I may have the free gyft and dyssposycion of the benefyces. **1673** TEMPLE *Ess. Ireland* Wks. 1731 I. 110 The Lieutenants of Ireland since the Duke of Ormond's Time have had little in their Disposition here. **1776** GIBBON *Decl. & F.* I. xii. 255 The choice of action or of repose is no longer in our disposition. **1860** TRENCH *Serm. Westm. Abb.* iii. 31 [He] had at his disposition no inconsiderable sums of money.

II. The way or manner in which a thing has been disposed, or is situated or constituted.

†**5.** *Astrol.* **a.** The situation of a planet in a horoscope, as supposed to determine the nature or fortune of a person, or the course of events. *Obs.*

1375 BARBOUR *Bruce* IV. 699 Astrology, Quhar-throu clerkis..May knaw coniunctione of planetis..And of the hevyn all halely How þat þe disposicioune Suld apon thingis virk heir doune. *c* **1386** CHAUCER *Knt's T.* 229 Som wikke aspect or disposition Of Saturne. *c* **1590** MARLOWE *Faust.* Wks. (Rtldg.) 88/1 A book where I might see all..planets..that I might know their motions and dispositions.

†**b.** The state of being 'disposed of' (see DISPOSE *v.* 8 a). *Obs.*

1647 LILLY *Chr. Astrol.* lxxxii. 447 See if the more ponderous Planet of the two, that is, the receiver of the Disposition be in any angle but the fourth.

†**c.** The nature or constitution of a planet or sign, in relation to its alleged influence or effects.

c **1386** CHAUCER *Wife's Prol.* 701 Mercurie loueth wysdam and science And Venus loueth ryot and dispence. And for hire diuerse disposicioun, Ech falleth in otheres exaltacioun. **1393** GOWER *Conf.* III. 114 His nativite Hath take upon the proprete Of Martis disposicion.

6. Natural tendency or bent of the mind, *esp.* in relation to moral or social qualities; mental constitution or temperament; turn of mind.

Possibly of astrological origin: cf. the description of dispositions as *saturnine, jovial, martial, venereal, mercurial*.

1387 TREVISA *Higden* (Rolls) III. 113 (Mätz.) Nouȝt by chaungynge of body, but by chaungynge of disposicioun of wit and of semynge. **1393** GOWER *Conf.* III. 19 After the disposition Of glotony and dronkeship. **1475** *Bk. Noblesse* 51 If suche prophesies and influence of the seide constellacions might be trew, yet..havyng a clene soule, may turne the contrarie disposicion that jugement of constellacion or prophesies signified. **1576** FLEMING *Panopl. Epist.* 266 Men of honeste and vertuous disposition. **1678** WANLEY *Wond. Lit. World* v. ii. §81. 472/2 A man he was of a fierce, bloody, and faithless disposition. **1779** J. MOORE *View Soc. Fr.* (1789) I. xvii. 128 Congenial with the phlegm and saturnine dispositions of the English. **1837** WHEWELL *Hist. Induct. Sc.* (1857) I. 108 The belief..that the motions of the stars, and the dispositions and fortunes of men, may come under some common conceptions and laws. **1841** JAMES *Brigand* i, His disposition was naturally cheerful and bright.

7. a. The state or quality of being disposed, inclined, or 'in the mind' (*to* something, or *to do* something); inclination (sometimes = desire, intention, purpose); state of mind or feeling in respect to a thing or person; the condition of being (favourably or unfavourably) disposed *towards.* (In *pl.* formerly sometimes = mental tendencies or qualities; hence nearly = sense 6.)

1393 GOWER *Conf.* III. 62 They take loggings in the town After the disposition Where as him thoughte best to dwelle. **1461** *Paston Lett.* No. 408 II. 35 If thei do it of her owne disposicion. **1526** *Pilgr. Perf.* (W. de W. 1531) 11 b, He requireth but onely a disposicyon in the persone..that he be repentaunt. **1600** SHAKS. *A.Y.L.* IV. i. 113 But come, now I will be your Rosalind in a more comming-on disposition. **1625** MEADE in Ellis *Orig. Lett.* Ser. I. III. 199 Those..that know best her dispositions are very hopefull his Majestie will have power to bring her to his own religion. **1690** LOCKE *Hum. Und.* II. xxiii. (1695) 156 Testiness is a disposition or aptness to be angry. **1754** CHATHAM *Lett. Nephew* iv. 28 Go on, my dear child, in the admirable dispositions you have towards all that is right and good. **1832** HT. MARTINEAU *Life in Wilds* ix. 121 There was a general disposition to remain. **1887** RUSKIN *Præterita* II. 253 A pleasant disposition to make the best of all she saw.

†**b.** A frame of mind or feeling; mood, humour.

1726–7 SWIFT *Gulliver* I. i. 31, I rose up with as melancholy a disposition as ever I had in my life. **1749** FIELDING *Tom Jones* X. iii, The footmen..were in a different disposition. **1764** FOOTE *Patron* III. Wks. 1799 I. 356 If he is admitted in his present disposition, the whole secret will certainly out.

†**8.** Physical constitution, nature, or permanent condition. *Obs.*

c **1477** CAXTON *Jason* 41 b, If ye juge the disposicion of my body after the colour of my face ye be gretly abused. **1555** EDEN *Decades* 29 Rather by the disposition of the earthe then constitucion of heauen. **1576** FLEMING *Panopl. Epist.* 365 Considering the weake disposition of your bodie. **1635** N. CARPENTER *Geog. Del.* II. xiv. 224 Hippocrates pronounced the people of the North to be of a leane and dry disposition. **1726** LEONI *Alberti's Archit.* I. 3/2 A constant unchangeable Disposition of Air above all the rest of the World. **1813** SIR H. DAVY *Agric. Chem.* (1814) 261 The disposition of trees may, however, be changed gradually in many instances.

9. a. Physical aptitude, tendency, or inclination (*to* something, or *to do* something).

1398 TREVISA *Barth. De P.R.* III. xix. (1495) 65 To make the wytte of smellynge perfyte it nedyth to haue..good dysposicions in the nosethryllis. **1541** R. COPLAND *Galyen's Terap.* 2 Aiij, We shall treate in this present boke the dysposycyons which augmenteth the vlcere. **1552** HULOET, Disposition to slepe or wake, *cataphora*. **1654** Z. COKE *Logick* (1657) 32 Disposition..sometimes it is largely used for all fitness to anything..as when water waxeth warm, it is said to have a disposition to heat. **1791** HAMILTON *Berthollet's Dyeing* I. I. II. i. 120 The different dispositions of wool, silk, etc. to unite with the colouring particles. **1804** ABERNETHY *Surg. Obs.* 97 The disposition to form wens prevails frequently in many parts of the body at the same time.

†**b.** Aptness or capacity for doing something; aptitude, skill. *Obs. rare.*

1600 E. BLOUNT tr. *Conestaggio* 27 Yet did he admire their order..their disposition to handle the pike, and their strict obedience. **1768** STERNE *Sent. Journ.*, *Montriul* (1775) I. 37 You can shave, and dress a wig a little, La Fleur!—He had all the dispositions in the world.

†**10. a.** Physical condition or state; state of bodily health. *Obs.*

c **1400** *Lanfranc's Cirurg.* 103, I foond þe sike of bettere disposicioun..& he spak bettere. **1541** R. COPLAND *Galyen's Terap.* 2 B iv b, Of other vlceres wherin no corrupte affection or dysposition (that the Grekes call Cacoetes) is adioyned. **1598** GRENEWEY *Tacitus' Ann.* VI. vi. 130 Cocceius Nerua..being in perfect disposition of body, resolued with him selfe to die. **1611** COTGR. s.v. *Habitude*, *L'habitude du corps*, the estate, plight, liking, or disposition of the bodie. **1633** T. STAFFORD *Pac. Hib.* xxx. (1821) 506 Being surprised by an ill disposition of health. **1732** ARBUTHNOT *Rules of Diet* 370 An inflammatory Disposition of the Coat of the Nerve.

†**b.** Normal or natural condition (of mind or body). *Obs. rare.* (Cf. *indisposition* = deranged condition.)

[*c* **1400** *Lanfranc's Cirurg.* 58 As soone as a membre is brouȝt to his kyndeli disposicioun.] **1581** PETTIE *Guazzo's Civ. Conv.* I. (1586) 19 This solitarinesse is profitable and necessary for the disposition of the minde, so verie often is it hurtfull to the health of the bodie. **1632** J. HAYWARD tr. *Biondi's Eromena* 36 The Pilot, seeing him restored to his disposition, caused [etc.].

11. *Comb.* in *Philos.*, as ***disposition-concept***, ***-term***, ***-word***.

1936 R. CARNAP in *Philos. Sci.* III. 440 Let us consider the question whether the so-called *disposition-concepts* can be defined. *Ibid.* 448 In the case of a disposition-term, the reduction cannot be replaced by a definition. **1949** G. RYLE *Concept of Mind* ii. 44 Many disposition-concepts are determinable concepts. **1958** *Aspects of Translation* 54 One may use the language of linguistic philosophers, and talk about disposition-words. **1965** P. CAWS *Philos. Sci.* viii. 54 Carnap..restricts the applicability of disposition terms.

dispo'sitional, *a.* [f. prec. + -AL[1].] Relating to disposition. Hence **dispositio'nality**; **dispo'sitionally** *adv.*

1846 WORCESTER cites J. JOHNSON. **1908** W. R. B. GIBSON *Probl. Logic* xiii. 129 We might refer to them as dispositional possibilities... To say that 'S can be P' is to say that S is potentially or dispositionally P. **1909** W. M. URBAN *Valuation* ii. 53 Actualisation of dispositional tendencies by acts of presumption, judgment, and assumption. **1921** R. M. JONES *Later Periods of Quakerism* II. xxiv. 970 In spite of these dispositional tendencies she rendered a remarkable service to the Society of Friends. **1949** G. RYLE *Concept of Mind* ii. 43 When we describe glass as brittle, or sugar as soluble, we are using dispositional concepts... To possess a dispositional property is not to be in a particular state, or to undergo a particular change; it is to be bound or liable to be in a particular state, or to undergo a particular change, when a particular condition is realised. **1956** A. J. AYER *Probl. Knowl.* iv. 137 The word 'remember' is used dispositionally, so that one can properly be said to remember things that one is not actually thinking of. **1958** *Listener* 27 Nov. 891/1 Our use of a dispositional verb like 'can'. **1963** A. PAP *Introd. Philos. Sci.* ii. 31 The so-called dispositional predicates,..designating a disposition to react in a characteristic way to a certain kind of stimulus. **1964** *Amer. Philos. Q.* I. 228 Goodman also construes dispositionality to be problematic or mystery-raising.

dispositioned (dɪspə'zɪʃ(ə)nd), *ppl. a.* [f. as prec. + -ED[2].] Having a (specified) disposition or turn of mind.

1646 SALTMARSH *Smoke in the Temple* 27 Not so unlike and contrary dispositioned and natured as you pretend. **1660** F. BROOKE tr. *Le Blanc's Trav.* 88 Happy in a sweet disposition'd, and a modest wife. **1767** H. BROOKE *Fool of Qual.* (1859) II. 150 (D.) Lord Clinton was indeed sweetly dispositioned by nature. **1804** J. LARWOOD *No Gun Boats* 9 An Assassin..dispositioned for midnight murder. **1826** R. H. FROUDE *Rem.* (1838) I. 31 A stumbling-block in the way of good-dispositioned men.

dispositive (dɪ'spɒzɪtɪv), *a.* (*sb.*) [In Caxton a. F. *dispositif, -ive* (13th c. in Hatz.-Darm.), ad. L. type **dispositīv-us*, f. *disposit-us*, pa. pple. of *dispōnĕre* to DISPOSE: see -IVE. In later use prob. immed. from L. or on L. analogies.]

A. *adj.* †**1.** Characterized by special disposition or appointment. *Obs. rare.*

1483 CAXTON *Gold. Leg.* 127 b/1 It is said that thys lyght was dipositif sodayne and celestyall.

2. That has the quality of disposing or inclining: often opposed to *effective*, and so nearly = preparatory, conducive, contributory: cf. B. 1.

1612 W. SCLATER *Chr. Strength* 13 Papists..allow to nature a power dispositiue, and ability to prepare it selfe to regeneration. **1616** BRENT tr. *Sarpi's Hist. Counc. Trent* (1676) 222 They did..deny all effective or dispositive virtue in the Sacraments. **1624** F. WHITE *Repl. Fisher* 546 Some causes are dispositiue, adiuuant, or impetrant. **1710** J. NORRIS *Chr. Prud.* ii. 80 That which makes a man act Prudently..(in a remote and dispositive sense). **1894** *Tablet* 20 Jan. 86 This new learning continued, by a sort of dispositive logic, to educate the English mind.

3. Having the quality or function of directing, controlling, or disposing of something; relating to direction, control, or disposal.

dispositive clause (*Sc. Law*): the clause of conveyance in a deed, by which the disposition of the property (see DISPOSITION 4) is expressed.

1613–18 DANIEL *Coll. Hist. Eng.* (1626) 29 It was not in the power of King Edward to collate [the Crown]..by any dispositiue and testamentary will. **1684** BATES *Duty of Resignation* (R.) Without..his dispositive wisdom and power, the whole frame would disband and fall into confusion. **1726** AYLIFFE *Parergon* 28 Sentences wherein dispositive and enacting Terms are made Use of. **1832** AUSTIN *Jurispr.* (1879) II. xliv. 781 When [the law] leaves a certain latitude to the parties, it is called dispositive or provisional; being to take effect only in case no disposition is made by the parties themselves. **1861** W. BELL *Dict. Law Scot.* 294/2 All the other clauses of the deed are merely auxiliary, or subservient to the dispositive clause, to which they are intended to give effect. **1868** *Act 31–32 Vict.* c. 101 Sched. B. No. 1 After the inductive and dispositive clauses, the deed may proceed thus.

†4. Of or pertaining to natural disposition or inclination. *Obs.*

1656 *Artif. Handsom.* 84 Not to be reduced to any rules or bounds of reason and religion; no, not under any intentionall piety, and habituall or dispositive holinesse. **1681** BAXTER *Apol. Nonconf. Min.* 124 Want of dispositive willingness or of a right will.

†**B.** *sb. Obs. rare.*

1. Something that disposes or inclines (see A. 2).

1629 H. BURTON *Babel no Bethel* 33 Their faith [is] but as a preparatiue or dispositiue to justification.

2. A dispositive document, law, or clause (see A. 3).

1677 TEMPLE *Let. to Coventry* Wks. 1731 II. 431 There was one essential Default in the very Dispositive; which was, The Omission of that Clause.

di'spositively, *adv.* ? *Obs.* [f. prec. + -LY².] In a dispositive manner.

†1. By way of or in regard to disposition, inclination, or tendency: opposed to *effectively*, *actually*; sometimes nearly = Potentially. *Obs.*

1475 *Bk. Noblesse* 50 If a constellacion or prophesie signified that suche a yere..there shulde falle werre, pestilence or deerthe of vitaile to a contree..it is said but dispositiflie and not of necessitie or certente. *c* **1624** LUSHINGTON *Resurr. Serm.* in *Phenix* (1708) II. 489 Not to organize the body (it was not dismembred nor any way corrupted, not so much as 'in fieri'—no, not dispositively). **1630** DONNE *Serm.* (1632) 39 Prayer actually accompanied with shedding of teares, and dispositively in a readines to shed blood..in necessary cases. **1646** SIR T. BROWNE *Pseud. Ep.* III. ix. 124 That axiome in Philosophy, that the generation of one thing, is the corruption of another, although it be substantially true concerning the forme and matter, is also dispositively verified in the efficient or producer. **1651** BAXTER *Inf. Bapt.* 92 It is sufficient that the Parent be virtually and dispositively at present a Believer. **1666** BOYLE *Orig. Formes & Qual.* (1667) 32 If there were no sensitive Beings, those Bodies that are now the Objects of our Senses, would be but dispositively, if I may so speak, endowed with Colours, Tasts, and the like, and actually but onely with those more Catholick affections of Bodies, Figure, Motion, Texture, &c.

†2. In a way that disposes. *Obs.*

1592 R. D. *Hypnerotomachia* 81 And thus touched with pleasant heates..they began to boyle and kindle my colde feare, and dispositively to adopt my altered heate to sincere love.

†3. At the disposition of some controlling power.

1616 R. CARPENTER *Past. Charge* 42 Euery instrument worketh dispositiuely at the command of the principall agent.

dispositor (dɪ'spɒzɪtə(r)). *Astrol.* [a. L. *dispositor* disposer, arranger, agent-n. from *dispōnĕre*: see DISPOSE. Cf. OF. *dispositor*, *-eur*, *-our* (Oresme, 14th c.)] A planet that 'disposes of' another (see DISPOSE *v.* 8 a); 'the lord of a sign in its relation to another planet'.

1598 G. C. *Math. Phis.* App. in *Dariot's Astrolog.* F. iv a, The qualitie and nature of the disease..generally..is to bee iudged of the nature of the signe of the 6 house, and the dispositor thereof. **1652** GAULE *Magastrom.* 141 For the planets (that lord it) are benefick, fortified in their proper houses..influences, irradiations, significators, dispositors, promissors. **1819** JAS. WILSON *Compl. Dict. Astrol.*, *Dispositor*, that planet which disposes of another.

†**di'spository**, *a. Obs. rare.* [f. L. *disposit-* ppl. stem of *dispōnĕre* to dispose: see -ORY.] Having the quality of disposing, fitting, or inclining: = DISPOSITIVE *a.* 2.

1629 H. BURTON *Babel no Bethel* 103 Preparatory and dispository workes to Iustification. **1641** HEYLIN *Hist. Episc.* I. (1657) 66 A dispository power.

‖**di'spositrix.** L. fem. of *dispositor* = she that disposes or arranges. In quot. used *attrib.* = Disposing, dispositive.

1677 GALE *Crt. Gentiles* II. IV. 388 If it be so, that the gubernatrix and dispositrix mind do thus dispose althings ..[on p. 473 the same passage is rendered 'gubernative dispositive mind'].

†**disposories**, *sb. pl.*, var. *desposories*, DESPONSORIES [Sp. *desposorios*] *Obs.*, betrothal.

1623 EARL OF BRISTOL *Let.* 28 Dec. in *Heylin's Laud* I. ii. (1668) 115 Letters which she intended to have written the day of her disposories to the Prince her Husband.

dispossess (dɪspə'zɛs), *v.* [ad. OF. *despossesser* to dispossess (in Godef.), f. *des-*, DIS- 4 + *possesser* to POSSESS. Cf. the parallel med.L. *dispossidēre*, 16th c. F. *desposseder*, mod.F. *déposséder*. For the development of sense 2, 2 b, cf. POSSESS.]

1. *trans.* To put (any one) out of possession; to strip of possessions; to dislodge, disseise, oust.

1565 *Child Marriages* (E.E.T.S.) 136 The said Roberte held possession in the said house till he was, bie order of Lawe, dispossessed. **1595** SHAKS. *John* I. i. 131 Shal then my fathers Will be of no force, To dispossesse that childe which is not his. **1667** MILTON *P.L.* VII. 142 The seat Of Deitie supream, us dispossest He trusted to have seis'd. **1765** H. WALPOLE *Otranto* iii. (1798) 49 His father and grandfather had been too powerful for the house of Vicenza to dispossess them. **1841** ELPHINSTONE *Hist. Ind.* II. 229 They were dispossessed by the Arghúns of Sind, who were, in their turn, expelled by Prince Cámrán.

b. To deprive (any one) of the possession *of* (a thing).

1494 FABYAN *Chron.* VII. 536 Yᵉ Sarazyns at this iourney were not dispossessyd of yᵉ cytie of Thunys. **1576** FLEMING *Panopl. Epist.* 273 Neverthelesse, I am not dispossessed of hope. **1603** SHAKS. *Meas. for M.* II. iv. 22 Why doe's my bloud thus muster to my heart..dispossessing all my other parts of necessary fitnesse? **1794** SULLIVAN *View Nat.* I. 299 Let a foreign body dispossess water of its coldness. **1845** S. AUSTIN *Ranke's Hist. Ref.* II. 389 The empire..seemed to be regarded as already dispossessed of all its rights.

refl. **1555** WATREMAN *Fardle Facions* II. xii. 278 To dispossesse them selues of all that euer thei haue. **1595** SHAKS. *John* IV. iii. 23 The king hath dispossest himselfe of vs. **1849** ROBERTSON *Serm.* Ser. I. viii. 117 We have also dispossessed ourselves of belief in the reality of retribution.

†c. with *from*, *out of*: To drive out (*from* a possession); to expel, banish. *Obs.*

1600 E. BLOUNT tr. *Conestaggio* 272 Having dispossessed F. from his charge, he began [etc.]. **1667** MILTON *P.L.* XII. 28 Who..will..quite dispossess Concord and law of Nature from the Earth. **1679** J. SMITH *Narrat. Pop. Plot* Ded. B b, Might your Popish Adversaries but once..dispossess you out of the hearts of your Subjects. **1772** *Ann. Reg.* 42/1 To make use of force, in dispossessing our people from Port Egmont.

†d. With double obj. (*of* omitted). *Obs. rare*⁻¹.

1607 SHAKS. *Timon* I. i. 138, I will choose Mine heyre from forth the Beggars of the world And dispossesse her all.

†2. To cast out (the evil spirit by which any one is possessed); to exorcize. *Obs.*

1618 ROWLANDS *Sacred Mem.* 34 Helpe, helpe, haue mercy, dispossesse this fiend. **1683** HICKES *Case Inf. Bapt.* 53 The true Disciples of Christ did then dispossess Devils. **1775** H. FARMER *Demoniacs N.T.* I. vii. 142 Writers, who.. represent the devil as being every day dispossessed by Christians.

b. To rid (the possessed person) *of* (an evil spirit); to free from demoniacal possession.

1599 HAKLUYT *Voy.* II. I. 65 There are many possessed men in those parts..who being dispossessed of the vncleane spirits, do presently beleeue in Christ who deliuered them. **1624** MASSINGER *Renegado* IV. iii, I cannot play the exorcist To dispossess thee. **1647** N. BACON *Disc. Govt. Eng.* I. x. (1739) 18 Then Exorcists, that served to dispossess such as were possessed by the Devil. **1676** KIDDER *Charity Dir.* 7 How many he..Dispossessed, and Raised. **1801** MAR. EDGEWORTH *Belinda* (1832) II. xxviii. 273 He was dispossessed of the evil spirit of gambling, as if by a miracle. **1845** G. OLIVER *Coll. Biog. Soc. of Jesus* 74 His fame for dispossessing obsessed persons becoming notorious.

3. *transf.* and *fig.* To dislodge, oust, drive out.

1598–9 E. FORDE *Parismus* II. (1661) 4 But Fortune..at an instant dispossessed their content. **1601** SHAKS. *Twel. N.* IV. ii. 64 Thou shalt hold th' opinion of Pythagoras..and feare to kill a Woodcocke, lest thou dispossesse the soule of thy grandam. **1676** HOBBES *Iliad* I. 451 And having thirst and hunger dispossest. **1830** HERSCHEL *Stud. Nat. Phil.* §68 Two kinds of prejudices, which..moreover, differ extremely in the difficulty of dispossessing them.

Hence **dispo'ssessed** *ppl. a.* (also *absol.*); **dispo'ssessing** *vbl. sb.* and *ppl. a.*; **dispo'ssess** *sb. U.S. colloq.*, the act of ejecting from possession, ejectment, as in ***dispossess proceedings***, ***d. warrant***, legal proceedings or warrant to eject a tenant (*Cent. Dict.*): cf. DISPOSSESSORY.

1597 BP. J. KING *Jonas* (1618) 76 Discountenancings, disturbings, dispossessings of them. **1599** MINSHEU, *Desposseydo*, dispossessed. *a* **1631** DONNE in *Select.* (1840) 96 We require..a dislodging, a dispossessing of the sin. **1628** EARLE *Microcosm.*, *Cook* (Arb.) 47 For that time hee is tame and dispossest. **1860** FROUDE *Hist. Eng.* V. 112 Thousands of dispossessed tenants made their way to London. **1901** *Macm. Mag.* Apr. 411/2 Throughout Ireland, on the whole, Protestants are the possessors, Catholics the dispossessed. **1909** *Englishwoman* Apr. 305 Woman rebelled because she belonged to the classes of the dispossessed. **1944** M. LASKI *Love on Super-Tax* i. 5 Spring as it came to the needy and the dispirited, to the fallen and the dispossessed.

dispossession (dɪspə'zɛʃən). [n. of action from DISPOSSESS; cf. mod.F. *dépossession*.]

1. The action of dispossessing or fact of being dispossessed; deprivation of or ejection from a possession. In *Law* = OUSTER.

1576 FLEMING *Panopl. Epist.* 379 And playd the arrant rebells, seeking not his dispossession onely, but also his destruction. **1660** R. COKE *Justice Vind.* 36 The dispossession and disinheritance of another. **1768** BLACKSTONE *Comm.* III. 201 The remedy by ejectment is in it's original an action brought by one who hath a lease for years, to repair the injury done him by dispossession. **1885** *Athenæum* 23 May 661/1 The dipossession of Huntley from the heritage.

†b. *concr.* Something of which one has been dispossessed. *Obs. nonce-use* (after *possession*).

1640 QUARLES *Enchirid.* I. 100 Warres, whose ends are not to defend your owne Possessions, or to recover your dispossessions, are but Princely Injuries.

2. The casting out of an evil spirit; exorcism.

1600 DARRELL (*title*), A True Narration..Wherein the doctrine of Possession and Dispossession of Demoniakes.. is particularly applied vnto Somers. **1647** TRAPP *Comm. Mark* ix. 28 The dispossession of the devil out of many persons..in Lancashire..is very famous. **1775** H. FARMER *Demoniacs N.T.* III. iii. 351 If by possession they intended only to describe a disorder..the removal of it was all they could intend by dispossession. **1863** S. J. ANDREWS *Life of our Lord* 233 Cures of dispossession were among the earliest and commonest of the Saviour's miracles.

†**dispo'ssessment.** *Obs. rare*⁻¹. [f. DISPOSSESS + -MENT.] The action of dispossessing or the fact of being dispossessed; loss.

1600 HEYWOOD *1st Pt. Edw. IV*, v. Wks. 1874 I. 73 My husband grieves (alas! how can he choose?) Fearing the dispossessment of his Jane.

dispo'ssessor. Also 7 -our. [f. DISPOSSESS + -OR.] One who dispossesses.

1593 NASHE *Christ's T.* (1613) 44 To oppugne the dispossessors of thy Deity. **1611** TOURNEUR *Ath. Trag.* III. iv. Wks. 1878 I. 95, I will not be Your dispossessour but your Gardian. I will supply your Father's vacant place. **1768** BLACKSTONE *Comm.* III. 180 If the dispossessor has any legal claim, he may afterwards exert it, notwithstanding a recovery had against him in these possessory actions. **1860** PUSEY *Min. Proph.* 228 The remnant of Zion, being delivered, would dispossess their dispossessors.

dispo'ssessory, *a.* [f. as prec. + -ORY.] Relating to dispossession or eviction.

1888 *Union Signal* (Chicago) 5 Apr., The number of distress and dispossessory warrants issued.

dis'post, *v.* [f. DIS- 7 + POST *sb.*: cf. obs. F. *desposter*, *-poester*, *-postir* to dispossess.] *trans.* To deprive of a post; to dismiss or drive from a post or position.

1577 BUCHANAN *Let. to Randolph* ['Master of the postes'] Wks. (1892) 59 Albeit I be on fut, and ye ryd the post; praying you als not to dispost my hoste at Newwerk, Jone of Kelsterne. **1609** J. DAVIES *Holy Roode* (1876) 12 (D.) Now, thinke thou see'st..This kindling Cole of flaming Charitie Disposted all in post. **1823** CHALMERS *Serm.* I. 225 It is God ..who alone can dispost it from this ascendency. **1827** SCOTT *Napoleon* xlvii, The..resolution of disposting the Austrian general by main force. **1851** *Fraser's Mag.* XLIII. 598 Lord George Bentinck died disposted.

dispost, obs. pa. t. and pa. pple. of DISPOSE.

disposure (dɪ'spəʊʒ(j)ʊə(r)). Now *rare.* [f. DISPOSE *v.* + -URE; cf. COMPOSURE.]

1. Arrangement, order; = DISPOSITION 1, 2.

a **1625** FLETCHER *Hum. Lieutenant* III. iv, She is so great a mistress of disposure. **1658** SIR T. BROWNE *Gard. Cyrus* iii. 47 The remarkable disposure of those yellow fringes about the purple Pestill of Aaron. **1704** SWIFT *Tale T.* Concl. (1710) 240 In my Disposure of Employments of the Brain, I have thought fit to make Invention the Master. **1824** *Examiner* 71/1 The disposure of the group is beautiful.

†b. Good order, orderly arrangement. *Obs.*

a **1637** B. JONSON *Underwoods, Epit. V. Corbet*, A life that ..was..all order and disposure still.

†2. Ordering, control, management, direction; dispensation; = DISPOSAL 1, DISPOSITION 3. *Obs.*

1569 COLMAN *Let.* in Strype *Ann. Ref.* I. lv. 609 Disposures..and crosses are very grievous to the flesh. **1625** K. LONG tr. *Barclay's Argenis* II. xvii. 119 Out of the placing of the Starres..out of their influence on Children..comes the whole disposure of their life and death. **1677** BATES *Chr. Relig. proved by Reason* v. (R.) In the disposures of providence. **1689** *Proc. Pres. Parl. Justified* 5 Dissatisfied with the Management and Disposure of Affairs.

3. The action of disposing of, making over, settling, etc.; bestowal, assignment; = DISPOSAL 2, 3; DISPOSITION 4.

a **1649** DRUMM. OF HAWTH. *Hist. Jas. I*, Wks. (1711) 3 Rendring the disposure thereof [revenue] chast, sincere and pure for expenses necessary and profitable. **1665** EVELYN *Mem.* (1857) III. 173 The disposure and assignment of this prodigious royal aid of £2,500,000. **1682** *Pennsylv. Archives* I. 50 Yᵉ Disposure of wᵉⁿ yoᵘ have already made of great Scopes of land. **1873** BROWNING *Red Cott. Nt.-cap* 168 Disposure of the commerce—that took time.

†4. Power or right to dispose of; = DISPOSAL 4, DISPOSITION 4 b. *Obs.*

1606 FORD *Honor Tri.* (1843) 13 Inchained to the disposure of his ladie. **1630** MASSINGER *Picture* I. ii, Surrendering up My will and faculties to your disposure. **1661** E. BURROUGHS *Plea conc. Quakers* 20 At the Will and Disposure of the Almighty we are. *a* **1693** URQUHART *Rabelais* III. iii. 38 To acquire Creditors is not at the Disposure of each Man's Arbitriment.

†**5.** Turn of mind; = DISPOSITION 6. *Obs.*

1613 CHAPMAN *Revenge Bussy d'Ambois* IV. Hij a, His sweet disposure, As much abhorring to behold, as doe Any vnnaturall and bloudy action.

dispotto, dispotical, obs. ff. DESPOT, -ICAL.

dispouse, var. form of DESPOUSE *v. Obs.*

†**dis'power,** *v. Obs. rare.* [DIS- 7 a.] *trans.* To deprive of power.

1656 S. H. *Gold. Law* 66 How could they do less having power, then desert and dispower him?

dispoyle, -spoyly, obs. ff. DESPOIL *v.*

†**dis'practice.** *Obs. rare.* [DIS- 9.] Discontinuance.

1673 PENN *Alex. Coppersm. Rebuked* 10 Well satisfied with any Member's Dispractice of an orderly Performance.

†**dis'praisable,** *a. Obs.* [f. DISPRAISE *v* + -ABLE. Cf. OF. *desprisable* reprehensible, f. *despriser* to dispraise.] Worthy of dispraise or blame.

c **1449** PECOCK *Repr.* III. viii. 325 He therbi be..preisable or dispreisable, doing honestli or doing dishonestli. **1553** GRIMALDE *Cicero's Offices* I. (1558) 49 Innumerable other diuersities ther be of nature and of maners no deal yet dispraysable. **1630** *R. Johnson's Kingd. & Commw.* 639 Onely in this it is dispraisable..it bringeth forth Inhabitants of savage..and inhumane behaviour. **16..** T. ADAMS *Wks.* (1861-2) II. 462 (D.) It is dispraisable either to be senseless or fenceless. **1755** JOHNSON *Dispraisible*, unworthy of commendation. *Dict.*

dispraise (dɪs'preɪz), *sb.* [f. DIS- 9 + PRAISE *sb.*; or f. DISPRAISE *v.* after *praise* sb. Cf. OF. *despriz, despris*, and see DISPRIZE *sb.*]

1. The action or fact of dispraising; the opposite of praise; expression of disparagement; blame, censure.

1509 HAWES *Past. Pleas.* XI. vi, The morall sense they cloke full subtyly, In prayse or dysprayse, as it is reasonable. **1580** NORTH *Plutarch* (1676) 218 He began to make a long Oration in his dispraise. **1667** MILTON *P.L.* XI. 167 To mee reproach Rather belongs, distrust, and all dispraise. **1783** HAILES *Antiq. Chr. Ch.* i. 3 Does not necessarily imply either praise or dispraise. **1852** TENNYSON *Death Dk. Wellington* 73 In praise and in dispraise the same, A man of well-attemper'd frame. **1852** MISS YONGE *Cameos* (1877) II. xix. 197 Charles VI would not hear a word in his dispraise.

2. with *a* and *pl.* An act or instance of dispraising or blaming. **b.** A cause of blame, discredit, or disgrace.

1535 COVERDALE *Wisd.* iv, *heading*, A dispraye of the wicked. **1580** SIDNEY *Arcadia* III. (1724) II. 718 Little did the melancholick Shepherd regard either his dispraises, or the other's praises. **1641** HINDE *J. Bruen* xli. 129 To bee praised of a man utterly unworthy of any praise himselfe, is a dispraise. **1754** RICHARDSON *Grandison* I. xxxvi. 257 How far from a dispraise in this humane consideration. **1872** HOWELLS *Wedd. Journ.* 33 As they twittered their little dispraises.

dispraise (dɪs'preɪz), *v.* Forms: 4-5 dispreise-n, 4-7 dispryse, 5 despreise, des-, dyspreyse, 5-6 dysprayse, 5-7 despraise, 6 dispreyse, -prease, 6-7 disprase, 4- dispraise. [a. OF. *despreisier, -preiser, -prisier*, = Pr. *desprezar, despreciar*, Sp. *despreciar*, It. *disprezzare*:—late L. or Romanic type **dispretiāre* for cl.L. *dēpretiāre*: see DEPRECIATE and DE- I. 6.

In OF., originally, the tonic stem had *-pris-*, the atonic *-preis-*, hence inf. *despreisier*, 3 sing. pr. *desprise*. But these distinctions were subseq. confused, and at length levelled under the *-pris-* form: thence Eng. DISPRIZE.]

1. *trans.* To do the opposite of *to praise*; to speak of with disparagement, depreciation, blame, or disapprobation; to blame, censure.

a **1300** *Cursor M.* 27585 (Cott.) We agh ilk [fallen] man upraise, and in vr hert vrself dispraise. *c* **1386** CHAUCER *Melib.* ¶105 (Harl.) Who-so wil haue Sapience schal no man desprayse. *c* **1400** *Rom. Rose* 1053 For to dispreisen, and to blame That best deserven love and name. **1494** FABYAN *Chron.* IV. lxix. 47 She disprayesd hym in that, that he worshypped a man yᵗ was nayled vpon a Crosse. **1547-64** BAULDWIN *Mor. Philos.* (Palfr.) 166 Doe not that thy selfe, which thou dispraisest in another. **1612** WOODALL *Surg. Mate* Pref. Wks. (1653) 12 Foxes dispraise the grapes they cannot reach. **1616** B. JONSON *Epigr.* I. lii. *To Censorious Courtling*, I rather thou should'st utterly Dispraise my Work, than praise it frostily. **1712** STEELE *Spect.* No. 288 ¶3 While they like my Wares they may dispraise my Writing. **1850** W. IRVING *Goldsmith* xxvi. 259 Johnson, who..rarely praised or dispraised things by halves. **1852** ROBERTSON *Lect.* 177 Men who cannot praise Dryden without dispraising Coleridge.

absol. **1483** CAXTON *Gold. Leg.* 235/1 To fore thys tyme I despreysed and scorned and wend there had ben none other lyf than this. *c* **1600** SHAKS. *Sonn.* xcv, That tongue that tells the story of thy daies..Cannot dispraise. **1650** FULLER *Pisgah* I. vi. 16 When he intends to praise or dis-praise, he will doe it to the purpose. **1878** MISS TYTLER *Anne Ascue* i. in *Sunday Mag.* 36 As for you or any other..I will not dispraise, because I know you not.

†**2.** To speak of depreciatingly or contemptuously; to depreciate, despise. *Obs.*

c **1386** CHAUCER *Melib.* ¶5 Whan Prudence had herd hire husbond avaunte him of his richesse..dispreising the power of his adversaries. **1475** *Bk. Noblesse* 59 Fabius despraised renommee and vayne glorie, but onlie gafe his solicitude, thought, and his bisy cure about the comon profit of Rome. *c* **1500** *Melusine* xx. 113 Dyspreyse not your enmyes though they be litel, but make euer good watche.

3. To bring dispraise upon, to cause to be depreciated or despised. *rare.*

1879 E. ARNOLD *Lt. Asia* VIII. (1881) 226 These riches shall not fade away in life, Nor any death dispraise.

Hence **dis'praised** *ppl. a.*; **dis'praising** *vbl. sb.* and *ppl. a.*; **dis'praisingly** *adv.*

c **1386** CHAUCER *Pars. T.* ¶423 In dispreisynge of hym that men preise. **1483** *Cath. Angl.* 101/2 Dispraysinge, *deprauacio.* **1526** *Pilgr. Perf.* (W. de W. 1531) 238 All yᵉ crymes of yᵉ tonge, as sclaunders, detraccyons..or dispraysynges, etc. **1552** HULOET, Disprayysed, *despectus, despicatus, obtrectatus.* **1604** SHAKS. *Oth.* III. iii. 72 When I haue spoke of you dispraisingly. **1839** *Fraser's Mag.* XIX. 31 [He] is dispraisingly sketched by the authoress.

dis'praiser. [-ER¹.] One who dispraises.

1532 TINDALE *Expos. & Notes* Wks. 194 Cursed be the..dispraysers of them that be good to bring them out of fauour. **1640** G. WATTS tr. *Bacon's Adv. Learn.* VI. iii. (R.) Praisers and dispraisers many times doe but aime at their own ends, and do not think all they say. **1880** RUSKIN in *19th Cent.* VIII. 201 Unbeliever, unmaker, and dispraiser.

Hence **dis'praiseress,** a female dispraiser.

1611 COTGR., *Despriseresse*, a disesteemeresse, despiseresse, or dispraiseresse of.

†**dis'praiseworthy,** *a. Obs. rare.* [f. DISPRAISE *sb.*, after *praiseworthy*.] Worthy or deserving of dispraise; blameworthy.

1553 GRIMALDE *Cicero's Offices* III. (1558) 137 If they bee dispraiseworthye who haue held their peace, what is to bee thought of those who haue used a vainnesse of talke?

disprave, bad form of DEPRAVE.

1402 HOCCLEVE *Letter of Cupid* 265 Than to deprave [*Speght's ed. Chaucer* disprave] wommen generally.

†**di'sprayer.** *Obs. rare.* [DIS- 9: cf. OF. *desprier* to unsay a prayer.] ? Deprecation.

1615 DANIEL *Queen's Arcadia* III. v. Wks. (1717) 194 That Sound of Words, that answers not the Tone Of my Disprayers in th' Accents of like Moan.

dispread, disspread (dɪ'sprɛd), *v. arch.* Forms: 6 dispred, despreed, 7- dispread, disspread. *Pa. t.* and *pple.* dispread; 6 despred, 6-7 dispred, 7- disspred, (pa. pple. *erron.* 7 dispreden, 8 -edden). [f. *di-*, DIS- 1 + SPREAD *v.*]

1. *trans.* To spread abroad or out; to extend, expand, dilate, open out.

1590 SPENSER *F.Q.* I. iv. 17 Drawne of fayre Pecocks, that excell in pride, And full of Argus eyes their tayles dispredden wide. **1591** —— *Virg. Gnat* 242 Looslie on the grassie greene dispredd. **1596** —— *F.Q.* V. xii. 13 Like as a tender Rose..Dispreds the glorie of her leaues gay. **1600** FAIRFAX *Tasso* I. xl. 9 Baldwine his ensigne faire did next despreed. **1616** SANDYS *Ps.* cxx. in Farr *S.P. Jas. I*, (1848) 80 A vine on wall disspred. **1639** G. DANIEL *Ecclus.* xxiv. 51 Dispreden farr, Farre as the Terebinth, my branches are. **1714** *Solomon's Song* in *Steele's Poet. Misc.* 242 While opening Buds their folded Leaves dis-spread. **1738** WESLEY *Psalms* XLV. iv, Dispread the Victory of thy Cross. *a* **1766** W. THOMPSON *Hymn to May* xxii. 3 Have ye not seen..Striding the clouds a bow dispredden wide? **1838** MRS. BROWNING *Vis Poets* 203 The lady stood beside his head, Smiling a thought, with hair dispread. **1863** W. LANCASTER *Praeterita* 64 The disunited, desolated hands Listless of use and nervelessly disspread.

2. *intr.* (for *refl.*)

1596 SPENSER *F.Q.* IV. vii. 40 His face they [his lockes] overgrew, And over all his shoulders did dispred. **1642** H. MORE *Song of Soul* I. I. xlix, She is the centre from whence all the light Dispreads. **1727-46** THOMSON *Summer* 209 Tyrant Heat, dispreading through the sky With rapid sway.

Hence **di'spread** *ppl. a.*; **di'spreading** *vbl. sb.*; **di'spreader,** one who spreads abroad.

1636 FEALTY *Clavis Myst.* ii. 15 Joseph of Arimathea..a great dispreader of the Gospel. **1642** H. MORE *Song of Soul* II. III. IV. x, Dispread exility Of slyer reasons fails. **1644** MILTON *Areop.* (Arb.) 48 Dispredders both of vice and error. *a* **1652** J. SMITH *Sel. Disc.* VII. vi. (1821) 361 The dispreadings and distended radiations of his love. **1890** *Spectator* 15 Feb., Prophets descend from the ceiling of the Sistine to become andirons, and their dispread limbs find a motive in the poker and tongs.

disprease, -preise, obs. ff. DISPRAISE.

dis'prejudice, *v. rare.* [DIS- 7 a.] *trans.* To free from prejudice.

1654 W. MOUNTAGUE *Devout Ess.* II. vii. §5 (R.) Those..will easilie be..disprejudiced in point of the doctrine.

dispre'pare, *v. rare.* [DIS- 6.] *trans.* To render unprepared.

1651 HOBBES *Leviath.* IV. xliv, A confederacy of deceivers that..endeavour..to extinguish in them [men] the light, both of nature and the Gospel; and so to disprepare them for the Kingdom of God to come.

†**dis'press,** *v. Obs.* [f. DIS- 1 + PRESS *v.*] *trans.* To press or force asunder or apart.

1605 TIMME *Quersit.* III. 156 Mercurial vapours thickened into Cloudes..and..not able to be dispressed. **1617** MARKHAM *Caval.* I. 83 The searing of the skinne..doth so seauer and dispresse it, that it will neuer after meete close together againe. *a* **1627** HAYWARD *Edw. VI* (1630) 92 Princes..in no case to endure their supreame authority to be forceably either oppressed or dispressed by their subjects.

dis'priest, *v. rare.* [DIS- 7 b.] *trans.* To deprive of the priesthood.

1563-87 FOXE *A. & M.* (1596) 131/2 If he did well in so dispreesting and discharactering Formosus. **1611** FLORIO, *Spretare*, to vnpriest, to dispriest.

disprince: see DIS- 7 b.

disprison (dɪs'prɪz(ə)n), *v.* [DIS- 7 c. Cf. obs. F. *desprisonner*, mod.F. *dép-*.] *trans.* To set free from prison. Hence **dis'prisoned** *ppl. a.*

1842 LYTTON *Zanoni* VI. vii, The disprisoned mind.

disprivacied (dɪs'praɪvəsɪd), *ppl. a.* [f. DIS- 7 a.] Deprived or bereft of privacy.

1848 LOWELL *Fable for Critics* Poet. Wks. 1890 III. 93 On the poet's dis-privacied moods..the pert critic intrudes.

disprivilege (dɪs'prɪvɪlɪdʒ), *v.* Also 7-8 **-edge.** [DIS- 7 a (or 6).]

1. *trans.* To deprive (a person) of privilege.

a **1617** BAYNE *On Eph.* (1658) 125 Our love must be shewed them..unlesse their foolish lewdness dis-priviledge them. **1670** PENN *Lib. of Consc.* iv. Wks. (1726) I. 452 So acting and believing, disprivilednes them for ever of that Recompence. **1882** *Trans. R. Hist. Soc.* X. 253 One ought not to dis-privilege a person without his knowledge.

†**2.** To annul or undo the privilege of. *Obs. rare.*

1622 H. SYDENHAM *Serm. Sol. Occ.* II. (1637) 141 Let not my zeale to the Priest disprivilege my allegiance to my King.

†**di'sprize,** *sb. Obs.* Also 6 **disprice.** [a. OF. *despris* 'disesteeme, contempt, disdaine' (Cotgr.), earlier *despriz* = It. *disprezzo*, Sp. *disprecio*:—late L. type **dispretium.* See DISPRIZE *v.* and cf. PRIZE, PRICE.]

Disparagement, depreciation, contempt.

1560 ROLLAND *Crt. Venus* II. 61 3e haif done greit dispric[e]. *c* **1636** JAMES *Iter Lanc.* (Cheth. Soc.) Introd. 36 In disprize of death.

disprize (dɪ'spraɪz), *v. Obs.* or *arch.* Forms: 5 despryse, 5-6 desprise, dispryse, 6 dyspryse, 7 disprise, 7- disprize. [a. late OF. *desprise-r* for original *despreisier* (tonic stem *desprise*): see DISPRAISE, which represents the earlier OF. form.]

1. *trans.* To depreciate, undervalue; to hold in small repute or in contempt. *arch.*

1480 CAXTON *Ovid's Met.* XII. xiv, He desprised Hector and his menace. **1484** —— *Chivalry* (Caxton) 80 Kynge Alysander in desprysing auarice and couetyse had alwey the handes stratched forthe for to gyue unto his knyghtes. **1606** SHAKS. *Tr. & Cr.* IV. v. 74 'Tis done like Hector; but securely done, A little proudly, and great deale disprising The knight oppos'd. **1644** QUARLES *Barnabas & B.* (1851) 147 And wilt thou more disprize the giver than the gift? **1886** [see DISPRIZED below.]

†**b.** To make of small account; to dishonour.

1508 A. CADIOU *Porteous of Noblenes* in *Compl. Scot.* (1801) Introd. 204 He desprisis his nobilnes that..kepis noght hym selue clene.

†**c.** To bring into depreciation. *Obs.*

a **1687** COTTON *Ode to Lydia* (T.) Dishevel, sunset, thy yellow hair, Whose ray does burnished gold disprize.

†**2.** To dispraise, disparage, decry; to speak of slightingly. *Obs.*

1514 BARCLAY *Cyt. & Uplondyshm.* (Percy Soc.) 4 The frosty wynter..Whiche men than praysed, they now dyspryse & hate. **1570** *Satir. Poems Reform.* xviii. 53 Thair fact and act all Scotland now disprysis. **1621** QUARLES *Argalus & P.* (1678) 4 Some trust to fame, some secretly disprize Her worth.

Hence **di'sprized** *ppl. a.*; **di'sprizing** *vbl. sb.* and *ppl. a.*

1500 *Burgh Rec. Edin.* 20 Oct. (Jam.) William Paterson [and] Patrick Lowiesoun convict be ane assyse vpoun the disprysing of William Todrig, baillie, invadand him with..drawin swordis. **1560** ROLLAND *Crt. Venus* II. 179 Bot be no way in Venus disprysing. **1602** SHAKS. *Ham.* III. i. 72 For who would beare..The pangs of dispriz'd Loue. **1886** DOWDEN *Shelley* I. iv. 154 Haunted by thoughts of his own disprized love.

dis'probabilize, *v. rare.* [f. DIS- 6 + PROBABILIZE.] *trans.* To deprive of probability, render improbable. Hence **dis'probabilizing** *ppl. a.*; **disprobabili'zation.**

1827 BENTHAM *Ration. Judic. Evid.* III. 13 The principal fact will be considered as being, in a greater or less degree, disprobabilized. *Ibid.*, The existence of this disprobabilizing fact. *Ibid.* 16 Notice cannot but be taken of the opposite effect, disprobabilization.

†**dispro'bation.** *Obs.* [DIS- 9, after *disprove.*] = DISAPPROBATION.

1647 M. HUDSON *Div. Right Govt.* II. vi. 110 The Books of Exodus and Numbers record ten several disprobations and murmurings of the people against Moses..Neither did the peoples disprobation of his just Power..unking David.

dis'probative, *a. rare.* [DIS- 10, after *disprove.*] That tends to disprove.

1823 BENTHAM *Not Paul* 23 A disprobative Circumstance. **1827** —— *Ration. Judic. Evid.* III. 16 Little need for considering the probative force (the disprobative force it will here be held).

disprofe, -proffe, obs. ff. DISPROOF.

†**dispro'fess,** *v. Obs. rare.* [DIS- 6.] *trans.* To renounce the profession of.

1590 SPENSER *F.Q.* III. xi. 20 His armes, which he had vowed to disprofesse, She..did about him dresse.

dis'profit, *sb. Obs.* or *arch.* [f. DIS- 9 + PROFIT *sb.*] The opposite of profit; disadvantage, detriment.

1494 FABYAN *Chron.* VII. 618 All was ruled by the quene & her counsayll, to the great disprofite of the kynge & his realme. **1596** DALRYMPLE tr. *Leslie's Hist. Scot.* VI. 330 Weiris ar begun, with gret slauchtir on baith sydes, disproffet and skaith. **1620** MARKHAM *Farew. Husb.* II. xxii. (1668) 120 You shall want their Company..which is both discomfort and disprofit. **1751** WESLEY *Wks.* (1872) XIV. 125 Adjectives signifying..disprofit..govern a Dative Case. **1837** CARLYLE *Mirabeau* Misc. (1872) V. 217 They fought much: with an eye to profit, to redress of disprofit.

†**b.** with *a* and *pl.* A disadvantage. *Obs.*

a **1568** COVERDALE *Bk. Death* I. viii. Wks. II. 56 All the aforesaid disprofits and griefs do justly vanish. **1651** HOBBES *Govt. & Soc.* x. §2. 149 All the profits and disprofits arising from government. **1671** H. M. tr. *Erasm. Colloq.* 219 Lest I should get for my self any profit by others disprofits.

dis'profit, *v. Obs.* or *arch.* [f. DIS- 6 + PROFIT *v.* (possibly from Fr.).]

1. *trans.* To bring disadvantage to; to injure, incommode, inconvenience.

1483 CAXTON *Gold. Leg.* 264/1 [He] commendyd hym to god prayeng that the pryson shold not disproufyte hym. **1532** in W. H. Turner *Select. Rec. Oxford* 113 The Towne is not profited by them, but..disprofited. **1660** tr. *Paracelsus' Archidoxis* II. 110* That which is Innate doth neither profit, or disprofit any one. **1837** CARLYLE *Fr. Rev.* II. v. vii, Of the whole two thousand there are not now half a score..that will profit or disprofit us. **1850** —— *Latter-d. P.* vii. (1872) 246.

†**2.** *intr.* (for *refl.*) To fail to profit; to receive disadvantage or injury. *Obs.*

1561 T. NORTON *Calvin's Inst.* IV. 88 He hath sene no worse menne than those that disprofited in monasteries.

Hence **dis'profited** *ppl. a.*, **dis'profiting** *vbl. sb.*

1599 MINSHEU, *Desaprovechado*, disprofited. **1632** SHERWOOD, A disprofiting, *Endommagement.*

†**dis'profitable,** *a. Obs.* [f. DIS- 10 + PROFITABLE: cf. obs. F. *desprofitable* (16th c. in Godef.).] Unprofitable; detrimental.

1548 HALL *Chron., Hen. VIII* (an. 19) (1809) 739 He had ..discharged 12 Articles whiche were moste grevous & disprofitable to the Frenche Kyng. **1572** R. H. tr. *Lavaterus' Ghostes* To Rdr. (1596) A iij, Profitable therefore it is..vnto many, and disprofitable vnto none.

disproof (dɪs'pruːf). Forms: 6 disprofe, -proufe, -prove, 6- disproof. [f. DIS- 9 + PROOF, after DISPROVE.] The proving of a thing not to be what is asserted; refutation, confutation; the evidence constituting such refutation.

1531 ELYOT *Gov.* I. xiv. (1883) 153 Therin they do diligently obserue the rules of Confirmation and Confutation, wherin resteth prouf and disproufe. **1533** MORE *Answ. Poysoned Bk.* Wks. 1099/2 These woordes haue ..in themselfe, neither any thyng in disprofe of the very eating of his flesh, nor for the profe yt he ment the beliefe of hys death. **1695** WOODWARD *Nat. Hist. Earth* I. 45 A fuller and more effectual Disproof of the recited opinions. **1825** SYD. SMITH *Wks.* (1859) II. 66/1 Such allegations..are scarce ever susceptible of specific disproof. **1884** tr. *Lotze's Metaph.* 194 Such a proof..has never been attempted; the burden of disproof has been thrown on the opposite view.

b. with *a* and *pl.* An instance of this; a disproving fact or piece of evidence.

a **1650** MAY *Satir. Puppy* (1657) 20 Lest he should betray himself to an eminent disproof. **1699** BENTLEY *Phal.* Pref. 51 A sufficient Disproof of this malicious Calumny. **1877** E. R. CONDER *Bas. Faith* v. 233 Lightly to pass over all.. irreconcilable facts as mere difficulties, not disproofs.

†**dis'property,** *v. Obs. rare.* [DIS- 7 b.] *trans.* To deprive of property: to dispossess.

1607 SHAKS. *Cor.* II. i. 264 He would Haue made them Mules, silenc'd their Pleaders, And dispropertied their Freedomes.

disproportion (dɪsprə'pɔəʃən), *sb.* [f. DIS- 9 + PROPORTION: perh. a. F. *disproportion* (16th c. in Hatz.-Darm.).]

Want of proportion in number, quantity, size, etc.; lack of symmetry or due relation of quantity or number between things or parts of the same thing; the condition of being out of proportion.

1555 EDEN *Decades* 190 The disproportion that they haue to all other beasts. **1642** FULLER *Holy & Prof. St.* III. xxii. 214 Let there be no great disproportion in age. *a* **1656** BP. HALL in Spurgeon *Treas. Dav.* Ps. cxliv. 3 The disproportion betwixt us and them [gnats] is but finite. **1752** JOHNSON *Rambler* No. 196. ¶3 The disproportion will always be great between expectation and enjoyment. **1878** *Masque Poets* 208 Evil perhaps being nothing more nor less Than good in disproportion or excess. **1880** DIXON *Windsor* III. xxxiii. 325 A sense of disproportion lifts men into mirth.

b. with *a* and *pl.*: An example of this; something out of proportion.

1597 DANIEL *Civ. Wars* I. xxxviii, Disproportions harmony do break. **1604** SHAKS. *Oth.* III. iii. 233 Foule disproportions, Thoughts vnnaturall. **1667** MILTON *P.L.* VIII. 27 Reasoning I oft admire, How Nature wise and frugal could commit Such disproportions. **1875** JOWETT *Plato* (ed. 2) III. 672 A leg too long, or some other disproportion.

dispro'portion, *v.* [f. the sb. Cf. F. *disproportionner.*] *trans.* To render or make out of due proportion.

1593 SHAKS. *3 Hen. VI*, III. ii. 160 Shee did corrupt frayle Nature with some Bribe..To shape my Legges of an vnequall size, To dis-proportion me in euery part. *a* **1631** DONNE *Lett.* (1651) 7 Nothing disproportions us..as murmuring. **1838** LYTTON *Alice* XI. viii, Statutes that disproportion punishment to crime. **1864** W. FAIRBAIRN in *Reader* 27 Feb. 270/1 It is even possible so to disproportion the top and bottom areas of a wrought-iron girder..as to cause it to yield with little more than half the ultimate strain.

dispro'portionable, *a.* [f. prec. + -ABLE.] Out of due or symmetrical proportion; disproportionate.

1589 PUTTENHAM *Eng. Poesie* III. xxiv. (Arb.) 283 So was the kings action proportionable to his estate and therefore decent, the Philosophers, disproportionable both to his profession and calling and therefore indecent. **1640** WILKINS *New Planet* vi. (1707) 209 Such an incredible Celerity, as is altogether disproportionable to its Bigness. *a* **1717** BLACKALL *Wks.* (1723) I. 136 Seeing..the good and evil things of this Life and of the next are so vastly disproportionable. **1760-72** tr. *Juan & Ulloa's Voy.* (ed. 3) I. 124 Its belly is, in largeness, very disproportionable to its body.

dispro'portionableness. [f. prec. + -NESS.] The quality of being out of proportion.

1651 BIGGS *New Disp.* ¶131 Consisting of crudities, disproportionablenesse. **1664** H. MORE *Myst. Iniq.* 336 From the disproportionableness of the seventh Age of the world to the rest. **1894** *Newspr.*, A correspondent..has submitted the word 'disproportionableness', as the longest in the English language.

dispro'portionably, *adv.* [f. as prec. + LY².] In a manner or to an extent which is out of due proportion; disproportionately.

1608 *Dispute Quest. Kneeling Sacrament* 3 Why doe wee.. disproportionably and unsutably..demeane our selues at the table and feast of our Lord Iesus. **1770** LANGHORNE *Plutarch* (1879) I. 176/2 His head was disproportionably long. **1838** LYTTON *Alice* 65 The room was almost disproportionably lofty.

dispro'portional, *a.* and *sb.* [f. DISPROPORTION + -AL¹; cf. F. *disproportionnel.*]

A. *adj.* = DISPROPORTIONATE.

1609 HOLLAND *Amm. Marcell.* Annot. G ij a, Then the length were disproportionall to the breadth. **1645** MILTON *Colast.* (1851) 371 To force the continuance of mariage between mindes found utterly unfit, and disproportional, is against nature. **1692** LOCKE *Educ.* §158 It is very disproportional to the Understanding of childhood.

B. *sb.* A disproportional quantity or number.

a **1696** SCARBURGH *Euclid* (1705) 192 Having finished his Explanations of..Proportionals, and Disproportionals.

Hence **dispro'portionalness** = next.

1730-6 in BAILEY (folio). In recent Dicts.

disproportio'nality. [f. prec. + -ITY.] The quality of being disproportional.

1642 H. MORE *Song of Soul* II. iii. III. lx, The world so's setten free From that untoward disproportionalitie. **1668** —— *Div. Dial.* II. xii. (1713) 125 That poison is nothing but disproportionality of particles to the particles of our own.. Bodies. **1818** BENTHAM *Ch. Eng.* 374 For..services of the occasional class..Pay, by disproportionality excessive.

dispro'portionally, *adv.* [f. as prec. + -LY².] In a manner or to an extent that is out of proportion.

1755 in JOHNSON. **1839** JOHNSTON in *Proc. Berw. Nat. Club* I. No. 7. 201 The eyes of the embryo, at this period disproportionally large. **1845** MᶜCULLOCH *Taxation* II. ix. (1852) 334 Disproportionally heavy taxes are the great cause of smuggling. **1880** T. W. WEBB in *Nature* XXI. 213 The satellites [of Mars]..are..so disproportionally minute, according to our limited ideas of proportion.

dispro'portionate, *a.* [f. DIS- 10 + PROPORTIONATE *a.* Cf. F. *disproportionné* (16th c.): see -ATE².] Out of proportion; failing to observe or constitute due proportion; inadequately or excessively proportioned. Const. *to.*

1555 EDEN *Decades* 189 His toonge..very longe and thynne and much disproportionate to his bodye. **1614** SELDEN *Titles Hon.* 135 Neither is this annointing much disproportionat to that. **1722** WOLLASTON *Relig. Nat.* ix. 181 A long repentance is a disproportionate price for a short enjoyment. **1862** H. SPENCER *First Princ.* II. iv. §53 (1875) 176 Effects extremely disproportionate to causes. **1867** FREEMAN *Norm. Conq.* (1876) I. iv. 246 Dwelling at an apparently disproportionate length on some subjects.

dispro'portionate, *v. Chem.* [Back-formation from next.] *intr.* To undergo disproportionation.

1934 in WEBSTER. **1946** *Nature* 9 Nov. 673/1 The monoethoxy compound..is unstable at room temperature, disproportionating rapidly into SiF_4 and (C_2H_5O) SiF_2... The triethoxy compound is the most stable of the three, having no tendency to disproportionate even at temperatures near its boiling point. **1950** A. F. WELLS *Structural Inorg. Chem.* v. 144 Many lower halides disproportionate into a mixture of metal and higher halide. **1964** J. W. LINNETT *Electronic Struct. Molecules* iii. 51 The ion contains an odd number of electrons and, in this environment, does not disproportionate to O_2 or O_2^-, both of which contain an even number of electrons.

†**dispro'portionated,** *a. Obs. rare.* [f. prec. + -ED¹.] = DISPROPORTIONATE *a.* Hence †**dispro'portionatedness** = DISPROPORTIONATENESS.

1572 J. JONES *Bathes of Bath.* II. 100 The qualitie [of Bath waters] especially disproportionated with as great a degree of heat..cannot be induced but by an especial heat. **1647** H. MORE *Song of Soul* Notes 391 No such vast excentricity as there, nor disproportionatednesse of Orbs and motions. **1668** —— *Div. Dial.* I. 23 That thinner Element being disproportionated to the Lungs of either Birds or Beasts.

dispro'portionately, *adv.* [f. as prec. + -LY².] In a manner or to an extent which is out of proportion, inadequate, or excessive.

1682 SIR T. BROWNE *Chr. Mor.* ii. 8 (T.) He.. disproportionately divideth his days. **1696** WHISTON *Th. Earth* IV. (1722) 294 Nothing should happen unseasonably, unfitly, disproportionately. **1705** BOSMAN *Guinea* 250 The Head disproportionately large. **1867** FROUDE *Short Stud., Criticism & Gospel* 161 Among the multitude the elements are disproportionately mixed.

dispro'portionateness. [f. as prec. + -NESS.] The quality of being out of proportion.

1668 H. MORE *Div. Dial.* II. xviii. (1713) 147 The Incongruity and Disproportionateness of the Use of them. **1819** COLERIDGE in *Lit. Rem.* (1836) II. 258 It would argue a disproportionateness, a want of balance. **1874** FARRAR *Christ* x. 119 Every one must have been struck..with the apparent disproportionateness between the cause and the effect.

disproportio'nation. *Chem.* [f. DISPROPORTION *sb.* or *v.* + -ATION.] A transfer of atoms or valency electrons between two or more identical molecules or ions, resulting in molecules or ions containing the same elements in different proportions or in different oxidation states.

1929 E. E. REID *Coll. Org. Chem.* xxxiv. 550 Reactions of this sort have received the name 'disproportionation'. **1939** *Jrnl. Amer. Chem. Soc.* LXI. 2769/2 The identification of tri-*p*-tolymethane..and a polymeric residue as the products of disproportionation of tri-*p*-tolylmethyl..makes it possible to suggest a mechanism for the reaction. **1946** *Nature* 9 Nov. 673/1 The disproportionation proceeds to about one third of completion, at which point an equilibrium is set up... Disproportionation occurs during the fluorination. **1960** *Times Rev. Industry* Sept. 55/1 Disproportionation of the monochloride into metallic aluminium. **1969** *Nature* 19 Apr. 257/1 Disproportionation of $MSiO_3$ composition into M_2SiO_4 olivine yields SiO_2.

dispro'portioned, *ppl. a.* [f. DISPROPORTION *v.* + -ED; cf. F. *disproportionné.*] Made or rendered out of proportion; disproportionate.

1597 HOOKER *Eccl. Pol.* v. lxxviii. (1611) 424 It argueth a disproportioned minde in them whom so decent orders displease. **1610** SHAKS. *Temp.* v. i. 290 He is as disproportion'd in his Manners As in his shape. **1699** BENTLEY *Phal.* 533. **1787** T. JEFFERSON *Writ.* (1859) II. 199 The women and children are often employed in labors disproportioned to their sex and age. **1851** MAYNE REID *Scalp Hunt.* xxviii, I gazed at the huge disproportioned heads.

†**b.** Inconsistent. *Obs.*

1604 SHAKS. *Oth.* I. iii. 2 *Duke.* There's no composition in this Newes, That giues them Credite. *1 Sen.* Indeed, they are disproportioned.

†**di'spropriate,** *v. Obs.* [f. DIS- 6 + L. *proprium* own, possession, property, after *appropriate, expropriate.*] *trans.* To deprive of the ownership (*of* something); to dispossess.

1613 PURCHAS *Pilgrimage* II. vii. 113 Who knoweth whether those Appropriations did not..dispropriate them of that which in a juster proprietie was given them?

disprovable (dɪs'pruːvəb(ə)l), *a.* [f. DISPROVE *v.* + -ABLE.]

†**1.** Reprehensible, to be disapproved. *Obs.*

1548 GEST *Pr. Masse*, The third and last cause why masse prayer is disprovable is by reason therin it is prayed [etc.]. **1579** FULKE *Refut. Rastel* 709 We receive them, or refuse them, as they be approuable or disprouable by the saide.. doctrine.

2. Capable of being disproved; refutable.

1685 BOYLE *Enq. Notion Nat.* 114 (L.) The incorruptibleness and immutability of the heavenly bodies is more than probably disproveable by the sudden and irregular generation, changes, and destruction of the spots of the sun. **1873** W. R. GREG *Enigmas of Life* Pref. 5 No disprovable datum is suffered to intrude.

disproval (dɪs'pruːvəl). *rare.* [f. DISPROVE + -AL¹.] The act of disproving; disproof.

1614 JACKSON *Creed* III. II. v. [vi.] §1. 47 Whither no European is likely to resort for a disproual of his relation. **1871** MORLEY *Voltaire* (1886) 250 A direct disproval of the alleged facts on which the system professes to rest.

disprove (dɪs'pruːv), *v.* Also 5 dis-, dyspreve, 7 disproove. *Pa. pple.* disproved; also disproven. [a. Of. *desprove-r, -prouver*, f. *des-*, L. *dis-* +

prover to PROVE. Early variants were DEPREVE, DEPROVE, q.v.

The OF. stressed-stem form *despruеve, -preuve*, gave the variant *dispreve*, whence (on the analogy of strong verbs, as *weave, woven*) the pa. pple. *disproven*.]

1. *trans.* To prove (an assertion, claim, etc.) to be false or erroneous; to show the fallacy or non-validity of; to refute, rebut, invalidate.

c **1380** WYCLIF *Sel. Wks.* III. 345 It is no nede to argue her for to disprove þis foli. **1386** *Rolls of Parlt.* III. 225/2 The which thyng..by an even Juge to be proved or disproved. *a* **1400** *Pistill of Susan* 294, I schal be proces apert disproue þis a-pele, For nede. *a* **1450** *Cov. Myst.* (1851) 315 Their owyn pepyl han dysprevyd Al that I have for the seyd or mevyd. **1594** HOOKER *Eccl. Pol.* II. vii. (1611) 72 Neither doth..the infirmity of men ouerthrow or disproue this. **1601** SHAKS. *Jul. C.* III. ii. 105, I speake not to disprooue what Brutus spoke, But heere I am; to speake what I do know. **1796** BP. WATSON *Apol. Bible* 346 A lesson which philosophy never taught, which wit cannot ridicule, nor sophistry disprove. **1814** CHALMERS *Evid. Chr. Revel.* ix. 251 There is a mighty difference between not proven and disproven. **1856** STANLEY *Sinai & Pal.* i. (1858) 53 No one can now prove or disprove the tradition. **1875** JOWETT *Plato* (ed. 2) III. 363 Nay, he replied, that is already disproven.

†**b.** To prove to be non-existent or fictitious.

c **1430** *Life St. Kath.* (1884) 29 How she dispreved hys goddes. *c* **1440** CAPGRAVE *Life St. Kath.* IV. 1576 Saturne, þe firste whom ye soo dispreue.

2. To prove (a person) to be untrue or erroneous in his statements; to convict (a person) of falsehood or error; to refute, confute. *Obs.* or *arch.*

1589 COGAN *Haven Health* ccxiv. (1636) 227 Some peradventure will disprove mee by their owne experience. **1604** SHAKS. *Oth.* v. ii. 172 Disproue this Villaine, if thou bee'st a man: He sayes, thou told'st him that his wife was false. **1633** HALL *Hard Texts, N.T.* 42 Ye Sadducees are in this palpably disproved. **1709** STRYPE *Ann. Ref.* I. lii. 560 One of these that did this was Dr. Calfhill, in two sermons preached in the same cathedral, the bishop present to hear himself disproved. **1749** CHESTERF. *Lett.* II. ccii. 267 Should you..happen to disprove me.

†**3.** To disallow authoritatively; to disapprove. Also *intr.* with *of*. *Obs.*

1477 NORTON *Ord. Alch.* vi. in Ashm. (1652) 100 That other [Art] is disproved and plainely forebod. **1494** FABYAN *Chron.* VII. 295 Let not the rudenesse of them hym lede For to dysproue thys ryme dogerell. **1594** HOOKER *Eccl. Pol.* II. viii. (1611) 78 Men are only not disproued or disallowed of God for them. **1628** VENNER *Tobacco* (1650) 406, I wonder why some disprove the taking of Tobacco after meals. **1720** *Wodrow Corr.* (1843) II. 539 For my share, I disprove the method of his licensing. **1824** MISS FERRIER *Inher.* viii, They have seen other things either better or worse, and can, therefore, either improve or disprove them.

Hence **dis'proved** *ppl. a.*, **dis'proving**, *vbl. sb.*

1587 GOLDING *De Mornay* i. 10 This also was a disproouing of the false Gods. **1598** BARRET *Theor. Warres* II. i. 25 Chaunging those disproued blacke Billes and Bowes into good Muskets. **1639** LD. DIGBY *Lett. conc. Relig.* (1651) 92 Credulity being so easie and naturall, Disproving so difficult.

disprove, obs. form of DISPROOF.

dis'provement. *rare.* [f. DISPROVE *v.* + -MENT.] The action or fact of disproving; a proving not to be true; disproof.

1662 J. CHANDLER *Van Helmont's Oriat.* Pref. to Rdr., They esteemed his disprovement of what the other had said, for a decision of the matter. **1886** *Pop. Sci. Monthly* XXVIII. 695 The scientific discovery..around which all Mr. Lawes's subsequent work centred was the disprovement of Liebig's mineral-ash theory.

dis'prover. [f. as prec. + -ER[1].] **a.** One who disproves; a refuter. †**b.** A disapprover (*obs.*).

a **1639** WOTTON *Dk. Buckhm.* in *Select. Harl. Misc.* (1793) 283 A concurrence of two extremes, within so short a time, by most of the same commenders and disprovers. **1682** H. MORE *Annot. Glanvill's Lux O.* 68 We may observe what a weak Disprover he is of Pre-existence.

dispro'vide, *v. arch.* [DIS- 6.] *trans.* To fail to provide for; to leave unprovided. Hence **dispro'vided** *ppl. a.*, unprovided, unsupplied, unfurnished (F. *dépourvu*).

152. BARCLAY *Sallust's Jugurth* (1557) 50 He shulde not hurt nor disprouyde them whyle he had vitail ynough of his owne prouyson. **1599** SANDYS *Europæ Spec.* (1632) 50 The Papacie is not disprovided of his instruments to worke upon these also. *a* **1691** BOYLE *Wks.* VI. 40 (R.) An impatient lutanist, who has his song book and his instrument ready, but is altogether disprovided of strings. **1864** CARLYLE *Fredk. Gt.* IV. 531 Much disprovided, destitute.

dispuile, dispulȝe, obs. ff. DESPOIL.

dispulp (dɪs'pʌlp), *v.* [f. DIS- 7a + PULP *sb.*] *trans.* To remove the pulp from.

1895 *Black & White* 6 Apr. 467/1 Dispulping coffee.

†**dis'pulverate**, *v. Obs. rare* [DIS- 5.] *trans.* To dissolve into dust.

1609 J. DAVIES *Holy Roode* (1876) 13 (D.) Confusion shall dispulverate All that this round Orbiculer doth beare.

dispume, -ation, var. ff. DESPUME, -ATION. So **dispu'matious** *a.*, characterized by despumation; foamy, frothy.

1819 H. BUSK *Vestriad* II. 85 The brawny Tritons..In dispumatious ranks, his progress wait.

†**di'spunct**, *a. Obs. rare.* [f. DIS- 4 + L. *punctus* pointed.] The reverse of punctilious; impolite, discourteous.

1599 B. JONSON *Cynthia's Rev.* v. ii, *Aso.* I'faith, master, let's go..Let's be retrograde. *Amo.* Stay. That were dispunct to the ladies.

dispunct (dɪ'spʌŋkt), *v. rare.* [f. L. *dispunct-* ppl. stem f. *dispungĕre* to prick or mark here and there, in med.L. to erase (Du Cange), f. DIS- 1 + *pungĕre* to mark, prick.] *trans.* To mark with points or pricks of the pen; hence: **a.** To mark for erasure or omission; **b.** To mark for distinction, to distinguish.

1563-87 FOXE *A. & M.* (1684) I. 798/1, I desire the Reder then so to take me, as though I did not deal here withal, nor speak of the matter, but utterly to haue pretermitted, and dispuncted the same. **1842** DE QUINCEY *Philos. Herodotus* Wks. IX. 207 All beyond Carthage, as Mauritania, etc... being dispuncted by no great states or colonies.

†**di'spunction.** *Obs. rare.* [n. of action from L. *dispungĕre*: see prec.] The action of marking off by points or pricks; erasure.

1637 JACKSON *Divers Sermons* Wks. 1844 VI. 44 The dispunction or inversion of points or letters. **1644** SIR E. DERING *Prop. Sacr.* D b, Another dispunction tells me.. that the very height of popery was the height of some designers, wherefore else should this line be blotted out?

dispunge (dɪ'spʌndʒ), *v.* Also -sponge. [f. *di-*, DIS- 1 + *spunge*, SPONGE *v.*, or L. *spongiāre* to wipe away with a sponge, f. *spongia* sponge. In sense there is evident association with EXPUNGE, L. *expungĕre* 'to prick out, strike out, erase' (which also appears in modern use to be influenced by 'sponge' and understood as 'to wipe out'); but no contact of sense appears with L. *dispungĕre* to check off (debits and credits), balance (accounts), weigh, try.]

1. *trans.* To discharge or pour down as from a squeezed sponge. *arch.* Hence **di'spunging** *vbl. sb.*

1606 SHAKS. *Ant. & Cl.* IV. ix. 12 Oh Soueraigne Mistris of true Melancholly, The poysonous dampe of night dispunge vpon me. **1876** C. WELLS *Joseph & His Brethren* I. v. 69 Mute and perpendicular Dispungings of the hollow-bosom'd clouds Gutter the fruitful surface of the earth.

†**2.** To wipe out, blot out, delete, EXPUNGE. *Obs.*

1622 SPARROW *Bk. Com. Prayer* Pref., Quarrels..about dispunging some Names out of the Diptychs. *a* **1639** SIR H. WOTTON *Hymn* in Farr *S.P. Jas. I* (1848) 250 Thou..that has dispong'd my score. **1662** STILLINGFL. *Orig. Sacr.* III. i. §13 They are to be dispunged out of the Census of such who act upon free principles of reason.

dispunishable (dɪ'spʌnɪʃəb(ə)l), *a. Law.* [a. AF. *dispunishable*, f. DIS- 10 + *punishable* = F. *punissable*.] Free from liability to punishment or penalty; not punishable.

[**1528** J. PERKINS *Profit. Bk.* ix. §619 Ce wast é dispunishable [tr. **1642** This wast is dispunishable].] **1577** STANYHURST *Descr. Irel.* in *Holinshed* (1587) II. 26/1 If this were in anie dispunishable wise raked vp in the ashes..some other would inkindle the like fire afresh. **1594** WEST *2nd Pt. Symbol.* §61 Until attornement hee is dispunishable of wast. **1628** COKE *On Litt.* 27 b, Tenant in tail after passibility is dispunishable for waste. **1639** *Of Nuisance to private Houses* 21 If water fall on my land, and I make a Sluice, and let it out of my land into another mans; this is dispunishable, for every man may doe this one after another. *a* **1734** NORTH *Exam.* II. v. §24 (1740) 329 The Person of the Sovereign is dispunishable and incoercible by Force. **1818** CRUISE *Digest* (ed. 2) IV. 82 If..long and unreasonable leases are the chief cause of dilapidations..much more would they be so, if they were made dispunishable for waste. **1882** LD. COLERIDGE in *Fortn. Rev.* Feb. 235 Seduction, which may be more wicked, is dispunishable.

†**di'spunished**, *ppl. a. Law. Obs. rare.* [f. DIS- 8 + PUNISHED, rendering AF. *despuni, depuny* (13-14th c.), f. F. *des-*, DIS- 4 + *puni* punished.] Unpunished, free from punishment.

1630 in Rushw. *Hist. Coll.* (1659) I. App. 53 In some cases, criminal offences shall be dispunished.

dispurple (dɪs'pɜːp(ə)l), *v. nonce-wd.* [f. DIS- 7a + PURPLE *sb.*] *trans.* To strip of the (imperial) purple; to deprive of sovereignty.

1877 BLACKIE *Wise Men* 347 'Tis fit we die with crowns upon our head Nor beg our way dispurpled to the grave.

†**dis'purpose**, *v. Obs. rare.* [f. DIS- 6 + PURPOSE *sb.*] *trans.* To defeat of its purpose.

1607 *Lingua* v. i, in Hazl. *Dodsley* IX. 433 She..seeing her former plots dispurposed, sends me to an old witch.

†**di'spurse**, *v. Obs.* [An alteration of DISBURSE after PURSE.] = DISBURSE, DEPURSE.

1593 SHAKS. *2 Hen. VI*, III. i. 117 Many a Pound of mine owne proper store..Haue I dis-pursed [*Fol.* 4 disbursed] to the Garrisons, And neuer ask'd for restitution. **1625-49** *Sc. Acts Chas. I* (1814) VI. 9 (Jam.) The estaits declaires they will sie the said John Kenneday..repayit of quhat he sall agrie for, dispurse, or give out for outreiking of the said ship.

†**dispur'vey**, *v. Obs.* Forms: 5 des-, dys-, -porvey, 5-6 -pourvey, 5- dispurvey. [a. OF. *desporveeir, -porveir, -porveer* (12th c. in Littré), f. *des-*, DIS- 4 + *porveeir* to provide: see PURVEY.]

trans. To rob or strip of provision; to render destitute. Chiefly in pa. pple, *dispurveyed* (= OF. *desporveii*, mod.F. *dépourvu*), unprovided, destitute.

c **1430** LYDG. *Bochas* I. x. (1544) 21 b, Thei be caught dispurueyed of defence. **1481-4** E. PASTON in *Paston Lett.* No 859 III. 280, I am not assartaynd how she is purveyde of mony..I woold not se her dysporveyd, yf I myght. **1485** CAXTON *Chas. Gt.* 69 Olyuer whyche was thus dyspourueyed of his hors. *c* **1489** —— *Sonnes of Aymon* xix. 418 They of mountalban be dyspurueyd of mete. **1530** PALSGR. 521/2, I dispourvey, I unprovyde. **1583** GOLDING *Calvin on Deut.* xcii. 570 Wee shall be dispurueied and stript out of all thinges. **1609** HEYWOOD *Brit. Troy* VI. xc. 133 They dispuruey their vestry of such Treasure As they may spare.

Hence †**dispur'veyed** *ppl. a.*, unprovided, unprepared. (= OF. *desporveü*.)

14.. LYDG. & BURGH *Secrees* 2417 Upon thy Enemy renne not sodeynly, Ne dispurveyed. **1483** CAXTON *Gold. Leg.* 101 b/1 And he despourueyd, deth cometh whyche taketh all fro hym. **1484** —— *Curiall* 14 To be drowned by theyr dyspourueyed aluysement. **1494** FABYAN *Chron.* VII. 422 [He] gatheryd hym an vnredy and dispurueyed hoost for the warre. **1580** BARET *Alv.* D 919 Dispurueied of frends: lacking frends, *Inops ab amicis.*

†**dispur'veyance.** *Obs. rare.* [f. prec., after PURVEYANCE.] Want of provisions; destitution.

1590 SPENSER *F.Q.* III. x. 10 Daily siege, through dispurvayance long And lacke of reskewes, will to parley drive.

disputa'bility. [f. next + -ITY.] The quality or fact of being disputable; a disputable matter.

1853 RUSKIN *Stones Ven.* III. iv. §3. 168 *note*, Their very disputability proves the state..above alleged. **1892** W. W. PEYTON *Mem. Jesus* vii. 205 History is a vast disputability.

disputable ('dɪspjuːtəb(ə)l, dɪ'spjuːtəb(ə)l), *a.* (*sb.*) [ad. L. *disputābilis* that may be disputed, f. *disputāre* to DISPUTE. Cf. 16th c. F. *disputable*.]

1. That may be disputed, questioned, or discussed; liable to be called in question, contested, or controverted; questionable.

1548 HALL *Chron.*, *Hen. IV* (an. 11) 30 Which thyng is nether materiall nor disputable. **1587** FLEMING *Contn. Holinshed* III. 1347/1 This is a matter disputable in Schooles. **1638** SIR T. HERBERT *Trav.* (ed. 2) 333 Of Japan ..Whether it bee an Ile or no, is disputable. **1658-9** *Burton's Diary* (1828) III. 114 It is disputable to me that all power is in the people. **1724** SWIFT *Drapier's Lett.* Wks. 1755 V. II. 38 Until any point is determined to be a law, it remains disputable by every subject. **1853** J. H. NEWMAN *Hist. Sk.* (1873) II. I. iii. 125 Let us put aside theories and disputable points.

†**2.** Ready or inclined to dispute; disputatious.

1600 SHAKS. *A.Y.L.* II. v. 36, I haue bin all this day to auoid him: He is too disputeable for my companie.

†**B.** as *sb.* A disputable matter. *Obs.*

1649 G. DANIEL *Trinarch.* The Author 7 The intricate pussle of Disputables. **1660** JER. TAYLOR *Duct. Dubit.* I. iv, This discourse of all the disputables in the world.

disputableness. [f. prec. + -NESS.] The quality of being disputable.

1660 FISHER *Rustick's Alarm* Wks. (1679) 279 Nothing that savours of more than Dubiousness and Disputableness it self. **1661** T. PHILIPS *Long Parlt. Rev.* (R.), The disputableness and unwarrantableness of their authority. **1685** H. MORE *Paralip. Prophet.* 42 Both..acknowledge an uncertainty and disputableness in some..Kings Reigns.

disputably, *adv.* [f. as prec. + -LY[2].] In a disputable manner or degree; questionably.

1836 LYTTON *Athens* (1837) I. 279 Linus and Thamyris, and, more disputably, Orpheus, are..precursors of Homer.

†**dispu'tacity.** *Obs.* [irreg. f. DISPUTATIOUS, as if *disputacious*: cf. *pugnacious, pugnacity*, and see -ACITY.] = DISPUTATIOUSNESS.

1660 H. MORE *Myst. Godl.* 472 Fruitlesse disputacity. **1672** *Mede's Wks., Life* 18 Addicted to a disingenuous humour of Disputacity. *a* **1711** KEN *Hymnotheo* Poet. Wks. 1721 III. 337 But Disputacity the Mind confounds.

disputant ('dɪspjuːtənt), *a.* and *sb.* [a. L. *disputānt-em*, pr. pple. of *disputāre* to DISPUTE: see -ANT.] **A.** *adj.* That disputes; disputing; engaged in dispute or controversy.

1671 MILTON *P.R.* IV. 218 Thou..there wast found Among the gravest Rabbies, disputant On points and questions fitting Moses' chair. **1711** SHAFTESB. *Charac.* IV. ii. (1737) III. 214 After the known way of Disputant Hostility. **1870** *Pall Mall G.* 5 Nov. 1 Time for disputant nations to recover their calmness..may possibly be secured.

B. *sb.* One who disputes or argues; *esp.* a public debater or controversialist.

1612 DEKKER *It be not good* Wks. 1873 III. 276 Hisse babling fooles, But crowne the deepe-braind disputant. *c* **1645** HOWELL *Lett.* (1650) II. 16 A quick and pressing disputant in logic and philosophy. **1791** BOSWELL *Johnson* an. 1763 (1831) I. 421 [Goldsmith]..was enabled to pursue his travels..partly by demanding at the Universities to enter the lists as a disputant. **1840** MILL *Diss. & Disc.* (1875) I. 408 Disputants are rarely..good judges.

disputation (dɪspjuː'teɪʃən). Also 4 -acioun, 4-6 -acion, -atioun, 5-6 dys-. [ad. L. *disputātiōn-em*, n. of action from *disputāre* to DISPUTE; perh.

immed. a. F. *disputation* (15th c. in Littré). The earlier word was DISPUTISOUN, of which *disputation* may be viewed as a refashioning after the L. original.]

1. The action of disputing or debating (questions, etc.); controversial argument; debate, discussion, controversy.

c **1450** *Merlin* 139 So indured longe the disputacion betwene hem tweyne. **1489** BARBOUR'S *Bruce* I. 250 Than mayss clerkis questioun, Quhen thai fall in disputacyoun. [*The original of 1375 had prob.* disputisoun.] **1526** *Pilgr. Perf.* (W. de W. 1531) 38 b, Let vs leue this disputacyon and reasonynge. **1561** T. NORTON *Calvin's Inst.* I. 30 For one litle wordes sake, they wer so whote in disputation. **1663** BUTLER *Hud.* I. I. 77 He'd run in Debt by Disputation, And pay with Ratiocination. **1758** JOHNSON *Idler* No. 19 ¶3 In the heat of disputation. **1880** MCCARTHY *Own Times* IV. lxiii. 427 He had a keen relish for theological disputation.

b. with *a* and *pl.* A discussion, a dispute.

1557 N. T. (Rhem.) *Rom.* xiv. 1 Him that is weake in the fayth, take vnto you, but not to enter into doubtful disputations of controuersies. **1570** DEE *Math. Pref.* 25, I was..by certaine earnest disputations..therto so prouoked. **1852** ROBERTSON *Serm.* Ser. IV. xix. (1876) 246 The church was filled with disputations. **1858** J. MARTINEAU *Stud. Chr.* 208 With one of these..to hold a disputation.

c. *spec.* An exercise in which parties formally sustain, attack, and defend a question or thesis, as in the mediæval schools and universities.

1551 T. WILSON *Logike* (1567) 61 a, That is called a disputacion or reasonyng of matters, when certaine persones debate a cause together, and one taketh part contrary vnto an other. **1612** BRINSLEY *Lud. Lit.* 281 [They] haue a disputation for the victorship once euery quarter of the yeare. **1726** AMHERST *Terræ Fil.* xx. 103 Academical disputations are two-fold, ordinary and extraordinary;.. extraordinary disputations I call those which are perform'd in the public schools of the university, as requisite qualifications for degrees. **1838** PRESCOTT *Ferd. & Is.* (1846) I. viii. 344 To visit the academies, where they mingled in disputation. **1870** JEVONS *Elem. Logic* xviii. (1890) 152 In former centuries it was, indeed, the practice for all students at the Universities to take part in public disputations, during which elaborate syllogistic arguments were put forward by one side and confuted by precise syllogisms on the other side.

attrib. **1760** GOLDSM. *Cit. W.* lxviii. ¶10, I have..drawn up a disputation challenge..to this effect.

†**2.** Written discussion or treatment of a question; a dissertation. *Obs.*

a **1533** FRITH (*title*), A Disputacion of Purgatorye; diuided into thre bokes. **1615** CROOKE *Body of Man* 45 This disputation concerning the number of the principall parts.

†**3.** Doubtful or disputable condition; doubt. *Obs.*

1549 ALLEN *Jude's Par. Rev.* 34 Let vs content..oure selfes with this, in this doubte and dysputacyon. **1689** *Prot. Garland* 2 For without all Disputation, I shall never trouble you.

†**4.** Interchange of ideas; discourse, conversation. *Obs.* (A doubtful sense.)

1596 SHAKS. *1 Hen. IV*, III. i. 206, I vnderstand thy Kisses, and thou mine, And that's a feeling disputation. **1599** —— *Hen. V*, III. ii. 101 Captaine Mackmorrice..will you voutsafe me, looke you, a few disputations with you.

disputatious (dɪspjuːˈteɪʃəs), *a.* Also 7–8 -acious. [f. prec.: see -OUS.] Characterized by, or given to, disputation; inclined to dispute or wrangle; contentious.

1660 H. MORE *Myst. Godl.* 69, I shall remit the disputacious to the mercy of School-Divines. **1768–74** TUCKER *Lt. Nat.* (1852) I. 61 In this divided disputatious world one must not expect to travel any road long without a check. **1818** SCOTT *Rob Roy* xii, The wine rendered me loquacious, disputatious, and quarrelsome. **1848** MRS. JAMESON *Sacr. & Leg. Art* (1850) 115 Those were disputatious days.

dispuˈtatiously, *adv.* [f. prec. + -LY².] In a disputatious manner; contentiously.

1864 in Webster. **1871** *Daily News* 18 Aug., [In railway accidents] injuries..may be disputatiously litigated.

dispuˈtatiousness. [f. as prec. + -NESS.] The quality of being disputatious.

1681 *Whole Duty Nations* 3 A scrupulosity, and Disputatiousness about Externals and Forms in Religion. **1796** LAMB *Lett.* (1888) I. 41 But enough of this spirit of disputatiousness. **1888** BRYCE *Amer. Commw.* I. 360 The inherent disputatiousness and perversity..of bodies of men.

disputative (dɪˈspjuːtətɪv), *a.* [a. late L. *disputātīv-us* (Cassiodorus), f. *disputāt-*, ppl. stem of *disputāre* to DISPUTE: see -ATIVE.]

1. Characterized by or given to disputation; disputatious.

1579 G. HARVEY *Letter-bk.* (Camden) 72 The disputative appetite of Doctor Busbye. **1630** B. JONSON *New Inn* II. ii, Thou hast a doctor's look, A face disputative, of Salamanca. **1787** MAD. D'ARBLAY *Diary* 6 Mar., I told him I was in no disputative humour. **1798** *Trifler* No. 23. 303 The cavils of the disputative. **1890** MISS S. J. DUNCAN *Soc. Departure* 57 The critic..most disputative of its positions.

†**2.** That is the subject of disputation or dispute; controversial; controverted. *Obs.*

1581 SIDNEY *Apol. Poetrie* (Arb.) 31 The Phylosopher.. teacheth a disputatiue vertue. **1589** NASHE *Pref.* to *Greene's Menaphon* (Arb.) 14, I had rather referre it, as a disputatiue plea to Diuines. **1708** LUTTRELL *Brief Rel.* (1857) VI. 270 [He] reported the method of ballotting in disputative elections.

3. Of or pertaining to disputation.

1664 H. MORE *Myst. Iniq.* Apol. 547 Which Knowledge of the Lord..is not certainly any Disputative Subtilty or curious Decision. **1873** BURTON *Hist. Scot.* VI. lxxii. 278 The oddest of all their disputative exhibitions.

Hence **diˈsputatively** *adv.*, in a disputative or contentious manner, disputatiously; **diˈsputativeness**, the quality of being disputatious.

1588 J. HARVEY *Disc. Probl.* 7, I..onely assay problematically, and as our schoolemen tearme it, disputatiuely, what may therin appeere most probable. **1836** G. S. FABER *Prim. Doctr. Election* (1842) 224 Disputativeness. **1842** —— *Provinc. Lett.* (1844) II. 203 In such a case of dogged disputativeness. **1860** READE *Cloister & H.* II. 316 'There, now', said Catherine, disputatively.

ˈdisputator. *rare.* [a. L. *disputātor*, agent-noun f. *disputāre*.] A disputer, a disputant.

1637 GILLESPIE *Eng. Pop. Cerem.* III. viii. 179 No man in the Councell ought to have a judiciarie voice, unlesse he bee withall a Disputator. **1845** S. AUSTIN *Ranke's Hist. Ref.* I. 447 How different a *disputator* was Johann Eck!

dispute (dɪˈspjuːt), *v.* Forms: 3–6 despute, 4 despuite, despout, dispite, 4–5 dispoyte, disputi(e, 4–6 dyspute, 6 dysspote, 4– dispute. [ME. *des-*, *dispute*, a. OF. *despute-r* (12th c. in Littré), mod.F. *disputer* (= Pr. *desputar*, Sp. *disputar*, It. *disputare*), ad. L. *disputāre* to compute, estimate, investigate, treat of, discuss, in Vulg. to dispute, contend in words; f. DIS- 1 + *putāre* to compute, reckon, consider.]

I. *intransitive.*

1. To contend with opposing arguments or assertions; to debate or discourse argumentatively; to discuss, argue, hold disputation; often, to debate in a vehement manner or with altercation about something.

a **1225** [See DISPUTING *vbl. sb.*]. *c* **1290** *S. Eng. Leg.* I. 94/72 For-to desputi a-ȝein a ȝong womman. *c* **1374** CHAUCER *Boeth.* v. metr. iv. 166 Þe porche ..of þe toune of athenis þer as philosophres hadde hir congregacioun to dispoyten. *c* **1400** *Apol. Loll.* Introd. 15 As if two persones dispitiden to gidre. **1551** T. WILSON *Logike* (1567) 1 a, *note*, Fower questions necessarie to bee made of any matter, before we despute. **1588** SHAKS. *L.L.L.* v. i. 69 Thou disputes like an Infant: goe whip thy Gigge. **1660** JER. TAYLOR *Worthy Commun.* Introd. 10 My purpose is not to dispute but to persuade. **1766** FORDYCE *Serm. Yng. Wom.* (1767) II. xi. 158 Be it your ambition to practise, not to dispute. **1845** S. AUSTIN *Ranke's Hist. Ref.* I. 445 He..took long journeys,—for example, to Vienna and Bologna,— expressly to dispute there.

b. Const. *about*, †*against*, †*of*, *on*, *upon* a subject; *with*, *against* an opponent.

a **1250** [See DISPUTING *vbl. sb.*]. *c* **1290** [See above]. *c* **1300** *Cursor M.* 8970 (Cott.) Quen þat þis sibele and þe kyng Disputed had o mani thing. *c* **1300** *Ibid.* 19739 (Edin.) Paul..faste disputid wiþ þe griues. *c* **1305** *Edmund Conf.* 255 in *E.E.P.* (1862) 77 As þis holi man in diuinite Desputede, as hit was his wone, of þe trinite. *a* **1420** HOCCLEVE *De Reg. Princ.* 379 Of our feithe wole I not dispute at alle. **1539** BIBLE (Great) *Acts* ix. 29 He spake and disputed agaynst the Grekes. **1597** SHAKS. *Rom. & Jul.* III. iii. 63 (Qo. 1) Let me dispute with thee of thy estate. **1604** —— *Oth.* I. ii. 75 Ile haue't disputed on. **1631** *Star Chamb. Cases* (Camden) 58 My Lord Keeper tould him it was noe tyme to dispute with the sentence, but to obey. **1648** SYMMONS *Vind. Chas. I*, 7 A Bill was proferred and disputed upon concerning a Fleet. **1655** STANLEY *Hist. Philos.* III. (1701) 77/1 Whosoever disputed with him of what subject soever. **1775** JOHNSON *Let. to Mrs. Thrale* 20 May, I dined in a large company.. yesterday, and disputed against toleration with one Doctor Meyer. **1847** EMERSON *Repr. Men, Napoleon* Wks. (Bohn) I. 378 The Emperor told Josephine that he disputed like a devil on these two points.

†**2.** To contend otherwise than with arguments (e.g. with arms); to strive, struggle. *Obs.*

1659 B. HARRIS *Parival's Iron Age* 131 He lost yet three Regiments more; whereby he was taught..that he must dispute lustily, to get any advantage upon him. **1828** SCOTT *F.M. Perth* xxix, Simon felt a momentary terror, lest he should have to dispute for his life with the youth.

II. *transitive.*

3. To discuss, debate, or argue (a question).

a. with *subord. cl.*

(Originally *intrans.*, the clause being a kind of cognate object, specifying the matter in dispute (cf. 'I dreamed that I saw', etc.); but at length *trans.*, and so *passive* in quots. 1736, 1850.)

1340 *Ayenb.* 79 Þe yealde filozofes þet zuo byzylyche desputede and zoȝten huet wes þe heȝeste guod ine þise lyue. **1382** WYCLIF *Mark* ix. 34 Thei disputiden among hem in the weie, who of hem schulde be more. **1538** STARKEY *England* I. ii. 54 To dyspute wych of thys rulys ys best..me semyth superfluouse. **1691** RAY *Creation* I. (1704) 70, I will not dispute what Gravity is. **1736** BUTLER *Anal.* II. i. Wks. 1874 I. 155 It may possibly be disputed, how far miracles can prove natural Religion. **1833** HT. MARTINEAU *Briery Creek* iv. 86 How long will the two parties go on disputing whether luxury be a virtue or a crime? **1850** MCCOSH *Div. Govt.* III. i. (1874) 331 It has often been disputed whether virtue has its seat among the faculties or the feelings.

b. with simple object (orig. representing or equivalent to a clause).

1513 MORE in Grafton *Chron.* (1568) II. 775 He sayde to her..that he would no more dispute the matter. **1526–34** TINDALE *Mark* ix. 33 What was it that ye disputed bytwene you by the waye? **1568** GRAFTON *Chron.* II. 553 Many doubts were moved and disputed. **1611** SHAKS. *Wint. T.* IV. iv. 411 Can he speake? heare? Know man from man? Dispute his owne estate? **1667** MILTON *P.L.* v. 822 Shalt thou dispute With him the points of libertie, who made Thee what thou art? **1820** SCOTT *Abbot* xxxvii, We may dispute it upon the road.

†**4.** To maintain, uphold, or defend (an assertion, cause, etc.) by argument or disputation; to argue or contend (that something is so). ? *Obs.*

1610 BP. CARLETON *Jurisd.* Pref., I haue disputed the Kings right with a good conscience, from the rules of Gods word. **1668** CULPEPPER & COLE *Barthol. Anat.* I. i. 3 The vapor growing into the like nature..as Casserus rightly disputes. **1713** SWIFT *Cadenus & Vanessa* 344 And these, she offer'd to dispute, Alone distinguish'd man from brute.

5. To argue against, contest, controvert.

a. To call in question or contest the validity or accuracy of a statement, etc., or the existence of a thing. The opposite of *to maintain* or *defend*.

1513 MORE in Grafton *Chron.* (1568) II. 811 Sith he is nowe king..I purpose not to dispute his title. **1651** HOBBES *Leviath.* II. xxix. 168 Men are disposed to..dispute the commands of the Commonwealth. **1701** DE FOE *True-born Eng.* Pref., As to Vices, who can dispute our Intemperance? **1770** *Junius Lett.* xxxvii. 182 The truth of these declarations ..cannot decently be disputed. **1783** COWPER *Alex. Selkirk* i, I am monarch of all I survey, My right there is none to dispute. **1824** J. S. MILL in *Westm. Rev.* I. 535 No one..will dispute to Johnson the title of an admirer of Shakspeare. **1885** Fox in *Law Rep.* 15 Q. Bench Div. 173 A bill of sale.. the validity of which is disputed by the trustee.

b. To controvert (a person).

1658–9 *Burton's Diary* (1828) III. 114 To dispute him here, is to question foundations. **1687** ? H. MORE *Death's Vis.* viii. *note* 32 (1713) 33 He would Dispute the Devil upon that Question. **1845** T. W. COIT *Puritanism* 280 Belknap could dispute Hutchinson about the quarrelsomeness of the Puritans in Holland.

6. To encounter, oppose, contest, strive against, resist (an action, etc.).

1605 SHAKS. *Macb.* IV. iii. 219 Dispute it like a man. **1720** *Independent Whig* (1728) No. 36. 320 [He] shall find no Mercy, if he disputes to bend to their Usurpations. **1737** *Col. Rec. Pennsyl.* IV. 251 Threatening to shoot the said Lowdon if he disputed doing what was required of him. **1748** *Anson's Voy.* II. xii. 265 They..seemed resolved to dispute his landing. **1884** *L'pool Mercury* 3 Mar. 5/2 The Soudanese..chose Teb..as the ground upon which to dispute the advance of the British troops on Tokar.

7. To contend or compete for the possession of; to contest a prize, victory, etc.

1654 LD. ORRERY *Parthen.* (1676) 575 If Parthenissa had been a spectator, she must have confest her self too well disputed. **1705** BOSMAN *Guinea* 14 The English..several times disputed the Ground with the Brandenburghers. **1734** tr. *Rollin's Anc. Hist.* (1827) I. Pref. 41 The poets disputed the prize of poetry. **1761** HUME *Hist. Eng.* III. lxi. 328 The battle of Warsaw..had been obstinately disputed during the space of three days. **1871** FREEMAN *Norm. Conq.* (1876) IV. xvii. 47 We..wonder..that every inch of ground was not disputed in arms.

III. 8. To move or influence by disputation; to argue *into* or *out of* something.

[Immediately from the intrans. sense 1; cf. 'to talk any one into' or 'out of'.]

1647 JER. TAYLOR *Lib. Proph.* Ep. Ded. 3 It would not be very hard to dispute such men into mercies and compliances. **1652** NEEDHAM *Selden's Mare Cl.* Ep. Ded. 5 To assert his own Interest and dispute them into a reasonable submission. **1695** *Preserv. Protest. Relig. Motive of Revolution* 12 The Roman Catholics would have disputed us out of our Religion. *a* **1732** ATTERBURY *Luke* xvi. 31 (Seager) One reason why a man is capable of being disputed out of the truth.

dispute (dɪˈspjuːt), *sb.* [f. the vb.; = F. *dispute*, It., Sp., Pg. *disputa*.]

1. The act of disputing or arguing against; active verbal contention, controversy, debate.

(In first quot. almost certainly the verb. infin.)

[*a* **1300** *Cursor M.* 20793 (Cott.) Disput, he [St. Jerome] sais, es na mister.] **1638** SIR T. HERBERT *Trav.* (ed. 2) 74 Without more dispute or delay [he] commands them all to execution. **1655** STANLEY *Hist. Philos.* III. (1701) 91/2 He was visited by his Friend, with whom he past the time in dispute after his usual manner. **1746** WESLEY *Princ. Methodist* 8 That once was in the Heat of Dispute. **1856** FROUDE *Hist. Eng.* (1858) I. i. 14 It is a common matter of dispute whether landed estates should be large or small. **1875** JOWETT *Plato* (ed. 2) IV. 31 We may make a few admissions which will narrow the field of dispute.

b. Phr. ***in dispute***: that is disputed, debated, in controversy. ***beyond, out of, past, without dispute***: past controversy, unquestionably, indisputably.

1659 B. HARRIS *Parival's Iron Age* 232 The Kingdom of Bohemia was..put out of dispute with Silesia, and Moravia. **1682** DRYDEN *MacFlecknoe* 5 Flecknoe..In prose and verse was owned without dispute Through all the realms of Nonsense absolute. **1698** FRYER *Acc. E. India & P.* 405 A thing beyond dispute. *a* **1704** LOCKE (J.), To bring as a proof an hypothesis which is the very thing in dispute. **1745** P. THOMAS *Jrnl. Anson's Voy.* 152 We, who could without Dispute sail much better. **1781** COWPER *Truth* 106 Which is the saintlier worthy of the two? 'Past all dispute, yon anchorite', say you. **1818** JAS. MILL *Brit. India* II. IV. vii. 263 The..necessity of such a fund..was pronounced to be without dispute. **1825** MACAULAY *Ess.*, *Milton* (1854) I. 17/1 To call a free parliament and to submit to its decision all the matters in dispute.

2. An occasion or instance of the same; an argumentative contention or debate, a controversy; also, in weakened sense, a difference of opinion; freq. with the added notion of vehemence, a heated contention, a quarrel.

1611 COTGR., *Dispute*, a dispute, difference, debate, altercation. 1638 PRYNNE *Briefe Relat.* 19 If I may be admitted a faire dispute, on faire termes.. I will maintaine.. the challenge against all the Prelates. 1696 tr. *Du Mont's Voy. Levant* 17 Being engag'd in a pretty warm dispute with some Officers. 1776 *Trial of Nundocomar* 96/1 There was a dispute between Bollakey Doss's widow and Pudmohun Doss. 1818 CRUISE *Digest* (ed. 2) V. 310 Disputes arose between [them] respecting the validity of this will. 1855 MACAULAY *Hist. Eng.* III: xvii, Disputes engender disputes. *Mod.* The dispute in the trade will, it is hoped, be settled without a strike.

†**b.** An oral or written discussion of a subject in which arguments for and against are set forth and examined. *Obs.*

1608 HIERON *Defence* III. 165 Thus.. am I come to an end of this dispute. 1655 STANLEY *Hist. Philos.* III. (1701) 120/1 He was the first that committed the disputes of Socrates his Master to writing. 1678 CUDWORTH *Intell. Syst.* I. i. §22. 21 His Lectures and Disputes concerning the Immortality of the Soul. 1725 tr. *Dupin's Eccl. Hist. 17th C.* I. v. 65 The Name also of Dispute was given to Sermons. 1831 BREWSTER *Newton* (1855) II. xv. 62 Trying to engage him in philosophical disputes.

†**c.** A logical argument. *Obs. rare.*

1594 HOOKER *Eccl. Pol.* III. xi. §10 These are but weake and feeble disputes for the inference of that conclusion. *Ibid.* III. xi. §18, I might have added.. their more familiar and popular disputes.

†**3.** Strife, contest; a fight or struggle. *Obs.*

1647-8 COTTERELL *Davila's Hist. Fr.* (1678) 25 They were taken prisoners without much dispute. 1659 B. HARRIS *Parival's Iron Age* 282 After four houres dispute, the Dutch endeavoured to get away. 1667 MILTON *P.L.* VI. 123 He who in debate of Truth hath won, Should win in Arms, in both disputes alike Victor. 1709 *Lond. Gaz.* No. 4540/5 The Bristol had a very warm Dispute with the aforesaid 2 Ships of the Enemy. *a* 1745 SWIFT *Stephen* in *Lett.* (1768) IV. 297 The Scots.. were.. after a sharp dispute, entirely defeated.

4. *attrib.*, as ***dispute benefit, pay***, pay to members of a trades' union while on strike or locked out.

1892 *Star* 1 Mar. 3/3 They have been receiving dispute pay from their union. 1895 *Daily News* 19 Aug. 5/2 Three-quarters of a million on dispute benefits, half a million on out-of-work benefits.

disputed (dɪ'spjuːtɪd), *ppl. a.* [f. prec. vb. + -ED[1].] That is made the subject of dispute, debate, or contention; debated, contested.

1611 COTGR., *Disputé*, disputed, debated. 1703 ROWE *Ulyss.* II. i. 928 The disputed Field at last is ours. 1719 DE FOE *Crusoe* (1840) I. xv. 264 Disputed points in religion. 1807 SCOTT *Fam. Let.* 15 May (1894) I. iii. 74 The tempest of disputed election was raging in every town.. through which I passed. 1855 MACAULAY *Hist. Eng.* IV. 127 All along the line.. there was long a disputed territory.

†**di'sputeful**, *a. Obs. rare.* [f. DISPUTE *sb.* + -FUL.] Given to disputing; disputatious.

1631 R. H. *Arraignm. Whole Creature* x. §3. 87 A doubtfull Didimist in this poinct, or a disputefull Scepticke.

di'sputeless, *a. rare*—[0]. [f. DISPUTE + LESS.]

1730-6 BAILEY (folio), *Disputeless*, without or free from dispute; also not apt to dispute. 1755 JOHNSON, *Disputeless*, undisputed, uncontrovertible. Hence in later Dicts.

disputer (dɪ'spjuːtə(r)). Also 5 -ar, 5-6 dys-. [f. DISPUTE *v.* + -ER[1].] One who disputes; one who is given to disputation or controversy; a disputant.

1434 MISYN *Mending of Life* 121 Hard sentens to disputars.. be left. 1529 *Supplic. to King* 23 The.. teaching of suche scole men & subtyll disputers. 1539 BIBLE (Great) *1 Cor.* i. 20 Where is the disputer of this worlde? 1643 MILTON *Divorce* II. iii. (1851) 70 In this controversie the justice of God stood upright ev'n among heathen disputers. 1725 WATTS *Logic* II. iii. §3 (6) Your great disputers and your men of controversy are in continual danger of this sort of prejudice. 1875 JOWETT *Plato* (ed. 2) I. 468 Great disputers.. come to think.. that they have grown to be the wisest of mankind.

disputing (dɪ'spjuːtɪŋ), *vbl. sb.* [f. as prec. + -ING[1].] The action of the vb. DISPUTE in various senses; disputation; debate; controversy.

a 1225 *Leg. Kath.* 561 Ah ȝet me þuncheð betere þ[t] ha beo ear ouercumen Wið desputinge. *a* 1250 *Owl & Night.* 875 Ȝif thu gest her-of to disputinge, Ich wepe bet thane thu singe. 1526-34 TINDALE *Acts* xv. 2 Ther was rysen dissencion and disputinge. 1548 HALL *Chron. Hen. VI* (an. 28) 159 b, Sober in communicacion, wyse in disputyng. 1649 JER. TAYLOR *Gt. Exemp.* Ep. Ded., Such is the nature of disputings, that they begin commonly in mistakes. 1881 MRS. HUNT *Childr. Jerus.* 111 Hills and rocks stand now as then, regardless of the disputings of East and West.

di'sputing, *ppl. a.* [f. as prec. + -ING[2].] That disputes; given to dispute, disputatious.

1645 MILTON *Tetrach.* (1851) 159 Many disputing Theologians. 1691 HARTCLIFFE *Virtues* 333 The Philosophy of the Disputing Greeks. 1762 GOLDSM. *Cit. W.* cxi. ⁋7 The stake, the fagot, and the disputing doctor in some measure ennoble the opinions they are brought to oppose.

†**di'sputisoun.** *Obs.* Forms: 3 desputisun, 4 -isoun, -eson, despitusoun, -esoun, disputiso(u)n, -isun, -eso(u)n, -pitesoun, -peticioun, 5 -petison. [a. OF. *desputeisun, -on, -aisun, -esun, -ison, -isson, disp-*, early ad. L. *disputātiōn-em*, with prefix and suffix conformed to their popular types: see -ATION, and cf. *oreisun*, ORISON. The regular ME. type, but superseded in 15th c. by the latinized DISPUTATION, q.v.]

= DISPUTATION.

c 1290 *S. Eng. Leg.* I. 279/56 A day þare was i-nome Of desputisun bi tweone heom. *a* 1300 *Cursor M.* 13925 (Cott.) And herd o þair disputisun. *c* 1330 R. BRUNNE *Chron.* (1810) 300 þe clergie of þe south mad a disputesoun, & openly with mouth assigned gode resoun. 1382 WYCLIF *Eccl.* iii. 11 To the disputisoun of them. —— *Rom.* xiv. 1 Take ȝe a syk man in bileue, not in deceptacioun [*gloss*, or dispeticiouns] of thouȝtis. *c* 1386 CHAUCER *Merch. T.* 230 As al day falleth altercacioun Bitwixen freendes in disputisoun [*MS. Harl.* dispiteson, 4 *MSS.* disputacion]. *c* 1450 LONELICH *Grail* xlv. 730 Tyl it happed vppon a day That theke dispetison ȝe comen & say.

dispys, dispyt(e, obs. ff. DESPISE, DESPITE.

disqualification (dɪsˌkwɒlɪfɪ'keɪʃən). [n. of action from DISQUALIFY: see -ATION.]

1. The action of disqualifying or depriving of requisite qualifications; *spec.* legal incapacitation; also, the fact or condition of being disqualified.

1770 BURKE *Pres. Discont.* (R.), The fault of overstraining popular qualities, and.. asserting popular privileges, has led to disqualification. 1789 *Constit. U.S.* I. §3 Removal from office, and disqualification to hold any office. 1878 LECKY *Eng. in 18th C.* II. vii. 405 Another deep line of disqualification was introduced into Irish life. 1887 BURY & HILLIER *Cycling* xi. 297 Furnishing false, misleading or incomplete information shall be a ground for disqualification [for cycle races]. 1899 J. D. CHAMPLIN *Young Folks' Cycl. Games & Sports* 696 Any contestant.. is liable to disqualification—subject to the discretion of the referee. 1935 *Encycl. Sports* 226/2 Disqualification... may ensue from a number of causes and may be permanent or temporary. 1954 F. C. AVIS *Boxing Ref. Dict.* 30 *Disqualification*, the dismissal from a contest through flagrant or persistent fouling. 1971 *Times* 21 Apr. 6/5 The disqualification [from driving] was set at six months. *Ibid.*, A driver.. appealed successfully, against the disqualification order.

2. That which disqualifies or prevents from being qualified; a ground or cause of incapacitation.

1711-14 *Spectator* (J.), It is recorded as a sufficient disqualification of a wife, that, speaking of her husband, she said, God forgive him. 1838 DICKENS *Nich. Nick.* xviii, I hope you don't think good looks a disqualification for the business. 1870 EMERSON *Soc. & Solit.* Wks. (Bohn) III. 5 In society, high advantages are set down to the individual as disqualifications.

disqualify (dɪs'kwɒlɪfaɪ), *v.* [f. DIS- 6 + QUALIFY. Cf. mod.F. *déqualifier*.] **a.** *trans.* To deprive of the qualifications required for some purpose; to render unqualified; to unfit, disable.

1723 [see DISQUALIFYING]. 1733 SWIFT *On Poetry, A Rhapsody* 41 Disqualify'd by fate To rise in church, or law, or state. 1736 —— *Let.* 22 Apr. Wks. 1814 XIX. 24 My common illness is of that kind which utterly disqualifies me for all conversation; I mean my deafness. [Cf. ib. 143 (1737) A long fit of deafness hath unqualified me for conversing.] 1753 HANWAY *Trav.* (1762) I. VII. xci. 416 Nor do their colder regions disqualify them for friendship. 1837 J. H. NEWMAN *Prophet. Off. Ch.* 180 What force prepossessions have in disqualifying us from searching Scripture dispassionately for ourselves. 1880 L. STEPHEN *Pope* iv. 109 Strong passions and keen sensibilities may easily disqualify a man for domestic tranquility.

b. *spec.* To deprive of legal capacity, power, or right; to incapacitate legally; to pronounce unqualified; = DISABLE *v.* 2.

1732 SWIFT *Sacr. Test* Wks. 1778 IV. 290 The church of England is the only body of Christians which in effect disqualifies those, who are employed to preach its doctrine, from sharing in the civil power, farther than as senators. 1741 MIDDLETON *Cicero* I. vi. 550 Disqualifying all future Consuls and Prætors, from holding any province, till five years after the expiration of their Magistracies. 1838 THIRLWALL *Greece* III. xxiv. 333 His youth did not disqualify him for taking part in the public counsels, as it did for military command. 1884 GLADSTONE in *Standard* 29 Feb. 2/6 Persons having such joint ownership.. ought not to be disqualified. 1887 BURY & HILLIER *Cycling* xi. 299 It shall be the duty of each competitor to see that he starts from his proper mark, and in default he may be disqualified for the race in question. 1897 *Encycl. Sport* I. 139/2 He [*sc.* the referee at boxing] can disqualify a competitor in the event of a foul. 1898 *Ibid.* II. 227/2 If a horse or his jockey jostle another horse or jockey, the aggressor is disqualified. 1908 *Times* 25 July 8/5 Partisans.. assisted him to the finish.. and the judges had no alternative but to disqualify him. 1963 BLOODGOOD & SANTINI *Horseman's Dict.* 63 An animal may be disqualified for a variety of reasons because either with, or without intent to defraud, it has been incorrectly described; because of carrying the wrong weight; of being doped, etc. 1971 *Times* 1 Apr. 4/4 He also pleaded guilty to driving a bus while disqualified. 1971 *Times* 29 Apr. 1/1 Mr. [Stirling] Moss.. was disqualified for six months and fined £35 by magistrates at Thame, Oxfordshire, for two offences.

c. *refl.* and *intr.* To represent or profess oneself to be disqualified; to deny or disparage one's own qualifications.

1754 RICHARDSON *Grandison* (1781) II. xxxi. 290 Disqualify now; can't you, my dear? Tell fibs.. Say you are *not* a fine girl. 1761 HUME *Hist. Eng.* II. xliii. 479 It is usual for the Speaker to disqualify himself for the office.

Hence **dis'qualified** *ppl. a.*

1718 *Freethinker* No. 69 ⁋10 In favour of the disqualified Gentlemen. 1726 AYLIFFE *Parergon* 116 Unworthy and disqualified Persons.

dis'qualifying, *ppl. a.* [f. prec. + -ING[2].] That disqualifies; incapacitating, disabling; self-depreciating.

1723 ARBUTHNOT in *Swift's Lett.* (1766) II. 31 Lord Whitworth, our plenipotentiary, had this disease, (which.. is a little disqualifying for that employment). 1754 RICHARDSON *Grandison* (1781) I. v. 23, I love not to make disqualifying speeches; by such we seem to intimate that we believe the complimenter to be in earnest. 1891 *Athenæum* 26 Dec. 874/2 The enforced retirement.. of many public servants when they have attained the disqualifying age.

dis'quality. *nonce-wd.* [DIS- 9.] Defect.

1863 LD. LENNOX *Biog. Remin.* II. 7 The latter quality, or, strictly speaking, disquality, rendering him a fair subject for a hoax.

disquamation, obs. f. DESQUAMATION. So **disqua'mator** (see quot.).

1656 BLOUNT *Glossogr.*, *Disquamation*, a scaling of fish, a taking off the shell or bark. 1674 *Ibid.* (ed. 4), *Disquamator*, a Chyrurgeon's or Apothecaries Instrument, to take off the scum, rind or bark of any thing.

disquantity (dɪs'kwɒntɪtɪ), *v.* [f. DIS- 7a + QUANTITY *sb.*]

1. *trans.* To lessen in quantity; to diminish.

1605 SHAKS. *Lear* I. iv. 270 Be then desir'd By her.. A little to disquantity your Traine. 1633 T. ADAMS *Exp. 2 Peter* iii. 9 [God] disquantitied his [Gideon's] forces from thirty-two thousand to three hundred.

2. To deprive of metrical quantity.

1866 LOWELL *Swinburne's Trag.* Prose Wks. 1890 II. 130 The Earl of Orford.. used to have Statius read aloud to him every night for two hours by a tipsy tradesman.. and found some strange mystery of sweetness in the disquantitied syllables.

†**di'square**, *v. Obs. rare.* [f. *di-* for DIS- 6 + SQUARE *v.*] *trans.* To put out of square, to place awry. Hence †**di'squaring** *vbl. sb.*

1604 T. WRIGHT *Passions* III. iii. 91 If there be but one eye.. out of square.. the first thing almost we marke, is the improportion or disquaring of that part.

†**dis'quarter**, *v.*[1] *Obs. rare.* [f. DIS- 6 or 7c + QUARTER.] *intr.* To leave one's quarters.

1654 EARL MONM. tr. *Bentivoglio's Warrs of Flanders* 65 In their quartering and disquartering, and particularly upon occasion of forrage, there happened almost continually some skirmishes between the soldiers of the two Armies.

†**dis'quarter**, *v.*[2] *Obs. rare.* [irreg. f. DIS- 1, in twain (or Gr. δίς twice) + QUARTER *v.*] *trans.* To halve or divide the quarters of.

1632 QUARLES *Div. Fancies* III. lxxviii. (1660) 132 If then, at most, the measur'd life of Man Be counted but a span, Being half'd, and quarter'd, and disquarter'd thus, What, what remains for us?

†**di'squatte**, *v. Obs.* Pa. t. & pple. disquatt. [f. *di-*, DIS- 1 + *squatte-n*, SQUAT *v.*, to crush, break (cf. TO-SQUATTE in same sense): perh. AF. had *desquater, -ir*, for OF. *esquater, -eir, -ir* to break.] *trans.* To break asunder, smash; to violate (a truce).

c 1380 WYCLIF *Serm.* Sel. Wks. I. 246 A woman shal disquatte his heed. 1480 CAXTON *Chron. Eng.* ccxxvi. 233 The whiche trewes he falsely and vntrewely by cauellacions losed and dysquatte. *Ibid.* ccxxix. 240 Thurugh lettyng of the pope and of the court of rome the forsayd couenaunts were disquatt and left of.

disqueat *v.*: see next.

disquiet (dɪs'kwaɪət), *v.* [f. DIS- 6 + QUIET *v.*] *trans.* To deprive of quietness, peace, or rest, bodily or mental; to trouble, disturb, alarm; to make uneasy or restless.

1530 PALSGR. 521/2, I disquyet, I trouble one of his rest, *je inquiete*.. He disquyeteth me horrybly a nyghtes with his revell. 1535 COVERDALE *Ps.* xxxviii. 5 Yee euery man.. disquieteth himself in vayne. 1555 EDEN *Decades* 95 After that the sea hathe byn disquyeted with vehemente tempestes. 1586 WARNER *Alb. Eng.* I. v. (1612) 18 Amidst their cheere, the solemne feast the Centaures did disqueat. 1693 *Mem. Cnt. Teckely* IV. 41 That Moldavia, Walaquia, and the Republick of Ragusa.. should not be disquieted by the Turks. 1796 H. HUNTER tr. *St.-Pierre's Stud. Nat.* (1799) I. 101, I disquieted myself to think that I had no powerful protector. 1844 THIRLWALL *Greece* VIII. lxi. 119 The Dardanians.. disquieted his northern frontier.

disquiet (dɪs'kwaɪət), *a.* Now *rare.* [f. DIS- 10 + QUIET *a.*] The reverse of quiet; unquiet, restless, uneasy, disturbed.

1587 T. UNDERDOWN *Æthiop. Hist. Heliod.* 69 A sea, which.. was very disquiet and troblesome. 1588 GREENE *Perimedes, Ditty* Wks. (Rtldg.) 292/2 Disquiet thoughts. 1596 SHAKS. *Tam. Shr.* IV. i. 171 Pray you husband be not so disquiet. 1611 SPEED *Hist. Gt. Brit.* VII. ix. (1632) 243 Egfred being by nature of a disquiet disposition. 1727 DE FOE *Hist. Appar.* vii. (1840) 120 Disquiet souls returning hither. 1848 THACKERAY *Van. Fair* lii, His mind was disquiet.

disquiet (dɪs'kwaɪət), *sb.* [Partly sb. use of the *adj.*, partly f. DISQUIET *v.*] Absence of bodily or mental quietness; disturbance; uneasiness, anxiety, worry; restlessness, unrest.

1581 PETTIE *Guazzo's Civ. Conv.* II. (1586) 68 b, To attaine to learning, there is not onelie required a will, but studie, watching, labour, and disquiet, which are irkesome thinges. **1599** SHAKS. *Much Ado* II. i. 268 All disquiet, horror, and perturbation followes her. **1614** RALEIGH *Hist. World* II. 260 Called by God..unto that rest which never afterward hath disquiet. **1641** *Termes de la Ley* (1708) 76 Making discord and disquiet to rise between his Neighbours. **1703** ROWE *Fair Penit.* II. ii. 580 This fond Paper would not give me A moment of Disquiet. **1845** S. AUSTIN *Ranke's Hist. Ref.* III. 235 The States of the Church and Naples were still in a state of universal disquiet and ferment. **1869** PHILLIPS *Vesuv.* iii. 58 The eleven months of disquiet may be regarded as one almost continual eruption.

†**b.** with *a* and *pl.* A disturbance; a disquieting feeling or circumstance. *arch.* or *Obs.*

1574 LD. BURGHLEY in Strype *Ann. Ref.* I. iv. 81 Anxieties and disquiets of mind. **1659** HAMMOND *On Ps.* cxliv. 12–14 Paraphr. 694 Without any disturbances or disquiets. **1698** FRYER *Acc. E. India & P.* 97 It is so mighty a Disquiet to the Governor, that he can never be at ease till he [etc.]. **1726–7** SWIFT *Gulliver* I. iv. 55 In the midst of these intestine disquiets. **1755** SMOLLETT *Quix.* (1803) IV. 135 My soul has been invaded by a thousand miseries, a thousand toils, and four thousand disquiets.

†**dis'quietal.** *Obs. rare.* [f. prec. vb. + -AL[1] 5.] The action of disquieting.

1642 H. MORE *Song of Soul* II. i. II. xxi, As when the flitting fire Grows full of wrath and rage, and gins to fume, And roars and strives 'gainst its disquietall.

†**disquie'tation.** *Obs. rare.* [f. DISQUIET *v.*; cf. F. *inquiétation*, med.L. *inquietātio*, in same sense, and see -ATION.] Disquieting; a cause of disquiet; disturbance.

1526 *Pilgr. Perf.* (W. de W. 1531) 92 b, The lacke or want therof is hurt notable to ony persone & disquietacyon to ony communalte.

dis'quieted, *ppl. a.* [f. as prec. + -ED[1].] Disturbed; rendered uneasy or restless. Hence **dis'quietedly** *adv.*, in a disquieted or uneasy manner; **dis'quietedness,** the state of being disquieted; uneasiness, disquietness.

1550 BALE *Image Both Ch.* I. (R.), Fleshlye cares, and disquieted consciences. **1645** J. COTTON (*title*), The Covenant of God's free Grace..comfortably applied to a disquieted soul. *a* **1680** CHARNOCK *Attrib. God* (1834) I. 337 Let us..examine the reason..as David did of his disquietedness. **1857** *Chamb. Jrnl.* VIII. 346 My mother's eyes rested..disquietedly upon the man's partly averted face.

disquieten (dɪs'kwaɪət(ə)n), *v.* [f. DIS- 6 + QUIETEN *v.*] = DISQUIET *v.*

1921 *Glasgow Herald* 9 Mar. 10 Her condition is disquietening. *Ibid.* 23 Sept. 7 In view of disquietening reports as to their activities in the Near East. **1928** L. ROSSITER *Sex Age* viii, She turned, bewildered and disquietened, from the sickening turmoil.

disquieter (dɪs'kwaɪətə(r)). [f. DISQUIET *v.* + -ER[1].] One who or that which disquiets; a disturber.

1564 BULLEYN *Dial. agst. Pest.* (1888) 110 A swarme of sedicious disquieters of the common wealth. **1575** TURBERV. *Faulconrie* 364 It also..kylles the flies, the dogges disquieters and enimies to his ease. **1600** SURFLET *Countrie Farme* II. li. 359 A procurer of vomit, and a disquieter of the stomacke. *a* **1660** HAMMOND *Serm.* i. (T.), The disquieters of the honour and peace of Christendom.

†**dis'quietful,** *a. rare.* [f. DISQUIET *sb.* + -FUL.] Full of or fraught with disquiet.

a **1677** BARROW *Serm.* Wks. 1687 I. xvi. 239 Love and pity of our selves should persuade us to forbear it [reviling], as disquietfull, incommodious, and mischievous to us.

disquieting (dɪs'kwaɪətɪŋ), *vbl. sb.* [f. DISQUIET *v.* + -ING[1].] The action of the vb. DISQUIET; disturbing; disturbance of peace or tranquillity.

1535 COVERDALE *Wisd.* xiv. 25 Manslaughter,.. disquyetinge of good men, vnthankfulnes, defylinge of soules. **1641** BAKER *Chron., Hen. I*, an. 1112 (R.) King Henry..was not without some little disquietings at home. **1883** *Athenæum* 1 Dec. 699/3 To the disquieting of his lawful spouse.

dis'quieting, *ppl. a.* [f. as prec. + -ING[2].] That disquiets or causes uneasiness; disturbing.

1576 FLEMING *Panopl. Epist.* 271 To expell the cause of that disquieting disease. **1691** HARTCLIFFE *Virtues* 17 The Troubles and Tumults of disquieting Passions. **1783** WATSON *Philip III*, II. 113 They were filled with the most disquieting apprehensions. **1894** *Times* 1 Sept. 8/4 Another disquieting feature of the present industrial situation.

disquietingly (dɪs'kwaɪətɪŋlɪ), *adv.* [f. DISQUIETING *ppl. a.* + -LY[2].] In a disquieting manner; also used to introduce a statement of a fact considered disquieting.

1901 'L. MALET' *Sir R. Calmady* IV. vii. 346 The creaking of a board, the rustle of a curtain,..were..disquietingly replete with possible meaning. **1922** *Public Opinion* 23 June 580/1 A tendency to change strangely and disquietingly. **1928** *Britain's Industr. Future* (*Lib. Ind. Inq.*) IV. xxvii. 398 In some industrial centres there is a disquietingly high percentage of registered unskilled workers between the ages of eighteen and twenty-five. **1970** *Nature* 28 Nov. 818/1 Disquietingly, no major known human teratogen..has been identified by prospective epidemiological analyses.

dis'quietist. [f. DISQUIET *sb.* + -IST.] A professed disturber of quiet; an alarmist.

1834 *New Monthly Mag.* XLI. 99 The most honest of agitators, the most disinterested of disquietists.

†**dis'quietive,** *a. Obs.* [f. DISQUIET *v.* + -IVE.] Tending to disquiet; of disquieting character.

1846 WORCESTER cites HOWE.

disquietly (dɪs'kwaɪətlɪ), *adv.* [f. DISQUIET *a.* + -LY[2].] In a disquiet or uneasy manner; †in a disquieting manner.

1605 SHAKS. *Lear* I. ii. 124 Machinations..and all ruinous disorders follow vs disquietly to our Graues. **1630** LENNARD tr. *Charron's Wisd.* Pref. A ij a, He that carrieth himself troubledly, disquietly, malecontent, fearing death, is not wise.

†**dis'quietment.** *Obs.* [f. DISQUIET *v.* + -MENT.] The action of disquieting; the fact or condition of being disquieted.

1606 TURNBULL in Spurgeon *Treas. Dav.* Ps. xv. 1 They are in continual perplexity..continual disquietment of their minds. **1662** STILLINGFL. *Orig. Sacr.* III. iii. §8 The passions, disquietments, and disappointments of men. **1689** *Col. Rec. Pennsylv.* I. 313 What a Spiritt has been raysed in ffrinds to his Disquietment there vpon y[t] account.

b. A disquieting circumstance or occurrence.

a **1658** O. SEDGWICK in Spurgeon *Treas. Dav.* Ps. xix. 12 Rebekah was weary of her life, not for any foreign disquietments, but because of domestic troubles.

disquietness (dɪs'kwaɪətnɪs). [f. DISQUIET *a.* + -NESS.] The quality or state of being disquiet; want of quiet; unrest; disturbance.

1535 COVERDALE *Prov.* xi. 29 Who so maketh disquyetnesse in his owne house, he shal haue wynde for his heretage. **1568** GRAFTON *Chron.* II. 553 A tumult and assembly was made, to the disquietnesse of the realme. **1615** T. ADAMS *Leaven* 117 In these dayes disquietnesse allowes no meditation, penurie no bookes. **1681** H. MORE *Exp. Dan.* 194 Enraged with everlasting disquietness.

†**dis'quietous,** *a. Obs.* [f. DISQUIET *sb.* + -OUS.] Fraught with disquiet; disquieting.

1618 BOLTON *Florus* III. ii (1636) 165 The troubles which brake out Northward, were farre more manifold, and horrible: no quarter is so disquietous. **1641** MILTON *Ch. Govt.* II. (1851) 142 This..subject..the touching whereof is so distastfull and disquietous to a number of men.

disquietude (dɪs'kwaɪətju:d). [f. DISQUIET *a.*, after QUIETUDE.] Disquieted condition or state; restlessness, disturbance, disquietness.

1709 ADDISON *Tatler* No. 97 ¶3 The Noise and disquietude of Business. **1753** N. TORRIANO *Gangr. Sore Throat* 24 She passed this Time very uneasily, with great Disquietude. **1844** THIRLWALL *Greece* VIII. lxi. 87 Antigonus must have viewed the alliance with great disquietude. **1869** PHILLIPS *Vesuv.* iii. 57 On the 3rd of September, the disquietude of Vesuvius returned.

b. with *a* and *pl.* A feeling, occasion, or cause of disquiet; a disquieting circumstance.

1711 ADDISON *Spect.* No. 256 ¶6 The Multitude of Disquietudes to which the Desire of it [Fame] subjects an ambitious Mind. **1726–7** SWIFT *Gulliver* III. ii. §13 (1865) These people are under continual disquietudes. **1885** *Manch. Exam.* 8 July 5/2 From the still unconquered Black Flags there are plenty of disquietudes to fear.

[**disquieture.** Error for DISQUIETNESS.

1860 FROUDE *Hist. Eng.* V. 435 (quoting letter of 1552 of Sir J. Crofts to Cecil) Such disquietures of mind. [The original MS. reads *disquyetnes*.]]

†**di'squiparancy.** *Logic. Obs.* [ad. med.L. *disquiparāntia* (F. Mayron *a* 1325, see Prantl III. 290, IV. 66) for *disæquiparāntia*, f. DIS- 4 + *æquiparāntia* (Tertull.): see EQUIPARANCE.] The relation of two correlates which are heteronymous, i.e. denoted by different names, as father and son: opp. to *equiparancy*.

1697 tr. *Burgersdicius his Logic* I. vii. 22 Relateds synonymous are usually called relateds of æquiparancy, as *friend*, *rival*, etc.; heteronymous of disquiparancy, as *father*, *son*, *master*, *servant*.

disquipa'ration. *rare.* [f. as prec. after L. *æquiparātiōn-em*, n. of action from *æquiparāre* to equalize.] = prec.

1894 FROUDE *Erasmus* 125 They define the personal or hypostatic union as the relation of a real disquiparation in one extreme with no correspondent at the other.

†**di'squire,** *v. Obs.* [ad. L. *disquīr-ĕre* to inquire diligently, f. DIS- 5 + *quærĕre* to search, seek.] *trans.* To inquire diligently, investigate.

1621 BP. MOUNTAGU *Diatribæ* II. 401 What the custome.. was, I doe not resolue, nor disquire. **1654** VILVAIN *Chronogr.* 16 Thus hav I..tired my head to disquire the truth of Times. **1654** —— *Theorem. Theol.* i. 24 Such are difficiler to discern or disquire their corporals, subject to sens.

So †**di'squiry** *Obs.*, investigation, inquiry.

1627 J. DOUGHTY *Sermon* (1628) 10 The Lord hath wholly exposed all the creatures to mans disquiry. **1650** DURYE *Just Re-prop.* 28 If..a regular way of disquiry may be followed. *Ibid.*, If they will engage to stand or fall to the issue of that disquiry.

'**disquisite, -it,** *v. rare.* [? a back-formation from *disquisition*.] *intr.* To make a disquisition.

1825 *New Monthly Mag.* XVI. 148 The same Creative Power..by which alone we ourselves at this moment breathe, think, or disquisite at all. **1893** LELAND *Mem.* II. 274 Here I would fain disquisit on Pike.

disquisition (dɪskwɪ'zɪʃɛn). [ad. L. *disquīsītiōn-em* inquiry, investigation, n. of action f. *disquīsīt-* ppl. stem of *disquīrĕre*: see DISQUIRE.]

1. Diligent or systematic search; investigation; research, examination.

1608–11 JOS. HALL *Medit. Vowes* II. §28 The disquisition of great truthes requires time. **1668** WILKINS *Real Char.* i, Others have applyed their disquisitions to some particular Letters. **1744** HARRIS *Three Treat.* (1841) 51 In this disquisition into human conduct. **1767** H. BROOKE *Fool of Qual.* (1859) I. 82 (D.) On their return from a disquisition as fruitless as solicitous, nurse declared her apprehensions that Harry had gone off with a little favourite boy. **1818** JAS. MILL *Brit. India* I. II. iv. 150 A subject..of less subtle and difficult disquisition. **1855** H. REED *Lect. Eng. Lit.* i. (1878) 42 To make it a topic of distinct disquisition.

†**b.** *ellipt.* A subject or topic for investigation; a question. *Obs. rare.*

1605 CAMDEN *Rem.* 214 Their growing vp, their flourishing..were a disquisition for the learned. **1660** R. COKE *Justice Vind.* 4 *margin*, The manner and order of attaining to Knowledge, is a subtil disquisition.

2. A treatise or discourse in which a subject is investigated and discussed, or the results of investigation set forth at some length; less correctly, a learned or elaborate dissertation *on* a subject.

1647 TRAPP *Comm. Matt.* xi. 17 Puzzling them with scholastical craggy disquisitions. *a* **1680** BUTLER *Rem.* (1759) I. 66 Unhappy Man..On hypothetic Dreams and Visions Grounds everlasting Disquisitions. **1794** SULLIVAN *View Nat.* II, In our foregoing disquisition we ventured upon the threshold of a Scythiac antediluvian hypothesis. **1840** MACAULAY *Ranke Ess.* (1854) II. 146 The constant subjects of their lively satire and eloquent disquisitions. **1873** G. C. DAVIES *Mount. & Mere* i. 3 A learned disquisition on the alleged cruelty of sport.

disquisitional (dɪskwɪ'zɪʃənəl), *a.* [f. prec. + -AL[1].] Of the nature of a disquisition.

1846 WORCESTER cites *Monthly Rev.* **1856** MASSON *Ess.*, *Story of 1770*, 199 Here the reader must permit me a little Essay or disquisitional Interleaf on the character and writings of Chatterton. **1861** *N. Brit. Rev.* May 196 [The 18th c.] sermons have no longer a voice of authority. They are disquisitional, explanatory or persuasive.

disqui'sitionary, *a.* [See -ARY.[1]] = prec.

1847 in CRAIG; and in later Dicts.

disqui'sitionist. [f. as prec. + -IST.] The author of a disquisition.

1838 *Fraser's Mag.* XVIII. 385 Many a disquisitionist on the character of Burns. **1878** BAGEHOT *Lit. Stud.* (1879) I. p. x, An arid disquisitionist on value and cost of production.

disquisitive (dɪ'skwɪzɪtɪv), *a.* (*sb.*) [f. L. *disquīsīt-* ppl. stem of *disquīrĕre* + -IVE.] Characterized by or given to disquisition; given to research or investigation; inquiring.

1647 TRAPP *Comm. 2 Cor.* xiii. 5 The disquisitive part belongs to us, the decisive to God. **1772** *Weekly Mag.* 22 Apr. 118/1 He..is a man of great disquisitive powers. **1796** COLERIDGE *Let.* in Mrs. Sandford *Poole & Friends* (1888) I. 185 My own shaping and disquisitive mind. **1889** W. L. COURTNEY *Life J.S. Mill* ii. 30 The disquisitive youth.

†**B.** *sb.* An inquiry or investigation. *Obs.*

1659 STANLEY *Hist. Philos.* III. IV. 11 The Sceptick's end is..Suspension in disquisitives.

di'squisitively, *adv. rare.* [f. prec. + -LY[2].] In a disquisitive manner; by investigation or examination.

1622 MALYNES *Anc. Law-Merch.* 262 By the mixt mettall Ore taking of disquisitively, or here and there.

disquisitor (dɪ'skwɪzɪtə(r)). [ad. L. **disquīsītor*, agent-n. from *disquīrĕre*: see -OR.] One who makes disquisition; an inquirer or investigator; the author of a disquisition.

1766 F. BLACKBURN *Confessional* 318 Let the Disquisitors answer for themselves. **1771** W. JONES *Zool. Eth.* 66 All the disquisitors that ever took the Law of Moses in hand. **1801** *Chron.* in *Ann. Reg.* 502 Because, say our profound disquisitors, all the seven sacraments confer grace. **1889** *Sat. Rev.* 2 Nov. 485/2 An academic disquisitor on political subjects.

disquisitorial (dɪskwɪzɪ'tɔərɪəl), *a. rare.* [f. prec. + -(I)AL.] Of or belonging to a disquisitor; investigating; inquiring.

1806 R. CUMBERLAND *Mem.* I. 189 (L.) When he came to exercise the subtlety of his disquisitorial powers upon it.

di'squisitory, *a. rare.* = prec.

1860 WORCESTER cites *Eclectic Rev.*

Disraelian (dɪz'reɪlɪən), *a.* [f. the name of Benjamin *Disraeli*, first Earl of Beaconsfield (1804–1881), Conservative statesman and prime minister.] Pertaining to or characteristic of Disraeli or his opinions, measures, or writings.

1880 T. W. Reid *Politicians of To-Day* I. 38 Perhaps no better word than 'impartiality' could be found to describe that peculiar quality of the Disraelian mind and character. **1901** *N. Amer. Rev.* Feb. 252 The great Disraelian Myth, which has changed the most un-English of all our Prime Ministers into an almost sacramental Symbol of Patriotism. **1927** *Observer* 11 Dec. 15/2 A devout Disraelian Tory. **1927** H. Miles tr. *Maurois's Disraeli* 296 Even abroad the altogether Disraelian boldness of this *coup* was extolled. **1962** *Daily Tel.* 12 Dec. 10/2 Seeking to give the Disraelian One Nation ideal more concrete expression.

† **dis'range**, *v. Obs.* Also 5 disrenge. [ad. OF. *desrengier*, *-rangier*, f. *des-*, DIS- 4 + *renc*, *reng*, now *rang* rank, order. Cf. DERANGE.] **a.** *trans.* To throw out of order or rank; to disarrange. **b.** *refl.* and *intr.* To fall out of rank.

1485 Caxton *Chas. Gt.* 226 They began to flee, disrenge & to be aferde. *c* **1530** Ld. Berners *Arth. Lyt. Bryt.* (1814) 162 Whan these iiii. knightes on horsbacke sawe Arthur, one of them dysranged hym selfe, and..ran at Arthur. **1610** Holland *Camden's Brit.* I. 317 The Englishmen..presently disranged themselues, and in disray preassed hard upon the enemies. **1775** R. Wood *Ess. Homer* 42 (Jod.) That delicate connexion and thread of circumstances, which are seldom disranged even by the smallest alteration without endangering his truth and consistence.

disrank (dɪs'ræŋk), *v.* [f. DIS- 7 c + RANK *sb.*]

† **1.** *trans.* To throw out of rank or into disorder. *Obs.*

1597 Daniel *Civ. Wars* VIII. xvi, The rangèd horse break out..Disrank the troops; set all in disarray. *a* **1616** Beaum. & Fl. *Lawes of Candy* I. i, I..Was he that first dis-rankt their woods of Pikes. **1654** Trapp *Comm. Ps.* l. 3 The army was dis-ranked and wandred any way.

† **b.** *intr.* (for *refl.*) To fall out of ranks, fall into disorder. *Obs.*

1605 Sylvester *Du Bartas* II. iii. I. *Abraham* 325 Too-too-tired, some at last dis-rank. **1629** J. Maxwell tr. *Herodian* (1635) 150 They disranke, and are routed.

† **2.** *transf.* and *fig.* (*trans.*) To disorder, disarrange, confuse. *Obs.*

1602 Dekker *Satiro-Mastix* K ij a, Out of thy part already; foil'd the scene; Disrank'd the lines. **1614** J. Cooke *Tu Quoque* in Hazl. *Dodsley* XI. 264 You shall march a whole day..and not disrank one hair of your physiognomy. **1628** Ford *Lover's Mel.* IV. ii, Throngs of rude divisions huddle on, And do disrank my brain from peace and sleep.

3. To deprive of one's rank, to reduce to a lower rank; to degrade.

1599 Daniel *Let. of Octavia* Arg. Wks. (1717) I. 69 He arms his Forces, either to reduce Antony to the Rank of his Estate, or else to disrank him out of State and all. **1615** A. Nicholes *Marr. & Wiving* vi. in *Harl. Misc.* (Malh.) III. 263 Thou wilt disrank thyself, or single out [a wife] from the too common shame and abuse in this kind [of women]. **1894** [see DISRATING].

Hence **dis'ranked** *ppl. a.*, **dis'ranking** *vbl. sb.*

1606 Marston *Fawne* I. i, Wilde longings, or the least of disranct shapes. **1627** May *Lucan* v. (1631) 24 The letter's lost in their disranked wings. **1629** J. Maxwell tr. *Herodian* (1635) 179 *note*, So the dis-ranking of the English lost all to the Normans.

† **dis'rapier**, *v. Obs.* [f. DIS- 7 a + RAPIER *sb.*] *trans.* To deprive of a rapier; to disarm.

1599 B. Jonson *Ev. Man out of Hum.* III. i, He that should offer to disrapier me now.

disrate (dɪs'reɪt), *v.* [f. DIS- 7 a + RATE *sb.*]

1. *trans.* To reduce (a petty officer or non-commissioned officer of marines) to a lower rating or rank.

1811 *Naval Chron.* XXV. 28 Having been disrated for some offence. **1829** Southey in *Q. Rev.* XLI. 406 He found it necessary to disrate Peter Hayles, the pirate. **1860** *Merc. Marine Mag.* VII. 85 This witness had been chief mate..but had been disrated..for drunkenness.

2. To remove (a ship) from its rate or class.

1885 Lady Brassey *The Trades* 246 The 'Tyrian', another 'yellow-fever ship', was disrated for the same reason.

3. *fig.* To remove from one's rank or position.

1854 *Chamb. Jrnl.* II. 200 He..had disrated himself from the genteel company of a ten-miles-wide circuit. **1883** G. Turner in *Gd. Words* Dec. 778/1 There is..no just reason for dis-rating 'which' from its old relation to persons as well as to things.

Hence **dis'rated** *ppl. a.*, **dis'rating** *vbl. sb.*

1833 Marryat *P. Simple* lvi, If you please, your honour, I'd rather take my disrating—I—don't wish to be chief boatswain's mate in this here business. **1891** *Daily News* 21 Nov. 4/6 What are the Tories going to do with all the disrated Liberal Secessionists? **1894** *Labour Commission* Gloss., *Disrating*, A nautical term for 'disranking', that is, reducing from a higher rank to a lower, such as lowering a man from A.B. to ordinary seaman, or from fireman to trimmer.

† **dis'rationate**, *v. Obs. rare.* [f. DIS- 6 + L. *rătiōn-em* reason + -ATE³.] *trans.* To deprive of its reason or rationality.

1668 C. Spelman in *Sir H. Spelman's De non Temer. Eccl.* (ed. 4) To Rdr. 18 Thou..must disrationate St. Paul's argument, who disswades the pollution of thy Body, because it is the Temple of the holy Ghost.

† **dis'ray**, *sb. Obs.* [var. of *desray*, DERAY, with the ordinary late ME. change of *des-* to *dis-*: see DIS- prefix, and cf. DISRAY *v.*] Disorder, confusion; = DERAY, DISARRAY.

13.. *K. Alis.* 4353 He gan make gret disray, And gradde ageyn to Darye. *c* **1450** *Merlin* 407 The Knyghtes..gan make soche a disray a-monge hem that noon a-bode other. *c* **1470** Harding *Chron.* LXVI. i, The realme to saue, and kepe out of disraye. **1609** Holland *Amm. Marcell.* XXIX. xii. 368 To come in manner of a sodaine tempest upon our armie..and to put it in disray. **1610** [see DISRANGE].

† **dis'ray**, *v. Obs.* [In sense 1, var. of DERAY, orig. *desray*, a. OF. *desreer*, *desrayer*, with the ordinary late ME. substitution of *dis-* for *des-*: cf. prec. In sense 3 identified with DISARRAY.]

1. *trans.* To put out of array or military order; to throw into disorder; = DISARRAY *v.* 1.

1300 *K. Alis.* 673 Now con Alisaundre of skyrmyng, And of stedes disrayng. **1609** Holland tr. *Amm. Marcell.* XXIV. i. 262 Least Archers running foorth might disray the rankes. *c* **1611** Sylvester II. iv. *Decay* 1124 Have these so yong and weak Disrayed your ranks? **1631** Weever *Anc. Fun. Mon.* 317 Guortimer..did here set vpon..the English Saxons, whom being disrayed, and not able to abide a second charge, he put all to flight.

2. To disorder the attire, or spoil the personal appearance of. In quot. *refl.*

1431 Lydgate *Chron. Troy* II. xiii. (*Paris to Helen*), And as a penitaunt in contrition Ye you disraye; alas why do ye so?

3. To deprive of personal array or attire; to despoil, strip; = DISARRAY *v.* 2.

1483 *Cath. Angl.* 100/2 (MS. A.), To disray or disgise [MS. M. disaray] *exornare.* **1599** Marston *Sco. Villanie*, II. vii. 208 Disrai'd Of that faire iem. **1608** Day *Law Trickes* I. i. (1881) 12 On the high Altar sacrifiz'd the Priests, Disray'd the Temple of the golden robes.

disrealise, in Udall 1548: see DISRELISH.

disrealize (dɪs'riːəlaɪz), *v. rare.* [f. DIS- 6 + REALIZE.] *trans.* To divest of reality, to idealize.

1889 *Sat. Rev.* 2 Mar. 261/1 The first and last rule of the poet should be..to pass every personal emotion through the sieve of the universal, to 'disrealize' everything, to bring it into union with the whole.

† **dis'reason**, *sb. Obs.* In 5 desrayson. [a. OF. *desraison*, f. *des-*, DIS- 4 + *raison* reason.] That which is contrary to reason or right; injustice.

1480 Caxton *Ovid's Met.* XII. xix, Certes it is to chyvalrye over grete blame, over grete tyrannye and desrayson.

† **dis'reason**, *v. Obs.* [Anglicized from OF. *desraisnier* or its latinized form *disrătiōnāre*, variants of OF. *deraisnier*, med.L. *dērătiōnāre*: see Du Cange, and cf. DERAIGN.] *trans.* To prove, assert, vindicate; = DERAIGN *v.* 1, 2.

(The prefix *des-*, *dis-*, was here a mere variant of *de-*, owing to the frequent equivalence and confusion of these prefixes (see DE- I. 6); but it appears to have been taken by the 17th c. legal antiquaries in the privative sense (DIS- 4); hence the erroneous explanation of *Disrationare* in Blount's Law Dict. 'contrarium ratiocinando asserere, vel quod assertum est ratiocinando destruere', and cf. J. C. Blomfield *Hist. Souldern* (1893) 12 *note*.)

1622 Malynes *Anc. Law-Merch.* 425 In which time the proprietarie may disreason the said recouerie, by disprouing the other parties surmises or allegations, prouing that the specialtie was paied whereupon the Attachment was grounded.

† **dis'reasonable**, *a. Obs. rare.* [ad. OF. *desraisonable* (Oresme, 14th c.), mod.F. *dé-*, f. *des-*, DIS- 4 + *raisonable*.] Devoid of reason, unreasonable, groundless.

1549 *Compl. Scot.* xv. 122 Thy complaynt is nocht disrasonabil. *Ibid.* xx. 169 The extreme disrasonabil abusione that rang amang the vniuersal pepil.

† **dis'reckon**, *v. Obs. rare.* [DIS- 6.] *intr.* To reverse reckoning; to reckon by deduction.

1561 Eden *Arte Nauig.* II. vi. 31 The dayes of the Moone beynge knowen, then vnrekenyng or disrekenynge backwarde, we shall knowe the daye. **1611** Florio, *Scomputare*, to disreckon.

† **disreco'mmend**, *v. Obs. rare.* [DIS- 6.] *trans.* = DISCOMMEND *v.* 3.

1691 Norris *Pract. Disc.* 217 The untunableness of one or two Instruments dis-recommends the whole Musical Consort.

disrecommendation (dɪsˌrɛkəmɛn'deɪʃən). [f. DIS- 9 + RECOMMENDATION.] That which is the reverse of a recommendation, or is unfavourable to any one's claims.

1752 Fielding *Amelia* Wks. 1775 XI. 44 The poverty of the person..is never, I believe, any forcible dis-recommendation to a good mind. *a* **1797** H. Walpole *Geo. II* (1847) II. vii. 211 He attained considerable weight in a Government where trifling qualities are no disrecommendation. *a* **1843** Southey *Doctor* Fragment (1862) 676 Add to these dis-recommendations that it is propounded in the coarsest terms of insolent assumption.

disregard (dɪsrɪ'gɑːd), *sb.* [f. DIS- 9 + REGARD *sb.*] **1. a.** Want of regard; neglect, inattention; in earlier use often, the withholding of the regard which is due, slighting, undue neglect; in later use, the treating of anything as of no importance.

1665 Glanvill *Scepsis Sci.* xiv. 89 We can be bold without resentment, yet it may be with an invincible disregard. **1733** Neal *Hist. Purit.* II. 478 The Bishops fell under a general disregard. **1795** Ld. Auckland *Corr.* (1862) III. 280 Acts..which tend to the levelling of thrones and conditions, and give to monarchs a more certain disregard and disrespect than all the labours..of the Jacobins. **1862** Merivale *Rom. Emp.* (1871) V. xlv. 318 Disregard and sympathy seemed to be equally distasteful to him.

b. Constr. *of* (*for*, *to*).

1716 Addison *Freeholder* 39 (Seager) A disregard of fame. *a* **1732** Atterbury *Prov.* xiv. 6 (Seager) A disregard for everything besides. **1736** Butler *Anal.* II. vi. 224 Profaneness and avowed Disregard to all Religion. **1875** Jowett *Plato* (ed. 2) I. 114 An extreme disregard of..historical accuracy. **1882** J. H. Blunt *Ref. Ch. Eng.* II. 484 His lawless disregard for the principles of the Reformation settlement.

2. (See quot. 1940.)

1940 *Manch. Guardian Weekly* 8 Mar. 192 What Mr. Elliot inelegantly but conveniently called 'disregards'—..the forms of income which are to be disregarded when the means of an applicant for supplementary pension are assessed. **1955** *Times* 15 June 3/6 There was a case for saying that the disregards in relation to pensions were not adequate. **1959** *Times* 25 June 14/4 The regulations dealt with..those disregards which related to earnings. The National Assistance Bill was necessary to give powers to deal with the other disregards.

disregard (dɪsrɪ'gɑːd), *v.* [f. DIS- 6 + REGARD *v.*] *trans.* To treat without regard, to pay no regard to. **a.** In earlier use, *esp.*, to treat without due regard, respect, or attention; to neglect unduly, to slight.

1641 Milton *Animadv.* To Postscr., Wks. (1847) 74/2 To take sanctuary among those churches which..formerly you have disregarded and despised. **1651** Baxter *Inf. Bapt.* 144 To make all the people disregard and despise the Gospel. **1760–72** tr. *Juan & Ulloa's Voy.* (ed. 3) I. 458 Quarries of fine stone; but these are utterly disregarded by the inhabitants. **1781** Gibbon *Decl. & F.* II. 85 Those who have attacked, and those who have defended..have alike disregarded two very remarkable passages of two orations pronounced under the succeeding reign.

b. In later use, *esp.*, to treat as of no importance, to pay no attention to.

1793 Holcroft *Lavater's Physiog.* xxi. 107 Desirous of private happiness he disregards public opinion. **1849** Macaulay *Hist. Eng.* II. 155 The king..advised the treasurer to disregard idle rumours. **1869** Dickens *Lett.* (1880) II. 421, I have had symptoms that must not be disregarded.

Hence **disre'garded** *ppl. a.* (whence **disre'gardedness**, state of being disregarded); **disre'garding** *vbl. sb.* and *ppl. a.*

1659 C. Noble *Mod. Answ. Immod. Q.* 6 To charge him with neglects and slightings and disregardings to his friends. **1659** D. Pell *Impr. Sea* 185 Unto which Ambassage the Queen of England..returned this bold, smiling, and disregarding answer. **1667** Flavel *Saint Indeed* (1754) 24 In the disregarded heart, swarms of vain foolish thoughts are perpetually working. **1791** Cowper *Iliad* VIII. 561 Then sullen nurse thy disregarded spleen. *a* **1854** Ld. Cockburn *Circuit Journ.* (1883) 95 Its surrounding bad taste and selfish disregardedness.

disre'gardable, *a.* [f. prec. + -ABLE.] That may be disregarded; unworthy of regard.

1661 *Grand Debate* 77 Till experience be proved to be disregardable. **1741** Richardson *Pamela* III. 152 An easy Fortune is..far from being disregardable.

disre'gardant, *a.* [f. DIS- 10 + REGARDANT, after prec. vb.] Paying no regard or attention; neglectful, disregarding.

1816 Southey *Poet's Pilgr.* I. 27 All disregardant of the Babel sound, A swan kept oaring near with upraised eye. **1880** Ruskin *Fors Clav.* Sept. VIII. 131, I understand you to be..disregardant, if not actually defiant, of the persons on whose capital you have been hitherto passively dependent for occupation.

disre'garder. [f. DISREGARD *v.* + -ER¹.] One who disregards.

1661 Boyle *Style of Script.* Pref. (1675) 10 Disregarders of the Scripture. **1864** H. Spencer *Illustr. Univ. Progr.* 110 In being considered a disregarder of public opinion.

disre'gardful, *a.* [f. DIS- 10 + REGARDFUL: cf. *disrespectful*.] The opposite of regardful; regardless, neglectful, careless.

a **1641** Bp. Mountagu *Acts & Mon.* 302 It was not probable he could be..so dis-regardfull of his owne state. *a* **1677** Barrow *Serm.* Wks. 1687 I. vii. 83 Will God..be so partial and fond to us, so disregardfull and injurious toward himself? **1748** Richardson *Clarissa* Wks. 1883 VIII. 372 Who..could be so disregardful of his own interest? **1882** A. B. Bruce *Parab. Teach. Christ* II. vi. (1891) 354 Love..disregardful of conventional barriers.

Hence **disre'gardfully** *adv.*, without regard, with neglect; **disre'gardfulness**.

1640 Bp. Hall *Chr. Moder.* 41/2 They..after many years vain hope were turned home disregardfully. *c* **1720** *Lett. fr. Mist's Jrnl.* (1722) II. 64 An Author..used too slightly and disregardfully. **1731** Bailey, *Disregardfulness*, neglectfulness. **1869** Mrs. Whitney *Hitherto* viii. 93 Not breaking in disregardfully; she always listened Mrs. Whistler through.

† **dis'regular**, *a.* [DIS- 10.] = IRREGULAR.
1649 EVELYN *Liberty & Servitude* iv. Misc. Writ. (1805) 21 Men.. who (not having more disregular passions) dispise honours, pleasures, riches.

disrelate (dɪsrɪ'leɪt), *v.* [See DISRELATED *ppl. a.*] *trans.* To sever the connection between, cause to have no connection.
1654 J. OWEN *Doctr. Saints Persev.* xv. 353 True Believers who only are the members of Christ disrelate themselves to him. **1895** *Westm. Gaz.* 25 Nov. 2/3 Something analogous to a sense of prudery has caused the author slightly to disrelate the two contestants for Lois. **1946** *New Republic* 29 Apr. 620 The vertical character of Thomas' vision tends to disrelate the components of immediate experiences.

disre'lated, *ppl. a.* [DIS- 10.] Unrelated; without relation or connexion. So **disre'lation**, absence of relation or connexion.
1893 *Westm. Gaz.* 15 May 3/2 Throughout his humour consists of the disrelation of his remarks to his age and size. *Ibid.*, When they utter disrelated speeches. **1894** *Ibid.* 26 Sept. 2/3 [He] looks on what goes before or comes after him as entirely disrelated.

disrelish (dɪs'rɛlɪʃ), *sb.* Also 7 **disrellish**. [f. DISRELISH *v.* or DIS- 9 + RELISH *sb.*] Distaste, dislike, aversion, some degree of disgust.
a **1625** FLETCHER *Nice Valour* I. i, Being once glutted, then the taste of folly Will come into disrelish. **1645** FULLER *Good Th. in Bad T.* (1841) 37 Dissensions.. will breed in pagans such a disrelish of our religion. **1667** MILTON *P.L.* x. 569 With hatefullest disrelish writh'd thir jaws With soot and cinders fill'd. **1717** POPE *Let. to Atterbury* 20 Nov., With a dis-relish of all that the world calls Ambition. **1791** BURKE *App. Whigs* Wks. VI. 202 Men.. have an extreme disrelish to be told of their duty. **1802** *Med. Jrnl.* VIII. 403 Her disrelish for food amounted to disgust. **1841** MIALL in *Nonconf.* I. 96 Conduct.. indicative of his disrelish for the whole subject.
b. Something which excites distaste or aversion.
1823 *New Monthly Mag.* IX. 104/2 The extraordinary nasal twang.. not to mention other disrelishes, we cannot get over.

disrelish (dɪs'rɛlɪʃ), *v.* [f. DIS- 6 or 7 a + RELISH *v.* or *sb.*]
† **1.** *trans.* To destroy the relish or flavour of; to render distasteful. *Obs.*
(The first quot. appears to belong here: *rellese*, *rellice* occur as 16th c. spellings of RELISH.)
1548 UDALL, etc. *Erasm. Par. Luke* xv. 130 b, Yet is it [the plentie or aboundance of the prodigal] marred and dis-realised with muche galle of sondrie griefes and sorowes. **1628** EARLE *Microcosm.* (1740) 86 Some musty proverb that disrelishes all things whatsoever. **1667** MILTON *P.L.* v. 305. **1691** NORRIS *Pract. Disc.* 140 'Tis like the Handwriting on the Wall, enough to spoil and disrelish the Feast. **1760** STERNE *Serm.* III. 374.
2. To have a distaste for, to find not to one's taste; to regard with disfavour; to dislike.
1604 SHAKS. *Oth.* II. i. 236 Her delicate tendernesse wil.. begin to heaue the gorge, disreelish and abhorre the Moore. **1642** MILTON *Apol. Smect.* Wks. 1738 I. 117 How long is it since he hath disrelish'd Libels? **1764** *Mem. G. Psalmanazar* 256 This excellent book, though.. disrelished by some weak Christians. **1799** G. WASHINGTON *Lett.* Writ. 1893 XIV. 151, I am not surprised that some members of the House.. should disrelish your report. **1886** STEVENSON *Kidnapped* xxvii. (1888) 281 He so much disrelished some expressions of mine that.. he showed me to the door.
† **3.** To prove distasteful to; to disgust. *Obs.*
1649 BP. HALL *Cases Consc.* III. vii. (1650) 230 Or preach some truth which dis-relishes the palate of a prepossessed auditor. **1659** *Lady Alimony* IV. vii. in Hazl. *Dodsley* XIV. 352 What might I say, That should disrelish Madam Caveare? **1708** J. PHILIPS *Cyder* I. 28 He tastes the bitter morsel, and rejects Disrelisht.
4. *intr.* To be distasteful, to 'go down badly.'
1631 [See DISRELISHING below]. **1647** SPRIGGE *Anglia Rediv.* IV. iv. 223 This much disrelished with the Lord Hopton. **1814** CARY *Dante Par.* XVII. 113, I learnt that, which if I tell again, It may with many wofully disrelish.
Hence **dis'relished** *ppl. a.*; **dis'relishing** *vbl. sb.*; **dis'relishing** *ppl. a.*, distasteful.
1631 BRATHWAIT *Whimzies* Ep. Ded. 8 Strong lines have beene in request, but they grew disrelishing. **1659** *Lady Alimony* II. v. in Hazl. *Dodsley* XIV. 314 A freedom from our disrelish'd beds. **1692** DRYDEN *St. Evremont's Ess.* 78 This first disrelishing of the Republick, had.. so much of Honesty that [etc.]. **1821** LAMB *Elia* Ser. I. *Imperf. Sympathies*, When once it becomes indifferent, it begins to be disrelishing. **1846** D. KING *Treat. Lord's Supper* iv. 89 A violated law and a disrelished salvation.

† **dis'relishable**, *a. Obs.* [f. prec. + -ABLE.] Such as to be disrelished or disliked; distasteful.
a **1670** HACKET *Abp. Williams* I. (1692) 78 (D.) That the match.. should be intended no more was disrelishable.

† **dis'relishment**. *Obs. rare.* [f. DISRELISH + -MENT.] A disliking; a distasteful matter.
1646 S. BOLTON *Arraignm. Err.* 354 An act of oblivion.. in which all disrelishments either in language or action, word or deed, may be buried up in silence.

disremember (dɪsrɪ'mɛmbə(r)), *v.* Chiefly *dial.* [f. DIS- 6 + REMEMBER *v.*] To fail to remember; to forget. (*trans.* and *absol.*)
1815 in *Doc. Hist. Amer. Industr. Soc.* (1910) IV. 25, I belonged to the Society about fifteen months; as to the constitution I disremember, the rules I recollect. **1834** M. EDGEWORTH *Tour in Connemara* (1950) 93 He had some outlandish name that was gone out of his head—that he disremembered. **1836** F. MAHONEY *Rel. Father Prout* (1859) 373 The.. lines of the author he feigns to disremember. **1848** MRS. GASKELL *M. Barton* ix. (1882) 23/1, I disremember rightly what I did. **1876** MISS CARY *Country Life* i. 13 If he did not dis-remember, he would look at it before he went to bed. **1880** OUIDA *Moths* vii, [American speaking] I disremembered to ask when the mails went out. **1880** *Antrim & Down Gloss.*, *Disremember*, to forget. [Also in Glossaries of Sussex, Berks, Hants, and in Bartlett *Dict. Amer.* (1860).] *c* **1885** G. M. HOPKINS *Poems* (1918) 52 Qúite Disremembering, dísmémbering! áll now. **1928** D. BYRNE *Destiny Bay* viii. 382 Either in Ohio or Illinois, I disremember which. **1938** M. K. RAWLINGS *Yearling* i. 13 'Do you mind what we said we'd do, full moon in April?' 'I disremember.'

disrepair (dɪsrɪ'pɛə(r)). [f. DIS- 9 + REPAIR *sb.*] The state of being out of repair, or in bad condition for want of repairs.
1798 *Telegraph* in *Spirit Pub. Jrnls.* (1799) II. 368 If our landlord should.. suffer our houses and fences to go entirely into disrepair. **1813** SCOTT *Rokeby* II. xvii, All spoke neglect and disrepair. **1816** —— *Old Mort.* v, It had been suffered to go considerably into disrepair. **1833** *Act 3-4 Will. IV*, c. 46 §104 Where any.. spouts.. drains or common sewers.. shall get into disrepair. **1854** H. MILLER *Sch. & Schm.* i. (1857) 8 It.. had now fallen greatly into disrepair.

† **disre'port**, *sb. Obs. rare.* [f. DIS- 9 + REPORT *sb.*] Evil report, report to any one's prejudice.
1640 FULLER *Joseph's Coat* viii. (1867) 193 Let us practise St. Paul's precept, 'by honour and dishonour, by good report and disreport'.

† **disreport**, *v. Obs. rare.* [f. DIS- 6 + REPORT *v.*] To give an evil report (of).
1653 R. BAILLIE *Disswasive Vind.* (1655) 81 Their forwardnesse to misreport, disreport, discovers much evill affection in their spirits.

dis,reputa'bility. [f. DISREPUTABLE *a.*: see -BILITY.] = DISREPUTABLENESS.
1854 DE QUINCEY *Autobiog. Sk.* Wks. II. 78 Why then should he court danger and disreputability? **1879** ARBER *Introd.* to *2nd Pt. Return fr. Parnass.* 16 The important testimony.. to the disreputability.. of the professional Actor. **1892** LOUNSBURY *Stud. Chaucer* III. vii. 250 To call a man a Goth conveyed.. a general sense of the disreputability of him about whom it was uttered.

disreputable (dɪs'rɛpjʊtəb(ə)l), *a.* (*sb.*) [f. DIS- 10 + REPUTABLE *a.*, after DISREPUTE.]
1. The reverse of reputable; such as to bring into disrepute or reflect discredit; discreditable.
1772 *Ann. Reg.* 27 He could not.. but be sensibly concerned for the present disreputable state of our law courts. *a* **1795** J. WEDGWOOD in *Darwin's Life & Lett.* (1887) I. 198 It would [not] be in any degree disreputable to his character as a Clergyman. **1871** FREEMAN *Hist. Ess.* Ser. I. vii. 200 One of the most disreputable of juggles.
2. Having a bad reputation; in bad repute; not of respectable character.
1828 WEBSTER, *Disreputable*.. as, disreputable company. **1844** DISRAELI *Coningsby* IV. iv. (L.), Nobody wants a second chamber, except a few disreputable individuals. **1861** GEO. ELIOT *Silas M.* v, There was Jem Rodney, a known poacher, and otherwise disreputable. **1867** MISS BRADDON *Run to Earth* i, The room was full of sailors and disreputable-looking women.
B. *sb.* A disreputable person.
1853 H. GREVILLE *Diary* (1884) 35 To clear his Court of the robbers and disreputables who surround him. **1862** SHIRLEY *Nugæ Crit.* iii. 172 Heine, one of the religious disreputables, was.. a mocker from his boyhood to his death. **1887** *Pall Mall G.* 23 Aug. 2/1 Where the.. drunkards and disreputables are well in evidence.

dis'reputableness. [f. prec. + -NESS.] The quality or state of being disreputable.
1710 W. HUME *Sacred Success.* 382 So that what people.. agree upon and determine.. shall respecting reputableness or disreputableness, have a very commanding force. **1860** *All Year Round* 142 That disreputableness of appearance which is one of their greatest sources of attraction.

dis'reputably, *adv.* [f. as prec. + -LY².] In a disreputable manner; discreditably.
1775 BURKE *Sp. Conc. Amer.* Wks. III. 29 Propositions are made.. somewhat disreputably, when the minds of men are not properly disposed for their reception. *Mod.* He is said to have behaved most disreputably on that occasion.

disrepu'tation. *Obs.* or *arch.* [DIS- 9.]
1. Privation or loss of reputation; bringing into disrepute; discrediting; dishonour, disgrace.
1601 FULBECKE *1st Pt. Parall.* Intr. iii, The sodaine and finall myserie, calamitie, and disreputation of that Common-weale. *a* **1617** HIERON *Wks.* II. 17 Those who vrge this to the dis-reputation of all that are affected well. **1651-3** JER. TAYLOR *Serm. for Year* I. xiv. 173 A disreputation of piety and a strict life. **1691-8** NORRIS *Pract. Disc.* (1711) III. 78 Are they not inwardly troubled.. when they hear anything said to their Disreputation? **1824** T. JEFFERSON *Writ.* (1830) IV. 387 He will.. bring disreputation on the institution. **1874** MOTLEY *Barneveld* I. vii. 320 To remove me from my post with disreputation.
† **b.** A discrediting circumstance, a discredit.
1609 BP. W. BARLOW *Answ. Nameless Cath.* 104 This reason.. is not onely a Calumniation against T.M. but a dis-reputation also to his Maiestie. **1651-3** JER. TAYLOR *Serm. for Year* (1678) 110 Intemperance.. is a Dishonour and disreputation to the person and the nature of the man. **1751** *Affect. Narr. Wager* 36 Humanity.. the want of which is a Disreputation to a Man's Character.
† **2.** Want of reputation, evil reputation; the condition of being in disrepute; discredited condition.
1633 T. ADAMS *Exp. 2 Peter* ii. 5 This vice.. is gotten already out of the disreputation of a sin. **1748** RICHARDSON *Clarissa* (1811) III. xxxvii. 221 The period in which our conduct or misconduct gives us a reputation or disreputation, that almost inseparably accompanies us throughout our whole future lives. **1770** LANGHORNE *Plutarch* (1879) II. 639/1 Eumenes, with the disreputation of having been only a secretary, raised himself to the first military employments.

disrepute (dɪsrɪ'pjuːt), *sb.* [f. DIS- 9 + REPUTE *sb.*] Loss or absence of reputation; ill repute, disesteem, discredit, dishonour.
1653 HOLCROFT *Procopius* Pref. A ij b, Belisarius then returned to Constantinople with disrepute. **1698** NORRIS *Pract. Disc.* IV. 18 The Holy things of Religion fell at length into Contempt and Dis-repute. **1758** *Phil. Trans.* L. 666 It was formerly in great credit as a pectoral, but is now quite in disrepute. **1857** BUCKLE *Civiliz.* I. ix. 573 It brings the administration of justice into disrepute. **1870** LOWELL *Among my Bks.* Ser. I. (1873) 89 A large and spacious house which lay under the disrepute of being haunted.

† **disre'pute**, *v. Obs.* [f. DIS- 6 + REPUTE *v.*] *trans.* **a.** To hold as of no reputation; to regard slightingly; to disesteem. **b.** To bring into discredit; to defame, disparage. **c.** To bring discredit or an evil name upon (by one's conduct).
1611 FLORIO, *Disreputare*, to disrepute, to disesteeme. **1625** BP. MOUNTAGU *App. Cæsar* II. vii. 183 You quote us the Homilies.. I think you dis-repute them. **1649** JER. TAYLOR *Gt. Exemp.* I. ad §1. 16 The Virgin was betrothed lest honorable marriage might be disreputed. **1651** —— *Holy Living* iv. ad §10 (1727) 335 O teach me to walk, that I may never disrepute the honour of my religion. *a* **1677** BARROW *Serm.* (1686) III. 380 Is it not infinitely better to be unjustly defamed by men, than to be disreputed by God? **1697** R. PEIRCE *Bath Mem.* II. ii. 272 Doubting that he would disrepute the Place.. by dying here.

disre'semble, *v. rare.* [a. OF. *desressembler* (in Godef.), f. *des-*, DIS- 4 + *ressembler.*] *trans.* Not to resemble; to be unlike.
So **disre'semblance**, want of resemblance.
1622 PEACHAM *Compl. Gent.* xiii. (1634) 130/1 To have blurred it out for some small disresemblance, either in the eye or mouth. **1654** LD. ORRERY *Parthen.* (1676) 24 One exceeding like the first.. and disresembling him in nothing [etc.].

† **disre'sent**, *v. Obs. rare.* [f. DIS- 6 + RESENT *v.* (which formerly meant 'to take well or ill').] *trans.* To have a feeling against, to take ill; = RESENT in its current sense.
1652 W. HARTLEY *Inf. Baptism* 12 The Lord.. dis-resented such performances as were tainted with wickedness.

disrespect (dɪsrɪ'spɛkt), *sb.* [f. DIS- 9 + RESPECT *sb.*; or perh. from DISRESPECT *v.*] Want of respect, courteous regard, or reverence.
1631 GOUGE *God's Arrows* III. §80. 336 Profanation of holy things.. manifesteth a disrespect of God himselfe. **1731** JOHNSON *Let. to G. Hickman* 30 Oct. in *Boswell*, This delay.. proceeded neither from forgetfulness, disrespect nor ingratitude. **1771** *Junius Lett.* liv. 285 My memory fails me, if I have mentioned their names with disrespect. **1849** MACAULAY *Hist. Eng.* II. 23 No expression indicating disrespect to the Sovereign.. was suffered to escape.
† **b.** With *a* and *pl.* An instance of this; an act showing disesteem or irreverence; 'an act approaching to rudeness' (J.). *Obs.*
1632 MARMION *Holland's Leaguer* IV. v, Howsoever I have found a disrespect from you, yet I forget it. **1647** CLARENDON *Hist. Reb.* I. §149 Any disrespect to any acts of state.. was in no time more penal. **1689** *Col. Rec. Pennsylv.* I. 314, I doe also fforgive yᵉ Disrespects and neglects of any persons. *a* **1714** M. HENRY *Wks.* (1835) II. 139 Their unkindnesses and disrespects to himself.

disre'spect, *v.* [f. DIS- 6 + RESPECT *v.*] *trans.* The reverse of *to respect*; to have or show no respect, regard, or reverence for; to treat with irreverence.
1614 WITHER *Sat. to King*, Juvenilia (1633) 346 Here can I smile to see.. how the mean mans suit is dis-respected. **1633** BP. HALL *Hard Texts N.T.* 11 If he love the one he must disrespect the other. **1683** CAVE *Ecclesiastici* 231 (Basil) To honor him, and dis-respect his Friend, was to stroke a man's head with one hand, and strike him with the other. **1706** HEARNE *Collect.* 26 Apr., He was disrespected in Oxford by several men who now speak well of him. **1852** L. HUNT *Poems* Pref. 27 As if.. sorrow disrespected things homely. **1885** G. MEREDITH *Diana* I. 257 You will judge whether he disrespects me.
Hence **disre'spected** *ppl. a.*, **-ing** *vbl. sb.*
1631 GOUGE *God's Arrows* I. §45. 75 A dis-respecting, despising, and vilifying of Gods mercies. **1640** GLAPTHORNE *Ladies Privil.* IV. Wks. 1874 II. 140, I meane not.. To save a dis-respected life. **1791** PAINE *Rights of Man* (ed. 2) I. 101 Reflecting how wretched was the condition of a disrespected man. **1876** G. MEREDITH *Beauch. Career* III. vi. 105 Treating her.. like a disrespected grandmother.

disrespectability (dɪsrɪ,spɛktə'bɪlɪtɪ). [f. next + -ITY, after *respectability*.] The quality of being disrespectable; the reverse of respectability.

1830 LYTTON *P. Clifford* vii, Committed..to the House of Correction on the charge of disrespectability. **1848** THACKERAY *Van. Fair* lxiv, Her taste for disrespectability grew more and more remarkable. **1893** W. WALLACE *Scot. Yesterd.* 60 An office which had an odour of disrespectability.

disrespectable (dɪsrɪˈspɛktəb(ə)l), *a.* [DIS- 10.] The opposite of respectable; not worthy of respect; not in accordance with standards of respectability.

1813 *Examiner* 22 Mar. 187/1 All distinction..between what is respectable and what is disrespectable would be at an end. **1822** SCOTT *Nigel* xvi, Well acquainted with the town ..but in a sort of disrespectable way. **1865** M. ARNOLD *Ess. Crit.* v. (1875) 223 Not only was he [Heine] not one of Mr. Carlyle's 'respectable' people, he was profoundly disrespectable.

disreˈspecter. *rare.* [f. DISRESPECT *v.* + -ER[1].] One who disrespects.

1661 BOYLE *Style Script.* (1675) 149 There..are but too many witty disrespecters of the Scripture. **1711** tr. *Werenfels' Disc. Logom.* 127 The Disrespecters of the Antients.

disrespectful (dɪsrɪˈspɛktfʊl), *a.* [f. DIS- 10 + RESPECTFUL, after *disrespect.*] The opposite of respectful; full of or manifesting disrespect.

a **1677** BARROW *Serm.* Wks. 1687 I. xxiii. 316 Offended with our injurious and disrespectfull behaviour toward him. **1681** E. SCLATER *Serm. at Putney* 26 The least disrespectfull word is Rebellion. **1741** RICHARDSON *Pamela* II. 320, I must say nothing..that is disrespectful or undutiful. **1859** DICKENS *T. Two Cities* II. xii, I will hear no disrespectful word of that young lady from any lips. **1884** SIR J. PEARSON in *Law Times Rep.* LI. 659/1 It would be disrespectful to the Court of Appeal.

fig. **1748** *Whitehall Even. Post* No. 405 Our Commerce.. still suffers much from these disrespectful Accidents.

disreˈspectfully, *adv.* [f. prec. + -LY[2].] In a disrespectful manner.

1671 CLARENDON *Hist. Reb.* IX. §110 The lord Wentworth ..talked very imperiously, and very disrespectfully..to some of the council. **1717** T. HOWEL *Desiderius* (ed. 3) 15 He has..withdrawn from the publick Stage of the World, where he has been disrespectfully treated. **1856** FROUDE *Hist. Eng.* I. 277 Prohibiting Tyndale's Testament, in the preface of which the clergy were spoken of disrespectfully.

disreˈspectfulness. [f. as prec. + -NESS.] The quality or fact of being disrespectful.

1672 *Life of J. Alleine* v. (1838) 48 Bearing with their dulness, rudeness, and disrespectfulness. **1863** MISS BRADDON *J. Marchmont* II. x. 229, I seemed to feel as if it was a sin and a disrespectfulness towards her to wear colours.

†**disreˈspective,** *a. Obs.* [f. DIS- 10 + RESPECTIVE; after *disrespect.*] = DISRESPECTFUL.

1623 WITHER *Hymns & Songs* (1856) 33 Disrespective we have been Of statutes, judgements, and decree. **1628** DIGBY *Voy. Medit.* (1868) 54, I restored my principall masters mate ..that I had turned before the mast for some disrespectiue misdemeanour. **1735–6** CARTE *Ormonde* I. 325 This rash and violent proceeding so disrespective to that nobleman.

Hence †**disreˈspectively** *adv.*, disrespectfully.

1636 BRATHWAIT *Roman Emperors* 360 He passed to another life at Prague, disrespectively there inhumed.

†**disreˈspondency.** *Obs. rare.* [DIS- 9.] Absence of response; the fact of not responding.

1657 COKAINE *Obstinate Lady* II. ii, Why..would you engage So much yourself to any of that sex, As for a disrespondency to lay Violent hands upon yourself?

†**disˈrest,** *sb. Obs.* [DIS- 9.] The opposite of rest; disquiet, unrest.

1567 TURBERV. *Ovid's Ep.* 19 b, The sorer is the cruell gashe, and breedes the more disrest. **1668** HOWE *Bless. Righteous* (1825) 103 Free from any molestation from without, or principle of disrest within. **1726** AMHERST *Terræ Fil.* xxxiii. 177 Violence, disrest, and an ill name, will be the rewards of your folly and obstinacy.

†**disˈrest,** *v. Obs. rare.* [f. DIS- 7 a + REST *sb.*] *trans.* **a.** To remove or dislodge from a place of rest. **b.** To deprive of rest; to disturb.

1696 in Church *Philip's War* (1867) II. 123 An Expedition to attack that Fort, and to disrest and remove the Enemy from that Post. **1726** PENHALLOW *Ind. Wars* (1859) 52 Our frontiers at home were as much disrested as ever.

disrestore *v.*: see DIS- 6.

†**disˈreverence,** *v. Obs.* [DIS- 6 or 7 a.] *trans.* The opposite of *to reverence*; to treat with irreverence; to deprive of reverence.

1529 MORE *Dyalogue* III. 84 a/1 To se his maieste disreuerenced. **1608** W. SCLATER *Malachy* (1650) 45 That we pollute not nor disreverence the Name God. *a* **1670** HACKET *Abp. Williams* I. (1692) 127 How is His glory dis-reverenced over all this land?

disreˈward, *v.* [DIS- 6 or 7 a.] *trans.* To reverse the act of rewarding; to deprive of reward.

1640 QUARLES *Enchirid.* II. xcvi, Beware of Pride..it disrewards goodnesse in it selfe, by vain glory.

†**disˈriegled,** *ppl. a. Obs.* [f. OF. *desreiglé* 'vnrulie, disordered..vnbridled' (Cotgr.) + -ED[1]. Cf. REGLE *v.*] Unruly, unregulated, outrageous.

1638 *Penit. Conf.* (1657) 342 It is a necessary duty to cut off enormity and disriegled inordinances.

disrobe (dɪsˈrəʊb), *v.* Also 6–7 -roab. [DIS- 6 or 7 a. Cf. OF. *desrober* in same sense.]

1. *trans.* To divest or strip of a robe or garment; to undress, strip. Const. *of*, *from.*

1590 SPENSER *F.Q.* I. iii. 17 The holy Saints of their rich vestiments He did disrobe. **1595** SHAKS. *John* II. i. 147 He.. That did disrobe the Lion of that robe. **1601** —— *Jul. C.* I. i. 69 Disrobe the Images. **1638** SIR T. HERBERT *Trav.* (ed. 2) 236 One holds his knee; a second disroabs him. **1648** MAYNE *Amorous War* IV. vi, Disrobe your upper parts. **1725** POPE *Odyss.* xx. 312 Dis-rob'd, their vests apart in order lay. **1847** TENNYSON *Princ.* Concl. 117 Lilia Disrobed the glimmering statue of Sir Ralph From those rich silks.

2. *refl.* and *intr.* To divest oneself of clothing; to undress.

1581 MULCASTER *Positions* xxxiv. (1887) 122 They disrobed themselues, and were chafed with a gentle kinde of rubber. **1603** *Order Coronation Jas. I* in Maskell *Mon. Rit.* (1846–7) III. 109 *note*, The king..there disrobeth himself of his upper garments. **1715–20** POPE *Iliad* v. 904 Pallas disrobes. **1807** CRABBE *Sir E. Grey* xx, They make the hypocrite disrobe. **1883** GILMOUR *Mongols* xviii. 211 You will notice as they disrobe, that each and all wear at their breast charms.

3. *transf.* and *fig.* To divest, strip.

1592 *Nobody & Someb.* in Simpson *Sch. Shaks.* I. (1878) 299 Archigallo shall be deposd, And thou disroab'd of all thy dignitie. **1638** SIR T. HERBERT *Trav.* (ed. 2) 330 Nutmeg.. at full ripnesse disroabs it selfe, and discovers..the Mace. **1751** SMOLLETT *Per. Pick.* (1779) IV. cii. 321 Desire to see her fair eyes disrobed of..resentment. **1878** G. MACDONALD *Phantastes* vii. 112 The very voice..seemed to disrobe the room of the strange look.

Hence **disˈrobed** *ppl. a.*; **disˈrobing** *vbl. sb.* and *ppl. a.*

1794 MRS. PIOZZI *Synon.* II. 302 Writers who delight not in disrobed meaning. **1813** SHELLEY *Q. Mab* ix. 171 Fear not ..death's disrobing hand. **1841** LANE *Arab. Nts.* I. 121 The first apartment is the..disrobing room. **1903** 'A. MCNEILL' *Egregious Eng.* 58 The bare business of robing and disrobing takes up pretty well half her waking day. **1912** L. A. HARKER *Mr. Wycherly's Wards* x, Neither of them cared a whit for Jane-Anne and her disrobings.

disˈrobement. [f. DISROBE + -MENT.] The action of disrobing or divesting of a covering.

1747 GOULD *Eng. Ants* 46 You may discern such Disrobements in the Cones of Silk-Worms. **1830** *Blackw. Mag.* XXVIII. 875 Damon watches the process of disrobement.

disˈrober. [f. as prec. + -ER[1].] One who or that which disrobes.

1654 GAYTON *Pleas. Notes* III. viii. 119 Disinchanters of Negromancers, disrobers of gypsies. **1882** SIR P. FELIS in *Society* 7 Oct. 18/1 The trees, swept bare by autumn's gale —That swift and merciless disrober.

disroof (dɪsˈruːf), *v.* [DIS- 7 a.] *trans.* To deprive of the roof; to unroof. Hence **disˈroofed** *ppl. a.*

1837 CARLYLE *Fr. Rev.* III. v. vii. (1872) 208 Ghastly châteaus stare on you by the wayside, disroofed, diswindowed. **1871** J. C. JEAFFRESON *Ann. Oxf.* II. x. 154 The disroofed and dismantled walls of the venerable fanes.

†**disˈroom,** *v. Obs. rare.* In 5 **dysrowme.** [f. DIS- 7 c + ROOM *sb.*] *trans.* To displace.

1489 CAXTON *Faytes of A.* I. xxiii. 71 Noon vpon peyne of deth shall dysrowme hym self.

disroost *v.*: see DIS- 7 c.

disroot (dɪsˈruːt), *v.* [f. DIS- 6 + ROOT *v.*] *trans.* To pull up by the roots; to uproot, unroot.

1800 *Trans. Soc. Encourag. Arts* XVIII. 368 Pine-suckers ..having disrooted and plunged them into old dust of bark. **1849** *Florist* 279 Repot the bottoms that have been disrooted. **1876** SWINBURNE *Erechtheus* (ed. 2) 178 And with one hand disroot All tender flower and fruit.

b. *transf.* To dislodge (anything) from the place where it is fixed.

1612 *Two Noble K.* v. vi, When neither curb would crack ..nor differing plunges Dis-root his rider whence he grew. **1774** GOLDSM. *Nat. Hist.* (1862) I. xii. 63 The sliding down of a higher piece of ground, disrooted from its situation. **1865** CARLYLE *Fredk. Gt.* VIII. XVIII. xii. 33 Daun..could not have disrooted Friedrich this season.

Hence **disˈrooting** *vbl. sb.*; **disˈrooter**, one who disroots.

1826 SCOTT *Jrnl.* 10 Oct., A kind of disrooting that recalls a thousand painful ideas of former happier journeys. **1883** *Encycl. Dict.*, Disrooter.

disˈround, *v. nonce-wd.* [DIS- 8.] *trans.* To deprive of roundness or rotundity; to unround.

1555 WATREMAN *Fardle Facions* I. iii. 33 [They] are of opinion that the circuite of the earth..disroundyng hym self, shooteth out thre corner wise.

†**disˈrout,** *v. Obs.* Also 6 **disrought.** [ad. OF. *desrouter* (13th c. in Littré), mod.F. *dérouter*, f. *des-*, DIS- 4 + OF. *route* band, company. Cf. ROUT *v.*] **a.** *trans.* To put to rout. **b.** *intr.* To be put to rout; to break up, become scattered.

1525 LD. BERNERS *Froiss.* II. cxxxix. [cxxxv.] 389 If they disrought and be out of ordre, they shall soone be taken vp. **1592** WYRLEY *Armorie* 63, I appoint to you..thence not buge vnlesse you plainly vewe Vs to disrout. **1626** *True Relat. Stratagem* in Arb. *Garner* I. 608 The Black Prince.. disrouted their mighty armies. **1630** J. TAYLOR (Water P.) *World runs on Wheels* Wks. II. 243/2 To disrowte their enemies, breaking their rankes and order.

†**disˈrout,** *sb. Obs. rare.* [a. OF. *desroute* rout, disorder, mod.F. *déroute*, f. *dérouter*: see prec.] The act of putting to rout; rout, defeat.

1623 tr. *Favine's Theat. Hon* II. xiii. 217 Were (after their disroute) brought to Julius Cæsar.

†**disˈroyalty.** *Obs. nonce-wd.* [f. DIS- 9 + ROYALTY.] Undoing of royal dignity.

1639 *R. Johnson's Kingd. & Commw.* 210 Kings of Denmarke..have thought it no disroyaltie to set up divers manufactures.

disˈruddered, *ppl. a. rare.* [DIS- 7 a.] Deprived of the rudder.

a **1788** in Croft *Let. to Pitt on Johnson's New Dict.* 58–9 At the 7249th of my additional words, I find *disruddered* ..'their gait like to that of a disruddered ship'.

†**disˈrulily,** *adv. Obs.* In 4 **disrewlilye.** [f. next + -LY[2].] In an unruly manner.

c **1400** *Rom. Rose* 4900 [Youthe]..makith hym love yvelle companye, And lede his lyf disrewlilye.

†**disˈruly,** *a. Obs. rare*[−0]. [In ME. ****disrewlie***, implied in prec. adv., a. OF. *desrieulé* unregulated, disordered, mod.F. *déréglé*.] Unruly.

1570 LEVINS *Manip.* 99/47 Disrulie, *irregularis.*

disrump (dɪsˈrʌmp), *v.*[1] [ad. L. *disrump-ĕre* (also *dīrumpĕre*) to break into pieces, burst asunder, f. DIS- 1 + *rumpĕre* to break.] To break up, burst asunder, DISRUPT (*trans.* and *intr.*).

(In quot. 1661, with a play upon the *Rump Parliament.*)

1581 T. NUCE *Seneca's Octavia* II. ii. 177 b, Let spouses age And curteous bashfull shame disrumpe your rage. **1661** *Sir H. Vane's Politics* 16 Upon the sad approach of that Scotch Army, our forlorn Society..became dis-rumped. **1886** *Sat. Rev.* 8 May 635/2 A caucus is a much worse monster than a dragon..and does not disrump so easily.

disˈrump, *v.*[2] *nonce-wd.* [DIS- 7 a.] *trans.* To deprive of the rump.

1654 GAYTON *Pleas. Notes* IV. v. 196 The Barber..parts with his taile-piece, and walks as one of the disrump'd [*printed* dirump'd] Poultry.

†**disˈrumpent,** *a. Obs.* [a. L. *disrumpent-em*, pr. pple. of *disrumpĕre*: see DISRUMP *v.*[1]] That bursts asunder.

1657 TOMLINSON *Renou's Disp.* 391 Vested with a membranous and frequently disrumpent barke.

disrupt (dɪsˈrʌpt), *ppl. a.* [ad. L. *disrupt-us*, pa. pple. of *disrumpĕre*: see DISRUMP *v.*[1] and cf. DIRUPT.] Burst or broken asunder; broken up. Chiefly as poetic *pa. pple.* = DISRUPTED.

1730–6 BAILEY (folio), *Disrupt*, broken or rent asunder. **1782** W. STEVENSON *Hymn to Deity* 16 Behind a watery cloud disrupt. **1850** MRS. BROWNING *Soul's Travelling* viii, Though at your feet The cliff's disrupt. **1885** G. MEREDITH *Diana* II. i. 3 Leaving them..disrupt, as by earthquake.

disrupt (dɪsˈrʌpt), *v.* [f. L. *disrupt-* ppl. stem of *disrumpĕre*: see DISRUMP *v.*[1]] Except in single quot. 1657, app. not in use before 19th c. Not in J., T., R., nor Webster 1828. Cf. the rare DIRUPT.]

1. *intr.* To burst asunder. *rare.*

1657 TOMLINSON *Renou's Disp.* 668 Almonds..may be.. agitated..over a slow fire, till the Involucrum disrupt.

2. *trans.* To break or burst asunder; to break in pieces, shatter; to separate forcibly.

1817 SCORESBY in *Ann. Reg., Chron.* 556 The most formidable fields..become disrupted into a thousand pieces. **1849** *Tait's Mag.* XVI. 423 We should..disrupt the bonds. **1879** TOURGEE *Fool's Err.* xxiii. 140 The attempt which was made to disrupt the government.

fig. **1865** *Pall Mall G.* 1 June 11 His very religious and philosophical thinkings being constantly disrupted by some whim or personal peculiarity.

Hence **disˈrupted, disˈrupting** *ppl. adjs.*

1819 *Blackw. Mag.* IV. 397 There is a concord and a harmony in the disrupted fragments of the cliffs. **1849** DANA *Geol.* ii. (1850) 107 These disrupting and transporting effects. **1876** PAGE *Adv. Text-Bk. Geol.* iv. 84 When igneous matter forces its way through the stratified rocks..it is termed disrupting. **1876** H. SPENCER *Princ. Sociol.* (1877) 704 There come into play disrupting influences. **1879** A. B. DAVIDSON *Expositor* 264 The reunion of the disrupted kingdom.

disˈruptable, *a. rare.* [f. DISRUPT *v.* + -ABLE.] Capable of being disrupted. Hence **disruptaˈbility.**

1820 C. R. MATURIN *Melmoth* (1892) III. xxx. 208 The intense and disruptable feeling. **1893** *Scott. Leader* 11 Oct. 3 As many points of disruptability as the mariner's compass has points.

dis'rupter, -or. [See -ER[1], -OR.] One who breaks up; one who causes disruption.

1881 *Sat. Rev.* 23 July 116/2 These eminent Disrupters had been passionate advocates for the nationality of the Church. **1886** PARNELL in *Pall Mall G.* 26 June 10/2 They denounced Mr. Gladstone as a betrayer of his country and a disruptor of the Empire.

dis'ruptic, *a. rare.* [f. L. *disrupt-* (see DISRUPT *v.*) + -IC.] Of or pertaining to the disruption or breaking up (of organic structures).

1889 GEDDES & THOMSON *Evol. of Sex* 88 The ascending, synthetic, constructive series of changes are termed 'anabolic'; the descending, disruptic series, 'katabolic'.

disruption (dɪs'rʌpʃən). [ad. L. *disruptiōn-em* (*dīruptiōn-em*), n. of action from *disrumpĕre* to burst or break asunder.]

1. The action of rending or bursting asunder; violent dissolution of continuity; forcible severance.

1646 SIR T. BROWNE *Pseud. Ep.* III. xvi. 145 Theophrastus ..conceiveth..that upon a full and plentifull impletion there may succeed a disruption of the matrix. **1684** T. BURNET *Th. Earth* I. 161 These great earthquakes and disruptions, that did such great execution upon the body of the earth. **1799** KIRWAN *Geol. Ess.* 251 These pillars did not assume the columnar form by crystallization, but by disruption. **1816** MISS SCHIMMELPENNINCK tr. *Tour La Grande Chartreuse* I. 10 At the sudden disruption of the masses of rock above. **1866** ROGERS *Agric. & Prices* I. xxiii. 601 On the final disruption of Guienne from the English crown.

2. A disrupted condition; a disrupted part or place, a rent.

1760–72 tr. *Juan & Ulloa's Voy.* (ed. 3) II. 88 They..rend the earth, and at every shock leave it full of disruptions. **1852** MISS YONGE *Cameos* (1877) III. xxv. 233 In the time of weakness and disruption. **1877** MORLEY *Crit. Misc., Carlyle* Ser. I. (1878) 199 The whole polity of Europe was left in such a condition of disruption as had not [etc.].

3. *spec.* ***the Disruption***: the name applied to the great split in the Established Church of Scotland, 18th May 1843, when 451 ministers left that Church and formed themselves into the Free Protesting (afterwards, simply, the Free) Church of Scotland.

The cause of their separation was the failure of the Church to maintain its complete independence in matters spiritual as against the interference of the Civil Courts (Court of Session), for which the Evangelical party had carried on a 'Ten Years' Conflict' against the 'Moderates'.

1843 CANDLISH *Speech* 30 Mar. in *Life* (1880) 293 All the people are concerned in making preparation for that disruption which is now inevitable. *Ibid.* 6 Sept. 315 The Free Church, since the Disruption has in a wonderful manner kept herself free from..attacks on the existing Establishment. **1886** J. H. BLUNT *Dict. Sects* 167/1 The standing outside the Establishment for a quarter of a century has much weakened the adherence..to the original views maintained at the Disruption.

attrib. **1871** J. MACKENZIE *Life Princ. Cunningham* xv. 192 The same contented cheerfulness dwelt in the poor abode of every Disruption minister. *Ibid.* 195 Dr. Cunningham visited this district in November of the Disruption year.

dis'ruptionist. [f. prec. + -IST.] One who favours disruption.

1886 *Sat. Rev.* 22 May 693/2 The disruptionists, with all Irish sedition to back them, will be powerless. **1886** *Athenæum* 11 Sept. 331/2 As to the origin of the [Homeric] poems Mr. Leaf seems to be a unionist by predilection, but a moderate disruptionist by conviction.

attrib. **1882** *Contemp. Rev.* Sept. 458 Disruptionist tendencies in some of the revolutionary schools of Russia.

disruptive (dɪs'rʌptɪv), *a.* [f. L. *disrupt-* ppl. stem: see DISRUPT *v.* and -IVE.]

1. Causing or tending to disruption; bursting or breaking asunder.

1862 J. SPENCE *Amer. Union* 92 None anticipated the great disruptive force that now convulses the country. **1874** STUBBS *Const. Hist.* (1875) I. ix. 255 The speedy development of disruptive tendencies.

b. *Electr.* (See quots.)

1842–3 GROVE *Corr. Phys. Forces* (1874) 80 The electrical disruptive discharge. **1870** R. M. FERGUSON *Electr.* 79 The term disruptive discharge is applied to all cases where discharge is accompanied with a disruption of the particles of the dielectric. **1880** J. E. H. GORDON *Electr. & Magn.* (1883) II. 187 It follows almost as a matter of course that all discharges in rarefied air are equally disruptive and discontinuous. **1892** *Pall Mall G.* 4 Feb. 6/3 Currents of still higher frequency and potential are obtained by passing the spark or disruptive discharge from a battery of Leyden jars through the primary circuit of an induction coil.

2. Produced by disruption: eruptive.

1876 PAGE *Adv. Text-Bk. Geol.* vii. 128 The disruptive character of these rocks.

Hence **dis'ruptively** *adv.*; **dis'ruptiveness**.

1870 R. M. FERGUSON *Electr.* 87 They discharge into each other disruptively. **1880** J. E. H. GORDON *Electr. & Magn.* (1883) II. 186 The character which was found to be fundamental in sensitive discharges, viz., disruptiveness, is common to both kinds of discharge.

dis'ruptment. *rare*$^{-1}$. [f. DISRUPT *v.* + -MENT.] Breaking off, disruption.

1834 *Fraser's Mag.* IX. 290 The disruptment of granite blocks from the summit of Mont Blanc.

disrupture (dɪs'rʌptjʊə(r)), *sb.* [f. DISRUPT *v.*, after RUPTURE.] The action of disrupting or bursting asunder; disruption.

1785 JEFFERSON *Notes Virginia* (1787) 27 The evident marks of their disrupture and avulsion from their beds by the most powerful agents of nature, corroborate the impression. **1796** MORSE *Amer. Geog.* I. 660 This disrupture discovered the vein of yellow metal at a great depth. **1804** WATT in *Phil. Trans.* XCIV. 308 Effected..by the apparent disrupture of rocks. **1828** *Hist. Europe* in *Ann. Reg.* 122/2 This disrupture of ordinary ties. **1884** BOWER & SCOTT *De Bary's Phaner.* 603 The consequent splitting and disrupture of the medullary sheath.

dis'rupture, *v.* [f. the sb.: cf. *rupture* vb.] *trans.* To break off or asunder; to divide by a rupture. Hence **dis'ruptured** *ppl. a.*

1828 WEBSTER cites *Med. Repos.* for *Disruptured.* **1834** M. SCOTT *Cruise Midge* (1859) 299 A huge mass of the grey cliff above was disruptured. **1838** POE *A.G. Pym* Wks. 1864 IV. 177 The ruins of the disruptured cliff. **1869** *Contemp. Rev.* XII. 184 These virtues exercise their beneficent influence in each portion of the disruptured church.

diss (dɪs). [a. Arab. *dīs*, the native name.] The Algerian name for a Mediterranean grass, *Ampelodesma* (*Arundo*) *tenax*, the fibrous stems of which are used for making cordage, etc.

1855 SIR W. HOOKER *Rept. on Veg. Prod. at Paris Exhib.* III. *Algeria* 35–7 Dis. **1871** *Policy of Alliance Assur. Co.*, On Merchandise (excluding Esparto, Alpha or Alfa, Diss.. Petroleum, and all Mineral and Rock Oils and their liquid products). **1895** *Guide to Museum of Econ. Bot., Kew* No. 2. 73 Diss.

diss, var. DIS *v.*

dissaf, -aiue, dissait(e, -at(e, obs. ff. DECEIVE, DECEIT.

†**dissaiff.** *Sc. Obs.* [Sc. form of DECEIVE.] Deception, deceiving.

c **1470** HENRY *Wallace* v. 612 And othir quhill he thocht on his dissaiff.

†**dis'saint,** *v. Obs.* [f. DIS- 6 or 7 b + SAINT.] *trans.* To make no longer a saint; to remove from the calendar of saints; to unsaint.

1612 T. JAMES *Corrupt. Script.* IV. 39 They may as well dissaint him hereafter (as saint him now).

dissaisin, obs. Sc. form of DISSEISIN.

†**dis'salt,** *v. Obs.* [DIS- 7 a.] *trans.* To free from salt.

1706 PHILLIPS (ed. Kersey), *Dissalted*, cleared from Salt, made fresh. **1721** in BAILEY.

dissar, dissard(e, var. DISOUR, DIZZARD.

dissatisfaction (dɪssætɪs'fækʃən). [f. DIS- 9 + SATISFACTION.] The fact or condition of being dissatisfied; discontent; 'want of something to complete the wish' (J.).

1640 in Rushw. *Hist. Coll.* III. (1692) I. 52 When..the Spanish Armada appeared in the Downs, to the great fear and dissatisfaction of the City. **1648** CROMWELL *Let.* 25 Nov., The dissatisfaction you take at the ways of some good men. **1791** MRS. RADCLIFFE *Rom. Forest* i, The chance of future trouble..occasioned some dissatisfaction. **1868** DICKENS *Lett.* (1880) II. 335 He..concluded (as usual) by giving universal dissatisfaction.

b. (with *pl.*) A feeling or expression of dissatisfaction or discontent.

c **1640** SANDERSON in Walton *Life* App. i, From the reading of it I went away with many and great dissatisfactions. **1662** H. MORE *Philos. Writ.* Pref. Gen. 12 Concerning my *Immortality of the Soul*, I shall take notice only of these two Dissatisfactions. **1723** BLACKMORE *True Hist. Conspir.* Pref. A viij a, The Conspirators..ingrafted their Treason on Public Dissatisfactions.

c. A cause or occasion of dissatisfaction or discontent; a dissatisfactory circumstance.

1702 W. J. *Bruyn's Voy. Levant* lxvii. 242 They had..the dissatisfaction of being obliged to return home, without having seen the Antiquities of Tadmor.

dissatisfactory (dɪssætɪs'fæktərɪ), *a.* [f. DIS- 10 + SATISFACTORY.] Not satisfactory; causing dissatisfaction or discontent; unsatisfactory; 'unable to give content' (J.).

c **1610** SIR J. MELVIL *Mem.* (1735) 109 Things which.. were dissatisfactory to her Subjects. **1779** T. JEFFERSON *Let.* Writ. (1893) II. 189 Their conduct..has been so dissatisfactory to the French minister that [etc.]. **1846** THACKERAY *Crit. Rev.* Wks. 1886 XXIII. 96, I don't know anything more dissatisfactory and absurd.

Hence **dissatis'factoriness**, the quality or condition of being dissatisfactory.

1677 HALE *Contempl.* II. 5 The shortness and uncertainty of sensible Enjoyments..their Poorness, Emptiness, Insufficiency, Dissatisfactoriness.

dissatisfied (dɪs'sætɪsfaɪd), *ppl. a.* [f. DISSATISFY + -ED[1].] Deprived of satisfaction; displeased; disquieted by the feeling of the insufficiency or inadequacy of something.

1675 tr. *Camden's Hist. Eliz.* an. 1599 [Essex] himself also was very much dissatisfied and displeased that the queen had..conferred on Sir Robert Cecyl the gainfull office of master of the wards. **1680** in Hacke *Collect. Voy.* II. (1699) 15 Very grateful to our dissatisfied Minds. *a* **1704** T. BROWN *Two Oxf. Scholars* Wks. (1730) I. 2 Infinitely dissatisfy'd with several things in the Church of England. **1827** LYTTON *Pelham* v, I had no reason to be dissatisfied with my success. **1875** JOWETT *Plato* (ed. 2) III. 227 Glaucon..was dissatisfied at Thrasymachus' retirement.

b. Exhibiting or expressing dissatisfaction.

1800 MRS. HERVEY *Mourtray Fam.* IV. 192 Lord Miramont's dissatisfied looks, and sullen silence. **1842** BARHAM *Ingol. Leg.*, *Row in Omnibus*, With a gloomy brow and dissatisfied air. **1883** O'DONOVAN *Merv* xxiv. 298 The horses were standing around in dissatisfied silence.

Hence **dis'satisfiedly** *adv.*, in a dissatisfied manner, with dissatisfaction; **dis'satisfiedness**, the condition of being dissatisfied, dissatisfaction.

1710 R. WARD *Life of H. More* 147 Seasons of Perplexity and Dissatisfiedness. **1805** MRS. INCHBALD *To Marry, or not* in *Br. Theatre* 3, *Hester.* Oh Madam..forgive this intrusion..*Mrs. M.* My dear, I must forgive all you do. (*Dissatisfiedly.*) **1880** RHODA BROUGHTON *Sec. Th.* I. viii, She remains dissatisfiedly mute.

dissatisfy (dɪs'sætɪsfaɪ), *v.* [f. DIS- 6 + SATISFY *v.*] *trans.* To deprive of satisfaction, to render unsatisfied; to fail to satisfy or fulfil the desires or wishes of; to displease, discontent, make unquiet in mind. Also *absol.*

1666 PEPYS *Diary* 23 July, The French are not yet joined with the Dutch, which do dissatisfy the Hollanders. **1673** *Lady's Call.* II. §2 ¶ 9. 68 Denying her self even the most innocent liberties, if she see they dissatisfy him. *a* **1726** COLLIER (J.), The advantages of life will not hold out to the length of desire, and, since they are not big enough to satisfy, they should not be big enough to dissatisfy. **1806** LD. GRENVILLE In Dk. Buckhm. *Crt. & Cab. Geo. III*, (1855) IV. 9 Doing enough to dissatisfy my own mind, and always too little to satisfy theirs. **1865** M. ARNOLD *Ess. Crit.* viii. (1875) 319 In all his production how much there is to dissatisfy us.

Hence **dis'satisfying** *ppl. a.*, that fails to satisfy, or renders unsatisfied.

1709 STEELE *Tatler* No. 180 ¶6 To follow such dissatisfying Pursuits. **1809** COLERIDGE *Friend* (1866) 338 After long and dissatisfying toils.

dis'saturate, *v.* [DIS- 6.] *trans.* To free (anything) *of* that with which it is saturated.

1866 LOWELL *Swinburne's Trag.*, Pr. Wks. (1890) II. 137 We cannot so dissaturate our minds of it.

dissava (dɪ'sɑːvə). Also **dissauva, dissave, dissuava.** [Sinhalese *disāwa.*] A governor of a district of Ceylon.

1681 R. KNOX *Hist. Rel. Ceylon* 35 He gives order to his *Dissava's* or Governors of the Countreys to..choose out Boyes. *Ibid.* 50 Next under the Adigars, are the *Dissauva's.* **1720** DEFOE *Capt. Singleton* 294 The King of the Country.. sent down a *Dissuava*, or General, with an Army. **1803** R. PERCIVAL *Ceylon* 258 The Dissauvas, as long as they hold their office, are allowed by the king a certain portion of land for their services. **1859** J. E. TENNENT *Ceylon* II. 91 The dissave of Oovah..placed himself at the head of the insurgents.

†**dis'savage,** *v. Obs.* [DIS- 8.] *trans.* To bring out of a savage condition; to tame, to civilize.

1631 CHAPMAN *Cæsar & Pompey* I. (D.), Those wilde kingdomes..Which I dissavag'd and made nobly ciuill.

dis'save, *v.* Also **dis-save.** [DIS- 6.] *intr.* to spend more than one's income, by drawing on savings or realising capital. So **dis'saving** *vbl. sb.*; **dis'saver**, one who dissaves.

1936 J. M. KEYNES *Gen. Theory Employment* vii. 82 No one can acquire an asset..unless..someone else parts with an asset of that value..someone else must be dis-saving an equal sum. **1946** *Economist* 13 Apr. 602/2 Nothing has been allowed for dis-saving, which must loom ever larger as increasing supplies of goods create opportunities for spending. **1950** *Daily Tel.* 6 Jan., A Federal Reserve report refers to people who spend more than they earn as 'dissavers'. **1952** *Times* 1 Dec. 7/2 The dissaving which estate duties do for them when they die. **1954** NEWLYN & ROWAN *Money & Banking* ix. 191 African holders of temporarily idle balances would tend to dissave in an effort to maintain their standards of consumption. **1971** *Daily Tel.* 23 July 17 In addition to..the encouragement to buy on credit there is a possibility of a substantial dis-saving.

dissave, -awe, -ayf, -ayte, etc., obs. ff. DECEIVE, DECEIT, etc.

dissaventure, var. of DISADVENTURE, *Obs.*

disscatter, var. of DISCATTER *v. Obs.*

dissceptre (dɪs'sɛptə(r)), *v.* Also 7 disceptre, 6–7 -er. [f. DIS- 7 a + SCEPTRE *sb.*] *trans.* To deprive of the sceptre, or of kingly authority.

1591 SYLVESTER *Du Bartas* I. vi. 615 Rebellious Flesh, whose rest-less Treason Strives to dis-throne and to discepter Reason. **1610** T. GODWIN *Moses & Aaron* I. xiii. 61 Prevent a possible deposing or disceptring. **1656** S. H. *Gold. Law* 55 This..people have de-thron'd, uncrown'd, and discepter'd me. **1886** W. ALEXANDER *St. Augustine's Holiday* 216 Disrobed, dissceptred..discrown'd.

dissch, obs. form of DISH.

dissease, obs. form of DECEASE, DISEASE.

†**dis'season**, *v. Obs.* Also 7 **diseason.**

I. [f. DIS- 6 + SEASON *v.*]

1. *trans.* To take away or change the flavour of.

1583 STANYHURST *Aeneis* I. (Arb.) 23 Foorth do they lay vittayls, with storme disseasoned heauy [*Cererem corruptam undis*]. **1613** JACKSON *Creed* I. xxix. §15 Seeing no hope of diseasoning the old and withered stockes, fit fewell for euerlasting flames. **1615** G. SANDYS *Trav.* 106 [The Red Sea]..would either drowne the countrey, or else by mixing with the Nilus, disseason his waters. **1621** —— *Ovid's Met.* XIV. (1626) 295 An oliue wild, which bitter fruit affords, Becomes dis-seasned with his bitter words.

2. To deprave the sense of taste of. *rare.*

1625 W. B. *True School War* To Rdr. 4 Like some Disseasoned Palats, thou doost nauseate at Plentie.

II. [f. DIS- 7 + SEASON *sb.*]

3. To render out of season, make unseasonable.

a **1628** F. GREVILLE *Poems Monarchy* D, Wks. Grosart I. 197 The second light of government, Which stories yield, and no time can disseason.

disseat (dɪs'siːt), *v.* [f. DIS- 6 or 7 c + SEAT *v.* or *sb.*] *trans.* To remove or eject from or as from a seat; to unseat; to remove from where it is seated or situated. Hence **dis'seated** *ppl. a.*

[That quot. 1605 belongs to this word is doubtful.]

[**1605** SHAKS. *Macb.* v. iii. 21 This push Will cheere me euer, or dis-eate [Fo. 2, 3, 4 disease] me now.] **1612** *Two Noble K.* v. iv, The hot horse..seekes all foule meanes..to dis-seate His lord, that kept it bravely. **1648** J. GOODWIN *Right & Might* 21 The disseated Parliament-men. **1684** tr. *Bonet's Merc. Compit.* XVI. 548 The Morbifick matter being disseated. **1822** C. O'CONOR *Chron. Eri* I. p. xxxi, This mighty conqueror who had dis-seated so many kings. **1833** LAMB *Elia* Ser. II. *Barrenness Mod. Art*, Disseat those woods and place the same figure among fountains..and you have a —Naiad! **1866** *Daily Tel.* 22 Feb. 4/5 Application..made..to disseat the member returned.

†**'dissecate**, *v. Obs. rare.* [f. L. *disseca-re* to cut in pieces, as if from a ppl. stem *dissecāt-* (cf. fut. pple. *secātūrus*) instead of the actual form *dissect-*.] = DISSECT *v.* So †**disse'cation** = DISSECTION.

1615 JACKSON *Creed* IV. §I. vii. §11 The anatomist's knife did lance and dissecate her living members. **1632** T. NASH *Quaternio* Ep. Ded., The Apothecary in his drugges, the anatomist in his dissecations.

†**dis'secret**, *v. Obs. rare.* [f. DIS- 8 + SECRET *a.*] *trans.* To deprive of secrecy, bring to light.

1640 G. WATTS tr. *Bacon's Adv. Learn.* II. xiii. §5 We must not put too much confidence, either in the concealeing our own designes, or the dissecreting the designes of the enimy.

dissect (dɪ'sɛkt), *v.* [f. L. *dissect-* ppl. stem of *dissecāre*, f. DIS- 1 + *secāre* to cut.]

1. *trans.* To cut asunder, cut in pieces, divide by cutting. *lit.* and *fig.* (Now more or less associated with 2 and 3.)

1607 TOPSELL *Serpents* (1653) 621 Young Chickens being dissected or cut in pieces when they are warm, ought to be laid to the stinged part. **1624** MASSINGER *Parl. Love* IV. v, To dissect thee, Eat thy flesh off with burning corrosives..were justice. **1638** SIR T. HERBERT *Trav.* (ed. 2) 178 Hee that dissected Gordions knot. **1783** W. F. MARTYN *Geog. Mag.* II. 131 This eminence is dissected into six terraces. **1805–17** R. JAMESON *Char. Min.* 166 The manner of dissecting this prism. **1886** F. B. JEVONS in *Jrnl. Hellenic Stud.* VII. 292 The aggregationists before them undertook to dissect the Iliad into its constituent lays.

2. *spec.* To cut up (an animal body, a plant, etc.) for the purpose of displaying the position, structure, and relations of the various internal parts; to anatomize.

1611 FLORIO, *Dissettare*, to desect or cut as an Anatomie. **1615** CROOKE *Body of Man* I. ix. (1631), They say, he [Galen] hath giuen vs onely the Anatomy of bruit Beasts, and not of Man, hauing neuer dissected a Mans body. **1671** GREW *Anat. Plants* I. i. §3 (1682) 2 If we take a Bean and dissect it. **1724** SWIFT *Reasons agst. Exam. Drugs* Wks. 1755 III. I. 127 The power given to physicians to dissect the bodies of malefactors. **1867** EMERSON *May-day*, etc. Wks. (Bohn) III. 422 Two doctors in the camp Dissected the slain deer.

absol. **1678** BUTLER *Hud.* III. iii. 477 Anatomists dissect and mangle, To cut themselves out work to wrangle. **1879** E. A. DAVIDSON in *Cassell's Techn. Educ.* II. 70 The teacher should obtain heads, hearts, &c. of sheep, oxen and other animals, and dissect in the presence of the boys.

b. *to dissect out*: to excise (an organ or a diseased part) so as not to remove any adjoining part with it.

1864–70 T. HOLMES *Syst. Surg.* II. 119 In dissecting out the cyst. **1894** *Lancet* 3 Nov. 1030, I made an incision..from the mouth over the prominent cyst wall and dissected the tumour out..The wall of the cyst was so thin that when nearly dissected out it ruptured.

3. *fig.* and *transf.* To take to pieces, so as to lay bare every part; to examine minutely part by part, to analyze; to criticize in detail.

a **1631** DONNE in *Select.* (1840) 114 That soul that is dissected and anatomized to God. **1647** CLARENDON *Hist. Reb.* I. §64 Persons of all conditions took great license in..dissecting all his infirmities. **1693** DRYDEN *Persius* Sat. I, Yet old Lucilius never fear'd the times; But lash'd the city, and dissected crimes. **1850** KINGSLEY *Alt. Locke* i, I never could dissect and map out my own being or my neighbour's as you analysts do. **1869** ROGERS *Pref.* to *Adam Smith's W.N.* I. 43 He dissected the pretensions of the great East India Company. **1875** JOWETT *Plato* (ed. 2) IV. 413 No other thinker has ever dissected the human mind with equal patience and minuteness.

†**4.** To analyze (chemically). *Obs.*

1808 J. BARLOW *Columb.* IV. 456 O'er great, o'er small extends his physic laws, Empalms the empyrean or dissects a gaz.

5. *Business.* To analyze an invoice or account of goods bought or sold, picking out the various items, and allotting them to the special departments to which they severally belong.

See DISSECTING *vbl. sb.*

di'ssected, *ppl. a.* [f. prec. + -ED[1].]

1. That has been cut up, divided into pieces, or anatomized.

dissected map or ***picture***, a map or picture mounted on a thin board and divided into variously shaped parts, to be put together as an exercise or puzzle.

1634 SIR T. HERBERT *Trav.* 184 Laying upon each piece of the dissected Betele, a little Arecca. **1638** *Ibid.* (ed. 2) 31 Not to be entred but by a long narrow dissected path or trench. **1667** *Phil. Trans.* II. 628 A dissected Head of a Sharke. **1807** SOUTHEY *Lett. from Eng.* vi. 69 They have..dissected maps which they combine into a whole. **1824** COL. L. STANHOPE *Greece* 10 She [Greece] is like a dissected map in the hands of children, all the pieces are there, but the children cannot make them fit. **18..** RUSKIN (O.), Or must every architect invent a little piece of the new style, and all put it together at last like a dissected map?

2. a. Of a divided form or structure; *spec.* in *Bot.* (of leaves): Cut into many deep lobes; much divided.

1652 GAULE *Magastrom.* 185 A little chin signes one envious..a dissected and retorted chin, libidinous. **1872** OLIVER *Elem. Bot.* II. 182 The finely-dissected leaves of Fennel. **1884** HENFREY *Elem. Bot.* (ed. 4) 62 When the leaves are subdivided a fourth time, or even where tripinnatisect leaves have filiform segments, the term dissected is usually employed.

b. *Physical Geogr.* Formed by the dissection of a once flat plateau or plain.

1902 W. M. DAVIS *Elem. Physical Geogr.* ix. 278 An excellent illustration of a well dissected upland is found in the Ozark plateau of southern Missouri. *Ibid.*, The maturely dissected surface has much less strength of relief than the plateau of West Virginia. **1949** W. G. MOORE *Dict. Geogr.* 51 *Dissected plateau*, a plateau into which a number of valleys have been carved by erosion; its origin as a plateau is patent, however, when the tops of the mountains and ridges are seen to be level against the skyline, showing that they once formed part of a continuous surface. **1965** A. HOLMES *Princ. Physical Geol.* (ed. 2) xix. 573 (*caption*) A maturely dissected plateau of the Gondwana cycle being invaded by the valley flats of the present cycle.

dissectible (dɪ'sɛktɪb(ə)l), *a. rare.* [f. L. *dissect-* ppl. stem (see the vb.) + -BLE.] Capable of being dissected.

1802 PALEY *Nat. Theol.* ix. Wks. 1830 IV. 101 Keill has reckoned up, in the human body, four hundred and forty-six muscles dissectible and describable.

dissecting (dɪ'sɛktɪŋ), *vbl. sb.* [f. DISSECT + -ING[1].] The action of the verb DISSECT. **a.** *gen.* and *Anat.*: see DISSECT 1–3. **b.** *Business*: see DISSECT 5.

1888 *Daily Tel.* 24 Aug. 7/8 Junior clerk wanted. Must be used to draper's counting house, and understand dissecting. **1893** *Daily News* 16 May 8/7 To Drapers.—Young lady wants re-engagement as Cashier and Bookkeeper. Used to dissecting.

c. *attrib.* and *Comb.*, as in ***dissecting-forceps***, ***-knife***, ***-microscope***, ***-room*** (i.e. used in anatomical dissection); **dissecting-clerk**, one employed in analyzing invoices and accounts of goods sold.

1767 GOOCH *Treat. Wounds* I. 176 Raising the vessel a little..with the point of the knife and dissecting forceps. **1854** R. WILLIS *Report* in Willis & Clark *Cambridge* (1886) III. 168 The present Dissecting-room of the Professor is removed altogether. **1882** SERJT. BALLANTINE *Exper.* ii. 15 Gaining a living by supplying the dissecting-table with its ghastly subjects. **1884** *Encycl. Dict.* (Cassell), *Dissecting-clerk.*

di'ssecting, *ppl. a.* [f. as prec. + -ING[2].] That dissects.

1854–67 C. A. HARRIS *Dict. Med. Terminol.*, *Dissecting abcess*, an abcess which insinuates itself between muscles, separating them from each other. *Ibid.*, *Dissecting Aneurism*, an aneurism in which the inner and middle coats of the artery are ruptured, and the blood passes between them and the outer coat. **1891** *Anthony's Photogr. Bull.* IV. 61 Brought to the dissecting eye of the prying student.

dissection (dɪ'sɛkʃən). [ad. L. *dissectiōn-em*, n. of action from *dissecāre*; used in med. or mod.L. Perhaps immed. a. F. *dissection* (Paré, 16th c.).]

†**1.** The action or process of cutting asunder or in pieces; division by cutting. *Obs.*

1611 COTGR., *Dissection*, a dissection; a cleauing in peeces. **1644** MILTON *Areop.* (Arb.) 70 There must be many schisms and many dissections made in the quarry and in the timber, ere the house of God can be built. **1669** GALE *Crt. Gentiles* I. II. ix. 141 As to the Dissection [after sacrifice], it was not made rashly, but with great Art. **1784** COWPER *Task* VI. 420 The spaniel dying for some venial fault, Under dissection of the knotted scourge.

2. *spec.* The methodical cutting up of an animal or a plant, for the purpose of displaying its internal structure.

1605 BACON *Adv. Learn.* I. v. §12 (1873) 43 Thus have I described and opened, as by a kind of dissection, those peccant humours. **1615** CROOKE *Body of Man* I. ix, Living dissections (as we call them) are then put in vse when we would find out some action or vse of a part which by the dead carkasse cannot be discerned. **1671** GREW *Anat. Plants* I. i. §28 (1682) 6 What Dissection cannot attain, yet an ocular inspection in hundreds of other seeds..will demonstrate. **1758** JOHNSON *Idler* No. 17 ¶8, I know not that by living dissections, any discovery has been made by which a single malady is more easily cured. **1850** HT. MARTINEAU *Hist. Peace* IV. xiv. (1877) III. 134 Murders for the sake of selling bodies for dissection. **1881** HUXLEY in *Nature* No. 615. 347 For hundreds of years..the dissection of human bodies was impeded, and anatomists were confined to the dissection of dead animals.

3. The action of separating anything into elementary or minute parts for the purpose of critical examination; a 'taking to pieces', a minute examination; detailed analysis or criticism.

1642 MILTON *Apol. Smect.* §4 Thus ends this Section, or rather dissection of himself, short ye will say both in breath and extent. **1654** WHITLOCK *Zootomia* 405 In the particular Dissection of mens Actions. **1796** MORSE *Amer. Geog.* II. 158 It is perhaps the best dissection of the human mind, that hath appeared in modern times. **1867** DEUTSCH in *Rem.* (1874) 1 Dissections of dogma and legend and ceremony.

†**4.** Chemical analysis. *Obs.*

1605 TIMME *Quersit.* I. xiii. 63 Mercury is extracted out of euery thing, first of all in his dissection or seperation into a watery vapour. **1794** S. WILLIAMS *Vermont* 90 By accurate dissection..it has been found that this ill scented fluid is entirely distinct from the urine.

5. *Business.* The analysis of invoices and accounts, in order that the various items may be entered to the account of the special departments to which they belong: see DISSECT *v.* 5.

6. *concr.* That which has been cut asunder or dissected, or is in a dissected condition; anything which is the result or produce of dissecting.

1581 SIDNEY *Apol. Poetrie* (Arb.) 48 All his [the Poet's] kindes are not onlie in their vnited formes, but in their seuered dissections fully commendable.

7. *Physical Geogr.* The breaking up by erosion of a flat surface such as a plateau or plain into hills, or flat uplands, and valleys.

1909 in *Cent. Dict.* Suppl. **1937** WOOLDRIDGE & MORGAN *Physical Basis Geogr.* xiii. 177 If the active deepening of the valleys is continued after the stage of mature dissection, the ridge-crests will remain sharp. **1968** R. W. FAIRBRIDGE *Encycl. Geomorphol.* 15/1 Deep canyon dissection is followed by secondary headward erosion of smaller tributaries.

8. *attrib.* and *Comb.*

1847 W. REEVES *Eccl. Antiq.* 66 *note*, The Dissection-room panic caused many to resort to this place. **1889** HUXLEY in *Pall Mall G.* 2 May, None of the ordinary symptoms of dissection poison supervened.

dissective (dɪ'sɛktɪv), *a.* [f. L. type **dissectīvus* (cf. *sectīvus*), f. *dissect-* ppl. stem: see -IVE.] Characterized by or having the quality of dissecting; serving to dissect.

1860 DICKENS *Lett.* (ed. 2) II. 110 The three people who write the narratives in these proofs have a dissective property in common. **1861** WILSON & GEIKIE *Mem. E. Forbes* v. 142 They were plainly anatomical dissective knives.

dissector (dɪ'sɛktə(r)). Also -er. [agent-n. in L. form, from L. *dissecāre* to DISSECT. Cf. F. *dissecteur*.] **a.** One who dissects, *esp.* anatomically.

1578 BANISTER *Hist. Man* I. 22 b, The most famous dissectors, and princes of Anathomy. **1615** CROOKE *Body of Man* 306 A most expert Chyrurgion, and the ordinary dissecter to the Colledge of Physitians at Monpelier. **1645** EVELYN *Diary*, The theatre [at Padua] for anatomie..is excellently contriv'd both for the dissector and spectators. **1794** *European Mag.* XXV. 454 Mr. Jones, dissector to St. Bartholomews Hospital. **1819** *P.O. Lond. Direct.* 305 Map-mounter and Dissecter. **1839** CARLYLE *Chartism* vii. in *Misc.* (1872) VI. 153 A determined despiser and dissector of cant. **1847** EMERSON *Repr. Men, Swedenborg* Wks. (Bohn) I. 316 Unrivalled dissectors..had left nothing for scalpel or microscope to reveal in human or comparative anatomy.

b. A dissecting instrument.

a **1860** A. R. SMITH *Med. Student* (1861) 6 He perpetually carries a Dublin dissector under his arm. **1910** *Practitioner* July 118 If the appendix..is concealed under massive granulations, careful search with swab, blunt dissector and the occasional use of scissors will rarely fail to bring it into view.

dissees(e, obs. form of DECEASE, DISEASE.

disseise, disseize (dɪs'siːz), *v.* Forms: 4 disseyse (-ceyse, 4–5 desese), 5–6 dis-, dyssease, (5 dysease, 6 decess, disseaze, -eize), 6–7 disseyze, 6– disseise, disseize. [ME. a. AF. *disseisir*, = OF. *dessaisir* to dispossess, f. *des-*, DIS- 4 + *saisir* to put (one) in possession, to take possession of, to SEIZE. In Pr. *dessazir*; med.L. *dissazire*, *-sasire*, *-sasiare*, also *dissaisire*, *-seisire*, *-seisiare* from OF.: see SEIZE.]

1. *trans. Law.* To put out of actual seisin or possession; to dispossess (a person) of his estates, etc., usually wrongfully or by force; to oust. Const. *of* (†*from*). Also *refl.*

[**1215** *Magna Carta* xxxix, Nullus liber homo capiatur vel imprisonetur aut disseisiatur [**1217** *inserts* (c. xxxv) de libero tenemento suo vel libertatibus]..nisi per legale judicium parium suorum. **1292** BRITTON II. xi. §2 Cestui est proprement disseisi qi a tort est engetté de acun tenement.] *c* **1330** R. BRUNNE *Chron.* (1810) 250 Our kyng Sir Edward ..Disseised him self of alle, ȝald it to Sir Jon. Bot Jon his homage salle mak or he be gon. **1357** *Lay Folks Catech.* 252 In case that we have..wittandly and willfalli gert our euen cristen..falsly be desesed of land or of lithe. *c* **1450** *St. Cuthbert* (Surtees) 7518 Of þair gudes falsly dissesid. **1494** FABYAN *Chron* VI. cxlix. 136 He..vexyd and dystourbed Ivore the duke and lorde of that countrey..lastly disceasyd hym of that lordeshyp. **1540** *Act 32 Hen. VIII*, c. 7. §7 Where..personnes..be dysseased, deforsed, wronged, or otherwyse put from their lawfull inheritance. **1628** *Petit. to King* in Rushw. *Hist. Coll.* (1659) I. 589 By the Statute called, The great Charter of the Liberties of England, It is declared and enacted; That no Freeman may be taken or imprisoned or be disseised of his Freeholds or Liberties, or his free Customs. **1641** [see DISSEISIN 1]. **1818** CRUISE *Digest* (ed. 2) I. 190 If a tenant in tail discontinues in fee, afterwards marries, disseises the discontinuee, and dies seised; his wife shall not have dower. **1819** I. MILNER *Milner's Hist. Ch. Christ* (1824) IV. 115 Wicliff asserted that temporal lords and patrons had a right to disseize the church of her emoluments in case of misbehaviour.

2. *transf.* and *fig.* **a.** To dispossess, deprive, rob; to deliver, rid (*of* anything).

c **1320** *Cast. Love* 1088 He ne ouȝte from wo disseysed be. *c* **1450** *Merlin* 229 It shall here-after be declared how that she was disceised of the seint Graal. **1590** SPENSER *F.Q.* I. xi. 20 He [the Dragon] so disseized of his gryping grosse. **1602** CAREW *Cornwall* 22 a, The Foxe planteth his dwelling in the steep cliffe..as in a maner it falleth out a matter impossible to disseyze him of this his ancient inheritance. **1700** BLACKMORE *Job* xxix. 17 My righteous hand broke fierce oppressors' jaws, And of their spoil disseiz'd their bloody paws. **1845** R. W. HAMILTON *Pop. Educ.* x. (ed. 2) 266 We repeat our protest against all attempts to disseize parents of their rights in their children.

†**b.** To oust, expel. *Obs.*

1627 MAY *Lucan* VII. 655 Through many wounds his life disseized, fled. **1675** HOBBES *Odyssey* XVI. 444 They..With gentle sleep their fear and care disseised.

Hence **dis'seised** *ppl. a.*, **dis'seising** *vbl. sb.*

1475 *Bk. Noblesse* 48 The unmanly disseising and putting oute of Fraunce, Normandie, Angew, and Mayne. **1611** COTGR., *Desemparement*, a disseising. **1675** tr. *Machiavelli's Prince* vii. (Rtldg. 1883) 50 All the disseized lords..he put to death. **1682** *Enq. Elect. Sheriffs* 18 If there be but the least flaw against them to countenance the dis-seizing them of their Rights.

disseise, obs. form of DECEASE, DISEASE.

1648 SYMMONS *Vind. Chas. I*, 98 The Honour of..our disseised Queen.

disseisee, -zee (dɪsˌsiːˈziː). *Law.* Also 6 -i, -ie, -ye. [f. DISSEISE *v.* + -EE; but the earlier form in *-ie* represented OF. *dessaisi* pa. pple. 'disseised'.] One who is disseised of his estate: correlative to DISSEISOR.

[**1377** *Act 1 Rich. II*, c. 9 Et eient desore les disseisiz lour recoverer vers les primers disseisours.] **1540** *Act 32 Hen. VIII*, c. 33 The disseisye or suche other personnes as..be thereby clerely excluded of their entre. **1574** tr. *Littleton's Tenures* 63 a, If the disseysi by his deede release al his righte ..to one of the disseisoures. **1594** WEST *2nd Pt. Symbol., Chancerie* §37 This release doth confirme his estate which the disseisee might else have defeated. **1602** FULBECKE *1st Pt. Parall.* 67 If the disseisie oute the disseisor with force. **1721** *St. German's Doctor & Stud.* 98 It is devised that the Disseisee shall release his right in the land. **1875** POSTE *Gaius* IV. §162 Restitution of seisin to a disseisee.

disseisin, disseizin (dɪsˈsiːzɪn), *sb.* Forms: 4 dysseysyne, 6 disseysin(e, -sceysen, -seissen, -sesin, -seison, -seizon, -season, dys-, 6–7 disseizen, 7 *Sc.* dissaisin), 6– disseisin, 8– disseizin. [a. AF. *disseisine* = OF. *dessaisine* (11th c.), f. *des-*, DIS- 4 + *saisine*, *seisine*, SEISIN, SASINE, formal possession, deriv. of *saisir* to SEIZE. (In med.L. *dissaisīna*, *disseisīna*.)]

1. *Law.* The act or fact of disseising; privation of seisin; usually, the wrongful dispossession (by forcible entry or otherwise) of the lands, etc. of another: since 15th c. not used of movable goods, nor in cases in which the dispossessed person was tenant at will or tenant for years.

[**1167** *Pipe Roll 12 Hen. II*, 65 Dissaisina super assisam regis. **1292** BRITTON II. i. §1 Homme a tort engitté ou desturbé de la peysible possessioun de soen fraunc tenement. Et cele violence est apelé disseisine et fresche force.] **1511–12** *Act 3 Hen. VIII*, c. 18 Preamb., Wrytte of entre uppon disseysen in the post before the Justices..of his Comen Benche. **1574** tr. *Littleton's Tenures* 57 b, Disseisin is properly where a man entreth into anye landes or tenementes where his entre is not leful, and putteth him out yt hath the franke tenement. **1641** *Termes de la Ley* 139 Disseissin upon Disseisin is when the Disseisour is disseised by another. **1670** BLOUNT *Law Dict.*, Disseisin is of two sorts, either Simple Disseisin, committed by day without force and arms, Or Disseisin by Force, for which see Deforceor and Fresh Disseisin. **1767** BLACKSTONE *Comm.* II. 195 A disseisin being a deprivation of that actual seisin, or corporal freehold of the lands, which the tenant before enjoyed. **1861** F. HALL in *Jrnl. Asiat. Soc. Bengal* 10 The disseizor, and..the abettor of disseizin. **1875** POSTE *Gaius* IV. Comm. (ed. 2) 631 It is certain that this interdict is not available for disseisin of movables. **1886** F. W. MAITLAND in *Law Q. Rev.* Oct. 485 The rightful tenant can be disseised, though the lord be not privy to the disseisin. **1889** J. B. AMES in *Harvard Law Rev.* III. 23 The word 'disseisin'..was rarely used with reference to personalty.

b. *novel, new, fresh disseisin*: disseisin of fresh or recent date. *Assise of Novel Disseisin*: an ordinance of Henry II, establishing an action at law for the recovery of the seisin of land by one who had himself been recently dispossessed; also the action thus established.

[*c* **1250** BRACTON 164 b, De beneficio principis succurritur ei per recognitionem assisae novae disseisinae multis vigiliis excogitatam et inventam.] *c* **1350** *Usages of Winchester* in *Eng. Gilds* 361 þe wryt þat me pledeth in þe Citee, by-fore Justyces, oþer by-fore baylyues of þe towne, beþ empne wrytes of newe dysseysyne. [**1383** *Act 7 Rich. II*, c. 10 Item est ordeignez & assentuz qassise de Novele Disseisine soit desore grante & faite de rent aderiere.] **1523** FITZHERB. *Surv.* xi. (1539) 17 The kynges wrytte of assise of nouell disseison. **1609** SKENE *Reg. Maj.*, *Stat. Robert I*, 22 He sall not tine nor amit his action or recoverance be the briefe of Novell dissaisin: sa lang as he may find the possessour leueand: or anie man committer of the dissaising, or was present at the committing thereof. **1670** BLOUNT *Law Dict.*, *Fresh disseisin*..signifies that Disseisin, which a man may seek to defeat of himself, and by his own power, without the help of the King or Judges, and which is not above fifteen dayes old. **1700** TYRRELL *Hist. Eng.* II. 1106 Disseisors that have redisseis'd those who have recovered Seisin..from them by Assize of Novel Disseisin. **1876** DIGBY *Real Prop.* ii. §9. 97 The Assize of novel disseisin was applicable where the demandant himself had been turned out of possession. **1895** POLLOCK & MAITLAND *Hist. Eng. Law* I. 124 Henry.. issued an ordinance and instituted a procedure: ordinance and procedure alike were known as the assize of novel disseisin.

†**2.** *transf.* and *fig.* Dispossession. *Obs.*

1586 FERNE *Blaz. Gentrie* 214 Ministers of the Gospell to whome the keyes of right do apperteine (for the others did by dissesin and tort hold possession of them) may execute that authoritie of the keys with all feare and diligence. **1606** WARNER *Alb. Eng.* XIV. lxxxvi. 355 Vntill the Picts.. Disseizen of the scottish Raigne within this Ile had made.

†**dis'seisin**, *v.* *Obs.* [f. prec. sb.] *trans.* = DISSEISE *v.*

1548 HALL *Chron.*, *Hen. V* (an. 8) 69 b, We shal not distroble, disseason or letten our father aforesaid, but that he holde and possede as long as he liveth..the croune and the dignitee royall of Fraunce. **1591** SYLVESTER *Du Bartas* I. ii. 974 Yet some (more crediting their eyes, then reason) From's proper place this Essence doe disseysin. **1600** HOLLAND *Livy* XXVII. xxxi. 652 He [Philip] went to Dymæ for to disseizen [*ad ejiciendum*] the garrison of the Ætolians. **1607** HIERON *Wks.* I. 365 A man past al feare of being disseisined of his expected inheritance.

disseisor, -zor (dɪsˈsiːzə(r), -ˌɔː(r)). Also 5–6 -our(e, 5 -er. [a. AF. *disseisour*, = OF. **dessaiseur*, f. *dessaisir* to DISSEISE. In med.L. *dissaisitor*, *-seizitor*, f. *dissaisire*, *disseisire*, to disseise.] One who disseises, or dispossesses another of his lands, etc.; a dispossessor.

[**1377** see DISSEISEE.] **1483** *Cath. Angl.* 101/2 A Disseiser, *disseisitor*. **1540** *Act 32 Hen. VIII*, c. 33 The diyng seased hereafter of any such disseasour..shall not be..demed.. any suche discent in the law. **1598** KITCHIN *Courts Leet* (1675) 265 If the Tenant be disseised and the Disseisor dieth seised, the Lord there cannot distrain. **1603** DRAYTON *Bar. Wars Bk.* III. lvi, Entering now by force, thou hold'st by might, And art disseisor of another's right. **1660** BOND *Scut. Reg.* 59 The King can do no wrong; Therefore cannot be a disseisor. **1788** BURKE *Sp. agst. W. Hastings* Wks. XV. 430 To call them disseizors, wrong doers, cheats, defrauders of their own son. **1861** [see DISSEISIN *sb.* 1]. **1886** F. W. MAITLAND in *Law Q. Rev.* Oct. 485 The disseisor will be seised whether the lord like it or not.

disseisoress (dɪsˈsiːzərɪs). Also 7–9 disseiseress. [f. prec. + -ESS. (The F. type would be *dissaiseresse*.)] A female disseisor.

1574 tr. *Littleton's Tenures* 125 b, Yf the husbande and the wife were of covin or consent that the disseisine should bee made, than..shee is a disseisouresse. **1641** *Termes de la Ley* 124 Shee shall bee adiudged in possession against the desseisee but as a disseiseresse, in respect of the deceit. **1642** PERKINS *Prof. Bk.* i. §46 A feme Covert may be a disseiseres. **1809** TOMLINS *Law Dict.* s.v. *Disseisin*, If he disseises another to her use, she is not a disseisoress, nor if the wife agrees to it during the coverture; yet, if after his death she agrees to it, she is a disseisoress. **1883** A. J. HORWOOD *Year Bks. 11–12 Edw. III*, 264 One cannot say that Katherine was a disseiseress.

†**dis'seisure, -zure.** *Obs.* [f. DISSEISE *v.* + -URE: cf. *seizure*.] The act of disseising; dispossession; = DISSEISIN.

1579 FULKE *Confut. Sanders* 685 The setting vp and worshipping of Images..was..a Disseisure of the true and spirituall worshippe of God. **1611** SPEED *Hist. Gt. Brit.* IX. ix. 47 To take reuenge for the spoyles and disseisures, which his hired enemies had made in his lands. **1718** HICKES & NELSON *J. Kettlewell* III. xi. 213 In Case of a Disseizure of the Right Owner.

disseit, obs. form of DECEIT.

dissel-boom (ˈdɪs(ə)lbuːm). *S. Africa.* Also disselboom. [Du. (pron. ˈdɪsəlboːm) = 'the beam or pole of a vehicle', f. *dissel* shaft + *boom* beam, boom.] The pole of a wagon.

1822 W. J. BURCHELL *Trav. S. Afr.* I. viii. 150 The pole (disselboom) is ten feet long, having at the end a strong iron staple. **1858** SIMMONDS *Dict. Trade*, *Disselboom*, the pole of a wagon in the Cape colony. **1881** FENN *Off to Wilds* xxix, The oxen were all secured to the dissel-boom and trek-tow. **1887** RIDER HAGGARD *Jess* viii, The tented cart, with its.. stout stinkwood dissel-boom. **1930** R. CAMPBELL *Adamastor* 65 In my last trek be thou the Star To whom I hitch my disselboom.

†**dis'self**, *v.* *Obs. nonce-wd.* [f. DIS- 7 + SELF *sb.*] To put (one) beside himself; to deprive of self-consciousness.

1606 SYLVESTER *Du Bartas* II. iv. I. *Tropheis* 1116 Whence comes This shiuering winter that my soule benums, Freezes my Senses, and dis-selfs me so With drousie Poppie, not my self to knowe?

disselie, obs. form of DIZZILY.

†**di'ssembill**, *a.* *Sc. Obs. rare.* [? corruption of F. *deshabillé*, or of a Sc. spelling of DISHEVEL *a.*] Undressed, unclothed.

c **1470** HENRY *Wallace* IX. 1917 That saw him bath dissembile and in weid.

†**di'ssemblable**, *a.* (and *sb.*) *Obs.* [a. OF. *dessemblable* (12th c.), in 14th c. *dissemblable*, f. *dessembler* to be unlike, DISSEMBLE *v.*[2], after *semblable* like.] Unlike, dissimilar, various. Hence *absol.* as *sb.*

1413 *Pilgr. Sowle* (Caxton 1483) I. iv. 5 Moche merueylous lyght I sawe of dissemblable maner. **1549** CHALONER *Erasm. on Folly* N j b, How amongs theim selves to be dissemblable [*inter se dissimiles*]. **1566** DRANT *Horace Sat.* IV. C ij b, Dissemblable to Sectans sorte [*Sectani dissimilis*]. **1589** PUTTENHAM *Eng. Poesie* III. xix. (Arb.) 238 Dissemblable and in effect contrary. **1603** FLORIO *Montaigne* I. xxxviii. (1632) 118 A man must imitate the vicious, or hate them..to resemble them is perilous, because they are many, and to hate many is hazzardous, because they are dissemblable. **1928** V. WOOLF *Orlando* iv. 161 What a phantasmagoria the mind is and meeting-place of dissemblables!

dissemblance[1] (dɪˈsɛmbləns). *arch.* [In sense 1, ad. OF. *dessemblance* (12th c.), mod.F. *dissemblance* unlikeness, f. *dessembler*, pr. pple. *dessemblant* unlike: see prec. and -ANCE. In sense 2, a later modification of DISSIMULANCE, after *dissemble*.]

1. Want of resemblance; unlikeness; difference; dissimilarity.

1463 *Craft of Lovers* xxi, Kepe wel true loue, forge no dissemblance [*so 1 MS.: 2 have* resemblance]. **1580** NORTH *Plutarch* (1676) 980 As touching other agreements and dissemblances which may be noted..in their life and behaviour [etc.]. **1658** OSBORNE *Adv. Son* (T.) Nor can there be a greater dissemblance between one wise man and another. **1883** I. TAYLOR *Alphabet* I. 100 The dissemblance of the hieroglyphic and Hieratic characters appears greater than it really is because in many cases they face in opposite directions. **1894** *Forum* (N.Y.) Nov. 317 To state the utter dissemblance between the Japanese and ourselves.

2. The action of dissembling, dissimulation.

1602 MARSTON *Antonio's Rev.* II. iv. Wks. 1856 I. 101 Thou that wants power, with dissemblance fight. **1633** P. FLETCHER *Purple Isl.* VIII. viii, Some touch-stone erring eyes to guide, And judge dissemblance. **1814** SOUTHEY *Roderick* xxiv, No time..is this for bravery As little for dissemblance. **1876** J. ELLIS *Caesar in Egypt* 18 Pothinus, in dissemblance deft, Bent low the knee.

†**dissemblance**[2]. *Obs. rare.* [a. OF. *dessemblance*, f. *dessembler* to separate: see DISSEMBLE *v.*[3]] Departure, dispersion.

1556 J. HEYWOOD *Spider & F.* ii. 33 Swifter then the star doth seeme to glaunce That assemblaunce turneth to dissemblaunce.

†**dissem'blation.** *Obs.* Also 6 -acion, 5 dissymbelatyon. By-form of DISSIMULATION, after *dissemble*.

c **1425** WYNTOUN *Cron.* VIII. xi. 55 He saw þat he mycht noucht The Town of were wyn..Undyr dissymbelatyoun. **1588** HUNSDON in *Border Papers* I. (1894) 305 But it is all dissemblacion, and that wee shall find if wee trust to them.

†**di'ssemble**, *sb.* *Obs. rare.* [f. DISSEMBLE *v.*[1]] The act of dissembling, dissimulation. (In quot. personified.)

c **1480** *Crt. of Love* 1191 Dissemble stood not fer from him in trouth, With party mantill, party hood and hose.

dissemble (dɪˈsɛmb(ə)l), *v.*[1] Also 6 dissimble, *Sc.* -sembill, dyssembul, -symble, 7 desemble. [app. a later form of DISSIMULE *v.*, through the intermediate stages *dissimill*, *dissimble*, influenced perh. by *resemble*. (There is no corresponding form in F.: cf. the next two words.)]

1. *trans.* To alter or disguise the semblance of (one's character, a feeling, design, or action) so as to conceal, or deceive as to, its real nature; to give a false or feigned semblance to; to cloak or disguise by a feigned appearance.

1513 MORE *Rich. III*, Wks. 65 Some..not able to dissemble their sorrow, were fayne at his backe to turne their face to the wall. **1552** *Bk. Com. Prayer, Morn. Pr.*, That we shoulde not dissemble nor cloke them [our sins] before the face of Almighty God. **1665** MANLEY *Grotius' Low C. Warres* 715 Among the Bodies..was found a Woman, who had dissembled her Sex, both in courage and a military Habit. **1709** *Tatler* No. 32 ¶4 With an Air of great Distance, mixed with a certain Indifference, by which he could dissemble Dissimulation. **1781** GIBBON *Decl. & F.* II. xlvi.

723 He dissembled his perfidious designs. **1850** PRESCOTT *Peru* II. 20 He was well pleased with the embassy, and dissembled his consciousness of its real purpose. **1860** EMERSON *Cond. Life, Behaviour* Wks. (Bohn) II. 385 How many furtive inclinations avowed by the eye, though dissembled by the lips!

†**2.** To disguise. *Obs.*

1508 DUNBAR *Tua mariit Wemen* 254, I wes dissymblit suttelly in a sanctis liknes. **1529** MORE *Dyaloge* IV. Wks. 283/1 Though he dissembled himselfe to bee a Lutherane whyle he was here, yete as sone as he gate him hence, he gate him to Luther strayght. **1601** SHAKS. *Twel. N.* IV. ii. 4 Ile put it on, and I will dissemble my selfe in't; and I would I were the first that euer dissembled in such a gowne. **1665** J. SPENCER *Vulg. Prophecies* 21 Their deformity appeared through the finest colors he could dissemble it with. **1697** DRYDEN *Æneid* XII. 340 Dissembling her immortal form, she [Juturna] took Camertus meen.

3. To pretend not to see or notice; to pass over, neglect, ignore.

c **1500** [see DISSEMBLING *vbl. sb.*]. *c* **1555** HARPSFIELD *Divorce Hen. VIII* (1878) 233, I will not urge..the Pope's..authority..I will dissemble that excellency. **1568** GRAFTON *Chron.* II. 823 Wherfore he determined to dissemble [HALL dissimule] the matter as though he knew nothing. **1579** LYLY *Euphues* (Arb.) 150 Some lyght faults lette them dissemble, as though they knew them not, and seeing them let them not seeme to see them. **1692** RAY *Dissol. World* III. viii. (1732) 395, I must not dissemble a great Difficulty. **1701** WALLIS 24 Sept. in Pepys *Mem.*, It hath been too late to dissemble my being an old man. **1703** ROWE *Ulysses* I. i. 75 Learn to dissemble Wrongs. **1761** HUME *Hist. Eng.* II. xlii. 451 Philip..seemed to dissemble the daily insults and injuries which he received from the English.

b. with clause: To shut one's eyes to the fact.

1554 RIDLEY *Lord's Supper* Wks. 41 It is neither to be denied, nor dissembled that..there be diuerse points wherein men..canne not agree. **1611** BIBLE *Transl. Pref.* 11 It cannot be dissembled, that..it hath pleased God [etc.]. **1692** RAY *Dissol. World* II. ii. (1732) 107, I must not dissemble or deny, that in the Summer-time the Vapours do ascend. *a* **1831** A. KNOX *Rem.* (1844) I. 54 It cannot be dissembled, that..the House of Commons seems to feel no other principle than that of vulgar policy. **1871** MORLEY *Voltaire* (1886) 8 No attempt is made in these pages to dissemble in how much he was condemnable.

c. *intr.* const. *with.*

a **1533** FRITH *Wks.* (1573) 51 These holy doctours..thought it not best..to condemne all thinges indifferently: but to suffer and dissemble wyth the lesse.

4. *absol.* or *intr.* To conceal one's intentions, opinions, etc. under a feigned guise; 'to use false professions, to play the hypocrite' (J.).

1523 LD. BERNERS *Froiss.* I. clxxx. 216 Therfore the duke dissembled for the pleasur of the prouost. **1535** COVERDALE *1 Macc.* xi. 53 He dyssembled in all that euer he spake. **1596** SHAKS. *Tam. Shr.* II. i. 9 Tel Whom thou lou'st best: see thou dissemble not. **1671** MILTON *P.R.* I. 467 The subtle fiend..Dissembled, and this answer smooth return'd. **1713** ADDISON *Cato* I. ii, I must dissemble, And speak a language foreign to my heart. **1852** LONGF. *Warden Cinque Ports* xi, He did not pause to parley nor dissemble.

b. const. *with*: To use dissimulation with.

1586 A. DAY *Eng. Secretary* I. (1625) 142, I dissemble not with you..for you shall finde it and prove it to be true. **1667** POOLE *Dial. betw. Protest. & Papist* (1735) 83, I will not dissemble with you, they do not. **1718** *Freethinker* No. 75 ¶3 He who dissembles with, or betrays, one Man, would betray every Man. **1829** SOUTHEY *All for Love* vi, Dissemble not with me thus.

†**5.** *trans.* To put on a feigned or false appearance of; to feign, pretend, simulate. *Obs.*

1538 STARKEY *England* I. iii. 91 Men may dyssembyl and fayne grete pouerty, where as non ys. **1581** J. BELL *Haddon's Answ. Osor.* 467 You were not your selfe ignoraunt, albeit you dissembled the contrary. **1660** F. BROOKE tr. *Le Blanc's Trav.* 304 This Creature..that can dissemble death so naturally. **1709** STEELE *Tatler* No. 83 ¶2 I'm lost if you don't dissemble a little Love for me. **1791** BOSWELL *Johnson* an. 1752 To suppose that Johnson's fondness for her was dissembled.

†**b.** with inf. or clause. *Obs.*

1654 R. CODRINGTON tr. *Hist. Ivstine* 60 The King dissembled that his Coat of Mayl was not fit for him. **1813** T. BUSBY tr. *Lucretius* IV. 913 Fancy..Lost friends, past joys, dissembleth to restore.

†**c.** To feign or pretend (some one) *to be* something. Also with ellipsis of the inf., or of both object and inf. *Obs.*

1634 FORD *P. Warbeck* I. i, Charles of France..Dissembled him the lawful heir of England. **1655** FULLER *Ch. Hist.* III. vii. §19 John Scott dissembled himself an English-man. **1660** F. BROOKE tr. *Le Blanc's Trav.* 176 Esteemed a Jew though he dissembled the Christian. *Ibid.* 246 Moores who dissembled Christians.

†**d.** *fig.* To simulate by imitation. *Obs.*

1697 DRYDEN *Æneid* VIII. 880, The gold dissembl'd well their yellow hair.

†**dissemble**, *v.*[2] *Obs. rare.* [a. OF. *dessembler*, *dissembler* to be unlike, f. *des-*, DIS- 4 + *sembler* to be like, to seem: the opposite of *ressembler* to resemble. Cf. DISSEMBLANCE[1] 1, -ABLE.] *trans.* To be unlike, to differ from, resemble not.

1586 T. B. *La Primaud. Fr. Acad.* (1589) 183 His end dissembled not his life. For, being hated of all and sought for to be slaine, he [Nero] killed himselfe.

†**di'ssemble**, *v.*[3] *Obs. rare.* [ad. OF. *dessembler* to separate, f. *des-*, DIS- 4 + stem of *as-sembler* to ASSEMBLE.] *intr.* To separate, disperse: = DISASSEMBLE.

1591 HORSEY *Trav.* (Hakl. Soc.) 177 The chieff bishops..assembled and disembled often tymes together, much perplexed and devided.

dissembled (dɪˈsɛmb(ə)ld), *ppl. a.* [f. DISSEMBLE *v.*[1] + -ED[1].]

1. Feigned, pretended, counterfeit.

1539 TONSTALL *Serm. Palm Sund.* (1823) 21 Leste he fall from his feyned & dissembled height. **1552** HULOET, Dissembled or fayned frend, *dissimulator*..*fictitius amicus.* **1697** DRYDEN *Virg. Eclog.* IV. 51 Nor Wool shall in dissembled Colours shine. **1805** SOUTHEY *Madoc in Azt.* ii, He..strove Beneath dissembled anger to conceal Visible grief.

†**2.** Disguised. *Obs.*

1631 *Celestina* II. 130 Melibea is but a dissembled Angell, that lives heere amongst us. **1643** SIR T. BROWNE *Relig. Med.* I. §53 Crosses, afflictions..have ever proved, the secret and dissembled favours of His affection.

dissembler (dɪˈsɛmblə(r)). [f. as prec. + -ER[1].] One who dissembles; one who conceals his real purposes under a false appearance; one who practises duplicity; a deceiver, hypocrite.

1526 *Pilgr. Perf.* (W. de W. 1531) 253 b, They iudged hym a dissembler and an ypocryte. **1592** SHAKS. *Rom. & Jul.* III. ii. 87 All periur'd, all forsworne, all naught, all dissemblers. **1649** MILTON *Eikon.* 11 A deep dissembler, not of his affections only, but of Religion. **1667** —— *P.L.* III. 681 So spake the false dissembler unperceiv'd; For neither Man nor Angel can discern Hypocrisie. **1741** RICHARDSON *Pamela* I. 163, I must put on the Dissembler a little, I see. **1864** PUSEY *Lect. Daniel* iii. 152 He was a thorough dissembler, able to hide his purpose and skilful to execute it.

di'ssembling, *vbl. sb.* [f. as prec. + -ING[1].] The action of the verb DISSEMBLE; dissimulation.

c **1500** *Lancelot* 1950 Al..ther gilt he knowith..and ȝhit he hyme with-drowith Them to repref..And this it is wich that dissemblyng hot. **1553** GRIMALDE *Cicero's Offices* III. xv, False pretending and also dissembling [*simulatio et dissimulatio*]. **1555** LATIMER in Strype *Eccl. Mem.* III. App. xxxvi. 102 Suche men had nede to take hede of their desemblings and clokings. **1643** MILTON *Divorce* II. viii, The perpetuall dissembling of offence. **1701** ROWE *Amb. Stepmoth.* II. i. 468 Flattery, the meanest kind of base dissembling. **1862** GOULBURN *Pers. Relig.* IV. iii. (1873) 273 Wilful dissembling of a generous emotion is the way to suppress it.

di'ssembling, *ppl. a.* [f. as prec. + -ING[2].] That dissembles; deceiving; hypocritical.

1526 *Pilgr. Perf.* (W. de W. 1531) 299 b, Yᵉ most vnkynde & dissemblynge disciple Iudas. **1535** COVERDALE *Prov.* x. 18 Dissemblynge lippes kepe hatred secretly. **1590** SHAKS. *Mids. N.* II. ii. 98 What wicked and dissembling glasse of mine, Made me compare with Hermias sphery eyne? **1707** *Curios. in Husb. & Gard.* 117 Double-hearted, dissembling, trickish..Men. **1875** MANNING *Mission H. Ghost* ii. 52 A cunning and dissembling Countenance.

dissemblingly (dɪˈsɛmblɪŋlɪ), *adv.* [f. prec. + -LY[2].] In a dissembling manner; in a way that disguises one's real character or purpose.

1546 BALE *Eng. Votaries* II. (1550) 50 b Thys Gualtherus colourably or dyssemblyngly reconcyled both Anselme and the Pope vnto hym, only to serue the tyme. **1586** T. B. *La Primaud. Fr. Acad.* (1589) 574 They obey not dissemblinglie, but of a free and willing minde. **1654** WHITLOCK *Zootomia* Pref. A vij b, I should own that which many Writers dissemblingly decline. **1857** *Chamb. Jrnl.* VIII. 200, I must quietly, dissemblingly, await the solution.

†**di'ssembly**[1]. *Obs.* [f. DISSEMBLE *v.*[1]: cf. next.] Dissembling, dissimulation.

c **1534** tr. *Pol. Verg. Eng. Hist.* (Camden) II. 198 Ther is no deceyt more depe and secrete than that which lurketh in the dissembly of understanding, or under soome colour of curtesy. **1588** ALLEN *Admon.* 21 [Elizabeth] dallied and abused by dissembly almost all the great personages of Europe, to whom..she proffered herself.

di'ssembly[2]. *nonce-wd.* [f. DISSEMBLE *v.*[3], after *assembly*.] The separation of an assembly.

1887 *Sat. Rev.* 10 Sept. 340 The hurried assembly and more hurried dissembly of some stolen meetings.

¶ It occurs in 16–17th c. as a perversion of *assembly*.

1599 SHAKS. *Much Ado* IV. ii. 1 Is our whole dissembly appeard? **1684** BAXTER *Twelve Argts.* §16. 27 Their usual Titles were, the Priestbyters, the Drivines, the Sinners of Westminster, the Dissembly men.

disseminate (dɪˈsɛmɪneɪt), *v.* [f. L. *dissēmināt-* ppl. stem of *dissēmināre* to spread abroad, disseminate, f. DIS- 1 + *sēmen, sēmin-* seed; cf. F. *disséminer* (14th c. in Littré).]

1. *trans. lit.* To scatter abroad, as in sowing seed; to spread here and there; to disperse (things) so as to deposit them in all parts.

1603 HOLLAND *Plutarch's Mor.* 1309 [Isis] applieth herselfe to engender the same, yea and to disseminate and sowe the..similitudes thereof. **1656** BLOUNT *Glossogr.*, *Disseminate*, to sow here and there, to spread abroad. **1665** HOOKE *Microgr.* 68 The tinging substance does consist of..particles..which are disseminated, or dispers'd all over the other. **1791** BOSWELL *Johnson* an. 1750 (1848) 67/2 Considering how universally those volumes are now disseminated. **1830–75** LYELL *Princ. Geol.* I. II. xix. 483 The action of tides and currents in disseminating sediment. **1859** DARWIN *Orig. Spec.* iii. (1873) 50 The mistletoe is disseminated by birds.

†**b.** To cause to ramify; to distribute. *Obs.*

1664 POWER *Exp. Philos.* I. 17 The liquours that circulate through the pipes and vessels disseminated through those parts. **1668** CULPEPPER & COLE *Barthol. Anat.* III. iii. 328 Seven pair of Nerves..disseminated into the whole outward Head.

c. In *pa. pple.* and *passive*, used of diffused situation, without implying the action: cf. DISPERSE 2.

1677 GREW *Anat. Seeds* IV. iii. §7 (1682) 201 In the Upper Coat, the Seed-vessels are disseminated. **1796** KIRWAN *Elem. Min.* (ed. 2) II. 291 Grey ore of manganese..occurs massive, disseminated, in nests or rifts. **1841** TRIMMER *Pract. Geol.* 73 A mineral which occurs in pieces not exceeding the size of a hazel-nut, imbedded or incorporated in another mineral, is said to be disseminated. **1869** *Pouchet's Universe* (1871) 16 The pantheists supposed life to be disseminated through all the interstices of matter.

2. *fig.* To spread abroad, diffuse, promulgate (opinions, statements, knowledge, etc.).

1643 SIR T. BROWNE *Relig. Med.* I. §23 This [the Bible] without a blow hath disseminated it selfe through the whole earth. **1670** G. H. *Hist. Cardinals* I. I. 13 To hear that Beast of a Priest disseminate such Doctrine. **1796** BP. WATSON *Apol. Bible* 2 The zeal with which you labour to disseminate your opinions. **1802** MAR. EDGEWORTH *Moral T.* (1816) I. xiii. 108 Disseminating knowledge over the universe. **1843** J. MARTINEAU *Chr. Life* (1867) 58 He disseminated the principles of peace.

3. *intr.* (for *refl.*) To diffuse itself, spread. *rare.*

1803 *Man in Moon* (1804) No. 3. 23 The..discipline and professional courage that would disseminate through the volunteer ranks.

Hence **di'sseminated** *ppl. a.*; *spec.* of a disease: dispersed or spread throughout an organ, a tissue, or the whole body.

1662 STILLINGFL. *Orig. Sacr.* III. ii. §17 Neither can I see how a disseminated vacuity can solve the difficulty. **1742** YOUNG *Nt. Th.* VI. 180 The least Of these disseminated orbs, how great! **1876** *Brit. Med. Jrnl.* 25 Nov. 675/2 (*heading*) A case of disseminated insular sclerosis. **1886** A. WINCHELL *Geol. Field* 295 To trace the train of events back to a disseminated cosmical dust. **1906** *Lancet* 17 Nov. 1351/1 A man suffering from Disseminated Sclerosis which resembled tabes dorsalis. **1932** *Discovery* Apr. 112/1 A single glance at the film gives information concerning creeping paralysis (disseminated sclerosis). **1963** H. BURN *Drugs, Med. & Man* (ed. 2) xviii. 181 Pemphigus and disseminated lupus erythematosus are cured by cortisone. **1964** S. DUKE-ELDER *Parsons' Dis. Eye* (ed. 14) xviii. 242 *Disseminated choroiditis.* In this type, small areas of inflammation are scattered over the greater part of the fundus behind the equator. *Ibid.* xxiii. 349 Acute disseminated encephalomyelitis.

dissemination (dɪˌsɛmɪˈneɪʃən). [a. L. *dissēminātiōn-em*, n. of action f. *dissēmināre* to DISSEMINATE; cf. mod.F. *dissémination.*] The action of scattering or spreading abroad seed, or anything likened to it; the fact or condition of being thus diffused; dispersion, diffusion, promulgation.

1646 SIR T. BROWNE *Pseud. Ep.* I. ii. 7 We..being now at greatest distance from the beginning of errour, are almost lost in its dissemination, whose wayes are boundlesse. **1759** B. STILLINGFL. *Misc. Tracts* (1775) 63 The dissemination of seeds, after they come to maturity. **1794** SULLIVAN *View Nat.* I. 185 All these facts manifest the general dissemination of the principle of fire. **1829** I. TAYLOR *Enthus.* x. 294 The extensive dissemination of the Scriptures. **1869** *Echo* 6 Apr., The courage of the missionaries in the dissemination of religious truth. **1874** COOKE *Fungi* 120 Forms of spores may be illustrated with their modes of dissemination.

di'sseminative, *a. rare.* [f. as DISSEMINATE *v.* + -IVE.] Having the quality of disseminating, or of being disseminated.

1660 JER. TAYLOR *Duct. Dubit.* IV. i. rule 5 §18 The effect of heresy is like the plague, infectious and disseminative.

disseminator (dɪˈsɛmɪneɪtə(r)). [a. L. *dissēminātor*, agent-noun from *dissēmināre* to DISSEMINATE.] One who or that which disseminates; one that spreads abroad or distributes seed or anything intended to be generally received.

1667 *Decay Chr. Piety* (J.), The disseminators of novel doctrines. **1777** G. FORSTER *Voy. round World* II. 337 The pigeon..is the same..as the disseminator of the true nutmeg at the Spice Islands. **1826** E. IRVING *Babylon* II. 391 Disseminators of the plague. **1875** JOWETT *Plato* (ed. 2) I. 350 The disseminators of this tale are the accusers whom I dread.

disseminule (dɪˈsɛmɪnjuːl). *Bot.* [Irreg. f. DISSEMIN(ATE *v.* + -ULE.] Any part of a plant that serves to propagate it, such as a seed or spore.

1904 F. E. CLEMENTS in *Bot. Surv. Nebraska* VII. 51 Disseminules designed to pass through a resting period are often brought into conditions where they germinate at once. **1932** FULLER & CONARD tr. *Braun-Blanquet's Plant Sociol.* i. 17 The numerical superiority of shoots and disseminules of certain species is certainly important here. **1960** N. POLUNIN *Introd. Plant Geogr.* iv. 97 In nature only a small proportion of the plant bodies which become dispersed, and which may conveniently be termed disseminules (diaspores), actually become established and effect migration.

dissence, var. of DESCENCE *Obs.*

†**dis'sense**, *v. Obs. rare.* [f. DIS- 7 + SENSE *sb.*] *trans.* To deprive of sensation.

1603 DRAYTON *Bar. Wars* III. vi, She a Potion made..That..could..quite dissense the Senses in an houre.

dissension (dɪˈsɛnʃən). Forms: 4 dissensiun, 5 -sion; also 4-6 disc-, dys-, des-, 4-5 -ciun, -cioun, 4-6 -cion, 5-9 -tion. [a. F. *dissension* (12th c. in Hatz.-Darm.), also *discencion*, etc., ad. L. *dissensiōn-em* disagreement, n. of action from *dissentīre*, ppl. stem *dissens-*; see DISSENT. Formerly, very frequently *dissention* (cf. *dissent*, *contention*), whence DISSENTIOUS.]

1. Disagreement in opinion; *esp.* such disagreement as produces strife or contention; discord; an instance of this, a violent disagreement or quarrel arising from difference of opinion.

a **1300** *Cursor M.* 22221 (Cott.) Bot if dissenciun bi-tide ..þat es bot if discord and strijf, Ouer all þis werld be runnun rijf. *Ibid.* 22238 (Gött.) First sal be dissensiun, er ante-crist sal cum in land. **1375** BARBOUR *Bruce* I. 48 Bot enwy..Amang thaim maid discencioun. **1382** WYCLIF *Acts* xv. 39 Forsoth dissencioun is maad, so that thei departiden atwyny. **1484** CAXTON *Fables of Æsop* III. xiii, Of the sheep whiche had werre and descencion with the wolues. **1526** TINDALE *1 Cor.* iii. 3 There is amonge you envyinge, stryfe and dissencion. **1607** WALKINGTON *Opt. Glass* x. (1664) 112 The procurer of a Civil Mutiny and Dissention. **1667** MILTON *P.L.* XII. 352 But first among the Priests dissension springs. **1777** ROBERTSON *Hist. Amer.* (1778) I. II. 131 He fomented the spirit of dissention in the island. **1876** J. H. NEWMAN *Hist. Sk.* II. I. ii. 31 There were dissensions.. existing within the Church, as well as without.

†**b.** Phr.: *in, upon, at dissension. Obs.*

1393 GOWER *Conf.* Prol. I. 30 Vpon dissencion Thei felle, and in diuision. *Ibid.* I. 304 Ovide..Maketh..mencion How they felle at dissencion. **1421** SIR HUGH LUTTRELL in Ellis *Orig. Lett.* Ser. II. I. 85 The two Remes that..han ben in discention. **1600** J. PORY tr. *Leo's Africa* II. 254 They are at..great dissention with the Arabians. **1654** tr. *Scudery's Curia Pol.* 7 Would they that I should..be at dissention with my own sonne?

†**2.** *Med.* Physical disturbance producing ailment. *Obs.*

1582 HESTER *Secr. Phiorav.* I. lx. 70 Difficultie of Urine maie also be caused of..dissention of the head. **1656** RIDGLEY *Pract. Physick* 232 It differs from obstruction because here is no great dissention, it is without pain or Feaver. **1725** BRADLEY *Fam. Dict.* s.v. *Worms*, Worms cause several accidents..as a dissention, wringings with a rumbling in the belly.

†**3.** Disagreement in matters of religious belief and observance; = DISSENT *sb.* 3. *Obs.*

1708 SWIFT *Sent. Ch. Eng. Man* Wks. ed. 1755 II. I. 59 What assurances can they [the clergy] have, that any compliances they shall make, will remove the evil of dissention? **1738** WARBURTON *Div. Legat.* II. vi. 238 In the Pagan World a tolerated Religion did not imply Dissention from the established, according to our modern ideas of Toleration. **1807** R. A. INGRAM (*title*), Causes of the Increase of Methodism and Dissention.

4. *attrib.*

1611 COTGR., *Sursemeur de noises*, a..dissention-sower.

dissensious: see DISSENTIOUS.

[**dissensse, disensse**, a freq. error, scribal or typographical, for *discusse*, DISCUSS.]

dis'sensualize, *v. rare.* [DIS- 6.] *trans.* To free from sensual quality or elements.

1854 LOWELL *Jrnl. in Italy* Prose Wks. 1890 I. 174 We had our table so placed that the satisfaction of our hunger might be dissensualized by the view from the windows.

dissent (dɪˈsɛnt), *v.* Also 5-6 dyss-, 6 dysc-, 6-7 disc-. [ad. L. *dissent-īre* to differ in sentiment, dissent, f. DIS- 1 + *sentīre* to feel, think; cf. F. *dissentir* (15th c. in Hatz.-Darm.).]

1. *intr.* To withhold assent or consent from a proposal, etc.; not to assent; to disagree with or object to an action. Const. *from*, †*to*.

c **1425** WYNTOUN *Cron.* VI. i. 36 Fra þis he dyssentyd hale. *c* **1430** LYDG. *Min. Poems* (1840) 44 (Mätz.) Dame July must nedes haf hir wille, If I dissente, and if I make affray, I have the wers. **1565** T. RANDOLPH in Ellis *Orig. Lett.* Ser. I. II. 199 Whear unto some among the Lords dyscented. **1696** LUTTRELL *Brief Rel.* (1857) IV. 146 Some lords entred their reasons for dissenting to the order. **1765** BLACKSTONE *Comm.* I. 105 The earls of Derby, as lords of Man, had maintained..authority..by assenting or dissenting to laws. **1827** JARMAN *Powell's Devises* II. 293 Where a trustee refuses either to assent or dissent, the Court will itself exercise his authority. **1830** D'ISRAELI *Chas. I*, III. ix. 207 Those who openly dissented from the acts which the King had carried through the Parliament.

2. To think differently, disagree, differ *from*, *in* (an opinion), *from*, †*with* (a person).

a **1536** TINDALE *Doctr. Treat.* (1848) 367 Where the first say 'bread and wine cannot be the very body and blood of Christ'; there they vary and dissent from them. *a* **1555** CRANMER *Wks.* I. 47 Wherein the popish priests dissent from the manifest word of God. **1565** SIR W. CECIL in Ellis *Orig. Lett.* Ser. II. II. 301 The Quenes Majesty will marry with none..that shall discent in Relligion. **1646** GAULE *Select Cases* 56 Hereupon it hath been somewhat dissented. **1654** TRAPP *Comm. Job* xxxiii. 32 Some are so eristical and teasty, that they will not..bear with any that dissent. **1710** ADDISON *Whig Exam.* No. 1 ¶14, I dissent with the Examiner upon certain phrases. *a* **1763** SHENSTONE *Ess.*, *Religion*, When misfortunes happen to such as dissent from us in matters of religion, we call them judgments. **1862** LD. BROUGHAM *Brit. Const.* xviii. 289 The points upon which they dissent from their neighbours. *a* **1871** GROTE *Eth. Fragm.* ii. (1876) 37 If the public dissent from our views, we say that they ought to concur with us.

b. *spec.* To differ in religious opinion; to differ from the doctrine or worship of a particular church, *esp.* from that of the established, national, or orthodox church.

c **1553** PHILPOT *Exam. & Writ.* (1842) 397 Our adversary saith we dissent from the church..With what church sayest thou that we dissent? **1597** HOOKER *Eccl. Pol.* v. i. §3 Every man ought to embrace the religion which is true, and to shun, as hurtful, whatsoever dissenteth from it, but that most, which doth furthest dissent. **1651** HOBBES *Govt. & Soc.* xvii. §26. 330 Those that came to Christianity..were not received into the Church without Baptisme; and those that dissented from the Church were depriv'd of the Churches Communion. **1653** HALES *Brevis Disquisitio* in *Phenix* (1708) II. 341 The whole Discipline of Manners is neglected..Only to dissent is counted a capital Crime. **1792** BURKE *Let. to Sir H. Langrishe* Wks. VI. 323 If mere dissent from the church of Rome be a merit, he that dissents the most perfectly is the most meritorious. In many points we hold strongly with that church. He that dissents throughout with that church will dissent with the church of England. **1808** SYD. SMITH *Wks.* (1867) I. 98 The Methodists have hitherto been accused of dissenting from the Church of England.

†**c.** *ellipt.* To differ as to, or from. *Obs.*

a **1619** FOTHERBY *Atheom.* I. iii. §2 (1622) 17 Though they doe dissent, what a God they ought to haue, yet they fully doe consent, that a God they ought to haue. *a* **1662** HEYLIN *Hist. Presbyt.* i. §29 The greater wonder..that..they should so visibly dissent him in the point of the Sabbath.

†**3.** To be at dissension or variance; to quarrel.

1538 BALE *God's Promises* I. in Hazl. *Dodsley* I. 289 They shall hereafter dissent; His seed with her seed shall never have agreement. **1602** FULBECKE *Pandectes* 37 Nowe they did discent by warre. **1614** BP. HALL *Recoll. Treat.* 584 Even the best Apostles dissented; neither knowledge, nor holynesse can redresse all differences. **1743** FIELDING *J. Wild* II. vi, I am ashamed to see men..so foolishly and weakly dissenting among themselves.

†**4.** To differ in sense, meaning, or purport; also, in more general sense, to differ in nature, form, or other respect. *Obs.*

1539 TAVERNER *Erasm. Prov.* 5 A certayne pleasaunt fable ..not much dissentynge from this purpose. **1611** BIBLE *Transl. Pref.* 8 The translation of the Seuentie dissenteth from the Originall in many places. **1634** SIR T. HERBERT *Trav.* 192 The people differ not in colour nor condition, from the other..but their Funerals dissent from the rest. **1659** STANLEY *Hist. Philos.* XII. (1701) 489/2 A God, whose Figure doth dissent From Men.

dissent (dɪˈsɛnt), *sb.* Also 7 desent. [f. prec.]

1. Difference of opinion or sentiment; disagreement; †dissension, quarrel (*obs.*).

1596 SPENSER *F.Q.* v. iv. 6 Artegall..Did stay awhile their greedy bickerment, Till he had questioned the cause of their dissent. **1628** T. SPENCER *Logick* 202, I finde no dissent betweene any parties touching this precept. **1655** H. VAUGHAN *Silex Scint.* II. 156 As if some deep hate and dissent..betwixt high winds and thee Were still alive. **1781** COWPER *Convers.* 97 Not that all freedom of dissent I blame ..A disputable point is no man's ground. **1867** CARLYLE *Remin.* (1881) II. 183 Cavaignac..accepting kindly my innumerable dissents from him.

2. Disagreement with a proposal or resolution; the opposite of *consent*.

1651 N. BACON *Disc. Govt. Eng.* II. xxix. (1739) 134 Nor can he interpose his Dissent; nor do they care much for his Consent. **1667** PEPYS *Diary* 21 Nov., The opposite Lords.. desired they might enter their dissents. **1705** J. LOGAN in *Pa. Hist. Soc. Mem.* X. 35 He and three Friends more entered not only their dissent but protest against it. **1827** JARMAN *Powell's Devises* II. 293 The onus of proof would be on the complaining party..to shew reasons for his dissent. **1878** MORLEY *Crit. Misc.*, *Vauvenargues* 3 Apart from formal and specific dissents like these.

3. *spec.* Difference of opinion in regard to religious doctrine or worship.

1585 ABP. SANDYS *Serm.* v. §3 Where dissent in religion is, there can hardly be consent in loue. Diuersitie of Religion sundered the Jewe and Gentile. **1676** MARVELL *Gen. Councils* Wks. 1875 IV. 151 He should not wonder at the dissents in the Christian religion, which were very small. *a* **1677** BARROW *Pope's Suprem.* (1687) 150 One Bishop excluding another from communion for dissent in opinion about disputable points. *a* **1742** BENTLEY *Serm.* (J.), What could be the reason of this general dissent from the notion of the resurrection? **1847-9** HELPS *Friends in C.* (1851) I. 25 Even religious dissent were less dangerous and more respectable than dissent in dress.

b. *esp.* The practical expression of disagreement with the form of religious worship which prevails or is authoritatively established in any country; nonconformity. Particularly applied to non-conformity with the established churches of England and Scotland, within the pale of the Reformed Churches.

1772 BURKE *Sp. Acts of Uniform.*, Dissent, not satisfied with toleration, is not conscience, but ambition. **1837** *Penny Cycl.* IX. 22/1 The origin of Protestant dissent from the church of England is usually traced back to the year 1548. **1840** MACAULAY *Ranke* Ess. (1854) 557/1 In this way the Church of Rome unites in herself all the strength of establishment and all the strength of dissent. *a* **1862** BUCKLE *Misc. Wks.* (1872) I. 577 In Scotland dissent assumed a very different..character than in England. **1873** H. SPENCER *Stud. Sociol.* ix. 238 The open expression of difference..to that which is authoritatively established, constitutes Dissent.

c. Put for: The dissenting or nonconformist section of the community.

1792 BURKE *Let. to Sir H. Langrishe* Wks. 1842 I. 549 Protestant dissent was one of the quarters from which danger was apprehended. **1849** MACAULAY *Hist. Eng.* ix. (L.), On this occasion the whole strength of dissent was put forth..with the whole strength of the establishment.

†**4.** Want of agreement or harmony; difference of sense, character, nature, meaning, quality, etc.

1603 FLORIO *Montaigne* III. ix. (1632) 537 The dissent or disparitie in the present manners of our state. **1611** SPEED *Theat. Gt. Brit.* xli. (1614) 81 [We] may attribute this unto a..hidden dissent betwixt this soile and these geese, as the like is betweene wolves and the squilla roots. *a* **1626** BACON (J.), Where the menstrua are the same, and yet the incorporation followeth not, the dissent is in the metals. **1626** BACON *Sylva* §255 *margin*, Experiments..touching the Consent and Dissent between Visibles and Audibles. **1638** SIR T. HERBERT *Trav.* (ed. 2) 330 The Mace in few dayes.. becom's tawny and unlike her former braverie: yet in that dissent, best pleases.

dissent, obs. form of DESCENT.

dissentaneous (dɪsɛnˈteɪniːəs), *a.* [f. L. *dissentāne-us* disagreeing, contrary (f. *dissentīre* to DISSENT) + -OUS.] Disagreeing, discordant; out of harmony; not in agreement, at variance *with*; contrary *to*.

1623 T. SCOTT *Highw. God* 47 It is easier to see flat contradictions and oppositions, then things only diuerse or dissentaneous. **1660** J. LLOYD *Prim. Episc.* Pref. 2 Unprofitable or dissentaneous to the edification and peace of the Church. **1674** R. GODFREY *Inj. & Ab. Physic* Pref., I knew I had wrote nothing dissentaneous with Truth. **1702** W. J. *Bruyn's Voy. Levant* xii. 55 Several other Fancies that they have, so dissentaneous to right Reason. **1876** M. COLLINS *Midnight to Midn.* ii. 27 A young gentleman of high cheek bones, dissentaneous eyes..calfless legs.

Hence **dissen'taneousness**, diversity of opinion.

1652 URQUHART *Jewel* Wks. (1834) 261 Who believed that God was best pleased with diversity of religions.. dissentaneousness of faith. **1727** BAILEY vol. II., *Dissentaneousness*, disagreeableness.

†**di'ssentany**, *a.* and *sb. Obs.* [ad. L. *dissentāne-us*: see prec.]

A. *adj.* = DISSENTANEOUS.

1586 BRIGHT *Melanch.* xii. 55 The consideration of the whol sort of dissentanie, and disagreeing things. **1645** MILTON *Tetrach.* (1851) 254 The parts are not discrete, or dissentanie. **1654** L. COKE *Logick* (1657) 147 Dissentany consecution, is, when from the truth of the one of the opposites is understood the falshood of the other; and contrary.

B. *sb.* (See quots.)

1656 S. H. *Gold. Law* 81 The distinct Bodies of Parliament and People make one Body of Dissentanies or things diverse. **1657** TOMLINSON *Renou's Disp.* 8 He opposes one contrary to another and one dissentany to another.

†**dissen'tation.** *Obs.* [irreg. f. DISSENT *v.* + -ATION.] Difference of opinion, dissension.

1613-16 W. BROWNE *Brit. Past.* II. ii, To leave their jars, Their strifes, dissentations, and all civil warres. **1623** COCKERAM II, Difference, discrepancy, dissentation.

dissenter (dɪˈsɛntə(r)). Also 7 -or, -our. [f. DISSENT *v.* + -ER[1].]

1. One who dissents in any matter: one who disagrees with any opinion, resolution, or proposal; a dissentient.

1647 CLARENDON *Hist. Reb.* II. §74 If the Question had been presently put, it was believed the number of the dissenters would not have appeared great. **1651** HOBBES *Govt. & Soc.* vi. §2. 87 If any one will not consent..the City retaines its primitive Right against the Dissentour, that is the Right of War, as against an Enemy. **1717** POPE *Let. to Lady M.W. Montagu* June, There is nothing like a coalition but at the masquerade; however, the Princess is a dissenter from it. **1728** MORGAN *Algiers* II. i. 211 Some think fit to be Dissenters; assuring us that Cæsaria stood elsewhere. **1869** SWINBURNE *Ess. & Stud.* (1875) 213 Mr. Arnold, with whose clear and critical spirit it is always good to come in contact, as disciple or as dissenter. **1875** GROTE *Plato* Pref. 7 These dissenters from the public will be more or less dissenters from each other.

2. One who dissents in matters of religious belief and worship: **a.** in the general sense.

1639 LD. G. DIGBY *Lett. conc. Relig.* (1651) 88 The dissentors may well have bin over-born or suppress't. **1644** in *Thomasson Tracts* (Br. Mus.) CLXXXVIII. No. 5. 36 By accommodation I understand an agreement of dissenters with the rest of the Church in practical conclusions. **1649** OWEN *Disc. Toleration* Wks. 1855 VIII. 193 The present differences which are between those dissenters who are known by the names of Presbyterians and Independents.. Neither party..dare avow the manner of worship by their dissenters embraced to be, as such, rejected by the Lord. **1678** DRYDEN *All for Love* Ded., Its discipline is..so easy, that it allows more freedom to dissenters than any of the sects would allow it. **1709** STRYPE *Ann. Ref.* I. xlii. 468 The application of the two leading dissenters here [Sampson, Dean of Ch. Ch., and Humfrey, Pres. of Magd. Coll., who refused to wear the Vestments] to those two eminent divines of the Church of Zurick.

b. One who dissents and separates himself *from* any specified church or religious communion, especially from that which is historically the national church, or is in some way treated as such, or regarded as the orthodox body.

1663 *Flagellum; or O. Cromwell* (ed. 2) 14 [Cromwell] began..at last to appear a publique Dissenter from the Discipline of the Church of England. **1673** in *Essex Papers* (Camden) I. 124 Complaints from some of ye Scotch Nation of their persecution..upon yᵉ score of Nonconformitie, divers of those people who are dissenters from yᵉ Church having bin..excommunicated. **1688–9** *Toleration Act 1 W. & M.* c. 18 § 13 Certain other Persons, Dissenters from the Church of England. **1793** CUTLER in *Life, etc.* (1888) II. 277 In Massachusetts the Congregationalists were the favorites of Government, and every other denomination was considered as dissenters from them. **1856** STANLEY *Sinai & Pal.* xiv. (1858) 462 Copt and Syrian, Georgian and Armenian, have..their own claims to maintain, as dissenters, so to speak, against the great Byzantine establishment. **1868** G. DUFF *Pol. Surv.* 54 The Persians happen to be Shiites, or dissenters—the Turks are Sunnites, or orthodox. **1882** SEELEY *Nat. Relig.* II. i. 124 The popular Christianity of the day..is for the artist too melancholy and sedate, for the man of science too sentimental and superficial..They become, therefore, dissenters from the existing religion.

c. *spec.* One who separates himself from the communion of the Established Church of England or (in Scotland) of Scotland. In early use including Roman Catholics, but now usually restricted to those legally styled ***Protestant Dissenters***. (Usually with capital D.)

Occasionally distinguished from *Nonconformist*, and restricted to those who not only dissent from the national church as it is actually constituted, but disagree with the principle of national or state churches.

1679–88 *Secr. Serv. Money Chas. & Jas.* (Camden) 98 To Benjᵃ Cranmer, of Hertford, bounty, in consideracion of his charge and service in prosecuting Dissenters in that county, £100. **1683** F. GODBURY *Pref.* to *Wharton's Wks.* 4 Dissenters (a Title Rebellious people pride themselves in, and love to be distinguished by). **1688** ABP. SANCROFT *Instructions* in D'Oyly *Life* vii, More especially that they have a very tender Regard to our Brethren the Protestant Dissenters. **1689** SIR G. SAVILE *Let. to Dissenter*, It is not so long since as to be forgotten, that the maxim was, It is impossible for a Dissenter not to be a Rebel. **1689** *Toleration Act 1 W. & M.* c. 18 § 11 Unlesse such person can produce two sufficient witnesses to testifie upon oath that they believe him to be a Protestant Dissenter. **1708** J. CHAMBERLAYNE *St. Gt. Brit.* I. III. i. (1743) 148 [After Papists] The other Dissenters..may be reduced into four classes, Presbyterians, Independents, Anabaptists, (or as they call themselves), Baptists, and Quakers. **1731** FIELDING *Lett. Writers* II. ii, Do you take me for a Dissenter, you rascal? **1821** T. JEFFERSON *Autobiog.* Writings 1892 I. 54 Although the majority of our citizens were dissenters..a majority of the legislature were churchmen. **1826** PETERSDORFF *Abr. Cases in Courts K.B. etc.* V. 432 *note*, Catholic and Protestant dissenters may plead the Acts of Toleration, and of 31 Geo. 3 to almost all prosecutions under these acts. **1839** *Eclectic Review* 1 Jan. 4 The Protestant Dissenters of English History, in whose favour the provisions of the 'Toleration Act' were originally intended to operate, consist of the three denominations which have branched from the original Nonconformists; viz., the Presbyterians, the Congregationalists (or Independents), and the Baptists. **1890** ATKINSON *Sp. in H. Com.* 22 July, I am not a Dissenter; I am a Nonconformist.

d. *fig.* and *transf.*

1827 LYTTON *Pelham* xxiii, Coxcombs and Coquettes are the dissenters of society. **1865** GROTE *Plato* I. ii. 88 There is no established philosophical orthodoxy, but a collection of Dissenters, small sects, each with its own following.

Hence **Di'ssenterage**, condition or rank of Dissenters. **Di'ssenterish** *a.*, having somewhat of the character of a Dissenter. **Di'ssenterism**, the principles and practice of Dissenters. **Di'ssenterize** *v. trans.*, to convert into a Dissenter.

1866 CARLYLE *Remin.* (1881) I. 82 The then *Dissenterage is definable to moderns simply as a 'Free Kirk, making no noise'. **1841** *Fraser's Mag.* XXV. 729 The volume looks..so *dissenterish and drab-coloured! **1864** MRS. OLIPHANT *Perpetual Curate* I. ii. 33 A kind of meddling, Dissenterish, missionising individual. **1809** BP. J. JEBB *Let.* in *Life, etc.* xxxv. 460 It..shews the interior of English *dissenterism, during a period of thirty very important years. **1847** W. E. FORSTER in Wemyss Reid *Life* (1888) I. 213 Men grumble at Romanism and Church of Englandism and Protestant Dissenterism. **1838** BP. S. WILBERFORCE in *Life* I. 128 Such men altogether escape us, they became wholly individualized and semi-*dissenterized. **1856** *Lit. Churchman* II. 94/1 A plan for the Protestantizing, and even Dissenterizing, the University.

dissenteries: see DYSENTERY.

†**di'ssentiate**, *v. Obs. rare.* [irreg. f. L. *dissentī-re* + -ATE³; after vbs. from L. sbs. in *-entia*.] *trans.* To move to dissension or discord.

1627 FELTHAM *Resolves* II. [I.] c. (1647) 313 One turbulent spirit will dissentiate even the calmest kingdom.

dissentience (dɪˈsɛnʃ(ɪ)əns). *rare.* [f. DISSENTIENT: see -ENCE.] The fact or condition of being dissentient; difference of opinion.

1864 CARLYLE *Fredk. Gt.* IV. 420 Dissentience on the Law of Thrift.

†**di'ssentiency.** *Obs. rare.* [f. as prec.: see -ENCY.] The quality of being dissentient.

1647 MANTON *Meat out of Eater* Wks. 1871 V. 391, I shall a little reflect upon our dissentiency and division.

dissentient (dɪˈsɛnʃ(ɪ)ənt), *a.* and *sb.* [ad. L. *dissentient-em*, pr. pple. of *dissentīre* to DISSENT.]

A. *adj.* Differing or disagreeing in opinion.

1651 HOWELL *Venice* 185 (2nd) If..ther will be still dissentient suffrages. **1847** LEWES *Hist. Philos.* (1867) I. 226 Several distinct and dissentient points of view opened. *a* **1871** GROTE *Eth. Fragm.* iv. (1876) 118 A young person is perplexed by the dissentient judgments he hears from different individuals.

b. *esp.* Dissenting from, or refusing assent to, the opinion or sentiment of the majority.

Dissentient Liberals, (in *Politics*) a term applied (by opponents) to those members of the Liberal party who in 1886 dissented from the action of the majority in adopting the principle of 'Home Rule' for Ireland as part of the political programme; called by themselves *Liberal Unionists*. Hence **di'ssentientism**.

1764–7 LYTTELTON *Hen. II*, I. 81 (Seager) All the vassals..swore fealty and homage to him without any one dissentient voice being heard. **1845** STEPHEN *Laws Eng.* (1874) II. Notes 346 They usually only set down their names as dissentient to a vote. **1849** MACAULAY *Hist. Eng.* II. 507 The authority of the two dissentient lords prevented several other noblemen from subscribing the address. **1888** GLADSTONE *Let. Mr. Ivory* 26 Oct., Not only Scotchmen in general, but such Scotchmen as were at one time dissentient. **1892** *Daily News* 25 Jan. 5/5 Lancashire will have nothing to do with dissentient Liberals..only Sir Henry James is left to keep up the pretence of Dissentientism in the whole county.

B. *sb.* One who differs or disagrees in opinion; one who differs from the opinion of the majority.

1621 BP. R. MOUNTAGU *Diatribæ* III. 415 To vilifie and traduce the Parts and Persons of all Dissentients. **1790** SIR W. JONES *Charge to Grand Jury*, Calcutta 10 June Wks. 1799 III. 42 When it has been found by a majority of your whole number, it is their counsel, which the dissentient must not disclose. **1823** T. JEFFERSON *Writ.* (1830) IV. 372 They would have left, there as here, no dissentients from their doctrine. **1868** HELPS *Realmah* xvi. (1876) 439 The voices of dissentients were drowned by the predominant shout. **1887** *Daily News* 18 July 5/1 Mr. Gladstone..presses the Dissentients with the awkwardness of their position.

di'ssenting, *vbl. sb.* [f. DISSENT *v.* + -ING¹.] The action of the vb. DISSENT; a differing in opinion; disagreement.

1594 HOOKER *Eccl. Pol.* I. x. § 14 Wherein the one part may haue probable cause of dissenting from the other. **1628** T. SPENCER *Logick* 50 Difference is a dissenting betweene the essence of two. **1655** FULLER *Ch. Hist.* II. ii. 29 He..Bad us to keep the holy Paschal Time, And count Dissenting for an hainous Crime.

di'ssenting, *ppl. a.* [f. as prec. + -ING².]

1. Differing or disagreeing in opinion, dissentient; also, †differing in sense, nature, character, etc.

1550 HOOPER *Serm. Jonas* Epist. Wks. (Parker Soc.) 442 The which doctrine is catholic..nothing dissenting, but agreeable with the prophets and apostles. **1627** SPEED *England* xxxiii. § 3 Whose natures thus dissenting [as to their soil] the Riuer Derwent doth diuide asunder. **1762** FALCONER *Shipwr.* I. 433 Dissenting reason strove To tame..the kindling flame of love. **1796** MORSE *Amer. Geog.* I. 329 A convention..ratified the constitution without a dissenting voice. *a* **1871** GROTE *Eth. Fragm.* iii. (1876) 51 Each of the dissenting schools of philosophy.

2. Differing in opinion on religious matters; *spec.* disagreeing with the established or prevailing doctrines or modes of worship; nonconformist.

Dissenting Brethren, a name applied to the five members of the Westminster Assembly, 1643–4, who advocated Congregational principles against the Presbyterian majority.

1644 *Jrnl. Ho. Commons* 23 Dec., Mr. Marshall delivered in the Reasons of the Dissenting Brethren against Presbyterial Government. **1649** in *Harl. Misc.* (*title*), The Dissenting Ministers' vindication of themselves. **1711** *Act 10 Ann* c. 2 § 9 A Preacher or Teacher of any Congregation of dissenting Protestants. **1766** ENTICK *London* IV. 366 The hall room is let out for a dissenting meeting. **1803** J. BUNTING 23 Sept. in *Life* (1859) I. x. 181 The Dissenting Ministers..are quite before us Methodists in [these] publications. **1843** *Penny Cycl.* XXVII. 247 The chiefs of the Independent party in the Assembly were Dr. Thomas Goodwin, Philip Nye, Jeremiah Burroughs, William Bridge, and Sidrach Simpson, often spoken of as the Five Dissenting Brethren. **1849** MACAULAY *Hist. Eng.* I. 177 It was made a crime to attend a dissenting place of worship.

di'ssentingly, *adv.* [f. prec. + -LY².] In a manner expressing dissent or disagreement.

1628 T. SPENCER *Logick* 239 Dissenting arguments onely are disposed: and dissentingly in the same manner as they are disposed in simple Axiomes. **1862** LEVER *Barrington* xlvi, Conyers shook his head dissentingly. **1864** *Gd. Words* 789/1 She may consent dissentingly.

dissentious (dɪˈsɛnʃəs), *a.* Now *rare.* Also 6 -cious, 6–7 -sious. [f. DISSENSION, and therefore more etymologically spelt *dissensious*: see -IOUS. But perh. orig. after OF. *dissencieux, -tieux*, from *dissencion, -tion*, obs. spellings of *dissension*. There are no other Eng. words in *-ensious*, while *-entious* is frequent, and naturally associates this word with *dissent, dissentient*, etc.]

Of, pertaining to, or characterized by, dissension or disagreement in opinion; *esp.* given to dissension, discordant, quarrelsome.

1560 P. WHITEHORNE tr. *Macchiavelli's Arte of Warre* (1573) 19 a, The disunited and discencious do agree. **1592** SHAKS. *Ven. & Ad.* 657 This carry-tale, dissentious Jealousy..Knocks at my heart. **1597** DALRYMPLE tr. *Leslie's Hist. Scotl.* x. 442 Tha began to be dissensious. **1615** G. SANDYS *Trav.* III. 206 The two brethren grew..dissentious about the deuision of their purchases. **1877** BLACKIE *Wise Men* 334 In violent plunges of dissentious rage. **1882–3** SCHAFF *Encycl. Relig. Knowl.* I. 354/2 As well fitted for harmonious as for dissentious action.

†**b.** Inclined to differ or dissent in religious or ecclesiastical matters. *Obs.*

a **1568** ASCHAM *Scholem.* II. (Arb.) 93 He..will..presume..in Religion, to haue a dissentious head, or in the common wealth, to haue a factious hart. **1579** TOMSON *Calvin's Serm. Tim.* 1032/1 We may not marueile if there be discentious persons in yᵉ Church, which go about to marre all order. **1676** *Life Muggleton* in *Harl. Misc.* I. 610 This Muggleton, an obstinate, dissentious, and opposive spirit.

†**c.** Of things: Differing, at variance, discordant; of the nature of dissension. *Obs. rare.*

1605 *Tryall Chev.* IV. i. in Bullen *O. Pl.* III. 322 Since he..first inkindled this dissensious brawle. **164.** CHAS. I. *Answ. to Earls Bristol & Dorset* 3 Severall and farre different conceptions, yet none dissentious from Truth.

†**di'ssentiously**, *adv. Obs. rare.* [-LY².] In a dissentious manner; with dissension.

c **1611** CHAPMAN *Iliad* II. 22 No more the Gods dissentiously imploy Their high-hous'd powers.

di'ssentism. *rare.* [f. DISSENT *sb.* + -ISM.] Religious dissent as a system; nonconformity.

1859 W. CHADWICK *Life De Foe* i. 44 The healthy growth of Protestant dissentism.

†**di'ssentive**, *a. Obs. rare.* [irreg. f. DISSENT *v.* + -IVE.] Inclined to be at discord.

1627 FELTHAM *Resolves* I. (ed. 2 II.) iv, A Lyer..is a Monster in Nature; for his Heart and Tongue, are Incongruous, and dissentiue.

dissentment (dɪˈsɛntmənt). [f. DISSENT *v.* + -MENT. Cf. 16th c. F. *dissentement*, mod.F. *-iment*.] Difference of opinion, dissentience, dissent.

1690 M. SHIELDS *Faithf. Contend.* (1780) 19 In which dissentment joined several societies. **1893** GLADSTONE *Sp. Belfast Deput.* 28 Mar., This dissentment between the sentiment of the propertied class and the national sentiment.

†**di'ssentory.** *Obs. rare.* [An erroneous form: cf. DESCENT 1 d, and DESCENSORY.]

1658 PHILLIPS, *Dissentory* (old word), a kind of still.

dis'separable, *a. rare.* [f. DIS- 10 + SEPARABLE.] Not to be dissevered; inseparable.

c **1825** BEDDOES *Poems, Torrismond* I. iii, Thou in my mind, and I in thine, shall be, And so disseparable to the edge Of thinnest lightning.

†**dis'separate**, *v. Obs. rare.* [f. DIS- 5 + SEPARATE *v.*] *trans.* To separate, dissever.

1550 NICOLLS *Thucyd.* 222 b, The shyppes that were in the myddeste of their battayle, remayned nakedde and disseparated frome those of the two poynctes.

dissepiment (dɪˈsɛpɪmənt). *Bot.* and *Zool.* [a. L. *dissæpimentum* that which separates, a partition, f. *dissæpīre* (*-sēpīre*): see DISSEPT.] A partition in some part or organ; a septum.

spec. **a.** *Bot.* A partition consisting of the coherent sides of adjacent carpels, separating the cells of a syncarpous ovary or fruit. (Partitions otherwise formed are called *spurious* or *false* dissepiments.) **b.** The middle part of a lamella of the pileus in hymenomycetous fungi: = TRAMA. **c.** *Zool.* One of the horizontal plates connecting the vertical septa in corals. **d.** One of the divisions between the body-segments of an annelid.

1727 BAILEY vol. II, *Dissepiment*, a middle Partition, whereby the Cavity of the Fruit is divided into Sorts of Cases or Boxes. **1760** JAS. LEE *Introd. Bot.* I. vi. (1776) 14 The partitions, which divide the capsule into sundry compartments, or cells, dissepiments. **1857** BERKELEY *Cryptog. Bot.* § 95. 116 The division of the protoplasm by dissepiments. **1861** J. R. GREENE *Man. Anim. Kingd., Cœlent.* 203 Each corallite has its chambers slightly interrupted by a few dissepiments. **1870** ROLLESTON *Anim. Life* 121 The muscular dissepiments dividing the body into compartments. **1870** BENTLEY *Bot.* 271 In the ovary of the Astragalus a spurious dissepiment is also formed.

dissepimental (dɪsɛpɪˈmɛntəl), *a.* [-AL¹.] Belonging to, or of the nature of, a dissepiment.

1857 BERKELEY *Cryptog. Bot.* § 242. 249 A close cellular tissue, in which the passage from dissepimental walls and threads is almost imperceptible. **1870** ROLLESTON *Anim. Life* 126 The muscular dissepimental walls of the segments.

†**di'ssept**, *v. Obs. rare.* [f. L. *dissæpt-* ppl. stem of *dissæpīre* to separate, part off, f. DIS- 1 + *sæpīre* (*sēpīre*) to hedge off, f. *sæpes* a hedge.] *trans.* To divide by a partition; to partition off.

1657 TOMLINSON *Renou's Disp.* 347 Certain aculeated cups..dissepted with little fences.

dissepulchred (dɪsˈsɛpəlkəd), *ppl. a. rare.* [DIS- 7.] Disentombed.

1800 W. TAYLOR in *Monthly Mag.* IX. 464 Like some dissepulchred half-waken ghost, Slow stretch a wither'd hand.

dissert (dɪˈsɜːt), *v.* [f. L. *dissert-* ppl. stem of *disserĕre* to discuss, treat, examine; also intr. to discourse, f. DIS- 1 + *serĕre* to bind, connect, join words, compose.]

†**1.** *trans.* To discuss, examine. *Obs.*

1623 COCKERAM, *Dissert*, to dispute on matters. **1641** R. BROOKE *Eng. Episc.* II. ii. 69 Either none seeme to state the Question right; or else, all seem to dissert it. **1721** STRYPE *Eccl. Mem.* I. xliii. 330 Thence they descended to dissert the single life of priests.

2. *intr.* To discourse upon a particular subject; to make a dissertation. (Now, *affected.*)

1657 TOMLINSON *Renou's Disp.* 651 We have abundantly disserted about the preparation of Medicaments. **1744** HARRIS *Three Treat.* Wks. (1841) 96 A venerable sage.. whom once I heard disserting on the topic of religion. **1752** CHESTERF. *Lett.* III. No. 289. 325 It is not amiss..to be able to dissert upon the growth and flavour of wines. **1823** BYRON *Juan* XII. xxxix, 'Tis always with a moral end That I dissert. **1855** THACKERAY *Newcomes* II. 255 Whilst George is still disserting Clive is drawing.

dissertate (ˈdɪsəteɪt), *v.* [f. L. *dissertāt-* ppl. stem of *dissertāre* to discuss, argue, debate, frequentative of *disserĕre* to DISSERT.] *intr.* To make a dissertation; to discourse; = prec. 2. (Unusual.)

1766 DERRICK *Lett.* (1767) II. 39 Why should I thus dissertate to you? **1811** L. HAWKINS *C'tess & Gertr.* I. 5 The first of these ladies, at thirteen..can dissertate on the various flavors. **1837** HAWTHORNE *Amer. Note-Bks.* (1883) 93 He had a good many old papers in his desk..which he produced and dissertated upon. **1868** BROWNING *Ring & Bk.* III. 270 He dissertated on that Tuscan house.

dissertation (dɪsəˈteɪʃən). [ad. L. *dissertātiōn-em* discourse, disquisition, n. of action f. *dissertāre* to DISSERTATE.]

†**1.** Discussion, debate. *Obs.*

1611 SPEED *Hist. Gt. Brit.* IX. xxii. (R.) As in a certaine dissertation had once with Master Cheeke it appeared. **1623** COCKERAM, *Dissertation*, a disputing on things. **1677** GALE *Crt. Gentiles* III. 27 Paul mentions some who had turned aside..to unprofitable dissertation or disputation. **1709** STRYPE *Ann. Ref.* I. xi. 137 [They] altogether refused..to engage in further dissertation with them.

2. A spoken or written discourse upon or treatment of a subject, in which it is discussed at length; a treatise, sermon, or the like; = DISCOURSE *sb.* 5.

1651 HOBBES *Govt. & Soc.* Title-p., A Dissertation concerning Man in his severall habitudes and respects. **1683** DRYDEN *Life Plutarch* 60 Observing this, I made a pause in my dissertation. **1728** POPE *Dunc.* III. Notes, He compos'd three dissertations a week on all subjects. **1762–71** H. WALPOLE *Vertue's Anecd. Paint.* (1786) I. 238 Vermander dedicated to Ketel a dissertation on the statues of the ancients. **1841** D'ISRAELI *Amen. Lit.* (1867) 476 Warton has expressly written a dissertation on that subject. **1879** GLADSTONE *Glean.* V. i. 77 The sermon is a dissertation, and does violence to nature in the effort to be like a speech.

Hence **disserˈtational** *a.*, belonging to or of the nature of a dissertation; **disserˈtationist**, one who makes a dissertation.

1844 DE QUINCEY *Logic of Political Economy* 36 This remark was levelled by the dissertationist..(I believe) at Ricardo. **1846** WORCESTER cites *Ch. Observ.* for *Dissertational.* **1865** *Reader* No. 113. 234/2 Dissertational, poetic, and rhetorical plays. **1866** *Spectator* 20 Oct. 1162/2 The dissertational language of so dry a piece of theoretic definition as the creed called the Athanasian.

dissertative (ˈdɪsəteɪtɪv), *a.* [f. L. ppl. stem *dissertāt-* (see DISSERTATE) + -IVE.]

Characterized by or given to dissertation.

1816 KEATINGE *Trav.* (1817) I. 10 *note*, It is not requisite to be of a peculiarly dissertative turn. **1858** H. MILLER *Rambl. Geol.* 407 That dissertative style of history..that, for series of facts, substitutes bundles of theories.

ˈdissertator. [a. L. *dissertātor* a disputant, f. *dissertāre.*] One who makes a dissertation.

1698 C. BOYLE *On Bentley's Phalaris* 114 (R.) Our dissertator learnedly argues [etc.]. **1718** POPE *Iliad* XIII. 1037 *note*, According to the grave manner of a learned dissertator. **1849** *Tait's Mag.* XVI. 789 How could I break up this conclave of dissertators?

dissertly, obs. var. of DISERTLY.

disserve (dɪsˈsɜːv), *v.* [f. DIS- 6 + SERVE *v.* Cf. F. *desservir* 'to clear a table' (whence our sense 2), 'to do any one a bad turn'; It. *diservire* to serve ill, 'to vnserve' (Florio).]

1. *trans.* To do the contrary of to *serve*; to serve badly, to do an ill turn to.

1618–29 RUSHW. *Hist. Coll.* (1659) I. 263 The Earl of Bristol did reveal unto his late Majesty..in what sort the said Duke had disserved him and abused his trust. **1637** LAUD *Sp. Star-Chamb.* 13 June 55 Nor hath any Kings Chappell any Prerogative..above any ordinary Church to dis-serve God in by any Superstitious Rites. **1748** RICHARDSON *Clarissa* Wks. 1883 VIII. 15, I have fulfilled your commands; and, I hope, have not dis-served my friend with you. **1874** PUSEY *Lent. Serm.* 69 He ended in deadly opposition to God, disserving God as greatly as he could.

2. To remove the 'service' from (a table).

1816 MARY A. SCHIMMELPENNINCK tr. *Lancelot's Tour Alet* I. 17 The table is served and disserved in the same manner.

disservice (dɪsˈsɜːvɪs), *sb.* [f. DIS- 9 + SERVICE; cf. F. *desservice* (16th c. in Littré), It. *diservizio*, 'a bad seruice, a shrewd turne, an ill office' (Florio).] The contrary of *service*; the rendering of an ill service or ill turn; injury, detriment.

1599 SANDYS *Europæ Spec.* (1632) 109 To ioyne with them in praysing the Creatour of the world, is no better than disseruice to his Maiestie. **1732** BERKELEY *Serm. to S.P.G.* Wks. III. 250 The making religion a notional thing hath been of infinite disservice. *a* **1754** FIELDING *Fathers* V. ii, It is not of any disservice to the young lady. **1852** J. H. NEWMAN *Scope Univ. Educ.* 413 That institution did both service and disservice to the ethical teaching of Catholicism.

b. With *a* and *pl.* An ill service or ill turn; an injury.

1611 COTGR., *Desservice*, a disseruice, ill office, misdeed. **1632** STRAFFORD in Browning *Life* (1891) 301 Since I cam heather, I haue hearde of many disseruices, but not any one seruice he hath paid backe vnto the Crowne. **1761** STERNE *Tr. Shandy* III. i, My uncle Toby's wish did Dr. Slop a disservice which his heart never intended. **1841** L. HUNT *Seer* (1864) 9 Among the disservices rendered us by fortune.

disˈservice, *v. rare.* [f. prec. sb.] *trans.* To render an ill service to; to disserve, to injure.

1837 WHITTOCK *Bk. Trades* (1842) 359 Mr. Tingry..has thus been disserviced;..portions of his work purloined.

disˈserviceable, *a.* [f. DIS- 8 + SERVICEABLE, after prec. sb.] Tending to do disservice; unhelpful, hurtful, detrimental.

1644 J. GOODWIN *Innoc. Triumph.* (1645) 93 [They] are.. in their natures disserviceable unto the common peace. **1710** NORRIS *Chr. Prud.* vii. 311 True sound Philosophy..is no way disserviceable, but very assistant to Religion. **1817** COLEBROOKE *Algebra* 199 Its presence in that multiplication would be highly disserviceable.

Hence **disˈserviceableness**, the quality of being disserviceable; **disˈserviceably** *adv.*, in a disserviceable manner; not serviceably.

1635 J. HAYWARD tr. *Biondi's Banish'd Virgin* 164 Hindered by..the disserviceablenesse of his owne horses. *a* **1670** HACKET *Abp. Williams* II. (1692) 17 I did nothing disserviceably to your majesty, or the duke. **1678** NORRIS *Coll. Misc.* (1699) 294 All action being for some End..its aptness to be commanded or forbidden, must be founded upon its serviceableness or disserviceableness to some end.

dissese, obs. form of DECEASE, DISEASE.

dissessor, obs. form of DISSEISOR.

dissete, var. of DISSITE *a. Obs.*

†**disˈsettle,** *v. Obs.* [DIS- 6.] *trans.* To undo the settled condition of; to unsettle, disturb.

1635 R. BOLTON *Comf. Affl. Consc.* (1640) 206 Did the sacred sence of those Divine Oracles dissettle thy noble faculties. **1659** in *Burton's Diary* (1828) IV. 442 These populous places..are..much dissettled by that unruly sect of people called Quakers. **1692** *Relat. Earthq. Lima* (1748) 332 The Country being broken all to pieces and dissettled.

Hence **disˈsettled** *ppl. a.*; **disˈsettledness.**

1664 H. MORE *Myst. Iniq.* II. II. ii. 465 Whose minde [is] ..distracted by the..unavoidable dissettledness in incredible..opinions. **1674** HICKMAN *Quinquart. Hist.* (ed. 2) 92 There is usually something of disorder cleaving to the best things that are done in dissettled times.

disˈsettlement. [f. prec. + -MENT.] The action of dissettling; the fact of being dissettled:

†**a.** Disturbance, unsettlement. *Obs.* **b.** Dislodgement or ejection from one's settled abode or place.

1654 CROMWELL *Sp. Dissol. Parlt.* 22 Subjecting us to Dissettlement in every Parliament. **1668** H. MORE *Div. Dial.* III. ii. (1713) 182 *margin*, His Relapse into Dissettlement of Mind. **1880** MASSON *Milton* VI. II. i. 232 The dissettlement of so many families, the breaking of old links.

dissever (dɪˈsɛvə(r)), *v.* Forms: 3–5 **desevir**, 3–6 **desever**, 5 **desevyr**, **deceuer**; 4– **dissever** (4–5 **dess-**, 4–6 **disc-**, 5–6 **dysc-**, **dyss-**, 4–5 **-evir**, 5–6 **-evyr**, 6 **-iver**, **-ivir**, **-yfer**). [a. AF. *deseverer*, *desceverer*, OF. *dessevrer*, *desevrer* (*disseverer*) (10th c. in Godef.), mod.F. (techn.) *desseuvrer*:—L. *dissēparāre*, f. DIS- 1, 5 + *sēparāre* to SEPARATE.]

1. *trans.* To separate (a person or thing *from* another or *from* a body, two or more things from each other); to divide, disjoin, sever, part, disunite.

c **1250** *Old Kent. Serm.* in *O.E. Misc.* 31 Þurch scab nis nacht man and wyman deseuird fram mannes felarede. **1382** WYCLIF *1 Chron.* xxv. 1 [Thei] deseuereden than in to the seruyce the sonys of Asaph. *c* **1400** MAUNDEV. (Roxb.) xxxiii. 149 Pissemyres..disseuerez þe fyne gold fra þe vnfyne. *c* **1450** *Mirour Saluacion* 2554 When thai his body and sawle with the crosse disseueryd. **1541** *Act 33 Hen. VIII*, c. 31 *heading*, Disseueringe the bishoprick of Chester..from the iurisdiction of Canturbury. **1550** COVERDALE *Spir. Perle* vii. Wks. 1844 I. 117 The kernel lieth mixed among the chaff, and afterwards are they dissevered asunder with the fan or windle. **1595** SHAKS. *John* II. i. 388 Disseuer your vnited strengths. **1681** H. MORE *Exp. Dan.* i. 6 A Stone cut out without hands, no man with Axe or Gavelock dissevering it. **1695** LD. PRESTON *Boeth.* v. 224 Mankind must of necessity ..be dissevered and disjoined from its Good. **1712–14** POPE *Rape Lock* III. 153 The meeting points the sacred hair dissever From the fair head for ever and for ever! **1827** LYTTON *Pelham* lvii, The difference in our politics had of late much dissevered us. **1877** FARRAR *Days of Youth* xix. 179, I have dissevered them from their context.

2. To divide into parts.

c **1400** *Destr. Troy* 1602 Thurgh myddis þe..toune meuyt a water, And disseuert þe Cite. **1417** *Searchers Verdicts* in *Surtees Misc.* (1890) 11 Chosen be the assent of partys for to dissevir a grounde of a tenement..betwix the Dene and Chipitre..of the ta party, and the Maistre and Freres..on the other party. **1571** DIGGES *Pantom.* II. xxi. Pja, The.. Pollygonium, which you shall diuide by the number of partes, whervnto ye would disseuer it. *a* **1845** HOOD *Public Dinner* ii, A goose that is oldish—At carving not clever—You're begged to dissever. **1854** J. SCOFFERN in *Orr's Circ. Sc.* Chem. 3 This mass may be dissevered into smaller parts.

†**b.** To break up, dissolve or disperse (a combination). *Obs.*

1393 GOWER *Conf.* I. 234 He that thoughte to dissever The compaignie of hem for ever. **1615** J. STEPHENS *Satyr. Ess.* 66 The very name of Crumwell was able to dissever insurrections.

3. a. *refl.* To separate, part from each; †to divide or disperse themselves.

c **1470** HENRY *Wallace* VIII. 757 A thousand archaris.. Disseueryt thaim amang the iiij party. **1501** *Plumpton Corr.* 156 We have desevered us. **1568** GRAFTON *Chron.* II. 87 They did many..famous actes..and many mo had like to have bene done, if they had not dissevered themselves.

b. *intr.* To separate, part, go asunder, depart.

c **1386** CHAUCER *Can. Yeom. Prol. & T.* 322 That futur temps hath maad men disseuere..from al þat euere they hadde. *c* **1422** HOCCLEVE *Learn to die* 404 To perseuere In vicious lyf & from it nat disseuere. *c* **1430** *Pilgr. Lyf Manhode* II. lix. (1869) 98, I sygh that my wey disseuerede and departed in twey weyes. **1568** GRAFTON *Chron.* II. 75 Neither he nor his sonne, should recede or dissever from Pope Alexander. **1621** G. SANDYS *Ovid's Met.* VIII. (1626) 160 Where His shields disseuer, thrusts his deadly speare. **1820** SHELLEY *Ode Lib.* x, As light may pierce the clouds when they dissever In the calm regions of the orient day!

Hence **diˈssevering** *vbl. sb.* and *ppl. a.*

c **1470** HENRY *Wallace* VII. 557 Our disseueryng I wald na Sotheroune saw. **1536–7** STARKEY *Let. Hen. VIII* in *England* p. lx, To thys dyssyferyng..schal neuer succede the brech of chrystyan charyte. **1610** HOLLAND *Camden's Brit.* I. 377 Pleasant..Islets lye dispersed by the sundry disseuerings of waters. *a* **1822** SHELLEY *Pr. Wks.* (1880) III. 57 Their dissevering and tyrannical institutions.

†**diˈssever,** *sb. Obs. rare.* [f. prec. vb.] The act of dissevering; severance.

1508 DUNBAR *Poems* vi. 22 *Semper ibi ad remanendum*, Quhill domisday, without disseuer.

disseverance (dɪˈsɛvərəns). Forms: see prec. vb. [a. OF. *dessevrance*, etc. (Godef.), f. *dessevrer* to DISSEVER: see -ANCE.] The action or fact of dissevering or separating; separation.

c **1374** CHAUCER *Troylus* III. 1375 (1424) That I was born allas what me is wo, That day of vs mot make desseueraunce. **1463** *Bury Wills* (Camden) 20 A deseueraunce maad of stoon wal ovir the entre, to parte the litil botrie vnder the gresys. **1586** A. DAY *Eng. Secretary* I. (1625) 86 To extinguish the cause of falling of the disseverance, or breach. **1832** *Fraser's Mag.* VI. 377 The disseverance of Belgium and Holland should be considered as matter of history.

disseveration (dɪsɛvəˈreɪʃən). [f. DISSEVER + -ATION.] = prec.

16.. *Cont. Knolles' Hist. Turks* 1434 E. (L.) Both will be the clearer by the disseveration. **1829** O'CONNELL in *Hist. Europe* in *Ann. Reg.* 127/1, I want no disseveration; but I want, and must have, a repeal of that cursed measure which deprived Ireland of her senate. **1882** A. C. LYALL *Asiatic Stud.* 5 This process is in India continually interrupted..by the religious element of disseveration.

dissevered (dɪˈsɛvəd), *ppl. a.* [f. as prec. + -ED[1].] Separated, disunited, divided.

1471 RIPLEY *Comp. Alch.* IV. in Ashm. (1652) 144 Of dysseveryd qualytes a Copulacyon. **1583** STANYHURST *Aeneis* II. (Arb.) 64 If Gods eternal thee last disseuered offal Of Troy determyn too burne. **1614** RALEIGH *Hist. World* II. iv. §10 They were a Nation apart and dissevered. **1795** COLERIDGE *Lines in Manner Spenser* 12 With thoughts of my dissevered Fair ingrost. **1835** BROWNING *Paracelsus* II. Wks. (1889) 65 Are we not halves of one dissevered world?

†**b.** *Math.* = DISCRETE 2. *Obs.*

1605 BACON *Adv. Learn.* II. viii. §2. 31 The one handling quantitie continued, and the other dissevered. **1654** Z. COKE *Logick* (1657) 29 Quantity is either continued, as greatness: dissevered, as number.

disseverment (dɪˈsɛvəmənt). [f. as prec. + -MENT; cf. obs. F. *dessevrement* (Godef.).] The action or process of dissevering; disseverance.

a **1603** T. CARTWRIGHT *Confut. Rhem. N.T.* (1618) 619 We uphold the difference of Minister and people by greater railes and disseverments of discretion both in calling and gifts. **1819** SCOTT *Leg. Montrose* vi, I could no more consent ..than the woman in the judgement of Solomon to the disseverment of the child. **1849** MURCHISON *Siluria* xiii. 327 Those disseverments which mark the separation of the Lower from the Upper Coal. **1885** MISS O'HANLON *Unforeseen* xxxviii, Since the day of their wretched disseverment.

disseyte, -eyue, obs. ff. DECEIT, DECEIVE.

disseyvaunt, var. of DECEIVANT *a. Obs.*

c **1450** *Bk. Curtasye* 208 in *Babees Bk.* 305 In swete wordis þe nedder was closet, Disseyuaunt euer and mysloset.

disˈshadow, diˈshadow, *v. rare.* [DIS- 7 a.] *trans.* To free from shadow or shade.

1610 G. FLETCHER *Christ's Vict.* xlii, Soon as he againe dishadowed is, Restoring the blind world his blemish't sight. **1873** A. & P. CARY *Memorial* 107 For out of heaven no bliss—Disshadowed lies, like this.

† **dis'shape, di'shape,** *v. Obs. rare.* [f. *di-*, DIS- 6 + SHAPE *v.*: cf. *misshape.*] *trans.* To put out of shape, disfigure.

1583 HARSNET *Serm. Ezek.* (1658) 131 Who so dishapes or defaces that Image..it is Capitale, a matter of life and Death.

disshe, obs. form of DISH.

dissheathe (dɪsˈʃiːð), *v. rare.* Also **disheathe.** [f. DIS- 6 + SHEATHE *v.*] *trans.* To draw out of a sheath; to unsheathe. (Also *intr.* for *refl.*)

1614 RALEIGH *Hist. World* III. iv. §3 Cambyses' sword dissheathing, pierced his owne thigh. **1840** BROWNING *Sordello* I. 274 Like the great palmer-worm..So fed Sordello, not a shard disheathed.

dissheviled, obs. form of DISHEVELLED.

† **dis'ship,** *v. Obs. rare.* [f. DIS- 6 + SHIP *v.*] *trans.* To remove from a ship.

1557 *Instr. Mariners Russia* in *Hakluyt* (1886) III. 164 The Captaine..shall..disship any artificer..or apprentice out of the Primrose into any other of the three ships.

† **dis'shiver,** *v. Obs.* Also 6 **di-**. [f. DIS- 1 + SHIVER *v.*] *trans.* To shiver in pieces; to shatter. **b.** *intr.* To become shattered, fall to pieces.

1586 W. WEBBE *Eng. Poetrie* (Arb.) 50 Shieldes dishyuering cracke. **1596** SPENSER *F.Q.* IV. i. 21 All within ..There were..Disshivered speares, and shields ytorne in twaine. *a* **1638** MEDE *Rem. Apoc.* x. Wks. (1672) III. 600 The Empire flourishing under one Monarch, not falling or disshivering.

disshort: see DISHORT.

disshroud (dɪsˈʃraʊd), *v. rare.* [f. DIS- 6 or 7 a + SHROUD *v.* or *sb.*] *trans.* To deprive of a shroud; *fig.* to unveil, expose.

1577 STANYHURST *Descr. Irel.* II. in *Holinshed* (1587) I. 15 As his negligence shall be in the one disshrow[d]ed, so his slanderous judgement maie be in the other reversed. **1868** BROWNING *Ring & Bk.* x. 2125 Like a ghost disshrouded, white the sea.

dissidence (ˈdɪsɪdəns). [ad. L. *dissidentia*, f. *dissidēre* to sit apart, disagree, f. DIS- 1 + *sedēre* to sit: see -ENCE. So in mod.F.] Disagreement (in opinion, character, etc.); difference, dissent.

1656 BLOUNT *Glossogr.*, *Dissidence*, discord or displacing. **1775** BURKE *Sp. Conc. Amer.* Wks. III. 53 But the religion most prevalent in our northern colonies is a refinement on the principle of resistance: it is the dissidence of dissent; and the protestantism of the protestant religion. **1847** LEWES *Hist. Philos., Comte* (1867) II. 592 In the sciences there is less dissidence, but there is the same absence of any general doctrine. **1863** GEO. ELIOT *Romola* III. xxxii, That dissidence between inward reality and outward seeming. **1874** GREEN *Short Hist.* viii. §7. 539 Among the farmers.. dissidence of every type had gained a firm foothold. **1891** *Times* 24 Feb. 9/5 Dissenting for the mere pleasure of dissidence.

† **'dissidency.** *Obs. rare.* [f. as prec.: see -ENCY.] = prec.

1670 *Conclave wherein Clement VIII was elected Pope* 3 The Cardinals..(were it either dissidency, or jealousie, or any other passion) were extreamly divided.

dissident (ˈdɪsɪdənt), *a.* and *sb.* [ad. L. *dissident-em*, pr. pple. of *dissidēre*: see DISSIDENCE. Cf. F. *dissident* (16th c.; adm. by Acad. 1798).]

A. *adj.* Disagreeing or differing (in opinion, character, etc.); at variance, different. Const. *from.*

c **1534** tr. *Pol. Verg. Eng. Hist.* (Camden) I. 257 These thinges are not altogether dissident from the trewthe. **1551** ROBINSON tr. *More's Utop.* II. (Arb.) 130 Sca[r]selie so farre frome vs..as our life and maners be dissident from theirs. **1617** COLLINS *Def. Bk. Ely* 283 A forme of prayer dissident from the common. **1837** CARLYLE *Fr. Rev.* III. VI. vii. (1872) 241 The dissident Armed-Forces have met. **1865** W. G. PALGRAVE *Arabia* I. 212 In most respects so dissident from the Wahhabee sectarians. **1890** LOWELL *Latest Lit. Ess.* (1892) 97 Men..dissident..in other respects, were agreed in resenting these impediments.

b. Dissenting in ecclesiastical matters.

1837 CARLYLE *Fr. Rev.* II. iii. iv. (1872) 101 Whereby come Dissident ejected Priests; unconquerable Martyrs according to some,..chicaning Traitors according to others.

c. Disagreeing in political matters; voicing political dissent, usu. in a totalitarian state.

1955 *Times* 10 May 10/1 Dispatches reaching Paris to-day report that the second of the two dissident sects, the Hoa Hao, are continuing their attacks on Viet Nam Army positions. **1967** *Ann. Reg. 1966* 211 On 8 February another dissident Soviet writer, Valery Tarsis, was allowed to leave for Britain. **1977** *Time* 8 Aug. 7/2 They violate the human rights of their own dissident citizens. **1984** CROUCH & PORTER *Understanding Soviet Politics through Lit.* p. ix, The distinctions that are often made between 'regime' and 'dissident' writers..can neglect the fact that there may be significant overlapping concerns.

B. *sb.* One who disagrees; a dissentient.

1789 H. WALPOLE *Let. to H. S. Conway* 15 July, Some may be seized by the dissidents, and whole provinces be torn from the crown. **1826** SCOTT *Rev. Kemble's Life* (1849) 153 The scruples of such dissidents from public opinion are real. **1886** G. ALLEN *Darwin* vii. 120 The magic of his name silenced the derisive whispers of the dissidents.

b. One who dissents from the established or dominant form of religion; a dissenter.

1790 *(title)*, An Address to the Dissidents of England on their late Defeat. **1809** SYD. SMITH *Wks.* (1859) I. 164/1 He did defend and support it; and did persecute all dissidents from its doctrine. **1855** MILMAN *Lat. Chr.* IV. 294 Leonists, Speronists, and dissidents of all other descriptions were incapable of holding places of honour. **1874** GREEN *Short Hist.* viii. §7. 538 Against dissidents from their own system, the Presbyterians were as bitter as Laud himself.

c. *spec.* Under the kingdom of Poland, the name (L. *dissidentes*) given to Protestants, members of the Greek Church, and other Christians, not of the established Roman Catholic Church.

1766 *Hist. Europe* in *Ann. Reg.* 11/2 Nothing could be granted to the dissidents; not even the toleration of their worship. **1767** CHESTERF. *Lett.* 5 May, I have a great opinion of the cogency of the controversial arguments of the Russian troops in favour of the Dissidents. **1837–9** HALLAM *Hist. Lit.* ii. II. §14 In the Polish diets the dissidents, as they were called, met their opponents with vigour and success.

d. In political contexts, one who openly opposes the policies of the government or ruling party, esp. in a totalitarian system.

1940 E. WILSON *To Finland Station* I. vii. 48 He took the position that the voters..had the right to confer power on whom they chose; that for a dissident like himself to refuse to submit to their choice would constitute an act of insurrection. **1949** KOESTLER *Promise & Fulfilment* IV. 246 The very term 'dissidents' had originated through Irgun's refusal to accept the authority of the Jewish Agency. **1970** *Ann. Reg. 1969* 197 Ivan Yakhimovich, once regarded as a model collective farm chairman but dismissed for criticizing the 1968 trial of four dissidents, was arrested in March. **1981** M. MCAULEY *Soviet Union since 1917* vii. 234 Dissidents range from left-wing communists to fervent Russian nationalists, from minority nationalists..to those who want socialism with a human face.

dissidiousness, var. DESIDIOUSNESS, *Obs.*

† **'dissidy.** *Obs. rare.* [ad. L. *dissidi-um* (now held to be error for *discidium*), f. *dissidēre*: see DISSIDENCE.] Disagreement, difference.

1657 TOMLINSON *Renou's Disp.* 281 Barbarism in speech doth not so much move me, as their dissidy in the very thing.

dissight (dɪsˈsaɪt, dɪˈsaɪt). [f. DIS- 9 + SIGHT *sb.* This form is more in accordance with analogy than the synonymous DESIGHT.] Something unpleasant to look upon, an unsightly object, an eyesore.

c **1710** C. FIENNES *Diary* (1888) 148 It would be..no dissight to yᵉ grace of yᵉ Streets. **1821** SOUTHEY *Vis. of Judgm.* Pref., This is noticed as merely a dissight, and of no moment. **1879** SIR G. G. SCOTT *Lect. Archit.* I. 234 Sufficient extension of abutment could not be obtained without inconvenience or dissight. **1881** MRS. A. R. ELLIS *Sylvestra* II. 24 [He] pulled down a picturesque old church to replace it by a regular and commodious dissight.

dis-'sighted, *ppl. a.* [DIS- 6.] = UNSIGHTED.

1825 *Sport. Mag.* XVI. 338/2 That the course be deemed to end..where one or both dogs get dis-sighted. [Cf. *ibid.* 268/2 If one or both dogs be unsighted.]

dis'sightly, *a. rare.* = UNSIGHTLY.

1777 T. CAMPBELL *Surv. S. Irel.* 104 Everything dissightly is..screened from the view. **1854** *Jrnl. R. Agric. Soc.* XV. II. 474 These make a turf look very dissightly.

† **dissig'nificative,** *a. Obs.*$^{-0}$ [DIS- 10.]

1721 BAILEY, *Dissignificative*, that serveth to signify something different from.

† **di'ssilience.** *Obs.*$^{-0}$ [see DISSILIENT and -ENCE.] The action of springing asunder.

1658 PHILLIPS, *Dissilience*, a leaping or bounding up and down, a falling asunder. **1721** BAILEY, *Dissilience*, a leaping down from off a place, or from one place to another: Also a leaping asunder.

dissiliency (dɪsˈsɪlɪənsɪ). *rare.* [see next and -ENCY.] The quality of being dissilient; tendency to spring asunder. *lit.* and *fig.*

1882–3 A. P. PEABODY in Schaff *Encycl. Relig. Knowl.* III. 1747 Not only dissent, but strong dissiliency was almost unanimously expressed by the Unitarian clergy.

dissilient (dɪsˈsɪlɪənt), *a.* [ad. L. *dissilient-em*, pr. pple. of *dissilīre* to leap or spring asunder, fly apart, f. DIS- 1 + *salīre* to leap.] Leaping asunder, springing apart; *spec.* in *Bot.* bursting open with force, as do some ripe capsules.

1656 BLOUNT *Glossogr.*, *Dissilient*, leaping down off a place, or hither and thither. **1793** T. MARTYN *Lang. Bot.*, *Dissiliens pericarpium*, a dissilient, bursting or elastic pericarp or fruit. **1830** W. PHILLIPS *Mt. Sinai* I. 120 Nature sprang Ofttimes dissilient from her destined course.

† **dissi'lition.** *Obs.* [n. of action f. L. *dissilīre* to leap asunder: cf. prec. and L. *salītio* a leaping.] A leaping or springing apart; a bursting.

1660 BOYLE *New Exp. Phys. Mech.* xxxvii. 312 The Dissilition of that Air was so great, that the small Viol seem'd to be full of Milk. **1669** —— *Contn. New Exp.* II. (1682) 166 The Glass broke..and made a great noise at its dissilition. **1685** —— *Effects of Mot.* Suppl. 143 The dissilition depended chiefly upon the peculiar texture of the Glass.

dissimilar (dɪˈsɪmɪlə(r)), *a.* (*sb.*) Also 7–8 **dissimular.** [f. DIS- 10 + SIMILAR: cf. F. *dissimilaire* (Paré, 16th c.), L. *dissimilis* unlike.]

Not similar or alike; different in appearance, properties, or nature; unlike. Const. *to* (less often *from*, rarely *with.*)

dissimilar whole (*Logic*), a whole composed of heterogeneous parts. ***dissimilar parts*** (in *old Anat.*), organs of the body composed of various 'similar parts' or tissues. Opposed to CONSIMILAR.

1621 BURTON *Anat. Mel.* I. i. II. iv, *Dissimular* parts are those which wee call *Organicall.* **1632** SHERWOOD, The dissimilar parts of the body, *les parties dissimilaires du corps* [not in Cotgr. 1611]. **1656** STANLEY *Hist. Philos.* v. (1701) 166 *Heterogeneous*, consist of dissimular parts. **1705** CHEYNE *Philos. Princ. Relig.* I. xxiv. (1715) 47 As well may the Ray be supposed to be dissimilar to the body of the Sun. **1779–81** JOHNSON *L.P.*, *Addison* Wks. III. 87 A poetical simile is the discovery of likeness between two actions, in their general nature dissimilar. **1802** MRS. E. PARSONS *Myst. Visit* II. 154 A wish of her own dissimilar with any expressed wish of his. **1819** W. TAYLOR in *Monthly Rev.* LXXXIX. 78 Short lucubrations, not dissimilar from those of the *Spectator.* **1848** C. BRONTË *J. Eyre* xii, A new picture..it was dissimilar to all the others hanging there. **1876** HUMPHREYS *Coin-Coll. Man.* vi. 69 An entirely new style of coinage..which..was ..dissimilar from the Roman.

† **b.** *Bot.* Applied to the cotyledonary or seed-leaves of a plant, as being unlike in form to the later-developed ordinary leaves. *Obs.*

1671 GREW *Anat. Plants* I. i. §42 These Dissimilar Leaves, for the most part Two, which first spring up, and are of a different shape from those that follow, being the very Lobes of the Seed. **1721** BAILEY, *Dissimilar leaves* (with Botanists) are the two first leaves of a Plant.

B. as *sb.* (in *pl.*) Dissimilar things.

1654 Z. COKE *Logick* (1657) 202 Dissimilars are wont chiefly to deserve explication. **1727–51** [see DISSIMILE]. **1869** GOULBURN *Purs. Holiness* viii. 67 If the dissimilars be not related to one another.

Hence † **dissimilarness** = next.

1727 BAILEY vol. II, *Dissimilarness*, unlikeness.

dissimilarity (dɪsɪmɪˈlærɪtɪ). [f. prec. after SIMILARITY: cf. F. *dissimilarité.*] Dissimilar quality or nature; unlikeness, difference; also, an instance of this, a point of difference.

1705 CHEYNE *Philos. Princ. Relig.* I. xxiv. (1715) 49 The acquired principle of dissimilarity must repel these Beings ..from their centre. **1806** SYD. SMITH *Elem. Sk. Mor. Philos.* (1850) 382 From their great dissimilarity with those which preceded them. **1841** ELPHINSTONE *Hist. Ind.* I. 97 Difference of habits and employments is..sufficient to create as great a dissimilarity as exists between the Bramin and the Súdra. **1850** F. FYSH in Spurgeon *Treas. Dav.* Ps. lxxxi. 6 Their dissimilarity to the Egyptians appears at the first view. **1882** FARRAR *Early Chr.* I. 296 It is vain to talk about difference of subject..as furnishing any explanation of these dissimilarities.

dissimilarly (dɪˈsɪmɪləlɪ), *adv.* [f. DISSIMILAR + -LY[2].] In a dissimilar or unlike manner; differently.

a **1770** SMART *Hop Garden* I. (R.) Chalky sides With verdant shrubs dissimilarly gay. **1869** J. T. SPRAGUE in *Eng. Mech.* 24 Dec. 341/1 Substances dissimilarly electrified attract each other.

† **di'ssimilary,** *a.* (*sb.*) *Obs.* [f. DIS- 10 + SIMILARY.] Dissimilar, unlike; heterogeneous.

1624 F. WHITE *Reply Fisher* 476 Similarie and dissimilarie parts make but one bodie. **1641** FRENCH *Distill.* v. (1651) 109 It appears there are dissimilary parts in water. **1660** R. COKE *Power & Subj.* 58 A body compounded of heterogeneous and dissimilary parts.

B. as *sb.* = DISSIMILAR *sb.*

1661 FELTHAM *Resolves* (ed. 8) II. lxxxi, In dissimilaries, there is a kind of natural contest that hinders all Prosperity.

dissimilate (dɪˈsɪmɪleɪt), *v.* Chiefly *Philol. rare.* [f. DIS- 4 + L. *simil-is* like, after ASSIMILATE.] **a.** *trans.* To make unlike. **b.** *intr.* To become unlike.

1841 CATLIN *N. Amer. Ind.* (1844) II. lviii. 234 It is far easier..for distinct tribes, or languages, grouped and used together, to assimilate than to dissimilate. **1876** DOUSE *Grimm's L.* vi. 45 The habit..of continually substituting *s*[1] for the *s* which they as continually hear about them, induces in their mind what I shall venture to call a 'Dissimilating Sentiment'. **1935** G. K. ZIPF *Psycho-Biol. of Lang.* (1936) 93 When *dh*..was dissimilated..to *d.* **1946** E. A. NIDA *Morphol.* 287 Vowels may assimilate and dissimilate.

dissimilation (dɪsɪmɪˈleɪʃən). [n. of action f. prec., after *assimilation.*] The action of making, or process of becoming, unlike: opp. to ASSIMILATION. Used *spec.* in: **a.** *Philol.* The differentiation of two identical sounds occurring near each other in a word, by change of one of them, as in It. *pelegrino* from Lat. *peregrinus.* **b.** *Biol.* Destructive metabolism; katabolism: opp. to ASSIMILATION 4.

In quot. 1830, used for the preparation of two dissimilar sets of papers, to be presented to either belligerent, as needed.

1830 GALT *Lawrie T.* II. v. (1849) 57 His misfortune might be..owing to the dissimilation of the ship's papers. **1874** SWEET *Eng. Sounds* 13 Dissimilation..by which two identical sounds are made unlike, or two similar sounds are made to diverge. **1885** STALLYBRASS *Hehn's Wand. Pl. & Anim.* 476 The modern Latin languages felt..the need of dissimilation.

di'ssimilative, *a.* [f. after prec. and *assimilative*: see -IVE.] Tending to or causing dissimilation: *spec.* in *Biol.* catabolic.
In recent Dicts.

dissimilatory (dɪ'sɪmɪlətərɪ), *a. Philol.* [f. DISSIMILATE *v.* + -ORY[2].] Pertaining to or produced by dissimilation.
1901 H. OERTEL *Lect. Stud. Lang.* iv. 232 The 'dissimilatory loss' of a repeated consonant is in no way similar to the syncope (haplology) of one of two similar syllables. *Ibid.* 234 Obscurity prevails with regard to the causes of dissimilatory substitution of similar sounds, such as *l* for *r*, or *n* for *l*. **1935** [see ABBREVIATORY *a.*]. **1945** *Mod. Lang. Notes* Dec. 546 *Danfords* is a good example of dissimilatory loss of *r*. **1952** *Archivum Linguisticum* IV. 35 It could also be argued that the dissimilatory process took the short cut from **morm* to **bhorm*.

dissimile (dɪ'sɪmɪliː), *sb.* [a. L. *dissimile*, neut. of *dissimilis* unlike; after SIMILE.] The opposite of 'simile'; a comparison setting forth the dissimilarity of things; a comparison or illustration by contrast: see DISSIMILITUDE 2.
1682 [see DISSIMILIES 1659]. **1727–51** CHAMBERS *Cycl.*, *Dissimilitude*, or *Dissimili*, in rhetoric, etc., an argument, wherein, from dissimilar, or unlike things, other dissimilars are deduced. **1826** H. N. COLERIDGE *West Indies* 179 No more to be compared to the last..than I to Hercules, a meeting house to a church, Westminster to Eton, or any other equally appropriate dissimile.

dissimile, -ill, etc., var. ff. DISSIMULE *v. Obs.*

†**di'ssimilies,** *sb. pl. Obs. nonce-wd.* [ad. L. *dissimilia* unlike things, neut. pl. of *dissimilis* unlike.] Unlike things; 'dissimilars'.
1659 O. WALKER *Oratory* vi. 63 *margin*, Dissimilies [1682 dissimiles] and Contraries, expressed..By Disjunction.

dissimilitude (dɪsɪ'mɪlɪtjuːd). [ad. L. *dissimilitūdo* unlikeness, difference, dissimilarity, f. *dissimilis* unlike: see -TUDE.]
1. The condition or quality of being unlike; unlikeness, difference, dissimilarity; diversity.
1532 MORE *Confut. Tindale* Wks. 682/2 There is speciall dissimilitude betwene the sinagoge and y[e] church. **1564** *Brief Exam.* * * * iv, Dissimilitude of life and diuersitie of maners. **1697** tr. *Burgersdicius his Logic* I. xxi. 84 Dissimilitude in a diversity either in quality or passion. **1764** REID *Inquiry* v. viii. Wks. I. 131/2 The colours are perfectly distinguishable, and their dissimilitude is manifest. **1876** J. H. NEWMAN *Hist. Sk.* II. I. iii. 50 It often happens that men of very dissimilar talents..are attracted together by their very dissimilitude.
b. with *a* and *pl.* An instance of dissimilarity.
1594 HOOKER *Eccl. Pol.* Pref. ii. §2 Whereupon grew marvellous great dissimilitudes. **1642** HOWELL *For. Trav.* (Arb.) 30, I knowe Nature delights and triumphs in dissimilitudes. **1759** JOHNSON *Rasselas* xxviii, New impressions..might wear away their dissimilitudes by long cohabitation. **1863** HAWTHORNE *Our Old Home, Leamington Spa* (1879) 53 Such places..bloom only for the summer-season, and offer a thousand dissimilitudes even then.
†**2.** *Rhet.* A figure of speech in which a comparison is made by contrast. *Obs.*
1589 PUTTENHAM *Eng. Poesie* III. xix. (Arb.) 248 The Tuskan poet vseth this Resemblance, inuring as well by Dissimilitude as Similitude. **1628** T. SPENCER *Logick* 128 This that I haue sayd..is sufficient to shew the..vse of similitudes, and dissimilitudes. **1696** PHILLIPS, *Dissimilitude*, unlikeness, whence a Form of Speech is so called wherein divers things are compared in a diverse Quality. **1727–51** [see DISSIMILE].

†**di'ssimulable,** *a. Obs.*[—0] [f. L. *dissimulāre* to dissemble + -BLE.] That may be dissembled.
1727 in BAILEY vol. II.

†**di'ssimulance.** Chiefly *Sc. Obs.* Also -simil-, -symil-. [ad. L. *dissimulāntia* a dissembling, f. *dissimulāre*: see DISSIMULE and -ANCE.] Dissembling, dissimulation.
1508 DUNBAR *Gold. Targe* 182 Quhen Venus had persauit this rebute, Dissymilance scho bad go mak persute. **1513** DOUGLAS *Æneis* IV. vi. 49 With dissimulance wenyt thow, wnfaithfull wycht, Thow mycht haif hid fra me sa fals a flycht. **1530** LYNDESAY *Test. Papyngo* 617 Dissimilance, flattry, nor fals reporte. **1596** DALRYMPLE tr. *Leslie's Hist. Scot.* x. 417 That al sal weil vnderstand his wil to be naiket and bair of ony couering of dissimulance towards the King. **1727** BAILEY vol. II, *Dissimulance*, dissembling.

dissimular, obs. form of DISSIMILAR.

†**di'ssimulate,** *a. Obs.* Also 5 -ait, 6 -at, disimilate. [ad. L. *dissimulāt-us*, pa. pple. of *dissimulāre*: see next.] Dissembled, feigned, pretended.
c **1450** HENRYSON *Mor. Fab.* 17 This feinȝet Foxe, false and dissimulate. **1533–4** *Act 25 Hen. VIII*, c. 12 Fals feined & dissimulate fables. **1556** J. HEYWOOD *Spider & F.* lxiii. 41 Fayre disimilate show. **1632** LITHGOW *Trav.* IV. 145 By his dissimulate behaviour, he crept in favour with Christians. **1653** R. BAILLIE *Dissuasive Vind.* (1655) 22 [He] speaks in a dissimulate and prevaricating way.
Hence †**di'ssimulately** *adv.*; also †**di's-simulateness.**
1549 *Compl. Scot.* xx. 182 ȝe sal be recompensit..for ȝour astuce dissymilitnes. **1556** J. HEYWOOD *Spider & F.* xxxiii. 24 The butterfly spake his thoughte..Thant [i.e. the ant] contrary talked dissimilately.

dissimulate (dɪ'sɪmjʊleɪt), *v.* [f. L. *dissimulāt-* ppl. stem of *dissimulāre*: see DISSIMULE.
Rare bef. the end of 18th c.; not in J., T., nor Webster 1828.]
†**1.** *trans.* To pretend not to see, leave unnoticed, pass over, neglect. *Obs. rare.*
a **1533** LD. BERNERS *Gold. Bk. M. Aurel.* ix. (R.) That al thyng be forgiuen to theim that be olde and broken, and to theim that be yonge and lusty to dissimulate for a time, and nothyng to be forgiuen to very yong children.
2. To conceal or disguise under a feigned appearance; to dissemble.
1610 BP. CARLETON *Jurisd.* 204 Frederick..being taken prisoner when he would haue dissimulated his estate, he was knowne by his picture. **1872** GEO. ELIOT *Middlem.* iii, Public feeling required the meagreness of nature to be dissimulated by tall barricades of frizzed curls and bows. **1882** STEVENSON *New. Arab. Nts.* (1884) 127 If ever..he described some experience personal to himself, it was so aptly dissimulated as to pass unnoticed with the rest.
b. *intr.* To practise dissimulation, to dissemble.
1796 MRS. HOWELL *Anzoletta Zadoski* I. 152 He could not so far dissimulate as to promise his concurrence. **1847** LYTTON *Lucretia* ii, All weakness is prone to dissimulate.
3. *Electr.* To conceal the presence of (electricity) by neutralizing it; cf. DISGUISE *v.* 8.
1838 FARADAY *Exp. Res. Electr.* §1684 The terms *free charge* and *dissimulated Electricity* convey therefore erroneous notions if they are meant to imply any difference as to the mode or kind of action. *Ibid.* The one [charge] is not more free or more dissimulated than the other. **1870** J. T. SPRAGUE in *Eng. Mech.* 11 Feb. 519/3 The negative electricity..neutralises the positive..which is thus bound or dissimulated.
Hence **di'ssimulated** *ppl. a.*; **di'ssimulating** *vbl. sb.* and *ppl. a.*
1794 MISS GUNNING *Packet* I. 56 The mask..was torn from..the dissimulating Mrs. Johnson. **1838** Dissimulated electricity [see 3 above]. **1843** BROWNING *Blot in Scutcheon* I. iii, Some fierce leprous spot Will mar the brow's dissimulating. **1874** MIVART *Evolution* in *Contemp. Rev.* Oct. 773 The long dissimulated Atheism of Mill is now avowed.

dissimulation (dɪˌsɪmjuː'leɪʃən). Also 4–6 -symul-, 5 -symyl-, 4–6 -acion, -acioun, -acyoun, -atyon. [a. OF. *dissimulation* (12th c. in Hatz.-Darm.), ad. L. *dissimulātiōn-em*, n. of action from *dissimulāre*: see DISSIMULE.]
1. The action of dissimulating or dissembling; concealment of what really is, under a feigned semblance of something different; feigning, hypocrisy.
c **1386** CHAUCER *Sompn. T.* 415 He wolde þat the frere had been on fire With his false dissymulacion. **1393** GOWER *Conf.* I. 74 O derke ypocrisie, Thurgh whos dissimulacion..I am þus wickedly deceived. **1494** FABYAN *Chron.* VI. ccv. 217 Thus with shame he ended, that in falshode and dissymylacion had contynued moche of his lyfe. **1538** STARKEY *England* II. ii. 191 Hys owne clyent..by hys dyssymulatyon and fare wordys was interteynyd in long sute. **1611** BIBLE *Rom.* xii. 9 Let loue be without dissimulation. **1710** STEELE *Tatler* No. 213 ⁋1 Simulation is a Pretence of what is not, and Dissimulation a Concealment of what is. **1780** COWPER *Table T.* 129 Smooth Dissimulation, skilled to grace A devil's purpose with an angel's face. **1856** FROUDE *Hist. Eng.* I. 238 An indifferent master of the tricks of dissimulation to which he was reduced.
b. with *a* and *pl.* An instance of this; an act of dissembling. *Obs.* or *arch.*
c **1384** CHAUCER *H. Fame* II. 179 Moo dissymulacions And feyned reparacions. *c* **1400** *Three Kings Cologne* 13 þe kyng Ezechias of verry Innocency of hert made a dissimilation. **1582** N. LICHEFIELD tr. *Castanheda's Conq. E. Ind.* lxiii. 129 a, All those dissimulations which he did vse.
†**c.** Dissimulated or disguised form. *Obs. rare.*
1671 MILTON *P.R.* I. 497 Satan, bowing low His gray dissimulation, disappeared Into thin air diffused.
†**2.** A fanciful name for a 'company' or flock of small birds. *Obs.*
1486 *Bk. St. Albans* F vj a, A Dissimulacion of breddis. **1688** R. HOLME *Armoury* II. 311/1 A flock of small Birds, or a dissimulation of Birds.

dissimulative (dɪ'sɪmjʊlətɪv), *a. rare.* [f. L. stem *dissimulāt-*: see DISSIMULATE *v.* and -IVE.] Given to, or characterized by, dissimulation.
1802 MRS. E. PARSONS *Myst. Visit.* IV. 163 Tired of the dissimulative life he had been compelled to observe. **1872** MISS BRADDON *R. Ainsleigh* xv, The man was past-master of all dissimulative arts.

dissimulator (dɪ'sɪmjʊleɪtə(r)). Also 6 -our. [ad. L. *dissimulātor* a dissembler, agent-n. from *dissimulāre*. Cf. mod.F. *dissimulateur*.] One who dissimulates or feigns; a dissembler.
1500–20 DUNBAR *Poems* xlix. 31 Off the falis fox dissimvlatour, Kynd hes every theiff and tratour. **1799** MRS. J. WEST *Tale of Times* III. 145 To drive the mean dissimulator from the affected decency of deism into the bold audacity of atheism. **1827** LD. LYTTON *Pelham* lxvii, Dissimulator as I was to others, I was like a guilty child before the woman I loved. **1867** SMILES *Huguenots Eng.* iii. (1880) 45 The Queen-mother, being a profound dissimulator, appeared still disposed to bargain with the Reformed.

†**di'ssimule,** *v. Obs.* Also 4–6 dissy-, 5 dissumule, -symyl, dyssymyl(e, 5–6 dyssymul, dissymyl(e, 6 dis- dyssimill, -symell, *Sc.* -simull, -symile, -semle, -semmil. [a. OF. *dissimule-r* (14th c. in Littré), ad. L. *dissimulāre* to disguise, conceal, dissemble, f. *dis-*, DIS- 4 + *simulāre* to feign, after *dissimil-is* unlike, different. By development of *b* after *m*, and vowel modification, this word was gradually changed into DISSEMBLE, q.v.]
1. *trans.* To alter the semblance of (one's feelings, actions, etc.) so as to conceal or deceive; to disguise under a feigned semblance; = DISSEMBLE *v.* 1.
c **1374** CHAUCER *Troylus* I. 322 His wo he gan dissimulen and hide. **1490** CAXTON *Eneydos* xvi. 65 They sholde doo this couertly, in dyssymulyng their goyng. *a* **1533** LD. BERNERS *Huon* lxxxii. 254 To dyssymell the matter vayleth not. *a* **1557** MRS. M. BASSET tr. *More's Treat. Passion* Wks. 1372/1 Enforsed either openly to professe their beliefe, or falselye to dissimull it. **1606** HOLLAND *Sueton.* 120 In part to dissimule and palliate his weakenesse.
b. with *inf. phrase.*
1388 WYCLIF *1 Sam.* x. 27 He dissymelide hym to here. **1570** BUCHANAN *Ane Admonitioun* Wks. (1892) 23 People..yat professis yame selffis in deid, and dissimulis in word to be ennemeis to God and to justice.
2. To alter the outward appearance of (a person or thing); to disguise; = DISSEMBLE 2.
1485 CAXTON *Chas. Gt.* I. ii. 14 Wherefore dyssymylest thou thy self lyke to the poure people. **1548** GEST *Pr. Masse* 120 A king renounceth to be honoured as a king when he dyssymeleth..hys personage and maiestye royall.
3. To pretend not to see or notice; to overlook, ignore; = DISSEMBLE 3.
(In quot. 1450, perh. 'to put any one off without answering.')
a **1450** *Knt. de la Tour* (1868) 100 The duk, that sawe her symplenes, beganne to lawghe and dissymyled her requeste. **1502** *Ord. Crysten Men* (W. de W. 1506) IV. xxi. 234 If he suffre & dyssymule ony grete euyll in his subgectes. **1537** *Inst. Chr. Man* L vj b, They..wol wynke therat, and dissimule it. **1636** B. JONSON *Discov.*, *Morbi* ix. 190 So in the church, some errors may be dissimuled with lesse inconvenience then they can be discover'd.
b. *intr.* with *with*, in same sense.
1558 Q. KENNEDIE *Compend. Tract.* in *Wodr. Soc. Misc.* 1844 I. 142 Magistratis dissimulis..with the faltis of the subjectis.
4. *absol.* or *intr.* To practise dissimulation; = DISSEMBLE 4.
c **1374** CHAUCER *Troylus* III. 385 (434) So wel dissimulen he kowde. *c* **1386** —— *Manciple's T.* 243 Dissimule as thou were deef, if that thou heere A Iangler. **1484** CAXTON *Curiall* 2 They that conne dyssymyle..use better theyr tyme in courtes than the other peple. **1513** DOUGLAS *Æneis* IV. vi. 21 And to dissymill [ed. 1555 dissemmil] gif ony askit quhy. **1624** *Brief Inform. Affairs Palatinate* 51 Vnto the Princes..he dissimuled, and would not be knowne of the same conditions.
b. const. *with.* (See also 3 b.)
1471 *Close Roll 10 Edw. IV*, 31 Mar., They dissimuled with his said Highness. **1582** N. LICHEFIELD tr. *Castanheda's Conq. E. Ind.* xxxvi. 86 a, He dissimuled therewith onely to see whether..he might lade there or no.
5. *trans.* To simulate, feign; = DISSEMBLE 5.
1483 CAXTON *Cato* F iij b, Thou oughtest..to make the a fole or to dyssymylle folye in tyme and in place whan the thynge requyreth it. **1570–1** *Act 11 Eliz.* (Bolton *Stat. Irel.* (1621) 311) His demaunds were yeelded to conditionally that it appeare to the world that he ment faithfully..which being dissimuled till the first of May [etc.].
b. with *subord. cl.* or *inf. phr.* = DISSEMBLE 5 b.
c **1430** *Pilgr. Lyf Manhode* IV. viii. (1869) 179 He taketh gladliche a fauce visage, and falsliche dissimuleth þat he is a briht angel. **1490** CAXTON *Eneydos* xix. 71 Why is it that I dyssymyle to go alle oute from my wyttes? **1553** EDEN *Treat. Newe Ind.* (Arb.) 36 People, dissimuling that thei desired to ioyne frendship with the Spaniardes.
6. *trans.* To feign, invent, make up falsely. *rare.*
1483 CAXTON *Gold. Leg.* 314 b/2 An illusion or an Inuencion dissimyled of his brethren the Freres.
¶**7.** In the later Wycliffite version used to represent *dissimulare* of the Vulgate, where the sense of the original is 'linger' and 'leave off, cease'.
1388 WYCLIF *Gen.* xix. 16 While he dissymelide [1382 hym denyinge] thei token his hond. —— *1 Sam.* xxiii. 13 Saul dissymylide [1382 laft] to go out.
Hence †**di'ssimuling** *vbl. sb.* and *ppl. a.* = DISSEMBLING.
c **1374** CHAUCER *Troylus* V. 1613 Whiche I shal with dissimulynge amende. *c* **1386** —— *Sqr.'s T.* 277 Swich subtil lookyng and dissymulynges. *c* **1515** *Cocke Lorell's B.* (Percy Soc.) 11 Dyssymulynge beggers. **1563** FOXE *A. & M.* 749 b, His subtile practises..and dissimuling conueiance.

†**di'ssimuled,** *ppl. a. Obs.* [f. prec. + -ED[1].] = DISSEMBLED.
1. a. Concealed under a specious disguise; disguised. **b.** Feigned, pretended, counterfeit.
1475 *Bk. Noblesse* (1860) 41 We have ben deceived and myschevid thoroughe suche dissimuled trewes. **1533–4** *Act 25 Hen. VIII*, c. 12 *heading*, Elizabeth Barton..under colour of hipocrisie, dissimuled sanctite, and false feined miracles, traitorously intended to distroy..the king. **1548** HALL *Chron.*, *Hen. V* (an. 39) 186 b, Brought up with a shepperd, in poore habite, and dissimuled behavior. **1585** T. WASHINGTON tr. *Nicholay's Voy.* I. xix. 22 b, That passe, which his knavery and dissimuled treason hadde wished for. **1624** T. SCOTT *Belg. Souldier* 24 The dissimuled peace of the Prouinces with the confederate Princes.
2. That has assumed a disguise; false; characterized by dissimulation.

1500-20 DUNBAR *Poems* xxvi. 47 Him followit mony freik dissymlit, With fenȝeit wirdis quhyte. **1549** *Compl. Scot.* vii. 71 Thai haue schauen them self ingrat, dissymilit, ande couuardis in the iust deffens of my veil fayr. *Ibid.* viii. 74.

† **di'ssimuler.** *Obs.* Also 4-5 -our, 5 discymuler, 6 -ar. [ME. *dissimulour*, f. DISSIMULE *v.* with AF. suffix -OUR = F. *-eur*, subseq. conformed to -ER¹.] = DISSEMBLER.

1386 CHAUCER *Nun's Pr. T.* 408 O false morderour..ffalse dissimylour. *c* **1398** —— *Fortune* 23, I knew hir ek a fals dissimulour. **1494** FABYAN *Chron.* VII. ccxxii. 247 A fare speker and great discymuler. **1526** TINDALE *Rom.* Prol. Wks. (Parker Soc.) I. 486 Such hypocrites and dissimulars. **1547-8** *Ordre Commvn.* 5 After the maner of dissimulers with God. [**1662** *Bk. Com. Prayer.*, *ibid.* dissemblers]. **1555** LATIMER *Serm. & Rem.* (1845) 441 If they be very dissimulers.

† **dis'sinew**, *v. Obs. rare.* [DIS- 7 a.] *trans.* To deprive of 'sinew' or vigour.

1640 G. WATTS tr. *Bacon's Adv. Learn.* VII. iii, Great.. Fortune..for most part loosens and dissinues mens minds. **1641** EARL MONM. tr. *Biondi's Civil Warres* I. i-iii, Effeminating the minde, and dissinewing the strength.

† **'dissipable**, *a. Obs.* [ad. L. *dissipābilis*, f. *dissipāre* to DISSIPATE.] That may be dissipated.

1603 HOLLAND *Plutarch's Mor.* 1041 A substance dissipable and apt to be dispersed. **1657** AUSTEN *Fruit Trees* I. 23 An idle life doth make the flesh soft and dissipable. **1696** WHISTON *Th. Earth* I. (1722) 54 Comets do not wholly consist of Vapours, exhalations, or such other dissipable matter. **1710** T. FULLER *Pharm. Extemp.* 237 Condensing and fixing the dissipable.

Hence † **dissipa'bility**, capability of being dissipated.

1659 H. MORE *Immort. Soul* (1662) 87 Not onely the fluidity of parts, but also their dissipability.

dissipate ('dɪsɪpeɪt), *v.* [f. L. *dissipāt-* ppl. stem of *dissipāre* to spread abroad, scatter, disperse, f. DIS- 1 + archaic vb. *supāre*, *sipāre* to throw, throw about, scatter. Cf. F. *dissiper* (14th c.).]

1. *trans.* To scatter; to drive or cause to go off in all directions; to disperse (that which has been concentrated). *arch.*

c **1534** tr. *Pol. Verg. Eng. Hist.* (Camden) 199 King Richerd..having gatherid a huge host..because he wold not dissypate his forces..resolvyd [etc.]. *a* **1635** NAUNTON *Fragm. Reg.* (Arb.) 24 She [Mary] both dissipated and persecuted the major part of her Brothers Councel. **1687** *Lond. Gaz.* No. 2270/6 They have pressed and dissipated the Ships Company..about 70 in number. **1725** POPE *Odyss.* VI. 160 A lion..Springs o'er the fence, and dissipates the fold. **1822** LAMB *Elia* Ser. I. *Mod. Gallantry*, To pick up her wandering fruit, which some unlucky dray has just dissipated. **1837** CARLYLE *Fr. Rev.* III. IV. v. (1872) 161 Several have dissipated themselves, whithersoever they could.

b. *intr.* (for *refl.*) To pass away in all directions; (of a company) to disperse.

1660 F. BROOKE tr. *Le Blanc's Trav.* 63 Those shelves of sand, which do dissipate, and are spent in the sea. **1679** *Lauderdale Papers* (1885) III. xciv. 163 The officers of the Dragoones required yᵐ in the King's names to Dissipate. **1704** ADDISON *Italy* 250 Woods that enclos'd the Lake, and hinder'd these noxious Steams from dissipating. **1837** CARLYLE *Fr. Rev.* I. IV. iii. (1872) 114 At sight of the.. Switzers, Saint-Antoine dissipates; hastily, in the shades of dusk.

† **2.** *trans.* To scatter in defeat; to disperse in flight, to rout. *Obs.*

1602 WARNER *Alb. Eng.* XII. lxxv, The once ship-bearing Ley, by Alfred slu'ste in Three, To dissipate the Dane Fleete. **1670** MILTON *Hist. Eng.* II. Wks. (1847) 493/1 The Legion..quickly broke and dissipated what oppos'd them. **1745-9** *Rep. Cond. Sir J. Cope* 120 Able to tell his Majesty ..that you have dissipated a Rebellion in Scotland. **1789** COWPER *Ann. Memorab.* 6 Chiefs, whose single arm could boast Prowess to dissipate a host.

3. To dispel by dispersion or minute diffusion (mist, clouds, etc.); to cause to disappear; to disperse or 'discuss' (humours, etc).

1532 MORE *Confut. Tindale* Wks. 401/2 They wil clerely dissipate and discusse the myst. **1601** HOLLAND *Pliny* II. 262 The root of marsh Mallow, doth dissipate and scatter all gatherings of humors to an impostume. **1696** tr. *Du Mont's Voy. Levant* 116, A thick and black Smoak..was dissipated in a Moment. **1732** ARBUTHNOT *Rules of Diet* 312 Restoring as much Water to the Blood as is dissipated by the Heat. **1810** SHELLEY *Zastrozzi* iv. Pr. Wks. 1888 I. 21 The rays of the lamp but partially dissipated the darkness. **1875** *Lyell's Princ. Geol.* I. II. cccxvii. 396 When the acid is dissipated in the atmosphere.

b. *fig.* and *transf.* To dispel (care, fear, doubt, or anything compared to cloud or darkness).

1691 HARTCLIFFE *Virtues* 165 Such Companions, as shall ..dissipate our sorrows with their innocent Mirth. **1710** STEELE *Tatler* No. 4 ¶8 [It] has dissipated the Fears of that People. **1828** D'ISRAELI *Chas. I*, I. iv. 78 Cool shades and exquisite viands in a moment dissipated heat and hunger. **1831** BREWSTER *Nat. Magic* v. (1833) 103 This illusion may be dissipated by a process of reasoning. **1855** MACAULAY *Hist. Eng.* IV. 381 To dissipate his melancholy by breathing the fresh air of that noble terrace.

c. *intr.* To pass away by minute dispersion or diffusion; to disappear.

1626 BACON *Sylva* §632 The Spirits doe but weaken and dissipate, when they come to the Aire and Sunne. **1640** HOWELL *Dodona's Gr.* (1645) 138 Libels neglected quickly find their own graves, and dissipat to ayr. **1758** J. S. *Le Dran's Observ. Surg.* (1771) 239 The Hardness sensibly dissipated. **1792** *Anecd. W. Pitt* I. xx. 323 In a few weeks..the public prejudice began to dissipate. **1878** B. TAYLOR *Deukalion* I. ii, Death and decay are things That dissipate beneath thy radiant eye.

4. *trans.* To disintegrate and reduce to atoms, dust, smoke, or impalpable form; to destroy or dissolve completely, undo, annul (material or immaterial objects).

c **1555** HARPSFIELD *Divorce Hen. VIII*, 45 This matrimony ..ought not in any wise to have been dissipated and dissolved. **1638** SIR T. HERBERT *Trav.* (ed. 2) 260 Fire is given to a trayne..and at length dissipates and blowes up the detested Syrian [an effigy]. **1647** JER. TAYLOR *Dissuas. Popery* ii. §4 (T.) The legate..revoked and dissipated all former grants. **1651** *Fuller's Abel Rediv.*, *Chytraeus* 419 The Wars..breaking forth..the University of Wittenburg was dissipated by reason of the same. **1692** RAY *Dissol. World* III. i. (1732) 303 Shall the Heavens and Earth be wholly dissipated and destroyed. **1798** MALTHUS *Popul.* (1817) I. 318 Violent hurricanes, by which whole harvests are dissipated. **1869** PHILLIPS *Vesuv.* iii. 45 The crater itself was dissipated in the convulsion.

b. *intr.* (for *refl.*) To become disintegrated; to moulder to dust or impalpable atoms.

1677 HALE *Prim. Orig. Man.* I. i. 33 If it gave over its work ..it would soon dissolve, dissipate and corrupt. **1880** DISRAELI *Endym.* ix, His whole position..seemed to dissolve, and dissipate into insignificant fragments.

5. *trans.* To scatter or consume wastefully (money, resources, faculties); to waste, squander.

1682 BURNET *Rights Princes* ii. 68 The Goods of the Church might not be dissipated. **1761** HUME *Hist. Eng.* I. viii. 175 The prelate had dissipated money beyond the income of his place. **1781** GIBBON *Decl. & F.* III. lxi. 550 The elder brothers dissipated their wealth in romantic adventures. **1852** THACKERAY *Esmond* I. ii, He had dissipated his small paternal inheritance. **1878** BOSW. SMITH *Carthage* 99 Rome could not yet afford so to dissipate her energy.

b. *intr.* (for *refl.*)

1622 F. MARKHAM *Bk. War.* v. vi. §2. 182 The Kings Treasure..which by any lavishnes of an..vnrestrained hand will soone dissipate.

6. *trans.* To scatter or distract (attention, thought, mental or practical activity) by variety of objects; to fritter away. The opposite of to *concentrate*.

1683 BURNET *More's Utopia* (1684) 191 Their Priests think that too much light dissipates the thoughts. **1751** JOHNSON *Rambler* No. 153 ¶4 That application which had hitherto been dissipated in general knowledge. **1769** BURKE *Corr.* (1844) I. 182 Various matters have so dissipated me as to hinder me from a vigorous pursuit of this object. *c* **1790** WILLOCK *Voy.* 285 The great variety..deranges and dissipates those powers, that in a state of nature have only one object. **1851** CARLYLE *Sterling* I. xii. (1872) 75 A gifted amiable being..in danger of dissipating himself into the vague. **1883** *Pall Mall G.* 18 Dec. 2 Thought may be dissipated into a number of aperçus.

7. *intr.* To practise dissipation; to engage in frivolous or (now usually) dissolute pleasures.

1836 T. HOOK *G. Gurney* II. 274, I was rather out of spirits, so I dissipated in a glass of negus and a biscuit. **1839** MARRYAT *Diary Amer.* Ser. I. II. 224 He dissipates awfully. **1859** SALA *Tw. round Clock* (1861) 408 The place is not harmless: people go there to dissipate, and do dissipate.

Hence **'dissipating** *vbl. sb.* and *ppl. a.*

1657 COWLEY *Dk. Buckhm.*, In dissipating Storms, and routed Battels they Did..constant with their Captain stay. **1818** G. S. FABER *Horae Mosaicæ* I. 214 The mixed and dissipating society of a palace. **1891** *Spectator* Mar., The education of the day is of a somewhat dissipating type.

† **'dissipate**, *ppl. a. Obs.* [ad. L. *dissipāt-us*, pa. pple. of *dissipāre*; or short for *dissipated*: see the vb.] = DISSIPATED.

1606 G. W[OODCOCKE] tr. *Hist. Ivstine* Ep. Ded. A iv a, So dissipate and large Countries, so rich and populous Citties. **1619** BAINBRIDGE *Descr. Late Comet* 10 The Sunne rayes were there alwayes more dissipate then in the Comet. **1715** *Wodrow Corr.* (1843) II. 101 The best of the rebels' men are dissipate and cut off. **1765** *Petit.* in *Westm. Gaz.* 28 Dec. (1894) 8/1 The means employed..in our youth for our instruction in religion and virtue are wholly dissipate.

'dissipated, *ppl. a.* [f. prec. vb. + -ED¹.]

1. Dispersed, scattered, dispelled, wasted, frittered away.

1609 BIBLE (Douay) *Isa.* xxxiii. 8 The wayes are dissipated, the passenger by the path hath ceased. **1659** PEARSON *Creed* (1839) 521 So did they think a resurrection of corrupted, dissolved, and dissipated bodies, to be.. impossible. **1683** HOWE *Let. to Lady Russell* in H. Rogers *Life* viii. (1863) 201 To recollect ourselves, and recover our dissipated spirits. *a* **1711** KEN *Hymns Festiv.* Poet. Wks. 1721 I. 387 At the great Day of all the Just, You shall collect the dissipated Dust. **1738** JOHNSON *London* 20 Of dissipated wealth the small remains. **1791** MRS. RADCLIFFE *Rom. Forest* (1806) III. xix. 195 Adeline..had now recollected her dissipated thoughts. **1871** MORLEY *Voltaire* (1886) 58 Freedom of thinking was only an empty watchword, the name for a dissipated fashion.

† **b.** Devoid of concentration.

1748 CHESTERF. *Lett.* (1792) II. clxxv. 150 Many young people are so light, so dissipated, and so incurious, that they can hardly be said to see what they see.

2. Given to or characterized by dissipation; dissolute.

1744 JOHNSON *L.P.*, *Savage* Wks. 1796 X. 400 An irregular and dissipated manner of life had made him the slave of every passion. **1784** COWPER *Task* III. 376 Who seeks A social, not a dissipated life. **1788** WESLEY *Serm.* lxxix. *Dissipation*, King Charles the second, one of the most dissipated mortals that ever breathed. **1848** C. BRONTE *J. Eyre* x, A dissipated young man. **1848** MRS. JAMESON *Sacr. & Leg. Art* (1850) 183 Augustine passed his restless youth in dissipated pleasures and desultory studies. **1865** ALFORD in *Life* (1873) 384 We are making out a dissipated week at the Macnaughten's.

'dissipater. Also 6 -our, 7 -or. [f. DISSIPATE *v.* + -ER¹: cf. F. *dissipateur* (15th c. in Littré), L. *dissipātor* disperser, destroyer.] One who or that which dissipates, disperses, or scatters; one that squanders or wastes.

1537 LATIMER *Serm. bef. Convocation* Wks. I. 35 Be these the faithful dispensers of goddis misteries, and nat rather fals dissipatours of them? **1633** AMES *Agst. Cerem.* I. 7 Sammay and Hilles, prophane dissipators of Gods Law. **1799** W. TAYLOR in *Monthly Rev.* XXVIII. 516 A dissipater of his patrimony. **1824** SCOTT *St. Ronan's* xv. **1894** BARING-GOULD *Deserts S. France* I. 86 The atmosphere when dry is the best..dissipater of the noxious elements.

dissipation (dɪsɪ'peɪʃən). [ad. L. *dissipātiōn-em*, n. of action from *dissipāre* to DISSIPATE. Cf. F. *dissipation* (16th c.).]

† **1.** The action of dissipating or dispersing; a scattering; the fact of being dispersed; dispersed condition. *Obs.*

1545 JOYE *Exp. Dan.* xii. (R.) Subuersions of empires & kingdoms, skatterings and dissipacions of nacions. **1605** SHAKS. *Lear* I. ii. 161 Banishment of friends, dissipation of cohorts, nuptial breaches. **1667** MILTON *P.L.* VI. 598 Foule dissipation follow'd and forc't rout. **1677** HALE *Prim. Orig. Man.* II. iii. 143 Peleg, in whose time the famous dissipation of Mankind and distinction of Languages hapned. **1760** C. JOHNSTON *Chrysal* (1822) II. 214 In this dissipation I fell to the lot of one of the officers.

b. *Optics.* The scattering or dispersion of rays of light. ***circle, radius of dissipation***: see quots.

1748 HARTLEY *Observ. Man* I. ii. 219 Narrow the Pupil of the Eye, i.e. lessen the Radius of Dissipation. **1753** CHAMBERS *Cycl. Supp.* s.v., *Circle of Dissipation*..is used for that circular space upon the retina, which is taken up by one of the extreme pensils of rays issuing from an object ..*Radius of Dissipation*, the radius of the circle of Dissipation. **1794** G. ADAMS *Nat. & Exp. Philos.* II. xvii. 283 The circular spaces..illuminated by pencils of rays.. are called circles of dissipation. **1867** J. HOGG *Microsc.* I. ii. 22 Produced by the central rays falling in a circle of dissipation, before they have come to a focus.

2. The passing away or wasting of a substance, or form of energy, through continuous dispersion or diffusion.

1615 CROOKE *Body of Man* 94 The substance of the whole body hath a necessary diffluence and dissipation, as well by the in bred heate..as also by the outward aire. *c* **1790** IMISON *Sch. Art* I. 62 In this case, the dissipation of the electricity is not so considerable. **1881** MAXWELL *Electr. & Magn.* I. 45 Coulomb investigated the law of dissipation. **1881** SIR W. THOMSON in *Nature* No. 619. 441 Losing..20 per cent of this [energy] by the generation and dissipation of heat through the conductor.

attrib. **1879** Dissipation-function [see DISSIPATIVITY].

3. Reduction to atoms or to an impalpable condition; complete disintegration or dissolution.

1597 HOOKER *Eccl. Pol.* v. lxv. §15 The dissipation of Idols ..they were fashioned of matter, subiect vnto corruption, therefore to grinde them to dust was easie. **1647** H. MORE *Philos. Poems, Democr. Platon.* Pref., The dissipation of the whole frame of Nature into dis-joynted dust. *a* **1656** BP. HALL *Rem. Wks.* (1660) 315 To hear of the least danger of the dissipation of your Church. **1680** H. MORE *Apocal. Apoc.* 189 An utter ruine and dissipation of this Idolatrous City. *a* **1711** KEN *Hymnarium* Poet. Wks. 1721 II. 52 Saints no Dissipation fear, Who to the Boundless one adhere. **1796** BURKE *Regic. Peace* IV. Wks. IX. 26 The dissipation of France into..a cluster of petty Republicks. **1875** E. WHITE *Life in Christ* III. xxi. (1876) 325 Another attempt to reconcile this expression of our Lord with the idea of dissipation of the soul.

4. Wasteful expenditure or consumption of money, means, powers, faculties, etc.; squandering, waste.

1639 T. BRUGIS tr. *Camus' Moral Relat.* 351 [Almsgiving] must be done fitly..Otherwise it were rather a dissipation then a distribution. **1677** HALE *Prim. Orig. Man.* I. i. 13 Means that our Faculties might use without dissipation, distraction, or too great astonishment. *a* **1715** BURNET *Own Time* (1766) I. 339 There had been such a dissipation of treasure. **1785** PALEY *Mor. Philos.* v. ix, Nothing but stupidity or the most frivolous dissipation of thought. **1893** W. LEWIN in *Bookman* June 85/2 Avoiding any wasteful dissipation of his powers.

5. Distraction of the mental faculties or energies from concentration on serious subjects: at first often with colourless sense, as the scattering or distraction of attention, or with laudatory sense, as the dispelling of melancholy or sadness; diversion, amusement; but later implying the frittering away of energies or attention upon frivolities, and thus gradually passing into sense 6; also, with *a* and *pl.*, a distraction; a diversion; a frivolous amusement.

1733 SWIFT *Let.* 28 May, I have begun two or three letters ..and been prevented from finishing them by a thousand avocations and dissipations. **1742** YOUNG *Nt. Th.* VIII. 949 While Noise, and Dissipation, comfort Thee. **1748** CHESTERF. *Lett.* II. clv. 55 I am going to Cheltenham tomorrow..for the dissipation and amusement of the journey. **1759** JOHNSON *Rasselas* xi, Change of place.. inevitably produces dissipation of mind. **1768** BEATTIE *Minstr.* II. xxvii, In the giddy storm of dissipation toss'd. **1788** WESLEY *Serm.* LXXIX. *Dissipation* Wks. 1872 VI. 445 We hear of the still increasing dissipations..the word..was hardly heard of fifty years ago..And yet it is so in every one's mouth, that it is already worn threadbare; being one of the cant words of the day. **1800** MRS. HERVEY *Mourtray Fam.* iv. 60 Nothing would be of so much service to her spirits, as a little dissipation. **1845** S. AUSTIN *Ranke's Hist. Ref.* v. ix. III. 289 He was not born for the amusements and dissipations of the world. **1876** OUIDA *Winter City* iii. 59 Art had remained with her rather an intellectual dissipation than a tenderness.

6. Waste of the moral and physical powers by undue or vicious indulgence in pleasure; intemperate, dissolute, or vicious mode of living.

1784 COWPER *Task* II. 770 A task That bids defiance to the united powers Of fashion, dissipation, taverns, stews. **1791** MRS. RADCLIFFE *Rom. Forest* i, In a few years his fortune and affection were equally lost in dissipation. **1837** DICKENS *Pickw. P.* ii, Tupman was not in a condition to rise, after the unwonted dissipation of the previous night. **1861** M. PATTISON *Ess.* (1889) I. 47 Severer penalties awaited drunkenness, dissipation, or dicing. **1894** SIR W. GREGORY *Autobiog.* v. 89 He died young, worn out by dissipation.

'dissipative, *a.* [f. L. *dissipāt-* ppl. stem: see DISSIPATE *v.* and -IVE.] Tending to dissipate, having the property of dissipating.

1684 tr. *Bonet's Merc. Compit.* v. 147 These concretes do breathe out..an Armoniack, or dissipative scent. **1839-44** TUPPER *Proverb. Philos.* (1852) 373 The dissipative fashions of society. **1873** H. SPENCER *Stud. Sociol.* xiii. 324 Certain actions which go on in the first are cumulative, instead of being, as in the second, dissipative. **1889** RUSSELL in *Nature* 21 Nov. 61 The apparently dissipative action of the air on London smoke.

Hence **dissipa'tivity** (in *Physics*), a quantity expressing the rate of dissipation of energy: also called *dissipation-function*.

1879 THOMSON & TAIT *Nat. Phil.* I. I. §345 [This] function of the velocities..has been called by Lord Rayleigh the Dissipation Function. We prefer to call it Dissipativity. It expresses the rate at which the palpable energy of our supposed cycloidal system is..dissipated away into other forms of energy.

†**'dissipe**, *v. Obs. rare.* [a. F. *dissipe-r*, or ad. L. *dissip-āre*.] = DISSIPATE *v. trans.* and *intr.*

1597 LOWE *Chirurg.* (1634) 381 The vaines of the head being opened, letteth generation, because of the animal spirits which dissipe. **1612** SYLVESTER *Panaretus*, I have oft seene armies dissiped.

†**'dissite**, *a. Obs.* [ad. L. *dissit-us* lying apart, f. DIS- 1 + *situs* placed, situate, pa. ppl. of *sinĕre* to allow, let, orig. (it is supposed) 'to let, put, lay, or set down'.] Situated apart; distant, remote.

1600 HOLLAND *Livy* XXVI. xx. 599 They [Carthaginians] had betaken themselves into their wintering harbours far dissite and remote asunder. **1610** —— *Camden's Brit.* (1637) 46 Britaine..Far dissite from this world of ours. **1615** CHAPMAN *Odyss.* VII. 270 His natural land (Without more toil or care, how far hence dissite Soever it can be) he may ascend. **1657** TOMLINSON *Renou's Disp.* 133 From the brain, or parts more dissite.

†**dis'situate**, *a. Obs. rare.* Also 6 disc-. [DIS- 1.] Removed from its situation or site, displaced. So †**dissituated** *ppl. a.*

1593 NASHE *Christ's T.* (1613) 75 No Trophy remaining, no stone but discituate. **1623** COCKERAM, *Discituated*, displaced, ouerturned.

disslander, var. DISCLANDER, *Obs.*

†**dis'sleep**, *v. Obs. rare.* [f. DIS- 7 + SLEEP *sb.*] *trans.* To rouse from sleep, swoon, or death.

1616 J. LANE *Cont. Sqr.'s T.* x. Argt. (1888) 161 Great murninge for Cambuscans losse of liefe: Kinge Thotobun him wondrouslie dissleepes.

dissocia'bility. *rare.* [f. next + -ITY.]

†**1.** The opposite of sociability; unsociableness.

1738 WARBURTON *Div. Legat.* II. vi, Universal prejudice had made men regard a refusal of this intercommunity as the most brutal of all dissociability. **1757** BRETT *Friendly Call to the Roman Catholics in Ireland* 12 (L.) This dissociability, this dogmatizing, cruel, enslaving principle, is that which makes popery so very dreadful.

2. Capability of being dissociated.

In recent Dicts.

dissociable (see below), *a.* [In sense 1, f. DIS- 10 + SOCIABLE, app. after F. *dissociable* (Montaigne, 16th c.) in same sense; in senses 2 and 3, f. L. *dissociāre* to dissociate: cf. L. *dissociābilis* that cannot be united.]

1. (dɪ'səʊʃəbl). The reverse of sociable, not companionable, unsociable.

1603 FLORIO *Montaigne*, There is nothing so dis-sociable and sociable as man, the one for his vice, the other for his nature. **1632** BURTON *Anat. Mel.* (ed. 4) III. iv. I. ii, His Janisary Jesuits, that dissociable society. **1711** ADDISON *Spect.* No. 3 ¶6 They came in two by two..matched in the most dissociable Manner. **1860** *Chamb. Jrnl.* XIV. 353 Our insular dissociable habits.

2. That tends to separate or dissociate. [= L. *dissociābilis* in active sense.] *rare.*

1835 KIRBY *Hab. & Inst. Anim.* I. ii. 57 The student of his own species might be tempted sometimes to roam, but the ocean would be truly dissociable. [After Horace's *oceano dissociabili*.] **1872** A. D. CARLISLE *Round World* xix. 230 The mild Pacific was the only [ocean] whose 'dissociable' influence was still unbroken.

3. (dɪ'səʊʃjəbl). Capable of being dissociated; separable.

1833 G. WADDINGTON *Hist. Ch.* xiii. 212 Two forms of worship essentially dissociable. **1853** *Fraser's Mag.* XLVII. 560 Elements not dissociable by human means. **1894** *Westm. Gaz.* 20 Dec. 7/2 Surely it is a dangerous thing to say that sport and betting are not dissociable.

Hence **di'ssociableness**, unsociableness.

1866 CARLYLE *Remin.*, *Irving* I. 90, I..had the character of morose dissociableness.

dissocial (dɪs'səʊʃəl), *a.* [f. DIS- 10 + SOCIAL *a.* Cf. rare L. *dissociālis* irreconcilable, repugnant.] The reverse of social; disinclined or unsuitable for society; unsocial.

1762 KAMES *Elem. Crit.* I. ii. 65 Where revenge flames so high as to have no other aim than the destruction of its object, it is no longer selfish; but in opposition to a social passion may be termed dissocial. *Ibid.* 91 Hatred and other dissocial passions. **1788** REID *Act. Powers* v. vi. 666 Without it man would be the most dissocial animal God has made. **1825** CARLYLE *Schiller* Misc. (1872) III. 91 His habits.. though far from dissocial, were solitary.

Hence **dissoci'ality** (dɪssəʊʃɪ'ælɪtɪ), the quality of being dissocial; **di'ssocialize** *v.*, to render dissocial.

1804 SOUTHEY in *Ann. Rev.* II. 210 Let us examine their practice, its dissocializing character [etc.]. **1811** T. JEFFERSON *Writ.* (1830) IV. 167 Why should we be dissocialized by mere differences in opinion? **1825** CARLYLE *Schiller* Misc. (1872) III. 82 Self-seclusion, dissociality and even positive misanthropy. **1826** SOUTHEY *Lett. to Butler* 405 Decrees of the most dissocializing and inhuman character.

dissociant (dɪ'səʊʃ(ɪ)ənt). [ad. L. *dissociānt-em*, pres. pple. of *dissociāre* to DISSOCIATE.] (See quot.)

1883 *Syd. Soc. Lex.*, *Dissociants*, a term applied in Microscopy to those agents which have the power to loosen the texture and to separate the elements of the structures which are placed in them, such as 'Müller's solution.'

di'ssociate, *ppl. a. rare.* [ad. L. *dissociāt-us*, pa. pple. of *dissociāre*: see next.] = DISSOCIATED.

1548 UDALL, etc. *Erasm. Par. John* xiv. (R.) You..whom I wil not suffre to be dissociate or disseuered from me. **1815** SHELLEY *Pr. Wks.* (1888) II. 193 Neither the dream could be dissociate from the landscape, nor the landscape from the dream. **1895** *Daily News* 1 Feb. 7/5 Nitrogen existed partly in an 'allotropic' or in a 'dissociate' form.

†**b.** *Astrol.* (see quot.).

1819 JAS. WILSON *Dict. Astrol.*, *Dissociate* signs, those that by being 1 or 5 signs distant, have no aspect to each other: thus ♈ is dissociate with ♓, ♉, ♍, and ♏.

dissociate (dɪ'səʊʃɪeɪt), *v.* [f. L. *dissociāt-* ppl. stem of *dissociāre* to separate from fellowship, f. DIS- 1 + *sociāre* to join together, associate: cf. prec., and see -ATE[3] 6.]

1. *trans.* To cut off from association or society; to sever, disunite, sunder. Const. *from*.

1623 COCKERAM, *Dissociate*, to separate. **1628** FELTHAM *Resolves* II. xxxvi, Grief..does dissociate man, and sends him with beasts to the lonelinesse of unpathed desarts. **1710** T. FULLER *Pharm. Extemp.* 296 These Earths mix in with it [the Bile] and dissociate it. **1768-74** TUCKER *Lt. Nat.* (1852) II. 313 Our very wants and desires, which first bring us together, have a tendency likewise to dissociate us. **1863** MISS BRADDON *Eleanor's Vict.* II. iv. 54 Eleanor Vane could not dissociate the two images. **1874** GREEN *Short Hist.* vi. §4. 303 It was the first time..that religion had formally dissociated itself from the ambition of princes and the horrors of war. **1888** LOWELL *Pr. Wks.* (1890) VI. 201 Done only by men dissociated from the interests of party.

b. *Chem.* To separate the elements of (a compound), *spec.* by heat: see DISSOCIATION 2.

1869 C. A. JOY in *Scientific Opinion* No. 58. 571/1 A part of the vapour of water is decomposed spontaneously or dissociated in the tube of porous clay. *Ibid.* 571/2 At the temperature of the fusion of silver, water is dissociated and no longer exists as water. **1880** CLEMENSHAW *Wurtz' Atom. Th.* 115 The vapour of calomel is dissociated at the high temperature at which its density is taken.

2. *intr.* (for *refl.*) To withdraw from association, cease to associate.

1866 MAURICE *Workm. & Franchise* 237 There is a tendency to dissociate, to separate, of which each man becomes very conscious, in whatever circle he finds himself.

Hence **di'ssociating** *ppl. adj.*

a **1691** BOYLE *Wks.* I. 373 (R.) The dissociating action even of the gentlest fire, upon a concrete.

dissociated (dɪ'səʊʃɪeɪtɪd), *ppl. a.* [f. DISSOCIATE *v.* + -ED[1].]

a. Cut off from associates or society; disunited, separated.

1611 COTGR., *Dissocié*, dissociated; separated or severed. **1882** SIEMENS *New Theory of Sun* in *19 Cent.* April, An inflowing stream of dissociated vapours. **1885** GRAY *Lett.* (1893) 776 In their limited but dissociated habitats.

b. *Psychol.* Characterized by the disjunction of associated mental connections or the disaggregation of consciousness; ***dissociated personality***, a pathological state of mind in which two or more distinct personalities exist in the same person. (Occas. used as active verb.)

1890 [see DISSOCIATION 3]. **1911** I. H. CORIAT *Abnormal Psychol.* 7 When an experience or complex has become dissociated, it tends to act automatically, and cannot be controlled by the will. **1912** B. HART *Psychol. Insanity* iv. 47 That the continuous stream of her thought had been interrupted by the sudden appearance of a 'dissociated system of ideas'. **1918** C. S. MYERS *Present-day Applic. Psychol.* 35 Irène had undergone a severe shock owing to the death of her mother... Shortly after, Irène began to develope a dissociated personality. **1919** M. K. BRADBY *Psycho-Anal.* 68 If we cannot readily recall such principles at will for a critical overhauling then we are in danger of becoming 'dissociated', of doing the thing and not knowing why we do it. *Ibid.* 70 It links up proverbial knowledge of human nature with the phenomena of 'dissociated personality'. **1922** *Encycl. Brit.* XXXII. 200/1 As a litle girl of three, 'Doris Fischer' was thrown down violently by her drunken father, and so sustained a psychic fracture, which 'dissociated' her into 'Margaret' and 'Real Doris'. **1924** W. B. SELBIE *Psychol. Relig.* 291 It is not necessary to presuppose a secondary personality or a dissociated consciousness. **1940** *Brit. Jrnl. Psychol.* July 11 Children.. who were apparently too dissociated for any expression of their energy in phantasy or cognition. **1957** R. L. MUNROE *Schools of Psychoanalytic Thought* III. xi. 483 Another way by which dissociated impulses may find partial discharge is through the process of sublimation.

dissociation (dɪsəʊʃɪ'eɪʃən, -sɪ'eɪʃən). [ad. L. *dissociātiōn-em*, n. of action f. *dissociāre* to DISSOCIATE: cf. F. *dissociation* (16th c. in Littré).]

1. The action of dissociating or the condition of being dissociated; severance; division; disunion.

1611 COTGR., *Dissociation*, a dissociation;..separation of fellowship. **1613-18** DANIEL *Coll. Hist. Eng.* (1626) 4 The Brittaines vnderstanding the misery of their dissociation. **1622** BACON *Hen. VII*, 88 Associations and Leagues; which commonly..turne to Dissociations and Diuisions. **1790** BURKE *Fr. Rev.* 276 It will add infinitely to the dissociation, distraction, and confusion of these confederate republics. **1877** E. CAIRD *Philos. Kant* I. 141 The association or dissociation of one feeling from another.

2. *Chem.* The direct separation of compound substances into their primary elements, or into less complex compounds; decomposition, *spec.* by the action of heat. Hence ***dissociation-point***, the temperature at which such decomposition takes place; ***dissociation constant***, the product of the concentrations of the dissociated ions in a solution divided by the concentration of the undissociated molecule when equilibrium has been reached.

Applied usually to the separation of a compound into its elements by the action of heat alone, without the intervention of any substance which breaks up the combination by its greater chemical affinity for one of the elements; but sometimes restricted to such a partial separation of the elements, that they reunite when the temperature is lowered below the dissociation-point. Others have used it in the wider etymological sense of direct separation of elements by any force, and applied THERMOLYSIS to dissociation by heat, as distinguished from ELECTROLYSIS or decomposition by electricity.

[**1857** Nov. 23 H. STE. CLAIRE DEVILLE in *Journal de l'Institut* (*title*), De la dissociation, ou décomposition spontanée des corps, sous l'influence de la chaleur.] **1869** C. A. JOY in *Scientific Opinion* (article), On Dissociation. **1872-5** WATTS *Dict. Chem.* VII. 636 As 'Dissociation' might be applied equally well to the separation of a mass into its constituent particles..by any other means, Mohr proposes to replace it by the more specific term 'Thermolysis'. **1874** GROVE *Corr. Phys. Forces* (ed. 6) 52 The term 'dissociation' has been applied..to other cases in which heat separates the constituents of a substance without any of them combining with another body. **1880** *Times* 1 Dec. 10 Mr. Norman Lockyer continues his researches on dissociation, as indicated in solar outbursts. **1880** *Nature* XXI. 445 The term dissociation-point is justified by analogy with the terms boiling-point and melting-point. **1891** *Jrnl. Chem. Soc.* LX. I. 257 The author..communicates his determination of the dissociation constants of some 60 organic substances of acid character. **1955** J. G. DAVIS *Dict. Dairying* (ed. 2) 418 The degree of dissociation is thus a measure of the strength of the acid or alkali, a very strong acid like hydrochloric or a very strong alkali like caustic soda being practically completely dissociated in dilute solution. The degree of dissociation is expressed in terms of the dissociation constant.

3. *Psychol.* **a.** The process or result of breaking up associations of ideas.

1890 W. JAMES *Princ. Psychol.* I. 506 What is associated now with one thing and now with another tends to become dissociated from either... One might call this the law of dissociation by varying concomitants. **1890** J. M. BALDWIN *Handbk. Psychol.* (ed. 2) 218 The part played by dissociation is evident. If there were no such breaking up of representations, imagination would be simply memory. **1925** E. & C. PAUL tr. *Janet's Psychol. Healing* I. xi. 676, I regard a memory, and especially a fixed idea,..as a system comprising a number of associated psychological phenomena... I have attempted to break up this system, to demolish it stone by stone; this is what I call the dissociation of a fixed idea. **1969** S. H. BARTLEY *Princ. Perception* (ed. 2) v. xii. 326 Dissociation brought about by local anaesthesia begins with effects upon the smallest nerve fibers and ends with the largest.

b. The disintegration of personality or consciousness; the state in which a person suffers from dissociated personality.

1897 E. PARISH *Halluc. & Illus.* 71 If we..seek for some quality common to all the various states in which hallucinations occur, we shall find that their most striking characteristic is the dissociation of consciousness. **1906** M. PRINCE *Dissociation of Personality* iii. 22 A dissociation of the mind, known as a state of hysteria or 'traumatic neurosis'... Sometimes the mental dissociation produces a complete loss of memory. **1908** *Brain* July 257 Cerebral dissociation..is at least one of the essential features of the hypnotic state. **1922** *Encycl. Brit.* XXXII. 200/1 Other cases of dissociation (e.g. the 'Watseka Wonder'). **1935** *Brit. Jrnl. Psychol.* Oct.

176 Many of the shamanistic phenomena which have been described,..can be explained by supposing varying degrees of dissociation. **1948** W. McDougall *Introd. Social Psychol.* (ed. 29) 84 Abnormal states of the brain, of which the relative dissociation obtaining in hysteria, hypnosis, normal sleep, and fatigue, is the most important. **1963** Langner & Michael *Life Stress & Mental Health* xv. 400 Such symptoms as fainting or amnesic periods (as well as alcoholism and drug addiction) are considered evidence of withdrawal by dissociation.

dissociative (dɪˈsəʊʃɪətɪv), *a.* [f. DISSOCIATE *v.* + -IVE.] Tending to dissociate; *spec.* in *Chem.* causing dissociation or direct decomposition.

1882 *Edin. Rev.* July 53 The resolution of carbonic acid into its elements..is one of the most familiar instances of this transformation of solar radiation into dissociative action. *Ibid.* 54 Their dissociative power..dependent upon their being made of compound molecules.

† **dissoˈciety.** *Obs. nonce-wd.* [DIS- 9.] The opposite of companionship; mutual aversion.

1602 W. Watson *Quodlib. Relig. & State* 104 So vertue and vice hauing such a dissocietie.

dissocioscope (dɪˈsəʊʃɪəʊskəʊp). *Chem.* [a. F. *dissocioscope*, f. L. *dissociāre* to DISSOCIATE + -SCOPE.] (See quot.)

1881 *Jrnl. Chem. Soc.* XL. 343 Apparatus for showing the Dissociation of Ammonium Salts. By D. Tommasi..This apparatus, to which the author gives the name 'dissocioscope', consists [etc.].

dissoconch (ˈdɪsəkɒŋk). *Zool.* [f. Gr. δισσός double + CONCH.] The shell of a mollusc in the veliger stage; also, the shell of an adult bivalve.

1888 Jackson in *Proc. Boston Soc. Nat. Hist.* XXIII. 543 In the oyster..this [*sc.* the earlier] shell is not single, but double-valved, and, therefore, deserves a distinct name, as it precedes the dissoconch or true shell.

dissogony (dɪˈsɒgənɪ). *Zool.* Also **-geny.** [ad. G. *dissogonie* (C. Chun 1888, in *Bibliotheca Zool.* I. 1. 64), f. Gr. δισσός double + γόνος offspring.] The phenomenon found among the Ctenophora, in which there are two periods of sexual maturity in the same individual, one in the larval and another in the adult form.

1896 R. Lydekker *R. Nat. Hist.* VI. 477 In at least one species (*Eucharis multicornis*) sexually mature larvæ, or larvæ which are capable of reproduction as such, also occur; these, when completely developed, become once more capable of reproduction as adults;—a method of multiplication which has been called dissogony. **1906** *Camb. Nat. Hist.* I. 419 To this series of sexual phenomena the name 'Dissogony' is given. **1911** *Encycl. Brit.* XVI. 224/2 The larva becomes sexually mature and lays eggs;..it then loses its generative organs and develops into the adult, which again develops reproductive organs (*dissogony*). **1940** L. H. Hyman *Invertebrates* I. viii. 677 All the ctenophores are hermaphroditic, and many have two periods of sexual maturity, one in the larva and a final one in the adult, with a degeneration of the gonads between the two phases. This peculiar phenomenon has been termed dissogeny.

dissolation, obs. var. of DESOLATION.

1422 tr. *Secreta Secret., Priv. Priv.* (E.E.T.S.) 192 His dissolacion radir þan his consolacioun he seth.

† **diˈssology.** *Obs. rare*⁻⁰. [ad. Gr. δισσολογία repetition, f. δίσσος double + λόγος word.]

1656 Blount *Glossogr., Dissology*, the speech of two.

dissolubility (dɪˌsɒljuːˈbɪlɪtɪ). [f. next + -ITY; in mod.F. *dissolubilité*.] The quality of being dissoluble; capability of being dissolved; †solubility in a liquid (*obs.*).

1611 Florio, *Dissolubilita*, a dissolubility. **1677** Hale *Prim. Orig. Man.* I. iii. 84 From the dissolubility of their parts. **1733** Cheyne *Eng. Malady* I. v. §4 (1734) 40 Mineral ..Salt..with its Dissolubility in Water. **1865** *Ch. Times* 12 Aug. 252/3 The theological objection to the dissolubility of marriage.

dissoluble (ˈdɪsəljuːb(ə)l, dɪˈsɒljuːb(ə)l), *a.* [ad. L. *dissolūbil-is* that may be dissolved, f. *dissolvĕre* to DISSOLVE: cf. F. *dissoluble* (14th c. in Hatz.-Darm.).] Capable of being dissolved.

1. Capable of being separated into elements or atoms; decomposable, disintegrable; capable of being destroyed by complete decomposition.

1534 More *Treat. Passion* Wks. 1285/1 The body being made of the earth, and mixte wyth other elementes, was of nature dyssoluble and mortall. **1665** Hooke *Microgr.* 105 Volatil sulphureous parts of dissoluble or combustible bodies. **1768–74** Tucker *Lt. Nat.* (1852) I. 314 Making the soul compounded, dissoluble, and perishable. **1839** J. H. Newman *Par. Serm.* VII. xii. 218 That which is material is dissoluble. **1868** Tennyson *Lucretius* 115 How then should the Gods Being atomic not be dissoluble?

†**2.** Capable of being dissolved in a liquid; soluble. *Obs.*

1641 French *Distill.* v. (1651) 165 The water..carryeth along with it some of the dissoluble parts of the mine. **1769** E. Bancroft *Guiana* 74 A yellowish gum, dissoluble in an aqueous menstruum. **1809** Pearson in *Phil. Trans.* XCIX. 339 That the whole of this oxide is not dissoluble in the acid.

3. Of a chain, knot, or anything that binds: Capable of being loosened or unfastened (see DISSOLVE 5); usually *fig.* of a 'tie', connexion, etc.: Capable of being undone (see DISSOLVE 10).

c **1600** Swinburne *Spousals* (1686) 225 The same Spousals were..dissoluble by occasion of Fornication. *a* **1639** Marmion *Antiquary* I. Dram. Wks. (1875) 205 If I stand link'd unto you, The Gordian knot were less dissoluble. **1645** Milton *Tetrach.* (1851) 170 That Mariage is indissoluble, is not Catholickly true; wee know it dissoluble for Adultery. **1803** Wordsw. *Depart. fr. Grasmere* 2 The gentlest Shade that walked Elysian plains Might sometimes covet dissoluble chains. **1878** Seeley *Stein* I. 209 The connexion of Austria with Germany was..far less easily dissoluble.

4. That may be dissolved, as an assembly or society.

1642 in Clarendon *Hist. Reb.* v. §289 Did not the people that sent them look upon them as a body but temporary, and dissoluble [ed. 1702 dissolvable] at his majesty's pleasure?

† **diˈssolubleness.** *Obs.* [f. prec. + -NESS.] The quality of being dissoluble; solubility.

1665 Hooke *Microgr.* 108 This Petrify'd substance..was differing from Wood..Fifthly, in its dissolubleness; for putting some drops of distill'd Vinegar upon the Stone, I found it..to yield..Bubbles. **1666** Boyle *Orig. Formes & Qual.* II. vii. 244 It acquir'd Dissolublenesse in *Aqua fortis*.

dissolute (ˈdɪsəl(j)uːt), *a.* (*sb.*) [ad. L. *dissolūtus* loose, disconnected, pa. pple. of *dissolvĕre* to loosen, disunite, DISSOLVE; cf. F. *dissolu*.

The appearance of the senses in Eng. does not correspond with their original development in Latin.]

†**1.** Having their connexion or union dissolved; disconnected, disjoined, disunited. *Obs.*

1541 R. Copland *Guydon's Quest. Chirurg.* C j, Nature.. wyl nat leue them [membres sparmatyf] thus dyssolute, reioyneth and knytteth them the best that she may. **1578** Banister *Hist. Man* I. 3 It were requisite, that the..bones should neither be dissolute and unioyned, nor yet altogether whole, and continuall. **1651** Hobbes *Leviath.* III. xlii. 278 The part excommunicated is no longer a Church, but a dissolute number of individuall persons. **1651** —— *Govt. & Soc.* vii. §10. 107 It is no longer a Court, or one Person, but a dissolute multitude without any supreme power.

†**2.** Relaxed, enfeebled, weak; wanting consistence or firmness of texture or temperament. *Obs.*

c **1450** tr. *De Imitatione* III. xlv, But I be holpen of þe & inwardly enformed, I am made all leuke & dissolute. **1577** Hanmer *Anc. Eccl. Hist.* (1619) 188 You loose hands, and dissolute knees, ye shall be strengthened. **1607** Topsell *Four-f. Beasts* (1658) 345 The flesh of the Alzabo..is of a slender and dissolute substance. **1684** tr. *Bonet's Merc. Compit.* IV. 120 This lax and dissolute consistency [of the blood]..makes it apt to dissolve into Serum. **1816** Coleridge *Statesm. Man.* 354 Vital warmth..relaxing the rigid, consolidating the dissolute, and giving cohesion to that which is about to sink down.

†**3.** Having the energies, attention, etc. relaxed; wanting firmness, strictness, or assiduity; loose, lax, slack, careless, negligent, remiss. *Obs.*

1382 Wyclif *Prov.* xix. 15 Slouthe sendeth in slep; and a dissolut [**1388** negligent] soule shal hungre. *c* **1430** Lydg. *Minor P.* (1840) 245 (Mätz.) Now passyng besy, now dissolut, now ydil. **1574** Whitgift *Def. Aunsw.* III. Wks. 1851 I. 330 Neither the law was then cruel, neither yet the gospel is now dissolute for the greatness of forgiveness. **1589** Hakluyt *Voy.* 188 Through meere dissolute negligence shee [a ship] perished on a sand. **1597** Hooker *Eccl. Pol.* v. lxxii. §18 To temper the minde, lest contrarie affection comming in place should make it too profuse and dissolute. **1619** W. Sclater *Exp. 1 Thess.* (1630) 459 Alas, how cold.. are our affections often? How dissolute our practice? How dull our memory?

†**4.** Unrestrained in behaviour or deportment; not subject to proper restraint; loose, wanton. (In quot. 1620, Wasteful, lavish.) *Obs.* (exc. as involved in 5).

c **1460** *Stans Puer* 20 (MS. *Harl.* 2251) in *Babees Bk.* 26 With dissolute [MS. *Lamb.* wantowne] laughters do thow non offence To-fore thy souerayn. **1526** *Pilgr. Perf.* (W. de W. 1531) 99 b, What cause hast yᵘ to be so dissolute & mery? **1616** Surfl. & Markh. *Country Farme* 117 This cattell is foolish and dissolute, easie to stray abroad hither and thither, contrarie vnto sheepe, which keepe together. **1620** Shelton *Don Quixote* II. iv, A great deal of Goods..of all which the young man remained a dissolute Lord. **1652** Needham tr. *Selden's Mare Cl.* 45 A rude sort of men, without Laws, without Government, free and dissolute [*liberum alque solutum*]. **1713** Berkeley *Guardian* No. 3 ¶ 1 It is a certain Characteristick of a dissolute and ungoverned mind to rail or speak disrespectfully of them.

b. Careless or lawless in style. Now *rare*.

1566 T. Stapleton *Ret. Untr. Jewel* Epist., Your maner of writing is..so Dissolut Loose and Negligent. **1619** W. Sclater *Exp. 1 Thess.* (1630) 559 Either hee is too profound, or too plaine..too dissolute, or too exact. **1718** Prior *Solomon* Pref., Heroic with continued rhyme..was found too dissolute and wild. **1771** H. Walpole *Vertue's Anecd. Paint.* IV. i. (R.) A loose, and, if I may use the word, a dissolute kind of painting. **1851** Ruskin *Stones Ven.* (1874) I. xvii. 184 The dissolute dulness of English Flamboyant.

5. That has thrown off the restraints of morality and virtue; lax in morals, loose-living; licentious, profligate, debauched. (Of persons, their actions, etc.) The current sense.

1513 Bradshaw *St. Werburge* I. 28 Dyssolute man folowyng sensualyte. **1548** Hall *Chron., Rich. III* (an. 2) 32 b, A woman geven to carnall affection, and dissolute livinge. **1598** Shaks. *Merry W.* III. iii. 204 Wee will yet haue more trickes with Falstaffe: his dissolute disease will scarse obey this medicine. **1671** Milton *P.R.* II. 150 Belial, the dissolutest Spirit that fell, The sensualest, and, after Asmodai, The fleshliest Incubus. **1729** Butler *Serm.* Wks. 1874 II. 15 The many untimely deaths occasioned by a dissolute course of life. **1874** Green *Short Hist.* vi. §1. 267 The nobles were as lawless and dissolute at home as they were greedy and cruel abroad.

B. *sb.* A dissolute person, a profligate. *rare.*

1608 Day *Hum. out of Br.* IV. iii, Did your euer conuerse with a more strаunger dissolute? **1824** Landor *Wks.* (1846) I. 177/2 Half the dissolutes in the parish. **1838** Southey *Poet's Pilgrim.* II. III. x. *note*, The homely but scriptural appellation..has been delicately softened down..Helen Maria Williams names her [Ch. of Rome] the Dissolute of Babylon.

¶ There are many instances of *dissolute* for *desolate* (†*dissolate*), mostly scribal or typographical errors, sometimes perh. owing to actual confusion.

1509 Hawes *Past. Pleas.* XXXVI. i, A place of dissolute darkenes. **1612** Brerewood *Lang. & Relig.* x. 83 Greece.. more dissolute then any region of Europe subject to the Turk. **1834** T. Crofton Croker *Fairy Leg. S. Irel.* 135 I got ashore, somehow or other..upon a dissolute island.

† **ˈdissolute,** *v. Obs. rare.* [f. DISSOLUTE *a.*] *trans.* To render dissolute.

1679 Prance *Addit. Narr. Pop. Plot* 29 The ready way to new-mould a Nation, is, first to dissolute and debauch it.

† **ˈdissoluted,** *ppl. a. Obs. rare.* [f. L. *dissolūt-us* (see DISSOLUTE *a.*) + -ED.] **a.** Dissolved. **b.** Loosened, unfastened, loose.

1606 G. W[oodcocke] tr. *Hist. Ivstine* 69 a, Protesting that al inueterate malice and displeasure, which hee had against him..was now dissoluted. *a* **1770** Smart *Temple of Dulness* (R.) Mad Mathesis; her feet all bare, Ungirt, untrimm'd, with dissoluted hair.

ˈdissolutely, *adv.* [f. DISSOLUTE *a.* + -LY².] In a dissolute manner.

†**1.** Loosely, slackly; carelessly, negligently; recklessly. *Obs.*

1553 Brende *Quintus Curtius* fol. 285 (R.) [They] merueiled..yᵗ he durst go so dissolutelye amonges those nacions..the barbarous people reputinge his rashenes, for an assured confidence. **1560** Becon *New Catech.* iv. *Prayer* Wks. 376 We nede not to come slackely and dissolutly, but rather diligently & earnestly vnto prayer. **1606** Holland *Sueton.* 19 Sulla..admonished the nobles oftentimes, To beware of the boy that went girded so dissolutely. **1736** Butler *Anal.* II. 314 Dissolutely to neglect their own greater Good, for the sake of a present lesser Gratification.

†**2.** Unrestrainedly, lavishly. *Obs.*

1561 T. Norton *Calvin's Inst.* I. Pref., They..thynke that God is not rightly worshypped, vnlesse altogether they be dissolutely set out with exquisite gorgeousnesse, or rather with outragious excesse. **1589** Puttenham *Eng. Poesie* III. xxiv. (Arb.) 297, I haue seene forraine Embassadours in the Queenes presence laugh so dissolutely. **1596** Shaks. *1 Hen. IV*, I. ii. 39 A Purse of Gold most resolutely snatch'd on Monday night, and most dissolutely spent on Tuesday Morning.

3. In a profligate manner; licentiously; in dissipation and debauchery.

1550 Crowley *Last Trump.* 619 To lyue..dissolutly, thou shouldste be vnto them offence. **1611** Bible *Wisd.* xii. 23 Men haue..liued dissolutely and vnrighteously. **1711** Strype *Parker* an. 1563 II. xvii, The queen's subjects lived dissolutely, vainly and luxuriously. **1859** Tennyson *Enid* 1124 Roisterers, Femininely fair and dissolutely pale.

ˈdissoluteness. [f. as prec. + -NESS.] The quality of being dissolute (in various senses).

†**1.** Remissness, negligence, carelessness. *Obs.*

1576 Fleming *Panopl. Epist.* 97 She chargeth Anthonie with dissolutenesse in duetie. *Ibid.* 356 This our dissolutenesse and negligence. **1619** W. Sclater *Exp. 1 Thess.* (1630) 558 Our dissoluteness hath beene too palpable, in praying God's blessing vpon our endeuours.

†**2.** Absence or abandonment of restraint; wantonness, excess, extravagance. *Obs.*

1580 J. Hatcher in Ellis *Orig. Lett.* Ser. I. III. 32 *note*, Which requireth rather diligence in study, then dissoluteness in plays. **1667** Marvell *Corr.* cciii. Wks. 1872–5 II. 401 The dissoluteness of grief, the prodigality of sorrow. **1690** Norris *Beatitudes* (1692) 51 All manner of odd Postures and Gestures up to the height of an Antick Dissoluteness.

3. Looseness of manners and morals; licentiousness, profligacy.

1549 Coverdale, etc. *Erasm. Par. Rev.* viii. (R.) A.. whyppe, whiche shoulde scourge and punyshe the christendome fallyng into synne and dyssolutenes. **1603** Florio *Montaigne* II. xii. (1632) 244 The dissolutenesse of the Prelates and people of those dayes. **1729** Shelvocke *Artillery* III. 170 People who would spend their lives in Debauchery and Dissoluteness. **1855** Macaulay *Hist. Eng.* IV. 456 The most dissolute cavaliers stood aghast at the dissoluteness of the emancipated precisian.

dissolution (dɪsəˈl(j)uːʃən). [In some senses a. F. *dissolution* (12th c. in Hatz.-Darm.), in others ad. L. *dissolūtiōn-em*, n. of action from *dissolvĕre* to break up, DISSOLVE.] The action of dissolving or fact of being dissolved, in various senses of the vb.

1. Separation into parts or constituent elements; reduction of any body or mass to elements or atoms; destruction of the existing condition; disintegration, decomposition.

1398 Trevisa *Barth. de P.R.* XIX. xlvii. (1495) 890 Though bytter thynges haue lesse hete than sharpe thynges of sauour yet it makith more dissolucion and departynge in the tonge. **1471** Ripley *Comp. Alch.* III. xiv. in Ashm. (1652) 142 Ells shall no kyndly Dyssolucyon be, Nor Putryfyyng shall thou none see. **1597** MORLEY *Introd. Mus.* 163 A hereditarie lepresie in a mans bodie is vncurable without the dissolution of the whole. **1667** MILTON *P.L.* XII. 459 When this worlds dissolution shall be ripe. **1736** BUTLER *Anal.* I. i. 21 The dissolution of flesh, skin and bones. **1829** SCOTT *Anne of G.* xxxiii, The vault where the long-descended Counts of Provence awaited dissolution. **1862** H. SPENCER *First Princ.* II. xii. §97 Dissolution is the absorption of motion and concomitant disintegration of matter.

b. In a theory of disease, opposed to *evolution*.
1883 HUGHLINGS JACKSON cited in *Syd. Soc. Lex.* **1894** —— *Factors of Insanities* 3, I have often urged that for the scientific study of maladies of the Nervous System, we should investigate them as Dissolutions (reversals of Evolution) of this or that part of the nervous system. *Ibid.* 8 Studying insanities as Dissolutions—as reversals of evolution—of the highest cerebral centres.

2. The reduction of a substance from the solid to the liquid form; liquefaction. Now only the melting into water or the like; formerly, also, = fusion.
1598 SHAKS. *Merry W.* III. v. 118 A man of my Kidney.. that am as subiect to heate as butter.. A man of continuall dissolution, and thaw. **1626** BACON *Sylva* §291 Metals give Orient and fine Colours in Dissolution. *a* **1661** FULLER *Worthies* (1840) I. 221 It happened in the year 1657, upon the dissolution of the great snow. **1779** J. MOORE *View Soc. Fr.* (1789) I. xxvi. 212 The rays of the sun.. occasion an unequal dissolution of the ice. **1802** ACERBI *Trav.* I. 396 Inundations.. caused by the dissolution of the ice and snow.

†**b.** Of the blood: see quots. *Obs.*
1727-51 CHAMBERS *Cycl., Dissolution of the blood* is an affection of that humour, directly opposite to coagulation. **1883** *Syd. Soc. Lex., Dissolution*.. formerly applied by the humoral physicians to a diminution of consistence of the blood.

3. The process of dissolving or condition of being dissolved in a liquid; solution. Now *rare* or *Obs.*
[**1558** see b.] **1641** FRENCH *Distill.* i. (1651) 10 *Dissolution*, is the turning of bodies into a liquor by the addition of some humidity. **1692** RAY *Dissol. World* iv. (1732) 54 The Dissolution of salt or sugar in water. **1707** *Curios. in Husb. & Gard.* 166 Aqua Fortis is the best for the Dissolution of Metals. **1838** DICKENS *Nich. Nick.* vii, Allowing for the dissolution of the sugar.

†**b.** *concr.* The result of this: the liquid with what is dissolved in it; a solution. *Obs.*
1558-68 WARDE tr. *Alexis' Secr.* 5a, To make a naturall dissolution of fine gold; and when you will take of it, take two parts of the said licor, and one part of the dissolution of ye gold. **1626** BACON *Sylva* §789 Dissolve the Iron in the Aqua Fortis: And weigh the Dissolution. **1707** *Curios. in Husb. & Gard.* 304 Dissolve it in.. Spirit of Nitre: set the dissolution to evaporate.

†**4.** Hurtful relaxation, softening, or weakening; enfeeblement. *Obs.*
c **1400** MAUNDEV. (1839) xv. 163 For the grete distresse of the hete.. for the gret dissolucioun of the Body. **1601** HOLLAND *Pliny* II. 288 The decoction.. helpeth the feeblenesse and dissolution of the sinewes. **1620** VENNER *Via Recta* viii. 166 Dolorous Gouts.. tortures and dissolutions of the limmes. **1651** JER. TAYLOR *Holy Living* ii. §1 A longing after sensual pleasures is a dissolution of the spirit of a man, and makes it loose, soft, and wandering. **1683** BURNET tr. *More's Utopia* 122 There must follow a Dissolution of Justice, the chief Sinew of Society.

5. The condition of being loose from due restraint; †excess, extravagance (*obs.*); laxity of behaviour or morals; dissolute living, dissoluteness (*arch.*).
c **1400** *Rom. Rose* 4901 It [youthe] ledith man now up now doun In mochel dissolucioun. **1482** *Monk of Evesham* (Arb.) 88 Them whiche wastyn the godys of the holy chyrche wherby they were made ryche in dyssolucyon of clothyng, in voluptuous metys and pompys of the world. **1526** *Pilgr. Perf.* (W. de W. 1531) 85b, Flye dissolucyon & wantonnesse. **1553** BECON *Reliques of Rome* (1563) 162* They for their vnthankefulnesse & dissolution of lyfe, were depriued of the holy communion. **1647** *Power of Keys* Pref. 2 Wickednesse and dissolution of manners was to be lookt on as the only heresy. **1651** J. TAYLOR *Holy Living* ii. §1 These tamed his youthful aptnesses to dissolution. **1707** NORRIS *Treat. Humility* vi. 271 Nothing more betrays.. dissolution of thought.. than a vain foppish dress. **1866** *Cornh. Mag.* Nov. 634 After the general peace of 1814, dissolution began to decrease in high places.

†**b.** with *pl.* An instance of this; a dissolute act or practice; an extravagance or excess. *Obs.*
c **1430** LYDG. *Bochas* (1558) II. xv. 1 Fleshly lustes and dissolutions. **1483** CAXTON *Gold. Leg.* 150b/1 Lerne to be stylle & teschewe all dissolucions. **1490** —— *Eneydos* vi. 23 He sheweth the dyssolucyons and peruerse condycyons that ben in the sexe femynyne. **1579** TOMSON *Calvin's Serm. Tim.* 130/2 That.. all dissolutions, vile and wicked actes be suppressed. **1651-3** JER. TAYLOR *Serm. for Year, Of Godly Fear* III. (1678) 61 Restraint of gaieties and dissolutions.

6. The relaxation or undoing of any tie, bond, or binding power; the dissolving of a connexion, union, etc. (Cf. DISSOLVE 10, 11.)
c **1534** tr. *Pol. Verg. Hist.* (Camden, No. 29) 5 Upon dissolution of that treatie. **1548** HALL *Chron., Edw. IV.* (an. 4) 195b, The cause of dissolucion of their amitie and league. **1651** J. TAYLOR *Holy Living* ii. §2 The loosing the bands of the tongue, and the very first dissolution of its duty is one degree of intemperance. **1840** *Penny Cycl.* XVII. 294/2 A marriage of a feme-sole trader is also a dissolution of a partnership at will. **1856** FROUDE *Hist. Eng.* (1858) I. ii. 120 Even if the marriage.. had never been questioned, he might justly have desired the dissolution of it.

7. The breaking up, dismissal, or dispersion of an assembly or association; the termination of the existence of a constituted body of persons (e.g. of the monasteries, and now esp. of Parliament).
1535 *Act 27 Hen. VIII*, c. 26. §26 Immediately vpon the prorogacion or dissolucion of this present parliament. **1651** HOBBES *Leviath.* II. xxii. 116 The Assembly may be punished.. by dissolution, or forfeiture of their Letters. **1659** B. HARRIS *Parival's Iron Age* 289 Some moneths before the dissolution of the Parliament. **1730** *Magna Brit.* V. 762/1 Herdwick Priors.. continued in the Monks Hands till the Dissolution. **1765** BLACKSTONE *Comm.* I. ii. 180 A dissolution is the civil death of the parliament. **1831** SIR J. SINCLAIR *Corr.* II. 373 Since the dissolution of the Board of Agriculture. **1862** LD. BROUGHAM *Brit. Const.* xiii. 184 The dissolution of the monasteries in Henry VIII's reign. **1874** GREEN *Short Hist.* viii. §2. 462 The conversion of the King was followed by a quiet dissolution of the Huguenot party.

8. Termination of life; death, decease.
Variously understood as 'departure or release from life', 'separation of the soul from the body', and 'disintegration of the body'. See DISSOLVE 6.
1522 MORE *De quat. Noviss.* Wks. 77 The disolucion and seueraunce of the soule fro the body. **1568** BIBLE (Bishops') *2 Tim.* iv. 6 The time of my dissolution [Gr. ἀναλύσεως, L. *resolutionis*; earlier Eng. vv., from Wycl. 1388 departing] is at hande. **1596-7** S. FINCHE in Ducarel *Hist. Croydon* App. (1783) 152 Thanks to Almightie God for Mr. Comptroller's dissolucion from the bondage of his corrupte bodie. **1641** HINDE *J. Bruen* lx. 201 Death is but a passage unto life, a dissolution of soule and body for a season. **1658** SIR T. BROWNE *Hydriot.* i. 2 Men have been most phantastical in the singular contrivances of their corporall dissolution. **1712** STEELE *Spect.* No. 263 ¶1 He waits the Day of his Dissolution with a Resignation mixed with Delight. **1750** JOHNSON *Rambler* No. 29 ¶12 It is absurd to be afraid of the natural dissolution of the body. **1827** J. W. CROKER 6 Aug. in *Croker Papers* (1884), His breathing is difficult, and.. there are all the symptoms of approaching dissolution. **1856** SIR B. BRODIE *Psychol. Inq.* I. iv. 131 Some die retaining all their faculties, and quite aware that their dissolution is at hand.

9. The action of bringing or condition of being brought to an end; undoing, termination, destruction, ruin; breaking up, disintegration, disorganization (of a connected system, etc.).
1528 GARDINER in Pocock *Rec. Ref.* I. l. 102 That realm were like to come to dissolution. *a* **1625** FLETCHER *Nice Valour* III. ii, I doubt not.. To see a dissolution of all bloodshed. **1677** HALE *Prim. Orig. Man.* II. x. 230 Down to the last Dissolution of their City under Titus. **1728** YOUNG *Love Fame* VI. (1757) 154 Such dissolution through the whole I find, 'Tis not a world, but chaos of mankind. **1855** MILMAN *Lat. Chr.* IX. iii. (1864) V. 241 He had but to wait the dissolution of Otho's power; it crumbled away of itself. **1883** S. F. SMITH *How Ch. Eng. washed her face* 21 The same dissolution of morals and irreligious spirit had existed.

†**b.** *Mus.* (See quot.) *Obs.*
1764 CROKER, etc. *Dict. Arts & Sc., Dissolution*, in music, is when a sound in the enharmonic genus is lowered three dieses; for thereby that genus is dissolved, and the music.. is chromatic.

†**10.** Solution, resolution (of a question, etc.). *Obs. rare.*
1549 *Latimer's 5th Serm. bef Edw. VI*, (Arb.) 132 *margin*, M. Latimer returneth to hys former question and to the dissolucion of the same.

disso'lutional, *a.* [f. prec. + -AL^1.] Of or pertaining to dissolution.
1889 J. M. ROBERTSON *Ess. towards Crit. Meth.* 4 Longinus.. has the note of that long dissolutional epoch. **1895** *Pall Mall G.* 6 July 2/2 The Factory Bill.. has passed in dissolutional and dissolute haste, and it can be amended, if necessary, at consolidating leisure.

disso'lutionism, [f. as prec. + -ISM.] The doctrine or principles of dissolutionists.
1894 SWINBURNE *Studies in Prose & Poetry* 102 Disunionism, dissolutionism, or communalism.

disso'lutionist. [f. as prec. + -IST.] One who advocates or aims at dissolution. Also *attrib.*
1882 *Pall Mall G.* 23 Sept. 1 The dissolutionist campaign of M. Gambetta's friends. **1882** *Fraser's Mag.* XXVI. 131 This is the reactionary, and in some degree dissolutionist, party in the Union.

†**disso'lutious**, *a. Obs. rare.* Inclined to dissoluteness.
1560 *Sheph. Kal.* vii. *Tree of Vices, Sloth* xiii, To draw and goe to such as be dissolutious Or that they doe and make dissolute.

dissolutive ('dɪsəl(j)uːtɪv), *a.* Now *rare.* [f. L. *dissolūt-* ppl. stem + -IVE: prob. immed. ad. med.L. *dissolūtīv-us* or F. *dissolutif.*]
1. Having the property of dissolving; producing dissolution or disintegration; dissolvent.
c **1400** *Lanfranc's Cirurg.* 210 To empostyms of blood þou mi3t do medicyns repercussifs & dissolutiuis sotilly. **1527** ANDREW *Brunswyke's Distyll. Waters* Rv, It hath vertue attractyfe and dyssolutyfe. **1662** J. CHANDLER *Van Helmont's Oriat.* 76 Air wants in it self a dissolutive principle of it self. *a* **1691** BOYLE *Wks.* V. 500 (R.) The air might promote the dissolutive action of the menstruum.

2. Pertaining to, or of the nature of, dissolution or disintegration.
1886 MYERS *Phantasms of Living* Introd. 43 We have induced [by hypnotism] a change of personality which is not per se either evolutive or dissolutive.

†**dissolutory**, *a. Obs. rare.* [f. as prec. + -ORY.] = prec. 1.
1757 tr. *Henckel's Pyritol.* 357 Fermentative, intestine, dissolutory motion.

di'ssolvable, *a.* Also -ible. [f. DISSOLVE *v.* + -ABLE: substituted (in part) for DISSOLUBLE from L. type *dissolūbilis.*] Capable of being dissolved; dissoluble.
1. Capable of being separated or reduced into its formative elements; decomposable.
1541 R. COPLAND *Guydon's Quest. Chirurg.*, For the substaunce seldom dyssoluable lyghtly it [the liver] oughte to haue medycyne somwhat styptyke. **1661** E. BORROUGHS *Plea to King conc. Quakers* Ded. 1 You are but men.. and your substance but dissolvable clay. **1677** HALE *Prim. Orig. Man.* I. iii. 86 Man that is even upon the intrinsick constitution of his nature dissolvible. *Ibid.* I. v. 112 A composition intrinsecally dissolvable. **1861** L. L. NOBLE *Icebergs* 114 It [an iceberg] is as dissolvable as the clouds from which it originally fell.

2. Capable of being liquefied or melted; fusible; soluble. ? *Obs.*
1653 H. MORE *Antid. Ath.* I. xi. (1712) 35 The Brains generally are easily dissolvable into a watery Consistence. **1668** WILKINS *Real Char.* 169 Dissolvable, by Water, or by Fire. **1711** STEELE *Spect.* No. 95 ¶3 Children, when crossed.. how dissolvable they are into Tears. **1733** CHEYNE *Eng. Malady* I. v. §3 (1734) 38 Salts.. hard, and dissolvible only by Water. **1794** SULLIVAN *View Nat.* I. 461 All the metals, excepting platina and gold, are dissolvable by aqua fortis.

3. Of a connexion, union, society, etc.: Capable of being undone or having its existence put an end to; terminable, destructible.
1681-6 J. SCOTT *Chr. Life* (1747) III. 392 The Obligations of divine Commands are dissolvable only by divine Countermands. **1702** [see DISSOLUBLE 4]. **1861** LOWELL *E Pluribus Unum* Prose Wks. 1890 V. 63 We are not a mere partnership, dissolvable.. by mutual consent.. but a nation.
Hence **dissolva'bility** (*-ibility* in Richardson 1836), **di'ssolvableness** (in Craig 1847).

dissolvant, obs. var. of DISSOLVENT.

†**di'ssolvative**, *a. Obs. rare.* [f. next + -ATIVE.]
a. Having the property of dissolving, dissolutive. **b.** That tends to dissolve readily.
1577 FRAMPTON *Joyful News* I. (1596) 8 Balsamo.. is dissoluatiue, and so it doeth consume.. swellinges. **1580** —— *Monardes Med. against Venom* 118 The use of good Meates easie and dissolvative.

dissolve (dɪ'zɒlv), *v.* Also 4-6 **dyssolve**, 5-6 **desolve**. [ad. L. *dissolv-ĕre* to loosen asunder, disunite, dissolve, f. DIS- 1 + *solvĕre* to loosen, SOLVE.] **I.** Transitive senses.
1. To loosen or put asunder the parts of; to reduce to its formative elements; to destroy the physical integrity; to disintegrate, decompose. (Now *rare* or *Obs.* exc. as associated with other senses.)
1382 WYCLIF *2 Cor.* v. 1 If oure erthely hous of this dwellyng be dissolued.. we han a bildyng of God, an hous not maad by hondis, euerlastinge. *c* **1400** *Three Kings Cologne* 123 þe bodyes of þes III kyngis wexed corrupt and were dissolued & turned in to powdre. **1500-20** DUNBAR *Poems* (Sc. T. S.) lxxiii. 244 Now cled in gold, dissoluit now in ass (= ashes). **1611** CORYAT *Crudities* 419 If it were a strong bridge, they could not dissolue it with so great expedition. **1722** WOLLASTON *Relig. Nat.* ix. §8. 195 Whether that soul.. can think at all when the body is quite dissolved. **1775** PRIESTLEY *Air* I. 266 Vegetable and animal substances dissolved by putrefaction.. emit phlogiston. **1841-4** EMERSON *Ess., Intellect* Wks. (Bohn) I. 134 Water dissolves wood, and iron, and salt.
fig. **1589** PUTTENHAM *Eng. Poesie* II. xiv. [xv.] (Arb.) 140 Make your choise of very few words dactilique, or.. dissolue and breake them into other feete. **1642** FULLER *Holy & Prof. St.* III. xxiv. 221 We may for a while dissolve our continued discourse into a dialogue.

2. To melt or reduce into a liquid condition.
a. To melt by heat; to fuse. Now *rare* or *Obs.*
1382 WYCLIF *2 Pet.* iii. 10 Elementes shulen be dissolued bi hete. *c* **1400** *Lanfranc's Cirurg.* 342 þe gummys schulen be.. dissolued wiþ fier. **1530** PALSGR. 522/1, I dissolve, as heate dothe lycour, whan it is frosen. **1600** HAKLUYT *Voy.* (1810) III. 48 Before the Sunne hath warmed the ayre, and dissolved the yce. **1793** SMEATON *Edystone L.* §274 The metal at each end having a considerable heat, it was found practicable to dissolve both the ends of the former masses.

b. To liquefy by contact with or immersion in a liquid; to diffuse the molecules of (a solid or gas) *in* a liquid so that they are indistinguishable from it; to melt (*in* something), make a SOLUTION of. (Predicated of a personal agent, or of the liquid.)
dissolve away, out: to remove or extract (from a compound mass) by dissolving.
[*c* **1380** WYCLIF *Sel. Wks.* III. 68 Men axen comounly, whi salt is dissolved þus, but cristal and oþere stoones ben not loosid as oþir salt.] **1460-70** *Bk. Quintessence* 9 Putte þanne yn þe watir corosyue Sal armoniac and þat watir wiþoute doute wol dissolue gold into watir. **1563** T. GALE *Antid.* II. 62 The Hammoniacum dissolued in Vineger. **1677** GREW *Solution of Salts* in *Anat. Plants, &c.* vii. (1682) 299 Two Ounces of Water will dissolve three Ounces of Loaf-Sugar. **1791** HAMILTON *Berthollet's Dyeing* I. I. I. i. 11 The iron may be dissolved in the muriatic acid. **1854** J. SCOFFERN in *Orr's Circ. Sc.* Chem. 24 Various salts.. may be dissolved out by lixiviation. **1873** A. W. WILLIAMSON *Chem. Students* (ed. 3) xiv. §87 At 15° C. water dissolves about twice its volume of chlorine gas. **1875** DAWSON *Dawn of Life* iv. 83 By dissolving away their shells with acid.

3. In various *fig.* applications of senses 1 and 2: *esp.* To melt or soften the heart or feelings of; to cause to 'melt' into tears, grief, etc.; to relax or enervate with pleasure, luxury, etc.; to immerse or absorb in some engrossing occupation. Chiefly in passive. (Now *rare* exc. in phr. ***dissolved in tears***, or in direct figures from sense 2 b.)

1509 HAWES *Past. Pleas.* xxxiv. xix, Her hardy harte she gan for to dissolve. 1632 MILTON *Penseroso* 165 In service high, and anthems clear, As may..Dissolve me into ecstasies. 1679 PENN *Addr. Prot.* I. 38 Dissolv'd in Pleasures, he worshipp'd no other God. 1707 WATTS *Hymn, 'Alas! and did my Saviour bleed?'* v, Dissolve my Heart in Thankfulness, And melt my Eyes to Tears. 1791 D'ISRAELI *Cur. Lit., Libraries,* Henry Rantzall..whose days were dissolved in the pleasures of reading. 1800 MRS. HERVEY *Mourtray Fam.* IV. 183 Mrs. Lenmer was dissolved in tears the whole evening. 1843 CARLYLE *Past. & Pr.* III. iii. (1872) 130 Action hangs, as it were, dissolved in Speech.

†4. To relax, weaken, enfeeble, in body or bodily strength. *Obs.*

c1400 *Lanfranc's Cirurg.* 16 To myche slepinge..feblip his vertewes..To myche wakynge dissolfip & consumep hys spirites. c1400 MAUNDEV. (Roxb.) xviii. 81 þe grete violence of hete, þat dissoluez þaire bodys. c1534 tr. *Pol. Verg. Hist.* (Camden, No. 29) 180 That sorceres Elyzabeth the quene..with her witchcraft hath so enchantyd me that by thanoyance thereof I am dissolvyd. 1563 *Homilies* II. *Agst. Gluttony,* Oft commeth sodaine death..by banquetyng sometyme the members are dyssolued.

5. To loosen, unfasten, detach, release, set free. (*lit.* and *fig.*) *arch.*

c1420 *Pallad. on Husb.* IV. 29 Yit must it [the vine-stalk] be dissolved ever amonge Oute of this bonde, lest it..Be letted to encrece. 1548 *Act 2-3 Edw. VI,* c. 23. §1 The partie who disired to be dissolved from the marriage. 1560 ROLLAND *Crt. Venus* IV. 458 Venus gart ane..Nimphe..Dissolue his handis quhilks..fast bundin war. 1606 G. W[OODCOCKE] tr. *Hist. Ivstine* 87 b, Occasion..to pull and dissolue their neckes out of the yoke. c1611 CHAPMAN *Iliad* VIII. 44 There his horse he check'd, Dissolved them from his chariot. 1727-46 THOMSON *Summer* 1310 As the soft touch dissolved the virgin zone. 1817 SHELLEY *Rev. Islam* I. xiii. 8 Dissolve in sudden shock those linked rings.

†6. To release from life; to cause the dissolution or death of; usually in *pass.* to die, depart. *Obs.*

Used chiefly with reference to *Phil.* i. 23, where the Vulgate has the passive *dissolvī* for the original active ἀναλῦσαι (here = 'depart'; also *trans.* = 'dissolve'). Various notions were app. attached to the expression by those who used it, some associating it with the dissolution of the bodily framework (cf. quots. 1382, 1400, 1722 in 1); some thinking of the dissolution of the union between soul and body, etc.

c1374 CHAUCER *Boeth.* I. pr. iii, Ofte a swifte houre dissoluep þe same man, þat is to seyne whan þe soule departip fro þe body. 1382 WYCLIF *Phil.* i. 23 Hauyng desyr for to be dissolued [*gloss,* or departid the soule fro body]. c1450 tr. *De Imitatione* I. xii, He desirip deþe, þat he miȝt be dissolued & be wip crist. 1565 JEWEL *Def. Apol.* (1611) 294 The Saints, which are dissolued, & reigne with Christ. a1592 H. SMITH *Serm. on Phil.* i. 23, Good cause had Paul to desire to be with Christ: yet he will not dissolve himself, but desireth to be dissolved. 1654 WHITLOCK *Zootomia* 566 Paul phraseth it, a Wish equall to the Gold searching Chymists endeavours, I desire to be dissolved, melted down. a1670 HACKET *Abp. Williams* II. (1692) 227 A squinancy..and a shortness of breath..which dissolved him in the space of twelve hours. 1736 WESLEY *Wks.* (1872) I. 37 O when shall I wish to be dissolved?

7. a. To cause to vanish or disappear from existence; to bring to nought, undo, destroy, consume.

c1374 CHAUCER *Boeth.* I. pr. iii. 10 þe clowdes of sorowe dissolued and don awey, I..receyuede mynde to knowe þe face of my fyciscien. 1548 HALL *Chron., Hen. VI* (an. 3) 88 b, To desolve the siege and raise the assault. 1563 W. FULKE *Meteors* (1640) 35 A great Circle about the Moone, betokeneth great cold..But if it vanish away and bee dissolved altogether, it is a signe of fayre weather. 1632 LITHGOW *Trav.* III. 120 Occasion..whereby the peace and happinesse of Thebes might be dissolved. 1769 SIR W. JONES *Palace of Fort.* Poems (1777) 18 Each gay phantom was dissolv'd in air. 1877 TYNDALL in *Daily News* 2 Oct. 2/5 That promise is a dream dissolved by the experience of eighteen centuries.

b. *Cinemat.* and *Television.* To cause (a picture) to become faint or fade away (*into* another); similarly *intr.* (cf. 13). Cf. DISSOLVING *ppl. a.* b. Hence as *sb.*, the act or process of dissolving a picture; a dissolving scene in a cinema film; a piece of apparatus with the aid of which this is produced.

[1845 *Poster for Assembly Rooms, Nottingham,* Dissolving Views & the Chromotrope.] 1912 F. H. RICHARDSON *Motion Picture Handbk.* (ed. 2) 378 A dissolving effect with one lens is an impossibility. 1915 *Ibid.* (ed. 3) 606 Dissolving moving picture. *Ibid.,* Many operators who run two machines dissolve one reel into the next. 1918 H. CROY *How Motion Pictures are Made* vii. 176 The second means of accomplishing a fade picture is by means of the dissolving shutter... The dissolving shutter is a mechanical device which, while the shutter is revolving, is closed by a blade slowly passing over the opening until it is entirely closed. *Ibid.* 178 The so-called 'dissolve', by which the figures of the scene gradually disappear while those of a succeeding scene slowly take their place. 1954 *Encounter* Aug. 52/1 The fade and the dissolve as means of visual transition from scene to scene. 1959 HALAS & MANVELL *Technique Film Animation* xix. 171 It [*sc.* the work book] must also show how each shot or sequence is to be punctuated, whether by a straight cut, a fade or a dissolve. 1960 N. KNEALE *Quatermass & Pit* I. 14 Dissolve..to a brass name-plate. *Ibid.* III. 86 Slow Dissolve..to the Rocket Group laboratory. 1970 *New Yorker* 31 Oct. 132/3 Their sexual bouts lead to quick dissolves.

†8. *Med.* To disperse (morbid humours), reduce (swellings), remove or assuage (pains or ailments). (Also *absol.*) *Obs.*

(Employed variously and vaguely according to context.)

c1400 *Lanfranc's Cirurg.* 136 Riȝt as þe mater of þe frenesie..bi emplastris wiþoutforþ I-leie is dissolued. *Ibid.* 238 Anoþer electuarie þat dissoluiþ akynge in ioyntis. 1577 FRAMPTON *Joyful Newes* I. (1596) 6 In griefes of swellinges..it [oil] taketh them away and dooth dissolue them. 1582 HESTER *Secr. Phiorav.* I. xxiii. 26 You must dissolue the Catarre first, and then helpe the Feuer. 1610 MARKHAM *Masterp.* II. clxxiii, It cleanseth and dissolueth, and also comforteth. 1657 W. COLES *Adam in Eden* liv, It is available in all cold Diseases..dissolving wind very powerfully.

9. a. To break up, dismiss, disperse (an assembly or collective body); to put an end to the association or connexion of; to terminate the existence of (a constituted body or association, e.g. of the monasteries, and now esp. of Parliament).

1494 FABYAN *Chron.* v. cxxxii. 116 When y[e] Kyng had orderyd his matiers..he dissoluyd this counceyll. 1548 HALL *Chron., Hen. VI* (an. 28) 159 b, To be perswaded to dissolve his armye. *Ibid.* (an. 39) 182 The kyng dissolved his Parliament. 1586 J. HOOKER *Girald. Irel.* in *Holinshed* II. 46/2 A religious house of Greie friers..since dissolued in king Henrie the eights time. 1758 JOHNSON *Idler* No. 26 ¶5 Our school was now dissolved. 1842 TENNYSON *Morte d'Arth.* 234 But now the whole Round Table is dissolved. 1863 H. COX *Instit.* I. vi. 33 Parliament shall not be dissolved on the death of the sovereign.

b. *ellipt.* = *dissolve parliament.*

1868 M. E. G. DUFF *Pol. Surv.* 16 He immediately dissolved and succeeded in throwing out most of the leading supporters of his predecessor.

10. a. To undo (a tie, bond, knot); to put an end to, bring to an end (a relation of union, connexion, or association, etc.).

c1380 WYCLIF *Sel. Wks.* III. 163 Ffor prestis ben weddid wiþ God by holdyng of his lawe, and þis bond is dissolvyd both in lif and offis. 1548 HALL *Chron., Hen. VI* (an. 2) 86 The..amitie betwene the Frenche and Scottishe nacions should be shortly broken and dissolved. 1558 BP. WATSON *Sev. Sacram.* xxvii. 173 The Knot of Matrimonie..can not be broken and dissolued. 1638 SIR T. HERBERT *Trav.* (ed. 2) 95 An excellent sympathy and union, till Ganganna dissolv'd it, having beene till then betwixt 'em. 1767 BLACKSTONE *Comm.* II. 187 It is advantageous for the joint-tenants to dissolve the jointure. 1776 GIBBON *Decl. & F.* I. xvi. 384 They dissolved the sacred ties of custom and education. 1841 LANE *Arab. Nts.* I. 63 When..the marriage is dissolved. 1853 C. BRONTE *Villette* iii. (1876) 18 The league..thus struck up was not hastily dissolved. a1897 *Mod.* They have dissolved partnership, and started each on his own account.

†b. To part, sunder (things united). *Obs.*

1598 SHAKS. *Merry W.* v. v. 237 She and I (long since contracted) Are now so sure that nothing can dissolue vs. 1608-11 BP. HALL *Medit. & Vowes* II. §49 It unites one Christian soule to another so firmely, that no outward occurrences..can dissolve them.

11. a. To undo (something formally ordained or established); to destroy the binding power, authority, force, or influence of; to annul, abrogate.

1526 *Pilgr. Perf.* (W. de W. 1531) 15 It dissolueth and loseth all vowes. 1671 MILTON *Samson* 1149 To frustrate and dissolve these magic spells. 1734 tr. *Rollin's Anc. Hist.* (1827) VIII. XIX. viii. 259 To dissolve and annul all we have enacted. 1805 SCOTT *Last Minstr.* III. xiii, The running stream dissolved the spell, And his own elvish shape he took. 1891 *Law Times* XC. 403/1 The Court of Appeal..dissolved an injunction granted by Justice Kekewich.

†b. To do away with as false or erroneous; to refute, confute. *Obs.*

1529 MORE *Dyaloge* 67 b/1 Whych obieccyon the author answereth and dyssolueth. 1551 T. WILSON *Logike* (1567) 84 b, The fault that is in the forme..maie be dissolued, when we shewe that the conclusion, is not well proued by the former proposicions. a1555 PHILPOT *Exam. & Writ.* (Parker Soc.) 414 All that these men are wont to allege..be all ready dissolved and..confuted. 1842 ABP. THOMSON *Laws Th.* §127 (1860) 271 We may dissolve (λύειν) the argument by showing its unfitness for proof because of some formal defect.

†c. To deny or reject the authority of. [repr. L. *solvere* of the Vulgate in *1 John* iv. 3.] *Obs.*

1382 WYCLIF *1 John* iv. 3 Ech spirit that dissolueth [*gloss,* or fordoith] Jhesu is not of God [so 1582 *Rhem.*; *Vulg.* qui solvit, *after a Gr. v.r.* ὃ λύει]. 1645 MILTON *Tetrach.* Matt. xix. 3 Our Lord..intended not to dissolve Moses.

12. To solve, resolve, explain (a question, doubt, etc.). *arch.*

1549 LATIMER *5th Serm. bef. Edw. VI,* (Arb.) 132 I wyll nowe..retourne to my question and dissolue it. 1607 TOPSELL *Four-f. Beasts* (1658) 14 All..that could not dissolve that riddle she presently slew. 1611 BIBLE *Dan* v. 16, I haue heard of thee, that thou canst make interpretations, and dissolue doubts. 1842 TENNYSON *Two Voices* 170 Thou hadst not between death and birth Dissolved the riddle of the earth.

II. Intransitive senses.

13. To lose its integrity or consolidation; to become disintegrated; to vanish or disappear gradually, come to an end. Now usually taken as *fig.* from sense 14, to melt away.

c1420 *Pallad. on Husb.* XI. 496 A multitude of reysons puld they take, And myghtely with yerdes first hem bete Until this with the grapes so desolve. 1481 CAXTON *Myrr.* III. vii. 142 All þ[e] world..shal desolue & faylle. 1526 *Pilgr. Perf.* (W. de. W. 1531) 254 His senewes and veynes brast, and the hole frame of the ioyntes of his body dissolued and losed. 1610 SHAKS. *Temp.* IV. i. 154 The great Globe it selfe, Yea, all which it inherit, shall dissolue, And like this insubstantiall Pageant faded Leaue not a racke behinde. 1660 F. BROOKE tr. *Le Blanc's Trav.* 265 It dissolved to nothing like a mist. 1791 D'ISRAELI *Cur. Lit., Lit. Jrnls.,* The unsuccessful author..dissolved away in his own weakness. 1820 SHELLEY *Ode to Liberty* xix, As summer clouds dissolve, unburthened of their rain. 1886 A. WINCHELL *Walks & Talks Geol. Field* 163 The illusion dissolves.

14. To become liquefied, to melt: **a.** with heat. Now *rare* or *Obs.*

c1450 *St. Cuthbert* (Surtees) 4480 þe paynyms pride it sall expire, And dissolue as wax at fyre. 1592 SHAKS. *Ven. & Ad.* 565 What wax so frozen but dissolves with tempering? 1697 DRYDEN *Virg. Georg.* I. 66 While Mountain Snows dissolve against the Sun. 1729 T. COOKE *Tales, Proposals, &c.* 40 The Wreck of Nature, the prodigious Day, When adamantine Rocks dissolv'd away. 1802-3 tr. *Pallas' Trav.* (1812) I. 9 The deep snow in the streets began to dissolve.

b. To become liquefied by contact with or immersion in a liquid; to melt; to become diffused in a liquid, forming a solution.

1638 SIR T. HERBERT *Trav.* (ed. 2) 297 The fruit [banana] put into your mouth, dissolves and yeelds a most incomparable relish. 1677 GREW *Solution of Salts* in *Anat. Plants* vii. (1682) 299 The Crystals of Tartar..will scarce at all dissolve in Water. 1718 QUINCY *Compl. Disp.* I. vi. 25 We find Sugar will dissolve in the strongest Solution of Common Salt that can be made. 1873 A. W. WILLIAMSON *Chem. for Students* (ed. 3) xi. §67 Olefiant gas dissolves considerably in water.

15. In various *fig.* applications of prec. senses: To become faint, faint away; to become softened in feeling, to 'melt' (into tears, etc.); to become resolved *into* something else, like a solid becoming liquid.

1605 SHAKS. *Lear* v. iii. 203, I am almost ready to dissolue, Hearing of this. 1672 CAVE *Prim. Chr.* III. ii. (1673) 250 He dissolved into tears. a1719 ADDISON tr. *Ovid* Wks. 1758 I. 177 The God dissolves in pity at her death. 1761 HUME *Hist. Eng.* III. lix. 279 He dissolved into a flood of tears. 1858 CARLYLE *Fredk. Gt.* (1865) II. v. v. 99 Full of alarm dissolving into joy.

16. Of an assembly or collective body: To break up into its individual constituents; to disperse; to lose its aggregate or corporate character.

1513 MORE in Grafton *Chron.* (1568) II. 795 The company dissolved and departed. 1548 PATTEN *Exped. Scotl.* in Arb. *Garner* III. 149 Our camp should, this day, dissolve. 1667 MILTON *P.L.* II. 506 The Stygian council thus dissolved. 1766 W. GORDON *Gen. Counting-ho.* 30 When a fixed company dissolves. 1847 TENNYSON *Princess* IV. 502 She, ending, waved her hands: thereat the crowd Muttering, dissolved.

17. To lose its binding force or influence.

1611 SHAKS. *Temp.* v. i. 64 The charme dissolues apace. c1750 SHENSTONE *Elegies* xi. 3 The charm dissolves; the aerial music's past.

dissolved (dɪˈzɒlvd), *ppl. a.* [f. prec. + -ED[1].]

1. Reduced to its elements, broken up, disintegrated, destroyed, annulled, dispersed, put an end to, etc.: see the verb.

1541 R. COPLAND *Guydon's Quest. Chirurg.* C j, Nature..engendreth a flesshe for to holde y[e] dissolued parties. 1586 A. DAY *Eng. Secretary* I. (1625) 52 The dissolued purpose of your good intention. 1634-5 BRERETON *Trav.* (Chetham Soc.) 157 We took up our lodging at Tinterden, a dissolved Abbey. 1659 PEARSON *Creed* (1839) 366 The temple of Christ's body was dissolved here, by the separation of his soul..the raising of the dissolved temple was the quickening of the body. a1831 A. KNOX *Rem.* (1844) I. 62 There could be no thought of re-submitting to the long dissolved chains. 1871 FREEMAN *Norm. Conq.* (1876) IV. xvii. 37 The lands of a dissolved monastery.

2. Melted; held in solution by a liquid: see DISSOLVE 2.

1707 *Curios. in Husb. & Gard.* 333 These dissolv'd Salts. 1839 G. BIRD *Nat. Phil.* 237 When various electrolytes are submitted in a dissolved, or fused state, to the action of the current from the voltaic battery. 1878 HUXLEY *Physiogr.* 116 All natural water..contains such dissolved salts.

†di'ssolveless, *a. Obs. rare.* [f. DISSOLVE + -LESS: cf. *quenchless, resistless,* etc.] That cannot be dissolved; indissoluble.

1721 CIBBER *Perolla* II, To cut this Gordian of dissolveless Love. —— *Lady's last Stake* Prol., Those dissolveless fetters.

dissolvent (dɪˈzɒlvənt), *a.* and *sb.* [ad. L. *dissolvent-em,* pr. pple. of *dissolvěre* to DISSOLVE. Cf. F. *dissolvant.*]

A. *adj.* Having the power to dissolve, disintegrate, liquefy, etc.; solvent. ? *Obs.*

1665 HOOKE *Microgr.* 104 Salt-peter..abounds more with those Dissolvent particles, and therefore..a small quantity of it will dissolve a great. 1691 RAY *Creation* (1714) 27 Being mingled with some dissolvent juices. 1777 MACBRIDE in *Phil. Trans.* LXVIII. 119 *note,* On the dissolvent Power of Quicksilver.

fig. 1840 MILL *Diss. & Disc., Enfranch. Women* (1859) II. 436 The companionship of women..often exercises a dissolvent influence on high faculties and aspirations in men. a1876 M. COLLINS in *Pen Sketches* I. 212 Neither was constructive like Shakespeare, nor dissolvent, like Heine.

B. *sb.* One who or that which dissolves.

1. *spec.* A substance having the power to dissolve or disintegrate other substances; a solvent, a menstruum; †formerly, in *Med.,* a substance having the power of 'dissolving' morbid concretions, etc. (see DISSOLVE 8). (Also 7–8 **dissolvant** as in F.)

1646 SIR T. BROWNE *Pseud. Ep.* II. iii. 68 If the menstruum or dissolvent be evaporated to a consistence. **1658** R. WHITE tr. *Digby's Powd. Symp.* (1660) 87 There is no dissolvant in the world that can well calcine..gold, but quicksilver. **1691** RAY *Creation* I. (1704) 115 Fire—the only Catholic Dissolvent. **1718** QUINCY *Compl. Disp.* 234 Several ..have flatter'd themselves, with obtaining..a universal Dissolvent. **1821** CRAIG *Lect. Drawing* vii. 399 The alkali.. being by nature a dissolvent of the ground.

2. *gen.* and *fig.*

1835 F. MAHONEY in *Fraser's Mag.* XI. 454 Wine is the great dissolvent of distrust. **1865** M. ARNOLD *Ess. Crit.* v. 186 Dissolvents of the old European system of dominant ideas and facts we must all be. **1874** MOTLEY *Barneveld* II. xv. 186 The only dissolvent of this Union was the intention to perpetuate slavery.

dissolver (dɪˈzɒlvə(r)). [f. DISSOLVE + -ER[1].] One who or that which dissolves.

1. One who or that which breaks up, disintegrates, destroys, puts an end to, etc.: see the verb.

1611 BIBLE *Dan.* v. 12 Dissoluing of doubts [*marg.* of a dissoluer]. **1641** MILTON *Prel. Episc.* (1851) 82 These men were the dissolvers of Episcopacie. *a* **1735** ARBUTHNOT (J.), Fire, and the more subtle dissolver, putrefaction. **1883** SIR M. WILLIAMS *Relig. Th. in Ind.* iii. 44 Rudra-Siva, the Dissolver and Reproducer.

2. A substance that dissolves another substance; a solvent: see DISSOLVE 2.

1651 BIGGS *New Disp.* ⁋ 80 Such dissolvers, as are wont to be made of Aqua fortis and Regis. *a* **1788** WESLEY *Serm.* lviii. Wks. 1811 IX. 114 It is the universal menstruum, the dissolver of all things under the Sun.

3. a. An apparatus for dissolving some substance. **b.** A contrivance for producing dissolving views: see DISSOLVING *ppl. a.* b. **c.** *Cinemat.* and *Television* An apparatus for dissolving a picture; also *attrib.*

1880 L. LOMAS *Alkali Trade* 226 The top of the dissolver being covered with thin sheet iron. **1892** *Daily News* 9 Feb. 3/5 Apropos of dissolving views, an automatic dissolver has been lately invented which will work in any single lantern. **1912** F. H. RICHARDSON *Motion Picture Handbk.* (ed. 2) 375 The lamps of a dissolver should each one be connected just as though the other one did not exist. *Ibid.* 377 To construct a home-made dissolver shutter. *Ibid.*, Your dissolver lens must be matched. **1915** *Ibid.* (ed. 3) 604 The upper dissolver lamp must be supplied with amperage equal to the projection machine arc.

dissolvible, var. of DISSOLVABLE.

diˈssolving, *vbl. sb.* [f. DISSOLVE + -ING[1].] The action of the verb DISSOLVE (q.v.), in various senses; dissolution.

1398 TREVISA *Barth. de P.R.* XVI. vi. (1495) 555 The cytrine auripigment..hath vertue of dyssoluyng and temprynge. **1577** HANMER *Anc. Eccl. Hist.* (1619) 31, I am now ready to be offered, and the time of my dissolving is at hand. **1726** LEONI *Alberti's Archit.* I. 64/1 Moist through the dissolving of the Salt. **1849** MACAULAY *Hist. Eng.* I. 270 Between the dissolving of one Parliament and the convoking of another.

diˈssolving, *ppl. a.* [f. as prec. + -ING[2].] That dissolves, in various senses: see the verb.

a. *trans.*

1620 VENNER *Via Recta* vii. 151 The roots haue..an opening and dissoluing faculty. **1821** SHELLEY *Prometh. Unb.* IV. 431 The dissolving warmth of dawn.

b. *intr.*

dissolving views, pictures produced on a screen by a magic lantern, one picture being caused gradually to disappear while another gradually appears on the same field.

1681–6 J. SCOTT *Chr. Life* (1747) III. 554 The Crack of the dissolving World, that is sinking into eternal Ruins. **1821** SHELLEY *Hellas* 1065 Faiths and empires gleam, Like wrecks of a dissolving dream. **1846** *Mech. Mag.* XLV. 486 The present method of exhibiting the dissolving views. **1886** A. WINCHELL *Walks & Talks Geol. Field* 278 The dissolving ice of the glacier.

Hence **diˈssolvingly** *adv.*

1822 MRS. E. NATHAN *Langreath* II. 322 A whining effort to be dissolvingly sentimental. **1832** TENNYSON *Eleanore* 128 A languid fire creeps Thro' my veins to all my frame, Dissolvingly and slowly.

dissonance (ˈdɪsənəns). [ad. L. *dissonāntia* dissonance, discrepancy, f. *dissonānt-em* DISSONANT: see -ANCE. Cf. F. *dissonance* (14th c. in Hatz.-Darm.)]

1. The quality or fact of being dissonant; an inharmonious or harsh sound or combination of sounds; = DISCORD 3 a, 4. *spec.* in *Music*, A combination of tones causing beats (cf. BEAT *sb.*[1] 8), and thus producing a harsh effect; also, a note which in combination with others produces this effect.

1597–8 BP. HALL *Sat.* Postscr., The Tralation of one of Persius his Satyrs into English, the difficultie and dissonance wherof shall make good my assertion. **1634** MILTON *Comus* 548 The..roar..filled the air with barbarous dissonance. **1660** tr. *Amyraldus' Treat. conc. Relig.* I. vii. 123 Making false Musick and committing dissonances. **1711** ADDISON *Spect.* No. 29 ⁋ 7 What is Harmony to one Ear, may be Dissonance to another. **1739** MELMOTH *Fitzosb. Lett.* (1763) 64 The harshness and dissonance of so unharmonious a sentence. **1795** SOUTHEY *Joan of Arc* VI. 180 With all the dissonance of boisterous mirth. **1875** OUSELEY *Harmony* viii. 95 The intruded new sound..is called a Dissonance. The chord in which the Dissonance is heard, is called a Discord. **1881** BROADHOUSE *Mus. Acoustics* 301 The various degrees of dissonance are produced by beats.

fig. **1875** HAMERTON *Intell. Life* v. vi. 196 Your shooting-coat, which was in tune upon the moors, is a dissonance amongst ladies in full dress.

2. Want of concord or harmony (between things); disagreement, incongruity; = DISCORD 2.

1571 HANMER *Chron. Irel.* (1633) 47 To reconcile the dissonance of varying writers. **1735** BERKELEY *Def. Free-th. in Math.* §43 The greatest dissonance, and even contrariety of opinions. **1826** KIRBY & SP. *Entomol.* xlvii. (1828) IV. 381 This puzzling variation and dissonance between the different tribes. **1871** TYNDALL *Fragm. Sc.* (1879) I. iii. 83 The molecules..are in dissonance with the luminous rays.

†**ˈdissonancy.** *Obs.* [ad. L. *dissonāntia*: see prec. and -ANCY.] Dissonant quality.

1. = DISSONANCE 1.

1657 W. RAND tr. *Gassendi's Life of Peiresc* II. 147 Certain Treatises of Consonancies and Dissonancies..and of musical composition or setting. **1711** SHAFTESB. *Charac.* IV. §2 (1737) I. 140 The rules of harmony will not permit it: the dissonancys are too strong. *Ibid.* (1737) II. 402 In musick [there is] the chromatick kind, and skilful mixture of dissonancys.

b. The combination of different sounds (in harmony). *nonce-use.*

1621 G. SANDYS *Ovid's Met.* x. (1626) 199 The Poet.. hauing tun'd his strings, In dissonancie musicall, thus sings.

2. = DISSONANCE 2. (The more usual sense.)

1584 R. SCOT *Discov. Witchcr.* x. iii. 144 A dissonancie in opinions about dreames. **1613** JACKSON *Creed* I. xxxii. §2. 229 Their stile, character, or dissonancie to Canonicall Scriptures. **1660** JER. TAYLOR *Duct. Dubit.* I. iv, Those things..haue no dissonancy from reason. **1702** C. MATHER *Magn. Chr.* v. II. (1852) 242 The objectors will find as much dissonancy from the scriptural example in their own practice. **1748** J. GEDDES *Compos. Antients* 351 He who loves not what he thinks good and honest..dwells with discord and dissonancy.

dissonant (ˈdɪsənənt), *a.* (*sb.*) [a. F. *dissonant* (13th c. in Littré), or ad. L. *dissonānt-em*, pr. pple. of *dissonāre* to disagree in sound, sound diversely, differ, f. DIS- 1 + *sonāre* to SOUND.]

1. Disagreeing or discordant in sound, inharmonious; harsh-sounding, unmelodious, jarring.

1573 G. HARVEY *Letter-bk.* (Camden) 117 Dissonant and iarring dittyes. **1597** MORLEY *Introd. Mus.* 71 *Phi.* Which distances make discord or dissonant sounds? *Ma.* All such as doe not make concords: as a second, a fourth, a seuenth. **1601** HOLLAND *Pliny* I. 9 As for the Moone, mortall men imagine..[to] helpe her in such a case when she is eclipsed by dissonant ringing of basons. **1774** J. BRYANT *Mythol.* I. 168 If the name was dissonant, and disagreeable to their ear, it was rejected as barbarous. **1876** tr. *Blaserna's Sound* vii. 109 To increase their resources..musicians have been obliged to have recourse to dissonant notes and chords.

2. Out of agreement, accordance, or harmony, in any respect; disagreeing, incongruous, discordant, at variance, different. Const. *from*, *to* (rarely *with*). (The earlier sense in English.)

1490 CAXTON *Eneydos* vii. 32 The maner of that countree ..was all dissonaunt & dishoneste in regarde to that of Dydo. **1514** CDL. BAINBRIDGE in Ellis *Orig. Lett.* Ser. II. I. 226 Thynges..that be dissonant..to your Graces honour or welthe of your Realme. **1613** PURCHAS *Pilgrimage, Descr. India* (1864) 151 Opinions not altogether dissonant from the Scriptures. **1613** JACKSON *Creed* I. ix. §1. 44 His conceit is not dissonant vnto the sacred storie. **1769** BURKE *Late State Nat.* Wks. 1842 I. 75 The interests..before that time jarring and dissonant, were..adjusted. **1792** A. YOUNG *Trav. France* 260 An air of poverty and misery..quite dissonant to the general aspect of the country. **1856** BRIMLEY *Ess., Angel in Ho.* 237 Very dissonant from the innermost spirit of the poem. **1857** HOLLAND *Bay Path* xxxiv. 407 [He] found himself dissonant with the spirit of the colony. **1861** MAINE *Anc. Law* iv. (1876) 84 An anomalous and dissonant jurisprudence.

B. *sb.* A dissonant element; a harsh sound of speech.

(In quot. 1579 the meaning is doubtful.)

1579 J. JONES *Preserv. Bodie & Soule* I. xxxi. 66 Haue ye Alphabet letters in Iuorie..or some other deuise conuenient ..to carry aboute with them, as first *a*, then *b*, after *c*, &c., then Consonants, after Dissonants, then Words, lastly Sentences. **1865** EMERSON in *Harper's Mag.* Feb. (1884) 461/1 Guttural consonants or dissonants.

dissonantal (ˌdɪsəˈnæntəl), *a.* [f. L. *dissonāntia* DISSONANCE + -AL.] = DISSONANT *a.*; employing or characterized by dissonance.

1946 R. BLESH *Shining Trumpets* (1949) i. 8 The ultra-modern polyphonal and dissonantal school of today. **1948** E. SITWELL *Notebk. on Shakes.* v. 29 The rocking up and down of the dissonantal *o*'s ('Crowne', 'Toe', 'top'). **1951** *Eng. Studies* XXXII. 68 Alliterative assonance—sometimes called para-rhyme, or dissonantal rhyme—is of course not unknown in English poetry before the twentieth century.

ˈdissonantly, *adv.* [f. DISSONANT *a.* + -LY[2].] In a dissonant manner; discordantly.

1799 E. DU BOIS *Piece of Fam. Biog.* II. 199 Not very dissonantly from the opinion of the reader. **1838** D. JERROLD *Men of Char., M. Clear* ii, The exclamation..broke somewhat dissonantly on the conference.

†**ˈdissonate**, *a. Obs.* [ad. L. *dissonāt-us*, pa. pple. of *dissonāre*.] = DISSONANT.

1548 GEST *Pr. Masse* 120 The worshyp and praying to Christ at the masse..is dissonate to the sacred Scripture. **1660** Z. CROFTON *St. Peter's Bonds abide* 34 Not onely different..but also dissonat to his doctrine. **1779–81** JOHNSON *L.P., Cowley* Wks. II. 66 His combination of different measures is sometimes dissonate and unpleasing.

ˈdissonate, *v. rare.* [f. L. *dissonātus* (see DISSONATE *a.*) and -ATE[3].] **a.** *intr.* 'To be dissonant or harsh: said of sounds' (*Cent. Dict.* Suppl. 1909). **b.** *trans.* To make dissonant.

1927 *Observer* 9 Oct. 14 From Adam de la Hale's sharp (and rising) fourth to Purcell's flat (and dissonating) seventh. **1961** *Times* 4 July 13/1 The piece is pleasant-sounding..'dissonated' by some violin harmonics held over moving chords.

[**dissoned.** Explained as: dissonant. Error for *distoned* in *Rom. Rose* 4248 (formerly ascribed to Chaucer).

1731 BAILEY, *Dissonid*, dissonant, disagreeing. *Chaucer.* **1881** OGILVIE (Annandale), *Dissoned.* Hence in some later Dicts.]

dissonous (ˈdɪsənəs), *a. rare.* [f. L. *disson-us* dissonant + -OUS.] Dissonant.

1715 M. DAVIES *Athen. Brit.* I. 284 Such dissonous concert of Canonical Musick.

Hence **ˈdissonously** *adv.*

1866 *Morn. Star* 18 Dec. 4/6 Unmistakeably (nay..most dissonously) the squelched rats will squeal.

†**disˈsort**, *v. Obs. rare.* [f. DIS- 6 + SORT *v.*] *intr.* Not to consort; to be out of place, be incongruous. Hence **disˈsorting** *ppl. a.*

1631 BRATHWAIT *Whimzies* 66 He [a jayler] holds nothing more unprofitable to one of his place than pitty, or more dissorting than compassion.

†**disˈsoul**, *v. Obs. nonce-wd.* [DIS- 7 a.] *trans.* To deprive of a soul.

1622 H. SYDENHAM *Serm. Sol. Occ.* II. (1637) 174 Man.. goeth..dis-soul'd by the frailtie of the body to the captivitie of a grave.

dissour, var. DISOUR.

disspaire, disspare, obs. ff. DESPAIR.

disspirit, dissple, obs. ff. DISPIRIT, DISPLE.

disspread: see DISPREAD.

†**disˈspur**, *v. Obs. nonce-wd.* [DIS- 7 a.] *trans.* To deprive (of spurs).

1603 DRAYTON *Bar. Wars* IV. ix, By a Varlet of his Spurres dis-spur'd.

†**disˈsquire**, *v. Obs. rare.* [DIS- 7 b.] *trans.* To deprive of the rank or title of squire.

1654 GAYTON *Pleas. Notes* III. vi. 109 It is in great Dispute ..whether this Launce-Bastinado..did dis-Squire Sancho.

†**disˈstanding**, *vbl. sb. Obs.* [f. DIS- 1 + STAND *v.*] A withstanding.

c **1485** *Digby Myst.* III. 196 A-ȝens vs þey can mak no dysstonddyng.

†**disˈstate**, *v. Obs.* Also 7 **distate**. [f. DIS- 7 + STATE *sb.*] *trans.* To remove (a thing) from its state or position; to deprive of state.

1605 DANIEL *Trag. Philotas* I. i. Wks. 1718 I. 318 Your Entertainments, Gifts and publick Grace That doth in jealous Kings distate the Peers. **1614** SYLVESTER *Bethulia's Rescue* v. 266 To supplant his throne, Bereave his sceptre.. and himself disstate. **1647** WARD *Simp. Cobler* 4 To distate the Truth of God and supplant the peace of the Churches.

dissuade (dɪˈsweɪd), *v.* Forms: 6–8 **disswade**, (6 **dysswade**, **disuade**, 6–7 **di-**, **deswade**), 6– **dissuade**. [ad. L. *dissuādē-re* to advise from or against, f. DIS- 1 + *suādēre* to advise, urge; cf. F. *dissuader* (16th c. in Hatz.-Darm.).]

1. *trans.* To give advice against (a thing); to represent as unadvisable or undesirable. ? *Obs.*

1513 MORE *Rich. III* Wks. 43 The quene..damning the time that euer shee dissuaded the gatheryng of power aboute the kinge. **1538** BALE *Thre Lawes* 11 Perswadynge all truth, dysswadynge all iniury. **1560** WHITEHORNE *Arte Warre* (1573) 65 a, To perswade or to diswade a thing vnto fewe is verye easie. **1611** E. GRIMSTONE *Hist. France* 1082 The Queene of Nauarre did much disswade this Alliance. **1667** MILTON *P.L.* IX. 293 Not diffident of thee do I dissuade Thy absence from my sight. **1725** POPE *Odyss.* IX. 578 My friends..With mild entreaties my design dissuade. **1818** JAS. MILL *Brit. India* II. v. iv. 438 The Nabob dissuaded any further preparations. **1842** SIR J. STEPHEN *Eccl. Biog., Founders Jesuitism* (1850) I. 205 His..friends anxiously dissuaded a journey so full of peril.

2. *trans.* To advise or exhort (a person) against; to disadvise, dehort (*from*). ? *Obs.*

c **1534** tr. *Pol. Verg. Hist.* (Camden, No. 29) 195 The duke dyd the lesse disswade kinge Richerd from usurping the kingdome. **1555** EDEN *Decades* Sect. I., Peter Martyr's *Dedication* (Arb. 63) Ascanius..dissuaded me from my purpose. But seeing that I was fully resolued to departe.. required me to wryte vnto hym. **1605** CAMDEN *Rem.* (1637) 246 Some disswaded him to hunt that day; but he resolved to the contrary. **1712** ADDISON *Spect.* No. 411 ⁋ 7 He particularly dissuades him from knotty and subtle Disquisitions. **1766** GOLDSM. *Vic. W.* xiii, My wife very strenuously insisted. Mr. Burchell on the contrary dissuaded her with great ardour. **1848** MOZLEY *Ess. Hist. & Theol.* (1878) I. 402 They dissuaded him from the contemplated step..but admitted..that, if he insisted upon it, they could not forbid it.

absol. **1598** BARRET *Theor. Warres* II. i. 29 To disswade from bad factions. **1793** *Trial of Fyshe Palmer* 55 Palmer dissuaded from the publication.

3. To divert or draw (a person) *from* a course or action by suasion or personal influence.

1576 FLEMING *Panopl. Epist.* 384 Yea I would (if I could) dissuade you from this intent. **1583** STUBBES *Anat. Abus.* II. (1882) 20 Which thing altogither dissuadeth them from their bookes. **1652–62** HEYLIN *Cosmogr.* Pref., Sufficient to disswade me from the undertaking. **1782** MISS BURNEY *Cecilia* v. iii, I have tried what is possible to dissuade him. **1823** F. CLISSOLD *Ascent Mt. Blanc* 8 Matthieu Balmat.. refused to accompany us; being dissuaded by his father. **1844** H. H. WILSON *Brit. India* II. 241 The Peshwa having been with difficulty dissuaded..from flying to Purandhar. **1847** EMERSON *Repr. Men, Plato* Wks. (Bohn) I. 290 He.. was easily dissuaded from this pursuit.

absol. **1805** SOUTHEY *Madoc in W.* xv, Gerald..sought.. to dissuade By politic argument.

Hence **di'ssuaded** *ppl. a.*, **di'ssuading** *vbl. sb.* and *ppl. a.*; also **di'ssuader**, one who or that which dissuades.

1546 BALE *Eng. Votaries* I. (R.) As though they were diswaders of marriage. **1552** HULOET, Disswaded, *abhortatus.* **1580** HOLLYBAND *Treas. Fr. Tong, Destournement*, a dissuading. **1586** A. DAY *Eng. Secretary* I. (1625) 82 Epistles Dehorting and Disswading. **1643** MILTON *Divorce* Introd. (1851) 9 A civil, an indifferent, a sometime disswaded Law of mariage. **1880** KINGLAKE *Crimea* VI. vi. 245 Carrying all the dissuaders along with it. **1883** M. ARNOLD *Lett.* (1895) II. 216, I relied on a dissuader from you. **1923** G. COLLINS *Valley of Eyes Unseen* 29 The other came on, and received a like dissuader from my right.

dissuadent (dɪ'sweɪdənt). *rare.* [ad. L. *dissuādēnt-em*, pr. pple. of *dissuādēre* to DISSUADE.] One who or that which dissuades.

1855 *Ess. Intuit. Mor.* 143 It sets forth as the dissuadent from Vice, the Pain of remorse.

dissuasion (dɪ'sweɪʒən). [ad. L. *dissuāsiōn-em*, n. of action f. *dissuādēre* to DISSUADE; or perh. a. F. *dissuasion* (14th c. in Hatz.-Darm.).] The action, or an act, of dissuading; advice or exhortation against something; dehortation.

1526 *Pilgr. Perf.* (1531) 289 But to this false disswasyon, it is soone answered. **1549** COVERDALE *Erasm. Par. Ephesians* Prol., With slaunderous dissuasions, & perplexe impertinent interpretations. **1597** BACON (*title*), A Table of Coulers, or apparances of good and euill, and their degrees as places of perswasion and disswasion. **1647** COWLEY *Mistress, Counsel* iv, Ev'n thy Dissuasions me persuade. **1823** DE QUINCEY *Lett. Educ.* i. (1860) 8 This chapter..is a dissuasion from Herder. **1863** GEO. ELIOT *Romola* I. xiii, He had not the courage to utter any words of dissuasion. **1868** BROWNING *Ring & Bk.* XII. 100 But for the dissuasion of two eyes..He had abstained, nor graced the spectacle.

†**b.** The condition of being dissuaded; a persuasion of the opposite. *Obs.*

1553 BALE *Gardiner's De Vera Obed.* (ed. 3) A v, He runneth post haste into a contrarye Dissuasion.

dissuasive (dɪ'sweɪsɪv), *a.* and *sb.* [f. L. type **dissuāsīv-us*, f. *dissuās-* ppl. stem of *dissuādēre*: see DISSUADE and -IVE; cf. F. *dissuasif, -ive.*]

A. *adj.* Tending to dissuade; characterized by dissuasion; dehortatory.

1609 W. M. *Man in Moone* (1849) 12 If I should extract the best counsell I coulde, being disswasive from your tobacco-taking, you would take it in snuffe. **1684** *Pennsylv. Archives* I. 88 Examples that have such a dissuasive power upon men. **1742** FIELDING *J. Andrews* III. ii, The dissuasive speech of Andromache. **1848** LYTTON *Harold* II. i, Despite all dissuasive ejaculations.

B. *sb.* A dissuasive speech or argument; that which tends or is intended to dissuade.

1629 tr. *Herodian* (1635) 25 This strong Disswasive of Pompeianus did..somewhat abate the edge of the young Emperour. **1664** JER. TAYLOR (*title*), A Dissuasive from Popery, addressed to the people of Ireland. **1711** ADDISON *Spect.* No. 92 ¶5 A Dissuasive from the Play-House. **1830** MACKINTOSH *Eth. Philos.* Wks. 1846 I. 86 The success of persuasives or dissuasives..must always be directly proportioned..to the strength of the principle addressed. **1894** BARING-GOULD *Kitty Alone* II. 123 To look with impatience..upon all dissuasives.

Hence **di'ssuasively** *adv.*, **di'ssuasiveness** *sb.*

1727 BAILEY vol. II, *Dissuasiveness*, dissuasive Quality. **1864** WEBSTER, *Dissuasively.* **1881** H. JAMES *Portr. Lady* xxiv, 'Ah, really, Countess', murmured Madame Merle dissuasively.

†**di'ssuasory**, *a. Obs.* [f. L. type **dissuāsōri-us*, f. *dissuāsor* dissuader: see -ORY. Cf. It. *disuasorio* 'disswading, discouraging' (Florio).] = DISSUASIVE *a.*

c **1555** HARPSFIELD *Divorce Hen. VIII*, 90 The said 18 chapter is partly dissuasory, partly teaching. **1586** A. DAY *Eng. Secretary* I. (1625) 128 Of Epistles Dehortatorie, and Disswasorie.

B. *sb.* = DISSUASIVE *sb.*

1844 JEFFREY *Contrib. Ed. Rev.* IV. 278 This person..has ill luck in all his dissuasories [orig. (in *Ed. Rev.* Oct. 1815, 362) dissuasions.]

†**dissub'jection.** *Obs. nonce-wd.* [DIS- 9.] The opposite of subjection; disobedience.

1673 O. WALKER *Educ.* 151 Dis-subjection to Laws and Magistrates.

dissub'stantiate, *v. nonce-wd.* [DIS- 6.] *trans.* To deprive of substance or substantiality.

1871 FRASER *Life Berkeley* x. 368 Hume and Positivism dissubstantiate spirits.

dissue, variant of DIZZUE.

†'**dissuetude.** *Obs. rare.* [ad. late L. *dissuētūdo* (Ambros. *c* 397) a becoming disaccustomed, disusing, f. *dissuēt-* ppl. stem of *dissuēscĕre* = *dēsuēscĕre*, to become unaccustomed to, f. DIS- 4 + *suēscĕre* to become used to.] = DESUETUDE.

a **1639** SPOTTISWOOD *Hist. Ch. Scot.* VI. (1677) 464 His long dissuetude of the Country-language..made him unuseful at first. **1755** JOHNSON s.v. *Disuse* 1, Cessation of use, dissuetude; want of practice.

dis'suitable, *a. rare.* [DIS- 10.] Not suitable, unsuitable. So **dis'suited** *ppl. a.*

1807 SOUTHEY *Espriella's Lett.* II. 195 The sort of frame through which it was seen [was] not dissuitable to the picture. **1820** —— *Lett.* (1856) III. 189 Hexameters..are in no respect dissuited to the genius of our language.

dissunder (dɪs'sʌndə(r)), *v.* [f. DIS- 1 or 5 + SUNDER *v.*] *trans.* To sunder, sever, dissever. Hence **dis'sundered** *ppl. a.*, separated, dissevered.

1580 T. M[ULCASTER] in *Baret's Alv.* To Rdr. i, Like Beé he manie a yeére did moile, In large wide fields, that far dissundred beé. **1615** CHAPMAN *Odyss.* I. 36 He himself solemniz'd a retreat To th' Aethiops, far dissunder'd in their seat. **1642** H. MORE *Song of Soul* I. III. xxv, Who can this strength dissunder? **1808** J. BARLOW *Columb.* IX. 450 Diffused o'er various far dissunder'd lands. **1855** SINGLETON *Aeneid* VIII. 438 The Gorgon..Her eyeballs rolling with dissundered neck.

dissury, obs. form of DYSURY.

†**dis'sweeten,** *v. Obs.* [DIS- 6.] *trans.* To deprive of sweetness; to unsweeten.

1622 W. WHATELEY *God's Husb.* II. 82 The gawdes of this world would not..beguile vs, the cumbers of this world would not..gawle vs, if wee did dis-sweeten the one..and dis-imbitter the other. **1647** TRAPP *Marrow Gd. Auth.* in *Comm. Epist.* etc. 656 An evil, unquiet conscience will extremely dissweeten a full cup of outward comforts. **1667** FLAVEL *Saint Indeed* (1754) 125 That fellowship is so dissweetened by remaining corruptions.

dissyde, obs. form of DECIDE.

dissyllabe: see DISYLLABE.

dissyllabic, -able, etc.: see DISYLLABIC, DISYLLABLE, etc.

dissymmetric (dɪssɪ'mɛtrɪk), *a.* = next.

1884 TYNDALL *Introd.* to *Life of Pasteur* 17 He may comfort himself by the assurance that the conception of a dissymmetric molecule is not a very precise one.

dissymmetrical (dɪssɪ'mɛtrɪkəl), *a.* [DIS- 10.] **a.** The opposite of symmetrical. **b.** Symmetrical, but in opposite directions, like the two hands.

In *Chem.* said *spec.* of crystals having two corresponding forms, but turned in different directions (like an object and its reflexion in a mirror); also of molecules in which the atoms are supposed to be thus arranged.

1867 G. MASSON tr. *Janet's Materialism* 75 Two substances are called dissymmetrical when they are absolutely similar in all respects, except that they are opposed to each other like the two hands in the human body. **1880** CLEMENSHAW *Wurtz' Atom. Th.* 303 The dissymmetrical compounds thus formed are..a mixture in equal proportions of dextro-rotatory and lævo-rotatory bodies. **1884** TYNDALL *Introd.* to *Life of Pasteur* 17 Pasteur invoked the aid of helices and magnets, with a view to rendering crystals dissymmetrical at the moment of their formation.

Hence **dissy'mmetrically** *adv.*

1880 CLEMENSHAW *Wurtz' Atom. Th.* 303 Dissymmetrically opposed compounds.

dissymmetry (dɪs'sɪmɪtrɪ). [DIS- 9.] **a.** Lack or absence of symmetry. **b.** Symmetry between two objects, disposed in opposite directions, such as the right and left hands or feet, or between crystals alike in all respects, save that their angles lie opposite ways.

1845 STOCQUELER *Handbk. Brit. India* (1854) 124 The larger vessels of the country, pleasant to look upon even for their strange dis-symmetry and their consequent unwieldiness. **1876** tr. *Schutzenberger's Ferment.* 6 In a remarkable lecture on molecular dissymmetry M. Pasteur had established an important distinction between artificial organic products. **1881** W. SPOTTISWOODE in *Nature* XXIV. 546 There is a dissymmetry at the two ends of a battery. **1895** *Daily News* 30 Sept. 7/2 Pasteur..propounded the theory that molecular dissymmetry, which is noticed when a beam of polarised light is caused by certain solutions to rotate, was characteristic of living matter and its products.

dissympathy (dɪs'sɪmpəθɪ). *nonce-wd.* [DIS- 9.] Absence of sympathy.

1860 WORCESTER cites JOHNSTON.

dis'synagogue, *v. nonce-wd.* [DIS- 7 c.] *trans.* To punish by casting out of the synagogue.

a **1655** VINES *Lord's Supp.* (1677) 225 The synagogues had a form of dissynagoguing offences.

distache, early form of DETACH *v.*

†**dis'tackle,** *v. Obs.* [f. DIS- 7 a + TACKLE *sb.*] *trans.* To deprive (a ship) of its tackle. Hence **dis'tackled** *ppl. a.*, deprived of tackle.

1589 WARNER *Alb. Eng.* II. Prose Add. (1612) 334 At length these instruments of their long wandrings..tossed their distackled Fleete to the shore of Libya.

distad ('dɪstæd), *adv.* [f. stem of DIST-ANT + *-ad*: cf. DEXTRAD.] In the direction of the end or distal part of a limb, etc.

1803 J. BARCLAY *New Anat. Nomen.* 166 Distad, towards the distant aspect. **1808** —— *Muscular Motions* 442 A small bone extending a short way distad on the leg. **1872** MIVART *Elem. Anat.* iv. (1873) 175 The phalanges..decreasing in length distad. **1882** WILDER & GAGE *Anat. Techn.* 27 Thus we say, the elbow is distad of the shoulder..the humerus extends distad from the shoulder.

distaff ('dɪstɑːf, -æ-). Forms: 1 distæf, 4–5 distaf, 5 dysestafe, 5–6 dystaf(fe, 6–7 distaffe, 5– distaff. *Pl.* distaffs (5–7 distaves). [OE. *distæf*, supposed to be for *dis-* or *dise-stæf*, the second element being the sb. STAFF; *dis* or *dise* is app. identical with LG. *diesse* (Bremen Wbch.) a bunch of flax on a distaff, and connected with DIZE, DIZEN 'to put tow on a distaffe' (Ray).]

1. A cleft staff about 3 feet long, on which, in the ancient mode of spinning, wool or flax was wound. It was held under the left arm, and the fibres of the material were drawn from it through the fingers of the left hand, and twisted spirally by the forefinger and thumb of the right, with the aid of the suspended spindle, round which the thread, as it was twisted or spun, was wound.

c **1000** ÆLFRIC *Gloss.* in Wr.-Wülcker 125/21 *Colus*, distæf. *c* **1386** CHAUCER *Nun's Pr. T.* 563 And Malkyn with a dystaf in hir hand. **1387** TREVISA *Higden* (Rolls) III. 33 Sardanapallus spynnynge reed selk at þe distaf. *c* **1475** *Pict. Voc.* in Wr.-Wülcker 794/14 *Hec colus*, a dysestafe. **1489** CAXTON *Faytes of A.* I. i. 2 Wymen comynly do not entremete but to spynne on the distaf. **1523** FITZHERB. *Husb.* §146 Let thy dystaffe be alwaye redye for a pastyme. **1621** BURTON *Anat. Mel.* III. iv. I. ii. (1651) 651 Tradesmen left their shops, women their distaves. **1675** HOBBES *Odyssey* (1677) 78 Others with their distaves sate to spin. **1697** DRYDEN *Virg. Georg.* IV. 475 One common Work they ply'd; their Distaffs full With carded Locks of blue Milesian Wooll. **1816** SCOTT *Bl. Dwarf* iii, Serving wenches..sate plying their distaffs. **1871** R. ELLIS *Catullus* lxiv. 311 Singly the left [hand] upbore in wool soft-hooded a distaff. **1876** ROCK *Text. Fabr.* 2 Spinning from a distaff is even now common..all through Italy.

b. In proverbial and figurative phrases. †*to have tow on one's distaff*: to have work in hand or trouble in store (*obs.*).

c **1386** CHAUCER *Miller's T.* 588 He hadde moore tow on his distaf Than Gerueys knew. *a* **1420** HOCCLEVE *De Reg. Princ.* 1226 Towe on my dystaf have I for to spynne More ..than ye wote of yit. **1525** LD. BERNERS *Froiss.* II. clxxiv. [clxx.] 520 In shorte space he shall haue more flax to his dystaffe than he can well spynne. **1546** J. HEYWOOD *Prov.* (1867) 60 If they fyre me, some of them shall wyn More towe on their distaues, than they can well spyn. **1853** C. BRONTE *Villette* xxv, The whole of my patience is now spun off the distaff.

2. The staff or 'rock' of a hand spinning-wheel, upon which the flax to be spun is placed.

1766 CROKER, etc. *Dict. Arts* s.v. *Spinning*, Performed on the wheel with a distaff and spindle. **1828** WEBSTER, *Distaff*, the staff of a spinning-wheel, to which a bunch of flax or tow is tied and from which the thread is drawn.

3. As the type of women's work or occupation.

c **1386** CHAUCER *Monk's Prol.* 19 She rampeth in my face And crieth..I wol haue thy knyf And thou shalt haue my distaf and go spynne. **1605** SHAKS. *Lear* IV. ii. 17, I must change names at home, and giue the Distaffe Into my Husbands hands. **1611** —— *Cymb.* v. iii. 34 Their owne Noblenesse, which could haue turn'd A Distaffe, to a Lance. **1659** B. HARRIS *Parival's Iron Age* 63 The women..so stoutly assailed the Town-House, that it was necessitated.. to make them retire to the distaffe. **1821** BYRON *Sardan.* II. i. 344, I blush that we should owe our lives to such A king of distaffs! *a* **1839** PRAED *Poems* (1864) I. 208 His delicate hand Seemed fitter for the distaff than the spear.

b. Hence, symbolically, for the female sex, female authority or dominion; also, the female branch of a family, the 'spindle-side' as opposed to the 'spear-side'; a female heir.

1494 FABYAN *Chron.* VII. 329 He wolde not haue so noble a lordshyp runne amonge, or to be deuydyd atwene so many dystauys [i.e. his four daughters]. **1602** CAREW *Cornwall* (1723) 152 b, M. Militon..whose sonne being lost in his trauaile beyond the seas, enriched 6 distaffs with his inheritance. **1644** HOWELL *Eng. Tears* (1645) 180 Some say the Crozier, some say the Distaffe was too busie. **1659** B. HARRIS *Parival's Iron Age* 51 The Kingdom is hereditary, and for want of an heir male, it falls to the Distaff. **1706** PHILLIPS (ed. Kersey) s.v. *Distaff*, The Crown of France never falls to the distaff. **1862** CARLYLE *Fredk. Gt.* (1865)

III. IX. i. 63 Old Anton being already fallen into the distaff, with nothing but three Granddaughters.

4. *attrib.* and *Comb.*, as ***distaff-business, -right, -woman***; **distaff side**, the female branch of a house or family; **distaff's** or **St. Distaff's day**, the day after Twelfth Day or the Feast of the Epiphany, on which day (Jan. 7) women resumed their spinning and other ordinary employments after the holidays; also called *rock-day*; **distaff cane**, a species of reed, the stems or canes of which are used for distaffs, arrows, fishing-rods, etc.; **distaff thistle**, a name of *Carthamus lanatus* (*Cirsium lanatum*), from its woolly flowering stems.

1593 SHAKS. *Rich. II*, III. ii. 118 Against thy State Yea Distaffe-Women manage rustie Bills. *a* **1633** LENNARD tr. *Charron's Wisd.* III. vii. §6 (1670) 409 This inconvenience followeth the friendship of married couples, that it is mingled with so many other strange matters, children, parents of the one side and the other, and so many other distaff-businesses that do many times trouble and interrupt a lively affection. **1648** HERRICK *Hesper.*, *St. Distaff's Day*, Partly worke and partly play Ye must on S. Distaff's day. [*Ibid.*, Give S. Distaffe all the right, Then bid Christmas sport good night.] **1715** PETIVER in *Phil. Trans.* XXIX. 234 This differs from the Distaff-Thistle in having its upper Stalks woolly like Cobwebs. **1869** HAZLITT *Prov. & Phrases* 304 On St. Distaff's Day, neither work nor play. **1884** MILLER *Plant-n.*, Distaff Cane, *Arundo Donax*. **1890** *Temple Bar Mag.* Nov. 311 'Is there insanity in Byng's blood?' Not certainly on the distaff side, the side of his eminently sane and wholesome mother. **1895** POLLOCK & MAITLAND *Hist. Eng. Law* II. 305 For a male to get a share by 'distaff right' [*iure coli*] was by no means uncommon.

distain (dɪ'steɪn), *v. arch.* Forms: 4 de-, disteign, 4–6 de-, disteyne, 5 destayne, 5–6 dysteyn, 5–7 distayn(e, 6 desteine, *Sc.* distene, (*pa. pple.* distaint), 6–7 destaine, distein(e, distaine, 6–9 destain, 6– distain. [a. OF. *desteindre* (stem *desteign-*), mod.F. *déteindre* = Pr. *destengner*, Sp. *desteñir*, Com. Rom. f. *des-*, DIS- 1 + L. *tingĕre* to dye, colour, TINGE. The prefix has been conformed to the L. type.]

1. *trans.* To imbue or stain (a thing) with a colour different from the natural one; to discolour, stain, dye, tinge.

1393 GOWER *Conf.* I. 65 Whan his visage is so desteigned. **1586** MARLOWE *1st Pt. Tamburl.* III. ii, The tears that so distain my cheeks. **1590** SPENSER *F.Q.* III. xlix. 9, I found her golden girdle cast astray Distaynd with durt and blood. **1612** DRAYTON *Poly-olb.* viii. 113 The Romans that her streame distained with their gore. **1704** OLDMIXON *Blenheim* iii. 11 Whose golden Sands are now distain'd with Blood. **1839** BAILEY *Festus* xxi. (1852) 382 Like autumn's leaves distained with dusky gold.

2. *transf.* and *fig.* To defile; to bring a blot or stain upon; to sully, dishonour.

1406 HOCCLEVE *Misrule* 340 Among an heep my name is now desteyned. **1436** *Pol. Poems* (Rolls) II. 159 Make fade the floures Of Englysshe state, and disteyne oure honnoures. **1594** SHAKS. *Rich. III*, v. iii. 322 You hauing Lands, and blest with beauteous wiues, They would restraine the one, distaine the other. *a* **1622** AINSWORTH *Annot. Song Sol.* v. 3, I washt my feet, how shall I them distaine? *c* **1750** SHENSTONE *Elegies* ix. 39 A soul distain'd by earth and gold. **1788** BURNS *Macpherson's Farewell* v, May coward shame distain his name, The wretch that dare not die! **1873** MORRIS *Love is Enough* 107 Surely no shame hath destained thee. **1873–4** DIXON *Two Queens* IV. xx. vi. 93 You would not that ..I should so distain mine honour or conscience.

†**3.** To deprive of its colour, brightness, or splendour; to dim; to cause to pale or look dim; to outshine. *Obs.*

c **1385** CHAUCER *L. G. W.* 216 Alceste is here that al that may desteyne. *Ibid.* 274 (Fairf. MS.) As the sonne wole the fire disteyne So passeth al my lady souereyne. **1633** P. FLETCHER *Purple Isl.* VI. ix, These lights the Sunne distain.

Hence **di'stained** *ppl. a.*, **di'staining** *vbl. sb.*

a **1483** *Liber Niger* in *Househ. Ord.* 69 Which mought be made..ne ware the adventure of distaynynge of all that other part. **1580** HOLLYBAND *Treas. Fr. Tong*, *Enlaidissement*, a dishonestie, a distayning, a defiling. **1590** MARLOWE *2nd Pt. Tamburl.* IV. i, Shame of nature, which Jaertis' stream..Can never wash from thy distainèd brows! **1838** LYTTON *Calderon* viii, Distained and time-hallowed walls.

†**di'stain**, *sb. Obs. rare*⁻¹. [f. prec. vb.] Tint, stain, colouring.

1581 RICH *Farewell* (1846) 133 To furnishe me with colours to make the perfect distaine of the beautie in your face.

†**di'stainted**, *pa. pple. Obs. nonce-wd.* [f. DIS- 5 + TAINT *v.*] Infected, corrupted.

1599 T. M[OUFET] *Silkwormes* 44 From egges of euery creature good, Sprang nought distainted but this little broode.

distal ('dɪstəl), *a.* [f. stem of DIST-ANT + -AL[1], after *dorsal*, *ventral*, etc.] *Anat.* Situated away from the centre of the body, or from the point of origin (said of the extremity or distant part of a limb or organ); terminal. Opp. to *proximal*.

1808 J. BARCLAY *Muscular Motions* 415 The bones of the distal phalanx. **1814** J. H. WISHART tr. *Scarpa's Treat. Hernia* p. xvi, Each pair of the extremities..have a proximal and a distal end; the former being that nearest the trunk, the latter that most remote. **1875** DARWIN *Insectiv. Pl.* x. 251 From the distal to the basal end of a leaf. **1881** MIVART *Cat* 37 The paw is the distal part of a limb.

b. *transf.*

1882 D. HOOPER in *Standard* 10 Oct. 2/2 The drainage-pipes are..very imperfectly..connected at their proximal or house termination, although they must, by the Act, be well connected at their distal or main drain termination. **1885** KLEIN *Micro-organ. & Dis.* (1886) 20 The distal end of the tube is introduced..into the neck of the sterilised flask. **1894** *Westm. Gaz.* 20 June 3/2 The distal message can be reproduced type-written.

Distalgesic (dɪstæl'dʒiːzɪk). *Pharm.* Also distalgesic. [f. *Dist(illers'* Co. Ltd., orig. maker's name + AN)ALGESIC *a.* and *sb.*] A proprietary name for a brand of pain-killer containing paracetamol and propoxyphene in tablet form.

1958 *Trade Marks Jrnl.* 30 July 767/2 *Distalgesic*... Pharmaceutical preparations for treating algesic conditions. The Distillers Company (Biochemicals) Limited. **1967** *Martindale's Extra Pharmacopoeia* (ed. 25) 793 *Distalgesic* (Dista Products), tablets each containing dextro-propoxyphene hydrochloride 32·5 mg. and paracetamol 325 mg. For the relief of pain. **1976** P. PARISH *Medicines* (1982) 185 There are numerous preparations prescribed by doctors which contain aspirin or paracetamol combined with a narcotic pain reliever (e.g., dextropropoxyphene combined with paracetamol in Distalgesic). **1980** *Daily Tel.* 26 June 3/4 When the bullying got on top of him Pte James Darkin, stationed at Simpson Barracks, Wooton, Northampton, took a dose of distalgesic.

distally ('dɪstəlɪ), *adv.* [f. DISTAL *a.* + -LY[2].] In a distal direction; at the distant or outer end.

1870 ROLLESTON *Anim. Life* 12 Their distally bifid transverse processes increase in size. **1872** MIVART *Elem. Anat.* 71 Ribs may also bifurcate distally.

distance ('dɪstəns), *sb.* Forms: 3 **destance**, 4 **-aunce, distawns**, 4–6 **distans, dis-, dystaunce**, 5 **dis-, dystawnce, distauns**, 3– **distance**. [a. OF. *destance*, *distance* (13th c. in Littré), ad. L. *distāntia* 'standing apart', hence 'separation, opening (between); distance, remoteness; difference, diversity', f. *distānt-em* pr. pple., DISTANT. By a further development, OF. *destance* had the sense 'discord, quarrel', which was also the earliest in Eng. In senses adopted directly from Latin, the form *distance* was used in OF., and this soon became the only form in Eng. The chronological appearance of the senses does not correspond to the logical development in L.]

I. [from OF. *destance* discord, quarrel.]

†**1. a.** The condition of being at variance; discord, disagreement, dissension; dispute, debate.

(After 1600, passing into the sense of 'estrangement, coolness'; cf. sense 8.)

1297 R. GLOUC. (1724) 511 The barons sende to the King Philip of France, That he hom sende socour in this luther destance. **1375** BARBOUR *Bruce* VII. 620 Emang thame sudanly Thair raiss debate and gret distans. **1393** GOWER *Conf.* III. 348 And thus we fellen in distaunce My prest and I. *a* **1400** *Octouian* 1523 He was y-take with greet destaunce And other kynges four. *c* **1430** LYDG. *Min. Poems* (1840) 60 (Mätz.) Triew people to sette at distaunce. *c* **1470** HARDING *Chron.* CLIII. i, In Wales Morgan made war & great distaunce. **1523** LD. BERNERS *Froiss.* I. ccclvii. 578 They were in suche vnyte, that there was no dystaunce amonge them. **1605** SHAKS. *Macb.* III. i. 115. **1667** PEPYS *Diary* (1877) V. 18 This..do breed a kind of inward distance between the King and the Duke of York. **1752** FIELDING *Amelia* II. ii, There was some little distance between them, which I hoped to have the happiness of accommodating.

†**b.** With *a* and *pl.* An instance of this; a quarrel, a disagreement; in later use, an estrangement. *Obs.*

c **1290** *Beket* 1267 in *S. Eng. Leg.* I. 142 A destaunce þare is isprongue liȝtliche in Engelonde, þat destourbez al þat lond. **1297** R. GLOUC. (1724) 570 Suþþe þer was at Londone a lute destance, ich wene. *c* **1330** R. BRUNNE *Chron.* (1810) 294 Bituex þe kyng of France & þe erle William Was þat tyme a distance. *c* **1430** LYDG. *Bochas* III. vii. (1554) 79 a, He told them plainly of a great distaunce..and a discencion. **1650** B. *Discolliminium* 30 It would allay and heale many great distances, and procure many..friends. **1666** PEPYS *Diary* 10 Sept., There have been some late distances between his lady and him.

†**c.** ***without distance***: without debate, discord, or opposition; often parenthetically qualifying the statement: Without dispute or contradiction, assuredly, 'ywis'. *Obs.*

c **1325** *Coer de L.* 2032 In March moneth, the Kyng of Fraunce Went to ship without distaunce. *c* **1400** *Cato's Morals* 320 in *Cursor M.* p. 1673, & þou se first chaunce, [co]me wiþ-out distaunce, first þou hit take. *c* **1430** *Syr Tryam.* 1017 And let owre londys be in pees, Wythowtyn any dystawnce. *c* **1460** *Towneley Myst.* 21 Sex hundreth yere and od have I, without distance, In erth..liffyd. **14..** *Cokwold's Daunce* 136 in Hazl. *E.P.P.* I. 44 After mete with out distans, The cokwolds schuld together dance.

II. [from L. *distāntia* in sense 'difference'.]

†**2.** Difference, diversity. *Obs.*

1382 WYCLIF *Deut.* i. 17 Noon shal be distaunce of persones. **1481** CAXTON *Myrr.* I. xiv. 46 She gyueth to one somme thyng that another hath not in hym, how be it that noman can perceyue any distaunce. **1556** *Aurelio & Isab.* (1608) G vij, There is yet founde in suche errour grete distance betwene affection and reason.

III. [from L. *distāntia*, F. *distance*, in the sense of 'being apart in space'.]

3. The fact or condition of being apart or far off in space; remoteness.

1594 CAREW *Huarte's Exam. Wits* (1616) 23 Places..that are not more than a little league in distance. **1660** HICKERINGILL *Jamaica* (1661) 54 Distance and absence usually enhanceth the affections of near friends. **1709** POPE *Ess. Crit.* 174 Which..Due distance reconciles to form and grace. **1799** CAMPBELL *Pleas. Hope* I. 7 'Tis distance lends enchantment to the view. **1820** SHELLEY *Let. to M. Gisborne* 287 Afar the Contadino's song is heard, Rude but made sweet by distance.

4. a. The extent of space lying between any two objects; the space to be passed over before reaching an object. With *a* and *pl.*, an intervening space.

c **1440** *Promp. Parv.* 123/1 Distawnce of place [*P.* or space] betwene ij thyngys, *distancia*. *a* **1541** WYATT in *Tottell's Misc.* (Arb.) 74 When I think vpon the distaunce, and the space: That doth so farre deuide me from my dere desired face. **1559** W. CUNNINGHAM *Cosmogr. Glasse* 10 The sterres kepe one uniforme distance in moving. **1608** D. T. *Ess. Pol. & Mor.* 96 Ther is too great a distance betweene us and thee. **1663** GERBIER *Counsel* 34 A Head [consists] of so many distances between the one Eye and the other. **1690** LOCKE *Hum. Und.* II. xiii. (R.) This space consider'd barely in length between any two beings, without considering anything else between them, is called distance. **1712** J. JAMES tr. *Le Blond's Gardening* 160 The Plants are spaced out..at three Foot Distances. **1860** TYNDALL *Glac.* I. x. 66 The width of the fissure seemed to be fairly within jumping distance. **1868** LOCKYER *Elem. Astron.* ii. §7 (1879) 38 Astronomers now know the distance of the Sun from the Earth. **1891** *Spectator* 28 Feb., The wedge-formation is abandoned..and the ducks fly in single file, though the 'distances' are always accurately kept.

†**b.** Lineal extent. *Obs. rare.*

1582 N. LICHEFIELD tr. *Castanheda's Conq. E. Ind.* xxix. 72 b, Whether it were a firme lande, as it did appeare..by the great distance of the Coast that they had found.

5. Technical applications of 4. **a.** *Milit.* The space between man and man when standing in rank; also the space between the ranks.

distance of divisions 'is the number of paces, of thirty inches each, comprised in the front of any division or body, and is nearly three-fourths of the number of files' (Stocqueler 1853). ***distance of the bastion*** (*Fortif.*), 'a term applied to the exterior polygon' (*ibid.*).

1635 BARRIFFE *Mil. Discip.* vi. (1643) 24 Distance is the space of ground, betweene man and man, either in file, or Ranke. **1690** S. SEWALL *Diary* 24 Mar. (1878) I. 316, I goe into the field, pray with the South Company, Exercise them in a few Distances, Facings, Doublings. **1833** *Regul. Instr. Cavalry* I. 67 *Take Distance*..A horse's length and half distance. *Ibid.* 122 The Files prove distance as directed. **1859** F. A. GRIFFITHS *Artil. Man.* (1862) 16 Open to quarter (or wheeling) distance from the front.

b. *Fencing.* A definite interval of space to be observed between two combatants.

1592 SHAKS. *Rom. & Jul.* II. iv. 21 He fights as you sing pricksong, keeps time, distance, and proportion, he rests his minum, one, two, and the third in your bosom. **1611** —— *Wint. T.* II. i. 233 In these times you stand on distance: your Passes, Stoccado's, and I know not what. **1684** R. H. *School Recreat.* 74 Being within Distance, approach with your first Motion. **1809** ROLAND *Fencing* 31 The words *measure* and *distance* are frequently used promiscuously, they being synonymous in Fencing.

c. *Horse-racing.* The space measured back from the winning-post which a horse must have reached, in a heat-race, when the winning horse has covered the whole course, in order not to be 'distanced' or disqualified for subsequent heats.

(The practice is obsolete in England, but not in U.S., where 'distances' varying according to the length of the course are in use in trotting and running races.)

1674 N. COX *Gentl. Recreat.* v. (1686) 75 A Horse-length lost by odds of Weight in the first Train, may prove a distance in the straight Course at last; for the Weight is the same every Heat tho his strength be not. **1723** *Lond. Gaz.* No. 6172/4 The Horse..that wins two Heats and saves his Distance a third too, wins the Plate. **1810** *Sporting Mag.* XXXVI. 241 When about two distances from home..his colt hung upon the former. **1875** 'STONEHENGE' *Brit. Sports* II. I. xiv. §2. 490 A round, flat course, short of two miles by a distance. **1894** *Standard* 20 Oct. 6/1 The 2000 yards—a mile and a distance, 'distance' being the term for a measurement of 240 yards—of the new Cambridgeshire course.

†**d.** *Mus.* An interval. *Obs.*

1551 ROBINSON tr. *More's Utop.* (Arb.) 116 No other liuinge creature..perceaueth the concordaunte and discordant distaunces of soundes, and tunes. **1684** R. H. *School Recreat.* 120 Two lesser Distances..named Semitones. **1797** *Monthly Mag.* III. 226 They exhibit the author as straining after novelty by eccentric distances, and by movements out of cathedral time.

e. In various technical phrases, as FOCAL *d.*, POLAR *d.*, ZENITH *d.*, etc.: see also these words.

1696 PHILLIPS, *Distance*..in Navigation..signifies the number of Degrees, Leagues, &c., that a Ship has fail'd from any purposed point; or the Distance in Degrees, Leagues, &c., of any two Places. **1727–51** CHAMBERS *Cycl.*, *Line of Distance*, in perspective, is a right line drawn from the eye to the principal point..*Point of Distance*, in perspective, is a point in the horizontal line at such distance from the principal point, as is that of the eye from the same. **1762** FALCONER *Shipwr.* I. 748 Thus height and polar distance are obtain'd, Then latitude and declination gain'd. **1795** *Gentl. Mag.* 541/1 Objects..placed beyond the focal distance. **1819** JAS. WILSON *Dict. Astrol.* 81 The distance of any place is found by subtracting the ascension of the preceding part, or its descension, from that of the succeeding part. **1832** *Nat. Philos., Electr.* vi. §87. 23 (Useful Knowl. Soc.) The distance between the conducting bodies requisite for the transfer of electricity through the air, or what is termed the striking distance. **1834** *Ibid.*, *Navig.* I. ii. §12 The lines which make with the meridian lines the angles called courses are called nautical distances. **1837** *Penny Cycl.* IX. 22/2 This common word.. is very frequently applied to angular distance, meaning the angle of separation which the directions of two bodies include.. In the apparent sphere of the heavens, distance always means angular distance. **1876** GWILT *Encycl. Archit.* Gloss., *Distance of the Eye*, in perspective, the distance of the eye from the picture in a line perpendicular to the plane thereof.

f. *Boxing.* Striking distance.

1805 *Sporting Mag.* XXVII. 130/1 He [*sc.* a boxer] was an excellent judge of his distance. **1808** *Ibid.* XXXII. 35/1 Dogherty commenced at a rally within distance with determined courage. *Ibid.* 35/2 Belcher, within distance, hit him a severe facer. **1888** F. W. J. HENNING *Recoll. Prize Ring* 44 At last Rooke got within distance and lashed out his left, catching Joe an ugly one on the ear. **1896** in J. C. Trotter *Boxing* 125 In the event of a competitor being knocked down, his opponent shall retire out of distance. **1897** *Encycl. Sport* I. 133/2 When out of distance, the left hand may be dropped.., but when within distance it must immediately be brought up to the proper position. *Ibid.* 135/2 After the blow is delivered you are to spring back well out of distance.

6. *fig.* Remoteness, or degree of remoteness, in any relation to which spatial terms are transferred or figuratively applied; e.g. in likeness, relationship, allusion, degree, etc. 'Ideal disjunction, mental separation' (J.).

1667 WOOD *Life* (Oxf. Hist. Soc.) II. 108 This.. was soe much resented that Mr. Vernon in a sermon at S. Marie's told the auditory at a distance of it [*i.e.* by a distant allusion]. **1698** FRYER *Acc. E. India & P.* 93 A Shiek is a Cousin too, at a distance. *a* **1715** BURNET *Own Time* (1823) I. 393 They did it at so great a distance, that.. there was no danger of misprision of treason. **1871** B. STEWART *Heat* §301 Some [substances] being near their melting-points, others at a great distance from them. **1875** MAINE *Hist. Inst.* ii. 30 The mistake.. I conceive to have been an effect of mental distance. **1876** MOZLEY *Univ. Serm.* iii. (1877) 67 The distance of an end raises the rank of the labour undergone for it.

†**7.** Position (high or low) with respect to others; class, rank. *Obs. rare.*

1655 FULLER *Ch. Hist.* VIII. ii. §33, I am not satisfied in what distance properly to place these persons. Some.. will account it too high, to rank them amongst Martyrs; and surely, I conceive it too low, to esteem them but bare Confessours.

8. Of relations of personal intercourse: Remoteness in intercourse, the opposite of intimacy or familiarity, arising from disparity of rank or station, or exclusiveness of feeling: hence, on the one part, **a.** Aloofness, 'stand-offness', excessive reserve or dignity; on the other, **b.** Deferential attitude, deference.

1597 SHAKS. *Lover's Compl.* 151 With safest distance I mine honour shielded. *Ibid.* 237 She.. kept cold distance, and did thence remove, To spend her living in eternal love. **1604** —— *Oth.* III. iii. 13 He shall in strangenesse stand no farther off, Than in a politique distance.

a. **1660** F. BROOKE tr. *Le Blanc's Trav.* 294 He was a benigne and courteous Prince, affectionate.. without state or distance. **1738** NEAL *Hist. Purit.* IV. 88 To let them see how little he valued those distances he was bound to observe for form sake with others. **1765** ORTON *Mem. P. Doddridge* viii. 199 He had contracted nothing of that moroseness and distance. **1818** JAS. MILL *Brit. India* II. v. vii. 620 They put on the forms of distance; and stood upon elevated terms. **1827** MACAULAY *Country Clergym. Trip* vi, No fleering! no distance! no scorn.

b. **1689** *Andros Tracts* II. 107 The Government expects to be treated with more Distance and Difference. **1699** BENTLEY *Phal.* 287 I'll observe the respect and distance that's due to him from his Scholar. *a* **1700** DRYDEN (J.), I hope your modesty Will know, what distance to the crown is due. **1742** FIELDING *J. Andrews* I. ix, Slipslop.. had preserved hitherto a distance to her lady.

c. *to keep one's distance*: to observe the due reserve and avoidance of familiarity which are proper to one's position. *to know one's distance*: to recognize what distance ought to be kept.

1601 SHAKS. *All's Well* V. iii. 212 She knew her distance, and did angle for mee, Madding my eagernesse with her restraint. **1624** MASSINGER *Parl. Love* II. iii, Pray you, keep your distance, And grow not rude. **1642** FULLER *Holy & Prof. St.* IV. xvi. 325 Teaching words their distance to wait on his matter. **1660** T. M. *Hist. Independ.* IV. 65 They intended to curb the Wallingford party, by teaching them manners, and to know their distance. **1727** POPE *Th. on Var. Subj.* Swift's Wks. 1755 II. I. 231 If a man makes me keep my distance, the comfort is, he keeps his at the same time. **1773** GOLDSM. *Stoops to Conq.* II, It won't do; so I beg you'll keep your distance. **1831** *Society* I. 12 Her mother.. treated him with bare civility, to make him, as she expressed it, keep his distance.

9. In prepositional phrases and constructions.

a. *at a distance, at d.*: remote, far away; also, at a specified interval of space (see also sense 6). So † *in distance* (*obs.*). *out of distance*: too far away, out of reach.

1638 SIR T. HERBERT *Trav.* (ed. 2) 52 The Distoore and other Lay-men (at 12 foot distance) surround the holy Diety. **1654** CODRINGTON tr. *Hist. Ivstine* 74 To those who at distance do observe it. **1655** FULLER *Ch. Hist.* IX. vi. §29 The wary Archbishop, not over-fond of his friendship, kept him at distance. **1697** DAMPIER *Voy.* I. 261 At a distance it appears like an Island. **1711** STEELE *Spect.* No. 96 ¶2 My Master.. has often been whipp'd for not keeping me at a distance. **1713** ADDISON *Guardian* No. 167 ¶8 At about a mile's distance from the black temple. *c* **1790** WILLOCK *Voy.* 305 At a safe distance from the scene of action. **1845** M. PATTISON *Ess.* (1889) I. 17 At no great distance from the Island City. **1847** TENNYSON *Princ.* VI. 67 Blanche At distance follow'd.

1563 W. FULKE *Meteors* (1640) 42 Not.. too farre off.. neither yet too neere.. but in a competent and middle distance. **1602** MARSTON *Antonio's Rev.* IV. i, Kept in distance at the halberts point. *a* **1613** OVERBURY *Newes from Sea* Wks. (1856) 181 A mans companions are (like ships) to be kept in distance, for falling foule one of another.

1641 BP. HALL *Rem. Wks.* (1660) 95 Those that are out of distance what noise so ever they make, are not heard. **1642** FULLER *Holy & Prof. St.* II. xvii. 114 He never demands out of distance of the price he intends to take. **1655** —— *Ch. Hist.* VI. i. §16 For skill in School-Divinity they beat all other Orders quite out of distance. **1815** JANE AUSTEN *Emma* II. xiv. 233 We are rather out of distance from the very striking beauties.

b. Also used without preposition as an adverbial adjunct of measure.

1577 B. GOOGE *Heresbach's Husb.* II. (1586) 99 Take heede.. that your trees stand a good distance a sunder. **1597** SHAKS. *2 Hen. IV*, IV. i. 226 Pleaseth your Lordship To meet his Grace, iust distance 'tweene our Armies? **1697** DAMPIER *Voy.* I. 116 A Rock a good distance from the shore. *a* **1719** ADDISON (J.), He lived but a few miles distance from her father's house. **1792** *Gentl. Mag.* 13/2 The bridge.. is some little distance from the main street.

10. *ellipt.* A point or place at a distance, the region in the distance. **a.** A point at a distance, a distant point. Chiefly in the phrases *from, to a distance*.

1782 COWPER *Progr. Err.* 202 Viewed from a distance.. Folly and Innocence are so alike. *c* **1790** WILLOCK *Voy.* 316, I found I was unable to walk to any distance. **1845** DARWIN *Voy. Nat.* i. (1890) 8 The rocks of St. Paul appear from a distance of a brilliantly white colour. *Mod.* Visitors from a distance have the preference. He has removed to a distance.

b. The remote part of the field of vision or perception; the distant or far-off region; esp. in the phr. *in the distance*.

1813 SHELLEY *Q. Mab.* II. 84 There was a little light That twinkled in the misty distance. **1847** TENNYSON *Princ.* IV. 63 A trumpet in the distance pealing news. **1856** KANE *Arct. Expl.* I. v. 46 All the back country apeared one great rolling distance of glacier. **1887** BOWEN *Virg. Æneid* I. 34 Scarce had Sicily's shores in the distance faded away. **1891** GLADSTONE in *Daily News* 28 Jan. 3/3 Viewed now, calmly, in the light of the golden distance.

c. *Painting*, etc. The distant part of a landscape; the part of a picture representing this.

middle distance, the part midway between the foreground and the remote region.

1706 *Art of Painting* (1744) 424 Accustom'd himself to take in a large extent of hills and distance. **1813** *Examiner* 10 May 299/2 His.. greyish green middle-distance, blue horizon, and grey sky, constitute a rich system of colour. **1865** KINGSLEY *Herew.* Prel. 18 Dark and sad.. autumn days, when all the distances were shut off. **1861** THORNBURY *Turner* (1862) I. 89 His distances were low, and his trees ill-formed. **1891** T. HARDY *Tess* I. ii, The atmosphere.. is so tinged with azure, that what artists call the middle distance partakes also of that hue.

11. a. *transf.* The extent or 'space' of time between two events; an interval, intervening period. (Now only in phr. *distance of time*, implying remoteness.)

c **1384** CHAUCER *H. Fame* I. 18 To knowe.. neyther the distaunce Of tymes of hem. **1494** FABYAN *Chron.* VII. 550 After a dystaunce or pause of tyme, the archebysshop.. stode vp and askyd [etc.]. **1622** SPARROW *Bk. Com. Prayer* (1661) 244 The Communion-Service is to be some good distance after the Morning Service. **1699** BENTLEY *Phal.* 404 From the Date of the Mosaic Law to the Prophecy of Ezekiel, there's a distance of 900 Years. **1774** FOOTE *Cozeners* III. Wks. 1799 II. 180 Take this draught three times a day, at two hours distance. **1820** SCORESBY *Acc. Arctic Reg.* I. 43 At the distance of eighteen to thirty years, from the time when the several navigations were performed. **1849** MACAULAY *Hist. Eng.* I. 455 An apprehension not to be mentioned, even at this distance of time, without shame and indignation. **1871** MORLEY *Voltaire* (1886) 172 The connection may be seen at our distance of time to have been marked and unmistakable.

b. *spec.* in *Boxing*, the scheduled length of a contest.

1934 L. HARVEY *Training & Self Defence* 112 If.. you can stay the full distance of a contest.. work to a schedule during the fight. **1936** *Times* 24 Nov. 6/6 A fearless fighter who had.. 'gone the distance' three times with the famous negro, Al Brown. **1958** *Times* 30 Sept. 15/1 This greater experience could be particularly valuable if the bout goes the distance.

12. *attrib.* and *Comb.*, as *distance-language*; *distance-softened*, *distance-veiled* adjs. Also **distance-block**, a block inserted between two objects to keep them a required distance apart; **distance-flag** (*Horse-racing*), a flag held by the man who is stationed at the distance-post; **distance-judge**, a judge stationed at the **distance-post**, a post (or flag) placed at the fixed 'distance' (see 5 c) in front of the winning post in a heat-race, to note what horses are 'distanced', through failing to reach this before the winner passes the winning-post; **distance learning**, education (esp. at tertiary level) in which contact between students and teacher is principally by correspondence or broadcast programmes, rather than face to face; **distance-piece** = *distance-block*; **distance-receptor** *Physiol.*, a sense organ, such as the eye or ear, that is responsive to stimuli from distant sources; **distance runner**, an athlete who competes in long- or middle-distance races; also **distance running; distance-signal**: see DISTANT 3 d; **distance-stand**, a stand erected at the distance-post on a race-course.

1894 H. DRUMMOND *Ascent of Man* 233 This new distance-language began again at the beginning, just as all Language does, by employing signs. **1972** T. DODDS (*title*) IEC Broadsheet on *distance learning no. 1. Multi-media approaches to rural education. **1977** *Proc. R. Soc. Med.* LXX. 684/2, I do not think that the distance learning pattern is suited to school-leavers. **1986** *Library Assoc. Rec.* Jan. 13/3 The Aberystwyth course did not get off the ground because most local authorities were unwilling to release staff for a whole year, and.. as a result Aberystwyth was considering offering the MEd degree as a distance-learning course. **1930** *Engineering* 4 July 9/3 The introduction of a distance piece between a piston and its crosshead. **1962** *Times* 7 Apr. 11/7 The fine toothed blades were separated by a distance-piece. **1809** *British Press* 6 Apr. in *Spirit Pub. Jrnls.* (1810) XIII. 63 Gibby and Premier.. were scarcely able to strike a trot in passing the distance-post. **1809** J. P. ROBERDEAN *Ibid.* 162 You a'n't near even the distance-post of notoriety. **1870** BLAINE *Encycl. Rur. Sports* III. iv. 371 In coming in on the right of the course, there should be two distance-posts; the first is to be erected two hundred and forty yards from the winning-post; the second a hundred and twenty from it. **1906** C. S. SHERRINGTON *Integrative Action Nerv. Syst.* ix. 324 It is in the leading segments that we find the 'distance-receptors'. **1927** HALDANE & HUXLEY *Animal Biol.* xii. 300 Since they [*sc.* gastropods] are free-moving, distance-receptors are wanted. **1965** MARSHALL & HUGHES *Physiol. Mammals* viii. 187 Exteroceptors.. may be divided into: teloreceptors or distance receptors, cutaneous receptors, and sometimes chemical receptors. [**1971** *Nature* 12 Feb. 491/2 The experimental evidence for the bursicles functioning as distance chemoreceptors came from a study of the escape response of [the marine snail] *Tegula funebralis* to the starfish *Pisaster ochraceus* Brandt.] **1911** *Encycl. Brit.* XXIII. 854/1 Hard daily training is necessary for a distance runner. **1976** *Sci. Amer.* June 110/3 For some years the faster sprinters have on the whole been Americans and the faster distance runners Europeans. **1935** *Encycl. Sports* 29/2 (*heading*) Distance running. **1985** *Christian Science Monitor* 26 Aug. 20/2 Slaney.. holds every American women's distance running record from 800 meters to 10,000. **1874** Distance signal [see DISTANT 3 d]. **1850** MRS. BROWNING *Poems* II. 196 You can hear that evermore Distance-softened noise. **1870** BLAINE *Encycl. Rur. Sports* III. iv. 372 So that the man in the distance-stand may clearly see the winning-post, and be ready to drop the distance-flag. **1883** A. J. MENKEN *Infelicia* 93 There cometh a hum, as of distance-veiled battle.

ˈdistance, *v.* [f. prec. sb. Cf. F. *distancer* (14th c. in Hatz.-Darm.).]

1. a. *trans.* To place at a distance; to separate by a space; to eloign. Also *fig.*

1578 BANISTER *Hist. Man* I. 19 The head is distaunsed from the body so much in man, for the cause of Aspera Arteria. **1624** T. SCOTT *Eng. Spanish Pilgr.* iii. 14 Furnished with some 50 beds, distanced onely by a partition of boards. *a* **1661** FULLER *Worthies, Hantshire* II. 1 Not to speak of the friendly Sea conveniently distanced from London. **1860** EMERSON *Cond. Life, Fate* 19 This insight.. distances those who share it from those who share it not. **1963** *Listener* 3 Jan. 21/2 Would it not be more true to say that the extreme formality.. distances the hatred for contemplation? **1963** *P.M.L.A.* LXXVIII. 296/1 Primarily Chaucer's narrative method serves to distance us from the characters. **1967** *Medium Ævum* XXXVI. 284 In *The Parlement of Foules* and in *Troilus and Criseyde* Chaucer takes great pains to distance himself as narrator from the action of the poem, and this hardly seems to be an ironic distancing.

†**b.** To fix the distance of. *Obs.*

1690 *Act 2 W. & M.* in *Lond. Gaz.* (1706) No. 4292/3 All Persons paying to any Lamps, distanced by two of Her Majesty's Justices of the Peace, are exempted from hanging out a Lanthorn and Candle. **1715** LEONI *Palladio's Archit.* (1742) I. 21 This manner of distancing the Column is.. call'd Systylos.

†**c.** To express the distance of. *Obs. rare.*

1650 FULLER *Pisgah* I. xiii. 40 The Hebrews distanced their places by severall measures.

2. To make to appear distant.

1695 DRYDEN tr. *Dufresnoy's Art Paint.* (J.), That which gives a relievo to a bowl, is the quick light, or white, which appears to be on the side nearest to us, and the black by consequence distances the object. **1864** LOWELL *Fireside Trav.* 198 Mountains, which the ripe Italian air distances with a bloom like that on unplucked grapes.

†**3.** *intr.* To be distant; to go to a distance. *Obs. rare.*

1614 T. ADAMS in Spurgeon *Treas. Dav.* Ps. cvi. 5 The less they distanced from the beginning, the poorer they were. **1658** J. WEBB tr. *Calprenede's Cleopatra* VIII. I. 7 Unable to hinder their distancing.. a great way from the place of combate.

4. a. *trans.* To put or leave at a distance by superior speed; to outstrip or leave behind in a race, or (*fig.*) in any competition.

1642 H. MORE *Song of Soul* II. iii. I. xxi, The Sun and all the starres that do appear She feels them in herself, can distance all. **1691** NORRIS *Pract. Disc.* 37 We are utterly Distanc'd in the Race. **1712** W. ROGERS *Voy.* 127 He distanc'd and tir'd both the Dog and the Men. **1851** LONGF. *Gold. Leg.* v. *Foot of the Alps*, Our fleeter steeds have distanced our attendants. **1856** LEVER *Martins of Cro' M.* 55 [He] had distanced all his competitors in his College career.

b. To put or leave (a place) at a distance by going away from it; to leave behind.

1873 MRS. CHARLES in *Sunday Mag.* Feb. 332 We heard the joyous voices sound louder and freer as they distanced the solemn precincts.

c. To keep at a distance from. ? *Obs.*

1786 MAD. D'ARBLAY *Diary* 28 Nov., I wished them well.. but I distanced them to the best of my power.

d. *Horse-racing.* To beat by a distance: see quot. 1803 and DISTANCE *sb.* 5 c.

1674 N. Cox *Gentl. Recreat.* v. (1686) 72 The hindmost Horse being bound to follow him, within a certain distance agreed on..and which ever Horse could distance the other won the Match. 1707 *Lond. Gaz.* No. 4363/4 Paying a Guinea Entrance (which is to go to the second Horse, distanc'd or not distanc'd). 1713 STEELE *Guardian* No. 6. ¶5 He puts in for the Queen's plate every year, with orders to his rider never to win or be distanced. 1803 M. CUTLER in *Life, etc.* (1888) II. 142 At a distance of about ten rods.. is another stage..called the distanced stage. If any horses in the race do not arrive at this stage before the foremost arrives at the stage from which they started, they are said to be distanced, and are taken out, and not suffered to run again in the same race.

fig. 1822 SCOTT *Nigel* i, Vincent beat his companion beyond the distance-post, in..dexterity of hand..and double-distanced him in all respecting the commercial affairs of the shop.

Hence **'distancing** *vbl. sb.* and *ppl. a.*

1658 J. WEBB tr. *Calprenede's Cleopatra* VIII. i. 7 To regret the distancing of Coriolanus, whom she fled, and whose Infidelity she detested. 1786 MAD. D'ARBLAY *Diary* 23 Dec., His appearance and air are dignified..but cold, and rather distancing. 1816 *Sporting Mag.* XLVII. 233 On account of such distancing superiority. 1945 *Kenyon Rev.* VII. 470 The distancing ('Verfremdung') which Brecht desires is complemented by his concreteness. 1949, 1956 [see ALIENATION 1 d]. 1958 R. WILLIAMS *Culture & Society* I. v. 87 The method..of documentary record..has..a slightly distancing effect. 1961 W. J. HARVEY *Art of G. Eliot* v. 116 George Eliot sometimes fails to achieve an adequate distancing of her experience.

distanced ('dɪstənst), *ppl. a.* [f. prec. + -ED[1].]

1. a. Put or set at a distance; remote, distant. Now only *fig.*

1654 tr. *Scudery's Curia Pol.* 135 Alexander the Great commanded Subjects (though remote and distanced) in the farthest parts. 1668 H. MORE *Div. Dial.* III. xxviii. 481 The distanced Singing of the chearful Birds. 1672 —— *Brief Reply* 91 In many thousand far distanced places at once. 1949 KOESTLER *Insight & Outlook* xix. 267 Interest becomes disinterested, as it were, distanced, almost completely detached from the aims of the original drive. 1962 W. NOWOTTNY *Lang. Poets Use* iv. 79 We take in the language of the last quatrain, so distanced from the language of common life, without recoil.

†**b.** At variance, differing in opinion. *Obs.*

1644 J. GOODWIN *Innoc. Triumph.* (1645) 54 Persons, not onely distanced in their judgements about Church-Government, but about the God-head of Christ.

2. a. Left behind, outstripped as in a race.

1713 GAY *Fan* Poems 1745 I. 31 The bounding damsel flies, Strains to the goal, the distanc'd lover dies. 1715-20 POPE *Iliad* XI. 200 Still slaughtering on, the king of men proceeds; The distanced army wonders at his deeds.

b. *Horse-racing.* Beaten by a distance: see DISTANCE *sb.* 5 c.

1737 BRACKEN *Farriery Impr.* (1757) II. 168 When they happen'd to ride a distanc'd Horse. 1870 BLAINE *Encycl. Rur. Sports* III. iv. 363 A distanced horse cannot start again.

'distanceless, *a.* [f. DISTANCE *sb.* 10 b + -LESS.] In which things in the distance are not visible.

1851 KINGSLEY *Yeast* i. (D.), A silent, dim, distanceless, rotting day in March.

distancy ('dɪstənsɪ). *rare.* [ad. L. *distāntia* DISTANCE: see -ANCY.]

†**1.** Disagreement, difference. *Obs.*

1628 T. SPENCER *Logick* 68 Dissenteth. This word.. signifieth a distancy, arising from a varietie.

†**2.** Distantness in space. *Obs.*

1642 H. MORE *Song of Soul* III. II. vi. (R.), Even absent things may be seen by phantasie; By sense things present at a distancie. 1647 —— *Philos. Poems, Infin. Worlds* xxxix, There is a distancy In empty space.

3. Distantness in manner.

1836 *Rand. Recoll. Ho. Lords* xiii. 277 A certain distancy and reservedness. 1883 *Chamb. Jrnl.* 690 He hid his feelings under the habitual mask of stolid distancy.

distannic (daɪ'stænɪk), *a. Chem.* [f. DI-[2] 2 + STANNIC.] Of or containing two equivalents of tin (*stannum*).

1873 *Fownes' Chem.* (ed. 11) 593 It forms distannic oxyhexethide.

distant ('dɪstənt), *a.* [a. F. *distant* (Oresme, 14th c.), ad. L. *distānt-em* standing apart, separate, distant, different, pr. pple. of *distāre* to stand apart: see DISTANCE.]

1. Separate or apart in space (by a specified interval). Const. *from.*

c 1391 CHAUCER *Astrol.* I. §17 It departeth the furste Moevable..in 2 ilike parties, evene distantz fro the poles of this world. 1546 *Mem. Ripon* (Surtees) III. 26 The same is distaunt from the paroch Church ccc Foote. 1559 W. CUNNINGHAM *Cosmogr. Glasse* 125 Within which draw an other Circle, a finger bredth distant. 1568 GRAFTON *Chron.* II. 1284 The armies..not distaunt by estimation above two myles. 1611 BIBLE *Exod.* xxxvi. 22 One board had two tenons, equally distant one from another. 1684 R. H. *School Recreat.* 46 Hold it even with the Muzzle of the Musket.. about an Inch distant. 1778 MISS BURNEY *Evelina* iv, This retired place, to which Dorchester, the nearest town, is seven miles distant. 1832 *Act 2-3 Will. IV*, c. 64 Sched. O. 38 A straight line drawn due east to a point one hundred yards distant.

2. Separated by an unspecified but large or considerable space; far apart, not close together. (Often used in *Nat. Hist.* of teeth, spines, hairs, leaves, spots, etc.)

1548 HALL *Chron., Hen. V* (an. 1) (R.), All other nacions were astonnied to se suche an honorable compaignie come from a countree so farre distant. 1577 B. GOOGE *Heresbach's Husb.* III. (1586) 154 b, His [a dog's] shoulder pointes well distant. *c* 1586 C'TESS PEMBROKE *Ps.* LXXII. vii, The woods, where enterlaced trees..Ioyne at the head, though distant at the knees. 1667 MILTON *P.L.* x. 362, I felt, Though distant from thee Worlds between, yet felt That I must after thee with this thy Son. 1760 ANNE STEELE *Hymn 'O for one celestial ray'* ii, Distant from thy blest abode. 1762 FALCONER *Shipwr.* I. 43 In distant souls congenial passions glow. 1828 STARK *Elem. Nat. Hist.* I. 465 Jaws armed with pointed and distant teeth.

3. a. Standing, lying, or taking place afar off; not near at hand, remote.

1590 SHAKS. *Mids. N.* II. ii. 60 So farre be distant, and good night sweet friend. 1697 DRYDEN *Virg. Georg.* III. 392 The Stallion..trembles for the distant Mare. 1710 POPE *Windsor For.* 401 Earth's distant ends our glory shall behold. 1712 W. ROGERS *Voy.* 2 Furnish'd with all Necessaries..for a distant Undertaking. 1747 GRAY (*title*), Ode on a Distant Prospect of Eton College. 1817 WOLFE *Burial Sir J. Moore* vii, We heard the distant and random gun That the foe was sullenly firing. 1850 KINGSLEY *Alt. Locke* i, Even the Surrey hills..Are to me a distant fairy land. 1879 HARLAN *Eyesight* viii. 105 Distant vision is a passive sensation not more exhausting than breathing.

†**b.** Long in extent. *Obs. rare.*

1705 BOSMAN *Guinea* 250 If the Trees be high, or the way any thing distant.

c. Of the eyes: Looking into the far-distance. *rare.*

1873 BLACK *Pr. Thule* xxi. 335 Her companion's pale face and troubled and distant eyes. 1877 —— *Green Past.* i, The large and tender eyes are distant and troubled.

d. ***distant signal***: *spec.* on railways: a signal placed some distance in advance of a home signal to give earlier intimation of what the latter indicates (orig. one placed some distance in advance of the point of danger); also called *distance signal.*

1820 SCORESBY *Acc. Arctic Reg.* III. 524 The sails of the ship are frequently used as distant signals. 1874 R. C. RAPIER *Signals Railw.* 15 A distance signal was put up at St. Margaret's, near Edinburgh, 250 yards in advance of the point of danger; and after this distant signals became general. *Ibid.* The Great Northern was, at its construction in 1852, completely fitted with distant signals of the semaphore type. *Ibid.* 46 Separate distant signal arms for each home signal. 1889 G. FINDLAY *Eng. Railway* 68 The distant signal is placed at varying distances behind the home signal, according to circumstances.

4. Far apart or remote in time.

1603 SHAKS. *Meas. for M.* II. i. 93 We had but two in the house, which at that very distant time stood, as it were in a fruit dish. 1732 BERKELEY *Alciphr.* VI. §8 The books of Holy Scripture were written..at distant times. 1757 GLYNN *Day of Judgem.* (Mason), Whom distant ages to each other's sight Had long denied. 1849 MACAULAY *Hist. Eng.* II. 148 The Parliament was again prorogued to a distant day. 1860 TYNDALL *Glac.* II. viii. 264 The glacier may also diminish in length at distant intervals.

5. a. *transf.* and *fig.* Remote in relations other than those of space and time. ***distant likeness***: a faint resemblance; the opposite of a close resemblance.

1538 STARKEY *England* I. iv. 108 A grete faute in our pollycy and much dystant from al cyuyle ordur. 1674 N. Cox *Gentl. Recreat.* v. (1686) 76 He may be far distant from that perfect State of Body. 1711 ADDISON *Spect.* No. 122 ¶9, I could still discover a distant Resemblance of my old Friend. 1777 SHERIDAN *Sch. Scand.* IV. iii, I haven't the most distant idea. 1866 ARGYLL *Reign Law* vi. (1871) 274 Is it only by distant analogy? 1891 *Leeds Mercury* 27 Apr. 4/7 Not even the most distant allusion was made to it.

b. *spec.* Remotely related in kinship.

a 1611 BEAUM. & FL. *Maid's Trag.* III. i, Good day, Amintor! for, to me, the name Of brother is too distant. 1768 STERNE *Sent. Journ.* (1778) II. 57 (*Sword*) Unlook'd for bequests from distant branches of his house. 1831 LYTTON *Godolph.* 5 A distant connexion of the deceased. 1868 FREEMAN *Norm. Conq.* (1876) II. App. 671 Not a sister, but a more distant kinswoman of the Emperor.

†**6.** Different in character or quality. *Obs.*

1659 HAMMOND *On Ps.* i. Heading to Paraphr. 5 The distant fate of pious and godless men. 1667 *Decay Chr. Piety* xix. ¶2 Is it fit she should have guardians and champions of a quite distant temper? 1705 STANHOPE *Paraphr.* I. 44 Distant opinions about the same Things. 1710 STEELE *Tatler* No. 26 ¶1 Enrolling all Men in their distant classes, before they presume to drink Tea or Chocolate in those Places.

7. Reserved in intercourse; standing aloof; not intimate or expressive of intimacy.

1709 STEELE *Tatler* No. 126 ¶1 The distant Behaviour of the Prude. 1766 GOLDSM. *Vic. W.* xxxi, He made Miss Wilmot a modest and distant bow. 1828 *Life Planter Jamaica* (ed. 2) 209 [He] obtained a very distant and stately reception. 1866 MRS. H. WOOD *St. Martin's Eve* x, She desired Eleanor to be very distant with him.

8. *Comb.* ***distant early warning*** (abbrev. D.E.W.) ***line***, a radar system installed in North America for the advance detection of missile attack; ***distant-water*** attrib.

1777 R. POTTER *Æschylus* (1779) I. 55 (Jod.) Train'd to bear The distant-wounding bow. 1788 ANNA SEWARD *Lett.* (1811) II. 181 The visits of distant-dwelling friends. 1955 *Times* 18 Aug. 6/3 Two task forces, totalling 3,000 men, now on their way to the Arctic regions of Canada, will be employed in erecting more than 50 radar stations there as part of the distant early warning (D.E.W.) line. Seven radar stations are known to be working in Greenland, besides those incorporated in the two newer warning lines across Canada, named Mid-Canada and Pine Tree. 1958 *Times* 21 July 9/6 The Distant Early Warning line in the far north is similarly run by civilians on private contract. 1958 *Listener* 3 July 6/1 The total catch of the distant-water fleet. 1960 *Times* 5 Feb. 5/1 The British distant-water fishermen are as vitally involved as anyone in the fishery limits dispute. 1962 J. TUNSTALL *Fishermen* ix. 218 In Hull all the ships are distant-water trawlers, whereas in the other ports there are more near and middle-water ships. *Ibid.* x. 228 By 1953 the restriction committee was called by the amusing title of 'The Distant Water *Development* Scheme'.

†**di'stantial,** *a. Obs.* [f. L. *distāntia* DISTANCE + -AL[1].] Distant, far-off; differing, diverse.

1648 W. MOUNTAGUE *Devout Ess.* I. xii. §1 (R.) How distancial are we from this ingenious coercion of our polluted fancies! 1656 BLOUNT *Glossogr.*, *Distantial*, differing or distant, far asunder, divers. 1676 H. MORE *Remarks* 145 Colligating..parts of the most distantial textures and consistencies. 1713 DERHAM *Phys. Theol.* VIII. iv. 402 Their Cornea and Optick Nerve..are only fitted to see distantial objects.

†**di'stantiate,** *v. Obs.* [f. L. *distāntia* DISTANCE + -ATE[3].] *trans.* To take the distance of.

1610 W. FOLKINGHAM *Art of Survey* II. v. 55 From conuenient distances in the same, distantiate euery By, dispersed in the Plot.

distantly ('dɪstəntlɪ), *adv.* [f. DISTANT + -LY[2].] In a distant manner.

1. At a distance in space or time; remotely, afar off.

1675 tr. *Camden's Hist. Eliz.* an. 1580 (R.), These Irish matters, though in time somewhat distantly acted, I have thought good to mention together. 1678 CUDWORTH *Intell. Syst.* 776 The Corporeal World is Distantly present, to the Intelligible. 1797 MRS. RADCLIFFE *Italian* xii, Ellena followed distantly in the Abbess's train.

b. Widely apart, at considerable distances.

1847 HARDY in *Proc. Berw. Nat. Club* II. No. v. 239 Head ..distantly and deeply punctured.

c. In a way expressing distance or remoteness.

1873 BLACK *Pr. Thule* xxvii. 454 Her eyes were looking somewhat distantly at the sea.

2. *fig.* Remotely (in other relations); not closely; not intimately.

a 1768 STERNE *Let.* iii. *to Miss L——* (R.), I..then most distantly hint at a droll foible in his character. 1822 BYRON *Werner* I. i. 194 *Iden.* Perhaps you are related to my relative ..*Jos.* We are, but distantly. 1828 WEBSTER, *Distantly*.. with reserve. 1848 C. BRONTE *J. Eyre* xi, I am distantly related to the Rochesters by the mother's side. *Mod.* He was distantly courteous.

'distantness. *rare.* [f. as prec. + -NESS.] The quality of being distant.

1731 BAILEY vol. II, *Distantness*, distance, a being distant from. *Mod.* He showed some distantness of manner.

†**dis'task,** *v. Obs. rare.* [DIS- 7 a.] *trans.* To relieve of a task, to exonerate.

1592 WARNER *Alb. Eng.* VIII. xliii. (1612) 207 On these doo vulgar Eares and Eyes so brimly waite and gaze, As they distaske our priuate Penne notorious Landes to blaze.

†**dis'tastable,** *a. Obs. rare.* [f. DISTASTE *v.* + -ABLE.] Distasteful. Hence **dis'tastably** *adv.*, with distaste or disgust.

1607 S. COLLINS *Serm.* (1608) 37 The broth which a strange root hath made distastable. 1625 tr. *Boccaccio's Decameron, Modell Wit* 41 b, Let him thinke that I can brooke those words as distastably, as you do or can his ill deeds.

distaste (dɪs'teɪst), *sb.* Also 7 **distast.** [f. DIS- 9 + TASTE *sb.*: prob. as a rendering of It. *disgusto*, OF. *desgoust*: see Florio and Cotgrave.]

1. Disrelish or dislike of food or drink; nausea; bad taste in the mouth. Now *rare* or *Obs.*

1598 FLORIO, *Sgusto*, disgust, distast, vnkindnes, dislike. 1614 BP. HALL *Recoll. Treat.* 1008 Moses was..in the same distaste of bitternes. 1635 BRATHWAIT *Arcad. Pr.* I. 200 Nor house, nor ground, nor any kind of wealth Can relish his distaste that has no health. 1753 N. TORRIANO *Gangr. Sore Throat* 28 [She] was seized..in the Evening, with a Distaste; she had a very uneasy and tumbling Night. 1849 C. BRONTE *Shirley* I. vi. 111 A positive crime might have been more easily pardoned than a symptom of distaste for the foreign comestibles.

2. Disinclination, dislike; (moderate) aversion, disgust, or repugnance.

1598 FLORIO, [see sense 1]. 1605 BACON *Adv. Learn.* I. i. §3 (1873) 8 Make application of our knowledge, to give ourselves repose and contentment, not distaste or repining. *a* 1628 F. GREVILLE *Sidney* (1652) 58 To raise a general distast in all men against the Government. *a* 1652 J. SMITH *Sel. Disc.* i. 17 Besides in wicked men there are sometimes distastes of vice. 1660 R. COKE *Power & Subj.* 59 For there is no native who is not in distaste with some body. 1726 SHELVOCKE *Voy. round World* (1757) 455 Which gave the ships company, such a distaste of Clipperton. 1816 KEATINGE *Trav.* (1817) I. 252 The Moors..have a distaste for the proselytes when made. *a* 1822 SHELLEY *Assassins* ii, Their predilections and distastes. 1869 J. MARTINEAU *Ess.* II. 5 An aversion more resembling a distaste than a conviction.

†**3.** Unpleasantness; annoyance, discomfort. *Obs.*

1611 B. JONSON *Poetaster* v. i, Our ear is now too much profaned, grave Maro, With these distastes, to take thy sacred lines. 1625 BACON *Ess., Adversity* (Arb.) 505 Prosperity is not without many Feares and Distastes. 1711 STEELE *Spect.* No. 4 ¶2 There are so many Gratifications attend this publick sort of Obscurity, that some little Distastes I daily receive have lost their Anguish.

†**4.** Offence, cause of offence or dislike. *Obs.*

1608 D. T. *Ess. Pol. & Mor.* 21 b, Court-Parasites..do labor upon the least distast that is offred, to procure an utter dislike. **1698** J. Fryer *Acc. E. India & P.* 156 To avoide giving distaste in not removing their Hats. **1709** Strype *Ann. Ref.* I. xxv. 280 At which Bishop Cheny took such distast. **1731** *Rape Helen* 24 *note*, Achilles would not go to battle for some distaste Agamemnon had given him.

†**5.** Mutual aversion, estrangement, difference, quarrel. *Obs.*

1621 Sir W. Aston in *Fortesc. Papers* 152 The King and his ministers have taken some distast. **1623** Bingham *Xenophon* 73 This was the only difference and distaste betwixt Cherisophus and Xenophon during this whole iourney. **1677** E. Smith in *12th Rep. Hist. MSS. Comm.* App. v. 38 They say he murdered himselfe..because of some distast betwixt his master and him. **1697** Dampier *Voy.* I. 433 All civil and quiet..No noise, nor appearance of distaste.

distaste (dɪsˈteɪst), *v.* Now *rare.* (Frequent in 17th c.) Also 7 **distast.** [f. dis- 6 + taste *v.*: prob. orig. an English rendering of It. (*di*)*sgustare*, or OF. *desgouster*: see Florio and Cotgr. In sense 5 used as f. dis- 7 a + taste *sb.*]

†**1.** *trans.* To dislike the taste of, have no taste for, disrelish (food, drink, etc.). *Obs.*

1586 Bright *Melanch.* xxxvi. 214 The tongue distasteth all things even of most pleasant relish. **1615** Latham *Falconry* (1633) 104 If you finde her any whit to distaste the water, then put into it..sugar-candie. **1641** French *Distill.* v. (1651) 144 It..may be given..to any that distast physick, in their milke. *a* **1661** Fuller *Worthies* (1840) III. 433 Distasting wholesome meat well dressed.

2. To have or conceive a mental distaste for or repugnance to (anything); to regard with aversion or displeasure; to have no taste for, disrelish, dislike.

1592 Davies *Immort. Soul* xxx. xxxv. (1714) 98 These do by fits her Fantasie possess; But she distastes them all within a while. **1621** Burton *Anat. Mel.* ii. iv. i. i. (1651) 363 The Romans distasted them so much that they were often banished out of their city. **1733** Neal *Hist. Purit.* II. 216 He was sorry that an established doctrine of the Church should be so distasted. **1805** Foster *Ess.* iii. 93 [He] should distaste the society of his class. **1893** Stevenson *Catriona* 60 A man ..whom I distasted at the first look, as we distaste a ferret or an earwig.

†**b.** with *obj. cl.* or *infin. phr. Obs.*

1596 Drayton *Legends* iii. 607 Who was so dull, that did not then distaste, That thus the King His Nobles should neglect? **1621** in L. Bacon *Genesis of New Eng. Ch.* (1874) xvi. 350 That you sent no lading in the ship is..worthily distasted. **1629** Gaule *Pract. The.* 161 How doe we abhorre and distast, to think him opprobriously debased.

†**3.** To offend the taste of; to disgust, nauseate.

1610 Heywood *Gold. Age* ii. Wks. 1874 III. 22 This meat distasts me, doth Lycaon..feed vs with humane flesh? **1636** Henshaw *Horæ Succ.* 21 Never refuse health because the Physicke that should procure it is bitter; let it distast me so it heale me. **1678** *Yng. Man's Call.* 155 Distempered stomacks, that are easily distasted.

†**b.** *absol.* or *intr.* To offend the taste; to cause disgust. *Obs.*

1604 Shaks. *Oth.* iii. iii. 327 Poysons, Which at the first are scarce found to distaste. **1613–6** W. Browne *Brit. Past.* ii. iii, Then least his many cherries should distast, Some other fruit he brings than he brought last. **1643** *5 Years K. James* in *Select. Harl. Misc.* (1793) 310 Poisons, that neither discolour nor distaste.

4. *trans.* To excite the dislike or aversion of; to be distasteful to; to displease, offend; *pass.* to be displeased or offended (*with*, *at*).

1597–8 Bacon *Ess.*, *Suitors* (Arb.) 44 Suters are so distasted with delaies, and abuses. **1638** Sir T. Herbert *Trav.* (ed. 2) 100 Yet loth in any thing to distaste the King. **1666** Pepys *Diary* 24 Oct., The Prince was distasted with my discourse..about the sad state of the fleet. **1702** Addison *Dial. Medals* ii. 35, I have sometimes however been very much distasted at this way of writing. **1709** J. Johnson *Clergym. Vade M.* ii. p. xiii, The Apostle..avoids the saying any thing that might distaste the Corinthians. **1833** I. Taylor *Fanat.* vi. 192 No enormity can distaste or alarm him. **1893** *Pall Mall G.* 18 Jan. 1/2 Threats and demonstrations so violent as to distaste the sympathies of many.

†**b.** *absol.* or *intr.* To cause displeasure or offence; to be distasteful. *Obs.*

1614 Sylvester *Du Bartas, Bethulia's Rescue* i. 21 Great-gracious Lady, let it not distaste That Ivdith made not.. more haste To kisse Your hands. *c* **1618** Fletcher *Q. Corinth* i. ii. **1654** Whitlock *Zootomia* Pref. A vij, If any thing that's good i' th' Book you see, Ascribe to God; but what distasts, to mee.

†**5.** *trans.* To destroy or spoil the taste or savour of; to render distasteful or tasteless. *Obs.*

1606 Shaks. *Tr. & Cr.* ii. ii. 123 Her brainsicke raptures Cannot distaste the goodnesse of a quarrell. **1617** Hieron *Wks.* II. 390 It is inough to sowre & to distaste the whole lumpe of our deuotions. **1646** J. Hall *Poems* Pref., Neither am I solicitous how they savour..and these I give over as already distasted. **1650** Trapp *Comm. Deuter.* xxviii. 15 If it distaste not his dough, or empty his basket.

Hence **dis'tasting** *vbl. sb.*

1591 Sylvester *Du Bartas* i. vii. 377 For a light surfet, or a small dis-tasting. **1654** Whitlock *Zootomia* 280 Suffer anything through..Indiscretion, or unadvised Distastings.

dis'tasted, *ppl. a.* [f. prec. + -ed[1].]

1. Disrelished, disliked. †**b.** Deprived of taste, tasteless, insipid (*obs.*).

a **1661** Fuller *Worthies* (1840) I. 362 To fight under so distasted a commander. **1662** Petty *Taxes* 15 To be spectators of these mistaken and distasted vanities.

2. Disgusted, offended; affected with nausea, disgust, or dislike.

1651 *Fuller's Abel Rediv.*, *Diazius* 143 In the eare Of the distasted Pope. **1655** Moufet & Bennet *Health's Improv.* (1746) 254 Weak, windy, distasted Stomachs. **1723** Pope *Let. to E. Blount* 27 June, The Spleenful, Ambitious, Diseas'd, Distasted..Souls wich this World affords.

distasteful (dɪsˈteɪstfʊl), *a.* [f. distaste *sb.*]

1. Disagreeable to the taste; causing disgust; 'nasty'.

1611 Florio, *Disgusteuole*, distastefull. *Disgustoso*, full of distaste, distastefull. **1621** Burton *Anat. Mel.* i. ii. iv. iii. (1651) 148 After a distasteful purge..at the very sight of physick he would be distempered. **1690** Dryden *Don Sebastian* iii. i. (R.), Why shou'd you pluck the green distasteful fruit. **1875** H. C. Wood *Therap.* (1879) 491 The potash salts are exceedingly distasteful.

2. Causing dislike; disagreeable, unpleasant, offensive.

1607 Drayton *Leg. Cromwell* (R.), For 'twas distasteful to my noble mind, That the vile world into my wants should look. **1615** J. Stephens *Satyr. Ess.* 240 He..is as willing to embrace any, as not to bee distastfull unto any. **1669** Dryden *Tyrannic Love* iv. i, None but a fool distasteful truth will tell. **1782** Pennant *Journ. fr. Chester* (R.), Freeing his country from so distasteful a minister. **1862** Ld. Brougham *Brit. Const.* xiii. 192 Persons distasteful to the Commons. **1895** J. Ambrose in *Law Times* XCIX. 546/1 His work must not be made distasteful to him through too much drudgery.

†**3.** Full of dislike; showing dislike or aversion; malevolent. *Obs.*

1607 Shaks. *Timon* ii. ii. 220 After distastefull lookes.. With certaine halfe-caps, and cold mouing nods, They froze me into Silence. **1639** T. Brugis tr. *Camus' Mor. Relat.* 144 Every one..soone growes distastfull of the prudent, because that he cannot be surprized. **1646** Sir T. Browne *Pseud. Ep.* iv. x. 204 The distastefull aversenesse of the Christian from the Jew.

dis'tastefully, *adv.* [f. prec. + -ly[2].]

1. In a distasteful manner, or to a distasteful degree: disgustingly, offensively, unpleasantly.

1631 Brathwait *Whimzies, Ruffian* 84 They..in the end grow distastefully rude to all the companie. *a* **1691** Boyle *Hist. Air* (1692) 166 The water..would grow distastefully hot. **1727** Bailey vol. II. pt. ii, Distastfully, *disagreeablement* F., *offensivè* L.

†**2.** With dislike or displeasure. *Obs.*

1627 J. Rous *Diary* (Camden) 11 In generall to speake distastfully of the voyage. **1638** Baker tr. *Balzac's Lett.* (1654) II. 16 Yet take not distastefully an officious injury.

dis'tastefulness. [f. as prec. + -ness.]

1. The quality of being distasteful; unpleasantness to the taste or mind, offensiveness.

1654 W. Mountague *Devout Ess.* ii. x. §2 (R.) The allaying and qualifying much of the bitter and distastefulness of our physick. **1654** Whitlock *Zootomia* 343 To leave the Distastfulnesse of Comparison. **1821** Lockhart *Valerius* III. xii. 296 There was something of distastefulness in the mirthful strains. **1840** Mill *Diss. & Disc.* (1859) I. 99 Speculation..has been falling more and more into distastefulness and disrepute among the educated classes.

†**2.** Dislike, aversion, repugnance. *Obs.*

a **1625** Earl Bristol *Let. to Jas. I* in *Cabala* Supp. 121 (T.) Out of a distastefulness of the former answer given. **1642** Rogers *Naaman* 466 It is a distastfulnesse of heart.

†**dis'taster.** *Obs.* [f. distaste *v.* + -er[1].] **a.** One who distastes or dislikes; a disliker. **b.** One who inspires with distaste or disgust.

a **1613** Overbury *A Wife* (1638) 183 A Distaster of the Time. **1623** N. Smith *Pref. Verse* in *Cockeram's Dict.*, Captious, yet wise seeming masters, Made by their curious eye, their owne distasters.

dis'tasting, *ppl. a.* [f. as prec. + -ing[2].] That distastes.

1. Feeling or showing distaste or dislike.

1654 Whitlock *Zootomia* 460 Slander, Backbiting, Detraction..entertaine them with..excusing Tongue, or distasting Silence. **1821** Lamb *Elia* Ser. i. *Old & New Schoolm.*, Doomed to read tedious homilies to distasting schoolboys.

2. Causing distaste; displeasing, offensive.

1603 Harsnet *Pop. Impost.* 53 For say anything distasting to them..ye shall be sure to have the Devil put upon you for your labour. **1671** Flavel *Fount Life* ii. 4 If there be something ravishing..there is also something distasting.

†**dis'tastive,** *a.* (*sb.*) *Obs.* [f. as prec. + -ive.]

1. Feeling or expressing distaste or dislike.

1611 Speed *Hist. Gt. Brit.* ix. xv. §10 (R.) Such fleering pick-thanks, that blow them [my faults] stronger into your unwilling and distastiue ear.

2. Disgusting, unpleasant, offensive.

1600 *Newe Metamorphosis* (Nares), Thus did they finishe their distastive songe. **1611** Speed *Hist. Gt. Brit.* ix. iii. §8 A Niding, a word of such disgrace, and so distastiue vnto the English. **1642** Sir E. Dering *Sp. on Relig.* x. 78 Some endeavours of mine..reported more distastive than before.

B. *sb.* Anything unpleasant or distasteful.

1654 Whitlock *Zootomia* 384 Pride..jealousie..or other Distastives incident to that part of advise, called Reproofe.

†**dis'tasture.** *Obs.* [f. as prec. + -ure.]

a. Disgust or loathing of food; nausea. **b.** Displeasure, vexation.

1611 Speed *Hist. Gt. Brit.* ix. xv. §46 His body wearied with watching, distasture, and want of rest. *Ibid.* ix. xxiii. §32 (R.) This duke..vpon this distasture impressed such dolour of minde..he liued not long after.

‖**distater** (daɪˈsteɪtə(r)). [f. di-[2] + stater[2].] An ancient Greek gold coin, of the value of two staters.

1895 *Daily News* 9 May 3/3 A Thurium distater, with head of Pallas to the right.

distaves, obs. pl. of distaff.

distearin (daɪˈstiːərɪn). *Chem.* [ad. F. *distéarine* (Berthelot 1854, in *Ann. de Chim. et de Phys.* 3rd Ser. XLI. 221), f. di-[2] + stearin.] A fat, the diglyceride of stearic acid. (Cf. stearin 1.)

1866 H. Watts tr. *Gmelin's Hand-bk. Chem.* XVII. 117 (*heading*) Distearin. **1873** C. H. Ralfe *Outl. Physiol. Chem.* 48 Stearic acid forms with glycerin 32 compounds, Monostearin, Distearin, and Tristearin. **1879** [see monostearin]. **1956** *Nature* 21 Jan. 146/2 These.. experiments indicated that..the distearin was preferentially precipitated by urea.

†**dis'tectured,** *ppl. a. Obs. nonce-wd.* [f. dis- 7 a + tecture.] Deprived of the roof; unroofed.

1632 Lithgow. *Trav.* viii. 352, I saw a distectured house.

distegous (ˈdɪstɪgəs), *a. rare.* [f. Gr. δι-, di-[2] + στέγ-η a covering, roof + -ous.] 'Having two ridges' (*Syd. Soc. Lex.* 1883).

distell, obs. Sc. form of distil.

distemonous (daɪˈstiːmənəs), *a. Bot.* [f. Gr. δι-, di-[2] + στήμων stamen + -ous.] Having two stamens; = diandrous.

1883 in *Syd. Soc. Lex.*

distemper (dɪˈstɛmpə(r)), *v.*[1] Now *rare.* Also 4 des-, 4–5 distempre, 4–6 dystemper. [f. med.L. **distemperāre*, f. dis- 4 + L. *temperāre* to proportion or mingle properly, to regulate, temper.

The verb in this sense is not recorded in OF., nor given in med.L. by Du Cange. But the latter has *distemperātus* = *male temperātus*, and also the cognate verbal sbs. *distemperāntia*, *distemperāmentum*; OF. has *destempré*, *-trempé* = *distemperātus*, immoderate, excessive, intemperate, deranged (in health), disordered; It. has *distemperare* to alter the natural temperament or temperature of, *distemperato* altered in natural temperament, intemperate, immodest, excessive; Sp. has *destemplar* to alter, disconcert, untune, refl. to be ill with a fever.]

†**1.** *trans.* To temper improperly by undue mixture of elements; to disturb or derange the due proportion of (elements, humours, etc.).

1340 *Ayenb.* 153 To þe bodye of man comeþ alle eueles uor þe destempringe of þise uour qualites, oþer of þise uour humours. *c* **1386** Chaucer *Pars. T.* ¶752 The fourthe is when, thurgh the grete habundance of his mete, the humours in his body been destempred.

†**2.** To disturb or derange the condition of the air, elements, weather, climate, etc. (chiefly in *passive*).

1387 Trevisa *Higden* vii. iv. (Rolls) VII. 311 Þat ȝere in Engelond was greet deeþ of beestes and distemperynge of þe ayer by þe whiche meny men deide [*Harl.* intemperance of the aier]. **1490–1612** [see distempered 1]. **1649** G. Daniel *Trinarch., Hen. IV*, v, 'Tis in mee now doubly Distempered; A Stormy Day and an vnquiet Age.

3. From the notion that attributed the 'humour' or 'temper' to the preponderance of one or other of the bodily humours:

To disturb or disorder the humour, temper, or feelings of; to put out of humour or temper; to render ill-humoured or ill at ease; to trouble, vex, 'upset'. *refl.* and *pass.* To be or become disturbed in mind; to 'put oneself out'. (Now *rare* or *Obs.*, exc. as *fig.* from 4.)

c **1386** Chaucer *Melib.* ¶270, I biseke yow..that ye wol nat..distempre youre herte, thogh I speke thyng that yow displese. *c* **1386** —— *Sompn. T.* 487 Sire..distempre yow noght..For goddes loue, youre pacience ye holde. **1581** J. Bell *Answ. Osor.* 28 b, Your excessive pride hath distempered and broken the gall of my patience. **1602** Shaks. *Ham.* iii. ii. 312. **1603** Harsnet *Pop. Impost.* 115 None but Children and fooles are distempered with Nicknames and Taunts. **1633** Bp. Hall *Hard Texts, N.T.* 312 Vainely distempering himselfe about idle and frivolous questions. **1670** Eachard *Cont. Clergy* 122 And what though churches stand at a little further distance? People may please to walk a mile without distempering themselves. **1813** Coleridge *Remorse* i. ii, Strange, that this Monviedro Should have the power so to distemper me!

4. Also, from the notion that diseases proceeded from a disturbance of the due proportion of the four humours:

To disorder or derange the physical or bodily condition of; to render unhealthy or diseased; to affect with a distemper; to sicken.

c **1380** Wyclif *Sel. Wks.* III. 157 Sum mon to lustfuly eetis or drinkes, and þat distemperes a mon in body and in soule. *c* **1400** *Lanfranc's Cirurg.* 31 He haþ noon oþir siįknesse wiþ him ne is nouȝt distemperid. *c* **1420** *Pallad. on Husb.* I. 273 They beth somer hoote and wyntir colde, That vyne, and grayne, and tre distempur wolde [nocent]. **1530** PALSGR. 522/1 This hote wether hath distempred him, I feare me he shall have an ague. **1597** SHAKS. *2 Hen. IV*, III. i. 41 It is but as a Body, yet distemper'd, Which to his former strength may be restor'd, With good aduice, and little Medicine. **1605** BACON *Adv. Learn* II. x. §2. 39 This variable composition of mans bodie hath made it as an Instrument easie to distemper. **1644** QUARLES *Barnabas & B.* 238 If every petty sickness distempers my body. **1769** *De Foe's Tour Gt. Brit.* II. 128 If any..are distempered, they are immediately put under proper Methods of Cure. **1833** CHALMERS *Const. Man* (1835) I. ii. 129 They would distemper the whole man.

b. To derange or disorder in brain or mind; to render insane.

c **1380** [see a]. **1581** PETTIE *Guazzo's Civ. Conv.* I. (1586) 4 To doubt yt youre braine is distempered. **1611** TOURNEUR *Ath. Trag.* v. ii, Griefe for his children's death distempers him. **1658** *Whole Duty Man* viii. §1. 68 If it be in danger to distemper our reason. *a* **1703** BURKITT *On N.T.*, *Mark* v. 20 They have power to distemper their minds. **1865** LECKY *Ration.* (1878) II. 27 Their imaginations, distempered by self-inflicted sufferings.

†**c.** *spec.* To intoxicate; *refl.* to get drunk. *Obs.*

1491 *Let.* in R. Davies *York Rec.* (1843) 224 We supposide he was distemperide awther with aill or wyn. **1530** PALSGR. 522/1 Distemper the nat with to moche drinke, for a dronken man is but a beest. **1568** T. NORTH tr. *Gueuara's Diall Pr.* IV. vii. 126 b, Wyne tempered with water, bringeth two commoditityes..hee shall not dystemper him self [etc.]. **1679** PENN *Addr. Prot.* I. 9 When the very Tasting of the several sorts of Wine..is enough to distemper a Temperate Head.

5. *transf.* and *fig.* To disorder or mar the condition of; to derange, confuse, put out of joint.

1494 FABYAN *Chron.* VII. 392 Contynuell rayne, whiche distemperyd the grounde in suche wyse that, the yere folowynge, whete was solde for xviii. d. a bushell. **1577** B. GOOGE *Heresbach's Husb.* IV. (1586) 180 b, [Honey] distempered with the sent of the flowres, ill seasoned in the Hives, and so often altred. **1601** SHAKS. *Twel. N.* II. i. 5 The malignancie of my fate, might perhaps distemper yours. **1650** FULLER *Pisgah* IV. iii. 44 Though barren for the main, and distempered with sterility, yet it [Desert of Paran] had some fertile intervalls. **1667** MILTON *P.L.* XI. 56 Sin, that first Distemper'd all things. **1879** [see DISTEMPERED *ppl. a.* 4].

†**6.** To deprive (a metal) of 'temper'. *Obs. rare.* [mod.F. *détremper* (1694 in Dict. Acad.).]

1795 PEARSON in *Phil. Trans.* LXXXV. 343 Wootz is not at all malleable when cold... It can be tempered and distempered, but not to a considerable extent of degrees.

Hence **di'stempering** *vbl. sb.* and *ppl. a.*

1340, **1387** [see above, senses 1, 2]. **1604** SHAKS. *Oth.* I. i. 99 Being full of Supper, and distempring draughtes. **1613–18** DANIEL *Coll. Hist. Eng.* (1626) 98 Their numbers growing so great, as bred many..distemprings betweene the nations. **1855** LYNCH *Rivulet* XXVII. i, To rid me of distempering heat.

di'stemper, *v.*[2] [ad. OF. *destemprer*, *-tremper* to dissolve in liquid, soak, mix = It. *distemperare* in same sense, med.L. *distemperāre* to soak, macerate (Du Cange), f. DIS- 1 or 5 + L. *temperāre* to mingle in due proportion, qualify, temper.

This is the ordinary sense in which *distemperāre* is found in med.L. and French; cf. DISTEMPER *v.*[1]. But It. *distemperare*, Sp. *distemplar* have senses corresponding to both our verbs.]

†**1.** *trans.* To treat with water or some other liquid; to mix with a liquid, so as to dissolve wholly or partly; to dilute, infuse; to soak, steep.

c **1400** *Lanfranc's Cirurg.* 66 Make poudre & distempere with þe white of an ey as þicke as hony. *Ibid.* 185 Distempere hem with vinegre & anoynte herwiþ. **1544** PHAER *Regim. Lyfe* (1553) D vij a, Take an ounce of cassia, an houre before dyner..distempered with a ptisane. **1607** TOPSELL *Four-f. Beasts* (1658) 305 Give the Horse thereof every morning..the quantity of a Hasel-nut distempered in a quart of Wine. *Ibid.* 329 Distemper it with the milk of a Cow. **1667** PETTY in Sprat *Hist. R. Soc.* 286 (T.) Colouring of paper, viz. marbled paper, by distempering the colours with ox-gall, and applying them upon a stiff gummed liquor.

2. *transf.* and *fig.* To dilute; to mix with something so as to weaken or impair; to allay. *Obs.* or *arch.* (Often run together with senses 4, 5 of DISTEMPER *v.*[1]: see quot. 1598.)

1592 SHAKS. *Ven. & Ad.* 653 Jealousy..Distempering gentle Love in his desire, As air and water do abate the fire. **1598** YONG *Diana* 366 At the first loue seldome affoords one little pleasure without distempering it in the end with sorrowe and care. **1643** MILTON *Soveraigne Salve* 5 Monarchy duely tempered is the best, but distempered by tyranny the worst. **1868** HAWTHORNE *Our Old Home, Pilgr. to Old Boston* (1879) 158 The May sunshine was mingled with water, as it were, and distempered with a very bitter east-wind.

3. *Painting.* To paint or colour in distemper. See DISTEMPER *sb.*[2]

1873 BREWER *Dict. Phr. & Fab.* (ed. 3) 230 s.v. *Distemper*, Applied to painting, the word is from..the French *détremper* (to soak in water), because the paints are mixed with water instead of oil. **1876** R. & A. GARRETT *House Decorat.* (1879) 43 Distempering or painting the wall above a shade lighter. **1881** YOUNG *Every man his own Mechanic* §1605 The difference between painting in oils and distempering is just this, that in the former the colouring matter is ground with oil and turpentine while in the latter it is mixed with size.

distemper (dɪˈstɛmpə(r)), *sb.*[1] Also 7 des-. [f. DISTEMPER *v.*[1]: partly after TEMPER *sb.*]

†**1.** 'A disproportionate mixture of parts; want of a due temper of ingredients'; 'want of due balance between contraries' (J.); distempered or disordered condition. *Obs.*

1607–12 BACON *Ess., Empire* (Arb.) 298 A true temper of governement is a rare thing; For both Temper and Distemper consist of contraryes. **1612** WOODALL *Surg. Mate* Wks. (1653) 207 A small distemper in the Animal salt of man is able to kill the strongest man. **1644** DIGBY *Nat. Bodies* I. xxxviii. (1645) 408 Their distemper from what they should be maketh the impression repugnant to their nature.

†**2.** A disordered or distempered condition of the air, climate, weather, etc.; inclemency. *Obs.*

1614 RALEIGH *Hist. World* I. iii. §8. 27 a, It was..a reasonable conjecture that those countreys..directly under it [the Æquinoctial] were of a distemper uninhabitable. **1655** *Let. to Hartlib* in *Ref. Commonw. Bees* 15 Exposed to theeves, vermin, and distempers of weather. **1660** SHARROCK *Vegetables* 86 The impediments which with us hinder the husbandmen..are either the distempers of the ground itself, or some evil accidents. **1856** EMERSON *Eng. Traits, Land* Wks. (Bohn) II. 17 The London fog aggravates the distempers of the sky.

3. Derangement or disturbance of the 'humour' or 'temper' (according to mediæval physiology regarded as due to disturbance in the bodily 'humours'; cf. TEMPER, TEMPERAMENT); a being out of humour; ill humour, ill temper; uneasiness; disaffection. (Now usually associated with sense 4; in quot. 1850 with allusion to metallic 'temper'.)

a **1555** LATIMER *Serm. & Rem.* (1845) 310, I check myself, lest whilst I aim at curing your distemper I stir up your bad humour; for..you are..more wrathful than is seemly. **1602** SHAKS. *Ham.* III. ii. 351 Good my Lord, what is your cause of distemper? **1608–11** BP. HALL *Medit. & Vowes* II. §83 A man of a lowly stomak, can swallow and digest contempt without any distemper. **1642** ROGERS *Naaman* 271 Although thou shouldest..dare the Lord with thy pride and distemper. **1665** HOWARD & DRYDEN *Ind. Queen* I. i, Compose these wild Distempers in your Breast. **1756** BURKE *Subl. & B.* Introd. Wks. I. 102 Then we must know the habits, the prejudices, or the distempers of this particular man. **1823** W. TAYLOR in *Monthly Mag.* LVI. 126 Let us talk of these things over a glass of nectar, without distemper and without prejudice. **1850** BLACKIE *Æschylus* I. 30 Like evil brass, His deep distemper he shall show By dints of trial.

4. Deranged or disordered condition of the body or mind (formerly regarded as due to disordered state of the humours); ill health, illness, disease.

1598 SHAKS. *Merry W.* IV. ii. 28 Any madnesse..seem'd but tamenesse, ciuility, and patience, to this his distemper he is in now. **1602** —— *Ham.* II. ii. 55 Your sonnes distemper. **1608** PR. OF WALES in Ellis *Orig. Lett.* Ser. I. III. 93, I am glad to have heard of your Maties recovery, before I understood of your distemper by the heat of the weather. **1695** HOWE in H. Rogers *Life* x. (1863) 289, I was confined by distemper to my bed. *a* **1716** SOUTH (J.), It argues sickness and distemper in the mind, as well as in the body, when a man is continually turning and tossing. **1781** COWPER *Expost.* 153 They saw distemper healed, and life restored, In answer to the fiat of his word. **1873** BROWNING *Red Cott. Nt.-cap* 278 Eccentricity Nowise amounting to distemper.

b. with *a* and *pl.* A disorder, a disease, an ailment (of body or mind).

1648 BOYLE *Seraph. Love* Ep. Ded. (1660) 3 My sight..is still so impair'd by a distemper in my eyes. **1659** STANLEY *Hist. Philos.* III. III. 18 All distempers of the mind, are, as I conceive, high madnesse. **1710** STEELE *Tatler* No. 103 ¶ 11 He was extremely afflicted with the Gout, and set his Foot upon the Ground with the Caution and Dignity which accompany that Distemper. **1756** NUGENT *Gr. Tour* III. 104 The mineral waters of this place are famous for curing many distempers. **1769** ROBERTSON *Chas. V*, III. XI. 274 A contagious distemper raged among his troops. **1856** R. A. VAUGHAN *Mystics* (1860) II. 131 The cloister breeds a family of mental distempers, elsewhere unheard of. **1860** EMERSON *Cond. Life, Behaviour* Wks. (Bohn) II. 392 There is one topic peremptorily forbidden to all well-bred..mortals, namely their distempers.

c. *spec.* A disease of dogs, characterized by catarrh, cough, and loss of strength. Also applied to various other diseases of animals.

1747 *Gentl. Mag.* 686 Dr. Barker's Method of treating the Distemper among Cows. **1781** P. BECKFORD *Hunting* (1802) 64 The distemper makes dreadful havock with whelps at their walks. **1816** TOWNE *Farmer & Grazier's Guide* 28 What is commonly denominated 'The Distemper' in Horses, proves generally to be a Catarrh. **1823** SCOTT *Let. to Miss Edgeworth* 22 Sept. in *Lockhart*, That fatal disorder proper to the canine race called par excellence, the distemper. **1887** *Times* 1 Feb. 9/6 Swine fever..being known in different parts of Great Britain by the names of pig typhoid, pig distemper [etc.].

†**d.** Intoxication. *Obs.*

1599 SHAKS. *Hen. V*, II. ii. 54 If little faults, proceeding on distemper, Shall not be wink'd at. **1607** *Drewill's Arraign.* in *Harl. Misc.* (Malh.) III. 55 Such plenty of wine as to cause distemper. **1650** FULLER *Pisgah* II. xiii. 279 Drunkards..in the fits of their distemper.

5. *transf.* and *fig.* Derangement, disturbance, or disorder (*esp.* in a state or body politic). (Now always with allusion to sense 4.)

1605 BACON *Adv. Learn.* I. iv. §3 (1873) 30 Here..is the first distemper of learning, when men study words and not matter. **1647** LILLY *Chr. Astrol.* lxxxiii. 448 In these sad times of our Civill Distempers. **1681** NEVILE *Plato Rediv.* title-p., An Endeavour is used to discover the present Politick Distemper of our own [Kingdom]. **1777** BURKE *Let. Affairs Amer.* Wks. III. 149 All struggle rather inflamed than lessened the distemper of the publick councils. **1849** MACAULAY *Hist. Eng.* II. 404 The distempers of the state were such as required an extraordinary remedy.

di'stemper, *sb.*[2] *Painting.* [f. DISTEMPER *v.*[2], after 16th c. F. *destrempe*, mod.F. *détrempe* in same sense, f. *des-*, *détremper*: see DISTEMPER *v.*[2]]

1. A method of painting, in which the colours are mixed with some glutinous substance soluble in water, as yolk of egg mixed with water, etc., executed usually upon a ground of chalk or plaster mixed with gum (***distemper-ground***): mostly used in scene-painting, and in the internal decoration of walls. Chiefly in such phrases as 'painting' or 'to paint in distemper' (It. *pingere a tempera*).

1632 PEACHAM *Compl. Gentl.* xiii. (1634) 141 He wrought in distemper (as we call it) or wet with size, sixe histories of patient Job, wherein are many excellent figures. **1658** PHILLIPS s.v., Painting in Distemper, or size..hath been ancientlier in use than that which is in oiled colours. **1666** PEPYS *Diary* (1879) VI. 4 There saw my picture of Greenwich finished to my very great content, though this manner of distemper do make the figures not so pleasing as in oyle. **1762–71** H. WALPOLE *Vertue's Anecd. Paint.* (1786) I. 44 They glued a linnen cloth upon the wall, and covered that with plaister, on which they painted in distemper. **1773** *Gentl. Mag.* XLIII. 216 Nor is there any strength in the shadows of the drapery, a defect that usually attends painting in fresco and distemper. **1837** *Penny Cycl.* IX. 22/2 *Distemper*, an inferior kind of colouring used for both internal and external walls..instead of oil colour, being a cheap substitute... Scene painting is executed in distemper. **1850** MRS. JAMESON *Leg. Monast. Ord.* (1863) 108 A small picture in distemper on panel. **1859** GULLICK & TIMBS *Paint.* 75 Oil-pictures are frequently executed partly in tempera, or, as it is now called, distemper—in other words, water-colours.

2. Also applied to the pigment prepared for this process, and to the ground on which it is executed. In *House-painting*, whiting mixed with size and water, with which 'ceilings are generally done; plastered walls, when not painted or papered, are also so covered' (Gwilt).

1837 [see 1]. **1839** W. B. S. TAYLOR tr. *Mérimée's Painting in Oil & Fresco* v. 220 The time required for priming, may be shortened..by making the first and second couches with distemper..let the last couch be merely oil, which has become viscous by exposure to the air; this will penetrate the distemper, and render it quite pliant. **1879** *Cassell's Techn. Educ.* IV. 229/1 *note*, Cobalt, raw umber, and white make a magnificent grey, both in oil-colours and in distemper (powder-colours mixed with size).

3. *attrib.* and *Comb.*, as ***distemper-brush***, ***-colour***, ***-painting***, ***-piece***; **distemper-ground**: see 1 above.

1837 *Penny Cycl.* IX. 22/2 Paper stainers employ distemper colour in printing and staining papers for walls. **1839** W. B. S. TAYLOR tr. *Mérimée's Painting in Oil & Fresco* v. 218 In the commencement of the art the canvasses were prepared like the panels with distemper grounds. **1841** W. SPALDING *Italy & It. Isl.* II. 242 Frescoes on the walls or distemper-pieces on the fixed altars. **1874** R. ST. JOHN TYRWHITT *Sketch. Club* 26 You pass out of pure water-painting into distemper-painting.

†**di'stemperance.** *Obs.* [a. OF. *destemprance*, *-trempance* intemperance (13th c. in Godef.) = med.L. *distemperāntia* (Du Cange), f. *dis-*, DIS- 4 + L. *temperāntia* TEMPERANCE.]

1. *gen.* Improper proportioning or mingling (of elements).

1340 *Ayenb.* 153 Ase to þe bodye of man comeþ alle eueles uor þe destempringe of þise uour qualities oþer of þise uour humours: alzuo of þe herte of þe manne comeþ alle þe uices and alle þe zennes be þe distemperance of þise þeawes.

2. Of the air, climate, weather: Intemperateness, inclemency; = DISTEMPERATURE 1.

c **1374** CHAUCER *Boeth.* III. pr. xi. 97–8 Þat þe vttereste bark [of trees] is put ayenis the destempraunce of þe heuene, as a defendowr. *c* **1430** *Life St. Kath.* (1884) 60 Tempest and alle distemperance of weder. **1494** FABYAN *Chron.* VII. 336 And this yere fell great dystemperaunce of wethyr. **1558** ABP. PARKER *Corr.* (1852) 52, I would wish ye were not much stirring abroad in the distemperance of the air. **1579** FENTON *Guicciard.* IX. (1599) 382 It was hard for him to remaine there, both for the want of victuals, and distemperance of the time, winter approching.

3. Disturbance of 'humour', temper, or mind; = DISTEMPER *sb.*[1] 3.

1574 HELLOWES *Gueuara's Fam. Ep.* 161 For any distemperaunce that may greeue you, or maye happen to anger you. **1602** DANIEL *Musophilus* cii, If..this nice wit, or that distemperance, Neglect, distaste, uncomprehend, disdain.

4. Distempered condition (of the 'humours', etc.); bodily or mental disorder, ailment.

1529 MORE *Comf. agst. Trib.* II. Wks. 1196/2 The dystemperance of either other, engendreth some tyme the distemperance of both twayne [soul and body]. **1573** ABP. PARKER in Ellis *Orig. Lett.* Ser. I. II. 268 My oft distemperance and infirmitie of bodye. **1576** NEWTON *Lemnie's Complex.* (1633) 128 When moisture is all wasted, a man falleth into a cold and dry distemperance, and finally thereby brought to his death. **1620** VENNER *Via Recta* vii. 114 Stomacks..subiect to vomiting through the distemperance of choler.

5. Lack or absence of moderation; excess, intemperateness; *spec.* excess in drinking or other indulgence, intemperance.

c **1374** CHAUCER *Boeth.* IV. pr. ii. 116 Certis so doþ distemperaunce to feble men, þat ne mowen nat wrastle aȝeins þe vices. **1398** TREVISA *Barth. De P.R.* V. xxviii. (1495) 139 The hondes ben drye by distemperaunce of heete and excesse that wastyth the moysture. **1500–20** DUNBAR *Poems* xlv. 18 To lufe in sic distemperance. **1547** BOORDE *Brev. Health* II. 26 All is thorowe distemperaunce of the bodye vsed the day before. **1576** NEWTON *Lemnie's Complex.* (1633) 178 Superfluity and distemperance of drinke. **1589** COGAN *Haven Health* cii. (1636) 100 The stomack is weake by distemperance of heat.

di'stemperate, *a. Obs.* or *arch.* [ad. med.L. *distemperāt-us* not properly proportioned, mingled, regulated, or ordered, immoderate, excessive (said of the weather, the bodily humours, etc.), f. DIS- 4 + L. *temperātus* tempered, proportioned, regulated, temperate, pa. pple. of *temperāre* to TEMPER.]

†**1.** Of the air or elements: Not temperate, not so tempered or regulated as to be conducive to health and comfort; excessive in some respect; inclement, stormy, unwholesome. *Obs.*

1398 TREVISA *Barth De P.R.* V. lxii. (1495) 179 Flesshe moost defendyth the rydge fro dystemperat ayre. **1594** CAREW *Huarte's Exam. Wits* xv. (1596) 264 Any temperat or distemperat region. **1647** FULLER *Good Th. in Worse T.* (1841) 90, I have endeavoured in these distemperate times to hold up my spirits, and to steer them steadily.. Now, alas! the storm grows too sturdy for the pilot.

†**2.** Of the bodily 'humours': Not properly tempered; disordered through excess or deficiency of some constituent; hence, of bodily or mental condition, etc., disordered, out of order; diseased, out of health; ill-conditioned. *Obs.*

1548 RECORDE *Urin. Physick* viii. 35 There remaineth yet somewhat of that distemperate trouble in the blood. **1604** J. BURGES in W. Covell *Briefe Answ.* (1606) 13 The Conscience soyled, is like a distemperate Locke, that no Key will open. **1614** JACKSON *Creed* III. xxiv. §4. 238 When they could not answere his reasons.. though most offensiue to their distemperate humor. **1623** WODROEPHE *Marrow Fr. Tongue* 295 (T.) Thou hast thy brain distemperate, and out of rule. **1658** *Whole Duty Man* xvi. §17. 133 Is it possible there can be (even to the most distemperate palate) any such sweetness in it.

3. Passing the bounds of moderation; immoderate, excessive; inordinate, intemperate; = DISTEMPERED 5. *Obs.* or *arch.*

1557 *Tottell's Misc.* (Arb.) 230 When I amid mine ease did fall to such distemperate fits. **1587** HARRISON *England* II. vi. (1877) I. 142 In over much and distemperate gormandize. **1598–9** E. FORDE *Parismus* I. (1661) 118 How can this distemperate sorrow procure your lost Friend? **1614** RALEIGH *Hist. World* I. (1634) 38 Against it Thomas Aquinas objecteth the distemperate heat. **1634** T. JOHNSON *Parey's Chirurg.* XXII. iv. (1678) 492 Humors putrefie either from fulness.. or by distemperate excess. **1847** BUSHNELL *Chr. Nurt.* II. iii. (1861) 276 A distempered or distemperate life.

†**di'stemperate**, *v. Obs. rare.* [f. ppl. stem of med.L. *distemperāre*: see DISTEMPER *v.*[1]] *trans.* To affect with distemper; to disorder, disease.

1547 BOORDE *Brev. Health* lxxiii. 25 b, It doth signifye that the lunges be out of order, and dystemperated. **1607** TOPSELL *Four-f. Beasts* (1658) 440 An extream.. inflammation and burning through all the parts of the body, which doth greatly distemperate and vex the same.

†**di'stemperately**, *adv. Obs.* [f. DISTEMPERATE *a.* + -LY[2]. (In 5 also *disatem-*, f. ATTEMPERATELY).] In a distemperate manner: immoderately, intemperately, excessively.

1398 TREVISA *Barth. De P.R.* XIX. lii. (1495) 893 Hete and coldnesse passyth not dystemperatly the fyrste gree. **1483** CAXTON *Gold. Leg.* 275/1 He wold not forbede them that wold edyffye yf that he sawe them not doo it dysatemperatly. **1607** WALKINGTON *Opt. Glass* 49 Distemperatly hote. **1653** A. WILSON *Jas. I*, 117 Not distemperately importuning them with Conjurations.

distemperature (dɪs'tɛmpərətjʊə(r)). Now *rare* and *arch.* [f. med.L. type **distemperātūra* (= OF. *destempreure*): cf. DISTEMPERATE and TEMPERATURE.] Distemperate or distempered condition.

1. A condition of the air or elements not properly tempered for human health and comfort; evil, deranged, or extreme 'temperature' (in the earlier sense of this word, including all atmospheric states); inclemency, unwholesomeness.

1531 ELYOT *Gov.* III. xxvi, The temperature or distemperature of the regions. **1584** PEELE *Arraignm. Paris* v, Woods Where neither storm nor suns distemperature Have power to hurt by cruel heat or cold. **1638** RAWLEY tr. *Bacon's Life & Death* (1650) 11 Surely their cloathing is excellent good against the distemperatures of the weather. **1665** SIR T. HERBERT *Trav.* (1677) 43 This distemperature by storms of Wind and Rain turns Summer into Winter. **1677** HALE *Prim. Orig. Man.* II. ix. 214 The same distemperature of the Air that occasioned the Plague, occasioned also the infertility or noxiousness of the Soil. **1860** TRENCH *Serm. Westm. Abb.* v. 49 Henceforth.. exposed to the sharp and wintry blasts and all those distemperatures of the air.

2. Disordered or distempered condition of the 'humours', or of the body; disorder, ailment.

1533 ELYOT *Cast. Helthe* I. ii. (1541) 3 To knowe the distemperature these sygnes folowyng wold be consydered. **1582** HESTER *Secr. Phiorav.* I. i. 1 Sicknesse or infirmitie is no other thyng then a distemperature of humours in the bodies of Creatures. **1590** SHAKS. *Com. Err.* v. i. 82 At her heeles a huge infectious troope Of pale distemperatures. **1621** BURTON *Anat. Mel.* I. ii. v. iii, This adventitious melancholy.. is caused by a hot and dry distemperature. **1685** J. SCOTT *Chr. Life* (1699) V. 458 A distemperature of the brain, and blood and spirits. **1753** CHAMBERS *Cycl. Supp.* s.v., Suckers are another Distemperature of trees arising from the tree itself. **1863** LD. LYTTON *Ring Amasis* II. 14 The effects of watching and the distemperature of an over-laboured brain.

3. Disturbance of mind or temper.

1571 GOLDING *Calvin on Ps.* To Rdr. 9, I wote not what distemperature had kindled up a sorte of leawd loyterers ageinst mee. **1592** SHAKS. *Rom. & Jul.* II. iii. 40 Thou art vprous'd with some distemprature. **1633** MARMION *Fine Companion* IV. vi, *Spr.* I hear she is run mad. *Aur.* Is, and the cause of her distemperature Is the reproach you put upon her honour. **1741** WARBURTON *Div. Legat.* II. 548 What I uttered through the distemperature of my passion. **1823** SCOTT *Quentin D.* xxxvii, Durward.. found the latter in a state of choleric distemperature. **1850** BROWNING *Easter Day* xxxiii. 8 A mere dream and distemperature.

4. *transf.* and *fig.* Derangement, disturbance, disorder (of society, the state, etc.). *arch.* or *Obs.*

1593 DRAYTON *Eclog.* VIII. 103 Since the Worlds distemp'rature is such. **1613–18** DANIEL *Coll. Hist. Eng.* (1626) 154 The distemprature of the time was such, as no sword could cure it. **1615** J. STEPHENS *Satyr. Ess.* 147 A curious clocke; which by the distemperature of one wheele, growes distempered in every one. **1711** SHAFTESB. *Charac.* v. iii. (1737) III. 321 In the present Distemperatures.. Partys are no good Registers of the Actions of the adverse Side.

5. Immoderateness, excess (esp. of heat or cold; cf. 1); excess in drinking or other indulgence, intemperateness, intemperance.

1572 J. JONES *Bathes Buckstone* 3 b, Nothing.. better.. Taketh away distemperature of heate.. then a dulce or pleasunt Bathe. **1605** *Bloudy Bk.* C, It shamed him not (after his distemperatures abroade) to bring queanes home with him. **1630** *R. Johnson's Kingd. & Commw.* 195 Princes .. following ill counsell and youthfull distemperature. **1875** LOWELL *Old Elm* Poet. Wks. 1890 IV. 82 The track it left seems less of fire than light, Cold but to such as love distemperature.

distempered (dɪ'stɛmpəd), *ppl. a.*[1] [f. DISTEMPER *v.*[1] + -ED; perh. immed. after OF. *destempré* immoderate, excessive, deranged, or med.L. *distemperātus* DISTEMPERATE.]

†**1.** Of the weather, air, etc.: Not temperate; inclement; = DISTEMPERATE *a.* 1. *Obs.*

1490 CAXTON *Eneydos* xii. 46 Considerynge the wynter that is alle dystempred. **1549** *Compl. Scot.* vi. 37 Situat maist comodiusly fra distempirit ayr ande corruppit infectione. **1594** CAREW *Huarte's Exam. Wits* xiv. (1596) 241 They inhabit places distempered, where men become.. ill conditioned. **1612** DRAYTON *Poly-olb.* i. 4 Muse, leaue the wayward Mount to his distempred heate.

†**2.** Of the bodily humours: = DISTEMPERATE 2. Hence, disturbed in humour, temper, or feelings; out of humour, vexed, troubled. *Obs.*

1595 SHAKS. *John* IV. iii. 21 Once more to-day well met, distemper'd Lords. **1631** WEEVER *Anc. Fun. Mon.* 212 His hastie distempered humour would breed great troubles in the State. **1635** BRATHWAIT *Arcad. Pr.* II. 136 The happy attemperature of his distempered humour. **1667** MILTON *P.L.* IX. 1131 From thus distemperd brest.. Adam.. Speech intermitted thus to Eve renewd. **1762** CHURCHILL *Ghost* IV, Why should the distemper'd Scold Attempt to blacken Men?

3. Disordered, diseased, affected with a distemper. **a.** Physically.

1440 *Generydes* (E.E.T.S.) 766 So sodenly.. All distemperyd and out of colour clene. *c* **1600** SHAKS. *Sonn.* cliii, I, sick withal.. thither hied, a sad distemper'd guest, But found no cure. **1688** BOYLE *Final Causes Mat. Things, Vitiated Sight* 271 When.. reading, she was fain to shut the distempered eye, and imploy only the other. **1718** J. CHAMBERLAYNE *Relig. Philos.* (1730) I. iv. §2 Sick and distempered People. **1784** COWPER *Task* III. 415 What is weak, Distempered, or has lost prolific powers, Impaired by age. **1825** WATERTON *Wand. S. Amer.* II. iii. 192 The insects which have already formed a lodgement in the distempered tree.

b. Mentally disordered, insane. Of persons (*obs.* or *arch.*); their brain, mind, fancy, feelings, actions, etc.

1594 HOOKER *Eccl. Pol.* II. v. §7 Speeches vttered in heat of distempered affection. **1633** G. HERBERT *Temple, Familie* v, Griefs without a noise.. speak.. louder, then distemper'd fears. **1651** HOBBES *Leviath.* III. xxxiv. 208 To a Distempered brain. **1667** MILTON *P.L.* IV. 807 Distemperd, discontented thoughts. **1692** LUTTRELL *Brief Rel.* (1857) II. 638 One Thomas, a distempered man.. was ordered to be sent to Bedlam for a madman. **1718** *Free-thinker* No. 82 ¶9 The Lives of most Men are but distempered Dreams. **1727** SWIFT *Further Acc. E. Curll* Wks. 1755 III. I. 161 His books, which his distempered imagination represented to him as alive. **1805** WORDSW. *Waggoner* IV. 82 As if the Warbler.. Upbraided his distempered folly. **1810** CRABBE *Borough* xxii, There they seized him—a distemper'd man. **1851** RUSKIN *Stones Ven.* (1874) I. xxv. 285 The visions of a distempered fancy. **1857** H. REED *Lect. Eng. Poets* II. xiv. 166 The darkened and distempered genius of Byron.

4. *transf.* and *fig.* Disordered, deranged, distracted, out of joint.

1605 SHAKS. *Macb.* v. ii. 15 He cannot buckle his distemper'd cause Within the belt of Rule. *a* **1628** PRESTON *Serm. bef. his Majestie* (1630) 18 We are wont to lay aside cracked vessels, and distempered watches as unusefull. **1649** BP. REYNOLDS *Hosea* Ep. 2 The.. difficulties under which this distempered Kingdom is now groaning. **1722** WOLLASTON *Relig. Nat.* i. 17 Such an irregular distemperd world. **1879** *Q. Rev.* Apr. 414 Those distempered times.

†**5.** Immoderate, inordinate, intemperate; = DISTEMPERATE 3. *Obs.*

1586 J. HOOKER *Girald. Irel.* in Holinshed II. 152/2 Verie temperat and modest, seldome or neuer in anie distempered or extraordinarie choler. **1644** LAUD *Wks.* (1854) IV. 121 He must answer for his own distempered language. **1665** SIR T. HERBERT *Trav.* (1677) 90 [He] died through distempered drinking.

†**6.** Of metal: Deprived of 'temper'. *Obs. rare.*

1796 PEARSON in *Phil. Trans.* LXXXVI. 446 Common annealed, or distempered steel.

Hence **di'stemperedly** *adv.*; also **di's-temperedness**.

a **1639** W. WHATELEY *Prototypes* II. xxxiv. (1640) 181 We must pray to God for such a measure of wisedome and patience, that crosses may not work so distemperedly upon us. **1649** *St. Trials, J. Lilburne* (R.), The distemperedness and invenomedness of spirit which is within you. **1832** J. WILSON in *Blackw. Mag.* XXXI. 257 Nature.. will not suffer such eyes to look distemperedly on her works.

†**di'stempered,** *ppl. a.*[2] *Obs.* [f. DISTEMPER *v.*[2]]

1. Diluted; weakened or impaired by dilution. (In quot. 1621 app. = Badly mixed or tempered. More or less influenced by DISTEMPERED *ppl. a.*[1])

1621–31 LAUD *Sev. Serm.* (1847) 72 If it be laid with 'untempered', or 'distempered morter', all will be naught. **1638** SIR T. HERBERT *Trav.* (ed. 2) 330 The Clove.. in the morne a pale greene, in the meridian a distempered red. **1743** *Lond. & Country Brew.* II. (ed. 2) 106 Great Quantities of distempered Beers, Ales, and other Liquors.

2. Painted in distemper.

1769 *Dublin Mercury* 23 Sept. 1/3 Colour rooms.. with fine blue.. or any other distempered colours.

di'stemperer. [f. DISTEMPER *v.*[2] + -ER[1].] One who paints in distemper.

1876 BROWNING *Pacchiarotto* 10 Our brave distemperer. **1881** *Instr. Census Clerks* (1885) 52 Colourer. Decorator. Distemperer. **1901** *Daily Chron.* 10 Sept. 9/7 Painter, Distemperer.—Good brush hand wants Work.

distempering: see under DISTEMPER *v.*[1] and [2].

†**di'stemperment.** *Obs.* [f. DISTEMPER *v.*[1] + -MENT. (OF. had *destemprement* = *mélange*.)] Distempered condition (of the air, or humours).

1582 HESTER *Secr. Phiorav.* III. lxiii. 87 Indispositions that come through distemperment of humours. **1661** FELTHAM *Resolves, Lusoria* XXIV. (1709) 584 Some sulphurous Spirit sent By the torne Air's distemperment.

†**di'stemperure.** *Obs.* [a. OF. *destemprure*, *-trempure* (Godef.), ad. L. type **distemperātūra*: see DISTEMPER *v.*[1] and -URE.]

= DISTEMPERATURE.

1. Distempered condition (of the elements, humours); = DISTEMPERATURE 1, 2.

1387 TREVISA *Higden* (Rolls) VI. 31 [In Paradise] þere is noon distemperure [*nulla intemperies*].

2. Intemperance, immoderation; = DISTEMPERATURE 5.

c **1380** WYCLIF *Sel. Wks.* III. 156 So, as temperure of iche bodily þing schulde norische a mon, distemperure þerinne may be calde glotorye.

†**di'stempre,** *a. Obs. rare.* [a. OF. *destempré* = L. *distemperātus* pa. pple.] = DISTEMPERED.

c **1374** CHAUCER *Boeth.* IV. pr. iii. 121 Yif he be distempre and quakiþ for ire.

distenant (dɪ'stɛnənt), *v.* [DIS- 7 a.] *trans.* To deprive of a tenant or occupier. So **dis'tenanted** *ppl. a.*, deprived of a tenant; unoccupied.

1594 NASHE *Unfort. Trav.* 8 Euerie vnder-foot souldior had a distenanted tun, as Diogenes had his tub to sleepe in. **1876** FARRAR *Marlb. Serm.* xxii. 211 The darkened and unspiritual intellect, may distenant creation of its God.

distend (dɪ'stɛnd), *v.* [ad. L. *distend-ĕre* to stretch asunder or out, swell out, extend, f. DIS- 1 + *tendĕre* to stretch. Cf. F. *distendre* (Paré, 16th c.) in sense 3.]

†**1.** *trans.* To stretch asunder, stretch out, extend; to spread out at full length or breadth. *Obs.*

c **1400** *Lanfranc's Cirurg.* 134 Mastik & þe white of an ey medlid togidere.. distende it vpon a clooþ & leie it on þe place. **1597** DANIEL *Civ. Wars* III. lxxx, As this sweet Prince distended lay. **1626** T. H. *Caussin's Holy Crt.* 101 God comming from Heauen.. to take humane flesh, to distend his imperiall robe vpon man. **1703** T. N. *City & C. Purchaser* 11 Those.. which keeping precisely the same heighth, shall yet be distended, one 4th part longer. **1834** *West Ind. Sketch Bk.* I. 43 Like.. the alternate movement of the distended legs of a pair of compasses.

fig. **1650** HOWELL tr. *Giraffi's Hist. Revolut. Naples* 82 The Archbishop was very busie in distending the Capitulations of the peeple for an accord. **1665** G. HAVERS *P. della Valle's Trav. E. India* 126 The King's discourse.. was distended to divers things.

†**b.** To stretch or extend beyond measure; to strain; to draw out of joint, to rack. *Obs. rare.*

1599 A. M. tr. *Gabelhouer's Bk. Physicke* 341/2 When anye mans Arme, or Legge is distended or else writhede. [Rendered 'out of ioynte' in the 'Exposition of wordes' on the flyleaf]. **1700** DRYDEN *Fables, Cock & Fox* 293 Stiff in denial, as the law appoints, On engines they distend their tortur'd joints.

†**2.** *intr.* To stretch out, extend; to spread out or abroad. *Obs.*

1581 STYWARD *Mart. Discipl.* II. 135 Seauen rankes of Pikes.. which did distend in length from the voward to the rereward. **1638** SIR T. HERBERT *Trav.* (ed. 2) 330 Leaves long and small, distending into many branches.

3. *trans. spec.* To stretch out any hollow thing, so as to enlarge its surface and capacity; to swell out or enlarge by pressure from within, as a bladder or an orifice with elastic sides; to expand, dilate by stretching.

1650 BULWER *Anthropomet.* 246 Giving her Children too much meat, that distended their stomacks. **1697** DRYDEN *Virg. Georg.* I. 130 The Warmth distends the Chinks. —— *Past.* IX. 41 May thy Cows their burden'd Bags distend. **1794** SULLIVAN *View Nat.* II. 21 When persons are immediately killed by lightning, their lungs are found distended. **1846** ELLIS *Elgin Marb.* I. 164 The veins of their faces and legs seem distended.

transf. and *fig.* **1742** YOUNG *Nt. Th.* IX. 1932 How such ideas of th' Almighty's pow'r.. distend the thought Of feeble mortals! **1824** DIBDIN *Libr. Comp.* 558 To distend it into three bulky tomes.

4. *intr.* To increase in bulk by internal stretching or swelling; to swell out, expand.

1667 MILTON *P.L.* I. 573 Now his heart Distends with pride. **1823** J. BADCOCK *Dom. Amusem.* 135 The bladder will distend. **1835** W. IRVING *Tour Prairies* 247, I could see his veins swell and his nostrils distend with indignation. **1875** BENNETT & DYER *Sachs' Bot.* III. iv. §14. 711 When wood distends on imbibition or contracts on dessication.

Hence **di'stending** *vbl. sb.* and *ppl. a.*

1633 P. FLETCHER *Purple Isl.* II. xxiv, Two parted Walls.. with wide distending space. *Ibid.* V. li, Stuffe.. Fit for distending or compression. **1823** ELLIS *Mem. J. Gordon* 77 The distending force of the water.

distended (dɪ'stɛndɪd), *ppl. a.* [f. prec. + -ED[1].] **a.** Spread out or extended in space; spread abroad; stretched. **b.** Dilated, expanded.

1597 DANIEL *Civ. Wars* VI. xii, That mighty Familie, The faire distended stock of Neviles kind. **1665** HOOKE *Microgr.* Pref. Bijb, I have, by the help of a distended wire, propagated the sound to a very considerable distance. **1697** DRYDEN *Virg. Georg.* III. 483 The still distended Udders. **1795** COWPER *Needless Alarm* 43 The huntsman, with distended cheek, 'Gan make his instrument of music speak. **1834** *West Ind. Sketch Bk.* II. 109 The boat resembled a huge sea-bird.. casting diamonds from its distended pinions. **1878** HUXLEY *Physiogr.* 221 This enclosed in the distended envelope furnished by the ovule, is the pea.

Hence **di'stendedly** *adv.*, in a distended or extended manner; extendedly.

1748 RICHARDSON *Clarissa* (1811) II. xviii. 121 A pinch taken with a dainty finger and thumb, the other three fingers distendedly bent.

di'stender. *rare.* [f. as prec. + -ER[1].] One who distends; an expander.

1831 *Examiner* 4/1 Not a retailer, even of anecdotes, he is a distender of them.

†**di'stendible,** *a. Obs.* Also 7 **-able.** [f. as prec. + -IBLE.] Capable of being distended; distensible.

1672 *Phil. Trans.* VII. 5137 The Veins only of plants being the parts probably distendable. **1732** *Hist. Litteraria* III. 350 Distendible, and ductile under the Hammer.

distensibility (dɪstɛnsɪ'bɪlɪtɪ). [f. next + -ITY.] The quality of being distensible; capability of being distended or stretched asunder.

1757 PARSONS in *Phil. Trans.* L. 355 As to the integuments and membranes of the body, their great distensibility is well known. **1835-6** TODD *Cycl. Anat.* I. 66/1 Qualities of.. distensibility and contractility. **1869** E. A. PARKES *Pract. Hygiene* (ed. 3) 408 India-rubber cloth loses in part its distensibility in very cold countries.

distensible (dɪ'stɛnsɪb(ə)l), *a.* [f. L. *distens-* ppl. stem of *distend-ĕre* to DISTEND + -IBLE.] Capable of being distended or dilated by stretching.

1828 in WEBSTER. **1836-9** TODD *Cycl. Anat.* II. 590/1 The tendinous zones are distensible. **1858** CARPENTER *Veg. Phys.* §110 The bark is sufficiently distensible to admit of the increase of the.. stems. **1881** GÜNTHER in *Encycl. Brit.* XII. 654/1 (*Ichthyol.*) A wide gullet and distensible stomach.

distensile (dɪ'stɛnsaɪl, -ɪl), *a.* [f. as prec. + -ILE, on L. type **tensil-is*.] = DISTENSIBLE. Also, capable of distending or causing distension.

1738 STUART *Muscular Motion* ii. 27 in *Phil. Trans* XL, If the vessel be distensile, it will distend it. *Ibid.* iii. 48 Carried on in extensile and distensile blood-vessels. **1879** *St. George's Hosp. Rep.* IX. 337 Over the whole of this tumour could be felt well-marked distensile pulsation. **1902** *Encycl. Brit.* XXXI. 560/2 As a result of these fibrous changes there is interference with the blood current, since the vessels become unyielding yet frangible, instead of distensile and elastic, tubes. **1907** *Practitioner* Nov. 621 This distensile force would have been amply sufficient to cause dilatation of the ventricular cavity. **1910** *Ibid.* Apr. 482 Forcible inflation under pressure may also be done by compressing the india-rubber tube between the distensile bulb and the proximal glass tube.

distension (dɪ'stɛnʃən). Also 7-9 **-tion.** [ad. L. *distensiōn-em*, var. of *distentiōn-em*, n. of action from *distendĕre* to DISTEND; perh. immed. a. F. *distension* (14th c. in Hatz.-Darm.).]

1. The action of distending; distended condition; expansion by stretching or swelling out.

1607 TOPSELL *Four-f. Beasts* (1658) 239 If a horse.. be weary, it is not safe to let him drinke.. except he first stale; for in such cases followeth distention. **1615** CROOKE *Body of Man* 77 Able to containe or keepe downe windie distensions. **1748** HARTLEY *Observ. Man* I. i. 36 All great Distentions are attended with Pain for a considerable time. **1802** PALEY *Nat. Theol.* x. §5 (1819) 160 Tubes.. kept in a state of perpetual distention by the fluid they enclose. **1850** B. TAYLOR *Eldorado* xxi. (1862) 215 The large sails.. motionless in their distension.

2. The action of stretching longitudinally, straightening out, or placing at full length; extension; straining, racking. Now *Obs.* or *rare.*

a **1625** BEAUM. & FL. *Double Marriage* III. iii, The rack has spoil'd her; the distensions of those parts have stopp'd all fruitfulness. **1671** FLAVEL *Fount. Life* xxvi. 79 A.. Reference to the Distention of all his Members upon the Tree. **1875** KINGLAKE *Crimea* (1877) V. i. 230 The alternate distension and contraction of the line.

†**b.** Stretching asunder or apart. *Obs. rare.*

1624 WOTTON *Archit.* (1672) 36 Our Leggs do labour more in Elevation then in Distention.

distensive (dɪ'stɛnsɪv), *a. rare.* [f. L. *distens-* ppl. stem + -IVE.] Capable of distending or being distended; distensible.

1836 SMART, *Distensive*, that may be distended. **1846** WORCESTER, *Distensive*, that distends or may be distended.

†**di'stent,** *sb. Obs.* [ad. L. *distentus* (*u-* stem) a stretching out, distending, f. ppl. stem of *distendĕre* to DISTEND.] Stretching out; outstretched extent; distension; breadth.

1613-18 DANIEL *Coll. Hist. Eng.* (1626) 34 The wide distent of these tumors, fed from many secret veines. **1614** RALEIGH *Hist. World* III. x. §4 The fronts of the two Armies were so vnequall in distent. **1624** WOTTON *Archit.* in *Reliq.* (1672) 32 [To] be distended one fourteenth part.. which addition of distent will confer much to their Beauty. **1659** B. HARRIS *Parival's Iron Age* 6 Poland is of very vast distent.

distent (dɪ'stɛnt), *ppl. a.* [ad. L. *distent-us*, pa. pple. of *distendĕre*. Commonly used as a pa. pple., = DISTENDED, on the analogy of such contracted pa. pples. as *sent*, *spent*.]

†**1.** Stretched out at full length or breadth; extended. *Obs.*

1590 SPENSER *F.Q.* II. vii. 5 Great heapes of gold that never could be spent; Of which some were rude owre.. others were new driven, and distent Into great Ingowes and to wedges square. **1773** J. ROSS *Fratricide* II. 296 (MS.) Thus murmur'd Earth's first-born.. Distent upon the ground.

2. Expanded by stretching; swollen out.

1605 DRAYTON *Man in Moon* (R.), The bright Latona.. her womb distent, With the great burden that by Jove she bare. **1728-46** THOMSON *Spring* 145 The big clouds with vernal showers distent. **1880** L. WALLACE *Ben-Hur* 360 Nostrils.. now distent, now contracted.

†**di'stent,** *v. Obs.* [f. L. *distent-* ppl. stem of *distendĕre*.] = DISTEND. (Perhaps only in pa. pple. *distended* = prec.)

1578 BANISTER *Hist. Man* v. 72 The intrels.. distented, or retched out by the thynges conteined. *c* **1720** W. GIBSON *Farrier's Dispens.* iii. I. App. (1734) 64 When the Stomack is moderately distented. *Ibid.* The Blood-vessels of the Brain being.. filled and distented. *Ibid.* xi. 255. *c* **1720** *Collect. Misc. Lett. fr. Miot's Jrnl.* (1722) II. 19 Bee's distented Thigh.

distention, var. form of DISTENSION.

dister: see DISTERR *v.*

†**di'sterminate,** *v. Obs.* [f. L. *disterminăt-* ppl. stem of *disterminăre* to mark off by boundaries, f. DIS- 1 = *terminăre* to bound, mark off: see TERMINATE *v.*] *trans.* To separate as a boundary does; to divide by a boundary; to bound, divide. Hence **di'sterminating** *ppl. a.*

1599 NASHE *Lenten Stuffe* 8 [The sands] clearely quitted, disterminated, and relegated themselues from his [the sea's] inflated capriciousnesse of playing the Dictator ouer them. **1611** CORYAT *Crudities* 441 This noble Rhene.. the fairest riuer of all Germany, which it disterminateth from France. **1652-62** HEYLIN *Cosmogr.* Introd. (1674) 13/1 A ridge of Hills.. disterminating Colchis from Armenia. **1676** BOYLE *New Exp.* I. in *Phil. Trans.* XI. 786 Whether some such .. Æthereal Fluid.. insinuated itself between our two Liquors, and made the Disterminating surface more specular.

†**di'sterminate,** *a. Obs. rare.* [ad. L. *disterminăt-us*, pa. pple. of *disterminăre*: see prec., of which it is also used as pa. pple. for *disterminated*.] Separated, marked off, divided.

1615 CHAPMAN *Odyss.* x. 106 The Læstrigonian state, That bears her ports so far disterminate. **1624** BP. HALL *Peacemaker* i. §3 (R.) There is one and the same church of Christ, however far disterminate in places.. however differing in rites and circumstances of worship. **1671** *True Nonconf.* 122 There can be nothing more clearly disterminat.

†**distermi'nation.** *Obs.* [ad. L. *disterminātiōn-em*, n. of action f. *disterminăre*: see prec.] Separation as by boundaries; division.

1647 HAMMOND *Power Keys* v. 117 This turning out of the Church, this Church-banishment, or distermination. **1657** REEVE *God's Plea* 133 Our discrepancy and distermination in good things is such, that it hath parted the community.

†**di'stermine,** *v. Obs. rare*[−0]. [ad. L. *disterminăre* to DISTERMINATE, after *determine*.]

1623 COCKERAM, *Distermine*, to diuide, to separate.

†**di'sterr,** *v. Obs. rare.* [f. DIS- 7 c + L. *terr-a* land. Cf. It. *disterrare*, OF. *desterrer* (11th c. in Hatz.-Darm.) 'to take out of the ground' (Cotgr.), mod.F. *déterrer*, formerly also, 'to deprive of land or country'.] *trans.* To banish from one's country; to exile. (Only in Howell.)

c **1645** HOWELL *Lett.* (1650) I. I. xxiv, The Moors, whereof many thousands were disterr'd and banished hence to Barbary. *Ibid.* I. III. xxxii, The Jews.. were all.. disterred and exterminated [from Spain].

†**di'stest,** *v. Obs. rare.* [f. DIS- 4 + L. *testāre*, *-ārī* to call to witness, f. *testis* witness.] *trans.* To undo or discredit the testimony of; to deprive of the right of being received in testimony.

1647 N. BACON *Disc. Govt. Eng.* I. xiii. 41 Æthelstan's Law gave it [power of sentence] and upon conviction.. distested the delinquents Oath for ever.

disteyne, obs. forms of DESTINY, DISTAIN.

†**dis'thatch,** *v. Obs. nonce-wd.* [DIS- 7 a.] *trans.* To deprive of thatch (in quot. *fig.*).

1654 GAYTON *Pleas. Notes* III. x. 141 Two Ancient Reverend Men, had almost disthatch'd their Faces.

disthene ('dɪsθiːn). *Min.* [mod. f. Gr. δι-, DI-[2] twice + σθένος strength. Named by Haüy, 1801, from its different electrical properties in two different directions.] A synonym of CYANITE 1.

1808 T. ALLAN *Names Min.* 26. *c* **1865** LIVINGSTONE in Chambliss *Livingstone & Stanley* x. 189 Great masses of kyanite or disthene. **1868** DANA *Min.* 375.

disthrone (dɪs'θrəʊn), *v.* [f. DIS- 7 c + THRONE *sb.*] *trans.* To remove from the throne; to DETHRONE. Also *fig.*

1591 SYLVESTER *Du Bartas* I. vi. 615 Our rebellious Flesh, whose rest-less Treason Strives to dis-throne and to dis-scepter Reason. **1603** HOLLAND *Plutarch's Mor.* 1197 Thrasibulus.. was disthroned and driven out of his dominions. **1666** J. SMITH *Old Age* To Rdr. (ed. 2) 4 Nothing can possibly disthrone them. **1876** GEO. ELIOT *Dan. Der.* III. xxvi, To be a queen disthroned is not so hard as some other down-stepping.

Hence **dis'thronement,** dethronement.

1883 *Hom. Monthly* Oct. 36.

†**dis'thronize,** *v. Obs.* [f. DIS- 6 + THRONE *sb.* + -IZE. Cf. *enthronize*.] = prec.

1583 STUBBES *Anat. Abus.* II. (1882) 60 That will go about to disthronize the mightie God.. of his regall throne. **1590** SPENSER *F.Q.* II. x. 44. **1615** T. ADAMS *Blacke Devill* 45 Man is by Christ advanced to that place whence God disthronized him. **1689** *Def. Liberty agst. Tyrants* 74 Kings convinced of loose Intemporancy were disthronized.

distich ('dɪstɪk), *sb.* Forms: 6-7 (**distichon**), **disticke**, 6-8 **distick**, 7 **distique**, **dystick**, 7-9 **distic**, 6- **distich**. Pl. **distichs** ('dɪstɪks) (also 7-8 **distiches**). [ad. L. *distichon*, a. Gr. δίστιχον distich, couplet (neut. of δίστιχος adj.: see next), f. δι- (DI-[2]) + στίχος row, line of verse. At first used in the Lat. form. The pl. *distiches* app. points to an obs. pronunciation ('dɪstɪtʃ).] A couple of lines of verse, usually making complete sense, and (in modern poetry) riming; a couplet.

1553 BECON *Reliques of Rome* (1563) 117* There is a godly Distichon fathered on S. Hierome. **1566** DRANT *Horace* To Rdr. 3 According to the tenour of this distichon. **1577-87** HOLINSHED *Chron.* III. 1206/2 Master Abraham Hartwell.. glanceth in a distich or twaine at the effect hereof. **1610** HOLLAND *Camden's Brit.* (1637) 284 A distichon engraven on her tombe. **1642** MILTON *Apol. Smect.* (1851) 292 Neither had I ever read the hobbling distick which he means. **1647** WARD *Simp. Cobler* 45, I shall compose halfe a dozen distichs. **1711** STEELE *Spect.* No. 43 ¶9 From among many other Distiches no less to be quoted on this Account, I cannot but recite the two following Lines. **1788** BURNS *Let. to W. Dunbar* 7 Apr., I have scarcely made a single distich since I saw you. **1891** DRIVER *Introd. Lit. O.T.* (1892) 341 By far the greater number of verses in the poetry of the Old Testament consist of Distichs.

distich ('dɪstɪk), *a. rare.* [ad. L. *distich-us*, a. Gr. δίστιχος of two rows, of two verses: see prec.] Arranged in two rows; = DISTICHOUS.

1788 JAS. LEE *Introd. Bot.* (ed. 4) 182 *Distich*, in two Rows, when the Branches are produced in a horizontal Situation. **1805-17** R. JAMESON *Char. Min.* (ed. 3) 211 Distic, when in a similar prism.. two rows of facets are arranged around each base. **1852** TH. ROSS *Humboldt's Trav.* I. xv. 477 A fine gramineous plant with distich leaves.

distichal ('dɪstɪkəl), *a.* (*sb.*) [f. L. *distichus* (see prec.) + -AL[1].]

1. *Pros.* Pertaining to, or of the form of, a distich; consisting of two lines of verse.

1778 BP. LOWTH *Transl. Isa.* Prelim. Diss. 1 The regular form of the Stanzas, chiefly Distichal, and the Parallelism of the Lines, were excellently well suited to this purpose. **1847** SIR T. D. LAUDER in *Tait's Mag.* XIV. 656 There exist numerous distichal prognostications. **1895** *Q. Rev.* Jan. 132 A distichal rhyme.

2. *Zool.* Applied to certain joints in the 'arm' of a crinoid; also as *sb.*: see quot. 1888.

1879 P. H. CARPENTER in *Trans. Linn. Soc., Zool.* II. I. 21 The distichal radii represent the primary arms of *Comatula* and *Pentacrinus*. *Ibid.* 24 Three distichals composing each primary arm and bearing the brachials directly. **1888** ROLLESTON & JACKSON *Anim. Life* 572 If the arms [of a Crinoid] branch twice, the joints between the first and second places of division are known as distichals; if thrice, the joints between the second and third places of division are designated palmars.

‖**distichiasis** (dɪstɪ'kaɪəsɪs). *Path.* [mod.L., f. *distichia*, a Gr. διστιχία a double row, f. δίστιχος (see DISTICH).] A malformation in which the eyelid has a double row of eyelashes.

[**1706** PHILLIPS (ed. Kersey), *Distichia*, a double Row of Hairs on the Eye-Lids.] **1875** H. WALTON *Dis. Eye* 673 The name of distichiasis has been given to this ideal state.

distichic (dɪ'stɪkɪk), *a.* [f. Gr. δίστιχ-ον DISTICH + -IC.] = DISTICHAL *a.* 1.

1882–3 SCHAFF *Encycl. Relig. Knowl.* III. 1955 A closed train of thought which is unrolled after the distichic and tristichic ground-form of the rhythmical period.

distichous ('dɪstɪkəs), *a.* [f. L. *distich-us* adj. (see DISTICH) + -OUS.] Disposed in two opposite rows; having parts so disposed, two-ranked; formerly, sometimes = dichotomous; *spec.* in *Bot.* arranged (alternately) in two vertical ranks on opposite sides of the axis, as in the glumes and grains of barley; in *Entom.* applied to antennæ having the joints similarly arranged.

1753 CHAMBERS *Cycl. Supp.* s.v. *Stalk*, If it [the stalk] part into two series of branches, it is expressed by the term *distichous*. **1819** *Mem. Sir J. E. Smith* (1832) II. 250 Perfectly distichous leaves. **1828** STARK *Elem. Nat. Hist.* I. 127 Tail round at its base, distichous at the extremity. **1839–47** TODD *Cycl. Anat.* III. 264/2 Having the hairs of the tail distichous. **1845** *Florist's Jrnl.* 69 Distichous flowers in a leafy spike. **1870** BENTLEY *Bot.* 137 A second variety of arrangement of alternate leaves is called distichous or two-ranked.

Hence '**distichously** *adv.*

1853 G. JOHNSTON *Nat. Hist. E. Bord.* I. 220 The spike is sometimes compound and distichously branched. **1870** HOOKER *Stud. Flora* 305 Statice, Sea-lavender.. spikelets, which are alternately distichously or secundly arranged. **1881** BENTHAM in *Jrnl. Linn. Soc.* XVIII. 325 The leaves are ..distichously imbricate on the short stem.

distil, distill (dɪ'stɪl), *v.* Inflect. **distilled, -illing.** Forms: 4–5 **distille**, 5–6 **destylle, dystyll**, 6 **distyll**, 6–7 **destil(l**, 5– **distill**, 7– **distil**. [ad. L. *distillāre*, more correctly *dēstillāre* to drip or trickle down, drop, distil, f. DE- I. 1 + *stillāre* to drop: cf. F. *distiller* (14th c. in Littré) = Pr. *distillar*, Sp. *destilar*, It. *distillare*.]

1. *intr.* To trickle down or fall in minute drops, as rain, tears; to issue forth in drops or in a fine moisture; to exude.

c **1400** MAUNDEV. (Roxb.) vii. 26 Þe liquour þat distilles oute of þe braunches. **1430** LYDG. *Chron. Troy* I. vi, Her teares on her chekes twayne Full pyteously gan to destylle. **1514** BARCLAY *Cyt. & Uplondyshm.* (Percy Soc.) p. lxxii, The sweat distilling with droppes aboundaunt. **1526** *Pilgr. Perf.* (W. de W. 1531) 258 [He] hath caused holy oyle to distyll out of yᵉ bones of his sayntes. **1612** CAPT. SMITH *Map Virginia* 7 Mountaines; from whence distill innumerable sweet and pleasant springs. **1659** D. PELL *Impr. Sea* 272 Fetch water out of the Seas.. to distill in silver showers upon the face of the whole Earth. **1704** POPE *Windsor For.* 54 Soft showers distill'd, and suns grew warm in vain. **1742** FIELDING *J. Andrews* I. xi, A thousand tears distilled from the lovely eyes of Fanny. **1810** SOUTHEY *Kehama* XI. v, The wine which from yon wounded palm.. Fills yonder gourd, as slowly it distills. **1853** KANE *Grinnell Exp.* v. (1856) 36 Water distilled in drops over the rocks.

b. To pass or flow gently. Chiefly *fig.*

1609 BIBLE (Douay) *Dan.* ix. 11 The malediction hathe distilled upon us.. because we have sinned. **1611** BIBLE *Deut.* xxxii. 2 My speach shall distill as the deaw. **1715–20** POPE *Iliad* I. 332 Words, sweet as honey, from his lips distill'd. **1830** SIR R. GRANT *Hymn*, '*O worship the King*' iv, Thy bountiful care.. sweetly distils in the dew and the rain. *a* **1853** ROBERTSON *Serm.* Ser. III. xxi. 281 The wisdom.. will distil in honeyed sweetness.

†**c.** To melt into, or become dissolved in, *tears*.

c **1374** CHAUCER *Troylus* IV. 491 (519) This Troylus in teris gan distille. *c* **1400** *Test. Love* I. Chaucer's Wks. (1561) 287 a/1 With that I gan in teares to distill.

d. To drip or be wet *with*.

1714 GAY *Trivia* III. 50 Till their arm'd Jaws distill with Foam and Gore. **1715–20** POPE *Iliad* XVII. 72 See his jaws distil with smoking gore. **1816** T. L. PEACOCK *Headlong Hall* xiii, Till his face.. distils with perspiration.

2. *trans.* To let fall or give forth in minute drops, or in a vapour which condenses into drops.

c **1400** *Lanfranc's Cirurg.* 265 Boile hem in a double vessel, & distille it in his eere flaisch [= tepidus]. **1494** FABYAN *Chron.* VI. clviii. 147 Hir eyen dystylled dropes of blode. **1509** HAWES *Joyf. Med.* ix. (Arb.) 72 The dewe of Joye.. Dystylled is nowe from the rose so red. **1601** HOLLAND *Pliny* II. 272 If by way of embrochation it be distilled from aloft vpon the head in a more thin and liquid substance. **1667** MILTON *P.L.* v. 56 His dewie locks distill'd Ambrosia. **1692** RAY *Dissol. World* 250 Trees do destil Water apace when Clouds or Mists hang about them. **1697** DRYDEN *Virg. Past.* VIII. 74 Fat Amber let the Tamarisk distill. **1758** J. S. *Le Dran's Observ. Surg.* (1771) 231, I distilled a few Drops of *Bals. Viride* into it [the Wound]. **1878** HUXLEY *Physiogr.* 53 The dew is distilled more abundantly upon the grass than upon the gravel.

3. *transf.* and *fig.* To give forth or impart in minute quantities; to infuse; †to instil.

1393 GOWER *Conf.* I. 3 A gentil herte his tonge stilleth, That it malice none distilleth Butt preyse. *c* **1480** *Crt. of Love* 23 Thy sugar droppes sweet of Helicon Distil in me, thou gentle Muse, I pray. **1577** FENTON *Gold. Epist.* 123 They shoulde haue distilled into their youth, doctrine, and rules of direction. **1630** SANDERSON *Serm.* II. 253 Solomon ..had this truth.. early distilled into him by both his parents. **1665** WALTON *Life Hooker* in *H.'s Wks.* (1888) I. 36 There was distilled into the minds of the common people such.. venomous and turbulent principles. **1841** MYERS *Cath. Th.* III. xxvii. 102 Distilling healing virtue into bitter waters. *a* **1881** ROSSETTI *Rose Mary* iii. 13 She felt the slackening frost distil Through her blood the last ooze dull and chill.

4. To subject to the process of distillation; to vaporize a substance by means of heat, and then condense the vapour by exposing it to cold, so as to obtain the substance or one of its constituents in a state of concentration or purity. Primarily said of a liquid, the vapour of which when condensed is again deposited in minute drops of pure liquid; but extended also to the volatilizing of solids, the products of which may be gaseous. See DISTILLATION 3.

1398 TREVISA *Barth. De P.R.* IV. vii. (1495) 90 Yf bloode be sodde and dystylled, therof we maye make talowe and grees. **1471** RIPLEY *Comp. Alch.* III. vii. in Ashm. (1652) 140 The Water.. Looke thou dystyll. **1577** B. GOOGE *Heresbach's Husb.* IV. (1586) 192 The water of the herbe steeped in White Wine, and destilled therewithal. **1787** WINTER *Syst. Husb.* 339 To distill a sufficient quantity of water. **1812–6** J. SMITH *Panorama Sc. & Art* II. 80 Water ..when distilled, is every-where of the same specific gravity. **1854** RONALDS & RICHARDSON *Chem. Technol.* (ed. 2) I. 157 Hill's process consists in distilling peat in the same way as wood. **1878** HUXLEY *Physiogr.* 73 If it is required to distil a liquid, the liquid is evaporated in a boiler, and the vapour conducted to the condenser, where it becomes sufficiently cooled to be deposited in drops.. Fresh water is thus being constantly distilled from the briny ocean.

b. To extract the essence of (a plant, etc.) by distillation; to obtain an extract of.

c **1400** MAUNDEV. (1839) v. 51 Some destyllen Clowes. **1590** SHAKS. *Mids. N.* I. i. 76 Earthlier happie is the Rose distil'd Then that which withering on the virgin thorne, Growes, liues, and dies in single blessednesse. **1633** G. HERBERT *Temple, Praise* iv, An herb destill'd, and drunk. **1750** JOHNSON *Rambler* No. 51 ¶4 The ladies.. begged me to excuse some large sieves of leaves and flowers.. for they intended to distill them. **1825** J. NEAL *Bro. Jonathan* III. 433 Of the hellish herbs.. that she hath distilled for us.

c. To transform or convert (*into* something) by distillation. Also *fig.*

a **1636** BEN JONSON *Sad Shepherd* I. ii, Two souls Distilled into kisses through our lips, Do make one spirit of love. **1792** J. BELKNAP *New Hampsh.* III. 205 Two or three vessels in a year would.. bring home molasses to be distilled into rum. **1822** LAMB *Elia* Ser. II. *Conf. Drunkard*, Draughts of.. wine which are to be distilled into airy breath to tickle vain auditors. **1847** EMERSON *Poems, Day's Ration* Wks. (Bohn) I. 482 All he distils into sidereal wine.

d. *absol.* To perform distillation.

1611 SHAKS. *Cymb.* I. v. 13 Hast thou not learn'd me how To make Perfumes? Distill? Preserue? **1800** tr. *Lagrange's Chem.* II. 403 Separate the salt, and distil at a gentle heat. **1838** T. THOMSON *Chem. Org. Bodies* 18 If we substitute 6 parts of alcohol for the 4 parts of water and distil, we obtain formic ether.

e. *fig.* To extract the quintessence of; to concentrate, purify.

1599 SANDYS *Europæ Spec.* (1632) 142 This man is very charie over that one remaining, and distilleth all other devises rather than set finger to that string. **1601** CORNWALLYES *Ess.* xii. (1632) Time hath distild our bloods. **1873** H. SPENCER *Stud. Sociol.* x. 267 Men who are distilled into the House of Commons, and then redistilled into the Ministry. **1889** *Spectator* 14 Dec. 830 We want a removable Secretary for school works, not a committee, which is only the public meeting over again, a little distilled.

f. To drive (a volatile constituent) *off* or *out* by distillation. Also *fig.*

1641 FRENCH *Distill.* iv. (1651) 105 Distill off the Water till no more will distill. **1800** tr. *Lagrange's Chem.* II. 225 If nitric acid be distilled from off this matter, you will obtain oxalic acid. **1874** L. STEPHEN *Hours in Library* (1892) II. v. 150 To make a Wycherley you must distil all the poetry out of a Fletcher. **1883** T. P. TEALE *Econ. Coal* 18 The coal.. as the volatile parts are distilled out, becomes a mass of red coke.

5. To obtain, extract, produce, or make, by distillation.

c **1400** MAUNDEV. (Roxb.) vii. 26 Þe licour þat es distilled of þam þai sell in steed of bawme. **1599** H. BUTTES *Dyets drie Dinner* B v, Strawberrie-water.. rudely distilled, betwixt two platters, and not in a limbeck. **1634** SIR T. HERBERT *Trav.* 150 They have Arack or Usquebagh, distilled from Dates or Rice. **1774** PENNANT *Tour Scotl. in 1772*, 165 A great quantity of whiskey is distilled. **1830** M. DONOVAN *Dom. Econ.* I. 43 Sir James Ware supposes that ardent spirit was distilled in Ireland earlier than in England.

b. *fig.*

1599 SHAKS. *Hen. V*, IV. i. 5 Ther is some soule of goodnesse in things euill, Would men obseruingly distill it out. *c* **1600** SHAKS. *Sonn.* cxix. 2 What potions have I drunk of Siren tears, Distill'd from limbecks foul as hell within. **1606** —— *Tr. & Cr.* I. iii. 350 A man distill'd Out of our Vertues. **1793** *Chron.* in *Spirit Pub. Jrnls.* (1799) I. 177 Books and papers were seized, that treason might be distilled out of them. **1830** TENNYSON *Sonn. to J.M.K.* 6 Old saws, Distill'd from some worm-canker'd homily. **1862** MERIVALE *Rom. Emp.* (1865) III. xxii. 34 The essence which the wisest of the Romans had distilled from the records of Greek philosophy.

6. *intr.* To become vaporized and then condensed into liquid; to undergo distillation; to drop, pass, or condense from the still. ***to distil over***: to pass over in the form of vapour which again condenses into a liquid.

c **1400** *Lanfranc's Cirurg.* 195 Make a fier aboute þe pott þat is aboue þe erþe & þere wole distille oile into þe pott þat is bineþe. **1471** RIPLEY *Comp. Alch.* III. vi. in Ashm. (1652) 140 Than Oyle and Water wyth Water shall dystyll. **1641** FRENCH *Distill.* i. (1651) 35 The oyle which first distils.. must be kept a part. **1812** SIR H. DAVY *Chem. Philos.* 265 The acid.. distils unaltered at 248° Fahrenheit. **1853** W. GREGORY *Inorg. Chem.* (ed. 3) 104 At this strength the acid distils over unchanged. **1878** HUXLEY *Physiogr.* 73 The liquid.. distils over in a state of purity.

fig. **1625** BACON *Ess., Religion* (Arb.) 425 The outward Peace of the Church, Distilleth into Peace of Conscience.

†**7.** *trans.* To melt, dissolve (*lit.* and *fig.*). *Obs.*

c **1470** HARDING *Chron.* Editor's Pref., My lord, distilde by kynde nature Thrugh besy age.. To such waykenesse he myght no more endure, Bot feel so in his grave. **1605** SYLVESTER *Dialog upon Troubles* x, Melt thee, distill thee, turne to wax or snow. *a* **1719** ADDISON (J.), Swords by the lightning's subtle force distill'd And the cold sheath with running metal fill'd.

[Cf. SHAKS. *Ham.* I. ii. 204 *Qq.* destilled, *Fol.* bestil'd.]

† **di'stil, di'still**, *sb. Obs.* [f. prec.] A vessel used in distillation; a still.

1822 BEWICK *Mem.* 74 Jars, retorts and distills.

† **di'stil-house.** *Obs.* [f. stem of DISTIL *v.*] A house constructed for the business of distilling, a distilling-house.

1682 *Lond. Gaz.* No. 1686/4 In Old-street is a very convenient Distill-House to be Lett. **1723** *Ibid.* No. 6202/4 A Distill-House, and Backs for working Mollosses. **1790** J. B. MORETON *West India Isl.* 55 The generality.. think attention to the distill-house a menial part of plantership. **1807** tr. *Goede's Trav.* III. 77 Distil-houses for brandy and other spirits.

distillable (dɪ'stɪləb(ə)l), *a.* (*sb.*) [f. DISTIL *v.* + -ABLE; cf. F. *distillable* (16th c. in Littré).]

A. *adj.* Capable of being distilled (*lit.* and *fig.*).

1611 COTGR., *Distillable*, distillable; fit or apt to be distilled. *a* **1691** BOYLE *Wks.* II. 225 (R.) Much of the obtained liquor coming from the distillable concretes. **1837** *Penny Cycl.* IX. 24/2 Distillable alcohol. **1851** CARLYLE *Sterling* I. iii. (1872) 91 Two.. octavos; stray copies of which ..may one day become distillable into a drop of History.

†**B.** *sb.* Something that may be distilled. *Obs.*

1669 W. SIMPSON *Hydrol. Chym.* 163 Which.. gives, amongst other distillables, that fetid empyreumatick oyl.

distillage (dɪ'stɪlədʒ). *rare.* [f. as prec. + -AGE 3.] The process or product of distilling.

1877 LANIER *Poems, Stirrup-cup* 5 David to thy distillage went.

† **di'stillant**, *a. Obs. rare.* [a. F. *distillant*, pr. pple. of *distiller*, or ad. L. *distillānt-em*, pr. pple. of *distillāre* to DISTIL.] Distilling.

1549 *Compl. Scot.* vii. 70 Vitht mony salt teyris distillant doune fra hyr piteous ene. **1606** J. HYND *Eliosto Libidinoso* 56 Watering the garden.. of her face with deaw from his distillant eyes.

distillate ('dɪstɪlət), *sb.* [ad. L. *distillāt-us*, pa. pple. of *distillāre*.] That which is distilled (see DISTIL *v.* 5); a product of distillation.

1864 in WEBSTER. **1869** E. A. PARKES *Pract. Hygiene* (ed. 3) 44 If the water be distilled, and if the distillate be tested for ammonia. **1869** *Advocate* 15 Dec., The more rapidly the distillate is sent over the better it will be. **1887** *Daily News* 25 Jan. 2/7 For the purposes of producing coal-tar distillates. **1888** B. W. RICHARDSON *Son of a Star* III. viii. 135 Their drink is the pure distillate of the skies.

distillation (dɪstɪ'leɪʃən). Also 6–8 **destillation.** [ad. L. *dē-*, *distillātiōn-em*, n. of action f. *dē-*, *distillāre* to DISTIL; cf. F. *distillation* (15th c. in Hatz.-Darm.).] The action of distilling or fact of being distilled.

1. The action of falling or flowing down drop by drop; gentle dropping or falling. (*lit.* and *fig.*)

14.. in *Pol. Rel. & L. Poems* (1866) 112 My blode alle split by distillacion. **1623** COCKERAM, *Distillation*, a dropping. **1694** F. BRAGGE *Disc. Parables* I. 4 This seed thus sown, is water'd with the dews of heaven, with the distillations of the Divine grace and blessing. **1833** CHALMERS *Const. Man* (1835) I. iv. 181 Cause distillation within the soul of the waters of bitterness.

†**2.** *Path.* A defluxion of rheum; a catarrh. *Obs.*

1533 ELYOT *Cast. Helthe* (1541) 78 a, Destyllation is a droppynge downe of a lyquyde mater out of the head, and fallynge eyther in to the mouth, or in to the nosethrilles, or in to the eyes. **1589** COGAN *Haven Health* ccxii. (1636) 217 Distillations from the head, commonly called rheumes. **1607** TOPSELL *Four-f. Beasts* (1658) 270 The Horse..is subject unto the distillation in his throat or parts thereabout. **1748** tr. *Vegetius' Distemp. Horses* 183 If the neck suffers by a Destillation or Defluxion of Humours. *a* **1755** G. WEST *Triumphs Gout* (Seager), Through th' obstructed pores the struggling vapour and bitter distillation force their way.

3. The action of converting any substance or constituent of a substance into vapour by means of heat, and of again condensing this by refrigeration into the liquid form, by means of an alembic, retort and receiver, or a still and refrigeratory; the extraction of the spirit, essence, or essential oil of any substance by the evaporation and condensation of its liquid solution; and, in a more generalized sense, the operation of separating by means of fire, and in closed vessels, the volatile parts of any substance from the fixed parts, in order to the collection of the products.

As shown by the etymology, the original application is to substances of which the distillates are condensed drop by drop into the liquid form; whether for the purpose of extracting the more volatile part of a substance, or of concentrating or purifying a volatile substance such as water by freeing it from matter held in suspension or solution. When no more heat is applied than just suffices to cause the liquid to pass over in drops, the process is called ***cold distillation***. ***Dry*** or ***destructive distillation***, the decomposition of a substance by strong heat in a retort, and the collection of the volatile matters evolved, as in the destructive distillation of coal in gas-making. ***fractional distillation***, the separation of two or more volatile liquids having different boiling-points, so that they pass over at different temperatures and can be collected separately, the more volatile first, and the less volatile in order afterwards. ***distillation by descent*** (*per descensum*), in *Old Chem.*, the name given to a method in which the fire was applied above, and the distillate drawn off beneath (see DESCENT 1 d). In opposition to this, the ordinary method was called ***distillation by ascent*** (*per ascensum*).

1393 GOWER *Conf.* II. 86 First of the distillation Forth with the congelation, Solucion, discention. **1527** ANDREW *Brunswyke's Distyll. Waters* Prol., I have chosen..the booke of distyllacyon of waters. **1559** MORWYNG *Evonym.* 1 Destillation, not distillation (as lerned doe write) is the drawing forthe of a thinner and purer humor out of a juise. **1626** BACON *Sylva* §99 The power of Heat is best perceived in Distillations, which are performed in close Vessels and Receptacles. **1673** RAY *Journ. Low C.* 66 The Chymical examination of these Waters by..Destillation. **1774** GOLDSM. *Nat. Hist.* (1776) I. 169 How far..it [water] may be brought to a state of purity by distillation, is unknown. **1802** PLAYFAIR *Illustr. Hutton. Th.* 34 The products obtained by the distillation of the common bituminous coal. **1806** *Gazetteer Scotl.* (ed. 2) 73 A considerable trade in the distillation of whisky. **1846** MCCULLOCH *Acc. Brit. Empire* (1854) I. 387 This is one of the counties in which illicit distillation was most prevalent. **1869** ROSCOE *Elem. Chem.* 47 All fresh water on the earth's surface has been derived from the ocean by a vast process of distillation. **1875** *Ure's Dict. Arts* (ed. 7) II. 48 Distillation consists in the conversion of any substance into vapour, in a vessel so arranged that the vapours are condensed again and collected in a vessel apart.

1683 ROBINSON in *Ray's Corr.* (1848) 137 Pitch is got from the Pinus by a kind of distillation *per descensum*. **1727–51** CHAMBERS *Cycl.* s.v., Distillation is twofold: 1°, *Per ascensum*, by ascent..2°, *Per descensum*, by descent; when the matter which is to be distilled is below the fire. **1831** T. P. JONES *Convers. Chem.* xxviii. 281 When organized substances are decomposed at a red heat in close vessels, the process is called destructive distillation. **1869** ROSCOE *Elem. Chem.* 317 It occurs in the dry distillation of wood, forming about one per cent. of the aqueous distillate. **1875** *Ure's Dict. Arts* (ed. 7) II. 48 In most cases of destructive distillation the bodies operated upon are solid, and the products liquid or gaseous; it is then called *dry distillation*. **1895** *Times* 19 Jan. 4/5 Our coal-gas..up to the present time ..obtained by destructive distillation of coal, hydrocarbon oils, or other organic substances.

b. *transf.* and *fig.*

1835 ARNOLD *Let.* in Stanley *Life & Corr.* (1844) I. vii. 425 The books of Livy..relate to a time so uninteresting, that it is hard even to extract a value from them by the most complete distillation. **1837** EMERSON *Nat., Amer. Schol.* Wks. (Bohn) II. 177 In proportion to the completeness of the distillation, so will the purity and imperishableness of the product be. **1894** J. RODWAY *Guiana Forest* iv. 76 Intermittent distillation [of perfume] is almost general in the white flowers of the tropics.

4. *concr.* The product of distilling: **a.** That which distils or forms by distilling (see sense 1). **b.** A distillate (*obs.*).

1598 SHAKS. *Merry W.* III. v. 115 And then to be stopt in like a strong distillation with stinking Cloathes. *c* **1600** —— *Sonn.* v. Were not summers distillation left A liquid prisoner pent in walls of glasse. **1616** R. C. *Times' Whistle* I. 57 The sunnes kinde heat, heavens fruitful distillation. **1678** R. R[USSELL] *Geber* II. I. IV. xiii. 119 Under that end of the Filter must be set another Vessel to receive the Distillation. **1746** HARVEY *Rep. Flower Garden* (1818) 88 What a sovereign restorative are these cooling distillations of the night.

c. *fig.* The extract, abstract; the refined or concentrated essence.

1649 MILTON *Eikon.* i. (1847) 280/1 Among..all those numberless volumes of their theological distillations. **1846** GROTE *Greece* I. xvi. (1862) I. 334 The narrative of Thucydides is a mere extract and distillation from their incredibilities. **1868** MILMAN *St. Paul's* ix. 228 That liturgy ..the distillation, as it were, and concentration, of all the orisons which have been uttered in the name of Christ.

†**di'stillative,** *a. Obs. rare*$^{-0}$. [f. L. *distillāt-* ppl. stem (see DISTIL) + -IVE.] = DISTILLATORY *a.* Hence **di'stillatively** *adv.*, by way of distillation, drop by drop.

1657 TOMLINSON *Renou's Disp.* 677 Liquor that will distillatively delabe.

†**'distillator.** *Obs.* Also 6 -our. [agent-n. in L. form f. *distillāre* to DISTIL; cf. F. *distillateur* (16th c.)] One who distils; a distiller.

1576 BAKER *Jewell of Health* 10b, The vapour may be annoyance to the Distillatour. **1644** J. GOODWIN *Innoc. Triumph.* (1645) 92 The most generous..lees, which gratifie their Distillator with the best strong waters. **1659** B. HARRIS *Parival's Iron Age* 59 The Empire had no need of a distillator, but rather of a good Operatour, to act powerfully.

distillatory (dɪˈstɪlətərɪ), *a.* and *sb.* [f. L. type **distillātōri-us, -um*, f. *distillāre*: see -ORY. Perh. after F. *distillatoire* (Paré, 16th c.).]

A. *adj.* Pertaining to, or employed in, distillation.

1576 BAKER *Jewell of Health* 164a, This poure into the distyllatorye bodie. **1594** PLAT *Jewell-ho.* III. 9 Some distillatorie vessell. **1631** R. H. *Arraignm. Whole Creature* xiii. §1. 171 Water, Wine, Milke, Distillatory waters. **1727** BRADLEY *Fam. Dict.* s.v. *Distillation of oil*, The Copper-Vessel being thus plac'd in the Furnace, fit to its Canal or distillatory Vessel the Recipient. **1871** NICHOLS *Fireside Sc.* 54 After the distillatory process..was completed. **1871** HARTWIG *Subterr. W.* xxx. 373 The ores are treated in 13 double distillatory furnaces, called alodels.

†**b.** ***distillatory plant***, the pitcher-plant. *Obs.*

1707 *Curios. Husb. & Gard.* 288 The Distillatory Plant.. grows not far from Colombo.

†**B.** *sb.* An apparatus for distillation; an alembic, retort, or still. *Obs.*

c **1460–70** *Bk. Quintessence* 4 Thanne must ȝe do make in þe furneis of aischin, a distillatorie of glas. **1599** A. M. tr. *Gabelhouer's Bk. Physicke* 22/1 Put al these together into a distillatory, and infuse theron thre pintes of Piony water. **1602** PLAT (*title*), Delights for Ladies, to adorne their Persons, Tables..and Distillatories with Beauties.. Perfumes and Waters. **1660** N. INGELO *Bentivolio & Urania* II. (1682) 4 They had a Room well appointed with Furnaces and Distillatories. **1730–6** BAILEY (folio) s.v. *Distillers Company*, Their armorial ensigns are..a distillatory double armed with two worms and bolt head receivers [etc.].

†**b.** Name of a collection of recipes for distilling. *Obs.*

1677 T. SHERLEY (*title*) Curious Distillatory [tr. Elsholt's Distillatoria curiosa] or the Art of Distilling Coloured Spirits, Liquors, Oyls, etc. from Vegetables.

distilled (dɪˈstɪld), *ppl. a.* [f. DISTIL *v.* + -ED[1].] That has undergone distillation; obtained, purified, or concentrated by distillation.

distilled water, water that has been vaporized and then again condensed in drops, so as to be freed from matters held in suspension or solution.

c **1460–70** *Bk. Quintessence* 10 Take þe beste vynegre distillid. **1502** *Ord. Crysten Men* (W. de W. 1506) I. ii. 10 Water of roses, or other water dystylled. **1577** B. GOOGE *Heresbach's Husb.* IV. (1586) 191 Restored to health, by the destilled water of this Thistell. **1626** BACON *Sylva* §347 So we see distilled Waters will last longer than raw Waters. **1732** ARBUTHNOT *Rules of Diet* 262 Distill'd Oils turn acrid. **1799** KIRWAN *Geol. Ess.* 358 Brisson dissolved 2 oz. of the purest common salt in 16 oz. of distilled water. **1854** J. SCOFFERN in *Orr's Circ. Sc.* Chem. 490 Neutral acetate of copper is known popularly by the absurd term distilled verdigris.

fig. **1876** GEO. ELIOT *Dan. Der.* III. xlviii. 353 A more thoroughly distilled sneer.

distiller (dɪˈstɪlə(r)). [f. as prec. + -ER[1].]

1. One who or that which distils: see the verb.

1577 FENTON *Gold. Epist.* 15 A distiller of waters. **1605** TIMME *Quersit.* III. 186 Thy vessell..must be such as the chymicall distillars do use. **1659** D. PELL *Impr. Sea* 266 This tree..is a very great distiller of water, which drops out of the leaves of it. **1821** SCOTT *Kenilw.* xi, He was a learned distiller of simples, and a profound chemist.

b. *spec.* One who extracts alcoholic spirit by distillation.

[**1638** The Distillers' Company (of London) incorporated.]

1639 (*title*), The Distiller of London, compiled and set forth for the sole use of the company of Distillers of London. *Ibid.* Pref. 10 Our duty requires us all (that are Distillers by profession and Trade) to acknowledge [etc.]. **1720** STRYPE *Stow's Surv.* II. v. xv. 237/1 Even the Distillers of Aqua Vitæ, and Vinegar-makers, did engross it up. **1830** M. DONOVAN *Dom. Econ.* I. 105 The chief use of yest is for raising bread, and exciting fermentation in malt infusions for brewers, distillers, and vinegar makers. **1846** J. JOYCE *Sci. Dial.* xviii. 182 A distiller's crane or syphon.

c. *fig.*

a **1631** DONNE *Ess.* (1651) 67 That late Italian Distiller and Sublimer of old definitions. **1713** POPE *Guardian* No. 92 ¶4 A great distiller of the maxims of Tacitus. **1895** *Daily News* 30 Dec. 6/3 The historic expression is the distilled essence of the ponderous sentence. Who was the distiller?

2. An apparatus for the distillation of salt water at sea; more fully called ***distilling apparatus*** or ***distilling condenser***.

1885 R. SENNETT *Marine Steam Engine* (ed. 2) 567 In some ships of the Royal Navy other kinds of distillers have been fitted. **1895** *Times* 1 Feb. 12/6 There are also in the engine-rooms two main-feed pumps, two evaporators and distillers, four bilge and fire engines.

Hence **di'stilleress**, a female distiller.

1841 *Fraser's Mag.* XXV. 599 An eminent private distilleress of that seducing liquor called potheen.

distillery (dɪˈstɪlərɪ). [f. prec.: see -ERY.]

†**1.** The action or art of distilling; = DISTILLATION 3. *Obs.*

1677 EVELYN *Mem.* (1857) II. 123 He and his lady (who is very curious in distillery) entertained me..very freely. **1757** W. THOMPSON *R.N. Advoc.* 44 Skill'd in that noble Science of Distillery. **1807** G. CHALMERS *Caledonia* I. II. vi. 309 Irish husbandry did not yet provide corn for the distillery of *aqua vitæ*.

2. A place for distilling; the establishment or works in which the distilling of spirits is carried on.

1759 B. MARTIN *Sure Guide Distillers* p. ii, A community which not only imports great quantities of..spirits from abroad, but employs such an extensive distillery at home entirely on that subject. **1765** *Ann. Reg.* 102 A large drain.. through which the water flowed a considerable way from a distillery. **1830** M. DONOVAN *Dom. Econ.* I. 253 The distillery was a very small thatched cabin. **1833** N. ARNOTT *Physics* (ed. 5) II. 195 An illicit distillery has been discovered by the exciseman happening..to look across a hole used as the chimney.

3. *attrib.* and *Comb*; **distillery-fed** (of cattle, etc.), fed on spent grains, wash, etc. obtained from a distillery.

1816 J. SCOTT *Vis. Paris* (ed. 5) App. 310 The new distillery apparatus of M. Adam. **1829** HEY *Gauger* in *Lond. Encycl.* (1829) VII. 323 A wash-back or other distillery utensil. **1861** *Times* 10 Oct., Distillery grains and wash are given [to cows], with straw-chaff and roots. **1881** *Chicago Times* 4 June, Fat distillery-fed bulls.

distilling (dɪˈstɪlɪŋ), *vbl. sb.* [-ING[1].] The action of the verb DISTIL; distillation.

1527 ANDREW *Brunswyke's Distyll. Waters* A j, Dystyllyng is none other thynge, but onely a puryfyeng of the grosse from the subtyll, and the subtyll from the grosse. **1628** GAULE *Pract. The.* (1629) 34 So doth my heart..sucke in the comfortable distillings of his Grace. **1770** MASSIE *Reas. agst. Tax on Malt* 7 The distilling..of Malt or of Corn.

b. *attrib.* and *Comb.*

1598 FLORIO, *Distilatoio*, a still or distilling house. **1757** (*title*) An Appeal to the Public concerning the Distilling Trade; with a rational Scheme to extirpate it from the Nation. **1837** *Penny Cycl.* IX. 24/1 The period in which they [mashing and fermentation] are carried on is by law kept quite distinct from the distilling period. **1894** *Times* 26 June 9/5 The representatives of the brewing and distilling interests.

di'stilling, *ppl. a.* [f. as prec. + -ING[2].] That distils: see the verb.

c **1485** *Digby Myst.* (1882) IV. 264 Gud Mawdleyn, mesure youre distillinge teres! **1592** SHAKS. *Ven. & Ad.* 66 Her cheeks..dew'd with such distilling showers. **1592** —— *Rom. & Jul.* IV. i. 94 Take thou this Violl..And this distilling liquor drinke thou off. **1634** SIR T. HERBERT *Trav.* 210 Divers Birds..would speed to sucke the distilling nectar. **1807** T. THOMSON *Chem.* (ed. 3) II. 203 With the assistance of a distilling heat, it dissolves in oils.

distilment (dɪˈstɪlmənt). [f. as prec. + -MENT.] The process of distillation; *concr.* the produce of this process, a distilled liquor. Also *fig.* (cf. *quintessence*).

1602 SHAKS. *Ham.* I. v. 64 Vpon my secure hower thy Vncle stole With iuyce of cursed Hebenon..And in the Porches of mine eares did poure The leaperous Distilment. **1611** S. PAGE *Panegr. Verse* in *Coryat's Crudities*, Put all your wits distillement in your pen. **1873** BROWNING *Red Cott. Nt.-cap* 245 For perfume, pour Distilment rare, the rose of Jericho, Holy-thorn. **1894** R. HUNTER *Lect. Germ. Th. Consumption* 10 A poisonous distillment of microbes.

†**dis'time,** *v. Obs. nonce-wd.* [DIS- 7 a.] *trans.* ? To put out of time; to mistime.

1650 W. BROUGH *Sacr. Princ.* (1659) 428 So sloth distimes the conscience.

distinct (dɪˈstɪŋkt), *ppl. a.* (*sb.*) Also 5 **destinct, distynte,** 5–6 **dis-, dystynct, distincte,** 6 **-stynke, -stincke.** [ad. L. *distinct-us*, pa. pple. of *distinguĕre* to separate, divide, DISTINGUISH; cf. F. *distinct, -te* (13–14th c. in Hatz.-Darm.).]

A. as *pa. pple.*

†**1.** Distinguished, differentiated. *Obs.*

c **1386** CHAUCER *Pars. T.* ¶754 (Ellesm.), In oother manere been distinct [*v.rr.* distynte, distinket] the speces of Glotonye after seint Gregorie. **1551** RECORDE *Pathw. Knowl.* I. Defin., That therby the whole figures may the better bee iudged, and distincte in sonder. **1667** MILTON *P.L.* VII. 536 For no place Is yet distinct by name.

†**2.** Separated into parts, divided. *Obs.*

1434 MISYN *Mending of Life*, þis boke is of mendynge of lyfe..destinct in-to xij chapiters. **1526** *Pilgr. Perf.* (W. de W. 1531) 1 This treatyse..is distincte and diuyded in to thre bokes.

¶ See also B. 4.

B. *adj.*

1. Distinguished as not being the same; separate, several, individual, not identical; = DIFFERENT 2. Const. *from*.

1382 [implied in DISTINCTLY 1]. **1447** BOKENHAM *Seyntys* (Roxb.) 149 That yche of these thyngys..To a dystynct persone approprat be. **1540** *Act 32 Hen. VIII*, c. 42 Twoo severall and distynct companyes..that is to say, both the Barbours and the Surgeons. **1665** HOOKE *Microgr.* 166 A large Feather..contains neer a million of distinct parts. **1796** WITHERING *Brit. Plants* II. 329 *Tamus.* Flowers m[ale] and f[emale] on distinct plants. **1838** THIRLWALL *Greece* IV. xxxii. 276 [The indictment] charged him with three distinct offences. **1885** F. TEMPLE *Relat. Relig. & Sc.* ii. 38 Absolute as distinct from relative knowledge.

b. Separate or apart so as to be capable of being distinguished, or as being different; not confounded with each other, or with something else.

a **1674** CLARENDON *Hist. Reb.* VIII. §35 The intention was, that the two armies, which marched out together, should always be distinct. **1733** POPE *Ess. Man* III. 229 The worker from the work distinct was known. **1816** J. SMITH *Panorama Sc. & Art* II. 699 If the first mark be erroneous, a second may be drawn at the distance of a hair's breadth from it, and still be a distinct line. **1888** BRYCE *Amer. Commw.* II. xlii. 113 Keeping the two systems [of common law and equity] distinct.

c. *Nat. Hist.*, *Pathol.*, etc. = DISCRETE *a.* 1 c. Said of markings or parts which are perceptibly separated from each other, as ***distinct spots, furrows, antennæ***, or from the contiguous parts, as ***distinct scutellum, thorax, tail***, etc.

1789 A. CRAWFORD in *Med. Commun.* II. 325 The smallpox..was of the distinct kind. **1810** R. THOMAS *Pract. Physic* (ed. 3) 167 [Smallpox] is distinguished into the distinct and confluent..in the former the eruptions are perfectly separate from each other.

2. Distinguished or separated from others by nature or qualities; possessing differentiating characteristics; individually peculiar; different in quality or kind; not alike. Const. *from*.

1523 *Act 14 & 15 Hen. VIII*, c. 3 Every warden..shal limitte distincte and seueral markes to euery of the said worstede weauers. **1594** HOOKER *Eccl. Pol.* I. x. §1 A distinct kind of law from that which hath been already declared. **1659** B. HARRIS *Parival's Iron Age* 72 These two Lords..as they were of a very contrary humour, so had they..a very distinct death. *a* **1698** TEMPLE *Ess., Const. & Int. Empire* Wks. 1731 I. 93 Flanders cannot be considered distinct from Spain in the Government. **1836** J. GILBERT *Chr. Atonem.* vi. (1852) 167 Holiness..is quite distinct from vindictiveness. **1845** M. PATTISON *Ess.* (1889) I. 1 Such history is a distinct species of composition, having its own principles.

3. Clearly perceptible or discernible by the senses or the mind; clear, plain, definite: **a.** to the senses.

1382-98 [implied in DISTINCTLY 2]. **1513** MORE *Rich. III*, Wks. 64/2 The voyce was neyther loude nor distincke. **1667** MILTON *P.L.* IX. 812 To see from thence distinct Each thing on Earth. **1784** COWPER *Task* IV. 162 The clear voice, symphonious yet distinct. **1813** SCOTT *Trierm.* III. Introd. ii, Distinct the shaggy mountains lie, Distinct the rocks, distinct the sky. **1827** KEBLE *Chr. Y.* 9th Sund. after Trin., God's chariot-wheels have left distinctest trace. **1856** SIR B. BRODIE *Psychol. Inq.* I. ii. 35 The transparency of the atmosphere renders distant objects unusually distinct.

b. to the mind or thought.

1606 SHAKS. *Tr. & Cr.* IV. v. 245 That I may giue the locall wound a name, And make distinct the very breach, where-out Hector's great spirit flew. **1668** HOWE *Bless. Righteous* (1825) 72 This somewhat distincter account of it. **1752** JOHNSON *Rambler* No. 208 ⁋11 When common words were..less distinct in their signification. **1860** TYNDALL *Glac.* II. xix. 328 The distinct expression of thoughts and convictions which had long been entertained. **1891** *Law Times Rep.* LXIII. 690/2 The defendant..had given distinct orders to Nunney never to lock anyone up.

c. In mod. use: That is clearly such; unmistakable, decided, pronounced, positive. (Cf. DISTINCTLY 2 b.)

1828 MACAULAY *Ess., Hallam's C.H.* (1854) 87/2 An act, not only of private treachery, but of distinct military desertion. **1871** FREEMAN *Norm. Conq.* IV. xviii. 229 Who.. would have a claim to a distinct preference at the next vacancy of the throne. **1873** BLACK *Pr. Thule* vi. 91 A most distinct dislike to Gaelic songs. **1887** *Punch* 19 Mar. 137/2 He is a distinct loss to the stage. **1892** W. MINTO in *Bookman* Nov. 57/1 His volume is a distinct enrichment of our literature.

d. Transferred to the mental impression or faculty by which something is perceived.

1654 Z. COKE *Logick* (1657) 5 The distinct knowledge of God is paramount the reach of the understanding..God.. is conceivable only..by himself. **1697** LOCKE *Let. to Stillingfl.* in Bourne *Life* (1876) II. xiv. 426 If your lordship has any better and distincter idea of substance than mine is. **1833** N. ARNOTT *Physics* (ed. 5) II. I. 225 The point of distinct vision is distinguishable from the retina around by being more transparent. **1892** W. B. SCOTT *Autobiog.* I. 3 The distincter memory of middle life.

†**e.** Capable of making clear distinctions; discerning, discriminating: = DISTINCTIVE *a.* 2. *Obs.*

1614 BP. HALL *Recoll. Treat.* 128 A distinct and curious head shall finde an hard taske, to define in what point the goodnes thereof consisteth. **1756-82** J. WARTON *Ess. Pope* (1782) I. iii. 120 Men of dry distinct heads, cool imaginations, and keen application.

4. Marked in a manner so as to be distinguished; decorated, adorned. (A Latinism, chiefly *poetic*, and somewhat participial in use.)

1596 SPENSER *F.Q.* VI. iii. 23 The place..was dight With divers flowres distinct with rare delight. **1667** MILTON *P.L.* VI. 846 From the fourfold-visag'd Foure, Distinct with eyes, and from the living Wheels, Distinct alike with multitude of eyes. **1715-20** POPE *Iliad* XIII. 768 The handle..Distinct with studs. **1817** SHELLEY *Rev. Islam* I. lv, A throne.. Distinct with circling steps which rested on Their own deep fire. **1830** TENNYSON *Arab. Nts.* 90 Dark-blue the deep sphere overhead, Distinct with vivid stars inlaid.

†**5.** = DISTINGUISHED 4. *Obs. rare.*

1756 W. TOLDERVY *Two Orphans* III. 85 An application made..to a person of distinction..and the reception that they met with from the said distinct person.

†**C.** *sb.* A separate or individual person or thing. *Obs. rare.*

1601 SHAKS. *Phœnix & Turtle* 27 Two distincts, division none: Number there in love was slain.

†**di'stinct**, *v. Obs.* Also 4 **destincti**, 5 **distinke**, 5-6 **dystynke**. [a. OF. *di-*, *destincter*, *-tinter* to distinguish (Godef.), f. *distinct* DISTINCT *a.*] = DISTINGUISH (in various senses); in *pa. pple.* sometimes = DISTINCT *a.*

1303 R. BRUNNE *Handl. Synne* 11590 A prest þat ys no clergye ynne, How can he weyl dystyncte þy synne? **1340** *Ayenb.* 152 To destincti be-tuene þe guode þinges and þe kueade. *c* **1386** [see DISTINCT *ppl. a.* A. 1, Distinket]. *c* **1400** *Rom. Rose* 6199 Ther can no wight distincte it so That he dare sey a word therto. **1526** *Pilgr. Perf.* (W. de W. 1531) 247 The consideracyon wherfore the foresayd hours be so distincted or diuyded in to vij tymes. **1541** R. COPLAND *Galyen's Terap.* 2 A iv b, It is an impertynent thynge to this worke to dystynke these thynges. **1546** GARDINER *Declar. Joye* 40 b, By distinctinge gods knowledge from his election. **1583** STUBBES *Anat. Abus.* II. (1882) 68 Be the churches, congregations, and assemblies there distincted into particulars. *Ibid.* 109.

Hence **di'stincted** *ppl. a.*, **di'stincting** *vbl. sb.*

1570 DEE *Math. Pref.* in *Rudd's Euclide* (1651) B iv b, The discretion, discerning, and distincting of things. *Ibid.*, Our Severalling, distincting, and numbring, createth nothing. **1575** T. ROGERS *Sec. Coming Christ* 47/1 Nor yet their earnefull plaintes abroade distincted voyces send.

†**di'stinctial**, *a. Obs. rare*$^{-1}$. [irreg. f. L. *distinct-* ppl. stem, perh. after *differential*, *partial*, *nuptial*, etc.] Capable of distinguishing.

1648 EARL WESTMORELAND *Otia Sacra* (1879) 59 What eye's so distinctiall, As for to single One out of them all?

di'stinctify, *v. rare.* [f. L. *distinct-us* DISTINCT + -FY.] *trans.* To make distinct. So **di,stinctifi'cation.**

a **1866** J. GROTE *Exam. Utilit. Philos.* xx. (1870) 337 The growth and distinctification of classes and interests. **1877** [quoted in] Proctor *Myths Astron.* 247 So could the same.. light, passed through the faintest focal object of a telescope, both distinctify (to coin a new word..) and magnify its feeblest component members.

distinction (dɪ'stɪŋkʃən). [a. F. *distinction* (12th c. in Littré), ad. L. *distinctiōn-em*, n. of action f. *distinguĕre* to DISTINGUISH.]

†**1.** The action of dividing or fact of being divided; division, partition; separation. (In quot. 1520, division of opinion, dissension.) *Obs.*

1387 TREVISA *Higden* (Rolls) I. 111 (Mätz.) For distinccioun of dyuers manere men þat woned þere. **1520** *Caxton's Chron. Eng.* v. 62/1 There was a great dystynccyon, for the Clergy entended to have chose Peres the archebysshop. **1586** A. DAY *Eng. Secretary* I. (1625) 144 There might also be made a distinction of love..one tearmed by the name of Friendship, and this other chalenging onely..Love. **1612** BRINSLEY *Pos. Parts* (1669) p. iii, Else distinctions of the Chapters are not observed. **1661** BOYLE *Style of Script.* (1675) 60 The distinction of chapters and verses now in use. **1668** DRYDEN *Ess. Dram. Poesy* (T.) The distinction of tragedy into acts. **1709-29** V. MANDEY *Syst. Math., Geogr.* 541 Part I. Of the Distinction of the Earth.

†**b.** Division of a sentence by stops, punctuation; a point or stop. *Obs.*

1552 HULOET, Distinction or poynte in sentence, *diastole, distinctio*. **1579** FULKE *Heskins' Parl.* 195 To corrupt it by.. wrong distinction or pointing. *a* **1637** B. JONSON *Eng. Gram.* II. ix, The distinctions of an imperfect sentence are two, a comma and a semicolon.

†**c.** *concr.* A partition, something that separates. *Obs.*

1578 BANISTER *Hist. Man* I. 13 Betwene euery tooth are euident distinctions, or hedges.

†**2.** One of the parts into which a whole is divided; a division, section; a class, category.

a **1225** *Ancr. R.* 12 þeos boc ich to dele on eihte distinctiuns, þet ȝe clepieð dolen. *c* **1400** tr. *Secreta Secret., Gov. Lordsh.* (E.E.T.S.) 42 Departand þis booke yn distinccons or bokes. **1586** A. DAY *Eng. Secretary* I. (1625) 20 His distinctions are Hortatorie and Dehortatorie; Swasorie and Disswasorie. **1677** HALE *Prim. Orig. Man.* II. x. 234 Persons..known to be of that Linage and Descent, and still continuing..in that Distinction. **1756** BURKE *Subl. & B.* v. ii, Words..are capable of being classed into more curious distinctions. **1848** KELLY tr. *Cambrensis Eversus* I. 373 He prepared to recite his work in Oxford..one of the three distinctions of the book being read each day.

†**b.** Class (in relation to status); rank, grade. ***of the first distinction***: of the highest rank; highly distinguished (cf. sense 8). *Obs.*

1719 SWIFT *To Yng. Clergym.* Wks. 1755 II. II. 3 Among the clergy of all distinctions. **1734** tr. *Rollin's Anc. Hist.* (1827) II. II. 88 Three hundred young Carthaginians of the first distinction. *a* **1763** SHENSTONE (Mason), Societies, ranks, orders, and distinctions amongst men.

3. The action of distinguishing or discriminating; the perceiving, noting, or making a difference between things; discrimination. With *a* and *pl.*, the result of this action, a difference thus made or appreciated.

a **1340** HAMPOLE *Psalter* lxv. 12 Sayand..i hafe nede of þe, noght þou of me, þis is a right distynccioun. **1382** WYCLIF *Rom.* iii. 22 The riȝtwysnesse of God is by the feith of Ihesu Crist on alle that bileuen in to hym; forsoth ther is no distynccioun. **1398** TREVISA *Barth. De P.R.* VIII. xvi. (1495) 323 The sonne hath vertue of dystynccion, for coloures and shappes of thynges by..the lyghte..of the sonne arne knowe and dystynguyd asondre. **1527** TINDALE *Treat. Justif. by Faith* Wks. I. 46 They rend and tear the scriptures with their distinctions. **1551** T. WILSON *Logike* (1567) 73 b, All suche argumentes must be auoided by distinction, that is, ye must declare the double meanyng in the twoo Proposicions. **1588** FRAUNCE *Lawiers Log.* I. iii. 17 b, This nice and frivolous distinction of Chaunce and Fortune. **1607** SHAKS. *Cor.* III. i. 323 He..is ill-school'd In boulted Language: Meale and Bran together He throwes without distinction. **1662** J. DAVIES tr. *Olearius' Voy. Ambass.* 78 Punish'd, without any distinction of Sex, Age, or Quality. **1677** LD. ORRERY *Art of War* 11 In some places..one may find a distinction from the Cohorts to the Centuries, and from the Centuries to the Manniples. **1709** STEELE *Tatler* No. 62 ⁋4 To cut off their Ears, or Part of them, for Distinction-sake. **1729** BUTLER *Serm.* Wks. 1874 II. 6 Every body makes a distinction between self-love, and the several particular passions. **1871** FREEMAN *Norm. Conq.* (1876) IV. xviii. 104, We may..see that a distinction is drawn between the rule of William himself and the rule of his oppressive lieutenants. **1891** *Speaker* 2 May 534/1 The old universities are open to all, without distinction of rank or creed.

b. Phr. ***a distinction without a difference***: i.e. one artificially or fictitiously made in a case where no real difference exists.

1579 FULKE *Heskins' Parl.* 207 The distinction remaineth without a difference. **1688** *Vox Cleri Pro Rege* 47 It seems his Power is absolute, but not arbitrary, which is..a distinction without a difference. **1771** *Junius Lett.* No. 59. 313 Your correspondent..seems to make a distinction without a difference. **1891** *Speaker* 2 May 532/2 The jugglery of words was never more successful than in this distinction without a difference.

4. The condition or fact of being distinct or different; difference. With *a* and *pl.*, an instance of this, a difference.

1435 MISYN *Fire of Love* 15 O godhede..is of iij. persones ..euynhede & onhede forsoth haueand after þe substance of þe godhede, not wantand distinccion of diuersite after þe propirte of þe name. **1532** MORE *Confut. Tindale* Wks. 492/2 The Jewes & the christen had other differences & dystinccions betwene them. **1678** NORRIS *Coll. Misc.* (1699) 288 It is a certain sign..of real distinction, when the idea of one thing..positively excludes the idea of the other. **1731** J. GILL *Trinity* i. (1752) 3 Denying a distinction of persons in the Godhead. **1847** EMERSON *Repr. Men, Plato* Wks. (Bohn) I. 300 His patrician tastes laid stress on the distinctions of birth. **1850** MCCOSH *Div. Govt.* III. i. (1874) 291 The.. process by which the distinction between good and evil is discovered.

5. The faculty of distinguishing or accurately observing differences; discernment, discrimination. ? *Obs.*

1606 SHAKS. *Tr. & Cr.* III. ii. 28, I doe feare..That I shall loose distinction in my ioyes. **1617** FLETCHER *Valentinian* I. iii, Yet take heed, worthy Maximus; all ears Hear not with that distinction mine do. **1654** COKAINE *Dianea* I. 4 The remotenesse of the place he was in afforded him not distinction to discerne from whence they came. **1768** STERNE *Sent. Journ.* (1778) II. 110 (Case of Consc.), I like a good distinction in my heart.

†**6.** The condition or quality of being distinctly or clearly perceptible; distinctness. *Obs.*

1589 PUTTENHAM *Eng. Poesie* II. iv. [v]. (Arb.) 87 There is no greater difference betwixt a ciuill and brutish vtteraunce then cleare distinction of voices;..the most laudable languages are alwaies most plaine and distinct. **1661** SOUTHWELL in *Phil. Trans.* XLIV. 220 Firing..I heard 56 Reiterations of the Noise. The first twenty were with some Distinction. **1709** BERKELEY *Th. Vision* §84 Able to view them..with the utmost clearness and distinction. **1712** STEELE *Spect.* No. 454 ⁋6 All the several Voices lost their Distinction, and rose up in a confused Humming.

7. Something that distinguishes or discriminates; a distinguishing quality, mark, or characteristic; a distinguishing name or title.

c **1374** CHAUCER *Boeth.* II. pr. v. 32 þat gemmes drawen to hem self..beaute..thorw the distinccon of hem self. **1729** BUTLER *Serm.* xi. Wks. 1874 II. 134 It may be spoken of as ..the distinction of the present [age] to profess a contracted spirit. **1772** COWPER *Let. to J. Hill* 4 Feb., The person was described as the Clerk of the House of Lords, without the addition of his proper distinction. **1828** D'ISRAELI *Chas. I*, I. iii. 31 From a slender volume of polemical divinity..our Sovereigns still derive one of their regal distinctions. **1848** RICKMAN *Goth. Archit.* 33 The capital is the great distinction of this order.

8. The action of distinguishing or treating with special consideration or honour; the showing of a preferential regard; with *a* and *pl.*, a mark of special appreciation or honour.

1715 DE FOE *Fam. Instruct.* I. iv. (1841) I. 87 She loves you to a distinction above every child she has. **1727** SWIFT *Gulliver* IV. x. 327 To give so great a mark of distinction to a creature so inferior as I. **1766** GOLDSM. *Vic. W.* x, The distinctions lately paid us by our betters awakened that pride which I had laid asleep. **1768** *Woman of Honour* III. 193 There is no great hazard of your distinction of him being lost upon him. **1780** HARRIS *Philol. Enq.* (1841) 394 For grammatical knowledge, we ought to mention with distinction the learned prelate, Dr. Lowth. **1810** SHELLEY *Zastrozzi* xv. Pr. Wks. 1888 I. 94 Julia rushed forwards, and, in accents of distinction, in a voice of alarmed tenderness, besought him to spare himself. **1816** J. SCOTT *Vis. Paris* Pref. (ed. 5) 30 The feeling..which procured him this distinction. **1855** PRESCOTT *Philip II*, I. III. iii. 343 Some were beheaded with the sword,—a distinction reserved..for persons of condition.

9. a. The condition or fact of being distinguished or of distinguishing oneself; excellence or eminence that distinguishes from others; honourable preeminence; elevation of character, rank, or quality; a distinguishing excellence.

1699 M. LISTER *Journ. Paris* 8 All the Houses of Persons of Distinction are built with Port-cocheres. **1748** *Relat.*

Earthq. Lima 55 Fifty select Persons, all Men of Distinction. **1756** [see DISTINCT *a.* 5]. **1828** SCOTT *F.M. Perth* xxiii, Various persons of distinction had come there in his train. **1867** SMILES *Huguenots Eng.* xii. (1880) 202 He had..served with distinction in the French army. **1887** T. FOWLER *Princ. Mor.* II. i. 12 The love of distinction or preeminence.. seems, in the great majority of men, to operate far more constantly and with far greater force than the love of knowledge. **1890** *Spectator* 14 June 829/1 Not only is distinctness from others not in itself distinction, but distinctness from others may often be the very opposite of distinction, indeed, a kind, and a very unpleasant kind, of vulgarity. **1891** *Speaker* 2 May 533/1 The book..has..more quality and distinction than four-fifths of the novels which come under our notice.

b. The condition or fact of distinguishing oneself by excellence in an examination, as of a degree awarded ***with distinction***; hence, a credit or acknowledgement of excellence awarded to candidates in some examinations who gain more than a certain mark, or otherwise impress the examiners with the high quality of their work; a mark or grade in this category.

? **1890** *Univ. Mississippi Catal. 1889–90* 33 The University now awards for excellent scholarship, distinctions as follows: 1. Diplomas 'with Special Distinction', to all students whose entire record averages 95 or upward. 2. Diplomas 'with Distinction', to all such whose entire record averages 90 or upward. **1922** *Bull. 31st Ann. Reg. 1921–22* (Stanford Univ.) 109 As a recognition of high scholastic attainment the Bachelor's degree may be granted 'with distinction' or 'with great distinction'. **1946** *Summary 57th Ann. Rep. 1945* (Assoc. Board R. Schools Music) p. i, Of the 3,662 candidates who passed, 8.85 per cent gained Distinction. **1985** *GCSE General Introd.* (Dept. of Educ. & Science) 14 The Government has proposed that Distinction and Merit Certificates should be introduced.

10. *Comb.*, as ***distinction-maker*** (see sense 3).

1701 J. LAW *Counc. Trade* (1751) 278 Speaking the same language, and if the distinction-makers would let them, having the same inclinations for the public and common good.

di'stinctional, *a. rare.* [f. prec. + -AL[1].] Relating to, or of the nature of, distinction.

1607 R. C. tr. *Estienne's World Wond.* xxxix. 327 The Decretals haue had their part..the Questionall, Distinctionall, Quodlibeticall bookes..theirs.

di'stinctity. *rare.* [f. L. *distinct-us* DISTINCT *a.* + -ITY.] The quality of being distinct.

1812 COLERIDGE in *Lit. Rem.* (1836) III. 2 The *pleroma* of being whose essential poles are unity and distinctity. **1829** *Ibid.* 123 Donne had not attained to the reconciling of distinctity with unity.

distinctive (dɪˈstɪŋktɪv), *a.* (*sb.*) [f. L. *distinct-* ppl. stem of *distinguĕre* (see DISTINCT, DISTINGUISH) + -IVE; cf. F. *distinctif, -ive* (1740 in Acad.).] **A.** *adj.*

1. a. Having the quality of distinguishing; serving or used to distinguish or discriminate; characteristic, distinguishing.

1583 STUBBES *Anat. Abus.* I. (1879) 73 Our Apparell was giuen vs as a signe distinctiue, to discern betwixt sex and sex. **1627–77** FELTHAM *Resolves* II. lvii. 278 'Tis one of the distinctive properties of Man from Beast, that he can reflect upon himself. **1828** D'ISRAELI *Chas. I*, I. vi. 156 Papist and Protestant now became distinctive names. **1856** RUSKIN *Mod. Paint.* III. IV. xvii. §9 Wordsworth's distinctive work was a war with pomp and pretence, and a display of the majesty of simple feelings and humble hearts. **1878** GLADSTONE *Prim. Homer* 9 The..distinctive office of the bard was to give delight. **1894** C. N. ROBINSON *Brit. Fleet* 319 A military organization, wearing a distinctive dress.

b. Applied *spec.* in *Linguistics* to a phonetic feature that is capable of distinguishing one meaning from another. Also ***distinctive-feature***, applied *attrib.* to a theory or system propounded by R. Jakobson of classifying linguistic elements in terms of their distinctive phonetic features.

1927 BLOOMFIELD & BOLLING in *Language* III. 129 Normally we symbolize only phonemes (distinctive features) so far as we can determine them. **1933** BLOOMFIELD *Lang.* v. 77 Part of the gross acoustic features are indifferent (non-distinctive), and only a part are connected with meanings and essential to communication (distinctive)... A feature that is distinctive in one language, may be non-distinctive in another language. **1942** BLOCH & TRAGER *Outl. Ling. Analysis* 38 Divide all phonetic differences observable in the language into two kinds: *distinctive differences* or *contracts*, capable of distinguishing one meaning from another; and *nondistinctive differences*, never used for this purpose. **1952** R. JAKOBSON et al. *Preliminaries to Speech Analysis* 3 The distinctive features are the ultimate distinctive entities of language since no one of them can be broken down into smaller linguistic units. The distinctive features combined into one simultaneous bundle form a phoneme. **1964** *Language* XL. 221 A problem wide open for experimentation is the psycholinguistic validation of 'distinctive-feature analysis'. **1965** *Ibid.* XLI. 168 A positional and articulatory distinctive-feature description has been more thoroughly exploited than any other in analyzing clusters. **1965** N. CHOMSKY *Aspects of Theory of Syntax* i. 55 Jakobsonian distinctive-feature theory. **1968** CHOMSKY & HALLE *Sound Pattern Eng.* 64 We take 'distinctive features' to be the minimal elements of which phonetic, lexical, and phonological transcriptions are composed.

2. Having the power of distinguishing or discriminating; discriminative; discerning. *rare.*

1646 SIR T. BROWNE *Pseud. Ep.* II. iii. 75 More judicious and distinctive heads. **1646** CRASHAW *Poems* 128 If with distinctive eye and mind you look. **1879** R. K. DOUGLAS *Confucianism* iii. 72 He..shows himself..accomplished, distinctive, concentrative, and searching.

3. Having a distinct character or position. *rare.*

1867 SMILES *Huguenots Eng.* xviii. (1880) 343 The refugees..at length ceased to exist as a distinctive people. **1877** J. C. COX *Ch. of Derbysh.* II. 417 Bonsall..was not a distinctive manor at the time of the Domesday Survey.

4. *Hebr. Gram.* Applied to accents used, instead of stops, to separate clauses.

1874 DAVIDSON *Hebr. Gram.* (1892) 27 These are the main distinctive accents, and by stopping at them..the reader will do justice to the sense.

B. *sb.* **1.** A distinguishing mark or quality; a characteristic.

1816 KEATINGE *Trav.* (1817) I. 189 The red umbrella, the distinctive of royalty here. **1836** CDL. WISEMAN *Sc. & Relig.* I. iii. 173 An intermediate class, possessing, to a certain degree, the distinctives of the extremes.

2. *Hebr. Gram.* A distinctive accent: see A. 4.

1874 DAVIDSON *Hebr. Gram.* (1892) 27 A distinctive of less power than Zakeph is Ṭiphḥâ. **1887** *Athenæum* 17 Dec. 820/1 As considerable attention is paid to the [Hebrew] accents, the author should know that *tiphca* is not a minor distinctive, but one of the four kings or great distinctives.

distinctively (dɪˈstɪŋktɪvlɪ), *adv.* [f. prec. + -LY[2].] In a distinctive manner.

1. With distinguishing operation or effect; in a way that makes a distinction; so as to distinguish; separately, severally.

1610 *Mirr. Mag.* 855 (R.) Her [Queen Elizabeth's] sweet tongue could speake distinctively Greek, Latin, Tuscane, Spanish, French, and Dutch. *a* **1677** BARROW *Serm.* Wks. 1686 II. xxxiv. 492 To what end also doth he distinctively assign a peculiar dispensation of operations to the Father, of ministeries to the Son, of gifts to the Holy Ghost? **1797** *Monthly Mag.* Jan. 52 He determined to blend, in a single tableau, all the different colourings of truth which he had long before pourtrayed distinctively. **1825** COLERIDGE *Aids Refl.* (1848) I. 168 Contemplated distinctively in reference to formal (or abstract) truth, it is the Speculative Reason. **1833** CHALMERS *Const. Man* (1835) I. ii. 129 Ere we see clearly and distinctively. **1841** MYERS *Cath. Th.* III. §38. 136 Not only..Facts..but also..what may be distinctively termed Truths, or technically Doctrines. **1863** E. V. NEALE *Anal. Th. & Nat.* 61 The individual rose has become to us one among many roses, each of which may be thought of as distinctively colored.

2. In a distinguishing manner; characteristically as distinct from others; peculiarly.

1871 FREEMAN *Hist. Ess.* (1872) 37 If we can suppose a distinctively Saxon settlement in the north. **1873–4** MOGGRIDGE *Ants & Spiders* Suppl. 168 The seeds of the distinctively spring and summer-flowering plants. **1881** *Sat. Rev.* 23 July 101/1 There is nothing distinctively Christian..in Gothic architecture. **1885** CLODD *Myths & Dr.* I. viii. 134 Legends and traditions..invested with a purity and majesty distinctively Hebrew.

¶**3.** ? Distinctly. *Obs.*

1632 SHAKS. *Oth.* I. iii. 155 (2. 3. 4. Fos.) Whereof by parcels she had something heard, But not distinctively [Qq. intentiuely, Fo. 1 instinctiuely].

di'stinctiveness. [f. as prec. + -NESS.]

1. The quality of being distinctive; distinctive force, tendency, operation, effect, or character.

a **1679** T. GOODWIN *Wks.* III. II. 13 (R.) The distinctiveness is imported..in the article put to each, *του πατρος* of the Father, *του υἱου* of the Son, *του ἁγιου πνευματος*, of the Holy Ghost. **1821** LOCKHART *Valerius* III. vi. 145 As if what I saw were still present in all the distinctiveness of reality. **1876** J. PARKER *Paracl.* I. vi. 94 Preaching should never lose its distinctiveness; it should stand apart. **1894** *Times* 6 Mar. 6/3 They have electric lights transcending in power and distinctiveness everything on this side of the.. Channel.

†**2.** Power of distinguishing or discriminating; discernment. *Obs.*

1667 DIGBY *Elvira* I. in Hazl. *Dodsley* XV. 22 Thou art an ass, and want'st distinctiveness 'Twixt love and love: that was a love of sport To keep the serious one in breath.

distinc'tivity. *rare.* [f. as prec. + -ITY.] = DISTINCTIVENESS.

1836 *Fraser's Mag.* XIII. 700 In similar connexion and distinctivity exist church and state, God and nature.

distinctly (dɪˈstɪŋktlɪ), *adv.* [f. DISTINCT *a.* + -LY[2].]

†**1.** In a distinct or separate manner; separately, individually, severally. *Obs.*

1382 WYCLIF *Ecclus.* i. 2 The grauel of the se, and the dropis of reyn, and the daȝes of the world, who distinctli hath noumbrede? **1425** *Found. St. Bartholomew's* 23 Sundry thyngys by ther propyr namys distynctly he callide. **1581** PETTIE *Guazzo's Civ. Conv.* II. (1586) 54, I will speake distinctlie of those two pointes. **1610** SHAKS. *Temp.* I. ii. 200 On the Top-mast, The Yards and Bore-spritt, would I flame distinctly, Then meete, and ioyne. **1737** WHISTON *Josephus, Antiq.* XVI. iv. §4 Their father..took each of them distinctly in his arms.

†**b.** ***distinctly from***: so as to be distinguished from; in contradistinction to. *Obs.*

a **1682** SIR T. BROWNE *Tracts* (1684) 16 Distinctly from that he chose plain Fare of Water and the gross Diet of Pulse.

2. In a distinct or clear manner; without confusion or obscurity; so as to be clearly perceived or understood; with clear perception or understanding; clearly, plainly.

1382 WYCLIF *Neh.* viii. 8 And thei radden in the boc of the lawe distinctli and apertli to vnderstonde. **1398** TREVISA *Barth. De P.R.* III. xvii. (1495) 62 Though a thinge be ryght tofore the eye, yf it be to ferre therfrom, it is not dystynctly knowe. **1535** COVERDALE *Isa.* xxxii. 4 The vnparfite tunge shal speake planely and distinctly. **1604** SHAKS. *Oth.* II. iii. 290, I remember a masse of things, but nothing distinctly. **1709** STEELE & ADDISON *Tatler* No. 103 ⁋13 He could see nothing distinctly. **1858** O. W. HOLMES *Aut. Breakf.-t.* xi. 110, I tried to speak twice without making myself distinctly audible. **1883** FROUDE *Short Stud.* IV. I. x. 112 They did not know, perhaps, distinctly what they meant to do.

b. In mod. use (chiefly with adjs. or adjectival phrases): In a way clear to the mind or perception; clearly, unmistakably, decidedly, indubitably. (Cf. DISTINCT *a.* 3 c.)

1858 KINGSLEY *Lett.* (1878) I. 21 An object which was distinctly not political. **1868** FREEMAN *Norm. Conq.* (1876) II. vii. 133 One would have thought that horses were distinctly in the way. **1873** BLACK *Pr. Thule* xiv. 217 The young American lady had distinctly the best of it. **1874** GREEN *Short Hist.* iii. §1. 114 The English court had become the centre of a distinctly secular literature. **1893** *Critic* (U.S.) 11 Mar. 147/1 Now the favorite slang word of literature is 'distinctly'. Heroines are now 'distinctly regal' in their bearing, and there is about the heroes a manner that is 'distinctly fine'.

distinctness (dɪˈstɪŋktnɪs). [f. as prec. + -NESS.]

1. The condition or quality of being distinct or different; separateness; individuality.

1668 H. MORE *Div. Dial.* III. x. (1713) 200 The opinion of the Immortality of the Soul and personal distinctness of the deceased in the other life. **1678** CUDWORTH *Intell. Syst.* 37 (R.) To assert the soul's immortality, together with its incorporeity or distinctness from the body. **1863** KINGLAKE *Crimea* (1876) I. viii. 116 The Turkish Government was.. sensible of the distinctness of the 'nations' held under its sway. **1890** [see DISTINCTION 9].

2. The condition or quality of being distinct or clear; clearness, plainness. **a.** As a quality of the object: Capability of being clearly perceived or understood.

1668 WILKINS *Real Char.* 413 The Character here proposed..the Facility, Comliness and Distinctness of it. **1794** HOME in *Phil. Trans.* LXXXV. 9 Judging of distinctness by the legibility of the letters. **1871** L. STEPHEN *Playgr. Eur.* xi. (1894) 271 In the evening light each ridge and peak..stands out with startling distinctness. **1875** JOWETT *Plato* (ed. 2) V. 105 To use the lyre on account of the distinctness of the notes.

b. As a quality of perception or thought: cf. DISTINCT *a.* 3 d.

1654 Z. COKE *Logick* (1657) 5 Our understanding cannot ..certainly determine to comprehend the natures of things with distinctnesse. **1794** HOME in *Phil. Trans.* LXXXV. 21 The distinctness with which an object is seen when the eye is first fixed upon it. **1837** WHEWELL *Hist. Induct. Sc.* (1857) I. 51 A degree of hesitation..which..shows the absence of all scientific distinctness of thought.

†**di'stinctor.** *Obs. rare.* [a. L. *distinctor*, agent-n. from *distinguĕre* to DISTINGUISH.] One who draws a distinction; a distinguisher.

1577 STANYHURST *Descr. Irel.* i. in *Holinsh.* (1587) II. 10/1 They would be named Ireland men, but in no wise Irish-men. But certes..such curious distinctors may be.. resembled to the foolish butcher, that offred to haue sold his mutton for fifteene grots, and yet would not take a crowne.

†**di'stincture.** *Obs. rare.* [f. DISTINCT *a.* + -URE.] = DISTINCTION, DISTINCTNESS.

1846 WORCESTER cites *Edin. Rev.*

†**di'stingue,** *v. Obs.* Also 4 distyng(e, 4–5 distingwe, 6 *Sc.* distuing. [ME. *disting-en, distingue-n*, a. F. *distingue-r* (13th c. in Littré), ad. L. *distinguĕre* to DISTINGUISH, f. *di-*, DIS- 1 + *stinguĕre* orig. 'to prick or stick', but found only in sense 'to extinguish'.] = DISTINGUISH (in various senses).

a **1340** HAMPOLE *Psalter* Prol., þis boke is distyngid in thris fyfty psalmes. *c* **1374** CHAUCER *Boeth.* II. pr. v. 47 Art þou distingwed and embelised by þe spryngyng floures? *c* **1380** WYCLIF *Serm.* Sel. Wks. II. 202 Here we moten distingue blame fro liȝt synne. *c* **1460** FORTESCUE *Abs. & Lim. Mon.* i. (1885) 110 In tho dayis *regimen politicum et regale*, was distyngued *a regimine tantum regale.* **1596** DALRYMPLE *Leslie's Hist. Scot.* IV. 387 Quairto thrie or four distuing or define J in this speiking.

‖**distingué** (distɛ̃ge), *a.* [F. *distingué* DISTINGUISHED, pa. pple. of *distinguer* to DISTINGUISH.] Distinguished (*esp.* in reference to appearance or manner); having an air of distinction.

1813 BYRON in Moore *Life* (1832) II. 290 (Stanf.) Every thing *distingué* is welcome there. **1833** C. HEATH *Bk. Beauty* (1837) 159 A tall, elegant, young man, of the most *distingué* appearance. **1841** THACKERAY *Misc. Ess.* (1885) 381 That snowy napkin coquettishly arranged round the kidneys gave them a *distingué* air. **1873** LOWELL *Lett.* (1894) II. 89 He is a *distingué* person in a high sense, with a real genius for looking like a gentleman.

distinguish (dɪˈstɪŋgwɪʃ), *v.* [f. F. *distinguer* or L. *distinguĕre* (see DISTINGUE), with the ending -ISH, etymologically appropriate to representatives of F. verbs in *-ir, -iss-ant.* Cf. EXTINGUISH.]

I. Transitive senses.

†1. To divide into parts or portions separate in space or time. *Obs.*

1609 BIBLE (Douay) *Exod.* xxxvi. 35 A veile of hiacinth.. with embrodered worke, varied and distinguished. 1610 *Histrio-m.* I. 200 The face of heaven..is distinguisht into Regions..fil'd with sundry sorts of starres. 1618 BOLTON *Florus* I. ii. 8 Hee..distinguisht the yeere into twelve Months. 1650 FULLER *Pisgah* II. vi. 149 In the third day.. this lower globe was distinguished into earth and water. 1695 WOODWARD *Nat. Hist. Earth* I. (1723) 6 The Stone.. was distinguished into Strata or Layers. 1709–29 V. MANDEY *Syst. Math., Geogr.* 540 Geography is a Doctrine shewing the Reason of Distinguishing, and Measuring the Earth.

†b. To divide or separate (*from* something else, or from each other). *Obs.*

1648 GAGE *West Ind.* xiii. 69 We cannot certainly avow this America to be continent, nor certainly affirme it to be an Island, distinguished from the old world. 1658 A. FOX *Wurtz' Surg.* II. xi. 89 The Midriffe, which distinguisheth the Lungs from the Breast. 1697 DRYDEN *Virg. Georg.* IV. 194 No Fences parted Fields, nor Marks nor Bounds Distinguish'd Acres of litigious Grounds.

†c. To divide by points; to punctuate. *Obs.*

1657 J. SMITH *Myst. Rhet.* 268 The Points or Notes used by the Learned in distinguishing writing..are not the least part of Orthography. 1699 BENTLEY *Phal.* 266 Thus the words are to be pointed, which have hitherto been falsly distinguish'd.

2. To divide into classes or species; to class, classify.

1581 J. BELL *Haddon's Answ. Osor.* 186 Your schoolemen do distinguishe into workes done, and works to be done. 1614 BP. HALL *Recoll. Treat.* 698, I might distinguish this service into habituall and actuall. 1762 GOLDSM. *Cit. W.* xxv. ¶3 The inhabitants were..distinguished into artisans and soldiers. 1774 —— *Nat. Hist.* (1862) I. IV. iii. 423 Mr. Buffon distinguishes this species into two kinds. 1831 R. KNOX *Cloquet's Anat.* 690 The branches which the radial artery gives to the forearm are distinguished into anterior, posterior, external, and internal.

3. To mark as different or distinct; to separate (things, or one thing *from* another) by distinctive marks; to indicate the difference of or between; to make or constitute a difference in, to differentiate.

1576 FLEMING *Panopl. Epist.* 236 Every several Epistle is distinguished with this mark (*). 1611 BIBLE *Transl. Pref.* 1 By the first [Ciuilitie] we are distinguished from bruit-beasts led by sensualitie. 1638 SIR T. HERBERT *Trav.* (ed. 2) 228 To tincture their nailes and faces with vermillion, serving..to distinguish them from the vulgar sort. 1781 GIBBON *Decl. & F.* III. 64 The deaths of his two rivals were distinguished only by the difference of their characters. 1876 J. PARKER *Paracl.* I. xvi. 250 The 'manifestation of the Spirit'..distinguishes human life from all other creaturedom below it.

b. To mark, as a distinctive mark or character does; to be a characteristic of; to characterize.

1600 J. PORY tr. *Leo's Africa* I. 3 Mount Atlas..beginneth westward at that place, where it distinguisheth the Ocean by the name of Atlanticus. 1662 J. DAVIES tr. *Olearius' Voy. Ambass.* 206 Square stones..set up-an-end, to distinguish the Graves of private Persons. 1780 HARRIS *Philol. Enq.* Wks. (1841) 456 Different portions of this age [the dark age] have been distinguished by different descriptions; such as *Sæculum Monotheleticum, Sæculum Eiconoclasticum,* &c. 1849 MACAULAY *Hist. Eng.* I. 321 He..was distinguished by many both of the good and of the bad qualities which belong to aristocrats.

4. To recognize as distinct or different; to separate mentally (things, or one thing *from* another); to perceive or note the difference between (things); to draw a distinction between.

1561 T. NORTON *Calvin's Inst.* III. 192 Can true repentance stande without faythe? No. But though they can not be seuered, yet they must be distinguished. 1590 SHAKS. *Com. Err.* I. i. 53 Two goodly sonnes..the one so like the other, As could not be distinguish'd but by names. 1684 R. H. *School Recreat.* 88 Endeavour to distinguish the Notes of a Peal of Bells, one from another while Ringing. 1713 BERKELEY *Hylas & P.* III. Wks. 1871 I. 322, I can distinguish gold, for example, from iron. 1809 W. IRVING *Knickerb.* III. ix. (1849) 191 It is scarcely possible to distinguish the truth from the fiction. 1887 MAX MÜLLER *Sc. Th.* 29 That very common error that things which can be distinguished can therefore claim an independent existence.

†b. To make a distinction in or with respect to; *esp.*, in scholastic use, to draw distinctions between various meanings of (a word or statement); hence, to do *away*, or *out of*, bring *into* (something) by making subtle distinctions. *Obs.*

1581 J. BELL *Haddon's Answ. Osor.* 168b, I deny the Major of this Arguement. In the Minor I distinguish this word Necessitie. *Ibid.* 186 So doe the schoolemen expound, and distinguishe it. 1643 MILTON *Divorce* II. xi. Wks. 1738 I. 196 That Proverbial Sentence..which also the Peripatetics do rather distinguish than deny. 1689–92 LOCKE *Toleration* iv. Wks. 1727 III. 465 You have distinguish'd yourself into a false Retreat. 1703 DE FOE *Let. to How* in *Misc.* 328 That..they be not distinguish'd out of their Reason and Religion by the Cunning and Artifice of Words. 1748 RICHARDSON *Clarissa* (1811) I. viii. 54 Thus by subtilty and cunning aiming to distinguish away my duty.

c. To separate as a distinct item.

1866 ROGERS *Agric. & Prices* I. xxi. 530 Items which used to be distinguished are lumped in one general sum. 1885 *Times* (Weekly ed.) 6 Mar. 14/1 To consider whether the cost of the railway could be distinguished from the other expenditure.

5. To perceive distinctly or clearly (by sight, hearing, or other bodily sense); to 'make out' by looking, listening, etc.; to recognize.

1593 SHAKS. *Lucr.* 1785 No man could distinguish what he said. 1605 —— *Lear* IV. vi. 215 Euery one heares that, which can distinguish sound. 1660 F. BROOKE tr. *Le Blanc's Trav.* 249 We saw the form of a body covered with linnen, without being able to distinguish more. 1726 *Adv. Capt. R. Boyle* 31 When they were near enough, I could distinguish them to be three handsome Women. 1791 MRS. RADCLIFFE *Rom. Forest* i, He distinguished the voices of men in the room above. 1856 SIR B. BRODIE *Psychol. Inq.* I. v. 182 An eagle..can distinguish objects at a distance at which they would be to us altogether imperceptible.

6. To single out, notice specially; to pay particular attention to, honour with special attention. *arch.*

1607 DAVIES *1st Let. to Earl Salisbury* (1787) 228 My Lord-Deputy..did presently distinguish the business that was to be done. 1702 ROWE *Tamerl.* Ded., I cannot help Distinguishing the last Instance very particularly. 1748 CHESTERF. *Lett.* (1792) II. cli. 35 His Polish Majesty has distinguished you. I hope you received that mark of distinction with respect and with steadiness. 1779 JOHNSON *Let. to Mrs. Thrale* 6 Apr., Do not let new friends supplant the old; they who first distinguished you have the best claim to your attention. 1848 DICKENS *Dombey* 363 If [they] would do him the honour to look at a little bit of a shrubbery..they would distinguish him very much. 1851 RUSKIN *Stones Ven.* (1874) I. Pref. ii. 12 The work of the Marchese Selvatico is ..to be distinguished with respect.

7. To make prominent, conspicuous, remarkable, or eminent in some respect. (In the quots. from Dryden, involving the notion of adornment; cf. DISTINCT *a.* 4.) Now usually *refl.* or *pass.*

1600 J. PORY tr. *Leo's Africa* II. 376 Nature having distinguished it with rivers, harbours and most commodious baies. 1692 DRYDEN *State Innoc.* IV. i, The ruddy fruit, distinguished o'er with gold. 1700 —— *Cymon & Iph.* 96 Not more distinguished by her purple vest Than by the charming features of her face. 1741 CHESTERF. *Lett.* (1792) I. lxxiv. 205 At dinner his awkwardness distinguishes itself particularly. 1776 GIBBON *Decl. & F.* I. xiii. 268 He had distinguished himself on every frontier of the empire. 1823 LAMB *Elia* Ser. II. *Poor Relation,* A peculiar sort of sweet pudding..distinguished the days of his coming. 1881 J. RUSSELL *Haigs* v. 108 Robert Haig distinguished himself in the battle by taking Lord Evers a prisoner.

II. Intransitive senses.

8. To make or draw a distinction; to perceive or note the difference between things; to exercise discernment; to discriminate. **a.** *absol.* (in quot. 1647, with clause.)

1612 BACON *Ess., Studies* (Arb.) 13 If his Wit be not Apt to distinguish or find differences, let him Study the Schoolemen. 1647 SALTMARSH *Sparkl. Glory* Ep. Ded. (1847) 7 Distinguishing to ye, that their Ordination was from the Bishops, as Ministers, not as Bishops. 1825 COLERIDGE *Aids Refl.* xxvi. (1836) 22 It is a dull and obtuse mind that must divide in order to distinguish; but it is a still worse, that distinguishes in order to divide. 1861 MAINE *Anc. Law* iii. (1876) 52 The propensity to distinguish characteristic of a lawyer.

b. with *between*: = 4. (The usual construction.)

1604 SHAKS. *Oth.* I. iii. 314 Since I could distinguish betwixt a Benefit, and an Iniurie. 1736 BUTLER *Anal.* II. vii. Wks. 1874 I. 261 A capacity of distinguishing between truth and falsehood. 1879 HARLAN *Eyesight* v. 64 A locomotive engineer who cannot distinguish between red and green, does not know the difference between danger and safety.

†c. ***to distinguish of***: to make distinctions with regard to (something), *esp.* in scholastic use (= 4b); to perceive or note the difference between (things) = 4, 8b; to judge of, discriminate between. ***to distinguish upon***: to make (scholastic or subtle) distinctions with regard to. *Obs.*

*a*1592 H. SMITH *Wks.* (1866–7) I. 97 To defend usury, they distinguish upon it, as they distinguish of lying. As they say, there is a pernicious lie, and an officious lie, and a merry lie, and a godly lie; so [etc.]. 1593 SHAKS. *2 Hen. VI,* II. i. 129 Sight may distinguish of Colours: But suddenly to nominate them all, it is impossible. 1646 H. LAWRENCE *Comm. Angells* 177 They have a certaine taste..by which they can distinguish of food. 1650 FULLER *Pisgah* I. vi. 14 The term navigable must be distinguished on. 1703 *Rules of Civility* 124 Able to judge and distinguish of Stiles.

†9. *intr.* (for *refl.*) To become distinguished or differentiated. *Obs. rare.*

1649 JER. TAYLOR *Gt. Exemp.* 199 (L.) The little embryo ..first distinguishes into a little knot, and that in time will be the heart, and then into a bigger bundle.

distinguishable (dɪˈstɪŋgwɪʃəb(ə)l), *a.* [f. prec. + -ABLE.]

1. Capable of being distinguished, separated, or discriminated from others or from one another; of which the difference can be perceived or noted.

1597 HOOKER *Eccl. Pol.* v. li. §1 They are by these their seuerall properties..distinguishable from each other. 1671 MILTON *P.R.* III. 424 A race..distinguishable scarce From Gentils, but by circumcision. 1739 HUME *Hum. Nature* I. vii. (1874) I. 326 Whatever objects are different are distinguishable. 1859 GEO. ELIOT *A. Bede* 29 Love of this sort is hardly distinguishable from religious feeling. 1894 F. HALL in *Nation* (N.Y.) LVIII. 427/2 Of the intransitive *part,* in its sense which is but slightly distinguishable from that of *depart* [etc.].

2. Capable of being divided or classified according to distinctive marks; divisible.

1658 SIR T. BROWNE *Hydriot.* i. (1736) 8 Two Pounds of Bones distinguishable in Skulls, Ribs, Jaws, Thigh-bones, and Teeth. *a*1704 LOCKE (J.), A simple idea..is not distinguishable into different ideas. 1844 H. H. WILSON *Brit. India* I. 433 The various tenures..[are] distinguishable into two principal classes. 1868 M. PATTISON *Academ. Org.* v. 122 The motive and design of college foundations is distinguishable chronologically into three periods.

3. Capable of being perceived by the senses or the mind; discernible, perceptible.

1611 TOURNEUR *Ath. Trag.* v. ii. Wks. 1878 I. 143 The very least Distinguishable syllable I speake. 1651 BIGGS *New Disp.* ¶301 Oftentimes but a gentle breath is felt, and sometimes scarce distinguishable. 1760 SWINTON in *Phil. Trans.* LII. 94 A very distinguishable Mock-Sun, opposite to the true one. 1850 ROBERTSON *Serm.* Ser. III. i. (1872) 10 Even in slander itself, perversion as it is, the interest of man in man is still distinguishable. 1853 KANE *Grinnell Exp.* xxxi. 271 The high land..took..a distinguishable outline.

†4. Worthy of distinction; eminent, remarkable, noteworthy. *Obs.*

1720 WELTON *Suffer. Son of God* I. Pref. 14 Distinguishable for their Singular and Exemplary Piety. 1740 MRS. M. WHITEWAY *Let. Pope* in *Swift's Wks.* 1778 XVIII. 229 Extolling your genius..or admiring your distinguishable virtue. 1762 tr. *Busching's Syst. Geog.* III. 172 The villa Hadriani is the most distinguishable and celebrated. 1824 L. MURRAY *Eng. Gram.* (ed. 5) I. 70 That which is nearly connected with us..becomes eminent or distinguishable in our eyes..though, in itself..of no particular importance.

†5. Serving to distinguish; distinctive. *Obs. rare.*

1665 MANLEY *Grotius' Low C. Warres* 297 Clear Daylight appearing, turned the Invention of their distinguishable Mark against themselves; for being thereby certainly known, they were as certainly slain.

Hence **di'stinguishableness**, the quality or fact of being distinguishable.

1730–6 BAILEY (folio), *Distinguishableness,* capableness of being distinguished. 1893 *Graphic* 4 Feb. 107/1 The chief merit of all the new coins is their distinguishableness one from another.

di'stinguishably, *adv.* [f. prec. + -LY[2].] In a distinguishable manner; in such a way as to be discriminated or perceived; perceptibly; †eminently, remarkably (*obs.*).

1704 in *Lond. Gaz.* No. 4057/2 Blessings..which make us distinguishably happy beyond any part of the World. 1705 F. HAUKSBEE in *Phil. Trans.* XXV. 2175 Parts of the Tubes ..were distinguishably Red. *a*1794 SIR W. JONES in *Asiatic Res.* (1799) IV. 264 We have both species..in this province; but they melt, scarce distinguishably, into each other.

distinguished (dɪˈstɪŋgwɪʃt), *ppl. a.* [f. DISTINGUISH *v.* + -ED[1].]

†1. Separate, individually distinct. *Obs.*

1609 TOURNEUR *Fun. Poem Sir F. Vere* 466 They want that competent required space For ev'ry power in a distinguished place To work in order. 1652 CRASHAW *Delights Muses* 88 She Carves out her dainty voice..Into a thousand sweet distinguish'd tones. 1715–20 POPE *Iliad* XII. 99 The forces part in five distinguish'd bands. 1813 T. BUSBY *Lucretius* I. 210 Distinguished seed each separate kind supplies.

†2. Clearly perceived or perceptible; clear, distinct; marked, pronounced. *Obs.*

1700 DRYDEN *Fables, Theodore & Hon.* 106 The noise.. approaching near With more distinguish'd notes invades his ear. 1703 ROWE *Ulyss.* I. i. 343 Mark him from the rest with most distinguish'd Hatred. 1782 MISS BURNEY *Cecilia* III. vii, Mrs. Delvile received her with the most distinguished politeness.

†3. Differentiated from others by character or quality; special, distinctive, characteristic. *Obs.*

1736 BUTLER *Anal.* II. vii. 376 The Jews..appear to have been in fact the people of God in a distinguished sense. 1794 SULLIVAN *View Nat.* II. 134 The various opinions..have respectively had their distinguished merits. 1813 T. BUSBY *Lucretius* I. *Comment.* vi, Amid this general praise..two expressions demand my distinguished notice.

4. a. Possessing distinction; marked by conspicuous excellence or eminence; remarkable, eminent; famous, renowned, celebrated; of high standing (social, scientific, or other). (Formerly of actions, occasions, reputation, etc.; now almost always of persons.) ***Distinguished Conduct Medal*** (abbrev. D.C.M.), a distinction, instituted in 1862, awarded to British warrant officers, non-commissioned officers, and men for distinguished conduct in the field. ***Distinguished Service Order*** (abbrev. D.S.O.), an order of distinction for British naval, military, and air force commissioned officers, instituted 9 Nov. 1886. Also ***Distinguished Service Cross*** (D.S.C.), ***Flying Cross*** (D.F.C.), ***Service Medal*** (D.S.M.), ***Flying Medal*** (D.F.M.): see quots.

1714 MANDEVILLE *Fab. Bees* (1724) 178 This awing of the multitude by a distinguished manner of living. 1724 WARBURTON *Tracts* (1789) 20 He has now three Children.. on whom he has bestowed the most distinguished Education. 1772 MISS WILKES *Let.* in *Wilkes' Corr.* (1805) IV. 103 My reception here was as distinguished as at Deal, and very handsome even at Portsmouth. 1800–24 CAMPBELL *Dream* vi, Worth itself is but a charter To be mankind's distinguish'd martyr. 1818 JAS. MILL *Brit. India* II. IV. v. 212 The making of a new Nabob, the most distinguished of all occasions for presents. 1849 MACAULAY *Hist. Eng.* I. 319 The modern country gentleman..receives a liberal education, passes from a distinguished school to a distinguished college. 1862 *Circ. Mem. 233* 25 Nov. in *Army List* (1863) Jan. 330 No retrospective action will be given to the warrant in question, so far as 'distinguished conduct' medals without Annuity or Gratuity are concerned. 1894 MRS. H. WARD *Marcella* II. 256 Four or five distinguished guests, including the Conservative Premier. 1914 *Times* 19 Oct. 8/5 His Majesty has been pleased to approve of the establishment of a medal, to be called the Distinguished Service Medal, to be awarded to chief petty officers, petty officers, men, and boys of all branches of the Royal Navy, to non-commissioned officers and men of the Royal Marines, and to all other persons holding corresponding positions in his Majesty's Service afloat, for distinguished conduct in war in cases where the award of the Conspicuous Gallantry Medal would not be applicable. His Majesty has further approved of the award of the Conspicuous Service Cross (to be designated in future the Distinguished Service Cross) to all officers below the rank of Lieutenant-Commander in addition to the officers previously eligible for this Decoration. **1918** *Times* 3 June 7/5 'The Distinguished Flying Cross', to be awarded to officers and warrant officers for acts of gallantry when flying in active operations against the enemy... 'The Distinguished Flying Medal', to be awarded to non-commissioned officers and men for acts of courage or devotion to duty when flying, although not in active operations against the enemy.

b. Having an air of distinction, stylish; = DISTINGUÉ.

1748 RICHARDSON *Clarissa* (1811) III. 357 Known by her clothes—her person, her features, so distinguished! **1826** DISRAELI *Viv. Grey* III. i. 91 Mr. Cleveland was tall and distinguished. **1873** MRS. H. KING *Disciples, Ugo Bassi* VII. (1877) 257 He was Though far from handsome, a distinguished man.. an ornament Of drawing-rooms.

Comb. **1852** JAMES *Agnes Sorrel* (1860) I. 225 He was a very.. distinguished-looking man.

distinguishedly (dɪˈstɪŋgwɪʃtlɪ), *adv.* [f. prec. + -LY².] In a distinguished manner; with distinction.

†**1.** Distinctly, specially, expressly. *Obs.*

1680 *Answ. Stillingfleet's Serm.* 9 Whether the Diocesan Bishop be distinguishedly named. **1746** W. HORSLEY *Fool* No. 63 ¶1 Then is there not any [trade] wherein the Operators so distinguishedly disagree. **1803** in *Spirit Pub. Jrnls.* (1804) VII. 155 His worth and his merits having been the more distinguishedly ascertained.

2. In a distinguished manner; with conspicuous or special excellence; eminently.

a **1745** SWIFT *4 Last Years of Queen* i. Wks. 1778 XII. 26 This address was presented.. and received an answer distinguishedly gracious. **1816** KEATINGE *Trav.* (1817) II. 149 An intended voyage by some person distinguishedly fitted for the undertaking. **1855** DORAN *Hanover Queens* II. iv. 76 There was no ship that bore herself.. more distinguishedly in the fray.

diˈstinguisher. [f. DISTINGUISH *v.* + -ER¹.] One who or that which distinguishes, in various senses: see the verb.

1599 PORTER *Angry Wom. Abingd.* in Hazl. *Dodsley* VII. 367 Mine ear, sound's true distinguisher. **1646** SIR T. BROWNE *Pseud. Ep.* VI. iv. 290 This distinguisher of times.. the Sun. **1763** JOHNSON in Boswell *Life* 19 July, A philosopher may know that it is merely a form of denial; but few servants are such nice distinguishers. **1863** J. G. MURPHY *Comm. Gen.* i. 18 The heavenly bodies become.. the distinguishers.. of day and night.. of seasons and years.

diˈstinguishing, *vbl. sb.* [-ING¹.] The action of the vb. DISTINGUISH, in various senses.

1587 GOLDING *De Mornay* xiv. 200 The vniting of all these powers together is with such distinctness, and the distinguishing of them is with such vnion. **1650** FULLER *Pisgah* I. viii. 22 The distinguishing of this land into seven nations. **1882** *Jrnl. Anthropol. Inst.* 369 Based on the distinguishing of differences.

diˈstinguishing, *ppl. a.* [f. as prec. + -ING².] That distinguishes.

1. Constituting a difference; serving to distinguish or mark off from others; distinctive, characteristic; sometimes in stronger sense, That renders (a person, etc.) distinguished or eminent.

1686 J. SCOTT *Chr. Life* (1747) III. 238 Such as freely submitted themselves to the distinguishing Laws of that Communion, by which they were separated from all other Nations. **1712** ADDISON *Spect.* No. 279 ¶4 Milton's chief Talent, and indeed his distinguishing Excellence, lies in the Sublimity of his Thoughts. **1795** NELSON in Nicolas *Disp.* (1845) II. 64 The command rests with me; and very probably I shall be ordered to hoist a Distinguishing Pendant. **1893** *Bookman* June 85/2 It is Mr. N.'s distinguishing merit that he knows what he can do, and.. does that efficiently.

2. That perceives differences or makes distinctions between things; discriminating.

1697 POTTER *Antiq. Greece* III. iv. (1715) 48 There is scarce any Passage in.. ancient Poetry, which does not.. disgust their curious and distinguishing palates. **1742** RICHARDSON *Pamela* III. 244 Encomiums given me by two Ladies of such distinguishing Judgment. **1846** TRENCH *Mirac.* xxix. (1862) 393 He loved with a distinguishing human affection 'Martha, and her sister, and Lazarus'.

†**3.** That confers distinction or special favour.

1670 *Devout Commun.* (1688) 195 The distinguishing goodness of the great and holy God.. in making me a reasonable creature, his servant, his son. **1719** DE FOE *Crusoe* (1840) I. vi. 105 The distinguishing goodness of the Hand which had preserved me.

diˈstinguishingly, *adv.* [f. prec. + -LY².] In a distinguishing manner; discriminatingly; in a way that serves to distinguish, by way of distinction, distinctively; markedly, specially, eminently.

a **1660** HAMMOND *Wks.* IV. 504 (R.), If we observe distinguishingly. **1691** BEVERLEY *Thous. Years Kingd. Christ* 4 The.. Constitution of the Church of England, as it is distinguishingly.. stiled. **1713-4** POPE *Let. to Addison* 30 Jan., Some calling me a Tory, because the Heads of that Party have been distinguishingly favourable to me. **1774** tr. *Helvetius' Child of Nature* II. 202 A man in his person distinguishingly favoured by Nature. **1856** OLMSTED *Slave States* 28 [They] seemed to me to have lost all distinguishingly African peculiarity of feature.

diˈstinguishment. Now *rare* or *Obs.* [f. DISTINGUISH + -MENT.]

1. The action of distinguishing or fact of being distinguished; distinction: also *concr.* something serving to distinguish. (Common in 17th c.)

1586 A. DAY *Eng. Secretary* I. (1625) 47 By distinguishment of all their properties and parts. **1611** SHAKS. *Wint. T.* II. i. 86 Least Barbarisme.. Should a like Language vse to all degrees, And mannerly distinguishment leaue out, Betwixt the Prince and Begger. **1651** BIGGS *New Disp.* ¶297 [They] have no sexuall distinguishments. **1709** *Brit. Apollo* II. Supernum. No. 6. 2/2 That one grand distinguishment of Nature. **1855** SINGLETON *Virgil* II. 372 Ye progeny of Daucus, full alike.. past distinguishment By their own parents. *Ibid.* 529.

†**2.** Clear discernment, distinct perception. *Obs.*

1642 SIR E. DERING *Sp. on Relig.* 86 When you can bring the object of one sence to fall under the notion and distinguishment of another sence; so that the eye may as well see a Name or sound, as the eare can heare it.

distinguo (dɪˈstɪŋgwəʊ). [L., = I distinguish.] A distinction in thought or reasoning.

1895 G. SAINTSBURY *Last Vintage* (1950) 176, I do not propose to deal with some correspondence which followed or to give any opinion on Mr. Gladstone's alleged practice of intimating dissent (or at any rate a sort of *distinguo*) by the syllable *ma*, which it seems was not intended for the bleat of an English sheep, but for the Italian equivalent of 'but' itself. **1920** *Contemp. Rev.* Mar. 364 When one hears that put in so unqualified a way, certain *distinguos* at once present themselves to the mind. **1945** R. G. COLLINGWOOD *Idea of Nature* 11 Renaissance cosmology had avoided this conclusion by a *distinguo*. The world of nature as it appears to our senses was admitted to be unknowable; but behind this world of so-called 'secondary qualities' there lay other things.. knowable because unchanging.

†**disˈtitle,** *v. Obs. rare.* [f. DIS- 7 a + TITLE *sb.*] *trans.* To deprive of title; to disentitle.

1599 B. JONSON *Cynthia's Rev.* IV. ii, That were the next way to dis-title myself of honour.

‖**ˈDistoma, ˈDistomum.** *Zool.* [mod.L., Gaertner 1775, f. Gr. δίστομος, -ον, double-mouthed, f. δι- twice + στόμα, pl. στόματα mouth. The form *distoma* has pl. *diˈstomata*; *distomum*, pl. *distoma*.

The etymological form is *Distomum* repr. Gr. δίστομον; *Distoma* as a neuter, with pl. *Distomata* is absurd, such a form as δίστομα, -όματα, being impossible in Gr. But *Distoma* as a fem. of modern formation, would be admissible.]

A genus of digenetic *Trematoda*, parasitic worms or flukes, having two suckers (whence the name), of which numerous species infest the alimentary canal, liver, etc., of vertebrates, the best-known being the liver-fluke (*D. hepaticum*) which causes rot in sheep. It is the typical genus of the family *Distomidæ*.

1851-60 MAYNE *Expos. Lex.*, *Distoma.*, *Zool.*, name of a genus of the Entozoa Trematodea, in which there is a sucker at the anterior extremity of the mouth, and a cup a little posterior to it on the venter. **1871** T. R. JONES *Anim. Kingd.* (ed. 4) 158 The now tailless animal assumes the appearance of a Distoma or fluke. **1876** tr. *Wagner's Gen. Pathol.* 120 The young.. in the distomata go through a complicated alternate generation connected with metamorphosis. **1884** *Public Opinion* 12 Sept. 331/1 Death caused by.. distoma. **1888** ROLLESTON & JACKSON *Anim. Life* 643 On the oral extremity of some species of *Distomum*.

attrib. **1885** W. ROBERTS *Urinary & Renal Dis.* III. xiii. (ed. 4) 650 We no longer doubt that the symptoms were produced by distoma-processes.

Hence **diˈstomian,** a member of the family *Distomidæ*, or group *Distomea*.

1876 *Beneden's Anim. Parasites* 45 Worms which have less freedom, like the Distomians, are sometimes both messmates and parasites.

distomatosis (ˌdaɪstəʊməˈtəʊsɪs, -stɒm-). *Path.* and *Vet. Sci.* [mod.L., ad. F. *distomatose* (A. A. Florance 1866, in *Diss. Faculté Méd. Strasbourg* XLI. 2), f. as DISTOMATOUS *a.*: see -OSIS.] = DISTOMIASIS.

1892 G. FLEMING tr. *Neumann's Parasites & Dis. Dom. Animals* II. iv. 516 The term *Distomatosis*.. or *Distomiasis*.. designates any affection due to Distomes. *Ibid.* 517 The distomatosis of herbivora has been known for a very long time under numerous designations, which have been applied almost exclusively to the ovine species. **1894** *Jrnl. Compar. Med. & Vet. Archives* XV. 162 An epizoötic of distomatosis. *Ibid.* 175 Three cases of pulmonary distomatosis in Kansas cattle. **1955** GAIGER & DAVIES *Vet. Path.* (ed. 4) xxxiii. 649 (*caption*) Distomatosis in liver of ox.

distomatous (dɪˈstɒmətəs), *a.* [f. mod.L. *distoma, -mat-*, or its elements (see DISTOMA, DISTOMUM) + -OUS.] Having two mouths or suckers; belonging to the genus *Distoma* of parasitic worms.

1877 HUXLEY *Anat. Inv. Anim.* iv. 204 The two lateral projections, characteristic of Distomatous Rediæ, appear.

†**disˈtomb,** *v. Obs. rare.* [DIS- 7 a.] *trans.* To take out of the tomb, to disentomb.

1628 GAULE *Pract. The.* (1629) 423 His power and vertue .. doth distombe him.

distome (ˈdɪstəʊm). [a. F. *distome*, ad. mod.L. *distoma*: see above.] An anglicized form of DISTOMA.

1876 *Beneden's Anim. Parasites* 84 An Egyptian distome, which lives in Man. **1888** ROLLESTON & JACKSON *Anim. Life* 648 Von Linstow met with in *Gammarus Pulex* a Distome encysted, a single Distome in each cell.

distomiasis (daɪstəʊˈmaɪəsɪs, -stɒm-). *Path.* and *Vet. Sci.* [mod.L., ad. F. *distomiase*, (Wiame 1862, in *Ann. de Méd. Vét.* 32), f. DISTOMA: see -IASIS.] (See quot. 1961.) = *liver-rot* (LIVER *sb.*¹ 7). Cf. FASCIOLIASIS.

1892 [see DISTOMATOSIS]. **1907** *Westm. Hosp. Rep.* XV. 60 Cerebral distomiasis displays itself with the irritative and paralytic phenomena of a cerebral neoplasm. **1961** *Brit. Med. Dict.* 449/1 *Distomiasis*, any infection by trematodes or flukes; the term is now obsolete since the worms formerly in the genus *Distoma* are now correctly placed in other genera. The term still survives in medical textbooks, with many qualifying adjectives.

†**diˈstoned,** *pa. pple. Obs. rare.* [as if from a verb **distone*: cf. obs. F. *destonner* 'to change or alter a tune' (Cotgr.).] Rendered out of tone or tune; inharmonious.

c **1400** *Rom. Rose* 4248 Discordaunt ever fro armonye And distoned from melodie.

distoor, var. form of DESTOUR.

distorn (dɪˈstɔːn), *pa. pple. rare.* [f. DIS- 1 + *torn*, pa. pple. of TEAR *v.*] Torn off, severed by tearing.

1859 MASSON *Brit. Novelists* iv. 277 Carrying in it some obscure ideas.. of the infinity whence it feels itself distorn.

†**diˈstorque,** *v. Obs. rare*⁻⁰. [ad. L. *distorquē-re*: see DISTORT.]

1623 COCKERAM, *Distorqued*, wrested.

†**diˈstorquement.** *Obs. rare.* [f. as prec. + -MENT.] Writhing, contortion.

1627-47 FELTHAM *Resolves* I. lxi. 188 Like the distorquements of a departed Conscience.

†**diˈstort,** *ppl. a. Obs.* [ad. L. *distort-us*, pa. pple. of *distorquēre*: see next.] Distorted (of which it may have been viewed as a shortened form); wry, awry.

1588 J. READ *Compend. Method* 66 Of the curing of a distort foote of a childe. **1596** SPENSER *F.Q.* V. xii. 36 Her face was ugly, and her mouth distort. **1605** A. WARREN *Selfishness World* in Farr. *S.P. Jas. I* (1848) 82 Thus I.. Homeward convert a distort countenance. **1642** H. MORE *Song of Soul* I. III. lxx, With monki's mouth distort.

distort (dɪˈstɔːt), *v.* [f. L. *distort-* ppl. stem of *distorquēre* to twist different ways, distort, f. DIS- 1 + *torquēre* to twist: cf. EXTORT.]

†**1.** *trans.* To twist, wrench, or turn to one side, or out of the straight position. *Obs.*

a **1631** DONNE *Litany* (R.), What distorted thee, And interrupted evenness with fits. **1646** SIR T. BROWNE *Pseud. Ep.* III. xx. 156 If you dip a pen in Aqua fortis.. and present it towards these points, they will.. decline the acrimony thereof, retyring or distorting them to avoid it. *c* **1720** GAY *Birth of Squire* 72 Headlong he falls, and on the rugged stone Distorts his neck.

2. a. To put out of shape or position by twisting or drawing awry; to change to an unnatural shape; to render crooked, unshapely, or deformed.

1634 [see DISTORTED]. **1751** JOHNSON *Rambler* No. 173 ¶1 Any action or posture, long continued, will distort.. the limbs. **1836** MARRYAT *Japhet* lxxiv, His features were distorted with extreme pain. **1860** TYNDALL *Glac.* I. i. 5 The fossils contained in slate-rocks are distorted in shape.

b. To alter the shape of any figure without destroying continuity, as by altering its angles; to represent by an image in which the angles or proportions of parts are altered, as by a convex mirror.

1812-6 J. SMITH *Panorama Sc. & Art* I. 429 A large object, seen through a lens which is very convex, appears more or less distorted. **1821** SHELLEY *Prometh. Unb.* IV. 383 A many sided mirror, Which could distort to many a shape of error. *Mod.* A mirror which distorts the features.

3. *fig.* To give a twist or erroneous turn to (the mind, thoughts, views); to pervert or misrepresent (statements, facts).

c **1586** C'TESS PEMBROKE *Ps.* CVII. xv, You whose conceites distorted be, Stand mute amazed at the sight. **1665** GLANVILL *Scepsis Sci.* xix. 118 Words.. distorted from their common use, and known significations. **1736** BUTLER *Anal.* I. v. Wks. 1874 I. 108 Both self love and particular affections .. distort and rend the mind. **1828** D'ISRAELI *Chas. I*, I. Pref. 5 To establish a pre-conceived theory.. the historian sometimes distorted facts. **1837** WHEWELL *Hist. Induct. Sc.* I. 58 The caprices of imagination distort our impressions.

4. *intr.* (for *refl.*) To become twisted or out of shape.

1680 OTWAY *C. Marius* V. ii, Old Ancharius.. was so violent.. That his beard bristled, and his face distorted.

1959 *New Scientist* 12 Nov. 942/3 The way in which the teeth distort is shown in Figure 3. **1962** *Which?* (Car Suppl.) Oct. 135/2 On the hill, the jack mounting points distorted slightly.

Hence **di'storting** *vbl. sb.* and *ppl. a.*

1610 BP. CARLETON *Jurisd.* 302 Which distorting of Scriptures is expresly censured by the said learned men. **1819** SHELLEY *Cenci* IV. i. 147 As From a distorting mirror. **1874** L. STEPHEN *Hours in Library* (1892) II. i. 5 Imperfect images refracted through..distorting media.

di'storted, *ppl. a.* [f. prec. vb. + -ED[1].]

1. Twisted out of shape; drawn awry; made crooked; represented with parts out of proportion, like the shadows falling obliquely on a surface.

1634 HABINGTON *Castara* (Arb.) 130 He who's lifted up by vice Hath a neighb'ring precipice Dazeling his distorted eye. **1715–20** POPE *Iliad* XVIII. 480 Wide with distorted legs oblique he goes. **1836** H. COLERIDGE *North. Worthies* Introd. Ess. (1852) 26 To..represent the opinions..not in the distorted perspective of their adversaries. **1838** DICKENS *Nich. Nick.* ii, He had fixed his eyes upon a distorted fir-tree.

2. *fig.* Turned awry; twisted, wrested.

1641 MILTON *Ch. Govt.* Pref. (1851) 96 The grosse distorted apprehension of decay'd mankinde. **1664** H. MORE *Myst. Iniq.* 448 You see how distorted..his Exposition is to the Text. **1818** CRUISE *Digest* (ed. 2) III. 411 The fifth depends upon a distorted authority, and violent assumption.

Hence **di'stortedly** *adv.*; **di'stortedness.**

1684 H. MORE *Answer* 407 There is not the least Incongruity or distortedness in Mr. Mede's way. *a* **1688** CUDWORTH *Immut. Mor.* IV. iv. (R.) To what purpose should they so violently and distortedly pervert the natural order? **1831** *Blackw. Mag.* XXIX. 1004 A glass that..would shew objects distortedly as well as dimly. **1885** L. OLIPHANT *Sympneumata* x. 152 The sad distortedness that she inherited in entering this world.

distorter (dɪ'stɔːtə(r)). [f. DISTORT *v.* + -ER[1].] One who or that which distorts.

1847 in CRAIG. **1851–60** MAYNE *Expos. Lex., Distortor,* a twister, or distorter. *Mod.* Bigotry is a distorter of the mental vision.

distortion (dɪ'stɔːʃən). [ad. L. *distortiōn-em,* n. of action f. *distorquēre* to DISTORT. Cf. F. *distorsion* (Paré, 16th c.).]

1. a. The action of distorting, or condition of being distorted, or twisted awry or out of shape; *spec.* a condition of the body or any limb, in which it is twisted out of the natural shape.

1581 MULCASTER *Positions* xxi. (1887) 90 The distortion or writhing of the mouth. **1622** WITHER *Mistr. Philar.* Wks. (1633) 622 Her dainty mouth [is] composed So as there is no distortion Misbeseemes that sweet proportion. **1764** REID *Inquiry* vi. §10. 152 They had never observed distortions of this kind in the eyes of children. **1804** ABERNETHY *Surg. Obs.* 202, I could not..perceive any distortion of the face to the opposite side. **1834** MEDWIN *Angler in Wales* II. 211 That..distortion generally known by the appellation of club-foot. **1887** G. H. DARWIN in *Fortn. Rev.* Feb. 266 Earthquake waves consist..of waves or vibrations of compression, and of distortion.

b. *Math.* and *Optics.* Any change of shape not involving breach of continuity, as the distortion of a circle into an oval, or that of a rectangle into a rhombus or rhomboid by alteration of the angles, lengthening or curving of certain lines, etc.

1879 *Cassell's Techn. Educ.* IV. 333/1 Refractive aberration, or in other words 'distortion', is common to many lenses, producing images wherein straight lines are represented as bulged inwards or outwards. **1885** OSBORNE REYNOLDS in *Proc. Brit. Assoc.* 898 The susceptibility of such a medium for a state in which the two sets of grains are in conditions of opposite distortions.

c. *concr.* A distorted form or image.

1820 SHELLEY *Witch of Atlas* lxii. 3 But other troubled forms of sleep she saw..Distortions foul of supernatural awe. **1851** NICHOL *Archit. Heav.* 59 Instead of an image of the object, will yield only a distortion. **1867** A. BARRY *Sir C. Barry* vii. 244 Some remains of the objectionable distortion at the entrance from S. Stephen's Hall.

2. A temporary twist awry, a twisting or writhing movement; a contortion.

1718 PRIOR *Power* 65 By his distortions he reveals his pains. **1752** JOHNSON *Rambler* No. 188 ¶4 What the Latins call, the Sardinian Laughter, a distortion of the face without gladness of heart.

3. a. *fig.* The twisting or perversion *of* words so as to give to them a different sense; perversion *of* opinions, facts, history, so as to misapply them.

1650 R. HOLLINGWORTH *Exerc. Usurped Powers* 51 Having vindicated this passage..from this authors distortion. **1745** WESLEY *Answ. Ch.* 37 What a frightful Distortion of my Words is this? **1849** MACAULAY *Hist. Eng.* II. 317 To bring together..by fraudulent distortions of law, an assembly which might call itself a parliament. **1874** L. STEPHEN *Hours in Library* (1892) I. vii. 246 He will be amused at the distortion of history.

b. *Psychol.* The alteration of repressed or unconscious elements before they appear in the conscious mind.

1910 *Amer. Jrnl. Psychol.* XXI. 304 The distortion in the dream-making is thus a means of evading the censor. **1925** A. & J. STRACHEY tr. *Freud's Coll. Papers* III. 361 Obsessional thoughts have undergone a distortion similar to that undergone by dream thoughts before they become the manifest content of a dream. **1957** R. L. MUNROE *Schools of Psychoanalytic Thought* III. xi. 482 The child whose personal experience was especially unfortunate..is especially prone to..distortion.

4. *Electr.* A change in the wave-form of a signal by an electronic device such as an amplifier or during transmission from one point to another, usually impairing the quality of its reproduction.

1887 O. HEAVISIDE in *Electrician* 3 June 80/1 The attenuation..increases so fast with the frequency, thus leading to a most prodigious distortion in the shape of irregular waves... Now the distortion and the attenuation, though different things, are intimately connected. *Ibid.* 24 June 143/2 'Distortion'..I chose myself as preferable to 'mutilation' and similar words. Its meaning is obvious. Make current-variations in a certain way at one place. If the current-variations at another place are similar, no matter how much attenuated they may be, there is no distortion. **1914** A. B. ROLFE-MARTIN *Wireless Telegr.* 117 It is found that, owing chiefly to dielectric losses in the condenser, the distortion has a still greater weakening effect on radiating power. **1962** SIMPSON & RICHARDS *Junction Transistors* xii. 276 Class B amplifiers must be used in push-pull arrangements if distortion-free amplification is to be obtained.

Hence **di'stortional** *a.*, of or pertaining to distortion; **di'stortionist**, one who practises or professes distortion: (*a*) a caricaturist; (*b*) one who professionally distorts his body; **di'stortionless** *a. Electr.*, not producing any distortion; also, not affected by distortion.

1864 *Sat. Rev.* 5 Nov. 563 Bunbury..was a mere caricaturist, or distortionist. **1885** OSBORNE REYNOLDS in *Proc. Brit. Assoc.* 898 The transmission of distortional waves becomes possible if the medium be composed of small grains with large grains interspersed. **1886** *Pall Mall G.* 6 Aug. 13/2 They play the rôle of distortionists..Their object is to draw money from the public by their piteous and excruciating positions. **1892** O. HEAVISIDE *Electr. Papers* II. 129 The distortionless system..brings the speed of the current into full view. **1921** *Jrnl. Inst. Electr. Engineers* Apr. 397/2 For satisfactory transmission of speech the circuit should also be practically 'distortionless'. **1937** *Proc. Inst. Radio Engineers* XXV. 321 It is possible to obtain distortionless reception of considerably higher levels of modulation if two side-band frequencies..are transmitted. **1962** SIMPSON & RICHARDS *Junction Transistors* xiii. 298 This is readily seen by considering any such distortion voltage as being produced by a fictitious generator added within the closed loop of a distortionless amplifier.

di'stortive, *a.* [f. L. *distort-* ppl. stem + -IVE: cf. L. *tortīv-us.*] Having the quality of distorting; producing or tending to distortion.

1823 SCORESBY *Whale Fishery* 166 The ships in the north-west..were..subject to a distortive influence; these appeared..elevated by refraction, like oblong black streaks, lengthened out. *Ibid.* 168 In its distortive effect.

‖**di'stortor.** *Anat.* [med.L. *distortor* a distorter (Du Cange).] (In full *distortor oris*), a name for the *Zygomaticus minor* muscle of the mouth, which distorts the face in laughter, etc.

1731 BAILEY vol. II., *Distortor,* a muscle of the mouth, the same as Zygomaticus. [In mod. Dicts.]

†**di'storture.** *Obs.* [f. DISTORT *v.* + -URE; after *torture.*] = DISTORTING, DISTORTION.

1613 JACKSON *Creed* II. xxiii. §3. 398 The infernal [*v.r.* internal] disturture of their proud affections. **1709** *Answ. Sacheverell's Serm.* 11 A Disturture of Words to a new Sense.

distourble, var. DISTURBLE *v. Obs.*

di'stract, *ppl. a. arch.* [ad. L. *distract-us,* pa. pple. of *distrahĕre* to draw in different directions, pull asunder, f. DIS- 1 + *trahĕre* to draw, drag. See also the earlier DISTRAIT from Fr.]

†**1.** Torn or drawn asunder, divided, separated; scattered; torn to pieces. (In quot. 1398 as *pa. pple.*) *Obs.*

1398 TREVISA *Barth. De P.R.* IX. xxv. (1495) 362 That the vertues that ben dystracte, sparplyd and made feble by daye wakyng maye be joynyd and rested by benefyce of nyghte. *c* **1400** *Destr. Troy* 3219 Distracte were þai stithly, & stonyt by dene. **1597** SHAKS. *Lover's Compl.* 231 To your audit comes Their distract parcels in combined sums.

†**2.** Drawn away, diverted; having the attention diverted. *Obs.*

1435 MISYN *Fire of Love* 73 þat with no cry or noys or any odyr þinge fro prayer [þai] may be distracte. **1514** BARCLAY *Cyt. & Uplondyshm.* (Percy) p. xlv, The hungry sewers..At euery morsell hath eye unto thy hande So much on thy morsell distract is their minde. **1553** BP. WATSON in Crowley *Soph. Dr. Watson* ii. (1569) 151 The priest..may haue his thoughtes distract to some other thing.

3. Perplexed or confused in mind by having the thoughts drawn in different directions. *arch.*

a **1340** HAMPOLE *Psalter* xxiv. 17, I am noght distracte in many thoghtes. **1432–50** tr. *Higden* (Rolls) I. 421 He..see in the aiere a meruellous thynge thro the whiche siȝhte he began to be distracte. **1581** MULCASTER *Positions* v. (1887) 31 Being distracte with diuersitie of thoughtes. **1671** MILTON *Samson* 1556, I recover breath, And sense distract, to know well what I utter. **1854** SYD. DOBELL *Balder* xxiii. 96 She flung her garlands down, and caught, distract, The skirts of passing tempests.

4. Deranged in mind; crazy, mad, insane. *arch.*

1481 *Will of Taylour* (Somerset Ho.), For seke & distracte people. **1578** LYTE *Dodoens* III. xciii. 448 To raue, and waxe distracte or furious. **1601** SHAKS. *Jul. C.* IV. iii. 155 With this she fell distract, And (her Attendants absent) Swallow'd fire. **1663** BUTLER *Hud.* I. i. 212 More peevish, cross, and splenetick Than Dog distract. **1779** SHERIDAN *Critic* III. i, My daughter..has gone Distract!

†**b.** as *pa. pple.* Driven mad, distracted. *Obs.*

1547 J. HARRISON *Exhort. Scottes* 227 What madnes or deuill..hath so..distracte oure myndes?

†**c.** phr. ***distract of one's wits***, etc.: cf. DISTRACT *v.* 6 b. *Obs.*

1470–85 MALORY *Arthur* XII. iv, He shold be distracte out of his witte. **1576** NEWTON *Lemnie's Complex.* (1633) 242 They that be distract of their right wits. **1578** LYTE *Dodoens* III. xxvi. 352 Melampus..cured with this herbe..the daughters of Prœtus, which were distract of their memories. **1601** F. GODWIN *Bps. of Eng.* 275 Rauing and taking on like a man distract of his wits.

distract (dɪ'strækt), *v.* [f. L. *distract-* ppl. stem of *distrahĕre*: see prec. As in many other verbs, the pa. pple. *distract,* repr. L. *distractus,* was in use before the finite vb., and with its expanded form *distracted,* prob. served to introduce the verb into use.]

†**1.** *trans.* To draw in different directions; to draw asunder or apart; to draw away; to separate, divide (*lit.* and *fig.*). *Obs.*

1600 E. BLOUNT tr. *Conestaggio* 20 The which he secretly feared, and his ministers greatly hoped for, so were their mindes distracted. **1609** BP. HALL *Recoll. Treat.* (1614) 646 His Godhead was never distracted eyther from soule or bodie. **1621** G. SANDYS *Ovid's Met.* VI. (1626) 117 [*Marsyas to Apollo*] Why doe you (oh!) me from my selfe distract? **1650** BULWER *Anthropomet.* 164 Whereby the Scapula is distracted and abscedes. **1651** HOBBES *Leviath.* II. xvii. 86 Being distracted in opinions.

†**b.** To carry away to other parts; to disperse.

16.. R. ASHLEY *Comparison, &c.*, I found the treatise to bee so well liked, that the former copies were for the most part alreadie distracted. **1617** MORYSON *Itin.* III. II. iii. 88 At Torg, where the best beere is brewed, and from thence distracted to other Cities. **1618** HALES *Gold. Rem.* (1688) 402 Foreign Books brought out of other Countries should not be distracted here without peculiar leave. *a* **1661** FULLER *Worthies* (1840) II. 415 The wits of the university were distracted into several counties, by reason of the plague therein.

2. To rend into parts or sections; to divide; usually implying disorder or disintegration. Now *rare* or *Obs.*

1585 ABP. SANDYS *Serm.* (1841) 380 A kingdom..divided and distracted into factions. **1623** BINGHAM *Xenophon* 108 The army of the Grecians [was] distracted into parcells. **1655** STANLEY *Hist. Philos.* III. (1701) 124/2 Philosophers who did not distract the Doctrine of their Master into Sects. **1698** FRYER *Acc. E. India & P.* 350 The Power was distracted among the Captains of the Conqueror. [**1888** *Pall Mall G.* 6 Oct. 6 The subject had to be distracted between two discussions.]

†**b.** *fig.* To 'pull to pieces', undo, spoil. *Obs.*

1413 *Pilgr. Sowle* (Caxton) II. xlvi. (1859) 52 Yet is my ioye in so moche dystracted that thou are not ther. **1695** LD. PRESTON *Boeth.* III. 143 By dissevering and segregating the Parts, that Oneness is distracted.

3. To draw or turn away from actual position, destination, or purpose; to turn aside, or in another direction; to divert. (Now only in *to* ***distract the attention, the mind,*** or the like.)

c **1380** WYCLIF *Sel. Wks.* III. 84 We schulden be war to kepe hem soundeli, for bodeli þingis distractiþ men to kepe hem riȝt. **1435** MISYN *Fire of Love* 65 On ee þai haue of waytynge, A-nodyr of trw sorow, qwhos lufe distractis þe wytt, peruertis & ouerturnes resone. **1612** W. SHUTE tr. *Fougasse's Venice* ii. 12 They might easily..distract him from the alliance with the French King. **1643** PRYNNE *Sov. Power Parl.* App. 166 The Emperour..swears, That he will alianate, distract, or morgage nothing of those things which appertain to the Empire. **1646** SIR T. BROWNE *Pseud. Ep.* II. ii. 62 The needle..being distracted, driveth that way where the greater & powerfuller part of the earth is placed. **1744** AKENSIDE *Pleas. Imag.* II. 52 Vice, distracting their delicious gifts To aims abhorr'd. **1874** CARPENTER *Ment. Phys.* I. v. (1879) 214 [This] distracts the mind from the sense of danger. **1878** R. W. DALE *Lect. Preach.* ii. 35 To drive away all thoughts that would distract their attention.

4. To draw in different directions; to divide attention, inclination, etc. (*between* different objects); to perplex or confuse by divergent aims or interests; to cause dissension or disorder in. (In mod. use often associated with senses 5, 6.)

1597–8 BACON *Ess., Followers & Friends* (Arb.) 38 To be gouerned by one is not good, and to be distracted with many is worse; but to take aduise of friends is euer honorable. **1638** SIR T. HERBERT *Trav.* (ed. 2) 216 Hee that sits above..distracted their designe. **1650** FULLER *Pisgah* II. 65 How is his tongue distracted between the Spirit of God and the spirit of gold. **1752** JOHNSON *Rambler* No. 196 ¶4 He stands distracted by different forms of delight. **1849** MACAULAY *Hist. Eng.* I. 542 The dissensions by which the little band of outlaws was distracted. **1855** *Ibid.* IV. 555 He was distracted between the fear of losing his ears and the fear of injuring his patron. **1874** GREEN *Short Hist.* vii. §8. 432 One of the endless civil wars which distracted the island.

5. To throw into a state of mind in which one knows not how to act; to perplex or bewilder greatly. (Often coloured by sense 6, which is, however, no longer used literally.)

1583 STANYHURST *Æneis* ii. (Arb.) 53 Thus then I distracted, with al hastning, ran to mye weapons. **1605** SHAKS. *Macb.* II. iii. 109 They star'd, and were distracted. **1667** MILTON *P.L.* IV. 18 Horror and doubt distract His troubl'd thoughts. **1771** MRS. GRIFFITH tr. *Viaud's Shipwreck* 198, I was so distracted with joy. **1856** DICKENS *Lett.* (1880) I. 434, I am at present distracted with doubts.

†**6.** To derange the mind or intellect of; to render insane, drive mad. *Obs.* in *lit.* sense: cf. 5.

1597 SHAKS. *2 Hen. IV*, II. i. 116 This is a poore mad soule ..poore hath distracted her. **1653** DOROTHY OSBORNE *Lett. to Sir W. Temple* xvii. (1888) 97 Sure, the poor woman is a little distracted, she could never be so ridiculous else. **1777** SHERIDAN *Trip Scarb.* I. i, Stay—thou'lt distract me. **1791** COWPER *Iliad* XXII. 66 Commis'rate also thy unhappy Sire Ere yet distracted.

†**b.** phr. *to distract of one's wit*, etc. *Obs.*

1602 T. FITZHERBERT *Apol.* 27 a, He dyed distracted of his sences. **1632** LITHGOW *Trav.* VIII. 355 Seeing them all madde and distracted of their wits with sorrow. **1633** BP. HALL *Hard Texts* 88 The view and sense of those judgments ..shall utterly distract thee of thy wits.

†**c.** *intr.* To become distracted, go mad. *Obs. rare.*

1768 ROSS *Helenore* 15 (Jam.) Like to distract, she..Cry'd Lindy, Lindy, waes me, are ye dead?

¶**7.** = DETRACT: cf. DISTRACTER, DISTRACTION 7.

†**di'stract**, *sb. Obs. rare.* [f. prec. vb.] A distraction.

1624 QUARLES *Div. Poems. Job* xv. iii, The man, whose soule is undistain'd with Ill, Stands onely free from the distracts of Care. **1632** —— *Div. Fancies* I. vi. (1660) 4 False hopes, true fears, vain joyes, and fierce distracts.

distracted (dɪ'stræktɪd), *ppl. a.* [f. DISTRACT *v.* + -ED[1].]

†**1.** Drawn apart, rent asunder; divided. *Obs.*

1598 FLORIO, *Distratto*, withdrawne, distracted, led away. **1600** J. PORY tr. *Leo's Africa* I. 2 Europe is of a more distracted and manifolde shape. **1601** SHAKS. *All's Well* v. iii. 35 To the brightest beames Distracted clouds giue way. **1631** GOUGE *God's Arrows* iii. §95. 365 Henry 7..married Elizabeth the heire of the house of Yorke, and therby united those two distracted houses. **1642** FULLER *Holy & Prof. St.* v. xv. 418 By putting together distracted syllables, and by piecing of broken sentences.

2. Driven hither and thither; agitated, disturbed, 'troubled'. *Obs.* exc. as *fig.* from senses 3–5.

1632 LITHGOW *Trav.* x. 505 There is a certaine place of sea, where these destracted tydes make their rancountering Randevouze. **1725** *Phil. Trans.* XXXIII. 427 Hard Gales of southerly Winds, attended with violent Squalls of Rain, and a distracted Sea. *a* **1845** HOOD *Forge* I. vi, Badly, madly, the vapours fly Over the dark distracted sky.

3. Mentally drawn to different objects; perplexed or confused by conflicting interests; torn or disordered by dissension or the like.

a **1633** AUSTIN *Medit.* (1635) 87 Having (according to my weake facultie, and distracted Studies) set downe what I thought most..observable. **1799** F. HERVEY *Nav. Hist.* II. 140 To settle the distracted affairs of that kingdom, Cromwell was appointed lord-lieutenant. **1821** LAMB *Elia* Ser. I. *Grace bef. Meat*, Savoury soup and messes.. moistening the lips of the guests with desire and a distracted choice.

4. Much confused or troubled in mind; having, or showing, great mental disturbance or perplexity.

1602 SHAKS. *Ham.* I. v. 97 Remember thee? I..while memory holds a seate In this distracted Globe. **1607** —— *Timon* III. iv. 115 You onely speake from your distracted soule. **1667** DRYDEN *Ind. Emperor* II. ii, Where shall a Maid's distracted Heart find Rest? **1822** *New Edin. Rev.* No. 3. 109 He bent over her, chiefly to hide her distracted countenance. **1857** BUCKLE *Civiliz.* I. vi. 304 The minds of men were too distracted for so deliberate a plan.

5. Deranged in mind; out of one's wits; crazed, mad, insane. Now *rare* in literal sense, exc. in such expressions as 'like one distracted'.

1590 SHAKS. *Com. Err.* v. i. 39 To fetch my poore distracted husband hence. **1657** HOWELL *Londinop.* 65 It [Bethlem] was an Hospital for distracted people. **1719** DE FOE *Crusoe* (1840) II. v. 107 They ran about..like distracted men. **1728** NEWTON *Chronol. Amended* i. 142 Athamas.. went distracted and slew his son. **1740** GRAY *Let.* Poems (1775) 95 The latter died distracted. **1772** SHERIDAN in *Sheridaniana* (1826) 38, I was in short almost distracted.

di'stractedly, *adv.* [f. prec. + -LY[2].] In a distracted manner; †disjointedly (*obs.*); with mental distraction, madly, like one distracted.

1597 SHAKS. *Lover's Compl.* 28 To euery place at once and no where fixt, The mind and sight distractedly commixt. **1601** —— *Twel. N.* II. ii. 22 She did speake in starts distractedly. **1608** T. MORTON *Pream. Encounter* 105 The whole being..distractedly quoted. **1715** JANE BARKER *Exilius* II. 39 Seeing him fall by her Hand, she cry'd out most distractedly. **1749** FIELDING *Tom Jones* XIV. iv, You have made her daughter distractedly in love with you. **1837** CARLYLE *Fr. Rev.* I. III. vi. (1872) 81 Monseigneur..does nothing but walk distractedly..cursing his stars. **1870** DISRAELI *Lothair* iv. 10 He was so distractedly fond of Lady Montairy.

di'stractedness. [f. as prec. + -NESS.] The condition of being distracted.

1580 SIDNEY *Arcadia* (1622) 327 A martiall noyse (raysed by the violence of Inuaders, and distractednesse of others). *a* **1691** BOYLE *Life* Wks. I. 41 (R.) The present distractedness of my mind.

di'stracter. [f. DISTRACT *v.* + -ER[1].] One who or that which distracts. In quot.: Something that detracts (*from*): cf. DISTRACT *v.* 7.

1653 H. MORE *Conject. Cabbal.* Pref. (1662) 3 Such Inspiration..is no distracter from, but an accomplisher and an enlarger of the humane faculties.

†**di'stractful**, *a. Obs.* [f. DISTRACT *sb.* or *v.* + -FUL.] Full of or fraught with distraction. Hence †**di'stractfulness.**

1636 HEYWOOD *Loves Maistresse* III. Wks. 1874 V. 130 Thanke thy sisters, they apparrell'd thee In that distractfull shape. *a* **1640** J. BALL *Power Godlines* (1657) 133 When they want comfort they fall into heavy dumps, and distractfulness. **1746** MORELL *Judas Macc.* I. 6 Distractful Doubt and Desperation, Ill become the chosen Nation.

distractibility (dɪstræktɪ'bɪlɪtɪ). [f. DISTRACTIBLE *a.* + -ITY.] The condition of being distractible; inability to give prolonged attention to a task or object; esp. in *Psychol.*, the tendency to have the direction of one's attention easily changed by chance stimuli.

1902 A. R. DEFENDORF tr. *Kraepelin's Clin. Psychiatry* 16 Distractibility is more marked in chronic nervous exhaustion. **1923** *Jrnl. Appl. Psychol.* VII. 358 This same group also showed a larger percentage of 'irritability', 'distractibility', ..and marked 'slowness of reaction' than did the other two groups. **1940** *Mind* XLIX. 69 The fluctuations and distractibility of attention are of obvious importance to applied psychologists. **1962** HENDERSON & GILLESPIE *Text-bk. Psychiatry* (ed. 9) vi. 109 Distractibility is a disorder of the attention in which the patient gives attention to every passing stimulus.

di'stractible, *a.* [f. as next + -IBLE.] Capable of being distracted.

1730–6 BAILEY (folio), *Distractible* (in Surgery) capable of being drawn aside. Hence **1775** in ASH.; and in mod. Dicts.

†**di'stractile**, *a. Obs.* [f. L. *distract-*, ppl. stem of *distrahĕre* to pull asunder + -ILE; cf. mod.F. *distractile* in *Bot.* (Littré).]

Capable of being drawn asunder or stretched, extensible; of or relating to stretching. (Cf. *contractile.*) In *Bot.* applied by Richard to anthers in which the cells are separated by a very long and narrow connective.

1709 F. HAUKSBEE *Phys. Mech. Exp.* v. (ed. 2) 117 These distractile Tubes will be..compress'd by that incumbent Weight. **1726** MONRO *Anat. Nerves* (1741) 36 Muscular Fibres are distractile, or capable of being stretched. **1747** LANGRISH *Muscular Motion* i. §31 in *Phil. Trans.* XLIV., This distractile Power must..be the Occasion of some Degree of Tension in them. **1835** LINDLEY *Introd. Bot.* (1848) I. 343 In Salvia..the connective has been called by Richard distractile.

di'stracting, *vbl. sb.* [f. DISTRACT *v.* + -ING[1].] The action of DISTRACT *v.*; distraction.

c **1440** HYLTON *Scala Perf.* (W. de W. 1494) I. xliii, To holde hym wythout forgetyng, distractyng or lettyng of ony creature. **1660** MILTON *Free Commw.* 451 To the retarding and distracting oft times of thir Counsels.

di'stracting, *ppl. a.* [f. as prec. + -ING[2].] That distracts; bewildering, maddening.

1632 LITHGOW *Trav.* IX. 402, I grew affrighted..for..the distracting noyse drew aye nearer and nearer us. **1749** FIELDING *Tom Jones* XV. iii, His mind was tost in all the distracting anxiety so nobly described by Shakespeare [*Jul. C.* II. i. 63–69]. **1799** tr. *Diderot's Nat. Son* II. 103 No one ..can conceive the heart-distracting misery I suffered. **1822** J. W. CROKER in *C. Papers* (1884) 12 Aug., I will..tell you this lamentable, this distracting story.

Hence **di'stractingly** *adv.*

1842 DICKENS *Amer. Notes* (1850) 67/2 A handsome city, but distractingly regular. **1859** GEO. ELIOT *A. Bede* 180 Hetty..had the same distractingly pretty looks..for everybody. **1879** MISS BRADDON *Vixen* III. 221 The ringing of imaginary wedding bells sounded distractingly in her ears.

distraction (dɪ'strækʃən). [ad. L. *distractiōn-em*, n. of action f. *distrahĕre* to pull asunder, DISTRACT; cf. F. *distraction* (1335 in Godef.).]

†**1. a.** A drawing or being drawn asunder; pulling asunder; forcible disruption, division, or severance.

1581 MULCASTER *Positions* xli. (1887) 248 The distraction of temporall, ciuill and Canon law being in many pointes very offensiue to our countrey. **1597** HOOKER *Eccl. Pol.* v. liii. §2 His two natures..are..as vncapable of confusion as of distraction. **1647** LILLY *Chr. Astrol.* clvi. 648 ♂ in the seventh in ferall Signes, argues death by Distraction, or by Ruine, or fall of Timber or Houses. **1837–8** SIR W. HAMILTON *Logic* xxv. (1866) II. 23 The parts which, by the distraction of the whole, come into view, are called the divisive members.

†**b.** A severed or divided form, drawn apart from others. *Obs.*

1606 SHAKS. *Ant. & Cl.* III. vii. 77 While he was yet in Rome, His power went out in such distractions, As beguilde all Spies.

†**c.** Dispersion, scattering. *Obs.*

1618 HALES *Gold. Rem.* (1688) 402 By reason of that great distraction of their Books and Papers.

†**d.** Violent stretching or extension. *Obs.*

c **1720** W. GIBSON *Farrier's Guide* II. xix. (1738) 65 A Distraction, or Rupture of the Vessels. **1737** BRACKEN *Farriery Impr.* (1756) I. 68 The Fibres..are in a State of Distraction, that is, they are drawn out into a greater length.

e. *Gr. Gram.* The resolution of a long vowel into two vowels, identical or differing only in quantity, as in ὁρόω for ὁρῶ, κράατος for κρᾶτος.

1891 MONRO *Homeric Gram.* (ed. 2) 51 These forms [ὁρόω, ὁράᾳς etc.] were regarded by the older grammarians as the result of a process called 'distraction', (the exact reverse of contraction), by which a long vowel, ᾱ or ω, could be separated into two distinct vowels (ᾱα, οω, &c.).

2. a. The drawing away (of the mind or thoughts) from one point or course to another; diversion of the mind or attention. Usually in adverse sense; less commonly = diversion, relaxation (as in Fr.).

1450–1530 *Myrr. our Ladye* 10 The harte owght to be kepte in tyme of these holy howres from dystraccyon, and from thynkynge on other thynges. **1526** *Pilgr. Perf.* (W. de W. 1531) 159 b, Harde it is to say one Pater noster without distraccyon of yᵉ mynde. **1611** BIBLE *1 Cor.* vii. 35 That you may attend vpon the Lord without distraction. **1699** BURNET *39 Art.* xii. (1700) 129 The distraction of their Thoughts in Devotion. **1749** CHESTERF. *Lett.* (1792) II. cxciv. 224, I know no one thing more offensive to a company, than that inattention and distraction. **1853** C. BRONTE *Villette* xxi, Considering sewing a source of distraction from the attention due to himself. **1853** MRS. JAMESON in G. Macpherson *Memoirs* (1878) 278 While attending on my mother, the compilation, printing, and illustrating furnish me with what the French call a *distraction*.

b. An instance or occasion of this. **c.** Something that distracts (or diverts) the mind or attention. Applied *attrib.* to behaviour of birds that is intended to distract the attention.

1614 BP. HALL *Recoll. Treat.* 158 A third, standing with the eyes..shut for feare of distractions. **1655** STANLEY *Hist. Philos.* I. (1701) 30/2 If he had not been constrained by seditious and other distractions to lay aside that study. **1849** ROBERTSON *Serm.* Ser. I. ii. 25 The cares of this world—its petty trifling distractions. **1859** WRAXALL tr. *R. Houdin* x. 136 Conjuring..was a mere distraction by which he amused his friends. **1943** *Trans. Linn. Soc. N.Y.* VI. 248 The instinctive response in face of danger to eggs and especially to young of drawing attention to the adult and away from the off-spring, is usually termed 'injury-feigning'. It would be better to call it 'nest-protecting display' (Murphy 1926) or distraction display. **1950** *Brit. Birds* XLIII. 1 The pseudo-sleeping figure occurs commonly in the Oyster-catcher's complex series of distraction-behaviour patterns. **1954** FISHER & LOCKLEY *Sea-Birds* vii. 173 But gannets, petrels and auks—birds clumsy on land—have no distraction display. **1961** BANNERMAN *Birds Brit. Isles* X. 213 Although distraction or 'injury feigning' displays are uncommon, they are sometimes elaborate, particularly by birds with chicks. *Ibid.*, 'Distraction flight' in which the cock or hen rises from the nest or near the chicks with fluttering flight.

3. a. The fact or condition of being drawn or pulled (physically or mentally) in different directions by conflicting forces or emotions.

1598 SHAKS. *Merry W.* III. v. 87 In her inuention, and Fords wiues distraction, they conuey'd me into a bucke-basket. **1633** T. JAMES *Voy.* 29 The ship did labour most terribly in this distraction of winde and waues. **1828** D'ISRAELI *Chas. I*, I. Pref. 4 Instead of the distraction of multifarious events..the philosopher discovered the inseparable connection of circumstances.

b. Disorder or confusion of affairs, caused by internal conflict or dissension; the condition of a community torn by dissension or conflict of parties.

1642 CHAS. I in Clarendon *Hist. Reb.* v. §386 To settle the Peace of the Kingdom, and compose the present Distractions. **1709** STEELE in *Lett. Lit. Men* (Camden) 344 My little affairs are in such distraction till I can come to an hearing in Chancery. **1780** BURKE *Sp. at Bristol* 9 Sept. Wks. III. 431 Your city, gentlemen, is in a state of miserable distraction. **1849** MACAULAY *Hist. Eng.* I. 134 The distractions of Ireland, he said, arose..from the differences between the Irish and the English. **1875** JOWETT *Plato* (ed. 2) III. 223 That body is..rendered incapable of united action by reason of sedition and distraction.

4. Violent perturbation or disturbance of mind or feelings, approaching to temporary madness. *to distraction*: to a degree which exemplifies or amounts to this; distractedly.

1606 SHAKS. *Ant. & Cl.* IV. i. 9 Giue him no breath, but now Make boote of his distraction. **1657** *Burton's Diary* (1828) II. 24 Pardon me if I speak confusedly, any man will justify my distraction in this. **1724** R. FALCONER *Voy.* II. (1769) 30 There was a sad Distraction amongst us in the Ship..for we had almost fell foul. **1802** *Noble Wanderers* I. 281 The Princess loves you to distraction. **1819** BYRON *Juan* I. cx, To contend with thoughts she could not smother, She seem'd, by the distraction of her air.

†**5.** Mental derangement; craziness, madness, insanity. *Obs.* (exc. as involved in prec.; cf. DISTRACT *v.* 5, 6, DISTRACTED 4, 5.)

c **1600** SHAKS. *Sonn.* cxix, In the distraction of this madding fever. **1702** C. MATHER *Magn. Chr.* II. vii. (1852) 145 A distempered melancholy at last issued in an incurable distraction. **1764** HARMER *Observ.* XII. iv. 159 The hermits of superstition..resemble Nebuchadnezzar in his distraction. **1794** SULLIVAN *View Nat.* I. 8 He traverses the whole circle of human imbecility and distraction.

6. In French-Canadian law: The diverting of costs from the client or party who would be in ordinary course entitled to them, and their ascription to his attorney or other person equitably entitled. [= F. *distraction*, in same use.]

18.. *Code of Civil Procedure of Lower Canada* Art. 484 (In 10th *Rept. of Codification Comm.* 1866), Attorneys ad Litem may demand and obtain distraction of their fees.

¶**7.** for DETRACTION.

c **1430** LYDG. *Min. Poems* 67 (Mätz.) Have in hate mowthes that ben double, Suffre at thy table no distractioun.

† **di'stractious**, *a. Obs.* [f. prec.: see -TIOUS.] Abounding in or fraught with distractions.
1667 WATERHOUSE *Fire Lond.* 104 In the time of the Fires raging, and of the distractious impetuosity. **1678** CUDWORTH *Intell. Syst.* Pref. 10 Which..would render His providences to humane apprehensions, laborious and distractious. **1691** RAY *Creation* (1714) 51 The former [opinion] would render the Divine Law operose, solicitous and distractious.

distractive (dɪˈstræktɪv), *a.* [f. L. ppl. stem *distract-* (see DISTRACT *v.*) + -IVE.] Of distracting quality or tendency.
1633 BP. HALL *Hard Texts* 212, I will walke free from all feares and distractive cares. **1643** MILTON *Divorce* II. xii. (1851) 93 How hurtfull and distractive it is to the house, the Church and Commonwealth. **1837** CARLYLE *Fr. Rev.* II. VI. vi. (1872) 248 Thou undefinable..self-distractive, self-destructive Legislative. **1855** —— *Misc., Prinzenraub* (1872) VII. 162 Johann Frederick..founding that imbroglio of little dukedoms..distractive to the human mind.
Hence **di'stractively** *adv.*, with distracting tendency or effect.
1831 CARLYLE *Sart. Res.* I. ii. (1872) 6 Maddest Waterloo-Crackers, exploding distractively and destructively, wheresoever the mystified passenger stands or sits. **1837** —— *Fr. Rev.* III. I. iv. (1872) 19 Whether the Flag..flapped soothingly or distractively.

† **di'stractly**, *adv. Obs. rare*⁻¹. [f. DISTRACT *a.* + -LY².] = DISTRACTEDLY.
c **1450** tr. *De Imitatione* III. liii, Forȝeue me..as ofte tymes as in my praier I þenke on eny oþer þinge þan on þe. I am wont to haue me þere ful distractly.

† **di'stracture.** *Obs.* [f. L. *distract-* ppl. stem (see DISTRACT *v.*) + -URE.] = DISTRACTION.
1622 R. HAWKINS *Voy. S. Sea* (1847) 192 The victory of the emperour Charles the Fifth, against the Protestant princes of Germanie, is imputed to their distractures arising from parity in command.

† **dis'trade**, *v. Obs. rare.* [f. DIS- 1 + TRADE *v.*] *trans.* To distribute by way of trade.
1623 LISLE *Ælfric on O. & N. Test.* To Rdr. 14 This creature [Camel]..is the best and only meanes..to conuey through the deserts, the sweet wares of happy Arabie, and so to distrade and retaile them among the Nations.

† **di'strage.** *Obs. rare*⁻¹. [f. *di-*, DIS- 5 + It. *strage*, L. *strāges* overthrow, slaughter, carnage.] A defeat with much slaughter.
c **1540** *Order in Battayll* B ij, After a dystrage, the hoste can not sodenely be apte to fyght: for wounds and mournyngs shal let them.

distrain (dɪˈstreɪn), *v.* Forms: 3–6 **destreyn(e**, 4–6 **des-**, **distrayne**, **distreyne**, (4 **-trene**, 4–5 **dystreyne**, 5 **-trayne**, 6 **-treine**), 5–8 **distrein**, 6–7 **distraine**, 6– **distrain**; *Sc.* 4–7 **des-**, **dys-**, **distrenȝe**, **-trinȝe**. [ME. a. OF. *destreindre*, *-aindre* 'to straine, presse, wring, vexe extremely, straiten' (Cotgr.), pres. stem *destreign-*, pa. pple. *destreint*; = It. *distrignere*, *-stringere* 'to distraine, distress, pinch, straiten' (Florio):—L. *distring-ĕre* to draw asunder, stretch out, detain, occupy, f. *dī-*, DIS- 1 + *stringĕre* to squeeze, draw tight. In med.L. and Romanic, the prefix lost its sundering force, being prob. confounded with *de-*, and *distringĕre* became merely intensive of *stringĕre*, as in mod.It.]

I. General senses: all *Obs.*

† **1.** *trans.* To press, compress, or grasp tightly; to squeeze; to clasp tightly. *Obs.*
c **1381** CHAUCER *Parl. Foules* 337 The gentyl faucoun that with his feet distraynyth The kyngis hand. *c* **1390** —— *Proverb*, Who so mychel wol embrace, Lytel þer-of he shal destreyne. **1483** CAXTON *Gold. Leg.* 372 b/1 Hit happed on a nyght that she distrayned her self by the throte that she was almost estrangled. **1600** FAIRFAX *Tasso* XII. xii. 215 The Prince..gently gan distraine Now him, now her, betweene his friendly armes.

† **b.** To confine, bind, restrain. *Obs.*
c **1374** CHAUCER *Boeth.* II. pr. vi. 42 (Camb. MS.) A man ..whiche þat visyous lustys holden destreyned with cheynes þat ne mowen nat be vnbownden. *c* **1386** —— *Pars. T.* ¶ 195 Oure lord Ihesu crist..after that he hadde be bytraysed of his disciple, and destreyned and bounde.

† **c.** *fig.* To hold captive, or in constraint. *Obs.*
c **1340** HAMPOLE *Prose Tr.* 18 Neuer-þe-lattere in þis maner felynge a saule may be distreynede by vayne glorye. *c* **1374** CHAUCER *Troylus* I. 355 Oþere besye nedes hym destrayned.

† **2.** *fig.* To hold in its grasp, as disease, sickness, love; to distress, oppress, afflict. *Obs.*
In quots. 1547, 1618 perhaps 'to strain'.
c **1374** CHAUCER *Troylus* III. 1479 (1528) No word for sorwe she answerede, So sore gan his partyng here destreyne. *c* **1430** LYDG. *Compl. Bl. Knt.* xx, And overmore distrayned with sicknesse Beside all this he was full grevously. **1483** CAXTON *Gold. Leg.* 266 b/1 The man of god ..destrayned his body by soo grete trauaill of fastynges and wakynges that he languyssed in contynuel maladye. *a* **1547** SURREY in *Tottell's Misc.* 14 Ragyng loue with extreme payne Most cruelly distrains my hart. *a* **1618** RALEIGH *Rem.* (1644) 121 Distrained with the wringing fits of his dying flesh.

† **3.** To control by force, restrain, subdue. *Obs.*
a **1400–50** *Alexander* 4244 A Kyng with-outen cunnyng, he can noȝt distreyne His subi[e]ctis. *c* **1530** *Spirituall Counsayle* H ij, Howe by his wysdome on the Crosse he hathe distrayned all the power of the devyll.

† **4.** To constrain, force, or compel (a person *to do* something). *Obs.* (Hence the legal sense 7.)
c **1374** CHAUCER *Troylus* V. 596 Distreyne here herte as faste to retorne, As þow dost myn to longen here to se. **1375** BARBOUR *Bruce* XII. 338 Thar gret vaward alsua Wes distrenȝeit the bak till ta. *c* **1386** CHAUCER *Pars. T.* ¶ 35 Penitence destreyneth a man to accepte benygnely euery peyne..enioyned. *c* **1400** tr. *Secreta Secret., Gov. Lordsh.* (E.E.T.S.) 62 Who destreyns þe to swere ofte?

† **5.** To strain out, express; to extract by pressing or straining. (In quot. 1563, *intr.* for *refl.*)
c **1400** tr. *Secreta Secret., Gov. Lordsh.* (E.E.T.S.) 85 His properte ys, to make stalworthe þe stomak, & destreyne & purge þe euyl and rotyn humours þat er in þe stomak. **1563** B. GOOGE *Eglogs* (Arb.) 117 The gryefe so sore, doth growe in euery parte, Destraynyng through the venomed vaines doth so torment the Hart. **1634** SIR T. HERBERT *Trav.* 150 Coffa or Coho, a drinke..blacke, thicke and bitter; distrained from Berries of that quality.

† **6. a.** To pull or tear off. **b.** To rend or tear asunder. [After L. senses.] *Obs.*
1382 WYCLIF *Ezek.* xvii. 22 Y shal take of the merewȝ of the heeȝ cedre, and I shal putte of the cop of his braunchis; the tendre I shal distreyne, [**1388** streyne, Vulg. *distringam*]. **1590** SPENSER *F.Q.* II. xii. 82 That same net so cunningly was wound, That neither guile nor force might it distraine.

II. *Law.* [The earliest use recorded, but etymologically a specific application of 4.]

† **7.** *trans.* **a.** To constrain or force (a person) by the seizure and detention of a chattel or thing, to perform some obligation (as to pay money owed by him, to make satisfaction for some wrong done by him or by his beasts, or to perform some other act, e.g. to appear in court); to punish by such seizure and detention for the non-performance of such obligation. (See DISTRESS *sb.* II.) *Obs.* exc. *Hist.*, or as included in c.
c **1290** *Beket* 758 in *S. Eng. Leg.* I. 128 Non Erchebishop of Caunturburi nas neuere i-somoned so, Ne so destreyned of no king [*v.r.* of nothing]. [**1292** BRITTON I. xxvii. [xxvi]. §1 Le viscounte face destreyndre les trespasours par lour avers et par lour chateus.] **1414** *Coldingham Papers* (1841) 86 Full power and autorite..the same tenantz and tenantdris til distreyn and hald, till all rerages and dettes..be assethid. **1512** *Act 4 Hen. VIII*, c. 19 §9 For none payment therof to destreyn the seid persones so beyng behynde by their goodes and catalles. **1568** GRAFTON *Chron.* II. 142 To make sommons, and distreyne for lacke of appearaunce, all and every Tenant of the sayd Abbot. **1671** F. PHILLIPS *Reg. Necess.* 467 He refused to give leave..to distrein the Bishop of St. Davids in Parliament time. **1895** POLLOCK & MAITLAND *Hist. Eng. Law* I. 335 After distraining the tenant by his chattels, the lord may obtain from his seignorial tribunal a judgment authorizing him to distrain the tenant by his land. *Ibid.* II. 574 Observe that [in the 13th c.], when words are correctly used, one does not distrain a thing; one distrains a man by (*per*) a thing.

b. with *inf.* or *subord. clause*, expressing the purpose.
c **1290** *Beket* 748 in *S. Eng. Leg.* I. 128 Seint thomas londes into is hond his men nome, Ase it were for-to destreynen him þat he to his court come. *c* **1315** SHOREHAM 72 Destrayned be he scholde, Be rytte To do hyt ȝyf that he may. **1609** SKENE *Reg. Maj.* 27 He may be distrenzied in his lands, to come to court. *a* **1626** BACON *Max. & Uses Com. Law* (1636) 20 Commanding him [the Sheriffe] to distraine them by their lands to appear at a certaine day. **1641** *Art. agst. Sir H. Davenport* in Rushw. *Hist. Coll.* III. (1692) I. 335 That he should distrain James Maleverer, Esq; to appear before the Barons of his Majesty's said Court of Exchequer. **1647** N. BACON *Disc. Govt. Eng.* I. lxx. (1739) 184 All such as ought to be Knights and are not, shall be distrained to undertake the weapons of Knighthood. **1767** BLACKSTONE *Comm.* II. 135 The widow shall pay nothing for her marriage, nor shall be distreined to marry afresh. **1895** POLLOCK & MAITLAND *Hist. Eng. Law* I. 334 The lord's handiest remedy is that of distraining his tenant to perform the services that are in arrear.

c. In later usage: To levy a distress upon (a person), in order by the sale of the chattels to obtain satisfaction for a debt, particularly for arrears of rent. (But the usual construction in this sense is *to distrain upon*: see 8 b.)
1768–74 TUCKER *Lt. Nat.* I. ii. §9 When Squire Peremptory distrained his tenant for rent perhaps he [etc.]. **1772** *Hist. Rochester* 46 Who had been distrained for the repair of the head of the bridge. **1818** CRUISE *Digest* (ed. 2) III. 201 A peer of the realm could never be arrested for debt; the law presuming that he had sufficient lands and tenements in which he might be distrained.

8. *absol.* or *intr.* To levy a distress. Const. *for* (a thing). Originally in order to compel the defaulter, by detention of the thing seized, to pay money due or perform an obligation; but in later use including the power to obtain satisfaction by sale of the chattels. See DISTRESS *sb.* 3.
c **1350** in *Eng. Gilds* (1870) 362 ȝif eny þo þat nymeþ rente of eny tenement in fraunchyse of þe Citee, and his rente holleche be by-hynde, oþer half oþer more and he ne fynde for to dystreyne. **1463** *Bury Wills* (Camden) 27 If my wil be nat devly executyd in eche part, they to haue pover to distreyne. **1512** FABYAN *Will* in *Chron.* Pref. 9, I geve full power over the said Church Wardeyns..to distreyn within any of the foresaid londs and tenements..and the distres so taken to withold and kepe till the said annuytie..be fully contented and paied. **1512** *Act 4 Hen. VIII*, c. 11 To distreyne for the same rentes in the seid Maners. **1552** in *Vicary's Anat.* (1888) App. iii. 152 It shalbe laufull for any offycer of the said Cytie to dystreine for the same [yearly rent]. **1648** MILTON *Observ. Art. Peace* Wks. 1738 I. 338 Any seven or more of them, in case of Refractories or Delinquency, may distrain and imprison. **1764** BURN *Poor Laws* 251 Where power is given to distrain, it seemeth reasonable that power should be given to come at the goods. **1863** FAWCETT *Pol. Econ.* II. vii. 237 The landlord had of course a legal right to distrain for the rent.

b. Const. *upon*, *on* a person or thing. (With indirect passive *to be distrained upon*.)
1605 CAMDEN *Rem.* (J.), I will not lend money to my superiour, upon whom I cannot distrain for the debt. **1689** *Col. Rec. Pennsylv.* I. 311 He was distreyned upon by Cornelius Empson, for Contrey Rates. **1812** *Examiner* 7 Sept. 570/2 He was..threatened..to be distrained on for the assessment and surcharge. **1861** PEARSON *Early & Mid. Ages Eng.* xxxiv. (L.), He or his heirs might distrain on them if this were neglected. **1891** *Punch* 25 Apr. 195/2 The total failure of my last attempt to distrain on the stock of a neighbouring farmer.
fig. *a* **1658** CLEVELAND *Gen. Poems, &c.* (1677) 2 The Airy Freebooter distrains First on the Violet of her Veins, Whose Tincture could it be more pure, His ravenous kiss had made it blewer. *a* **1678** MARVELL (J.), Blood, his rent to have regain'd Upon the British diadem distrain'd.

9. *trans.* To seize (chattels, etc.) by way of distress; to levy a distress upon. *arch.*
1531 *Dial. on Laws Eng.* II. xxvii. (1638) 112 A pound..to put in beasts that bee distrained. **1593** SHAKS. *Rich. II*, II. iii. 131 My Fathers goods are all distraynd, and sold. **1671** F. PHILLIPS *Reg. Necess.* 490 The Laws or reasonable Customs of England will not permit a Horse to be destrained when a Man or Woman is riding upon him. *a* **1713** ELLWOOD *Autobiog.* (1714) 66 If you have no Money, you have a good Horse under you; and we can Distrain him for the Charge. **1765** BLACKSTONE *Comm.* I. 256 All process whereby the person of any embassador..may be arrested, or his goods distreined or seised, shall be utterly null and void. **1848** WHARTON *Law Lex.* 186 All chattels and personal effects, found upon the premises, may be distrained, whether they belong to the tenant or to a stranger.

† **10.** Extensions or loose uses of the legal senses. **a.** To deprive (a person) of (something). *Obs.*
1530 PALSGR. 522/1, I distrayne a persone of his lybertye, or plucke some thynge from hym that belongeth him.

† **b.** To seize, confiscate, annex. *Obs.*
1591 SHAKS. *1 Hen. VI*, I. iii. 61 Here's Beauford, that regards nor God nor King, Hath here distrayn'd the Tower to his vse. **1676** HOBBES *Iliad* XI. 622, I then went his Cattle to destrain, And take amends for those he took of mine. **1727** A. HAMILTON *New Acc. E. Ind.* I. viii. 86 They first built a Sconce..both to secure themselves from sudden Attacks or Surprize, as well as to hold what they might distrain from the poor Peasants.

Hence **di'strained** *ppl. a.*; **di'straining** *vbl. sb.* and *ppl. a.*
c **1380** WYCLIF *Sel. Wks.* III. 302 Stelyng of chartris, and distreynyng of ȝonge eiris. **1530–1** *Act 22 Hen. VIII*, c. 12 If any such person..distreined appere not at the day and place conteyned in suche distresse. **1672–3** MARVELL *Reh. Transp.* I. 244 They reckon there would be little got by distraining. **1887** *Spectator* 4 June 760/1 To give instant warning of the approach of the distraining parties. **1895** *Daily News* 25 Jan. 5/3 The Judge..has been saying some severe things on the subject of distraining bailiffs.

† **di'strain**, *sb. Obs.* [f. prec. vb.]
1. = DISTRAINT.
c **1450** *Eng. Misc.* (Surtees) 59 No distreyn yᵗ is made wᵗ in yᵉ sayd Burgage.
2. Restraint, control.
c **1531** LATIMER *Serm. & Rem.* (1845) 329 The kings highness..did decree that all admitted of universities should preach throughout all his realm as long as they preached well, without distrain of any man. **1598** FLORIO, *Distretta*, a destraine, a trouble, an inconvenience.

distrainable (dɪˈstreɪnəb(ə)l), *a.* [a. AF. *destreynable* = OF. *destreign-*, *destraignable*, f. stem of prec. vb.: see -ABLE.]
1. Liable or subject to distraint; liable to be distrained or distrained upon: **a.** of a person.
[**1292** BRITTON I. ii[i]. §7 Si troeffe deus pleges suffisauntz et destreynables al viscounte del pays.] **1865** NICHOLS *Britton* II. 341 It is sufficient to make the summons in the fee where he is distrainable.
b. of chattels.
1588 FRAUNCE *Lawiers Log.* I. xvi. 60 His [the King's] goodes and cattels are under no tribute, toll, or custome, nor otherwise distreignable. **1641** *Termes de la Ley* 124 Else they [beasts] be not distreinable for rent or service. **1768** BLACKSTONE *Comm.* III. 7 Instead therefore of mentioning what things are distreinable, it will be easier to recount those which are not so. **1889** *Law Times* LXXXII. 223/2 There were other distrainable goods in the house available to satisfy the claim for rent.
2. Capable of being distrained for, or recovered by distress.
1791 G. WASHINGTON *Let.* Writ. 1891 XII. 76 All the rents become due on or before the first day of January in every year, and distrainable at the expiration of a certain number of days thereafter. **1895** *Times* 17 Jan. 14/4 Subject to distrainable rent.

† **di'strainant.** *Obs.* [a. AF. *destreynaunt* = OF. *destreignant*, pr. pple. of *destreindre* to DISTRAIN.] = DISTRAINER.
[**1292** BRITTON I. xxviii. [xxvii]. §17 Devers les chiefs seignurs destreynauntz.] **1553** *Act 7 Edw. VI*, c. 1 §11 The Kings Debts and Duties being first paid, and the Distrainant answered of reasonable Costs.

distrainee (dɪˌstreɪˈniː). [f. DISTRAIN *v.* + -EE.] One who is distrained.

1875 MAINE *Hist. Inst.* ix. 272 He appeared virtually as a plaintiff like the distrainee in our Action of Replevin.

distrainer (dɪˈstreɪnə(r)). [f. as prec. + -ER¹.] One who distrains; = DISTRAINOR.

1607 COWELL *Interpr.* s.v. *Distresse*, The effect..is, to driue the party distreined to replevie the distresse, and so to take his action of trespasse against the distreiner. **1736** in JACOB *Law Dict.* (ed. 3). **1863** MRS. C. CLARKE *Shaks. Char.* xiv. 363 Thou mightst have become a distrainer for rent, or a surcharger of taxes. **1880** MUIRHEAD *Gaius* Digest 535 The distrainer had to use certain words of style. **1893** *Law Times* XCIV. 600/2 A sheriff's officer may break open outhouses, though a distrainer may not.

di'strainment. [f. as prec. + -MENT.] The action or fact of distraining; distraint.

1756 T. AMORY *J. Buncle* (1825) I. 47 As I was ever liable to distrainment, I took my leave. **1882** WEEDEN *Soc. Law Labor* 151 Many families have been ruined by this distrainment. **1886** *Pall Mall G.* 24 Apr. 4/1 The only means of enforcing rent is by ejectment, as seizures and distrainments cannot be carried out in the district.

distrainor (dɪˈstreɪˌnɔː(r)). [f. DISTRAIN *v.*, after AF. *destreinor* (Year-bks. Edw. II).] One who distrains or levies a distress: a more technical form than *distrainer*, and correlative to *distrainee*.

1767 BLACKSTONE *Comm.* II. 453 If a landlord distreins goods for rent, or a parish officer for taxes, these for a time are only a pledge in the hands of the distreinors. **1875** POSTE *Gaius* IV. §29 In all these cases the distreinor used a set form of words. **1875** MAINE *Hist. Inst.* ix. 263 The impounded beasts, when the pound was uncovered, had to be fed by the owner and not by the distrainor.

distraint (dɪˈstreɪnt). [f. DISTRAIN *v.*, perh. after OF. *destrainte* (13–16th c. in Godef.), *destraincte* 'a restraint of libertie' (Cotgr.), fem. sb. from pa. pple.: cf. CONSTRAINT.] The action of distraining (in the legal sense); = DISTRESS *sb.* 3.

1730–6 in BAILEY (folio). **1833** HT. MARTINEAU *Loom & Lugger* I. vii. 115 There would be a distraint for penalties. **1869** *Daily News* 25 Aug., The bailiffs shortly afterwards entered the house, and..made a distraint which almost stripped it of furniture. **1874** GREEN *Short Hist.* viii. §10. 571 Payment of taxes..was enforced by distraint. **1875** MAINE *Hist. Inst.* ix. 262 The distraint of cattle for damages still retains a variety of archaic features.

b. *distraint of knighthood*: compulsion to accept knighthood (in consequence of tenure of a knight's fee, or an estate worth £20 a year). (See DISTRAIN *v.* 7 b, quot. 1647.)

1875 STUBBS *Const. Hist.* II. xv. 281 The distraint of knighthood was..a link between the two branches of the national force.

†**di'strait,** *sb. Obs.* [later form of *destrait*, DESTRAYT, OF. *destreit*, mod.F. *détroit*:—L. *district-um*.] **a.** A narrow passage (of land or water); an isthmus or strait; **b.** a strait or difficult situation; **c.** a district.

1480 CAXTON *Ovid's Met.* XIV. vi, [The winds] remysed us in to the cruel dystraytis of Eolus. *c* **1477** —— *Jason* 42 b, I had leuer to receyue and passe the distrait of dethe. **1562** J. SHUTE *Cambine's Turk. Wars* 7 b, If this distraite of yᵉ land were cut through, Peloponesso shold be an isle.

di'strait, *a.* [a. F. *distrait* (in 16th c. also *distraict*), pa. pple. of *distraire* to DISTRACT. The form *distrat* appears to connect this with DISTRACT.]

†**1.** Distracted in mind; excessively perplexed or troubled. *Obs.*

c **1374** CHAUCER *Boeth.* III. pr. viii. 80 þou shalt ben so destrat by aspre þinges þat þou shalt forgone sykernesse. **1440** J. SHIRLEY *Dethe K. James* (1818) 17 The other ladyes ..cryyng and wepyng, all distraite made a pitous and lamentable noyse. *c* **1450** tr. *De Imitatione* II. i, So muche is a man lette and distraite, as þinges are drawen to him.

2. Having the attention distracted from what is present; absent-minded. [from mod.F., and usually treated as an alien word (distrɛ, diːˈstreɪ) with F. fem. *distraite* (distrɛt, diːˈstreɪt).]

[**1711** BUDGELL *Spect.* No. 77 ¶ 1 One of those Sort of Men who are very often absent in Conversation, and what the French call *a reveur* and *a distrait*.] **1748** CHESTERF. *Lett.* (1774) I. cxxxiii. 325, I took care never to be absent or *distrait*. **1771** MRS. E. GRIFFITH *Lady Barton* I. 72 He.. sometimes appears gloomy and distrait. **1788** *Walpoliana* xlii. 21 Oh, Madam (exclaimed the *distrait* prelate), he had such a brimstone of a wife! **1824** BYRON *Juan* XVI. xxx, So much distrait was he. **1849** THACKERAY *Pendennis* xxvii, She was very *distraite*. **1857** KINGSLEY *Two Y. Ago* xxvi, She.. tried to make her talk; but she was *distrait*, reserved. **1883** E. INGERSOLL in *Harper's Mag.* Feb. 431/2 This knowledge.. kept her *distrait*.

†**3.** as *pa. pple.* Torn to pieces, divided. *Obs.*

1579 E. K. *Gloss.* in *Spenser's Sheph. Cal.* June 25 All Italy was distraict into..Factions.

†**distrami'nation.** *Obs. rare.* [f. *di-*, DIS- 4 + L. *strāmen* (*strāmin-*) anything strewn, straw: see -ATION.] Unthatching, stripping of thatch.

1654 GAYTON *Pleas. Notes* III. x. 141 Two Ancient Reverend Men had almost disthatch'd their Faces, and could neither of them sue for distraminations.

distrammel (dɪˈstræməl), *v. rare.* [DIS- 6.] *trans.* To rid of trammels; to untrammel.

1856 R. A. VAUGHAN *Mystics* (1860) I. 105 The native soul, distrammelled of dim earth, Doth know herself immortal, and sits light Upon her temporal perch.

distraught (dɪˈstrɔːt), *ppl. a. arch.* Also 4–7 des-, 5 dys-, 6 distraghte, 7 distrought. [modification of DISTRACT *ppl. a.*, L. *distract-us*.

Not of ordinary phonetic origin, but due app. to association with other pa. pples. in *-ght*, as *caught*, *taught*, *bought*, *brought*, *sought*, *thought*, *wrought*. Perh. more immediately influenced by *straught*, pa. pple. of STRETCH; as the latter had also the form *streight*, *straight*, it may be that *distraught* = *distreight* = DISTRAIT.]

1. Mentally distracted, by being drawn or driven in diverse directions or by conflicting emotions; deeply agitated or troubled; = DISTRACTED 4.

1393 GOWER *Conf.* I. 218 Wherof his herte is so distraught. *Ibid.* 279 Many a good felawe Hath be destraught by sodein chaunce. *c* **1491** *Chast. Goddes Chyld.* xxvii. 79 Some ben so ferforth distraught..that whan they come ayen to hemself it is clene fro her mynde where they left. **1591** SPENSER *Ruines of Time* 578, I in minde remained ..Distraught twixt feare and pitie. **1608–11** BP. HALL *Medit. & Vowes* I. §92 The worldling standes amazed and distraught with the evill. **1610** G. FLETCHER *Christ's Tri.* (1632) 44 With present fear, and future grief distraught. **1848** LYTTON *Harold* I. i, Her mind is somewhat distraught with her misfortunes. **1877** L. MORRIS *Epic Hades* I. 17, I lay awake Distraught with warring thoughts.

2. Driven to madness; mentally deranged; crazy: = DISTRACTED 5.

1592 SHAKS. *Rom. & Jul.* IV. iii. 49. **1594** —— *Rich. III*, III. v. 4 And then againe begin, and stop againe, As if thou were distraught, and mad with terror. **1598** STOW *Surv.* (1842) 167/2 One house, wherein sometime were distraught and lunatic people. **1652** GAULE *Magastrom.* 90 Fools, madmen, melancholy, fanatic, distraught. **1828** SCOTT *F.M. Perth* xix, 'Are ye distraught, lassie?' shouted Dorothy. **1886** HALL CAINE *Son of Hagar* III. v, Hugh Ritson rushed here and there like a man distraught.

†**b.** Const. *of*, *in* (wits, senses, etc.). *Obs.* (In senses 1 and 2.)

1556 *Aurelio & Isab.* (1608) F, Folkes distraghte of wisdome. **1583** T. WATSON *Centurie of Loue* lxxxix. (Arb.) 125 Loue is distraught of witte, and hath no end. **1653** H. COGAN tr. *Pinto's Trav.* viii. 23 Like a man distraught of his wits I cast myself at the feet of the Elephant. **1657** HOWELL *Londinop.* 66 In this place [Bethlem] people that be distraught in their wits.

†**3.** *lit.* Pulled asunder, drawn in different directions. (Spenserian use.) *Obs.*

1596 SPENSER *F.Q.* IV. vii. 31 [An arrow] in his nape arriving, through it thrild His greedy throte, therewith in two distraught. *Ibid.* V. v. 2 A Camis..Trayled with ribbands diversly distraught. **1604** R. CAWDREY *Table Alph.*, *Distraught*, drawne into diuers parts. **1642** H. MORE *Song of Soul* II. ii. II. x, By distrought distension.

4. As *pa. pple.* of DISTRACT, or DISTRAUGHT *v.*

1581 PETTIE *Guazzo's Civ. Conv.* I. (1586) 40 b, [They] have bene distraught of their right understanding. **1625** K. LONG tr. *Barclay's Argenis* II. xxi. 139 What fury..hath distraught you of your wits? **1816** SOUTHEY *Lay of Laureate* Epil. 2 Have fanatic dreams distraught his sense?

†**di'straught,** *sb. Obs. rare.* [f. prec.] = DISTRACTION.

1610 ROWLANDS *Martin Mark-all* 31 They wil bring you out of the way, through distraught and feare.

†**di'straught,** *v. Obs.* [Improperly used as a variant of DISTRACT *v.*, on the analogy of *distraught* and *distract* ppl. adjs.] = DISTRACT *v.*

1579 G. HARVEY *Letter-bk.* (Camden) 59 There never happenid any on thinge..that did ever disorder and distraute the power of my mynde so mutche. **1593** NASHE *Christ's T.* (1613) 44 The zeale of thee distraughteth me.

†**di'straughted,** *ppl. a. Obs.* [Altered from DISTRACTED: see prec.] = DISTRACTED.

1572 R. H. tr. *Lauaterus' Ghostes* (1596) 10 In those men, which be..distraughted of their wittes. **1596** SPENSER *Hymn Heavenly Beauty* 14 That immortall beautie..Which in my weake distraughted mynd I see. **1603** KNOLLES *Hist. Turks* (1621) 41 His base determination..all wondering at, as proceeding from a distraughted minde.

†**di'straughtful,** *a. Obs. rare.* [see prec.] By-form of DISTRACTFUL.

1594 *2nd Rep. Faustus* in Thoms *Prose Rom.* (1858) III. 318 In a distraughtful fury.

distraughtly (dɪˈstrɔːtlɪ), *adv.* [f. DISTRAUGHT *a.* + -LY².] In a distraught manner.

1926 *Chamber's Jrnl.* June 383/1 She strove, strove distraughtly to shriek, to move. **1958** S. SPENDER *Engaged in Writing* 32 Botor's long..hair had been shoved distraughtly ..across his head.

†**di'straughtness.** *Obs. rare.* [f. DISTRAUGHT *a.* + -NESS.] Distractedness, distraction.

1576 NEWTON *Lemnie's Complex.* (1633) 30 Hence proceedeth..roving dotage, and distraughtnesse of right wits.

†**di'straughture.** *Obs. rare*⁻¹. [See DISTRAUGHTED.] By-form of DISTRACTURE, distraction.

1594 *2nd Rep. Faustus* in Thoms *Prose Rom.* (1858) III. 317 Which were witnesses of his distraughture.

†**di'stream,** *v. poetic. Obs. rare.* [f. *di-*, DIS- 1 + STREAM *v.*] *intr.* To flow away in a stream; to stream down or away. Hence **di'streaming** *ppl. a.*

1630 BRATHWAIT *Eng. Gentlem.* (1641) 226 Let the dolefull remembrance thereof produce torrents of teares from your distreaming eyes. *c* **1750** SHENSTONE *Elegies* xv. 4 A swelling tear distream'd from ev'ry eye. *Ibid.* xix. 71 O'er that virtuous blush distreams a tear.

†**dis'treasure,** *v. Obs. rare.* [DIS- 7 a.] *trans.* To despoil of a treasure.

1640 QUARLES *Enchirid.* IV. xxi, Distreasure him of his ill-got Wealth.

†**di'stree,** *v. Obs. nonce-wd.* [DIS- 7 a.] *trans.* To deprive or strip of trees.

a **1638** MEDE *Disc. Josh.* xxiv. 26 Wks. (1672) I. 68 Of some of the Proseucha's they cut down the Trees..Mark here, They dis-tree'd the Proseucha's.

distrein(e, obs. forms of DISTRAIN.

†**di'strempe,** *v. Obs. rare*⁻⁰. To distemper.

c **1532** DEWES *Introd. Fr.* in *Palsgr.* (1852) 941 To distrempe, *destrempér*.

distress (dɪˈstrɛs), *sb.* Forms: 3–6 **destresse**, 4–7 **distresse**, (4 **destres**, 4–7 **distres**, 5 **distryss(e**, 5–6 **dystresse**, 6 **dystres**), 7– **distress**. [ME. a. OF. *destrece*, *-stresce*, *-stresse*:—late pop. L. **districtia*, f. *district-us*, pa. pple. of *distringĕre* to DISTRAIN (like *angustia* from *angustus*); *distress* is the fact of distraining or condition of being distrained, in the various senses of the vb.]

I. †**1. a.** The action or fact of straining or pressing tightly, strain, stress, pressure; *fig.* pressure employed to produce action, constraint, compulsion; less usually, pressure applied to prevent action, restraint. *Obs.* exc. in *dial.* (in which the primary sense is still used.)

13.. *Cursor M.* 28360 (Cott.) And i, prest, funden vte of distresse, In dedly sin has sungen messe. *c* **1384** CHAUCER *H. Fame* III. 497 This Eolus with harde grace helde the wyndes in distresse And gan hem vnder him to presse. *a* **1400** in *Eng. Gilds* (1870) 361 He sheweþ wiþoute dystresse, weiþer he be of fraunchyse oþer ne be, and be of towne. *c* **1420** *Pallad. on Husb.* IV. 79 Swathe a tender vyne in bondes softe: Ffor bonde to hardde wol holde it in distresse. *c* **1450** *Chester Pl.* (Shaks. Soc.) II. 52 God I take to wittnes That I doe this by destresse. **1481** CAXTON *Myrr.* II. xxii. 114 The ayer that is shette fast within, the whiche is enclosed in grete distresse. **1590** SPENSER *F.Q.* I. i. 32 In wastfull wildernesse..by which no living wight May euer pass, but thorough great distresse. [**1876** *Surrey Provincialisms*, *Distress*, strain; e.g. 'Slacken they there ropes before you go, and then there won't be no distress on the [rick-]cloth'. **1879** MISS JACKSON *Shropsh. Word-bk.*, *Distress*, strain; stress; application of force. 'Theer wunna be no distress on that theer 'edge tin [= till] after 'arvest.']

†**b.** The overpowering pressure *of* some adverse force, as anger, hunger, bad weather; stress (of weather, etc.). *Obs.*

1485 CAXTON *Chas. Gt.* 187 By destresse of angre he took a staffe for to smyte the messager. **1486** *Bk. St. Albans* C j b, In grete destresse of hungre. **1568** GRAFTON *Chron.* II. 87 Driven by distresse of weather about the partes of Austria. **1588** GREENE *Pandosto* (1607) 43, I was sayling, and by distresse of weather, I was driuen into these coasts. **1793** SMEATON *Edystone L.* Contents 10, Driven westward, by distress of weather. *Ibid.* 12 Without any distress of weather, the Buss got loose.

2. a. The sore pressure or strain of adversity, trouble, sickness, pain, or sorrow; anguish or affliction affecting the body, spirit, or community.

1297 R. GLOUC. (1724) 460 þe kyng, þat so defended hym, as in such destresse. *c* **1330** R. BRUNNE *Chron. Wace* (Rolls) 3472 þan were þey boþe in hard destres. *c* **1385** CHAUCER *L.G.W.* 664 *Cleopatra*, To egipt is sche fled for dred & for destresse. *c* **1400** *Rom. Rose* 4997 Peyne and Distresse, Syknesse and Ire, and Malencoly..Ben of hir paleys senatours. **1413** *Pilgr. Sowle* (Caxton 1483) IV. xx. 65 Ye knoweth my comforteles dystresse. **1600** SHAKS. *A. Y. L.* II. vii. 90 Art thou thus bolden'd man by thy distres? **1611** BIBLE *1 Kings* i. 29 As the Lord liueth, that hath redeemed my soule out of all distresse. *a* **1656** BP. HALL *Rem. Wks.* (1660) 2 Being in great distress of Conscience. **1667** MILTON *P.L.* XII. 613 With sorrow and hearts distress Wearied I fell asleep. **1818** JAS. MILL *Brit. India* II. v. viii. 627 The Company's finances, always in distress. **1853** J. H. NEWMAN *Hist. Sk.* (1873) II. II. iii. 252 This event..filled him with the utmost distress and despondency. **1867** DICKENS *Lett.* (1880) II. 273 There is great distress here among the poor.

b. with *a* and *pl.* A sore trouble, a misfortune or calamity that presses hardly; esp. in *pl.* straits, distressing or strained circumstances.

1549 COVERDALE, etc. *Erasm. Par.*, *Rom.* viii. (R.), That in all our distresses we may boldly speake vnto God. **1588** (*title*), Copie of a Letter sent out of England to Don Bernardin Mendoza..Whereunto are adioyned certaine late Advertisements, concerning the losses and distresses happened to the Spanish Navie. **1605** SHAKS. *Macb.* IV. iii. 188. **1659** B. HARRIS *Parival's Iron Age* 285 So many storms, that both men, and horses felt excessive distresses. **1691** WOOD *Ath. Oxon.* II. 53 His distresses made him stoop so low as to be an Abcdarian. **1783** BURKE *Sp. on E. India Bill* Wks. IV. 129 Want of feeling for the distresses of mankind. **1842** TENNYSON *Dora* 47 Then distresses came on him.

c. *Naut.* 'A term used when a ship requires immediate assistance from unlooked-for damage or danger' (Smyth *Sailor's Word-bk.*).

1659 D. PELL *Impr. Sea* 291 Firing of Guns, which is commonly a signal of that ships distress that fires. **1697** DAMPIER *Voy.* I. 394 Any Ship in distress may be refreshed and recruited here. **1726** SHELVOCKE *Voy. round World* (1757) 320, I returned to our ships again, and made signals of distress. **1745** P. THOMAS *Jrnl. Anson's Voy.* 156 They fired four Guns as Signals of Distress. **1839** LONGF. *Wreck of Hesp.* xi, Some ship in distress, that cannot live In such an angry sea!

d. 'Distressed' or exhausted condition under extreme physical strain. (Also *fig.*)

1803 *Sporting Mag.* XXII. 21/2 Fifth Round... Firby began to exhibit symptoms of distress. **1836** *Spirit of Times* 27 Feb. 13/2 She showed some symptoms of distress and the backers of the field thought there was still a chance. **1861** A. TROLLOPE *La Beata* I. 162 (Hoppe) The lady arrives at the top [of the stairs] with very visible signs of 'distress' in wind and limb. **1887** H. D. TRAILL in *Macm. Mag.* July 177/1 Their patience, which is already showing manifest signs of distress, will be completely 'pumped' before long.

II. *Law.*

3. a. The action of distraining; the legal seizure and detention of a chattel, originally for the purpose of thereby constraining the owner to pay money owed by him or to make satisfaction for some wrong done by him, or to do some other act (e.g. to appear in court); according to later practice, in order that out of the proceeds of its sale (if not redeemed within a fixed period) satisfaction may be obtained of some debt or claim, now, especially, for rent unpaid.

c **1290** *Beket* 761 in *S. Eng. Leg.* I. 128 On me nast þu power non swych destresse for-to do. *c* **1330** R. BRUNNE *Chron.* (1810) 186 And neuer þorgh no distresse suld clayme þer of no right. **1543** tr. *Act 51 Hen.* III. (1266) *De Destrictione Scaccarii* (Berthelet), And if he brynge the tayle of any shyriffe or baylyffe, of payment made to them of the thyng demaunded..then the distresse shal sease. **1613** SIR H. FINCH *Law* (1636) 135 Distresse is a taking of chattels.. found upon the same land..for satisfaction of arerages. **1614** RALEIGH *Hist. World* III. (1634) 113 The Phocians not meaning so to lose their Rent, made a distresse by strong hand. **1768** BLACKSTONE *Comm.* III. 6 A distress..the taking of a personal chattel out of the possession of the wrongdoer into the custody of the party injured, to procure a satisfaction for the wrong committed. **1794** GODWIN *Cal. Williams* 46 The squire..took the earliest opportunity of seizing on his remaining property in the mode of a distress for rent. **1818** CRUISE *Digest* (ed. 2) III. 299 A right to enter on the lands, to seize the cattle and other personal chattels found there, and to sell them for payment of the rent; which is called a distress. **1836** DICKENS *Sk. Boz* v, I put in a good many distresses in my time (continued Mr. Bung). **1875** MAINE *Hist. Inst.* ix. 250 The branch of the law which we now call the Law of Distress.

b. ***double, grand, finite, infinite, personal, real distress***: see quots.

1641 *Termes de la Ley* 125 Distresse..is divided first into finite and infinite, finite is that which is limited by Law, how often it shall bee made to bring the party to tryall of the action, as once or twice. Distresse infinite is without limitation untill the party comes, as against a Jurie that refuseth to appeare upon certificate of assise. **1670** BLOUNT *Law Dict.*, *Distress Personal* is made by distreining a Mans movable Goods..*Distress Real* is made upon immovable Goods..A *Grand Distress* is that which is made of all the Goods and Chattels that the party hath within the County. **1768** BLACKSTONE *Comm.* III. 231 A distress..that has no bounds with regard to it's quantity, and may be repeated from time to time, until the stubbornness of the party is conquered, is called a *distress infinite*. **1861** W. BELL *Dict. Law Scot.* s.v. *Double Distress*, Where arrestments have been used by two or more creditors, in order to attach the funds of their debtor in the hands of a third party, such arrestments constitute what is called *double distress*.

†**c.** The right or power of distraining, the seigniory of a district. *Obs. rare.*

[**1292** BRITTON VI. iv. §12 Si celi garraunt ne soit mie en la destresce le viscounte de cel pays. *tr.* If the warrant is not situated within the distress (= district) of the sheriff of that country.] *a* **1658** CLEVELAND *Rustic Rampant* Wks. (1687) 459 The other Growtnolls of the Neighbourhood, subject to the Distress, or Seigniory of Saint Albans.

4. a. The chattel or chattels seized by this process.

[**1292** BRITTON I. xxviii. §2 Pur qe bestes et autres destresces ne soint mie trop loungement detenues enparkez.] **1411** *E.E. Wills* (1882) 20 Takynge a distresse in defawte of payment. **1512** *Act 4 Hen. VIII*, c. 11 If..no distresse sufficient there can be founde. **1568** GRAFTON *Chron.* II. 128 It was agreed..that the distresses taken for the same should be restored, and if any were perished by keping, then the Abbot to make them good. **1641** *Termes de la Ley* 124 Distresse is the thing which is taken and distrained upon any land for rent behinde, or other duty, or for hurt done. **1700** TYRRELL *Hist. Eng.* II. 1109 Neither the Beasts nor any other Distress..shall be sold..within fifteen days. **1886** REDMAN & LYON *Law Landlord & T.* (ed. 3) 238 The Landlord acquires no property in the distress, and it is an abuse of his power if he use the distress, except in the case of milch cows, which may be milked.

†**b.** *Old Law of Scotl.*: see quots. *Obs.*

1456 *Sc. Acts Jas. II*, c. 9 Item of gret stalls..of yᵉ quhilke yai haif use to tak yᵉ distress for the continuacione of yᵉ fare The quhilk distresses air to be delieuryt agane at the court of yᵉ fayr gif yᵉ persone has done na defalt nor distrubling in yᵉ fayr. **1710** *Summary View of Feudal Law* s.v., Distresses were pledges taken by the Sheriff from those who came to Fairs for their good behaviour; which at the end of the Fair or Mercat were delivered back, if no harm was done.

III. 5. *attrib.* and *Comb.*, as (sense 2 c) ***distress call, light, message, signal, signalling***, etc.; **distress committee**, a committee set up to help people in distressed circumstances; **distress-gun, -rocket**, signals of a ship in distress; **distress-sale**, a sale of distrained goods; **distress-warrant**, a warrant authorizing a distress; **distress work**, work provided for people in distress.

1826 SYDNEY SMITH *Memoir* (1855) II. 272 We hear nothing here but of distress bazaars and the high price of hay. **1913** *Year-bk. Wireless Telegr. & Teleph.* 319 Accumulators, enabling the ship to issue distress calls. **1970** *Times* 9 Dec. 1/1 (*headline*) Sea search after distress call. **1905** *Daily Chron.* 21 Sept. 1/7 The establishment of distress committees. **1891** *Pall Mall G.* 13 Oct. 4/3 The boat was launched one hour after the vessel showed distress flares. **1823** JOANNA BAILLIE *Poems* 199 The drear distress-gun moaning. **1885** *Encycl. Brit.* XVIII. 818/1 Inextinguishable distress-lights. **1921** *Discovery* Apr. 92/2 A distress message is preceded by a signal consisting of three dots, three dashes, and three dots sent as one sign, and repeated at short intervals. This is usually alluded to as the S.O.S. signal. **1868** LOWELL *Dryden* Pr. Wks. 1890 III. 139 Distress-rockets sent up at intervals from a ship just about to founder. **1883** *Pall Mall G.* 5 Apr. 10/1 This meeting desires to call public attention to the exaction of extraordinary tithes by the distress sale effected this day. **1873** *Porcupine* 6 Sept. 361/1 It is necessary for all craft to carry a gun for use in making distress signals. **1913** *Year-bk. Wireless Telegr. & Teleph.* 318 Distress Signalling. **1888** *Union Signal* (Chicago) 5 Apr., The number of distress and dispossessory warrants issued. **1905** *Daily Chron.* 13 Nov. 4/4 The distress work is not provided except in emergencies.

distress (dɪˈstrɛs), *v.* *Pa. t.* and *pa. pple.* **distressed**; also **distrest**. [a. AF. *destresse-r* (Statutes of Edw. III) = OF. *destresser*, orig. *destrecier*: late L. *districtiāre*, f. *district-us*: see prec. (See also senses 5 and 6.)]

1. *trans.* To subject to severe strain or pressure (physical, financial, or other); to put to sore straits, to embarrass; now *esp.* to afflict or exhaust, as painful exertion which puts a severe strain upon the physical powers.

13.. *E.E. Allit. P.* B. 880 þay þrobled & þrong & þrwe vmbe his erez, & distressed hym wonder strayt with strenkþe in the prece. **1483** *Cath. Angl.* 102/1 To Distresse; *vbi* to Stresse [To Stresse, *distringere*]. **1530** PALSGR. 522/2, I distresse, I put a thynge to an utter profe to trye whether it wyll holde, or endure, or not, *je destraigns*. **1570** LEVINS *Manip.* 85 To Distresse, *distrahere*. **1578** T. PROCTOR *Gorg. Gallery, Pyramus & Thisbie*, Distrest with woodlike rage, the words he out abrade. **1600** E. BLOUNT tr. *Conestaggio* 30 Seeing his souldiors distressed for water, he commanded them to lande and refresh themselves. **1611** BIBLE *2 Cor.* iv. 8 Wee are troubled on euery side, yet not distressed [**1881** R. V. straitened]. **1661** BOYLE *Spring of Air* II. iii. (1682) 38 Being sufficiently distressed by Avocations of several sorts. **1714** SWIFT *Pres. St. Affairs* Wks. 1755 II. I. 209 [The ministry] have been frequently deserted or distressed upon the most pressing occasions. **1771** GOLDSM. *Hist. Eng.* III. 228 The..servants of the crown..distressed their private fortunes to gratify their sovereign. **1791** 'G. GAMBADO' *Ann. Horsem.* xii. (1809) 113 But Looby [racehorse] being distrest by the severity of this, and the first heat, was forc'd to submit to his adversary..by half a neck. **1825** MRS. SHERWOOD *Old Times* I. (Houlston Tracts I. No. 24. 10) Does he not often distress himself in order to pay a good round sum to have him properly instructed? **1868** DICKENS *Lett.* (1880) II. 339 The railway journeys distress me greatly. **1886** *Times* 5 Apr. 7/2 Several of the oarsmen were fearfully distressed.

b. *transf.* and *fig.*

1721 PERRY *Daggenh. Breach* 7 Sullage..carry'd out without the Mouth of the Thames..there subsides..and distresses the Entrance into the Port. *Ibid.* 20 The.. Inconveniences which distress that Port. **1794** GODWIN *Cal. Williams* 25, I have seen..too many pastoral ditties distressed in lack of a meaning.

†**2. a.** To crush in battle, overwhelm, coerce. **b.** To harass or put to straits in war. *Obs.*

1489 CAXTON *Faytes of A.* I. viii. 21 Men ynoughe for to dystresse bothe hym and his grete oost. **1494** FABYAN *Chron.* IV. lxxi. 50 [He] was purposed to haue frayed with the sayd Maximus, and to haue distressed hym. *Ibid.* v. lxxix. 57 They than manfully issued out, & gaue to yᵉ Frenschmen harde batayll, but fortune was to theim frowarde, so that they were distressyd. **1568** GRAFTON *Chron.* II. 1308 At the length the rebels were distressed, taken and executed. **1630** *R. Johnson's Kingd. & Commw.* 245 The Duke of Savoy..on the other side distressing Genoa with an Armie. *a* **1656** USSHER *Ann.* VI. (1688) 259 But he passing the River, quickly distressed and routed them. **1709** STEELE *Tatler* No. 29 ¶3 Taking her as we do Towns and Castles, by distressing the Place. **1727** A. HAMILTON *New Acc. E. Ind.* I. xii. 137 The Portugueze large Cannon from their Walls disturbed and distrest his Camp. **1796** MORSE *Amer. Geog.* I. 290 Anson, with a squadron of ships..distressed the Spanish settlements on the western shore of America.

3. To constrain by force or infliction of suffering (*to do* a thing, *into*, *out of* something).

a **1400–50** *Alexander* 2781, I am depely distryssyd þis dede for to wirke. **1727** A. HAMILTON *New Acc. E. Ind.* I. ii. 18 They could have easily distressed the Boats Crews out of the Woods. **1742** YOUNG *Nt. Th.* II. Pref. (1787) 141 Yet is it an error into which bad men may naturally be distressed. **1788** A. HAMILTON *Federalist* (Webster 1828), Men who can neither be distressed nor won into a sacrifice of duty. **1829** W. IRVING *Granada* I. vi. 53 Muley Aben Hassan.. attempted to distress it [the city] into terms, by turning the channel of the river which runs by its walls.

4. To cause pain, suffering, agony, or anxiety to; to afflict, vex, make miserable. Now chiefly *refl.* or *passive*: cf. DISTRESSED *ppl. a.*

1586 [see DISTRESSED.] **1611** BIBLE *2 Sam.* i. 26, I am distressed for thee, my brother Ionathan, very pleasant hast thou beene vnto me. **1641** J. JACKSON *True Evang. T.* I. 77 We must not vexe ourselves..nor distresse ourselves with bootlesse problemes. **1741** MIDDLETON *Cicero* II. IX. 336 To ..take all measures of distressing him. **1800** MRS. HERVEY *Mourtray Fam.* III. 205 'Why'..said she, weeping..'why distress me thus?' **1884** FORBES in *Eng. Ill. Mag.* Jan. 235 The Emperor had asked where he was without a satisfactory answer, whereat honest Bazaine was sore distressed. *Mod.* The tone of your letter greatly distresses me. Do not distress yourself about the child, he is safe.

†**5.** To rob (of baggage, etc.); to plunder. Cf. DETRUSS, DISTRUSS. *Obs.*

[App. repr. OF. *destrousser*, perh. confounded with *destroisser* = *destresser*.]

c **1489** CAXTON *Sonnes of Aymon* iv. 116 All they.. that bare ony vytaylles, they were dystressed by theym [tous ceulx q' portoient viures estoient destroussey]. *Ibid.* He was ..dystressed of suche vytaylles as he hadde. **1546** *St. Papers Hen. VIII*, XI. 17 Our men distressed almost all their victualles. **1568** GRAFTON *Chron.* II. 373 [He] set upon them, and distressed them and their shippes and so brought them into dyverse Partes.

6. To levy a distress upon, subject to a distress-warrant; = DISTRAIN *v.* 7.

[Quot. 1440 may be in sense 1: in the later quots. the vb. seems to be a deriv. of the sb.]

c **1440** *Jacob's Well* iv. 28 Alle þo lay-men, þat..ony swych clerk arestyn, or dystressin, or enprisoun wrongfully. **1609** SKENE *Reg. Maj.* 78 The distres (or gudes poynded) sall remaine in the possession of the complainer, vntil it be discussed, quhither he is lawfullie or vnlawfullie distressed. **1707** J. JOHNSON *Clergym. Vade M.* 248 Quakers, who are liable to be distress'd. **1771** SMOLLETT *Humph. Cl.* (1815) 14, I will not begin at this time of day to distress my tenants, because they are unfortunate, and cannot make regular payments. **1823** *Blackw. Mag.* 703 His generous chief distresses him to the very blankets on his bed.

absol. **1811** *Monthly Mag.* XXXIV. 596 He..replied that the landlord might distress for the rent.

7. To damage (a piece of furniture, painting, etc.) deliberately, so as to make it appear older and often to render it more valuable as an 'antique'; hence, to introduce the effect of wear or age on to (a new material, etc.), esp. for a fashion garment. Cf. DISTRESSED *ppl. a.* d.

1943 H. READ *Politics of Unpolitical* iv. 55 In extreme cases he must 'distress' the piece—that is to say, employ a man to throw bolts and nails at the chair until it has been knocked about enough to look 'antique'. **1971** *Times* 8 Apr. 5/3 The forger..can..take a new piece of wood and 'distress' it by burning, warping and drilling 'worm holes' in it. **1981** *Times* 29 Apr. 16/3 Most of his paintings have gilded backgrounds, which he 'distresses', or burnishes, producing a slightly worn appearance. **1986** *Sunday Express Mag.* 12 Oct. 51/1 Fireplaces..are treated like pieces of furniture and distressed, stippled, hand-marbled and fussed with.

Hence **di'stressing** *vbl. sb.*

1599 MINSHEU, A distressing, *aprietamiento*. **1603** KNOLLES *Hist. Turks* (1638) 28 He put to sea a huge fleet.. for the distressing of the sea towns. **1633** P. FLETCHER *Purple Isl.* III. xix, So when a tyrant raves, his subjects pressing, His gaining is their losse, his treasure their distressing.

distressed (dɪˈstrɛst, *poet.* -ˈɛsɪd), *ppl. a.* Also 6–9 **distrest**. [f. prec. + -ED¹.] **a.** Afflicted with pain or trouble; sorely troubled; in sore straits. Applied *spec.* to a person living in impoverished circumstances.

1586 B. YOUNG *Guazzo's Civ. Conv.* IV. 219 Bitter teares, which copiouslie..fell from my distressed eies. **1597** HOOKER *Eccl. Pol.* v. lxvii. §12 That poore distressed woman commyng vnto Christ. **1601** CORNWALLYES *Disc. Seneca* (1631) 43 To heare the distresseds petitions. **1632** LITHGOW *Trav.* II. 51 Giving comfort to our distressed bodies. **1719** DE FOE *Crusoe* (1840) II. ii. 32 This distressed ship's crew. **1729** BUTLER *Serm.* Wks. 1874 II. 64 We..compassionate the distressed. **1838** THIRLWALL *Greece* IV. 311 His distrest countrymen. **1844** C. RIDLEY *Let.* (1958) xv. 180 Little round mats..which she works at all the evening as if she were a distressed gentlewoman. **1867** SMILES *Huguenots Eng.* vi. (1880) 89 Invitations to the distressed Flemish artizans to come over and settle in England. **1932** R. LEHMANN *Invit. Waltz* III iv. 202 It's all right, Aunt Sybil, I swear. Don't look so like a distressed gentlewoman. **1935** E. BOWEN *House in Paris* I. i. 19 A 'distressed lady'..jotting down what she spent. **1967** *Daily Mail* 17 Nov. 10/1 A field on the other side of Oxfordshire belonging to the Distressed Gentlefolks Aid Association. **1971** *Daily Tel.* 16 July 7/4 Distressed gentlefolk, daughters of a Harley Street surgeon whose legacy..could not or would not foresee inflation and a dearth of husbands.

b. Of actions or conditions: Pertaining to or showing distress; in straits, sorely straitened. ***distressed area***, a region where there is much unemployment.

c **1592** BACON *Confer. Pleasure* (1870) 22 Consider how benigne eare and correspondence she gaue to the distressed requestes of that king. **1625–49** *Declar. of Chas. I*, App. in Rushw. *Hist. Coll.* (1659) I. 1 The distressed extremities of Our dearest Uncle the King of Denmark. **1754** MRS. DELANY *Let. to Mrs. Dewes* 16 May, It would be unkind in me to leave her in the distrest way she is in. **1785** J. TRUSLER *Modern Times* I. 168 Their poverty and distressed situation. **1928** *Britain's Industr. Future* (*Liberal Ind. Inquiry*) I. ii. 20 The continued depression of these industries entails the unemployment, on a large scale, of many..workers..and raises acute problems in a number of distressed areas. **1936** *Discovery* Nov. 355/2 The development of newer industries is vital to the recovery of our distressed areas, which remain the one black spot in the otherwise remarkable position of Great Britain. **1942** *Times Weekly* 2 Dec. 15 If their 400 hat factories became derelict they would be a distressed area.

c. Upon which a distress is levied.

1896 *Westm. Gaz.* 24 June 3/1 The Government had never said they could discriminate between land distressed and land not distressed.

d. Of furniture: see quot. 1940. Also applied to decorative materials and paintings. orig. *U.S.*

1940 J. JUDSON *What Every Woman should know about Furniture* 33 If you're a real antique lover you can even buy pieces with 'distressed' finish—that is, with simulated marks of age and wear. **1966** *Daily Tel.* 4 Oct. 13/5 'We're using a lot of distressed furniture,' said the American designer solemnly... The current vogue in America is for furniture that has been bashed or scarred to make it look like English antique. **1967** *Boston Sunday Globe* 23 Apr. 23 (Advt.), Traditional lamps..rendered in..distressed wood finishes. **1967** L. J. BRAUN *Cat who ate Danish Modern* ii. 15 A sofa covered in distressed pigskin, like the hides of retired footballs. **1970** K. BENTON *Sole Agent* xi. 125 The rusty gleam of panels of 'distressed' mirror in a pair of double doors. **1970** *Cabinet Maker & Retail Furnisher* 16 Oct. 129/1 Heavily-distressed oak lowboy..has 12 full-working drawers with antiqued brass handles. **1984** *Times* 6 Mar. 10 (*caption*) Antiqued, toughened and distressed leathers give new interest to the uppers.

distressedly (dɪˈstrɛsɪdlɪ), *adv.* [f. prec. + -LY².] In a distressed or sorely troubled manner.

1890 *Temple Bar Mag.* Aug. 466 Her poor wandering brain is still distressedly labouring. **1893** MCCARTHY *Dictator* I. 178 Hamilton began distressedly. **1894** *Temple Bar Mag.* CI. 199 Emma is distressedly silent.

diˈstressedness. [f. as prec. + -NESS.] The quality or condition of being distressed; distress.

1592 WYRLEY *Armorie* 154 For fellowes many in distressednes Is to the greeuance much releasment. **1617** HIERON *Wks.* II. 380 Those extraordinary fits of distressednesse, with which God is pleased to exercise some of His. **1625** SANDERSON *Serm.* I. 133 Compassion to the poverty or distressedness of any.

diˈstresser. [f. DISTRESS *v.* + -ER¹.] One who distresses.

1617 AINSWORTH *Annot. Ps.* xxiii. 5 Thou fournishest before me, a table, in presence of my distressers. —— *Annot. Pentat.* Gen. xiv. 20 Enemies or Distressers.

diˈstressful, *a.* [f. DISTRESS *sb.* + -FUL.] Full of or attended with distress. (A literary and chiefly poetical word; not colloquial.)

1. Fraught with, causing, or involving distress; distressing; painful.

1591 SHAKS. *1 Hen. VI*, v. iv. 126 To ease your Countrie of distressefull Warre. **1604** —— *Oth.* I. iii. 157 Of some distressefull stroke That my youth suffer'd. **1750** JOHNSON *Rambler* No. 78 ¶5 What is above all distressful and alarming, the final sentence. **1820** SCORESBY *Acc. Arctic Reg.* II. 207 Night, a tempestuous sea, and crowded ice, must probably produce as high a degree of horror in the mind of the navigator, who is..subjected to their distressful influence, as any. **1860** J. P. KENNEDY *Horse Shoe R.* xix. 228 Subjects of distressful uncertainty.

†**b.** Attended with distress, gained by severe toil. *Obs. rare.*

1599 SHAKS. *Hen. V*, IV. i. 287 Who with a body fill'd, and vacant mind, Gets him to rest, cram'd with distressefull bread.

2. Of persons, their actions, state, etc.: Full of distress; marked by or indicating distress or suffering; in great distress, sorely distressed.

1601 MUNDAY, etc. *Downfall Earl of Huntington* I. iv b, Looke if you see not a distressefull man, That to himselfe intendeth violence. **1715–20** POPE *Iliad* XVII. 293 Wide The field re-echo'd the distressful sound. **1781** COWPER *Conversation* 116 Fix on the waistcoat a distressful stare. **1868** BROWNING *Ring & Bk.* IX. 969 At a safe distance, both distressful watch. **1883** *Fortn. Rev.* June 873 The most distressful districts lie in the west.

diˈstressfully, *adv.* [f. prec. + -LY².] In a distressful manner; in sore distress; distressedly.

1593 NASHE *Christ's T.* (1613) 44 Distressefully am I diuided from thee. **1611** COTGR., *Miserablement*, miserably, wretchedly..distressefully. **1775** JOHNSON *Let. to Mrs. Thrale* 17 June, I am distressfully and frightfully deaf. **1879** G. MEREDITH *Egoist* III. xiii. 284 Laetitia distressfully scribbled a line..to deliver to him.

diˈstressfulness. [f. as prec. + -NESS.] The quality of being distressful; painfulness.

1890 *Sat. Rev.* 23 Aug. 242/1 We cannot but smile a little at the vehemence of the actions..at the truly English distressfulness of the manner of taking amusement.

diˈstressing, *ppl. a.* [f. DISTRESS *v.* + -ING².] That distresses or causes distress; see the verb.

c **1586** C'TESS PEMBROKE *Ps.* LX. vi, Against distressing foes Let us thy succour finde. **1719** DE FOE *Crusoe* (L.), Under these distressing circumstances what could I do? *a* **1859** MACAULAY *Hist. Eng.* (1861) V. 228 The heat of a distressing midsummer day.

diˈstressingly, *adv.* [f. prec. + -LY².] In a distressing manner; distressfully, painfully.

1786 MISS CLAYTON in *Mrs. Delany's Corr.* Ser. II. III. 411 It was serious, but not distressingly so. **1865** LIVINGSTONE *Zambesi* xx. 408 Our progress up was distressingly slow. **1870** PROCTOR *Other Worlds* vii. 170 Prolonged and bitter frosts, contrasting so distressingly with the imagined geniality of his summer weather.

distrest, var. *distressed*, pa. t. and pple. of DISTRESS *v.*

distreyne, obs. form of DISTRAIN *v.*

†**diˈstribue,** *v. Obs.* [a. F. *distribue-r*, ad. L. *distribu-ĕre* to DISTRIBUTE.] = DISTRIBUTE.

c **1477** CAXTON *Jason* 70 b, Only for to haue distribued this so noble a londe. **1483** —— *Cato* E ij b, I counceyl the..that thou ne gyue ne distrybue thy goodes to thy children.

diˈstribuend. [ad. L. *distribuend-um*, neut. of *distribuend-us* 'to be distributed', gerundive of *distribuĕre*.] That which is to be distributed.

1874 SIDGWICK *Meth. Ethics* xi. 330 The social distribuend includes not merely the means of obtaining pleasurable passive feelings.

distribulance, var. DISTROUBLANCE. *Obs.*

distributable (dɪˈstrɪbjuːtəb(ə)l), *a.* Also 7 -ible. [f. DISTRIBUTE *v.* + -ABLE.] Capable of being distributed; see the verb.

1654 Z. COKE *Logick* (1657) 10 Words..significative..of the parts of the whole distributible. **1655** FULLER *Ch. Hist.* XI. vii. §99 The money gathered at the offertory, distributable by the English Liturgy to the poor alone. **1823** J. BADCOCK *Dom. Amusem.* 161 Imparting the full amount of the distributable carbon to the oxygen of the atmosphere. **1827** WHATELY *Logic* i. §5 *note*, He might have said that in such a proposition as the above the predicate is distributable, but not that it is actually distributed.

distributary (dɪˈstrɪbjuːtərɪ), *a.* and *sb.* [f. L. ppl. stem *distribūt-* (see DISTRIBUTE *v.*) + -ARY.]

A. *adj.* †**1.** Distinct, several. *Obs.*

1541 R. COPLAND *Guydon's Quest. Chirurg.*, For howe many distributary intencyons were they created?

2. Distributive; 'that distributes, or is distributed' (Worcester). *spec.* in ***distributary canal, channel, river.***

1846 WORCESTER cites WILLIAMS. **1926** *Spectator* 24 Apr. 756/2 To excavate additional distributary canals and field channels. **1954** W. D. THORNBURY *Princ. Geomorphol.* xxii. 584 Shoestring sands may be..river channel fillings, delta distributary channel fillings, [etc.].

B. *sb.* **a.** Something whose function is to distribute; applied to branch canals distributing water from a main one. (Cf. *tributary*.)

1886 J. T. WHEELER *India under Brit. Rule* 175 The Ganges canal..runs along the Doab..throwing out distributaries at intervals. **1891** *Cornh. Mag.* May 553 The great canal, of which the small channel..was a distributary.

b. A river branch which flows away from the main stream without returning to it, as in a delta; a similar branch of a glacier.

1863 J. FERGUSSON in *Q. Jrnl. Geol. Soc.* XIX. 328 One consequence of any such alteration in the course of the main stream is, that the initial or terminal oscillation of any tributary or distributary is continually altering its position. **1881** *Times* 16 Aug. 3/6 [A river's] breaking up into distributaries as it approaches the sea. **1954** W. D. THORNBURY *Princ. Geomorphol.* vii. 173 A river crosses its delta through a number of channels known variously as distributaries, mouths, or passes. **1957** G. E. HUTCHINSON *Treat. Limnol.* I. i. 76 The possibility that the glacier that filled the basin had a western distributary which cut the present outlet.

†**diˈstribute,** *pa. pple. Obs.* Also -ut. [ad. L. *distribūt-us*, pa. pple. of *distribuĕre*: see next.] Distributed (of which it was prob. at length regarded as a contracted form).

1434 *E.E. Wills* (1882) 99 To be distribute among porefolk. **1538** STARKEY *England* II. ii. 183 By them al byschoprykys and al hye offyce of dygnyte schold be dystrybut. **1552** ABP. HAMILTON *Catech.* (1884) 98 To be distrubit [? distribut] to thaim self. **1562** *Wills & Inv. N.C.* (Surtees 1835) 203 Sex pounds thirteyne shillings forpence to be distribute emongst ye poore of the parishe.

distribute (dɪˈstrɪbjuːt), *v.* Also 5–8 des-, 6 dys-; 5–6 *pa. t.* and *pple.* distribut. [f. L. *distribūt-* ppl. stem of *distribuĕre*, f. DIS- 1, in various directions + *tribuĕre* to assign, grant, deliver.]

1. *trans.* To deal out or bestow in portions or shares among a number of recipients; to allot or apportion as his share to each person of a number.

1460 CAPGRAVE *Chron.* 32 Josue..disposed and distribut the lond of behest to the puple. **1485** CAXTON *Chas. Gt.* 176 There he abode thre dayes in departyng & destrybutyng the goodes. **1574** tr. *Littleton's Tenures* 30 a, To distribut in almes to an hundred poore men an hundred pence. **1613** SHAKS. *Hen. VIII*, V. iv. 20 As much [beating] as one sound Cudgell of foure foote..could distribute, I made no spare Sir. **1736** BUTLER *Anal.* I. iii. Wks. 1874 I. 60 Happiness and misery..may sometimes be distributed by way of mere discipline. **1840** HOOD *Up Rhine* 37 Pray distribute my kindest regards amongst all friends. **1855** MACAULAY *Hist. Eng.* III. 546 The doctrine generally received..was that it was shameful to receive bribes, but that it was necessary to distribute them.

absol. **1526–34** TINDALE *1 Cor.* vii. 17 But even as God hath distributed to every man..so let him walke. **1611** BIBLE *Rom.* xii. 13 Distributing to the necessity of Saints.

†**b.** To dispense, administer (justice, etc.). *Obs.*

1607 SHAKS. *Cor.* III. iii. 99 Not in the presence of dreaded Justice, but on the Ministers That doth distribute it. **1698** FROGER *Voy.* 125 The Power of distributing Justice is vested in him. **1746** JORTIN *Chr. Relig.* iii. (R.), He will distribute rewards and punishments to all, proportionably to their behaviour in the days of their mortality.

2. To spread or disperse abroad through a whole space or over a whole surface; properly, so that each part of the space or surface receives a portion; less definitely, to spread generally, scatter. (In *pass.* often with reference merely to situation, with no idea of motion: cf. *diffused*, *dispersed*.)

c **1511** *1st Eng. Bk. Amer.* (Arb.) Introd. 33/1 They shall be dystributed or parted thorough all the world. **1615** J. STEPHENS *Satyr. Ess.* 229 A Spend-thrift..will promise much and meane nothing: for he distributes his words as commonly as Printers. **1620** VENNER *Via Recta* vii. 109 Those that are of a soft substance, are easily digested, and distributed. **1736** *Nature Display'd* III. 431 This subtle and active Element [fire] is distributed in great Abundance all round the Earth. **1875** *Ure's Dict. Arts* III. 657 (Printing Machine) The mechanism for supplying the ink, and distributing it over the form. **1889** A. R. WALLACE *Darwinism* 340 Mammalia may be said to be universally distributed over the globe. **1890** WORMELL *Electr. in Serv. Man* 49 On [non-spherical] shapes electricity is not uniformly distributed.

b. Said of the ramification of vessels, pipes, etc.

1659 *Vulg. Errors Censured* 32 Nerves..divided into.. Filaments, distributed after a most exact order throughout the whole Body. **1804** ABERNETHY *Surg. Obs.* 20 The vessels are distributed in their usual arborescent manner. **1869** E. A. PARKES *Pract. Hygiene* (ed. 3) 15 Water should be distributed not only to every house, but to every floor.

3. To divide (a whole or collective body) into parts having distinct characters or functions; to divide and arrange.

1553 EDEN *Treat. Newe Ind.* (Arb.) 25 He hath in his courte twelue thousand horsemen, whiche..distribute their wayting dayes after this order. **1611** BIBLE *2 Chron.* xxiii. 18 The Leuites, whom Dauid had distributed in the house of the Lord, to offer the burnt offrings of the Lord. **1643** 5 *Years Jas. I* in *Select. Harl. Misc.* (1793) 311, I will break and distribute the proofs. **1659** HAMMOND *On Ps.* civ. 8 Paraphr. 511 The earth [being] distributed into mountains and valleys. **1710** PRIDEAUX *Orig. Tithes* i. 13 The Law of Moses is usually distributed into these three parts: 1 The Moral, 2 The Ceremonial, and 3 The Judicial. **1776** GIBBON *Decl. & F.* i, That great peninsula [Spain]..was distributed by Augustus into three provinces. **1849** MACAULAY *Hist. Eng.* I. 294 The Life Guards..were then distributed into three troops.

4. To divide and place in classes, or other divisions; to classify.

1664 EVELYN *Kal. Hort.* (1729) 22 These we have distributed into the three following Classes. **1725** WATTS *Logic* I. vi. §10 A Politician distributes Mankind according to their civil Characters, into the Rulers and the Ruled. *Ibid.* II. ii. §7 Propositions..are distributed into true and false. **1857** HENFREY *Elem. Course Bot.* II. ii. §386 By the Linnean plan, the Flowering plants of Britain..are..distributed into 22 well-marked classes.

†**b.** *Arith.* = DIVIDE. *Obs.*

1593 FALE *Dialling* 27 b, The product 9101921907 I distribute by the whole Sine: and the quotient 91019 giveth an ark 65.ᵈ. 32.ᵐ, the Elevation of the Meridian. **1709–29** V. MANDEY *Syst. Math., Arith.* 16 To Divide one Number by another, or to Distribute one into another.

5. To separate and allocate to distinct places or compartments. *spec.* in *Printing*. To remove (type that has been 'composed' or set up) from the forme, and return each letter into its proper box or compartment in the case. Also *absol.*

1615 [See sense 2.] **1683** MOXON *Mech. Exerc.* II. 207 The compositer seeks ..for a riglet, a little longer than the line of the page he is to destribute, or else he cuts a riglet to that length (this riglet is called a destributing stick). **1736** *Nature Display'd* III. 364 The Types..being again distributed into their Boxes, serve to do the same Office to several others. **1808** *Post-Off. Law with Instruct.* (U.S.), Distributing offices, where the postmasters open the mails addressed Northern, Southern, etc., and distribute the letters into proper mails. **1888** J. SOUTHWARD in *Encycl. Brit.* XXIII. 701 (*Typography*) The operation of distributing the types is the converse of that of composing: it is de-composing the forme and returning the several letters to their proper boxes in the case. **1891** *Athenæum* 24 Oct. 558/1 The work is..published in a limited edition, and the type has been distributed. *Mod.* A compositor who distributes rapidly.

6. *Logic.* To employ (a term) in its full extension, so that it includes every individual of the class. See DISTRIBUTION 4 b.

[**1692** ALDRICH *Artis Logicæ Rud.* iii. §3. 5 Quare medium in præmissis semel ad minimum distribui debet. —— §3. 12 Distribuas medium; nec quartus terminus adsit.] **1827** WHATELY *Logic* ii. III. §2 The middle term..must be distributed once, at least, in the premisses. **1847** DE MORGAN *Formal Logic* vii. 137. **1849** MANSEL *Aldrich's Logicæ* 59 To say [as Aristotle does] that the major premise in fig. 1 must be universal, or one premise in fig. 2 negative, is equivalent to a rule for distributing the middle term. **1849** ABP. THOMSON *Laws of Thought* (1860) §77. 130. **1864** BOWEN *Logic* vii. 181. **1887** FOWLER *Elem. Deduct. Logic* iv. (ed. 9) 34 All universal propositions distribute their subject, whereas particular propositions do not. All negative propositions distribute their predicate, whereas affirmative propositions do not.

7. *Grammar.* To make distributive (in sense).

1876 MASON *Eng. Gram.* (ed. 21) §173 b, In 'they loved each other', *each* is in the nominative case, in the attributive relation to *they*, which it distributes in sense.

Hence **diˈstributed, diˈstributing** *ppl. adjs.*; **diˈstributedly** *adv.* ***distributed term, middle*** (see sense 6 above).

1641 MILTON *Ch. Govt.* vi. (1851) 123 That beneficent and ever distributing office of Deacons. [**1692** ALDRICH *Art. Log. Rud.* iii. §3. 4 Medium non distributum est anceps.] **1826** G. S. FABER *Difficulties of Romanism* I. iv. (1853) 114 Adoration paid to the elements after consecration, on the avowed ground, that those elements, jointly and severally, unitedly and distributedly, have now become the Supreme Being himself. **1827** WHATELY *Logic* i. §5 A term is said to be 'distributed' when it is taken universally, so as to stand for everything it is capable of being applied to. **1844** *Ibid.* ii. III. §2 Then the conclusion.. would have its predicate—the Major term—distributed, which was undistributed in the premiss. **1889** *Spectator* 9 Nov., To avoid the loss of time inherent in distributed workshops.

distribu'tee. *Law.* [f. prec. vb. + -EE.] A person to whom a share falls in the distribution of the estate of an intestate.

1870 PINKERTON *Guide* 45 Where an Administrator has money belonging to a distributee, whose residence is known, it is his duty to give notice of his readiness to pay it over. **1891** R. LINN in *N. & Q.* 3 Oct. 269 An Act of Congress was passed for the relief of the distributees of Col. Linn.

distributer: see DISTRIBUTOR.

distributible, obs. form of DISTRIBUTABLE.

di'stributing, *vbl. sb.* [-ING[1].] The action of the verb DISTRIBUTE; distribution.

1663 GERBIER *Counsel* 25 To be discreet in the distributing of them to some Carpenters. **1663** *Roy. Proclam.* 25 May in *Parl. Rep. Secr. Comm.* (1844) No. 582. 89 The conveying of letters, or the distributing of the same. **1888** J. SOUTHWARD in *Encycl. Brit.* XXIII. 701 (*Typography*) There is hardly any operation which so strikes a spectator as distributing, for a competent distributor literally showers the types into their receptacles.

b. *attrib.*

1683 Distributing stick [see DISTRIBUTE *v.* 5]. **1808** Distributing office [*ibid.*]. **1842** *Specif. Clay & Rosenborg's Patent* No. 9300. 2 The arranging or distributing machine. **1853** *Specif. Mitchel's Patent* No. 1287. 5 The types are to be taken in rows from the distributing machine. **1874** KNIGHT *Dict. Mech.* I. 710/2 The least that a distributing-reservoir should hold is half the daily demand. *Ibid., Distributing-roller* (Printing), a roller on the edge of an inking-table for distributing ink to the printing-roller. **1884** *Pall Mall G.* 17 Oct. 1/2 Goods..from that distributing centre [Hong Kong] are sent off to almost every market in China. **1888** J. SOUTHWARD in *Encycl. Brit.* XXIII. 701 (*Typography*) Distributing machines..in which the distributing is to a certain extent done automatically. **1891** *'Lightning' Gloss. Electr. Terms, Distributing Boards*, large blocks of paraffined wood, slate or similarly insulating material upon which are mounted the various switches, fuses, &c., connected with main or branch wires.

distribution (dɪstrɪ'bjuːʃən). [a. F. *distribution*, earlier *-cion* (13th c. in Hatz.-Darm.), ad. L. *distribūtiōn-em*, n. of action f. *distribuĕre* to DISTRIBUTE.] The action of distributing.

1. a. The action of dividing and dealing out or bestowing in portions among a number of recipients; apportionment, allotment.

1382 WYCLIF *Heb.* ii. 4 God witnessynge by sygnes, wondris..and distribucions [**1388** departyngis] of the Hooly Gost. **1413** *Pilgr. Sowle* (Caxton 1483) IV. xxxiv. 82 They taken hede of alle makynge suche distribucions, so that eueriche haue that hym oweth. **1538** STARKEY *England* II. ii. 183 The inequalyte of dystrybutyon of the commyn offyceys. **1662** STILLINGFL. *Orig. Sacr.* I. v. §8 Joseph.. made a new distribution of the whole Land. **1729** BUTLER *Serm.* Wks. 1874 II. 36 All shall be set right at the final distribution of things. **1770** *Junius Lett.* xxxix. 198 The crown..will lose nothing in this new distribution of power. **1894** *Times* 21 Dec. 11/5 The annual distribution of prizes and certificates to the pupils.

b. *Pol. Econ.* (*a*) The dispersal among consumers of commodities produced: this being, as opposed to *production*, the business of commerce. (*b*) The division of the aggregate produce of the industry of any society among its individual members, as in 'the unequal distribution of the fruits of industry'.

1793 tr. A. R. J. Turgot (*title*) Reflections on the formation and distribution of wealth. **1848-65** MILL *Pol. Econ.* Contents I. ii. §6 Labour employed in the transport and distribution of the produce. *Ibid.* Prelim. Remarks (1872) 12/2 The diversities in the distribution of wealth are still greater than in the production. *Ibid.* 14/2 The laws of Production and Distribution..are the subject of the following treatise. *Ibid.* II. i. §3 A system of community of property and equal distribution of the produce. *Mod.* By the system of middlemen which now prevails the cost of distribution is disproportionately great compared with that of production.

2. a. The action of spreading abroad or dispersing to or over every part of a space or area; the condition or mode of being so dispersed or located all over an area; sometimes without implying actual dispersal from a centre.

†In older Physiology (esp. before the discovery of the circulation of the blood), applied to the dispersal of the assimilated food to all parts of the body.

1589 PUTTENHAM *Eng. Poesie* III. xxv. (Arb.) 309 Helping the naturall concoction, retention, distribution, expulsion, and other vertues, in a weake and vnhealthie bodie. **1620** VENNER *Via Recta* v. 90 It is..hard of concoction, and of very slow distribution. **1727-51** CHAMBERS *Cycl.* s.v., The distribution of the food throughout all the parts of the body, is one of the wonders in nature. **1860** TYNDALL *Glac.* I. iii. 31 This distribution of temperature must..have some influence on the shape of the [hail] stone. **1875** *Ure's Dict. Arts* III. 657 (*Printing-machine*) There are three or four small rollers of distribution..by [a] compound movement they are enabled..to effect a perfect distribution of the ink along the table. **1877** HUXLEY *Anat. Invert.* 19 Certain areas of the earth's surface are inhabited by groups of animals and plants which are not found elsewhere..Such areas are termed *Provinces of Distribution.* **1885** DAVIDSON *Logic of Definition* x. 296 This Order..has such and such a geographical distribution. **1889** A. R. WALLACE *Darwinism* 340 How animals and plants have acquired their present peculiarities of distribution.

b. The occurrence of linguistic elements in a language, in terms of their characteristic position or context (see quots.).

1933 BLOOMFIELD *Lang.* v. 81 Non-distinctive features occur in all manner of distributions. **1951** Z. S. HARRIS *Meth. Struct. Ling.* ii. 15 The distribution of an element is the total of all environments in which it occurs. **1953** C. E. BAZELL *Ling. Form* 6 And if distribution is (as will generally be granted) the surest clue to semantics, it is neither a semantic unit, nor the basis of semantic analysis. **1964** R. A. HALL *Introd. Ling.* v. 26 By distribution, we mean the conditions under which the various elements (allophones, allomorphs, etc.) occur.

3. a. The orderly dividing of a mass or collective body into parts with distinctive characters or functions; the orderly arrangement of the parts into which any whole is divided; division and arrangement; classification.

1605 BACON *Adv. Learn.* I. vi. §5 (1873) 45 So in the distribution of days we see the day wherein God did rest and contemplate his own works, was blessed. **1668** HALE Pref. to *Rolle's Abridgm.* 6 The Common-Law..wants method, order, and apt distributions. **1712** J. JAMES tr. *Le Blond's Gardening* 201 Care should be taken in this Distribution, that the Fountains be disposed in such manner, that they may be seen almost all at a time. **1790** BURKE *Fr. Rev.* Pref. 4 A commodious division and distribution of his matter. **1856** EMERSON *Eng. Traits, Relig.* Wks. (Bohn) II. 96 The distribution of land into parishes.

b. *concr.* A division.

1829 SOUTHEY *O. Newman* vii, Omitting The minor distributions (which are many And barbarous all) suffice it to name these..the Pequods first; The Narhagansets [etc.].

c. *Statistics.* The way in which a particular measurement or characteristic is spread over the members of a class.

1854 *Amer. Jrnl. Sci. & Arts* 2nd Ser. XVII. 396 The very cause which determined the distribution of the atomic weights according to a numerical law. **1886** *Jrnl. Anthrop. Inst.* XV. 351 (*title*) The comparative distribution of Jewish ability. **1895**, etc. [see *frequency distribution* s.v. FREQUENCY 6 b]. **1959** *Chambers's Encycl.* XIII. 150/1 Further examples ..are distributions according to income, volume of trade, height and weight. **1971** *Nature* 18 June 416/3 The NSF survey gives the following distribution of graduate students by area of science..: physical sciences 18 per cent.., social sciences 21 per cent [etc.].

4. *Logic.* †**a.** In the earlier English writers used for what is now called DIVISION, i.e. the logical division of a genus (a logical whole) into the several species included under it; less properly, the partition of a whole into the integral or constituent parts contained in it. *Obs.*

1588 FRAUNCE *Lawiers Log.* I. xiii. 56 b, A distribution is when the whole is distributed into his partes. **1628** T. SPENCER *Logick* 143 When we say, a man hath two parts, soule and bodie: Living Creatures are reasonable, and vnreasonable, then we make a distribution. **1698** NORRIS *Pract. Disc.* (1707) IV. 194 Then he would have given us a full distribution of Immorality, to which all the instances of it might be reduced. **1725** WATTS *Logic* I. vi. §10 The word distribution is most properly used, when we distinguish an universal whole into several kinds of species.

b. More recently, after Scholastic usage of Latin *distribuere, distributio*: The application of a term to each and all of the several individual instances included in its denotation or extension; the acceptation of a term in a general sense including every individual to which it is applicable.

Said of a term qualified explicitly or implicitly by such marks of universality (*signa universalia*) as *all, each, every, any*, etc.; the one simple common term being treated as 'distributed' over all its significates; e.g. in *every man*, the term *man* is spread out over, or dispersed among, this, that, and every other individual man.

This use of *distributio* (which turns on the question discussed in Plato, *Parm.* 130 seqq.), first appears in the Schoolmen of the 13th cent., as Shyreswod, and especially Petrus Hispanus (1226-1277), of whose *Summulæ* the 7th chapter deals with the properties of terms, including Distribution, as an appendix to the exposition of the *Organon*, and with special reference to the solution of sophisms. The term apparently came into English logic through the medium of Aldrich: see DISTRIBUTE *v.* 6.

(The speculation in Latham's Johnson s.v. *Distributed* is wholly gratuitous, and ignores the history of the word.)

[*c* **1250** PETRUS HISP. *Summulæ* vii. 5. 1 Distributio est multiplicatio termini communis per signum universale facta, ut cum dicitur 'omnis homo', iste terminus 'homo' distribuitur sive confunditur pro quolibet suo inferiori.] **1827** WHATELY *Logic* i. §5 *'All* food', or *every* kind of food, are expressions which imply the distribution of the term 'food'; '*some* food' would imply its non-distribution. **1849** MANSEL *Aldrich's Logicæ* iii. §3. 4 *note, Distribution* is not an Aristotelian term. It forms part of what the Schoolmen call *parva logicalia*; a kind of appendix to analyses of the Organon; containing matters, some evolved from.. Aristotle, others complete innovations..The syllogistic rules concerning distribution are of course implied in Aristotle's account of each figure, though not enumerated separately, as common to all. **1864** BOWEN *Logic* v. 126 The distribution of the Subject depends upon the Quantity of the Judgment. **1887** FOWLER *Elem. Deduct. Logic* (ed. 9) iv. 34 The distribution or non-distribution of an attributive, as 'human', 'red', etc., follows that of the corresponding common term, 'human being', 'red thing', etc.

5. *Rhet.* (See quots.)

1553 T. WILSON *Rhet.* (1567) 95 a, It is also called a distribution, when we deuide the whole into seuerall partes, and saie we haue fower pointes, wherof we purpose to speake, comprehending our whole talke within compasse of the same. **1727-51** CHAMBERS *Cycl., Distribution*, in rhetoric, is a kind of description; or a figure whereby an orderly division and enumeration is made of the principal qualities of a subject.

6. *Arch.* The arrangement of the several parts of a building, esp. of the interior divisions or apartments. (Cf. DISPOSITION 1 d.)

[**1624** WOTTON *Archit.* 120 *Distributio* is that vsefull Casting of all Roomes for Office, Entertainement, or Pleasure, which I haue handled before.] **1727-51** CHAMBERS *Cycl., Distribution of the plan*, denotes the dividing, and dispensing the several parts, and members, which compose the plan of a building. **1876** GWILT *Encycl. Archit.* §2489 Distribution and disposition are the first objects that should engage the architect's attention, even of him whose great aim is to strike the attention by ornament, which can never please unless its source can be traced to the most convenient and economical distribution of the leading parts.

7. *Printing.* The action or process of distributing type: see DISTRIBUTE *v.* 5.

1727-51 CHAMBERS *Cycl., Distribution*, in printing, the taking a form asunder, separating the letters, and disposing them in the cases again, each in its proper cell. **1875** *Ure's Dict. Arts* III. 651 Distribution is performed four times faster than composition.

8. *Steam-engine.* 'The steps or operations by which steam is supplied to and withdrawn from the cylinder at each stroke of the piston; viz., admission, suppression or cutting off, release or exhaust, and compression of exhaust steam prior to the next admission' (Webster 1864).

9. *attrib.*, as **distribution board** *Electr.*, an insulated panel carrying terminals, fuses, etc., for controlling a number of subsidiary electrical circuits; **distribution map** (see quot. 1951).

1907 *Installation News* Apr. 11/2 The ordinary type of distribution board where the switches and fuses are enclosed under one cover. **1933** *Archit. Rev.* LXXIV. 202 Most buildings are now wired on the 'distribution board' method which collects all fuses together. **1947** J. & C. HAWKES *Prehist. Brit.* vii. 177 For all work of this kind..the prehistorian uses distribution-maps. In these the find-spots ..are plotted on a map. **1951** *Oxf. Jun. Encycl.* IV. 254/1 In recent years new kinds of maps have been developed to show such things as the distribution of rainfall, temperature, population, crops, and other things of importance and interest. These are called distribution maps, or statistical maps.

distri'butional, *a.* [f. prec. + -AL[1].] Of or pertaining to distribution, *esp.* to the geographical distribution of animals or plants. Hence **distri'butionally** *adv.*

1864 HUXLEY *Lect. Compar. Anat.* i. 2 The student of the geographical distribution of animals..would..dispose the contents of a Zoological Museum in a totally different manner: basing his classification not upon organs, but on distributional assemblages. **1880** A. R. WALLACE *Isl. Life* II. xix. 399 The mode of solving distributional problems. **1933** A. M. WOODBURY in *Ecol. Monogr.* III. 168 (*heading*) Distributional Units. **1936** *Amer. Speech* XI. 171/1 Mr. Zipf has succeeded in defining distributional factors and in demonstrating their significance in language. **1947** *Int. Jrnl. Amer. Linguistics* July 171 This procedure allows meanings to be catalogued in terms of distributionally defined units. **1951** Z. S. HARRIS *Meth. Struct. Ling.* ii. 16 Two utterances or features..distributionally equivalent. **1953** C. E. BAZELL *Ling. Form* 83 The view of traditional grammar that *he eats* and *he is eating* stand in immediate opposition is fully confirmed by distributional criteria. **1958** C. F. HOCKETT *Course Mod. Ling.* xix. 174 The..problems below are in what may be called pure distributional analysis. **1963** J. LYONS *Structural Semantics* ii. 11 The lexeme is a formal unit of grammatical analysis, established distributionally.

†**distri'butioner.** *Obs.* [f. as prec. + -ER[2] 2.] One who makes distribution; a distributor.

1650 ELDERFIELD *Tythes* 34 The only..distributioner that hath both given and setled several men in their several proprieties. *Ibid.* 43 Distributioners of property.

distri'butionist. *rare.* [f. as prec. + -IST.] One who advocates a system of distribution.

1836 DICKENS *Sk. Boz* (1837) I. 69 The distributionists trembled, for their popularity was at stake.

distributism (dɪs'trɪbjʊtɪz(ə)m). [f. DISTRIBUTE *v.* or DISTRIBUT(IVE *a.* + -ISM.] The theory or practice of the 'distributive state' (see DISTRIBUTIVE *a.*); = AGRARIANISM 1. So **di'stributist** *a.* and *sb.*; also **di'stributivism** (*rare*).

1915 E. BARKER *Pol. Thought in Eng.* viii. 223 Mr. Belloc's Distributivism. **1918** *Irish Theol. Q.* Jan. 102 Industrialism *versus* the distributist state—return to agriculture and handicrafts. **1926** G. K. CHESTERTON *Outl. Sanity* i. 30 Disquisitions throwing doubt on the detailed perfection of a Distributist State. *Ibid.* vi. 224 Several things that may bring us a stage nearer to Distributism. *Ibid.*, I do not claim that all Distributists would agree with me. **1933** T. S. ELIOT *Use of Poetry* iv. 73 Wordsworth then proceeds to expound a doctrine which nowadays is called distributism. **1953** *Universe* 31 July 6/4 It is Distributist to advance schemes of real co-operation among owner-producers. **1964** *English Studies* XLV (Suppl.). 214 It was Chesterton the Distributist and advocate of 'three acres and a cow'.

distributival (dɪˌstrɪbjuːˈtaɪvəl), *a. Gram.* [f. DISTRIBUTIVE + -AL[1]: cf. *adjectival.*] Of or pertaining to a distributive.

1868 KEY *Philol. Ess.* 4 In the passages..referred to, the distributival sense [of ἀνά] seems to prevail.

distributive (dɪsˈtrɪbjʊtɪv), *a.* and *sb.* [a. F. *distributif, -ive*, ad. L. *distribūtīv-us* (Priscian) apportioning, f. *distribūt-* ppl. stem: see DISTRIBUTE.]

A. *adj.* **1. a.** Having the property of distributing; characterized by dispensing, bestowing, or dealing out, in portions; given to or engaged in distribution.

distributive finding of the issue: a finding by a jury which is in part for plaintiff and in part for defendant (Wharton *Law Lexicon*).

1475 *Bk. Noblesse* 85 Wolde..God that every harde covetouse hert were of suche largesse and distributif of here meveable good and tresoure to the comon wele. **1732** BERKELEY *Alciphr.* III. §14 To endeavour to destroy the belief of..a distributive Providence. **1821** *Blackw. Mag.* IX. 323 A ready ‘Shelty’ stands in waiting by, Around the board distributive to fly. **1837** CARLYLE *Fr. Rev.* III. III. i. (1872) 100 The distributive Citoyennes are of violent speech and gesture.

b. Of, pertaining to, or designating a political system or state in which personal property is owned by the largest possible number of people.

1912 BELLOC *Servile State* 6 A reaction towards a condition of well-divided property or the *Distributive State*. *Ibid.* iii. 50 The State..was an agglomeration in which the stability of this *distributive* system (as I have called it) was guaranteed by the existence of co-operative bodies. **1919** G. B. SHAW *Matter with Ireland* (1962) 212 An economic Utopia which Mr Chesterton and Mr Belloc call the Distributive State. **1925** R. H. TAWNEY *T. Wilson's Disc. Usury* 19 Elizabethan England..is still, in a convenient modern phrase, a Distributive State.

2. a. Characterized by distributing or diffusing itself; having a tendency to diffusion.

1627–77 FELTHAM *Resolves* I. lxxxvi. 132 Wisdom and Science are worth nothing, unless they be distributive, and declare themselves to the world. Wealth in a Misers hand is useless. **1873** B. STEWART *Conserv. Force* iv. 106 If we reflect that heat is essentially distributive in its nature.

b. ***distributive fault***, a fault in which the displacement is distributed among several parallel planes at short distances from one another instead of being confined to a single plane.

1904 CHAMBERLIN & SALISBURY *Geol.* (1905) I. 494 Sometimes the faulting is distributed among a series of parallel planes,..thus giving rise to a distributive fault. **1955** W. L. RUSSELL *Struct. Geol. for Petroleum Geologists* v. 113 Step and distributive faults consist of a number of parallel breaks, each with a throw in the same direction.

3. a. Of, belonging to, or arising from, distribution.

1616 SURFL. & MARKH. *Country Farme* 363 The distributiue vertue of the Trees being occupied about many, must needs haue the lesse for euerie one, whereas when it hath but a few to feed, it dealeth the more bountifully. **1771** *Contemplative Man* I. 60 All the Sisters agreed..that Mrs. Barnes's distributive Share of her Father's Effects should be entrusted to Mr. Crab. **1813** G. EDWARDS *Meas. True Pol.* 13 A Local Agency appropriated to each distributive circle of the Kingdom. **1879** *Daily News* 16 Apr. 3/6 To use..the profits derived from the distributive business on manufacturing industry.

b. ***distributive justice***, one of the two divisions of Justice, according to Aristotle (the other being COMMUTATIVE); that which consists in the distribution of something in shares proportionate to the deserts of each among the several parties.

[The old Latin version of Aristotle's *Ethics* c 1250 renders διανεμητικὸν δίκαιον by *distributivum justum*; Aquinas, in his commentary on the text, has *distributiva justitia*.]

1531 ELYOT *Gov.* III. i, Justice..is..described in two kyndes or spices. The one is named iustyce distributiue, which is in distribution of honour, money, benefite, or other thinge semblable..Justice distributiue hathe regarde to the persone. **1581** J. BELL *Haddon's Answ. Osor.* 192 Neither doth God therfore offend in Justice distributive, if he have mercy on whom hee will have mercy: or if hee doe harden whom he will harden. **1586** T. B. *La Primand. Fr. Acad.* I. 370 Distributive justice consisteth in giving to everie one according to his desert, whether it be honor and dignitie, or punishment. *a* **1680** BUTLER *Rem.* (1759) II. 488 Nature..in her distributive Justice endeavours to deal as equally as possibly she can with all Men. **1791** PAINE *Rights of Man* (ed. 4) 74 Their ideas of distributive justice are corrupted at the very source.

c. Hence, applied to that part of substantive law, which is concerned with the determination of rights, as distinguished from the corrective, penal, or vindicative part.

1651 HOBBES *Govt. & Soc.* xiv. §6. 216 The civill Law (according to the two offices of the Legislator, whereof one is to judge; the other to constrain men to acquiesce to his judgements) hath two parts; the one distributive, the other vindicative, or penall. By the distributive it is, that every man hath his proper Right. *Ibid.* §7 The first of them [parts of a Law] which is called distributive, is Prohibitory, and speaks to all, the second which is styled vindicative, or pœnary, is mandatory, and onely speaks to publique Ministers. **1678** YOUNG *Serm. at Whitehall* 29 Dec. 7 The Civilians distinguishing a Law into parts, the Preceptive Part, which enjoyns the Duty, and the Distributive Part, which assigns the Punishment or the Reward.

4. Expressing distribution or division among individuals; *spec.* in *Gram.* Having reference to each individual of a number or class, as distinguished from the whole number taken together.

distributive adjectives, the words *each*, *either*, *neither*, *every* (the three first of which can also be used pronominally). ***distributive numerals***, in Latin, *singuli*, one by one, *bini*, two by two, etc.

1520 WHITINTON *Vulg.* (1527) 5 b, Nownes distributives: as *nullus*, *neuter*. **1530** PALSGR. Introd. 29, I speke also amongest the pronownes of nownes partityves and distributyves as *tout*, *nul*..*chascun*. *a* **1653** GOUGE *Comm. Heb.* i. 5 The distributive particle *which* (unto which of the Angels) implieth a number of Angels. **1818–48** HALLAM *Mid. Ages* (1872) II. 359 Dr. Lingard has clearly apprehended..the distributive character of the words *eorl* and *ceorl*. **1824** L. MURRAY *Eng. Gram.* (ed. 5) I. 247 The distributive adjective pronouns, *each*, *every*, *either*, agree with the nouns..and verbs, of the singular number only. **1881** E. ADAMS *Elem. Eng. Lang.* 68 Distributive numerals signify how many at a time. There are no separate forms to express them in English.

5. *Logic.* Referring to each individual of a class separately, and not to the whole class as made up of these individuals. Opposed to *collective*.

1725 WATTS *Logic* III. iii. §1 This sort of sophisms is committed when the word *all* is taken in a collective and a distributive sense, without a due distinction. **1863** E. V. NEALE *Anal. Th. & Nat.* 253 A defect..pointed out by the sagacity of Sir William Hamilton, namely, the absence of the distributive words ‘all’ or ‘some,’ in the predicates of its formal judgments.

6. *Math.* Operating (or expressing operation) upon every part in operating upon the whole; as ***distributive formula, function, operation, principle, symbol.***

1855 CARMICHAEL *Calculus of Operations* 8 A symbol Φ is said to be distributive when, u and v being two distinct subjects, $\Phi\ (u + v) = \Phi\ u + \Phi\ v$. *Ibid.* 11 Any algebraic function of a distributive symbol is itself also distributive.

B. *sb.* **1.** *Gram.* A distributive word: see A. 4.

1530 PALSGR. 74 Pronownes, unto whiche I joyne.. partityves, distributyves and numeralles. **1612** BRINSLEY *Pos. Parts* (1669) 102 All Relatives, Interrogatives, Distributives, Indefinites..do lack the Vocative case. **1874** MORRIS *Hist. Eng. Gram.* 98 *Distributives* express how many at a time, as *one by one*, *one and one*, *by twos*, *two each*, etc.

†**2.** That which is distributed. *Obs.*

a **1635** NAUNTON *Fragm. Reg.* (Arb.) 52 Parents..though they may expresse more affection to one in the abundance of bequests, yet cannot forget some Legacies, just distributives, and dividents to others of their begetting.

distributively (dɪsˈtrɪbjʊtɪvlɪ), *adv.* [f. prec. + -LY[2].] In a distributive manner or sense.

a. By way or by means of distribution.

1626 T. H. *Caussin's Holy Crt.* 42 He..distributiuely sowed it, vpon all the creatures of the earth. **1660** MILTON *Free Commw.* (1851) 450 Communicating the natural heat of Government and Culture more distributively to all..parts.

b. *Law.* So as to be distributed between two parties, each obtaining part of his plea.

1848 WHARTON *Law Lex.* 187 There are cases in which an issue may be found distributively, *i.e.* in part for plaintiff and in part for defendant.

c. In relation to each individual of a number separately; opposed to *collectively*.

1597 HOOKER *Eccl. Pol.* v. xlviii. §12 Wee cannot be free from all sinne collectiuely..yet distributiuely..all great and grieuous actuall offences..may and ought to be..auoyded. **1652** T. WHITFIELD *Doctr. Armin.* 66 The word *all* is here to bee taken not distributively for every particular man, but collectively for all sorts, states, and conditions of men. **1697** tr. *Burgersdicius his Logic* II. xxvi. 123 This Fallacy consists in the Word *All*, which if Collectively taken, the Major indeed will be true, but the Minor false. If the Word *All* is taken Distributively, the Major will be false. **1876** BANCROFT *Hist. U.S.* V. xlviii. 75 In Parliament, as the common council, the whole empire was represented collectively, though not distributively. **1889** ILLINGWORTH *Probl. Pain* in *Lux Mundi* (ed. 10) 114 The mass of animal suffering..is felt distributively. No one animal suffers more because a million suffer likewise.

d. *Logic.* In a sense in which the term is applied to each and every individual of a class. See DISTRIBUTION 4 b.

1773 E. BENTHAM *Introd. Logick* II. i. 39 The predicate of the former (Six) is affirmed of all the Planets taken collectively: that of the latter (opake Bodies) is affirmed distributively. **1834** WHATELY *Elem. Logic* (ed. 5) III. §II. 215 The middle term is used in one Premiss collectively, in the other, distributively. **1843** MILL *Logic* I. iv. §4. 114 When a general name stands for each and every individual which it is a name of, or in other words, which it denotes, it is said by logicians to be distributed, or taken distributively. **1864** BOWEN *Logic* v. §2 (1870) 121 A Universal Judgment is one in which the Predicate is affirmed of the whole Subject taken distributively. Thus *all men* (i.e. *each* and *every* man) *are mortal*.

diˈstributiveness. [f. as prec. + -NESS.] The quality of being distributive.

1661 FELL *Dr. Hammond* §2 (T.) That practice [of carving at the table] had another more immediate cause, a natural distributiveness of humour, and a desire to be employed in the relief of every kind of want of every person. **1884** SIR C. BOWEN in *Law Times Rep.* LII. 163/2 A great many other sections, where distributiveness is necessary.

distributivity (dɪsˌtrɪbjʊˈtɪvɪtɪ). [f. DISTRIBUTIVE *a.* + -ITY.] The character or quality of being distributive.

1940 W. V. QUINE *Math. Logic* 60 Distributivity always justifies an operation analogous to that of ‘multiplying through’ in arithmetic. **1947** H. REICHENBACH *Elem. Symb. Logic* II. §11. 47 The laws of commutativity, associativity, and distributivity supply the reason that these manipulations closely resemble algebraic transformations. **1965** PATTERSON & RUTHERFORD *Elem. Abstract Algebra* iii. 73 Associativity of multiplication in $M_{p,p}$ is a consequence.. of distributivity of multiplication over addition for real numbers.

distributor (dɪsˈtrɪbjʊtə(r)). Also 6 -our, 6–9 -er. [orig. f. DISTRIBUTE *v.* + -ER; conformed to L. *distribūtor*, agent-n. f. *distribuĕre*: cf. F. *distributeur* (14th c. in Hatz.-Darm.).] **1.** One who distributes: see the verb.

1526 *Pilgr. Perf.* (W. de W.) II. xxxi. 105 b, So true & feythfull a distributer of the counselles & graces of god. **1548** UDALL, etc. *Erasm. Par. Matt.* iii. 17 (R.) My derelye beloued sonne, the..distributer of my goodnes towardes you. **1578** *Chr. Prayers* in *Priv. Prayers* (1851) 559 Faithful distributours of right and justice to the poor commons of this Realm. **1614** B. JONSON *Barth. Fair* v. ii, A deuourer, in stead of a distributer of the alms. **1738** WARBURTON *Div. Legat.* I. 70 The equal Distributer of Rewards and Punishments. **1752** JOHNSON *Rambler* No. 204 ⁋2 Seged.. the distributor of the waters of the Nile. **1884** H. SPENCER in *Contemp. Rev.* July 42 Entire classes of producers and distributors, which have arisen through division of labour. **1888** [see DISTRIBUTING].

2. a. That which distributes; an appliance for distributing.

1853 *Catal. R. Agric. Soc. Show* 76 The best broadcast manure distributor exhibited. **1864** *Jrnl. R. Agric. Soc.* XXV. II. 525 Put manure on with distributor. **1881** HUXLEY in *Nature* No. 615. 345 The parts of the machine are merely passive distributors of that power.

b. *spec.* An electric cable from which lines run to the premises of individual consumers.

1901 C. H. WORDINGHAM *Central Electr. Stations* xviii. 186 The system of distributors should be as flexible as possible, since it is always preferable to lay them under the footways and near the buildings. **1929** G. W. STUBBINGS *Underground Cable Systems* vi. 71 The pressure drop in a distributor is fixed by the statutory limitations; in a feeder it is governed by economic conditions only. **1967** H. COTTON *Adv. Electr. Technol.* iii. 101 The main consideration in the design of distributors is the voltage drop.

c. A device in an internal combustion engine that passes the current to each sparking plug in turn so as to maintain the correct firing order of the cylinders; also *attrib.*

1905 T. H. HAWLEY *Motor Ignition Appliances* v. 29 The high-tension discharge from B, instead of going to the sparking plug direct, must first find the path open through the four-point distributor D. **1925** *Morris Owner's Man.* iv. 44 The distributor, the distributor rotating arm, and—at the driving end of the magneto—the end cover, should..be removed, wiped clean, and polished with a fine dry cloth. **1964** J. GRIFFITHS *Your Car* xi. 119 The distributor itself is simply a kind of switch, with a rotating arm that conveys the high-voltage supply from the coil to each of the sparking plugs. *Ibid.*, The contact breaker, condenser, and rotor arm are all part of the distributor unit, and are revealed by lifting off the distributor cap.

3. †Applied by Puttenham to the figure of speech whereby the elements of a description, or the like, are set forth one by one. *Obs.*

1589 PUTTENHAM *Eng. Poesie* III. xix. (Arb.) 230 A figure very meete for Orators..when we may..vtter a matter in one entier speach..and will rather do it peecemeale and by distribution of euery part..and therefore I name him the distributor. *Marg.* Merismus, or the Distributer.

Hence **diˈstributorship**, office of distributor.

1825 *New Monthly Mag.* XVI. 60 How did he get his stamp distributorship?

diˈstributory, *a. rare.* = DISTRIBUTIVE *a.* (3).

1827 JARMAN *Powell's Devises* II. 209 Until her distributory share were exhausted.

diˈstributress. [f. DISTRIBUTOR + -ESS.] A female distributor.

1632 J. HAYWARD tr. *Biondi's Eromena* 85 Being so bountifull a distributresse of your courtesies. **1634** SIR T. HAWKINS tr. *Manzini's Pol. Observ.* 28 Discretion ought to be the distributresse of these treasures. **1830** *Blackw. Mag.* XXVII. 423 The fair distributress.

†**ˈdistricate,** *v. Obs. rare*[−0]. [f. DIS- 1 + L. *trīcæ* perplexities, embarrassments: after *extricate*.] = DISINTRICATE. So †**distriˈcation.**

1632 SHERWOOD, To districate, *extriquer*. **1656** BLOUNT *Glossogr.*, *Districate*, to rid out of trouble or incumbrance. **1658** PHILLIPS, *Districation*, a ridding out of trouble.

†**diˈstrict,** *a. Obs.* [ad. L. *district-us* severe, strict, pa. pple. of *distringĕre* to draw asunder, strain: see DISTRAIN and STRICT.] Strict, stringent, rigorous; severe; exact.

1526 *Pilgr. Perf.* (W. de W. 1531) 263 b, Impossyble to perseuer & contynue in thy district or sharpe exercyse of vertues. **1583** STUBBES *Anat. Abus.* I. (1877) 46 Aristotle is so district in this point. **1656** SANDERSON *Serm.* Pref. (1689) 61 The most diligent, district, and unpartial search. **1700** H. J. *Salvab. Heathen* 26 A Righteousness consisting in a Condecency of his Goodness and Mercy, and not in the Rule of his district Holiness.

district ('dɪstrɪkt), *sb.* [a. F. *district* (16th c. in Littré) ad. med.L. *district-us* (1) the constraining and restraining of offenders, the exercise of justice, (2) the power of exercising justice in a certain territory, jurisdiction, (3) the territory under the jurisdiction of a feudal lord; f. L. *district-* ppl. stem of *distringĕre*: see DISTRAIN.

(The explanation of the 17th c. legal antiquaries, 'the territory within which the lord may *distrain*', is much narrower than the notion involved in *districtus*.)]

†**1.** *Law.* The territory under the jurisdiction of a feudal lord. *Obs.*

1611 Cotgr., *District*, a district; the liberties, or precincts of a place; the territorie, or circuit of countrey, within which a Lord, or his Officers may iudge, compell, or call in question, the inhabitants. [**1641** *Termes de la Ley* 125 *Districtus* is sometimes used for the circuit or territory, within which a man may be thus compelled to appeare.] **1670** Blount *Law Dict.*, *District*, is the place in which a Man hath the power of distreining, or the Circuit or Territory wherein one may be compelled to appear.. Where we say, *Hors de son Fee*, others say, *Extra districtum suum.*

2. A portion of territory marked off or defined for some special administrative or official purpose, or as the sphere of a particular officer or administrative body civil or ecclesiastical; e.g. a ***police***, ***postal***, or ***registration district***; the ***Metropolitan district***, ***London postal district***, that of a *Local Board* or *Urban Sanitary Authority*.

1664 Jer. Taylor *Dissuas. Popery* I. II. §1 (R.) The decrees of general councils bind not but as they are accepted by the several churches in their respective districts and dioceses. **1712** Addison *Spect.* No. 403 ¶2 The several Districts and Parishes of London and Westminster. **1834** S. Gobat *Abyssinia* 367 As soon as the son of a great man has learned to read.. his father gives him a district of a greater or less extent. **1847** *Act 10 Vict.* c 15 §43 Any offence which shall take place within the Metropolitan Police District. **1861** Flo. Nightingale *Nursing* 28 In healthy 'registration' districts, the mortality is low.

3. *spec.* **a.** in England: A division of a parish, having its own church or chapel and resident clergyman, constituted under the Church Building Acts, from 58 Geo. III, c 45 onwards. Hence ***district chapel***, ***church***, ***parish***. (See CHAPEL 3 b.) ***Peel district***: an ecclesiastical division formed under 6 and 7 Victoria, c. 37, 'having a minister licensed by the bishop and vested with limited powers'.

These ecclesiastical districts originally constituted perpetual curacies; they are now mostly for ecclesiastical purposes distinct parishes, being vicarages or rectories according to the status of the benefice out of which they have been taken.

1818 *Act 58 Geo. III*, c. 45 §21 In any case in which the said Commissioners shall be of opinion that it is not expedient to divide any populous Parish or Extra Parochial Place into such complete, separate, and distinct Parishes as aforesaid, but that it is expedient to divide the same into such Ecclesiastical Districts as they.. may deem necessary for the Purpose of affording Accommodation for the attending Divine Service.. to Persons residing therein. *Ibid.* §24 The churches and chapels respectively assigned to such Districts shall, when duly consecrated for that Purpose, become and be the District Parish Churches of such District Parishes. **1822** *Act 3 Geo. IV*, c. 72 §10 To act on the Vestry of such District or Division, and of the Church or Chapel thereof. **1855** Timbs *Curiosities of London* (1867), St. Peter's, Saffron-hill, a district church of St. Andrew's, Holborn. **1856** Walbran *Ripon, etc.* 110 A district parish has.. been assigned to this Church. **1866** J. M. Dale *Clergyman's Legal Handbk.* (ed. 4) 34 Upon the new church being consecrated in the Peel district, it becomes a 'new parish for ecclesiastical purposes'. *Ibid.* 35 The patronage of the Peel districts and parishes, until otherwise assigned, rests with the Crown and the bishop alternately.

b. One of the urban or rural subdivisions of a county, constituted by the Local Government Act of 1894, and having an Urban or Rural District Council.

1895 *Whitaker's Almanac* 667 (*Parish Councils Act*) The whole country will be divided into districts, some of which are borough urban districts, some urban districts other than Boroughs, and some rural districts, each of which will have its own council. Rural districts in most cases comprise a large number of parishes. *Ibid.* 669 Rural districts are those areas which occupy the whole of the country outside London other than so much as is included in any borough or any other urban district.

c. In British India: A division or subdivision of a province or presidency, constituting the most important unit of civil administration, having at its head an officer called 'Magistrate and Collector', or 'Deputy-Commissioner'. It corresponds to the *Zillah* of earlier times.

Generally, four or more 'districts' constitute a 'division' under a 'commissioner'; but in Madras presidency the districts themselves are the primary divisions.

1776 *Trial Jos. Fowke* 2/1 (Stanf.) Having a demand on the Dewan of the Calcutta District for.. 26,000 rupees. **1818** Jas. Mill *Brit. India* (1840) V. 422 (Y.) In each district, that is in the language of the country, each Zillah.. a Zillah Court was established. **1848** G. Wyatt *Revelat. Orderly* (1849) 67 The Planters.. in the Chumparan district. **1885** Hunter *Imp. Gaz. India* IV. 416 Farakhābād bears the reputation of being one of the healthiest Districts in the Doāb. **1886** Yule & Burnell *Anglo-Ind. Gloss.* 749 *Zillah*.. is the technical name for the administrative districts into which British India is divided, each of which has in the older provinces a Collector, or Collector and Magistrate combined, a Session Judge, &c., and in the newer provinces, such as the Punjab.. a Deputy Commissioner.

d. In U.S. used in various specific and local senses: e.g. a political division = election constituency, as an ***assembly***, ***congressional***, ***senate district***.

In some States the chief subdivision of a county (*civil, magisterial, militia, justice's district*), called in other States *townships* or *towns*. Formerly, in South Carolina = county; elsewhere, a division of a State containing several counties. Also, a division of the country, directly under the control of Congress, and having no elective franchise, as the federal District of Columbia; the District of Alaska (formerly Russian America).

1800 M. Cutler in *Life, Jrnls. & Corr.* (1888) II. 40 Much said about my being elected member for this district in Congress. **1802** R. Brookes *Gazetteer* (ed. 12), *Fayette*, a district of N. Carolina, comprehending the counties of Moore, Cumberland, Sampson, Richmond, Robeson, and Anson. *Fayetteville*, a town of N. Carolina, in Cumberland county, capital of the district of Fayette. **1809** Kendall *Trav.* I. ii. 10 The town-proper was of course the collection of dwellings; but, in the vulgar acceptation the same word embraced the entire district or township. **1890** M. Townsend *U.S.* 138 The District of Columbia (including the national capital of Washington); the District of Alaska.

e. The portion of country or of a town allotted to or occupied by any person as the sphere of his operations; particularly, a section of a parish allotted to a lay 'visitor', working under the clergyman. Also, *spec.* the area served by a maternity hospital or a midwife for home confinements; colloq. phr. ***on the district***: see quot. 1933.

1854 C. M. Yonge *Castle Builders* v. 64 The Miss Shaws.. have undertaken to get.. a district appointed for us to visit. *Ibid.* v. 66 Several excellent persons.. had attempted visiting and instructing the poor in his [*sc.* the vicar's] district. **1863** Mrs. Carlyle *Lett.* III. 162 Visiting about in their 'district', and attending all sorts of meetings. **1888** A. T. Quiller-Couch in *Echoes fr. Oxford Mag.* (1890) 104 There's no one to visit your 'district' Or make Mother Tettleby's soup. *a* **1897** *Mod.* For this purpose the town has been divided into districts, and two canvassers appointed to each. **1933** Partridge *Slang To-day & Yesterday* II. iii. 191 'Each of the London teaching hospitals undertakes the care of the parturient poor in its own district.'.. A student engaged on his three or six months' course of such midwifery is said to be 'on the district'. **1961** *Observer* 7 May 35/3 The different conditions which exist in maternity hospitals and on the district. **1964** G. L. Cohen *What's Wrong with Hospitals?* v. 87 'I'm me own boss on the district,' Nurse Bailey.. expounded the advantages of domiciliary work. *Ibid.* 109 Midwives on the District recommend bed-rest but cannot enforce it.

f. A territorial division of the Methodist communions comprising a number of circuits.

1831 J. M. Peck *Guide for Emigrants* 258 There are three districts, the Illinois, the Kaskaskia, and the Wabash districts, over each of which is a presiding Elder. **1839** [see CIRCUIT *sb.* 6]. **1885** [see *district meeting*, sense 6]. **1970** B. Drewery in S. G. F. Brandon *Dict. Compar. Relig.* 440/2 The Methodist constitution.. forms series of concentric circles, from the local chapels organised into 'circuits', each with a team of Ministers under the 'Superintendant', the Districts under 'Chairman', and the central authority of the annual Conference of 650.

g. With capital initial: short for the London ***Metropolitan District Railway***; also *pl.* shares in this railway. Also *attrib.*

1886 [see GAS *v.* 1]. **1898** *Westm. Gaz.* 29 Nov. 8/1 We cannot find any sufficient reason for the recent rise in Districts. **1902** *Ibid.* 29 May 7/3 To travel on the District from Ealing to the Mansion House and back, third-class, will in the future cost 8d. **1909** *Ibid.* 16 July 10/3 Districts were also good in tone at 17⅝. **1911** W. Owen *Lett.* (1967) 80 Transported to the other side of London by those wretched District trains. **1959** *Chambers's Encycl.* XI. 500/1 The District owned the south side of the Inner Circle from Mansion House to South Kensington... District trains reached Uxbridge over the Metropolitan.

4. Any tract of country, usually of vaguely defined limits, having some common characteristics; a region, locality, 'quarter'.

1712 Blackmore *Creation* II. (R.) These districts which between the tropics lie.. Were thought an uninhabitable seat. **1776** Gibbon *Decl. & F.* i, The most extensive and flourishing district, westward of Mount Taurus and the river Halys, was dignified by the Romans with the exclusive title of Asia. **1865** Lyell *Elem. Geol.* (ed. 6) 79 Districts composed of argillaceous and sandy formations. **1889** A. R. Wallace *Darwinism* 222 Species [of birds] which inhabit open districts are usually protectively coloured. *a* **1897** *Mod.* The roughest carriage road in the Lake district. A manufacturing district; a purely agricultural district.

†**5.** *fig.* Sphere of operation; province, scope. (In quot. 1704 used in *pl.* = limits, bounds.) *Obs. rare.*

[**1677** Hale *Prim. Orig. Man.* I. i. 28 This Principle of Life, Sense, and Intellection in Man called the Soul, hath the Body as its Province and Districtus, wherein it exerciseth these Faculties and Operations.] **1704** Swift *Mech. Operat. Spirit* Misc. (1711) 283 The first and the last of these I understand to come within the Districts of my Subject.

6. *attrib.* and *Comb.*, in sense 'of, belonging to, or allotted to a particular district'; as ***district-chapel***, ***church***, ***parish***: see 3 a.; ***district-judge***, ***school***, ***-superintendent***, ***-surveyor***, ***-visiting***, ***-visitor*** (whence *district-visit v.* (*humorous*).); **district-attorney** (*U.S.*), the local prosecuting officer of a district; **district-council**, the local council of an Urban or Rural District as constituted by the Parish Councils Act of 1894; hence **district-councillor**; **district-court** (*U.S.*), a court of limited jurisdiction, having cognizance of certain causes within a district, presided over by a district-judge; **district heating**, a method of supplying heat or hot water from a single source to a number of separate buildings or a whole district; **district nurse**, a nurse who serves a rural or urban district; so ***district nursing***; **district officer**, a representative of the Government in a colonial district; **district system** *U.S.*, a system of electing members to the House of Representatives by electing one member for each district of a State (see sense 3 d).

1888 Bryce *Amer. Commw.* II. II. xlix. 255 The local prosecuting officer, called the district attorney. **1839** *Act 2 & 3 Vict.* c. 93 An Act of the Establishment of County and District Constables. **1894** *Times* 19 Dec. 6/3 Returned at the head of the poll for the urban district council.. The village shoe-maker heads the poll for both the parish and the rural district council. **1895** *Whitaker's Almanac* 669 (*Parish Councils Act*) Urban District Councils are but urban sanitary authorities under a new name, and elected on the same system as town councils in boroughs. Rural District Councils are a new body, and take over the functions which guardians of the poor, acting as rural sanitary authorities, discharged in rural sanitary districts. *Ibid.* 670 The elections of guardians, and of urban and rural district councillors, are to take place under rules issued by the Local Government Board. **1802** A. Hamilton *Wks.* (1886) VII. 301 It abolishes the District Courts of Tennessee and Kentucky. **1908** A. G. King *Pract. Steam & Hot Water Heating* xxiii. 288 District Heating. This type, if it may be so termed, of steam and hot-water heating owes its inception to.. Mr. Birdsall Holly, of Lockport, N.Y. **1913** A. M. Greene *Elem. Heating & Ventil.* xi. 279 District heating or heating from a central station.. has been extended to heat towns or portions of towns. **1943** *Archit. Rev.* XCIII. 102/3 The district heating pipes by which a house and a whole estate.. can be centrally heated. **1970** *Daily Tel.* 7 Dec. 8/4 District heating costs more to install than individual heating systems but running costs are substantially less. **1828** Webster, *District-judge*, the judge of a district court. *District-school*, a school within a certain district of a town. *New England.* **1833** F. J. Shore *Notes Indian Affairs* (1837) I. 136 There were kazees.. who may be designated district judges. **1885** *Minutes Wesleyan Conference* 370 The Chairmen of Districts in their several District meetings. **1883** *Cassell's Family Mag.* Apr. 314/1 *District Nurses.*—Some seven or eight years ago, an Association was formed in London for providing a body of skilled and trained nurses to nurse the sick poor at their own homes. **1894** Mrs. H. Ward *Marcella* II. III. iv. 313 Marcella's Association allowed its District Nurses to live outside the 'home' of the district on certain conditions. **1957** *New Yorker* 12 Jan. 28/3 Terrified of infections and vaccines, she barred the door to the district nurse. **1883** *Cassell's Family Mag.* Apr. 314/2 She.. receives training in the practice of district nursing for a period of six months. **1956** in A. Pryce-Jones *New Outl. Mod. Knowledge* 220 So much can now be provided by way of meals, home helps, and district-nursing services. **1861** *Statem. Mat. & Moral Progr. India 1859–60* IV. xiv. §6 in *Parl. Papers* [265] XLVII, Appeal cases, exceeding in value 1,000 Rupees, do not come before the District Officers. **1931** A. R. Radcliffe-Brown *Method in Social Anthropol.* (1958) I. iii. 92 An officer of one of the African colonies.. was asked if it would be a good thing to give a training in anthropology to those who would ultimately become district officers. **1867** Smyth *Sailor's Word-bk.*, *District Orders*, those issued by a general commanding a district. **1793** F. Asbury *Jrnl.* 7 Mar. (1852) II. 186 Building a house for conference, preaching, and a district school. **1854** M. J. Holmes *Tempest & Sunshine* viii. 111 He handed him five hundred dollars, telling him.. to send her for two years to the district school. **1946** Partridge & Bettman *As We Were* 19 Only in the backward regions of the country does the district school still survive. **1889** G. Findlay *Eng. Railway* 14 In the more important districts the District Superintendents are relieved of the management of the goods business by 'District Goods Managers'. **1823** P. Nicholson *Pract. Build.* 368 The District-Surveyors are elected by the Magistrates. **1855** *Act 18 & 19 Vict.* c. 122 §49 There shall be paid to the district surveyors.. such other fees.. as may from time to time be directed by the Metropolitan Board of Works. **1816** *Deb. Congress U.S.* 20 Mar. (1854) 214 Under the district system, .. the weight of Pennsylvania, great as she is, dwindled down to a solitary vote. **1902** *Encycl. Brit.* XXXIII. 581/2 The House of Representatives is composed of members elected by popular vote... Each State is at liberty under the Constitution to adopt either the 'general ticket' system, *i.e.*, the plan of electing all its members by one vote over the whole State, or to elect them in one-membered districts (the 'district system'). **1854** C. M. Yonge *Castle Builders* vi. 78, I read to him about your plans for district visiting. **1935** *Scrutiny* IV. 116 No amount of observation of the district-visiting kind.. will produce a convincing substitute for adequate response to the quality of the working-class life. **1850** Kingsley *A. Locke* II. xii. 183 Katie had never heard of her before—'some district visitor' or other? **1870** Miss Bridgman *Ro. Lynne* I. iv. 43 'What are the duties of a district-visitor?'.. 'She scolds the men for frequenting public-houses, abuses the women for being idle and slatternly.' *Ibid.* 44 When I am ill, I shall.. be 'district-visited'.

'**district**, *v.* orig. and chiefly *U.S.* [f. prec. sb.] *trans.* To divide or organize into districts. Hence '**districting** *vbl. sb.*

1792 *Mass. Acts & Laws* (1895) 184 Resolve for districting the commonwealth, for the purpose of choosing federal representatives. **1828** Webster, *Districted*, divided into districts or definite portions. *Districting*, dividing into limited or definite portions. **1855** Motley *Dutch Rep.* Introd. xii. (1866) 40 The Netherlands like other countries are districted and farmed. **1869** *Daily News* 2 Sept., The town is in the hands of certain groups of lawyers, and is districted by them. **1882** *Ibid.* 16 June 5/4 Towns must be districted between them [electric-lighting Companies] as London is between gas and water Companies. **1888** in Bryce *Amer. Commw.* II. App. 648 Until such districting as herein provided for shall be made. **1891** W. K. BROOKS *Amer. Oyster* 195, I believe that the districting plan is neither a real remedy nor the best method for arresting the destruction.

† **di'striction.** *Obs.* [a. OF. *distriction* rigour, severity, arbitrary control (Godef.), ad. L. *districtiōn-em*, n. of action f. *distringĕre*: see DISTRAIN, DISTRICT *a.*] Strictness, severity, rigour.

c **1450** tr. *De Imitatione* III. x, I ȝaue all, & I wol haue all ayen, & wiþ districcion I require þankinges. *a* **1631** DONNE *Serm. John* v. 22 (1634) 10 Earthly judges have their districtions, and so their restrictions; some things they cannot know. **1660** R. COKE *Power & Subj.* 191 Justice and Secular distriction are necessary for the most part in Divine Laws and Secular Institutes.

[The erroneous sense 'Sudden display' in J., copied in later Dicts., is founded on a mistaken quotation of *distinction* as *distriction* in **1697** COLLIER *Ess. Mor. Subj.* II. xii. 118.]

† **di'strictly,** *adv. Obs.* [f. DISTRICT *a.* + -LY².] Strictly, stringently, severely.

1563-87 tr. *Pope Urban's Let.* in Foxe *A. & M.* (1596) 218 (R.) We send our mandats againe vnto your brotherhood.. districtlie..commanding you, that [etc.]. *a* **1665** J. GOODWIN *Filled w. the Spirit* (1867) 124 They..would not have been so districtly and austerely abstemious. **1678** H. MORE *Lett. Sev. Subjects* (1694) 28 He..has not had leisure to observe things so closely and districtly.

† **di'strictness.** *Obs. rare.* [f. as prec. + -NESS.] Strictness, precision, exactitude.

1586 A. DAY *Eng. Secretary* II. (1625) 59 [It] challengeth no such districtnesse..as was required in the other. *Ibid.* 110, I doe in all things commend fidelity and trust to be performed where by districtnesse it is challenged.

di'strictual, *a. rare.* [f. med.L. *districtu-s* DISTRICT + -AL¹.] Of or belonging to a district.

1849 J. M. KEMBLE *Saxons in Eng.* II. 106 We find no traces of any districtual or missatic authority to whom these officers could account.

† **di'strife.** *Obs. rare.* [f. DIS- 1 or 5 + STRIFE.] Strife, contention.

c **1450** *Merlin* 536 He wolde not haue..distrif be-twene hem two.

‖ **distringas** (dɪ'strɪŋgæs). *Law.* [a. L. *distringās* 'thou shalt distrain', 2 pers. pres. subj. of *distringĕre*, in med.L. sense, being the first word of the writ.] The name of a writ directing the sheriff to distrain in various cases.

The main forms are, in Common Law: **a.** The *distringas* to compel appearance, where defendant has a place of residence in England or Wales. **b.** The *distringas in detinue*, to compel the defendant to deliver goods by distresses upon his chattels. **c.** *distringas juratores*, empowering the sheriff to distrain defaulting jurors to compel their appearance. In Equity: **d.** A process issued against a corporation aggregate in cases of disobedience to the summons or directions of the court. **e.** An order of the Chancery Court by which the Bank of England or other public company is restrained from permitting a transfer of stock or shares in which a party claims to be interested, or from paying any dividend on it.

1467 *Ord. Worcester* in *Eng. Gilds* 391 That no seriaunt [take] of eny citizen for servynge of a venire facias, habeas corpore and destringas, for alle but vj d. **1607** MIDDLETON *Phœnix* II. iii. Wks. 1885 I. 157 Get your distringas out as soon as you can for a jury. **1641** *Art. agst. Sir H. Davenport* in Rushw. *Hist. Coll.* III. (1692) I. 336 Writs of Distringas.. ..directed to the several High Sheriffs of the said County of York; whereby the said Sheriffs were commanded further to distrain the said James Maleverer to appear as aforesaid. **1641** *Termes de la Ley* 125 Distringas is a Writ directed to the Sheriffe or any other officer, commanding him to distreine for a debt to the King, &c. or for his appearing at a day. **1714** SCROGGS *Courts-Leet* (ed. 3) 172 An Attachment or Distringas to attach his Goods. **1768** BLACKSTONE *Comm.* III. xxvii. (Jod.), The process against a body corporate is by distringas to distrain them by their goods and chattels, rents, and profits, till they shall obey the summons or directions of the court. **1857** J. T. SMITH *Parish* 50 A distringas shall issue against the inhabitants to make them repair it [bridge, highway etc.].

Hence **distringas** *v. trans.*, to restrain by a distringas.

1895 *Law Times* XCIX. 533/2.

‖ **distrix** ('dɪstrɪks). *Med.* [mod.L., f. Gr. δίς twice (DI-²) + θρίξ hair.] A disease of the hair, in which it splits and divides at the end.

1811 in HOOPER *Med. Dict.* **1822** J. M. GOOD *Study Med.* (1834) IV. 517 The terms athrix and distrix..express two of the species under this genus.

distrou, distrowe, etc., obs. ff. DESTROY.

† **di'stroublance.** *Obs.* Forms: 5 distroblans, -troybulance, -trublance, 5-6 -troublance, -tribulance. [f. next + -ANCE; prob. after a corresponding F. form: cf. the earlier DISTURBLANCE.] Disturbance, molestation.

a **1400** *Burgh Laws* l. (*Sc. Stat.* I) Na greyff nor na distroblans [*molestia*]. *c* **1425** WYNTOUN *Cron.* VIII. xliv. 4 Makand fellown Distroybulance. **1487** JAS. III *Let.* in C. Innes *Sk. Early Sc. Hist.* (1861) 393 Mak him nane impediment, letting nor distroublance. **15..** *Exam. W. Thorpe* in Arb. *Garner* VI. 80 They..may..be the more fervent [when] that all their outward wits be closed from all outward seeing and hearing, and from all distroublance and lettings. **1572** in *Muniments Burgh of Irvine* (1891) II. 17 The saidis provest and baillies..sall..cognosce and decerne thair apoun the wrang and distribulance of the burgh.

† **di'strouble,** *v. Obs.* Also des-, dys- -troble, -trowbel, -truble, -trubill, -trybul. [ME. a. OF. *destrobler*, *-troubler*, f. *des-*, L. *dis-* + *trobler*, *troubler* to TROUBLE. An etymologically earlier OF. form of the latter was *torbler*, *turbler*, *tourbler* (:—L. **turbulāre*), whence the earlier ME. type *desturble*, *-tourble*, DISTURBLE. *Trouble* had become at an early date the prevalent form of the simple vb., and *distrouble* gradually superseded *disturble*, but itself scarcely survived to 1600. Sc. *distrybul*, *distribulance*, etc., were app. associated with L. *tribulāre* to afflict, oppress.]

trans. To disturb, trouble greatly.

c **1369** CHAUCER *Dethe Blaunche* 524, I am ryght sory yif I have oughte Destroubled yow out of your thoughte. *c* **1375** *Sc. Leg. Saints, Alexis* 421 þu has distrybulyt me. *a* **1400-50** *Alexander* 3167* As wawes of þe wild see when wynd þaim distrobles. **1413** *Pilgr. Sowle* (Caxton 1483) III. iv. 53 Thus haue ye by your fals confederacy destroubled my Royamme. *c* **1500** *Lancelot* 1292 Furth he goith, distrublit in his hart. **1565** GOLDING *Ovid's Met.* XIII. (1593) 320 A brooke with raine distroubled new. **1609** SKENE *Reg. Maj.* 101, I defend ..that na man distrouble this court vnlawfullie, vnder the paine that may follow. [W. TENNANT *Papistry Storm'd* (1827) 102 Me had thir Lollards no distrubill'd My denner had been nearly doubl'd.]

Hence † **di'stroubled** *ppl. a.*, † **di'stroubling** *vbl. sb.*

1375 BARBOUR *Bruce* v. 216 The persy..went vith thaim ..his castell till, Vithout distrowbilling or Ill. **1491** CAXTON *Vitas Patr.* (W. de W. 1495) I. xliv. 75 a/1 She..hathe noo dystrowblynge ne empeshement. **1590** SPENSER *F.Q.* III. iv. 12 Coosen passions of distroubled spright.

† **di'strouble,** *sb. Obs. rare.* [f. prec. vb.] Disturbance, molestation.

c **1450** *Merlin* 545 No distrouble thei ne hadde till thei com to Roestok. **1483** CAXTON *Gold. Leg.* 306/1 To constrayne Impedymentes & destroubles [L. *infestantia*].

† **di'stroubler.** *Obs.* [f. prec. *v.* + -ER: cf. DISTURBLER.] One who troubles or disturbs.

c **1440** *Promp. Parv.* 123/2 Dystrobelar of þe pece [*v.r.* disturbeler], *turbator, perturbator.* **15..** *Exam. W. Thorpe* in Arb. *Garner* VI. 56 All such distroublers of Holy Church.

distrue, distruie, obs. ff. DESTROY.

† **dis'truss,** *v. Obs.* [ad. OF. *destrousser* to unpack (mod.F. *détrousser* to unfasten), f. *des-* (DIS- 4) + *trousser* to pack, TRUSS.]

trans. To strip or plunder; hence, to deafeat, rout. Also *fig.*

c **1430** LYDG. *Bochas* VI. vi. (1554) 144 a, The distrussing of hys chiualrie. *Ibid.* VI. ix. (1554) 155 a, Pompey.. Distrussed was, by sodeyn death. **1476** SIR J. PASTON in *Paston Lett.* No. 776 III. 162 The Swechys..berded hym at an onsett place, and hathe dystrussyd hym. **1527** *St. Papers Hen. VIII*, I. 238 Monʳ Mont had distrussed, taken, and brent 2 grete carrikes of Ieane [Genoa].

b. To seize or carry off as plunder.

1548 HALL *Chron., Hen. VIII*, (an. 5) (1809) 539 So thei distrussed the victailes and caused Sir Nicholas Vaux..to flei toward Guisnes.

distrust (dɪs'trʌst), *sb.* [f. DIS- 9 + TRUST *sb.*: cf. next.] Absence or want of trust; lack of confidence, faith, or reliance; doubt, suspicion.

1513 MORE in Grafton *Chron.* (1568) II. 809 Eche..in such hatred and distrust of other. **1581** PETTIE *Guazzo's Civ. Conv.* I. 19 b, Through distrust in himselfe, or for some other defect. **1659** B. HARRIS *Iron Age* 291 The Germans, by their dissentions, and distrusts, have very much weakned the Empire. **1752** JOHNSON *Rambler* No. 194 ¶10 So little distrust has my pupil of his own abilities. **1798** SOUTHEY *Sonnets* xi, Beware a speedy friend, the Arabian said, And wisely was it he advised distrust. **1849** MACAULAY *Hist. Eng.* I. 258 A deep mutual distrust which had been many years growing..made a treaty impossible.

b. The fact of being distrusted; loss of credit.

1667 MILTON *P.L.* XI. 166 To mee reproach Rather belongs, distrust and all dispraise.

c. Breach of trust, the proving false to trust.

1667 MILTON *P.L.* IX. 6 Foul distrust and breach Disloyal on the part of Man, revolt, And disobedience.

distrust (dɪs'trʌst), *v.* [f. DIS- 6 + TRUST *v.*; perh. after L. *diffidere*. Found intrans. in Lydgate, but app. not in ordinary use till the 16th c.]

† **1.** *intr.* **a.** with *of*: To have a doubt or dread of; to suspect. [Cf. OF. *difier de.*] *Obs.*

1430 LYDG. *Chron. Troy* I. vi, I durst not, distrustyng of myschyefe, Accomplyshe it whan it came to the prefe.

† **b.** with *of, in, to*: To be without confidence in.

1576 FLEMING *Panopl. Epist.* 25 To write more touching this point, I..am ashamed, least I should seeme to distrust of your wisedome. **1582** N. LICHEFIELD tr. *Castanheda's Conq. E. Ind.* lxxi. 144 Howe sadde and heauie..he went away distrusting in the victory. **1654** R. CODRINGTON tr. *Ivstine* 231 Distrusting to their arms. *Ibid.*, Distrusting to the Macedons. **1671** H. M. tr. *Colloq. Erasm.* 208 Distrusting in mine own strength, I wholly rely upon him.

† **c.** with *for*: To doubt or fear for the safety of. *Obs.*

1693 *Mem. Ct. Teckely* I. 3 *marg.*, The Hungarians distrust for their Civil Priviledges.

2. *trans.* To do the opposite of trusting; to withhold trust or confidence from; to put no trust in, or reliance on, the statements or evidence of.

1548 UDALL, etc. *Erasm. Par.* Matt. v. (R.), He yᵗ requireth yᵉ othe doeth distrust that other partie. **1601** SHAKS. *Twel. N.* IV. iii. 13, I am readie to distrust mine eyes, And wrangle with my reason that perswades me To any other trust. **1710** BERKELEY *Princ. Hum. Knowl.* §88 We see philosophers distrust their senses, and doubt of the existence of heaven and earth. **1776** GIBBON *Decl. & F.* I. xix. 506 He feared his generals, and distrusted his ministers. **1850** PRESCOTT *Peru* II. 241 Any one who has occasion to compare his narrative with that of contemporary writers will find frequent cause to distrust it.

absol. **1602** SHAKS. *Ham.* III. ii. 175 Though I distrust, Discomfort you (my Lord) it nothing must.

b. To entertain doubts concerning; to call in question the reality, validity, or genuineness of; not to rely upon.

1586 A. DAY *Eng. Secretary* I. (1625) 87 Thy knowne good will..assureth me not to distrust the same at thy hands. **1611** BIBLE *2 Macc.* ix. 22 Not distrusting mine health, but hauing great hope to escape this sicknes. **1781** GIBBON *Decl. & F.* III. 63 A tyrant, whose..officers appeared to distrust, either the justice, or the success, of his arms. **1875** JOWETT *Plato* (ed. 2) I. 28, I altogether distrust my own power of determining this.

† **c.** with *inf.* Not to trust, to have no confidence. *Obs.*

1626 C. POTTER tr. *Sarpi's Hist. Quarrels* 144 The Pope, distrusting to obtaine from Spaine that which he desired. **1642** MILTON *Apol. Smect.* Wks. 1738 I. 103, I shall not distrust to be acquitted of presumption.

† **3.** with *infin. phr.* or *clause*: To have suspicion; to suspect. *Obs.*

1628 WITHER *Brit. Rememb.* Pref. 190 Distrust, that we discry their secret'st plots. **1660** F. BROOKE tr. *Le Blanc's Trav.* 292 The Arabians, whom he distrusted to be of his nephews party. **1707** *Curios. in Husb. & Gard.* 331, I distrust that Monconys had added something of his own to what Kircherus told him.

Hence **dis'trusted** *ppl. a.*, **dis'trusting** *vbl. sb.* and *ppl. a.*

1549 COVERDALE, etc. *Erasm. Par.* Jas. i. 6 (R.), Let him ask without distrusting, without doubt or wauering. **1611** FLORIO, *Sfidato*, challenged, defied, distrusted. **1614** BP. HALL *Recoll. Treat.* 97 A base and distrusting mind. **1651** JER. TAYLOR *Holy Dying* iv. §1 (R.), God hath created the physician for thine [need]: therefore use him..without uncivil distrustings. **1837** ROBT. WILSON *Pleas. Piety* II. 34 Distrusting Man! Behold this marvellous sight.

dis'truster. [f. prec. vb. + -ER¹.] One who distrusts.

1636 HENSHAW *Horæ Succ.* 127 When our Saviour would put to silence the distrusters of his time. **1889** *Forum* (U.S.) Jan. 502 Distrusters of human nature. **1893** *Westm. Gaz.* 22 Nov. 7/2 Distrusters of trades unions.

distrustful (dɪs'trʌstfʊl), *a.* [f. DISTRUST *sb.* + -FUL.]

1. Full of or marked by distrust in oneself or others; wanting in confidence, diffident; doubtful, suspicious, incredulous.

1591 SHAKS. *1 Hen. VI*, I. ii. 127 Distrustfull Recreants, Fight till the last gaspe: Ile be your guard. *a* **1600** HOOKER *Serm. Faith in Elect* Wks. 1888 III. 473 By distrustful and doubtful apprehending of that, which we ought stedfastly to believe. **1654** TRAPP *Comm. Ps.* xxvii. 1 Faith fortifieth the heart against distrustful fears. **1748** CHESTERF. *Lett.* (1792) II. clxi. 82 Being justly distrustful that men in general look upon them in a trifling light. **1810** SOUTHEY *Kehama* VI. vi, Distrustful of the sight, She moves not, fearing to disturb The deep and full delight. **1856** KANE *Arct. Expl.* II. x. 103, I became..distrustful as to the chance of our ever living to gain the open water.

2. Causing or giving rise to distrust. (Cf. *suspicious, fearful, doubtful*, in analogous use.) *rare.*

1618 *Hist. P. Warbeck* in *Select. Harl. Misc.* (1793) 70 Loth to remain amongst such distrustful enemies, he quietly returned to his most assured friend, the lady Margaret. **1685** *Lond. Gaz.* No. 2100/5 In despight of all Turbulent, Seditious, and Distrustful Principles. **1840** DICKENS *Old C. Shop* xv, Places that had shown ugly and distrustful all night long, now wore a smile.

dis'trustfully, *adv.* [f. prec. + -LY².] In a distrustful manner; with distrust; suspiciously.

1611 COTGR., *Souspeçonneusement*, suspitiously, distrustfully. **1612** T. TAYLOR *Comm. Titus* ii. 12 Neither be so distrustfully prouident, as though thou hadst no father to prouide for thee. **1653** MILTON *Psalms* iii. 5 Many are they That of my life distrustfully thus say, 'No help for him in God there lies'. **1859** DICKENS *T. Two Cities* I. ii, The guard ..and the two other passengers eyed him distrustfully.

dis'trustfulness. [f. as prec. + -NESS.] The quality or state of being distrustful; want of confidence, diffidence; suspiciousness.

1577 tr. *Bullinger's Decades* (1592) 500 Originall sinne, that is the hatred of God..foolishnesse, distrustfulnesse, desperation. **1631** GOUGE *God's Arrows* III. §80. 336 Distrustfulnesse, and doubting of good successe. **1860** W. COLLINS *Wom. White* III. iv. 444 Whom the ceaseless distrustfulness of their governments had followed privately.

† **dis'trustiness.** *Obs. rare*⁻¹. [f. an assumed adj. **distrusty* (f. DIS- 10 + TRUSTY) + -NESS.] = prec.

1579 TWYNE *Phisicke agst. Fort.* II. cxix. 321 a, He applied him selfe vnto the want of fayth in him, with whom he communed, or the distrustinesse of the time in which he liued.

† **dis'trustless,** *a. Obs.* [f. DISTRUST *sb.* + -LESS.] Void of distrust, doubt, or suspicion; confident; unsuspecting.

1611 SPEED *Hist. Gt. Brit.* IX. viii. §48 [This] made him distrustlesse of attaining easily his wished successe. **1615** G. SANDYS *Trav.* IV. 234 Droue the distrustlesse Turkes..into the sterne. **1728** MORGAN *Algiers* I. Pref. 13 Distrustless Hans was seized on. *a* **1763** SHENSTONE *Economy* I. 66 Poets ..distrustless, scorn the treasured gold.

distruy(e, distrye, obs. forms of DESTROY.

distuing, var. DISTINGUE *v. Obs.*

distune (dɪs'tjuːn), *v.* [f. DIS- 6 or 7 + TUNE.] *trans.* To put out of tune. Hence **di'stuned** *ppl. a.*

c **1484** CAXTON *Lyfe Our Ladye* D iv/2 (R. Supp.), The clapper of his distuned belle. **1598** SYLVESTER *Du Bartas* II. i. *Furies* Argt., Their Harmonie dis-tuned by His iarre. **1664** J. WILSON *Andronicus Comnenius* II. iii, Distune a viol, And you may set it to what tone you please. **1755** PEARSALL *Contempl. Harvest* (ed. 2) I. 177 His harp..distuned in every string. **1887** SWINBURNE *Locrine* IV. i. 209 A broken chord Whose jar distunes the music.

fig. **1586** A. DAY *Eng. Secretary* I. (1625) 96 Where the spirits are so distuned. **1667** FLAVEL *Saint Indeed* (1754) 94 It [anger] distunes the spirit for duty. **1801** LAMB *J. Woodvil* IV, O most distuned and distempered world. **1887** SWINBURNE *Locrine* I. i. 292 What thought distempers and distunes thy woe?

disturb (dɪ'stɜːb), *v.* Forms: 3–6 des-, dys-, 4–6 dis-, -torbe, -tourbe, -turbe, 6 distowrb, -trub, -troub, 6– disturb. [ME. *destorben, destourben,* a. OF. *destorbe-r, -turbe-r, -tourbe-r,* = Pr., OSp. *destorbar* (Sp. *disturbar*), It. *disturbare, sturbare*:—L. *disturbāre* to throw into disorder, disturb, f. DIS- 5 + *turbāre* to disorder, disturb, f. *turba* tumult, turmoil, crowd.]

1. a. *trans.* To agitate and destroy (quiet, peace, rest); to break up the quiet, tranquillity, or rest of (a person, a country, etc.); to stir up, trouble, disquiet.

c **1290** *Beket* 1268 in *S. Eng. Leg.* 142 A destaunce þare is i-sprougue, liȝtliche in Engelonde, þat destourbez al þat lond. **1297** R. GLOUC. (1724) 90 þe kynges neuew, þo he herde þis, Was wroþ, and destourbede al þe court y wys. **1387** TREVISA *Higden* (Rolls) II. 347 Jupiter þat was ful cruel and desturbed þe pees. **1467** in *Eng. Gilds* (1870) 408 Wherby the kynges pes be dysturbed. **1530** PALSGR. 522/1, I have a sewte to you, but I dare nat distourbe you. *Ibid.* 523/1, I distroube, I troubyll. **1592** SHAKS. *Rom. & Jul.* I. i. 98 Three ciuill Broyles..Haue thrice disturb'd the quiet of our streets. **1697** DRYDEN *Virg. Georg.* IV. 279 No buzzing Sounds disturb their Golden Sleep. **1701** DE FOE *True-born Eng.* I. 9 No Nonconforming Sects disturb his Reign. **1882** PEBODY *Eng. Journalism* xxiii. 185 Burmah was disturbed, and a correspondent was instantly despatched to Mandalay. **1885** MARQ. SALISBURY *Speech* 4 Nov., Lord Granville says that I have disturbed the Sleeping lion.

b. To throw into a state of physical agitation, commotion, or disorder; to agitate.

1599 H. BUTTES *Dyets drie Dinner* B iij, Mulberries.. Breede winde: disturbe the stomacke. **1650** H. VAUGHAN *Silex Scint.* I. (1858) 105 The famous fan Purging the floor which chaff disturbs. **1665** SIR T. HERBERT *Trav.* (1677) 24 The sea raged and seemed disturbed as it is under London-bridge. **1817–18** SHELLEY *Rosalind & H.* 838 Like an image in the lake Which rains disturb.

c. To move anything from its settled condition or position; to unsettle.

1664 EVELYN *Kal. Hort.* (1729) 215 Disturb not their Beds, but hand-weed them. **1815** SHELLEY *Alastor* 261 With lightning eyes, and eager breath, and feet Disturbing not the drifted snow. **1856** EMERSON *Eng. Traits, Lit.* Wks. (Bohn) II. 103 A strong common sense, which it is not easy to unseat or disturb, marks the English mind for a thousand years. *Mod.* Do not disturb the plants after they show signs of bloom. Plant it in some permanent position where it will not be disturbed.

d. *refl.* To put oneself out by moving, etc. (e.g. in order to assist a person).

1831 T. L. PEACOCK *Crotchet Castle* iii, The stranger was rising up, when Mr. Crotchet begged him not to disturb himself. **1888** MRS. H. WARD *R. Elsmere* xiii, 'Can I find anything for you?' he said springing up. She hesitated a moment, then..she said..: 'Pray don't disturb yourself. I know exactly where to find it.'

2. To agitate mentally, discompose the peace of mind or calmness of (any one); to trouble, perplex.

c **1305** *Edmund Conf.* 369 in *E.E.P.* (1862) 80 þer ne ful noȝt a reynes drope to desturbi a manes mod. **1382** WYCLIF *Eccl.* vii. 8 [7]Chaleng disturbeth [**1388** disturblith] the wise man. *a* **1400–50** *Alexander* 5159 þan was ser Candoile in þat cas kenely distourbid. **1567** DRANT *Horace Epist.* VI. C viij, Both parties are distrubde with feare. **1684** R. H. *School Recreat.* 85 Let not this or any other Pastime disturb your Minds. **1752** JOHNSON *Rambler* No. 204 ¶13 Having been first disturbed by a dream, he afterwards grieved that a dream could disturb him. **1856** FROUDE *Hist. Eng.* (1858) I. ii. 150 She was not a person who would have been disturbed by the loss of a few Court vanities.

3. a. To interfere with the settled course or operation of; to put out of its course; to interrupt, derange, hinder, frustrate.

c **1290** *Beket* 380 in *S. Eng. Leg.* I. 117 þe loue was euere gret i-nouȝ bi-tweone seint thomas And þe Kinge, for-to þe feond destourbede hit, allas! *c* **1380** *Sir Ferumb.* 2456 þe þef þer riȝt scholde haue leyen by ys lef, Nad he come þo as god wolde & distorbed þat myschef. *c* **1400** MAUNDEV. (Roxb.) xxi. 98 Men may ga sauely and sikerly thurgh his land and na man be so hardy to disturbe þam. **1513** MORE in Grafton *Chron.* (1568) II. 788 She devised to disturbe this mariage. **1626** BACON *Sylva* §224 Sounds that moue in Oblique and Arcuate Lines must needs encounter and Disturbe the one the other. **1784** COWPER *Task* II. 492 Praise..Is oft too welcome, and may much disturb The bias of the purpose. **1875** JOWETT *Plato* (ed. 2) IV. 42 In a mathematical demonstration an error in the original number disturbs the whole calculation which follows. **1883** SIR W. WILLIAMS in *Law Times Rep.* XLIX. 139/2 No sufficient grounds have been shown for disturbing that judgment or for granting a new trial.

† **b.** with *inf.* To hinder by interference. *Obs.*

c **1386** CHAUCER *Melib.* ¶11 He is a fool that destourbeth the mooder to wepen in the deeth of hire childe, til sche haue wept hir fille, as for a certein tyme. *c* **1391** —— *Astrol.* I. §2 This ring rennyth..in so Rowm a space that hit disturbith nat the instrument to hangen aftur his rihte centre.

† **4. a.** With *of, from*: To deprive *of*; to drive, turn, or draw away *from*, by disturbance. *Obs.*

a **1225** *Ancr. R.* 162 He..þet no muruhðe, ne noise, ne þrung of folc ne muhte letten him of his beoden, ne disturben him of his god. *c* **1305** *Edmund Conf.* 417 in *E.E.P.* (1862) 82 Ne let noman in gon To desturbi me of mie studie. *c* **1386** CHAUCER *Pard. Prol. & T.* 12 (Ellesm.) That no man be so boold..Me to destourbe [so *Hengwrt, Corpus, Harl.* 7334; *Lansd.* destorble, *Bodl.* 686 distrouble] of Cristes hooly werk. **1658** ROWLAND *Moufet's Theat. Ins.* 899 Bees are most patient of labour in the day time, but most impatient of being scared in the night, and of being disturbed of their rest. **1667** MILTON *P.L.* I. 168 So as perhaps Shall grieve him..and disturb His inmost counsels from their destind aim.

b. *Law.* To deprive of the peaceful enjoyment or possession *of*. See DISTURBANCE 4.

[**1292** BRITTON II. xxv. §i, Ceux qi de commune sount engittez ou destourbez. *transl.* Those who are ejected or disturbed of their common.] **1541** *Act 33 Hen. VIII*, c. 32 The vicar of the parishe..wolde now disturbe the said tenauntes and inhabitauntes of their saide parishe church. **1865** NICHOLS *Britton* I. 285 If one of the parceners be ejected or disturbed of his seisin. **1870** FISHER *Digest Rep. Cases* II. 3319 An action against a stranger for disturbing the plaintiff in his pew.

† **di'sturb,** *sb. Obs.* [f. the vb.] An act of disturbing; a thing that disturbs; disturbance.

[**1594** SHAKS. *Rich. III*, IV. ii. 73 Foes to my Rest, and my sweet sleepes disturbers [*Qq.* disturbes].] **1597** DANIEL *Civ. Wars* VI. xlvii, From all Disturbs to be so long kept free. **1667** MILTON *P.L.* VI. 549 Instant without disturb they took Allarm, And onward move Embattelld.

disturbance (dɪ'stɜːbəns). [a. OF. *destorbance, destour-, destur-* (12th c. in Godef.), f. *destourber* to DISTURB: see -ANCE.] The action of disturbing or fact of being disturbed.

1. The interruption and breaking up of tranquillity, peace, rest, or settled condition; agitation (physical, social, or political).

1297 R. GLOUC. (1724) 436 þe erl Tebaude de Bleys.. dystourbed þe peys, And þoru Kyng Henryes rede made destourbance. **1398** TREVISA *Barth. De P.R.* XVII. clxxxvi. (1495) 727 Of suche dystourbance and stryfe and contrarynesse comyth stronge boyllyng and dureth vnto the hete hath maystry. **1467** *Ord. Worcester* in *Eng. Gilds* 388 Disturbaunce of the seid pease. **1576** FLEMING *Panopl. Epist.* 334 That hee might live quietly in Rome: for..some there were that sought his disturbaunce. **1662** J. DAVIES tr. *Mandelslo's Trav.* 256 Such as tend to the disturbance of the publick peace. **1665** SIR T. HERBERT *Trav.* (1677) 30 The Sea was..smooth, and no disturbance by wind to curl the waves, or to make it frothy. **1741–2** H. WALPOLE *Lett. H. Mann* (1834) I. xviii. 63 The..election passed without any disturbance. **1855** BAIN *Senses & Int.* I. ii. §2 In most cases of bodily irritation we can assign the place or seat of the disturbance. **1860** TYNDALL *Glac.* I. vii. 49 The slightest disturbance was sufficient to bring them down.

b. with *a* and *pl.*: An instance of this; *spec.* a breach of public peace, a tumult, an uproar, an outbreak of disorder.

atmospheric disturbance, a change in atmospheric conditions putting an end to calm weather.

1297 R. GLOUC. (1724) 514 Tho bigan ther in this lond a newe destourbance. **1598** FLORIO, *Sturbo, sturbamento*, a trouble, a vexation, a disturbance. **1608** SHAKS. *Per.* III. ii. 37, I can speak of the disturbances That nature works, and of her cures. **1667** MILTON *P.L.* x. 897 Innumerable Disturbances on Earth through Femal snares. **1844** H. H. WILSON *Brit. India* II. 98 With their apprehension the disturbances ceased. **1875** *Chamb. Jrnl.* CXXXIII. 8 Telegraphic intelligence of storms or atmospheric disturbances. **1880** *Daily News* 30 Oct., A disturbance will arrive on the North British and Norwegian Coasts.. attended by..strong winds or gales, rain or snow.

2. Interruption of mental tranquillity or equanimity; mental agitation, excitement, discomposure.

1387 TREVISA *Higden* (Rolls) III. 207 (Mätz.) Pictagoras wiþ harpe and strenges cessede þe destourbaunce of wittes. **1398** —— *Barth. De P.R.* V. v. (1495) 108 In the eyen is seen and knowen the distourbaunce and gladnesse of the soule. **1576** FLEMING *Panopl. Epist.* 204 To any ones disturbaunce and vexation. **1665** SIR T. HERBERT *Trav.* (1677) 23 To allure the hearts of greedy men, to afford them disturbance. **1751** JOHNSON *Rambler* No. 126 ¶7 One whose reigning disturbance was the dread of house-breakers. **1858** J. MARTINEAU *Stud. Chr.* 271 The dislike felt by the comfortable classes towards the trouble of thought and the disturbance of thought.

3. Interference with the regular or due course or continuance of any action or process; molestation.

c **1340** *Cursor M.* 7700 (Trin.) Saul souȝte dauid to quelle Often fel so þe chaunce Was þere but goddes disturbaunce. **1393** GOWER *Conf.* I. 181 Envie..began to travaile In disturbaunce of this spousaile. *c* **1400** *Beryn* 3981 A saff condit..That he may com & pas withouten disturbaunce. **1513** MORE in Grafton *Chron.* II. (1568) 766 This demeanor attempted..against the king..in the disturbance of his coronation. **1578** T. N. tr. *Conq. W. India* 102 To withstand his men from disturbance of his enterprise. **1711** ADDISON *Spect.* No. 262 ¶6 That he may let the ship sail on without disturbance. **1851** RUSKIN *Stones Ven.* (1874) I. xx. 218 We are to follow the labour of Nature, but not her disturbance.

4. *Law.* (See quot. 1765–9.)

[**1292** BRITTON II. xi. §7 Et ausi est home disseisi quel houre qe ly ou sa meyné soit destourbé de user sa peissible seisine par autre qi i cleyme fraunc tenement par teles destourbances.] **1598** *Child Marriages* 164 He, the said Robert Fletcher, shall..enioie the same shop as tenant.. without the lett or disturbans of the said John Allen, his executors, or Assignes. **1613** SIR H. FINCH *Law* (1636) 291 An assise which may bee either of his owne or his ancestors possession called an assise of darrein presentment is upon a disturbance when himselfe or his ancestor did last present. **1765–9** BLACKSTONE (Mason), Disturbance is a wrong done to some incorporeal hereditament, by hindering or disquieting the owners in their regular, and lawful enjoyment of it. **1768** —— *Comm.* III. 236 Disturbance of franchises happens, when a man has the franchise of holding a court-leet, of keeping a fair or market [etc.] and he is disturbed or incommoded in the lawful exercise thereof. **1848** WHARTON *Law Lex.*, *Disturbance*..There are five sorts of this injury, viz., disturbance of (1) franchise, (2) common, (3) ways, (4) tenure, and (5) patronage.

† **di'sturbancy.** *Obs. rare.* [f. prec. or next: see -ANCY.] Condition or state of disturbance.

1597 DANIEL *Civ. Wars* VIII. xcix, As exiles even from your homes You live perpetuall in disturbancy. **1603** —— *Epist.* Poems (1717) 350 Some Hearts are blinded so, that they Have divers Doors whereby they may let out Their Wills abroad without Disturbancy.

disturbant (dɪ'stɜːbənt), *a.* and *sb.* [ad. L. *disturbānt-em*, pr. pple. of *disturbāre* to DISTURB: see -ANT. Cf. AF. *destourbant.*]

A. *adj.* That disturbs; agitating, disquieting.

a **1617** BAYNE *On Eph.* (1658) 12 Disturbant aberrations deprived us of all peace. **1645** *Arraignm. Persecution* 30 Their Religion though different was not disturbant to the State. **1702** C. MATHER *Magn. Chr.* VII. ii. (1853) II. 497 These things were..disturbant and offensive. **1829** SOUTHEY *O. Newman* ix, Had they from such disturbant thoughts been free. **1856** RUSKIN *Mod. Paint.* III. IV. iv. §12. 52 The fantasy which I have just been blaming as disturbant of the simplicity of faith.

B. *sb.* One who disturbs; a disturber. **a.** *Law.* = DISTURBER 2.

1865 NICHOLS *Britton* II. 172 In cases of contumacy; as, where the tenant or the disturbant [*le tenaunt ou le destourbant*] appears in court, and contemptuously departs.

b. = DISTURBER 1.

1894 *Catholic News* 16 June 7/2 The disturbants gained admission to the park by a wicket.

Hence † **di'sturbantly** *adv.*, by way of disturbance. *Obs.*

a **1617** BAYNE *On Eph.* (1658) 138 They are not able disturbantly to assail us.

† **distur'bation.** *Obs.* [ad. L. *disturbātiōn-em*, n. of action from *disturbāre* to DISTURB.] The action of disturbing; = DISTURBANCE.

1529 *Will of Sir J. Digby, Leicestersh.* (MS.) Without lett or interruption or disturbacon of the said John Digby. **1590** R. HICHCOCK *Quintessence Wit* 54 b, To deliuer their owne kingdomes from those disturbations. **1658** A. FOX *Wurtz' Surg.* II. v. 59 Tarrying would prove..prejudicial to the wounded, by reason of his bleeding, and other disturbations.

di'sturbative, *a. rare.* [f. L. *disturbāt-* ppl. stem + -IVE: see -ATIVE.] Of disturbing tendency or character.

1842 MISS COSTELLO *Pilgr. Auvergne* I. 77 Our journey, independently of the disturbative character of our driver, was pleasant. **1846** —— *Tour Venice* 143 Monza, which formerly had a monastic character of quiet silence, is now noisy and disturbative.

disturbed (dɪ'stɜːbd, -ɪd), *ppl. a.* [f. DISTURB *v.* + -ED[1].] **a.** Disquieted; agitated; having the settled state, order, or position interfered with.

1592 SHAKS. *Ven. & Ad.* 340 He..Looks on the dull earth with disturbed mind. **1601** —— *Jul. C.* I. iii. 40 This disturbed Skie is not to walk in. **1763** SCRAFTON *Indostan* (1770) 50 He had ever after a disturbed imagination. **1830** D'ISRAELI *Chas. I*, III. i. 9 Four years of a disturbed reign had taught the Sovereign some lessons. **1838** J. W. CROKER in *C. Papers* (1884) II. xx. 323 Rheumatism in his neck.. gives him a disturbed air. **1860** TYNDALL *Glac.* II. xvii. 315 Crevasses..in the more disturbed portions of glaciers.

b. *spec.* in *Psychiatry*, emotionally or mentally unstable or abnormal; also (orig. *U.S.*), designed for or occupied by disturbed patients.

1904 T. JOHNSTONE tr. *Kraepelin's Lect. Clin. Psychiatry* iii. 25 A few weeks before his admission he had some attacks of apprehension, and then became disturbed, ill-balanced and absent-minded. **1935** W. SEABROOK *Asylum* xiv. 220 A disturbed hall as seen through the eyes of a disturbed patient. **1960** *Guardian* 9 Nov. 6/5 The standards she set were too high for the child, who became disturbed and began to pilfer. **1964** G. L. COHEN *What's Wrong with Hospitals?* viii. 164 Only by segregating those considered dangerous in a 'disturbed ward'—the erstwhile refractory section—can hospitals give the rest a parcelled-out freedom. **1970** *Guardian* 21 May 26/2 The centre.. has kept its belief that disturbed people could respond to.. a small community .. where they would never be regarded as patients.

Hence **di'sturbedly** (-ɪdlɪ) *adv.*; **di'sturbedness.**

1731 BAILEY (ed. 5), *Disturbedly*, interruptedly. *Ibid.*, *Disturbedness*, disorderliness, interruption. **1807** SOUTHEY *Espriella's Lett.* III. 339 The dog is uneasy.. and the cat wanders disturbedly from room to room.

disturber (dɪ'stɜːbə(r)). Also 3–5 -our, 6–9 -or. [ME. a. AF. *destourbour* = OF. *destorbeor*:—L. type **disturbātōr-em*, agent-n. from *disturbāre* to DISTURB.]

1. A person or thing that disturbs, disquiets, or interferes with peace or quiet; one who causes tumult or disorder; a troubler.

c **1290** *Beket* 1102 in *S. Eng. Leg.* I. 138 He was fals and for-swore: and destourbour of þe londe. **1548** *Act 2 & 3 Edw. VI*, c. 23. §2 Inflicting all such Pains upon the Disobedients and Disturbers [of matrimony]. **1588** SHAKS. *Tit. A.* IV. iv. 6 How euer these disturbers of our peace Buz in the peoples eares. **1674** R. GODFREY *Inj. & Ab. Physic* 8 That are rather disturbers than aiders of Nature. **1709** WYCHERLEY *Let. to Pope* 1 Apr., There I can have you without Rivals or Disturbers. **1764** WESLEY *Jrnl.* 10 Sept., Only one man, a common disturber, behaved amiss. **1883** FROUDE in *Contemp. Rev.* XLIV. 14 Little inclined.. to favour a disturber of the public peace.

2. *Law.* (also *disturbor.*) One who disquiets or hinders another in the lawful enjoyment of his right: see esp. quot. 1767.

1498–9 *Plumpton Corr.* 133 To have a spoliacion in the spirituall court agaynst the preyst that now occupyeth, because he is one disturber. **1726** AYLIFFE *Parergon* 41 When a Bishop refuses a Clerk for Insufficiency, and the Patron thereupon presents another, such Bishop shall be deemed a Disturber, if he afterwards within the six months presents the first Clerk presented to him. **1767** BLACKSTONE *Comm.* II. 278 If the bishop refuse or neglect to examine and admit the patron's clerk, without good reason assigned or notice given, he is stiled a disturber by the law, and shall not have any title to present by lapse. **1865** NICHOLS *Britton* IV. i. §2 Unless the disturbor or deforceor [*le destourbour ou deforceour*] can shew plain reasons to the contrary.

di'sturbing, *vbl. sb.* [f. DISTURB *v.* + -ING[1].] The action of the verb DISTURB; disturbance. (Now only *gerundial.*)

1340 *Ayenb.* 225 Alneway he may bleue ine his spoushod yef þer ne is non oþer destorbinge. **1382** WYCLIF *Ps.* xxx. 21 Thou schalt hide them in the hid place of thi face; fro the disturbyng of men [Vulg. *conturbatione*; **1388** disturblyng]. **1597** J. KING *On Jonas* (1618) 76 Discountenancings, disturbings, dispossessings of them. [**1776** G. SEMPLE *Building in Water* 51 The disturbing our Stages, Utensils, &c.]

di'sturbing, *ppl. a.* [f. as prec. + -ING[2].] That disturbs; see the verb.

1592 SHAKS. *Ven. & Ad.* 649 Where Love reigns, disturbeing Jealousy Doth call himself Affection's sentinel. **1812–6** PLAYFAIR *Nat. Phil.* (ed. 3) II. 259 From the disturbing force in the direction of the radius vector, he determined the Moon's nearest approach to the Earth, and farthest recess from it. **1875** JOWETT *Plato* (ed. 2) III. 3 This uncertainty.. is a disturbing element.

Hence **di'sturbingly** *adv.*, disquietingly.

1880 *New Virginians* I. 200 The old man groaned.. louder and more disturbingly. **1886** H. JAMES *Bostonians* II. II. xxiv. 120 She was so disturbingly beautiful.

†**di'sturblance.** *Obs.* [f. next + -ANCE: prob. from a corresponding AF. form: cf. DISTROUBLANCE.] = DISTURBANCE.

c **1330** R. BRUNNE *Chron. Wace* (Rolls) 8141 Seys now hym al þe desturblance, & where-of comeþ þat wonder chaunce. *c* **1430** *Pilgr. Lyf Manhode* II. v. (1869) 77 Þe disturblaunce cometh of þin ouertrowinge. *c* **1449** PECOCK *Repr.* 401 Grete.. disturblauncis and debatis. *c* **1450** *St. Cuthbert* (Surtees) 4629 Wha so did þaim disturblaunce.

†**di'sturble,** *v. Obs.* Also des-, -tourble. [ME. a. OF. *destorbler, -turbler, -tourbler*, f. *des-* DIS- 1 + *torbler, turbler, tourbler*, early forms of *trobler, troubler* to TROUBLE (:—L. **turbulāre*, f. *turbula, turbāre*). In the simple verb, the form *trouble* was from the first prevalent; in the derivative, *des-, disturble* was the earlier form, and (supported by DISTURB) survived to *c* 1500, when it yielded to DISTROUBLE (q.v.).]

trans. To disturb, trouble.

c **1330** R. BRUNNE *Chron. Wace* (Rolls) 1106 Þat þey ne go nought vs to wrye, Ne desturble me my weye. *c* **1380** WYCLIF *Sel. Wks.* III. 134 Ire distourblis monnis witte. **1382** —— *Matt.* xiv. 26. *c* **1400** *Three Kings Cologne* 57 All þe citee was gretlich desturbled of her sodeynlich comyng. *c* **1440** *Promp. Parv.* 123/1 Dysturbelyn [distroublyn, P.], *turbo, conturbo.* **1480** CAXTON *Chron. Eng.* lxi. 45 They ne were distourbled of noo man ne lette.

Hence †**di'sturbling** *vbl. sb.*; †**di'sturbler.**

c **1330** R. BRUNNE *Chron.* (1810) 254 Edward.. salle gyue Philip þe Kyng Alle holy Gascoyn, withouten disturblyng. **1440** Disturbler [see DISTROUBLER]. *c* **1449** PECOCK *Repr.* II. ii. 139 Scisme sowers and disturblers of the peple. **1481** CAXTON *Godfrey* xviii. 48 They.. had passed the water agayn, yf they had not.. so grete distourblyng.

di'sturbor: see DISTURBER 2.

†**di'sturdison.** *Obs. rare.* [app. derived, with change of prefix, from OF. *estordison, estourdison* (:—L. type **exturditiōn-em*), from *estordir*, mod.F. *étourdir*, to stun, stupefy.] Stunned or stupefied condition; a state of unconsciousness caused by a blow or the like.

c **1450** *Merlin* 266 Withynne a while a-roos the saisne fro disturdison, and saugh hem a-boute hym. *Ibid.* 268 The saisnes a-bode a-boute her lorde that was caste down and so diffouled vnder horse feet, whereof he was so sorowfull whan he a-roos from disturdison.

dis'turf, *v. rare.* [DIS- 7 a.] *trans.* To deprive of turf.

1858 LYTTON *What will he do* II. xi, The play-ground [was] disturfed to construct fortifications.

†**dis'turn,** *v. Obs.* Also 4–5 des-, 5–6 dys-, -torn(e, -tourn(e. [a. OF. *destourne-r*, in 11th c. *desturner* (mod.F. *détourner*, whence DETURN), f. *des-, dé-* (DE- I. 6) + *tourner* to TURN.] *trans.* To turn aside or away; to avert, divert, pervert.

c **1374** CHAUCER *Troylus* III. 669 (718) Thy fader prey al þilke harme disturne Of grace. **1483** CAXTON *Gold. Leg.* 138 b/2 Dyuerse thoughtes and occasions by whyche they be dystorned for to do wel. **1490** —— *Eneydos* xxi. 75 She.. dystourned her eyen from the lyghte. **1537** STARKEY in Strype *Eccl. Mem.* I. App. lxxxi. 195 You could never have distorned your wit and eloquence.. to spot your honour and name. *a* **1631** DONNE *Lament. Jeremy* II. xiv, Which might disturne thy bondage.

disturnpike (dɪs'tɜːnpaɪk), *v.* [DIS- 7 b.] *trans.* To free (a road) from turnpikes; to make no longer a turnpike-road. Hence **dis'turnpiked** *ppl. a.*, **dis'turnpiking** *vbl. sb.*

1872 *Daily News* 26 June, On Monday next, 1st July, the remainder of the metropolis roads north of the Thames will be 'disturnpiked.' **1881** *Times* 29 Mar. 9 The disturnpiking of main roads had seriously increased local burdens. **1882** *St. James' Gaz.* 2 June, To maintain milestones on disturnpiked roads. **1883** M. D. CHALMERS *Local Govt.* 133 Until 1878, when a road was disturnpiked, it became an ordinary highway; but by the Act of that year it was provided that all roads disturnpiked after 1870 should be main roads.

†**dis'tutor,** *v. Obs. rare.* [DIS- 7 b.] *trans.* To deprive of the position of tutor.

1691 WOOD *Ath. Oxon.* II. 391 Being found guilty of a strange singular and superstitious way of dealing with his Scholars.. he was distutor'd in the month of May 1634.

dis'twine, *v. rare.* [DIS- 6.] *trans.* To disentwine, unfasten.

1562 PHAER *Æneid* IX. Ccj, Those fal did Rutils whelme and brake their tortais roof distwynde.

distyle ('daɪstaɪl), *sb.* (*a.*) *Arch.* [f. DI-[2] + Gr. στῦλ-ος column, pillar: so mod.F. *distyle* sb.] A porch having two styles or columns. Also *attrib.* or as *adj.* ***distyle in antis***: see quot. 1865.

1840 *Penny Cycl.* XVIII. 412/2 The octagonal structure called the Tower of the Winds,.. which has a small prostyle portal on two of its faces,.. each consisting of a simple distyle, or two columns and their entablature, surmounted by a pediment. *Ibid.* 425/2 Converting the insulated piers below into columns of short and massive proportions, so as to produce a distyle in antis. **1865** J. FERGUSSON *Hist. Archit.* I. 167 A group of pillars 'distyle in antis' as it is technically termed, viz., two circular pillars between two square piers. *Ibid.* 176 There are three other distyle halls or gates on the platform.

distylous (daɪ'staɪləs), *a. Bot.* [f. as prec. + -OUS.] Having two styles.

1883 in *Syd. Soc. Lex.*

distyne, obs. form of DESTINY.

disulphate (daɪ'sʌlfət, -eɪt). *Chem.* [f. DI-[2] + SULPHATE.]

†**1.** In earlier use, a salt containing one equivalent of sulphuric acid to two of base. *Obs.*

1838 T. THOMSON *Chem. Org. Bodies* 228 Solution of disulphate of cinchonina. *c* **1865** J. WYLDE in *Circ. Sc.* I. 417/1 Quinine,.. as a disulphate, has been.. substituted.

2. A salt containing two equivalents of sulphuric acid to one of base (*Syd. Soc. Lex.*).

3. Applied by some to a sulphate containing a hydrogen atom replaceable by a basic element or radical; an acid sulphate (*Cent. Dict.*).

4. A salt of disulphuric acid, a pyrosulphate.

1877 ROSCOE & SCHORL. *Chem.* I. 345 The name disulphuric acid $H_2S_2O_7$ has been given to this substance, as it forms a series of very stable salts; thus sodium disulphate $Na_2S_2O_7$ is obtained by heating the acid sodium sulphate $HNaSO_4$, so long as water is given off.

disulphide (daɪ'sʌlfaɪd). *Chem.* [f. DI-[2] + SULPHIDE.] A compound in which two atoms of sulphur are united with another element or a radical, as ***carbon disulphide***, CS_2. †Formerly, a compound having one atom of sulphur united to two of another element, as ***disulphide of copper*** = cuprous sulphide, Cu_2S.

1863–72 WATTS *Dict. Chem.* II. 74 Hemisulphide of copper, or Cuprous Sulphide, Cu_2S, also called Disulphide of copper. Found native as *Copper-glance.* **1869** ROSCOE *Elem. Chem.* 128 When deposited from solution in carbon disulphide, sulphur crystallizes in the ordinary natural or octahedral form. **1895** *Edin. Rev.* Oct. 409 Carbon disulphide took it up more freely.

disulpho- (daɪ'sʌlfəʊ). *Chem.* [See DI-[2] 2 and SULPHO-.] In composition, denominating acids derived from two molecules of sulphurous acid.

Hence **disul'phonic** *a.*

1868 WATTS *Dict. Chem.* V. 551 There is a group of acid ethers, $(SO)_2{\cdot}R''H_2{\cdot}O_4$, derived from a double molecule of sulphurous acid, $H_4S_2O_6$, by substitution of a diatomic alcohol-radicle for half the hydrogen. These are the so-called disulpho-acids, which may also be formulated as compounds of hydrocarbon with 2 at[oms of] SO_3. **1869** ROSCOE *Elem. Chem.* 423 When disulpho-anthraquinic acid is formed. **1881** WATTS *Dict. Chem.* VIII. 1857 Anthracene treated with sulphuric acid yields two disulphonic acids.

di'sulphuret. *Chem.* [See DI-[2] 2 and SULPHURET.] = DISULPHIDE (in obs. and current senses).

1854 J. SCOFFERN in *Orr's Circ. Sc., Chem.* 491 The application of heat drives off one equivalent of its sulphur and converts it into the disulphuret. *Ibid.* 500 Sub- or Di-sulphuret of Mercury.

disulphuric (daɪsʌl'fjʊərɪk), *a. Chem.* In ***disulphuric acid***, the same as pyrosulphuric or Nordhausen sulphuric acid, $H_2S_2O_7 = 2(SO_2OH) + O$. Its salts are *pyro-* or *di-sulphates.* (So called because the molecule represents two molecules of sulphuric acid deprived of one of water.)

1875 WATTS *Dict. Chem.* VII. 1140.

†**disu'nanimous,** *a. Obs. rare.* [DIS- 10.] Not unanimous; divided in mind.

1728 MORGAN *Algiers* I. v. 166 So degenerate, so effeminate, and so disunanimous were they grown.

dis'uniform, *a.* [DIS- 10.] The opposite of uniform; without uniformity.

1687 NORRIS *Coll. Misc.* 261 The Sun shines upon the Earth with a disuniform and unequal light. **1710** —— *Chr. Prud.* iii. 115 All is disuniform, because there is nothing to unite or regulate them. **1737** H. COVENTRY *Phil. to Hyd.* II. (T.) Confused heaps and disuniform combinations.

disuni'formity. [DIS- 9.] Want or absence of uniformity; variety of form or appearance.

1710 NORRIS *Chr. Prud.* vii. 326 If it (the body) be evil, it will be as full of darkness, all confusion and disuniformity. **1876** *Daily News* 18 Mar., We laughed at their equipment.. their disuniformity of costume.

disunify (dɪs'juːnɪfaɪ), *v.* [DIS- 6.] *trans.* To do the opposite of unifying; to keep from unity. Hence **dis'unifying** *ppl. a.*

1891 *Cycl. Temperance & Prohibition* 393/1 As a result of this disunifying measure.

disunion (dɪs'juːnɪən). [DIS- 9]

1. Rupture of union; separation, severance; disjunction.

1598 MARSTON *Pygmal.* v. 156 Chaos returne, and with confusion Inuolue the world with strange disunion. **1623** COCKERAM, *Disunion*, a seuering. **1634** WITHER *Emblemes* 177 When disunion is begunne It breedeth dangers, where before were none. **1775** DE LOLME *Eng. Const.* Advt. (1784) 12 A disunion of the empire was endeavoured to be promoted. **1792** G. WASHINGTON *Lett.* Writ. 1891 XII. 204 Foreigners would.. believe that inveterate political dissensions existed among us, and that we are on the very verge of disunion; but the fact is otherwise. **1820** SCORESBY *Acc. Arctic Reg.* II. 346 Three boats.. were secured [to the fast-boat] by means of a rope, and towed without danger of disunion. **1884** *Act 47 & 48 Vict.* c. 66 (*title*) An Act to provide for the disunion of the Sees of Gloucester and Bristol.

attrib. [cf. DISUNIONIST a.] **1848** LOWELL *Lett.* (1894) I. 125, I do not agree with the abolitionists in their disunion and non-voting theories. *a* **1857** in *Pall Mall G.* 29 May (1865) 2 New York Dis-Union Anti-Slavery Convention —To be held at Albany in February, 1857.

2. Absence or want of union; disunited or separated condition; dissension.

1601 HOLLAND *Pliny* I. 115 In this disunion, as it were, appeareth yet a brotherly fellowship and vnitie. **1659** B. HARRIS *Parival's Iron Age* 287 By dis-union of wils amongst his friends. **1711** SHAFTESB. *Charac.* v. iii. (1737) III. 319 The Inconveniences which the Dis-union of Persuasions and Opinions accidentally produces. **1807** G. CHALMERS *Caledonia* I. III. ii. 335 Ages of disunion and disaster. **1838** THIRLWALL *Greece* III. xxv. 404 He complained.. of the disunion of the Sicilian Greeks.

disunionist (dɪs'juːnɪənɪst). [f. prec. + -IST.] One who advocates or works for disunion: *spec.* **a.** In U.S. politics, One of those who, before or during the civil war of 1861–65, advocated a dissolution of the Union. **b.** In English politics, applied controversially to an advocate of the repeal or modification of the Act of Union with Ireland.

1846 WORCESTER cites NORTH. **1852** *Blackw. Mag.* LXXII. 47 The population is divided really into Unionists, or Compromise-men, and Disunionists, or Abolitionists. **1854** L. OLIPHANT *Let.* in *Life* (1891) I. iv. 124 There are the Whigs and Democrats, and Filibusters.. Disunionists and Federalists. **1861** LOWELL *E Pluribus Unum* Prose Wks. 1890 V. 52 It is time that we turned up our definitions in some more trustworthy dictionary than that of.. disunionists and their..accomplices. **1889** *Catholic Household* 5 Oct. 10/2 The Disunionists..seem to revel in fiery invective of a zoological character.

c. *attrib.* or as *adj.*

1884 GOLDW. SMITH in *Contemp. Rev.* Sept. 317 The disunionist movement in Ireland. **1888** BRYCE *Amer. Commw.* II. III. lvi. 377 The disunionist spirit of the South which led to the war.

So **dis'unionism**, the doctrine of disunionists.

1894 SWINBURNE *Stud. Prose & Poetry* 102 Disunionism, dissolutionism, or communalism.

disunite (dɪsjuː'naɪt), *v.* [f. DIS- 6 + UNITE.]

1. *trans.* To undo the union of; to disjoin:

a. from material union.

1598 FLORIO, *Disgiongere*..to disioyne, to disunite, to deuide. *a* **1631** DONNE in *Select.* (1840) 178 A corner-stone, that unites things most disunited. **1725** POPE *Odyss.* III. 582 The beast they then divide, and disunite The ribs and limbs. **1830** LYELL *Princ. Geol.* (1875) I. II. xvii. 406 The Alkali, when disunited from the Silica, would readily be dissolved.

b. (more frequently) from immaterial union; To separate from alliance, conjoint action, etc.; to set at variance, alienate.

1560 [see DISUNITED below]. **1606** SHAKS. *Tr. & Cr.* II. iii. 109 Their fraction is more our wish than their faction; but it was a strong counsell that a Foole could disunite. **1641** MILTON *Reform.* II. (1851) 55 Goe on both hand in hand, O Nations never to be dis-united. **1685** DRYDEN *Albion & Albanus* II. Wks. 1883 VII. 257 Disturb their union, disunite their love. **1794** SOUTHEY *Wat Tyler* II. i, They will use every art to disunite you..Whom in a mass they fear. **1852** MISS YONGE *Cameos* (1877) IV. v. 62 That her father was not disunited from his first wife.

2. *intr.* (for *refl.*) To sever or separate oneself; to part; to fall or come asunder.

1675 G. R. tr. *Le Grand's Man Without Passion* 146 The Spirit must disunite from the senses. *a* **1716** SOUTH (J.), The several joints of the body politick do separate and disunite. **1818** SHELLEY *Rosalind & Helen* 984 Strains of harmony, That mingle in the silent sky, Then slowly disunite. **1827** AIKMAN *Hist. Scot.* III. IV. 435 The supplicants..refused to disunite.

3. *Manège.* (See quots.)

1727 BAILEY vol. II. s.v., (With Horsemen) A Horse is said to disunite, that drags his Haunches, that Gallops false. **1833** *Regul. Instr. Cavalry* I. 57 Cantering with the near fore, followed by the off hind, or off fore, followed by the near hind, is 'disunited'.

Hence **disu'nited** *ppl. a.* (whence **disu'nitedly** *adv.*): **disu'niting** *vbl. sb.* and *ppl. a.*

1560 WHITEHORNE *Arte Warre* (1573) 19a, The disunited and discencious do agree. **1611** FLORIO, *Disunimento*, a disuniting. **1651** HOBBES *Leviath.* II. xviii. 88 The confusion of a disunited Multitude. **1680** S. MATHER *Iren.* 16 The severity of this dis-uniting principle. **1844** THIRLWALL *Greece* VIII. 21 A number of feeble disunited hordes. **1854** J. S. C. ABBOTT *Napoleon* (1855) II. xxvi. 490 The disuniting of the army. **1871** R. ELLIS *Catullus* lxiii. 84 So in ire she spake, adjusting disunitedly then her yoke.

†**disu'nite,** *ppl. a. Obs.* [Short for *disunited*, after L. *ūnītus* united.] = DISUNITED.

1642 H. MORE *Song of Soul* III. II. xviii, Sith the soul from them is disunite.

disu'niter. *rare.* [f. prec. vb. + -ER[1].] One who or that which disunites.

1755 JOHNSON, *Divider*..3. A disuniter; the person or cause that breaks concord.

†**disu'nition.** *Obs. rare.* [f. DISUNITE *v.*, after *unition.*] The action of disuniting; disjunction, separation, disunion.

1611 COTGR. *Abstraict*, a seperation, disunition, disiunction. [**1702** *Clarendon's Hist. Reb.* XIV. §149 III. 444 Disunition [*other edd.* disunion] and distinction of Parties.]

disunity (dɪs'juːnɪtɪ). [DIS- 9.] Want of unity; a state of separation, physical, political, social, or sentimental; dissension, discord.

1632 LITHGOW *Trav.* x. 474 Diversities of Doctrine..and hundreds of like disunities. **1767** *Misc.* in *Ann. Reg.* 209/2 By the disunity of your nation, all the nations insult you. **1884** *Contemp. Rev.* June 794 It is hard to tell the price London pays for its disunity.

†**disuni'versity,** *v. Obs. nonce-wd.* [DIS- 7a.] *trans.* To deprive of a university.

1665 EVANS in Worthington *Diary* (1855) II. I. 179 Cambridge is almost dis-universitied, and either there will be no winter term, or nothing to do in it.

disur, var. DISOUR *Obs.*

disury, obs. form of DYSURY.

†**dis'usage.** *Obs.* [f. DISUSE *v.*, after *usage*; cf. obs. F. *desusage* (Cotgr.).] Discontinuance of a usage or practice; = DISUSE *sb.* 1.

1475 *Bk. Noblesse* 26 That good courages of hertis be not mynissed..for disusage and levying armes for a litille season. **1594** HOOKER *Eccl. Pol.* IV. xiv. §3 To be abolished by disusage through tract of time. **1607** *Schol. Disc. agst. Antichr.* II. viii. 102 Nor [can] an angrie Iudge condemne vs for any thing else, then for disvsage of a trifle. **1712** PRIDEAUX *Direct. Ch.-wardens* (ed. 4) 104 After so long a disusage it would be in vain to attempt it.

disusance (dɪs'juːzəns). *rare.* [f. as prec. after *usance.*] The fact of disusing; = DISUSE *sb.* 1.

1685 COTTON tr. *Montaigne* III. 513 By disusance for ever to lose the commerce of the common life. **1880** H. C. COOTE *Eng. Gild Knts.* 15 Disusance, compulsory rather than voluntary, had extinguished them both.

disuse (dɪs'juːs), *sb.* [f. DIS- 9 + USE *sb.*]

1. Discontinuance of use, practice, or exercise; prolonged cessation from an action or practice.

1552 HULOET, Disusage or disuse, *desuetudo.* **1603** HOLLAND *Plutarch's Mor.* 1255 Fashions..well enough knowen, though they be not practised: mary, strange they be by reason of disuse. **1646** SIR T. BROWNE *Pseud. Ep.* IV. vi. 194 Nor is there any who from disuse did ever yet forget it. **1738** *Oxford Methodists* 9 The general disuse of a duty could not by any means excuse the neglect of it. **1859** DARWIN *Orig. Spec.* v. (1873) 108 Structures which can be best explained by the effects of disuse. **1885** *Law Times* 23 May 68/2 His fine abilities rusting from disuse.

†**b.** The being or becoming unused or unaccustomed (*to*); unaccustomedness. *Obs.*

1570 LEVINS *Manip.* 194/43 Disuse, *desuetudinis.* **1580** HOLLYBAND *Treas. Fr. Tong*, *Desaccoustumance*, disuse. **1726** SHELVOCKE *Voy. round World* (1757) 419 It appeared to us to proceed more from disuse than disinclination to work. **1733** SWIFT *Apol.* 135 Wks. 1755 IV. I. 213 Frighten'd at a scene so rude, Through long disuse of solitude. **1792** MAD. D'ARBLAY *Diary* V. VIII. 369, I pleaded..my disuse to the night air at this time of the year.

c. The condition or state of being no longer in use; desuetude.

1699 BENTLEY *Phal.* 455 The other acceptation of the word falling into disuse. **1705** BOSMAN *Guinea* 371 This Custom, which is..grown in disuse for several years past. *a* **1771** GRAY in *Corr. w. N. Nicholls* (1843) 301 Many of them have gradually dropped into disuse. **1889** I. TAYLOR *Orig. Aryans* 126 The pile dwellings, being no longer needed, gradually fell into disuse.

†**2.** The quality of being of no use; uselessness. *Obs. rare*[−1].

1627–77 FELTHAM *Resolves* I. xxxvi. 60 Grief is like Ink poured into water, that fills the whole Fountain full of blackness and disuse.

disuse (dɪs'juːz), *v.* Also 6 *Sc.* disose. [f. DIS- 6 + USE *v.*]

†**1.** *trans.* To make (a person) unaccustomed or unused to anything; to cause to lose a habit; to disaccustom. Chiefly in *passive*: cf. DISUSED *ppl. a.* 1. Const. *from*, *of*, *to*, or *infin. Obs.*

1375 BARBOUR *Bruce* XIX. 183 Quhen thai thus diswsyt ar, Than may ȝhe move on thame ȝour wer. **1513** DOUGLAS *Æneis* VI. xiv. 16 He sall..men steir, Quhilk lang hes bene disosit fra the weir, To armis and triumphe of victory. *a* **1618** RALEIGH *Maxims St.* in *Rem.* (1661) 40 They are to be dis-used from the practise of Arms. *a* **1640** W. FENNER *Christ's Alarm* II. (1657) 25 If sinne be yielded unto, it will disuse a man of Gods Ordinances. *a* **1791** BLACKLOCK *On Melissa's Birth-day* (R.) With Bion long disus'd to play.

2. To discontinue the use or practice of (a thing); to cease to use.

1487 *Act 3 Hen. VII*, c. 2 Which lawe by negligence is disused. **1549** *Compl. Scot.* Prol. 17 Gyf sic vordis suld be disusit..than the phrasis of the antiquite vald be confundit. **1690** NORRIS *Beatitudes* (1694) I. 199 They..condemn and disuse many things meerly because we approve and use them. **1727** SWIFT *What passed in Lond.* Wks. 1755 III. I. 181 Now I reflected..that I had disused family prayers for above five years. **1868** M. PATTISON *Academ. Org.* v. 193 Other universities..have disused the term 'Arts'. **1874** PARKER *Goth. Archit.* I. vi. 197 In many later examples these sub-arches are entirely disused.

†**3.** To make a wrong use of; to misuse, abuse. *Obs.*

c **1380** WYCLIF *Serm.* Sel. Wks. I. 1 A riche man þat dis-uside his richesse in pride and in glotonye. *Ibid.* III. 355 He ..disuside þe ȝiftis of God. *c* **1430** LYDG. *Bochas* II. (1558) *Lenuoy* 17 All olde abusion Of ceremonies falsly disusyng. *c* **1440** *Promp. Parv.* 123/2 Dysvsyn, or mysse vsyn a-ȝenste resone, *abutor.*

Hence **dis'using** *vbl. sb.*

1605 *Clergy Lincoln agst. Liturgy* 69 This may..appear by their long disuseing, or seldom useing of them. **1611** COTGR., *Desusitation*, a disusing, discontinuing.

disused (dɪs'juːzd), *ppl. a.* [f. prec. + -ED[1].]

†**1.** Of persons: Not used or accustomed; out of the habit. *Obs.*

1530 PALSGR. 523/1, I can nat shote nowe but with great payne, I am so disused. **1656** BAXTER *Reformed Pastor* v. 85 Many disused persons can mutter out some honest requests in secret. **1748** *Anson's Voy.* II. vii. 214 Being now in a rainy climate, which we had been long disused to. *a* **1763** SHENSTONE *Progress Taste* I. 59 Disus'd to speak, he tries his skill, Speaks coldly, and succeeds but ill.

2. No longer used; fallen out of use; obsolete.

1611 COTGR., *Disusité*, disused, grown out of vse. **1630** SANDERSON *Serm.* II. 261 Some dis-used statute. **1674** BOYLE *Excell. Theol.* II. v. 222 Our ignorance..of the dis-used languages wherein they are delivered. **1864** BOWEN *Logic* vii. 220 A different and now disused meaning.

†**dis'user.** *Obs. rare.* [f. prec. vb., after *user.*] Disuse, lapse of use.

1710 PRIDEAUX *Orig. Tithes* v. 285 A Law grows antiquated by disuser when..the Government drops the Execution of it.

disutility (dɪsjuː'tɪlɪtɪ). [DIS- 9.] The opposite of utility; injuriousness, harmfulness.

1879 JEVONS *Pol. Econ.* iii. (1888) 58 For the abstract notion, the opposite or negative of utility, we may invent the term 'disutility', which will mean something different from inutility, or the absence of utility. It is obvious that utility passes through inutility before changing into disutility, these notions being related as +, 0 and −. **1886** *Academy* 22 May 355/3 The fatigues of the evening lecture painfully illustrated the Jevonian theory of the 'final disutility' of labour.

disutilize (dɪs'juːtɪlaɪz), *v.* [DIS- 6.] *trans.* To deprive of utility, render useless.

1856 MRS. BROWNING *Aur. Leigh* II. 1062 Death's black dust..Annulled the gift, disutilised the grace, and left these fragments.

†**dis'vail,** *v. Obs. rare.* [f. DIS- 6 + VAIL *v.*: cf. in same sense *disavail.*] *trans.* To be the reverse of advantageous to; to be hurtful to.

14.. LYDG. & BURGH *Secrees* 1638 Sleap before mete, ovir moche travaylle, With fretyng wratthe, gretly doon disuaylle. *Ibid.* 2006 Moche to Ete..Of the body ech membre doth disvaylle.

disvail(e, obs. form of DISVEIL.

†**dis'valedge,** *v. Obs. rare.* [ad. It. *svaligiare* to rob, strip, f. *s-* = DIS- 4 + *valigia* port-manteau, valise.] = next.

1598 BARRET *Theor. Warres* v. i. 148 Whosoeuer shall disualedge or spoile any of the Princes friends.

†**dis'valise,** *v. Obs. rare.* [ad. obs. F. *desvaliser*, 'to rob, despoyle, rifle; to depriue of cloake-bag, bag, and baggage' (Cotgr.), mod. F. *dévaliser*, f. *des-*, DIS- 4 + *valise* portmanteau.] *trans.* To strip (any one) of his baggage; to rob, plunder.

1672 MARVELL *Reh. Transp.* I. 134 We have had the Titles ..of Mr. Bayes his six Playes. Not but that, should we disvalise him, he hath..a hundred more as good in his budget.

†**disvalu'ation.** *Obs.* [f. DISVALUE *v.* after *valuation.*] The action of disvaluing; depreciation.

1617 MORYSON *Itin.* II. III. i. 271 The disualuation of the mixed coyne now currant. *a* **1626** BACON *War w. Spain* in *Harl. Misc.* (Malh.) IV. 147 What can be..more to the disvaluation of the power of the Spaniards? **1647** M. HUDSON *Div. Right Govt.* II. ii. 79 Such disvaluations and disertions of worldly and Natural gifts.

disvalue (dɪs'væljuː), *v.* Now *rare.* (Frequent in 17th c.) Also 7 -valewe, [f. DIS- 6 + VALUE *v.*] *trans.* To make or treat as of no value, depreciate, disparage. Hence **dis'valuing** *vbl. sb.*

1603 SHAKS. *Meas. for M.* v. i. 221 For that her reputation was dis-valued In leuitie. **1605** BACON *Adv. Learn.* II. xxiii. §31. 111 It is..necessary that vertue be not disualewed and imbased vnder the iust price. *a* **1639** W. WHATELEY *Prototypes* I. iii. (1640) 12 It is an extreame disvaluing of Christ's righteousnesse, and underprizing of God's mercies in Christ. **1649** G. DANIEL *Trinarch., Rich. II*, cclxxxv, The King disvalued The Peer'age of the Kingdome. **1678** *Lively Orac.* 243 The disvaluing of this Divine Book. *a* **1876** M. COLLINS in *Pen Sketches* (1879) II. 177 Perhaps his pen disvalueth Froude upon Elizabeth.

dis'value, *sb.* [f. prec. vb., after *value* sb.]

†**1.** Depreciation, disparagement. *Obs.*

1603 B. JONSON *Sejanus* III. i, Nor is't the time alone is here disprised, But the whole man of the time, yea, Caesar's self Brought in disvalue. **1644** *Charge agst. Visct. Wilmott* in R. Symonds *Diary Civ. War* (Camden) 108 A disvalew and contempte of his Majesties person. **1678** *Lively Orac.* viii. §26. 315 There can scarce be a greater instance of contempt and disvalue.

2. *Philos.* Negative value. Hence **dis'valuable** *a.*, having negative value; bad, evil, or noxious.

1925 C. D. BROAD *Mind & its Place* xi. 504 Intrinsically good states..may have a great instrumental disvalue. **1929** J. LAIRD *Idea of Value* p. xvi, In the technical usage of philosophy, economics, aesthetics and certain other such studies, 'value' is usually taken to mean both value and disvalue. It is therefore contrasted with non-value, or with that which is neither good nor bad. **1942** *Mind* LI. 185 Having value sometimes means having positive as opposed to negative value, and sometimes means being either valuable or disvaluable. **1963** J. N. FINDLAY *Meinong's Theory* (ed. 2) ix. 291 When things are given as actual or non-actual, we experience their values or disvalues by serious feelings and unserious desires.

†**dis'vantage,** *sb. Obs.* [f. DIS- 9 + VANTAGE *sb.* Cf. It. *disvantaggio* (Florio), disadvantage.] = DISADVANTAGE.

1591 HARINGTON *Orl. Fur.* XXIV. li. (1634) 193 Zerbino.. voided all the blowes with much facilitie, Though having great disvantage in the blade. *a* **1619** FOTHERBY *Atheom.* I. ii. §1 (1622) 8 It is good..for euery man, to vnderstand, not only his aduantages, but also his disuantages.

† **dis'vantage**, *v. Obs. rare.* [f. DIS- 6 + VANTAGE *v.*; cf. It. *disvantaggiare* (Florio).] *trans.* To disadvantage; to be disadvantageous to.

1567 DRANT *Horace Epist.* A vj, As yeares do helpe vs mightely whilst we cum at a staye, So after they disuantage vs, and breake vs to decaye.

† **disvan'tageous**, *a. Obs. rare.* [f. DISVANTAGE *sb.*, after *advantageous*. Cf. It. *disvantaggioso* (Florio).] Disadvantageous.

1622 DRAYTON *Poly-olb.* xxii. (R.) Had not his light horse by disvantageous ground Been hindered, he had struck the heart of Edward's host.

† **dis'veil**, *v. Obs.* Also 7 **disvaile**. [f. DIS- 6 or 7 + VEIL *v.* or *sb.* Cf. F. *dévoiler*, in 16th c. *desvoiler* (Cotgr.).] *trans.* To strip of a veil; to unveil, unmask. Hence **dis'veiled** *ppl. a.*

1611 FLORIO, *Sbendare*, to vnmaske, to disuaile. **1621** BP. MOUNTAGU *Diatribæ* I. 17 You..plainly dis-vaile your contrary purpose and intent. **1867** MRS. OLIPHANT tr. *De Montalembert's Monks of West* V. 285 A disveiled nun married to an apostate priest.

† **dis'velop**, *v. Obs.* Also 6-7 **-vellop(e**. [ad. 14-16th c. F. *desveloper*, in mod.F. *développer*: see DEVELOP.] The earlier form of DEVELOP, occurring chiefly in the literal sense: To unfold, unfurl, display heraldically. Hence **dis'veloped** *ppl. a., Her.* displayed. **dis'veloping** *vbl. sb.*

1592 WYRLEY *Armorie, Ld. Chandos* 79 The Prince and King as two that all us rules Disuellope siluer a sharpned pile of gules. **1610** GUILLIM *Heraldry* IV. xiii. (1611) 223 With..my disuellopped pennon me before. *Ibid.* IV. xiii. (1660) 328 Disvellopping is the proper term for spreading or displaying of the Martial Ensign. **1659** *Unhappy Marksm.* in *Harl. Misc.* (Park) IV. 3 (D.) Since the time wherein those black thoughts disveloped themselves by action. **1727-51** CHAMBERS *Cycl.*, *Disveloped*, in heraldry, is used much in the same sense with displayed.—Thus colours, said in an army to be flying, are, in heraldry, said to be disveloped. **1755** JOHNSON, *To disvelop*, to uncover. *Dict.*

dis'venerate, *v. nonce-wd.* [f. DIS- 6.] *trans.* To regard without veneration.

1826 R. H. FROUDE *Rem.* (1838) I. 199, I venerate ——, but dislike him; I like ——, but disvenerate him.

† **dis'venture**. *Obs.* [ad. Sp. *desventura* misfortune, f. *des-*, DIS- 4 + *ventura* VENTURE.] A misadventure, misfortune.

1612-20 SHELTON *Quix.* I. III. vi. (R.), Adventures, or rather disventures, never begin with a little. **1718** MOTTEUX *Quix.* (1733) I. 40 Many times my Uncle would read you those unconscionable books of Disventures.

† **dis'venturous**, *a. Obs.* [f. prec. + -OUS.] Unfortunate, disastrous.

1742 JARVIS *Quix.* II. IV. xvi. (D.) Would to God this disventurous adventure that threatens us may end in no worse.

† **dis'vest**, *v. Obs.* [DIS- 6.] *trans.* To divest, unrobe, strip.

1627 HAKEWILL *Apol.* IV. v. (1630) 486 The Earth, disvested of the vegetables which apparelled her. **1655** tr. *De Moulines' Francion* vii. 26 His Friend..caused him to disvest himself.

† **dis'vesture**, *v. Obs. rare.* [DIS- 7 a.] *trans.* To strip of one's vesture; to unrobe.

1563-87 FOXE *A. & M.* (1596) 178/1 The prelats..then disuestured him, taking from him his purple and his scepter.

† **dis'vigorate**, *v. Obs. rare.* [f. DIS- 6 + L. *vigor* strength, after *invigorate*.] *trans.* To deprive of vigour or strength.

1694 WESTMACOTT *Script. Herb.* (1695) 112 A pungent Volatile Salt, and a subtil Sulphur, which disvigorate and destroyeth Acids.

† **dis'virgin**, *v. Obs. rare*$^{-0}$. [f. DIS- 7 b; cf. OF. *desvirginer*.] *trans.* To devirginate.

1611 FLORIO, *Dispucellare*, to disuirgine. *Ibid.*, *Disuerginare*, to vnmaiden, to disuirgin.

dis'visage, *v. rare.* [ad. OF. *desvisage-r* to damage the face of, deface, mod.F. *dévisager*; f. *des-*, DIS- 4 + *visage* VISAGE.] *trans.* To mar the visage or face of; to deface, disfigure.

1603 FLORIO *Montaigne* III. xiii. (1632) 620, I had a quartan ague which..had altogether disvisaged and altered my countenance. **1611** FLORIO, *Suisáre*, to vnface, to disuisage. Also to slash or gash ouer the face. **1881** DUFFIELD *Don Quix.* I. 365 The knight..remained so disvisaged.

† **dis'visor**, *v. Obs.* In 6 **-ser**, 7 **-zor**. [DIS- 7 a.] *trans.* To remove the visor from, to uncover (a visored face). Also *intr.* for *refl.* Hence **dis'visored** *ppl. a.*, **dis'visoring** *vbl. sb.*

1548 HALL *Chron., Hen. VIII* (an. 12) 79 The kynges moste noble grace never disvisered nor breathed tyll he ranne the five courses. *Ibid.* 80 b, At thinstance of the Frenche quene and her ladies these maskers and revelers them disvisered, shewyng them what persones they were. *Ibid.* 83 b, Eche compaigny passed by other without any countenaunce makyng or disviseryng. **1621** BP. MOUNTAGU *Diatribæ* I. 261 With open Mouth, & disvizored Face.

dis'voice, *v. rare.* [DIS- 7 a.] *trans.* To deprive of voice, render voiceless or mute.

1865 LOWELL *Ode at Harvard Commemoration* ix, Before my musing eye The mighty ones of old sweep by, Disvoicèd now and insubstantial things, As noisy once as we.

† **dis'vouch**, *v. Obs. rare.* [DIS- 6.] = DISAVOUCH, DISAVOW.

1603 SHAKS. *Meas. for M.* IV. iv. 1 Euery Letter he hath writ, hath disuouch'd other.

† **dis'vow**, *v. Obs. rare.* [f. DIS- 6 + VOW *v.*; cf. OF. *desvouer*, *-voer* (Godef.).] = DISAVOW.

1502 *Ord. Crysten Men* (W. de W. 1506) IV. xxix. 344, I you refuse & dysuowe.

dis'vowelled, *ppl. a. nonce-wd.* [f. DIS- 7 a + VOWEL *sb.*] Rendered vowelless; that does not pronounce vowels.

1849 LYTTON *K. Arthur* IV. xvii, O guttural-grumbling and disvowell'd man.

disvulnerability (dɪsˌvʌlnərəˈbɪlɪtɪ). [DIS- 9.] The faculty of abnormally rapid recovery from wounds and injuries.

1890 H. ELLIS *Criminal* iii. 113 This insensibility shows itself also in disvulnerability, or rapid recovery from wounds. **1894** —— *Man & Woman* 122 Disvulnerability is the term, first used by Professor Benedikt, to signify the quick repair of wounds and comparative freedom from ill consequences after severe injuries. **1894** A. GRIFFITHS *Secr. Prison-Ho.* 27 Disvulnerability..is another quality possessed by the criminal.

† **dis'wall**, *v. Obs. rare.* [DIS- 7 a.] *trans.* To deprive of its wall, to dismantle.

1627 SPEED *England* iv. §5 Hay upon Wye..was diswalled, depopulated, and burnt.

† **dis'ware**, *a. Obs. rare.* [f. DIS- 10 + WARE *a.*] Not aware, unaware; not on one's guard.

c **1400** *Beryn* 3046 Howe hanybald led Geffrey, disware of his entent. *Ibid.* 3266 Be-twene hope & drede, disware how it shuld goon. *c* **1430** LYDG. *Bochas* III. v. (1558) 7, I full disware to make purueyaunce, Agayne hys commynge.

disware, var. of DISWERE, *Obs.*, doubt.

† **dis'warn**, *v. Obs. rare.* [f. DIS- 1 + WARN *v.*] *trans.* To warn against a course, warn off *from* something.

1607 TOPSELL *Serpents* (1658) 708 Wondering..what Shepheards or Hunters, or other men might be in that place to diswarn him from his game. **1622** LD. KEEPER WILLIAMS *Let. to Dk. Buckhm.* Sept. in *Cabala* 73 (T.) My Lord Brook diswarning me..from coming to Theobalds this day.

dis'warren, *v.* [DIS- 7 b. Cf. DE-AWARREN *v.*] *trans.* To deprive of the character of a warren; to render no longer a warren.

1727 W. NELSON *Laws conc. Game* (1736) 32 When a Warren is diswarrened, or broke up and laid in Common. **1796** W. MARSHALL *W. England* I. 271 A small one [rabbit warren] that has been diswarrened. **1800** D. LYSONS *Suppl. to Environs Lond.* 241 Staines forest was diswarrened and disforested by the King's charter in 1227.

† **dis'waryed**, *a. Obs. rare.* [f. AF. *deswaré, OF. *desguaré, *desgaré = OF. *esgaré*, *esward*, mod.F. *égaré*. See DESWARRÉ.] Strayed, gone astray, having lost his way.

? **13..** *Cast. Love* (Halliw.) 429 As a diswaryed mon mysrad, On uche half he his myslad.

† **dis'weapon**, *v. Obs.* [DIS- 7 a.] *trans.* To deprive of weapons; to disarm. Also *fig.*

1602 MIDDLETON *Blurt* II. i. Wks. (1885) I. 29 Camillo and his men set upon him, get him down, disweapon him. **1618** BOLTON *Florus* I. xxiii. 65 If his mother Veturia..had not disweapon'd him with weeping. **1652-62** HEYLIN *Cosmogr.* I. (1682) 118 Posthumius so disweaponed them, that he scarce left them Instruments to plough the earth.

diswench: see DIS- 7 a.

† **di'swere**. *Obs.* Also **dys-**, **-ware**, **-wary**, **-weare**. [f. DIS- 5 + WERE *sb.*³ doubt, hesitation.] Doubt. ***wythout diswere***, without doubt, 'ywis': common as a metrical tag.

c **1420** *Liber Cocorum* (1862) 25 Lay þo tenche opon a platere fayre, Do on þat browet withouten disware. *c* **1440** *Promp. Parv.* 123/2 Dyswere, or dowte, *dubium*. *c* **1450** *Cov. Myst.* 383 Seynt Ihon the Evangelist wrot and tauht, as I lere, In a book cleped Apocriphun, wythoutyn dyswary. *c* **1450** *Bk. Curtasye* 436 in *Babees Bk.*, Gromes palettis shyn fyle and make litere, ix fote on lengthe with-out diswere. *a* **1500** H. BRERETON *Song, Lady Bessy* (Way *Promp. Parv.*), You promised..To him to be both true and just, And now you stand in a disweare.

diswhip (dɪsˈhwɪp), *v. nonce-wd.* [f. DIS- 7 a + WHIP *sb.*] *trans.* To deprive of a whip. Hence **dis'whipped** *ppl. a.*

1837 CARLYLE *Fr. Rev.* II. I. i, Is it neither restored Father nor diswhipped Taskmaster that walks there?

diswig (dɪsˈwɪg), *v.* [DIS- 7 a.] *trans.* To deprive of a wig.

1780 in *Mrs. Delany's Corr.* Ser. II. II. 533 They had diswigged Lord Bathurst. **1861** SALA in *Temple Bar Mag.* II. 22 She had publicly diswigged the dancing-master.

dis'window, *v. rare.* [DIS- 7 a.] *trans.* To deprive of windows.

1837 CARLYLE *Fr. Rev.* III. v. vii. (1872) 208 Ghastly châteaus stare on you..disroofed, diswindowed.

diswing (dɪsˈwɪŋ), *v. rare.* [DIS- 7 a.] *trans.* To deprive of wings.

1837 CARLYLE *Diamond Necklace* iii, Misc. Ess. (1872) V. 142 A butterfly, now diswinged and again a worm.

† **dis'wit**, *v. Obs.* [f. DIS- 7 a + WIT *sb.*] *trans.* To deprive of wit. Hence **dis'witted** *ppl. a.*, bereft of one's wits, crazed.

1599 T. M[OUFET] *Silkwormes* 34 Diswitted dolts that huge things wonder at. **1627** DRAYTON *Agincourt* 121 But ranne her selfe away alone..As she had beene diswitted.

† **dis'wont**, *v. Obs.* [f. DIS- 6 + WONT *v.*] *trans.* To render unaccustomed or unused; to disaccustom. Hence **dis'wonted** *ppl. a.*, unwonted, unaccustomed, unusual.

1600 HOLLAND *Livy* XLI. xxiii. 1111 This diswonted voiage and unaccustomed expedition [*itineris insoliti*]. **1627-47** FELTHAM *Resolves* I. xvii. 58 Why should a diswonted unkindnesse make me ingrate for wonted benefits? **1634-5** BRERETON *Trav.* (Chetham 1844) 105 They inure themselves to..hardship, and will not diswont themselves.

diswood (dɪsˈwʊd), *v.* [f. DIS- 7 a + WOOD *sb.*] *trans.* To deprive of wood or trees.

1611 FLORIO, *Sbascare*, to vnwood, to lope, to cut downe or fell wood, trees or branches, to diswood. **1878** G. R. L. MARRIOTT tr. *E. de Laveleye's Prim. Property* 82 Almost all the gorges..are diswooded to a terrible extent.

† **dis'workmanship**. *Obs. nonce-wd.* [DIS- 9.] Bad or defective workmanship.

1610 HEYWOOD *Apol. for Actors, Addr. to Printer* (1612) 62 When I would have taken a particular account of the *errata*, the printer [of 'Britaines Troy'] answered me hee would not publish his owne disworkemanship, but rather let his owne fault lye upon the necke of the author.

† **dis'worship**, *sb. Obs.* [f. DIS- 9 + WORSHIP *sb.*]

1. The opposite of worship; the withholding of esteem, regard, or honour; dishonour, disgrace, discredit.

a **1400-50** *Alexander* (E.E.T.S.) p. 280 Besechyng þat..by no maner of the delectacion he suffre me do þat thyng þat is ayen your profectez ne to my disworship. **1489** CAXTON *Faytes of A.* III. ix. 186 It is the captaynes dysworship whan suche felawes he has chosen. **1576** FLEMING *Panopl. Epist.* 395 Your vertue hathe done you more honour, then your fortune hathe wrought you disworship. **1644** MILTON *Divorce* I. iv. 128 Adultery..a thing which the rankest politician would think it shame and disworship that his laws should countenance.

b. with *a* and *pl.*: A disgrace, a dishonour.

1465 SIR J. PASTON in *Paston Lett.* No. 531. II. 245 Wheche wer a gret dysworchep to my Lord. **1600** HOLLAND *Livy* 881 (R.) It were a great disworship and shame even for them, that there should remaine in bondage any [etc.].

2. Alleged term for a 'company' of Scots.

1486 *Bk. St. Albans* F vij, A Disworship of Scottis.

† **dis'worship**, *v. Obs.* [f. DIS- 6 + WORSHIP *v.* or f. prec.] *trans.* The reverse of *to worship*; to do 'disworship' or dishonour to; to dishonour.

a **1450** *Knt. de la Tour* (1868) 76 This fals traitour wolde haue rauisshed and disworshipped me here. **1483** *Cath. Angl.* 102/1 To Disworschippe, *dehonorare*. **1519** HORMAN *Vulg.* 59 b, Nothyng..that shulde disworshyp or abate the laude of thy dedes. **1549** COVERDALE *Erasm. Par. 1 Cor.* xii. 34 By the uncomlynesse of any parte, the whole body is diswurshypped. **1610** HEALEY *St. Aug. Citie of God* 176 Therefore was this godde dis-worshipped without the citty.

Hence **dis'worshipping** *vbl. sb.*, dishonouring.

1529 MORE *Dyaloge* II. 63 a/2 Dyspytynge and dysworshyppynge of sayntys.

† **dis'worshipful**, *a. Obs.* [f. DISWORSHIP *sb.*, after *worshipful*.] Fraught with disworship; dishonourable.

1539 TAVERNER *Erasm. Prov.* (1552) 29 [They] meruayled why he wolde take so vyle and dysworshypfull an offyce upon hym [etc.]. **1564** HAWARD *Eutropius* IV. 46 Concluded a dysworshipfull peace wyth him.

† **dis'worth**, *v. Obs. rare.* [DIS- 7 a.] *trans.* To deprive of worth; to render worthless or unworthy.

1627 FELTHAM *Resolves* I. [II.] xl. 126 Nothing more disworthes man than Cowardice.

disy, disyn, obs. ff. DIZZY, DIZEN.

† **dis'yellow**, *v. Obs. nonce-wd.* [DIS- 7 a.] *trans.* To remove the yellow from; to rid of jaundice.

1586 WARNER *Alb. Eng.* II. x, Her crooked joynts (which long ere then, supported, scarcely stood) She brought unto a wallowing place, disiellowing so her bloud.

† **'disyllabe, dissyllabe,** *a. Obs. rare.* [a. F. *dissyllabe* (16th c. in Godef. *Supp.*), ad. L. *disyllabus*, a. Gr. δισύλλαβος of two syllables, f. δι-, DI-[2] twice + συλλαβή syllable. For spelling, see next.] = DISYLLABIC.

a **1637** B. JONSON *Eng. Gram.* I. vii, All verbes dissyllabes ending in el, er, ry, and ish, accent *in prima.*

disyllabic, dissyllabic (daɪ-, dɪsɪˈlæbɪk). *a.* (and *sb.*) [a. F. *dissyllabique* (16th c.), f. L. *disyllab-us* (see prec. and -IC): after SYLLABIC.

In this and the following related words, as also in *trisyllable*, etc., the non-etymological spellings *diss-*, *triss-*, were originally taken over from French (*dissyllabe, trissyllabe*, etc.), in which, according to Darmesteter, the function of the *ss* is 'to express the hard sound of the *s*'. In English, *trissyllable*, though frequent in 17–18th c., was early corrected in the Dictionaries and altered to *trisyllable. Dissyllable* was universal in 17–18th c., and (app. either under the erroneous impression that it contains, not the Greek prefix δι-, but the word δίς, or from association with words in the Latin prefix *dis-*, as *disseminate, dissimulate, dissonant*, etc.), is still the spelling of the majority. But classical scholars now prefer the etymological form, which has also been approved by the Philological Society.]

Consisting of two syllables. Also as *sb.*

a **1637** B. JONSON *Eng. Gram.* I. vii, In all nounes dissyllabick. **1812** BYRON *Waltz* xiii, *note*, There are several dissyllabic names. **1840** MRS. F. TROLLOPE *Widow Married* iv, The postman's speaking dissyllabic signal. **1871** EARLE *Philol. Eng. Tongue* § 119 The elongation of this vowel has in a few instances produced a disyllabic word out of an old monosyllable. **1934** JESPERSEN *Essent. Eng. Gram.* iv. 41 *Fire* and *hire* are disyllabics as early as in Shakespeare. **1935** CURME *Gram. Eng. Lang.* II. 341 The dissyllabics, *often* and *early*.

disy'llabically, diss-, *adv.* [f. prec. + -AL[1] + -LY[2].] In a disyllabic manner; as two syllables.

1878 H. H. VAUGHAN *Shaks. Readings* 321 A word which is with us now simply a monosyllable, articulated by Shakespeare disyllabically.

disy'llabify, diss-, *v.* [f. L. *disyllab-us* (see above) + -FY.] *trans.* = DISYLLABIZE. So **disyˌllabifi'cation.**

1846 WORCESTER cites *Christian Observer* (for both words).

di'syllabism, diss-. [f. as next + -ISM: cf. F. *dissyllabisme.*] Disyllabic character or state.

1885 *Encycl. Brit.* XVIII. 774 (*Philology*) We do not yet know that all dissyllabism, and even that all complexity of syllable beyond a single consonant with following vowel, is not the result of combination or reduplication.

disyllabize, diss- (daɪ-, dɪˈsɪləbaɪz), *v.* [f. L. *disyl'labus*: see DISYLLABE and -IZE.] *trans.* To make disyllabic.

1870 E. A. ABBOTT *Shaks. Gram.* §484 Whether the word is dissyllabized, or merely requires a pause after it, cannot.. be determined. **1886** J. B. MAYOR *Eng. Metres* iii. 36 Monosyllables, in which 'r' follows a vowel, are often disyllabized in Shakespeare.

disyllable, dissyllable (daɪ-, dɪˈsɪləb(ə)l), *sb.* (*a.*) Also 6 dissill-, 7 dyssyll-. [f. F. *dissyllabe*, in 16th c. *dissillabe* (see above); after SYLLABLE, F. *syllabe.* For spelling, see DISYLLABIC.]

A. *sb.* A word, or metrical foot, consisting of two syllables.

1589 PUTTENHAM *Eng. Poesie* II. xii[i]. (Arb.) 128 For wordes monosyllables.. if they be tailed one to another, or th'one to a dissillable or polyssillable ye ought to allow them that time that best serues your purpose and pleaseth your eare most. **1668** WILKINS *Real Char.* 416 Expressed.. in Dyssyllables by repeating the second Radical Consonant after the last Vowel. **1874** SWEET *Eng. Sounds* 47 Dissyllables ending in a vowel.. are almost always lengthened. **1883** LIDDELL & SCOTT *Greek-Eng. Lex.* δισυλλαβέω.. to use as a disyllable. **1887** EARLE *Philol. Eng. Tongue* (ed. 4) §174 The plural 'aches'.. appears as a disyllable in Shakspeare, Butler, and Swift. **1889** R. ELLIS *Comment. on Catullus* p. xxvii, In the short elegy to Hortulus the pentameter ends four times with a disyllable, four times with a trisyllable.

B. as *adj.* = DISYLLABIC.

1749 *Numbers in Poet. Comp.* 17 They are compounded of two dissyllable Feet. **1824** L. MURRAY *Eng. Gram.* (ed. 5) I. 348 Dissyllable nouns in *er*: as, 'Cánker, bútter', have the accent on the former syllable.

disyntheme (daɪˈsɪnθiːm). *Math.* [f. DI-[2] + SYNTHEME.] A system of groups of elements, each of the groups being formed of a certain number of elements, so that each occurs just twice among all the groups. Thus 1·2, 2·3, 3·4, 1·4 is a duadic disyntheme—that is, one composed of pairs.

1879 SYLVESTER in *Amer. Jrnl. Math.* II. 94 When a disyntheme is formed by means of cycles all of an even order, it will be resolvable into a pair of single synthemes, and in no other case. *Ibid.*, *Duadic disyntheme*, Any combination of duads, with or without repetition, in which each element occurs twice and no oftener.

disyoke (dɪsˈjəʊk), *v. rare.* [f. DIS- 6 + YOKE *v.*] *trans.* To unyoke; to free from the yoke.

1847 TENNYSON *Princ.* II. 127 Who first had dared To leap the rotten pales of prejudice, Disyoke their necks from custom.

dit, *sb.*[1] *arch.* Also 6 ditt. [app. taken by Spenser from ME. *dit* = DITE *sb.*[1], and erroneously pronounced with short vowel, perh. by association with *ditty*. Thence in later verse.] A poetical composition; a ditty: see DITE *sb.*[1]

1590 SPENSER *F.Q.* II. vi. 13 No song but did containe a lovely ditt. [cf. *a* **1592** T. WATSON *Tears Fancie* li. Poems (Arb.) 204 No song but did containe a louelie ditt.] **1861** MRS. BROWNING *Paraphr. Monnus* Last Poems 125 A Hamadryad sang a nuptial dit Right shrilly.

dit (dɪt), *sb.*[2] Chiefly *U.S.* Also **di** (dɪ). [Imitative.] In Morse telegraphy, etc.: = DOT *sb.*[1] 5 e. Cf. DAH *sb.*[2]

When a message is being described, *di* is used for a dot appearing at the beginning or in the middle of a character string, and *dit* for one at the end, as *di-di-dah-dah-di-dit* 'question mark'.

1942, 1957 [see DAH *sb.*[2]]. **1968** *Radio Communication Handbk.* (ed. 4) xx. 2/1 The space between parts of the same letter should be equal to one di (dit). **1977** *Sci. Amer.* Dec. 42/3 The tapes offer a meticulous set of graded dit-dah practice sessions, half an hour each at 5, 7.5, 10 and 13 words per minute.

dit (dɪt), *v.* Now only *Sc.* and *dial.* Forms: 1 **dyttan**, 3–4 **dutte(n(*ü*)**, 3–6 **ditt(e**, 4–6 **dytt**, 4– **dit.** *Pa. t.* and *pple.* **ditted**, *Sc.* **dittit**; also pa. t. 3 **dutte**; pple. 4–9 **dit**, 5 **dytt.** [OE. *dyttan* to close, shut:—OTeut. type **duttjan*, prob. f. **dutto*m, OE. *dott*, a small lump, a clot, a plug: see DOT, DOTTLE. Cf. FORDIT.]

1. *trans.* To stop up, close up, shut (an opening); to fill *up* (a hole or gap). *lit.* and *fig.*

c **1000** *Ags. Gosp.* Luke xi. 53 Ongunnun ða farisei.. his muð dyttan. *c* **1000** *Ags. Ps.* lvii. 4 Anlic nædran.. seo.. dytteð hyre earan. *c* **1200** *Trin. Coll. Hom.* 199 We.. swo ditteð þe eare and noht ne hercnið. *c* **1200** ORMIN 18633 Onnʒæn þatt laþe læredd folc Forr þeʒʒre muþ to dittenn. *a* **1225** *Ancr. R.* 82 Me schulde dutten [*v.r.* ditten] his muð.. mid herde fustes. *c* **1340** *Gaw. & Gr. Knt.* 1233 þe dor drawen & dit with a derf haspe. **1375** BARBOUR *Bruce* VI. 168 The vpcom wes then Dittit with slayn hors and men. *c* **1460** *Towneley Myst.* (Surtees) 194 Ayther has thou no wytt Or els ar thyne eres dytt. **1572** *Satir. Poems Reform.* xxxiii. *Lament. of Lady Scotl.* 196 Dit the mouths of thame that sa dois speik. **1647** H. MORE *Cupid's Conflict* lv. Philos. Poems 173 Foul sluggish fat ditts up your dulléd eye. *a* **1758** RAMSAY *Scots Prov.* (1776) 77 When a's in and the slap dit, Rise herd and let the dog sit. **1871** W. ALEXANDER *Johnny Gibb* (1873) 140 Ye wud 'a keepit by the aul' proerb that says, 'Dit your mou' wi your meat'.

2. To stop or obstruct the course or way of.

a **1300** *Cursor M.* 11942 (Cott.) Wit nith and enst and iuel witt þe water wissing can he ditt. *Ibid.* 24003 (Cott.) Mi teres all mi sight þai ditte. **1362** LANGL. *P. Pl.* A. VII. 178 An Hep of Hermytes henten heom spades And doluen drit and donge to dutte honger oute. *c* **1460** *Towneley Myst.* (Surtees) 14 Almost had myne breth beyn dit. **1513** DOUGLAS *Æneis* v. xiii. 96 The riueris dittit with deid corsis wox reid. **1818** SCOTT *Hrt. Midl.* xxx, It.. sweeps away a' my gude thoughts, and dits up my gude words.

dit, early form of DITE *sb.*[1] *Obs.* composition.

‖ **dita** (ˈdiːtə). [The native name.] The bark of a forest tree found in the Philippine Islands, *Echites (Alstonia) scholaris.* Usually **dita-bark.**

1876 *Pharmaceut. Jrnl.* Ser. III. VI. 142 Under the name 'Dita' the natives of the Philippines indicate the bark of the *Echites scholaris*, Linn. (*Alstonia scholaris*, Brown.), a stately forest tree. *Ibid.* The fame of dita bark as a remedy is of old standing, since in 1678 it was mentioned by Rheede and afterwards in 1741 by Rumphius. **1879** WATTS *Dict. Chem.* VIII. 688 Dita bark usually consists of irregular curved fragments from 40 to 60 mm. long, 15 mm. wide and 1 mm. thick, covered externally with a thin leather-coloured cortical layer.

Hence **ditamine** (ˈdɪtəmaɪn), **ditaine** (ˈdɪteɪaɪn), *Chem.* [see AMINE, -INE], the characteristic amine or alkaloid of dita-bark, $C_{16}H_{19}NO_2$.

1876 *Pharmaceut. Jrnl.* Ser. III. VI. 143 Ditain was prepared by Gruppe in a manner similar to that in which quinine is prepared. **1879** WATTS *Dict. Chem.* VIII. 688 Gorup-Besanez afterwards extracted from ditaïn a crystallisable substance which proved to be an alkaloïd, but which.. he did not completely examine. *Ibid.*, Ditamine is easily soluble in ether [etc.].

dital (ˈdaɪtəl). [f. It. *dito* finger, after *pedal*: cf. It. *ditale* glove-finger, finger-stall, thimble.]

The name given to a kind of stop to be pressed by the thumb, by which the pitch of a guitar- or lute-string can be raised by a semitone. *dital harp*, an instrument invented by Edward Light in 1798, and patented with improvements in 1816, intended to be an improvement of the guitar. It was fitted with ditals.

1816 *Specif. E. Light's Patent* No. 4041. 2 To the harp lute at present in use I apply certain pieces of mechanism which I call ditals or thumb keys. **1880** GROVE *Dict. Mus.* s.v. *Dital harp*, Called 'ditals' or 'thumb-keys', in distinction from 'pedals' or 'foot-keys'.

ditanie, -ny, ditayne, obs. ff. DITTANY.

† **di'tation.** *Obs.* [n. of action f. L. *dītāre* to enrich, f. *dīves, dīt-* rich] Enrichment.

1612–15 BP. HALL *Contempl.*, *N.T.* I. v, After all the presents of these eastern worshippers who intended rather homage, than ditation, the blessed virgin comes, in the forme of poverty, with her two doves. **1615** T. ADAMS *Lycanthropy* 29 They grudge not the Merchants wealth, nor envy the ditation of Lawyers. **1659** FELTHAM *Low Countries* Resolves, etc. (1677) 60 War.. the worlds ruine.. is to them prosperity and Ditation.

ditch (dɪtʃ), *sb.*[1] Forms: 1–3 dic, 2–7 dich(e, 4–6 dych(e (4 dicche), 5–7 ditche (6 deche, dytch), 6– ditch. [OE. *dic*, which has also given DIKE *sb.*[1], q.v.

The analogy of other words, e.g. ME. *like, liche*, (dead) body, *like, liche*, adj., *-rik, -riche*, suffix in *kinrik, kyneriche*, etc., *ik, ich*, I, *pik, piche*, pitch, *stike, stiche*, stitch, leads us to expect *dike* as the northern, *dich* as the southern repr. of OE. *dic.* The ME. evidence favours this; but in modern use, both forms occur in nearly all parts of the country, with various differentiation of meaning. Generally, *ditch* is a hollow channel or deep furrow, wet or dry, but in some parts (see sense 4) it is an embankment or raised fence; usually *dike* or *dyke* is a bank or wall, but in many parts it is a wide and deep channel for running water. The existence of *dick* or *deek* in this sense in Kent, Sussex, and other southern counties, is remarkable. The use of *dike, dyke*, for a sea-wall or embankment in the eastern counties, may possibly have been introduced from Holland: cf. the title DIKE-GRAVE.]

1. a. An excavation narrow in proportion to its length; a long and narrow hollow dug in the ground; the trench or fosse of a fortification, etc.

[**847**–*c* **1205** see DIKE *sb.*[1] I.] **1045** *Charter Eadweard* in *Cod. Dipl.* IV. 98 (written after 1200) Of ðam paðe on ðane greatan þorn ðe stynt wið Grimes dic; andlang ðære diche on ðone haran þorn. *a* **1200** *Moral Ode* 41 þes riche Men weneð bon siker þurh walle and þurh diche. *c* **1205** LAY. 15900 þa dich wes idoluen seoue vet depre. *c* **1290** *S. Eng. Leg.* I. 55/70 He wende and hudde him in a Dich. *c* **1340** *Cursor M.* 9899 (Trin.) A deep diche [*v.rr.* dik, dick] is þere aboute. *c* **1430** LYDG. *Bochas* III. 94 a, Cincinnatus.. Made dyches to geat his Sustenaunce. **1494** FABYAN *Chron.* VI. cli. 138 He also.. made a famous dyke atwene Walys and the vtter bondys of Mercia.. the which, to this day, is namyd Offedych. **1553** EDEN *Treat. Newe Ind.* (Arb.) 13 They moued neare vnto the trenche or ditche of the castell. **1606** SHAKS. *Ant. & Cl.* V. ii. 57 Rather a ditch in Egypt Be gentle graue vnto me. **1665** BOYLE *Occas. Refl.* V. vii. (1845) 324 One must search the Ditches amongst Briars and Weeds.. to find Medicinable Herbs. **1776** GIBBON *Decl. & F.* (1846) I. i. 17 The rampart.. was.. defended by a ditch of twelve feet in depth as well as in breadth. **1829** COL. HAWKER *Diary* (1893) II. 3 The most impregnable fences I ever met with, and blind ditches, six feet deep, to half the fields. **1879** *Cassell's Techn. Educ.* IV. 136/2 The ditch of a permanent work provides the earth to form the rampart.

b. *Salt-making* (*Cheshire*). See quot.

1884 *Cheshire Gloss., Ditch*, salt-making term. The space in the 'hot-house' between two raised flues for putting lump salt in to complete its stoving and drying.

c. Calcutta, so called in allusion to the Mahratta Ditch (see MAHRATTA 3). *slang.*

1886 YULE & BURNELL *Hobson-Jobson* 246/2 *Ditch*; and *Ditcher*, disparaging sobriquets for Calcutta and its European citizens.

d. The trench or piece of ground immediately surrounding a bowling green.

1861 *Chambers's Encycl.* II. 289/1 If a bowl.. strikes the jack, and then rolls into the ditch, it reckons as if on the green. **1886** T. TAYLOR *Rules of Bowling* 16 When the jack is run into the ditch by a bowl in the regular course of the game. **1902** *Encycl. Brit.* XXVI. 328/1 There is no excuse for short play on the part of the first players; their bowls would be far better in the ditch. **1962** *Bowls* (*Know the Game*) 3/2 The green must be level and surrounded by a ditch and bank.

2. a. *esp.* Such a hollow dug out to receive or conduct water, esp. to carry off the surface drainage of a road, a field, etc.

On the borders of fields, etc., often serving the double purpose of carrying off surface water, and of forming an effective protective fence. The latter purpose is in marshy ground often served by a ditch alone, but elsewhere usually in combination with a hedge.

1297 R. GLOUC. (1724) 409 Alle þe wateres.. aboute þe toun þere, And dyches and puttes, rede of blode were. *c* **1305** *St. Kenelm* 364 in *E.E.P.* (1862) 57 þis bodi.. in a foul dich me drouʒ In þe fouleste þat þere was neʒ. **13..** *E.E. Allit. P.* A. 606 He lauez hys gyftez as water of dyche. **1484** CAXTON *Fables of Æsop* II. ii, There were frogges whiche were in dyches and pondes at theyre lyberte. **1582** N. LICHEFIELD tr. *Castanheda's Conq. E. Ind.* lix. 122 b, There was cast about the same a Caue or Ditch, which alwaies was full of water. **1697** DRYDEN *Virg. Georg.* IV. 687 All these Cocytus bounds.. With muddy Ditches, and with deadly Weeds. **1756** C. LUCAS *Ess. Waters* II. 140 The overflowings of this spring fill all the.. ditches with a light, pale ochre. **1845** JAMES *A. Neil* vii, Ditches enough to drain the sea. **1881** RAYMOND *Mining Gloss., Ditch*, an artifical watercourse, flume, or canal, to convey water for mining. A flume is usually of wood; a ditch, of earth.

b. Extended rhetorically to any watercourse or channel, including those of natural formation.

1589 PUTTENHAM *Eng. Poesie* III. xxiii. (Arb.) 277 Thy maister durst not haue sent me These words, were it not for that broad ditch [*i.e.* the English Channel] betweene him and me. **1608** E. GRIMSTONE *Hist. France* (1611) 364 That great ditch of the sea is sufficient to distinguish these two Monarchies. **1660** F. BROOKE tr. *LeBlanc's Trav.* 251 This branch.. is much about the rate of the ditch or channel of Pisa at Livorne. **1842** DICKENS *Amer. Notes* II. iv, The Mississippi.. an enormous ditch sometimes two or three miles wide, running liquid mud. **1874** KINGSLEY *Lett.* (1878) II. 432 Across the rude rushing muddy ditch, the Mississippi.

c. (*a*) *Naval slang.* The sea; (*b*) *R.A.F. slang.* The English Channel or the North Sea.

1922 *Man. Seamanship* I. i. 33 A smart seaman would not talk officially of the sea by a favourite slang expression 'the ditch'. **1925** FRASER & GIBBONS *Soldier & Sailor Words* 78 'He fell into the ditch', *i.e.* overboard. **1945** PARTRIDGE *Dict. R.A.F. Slang* 23 *The Ditch*, the sea; especially the English Channel. (Adopted from nautical slang.)

†3. Any hollow dug in the ground; a hole, pit, cave, den. *Obs.*

c **1275** *Passion of our Lord* 80 in *O.E. Misc.* 39 Hit is iwrite þat myn hus is bede hus icleped. And ye þeouene dich hit habbeþ y-maked. c **1320** *Seuyn Sag.* (W.) 1279 The wise man dede make a dich, Ful of lim and of pich, That yif he agen wald come, That the traitour ss cholde bi nome. **1340** *Ayenb.* 57 þe tauerne is a dich to þieues. c **1420** *Pallad. on Husb.* I. 76 Make a dyche, and yf the moolde abounde And wol not in agayn, it is fecounde. **14..** *Voc.* in Wr.-Wülcker 584 *Fovea*, a dyche.

4. A bank or mound formed by the earth thrown up in digging a hollow or trench; an embankment; = DIKE *sb.*[1] 5, 6. Now only *dial.*

1568 GRAFTON *Chron.* II. 1301 [They] brake downe those inclosures, and cast downe ditches. **1590** R. PAYNE *Descr. Irel.* (1841) 9 Let the slope side of your ditch be towardes your warraine. **1635** *N. Riding Rec.* IV. 36 Stopping the highway by casting upp a great ditche. **1666** in Picton *L'pool Munic. Rec.* (1883) I. 315 Roger Bushell shall throwe down that new ditch hee hath made. **1880** *Antrim & Down Gloss.*, *Ditch*, a fence, generally of earth. **1892** E. J. HARDY in *Sund. Mag.* Sept. 600 It is not true, then, that [in Malta] the mosquitoes are so large that they sit on ditches and bark at you.

5. Phrases. ***to fall*** or ***lead into a ditch***; ***to die in a ditch***. ***the last ditch***, the last line of defence; ***to die in the last ditch***, to die, resisting to the last (see DIE *v.*[1] 3); so ***to be driven to the last ditch***, i.e. to the utmost extremities. ***to lay*** (***put***) ***under the ditch*** (U.S.), to intersect with ditches so as to irrigate.

c **1380** WYCLIF *Serm.* Sel. Wks. II. 25 Foolis and sinful men lede oþer foolis into þe diche. **1382** —— *Matt.* xv. 14 ȝif a blynd man ȝeue ledynge to a blynd man, bothe fallen doun in to the diche. c **1440** *Gesta Rom.* lxx. 326 (Harl. MS.) The stiward is fallyn in his owne diche, by þe right wisdom of god. **1683** BURNET tr. *More's Utopia* (1684) 39, I..shew him the Ditch into which he will fall, if he is not aware of it. a **1715** To die in the last ditch [see DIE *v.*[1]3]. **1798** in *Proc. Amer. Antiq. Soc.* IX. III. 324 In War We [Citizens of Westmoreland, Virginia] know but one additional Obligation, To die in the Last Ditch or uphold our Nation. **1821** T. JEFFERSON *Writ.* (1892) I. 122 A government.. driven to the last ditch by the universal call for liberty. **1874** BLACKIE *Self-Cult.* 48 He who abstains from it [whisky].. will never die in a ditch. **1890** *Spectator* 29 Mar. 426/1 Although the discussion will be harrassing, the resistance will not be to the last ditch. **1892** *Harper's Mag.* June 93/1 Three-fifths of it [the soil] can be laid under the ditch. *Ibid.* 95/1 This scheme looks forward to putting 30,000 acres under the ditch.

6. *attrib.* and *Comb.* **a.** simple attrib., 'Of, belonging to, found in, working at, a ditch', as ***ditch-back***, ***-bank***, ***-bottom***, ***-dog***, ***-labourer***, ***-side***, ***-work***, ***-world***. **b.** 'Of the quality of a ditch, dirty, vile, worthless', as ***ditch constable***. **c.** objective, as ***ditch-digger***. **d.** Special combs.: **ditch-delivered** *pa. pple.*, brought forth in a ditch; **ditch-drawn**, drawn from a ditch; **ditch measure**, see quot. 1670, and PERCH. Also in various names of plants growing in ditches, as **ditch-bur**, *Xanthium strumarium*; **ditch-down**, the reed-mace, *Typha latifolia*; **ditch-fern**, *Osmunda regalis*; **ditch-grass** (U.S.), *Ruppia maritima*; **ditch-reed**, *Phragmites communis*. Also DITCH-WATER.

1869 *Lonsdale Gloss.*, **Ditch-back*, a fence. **1776** WITHERING *Brit. Plants* (1796) III. 527 White Dead Nettle. On rubbish, cornfields, and *ditch-banks. **1548** TURNER *Names of Herbes* 81 *Xanthium* is called in english *Dichebur or Clotbur. **1608** MIDDLETON *Mad World* v. ii. Wks. (Bullen) III. 350 I'll make you an example for all *ditch constables. **1605** SHAKS. *Macb.* IV. i. 31 Birth-strangled Babe, *Ditch-deliuer'd by a Drab. **1605** —— *Lear* III. iv. 138 Poore Tom, that..swallowes the old Rat, and the *ditch-Dogge. **1611** COTGR., *Typhe*, water-Torch, Cats-tayle, Reed Mace, *Ditch Downe, the marsh beetle or pestle. **1889** *Sat. Rev.* 23 Mar. 335/2 The *ditch-drawn missiles they fling about them. **14..** *MS. Gloss.* Sloane 5 fol. 40b in *Sax. Leechdoms* III. 321 *Diche fern, *Osmunda*. **1869** BLACKMORE *Lorna D.* iv, Here was no *ditch-labourer. **1670** J. SMITH *Eng. Improv. Reviv'd* 25 If the fence be measured by Wood, Hedge, or *Ditch measure, allowing 18 foot to the Perch. c **1440** *Gesta Rom.* viii. 21 (Harl. MS.) The fond knyȝt thei cast in a *dich place. **1843** *Zoologist* I. 100 By *ditch-sides and mill-pond streams. **1562** PHAER *Æneid* IX. Aaiij b, Doth *dichworks giue them pryde? **1890** *Pall Mall G.* 4 Sept. 3/1 Frogs and minnows..and all the wonderful, mysterious *ditch-world that children love!

ditch, *sb.*[2]: see under DITCH *v.*[2]

ditch (dɪtʃ), *v.*[1] [f. DITCH *sb.*[1] OE. had *dícian*, but this would regularly give *dike*: cf. *lícian*, like.]

1. *intr.* To construct a ditch or ditches.

1377 LANGL. *P. Pl.* B. XIX. 232 Somme he tauȝte to tilie to dyche and to thecche. **14..** *Voc.* in Wr.-Wülcker 584 *Fosso*, to dyche. **1523** FITZHERB. *Husb.* §123 It is lesse cost..to quyckeset, dyche, and hedge, than to haue his cattell goo before the herdeman. **1776** J. Q. ADAMS in *Fam. Lett.* (1876) 195 The practice..of ditching round about our enemies. **1860** EMERSON *Cond. Life, Fate* Wks. (Bohn) II. 314 They are ferried over the Atlantic, and carted over America, to ditch and to drudge.

2. *trans.* To surround with a ditch; to cast a ditch *about*, *around*, *esp.* for the purpose of defence, fortification, or fixing a boundary.

13.. *K. Alis.* 2658 That cite was..Wel y-walled, and well y-dyched. c **1386** CHAUCER *Knt.'s T.* 1028 The circuit..a myle was aboute, Walled of stoon, and dyched al witoute. **1520** *Caxton's Chron. Eng.* VII. 118 b/2 He made..a fayre towne of pavylyons, and dyched them all aboute. **1523** FITZHERB. *Husb.* §123 Seuerall closes and pastures..the whiche wolde be wel quyckesetted, dyched, & hedged. **1548** HALL *Chron.*, *Hen. VIII* (an. 12) 77 b, The Campe was.. ditched rounde aboute. **1670** MILTON *Hist. Eng.* II. (1851) 42 Towns then in Britain were only Wooddy places Ditch't round. **1788** *Filey Inclos. Act* 14 The several parcels of land ..shall be inclosed, hedged, ditched, or fenced. **1848** PETRIE tr. *A.S. Chron.* 89 They ditched the city around [*anno* 1016 bedicodon þa burh utan].

3. a. To dig ditches or furrows in for purposes of drainage or irrigation; to provide with ditches.

1393 GOWER *Conf.* I. 153 The erthe..men it delve and diche And eren it with strength of plough. **1565-73** COOPER *Thesaurus*, *Agrum fossione concidere*..to trench or ditch the grounde to avoyde water. **1598** BARRET *Theor. Warres* IV. i. 99 Whether the countrey be stony, plaine field, or ditched. **1747** FRANKLIN *Let.* Wks. 1887 II. 80 Eighty acres [of meadow], forty of which had been ditched and mowed. **1837** HOWITT *Rur. Life* II. iii. (1862) 110 Set two men to ditch the five roods. **1837** HT. MARTINEAU *Soc. Amer.* III. 325 Papa said he might be compelled to ditch rice fields, but he never would undertake to teach children again.

b. To cut furrows in (stone).

1865 *Morn. Star* 18 Apr., It is driven by manual power, and is intended for cutting or 'ditching' the stone in the quarry.

†**4.** *intr.* Of the earth: To become ditched; to open up into furrows or chasms. *Obs.*

1483 CAXTON *Gold. Leg.* 424/1 There cam a woman which meruaylled moche how therthe claue & dyched by hit self onelye by the touchying of the holy mannes Staffe.

5. To clean out, scour (a ditch); to cast up and repair (the banks of a ditch or hedge).

1576 *Act 18 Eliz.* c. 10. §4 All and euery person and persons that shall not repaire, diche, or scoure any hayes, fences, diches, or hedges adioyning to any high way. *Ibid.* §6 Upon paine of forfeiture..for euery rod not so ditched and scoured xii.d. **1874** R. JEFFERIES in *Toilers of Field* (1893) 95 The Master has given him a hedge to cut and ditch. [**1888** ELWORTHY *W. Somerset Word-bk.*, *Dik*,..to make good the sides and top of a hedge, which in this district is usually a high bank; i.e. to throw up the parings upon the top.]

6. a. *trans.* To throw into or as into a ditch; *esp.* in U.S., to throw (a train) off the line or track.

1816 *Sessions' Papers* May/June 248/2 When I got up, they cried..ditch him, and I was immediately thrown into the ditch. **1877** J. A. ALLEN *Amer. Bison* 470 After having trains ditched twice in one week, conductors learned to have ..respect for the idiosyncrasies of the buffalo. **1881** *Philad. Rec.* No. 3438. 1 A..train..struck a drove of cattle..on Saturday. The engine was ditched and turned on its side.

b. *slang.* (*a*) *trans.* To bring (an aircraft) down into the sea in an emergency. (*b*) *intr.* To come down into the sea in an emergency. Cf. DITCH *sb.*[1] 2 c. Hence **ditching** *vbl. sb.*

1941 *Times Weekly* 15 Oct. 19 The pilot..must 'ditch' his aircraft in the sea, near enough to a ship for him to be picked up. **1941** in A. G. Smith et al. *Investigations Behaviour Aircraft* (1957) 23/2 Hudson ditching trials. **1943** REDDING & LEYSHON *Skyways to Berlin* xv. 100, I..got ready to ditch the plane. *Ibid.*, We had had ditching practice. *Ibid.* 101 There is a standard procedure in ditching. **1944** *Times* 20 Mar. 5/7 The crews run over the 'ditching' procedure to be followed should they have to come down on the sea. **1958** *Daily Mail* 15 Aug. 2/5 If an airliner is ditched, it should give a Mayday call. **1962** D. SLAYTON in *Into Orbit* 23 Most flyers have had to learn some kind of ditching technique in case they make a forced landing over water.

c. *transf.* and *fig.* To defeat, frustrate; to abandon, discard; to jilt. (See also quot. 1899.) *slang* (orig. *U.S.*).

1899 'J. FLYNT' *Tramping with Tramps* (1900) 393 *Ditch*, or *be ditched*, to get into trouble, or to fail at what one has undertaken. To be 'ditched' when riding on trains means to be put off, or to get locked into a car. **1911** *Springfield* (Mass.) *Republican* 31 Aug. 1 Its enactment into law would have ditched them in their present reciprocity campaign. **1921** T. WOLFE *Let.* 13 Nov. (1956) 22, C. is going to see a girl in Brookline that he met in the bank last summer and it seems the Ohio girl has been ditched. **1923** *Saucy Stories* 1 Mar. 74/1, I was gonna ask you to hop over to a dance... Can't you ditch the other guy? **1924** G. C. HENDERSON *Keys to Crookdom* 104 After they have committed the hold-up, they 'ditch' the stolen motor vehicle. **1926** J. BLACK *You can't Win* vii. 85 We got 'ditched' off our train at Port Costa, and crawled into a hay car for the night. **1946** 'S. RUSSELL' *To Bed with Grand Music* ii. 27 Let's ditch the others and go and dance privately. **1948** L. A. G. STRONG *Trevannion* 186 The one who scuppered his parents and ditched his wife. **1950** T. S. ELIOT *Cocktail Party* II. 117 It isn't simply the end of an illusion In the ordinary way, or being ditched. **1958** P. KEMP *No Colours or Crest* viii. 175 Davis..was struggling to carry the heavy wireless set; I shouted to him to ditch it and save himself.

7. ***to ditch in***, ***out***: to enclose, or shut out, by means of a ditch; ***to ditch up*** = 2.

1545 ASCHAM *Toxoph.* (Arb.) 96 The more vnreasonable is theyr dede whiche would ditche vp those feeldes priuatly for ther owne profyt. **1555** LATIMER *Serm. & Rem.* (1845) 282 Indeed they ought *regere*..Not as they will themselves: but this *regere* must be hedged in and ditched in. **1630** *R. Johnson's Kingd. & Commw.* 39 To hedge and ditch out their incroaching neighbours.

Hence **ditched** *ppl. a.*, furnished with a ditch; also with *adv.*, as ***ditched-in***, enclosed with a ditch.

1810 *Sporting Mag.* XXXV. 139 Four-mile heats..over the new ditched-in Course. **1895** *United Service Mag.* July 430 The ditched parapet.

ditch, *v.*[2] *dial.* Also deech. [OE. *décan*, ME. *dēche* to smear, daub: app. unknown to the other Teutonic langs. It is notable that this verb, used in OE. and in modern dialects, is known to us, during the intervening 900 years, only in the 15th c. transl. of *Palladius on Husbandry*: see DECHE. The modern *ditch* shows a recent shortening of (iː) to (ɪ).] *trans.* To smear, daub, plaster, impregnate, esp. with dirt which hardens and becomes 'ingrained'.

a **1000**, c **1420** [see DECHE *v.*]. **1790** W. MARSHALL *Midl. Counties* Gloss. (E.D.S.) *Ditch*, to stick to, as the clamminess of mow-burnt hay sticks to the cutting knife. **1860** (*Northamptonsh.*) 'His face and hands are ditched with dirt.' **1872** BESANT & RICE *Ready-Money Mortiboy* xxi, Smearing his coarse hands with spirits, to get off the dirt with which they were ditched. **1881** *Leicester Gloss.* s.v., The touch-'ole were reg'lar ditched up. **1896** *Academy* 29 Feb. 178/3 *Deech't*.

b. *intr.* for *refl.*

1881 *Leicester Gloss.*, *Ditch*..to get dirty; filled with dirt. 'My hands never ditch', i.e. the dirt does not get grained into them so that it will not wash off.

Hence **ditch** *sb.*[2] *dial.* 'dirt grained into the hands, or in cracks, crevices, etc.' (*Leicester Gloss.*).

1847-78 HALLIWELL, *Ditch*, grimy dirt. **1881** *Leicester Gloss.* s.v., I want to get off the ditch.

ditcher ('dɪtʃə(r)). [f. DITCH *v.*[1] + -ER[1].]

1. One who makes and repairs ditches.

c **1430** LYDG. *Min. Poems* (1840) 211 (Mätz.) Dichers, delverys, that greet travaylle endure. **1464** *Mann. & Househ. Exp.* 261 My mastyr payed to John Wodeman, the dycher, iij.s. iiij.d. **1602** SHAKS. *Ham.* v. i. 33 There is no ancient Gentlemen, but Gardiners, Ditchers and Graue-makers; they hold vp Adams Profession. **1730** SWIFT *Panegyrick on Dean* 156 Our thatcher, ditcher, gard'ner, baily. **1848** MILL *Pol. Econ.* I. ii. §1 The hedgers and ditchers who made the fences..for the protection of the crop.

2. A machine used to make ditches; a ditching-machine.

1846 *Rep. Comm. Patents* (*U.S. Pat. Off.*) (1847) 256 Having thus fully described my improved ditcher what I claim therein as new..is [etc.]. **1862** *Times* 12 June, In addition to the agricultural machines..a ditcher, which will cut a ditch of any depth or width, lift out the earth, and deposit it in any given place. **1874** KNIGHT *Dict. Mech.* I. 711 A rotary ditcher.

attrib. **1887** *Sci. Amer.* 30 July 74/1 A combined cultivator and potato digger..It has a plow or ditcher shovel formed from a plate of metal.

3. (See quot. 1890.)

1877 A. ARNOLD *Through Persia* II. xiv. 251 Huge iron vessels, long and narrow, built for the Suez Canal, and locally known as 'ditchers'. **1884** *Pall Mall G.* 19 Nov. 1/2 In time of war the 'ditchers' would be bound to coal..at Sierra Leone. **1890** *New Rev.* Feb. 153 Steamers specially built for the passage of the Suez Canal, and hence called 'Ditchers'.

4. A bowl which runs or is driven off the green. Cf. DITCH *sb.*[1] 1 d.

1886 T. TAYLOR *Rules of Bowling* 17 A bowl which runs off the green..and which has not previously touched the jack, is called a 'ditcher', and must be immediately removed to the bank. **1948** G. T. BURROWS *All about Bowls* xiv. 86 *Ditcher*, a bowl that runs on into the ditch or is driven there or is turned quickly into the pebbles, for reasons of strategy.

5. A resident in Calcutta (cf. DITCH *sb.*[1] 1 c). *slang.*

1886 [see DITCH *sb.*[1] 1 c]. **1909** *Westm. Gaz.* 17 June 8/1 The existence of the unfortunate ditchers left to themselves in the off season. **1923** *United Free Ch. Miss. Rec.* June 248/1 Residents in Calcutta are sometimes referred to..as 'Ditchers'.

ditching ('dɪtʃɪŋ), *vbl. sb.* [f. as prec. + -ING[1].] The action of the verb DITCH. **a.** The making and repairing of ditches.

c **1380** WYCLIF *Serm.* Sel. Wks. I. 28 For dichying and hegging and delvynge of tounes. **1523** FITZHERB. *Husb.* §123 In quickesettynge, dychynge and hedgynge. **1767** A. YOUNG *Farmer's Lett. to People* 245 When the ditching is done, the next work is to land-drain the whole fields. **1868** ROGERS *Pol. Econ.* xii. (1876) 159 Rough draining, ditching, and ridging were used in wet soils.

b. *Sculpture.* (See quot.)

1886 *Pall Mall G.* 1 June 14/1 On being asked the way he prepared his models he continued:—I first draw the subject in crayon..and then transfer the lines to clay. Then I begin an operation known as 'ditching,' which consists of digging up around the outlines of the figures and objects until they stand out in rough relief.

c. Of aircraft: see DITCH *v.*[1] 6 b.

d. *Comb.*, as ***ditching-machine***, ***-plough***, ***-tool***.

1874 KNIGHT *Dict. Mech.*, *Ditching-plow*, a plow having a deep, narrow share for cutting drains and trenches, and means for lifting the earth and depositing it at the side or sides of the excavation. **1880** J. W. HILL *Illustr. Guide Agric. Implem.* 500 Fowler's ditching machine..for opening wide drainage or irrigation ditches.

'ditchless, *a.* [f. DITCH *sb.*[1] + -LESS.] Without a ditch.

1876 T. HARDY *Ethelberta* (1890) 27 The glazed high-road which stretched, hedgeless and ditchless..lying like a riband unrolled across the scene. **1892** A. G. LEE *Hist. Columbus* (Ohio) I. 29 Skirted by a ditchless wall of earth and stone.

'ditchlike, *a.* [f. as prec. + LIKE *a.*] Like or resembling a ditch.

a **1743** SAVAGE *London & Bristol* (R.), Thy cliffs a ditch-like river laves, Rude as thy rocks and muddy as thy waves. **1890** BOLDREWOOD *Colonial Ref.* (1891) 185 A sombre water-course, the ditchlike banks of which dropped perpendicularly through the clay.

'ditch-water. The stagnant, stale, or foul water which collects in a ditch. Chiefly in the phrases: †*as digne as d.* (see DIGNE 4); †*as light* (i.e. easy) *as d.*; *as dull as d.*

c**1394** *P. Pl. Crede* 375 þey ben digne as dich water þat dogges in baytеþ. c**1425** *Craft Nombrynge* (E.E.T.S.) 16 þen worch forth in þe oþer figurys till þou come to þe ende, for it is lyght as dyche water. **1819** SHELLEY *Cenci* II. i. 67 Ditch water, and the fever-stricken flesh Of buffaloes. **1844** W. H. MAXWELL *Sports & Adv. Scotl.* (1855) 17 The people..are as 'dull as ditch-water'. **1893** G. TRAVERS *Mona Maclean* I. 203, I find them dull as ditch-water.

attrib. **1826** H. N. COLERIDGE *West Indies* 295 In virtue of their freckled ditchwater faces.

Hence **'ditchwaterly** *adv.* = 'as ditch-water' (see above); **'ditch,watery** *a.*, of the quality of ditch-water, dull as ditch-water; whence **'ditch,wateriness.** (*nonce-wds.*)

1840 *Fraser's Mag.* XXI. 19 If it be so prepared as to be piquant, then, it is of small consequence what may be its ditch-wateriness. **1859** SALA *Gas-light & D.* xxiv. 270 How wofully tired, and ditchwaterly dull they look.

'ditchy, *a.* [f. DITCH *sb.*[1] + -Y[1].] Of the nature of a ditch; abounding in ditches or deep furrows.

1786 T. TWINING in L. Twining *Recreat. & Studies* (1882) 135 If the Seine were a little less ditchy. **1888** *Bradford Cycle Co. Prospectus* 2 The very pleasant swinging sensation one feels when riding ditchy roads..is wonderful compared to the bumping..on an ordinary-type safety.

†**dite,** *sb.*[1] *Obs.* (After 1500 only *Sc.*) Also 5 **dete, dit,** 5-6 **dyt(e,** *Sc.* **dyit.** [a. OF. *dit* (12th c. in Littré) saying, speech:—L. *dict-um* that which is said, saying, word, f. *dīcĕre* to say; cf. DICT. (The final *e* was app. a phonetic expedient to indicate the length of the *ī*; but in some 15th c. instances, it is difficult to say whether *dite* stands for this, or for *ditty*. See also DIT *sb.*[1])]

1. Something indited or composed and put in writing; a composition, writing; a written message, letter, 'passage', etc. *to put in dite*: to put in writing, put on record.

1340-70 *Alex. & Dind.* 819 Sone sente he again his sel & his lettrus..To dindimus þe dere king þat þe dite radde. c**1425** WYNTOUN *Cron.* VIII. xix. 1 Here Wyntown poyntis in þis Dyte Quhat he gert of þis Tretis wryt. c**1470** HENRY *Wallace* v. 540 Maister Jhone Blayr..That fyrst compild in dyt the Latyne buk Off Wallace lyff. **1535** STEWART *Cron. Scot.* I. 474 In haist ane epistill he gart write..contenand this same dyte. **1578** *Ps.* cvi. in *Scot. Poems 16th C.* II. 107 Thy magnitude I will it put in dyte.

2. A composition in poetic form, or intended to be set to music; a song, a ditty.

a**1325** *Prose Psalter* xxxix [xl]. 4 And he laide gode worde in my mouþe, dite to our Lord [Vulg. *carmen Deo nostro*]. c**1386** ? CHAUCER *Balade of Compleynt* 16 Beseching you.. Taccepte in worth this litel povre dyte. c**1470** HENRY *Wallace* XI. 1431 All worthi men at redys this rurall dyt, Blaym nocht the buk. **1567** *Satir. Poems Reform.* iii. 156 Sho the cause is of my wofull dyte.

3. Manner or mode of composition; form of speech; diction, language. *Sc.*

c**1425** WYNTOUN *Cron.* IV. Prol. 3 A Tretys made to be publik, Fourme of dyte and fayre spekyng. **1535** STEWART *Cron. Scot.* (1858) I. 4 The kingis grace I knaw is nocht perfite In Latyn toung, and namelie in sic dyte It wilbe tedious..To reid the thing he can nocht vnderstand. **1549** *Compl. Scot.* vi. 68 The guhilk dreyme i sal reherse in this gros dyit.

4. Clamour, vociferation. *rare.*

c**1400** *Destr. Troy* 5788 Cloudis with the clamour claterit aboue, Of the dit & þe dyn, þat to dethe went. *Ibid.* 11946 The dyn & the dite was dole for to here. *Ibid.* 1347, 8680.

dite, *sb.*[2] Also dit. Phr. *not to care a dit(e)*: not to care at all. Cf. DOIT 2.

1907 *Westm. Gaz.* 7 Sept. 13/1 'Don't care a dite,' Sylvia said despondently. **1920** *Blackw. Mag.* Oct. 488/2 'I suppose your major won't mind that?' 'Not a tuppenny dit.'

†**dite,** *v.* *Obs.* Also 5-6 **dyt(e.** [a. OF. *diter*, earlier *ditier* (12th c. in Hatz.-Darm.), to write, compose:—L. *dictāre*, freq. of *dīcĕre* to say, tell (see DICTATE), mod.F. *dicter*. Perh. in some cases aphetic form of *endite*, INDITE. After 1500 mainly *Sc.* In early examples often difficult to distinguish from DIGHT *v.*, senses 1, 2, 6.]

1. *trans.* To compose or put in words (a set speech, poem, or writing); to indite. (Also *absol.*)

a**1300** *Sat. People Kildare* xiv. in *E.E.P.* (1862) 155 Worþ hit wer þat he wer king þat ditid þis trie þing. c**1440** *Promp. Parv.* 123/2 Dytyn or indytyn letters and speche, *dicto*. c**1450** HENRYSON *Mor. Fab.* 16 So different are they in properties..My cunning is excluded for to dyte. **1535** COVERDALE *Ps.* xliv. 1 My hert is dytinge of a good matter. **1549** *Compl. Scot.* x. 82 Quhou beit that the said poietical beuk be dytit oratourly. **1603** JAS. I in Ellis *Orig. Lett.* Ser. I. III. 80, I suspecte ye have rather written then dyted it.

2. = DICTATE. **a.** To utter or pronounce to a person (what he is to write). **b.** To prescribe, lay down, impose, order.

The first quot. is doubtful; it may belong to DIGHT *v.* 2.
a**1490-50** *Alexander* 3462 Aȝt daies all bedene he dites in his pistill For reuerence of Rosan to revell & halowe. **1536** BELLENDEN *Cron. Scot.* (1821) I. 196 Origenes, ane singular man..with sa properant ingine, that he wald dite fastar than sevin practicians might suffice to write. **1563** DAVIDSON *Answ. Kennedy* in *Wodr. Soc. Misc.* (1844) 201 That quhilk the Haly Spirit dytit to them. a**1598** R. ROLLOCK *Wks.* (1844) II. ix. 103 Pilate insisted earnestly to get Jesus, whom his conscience dited to be innocent, set free. **1643** R. BAILLIE *Lett. & Jrnls.* (1841) II. 71 Dr. Strong dytes..his notes on the hard places of Scripture.

3. To summon, indict.

c**1440** *Promp. Parv.* 123/2 Dytyn or indytyn for trespace, *indicto*. c**1450** HENRYSON *Mor. Fab.* 43 Ane Schiref stout Whilk..hes with him ane cursed assyse about, And dytes all the poore men vpon land. ? a**1500** *Thrie Priests Peblis* (Jam.) Thay dyte your Lords, and heryis up your men. **1775** S. J. PRATT *Liberal Opinions.* (1783) I. 157 The grocer..would dite them for a nuisance.

dite, obs. form of DIGHT, DITTY.

†**'ditement**[1]. *Obs.* [f. DITE *v.* + -MENT: cf. OF. *ditement* (L. type **dictāmentum*); but perh. often aphetic f. *inditement*, INDICTMENT.]

1. A written or spoken composition; = DITE *sb.*[1] 1. *Sc.*

1556 LAUDER *Tractate* 530, I wald beseik ȝour Maiesteis, My dytement did ȝov not displeis. **1562** WINȜET *Cert. Tractates* iii. Wks. 1888 I. 25 Ane form of ditement maid for caus of exercise and priuat studie, as vsis to be in sculis. **1629** MOORE OF ROWALLAN *True Crucifix* 22 (Jam.) Which holy ditements..Might serve his glorious image to present.

b. Inditing; dictation. *Sc.*

1599 JAS. I. *Βασιλ. Δωρον* 8 Some of them [apocryphe books] are no wais like the ditement of the Spirit of God.

2. A summons, an indictment.

a**1308** *Pol. Songs* (Camden) 198 That seli asse, That trespasid noȝt, no did no gilte..in the ditement was i-pilt. **1502** *Plumpton Corr.* 171 Anthony Cliforth gave in the bill of dytement against my sone.

†**'ditement**[2]. *Obs. rare.* [for **dightment*, f. DIGHT *v.* + -MENT.] That with which one is 'dight' or arrayed; raiment, array.

1603 HARSNET *Pop. Impost.* 93 These Priests ditements being severally so many infernal serpents and scorpions to sting and bite the Devil.

†**'diter.** *Obs.* Also 4-5 **-our,** 5 **-ar.** [ME. (and AF.) *ditour* = OF. *diteor, ditor, ditur* author, composer, public crier, etc.:—L. *dictātōr-em* (see DICTATOR), agent-n. f. *dictāre*: see DITE *v.* But in sense 1, perh. a direct deriv. of the vb.]

1. One who indites; author, writer, composer.

1388 WYCLIF *Esther* viii. 9 The dyteris and writeris of the kyng weren clepid. **1535** COVERDALE *2 Sam.* xxiii. 1 A pleasaunt dyter of songes of Israel. **1585** *Animadv. Kirk* in J. Melvill's *Diary* (1842) 234 For the Saxt Act, the dytter thairof apeires to be verie cairfull.

2. An orator, rhetorician.

1387 TREVISA *Higden* (Rolls) II. 373 Advoketes and ditoures [*oratores*]. *Ibid.* III. 163 Of þis happe spekeþ a dytour [*Caxt.* or ret[or]ycyon, orig. *exclamator quidam*.]

3. A summoner, indicter.

1303 R. BRUNNE *Handl. Synne* 338 What shal we sey of þys dytours..þat for hate a trewman wyl endyte. c**1400-20** *Judicium* (1822) 6 Of backbytars and fals quest dytars.

diter, obs. form of DIGHTER.

diterpene (daɪ'tɜːpiːn). *Chem.* [f. DI-[2] 2 + TERPENE.] Any terpene with the formula $C_{20}H_{32}$; also, any of the simple derivatives of such a hydrocarbon, differing in their substituents or their degree of saturation from the diterpenes proper. Hence **di'terpenoid,** a term used in place of *diterpene* when this is restricted to compounds of the formula $C_{20}H_{32}$ only; also *attrib.* or as *adj.*

1902 F. J. POND tr. *Heusler's Chem. Terpenes* 431 Very many diterpenes are known, but they have never been thoroughly characterized. **1949** *Q. Rev.* (*Chem. Soc.*) III. 36 A full understanding of the chemistry of the diterpenoids has been developed only in the last twenty years. *Ibid.* 37 (*heading*) Diterpenoid resin acids. **1953** E. H. RODD *Chem. Carbon Compounds* II. xii. 489 The diterpenoids (C_{20}) and triterpenoids (C_{30}) are mostly obtained from plant or tree gums and resins which, unlike the essential oils, are not volatile in steam. **1956** *Chem. & Ind.* 3 Nov. 1275 (*heading*) The preparation of an intermediate for the synthesis of bicyclic diterpenes. **1956** I. L. FINAR *Org. Chem.* II. viii. 324 Phytol, $C_{20}H_{40}O$,..is an acyclic diterpene.

ditetragonal (daɪtɪ'trægənəl), *a.* *Cryst.* [f. DI-[2] 1 + TETRAGONAL.] Having eight angles, of which the first, third, fifth, and seventh, are equal to one another, and the second, fourth, sixth, and eighth, also equal to one another, but those of the one set not equal to those of the other; as a *ditetragonal pyramid* or *prism*. Cf. DIHEXAGONAL.

1879 RUTLEY *Study Rocks* x. 109 The form assumed by leucite is a combination of a di-tetragonal pyramid..with a tetragonal pyramid. **1895** STORY-MASKELYNE *Crystallogr.* v. §112. 129 When the symmetry is complete it is ditetragonal. *Ibid.* vii. §200. 248 The ditetragonal prism.

†**di-tetra'hedral,** *a.* *Cryst.* *Obs.* [f. DI-[2] 1 + TETRAHEDRAL.] Having the form of a tetrahedral prism with dihedral summits.

1805-17 R. JAMESON *Char. Min.* (ed. 3) 203 It represents a four-sided prism, bevelled on the extremities. Example, Di-tetrahedral tremolite.

diteyne, obs. form of DITTANY.

dith, diþ, obs. form of DEATH *sb.*

dithallious (daɪ'θæliəs), *a.* *Chem.* [f. DI-[2] + THALLIOUS (f. THALLIUM + -OUS).] Applied to thallious salts which contain two equivalents of thallium. See THALLIOUS.

1868 WATTS *Dict. Chem.* V. 755 The dithallious salt. **1873** *Fownes' Chem.* (ed. 11) 413 Dithallious orthophosphate.

dithecal (daɪ'θiːkəl), *a.* *Bot.* [f. as next + -AL[1].] = next.

1883 *Syd. Soc. Lex.*, *Dithecal anthers*, anthers in which the septa between the two loculi of each anther-lobe have been absorbed, so that there are two cells or cavities only.

dithecous (daɪ'θiːkəs), *a.* *Bot.* [f. Gr. δι-, DI-[2] twice + θήκη case + -OUS.] Consisting of two cells or small receptacles; bilocular.

1880 GRAY *Struct. Bot.* vi. §6. 254 The normal anther is two-celled, bilocular, or dithecous.

ditheism ('daɪθiːɪz(ə)m). [f. DI-[2] + THEISM.] Belief in two supreme gods; religious dualism; *esp.* the belief in two independent antagonistic principles of good and evil, as in Zoroastrianism and Manicheism. Also applied (controversially) to forms of belief in which it is asserted or implied that Jesus Christ is not of one substance with God the Father, as in Arianism and Socinianism.

1678 CUDWORTH *Intell. Syst.* I. iv. §13. 213 The fore-mentioned Ditheism, or opinion of two gods, a good and an evil one. **1719** WATERLAND *Vind. Christ's Divinity* 84 The common Answer to the Charge of Tritheism, or Ditheism, as well of the Post-Nicene, as Ante-Nicene Fathers, was, that there is but one Head, Root, Fountain, Father of all; not in respect of Authority only, but of Substance also. **1854** MILMAN *Lat. Chr.* I. 45 Callistus..hoped to elude the charge on one side of Patripassianism, on the other of Ditheism. **1895** A. C. HEADLAM in *Expository Times* Mar. 266 The Father and the Son are..one in their action, one in their purpose..If we are to realize..the Atonement, we must put aside all idea of ditheism or tritheism.

ditheist ('daɪθiːɪst). [f. DI-[2] + THEIST.] One who holds the doctrine of DITHEISM.

1678 CUDWORTH *Intell. Syst.* I. iv. §13. 213 These Ditheists..had it not been for this business of evil..would never have asserted any more principles or gods than one. **1720** WATERLAND *Eight Serm.* Pref. 36 They do by.. Implication, tho' not in Intention, make two supreme Gods; and consequently are practical Ditheists.

ditheistic (,daɪθiː'ɪstɪk), *a.* [f. prec. + -IC.] Of or pertaining to ditheism. So **dithe'istical** *a.*

1678 CUDWORTH *Intell. Syst.* I. iv. §13. 213 The chiefest.. Assertors of which Ditheistick Doctrine of..a Good God and an Evil Dæmon, were the Marcionites and the Manicheans. **1750** BOLINGBROKE *Authority in Relig.* IV. xxvii, I have spoken somewhere of the ditheistical doctrine. **1890** HATCH *Influence Grk. Ideas Chr. Ch.* viii. 228 The ditheistic hypothesis was more difficult than the difficulties which it explained.

dithematic (daɪθiː'mætɪk), *a.* [f. DI-[2] + THEMATIC.] Of a word: containing two significant themes or stems. Also as *sb.*

1916 E. WEEKLEY *Surnames* 26 These Teutonic names were originally all dithemetic [*sic*]. **1922** —— in *N. & Q.* 12th Ser. XI. 52/2 Some old Teutonic dithematic. **1927** *Englische Studien* 10 Nov. 76 In the course of the tenth century dithematic names, such as *Wulfstan*, *Æthelstan* and *Ælfred*, are used almost exclusively among the higher classes of society.

dither ('dɪðə(r)), *v.* [A phonetic variation of DIDDER, q.v.; cf. *father, mother, feather, hither, gather*, in which *-ther* represents earlier *-der*.]

1. *intr.* Orig. chiefly *dial.*, to tremble, quake, quiver, thrill. Now also in gen. colloq. use: to vacillate, to act indecisively, to waver between different opinions or courses of action.

1649 *Depos. Cast. York* (Surtees) 29 He saw the said Sara Rodes..her body quakeing and dithering about halfe a quarter of an hower. **1666** tr. *Horace Odes* I. xxiii, So tremulous is she Dith'ring both in heart and knee. **1820** CLARE *Rural Life* (ed. 3) 47 Needy Labour dithering stands. **1828** in *Craven Gloss.* **1891** MRS. L. ADAMS *Bonnie Kate* II. iii. 85 Kate would not be there to hear it [the organ] boom, and thrill, and 'dither'. [In most dialect glossaries as far south as Shropsh., Leicester, Northamp.] **1908** 'I. HAY' *Right Stuff* i. 6 If there is a viva-voce, be sure to speak up and give your answers as though you were sure of them... The one thing the examiners will not thole is a body that dithers. **1923** H. C. BAILEY *Mr. Fortune's Practice* iii. 81 All newspapers are run by madmen, but the 'Watchman' merely dithers. **1927** *Manch. Guardian Weekly* 16 Dec. 463/1 While Governments dither and talk limply of disarmament and peace large numbers of normally inarticulate citizens grow increasingly restive. **1930** J. B. PRIESTLEY *Angel Pavement* vii. 359 'I don't know what on earth you're trying to say,' she told him... 'Oh, don't dither so much, silly.' **1932** C. WILLIAMS *Greater Trumps* x. 168 She re-ordered her thoughts; this was mere dithering. **1938** E. BOWEN *Death of Heart* II. v. 255 The lady..was already dithering round a table of new novels. **1948** 'N. SHUTE' *No Highway* i. 27, I don't think it [*sc.* a tailplane] had any continuous movement—it wasn't dithering all the time. **1959** *Times* 14 Dec. 13/4 She was the first producer we had ever had who never dithered about which was Up Stage and which Down.

2. To confuse, perplex, make nervous (esp. in *pass.*). So **'dithered** *ppl. a.*, confused, perplexed; also (*Austral.*), drunk.

1919 MASEFIELD *Reynard* 98 He's done: he's dithered. **1932** N. LINDSAY *Cautious Amorist* v. 70 Dithered we [w] as already by the booze we had ashore. **1936** D. G. SMITH *Call it a Day* II. ii. 75 It's these girls in the shops. They just dither you. **1948** V. PALMER *Golconda* xvii. 140 I've seen him so dithered by printed words he didn't know whether it was this week or next. *Ibid.* v. 32 They have a right to know what the prospects here actually are. At present they are dithered by rumours.

Hence **'dithering** *vbl. sb.* and *ppl. a.*; **dithering-grass**, quaking-grass, *Briza media.*

1821 CLARE *Vill. Minstr.* II. 193 How have I joy'd, with dithering hands, to find Each fading flower. **1878–86** BRITTEN & HOLLAND *Plant-n.*, Dithering Grass, *Briza media.* Lanc. **1890** R. KIPLING *Soldiers Three* 65 Thomas in bulk can be worked up into dittering, rippling hysteria.

'dither, *sb.* [f. prec. vb.] **a.** The action of dithering; vibration.

1878 F. W. WILLIAMS *Midl. Railw.* 651 The firmness with which one has to stand on the footplate in order to resist the 'dither'of the engine. **1888** *Engineer* 24 Feb. 163/3 The range of the reciprocation of the tool..is not much more than a vibration or dither.

b. A state of tremulous excitement or apprehension; chiefly in phr. ***all of a dither***; also, vacillation; a state of confusion. *colloq.* or *dial.*

1819 'P. BOBBIN' *Sequel to Lanc. Dial.* 6 (E.D.D.), I'm aw on o' dither, if th' wynt bo sturs a twig. **1891** C. WORDSWORTH *Rutland Words* 11 Those children keep me in the dithers, they do. **1899** WATTS-DUNTON *Aylwin* xii. 331 The sight o' both on us..might make the poor body all of a dither if she was very ill. **1929** J. B. PRIESTLEY *Good Comp.* III. ii. 500 They'll rehearse all right... When it comes to the night, all of a dither. **1931** E. SACKVILLE-WEST *Simpson* III. xvii, She quickly pulled herself together, feeling that such a state of dither would not, if she showed it, illustrate her name. **1939** N. MARSH *Overture to Death* xxi. 243 Eleanor was thrown into a dither by finding us there together. **1957** S. JAMESON *Cup of Tea for Mr. Thorgill* ii. 31 Always in a dither of enthusiasm and misplaced devotion—and what a bore that is! **1958** *Sat. Rev. Lit.* 31 May 8/3 She came up with Stanley Baldwin and his policy of delusion and dither, which left England nearly helpless against Hitler. **1970** M. PEREIRA *Pigeon's Blood* xi. 127 Such brains are usually characterised by two things: the speed with which they can reach vital decisions; and the speed with which they can grasp how to implement such decisions. A total absence of dither, if you like.

dithery ('dɪðərɪ), *a.* orig. *dial.* [f. DITHER + -Y[1].] Dithering, trembling.

[**1866** E. L. LINTON *Lizzie Lorton* III. ix. 245 A puir lile diddery doddery horphan.] **1887** T. DARLINGTON *Folk-Speech S. Cheshire* 172, I went queite sick an' dithery. **1931** J. CANNAN *High Table* xi. 175 Learned and famous though he was, he was all dithery over having two young nobodies to dine. **1942** J. D. CARR *Seat of Scornful* xiii. 135 She'd already sounded all wild and dithery, but now was worse.

dithing ('dɪðɪŋ), *vbl. sb. dial.* Also dithying, *ppl. a.* [Cf. DITHER *v.*] Quivering, trembling.

1818 R. WILBRAHAM *Gloss. Cheshire* 14 *Dithing*, a trembling or vibratory motion of the eye, from dither or didder. **1913** MASEFIELD *Daffodil Fields* 66 Red dithying sparks flew..from the fire's heart. **1916** BLUNDEN *Pastorals* 34 Such gusts of rain..dashed on the belfry tower..And roused the dithying goblin on the vane.

dithionic (daɪθaɪ'ɒnɪk, dɪθɪ'ɒnɪk), *a. Chem.* [f. DI-[2] + θεῖον sulphur + -IC. (The formative *-thionic* is used for a group of compounds containing H_2O_6, in combination with two or more atoms of sulphur.)] In ***dithionic acid***, a synonym of hyposulphuric acid, $H_2S_2O_6$, a dibasic acid not isolated in the pure state, but forming crystallizable salts, called **dithionates** (daɪ'θaɪənət).

1854 J. SCOFFERN in *Orr's Circ. Sc.* Chem. 285 Hyposulphuric acid (*Dithionic acid*). **1868** WATTS *Dict. Chem.* V. 637 Dithionic Acid, when concentrated as highly as possible, is an inodorous, strongly acid, hydrated liquid, of specific gravity 1·347; on attempting to concentrate it further, it resolved into sulphuric acid and sulphurous oxide ..The dithionates are permanent at ordinary temperatures. **1883** *Hardwich's Photogr. Chem.* 97 All the acids being unstable with the exception of the Dithionic.

dithizone (daɪ'θaɪzəʊn). *Chem.* [ad.G. *dithizon* (H. Fischer 1929, in *Zeitschr. f. angew. Chem.* XLII. 1025), f. *di*phenyl*thio*carba*zone*.] The crystalline compound diphenylthiocarbazone, $C_{13}H_{12}N_4S$, which is used as a reagent for the estimation and separation of lead and other metals.

1929 *Brit. Chem. Abstr.* A. 1412/2 (*heading*) Detection of heavy metals by means of 'dithizone'. *Ibid.*, Dithizone forms coloured complex compounds with many metals. **1956** *Nature* 31 Mar. 620/1 Phosphate adsorption followed by dithizone extraction. **1957** G. E. HUTCHINSON *Treat. Limnol.* I. xv. 820 The zinc extractable by dithizone from the waters of Japanese mountain lakes varied from 1·3 to 5 mg. m.[−3]. **1958** *Oxf. Univ. Gaz.* 23 Apr. 880 Some new metal-dithizone complexes.

dithyramb ('dɪθɪræmb). [ad. L. *dīthyrambus*, a. Gr. διθύραμβος (origin unknown). In F. *dithyrambe.* Also used in the Latin form.] *Gr. Antiq.* A Greek choric hymn, originally in honour of Dionysus or Bacchus, vehement and wild in character; a Bacchanalian song.

1603 HOLLAND *Plutarch's Mor.* 1358 According as Aeschylus saith: The Dithyrambe with clamours dissonant Sorts well with Bacchus. **1847** GROTE *Greece* II. xxix. IV. 118 The primitive Dithyrambus was a round choric dance and song in honour of Dionysus. **1873** SYMONDS *Grk. Poets* v. 118 The Dithyramb never lost the tempestuous and enthusiastic character of Bacchic revelry.

b. *transf.* A metrical composition having characteristics similar to this.

1656 S. HOLLAND *Zara* III. iii. 153 The Musick having charmed their sences with a Celestiall Dithyramb [*pr.* Dyrathamb]. [**1727–51** CHAMBERS *Cycl.* s.v., Some.. modern writers, have composed Latin pieces of all kinds of verse indifferently..without any order, or distribution into strophes, and call them *dithyrambi.*] **1859** A. A. BONAR in Spurgeon *Treas. Dav.* Ps. vii. *heading*, Ewald suggests, that it [Shiggaion] might be rendered 'a confused ode', a Dithyramb. **1860** ADLER *Fauriel's Prov. Poetry* i. 8 Martial dithyrambs, full of ardor and highmindedness.

c. A speech or writing in vehement or inflated style.

1863 GEO. ELIOT *Romola* xxxix, What dithyrambs he went into about eating and drinking. **1863** *Sat. Rev.* 153 M. Victor Hugo, in *Les Misérables*, has poured forth a rhapsody, or dithyramb, or whatever, under a classical name, expresses exaggerated and inflated nonsense. **1877** MORLEY *Crit. Misc.* Ser. II. 4 Mr. Carlyle..has reproduced in stirring and resplendent dithyrambs the fire and passion..of the French Revolution.

dithyrambic (dɪθɪ'ræmbɪk), *a.* and *sb.* [ad. L. *dīthyrambic-us*, a. Gr. διθυραμβικός, f. διθύραμβος: see prec. In F. *dithyrambique.*]

A. *adj.* Pertaining to, or of the nature of, a dithyramb; composing dithyrambs.

1603 HOLLAND *Plutarch's Mor.* 1358 To Bacchus they do chant..certeine Dithyrambicke ditties and tunes. **1656** COWLEY *Pindar. Odes, Praise Pindar* ii, So Pindar does new Words and Figures roul Down his impetuous Dithyrambique Tide. **1853** GROTE *Greece* II. lxxxiii. XI. 36 The dithyrambic poet Philoxenus. **1854** LONGF. *Epimetheus* ii, With dithyrambic dances.

b. *transf.* Resembling a dithyramb in irregularity of style; wild, vehement, boisterous.

c **1611** SYLVESTER *Du Bartas* II. iv. III. Schisme 547 Ba'l's bawling Priests..howling chaunt these Dithyrambik charms. **1689–90** TEMPLE *Ess. Poetry* Wks. 1731 I. 245 The common Vein of the Gothick Runes was what is termed Dithirambick. **1692** BENTLEY *Boyle Lect.* ix. 329 Dithyrambic liberty of Style. **1838** PRESCOTT *Ferd. & Is.* (1846) II. xx. 208 A flow of lofty dithyrambic eloquence.

B. *sb.* **a.** A dithyrambic verse; a dithyramb. **b.** Something resembling a dithyramb in style. **c.** A writer of a dithyramb.

1646 SIR T. BROWNE *Pseud. Ep.* VII. xiv. 367 Philoxenus.. went off from the Dorik Dytherambicks unto the Phrygian Harmony. **1674** BLOUNT *Glossogr.* (ed. 4), The Poets, who composed such Hymns, were called Dithyrambicks. **1828** CARLYLE *Goethe's Helena* Misc. Ess. 1872 I. 163 He concludes with another rapid dithyrambic describing the Peninsula of Greece. **1850** MAURICE *Mor. & Met. Philos.* (ed. 2) 126 [Plato] had been a writer of dithyrambics.

† **dithy'rambical**, *a. Obs. rare.* = prec. adj.

1624 GATAKER *Transubst.* 94 Writing rather like a Dithyrambicall Poet..then like a sober and sound Divine.

dithyrambically (dɪθɪ'ræmbɪkəlɪ), *adv.* [f. DITHYRAMBIC *a.*: see -ICALLY.] In or as in dithyrambs; with dithyrambic or 'lyrical' expression.

1891 SYMONDS *Biogr.* (1895) II. 332 Tell me if you would like me to write what I think about their excellence—not dithyrambically, as here, but soberly as art requires. **1905** *Spectator* 11 Mar. 371/1 M. Santos-Dumont writes interestingly, if dithyrambically, of the future of the airship.

dithyrambist (dɪθɪ'ræmbɪst). [f. DITHYRAMB + -IST.] A composer or utterer of dithyrambs.

1885 *Spectator* 30 May 704/1 The great dithyrambist to whom France is about to pay the last honours.

dithyrous ('dɪθɪrəs), *a.* [f. Gr. δίθυρος having two doors, (f. δι-, DI-[2] + θύρα door) + -OUS.] 'Having two valves'. *Syd. Soc. Lex.* 1883.

† **'diting**, *vbl. sb. Obs.* [f. DITE *v.* + -ING[1].]

1. The action of the the verb DITE: inditing.

1382 WYCLIF *Wisd.* Prol., That diting the more smelleth fair Grec speche. *c* **1400** *Destr. Troy* 7392 Dares in his dytyng of his dedis tellis. *c* **1440** *Promp. Parv.* 123/2 Dytynge, or indytynge of curyowse speche, *dictamen.* *a* **1605** POLWART *Flytyng w. Montgomerie* 224 Thy doytit dytings soone denie.

2. Indictment.

c **1440** *Promp. Parv.* 123/2 Dytynge, or indytynge of trespace, *indictacio.*

diting, obs. form of DIGHTING.

† **dition** ('dɪʃən). *Obs.* Also 6 dicion. [a. OF. *dicion* (*dition*), ad. L. *diciōn-em* (in later transcription *ditiōn-em*) command, rule, sway, authority; perh. from root *dic-* of *dīcĕre* to declare, tell, say, etc. Cf. CONDITION.]

1. Rule, sway, jurisdiction, command.

1538 LELAND *Itin.* I. 70 Northalvertonshir is holely of the Dition of the Bishop of Duresme. **1633** BP. HALL *Hard Texts* Luke ii. 1 Under the Roman dition and jurisdiction. **1654** VILVAIN *Epit. Ess.* v. vi, Cambry twelv Shires contains under one dition.

2. The country or region under any particular rule; a dominion, empire.

1542 UDALL *Erasm. Apoph.* 256 a, A dicion or royalme descended and come to his possession. **1545** JOYE *Exp. Dan.* iv. H iv b, Caste oute of theyr dicions empyres and realmes. **1685** H. MORE *Paralip. Prophet.* 64 Herodes Palaestinus.. was banished beyond the Alpes, and part of his Dition laid to the Publick.

¶ **3.** Used by T. Adams app. in sense 'enrichment, resources': perh. by confusion with DITATION, and with play on *addition*, *condition.*

1615 T. ADAMS *Black Devill* 25 A mutinous rebell *viresque acquirit eundo*: he still enlargeth his own Dition. **1633** —— *Exp. 2 Peter* i. 11 Rich men scorn to be beggars, their dition admits no such condition.

† **'ditionary**, *a.* and *sb. Obs.* [f. prec. + -ARY.]

A. *adj.* Under dominion; subject, tributary.

1629 CHAPMAN *Juvenal* v. 180 Now our markets their chief purveyance owe To some remote and ditionary coast.

B. *sb.* One who is under rule; a subject.

1555 EDEN *Decades* 18 The ditionaries of Cannaboa. *Ibid.* 23 All the princes which dwell betwene the Weste ende and his palaice are ditionaries. [**1577** Objected to by R. Willes in his re-edition of Eden's *Hist.* Pref. to Rdr.]

ditokous ('dɪtəʊkəs), *a. Zool.* [f. Gr. διτόκος having two at a birth (f. δι-, DI- + τόκος a bringing forth, offspring) + -OUS.] **a.** Producing two at a birth; having twins. **b.** Laying only two eggs in a clutch, as pigeons. **c.** Producing young of two kinds, as some worms.

In recent Dicts.

ditolyl (daɪ'təʊlɪl). *Chem.* [DI-[2].] An aromatic hydrocarbon, a crystalline substance of the constitution $2(C_6H_4{\cdot}CH_3)$: see TOLYL.

1877 WATTS *Fownes' Chem.* II. 564 Ditolyl..forms monoclinic crystals, easily soluble in hot alcohol, melting at 121°. **1878** *Pharmaceut. Jrnl.* Ser. III. VIII. 379 Two liquid ditolyls boiling about 275° and 285° were obtained.

diton, var. of DITTON, *Obs.*, a phrase.

ditone ('daɪtəʊn). *Mus.* [ad. Gr. δίτον-ον the ancient major third, neuter of δίτονος, f. δι-, DI-[2] + τόνος TONE.] An interval containing two whole tones; a major third; *esp.* the Pythagorean major third in ancient Greek music, consisting of two major tones (ratio 81:64).

1609 DOULAND *Ornith. Microl.* 18 A Ditone is a perfect third: so called, because it containes..two Tones. **1694** W. HOLDER *Harmony* (1731) 98 In the Enharmonic Kind [the Ancients used] only Diesis, or quarter of a Tone, and Ditone, as the Degrees whereby they made the Tetrachord. **1818** *Gentl. Mag.* May 416/1 The Enharmonic [Scale proceeded] by the semitone and ditones (or combinations of two whole tones).

Hence † **di'tonean** *a.*, containing a ditone. *Obs.*

1728 R. NORTH *Mem. of Music* (1846) 20 The Ditonean scale as they used it is not without this fault.

ditrematous (daɪ'triːmətəs), *a. Zool.* [f. mod.L. *Ditrēmata* neut. pl. (f. Gr. δι-, DI[2] + τρῆμα, τρηματ- opening) + -OUS.] Of or pertaining to the *Ditremata*, a division of gastropod molluscs, having the external male and female orifices widely separate; also, having the anal and genital orifices distinct, as in *Ditrema*, a genus of fishes.

In recent Dicts.

ditremid (daɪ'triːmɪd). *Zool.* [f. mod.L. *Ditremid-æ* sb. pl., f. *Ditrema*: see prec.] A fish of the family *Ditremidæ*, of which *Ditrema* (see prec.) is the typical genus. So **di'tremoid** *a.*, of or pertaining to this family of fishes.

di-tri-, a compendious way of expressing *di- or tri-*, *di- and tri-*, in composition, as ***di-trichotomous*** = dichotomous or trichotomous, ***di-trimerous*** (abbreviated 2-3 *-merous*, cf. 2-3 *-fid*, 2-3 *-celled*, etc.).

1838 LOUDON *Encycl. Plants* (1841) 57 *Trichodium caninum*, Branches of panicle di-trichotomous roughish, glumes acute. **1847** CRAIG, *Ditrichotomous*, divided into twos or threes; having the stems continually dividing into double or treble ramifications; the term is sometimes applied to a panicle of flowers. [So in later Dicts.]

ditriglyph (daɪ'traɪglɪf). *Arch.* [a. F. *ditriglyphe* (Dict. de Trevoux), f. DI-[2] + *triglyphe.*]

1. 'The space between two triglyphs'.

1727–51 CHAMBERS *Cycl.* **1731** BAILEY vol. II. **1754** *Dict. Arts & Sc.* II. 947. **1830** 'R. STUART' *Dict. Archit.* II. 11 *Ditriglyph*, the intervening space between two triglyphs. [Cf. LITTRÉ s.v. *Ditriglyphe.*]

2. A certain interval (viz. $5\frac{1}{2}$ modules) between columns of the Doric order (nearly but not quite equal to that of the diastyle intercolumniation in the other orders, which is 6 modules), admitting the use of two triglyphs in the frieze, between those over the columns.

(This sense app. began with quot. 1791, in which it was perhaps an attrib. or adj. use of 1.)

1791 SIR. W. CHAMBERS *Civil Archit.* (ed. 3) 80 Setting.. aside the pycnostyle and systyle dispositions,..the diastyle intercolumniation..may be employed..in all the orders, excepting the Doric; in which the most perfect interval is the ditriglyph. **1830** 'R. STUART' *Dict. Archit.* II. 11 *Ditriglyph*, in intercolumniations, the placing of two triglyphs over the intercolumn, so that a triglyph being placed over each of the two outermost columns, will form the ditriglyph. **1842** GWILT *Encycl. Archit.* 717. **1850** J. H. PARKER *Gloss. Terms* (ed. 5) 166 *Ditriglyph*, an interval between two columns, admitting two triglyphs in the entablature; used in the Doric order.

3. *attrib.* or *adj.* = next.

1819 P. NICHOLSON *Dict. Archit.* I. 389 *Ditriglyph*, having two triglyphs over the intercolumn.

So **ditri'glyphic** *a.*, having two triglyphs in the space over the intercolumniation.

1837 *Penny Cycl.* VII. 218 The centre intercolumn..in the Propylæa at Athens, where a ditriglyphic arrangement is employed.

ditrigonal (daɪ'trɪgənəl), *a. Cryst.* [f. DI-² + TRIGONAL.] Having six (dihedral) angles, of which the first, third, and fifth are equal, and also the second, fourth, and sixth, but those of the one set not equal to those of the other. (Cf. DIHEXAGONAL, DITETRAGONAL.)

1878 GURNEY *Crystallogr.* 60 Some minerals..appear to possess a truly hexagonal and not merely a trigonal or ditrigonal symmetry. **1895** STORY-MASKELYNE *Crystallogr.* v. §116. 133 A form with six poles grouped round the axis, that may be viewed as an axis of ditrigonal symmetry. *Ibid.* vii. §244. 293 The ditrigonal scalenohedron.

Hence **di'trigonally** *adv.*

1895 STORY-MASKELYNE *Crystallogr.* vii. §246. 296 The summit-quoins are symmetrical ditrigonally on the axis.

ditrochee (daɪ'trəʊkiː). *Pros.* [ad. L. *ditrochæus*, a. Gr. διτρόχαιος, f. δι-, DI-² + τροχαῖος TROCHEE. Oftener used in the L. form.] A foot consisting of two trochees; a double trochee: = DICHOREE. So **ditro'chean** *a.*, containing two trochees.

[**1706** PHILLIPS (ed. Kersey), *Ditrochæus*, a Foot in Greek or Latin Verse which consists of Two Trochees; as Cāntĭlēnă.] **1855** *Sat. Rev.* I. 3/2 Does Absolute Wisdom take pleasure in forced and far-fetched *àpropos*, or does it delight in ditrochees? **1846** WORCESTER, *Ditrochean*, containing two trochees. *Edin. Rev.*

ditroite ('dɪtrəʊaɪt). *Min.* [f. *Ditro* in Transylvania + -ITE.] (See quot. 1868.)

1868 DANA *Min.* 328 A rock composed of orthoclase, elæolite, and sodalite, from Ditro in Transylvania, is the ditroÿte of Tschermak. **1879** RUTLEY *Study Rocks* x. 108 It is a component of the rock named ditroite, in which it occurs associated with sodalite [etc.].

ditsy ('dɪtsɪ), *a. U.S. slang.* Also **ditzy**. [Origin unknown; perh. corruption of DICTY *a.*]

a. = DICTY *a.* a, b. Also, fussy, intricate.

1978 *Detroit Free Press* 5 Mar. (Spring Fashion Suppl.) 23/1 Forget about delicate chains, a ring on every finger, clanking bangles and ditsy earrings. **1979** OBERMAN & STECKLER *I could have been Contender* ii. 8 A ditsy manicurist who's crazy about cats and lives alone. **1981** *N.Y. Times* 3 Dec. c8/5 They'll cook and clean for a week before a party and worry over the ditsy little touches, the table, the flowers, the matching guest towels. **1985** *Ibid.* 29 Jan. C13/3 She also has a big repertory of comic voices, ranging from..a maternal croon to a ditsy English matron's stiff-upper-register.

b. (Esp. of a woman) stupid, scatterbrained; cute.

1980 *Maledicta* III. II. 245 In this new age of the New Woman, the only old-fashioned *girl* left may be the *drag queen* who apes a *ditzy*, decorative female largely obsolete, much as Mae West (darling of female impersonators) recalls the woman of a past time. **1981** *Time* 12 Jan. 45/1 Bob Newhart plays the President of the United States: Madeline Kahn is his dipso wife, Gilda Radner his ditsy daughter. **1982** *Christian Science Monitor* 26 Mar. 15/1 It is filled with charmingly 'dotty' and 'ditsy' people who engage in generally 'gaga' relationships. **1984** *Washington Post* 20 May H13/1 Willie Scott..is a ditsy blond who sings at a Shanghai nightclub. **1985** *N.Y. Times* 31 Jan. A22/2 According to a wholly unscientific sample, this decade's terms [for 'dumb'] so far include, besides airhead, retard, ditsy and wifty. **1987** *Los Angeles Times* 7 June 16 What do father and daughter think of television's flashy detectives? Maddie and David on 'Moonlighting': 'They never work. They're ditzy.'

Hence (as a back-formation) **ditz**, one who is 'ditsy', scatterbrained, or cute.

1984 *N.Y. Times* 9 Feb. 19/1 Miss Alexander's portrayals of Anna ranged from 'a complete ditz' to playing her 'as Astarte'. **1985** *Guardian* 22 June 12/4 Meryl Streep is serious, Suzanne Somers isn't. That's the way they're seen ... I don't think Miss Somers does ditsy tap dances when she gets home. I've been both. I used to be a ditz. Now I'm talented.

ditt, obs. form of DIT *sb.*¹ and *v.*

dittander (dɪ'tændə(r)). ? *Obs.* [Of the same origin as DITTANY; the form *ditaundere* appears to be Anglo-F. (cf. OF. *ditan*), but its terminal part is unexplained.]

1. A name for Pepperwort, *Lepidium latifolium*: = DITTANY 4.

[*c* **1265** *Voc. Plants* in Wr.-Wülcker 556/34 *Diptannum*, ditaundere.] **1578** [see DITTANY 4]. **1597** GERARDE *Herbal* II. vii. §2. 188 The Englishmen [call it] Dittander, Ditany, and Pepperwoort. **1671** SALMON *Syn. Med.* III. xxii. 419 Piperitis, Λεπίδιον, Dittander. **1832** *Veg. Subst. Food* 195 Dittander..The leaves..are..hot and acrid..whence..the name of 'poor man's pepper'.

†**2.** Dittany of Crete: = DITTANY 1. *Obs.*

1607 TOPSELL *Serpents* (1658) 619 Things that..will likewise defend and keep us from venomous creatures: as for example; Southernwood, Dittander, Fleabane, Calamint. **1611** COTGR., *Dictame de Candie*, dittanie of Candia, the right Dittander. **1658** PHILLIPS, *Dittany*, or *Dittander*, a herb growing abundantly in Dicte, a Promontory of Creet.

dittany ('dɪtənɪ). Forms: 4 ditoyne, 5 dytan(e, diteyne, di-, dytayne, detane, 5–6 detany, -ie, 6 ditanie, dittayne, ditten, 6–7 ditany, dittani(e, (7 dittamy, diptani), 6– dittany. Also *β.* 6–7 dictam, 7 dictamne, dictamen; *γ.* (in Lat. forms) 6 dictamus, dictanum, (dictamion), 6–7 dictamnus, dictamnum. [repr. OF. *ditan* (12th c. in Hatz.-Darm.), *ditain, diptam, dictam*, later *diptame, dictame, -amne*:—med.L. *dictamus, -um*, L. *dictamn-us, -um*, Gr. δίκταμνον, reputed to be f. Δίκτη, the mountain Dicte in the island of Crete, where (among other places) the herb grew. It is not easy to account for the English forms in *-ayne, -any*. But the word suffered great perversion in other langs. also: thus med.L. had also *diptamnus, diptamus, diptanus, ditanus*, etc.: cf. also Pr. *diptamni* (Littré), It. *dittamo*.]

1. A labiate plant, *Origanum Dictamnus*, called also *Dictamnus Creticus* or ***dittany of Crete***; formerly famous for its alleged medicinal virtues.

1398 TREVISA *Barth. De P.R.* XVII. xlix. (1495) 632 Diptannus..is of so grete vertue that it dryueth and putteth out yren out of the body, therfore beestys smyte wyth arowes ete therof. *a* **1400** *Pistill of Susan* 114 Daysye and Ditoyne, Ysope and Aueroyne. **1513** DOUGLAS *Æneis* XII. vii. 74 Venus..Caucht rewth and piete of hir sonnys diseis, And from the wod of mont Ida in Creit, Vp hes scho pullit dictam, the herb sweit. **1546** LANGLEY *Pol. Verg. De Invent.* I. xvii. 31 b, As the Harte stryken with an arrow driueth it out with Detany. **1591** HARINGTON *Orl. Fur.* XIX. xvii, An herb whose vertue was to staunch the blood, As Dittany. **1794** MARTYN *Rousseau's Bot.* xxii. 310 Dittany of Crete has the small purple flowers collected in loose nodding heads. **1870** MORRIS *Earthly Par.* I. II. 484 Fresh dittany beloved of wild goats.

b. *fig.* (From the supposed power of Cretan dittany to expel weapons.)

1623 SIR E. DIGBY *Sp.* in Rushw. *Hist. Coll.* (1659) I. 134 We shall receive from his Royal Hand that Dictamen which must expel these Arrows that hang in the sides of the Commonwealth. **1624** BP. HALL *Serm.* v. 190 The shaft sticks still in thee;..None but the Sovereign Dittany of thy Saviour's Righteousness can drive it out. **1639** T. BRUGIS tr. *Camus' Mor. Relat.* 297 But this newes..was a forcible dittany to drive this arrow out of the wound. **1860** TRENCH *Serm. Westm. Abb.* xv. 179 The arrow which drinks up his spirit, there is no sovereign dittany which will cause it to drop from his side.

†**2.** Applied to another labiate, *Marrubium Pseudodictamnus*, also called ***bastard dittany***. *Obs.*

1552 HULOET, Dittayne, called false dittayne, herb, *condris.* **1578** LYTE *Dodoens* II. lxxxviii. 267 The second kinde which is called Pseudodictamnum, that is to say Bastarde Dictam, is much like vnto the first..sauing that it is not hoate. **1611** COTGR., *Dictame bastard*, Bastard Dittanie; somewhat resembles the right one. **1671** SALMON *Syn. Med.* III. xxii, *Pseudo-dictamnus*..Bastard Dittany.

3. The English name for the genus *Dictamnus* (N.O. *Rutaceæ*); esp. *D. Fraxinella* (***bastard dittany***), and *D. albus* (***white dittany***).

[**1551** TURNER *Herbal* I. O iv, Dictamnus growith no where ellis that I knowe of, sauynge only in Candye..Many haue abused fraxinella for thys herbe.] **1605** TIMME *Quersit.* III. 177 Take..of white diptani,..of goates beard,..of each one handfull. **1611** COTGR., *Dictame blanc*, tragium, fraxinella; called also bastard, or false Dittanie; and oft mistaken..for the right Dittanie. **1794** MARTYN *Rousseau's Bot.* xix. 266 White Dittany or Fraxinella. **1866** *Treas. Bot.*, Dittany, Bastard, *Dictamnus Fraxinella*.

†**4.** Erroneously applied to Pepperwort, *Lepidium latifolium* (N.O. *Cruciferæ*): see DITTANDER 1.

1548 TURNER *Names of Herbes* 34 Some cal Lepidium also Dittany. **1573** TUSSER *Husb.* xlv. (1878) 97 Detanie, or garden ginger. **1578** LYTE *Dodoens* v. lxvi. 631 *heading*, Of Dittander Dittany, but rather Pepperwurt.

5. Applied to various plants resembling the above in appearance or properties; *esp.* in U.S. to *Cunila Mariana* (N.O. *Labiatæ*).

1676 T. GLOVER *Virginia* in *Phil. Trans.* XI. 629 Here is also an herb which some call Dittany, others Pepper-wort; it is not Dittany of Candia, nor English Dittander. **1693** J. CLAYTON *Acc. Virginia* in *Misc. Cur.* (1708) III. 352 They fetched some of the Herb which they call Dittany, as having a great Traditionary Vertue for the Cure of Poisons. **1712** tr. *Pomet's Hist. Drugs* I. 26 Snake-Root is called by some Dittany. **1854–67** C. A. HARRIS *Dict. Med. Terminol.*, *Cunila Mariana*, dittany; mountain dittany; stone-mint; a plant possessing stimulant, carminative, and aromatic properties.

dittay ('dɪteɪ, 'dɪtɪ). *Sc. Law.* Also 5 **dyttay**; cf. also DITTY 5. [a. OF. *dité, ditté*, and thus the same word as DITTY, but prob. of later introduction in Sc., and in consequence preserving later the Fr. pronunciation, represented by final *-ay*.]

The matter of charge or ground of indictment against a person for a criminal offence; also, the formulated indictment. ***to take up dittay***, to obtain 'information and presentments of crime in order to trial' (Bell *Dict. Law Scot.*).

c **1470** HENRY *Wallace* I. 274 A gret dyttay for Scottis thai ordand than. **1535** STEWART *Cron. Scot.* II. 192 Befoir the air ane dittay for to tak In euirilk schyre. **1571** *Satir. Poems Reform.* xxviii. 182 The Justice Clerk my dittay red perqueir. *a* **1605** MONTGOMERIE *Flyting w. Polwart* 77 Thy dittay was death: thou dare not deny it. **1609** SKENE *Reg. Maj.* 6. **1637** RUTHERFORD *Lett.* (1862) I. 431 As many sentences as I uttered, as many points of dittay shall there be, when the Lord shall plead with the world. **1743** *J. Chamberlayne's St. Gt. Brit.* II. III. v. 412 The method of taking up offenders by dittay..abolished. **1753** W. STEWART in *Scots Mag.* Mar. 135/2 This letter..is brought as a point of dittay against the pannel. **1818** SCOTT *Hrt. Midl.* xii, Here's the dittay against puir Effie: Whereas [etc.].

fig. **1831** *Westminster Rev.* XIV. 50 All that he says under this head of dittay, consisting of a string of *niaiseries* unworthy of a schoolboy.

ditten, obs. var. of DITTANY.

dittied: see DITTY *v.*

ditto ('dɪtəʊ), *sb.* [a. It. *ditto* (Florio), *detto* said, spoken, aforesaid (:—L. *dictus, -um*). Used in It. with a sb. like 'said' in Eng.: (*il*) *detto libro* '(the) said book'; also, absolutely, to avoid repetition of the name of a month, thus (*Vocab. Della Crusca*) 'Sotto li 22 di dicembre mi fu significato ..che per li 26 detto..io dovessi' etc. (on the 22nd December it was signified to me..that by the 26th aforesaid (*ditto*)..I should have, etc.). This was the original sense in which the word was adopted in English, where it has been transferred to other uses, quite unknown to Italian.]

†**1.** In or of the month already named; said month. *Obs.*

1625 PURCHAS *Pilgrims* x. ix. §4 The eight and twentieth ditto, I went.. to the Generals Tent. **1677** HENCHMAN in W. Hubbard *Narrative* (1865) I. 237 They, 27 ditto, brought in two Squaws, a Boy and a Girl. [By *ditto* is meant June, the date June 30 having just been mentioned.]

2. By extension: The aforesaid, the same; used, in accounts and lists (where also abbreviated *dº, do.*, or expressed by two dots or commas, or a dash) to avoid repetition of a word or phrase appearing above; hence in commercial, office, and colloquial language.

1678 PHILLIPS, *Ditto* (Italian, said) [**1706** *adds* the aforesaid or the same] a word used much in Merchants Accompts, and relation of Foreign news; and signifieth the same place [ed. **1696** the same Commodity or Place] with that immediately beforementioned. **1712** ARBUTHNOT *John Bull* IV. ii, To Esquire South's accompt for *post Terminums* To ditto for *Non est factums*. **1752** J. LOUTHIAN *Form of Process* (ed. 2) 261 To the Clerk for every Petition or Answer 0 12 0 To *ditto* for Letters of Intimation or Liberation..0 18 0. **1759** VERRAL *Cookery* 105 (Stanf.) Parsley roots, and leaves of ditto. **1776** G. SEMPLE *Building in water* 67 C. Thorough Foundation of Masonry..D. Low-water mark (three Feet above ditto Foundation). **1814** COL. HAWKER *Diary* (1893) I. 116 Buonaparte's crown..ditto of Charlemagne. **1840** DICKENS *Barn. Rudge* lii, Came in yesterday morning rather the worse for liquor, and was ..*ditto* last night. **1878** *Lloyd's Weekly* 19 May 5/2 (Stanf.) Mrs. Brown (who is also possessed of ditto ditto ditto).

b. *to say ditto to*: to acquiesce in or express agreement with what has been said by (another); to endorse the statements or conclusions of.

1775 in Prior *Life of Burke* (1825) I. 284 His brother candidate Mr. Cruger, a merchant..at the conclusion of one of Mr. Burke's eloquent harangues, finding..nothing to add ..exclaimed..in the language of the counting-house, 'I say ditto to Mr. Burke'. **18..** W. E. NORRIS (Dixon), His wife's convictions resembled those of the wise and unassuming politician who was content to say ditto to Mr. Burke. **1894** MRS. H. WARD *Marcella* II. 8 Two people who are going to be married ought to say ditto to each other in everything.

3. Hence as *sb.* **a.** A duplicate or copy; an exact resemblance; a similar thing.

1776 J. Q. ADAMS in *Fam. Lett.* (1876) 209 Canteens, camp kettles, blankets, tents, shoes, hose, arms, flints, and other dittoes. **1818** LADY MORGAN *Fl. Macarthy* (1819) III. i. 67 (Stanf.) Judge Aubrey, just the ditto of herself. **1880** MRS. PARR *Adam & Eve* xii. 173 Aunt and uncle and my mother..think his ditto was never made. **1885** L. OLIPHANT *Haifa* (1887) 236 The upper fragment..the ditto of which is to be found at Irbid.

b. Cloth of the same material; chiefly plural, in ***suit of dittos***: a suit of clothes of the same material and colour throughout.

1755 *Connoisseur* (1774) III. No. 77 ¶3 A snuff-coloured suit of ditto with bolus buttons. **1787** *Microcosm* (1793) II. No. 29 ¶16 To..rescue a suit of Dittos from revilings. **1817** BELOE *Sexagenarian* (1818) 52 His suit of clothes was made of what the young men of that day called Ditto. **1834** SOUTHEY *Doctor* II. lvi. 191 A sober suit of brown or snuff-coloured dittos such as beseemed his profession. **1883** PAYN *Thicker than Water* ix, He was never seen in dittos even in September.

c. A succession of the same thing; a repetition.

1887 CLELAND *True to a Type* I. 112 Picnics..form an ever-recurring ditto.

4. *attrib.* and *Comb.*, as ***ditto-suit***; ***ditto-saying*** adj.

1892 *Pall Mall G.* 5 May 7/1 Knots..that cannot be untied by loud banality or ditto-saying Gladstonianism. **1893** *Daily News* 5 Apr. 7/1 No change is recorded in ditto suits.

¶ For DITTY *sb.* 3.

a **1679** T. GOODWIN *Object. Justif. Faith* I. ix. Wks. 1697 IV. 49 The declared *Ditto* of his Song.

Hence **'ditto** *v.*, (*a*) to produce a 'ditto' or duplicate of; to match; (*b*) to say or do the same as another person; to agree; **'dittoism**, **'dittoship**, exact repetition or reproduction; sameness.

1837–40 HALIBURTON *Clockm.* (1862) 162 Where will you ditto our fall? It whips English weather by a long chalk. **1869** BUSHNELL *Wom. Suffrage* vii. 16 When a woman has set herself up for a practical dittoship with men. **1884** A. A.

PUTNAM *10 Years Police Judge* vii. 42 The wear and tedium of court-house dittoism. **1890** *Army and Navy Gaz.* 4 Jan., 'Dittoing' the ships of other powers. *Ibid.*, What is the *Dupuy de Lôme* to be 'dittoed' with? **1894** H. GARDENER *Unofficial Patriot* 299 They are sulking in their tents and we are dittoing in ours. **1901** *Westm. Gaz.* 22 Mar. 2/1 No, Mr. Balfour knew nothing of Lord Lansdowne's communication. 'Nor I,' dittoed Lord Cranborne. **1922** JOYCE *Ulysses* 621 Quite so, Mr Bloom dittoed.

'dittogram. [f. Gr. *διττό-ς* twofold, double + *γράμμα*: see -GRAM.] A letter or series of letters unintentionally repeated by a scribe in copying; = DITTOGRAPH.

1881 *Athenæum* 16 July 77/2 The *mora* of 'moram' may be a dittogram from *-m o*rationis.

'dittograph, *v.* [f. the sb.] *pass.* To be repeated by dittography. Hence **'dittographing** *vbl. sb.*

1897 *Expositor* June 409, x. 22*c* is certainly 'dittographed' from *v.* 22*a*. **1906** S. R. DRIVER *Jeremiah* 349 The ה at the end..is simply dittographed from the following [word]. **1943** C. L. WRENN in *Trans. Philol. Soc.* (1944) 20 The *-i* of *maegsibbi* seems obviously to be a mere dittographing of the *i* of *affectui*.

dittography (dɪ'tɒgrəfɪ). [f. as DITTOGRAM + -GRAPHY; cf. Gr. *διττογραφούμενον* a double reading.] In *Palæography* and *Textual Criticism*: Double writing; the unintentional repetition of a letter or word, or series of letters or words, by a copyist. So **'dittograph,** a letter or series of letters thus repeated; **ditto'graphic** *a.*, of the nature of a dittograph.

1874 T. H. KEY *Language* 407 *note*, The letters in italics stand, probably, for *probeidem*, i.e. a dittograph for *probe* and *pridem*. **1876** H. SWEET *A.S. Rdr.* Notes (1879) 202 The *ge* may be merely a scribal error—a repetition (dittography) of the preceding *ge*. **1882** *Athenæum* 7 Oct. 456/3 They committed errors through confusing sounds..through dittography and repetition of letters. **1885** *Ibid.* 11 July 46/2 If the כ of כמריבי is considered as dittographic of the כ of the word ועמכ which precedes. **1889** *Sat. Rev.* 26 Jan. 108/1 Mistakes that arose from the haplography, dittography, homœoteleuton, and all the other malfeasances of the much-abused Scribes. **1893** J. COOK WILSON in *Classical Rev.* Feb. 34/1 *Οὐδείς* before *φησι* may be a dittograph of *οὐδ' εἰ* after *φησι*.

dittology (dɪ'tɒlədʒɪ). [ad. Gr. *διττο-, δισσολογία* repetition of words, f. *διττολόγος*, f. *διττός, δισσός* double: see -(O)LOGY.] A twofold or double reading or interpretation.

1678 PHILLIPS, *Dittology* (Gr.) Double reading, such as divers Texts of Scripture will admit of. **1730** T. BOSTON *Mem.* XII. 474 Thinking on the sacred name *Jehovah* I had fallen into a notion of its being a dittology standing for *Jehovah Elohim*. **1859** F. HALL *Vásavadattá* Pref. 11 There is scarcely a doubt of..the assumption that Subandhu designs a dittology.

†**'ditton.** *Obs.* Also 6 *Sc.* **dytone,** 7 **diton.** [a. F. *dicton* (in 16th c. pronounced *diton*, acc. to Palsgrave p. 23, and Beza), a word or phrase become proverbial:—L. *dictum* a saying: see DICTUM.] A phrase, an expression; *esp.* one of the nature of a motto or proverb.

1572 *Satir. Poems Reform.* xxx. ad fin., Finis with the Dytone Quod Sempill. **1606** BIRNIE *Kirk-Buriall* (1833) 17 Inscryving their tombes with a trigram of D.M.S. a diton that meaned, *Diis manibus Sacrum*. **1631** A. CRAIGE *Pilgr. & Herm.* 7 On the greene growing Barke of each blooming Tree, This Diton indorsed shall well written bee. **1653** URQUHART *Rabelais* II. xxvii. (1694) 163, Pantagruel for an eternal Memorial wrote this victorial Ditton.

ditty ('dɪtɪ), *sb.* Forms: 4 **dittee,** 4–5 **dite, ditee, dyte, dytee,** (5 **dete, dety, dytte**), 6–7 **ditie, dittie,** (6 **detie, diti, ditte, dytie, dytty**), 6– **ditty.** *β.* 5 **dictee, dyctee,** 6 **dictie, dyctye.** [ME. *dite, ditee*, a. OF. *dité, ditté*, orig. *ditié*, in 17th c. *dictié*, composition, treatise:—L. *dictāt-um* thing dictated, lesson, exercise, neut. pa. pple. of *dictāre* to DICTATE.]

†**1.** A composition; a treatise: = DITE *sb.*[1] 1.

1387 TREVISA *Higden* (Rolls) III. 361 Ditee of Troye, þe whiche he [Aristotle] bytook Alisaundre [*Higd.* Iliadis dictamen quod dedit Alexandro.] *c* **1400** *Rom. Rose* 5289 Of this unyte spak Tulius in a ditee [Cicero *De Amicitia*].

2. A composition intended to be set to music and sung; a song, lay; now, a short simple song; often used of the songs of birds, or applied depreciatively.

a **1300** *Sat. People Kildare* ix. in *E.E.P.* (1862) 154 Swiþe wel ȝe vnder-stode þat makid þis ditee so gode. **1382** WYCLIF *Exod.* xv. 1 Thanne Moyses soong..this ditee to the Lord. —— *Prov.* xxv. 20 That singeth dites with peruerted herte. *c* **1485** *Digby Myst.* IV. 795 Sum dolorose ditee. **1589** PUTTENHAM *Eng. Poesie* I. xxx. (Arb.) 72 All the commended fourmes of the auncient Poesie, which we..do imitate and vse vnder these common names: enterlude, song, ballade, carroll and ditty. **1599** SHAKS. *Pass. Pilgr.* 199 The lark..doth welcome daylight with her ditty. **1625** *Gonsalvio's Inquis.* 194 Filthie and slanderous dities sung by boyes in his dispraise. **1667** MILTON *P.L.* XI. 584 To the Harp they sung Soft amorous Ditties. **1712** HENLEY *Spect.* No. 396 ¶2 Penning a Catch or a Ditty, instead of inditing Odes, and Sonnets. *a* **1800** COWPER *Poplar Field* iii, The blackbird has fled..And the scene..Resounds with his sweet-flowing ditty no more. **1810** SCOTT *Lady of L.* II. xviii, Distinct the martial ditty flowed. **1885** R. BUCHANAN *Annan Water* xxv, After each ditty she went round with a plate collecting coppers.

†**b.** Any composition in verse; a poem, ballad.

1387 TREVISA *Higden* (Rolls) IV. 309 A Greek..usede to make noble ditees in preysinge of Cesar. *c* **1430** LYDG. *Min. Poems* (1840) 25 (Mätz.) The aureat dytees..Of Omerus in Grece. *c* **1510** BARCLAY *Mirr. Gd. Manners* (1570) A iij, My ditties indited may counsell many one. **1589** PUTTENHAM *Eng. Poesie* III. xix. (Arb.) 225 Our poet in his short ditties ..will..conclude..his Epigram with a verse or two, spoken in such sort, as [etc.]. **1614** BP. HALL *Recoll. Treat.* 124 Not the worst of the heathen Emperors made that monefull dittye on his deathbed.

†**3.** The words of a song, as distinguished from the music or tune; also, the leading theme or phrase; hence, Subject, matter, theme, 'burden'.

1552 HULOET, Dittye synger, or he that beareth yᵉ fote of the song, *præsentor*. **1561** BP. PARKHURST *Injunctions*, That the songe in the Churche be..so deuised and vsed that the ditte may plainly be vnderstand. **1580** SIDNEY *Ps.* XIII. v, Still, therefore, of thy graces shall be my Songs ditty. **1600** SHAKS. *A.Y.L.* v. iii. 36 There vvas no great matter in the dittie, yet yᵉ note was very vntunable. **1641** J. JACKSON *True Evang. T.* III. 175 The Dity of that hymne, or Caroll, [was] Peace on earth. **1654** WHITLOCK *Zootomia* 485 Hymnes and Spirituall Songs, where Humane Invention cometh in for Ditty and Notes. **1672** SIR T. BROWNE *Lett. to Friend* §25 To be dissolved and be with Christ was his dying ditty.

†**4.** That which is said; speech. *Obs. rare.*

1483 CAXTON *Gold. Leg.* 275/2 Whan he spack for his frende he attempred soo the maner of his dytee that he was not ouer hastyng hym self.

†**5.** = DITTAY. (Anglicized spelling of the Sc. law term.) *Obs.*

1634 RUTHERFORD *Lett.* (1862) I. 134 If you can learn a ditty against C., try, and cause try, that ye may see the Lord's righteous judgement upon the devil's instruments. **1649** BP. GUTHRIE *Mem.* (1702) 47 The Scottish Bishops.. did accuse the Earl of Traquair..and gave in great Ditties against him. **1657** HUTCHESON *Expos. John* iii. 17 Albeit Christ may be eventually for the falling of many, and his coming will afford sad matter of ditty against them.

†**'ditty,** *v. Obs.* [f. prec. sb.: cf. OF. *ditier* to write, compose, DITE.] **a.** *intr.* To sing a ditty; *trans.* to sing as a ditty; also, to celebrate in song. **b.** To fit or adapt words to (music): cf. prec. 2. Hence **'dittied** *ppl. a.*, **'dittying** *vbl. sb.*

1597 MORLEY *Introd. Mus.* 172 You must have an especiall care of causing your parts [of a ditty] giue place one to another..nor can you cause them rest till they haue expressed that part of the dittying which they haue begun. *Ibid.* 178 One of the greatest absurdities which I haue seene committed in the dittying of musicke. **1602** MARSTON *Antonio's Rev.* II. ii, Such Songs..I often dittied till my boy did sleepe. **1633** G. HERBERT *Temple, Providence* iii, Beasts fain would sing; birds dittie to their notes. **1633** P. FLETCHER *Purple Isl.* I. viii, Which bears the under-song unto your chearfull dittying. **1633** —— *Poet. Misc.* 65 My Fusca's eyes, my Fusca's beauty dittying. **1634** MILTON *Comus* 86 With his soft Pipe, and smooth-dittied song. **1768** S. BENTLEY *River Dove* 8 Heard is the love-ditty'd Strain. **1797** T. PARK *Sonnets* 97 Many a little dittied tale.

'ditty-bag. [Origin obscure: according to Smyth *Sailor's Word-bk.* it 'derives its name from the *dittis* or Manchester stuff of which it was once made'; but no evidence of this is given, nor is anything known of the stuff alleged.] A bag used by sailors to contain their smaller necessaries.

c **1860** H. STUART *Seaman's Catech.* 81, 1 ditty bag, to contain two dozen of clothes stops, needles, thread, scissors, tape, thimbles, and buttons. **1885** RUNCIMAN *Skippers & Sh.* 159 He had a lumpy canvas bag—a dittey-bag they call it—on his shoulders.

So **'ditty-box,** a box serving the same purpose, used by fishermen.

1883 *Pall Mall G.* 2 June Suppl., A 'ditty-box' is an American fisherman's receptacle for all sorts of odds and ends together with implements of every-day use. **1883** *Fisheries Exhib. Catal.* 198 Fishermen's tools, 'ditty-boxes,' ..coopering tools, [etc.].

‖**diuca** (diː'uːka, daɪ'(j)uːkə). *Ornith.* [Native name in Chili.] A Chilian finch, *Diuca grisea*.

1893 W. H. HUDSON *Idle Days Patagonia* i. 15 The diucas were sure prophets.

diureide (daɪ'jʊəriːaɪd). *Chem.* [f. DI-[2] + UREIDE.] A compound of two urea-residues with an acid radical.

1877 WATTS *Fownes' Chem.* II. 400 The 4- and 5-carbon diureides (including uric acid itself) are formed by the union of one molecule of a bibasic acid and 2 molecules of urea, with elimination of 4 molecules of water, and accordingly contain one diatomic acid residue and two urea-residues, $CO \cdot 2(NH)$.

‖**diuresis** (daɪjʊ'riːsɪs). *Med.* [mod.L. *diūrēsis*, a. Gr. **διούρησις*, f. *διά* through + *οὔρησις* urination. Cf. F. *diurèse*.] Excretion or evacuation of urine, especially when excessive.

1681 tr. *Willis' Rem. Med. Wks.* Vocab., *Diuresis*, evacuation by urin. **1710** T. FULLER *Pharm. Extemp.* 81 It [the decoction] turns off Feculencies by..Diuresis. **1879** KHORY *Princ. Med.* 31 Diuresis may be due to an abnormal condition of the passages, to nervous influence.

diuretic (daɪjʊ'retɪk), *a.* and *sb. Med.* Also 5 **duretick, -ik, duritik,** 6 **diuretike, dyurytyke,** (7 **diuretique**), 7–8 **diuretick(e.** [ad. L. *diūrētic-us*, a. Gr. *διουρητικός* promoting urine, f. *διουρεῖν* to urinate: see prec. Cf. F. *diurétique* (14th c. in Hatz.-Darm.).]

A. *adj.* Having the quality of exciting (excessive) excretion or discharge of urine.

c **1400** *Lanfranc's Cirurg.* 276 A decoccioun of herbis þat ben mollificatif & duretik. **1541** R. COPLAND *Galyen's Terap.* 2 H ij b, It must be myxed..with some dyurytyke medycamentes. **1646** SIR T. BROWNE *Pseud. Ep.* II. v. 84 Inwardly received it may be very diuretick, and expulse the stone in the kidnyes. **1732** ARBUTHNOT *Rules of Diet*, All salts whatsoever are diuretick. **1885** *Manch. Exam.* 4 May 5/2 The salts of potash which it contains are diuretic.

†**b.** Of persons: Urinating excessively. *Obs.*

1768 *Life Sir B. Sapskull* II. 97. **1812** *Morn. Chron.* 11 Apr.

B. *sb.* A substance having the property of promoting excretion or evacuation of urine.

c **1400** *Lanfranc's Cirurg.* 279 þou schalt make him a clisterie of duritikis. **1658** ROWLAND *Moufet's Theat. Ins.* 912 Galen placeth it amongst Diureticks. **1704** SWIFT *T. Tub* Wks. 1760 I. 109 Laughter..the most innocent of all diureticks. **1732** ARBUTHNOT *Rules of Diet* 256 Stimulatory Diureticks. **1875** H. C. WOOD *Therap.* (1879) 477.

†**diu'retical,** *a.* (*sb.*) *Obs. Med.* [f. as prec. + -AL[1].] = prec. **A.** *adj.*

1601 HOLLAND *Pliny* II. 444 The egs or spawn that the Cuttill fish doth cast be diureticall, and prouoke vrine. **1646** SIR T. BROWNE *Pseud. Ep.* II. v. 92 That Bezoar is Antidotall, Lapis Judaicus diureticall..we will not deny. **1685** *Phil. Trans.* XV. 983 Scaliger's Story of the sound of the bagpipe being too diuretical upon a Knight of Gascony.

B. *sb.*

1658 A. FOX tr. *Wurtz' Surg.* III. vii. 236 To this purpose are..used..all manner of diureticals.

Hence †**diu'retically** *adv.*, in a diuretic way, by diuresis; †**diu'reticalness,** diuretic property.

1644 HAMMOND *Loyal Convert* 13 Physicians evacuatethe Body..sometimes by Phlebotomie..sometimes diuretically. **1662** H. STUBBE *Ind. Nectar* iii. 65 Its deobstructing faculty, and its diureticalness. **1751** SMOLLETT *Per. Pic.* lxv, Peregrine's nerves were diuretically affected.

diuretin (daɪjʊ'riːtɪn). *Chem.* [f. as prec. + -IN.] A crystalline compound derived from coal-tar, used as a diuretic.

1890 *Lancet* 11 Oct. 783/2 Diuretin has produced well-marked diuresis in many cases of dropsy.

†**di'urn(e,** *a. Obs.* Also 4–5 **dyurne, diourne.** [ad. L. *diurn-us* of or belonging to a day, daily, f. *diēs* a day. Cf. F. *diurne*.] = DIURNAL *a.*

c **1386** CHAUCER *Merch. T.* 551 Parfourmed hath the sonne his Ark diurne. **1500–20** ? DUNBAR *Poems* (1893) 329 Phebus, the radius lamp divrn. **1603** SIR C. HEYDON *Jud. Astrol.* xxi. 432 The Moone by her diurne rapt motion from East to West commeth to the nine a clocke point in the morning.

diurnal (daɪ'ɜːnəl), *a.* and *sb.* [ad. L. *diurnāl-is* daily, f. *diēs* day. Cf. F. *diurnal* (admitted by the Academy 1694), It. *giornale* (Florio 1598: now only sb.) and see JOURNAL.]

1. Performed in or occupying one day; daily. Chiefly of the motion of the heavenly bodies.

c **1430** LYDG. *Compl. Bl. Knt.* (R.) Bicause that it drew to the night And that the sonne his arke diurnall Ypassed was. **1559** W. CUNNINGHAM *Cosmogr. Glasse* 54 Phebus..was entred his chariot, minding to finishe his diurnall Arcke. **1697** DRYDEN *Virg. Georg.* Ded. (1721) 179 The Diurnal Motion of the Sun. **1725** POPE *Odyss.* IV. 804 The joyous sun His twelfth diurnal race begins to run. **1890** C. A. YOUNG *Elem. Astron.* §363 No spots are visible from which to determine the planet's [Uranus's] diurnal rotation.

2. Of or belonging to each day; performed, happening, or recurring every day; daily. Of periodicals: Published or issued every day. *arch.*

1594 BLUNDEVIL *Exerc.* I. xxviii. (ed. 7) 77 The diurnall excesse of the Moones Motion from the Sun. **1638** WOTTON *Let. to Milton* 10 Apr. in *Reliq. Wotton.*, Genoa, whence the passage into Tuscany is as diurnal as a Gravesend Barge. **1711** ADDISON *Spect.* No. 101 ¶7 The Spectator published those little Diurnal Essays which are still extant. **1815** W. H. IRELAND *Scribbleomania* 234 The subject having been so recently before the public in all the diurnal prints. **1818** SCOTT *Hrt. Midl.* ix, The Laird's diurnal visits. **1848** LOWELL *Fable for Critics* Poet. Wks. 1890 III. 33 They're all from one source, monthly, weekly, diurnal.

3. Of or belonging to the day as distinguished from the night; day-: opp. to *nocturnal*. In *Zool.*, *spec.* of animals active only during the day.

1623 COCKERAM, *Diurnall*, of or belonging to the day. **1649** JER. TAYLOR *Gt. Exemp.* II. vii.[viii]. §4 The houses of prayer which the Jewes had..for their diurnall and nocturnal offices. *c* **1750** (*title*) Complete Modern London Spy, or a Real, New and Universal Disclosure of the Secret, Nocturnal and Diurnal Transactions in London and Westminster. **1874** WOOD *Nat. Hist.* 287 This..bird is.. very late in returning to rest, later indeed than any of the diurnal birds. **1875** BENNETT & DYER tr. *Sachs' Bot.* 784 The expanded position [of leaves or petals] is called that of growth or the diurnal position, the opposite one that of sleep or the nocturnal position.

†**4.** Of or pertaining to the (particular) day (of the week). *Obs. rare.*

1659 PEARSON *Creed* (1839) 375 The obligation of the day which was then the sabbath, died and was buried with him, but in a manner by a diurnal transmutation revived again at his resurrection.

5. Lasting for a day only; ephemeral. *rare.*

1866 *Treas. Bot.*, *Diurnal*, enduring but for a day, as the flower of Tigridia.

B. *sb.*

1. *Eccl.* A service-book containing the day-hours, except matins (this being a night office); †thence, a book for devotional exercises; a book of devotion (*obs.*).

[**1512** (*title*) Diurnale ad usum Sarum. **1549** *Act 3 & 4 Edw. VI*, c. 10 §1 All Books called.. Cowchers, Journales, Ordinales.. shall be.. abolished.] ? *a* **1550** (*title*) A Dyurnall for Deuoute Soules, to ordre themselfe therafter. **1686** (*title*) The Christian Diurnal of Father Nicholas S.J. Revised and much augmented and translated into English by S[ir] T. H[awkins]. **1846** W. MASKELL *Mon. Rit. Eccl. Ang.* I. p. cxxx. (On Service books).

2. A book for daily use, a day-book, diary; *esp.* a record of daily occurrences, a journal. *arch.*

1600 HAKLUYT *Voy.* (1810) III. 301 The diurnall of our course, sayling thither and returning. **1660** F. BROOKE tr. *Le Blanc's Trav.* 320, I ever carried with me a little memorial or diurnall, where I set down all the curiosities I met with. **1824** SCOTT *Redgauntlet* Let. x, Let me proceed in my diurnal.

3. A newspaper published daily; also *loosely*, any newspaper published at short periodical intervals; a journal. *Obs.* exc. *Hist.*

1640 *St. Trials, Abp. Laud* (R.), I found myself aggrieved at the Diurnal, and another pamphlet of the week, wherein they print whatsoever is charged against me, as if it were fully proved. **1646** MRQ. WORC. in Dircks *Life* ix. (1865) 147, I.. perused all the diurnals for more than a quarter of a year. **1710** STEELE *Tatler* No. 204 ¶4 We Writers of Diurnals are nearer in our Styles to that of common Talk than any other Writers. [The *Tatler* was published three times a week.] **1823** SCOTT *Peveril* xxvii, It was in every coffee-house, and in half the diurnals.

attrib. **1644** *Mercurius Brit.* 4–11 Jan., A Diurnall maker, a paper-intelligencer. **1654** CLEVELAND (*title*) A Character of a Diurnal-Maker.

4. A diurnal bird, butterfly, or moth.

In recent Dicts.

Hence **di'urnalness**, diurnal quality.

1727 BAILEY vol. II, *Diurnalness*, the happening daily.

di'urnalist. *Obs.* or *arch.* [f. prec. sb. + -IST.] A writer of a diurnal; a journalist.

1649 BP. HALL *Cases Consc.* IV. ix. (1650) 368 By the relation of our Diurnalists. **1674** HICKMAN *Quinquart. Hist.* (ed. 2) 116 The Diurnalists and Intelligencers. **1837** CARLYLE *Fr. Rev.* II. VI. v. (1872) 238 The Day-historians, Diurnalists or Journalists as they call themselves.

†**di'urnaller.** *Obs.* [f. as prec. + -ER¹.] = prec.

1661 R. BAILLIE *Lett. & Jrnls.* (1841) III. 468 Tom Sincerfe the diurnaller, a profane atheisticall papist.

di'urnally, *adv.* [f. DIURNAL *a.* + -LY².] In a diurnal way; every day; day by day; daily.

1599 A. M. tr. *Gabelhouer's Bk. Physicke* 22/1 Administer heerof to the Patient, a spoonefull, which diurnallye he may vse. **1664** H. MORE *Myst. Iniq., Apol.* 483 The Earth is moved annually and diurnally about the Sun. **1709** STEELE *Tatler* No. 56 ¶2 As we make these Enquiries, we shall diurnally communicate them to the Publick. **1758** J. S. tr. *Le Dran's Observ. Surg.* (1771) 323 Fits of an irregular Fever, which returned diurnally. **1869** R. A. PROCTOR in *Eng. Mech.* 31 Dec. 372/2 The idea that the stars revolve diurnally round the polar axis.

†**di'urnary.** *Obs.* [ad. L. *diurnāri-us* diary-keeper, journalist, f. *diurnus* daily, DIURN.]

1727–51 CHAMBERS *Cycl., Diurnary*, an officer in the Greek empire, who wrote down, in a book for that purpose whatever the prince did, ordered, regulated, &c., every day.

diur'nation. [f. L. *diurn-us* daily, DIURN + -ATION; after *hibernation*.] The habit of some animals, of sleeping or remaining quiescent during the day, as contrasted with their activity at night.

1836–9 MARSHALL HALL *Hibernation* in Todd *Cycl. Anat.* II. 767 The bat, which is a crepuscular or nocturnal feeder, regularly passes from its state of activity to one which may be designated diurnation. **1883** in *Syd. Soc. Lex.*

†**diu'turn,** *a.* *Obs.* [ad. L. *diūturn-us* of long duration, lasting, f. *diū*, *diūt-* long, for a long time. Cf. also obs. F. *diuturne*, It., Sp. *diuturno*.] = next.

1541 R. COPLAND *Galyen's Terap.* 2 E iv b, These vlceres here all are called Cacoethe, inueterate, and diuturnes. **1644** DIGBY *Nat. Bodies* II. (1645) 136 Diseases and poysons by diuturne use, doe.. temper to themselves those bodies, which are habituated to them.

diuturnal (daɪ(j)uː'tɜːnəl), *a.* Now *rare.* [ad. L. type **diūturnāl-is* (cf. *diūturnāliter* in Du Cange), f. *diūturn-us*: see prec. and -AL¹.] Of long duration, lasting.

1599 A. M. tr. *Gabelhouer's Bk. Physicke* 109/1 Diuturnalle coughinge is almost accountede incurable. **1694** tr. *Milton's Lett. State* Dec. an. 1657 Those things, by which the Peace between us may be preserv'd entire and diuturnal. **1830** *Fraser's Mag.* I. 344 Lift up, O Hell! thy diuturnal gate, But not eternal.

diu'turnity. Now *rare.* [ad. L. *diūturnitāt-em* long duration, f. *diūturn-us* DIUTURN.] Long duration or continuance; lastingness.

1432–50 tr. *Higden* (Rolls) I. 183 Dredenge to lose multiplicacion off childer by diuturnite of batelle. **1581** J. WALKER in *Confer.* IV. (1584) D d b, It is greater.. in diuturnitie, because it neuer dieth, nor hath any ende. **1684** tr. *Bonet's Merc. Compit.* IX. 339 Being tired by the diuturnity and violence of the pain. **1726** AYLIFFE *Parergon* 123 A Fourth.. Proof arises from Length and Diuturnity of Time. **1829** LAMB *Let. to W. Wilson* 15 Nov. (1837) II. 247 I promise myself, if not immortality, yet diuturnity of being read.

‖**div** (diːv). Also **dive, deev, dev, dew.** [Pers. *dīv*, *dīw*, formerly *dēv*:—Zend *daēva*, = Skr. *dēva* god: see DEVA.] An evil spirit or demon of Persian mythology; a devil; an evil genius.

The Indo-Iranian language had two words expressive of divinity: *asuria* and *dēva*. In the separate development of the languages, *dēva* became in Sanskrit the general name for gods, while the *Asuras* became the enemies of the gods. In the Zend-Avesta, on the other hand, *Ahura*, i.e. *Asura* (originally 'Lord' in Indo-Iranian) came to mean the supreme God *Ahura Mazda*, while *daēva* (Persian *dēv* or *dīv*) became the general name of an evil spirit, a fiend, demon, or devil, for which there had originally been no generic name.

1777 J. RICHARDSON *Dissert. East. Nations* 142 The Dives are pictured as hideous in form and malignant in mind. **1843** J. WILSON *Pársi Relig.* 150 Ahriman, this chief of death, this chief of the Dews. **1855** SMEDLEY *Occult Sciences* 50 The div of ancient Persia.. is supposed to be the same as the European devil of the middle ages. **1878** HAUG *Relig. of Parsis* (ed. 2) 268. **1883** E. O'DONOVAN *Story of Merv* xviii, Ghouls and divs, and various other kinds of evil spirits. **1893** MAX MÜLLER *Theosophy* vi. 181. **1895** J. DARMESTETER *Zend-Avesta* (ed. 2) Introd. 51 Daêva is generally understood as a 'dream', and that is the meaning it has in the derived *dêv* and in most of the Zend texts generally.. but it must also have applied to false gods.

div, Sc. and north. dial. f. DO *v.*, in pres. indic.

‖**diva** ('diːva). [It. *diva* goddess, lady-love, 'fine lady':—L. *diva* goddess, female divinity, fem. of *dīvus* divine, god, deity.] A distinguished female singer, a prima donna.

1883 BLACK in *Harper's Mag.* Feb. 465/2 The latest *diva* of the drama. **1894** *Tablet* 7 Apr. 531 Operatic singers of the other sex are to be engaged, but no diva.

divagate ('daɪvəgeɪt), *v.* [f. L. *dīvagāt-*, ppl. stem of *dīvagārī* to wander about, f. DI-¹, DIS- 1 + *vagārī* to wander.] *intr.* To wander about; to stray from one place or subject to another.

1599 A. M. tr. *Gabelhouer's Bk. Physicke* 203/1 [A prescription] agaynste divagatinge payne. **1852** *Fraser's Mag.* XLV. 171 Sir James had divagated into the question of Eternal Punishment. **1892** STEVENSON *Across the Plains* vi. 200 So does a child's balloon divagate upon the currents of the air.

divagation (daɪvə'geɪʃən). [n. of action f. L. *dīvagārī*: see prec. and -TION: cf. F. *divagation* (16– 17th c. in Hatz.-Darm.).] The action of divagating; a wandering or straying away or about: deviation; digression.

1560 *Bk. Discipl. Ch. Scot.* ix. (1621) 59 This skipping and divagation from place to place of Scripture. **1664** H. MORE *Myst. Iniq.* II. I. xi. 272 That the phancy may make no divagation. **1855** *Ess. Intuit. Mor.* 149 The illogical divagations of their adherents. **1881** *Sat. Rev.* 1 Jan. 13 Her divagations from the proper purpose of her life will be forgotten. **1883** STEVENSON *Silverado Sq.* ii. 78 With that vile lad to head them off on idle divagations.

†**di'vage,** *v.* *Obs. rare*⁻⁰. = DIVAGATE.

1623 COCKERAM, *Diuage*, to wander from place to place.

di'vaguely, *adv.* *nonce-wd.* [f. *vaguely*, under the influence of *divagate*.] In a wandering or aimless manner.

1857 READE *Course True Love* iii. 67 They drifted divaguely over the great pacific ocean of feminine logic.

†**'dival,** *a.* *Obs. rare*⁻⁰. [ad. L. *dīvāl-is* divine, f. *dīvus* deity.]

1656 BLOUNT *Gl., Dival*, divine, belonging to the Gods.

divalent ('daɪvələnt, 'dɪv-), *a.* *Chem.* [f. DI-² twice + L. *valēnt-em*, pr. pple. of *valēre* to be worth.] Combining with two atoms of hydrogen or other univalent element or radical; having two combining equivalents; also *bivalent*.

A *diatomic* element, e.g. OXYGEN, is divalent; so is the highly complex molecule C_5H_{10} = $(CH_3)_2{\cdot}C{\cdot}(CH_2)_2$, which has two combining powers unsaturated.

1869 ROSCOE *Elem. Chem.* 183 Calcium, Strontium, Barium. The metals of this class are divalent. **1870** F. HURTER in *Eng. Mech.* 11 Feb. 524/2 Oxygen is called divalent, or bivalent, because it can hold two atoms of a monogenous element. **1881** *Academy* 15 Jan. 47/1 In like manner the term 'divalent' may be given to such atoms as are equal in combining power to two atoms of hydrogen.

Divali, var. DEWALEE.

divan (dɪ'væn, daɪ-, 'daɪvæn). Also 6 **douan**, 7 **dyvan, divano**, 7–8 **duan(a**, 7–9 **diwan**, 9 **dewan, deewan.** [A word originally Persian, *dēvān*, now *dīwān*, in Arabic pronounced *dīwān*, *diwān*; in Turkish *divān*, whence in many European langs., It. *divano*, Sp., Pg., F. *divan*. Originally, in early use, a brochure, or fascicle of written leaves or sheets, hence a collection of poems, also a muster-roll or register (of soldiers, persons, accounts, taxes, etc.); a military pay-book, an account-book; an office of accounts, a custom-house; a tribunal of revenue or of justice; a court; a council of state, senate; a council-chamber, a (cushioned) bench. The East Indian form and use of the word is given under DEWAN. Another European form, older than *divan*, and app. directly from Arabic, is It. *dovana*, *doana*, now *dogana*, F. *douane* (in 15th c. *douwaine*), custom-house: see DOUANE.]

1. a. An Oriental council of state; *spec.* in Turkey, the privy council of the Porte, presided over by the Sultan, or in his absence by the grand vizier.

1586 T. B. *La Primaud. Fr. Acad.* I. 679 In Turkie the councell is kept fower daies in a week by the bassaes wheresoever the prince sojourneth.. In this councell called diuan.. audience is open to euery one. **1599** HAKLUYT *Voy.* II. i. 305 Requesting the ambassador within an houre after to goe to the Douan of the Vizir. **1603** KNOLLES *Hist. Turks* (1638) 252 Mahomet being dead, the three great Bassa's.. called a Divano or counsel for the wars, as if the King had bin aliue. **1625** PURCHAS *Pilgrims* IX. xii. §6 He comes no more at the Duana, except hee bee called. **1687** *Lond. Gaz.* No. 2230/1 Proposals have been made for these two Months last past in the Divan. **1753** HANWAY *Trav.* (1762) II. IX. ii. 216 The divan declared for the continuation of the peace. **1813** BYRON *Br. Abydos* II. xviii, In full Divan the despot scoff'd. **1843** *Penny Cycl.* XXV. 366/2 Upon its conquest by the Turks, Tunis was governed by a Turkish basha and a divan, or council of military men. **1850** W. IRVING *Mahomet* II. lvii. 487 The Moslem Caliph at Damascus had now his divan, in imitation of the Persian monarch.

b. *transf.* A council in general.

1619 PURCHAS *Microcosm.* lxxviii. 770 This (what Diuano would haue done it?) is too weightie. **1667** MILTON *P.L.* x. 457 The great consulting Peers, Rais'd from their dark Divan. **1725** POPE *Odyss.* IV. 903 The consult of the dire Divan. **1763** H. WALPOLE *Lett.* (1857) IV. 130 (Stanf.) Of the British Senate, of that august divan whose wisdom influences, [etc.]. **1818** SCOTT *Rob Roy* xii, To meet the family.. in full divan. *a* **1849** J. C. MANGAN *Poems* (1859) 324 The changeless decree of Heaven's Deewàn.

2. The hall where the Turkish divan is held; a court of justice; a council-chamber.

1597 R. WRAG in Hakluyt *Voy.* (1598) II. I. 305 Certaine Chauses conducted him to the Douan, which is the seat of Justice. **1634** SIR T. HERBERT *Trav.* 157 The rigour of the Caddies or Causae in the Divanoes, or Judgement Hals. **1662** J. DAVIES tr. *Mandelslo's Trav.* 46 Under this Gate is the Diwan, or the place of publick Judicature. **1717** LADY M. W. MONTAGU *Poems, Chiosk of Brit. Palace, Pera*, 'Till at the dread Divan the slow procession ends. *c* **1850** *Arab. Nts.* (Rtldg.) 548 The officers of state went into the divan, or hall of audience, where the sultan always assisted in person.

3. Orig., a long seat consisting of a continued step, bench, or raised part of the floor, against the wall of a room, which may be furnished with cushions, so as to form a kind of sofa or couch. Now usually, a low bed or couch with no back or ends.

1702 W. J. *Bruyn's Voy. Levant* ix. 32 Their greatest Magnificence consists in their Divans or Sofas. **1703** MAUNDRELL *Journ. Jerus.* (1732) 29 These Duans.. are a sort of low stages.. elevated about sixteen or eighteen inches or more above the floor, whereon the Turks eat, sleep, smoke, receive visits, say their prayers, etc. **1764** HARMER *Observ.* XIX. vi. 265 The Hebrew word *mittah*, which is here translated 'bed' may be understood of a divan. **1813** *Edin. Rev.* XXI. 133 The divan is that part of the chamber which is raised by a step above the rest of the floor, and which, is commonly surmounted by a couch.. placed along the wall. **1840** DICKENS *Old C. Shop* xi, The bed being soft and comfortable, Mr. Quilp determined to use it, both as a sleeping place by night and as a kind of Divan by day. **1863** MARY HOWITT *F. Bremer's Greece* II. xiv. 103 The Aga conducted me to the divan where he himself sat. **1919** W. S. MAUGHAM *Moon & Sixpence* xxix. 129, I had a divan in my sitting-room, and could very well sleep on that. **1954** 'V. H. COLLINS' *One Word & Another* 47 A *divan* is an upholstered piece of furniture... It can be used as a *bed* (often called *divan-bed*) in a bedroom, or as a *settee* in the day and a *bed* at night. **1965** M. FORSTER *Bogeyman* x. 175 The cover over her divan was red and white striped cotton.

4. A room having one side entirely open towards a court, garden, river, or other prospect.

1678 J. PHILLIPS tr. *Tavernier's Voy.* (1684) II. 49 The Palace at Agra. On the side that looks towards the River, there is a Divan, or a kind of out-jutting Balcone, where the King sits to see his Brigantines. **1759** *Lond. Mag.* XXVIII. 605 In Surat.. They [the Moors] have generally a kind of saloon which they call a *diwan*, entirely open on one side to the garden. **1841** ELPHINSTONE *Hist. Ind.* I. 307 The great rooms of state are upstairs.. open at one side like Mahometan divans.

5. A name sometimes given to a smoking-room furnished with lounges, in connexion with a cigar-shop or bar, as ***cigar-divan***; hence, a fancy name for a cigar-shop.

1848 DICKENS *Dombey* xxii, Mr. Toots had furnished a choice set of apartments: had established among them a sporting bower; and a divan which made him poorly. **1855** TROLLOPE *Warden* xvi, Mr. Harding had not a much correcter notion of a cigar divan than he had of a London dinner-house. **1880** DISRAELI *Endym.* xx, Mr. Trenchard.. said to Endymion, 'We are going to the divan. Do you smoke?'

‖**6.** A Persian name for a collection of poems (Persian, Arabic, Hindustani, Turkish); *spec.* a series of poems by one author, the rimes of which usually run through the whole alphabet. [From the original sense 'collection of written sheets', perh. influenced by later uses of the word.]

1823 tr. *Sismondi's Lit. Eur.* (1846) I. ii. 61 A perfect divan, in their eyes, was that in which the poet had regularly pursued in his rhymes, all the letters of the alphabet. *a* **1827** J. M. GOOD in Spurgeon *Treas. Dav.* (1882) VI. 6 Persian poets..distinguish their separate poems..by the name of gazels, and the entire set..by that of diwan. **1837** *Penny Cycl.* IX. 42/1. **1877** *Encycl. Brit.* VII. 292/2 The most important diwans are those of..Hafiz, Saadi, and Jami among the Persians. The plan has been imitated by Goethe in his 'West-östlicher Divan'. **1886** *Athenæum* 18 Dec. 820/1 Complete Divans of the great poetical triumvirate, Solomon ibn Gabirol, Moses ibn Ezra, and Jehuda Halevi.

7. *Comb.*, as ***divan-bed***, ***-cover***, ***-day***, ***-hall***, ***-seat***, ***-sofa***.

[**1919** F. Hurst *Humoresque* 99 A leather-and-oak 'davenbed' had obviously and literally been dragged to the least conspicuous corner.] **1933** *Discovery* Aug. 254/2 There is a divan-bed opposite the window. **1932** D. C. Minter *Mod. Needlecraft* 217/2 Box-shape divan cover. **1677–8** J. Phillips tr. *Tavernier's Grd. Seignior's Serag.* (1684) 24 (Stanf.) The Divan-days (that is to say, upon Council-days). *Ibid.* 27 The Divan-Hall. **1898** G. B. Shaw *Philanderer* 11, There are circular recesses at each side of the fireplace, with divan seats running round them. **1893** Divan sofa [see settee³ a].

Hence **divaned** *a.*, furnished with divans (sense 3).

1847 Disraeli *Tancred* v. ii, Some strolled into the divaned chambers. **1852** G. W. Curtis *Wanderer in Syria* 300 Alcoves..divanned with luxurious stuffs.

divanship: see dewan.

†**divapo'ration.** *Obs.* [f. di-¹, dis- 1 + vaporation.] The driving out of vapours by heat; evaporation.

1612 Woodall *Surg. Mate* Wks. (1653) 270 Divaporation is exhalation by fire of vapour, remaining in liquid substances, till all aquosity be consumed. **1706** in Phillips (ed. Kersey). **1721–1800** in Bailey. **1823** in Crabb *Technol. Dict.* Hence in mod. Dicts.

So **di,vapori'zation**.

In recent Dicts.

divaricate (dɪ-, daɪˈværɪkeɪt), *v.* [f. L. *dīvaricāt-*, ppl. stem of *dīvaricāre* to stretch asunder, f. di-¹, dis- 1 + *varicāre* to stretch (the legs) asunder, straddle, f. *varic-us* straddling.]

1. *intr.* To stretch or spread apart; to branch off or diverge from each other or from any middle line.

1623 Cockeram, *Diuaricate*, to step, to stride wide. **1656** Hobbes *Six Less.* Wks. 1845 VII. 195 Two lines may be made to divaricate..when having one end common and immoveable, they depart one from another at the other ends circularly, and this is called simply an angle. **1671** Grew *Anat. Plants* i. iv. (1682) 29 All its Parts, upon their shooting forth, divaricate from their perpendicular. **1740** Dyche & Pardon, *Divaricate*, to straddle wide, as those who are bow-legged do. **1779–81** Johnson *L.P.*, *Dryden* Wks. II. 387 While they [languages] run on together, the closest translation may be considered as the best; but when they divaricate, each must take its natural course. **1830** James *Darnley* (1846) 4 At the spot where these two [roads] divaricated, the horseman stopped. **1884** *19th Cent.* Feb. 333 The different races of plants and animals have come to divaricate from each other.

b. *Bot.* and *Zool.* To branch off at a wide angle; to diverge widely from the main stem: see divaricating *ppl. a.*

c. To ramify into divergent branches.

1672 Newton in *Phil. Trans.* VII. 5097 Irregularly refracted and made to divaricate into a multitude of other colours. *a***1728** Woodward *Nat. Hist. Fossils* 90 The partitions are striated across..one of them also divaricates into two, and another into several small ones. **1825** C. Butler *Roman-Cath. Ch.* 120 Here they divaricate into the Transalpine and Cisalpine opinions.

2. *trans.* To stretch or open wide apart or asunder (as the legs, fingers, limbs of a compass, etc.).

1672–3 Marvell *Reh. Transp.* i. 160 The incorrigible scold, that..streatched up her hands with her two thumb nails in the knit-cracking posture, or with two fingers divaricated, to call the man still in that language lousy rascal and Cuckold. *Ibid.* ii. Wks. II. 362, I took my compasses, and divaricating them for experiment, I drew the circular line. **1861** Hulme tr. *Moquin-Tandon* ii. vii. i. 336 Three small tubercles..capable of being alternately divaricated and approximated.

3. To cause to spread or branch out in different directions. ? *Obs.*

1670 *Phil. Trans.* V. 2061 A Congeries or Heap of innumerable Filaments, divaricated out of the Solider substance of the Brain. **1679** Evelyn *Sylva* (ed. 3) viii. ¶ 1 Putting a tile-shard under the nuts, when first set, to Divaricate and spread the roots. **1698** Fryer *Acc. E. India & P.* 386 Its Course was not broken, but divaricated into two Streams. **1738** Warburton *Div. Legat.* ii. App. Wks. 1811 II. 259 Refracted and divaricated, in passing through the medium of the human mind.

4. *fig.* To separate mentally, distinguish (one thing *from* another). *rare.*

1868 E. Edwards *Raleigh* I. xxviii. 714 [He] had too much intellect..not to be able to divaricate populace from people quite as sharply as did Ralegh.

di'varicate, *a.* [ad. L. *dīvaricāt-us*, pa. pple. of *dīvaricāre* to divaricate.] Spreading apart at a considerable angle; widely divergent; *spec.* applied (in *Bot.* and *Zool.*) to branches which diverge from the stem, etc. almost at right angles; and (in *Entom.*) to wings which spread apart at the tips when in repose.

1788 Jas. Lee *Introd. Bot.*, Explan. Terms (ed. 4) 382 *Divaricati*, divaricate, Branches shooting from the Trunk, so as to form an obtuse angle. **1823** Crabb *Technol. Dict.*, *Divaricatus* (*Bot.*) divaricate..standing out wide, an epithet for branches, a panicle, petiole, and peduncle. **1830** Lindley *Nat. Syst. Bot.* 173 Cotyledons divaricate. **1856–8** W. Clark *Van der Hoeven's Zool.* I. 311 Wings divaricate, sometimes very short.

b. Divergent in opinion or practice. *rare.*

1855 Bailey *Mystic* 57 The universe Contentiously divaricate, he shews Made one in spirit with eternity.

Hence **di'varicately** *adv.*, in a divaricate or wide-branched manner.

1846 Dana *Zooph.* 390 Divaricately ramose. **1854** Woodward *Mollusca* 295 Shell trigonal, divaricately sculptured.

di'varicated, *ppl. a.* [f. prec. vb. + -ed.] Widely divergent from each other or from a stem; widely or greatly branched; divaricate.

1665–6 *Phil. Trans.* I. 301 Its Tail being..divaricated towards the End. **1757** *Phil. Trans.* L. 68 The stalk..is much divaricated and branched. **1837** Howitt *Rur. Life* vi. vi. (1862) 463 Mistletoe..the beauty of its divaricated branches of pale-green. **1864** Huxley in *Reader* 5 Mar., The great toe is widely divaricated from the others. **1875** Whitney *Life Lang.* ix. 174 The languages in question are the divaricated representatives of a single tongue.

di'varicating *ppl. a.* [f. as prec. + -ing².] That divaricates or branches off in different directions; spreading out, diverging.

1835 Lindley *Introd. Bot.* (1848) I. 154 More correctly named divaricating hairs. **1874** Coues *Birds N.-W.* 14 It would seem to have two divaricating lines of migration. **1885** H. O. Forbes *Nat. Wand. E. Archip.* vi. ii. 431 High trees whose trunk was divided into four divaricating arms.

Hence **di'varicatingly** *adv.*

1870 Hooker *Stud. Flora* 374 Stem dichotomously and divaricatingly branched.

divari'cation. [n. of action f. divaricate *v.* (or its L. original): see -ation.]

1. The action of stretching apart; the stretching of the legs, straddling.

1650 Fuller *Pisgah* v. xix. 178 So that the Priests, not striding, but pacing up thereon, were not necessitated to any divarication of their feet. **1709–29** V. Mandey *Syst. Math.*, *Geom.* 139 The Quantity of an Angle, is the greater or lesser Divarication of the Legs. **1835–6** Todd *Cycl. Anat.* I. 157/1 A force..which can..cause a divarication of the bones of the leg.

2. The action of separating or branching out in different directions, spreading out, divergence.

1578 Banister *Hist. Man* v. 68 Where [of Veynes] such distribution, and divarication ought to be made. **1671** Grew *Anat. Plants* i. vii. (1682) 49 [Branches] by their co-arcture and divarication where they are inosculated. **1837** Lockhart *Scott* Dec. an. 1804 The gradual divarication of the two great dialects of the English tongue. **1884** Bower & Scott *De Bary's Phaner.* 439 The divarication of their branches in the parenchyma of the leaf.

3. *concr.* **a.** The point at which branching takes place. **b.** That which divaricates from a centre; a divaricating nerve or vein; a ramification.

1664 Power *Exp. Philos.* i. 65 They may be transmitted to the Brain, and its divarications. **1691** Ray *Creation* (1714) 55 Dogs..running before their Masters will stop at a Divarication of the way. **1794** J. E. Smith *Eng. Bot.* III. 205 Flowers mostly at the divarications of the branches.

4. *transf.* Divergence of opinion; disagreement; divergence from a fixed standard of opinion, etc.

1646 Sir T. Browne *Pseud. Ep.* vi. xi. 331 To take away all doubt or any probable divarication, the curse is plainely specified in the Text. **1651** Biggs *New Disp.* ¶ 185 Which is drawn from the divarications of the cubit. **1856** Ferrier *Inst. Metaph.* i. xiv. 91 The divarication of the two systems—our popular psychology on the one hand..and our strict metaphysics on the other hand. **1865** J. H. Stirling *Secr. Hegel* I. 152 How reconcile ourselves to the discrepancy and divarication?

di'varicator. [agent-noun in L. form from divaricate *v.*] That which divaricates; a muscle which draws parts asunder, as the muscle which opens the shells of Brachiopods. Also *attrib.*

1870 Rolleston *Anim. Life* 234 Divaricator muscle, passing from hinge process in the dorsal valve into the peduncle. **18..** Huxley (Cent.), Divaricators of the wall of the sac. **1888** Rolleston & Jackson *Anim. Life* 693 In the hinged Brachiopoda..the dorsal valve is furnished with a projecting cardinal process to which are attached the divaricator muscles.

†**divast,** *a. Obs. rare*⁻¹. [incorrect form for *devast*: cf. L. *dēvast-us* 'frightfully large', and devast *v.*] Devastated, laid waste.

1677 T. Harvey *Owen's Epigrams* 89 Time will come when the' earth shall lie divast.

dive (daɪv), *v.* Forms: α. 1 dúfan, 2 duven; β. 1 dýfan, 2–3 duve(n (y), 3 diven, 3–6 (9 *dial.*) deve, deeve (6 deave), 4–6 dy(e)ve, 7–9 dieve, 6– dive. Pa. t. α. 1 déaf, 2–3 deæf, 3 def, 9 *N.Amer.* and *Eng. dial.* dove; β. 1 dýfde, 3 defde, 7– div'd, 6– dived. [OE. had two verbs: (1) the primary strong vb. *dúfan*, pa. t. *déaf*, pl. *dufon*, pa. pple. *dofen*, intr. to duck, dive, sink; (2) the derivative causal weak vb. *dýfan*, *dýfde*, *ȝedýfd* to dip, submerge. Already in 12th c. these had begun to be confounded, the primary *dūven* (pa. t. *deæf*, *dêf*, pa. pple. *doven*) being used also trans., and the causal *dȳven* intrans., so that the two became synonyms, and before 1300 the strong vb. became obs., *dȳven* (s.w. *düven*, s.e. *dēven*, midl. and north *dīven*) remaining, chiefly in the intrans. sense of the OE. strong vb. Of the compound *bedive*, the pa. pple. bedoven came down to 16th c. in Sc. Only traces of this verb are found in the cognate langs.: ON. had *dýfa* to dip (also in same sense *deyfa*); MDu. had *bedûven*, pa. pple. *bedoven*, mod.Du. *beduiven* = OE. *bedúfan*. These belong to an OTeut. ablaut series *deub-*, *daub-*, *dub-*, secondary form of *deup-*, *daup-*, *dup-*, to dip, submerge:—pre-Teut. stems (weak-grade) *dhup-*, *dhub-*, respectively.

The s.e. *deven* gave the later *deeve*, *deave*, *dieve*; the modern dial. pa. t. *dove* is app. a new formation after *drive*, *drove*, or *weave*, *wove*.]

I. *intr.* **1. a.** To descend or plunge into or under water or other liquid. (Usually, unless otherwise stated, to plunge head-foremost.)

*a***1000** *Riddles* lxxiii. 4 (Gr.) Ic..deaf under yðe. *c***1220** *Bestiary* 539 Sone he [the whale] diueð dun to grunde, He drepeð hem alle wið-uten wunde. **1377** Langl. *P.Pl.* B. xii. 163 þat one hath connynge..and can swymmen and dyuen. ?*a***1400** *Balade in Jyll of Breyntford, &c.* (1871) 35 To dompe als deepe as man may dyeve þus holde I bett þan labour as a Reve. *c***1440** *Promp. Parv.* 124/1 Dyvyn vnder þe weter, *subnato.* **1555** Eden *Decades* 95 They durste not aduenture to dyue to the bottome. **1567** Maplet *Gr. Forest* 102 Those birds that deeuing downe to the waters to ketch fish, drowne themselues. **1660** Boyle *New. Exp. Phys. Mech.* Digress. 375 Those that dive for Pearles in the West Indies. **1774** Goldsm. *Nat. Hist.* (1776) VI. 69 [The cormorant] from a vast height drops down to dive after its prey. **1834** McMurtrie *Cuvier's Anim. Kingd.* 71 These animals..close their nostrils when they dive by a kind of valve. **1855** Longfellow *Hiawatha* vii. 96 Straight into the river Kwasind Plunged as if he were an otter, Dove as if he were a beaver. **1857** *Canad. Jrnl. Industry Sci. & Art* II. Sept. 351 In England when a swimmer makes his first leap, head foremost, into the water he is said to *dive*, and is spoken of as having *dived*... Not so however, is it with the modern refinements of our Canadian English. In referring to such a feat here, it would be said, not that he *dived*, but that he *dove*. **1867** Hayes *Open Polar Sea* xxxvi, The whole herd..dove down with a tremendous splash. *a***1940** F. Scott Fitzgerald *Last Tycoon* (1949) v. 119 He dove in and saved her life.

b. *transf.* To descend with similar motion into the earth, an abyss, etc.

*a***1225** *St. Marher.* 17 Ah flih sorhfule thing ut of min ehsihðe, ant def thider [into hell]. **1610** Shaks. *Temp.* i. ii. 191, I come To answer thy best pleasure; be't..to diue into the fire. **1615** Chapman *Odyss.* x. 245, The reason, how the man-enlightning sunne Diues vnder earth. **1725** Pope *Odyss.* xxii. 104 The fierce soul to darkness dived and hell. **1882** *N.Y. Herald* 14 Mar. 4/5 Women dove headlong from the crosstrees into friendly and convenient nets.

c. Of a submarine: to submerge.

1872 tr. *Verne's Twenty Thousand Leagues under Sea* (1874) ii. iv. 168, I quite approved of the *Nautilus* entering it [*sc.* the gulf]. Its speed was lessened: sometimes it kept on the surface, sometimes it dived to avoid a vessel. **1902** *Encycl. Brit.* XXXII. 575/2 An officer..dived with her [*sc.* a submarine] in water about 16 ft. deep. **1955** *Oxf. Jun. Encycl.* VIII. 49/2 When a submarine is to dive beneath the surface, its buoyancy is reduced by allowing water to enter large tanks..inside the hull.

d. *Aviation.* To descend or fall precipitously with increasing momentum.

1908 H. G. Wells *War in the Air* iv. §5 He could feel the airship diving down, down, down. **1914** Rosher *In R.N.A.S.* (1916) 37, I switched on and off, and dived down through the opening to 1,000 feet. **1916** H. Barber *Aeroplane Speaks* 136 *Dive*, to descend so steeply as to produce a speed greater than the normal flying speed. **1959** *Chamber's Encycl.* I. 115/1 There also exists a diving altitude above which the jet comes into its own.

Hence **'dive-bomb** *v. trans.*, to attack with bombs at a low level after diving. Also *transf.* So **dive-bomber** (= G. *sturzkampfflugzeug*), a dive-bombing aircraft; **dive-bombing** *vbl. sb.* and *ppl. a.*

1935 *Evening News* 11 July 7/1 In dive-bombing, which is the most accurate form of aerial attack on surface targets yet devised, the aircraft is aimed bodily at the target in the course of an almost vertical dive, which is maintained for several thousands of feet. **1936** *Jrnl. R. Aeronaut. Soc.* XL. 720 Dive bombing is limited to low altitude and suffers from insufficient penetration, although the aiming is probably good. **1937** *Flight* 4 Nov. c/1 (*caption*) Great Lakes dive bombers of the U.S. Marine Corps. **1939** *Times* 29 Sept. 10/4 The North Sea Attack. Failure of German Dive-Bombers. **1940** *Ibid.* 8 July 3/4 The aircraft..delivered a dive-bombing attack. *Ibid.* 23 July 2/4 Patrolling off the South Coast, three Hurricane pilots spotted 16 Me. 110s flying line astern to dive-bomb a convoy. **1958** A. J. Toynbee *East to West* xxxi. 94 They [*sc.* hawks] ignored his impertinence and dive-bombed us thick and fast. **1971** P. C. Smith *Stuka at War* iv. 38 The dive-bombers blasted a coastal gun battery on the Isle of Wight.

†**2.** Of things: To sink deeply into water or the like; to penetrate into any body. *Obs.*

*c***1205** Lay. 6505 þæt þ et sweord in deæf. *a***1225** *Juliana* 29 Euch dunt defde in hire leofliche lich. *Ibid.* 76 & wið þat ilke beide & def duueling dun to þer eorðe. *a***1225** *Ancr. R.* 282 A bleddre ibollen ful of winde ne dueð nout into þeos deope wateres. **1567** Maplet *Gr. Forest* 111 The Spider..of the water. This laste is of such nimblenesse that running vpon the water neuer drowneth nor deaueth. **1595** Shaks. *John* v. ii. 139 To diue like Buckets in concealed welles. **1607** —— *Timon* iv. i. 2 O thou Wall..diue in the earth, And fence not Athens.

3. a. To penetrate with the hand *into* any recess; to plunge the hand *into* water, etc., or *into* a vessel, *esp.* for the purpose of taking something out. **b.** *slang.* To pick pockets.

a **1700** B. E. *Dict. Cant. Crew, Dive,* to pick a Pocket. **1714** GAY *Trivia* II. 89 She'll lead thee with delusive Smiles along, Dive in thy fob, and drop thee in the throng. **1821** LAMB *Elia* Ser. I. *Old Bencher's I.T.*, He took snuff.. diving for it under the mighty flaps of his old-fashioned waistcoat pocket. **1889** JESSOPP *Coming of Friars* ii. 53, I at once dived into one of the boxes, and then spent half the night in examining some of its treasures.

†**c.** *spec.* To plunge a fork into a large pot containing portions of meat, having paid for the privilege of taking whatever the fork brings up. *Obs.*

1748 SMOLLETT *Rod. Rand.* xiii, Diving, practised by those who are.. inclined to live frugally.. Many creditable people.. dive every day.

4. *fig.* To enter deeply or plunge *into* (a matter); to penetrate.

1583 STANYHURST *Æneis* ii. (Arb.) 44 But Capys and oothers diuing more deepelye to bottom.. Dyd wish thee woodden monster weare drowned. **1593** SHAKS. *Rich. II*, I. iv. 25 He did seeme to diue into their hearts With humble and familiar courtesie. **1630** PRYNNE *Anti-Armin.* 10 Into the grounds and causes of which euery meane capacity may diue. **1754** SHERLOCK *Disc.* (1759) I. iii. 136 The vain Attempts of Men to dive into.. the Mysteries of God. **1845** M. PATTISON *Ess.* (1889) I. 23 The king.. had been diving into the collection of the canons.

5. To dart suddenly down or into some place or passage; to dart out of sight, disappear.

1748 SMOLLETT *R. Random* I. xiii. 102 Walking a few paces, [he] dived into a cellar, and disappeared in an instant. **1844** DICKENS *Mart. Chuz.* viii, Mr. Pecksniff.. dived across the street. **1873** BURTON *Hist. Scot.* VI. lxxi. 248 The Highlanders.. had dived into their mountain recesses. **1891** N. GOULD *Double Event* 27 He dived into the nearest restaurant. **1893** C. KING *Foes in Ambush* 8 He.. dove out of sight. **1893** Q. [COUCH] *Delectable Duchy* 19 Where a straight pathway dived between hazel-bushes and appeared again twenty feet above. **1970** *Toronto Daily Star* 24 Sept. 17/4 Forest Hill struck first when Mike Brown dove on a loose ball.

II. *trans.* [In early use OE. *dýfan*; from 16th c. a new construction].

6. a. To dip, submerge, or plunge (a person or thing) *in*, or *into* a liquid, or the like. *arch.*

c **900** tr. *Bæda's Hist.* v. xiii. [xii]. (1891) 436 He hine on ðam streame sencte and dyfde. *a* **1000** *Riddles* xxvii. 3 (Gr.) Mec feonda sum.. dȳfde on wætre. *c* **1200** *Trin. Coll. Hom.* 43 Louerd ne þaue þu þat storm me duue. *Ibid.* Woreldes richeise wecheð orgel on mannes heorte, and deuð him on helle . alse storm doð þat ship in þe watere. **1594** HOOKER *Eccl. Pol.* IV. xii. §3 To diue an infant either thrice or but once in Baptisme. **1605** VERSTEGAN *Dec. Intell.* ii. (1628) 45 The Germans vsed to take their new-born children and to diue them in riuers. **1662** SIR W. DUGDALE *Hist. Imbanking & Draining* (1772) 231 Thenceforth, neither flax or hemp should be dieved in the said sewers. **1854** SYD DOBELL *Balder* xxii. 84 Spout thee to heaven, and dive thee to the deep!

b. To plunge (the hand or anything held) *into.* (A trans. variant of 3.)

c **1590** GREENE *Fr. Bacon* i. 81 She turned her smocke ouer her lilly armes, And diued them into milke to run her cheese. **1878** T. P. BIGG-WITHER *Pioneer. Brazil* I. 266 The Camaradas dive their own spoons into the bag and commence to eat from it all together. **1891** *Blackw. Mag.* Mar. 314 She had 'dieved' her kettle into the snow instead of filling it at the pump. **1893** Q. [COUCH] *Delectable Duchy* 42 He dived a hand into his tail pocket.

†**c.** *transf.* and *fig.* To plunge, cause to sink.

1649 DRUMM. OF HAWTH. *Hist. Jas.* IV. Wks. (1711) 78 By largesses, banqueting, and other magnificence, diving himself in debt. **1672** MARVELL *Reh. Transp.* I. 55 The River dives it self under ground. **1771** *Muse in Min.* 14 Nurse of nature.. Dive me in thy depths profound.

7. To penetrate or traverse by diving; to dive into or through. Now *rare.*

1615 CHAPMAN *Odyss.* v. 459 She.. Turn'd to a cormorant, div'd, past sight, the main. *c* **1650** DENHAM *Old Age* 794 The Curtii bravely dived the gulf of flame. **1772** *Poetry* in *Ann. Reg.* 224 She fish'd the brook,—she div'd the main. **1813** T. BUSBY *Lucretius* I. 1015 To those who seldom dive the well of truth. **1847** EMERSON *Poems* (1857) 42 He dives the hollow, climbs the steep.

8. *slang.* To pick (pockets).

1621 B. JONSON *Gipsies Metamorph.* Wks. (Rtldg.) 619/2 Using your nimbles [fingers], In diving the pockets.

dive (daɪv), *sb.* [f. DIVE *v.*]

1. a. The act of diving; a darting plunge into or through water or the like. *lit.* and *fig.*

The Amateur Swimming Association distinguishes between a dive and a plunge. The latter is defined as a standing dive made head-first from a firm take-off, free from spring. The plunger does not add any further impetus, but allows himself to progress till all forward motion ceases, when he raises his face above water. A dive may be running, from a spring-board, and with propulsion added on reaching the water.

1700 T. BROWN *Amus. Ser. & Com.* 126 A Pick-Pocket; who made a Dive into my Pocket. **1804** *Miniature* No. 19 ¶2 Upon taking too profound a dive into the Bathos, he was.. unfortunately drowned. **1828** *Boy's Own Bk.*, '*Swimming*' 107 (The Dolphin) This is taking a dive from the surface of the water by turning heels upwards for that purpose, instead of leaping from a bank or elsewhere. **1875** TALMAGE *Tea-Table* iii, I first take a dive into the index, a second dive into the preface. **1893** *Badminton Libr., Swimming* 107 The usual high dive is a mere drop at a down-ward angle. **1893** EARL DUNMORE *Pamirs* II. 270 He [the hawk].. gave a sort of dive underneath him.

b. *Aviation.* A precipitate descent. (Cf. *nose-dive* and DIVE *v.* 1 d).

1914 ROSHER *In R.N.A.S.* (1916) 13 When in the air, he bawls in your ear, 'Now when you push your hand forward, you go down, see!' (and he pushes your hand forward and you make a sudden dive). **1915** *War Illustr.* 27 Feb. 46/2 The excitement of the dive,.. and the swift upward leap of the machine. **1936** *Discovery* Mar. 73/2 The pilot cannot pull the nose of his aeroplane up so quickly that he stalls it with the subsequent danger of a steep dive or spin. **1970** D. L. BROWN *Miles Aircraft since 1925* 111 He opened the throttle wide and put the nose down into a steep dive.

c. Of a submarine: submerging, submersion.

1915 W. E. DOMMETT *Submarine Vessels* iv. 42 When preparing for a dive, the.. valves are tried. **1962** G. WELLER *All about Submarines* (1963) iii. 36 On *Hunley's* first dive, the flames of her lantern flickered low after only a half-hour... On the next trip the submarine stayed down five times as long.

2. *transf.* A sudden dart into a place or across a space, *esp.* so as to disappear.

a **1897** *Mod.* He made a dive into the nearest shop.

3. *colloq.* (orig. *U.S.*) An illegal drinking-den, or other disreputable place of resort, often situated in a cellar, basement, or other half-concealed place, into which frequenters may 'dive' without observation.

1871 *N.Y. Herald* 6 July 8/2 One of the gayly decorated dives where young ladies.. dispense refreshments to thirsty souls. **1882** *Society* 11 Nov. 7/2 The proprietor of a New York 'dive'. **1883** H. H. KANE in *Harper's Mag.* Nov. 945/1 Those who frequent the opium-smoking dives. **1885** *Referee* 10 May 3/3 A grand entrance takes the place of the tavern, which is relegated to down below, and is called a 'dive'. **1886** E. W. GILLIAM in *N. Amer. Rev.* July 33 There are 150 gambling dives, the approaches to which are so barricaded as to defy police detection. **1887** *Boston Jrnl.* 24 Apr. 2/4 Ordinary saloons and unlicensed dives did a rushing trade. **1892** STEVENSON & OSBOURNE *Wrecker* viii, I visited Chinese and Mexican gambling-hells, German secret societies, sailors' boarding-houses, and 'dives' of every complexion of the disreputable and dangerous. **1897** *Daily News* 17 Apr. 3/1 From highway into byway they go; now up into tottering garret, then down into dim dive. **1910** *Westm. Gaz.* 25 Jan. 4/1 This dingy 'dive' can boast of many glorious memories. **1940** AUDEN *Another Time* 112, I sit in one of the dives On Fifty-Second Street. **1958** *Spectator* 4 July 8/3 The degenerate dives of Berlin.

4. *attrib.* and *Comb.* **dive brake** (see quot. 1962); **dive-keeper** *U.S.*, a person who keeps a 'dive' (sense 3).

1940 C. GARDNER *A.A.S.F.* 238 The 87's, with their dive-brakes on, came down vertically to about 600 feet. **1954** *Economist* 11 Sept. (Suppl.) 3/1 The Hawker factories producing Hunters contain two or three hundred complete and half-complete machines waiting for their new dive brakes. **1962** *Gloss. Aeronaut. Terms* (*B.S.I.*) v. 5 *Dive brake*, any device primarily used to increase the drag of an aircraft at will. **1887** *Chicago Tribune* 4 May 3/1 Consternation has seized the divekeepers. **1910** S. E. WHITE *Rules of Game* I. xvi, One of the saloon keepers at Twin Falls... This dive-keeper.. had offered transportation.

dive, variant of DIV.

dive-bomb, -bomber, -bombing: see DIVE *v.* 1 d.

'dive-dap, -dop. *Obs.* exc. *dial.* Forms: 1 dufedoppa, 3 douedoppe(n, 4 dyuedap, deuedep, 6 dyuendop, 9 *dial.* **dive dop, dive an'** dop. [OE. *dufedoppa*, f. *dúfan* to dive, duck + *doppa*, agent-n. f. ablaut stem *déop-*, *déap-*, *dup-* (*dop-*) to dip: cf. *dop-enid* dipping-duck, coot, *dop-fugel* dipping-fowl, diver; also the derivative vb. *doppettan* to dip often. The first element appears to have been changed to *dyve-* when the strong form of the vb. became obsolete: see DIVE. Some later forms are due to 'popular etymology'.] = next.

a **1000** *Lamb. Ps.* ci[i]. 6 (Bosw.) Gelic ȝeworden ic eom niht-hræfne oððe dufedoppan westennes. *c* **1290** *S.E. Leg.* I. 452/127 He saiȝh douedoppene fisches cachche. **1382** WYCLIF *Lev.* xi. 17 An owle, and a deuedep [**1388** dippere; Vulg. *mergulum.*] —— *Deut.* xiv. 17 Vnclene [briddis] eete ȝe not, that is,.. a dyuedap, a pellican, and a nyȝt crowe. *a* **1529** SKELTON *Phyllyp Sparowe* 450 With the wilde mallarde; The dyuendop to slepe. **1885** SWAINSON *Prov. Names Brit. Birds* 216 Divedapper or Divedop (Lincolnsh.).. Dive an' dop (Norfolk).

'dive-dapper. *Obs.* exc. *dial.* Also 6 dive-doppel, 6–7 dive-dopper. [The form *dive-doppel* is app. a dim. of *divedop*, *-dap*; the form in *-dapper*, *-dopper*, is assimilated to agent-nouns in -ER.] A small diving waterfowl; a dabchick; = DIDAPPER; also applied to other diving water fowls.

1559 BECON *Display. Popish Mass* Prayers, etc. (1844) 276 Then once again kneel ye down, and up again, like dive-doppels, and kiss the altar. **1592** SHAKS. *Ven. & Ad.* 86 Vpon this promise did he raise his chin, Like a diuedapper peering through a waue. **1605** DRAYTON *Man in Moone* 187 And in a Creeke where waters least did stirre, Set from the rest the nimble Divedopper. **1659** D. PELL *Impr. Sea* 383 *note*, The black dive-dappers in the salt-waters. **1783** *Ainsworth's Lat. Dict.*, A didapper, or dive dapper, *mergus.* **1885** [see DIVE-DAP].

b. Applied, ludicrously, to a person.

1607 MIDDLETON *Trick to catch Old One* IV. v. Wks. (Bullen) II. 340 Behold the little dive dapper of damnation, Gulf the usurer. **1654** TRAPP *Comm. Ps.* xxix. 3 Yet your dive-dappers duck not at this rattle in the air.

Hence **'dive-dopping** *ppl. a.* (*nonce-wd.*), diving or ducking like a dabchick.

1615 J. STEPHENS *Satyr. Ess., Informer* (1857) 193 He is worse then an Otter-hound for a dive-dopping Ale-house keeper: and hunts him out unreasonably.

divel, obs. form of DEVIL.

diveli'nation. *nonce-wd.* [f. *devil* and *divination.*] Divination by aid of the devil.

1591 HORSEY *Trav.* (Hakl. Soc.) 199 To receive and bring from them [witches] their divelinacions or oracles.

†**di'vell,** *v. Obs.* [ad. L. *dīvell-ĕre* to tear or rend asunder, f. *dī-*, *dis-*, DIS- 1 + *vellĕre* to tear. Cf. DIVULSE.] *trans.* To tear, rend, or pull asunder. Hence **di'velling** *ppl. a.*, divellent.

1627–47 FELTHAM *Resolves* I. [11]. xlvii. 147 How the antient society of the body and the soul is divelled. **1646** SIR T. BROWNE *Pseud. Ep.* III. xxv. 174 They [eyelids] begin to separate, and may be easily divelled or parted asunder. **1801** CHENEVIX in *Phil. Trans.* XCI. 223 A new order of divelling affinities.

divellent ('dɪ-, daɪ'vɛlənt), *a.* [ad. L. *dīvellent-em*, pr. pple. of *dīvellĕre* to DIVELL.] Drawing asunder; decomposing, separative.

1782 KIRWAN in *Phil. Trans.* LXXIII. 40 In all decompositions we must consider, first, the powers which resist any decomposition.. and, secondly, the powers which tend to effect a decomposition and a new union. The first I shall call *quiescent* affinities, and the second sort *divellent.* **1805** CHENEVIX in *Phil. Trans.* XCV. 108 The application of two divellent forces. **1850** DAUBENY *Atom. Th.* x. (ed. 2) 351 Unstable equilibrium.. with the divellent and quiescent attractions so nearly balanced, that nothing but the inertia of the atoms tends to maintain the existing combination.

divellicate (daɪ'vɛlɪkeɪt), *v.* [f. L. *dī-*, *dis-*, DIS- 1 + ppl. stem of *vellicāre* to pluck, twitch, pinch, deriv. of *vellĕre* to pluck, pull: cf. DIVELL.] *trans.* To tear asunder, pull to pieces. Also *fig.*

1638 SIR T. HERBERT *Trav.* (ed. 2) 101 To reduce all Majesty (too long divellicated) to the proper station. **1749** FIELDING *Tom Jones* VII. xiii, The interior membranes were so divellicated, that the os, or bone, very plainly appeared. **1752** —— *Amelia* v. vi, My brother told me you had used him dishonestly, and had divellicated his character behind his back. **1837** *Blackw. Mag.* XLII. 234 Three out of the fifteen were divellicated from the parent stem.

†**di'ventilate,** *v. Obs. rare*$^{-0}$. [F. L. *dīventilāre*, f. *ventilāre* to fan, winnow, toss in the air.] (See quot.) Hence †**diventi'lation.**

1656 BLOUNT *Glossogr.*, *Diventilate*, to fan or winnow,.. also to turn out of one hand into another. **1658** PHILLIPS, *Diventilation*, a winnowing, or tossing to and fro.

diver ('daɪvə(r)). [f. DIVE *v.* + -ER[1].]

1. A person who dives under water. *spec.* One who makes a business of diving in order to collect pearl-oysters, to examine sunken vessels, etc.

1506 GUYLFORDE *Pylgr.* (Camden) 76 The rother.. by suttell crafte of a dyuer, was set perfaytly in her place the same nyght. The sayde dyuer dyde all that busynes beynge vnderneth the water. **1555** EDEN *Decades* 95 They had certeyne dyuers or fysshers exercised from theyr youthe in swymmynge vnder the water. **1622** R. HAWKINS *Voy. S. Sea* (1847) 227 Eight negroes, expert swimmers, and great deevers, whom the Spaniards call *busos.* **1695** WOODWARD *Nat. Hist. Earth* (1723) 27 Dyvers, and Fishers for Pearls. **1893** *Badminton Libr., Swimming* 99 If deep diving be often indulged in.. a curious disease, known as 'Diver's paralysis' is likely to be contracted.

b. An animal expert in diving. (Cf. 2.)

1694 *Acc. Sev. Late Voy.* II. (1711) 90 This Bird is a Diver. **1735** SOMERVILLE *Chase* IV. 445 This artful Diver [the Fox] best can bear the Want of vital Air. **1847** CARPENTER *Zool.* §455 Most of them [Ducks], too, are good divers.

c. *fig.* One who 'dives' into a subject, etc.

1624 WOTTON *Archit.* A diver into causes, and into the mysteries of proportion. **1654** W. MOUNTAGUE *Devout Ess.* II. iv. §3 (R.) Diuers in the deep of providence.

2. A name given to various water birds remarkable for their power of diving. **a.** *spec.* The common name of the *Colymbidæ*, noted for the time they remain and the distance they traverse under water; species are the ***great northern d.***, the ***black-throated d.***, the ***red-throated d.***, etc. **b.** The little grebe, dabchick, or dive-dapper and other species of grebe. **c.** Various species of *Anseres*: ***black diver***, the common scoter, ***dun diver***, the female and young male merganser.

c **1510** BARCLAY *Mirr. Gd. Manners* (1570) F iij, When shall the diuer leaue in waters for to be? **1552** HULOET, Diuer byrde. **1678** RAY *Willughby's Ornith.* 341 The greatest speckled Diver or Loon: *Colymbus maximus caudatus. Ibid.* 366 The black Diver or Scoter: *Anas niger minor.* **1766** PENNANT *Zool.* (1812) II. 213 The Dun Diver, or female [Merganser] is less than the male. **1774** GOLDSM. *Nat. Hist.* VI. viii. VI. 98 The first of this smaller tribe is the Great Northern Diver. **1789** G. WHITE *Selborne* II. xlii. (1853) 272 Divers and auks walk as if fettered. **1828** STARK *Elem. Nat. Hist.* I. 321 Little Auk, or Small Black and White Diver. **1862** ANSTED *Channel Isl.* II. ix. (ed. 2) 207 The great northern, the black-throated, and the red-throated divers visit us regularly each winter.

3. A pick-pocket; see also quot. 1608.

1608 DEKKER *Belman of Lond.* Wks. 1884–5 III. 140 The Diuer workes his Iugling feates by yͤ help of a boy, (called a Figger) whom hee thrusts in at a casement.. this Figger deliuers to the Diuer what snappings he findes in the shop or chamber. **1611** MIDDLETON & DEKKER *Roaring Girle* v. i.

Wks. (Bullen) IV. 133 A diuer with two fingers, a picke-pocket. **1706** E. Ward *Hud. Rediv.* I. i. 24 So expert Divers call aloud, Pray mind your Pockets, to the Crowd. **1887** Baumann *Londismen* p. v, Are Smashers and divers.. Not sold to the beaks By the coppers an' sneaks?

4. Something made to plunge under water.

1799 G. Smith *Laboratory* I. 22 The water-crackers, or divers, are commonly rammed in cases. **1820** Scoresby *Acc. Arct. Reg.* I. 186 This instrument which I called a marine diver.. With this.. I completed a series of experiments on submarine temperature.

b. **1884** *Chesh. Gloss.*, *Divers*, the larger blocks of burr stone used for making river embankments.

Hence **'diver-like** *a.* and *adv.*

1791 Cowper *Iliad* xvi. 906 He, diver-like, from his exalted stand Behind the steeds pitch'd headlong.

†**'diver**, *v. Obs.* [app. related to daver *v.*, and Du. *daveren* to shake, quake, LG. *dȧveren*, *dâveren* (Mätz.); but the phonology is obscure.] *intr.* To shake, quake.

a **1225** *Leg. Kath.* 619 Ha ne schulden nowðer diuerin ne dreden. *a* **1225** *St. Marher.* 16 Speoken i ne dar nawt, ah diueri ant darie drupest alre þinge. *a* **1240** *Wohunge* in *Cott. Hom.* 283 Tu þat al þe world fore mihte drede and diuere.

†**'diverb.** *Obs.* [f. *di-* (? di-² two, twice) + L. *verbum* word: cf. L. *dīverbium* 'the colloquial part of a comedy, the dialogue', to which, however, the Eng. use shows no approach.] A proverb, byword; a proverbial expression.

(Often used, and app. introduced by Burton; Richardson explains 'an antithetical proverb or saying, in which the parts or members are contrasted or opposed'; but this is hardly applicable to all Burton's diverbs.)

1621–51 Burton *Anat. Mel.* II. ii. iv. (1676) 178/2 You may define *ex ungue leonem*, as the diverb is, by his thumb alone the bigness of Hercules. *Ibid.* II. iii. vii. 220/1 Durum & durum non faciunt murum, as the diverb is. *Ibid.* III. i. ii. 364/1 England is a paradise for women, and hell for horses; Italy a paradise of horses, hell for women, as the diverbe goes. **1678** Bp. Wetenhall *Office of Preaching* 793 What do we mean by the usual diverb, the Italian Religion? **1689** Hickeringill *Ceremony-Monger* Wks. (1716) II. 498 Verifying the Proverb, A great Head and little Wit; not that the Diverb is always true, but it is often so.

diverbal (daɪˈvɜːbəl), *a. rare.* [f. di-² + verbal; or ? f. prec.] Relating to two words.

1825 *New Monthly Mag.* XVI. 30 It may.. be asserted of this di-verbal allusion, that it is too good to be natural.

†**di'verberate**, *v. Obs.* [f. L. *dīverberāt-* ppl. stem of *dīverberāre* to strike or cleave asunder, f. *dī-*, dis- 1 + *verberāre* to beat, scourge, whip.] *trans.* To cleave asunder; to strike through.

1609 J. Davies *Holy Roode* cxlvii, These cries for.. blood diuerberate The high resounding Heau'n's convexitie. **1656** Blount *Glossogr.*, *Diverberate*.. to strike, beat or cut.

Hence **diverbe'ration**, beating.

1651 *Raleigh's Ghost* 311 Praise (which is but an idle diverberation or empty sound of ayre). **1658** Phillips, *Diverberation*, a violent beating. **1684** tr. *Bonet's Merc. Compit.* x. 352 Aquapendent mentions this diverberation.

diverge (dɪˈvɜːdʒ, daɪ-), *v.* [ad. mod.L. *dīvergĕre*, f. *dī-*, dis- 1 + *vergĕre* to bend, turn, incline, verge. Cf. F. *diverger*, Sp., Pg. *divergir*.]

1. *intr.* To proceed in different directions from a point or from each other, as lines, rays of light, etc. The opposite of converge 1.

1665 Hooke *Microgr.* 69 The Rays.. will after the refraction.. diverge and spread. **1704** Newton *Optics* I. axiom vi, Homogeneal Rays.. shall afterwards diverge from so many other points, or be parallel to so many other lines, or converge to so many other points. **1782** Cowper *Hope* 303 Ethelred's house, the centre of six ways, Diverging each from each, like equal rays. **1816** Keatinge *Trav.* (1817) II. 232 The mountains here diverge, in a fan-like form. **1851** Richardson *Geol.* (1855) 148 The anticlinal line is that elevated central point from which the strata diverge.

b. *transf.* and *fig.* To take different courses; to turn off *from* a track or course; to differ in opinion or character; to deviate from a typical form or normal state.

1856 E. A. Bond *Russia at close 16th C.* (Hakl. Soc.) Introd. 27 Brought up to the practice of medicine, he diverged to the profession of astrology. **1856** Dove *Logic Chr. Faith* v. i. §2. 264 We may diverge, either into the region of morals.. or into the region of matter. **1860** Tyndall *Glac.* I. iii. 31, I diverged from the track. **1867** J. Martineau *Ess.* II. 377 This is the point.. at which Aristotle diverges from Plato.

c. *Math.* Said of an infinite series the sum of which increases indefinitely as the number of terms is increased. Opp. to converge 1 c.

1796 Hutton *Math. Dict.* II. 436 When the terms grow larger and larger, the Series is called a *diverging* one, because that by collecting the terms continually, the successive sums diverge, or go always farther and farther from the true value or radix of the Series.

2. *trans.* To cause (lines or rays) to branch off in different directions; to make divergent, deflect.

1748 *Phil. Trans.* XLV. 187 The electrified Jet or Stream .. is diverged into several divergent Rays. **1758** J. Dollond in *Phil. Trans.* L. 740 In general the crown glass seems to diverge the light rather the least. *c* **1865** J. Wylde in *Circ. Sc.* I. 260/1 An electric current diverges a magnetic needle. **1879** H. Grubb in *Proc. R. Dubl. Soc.* 184 The makers [of stereoscopes] have got so accustomed to diverging their eyes, that.. they require little or no divergent power.

di'vergement. [f. prec. + -ment.] The action of diverging; divergence.

1766 G. Canning *Anti-Lucretius* iv. 257 Then Epicurus had not been constrain'd His lame absurd Divergement to have feign'd. **1835** Kirby *Hab. & Inst. Anim.* I. App. 359 It .. can fix itself.. also by the divergement of its lobes. **1835** —— *Power, etc. God* (1852) II. 15 Obliged to retrograde, and begin a branch, from the point of its divergement.

divergence (dɪˈvɜːdʒəns, daɪ-). [ad. mod.L. *dīvergentia* (f. *dīvergĕre*) or a. F. *divergence* (17th c. in Hatz.-Darm.): see divergent and -ence.]

1. The action of diverging: moving off in different directions from the same point (called the *point of divergence*), so that the intervening distance continually increases. The opposite of *convergence*.

1656 Hobbes *Six Less.* iii. Wks. 1845 VII. 252 That angle which is generated by the divergence of two straight lines. **1657** Wallis *Corr. of Hobbes* ix. 81 Doth it remain the same angle, the same quantity of divergence? **1713** Derham *Phys. Theol.* iv. ii. (Seager) The convergences and divergences of the rays. **1870** R. M. Ferguson *Electr.* 34 This divergence from the true north.

b. *ellipt.* for *amount* or *degree of divergence*.

1880 Gray *Struct. Bot.* iv. §1. 121 This angular divergence (i.e. the angular distance of any two successive leaves). **1882** Vines *Sachs' Bot.* 608 The stamens stand in one or two turns with the divergence $\frac{8}{21}$ or $\frac{13}{34}$.

2. *transf.* and *fig.* The departure from each other of two paths, courses, modes of action, or processes; continuous departure or deviation from a standard or norm.

1839 Alison *Hist. Europe* (1849–50) VII. xliv. §84. 370 Augereau's divergence had been occasioned by something more than the snow-storm. **1858** Gladstone *Homer* II. 140 The natural divergence of the two traditions. **1871** L. Stephen *Playgr. Eur.* iv. iii. 232 There was the widest divergence of opinion as to our probable fate. **1888** Bryce *Amer. Commw.* II. ii. xl. 88 *note*, An illustration of the divergences between countries both highly democratic.

3. *Math.* **a.** Of a series: the action of diverging (diverge *v.* 1 c), or fact of being divergent. **b.** In fluid motion, the decrement of density at any point. In quaternions, the negative of the scalar part of the result of operating with the Hamiltonian operator upon a vector function (which serves to measure such decrement).

1858 Todhunter *Algebra* xl. *heading*, Convergence and Divergence of Series.

di'vergency. [f. as prec.: see -ency.]

1. The quality or state of being divergent; the amount or degree of divergence.

1709 Berkeley *Th. Vision* §6 The apparent distance still increasing, as the divergency of the rays decreases. *c* **1790** Imison *Sch. Art* I. 86, I.. present it to the balls in their diverging state.. if it increase their divergency.. it shews their electricity to be.. negative. **1831** Brewster *Optics* i. §16. 7 The rays will have the same divergency after reflexion as they had before it.

b. *transf.* and *fig.*

1860 Westcott *Introd. Study Gosp.* vii. (ed. 5) 350 General agreement will be diversified by characteristic divergencies. **1879** Proctor *Pleas. Ways Sc.* xiii. 327 That divergency which.. characterizes the relationship between man and the anthropoid ape.

2. *Math.* Divergent character or quality (of a series).

1837 *Penny Cycl.* VII. 486/1 Of series of positive terms which diminish without limit, a test of convergency or divergency may frequently be given as follows. **1887** Hall & Knight *Higher Algebra* §279. 230 Rules by which we can test the convergency or divergency of a given series without effecting its summation.

3. = divergence 1.

1727–51 Chambers *Cycl.* s.v. *Virtual Focus*, Also called point of dispersion, or divergency. **1833** Chalmers *Const. Man* (1835) I. iii. 156 The point of departure or divergency.

divergent (dɪˈvɜːdʒənt, daɪ-), *a.* [ad. mod.L. *dīvergent-em*, pr. pple. of *dīvergĕre* to diverge: cf. F. *divergent* (17th c. in Hatz.-Darm.).]

1. Proceeding in different directions from each other or from a common point; departing more widely from each other; diverging.

1696 Phillips, *Divergent*, a Term in Opticks, said of the Beams, which having suffered the Refraction, separate one from the other. **1796** Morse *Amer. Geog.* I. 590 Lines.. so combined as to meet at certain given points, with the divergent avenues. **1829** Southey *Sir T. More* Ded. x, Central plains, Whence rivers flow divergent. **1869** Tyndall *Notes Lect. Light* §92 If these divergent rays be produced backwards, they will intersect behind the mirror. **1871** Darwin *Desc. Man* II. xix. 345 The Siamese have small noses, with divergent nostrils.

2. *transf.* and *fig.* **a.** Following different routes, lines of action, or of thought; deviating from each other or from a standard or normal course or type.

1801 W. Dupré *Neolog. Fr. Dict.* 93 Questions divergent (or which diverge) from themselves. **1832** Southey in *Q. Rev.* XLVIII. 240 Thence arise divergent opinions. **1875** Gladstone *Glean.* (1879) VI. iii. 144 Were the question between historical Christianity and systems opposed to or divergent from it.

b. *Psychol.* Of thinking, reasoning, etc.: of a kind that produces a wide variety of possible answers to a problem. So **di'verger**, one who thinks in this way.

1956 J. P. Guilford in *Psychol. Bull.* LIII. iv. 274 Production factors fall into two groups—convergent-thinking factors and divergent-thinking factors. Such a distinction seems not to have been emphasized in prior literature on thinking. **1966** L. Hudson *Contrary Imaginations* iii. 38 With new tests, it seems vital that we should avoid question-begging if we possibly can. For this reason, I propose to name them technically. The 'High IQ' I shall call a converger; the 'High Creative', a diverger, and the two styles of reasoning, convergent and divergent, respectively. **1970** *Nature* 25 July 420/2 If you are better at conventional IQ tests than at 'open-ended' tests.. you are a converger; if not, you are a diverger.

3. Of, pertaining to, characterized or produced by, divergence.

(*divergent squint*: strabismus in which the axes of the eyes diverge.)

1831 Brewster *Optics* iv. 34 The divergent point of diverging rays. **1870** T. Holmes *Surg.* (ed. 2) III. 248 Strabismus may be either convergent or divergent. **1879** [see diverge *v.* 2].

4. *Math.* Applied to an infinite series of terms, the sum of which becomes indefinitely greater as more and more terms are taken. (Opp. to convergent *a.* 2.)

Sometimes used to include *oscillatory* series, or such as oscillate from one value to another, as the series of 1 − 1 + 1 − 1 + 1.., the sum of which oscillates between 0 and 1.

1837 *Penny Cycl.* VII. 486/1 Series of increasing terms are certainly divergent. **1858** Todhunter *Algebra* xl. §557 An infinite series in which all the terms are of the same sign is divergent if each term is greater than some assigned finite quantity however small.

divergenti'florous, *a. Bot.* [f. L. *dīvergent-em* + *-flōrus*, f. *flōrem* flower; cf. F. *divergentiflore*.] Having diverging flowers.

1883 in *Syd. Soc. Lex.*

di'vergently, *adv.* [f. divergent + -ly².] In a divergent manner; divergingly.

1812–16 J. Smith *Panorama Sc. & Art* I. 485 Pencils of rays, which, after their crossing.. proceed divergently. **1840** *Blackw. Mag.* XLVII. 778 Variations.. [which] like those of the compass, point, not divergently, but with wavering trepidations in the same direction.

divergi-, combining form abbreviated from *divergenti-* (see above); e.g. **divergi'nervious** *a. Bot.*, having diverging nerves; **divergi'venate** *a. Bot.*, having diverging veins.

1883 in *Syd. Soc. Lex.*

di'verging, *ppl. a.* [f. diverge *v.* + -ing².]

1. Proceeding in different directions from a common point, so as to become more and more widely separate; turning off from the straight course.

1706 Phillips (ed. Kersey), *Divergent* or *Diverging* Rays .. are those Rays which.. continually depart one from another. **1796** Kirwan *Elem. Min.* (ed. 2) I. 35 These are straight or curved, parallel or diverging, or stellated. **1804** Windham *Diary* in Rye *Cromer* (1889) 75 A diverging ball struck their Capt. Tremlett.. on the foot. **1875** Jowett *Plato* (ed. 2) IV. 387 Thus, after wandering in many diverging paths, we return to common sense.

fig. **1860** Emerson *Cond. Life, Fate* Wks. (Bohn) II. 312 Uterine brothers with this diverging destination. **1862** Stanley *Jew. Ch.* (1877) I. xviii. 350 Two diverging epochs.

2. *Math.* = divergent 4.

1795 Hutton *Math. Dict.* II. 439/1 *Diverging Series*, is one whose terms continually increase, or that has the successive sums of its terms diverging, or going off always the farther, from the sum or value of the Series. **1807** —— *Course Math.* II. 300 The series produced may be a converging one, rather than diverging.

Hence **di'vergingly** *adv.*, in a diverging manner; with divergence; divergently.

1796 Kirwan *Elem. Min.* (ed. 2) I. 159 Fracture, parallel, or divergingly. **1811** Pinkerton *Petral.* I. 308 Of a divergingly striated texture. **1828** *Chem.* in *Ann. Reg.* 529/1 Rays which issue divergingly.

divers (ˈdaɪvəz), *a.* [ME. *divers*, *diverse*, a. OF. *diviers*, *divers*, fem. *-erse* (11th c. in Littré) different, odd, wicked, cruel, = It., Sp., Pg. *diverso*:—L. *divers-us* contrary, different, unlike, separate, orig. 'turned different ways', pa. pple. of *dīvertĕre* to divert. The spelling was in ME. indifferently *divers* and *diverse*. The stress was orig. as in OF. on the last syllable, but in conformity with English habits, was at a very early date shifted to the first, though, as with other words from French, both pronunciations long co-existed, esp. in verse. After *'divers* became the established prose form, esp. in sense 3, in which the word is always plural, the final *s* came, as in plural nouns, to be pronounced as *z*, and the word to be identical in pronunciation with the plural of *diver*.]

†**1.** Different or not alike in character or quality; not of the same kind. *Obs.* in this form since *c* 1700, and now expressed by diverse *a.* 1. *Obs.*

c **1250** *Kent. Serm.* in *O.E. Misc.* 35 So as we habeþ i-seid of diuers wordles.. so we mowe sigge of þo elde of eueriche men. *a* **1300** *Cursor M.* 11054 (Cott.) Bot þat mensking þam bi-tuin, Was sum-quat diuers, als i wene. *c* **1384** Chaucer *H. Fame* iii. 484 Bid him bring his clarioun That is ful dyvers of his soun. *c* **1400** *Lanfranc's Cirurg.* 32 Also þese woundis han dyuers [*MS.* B. dyverse] cause. **1513**

BRADSHAW *St. Werburge* I. 58 Dyvers men dyvers in lyvynge these be. **1568** BIBLE (Bishops') *Prov.* xx. 23 Diuers weightes are an abomination vnto the Lord. **1625** (*title*) Free Schoole of Warre, or a Treatise whether it be lawful to beare Arms for the Service of a Prince that is of divers Religion. **1691** RAY *Creation* I. (1704) 67 The divers Figures of the minute Particles.

†**b.** Const. *from*: Different (in kind, etc.) *from*.

c **1374** CHAUCER *Boeth.* III. pr. x. 71 (Camb. MS.) But that it is diuers from hym by wenynge resoun. *c* **1400** *Lanfranc's Cirurg.* 119 Brekynge of boonys in þe heed is dyuers in perels fro brekinge of oþere boonys. **1568** BIBLE (Bishops') *Esther* iii. 8 Their lawes are diuers from al people. **1611** BIBLE *Esther* i. 7 The vessels being diuers one from another. **1678** OWEN *Mind of God* viii. 247 Openly divers from that exhibited therein.

†**2.** Differing from or opposed to what is right, good, or profitable; perverse, evil, cruel; adverse, unfavourable. [Cf. OF. *divers.*] *Obs.*

1340 *Ayenb.* 68 Wyþstondynge is a zenne þet comþ of þe herte þet is rebel and hard and rebours and dyuers. *a* **1450** *Knt. de la Tour* (1868) 88 An euelle quene and diuers and to cruelle..Gesabelle. **1523** LD. BERNERS *Froiss.* I. iv. 3 Ryght wyld and diuers of condicions. **1581** *Satir. Poems Reform.* xliv. 156 Diuers in maners, vnhappy, fals, forlorne. [**1613** SHAKS. *Hen. VIII*, v. iii. 18 New opinions, Diuers, and dangerous, which are Heresies.]

3. Various, sundry, several; more than one, some number of. Referring originally and in form to the variety of objects; but, as variety implies number, becoming an indefinite numeral word expressing multiplicity, without committing the speaker to 'many' or 'few'. Now somewhat *archaic*, but well known in legal and scriptural phraseology.

a. with the notion of *variety* the more prominent: Different, various. **b.** with that of *indefinite number* more prominent: Several, sundry. (In many cases both notions are equally present, and the word might be rendered 'several different'. Cf. the sense-history of *several*, *sundry*, *various*, all of which have come to be vague numerals.)

a. 1297 [see DIVERSE *a.* 5 a]. **1340** HAMPOLE *Pr. Consc.* 3144 Alle þe fire þat es þar-in, Es bot a maner of fyre..And noght divers fires, les and mare. **1382** WYCLIF *Mark* i. 34 He helide many that weren trauelide with dyuers [ποικίλαις] soris. *c* **1440** *Ipomydon* 86 Of dukis, erlis and barons, Many there come frome dyvers townes. **1557** N. T. (Genev.) *Heb.* i. 1 At sondrie tymes and in diuers maners. **1589** COGAN *Haven Health* cxcviii. (1636) 186 Divers meates require divers sawces, and divers men have divers appetites. **1669** BUNYAN *Holy Citie* 204 The word Sun is in Scripture taken divers ways. **1772–84** COOK *Voy.* (1790) V. 1552 Fish of divers sorts. **1845–6** TRENCH *Huls. Lect.* I. vi. 98 We have the divers statements of St. Paul and St. James—divers but not diverse. **1875** JOWETT *Plato* (ed. 2) I. 408 This heavenly earth is of divers colours.

b. 1393 GOWER *Conf.* III. 232 Thus to se Divers ensamples how thy stonde. **1513** MORE in Grafton *Chron.* (1568) II. 807 The Citizens..made divers dayes playes and Pagiaunts. **1585** T. WASHINGTON tr. *Nicholay's Voy.* I. vii. 5 Too whom..came running divers other Turkes to recover him. **1614** RALEIGH *Hist. World* I. (1634) 113 If Nimrod tooke divers yeeres to find Shinaar. **1751** SMOLLETT *Per. Pic.* lxvi, The old gentleman..made divers ineffectual efforts to get up. **1818** CRUISE *Digest* (ed. 2) III. 172 The two Chief Justices, the Chief Baron, and divers other Justices there present. **1827** JARMAN *Powell's Devises* II. 195 Seised in fee of divers freehold lands. **1840** BARHAM *Ingol. Leg., Witches' Frolic* 449 Conspiring with folks to deponents unknown, With divers, that is to say, two thousand, people. **1860** MRS. CARLYLE *Lett.* III. 36 There are directions to be given to divers workmen before I start.

c. *absol.*, and with *of*: Several, many. *arch.*

c **1450** [see DIVERSE *a* 5 c]. **1526–34** TINDALE *Mark* viii. 3 Diuers of them came from farre. **1533** FRITH *Answ. More* (1829) 174 Such fantastical apparitions do appear to divers. *a* **1618** RALEIGH *Mahomet* (1637) 86 Hope of gaine provoked divers to make search for him. **1628** HOBBES *Thucyd.* I. xiii, He subdued divers of the islands. **1684** *Scanderberg Rediv.* iii. 38 The General..slew divers, and forced the rest to fly.

†**4.** as *adv.* = DIVERSELY. Cf. DIVERSE *a.* 6.

1597 DANIEL *Civ. Wars* II. lxiii, Divers-speaking zeele. **1667** MILTON *P.L.* IV. 234 The neather flood, Which..now divided..Runs divers. **1715–20** POPE *Iliad* XVI. 347 His troops..Fly divers.

diverse (dɪ-, daɪ'vɜːs, 'daɪvəs), *a.* [In origin identical with DIVERS; but in later use prob. more immediately associated with L. *dīversus* (cf. *adverse*, *inverse*, *obverse*, *perverse*, *reverse*). Hence, no longer (since *c* 1700) used in the merely vague numerical sense of *divers*, but always distinctly associated with *diversity*.]

1. Different in character or quality; not of the same kind; not alike in nature or qualities. (Formerly also written *divers*: see DIVERS 1.)

1297 R. GLOUC. (Rolls) 657 Suþþe þoru diuerse tonge me clupeþ it seuerne. **1387** TREVISA *Higden* (Rolls) I. 25 Take hede of eyȝte dyuerse manere of accountynge of ȝeres. *c* **1430** LYDG. *Hors, Shepe & G.* (Roxb.) 4 The thirde was white..The fourth diuerce of colours. **1592** WEST *1st Pt. Symbol.* §50 H, Wordes of diuerse or doubtfull significations. **1647–8** COTTERELL *Davila's Hist. Fr.* (1678) 30 From the diverse sense, that men had of this proceeding. **1822** COLERIDGE *Lett. Convers., etc.* II. 83 The subjects of the Lectures are indeed very different, but not, in the strict sense of the term diverse: they are various rather than miscellaneous. **1841–71** T. R. JONES *Anim. Kingd.* (ed. 4) 798 With habits so diverse, we may well expect corresponding diversity in their forms. **1865** R. W. DALE *Jew. Temp.* ix. (1877) 95 These diverse but not antagonistic spiritual forces.

b. Const. *from* (†*to*).

c **1400** MAUNDEV. (Roxb.) xii. 54 Þaire clething also es diuerse fra oþer men. *a* **1568** ASCHAM *Scholem.* (Arb.) 157 A certaine outlandish kinde of talke, strange to them of Athens, and diuerse from their writing. **1570** *Act 13 Eliz.* c. 29 Any Name contrary or dyverse to the name of the now Chauncellor. **1611** BIBLE *Esther* iii. 8 Their lawes are diuerse from all people. **1754** EDWARDS *Freed. Will* I. iv. 25 Against, or diverse from present Acts of the Will. **1836** J. GILBERT *Chr. Atonem.* i. (1852) 11 A procedure..very diverse from that which he has universally prescribed.

2. Differing from itself under different circumstances at different times, or in different parts; multiform, varied, diversified.

a **1541** WYATT *Poet. Wks.* (1861) 153 And beareth with his sway the diverse Moon about. **1656** RIDGLEY *Pract. Physick* 11 An eschar..of a diverse colour like a rainbow. **1875** JOWETT *Plato* (ed. 2) IV. 19 Enlarging on the diverse and multiform nature of pleasure.

†**3.** Different from, or opposed to what is right, good, or profitable: perverse, adverse. *Obs.*

1393 GOWER *Conf.* III. 49 He found the see diverse With many a windy storm reverse. *Ibid.* III. 295 Fortune..as I shall reherce..was to this lord diverse. *a* **1450** *Knt. de la Tour* (1868) 104 But kinge herode was diuerse, couettous, and right malicious. **1483** CAXTON *G. de la Tour* F vj b, An euylle cruell and dyuerse quene.

†**4.** Turning or impelling in different directions; diverting, distracting. (In Spenser.) *Obs. rare.*

1590 SPENSER *F.Q.* I. i. 10 In diverse doubt they been. *Ibid.* II. ii. 3 And into diverse doubt his wavering wonder clove.

†**5.** = DIVERS 3, with its varieties **a.** and **b.** *Obs.* (rare in this spelling after 1700).

a. 1297 R. GLOUC. (1724) 378 Þe kyng hem sende her & þer..To dyuerse men, to vynde hem mete. *c* **1340** *Cursor M.* 1034 (Trin.) Foure stremes passynge into dyuerse remes. **1450–1530** *Myrr. our Ladye* 209 How aungels and men desyred her byrthe for diuerse causes. *a* **1592** H. SMITH *Serm.* (1637) 777 They thought that there were diverse Gods, as there were diverse Nations, diverse trades, diverse languages, diverse and sundry kinds of all things. **1688** R. HOLME *Armoury* II. 68/1 The double Daisies are of diverse Sorts.

b. 1386 *Rolls of Parlt.* III. 225/1 The forsaid Nichol.. ayein the pees, made dyverse enarmynges bi day and eke bi nyght. **1428** *Surtees Misc.* (1890) 10 Wele knawen to diverses gude men of yis cite. **1548** HALL *Chron., Hen. VI* (an. 29) 162 The toune of Acques, in the whiche be diverse hote bathes. *a* **1568** ASCHAM *Scholem.* Pref. (Arb.) 18 Diuerse Scholers of Eaton be runne awaie from the Schole. **1601** CHESTER *Loves Martyr* title-p., Collected out of diuerse Authenticall Records. **1728** MORGAN *Algiers* I. Pref. 6 Towards the close of this History and in diverse other parts of it.

†**c.** *absol.* = DIVERS 3 c. *Obs.*

c **1450** *St. Cuthbert* (Surtees) 3638 He..had made diuerse hale and fere. **1559** W. CUNNINGHAM *Cosmogr. Glasse* 172 Many perticuler Regions as Englande..Denmarke, Greece, and diverse, unto the number..of 34. **1568** GRAFTON *Chron.* II. 1309 With the losse of diverse of his company. **1605** BACON *Adv. Learn.* II. vi. §1. 22 [It] hath been excellently handled by diverse. **1706** H. MAULE *Hist. Picts* in *Misc. Scot.* I. 37 Diverse of our historians attribute this victory to the valour of the King.

†**6.** as *adv.* = DIVERSELY. *Obs.*

1708 J. PHILIPS *Cyder* I, The gourd And thirsty cucumber ..with tendrils creep Diverse. **1729** POPE *Dunc.* (ed. 2) II. 114 His papers light, fly diverse, tost in air.

7. *Comb.* adverbial or parasynthetic, as *diverse-coloured*, *-natured*, *-shaped*, etc.

1551 BIBLE *Judg.* v. 30 (R.) Dyuerse coloured browdered work. **1606** SHAKS. *Ant. & Cl.* II. ii. 208 Smiling Cupids, With diuers coulour'd Fannes. **1697** J. SERGEANT *Solid Philos.* 11 Diverse-natured parts. **1875** W. MCILWRAITH *Guide Wigtownshire* 100 Diverse-shaped parterres.

†**di'verse**, *v. Obs.* Also 4–6 dyverse (6 *pa. t.* diverst). [a. OF. *diverse-r* to change, vary, diversify: -med.L. *dīversā-re* to turn, drive about, freq. of *dīvertĕre* to DIVERT, or f. *dī-*, DIS- 1 + *versāre* to turn about.]

1. *trans.* To render diverse or different; to vary, change, diversify. (Also *refl.* = *intr.*)

1340 *Ayenb.* 124 Þise uour uirtues..mochel ham diuerseþ ine hire workes. *c* **1374** CHAUCER *Troylus* III. 1703 (1752) Þe world with feyth which þat is stable Dyverseth so his stoundes concordynge. **1382** WYCLIF *Acts* xv. 9. *c* **1400** *Lanfranc's Cirurg.* 331 For þis cause þou muste diuerse þi medicyns. **1530** PALSGR. 523/1, I dyverse, I make difference, *je diversifie.* *a* **1634** RANDOLPH *Amyntas* IV. 9 The sentence now is past..It cannot be divers'd.

2. *intr.* To be or grow diverse, different, or varied; to vary, change, become diversified; to differ (*from*).

c **1340** *Cursor M.* 2262 (Trin.) Her tonges dyuersed fro þat day. **1382** WYCLIF *1 Cor.* xv. 41 A sterre diuersith from a sterre in clerenesse. *c* **1400** *Lanfranc's Cirurg.* 233. *c* **1460** FORTESCUE *Abs. & Lim. Mon.* i. (1885) 109 Ther bith ij kyndes off kyngdomes..thai diuersen in that the first kynge mey [etc.]..The secounde kynge may not rule his peple by other lawes than such as thai assenten unto.

3. *intr.* To turn aside, diverge, be diverted. *rare.*

1590 SPENSER *F.Q.* III. iii. 62 The Redcrosse Knight diverst: but forth rode Britomart.

Hence **di'versed** *ppl. a.*, diversified, different.

1393 GOWER *Conf.* Prol. I. 3 Men se the world..In sondry wyse so diversed. *c* **1420** *Pallad. on Husb.* I. 784 Dyversed wittes dyversely devyse.

diversely (dɪ-, daɪ'vɜːslɪ, 'daɪvəslɪ), *adv.* [f. DIVERSE *a.* + -LY[2].] In a diverse manner, in a different way; differently, otherwise; in diverse ways or directions, variously; with diversity. See also DIVERSLY.

a **1300** [see DIVERSLY 1]. *c* **1325** *Poem Times Edw. II*, 255 in *Pol. Songs* (Camden) 335 Nu ben theih so degysed and so diverseliche i-diȝt. *c* **1380** WYCLIF *Sel. Wks.* III. 432 Þei lyveden diverseliche fro þise newe sects. *c* **1386** CHAUCER *Sqr.'s T.* 194 Diuerse folk diuersely [*v.r.* dyuersly] they demed. **1485** CAXTON *Chas. Gt.* 1 The helthe of euery person proceedeth dyuercely. **1526** FRITH *Disput. Purgatory* 167 Infernus, which is diversely taken in Scripture both for death, for a grave, and for hell. **1690** LOCKE *Hum. Und.* II. i. (1695) 42 Being surrounded with Bodies, that perpetually and diversely affect us. **1732** POPE *Ess. Man* II. 97 On Life's vast ocean diversely we sail. **1862** MERIVALE *Rom. Emp.* (1871) V. xl. 23 The seven hills of Rome have been diversely enumerated.

di'verseness. Now *rare*. Also **diversness.** [f. as prec. + -NESS.]

1. The quality or state of being diverse; difference, diversity, variety.

c **1340** *Cursor M.* 25160 (Fairf.) Wiþ þis worde ours we vnderstande al diuersenes of our erande. *a* **1541** WYATT *Change in minde* in *Tottell's Misc.* (Arb.) 37 You, this diuersnesse that blamen most, Change you no more. **1862** F. HALL *Hindu Philos. Syst.* 114 The diverseness of the condition of souls is owing to the diverseness of their works.

†**2.** Adverseness, frowardness. *Obs. rare.*

1580 BARET *Alv.* F 1154 Waiwardnesse, frowardnesse, diuersnesse to please, *morositas.*

diversi-, combining element, f. L. *dīvers-us* DIVERSE, as in *dīversicolor*, *dīversicolōrus*: used in some English words, chiefly technical, as **diver'sicolor, di'versicoloured** *adjs.*, of varied colours. **diversi'florate, diversi'florous** *adjs.*, bearing flowers of different kinds. **diversi'foliate, diversi'folious** *adjs.*, having leaves of different kinds. **diversi'pedate** *a.*, having varied feet. **diversi'sporous** *a.*, having spores of different kinds.

1756 C. LUCAS *Ess. Waters* I. 137 It throws up a diversicolored pellicle, in which orange appeared to predominate. **1866** *Treas. Bot.*, *Diversiflorous.* **1883** *Syd. Soc. Lex.*, *Diversicolor..Diversiflorate..Diversifoliate ..Diversipedate..Diversisporous.*

di'versifiable, *a. rare.* [f. DIVERSIFY + -ABLE: so in F.] Capable of being diversified.

1674 BOYLE *Grounds Corpusc. Philos.* 11 Since a single particle of matter..be diversifiable so many ways. *a* **1691** —— *Wks.* IV. 281 (R.) The almost infinitely diversifiable contextures of all the small parts.

Hence **diversifia'bility.**

1871 EARLE *Philol. Eng. Tongue* §250 They have a relative diversifiability of states and powers and functions.

†**di'versificate,** *v. Obs. rare.* [f. ppl. stem of med.L. *dīversificāre* (Du Cange) to render unlike, to DIVERSIFY.] = DIVERSIFY.

1604 T. WRIGHT *Passions* v. ii. 171. **1622** H. SYDENHAM *Serm. Sol. Occ.* (1637) 22 Variety of sounds diversificate passions, stirring up in the heart many sorts of joy or sadnesse according to the nature of tunes.

diversification (dɪˌvɜːsɪfɪ'keɪʃən, daɪ-). [n. of action f. med.L. *dīversificāre* to DIVERSIFY: cf. F. *diversification* (14th c. in Littré).] **a.** The action of diversifying; the process of becoming diversified; the fact of being diversified; the production of diversity or variety of form or qualities.

1603 HOLLAND *Plutarch's Mor.* 1027 They be passions, accidents, and diversifications of elements. **1681** H. MORE *Exp. Dan* i. 14 Which diversification..need not be expressed. **1776** JOHNSON *Let. to Boswell* 16 Nov. in Boswell *Life*, Such an effort annually would give the world a little diversification. **1831** BREWSTER *Nat. Magic* xi. (1833) 288 He at first was perplexed about the diversification of the pattern. **1859** DARWIN *Orig. Spec.* iv. (1872) 90 In the Australian mammals, we see the process of diversification in an early and incomplete stage of development.

b. A diversified condition, form, or structure.

1677 HALE *Prim. Orig. Man.* IV. ii. 305 Animals..that yet possibly are not of the same Species, but have accidental diversifications. **1796** KIRWAN *Elem. Min.* (ed. 2) I. 48 The minuter diversifications are called varieties.

c. *Econ.* The spread of investment over a variety of enterprises, or the production of a variety of different articles, services, etc., often as a safeguard against the effects of fall in demand for a particular product.

1939 S. R. DENNISON *Location of Industry* I. ii. 38 Industrial diversification will result in the development of subsidiary and complementary industries, and also of entirely new lines of manufacture. **1944** A. CAIRNCROSS *Introd. Econ.* II. vi. 76 Such diversification makes the firm less vulnerable to sudden changes and allows it to remain a going concern where smaller, less diversified concerns would be forced to give up business. **1971** *Brit. Printer* Jan. 104/1 A stone-layer, named Hans Rüegger, venturing into an early example of diversification, added a printing shop to his business.

di'versified, *ppl. a.* [f. DIVERSIFY + -ED[1].] Rendered diverse; varied in form, features, or character; variegated.

1611 COTGR., *Bigarré*, diuersified, varied, mingled, of many colours. **1669** WOODHEAD *St. Teresa* II. vii. 59 Let the singing be not in diversifyed notes, but in one and the same tone. **1799** J. ROBERTSON *Agric. Perth* 360 Views of that charming lake and of the diversified scenery around its wooded banks. **1878** HUXLEY *Physiogr.* 219 Deep-seated points of agreement among the diversified forms of life.

di'versifier. *rare.* [f. DIVERSIFY + -ER[1].] One who or that which diversifies.

1894 H. DRUMMOND *Ascent of Man* 253 The first moral and intellectual diversifiers of men are to be sought for in geography and geology.

diversiflorous, -folious: see DIVERSI-.

diversiform (dɪ-, daɪ'vɜːsɪfɔːm), *a.* [f. DIVERSI- + -FORM. So mod.F. *diversiforme.*] Of diverse or various forms; differing in form.

1660 STANLEY *Hist. Philos.* IX. (1701) 379/2 It is all one.. if it be called biform or æqualiform or diversiform. **1844** J. G. WILKINSON tr. *Swedenborg's Anim. Kingd.* II. ii. 51 To diminish and enlarge these diversiform apertures of the glottis. **1882** *Fraser's Mag.* XXV. 769 The diversiform aspects of strange superstitions.

diversify (dɪ'vɜːsɪfaɪ, daɪ-), *v.* [a. OF. *diversifie-r* (13th c. in Hatz.-Darm.), ad. med.L. *dīversificāre* to render unlike (Du Cange), f. *dīversus* DIVERSE + *-ficāre* vbl. formative, see -FY.]

1. a. *trans.* To render diverse, different, or varied, in form, features, or qualities; to give variety or diversity to; to variegate, vary, modify.

1490 CAXTON *Eneydos* vi. 24 Bochace.. hath transposed or atte leste dyuersifyed the falle and caas of dydo otherwyse than vyrgyle. **1541** R. COPLAND *Guydon's Quest. Chirurg.*, The bones of the body.. be deuersyfyed in dyuers maners. **1665** HOOKE *Microgr.* 17 This adventitious or accidental pressure.. must diversify the Figure of the included heterogeneous fluid. **1704** POPE *Windsor For.* 145 Swift trouts, diversify'd with crimson stains. **1855** MACAULAY *Hist. Eng.* III. 505 The course of parliamentary business was diversified by another curious and interesting episode.

†**b.** To make different, to differentiate *from.*

1594 CAREW *Huarte's Exam. Wits* (1616) 98 Whether it could haue.. beene able to diuersifie them from those who came with them. **1661** FELTHAM *Resolves* (ed. 8) II. lxxxi, We diversifie our selves from him [God], we fight against his love. **1712** ADDISON *Spect.* No. 409 ¶3 Ways of expressing himself which diversify him from all other Authors.

c. *Econ.* To introduce or use diversification in (see DIVERSIFICATION). Also *intr.*, to engage in diversification.

1939 S. R. DENNISON *Location of Industry* I. iii. 72 As industry becomes diversified, as the needs of consumers grow.., then the market exerts a stronger attraction. **1944** A. CAIRNCROSS *Introd. Econ.* II. vi. 76 Firms may seek to spread their risks by diversifying their output, or markets, or sources of supply, or processes of manufacture. **1967** *Times Rev. Industry* Apr. 39/1 Westland Engineers itself diversified when it bought up Unique Balance Company, making sash balances for windows. **1971** *Guardian* 6 Mar. 1/1 An explosives firm at Great Oakley, near Harwich, has decided to 'diversify' into potato chips. Its factory was threatened with closure unless a new product was introduced.

†**2. a.** *intr.* or *absol.* To produce diversity or variety. **b.** *intr.* (for *refl.*) *Obs.*

1481 CAXTON *Myrr.* III. xxiv. 189 How nature werketh, and.. how she dyuersefyeth in euerych of her werkes. *a* **1680** GLANVILL tr. *Fontenelle's Plurality Worlds* (1695) 89 How Nature diversifies in these several Worlds. **1815** MAD. D'ARBLAY *Diary* (1846) VII. 222 Prospects eternally diversifying varied our delighted attention.

Hence **di'versifying** *vbl. sb.* and *ppl. a.*

1611 COTGR., *Bigarrément*, a variation, or diuersifying, as in colours. **1753** CHAMBERS *Cycl. Supp.*, *Diversifying*, in rhetoric, is of infinite service to the orator; it.. may fitly be called the subject of all his tropes and figures. **1837** PRICHARD *Phys. Hist. Man.* (ed. 3) II. 226 The diversifying process.. may have given rise to differences.

diver'siloquent, *a.* *rare*[—0]. [f. DIVERSI- + L. *loquent-em* speaking.] (See quots.)

1656 BLOUNT *Glossogr.*, *Diversiloquent*, that varieth or speaks diversly. **1848** CRAIG, *Diversiloquent*, speaking in different ways. Hence in mod. Dicts.

diversion (dɪ'vɜːʃən, daɪ-). [ad. med.L. *dīversiō* (vox Medicorum: Du Cange), n. of action f. L. *dīvertĕre* to DIVERT. Cf. F. *diversion*, in medical use in 13-14th c. (Littré), in military and other uses in 16th c., perh. the immediate source of the English, but not in Cotgr. 1611.]

1. a. *lit.* The turning aside (*of* anything) from its due or ordinary course or direction; a turning aside of one's course; deviation, deflection.

1626 BACON *Sylva* §414 In Retention of the Sap for a time, and Diversion of it to the Sprouts. **1660** HICKERINGILL *Jamaica* (1661) 65 This Diversion is somewhat out of our way to Jamaica. **1871** TYNDALL *Fragm. Sc.* (1879) II. i. 2 A diversion of the Rhone.. would.. have been of incalculable benefit. **1871** L. STEPHEN *Playgr. Eur.* x. (1894) 245, I made a diversion towards the valley. **1872** YEATS *Growth Comm.* 180 Fearing the diversion of trade. **1883** *Nature* 8 Mar. 437 Due to its diversion into some other than the usual channel.

†**b.** *Med.* A turning away of the course of the humours by means of medicinal applications. *Obs.*

1656 RIDGLEY *Pract. Physick* 17 To use diversion, evacuation, and strengthening. **1727-51** CHAMBERS *Cycl.*, *Diversion* in Medicine, the turning of the course or flux of humours from one part to another, by proper applications.

c. An alternative route by-passing a road that is temporarily closed.

1955 *Times* 29 Aug. 5/1 One of the hazards for the motorist is finding a way round the many places where the road is up with the aid of, sometimes in spite of, what has become almost a Viennese institution—the Umleitung or diversion. **1958** 'A. GILBERT' *Death against Clock* xii. 167 When you put up your road blocks, then I have to take the diversion.

2. *transf.* and *fig.* **a.** The turning aside (of any person or thing) from a settled or particular course of action, an object, or the like.

1600 E. BLOUNT tr. *Conestaggio* 10 Turning all his resolutions upon Affrick.. But this diversion whereunto they perswaded the King, was cause of great ruines. **1626** DONNE *Serm. Ps.* lxiv. 10 A diversion, a deviation, a deflection.. from this rectitude, this uprightness. **1797** BURKE *Regic. Peace* III. Wks. VIII. 343 If the war has been diverted from the great object.. this diversion was made to encrease the naval resources and power of Great Britain.

†**b.** A turning aside from the business in hand, or from one's regular occupation; avocation. *Obs.*

1637 LAUD *Wks.* (1857) VI. 37 Considering my many diversions and the little time I could snatch from other employment. **1662** LIGHTFOOT *Broughton's Wks.* Pref. 2. **1675** MARVELL *Corr.* Wks. II. 456 The Lords have agreed for.. another conference.. these and other diversions withhold them from proceeding in their Committee of their Test.

c. A turning aside or diverting of the attention.

1667 *Decay Chr. Piety* ii. ¶7 An artifice of diversion, a sprout of that first fig-tree which was to hide the nakedness of lapsed Adam. **1796** BURKE *Regic. Peace* I. Wks. VIII. 155 The.. diversion.. was the suggestion of a treaty proposed by the enemy. **1814** SCOTT *Wav.* iv, Charging them to make good with their lives an hour's diversion, that the king might have that space for escape.

3. *Mil.* A manœuvre to draw off the enemy's attention from the operation on which they are engaged, by a movement or attack in an unexpected quarter.

1647 CLARENDON *Hist. Reb.* II. §88 The forces.. which were raised to make a diversion in Scotland. **1659** B. HARRIS *Parival's Iron Age* 45 The Prince.. bethought himself.. of sending his brother to Venlo, so to make a powerfull diversion. **1801** WELLINGTON in Gurw. *Desp.* I. 299 My determination is to make the most powerful diversion which may be practicable on the coasts of the Red Sea.

4. a. *spec.* The turning away of the thoughts, attention, etc., from fatiguing or sad occupations, with implication of pleasurable excitement; distraction, recreation, amusement, entertainment.

1653 H. COGAN tr. *Pinto's Trav.* xliv. 174 My long indisposition.. hath great need of some diversion. **1671** LADY MARY BERTIE in *12th Rep. Hist. MSS. Comm.* App. v. 22, I.. am glad you had so good diversion in drawing valentine. **1706** ESTCOURT *Fair Examp.* II. ii, Will you allow her no Diversion? **1710** STEELE *Tatler* No. 89 ¶4 Diversion, which is a kind of forgetting our selves, is but a mean Way of Entertainment. **1814** JANE AUSTEN *Mansf. Park* xvii, All were finding employment in consultations.. or diversion in the playful conceits they suggested.

b. with *a* and *pl.* An amusement, entertainment, sport, pastime.

1648 EVELYN *Diary* 5 Feb., Saw a Tragie-comedy acted in the Cockpit, after there had been none of these diversions for many years during the warr. **1725** DE FOE *Voy. round World* (1840) 254 If wild and uncouth places be a diversion to you, I promise your curiosity shall be fully gratified. **1843** LYTTON *Last Bar.* I. i, Open spaces for the popular games and diversions. **1875** J. CURTIS *Hist. Eng.* 154 Among the in-door diversions were draughts, chess, etc.

c. *Comb.* as ***diversion-monger.***

1744 ELIZA HEYWOOD *Female Spect.* (1748) I. 212 Our diversion-mongers.. every day contriving new entertainments.

†**5.** Diverse condition, diverseness. *Obs. rare.*

14.. WYNTOUN *Chron.* (ed. Laing) III. 166 (Wemyss MS.) For diversion [*v.r.* syndrynes] of thar changeing.

6. *attrib.* and *Comb.*: **diversion-cut**, a channel made to divert impure water past a reservoir; **diversion weir**, a weir erected to divert water from a river to the head of an irrigating canal.

a **1877** KNIGHT *Dict. Mech.*, *Diversion-cut*, a channel to divert past a reservoir a stream of impure or turbid water which would otherwise flow into the reservoir. A by-wash. **1893** *Ann. Rep. U.S. Geol. Surv. 1892-3* III. 231 One of the latest.. diversion weirs constructed in this country is that built at the head of the Turlock and Modesto canals.

di'versionary, *a.* [f. prec. + -ARY[1].] Pertaining or tending to a diversion; divertive.

1846 LANDOR *Wks.* II. 179 What a farce in the meanwhile is the diversionary talk about the abolition of the slave-trade! **1957** P. WORSLEY *Trumpet shall Sound* vii. 142 Diversionary action was sometimes taken. **1958** *Times Lit. Suppl.* 21 Nov. 677/2 The book tells the story in great detail.. explaining.. why the diversionary bombing failed. **1960** *Times* 12 Aug. 6/3 Waddington is not only a V-bomber base but a diversionary airfield for civil aircraft.

diversionist (dɪ'vɜːʃənɪst, daɪ-). [f. DIVERSION + -IST; cf. Russ. *diversánt.*] In Communist usage: a saboteur; also, one who conspires against the government. Also *attrib.* or as *adj.* Hence **di'versionism**, the activity of a diversionist.

1937 *Daily Tel.* 28 Aug. 12/3 A woman railway worker.. has been sentenced to be shot.. for 'putting sulphuric acid in the water bottles' of three trains bound for Moscow... Her sub-bottle-washer and fellow 'diversionist'.. was sentenced to 10 years' imprisonment. **1949** F. MACLEAN *Eastern Approaches* I. ii. 24 For some years past numerous politicians and others had met with this fate, variously branded as 'Trotskists', 'wreckers', 'Fascist spies', 'diversionists' and so on. **1951** KOESTLER *Age of Longing* I. vi. 110 We have proofs that Nadesha Filipovna was one of the leaders of this diversionist conspiracy. **1955** *Reporter* 16 June 3/1 Will *Pravda's* rash critic now be found to have indulged in right-wing diversionism and petty-bourgeois wrecking? **1955** *Times* 1 July 10/6 He pleaded Guilty to political crimes and diversionist activity, but denied collaborating with the Gestapo during the war.

di'versitude. *rare.* [f. DIVERSE *a.*] = next.

1870 E. MULFORD *Nation* xviii. 344 No diversitude in thought and action.

diversity (dɪ'vɜːsɪtɪ, daɪ-). Also 4-6 -te(e, 4-5 dyverste. [a. OF. *diverseté*, *diversité* (12th c. in Hatz.-Darm.) difference, oddness, wickedness, perversity:—L. *dīversitāt-em* contrariety, disagreement, difference, f. *dīversus* DIVERSE.]

1. a. The condition or quality of being diverse, different, or varied; difference, unlikeness.

a **1340** HAMPOLE *Psalter* cl. 4 þai sown all samyn in acordandist dyuersite. *c* **1386** CHAUCER *Man of Law's T.* 122 Ther was swich diuersitie Bitwene hir bothe lawes. *c* **1400** *Lanfranc's Cirurg.* 32 Alle þese ben dyverse, after þe dyverste of here cause. **1494** FABYAN *Chron.* II. xlv. 29 The dyuersytie of that one from yᵉ other. **1530** PALSGR. 76 Dyversite of gendre is expressed onely in pronownes of the thirde persone. **1614** RALEIGH *Hist. World* II. xxii. §9 Diversitie of circumstance may alter the case. **1628** T. SPENCER *Logick* 240 A discrete Axiome is then framed according to Art, when the partes of it doe dissent by diversitie, not as opposites. **1697** tr. *Burgersdicius his Logic* I. xxi. 81 Diversity is that affection by which things are distinguished one from the other. And is either real, rational, or modal. **1790** BURKE *Fr. Rev.* 51 Through that diversity of members and interests, general liberty had as many securities as there were separate views in the several orders. **1882** FARRAR *Early Chr.* I. 247 Unity does not exclude diversity—nay more, without diversity there can be no true and perfect unity.

b. with *a* and *pl.* An instance of this condition or quality; a point of unlikeness; a difference, distinction; a different kind, a variety.

c **1340** HAMPOLE *Prose Tr.* (1866) 35 ȝit es þer a dyuersite by-twyx gastely and bodily dedis. **1481** CAXTON *Myrr.* I. xiv. 45 In the persones ben so many dyuersetees, & facions not lyke. **1665** RAY *Flora* I. vii. 42 The White lily affordeth three diversities, two besides the common kind. **1731** POPE *Ep. Burlington* 84 A waving Glow the bloomy beds display, Blushing in bright diversities of day. **1811** PINKERTON *Petral.* I. 386 The colours being merely regarded as varieties: though some, from their rarity and singularity.. ought rather to form diversities. **1859** MILL *Liberty* iii. (1865) 39/2 People have diversities of taste.

†**c.** Divers manners or sorts: a variety. *Obs.*

1382 WYCLIF *Exod.* xxxi. 5 Forgid of gold, and of siluer.. and dyuerste [1388 dyuersite] of trees. —— *Ps.* xliv. 15 The doȝter of the King.. in goldene hemmes, aboute wrappid with diuersitees [*circumamicta varietatibus*]. **1610** SHAKS. *Temp.* v. i. 234 Roring, shreeking.. And mo diuersitie of sounds, all horrible.

2. *Law.* (See quot.)

1848 WHARTON *Law Lex.*, *Diversity*, a plea by a prisoner in bar of execution, alleging that he is not the same who was attainted; upon which a jury is.. impanelled to try the collateral issue thus raised, viz., the identity of the person.

†**3.** Contrariety to what is agreeable, good, or right; perversity, evil, mischief. *Obs.*

1483 CAXTON *G. de la Tour* F vij, This quene.. made unto the peple grete dyuersytees [*moult de diversitez*]. *c* **1485** *Digby Myst.* (1882) III. 1308 Wethyr it be good ar ony deversyte. **1513** BRADSHAW *St. Werburge* I. 2395 In all his realme was no dyuersyte, Malyce was subdued. **1523** LD. BERNERS *Froiss.* I. xvii. 18 They carey with them no cartis.. for yᵉ diversities [Fr. *diversités*] of yᵉ mountaignes.

4. diversity factor *Electr.* (see quot. 1943).

1905 *Fabian Tract* CXIX. 6 When we speak of a good diversity factor we mean that the generating station is so happily situated that it meets a regular and constant maximum demand for diverse purposes... A continuous 'diversity factor' makes a good 'load factor'. **1916** *Standardization Rules Amer. Inst. Electr. Engin.* 17 *Diversity Factor*, the ratio of the sum of the maximum power demands of the subdivisions of any system or parts of a system to the maximum demand of the whole system or of the part of the system under consideration, measured at the point of supply. **1930** *Sci. Abstr.* B. XXXIII. 388 Nomograms for determining the diversity factor of a network having a number of loads of different magnitudes and durations. **1943** *Gloss. Terms Electr. Engin.* (*B.S.I.*) 90 *Diversity factor*, .. the ratio of the sum of the maximum demands of the several consumers or loads to their maximum simultaneous demand.

5. *Radio.* Applied *attrib.* to a system of reception in which, in order to reduce the effects of fading, a signal is received simultaneously by several channels, the signal or combination of signals of best quality being automatically selected.

1930 *Proc. Inst. Radio Engin.* XVIII. 1738 The R.C.A. receiving stations now employ the diversity system, usually with three antenna groups for a single unit. **1938** *Admiralty Handbk. Wireless Telegr.* II. R. §54 *Diversity reception.* This is the name given to various schemes that may be utilised at a receiving station... If a signal fades at one place, it may be quite strong at another a few hundred feet away. **1960** *Electr. Comm.* XXXVI. 123/1 Techniques of diversity reception have advanced rapidly... Two or more [radio] signals are separately received at different frequencies or over different paths.

† **di'versive**, *a. Obs.* [f. L. *dīvers-*, ppl. stem of *dīvertĕre* to DIVERT: see -IVE.] Tending to divert or cause diversion; divertive.

1693 *Mem. Cut. Teckely* II. 103 Contenting themselves with only pillaging, did nothing diversive. **1704** tr. *Boccalini's Adv. fr. Parnass.* III. 274 That Cankar, which her Enemies term'd a Diversive Issue.

† **diver'sivolent**, *a. Obs. rare.* [f. DIVERSI- + L. *volent-em* wishing.] Desiring strife or differences.

1612 WEBSTER *White Devil* III. i. Plays (1888) 44 This debauched and diversivolent woman. *Ibid.* 57 Your diversivolent lawyer, mark him.

diversly ('daɪvəzlɪ), *adv.* [f. DIVERS *a.* + -LY[2]. Formerly not distinguishable from *diversely*.]

1. In divers ways, variously; formerly, Differently, DIVERSELY (of which this was a common spelling before 1700); in some recent writers = In several or sundry ways.

a **1300** *Cursor M.* 21807 (Cott.) Þis tale.. Mani telles diuersli [*Fairf.* diuerseli] For þai find diuers stori. *c* **1384** CHAUCER *H. Fame* III. 810 Somme folke have desired fame Diversly. **1393** LANGL. *P. Pl.* C. xvi. 79 Alle we ben brethren þauh we be diuersliche cloþede. **1526** TINDALE *Heb.* i. 1 God in tyme past diversly and many wayes [etc.]. **1594** SPENSER *Amoretti* liv, Disguysing diuersly my troubled wits. **1614** RALEIGH *Hist. World* II. iii. §6 Divers have diversly set downe the forme of the Hebrew yeare. **1639** HORN & ROB. *Gate Lang. Unl.* lxiv. §669 Stubborn enemies ..are torn in peeces of horses, diversly driven. **1791–1823** D'ISRAELI *Cur. Lit., Jews of York*, They flew diversly in great consternation. *a* **1834** COLERIDGE *Confess. Enquir. Spirit* iii. (1853) 64 One spirit, working diversly, now awakening strength, and now glorifying itself in weakness. [See Author's *Note.*] **1881** SWINBURNE *Mary Stuart* III. i. 112 Men's minds Are with affections diversly distraught.

†**2.** [= OF. *diversement*.] Wickedly, evilly, perversely. *Obs. rare.*

1523 LD. BERNERS *Froiss.* I. vi. 4 This sayd kyng gouerned right diuersly his realme by y^e^ exortacion of Sir Hewe Spencer.

diversness, obs. var. of DIVERSENESS.

† **di'versory**, *sb. Obs.* [ad. L. *dī-*, properly *dēversōri-um*, lodging-place, inn, f. *dēvertĕre* to turn aside, turn in, resort, lodge: cf. OF. *diversoire* (12th c.), It *diversorio* 'an Inne, an hostery.' See DEVERSARY.] A place to which one turns in by the way; a temporary lodging-place or shelter.

c **1410** LOVE *Bonavent. Mirr.* vi. (Gibbs MS.), A comun place..þat was heled aboune men for to stonde þere for þe reyne & was icleped a dyuersorie. **1615** CHAPMAN *Odyss.* XIV. 536 Since the man.. In my stall, as his diversory, stay'd. **1681** tr. *Willis' Rem. Med. Wks.* Vocab., *Diversory*, a diverting place, or a place to turn of one side out of the way.

di'versory, *a. rare*[−0]. [f. L. *dīvers-* ppl. stem of *dīvertĕre* to DIVERT + -ORY.] Serving to divert, divertive.

1864 in WEBSTER. NORTH in *Cent. Dict.*

divert (dɪ'vɜːt, daɪ-), *v.* Also 6 dyvert(e. [a. OF. *divertir* (14–15th c. in Hatz.-Darm.) = It. *divertire*, Sp. *divertir*, ad. L. *dīvertĕre* to turn in different directions, turn out of the way, with which is also blended L. *dēvertĕre* to turn away or aside.]

1. *trans.* To turn aside (a thing, as a stream, etc.) from its (proper) direction or course; to deflect (the course of something); to turn *from* one destination or object *to* another.

1548 HALL *Chron., Hen. IV* (an. 9) 28 b, They heryng of his armie, were diuerted to the partes of Britayn. **1649** MILTON *Eikon.* xxii, [Since] it was proclaim'd that no man should conceal him, he diverted his course. **1699** WALLIS in *Pepys' Diary* VI. 209 The old Channel..for diverting the Thames whilst London Bridge was building. **1709** ADDISON *Tatler* No. 161 ¶8 My Eyes were soon diverted from this Prospect. **1794** SULLIVAN *View Nat.* II. 28 We read of irons, which being fixed in earth, diverted the stream of lightning. **1843** ARNOLD *Hist. Rome* III. 170 Some of the reinforcements..were afterwards diverted to other services. **1873** *Act 36–7 Vict.* c. 83 Preamb., To make good to the said Fund the sum so improperly diverted from it.

†**b.** In medical use: cf. DIVERSION 1 b. *Obs.*

1541 R. COPLAND *Galyen's Terap.* 2 Bj, Whan the humours that gathereth in the vlcerate partyes is nat very fer of..it behoueth to dyuert & dryue away that is in restreynyng. **1541** —— *Guydon's Quest. Chirurg.*, Applyed ..vnder the brestes for to staunche and dyuerte the floures of women. **1651** WITTIE tr. *Primrose's Pop. Err.* IV. §472. 401 That..the Physicians use..revulsions, and diverting remedies.

†**c.** *refl.* To turn aside; to betake oneself (*to* something different). *Obs.*

1577 HANMER *Anc. Eccl. Hist.* (1619) 134 They diverted themselves, and fled from their most loving and dearest friends. **1605** *Tryall Chev.* I. iii. in Bullen *O. Pl.* III. 282 Which way soever I divert my selfe Thou seemst to follow with a loving eye. **1656** STANLEY *Hist. Philos.* IV. (1701) 143/1 He [Bion] diverting himself to Philosophy.

2. *intr.* (for *refl.*) To turn aside out of one's course; to deviate, digress (*lit.* and *fig.*). (The earliest sense exemplified; now *arch.*)

1430 LYDG. *Chron. Troy* I. vi, If that I shulde..Fro this my purpose by any way diuerte. —— *Thebes* II. (R.), [He] List not once aside to diuert But kept his way. **1548** HALL *Chron., Rich. III*, (an. 3) 46 That when they approched the marches..they should dyverte and take the next weye into Fraunce. **1641** EVELYN *Diary* 1 Sept., As I returned, I diverted to see one of the Prince's palaces. **1703** MAUNDRELL *Journ. Jerus.* 33 We diverted a little out of the way to see it. **1774** BP. HALLIFAX *Anal. Rom. Law* (1795) Pref. 23 Studies..from which..I should never have diverted. **1804** NELSON 10 Feb. in Nicolas *Disp.* (1845) I. 413 Captain Richardson cannot divert from the immediate prosecution of my orders. **1895** W. MUNK *Life Sir H. Halford* 10 He..was bred to physic, but he diverted to the diplomatic line.

†**b.** To withdraw oneself, separate *from*; to part. (Also *refl.*) *Obs. rare.*

c **1555** HARPSFIELD *Divorce Hen. VIII* (1878) 293 The King might divert and divorce himself from Queen Katherine. **1604** R. CAWDREY *Table Alph.* (1613), *Diuert*, turne from to another. **1705–14** FORBES in M. P. Brown *Suppl. Decis.* (1824) V. 60 (Jam.) In case they should divert, and live separately.

3. *trans.* (*transf.* and *fig.*) To turn aside the course or tendency, or interrupt the progress, of (an action, design, feeling, etc.); to avert, ward off, turn in another direction.

1548 HALL *Chron., Hen. VI* (an. 38) 174 [They] studied to divert and turne from them, all mischief or infortunitie. **1599** SHAKS. *Hen. V*, II. Prol. 15 The French..Seeke to diuert the English purposes. **1649** MILTON *Eikon.* xi. 110 Which Omen..God hath not diverted. **1732** POPE *Ep. Bathurst* 51 Could France..divert our brave designs? **1862** SIR B. BRODIE *Psychol. Inq.* II. ii. 70 Persevering labour, not diverted from one object to another. **1874** GREEN *Short Hist.* vi. §4. 303 The indignation of the New Learning was diverted to more practical ends.

†**4.** (?) To turn awry, or away from the straight. *Obs. rare.*

1606 SHAKS. *Tr. & Cr.* I. iii. 99 Frights, changes, horrors, Diuert, and cracke, rend and deracinate The vnity, and married calme of States Quite from their fixture.

5. To draw off (a person) *from* a particular course, design, etc.; to cause (the mind, attention, etc.) to turn *from* one channel to another; to distract.

c **1600** SHAKS. *Sonn.* cxv, Time whose milliond accidents ..Diuert strong mindes to the course of altering things. **1667** MILTON *P.L.* IX. 814 Other care..May have diverted from continual watch Our great Forbidder. **1704** HEARNE *Duct. Hist.* (1714) I. 397 Presently after which Augustus was diverted by a Revolt of the Armenians. **1782** COWPER *Let.* 11 Nov., Less profitable amusements divert their attention. **1853** C. BRONTE *Villette* xi, She had an important avocation ..to fill her time, divert her thoughts, and divide her interest. **1874** L. STEPHEN *Hours in Library* (1892) I. i. 5 People are diverted from the weak part of the story by this ingenious confirmation.

b. *Mil.*: see DIVERSION 3.

1600 E. BLOUNT tr. *Conestaggio* 309 To divert the Spanish forces. **1665** MANLEY *Grotius' Low C. Warres* 596 It was necessary first to divert the Enemy to some other part.

6. To draw away from fatiguing or serious occupations; pleasurably to excite the mind or attract the attention; to entertain, amuse.

1662 J. DAVIES tr. *Olearius' Voy. Ambass.* 278 Paste and Sugar..which were brought to the Table, rather to divert the Eye, than to sharpen the Appetite. **1709** STEELE *Tatler* No. 106 ¶1, I had neither Friends or Books to divert me. **1858** HAWTHORNE *Fr. & It. Jrnls.* I. 259 The people.. seemed much diverted at our predicament.

b. *refl.* To entertain, amuse, recreate oneself; to give oneself to diversion. Now *rare.*

1660 R. COKE *Justice Vind.* 12 When they are alone, and seek company to divert themselves, so to elude the length of time. *c* **1665** MRS. HUTCHINSON *Mem. Col. Hutchinson* 22 He ..often diverted himself with a viol. **1719** DE FOE *Crusoe* (1840) I. xi. 182, I used frequently to visit my boat.. sometimes I went out in her to divert myself. **1800** *Med. Jrnl.* IV. 285 [He] was diverting himself with some of his companions at the rural diversion of hop, spring, and leap.

†**c.** *intr.* (for *refl.*) = prec. *Obs. rare.*

1670 G. H. *Hist. Cardinals* II. III. 177 He apply'd himself to divert amongst other young men, rather than to converse amongst books.

†**7.** *trans.* To cause (time) to pass pleasantly; to while away. *Obs.*

1707 J. STEVENS tr. *Quevedo's Com. Wks.* (1709) 214 They diverted the Afternoon playing at All-Fours. **1726** SHELVOCKE *Voy. round World* (1757) 395, I urged that.. going to California would divert our time. **1773** MRS. CHAPONE *Improv. Mind* (1774) I, How trifling is the talent of diverting an idle hour.

Hence **di'verted** *ppl. a.*

1600 SHAKS. *A.Y.L.* II. iii. 37, I rather will subiect me to the malice Of a diuerted blood and bloudie brother. **1608** CHAPMAN *Byron's Trag.* IV. Wks. 1873 II. 278 Their diverted ears, Their backs turned to us. **1812** L. HUNT in *Examiner* 7 Dec. 771/1 How is he to hold the balance with diverted eyes, and a hand that is trembling with passion?

di'verter. Also divertor. [f. prec. + -ER[1], -OR.]

a. *gen.* One who or that which diverts: see the verb.

1621–51 BURTON *Anat. Mel.* II. ii. IV. 282 'Tis the best Nepenthe, surest cordiall, sweetest alterative, present'st diverter. **1661** WALTON *Angler* (ed. 3) 42 Angling was..A rest to his mind, a cheerer of his spirits, a diverter [*ed.* 1 divertion] of sadness. **1727** *Philip Quarll* 204 Seeing his beloved Diverters carrying away by those Birds of Prey, he runs in for his Bow. *a* **1897** *Mod.* A diverter of young people.

b. *Electr.* Any of several devices that provide an alternative path for an electric current or for magnetic field lines; *spec.* (*a*) a resistance placed in parallel with the series winding of a series- or compound-wound d.c. motor or generator in order to alter the size of the current through the windings; (*b*) a device that protects a transmission line or associated equipment from surges by providing a path to earth for the surge current.

1891 J. W. URQUHART *Dynamo Constr.* xvii. 242 A device, having for its object the controlling of the magnetic intensity was formerly employed in the case of magneto machines. It consisted in placing a 'divertor'..of soft iron partially across the limbs of the magnet, so as to magnetically short-circuit the magnet. **1909** HAWKINS & WALLIS *Dynamo* (ed. 5) I. xvi. 542 Where it may be necessary to alter the amount of compounding..a diverter is employed just as with a series-wound dynamo. **1934** J. HENDERSON *Automatic Protective Gear* v. 63 When the straight-through fault current reaches an abnormal value..the diverter relay operates instantaneously. **1946** *Nature* 23 Nov. 742/1 Their development was first stimulated by the requirements of surge diverters (lighting arresters) for overhead power transmission lines. **1965** B. J. CORY *High Voltage Direct Current Convertors & Systems* viii. 213 Diverters are installed to protect this item from overvoltages that would arise on account of arc-quenching. **1968** J. F. WHITFIELD *Electr. Installations Technol.* viii. 167 Terminal voltage is adjusted by means of the divertor resistance.., which carries part of the current, thus reducing field current and terminal voltage.

di'vertible, *a. rare.* [f. L. *dīvert-ĕre* to DIVERT + -IBLE.] Able or liable to be diverted. Hence **diverti'bility**, capability of being diverted.

1881 *Fair Trade Cry* 11 The divertibility of trade is proved by its diversion. **1904** W. JAMES in *Atlantic Monthly* July 103/2 He who had the keenest eye for instances and illustrations, and was least divertible by casual side-curiosity, would score the quickest triumph. **1928** *Manch. Guardian Weekly* 31 Aug. 178/3 [Flood-water] will be divertible into the parallel valley of the Atchafalaya River.

† **di'verticle.** *Obs.* Also 7 -icule. [ad. L. *dīverticul-um*: see below. In F. *diverticule*.]

1. A byway or bypath; a turning out of the main way or straight course. Also *fig.*

1570–6 LAMBARDE *Peramb. Kent* (1826) 234 Neither of them standeth in the full sweepe..of those Rivers, but in a diverticle, or by way. **1634** T. JOHNSON *Parey's Chirurg.* II. (1678) 37 The first entrance..is not streight, but full of many diverticles and crooked paths. **1677** GALE *Crt. Gentiles* IV. 55 Who made the heart, and knows al the diverticules or turnings and windings of it. **1782** T. WARTON *Hist. Kiddington* 52 (T.), I suspect there was a diverticle of the Akeman shooting from Whichwood towards Idbury.

2. = DIVERTICULUM 2.

1847 CRAIG, *Diverticle*..in Anatomy, any hollow appendage which belongs to and communicates with the cavity of the intestinal canal, and terminates in a *cul-de-sac*.

diver'ticular, *a.* [f. L. *dīverticul-um*: see below and -AR[1].] Pertaining to or of the nature of a diverticulum.

1849–52 TODD *Cycl. Anat.* IV. 847/1 A left gall-bladder.. is [a] diverticular production of the gall-duct. **1878** BELL *Gegenbaur's Comp. Anat.* 49 A diverticular outgrowth.

diver'ticulate, *a.* [f. DIVERTICULUM + -ATE[2].] Provided with a diverticulum. Also, in same sense, **diver'ticulated** *a.*

1870 ROLLESTON *Anim. Life* 130 The diverticulate portion of the digestive tract.

diverticulectomy (daɪvəˌtɪkjʊ'lɛktəmɪ). *Surg.* [f. DIVERTICUL(UM + -ECTOMY.] The excision of a diverticulum.

1926 YOUNG & DAVIS *Young's Pract. Urology* II. xvi. 335 *Diverticulectomy.* This term is applied to operations for the removal of vesical diverticulum. **1928** J. S. HORSLEY *Operat. Surg.* (ed. 3) xxx. 837 Approach to the bladder for resection of the bladder wall, diverticulectomy, for stone or for drainage is frequently indicated. **1961** *Lancet* 30 Sept. 744/1 Vesical diverticulectomy.

diverticulitis (daɪvətɪkjʊ'laɪtɪs). *Path.* [f. DIVERTICUL(UM + -ITIS]. Inflammation of a diverticulum, esp. in the intestine.

1900 in DORLAND *Med. Dict.* 211/2. **1923** R. KNOX *Radiogr. & Radio-Therap.* (ed. 4) I. 364 (*heading*) Diverticulitis of the colon. **1939** *Times* 3 Mar. 14/4 Lord Ashfield, who is..suffering from diverticulitis, underwent an operation yesterday. **1969** N. S. PAINTER in B. C. Morson *Dis. Colon, Rectum & Anus* xvii. 201 When diverticula are causing no symptoms or only minimal symptoms the disease is called diverticulosis and when one or more diverticula are inflamed the condition is called diverticulitis.

diverticulosis (daɪvətɪkjʊ'ləʊsɪs). *Path.* [mod.L., a. G. *diverticulosis* (F. de Quervain 1914, in *Deut. Zeitschr. f. Chirurgie* CXXVIII. 81), f. DIVERTICUL(UM + -OSIS.] The presence of diverticula, esp. in the intestine.

1917 *Amer. Jrnl. Roentgenology* IV. 381/2 Both carcinoma and diverticulosis are important causes of pelvic colon obstruction. **1956** A. S. TILL in H. Souttar *Textbk. Brit. Surg.* I. xi. 352 (*heading*) Diverticulosis of the small intestine. **1969** [see prec.].

‖**diverticulum** (daɪvə'tɪkjʊləm). Pl. -a. [L. *dī-dēverticulum* a byway, bypath, deviation, wayside shelter or lodging; f. *dēvertĕre* to turn down or aside, f. DE- I. 1 + *vertĕre* to turn.]

†**1.** A byway; a way out, means of exit. *Obs.*

1647 W. STRONG *Trust & Acc. Steward* 19 Some..love diverticulaes and turne aside unto crooked waies. **1695** WOODWARD *Nat. Hist. Earth* III. §13 (1723) 159 Were it not for these Diverticula, whereby it [fire] thus gains an Exit, 'twould..make greater Havock than now it doth.

2. A smaller side-branch of any cavity or passage; in *Anat.* applied usually to a blind tubular process; in *Pathol.* to a malformation having this character.

1819 *Pantologia, Diverticulum,* a mal-formation or diseased appearance of intestine, in which a portion of intestine goes out of the regular course of the tube. **1822** in CRABB *Technol. Dict.* **1871** DARWIN *Desc. Man* I. i. 27 The cæcum is a branch or diverticulum of the intestine, ending in a cul-de-sac. **1880** MIVART in *Contemp. Rev.* 285 The South Pacific, of which all other oceans and seas may be regarded as diverticula or reaches.

‖**divertimento** (diverti'mento, dɪˌvɜːtɪ'mɛntəʊ). Pl. -ti (-tɪ), -tos. [It. = diversion, pastime, pleasure.] †**a.** Diversion, amusement. *Obs.*

1759 GOLDSM. *Polite Learn.* iii. (Globe) 425/2 Where.. abbés turned shepherds, and shepherdesses without sheep indulge their innocent *divertimenti*!

b. *Mus.* (*a*) A composition designed primarily for entertainment, esp. a suite of movements for a chamber ensemble. (*b*) An arrangement of, or fantasia on, airs from an opera, etc.

1823 *Spirit Pub. Jrnls.* (1824) 198 Haydn composed..20 divertimentos for various instruments. **1880** GROVE *Dict. Mus., Divertimento,* a term employed for various pieces of music. **1887** *Athenæum* 9 Apr. 489/3 (Stanf.) We find five large serenades and divertimenti for wind instruments. **1948** H. ULRICH *Chamber Music* (1966) v. 122 Various versions of the divertimento differed widely in the number of movements, but all had two features in common: their light, cheerful content and their derivation from the three-movement *sinfonia*. **1955** *Times* 14 May 4/5 We would have been glad to hear one of Mozart's earlier symphonies, or larger divertimenti. **1957** AUDEN & KALLMAN *Magic Flute* 58 And even those *Divertimenti* which He wrote to play while bottles were uncorked.

di'verting, *vbl. sb.* [-ING[1].] The action of the verb DIVERT; diversion. Also *attrib.*

1611 FLORIO, *Diuertita,* a diuerting, a remouing. *a* **1612** DONNE *Βιαθανατος* (1644) 213 All darke and dangerous Secessions and divertings into points of our Freewill, and of Gods Destiny. **1617** HIERON *Wks.* II. 237 To obtaine of God the diuerting or turning by of some great iudgements. **1681** [see DIVERSORY *sb.*]. **1895** *Daily Chron.* 19 Jan. 5/5 The diverting of the water to the old workings.

di'verting, *ppl. a.* [f. as prec. + -ING[2].] That diverts or turns aside; distracting; amusing.

1651 BAXTER *Inf. Bapt.* 224 To thrust in mens names and words..was unseasonable and diverting. **1700** S. L. tr. *C. Fryke's Voy. E. Ind.* 168 Their Comedies..are very diverting. **1782** COWPER (*title*) The Diverting History of John Gilpin. **1871** MORLEY *Voltaire* (1886) 144. **1878** H. H. GIBBS *Ombre* 1 Ombre..the most diverting..of games.

Hence **di'vertingly** *adv.*; **di'vertingness.**

1697 COLLIER *Immor. Stage* vi. (1730) 168 The Divertingness of it. **1701** STRYPE *Life Aylmer* xiv. (R.), He ..then added, divertingly, that this argument therefore arose of wrong understanding the word. **1837** *Fraser's Mag.* XV. 339 Her sensibility appears to be strangely—we had almost said divertingly—acute.

†**divertise,** *v. Obs.* Also 7 -ize. [f. F. *divertiss-* lengthened stem of *divertir* to DIVERT: cf. *advertise,* and see -ISE. Stressed by Bailey *di'vertise*; Johnson has *diver'tise.*]

1. *trans.* = DIVERT 1 b.

1597 LOWE *Chirurg.* (1634) 338 Let it [the ulcer] bleed well, to divertize the fluxion.

2. To distract the attention of: to draw off; = DIVERT 5.

1648 EVELYN *Mem.* (1857) III. 17 If the army were but conveniently divertised, both this city and the adjacents to it would be so associate as [etc.]. **1652** J. WRIGHT tr. *Camus' Nat. Paradox* 161 Every one's attentions were divertised according to their different inclinations.

3. To entertain, amuse; = DIVERT 6. Chiefly *refl.*: To enjoy oneself, make merry.

1651 tr. *De-las-Coveras' Don Fenise* 32 The ordinary entertaines wherewith I divertised my selfe. **1671** tr. *Frejas' Voy. Mauritania* 63 The King..bad him take care to divertise me. **1673** WYCHERLEY *Gentl. Danc. Master* I. ii, I think we had better..divertise the gentleman at cards till it be ready. **1696** AUBREY *Misc.* (1721) 62 Sir Roger L'Estrange was wont to divertise himself with Cocking in his Father's Park.

Hence **divertising** *ppl. a.*, entertaining, amusing.

1655 *Theophania* 84 His humour [was] so divertising. **1667** PEPYS *Diary* 28 May, To hear the nightingale and other birds, and here fiddles, and there a harp, and here a Jew's trump, and here laughing, and there fine people walking, is mighty divertising. **1694** CROWNE *Married Beau* I. 5 The compliment is not divertising.

divertisement (dɪ'vɜːtɪzmənt). *arch.* [ad. F. *divertissement* (15th c.) action of diverting, diversion, f. *divertiss-*: see prec. and -MENT.]

1. The action of diverting or fact of being diverted; recreation, entertainment, = DIVERSION 4.

1651 HOBBES *Govt. & Soc.* Ep. Ded., Some for divertisement, and some for businesse. **1719** LONDON & WISE *Compl. Gard.* 287 Nature now affect[s] no better divertisement than to be amazing us with Miracles of fertility. **1854** J. S. C. ABBOTT *Napoleon* (1855) I. i. 21 He left the bat and the ball..and in this strange divertisement found exhilarating joy. **1894** J. WINSOR *Cartier to Frontenac* 200 Half trader, half explorer, wholly bent on divertisement.

2. with *a* and *pl.* An instance of this; an entertainment, amusement; = DIVERSION 4 b.

1642 HOWELL *For. Trav.* xix. (Arb.) 80 In this variety of studies and divertisments. **1707** *Lond. Gaz.* No. 4314/3 There will be..Foot-Matches, and other Divertisements. **1801** STRUTT *Sports & Past.* III. iv. 187 The juggler's exhibition..consists of four divertisements. **1865** M. PATTISON *Ess.* (1889) I. 352 The divertisements of his leisure.

b. = DIVERTISSEMENT 2.

1667 PEPYS *Diary* 7 Jan., A most excellent play in all respects, but especially in divertisement, though it be a deep tragedy. **1803** *Edin. Rev.* II. 180. **1822** T. MOORE *Mem.* (1853) III. 314 Too late for the divertisement in the opera.

‖**di'vertissant,** *a. Obs.* Also 8 **divertisant.** [F. *divertissant,* pr. pple. of *divertir* to DIVERT.] Diverting, entertaining, pleasing.

1645 EVELYN *Diary* 31 Jan., One of the most divertissant and considerable vistas in the world. **1664** —— *Sylva* (1679) 27 These sweet, and divertissant Plantations. **1730–6** BAILEY (folio), *Diver'tisant,* diverting.

‖**divertissement** (divɛrtismɑ̃). [F. = diversion, also 'a ballet-interlude, piece of music for several instruments' (Littré).]

1. An entertainment; = DIVERTISEMENT 2.

1804 *Edin. Rev.* V. 86 The whole party..were called upon to repeat the *divertissement* in a more public..manner. **1816** BYRON in Moore *Life* (1832) III. 328 (Stanf.) All kinds of concerts and divertissements on every canal of this aquatic city. **1887** *Pall Mall G.* 23 Sept. 3/1 Novels, tales, and adventures of every kind. It is by these divertissements that the taste for reading is first developed.

2. A kind of ballet; a short ballet or other entertainment given between acts or longer pieces (= F. *entr'acte*); formerly also a piece of music containing several movements.

c **1728** EARL OF AILESBURY *Mem.* (1890) 710 She hath nothing in her head but plays, operas, and all divertissements. **1794** MATHIAS *Purs. Lit.* (1798) 257 Messrs. Fox, Sheridan, and Grey, are preparing a new Serious Divertissement, or Pas de Trois, with new scenes, dresses, and decorations, called, '*Le Directoire Executif*'. **1840** MOORE *Lalla R.* Pref. (1850) 14, I must not omit to notice the splendid *Divertissement* founded upon it. **1880** GROVE *Dict. Mus., Divertissement,* a kind of short ballet.. Also a pot-pourri or piece on given *motifs*..The term is no longer used. **1888** *Times* 26 June 12/2 Advt., The new grand spectacular ballet divertissement.

divertive (dɪ'vɜːtɪv, daɪ-), *a.* Now *rare.* [f. DIVERT + -IVE; cf. It. *divertivo* (Florio).] Tending to divert; having the property of diverting or producing diversion; distractive; amusing, entertaining.

1598 FLORIO, *Diuertiua,* diuertiue or remouing. *Guerra diuertiua,* diuertiue war. **1661** FELTHAM *Resolves* (ed. 8) II. xxi, By reason of..the divertive crowd of other occasions, Rich men haue not leisure. **1670** E. R. *Animadv. Glanvill's Ne Plus Ultra* 7 Something so charming and divertive in this discourse. **1707** J. JOHNSON *Clergym. Vade M.* App. xii, Several Inscriptions that are Real, but Jocular and Divertive. **1831** *Fraser's Mag.* III. 28 Greatly divertive to the inward man.

†**di'vertment.** *Obs.* [-MENT.] Diversion.

1613–18 DANIEL *Coll. Hist. Eng.* (1626) 83 The prosequution..thereof was neyther by him or his successors (hauing other diuertments) euer throughly accomplished. **1635** A. STAFFORD *Fem. Glory* (1869) 116 The manifold divertments incident to your Sexe.

divertor, var. DIVERTER.

‖**Dives** ('daɪviːz). [L. *dīves* rich, a rich man.]

1. The Latin word for 'rich (man)', occurring in the Vulgate, Luke xvi; whence commonly taken as the proper name of the rich man in that parable; and used generically for 'rich man'. Hence **'Divesdom,** the condition of being a 'Dives'.

c **1386** CHAUCER *Sompn. T.* 169 Lazar and diues lyueden diuersly. **1393** LANGL. *P. Pl.* C. IX. 279 Diues for hus delicat lyf to þe deuel wente. **1493** H. PARKER (*title*) Diues and Pauper. **1588** LUPTON (*title*) A Dreame of the Deuill and Diues. **1614** T. ADAMS *Devil's Banquet* 281 Euery one had rather be a Diues, then a Diuus: a rich sinner, then a poore Saint. **1640** BASTWICK *Lord Bps.* vi. F b, Doe not our Diveses, our rich Lord Prelates..goe in their Purple, Satten, Velvet? **1848** THACKERAY *Van. Fair* lvii, There must be rich and poor, Dives says, smacking his claret. **1891** *Pall Mall G.* 6 Oct. 7/2 Pleading and entreating with the Christian Diveses, of which the land is so full, for the tiny Lazarus lying hard by their gate.

1822 BESANT *All Sorts* xxviii, Pauperdom, Divesdom, taxes, and all kinds of things.

2. *Law. dives costs*: costs on the higher scale.

Under an old practice of the Court of Chancery, a plaintiff who sued *in forma pauperis* (and who therefore if he failed in his action could not be condemned to pay the defendant's costs) was sometimes, in case the action was successful, allowed to recover from the defendant only 'pauper costs', which were costs taxed on a low scale; while in other cases he was allowed to recover what by way of contrast were called 'dives costs', taxed on the ordinary scale.

1849 *Consol. Orders in Chancery* xl. 5 Such costs shall be taxed as dives costs unless the Court shall otherwise direct. **1885** SIR C. S. C. BOWEN in *Law Rep.* 14 Q. Bench Div. 870 In 1701 Lord Somers allowed a pauper 'dives costs', that is, costs like other suitors. *Ibid.* 871.

divest (dɪ'vɛst, daɪ-), *v.* [A refashioning, after L. analogies, of earlier DEVEST from French. OF. *desvestir,* through its later form *devestir,* gave *devest* immediately, while its mediæval latinization *disvestire,* rectified to *dīvestīre* (after ancient L. *dīvellĕre, dīvertĕre,* etc.) has given *divest,* and this, through the general preference for the Latin over the French forms of the prefixes has supplanted *devest,* except in legal use, where both are found.]

1. *trans.* To unclothe, undress, disrobe; to strip *of* clothing, or of any covering, ornament, etc.

[**1583–1809**: see DEVEST 1, 2.] **1795–1814** WORDSW. *Excursion* VI. 161 A leafy grove Discoloured, then divested. **1847** DICKENS *Haunted M.* ii, Divesting herself of her out-of-door attire. **1859** LANG *Wand. India* 327 Having divested himself of the dust with which he was covered. **1870** E. PEACOCK *Ralf Skirl.* I. 32 Some of the Gothic windows had been divested of their tracery.

2. *fig.* To strip (a person or thing) *of* possessions, rights, or attributes; to denude, dispossess, deprive; less usually in good sense, to free, rid.

[**1563–1686**: see DEVEST 3.] **1648** *Hunting of Fox* 36 A prevailing Faction..hath divested him of all his Rights. **1769** E. BANCROFT *Nat. Hist. Guiana* 136 [Monkeys] are frequently tamed..but they can never be divested of a mischievous disposition. **1818** JAS. MILL *Brit. India* II. IV. v. 204 Divesting him of the government. **1882** FARRAR *Early Chr.* II. 105 He divests them of their antithetical character.

b. *refl. to divest oneself of*: to strip or dispossess oneself of; to put off, throw off, lay aside, abandon, rid oneself of.

1605 SHAKS. *Lear* I. i. 50 Now we will diuest vs both of Rule, Interest of Territory, Cares of State. **1767** BLACKSTONE *Comm.* II. v. 70 He agreed to divest himself of this undoubted flower of his crown. **1823** KEBLE *Serm.* iii. (1848) 66 Divesting ourselves, for a moment, of all impressions received from other kinds of evidence. **1856** DOVE *Logic Chr. Faith* v. i. §2. 300 We have a moral nature from which we cannot divest ourselves.

3. To put off (clothes, or anything worn or represented as worn); to lay aside, abandon. Now *rare.*

[**1566–1765**: see DEVEST 4.] **1639** G. DANIEL *Vervic.* 708, I endeavour To put of Man, and ffrailtie to divest. **1673** *Lady's Call.* II. §4 ¶ 10. Knowing how hardly we can divest our voluptuousness and ambition. **1835** BROWNING *Paracelsus* I. 23, I will divest all fear.

4. *Law.* To take away (property, etc., vested in any one); to alienate, convey away; = DEVEST 5.

[**1574–1848**: see DEVEST 5.] **1789** *Durnford & East's Law Rep.* III. 467 The assignees putting his mark on them could not divest the consignor's right. **1818** CRUISE *Digest* (ed. 2) XXXV. xiii. §5 No estate or interest can be barred by a fine, unless it is divested out of the real owner, either before the fine is levied, or by the operation of the fine itself. **1845** STEPHEN *Comm. Laws Eng.* (1874) II. 145 The property of a bankrupt is..made liable to be divested from him and distributed.

5. *Econ.* To sell off (a subsidiary company); to dispose of, cease to hold (an investment). Also *absol.* orig. *U.S.*

1961 *Atlantic Reporter* (1962) CLXXV. 2nd Ser. 37/1 He might have, if not repulsed, divested American Screw from Noma. **1973** *N.Y. Law Jrnl.* 30 July 3/5 A 1966 decree requiring Von's Grocery Stores to divest a certain number of required stores..resulted in divestment of its forty least profitable outlets. **1978** *Washington Post* 28 Feb. D8 More than 400 students and faculty..have asked the school's board of trustees to divest $20 million in stock in 22 American corporations. **1982** *Daily Tel.* 16 Jan. 23/2 Colgate has been..divesting some of the activities not in its main business. **1984** *Times* 3 May 25/2 Mr Saul Steinberg's US-based Reliance group of companies has also decided to divest. **1986** *Christian Science Monitor* 5 Mar. 3 She advises American people to divest their investments in South Africa.

¶ *catachr.* To vest, invest.

1638 SIR T. HERBERT *Trav.* (ed. 2) 343 When Apollo divests himselfe in his most ardent splendour. *a* **1662** HEYLIN *Hist. Presbyt.* (1670) 333 That authority which was divested by God in His Majesty's person.

Hence **di'vesting** *vbl. sb.*, **di'vested** *ppl. a.* (The latter is found loosely used for: Devoid *of.*)

1712 PRIDEAUX *Direct. Ch.-wardens* (ed. 4) 80 This would be a Divesting of themselves. **1742** *Mem. Lady H. Butler* II. 184, I..was entirely divested of the vanity of wishing to shine in borrowed ornaments. **1815** W. H. IRELAND *Scribbleomania* 308 *note,* By no means divested of a literary talent at retort.

†**di'vest,** *pa. pple.* Short for DIVESTED. *rare.*

a **1679** LD. ORRERY *Herod Gt.* iv, As those who bore them ..Seem'd, by their Looks, of more than Life divest.

di'vestible, *a. rare.* [f. DIVEST *v.*: see -BLE.] Capable of being divested.

1648 BOYLE *Seraph. Love* i. (1700) 2 Liberty being too high a Blessing to be divestible of that nature by circumstances.

di'vestitive, *a.* [f. as next: see -IVE.] Having the property or function of divesting.

1802–12 BENTHAM *Ration. Judic. Evid.* (1827) I. 43 Ablative, or say divestitive facts. **1832** AUSTIN *Jurispr.* (1879) II. lv. 914. **1875** POSTE *Gaius* I. Introd. (ed. 2) 3 Title ..is a fact Investitive or Divestitive of Rights and Obligations.

divestiture (dɪ'vɛstɪtjʊə(r), daɪ-). Also 7 de-. [f. mod.L. *dīvestīt-* ppl. stem of *dīvestīre* to DIVEST: cf. *investiture,* and see -URE. Cf. F. *dévestiture.*] The act of divesting.

1. Deprivation of a possession or right; dispossession; alienation: see DIVEST 2, 4.

1601 Bp. W. Barlow *Defence* A iij b, By the diuestiture of the accusers from their places. **1640** Bp. Hall *Episc.* ii. xv, He is sent away without remedy with a devestiture from his pretended orders. **1794** Mrs. Piozzi *Synon.* I. 146 Proud honour that shrinks from the idea of divestiture. **1883** Ld. Craighill in *Law Rep.* 9 App. Cases 312/2 There was only a conditional divestiture of the truster.

2. Putting off of clothing; also *fig.*

1820 Lamb *Elia* Ser. i. *Christ's Hosp. 35 Years Ago*, The effect of this divestiture. **1875** Lightfoot *Comm. Col.* ii. 15 The ἀπέκδυσις..is a divestiture of the powers of evil, a liberation from the dominion of the flesh.

3. *Econ.* = divestment b. See divest *v.* 5. Also *attrib.* Chiefly *U.S.*

1961 *U.S. Rep.* CCCLXVI. 342 The plan called for divestiture by du Pont of its 63,000,000 shares of General Motors stock. **1972** *Bankers Mag.* (Boston, Mass.) Winter 31/1 It..has so many legal implications tied to each and every divestiture and forced sale. **1976** *Billings* (Montana) *Sunday Gaz.* 20 June 1-F/3 Divestiture, as the breakup of the present oil industry structure is called, has thus become one of the hottest and most controversial issues in Washington. **1977** *N.Y. Rev. Bks.* 29 Sept. He had to ask for an extension on the divestiture requirements of Carter's regime. **1982** *Times* 21 July 15/7 A European Commission investigation..could have the drastic outcome of forcing divestiture. **1984** *Christian Science Monitor* 2 Mar. 4/3 Massachusetts; Washington, D.C.; and Philadelphia passed blanket divestiture bills.

divestment (dɪˈvɛstmənt, daɪ-). [f. divest + -ment.] The action of divesting or state of being divested; divestiture.

[**1647** see devestment. **1664** H. More *Myst. Iniq.* 407 Their Devestment of all Political Power.] **1756** Richardson *Corr.* (1804) II. 92. *a* **1831** A. Knox *Rem.* (1844) I. 99 The Apostle..would that we have poverty amidst our riches, and divestment in the midst of our possessions. **1854** M. J. Routh in Burgon *Lives 12 Gd. Men* (1888) I. 101 To effect the divestment of a body thus bound.

b. *spec.* in financial contexts, the policy or practice of selling off subsidiary interests or withdrawing from investments. orig. *U.S.* Cf. disinvestment and divestiture 3.

1955 *U.S. Congr. House Hearings Comm. Banking & Currency: Control & Regulation Bank Holding Companies* 509, I recommended the divestment of this whole thing [*sc.* Bank of America stock]. **1973** [see divest *v.* 5]. **1978** *Business Week* 3 July 7 Students demand 'divestment' by American business interests. **1981** *Times* 14 May 24/8 There will be a £1.25m write-down of shareholders' funds in the accounts, reflecting the now-completed divestment of the Leisure Products division. **1986** *Marketing* 11 Sept. 12/3 The trend towards conglomeration will be followed by one towards divestment.

divesture (dɪˈvɛstjʊə(r), daɪ-), *sb.* [f. divest + -ure: cf. also devesture.] The act of divesting; putting or stripping off; unclothing; divestiture.

1648 Boyle *Seraph. Love* iv. (1660) 27 When their divesture of Mortality dispenses them from those..Duties. **1865** *Ess. Soc. Subj.* 150 Hasty divesture of prejudice.

So **diˈvesture** *v.*, to strip of a vesture, unrobe.

1854 Syd. Dobell *Balder* xxiii. 117 Dethroned, discrowned, divestured.

divet, var. of divot.

divi, colloq. abbreviation of dividend; see also divvy *sb.*

divice, obs. form of device.

†**diˈviciate**, *v. Obs. rare.* [f. di-¹ or ? de- + L. *vitiāre* (*viciāre*) to spoil, injure, mar, f. *vitium* blemish.] *trans.* To corrupt, defile.

c **1470** Harding *Chron.* cvii. vii, The women euer they diuiciate In euery place.

dividable (dɪˈvaɪdəb(ə)l), *a.* [f. divide *v.* + -able.]

1. Capable of being divided; divisible.

1587 Golding *De Mornay* vi. 72 God..is one in himselfe, and in no part diuidable. **1628** Coke *On Litt.* i. 386 b, Lands in the County of Kent, that are called Gauelkinde, which lands are diuidable betweene the brothers. *a* **1774** Z. Pearce *Serm.* (1779) I. ii. (R.), To make them hard and not easily dividable. **1890** *Illustr. Lond. News* 20 Sept. 363/3 All that comrades had..was equally dividable.

†**2.** Having the function of dividing. *Obs.*

1606 Shaks. *Tr. & Cr.* i. iii. 105 Peacefull Commerce from dividable shores.

Hence **diˈvidableness**, divisibility.

1674 R. Godfrey *Inj. & Ab. Physic* 36 Denying the dividableness of Mercury.

dividant, var. of divident, *Obs.*

divide (dɪˈvaɪd), *v.* Also 4–6 di-, dy-, devyde, dyvide, 4–7 devide, 5 *Sc.* dewyd(e, dewid. [ME. *de-*, *dividen*, ad. L. *dīvidĕre* to force asunder, cleave, apportion, distribute, separate, remove): cf. It. *dividere*, Sp., Pg. *dividir*; F. has *diviser* (OF. *deviser*): see devise.]

I. Transitive senses.

1. a. To separate (a thing) into parts, or (a number or collective body) into smaller groups; to split up, cleave; to break or cut asunder.

c **1374** Chaucer *Boeth.* iii. pr. ix. 65 (Camb. MS.) Thylke thing þat symply is o thing, with-owten any deuysyon, the errour and folye of mankynde departeth and deuydeth it. **1382** Wyclif *1 Kings* iii. 25 Deuydith, he seith, the quyk child in two parties. *c* **1470** Henry *Wallace* ix. 1046 Hys power sone he gart dewyd in twa. **1579** Fulke *Heskins' Parl.* 158 We breake and deuide this holy breade. **1611** Bible *Dan.* v. 28 Thy kingdome is diuided, and giuen to the Medes and Persians. **1712–14** Pope *Rape Lock* iii. 148 The Peer now spreads the glitt'ring Forfex wide, T'inclose the Lock; now joins it, to divide. **1776** *Jrnl. U.S. Congress* 17 July, If a question in a debate contains more parts than one, any member may have the same divided into as many questions as parts. **1849** Macaulay *Hist. Eng.* I. 552 Argyle divided his mountaineers into three regiments.

b. *to divide the hoof*: to have divided or cloven hoofs. (A Hebraism of Scripture.)

1382 Wyclif *Lev.* xi. 7 A sowe that al be it that sche dyuidith [**1388** departith] the clee, she chewith not kude. **1611** Bible *ibid.*, The swine, though he diuide the hoofe and be clouen footed, yet hee cheweth not the cud. **1674** N. Cox *Gentl. Recreat.* iii. (1677) 3 All sorts of greater Fowl, viz. those who divide the Foot.

c. To penetrate by motion through, pass through or across, 'cleave'; also *transf.* to make (a path) *through.* (*poet.* and *rhet.*)

1590 Spenser *F.Q.* i. xi. 18 He..with strong flight did forcibly divyde The yielding ayre. **1855** Tennyson *Maud* i. i. 16, I heard The shrill-edged shriek of a mother divide the shuddering night. **1872** Spurgeon *Treas. Dav.* Ps. lxvi. 6 To divide a pathway through such a sea.

†**d.** To determine, decide. *Obs. rare.*

1596 Dalrymple tr. *Leslie's Hist. Scot.* viii. (1890) 74 The Erle Douglas..bidis outher ȝeild him selfe, or the morne diuyde it with the sworde.

e. phr. ***divide and rule*** (occas. ***govern***) [tr. L. *divide et impera* (also used)]: a statement of the policy of not allowing subject peoples or factions to make common cause.

1602 W. Watson *Decacordon* iii. 69 According to Machiauels rule of *divide & impera.* **1606** J. Hall *Meditations* i. 109 For a Prince, that he may have good successe against either rebels or forraine enemies, it is a sure axiome, Divide and rule. **1870** Brewer *Dict. Phr. & Fable* 231/1 *Divide and Govern.* Divide a nation into parties, or set your enemies at loggerheads, and you can have your own way. A maxim of Machiavelli. **1932** Kipling *Limits & Renewals* 91 Divide and rule—especially with Hebrews. **1936** P. Fleming *News from Tartary* v. iii. 198 There has really been no need for the Chinese to put their immemorial colonial policy of *Divide et impera* into practice; nature has done it for them. **1948** B. Stevenson *Home Bk. Proverbs* (1959) 1014/1 'Divide et impera'..was the motto of Philip of Macedon and of Louis XI of France, in dealing with his nobles. It was the traditional motto of Austria. Polybius, Bossuet, and Montesquieu used it, but it is generally ascribed to Machiavelli. **1962** *Listener* 26 Apr. 718/2 True to their traditional 'divide and rule' policy British diplomats tried to deepen the differences between the Kenya African National Union and the Kenya African Democratic Union.

2. To separate into branches; to cause to ramify.

c **1400** *Lanfranc's Cirurg.* 26 Þat þe spirit of lijf myȝte be brouȝt bi hem to al þe bodi þese arteries ben devyded many weiss. *Ibid.* 158 Þis veyne..strecchiþ to þe vttere partie of þe schuldre & þere is dyuydid. **1659** B. Harris *Parival's Iron Age* 165 This Fort stood upon a point, which divided the Rheyn into his Arms or Branches. **1853** Kane *Grinnell Exp.* l. (1856) 478 The rod or staff is divided at right angles in two pieces.

3. a. To separate or mark out (a continuous whole) into parts (in fact, or in thought); to make to consist of parts, or to distinguish the parts of. Said of a personal agent, or of a line or boundary; usually with the number of parts specified. Most freq. in *pass.*; sometimes referring chiefly to condition, and so nearly = to consist of (so many) parts.

c **1380** Wyclif *Sel. Wks.* II. 407 Crist devydiþ al mankynde in þre partis. *c* **1400** *Lanfranc's Cirurg.* 108 Dyuers men..dyuyden þe brayn panne diuerslych; summen noumbren mo boonys þan summe oþir speken of. **1450–1530** *Myrr. our Ladye* 3 Thys boke ys deuyded in to thre partes. **1665** Hooke *Microgr.* Pref. F b, A Ruler divided into inches and small parts. **1667** Milton *P.L.* iv. 688 Thir songs Divide the night, and lift our thoughts to Heaven. **1777** J. Ramsden (*title*) Description of an Engine for dividing Straight Lines on Mathematical Instruments. **1797** *Encycl. Brit.* III. 43 Barry-Pily, is when a coat is divided by several lines drawn obliquely from side to side. **1838** *Penny Cycl.* XI. 338/1 Graduation is the name commonly applied to the art of dividing mathematical and astronomical instruments. **1864** Tennyson *En. Ard.* 733 A little garden..all round it ran a walk Of shingle, and a walk divided it.

b. *Billiards.* To distinguish (the ball) into distinct parts or points to be aimed at.

1856 Crawley *Billiards* (1859) 44 The old and more usual style of play is to divide the object ball..striking your own ball full in the centre; by the side stroke just the reverse plan is adopted, and you divide your own ball and strike the object ball full.

4. a. To separate into classes; to distinguish the kinds of; to class, classify. †**b.** Formerly, in scholastic use, To draw distinctions with regard to; also *absol.*: = distinguish 4 b, 8.

1551 T. Wilson *Logike* (1567) 15 a, I would diuide this worde *Canis* into a Dogge, a fishe of the sea, and a starre in the Elemente, thus might I saie, *Canis* is either a Dogge that liueth vpon the yearth, or a fishe, [etc.]. *Ibid.* 50 b, Comparations are deuided twoo maner of wayes, for, either thei bee equall, or not equall. *a* **1763** Shenstone *Ess.* 225 Mankind, in general, may be divided into persons of understanding, and persons of genius. **1845** R. W. Hamilton *Pop. Educ.* iii. (ed. 2) 37 We commonly divide the people into agricultural and manufacturing.

5. a. To separate (a thing) *from* something else, or (things) from each other; to cut off, sunder, part.

c **1380** Wyclif *Wks.* (1880) 426 If þe pope & alle his clerkis weren dyuydid fro cristis chirche. **1382** —— *2 Sam.* i. 23 Saul and Jonathas loueli..in deeth thei ben not deuydide. **1480** Caxton *Chron. Eng.* ccxliii. (1482) 293 The kyng made hem to goo out of the feld at ones, and so they were deuyded of hyr batayles. **1581** Sidney *Apol. Poetrie* (Arb.) 42 The people..had..deuided themselues from the Senate. **1634** Milton *Comus* 279 Could that divide you from near-ushering guides? **1700** S. L. tr. *Fryke's Voy. E. Ind.* 16 The sick were divided from the rest. **1856** Emerson *Eng. Traits, Land* Wks. (Bohn) II. 18 The sea which..divided the poor Britons utterly from the world.

b. To separate mentally, distinguish *from. rare.*

1859 Tennyson *Geraint & Enid* 686 Enid..all confused at first, Could scarce divide it from her foolish dream.

6. To separate or mark off (a thing) *from* something adjacent, or (adjacent things or parts) from one another; to establish or constitute a boundary between. (Said of a personal agent, or of the boundary, etc.) *lit.* and *fig.*

1382 Wyclif *Gen.* i. 4 God..deuydid liȝt fro derknessis. *Ibid.* 6 Be maad a firmament in the myddel of watres, and dyuyde it watres fro watrys. **1393** Gower *Conf.* III. 86 Thus danz Aristoteles These thre sciences [theorique, rhetorique, practique] hath devided. *c* **1510** More *Picus* Wks. 19/2 The partes & lots of enheritances were of old time met oute & deuided by cordes or ropes. **1632** Lithgow *Trav.* iii. 95 A partition wall..dividing the little roome from the body of the Chappell. **1732** Pope *Ess. Man* i. 226 What thin partitions Sense from Thought divide. **1850** Tennyson *In Mem.* xlvii. 6 Eternal form shall still divide The eternal soul from all beside.

7. To separate (persons) in opinion, feeling, or interest; to cause to disagree, set at variance, produce dissension in or among; to distract or perplex (a person) by conflicting thoughts or feelings.

c **1380** Wyclif *Sel. Wks.* III. 365 Þes newe ordris ben dividid in þer love. **1393** Gower *Conf.* I. 7 Þe regnes ben diuided, In stede of loue is hate guided. **1526–34** Tindale *Luke* xii. 52 Ther shalbe five in one housse devided, thre agaynst two, and two agaynst thre. **1650** T. B[ayley] *Worcester's Apoph.* 77 The Marquess, was much divided within himself. **1736** Butler *Anal.* ii. viii. Wks. 1874 I. 300 Men are divided in their opinions, whether our pleasures over-balance our pains. **1831** Brewster *Newton* (1855) II. xxi. 255 The fluxionary controversy had at this time begun to divide the mathematical world.

8. a. To distribute among a number; to deal out, dispense. Const. †*to* (obs.), *among*, *between*, *up*.

1377 Langl. *P. Pl.* B. xix. 210, I will dele..& dyuyde grace To alkynnes creatures. *c* **1380** Wyclif *Serm.* Sel. Wks. II. 190 Crist..wolde not juge ne devide heritage among men. *c* **1470** Henry *Wallace* x. 995 The castellis off Scotland King Eduard haill has tane in his awin hand: Deuidyt syn, to men that he wald lik. **1526–34** Tindale *1 Cor.* xii. 11 The silfe same sprete, devydynge to every man severall gyftes, even as he will. **1651** Hobbes *Leviath.* iii. xxxvi. 230 God divided the land of Canaan amongst the Israelites. **1710** Prideaux *Orig. Tithes* iii. 145 The Ministers, had their Stipends divided to them out of these Offerings. **1849** Macaulay *Hist. Eng.* I. 319 Of the rent, a large proportion was divided among the country gentlemen. **1914** E. Cannan *Wealth* v. 82 Even the pasture was divided up with the small exceptions which we see in the 'commons' of the present day.

b. To take or have a portion of (something) along *with* another or others; to share.

1526 Tindale *Luke* xii. 13 Master, bid my brother deuide the enherytaunce with me. **1591** Shaks. *1 Hen. VI*, i. vi. 18 Tis Ioane, not we, by whom the day is wonne, For which, I will diuide my crowne with her. *c* **1630** Milton *Passion* i, Erewhile of music and ethereal mirth..My muse with angels did divide to sing. **1697** Dryden *Alexander's Feast* 168 Let old Timotheus yield the prize, Or both divide the crown. **1842** Tennyson *Walking to the Mail* 69 These two parties still divide the world—Of those that want, and those that have.

absol. **1607** Shaks. *Cor.* i. vi. 87 Make good this ostentation, and you shall Diuide in all, with us.

†**c.** To give forth in various directions. *Obs.*

1594 Spenser *Amoretti* vi, When it once doth burne, it doth diuide Great heat. *a* **1687** Waller *Her Chamber* Poems (1893) 26 While she..like Phœbus so divides her light, And warms us, that she stoops not from her height.

†**d.** To assign severally to different places or posts; to allocate. *Obs.*

1600 E. Blount tr. *Conestaggio* 315 To devide the souldiers and munition into their severall places. **1700** S. L. tr. *Fryke's Voy. E. Ind.* 124 There Men are all divided, so many to each Boat, and so they go to the Oyster-Banks. **1718** Watts *Ps.* i. (L.M.) v, The dreadful judge with stern command Divides him to a different place.

e. To distribute (attention, etc.) between different objects; to direct to different things.

1611 Shaks. *Wint. T.* iv. iv, Me thinkes I see Leontes..ore and ore diuides him, 'Twixt his vnkindnesse, and his Kindnesse. **1737** Pope *Hor. Epist.* ii. ii. 291, I, who at some times spend, at others spare, Divided between carelessness and care. **1814** Scott *Ld. of Isles* iv. xxiii, The bell's grim voice divides thy care, 'Twixt hours of penitence and prayer! **1842** Tennyson *Morte D' Arth.* 60 Both his eyes were dazzled, as he stood, This way and that dividing the swift mind, In act to throw. [Cf. Virgil *Æn.* iv. 285.] **1860** Tyndall *Glac.* ii. xi. 290 The guide's attention had been divided between his work and his safety.

9. *Math.* **a.** *to divide* a number or quantity *by* another: to find how many times the latter is contained in the former; to perform the process of division on. (Also *absol.*)

c **1425** *Craft Nombrynge* (E.E.T.S.) 25 Þou schalt deuide ..þe noumbre..by þe neþer figures. **1509** Hawes *Past. Pleas.* xv. v, Who knewe arsmetryke in every degre..Bothe to detraye and to devyde and adde. **1542** RECORDE *Gr. Artes* 47. **1652** *News fr. Low-Countr.* 8 Podex can cast, can clear a summe, Adde, Multiply, Subtract, Divide. **1827** HUTTON *Course Math.* I. 8, 8 ÷ 4, denotes that 8 is to be divided by 4.

b. Of a number or quantity: To be a divisor or factor of (another number or quantity); to be contained an exact number of times in; to measure.

1709–29 V. MANDEY *Syst. Math., Arith.* 4 A Number is said to measure a Number, when one so exactly divides the other, that nothing remains. *Mod.* 9 divides 36. $x + y$ divides $x^n + y^n$ when n is odd.

†**c.** To take the difference of the terms of a given ratio, and make a new ratio by comparing this difference with either term of the original one. *Obs.* The phrase 'by dividing' is now expressed by the Lat. *dividendo.* See also DIVIDED 5.

1726 tr. *Gregory's Astron.* I. 402 By compounding and dividing them, you will have the Ratio of $SA + SP$ to SP, and $SA - SP$ to SP.

10. To part (a legislative assembly, etc.) into two groups which are counted in order to ascertain the number voting on each side of a question. Also *absol.* and *intr.*

1554 *Jrnl. Ho. Com.* 19 Apr., I. 34 Upon the Question for the Bill, the House did divide. **1604** *Ibid.* 24 Mar., I. 152 The Voice seeming doubtful, the House was divided. **1647** CLARENDON *Hist. Reb.* IV. §52 The House being then divided upon the passing or not passing it, it was carried for the affirmative by nine voices and no more. *a* **1794** GIBBON (Webster 1828), The emperors sat, voted, and divided with their equals. **1801** G. ROSE *Diaries* (1860) I. 335 Opposition were afraid to divide upon it. **1885** *Manch. Exam.* 15 May 6/2 The House..divided, when Mr. Gladstone's motion was carried by 337 to 38. *Mod.* The honourable member proceeded amid cries of 'Divide!' 'Divide!' *Mod.* Mr. B. expressed his intention of dividing the House on the motion.

†**11.** *Mus.* **a.** *trans.* To perform with 'divisions'; **b.** *intr.* To perform or execute 'divisions'; to descant: see DIVISION 7. *Obs.*

1590 SPENSER *F.Q.* I. v. 17 Most heauenly melody About the bed sweet musicke did diuide. **1609** *Ev. Woman in Hum.* III. i. in Bullen *O. Pl.* IV, What heavie string doost thou devide upon? **1618** FLETCHER *Loyal Subj.* II. ii, You will divide too shortly; Your voice comes finely forward.

12. Of a horse: (?) To distribute his legs and feet as they touch the ground; to keep them clear of each other in walking, trotting, etc. Also *absol.*

1737 BRACKEN *Farriery Impr.* (1757) II. 23 How a Horse ought to devide his Legs. *Ibid.* 38 Horses that devide all four well. *Ibid.* 93 The truest way to know whether he be a firm compact Nag, and divide well.

II. Intrans. senses. (See also 4 b, 9, 10, 11 b, 12.)

13. *absol.* To make separation or distinction (*between*). (In quot. 1377, To make distinctions, as in logic: = DISTINGUISH 8; cf. DIVISION 3, 6.)

1377 LANGL. *P. Pl.* B. XIX. 234 Somme he tauȝte..to dyuyne and diuide. **1382** WYCLIF *Isa.* lix. 2 ȝoure wickidnesses deuydeden betwe ȝou and ȝoure God. **1607–12** BACON *Ess., Wisdom for a Man's Self* (Arb.) 182 Diuide with reason betweene Self-loue, and Society: and be so true to thy self as thou be not false to others. **1661** CRESSY *Refl. Oathes Suprem. & Alleg.* 61 Justice requires that we should divide between the innocent and the guilty.

14. a. *intr.* (for *refl.*) To become divided, undergo division; to become separated into parts, or from something else or each other; to part; to cleave, break up, go to pieces; to branch, ramify.

1526 *Pilgr. Perf.* (W. de W. 1531) 14 Whan we come to the yeres of discrecyon, than we deuyde in two partes, two companyes & two wayes. **1593** SHAKS. *Lucr.* 1737 Bubbling from her breast, it [the blood] doth divide In two slow rivers. **1605** —— *Lear* I. ii. 15 Loue cooles, friendship falls off, brothers diuide. **1667** MILTON *P.L.* VI. 569 To Right and Left the Front Divided, and to either flank retir'd. **1734** WATERLAND *Script. Vind.* ad fin. (T.), Commentators and criticks have divided upon this matter. **1855** TENNYSON *Brook* 73 Her hair In gloss and hue the chestnut, when the shell Divides threefold to show the fruit within. **1878** HUXLEY *Physiogr.* 144 [The river] divides and subdivides, till at last it is split up into a network of channels.

b. *Camb. Univ.*: see DIVISION 1 c.

1797 *Camb. Univ. Calendar* 235 February..23. Lent Term divides. **1895–6** *Ibid.* October 1, Michaelmas Term begins. Oct. 20, End of first quarter of Mich. Term. Nov. 9, Michaelmas Term divides. Nov. 29, End of third quarter of Mich. Term. Dec. 19, Michaelmas Term ends.

di'vide, *sb.* [f. prec. vb.]

1. The act of dividing, division: †**a.** Separation; **b.** Distribution among a number of persons.

1642 *Preparative for Fast* 4 This divide and scatter, if it be not prevented, will be no small curse. **1873** *Contemp. Rev.* XXI. 749 In these [friendly societies]..the hope of a 'divide', as it is often termed, tends to keep up the figure of contributions. **1893** MCCARTHY *Red Diamonds* II. 27 There is to be the big divide next New Year, but I shan't be in it.

2. In N. Amer., Austral., etc.: A ridge or line of high ground forming the division between two river valleys or systems; a watershed; *the Great* (*Continental*) *Divide*, that of the Rocky Mountains; *fig.* a dividing or boundary line; *spec.* the boundary between life and death.

1807 PIKE *Sources Mississ.* II. (1810) 136 Struck and passed the divide between the Grand river and the Verdegris river. **1868** *Congress. Globe* 14 July 4068/1 The doctrine of political equality forms the great 'divide' between parties now as heretofore. **1869** W. J. PALMER *Surv. across Continent* 171 The great Continental Divide at Arkansas Pass. **1872** J. H. TICE *Over Plains* 214 [Tales] of those who long since 'have gone over the Divide'. **1887** R. MURRAY *Geol. & Phys. Geog. Victoria* 6 The 'Main Divide' of Victoria, forming the watershed line between the Murray River system on the north, and the numerous streams debouching on the southern coast. **1890** *Century Mag.* Mar. 771/1 In central Colorado the 'Continental Divide' is a wilderness of desolate peaks. **1893** SELOUS *Trav. S.E. Africa* 377, I could take the expedition..along the great divide which forms the watershed. **1907** C. E. MULFORD *Bar-20* xxiii. 226 Snip! goes his bill an' th' snake slides over th' Divide. **1908** —— *Orphan* xi. 139 If he was killed, he would have company across the Great Divide. **1909** *Daily Chron.* 16 Sept. 1/2 He was good to Ruth, and she, too, loved him. But between them still was 'the great divide'. She could not forget that he had bought her for a string of nuggets. **1955** C. S. LEWIS *Let.* 25 June (1966) 263 Instead of saying the Great Divide came between the Middle Ages and the Renaissance, I said..that it didn't. **1965** *Listener* 16 Sept. 414/2 This is the divide between Barth and Aquinas, it is the divide between the conservative evangelical tradition and liberal theology, it is the divide between Biblicism and the Bishop of Woolwich.

di'vided, *ppl. a.* [f. DIVIDE *v.* + -ED[1].]

1. Separated into parts. **a.** Split, cut, or broken into pieces; †incomplete, imperfect (quot. 1595).

1565–73 COOPER *Thesaurus, Abscissus*..deuided, broken. **1595** SHAKS. *John* II. 439 And she a faire diuided excellence, Whose fulnesse of perfection lyes in him. **1831** BREWSTER *Optics* xiv. 113 A plate of glass covered with..dust in a finely divided state.

b. Marked out into parts; marked by divisions, graduated; consisting of distinct parts; in *Bot.* (of leaves, etc.) cut into segments.

1674 N. COX *Gentl. Recreat.* III. (1677) 71 Divided-footed-Fowl. **1715** DESAGULIERS *Fires Impr.* 95 A divided Box. **1776** WITHERING *Brit. Plants* (1796) I. 24 The Species are..arranged according as the Leaves are divided, or not divided. **1831** BREWSTER *Optics* xxvii. §131 A goniometer, or other divided instrument.

†**c.** Said of the moon in the phase at which half the disk is illuminated; = DICHOTOMIZED 2.

1822 T. TAYLOR *Apuleius* 292 [The moon] cornicular, or divided, or gibbous, or full.

d. ***divided skirt***: see SKIRT *sb.* 1.

2. a. Separated from something else, or from each other; situated apart; separate.

1658 SIR T. BROWNE *Hydriot.* ii. 8 The Province of Britain in so divided a distance from Rome. **1677** HALE *Prim. Orig. Man.* II. iii. 140 Possibly the first divided King of Babylon was that Nabonassar. **1694** *Acc. Sev. Late Voy.* II. (1711) 105 Those Birds that have divided Claws.

b. *Mus.* Said of voices or instruments, usually in unison, to which independent parts are temporarily assigned in the course of a piece.

1880 STAINER & BARRETT *Dict. Mus. Terms, Divisi*, divided. A direction that instruments playing from one line of music are to separate and play in two parts.

3. Separated in opinion or interest; discordant, at variance; split into parties or factions.

1594 SHAKS. *Rich. III*, I. iv. 244 He little thought of this diuided Friendship. **1614** BP. HALL *Recoll. Treat.* 129 The unstable vulgar..whose divided tongues, as they never agree with each other; so seldome..agree long with themselves. **1781** GIBBON *Decl. & F.* III. xxx. 136 A divided court, and a discontented people. **1855** MACAULAY *Hist. Eng.* IV. 454 Divided and tumultuous assemblies. **1871** BLACKIE *Four Phases* i. 113 Any charm that might save a jury from the pain of giving a divided verdict.

4. Distributed or parted among a number of things or persons; directed to different objects.

1607 SHAKS. *Timon* I. ii. 49 The fellow that..pledges the breath of him in a diuided draught. **1764** GOLDSM. *Trav.* 415 Where beasts with man divided empire claim. *c* **1845** C. MACKAY *Candid Wooing* iii, Accept then a divided heart. **1869** FREEMAN *Norm. Conq.* III. xii. 249 The difficulties into which he was brought through this divided allegiance.

†**5.** *Math.* ***divided ratio***: see DIVIDE *v.* 9 c.

1660 BARROW *Euclid* v. def. 15, Divided ratio is when the excess wherein the antecedent exceeds the consequent, is compared to the consequent. **1827** HUTTON *Course Math.* I. 325 Divided ratio, is when the difference of the antecedent and consequent is compared, either with the antecedent or with the consequent.—Thus, if 1:2::3:6, then, by division, 2−1:1::6−3:3, and 2−1:2::6−3:6.

di'videdly, *adv.* [f. prec. + -LY[2].] In a divided manner; separately, apart; in separate parts.

1607 S. COLLINS *Serm.* (1608) 2 Either iointly all at once, or diuidedly by themselues. **1627** *Lisander & Cal.* VI. 100 They..went out after them, but dividedly, the better to finde them. **1678** CUDWORTH *Intell. Syst.* 783 (R.) If therefore, God be every where: it cannot possibly be, that he should possibly be so dividedly; because then himself would not be every where, but only a part of him here and a part of him there. **1867** ATWATER *Logic* 168 The middle term is taken dividedly or distributively.

†**b.** *Math.* By 'dividing' the ratio: see prec. 5.

1706 W. JONES *Syn. Palmar. Matheseos* 70 If A:a::B:b, Then..Dividedly, A−a:a::B−b:b. **1827** HUTTON *Course Math.* I. 218 When four quantities, *a, ar, b, br*..are proportional; then..Dividedly, *a:ar−a::b:br−b.*

di'videdness. [f. as prec. + -NESS.] The fact or condition of being divided.

1656 BAXTER *Refd. Pastor* (1862) 234 Our dividedness and unaptness to close for the work. **1871** H. B. FORMAN *Living Poets* 400 The failure..has arisen from dividedness of motive. **1877** E. CAIRD *Philos. Kant* II. xvi. 569 Infinite dividedness..or composition which is not of simple parts.

†**'dividence.** *Obs. rare.* [f. L. *dīvident-em*, pr. pple. of *dīvidĕre* to DIVIDE; prob. after It. *dividenza* (Florio 1611).] The action of dividing; division.

1598 FLORIO, *Partigione*, a partition, a diuidence. **1611** *Ibid., Diuidenza*, a diuidence, a distinction. **1603** —— *Montaigne* I. xxvii. (1632) 90 This commixture, dividence, and sharing of goods.

dividend ('dɪvɪdənd). Also 6–7 *erron.* dividente, -ent. [a. F. *dividende*, in sense 4 (1300 in Anglo-Fr.), ad. L. *dīvidend-um* (that) which is to be divided, absol. use of neuter gerundive of *dīvidĕre* to DIVIDE. In early use often erroneously *dividente*, *divident* (*-end* being an unusual, and *-ent* a well-known ending), but in 17th c. conformed to the L. type. (The sense development is not clear, senses 3 and 4 being the earliest found.)]

1. *Math.* A number or quantity which is to be divided by another. (Correlative to DIVISOR.)

α. **1542** RECORDE *Gr. Artes* 126 b, Then begynne I at the hyghest lyne of the diuident, and seke how often I may haue the diuisor therin. **1608** R. NORTON *Stevin's Disme* B ij, The number to be diuided (or diuident) and the number to diuide (or diuisor).

β. **1557** RECORDE *Whetst.* Z j, I see noe soche denomination in the diuidende. **1594** BLUNDEVIL *Exerc.* I. v. (ed. 7) 14 The dividend. 487. (9. the quotient.) **1674** JEAKE *Arith.* (1696) The divisor. 53.
31 Proceed as before to the end of the Dividend. **1806** HUTTON *Course Math.* I. 16 The usual manner of placing the terms, is, the dividend in the middle, having the divisor on the left hand, and the quotient on the right, each separated by a curve line. *c* **1865** *Circ. Sc.* I. 437/1.

2. A sum of money to be divided among a number of persons; *esp.* the total sum payable as interest on a loan, or as the profit of a joint-stock company, divided periodically among the holders (usually reckoned at a certain rate per cent.); also, the sum divided among the creditors of an insolvent estate. ***to declare a dividend***: DECLARE *v.* 5 d.

1623 W. SCLATER *Quaest. Tythes Revised* 152 Will you moove doubt whether Tithes entered the common Diuidend? **1643** MILTON *Soveraigne Salve* 11 Profits and emoluments accrewing may make a dividend sufficient to draw to some unjust act. **1684** *Lond. Gaz.* No. 1948/4 The Creditors of Benjamin Hinton..are desired to meet..to receive an Accompt of their Trustees, and to advise of a Divident. **1710** *Lond. Gaz.* No. 4744/3 Warrants for the said Dividend will be delivered. **1776** ADAM SMITH *W.N.* (1869) I. II. ii. 320 For some years past the Bank dividend has been at five and a half per cent. **1863** FAWCETT *Pol. Econ.* II. x. (1876) 271 Two-fifths of these profits form a fund from which the annual dividend on capital is paid.

3. *transf.* A portion or share of anything divided; *esp.* the share (of anything divided among a number of persons) that falls to each to receive or pay. †**a.** *gen. Obs.* exc. as *fig.* from b.

α. **1477** NORTON *Ord. Alch.* vi. in Ashm. (1652) 97 Another Furnace..serving for Seperation of dividents. **1563–70** FOXE *A. & M.* (1583) 116 What portions or diuidentes ought to be made thereof. *Ibid.* 1513 The Kings subsidie..is committed vnto me in the Kings Roll a whole Summe in grosse, to be receyued of the Canons Residentiaries for their Diuident, who..cannot agree in deuiding. **1593** NASHE *Christ's T.* 81 Security the last deuident of Delicacy, it [sloth] includeth in it. **1661** J. STEPHENS *Procurations* 108 Which otherwise rested upon the Priest or Clerks or that Church to do from the allotted divident.

β. **1600** HOLLAND *Livy* XXXIII. xlvi. 850 The financies and revenues..were shared out in dividends between some certaine of the head citizens. **1670** NARBOROUGH *Jrnl.* in *Acc. Sev. Late Voy.* I. (1711) 28 Divided all things equally ..the Boys Dividend being as large as my own. **1779–81** JOHNSON *L.P., Waller* Wks. II. 264 The Panegyrick upon Cromwell has obtained..a very liberal dividend of praise. **1806–7** J. BERESFORD *Miseries Hum. Life* (1826) XX. i. 266 What proportional dividend of man is a Stay maker?

b. *spec.* The portion of interest on a loan, or profit from a joint-stock company, received by an individual holder as his share; the amount received by an individual creditor from an insolvent estate. Also *fig.*

1690 *Lond. Gaz.* No. 2596/4 Sir Edward Dering Deputy-Governor of the Hudsons Bay Company..Presented to his Majesty a Dividend in Gold, upon His Stock in the said Company. **1827** JARMAN *Powell's Devises* (ed. 3) II. 337 A testatrix gave to trustees certain bank stock, upon trust to pay the dividends to her daughter M. for life. **1884** ACLAND & JONES *Working Men Co-operators* iii. 32 It is on the amount of her purchases at the shop that her dividend or share of profits is declared. **1965** *Listener* 16 Sept. 402/2 Nothing in fact will pay better dividends in the long run than a determined effort to discover what is actually going on in the Health Service.

†**4.** The action of dividing among a number of persons; distribution (*esp.* of profits, or assets.) *Obs.*

[**1300** *Act 28 Edw. I*, Super Cartas ii, Et des choses issint par eus prises..soit faite dividende entre les prenours & les gardeins des feires.]

α. **1535** LATIMER *Fruitf. Serm.* i. Eph. vi. 10 By these meanes a diuident [ed. **1635** devision] of the spoyle was made. **1570** LEVINS *Manip.* 67/32 A diuident, *diuidentia*. **1634** in *4th Rep. Hist. MSS. Comm.* 126/2 The divident of corne is managed according to the ancient custome.

β. **1647** N. BACON *Disc. Govt. Eng.* I. lxvii. (1739) 165 Paying the Debts, and making Dividend of the overplus into the reasonable parts. **1675** *Art Contentm.* IX. iii. 224 If there were a common bank made of all mens troubles, most men would rather chuse to take those they brought, then to venter upon a new dividend. **1726** *Adv. Capt. R. Boyle* 292 So we resolv'd to steer for Zant..and there make Dividend of our Prize Money and Goods.

5. *attrib.* and *Comb.* **dividend-stripping** (see quot. 1959); hence ***dividend-stripper***; **dividend warrant**, the documentary order or authority on which a shareholder receives his dividend.

1716 *Lond. Gaz.* No. 5479/4 Lost..a Dividend Warrant on the South Sea Company. **1860** *All Year Round* No. 54. 88 He might be seen at the Bank of England about Dividend times. **1884** *Harper's Mag.* May 897/2 The dividend warrants are sent..by post. **1958** *Times* 22 Apr. 10/3 Nothing in the Budget created more concern among many Conservative backbenchers than the retrospective effect of the proposal by the Chancellor of the Exchequer to make the tax evading practice of 'dividend stripping' illegal—with effect from October, 1955. **1958** *Punch* 25 June 839/2 What Odhams and the *Daily Herald* had done was not indeed exactly the same as what the dividend-strippers had done, and Mr Houghton may have been right in saying that the object of that exercise was not to avoid taxation. **1959** *Times* 8 Apr. 17/2 Dividend-stripping (which is essentially a finance company operation for offsetting a dealing loss against tax reclaimed from dividends accumulated by the company which is the subject of the deal) was stopped some time ago.

'dividendless, *a.* [See -LESS.] Without dividends.

1899 *Westm. Gaz.* 26 Jan. 8/1 If the Hyderabad-Deccan Company were in its infancy instead of having laboured on through thirteen years of a dividendless career. *Ibid.* 2 Mar. 8/1 The dividendless stock of the District Railway. **1920** *Glasgow Herald* 4 Sept. 10 It may be noted that shareholders again go dividendless. **1938** *Times* 18 Aug. 16/2 Not only they but also the Preference stockholders..go dividendless.

†**'divident**, *a.* and *sb.* Also 7 **-ant**. [ad. L. *divident-em*, pr. pple. of *dīvidĕre* to DIVIDE.]

A. *adj.* **1.** Dividing; distributive.

1660 BURNEY *Κερδ. Δωρον* Ep. Ded. (1661) 4 The divident and impartial justice of our Sovereign Lord.

2. Divided, separate. (In Shaks. *di'vidant.*)

1607 SHAKS. *Timon* IV. iii. 5 Twin'd brothers of one Wombe, Whose procreation..and birth Scarse is diuidant.

B. *sb.* One who or that which divides; something that separates or forms the boundary between two regions, etc.; in *Arith.* = DIVISOR.

c **1450** *Chester Pl.* ii. 19 Now will I make the fyrmament.. for to be a divident to twyne the waters aye. **1513** BRADSHAW *St. Werburge* I. 249 This Offa..made a depe dytche for a sure dyuydent Bytwene Englande and Wales. **1571** DIGGES *Pantom.* I. xviii. E iv b, Multiply the third distance by the second, and the product diuide by your diuident or diuisor. **1656** J. HARRINGTON *Oceana* (1700) 47 'Divide', says one [girl] to the other, 'and I will chuse'..The divident, dividing unequally, loses, in regard that the other takes the better half; wherefore she divides equally.

divident, -e, frequent early f. DIVIDEND, q.v.

divider (dɪˈvaɪdə(r)). [f. DIVIDE *v.* + -ER[1].] One who or that which divides, in various senses.

1. One who or that which separates a whole into parts or portions.

1591 PERCIVALL *Sp. Dict.*, *Ochavero*, a deuider into eight parts. **1644** DIGBY *Nat. Bodies* I. ix. 78. **1674** JOSSELYN *Voy. New Eng.* 54 The Sun and Moon..the dividers of time into dayes and years. **1774** *Hist.* in *Ann. Reg.* 2/2 The dividers of Poland. **1862** F. HALL *Hindu Philos. Syst.* 239 Two several dividers of intelligence.

2. One who distributes, a distributor; one who shares something with another.

1526-34 TINDALE *Luke* xii. 14 Who made me a iudge or a devider over you? **1587** GOLDING *De Mornay* i. 3 There is a devider or distributer of these things. **1802** *Noble Wanderers* II. 88 Roused from the stupor of her affliction by this little divider of her cares.

†**3.** One who makes philosophical distinctions (cf. DIVIDE *v.* 4 b); one who classifies. *Obs.*

1588 FRAUNCE *Lawiers Log.* I. xiii. 57 Plato..compareth inartificial dividers to bungling cookes, who in stead of artificiall carving, use rudely to breake and dismember things. **1610** HEALEY *St. Aug. Citie of God* VI. ii. (1620) 227 Who was euer a more curious inquisitor of these things..a more elegant diuider, or a more exact recorder?

4. One who or that which disunites, separates, or parts; a causer of dissension or discord.

1643 MILTON *Divorce* II. xxi, Hate is of all things the mightiest divider. **1724** SWIFT *Drapier's Lett.* iv, Money, the great divider of the world, hath..been the great uniter of a most divided people. **1870** H. MACMILLAN *Bible Teach.* xv. 295. **1871** PALGRAVE *Lyr. Poems* 56 They swear that death the divider Shall only unite them more.

†**5.** *Arith.* = DIVISOR. *Obs. rare.*

1797 *Monthly Mag.* 130 By my method of dividers, other numbers might have been assumed for the value of *y*.

6. *pl.* **a.** Dividing compasses; a kind of compasses worked by means of a screw fastened to one leg and passing through the other; used for measuring or setting off very small intervals. **b.** A simple pair of compasses with steel points.

1703 MOXON *Mech. Exerc.* 316 You may in small Quadrants divide truer and with less trouble with Steel Dividers, (which open or close with a Screw for that purpose,) then you can with Compasses. **1875** BEDFORD *Sailor's Pocket-bk.* v. (ed. 2) 195 Chart, scale, and dividers. **1879** *Cassell's Techn. Educ.* I. 12 Compasses which have both points of steel are called 'dividers'. **1881** *Metal World* No. 14. 218 A pair of 4½ in. or 5 in. plain dividers, or what are called hair dividers.

7. *Farming.* (See quot.)

1874 KNIGHT *Dict. Mech.*, *Divider* (Husbandry), the prow or wedge-formed piece on a reaping-machine, which divides the grain to be cut from the standing grain.

8. *Mining. pl.* Timbers or scantling put across a shaft to divide it into compartments: also called *buntons.* (Raymond *Mining Gloss.*)

9. A partition or screen; *spec.* a piece of furniture or the like dividing a room into two parts; freq. ***room-divider***.

1959 D. BARTON *Loving Cup* 95 Alastair slid back a panel in a walnut room divider and brought out brandy and glasses. *Ibid.* 96 Climbing plants trailing up the room divider. **1960** *House & Garden* May 59 Divider (with glass shelves), £30. **1967** E. SHORT *Embroidery & Fabric Collage* iii. 80 A feature of modern open-plan living-rooms is often the room divider, screening the dining area or study from the main sitting room. **1970** *Harper's Bazaar* Oct. 17/2 The restaurant is spacious with raffia'd dividers between the tables.

dividing (dɪˈvaɪdɪŋ), *vbl. sb.* [f. DIVIDE *v.* + -ING[1].] The action of the verb DIVIDE; division.

1526-34 TINDALE *Heb.* iv. 12 Euen vnto the diuidynge a sonder of the soule and the sprete. **1663** GERBIER *Counsel* C ij a, Their Jurisdiction extends as far as the deviding of the Seas neere Rochel. **1719** DE FOE *Crusoe* (1840) II. vi. 124 That there might be no dispute about dividing. **1882** *Garden* 4 Feb. 86/3 Alocasias..bear dividing freely.

di'viding, *ppl. a.* [f. as prec. + -ING[2].] That divides, in various senses; that cleaves into parts; †'running divisions' in singing (quot. 1639; see DIVISION 7); that separates regions, parts, etc.

Now often written with hyphen in certain phrases or combinations, as *dividing-line*, *-point*, where it may be taken as the *vbl. sb.* used *attrib.* *dividing-engine*, a machine for graduating or dividing a circle into a number of equal parts, or for cutting the circumference of a wheel into a number of teeth. *dividing ridge* = DIVIDE *sb.* 2.

1620 QUARLES *Jonah* (1638) 34 Horrid claps of heavens-dividing thunder. *a* **1639** CAREW *Poems* Wks. (1824) 129 In your sweet dividing throat, She [the nightingale] winters and keepes warme her note. **1807** P. GASS *Jrnl.* 237 We came to the dividing ridge between the waters of the Missouri and Columbia. **1838** *Penny Cycl.* XI. 338/1 The invention by Ramsden of his dividing engine. *Ibid.* 338/2 The dividing tool employed by Graham was the beam-compass. **1866** J. MARTINEAU *Ess.* I. 251 The true dividing-line. **1874** KNIGHT *Dict. Mech.* s.v., Ramsden's circular dividing-engine consisted of a large wheel moved by a tangent screw. **1884** F. J. BRITTEN *Watch & Clockm.* 88 [A] Dividing plate ..[is] the circular brass plate in a wheel-cutting engine, in which holes are drilled as a register for the proper division of the wheel teeth.

Hence **di'vidingly** *adv.*, so as to divide.

1580 HOLLYBAND *Treas. Fr. Tong*, *Divisément*, diuidingly, separately. **1847** in CRAIG.

‖**Divi-divi** (ˈdɪvɪdɪvɪ). [The native Galibi or Carib name.] The commercial name of the curled pods of *Cæsalpinia coriaria*, a tree found in tropical America and the West Indies; they were introduced to Europe from Caracas in 1768, and are highly astringent, and much used in tanning. Also the tree itself. **b.** The similar pods of *C. tinctoria* used in Lima for making ink (*Cent. Dict.*).

[**1763** JACQUIN *Stirp. Amer. Hist.* 124 Legumina..ab Hispanis et barbaris..nuncupata *Libi dibi.* **1832** G. DON *Dichlamydeous Pl.* II. 432 *Libidibi* is the name of the legume at Curaçao.] **1843** *Pharmaceut. Jrnl.* II. 600 Divi-divi, imported from Carthage, is the pod of a leguminous shrub. **1853** LINDLEY *Veg. Kingd.* 550 In the Dividivi or Libidibi pods..we have one of the most astringent of known substances.

dividual (dɪˈvɪdjuːəl), *a.* (*sb.*) [f. L. *dīvidu-us* divisible, separated + -AL[1].]

1. That is or may be divided or separated from something else; separate, distinct, particular.

1598 FLORIO, *Diuisible*, separable, diuiduall. **1612** *Two Noble K.* I. iii, The true love 'tweene mayde and mayde may be More then in sex dividual [*printed* individuall]. **1667** MILTON *P.L.* XII. 85 True Liberty..which always with right reason dwells Twinn'd, and from her hath no dividual Being. **1740** WARBURTON *Div. Legat.* VI. vi, The two.. scarce dividual. **1836** *Blackw. Mag.* XL. 536 A union of the mind's dividual acts. **1856** T. AIRD *Poet. Wks.* 147 The Seasons..Come and go with sweet dividual change.

2. Capable of being divided into parts, divisible; divided into parts, fragmentary.

a **1619** FOTHERBY *Atheom.* I. vii. §1 (1622) 50 Some make their god of Atomes, and indiuidual moates; some of diuidual numbers; as Epicurus, and Pythagoras. **1635** BARRIFFE *Mil. Discip.* iv. (1643) 13 Where any one would shew much variety of exercise, then 8..will be the more pliant and dividuall number [of soldiers.]. *a* **1650** MAY *Satir. Puppy* (1657) 10. **18..** LOWELL *Ambrose* Poet. Wks. (1879) 772 'Believest thou then'..Cried he, 'a dividual essence in Truth?'

3. Divided or distributed among a number; shared, participated, held in common.

1667 MILTON *P.L.* VII. 382 The moon..her reign With thousand lesser Lights dividual holds. **1735** H. BROOK *Univ. Beauty* IV. 132 While thro' the pores nutritive portions tend, Their equal aliment dividual share. **1818** COLEBROOKE *Obligat. & Contracts* I. 141 The rule holds when the obligation is dividual.

†**B.** *sb. Obs.* **1.** That which is dividual; something divided or capable of being divided.

1668 H. MORE *Div. Dial.* Schol. (1713) 553 This is that of Gregory Nazianzen, ἀμέριστος ἐν μεμεριομένοις ἡ θεότης, The Individual Divinity in Dividuals.

2. *Math.* In the process of division: One of the several parts of the dividend, each of which yields successively one figure or term of the quotient.

1704 J. HARRIS *Lex. Techn.* **1706** PHILLIPS (ed. Kersey), *Dividuale* (in *Arithm.*) is a Number in the Rule of Division, comprehending part of the Dividend distinguished by a Point; whereof the Question must be ask'd, How often the Divisor is contain'd in it? **1811** *Self Instructor* 62 A new dividend, or dividual, to work upon.

Hence **di'vidualism, dividu'ality** (used as the opposites of *individualism, individuality*).

1803 SYD. SMITH *Wks.* (1869) 23 The chances..do not depend solely upon their dividuality. **1883** F. GALTON *Hum. Faculty* 169 Individualism is changed to dividualism. *Ibid.* 207 Dividuality replaces individuality.

di'vidually, *adv.* [f. prec. + -LY[2].] In a dividual manner; separately.

1633 EARL MANCH. *Al Mondo* (1636) 6 Meditation is..as hee that smells the Violet, the Rose, the Jessamie, and the Orenge flowers dividually..But Contemplation is a water compounded of them all. **1805** WORDSW. *Prelude* XIV. 209 They are each in each, and cannot stand Dividually. **1821** COLERIDGE in *Blackw. Mag.* X. 247 We are compelled to express it dividually, as consisting of two correlative terms.

dividuity (dɪvɪˈdjuːɪtɪ). *rare.* [ad. rare L. *dīviduitātem*, n. of quality f. *dīviduus*: see next and -ITY.] Dividuous quality or state.

1656 BLOUNT *Glossogr.*, *Dividuity*, a division, also an aptness to divide. *a* **1834** COLERIDGE *Lit. Rem.* (1838) III. 108 This mysterious dividuity of the good and the evil will.

dividuous (dɪˈvɪdjuːəs), *a. rare.* [f. L. *dīvidu-us* (see DIVIDUAL) + -OUS.]

1. Capable of being divided, divisible (= DIVIDUAL 2); characterized by division.

1766 G. CANNING *Anti-Lucretius* v. 397 The Mind, of separate parcels uncompos'd, Though in dividuous Body now inclos'd. *c* **1800** COLERIDGE *Mahomet*, The ruinous river Shatters its waters abreast, and..Rushes dividuous. **1820** SHELLEY *Ode to Liberty* iv, The..cloud-like mountains, and dividuous waves Of Greece.

2. Separable, non-essential (= DIVIDUAL 1).

1816 COLERIDGE *Lay Serm.* 343 The accidental and dividuous in this quiet and harmonious object is subjected to the life and light of nature which shines in it.

†**'divify**, *v. Obs. rare.* [f. L. *dīvus* godlike (see DIVINE *a.*) + -FY.] *trans.* To raise to the rank of a divinity, invest with divine dignity, DEIFY. So †**divifi'cation**, *Obs.*

1615 JACKSON *Creed* IV. II. iv. §7 The divifications ascribed unto them, as their enrolments in the catalogue of former saints, adoration of relics, and the like. **1652** SPARKE *Prim. Devot.* (1663) 4 [They] divifie such as never were holy men.

di'vinable, *a. rare.* [f. DIVINE *v.* + -ABLE.] Capable of being divined or conjectured.

1816 J. SCOTT *Vis. Paris* (ed. 5) 5 Travelling for no definite, nor even divinable purpose.

†**'divinail.** *Obs.* Also 4-5 **de-, dy-, -al(e, -aile, -aille, -ayle, deuenayle.** [a. OF. *de-, divinail, -al* masc., and *devinaille, -nalle, -gnaille* fem. (Godef.) a thing divined, a conjecture, prediction, DIVINATION, repr. L. types **dīvīnāle* sing., **dīvīnālia* pl., of *dīvīnālis*: see next and -AL[1] 4, 5.]

1. Divining, soothsaying, divination.

c **1386** CHAUCER *Pars. T.* ¶531 Hem þat bilieuen in diuynailes [*v. rr.* dyuynayles, -ales, -alis, divynailles, deuenayles] as by flight or by noyse of briddes or of beestes. *c* **1430** LYDG. *Bochas* II. xiii. (1554) 51 b, Her clerkes in theyr diuinayle Tolde it was token of seruage and trauayle. **1484** CAXTON *Chivalry* 87 The deuynaylles of them that by the flyght of byrdes deuynen.

2. Something to be divined, a riddle.

c **1430** LYDG. *Bochas* I. ix. (1544) 18 a, The serpent him.. would assaile With a problem..Called of some men an uncouthe deuinaile. *c* **1430** —— *Thebes* I. (R.), To slea all tho ..that did faile, To expoune, his misty deuinale. **1483** CAXTON *G. de la Tour* G ij b, Sayeng that they myȝt not arede a certayne deuynal.

†**'divinal**, *a. Obs.* [ad. med.L. *dīvīnāl-is*, f. *dīvīn-us* DIVINE: see -AL[1] 3.] Pertaining to divination; divinatory, magical.

1494 FABYAN *Chron.* 6 All these were Mynystris of God immortale, And had in theym no power dyuynall. **1503** HAWES *Examp. Virt.* viii. (Arb.) 38 A myrrour of lernyng that was dyuynall. **1513** DOUGLAS *Æneis* IX. i. 52 Wyth wordis augurall, Eftyr thar spaying ceremonis diuynal.

divination (dɪvɪˈneɪʃən). [a. OF. *divination* (13th c. in Hatz.-Darm.), ad. L. *dīvīnātiōn-em*, n. of action f. *dīvīnāre* to DIVINE.]

1. The action or practice of divining; the foretelling of future events or discovery of what is hidden or obscure by supernatural or magical means; soothsaying, augury, prophecy. With *a* and *pl.*, an exercise of this, a prophecy, an augury.

c **1374** CHAUCER *Boeth.* v. pr. iv. 125 (Camb. MS.) Marchus tullius, whan he deuynede the dyuynaciouns, þat is to seyn in his book þat he wroot of diuinaciouns. **1382** WYCLIF *Acts* xvi. 16 Sum wenche hauynge a spirit of dyuynacioun. **1387** TREVISA *Higden* (Rolls) III. 57 Eiþer seide þat [he] hadde þe better dyuynacioun of foules [*felicius augurium*]. **1555** EDEN *Decades* 309 To speke of thynges that shalbe, longe before they are, is a kynde of diuination.

1579–80 NORTH *Plutarch* (1895) 80 The flying of birds, which doe geue a happy divination to things to come. **1662** STILLINGFL. *Orig. Sacr.* II. iv. §1 The Gentiles hearkend unto Oracles and Divinations. **1712** ADDISON *Spect.* No. 505 ¶5 Among the many pretended arts of divination, there is none which so universally amuses as that by dreams. **1879** D. M. WALLACE *Australas.* v. 103 Divination is made by examination of the state of the body internally.

attrib. **1877** W. JONES *Finger-ring* 100 The annexed illustrations, representing divination rings, are taken from Liceti.

2. In a weaker sense: Prevision or guessing by happy instinct or unusual insight; successful conjecture or guessing.

1597 SHAKS. *2 Hen. IV*, I. i. 88 Tell thou thy Earle, his Diuination lies. **1614** RALEIGH *Hist. World* III. vii. §5 Whether he or they would have bin contented with an equall share..were perhaps a divination unnecessary. **1685** KEN *Serm.* Dan. x. 11 Wks. (1838) 169 It was such divination, such sagacity as this which interpreted to him [Daniel] all the dreams of human life. **1856** EMERSON *Eng. Traits, Lit.* Wks. (Bohn) II. 113 Richard Owen..adding sometimes the divination of the old masters to the unbroken power of labour in the English mind.

3. *Rom. Law.* (See quot. 1868.)

1823 in CRABB *Technol. Dict.* **1868** SMITH *Dict. Gr. & Rom. Antiq.* s.v. *Divinatio*, If in any case two or more accusers came forward against one and the same individual, it was, as the phrase ran, decided by divination, who should be the chief..accuser..The judices had, as it were, to divine the course which they had to take.

¶ *catachr.* Divine condition or state, divinity.

1603 HOLLAND *Plutarch's Mor.* 1327 Of Dæmons some few..came to participate the divination of the gods.

'divinator. *Obs.* or *arch.* Also 7 -our. [ad. L. *dīvīnātor*, *-ōrem* soothsayer, agent-n. from *dīvīnāre* to DIVINE: cf. F. *divinateur*.] One who divines; a diviner, soothsayer.

1607 TOPSELL *Serpents* (1658) 688 The Egyptians hold opinion that the Crocodile is a divinator. *a* **1610** HEALEY *Epictetus' Man.* xxxix. (1636) 60 When thou goest unto a divinatour. **1621** BURTON *Anat. Mel.* III. iv. I. i. (1652) 638 Of this number are all Superstitious Idolaters..Divinators, Prophets, Sectaries and Scismatiques. **1884** *Science* 19 Dec. 559/2 In the leading paper of Cambridge, Mass...a professed divinator has kept for years a large, businesslike, and soberly worded advertisement of his services.

divina'torial, *a. rare.* [f. as next + -AL[1].] Conjectural.

1860 M. PATTISON *Ess.* (1889) I. 167 Divinatorial criticism has often undertaken to work wonders by conjecture operating upon collation of MSS.

divinatory (dɪˈvɪnətərɪ), *a.* [f. L. type **dīvīnātōri-us*, f. *dīvīnātōr-em*: see DIVINATOR and -ORY.] Pertaining to a diviner or to divination; prophetic, divining. **b.** Conjectural.

1569 J. SANFORD tr. *Agrippa's Van. Artes* 44 b, An other kinde of Astrologie..called Diuinatorie, or Judiciall. **1616** GATAKER *Lots* (1619) 269 These are those that are most commonly tearmed Diuinatorie Lots. **1664** EVELYN *Sylva* 35 The use of the Hasel is..for..Divinatory Rods for the detecting and finding out of Minerals. **1828** MISS BERRY *Soc. Life Eng. & Fr.* (1831) 395 A peasant of Burgundy.. appeared with the exploded notion of the divinatory wand to discover hidden sources of water. **1838** SIR W. HAMILTON *Logic* xxxiv. (1866) II. 199 Here the conjectural or divinatory emendation comes into play.

†di'vinatrice, *a. Obs. rare.* [a. F. *divinatrice*, fem. of *divinateur*, ad. L. *dīvīnātrīcem*, fem. of *dīvīnātor*: see above.] That divines, divining.

a **1535** MORE *Ruful Lamentacion* (R.) Lo where to commeth thy blandishyng promyse, Of false astrology and diuinatrice.

divine (dɪˈvaɪn), *a.* and *sb.*[1] Forms: 4–6 devin(e, de-, dyvyn(e, 5–6 divyne, *Sc.* de-, dywyne, 6 dyvine, 7 divin, 4- divine. [ME. *devine*, *divine*, a. OF. *devin* (12th c. in Hatz.-Darm.), later *divin*:—L. *dīvīnus* pertaining to a deity. In med.L. *dīvīnus* bore the sense of *theologus*. OF. *devin* was the word of popular formation; *divin* was a learned assimilation to the ancient L. type, which in F. became the accepted form for the adj., and in English for all senses: cf. DIVINE *sb.*[2]]

A. *adj.*

1. Of or pertaining to God or a god.

c **1374** CHAUCER *Boeth.* v. pr. ii. 118 (Camb. MS.) The speculacion or lookynge of the deuyne thoght. **1388** WYCLIF *Deut.* i. 13 ȝyue ȝe of ȝou men wise in dyuyn thingis. **1526** *Pilgr. Perf.* (W. de W. 1531) 3 b, The diuyne nature or godhed. **1590** SPENSER *F.Q.* I. x. 67 So darke are earthly things compar'd to things divine. **1644** MILTON *Areop.* (Arb.) 51 Many..complain of divin Providence for suffering Adam to transgresse. **1709** POPE *Ess. Crit.* 525 To err is human, to forgive divine. **1878** R. W. DALE *Lect. Preach.* 290 Divine acts are not less Divine because they do not happen to be recorded in the Canonical Scriptures.

2. Given by or proceeding from God; having the sanction of or inspired by God.

divine right, a right conferred by or based on the ordinance or appointment of God. ***divine right of kings***, that claimed according to the doctrine that (legitimate) kings derive their power from God alone, unlimited by any rights on the part of their subjects. In English History, the phrase came into specific use in the 17 c., when the claim was prominently made for the Stuart kings.

c **1386** CHAUCER *Monk's T.* 67 By precept of the Messager diuyn. *c* **1425** WYNTOUN *Cron.* I. i. 2 Dywyne Scrypture. *c* **1450** HENRYSON *Test. Cres.* (R.) Ye gaue me ones a diuine responsaile That I should be the floure of loue in Troye. **1567** *Satir. Poems Reform.* iii. 128 Quhome God did place be ordinance dewyne. *a* **1600** HOOKER *Eccl. Pol.* VIII. ii. §6 Unto kings by human right, honour by very divine right, is due. **1625** BURGES *Pers. Tithes* 2 Whether Tithes be perpetually due to the Ministers of the Gospell by Diuine Right. **1642** MILTON *Apol. Smect.* ii. Wks. (1847) 85 The divine right of episcopacy was then valiantly asserted. **1640** *Const. & Canons* i. B iv b, The most High and Sacred order of Kings is of Divine right, being the ordinance of God himself. **1742** POPE *Dunc.* IV. 188 The Right Divine of kings to govern wrong. **1767** BLACKSTONE *Comm.* II. iii. 25, I will not put the title of the clergy to tithes upon any divine right, though such a right certainly commenced, and I believe as certainly ceased, with the Jewish theocracy. **1835** J. WATERWORTH *Exam. Princ. Protestantism* 95 Did this unrivalled Biblist acknowledge any writings as divine, which the Jews did not receive as canonical? **1865** SEELEY *Ecce Homo* iv. (ed. 8) 31 In obedience to an irresistible divine impulse. **1871** MORLEY *Voltaire* (1886) 63 The apologies of Jesuit writers for the assassination of tyrants deserve an important place in the history of the doctrine of divine right.

3. Addressed, appropriated, or devoted to God; religious, sacred.

divine service, the public worship of God, ***divine office***, the stated office or service of daily prayer; the canonical hours.

c **1380** WYCLIF *Wks.* (1880) 41 Do clerkis deuyn officis after þe ordre of þe holy Chirche of rome. *c* **1386** CHAUCER *Prol.* 122 Fful weel she soong the seruice dyuyne. **1500–20** DUNBAR *Poems* x. 27 Do ȝour obseruance devyne To him that is of kingis king. **1549** *Bk. Com. Prayer* Pref., The common prayers in the Churche, commonlye called diuine seruice. *c* **1600** SHAKS. *Sonn.* cviii. 5 Yet, like prayers divine, I must each day say o'er the very same. **1674** PLAYFORD *Skill Mus.* I. 71 The Tunes of Psalms are of general use, all who are true Lovers of Divine Musick, will have them in estimation. **1682** STODDON (*title*) An Essay on a Question relating to Divine Worship. **1720** WATTS (*title*), Divine Songs, attempted in easy language, for the use of children. **1848** WHARTON *Law Lex., Divine Service, tenure by*, an obsolete holding, in which the tenants were obliged to do some special divine services in certain, as to sing so many masses, to distribute such a sum in alms, etc. **1880** *Dict. Chr. Antiq.* s.v. *Divine office*, Offices for the several hours of prayer, which together constitute the Divine Office, as distinguished from the liturgy. **1889** FARRAR *Lives Fathers, Ambrose*, xv. §3 II. 169 Theodosius..as a penitent.. abstained from presenting himself at divine service.

4. a. Partaking of the nature of God; characteristic of or consonant to deity; godlike; heavenly, celestial.

c **1374** CHAUCER *Boeth.* v. pr. ii. 118 (Camb. MS.) Why in the souereynes dyuynes substaunces, þat is to seyn in spiritz, Iugement is more cleere. **1393** GOWER *Conf.* II. 167 Men saiden, that she was divine, And the goddess of sapience. **1500–20** DUNBAR *Poems* xxv. 113 All the hevinly court devyne. **1594** HOOKER *Eccl. Pol.* I. viii. §6 The diuiner part in relation vnto the baser of our soules. **1632** MILTON *Penseroso* 12 Hail, divinest Melancholy! Whose saintly visage is too bright To hit the sense of human sight. **1667** —— *P.L.* III. 40 Or flocks, or herds, or human face divine. **1697** DRYDEN *Alexander's Feast* 171 At last divine Cecilia came. **1850** TENNYSON *In Mem.* Prol. iv, Thou seemest human and divine, The highest, holiest manhood, thou. **1882** FARRAR *Early Chr.* I. 97 The strains..of divinest music in which the voice of inspiration died away.

†b. Immortal; beatified. *Obs.*

1593 SHAKS. *Rich. II*, I. i. 38 For what I speake, My body shall make good vpon this earth, Or my diuine soule answer it in heauen. **1632** HEYWOOD *2nd Pt. Iron Age* IV. Wks. 1874 III. 409 Thou lyest downe mortall, who must rise diuine.

5. In weaker sense: More than human, excellent in a superhuman degree. **a.** Of persons: Of more than human or ordinary excellence; pre-eminently gifted; in the highest degree excellent.

1552 HULOET, Divine or immortall, *nectareus*. **1591** SHAKS. *1 Hen. VI*, I. vi. 4 Diuinest Creature..How shall I honour thee for this success? *a* **1635** CORBET *Poems* (1807) 18 Nothing did win more praise..Then did their actors most divine. **1680** CROWNE *Misery Civ. War* Prol., For by his feeble skill 'tis built alone, The Divine Shakespear did not lay one stone. **1711** STEELE *Spect.* No. 146 ¶3 The divine Socrates is here represented in a Figure worthy his great Wisdom and Philosophy. **1795–1814** WORDSW. *Excursion* I. 250 That mighty orb of song, The divine Milton. **1875** JOWETT *Plato* (ed. 2) I. 473 That would clearly contradict the divine Homer.

b. Of things: Of surpassing beauty, perfection, excellence, etc.; extraordinarily good or great. Freq. in trivial use.

c **1470** HENRY *Wallace* VI. 348 Thai..In cartis brocht thar purwiance dewyne. **1561** T. NORTON *Calvin's Inst.* I. xiii. §9, I graunt..that oftentimes a thing is called Diuine or of God, that is notable by any singular excellence. **1592** SHAKS. *Rom. & Jul.* III. ii. 77 Beautifull Tyrant, fiend Angelicall.. Dispised substance of Diuinest show. **1655** H. VAUGHAN *Silex Scint.* 85 Blackness sits On the divinest wits. **1757** A. COOPER *Distiller* III. xlvii. (1760) 212 Recipe for a Gallon of Divine Water. **1818** *La Belle Assemblée* XVII. 40/6, I have had the divinest cornette sent me. **1826** H. N. COLERIDGE *West Indies* 147 The champagne at eighteen dollars really divine. **1870** L. M. ALCOTT *Old-Fashioned Girl* (1874) iii. 42 Your foot is perfectly divine in that boot. **1877** KATE THOMPSON *Publ. Pict. Gall. Rembrandt*, The great master of the Dutch school..preeminent by his wonderful and Divine talents. **1960** R. DANIEL *Death by Drowning* iv. 45 I've just bought a divine swim suit.

6. Connected or dealing with divinity or sacred things; sacred. *Obs.* or *arch.*

1548 HALL *Chron., Hen. VI* (an. 9) 115 b, All auncient writers, as well devine, as prophane. **1603** OWEN *Pembrokesh.* (1891) 235 A famouse Doctour of divinitie as appeareth by his devyne works. **1605** BACON *Adv. Learn.* I. Ded. §2. 2 A rare Conjunction, as wel of divine and sacred literature, as of prophane and humaine. **1720** WATTS *Divine Songs* Pref., This may sometimes give their thoughts a divine turn, and raise a young meditation. [**1840** CARLYLE *Heroes* iii. (1872) 85, I give Dante my highest praise when I say of his Divine Comedy that it is..genuinely a Song.]

†7. Forboding, prescient. [a Latinism.] *rare.*

1667 MILTON *P.L.* IX. 845 Yet oft his heart, divine of somthing ill, Misgave him.

8. *Comb.*, as ***divine-human***, human and divine; ***divine-looking*** adj.; ***divine proportion***, literal translation of the term used by L. Pacioli for *golden section*: see GOLDEN *a.* 5 d.

1884 *Chr. World* 11 Sept. 688/2 The animal-human is very obstructive to the Divine-human. **1892** WESTCOTT *Gospel of Life* 254 [Christianity] is summed up in the facts of a divine-human life. **1893** *Tablet* 9 Dec. 933 The Divine-human Mediator in heaven. **1937** F. SCOTT FITZGERALD *Let.* 8 Oct. (1964) 18 I'm glad Stanley is divine-looking; sorry Andrew is repulsive. [**1509** L. PACIOLI (*title*) De divina proportione.] **1920** R. C. ARCHIBALD in J. Hambidge *Dynamic Symmetry* 152 'Divine proportion' was used by Fra Luca Pacioli in 1509 and possibly earlier by Pier della Francesca. **1951** [see GOLDEN *a.* 5 d]. **1974** *Encycl. Brit. Macropædia* XIII. 874/2 The Neo-Impressionists Georges Seurat..and Paul Signac based the linear pattern of many of their compositions upon the principle of this 'divine proportion'.

†B. *sb.*[1] *Obs.* [absolute uses of the adj., or its F. original.]

1. Divine service.

1480 *Will of Vavesour* (Comm. Crt. Lond.), To sing Devyne for my sowle. **1606** *Sc. Acts Jas. VI* (1814) 327 (Jam.) Twa clerkis to serue in the divines within the College kirk of Creichtoun.

2. Divinity, theology.

1303 R. BRUNNE *Handl. Synne* 2890 Seynt austyn þat was a clerk of dyuyne. *Ibid.* 11411 A master of dyuyne. **1362** LANGL. *P. Pl.* A. Prol. 90 Bisschops Bolde and Bachilers of diuyn. *c* **1400** *Rom. Rose* 6490, I wole fillen..My paunche of good mete and wyne, As shulde a maister of dyvyne.

3. Soothsaying; conjecture; DIVINATION.

c **1330** R. BRUNNE *Chron.* (1810) 282 Merlyn, in his deuyn, of him has said, þat þre regions, in his bandons, salle be laid. —— *Chron. Wace* (Rolls) 8092 On þis manere myghte Merlyn Be geten & born, by oure deuyn.

4. Divine nature, divinity.

1393 GOWER *Conf.* II. 132 Bachus..Accordant unto his divine A prest..He had.

divine (dɪˈvaɪn), *sb.*[2] Also 4–5 devine, -vyne, dy-. [a. OF. *devin* soothsayer (13th c. in Littré), also later *devin*, *divin* theologian (15th c. in Godef.); the former the popular descendant of L. *dīvīn-us* soothsayer (become **devin-us* in late L.); the latter repr. med.L. *dīvīnus* doctor of divinity, theologian; both subst. uses of L. *dīvīnus* adj. In both senses confirmed in Eng. to the L. spelling.]

†1. A diviner, soothsayer, augur; a prophet, seer.

13.. *E.E. Allit. P.* B. 1302 Dere Daniel also, þat watz deuine noble. **1340** *Ayenb.* 19 þe deuines and þe wichen and þe charmeresses þet workeþ be þe dyeules crefte. *c* **1374** CHAUCER *Troylus* I. 66 A gret Deuyn þat cleped was Calkas ..Knew wel þat Troye sholde destroyed be By answere of his god. *c* **1430** LYDG. *Bochas* II. i. (1554) 42 b, Saul had cast out all diuines From Israell, and eche diuineresse. **1525** LD. BERNERS *Froiss.* II. ccxx [ccxvi]. 680 *note*, Of these deuins, arioles, and charmers, there were certayne brente at Parys. **1577–87** HOLINSHED *Chron.* I. 2/2 To deriue the name of their diuines called Magi from him [Magus].

2. One who has officially to do with 'divine things'; formerly, any ecclesiastic, clergyman, or priest; now, one skilled in divinity; a theologian.

c **1380** WYCLIF *Serm.* Sel. Wks. I. 376 Bastard dyvynes seien..þat þes wordis of Crist ben fals. **1388** —— *Bible* Prol. xiii. 51 Dyuynys that schulden passe othere men in clennesse and hoolynesse. *c* **1450** *St. Cuthbert* (Surtees) 7503 He was a clerke and gude deuyne. **1596** SHAKS. *Merch. V.* I. ii. 16 It is a good Diuine that followes his owne instructions. **1662** GAUDEN (*title*) The works of Mr. Richard Hooker, that learned godly judicious and eloquent Divine. **1791** BOSWELL *Johnson* 30 Aug. an. 1780, He wrote a young clergyman..the following..letter, which contains valuable advice to Divines in general. **1847** EMERSON *Poems, Problem* Wks. (Bohn) I. 401 Taylor, the Shakespeare of divines. **1874** L. STEPHEN *Hours in Library* (1892) I. ix. 305 We see in him the gentle mystic rather than the stern divine.

†b. Applied to non-Christian writers on theology, and to the priests of heathen religions. *Obs.*

1387 TREVISA *Higden* (Rolls) III. 219 (Mätz.) Among alle manere of philosofres þey þat were icleped deuynes [*qui theologi vocabantur*] bere þe prys. **1587** GOLDING *De Mornay* x. 144 Pythagoras and all the old Diuines affirme, that God or the onely One is the beginner of all things. **1611** SHAKS. *Wint. T.* III. i. 19 The Oracle (Thus by Apollo's great Diuine seal'd vp).

divine (dɪˈvaɪn), *v.* Also 4–5 devine, -vyne, dyvyne, -yne. [a. F. *devine-r* (12th c.) to recount, signify, wish, prophesy, ad. L. *dīvīnāre* to foretell, predict, after *devin* divine: see prec.]

I. Transitive senses.

†1. To make out or interpret by supernatural or magical insight (what is hidden, obscure, or unintelligible to ordinary faculties); hence, in later use, to interpret, explain, disclose, make known. *Obs.*

13.. *E.E. Allit. P.* B. 1561 þat con dele wyth demerlayk, & deuine lettres. **1362** LANGL. *P. Pl.* A. VIII. 138 Daniel deuynede þe Dremels of a Kyng. **1393** *Ibid.* C. I. 217 What this metals by-meneþ Diuine ȝe. *Ibid.* XXII. 240 He tauhte.. somme to dyuyne and dyuyde, numbres to kenne. *a* **1400–50**

Alexander 1905 Now þou..graithis me trouage, With all þis dignites be-dene þat I diuined haue. *c* **1500** *Blowbol's Test.* in Halliw. *Nugæ Poet.* 5 The cause why I shall to you devyne. *a* **1625** FLETCHER *Nice Valour* II. i, I can..Divine my mind to you.

b. To discover or indicate by means of the divining rod. *nonce-use.*

1890 *Pall Mall G.* 9 June 6/3 The boy has now been engaged to go to Australia to 'divine' the underground water and minerals of its arid and auriferous regions.

2. To make out by sagacity, intuition, or fortunate conjecture (that is, in some other way than by actual information); to conjecture, guess.

c **1374** CHAUCER *Troylus* v. 288 He koude wel dyuyne That Troilus al nyght for sorwe wook. *c* **1386** —— *Shipman's T.* 224 Wyf..litel kanstow deuyne The curious bisynesse that we haue. *c* **1450** *St. Cuthbert* (Surtees) 6706 How it strekys kan I noȝt deuyne. **1530** PALSGR. 514/2 He were a wyse man that coulde devyne what they talke of nowe. **1696** tr. *Du Mont's Voy. Levant* 44 Nor cou'd I divine the Meaning of it. **1786** T. JEFFERSON *Writ.* (1859) II. 37 He could not divine the cause of this extraordinary change. **1847** EMERSON *Repr. Men, Swedenborg* Wks. (Bohn) I. 312 In common parlance, what one man is said to learn by experience, a man of extraordinary sagacity is said, without experience, to divine. **1863** MRS. OLIPHANT *Salem Ch.* ii. 28 He began to divine faintly..that external circumstances do stand for something.

3. To have supernatural or magical insight into (things to come); to have presentiment of; hence *gen.* to predict or prophesy by some kind of special inspiration or intuition.

c **1374** CHAUCER *Troylus* IV. 361 (389) But who may al eschewe or al deuyne? *c* **1400** MAUNDEV. (Roxb.) viii. 29 Oþer thinges þai pronostic and diuines by þe colours of þa flawmes. **1555** EDEN *Decades* 47 They diuined the destruction of theyr country. **1594** SHAKS. *Rich. III*, III. ii. 18 To shun the danger that his Soule diuines. **1663** BUTLER *Hud.* I. ii. 833 None..could divine To which side Conquest would incline. **1790** BURKE *Fr. Rev.* Wks. V. 374 Truly it is not easy to divine what that army may become at last. **1855** BAIN *Senses & Int.* III. ii. §23 To infer beforehand, or divine, the characters that we should find.

†**4.** Of things: To point out, foreshow, prognosticate, portend. *Obs.*

1596 DRAYTON *Leg.* IV. 69 This prodigious sign..some strange Newes though ever it divine, yet forth them not immediately it brings. **1657** COKAINE *Obstinate Lady* I. ii, What envious star when I was born divin'd This adverse Fate? **1712** SWIFT *Sid Hamet* 22 A certain magick rod..divines Whene'er the soil has golden mines. **1847** EMERSON *Poems, Initial Love* Wks. (Bohn) I. 457 All things wait for and divine him.

†**5.** To think or conceive of, devise, contrive, by special inspiration or extraordinary sagacity. *Obs.*

1393 LANGL. *P. Pl.* C. XII. 265 Dauid þe doughty..deuynede how Vrye Mighte slilokeste be slayn. *c* **1450** HENRYSON *Mor. Fab.* 11 All courses that Cookes could deuyne. **1500–20** DUNBAR *Poems* lxxxiv. 15 The lustiast ladie that nature can devyne. **1598** YONG *Diana* 225 So much force had one God..ouer each others soule, diuining the great and inuiolable friendship that should be betweene him and me.

†**6.** To render divine; to canonize; to divinize.

1591 SPENSER *Daphn.* 214 Living on earth like Angell new divinde. **1591** —— *Ruines of Time* 611 Th' Harpe..out of the River was reard And borne above the cloudes to be divin'd. **1622** DRAYTON *Poly-olb.* xxiv. 191 Leaving these divin'd, to Decuman we come..who was crown'd with glorious martyrdom.

†**b.** To call or style divine. *Obs.*

1621 BP. MOUNTAGU *Diatribæ* II. 353 Your nobling and diuining him elswhere.

II. Intransitive senses.

7. To use or practise divination; to obtain insight into what is future or unrevealed by auguries, portents, magical or occult devices; to soothsay.

c **1374** CHAUCER *Troylus* II. 1696 (1745) The folk deuyne at waggynge of a stre. **1382** WYCLIF *Gen.* xliv. 5 The coppe..in the which my Lord is wonte to dyuyne. **1388** —— *Isa.* xliv. 25 Dyuynours that dyuynen by sacrifices offrid to feendis. **1398** TREVISA *Barth. De P.R.* XV. lii. (1495) 507 Some in Ethiopia..haue an hounde for theyr kynge, and dyuyne by his meuynge. **1609** BIBLE (Douay) *Lev.* xix. 26 You shal not divine, nor observe dreames. **1698** FRYER *Acc. E. India & P.* 372 They go to some learned Doctor, who Divines by the Alcoran. **1726** DE FOE *Hist. Devil* II. vi. **1835–49** LANE *Mod. Egypt.* II. 111 They [Gypsies] mostly divine by means of a number of shells, with a few pieces of coloured glass, money, etc., intermixed with them.

8. To foretell by divine or superhuman power; to prophesy. *arch.*

1362 LANGL. *P. Pl.* A. VIII. 143 As Daniel diuinede hit fel in dede after. **1606** SHAKS. *Ant. & Cl.* II. vi. 123 If I were bound to Diuine of this vnity, I wold not Prophesie so. **1860** EMERSON *Cond. Life* i. (1861) 19 We are as lawgivers; we speak for Nature; we prophesy and divine. **1887** BOWEN *Virg. Æneid* II. 246 Cassandra of coming evil divined.

9. To conjecture (as to the unknown or obscure); to make an inference by conjecture, insight, intuition, or other means than actual information.

1362 LANGL. *P. Pl.* A. XI. 138 þe deppore I diuinede þe derkore me þouȝte. *c* **1386** CHAUCER *Wife's Prol.* 26 Men may deuyne and glosen vp and doun. **1604** SHAKS. *Oth.* I. ii. 39 Something from Cyprus, as I may diuine. **1851** CARLYLE *Sterling* II. ii. (1872) 100 The meanest have a dignity..and hence, as I divine, the startling whirl of incongruous juxtaposition.

†**b.** with *of, on, upon*: To make conjectures about or concerning; to augur from. *Obs.*

c **1374** CHAUCER *Troylus* III. 409 (458) Lest ony wyght dyuynen or deuyse Wolde of hem two. *c* **1386** —— *Knt.'s T.* 1657 The paleys ful of peples..Dyvynynge of thise Thebane knyghtes two. **1513** MORE in Grafton *Chron.* (1568) II. 766 The people diverslye devinyng upon this dealing. *a* **1592** GREENE *Jas. IV*, v. v, Whereon divine you, Sir? **1603** KNOLLES *Hist. Turks* (1621) 857 Thereof would diversely divine every man according to his own fantasie. **1653** HOLCROFT *Procopius* I. 29 The Romans divining upon it, were confident of the Emperours prevailing in this Warr. **1725** POPE *Odyss.* I. 144 At chess they vie, to captivate the queen; Divining of their loves.

Hence **di'vined** *ppl. a.* (in quot., Made divine).

1624 QUARLES *Sion's Sonn.* in Farr *S.P. Jas. I* (1848) 140 The glory of thy divined place No age can injure, nor yet time deface.

† **di'vinely**, *a.* [f. prec. adj. + -LY[1].] Divine.

c **1400** *Test. Love* III. (R.) Philosophy is knowing of deuinely and manly things ioyned with study of good liuing. **1530** RASTELL *Bk. Purgat.* II. xi, The infinyte dyvynely Substaunce.

divinely (dɪ'vaɪnlɪ), *adv.* [f. DIVINE *a.* + -LY[2].] In a divine manner or way.

1. By or as by the agency or power of God.

1594 SPENSER *Amoretti* lxi, As she is, divinely wrought, And of the brood of Angels hevenly borne. **1662** STILLINGFL. *Orig. Sacr.* II. vi. §2 Whatever comes under Divine knowledge, may be Divinely revealed. *a* **1707** BEVERIDGE *Serm.* I. xviii. (R.) In his divinely-inspired judgment. **1850** TENNYSON *In Mem.* lxiv. 2 As some divinely gifted man. **1876** J. PARKER *Paracl.* I. iii. 23 If the Bible is divinely inspired, it follows that it is divinely authoritative.

2. As or like God; in a godlike manner; with an excellence or perfection more than human. Also in trivial use: excellently, extremely well.

1582 HESTER *Secr. Phiorav.* III. iv. 9 Because this composition worketh diuinely, I called it Angelico. **1585** T. WASHINGTON tr. *Nicholay's Voy.* IV. xxiii. 139 Cleere and fayre fountaines dyvinely wrought. **1667** MILTON *P.L.* IX. 489 Shee fair, divinely fair, fit love for Gods. **1728** YOUNG *Odes to King* Wks. 1757 I. 173 Its stream divinely clear, and strong. **1822** W. IRVING *Braceb. Hall* 35 An elegant young man..who danced a minuet divinely. **1832** TENNYSON *Dream Fair Wom.* 87 A daughter of the Gods, divinely tall And most divinely fair. **1927** L. MAYER *Just between us Girls* vii. 43 Honestly those nobilities *can* make love divinely. **1928** E. WAUGH *Decline & Fall* I. ix. 98 He plays just too divinely. **1929** E. BOWEN *Last Sept.* xvii. 227 You do dance divinely. **1930** H. WOLFE *Uncelestial City* III. 124 My dears, too grim, too psycho-analytically ungodly, and altogether too divinely Jim.

†**3.** In a holy or pious manner. *Obs.*

1594 SHAKS. *Rich. III*, III. vii. 62 He is..with two right reuerend Fathers Diuinely bent to Meditation. **1595** —— *John* II. i. 237 This right hand, whose protection Is most diuinely vow'd vpon the right Of him it holds. **1682** NORRIS *Hierocles* 8 They proceed from a divinely disposed mind.

†**4.** After the manner of divinity. *Obs.*

1607 TOPSELL *Serpents* (1658) 591, I purpose not to follow these things Philosophically..but rather Divinely.

† **di'vinement.** *Obs.* [f. DIVINE *v.* + -MENT.] The action of divining; divination.

1579–80 NORTH *Plutarch* (1676) 33 That which they write of Romulus divinements, maketh great difference between him and Theseus. *Ibid.* 589 Priests and Soothsayers, that did sacrifice and purifie, and tend upon divinements.

divineness (dɪ'vaɪnnɪs). [-NESS.]

1. The quality or state of being divine; divine nature, character, or origin; divinity, sacredness.

1579–80 NORTH *Plutarch* (1676) 84 The common nature of man, that hath in it both Divineness, and sometimes beastly brutishness. **1587** GOLDING *De Mornay* xxxii. 507, I haue..prooued the trunesse and diuinenesse of the Scriptures. **1640** BP. REYNOLDS *Passions* i. 2 Their admirable Motions and Order, in which the Heathen have acknowledged a Divineness. **1718** *Free-thinker* No. 54 ¶11 The real Excellency and Divineness of Virtue. **1843** CARLYLE *Past & Pr.* III. xii, In all true Work..there is something of divineness.

2. Superhuman or supreme excellence.

1580 SIDNEY *Arcadia* (1622) 321 Besought him to repeate it againe, that..his minde might bee the better acquainted with the diuinenesse thereof. **1611** SHAKS. *Cymb.* III. vii. 45 Behold Diuinenesse No elder then a Boy.

diviner (dɪ'vaɪnə(r)). Forms: 4–5 devinor, -vynour, dyvynour, 5–7 divinour, 5– diviner. [ME. and AF. *devinour, divinour* = OF. *devineor, -eour, -ur* (12th c. in Hatz.-Darm.), agent-n. from F. *deviner* to DIVINE, corresponding to L. *dīvīnātōr-em* DIVINATOR. Down to 1500 regularly stressed ˌ*devi'nour*, '*deviˌnour*. In sense 2, app. f. F. *devin, divin* sb.: cf. *philosoph-er*.]

1. One who practises divination; a soothsayer, prophet, seer; a magician, sorcerer.

c **1330** R. BRUNNE *Chron. Wace* (Rolls) 8107 þus seide alle my dyuinours. **1382** WYCLIF *Deut.* xviii. 10 Ne be foundun in thee..that askith dyvynours. **1388** —— *Jer.* xxvii. 9 Dyuyneris by chiteryng and fleyng of briddis. **1483** CAXTON *Gold. Leg.* 234 b/2 The deuynour had told hym that he shold deye within fyue dayes. **1545** JOYE *Exp. Dan.* v. (R.) He fled to his wyse men of the worlde, to his diuiners and charmers. **1610** HOLLAND *Camden's Brit.* I. 649 The..Divinour or Prophet of the Britans, I mean Merlin. **1681** DRYDEN *Abs. & Achit.* 238 The People's Pray'r, the glad Diviner's Theme, The Young men's Vision and the Old men's Dream! **1723** POPE *Odyss.* I. 524 Vain diviner's dreams divert her fears. **1860** HOOK *Lives Abps.* (1869) I. v. 223 The bishops..were required..to banish..diviners and fortune-tellers. **1881** *Folk-lore Record* IV. 106 Very lately an eminent man..employed a diviner to look for mines on his property with a divining rod.

b. A successful conjecturer or guesser.

1690 LOCKE *Hum. Und.* II. i. (1695) 48 He must be a notable Diviner of Thoughts, that can assure him, that he was thinking. **1856–61** MAURICE *Critics* in *Friendship Bks.* xiii. (1874) 377 Richard Bentley was one of the subtlest diviners of the meaning of obscure passages.

†**2.** A divine, a theologian. *Obs.*

1377 LANGL. *P. Pl.* B. x. 452 þe doughtiest doctour and deuynoure of þe trinitee Was augustyn þe olde. *Ibid.* XIII. 114 Sire doctour..What is dowel and dobet? ȝe deuynours knoweth. **1393** *Ibid.* C. XVI. 85 This doctor and diuinour and decretistre of canon. **1552** HULOET, Diuinour or wryter of holy scripture, *agiographus.*

†**b.** = DIVINE *sb.*[2] 2 b; also, a wise man, sage.

1387 TREVISA *Higden* (Rolls) III. 65 Thales..þis naturel philosofer and dyuynour. *a* **1400–50** *Alexander* 1545 Doctours & diuinours & othire dere maistris.

divineress (dɪ'vaɪnərɪs). Also 4–6 de-, (5 -ourese). [a. OF. *devineresse* (12th c. in Hatz.-Darm.), fem. of *devineur* DIVINER: see -ESS.] A female diviner; a prophetess; a sorceress, witch.

c **1374** CHAUCER *Troylus* v. 1522 þow sorceresse With al þi fals gost of prophesie Thow wenest ben a grete deuyneresse! **1440** J. SHIRLEY *Dethe K. James* (1818) 14 The said woman of Yreland, that clepid herself a dyvenourese. **1480** CAXTON *Ovid's Met.* XIII. vi, And Cassandra, hys doughter, the devyneresse. *a* **1533** LD. BERNERS *Gold. Bk. M. Aurel.* xxvi. (1546) M ij, A woman diuineresse, or contrary, a sothsayer. **1681** H. MORE *Postscript to Glanvill's Sadducismus* I. (1726) 24 Do the office of a Divineress, or a Wise-woman. **1837** CARLYLE *Fr. Rev.* III. v. ii. (1872) 177 A black Divineress of the Tropics prophesied..that she should be a Queen. **1848** J. A. CARLYLE tr. *Dante's Inferno* xx, The wretched women who..made themselves divineresses.

† **divinesse.** *Obs.* [Compressed variant of *divineness*; perh. with some thought of F. *-esse*, as in *richesse* and Eng. *idlesse*: cf. *profaness, proness*, etc.] **a.** Divination. **b.** Divineness, divinity; divine quality or character.

1594 CAREW *Huarte's Exam. Wits* iv. (1596) 46 The first who tearmed these maruellous matters by the name of diuinesse was Hippocrates; and that if any such point of diuinesse bee found in the disease, that it manifesteth also a prouidence. **1605** BACON *Adv. Learn.* II. iv. §2. 18 Poesie..was euer thought to haue some participation of diuinesse. *Ibid.* §4. 19 Enquirers into truth..will despise those delicacies and affectations, as indeede capable of no diuinesse.

diving ('daɪvɪŋ), *vbl. sb.* [f. DIVE *v.* + -ING[1].]

a. The action of the verb DIVE, in its various senses.

1398 TREVISA *Barth. De P.R.* XII. xxvi. (1495) 429 By manere of plungynge and of dyuynge. **1614** ROWLANDS *Fooles Bolt* 37 A common Scould, her furious heate must coole: Wash'd by her diuing in a Cucking stoole. **1743–5** R. POCOCKE *Trav.* (Camden) II. 129 The curious manner of diveing which they lately began, in order to raise what they could of the wreck. **1854** *(title)* Divings into Scripture and Sprinkling of Wisdom for Little Folk.

b. *attrib.* and *Comb.*, as **diving-bladder, -boat, -engine, -helmet, -machine, -suit,** DIVING-BELL, etc.; **diving-board**, a board projecting some distance over the water, from which a swimmer dives; **diving-plane**, a horizontal rudder on a submarine for steering the vessel up or down; also a similar device fitted to instruments used in oceanography.

1601 BP. W. BARLOW *Defence* 143 The diuing poole of Bethesda. **1661** Diving-engine [see DIVING-BELL]. **1693** *Lond. Gaz.* No. 2842/3 Letters Patents..for a Diving-Engine. **1752** JOHNSON *Rambler* No. 199 ¶3 The first experiment in nineteen diving engines of new construction. **1753** CHAMBERS *Cycl. Supp.*, *Diving Bladder*, a term used by Borelli for a machine..contrived for Diving under the water to great depths..The objections all other diving machines are liable to are obviated. **1802** *Naval Chron.* VII. 270 The Diving-boat..will be capacious enough to contain eight men. *a* **1825** FORBY *Voc. E. Anglia*, *Deving-pond*, a pond from which water is drawn for domestic use, by dipping a pail. **1839** COL. HAWKER *Diary* (1893) II. 163 Inflating air into the diving machine, or rather diving dress, of the man who was working no elder then the sea. **1875** *Ure's Dict. Arts* s.v. *Diving-dress*, The diving helmet is, in principle, similar to the bell. **1893** SINCLAIR & HENRY *Swimming* iv. 108 A spring diving-board is generally used for running headers. **1908** J. LONDON *Let.* 26 Oct. (1966) 264, I supply it with..diving-suits and boats. **1915** KIPLING *Fringes of Fleet* 29 A mine and chain had jammed under her [*sc.* the submarine's] forward diving-plane. *c* **1938** L. MUMFORD *City Development* (1946) 112 The curve of a diver's body as he leaps from the diving-board. **1943** C. S. LEWIS *Perelandra* ii. 27 If they have a scientific civilisation they may have diving-suits. **1959** H. BARNES *Oceanogr. & Marine Biol.* i. 31 *(caption)* Small high-speed Plankton Indicator... All models except the last have their own diving planes. **1959** *Jane's Fighting Ships 1959–60* 414 She incorporates several novel features including hydro-wings or diving planes fitted to the conning tower 'fin'.

'diving, *ppl. a.* [f. as prec. + -ING[2].]

That dives, in various senses of the vb.

1602 FULBECKE *2nd Pt. Parall.* Ded. 1 The industrious search of some diuing braine. *a* **1639** WOTTON in *Reliq. Wotton.* 402 (R.) Let the diving Negro seek For gemms hid in some forlorn creek. **1712** GAY *Trivia* III. 80 Guard well thy pocket, for these syrens stand To aid the labours of the diving hand.

b. In names of various animals.

diving-buck or **goat**, a S. African antelope (*Cephalophus mergens*), the *duyker-bok* of the Boers; **diving-duck**, the golden-eye duck (*Clangula glaucion*); **diving-pigeon**, the lack guillemot or doveky (*Uria Grylle*); **diving-spider**, *Argyroneta aquatica*, which lives in a nest filled with air under water.

1694 *Acc. Sev. Late Voy.* II. (1711) 84 The first Diving Pigeon I got.. at Spitzbergen. **1786** SPARRMAN *Voy. Cape G.H.* II. 243 The duyker-bok, or diving goat.. rising in its leap with its neck erect, and in its descent bringing it down between its legs.. had the appearance of diving and gave rise to its name. **1813** COL. HAWKER *Diary* (1893) I. 89, I got a diving duck, and should have had more shots. **1885** SWAINSON *Prov. Names Birds* 161 Diving duck (Shetland Isles). *Ibid.* 218 Diving pigeon.

ˈdiving-bell. [f. DIVING *vbl. sb.* + BELL *sb.*[1] 5.]

a. A strong heavy vessel, originally bell-shaped, with the bottom open, in which persons may descend into deep water, respiration being sustained by the compressed air at the top, or by fresh air supplied by a forcing pump from above.

1661 EVELYN *Diary* 19 July, We tried our Diving-Bell, or Engine, in the water-dock at Deptford.. it was made of cast lead, let down with a strong cable. **1693** *Phil. Trans.* XVII. 896 Means of weighing up sunken Vessels.. and taking out the Goods by means of the Diving Bell. **1713** DERHAM *Phys. Theol.* IV. iii. *note* (R.), One of the divers blew an horn in his diving-bell, at the bottom of the sea. **1774** GOLDSM. *Nat. Hist.* (1776) I. 241 The great diving-bell improved by Doctor Halley, which was large enough to contain five men. **1874** BURNAND *My Time* xxiv. 212 Breathing with as much difficulty.. as he might have experienced in a diving-bell.

attrib. **1874** KNIGHT *Dict. Mech.* I. 713/2 A diving-bell company was formed in England in 1688. *Ibid.* 715/1 *Diving-bell Pump*, a pump having a casing divided by a vertical partition into two chambers, which are provided with inwardly and outwardly opening valves.

b. The air-filled web in which the water-spider lives under water.

1854 [see WATER-SPIDER]. **1961** *Listener* 7 Dec. 986/2 A water-spider beside its 'diving-bell', a bubble of air contained in a web.

divinify (dɪˈvɪnɪfaɪ), *v.* [f. L. *dīvīn-us* DIVINE + (-I)FY; cf. *deify*, etc.] *trans.* To render divine; to regard as of divine nature, rank, or origin; to divinize. Hence **diˈvinified** *ppl. a.*

1633 A. H. *Parthenia Sacra* 204 (T.) My beloved is white and red.. white, for his blessed and divinified soul. **1660** STANLEY *Hist. Philos.* IX. (1701) 395/1 Good the Civil Virtues render a Man, but the Sciences conducing to the Divine Virtue divinifie. **1855** BAILEY *Mystic* 32 And knew himself divinified. **1892** AGNES M. CLERKE *Fam. Stud. Homer* 45 The same constellation.. under a divinified aspect.

diˈvining, *vbl. sb.* [f. DIVINE *v.* + -ING[1].]

1. The action of the verb DIVINE:

a. Soothsaying, prophecy, divination. **b.** Conjecture, guessing.

c **1340** HAMPOLE *Prose Tr.* (1866) 9 In þis comandement es forbodyn to gyffe trouthe till socerye or till dyuynyngez by sternys. *c* **1374** CHAUCER *Boeth.* V. pr. iii. 122 (Camb. MS.) Elles what difference is ther bytwixe the prescience and thilke Iapeworthi dyuynenge of tyresye the dyuynor? **1483** *Cath. Angl.* 102 A Dyuynynge be fyre, *piromancia*. A Diuinynge be water, *idromancia*. **1646** J. GEREE (*title*) Astrologo-Mastix, or a Discovery of the Vanity and Iniquity of Judiciall Astrology or Divining by the Starres. **1860** PUSEY *Min. Proph.* Jonah i. 7 The lot for divining.. is wrong, except by direct inspiration of God.

2. *attrib.*, as *divining-rod, -staff, -stick, -wand*: a rod, etc., used in divination; *spec.* a forked stick, by means of which certain persons are reputed to have the power of tracing and indicating subterraneous supplies of water and mineral veins. See quots.; also DOWSING-ROD.

1656 COWLEY *Pindar. Odes, To Mr. Hobs* iii, With fond Divining-Wands, We search among the dead For Treasures buried. *Ibid.* Note, *Virgula Divina*; or a Divining-Wand is a two-forked branch of an Hazel-Tree.. used for the finding out either of Veins, or hidden Treasures of Gold or Silver; and being carryed about, bends downwards (or rather is said to do so) when it comes to the place where they lye. **1712** J. JAMES tr. *Le Blond's Gardening* 188 To find out Water by the Help of a Hasel-Wand, called a Divining-Stick. **1751** *Gentl. Mag.* Nov. (Brand *Pop. Antiq.*) So early as Agricola the divining Rod was in much request, and has obtained great credit for its discovering where to dig for Metals and Springs of Water.. lately it has been revived with great success. **1816** SCOTT *Antiq.* xvii. **1883** P. ROBINSON in *Harper's Mag.* Oct. 708/1 The divining-rod finds its professors and disciples.. in every part of the world. **1888** ELWORTHY *W. Somerset Word-bk., Dowse*, to use the divining-rod for the purpose of finding springs of water.

diˈvining, *ppl. a.* [f. as prec. + -ING[2].] That divines, foresees, or conjectures; soothsaying, prophesying, conjecturing, guessing, etc.

1382 WYCLIF *1 Kings* xxviii. 7 There is a womman havynge a dyvynynge spirite in Endore. **1593** SHAKS. *3 Hen. VI*, IV. vi. 69 If secret Powers suggest but truth To my diuining thoughts. **1697** DRYDEN *Æneid* VI. 54 The mad divining dame, The priestess of the god, Deiphobe her name. **1876** GEO. ELIOT *Dan. Der.* V. xxxix, This dreadfully divining personage—evidently Satan in grey trousers.

†**diviˈnipotent,** *a. Obs. rare*$^{-0}$. [ad. L. *dīvīnipotent-em* mighty in divination.]

1656 BLOUNT *Glossogr., Divinipotent*, that hath power in divine things. **1727** in BAILEY vol. II.

†**diˈvinister.** *Obs. rare.* [f. DIVINE *v.*, or *divinour*, DIVINER *sb.*: see -ISTER.] A diviner.

c **1386** CHAUCER *Knt.'s T.* 1953 Therfore I stynte, I nam no divinistre.

†**diˈvinitize,** *v. Obs. rare*$^{-1}$. [irreg. f. DIVINITY + -IZE.] = DIVINIZE.

1649 J. E. tr. *Behmen's Epist.* Pref. 9 We.. Divinitize our knowledge into an effectual working Love.

divinity (dɪˈvɪnɪtɪ). Forms: 4-6 de-, dy-, divinite, 4-7 -tie. [ME. *de-, divinite*, a. OF. *devinité, -eté, -iteit* (12th c. in Hatz.-Darm.) theology, ad. L. *dīvīnitāt-em* godhead, divination, excellence, f. *dīvīn-us* DIVINE: see -ITY.]

1. The character or quality of being divine; divineness, godhood; divine nature; Deity, Godhead.

c **1374** CHAUCER *Boeth.* I. pr. iv. 7 (Camb. MS.) Thow desputedest.. towching deuynyte and mankynde. *c* **1450** *Mirour Saluacioun* 272 In crist warre flesshe and sawle and verray divinitee. **1581** FULKE in *Confer.* III. (1584) Y, The humanitie of Christ after it was assumpted by the Diuinitie, was absorpte of the same. *c* **1610-15** *Women Saints, Agnes* (1886) 147 Diuinitie dwelleth not in stones but in heauen. **1667** MILTON *P.L.* IX. 1010 They feel Divinitie within them breeding wings. **1784** COWPER *Task* VI. 877 The veil is rent .. That hides divinity from mortal eyes. **1884** RUSKIN *Pleas. Eng.* 17 *note*, Arianism consists not in asserting the subjection of the Son to the Father, but in denying the subjected Divinity.

2. a. *concr.* A divine being; a god, a deity. *the Divinity*: the Deity, the Supreme Being, God.

c **1386** CHAUCER *Sec. Nun's T* 316 Whil we seken thilke diuinitee That is yhid in heuene. **1398** TREVISA *Barth. De P.R.* I. (1495) 8 Cryst Iesus very god and man is.. moost blessyd and inestymable dyuynyte or deyte for all mankynde. **1602** SHAKS. *Ham.* V. ii. 10 There's a Diuinity that shapes our ends, Rough-hew them how we will. **1777** ROBERTSON *Hist. Amer.* (1778) II. VII. 302 Its divinities were clothed with terror. **1796** H. HUNTER tr. *St. Pierre's Stud. Nat.* (1799) II. 76 It's last and only end is the Divinity himself. **1865** SEELEY *Ecce Homo* iv. (ed. 8) 31 Their national Divinity had been their king. **1875** WHITNEY *Life Lang.* v. 80 Mercury.. the swift messenger of the divinities.

b. *fig.* An object of adoration, an adorable being.

1648 BOYLE *Seraph. Love* vi. (1700) 49 A Lover, naming what he worships, a Divinity. **1749** SMOLLETT *Gil Blas* III. ix, I perceived the divinity seated on a large sattin couch —in a genteel deshabille. **1849** THACKERAY *Pendennis* vii, Composing a most flaming and conceited copy of verses to his divinity.

3. Divine quality, virtue, or power; god-likeness, divineness.

1510-20 *Everyman* in Hazl. *Dodsley* I. 133 These seven.. Gracious sacraments of high divinity. **1590** SPENSER *F.Q.* III. v. 34 The goodly Maide, ful of divinities And gifts of heavenly grace. **1598** SHAKS. *Merry W.* V. i. 3 There is Diuinity in odde Numbers, either in natiuity, chance, or death. **1681-6** J. SCOTT *Chr. Life* (1747) III. 71 These miraculous Signs of the Divinity of the Christian Doctrine. **1847** TENNYSON *Princ.* III. 207 To lift the woman's fall'n divinity Upon an even pedestal with man.

4. a. The science of divine things; the science that deals with the nature and attributes of God, His relations with mankind, etc.; theology; the theological faculty in Universities. (The earliest sense in English.)

divinity hall, (Scotland, etc.), a theological hall or college. *c* **1305** *Edmund Conf.* 238 in *E.E.P.* (1862) 77 To diuinite as god wolde þis gode man him drouȝ. **1387** TREVISA *Higden* (Rolls) I. 5 Of þe þre vertues of deuynyte [*theologicarum virtutum*]. *c* **1400** MAUNDEV. (1839) xiii. 144 Athanasius was a gret Doctour of Dyvynytee. **1439** *E.E. Wills* (1882) 118, I woll that the maister of devenyte haue xx li. **1556** *Chron. Gr. Friars* (Camden) 40 William Thurston abbot of Fowntens and bachelar of devinite.. hongyd, heddyd and qwarterd. **1599** SHAKS. *Hen. V*, I. i. 38 Heare him but reason in Diuinitie. **1690** LOCKE *Govt.* II. viii. §112 They never dream'd of Monarchy being *Jure Divino*.. till it was revealed to us in the Divinity of this last Age. **1722** DE FOE *Moll Flanders* (1840) 303 The ordinary of Newgate.. talked a little in his way, but all his divinity ran upon confessing my crime, as he called it. **1833** COLERIDGE *Table-t.* 14 Mar., Divinity is essentially the first of the professions, because it is necessary for all at all times. **1849** MACAULAY *Hist. Eng.* I. iv. 498 Three poor labouring men, deeply imbued with this unamiable divinity.

b. Applied also to the theological systems of heathen nations or philosophers.

1669 GALE *Crt. Gentiles* I. I. ii. 12 Plato acknowlegeth that he received the.. choicest of his Divinitie from the Phenicians. **1754** SHERLOCK *Disc.* (1759) I. iv. 145 The Religion and Divinity of the Vulgar in the Days of Heathenism. **1855** MILMAN *Lat. Chr.* (1864) II. IV. vii. 365 He.. was versed in all the divinity of the Greeks.

†**5.** = DIVINATION I. *Obs. rare.*

1481 CAXTON *Myrr.* I. xiii. 39 By this Arte and science [Astronomye] were first emprysed.. alle other sciences of decrees and of dyuinyte. **1601** HOLLAND *Pliny* I. 28 This diuinitie or fore-telling of Anaxagoras.

6. *attrib.* (*esp.* in reference to the Faculty of Divinity at the Universities), as *divinity act, book, chair, lecture, man, school*, etc.; **divinity-calf** (*Bookbinding*), dark brown stained calf decorated with blind stamping, without gilding: used for theological works; (Zaehnsdorf, *Hist. Bookb.* 1895); **divinity fudge** *U.S.*, a type of home-made fudge.

1548 UDALL *Erasm. Par.* Pref. (R.) A full library of all good diuinity-books. *a* **1555** LATIMER *Serm. & Rem.* (1845) 291 We.. appointed you to appear before us.. in the divinity school, a place for disputations. **1641** 'SMECTYMNUUS' *Answ.* v. (1653) 22 Such as were able to preach, or keepe a Divinitie Act. **1670** EACHARD *Cont. Clergy* 97 If a young divinity-intender has but got a sermon of his own or of his father's.. he gets a qualification. *c* **1680** HICKERINGILL *Wks.* (1716) I. 79 The Tongues and Pens of the thriving Divinity-men. **1691-8** NORRIS *Pract. Disc.* (1711) III. 83 Acceptable.. from the Pulpit as from a Divinity-Chair. **1709** HEARNE *Collect.* 6 Nov., The Divinity-Bedell's Staff. **1785** J. TRUSLER *Mod. Times* I. 138 A register office for parsons, a kind of divinity-shop.. for hiring of preachers. **1846** MCCULLOCH *Acc. Brit. Empire* (1854) II. 341 Attendance on divinity lectures is requisite. **1913** E. H. GLOVER '*Dame Curtsey's*' *Bk. Candy Making* 34 Divinity Fudge. Three and one-half cups of granulated sugar, one-half cup of 90 per cent corn syrup, [etc.]. **1970** *New Yorker* 5 Sept. 36/3 My mother stayed out of the kitchen as much as possible, except for making divinity fudge perhaps once a year.

diˈvinityship. [f. prec. + -SHIP.]

1. The status or personality of a divinity; deityship, godship.

1689 HICKERINGILL *Wks.* (1716) II. 423 The Keys of the Church, to which he has as good right as your D.D. Divinityship. **1788** *Disinterested Love* I. 19 'Tis to her divinityship I pay my adoration. **1811** SHELLEY *Let. to E. Hitchener*, Truth is my God.. yours is reducible to the same simple Divinityship. **1834** L. HUNT *Town* (1858) 398 The first time he [Henry VIII] had discovered the possibility of such an impiety towards his barbarous divinityship.

2. Knowledge of or skill in divinity.

1762 STERNE *Tr. Shandy* VI. xxxvi, Plato's opinion, which with all his divinityship,—I hold to be damnable.

diviniˈzation. [f. next + -ATION.] The action of divinizing, or condition of being divinized.

1840 MILL *Diss. & Disc., Grecian Hist.* (1859) II. 310 The basis of that was a *bona fide* personification and divinization of the occult causes of phenomena. **1873** M. ARNOLD *Lit. & Dogma* (1876) 38 The glorification and divinisation of this natural bent of mankind.

divinize (ˈdɪvɪnaɪz), *v.* [ad. F. *diviniser* (16th-17th c. in Hatz.-Darm.) to render divine, deify, f. *divin* DIVINE: see -IZE.]

1. *trans.* To make or render divine; to deify.

1656 BLOUNT *Glossogr., Divinize*, to make divine or heavenly. *a* **1743** A. M. RAMSAY *Nat. & Rev. Relig.* II. 401 (R.) The predestinarian doctors have divinized cruelty, wrath, fury, vengeance, and all the blackest vices. **1890** NEWELL *St. Patrick* 70 He divinised the powers of nature because he feared them.

†**2.** *intr.* To become divine; to act as a divine being. *Obs. rare.*

1685 *Gracian's Courtiers Orac.* 163 By Divinizing, one gets Respect, by Humanizing, Contempt.

Hence **ˈdivinized** *ppl. a.*; **ˈdivinizing** *vbl. sb.*

1837 *Tait's Mag.* IV. 459 This divinizing of 'myself'—this deification of the individual man. **1839** BAILEY *Festus* (1854) 164 The form Of Divinized humanity.

diˌvino-poˈlitical, *a. nonce-wd.* Of or pertaining to divine polity.

1668 H. MORE *Div. Dial.* V. x. (1713) 437 The meaning of Ezekiel's Mercavah is not Physical, but Moral, Spiritual, or Divino-political, if I may so speak. **1684** —— *An Answer* 241 The Divino-political sense of that Vision.

‖**divisa** (dɪˈviːsə). [Sp., device, emblem (cf. DEVICE).] In *Bull-fighting*: coloured ribbons denoting the breeder of a bull.

1932 R. CAMPBELL *Taurine Provence* ii. 45 To seize the divisa (or cocarde) and present it to the lady of one's affections is the summit of gallantry. **1967** MCCORMICK & MASCAREÑAS *Compl. Aficionado* ii. 52 An attendant placed a short barb with the *divisa* of the ganaderia in the toro's *morillo*.

divis(e), obs. forms of DEVICE, DEVISE.

†**diˈvise,** *sb. Obs.* [a. OF. *de-, divise*, ad. late L. *dīvīsa* (med.L. in Du Cange) division, boundary, fem. sb. from pa. pple. of *dīvidĕre*: see DEVISE, and cf. the town name *Devizes*, formerly 'The Devizes', med.L. *Divisæ*.] Boundary; *pl.* bounds.

c **1575** BALFOUR *Practicks* (1754) 434 (Jam.) Divisis betwix sic landis pertening to sic ane man, on the ane part, and sic landis pertening to sic ane uther man on the uther part. *Ibid.* 438 Divises, meithis and merchis.

†**diˈvise,** *a. Obs.* Also 5 de-. [ad. L. *dīvīs-us*, pa. pple. of *dīvidĕre* to DIVIDE: cf. OF. *devis* divided.] Divided; separate, distinct.

c **1420** *Pallad. on Husb.* IV. 416 In March orenge is sette in sondry wyse: Thai loveth lande that rare is and divise. **1677** GALE *Crt. Gentiles* II. IV. 255 The Author of the Book .. [says] 'the name One is truely said of that which is indivise in it self and divise as to althings else'.

Hence †**diˈvisely** *adv.*, separately (*obs.*).

c **1449** PECOCK *Repr.* III. xviii. 398 Ioyntli and deviseli. **1552** HULOET, Diuisely, *seorsum, seorsus, separatim.*

diviser, obs. form of DEVISER, DIVISOR.

‖**divisi** (dɪˈviːzɪ). [It., lit. 'divided', *pa. pple. pl.* of *dividere* to DIVIDE.] A musical direction (see quot. 1876).

1740 GRASSINEAU *Mus. Dict.* 65 *Divisi*, signifies, divided into two or more parts. **1876** STAINER & BARRETT *Dict. Mus. Terms* 135/2 *Divisi*,.. a direction that instruments playing from one line of music are to separate and play in two parts. **1929** *Melody Maker* Mar. 310/1 Six first violins (playing three *divisi* parts). **1940** G. JACOB *Orchestral Technique* (ed. 2) x. 100 In quiet passages use 'divisi' rather than double-stops.

divisibility (dɪvɪzɪˈbɪlɪtɪ). [f. next + -ITY: cf. F. *divisibilité* (15th c. in Godef. *Suppl.*).]

1. The quality of being divisible; capacity of being divided into parts, or among a number of persons.

1644 Digby *Nat. Bodies* II. viii. (1645) 15 Divisibility, or a capacity to be divided into partes. **1691** Norris *Pract. Disc.* 52 That endless..Controversy concerning..the infinite Divisibility of Quantity. **1710** Berkeley *Princ. Hum. Knowl.* §47 The infinite divisibility of Matter is now universally allowed. **1831** Lardner *Pneumat.* iii. 237 Numerous physical analogies favour the conclusion, that the divisibility of matter has a limit.

2. *Math.* Capacity of being divided without remainder.

divisible (dɪˈvɪzɪb(ə)l), *a.* (*sb.*) Also 6–7 **de-**. [ad. L. *dīvīsibil-is* (Tertullian, 3rd c.), f. *dīvīs-* ppl. stem of *dīvidĕre* to DIVIDE: cf. F. *divisible* (Oresme, 14th c.).] Capable of being divided.

1. Capable of being divided into parts (actually, or in thought); capable of being divided into kinds or classes, distinguishable; capable of being divided or distributed among a number.

1552 Huloet, Deuisible, or able to be parted or deuided, *deuiduus*. **1597** Hooker *Eccl. Pol.* v. lv. §7 In as much as that infinite word is not diuisible into parts, it could not in part, but must needs be wholly incarnate. **1665** Hooke *Microgr.* 2 Certainly the quantity or extension of any body may be divisible *in infinitum*, though perhaps not the matter. **1777** Priestley *Matt. & Spir.* (1782) I. iii. 38 Every particle of matter is infinitely divisible. **1881** Mivart *Cat* 14 The Cat's entire frame is divisible into head, neck, trunk, tail, and limbs. **1891** *Law Times* 106/2 The beneficial interest..is to be divisible amongst the next of kin.

2. *Math.* Of a number or quantity: †**a.** To be divided; forming the dividend (*obs.*). **b.** Capable of being divided without remainder (*by*).

1579 Digges *Stratiot.* 9 The number divisible. **1709–29** V. Mandey *Syst. Math., Arith.* 23 Because 4869 [i.e. 4 + 8 + 6 + 9] make 27, a number divisible by 9, therefore also 4869 may be divided by 9. **1727–51** Chambers *Cycl.* s.v. *Number, Primitive*, or *prime Number* is that, which is only divisible by unity..*Compound Number* is that divisible by some other number besides unity; as 8, divisible by 4, and by 2. *Mod.* A number is divisible by 9 if the sum of its digits is divisible by 9.

†**B.** *sb.* A divisible body. *Obs.*

1665 Glanvill *Scepsis Sci.* v. (R.), The composition of bodies, whether it be of divisibles or indivisibles.

Hence **diˈvisibleness**, divisibility; **diˈvisibly** *adv.*, in a divisible manner, so as to be divisible; †in small portions (*obs.*).

1558 Bp. Watson *Sev. Sacram.* vii. 40 Gods onely begotten sonne goeth into euery man diuisiblye that receyueth him. **1649** Jer. Taylor *Gt. Exemp.* Ad Sect. v. §7 The use of reason comes at no definite time, but insensibly and divisibly. *a* **1691** Boyle (J.), Naturalists disagree about ..the indefinite divisibleness of matter. —— *Wks.* I. 376 (R.) The divisibleness of nitre into fixed and volatile parts.

division (dɪˈvɪʒən). Forms: 4–6 **devi-, divisioun**, etc. (with usual interchange of *i* and *y*, *-on* and *-oun*), 4 **deveseoun, devyseoun**, 5 *Sc.* **dywysiown**, 5–7 **divisione**, 4– **division**. [ME. *de-, divisioun*, a. OF. *devisiun, division*, ad. L. *dīvīsiōn-em*, n. of action f. *dīvidĕre* to DIVIDE.]

I. As an action or condition.

1. a. The action of dividing or state of being divided into parts or branches; partition, severance.

c **1374** Chaucer *Boeth.* III. pr. xi. 77 (Camb. MS.) But fyr [fleeth] and refuseth alle deuysyon. *Ibid.* III. pr. ix. [see DIVIDE *v.* 1]. *c* **1400** *Lanfranc's Cirurg.* 26 þese arteries ben deuydid many weies; whos dyuysiouns man mai nouȝt conseyue bi his witt. **1559** W. Cunningham *Cosmogr. Glasse* 111 By.. the devision of th' Earth into zones. **1601** Shaks. *Twel. N.* v. i. 229 How haue you made diuision of your selfe? **1634** Sir T. Herbert *Trav.* 136 Babylon..there first hapned the division of Languages from one..to seventie two. **1726** tr. *Gregory's Astron.* I. 237 The Division of Time into Hours, Days, and Weeks. **1840** Lardner *Geom.* ix. 109 Let the line..be divided into three parts, at C and D..and, from the points of division C and D let perpendiculars be drawn. **1875** Jowett *Plato* (ed. 2) III. 2 The division into books..is probably later than the age of Plato.

b. Separation, partition, parting.

1535 Coverdale *2 Esdras* vi. 41 To make a deuysion betwixte the waters, that the one parte might remayne aboue, and the other beneth. **1634** Massinger *Very Woman* II. i. Plays (1868) 499/1 We may meet again, But death's division is for ever, friend. **1864** Tennyson *Higher Pantheism* 6 This weight of body and limb, Are they not sign and symbol of thy division from Him?

c. *Camb. Univ.* The partition of the term into two halves; the point of time at which the term is thus divided.

1803 *Gradus ad Cantab.* s.v. *Term-Trotters*, Young men who contrive to be *in* College the night before the division of the term, and *out* of it the morning after the close. **1852** Bristed *Eng. University* 63 After 'division' in the Michaelmas and Lent Terms, a student, who can assign a good plea for absence to the College authorities, may go down. **1896** W. Aldis Wright in *Letter*, The division of term still marks a period for certain purposes.

†**d.** 'Methodical arrangement, disposition' (Schmidt). *Obs.*

1604 Shaks. *Oth.* I. i. 23 A Fellow..That neuer set a Squadron in the Field, Nor the deuision of a Battaile knowes More then a Spinster.

e. *Hort.* The propagation of perennial plants by splitting clumps into parts capable of rooting themselves.

1805 T. A. Knight *Rep. Committee Hort. Soc. Lond.* 5 Almost every plant, the existence of which is not confined to a single summer, admits of two modes of propagation; by Division of its Parts, and by Seed. **1841** J. Loudon *Ladies' Compan. Flower Garden* 86/1 Plants are said to be propagated by division when they are taken up and separated into portions. **1915** T. W. Sanders *Pop. Hardy Perennials* I. 24 By division, the simplest of all methods, we can easily obtain strong plants of any perennial. **1971** E. Coxhead *One Woman's Garden* vii. 54, I started with one plant and by division now have three.

f. *Biol.* The spontaneous separation or breaking up of a cell into two or more approximately equal parts that constitute daughter-cells, usu. involving division of the nucleus (if any) followed by the breaking up of the cell as a whole; freq. as ***cell division***. As a mode of reproduction of simple organisms usu. termed FISSION or *schizogony*.

1880 *Encycl. Brit.* XII. 13/1 Four types of Cytogenesis may be distinguished: (1) Rejuvenescence; (2) Conjugation; (3) Free-cell formation; and (4) Division. **1896** E. B. Wilson *Cell* ii. 45 In the multicellular organism all the tissue-cells have arisen by continued division from the original germ-cell, and this in its turn arose by the division of a cell pre-existing in the parent-body. **1901** T. H. Morgan *Regeneration* 149 The breaking up of lumbriculus or of a planarian into pieces that form new individuals is a typical example of division. **1920** L. Doncaster *Introd. Study Cytol.* xv. 247 The differentiation of the germ-layers is not conditioned by differential nuclear division, but by unequal division of the cytoplasm. **1940** Parker & Haswell *Text-bk. Zool.* (ed. 6) I. II. 89 Multiplication [of *Paramecium*] takes place by binary fission (*D*), the division of the body being preceded by that of both nuclei. **1964** G. H. Haggis et al. *Introd. Molecular Biol.* i. 13 A remarkable bubbling of the cytoplasm occurs, and this becomes furiously active in the later stages of cell division. After division the movement dies away and the daughter cells spread out, [etc.]. **1970** Ambrose & Easty *Cell Biol.* i. 20 Cell division is the way in which reproduction occurs in most simple unicellular organisms.

2. The action of distributing among a number; distribution, partition, sharing.

division of labour, in *Pol. Econ.*, the division of a process of manufacture or an employment into parts, each of which is performed by a particular person.

c **1380** Wyclif *Sel. Wks.* III. 341 God wolde suffre no lenger þe fend to regne oonli in oo siche preest, but, of synne þat þei hadden do, made devisioun amongis two. **1484** Caxton *Fables of Æsop* I. vi, It is not good to have partage and dyuysyon with hym which is ryche & myghty. **1555** Eden *Decades* Contents (Arb.) 45 The debate and strife betwene the Spanyardes and Portugales for the diuision of the Indies. **1601** Shaks. *Twel. N.* III. iv. 380 Ile make diuision of my present with you: Hold, there's halfe my Coffer. **1776** Adam Smith *W.N.* I. i. *heading*, Of the Division of Labour. The greatest improvement in the productive power of labour, and [etc.]..seem to have been the effect of the division of labour. **1878** Jevons *Prim. Pol. Econ.* 33 Even in a single family there is division of labour: the husband ploughs, or cuts timber; the wife cooks, manages the house, and spins or weaves; the sons hunt or tend sheep; the daughters employ themselves as milkmaids.

†**3.** The action of distinguishing, or of perceiving or making a difference; distinction. *Obs.*

c **1398** Chaucer *Fortune* 33, I haue the tawht deuisyoun by-twene Frend of effect and frende of cowntenaunce. *c* **1500** *Lancelot* 1648 That Iustice be Elyk [= alike] Without diuisione baith to pur and ryk. **1553** T. Wilson *Rhet.* 4 b, The division is an openyng of thynges wherin we agree and rest upon, and wherein we sticke, and stande in traverse. **1611** Bible *Exod.* viii. 23, I will put a division between my people and thy people.

4. The fact of being divided in opinion, sentiment, or interest; disagreement, variance, dissension, discord; an instance of this, a disagreement.

1393 Gower *Conf.* III. 381 Division..many a noble worthy town..Hath brought to great adversite. *c* **1477** Caxton *Jason* 71, I praye you..that ye kepe you from all dyuysion and roncour. **1526–34** Tindale *Rom.* xvi. 17 Marke them which cause division..and avoyde them. **1611** Bible *1 Cor.* xi. 18, I heare that there be diuisions [Wycl. & *Geneva*, dissensions] among you. **1665** Sir T. Herbert *Trav.* (1677) 190 A bone of division betwixt the Turk and Persian. **1712** W. Harrison in *Swift's Corr.* 16 Dec., To sow division between us. **1847** Tennyson *Princess* III. 62 Betwixt these two Division smoulders hidden.

5. *Math.* **a.** The action or process of dividing one number or quantity by another, i.e. of finding how many times the latter is contained in the former, or, more generally, of finding a quantity (the *quotient*) which multiplied by the latter (the *divisor*) will produce the former (the *dividend*); the inverse of multiplication; a rule or method for doing this.

long division (in *Arith.*), the method usually adopted when the divisor is greater than 12, in which the products of the divisor by the several terms of the quotient are successively set down and subtracted from the corresponding portions of the dividend. ***short division***: the method used when the divisor is 12 or less, in which the quotient is set down directly, without writing the successive products. COMPOUND *d.*, SIMPLE *d.*: see these words. ***complementary, direct***, and ***scratch d.***, ancient or obsolete methods of performing arithmetical division.

c **1425** *Craft Nombrynge* (E.E.T.S.) 25 þou schalt deuide alle þe nounbre þat comes of þe multiplicacion by þe neþer figures..but ȝet þou hast not þe craft of dyuision. **1542** Recorde *Gr. Artes* 126 a, If you would prove Multiplycation, the surest way is by Dyuision. *Ibid.* (1575) 148 Diuision is a distributing of a greater summe by the vnities of a lesser, Or Diuision is an Arithmeticall producing of a thirde number..which..shall so often conteyne an vnit, as the greater of the twoo propounded numbers doth containe the lesser. **1690** Leybourn *Curs. Math.* 18 The ways of performing Division are divers. **1706** W. Jones *Syn. Palmar. Matheseos* 25 Division is a Manifold Subduction; or the taking of one Number..out of another, as often as possible. **1823** H. J. Brooke *Introd. Crystallogr.* 299 The division..is effected by subtracting the logarithm of the latter fraction from that of the former.

†**b.** The process of 'dividing' a ratio, i.e. substituting the difference of its terms for either of them. *Obs.* (Now expressed by *dividendo*: cf. COMPOSITION 5 c.)

1695 Alingham *Geom. Epit.* 19 If A: B:: C: D then by Division of reason it will be as A − B: B:: C − D: D. **1827** Hutton *Course Math.* I. 325 The term Divided, or Division, here means subtracting, or parting; being used in the sense opposed to compounding, or adding, in def. 86.

6. *Logic*, etc. **a.** The action of dividing into kinds or classes; separation of a genus into species, called ***substantial division***, or ***division per se***; classification; *esp.* in scholastic logic, a rough kind of classification based on ordinary knowledge, not on methodical investigation. Also, less strictly, **b.** Enumeration of the parts of a whole, partition, called ***partible division***. **c.** Distinction of the various significations of a term: called ***nominal division***, in opposition to which the two preceding are also called ***real division***.

1551 T. Wilson *Logike* (1567) 83 b, Euery man is either wastfull or couetous..This diuision is not good, for, many men offende in neither. **1597** Morley *Introd. Mus.* Annot., As for the diuision, Musicke is either speculatiue or practicall. **1656** Stanley *Hist. Philos.* v. (1701) 181/2 Of Divisions, one is a distribution of the Genus into Species, and of the whole into parts;..Another is of a word into divers significations, when the same may be taken several ways. **1839** G. Bird *Nat. Philos.* 32 Absolute motion.. relative motion..Besides these, there are some other divisions of motion..[as] uniform..accelerated..retarded. **1842** Abp. Thomson *Laws Th.* lv. (1860) 82 Division is the enumeration of the various co-ordinate species of which a proximate genus is composed. **1864** Bowen *Logic* iv. 99 Division resolves the Extension [of a Concept] into its constituent Genera and Species.

†**7.** *Mus.* **a.** The execution of a rapid melodic passage, originally conceived as the dividing of each of a succession of long notes into several short ones; such a passage itself, a florid phrase or piece of melody, a run; *esp.* as a variation on, or accompaniment to, a theme or 'plain song'; hence often nearly = DESCANT *sb.* Phr. ***to run division***: to execute such a passage or variation; also *fig.* (cf. DESCANT *v.*) *Obs.*

1589 R. Harvey *Pl. Perc.* (1590) 21 Diuisions framde with such long discords, and not so much as a concord to end withall, argues a bad eare. *c* **1592** Marlowe *Jew of Malta* IV. iv, That kiss again! She runs division of my lips. **1596** Shaks. *1 Hen. IV*, III. i. 209 Ditties..Sung by a faire Queene..With ravishing Diuision to her Lute. **1628** Ford *Lover's Mel.* I. i, He could not run division with more art Upon his quaking instrument. **1674** Playford *Skill Mus.* II. 101 A Bass-Viol for Divisions must be of less size. **1737** Bracken *Farriery Impr.* (1756) I. 308 Time will not permit me to run Divisions upon each of the Symptoms. **1779** Sheridan *Critic* I. i, Signoras..gargling glib divisions in their outlandish throats. **1840** *Penny Cycl.* XVI. 21/2 s.v. *Music*, In the fine chorus..when the line 'Hark! how the thund'ring giant roars' occurs, he makes the bases roar in a long division, till they nearly gasp for breath.

†**b.** *fig.* Variation, modulation. *Obs.*

1605 Shaks. *Macb.* IV. iii. 96 The King-becoming Graces ..I haue no rellish of them, but abound In the diuision of each seuerall Crime, Acting it many wayes.

8. The separating of the members of a legislative body, etc. into two groups, in order to count their votes; in the British Houses of Parliment effected by their passing into separate lobbies, the numbers on each side being counted by tellers.

1620 *Jrnl. Ho. Com.* 13 Feb. I. 520 Question whether the I or Noe to go out. The Noe yielded, before Division of the House. **1771** *Gentl. Mag.* XLI. 103 The Minority on the division was 101. **1794** *Ibid.* LXIV. II. 727 The question.. was then put and negatived without a division. **1871** M. Collins *Mrq. & Merch.* II. iv. 115 He was in every division, and sat out every debate.

II. What produces, or is produced by, dividing.

9. Something that divides or marks separation; a dividing line or mark; a graduated scale (quot. 1669); a boundary; a partition.

c **1391** Chaucer *Astrol.* I. §19 Thise same strikes or diuisiouns ben cleped Azymuthz. And they deuyden the Orisonte of thin astrelabie in 24 deuisiouns. **1559** W. Cunningham *Cosmogr. Glasse* 6 Noting and observing certaine divisions, answering unto .v. principall paralelles. **1669** Sturmy *Mariner's Mag.* v. 76 On one side the slit you must place a Division of Inches, and every Inch into 10 Parts Divided. **1715** Desaguliers *Fires Impr.* 51 The Funnel.. shou'd have several divisions to cut the Wind. **1797** *Monthly Mag.* III. 144 A moveable circle, on which are engraved divisions respecting the periodical revolution of the moon.

10. a. One of the parts into which anything is or may be divided; a portion, section.

By the Judicature Act of 1873, the Courts of King's (Queen's) Bench, Common Pleas, Chancery, etc,. became 'divisions' of the High Court of Justice, e.g. Chancery Division, King's Bench Division, Probate and Admiralty Division.

c **1374** CHAUCER *Compl. Mars* 273 To yow hardy knyghtis of renoun, Syn that ye be of my deuisioun. **1382** WYCLIF *2 Chron.* xxxi. 2 Ezechias..sette prestis companyes and Levytis bi their devysiouns, echone in propre office. **1577** B. GOOGE *Heresbach's Husb.* I. (1586) 35 b, The leafe jagged in five divisions like a starre. **1711** ADDISON *Spect.* No. 225 ¶5 If we look into particular Communities and Divisions of Men..it is the discreet Man..who guides the Conversation. **1719** SWIFT *To Yng. Clergyman* Wks. 1755 II. II. 10 Desiring you to express the heads of your divisions in as few and clear words as you possibly can. **1840** *Penny Cycl.* XVIII. 335/2 The total number of the [metropolitan police] force is 3486, who are placed in divisions, each division being employed in a distinct district. **1865** W. L. C. *Etoniana* vii. 117 Forms, or divisions, as they are termed at Eton. **1874** DEUTSCH *Rem.* 265 Our document contains six principal divisions.

b. *spec.* A portion of a country, territory, county, district, etc., as marked off for some political, military, administrative, judicial, or other purpose; e.g. the ***parliamentary*** or ***petty sessional divisions*** of the counties of the United Kingdom, the ***military divisions*** of the United States; the ***administrative divisions*** of the presidencies (except Madras) and provinces of British India, presided over by a commissioner, and subdivided into 'districts'.

1640–1 *Kirkcudbr. War-Comm. Min. Bk.* (1855) 73 The Committie ordaines that everie captaine, within this divisione, bring in all the runawayes to the next Committie day. **1709** LUTTRELL *Brief Rel.* (1857) VI. 463 The constable ..was out of his division. **1778** *Eng. Gazetteer* (ed. 2) s.v. *Truro*, The quarter-sessions for its S. and W. divisions being generally held here. **1802** BROOKES *Gazeteer* (ed. 12), *Kesteven*, one of the three divisions of Lincolnshire. **1835** *Penny Cycl.* IV. 479/2 (*Blackburn*) A sort of supreme authority is vested in two officers..called high-constables, one for the higher and the other for the lower division of the hundred. **1837** *Ibid.* VIII. 456/2 (*Devonshire*) The county is divided into two parts for the purpose of parliamentary representation: each division sends two members. **1881** *Imp. Gaz. India* I. 531 Benares—a Division under a Commissioner in the North Western Provinces comprising the six Districts of Azamgarh, [etc.]. **1895** *Oxford Direct.* Oxford, the capital of and a polling place for the Mid division of the county..is locally in the hundred and petty sessional division of Bullingdon.

c. *Mil.* and *Naut.* A portion of an army or fleet, consisting of a definite number of troops or vessels, under one commanding officer; also applied to a definite portion of a squadron or battalion (see quots.); also, a portion of a ship's company appropriated to a particular service; in *pl.*, the parade of a ship's company according to its divisions.

1597 SHAKS. *2 Hen. IV*, I. iii. 70 His diuisions..Are in three Heads: one Power against the French, And one against Glendower: Perforce a third Must take vp vs. **1623** BINGHAM *Xenophon* 108 When day-light appeared, euery Coronell led his Diuision or Regiment to a village. **1730–6** BAILEY (folio), *Division* (in *Marit. Affairs*) the third part of a naval army or fleet, or of one of the squadrons therof under a general officer. **1796** *Instr. & Reg. Cavalry* 1 Each Squadron is to be told off—by Half squadrons. Four divisions. Eight sub-divisions. **1810** WELLINGTON in Gurw. *Desp.* VI. 79 An army composed of divisions. **1832** *Regul. Instr. Cavalry* III. 45 *Division*—In its strict sense, the fourth part of a Squadron. Divisions are numbered 1st, 2d, 3d, and 4th from the right. **1867** SMYTH *Sailor's Word-bk.*, *Division*, a select number of ships in a fleet or squadron distinguished by a particular flag, pendant, or vane. **1879** *Cassell's Techn. Educ.* IV. 320 Two or three battalions are usually formed into a brigade, two brigades into a division. **1915** 'BARTIMEUS' *Tall Ship* iii. 54 Nine o'clock, sir; all ready for divisions. *Ibid.* 55 A moment later the bugle overhead blazed forth 'Divisions'. **1947** B. MASON in D. M. Davin *N.Z. Short Stories* (1953) 338 It was Sunday, and we began to make ourselves 'tiddly' for Divisions. **1971** *Daily Tel.* 18 Jan. 10/3 'Divisions', or the muster and inspection of the ship's company each morning in harbour, long regarded as sacrosanct, now seldom occurs more than once a week.

d. *Nat. Hist.* A section of a larger group in classification: used widely of groups of higher or lower grade, as the divisions of a kingdom, class, order, family, or genus.

1833 *Penny Cycl.* I. 501/2 Cuvier..laid down the following general table of the animal kingdom: Four divisions: Vertebrated animals. Molluscous animals [etc.]. **1857** HENFREY *Bot.* II. ii. 203 Jussieu established his primary divisions of the Vegetable Kingdom on characters which.. define really natural groups..On these characters stood the three divisions, *Acotyledons*, *Monocotyledons*, and *Dicotyledons*. *Ibid.* II. iii. 218 Subkingdom I. *Phanerogamia* ..Division I. *Angiospermia*. **1888** ROLLESTON & JACKSON *Anim. Life* 359 Amniota..Three classes are included in this division of Vertebrata, the *Mammalia*, *Aves*, and *Reptilia*.

e. A section of a railway line. Also *attrib.* *U.S.*

1858 W. P. SMITH *Gt. Railway Celebrations* 98 The opening of the Western Division of the O. and M. Railroad. **1887** C. B. GEORGE *40 Yrs. on Rail* xii. 254 My plan..is to have a book to be called the division book kept by each company. **1891** C. ROBERTS *Adrift Amer.* 71 Every line in the United States is divided into divisions of various lengths... Each division is under the supervision of a man who is called a division road master. *Ibid.* 96 Wallace was a division terminus. **1892** A. C. GUNTER *Miss Dividends* 10 This citizen soldier..had been one of the division engineers of the Union Pacific Railway.

f. Any of the two or three grades of imprisonment to which certain misdemeanants could be sentenced with a view to separating hardened criminals from less serious offenders. *Obs.* exc. *Hist.*

1865 *Act 28 & 29 Vict.* c. 126 §67 In every Prison to which this Act applies Prisoners convicted of Misdemeanor, and not sentenced to Hard Labour, shall be divided into at least Two Divisions, One of which shall be called the First Division; and..a Misdemeanant of the First Division shall not be deemed to be a Criminal Prisoner within the Meaning of this Act. **1898** *Act 61 & 62 Vict.* c. 41 §6 Prisoners..not sentenced to penal servitude or hard labour, shall be divided into three divisions... Where a person is.. sentenced to imprisonment without hard labour, the court may direct that he be treated as an offender of the first division or as an offender of the second division. If no direction is given by the court, the offender shall..be treated as an offender of the third division. **1918** A. HUXLEY *Let.* 30 Apr. (1969) 150 His trial takes place to-morrow, the appeal, which won't, I imagine, do any good except perhaps to change his six months from second to first division. **1947** *Rep. Commissioners of Prisons 1945* 64 in *Parl. Papers 1946–7* (Cmd. 7146) XIV. 155 The provisions of this Bill [*sc.* the Criminal Justice Bill, 1938], so far as concerns the prison system, proposed..the abolition of sentences of Penal Servitude and imprisonment with Hard Labour, and of the Triple Division of Offenders.

g. In the Civil Service, the technical designation of the several grades of clerks.

1876 *London Gaz.* 12 Feb. 638/2 A Lower Division of the Civil Service shall be constituted. It shall consist of Men Clerks and of Boy Clerks, engaged to serve in any Department of the State to which they may, from time to time, be appointed or transferred. *Ibid.* 639/1 Promotion from the Lower to the Higher Division of the Service shall not be made without a special certificate from the Civil Service Commissioners. **1892** S. SAVILL *Civil Service Coach* 2 The salaries of Clerks in the Second Division..shall commence at 70*l.* per annum. **1898** *Guide Employm. Civil Service* 15 Second Division Clerkships... The Second Division forms at present the rank and file of the permanent Civil Service. **1959** *Chambers's Encycl.* III. 605/1 There is a Civil Service Clerical Association and a First Division Association (the latter representing the administrative grade and taking its name from the old name for that grade).

h. In Association Football, a group of teams in competition, usu. forming part of a league.

1899 OAKLEY & SMITH *Football* iii. 170 A Second League has been formed, and the number of clubs admitted to the First League or Division has been enlarged. **1908** 'BEDOUIN' *Scottish League Football* 24 The Second Division of the League was created in 1894–5. **1912** A. BENNETT *Matador of Five Towns* 9 If Knype drop into the Second Division..it'll be all up with first-class football in the Five Towns! **1966** *Listener* 20 Jan. 88/1 Ipswich Town topped the First Division for a season without ever seeming of international calibre. **1971** *Times* 13 Apr. 7/1 Leicester, in essence, are a first division club.

†**11.** *Mus.* A florid melodic passage: see 7. *Obs.*

III. 12. *attrib.* and *Comb.*, as ***division-bell***, ***-list***, ***-lobby*** (sense 8), ***-maker***, ***-making***, etc.; **division-mark** (*Mus.*), a slur enclosing a numeral, placed over or under a group of notes not in the ordinary rhythm of the piece, (e.g. a triplet), and showing the number of notes; **division-plate** (see quot. 1874); †**division-viol**, a smaller kind of 'bass-viol', adapted for playing 'divisions' (sense 7); the same as *viola da gamba* (*obs.*).

1530 PALSGR. 408 Nouther the erthe nor the Gaulles suffre nothyng by this devysion makyng. **1656** WOOD *Life* (Oxf. Hist. Soc.) I. 208 J. Procter..was a rare musicion, especiall for the Lyra violl and also for the division violl. **1667** C. SIMPSON (*title*) The Division-Viol; or the Art of playing extempore upon a Ground. **1843** CARLYLE *Past & Pr.* II. ix. (1845) 119 Parliamentary traditions, division lists, election-funds. **1874** KNIGHT *Dict. Mech.*, *Division-plate*, the disk or wheel in the gear-cutting lathe, which is pierced with various circular systems of holes; each circle represents the divisions of a circumference into a given number of parts. **1880** STAINER & BARRETT *Dict. Mus. Terms*, *Division viol*, a violin with frets upon the finger-board. **1894** *Times* 1 Oct. 6/1 Brigade drill, five days; division drill and manœuvres, four and a half days.

Hence **di'visionist**, one who favours or advocates division; **di'visionless** *a.*, without divisions, (in quot., Not taking part in a division).

1884 McCARTHY *Eng. under Gladstone* ii. 37 A youthful ambition to be divisionless. **1889** *Columbus* (Ohio) *Disp.* 15 Jan., The divisionists are embarassed by the absence from the house..of [three members] in favour of division.

divisional (dɪˈvɪʒənəl), *a.* (*sb.*) [see -AL[1].]

1. a. Of the nature of division; pertaining to, or serving for, division; characterized by division.

1738 A. HILL *Let. to Ld. Bolingbroke* 31 July, Wks. 1753 I. 289 Let this divisional contract between us support, and encourage a correspondence. **1796** MORSE *Amer. Geog.* I. 447 The divisional line between Connecticut and Massachusetts. **1830** LYELL *Princ. Geol.* (1875) II. III. xlviii. 575 A divisional structure, like that..derived from plates of mica. **1839** BAILEY *Festus* (1854) 172 Time is divisional; eternity, all unitive. **1861** CRAIK *Hist. Eng. Lit.* I. 260 Separated by a point, or other divisional mark.

b. Of a lower denomination which exactly divides or measures the higher; fractional; forming an aliquot part of the standard. Also as *sb.* an aliquot part, a submultiple.

1826 BENTHAM in *Westm. Review* VI. 504 Successive divisional operations, performed upon the same integral subject-matter. **1880** *Libr. Univ. Knowl.* (N.Y.) IX. 764 Prefixing the Greek words..for multiples, and the Latin *deci*, *centi*, and *milli* for divisionals. **1892** *Daily News* 5 Sept. 5/1 A new issue of divisional money is contemplated.

2. Of or belonging to a division, section, or portion: see DIVISION 10. ***Divisional Court***: a court constituted by two or more judges of the High Court to try cases from one of the divisions (see DIVISION 10 a), when such cases are not suitable to be heard by a single judge.

1845 STOCQUELER *Handbk. Brit. India* (1854) 296 Wattair, a military station, the head-quarters of the divisional command. **1846** GROTE *Greece* I. xviii. II. 17 A population ..without any special and recognised names either aggregate or divisional. **1873** *Act 36 & 37 Vict.* c. 66 §40 Such causes and matters as are not proper to be heard by a single judge shall be heard by divisional courts of the high court, which shall for that purpose exercise all or any part of the jurisdiction of the high court. **1875** KINGLAKE *Crimea* (1877) V. i. 95 The divisional commander and his brigadier. **1896** *Times* (weekly ed.) 17 Apr. 292/2 The police divisional surgeon. **1928** *Daily Mail* 3 Aug. 10/6 In recent years the trend of decisions is very different and reached its culminating point in the Divisional Court this year. **1939** BISHOP & SACHS *ABC of Divorce Practice* 4 The President of the Probate, Divorce and Admiralty Division, with other Judges attached thereto are the permanent Judges of the Divorce Division and a Divisional Court..is constituted by two of these Judges or by any two Judges of the High Court, sitting together.

Hence **di'visionally** *adv.*, in relation to division, or to a division.

1872 *Daily News* 26 Aug., To accustom themselves and their respective commands to work divisionally. **1887** LECKY *Eng. in 18th C.* VI. xxv. 580 Throwing the greatest part of the borough representation into the counties, collectively or divisionally.

di'visionary, *a. rare.* [f. DIVISION + -ARY[1].] = DIVISIONAL.

1815 *Q. Rev.* (F. Hall). **1828** in WEBSTER. **1858** G. P. SCROPE *Geol. etc. France* (ed. 2) 171 The three chief modifications of divisionary structure. **1891** *Times* 30 Dec. 3/5 Silver can serve all the purposes of the divisionary money.

†**di'visionate**, *v. Obs. nonce-wd.* [f. as prec. + -ATE[3].] *trans.* To make division of, divide.

a **1586** SIDNEY *Wanstead Play* Wks. (1674) 622 (D.) [Pedantic schoolmaster speaking] First, you must divisionate your point [of argument], quasi you should cut a chees into two particles..which must also be subdivisionated into three equal species.

†**di'visioner**. *Obs.* [f. as prec. + -ER[1] 1.] One who makes a division.

1616 R. SHELDON *Miracles Antichr.* 181 (T.) The divisioner, which was Freeman the Ignatian, and the other priests, thought that I knew nothing of the grand present.

divisionism (dɪˈvɪʒənɪz(ə)m). [f. DIVISION + -ISM.] The practice of painting with pure colours, and of achieving the effect of mixed colours by the juxtaposition on the canvas of contrasting colours instead of by mixing the desired shade on the palette. Hence **di'visionist**, a painter who follows this practice; also *attrib.* or as *adj.*

1901 L. VILLARI *Giovanni Segantini* 53 His 'divisionist' drawings. *Ibid.* 73 In this replica he began to apply the system of divisionism. **1920** *Times Lit. Suppl.* 18 Nov. 745/4 Cézanne, with his insistence upon the volumes of objects, rebelled against the disintegration of form which was the logical consequence of divisionism. **1921** *Edin. Rev.* Apr. 304 The most enthusiastic Divisionist discovered there were limits beyond which his theories could not be put into practice. **1926** F. RUTTER *Evol. Mod. Art* 41 A Divisionist painter desiring a grey..places on his canvas little touches, say, of pure violet in juxtaposition to little touches of a yellowish green. **1949** KOESTLER *Insight & Outlook* 391 The great influence which Seurat's system of 'divisionism' exerted on painters of his generation. **1970** *Oxf. Compan. Art* 318/2 Notable precursors of Divisionism were Watteau and Delacroix. **1971** *Listener* 4 Mar. 274/1 Pointillist or divisionist in detail.

divisive (dɪˈvaɪsɪv), *a.* [f. L. type *dīvīsīv-us, f. *dīvīs-*: see DIVISE and -IVE. Cf. F. *devisif*, *-ive* (16th c. in Hatz.-Darm.).]

1. Having the quality or function of dividing; causing or expressing division or distribution; making or perceiving distinctions, analytical.

1603 HOLLAND *Plutarch's Mor.* 1341 Dualitie, which is a divisive nature. *a* **1638** MEDE *Treat. Daniel's Weeks* Wks. III. (1672) 700 The Hebrews want those numbers which the Grammarians call Distributive or Divisive, *Terni*, *quaterni*, *quini*..&c. **1659** STANLEY *Hist. Philos.* III. III. 82 The common Sciences, as the demonstrative, the definitive, the divisive. *a* **1688** CUDWORTH *Immut. Mor.* IV. iii. (R.) With its subtle divisive power. **1831** CARLYLE *Schiller* Misc. Ess. 1872 III. 110 As the one spirit was intuitive, all-embracing ..so the other was scholastic, divisive.

2. Producing or tending to division, disunion, dissension, or discord.

1642 *Declar. Lords & Com. to Gen. Ass. Ch. Scot., Lond.* 11 Divisive motions against the Course of Reformation. **1649** MILTON *Observ. Art. Peace, Belfast Presbyt.* Wks. (1847) 261/1 Broachers of national and divisive motions. **1653** BAXTER *Chr. Concord* 6 We are not so unconscionably self-conceited or divisive, as to think we must..reject all those..that differ..from us. **1711** *Act of Genl. Assembly of Ch. of Scotl.* (Subscription Formula, Question 6) Do you promise that you shall follow no divisive courses from the present establishment of the Church? **1829** CARLYLE *Voltaire*, Misc. (1872) II. 147 Vanity is of a divisive, not of a uniting nature.

Hence **di'visively** *adv.*, in a divisive manner, by way of division; **di'visiveness**, the quality of being divisive, tendency to divide or split up.
*a*1600 HOOKER *Eccl. Pol.* VIII. iv. §6 Kings..are in authority over the Church, if not collectively, yet divisively understood; that is over each particular person within that Church. 1602 WARNER *Alb. Eng.* Epit. (1612) 353 Seuerall parts or Colonies, held, deuisiuely, by seauenteene different peoples. 1837 CARLYLE *Fr. Rev.* III. III. i. (1872) 100 So invincible is man's tendency to unite, with all the invincible divisiveness he has! 1887 *Pall Mall G.* 29 Oct. 2/2 This, surely, of all times is not the hour for divisiveness. Every soldier is wanted..Every voice calls for union.

divisor (dɪ'vaɪzə(r)). Also 5 -er, -our. [ad. L. *dīvīsōr-em*, agent-n. from *dīvidĕre* to DIVIDE; perh. in early instances a. F. *diviseur* (15th c. in Hatz.-Darm.).]
1. *Math.* A number or quantity by which another is to be divided. (Correlative to DIVIDEND.)
*c*1430 *Art Nombryng* (E.E.T.S.) 12 The last figure of þe nombre of the dyvyser. *Ibid.*, Yf it happe..þat þe last of the divisor may not so oft be withdraw of the figure above his hede. 14.. *Mann. & Househ. Exp.* 439, clx. roddes is one acre; wher fore he must ever be your devysour. 1674 JEAKE *Arith.* (1696) 30 This Remain is always less than the Divisor. 1806 HUTTON *Course Math.* I. 64 Division of Vulgar Fractions..invert the terms of the divisor, and multiply the dividend by it.
b. A number or quantity that divides another exactly; a measure, factor.
common divisor, a number or quantity that divides each of two or more numbers or quantities without a remainder; = common measure or factor.
1557 RECORDE *Whetst.* G ij b, Take any twoo square nombers, that will admitte one diuisor. 1858 TODHUNTER *Algebra* vi. §106 The term *greatest common measure* is not very appropriate in Algebra..It would be better to speak of the *highest common divisor* or of the *highest common measure.* 1859 BARN. SMITH *Algebra* (ed. 6) 290 The Highest Common Divisor of the expressions.
attrib. 1817 COLEBROOKE *Algebra* 229 The divisor quantity.
†**2.** One who divides; a person appointed to divide property. *Obs. rare.*
1542 *Richmond. Wills* (Surtees) 31 The iiij men divisores and prycers of this forsayd Inventory.

divi'sorial, *a. rare.* [f. as next + -AL[1].] Characterized by dividing.
1882 ELWES tr. *Capello & Ivens' Benguella* II. vii. 148 The divisorial line of the waters of the two rivers.

divisory (dɪ'vaɪzərɪ), *a.* [ad. med. or mod.L. *dīvīsōri-us*, f. *dīvīsor*: see above and -ORY.] Pertaining to division or distribution among a number.
1614 RALEIGH *Hist. World* II. xvi. §2. 467 Diuers sorts of lots..as in the diuision of grounds or honours; and in things to be vnder-taken: the two first kindes were called diuisorie; the third diuinatorie. 1656 FULLER *Notes on Jonah* (1657) 39 Lots were of three natures, 1st. divinatorie, 2nd. Divisorie, 3[rdly]. consultory. 1710 *Brit. Apollo* III. No. 65. 1/2. 1880 MUIRHEAD *Gaius* Digest 442 The divisory actions were the *a. familiae erciscundae* for partitioning an inheritance, *communi dividundo* for dividing common property, and *finium regundorum* for settling boundaries. 1885 LORENZ tr. *Van der Kessel's Select Thesis* ccclxi, In divisory contracts made..between a surviving parent and the relatives of the ward.

†**di'vitiate**, *v. Obs.* [f. L. *dīvitiæ* riches + -ATE[3].] *trans.* To enrich.
1627 FELTHAM *Resolves* I. lxxiv, Not possession, but use divitiates a man more truely. 1656 in BLOUNT *Glossogr.*

†**diviti'osity.** *Obs.*[-0] [ad. med.L. *dīvitiōsitās*, f. *dīvitiōsus* abounding in riches: see -ITY.] 'Abundance of riches' (Blount *Glossogr.* 1656).

divitism ('daɪvɪtɪz(ə)m). *nonce-wd.* [f. L. *dīvit-* (*dīves*) rich + -ISM.] The condition of being rich.
1890 *Contemp. Rev.* Mar. 230 Pauperism and divitism would disappear.

divoit, obs. Sc. form of DEVOUT.

divolve, erroneous form of DEVOLVE *v.*

divorce (dɪ'vɔəs), *sb.* Also 4-5 de-, dy-, divors, 4-6 de-, dyvorse, 4-7 devorce, 5 devourse, 5-7 divorse, 6 dyvorce. [a. F. *divorce* (14th c. in Hatz.-Darm.) = It. *divorzio*, Sp., Pg. *divorcio*:—L. *dīvortiu-m* (*divertium*) separation, dissolution of marriage by consent, n. of action f. *dīvertĕre* (earlier *dīvortĕre*) to turn aside, spec. of a woman, to separate from or leave her husband.]
1. Legal dissolution of marriage by a court or other competent body, or according to forms recognized in the country, nation, or tribe.
Formerly and still often (e.g. historically or anthropologically) used in the widest sense; hence, including the formal putting away of, or separation from, a spouse by a heathen or barbarian; the pronouncing a marriage to have been invalid from the beginning owing to fraud, or to legal, canonical, or physical incapacity of the parties, as in the 'divorce' of Henry VIII from Catherine (now called in English Law *decree of nullity*), and the 'divorce *a mensa et thoro*' (from bed and board), long the only 'divorce' recognized by English law, but now, since 1857, called 'judicial separation'. But, in strict legal use, now applied in English-speaking countries only to the dissolution by decree of court of what was in itself a legal marriage, upon grounds sanctioned by the law, and upon evidence accepted by the court.
1377 LANGL. *P. Pl.* B. II. 175 Owre synne to suffre, as auoutrie and deuo[r]ses. 1393 *Ibid.* C. XXIII. 139 He made leel matrimonye Departe er deþ come and a deuors shupte. *c*1400 *Apol. Loll.* 72 Be ware of making of mariagis, & of diuorsis or dipartingis. 1520 *Caxton's Chron. Eng.* VII. 80/1 In the same yere was made a dyvorce bytwene the kynge of Fraunce and the quene his wyfe. 1611 BIBLE *Jer.* iii. 8, I had put her away and giuen her a bill of diuorce. 1613 SHAKS. *Hen. VIII*, III. ii. 31 The Cardinall did intreat his Holinesse To stay the Iudgement o' th' Diuorce. 1709 ADDISON *Tatler* No. 20 ¶2 A Method of obtaining a Divorce from a Marriage, which I know the Law will pronounce void. 1765-9 BLACKSTONE *Comm.* (1793) 559 In cases of total divorce, the marriage is declared null, as having been absolutely unlawful *ab initio*..for which reason..no divorce can be obtained, but during the life of the parties. 1893 EARL DUNMORE *Pamirs* I. 337 This..widow marries the first man that takes her fancy: as..she can get a divorce for the modest sum of threepence-halfpenny.
2. *transf.* and *fig.* Complete separation; disunion of things closely united.
*c*1380 WYCLIF *Serm.* Sel. Wks. I. 26 Anticrist haþ so weddid þes goodis wiþ preestis þat noon may make þis dyvors. *c*1450 *St. Cuthbert* (Surtees) 4775 Bischope Eardulphe..To þe blisse of heuen wende, Fra þis werlde made deuorse. *c*1532 DEWES *Introd. Fr.* in *Palsgr.* 1050 To suffre devorce or departyng betwene his soule and his body. 1599 SHAKS. *Hen. V*, v. ii. 394 To make diuorce of their incorporate League. 1680 BOYLE *Scept. Chem.* I. 41 Without ..having their coherence violated by the divorce of their associated parts. 1726 AYLIFFE *Parergon* 110 'Tis hard to make a Divorce between things that are so near in Nature to each other, as being convertible Terms. 1852 H. ROGERS *Ecl. Faith* (1853) 304 The divorce between the ' spiritual faculties' and the intellect..is impossible.
†**3.** That which causes divorce or separation.
1592 SHAKS. *Ven. & Ad.* 932 Hateful divorce of love',—thus chides she Death. 1607 —— *Timon* IV. iii. 382 [To the Gold] O thou sweete King-killer, and deare diuorce Twixt naturall Sunne and sire.
4. *attrib.*, as *divorce-court*, etc.
*a*1806 HORSLEY *Sp. Adultery Bill* (R.), Expatiating.. upon..the perversion as well as the abuse of many divorce-bills which had passed the legislature. 1837 *Penny Cycl.* IX. 40/1 Divorce bills have not improperly been called the privilege of the rich. 1891 *Law Times* XCII. 104/2 A point of Divorce law and practice. 1905 *Macm. Mag.* Nov. 57 Is it an ill thing that the newspapers should publish detailed reports of divorce-suits? 1945 Divorce case [see AT *prep.* 40]. 1955 M. GLUCKMAN *Custom & Conflict in Afr.* iii. 79 Social factors and not only personal disharmonies may control divorce-rates in Western society. 1960 *Spectator* 23 Sept. 444 Where people aren't brittle and promiscuous and divorce-prone.

divorce (dɪ'vɔəs), *v.* Forms: see prec. [a. F. *divorce-r* (14th c. in Hatz.-Darm.):—med.L. *dīvortiāre* to dissolve a marriage (Du Cange), f. L. *dīvortium*: see prec.]
1. *trans.* To dissolve the marriage contract between (husband and wife) by process of law; to separate by divorce *from.*
1494 FABYAN *Chron.* v. cxiii. 86 The Kynge..sayde if y[t] were true, she shuld frome hym be deuorcyd. 1536 WRIOTHESLEY *Chron.* (1875) I. 41 The King was diversed from his wife Queene Anne. 1556 *Chron. Gr. Friars* (Camden) 70 The byshoppe of Wynchester that was than was devorsyd from hys wyffe in Powlles, the whyche was a bucheres wyff of Nottynggam, and gave hare husbande a sartyne mony a yere dureynge hys lyffe. 1613 SHAKS. *Hen. VIII*, IV. i. 32 By the maine assent Of all these Learned men, she was diuorc'd, And the late Marriage made of none effect. *a*1734 NORTH *Exam.* II. iv. §57 (1740) 260 When that extraordinary Law passed, to divorce the Earl of Ross from his Wife. 1771 HOOKE *Rom. Hist.* XI. iv, Scribonia was divorced from him [Octavius] the very day she was brought to bed of the famous Julia.
b. *refl.*
1593 SHAKS. *3 Hen. VI*, I. i. 247, I here diuorce my selfe, Both from thy Table, Henry, and thy Bed. 1886 F. M. CRAWFORD *Lonely Parish* xiv, Mrs. G...seemed never to have thought of divorcing herself from her husband.
c. *intr.* (for *refl.*)
1643 MILTON *Divorce* I. iv, The reasons which now move him to divorce, are equal to the best of those that could first warrant him to marry. *a*1649 DRUMM. OF HAWTH. *Hist. Jas. V*, Wks. (1711) 100 King Henry, impatient of delays and amorous, divorceth from his own queen, and marrieth Anne Bullen. 1875 POSTE *Gaius* I. Comm. (ed. 2) 116 Justinian enacted that a man or a woman who divorced without a cause should retire to a cloister.
2. *trans.* To put away (a spouse); to repudiate.
1387 [see DIVORCING below]. 1526-34 TINDALE *Matt.* v. 32 Whosoever maryeth her that is devorsed breaketh wedlocke. *c*1550 CHEKE *Matt.* v. 31 Whosoever divorceth his wife let him give her a diuorsment bil. *a*1656 BP. HALL *Rem. Wks.* (1660) 161 Another allows a man to divorce that wife he hath upon sleight occasions, and to take another. 1771 HOOKE *Rom. Hist.* Index, Antony..divorces his wife, and marries Fulvia..Declares Cleopatra his wife. Divorces Octavia. 1837 *Penny Cycl.* IX. 40/1 By the Mohammedan law a man may divorce his wife orally and without any ceremony..He may divorce her twice, and take her again without her consent; but if he divorce her a third time..he cannot receive her again until she has been married and divorced by another husband.
3. To dissolve (a marriage or union). *arch.*
1580 SIDNEY *Arcadia* III. Wks. 1724 II. 545 The cruel villain forced the sword..to divorce the fair marriage of the head and body. 1643 MILTON *Divorce* I. x, An unlawful marriage may be lawfully divorced. 1873 BROWNING *Red Cott. Nt.-Cap* 243 When death divorces such a fellowship.
4. *fig.* To separate; to sever, cut off, part.
1430 LYDG. *Chron. Troy* II. xx, Howe his goste and he were deuorced. 1570-6 LAMBARDE *Peramb. Kent* (1826) 89 It was sometime divorced from the continent by a water. 1594 HOOKER *Eccl. Pol.* II. v. §5 Were it consonant vnto reason to diuorce these two sentences? 1659 B. HARRIS *Parival's Iron Age* 29 The King divorced himself from the Church of Rome. 1784 COWPER *Task* I. 748 Till..knees and hassocks are well nigh divorced. 1871 TYNDALL *Fragm. Sc.* (1879) II. ix. 192 Divorced from matter, where is life?
†**b.** *intr.* (for *refl.*) *Obs.*
1687 DRYDEN *Hind & P.* III. 205 Divorcing from the Church to wed the dame.
5. *trans. fig.* To put away, remove, dispel; to repudiate.
*a*1592 MARLOWE & NASHE *Dido* III. ii, Fair queen of love, I will divorce these doubts. 1593 SHAKS. *Rich. II*, v. iv. 9 The man That would diuorce this terror from my heart. 1675 tr. *Machiavelli's Prince* xii. (Rtldg. 1883) 77 In time of peace they [mercenaries] divorce you. 1712 BLACKMORE *Creation* VI, The pipe distinguished by its gristly rings To cherish life aerial pasture brings, Which the soft-breathing lungs with gentle force Constant embrace by turns, by turns divorce. 1865 SWINBURNE *Poems & Ball.*, *Rococo* 30 Say March may wed September And time divorce regret.
Hence **di'vorced** *ppl. a.*; **di'vorcing** *vbl. sb.*
1387 TREVISA *Higden* (Rolls) VII. 139 Guynuld..gaf to her housbonde a perpetuel dyvorsynge and forsakynge. 1535 COVERDALE *Lev.* xxi. 14 No wedowe, ner deuorsed, ner defyled..but a virgin of his awne people shal he take to wife. 1642 MILTON *Apol. Smect.* xi. Wks. (1847) 95 1 Why do we not say as to a divors't wife. 1645 —— *Tetrach.* Deut. xxiv. 1-2, The divorcing of an Israelitish woman was as easy by the law as the divorcing of a stranger. 1861 MRS. H. WOOD *East Lynne* II. xi, To marry a divorced woman.

divorceable (dɪ'vɔəsəb(ə)l), *a.* In 7 divorcible. [f. DIVORCE *v.* + -ABLE.] Capable of being divorced; liable to divorce.
1645 MILTON *Colast.* Wks. (1847) 229/2 It can be no human society, and so not without reason divorcible. 1737 STACKHOUSE *Hist. Bible, N.T.* (1765) V. III. 336 *note*, If she found not grace in her husband's eyes, she was divorceable. 1813 BYRON in Moore *Life* (1866) 215 Lady —— and her daughter Lady —— both divorceable.

divorcee (dɪ,vɔə'siː). [f. DIVORCE *v.* + -EE. Often used in the Fr. forms *divorcé* masc., *divorcée* fem. (divɔrse), pa. pple. used subst. of *divorcer* to divorce.] A divorced person.
1813 MAR. EDGEWORTH *Patron.* (1833) I. 71 (Stanf.) The mother was a *divorcée.* 1877 READE *Woman Hater* ii. (1883) 13 (Stanf.) He was now a *divorcé.* 1880 *Daily News* 1 Oct. 6/1 The Church would..refuse to sanction..any civil marriage between divorcees and co-respondents. 1884 MRS. C. PRAED *Zero* xviii, Divorcées were in the ascendant.

di'vorceless, *a.* [f. DIVORCE *sb.* + -LESS.] Not practising or liable to divorce.
1595 CHAPMAN *Coronet* st. iv in *Ovid's Banquet* sig. F1[r], And in th' vntainted Temple of her hart Doth the diuorceless nuptials celebrate Twixt God and her. 1825 COLERIDGE *Aids Refl.* Aph. xxxvi. (1848) I. 86 Contemplate the filial and loyal Bee; the home-building, wedded, and divorceless Swallow. 1914 H. G. WELLS *Englishman looks at World* xv. 207 There was a time in this country when our marriage was a practically divorceless bond.

divorcement (dɪ'vɔəsmənt). [f. DIVORCE *v.* + -MENT.]
1. The action of divorcing, or the fact of being divorced; dissolution of the marriage tie; divorce.
1526-34 TINDALE *Matt.* v. 31 Let hym geue her a testymonyall also of the devorcement [*c*1550 CHEKE a diuorsment bill; 1611 a writing of diuorcement]. 1568 GRAFTON *Chron.* II. 96 A devorcement was made, betwene king John and Avis his wife. 1627 SPEED *England, Ireland* I. §18 Their wiues were many, by reason of diuorcements. 1702 ECHARD *Eccl. Hist.* (1710) 494 She procured a divorcement from him. 1823 J. D. HUNTER *Captivity N. Amer.* 231 Marriage, widowhood, polygamy, divorcements.
2. The severance of any close relation; complete separation.
1551 T. WILSON *Logike* (1567) 21 b, How then canst thou make a diuorsment, betwixte honestie and profite? 1593 R. HARVEY *Philad.* Ded. 2 Diuorcement of heartes. 1822 BYRON *Werner* IV. i. 331 After twelve years divorcement from my parents. 1894 *The Voice* (N.Y.) 24 May, The eternal divorcement of church and saloon is..approaching.

divorcer (dɪ'vɔəsə(r)). [f. as prec. + -ER[1].]
1. a. One who divorces or puts away in legal form a wife or husband. **b.** One who or that which divorces or separates husband and wife.
1613 DRUMM. OF HAWTH. *Cypress Grove* (J.), Death is the violent estranger of acquaintance, the eternal divorcer of marriage. 1644 MILTON *Jdgm. Bucer* (1851) 318 They think it follows that second marriage is in no case to be permitted either to the Divorcer, or to the Divorced. 1831 CARLYLE in Froude *Life* II. 189 Rutherford sate also within the ring with Dr. Lushington (the divorcer).
2. *fig.* One who or that which severs or parts persons or things closely united.
*c*1611 CHAPMAN *Iliad* XVI. 759 Patroclus..was from his own [life] divorced, And thus his great divorcer braved: [etc.]. 1822 LAMB *Elia* Ser. I. *Distant Corr.*, Since then the old divorcer [death] has been busy. 1827 HOOD *Hero & Leander* xviii, That cold divorcer will be twixt them still.

divorcive (dɪ'vɔəsɪv), *a.* Also -sive. [f. as prec. + -IVE.] Causing or leading to divorce.
1643 MILTON *Divorce* I. i, The grave and pious reasons of this divorsive Law. *Ibid.* II. xviii (1738) Divorcive Adultery.

† **di'vorcy, di'vorcie.** *Obs.* [ad. L. *dīvorti-um*, med.L. *dīvorci-um*: see above.] = DIVORCE *sb.*

1565 CDL. ALLEN in Fulke *Confut. Purg.* (1577) 12 Often diuorcies, and perpetuall change for nouelty. *Ibid.* 15.

† **di'vorsion.** *Sc. Obs. rare.* [f. med.L. *dīvortiōn-em*, n. of action f. *dīvortĕre, divertĕre*: see DIVORCE *sb.*] Divorcing, DIVORCE.

1596 DALRYMPLE tr. *Leslie's Hist. Scot.* IX. 205 Anent the controuersie of diuorsioun and pairteng betuene him and her.

† **di'vort,** *v. Obs. rare.* [ad. L. *dīvort-ĕre*, archaic var. of *dīvertĕre* to turn aside; cf. DIVORCE *sb.*] *intr.* To turn away, separate (*from* a spouse).

1581 NUCE *Seneca's Octavia* I. iv, She causeth Make from spouse for to divort.

divot ('dɪvət), *sb. Sc.* and *north. dial.* Forms: 6 **diffat, -et, devait,** (dovet), 7-8 **devot,** 7-9 **divet** (7 divott, 8 diviot), 7- **divot.**

1. a. A slice of earth with the grass growing upon it, a turf, a sod, such as are used in the north for roofing cottages, forming the edges of thatched roofs, the tops of dry-stone walls, etc.

The thicker, more earthy sods used in building walls or dikes, are called *fails*; hence the common collocation *fail* and *divot*. The digging and throwing up of either is 'casting': see CAST *v.* 28.

1536 BELLENDEN *Cron. Scot.* (1821) I. 179 Gret strenthis of treis, stanis and devaitis. *a* **1670** SPALDING *Troub. Chas. I* (1829) 27 This kiln was first covered with divots. **1771** PENNANT *Tour Scotl.* (1790) 132 The houses..are formed with loose stones and covered with clods which they call devots. *c* **1817** HOGG *Tales & Sk.* V. 214 A coverlet worked as thick as a divot. **1843** T. WILSON *Pitman's Pay* Note (Northumbld. Gloss.), The cottages on the Fell were all covered with divots. *a* **1852** MACGILLIVRAY *Nat. Hist. Dee Side* (1855) 193 [He] conducted us to his Museum, a little hut, built of stones and roofed with divots. **1895** CROCKETT *Men of Mosshags* 150 Clodding him with divots of peat and sod.

b. As a material.

1536 BELLENDEN *Cron. Scot.* (1821) I. 172 He beildit ane huge wall of fail and devait. **1541** *Ld. Treas. Accts.* in Pitcairn *Crim. Trials* (1830) I. 312 Theking of the Tour with brwme and dovet. *a* **1575** *Diurnal of Occurrents* (1833) 322 The toun of Edinburgh begane to big thair fortressis of diffet and mik. **1605** *Feu Contract* in J. Mill *Diary* (1889) 193 To cast faill and devot on the ground of Sumburgh.. according to use and wont. **1730** *Crt. Bk. of Barony of Urie* (1892) 133 The said turf or divot so cast to be forfeit. **1861** SMILES *Engineers* II. *Rennie* i. 102 To fetch a load of 'divot' from Gladsmuir, or of coal from the nearest colliery.

c. *Sc. Law. fail (feal) and divot*, 'a rural servitude, importing a right in the proprietor of the dominant tenement to cut and remove turf for fences or for thatching or covering houses or the like purposes, within the dominant lands' (Bell *Dict. Law Scot.*).

1593 *Sc. Acts Jas. VI* (1597) § 161 That the saidis glebes be designed with freedome of foggage, pastourage, fewall, faill, diffat, loning, frie ischue and entrie. **1693** STAIR *Instit. Law Scot.* II. vii. § 13 (ed. 2) 288 A Servitude of Pasturage introduced by Fourty years peaceable Possession of the Pasturage, was not to be extended to Feal and Divet. **1754** ERSKINE *Princ. Sc. Law* (1809) 223 We have two predial servitudes..viz. that of fuel or feal and divot, and of thirlage. **1773** —— *Instit. Law Scot.* I. II. ix. § 17. **1814** SCOTT *Wav.* xlii, Rights of pasturage—fuel—feal and divot.

d. *Golf.* A piece of turf cut out with a club by a player in making a stroke.

1886 H. G. HUTCHINSON *Hints on Golf* 9 With an iron club an unskilful player is more likely to cut fids of turf—*golficè*, 'divots'—out of the green. **1890** —— *Golf* x. 272 A divot well replaced is, in most conditions of the ground, as a divot that has never been cut. **1935** O. NASH *Primrose Path* (1936) 105 The wretched golfer, divot-bound.

2. *Comb.*, as **divot-cast**, as much (land) as one divot might be 'cast' or cut off; **divot-seat**, one made of divots; **divot-spade**, a spade for casting turf, a flaughter-spade.

1725 RAMSAY *Gent. Sheph.* II. i, There you may see him lean, And to his divot-seat invites his frien'. **1818** HOGG *Brownie of Bodsbeck* II. 153 (Jam.) The old shepherd was sitting on his divot-seat, without the door. **1818** SCOTT *Hrt. Midl.* xii, He hasna a divot-cast of land in Scotland.

'**divot,** *v. Sc.* [f. prec. sb.] **a.** *trans.* To cover with divots; **b.** *intr.* 'To cast or cut divots' (Jam.).

1696 *Banff Burgh Rec.* in Cramond *Ann. Banff* (1893) II. 176 To repaire the thatch by divoteing the house.

divot, obs. Sc. form of DEVOUT.

† **di'vulgate,** *ppl. a. Obs.* [ad. L. *dīvulgāt-us*, pa. pple. of *dīvulgāre* to DIVULGE.] Made public, spread abroad. (Chiefly used as pa. pple. = divulged.)

a **1440** *Found. St. Bartholomew's* (E.E.T.S.) 19 This dede anoon was dyvulgate by all the Cyte. **1513** DOUGLAS *Æneis* Dyrectioun, ad fin., Every burell rude poet divulgait. **1536** BELLENDEN *Cron. Scot.* (1821) I. 210 The fame of this unhappy battall, divulgat in the cuntre. **1574** HELLOWES *Gueuara's Fam. Ep.* (1577) 216 It was diuulgate through all Rome.

divulgate (dɪ'vʌlgeɪt, daɪ-), *v.* Also 6 **de-**. [f. L. *dīvulgāt-*, ppl. stem of *dīvulgāre* to DIVULGE. Pa. pple. and (in Sc.) pa. t. in 16th c. often *divulgat(e*: see prec.] *trans.* To make commonly known; to publish abroad.

1530 PALSGR. 523/2, I dyvulgate a mater, I blowe it abrode ..I thought full lytell he wolde have dyvulgate this mater. **1531** ELYOT *Gov.* Proem, I am violently stered to deuulgate or sette fourth some part of my studie. **1623** HART *Arraignm. Ur.* III. vi. 119, I hope that honest and ingenuous Physitians will..abstaine from divulgating abroad their billes or bookes. **1824** LANDOR *Imag. Conv.* Wks. 1846 I. 362, I know not whether the facts have been divulgated. **1878** BESANT & RICE *Monks of Th.* xxv, Why should she wish her choice to be divulgated?

Hence **di'vulgated** *ppl. a.*, **di'vulgating** *vbl. sb.*; also **di'vulgater, -ator.**

1537 THROGMORTON *Let. to Cromwell* in Froude *Hist. Eng.* (1858) III. 228 The divulgating of the censures. **1599** JAS. I *Βασιλ. Δωρον* To Rdr., The un-timous divulgating of this booke. **163.** M. PARKER *Harry White's Humour* (N.), To that great promulgater And neat divulgater Whom the citie admires. **1842** *Blackw. Mag.* LII. 659 Our divulged and divulgated attachment to the *veneranda rubigo.*

divulgation (dɪvʌl'geɪʃən, daɪ-). Also 6 **de-**. [ad. L. *dīvulgātiōn-em*, n. of action f. *dīvulgāre* to DIVULGE: cf. F. *divulgation* (16th c.).]

† **1.** The action of publishing or making known abroad; publication. *Obs.*

c **1540** tr. *Pol. Verg. Eng. Hist.* (Camden) I. 25 The first springe and divulgation of the hollie Gospell. **1548** HALL *Chron., Hen. VII* (an. 7) (1809) 463 This Devulgacion that Richard sonne of Kyng Edward was yet lyvyng. **1727** WOODWARD *Will* in *A. Sedgwick's Life & Lett.* (1890) I. 186 To prejudice the sale and divulgation of any of the said copies. *c* **1800** K. WHITE *Rem.* (1837) 398 A rule of moral conduct, such as the world never had any idea of before its divulgation. **1823** BENTHAM in *Parr's Wks.* (1828) VIII. 7 That they will oppose no obstruction to the divulgation of it.

2. The divulging or revealing of something private or secret; revelation, disclosure.

1610 HEALEY *St. Aug. Citie of God* 280 Had they beene honest, they would not have feared divulgation. **1638** J. R. in *Featly's Strict. Lyndom.* II. 66 Divulgation of secret Mysteries. **1860** *Times* 17 Dec. 6/5 His organ for the divulgation of Cabinet secrets.

divulgatory (dɪ'vʌlgətərɪ), *a.* [f. L. *dīvulgāt-*, ppl. stem of *dīvulgāre* to divulge + -ORY.] Tending to publish or make known.

18.. EMERSON *Sp., Free Relig. Assoc.* (Cent.), Nothing really is so self-publishing, so divulgatory, as thought.

divulge (dɪ'vʌldʒ, daɪ-), *v.* Also 5 **dy-**. [ad. L. *dīvulgā-re* to spread abroad among the people, make common, f. *dī-*, DIS- 1 + *vulgāre* to make common, publish; cf. F. *divulguer* (14th c.), but the palatalized *g* in English is abnormal.]

† **1.** *trans.* To make publicly known, to publish abroad (a statement, etc.). *Obs.*

1460 CAPGRAVE *Chron.* 1 It is somewhat divulgid in this lond, that I have aftir my possibilitie be occupied in wryting. **1490** CAXTON *Eneydos* vi. 25 Fame of his ouurages hath ben dyuulged. **1548** HALL *Chron., Hen. IV* (an. 3) 20 Whiche fraude the Kyng caused openly to be published and divulged. **1669** GALE *Crt. Gentiles* I. II. i. 4 Their fables they divulge, first by Hymns and Songs. **1768** H. WALPOLE *Hist. Doubts* 14 It is impossible to believe the account as fabricated and divulged by Henry the Seventh. **1791** COWPER *Iliad* I. 133 Among the Danai thy dreams Divulging.

† **b.** To proclaim (a person, etc.) publicly. *Obs.*

1598 SHAKS. *Merry W.* III. ii. 42, I will divulge Page himselfe for a secure and wilfull Acteon. **1671** MILTON *P.R.* III. 60 When God..with approbation marks The just man, and divulges him through Heaven To all his angels.

† **c.** To publish (a book or treatise). *Obs.*

1566 in Strype *Ann. Ref.* I. xlviii. 517 That treatise..so publickly by print divulged and dispersed. **1644** MILTON *Areop.* (Arb) 53 Ye must repeal and proscribe all scandalous and unlicenc't books already printed and divulg'd. **1709** STRYPE *Ann. Ref.* I. lvii. 629 Divers other articles.. propounded and divulged abroad by the said Cartwright.

2. To declare or tell openly (something private or secret); to disclose, reveal.

1602 MARSTON *Ant. & Mel.* Induct. Wks. 1856 I. 4, I will ding his spirit to the verge of hell, that dares divulge a ladies prejudice. **1671** MILTON *Samson* 201 Who..have divulg'd the secret gift of God To a deceitful woman. **1797** MRS. RADCLIFFE *Italian* xxvi, Command him to divulge the crimes confessed to him. **1849** MACAULAY *Hist. Eng.* I. ii. 268 Cowardly traitors hastened to save themselves, by divulging all..that had passed in the deliberations of the party.

† **3.** *transf.* To make common, impart generally. [A Latinism.] *Obs. rare.*

1667 MILTON *P.L.* VIII. 583 The sense of touch..would not be To them made common & divulg'd.

4. *intr.* (for *refl.*) To become publicly known. *rare.*

1602 SHAKS. *Ham.* IV. i. 22 To keepe it [a disease] from divulging, let's it feede Euen on the pith of life. **1890** CHILD *Ballads* VII. cxciv. 29 Nothing seems to have been done to keep the murder from divulging.

Hence **di'vulged** *ppl. a.*; **di'vulging** *vbl. sb.* and *ppl. a.*

1601 SHAKS. *All's Well* II. i. 174 A divulged shame Traduc'd by odious ballads. **1604** *St. Trials, Hampton Crt. Confer.* (R.), There is no such licencious divulging of these books. **1607** TOPSELL *Four-f. Beasts* (1658) 555 That which divulged fame doth perswade the believers. **1614** T. ADAMS *Devil's Banquet* 338 Cease your obstreperous clamours, and divulging slanders. **1883** *Daily News* 20 July 6/2 An action brought for alleged divulging of telegrams.

† **di'vulge,** *sb. Obs.* [f. prec. vb.] The act of divulging or publishing abroad.

1619 LUSHINGTON *Repet. Serm.* in *Phenix* (1708) II. 478 Our modern News..is forg'd in Conventicles..and the Divulge committed to some vigilant and watchful Tongue.

di'vulgement. [f. as prec. + -MENT.] The action of divulging. Also, †*concr.* in *pl.*

1632 LITHGOW *Trav.* x. 497 Rossay that kisseth the devulgements of the River. *c* **1817** HOGG *Tales & Sk.* II. 84 Anxious and acrimonious act of divulgement. **1850** DAUBENY *Atom. The.* xiv. (ed. 2) 459 Divulgement would be considered as the deepest of crimes. **1876** MOZLEY *Univ. Serm.* xii. (1877) 226 It would not admit of unqualified divulgement of such truth as this.

divulgence (dɪ'vʌldʒəns, daɪ-). [f. DIVULGE *v.* + -ENCE: app. by form-association with *indulgence*, etc.] The action of divulging; disclosure.

1851 DICKENS *Our School* in *Househ. Words* 11 Oct. 51/2 The Chief 'knew something bad of him', and on pain of divulgence enforced Phil to be his bondsman. **1875** LIGHTFOOT *Comm. Col. & Philem.* (1876) 92 Their whole organisation was arranged so as to prevent the divulgence of its secrets to those without.

di'vulger. [f. as prec. + -ER[1].] One who divulges: † **a.** a publisher (*obs.*); **b.** a discloser.

1606 *Proceed. agst. Garnet, etc.* M iv b (T.), The first devisers, and divulgers of this scandalous report. *c* **1611** CHAPMAN *Iliad* XIX. Comment., Our Commentators..will by no means allow the word *κάπρος* here for Homer's, but an unskilfulness in the divulger. **1749** FIELDING *Tom Jones* III. ix, Like other hasty divulgers of news, he only brought on himself the trouble of contradicting it. **1782** V. KNOX *Ess.* vi. (R.), Those secrets, which..the confidence of a friend has made known to the treacherous divulger of them.

† **di'vulse,** *v. Obs.* [f. L. *dīvuls-*, ppl. stem of *dīvellĕre* f. *dī-*, DIS- 1 + *vellĕre* to pluck, pull: cf. *convulse.*] *trans.* To tear apart or asunder.

1602 MARSTON *Ant. & Mel.* I. Wks. 1856 I. 9 Vaines, synewes, arteries..Burst and divul'st with anguish of my griefe. **1633** T. BANCROFT *Glutton's Feaver* B iv, My sinewes all divul'st with passion fell. **1691** BEVERLEY *Thous. Years Kingd. Christ* 36 No part that can be divuls'd One from Another, but All Lying Close in a Line.

divulsion (dɪ'vʌlʃən, daɪ-). [a. F. *divulsion* (Montaigne, 1580) or ad. L. *dīvulsiōn-em*, n. of action f. *dīvellĕre*: see prec.] The action of tearing, pulling, or plucking asunder; the condition of being torn apart (*from* something); a rending asunder, violent separation, laceration. Also *fig.*

1603 HOLLAND *Plutarch's Mor.* 1340 That natures parmanent and divine should cohere unto themselves inseparably, and avoid as much as is possible all distraction and divulsion. **1605** G. POWEL *Refut. Epist.* 40 It..causeth diuulsion and distraction of affections. **1624** T. SCOTT *Aphor. of State* 2 The divulsion of the Easterne Empire from the Westerne. **1684** T. BURNET *Th. Earth* I. 137 Others [islands] are made by divulsion from some continent. **1885** G. H. TAYLOR *Pelv. & Hern. Therap.* 80 To sever such adhesions by sudden, forcible divulsion, is painful.

divulsive (dɪ'vʌlsɪv), *a.* [f. L. *dīvuls-*: see above and -IVE.] Tending to tear apart or asunder.

c **1605** ROWLEY *Birth Merl.* III. vi, Let tortures and divulsive racks Force a confession from them. **1799** KIRWAN *Geol. Ess.* 96 The divulsive force that separated Britain from Germany, seems to have been directed from north to south. **1837** CARLYLE *Fr. Rev.* II. I. xii, Long years of vinegar: perhaps divulsive vinegar, like Hannibal's.

Divvers ('dɪvəz). *Oxford University slang.* [f. first syllable of DIVINITY + -ER[6] + -S (representing the pl. *moderations*).] Formerly, divinity moderations, the first public examination in Holy Scripture.

1905 *'Varsity* 30 Nov. 109/3 Those who are in for 'Divvers' should make sure of knowing all about St. Stephen's Speech. **1913** *Isis* 8 Feb. 184/2 Honour Mods. and Divvers behind him and Groups before. **1949** L. A. G. STRONG *Maud Cherrill* 12 An obsolete examination known to generations of undergraduates as Divvers. **1969** G. SMITH in *Lett. of A. Huxley* 11 H. passes the Examination in Holy Scripture ('Divvers'), which he has previously failed.

'**divvy, (divi.),** *sb.* Colloq. abbreviation of DIVIDEND. Hence '**divvy** *v. colloq.*, to 'go shares'. Freq. *to divvy (up)*, to divide (up).

1872 in *Amer. Speech* (1952) XXVII. 77 A fraudulent 'divy'. **1877** L. GROVER in Goldberg & Heffner *America's Lost Plays* (1940) IV. 203 We divvy a cool $20,000. **1880** A. A. HAYES *New Colorado* (1881) xi. 156 The two men, unsuspicious of danger were 'divvying up' the spoils in the middle of the road. **1884** J. HAY *Bread-winners* x. 150 'You surely do not intend—' 'To strike Saul for a divvy?' **1890** G. B. SHAW *Fab. Ess. in Socialism* 88 It degenerated into mere 'divvy' hunting and joint-stock shop-keeping. **1890** *Nation* (N.Y.) 10 Apr. 291/1 Where the chiefs have large families, and the 'divvies' are inadequate for their support. **1893** A. KENEALY *Molly & Her Man of War* 4 We even went so far as to 'divvy up'. **1894** *Westm. Gaz.* 3 Oct. 6/1 Co-operators tried to get as much as they could out of the servants, in order to increase the 'divi'. **1926** KIPLING *Debits & Credits* 156, I pinched 'em an' divvied with Macklin. **1936** 'R. HYDE' *Passport to Hell* xv. 227 They didn't divvy up with the spoils like our crowd would have done. **1938** J. RICE *Somers Inheritance* IV. vii. 264 It says here his money is to be divvied up. How'd you like a cut-in? **1957** *Times Lit. Suppl.* 20 Dec. 766/5 The problem of 'divvying-up' the spoils of automation.

divvy (ˈdɪvɪ), *a. slang.* [f. first syllable of DIVINE (A. 5 b) + -Y[1]; cf. DEEVY *a.*] Extremely pleasant, 'divine', 'heavenly'.

1903 *Daily Chron.* 1 Aug. 8/1, I heard one of them say that 'the dimpy was divvy', and this, when translated, meant that a certain dinner party was divine. **1924** F. M. FORD *Some do Not* I. ii. 48 The only divvy moment was when you stood waiting in the booking-office for the young man to take the tickets.

Diwali, var. DEWALEE.

diwan: see DEWAN, DIVAN.

diwyse, obs. Sc. form of DEVISE.

Dix (diːs). [Fr., = ten.] The lowest trump in Bezique and other card games; also, in Pinocle, a certain score of ten points, or the trump entitling the player to it.

1908 R. F. FOSTER *Pinochle* 5 In two-hand, any player holding the dix may exchange it for the trump card immediately after winning a trick. **1952** E. KEMPSON et al. *Hoyle Up-to-Date* 151 A player holding a dix may count it merely by showing it upon winning a trick.

‖**dix-huitième** (dizɥitjɛm), *a.* [Fr., = eighteenth.] Of or belonging to the eighteenth century. Also as *sb.*

1920 *Times Lit. Suppl.* 26 June 538/1 In a charming and characteristically dix-huitième manner. **1926** A. HUXLEY *Essays New & Old* 87 The more sophisticated find their *dix-huitième* in the original French documents..or in the ironic pages of Mr. Lytton Strachey. **1926** —— *Jesting Pilate* I. 166 The *dix-huitième* parody of Chinese art. **1936** F. R. LEAVIS *Revaluation* iii. 68 The post-war cult of the *dix-huitième*.

dixie[1] (ˈdɪksɪ). Also **dechsie, dixey, dixy.** [Hind. *degchi, -cha*, a. Hindi *degachī, -chā*, Punjabi *dekachī, degāchī, -chā*, ad. Pers. *degcha*, dim. of *deg, dīg* iron pot, kettle, cauldron.] An iron kettle or pot, used by soldiers for making tea or stew.

[**1879** MRS. A. E. JAMES *Ind. Househ. Managem.* 40 Six dechsies and covers. *Ibid.* 45 A few *dechsies* (copper pots).] **1900** *Westm. Gaz.* 29 Mar. 8/1 On halting at Klip Drift we immediately got down our dizies [*sic*] and made tea for all. **1900** *Daily News* 10 July 3/2 The 'billy' is what Tommy calls a 'dixie'. **1901** *Westm. Gaz.* 26 June 8/1 With much difficulty water was procured from a spruit over a mile away, and the 'dixey' boiled. **1916** H. G. WELLS *Mr. Britling* II. iv. §14 They shelled us again next day and our tea dixy was hit. **1916** *Anzac Bk.* 41/2 Tea made in the stew dixie, and tasting more of dixie and stew than of tea. **1942** C. BARRETT *On Wallaby* iv. 71, I returned with..a dixie much the worse for wear.

Dixie[2] (ˈdɪksɪ). *U.S.* [Origin obscure: see Mathews *Dict. Amer.*]

1. The southern United States; the South. Also ***Dixie('s) Land, Dixieland.***

1859 D. D. EMMETT *Dixie's Land*, Away! away! away down South in Dixie. *Ibid.*, In Dixie Lann whar I was bawn in, Arly on one frosty mawnin. **1859** *N.Y. Herald* 4 Apr., [Bryant's Minstrels are giving] Dixie's Land, another new Plantation Festival. **1861** G. P. PUTNAM *(title)* Before and after the battle; a day and night in 'Dixie'. **1864** W. PITTENGER *Daring & Suffering* 35 That coat..I wore all through Dixie. **1866** C. H. SMITH *Bill Arp* 139 I'm a good Union reb, and my battle cry is Dixie and the Union. **1901** W. PITTENGER *Gt. Locom. Chase* 101 Now I will succeed, or leave my bones in Dixie. **1903** *N.Y. Times* 10 Dec. 5 Nearly 400 exiles from Dixie Land gathered at the annual dinner of the Southern Society. **1948** *Daily Ardmoreite* (Ardmore, Okla.) 15 July 1/8 The 20-minute show Dixieland put on.. was more liberally sprinkled with rebel yells.

b. The music or words of the song of 'Dixie', written by D. D. Emmett in 1859.

1860 E. COWELL *Diary* (1934) 231 The irrepressible 'Dixie' predominates, but sentimental ditties are in high favor. **1904** *Minneapolis Times* 23 June 8 The orchestra in a Georgia theatre quieted a panic-stricken crowd by playing 'Dixie'. **1911** H. S. HARRISON *Queed* xxi. 261 From far away floated the strains of 'Dixie', crashed out by forty bands.

c. ***Dixieland***: used *attrib.* or quasi-*adj.* to designate a type of jazz music originally played in the southern United States, characterized by a strong rhythm of two beats to the bar and collective improvisation. Also *ellipt.* Hence **'Dixielander**, one who plays Dixieland jazz.

[**1919** *Punch* 16 Apr. 293/1 'The Original Dixie Land Jazz Band has arrived in London,' says an evening paper.] **1927** *Melody Maker* June 553/1 A dance band..need not be merely the type of 'Dixieland' jazz band. **1934** S. R. NELSON *All about Jazz* i. 25 The Dixielanders are not so démodé as one would think. *Ibid.* vi. 141 'The Jazz Band' was a 'Dixieland' combination playing modernized 'Dixieland' style. **1937** *Étude* Dec. 835/1 *Dixieland*, the original, New Orleans jazz as developed by the famous 'Dixieland Five'. **1939** W. HOBSON *Amer. Jazz Music* 210 Dorsey plays a strong bass-part foundation in the style known as 'Dixieland'. **1946** *Amer. Jazz* No. 1. 13/1 The results are probably nearer to the earliest Dixieland (containing a coloured element) than anything waxed in recent years. **1950** A. LOMAX *Mr. Jelly Roll* (1955) iii. 126 The all-white Original Dixieland Jazz Band of 1917 (by chance the first band to record jazz) is generally reckoned the originator of 'Dixieland'. *Ibid.* iv. 179 The white New Orleans Dixielanders. **1970** *Melody Maker* 12 Sept. 35/7, I strongly suspect it will still be possible, somewhere or other, to listen to live Dixieland in 1999.

2. (See quot. 1873[2].) Also *attrib.*

1873 J. H. BEADLE *Undevel. West* xxx. 660 'Dixie wine' as the Mormons call it, is rather strong and pungent. *Ibid.* 661 All that part of Mormondom south of the rim of the Great Basin is called Dixie, and extends some distance into Arizona. **1894** *Irrigation Age* Jan. 38/1 The famous 'Dixie Land', comprising the counties of Millard, Washington and Beaver. **1942** W. STEGNER *Mormon Country* 345 Dixie sleeps peacefully all winter with hardly a Gentile intruder.

Dixiecrat (ˈdɪksɪkræt). *U.S. colloq.* [f. DIXIE[2] + DEMO)CRAT 2.] A member of a group of southern United States Democrats who seceded from the Democratic Party in 1948 because they opposed its policy of extending civil rights; a States' Rights Democrat. Also *attrib.* Hence **ˌDixieˈcratic** *a.*; **ˈDixiecratism.**

1948 *Birmingham* (Ala.) *News* 22 May 5 Truman finds some Dixiecrats supporting him on A-veto stand. **1948** *Tuscaloosa* (Ala.) *News* 14 July 4/1 States Rights' walkout delegates..will..select a 'Dixiecratic' nominee for President. **1948** *N.Y. Times* 5 Sept. 5/2 The States Rights Democrats have Bill Weisner, telegraph editor of the Charlotte News, to thank for putting Dixiecrat into the American vocabulary. Mr. Weisner was writing a headline on a story about the States Rights Democrats which would not fit. Dixiecrats would. **1948** *Economist* 18 Sept. 464/1 Democrats will be able to express their sense of outrage by voting for the Dixiecrats—the..name given to the rebellious States Rights' Democrats. *Ibid.*, The Dixiecrat candidate. **1949** *Tuscaloosa* (Ala.) *News* 17 Dec. 4/3 Byrnes' conversion to Dixiecratism.

‖**dixit** (ˈdɪksɪt). [L. *dixit* = he has said, perf. t. of *dīcere* to say; the usual expression is *ipse dixit* (q.v.).] An utterance (quoted as) already given.

1628 EARLE *Microsm., Sceptic in Relig.* (Arb.) 66 He hates authority as the tyrant of reason, and you cannot anger him worse than with a father's *dixit*. *a* **1734** NORTH *Exam.* III. viii. §80. (1740) 645 (Stanf.) On no better Ground than this Man's *Dixit*. **1812** *Examiner* 24 Aug. 543/2 The point..did not depend on Lord Moira's dixit.

diz: see DIZZ.

‖**dizain** (dɪˈzeɪn). *Obs.* Also 6 **di-, dyzaine,** 7 **dixain.** [a. F. *dizain* (15th c. in Hatz.-Darm.), f. *dix* ten.] A poem or stanza of ten lines.

The meaning in the first quot. is doubtful.

[*a* **1400–50** *Alexander* 4307 In all oure diȝans on daies þat duke we comend.] **1575** GASCOIGNE in Haslewood *Eng. Poets & Poesy* (1815) II. 7 (Stanf.) There are Dizaynes.. which are of ten lines. **1580** SIDNEY *Arcadia* II. (1622) 217 Strephon againe began this Dizaine, which was answered vnto him in that kinde of verse which is called the crowne. **1602** J. MELVILL *Diary* (1842) 501 [Title of poem] Dixain. **1656** in BLOUNT *Glossogr.*

‖**dizdar, disdar** (ˈdiːzdɑː(r)). [Pers. and Turkish *dīzdār*, f. Pers. *dīz* castle + *dār* holder.] The warden of a castle or fort.

1768 *Gentl. Mag.* XXXVIII. 155/1 That gentleman introduced him to the Disdar, or commandant of the citadel. **1812** BYRON *Ch. Har.* II. xii. *note*, The Disdar was the father of the present Disdar. **1846** ELLIS *Elgin Marb.* I. 2 The Disdar of the Acropolis.

†**dize**, *v. dial. Obs.* = next (sense 1).

1674 RAY *N.C. Words* 14 *To Dize*, to put tow on a distaffe. **1787** in GROSE. **1847** in HALLIWELL.

dizen (ˈdaɪz(ə)n, ˈdɪz(ə)n), *v.* Also 6 **disyn, dysyn,** 7 **disen,** 9 **dizzen.** [Found only from 1530: but evidently the verb belonging to *dis-, dise-*, in DISTAFF, and LG. *diesse* the bunch of flax on a distaff. It is remarkable that neither the vb., nor the sb. as a separate word, has been found in OE. or ME., and that on the other hand no vb. corresponding to *dizen* is known in LG. or Du.]

†**1.** *trans.* To dress or attire (a distaff) with flax, etc. for spinning. *Obs.*

1530 PALSGR. 519/2, I dysyn a dystaffe, I put the flaxe upon it to spynne..And I had disyned my distaffe, I durste drinke with the best of you. **1575** LANEHAM *Let.* (1871) 47 The spindel and rok, that waz dizend with purpl sylk.

2. To dress (with clothes), *esp.* to attire or array with finery, to deck *out* (*up*), bedizen. (In later use mostly contemptuous.)

1619 FLETCHER *M. Thomas* IV. vi, Come quickly, quickly, paint me handsomely..Com Doll, Doll, disen me. **1621** —— *Pilgrim* IV. iii, I put my clothes off, and I dizen'd him. **1706** E. WARD *Hud. Rediv.* II. v, Lasses..Sate dizen'd up. **1729** SWIFT *Grand Question* Wks. 1755 IV. I. 106, I had dizen'd you out like a queen. **1730–6** BAILEY (folio), *Dizen*, to dress, to deck or trim, commonly us'd by way of raillery. **1774** GOLDSM. *Retal.* 67 Comedy wonders at being so fine: Like a tragedy-queen he has dizen'd her out. **1870** EMERSON *Soc. & Solit., Work & Days* Wks. (Bohn) III. 72 'Tis the vulgar great who come dizened with gold and jewels. [In most northern dial. glossaries, usually *dizzen* with *i* short.]

b. *transf.* and *fig.* To deck out, adorn.

1806–7 J. BERESFORD *Miseries Hum. Life* (1826) xx. 252 Here the Muse dizens My dirge with orisons. **1870** EMERSON *Soc. & Solit., Clubs* Wks. (Bohn) III. 94 The fact they had thus dizened and adorned was of no value. **1889** BROWNING *Reverie* 105 Herb and tree Which dizen thy [Earth's] mother-breast.

Hence **ˈdizened** *ppl. a.*; **ˈdizenment**, condition of being dizened, bedizenment.

1775 S. J. PRATT *Lib. Opinions* (1783) IV. 170 You fine dizen'd-out hussey. **1821** JOANNA BAILLIE *Metr. Leg., Colum.* xxvii. 10 Standing in dizen'd rows. **1864** CARLYLE *Fredk. Gt.* XVI. i. VI. 137 Foul creatures in high dizenment. *Ibid.* Indeed there was in that man what far transcends all dizenment.

†**ˈdizener.** *Obs.* Also 5–6 **disener.** [a. 15th c. F. *disenier* (later *dizeinier, dizainier*), f. OF. *dizeine*, later *dizaine* group of ten, in med.L. *decēna*, Sp. *decena*, Pr. *desena*, whence also med.L. *decēnārius*, OF. *decenier*: see DECENER, and cf. *douzener*, DOZENER.] A foreman or captain of a group of ten men; = DECENER 1.

[**1292** BRITTON I. xiii. [xii] . § 1 Qe touz soint en dizeyne et pleviz par dizeyners. *transl.* That every one be in some tithing and pledged by their tithingmen.] **1489** CAXTON *Faytes of A.* II. xxx. I vij, Eueryche of hem shal haue vndre hym a dyzener of carpenters and a dyzener of helpers and also thre diseners of laborers for to make the same. **1555** WATREMAN *Fardle Facions* II. x. 211 Their capitaines ouer ten, whiche, by a terme borowed of the Frenche, we calle Diseners.

dizoic (daɪˈzəʊɪk), *a. Zool.* [f. Gr. δι- DI-[2] + ζῷον animal + -IC.] Producing two young; applied to a spore producing two sporozoites.

1901 [see POLYZOIC *a.* 1 b]. **1903** [see MONOZOIC *a.* 2].

dizygotic (daɪzaɪˈgɒtɪk), *a. Biol.* [f. DI-[2] + ZYGOTE + -IC.] Of twins: derived from two separate ova (and therefore not identical).

1930 *Nature* 15 Nov. 766 Dizygotic twins are..on the whole inferior to their brothers and sisters in the physical measurements, but this is certainly not the case with monozygotic twins. **1952** *New Biol.* XII. 27 Ordinary fraternal or dizygotic twins are due to the independent fertilization of two separate ova and may be of the same or of different sex. **1966** *Lancet* 24 Dec. 1401/2 The frequency of monozygotic twins ranges from 1·9 to 6·9 per 1000 births, but of dizygotic twins from 2·7 to 32·2 per 1000.

dizz (dɪz), *v.* [Back-formation from DIZZY, on the analogy of *craze, crazy*, etc.] *trans.* To make dizzy or giddy. Hence **dizzed, ˈdizzing** *ppl. adjs.*; also **dizz** *sb.*, the act of 'dizzing'.

1632 SHERWOOD, To dizze, *estourdir*. **1654** GAYTON *Pleas. Notes* IV. xv. 253 He [a horse] is dizzed with the continuall circuits of the Stables. **1814** T. L. PEACOCK *Wks.* (1875) III. 133 In spite of all the diz and whiz, Like parish-clerk he spoke. **1834** MEDWIN *Angler in Wales* II. 304 Or wheel in dizzing mazes round and round.

†**dizzard** (ˈdɪzəd). *Obs.* or *arch.* Forms: 6 **disarde, dysarde, diserde, dissarde, dyzerde, dyzert,** 6–7 **dizard(e, dissard(e,** 6–8 (9 *arch.*) **disard, dizzard.** [First found *c* 1520. Perh. a modification of earlier DISOUR, by assimilation to words in -ARD. See the intermediate forms in *-er, -are, -ar* in sense 1. In later use, *esp.* in sense 2, app. associated with DIZZY.]

1. = DISOUR; a jester, a 'fool'.

[**1502** *Priv. Purse Exp. Eliz. of York* (1830) 53 A disare that played the Sheppert before the Quene. **1526** SKELTON *Magnyf.* 119 In a cote thou can play well the dyser. Ye, but thou can play the fole without a vyser. **1530** PALSGR. 214/1 Dissar a scoffer, *saigefol*.]

a **1529** SKELTON *Image Ipocr.* 364 To goe gaye With wonderful aray As dysardes in a play. **1540–1** ELYOT *Image Gov.* (1556) 8 b, To minstrels, players of enterludes, and disardes. **1576** NEWTON *Lemnie's Complex.* (1633) 210 Such commonly are Dizards, Gesturers, Stage-players, [etc.]. **1578** N. BAXTER *Calvin on Jonah* Ep. ded. 3 In the Iestes of Skoggen the King's dizzard. **1618** *Crt. & Times Jas. I* (1849) II. 90 Archy, the Dizzard.

2. A foolish fellow, idiot, blockhead.

1547 *Homilies* I. *Contention* II. (1859) 138 Shall I be such an idiot and diserde to suffre euery man to speake vpon me what thei list. **1607** WALKINGTON *Opt. Glass* iii. 17 Who seeing his deformed countenance called him an idiot and a dissard. **1791–1823** D'ISRAELI *Cur. Lit., Acajou & Zir*, One may be as great a dizzard in resolving a problem as in restoring a reading. **1886** M. K. MACMILLAN *Dagonet the Jester* ii. 100 They flattered the wantonness of young lords and old wealthy disards.

attrib. **1546** BALE *Eng. Votaries* I. (1550) 63 b, The craftye knave lyed falselye, and so mocked hys kynge, to make of hym a very dysarde fole. **1566** DRANT *Horace Sat.* III. B iv b, We call him goose, and disarde doulte.

†**ˈdizzardly**, *a. Obs.* [f. prec. + -LY[1].] Like a dizzard, silly, idiotic.

1594 R. WILSON *Cobler's Proph.* A iv, This prating asse, this dizzardly foole. **1607** TOPSELL *Serpents* (1658) 739 These dizzardly people think to make these Lizards.. vigilant for their welfare.

dizzen (ˈdɪz(ə)n), *v. rare.* [f. stem of DIZZY + -EN[5]: cf. DIZZ.] **a.** *trans.* To make dizzy. **b.** *intr.* ? To dance giddily.

1835 *Fraser's Mag.* XI. 294 Down flowing from its dizzening height, One dazzling gush of liquid light. **1882** *Blackw. Mag.* May 569 The life of a myriad insect-wings In the wet grass buzz and dizzen.

dizzen, var. DIZEN; Sc. f. DOZEN.

dizzily (ˈdɪzɪlɪ), *adv.* [f. DIZZY *a.* + -LY[2].] In a dizzy or giddy manner.

[*a* **1000** *Sal. & Sat.* 228 (Gr.) Se Godes cunnaþ ful dyslice.] *c* **1175** *Lamb. Hom.* 119 þa þe heom duseliche folȝiað. **1375** BARBOUR *Bruce* II. 422 He gert him galay disyly. *Ibid.* VII. 210 He valknyt and raiss all desaly. **1501** DOUGLAS *Pal. Hon.* I. xxvi, My daisit heid fordullit disselie. **1801** SOUTHEY *Thalaba* IX. vii, Dizzily rolls her brain. **1871** R. ELLIS *Catullus* cv. 2 They with pitchforks hurl Mentula dizzily down.

dizziness (ˈdɪzɪnɪs). [f. DIZZY *a.* + -NESS.] The state or condition of being dizzy or giddy.

c **900** tr. *Bæda's Hist.* II. v. (1891) 112 Wæron heo mid elreorde dysignesse onblawne. *c* **1000** *Ags. Gosp.* Mark vii. 22 Innan of manna heortan..cumað..dysinessa.. stuntscipe. **1375** BARBOUR *Bruce* XVIII. 133 Schir philip of his desynaiss ourcome. **1562** TURNER *Herbal* II. 35 b, Rosemari is..good to withstand..yᵉ dusines of yᵉ heade. **1583** GOLDING *Calvin on Deut.* xxi. 123 Yet..needes must they..bee stricken with the spirit of disinesse and be carried away by the diuill. **1675** WOOD *Life* (Oxf. Hist. Soc.) II. 324 Men were taken with a disiness in the head. **1861** *Sat. Rev.* XI. 635/1 Freedom from dizziness while standing at a great height on a narrow base.

†**dizzue** (ˈdɪzjuː, ˈdɪʒ(j)uː), *v. Obs.* Also **dyzhu**. [from Cornish: see quot.]

1778 W. PRYCE *Min. Cornub.* Gloss., *Dizzue* (from Dyzhui, to discover unto, Cornish). To Dizzue the Lode, is this: If it is very small and rich, they commonly only break down the country or stratum on one side of it, by which the Lode is laid bare, and may be afterwards taken down clean.

Hence ˈ**dizzued** *ppl. a.*, ˈ**dizzuing** *vbl. sb.*; also ˈ**dizzue** *sb.*

1778 W. PRYCE *Min. Cornub.* 162 This separation or breaking the bad from the good Ore, they call Dyzhuing the leader, or making a Dyzhu; and the good Ore that is thus exposed, is called a Dyzhu. *Ibid.* Gloss. s.v., Afterwards they break the Dizzue or best part, and reserve it to be separately handled and dressed.

dizzy (ˈdɪzɪ), *a.* Forms: 1 **dysiȝ, dyseȝ,** 2–3 **dysiȝ, dusiȝ,** 3 **dusi(e (y),** 2–6 **desi(e);** 4–6 **dys(s)y,** (6 **dusey**), 6–7 **dis(s)ie, -y;** 6–7 **diz(z)ie,** 7– **dizzy.** [OE. *dysiȝ, dyseȝ* foolish, stupid = OFris. *dusig*, MDu. *dosech, dösech*, LG. *dusig, dösig, dusig* giddy, OHG. *tusig, tusic* foolish, weak, a common WGer. adj. in *-ig* (-Y), from a root *dus-* found also in LG. *dusen* to be giddy, OE. *dyslíc, dyselíc* foolish, stupid, and in a different ablaut grade with long vowel in LG. *dûsel* giddiness, MDu. *dûzelen*, Du. *duizelen* to be giddy or stupid. See early ME. derivatives under DUSI-.]

1. a. Foolish, stupid. Now only *dial.* (Not in general use since 13th c.)

c **825** *Vesp. Hymns* vii, Swe folc dysiȝ. *c* **950** *Lindisf. Gosp.* Matt. vii. 26 Gelic bið were dysȝe se ðe ȝetimberde hus his ofer sonde [*c* **1160** *Hatton* desien men]. **971** *Blickl. Hom.* 41 Geþenc, þu dyseȝa mon. *c* **1175** *Lamb. Hom.* 117 þer þe dusie mon bið priste and þer þe dwolunge rixað. *a* **1225** *Ancr. R.* 182 Nolde me tellen him alre monne dusiȝest? *a* **1250** *Owl & Night.* 1466 Dusi luve ne last noht longe. *a* **1275** *Prov. Ælfred* 479 in *O.E. Misc.* 131 Wurþu neuere so wod, ne so desi of þi mod. **1876** *Whitby Gloss.*, *Dizzy*, half-witted. **1893** BARING-GOULD *Cheap Jack Z.* II. 45 Such dizzy-fools that they put their money there.

†**b.** *absol.* A foolish man, a fool. *Obs.*

c **825** *Vesp. Psalter* xci. 6 Dysiȝ ne onȝiteð ða. *c* **1175** *Lamb. Hom.* 33 Hwet seið þe dusie. *Ibid.* 105 Wreððe hafð wununge on þes dusian bosme. *a* **1225** *Leg. Kath.* 599 Ha ne stod neauer, ear þene þes dei, bute biforen dusie.

2. Having a sensation of whirling or vertigo in the head, with proneness to fall; giddy.

c **1340** HAMPOLE *Pr. Consc.* 771 Than waxes his hert hard and hevy. And his heved feble and dysy. **1526** SKELTON *Magnyf.* 1052, I daunce up and down tyll I am dyssy. **1568** TURNER *Herbal* I. 20 [Wolfesbayne] maketh [men] dusey [ed. **1551** dosey] in the head. **1581** MULCASTER *Positions* xvi. (1887) 73 For feare they be disie when they daunce. **1653** H. COGAN tr. *Pinto's Trav.* xiii. 40 They were so exceeding dizzy in the head that they would fall down. **1852** MRS. CARLYLE *Lett.* II. 200 With my heart beating and my head quite dizzy.

fig. **1726–46** THOMSON *Winter* 122 The reeling clouds Stagger with dizzy poise, as doubting yet Which master to obey.

3. a. Mentally unsteady or in a whirl; **b.** Wanting moral stability, giddy.

1501 DOUGLAS *Pal. Hon.* Prol. 101 My desie heid quhome laik of brane gart vary. **1599** *Broughton's Lett.* ii. 9 Meere buzzings of your owne conceited dizzie braine. **1671** MILTON *P.R.* II. 420 At thy heels the dizzy multitude. **1780** COWPER *Table Talk* 607 He..dizzy with delight, profaned the sacred wires. **1875** JOWETT *Plato* (ed. 2) I. 61 My head is dizzy with thinking of the argument. **1878** J. H. BEADLE *Western Wilds* xxxv, Dance houses and saloons multiplied and 'dizzy doves' gave an air of abandon to the streets. **1879** MISS JACKSON *Shropsh. Word-bk.*, *Duzzy*, stupid; confused. 'I'm mighty duzzy this morning.' **1888** *Texas Siftings* 29 Sept. (Farmer), Professional beauties or maidens, commonly called dizzy blondes. **1889** *Kansas Times & Star* 4 Nov., Many of the local clergy last night warned the church members..against a 'Dizzy Blonde' company coming to one of the theaters soon. **1938** G. HEYER *Blunt Instrument* ix. 166 The dizzy blonde herself. **1945** [see DOG *sb.*[1] 17 q].

c. Startling, astonishing, vivid. *slang.*

1896 ADE *Artie* xvii. 158 They was out there in them dizzy togs cuttin' up and down the track. **1897** *Daily News* 10 Aug. 5/2 Four straw hats with 'dizzy bands'. **1923** R. D. PAINE *Comr. Rolling Ocean* v. 84 When she limped into Brest a week overdue, the admiral called it a dizzy miracle.

4. Accompanied with or producing giddiness.

1605 SHAKS. *Lear* IV. vi. 12 How fearefull And dizie 'tis, to cast ones eyes so low. **1643** MILTON *Divorce* Ded., Did not the distemper of their own stomachs affect them with a dizzy megrim. **1812** S. ROGERS *Columbus* I. 24 The very ship-boy on the dizzy mast. **1855** MACAULAY *Hist. Eng.* IV. 561 He began..to climb..towards that dizzy pinnacle.

5. Arising from or caused by giddiness; reeling.

1715–20 POPE *Iliad* v. 381 Lost in a dizzy mist the warriour lies. **1740** PITT *Æneid* XII. (R.), A dizzy mist of darkness swims around. **1781** COWPER *Hope* 518 The wretch, who once..sucked in dizzy madness with his draught. **1863** GEO. ELIOT *Romola* II. vii, Thought gave way to a dizzy horror, as if the earth were slipping away from under him.

6. *fig.* Whirling with mad rapidity.

1791 COWPER *Iliad* XXI. 10 Push'd down the sides of Xanthus, headlong plung'd, With dashing sound into his dizzy stream. **1795–1814** WORDSW. *Excursion* VIII. 179 The ..stream, That turns the multitude of dizzy wheels.

7. Dull of hearing. *dial.*

1879 MISS JACKSON *Shropsh. Word-bk.*, *Duzzy*, deafish. "E's lother duzzy; e doesna 'ear very well.'

8. *Comb.*, as **dizzy-eyed, -headed.**

1591 SHAKS. *1 Hen. VI*, IV. vii. 11 Dizzie-ey'd Furie.. Suddenly made him from my side to start. **1611** COTGR. *Estourdi*, dulled, amazed..dizzie-headed. **1654** TRAPP *Comm. Ps.* cvii. 33 A company of dizzy-headed men.

dizzy (ˈdɪzɪ), *v.* [OE. had *dysiȝan, -eȝian, dysian* to be foolish, to act or talk foolishly = OFris. *dusia*, whence the intr. sense 1; but the trans. sense seems to be a later formation, f. the adjective in its modern form and sense.]

†**1.** *intr.* To act foolishly or stupidly. *Obs.*

c **888** K. ÆLFRED *Boeth.* v. §2 þonne dyseȝaþ se þe þonne wile hwilc sæd oþfæstan þam dryȝum furum. *a* **1275** *Prov. Ælfred* 466 in *O.E. Misc.* 131 Ac [gif] he drinkit and desiet þere a morȝe, so þat he fordrunken desiende werchet.

†**b.** To talk foolishly, blaspheme (in *OE.*).

c **1000** *Ags. Gosp.* Mark ii. 7 Hwi spycð þes þus . he dyseȝað. *Ibid.* Luke xxii. 65 Maneȝa oðre þing hiȝ him to cwædon dysiȝende.

2. *trans.* To make dizzy or giddy; to cause (any sense) to reel; to produce a swimming sensation in, to turn the head of.

1501 DOUGLAS *Pal. Hon.* Prol. 109 And with that gleme sa desyit was my micht. **1606** SHAKS. *Tr. & Cr.* v. ii. 174 Not the dreadfull spout..Shall dizzie with more clamour Neptunes eare In his discent, then [etc.]. **1663** COWLEY *Cutter of Coleman St.* v. xiii, You turn my Head, you dizzy me. **1785** MRS. A. GRANT *Lett. fr. Mountains* (1813) II. xix. 99 It dizzies one to look down from the tower. **1820** SOUTHEY *Lodore*, Confounding, astounding, Dizzying and deafening the ear with its sound.

3. To render unsteady in brain or mind; to bewilder or confuse mentally.

1604 SHAKS. *Ham.* v. ii. 119 (Qo. 2) To deuide him inuentorially would dosie [Qo. 3 dazzie, Qq. 4 & 5 dizzie] th' arithmaticke of memory. **1801** HEL. M. WILLIAMS *Sk. Fr. Rep.* I. i. 7 That wild and chimerical equality, the fumes of which dizzy the head of the demagogue. **1852** MRS. STOWE *Uncle Tom's C.* xxi, Giving her so many..charges, that a head less systematic and business-like than Miss Ophelia's would have been utterly dizzied and confounded.

absol. **1864** J. H. NEWMAN *Apol.* 378 All this is a vision to dizzy and appal.

Hence ˈ**dizzied** *ppl. a.*, ˈ**dizzying** *vbl. sb.* and *ppl. a.*

1804 J. GRAHAME *Sabbath* 20 The dizzying mill-wheel rests. **1823** CHALMERS *Serm.* I. 343 In the din and dizzying of incessant labour. **1853** FELTON *Fam. Lett.* xiv. (1865) 136 The dizzying effect of height. **1870** MORRIS *Earthly Par.* II. III. 242 With dizzied head upon the ground he fell.

dizzyingly (ˈdɪzɪɪŋlɪ), *adv.* [f. DIZZYING *ppl. a.* + -LY[2].] In a dizzying manner; amazingly.

1925 A. S. M. HUTCHINSON *One Incr. Purpose* III. xvi. 335 Not hurtingly now, but, mysteriously, dizzyingly. **1952** DYLAN THOMAS *Let.* 21 Nov. (1966) 383 Forgive me for not answering your dizzyingly kind letter long before this. **1957** *New Yorker* 26 Oct. 71/1 This was a dizzyingly far cry from the small provincial company that London had hoped might be willing to accept him. **1964** *Rev. Eng. Stud.* XV. 315 But were the ordinary people who watched mysteries really so dizzyingly other-worldly?

Dizzyite (ˈdɪzɪaɪt). [f. *Dizzy*, nickname of Benjamin Disraeli (see, e.g., *Punch* 3 Apr. 1852, p. 139) + -ITE[1].] A follower or admirer of Disraeli (cf. DISRAELIAN *a.*)

1903 W. MEYNELL *Disraeli* I. 61 Dizzyites..must marvel that one who received this close confidence could afterwards be jaunty at the expense of the dead woman whom Disraeli 'so truly loved'. *Ibid.* II. 483 If Disraeli bore his traducers no grudge, it would be superfluous indeed for true Dizzyites to bear them any.

dj- is not an English combination, but is sometimes put to represent the Arabic letter *jim*, = English *j* (dʒ), in Arabic, Turkish, or Berber words, which have come to us through a French channel, or are spelt in imitation of French orthography; e.g. **djebel**, a mountain or hill, **djerid** or **djereed**, a javelin, **djin**, genii or familiar spirits, **djubbah**, an outer garment. So far as these come under the scope of this Dictionary, they will be found under J; for **djowr**, an infidel, see GIAOUR.

djati (ˈdʒɑːtɪ). Also **d'jatti, jati.** [Malay *jātī.*] The teak tree, *Tectona grandis.*

1908 *Westm. Gaz.* 9 June 5/3 Java teak, known as d'jatti. **1940** E. J. H. CORNER *Wayside Trees of Malaya* II. Pl. 215 (*caption*) Teak, *Jati, Tectona grandis* in the Residency Grounds, at Penang.

djebba, djibba(h), varr. JIBBAH.

D.N.A., DNA, see DEOXYRIBONUCLEIC ACID.

do (duː), *v.* Forms and inflexions: see below. [A common WGer. strong vb. (wanting in Gothic and Norse): OE. *dón* = OFris. *dua*, OS. *dôn, duon, dôan, duan* (MDu. & Du. *doen*, MLG. & LG. *dôn, duon*), OHG. *tôn, tôan, tuon, tuoan, tuen* (MHG. *tuon*, Ger. *thun, tun*); Pa. t., OE. *dyde*, pl. *dédon, dǽdon, dydon* = OFris. *dede*, pl. *dêden*, OS. *deda*, pl. *dâdun, dêdun* (MDu. *dede*, Du. *deed*, pl. *deden*, MLG. & LG. *dêde*, pl. *dêden*), OHG. *teta*, pl. *tâtum* (MHG. *tete, tâte*, pl. *tâten*, Ger. *that, tat*, pl. *thaten, taten*); Pa. pple., OE. *ȝedón, ȝedén* = OFris. *dên*, OS. *gidôn, -dôen, -duan*, ODu. *dân*, (MDu. *gedân*, Du. *gedaan*), OHG. *(ge)tân*, Ger. *gethan, getan*; OTeut. types *dôn, deda, dǣno-*: *dôno-*, from verbal stem *dǣ-*: *dô-* (appearing also in DEED, DOOM, -DOM), the Germanic representative of the Aryan verb stem *dhē-*: *dhō-*, to place, put, set, lay, in Skr. *dhā-*, OPers. *dā-*, Gr. *θη-* (pres. *τίθημι*, deriv. sb. *θωή* a penalty imposed), L. *-dĕre* in *abdĕre* to put away, *condĕre* to put together, *dēdĕre* to lay down, OSlav. *dête, dêyati*, Lith. *dėti*, Lett. *dêt* to put, lay.

The vocalization of the Germanic vb., esp. the present stem *dō-* beside the Gr. *θη-* and Slav.-Lith. *dē-*, has been variously explained (see e.g. Streitberg *Urgerm. Gramm.* 329). The pret. *deda* is generally held to be a reduplicated form corresponding to Skr. *dadhāu*:—orig. **dhedhō*. The 1st p. sing. pres. indic. had originally the *m* of primitive verbs in *-mi*, Skr. *-mi*, Gr. *-μι*, L. *-m*: viz. OE. *dóm* (later *dó*), OS. *dôm* (*dôn*), OHG. *tôm, tuom* (later *tuon*). This verb is considered by many philologists to be the source of the formative suffix of the pa. t. of weak verbs in the Germanic languages, including Norse and Gothic; in the latter the plural endings *-dêdum, -dêdup, -dêdun*, are the forms which the pl. of the pret. *deda* would have in Gothic.

OE. deviates from the other WGer. langs. in the past *dyde*, for OS. *deda*, OHG. *teta*; the *y* is now generally explained as a special OE. representation of an Indo-germanic weak vowel. Thence the pl. *dydon*; the plural corresp. to OS. *dâdun*, modG. *thaten*, was Anglian *dédon* (also *dǽdon*, in Cædmon, etc.). In ME. *dyde, dydon* were represented by *dude, -en* (*ü*), midl. & north. *diden, dide*, now *did*; but *dēden* (with a sing. *dēde* derived from it like modG. *that* from pl. *thaten*) came down in some dialects to 15th c. In the pres. ind., the 2nd and 3rd pers. sing. in OE. had umlaut, *dǽst, dǽð, dést, deð*, and these forms survived in s.w. till the 15th c.; but ONorthumbrian had, without umlaut, *dóas, dóæð, dóas*, and in ME. the forms *dōst, dōth* (*dōs*) are found in north. & midl. from the 12th c. The pa. pple. in OE. is known only with the prefix *ȝe-*, which in ME. remained in the south as *y-, i-*. (Forms with *ȝe-* are found also in the pa. t., and occasionally other parts, which, however, are more properly referred to a derivative vb. OE. *ȝedón*, ME. *ido, ydo*). The final *-n* of the pple. was generally dropped in the south in ME., esp. in the forms *ydo, ido*, whence the *ado* (əˈduː) of modern s.w. dialects.]

A. Inflexional Forms.

1. *Infinitive.*

a. *Simple Infinitive*, do (duː, dʊ). Forms: 1 **dón** (*north.* **dóan, dóa, doe**); 2–5 **don** (4–5 **doon,** 4 **doyne, doun,** 4–6 **done,** 5 **doone**); 2– **do** (4–7 **doo,** 6–7 **dooe, doe,** *Sc.* 6 **du, dw,** 9 **dui, dee**).

Beowulf 2349 (Th.) Swa sceal man don. *c* **950** *Lindisf. Gosp.* Mark x. 17 Huæd sceal ic doa? —— xiv. 7 Gie maȝon him wæl doe. **1131** *O.E. Chron.*, Swa swa hi scoldon don. *c* **1175** *Lamb. Hom.* 73 Ne mei na man do þing þet beo god iqueme. **1297** R. GLOUC. (1724) 47 Gret wrong þou woldest don vs. **13..** *Guy Warw.* (A.) 1309, I schal him in mi prisoun do. *c* **1374** CHAUCER *Boeth.* I. pr. ii. 9 þat he may so done. **1411** *Rolls of Parlt.* III. 651/1 The same..schall so doon to hem. **1548** HALL *Chron.*, *Hen. V* (an. 10) 78 b, We might lawfully so dooe. **1577** B. GOOGE *Heresbach's Husb.* I. (1586) 46 In what sort shall he best doo it. **1594** SPENSER *Amoretti* xlii, Let her..doe me not..to dy. **1653** H. COGAN tr. *Pinto's Trav.* x. 31 What he would have me do. *Mod.* Who saw him do it?

b. *Dative Infinitive* (with *to*) to do (tʊ duː); in OE. **to dónne** (**dóanne, dóenne**), ME. **to donne, to done, to don** (**to donde, to doinde**).

c **1000** *Ags. Gosp.* Matt. xii. 12 Hyt ys alyfed on restedaȝum wel to donne [*Lindisf. G.* wel doa; *Rushw.* god to doanne]. **1154** *O.E. Chron.* an. 1137 Alse he ment to don. *c* **1175** *Lamb. Hom.* 109 ȝif he seolf nule don swa swa he heom techeð to donne. *a* **1200** *Moral Ode* 19 Arȝe we beoþ to done god. *c* **1200** *Trin. Coll. Hom.* 139 He was send.. to donde þrefolde wike. *Ibid.* 219 He ne turnde..to doinde.. nan þer þinge. *c* **1305** *St. Kath.* 82 in *E.E.P.* (1862) 92 þan we hire..makede to do sacrefise. *c* **1374** CHAUCER *Boeth.* III. pr. xii. 102, I haue lytel more to done. **1387** TREVISA *Higden* (Rolls) I. 87 (Mätz.) More redy for to doo than for to speke. *c* **1420** *Metr. Life St. Kath.* (Halliw.) 3 To dethe hyt for to doone! **1534** TINDALE *Mark* v. 7 What haue I to do [**1611** to doe] with the? **1548** HALL *Chron.*, *Hen. V*, (an. 8) 71 b, Men that enforce theim for to doen or to ymagine wronges. **1556** *Aurelio & Isab.* (1608) K vij, So am I constrainede to doo it. **1644** MILTON *Areop.* (Arb.) 32 Which if I now should begin to doe. *Mod.* What are you going to do?

2. *Indicative Present.*

a. *1st pers. sing.* do. Forms: 1 **dóm** (**dóam**), **dó** (**dóa**); 2– **do** (4–6 **doo,** 6–7 **doe**).

c **950** *Lindisf. Gosp.* Matt. xxvii. 22 Hwæt ðonne dóm ic of ðæm hælend? [*c* **975** *Rushw. G.* ibid., Hwæt dom ic þanne be hælend? *c* **1000** *Ags. G.* ibid., Hwæt do ic?] *a* **950** *Lindisf. Gosp.* John xiv. 14 Ðis ic doam *vel* ic uyrco. [*c* **975** *Rushw. G.* ibid., Ðis dom ic.] *c* **1000** ÆLFRIC *Gram.* xxxiii. (Z.) 210 Ic do oððe wyrce. **1388** WYCLIF *John* xiii. 7 What Y do thou wost not now. *c* **1400** *Melayne* 361, I doo yowe wole to wytt. **1535** COVERDALE *1 Sam.* iii. 11 Beholde I do a thinge. **1610** SHAKS. *Temp.* I. ii. 52 That I doe not.

b. *2nd pers. sing.* doest (ˈduːɪst), dost (dʌst).

Forms: 1 **dǽst, dést** (*North.* **dóas, dóæs, dóes**), 2–4 **dest,** 2– **dost** (3–7 **dust,** 4–5 **doist,** 7 **doost;** 3–4 *north.* **dos,** 4 **dose, duse,** 5 **doyse**), 6– **doest** (6 **doeste, doiste,** 7 **do'st**). In late use, the form *doest* is confined to the principal verb, *dost* is usually auxiliary.

c **950** *Lindisf. Gosp.* Matt. vi. 2 Ðonne ðu doas ælmessa. —— John vi. 30 þæt ðu doæs. *c* **975** *Rushw. G.* ibid., Hwæt ðu does. *c* **1000** ÆLFRIC *Gen.* xii. 18 Hwi dest þu wið me swa? *c* **1160** *Hatton G.* John vi. 30 Hwæt dest þu? *c* **1175** *Lamb.*

Hom. 23 þa dedbote þe þu dest. *Ibid.* 67 ȝef þu þus dost. *c* **1200** ORMIN 15587 þu.. þatt dost tuss þise dedess. **1297** R. GLOUC. (1724) 428 þou ne dust noȝt as þe wyse. *c* **1300** *Havelok* 2390 Wat dos þu here? **1375** *Cantic. de Creatione* 230 þou vs dest so mochel wo. *c* **1385** CHAUCER *L.G.W.* 315 What dostow here? *c* **1460** *Towneley Myst.* (Surtees) 3 So thynke me that thou doyse. **1534** TINDALE *John* vii. 3 Thy workes that thou doest [so all 16–17th c. vv., *Wyclif* doist]. *Ibid.* ix. 34 And dost thou teache vs? [so **1539** *Cranm.*; but **1557** *Geneva*, **1582** *Rhem.*, **1611** have 'doest']. **1610** SHAKS. *Temp.* I. ii. 78 Do'st thou attend me? **1611** BIBLE *1 Kings* xix. 9 What doest thou here, Eliiah? —— *John* xiii. 27 That thou doest [TINDALE dost], doe quickly. **1653** HOLCROFT *Procopius* IV. 153 Doest thou run after thine owne Master? *Mod. poetic.* Why dost thou weep?

c. *3rd pers. sing.* does (dʌz); *arch.* doth (dʌθ), doeth ('duːɪθ).

Forms: α. 1 (dœ̄ð, dóæð), déð, 2–5 deþ (2 deaþ, dieþ, 3 deeþ, 5–6 dethe), 3–5 doþ (4 doith, 5–6 dooth), 5– doth, 6–7 doeth (6 dothe). β. 1 *north.* dóas, dóes, 3–4 *north.* dos, dus, (4 dotz, 5 duse, doys), 5–6 dois, dose (6 doose), 6– does. γ. 6– do (doe). The orig. northern form *does* superseded *doth, doeth*, in 16–17th c. in general use; the latter being now liturgical and poetic. The form *he do* is now s.w. dial., and *he don't* is vulgar.

α. *c* **1000** *Ags. Gosp.* Matt. v. 19 Se þe hit deð [*c* **950** *Lindisf. G.* doeð]. *a* **1175** *Cott. Hom.* 233 Hwat deð sí moder hire bearn?.. hi hit.. dieð under hire arme. *c* **1175** *Lamb. Hom.* 51 Al swa me deað bi þe deade. *c* **1200** *Trin. Coll. Hom.* 53 He doð alse holie write seið. *c* **1320** *Cast. Love* 1468 Vnwrestlyche he deeþ. **1340** *Ayenb.* 68 In al þet god deþ. *c* **1340** *Cursor M.* 11838 (Trin.) þis caitif.. Dooþ [*v.r.* dos] him leches for to seke. **1382** WYCLIF *John* iii. 21 Ech man that doith yuele. *c* **1500** *Melusine* lxii. 371 Yf a man doeth as wel as he can. **1559** *Primer in Priv. Prayers* (1851) 35 God .. Which doth all in order due. **1569** GOLDING *Heminges Post.* 27 The thing that Christ dothe here, is that he dothe Peter to understand. **1587** GOLDING *De Mornay* xi. (1617) 166 He doeth thee to understand. **1588** SHAKS. *L.L.L.* I. ii. 50 It doth amount to one more then two. **1721** *St. German's Doctor & Stud.* 21 He that doth against them, doth against justice. **1819** SHELLEY *Cenci* IV. iv. 4, I must speak with Count Cenci; doth he sleep?

β. *c* **950** *Lindisf. Gosp.* Matt. vi. 3 Nyta winstra ðin huæt wyrcas *vel* doas suiðra ðin. *Ibid.* vii. 24 Se ðe.. does ða ilco. *Ibid.* viii. 9 Ic cueðo.. ðeua minum, do ðis, and [he] does [*Rushw.* he doeþ]. *a* **1300** *Cursor M.* 5208 He dus [*v.r.* dos] nakins þing. *c* **1340** *Ibid.* 2908 (Fairf.) Hit dose [*v.r.* dos] mony in syn to fal. *a* **1375** *Joseph Arim.* 233 He dos as he bad. *c* **1450** *St. Cuthbert* (Surtees) 7291 Wha so dose agayne þe saynte. **1555** ABP. PARKER *Ps.* xxii, My hart.. doth melt and pyne, as waxe by fier dose. **1596** SHAKS. *1 Hen. IV*, III. i. 172 Faith he does. **1601** —— *All's Well* IV. iii. 236 Our Interpreter do's it well. *Ibid.* 317 Why do's he aske? **1661** MARVELL *Corr.* xxi. Wks. 1872–5 II. 54 Longer then your business usually dos. **1662** STILLINGFL. *Orig. Sacr.* II. iii. §2 The person that does them.

γ. **1547** BALE *Sel. Wks.* (1849) 234 No goodly institution, nor ordinance.. do this faithful woman contemn. *a* **1553** PHILPOT *Exam. & Writ.* (1842) 333 He.. do confess himself to speak of this third kind. **1559** W. CUNNINGHAM *Cosmogr. Glasse* 6 Geographie doe deliniat, and set out the universal earth. **1660** PEPYS *Diary* (1875) I. 62 Sir Arthur Haselrigge do not yet appear in the House. **1670** in *Coll. Rhode Isl. Hist. Soc.* (1902) X. 102 Evidence of.. River being more than 11 Miles Long but how Much More dont say. **1741** RICHARDSON *Pamela* I. 65 He don't know you. **1774** P. V. FITHIAN *Jrnl.* (1900) 202 A Sunday in Virginia dont seem to wear the same Dress as our Sundays to the Northward. **1813** J. K. PAULDING *John Bull & Br. Jon.* ii. 9 The old saying that a man don't know when he is well off. **1831** FONBLANQUE *Eng. under 7 Administ.* (1837) II. 100 God don't suffer them now. **1835** R. M. BIRD *Hawks of Hawk-Hollow* I. xi. 143, I wonder she don't sing; for a speaking voice, she has the richest *soprano*. **1862** O. W. NORTON *Army Lett.* (1903) 120 It don't take ten thousand acres here to support one family. *a* **1897** *Mod. s.w. dial.* He du zay. That he du. **1918** A. HUXLEY *Let.* 28 June (1969) 157, I only hope that this letter will reach you, though your loss will not be very great if it dont. **1946** K. TENNANT *Lost Haven* (1947) i. 15 A man what don't profit from all a woman's telling and hiding the bottles ain't worth the trouble.

d. *plural*; do.

Forms: α. 1 dóð, dó (we, etc.), (dóað, dóeð), 2–4 doþ. β. 3–4 don, (4–5 done), 6– do (5–6 doo, 6–7 doe, dooe, 7– *interr.* d'ye). γ. *north.* 1 dóas, dóes, 3–6 dos, 4 dose, dus, 4–5 duse, 6 dois.

α. *c* **975** *Rushw. Gosp.* Matt. v. 46 Ah gæfel-ȝeroefe þæt ne doeþ. *Ibid.* 47 Hwæt doaþ ȝe marae? *c* **1000** *Ags. Gosp.* Matt. v. 47 Gyf ȝe ðæt doþ. *Ibid.*, Hwæt do ȝe mare? *c* **1175** *Lamb. Hom.* 9 Bet.. þene we doþ. **1340** *Ayenb.* 69 Hi doþ.. þe contrarye.

β. *c* **1200** *Trin. Coll. Hom.* 19 þese two þing don alle heðen men. **1382** WYCLIF *Mark* vii. 8 Manye oþere thingis lyke to þes ȝe don [**1388** doon; **1534** TINDALE—**1611** ye do; **1582** *Rhem.* you doe]. **1426** AUDELAY *Poems* 12 Thai done hym deme. **1576** FLEMING *Panopl. Epist.* 89 What you doe, and what other do. **1584** PEELE *Arraignm. Paris* I. iii, As done these fields and groves. **1660** JER. TAYLOR *Worthy Commun.* I. §2. 39 We do it also, and doe it much more. **1730** A. GORDON *Maffei's Amphith.* 108 Why don't they consider? *a* **1832** BENTHAM *Mem.* Wks. 1843 X. 246 How d'ye do?

γ. *c* **950** *Lindisf. Gosp.* Matt. v. 46 Bær-suinnigo ðis doas. *Ibid.* 47 Gie doas *vel* wyrcas. *c* **1340** HAMPOLE *Pr. Consc.* 4146 Swilk men.. þat mykel dus [*v.r.* dose] ogayns Goddes lawe. *c* **1400** Duse [see 24 d]. **1533** Dois [ibid.]. *Mod. north. dial.* Them that does it.

3. *Indicative Past.*

a. *1st and 3rd pers. sing.* did.

Forms: 1–2 dyde, 2–5 dide, dude (y), dede, 5 dode, 4–6 dyde, dyd, 4– did (4 dud, 4–5 didd, 5–6 didde).

a **1000** *Cædmon's Gen.* 2691 (Gr.) Ne dyde ic for facne. *a* **1131** *O.E. Chron.* an. 1123 þis he dyde. *Ibid.* an. 1127 Se king hit dide. *c* **1175** *Lamb. Hom.* 95 He dude þet heo weren birnende. *c* **1250** *Gen. & Ex.* 762 Quer abram is bigging dede. *c* **1330** R. BRUNNE *Chron.* (1810) 221 Sir Rauf.. did þer his endyng. **13..** *Cursor M.* 1608 He to pin him-selfen did [*G.* didd, *Tr.* didde]. *c* **1340** *Ibid.* 6270 (Trin.) þe brode watir he dud him ynne [earlier MSS. did, dide]. **1387** TREVISA *Higden* (Rolls) I. 215 þerynne Romulus dede his owne ymage. *c* **1420** *Chron. Vilod.* 501 He dude also. *Ibid.* 936 To his mowthe þo his hond he dode. *c* **1430** *Syr Tryam.* 495 He dyd hym faste away. **1461** CL. PASTON in *Paston Lett.* No. 367 I. 540, I dede.. Hauswan goo to my Lord. **1590** SPENSER *F.Q.* II. i. 33 All I did, I did but as I ought.

b. *2nd pers. sing.* didst.

Forms: α1 dydes(t, 2–5 dides(t, dudest, 5 dydest, 6–7 diddest, 6– didst. β. 3–4 dides-(tou), dedes-, dudes-; γ. *north.* 4 did.

a **1000** *Andreas* 929 (Gr.) Ðu ondsæc dydest. *a* **1225** *Ancr. R.* 306 þis þu dudest þer. *c* **1230** *Hali Meid.* 9 þat tu euer dides te into swuch þeowdom. **13..** *Cursor M.* 10484 Als þou did [*v.rr.* diddist, dudest] quilum dame sarra. *Ibid.* 12626 Qui did þu þus? [*Trin.* didestou þus]. **1382** WYCLIF *2 Sam.* xii. 12 þou didist hidyngli. *c* **1450** *Merlin* 41 Thow dedist their brother to be slain. **1545** *Primer Hen. VIII, Litany*, The noble workes that thou diddest in their daies. **1611** BIBLE *2 Sam.* xii. 12 Thou diddest it secretly. *Ibid. Ps.* xliv. 1 What worke thou didst in their dayes. **1819** SHELLEY *Julian & M.* 459 Thou.. didst speak thus and thus.

c. *plural* did.

Forms: 1 dydon (-un), *poet. Angl.* dédon (*WS.* dǣdon), 2 didon, 2–5 diden, duden, deden (2 dedeun, 4 didyn, diddyn), 2–6 dide, 3–5 dude, dede (4–6 didde), 4– did (4 dud, 5–6 dyd).

a **1000** *Cædmon's Gen.* 722 (Gr.) þæt hie to mete dædon ofet unfæle. *Ibid.* 1944 He ne cuðe hwæt þa cynn dydon. *c* **950** *Lindisf. Gosp.* Matt. xxvi. 19 And dedon ða ðeȝnas suæ bibeod him ðe hælend. *Ibid.* xxviii. 15 Hia.. dedon suæ weron ȝelæred [*Rushw.* dydun, *Ags. G.* dydon, *Hatt.* dyden]. *a* **1132** *O.E. Chron.* an. 1129 Swa swa hi ear didon. **1154** *Ibid.* an. 1137 Sume hi diden in crucethus.. and dide scearpe stanes þer inne. *c* **1175** *Lamb. Hom.* 91 Heo.. swa duden. *c* **1250** *Gen. & Ex.* 1059 He so deden als he hem bad. *c* **1330** R. BRUNNE *Chron.* (1810) 201 Alle þat did þat dome. *c* **1340** *Cursor M.* 17411 (Trin.) ȝe duden him vndir lok & sele. *c* **1380** WYCLIF *Sel. Wks.* III. 109 More.. þan þey dude. **1387** TREVISA *Higden* (Rolls) IV. 353 þey dede [*v.rr* . dude, dide] hym in to þe see. *c* **1400** MAUNDEV. (Roxb.) xi. 42 þai did Criste to deed. *Ibid.* xv. 67 Him didd þe Iews on þe crosse. *c* **1400** *Destr. Troy* 1381 Dydden all to the dethe. *Ibid.* 11960 Dyden. **1426** AUDELAY *Poems* 10 Thus we dydon myschyvysly. **1530** *Compend. Treat.* (1863) 59 So diden ye apostles. **1548** HALL *Chron., Hen. V* (an. 8) 72 b, Why did thei take it? **1659** BAXTER *Key Cath.* xxxv. 252 The rest.. did what they did.

d. *colloq., dial.*, and *U.S.* done.

1847 in D. Drake *Pioneer Life Kentucky* (1870) iii. 63 The weavil.. 'done' great injury to that grain. **1848**, etc. [see E.D.D.]. **1849** N. KINGSLEY *Diary* (1914) 56 Anna done the fair thing last night. **1850** *Ibid.* 117 [We] worked in the old place and done middling well. **1873** 'MARK TWAIN' & WARNER *Gilded Age* xxxiii. 307, I think it done him good. **1924** W. M. RAINE *Troubled Waters* xxi. 226 The little boss done right not to take that Cheyenne bid for the doggies. **1969** *Listener* 4 Sept. 312/3 After what they've done to me, I never could forgive them. And I never done anybody any harm.

4. *Subjunctive Present.*

a. *singular* do. Forms: 1 dó, (dóe, dóa), 2– do (5–7 doo, doe).

c **950** *Lindisf. Gosp.* Mark x. 35 þætte.. ðu doe us. *c* **975** *Rushw. Gosp.* Matt. vi. 3 Nyte se winstrae hond þin hwæt þin sio swiþre doa. *c* **1000** *Ags. Ps.* (Th.) lxxv. 6 Ðæt he do ealle hale. *a* **1225** *St. Marher.* 20 Ich bidde.. þæt tu do baldeliche. **13..** *Cursor M.* 23904 þar-of.. scho do hir will. *c* **1400** MAUNDEV. (1839) iv. 32 3if ony man do thereinne ony maner metalle. **1577** B. GOOGE *Heresbach's Husb.* I. (1586) 15 b, That he doo not thinke himselfe wyser then his maister. **1581** SAVILE *Tacitus Hist.* I. vii. (1591) 5 Doe he wel doe he ill, al is ill taken. *Mod.* If he do anything unexpected.

b. *plural* do. Forms: 1 dón (dóen, dóan, dóe), 2–5 don, 4–5 doon, 3– do (5–7 doo, doe).

a **1000** *Father's Instr.* (Cod. Ex.) 70 Ðeah hi wom dón. **13..** *Cursor M.* 23760 (Fairf.) If we bleþeli after him do. *c* **1385** CHAUCER *L.G.W.* 1988 *Ariadne*, That we doon the gayler.. To come. *Mod.* What if we do?

5. *Subjunctive Past.* did.

Forms: *sing.* 1 dyde (dḗde); 2– (as Indicative). *plural* 1 dyden, dyde; 2– (as Indic.).

a **900** *Martyrol.* in *O.E.T.* 178/36 Ða fræȝn se.. for hwon he suæ dede. *c* **950** *Lindisf. Gosp.* John xv. 24 Gif ic ne dyde. —— Matt. xii. 16 Dedon *vel* dydon [*Rushw.* dydun]. *c* **1000** *Ags. Gosp.* Matt. xi. 21 Hi dydun dæd-bote [*Lindisf., Rushw.* dydon, *Hatt.* hyo deden]. **1556** *Aurelio & Isab.* (1608) K vij, If I didde it not. *Mod.* If you did that, you would be blamed.

6. *Imperative* do. **a.** *sing.* Forms: 1 dó (dóa, dóe), 2– do (5–7 doo, doe, dooe).

a **1000** *Cædmon's Gen.* 2225 (Gr.) Do swa ic ðe bidde. *c* **1000** *Ags. Gosp.* Luke x. 37 Ga and do eall-swa [*Lindisf.* gaa and ðu dóo onȝelic]. *a* **1300** *Cursor M.* 15306 Fra mi fete do þin hand. *c* **1400** *Melayne* 308 To dedis of armes hym doo. **1611** BIBLE *Jer.* xliv. 4 Oh doe not this abominable thing. *Mod.* Do your best.

b. *plural.* Forms: α. 1 dóð (dóeð, -æð, -að, dóas), 2–3 doþ, 4 dothe, 4–5 dooth. β. 4– do (5–7 doo, doe). γ. *north.* 3–4 dos (dus), 4–5 dose.

α. *c* **1000** *Ags. Gosp.* Matt. iii. 3 Doþ his siðas rihte. *c* **1340** *Cursor M.* 16281 (Laud) Dothe hym on rode. *c* **1350** *Will. Palerne* 3807 Doþ your dede to-day. *c* **1400** A. DAVY *Dreams* 154 Dooþ me into prison.

β. *c* **1340** *Cursor M.* 4893 (Fairf.) Do folow ham. **1611** BIBLE *Matt.* vii. 12 Doe [*earlier 16th c. vv.* do] ye even so to them. **1682** NORRIS *Hierocles, Golden Verses* 32 That doe.

γ. *c* **950** *Lindisf. Gosp.* Matt. iii. 2 Hreonisse doas *vel* wyrcas. —— John vi. 10 Does þætte ða menn ȝesitta. *a* **1300** *Cursor M.* 2792 Tas and dos [*Fairf.* take an and do] your will wit paa. *c* **1300** HAVELOK 2592 Dos me als ich wile you lere. *c* **1340** *Cursor M.* 5090 (Fairf.) Make you redy.. and dose you hame.

7. *Present Participle* doing ('duːɪŋ).

Forms: α. 1 dónde (dóende), 2–3 donde, 4 doinde, 4–6 doinge, doynge, 6– doing. β. *north.* 3–5 doande, 4–6 doand.

c **950** *Lindisf. Gosp.* John, Cont. x, Efne ȝelic hine.. doende gode. *c* **1000** *Ags. Gosp.* Matt. xxiv. 46 Hys hlafurd hyne ȝemet þus dondne [*Lind.* doende, *Rushw.* dónde, *Hatt.* doende]. *c* **1275** LAY. 5872 Her solle þe wel donde euere worþe riche. *c* **1300** *Beket* 277 Evere doinge he was. *Mod.* What was he found doing?

8. *Past Participle* done (dʌn).

Forms: α. 1 ȝedón (-dœ́n, -dén, -dóen, -dóan), 2–3 idon, 3–5 ydon, ido, ydo (5 ydoo, edoone). β. 3–7 don, 4– done (4 doun, dun(e, 5 doon, *north.* doyne, 5–6 doone, doen, 6 dooen, downe, *Sc.* 6–dune). γ. 4–6 do, 5 doo, doe.

α. **1123** *O.E. Chron.*, Swa mycel hearm þær wæs ȝedon. *c* **1305** *St. Edward* 19 in *E.E.P.* (1862) 107 þulke ring is ȝut .. for relik ido. *c* **1420** *Chron. Vilod.* 377 Had y don meyte in a dysshe. *Ibid.* 580 Hit was þo y do. **1440** J. SHIRLEY *Dethe K. James* (1818) 26 That edoone the hangmane was commandid.. to kut of that hand. *c* **1440** *Partonope* 6794 How he hadde follyly I do.

β. *a* **1131** *O.E. Chron.* an. 1126, þæt wæs eall don ðurh his dohtres ræd. *a* **1300** *Cursor M.* 2996 Qui has þou þusgat don? **13..** *Ibid.* 16762 + 22 Til end þis dede is doyn. —— *Ibid.* 16812 Thingez þat are doyne. —— *Ibid.* 20065 Crist was doun on þe rode. *c* **1350** *Will. Palerne* 937 Y-wisse, y am done. *c* **1380** WYCLIF *Serm.* Sel. Wks. I. 271 Bifore alle þingis ben doone. *c* **1420** *Pallad. on Husb.* I. 4 As sum have doon. *c* **1425** WYNTOUN *Cron.* VI. xii. 28 þan wes he dwne. **1432–50** tr. *Higden* (Rolls) I. 193 What scholde be doen. **1535** FISHER *Wks.* (1876) 380 He hath.. don al this. **1555** EDEN *Decades* 182 After he hath dooen thus. **1558–68** WARDE tr. *Alexis' Secr.* 2 a, That doen, take a pound.. of Aloes. **1577** B. GOOGE *Heresbach's Husb.* IV. (1586) 174 b, All is dasht, and done. **1594** PLAT *Jewellho.* I. 5 To have been doone by Abimelech. **1674** tr. *Scheffer's Lapland* 7 Which don, he rises up. **1860–1** FLO. NIGHTINGALE *Nursing* 24 [To see] that what ought to be done is always done.

γ. **13..** *Cursor M.* 2413 (Trin.) Sir she seide hit shal be do. *c* **1380** WYCLIF *Serm.* Sel. Wks. I. 337 3if Eve hadde do so. *c* **1449** PECOCK *Repr.* Prol. 1 So that it be do with honeste. **1482** *Monk of Evesham* (Arb.) 49 Thyngys that y schulde haue doo. **1509** *Act 1 Hen. VIII*, Pref., The kynge.. hath do to be ordeined. **1522** *World & Child* in Hazl. *Dodsley* I. 252 Many a lord have I do lame.

9. *Verbal sb.* DOING, q.v.

B. Signification.

General scheme of arrangement—I. Transitive senses (*To put. **To bestow, render. ***To perform, effect). II. Intransitive: To put forth action, to act. III. Causal and Auxiliary uses (*Causal. **Substitute. ***Periphrastic). IV. Special uses of certain parts (Imperative, Infinitive, Pres. pple., Past pple.). V. Special uses with prepositions (e.g. *do for*). VI. In combination with adverbs (e.g. *do off*).

I. Transitive senses.

* To put, place. (Cf. the adv. combinations *do on, off, in, out*, etc. in VI.)

1. To put, place. **a.** *lit. Obs.* exc. *dial.*

c **897** K. ÆLFRED *Gregory's Past.* xlix. (E.E.T.S.) 383 Ðæt mon his sweord doo ofer his hype. *c* **1000** *Ags. Gosp.* Matt. ix. 17 Hiȝ doð niwe win on niwe bytta. **1154** *O.E. Chron.* an. 1137 Me dide cnotted strenges abuton here hæued. *c* **1175** *Lamb. Hom.* 85 þet corn me deð in to gerner. *c* **1250** *Gen. & Ex.* 2586 Euerilc knape child.. ben a-non don ðe flod wið-in. *a* **1300** *Cursor M.* 13846 (Cott.) þat he be tan, and don in band. *c* **1300** *Ibid.* 20112 (Edin.) Amang þe nunnis.. he hir dide. *c* **1400** *Sowdone Bab.* 1363 Take myn hawberke and do it on the. *c* **1440** *Anc. Cookery* in *Househ. Ord.* (1790) 425 Do hom in a pot and seth hom, and do therto gode broth. **1460** CAPGRAVE *Chron.* 43 Ozias.. presumed to do upon him the prestis stole. **1563–87** FOXE *A. & M.* (1684) II. 440 If I would not tell where I had done him. **1600** W. VAUGHAN *Directions for Health* (1633) 117 Take a gallon.. of pure water, and do it into a pot. **1606** HOLLAND *Sueton.* 120 He tooke of his Ring.. then afterwardes did it uppon his finger agaime. **1877** E. PEACOCK *N.W. Lincolns. Gloss.* 89/1 Where hes ta done it? I've look'd high an' low for it.

†**b.** *fig. Obs.*

c **1230** *Hali Meid.* 7 Deð hire in to drecchunge to dihten hus & hinen. *a* **1300** *Cursor M.* 15235 (Cott.) þat sal þis ilk night be don.. to mikel pine. *c* **1305** *Judas Iscariot* 46 in *E.E.P.* (1862) 108 þe quene vpe him hire hurte dude. *a* **1325** *Prose Psalter* xxxix. [xl]. 15 Ne do nouȝt, Lord, þy mercy fer fra me. **1393** LANGL. *P. Pl.* C. xxi. 93 Ich do me in ȝoure grace. *c* **1460** *Towneley Myst.* (Surtees) 16 And thou thus dos me from thi grace. **1535** STEWART *Cron. Scot.* (1858) I. 225 He did him in his will. **1598** *Mucedorus* in Hazl. *Dodsley* VII. 222 Take him away, and do him to execution straight.

c. *to do to death*: orig. to put to death; now, often with emphasis on the *do*, implying a slow or protracted process. *arch.* (Cf. DEATH *sb.* 12.)

a **1175** *Cott. Hom.* 229 Hu hi michte hine to deaðe ȝedon. *a* **1225** *Leg. Kath.* 2131 Ichulle.. don þe to deaðe. *a* **1300** *Cursor M.* 13961 (Cott.) þe Iues.. soght iesu at do to ded. *c* **1449** PECOCK *Repr.* 564 Men for her trespacis ben doon into her Deeth. **1579–80** NORTH *Plutarch* (1676) 1004 The putting away and doing his Wife Octavia to death. **1599** SHAKS. *Much Ado* v. iii. 3 Done to death by slanderous tongues. **1868** FREEMAN *Norm. Conq.* (1876) II. viii. 302 That brother had been done to death by English traitors.

†**d.** *to do of*: to put out of, deprive of, rid of, 'do out' of. *to do of dawe, adawe*: see DAY *sb.* 17. *to do of live*: see LIFE. *Obs.*

c **1305** *St. Lucy* 95 in *E.E.P.* (1862) 104 Ne mai no womman.. of hire maidenhod beo ido. **13..** *Cursor M.* 5944 (Cott.) Drightin sua þam did of all.

†**2.** *refl.* To put or set oneself; to betake oneself, proceed, go. *Obs.*

a **1225** *Ancr. R.* 430 Me were leouere uorto don me touward Rome. *a* **1300** *Cursor M.* 12832 (Cott.) He did him þan to flum iordan. *c* **1300** *St. Brandan* 33 We dude ous in a schip. **13..** *Guy Warw.* (A.) 343 On his knes he him dede Bifor Felice. *c* **1340** *Gaw. & Gr. Knt.* 1368 Ho dos hir forth at þe dore. *c* **1350** *Will. Palerne* 2061 He deraied him as a deuel & dede him out a-ȝeine. *c* **1425** *Seven Sag.* (P.) 2416 He dyde hym anoon to ryde. *c* **1435** *Torr. Portugal* 1521 Of the valey he did hym swith.

†**b.** *intr.* To proceed, go. See *do way* (53). *Obs.*

a **1300** *Cursor M.* 6140 'Dos now forth', þai said in hi.

†**3.** *trans.* To apply, employ, lay out, expend. *Obs.* ***to do cost***: see COST *sb.*² 5.

1411 *E.E. Wills* (1882) 17 Y wille þat þe surplus be don for my soule. **1434** *Ibid.* 101 Sell hit, & do hit for the loue of god. **1522** *Bury Wills* (1850) 117 The mony..to be don for my sowle and hys.

b. To settle, invest. *Obs.*

c **1330** R. BRUNNE *Chron.* (1810) 31 Who felle to haf þe lond, on þam it suld be don.

** To bestow, impart, grant, render, give (a thing to a person); to cause to befall or come.

Orig. with dative of the recipient or person affected, and accusative of that which is imparted or caused: e.g. 'it did him credit'. But in later use the dative is largely replaced by *to* and prepositional object, and then changes places with the verbal object: 'it did credit *to* his good sense'.

(The primary notion here appears to have been that of *putting* (or *bestowing*) something to a person, being closely related to prec. section, in which a person is put to or into something.)

4. To impart to, bring upon (a person, etc.) some affecting quality or condition; to bestow, confer, inflict; to cause by one's action (a person) to have (something). In later use, associated more closely with the notion of performance, as in 6, e.g. ***to do any one a service*** = to perform some action that is of service to him.

a **1000** *Martyrol.* 7 May (E.E.T.S.) 78 Se ȝedyde dumbum men spræce. *c* **1000** *Ags. Ps.* (Th.) cxlii[i]. 10 þu me god dydest. **1154** *O.E. Chron.* an. 1137 Alle þe pines þe hi diden wrecce men. *c* **1205** LAY. 481 Heo willeð þe freonscipe don. *a* **1225** *Ancr. R.* 124 þu dest me god. *a* **1300** *Cursor M.* 13666 (Cott.) He thoght him do solace. *Ibid.* 20079 (Cott.) þai me do þis mikel scham. *Ibid.* 20274 (Cott.) It dos me god þat i yuu se. *c* **1400** MAUNDEV. (Roxb.) iv 12 Scho duse na man harme. **1523** LD. BERNERS *Froiss* I. ccvii. 244 The which dyd them great trouble. **1535** COVERDALE *2 Macc.* ix. 7 It brussed his body, & dyd him greate payne. **1675** WOOD *Life* (Oxf. Hist. Soc.) II. 316 It..did me a great deal of good. **1773** GOLDSM. *Stoops to Conq.* v, Sure he'll do the dear boy no harm. **1819** SOUTHEY *Lett.* (1856) III. 112 The book does him very great credit.

b. To render, administer, pay, extend, exhibit, show ***to a person*** (justice, worship, thanks, etc.).

a **1000** CYNEWULF *Christ* 1567 Hy to sið doð gæstum helpe. *c* **1000** *Ags. Ps.* (Th.) cviii. 21 Do me þine..mycle mildheortnesse. **1154** *O.E. Chron.* an. 1140 Alle diden him manred. *c* **1300** *Cursor M.* 24058 (Edin.) Vs al to don sucour. *c* **1340** *Ibid.* 15047 (Trin.) þat we þe do suche worshepe as we may. *c* **1400** MAUNDEV. (Roxb.) xxiv. 113, I schall do þe an euill turne. *c* **1450** *Merlin* 5 They moste do hir the lawe. *c* **1477** CAXTON *Jason* 11 To doo her ayde ayenst her ennemyes. **1523** LD. BERNERS *Froiss.* I. cxxxiii. 161 Than the kyng dyd them that grace, that he suffred them to passe. **1703** ROWE *Ulyss.* I. i, To do him right He was a Man indeed. **1776** *Trial of Nundocomar* 73/1 The Gentlemen of the Audawlet would do him justice. **1847** MARRYAT *Childr. N. Forest* xiii, I did a gipsy a good turn once.

5. With the indirect object governed by *to*; thus passing into 6.

a **1300** *Cursor M.* 17288 + 257 (Cott.) A grete honour to wymmen did he in þat cas. *c* **1340** *Ibid.* 5980 (Fairf.) þe folk of egipte þat maste to bestes done worshepe. *c* **1385** CHAUCER *L.G.W.* 1601 *Hypsip. & Medea*, He made hire don to Iason cumpaynye At mete. *c* **1420** *Chron. Vilod.* 493 Of þe desplesaunce þᵗ ychave do to ȝow. **1509** HAWES *Past. Pleas.* XXXIII. xxviii, These ladies unto me did great pleasaunce. **1587** GOLDING *De Mornay* iii. 36 If due Iustice vnto you were doone. **1660** PEPYS *Diary* (1890) 17 Which..he did to do a courtesy to the town. **1711** ADDISON *Spect.* No. 70 ¶5 Persons..which do Honour to their Country. **1878** S. WALPOLE *Hist. Eng.* I. 158 A day's sport which would have done credit to these modern days.

*** To put forth (action or effort of any kind); to perform, accomplish, effect. (Now the leading trans. use.)

Since every kind of action may be viewed as a particular form of *doing*, the uses of the verb are as numerous as the classes of objects which it may govern. Only the general senses can here be exhibited; the phrases formed by the verb with special substantive objects, are treated under the words concerned; e.g. *to do honour, the honours of*: see HONOUR.

6. To perform, execute, achieve, carry out, effect, bring to pass. (With an object denoting action.) e.g. *to do work, a thing, that, it, what?* etc.

a **1000** *Guthlac* 61 (32) [Hi] þa weorc ne doð. *a* **1000** *Boeth. Metr.* xiii. 79 (Gr.) Hio sceal eft don þæt hio ær dyde. **1123** *O.E. Chron.*, þis he dyde eall for þes biscopes luuen. *a* **1225** *Leg. Kath.* 748 Heo ne duden nawiht. *a* **1300** *Cursor M.* 13473 (Cott.) He..Wist well wat he had to don. **1382** WYCLIF *John* x. 37 If I do not the workis of my fadir, nyle ȝe bileue to me. *c* **1450** *St. Cuthbert* (Surtees) 4156 Of diuers miracles þat Cuthbert did. **1581** MULCASTER *Positions* i. (1887) 2 Neither I haue don so much as I might. **1611** BIBLE *Transl. Pref.* 2 He did neuer doe a more pleasing deed. **1711** ADDISON *Spect.* No. 93 ¶1 Our Lives..are spent either in doing nothing at all, or in doing nothing to the purpose. **1847** MARRYAT *Childr. N. Forest* iv, Humphrey will..do all the hard work.

b. ***to do good, evil, right, wrong***, etc.

c **1000** *Ags. Ps.* lxi[i]. 9 Ge woh didon. **1154** *O.E. Chron.* an. 1140 Ware se he com he dide mare yuel þanne god. *c* **1300** *Cursor M.* 29167 (Cott. Galba) þam aw here to do right. **1382** WYCLIF *Eccl.* vii. 21 Ther is not forsothe a riȝtwis man in the erthe, that do good, and not synne. **1513** DOUGLAS *Æneis* III. i. 105 Quhat wickitnes or mischeif may be do. **1526–34** TINDALE *Matt.* xxvii. 23 What evyll hath he done? **1847** MARRYAT *Childr. N. Forest* xxv, Surely I have done wrong.

c. To commit (sin, crime, etc.); to perpetrate. *Obs.* or *arch.*

a **1000** *Father's Instr.* 70 (Cod. Ex. lf. 81 a) Ðeah hi wom don. **1297** R. GLOUC. (1724) 369 þulke robberye, þat hym þoȝte he adde ydo. *a* **1300** *Cursor M.* 5173 (Gött.) ȝe gabb, and certis, ȝe do gret sin. *c* **1440** *Promp. Parv.* 126/2 Do mawmentrye, *ydolatro.* **14..** *Circumcision* in *Tundale's Vis.* (1843) 98 As thow dydest neuer trespace. **1539** BP. HILSEY *Primer* 111, Thou shalt do no murder. **1686** in Picton *L'pool Munic. Rec.* (1883) I. 271 Severall abuses done by such as sell rootes. *a* **1745** SWIFT *Rules conc. Servants* Wks. 1745 VIII. 7 When you have done a fault, be pert and insolent.

d. To execute, administer, practise (a function, office, or duty).

c **1000** *Ags. Ps.* (Th.) cxxxix. 12 Gode deð drihten domas. **1154** *O.E. Chron.* an. 1140 He dide god iustise and makede pais. *a* **1300** *Cursor M.* 9708 (Cott.) Rightwisli to do iustise. *Ibid.* 27272 Queþer þai þair mister leli do. **1715** LEONI *Palladio's Archit.* (1742) I. 99 The judges attended to do justice. **1847** MARRYAT *Childr. N. Forest* xxvii, As many of your countrymen as you may consider likely to do good service. **1892** GARDINER *Stud. Hist. Eng.* 21 Justice was done between man and man.

e. With various extensions of the predicate expressing the relation of the action to another person or thing; now esp. with *with*. Often blending with 5.

c **1000** *Ags. Ps.* (Th.) lxxxv. 16 Do ȝedefe mid me, Drihten, tacen. **1154** *O.E. Chron.* an. 1137 Na god ne dide me for his saule þar of. *c* **1175** *Lamb. Hom.* 121 þere muchele mildheortnesse þe he dude on us. *a* **1300** *Cursor M.* 19325 (Cott.) þai durst na uiolence to þam do. **1382** WYCLIF *John* xvi. 3 And thei schuln do to ȝou thes thingis, for thei han not knowe the fadir, nether me. *c* **1400** MAUNDEV. (1839) xxx. 300 So riche þat þei wyte not what to done with hire goldes. *c* **1480** *Crt. Love* 46 Love arted me to do my observaunce To his estate. **1535** COVERDALE *1 Chron.* xx. [xix]. 2, I wil do mercy vpon Hanun the sonne of Nahas. **1644** MILTON *Areop.* (Arb.) 37 Then began to be consider'd..what was to be don to libellous books. **1719** DE FOE *Crusoe* II. ii, We knew not what to do with this poor girl. **1820** *Edin. Rev.* XXXIII. 93 They are so happy that they know not what to do with themselves. **1843** *Fraser's Mag.* XXVIII. 729 What is to be done with Ireland now? **1858** BULWER-LYTTON (*title*) What will he do with it? **1890** SIR N. LINDLEY in *Law Times Rep.* LXIII. 690/1, I think an injustice has been done to the plaintiff. *c* **1920** D. H. LAWRENCE *Phoenix II* (1968) 116 And what are you doing with yourself these days, Mr. Noon?

f. ***to have done it***: to have acted extremely foolishly; to have made a mess of things; ***that does*** (or ***did***) ***it***: that is (or was) the last straw. *colloq.*

1837 DICKENS *Pickw.* xxxv. 391 Well, young man, now you *have* done it. **1842** S. LOVER *Handy Andy* xlii. 320 By the powers, you *have* done it this time! **1857** DICKENS *Dorrit* I. viii. 62 'You've done it,' observed Tip; 'you must be sharper than that, next time.' **1883** G. M. HOPKINS *Let.* 28 Sept. (1938) 164, I began to fear I had, as people say, 'done it this time'. **1914** 'E. BRAMAH' *M. Carrados* 82 'Now you've done it,' commented Mr. Carlyle. **1930** BELLOC *New Caut. Tales* 45 His father made a fearful row. He said 'By Gum, you've done it now!' **1946** W. F. BROWN *Through Windows* xiii. 64 Again I did not go and pleaded the same reason. That apparently did it, as they say—she stopped asking me to lunch parties.

g. ***it is not*** (freq. ***isn't***) ***done***: it is forbidden by custom, opinion, or propriety; it is bad form. *colloq.*

1879 E. GOSSE in Charteris *Life & Lett.* (1931) 126 We haven't the originality to think of dying. It's never done here, in our set. **1911** R. W. CHAMBERS *Common Law* i, 'You know,' he said, 'models are not supposed to come here unless sent for. It isn't done in this building.' **1926** E. M. DELL *Black Knight* I. viii, 'Oh, but you couldn't—you couldn't—live there by yourself!' protested Joyce. 'It isn't done, Ermine. It wouldn't be fitting.' **1928** *Observer* 29 Jan. 22/1 Undergraduates regard the conduct of the night of December 13 as the sort of thing that 'isn't done'. **1932** *Times Lit. Suppl.* 5 May 318/4 A first-class book made up of things which emphatically are 'not done'. **1963** A. HERON *Towards Quaker View of Sex* 56 When it is 'not done' to discuss sexuality—as in many Western sub-cultures. **1971** P. WORSTHORNE *Socialist Myth* viii. 188 That kind of behaviour simply is not done, simply is not cricket.

7. To perform duly, carry out, execute. (With obj. expressing command, duty, etc.)

c **825** *Vesp Psalter* cxliii. 10 Lær mec doan willan ðinne. *a* **1000** *Cædmon's Gen.* 142 Druȝon and dydon drihtnes willan. *a* **1300** *Cursor M.* 3414 (Cott.) Gladli his biding he didd. *c* **1385** CHAUCER *L.G.W.* 1644 *Hypsip. & Medea*, And doth his oth & goth with hire to bedde. ? *a* **1525** *Hickscorner* in Hazl. *Dodsley* I. 177 Do my counsel, brother Pity. **1557** N. T. (Genev.) *Matt.* vi. 10 Thy wil be done [TIND. fulfilled]. **1653** HOLCROFT *Procopius* II. 50 They did his commands with alacrity. **1712** J. JAMES tr. *Le Blond's Gardening* 204 Take out the Dirt that hinders the Water from doing its Office. **1872** E. PEACOCK *Mabel Heron* I. i. 5 Servants who did his bidding.

b. To perform duly, celebrate (a ceremony, etc.).

c **1000** *Soul's Compl.* 69 þonne haleȝe menn gode.. lofsong doð. *a* **1300** *Cursor M.* 28251 (Cott.) In kyrk..quen goddis seruis was to do. *c* **1400** *Destr. Troy* 1413 All þere lordes Didyn sacrifice solempne vnto sere goddes. **1463** *Bury Wills* (Camden) 28 Whan the messe is do on my yeerday. **1483** CAXTON *Gold. Leg.* 219 b/2 To don penaunce here for our synnes. **1548** HALL *Chron.*, *Hen. V* (an. 8) 75 b, The coronacion of his Quene and spouse..which was doen the daie of S. Mathy. **1583** RICH *Phylotus & Em.* (1835) 23 The Mariage rites that are to bee doen in the Churche. **1875** STUBBS *Const. Hist.* III. xviii. 127 She..submitted to the correction of the bishops, and did penance.

†**c.** To execute, discharge, deliver (a message, etc.). *Obs.*

1523 LD. BERNERS *Froiss.* I. lxxvi, 97 They loked among them who shulde do yᵉ message. **1580** SIDNEY *Arcadia* (1622) 55 A Gentleman desired leaue to doe a message from his Lord vnto him. **1596** J. DEE in *Lett. Lit. Men* (Camden) 88 To Mr. Boston..I wold full fayne have my commendations done. **1678** BUNYAN *Pilgr.* I. 144 We will do him word of this thy behaviour. **1706–7** FARQUHAR *Beaux Strat.* III. ii, Do my bassemains to the gentleman.

8. (In *pa. pple.* and *perf. tenses.*) To accomplish, complete, finish, bring to a conclusion. ***to be done***, to be at an end.

a **1300** *Cursor M.* 20319 (Cott.) Mi ioi es don euerilk dele. *c* **1320** R. BRUNNE *Medit.* 131 Whan þe soper was do, cryst ros anone. *a* **1450** *Knt. de la Tour* (1868) 145 Alle the.. seruice is songe & doo. *c* **1489** CAXTON *Sonnes of Aymon* i. 56 He knewe well that it was doon of [= all up with] hym. **1548–9** (Mar.) *Bk. Com. Prayer* 127 b, When the Clerkes have dooen syngyng. **1568** GRAFTON *Chron.* II. 21 Before his funerall obsequy was finished and done. **1697** DRYDEN *Virg. Past.* IX. 73 Now the Chime of Poetry is done. *a* **1745** SWIFT *Direct. Servants* Wks. (1869) 566/2 When dinner is done. **1887** RIDER HAGGARD *Jess* xv, By the time that the horses had done their forage.

b. *to be done* is used of the agent instead of 'to have done', in expressing state rather than action. (Chiefly *Irish, Sc., U.S.*, and *dial.*)

1766 AMORY *Buncle* (1770) IV. 119, I was done with love for ever. **1771** T. JEFFERSON *Let. T. Adams* in *Harper's Mag.* No. 482. 206 One farther favor and I am done. **1776** BENTHAM *Wks.* (1838–43) X. 77 The rogue is pressing me so, I must be done. **1835** MARRYAT *Jac. Faithf.* xiii, One little bit more, and then I am done. **1876** H. B. SMITH in *Life* (1881) 404 After this is done I am done. **1876** RUSKIN *Fors. Clav.* VI. lxvi. 192 Let us be done with the matter. **18..** *Lit. World* (Boston) X. 400 The mills of the gods are not yet done grinding. **1883** *Century Mag.* XXV. 767/1 'Going..at twenty-four thousand dollars! Are you all done?' He scanned the crowd.

9. To put forth, exert, use (diligence, endeavour, etc.) in effecting something. ***to do one's best, cure, devoir, diligence, endeavour, might, pain***, etc.: see these words.

a **1300** *Cursor M.* 14480 (Cott.) þai did þair pain þat he and lazar war bath slain. *c* **1330** *Assump. Virg.* (B.M. MS.) 7 Aungeles donn here myȝt To serue hure boþe day & nyȝt. *c* **1440** *Generydes* 68 They dede ther besy payne. **1509** HAWES *Past. Pleas.* I. xvii, To reade their names I did my busy cure. **1523** LD. BERNERS *Froiss.* I. clxxxii. 216 Shame haue he that dothe nat his power to distroy all. **1611** BIBLE *2 Tim.* iv. 9 Doe thy diligence to come shortly vnto me. **1724** DE FOE *Mem. Cavalier* (1840) 76 They bade the Swedes do their worst. **1843** *Fraser's Mag.* XXVIII. 328, I shall do my utmost to serve her. **1872** BLACK *Adv. Phaeton* vi. 82 The Lieutenant did his best to amuse her.

10. To produce, make, bring into existence by one's action.

1580 FULKE (*title*), Stapleton and Martiall..confuted.. Done and directed to all those that love the truth and hate superstitious vanities. **1583** HOLLYBAND *Campo di Fior* 357 We have done five or six copies in the same paper. **1601** CHESTER *Loves Martyr*, etc. 165 [169] Done by the best and chiefest of our moderne writers. **1703** MOXON *Mech. Exerc.* 239 The Rough or Plain Work, is done with the Grey Kentish Bricks. **1810** *Sporting Mag.* XXXVI. 73 This method of *doing* (as it is called) a paper, is disgraceful. **1858** CARLYLE *Fredk. Gt.* (1865) I. II. viii. 98 Otto IV..had an actual habit of doing verse. **1860–1** FLO. NIGHTINGALE *Nursing* 58 The sun is a painter. He does the photograph.

11. To operate upon or deal with (an object) in any way. The most general word expressing transitive action; and so, familiarly substituted for any verb the action of which is of a nature to be readily inferred from the subject or object, or both combined. In *Slang*, employed euphemistically to avoid the use of some verb plainly naming an action. Among the great variety of uses, the following are some of the chief:

a. To do work upon or at, repair, prepare, clean, keep in order, etc; to decorate, furnish. With person as obj. (*colloq.*) = to operate on, attend to, etc.

c **1515** *Cocke Lorell's B.* (Percy Soc.) 12 Some yᵉ lodysshestone dyd seke, some yᵉ bote dyd. **1691** T. H[ALE] *Acc. New Invent.* p. xxi, If they had done the other nineteen as that twentieth Ship was done [i.e. sheathed]. **1778** MISS BURNEY *Evelina* xxi, I did my hair on purpose. **1848** J. H. NEWMAN *Loss & Gain* (1876) 170 A gardener..whose wife (what is called) *did* his lodgers. **1881** GRANT WHITE *Eng. Without & Within* xvi. 388 *Do* is made a word of all work.. Women do their back hair, and do everything that they arrange. 'I have got these flowers to do'—meaning to arrange in a vase. **1883** *Leisure H.* 84/1 The Chinaman who usually 'does' my room. *a* **1897** *Mod.* The man who does our garden. The paper-hanger who did this room, has done it very well. **1898** A. E. T. WATSON *Turf* i. 21 Almost all these horses have their own boys, who ride at exercise, and, as the phrase goes, 'do' them, that is to say, groom and attend to them in their stables. **1901** *Daily Chron.* 16 Oct. 5/2 The [vaccinated] man who..has been 'done in the leg'. **1902** MRS. C. S. PEEL *How to keep House* iv. 42 Do flowers, write *menus*, do house accounts and see housemaid. **1919** D. ASHFORD *Young Visiters* (1951) v. 33 A small but handsome compartment done in dark green lether with crests on the chairs. **1929** P. GUEDALLA *Missing Muse* 147 The explorers ..went below and began to do their hair. **1960** C. DAY LEWIS *Buried Day* 116 Confirmation was habitually referred to as 'getting done'. We were 'done', according to our age group, in batches—like loaves. **1960** *Housewife* Apr. 29/2 She has 'done the flowers' at innumerable society dinners. **1962** R. HYMAN *Mod. Dict. Quots.* 146 Can I do you now, sir?—Mrs. Mop (Itma, B.B.C. Radio Programme, 1939–1949).

b. To prepare or make ready as food; to cook; to preserve, pickle, etc.

1660 PEPYS *Diary* 2 Mar., We had..a carp and some other fishes, as well done as ever I eat any. **1796** MRS. GLASSE *Cookery* xix. 304 Red currants are done the same way. **1822** LAMB *Elia* Ser. I. *Roast Pig*, How equably he twirleth round the string. Now he is just done. **1885** *Manch. Exam.* 16 Sept. 5/2 [She] will have an extra bloater or a mutton chop done to a turn. *a* **1897** *Mod.* (U.S.) *Advertisement*, Young woman as dinner or order cook: capable of doing pastry.

c. To work at or out, solve, translate, review, depict, etc.

1780 JOHNSON *Let. to Mrs. Thrale* 9 May, My Lives creep on..I have done Addison, Prior..and almost Fenton. **1813** MACAULAY in *Life & Lett.* (1880) I. 41, I do Xenophon every day. **1855** THACKERAY *Newcomes* iii, He had done [sketched] me and Hannah too. **1866** *Reader* 3 Nov. 914 The gentle man who 'does' the French books for the Athenæum. **1883** R. BUCHANAN *Love me for ever* II. iii. 92 There Amos often sat and did his accounts. **1887** L. CARROLL *Game of Logic* iv. 96 Not one syllable of lessons do they ever do after their one o'clock dinner. *a* **1897** *Mod.* A class of boys doing arithmetic while another is doing Euclid. I cannot do this problem. Show me how to do this sum.

d. To enact, act; to play the part of. Also *colloq.*, to act or behave in a manner characteristic of (a specified person, etc.).

1599 SHAKS. *Much Ado* II. i. 122 You could neuer doe him so ill well, vnlesse you were the very man. **1660** PEPYS *Diary* 11 Oct., To the Cockpitt to see 'The Moore of Venice', which was well done. **1709** STEELE *Tatler* No. 4 ¶4 A great Part of the Performance was done in Italian. **1770** FOOTE *Lame Lover* II. Wks. 1799 II. 80, I shall do Andromache myself. **1830** *Fraser's Mag.* I. 131 He was too poor to do comet; but he did fire-fly with some brilliancy. **1857** HUGHES *Tom Brown* I. vii, East still doing the cicerone. **1883** *Century Mag.* XXV. 755/1 He did not seem to do the host. **1934** *Tit-Bits* 31 Mar. 12/3 'To do a Gaynor' means to smile upwards through eyes swimming with tears, a tribute to Janet Gaynor's ability to switch on the 'sunshine through the tears'. 'To do a Garbo', on the other hand, means to be proud, aloof, and unbending. **1943** N. BALCHIN *Small Back Room* 28 We do all the work and then R. B. sails in and does a God Almighty on us. **1960** L. COOPER *Accomplices* I. vi. 58 He's a fiend about it—not that he does a McCarthy or rants. **1963** *Times* 20 Apr. 9/4 Already those responsible for premises or institutions under threat of closure and persons haunted by the now inevitable word redundancy are saying 'They're doing a Beeching on us'.

e. To finish up, exhaust, undo, ruin, 'do for'. Also colloq. phr. ***done to the wide*** or ***the world***: absolutely done for, defeated, etc. Also *slang*, to beat up; to defeat; to finish up; to kill. Cf. sense 45 b below.

c **1350** *Will. Palerne* 937 And but he wiȝtly wite, y-wisse, y am done. *a* **1400–50** *Alexander* 3713 How we haue done ser Dary & drepid his kniȝtes. **1542** UDALL *Erasm. Apoph.* 364 A man euen with veray age almoste clene dooen. **1666** DRYDEN *Ann. Mirab.* lxx, The Holland fleet, who, tired and done, Stretch'd on their decks like weary oxen lie. **1780** *Sessions' Paper* 611/2 He..got one of our cutlasses, which was drawn;..and said, 'D—n my eyes, here is one of Akerman's bloody thieves, let us do him first.' **1794** *Sporting Mag.* III. 260/2 Much skill was displayed by both the combatants... Dame Fortune..at length favoured the tin-man, who, in the language of the schools, *did his man.* **1796** GROSE *Dict. Vulgar T.* (ed. 3), *Do*,..to overcome in a boxing match; witness those laconic lines written on the field of battle, by Humphreys to his patron—'Sir, I have done the Jew.' **1812** *Examiner* 9 Nov. 719/2 Oh, Charles, you have done me. **1841** P. MCFARLANE *Sp.* 25 Aug., If we shrink, we are done. **1892** *Black & White* 14 May 623/2 It was a decimal that did me in the Little-Go. **1893** DUNMORE *Pamirs* I. 90 It was a..trying march to-day for men and horses, and both were pretty well done by the time we got in. **1905** CONAN DOYLE *Return of S. Holmes* 218 'You've done me,' he cried, and lay still. **1922** *Daily Mail* 6 Dec. 11 He came again after appearing 'done to the world' more than once. **1925** FRASER & GIBBONS *Soldier & Sailor Words*, *Done to the wide*, utterly beaten. **1948** L. A. G. STRONG *Trevannion* 3 If I do Sid, I'm to have a go at Sailor Berridge. **1954** M. PROCTER *Hell is City* II. ii. 47 I'll do you if it's my last act in life. I'll swing for you with pleasure. **1959** *Encounter* Aug. 33/2, I..told him..I'd do him if I ever saw his face again. **1959** I. & P. OPIE *Lore & Lang. Schoolch.* x. 195 'I'll clout you', 'I'll do you', or 'I'll do you up' (a threat of sinister implication in London S.E.).

f. To hoax, cheat, swindle, overreach. *slang.* Also *to do in the eye* (see EYE *sb.*[1] 2 k).

1641 BEST *Farm. Bks.* (Surtees) 136 And I can doe, My master too, When my master turnes his backe. **1768** GOLDSM. *Good-n. Man* II. i, If the man comes from the Cornish borough, you must do him. **1801** *Sporting Mag.* XVIII. 100 To do any one, to cheat him. **1830** DISRAELI in *Edin. Daily Rev.* 12 May (1885) 2/8 He did the Russian Legation at écarté. **1887** SIMS *Mary Jane's Mem.* 106 If you are too suspicious of servants..they take a pleasure in 'doing' you, to use a common saying.

g. To accomplish (a given distance) in travelling; to achieve; to travel at (a certain speed, etc.).

1808 *Sporting Mag.* XXXIII. 146/2 The Captain did the first mile in five minutes and a second. **1824** T. MOORE *Mem.* (1853) IV. 179, [I] did the four miles in less than twenty minutes. **1890** *Nature* 13 Mar. 435 The 105½ miles between Grantham and London are continuously 'done' in 117 minutes. **1919** C. MACKENZIE *Early Life Sylvia Scarlett* II. i. 273 Good engine this. We're doing fifty-nine or an unripe sixty. **1919** G. B. SHAW *Augustus does his Bit* 228 The old cars only do twelve miles to the gallon. Everybody has to have a car that will do thirty-five now. **1963** M. PROCTER *Moonlight Flitting* i. 6 'That's a Rolls-Royce, isn't it?' 'Yes. It's practically new. Only done about a thousand.' **1966** J. MILES in T. Wisdom *High-Performance Driving* vii. 70 A Ford Zodiac and a caravan..doing 25 m.p.h. and taking up a lot of road. **1967** 'L. BRUCE' *Death of Commuter* vi. 62 What do you reckon to do to the gallon?

h. To go over as a tourist, visit, see; to attend (an entertainment). *colloq.*

1817 LADY GRANVILLE *Let.* June (1894) I. 119 We shall then meet them at Basle, do the Rhine, stay two or three days at Brussels, and home. **1830** MARRYAT *King's Own* xlii, Captain Hall..has..*done* North and South America. **1844** J. T. HEWLETT *Parsons & W.* xvi, We..as he used to call it, '*did* a bit of continent' together. **1854** R. DOYLE *Brown, Jones, and Robinson* 8 They 'do' Cologne Cathedral. **1857** J. F. MAGUIRE *Rome* 8 Some of the latter evidently went to the Pope's Chapel as they had gone the previous night to the Opera, to hear the music, or to 'do' it, as they would the Coliseum. **1861** *Court Life at Naples* II. 115 Travellers, zealously bent on *doing* the country and all the sights. **1890** E. DOWSON *Let.* 4 Mar. (1967) 139, I rather want..to do a St. James's Ballad Concert. **1932** D. L. SAYERS *Have his Carcase* xviii. 239 We could go and do a show together. **1951** M. KENNEDY *L. Carmichael* II. i. 85 People over a wide area would..dine and do a show, as they do at Stratford. **1955** *Times* 25 Aug. 12/3 During siesta the only activity comes from tourists 'doing' St. Peter's, the Colosseum, and the Trevi Fountain before sunstroke or tea. **1966** AUDEN *About House* 20 This unpopular art..Cannot be 'done' like Venice Or abridged like Tolstoy.

i. To serve out (a term of punishment). *slang.*

1865 *Daily Tel.* 1 Mar. 3/3, 'I was doing time'..(A cant term for serving a sentence in prison). **1889** BOLDREWOOD *Robbery under Arms* (1890) 316 Men that have 'done time'. **1892** SAINTSBURY in *Academy* 30 Jan. 106/3 Tuer is a criminal..and..does his five years.

j. With adjectives (in its origin an ellipt. use of d): as ***to do the amiable, civil, grand, lazy, polite*** (person); but at length sometimes with *thing* understood. *colloq.*

1836–9 DICKENS *Sk. Boz, Steam Excursion* 234/1 He used to..flatter the vanity of mammas, do the amiable to their daughters. **1856** WHYTE MELVILLE *Kate Cov.* iii, John 'doing the polite', and laughing as he..introduced 'Captain Lovell' and 'Miss Coventry'. **1864** SALA in *Daily Tel.* 24 Aug., Honestly doing the lazy, and luxuriating in the..bounteous summer. **1873** TRISTRAM *Moab* xiii. 231 Doing the civil most oppressively. **1875** R. H. R. *Rambles in Istria* 195 One confesses, goes to mass, and does the proper.

k. In elliptical expressions, as ***to do the outside edge***, i.e. to practise skating on the outside edge.

1885 *Graphic* 3 Jan. 3/2 To polish up their skates, and to dream..of doing the outside edge almost before Candlemas is over.

l. To arrest; to catch or seize hold of; to charge; to convict. *slang.*

1784 *Sessions' Paper* Jan. 221/1 He stepped on one side of me and said, 'You have not done me yet.' I immediately pursued him. **1812** J. H. VAUX *Flash Dict.*, *Done*, convicted; as, he was *done* for a *crack*, he was convicted of house-breaking. **1936** G. INGRAM *Muffled Man* vi. 91 Blow me if one of your tribe [*sc.* policemen] don't go and do me, and I get found a quid. **1963** *Guardian* 23 Feb. 4/4 'This is a murder charge. There is no certainty that you will be done for murder.'..He did not say that Kelly would only be 'done' for robbery and not murder. **1968** 'R. SIMONS' *Death on Display* iii. 44 I'm goin' straight. Last time I was done was two years ago, and I ain't been tapped on the shoulder since.

m. To look after or provide food for (an animal). *dial.* and *N.Z.*

1890 S. S. BUCKMAN *Darke's Sojourn* viii. 72 Nobody can't be expected to do a flock on no vittles. **1916** *N.Z. Jrnl. Agric.* 20 Sep. 174 Ewes have been..'well done by' during the winter. **1923** W. PERRY *Sheepfarming in N.Z.* viii. 116 Besides the usual pasture, roots and green feed given to the flock it is often found profitable to 'do' the show sheep especially well. **1950** *N.Z. Jrnl. Agric.* Oct. 347/2 The successful management of a sheep run calls for..an appreciation of the carrying capacity of tussock land to 'do' sheep well without either overstocking or understocking.

n. To provide food, etc., for (a person); to treat or entertain (*well*). Also, ***to do oneself well***: to make liberal provision for one's creature comforts; ***to do*** (a person) ***proud***: see PROUD *a.* 10 b. *colloq.*

1897 *Punch* 23 Oct. 185/1 The nightmare of an artist who does himself not wisely but far too well, at an unnecessary supper. **1902** *Daily Chron.* 16 Aug. 3/4 For ten francs a day one is done well there. **1902** *Westm. Gaz.* 25 Aug. 2 His Majesty has been to Westminster Abbey, and the Crystal Palace,..and Madame Tussaud's—really we think that on the whole we have done him very well. *Ibid.* 22 Oct. 3/3 The man who had done himself fairly well on everyday cooking. **1928** *Daily Express* 7 Sept. 1/1 They do you well, with plenty of eggs, cream, [etc.]. **1940** G. D. H. & M. COLE *Murder at Munition Works* iv. 55 The Chief Constable will bear me out that they do one quite well there.

o. To spend completely. *Austral.* and *N.Z. slang.*

1928 *Bulletin* (Sydney) 15 Feb. 35/1 He grumbled:'..I'd just as soon ha' done me brass on goats.' **1931** V. PALMER *Separate Lives* 218, I did my last frog [*sc.* franc] on a feed at the estaminet to-night. **1959** G. SLATTER *Gun in Hand* v. 71 Could you lend me a few bob to put on?.. She was always doing her money cold on the donks. **1969** 'A. GARVE' *Boomerang* i. 24 Right now I've done my money, but as soon as I can raise the fare I'll be getting back.

p. To take (a hallucinogenic or other drug); to smoke (marijuana). *slang* (chiefly *U.S.*).

[**1969** R. D. LINGEMAN *Drugs from A to Z* 66 *Do up* (analogous to fix; from tie up, to tie a cord around an arm to distend the vein, thus making an injection easier), to inject heroin.] **1971** E. LANDY *Underground Dict.* 67 *Do a drug*, use any drug; get stoned, high—e.g. *Let's do some grass.* **1977** MCKNIGHT & TOBLER *Bob Marley* v. 66 Bunny Livingstone spent a year in jail during the late sixties for doing dope. **1977** *Amer. Speech* 1975 L. 58 *Do*, 1: take (a drug) 'What are you doing, uppers?' 2: smoke (marijuana) 'We did some fantastic weed the other night.' **1985** *New Yorker* 29 July 77/2 Their lives..involve..smoking (tobacco, marijuana, cloves), drinking (everything), and doing drugs—mainly cocaine.

q. In many other expressions, for which see the specific words.

12. With noun of action as object, the two being equivalent to a cognate verb of action, as ***to do writing*** = *to write*, ***to do repairs***, = *to repair things.*

So *to do* BATTLE, SLAUGHTER, etc. q.v.

c **1511** *1st Eng. Bk. Amer.* (Arb.) Introd. 35/1 He comyth ..euery yere in his chirche and doth a sermon. **1525** LD. BERNERS *Froiss.* II. clxii. [clviii]. 449 There the kynge kneled downe and dyd his prayers. **1611** SHAKS. *Cymb.* III. v. 38 The Cure whereof, my Lord, 'Tis time must do. *c* **1750** CHATHAM *Lett. Nephew* i. 1 Your translation..is..done.. with much spirit. **1885** *Law Reports* 15 Q. Bench Div. 316 To do trifling repairs to waggons. **1894** DOYLE *S. Holmes* 58, I was sitting doing a smoke.

13. To translate or render *into* another language or form of composition.

1660 BOYLE *New Exp. Phys. Mech.* Pref. 15 He has already provided, that this piece shall shortly be done into Latine. **1710** STEELE *Tatler* No. 230 ¶2 Books.. not translated, but ..Done out of French, Latin, or other Language, and Made English. **1727** POPE, etc. *Art of Sinking* 121 A chapter or two of Burnet's theory..well circumstanced and done into verse. **1831** MACAULAY *Ess.*, *Boswell's Johnson* (1854) 189/1 When he wrote for publication, he did his sentences out of English into Johnsonese.

†**14.** In *passive*, rendering L. *fieri, factum esse*: To be brought about, come to pass, happen. *Obs.*

1382 WYCLIF *Matt.* xxvi. 1 It is don, whenne Jhesus hadde eendid alle these wordis, he seide to his disciplis. **1388** —— *Isa.* xxxvii. 1 It was don, whanne kyng Ezechie hadde herd, he to-rent hise clothis.

II. Intransitive senses.

15. To put forth action, exert activity of any kind whatever; to act (in some specified way). Now a leading sense of the verb.

a **1000** *Cædmon's Gen.* 2225 (Gr.) Do swa ic ðe bidde. **1154** *O.E. Chron.* an. 1137 Næure hethen men ne diden werse þan hi diden. *c* **1205** LAY. 1806 Als his men duden. *a* **1225** *Ancr. R.* 122 Þenc, dude he so? *c* **1380** WYCLIF *Sel. Wks.* III. 514 Neiþer þe kyng ne his counsayl deede unriȝtfully. **1426** AUDELAY *Poems* 9 To do as thou woldest me dud by the. **1465** MARG. PASTON in *Paston Lett.* No. 500 II. 178 Send me word how ye wyll that I doo there in. **1539** TAVERNER *Erasm. Prov.* (1552) 51 When ye are at Rome, do as they do at Rome. **1710** STEELE *Tatler* No. 138 ¶1 It is almost a standing Rule to do as others do, or be ridiculous. **1797** MRS. RADCLIFFE *Italian* vi, He had done imprudently to elect her for the companion of his whole life. **1847** TENNYSON *Princess* IV. 506 You have done well and like a gentleman. **1896** F. HALL in *Nation* (N.Y.) LXII. 223/3 An example which others..would do wisely to copy.

b. To proceed in an emergency or juncture; to have recourse to some procedure or action; to contrive, manage; to make shift to live *on* (a limited income).

c **1300** *Cursor M.* 28707 (Cott. Galba) When slike wrake on a syn was tane, how sall he do [that] has many ane. **1593** SHAKS. *Rich. II*, II. ii. 104 How shall we do for money for these warres? *a* **1761** RICHARDSON (Ogilvie), How shall I do to answer as they deserve your two last letters? *a* **1897** *Mod.* How do you do for fresh provisions? **1924** R. MACAULAY *Orphan Island* xviii. 237 'Is that a good living wage?' he asked her; and she answered that they could just do on it, no more, with what she herself earned.

16. To perform deeds; to exert oneself; to work. (As opposed to doing nothing, talking, etc.) Hence ***do or die*** as adj. phr., expressing determination not to be deterred by any danger or difficulty.

1375 BARBOUR *Bruce* III. 585 For all war doand, knycht and knawe. **1535** COVERDALE *1 Chron.* xxiii. 16 Get the vp, and be doynge. **1621** FLETCHER *Isl. Princess* II. ii. Let's meet, and either do or die. **1724** RAMSAY *Tea-t. Misc.* (1733) I. 7 He could neither say nor do. **1793** BURNS *Scots wha hae* vi, Liberty's in every blow! Let us do, or die. **1809** T. CAMPBELL *Gertrude of Wyoming* III. xxxvii. 71 To-morrow let us do or die! **1850** CARLYLE *Latter-d. Pamph.* v. (1872) 157 All human talent..is a talent to do. **1863** L. M. ALCOTT *Hospital Sk.* i. 13 The head..fermented with all manner of high thoughts and heroic purposes 'to do or die',—perhaps both. **1879** *Boy's Own Paper* 18 Jan. 2/2 Never soldier went into action with a more solemn do-or-die feeling than that with which I took my place on the field that afternoon. **1884** W. C. SMITH *Kildrostan* 58 You have but to say, and they will do. **1902** *Westm. Gaz.* 1 Mar. 4/1 She dips the first pen into the ink with a do-or-die expression. **1907** *Daily Chron.* 26 Sept. 4/6 The dominant motive with all was hatred of the foreign yoke, and the 'do-or-die' determination to shake it off. **1947** *People* 22 June 7/4 His hands grip the handlebars tightly, his face is grim with a do-or-die look. **1971** *Rand Daily Mail* 27 Mar. 23/6 Highlands Power..face a do-or-die effort from the Pretoria team.

b. *euphem.* To copulate (with). Phr. ***to do it*** [IT *pron.* 9], used *colloq.* in the same sense. See DOING *vbl. sb.* 1 b.

1913 D. H. LAWRENCE *Sons & Lovers* II. vii. 162 Do you think we *spoon* and do? We only talk. **1922** JOYCE *Ulysses* 724 Not that I care two straws who he does it with. **1954** R. BISSELL *High Water* xvii. 181 Them island girls they'd rather do it than eat. **1959** A. SINCLAIR *Breaking of Bumbo* II. x. 106 You don't *do her*? And you eat in *Chelsea*? There's something queer about you. **1967** V. CANNING *Python Project* viii. 157 Some service-man..did your mother in Cyprus..and then..made an honest woman of her.

17. In perfect tenses: To make an end, to conclude. ***have done!*** make an end. ***to have done***

with, to cease to have to do with; to desist or cease from.

1303 R. BRUNNE *Handl. Synne* 31 Comyþ alle home, and hauyþ doun. *c* **1305** *St. Katherine* 279 (1862) Do what þu wolt and hane ido: and bring þi wille to ende. *c* **1400** *Melayne* 164 Hafe done! late semble the folke of thyne! **1530** PALSGR. 525/2 Nay, and you double ones, I have done with you. **1538** STARKEY *England* I. iii. 77 [They] ete them when they haue downe. **1592** SHAKS. *Rom. & Jul.* III. v. 205 Do as thou wilt, for I haue done with thee. **1596** —— *Tam. Shr.* III. ii. 118 Ha done with words, To me she's married, not vnto my cloathes. **1668** PEPYS *Diary* 17 Nov., To make clean the house above stairs; the upholsterers having done there. **1712** HEARNE *Collect.* (Oxf. Hist. Soc.) III. 404 After we had done in the Kitchin the woman carried us to the East Part of the House. **1803** C. K. SHARPE *Corr.* (1888) I. 191, I wish the French would come, and have done.

18. To fare, get on (in some way). ***to do well***: to be prosperous in one's doing or proceedings; to prosper, thrive, succeed. **a.** of persons.

a **1300** *Cursor M.* 13492 (Cott.) 'We sal', he said, 'do nu ful wele'. **1375** BARBOUR *Bruce* II. 128 God..Graunt that he thow passis to, & thow sa weill all tyme may do, That ȝe ȝow fra ȝowr fayis defend! *c* **1489** CAXTON *Blanchardyn* xxxi. 116 Daryus demaunded of his fader how they of þe cytye dyd. *a* **1533** LD. BERNERS *Huon* lxv. 223, I pray you shewe me how you haue done syn my departure. **1768** STERNE *Sent. Journ.* (1778) II. 14 (*Passport*) Let me go to Paris..and I shall do very well. **1832** HT. MARTINEAU *Homes Abroad* i. 2 The farmers were doing badly. **1879** TROLLOPE *Thackeray* 56 He had done well with himself, and had made and was making a large income. **1886** STEVENSON *Dr. Jekyll* i, The inhabitants were all doing well..and all emulously hoping to do better still.

b. of things.

1525 LD. BERNERS *Froiss.* II. i. 174 So they had done, if the iourney had done amysse. **1577** B. GOOGE *Heresbach's Husb.* I. (1586) 31 It dooth best in good grounde. **1600** SHAKS. *A. Y. L.* III. v. 111 Words do well When he that speakes them pleases those that heare. **1605** —— *Macb.* v. viii. 3. **1823** J. BADCOCK *Dom. Amusem.* 161 Some fruits do best that are put away in a half ripe state. **1847** *Jrnl. R. Agric. Soc.* VIII. II. 447 Flax does well after wheat, and wheat does well after flax. *Mod.* I am glad your affairs are doing well.

19. *spec.* With regard to health or condition: To be (in health), find oneself, feel, fare (well or ill).

[Arising out of 18, and in early instances not easy to separate from it. Cf. MDu. *doen*, in same use; also OF. *Comment le faites vous?* Lat. *Quid agis?* ModGr. πῶς πράσσεις; how do you do?]

1463 MARG. PASTON in *Paston Lett.* No. 480 II. 142, I wold ye shuld send me word howghe ye doo. **1535** PALSGR. 524/1, I do, I fare well or yvell touchynge my helth. **1563–87** FOXE *A. & M.* (1684) III. 253 God be thanked for you, How do you? **1597** SHAKS. *2 Hen. IV*, III. ii. 70 How doth the good Knight? may I aske how my Lady his Wife doth? **1597** MORLEY *Introd. Mus.* 2 *Phi.* How haue you done since I sawe you? *Ma.* My health, since you sawe mee, hath beene ..badd. **1709** STEELE *Tatler* No. 10 ¶ 1 He asked Will..how he did? **1709** STEELE & ADDISON *ibid.* No. 114 ¶ 1 Child, How does your Father do? **1745** CHESTERF. *Lett.* I. ciii. 284. **1799** SHERIDAN *Pizarro* Prol. (1883) 180 Nodding to booted beaux—'How do, how do?' **1826** DISRAELI *Viv. Grey* IV. v, All..asked him 'how the Marquess did?' **1854–6** PATMORE *Angel in Ho.* I. II. ix. (1879) 225 Learn of the language 'How d'ye do?' And go and brag that they've been there.

20. To 'work', 'act', operate, or turn out (in some way); to do what is wanted; to succeed, answer, or serve; to be fitting or appropriate; to suffice. ***that will do*** (***that'll do***): that is sufficient.

[The unfortunate conjecture of Latham (followed in subsequent dictionaries) that *do* here represents OE. *duȝan*, DOW, and is thus a distinct verb, is entirely erroneous.]

1596 SHAKS. *1 Hen IV*, II. iv. 188, I neuer dealt better since I was a man: all would not doe. **1618** BOLTON *Florus* IV. ii. (1636) 262 As if she tride how it would do. **1750** CHESTERF. *Lett.* (1792) III. No. 226. 24 Adieu, my dear! I find you will do. **1762** FOOTE *Lyar* III. Wks. 1799 I. 314 No, no, Mr. Mandeville, it won't do. *c* **1805** MAR. EDGEWORTH *Wks.* (Rtldg.) I. 48 She had long since prophesied he would not do for them. **1818** CRUISE *Digest* (ed. 2) II 322 The right ..must be a present right; a future one will not do. **1848** LOWELL *Biglow P.* Poet. Wks. (1879) 179 The present Yankee..not so careful for what is best as for what will *do*. **1861** NEALE *Notes Dalmatia*, etc. 70, I cannot say much for our inn; but it did. **1869** FREEMAN *O. Eng. H. for Child.* xi. §2. 277 Perhaps it would hardly have done to send him. *a* **1897** *Mod.* That will do, thank you.

b. Hence *trans.* To do for, suffice for, satisfy (a person). *colloq.*

1846 *Congress. Globe* 20 July 1118, I have just enough [money] to do me to the end of the session. **1880** *Congress. Rec.* 22 Jan. 491/1, I should like to have ten minutes, but it will do me just as well in the morning. **1925** W. DEEPING *Sorrell & Son* xiii, 'What's it to be, Do? An orange cocktail?' 'Yes, that will do me.' **1928** GALSWORTHY *Swan Song* I. iv. 25 Leicester Square would do me all right. **1951** J. B. PRIESTLEY *Festival at Farbridge* 325 That'll do me. Not choosy. **1965** F. SARGESON *Memoirs of Peon* i. 12 The reverse side..did me to draw and paint on.

III. Causal and auxiliary uses. * *Causal.*

†**21.** With *that* and subord. clause: To make it so that, produce the effect that; to cause (*that* a person or thing shall do something). *Obs.*

c **897** K. ÆLFRED *Gregory's Past. Care* xxi. (1871) 207 Ic ȝedo ðæt ðu forgitst. *c* **1000** *Ags. Gosp.* Matt. v. 45 Se þe deð þæt his sunne up aspringð ofer þa godan & ofer þa yfelan. *c* **1175** *Lamb. Hom.* 95 He dude þet heo weren birnende on godes willan. *c* **1250** *Gen. & Ex.* 224 God dede ðat he on sweuene cam. *c* **1386** CHAUCER *Knt.'s T.* 1547 Do that I tomorwe haue victorie.

22. With *obj.* and *infin.* (the obj. being logical subject of the infin.): To make or cause a person, etc., to do something. †**a.** with *simple infin.*; e.g. 'he did them come'. ***to do him die***: to cause or make him die, to put him to death. *Obs.* or *arch.*

c **825** *Vesp. Psalter* xxxviii. 12 Aswindan þu didest..sæwle his. *Ibid.* ciii. 32 Se ȝelocað in eorðan & doeð hie cwaecian. *c* **1000** *Ags. Ps.* (Th.) ciii. 30 He..deð hi for his eȝsan ealle beofian. **1154** *O.E. Chron.* an. 1140, þe biscop of Wincestre ..dide heom cumen þider. *c* **1250** *Gen. & Ex.* 3608 Min engel of Sal ic don ðe bi-foren gon. *a* **1300** *Cursor M.* 3071 (Cott.) þe barn sco dide drinc o þat wel. *c* **1386** CHAUCER *Frankl. T.* 609 In yow lith al to do me lyue or deye. **1460** CAPGRAVE *Chron.* 264 The Kyng..ded his officeres arestin ..his uncil the Duke of Gloucetir. **1590** SPENSER *F.Q.* II. vi. 7 Sometimes, to do him laugh, she would assay To laugh. **1621** AINSWORTH *Annot. on Ps.* lix. 1 To kill him or to doe him die. [**1886** BURTON *Arab Nts.* I. 11 So he carried her to the place of execution and did her die.]

†**b.** with *dative infin.* *Obs.* or *arch.*

a **1300** *Cursor M.* 11222 (Cott.) He..did þe dumb asse to speke. *c* **1300** *Harrow. Hell* 124 Y shal..do the to holde gryht [= gryþ]. ? *a* **1366** CHAUCER *Rom. Rose* 1063 An hundred have [they] don to dye. *c* **1450** *Merlin* 29 The kynge dide hem to swere. *a* **1547** SURREY *Æneid* II. 140 Oft the boisteous winds did them to stay. **1599** H. BUTTES *Dyets drie Dinner* P iij b, Who smoke selleth, with smoke be don to dy. [**1886** BURTON *Arab. Nts.* I. 10 He shall do you to die by the illest of deaths.]

c. ***to do*** (one) ***to wit***, ***know***, or ***understand***: to cause (one) to know; to give (one) to understand; to make known to; to inform. *arch.*

a **1131** *O.E. Chron.* an. 1127 Se ilce Heanri dide þone king to understandene þæt he hæfde [etc.]. *c* **1205** LAY. 27150 And sone duden him to witen Whuder he wolde wenden. **1340–70** *Alex. & Dind.* 224 And þat ȝour doctours dere don ȝou to know. *c* **1449** PECOCK *Repr.* Prol. 1 First openyng or doing to wite, thanne next blamyng. *c* **1460** *Towneley Myst.* (Surtees) 69 Syr, I am done to understand, That a qweyn here..Shalle bere a chyld. *a* **1540** T. CROMWELL in Burnet *Hist. Ref.* (1681) II. 192, I commend me to your Lordship, doing you to understand that I have received your letters. **1610** in Picton *L'pool Munic. Rec.* (1883) I. 121 You shall.. do the Maior of this towne to wete thereof. **1674** N. FAIRFAX *Bulk & Selv.* 22 We are done to wit, that 'tis an infinite not infinite. **1828** SCOTT *F.M. Perth* xxxi, We..do thee, Sir Patrick Charteris.. to know, that [etc.].

†**d.** with *passive infin.* (with or without '*to*'): e.g. 'to do him (to) be slain'. *Obs.*

a **1300** *Cursor M.* 15468 (Cott.) To do his lauerd be tan. *c* **1380** *Sir Ferumb.* 1853 Othre relyqes dere, þat þou dudest a-way be born. **1483** CAXTON *Gold. Leg.* 180 b/2 That in no wyse she shold shewe ne doo be knowen that she were a woman. **1530–1** *Act 22 Hen. VIII*, c. 12 Euery of them shall do the sayde seales to be made.

†**23.** With the logical subject of the inf. omitted; the infinitive being (usually) *trans.* with its own object. E.g. ***do bind him*** = make somebody bind him, cause him to be bound, have him bound [= Fr. *faire lier*, Ger. *binden lassen*]. *Obs.*

c **1250** *Kentish Serm.* in *O.E. Misc.* 26 þo dede he somoni alle þo wyse clerekes. *a* **1300** *Cursor M.* 10355 'Maria' sal þou do hir call. *c* **1386** CHAUCER *Sqr.'s T.* 38 He leet the feeste of his Natiuitee Doon cryen. **1393** LANGL. *P. Pl.* C. IV. 140 In þe castel of corf ich shal do þe close. *c* **1450** *Merlin* 57 The kynge dide do make this dragon..and lete it be born before hym. **1463** *Bury Wills* (Camden) 26 He shal yeerly pay or do paye all the pencyowns. **1541** *Act 33 Hen. VIII*, in Bolton *Stat. Irel.* (1621) 209 Every such person..shall doe make a seale engraved with the name of the Castle..which he keepeth.

b. with *dative infin.* *Obs.*

a **1300** *Cursor M.* 1936 (Cott.) Noe did to rais an auter suyth [*Fairf.* gert to raisse, *Trin.* let reise]. *c* **1450** *Merlin* 27 Than [he] did to brynge ston and morter.

c. *passive.* To be caused to be done. *Obs.*

? *a* **1366** CHAUCER *Rom. Rose* 413 Another thing was doon ther write. [*Passive of* '(thei) dide write another thing'.]

** As a *substitute* for other verbs.

24. Put as a substitute for a verb just used, to avoid its repetition. **a.** Without construction, and so intransitive (as in 15), whether the verb which it represents is intr. or trans.

c **1000** ÆLFRIC *Man. Astron.* (Wright) 2 [Seo sunne] scinð under þære eorðan on nihtlicre tide swa heo on dæȝ deð bufan urum heafdum. *c* **1000** —— *Judg.* xvi. 30 He miccle ma on his deaþe acwealde þonne he ær cucu dyde. *a* **1131** *O.E. Chron.* an. 1127 þær he wunede eall riht swa drane doð on hiue. *c* **1175** *Lamb. Hom.* 111 Summe lauerdes..god gremiað, swa saul þe king dude. *c* **1340** *Cursor M.* 13950 (Fairf.), I haue him knawen & sal do [*Trin.* haue done] euer. **1411** *Rolls of Parlt.* III. 650/2 He ne hath noght born hym as he sholde haue doon. **1527** R. THORNE in Hakluyt *Voy.* (1589) 252 If as the king of Portingall doth, he would become a merchant. *c* **1682** J. COLLINS *Making Salt* 141 We pay double the price we formerly did. **1835** URE *Philos. Manuf.* 306 If competition advances..as it has done for several years. **1879** BAIN *Higher Eng. Gram.* 176 He speaks as well as you do.

b. In some (esp. late) instances *do*, *did*, is to be explained as an elliptical use of the periphrastic form: see 26.

1610 SHAKS. *Temp.* II. i. 195 It sildome visits sorrow, when it doth, it is a Comforter. **1816** J. WILSON *City of Plague* II. iv, Spoke they not of a burial-place? They did. **1823** BYRON *Let. to Kinnaird* 18 Jan., I *will* economise, and *do*. **1830** *Fraser's Mag.* I. 749, I think I said that before. Yes, I did.

c. With the construction of the verb which it represents, and thus often *trans.* (as in 6).

c **1175** *Lamb. Hom.* 65 Vre gultes..bon us forȝeuen Al swa we doþ alle men þet liuen. *Ibid.* 93 Nu luȝe þu na monnum, ac dudest gode. *a* **1200** *Moral Ode* 304 And warnie his frend ..swo ich habbe ido mine. *a* **1225** *Ancr. R.* 54 ȝet ne seið hit nout þæt heo biheold wepmen; auh deð wummen. *c* **1320** *Song Husbandm.* 57 in *Pol. Songs* (Camden) 152 He us honteth ase hound hare doth on hulle. *c* **1340** *Cursor M.* 5672 (Trin.) Woltou me sle..As þou didest þe egipcian not ȝore? *c* **1394** *P. Pl. Crede* 357 Wouȝ halwen þei chirches And deleþ in devynitie as dogges doþ bones. **1526** *Pilgr. Perf.* (W. de W. 1521) 301 They did leade the bounden as they do theues. **1626** L. OWEN *Spec. Jesuit.* (1629) 18 These diseases doe alwaies accompanie the Iesuites, as a dogge doeth a Butcher. **1766** GOLDSM. *Vic. W.* i, I..chose my wife, as she did her wedding-gown..for such qualities as would wear well. **1880** L. WALLACE *Ben-Hur* VI. iii. 144 Thank thou thy God..as I do my many gods.

d. The following serve to connect the substitute use with senses 6 and 15.

(*to do so* = to act thus; *to do it* = to perform this act.)

a **1000** *Cædmon's Gen.* 2586 (Gr.) Waldend usser ȝemunde wærfæst þa Abraham arlice, swa he oft dyde. *c* **1000** *Ags. Gosp.* Mark viii. 6 [He] sealde his leorning-cnihtum þæt hi toforan him asetton, hi swa dydon. *c* **1297** R. GLOUC. (1724) 377 þat folc com..And robbede & destrude, as hii were ywoned to done. *c* **1380** *Sir Ferumb.* 932 Roland prikede is stede..so dude scot Gwylmer, So dude Geffray and Aubrys. *c* **1400** MAUNDEV. (Roxb.) iii. 10 þai sell benificez of haly kirk, and so duse men in oþer places. **1533** BELLENDEN *Livy*, Tak away that odius name..and, gif you dois it plesandlie, thy cieteyanis sal, [etc.]. **1560** BECON *New Catech.* Wks. 94 If a man maim his neighbour as he hath done. **1615** BEDWELL *Moham. Imp.* A ij b, If any man shall.. say, as the consistorie..did by the Talmud, That it were better that such foolish fables..were..suppressed. **1678** BUTLER *Hud*, III. iii. 244 For those that fly may fight again, Which he can never do that's slain. **1793** BEDDOES *Sea Scurvy* 52 Thay may acquire this principle..but we have no direct experience of their doing so. **1818** CRUISE *Digest* (ed. 2) V. 561 Whoever wanted to surrender must..do it in person. **1826** DISRAELI *Viv. Grey* v. v, In passing through the bazaar one morning, which he seldom did.

*** As a *Periphrastic Auxiliary* of the present and past Indicative, and Imperative. (Formerly sometimes of the Infinitive.)

(For a detailed treatment of this, see '*Das Umschreibende Do in der Neuenglischen Prosa*' by Hugo Dietze, Jena, 1895.)

As auxiliary of the *Indicative* (*present* and *past*).

Examples of this are found already in OE. (as in MDu., O. & MLG., mod.Ger. dialects). It is more frequent in ME., but became especially frequent after 1500, first as a simple periphrastic form without perceptible difference of sense, in which use it has in the s.w. dialects practically taken the place of the simple form of the verb (e.g. *I dŭ zay* for *I say*, *he dŭ zim* for *he seems*). But in standard English it is now regularly used only where, for the sake of emphasis, or of word position, it is advantageous to have the verb in two words, so that the auxiliary may receive the stress or be separated from the main verb, like the auxiliaries of the perfect and future tenses, to which the periphrastic present and past is exactly parallel in use. Thus *Simple Affirmative* after certain conjunctive adverbs: 'So quietly did he come that..' (like 'So quietly has he come'). *Emphatic*: 'He *did* drink', 'and drink he *did* (like 'I *will* go', 'and go I *will*'). *Interrogative*: 'Do you hear?' (like 'Will you hear?'). *Negative*: 'They do not speak' (like 'They will not speak,' 'They have not spoken'.)

25. In *Affirmative* sentences.

a. Originally, simply periphrastic, and equivalent to the simple tense. Found in OE., frequent in ME., very frequent 1500–1700, dying out in normal prose in 18th c.; but still retained in s.w. dialects; also as an archaism in liturgical and legal use, and as a metrical resource in verse.

c **893** K. ÆLFRED *Oros.* I. x. §5 Æftre ðæm hie dydon æȝþer ȝe cyninga ricu settan ȝe niwu ceastra timbredon. **1297** R. GLOUC. (1724) 320 þys lond..ofte he dude bytraye. *c* **1420** *Chron. Vilod.* 315 In hurre lyff, as we don rede. *c* **1489** CAXTON *Blanchardyn* xlvii. 180 She ded call after hym ryght pyteousli. **1526–34** TINDALE *John* i. 45 Of whom Moses in the lawe and the prophetes dyd wryte. **1548–9** (Mar.) *Bk. Com. Prayer* Collect 1st Sund. Lent, O Lord, whiche for oure sake dyddeste faste fortye dayes and fourtie nightes. **1557** *Bury Wills* (Camden) 148 He do knowe the men that do owe me the sayd monie. **1615** BEDWELL *Moham. Imp.* III. §120, I do pity the case in which I do see they are. **1673** RAY *Journ. Low C.* Pref., Which doth sufficiently evince they were not of that Original. *c* **1710** C. FIENNES *Diary* (1888) 192 He did design a new house. **1748** CHESTERF. *Lett.* (1792) II. clvi. 56 Good-breeding, and good-nature, do incline us rather to help and raise people up. **1787** WINTER *Syst. Husb.* 54 The vernal heat of the sun does also influence them. **1818** CRUISE *Digest* (ed. 2) III. 22 This being no more than the law doth appoint. **1838** LONGF. *Reaper & Fl.* vi, The flowers she most did love.

β. Also employed as an auxiliary to itself as independent vb., or (formerly) in its substitute and causal uses.

a **1400** *Octouian* 901 The kyng hym louede..So dede al do that in Paris were. **14..** HOCCLEVE in *Anglia* V. 30 Thogh thow no lenger do do by my reed. **1490** CAXTON *Eneydos* Prol. 2 My lorde abbot..ded do shewe to me late certayn euydences. *c* **1500** *Melusine* xix. 103 A grete toure & bigge, whiche Julius Cesar dide doo make. **1667** PEPYS *Diary* 29 July, He and the Duke of York do do what they can to get up an army.

b. Still used, instead of the simple tense form, in those constructions in which the ordinary order of pronoun and verb is inverted; the use of the periphrastic form allowing the main verb to retain its final position as in the perfect and future.

c **888** K. ÆLFRED *Boeth.* vi, Swa doþ nu þa þeostro þinre ȝedrefednesse wiþstandan minum leohtum larum. *c* **1250** *Gen. & Ex.* 1518 An time dede ysaac flen. **1551** ROBINSON tr. *More's Utop.* (Arb.) 145 This lawe did kynge Utopus make. **1579** LYLY *Euphues* (Arb.) 45 Ah Euphues little dost thou know [etc.]. **1588** SHAKS. *L.L.L.* I. i. 249 There did I see that low-spirited Swaine. **1598** BACON *Ess.*, *Atheism* (Arb.) 121 In vayne doth he striue. **1644** MILTON *Areop.* (Arb.) 33 Thus did Dion..counsell the Rhodians. **1692** LOCKE *Educ.* (1749) 205, I should not say this..did I think that [etc.]. **1749** FIELDING *Tom Jones* (Tauchn.) I. 216 Such vengeance did he mutter forth. **1766** GOLDSM. *Vic. W.* xiv, Nor did she seem to be much displeased. **1849** DICKENS *Dav. Copp.* (Tauchn.) I. 90 Not a single word did Peggotty speak. **1850** HAWTHORNE *Scarlet L.* 194 Never did mortal suffer what this man has suffered. *Mod.* How bitterly did I repent! Well do I remember the scene.

c. Now the normal *Emphatic* form of the present and past Indicative.

The stress is placed upon the auxiliary, as in the perfect and future tenses. There may be inversion of order as well.

1581 PETTIE *Guazzo's Civ. Conv.* I. (1586) 27b, But these same..doe manye times more offend..than those who doe commit them [**1738** *Guazzo's Art. Conv.* 52 Than those who actually commit them]. **1599** SHAKS. *Much Ado* II. iii. 204. **1601** —— *Twel. N.* III. i. 32 *V.* Thou art a merry fellow and car'st for nothing. *C.* Not so, sir, I do care for something, but..I do not care for you. **1683** WYCHERLEY *Co. Wife* v. ii, *H.* Art thou sure I don't know her? *P.* I am sure you do know her. **1689** SHERLOCK *Death* ii. §1 (1731) 61 And yet die they all did. **1773** GOLDSM. *Stoops to Conq.* II, I do stir about a good deal, that's certain. **1826** DISRAELI *Viv. Grey* II. v, The floodgates of his speech burst, and talk he did. *Ibid.* IV. iv, Why, Mr. Grey, I do declare you are weeping. **1832** TENNYSON *Death Old Year* iii, We did so laugh and cry with you. **1838** DICKENS *Nich. Nick.* ix, But we *do* want him. **1863** BRIGHT *Sp. Amer.* 26 Mar., But these concessions failed, as I believe concessions to evil always do fail. **1890** *Illustr. Lond. News* Xmas No. 2/1, I *do* wish you would let me sleep. *Mod.* Tell us what he did do.

†**d.** In ME. the main verb was sometimes put in the same tense and person: cf. 30 a. β.

c **1205** LAY. 9385 Aras þer þe to-nome, swa doð a feole wise to-nome ariseð. **1387** TREVISA *Higden* (Rolls) I. 155 Thalestris..did wroot to kyng Alexandre in þis manere. *c* **1460** *Towneley Myst.* (Surtees) 15 Whi brend thi tend so shyre, Ther myne did bot smoked? **1483** CAXTON *G. de la Tour* D viij, He dyd made to rayne fourty dayes.

26. In *Interrogative* sentences.

The periphrastic form with *do, did*, is now the normal form. Its use allows the pronoun to be placed between the auxiliary and main verb, instead of coming after the latter: e.g. 'Did he recognize her?' instead of 'Recognized he her?'

In monosyllabic verbs, the simple form may still be used; it is always used in *be* and usually in *have*, though very recently (esp. in U.S.) we find *do you have? did you have?*

c **1386** CHAUCER *Monk's T.* 442 Fader why do ye wepe? *c* **1450** *Cov. Myst.* 196 Dude ȝe hym se? **1549** LATIMER *3rd Serm. bef. Edw. VI* (Arb.) 84 Did ye se any greate man? **1557** N.T. (Genev.) *John* xvi. 31 Now do you beleue? [**1611** Do ye now believe?] **1610** SHAKS. *Temp.* I. ii. 250 Do'st thou forget From what a torment I did free thee? **1738** *Guazzo's Art Conv.* 76 Do'st think I never saw a Crane before? **1773** GOLDSM. *Stoops to Conq.* III, What d'ye call it? **1852** MRS. STOWE *Uncle Tom's C.* viii, 'Why, Sam, what *do* you mean?' said Mrs. Shelby, breathless.

27. In *Negative* sentences.

The periphrasis with *do, did*, is now the normal form with *not*. Its use allows the negative to come after the auxiliary, instead of following the principal verb: e.g. 'We did not recognize him' instead of 'We recognized him not'.

The introduction of the periphrastic *do not, did not*, was connected with the obsolescence of the earlier usage which placed the negative particle first, 'we ne sungen'.

The simple form is still retained with *be, have* ('do', 'did not have', is colloquial and recent, chiefly in U.S.), and is frequent with monosyllabic words as *dare, need*; with other verbs it is always possible, and not being the ordinary form has an impressive rhetorical effect.

c **1489** CAXTON *Sonnes of Aymon* xxii. 472 It is to late to repente me that I dyde not doo. *c* **1489** —— *Blanchardyn* xli. 153 Whan ye dyde not knowe hym. **1564** GRINDAL *Rem.* (1843) 22, I do not doubt but that God revealed..other parts. **1664** EVELYN *Kal. Hort.* (1729) 224 When it does not actually freeze. **1719** DE FOE *Crusoe* II. iii, They did not take their measures with them, as I did by my man Friday. **1776** *Trial of Nundocomar* 73/2 If you do not give a plain answer ..you will be committed. **1889** J. FISKE *War of Independence* 139 The popular histories do not have [= have not] much to say about these eighteen days. *Mod.* We do not know.

28. In *Negative Interrogative* sentences.

Now the normal form, as in 26 and 27.

1581 PETTIE *Guazzo's Civ. Conv.* I. (1586) 11 Doe you not thinke that these men may be called wise? [**1738** *Guazzo's Art Conv.* 19 Don't you think that these men may be called Wise?] **1638** CHILLINGW. *Relig. Prot.* I. iii. §4 Doe not they agree in those things? **1655** STANLEY *Hist. Philos.* III. (1701) 124/1 Did he not aim at your hurt? **1796** H. HUNTER tr. *St. Pierre's Stud. Nat.* (1799) I. 387 Do we not see there.. talents distracted? **1841** LANE *Arab. Nts.* I. 83 Dost thou not believe that I was in it?

29. In colloquial speech *do not* (senses 27, 28), is usually contracted to *don't* (dəʊnt), *does not* to *doesn't* (vulgar *don't* from *do not* 3rd sing.: see A 2 c. γ.), *did not* to *didn't*. The dialectal forms are numerous: Sc. *dinna, disna, didna*, north. Eng. *dunno, dunnot*.

1672 WYCHERLEY *Love in Wood* II. i, Don't you know me? **1687** CONGREVE *Old Bach.* I. iv, Faith, I don't know. **1706** FARQUHAR *Recruit. Off.* IV. iii, Don't the moon see all the world? **1713** ADDISON *Cato* II. ii, You don't now thunder in the capitol. **1713** R. NELSON *Life Bull* 81 Why, said the Preacher, Solomon don't say so. **1731** *Keller's Rules for Thorow Bass* in Holder *Harmony* 168 Play common Chords on all Notes where the following Rules dont direct you otherwise. **1762** *Gentl. Mag.* 38 It don't regard the present war. **1775** SHERIDAN *Rivals* v. ii, Didn't you stop? **1818–60** ABP. WHATELY *Commpl. Bk.* (1864) 216, 'I *don't* think so'.. is good English. But we should not say 'he *don't* think so', but he *doesn't* think so. **1939** JOYCE *Finnegans Wake* 198 Didn't you spot her?

b. Colloq. phr. ***no, you don't***: you will not be allowed to do what you intend; I shall prevent you from doing (something implied).

1884 *Boy's Own Paper* 4 Oct. 2/2 'No, you don't!' muttered Soady, starting his melody. **1912** P. NASH *Let.* 21 Aug. in Bottomley & Nash *Poet & Painter* (1955) 48, I started a new outdoor drawing—but the devil or someone said 'no you don't', and at half hour intervals I was interrupted by heavy rain. **1926** B. A. MCKELVIE *Huldowget* ii. 27 'No, you don't,' exclaimed Collishaw, and he caught the girl's arm and gently drew it aside. **1952** W. G. HARDY *Unfulfilled* 176 But then Barty started toward Pam, his face blazing, his fist up and Peter jumped forward. 'No, you don't.'

30. As auxiliary of the *Imperative*.

a. In the Imperative *positive*, adding force to entreaty, exhortation, or command (this usually with the pronoun inserted as 'do you go at once!'); in early times, down to *c* 1600, it was sometimes merely periphrastic.

The main verb is in OE. found both in the Infinitive (α) and the Imperative (β); the Imperative is usual in early ME.; in later use (γ) the forms are indistinguishable, but it is usually viewed as Infinitive, as in 25.

α. *c* **1000** *Ags. Ps.* (Th.) cxviii[i]. 25 Do me æfter þinum wordum wel ȝecwician [L. *vivifica me*].

β. *c* **1000** *Ags. Gosp.* John viii. 11 Do ga, and ne synya þu næfre ma. *c* **1160** *Hatton G. ibid.*, Dó ga [L. *vade*]. *a* **1225** *Juliana* 39 Do swiðe sei me. *a* **1225** *Ancr. R.* 398 Gif þi luue nis nout for to ȝiuen, auh wult allegate þet me bugge hire, do seie hu! *a* **1300** *Cursor M.* 4893 Dos folus þam [*F.* do folow]. *Ibid.* 23159 Dos fles heþen, yee maledight! [*Edin.* do fles, *Trin.* do fleeþ]. *c* **1340** *Gaw. & Gr. Knt.* 1533 Dos techez me of your wytte.

γ. *c* **1440** *York Myst.* xxxiii. 262 Do stiffeley steppe on þis stalle. **1582** BENTLEY *Mon. Matrones* III. 342 Doo you let all men to vnderstand, that this is God. **1591** SPENSER *M. Hubberd* 1331 Arise, and doo thy selfe redeeme from shame. **1606** SHAKS. *Tr. & Cr.* v. ii. 105, I, come: O Ioue! doe, come! **1722** DE FOE *Col. Jack* (1840) 31 Do you go. **1749** FIELDING *Tom Jones* (Tauchn.) II. 15 Do tell me what I can have for supper. **1768–74** TUCKER *Lt. Nat.* (1852) I. 442 None of your coaxing and cajoling, your 'Pray Sirs', and 'Do Sirs'. **1813** DICKENS *Christmas Carol* iii, Do go on, Fred. **1884** JEAN MIDDLEMASS *Poisoned Arrows* III. i. 7 'Do, do be calm', said Camilla.

b. For emphasis, *do* is also added to the main Imperative.

1611 SHAKS. *Wint. T.* v. iii. 144 Giue me the lie, do. **1775** SHERIDAN *Duenna* II. iv, Get in, do. **1838** DICKENS *O. Twist* lii, Let me say a prayer. Do! **1930** D. L. SAYERS *Strong Poison* ix. 112 'Ev another crumpet, do, Mr. Bunter.

c. In ***do but*** ——, *do* was perhaps not originally auxiliary, but a main verb = *ne do but, do nought but* ——: cf. BUT *conj.* 6.

1604 DEKKER *Honest Wh.* IV. i. Wks. (1888) 107 Do but think what sport it will be. **1638** HEYWOOD *Wise Wom. Hogsd.* IV. iv. Wks. (1888) 311 Do but wait here. **1768** GOLDSM. *Good-n. Man* v, Do but hear me. **1832** CARLYLE in *Fraser's Mag.* V. 260 Do but open your eyes.

d. In the Imperative *negative, do not*, colloq. contracted *don't* (dəʊnt), is now the normal form. Colloq. phr. ***don't*** —— ***me***: do not use the word —— or mention the name of —— to me.

(The simple forms, now archaic, may still be used impressively, as *be not, say not, think not, withhold not*.)

1590 SHAKS. *Mids. N.* III. ii. 306 Good Hermia, do not be so bitter with me. **1599** —— *Much Ado* III. i. 87 O doe not doe your cosin such a wrong. **1672** WYCHERLEY *Love in Wood* III. ii, Don't speak so loud. **1687** CONGREVE *Old Bach.* II. viii, Don't come always, like the devil, wrapped in flames. **1705** VANBURGH *Mistake* I. i, Hold, master, don't kill him yet. **1807** ANNA PORTER *Hungar. Bro.* vi. (1832) 66 Do not you add to the idle race. **1829** [see DEAR *v.* 3]. **1840** DICKENS *Barn. Rudge* 6 Don't you speak. **1870** TROLLOPE *Vicar of Bullhampton* xli. 263 'But, Mrs. Brattle——' 'Don't Mrs. Brattle me, Mr. Fenwick, for I won't be so treated.' **1892** C. M. YONGE *Cross Roads* x. 112 'Emmie!' 'Don't Emmie me!' *a* **1897** *Mod.* Mr. Punch's celebrated advice to those about to marry—'Don't'.

†**31.** As auxiliary of other parts of the verb. The 16th c. Scottish poets extended the periphrastic use to the infinitive and pples.: thus, ***to do incres*** = to increase, ***done discus*** = discussed, ***doand proclame*** = proclaiming. Traces of this occur elsewhere.

1508 DUNBAR *Lament for Makaris* 49 He hes done petuously devour The noble Chaucer, of makaris flouir. *a* **1520** —— *Thistle & Rose* 24 The lark hes done the mirry day proclame. **1513** DOUGLAS *Æneis* XIII. x. 103 Onto his ceptre thou sall do succeid. **1556** LAUDER *Tractate* 23 No geir sulde do the faltour bye. *Ibid.* 340 As I afore haue done discus. **1578** *Scot. Poems 16th C.* II. 189 And many other false abusion The Paip hes done invent. **1597** *Regul. Manor Scawby Lincolnsh.* (MS.), That the Carrgraues shall doe execute theire office truely.

b. *done*: used in *U.S. dial.* (chiefly *Southern*) as a perfective auxiliary or with adverbial force in the sense 'already; completely'.

1827 A. SHERWOOD *Gaz. Georgia* 139 *Done said it*, for has said it. *Done did it*, for has performed, or done it. **1836** *Spirit of Times* (N.Y.) (1846) 22 (Th.), He had done gone three hours ago. *Ibid.* 94 I'd done got the licker, and I was satisfied. **1853** 'P. PAXTON' *Yankee in Texas* 114 Of Alabama origin..is that funny expression, 'done gone', 'done done', implying 'entirely gone', and 'entirely done'. **1854** M. J. HOLMES *Tempest & Sunshine* ii. 24 I've done let my best horse and nigger go off with a man from the free States. **1873** J. H. BEADLE *Undevel. West* xix. 356 People have done forgot they had any Injun blood in 'em. **1887** *Century Mag.* Nov. 96/1 'You done had supper?' she asked. **1917** H. T. COMSTOCK *Man thou Gavest* 300, I done told Burke I—I was going to prove myself. **1938** M. K. RAWLINGS *Yearling* vii. 65 You couldn't see 'em. There ain't none left. They've done left here, jest like the Injuns. **1945** E. T. WALLACE *Barington* 18, I don't know what you need with another boy. You done got four.

IV. Special uses of certain parts of the verb.

†**32.** *do*, the imperative, was used absolutely, as a word of encouragement or incitement = Go on! go it! (Cf. L. *age*; also 30 b.) *Obs.*

c **1440** *York Myst.* xxviii. 297 Do, do, laye youre handes Belyue on þis lourdayne. **1590** SHAKS. *Mids. N.* III. ii. 237, I, doe, perseuer, counterfeit sad lookes. **1610** —— *Temp.* IV. 239 Doe, doe; we steale by lyne and leuell.

33. *to do* (formerly in north. dial. *at do*: see ADO), the dative infinitive, is used *predicatively* after the verb *to be*, also *attributively* after a sb. = Proper or necessary to be done, hence, †the thing to be done, necessary, needful (*obs.*). [= MDu. *te doene*, MLG. *to dônde, to dôn*, needful.] ***what's to do?*** what is the matter? †***to have somewhat to do***: to have something the matter with one (*obs.*).

c **1290** *Beket* 476 in *S. Eng. Leg.* I. 120 'We schullen do' seint Thomas seide 'al þat is to done.' *c* **1340** *Cursor M.* 1651 (Trin.) Wreche to take hit is to done [= It is necessary to take vengeance]. *c* **1420** *Pallad. on Husb.* I. 11 What is to rere or doon in everything. **1523** LD. BERNERS *Froiss.* I. ccxlii. 357 If it were to do agayn. *a* **1533** —— *Huon* cxxxix. 521, I can not beleue but that my wyfe hath sumwhat to do. **1603** SHAKS. *Meas. for M.* I. ii. 114 What's to doe heere, Thomas Tapster? let's withdrawe. **1605** —— *Macb.* v. vii. 28 And little is to do. **1708–1774** The devil and all to do [see DEVIL *sb.* 22 g].

b. Hence it has passed into a *subst. phrase* = ADO, work, business, bustle, fuss.

1570–6 LAMBARDE *Peramb. Kent* (1826) 211 The husband (with much to doe) consented to the condition. **1675** EVELYN *Mem.* (1857) II. 103 What a to-do is here! **1782** PRIESTLEY *Corrupt. Chr.* III. II. 141 There was much to do about..readmission. **1830** GALT *Laurie T.* IV. v. (1849) 159 In the midst of the bustle and to-do. **1882** STEVENSON *Stud. Men & Bks.* 224 Many a to-do with blustering Captains.

c. ***to have to do***, to have something to do, to have business, or concern. ***what has he to do?*** what business has he...? *arch.* and *dial.*

? *a* **1500** *Sir Penny* in Ritson *Anc. Songs & B.* (1877) 116 If I have to don fer or ner And Peny be myn massangar. **1530** PALSGR. 596/2 If I kembe my heed tyll to morowe what have you to do? **1570–6** LAMBARDE *Peramb. Kent* (1526) p. xii, All these Nations have had to doe within this our Countrie. **1603** HOLLAND *Plutarch's Mor.* 135 Neither any man hath to doe, to forbid and warne them. **1611** BIBLE *Ps.* l. 16 What hast thou to doe, to declare my Statutes? **1748** RICHARDSON *Clarissa* (1811) I. 187 What has he to do to controul you?

d. ***to have to do with*** (in ME. also *to do of, at do with*): to have dealings or business with; to have connexion or intercourse (of any kind) with; to have relation to.

c **1175** *Lamb. Hom.* 77 Na mon..mid me flesliche nefde to done. *c* **1205** LAY. 19056 The king hire wende to, & hæfde him to done wið leofuest wimmone. *a* **1300** *Cursor M.* 14974 (Cott.) þe lauerd has Wit þam for to do. *Ibid.* 16487 (Gött.) Han we noght þar-of to do. *c* **1460** *Towneley Myst.* (Surtees) 76, I had never with the to do, How shuld it [that chyld] then be myne? **1555** EDEN *Decades* 34 He wolde not haue to doo with suche myscheuous men. **1630** WADSWORTH *Sp. Pilgr.* viii. 90, I neuer had any thing to doe with the said Duke. **1711** STEELE *Spect.* No. 33 ¶1 Insolent towards all who have to do with her. **1830** *Fraser's Mag.* I. 203 It has nothing to do with the purpose. **1875** JOWETT *Plato* (ed. 2) V. 34 All law has to do with pleasure and pain.

34. *doing*, the pres. pple., is used in the sense 'in action, at work, actively engaged, busy'.

1375, 1535 [see 16]. **1838** LONGF. *Psalm of Life* ix, Let us then be up and doing.

†**b.** ***to be doing with***: to be engaged with, at work with, engaged in active hostilities with. *Obs.*

1601 HOLLAND *Pliny* I. 106 As if he would now and then be doing with the seas. **1608** GOLDING *Epit. Frossard* II. 127 The truce..being expired, the French King had a meruailous desire to bee doing with the King of England. **1724** DE FOE *Mem. Cavalier* (1840) 268 Our general would fain have been doing with him again.

c. *to be doing* [in which an early passive use of the present pple. (cf. northern *doand*, *a* 1300, and mod.Sc.) seems to have blended with *a-doing*, i.e. the verbal sb. governed by the prep. *a* = on, in] is used with a passive signification (= the passive of senses 6–12), for which in more recent use the passive form *being done* is often substituted. ***nothing doing***: *lit.* nothing being done, or transacted; no business on foot; hence (*slang* or *colloq.*) an announcement of refusal of a request or offer, failure in an attempt, etc.

a **1300** *Cursor M.* 26812 (Cott.) þat þere er dedis doand neu, þat þai agh sare wit resun reu. **1526** TINDALE *Col.* iv. 9 All thynges which are adoynge here. *a* **1592** H. SMITH *Wks.* (1867) II, Sin, which is here expressed (while it is a-doing) to be, not bitter, but sweet. **1666** PEPYS *Diary* 22 Aug., My closett is doing by upholsters. *a* **1715** BURNET *Own Time* (1766) I. 152 While these things were doing. **1749** LADY M. W. MONTAGU *Let. to C'tess Bute* 7 May, What is doing among my acquaintance at London. **1827** DE QUINCEY in *Blackw. Mag.* Feb. 211/2 Complaining 'that there was nothing doing'. **1858** *Leisure Hour* 25 Mar. 186/2 There's nothing doing now. **1870** *Porcupine* 26 Mar. 503/3 A friend of mine hailed an outfitter the other day, 'How is business?' 'Nothing doing.' **1910** *N. Y. Even. Post* 13 Dec. 7 Spottford offered the porter a dime. The negro waved it aside and said: 'Nothing doing; my price is a quarter at least.' **1915** 'I. HAY' *First Hundred Thou.* xx. 302 'Na pooh!'..also means, 'Not likely!' or 'Nothing doing!' **1928** *Boston Even. Transcript* 30 Mar. 15/7, I looked in the dictionaries. 'Nothing doing!' **1930** W. S. MAUGHAM *Gent. in Parlour* x. 46 Then my girl asked me to marry her... I told her there was nothing doing. **1937** —— *Theatre* xii. 107 He can hardly expect me to ask him to come and sleep in here... Nothing doing, my lad. **1947** *People* 22 June 1/1 It was suggested that she should come incognito. Nothing doing.

35. *done*, the pa. pple., is used esp. in the sense 'accomplished, finished, brought to an end': see 8. Hence **a.** in dating an official document.

1833 *Fraser's Mag.* VII. 49 'Done at Battle, in the County of Sussex'; signed as our ambassador at Paris would sign a treaty of peace.

b. as the word for the acceptance of an offer, esp. of a wager.

1596 SHAKS. *Tam. Shr.* v. ii. 74 A match; 'tis done. **1610** —— *Temp.* II. i. 32 Done: The wager? **1719** D'URFEY *Pills* II. 54 Gad Dam-me cries Bully, 'tis done. **1771** P. PARSONS *Newmarket* II. 149 'Squib against Janus, ten guineas to eight.' 'Done, sir, done.' **1833** *Fraser's Mag.* VIII. 614 'I'll lay you five guineas I have.' 'Done!' **1844** DICKENS *Mart. Chuz.* xxvii, 'Dine with me to-morrow'..'I will', said Jonas. 'Done!' cried Montague.

V. With prepositions in specialized senses.

†**36. do after** ——. To act in obedience to or compliance with: see AFTER *prep.* 12. *Obs.*

1388 [see AFTER *prep.* 12]. *a* **1450** *Knt. de la Tour* (1868) 21. Y tolde her..but she wolde not do after me.

37. do by ——. To act towards or in respect of; to deal with: see BY *prep.*, 26. (With *indirect passive.*)

c **1175** *Lamb. Hom.* 51 Þenne do we bi ure sunne al swa me deað bi þe deade. **1387** TREVISA *Higden* (Rolls) V. 213 If a man..doþ wel by hym as þey he were his own childe. **1408** *E.E. Wills* (1882) 15 That he do be me, as he wolde y dede by hym. **1667** PEPYS *Diary* (1879) IV. 317 My Lord Arlington hath done..like a gentleman by him. **1865** KINGSLEY *Herew.* ix, To do as he would be done by.

38. do for——. (With *indirect passive*; esp. in b.)

a. To act for or in behalf of; to manage or provide for; to attend to. Now *colloq.*

1523 LD. BERNERS *Froiss.* I. ccccxiii. 723 God dyde for them..to abate the pride of the flemynges. **1526** TINDALE *Luke* vi. 33 Yf ye do for them which do for you what thanke are ye worthy of? **1658** T. WALL *Charac. Enemies Ch.* (1659) 2 When God does for man, he expects that man should do for God. **1712** STEELE *Spect.* No. 426 ¶3 Men who would do immoderately for their own offspring. **1844** J. S. HEWLETT *Parsons & W.* xliii, The slip-shod maid who 'did' for the lodgers. **1914** B. STOKER *Dracula's Guest* 21 He..got..the name of an old woman who would probably undertake to 'do' for him. **1936** A. CHRISTIE *Cards on Table* xiv. 136 The superintendent's researches..led him..to Mrs. Astwell—who 'did' for the ladies at Wendon Cottage.

b. To ruin, damage, or injure fatally, destroy, wear out entirely. *colloq.* Now freq. in *pass.* Also ***done-for*** adj.

1740 *Sessions' Paper* 9 July 190/2 D-mn you, I'll *do* for you. **1752** FIELDING *Amelia* VI. iv. (Farmer) He said he would do for him..and other wicked, bad words. **1803** NELSON 28 Dec. in Nicolas *Disp.* (1845) V. 334 The Kent is almost done for, and she is going to Malta. **1811** JANE AUSTEN *Sense & Sens.* xli. (Farmer) He has done for himself completely! shut himself out for ever from all decent society. *a* **1817** JANE AUSTEN *Persuasion* (1818) xi. 279 Give Anne your arm... She is rather done for this morning. **1847** J. S. ROBB *Squatter Life* 128 They found Sam holding the straw figure in his arms, and looking in a state of stupor at the horse; he thought his master was 'done for'. **1876** C. D. WARNER *Wint. Nile* i. 18 The railway up the Nile had practically 'done for' that historic stream. **1950** J. CANNAN *Murder Included* i. 12 These doomed and done-for ladies and gentlemen.

39. do to ——, **unto** ——. **a.** To act or behave to; to treat. (With *indirect passive.*)

14.. *Tundale's Vis.* 1704 Pore pylgrymis..Too whom of hys charyte he dyd. **1549** *Bk. Com. Prayer*, Catechism, To do to all men as I would they should do to me. **1748** G. WHITE *Serm.* (MS.) We should..do as we have been done unto.

b. Colloq. phr. *to do something* (or *things*) *for* or *to*: to improve; to render more pleasing or attractive.

1942 D. POWELL *Time to be Born* (1943) ii. 43 The bathing-suit would have to be..very carefully cut indeed to 'do things for her'. **1960** *Daily Express* 21 Jan. 1/3 A beret always seems to *do* something to generals. **1961** *Sunday Express* 12 Nov. 18/7 Here it is—a suit that does things for a woman. **1961** *Guardian* 13 Dec. 6/6 A coffee flavoured liqueur..really does something to the ice-cream.

40. do with ——.

a. To deal with, meddle with, have to do with. (Cf. 33 d.)

a **1300** *Cursor M.* 26833 (Cott.) Namli wit fals scrift doand. **1470–85** MALORY *Arthur* III. v, I maye not doo therwith said the kynge. **1607** TOURNEUR *Rev. Trag.* I. i. Wks. 1878 II. 5 And thou his Dutchesse that will doe with Diuill. *a* **1897** *Mod.* She has grown old and difficult to do with.

b. To get on with, put up with, manage with. (With *indirect passive.*)

1815 JANE AUSTEN *Emma* (1866) 207 A mind lively and at ease can do with seeing nothing. **1842** *Penny Cycl.* XXII. 128/2 Persons in middle life can do with less sleep than children or very old persons. **1891** *Law Times* XC. 443/1 We ..could well do with a little leaven of the Nisi Prius leader. *a* **1897** *Mod.* He does with very few books. I think ten as many as can well be done with. I am busy, I cannot do with you here.

c. *I* (*you*, etc.) *could do with*: I could make use of or profit from; I should be glad to have; I need. *colloq.*

1783 R. BENSON *Let.* 3 Nov. in T. W. Thompson *Wordsworth's Hawkshead* (1970) 335, I cd. also do with some Apples. **1859** GEO. ELIOT *A. Bede* II. xxv. 197 Well, I could do wi't, if so be ye want to get rid on't. **1936** J. B. PRIESTLEY *They walk in City* vi. 140 Ah'll pay up, ay, an' Ah'll give it to t'lad. He could do wi' it. *Ibid.* xii. 376, I could do with a cup of tea and a smoke. **1941** *Punch* 18 June 584/2 'If ever there was a man who could do with a little assistance—.' 'Just independent perhaps.' **1955** M. GILBERT *Sky High* xiv. 205 You look as if you could do with a wash and brush up.

41. do without ——. To do one's business or get on without; to dispense with. (With *indir. pass.*)

1713 ADDISON *Cato* II. vi, Come 'tis no matter, we shall do without him. **1849** RUSKIN *Sev. Lamps* vii. §5. 189 But there are some things which..all the real talent and resolution in England, will never enable us to do without. **1884** W. C. SMITH *Kildrostan* I. ii. 238, I daresay..you did without a frock, Until those debts were paid. *Mod.* Among things that must be done without.

VI. With adverbs: forming the equivalents of compound verbs in other languages: e.g. *do about*, L. *circumdăre*; *do off*, L. *exuĕre*. (Chiefly *trans.* with *passive.*)

†**42. do about.** To surround, enclose. ? *Obs.*

1657 R. LIGON *Barbadoes* (1673) 89 A little platform.. done about with a double rayle.

†**43. do abroad.** To diffuse, promulgate, publish.

c **1290** *Beket* 1764 in *S. Eng. Leg.* I. 157 To don þe sentence al a-brod.

44. do away.

†**a.** *trans.* To put away, dismiss, remove. *Obs.*

c **1205** LAY. 3387 Do we awai þane twenti, a tene beoð inohȝe. *a* **1300** *Cursor M.* 3028 (Cott.) Yon bastard Do him a-wai. *c* **1400** MAUNDEV. (1839) xxii. 235 He byddethe hem to don here hond a wey. **1486** *Bk. St. Albans* C ij b, Cast it out and doo away the bonis. **1596** SPENSER *F.Q.* VI. xi. 29 Doe feare away, and tell.

b. To put an end to, abolish, destroy, undo.

c **1230** *Hali Meid.* 11 Do þu hit eanes awei, ne schal tu neauer nan oðer..acoueren. *a* **1340** HAMPOLE *Psalter* Prol., It dos away & distroys noy and angire of saule. *c* **1440** *Promp. Parv.* 126/1 Doon a-wey..*deleo.* **1450–1530** *Myrr. our Ladye* 294 Thou that doest away the synnes of the worlde. **1480** CAXTON *Descr. Brit.* 8 Kynadius kyng of scotland dyde away the pictes. **1552** HULOET, Do awaye or vndo, *abrogo.* **1631** GOUGE *God's Arrows* ii. §25. 168 Sundry and ancient demaines of husbandmen were in a manner quite done away. **1794** SOUTHEY *Wat Tyler* II. iii, Your grievances shall all be done away. **1804** *Med. Jrnl.* XII. 47 To do away every jealousy. **1855** PRESCOTT *Philip II*, I. II. vii. 214 Necessary to do away this impression.

c. *intr. do away with*: a later substitute for prec. (With *indirect passive.*)

1789 ROMILLY in *Bentham's Wks.* X. 225 Doing away with ..the amenability to law. **1832** *Fraser's Mag.* V. 149 This does away with much of the disgustfulness. **1891** *Law Times* XCI. 204/2 The Act of Parliament which does away with the distinctions. *Mod.* A practice which has since been done away with.

†**d.** *do away!* (Imperative): see *do way*, 53.

†**45. do down. a.** To put down; to take down; to lower; to subdue; to depose. *Obs.*

c **1330** R. BRUNNE *Chron.* (1810) 90 To wend with Sir Dunkan, & do Dufnald doune. *c* **1340** *Cursor M.* 19167 (Fairf.) Euer wiþ conquest ȝe do vs doun. **1382** WYCLIF *Gen.* xxxviii. 19 The abite doon doun that she toke. —— *Mark* xv. 36 Se we if Hely come for to do hym down. *c* **1430** *Freemasonry* 603 Furst thou most do down thy hode. **1587** TURBERV. *Trag. T.* (1837) 221 And do their wrathfull weapons down.

b. To overcome, master, get the better of, bring to grief; to 'do' (sense 11 f). *colloq.*

1911 H. S. WALPOLE *Mr. Perrin & Mr. Traill* viii. 154 He saw nothing but a spiteful and malignant world trying, as he phrased it, to 'do him down'. **1922** D. H. LAWRENCE *England, my England* 257 Poor Fanny! She was such a lady, and so straight and magnificent. And yet everything seemed to do her down. **1923** *Daily Mail* 12 Mar. 6 Sir Arthur Griffith-Boscawen..said they had been done down by what had been rightly called an act of treachery. **1936** L. A. G. STRONG *Last Enemy* 13 To get your rights from Fosdyke was to cheat him, since he had never meant you to have them... It was a real injury to stop him from doing you down. **1958** *Economist* 29 Nov. 784/1 School for them is the great game of doing down, or being done down by, the teacher.

†**46. do in.** To put in. *Obs.*

a **1300** *Cursor M.* 11411 (Cott.) Ilk yere quen þair corns war in-don [G. in done]. *a* **1375** *Joseph Arim.* 40 Make a luytel whucche Forte do in þat ilke blod.

b. To spend completely (cf. sense 11 o). *slang* (chiefly *Austral.* and *N.Z.*).

1889 *Referee* 19 May 2/1 A young fellow..rushes to 'do in' every spare fiver or tenner that comes into his possession. **1909** T. H. THOMPSON *Ballads about Business* 27 I'd..never make for home again until I'd 'done it in'. **1930** V. PALMER in *Bulletin* (Sydney) 19 Feb. 51/1 Now he's done his money in.

c. To bring disaster upon, do a great injury to, ruin; often, to murder, kill. *slang.*

1905 *Daily Chron.* 22 May 6/3, I heard people tell her to do me an injury, throw glasses at me, and 'do me in'. **1906** *Ibid.* 11 Dec. 4/4 It seems funny that the first blooming order I got in Enfield I should be done in. **1914** G. B. SHAW *Pygmalion* 111 in *Nash's Mag.* Dec. 308 My aunt died of influenza: so they said... But it's my belief they done the old woman in. **1918** W. J. LOCKE *Rough Road* vi, If you engage a second-rate man..who isn't used to this make of car, he'll do it in for you pretty quick. **1919** J. B. MORTON *Barber of Putney* xiv. 235 'Yes,' said Graves. 'That's what did my nerves in. Still sleep bad.' **1928** GALSWORTHY *Swan Song* I. ix. 66 That house had 'done in' her father. **1963** *Listener* 4 Apr. 585/2 These were professional killers who 'did in' John Regan.

d. To exhaust, wear out; freq. ***done in***, exhausted. *colloq.*

1917 S. MCKENNA *Sonia* v. 245 Loring mopped his forehead. 'I feel absolutely done in,' he murmured. **1955** E. HILLARY *High Adventure* 143 For the first time I really feel a bit done in.

47. do off.

a. To put off, take off, remove (what is on); to DOFF. *arch.*

Beowulf 1346 (Th.) He him of dyde isern-byrnan. *c* **1000** *Sax. Leechd.* II. 86 Do þonne of þa rinda. *c* **1250** *Gen. & Ex.* 2781 Moyses, moyses, do of ðin s[h]on. *c* **1340** *Cursor M.* 20211 (Trin.) Of dud she hir cloþes. *c* **1430** *Pilgr. Lyf. Manhode* I. cxxxvi. (1869) 71 Dauid dide of the armure. *a* **1533** LD. BERNERS *Huon* x. 27 Huon..dyd of his brothers gowne. **1554** *Interlude Youth* in Hazl. *Dodsley* II. 19 Every poor fellow..Will do off his cap, and make you courtesy. **1606** HOLLAND *Sueton.* 156 As wee use to veile bonet or do of our hats. **1870** MORRIS *Earthly Par.* I. I. 313 He did off all his rich array.

b. To sketch off, hit off. *rare.*

1879 SHAIRP *Burns* viii. 195 In this..poem you have the whole toiling life of a ploughman and his horse, done off in two or three touches.

48. do on. To put on; to DON. *arch.*

c **1000** *Sax. Leechd.* II. 32 Haran ȝeallan do wearmne on. *c* **1205** LAY. 1701 Brutus hehte his beornes don on heora burnan. *a* **1300** *Cursor M.* 20214 (Cott.) A new smock scho did hir on [*v.r.* on she dude]. *c* **1460** *Urbanitatis* 12 in *Babees Bk.* (1868) 13 Holde of þy cappe..Tylle þou be byden hit on to do. **1535** COVERDALE *Song Sol.* v. 3, I haue put off my cote, how can I do it on agayne? **1582** N. T. (Rhem.) *Rom.* xiii. 14 Doe ye on our Lord Jesus Christ. **1606** HOLLAND *Sueton* 185 He did the diademe on. **1828** SCOTT *F.M. Perth* xxix, 'I did on my harness,' said Simon.

49. do out.

†**a.** To put out, expel, extirpate, remove. *Obs.*

c **1250** *Gen. & Ex.* 3012 Ðis fleȝes fliȝt vt is don. *c* **1440** *Gesta Rom.* xi. 35 (Harl. MS.) His yen were don out.

†**b.** To put out (a light), extinguish, DOUT.

c **1440** *Promp. Parv.* 126/2 Doon owte, or qwenchyn (liȝth),..*extinguo.* *c* **1450** *St. Cuthbert* (Surtees) 1856 þe fire with water oute to do. **1572** R. H. tr. *Lavaterus' Ghostes* (1596) 44 Having the candles done out. *a* **1652** BROME *Novella* I. ii. Wks. 1873 I. 111 Doe out the uselesse taper.

c. To clean out, sweep out.

1728 VANBR. & CIB. *Prov. Husb.* II. i. 37 Are all the Rooms done out? **1881** A. B. EVANS *Leicestersh. Words* 139 Ye're ollus a-doin' out the house of a Saturday! *a* **1897** *Mod.* The woman who does out his office. **1910** A. BENNETT *Clayhanger* III. i. 326 Once a week..his room was 'done out'. **1955** J. CANNAN *Long Shadows* iii. 44 'E's not arriving till.. this afternoon but I did the room out yesterday.

†**d.** *to do out of*: to put or take away out of.

a **1225** *Juliana* 30 þohte þat he walde anan don hire ut of dahene. *c* **1250** *Gen. & Ex.* 381 He ben don ut of paradis. *c* **1400** MAUNDEV. (Roxb.) Pref. 2 To do it oute of straunge men handes. **1496** *Dives & Paup.* (W. de W.) Introd. ii. 22/1 I do the out of doubte. **1660** BOND *Scut. Reg.* 39 They have undone themselves by doing thee out of thy Kingdom.

e. *to do* (any one) *out of*: to deprive or dispossess of; now *esp.* to deprive of by sharp practice or fraud.

1825 T. CREEVEY *Creevey Papers* (1963) xii. 209 Mrs. Taylor and I having done Mylord and Mylady out of £3. apiece at Ecarté. **1831** DISRAELI *Yng. Duke* IV. vi, Who boasted of having done his brothers out of their..£5000. **1840** R. BARHAM in *Bentley's Misc. Mar.* 269 Rubuked 'em For unhandsomely doing him out of his Dukedom. **1929** H. S. WALPOLE *Hans Frost* II. i. 118 Your aunt's so unselfish, she'd do herself out of anything.

50. do over. a. To overlay, overspread, cover, coat.

1611 COTGR., *Ardiller*..to dawbe, or do eouer, with clay. **1703** MOXON *Mech. Exerc.* 243 [It] is done over with Linseed Oil. **1725** BRADLEY *Fam. Dict.* s.v. *Tapestries*, Rub out the Chalk with which you have done it all over. **1870** MORRIS *Earthly Par.* III. IV. 6 A mighty club with bands of steel done o'er.

b. To cheat, swindle, get the better of. *slang.*

1781 G. PARKER *View of Society* II. 43 And now, Hostler, can't you tell me how you have *done 'em over*? **1789** —— *Life's Painter* v. 44 His huntsman was his prime-minister.. who could, at any time, *do him over*, as they phrased it, for half-a-crown or half-a-guinea. **1930** 'A. ARMSTRONG' *Taxi* xii. 164 'Pinching (or knocking) a job off the rank', means cruising near a rank head and snapping up a fare who would otherwise have taken a cab from the standing. To 'do the rank over' has the same meaning. **1939** H. HODGE *Cab, Sir?* xv. 219 'Doing a man over', or 'doing the rank over', is ..'wrongfully..taking away the fare from any other driver who..appears to be fairly entitled to it'.

c. To disable, wear out, tire out. *colloq.*

1789 W. DUNLAP *Darby's Return* 13 For while we were watching, like sportsmen for plover, The linen took fire—and did us all over. *Ibid.* 14 We sneak'd into town;—very fairly done over. **1837** DICKENS *Pickw.* xxxviii. 417 He's in a horrid state o' love; reg'larly comfoozled, and done over vith it. **1853** 'P. PAXTON' *Yankee in Texas* 96 [The dogs] were completely done over and used up.

d. To handle (a person) roughly. *Austral.* and *N.Z. slang.*

1866 *Maungatapu Murders* 17 Since we are going to do these people [*sc.* their murder/robbery victims] over..I think we had better prevent him from doing us any harm. **1953** A. UPFIELD *Murder must Wait* ix. 81 'Done over properly, wasn't he?' 'From appearances, yes. Mitford must be a rough place.'

e. To copulate with; to seduce. *slang.*

1873 HOTTEN *Slang Dict.* 145 *Done over*..also means among low people seduced. **1961** R. AMATO in C. K. Stead *N.Z. Short Stories* (1966) 233 All the sailors..want to marry the girl they've done over. **1961** *John o' London's* 3 Aug. 163/2 A truly Moravian rape-scene in a ruined church, with Cesira and Rosetta both done over by a screeching pack of Moroccan *goums*.

f. To decorate, refurbish; = *make over* (MAKE *v.*[1] 92 d).

1905 E. WHARTON *House of Mirth* I. i. 10 It must be pure bliss to arrange the furniture just as one likes... If I could only do over my aunt's drawing-room I know I should be a better woman. **1908** *Smart Set* Sept. 84/1 If only somebody would 'do over' Browning into English. **1941** J. P. MARQUAND *H. M. Pulham* xxxiv. 386 We ought to keep this as the spare room and do the nursery over.

51. do to.

†**a.** To put to, add, apply. *Obs.*

c **1000** *Sax. Leechd.* II. 28 Do huniȝ to and baldsamum. *c* **1380** WYCLIF *Sel. Wks.* III. 70 þis vers had Cristen men doon to. *c* **1420** *Pallad.* III. 926 Askes and shalkes do to.

†**b.** To put to, shut (a door, a book). *Obs.*

1562 *Great Curse* in Becon *Reliq. Rome* (1563) 254 b, Do to the boke. Quenche the candle. Ring the Bell.

52. do up.

†**a.** To put up; to raise; to open. *refl.* To get up, arise. *Obs.*

c **1205** LAY. 1704 Vp heo duden heora castles ȝaten. *Ibid.* 5714 Doð vp an waritreo þer on heo scullen winden. *c* **1305** *Land Cokaygne* 160 in *E.E.P.* (1862) 160 Hi doth ham up, and forth hi fleeth. *c* **1386** CHAUCER *Miller's T.* 615 Vp the wyndowe dide he hastily.

b. To repair, restore, put into proper order.

1666 WOOD *Life* (Oxf. Hist. Soc.) II. 79 To my taylor for dying and doing up my puff suit. **1766** GOLDSM. *Vic. W.* xi, They can do up small clothes. **1829** COL. HAWKER *Diary* (1893) II. 4[I] found the gun.. newly done up. **1884** BESANT *Ch. Gibeon* I. x, But who is to do up your room every day?

c. To put up, fasten up (a parcel), wrap up. Also, to dress up. *colloq.*

1806–7 J. BERESFORD *Miseries Hum. Life* (1826) XII. i, Labouring in vain to do up a parcel, with.. weak, bursting paper. **1882** *Century Mag.* XXIV. 842/2 The peasants are bundles done up in fur caps. **1897** M. KINGSLEY *Trav. W. Afr.* 21 Here and there in the street you come across a black man done up in a tweed suit, or in a black coat and tall hat. **1946** R. LEHMANN *Gipsy's Baby* 10 The younger ones could not be said to be dressed, in the accepted sense. They were done up in bits of cloth, baize or blanket.

d. To disable, wear out, tire out. (Chiefly in *pa. pple.*) *colloq.*

1803 NELSON 27 Dec. in Nicolas *Disp.* (1845) V. 332 The Kent being done up. **1812** *Sporting Mag.* XXXIX. 55 Horses and riders were completely done up. **1831** JANE PORTER *Sir E. Seaward's Narr.* I. 119 We were often languid, what I called 'done up'.

e. To ruin financially; to 'smash up'. Also, to ruin other than financially; to get the better of; to settle or finish; to beat up. *colloq.*

1785 GROSE *Dict. Vulgar T.*, *Done up*, ruined by gaming, and extravagances, (*modern term*). **1801** *Sporting Mag.* XVIII. 100 *Done up*..Ruined by gaming. **1833** *Fraser's Mag.* VIII. 113 They have reformed them [the West Indies] so totally, that they are done up. **1835** COLERIDGE *Table-t.* I. 5 It is not easy to put me out of countenance,.. yet once I was thoroughly *done up*, as you would say. *a* **1846** B. R. HAYDON *Autobiogr.* (1927) III. xvi. 317 Lord Elgin saw Knight was done up, and done up was the whole clique. *a* **1849** MAR. EDGEWORTH *Stories Irel.* i, There was a pleasure in doing up a debtor which none but a creditor could know. **1854** A. E. BAKER *Gloss. Northants Words* I. 192 *Done-up* , ruined in circumstances. 'They can't go on much longer, they're quite *done up*.' **1887** *Lantern* (New Orleans) 30 Apr. 2/2 The idea of this gang jumping on J. C. Matthews and doing him up. **1894** *Harper's Mag.* LXXXIX. 389/1 They lame Bob Griffiths fer life. And then they do up Buck. Shoot a hole through his spine. **1904** W. H. SMITH *Promoters* ii. 54 The thing to do is to do up your competitor. **1906** 'O. HENRY' *Four Million* 121 I have many times told you those Dagoes would do you up. **1962** 'R. SIMONS' *Killing Chase* vi. 77 Some of the boys did me up last night.

†**53. do way** (in Imperative). *Obs.*

a. *trans.* To put away; to leave off, abandon, have done with.

a **1300** *Cursor M.* 13049 (Cott.) Do wai fra þe yon wicked womman. *a* **1325** *Prose Psalter* I[i]. 2 Do way my wickednes. *a* **1541** WYATT *Poet. Wks.* (1861) 4 Arise for shame, do way your sluggardy. **1578** *Scot. Poems 16th C.* II. 163 Idolatrie do way, do way.

b. *absol.* or *intr.* To leave off, let alone, cease.

a **1300** *Cursor M.* 3667 (Cott.) 'Do wai, leue son,' rebecca said, 'þat malison on me be laid.' *c* **1340** *Ibid.* 5976 (Trin.) Do wey þei seide hit is not so. *c* **1475** *Rauf Coilȝear* 436 'Do way', said Schir Rolland, 'me think thow art not wise.' **1514** BARCLAY *Cyt. & Uplondyshm.* (Percy Soc.) p. xi, Do way, Coridon, for Gods love let be.

†**54. do withal.** *intr.* To do to the contrary; to withstand; to help it. (In negative and interrog. sentences.) *Obs.*

1470–85 MALORY *Arthur* X. xxii, It was his owne desyre.. and therfore I myghte not doo with alle for I haue done alle that I can and made them at accord. *c* **1570** *Pride & Lowl.*, It was agreed The craftes man could not do there withall. **1596** MUNDAY tr. *Silvayns Orator* 269 But what can a woman doe withall, if men doe love her? **1611** CHAPMAN *May-day* A iv, It is my infirmity, and I cannot doe withall, to die for 't.

55. *Comb.* in *attrib. phr.* as *do-as-you-please*, DO-IT-YOURSELF.

1923 D. H. LAWRENCE *Kangaroo* ii. 24 The sense of do-as-you-please liberty. **1963** *Listener* 10 Jan. 73/2 The opportunities for enjoying the kind of do-as-you-please holiday that more and more Russians.. now take for granted every year.

do (du:), *sb.*[1] Also 6–7 doe, 7 doo. [f. DO *v.*]

†**1.** Commotion, stir, trouble, fuss, ADO; usually in phr. *a deal of do. Obs.* (Common in 17th c.)

[Arising in part from erroneous resolution of *ado* into *a do*.]

[**1586** FERNE *Blaz. Gentrie* 71 It maketh me laugh to see what a doe this Herat maketh of nothing.] **1599** MARSTON *Sco. Villanie* I. iv, Without much doe. **1601** DENT *Pathw. Heaven* 358 What a marriage, what a meeting, what a doe. **1631** *Celestina* I. 9 Heer's a deal of doo indeede! **1666** PEPYS *Diary* 31 Mar., To my accounts,.. but Lord! what a deal of do I have to understand any part of them. **1708** MOTTEUX *Rabelais* IV. lxiv. (1737) 262 We find a..Parasite making a heavy do, and sadly railing.

2. a. The action of doing, or that which is done; deed, action, business. Chiefly in phr. *to do one's do*, i.e. what one has to do, or what one can do. (Common *c* 1650–80; now *rare* or *arch.*)

1631 J. BURGES *Answ. Rejoined* 475 Howbeit once, for a full-doe, I desire..to make it appeare [etc.]. **1650** CROMWELL *Let.* 4 Sept., Surely it's probable the Kirk has done their doo. **1664** BUTLER *Hud.* II. III. 952 No sooner does he peep into The World, but he has done his doe. **1669** GALE *Jansenisme* 105 The will, and the doe. **1850** CARLYLE *Latter-d. Pamph.* iv. 54 [He] can very well afford to let innumerable ducal Costermongers.. say all their say about him, and do all their do.

b. Something done in a set or formal manner; a performance; *esp.* an entertainment or show; a party; hence (orig. *jocular*), a military engagement, raid, or other 'show'. Orig. *dial.* or *vulgar*.

a **1824** J. BRIGGS *Remains* (1825) 243 Such individuals should have their feast (or *do*, as it is called). **1828** *Craven Dialect*, *Do*,.. a fete, 'a feaful grand do'. **1831** *Lincoln Herald* 15 July 4/3 At the great Do, or Doment, (as it was called in other days; and is now, in some places,) in honor of the Whig Ministry. **1890** *Placard*, (Winterton, Lincolnsh.) Barkworth's 'Do'..the most popular of local entertainments. **1894** HALL CAINE *Manxman* 260 ''Lowed her out to see the do, it's like'. **1915** 'BOYD CABLE' *Between Lines* 110 We are about the first Terrier lot to be in a heavy 'do' in the forward trenches. **1925** FRASER & GIBBONS *Soldier & Sailor Words* 78 *Do*, an event. A stunt. An attack, etc. *E.g.*, 'When is the do coming off?'; 'The Somme do'; 'The Havrincourt do', etc. **1955** *Times* 18 May 14/2 Miss Margaret Herbison broadcast on behalf of the Labour Party last night a talk which she described as a 'family do'. **1958** M. KERR *People of Ship St.* ix. 108 Her family has a 'do' every year on the anniversary of the day her mother's father died. *Ibid.*, Christmas 'dos' are especially important.

c. Usu. in *pl.* Dealing, treatment; esp. in phr. *fair do's. colloq.* (orig. *dial.*).

1859 HUGHES *Scour. White Horse* vi. 122 Only seemed to want what they called 'fair doos' . **1862** C. C. ROBINSON *Dial. of Leeds* 282 'A shabby dew', says a man who has had twopence given him for getting a waggon-load of coals in. 'A fairish dew', says another who has got a shilling and a lot of victuals away with him for the same. **1941** L. A. G. STRONG *Bay* 168 Come on, Doctor. Fair do's. **1951** 'A. GARVE' *Murder in Moscow* i. 15 There's no 'nobs' there; it's fair do's for everybody. **1952** A. STUART in J. C. Trewin *Plays of Year* V. 114 It's fair dos. I need you and you need me. **1953** S. BECKETT *Watt* i. 8 The lady now removing her tongue from the gentleman's mouth, he put his into hers. Fair do, said Mr Hackett. **1960** *She* Dec. 74/3 If *she* wants to go out agree to take her this year providing she will stay at home the next, to please you. That would be 'fair do's'.

3. A cheat, fraud, swindle, imposture. *slang.*

1835 DICKENS *Sk. Boz, Broker's Man* (D.), I thought it was a do to get me out of the house. **1837** —— *Pickw.* xlviii, 'A disgraceful imposition', observed the old lady. 'Nothing but a do', remarked Martin. **1854** R. DOYLE *Brown, Jones, and Robinson* 15 Expressing his opinion that the whole concern is a 'do' and a 'sell'.

4. An injunction to do (something specified). Only when coupled with *don't*: see DON'T.

1902 'STANCLIFFE' (*title*) Golf do's and don'ts. **1920** G. C. BAILEY *Complete Airman* 190 Between this and the next lesson the pupil should be encouraged to think well over the 'dos' and 'don'ts' of his trip. **1962** Y. OLSSON in F. Behre *Contrib. Eng. Syntax* 91 There are certain do's and don'ts that he should keep in mind.

5. A success, a 'go'; esp. in phr. *to make a do of it. Austral.* and *N.Z. colloq.*

1902 *N.Z. Illustr. Mag.* V. 381/1 Your poor, rough, back section. It has been forfeited twice, and you'll never make a do of it. **1945** *N.Z. Geographer* I. I. 36 High-country men.. take to the back-country because they can make a better 'do' of it than on a mixed farm down-country. **1947** D. M. DAVIN *Gorse blooms Pale* 91 Another go at making a do of things with his wife.

¶ See also DERRING-DO.

do (dəʊ), *sb.*[2] *Mus.* [arbitrary.] The syllable now commonly used in solmization instead of UT, to denote the first note (key-note) of the scale (*movable do*); or in some cases the note C, the key-note of the 'natural' scale (*fixed do*). (In *Tonic Solfa* commonly spelt *doh.*)

1754 *Dict. Arts & Sc.* II. 957 *Do*, in music, a note of the italian scale, corresponding to *ut* of the common gamut. **1842** BARHAM *Ingol. Leg.*, *Netley Abbey* 32 Then, you know, They'd a moveable Do, Not a fixed one as now. **1880** GROVE *Dict. Mus.*, *Do*, the syllable used in Italy and England in solfaing instead of *Ut*..said by Fétis to have been the invention of G. B. Doni.. who died 1669.

do., abbreviation of DITTO *sb.*

1730–6 BAILEY (folio), *Do*, is frequently us'd by merchants and tradesmen for Ditto.

do, doa, obs. forms of DOE.

‖**doab, duab** ('dəʊəb, 'du:əb). [Pers. and Urdū *dōāb*, lit. 'two waters'; used in India of the tongue of land between the Ganges and Jumna, and of similar tracts in the Punjab, etc.] The 'tongue' or tract of land between two confluent rivers.

1803 WELLINGTON *Disp.* (1844) I. 605 (Stanf.) That you should transport your company.. into the dooab between [that river] and the Godavery. **1824** HEBER *Jrnl.* (1828) II. 4 An eligible method of travelling in the Dooab. **1835** BURNES *Trav. Bokhara* (ed. 2) III. 319 Cotton.. is chiefly produced in the 'doab', between the Sutlege and Beas Rivers. **1854** R. G. LATHAM *Native Races Russian Emp.* 177 The Doab, Entre Rios, or Mesopotamia, bounded by the rivers Obi and Irtish. **1859** R. F. BURTON *Centr. Afr.* in *Jrnl. Geog. Soc.* XXIX. 72 Khutu proper.. begins with a Doab. *Note.* This useful word, which means the land about the bifurcation of two streams, has no English equivalent ..[and] might be naturalized with advantage.

doable ('du:əb(ə)l), *a.* [f. DO *v.* + -ABLE.]

1. That can be done; practicable.

c **1449** PECOCK *Repr.* I. vii. 37 A lawe.. which is doable and not oonli knoweable. **1611** COTGR., *Faisable*..doeable, effectable. **1843** CARLYLE *Past & Pr.* Proem iii. 23 A right noble instinct of what is doable and what is not doable never forsakes them. **1883** STEVENSON *Silverado Sq.* 112.

2. Capable of being 'done' or victimized: see DO *v.* 11 f.

1852 R. S. SURTEES *Sponge's Sp. Tour* x, Every man has his weak or 'do-able' point.

doagh, doach (do:x). *Sc.* [Derivation unknown.] A salmon-weir.

1794 *Statist. Acc. Scot.* XI. 10 The number of salmon.. caught in the doaghs or cruives.. is almost incredible. **1895** CROCKETT *Men of Mosshags* 203, I came down the west side of the water of Ken, by the doachs.

†**do'aire.** *Obs.* [a. OF. *doaire* (11th c. in Littré), *douaire* dower.] District allotted, province assigned, after the fashion of a dower.

1393 GOWER *Conf.* III. 127 Tho Signes.. most.. worth In governance of that doaire, Libra thei ben and Sagittaire.

doak, doal(e, obs. forms of DOKE, DOLE.

do-all ('du:ɔ:l). [f. DO *v.* + ALL.] One who manages the whole business; a factotum. Also *attrib.*

1633 D. ROGERS *Treat. Sacraments* II. 7 It is conscience which is the do-all in the soule. **1655** FULLER *Ch. Hist.* II. v. §20 Dunstan was the Do-all at Court, being the Kings Treasurer, Chancellour, Counsellour, Confessour, all things. **1701** J. JACKSON *Let.* in *Pepys' Diary* (1879) VI. 233 The Cardinal is the do-all. **1816** JANE AUSTEN *Emma* I. i. 19 A something between the do-nothing and the do-all. **1964** G. L. COHEN *What's Wrong with Hospitals?* i. 21 Medical advance soon prevented the do-all doctor from subsisting alone. He leaned increasingly on hospital resources.

doand, obs. f. *doing*, pr. pple. of DO *v.*

doar, obs. form of DOR, DOER.

doat, -er, -ing, etc.: see DOTE, etc.

doaty, var. DOTEY.

doaty, *a.*, var. DOTY *a.*

dob (dɒb), *v.* [variant of DAB.]

1. = DAB *v.*[1] 3.

1821 J. W. MASTERS *Dick & Sal* lxxxii. in *Kent. Dial.*, So den I dobb'd him down the stuff. **1881** *Cheq. Career* 251 She deliberately lifted up her off hind-leg, and 'dobbed' it down into the milk-pail.

2. To betray, inform against. Const. *in.* *Austral. slang.*

1959 BAKER *Drum* (1960) 105 *Dob in*, to betray, to focus blame on another; esp. *to dob someone in.* **1963** E. THOMPSON *Lawyer & Carpenter* vi. 100 Any time you run outside the law, I won't dob you in, either. **1964** *Punch* 18 Nov. 750/2 Those Canberra wowsers have really dobbed us in this time. **1970** M. KELLY *Spinifex* vii. 113 You won't dob me into the demons.

dob, obs. form of DUB *v.*

dobash, variant of DUBASH.

dobber[1] ('dɒbə(r)). *U.S. local.* [a. Du. *dobber* float, cork.] The float of an angler's fishing-line.

1809 W. IRVING *Knickerb.* II. v. (1849) 113 He floated on the waves.. like an angler's dobber.

dobber[2] ('dɒbə(r)). Chiefly *dial.* [f. *dob*, dial. var. *dab* a lump (DAB *sb.*[1]); cf. DABBER 2.] A large marble.

1874 E. WAUGH *Chimney Corner* (1879) 116 He's as numb as a clay dobber. **1875** NODAL & MILNER *Gloss. Lancs. Dial.* 107 *Dobber*.. a large marble. **1934** J. O'HARA *Appt. Samarra* vii. 186 There was a game of marbles called Dobbers, played with marbles the size of lemons. You played it in the gutter .. throwing your Dobber at the other fellow's. **1961** *Times* 17 Apr. 12/6 Bending down to bowl along the pitch to the ring of marbles with what we called a 'dobber'.

dobbin ('dɒbɪn). [the proper name *Dobbin* (dim. of *Dob*, altered forms of *Robin*, *Rob*, dim.

of *Robert*) as a pet name. Sense 2 may be a distinct word; there are other dialectal uses.]

1. An ordinary draught or farm horse; sometimes *contemptuously*, an old horse, a jade.

1596 SHAKS. *Merch. V.* II. ii. 100 Thou hast got more haire on thy chin, then Dobbin my philhorse has on his taile. **1862** SALA *Accepted Addr.* 229 The dappled dobbins wink lazily. **1871** MISS MULOCK *Fair France* 5 Bits of shiny brass.. jangling about their fore legs, in a fashion which British Dobbin would never submit to.

b. *attrib.*, as **dobbin-cart**, an Irish four-wheeled carriage used for travelling, and generally drawn by two horses; **dobbin-wheels**, the large hind wheels of a timber cart (*Cheshire Gloss.* 1884).

2. A small drinking-vessel.

1792 *Gentl. Mag.* LXII I. 179 A.. quantity of plate.. 10 silver tankards, 9 cans, 14 silver dobbins. **1821** J. MARSDEN *Sketches Early Life* (ed. 3) 92 A little bread and cheese and a dobbin, or about a gill of Welsh ale.

dobby, dobbie (ˈdɒbɪ). [perh. a playful application of the proper name *Dobbie*, dim. of *Dob*, altered forms of *Robbie*, *Rob*; cf. DOBBIN.]

1. A silly old man, a dotard, a booby. *dial.*

1691 NICHOLSON *Gloss. North.* in Ray *N.C. Words* 140 A Dobby, *Stultus, Fatuus.. senex decrepitus & delirans.* **1787** in GROSE *Provinc. Gloss.*

2. A household sprite or apparition supposed to haunt certain premises or localities; a brownie. *dial.* (In Sussex called *Master Dobbs.*)

1811 J. B. S. MORRITT *Let. to Scott* 28 Dec. in *Lockhart*, She.. became a ghost.. under the very poetic *nom de guerre* of Mortham Dobby. **1822** W. IRVING *Braceb. Hall* xvi. 136 An ancient grange.. supposed.. to be haunted by a dobbie. **1823** SCOTT *Peveril* x, The Dobby's Walk was within the inhabited domains of the Hall.

3. *Weaving.* An attachment to a loom for weaving small figures (i.e. from twelve to thirty-six threads) similar in principle to the Jacquard attachment. Hence ***dobby-loom***, ***-machine***; *dobby-weave* attrib.

1878 A. BARLOW *Weaving* xxvi. 279 A small Jacquard machine, or dobby, was introduced in the silk trade in 1830 by Mr. S. Dean. **1882** *Standard* 7 Sept. 2/3 The 'dobbies'—a modification of the Jacquard—were also shown. **1961** *Guardian* 30 Jan. 5/5 Some attractive suitcases.. have 'dobby-weave' linings.

4. In full ***dobby-horse***. A wooden figure of a horse. Cf. HOBBY-HORSE *sb.* 2, 4 b.

1879 J. C. CLOUGH *B. Bresskittle* 9 (E.D.D.), Theer were shows an.. dobby horses. **1886** R. HOLLAND *Gloss. Chester* 101 *Dobby-horse*, a hobby-horse. An imitation horse which figures in the play performed by the 'Soulers'. **1933** E. K. CHAMBERS *Eng. Folk-Play* 214 Cheshire with a 'Dobby-Horse'.. and.. there are similar rites with animals other than a Horse. **1937** J. B. PRIESTLEY *I have been here Before* II. 63 He says we all go round and round like dobby horses. **1968** D. BRAITHWAITE *Fairground Architecture* iii. 46 Early horse roundabouts, known as 'Dobbies',.. were being produced at King's Lynn certainly in the early 1870's. *Ibid.* 158/1 Steam-driven 3-abreast Dobby Horses.

dobchick(in, obs. forms of DABCHICK.

dobe, 'dobe (ˈdəʊbɪ). *U.S.* Also dobbie, dobie, doby, etc. Colloq. shortenings of ADOBE. Also *attrib.* and *Comb.*

1838 M. WHITMAN *Let.* 12 Mar. in *Overland to Pacific* (1936) VI. 294, I had walled the cellar with dobies. *Ibid.* 30 Oct. 327 The erection of a Doby house. **1842** J. WILLIAMS *Tour to Oregon* (1921) 84 Some of them build their houses with what they call 'dobbeys', made of mud, in the shape of brick. **1845** J. CLYMAN *Diary* 12 July (1928) 168 A strong doba or mud walled fort. **1854** *Fort Benton Jrnl.* 10 Oct. in *Montana Hist. Soc. Contrib.* (1940) X. 2 Men commenced Dobbie making. *Ibid.* 13 Oct. 3 Had Dobbie makers make up their mud into bricks. **1865** [see ADOBE 1]. **1883** E. W. NYE *Baled Hay* 135 The dobe pig pens.. are not true to nature. **1885** *Outing* (U.S.) VII. 52/1 Half sand and the other half 'doby'-mud. **1891** C. ROBERTS *Adrift Amer.* 86 These bricks.. although they are spelt 'adobes', I always heard.. spoken of as 'dobies'. **1897** *Outing* (U.S.) XXIX. 582/1 The afternoon monsoon.. howls.. as if it would tear the stubborn little 'dobe shanties off the earth. **1904** 'O. HENRY' *Cabbages & Kings* iv. 73 Grass huts, 'dobes, five or six two-story houses. *Ibid.* vi. 104 A 'dobe house in a dirty side street. **1951** STEINBECK *Burning Bright* I. 1 The close-cut barley stubble stood in bunches with the black 'dobe earth between.

dobee, -ie, var. ff. DHOBI, Indian washerman.

Dobermann (ˈdəʊbəmæn). [Name of Ludwig *Dobermann*, a nineteenth-century German dog-breeder of Thuringia. See also PINSCHER.] In full ***Dobermann pinscher***. A kind of German hound with a smooth coat and docked tail.

1917 *Policeman's Monthly* Jan. 5/3 Nowadays four breeds of dogs are being used for police purposes: the Continental Sheepdog, the Airedale Terrier, the Doberman Pinscher and the Rottweilers. **1922** R. LEIGHTON *Compl. Bk. of Dog* viii. 119 The Germans pride themselves upon their sheepdogs, no less than upon their Boxers, their Dobermann Pinschers, their Saufangers, and Teckels. **1928** *Sunday Express* 24 June 11 A German named Dobermann, of Aplolba, Thuringia.. spent his life experimenting with different breeds, and at last, in the middle of the last century, he produced specimens of the 'Dobermann Pincher'—and died before disclosing his secret. **1959** *Times* 16 Jan. 1/7 Home Wanted for 18 month Dobermann Pinscher bitch.

dobeying (ˈdəʊbɪɪŋ). *Naval slang.* Also **dhobeying.** [f. DHOBI + -ING[1].] Washing clothes, doing laundry.

1929 in F. C. BOWEN *Sea Slang* 37. **1940** *Illustr. London News* CXCVII. 160 (*caption*) Destroyer-men doing their 'dobeying' on deck. **1955** *Times* 2 June 2/6 Some of the early plays.. are the stuff of their lives; swabbing and dobeying being more natural than all the heroics.

dobie, doby, varr. DOBE.

‖**ˈdobla.** *Obs.* exc. *Hist.* [Sp.: cf. *doble* double.] An obsolete Spanish gold coin.

[**1599** MINSHEU, *Dobla*, a peece of money called a double containing 23 rials and a halfe, of English money ten shillings ten pence halfepenie.] **1829** W. IRVING *Granada* i. (1850) 22 (Stanf.) An annual tribute of twelve thousand doblas or pistoles of gold. **1838** PRESCOTT *Ferd. & Is.* II. II. v. 343 A substantial donative of gold doblas.

doble, dobler, doblet(te, obs. ff. DOUBLE, etc.

‖**Dobos Torte** (ˈdɒbɒʃ ˈtɔːtə). Also with small initials; **Dobos Torta, Dubosch Torte.** Pl. **Dobos Torten.** [G. *dobostorte*, f. the name of József C. *Dobos* (1847–1924), Hungarian pastry chef, who first displayed the cake at an exhibition in 1885 + *torte* TORTE 2 a, tart; cf. Hungarian *dobostorta* (1896).] A rich cake made of alternate layers of sponge and chocolate or mocha cream, with a crisp caramel topping.

1915 W. H. BROOKS *Mod. Pract. Cake Baking* xvii. 63 (*heading*) Dubosch Torten. **1943** I. S. ROMBAUER *Joy of Cooking* (ed. 3) 564/1 *Dobos Torte*, the many tiered Hungarian chocolate cake that looks rich, is rich, and enriches all who eat it. **1961** [see LINZERTORTE]. **1970** 'E. QUEEN' *Last Woman* II. 102 A Dobos Torta which decided Ellery to make Bucharest his next continental port of call. **1978** *Washington Post* 16 Mar. Va.12/4 We agreed to taste some of the desserts: a rum punch cake and dobos torta. **1980** *N.Y. Times Mag.* 19 Oct. 129/3 A county with as many layers of government as a dobos torte is made to order for subtle political maneuvering, and it doesn't come cheap.

dobro (ˈdɒbrəʊ, dəʊ-). orig. *U.S.* [f. the name of its Czech-American inventors, the *Do*(*pěra Bro*(*thers*; the coincidence with Czech *dobro* (the) good, a good thing, may also help to explain the choice of this form.] The name (proprietary in the U.S.) for a type of acoustic guitar with steel resonating discs fitted inside the body under the bridge, popular for playing country and western music.

1952 *Official Gaz.* (U.S. Patent Office) 26 Feb. 921/1 Valco Manufacturing Company, Chicago.... Filed July 14, 1947. *Dobro*, for string musical instruments.... Claims use since November 1929. **1969** *Rolling Stone* 28 June 17/1 The traditional country sound is characterized by guitar, fiddle and banjo, augmented by harmonica, zither, dobro or bass. **1970** J. LENNON in J. Wenner *Lennon Remembers* 182, I remember the first guitar I ever saw. It belonged to a guy in a cowboy suit in a province of Liverpool, with stars, and a cowboy hat and a big dobro. **1972** *Official Gaz.* (U.S. Patent Office) 31 Oct. 269/1 Edgar E. Dopera.... Original Musical Instrument Company, Inc., Long Beach, Calif. Filed June 9, 1971. *Dobro.* For guitars and banjos. **1976** *National Observer* (U.S.) 5 June 20/5 These country people have rough but honest faces, look to have the moral fiber of birch, love strangers, play fiddles and dobros, [etc.]. **1984** *Washington Post* 24 Dec. B7/6 The ornate surface of Ben Eldridge's banjo and the brittle precision of John Duffey's mandolin were answered by the warm and elastic dobro of Mike Auldridge.

dobson (ˈdɒbsən). *U.S.* An angler's name for the larva of *Corydalus cornutus*, a North American neuropterous insect allied to the May-fly, also of other species of the family *Sialidæ*.

1889 in *Century Dict.*

dobule (ˈdɒbjuːl). *Ichthyol.* [ad. mod.L. *Dobula* (Gesner).] A North American species of dace (*Leuciscus dobula*).

[**1753** CHAMBERS *Cycl. Supp.*, *Dobula.*] **1864** in WEBSTER.

doc (dɒk). Colloq. abbrev. of DOCTOR *sb.*

?**1850** E. Z. C. JUDSON *Three Years After* vii. 29/2 'Where's the Doc?' asked the old lady. **1854** R. GLISAN *Jrnl. Army Life* 24 Nov. (1874) 149 Don't you think, Doc., ague makes a fellow powerful weak? **1887** F. FRANCIS *Saddle & Mocassin* viii. 146 Anyhow, Doc Gilpen the Marshal jumped him [= took him to task]. **1904** G. H. LORIMER *Old Gorgon Graham* 173 Doc was cribbing those powerful Sunday evening discourses from a volume of Beecher's sermons. *a* **1918** W. OWEN *Coll. Poems* (1963) 72 The Doc.'s well-whiskied laugh. **1920** C. E. MULFORD *J. Nelson* vi. 60 I'd like to shake hands with th' coyote that lugged th' Doc off to fix that laig. **1964** A. CHRISTIE *Caribbean Mystery* xxiii. 230 Molly's practically herself again. The doc says she can get up to-morrow.

‖**Doccia** (ˈdɒtʃɪə). The name of a town near Florence, Italy, used *attrib.* of a variety of porcelain produced there.

1857 J. MARRYAT *Hist. Pott. & Porc.* (ed. 2) xiv. 331 The early pieces of Doccia porcelain show a close imitation of the white Oriental. **1900** F. LITCHFIELD *Pott. & Porc.* vii. 139 Doccia china is generally found in parts of table services. **1960** R. G. HAGGAR *Conc. Encycl. Continental Pott.* 138/1 Doccia was a hybrid porcelain akin to hard-paste, grey like most Italian porcelain in colour, badly turned out, often showing fire cracks and other technical faults.

doce, var. of DOSS. *Obs.*

†**doceaˈmur.** *Obs.* [F. *douce amour*, sweet love.] Sweetheart.

c **1320** *Sir Beues* 161 He hire clepede doceamur.

doced (in Phillips), var. of DOUCET, *Obs.*

docent (ˈdəʊsənt), *a.* and *sb.* [ad. L. *docēnt-em*, pr. pple. of *docēre* to teach.]

A. *adj.* That teaches or instructs; teaching.

1639 LAUD *Agst. Fisher* §33 (L.) The church here is taken .. as it is docent and regent. **1845** R. W. HAMILTON *Pop. Educ.* ix. (ed. 2) 231 Special reasons may be found against the docent authority and right of any Established Church.

B. *sb.* In some American universities and colleges, a recognized teacher or lecturer not on the salaried staff; usually a post-graduate student who is allowed to lecture in some special branch. [Cf. Ger. *privat-docent*, private teacher, recognized by a university.]

1880 *Nation* (N.Y.) XXX. 347 The young docents, whose specialty is Semitic philology. **1890** *Boston* (Mass.) *Jrnl.* 13 Sept. 4/1 Docent in Psychology at Clark University, Worcester. **1893** *Register Chicago Univ.*, Docent in Spanish, Docent in Chemistry, Docent in Biblical Literature, [etc.].

docer(e, obs. form of DOSSER.

‖**Docetæ** (dəʊˈsiːtiː), *sb. pl. Eccl. Hist.* [med.L. a. Gr. Δοκηταί, f. δοκέ-ειν to seem, appear.] An early sect of heretics, who held that Christ's body was not human, but either a phantom, or of real but celestial substance.

1818–21 J. PYE SMITH *Script. Test. Messiah* (1829) III. IV. 134 The doctrines of the Docetæ. **1831–3** E. BURTON *Lect. Eccl. Hist.* xii, The earliest Gnostics.. called Docetæ, believed the body of Jesus to have been.. either a mere optical illusion, or.. something ethereal and impalpable.

Docete (ˈdəʊsiːt). [Anglicized form.] = DOCETIST.

1781 GIBBON *Decl. & F.* II. xxi. 241 The Gnostics, who were distinguished by the epithet of *Docetes.* **1788** *Ibid.* IV. xlvii. 537 The *Docetes*, a numerous and learned sect of Asiatics. **1894** J. R. ILLINGWORTH *Pers. Hum. & Div.* i. 11 Had Christ been.. a mere appearance as with the Docetes.

docetic (dəʊˈsɛtɪk, -ˈsiːtɪk), *a.* See also **doketic.** [f. DOCETÆ *sb. pl.* + -IC.] Of or pertaining to the *Docetæ*.

1846 TRENCH *Mirac.* xvii. (1862) 289 It is a docetic view of the person of Christ, which conceives of his body as permanently exempt from the law of gravity. **1855** MILMAN *Lat. Chr.* IV. vii. *note*, An argument for Christ's real humanity against the Docetic sects.

Hence **doˈcetically** *adv.*, according to the *Docetæ*.

1887 E. JOHNSON *Antiqua Mater* 178 Christ actually and not merely docetically risen in the flesh. **1894** MITCHELL tr. *Harnack's Hist. Dogma* v. 270 *note*, He taught docetically about Christ.

Docetism (dəʊˈsiːtɪz(ə)m). [f. as prec. + -ISM.] The doctrine or views of the *Docetæ*.

1846 GEO. ELIOT tr. *Strauss's Life of Jesus* I. I. v. 274 To say.. that the food which he took did not serve for the nourishment.. of his body by real assimilation.. would strike every one as Docetism. **1855** MILMAN *Lat. Chr.* IV. vii, A kind of Docetism—asserting the unreality of the body of the Saviour. **1879** FARRAR *St. Paul* II. 517 *note*, There may be a silent condemnation of incipient Docetism in ἄνθρωπος (1 Tim. ii. 5).

So **Docetist** (dəʊˈsiːtɪst), a follower of docetic teaching. **docetistic** (dɒsiːˈtɪstɪk), *a.* = DOCETIC. **docetize** (dəʊˈsiːtaɪz), *v. trans.*, to represent docetically, regard as phantasmal.

1880 *Encycl. Brit.* XI. 736 These Docetists.. had a whole series of successors in the early church. **1886** *Q. Rev.* Oct. 129 Basilides docetized the humanity.

doch-an-dorris, doch-an-dorroch, doch and dorus, etc., varr. DEOCH AN DORIS.

dochmiac (ˈdɒkmɪæk), *a.* and *sb. Gr. Pros.* [ad. Gr. δοχμιακός, f. δόχμιος pertaining to a δοχμή or hand's-breath.]

A. *adj.* Of the nature of a *dochmius*; composed of *dochmii*, i.e. of pentasyllabic feet of which the typical form is ∪ – – ∪ –. **B.** *sb.* A foot or verse of this description. Hence **dochˈmiacal** *a.*, connected with (in quot., learned in) dochmiac verse.

1775 ASH, *Dochmaic a.* and *sb.* **1821** *Blackw. Mag.* VIII. 683 'The most dochmiacal Seidlerus'. That most facete scholar being particularly sublime upon the dochmius. **1844** BECK & FELTON tr. *Munk's Metres* 255 The dochmiac systems are very frequent in the Greek dramatists. **1867** R. C. JEBB *Sophocles' Electra* (1870) 22/1 The normal dochmiac. *Ibid.* 25/1 A dochmiac verse.

docht, obs. pa. t. of DOW *v.*

dochter, obs. form of DAUGHTER.

dochtie, -ilie, obs. ff. DOUGHTY, -ILY.

dociˈbility. ? *Obs.* [f. next + -ITY; cf. late L. *docibilitās* (Isidore), f. *docibilis* DOCIBLE.]

Capacity or aptness for being taught; teachableness.

Coleridge differentiates *docibility* 'aptness to be taught' from *docility* 'willingness to be taught'.

1607 TOPSELL *Four-f. Beasts* (1658) 162 This beast is..of ..wonderful meekness and docibility. *a* **1691** BOYLE *Wks.* VI. 446 (R.) To persons of docibility, the real character may be easily taught in a few days. **1825** COLERIDGE *Aids Refl.* (1848) I. 148 Humility is the safest ground of docility and docility the surest promise of docibility.

docible (ˈdɒsɪb(ə)l), *a. Obs.* [ad. L. *docibil-is* teachable, f. *docēre* to teach: see -BLE.]

1. Apt to be taught; teachable, docile; submissive to teaching or training, tractable.

1549 LATIMER *2nd Serm. bef. Edw. VI* (Arb.) 70 Lorde, sayed he, *Da mihi cor docile.* He asked a docible herte. **1601** HOLLAND *Pliny* I. 293 Linnets..be very docible. **1644** MILTON *Educ.* Wks. (1847) 99/2 Their tenderest and most docible age. **1783** HAILES *Antiq. Chr. Ch.* iv. 147 A young and docible philosopher.

†**b.** Const. *of, to, in. Obs.*

1617 BP. HALL *Quo Vadis* iii, This age..is therfore more docible of euill. **1632** J. HAYWARD tr. *Biondi's Eromena* 188 The Prince, docible in such like disciplines. **1768–74** TUCKER *Lt. Nat.* (1852) II. 532 Persons..most docible to instruction.

2. Capable of being imparted by teaching.

1659 STANLEY *Hist. Philos.* III. III. 82 Corporealls are not docible nor admit certain knowledge. *a* **1670** HACKET *Abp. Williams* I. (1692) 28 Learning anything that is docible.

ˈdocibleness. ? *Obs.* [f. prec. + -NESS.] The quality of being docible or teachable; docibility.

1638 BAKER tr. *Balzac's Lett.* (1654) III. 122, I have at least docibleness enough to learne of them that which I know not. **1653** H. MORE *Antid. Ath.* II. viii. (1662) 64 The horse's..Speed..his docibleness and desire of glory and praise.

docile (ˈdəʊsaɪl, ˈdɒsɪl), *a.* [a. F. *docile* (16th c. in Hatz.-Darm.), ad. L. *docilis* easily taught, f. *docēre* to teach.]

1. Apt to be taught; ready and willing to receive instruction; teachable.

1483 CAXTON *Gold. Leg.* 71 b/2 Gyue to me thy seruaunt a herte docyle. **1585** JAS. I. *Ess. Poesie* (Arb.) 54 The cause why (docile Reader) I haue not dedicat this short treatise, [etc.]. **1616** B. JONSON tr. *Horace Art Poetrie* Wks. (Rtldg.) 735/2 The docile mind may soone thy precepts know. **1629** DONNE *Serm. Matt.* vi. 21 A parrot, or a stare, docile birds, and of pregnant imitation. **1751** JOHNSON *Rambler* No. 147 ¶3 Flattering comparisons of my own proficiency with that of others..less docile by nature. **1845** S. AUSTIN *Ranke's Hist. Ref.* III. 495 His docile and intelligent pupil.

b. Submissive to training; tractable, manageable.

1774 GOLDSM. *Nat. Hist.* (1776) III. 21 The bison breed is also more expert and docile than ours. **1835** URE *Philos. Manuf.* 150 This..work..is now discharged by young children..substituting cheap and docile labour for what is dear, and sometimes refractory. **1891** E. PEACOCK *N. Brendon* II. 78 The docile wife would obey without a murmur.

c. Const. *to*, or *inf. rare.*

1647 R. STAPYLTON *Juvenal* xiv. 255 To fall Into foule vices we are docill all. **1718** PRIOR *Solomon* III. 478 Soon docile to the secret acts of ill With smiles I would betray. **1862** CARLYLE *Fredk. Gt.* (1865) III. IX. i. 69, I am docile to follow your advice.

2. *transf.* of things: Yielding readily to treatment; easily managed or dealt with; tractable.

1795 tr. *Rapin's Gardens* 278 Docil Cypresses, dispos'd with ease, Take whatever handsome form you please. **1881** P. BROOKS *Candle of Lord* I The docile wax acknowledges that the subtle flame is its master. **1884** L. HAMILTON *Mexican Handbk.* 95 The ores are docile and contain ruby-silver and sub-sulphides.

Hence ˈ**docilely** *adv.*

1868 LOCKYER *Guillemin's Heavens* (ed. 3) 40 The Sun.. now tells his own story..so docilely. **1876** T. HARDY *Ethelberta* (1890) 42 'Thank you', said Picotee, docilely.

docility (dəʊˈsɪlɪtɪ). [ad. F. *docilité* (15th c. in Hatz.-Darm.), ad. L. *docilitāt-em*, f. *docilis* DOCILE.] Docile quality. **a.** Aptness to be taught; readiness to receive instruction; teachableness.

1560–78 *Bk. Discipl. Ch. Scot.* (1621) 41 Tryall being taken whether the spirit of docility be in them [children of the poore] found, or not. *a* **1619** FOTHERBY *Atheom.* II. xiv. §5 (1622) 360 Nature may giue the gift of docility to vs: but God giueth the gift of docility to it. **1748** HARTLEY *Observ. Man* II. iv. 379. **1750** JOHNSON *Rambler* No. 70 ¶1 He that has neither acuteness nor docility..is a wretch without use or value. **1849** MACAULAY *Hist. Eng.* I. ii. 173 Tact and docility made no part of the character of Clarendon. To him England was still the England of his youth.

b. Amenability to training or treatment; submissiveness to management; tractability, obedience.

1603 HOLLAND *Plutarch's Mor.* 787 (R.) That which the elephant learneth..whose docility is exhibited unto us in the theaters. **1796** MORSE *Amer. Geog.* II. 525 The docility of these birds in employing their..powers, at the command of the fishermen. **1814** SOUTHEY *Roderick* xxv, Roderick's own battle-horse..from his master's hand had wont to feed, And with a glad docility obey His voice familiar. **1885** R. BUCHANAN *Annan Water* xxx, Marjorie bore her lot with exemplary docility and characteristic gentleness.

†ˈ**docilize,** *v. Obs.*$^{-0}$ [f. DOCILE + -IZE.] *trans.* 'To make docible, teachable, tractable' (Blount *Glossogr.* 1656).

docimastic (dɒsɪˈmæstɪk), *a.* [ad. Gr. δοκιμαστικός pertaining to examination or scrutiny, f. δοκιμάζειν to essay, examine, scrutinize: cf. mod.L. *docimasticus* (in *ars docimastica*), F. *docimastique.*] Of or pertaining to docimasy; proving by experimental tests; *spec.* of or pertaining to the assay of metals.

1758 A. REID tr. *Macquer's Chem.* I. 177 The Docimastic art..in making small Assays of ores. **1776** *Phil. Trans.* LXVI. 266 Platina mixed with lead was put..in a docimastic furnace. **1802** CHENEVIX *ibid.* XCII. 327 A revolution in docimastic chemistry. **1878** tr. *Lacroix's Sc. & Lit. Mid. Ages* 127 The chemical part..the docimastic part.

dociˈmastical, *a. rare*$^{-0}$. [f. as prec. + -AL[1].] = prec.

1753 CHAMBERS *Cycl. Supp.* s.v., Docimastical experiments, see Assaying.

docimasy (ˈdɒsɪməsɪ). [mod. ad. Gr. δοκιμασία examination, scrutiny, n. of action f. δοκιμάζειν to examine: cf. mod.L. *docimasia*, F. *docimasie.*]

1. *Gr. Antiq.* A judicial inquiry (esp. at Athens) into the character and antecedents of aspirants for public office or citizenship.

2. The art or practice of assaying metallic ores, i.e. of separating the metallic substance from foreign admixture, and determining the nature and quantity of constituent metal.

[**1801** CHENEVIX in *Phil. Trans.* XCI. 197 *note*, Carbone can be of no consequence..in humid docimasia.] **1802** *Paris as it was* II. lxix. 381 To naturalize in France mineralogy, docimacy, and metallurgy. **1878** tr. *Lacroix's Sc. & Lit. Mid. Ages* 178 The applications of chemistry to..docimacy.

3. The art of ascertaining the properties and purity of drugs; also of determining by physiological tests whether a child has been born alive or not.

1847 in CRAIG.

docimology (dɒsɪˈmɒlədʒɪ). [f. Gr. δόκιμος examined, tested + -LOGY.] A treatise on the art of assaying metallic substances, or on certain questions in obstetrics; see prec.

1847 in CRAIG.

docious (ˈdəʊʃəs), *a. U.S. local.* [Related to next.] Docile, amenable to order.

a **1860** *N.Y. Spirit of Times, Western Life* (Bartlett), I was so mad..I can hardly keep my tongue docious now to talk about it.

docity (ˈdɒsɪtɪ). *dial.* Also 7 **dossety**, 9 **dossity.** [Origin doubtful: supposed to be an alteration of *docility.*] Docility; quickness of comprehension; 'gumption'.

1682 MRS. BEHN *False Count* II i, With good instructions I shall improve; I thank Heaven, I have Dossety, or so. **1687** —— *Lucky Chance* II. i, Were you a rascal of Docity you wou'd invent a way. **1746** [see DACITY]. **1758** WESLEY *Wks.* (1872) XII. 155, I cannot help it, if people have no docity. **1787** GROSE *Provinc. Gloss., Docity*, docility, quick comprehension. *Glouc.* **1825** MRS. E. HEWLETT *Cottage Comforts* vi. 40 If she has but..docity or gumption, that is, if she has got the use of her wits and the use of her hands. **1838** HALIBURTON *Clockm.* I. 243 She's all docity jist now, keep her so. **1886** *S.W. Linc. Gloss.* s.v., She seems to have no mind, no dossity whatever.

dock (dɒk), *sb.*[1] Forms: 1 **docce**, 4–5 **dokke, dok**, 4– **dock.** [OE. *docce*, pl. and inflected sing. *doccan*; app. Common WGer. or OTeut.: cf. MDu. *docke*, in comb. *docke-blaederen* 'petasites', Ger. *docken-blätter* the common dock, ODa. *ådokke* = OE. *éadocce* water-dock; also OF. *doque, doke, docque*, mod.Norm. *doque*, the Patience dock or Monk's rhubarb. So Gael. *dogha* burdock.]

1. The common name of various species of the genus *Rumex* (N.O. *Polygonaceæ*), coarse weedy herbs with thickened rootstock, sheathing stipules, and panicled racemes of inconspicuous greenish flowers. **a.** Without qualifying word usually the common dock (*R. obtusifolius*), well known as the popular antidote for nettle-stings.

c **1000** *Sax. Leechd.* II. 218 Sume betan oþþe doccan on ȝeswettum wine seoþað. **1398** TREVISA *Barth. De P.R.* XVII. xciii. (1495) 661 Al manere Dockys heele smytynge of Scorpions. **14..** *Lat. & Eng. Voc.* in Wr.-Wülcker 602/1 *Perdilla*, a dokke. **1562** TURNER *Herbal* II. 121 a, We have the great kinde of Dock, which the vnlearned toke for Rebarbe. **1599** SHAKS. *Hen. V*, v. ii. 52 Hatefull Docks, rough Thistles, Keksyes, Burres. **1611** SPEED *Hist. Gt. Brit.* IX. xvii. (1632) 876 Yet found no docke to rub out the smart. **1728** SWIFT *Pastoral Dial.* Wks. 1755 III. II. 203 Cut down the dock, 'twill sprout again. **1879** HESBA STRETTON *Through Needle's Eye* I. 60 The grounds and gardens..were overgrown with nettles and docks.

b. With descriptive epithet: **fiddle dock**, from the shape of the leaves, *R. pulcher*; **golden dock**, *R. maritimus*; **patience** or **passions dock**, *R. patientia*; also locally applied to *Polygonum bistorta*; **red dock**, *R. sanguineus*; **sharp** or **sour dock**, *R. acetosa*, sorrel; **swamp dock**, *R. verticillatus*; **water dock**, *R. hydrolapathum*; **white dock**, *R. salicifolius*; **yellow dock**, *R. crispus.* Many species were already distinguished in OE.

c **1000** *Sax. Leechd.* I. 132 *Herb.* xxxiv, Wudu docce [MS. Harl. 5294 Sur docce]..þas wyrte þe man lapatium & oðrum naman wudu docce nemneð. *Ibid.* II. 122 þa fealwan doccan nær þa readan. *Ibid.* III. 304 *Durh. Gloss., Oxilapathum*, scearpe docce. *c* **1400** *Test. Love* III. ix. (1532) 360 The frute of the soure docke. **1483** *Cath. Angl.* 103/1 A redi Dok, *lappacium.* **1548** TURNER *Names of Herbes* 69 In english Waterdocke or sharpdocke. **1578** LYTE *Dodoens* v. ix. 558 The sharpepoynted Docke or Patience, groweth in wette moyst medowes. **1597** GERARDE *Herbal* II. lxxxi. 387 Soure Docke called Sorrel. **1601** HOLLAND *Pliny* XIX. vi. (R.), The root of the hearb patience or garden docke..is knowne to run downe in the ground three cubits deepe.

2. Also in the popular names of other coarse plants of similar habit, as **dove dock**, coltsfoot (*Tussilago farfara*); **round dock**, common mallow (*Malva sylvestris*); **spatter dock**, yellow pond-lily (*Nuphar advena*); **velvet dock**, mullein (*Verbascum thapsus*). Also BURDOCK, CAN-DOCK, ELF-DOCK, etc.

c **1000** ÆLFRIC *Gloss.* in Wr.-Wülcker 136 *Nimphea*, eadocca. **1712** tr. *Pomet's Hist. Drugs* I. 27 The great, common round Dock, which many People cultivate.

3. phr. *in dock, out nettle*: orig. a charm uttered to aid the cure of nettle-stings by dock-leaves; †hence, in allusion to the full phrase used, a proverbial expression for changeableness and inconstancy (*obs.*).

The charm to be repeated during the rubbing process is 'Nettle in, dock out, Dock in, nettle out, Nettle in, dock out, Dock rub nettle out' (*N. & Q.* Ser. I. III. 133).

c **1374** CHAUCER *Troylus* IV. 433 (461) But kanstow pleyen raket to and fro, Netle In, dokke out, now this now þat, Pandare? *a* **1553** UDALL *Royster D.* II. iii. (Arb.) 34, I can not skill of such chaungeable mettle, There is nothing with them but in docke out nettle. **1623** MIDDLETON *More Dissemblers* IV. i. 233 Is this my in dock, out nettle? *a* **1626** BP. ANDREWES *Serm.* 391 (N.) Off and on, fast or loose, in docke, out nettle, and in nettle, out docke. **1715** tr. *C'tess D'Aunoy's Wks.* 430 They had been in Dock out Nettle above forty and forty Times.

4. *attrib.* and *Comb.*, as *dock-leaf, -root*; also **dock-bur**, the flower-head of the burdock; **dock-cress**, nipplewort (*Lapsana communis*); **dock-fork, -iron**, a tool for digging out the roots of docks; **dock-nettle**, the lesser stinging nettle (*Urtica urens*); **dock-sorrel**, the sour dock, (*Rumex acetosa*); **dock-worm**, a grub found on docks, used as a bait by anglers.

1632 SHERWOOD, The *dock-burre or burre-docke, *Bardane.* **1726** SHELVOCKE *Voy. round World* 55 The sea-egg ..nearly resembles a dock-burr. **1597** GERARDE *Herbal* II. xvi. (1633) 255 *Docke Creeses is a wilde wort or pot herbe. **1850** *Beck's Florist* Feb. 39 Eradicating this weed with a small instrument like a *dock-fork. **1846** J. BAXTER *Libr. Pract. Agric.* (ed. 4) II. 389 The root must be completely taken out by the *dock-iron. **1613–16** W. BROWNE *Brit. Past.* II. ii. (R.), He suckt it with his mouth..and softly gan it binde With *dock-leaves. *c* **1265** *Voc. Plants* in Wr.-Wülcker 557/39 *Dormentille, i.* ortie griesche, *i.* *docnettle. **1886** MARY LINSKILL *Haven under Hill* in *Good Words* 301 The *dock-sorrel stood with its maroon spires in the air. **1653** WALTON *Angler* iv. 95 The Flagworm, the *Dockworm, the Oakworm.

dock (dɒk), *sb.*[2] Forms: 4 **dok**, 6–7 **docke**, 6– **dock.** [Identical with mod.Icel. *dockr* short stumpy tail (Haldorssen). Ulterior etymology obscure. Cf. Fris. *dok* bundle, bunch, ball (of twine, straw, etc.), LG. *dokke* bundle (of straw, thread), skein of yarn, mod.G. *docke* bundle, skein, plug, peg.]

1. The solid fleshy part of an animal's tail.

c **1340** *Gaw. & Gr. Knt.* 193 þe tayl..bounden bothe wyth a bande of a bryȝt grene, Dubbed wyth ful dere stonez, as þe dok lasted. **1601** HOLLAND *Pliny* I. 352 Asses haue the said docke or rumpe longer than horses. **1646** SIR T. BROWNE *Pseud. Ep.* III. xvii. 150 We conjecture the age of Horses from joynts in their dockes. **1856** *Farmer's Mag.* Jan. 59 Hips wide, and rumps and docks good.

2. a. A piece of leather harness covering the clipped tail of a horse. **b.** The crupper of a saddle or harness; see also quot. 1874.

c **1340** [see prec.]. **1617** MARKHAM *Caval.* v. 31 You shall buckle on his breastplate and his crooper..then you shall lace on his saker or docke. **1753** CHAMBERS *Cycl. Supp.*, *Dock*, in the manege, is used for a large case of leather.. which serves it [the tail] for a cover. The French call the Dock, *troussequeue.* **1787** GROSE *Provinc. Gloss., Dock*, a crupper to a saddle. *Devon.* **1874** KNIGHT *Dict. Mech., Dock* ..the divided piece forming part of the crupper, through which the horse's tail is inserted. **1888** *W. Somerset Word-bk. Dock*, the crupper of either saddle or harness.

†**3.** *transf.* of human beings: The rump, buttocks. *Obs.*

1508 KENNEDY *Flyting w. Dunbar* 484 A rottyn crok, louse of the dok. **1684** *Frost of 1683–4*, 22 One's heels fly up, and down he's on his dock.

†**b.** The skirts or 'tails' of clothes. *Obs.*

1522 *World & Child* in Hazl. *Dodsley* I. 247, I will not go to school..For there beginneth a sorry feast, When the master should lift my dock. **1557** TUSSER *100 Points Husb.* xxvii, The drier, the les maidens dablith their dockes.

†**4.** The fleshy part of a boar's chine between the middle and the buttock. *Obs.*

1678 in PHILLIPS. Thence in later Dicts.

†**5.** The poop or stern of a ship. *Obs. rare.*

c **1565** LINDESAY (Pitscottie) *Chron. Scot.* (1728) 108 She bare many canons..two behind in her dock. **1570** LEVINS *Manip.* 158/13 Dock of a ship, *puppis*.

6. A cut end of anything, e.g. of hair, (?) of a tree-trunk (Tusser); a stump; an end cut off. Now *dial.*

1573 TWYNE *Æneid* x. Dd iij b, His heare down shadowing shed, but gold embroyding bynds their docks. **1573** TUSSER *Husb.* xvii. (1878) 37 For chimney in winter, to burne vp their docks. **1755** JOHNSON, *Dock*, the stump of the tail, which remains after docking. **1892** BARING-GOULD *Strange Survivals* v. 112 [To] prevent..the red-hot dock [of a wick] from spluttering on to the carpet.

†7. [f. DOCK *v.*[1]] The act of cutting off; amputation. *Obs.*

1667 WATERHOUSE *Fire Lond.* 133 The amputation and dock of one member forces the bloud. **1727–51** CHAMBERS *Cycl.*, *Dock, Docking*, in law, a means or expedient for cutting off an estate tail.

dock (dɒk), *sb.*[3] Forms: 6 dok, 6–7 docke, 6– dock. [Found early in 16th c., also in 16th c. Du. *docke*, mod.Du. *dok*. From Du. and Eng. it has passed into other langs., Da. *docke*, Sw. *docka*, mod.Ger. *dock*, *docke*, mod.F. *dock*, in 1679 *doque*. Ulterior origin uncertain.

It has been variously compared with rare Icel. *dökk*, *dökð* pit, pool, Norw. *dokk* hollow, low ground, med.L. *doga* ditch, canal (Du Cange), Gr. δοχή receptacle. See Skeat, E. Müller; also Grimm, and Diez s.v. *Doga*.]

†1. The bed (in the sand or ooze) in which a ship lies dry at low water; the hollow made by a vessel lying in the sand. *Obs.*

1513 DOUGLAS *Æneis* x. vi. 22 Lat euery barge do prent hyr self a dok. **1583** STANYHURST *Æneis* I. (Arb.) 35 Graunt foorth thy warrant in docks oure nauye too settle [L. *liceat subducere classem*]. **1627** CAPT. SMITH *Seaman's Gram.* i. i, A wet docke is any place where you may hale in a ship into the oze out of the tides way, where shee may docke her selfe. **1633** T. JAMES *Voy.* 80 Shee at a high water would fleet in her docke, though she were still dockt in the sands, almost foure foot.

†2. (Apparently) A creek or haven in which ships may lie on the ooze or ride at anchor, according to the tide. *Obs.*

1538 LELAND *Itin.* I. 53 Robyn Huddes Bay, a Dok or Bosom of a Mile yn lenghth. **1579–80** NORTH *Plutarch* (1656) 536 When he had taken them [the pyrates ships] he brought them all into a Dock.

†3. A trench, canal, or artificial inlet, to admit a boat, etc. *Obs.*

(Sense in first quot. doubtful.)

1634–5 BRERETON *Trav.* (Chetham) 45 A chest bored full of holes..placed in a dock prepared for it..Herein were fish kept. **1648** GAGE *West Ind.* 40 The Dock or Trench being thus finished, the Vergantines were calked. **1719** DE FOE *Crusoe* I. ix, I..resolv'd to cut a Dock, or Canal, to bring the Water up to the Canoe.

4. a. An artificial basin excavated, built round with masonry, and fitted with flood-gates, into which ships are received for purposes of loading and unloading or for repair.

dry or *graving dock*, a narrow basin into which a single vessel is received, and from which the water is then pumped or let out, leaving the vessel dry for the purpose of repair. (Sometimes also used for building ships.) *wet dock*, a large water-tight enclosure in which the water is maintained at the level of high tide, so that vessels remain constantly afloat in it. *floating dock*, a large floating structure that can be used like a dry dock.

1486 *Naval Accts. Hen. VII* (1896) 23 About the bringing of the same ship into her dokke. **1488** *Ibid.* 26 Keping the said Ship at Erith in her dokke. **1495** *Ibid.* 137 The Reparalyng, fortifying, and amendyng the dokke for the Kynges shippes at Portesmouth, makyng of the gates, & fortifying the hede of the same dokke. **1552** HULOET, Docke where shippes be layed vp and made, *nauale*. **1569** STOCKER tr. *Diod. Sic.* II. xxiv. 76 Antigone..likewise caused iii mightie Docks to be cut out to build the sayd shippes in. **1591** PERCIVALL *Sp. Dict.*, *Astillero*, a docke to build ships in, *nauale*. **1627** CAPT. SMITH *Seaman's Gram.* i. 1 A Docke is a great pit or creeke by a harbour side..with two great floud-gates built so stronge and close, that the Docke may be dry till the ship be built or repaired..and this is called a dry Docke. **1661–2** PEPYS *Diary* 25 Jan., Sir N. Crisp's project of making..about Deptford..a wett-dock to hold 200 sail of ships. **1758** *Descr. Thames* 268 Docks are small Harbours cut into the Land. **1849** MACAULAY *Hist. Eng.* I. iii. 344 Her endless docks, quays, and warehouses are among the wonders of the world. **1868** *Daily News* 2 Sept., Mr. Campbell's..plan of an iron floating dry dock.

fig. **1642** MILTON *Apol. Smect.* viii. (1851) 297 He must cut out large docks and creeks into his text to unlade the foolish frigate of his unseasonable autorities.

b. *transf.* with preps., *in* (or *out of*, etc.) *dock*, in hospital, undergoing treatment; (of a vehicle) laid up for repairs. *colloq.*

1785 GROSE *Dict. Vulgar T.* s.v. *Dock*, He must go into dock, a sea phrase, signifying that the person spoken of, must undergo a salivation. **1848** in *Amer. Speech* (1935) X. 40/1 *Hauled into dock*, sick at home. **1919** *Athenæum* 11 July 582/2 'Dock', hospital, is..probably from 'in dock'. *Ibid.* 22 Aug. 791/2 While 'in dock' (*i.e.* in hospital) one lay upon 'biscuits'. **1939** 'G. ORWELL' *Coming up for Air* I. i. 11 The old car..was temporarily in dock. **1960** *News Chron.* 16 Feb. 6/5 He's just out of dock after the old appendix. **1963** 'R. EAST' *Pin Men* ii. 52 If Father's car hadn't been in dock.

c. In full *scene-dock* (see SCENE 13).

1898 SACHS & WOODROW *Mod. Opera Houses* III. Suppl. I. 24 At each side of the stage the counterweight boxes practically form enclosing walls with a number of openings leading to a series of 'scene' docks on each side. The arrangement of these side docks..is essentially of French origin, and they afford a very ready means for the disposal of scenery which has to be quickly removed from the stage. *Ibid.* 34 There is a dock for each sequence of 'traps', so that the 'wings' belonging to each 'entrance' can always be kept in the dock opposite it. **1952** W. GRANVILLE *Dict. Theatr. Terms* 158 *Scene-dock*, usually shorted, by stage carpenters, to *dock*. A stowage space at the back, or side, of the stage.

5. (Often *pl.*) a. A range of dock-basins (sense 4 a) together with the adjoining wharfs, warehouses and offices (*commercial docks*). b. The whole establishment of similar basins and adjoining work-shops, etc., concerned with the building, outfit, and repair of ships; a dockyard (*naval docks*).

1703 *Lond. Gaz.* No. 3912/2 Timber..for the use of her Majesty's Dock at Plimouth. **1770** WESLEY *Jrnl.* 12 Oct., I walked round the Dock [at Portsmouth], much larger than any other in England. **1848** DICKENS *Dombey* ix, Captain Cuttle lived..near the India Docks. **1875** JOWETT *Plato* III. 698 The docks were full of triremes and naval stores.

6. *Railways.* An enclosure in a platform into which a single line of rails runs and terminates.

7. *attrib.* and *Comb.*, as *dock-boot*, *-constable*, *-head*, *-house*, *-labourer*, *-man*, *-side*, *-sill*, *-space*, *-trade*, *-warehouse*, etc.; also **dock-company**, the company or corporate body owning a dock; **dock-charges**, **dock-dues**, charges made for the use of a dock; **dock-glass**, a large wine-glass originally designed for wine-tasting; **dock-master**, the superintendent or manager of a dock; **dock-port**, a port that has a (naval) dock; **dock-rent**, the charge made for warehousing goods in a dock; †**dock-silver** (*Sc.*), dock-dues; **dock-walloper** (*U.S.*), a casual labourer engaged at docks and wharfs; **dock-warrant**, a certificate given to the owner of goods warehoused in a dock. Also DOCKYARD.

1883 *Fisheries Exhib. Catal.* 10 Sea Boots, *Dock Boots. **1891** *Daily News* 28 Dec. 3/6 The deceased..was seen safely aboard the vessel by a *dock constable. **1837** *Penny Cycl.* IX. 44/2 Amount of *Dock Dues. **1920** G. SAINTSBURY *Notes on Cellar-Book* i. 9 The large, slightly pinched-in '*dock-glass', half filled, suited it as indeed it does almost any wine. **1953** *Word for Word* (Whitbread & Co.) 18/1 *Dock glass*, a goblet holding exactly a quarter of a pint, used originally by Excise Officers for wine tasting in the docks. **1497** *Naval Accts. Hen. VII* (1896) 143 The dokke, the *dokke hedde & gates of the same. **1657** *Rec. Early Hist. Boston* (1877) II. 142 To sett up a building att the west end of the house..by the dock head. **1736** *Ibid.* (1885) XII. 139 The Watch House at the Dockhead. **1880** *Times* 17 Dec. 5/6 The Hartlepool..in entering dock struck the dockhead. **1661** PEPYS *Diary* 10 Apr., In the morning, to see the *Dock-houses. **1878** JEVONS *Prim. Pol. Econ.* 59 *Dock-labourers..are simply strong men without any particular skill. **1755** B. MARTIN *Misc. Corr.* Oct. 171 Orders..that he should..form the *Dockmen into a Regiment. **1736** in Picton *L'pool Munic. Rec.* (1886) II. 146 Mr. Steers the *Dockmaster. **1758** *M.P.'s Let. on R.N.* 42 Wages may be paid..at any *Dock-Port. **1887** *Times* 25 Aug. 4/5 [They] arrived at the *dockside. **1858** *Merc. Marine Mag.* V. 174 The *dock sill is 3 feet 6 inches above low water-mark. **1641** *Stirling Charters* (1884) 151 (Jam. Suppl.) Heavin silver et *dock silver. **1860** BARTLETT *Dict. Amer.*, **Dock walloper*, a loafer that hangs about the wharves. New York. **1879** *Lumberman's Gaz.* 15 Oct., Dockwollopers are paid 40 to 45 cents an hour. **1875** JEVONS *Money* (1878) 207 The holder of a *dock-warrant has a prima-facie claim to the..hogsheads of sugar, or other packages named thereon.

dock (dɒk), *sb.*[4] [The same word as Fl. *dok* rabbit-hutch, fowl-pen, cage; '*Docke* = *keuie*, *renne*,' i.e. cage, fowl-pen, fowl-run (Kilian). In Eng. prob. at first a word of rogues' cant.

Used by Warner and Ben Jonson 1586–1610; but an unknown word to Jonson's editors, Whalley 1756, Gifford 1816. Absent from the 18th c. dictionaries, and from Todd, Webster 1828, Richardson; and after 1610, known to us only in BAIL-DOCK, till the 19th c., in which it has become familiar, largely through the writings of Dickens.]

1. The enclosure in a criminal court in which the prisoner is placed at his trial: it was formerly filled with the prisoners whose trial was put down for the day. Cf. BAIL-DOCK.

1586 WARNER *Alb. Eng.* III. xviii, Sterne Minos and grim Radymant discend their duskie roomes, The docke was also Cleare of Gosts, adiorn'd to after-doomes. **1610** B. JONSON *Alch.* v. iv, Here will be officers, presently; bethinke you, Of some course sodainely to scape the dock: For thether you'll come else. **1824** *Ann. Reg.* LXVI. 40 The prisoner, after receiving the congratulations of several of his friends, bowed, and retired from the dock. **1838** DICKENS *O. Twist* xliii, A dirty frowsy room..with a dock for the prisoners on the left hand. **1882** SERJT. BALLANTINE *Exper.* xliii. 396 [He] had to appear and surrender into the dock.

attrib. **1838** DICKENS *O. Twist* xliii, A jailer stood reclining against the dock-rail.

2. Special Comb.: **dock brief**, a brief handed direct to a barrister in court, who has been selected by a prisoner, standing in the dock, to defend him. (Cf. DOCKER[3].)

1909 *Daily Chron.* 30 Apr. 6/7 The 'dock brief'..is the only exception to the rule that briefs must come through a solicitor. **1928** *Daily Tel.* 10 Jan. 9 Barristers who are not anxious to accept dock briefs are entitled to leave the court on hearing a prisoner ask for one.

dock (dɒk), *v.*[1] [f. DOCK *sb.*[2]]

1. *trans.* a. To cut short in some part, *esp.* in the tail, hair, or similar appendage; to curtail.

c **1386** CHAUCER *Prol.* 590 His tope was doked lyk a preest biforn. **1408** *Will of de Brugge* (Somerset Ho.), Equum meum nigrum dokkede. *c* **1440** *Promp. Parv.* 125/2 Dockyd by þe tayle, *decaudatus*. **1564** BECON *Early Wks.* Gen. Pref. (1843) 7 Admitting him unto the ministry..without docking, greasing, shaving. **1673** E. BROWN *Acc. Trav.* 72 They have very good Horses..but they never dock them, but their tayls grow out at length. **1754** RICHARDSON *Grandison* (1781) I. xxxvi. 256 His horses are not docked: their tails are only tied up. **1813** *Sporting Mag.* XLI. 60 He related..his docking a defaulter in payment..He..cut off his long hair close to the scalp.

b. *spec.* To shorten (the tail of a horse, dog, etc.) by cutting off one or more of the extreme caudal vertebræ. Also *absol.*

1419 in Ellis *Orig. Lett.* Ser. II. I. 78 *note*, Y wolde breke his Sege, and make hem of Roon dokke hys tayle. **1530** PALSGR. 523/2 Docke your horse tayle, and make hym a courtault. **1778** JOHNSON 3 Apr. in *Boswell*, His tail then must be docked. That was the mark of Alcibiades's dog. **1802** BINGLEY *Anim. Biog.* (1813) I. 494 The barbarous custom of docking the tails..is in this country very prevalent. **1876** MISS CARY *Country Life* 189 I'm a going to ..learn to nick and dock.

2. *transf.* and *fig.* a. To cut short or abridge by taking away a part; to lessen, curtail, subject to limitation in some respect; to deprive, divest *of* (†*from*) some part or appendage.

c **1380** WYCLIF *Sel. Wks.* III. 180 þei docken Goddis word, and tateren it bi þer rimes. *c* **1422** HOCCLEVE *Jereslaus' Wife* 541 If thow fynde þat I gabbe, Of my promesse thanne dokke me. **1693** W. FREKE *Sel. Ess.* xix. 109 Docking it [learning] from its superfluous Pedantry. **1771** T. JEFFERSON *Lett.* Writ. 1892 I. 387 Dock the invoice of such articles as ..I may get in the country. **1871** BROWNING *Pr. Hohenst.* 1374 Dock, by the million, of its friendly joints, The electoral body short. **1889** *Spectator* 26 Oct., Wages..will be pretty sharply docked by rent. **1892** F. HALL in *Nation* (N.Y.) LV. 335/1 A participial adjective docked of its termination.

b. To make a deduction from (a person's pay) as a fine, subscription, etc.; also with the person as object. *colloq.* (orig. *dial.*).

1822 COBBETT *Weekly Reg.* 13 Apr. 81 Hence arose numerous schemes for *docking* you in this quarter. **1891** C. WORDSWORTH *Rutland Words.* s.v., Mr. A—— has docked his men as last Saturday, I suppose. **1891** *Harper's Mag.* Nov. 888/2 Each man was 'docked', or charged, seventy-five cents a month for medical services. **1901** MERWIN & WEBSTER *Calumet 'K'* vii. 128 Every man that drops anything into the bins gets docked an hour's pay. *Ibid.*, I guess we won't take the trouble to dock you. **1937** V. BARTLETT *This is my Life* xi. 170, I should find my salary docked or stopped altogether.

3. To cut away, cut off; also = DAG *v.*[1] 3.

c **1380** WYCLIF *Wks.* (1880) 430 þei wolden teche sum & sum hide & docke sum [of God's law]. **1855** THACKERAY *Newcomes* II. 45, I see you have shaven the mustachios off.. I thought I had best dock them. **1888** ELWORTHY *W. Somerset Word-bk.*, *Dock*, to cut off the wool clotted with dung from around a sheep's tail.

4. *Law. to dock the entail*: to cut off or put an end to the entail; to break the prescribed line of succession to an estate; also *fig.*

a **1626** BACON *Max. & Uses Com. Law* (1635) 47 These notable Statutes..do dock intailes. **1723** STEELE *Consc. Lovers* III, He could not dock the entail. **1854** LOWELL *Jrnl. in Italy* Pr. Wks. 1890 I. 124 A poor relation whose right in the entail of home traditions has been docked by revolution.

Hence **'docking** *vbl. sb.*; also *attrib.*

1727–51 [see DOCK *sb.*[2] 7]. **1741** *Compl. Fam. Piece* III. 449 So many Horses die with Docking. **1865** YOUATT *Horse* xxii. (1872) 466 The veterinary surgeon with his docking-machine cuts through the tail at one stroke.

dock (dɒk), *v.*[2] [f. DOCK *sb.*[3]]

†1. *trans.* To bring or put (a ship) into station or anchorage in a roadstead, etc. *Obs.*

1514 BARCLAY *Cyt. & Uplondyshm.* (Percy Soc.) 29 Now are they..sparcled abrode, Lyke wyse as shyppes be docked in a rode. **1615** *Trade's Incr.* in *Harl. Misc.* (Malh.) III. 296 Two more [ships] are docked up there, as pinnaces, to trade up and down.

†2. To bring or put (a vessel) ashore where it may rest in the ooze, or in some trench, or creek: cf. DOCK *sb.*[3] 1. *Obs.*

1596 SHAKS. *Merch. V.* I. i. 27 And see my wealthy Andrew dockt [*early edd.* docks] in sand. **1627**, **1633** [see DOCK *sb.*[3] 1]. **1669** STURMY *Mariner's Mag.* v. 81 To weigh Ship..that hath not lain too long, and docked it self in Oaze. **1751** R. PALTOCK *P. Wilkins* xv, When I had docked my boat, I would accompany her. [Cf. xii, I sought for a convenient place to stow my boat in..Having pitched upon a swampy place..I soon cut a trench from the lake.]

3. a. To take, bring, or receive (a ship) into a dock (in the modern sense); cf. DOCK *sb.*[3] 4.

1600 PORY tr. *Leo's Africa* II. 376 Arsenals, or places for the building, repairing, docking, and harbouring of.. gallies. **1662** PEPYS *Diary* 21 July, We..saw the manner and trouble of docking such a ship. **1795** *Hull Advertiser* 3 Oct. 1/4 A grand dock-yard..sufficient to dock and re-fit 30 sail of the line. **1861** *Sat. Rev.* 14 Dec. 608 A British man-of-war was lying there waiting to be docked.

b. *intr.* (for *refl.*) To come into dock.

1892 *Daily News* 4 Nov. 3/1 Water..must be pumped out before she can dock.

4. *trans.* To furnish or lay out with docks.

1757 W. SMITH *Hist. New York* 187 The Ships lie off in the Roads, on the East Side of the Town, which is docked out. **1861** *Sat. Rev.* 14 Dec. 615 The cutting of the.. Caledonian Canal, the docking of London and Liverpool.

5. *trans.* To join (a space vehicle) to another in space; also *intr.*, to become joined. Const. *with*. Freq. as DOCKING *vbl. sb.* Hence **docked** *ppl. a.*[3]

1951 *Jrnl. Brit. Interplanetary Soc.* X. 299 The idea of 'docking' a spaceship inside..a space-station is suicidal lunacy. **1960**, etc. [see DOCKING *vbl. sb.* below]. **1961** W. SCHROEDER *Terminal Guidance Scheme for Docking Satellites* (Amer. Rocket Soc. Paper 1952–61) 5/1 While such a solution requires the minimum expenditure of fuel, it is unsatisfactory because of the time required to dock. **1969** *Daily Tel.* 17 Jan. 1/2 Tass did not say whether an airlock connection allowed the crew to move from one docked capsule to the other, internally. **1969** *Guardian* 22 July 1 Astronauts Neil Armstrong and Edwin Aldrin soared up and away from the moon's surface to dock with the command module. **1971** *Times* 26 Apr. 1/6 Soyuz 10 was docked with Salyut at 02.47 B.S.T. yesterday.

Hence ˈ**docking** *vbl. sb.*; also *attrib.*

1600 [see 3 a above]. **1691** T. H[ALE] *Acc. New Invent.* 28 Their Ransackings, Groundings, Dockings, and Repairings. **1799** NELSON 12 Sept. in Nicolas *Disp.* (1845) IV. 11 The Seahorse..requires docking. **1886** *Law Times* LXXX. 284/1 [She] carried the usual docking signal of two bright lights aft. **1960** A. W. NELSON in *Amer. Rocket Soc. Paper* No. 1493–60. 9/1 The two are in essentially identical orbits and only a few hundred feet or so apart. Now the final 'parking' or 'docking' must be accomplished. **1961** W. SCHROEDER *Terminal Guidance Scheme for Docking Satellites* (Amer. Rocket Soc. Paper 1952–61) 1/1 It appears extremely likely that in the very near future a number of missions will require the docking of two vehicles in space. *Ibid.* 2/2 The propulsion system consists of two canted engines on the aft or docking end..and a single main engine on the nose. **1962** K. W. GATLAND *Astronautics in Sixties* xi. 344 Although initially radar and other homing devices may be relied upon to achieve linkage of the spacecraft,.. experiments will be performed..to see if manual control of the docking procedure is possible. **1965** *New Scientist* 23 Dec. 851/2 Five such rendezvous and docking experiments in space are planned in 1966. **1966** *Times* 6 June 1/6 The target satellite's protective shroud hanging on to the docking collar. **1971** *Ibid.* 21 June 1/2 If his background is in docking, that is an expert in the orbital problems of bringing the space station and the module together at a certain time and place, he will be invaluable.

dock, *v.*[3] *Biscuit-making.* [Origin unknown.] *trans.* To pierce (a biscuit) with holes.

1840 [Remembered as the term in regular use. G. Palmer.] **1875** *Ure's Dict. Arts* I. 343 The biscuit was then docked, that is, pierced with holes by an instrument adapted to the purpose. *Ibid.* 346 A stamping and docking frame.. The stamps or cutters in the frame being internally provided with prongs..dock the cakes, or cut pieces, with a series of holes, for the subsequent escape of the moisture, which, but for these vents, would distort and spoil the cake or biscuit when put in the oven.

dock, *v.*[4] *nonce-wd.* [f. DOCK *sb.*[4]] *trans.* To place (a prisoner) in the dock.

1895 *Pall Mall G.* 2 Dec. 2/3 They [jury] did so on Saturday at Riom, when and where a lady was docked for disposal.

dockage[1] (ˈdɒkɪdʒ). [f. DOCK *sb.*[3] + -AGE.]

a. Charges made for the use of docks. **b.** Docks collectively, dock accommodation. **c.** The berthing of vessels in docks.

1708 *Deed* 9 Apr. in *New Engld. Hist. Gen. Reg.* (1879) 402 The privilidge of Dockage and Wharffage. **1788** CLARKSON *Impol. Slave Tr.* 121 These vessels pay their dockage. **1864** *Daily Tel.* 3 May, With regard to the dockage of the iron fleet. **1893** *Critic* (U.S.) 25 Mar. 186/1 An interesting study [in water-colour] of dockage in New Orleans.

ˈ**dockage**[2]. [f. DOCK *v.*[1] + -AGE.] The action of docking; deduction.

1886 *Philad. Times* 20 Mar. (Cent.), I do not find..in the time-book a single instance of dockage. **1887** *Contemp. Rev.* May 699 Dishonest dockage for dirt and chaff.

docked (dɒkt), *ppl. a.*[1] [f. DOCK *v.*[1] + -ED[1].] Cut short, curtailed; with short or shortened tail.

1408 [see DOCK *v.*[1] 1]. *c* **1440** *Promp. Parv.* 125/2 Dockyd, lessyd or obryggyd, *abbreviatus.* **1830** CARLYLE *Richter* Misc. (1872) III. 26 Besides the docked cue, he had shirts *a la Hamlet.* **1861** SALA *Dutch Pict.* xii. 187 A grey horse, with a docked military tail.

docked, *ppl. a.*[2] [f. DOCK *sb.*[2] 3 + -ED[2].] Having buttocks; in ***strong-docked***, 'that has strong Reins and Sinews, lusty, stout' (Phillips 1706).

a **1652** BROME *New. Acad.* II. i, She's a tight strong dock't Tit. **1709** *Brit. Apollo* II. No. 12. 3/1 A Strong dock'd Bucksome Quean.

docken (ˈdɒk(ə)n). *Sc.* and *north. dial.* Also 5 doken, -an, 8 dockan, 9 docking. [app. repr. OE. *doccan*, early ME. **dokken*, pl. and inflected form of *docce*, DOCK *sb.*[1]] = DOCK *sb.*[1] 1.

1423 JAS. I *Kingis Q.* cix, Als like ȝe bene, as..doken to the fresche dayesye. **1483** *Cath. Angl.* 103/1 A Dokan, *paradilla.* **1721** KELLY *Scot. Prov.* 184 (Jam.), 'I wo'd be very loth And scant of cloth, To sole my hose with dockans.' The return of a haughty maid to them that tell her of an unworthy suitor. **1724** RAMSAY *Tea-t. Misc.* (1733) I. 21 Wad ye compare ye'r sell to me, A docken till a tansie? **1863** ROBSON *Bards of Tyne* 138 Amang these green dockings.

b. *attrib.* Of or like a dock-leaf; dock-like.

1852 R. S. SURTEES *Sponge's Sp. Tour* xliv. 245 His great red docken ears.

docker[1] (ˈdɒkə(r)). [f. DOCK *sb.*[3] + -ER[1].]

1. A dweller in or near a dock; *spec.* an inhabitant of Devonport, formerly Plymouth Dock.

1762 JOHNSON in Boswell *Life* Visit Devonsh., I am against the Dockers: I am a Plymouth-man. **1870** R. N. WORTH *Hist. Devonport* ix. 100 The oldest living Docker.

2. A labourer in the docks.

1887 *Pall Mall G.* 19 Sept. 2/2 A trade union for dockers. **1889** *Times* 11 Dec. 9/3 Gross intimidation during the dockers' strike.

ˈ**docker**[2]. [f. DOCK *v.*[1] and [3] + -ER[1].]

1. One who docks the tails of horses, etc.

1810 *Sporting Mag.* XXXV. 263 Croppers, dockers, nickers and trimmers. **1844** J. T. HEWLETT *Parsons & W.* iii, You..mane-and-tail docker.

2. A stamp used for 'docking' or perforating the dough for biscuits.

1874 in KNIGHT *Dict. Mech.*

ˈ**docker**[3]. [f. DOCK *sb.*[4] + -ER[1].] (See quot.)

1889 in BARRÈRE & LELAND *Dict. Slang.* **1891** *Strand Mag.* II. 89/1 Many young advocates do a brisk trade in what are termed 'dockers'. **1892** *Pall Mall G.* 28 Jan. 6/1 Dock cases, 'dockers', as they are called—cases in which you are retained by the prisoner in the dock. **1928** *Daily Tel.* 17 Jan. 10/6 A dock brief... Sometimes it is called a 'docker'.

docket (ˈdɒkɪt), *sb.*[1] Also 5 doket, 5–9 dogget(t, 6–8 docquett, 6–9 docquet. [Found since 15th c.: derivation and original sense obscure.

It has been suggested to be a derivative of DOCK *v.*[1], the suffix being either the dim. -ET[1] (cf. *pocket*), or a var. of the -ED of pa. pple. But neither view is free from serious objections.]

†**1.** (?) *Obs.*

c **1460** *Towneley Myst.* (Surtees) 313 May he dug hym a doket, A kodpese like a pokett.

†**2.** A brief, summarized statement; an abstract or abridgement; a digest, minute. *Obs.* exc. *Hist.*

a **1483** *Liber Niger* in *Househ. Ord.* 25 Lett it alwey be remembered to make in the kinges doggettes both venit and recessit as often as it pleseth the King the prince to come or goe. **1526** *Ibid.* 229 The Clerke of the Green Cloth shall.. ingrosse and cast up all the particuler Breifments of the House..and the same, soe cast up..enter in the Parchment docquett, called the Maine Docquet. *Ibid.* 234 The Clerk of the Spicery..doe dayly make the Briefments or docquets of the expence of his office. **1555** *Act 2 & 3 Phil. & Mary* c. 6 That every person..auctorised to..purveye any Beefes, Wethers, Lambes [etc.]..shall make a Docket or Briefe in writing..conteyning all & every suche Beefe, Wethers, Lambes [etc.] **1641** *Termes de la Ley* 126 Docket is a little peece of paper or parchment written, that conteineth in it the effect of a greater writing. **1643** in Clarendon *Hist. Reb.* VII. §347 Several proportions of arms mentioned in a docquet then sent inclosed in our said letters. **1858** DORAN *Crt. Fools* 219 The warrant..may have been preserved, and probably also a docket or short minute of it.

3. *spec.* The abstract of the contents of a proposed Letter-patent, written upon the King's bill which authorized the preparation of such letter for the Great Seal, and also copied into a Register or Docket-book.

1552 in *St. Papers, Domestic* (MS.), Docquets I. [King's Bills endorsed 'Docquet']. **1576** *Ibid.*, A docquet of the contents of her ma[ties] lettres patentes graunted the xvth of June. **1580, 1590** *Ibid.* **1660** PEPYS *Diary* 13 July, My patent ..being done, we carried it..to Mr. Beale for a Dockett. **1662–3** *Ibid.* 28 Feb., I did see the docquet by which Sir W. Pen is made the Comptroller's assistant. **1686** EVELYN *Diary* 12 Mar., A docquet was to be seal'd importing a lease of 21 yeares to one Hall. *Ibid.* 5 May, We should be requir'd to passe a doquett dispensing with Dr. Obadiah Walker and four more..to hold their masterships, fellowships, and cures. *a* **1837** W. H. BLACK *Docquets of Lett. Pat. Chas. I, 1643–6* (Recd. Commiss., unpubl.) Pref. vii, The Docquet books..present in the form of a Register or Journal short abstracts of all instruments that were prepared for the great seal in the offices to which they respectively belong.

4. *Law.* A memorandum or register of legal judgements.

1668–9 PEPYS *Diary* 12 Mar. (1879) VI. 20 To the Crowne Office, where we..did take short notes of the dockets. **1687** DR. HEDGES in *Magd. Coll. & Jas. II* (Oxf. Hist. Soc.) 204 The Steward ask'd for a docket of yᵉ fines. **1692** *Act 4 Will. & Mary* c. 20 §1 Every Clerk of the Doggets of the Court of Kings Bench..shall..put into an Alphabeticall Doggett by the Defendants names a particular of all Judgments for Debt. **1809** TOMLINS *Law Dict.* s.v. *Docket or Dogget*, When rolls of judgments are brought into C.B. they are docketted, and entered on the docket of that term; so that upon any occasion you may soon find out a judgment, by searching these dockets, if you know the attorney's name. *Ibid.* s.v. *Judgment*, By rule of Michaelmas, 42 Geo. 3 (2 East. 136) no Judgment can be signed upon any warrant authorising any attorney to confess Judgment, without such warrant of attorney being delivered to and filed by the Clerk of the Dockets; who is ordered to file the warrants in the order in which they are received.

5. *Law.* A list of causes for trial, or of names of persons having causes pending. Hence phr. ***on the docket.*** (*U.S.*)

1790 DALLAS *Amer. Law Rep.* I. 382 The plea entered on the docquet. **1800** ADDISON *Amer. Law Rep.* 14 Only one cause appeared on the docquet. **1828** WEBSTER, *Docket*,..3. An alphabetical list of cases in a court, or a catalogue of the names of the parties who have suits depending in a court. In some of the States, this is the principal or only use of the word. **1864** *Ibid.* s.v., *On the docket*, in hand; under consideration; in process of execution or performance. (Colloq.)

†**6.** In phr. ***to strike a docket***: see quots. *Obs.*

1809 R. LANGFORD *Introd. Trade* 115 The person has subjected himself to being a bankrupt: if so, he is made one, which is termed striking a docket. **1823** CRABB *Technol. Dict.* s.v., 'To strike a docket' is said of a creditor who gives bond to the Lord Chancellor, proving his debtor to be a bankrupt; in consequence of which a commission of bankruptcy is taken out against him. **1835** HOOD *Dead Robbery* i, Of all the causes that induce mankind To strike against themselves a mortal docket. **1848** WHARTON *Law Lex.*, *Docket* or *Dogged*..the entry made by the secretary of bankrupts, when a petitioning creditor's affidavit of debt is lodged with him for the purpose of issuing a fiat in bankruptcy, technically called 'striking a docket'. **1852** THACKERAY *Esmond* III. iv, Esmond..having fairly struck his docket in this love transaction, determined to put a cheerful face on his bankruptcy.

7. An endorsement on a letter or other document, briefly indicating its contents or subject; a label affixed for a similar purpose; a written direction, a ticket.

1706 PHILLIPS (ed. Kersey), *Docket*, a little Bill ty'd to Goods or Wares, and directed to the Person and Place they are to be sent to. **1839** LADY GRANVILLE *Lett.* 11 Feb. (1894) II. 282 You may find your delightful tour safe in red tape and docket. **1840** HOOD *Up Rhine* 76 Tourists..Provided with passport, that requisite docket. **1883** I. TAYLOR *Alphabet* I. 253 On the outer edge of these tablets a docket is occasionally inscribed..containing a brief reference to the contents, evidently for the purpose of enabling the keeper of the records to find any particular document. **1886** *Cheshire Gloss.*, *Docket*, hatting term. The wage ticket of workpeople.

8. a. A warrant from the Custom House on entering goods, certifying the payment of the duty. **b.** A form of certificate giving particulars of the bales, marks, ship's name, etc., of cotton sold for future delivery, the presentation of which at the Cotton Clearing-house entitles the presenter to obtain a delivery order.

The dockets show the amount of cotton tendered on each Tendering Day at the Clearing House. When the same 'form' is used on a second Tendering Day, it is called a ***letter-docket.***

1712 SWIFT *Jrnl. to Stella* 13 Mar., He dreams of nothing but cockets, and dockets, and drawbacks and other jargon, words of the custom-house. **1887** *Times* 27 Aug. 11/6 (Cotton Market) The tenders were 2,100 bales of which 100 [were] letter dockets.

9. *attrib.* and *Comb.*, as ***docket-book*** (see sense 3), ***-rolls, -warrant.***

1643 *St. Trials, Abp. Laud* 13 Mar., For Worcester, there is no proof but the Docket-book. **1659** RUSHW. *Hist. Coll.* I. 637 There were then entred in the Docket Book, several Conge D'esliers and Royal assents for Dr. May to be Bishop of Bath and Wells [etc.]. **1690** J. PALMER in *Andros Tracts* I. 34 As appears by the Dogget-Book of the Council. **1762–71** H. WALPOLE *Vertue's Anecd. Paint.* (1786) II. 12, I found the minute of the docquet warrant for this among the Conway papers. **1888** W. RYE *Records & Rec. Search.* 48 *note*, Calendars and indexes of the Docket Rolls of the Common Pleas. *Ibid.* Index, Doggett or Docket Books (indexes to Common Law Judgment Rolls).

†ˈ**docket**, *sb.*[2] *Obs.* ? = DOCK *sb.*[2] 1.

c **1590** GREENE *Jas. IV*, Wks. (Rtldg.) 193 Properties of a lion, a broad breast, a stiff docket.

ˈ**docket**, *v.* [f. DOCKET *sb.*[1]]

†**1.** *trans.* To furnish or inscribe with a docket.

1615 BACON *Let. to King* 12 Aug. in Rawley *Resuscitatio* (1657) Your Majesty shall shortly receive the Bill, for the Incorporation of the New Company: together with a Bill, for the Privy Seal, being a Dependancy thereof. For this Morning I subscribed, and docketted them both. **1621** LD.-KEEPER WILLIAMS in *Fortesc. Papers* (Camden) 169, I could not all yesterday get the Clarke of the Signet to docquet the same. **1833** *Act 3 & 4 Wil. IV*, c. 46 §69 The Lists of Occupiers..or a Copy thereof docqueted and signed by the Preses of any Meeting of the said Commissioners.

2. *Law.* To make an abstract of (judgements, etc.) and enter them in a list or index.

1692 *Act 4 Will. & Mary* c. 20 §2 No Judgment not doggetted and entred in the Bookes..shall affect any Landes or Tenementes as to Purchasers or Mortgagees. **1809** TOMLINS *Law Dict.* s.v. *Judgment*, Which Judgment..is.. binding; provided the same..be regularly docketed; that is, abstracted and entered in a book. **1818** CRUISE *Digest* II. 58 It is said by Sir J. Jekyll, that judgements cannot be docketed after the time mentioned in the act. **1868** *Act 31 & 32 Vict.* c. 101 §22 Such assignation..may not have been docqueted with reference to such warrant.

3. To endorse (a letter or document) with a short note of its contents, writer, date, or the like.

1750 CHESTERF. *Let.* 5 Feb. (1870) 175 Whatever letters and papers you keep, docket and tie them up in their respective classes so that you may instantly have recourse to any one. **1779** FRANKLIN *Lett.* Wks. 1889 VI. 328 Returning immediately all the others, docketed and catalogued, as you please. **1851** *Ord. & Regul. R. Engineers* ii. 4 These..official Returns, are to be properly docketed and addressed on the back. **1887** T. A. TROLLOPE *What I remember* I. xi. 229 Letters..carefully docketed with the date by my father.

b. *transf.* and *fig.*

1856 R. A. VAUGHAN *Mystics* IX. i. (1860) II. 117 Every emotion was methodically docketed; every yearning of the heart minutely catalogued. **1883** E. PENNELL-ELMHIRST *Cream Leicestersh.* 244 The Season that is now filed and docketed with the past. **1894** SALA *Lond. up to Date* xx. 300 Plans..docketed, and consigned to their proper imaginary pigeon-holes.

Hence ˈ**docketed** *ppl. a.*, ˈ**docketing** *vbl. sb.*

1810 LADY GRANVILLE *Lett.* 29 Aug. (1894) I. 11 Having embarked me at last in a regular docketted correspondence. **1865** CARLYLE *Fredk. Gt.* VII. XVII. viii. 86 In this docketing it lay, sealed for many years. **1866** R. CHAMBERS *Ess.* Ser. I. 152 A set of docketed papers, tied up with red tape.

docking-iron = *dock-iron*; see DOCK *sb.*[1] 4.

1780 W. CURTIS *Flora Lond.* III. 22 For its [dock's] destruction an instrument called a Docking Iron has been invented.

dockize (ˈdɒkaɪz), *v.* [f. DOCK *sb.*[3] + -IZE.] *trans.* To transform (a river) into a range of docks. Hence ˈ**dockized** *ppl. a.*, ˈ**dockizing** *vbl. sb.*

1877 A. FORROW *Thames & its Docks* 61 Could the good people of Bristol be induced to dockise that very erratic stream. **1881** *Nature* XXIV. 17 The process called 'dockising', or damming a river at its mouth. **1891** *Pall Mall G.* 2 Dec. 5/9 The proposed 'dockized' portion.

So **docki'zation**, conversion into docks.

1893 DE RIDDER (*title*) Dockization v. docks. Letter.. to the Mayor.. of Bristol. **1895** *Chamb. Jrnl.* 140 The dockisation scheme.. a proposal to construct a dam across the mouth of the Avon.

Dockland, dockland ('dɒklænd, -lənd). A name, originally journalistic, for the districts about the London docks.

1904 *Daily Chron.* 21 Sept. 6/2 Clarkson-street School.. is situated in the heart of Dockland. **1922** *Weekly Dispatch* 19 Nov. 8 For him there is glamour even in the mean streets of dockland. **1922** *Daily Mail* 12 Dec. 7 The Dockland Mission, formerly known as the Malvern Mission, in Canning Town. **1929** *Times* 7 Feb. 9/4 His work there won the whole-hearted love and devotion of Dockland.

docksman ('dɒksmən). [f. *docks* (see DOCK *sb.*[3] 5) + MAN *sb.*[1]] A man employed at a dock or docks; *spec.* see quot. 1921.

1921 *Dict. Occup. Terms* (1927) §745 *Docksman*, one of a team of men who open and shut dock gates by means of capstan. **1929** *Daily News* 25 July 5/6 The former Cardiff docksman.

dock-tail, *a.* = next.

1785 *Criticisms on Rolliad* xvii, May thy dock-tail pair Unharm'd convey thee with sure-footed care.

'dock-tailed, *ppl. a.* [f. stem of DOCK *v.*[1] + TAILED.] Having its tail docked or cut short.

1824 MISS MITFORD *Village* Ser. I. 200 That still wretcheder apology for a coat, a dock-tailed jacket. **1852** R. S. SURTEES *Sponge's Sp. Tour* (1893) 189 A dock-tailed waggon horse.

dockyard ('dɒkjɑːd). [f. DOCK *sb.*[3] + YARD.] A more or less spacious enclosure, adjoining the sea or a river, in which ships are built and repaired, and all kinds of ships' stores are prepared or brought together; *esp.* in British use, applied to the Government establishments of this character for the use of the navy, in U.S. called *navy-yards*. Also *attrib.*, as **dockyard man, dockyard-man**, a man permanently employed in a Government dockyard; also (*colloq.*) **dockyard matey**.

1704 *Lond. Gaz.* 4080/3 [He] landed at the Dock-Yard at Blackwall. **1768–74** TUCKER *Lt. Nat.* (1852) II. 32 Peter the Great.. worked with a hatchet among the carpenters in our dock-yards. **1801** NELSON *Let.* 31 July (1845) 433 The Vessels should be.. ready for the Dock-yard men to be put on board. *a* **1821** KEATS *Robin Hood* 44 All his oaks, Fall'n beneath the dock-yard strokes, Have rotted on the briny seas. **1829** W. N. GLASCOCK *Sailors & Saints* III. 95 The 'Dock-yard-Maties'—a class of men, whose hostility, and turbulent insolence to naval officers.. is proverbial. **1833** MARRYAT *P. Simple* xi, The dock-yard boat with all the pay clerks and the cashier.. came. **1833** Dock-yard matey [see MATEY *sb.*]. **1837** DICKENS *Pickw.* ii, Soldiers, sailors,.. and dockyard men. **1840** THIRLWALL *Greece* VII. 297 Three dockyards were speedily established in Phœnicia. **1906** *Outlook* 20 Nov. 495/2 Dockyardmen who are in danger of losing that *otium cum dignitate* which they have regarded as their perquisite. **1909** *Pall Mall Gaz.* 12 Apr. 3/2 Naval men, or dockyard-men, which practically amounts to the same thing, raised Torpedo-boat No. 99 after she was sunk off Berry Head. **1918** 'TAFFRAIL' *Little Ship* ii. 26 The dockyard-maties had slapped on the service gray paint over coal-dust and dirt alike. **1942** N. MONSARRAT *H.M. Corvette* i. 11 Aft, the Torpedoman was arguing.. with a welder, a Clydeside dockyard-matey.

docoglossate (dɒkəʊ'glɒsət), *a.* *Zool.* [f. mod.L. *Docoglossa* (f. Gr. δοκός balk, bar + γλῶσσα tongue) + -ATE[2].] Of or pertaining to the *Docoglossa*, a group of gastropod molluscs having transverse rows of beam-like teeth on the lingual ribbon.

1884 T. GILL in *Science* IV. 335 The docoglossate Gastropoda.

docquet(t, obs. form of DOCKET.

†**doct**, *a.* *Obs. rare*[−1]. [ad. L. *doct-us*, pa. pple. of *docēre* to teach.] Learned.

1708 MOTTEUX *Rabelais* (1737) V. 233 Doct Verbocination is imbib'd.

†**doc'tiloquent**, *a.* *Obs. rare*[−0]. [f. L. *doct-us* learned + *loquent-em*, pr. pple. of *loquī* to speak; cf. L. *doctiloquus*.] 'That speaks learnedly' (Blount *Glossogr.* 1656). So **doc'tiloquous** *a.*, 'speaking learnedly' (Bailey vol. II. 1727).

doctor ('dɒktə(r)), *sb.* Forms: 4–7 doctour, (4–5 -ur, -oure, 5 doktor), 5– doctor. [a. OF. *doctor* (-*ur*, -*our*, -*eur*), ad. L. *doctor*, -*ōrem* teacher, agent-n. from *docēre* to teach.]

1. a. A teacher, instructor; one who gives instruction in some branch of knowledge, or inculcates opinions or principles. (Const. *of*.) Now *rare*.

1387 TREVISA *Higden* (Rolls) II. 43 Seynt Austyn þe firste doctour [= *prothodoctor*] of Englischemen. **1485** CAXTON *Chas. Gt.* 1 Saynt Poul, doctour of verite. **1548** UDALL, etc. *Erasm. Par. Matt.* i. 20 The heauenly doctour Christe Jesus. **1557** N. T. (Genev.) *Matt.* xxiii. 10 Be not called Doctors, for ther is but one your Doctor, and he is Christe. **1665** *Phil. Trans.* I. 73 One of the most zealous Doctors of the contrary Opinion. **1790** BURKE *Fr. Rev.* 32 These new Doctors of the rights of men. **1864** J. H. NEWMAN *Apol.* App. 77 St. Augustine.. is the doctor of the great and common view that all untruths are lies.

†**b.** *spec.* (*Sc.*) An assistant-master in a school.

1630 *Burgh Recds. Perth* in Grant *Burgh Sch. Scot.* 147. **1640** *Burgh Recds. Edin.* ibid. 147 For the tryell of the maister and doctors in teatching. **1695** SIBBALD *Autobiog.* (1834) 129 Mr. Heugh Wallace was master. Mr. Francis Cockburn, Mr. Samuel Macom and Mr. John Wardlaw were doctors of the [Edinburgh High] school.

2. a. One who, by reason of his skill in any branch of knowledge, is competent to teach it, or whose attainments entitle him to express an authoritative opinion; an eminently learned man. *arch.*

c **1340** *Cursor M.* 12577 *heading* (Fairf.), Ihesus disputed wiþ þe doctours. *c* **1391** CHAUCER *Astrol.* Prol., An introductorie aftur the statutz of owre doctours. *?a* **1400** *Morte Arth.* 145 Dukes and duspers and doctours noble. *c* **1510** MORE *Picus* Wks. 3/1 He scrupulously sought out all the famous doctours of his time. **1732** POPE *Ep. Bathurst* 1 Who shall decide, when Doctors disagree? **1841–4** EMERSON *Ess.*, *Intellect* Wks. (Bohn) I. 135 The wisest doctor is gravelled by the inquisitiveness of a child.

†**b.** *transf.* One who is eminently skilled in a particular art or craft. *Obs.*

1548 HALL *Chron.*, *Hen. V* (an. 10) 82 This kyng.. in marcial affaires a very doctor. **1602** ROWLANDS *Greenes Ghost* 18 He indeed was a doctor in his arte [of Cutpurses].

3. *spec.* applied to: **a.** *the Doctors of the Church*, certain early 'fathers' distinguished by their eminent learning, so as to have been teachers not only in the Church, but of the Church, and by their heroic sanctity; *esp.* in the Western Church, the four, Ambrose, Augustine, Jerome, Gregory (so named in the canon law), and, in the Eastern Church, the four, Athanasius, Basil, Gregory of Nazianzum, and Chrysostom. **b.** The leading Schoolmen of mediæval philosophy.

1303 R. BRUNNE *Handl. Synne* 11007 Seynt Gregory.. telleþ mo hymself a lone þan alle þe doctours do echone. **1362** LANGL. *P. Pl.* A. XI. 294 þe dougtiest doctour.. austyn þe olde and hiȝeste of þe foure. *a* **1440** *Sir Degrev.* 1447 Austyn and Gregory, Jerome and Ambrose.. the foure doctorus. **1552** ABP. HAMILTON *Catech.* (1884) 46 Autentyk doctours apprevit be the auctorite of haly kirk.. as Hierome, Ambrose.. Chrisostome. **1788** REID *Aristotle's Log.* iv. §6. 97 The Scholastic Doctors.. tortured.. the modal syllogisms. **1855** MILMAN *Lat. Chr.* XIV. iii. (1867) IX. 119 Doctors, who assumed the splendid titles of the Angelical, the Seraphic, the Irrefragable [Aquinas, Bonaventura, Alexander Hales].

4. a. One who, in any faculty or branch of learning, has attained to the highest degree conferred by a University; a title originally implying competency to teach such subject or subjects, but now merely regarded as a certificate of the highest proficiency therein.

The degree is now often conferred by Universities as an honorary compliment upon distinguished statesmen, authors, divines, etc.: *Doctor of Civil Law* by Oxford and Durham, *Doctor of Laws* by Cambridge, Dublin, etc., *Doctor of Divinity*, *Doctor of Philosophy*, etc., by many Universities. ***Lambeth Doctor***: one on whom the Archbishop of Canterbury has conferred the degree.

1377 LANGL. *P. Pl.* B. XV. 373 Doctoures of decres and of diuinitie maistres. *a* **1400–50** *Alexander* 234 A clerke.. diȝt as a Doctour in drabland wedis. **1529** MORE *Comf. agst. Trib.* II. Wks. 1170/1 You y[t] haue bene at lerning so long, and are doctor. **1551** T. WILSON *Logike* (1567) 33 a, I heard ones a doctour of Diuinitie, whiche was not so greate in knowlege as he was in title. **1654** WHITLOCK *Zootomia* 107 Many Medicasters, pretenders to Physick, buy the degree of Doctor abroad. **1684** *Lond. Gaz.* No. 1945/4 Dr. Nic. Stagins.. was.. admitted to the Degree of Doctor of Musick. **1710** HEARNE *Collect.* 4 Feb., Dr. West's (he is only a Lambeth Doctor) sermon. **1791** BOSWELL *Johnson* an. 1765, Trinity College, Dublin, at this time surprised Johnson with a spontaneous compliment of the highest academical honours, by creating him Doctor of Laws. **1843** MIALL in *Nonconf.* III. 737 To make Prince Albert a doctor of laws.

b. Prefixed, as title, to the name (now usually abbreviated *Dr.*), and in addressing a person.

c **1450** *St. Cuthbert* (Surtees) 7004 Jarow.. Whare doctour bede leuyd and dyed. **1455** *Paston Lett.* No. 257 I. 350 Oon Doktor Grene, a preest. **1501** *Bury Wills* (Camden) 90 Mast[r] Doctor Curteys, the prior of the Fryers Austyns in Norwysche. **1598** SHAKS. *Merry W.* I. iv. 3 My master, master Docter Caius. *a* **1656** BP. HALL *Rem. Wks.* (1660) 10 The Master of the Colledge Mr. Dr. Chaderton. **1778** in Boswell *Johnson* 17 April, Why, doctor, you look stout and hearty. **1882** EDNA LYALL *Donovan* iii, Dr. Tremain was standing by the window. **1895** IAN MACLAREN *Auld Lang Syne* II. v. 113 Doctor Davidson motioned to the Free Church minister to take his place at the head.

†**c.** ***Doctor of the Chair***: a professor in a university; cf. CHAIR *sb.* 6. *Obs.*

a **1634** RANDOLPH *Muses' Looking-Glass* II. iv. Wks. (1875) 213 Thou shalt be doctor o' th' chair. **1659** RUSHW. *Hist. Coll.* I. 62 A Sermon preached by Robert Abbot, Doctor of the Chair in Oxford.

5. Hence used with express or implied specification of: **a.** One who is proficient in knowledge of theology: a learned divine.

a **1375** *Lay Folks Mass Bk.* App. iv. 148 þus Doctours han I-souht. **1377** [see 4]. **1393** LANGL. *P. Pl.* C. XII. 97 For doctor he is yknowe And of scripture þe skylful. **1550** BALE *Apol.* 50 (R.) Y[e] best of your doctours in expownynge the Scriptures. **1680** OTWAY *Orphan* II. i, Thanking a surly Doctor for his Sermon. **1871** MORLEY *Voltaire* (1886) 244 He heard only the humming of the doctors as they served forth to congregations of poor men hungering for spiritual sustenance the draff of theological superstition.

b. One who is proficient in knowledge of law.

Till 1857 barristers practising in the Court of Arches were required to take the degree of doctor. For the honorary doctors of law, see 4.

1377 LANGL. *P. Pl.* B. XV. 238 þat conscience and cryst hath yknitte faste, þei vndon it vnworthily þo doctours of lawe. *c* **1460** J. RUSSELL *Bk. Nurture* 1024 Doctour of bothe lawes, beynge in science digne. **1588** J. UDALL *Diotrephes* (Arb.) 12 Why did you not rather take some doctour of the Arches? **1596** SHAKS. *Merch. V.* IV. i. 144 This Letter from Bellario doth commend A yong and Learned Doctor in our Court. **1845** M. PATTISON *Ess.* (1889) I. 23 With the gravity of a doctor expounding ecclesiastical law.

6. a. *spec.* A doctor of medicine; in popular current use, applied to any medical practitioner. Also, a wizard or medicine-man in a primitive tribe.

[**1377** LANGL. *P. Pl.* B. XVIII. 362 þe bitternesse þat þow hast browe brouke it þi-seluen, þat art doctour of deth, drynke þat þow madest! *c* **1386** CHAUCER *Prol.* 411 Wiþ vs þere was a Doctur of Phesike.] *c* **1400** *Lanfranc's Cirurg.* 73 Of rasis auicen & galion & of oþere doctouris. **1598** SHAKS. *Merry W.* III. i. 106 Shall I loose my Doctor? No: hee giues me the Potions and the Motions. **1699** DRYDEN *Ep. to J. Driden* 71 So liv'd our Sires, ere doctors learn'd to kill. **1725** DE FOE *Voy. round World* (1840) 182 Our doctors themselves (so we call the surgeons at sea). **1783** AINSWORTH *Lat. Dict.* (Morell) II, *Veterinarius*, a farrier, a horse doctor. **1858** *Compendium of Kaffir Laws & Customs* 123 Doctors are not entitled to fees, except a cure is performed, or the patient relieved. **1872** GEO. ELIOT *Middlem.* xv, A common country doctor. **1884** GILMOUR *Mongols* 180 They apply to the missionary in his capacity of doctor.. and.. want him only in so far as he is a doctor.

b. *fig.* Applied humorously to any agent that gives or preserves health; esp. in the West Indies, S. Africa, and W. Australia, a cool sea-breeze which usually prevails during part of the day in summer. *colloq.*

1660 HOWELL *Parly of Beasts* 23 (D.) After those two, Doctor Diet and Doctor Quiet, Doctor Merriman is requisit to preserve health. **1740** *Hist. Jamaica* ii. 21 The People here give it [the sea-breeze] the name of Doctor, and truly it deserves the Title. **1823** *Spirit Pub. Jrnls.* (1824) 55 Each horseman gulped down a doctor, to counteract the effects of the raw morning air. **1844** *Knickerbocker* XXIII. 46 [In St. Augustine] we were beginning the summer custom of gathering every morning to meet the 'doctor' (sea-breeze) on the square. **1856** F. FLEMING *Southern Africa* iv. 62 The South-easter, from blowing all pestilent vapours and effluvia out to sea.. has obtained the local epithet of '*the Doctor*'. **1861**, etc. [see *Cape doctor*, CAPE *sb.*[2] 4].

c. One who mends or repairs; esp. with a qualifying word; also *transf.*; *spec.*, see quot. 1899. *colloq.*

1899 *Daily News* 2 Mar. 9/1 The owner, nervous about a vessel, wants a further insurance, and the 'doctor' procures it for him... The 'doctor' is a broker who deals particularly with the overdue vessels. **1922** A. HADDON *Green Room Gossip* iv. 97 Miss Platt is a professional play-reader and 'play doctor'. **1938** M. LANE *E. Wallace* IV. i. 319 Du Maurier was a skilful 'play doctor', and the final script.. bore only a family resemblance to the drama which Edgar had written at top speed.

d. Colloq. phr. ***what the doctor ordered***, transf. and fig.: something beneficial or desirable; ***you are*** (freq. ***you're***) ***the doctor***: you are the expert; it is for you to decide.

1907 'O. HENRY' *Trimmed Lamp* (1915) 95 You are the lady doctor. **1914** *Dialect Notes* IV. 71 She thought Ezry was jest *what the doctor ordered*. **1920** R. MACAULAY *Potterism* I. iv. 50 Very well, mother. You're the doctor. [**1922** JOYCE *Ulysses* 257 And what did the doctor order today?.. I think I'll trouble you for some fresh water and a half glass of whisky.] **1948** G. VIDAL *City & Pillar* I. i. 16 The waiter brought her a drink. 'Just what the doctor ordered,' she said, smiling at him. **1950** WODEHOUSE *Nothing Serious* 61 'You admired my little friend?' 'She is what the doctor ordered.' **1962** 'H. HOWARD' *Double Finesse* ix. 106 You're the doctor. Go ahead and open it. **1969** C. YOUNG *Todd Dossier* 120 The thing to do now was relax.. and forget about it. 'Okay, you're the doctor,' Charlie said.

7. *transf.* A name given to various mechanical appliances, usually for curing or removing defects, regulating, adjusting, or feeding.

a. *Calico-printing* and *Paper-making*. A thin blade of metal used to remove superfluous colour, loose threads, dust, etc. from the cylinder (a calico-printing machine has a ***colour-doctor***, a ***lint-doctor***, and a ***cleaning-doctor***; see quots.). **b.** A tool used for soldering. **c.** An auxiliary steam-engine for feeding the boiler; a donkey-engine. **d.** *Electro-plating*. **e.** *Photo-gravure*. Also ***doctor blade***.

1796 *Specif. Wild & Ridge's Patent* No. 2134 (*title*), Manufacturing.. steel doctors for printers. **1833** J. HOLLAND *Manuf. Metal* II. 316 A heated doctor, or soldering bit. **1837** WHITTOCK *Bk. Trades* (1842) 96 (Calico-printer) The polished surface is cleared by the scraper called the 'doctor'. **1874** KNIGHT *Dict. Mech.*, *Doctor*.. (*Calico-printing*).. The cleaning-doctor, which wipes clean the surface of the roller. **1875** *Ure's Dict. Arts* I. 590 The lint-doctor, whose office it is to remove any fibres which may have come off the calico in the act of printing. *Ibid.* 603 The superfluous colour is.. wiped off by the colour doctors.. These doctors are thin blades of steel or brass, which are mounted in doctor-shears, or plates of metal screwed together with bolts. **1886** A. WATT *Electro-Deposition* xiv. 184 The pad, or 'doctor', as it is sometimes called, is dipped in the gold solution and applied to the part to be gilt. **1926** C. N. BENNETT *Elem. Photogravure* xviii. 117 Rapid rotary gravure [was] made definitely commercial, by the introduction of what is known as 'doctor wiping'. *Ibid.* 118 One side of the doctor is clamped firmly in a 'carriage' or holder, while the free, or 'wiping', edge is caused to press upon the printing cylinder at a slight angle. **1930** H. M. CARTWRIGHT *Photogravure* vii. 92 The cylinder receives ink from the inking or 'furnishing' roller... The ink is removed from the cylinder surface by means of the doctor. **1943** *Gloss. Terms Electr. Engin.* (*B.S.I.*) 101 *Doctor*, an anode covered with fabric or sponge saturated with the plating solution and applied locally to the article to be plated, which is made the cathode. **1961** T. LANDAU *Encycl. Librarianship* (ed. 2) 119/2 *Doctor blade*, a flexible knife which removes surplus ink from engraved plate in intaglio printing, *e.g.* photogravure. **1967** KARCH & BUBER *Offset Processes* 536 *Doctor blade*, a 'knife' of rigid plastic or thin sheet-metal which presses against the gravure press cylinder, and which wipes away ink from the surface of the cylinder.

8. A fish of the genus *Acanthurus*: also called ***doctor-fish*** and ***surgeon-fish***: see quot. 1850.

1833 *Penny Cycl.* I. 68 The name of 'Doctors', by which they are well known to the English sailors and colonists. **1834** M. G. LEWIS *Jrnl. W. Ind.* 50 Its name is the 'Doctor Fish'. *c* **1850** *Nat. Encycl.* I. 97 Termed Doctors.. because they are armed on each side of the tail with a sharp moveable spine like a lancet, which they use with great effect.

9. *Angling.* A kind of artificial fly.

1860 C. M. YONGE *Hopes & Fears* I. II. iv. 229 The doctor .. and all her other radiant fabrications of .. feathers. **1867** F. FRANCIS *Angling* x. (1880) 341 The Doctor.. is a very general and deserved favourite. **1895** *Daily News* 22 Aug. 6/2 With fine tackle and a very small Blue Doctor.

10. Something used to 'doctor' or adulterate food or drink; e.g. a liquor mixed with inferior wine to make it more palatable, or with light-coloured wine (as sherry) to darken it; hence, a name for brown sherry. (*slang* or *colloq.*)

1770 C. JENNER *Placid Man* I. 84 The governor was as happy if he drank his Doctor next to a man who talked to him upon any thing. **1785** GROSE *Dict. Vulg. Tongue* (Farmer), *Doctor*, a composition used by distillers to make spirits appear stronger than they really are. **1828** G. SMEATON *Doings in London* (Farmer), Maton, in his 'Tricks of Bakers Unmasked', says alum, which is called the Doctor .. is sold to the bakers at fourpence per pound.

11. (*Naut.*) A ship's cook; (*U.S.* and *Australian*) the men's cook at a station or camp. (*colloq.*)

1821 *Massachusetts Spy* 1 Aug. (Th.), The cook, at sea, is generally called doctor. **1835** J. H. INGRAHAM *South-West* I. vi. 69 All [the crew] neatly dressed in white trousers and shirts, even to the sable 'Doctor' and his 'sub'. **1860** BARTLETT *Dict. Amer.*, *Doctor*, the cook on board a ship. **1867** SMYTH *Sailor's Word-bk.*, *Doctor*.. a jocular name for the ship's cook. **1892** LENTZNER *Australian Word-bk.* 20 *Doctor, the* (up-country), the men's cook on a station. **1893** FUNK *Standard Dict.*, *Doctor*.. 6. (Local, U.S.) The cook in a logging-camp. **1902** W. S. WALKER *Zealandia's Guerdon* v. 55 'Cook-shop for all hands'... Close by this building is the 'doctor's'—cook's—residence.

12. *Old slang.* A false or loaded die.

a **1700** B. E. *Dict. Cant. Crew*, *Doctor*, a false Die, that will run but two or three Chances. *They put the Doctor upon him*, they cheated him with false Dice. **1721** CIBBER *Woman's Wit* I, The old Rogue.. wou'd ha' put the Doctor upon me .. (unknown to him) I flung away the Doctor, and clapt into the Box a Pair of true Mathematics. **1749** FIELDING *Tom Jones* VIII. xii. **1774** FOOTE *Cozeners* I. Wks. 1799 II. 153. **1801** *Sporting Mag.* XVIII. 7 Loaded a couple of the Doctors for throwing a seven and nine.

13. *Comb.*, as ***doctor-farrier***, ***-like*** (adj. and adv.), ***-maker***, ***-monger***; **doctor-box**, a form of colour-box in a calico-printing machine, of which the 'doctor' (7 a) forms the bottom; **doctor's curse** (see quot.); **doctor-fish** = sense 8; **doctor-gum**, 'a South-American gum, also called *Log-gum* usually considered to be a product of *Rhus metopium*' (Cent. Dict.); **doctor's gum**, the West Indian tree *Rhus metopium*; also, see quot. 1887; **doctor-shears** (see 7 a); **doctor's stuff** (*colloq.*), medicine, physic (also ***doctor-stuff***). See also DOCTORS' COMMONS.

1821 COL. HAWKER *Diary* (1893) I. 226, I.. took the *doctor's curse, or, in other words, a dose of calomel. **1638** FORD *Fancies* v. ii, Some *doctor-farriers are of opinion that the mare may cast a foal. **1858** *Doctor's gum [see HOG GUM]. **1887** C. A. MOLONEY *Forestry W. Afr.* 279 Hog or Doctor's gum, Gamboge tree (*Symphonia globulifera*). **1549** CHALONER *Erasm. on Folly* M j b, This Definicion.. was not ..*doctourlike sette foorth by hym. **1654** GATAKER *Disc. Apol.* 41, I told them merilie, They must first make me a Doctor-like maintenance, ere I would take the degree of Doctor. **1884** *Chr. World* 10 Jan. 17/5 A '*doctor-maker' is the maker of a particular metal plate called a 'doctor'. *c* **1449** PECOCK *Repr.* I. xvi. 87 Summe of þou ben clepid *Doctour mongers. **1772** GRAVES *Spirit. Quix.* x. xvii. (D.), The man said.. he could not take *Doctor's stuff, if he died for it. **1856** KANE *Arct. Expl.* I. xv. 171 Like doctor-stuff generally, it is not as appetizing as desirable.

Hence (*nonce-wds.*) **'doctordom**, the world of doctors, doctors collectively. **'doctorhead**, **'doctorhood**, the position or rank of a doctor. **'doctorless** *a.*, without a doctor.

1541 BARNES *Wks.* (1573) 542/2 Thinketh your doctourhed that the children of Israell.. could not haue made.. excuse? **1849** THACKERAY *Pendennis* vi, A match for all the Doctors in Doctordom. **1870** *Daily News* 5 Dec., The shibboleth of doctorhood. **1885** *Athenæum* 12 Dec. 764 Our butcherless, bakerless.. doctorless.. and altogether comfortless jungle.

doctor ('dɒktə(r)), *v. colloq.* [f. prec. sb.]

1. *trans.* To confer the degree or title of Doctor upon; to make a Doctor.

1599 SANDYS *Europæ Spec.* (1632) 117 Which Church hath now fully.. delivered her mind in the late Councell of Trent; whereto all that are solemnly doctored in Italy must subscribe. *a* **1744** POPE *Let. to Swift* Wks. 1751 IX. 341 (Jod.), I will be doctored with you, or not at all. **1873** LOWELL *Lett.* (1894) II. 108, I have been over to Oxford to be doctored, and had a very pleasant time of it. **1891** *Sat. Rev.* 20 June 730/1 Cambridge on Tuesday 'doctored' among others her new High Steward.

2. a. To treat, as a doctor or physician; to administer medicine or medical treatment to.

1737 BRACKEN *Farriery Impr.* (1757) II. 47 Rather than suffer a good serviceable Creature to be doctor'd out of his Life by the common Farrier. **1832** COL. HAWKER *Diary* (1893) II. 38 Brodie.. prescribed for me and sent me off to doctor myself. **1842** C. WHITEHEAD *R. Savage* (1845) I. xi. 156 We'll doctor him up while you're gone.

b. *transf.* To repair, patch up, set to rights.

1829 ALFORD in *Life* (1873) 50 Wasted most of the morning in doctoring a clock. **1833** R. H. FROUDE *Rem.* (1838) I. 317 Can these [verses] be doctored into any thing available?

c. To castrate (an animal).

1902 F. SIMPSON *Cats* ii. 30 It is necessary.. to have your male cat doctored when he arrives at years of discretion. **1958** *Amer. Speech* XXXIII. 165 *Doctor*, to castrate [in Australian stockmen's language]. **1960** T. CLARKE in J. Pudney *Pick of Today's Short Stories* XI. 80 If that cat's a Tom,.. I'd better get it doctored. **1970** C. KERSH *Aggravations of Minnie Ashe* v. 63 He had been paid 'good English money' to doctor our cat.

3. *fig.* To treat so as to alter the appearance, flavour, or character of; to disguise, falsify, tamper with, adulterate, sophisticate, 'cook'.

1774 FOOTE *Cozeners* III. Wks. 1799 II. 188, I wish we had time though to doctor his face. **1820** *Edin. Rev.* XXXIII. 138 Directions for.. doctoring all sorts of wines. **1847** DE QUINCEY *Sp. Mil. Nun* xxi. (1853) 66 Modes of doctoring dice. **1866** *Pall Mall G.* 3 Jan., A serious doubt arises.. as to the trustworthiness of.. the narratives thus doctored. **1884** *St. James's Gaz.* 5 Dec. 6/1 By a few touches of a file on the milled edge, a coin can be so 'doctored' as to fall almost invariably heads or tails at will.

4. *intr.* **a.** To practise as a physician.

(Usually in *vbl. sb.* or *pr. pple.*)

1865 MRS. WHITNEY *Gayworthys* ii, Preaching ran in the King family; as politics or doctoring, sailoring or soldiering run in some others. **1885** *Harper's Mag.* Jan. 205/1, I know more about doctoring.

b. To take medicine, undergo medical treatment.

In recent Dicts.

Hence **'doctored** *ppl. a.*, **'doctoring** *vbl. sb.*; also **'doctorer**, one who doctors.

1533 SIR T. MORE *Apol.* xlv. Wks. 915/2 If this pacifyer's doctoring [i.e. citing of doctors] wer a good profe. **1832** BABBAGE *Econ. Manuf.* xv. (ed. 3) 135 A mode of preparing old clover and trefoil seeds by a process called 'doctoring'. **1851** THACKERAY *Eng. Hum.* iii. (1858) 143 Most men's letters.. are doctored compositions. **1882** T. W. KNOX in *Harper's Mag.* Dec. 38/1 The high-priced wines.. need no doctoring. **1885** MRS. C. PRAED *Head Station* 15 Serving out doctored grog. **1887** THRING in *Jrnl. Educ.* June 297 Any master of language, as distinct from a doctorer of words.

doctoral ('dɒktərəl), *a.* [f. as prec. + -AL[1]: cf. F. *doctoral*, It. *dottorale*.]

1. Of or belonging to a doctor (i.e. a man of eminent learning, a professional teacher, or one who has received the degree of Doctor).

1563-87 FOXE *A. & M.* Let. Bp. Hereford an. 1391 (R.), The golden laurell of teaching doctorall, is not from aboue indifferently euery mans gift. **1644** MILTON *Jdgm. Bucer* Wks. 1738 I. 278 O that I could set him living before ye in that Doctoral Chair, where once the learnedest of England, thought it no disparagement to sit at his feet! **1651** BAXTER *Inf. Bapt.* 121 The Authority of Synods in matters of Faith is Doctorall and declarative, and not decisively Judiciall. **1849** MACAULAY *Hist. Eng.* II. 277 To receive from an university the privilege of wearing the doctoral scarlet.

†**b.** Holding the position of a doctor or teacher.

a **1603** T. CARTWRIGHT *Confut. Rhem. N.T.* (1618) 575 When the elder Doctors.. faile them, they might goe to Sorbona.. to furnish them of Doctorall witnesses. **1604** TOOKER *Fabrique of Ch.* 55 The Elders Doctorall or Pastorall are worthy of double honour.

2. Belonging to or characteristic of a physician or medical man. (*nonce-use.*)

1892 STEVENSON *Across the Plains* 17 A native.. pronounced it, with a doctoral air, 'a fever and ague morning'.

Hence **'doctorally** *adv.*, in the manner of a doctor; as a doctor.

1580 G. HARVEY *Three Witie Lett.* 12 Very solemnly pawsing a whyle, most gravely, and doctorally [I] proceeded as followeth. **1627** HAKEWILL *Apol.* IV. x. §2 (1630) 428 The Physitions dayly resorted to him to touch his pulse, and consider in Colledge of his desease, doctorally at their departure. *a* **1660** HAMMOND *Wks.* IV. 671 (R.) Sinning doctorally, and magisterially.. even setting up a school of Atheism.

doctorand ('dɒktərænd). Also in L. form **docto'randus** (pl. -i). [G., ad. med.L.] A candidate for a doctor's degree.

1912 R. S. RAIT *Life Med. Univ.* ii. 32 When our young English Doctorand received the permission of his Rector to proceed to his degree. **1921** *Edin. Rev.* Jan. 72 Increasing numbers of *doctorandi* sought admission to his laboratory.

doctorate ('dɒktərət), *sb.*[1] [ad. med.L. *doctōrāt-us*, f. *doctor* DOCTOR: see -ATE[1]. Cf. F. *doctorat* (16th c.).] The degree of Doctor.

1676 W. ROW *Contn. Blair's Autobiog.* xii. (1848) 373 Make the doctorate a stirrup to mount him to Prelacy. **1775** JOHNSON *Let. to Boswell* 7 Feb., No man not a Doctor can.. practice Physick but by Licence particularly granted. The Doctorate is a licence of itself. **1858** MASSON *Milton* I. 119 The Doctorates of Law and Medicine. **1882-3** SCHAFF *Encycl. Relig. Knowl.* I. 651 The evolution of the doctorate as a third university degree above that of master cannot be distinctly traced.

†**'doctorate,** *ppl. a.* and *sb.*[2] *Obs.* [ad. med. or mod.L. *doctōrāt-us* made a doctor: cf. *doctōrandus* in Du Cange.] **a.** *ppl. a.* Made a doctor. **b.** *sb.* One who has received the degree of Doctor.

1591 GREENE *Disc. Coosnage* II. (1592) 20 One.. that for his skill might haue been Doctorat in his misterie. **1651** *Life Father Sarpi* (1676) 15 Master, (which is the Title of the Doctorates in Theology).

doctorate ('dɒktəreɪt), *v.* Now *rare.* [f. med. or mod.L. *doctōrāre* to make doctor: see -ATE[3].]

trans. To confer the degree of Doctor upon; also *absol.* to confer the degree of Doctor.

1611 FLORIO, *Addottoráre*, to take or giue the degree of a doctor, to doctorate. **1637-50** ROW *Hist. Kirk* (1842) 261 They behoued to be doctorated. *a* **1661** FULLER *Worthies* I. (1662) 237 Going afterwards to Oxford he was doctorated in Divinity. **1774** WARTON *Hist. Eng. Poetry* III. xl. 395 Afterwards doctorated in medicine at Oxford. **1886** LAURIE *Universities* vii. 123 Even after Salernum had a teacher of law.. it could not doctorate in law.

doctoress: see DOCTRESS.

doctorial (dɒk'tɔərɪəl), *a.* [f. L. type **doctōri-us* (cf. *senātōrius*, *tūtōrius*, etc.) + -AL[1].] Of or belonging to a doctor: = DOCTORAL.

1729 *Wodrow Corr.* (1843) III. 453, I cannot account for the doctorial degrees given all to Non-subscribers by the College of Edinburgh. *c* **1730** J. EARLE in *Calamy's Life* II. 513 So, when our Universities Doctorial honours give, 'Tis not our merit they declare, But their prerogative. **1843** LEFEVRE *Life Trav. Physic.* I. I. vi. 105 Had not my doctorial title been specified in my passport.

Hence **doc'torially** *adv.*, as a doctor.

1858 TROLLOPE *Dr. Thorne* iii, That a doctor should not laugh at all when called in to act doctorially.

doctorism ('dɒktərɪz(ə)m). [f. DOCTOR *sb.* + -ISM.] The principles or practice of doctors; a saying characteristic of a doctor.

1661 K. W. *Conf. Charac.*, *Detracting Empirick* (1860) 66 Hocus pocusses of doctorisme. **1825** LOCKHART *Let.* 19 Nov. in Smiles *Life J. Murray* (1891) II. xxvii. 224 The Doctors uttering doctorisms on the occasion.

'doctorize, *v. rare.* [f. as prec. + -IZE.] *trans.* To confer the degree of Doctor upon; to doctor.

1600 E. BLOUNT *Hosp. Incur. Fooles* 13, I meane to returne to my towne of Tripalda, doctorized thus by your grace and favour. **1850** PRESCOTT *Let. to G. Ticknor* 26 June in *Life*, Lord Northampton and I were Doctorized in due form.

Hence **doctori'zation**, the conferring of a doctor's degree.

In recent Dicts.

doctorly ('dɒktəlɪ), *a.* [f. as prec. + -LY[1].] Like, characteristic of, or befitting a doctor; having the position or character of a doctor.

1563-87 FOXE *A. & M.* Life Tindale (R.), The doctourly prelates. *Ibid.* (1596) 1526 (R.) This doctourlie disputation. **1657** TOMLINSON *Renou's Disp.* Pref., With a Doctorly arrogance. **1888** FREEMAN in W. R. W. Stephens *Life & Lett.* (1895) II. 386, I am still writing upstairs, in a gown scarlet but not doctorly.

Doctor Martens. Also Marten's, etc. [f. the name of its inventor: see quot. 1977.] A proprietary name for a type of heavy laced walking boot or shoe with a cushioned sole. Also **Doc Martens.**

1977 *Trade Marks Jrnl.* 23 Mar. 599/1 Dr. Martens... Use claimed from the year 1965... 998,025 Soles for boots and for shoes. Ing. Herbert Funck and Klaus Maertens.. Munchen-Pasing, Haidelweg 20, and Seeshaupt (Oberbayern), An der Ach, Federal Republic of Germany. **1978** *New Musical Express* 3 June 54/2, I imagine the band felt well pleased driving home at three in the morning while all the non-sexist ladies were tucked up in bed with their Doctor Martins and old mens shirts. **1983** *N.Y. Times* 11 Oct. C11/1 The new look is.. everything in gray and black, with stiletto heels on girls and Doctor Marten's ankle boots on guys. **1984** S. TOWNSEND *Growing Pains A. Mole* 156 Today I drew some money out of my Building Society account, and bought my first pair of Doc Marten's. They are bully-boy brown and have got ten rows of lace holes.

Doctors' Commons. [See COMMONS 3 b.] The common table and dining-hall of the Association or College of Doctors of Civil Law in London; hence, the buildings occupied and used by these as an incorporated Society and now the name of the site of these, to the south of St. Paul's Cathedral.

The Society was formed in 1509, by civilians entitled to plead in the Court of Arches. In 1768 they were incorporated under the name of 'the College of Doctors of Laws [of Oxford and Cambridge] exercent in the Ecclesiastical and Admiralty Courts'. In the buildings of Doctors' Commons were held five courts, viz. the Court of Arches, Prerogative Court of Canterbury, Court of

Faculties or Dispensations, Consistory Court, and High Court of Admiralty; the business included all matters of ecclesiastical law, prosecutions for heresy, divorce suits, licences for marriage, testamentary affairs, Admiralty and Prize cases, etc. The Society was dissolved in 1858 and the buildings were taken down in 1867. Literary references to Doctors' Commons in later times usually refer to the registration or probate of wills, to marriage licences, or to proceedings for divorce.

1680 J. GODOLPHIN *Repertor. Canon.* (ed. 2) App. 10 Doctors of the Civil Laws to the Number of Thirteen in all, assembled together in the common Dining-Hall of Doctors Commons in London. *a* **1690** BP. T. BARLOW *Rem.* 365 (T.) A dignitary of our church.. had been at Doctors-Commons; and there fee'd one of the doctors, who is a judge of one of those courts where matrimonial causes are consulable. **1705** HICKERINGILL *Priest-cr.* IV. (1721) 210 Another calls to the Bumbailiffs, the Jaylors, Doctor's-Commons, and the Hangman. **1708** MRS. CENTLIVRE *Busie Body* IV. iv, With this Proviso that he To-morrow Morning weds me. He is now gone to Doctors-Commons for a Licence. **1813** BYRON *Waltz* xiii, Search Doctors' Commons. **1819** —— *Juan* I. xxxvi, No choice was left his feelings or his pride, Save death or Doctors' Commons. **1854** PHILLIMORE *Internat. Law* Pref. (1873) 37.

doctorship ('dɒktəʃɪp). [f. DOCTOR *sb.* + -SHIP.]

1. The degree of Doctor; = DOCTORATE *sb.*[1]

1586 FERNE *Blaz. Gentrie* 33 Invested with the degree of Doctorship. **1647** CLARENDON *Hist. Reb.* I. §189 After he had received all the graces and degrees, the proctorship and the doctorship. **1807** W. TAYLOR in *Ann. Rev.* V. 178 They coveted doctorship. **1891** *Nation* (N.Y.) 17 Dec. 464/3 A thesis written for the doctorship in letters.

2. The position, character, or function of a doctor, teacher, or learned man; teaching, instruction; eminent learning or scholarship.

1598 FLORIO, *Dottoraggine*, doctorship. *a* **1603** T. CARTWRIGHT *Confut. Rhem. N.T.* (1618) 299 They were taught of the Holy Ghost, through the immediate Mastership or Doctorship of Christ. **1739** 'R. BULL' tr. *Dedekindus' Grobianus* 252 Your Worship and your Doctorship display. **1838** *Fraser's Mag.* XVII. 703, I must here break off, fascinating as is German doctorship, soothing as is German dullness.

3. The function or practice of a physician; medical skill or attendance.

1640 BROME *Antipodes* Epil., Whether my cure be perfect yet or no, It lies not in my doctor-ship to know. **1856** *Tait's Mag.* XXIII. 515 Would the sick be less likely to recover.. under gratuitous doctorship?

4. The personality or dignity of a doctor; used humorously or ironically as a title.

1610 BP. HALL *Apol. Brownists* 25 Why then doth his Doctor-shippe parallell these two? **1709** *Brit. Apollo* II. No. 19. 3/2 A poor Fidler.. Your Doctorship here does Petition. **1823** *Examiner* 787/2 His Reverend Doctorship.

doctress ('dɒktrɪs), **doctoress** ('dɒktərɪs). Also 7 doctrisse. [f. DOCTOR: prob. in part a. F. *doctoresse* (15th c.), or repr. a mod.L. **doctrissa*; see -ESS.] A female doctor. (Now only used when sex is emphasized; in which case also *woman-doctor*, *lady-doctor*, are more common.)

1. A female teacher; a woman of eminent learning; a woman who has a doctoral degree. ?*Obs.*

(In the last sense, *doctor* is now applied to both sexes.)

α. **1549** CHALONER *Erasm. on Folly* R iv a, I must be borne with, beyng but a younge doctresse. **1612** CHAPMAN *Widdowes T.* Plays 1873 III. 29 Thou speak'st like a Doctrisse in thy facultie. **1635** A. STAFFORD *Fem. Glory* (1869) 124 Who being a Doctresse, scorn'd not to be a Disciple. **1741** LADY POMFRET *Lett.* (1805) III. 179 The famous doctress signora Laura Bassi. **1882** *Knowledge* No. 17. 362 Doctress Kingsford.. and some of her *confrères* appear to misinterpret the position which I have assumed.

β. **1626** tr. *Boccalini* 71 (T.) Glorying.. to be called the doctoress of all nations. **1689** EVELYN *Let. to Pepys* 12 Aug., Hellen Cornaro.. received the degree of Doctoresse at Padua.

b. Applied to things personified as feminine.

1577 STANYHURST *Descr. Irel.* in *Holinshed* VI. Ep. Ded., The learned.. adiudged an historie to be the life of memorie, the doctresse of behaviour. **1589** *Almond for Parrat* 7 That long tongd doctresse Dame Law.

2. A female physician or medical practitioner.

α. **1577** B. GOOGE *Heresbach's Husb.* (1586) 191 b, The women.. take upon them to bee great doctresses in physicke. **1718** QUINCY *Compl. Disp.* 104 Shavings of Hartshorn is much more in Esteem amongst Family Doctresses. **1801** BLOOMFIELD *Rural T.* (1802) 35 His Wife, the Doctress of the neighb'ring Poor. **1879** MISS DRURY *Called Resc.* I. vi. 148 Her young friend's skill as a bird and dog doctress.

β. **1683** TRYON *Way to Health* 66 Unless the excellent Lady Sobriety be their Doctoress. **1830** *Fraser's Mag.* I. 34 Let the healing doctoress come.

3. *humorously.* A doctor's wife or daughter. (Cf. Ger. *Frau Doktorin.*)

1748 GRAY *Let. to Dr. T. Wharton* Wks. 1884 II. 185 After having made my compliments to the god-mothers of the little Doctress. **1810** *Sporting Mag.* XXXV. 8 The doctor.. came accompanied by his lady Mrs. Doctoress Savage. **1870** MISS BROUGHTON *Red as Rose* I. 253 The Doctor and the Doctress are issuing from the brass-knockered hall door.

†**doc'trice.** *Obs.* [ad. L. *doctrix*, *-trīc-em* female teacher, fem. of *doctor*; perh. through an obs. F. **doctrice.*] A female teacher: in quots. used of things personified; = prec. 1 b.

c **1450** tr. *De Imitatione* III. lx, þi grace.. is maistresse of trouþe, doctrice of discipline, liȝt of þe herte. **1548** UDALL *Erasm. Par. Luke* i. 27 The Jewish tongue.. being.. the doctrice and auauncer of carnall obseruaunces. **1577** J. KNEWSTUB *Confut. Heresies* (1579) 18 a, Marie.. signifieth with him a doctrice.

†**'doctrinable,** *a. Obs. rare.* [f. DOCTRINE *sb.* or *v.* + -ABLE.] Fit for instruction; instructive.

1581 SIDNEY *Apol. Poetrie* (Arb.) 36 Then certainely is more doctrinable the fained Cirus of Xenophon then the true Cyrus in Iustine.

doctrinaire (dɒktrɪ'nɛə(r)), *sb.* (*a.*) [a. F. *doctrinaire* (14th c.), ad. L. type **doctrīnārius*, f. *doctrīna* DOCTRINE: see -ARY.] **A.** *sb.*

1. *Fr. Hist.* One of a political party which arose in France soon after 1815, 'having for their object and doctrine the establishment and preservation of constitutional government, and the reconciliation of authority and liberty, royalty and national representation.' (Townsend *Manual of Dates.*)

They were looked upon by members of the two extreme parties as speculative politicians holding a 'doctrine' not within the range of practical politics.

1820 *Edin. Rev.* XXXIV. 38 (Stanf.) There is at Paris a small set of speculative politicians called *doctrinaires.* **1834** *Spectator* 15 Nov. 1086/2 Do not be cajoled by any stupid stories.. about the Doctrinaires going out of office on any question of principle. **1848** W. H. KELLY tr. *L. Blanc's Hist. Ten Y.* II. 296 M. Guizot.. was a doctrinaire. But though that designation had no political meaning; though it expressed a manner of being, rather than a manner of thinking, still there adhered to it some indescribable tincture of unpopularity which was totally indelible.

2. Hence, One who holds some doctrine or theory which he tries to apply without sufficient regard to practical considerations; a pedantic theorist. (Often applied as a term of reproach by 'practical' men, to those whom they consider talking or writing theorists.)

1831 *Edin. Rev.* LII. 454 (Stanf.) A system may be the truest possible whilst argued on *in vacuo*, in the cabinet of a *Doctrinaire.* **1859** HELPS *Friends in C.* Ser. II. II. x. 265 The way to answer these doctrinaires is to turn to facts. **1871** GR. DUFF *Teachings Cobden*, Those are only justly called doctrinaires who insist on acting in season and out of season upon the doctrines which they profess. **1887** JESSOPP *Arcady* vii. 197 They got astride of this favourite hobby-horse of the doctrinaires. **1888** LOWELL *Pr. Wks.* (1890) II. 193 Practical politicians, as they call themselves,.. have substituted *doctrinaire* for *pedant* as the term of reproach.

B. *adj.* Pertaining to, or of the character of, a doctrinaire; wedded to a particular doctrine or theory and seeking to apply it in all circumstances; merely theoretical or speculative.

1834 *Spectator* 22 Nov. 1112/2 A Cabinet.. with an old.. employé of the Empire at the head, and a Doctrinaire Minister of Justice at the tail. **1873** H. SPENCER *Stud. Sociol.* xv. 362 The re-iterations of doctrinaire politicians. **1879** M. PATTISON *Milton* 120 Would Milton take his stand upon doctrinaire republicanism? **1880** DISRAELI *Endym.* i, Don't you be too doctrinaire.. you and I are practical men.

doctrinairism (,dɒktrɪ'nɛərɪz(ə)m). [f. prec. + -ISM.] The principles or practice of a doctrinaire; pedantic adhesion to a doctrine or theory without regard to practical considerations; doctrinarianism.

1836 R. H. FROUDE in *J. H. Newman's Lett.* (1891) II. 151 The imputation of a little doctrinaireism. **1837** *Tait's Mag.* IV. 454 Eclecticism, or Doctrinairism, is a philosophy marvellously suited to profit from such circumstances. **1852** *Fraser's Mag.* XLVI. 353 The largeness of his views saved him from mere doctrinairism. **1878** SEELEY in *Macm. Mag.* Jan. 179/1 The same public which despises doctrinairism in politics, is just as decided and united in despising everything but doctrinairism in religion.

doctrinal ('dɒktrɪnəl, dɒk'traɪnəl), *a.* and *sb.* [The sb. was a. F. *doctrinal* (13th c. in Littré); the adj. was perh. more directly ad. late L. *doctrīnāl-is* (Isidore), f. *doctrīna* learning, doctrine: see -AL[1].

The historical pronunciation, from L. *doctrīnālis*, Fr. and ME. *doctri'nal*, is '*doctrinal* (so Bailey, Todd); *doc'trīnal* (J.) passes over the actual L., Fr. and ME. words, to reach the ulterior *doctrīna.*]

A. *adj.*

1. Of or pertaining to doctrine; containing or inculcating a doctrine or doctrines. ***Doctrinal Puritans***, those whose puritanism had reference to doctrines rather than discipline or ceremonial.

1570 LEVINS *Manip.* 14/15 Doctrinall, *doctrinalis.* **1611** BIBLE *Transl. Pref.* 11 Not in doctrinall points that concerne saluation. **1647** CLARENDON *Hist. Reb.* I. §191 He had some doctrinal Opinions which they liked not. **1732** NEAL *Hist. Purit.* I. 579 The Calvinists were.. branded with the character of Doctrinal Puritans. **1751** JENNINGS & DODDRIDGE *Pref. to Watts' Improv. Mind* II, A doctrinal controversy. **1856** FROUDE *Hist. Eng.* I. 115 If he believed that in their doctrinal conservatism they knew and meant what they were saying.

†**b.** Derived from instruction. *Obs. rare.*

1628 HOBBES *Thucyd.* II. xxxix, When.. upon natural rather than doctrinal valour [μὴ μετὰ νόμων τὸ πλεῖον ἢ τρόπων ἀνδρίας] we come to undertake any danger.

†**2.** Serving to teach or instruct; instructive, didactic. *Obs.*

1597 HOOKER *Eccl. Pol.* v. xxi. §3 The word of God.. serueth then only in the nature of a doctrinall instrument. *a* **1632** G. HERBERT *Country Parson* xxviii, In a doctrinal way, saying to the contemner, Alas, why do you thus? **1641** MILTON *Ch. Govt.* II. (1851) 146 Whether those Dramatick constitutions, wherein Sophocles and Euripides raigne shall be found more doctrinal and exemplary.

B. *sb.*

†**1.** The title of a text-book on grammar by Alex. de Villedieu; by extension, a book of instruction in any subject; a text-book. *Obs.*

c **1450** *Cov. Myst.* 189 In alle this scyens is non us lyke, In Caton, Gryscysme, nor Doctrynal [*rime* over alle]. **1481-3** [see CATON]. **1509** BARCLAY *Shyp of Folys* (1874) I. 144 If he have onys red the olde doctrinall [*rime* all]. **1531** ELYOT *Gov.* I. xiii, Comedies.. they suppose to be a doctrinall of rybaudrie. **1534** —— (*title*) Doctrinal of Princes. **1653** URQUHART *Rabelais* I. xiv, An old coughing fellow.. who read unto him Hugotio, Hebard, Grecisme, the doctrinal.

b. *transf.* An instructor. *Obs. rare.*

1503 HAWES *Examp. Virt.* xiii. (Arb.) 55 Also saynt Ierome the noble cardynall.. Whiche euermore was a good doctrynall.

2. *pl.* Matters or points of doctrine or instruction.

1619 S. WARD in *Ussher's Lett.* (1686) 68 Our consent was only asked for Doctrinals, not for matters touching Discipline. **1681** BAXTER *Apol. Nonconf. Min.* 48 We differ in Doctrinals as well as in Ceremony. **1718** *Wodrow Corr.* (1843) II. 398 The.. controversy about doctrinals is again revived. **1876** J. G. WILKINSON *Hum. Sc. & Div. Revel.* lxv. 212 Doctrinals are the indispensable readers of all reality.

Hence **doctrinalism**, the laying of stress on doctrinal matters; **doctrinalist**, a strict adherent to doctrine; **doctri'nality**, doctrinal character.

1846 DE QUINCEY *Christianity* Wks. XII. 278 The doctrinality of our religion. **1860** FROUDE *Hist. Eng.* V. 356 The Papists were put out of the way. The doctrinalists were promoted to honour. **1869** *Ibid.* (1870) XII. 550 Theological doctrinalism passed out of fashion. **1894** *Thinker* V. 447 Driven.. into the other extreme of rigid doctrinalism.

doctrinally (see prec.), *adv.* [f. prec. + -LY[2].]

In a doctrinal manner or form; in respect of, or as a matter of, doctrine; by way of teaching.

1633 AMES *Agst. Cerem.* II. 371 Writing on the second Commandement doctrinally. **1679** PENN *Addr. Prot.* II. iii. (1692) 87 Christ Jesus himself and his Apostles.. have doctrinally laid it down. **1706** DE FOE *Jure Div.* Pref. 30 If my Opinion be really in it self, Doctrinally Sound. **1869** HADDAN *Apost. Succ.* iii. (1879) 58 Churches organically complete but doctrinally corrupt.

Doctrinarian (dɒktrɪ'nɛərɪən), *sb.* and *a.* [f. L. type **doctrīnāri-us* (DOCTRINAIRE) + -AN.]

A. *sb.* †**1.** *pl.* The Brethren of Christian Doctrine, or Christian Brothers (F. *doctrinaires*), a lay order instituted at Rheims in 1680 by J. B. de la Salle, to teach gratuitously the principles of religion and the elements of primary instruction. *Obs.*

1747 *Gentl. Mag.* 570 Other amphibious kinds, which are neither Regulars nor Seculars, as Jesuits, Oratorians, Doctrinarians, Lazarists. **1794** BARRUEL *Hist. Clergy Fr. Rev.* (1795) 161 [He] had been educated in a secular congregation by the Doctrinarians.

2. = DOCTRINAIRE *sb.*

1836 J. H. NEWMAN *Discuss. & Argts.* (1872) 19 Protestantism is embodied in a system; so is Popery: but when a man takes up this Via Media, he is a mere doctrinarian—he is wasting his efforts in delineating an invisible phantom. **1840** T. HOOK in *New Monthly Mag.* LX. 164 England has its sect of doctrinarians as well as France.

B. *adj.* = DOCTRINAIRE *a.*, DOCTRINARY.

1878 E. JENKINS *Haverholme* 101 A stiff and doctrinarian politician of the Whig school.

Hence **doctri'narianism**, doctrinairism.

1877 D. M. WALLACE *Russia* v. 82 The latest products of French doctrinarianism.

doctrinary ('dɒktrɪnərɪ), *a.* [ad. F. *doctrinaire*: see above and -ARY[1].] Holding an abstract doctrine and seeking to apply it in all circumstances; = DOCTRINAIRE *a.*

1850 HARE *Mission Comf.* 284 Arguing against the doctrinary school. **1860** J. P. KENNEDY *Swallow B.* ii. 33 His .. doctrinary republicanism. **1893** *Nat. Observer* 15 Apr. 535/1 Doctrinary pedants.

Hence **doctri'narity**, quality of a doctrinaire.

a **1869** LD. STRANGFORD *Lett. etc.* 235 (D.) Excess in doctrinarity and excess in earnestness are threatening to set their mark on the new political generation.

'doctrinate, *v. arch.* [f. med.L. *doctrīnāre*, *-īnāt-* to teach, instruct, f. *doctrīna*: see -ATE[3] 5.] *trans.* To teach or instruct; = DOCTRINE *v.* a.; *absol.* To give instruction (*on* a subject).

1631 HEYWOOD *Eng. Eliz.* (1641) 33 They were doctrinated and instructed, either in language, or some of the liberall sciences. **1638** SIR T. HERBERT *Trav.* (ed. 2) 46 They are of Pythagora's doctrinating.. in beleeving the Metempsychosis of the soule. **1651** *Fuller's Abel Rediv., Chytraeus* 421 Most profoundly by him doctrinated. **1840** MARRYAT *Olla Podr.* (Rtldg.) 282 On that.. you have not yet doctrinated.

doctrine ('dɒktrɪn), *sb.* Also 4-6 doctryn(e, 6-8 doctrin. [a. F. *doctrine* (12th c.), ad. L. *doctrīna* teaching, learning, f. *doctor* teacher, DOCTOR: cf. *pistrīna* bakery, f. *pistor* baker.]

†**1.** The action of teaching or instructing; instruction; a piece of instruction, a lesson, precept. *Obs.*

1382 WYCLIF *2 Tim.* iv. 2 Arguwe, or proue, biseche, blame in al pacience and doctryn. *c* **1391** CHAUCER *Astrol.* Prol., I..have hit translated in myn englissh only for thi doctrine. **1485** CAXTON *Chas. Gt.* 1 Al thynges that ben reduced by wrytyng ben wryton to our doctryne. **1526–34** TINDALE *Mark* iv. 2 He..sayde vnto them in his doctrine [so **1611**; **1881** (R.V.) teaching]: Herken to. **1645** USSHER *Body Div.* (1647) 56 The Commandement..was a doctrine to teach Pharoah what he must have done. **1710** STEELE *Tatler* No. 11 ¶2 Doctrines on this Occasion..are the most..empty of all the Labours of Men.

b. Public instruction; preaching. *Obs.*

1560–78 *Bk. Discipl. Ch. Scot.* (1621) 40 Where the people convene to the doctrine but once in the week. *a* **1572** KNOX *Hist. Ref.* Wks. 1846 I. 250 After doctrin, he lyikwiese ministrat the Lordis Table. **1600** J. MELVILL *Diary* (Wodrow Soc.) 33, I saw him everie day of his doctrine go hulie and fear..to the Paroche Kirk.

2. That which is taught. **a.** In the most general sense: Instruction, teaching; a body of instruction or teaching.

1382 WYCLIF *Tit.* ii. 10 In alle thingis schewing good feith, that thei ourne in alle thingis the doctryn of oure sauyour God. *c* **1400** MAUNDEV. (1839) xii. 133 The Gospelles, in the which is gode doctryne. **1483** CAXTON *Cato* 3 In this smal lytyl booke is conteyned a short..doctryne for all maner of peple. **1500–20** DUNBAR *Poems* xli. 7 Be rewlyt rycht and keip this doctring. **1502** *Ord. Crysten Men* (W. de W. 1506) Prol. 2 Foloweth a shorte doctryne..in yᵉ whiche shall be spoken..of fyue thynges. **1526–34** TINDALE *Matt.* xvi. 12 He bad not them beware of the leven of breed: but of the doctrine of the Pharises. **1845** S. AUSTIN *Ranke's Hist. Ref.* II. 179 They next proceeded to consider the points of doctrine and life. **1851** ROBERTSON *Serm.* Ser. II. 110 In Scripture, doctrine means broadly, teaching: anything that is taught is doctrine.

b. *esp.* That which is taught or laid down as true concerning a particular subject or department of knowledge, as religion, politics, science, etc.; a belief, theoretical opinion; a dogma, tenet.

1382 WYCLIF *Matt.* xv. 9 Techynge the doctrines and maundements of men. **1485** CAXTON *Paris & V.* Prol., The book of his doctrines. **1509** FISHER *Fun. Serm. C'tess Richmond* Wks. (1876) 308 To publysshe the doctryne & fayth of cryste Ihesu. **1605** BACON *Adv. Learn.* II. xxv. §20. 116 The doctrine of the nature of God. **1712** ADDISON *Spect.* No. 269 ¶10 To vent among them some of his Republican Doctrines. **1725** WATTS *Logic* IV. ii. Rule 6, The doctrine of the sacred Trinity. **1778** BURKE *Corr.* (1844) II. 242 That doctrine of the equality of all men, which has been preached by knavery, and so greedily adopted by malice, envy, and cunning. **1860** WESTCOTT *Introd. Study Gosp.* viii. (ed. 5) 405 Difficulties in applying the great doctrine of gravitation. **1893** SIR J. W. CHITTY in *Law Times Rep.* LXVIII. 430/1 To hold that mere oral assent to the new lease operates as a surrender in law would be a most dangerous doctrine.

c. ***Monroe doctrine*** (U.S. politics): the name applied (since about 1848) to a principle or series of principles of policy put forward in, or deduced from, the Message of President Monroe to Congress, 2 Dec. 1823.

In this it was declared that 'we should consider any attempt' on the part of the Allied European Powers 'to extend their system to any portion of this hemisphere as dangerous to our peace and safety'; that 'any interposition, for the purpose of oppressing' the recently revolted Spanish-American colonies, 'or controlling in any other manner their destiny, by any European Power' would be viewed 'as the manifestation of an unfriendly disposition towards the United States'; and that 'the American continents should no longer be subjects for any new European colonial settlement'.

1848 I. E. HOLMES in *Congress. Globe* 29 Apr. 711 The President [Polk] had taken the opportunity of reiterating a doctrine which was said to be the doctrine of Mr. Monroe. **1858** *Sun* (Balt.) 30 Oct. (Bartlett), If we now fall back on the Monroe doctrine, we shall see the difference between an abstraction and its application in practice. **1866** LOWELL *Seward-Johnson Reaction* Prose Wks. 1890 V. 323 The South should put in practice at home that Monroe Doctrine of which it has always been so clamorous a supporter. **1895** MRQ. OF SALISBURY *Disp.* 26 Nov. (*Times* 18 Dec. 7/2) The application of the Monroe doctrine to the question of the boundary dispute between Venezuela and the colony of British Guiana. **1896** *Daily News* 7 Mar. 4/6 It was during this contest between Spain and her insurgent colonists that President Monroe, in 1823, at the instigation of Mr. Canning, laid down in a Message to Congress the famous 'doctrine' which bears his name.

3. A body or system of principles or tenets; a doctrinal or theoretical system; a theory; a science, or department of knowledge. ? *Obs.*

1594 WEST *2nd Pt. Symbol.* §100 F, I haue..laid downe the doctrine of Instruments. **1666–7** PEPYS *Diary* 16 Feb., [He] understands the doctrine of musique. **1667** PRIMATT *City & C. Build.* 160 Measure the same by the Doctrine of Triangles. **1709–29** V. MANDEY *Syst. Math., Astron.* Pref. 248 Astronomy is a Doctrine or Science. **1754** CHATHAM *Lett. Nephew* 48 A..notion of..the solar system: together with the doctrine of comets. **1836–7** SIR W. HAMILTON *Metaph.* (1877) I. viii. 130 Psychology therefore, is the discourse or doctrine treating of the human mind.

†**4.** Learning, erudition, knowledge. *Obs.*

c **1400** *Beryn* 1245 Thow art xx wynter, and nauȝt hast of doctryne. **1483** CAXTON *Cato* Gj, The man whiche is without doctryne is like thymage of deth. **1563–7** BUCHANAN *Reform. St. Andros* Wks (1892) 12 The principal to be ane man of..sufficient doctrine to supple the regentis absens in redyng. **1601** SHAKS. *All's Well* I. iii. 247 The Schooles Embowel'd of their doctrine.

†**5.** Discipline. *Obs. rare.*

a **1483** *Liber Niger* in *Househ. Ord.* 78 These officers should be marked and ordered after theyre..behaviour..or elles to be at the doctryne conveniente in the countynghouse. *a* **1533** LD. BERNERS *Gold. Bk. M. Aurel.* (1546) Pv, The doctrine of sones and doughters was enlarged, and theyr bridell let go at libertee.

6. *attrib.* and *Comb.*

a **1716** SOUTH *Serm.* V. 31 To give those doctrine and use-men, those pulpit-engineers their due. **1879** BARING-GOULD *Germany* II. 194 When the excitement of doctrine-smashing was over, the laity grew listless.

†**'doctrine**, *v. Obs.* [a. OF. *doctrine-r*, ad. med.L. *doctrināre*, f. *doctrīna*: see DOCTRINATE.] *trans.* **a.** To teach or instruct (a person); **b.** To teach, give instruction in (a science, etc.).

1475 *Bk. Noblesse* 77 Henry duke of Lancastre..had sent to hym..yong knightis, to be doctrined, lerned, and broughte up..in scole of armes. **1530** PALSGR. 523/2, He hath ben well doctryned: *il a esté fort bien endoctriné*. **1549** *Compl. Scot.* vi. 46 Phisic, astronomye and natural philosophie, var fyrst prettikit and doctrinet be vs. **1648** GAGE *West Ind.* xvii. (1655) 112 They doctrined me as a novice.

Hence **'doctrined** *ppl. a.*

1627 W. SCLATER *Exp. 2 Thess.* (1629) 137 Take view of their doctrined practises, in deuotion to God, Carriage to men, to our selues.

doctrinism ('dɒktrɪnɪz(ə)m). [f. DOCTRINE *sb.* + -ISM.] Adherence to, or setting forth of, doctrine. So **'doctrinist**, one who propounds, or adheres to, doctrine.

1840 G. S. FABER *Regeneration* 328 Our aim is to be Primitive, not Tridentine, Doctrinists. **1872** TULLOCH *Ration. Theol.* I. ii. 43 The most memorable exception to this fair and conciliatory doctrinism of the Church of England..is to be found in the famous Lambeth Articles. **1883** *Manch. Guard.* 13 Oct. 7/4 The mere doctrinism of the Congress being inadequate for the requirements of the age. **1891** G. MACDONALD *There & Back* II. xxxv. 226 Neither ascetic nor mystic nor doctrinist..she believed in God.

doctrinize ('dɒktrɪnaɪz), *v.* [f. DOCTRINE *sb.* + -IZE.] *intr.* To form doctrines or theories; to speculate, theorize. Hence **doctrini'zation**.

1836 R. M. MᶜCHEYNE *Jrnl.* in *Mem.* (1866) 55 The error of those who speculate or doctrinize about the Gospel. **1852** *Fraser's Mag.* XLV. 570 Stories about animals..are generally spoiled by the same mistaken doctrinization.

†**'doctrix.** *Obs.* [a. L. *doctrix*, fem. of *doctor* DOCTOR.] A female doctor: = DOCTRESS.

1604 PARSONS *3rd Pt. Three Convers. Eng.* xv. 254 Alice Driuer, a famous doctrix. **1635** PAGITT *Christianogr.* I. ii. (1636) 53 This country of Palestine is called..the nurse of the prophets, the doctrix of the Apostles. **1746** in Edgar *Old Ch. Life Scot.* (1885) 270 *note*, In 1746 a 'doctrix' was consulted in Galston about the recovery of a sick child.

'docudrama. orig. *N. Amer.* Also **docu-drama.** [f. DOCU(MENTARY *a.* + DRAMA.] A dramatized film (usu. for television) which is based on a semi-fictional interpretation of real events; a documentary drama.

1961 *Britannica Bk. of Year* 537/2 *Docudrama*, a documentary drama. **1975** *Toronto Star* 12 July G1/1 CBC producer Ralph Thomas and director Peter Pearson were completing under wraps the most controversial of the network's five new hour-long 'docu-dramas' series. **1977** *TV Guide* (U.S.) 5 Feb. 22/1 Unfortunately, as in most docudramas, fiction and wishful thinking often are mixed up with facts. **1981** *Listener* 17 & 24 Dec. 790/2 In the excellent docudrama film, *This is Elvis*, there is a painful sequence..when Elvis..attempts to sing 'Are You Lonesome Tonight?'. **1985** *Times* 6 Apr. 8/6 Dramatized documentaries—or 'docu-dramas'—are suspect.

document ('dɒkjʊmənt), *sb.* [a. OF. *document* lesson, written evidence (12th–13th c. in Hatz.-Darm.), ad. L. *document-um* lesson, proof, instance, specimen, in med.L. also written instrument, charter, official paper, f. *docēre* to teach.]

†**1.** Teaching, instruction, warning. *Obs.*

c **1450** HENRYSON *Mor. Fab.* 58 Despysing thus her hailsome document, The fowles..tuke their flight. **1503** HAWES *Examp. Virt.* Prol. iii, All that is wryten is to oure document. **1660** *Trial Regic.* 147 Punishment goes to the prisoner, but examples to the document of all others. **1793** J. WILLIAMS *Life Ld. Barrymore* 101, I have heard much document from the Grey Beards of society, delivered to prove [etc.].

†**2.** An instruction, a piece of instruction, a lesson; an admonition, a warning. *Obs.*

1549 T. SOME *Latimer's Serm. bef. Edw. VI*, Ded., In them are frutefull and godlye documentes. **1620** tr. *Boccaccio's Decameron* 80 b, These were his daily documents to his young wife. **1751** JOHNSON *Rambler* No. 87 ¶10 There are..few to whom it is not unpleasing to receive documents. **1769** SIR J. REYNOLDS *Disc.* ii. (1876) 328 Even bad pictures themselves supply him with useful documents. *c* **1800** LANDOR in *Parr's Wks.* (1828) VIII. 48, I will give him some documents which shall enlighten his judgment at the expence of his skin.

†**3.** That which serves to show, point out, or prove something; evidence, proof. Chiefly with *dependent cl. Obs.*

1459 *Charters of Peebles* (Burgh Rec. Soc. 1872) 132 And than be verray document of thaim that herd and saw the begyning of that bargan the gud men..fand [etc.]. **1533** BELLENDEN *Livy* IV. (1822) 353 Ane notabil document, that pluralite of capitanis are unproffittabil in battal. **1614** RALEIGH *Hist. World* V. iii. §21. 490 This may serue as a document of Fortunes instabilitie. **1769** *Junius' Lett.* xxvii. ¶5 Sufficient care was taken to leave no document of any treasonable negociation. **1847** EMERSON *Repr. Men, Napoleon* Wks. (Bohn) I. 374 The best document of his relation to his troops is the order of the day..in which [etc.].

4. Something written, inscribed, etc., which furnishes evidence or information upon any subject, as a manuscript, title-deed, tomb-stone, coin, picture, etc.

1727–51 CHAMBERS *Cycl.*, *Document*, in law, some written monument produced in proof of any fact asserted..The antiquity of the foundation of such a church is proved by a number of authentic documents. **1755** MAGENS *Insurances* I. 340 As an Authentic Document was required of the foregoing Declaration, I signed and sealed this to serve where occasion shall require. **1810** WELLINGTON in Gurw. *Desp.* VI. 290, I had got..the emplacement of the whole French army of the 1st June which is a very curious document and gives a tolerable notion of their whole force in Spain. **1850** MRS. JAMESON *Leg. Monast. Ord.* (1863) 401 These frescoes..have become invaluable as documents. **1877–9** F. WHARTON *Law of Evid.* I. II. ix. §614. 586 A 'document'..is an instrument on which is recorded, by means of letters, figures, or marks, matter which may be evidentially used.

b. *spec.* The bill of lading and policy of insurance handed over as collateral security for a foreign bill of exchange; hence ***document-bill***.

1858 SIMMONDS *Dict. Trade*, *Document-bill*, an Indian bill of exchange drawn on London, having as collateral security the bill of lading and policy of insurance on the goods; against a part of the estimated value of these the bill is drawn.

document ('dɒkjʊmɛnt), *v.* [f. prec. sb.: cf. F. *documenter*.] †**1.** *trans.* To teach, instruct. *Obs.*

1648 *Scottish Mist Dispel'd* 32 Upon this principle you document the Parliament of England about the Kings power in making laws. **1682** BUNYAN *Holy War* 217 That they might be documented in all good and wholesome things. **1739** 'R. BULL' tr. *Dedekindus' Grobianus* 271 The Monarch documents him in his Part.

b. To give a 'lesson' to; to instruct or admonish in an authoritative or imperious manner. *Obs.*

1690 DRYDEN *Don Sebastian* IV. ii, I am finely documented by my own daughter! **1778** FRANKLIN *Let.* Wks. 1889 VI. 161 Your letters..in which you, with magisterial airs, schooled and documented me, as if I had been one of your domestics. **1802** MARIAN MOORE *Lascelles* I. 126 She..entreated Mrs. Carisbrook to send them [the girls] to her..that she might document them.

2. To prove or support (something) by documentary evidence.

1711 *Countrym. Let. to Curat* 31 The Historical deduction before given (sufficiently documented from your own Writers). **1780** *Blue Blanket* 4 (Jam.) This city was so often destroyed, her monuments and charters lost, that her original cannot well be documented. **1825** ANDERSON *Hist. Acc. Fam. Fraser* 79 They are documented in a charter of confirmation of the lands of Wester Logy.

3. To provide with documents. **a.** To furnish (a ship) with the 'papers' or documents required for the manifestation of its ownership and cargo.

1828 WEBSTER s.v., A ship should be documented according to the directions of law. **1848** ARNOULD *Mar. Insur.* (1866) I. I. i. 8 By sailing his ship imperfectly or improperly documented, he forfeits his right to protection under the policy. **1884** R. WHEATLEY in *Harper's Mag.* June 60/1 To enable such vessels..to be documented and receive an American register.

b. To furnish (a person) with evidence; to keep informed or instructed.

1807 W. TAYLOR in *Ann. Rev.* V. 165 A..corroboration to the statements of that courageous and documented historiographer. **1892** *Nation* (N.Y.) 8 Sept. 187/1 It was for a novel..that he was 'documenting himself'. **1894** *Daily News* 20 Dec. 5/4 Statesmen who want to be, as they say here, 'well documented' to resist possible attacks.

Hence **'documented** *ppl. a.*, **'documenting** *vbl. sb.*; †**'documentor**, an indicator.

1684 tr. *Agrippa's Van. Arts* lxxxi. 277 There be many of smaller Animals also that claim a Prerogative in the Shields of great men, provided they be the Documentors of mischief: such as Coneys, Moles, Frogs, Locusts, Mice, Serpents. **1801** MAR. EDGEWORTH *Belinda* (1857) 4 After the course of documenting which she had gone through. **1803** W. TAYLOR in *Ann. Rev.* I. 256 A full, a documented, a well-proportioned account. **1886** *American* XII. 286 There were 256 disasters to documented vessels.

documental (ˌdɒkjʊ'mɛntəl), *a.* [f. L. *document-um* DOCUMENT *sb.* + -AL¹.]

†**1.** Pertaining to teaching or instruction; instructive; didactic. *Obs.*

c **1575** (*title*) Documental Sayings as those same were spoken forth by H[enrick] N[iclas]. **1610** HEALEY *St. Aug. Citie of God* VI. ii. (1620) 227 Varro..though he be not eloquent yet is he so documental and sententious.

2. Of or pertaining to documents; documentary.

1825 COLERIDGE *Aids Refl.* (1848) I. 277 The documental proofs of the same. **1883** H. M. KENNEDY tr. *Ten Brink's E.E. Lit.* 37 The collection of documental material. **1892** R. DUNLOP in *Academy* 10 Sept. 207/3, I think one ought to say 'documentary' and not 'documental' evidence.

documentalist (ˌdɒkjʊ'mɛntəlɪst). [f. DOCUMENTAL *a.* + -IST.] A person engaged in documentation (see DOCUMENTATION 3 b).

1939 *Nature* 23 Sept. 560/1 The Section devoted to the Division of Work between Libraries and Documentalists. **1948** S. C. BRADFORD *Documentation* 11 The documentalist is enabled to put before the creative specialist the existing literature, bearing on the subject of his investigation, in order that he may be saved from the dissipation of his genius upon work already done.

documentary (ˌdɒkjʊˈmɛntərɪ), *a.* [f. as DOCUMENTAL *a.* + -ARY[1]: cf. F. *documentaire.*]

1. Of the nature of or consisting in documents. **1802–12** BENTHAM *Rat. Judic. Evid.* (1827) I. 54 Documentary evidence. **1831** CARLYLE *Sart. Res.* II. iii, Various fragments of Letters and other documentary scraps. **1855** MACAULAY *Hist. Eng.* IV. 178 They were in possession of documentary evidence which would confound the guilty. **1861** M. PATTISON *Ess.* ('89) I. 30 Going back beyond the printed annalists to original and documentary authorities.

2. Affording evidence, evidential. *rare.* **1843** CARLYLE *Past & Pr.* I. iii, It is an authentic..fact, quietly documentary of a whole world of such.

3. Relating to teaching or instruction. *rare.* **1871** EARLE *Philol. Eng. Tongue* §52 Long before 1250 we get traces of the documentary use of French.. Trevisa says it was a new thing in 1349 for children to construe into English in the Grammar schools.

4. Factual, realistic; applied esp. to a film or literary work, etc., based on real events or circumstances, and intended primarily for instruction or record purposes. Also *ellipt.* as *sb.* **1926** *N. Y. Sun* 8 Feb. 18/1 'Moana', being a visual account of events in the daily life of a Polynesian youth and his family, has documentary value. **1930** P. ROTHA *Film till Now* I. ii. 65 The Documentary or Interest Film, including the Scientific, Cultural and Sociological Film. **1932** *Cinema Q.* I. I. 67 Documentary is a clumsy description, but let it stand. The French who first used the term only meant travelogue. **1932** *Film in National Life* (*Rep. Comm. Educ. & Cult. Films*) viii. 115 §174 A deliberate documentary film must be a transcript of real life, a bit of what actually happened, under approximately unrehearsed conditions. **1934** *Punch* 26 Dec. 720/1 Most documentary films seem to hinge upon the exposition of some staple industry. **1935** R. SPOTTISWOODE *Gram. of Film* 288 The documentary as he defines it is still flourishing. **1936** *Times Lit. Suppl.* 25 Jan. 72/3 The documentary film—or, *tout court*, 'documentary'. **1941** [see ACTUALITY 4 b]. **1947** J. HAYWARD *Prose Lit. since 1939* 32 'Mass-Observation', whose intriguing 'documentaries' of the British people at work and play contain the crude substance of innumerable novels, biographies, and essays. **1957** V. J. KEHOE *Film & T.V. Make-Up* i. 17 Some producers do not like the smoothness of the face created by the use of make-up. They strive to achieve what is termed a *documentary* effect..by the lack of make-up on men (even at times, on women). **1957** *Listener* 18 July 103/1 Mr. Owen's 'documentary', as he calls his attractive book, reveals him as an acute observer. **1962** *Observer* 8 July 20/4 Henry Cecil's light legal documentary fiction.

Hence **docu'mentarily** *adv.*, in the way of a document; from a documentary point of view; **docu'mentarist**, one who makes documentary films. **1857** RUSKIN *Pol. Econ. Art* ii. (1868) 126 These copies.. would be historically and documentarily valuable. **1953** *New Statesman* 10 Oct. 419 A documentarist of sensation. **1959** *Times* 3 Nov. 15/3 The most ruthless of documentarists. **1961** *Times* 1 June 6/4 It is a film about film-making... A simple, puppyish documentarist has moved into the 'pad' of a group of junkies. **1962** *Times* 26 Apr. 8/5 The Swedish documentarist..in his new film.

documentation (ˌdɒkjʊmɛnˈteɪʃən). [ad. med.L. *documentātiōn-em* admonition, n. of action f. **documentāre* to DOCUMENT.] The action of documenting or fact of being documented.

†**1.** Instruction, admonition, 'lecturing'. *Obs.* **1754** RICHARDSON *Grandison* VI. xxv. 143 Not another word of your documentations, dame Selby, I am not in a humour to bear them. **1844** *Blackw. Mag.* LV. 199 No end to these chartered documentations of the sex!

2. The furnishing of a ship with the requisite 'papers'. **1884** *Harper's Mag.* June 60/2 In the registration of a new vessel, the production..of the certificate of measurement.. is required in order to documentation.

3. a. Preparation or use of documentary evidence and authorities.

In reference to realistic fiction, applied to the faithful reproduction of historical or objective facts.

1888 *Athenæum* 17 Mar. 342 Is art simply an affair of documentation, as the phrase of the day goes? **1893** *Spectator* 23 Dec. 919/1 M. Zola..has great industry and is very painstaking in 'documentation'. **1895** *Westm. Gaz.* 4 July 2/1 There is so much to read up, such documentation to be exercised.

b. The accumulation, classification, and dissemination of information (see quot. 1948); the material so collected. [**1905** *Publ. Office Internat. de Bibliographie* LXIX (*title*) L'Organisation rationnelle de l'information et de documentation en matière économique. Rapport présenté ..par P. Otlet.] **1927** D. P. MYERS in *Libraries* XXXII. 107 (*title*) International documentation, its classification and purpose. **1938** *Rep. World Congr. Universal Documentation, 1937* 32 The documentation centre at the Science Library. **1940** *Proc. Brit. Soc. Internat. Bibliogr.* I. II. 11 The co-ordination of documentation. **1948** S. C. BRADFORD *Documentation* 9 Documentation is the process of collecting and subject classifying all the records of new observations and making them available, at need, to the discoverer or the inventor. **1967** *FID News Bull.* XVII. 70/1 The advent of a new discipline of science called *documentation*,..*scientific information*, *information science*, etc., is a commonly recognized fact.

†**'documentize**, *v. Obs.* [f. DOCUMENT *sb.* + -IZE.] *trans.* **a.** To teach, instruct, give a lesson to. **b.** To furnish with evidence. Hence **'documentizing** *vbl. sb.* **1599** NASHE *Lenten Stuffe* 21 Those that be scrutinus..let them reuolue the Digests of our English discoueries..and be documentized most locupleatly. **1647** *Maids' Petition* 5 Bulcher..with his newly hatcht errors will documentise our Bulwarks alive or dead. **1682** MRS. BEHN *City Heiress* I. i, You'd best carry your nephew..to Church; he wants a little documentizing that way. *a* **1734** NORTH *Exam.* II. iv. §122. (1740) 294 Being, as he said, well documentised. **1754** RICHARDSON *Grandison* VI. xxv. 143, I am to be closetted, and to be documentized.

dod, *sb.*[1] and *int. dial.* or *vulgar.* In asseverations; originally a deformation of *God.* (Cf. ADOD; also DAD[3], BEDAD.) **1676** ETHERIDGE *Man of Mode* II. i, A Dod she's too serious. **1855** HALIBURTON *Nat. & Hum. Nat.* 60 (Bartlett) I'll cut and run, and dot drot me if I don't. **1892** *Northumbld. Gloss.* s.v., Dod! but yor a queer fellow! **1893** STEVENSON *Catriona* 14 And, dod! I believe the day's come now.

dod (dɒd), *sb.*[2] *dial.* [Cognate with early mod. Du. *dodde* in same sense ('caulis et spica typhæ palustris' Kilian); also a stalk, staff, club ('a little broach or spit, a reed' Hexham).] The Reed-Mace or Cat's-tail, *Typha latifolia.* *a* **1661** FULLER *Worthies, Northampton* II. (1662) 290 Dods, Waterweeds (commonly called by children Cats Tales). **1847–78** HALLIWELL, *Dod*, the fox-tail reed. *North.* **1864** *Alnwick Mercury* 1 Mar. (Britten & Holland), Dod is the Reedmace (*Typha latifolia*, L.) in the north of England. **1882** FRIEND *Devonshire Plant-n.*

dod, dodd, *sb.*[3] *north. dial.* [Evidently related to DOD *v.*[1]; app. a specific application of a sb. of which the primary sense was 'rounded head': cf. also DODDY.]

In North of England and South of Scotland a frequent term for a rounded summit or eminence, either as a separate hill, or more frequently a lower summit or distinct shoulder or boss of a hill.

Rarely applied to a lower buttress when not rounded, as Skiddaw Dod. Usually forming part of a proper name, like the equivalent Welsh *Moel* (*Foel*), but also an appellative.

[**1843** *Penny Cycl.* XXVII. 248/2 (*Westmoreland*) Of which [branch] Dod Hill, Place Fell..and Swarth Fell are summits.] **1878** *Cumbld. Gloss.*, *Dod*, a round topped fell, generally an offshoot from a larger or higher mountain. **1879** JENKINSON *Guide Eng. Lakes* 233 There are many hills in the district known by the appellation of Dodd, and they are generally small and attached to large mountains. **1882** J. HARDY in *Hist. Berw. Nat. Club* IX. 452 *Pike, crag, law, head, know, dod, edge, rig*..predominate in the nomenclature of the Redesdale eminences. **1886** G. A. LEBOUR *Geol. Northumb. & Durh.* (ed. 2) 24 Sand and gravel 'dodds'. **1892** *Northumbld. Gloss.*, *Dodd*, a blunt hill, a butt end of a hill. Its occurrence is noted thirteen times in place-names in Northumberland.. The truncated chimney or ventilator of a malt-kiln is called the kiln-dodd.

dod, *sb.*[4] *Sc.* [Gaelic *dod* peevishness.] A slight fit of ill-humour; sullenness, peevishness. **1808** in JAMIESON. **1823** GALT *Entail* II. 143 (Jam.) When she happens, poor body, to tak the dods now and then. **1823** MISSES CORBETT *Petticoat Tales* I. 250 (Jam.) Her father has ta'en the dods at him.

†**dod, dodd**, *a.* and *pa. pple. Obs.* Short for DODDED, q.v. *c* **1449** PECOCK *Repr.* II. i. 135 He wole haue hise heer schorne of and his heed to be dod. **1641** BEST *Farm. Bks.* (Surtees) 99 White-wheat massledine will outsell dodd-reade massledine..grey wheate and long reade will outsell dodde read oftentimes. **1674–91** RAY *N.C. Words* 21 Dodred Wheat; is red Wheat without beards.

dod (dɒd), *v.*[1] *Obs.* exc. *dial.* [ME. *dodden*, app. from the same root as DOD *sb.*[3]: cf. DODDY.

Wedgwood compares Fris. *dodd*, *dadde*, lump, clump, bunch; but the connexion is doubtful.]

trans. To make the top or head of (anything) blunt, rounded, or bare; hence, to clip or poll the hair of (a person); to deprive (an animal) of its horns; to poll or lop (a tree), etc.; also *fig.* to behead. *a* **1225** *Ancr. R.* 422 Ʒe schulen beon i-dodded [= have your hair cut] four siðen iðe ʒere, uorto lihten ower heaued. *a* **1307** *Pol. Songs* (Camden) 192 Hue nolden take for huem raunsoun ne ware; Hue doddeth of huere hevedes, fare so hit fare. **1382** WYCLIF *Lev.* xix. 27 Ne ʒe shulen in rownde dodde heer, ne shave beerde. —— *2 Sam.* xiv. 26 Onys in the ʒeer he was doddid, for the heere heuyde hym. *c* **1440** *Promp. Parv.* 125/1 Doddyn trees, or herbys, and oper lyke, *decomo, capulo.* **1683** MERITON *Yorke-sh. Dialect* 6 We mun dod our Sheepe. **1825** BROCKETT *N.C. Words*, *Dodd*, to cut wool from and near the tails of sheep.—*Doddings*, the cuttings. *Dod*, to lop, as a tree, is an old word.

Hence **'dodding** *vbl. sb.*, the action of clipping the hair; tonsure; in *pl.*, the wool clipped from a sheep. *a* **1225** *Ancr. R.* 14 Of ower doddunge..& of ower blod letunge. **1825** [see above]. **1847–78** HALLIWELL, *Doddings*, the fore-parts of a fleece of wool. *North.*

dod, *v.*[2] *Obs.* exc. *dial.* [variant of DAD *v.*] *trans.* To beat, knock. *a* **1661** FULLER *Worthies* I. (1662) 47 Our husbandmen in Middlesex make a distinction between dodding and threshing of wheat, the former being only the beating out of the fullest and fairest grain.. Our comment may be said to have dodded the Sheriffes of several Counties. **1883** *Gd. Words* 574 He..dodded our heids down on the desk.

dod- (DOD *sb.*[1]), used as an intensive with verbs and pa. pples. *U.S. colloq.* See also DODGAST *v.* DOD-ROT *v.* **1829** *Yankee* Apr. 131/2 Dod burn the boy! what's he arter? **1835** A. B. LONGSTREET *Georgia Scenes* 231 I'll be dod blamed if I do. **1883** 'MARK TWAIN' *Life on Miss.* 220 He ejaculated: 'Well, I'll be dod-derned.' *Ibid.*, 'Dod-dern' was the nearest he ventured to..swearing. **1908** C. E. MULFORD *Orphan* xiii. 164 'Dod-blasted postage stamp of a pelt,' he grumbled.

dodart, obs. var. of DOTARD.

†**'doddard.** *Obs. rare.* [app. f. DOD *v.*[1] to poll (trees) + -ARD; the formation being parallel to *poll-ard*: cf. DODDLE *sb.*, DODDEREL in same sense. But it may have been merely a modification of *dottard*, DOTARD (found earlier in same sense) with fanciful assimilation to DOD *v.*[1] and its derivatives: see DODDERED.] A tree that has lost its head of branches by decay. In quot. *attrib.* = DOTARD B. 2. **1693** DRYDEN *Persius* v. (R.), Another shakes the bed.. Till..chalk is in his crippled fingers found; Rots like a doddard oke, and piecemeal falls to ground.

'dodded, *ppl. a. north. dial.* [f. DOD *v.*[1]] Polled, lopped; hornless; awnless. *c* **1440** *Promp. Parv.* 125/1 Doddyd, wythe-owte hornysse ..*incornutus. Ibid.*, Doddyd, as trees. **1641** BEST *Farm. Bks.* (Surtees) 6 Signes of a Goode Ewe. Lett her be dodded. **1674–91** RAY *N.C. Words* 21 Dodded Sheep, i.e. Sheep without Horns. **1819** *Edin. Advertiser* 24 Aug. (Jam.), Extensive sale of improved dodded cattle. **1892** *Northumbld. Gloss.*, *Dodded corn*, is corn without beards.

dodder (ˈdɒdə(r)), *sb.* Also 3–6 **doder.** [perh. Common WGer., though not known in OE., OS., or OHG. ME. *doder* = MLG. *doder*, *dodder*, MHG. *toter*, mod. Ger. *dotter*, Du. and Da. *dodder*, Sw. *dodra*. Similarity of form has suggested connexion with Ger. *dotter*, MHG. *toter*, OHG. *totoro*, *tutaro*, MDu. *doder*(*e* yolk of an egg, as if with reference to the colour of the flower-clusters of *Cuscuta europæa*; but this is a doubtful conjecture.]

1. The common name of the genus *Cuscuta*, N.O. *Convolvulaceæ*, comprising slender leafless plants, like masses of twining threads, parasitic on flax, clover, thyme, furze, and other plants. *c* **1265** *Voc. Plants* in Wr.-Wülcker 557/11 *Cuscute*, doder. *a* **1387** *Sinon. Barthol.* 17 *Cuscute*, *podagra lini*, doder. *c* **1450** *Alphita* 154 *Rasta lini*..doder *uel* haynde. **1551** TURNER *Herbal* I. H v b, Doder groweth out of herbes, and small bushes, as miscelto groweth out of trees. **1578** LYTE *Dodoens* III. lviii. 398 Doder is a strange herbe without leaves and without roote, lyke unto a threed, muche gnarled and wrapped togither. **1640** PARKINSON *Theat. Bot.* 11 Wee call those strings generally by the name of Dodder. **1871–2** H. MACMILLAN *True Vine* v. 227 The dodder..is a mere mass of elastic, pale red, knotted threads, which shoot out in all directions over the vine.

2. Applied locally to some choking or climbing weeds: see quots. **1878** *Cumbld. Gloss.*, *Dodder*..the corn spurrey plant, *Spergula arvensis.* **1884** *Cheshire Gloss.* s.v. *Dother*, In Mid-Ches. *Polygonum Convolvulus* is called dother.

3. = DOD *sb.*[2] *dial.* **1891** *Rutland Gloss.*, *Dodders*, coarse reeds and rushes in swampy land.

†**'dodder**, *a. Obs.* [f. DOD *v.*[1]] = DODDED. **1614** MARKHAM *Cheap Husb.* III. i. (1623) 104 Let them have by no meanes any hornes, for the dodder Sheepe is the best breeder. **1868** [see DOTTEREL 3].

dodder (ˈdɒdə(r)), *v.* [A variant of or parallel formation to DADDER, q.v. Cf. also TOTTER.]

1. *intr.* To tremble or shake from frailty. **1617** MINSHEU *Ductor*, Dodder grasses..so called because with the least puff or blast of wind it..doth as it were dodder and tremble. **1785** [E. PERRONET] *Occas. Verses*, *What is Life?* 173 Where wisdom dodders, and where wanders peace. **1825** BROCKETT *N.C. Words*, *Dodder*, *Dother*, to shake, to tremble; to nod, as in the palsy of decrepitude. **1894** *Cornh. Mag.* Mar. 285 He doddered as he spoke.

†**2.** To nod (in sleep). *Obs.* **16..** *Poem* (N.) She dodders all day, While the little birds play; And at midnight she flutters her wings.

3. To proceed or move unsteadily or with tottering gait; to totter; to potter. **1819** MISS MITFORD in L'Estrange *Life* (1870) II. 58 One has such pleasure in doddering along the hedgerows. **1862** SALA *Ship Chandler* iii. 48 [He] was permitted to dodder about books and accounts of no great moment. **1885** *Spectator* 21 Nov. 1544 We must either set [one] up..once and for all, or dodder along for another half century with our miserable muddle. **1894** MRS. H. WARD *Marcella* III. 201 Old Alresford, too, was fast doddering off the stage.

Hence **'doddering** *ppl. a.*, that dodders; now freq. mentally feeble or inept; futile, footling; **'doddering-grass**, quaking-grass (Britt. & Holl.); **'dodderingness.** **1745** W. THOMPSON *Sickness* IV. (R.), The sailor hugs thee to the doddering mast. **1871** MISS BRADDON *Lovels* xlii, A little old grey-headed man, who..had an ancient doddering manner. **1892** *Northumbld. Gloss.*, *Dodderin'-dicks*, the quivering heads of the..quaking grass. **1908** *Fabian News*

XIX. 82/2 Mr. Justin McCarthy, in his rather doddering introduction, explicitly warns us against Mr. Sheehy-Skeffington's portraiture of Davitt as an anti-clerical politician. **1915** WODEHOUSE *Something Fresh* iii, The amiable dodderingness which marked every branch of his life. **1921** G. B. SHAW *Back to Methuselah* IV. III. 203 He was a doddering old ass. **1926** *Brit. Weekly* 23 Sept. 519/3 Your puir, toom, dodderin', fushionless kirk.

doddered (ˈdɒdəd), *ppl. a.* [app. originally a deriv. of DOD *v.*[1] to poll or take the top off (a tree).

It is not clear whether it was a contaminated form of DODDED 'polled', or a mistaken spelling of DODDARD *sb.*, 'doddered oak' for 'doddard oak' (cf. *pollard willow*); while the matter is complicated by the earlier use of *dottard* or *dotard* (see DOTARD 2) in the same sense. In later use there has been unintelligent association with DODDER *sb.*, and perhaps with DODDER *v.*, and its cognates. It is doubtful whether senses 2 and 3 belong originally to this word.]

1. A word conventionally used (? after Dryden) as an attribute of old oaks (rarely other trees); app. originally meaning: Having lost the top or branches, esp. through age and decay; hence, remaining as a decayed stump. Johnson explained it as 'Overgrown with dodder: covered with supercrescent plants'; and this explanation, which was manifestly erroneous, since neither dodder nor any plant like it grows upon trees, has been repeated in the dictionaries, and has influenced literary usage, in which there is often a vague notion of some kind of parasitical accretion accompanying or causing decay.

1697 DRYDEN *Virg. Past.* IX. 9 From the sloaping mountain to the Vale, And dodder'd Oak [*veteres, jam fracta cacumina, fagos*]. **1700** —— *Pal. & Arc.* III. 905 The peasants were enjoined Sere-wood, and firs, and doddered oaks to find. **1725** POPE *Odyss.* XX. 200 The dodder'd oaks Divide, obedient to the forceful strokes. *a* **1748** THOMSON (Ogilvie), Rots like a dodder'd Oak. **1813** SCOTT *Rokeby* VI. iii, He passes now the doddered oak, Ye heard the startled raven croak. **1850** H. MILLER *Footpr. Creat.* x. (1874) 197 Doddered trunks of vast size, like those of Granton and Craigleith. **1853** C. BRONTE *Villette* xii, Nasturtiums clustered beautifully about the doddered orchard giants. **1878** F. S. WILLIAMS *Midl. Railw.* 2 Doddered willows by the watercourses. **1880** DISRAELI *Endym.* xxxiv, Sometimes they stood before the vast form of some doddered oak.

b. as *pa. pple.* So **'doddering** *pr. pple.*, becoming doddered.

1697 DRYDEN *Æneid* II. 703 Near the hearth a laurel grew, Dodder'd with age [*veterrima laurus*]. **1766** *Poetry* in *Ann. Reg.* 235 The doddering oaks forewarn me of decay.

2. *dial.* [Cf. DODDER *v.*]

1847–78 HALLIWELL, *Doddered*, confused, shattered, infirm. **1876** *Whitby Gloss.*, *Dodder'd*, shattered, dilapidated.

3. Of persons: Decayed or impaired with age.

1893 STEVENSON *Catr.* XV. 173 Auld feckless doddered men.

dodderel, -ril. *dial.* [f. DOD *v.*[1]: cf. DODDERED, also DOTTEREL (in same sense).] (See quots.)

1847–78 HALLIWELL, *Dodderel*, a pollard. *Warw.* **1881** *Leicestersh. Gloss.*, *Dodderil*, a pollard tree. **1891** *Rutland Gloss.* s.v., The boundary is by yon old dodderil oak.

dodderer (ˈdɒdərə(r)). [f. DODDER *v.* + -ER[1].] One who dodders; one infirm in body or mind; a feeble or inept person.

1907 G. B. SHAW *John Bull's Other Island* III. 65 We're not all foostherin oul doddherers like Mat. **1917** W. J. LOCKE *Red Planet* xi. 131 Do you think I'm a blind dodderer? **1926** *Public Opinion* 23 Apr. 420/1, I am constantly meeting ponderous dodderers who are sure civilisation is in rapid decay. **1930** *Punch* 14 May 551, I see now that I have been a difficult old dodderer upon this subject.

'dodder-grass. *dial.* [f. DODDER *v.*] Properly, Quaking-grass, *Briza media*; also called *doddering-grass*, *doddle grass*, *doddering dicks*, etc. Sometimes loosely applied locally to species of *Bromus*, *Festuca*, *Poa*, or other loose-panicled grasses.

1617 [see DODDER *v.* 1]. **1736** PEGGE *Kenticisms* s.v. *Dawther*, A certain long shaking-grass is called dodder-grass or dawther in Kent. [App. some *Bromus*.] **1875** *Sussex Gloss.*, *Doddlegrass*, *Briza media*, or quaking grass, called in the north 'doddering dick'. **1878–86** BRITTEN & HOLLAND *Plant-n.*, Dodder Grass, *Briza media*. *Cumb.*; *Kent.*

doddery (ˈdɒdərɪ), *a.* [f. DODDER *v.* + -Y[1].] Apt to tremble or totter, from age or infirmity; shaky.

1866 [see DITHERY *a.*]. **1919** J. BUCHAN *Mr. Standfast* xvii, When he got on his feet he was as doddery as an old man. **1921** *Chambers's Jrnl.* May 325/1 The old man..seemed to have become very doddery as he descended from the buggy. **1963** H. CALISHER *Textures of Life* ii. 35 Its thick-walled ambling waste of space and doddery pediment.

doddle (ˈdɒd(ə)l), *sb.*[1] and *a.* *Obs.* exc. *dial.* [f. DOD *v.*[1]: cf. DODDARD. Whether orig. *sb.* or *a.* is not clear.]

A. *sb.* A pollard.

B. *adj.* Pollard, of which the top has been cut off.

1601 HOLLAND *Pliny* XXVI. II. 251 It..growth at the foot of old trees. (*Marg.* Yea also in the head of doddle oaks.) **1887** JESSOP *Arcady* 55 Its huge hedgerow with the 'doddles' or pollards, which afforded firing for rich and poor.

†**'doddle,** *sb.*[2] *Obs.* [f. DODDLE *v.*] ? A doddling or infirm person.

1681 OTWAY *Soldier's Fort.* I. i, Is your Piece of Mortality such a doting Doddle? is he so very fond of you?

'doddle, *sb.*[3] *colloq.* [? f. DODDLE *v.* 2.] Something that is easy or requires little effort; a 'walk-over'; (see also quot. 1937).

1937 PARTRIDGE *Dict. Slang* 229/2 *Doddle*, money very easily obtained. **1966** M. WOODHOUSE *Tree Frog* xv. 122 If the climb had reached any level of difficulty higher than Moderate, which is the Climbers' Club's polite way of labelling a gumshoe doddle, we'd have died. **1970** A. DRAPER *Swansong for Rare Bird* vi. 40 Probation was a doddle really, and it didn't make much difference to me.

doddle (ˈdɒd(ə)l), *v.* [var. of DADDLE: cf. also DODDER *v.*, and with sense 2 TODDLE.]

†**1.** *trans.* To shake, nod (the head). *Obs.*

1653 URQUHART *Rabelais* I. xxii. (1694) I. 85 Mumbling with his Mouth, nodding and dodling his Head.

2. *intr.* To walk with short, infirm, or unsteady steps, to toddle; to totter; to dawdle.

1761 GRAY *Let.* 24 Sept. Wks. 1884 III. 114 The old Bishop of Lincoln, with his stick, went doddling by the side of the Queen. **1847–78** HALLIWELL, *Doddle*, to totter; to dawdle. *North.* **1869** in *Lonsdale Gloss.* **1875** in *Sussex Gloss.* **1884** *Spectator* 6 Dec. 1614 A pretty girl..with a quantity of little pigs doddling about in front of her.

Hence **'doddled, 'doddling** *ppl. adjs.*; **'doddlish** *a.* (*dial.*), feeble, infirm.

1847–78 HALLIWELL, *Doddleish*, feeble. *Sussex.* **1874** BURNAND *My Time* xxxiv. 369 A doddling old grandfather. **1875** *Sussex Gloss.*, *Doddlish*, infirm. **1893** H. M. DOUGHTY *Our Wherry in Wendish Lands* 321 The doddled old küster so bothered us.

doddy, doddie (ˈdɒdɪ), *sb.* [f. DOD *v.*[1]]

1. A cow or bull without horns; *attrib.* = DODDED, as 'a black doddy cow'. *Sc.*

1808 in JAMIESON. **1827** SCOTT *Two Drovers* ii, They were something less beasts than your drove, doddies most of them. **1892** *Scott. Leader* 1 Jan. 3 A very fine herd of the favourite 'Doddies'.

†**2.** Shortened form of DODDYPOLL. *Obs.*

a **1590** *Marr. Wit & Wisd.* (N.), Now purpose I soundly Trick this pretty doddy, And make him a noddy.

doddy (ˈdɒdɪ), *a.* *Sc.* [f. DOD *sb.*[4] + -Y.] Pettish, cross, ill-tempered.

1808 in JAMIESON. **1823** GALT *Entail* I. xx. 166 Colley is as doddy and crabbit to Watty as if he was its adversary.

†**'doddy-pate.** *Obs.* [f. as next + PATE.] = next.

c **1500** *Maid Emlyn* 19 [She] Made hym a fole, And called hym dody-pate.

†**doddypoll** (ˈdɒdɪpəʊl). *Obs.* Forms: *α.* 5 dotty-, doty-, dote-, 6 doti-, dotti-, -pol(e, -poll(e. *β.* 6 dody-, doddye-, 6–7 dodi-, 7–8 doddy-, doddi-, -pole, -poll, etc. [app. originally f. DOTE *v.* to be foolish or silly, subseq. referred to DOD *v.*[1], as if 'having a dodded poll': cf. *roundhead.*] A stupid person; blockhead, fool.

1401 *Pol. Poems* (Rolls) II. 99 Ȝit, Dawe Dotypolle, thou justifiest this harlotrie. *c* **1422** HOCCLEVE *Min. Poems*, *Jonathas* 49 A lewde dotepol, straw for his wit! *c* **1460** *Towneley Myst.* (Surtees) 145 Fy, dotty-pols, with youre bookes. **1549** LATIMER *3rd Serm. bef. Edw. VI* (Arb.) 84 What ye brain-sycke fooles, ye hoddy peckes, ye doddye poulles!..are you seduced also? **1581** J. BELL *Haddon's Answ. Osor.* 29 b, No man..besides this Doctour Dottipoll. *a* **1652** BROME *Eng. Moor* II. i. Wks. 1873 II. 18 All the Doddy-poles in Town. **1767** STERNE *Tr. Shandy* IX. xxv, Shall I be called as many blockheads, numsculls, doddy-poles, dunderheads.

Hence †**'doddy-polled** *a.* *Obs.*

1708 MOTTEUX *Rabelais* V. xlvi, Thou doddipol'd Ninny.

dode, obs. pa. t. of DO *v.*

dodeca-, dodec-, Gr. δώδεκα twelve, an initial element in numerous technical words: see below. Also **do'decafid** *a.* [L. *-fidus* -cleft], divided into twelve segments (*Syd. Soc. Lex.* 1883). **dode'camerous** *a.* [Gr. μέρος part], consisting of twelve parts or divisions (*Syd. Soc. Lex.*). **ˌdodeca'partite** *a.* [L. *partīt-us* divided] = prec. **ˌdodeca'petalous** *a. Bot.*, having twelve petals. **ˌdodeca'semic** *a. Pros.* [Gr. δωδεκάσημος of twelve times (in music), f. σῆμα sign, mark], consisting of 12 moræ or units of time, as a *dodecasemic foot*. (In recent Dicts.)

1879 SIR G. G. SCOTT *Lect. Archit.* II. 197 If all sides had the threefold division, it would have become dodecapartite. **1847** CRAIG, *Dodecapetalous*, having twelve petals.

†**'dodecade.** *Obs.* Also do'decady. [f. Gr. δώδεκα twelve, after DECADE: cf. F. *dodécade* in Littré.] A group, set, or series of twelve.

c **1624** LUSHINGTON *Recant. Serm.* in *Phenix* (1708) II. No. 26. 494 The 12 disciples answering the 12 patriarchs.. that both the Testaments, the New and Old, should be founded upon dodecadies. **1686** GOAD *Celest. Bodies* III. ii. 436 We have..a Dodecade of such Rarities.

dodecadrachm (dəʊˈdɛkədræm). *Numism.* [ad. Gr. δωδεκάδραχμος, f. δώδεκα twelve + δραχμή DRACHMA.] An ancient Greek gold coin of the value of 12 drachmas.

1881 *Athenæum* 3 Dec. 748/1 Of the 27 gold coins exhibited one is the dodecadrachm of Queen Berenice II.

dodecagon (dəʊˈdɛkəgən). *Geom.* [ad. Gr. δωδεκάγωνον, f. δώδεκα twelve + -γωνος angled, γωνία angle; cf. F. *dodécagone* (1690 in Hatz.-Darm.).] A plane figure having twelve sides and twelve angles. ***regular dodecagon***, one that has all its sides and all its angles equal.

1658 PHILLIPS, *Dodecagon* (Greek), a Geometrical figure of 12 Angles. **1861** THORNBURY *Turner* (1862) I. 51 He draws trees when he should draw dodecagons.

Hence **dode'cagonal** *a.*, of or pertaining to a dodecagon; twelve-sided.

1851–60 in MAYNE *Expos. Lex.*

‖**Dodecagynia** (ˌdəʊdɪkəˈdʒɪnɪə). *Bot.* [mod.L. (Linnæus 1735), f. Gr. δώδεκα twelve + γυνή woman, female, taken by Linnæus in sense of 'female organ, pistil'.] An order in some classes of the Linnæan sexual system, comprising plants having either eleven or twelve pistils.

1762 in HUDSON *Flora Anglica.* **1794** MARTYN *Rousseau's Bot.* x. 110. **1857** HENFREY *Elem. Bot.* I. ii. 197.

Hence **do'decagyn**, a plant of *Dodecagynia*; **dodeca'gynian, -'gynious, dode'cagynous** *adjs.*

1828 WEBSTER, *Dodecagyn*, a plant having twelve pistils. *Ibid.*, *Dodecagy·nian*, having twelve pistils. **1864** *Ibid.*, *Dodecagynous*, having twelve styles. **1883** *Syd. Soc. Lex.*, *Dodecagynious*..twelve-pistilled.

dodecahedral (ˌdəʊdɪkəˈhiːdrəl), *a.* Also dodecaedral. [f. DODECAHEDR-ON + -AL[1].] Having the form of a dodecahedron; twelve-sided.

1796 KIRWAN *Elem. Min.* (ed. 2) I. 207 Transparent, and of a dodecaedral figure. *Ibid.* II. 8 It often gives dodecahædral crystals. **1870** BENTLEY *Bot.* 14 In a perfectly regular arrangement..we have dodecahedral cells.

So **ˌdodeca'hedric** *a.* = prec.

1878 LAWRENCE tr. *Cotta's Rocks Class.* 34 Cleavage indistinct, dodecahedric. **1881** RUSKIN *Love's Meinie* I. iii. 126, I retain, therefore, my dodecahedric form of catechism.

dodecahedron (ˌdəʊdɪkəˈhiːdrən). *Geom.* Also 6–9 dodecaedron, 6–8 -um. [a. Gr. δωδεκάεδρον, neuter of δωδεκάεδρος, f. δώδεκα twelve + ἕδρα seat, base, face. Cf. F. *dodécaèdre* (16th c.).]

A solid figure having twelve faces: *esp.* the ***regular dodecahedron***, see quots. 1570, 1653.

1570 BILLINGSLEY *Euclid* XI. def. xxiv. 319 A Dodecahedron is a solide or bodily figure contained vnder twelue equall, equilater, and equiangle Pentagons. **1653** H. MORE *Antid. Ath.* II. (1662) 147 There are Five regular Bodies in Geometry..the Cube, the Tetraedrum, the Octaedrum, the Dodecaedrum, and the Eicosaedrum. **1850** DAUBENY *Atom. The.* vi. (ed. 2) 171 Phosphorus crystallizes in regular dodecaedrons. **1878** GURNEY *Crystallogr.* 85 A form consisting of twelve similar rhombuses..is..called the rhombic dodecahedron.

‖**Dodecandria** (dəʊdɪˈkændrɪə). *Bot.* [mod.L. (Linnæus 1735), f. Gr. δώδεκα twelve + ἀνδρ-, stem of ἀνήρ man, male: see DECANDRIA.] The eleventh class in the sexual system of Linnæus, comprising plants having from twelve to nineteen stamens not cohering.

1753 CHAMBERS *Cycl. Supp.*, *Dodecandria*..a class of plants which have hermaphrodite flowers, with twelve stamina or male parts in each. **1762** in HUDSON *Flora Anglica.* **1794** MARTYN *Rousseau's Bot.* ix. 89.

Hence **dode'cander**, a plant of the class *Dodecandria*; **dode'candrian** *a.*, belonging to that class; **dode'candrous** *a.*, having twelve stamens.

1806 J. GALPINE *Brit. Bot.* 40 Lythrum..Flowers spiked, dodecandrous. **1828** WEBSTER, *Dodecander*, *Dodecandrian*, [cited from LEE]. **1870** BENTLEY *Bot.* 246 A flower having 12 stamens is Dodecandrous.

'dodecane. *Chem.* [f. DODECA- + -ANE.] A paraffin of the composition $C_{12}H_{26}$.

1875 WATTS *Dict. Chem.* VII. 891 Dodecane..Boiling point 202° [C.]. **1877** —— *Fownes' Chem.* (ed. 12) II. 50.

dodecaphonic (ˌdəʊdɪkəˈfɒnɪk, dəʊˌdɛkəˈfɒnɪk), *a. Mus.* [Gr. δώδεκα twelve + PHONIC *a.*] Of, relating to, or using, the twelve-note system, a method of composition formulated by Arnold Schönberg. Hence **do'decaphonism** (also ˌdəʊdɪˈkæfənɪz(ə)m), **do'decaˌphony** (-ˌfəʊnɪ, also ˌdəʊdɪˈkæfənɪ), the twelve-note system; **dodecaphonist** (dəʊˈdɛkəfənɪst, ˌdəʊdɪˈkæfənɪst), a composer using this system.

1950 L. O. SYMKINS in *Étude* Sept. 12 (*title*) Schœnberg's new world of dodecaphonic music. **1951** *Musical Q.* XXXVII. 95 We dislike Schœnbergism, atonalism, dodecaphonism, and the rest. **1952** *Ibid.* XXXVIII. 604 Schollum's Second Sonata is in its combination of linearity, Romantic expressiveness, and dodecaphony a mixture of styles. **1953** *N.Y. Times* 2 Feb. 18/8 Like the majority of dodecaphonists, he presents music governed by strict logic and organization. **1955** *Oxf. Compan. Mus.* (ed. 9) 698/1 All the twelve notes of the octave are employed in every composition, and all the notes are treated in such a way as to enjoy an equal footing... Theorists of the Schönberg school prefer to call his method not a chromatic one but 'Dodecaphonic'. **1955** *Times* 11 May 7/6 Dallapiccola's music, written before his conversion to dodecaphony, never failed to heighten the emotion. **1970** *Daily Tel.* 20 May 16/5 No amount of explaining could trace dodecaphony in Tippett's 2nd Symphony.

dodecarch, dodek- (ˈdəʊdɪkɑːk). *Anc. Hist.* [ad. Gr. δωδεκάρχ-ης, f. δώδεκα twelve + -αρχης ruler.] One of a ruling body of twelve.

1882-3 SCHAFF *Encycl. Relig. Knowl.* I. 707 Psammeticus I., one of the dodekarchs.

dodecarchy (ˈdəʊdɪkɑːkɪ). [f. as prec. + Gr. -αρχία rule: cf. DECARCHY.] Government by twelve rulers or kings; a ruling body of twelve.

1662 STILLINGFL. *Orig. Sacr.* I. v. §8 So that Egypt was anciently a dodecarchy, as England in the Saxons' time was a heptarchy. **1862** STANLEY *Jew. Ch.* (1877) I. xiii. 246 It was ..a dodecarchy, of which the supremacy passed..first to one tribe and then to another. **1876** S. BIRCH *Rede Lect. Egypt* 39 Psammetichus..seized the moment to reduce the Assyrian Dodecarchy under his sway.

dodecastyle (ˈdəʊdɪkəstaɪl). [f. Gr. δώδεκα twelve + στῦλος column. So mod.F. *dodécastyle*.] A portico or colonnade of twelve columns.

1825 GWILT *Chambers's Civil Archit.* 413 *Dodecastyle*, a Building having twelve Columns in front. **1853** *Encycl. Brit.* III. 509/1 The Chamber of Deputies in Paris has a true dodecastyle.

ˌdodecaˈsyllable. [f. Gr. δώδεκα twelve + SYLLABLE.] **a.** *Pros.* A line or verse of twelve syllables. **b.** 'A word of twelve syllables' (Worcester, 1846). So **dodecasyˈllabic** *a.*, of or containing twelve syllables.

1753 CHAMBERS *Cycl. Supp.* s.v. *Alexandrin*, Alexandrins are otherwise called dodecasyllables; and are peculiar to the modern poetry. **1831** W. H. MILL *Christa Sangitá* Pref. 11 Distinguishing only the Benedictus or hymn of Zacharias by a lyric dodecasyllable measure. **1882-3** SCHAFF *Encycl. Relig. Knowl.* 2286 A sermon in verse, heptasyllabic, octosyllabic, or dodecasyllabic.

†**dodecaˈtemory.** *Astron. Obs.* Also 7 dodecatemorion. [ad. Gr. δωδεκατημόριον a twelfth part, f. δωδέκατ-ος, -η, -ον twelfth + μόριον piece, portion.] A twelfth part; a term formerly applied to each of the twelve divisions of the Zodiac.

1603 SIR C. HEYDON *Jud. Astrol.* xviii. 374 The dodecatemories of the Zodiack. **1674** JEAKE *Arith.* (1696) Bij, The mildest Dodecatemorie springs In beauteous Orient. *a* **1700** CREECH (J.), 'Tis dodecatemorion thus describ'd: Thrice ten degrees, which every sign contains. **1727-51** CHAMBERS *Cycl.*, *Dodecatemory*..The term is chiefly applied to the twelve houses, or parts of the zodiac of the primum mobile; to distinguish them from the 12 signs.

doˈdecuplet. *Mus.* [f. DODEC(A- + ending of OCTUPLET, etc.] 'A group of twelve notes to be played in the time of eight' (Stainer and Barrett *Dict. Mus. Terms* 1880).

dodecyl (ˈdəʊdɪsɪl, dəʊˈdiːsaɪl). *Chem.* [f. DODEC(ANE + -YL.]. The univalent hydrocarbon radical $C_{12}H_{25}-$, derived from dodecane by the loss of one hydrogen atom.

1889 MUIR & MORLEY *Watts' Dict. Chem.* II. 413/2 Dodecyl alcohol $C_{12}H_{25}OH$. **1963** A. J. HALL *Textile Sci.* vi. 294 Thus two very popular synthetic detergents in use today are dodecyl benzene sulphonate [etc.].

†**dodeˈmusyd,** *ppl. a. Obs. rare.* [The first element is possibly as in *doddypoll*; the second appears to be from *muse* v., in ME. to be amazed.]

c **1450** *Cov. Myst.* 395 Ye dodemusyd prynces faste you aray, Or I make avow to Mahomed youre bodyes schul blede.

doderell, var. of DOTTEREL, plover.

dodgast (ˈdɒdgɑːst, -gæst), *v. U.S. colloq.* [f. DOD- + *gast*, prob. for BLAST *v.* 10. Cf. DOD-ROT *v.*] In imprecatory and expletive use: to 'confound', 'curse'. Chiefly in ˈ**dodgasted** *ppl. a.*

1888 *Detroit Free Press* (Farmer), It's a dodgasted funny thing,..but it's a fact. **1908** C. E. MULFORD *Orphan* ix. 103 What can we do when our cayuses are so dod-gasted tired? **1909** *N.Y. Observer* 2 Sept. 319/2 Well, dodgast you, get in the stern there. **1914** W. J. LOCKE *Fort. Youth* xxi, It's a pity, sonny—a dodgasted pity!

dodge (dɒdʒ), *v.* [Known only from 16th c.; origin unascertained. The primary meaning and sense-development are also uncertain.

Wedgwood and Skeat compare an alleged dial. Sc. *dodd* to jog (cf. sense 11 below), which Skeat would also identify with the base of *dodder*, *doddle*. This might perhaps pass for the sense, but the phonetic development is not evident; cf. however *sled*, *sledge*.]

1. *intr.* **a.** To move to and fro, or backwards and forwards; to keep changing one's position or shifting one's ground; to shuffle.

1704 STEELE *Lying Lover* II. i. 18 Don't stand staring, and dodging with your feet, and wearing out your Livery Hat with squeezing for an excuse. **1720** J. QUINCY *Hodges' Hist. Acc. Plague* 189 Whenever a Buboe is uncertain and dodges, sometimes appearing and then going back. **1750** *Phil. Trans.* XLVI. 324 The Dragon fly..in a hovering Posture, dodging up and down in the Water. **1820** W. IRVING *Sketch Bk.* I. 60 Whenever he went dodging about the village.

†**b.** To use shifts or changes of position (*with* a person, etc.), so as to baffle or catch him. *Obs.*

1631 MILTON *Univ. Carrier* i. 8 He had, any time this ten years full, Dodged with him betwixt Cambridge and the Bull. **1677** W. HUBBARD *Narrative* Postscr. 7 He began to dodge with his pursuers. **1724** DE FOE *Mem. Cavalier* II. 182 The King..had been dodging with Essex eight or ten Days. **1816** SCOTT *Old Mort.* xxxvi, Do you think we can stand here all day to be turning and dodging with you, like greyhounds after a hare?

c. To move to and fro *about*, *around*, or *behind* any obstacle, so as to elude a pursuer, a missile, or a blow, or to get a sudden advantage of an enemy.

1681 R. KNOX *Hist. Ceylon* 22 Trees, about which they may dodg. **1756** *Gentl. Mag.* XXVI. 426 Dodging behind the mizzen mast, and falling down upon the deck at the noise of the enemy's shot. **1845** DARWIN *Voy. Nat.* iv. (1879) 77 He was obliged to dodge round his horse. **1859** TENNENT *Ceylon* VIII. iii. II. 331 Amongst full grown timber, a skilful runner can escape an elephant by dodging round the trees.

2. *intr.* †**a.** To go this way and that way in one's speech or action; to be off and on; to parley, palter, haggle about terms. *Obs.*

1568 JEWEL *Answ. Harding's Detect. Foul Err.* in *Def. Apol.* (1611) 127 If yee doubt heereof, leaue dodging in your note Bookes, and read S. Cyprian, and ye shall find it. **1577** STANYHURST *Descr. Irel.* iii. in *Holinshed* II. 25/1 The merchant and he stood dodging one with the other in cheaping the ware. **1684** tr. *Bonet's Merc. Compit.* IX. 335 If the Disease go not off presently, we must not stand dodging, but give a gentle purging potion. *a* **1763** BYROM *Careless Content* (R.), For lack or glut, for loss or gain, I never dodge, nor up nor down.

b. To play fast and loose, change about deceitfully; to shuffle *with* a person; to prevaricate.

1575 J. STILL *Gamm. Gurton* v. ii. in Hazl. *Dodsley* III. 254 Fie, dost but dodge. **1614** RALEIGH *Hist. World* v. iii. §12. 418 They did him no manner of good, but rather dodged with him, euen in the little courtesie which they most pretended. **1708** PRIOR *Turtle & Sp.* 109 With Fate's lean tipstaff none can dodge. **1859** SMILES *Self-Help* xiii. (1860) 340 He does not shuffle nor prevaricate, dodge nor skulk.

†**c.** *to dodge it*: to haggle. *Obs.*

1652 URQUHART *Jewel* Wks. (1834) 267 That frankness of disposition..not permitting him to dodge it upon inches and ells.

3. *trans.* To play fast and loose with; to baffle or parry by shifts and pretexts; to trifle with.

1573 G. HARVEY *Letter-bk.* (Camden) 15 Thus was I doggid and dodgid on everi side. **1663** J. SPENCER *Disc. Prodigies* (1665) 256 Loth to be dodged and abused with endless uncertainties and dissimilitudes. **1697** *Occas. Conformity* 27 To make the matter a Game, to dodge Religions, and go in the Morning to Church, and in the Afternoon to the Meeting. **1855** TENNYSON *Sea Dreams* 145 He dodged me with a long and loose account. **1868** E. EDWARDS *Raleigh* I. xxiv. 559 The Crown lawyers had again to dodge the case..by a trick of their craft.

4. To avoid an encounter with (a person or thing) by changes of position, shifts, or doublings; to elude (a pursuer, etc.) by shifts or sideward movements.

1680 OTWAY *C. Marius* IV. ii. Wks. 1727 II. 239 Asunder we may dodge our Fate. **1713** DERHAM *Phys. Theol.* IV. xiv. (1723) *note*, The Doublings of the Hare..to dodge and deceive the Dogs. **1893** E. B. KNIGHT *Where three Empires meet* xxiv. 366 Rocks..would come rolling down upon us, and had to be nimbly dodged. **1893** FORBES-MITCHELL *Remin. Gt. Mutiny* 19 Where blows aimed at the victims had evidently been dodged.

5. To follow stealthily, and with shifts to avoid discovery, as by keeping behind intervening objects. (Cf. DOG *v.* 1.)

1727 FIELDING *Love in Sev. Masq.* Wks. 1775 I. 58 *La.* Promise not to dodge us. *Wi.* Not even to look after you. **1814** MAD. D'ARBLAY *Wanderer* IV. 51 If they saw any suspicious persons dodging them. **1840** LADY C. BURY *Hist. Flirt* xi, I will never quit you..I will dodge your steps.

6. To move (a thing) to and fro, or up and down; to lead (an examinee) to and fro in a subject of examination and not straight on.

1820 *Sporting Mag.* VI. 266 Two pieces of wood had been introduced between the hoof and the shoe; after replacing the shoe again the horse was dodged, and discovered to be perfectly sound. **1861** DICKENS *Gt. Expect.* viii, He said, pompously, 'Seven times nine, boy'! and how should I be able to answer, dodged in that way? **1880** *Daily Tel.* 7 Oct., It would be absolutely childish to go on dodging the Fleets about from Cattaro to Volo [etc.].

7. *intr. Change-ringing.* Said of a bell rung in a chime, when, instead of following in its regular ascending or descending order, as in plain hunting, it is shifted one place in the opposite direction, and then in the next round back again to resume its course, until another dodge occurs.

1684 R. H. *School Recreat.* 101 In this Bob, when the Treble leaves the two Hind Bells, they dodge 'till it comes there again, and 'till the Treble gives Way for the dodging again of the said two Hind Bells, the two first Bells dodge, but after cease dodging, when the two Hind Bells dodge. **1872** ELLACOMBE *Ch. Bells Devon* ii. 29. **1880** GROVE *Dict. Music* s.v. *Changes*, The first three bells go through the six changes of which they are capable..while the bells behind 'dodge'.

8. *intr.* (*techn.*) To occupy positions alternately on the one side and the other of a medial line.

1874 KNIGHT *Dict. Mech.*, *Dodging*, said of mortises, when they are not in the same plane at the hub. By spreading the butts of the spokes where they enter the hub, dodging on each side of a median line, alternately, the wheel is stiffened against a lateral strain.

9. *trans. Photogr.* To use any artifice to improve (the negative) for printing.

1883 *Hardwick's Photogr. Chem.* (ed. Taylor) 335 The important operations of 'dodging' and 'printing-in'. **1889** *Anthony's Photogr. Bulletin* (U.S.A.) II. 349 That 'dodging' had been resorted to to make the tree print well.

10. *trans. Salt-making* (*Cheshire*). (See quot.)

1884 *Cheshire Gloss.*, *Dodging*, salt-making term. Knocking scale off the plates over the fire.

11. *trans.* and *intr.* (*dial.*) To jog (see quots.).

1802 SIBBALD *Chron. Sc. Poet.* Gloss. (Jam.), *Dodge*, to jog, or trudge along. **1825** BROCKETT *N.C. Wds.*, *Dodge*, to jog, to incite. **1869** *Lonsdale Gloss.*, *Dodge*, (1) to jog, incite. **1877** *Holderness Gloss.*, *Dodge-on*, to go along, making the best of an affliction..'Hey! it a bad job, but Ah mun dodge-on somehow or other'.

†**12.** *trans.* To insinuate *into* by a dodge. *Obs.*

1687 R. L'ESTRANGE *Answ. Diss.* 47 A Paradox of Conscience Dodg'd into a Popular Scheme of Government!

13. *to dodge Pompey*: (*a*) to evade work (*Naval slang*); (*b*) see quot. 1930 (*Austral. slang*).

1929 F. BOWEN *Sea Slang* 38 *Dodging Pompey*, avoiding work on shipboard. Originally a naval phrase entirely. **1930** BILLIS & KENYON *Pastures New* iii. 46 Browne detailed the laws passed, not to encourage the overlander, but rather to counteract his habit of stealing grass—'dodging Pompey', as it was known. **1961** F. H. BURGESS *Dict. Sailing* 73 *Dodging Pompey*, skulking, or avoiding work by the use of any semi-legitimate excuse.

dodge (dɒdʒ), *sb.*[1] [f. prec. vb.]

†**1.** The act of slipping aside so as to elude a person or thing; the 'slip', the 'go-by'. *Obs.* or *dial.*

1575 J. STILL *Gamm. Gurton* II. i. in Hazl. *Dodsley* III. 193 There was a fouler fault, my Gammer ga' me the dodge. **1606** *Wily Beguiled* ibid. IX. 256 Shall I trouble you so far as to take some pains with me? I am loth to have the dodge. **1749** FIELDING *Tom Jones* VII. iv, I was hard run enough by your mother for one man; but after giving her a dodge, here's another..follows me upon the foil. **1880** MRS. PARR *Adam & Eve* II. 116 He was forced to avoid him by giving a sudden dodge to one side.

2. a. A shifty trick, an artifice to elude or cheat.

1638 FEATLY *Strict. Lyndom.* I. 201, I have beate the Iesuit heretofore out of this dodge. **1681** H. MORE *Exp. Dan.* Pref. 64 To put a dodge upon the Protestants to weaken their Faith. **1837** DICKENS *Pickw.* xvi, 'It was all false, of course?' 'All, sir', replied Mr. Weller, 'reg'lar do, sir; artful dodge.' **1860** BRIGHT *Sp. Church Rates* 27 Apr., I am altogether against any kind of dodge by which this matter may be..settled.

b. *on the dodge*: engaged in crooked or dishonest proceedings.

1904 'O. HENRY' *Heart of West* (1912) xi. 214 I've been on the dodge for a month, and I'd like to rest up. **1920** J. M. BARRIE *Kiss for Cinderella* I. 26 If you wanted to get into Buckingham Palace on the dodge, how would you slip by the policeman?

3. *colloq.* and *slang.* A clever or adroit expedient or contrivance (cf. *trick* in similar use): vulgarly extended to a machine, a natural phenomenon, etc.

1842 E. FITZGERALD *Lett.* (1889) I. 111 The alternation of green and corn crops is a good dodge. **1849** THACKERAY *Pendennis* xxix, [They] have many harmless arts..and innocent dodges (if we may be permitted to use an excellent phrase that has become vernacular since the appearance of the last dictionaries). **1855** SMEDLEY *H. Coverdale* iii, I'd start to America, and do Niagara, and all the other picturesque dodges [etc.]. **1867** LD. MALMESBURY *Memoirs of an Ex-Minister* (1884) II. 376 To show us how to light a good fire by some dodge of lighting the wood at the back.

4. *Change-ringing.* See quot. 1684, and cf. DODGE *v.* 7.

1684 R. H. *School Recreat.* 93 The..Meaning of a Dodge is this; any Bell that is coming down, and is to make a Dodge, must move up again one Bell higher, and any Bell that is going up, and is to make a Dodge, must come down one Bell lower, and then up or down as the Course of such Bell requires. **1880** GROVE *Dict. Music* s.v. *Changes*, In change-ringing terms, the 4th and 5th [bells] are said to 'make places', and the 2nd and 3rd are said to make a 'double dodge'.

dodge, *sb.*[2] *north. dial.* A large irregular piece, a lump.

1562 *Wills & Inv. N.C.* (Surtees 1835) 207, j dodge of iron viij[d]. Fowr axes xvj[d]. **1825** JAMIESON, *Dodge*, a pretty large cut or slice of any kind of food. *Dodgel*, a large piece or lump. [**1895** Still in use.]

Dodgem (ˈdɒdʒəm). Also Dodge-Em, and with small initial(s). [f. DODGE *v.* 4 + 'EM.] Esp. in *pl.*, a fairground amusement consisting of a number of small electrically-powered cars steered about in an enclosure. Also *attrib.*, as *dodgem car*.

1921 *Sci. Amer.* 15 Oct. 269/1 A device known as the 'Dodge-Em' is a clever piece of..work. Small cars, fitted with steering wheels, are placed on a polished..floor. A trolley connects each little car with an electrically charged mesh..overhead... The steering is only relative and it requires extreme ability to dodge the other fellow's car. **1937** *Night & Day* 23 Sept. 27 The big outfits—the Giant Racers, Over the Falls, the Helter-Skelter, the Dodge 'Ems. **1945** *Archit. Rev.* XCVII. 53 The sparks flying from the Dodgems. **1947** 'N. SHUTE' *Chequer Board* x. 278 Among the hurly-burly of his swings and roundabouts and flip-flops and dodgem cars. **1952** N. COWARD *Relative Values* I. ii. 28 What on earth's a Dodgem?.. One of those little motor cars you go on in Margate and bang into everybody. **1968** D. BRAITHWAITE *Fairground Architecture* i. 20 The transport revolution has been reflected in a succession of devices from ..'Dodg'em Cars'..to present day 'Space-Cruisers' and 'Hurricane Jets'. *Ibid.* vi. 103 'Dodg'ems' have been the most consistently popular ride on the fairground.

dodger ('dɒdʒə(r)), *sb.* [f. DODGE *v.* + -ER[1].]

1. One who dodges, in various senses of the vb.; in early use, *esp.* a haggler; later, *esp.* one who practises artful shifts or dodges.

1568 T. HARDING *Detect. Foul Err.* 226 By this a man may know what a Dodger you are, and whence your great bookes procede. **1598** FLORIO, *Auarone*, a pinch penie, a paltrer, a dodger, a miser, a penie father. **1611** COTGR., *Cagueraffe*, a base micher, scuruie hagler, lowsie dodger. **1704** HEARNE *Duct. Hist.* (1714) I. 156 Tacitus has no good Morals; He is a great Dodger..he always speaks more out of Policy than according to Truth. **1824** SCOTT *St. Ronan's* xxviii, 'A shy cock, this Frank Tyrrel..a very complete dodger!..I shall wind him, were he to double like a fox.' **1838** DICKENS *O. Twist* viii, Among his intimate friends he was better known by the sobriquet of 'The artful Dodger'.

2. a. *U.S.* A hard-baked corn-cake.

1831 J. M. PECK *Guide for Emigrants* II. 152 Dodgers are masses [of corn meal] like small loaves of bread, prepared in a similar manner [i.e. with water or milk], and baked in the spider or skillet. **1832** MRS. F. TROLLOPE *Dom. Mann. Amer.* I. 83 Hoe cake, johnny cake, waffle cake, and dodger cake. **1852** MRS. STOWE *Uncle Tom's C.* iv, Corn-cake, in all its varieties of hoe-cake, dodgers, muffins. **1882** *Garden* 13 May 327/1, I prospered rarely in the South on 'dodgers'.

b. A sandwich; bread, food. *Austral.* and *Services' slang.* Also *dial.* (cf. DODGE *sb.*[2]).

1919 DOWNING *Digger Dial.* 19 *Dodger*, bread. **1925** FRASER & GIBBONS *Soldier & Sailor Words* 79 *A dodger*..a sandwich. **1941** BAKER *Dict. Austral. Slang* 24 *Dodger*, food of any kind. Also, a 'yunk of dodger', a slice of bread. **1957** 'N. CULOTTA' *They're a Weird Mob* (1958) 51 Smack us in the eye with another hunk o' dodger. **1966** 'L. LANE' *ABZ of Scouse* II. 27 *Dodger*, bread or sometimes crude cake. 'Gimme a slice er dodger.'

3. *U.S.* A small handbill or circular.

1884 *Fargo* (Dakota) *Broadaxe* 7 Apr., With dodgers of warning distributed at the different polling-places. **1888** *Boston Jrnl.* 11 Feb. 5/4, I never in my life used such a thing as a poster, a dodger or a handbill.

4. *Salt-making.* (See quot.) Cf. DODGE *v.* 10.

1884 *Cheshire Gloss.*, *Dodger*, salt-making term; a long-headed hammer with a long handle, used for knocking off the scale or incrustations of lime or dirt on the pan bottoms when the pan is at work; also called *Dodging Hammer*.

5. On a ship: a screen to afford protection from spray, etc. Also, a protective shield used on a rocket, etc.

1898 C. HYNE *Capt. Kettle* x. 260 Under shelter of the dodgers on the upper bridge. *Ibid.* 262 Kettle hung on behind the canvas dodgers at the weather end of the bridge. **1942** MASEFIELD *Generation Risen* 42 Sprays are freezing on the dodger. **1956** *Jrnl. Brit. Interplan. Soc.* XV. 126 A dodger or shield had been placed at some distance from the thrust-balance. **1959** P. MCCUTCHAN *Storm South* vi. 75 Wynton took..shelter..behind a canvas dodger secured to the weather mizzen rigging.

dodger ('dɒdʒə(r)), *a. Austral. slang.* [Orig. unknown.] Good, excellent.

1941 in BAKER *Dict. Austral. Slang* 24. **1953** D. STIVENS *Gambling Ghost* 1 Instead of having to risk a knock on the Pearly Gates everything was dodger.

dodgery ('dɒdʒərɪ). [f. DODGE *v.* or *sb.* + -ERY.] The employment of dodges; trickery.

a **1670** HACKET *Abp. Williams* I. (1692) 98 When he had put this dodgery strongly upon those at London. **1865** DICKENS *Mut. Fr.* III. i, What dodgery are you up to next?

'**dodging**, *vbl. sb.* [f. DODGE *v.* + -ING[1].] The action of the verb DODGE, in various senses.

1593 *Tell-Troth's N.Y. Gift* 16 The dodging of an old beldam. *a* **1677** BARROW *Serm. Upright Walking* Wks. 1687 I. 65 Versatile whifflings and dodgings..and the like. **1880** GROVE *Dict. Music* s.v. *Changes*, At the end of each six changes one of the bells going up to take part in the dodging, and another coming down to take its place in the changes.

'**dodging**, *ppl. a.* [f. as prec. + -ING[2].] That dodges, in the various senses of the verb.

1625 W. PEMBLE *Justific. by Faith* (1629) 148 Tricks of wit and dodging Distinctions to avoid the accusations of conscience. **1648** MILTON *Tenure Kings* (1649) 30 Som dodging Casuist with more craft then sinceritie. **1735** SOMERVILLE *Chase* IV. 115 The Brakes Where dodging Conies sport. **1775** BURKE *Corr.* (1844) II. 63 Their irresolute and dodging motions. **1880** GROVE *Dict. Music* s.v. *Changes*, The bells..have a dodging course.

Hence '**dodgingly** *adv.*, in a dodging manner.

1599 MINSHEU, *Cavilosaménte*, dodgingly, contentiously, deceitfully, fraudulently.

dodging, var. of DOTCHIN, Chinese steelyard.

dodgy ('dɒdʒɪ), *a.* [f. DODGE *sb.*[1] + -Y[1].] Full of or addicted to dodges; evasive, tricky, artful. Also (*colloq.*) of things: difficult, awkward, tricky. Hence '**dodgily** *adv.*, '**dodginess**.

1861 WYNTER *Soc. Bees* 237 Beggars divide themselves in several classes:—the humourous, the poetical, the sentimental, the dodgey, and the sneaking. **1870** FURNIVALL in *Bk. Curtasye* 698 in *Babees Bk.* marg., A towel folded dodgily. **1871** *Daily News* 22 Sept., 'Dan Lysons' and his dodginess are on everybody's lips. **1896** *Ibid.* 16 Oct. 6/3 The pious purpose perhaps justified the dodgy means. **1898** G. B. SHAW *Mrs. Warren's Prof.* I, Take care of your fingers: theyre rather dodgy things, those chairs. **1916** D. H. LAWRENCE *Let.* 13 Jan. (1948) 67 The roads are too dodgy to be grasped. **1959** *Times Lit. Suppl.* 7 Aug. p. xii/2 Docketing and definition are dodgy businesses. **1960** H. PINTER *Room* 108 It'd be a bit dodgy driving tonight.

dodipate, -pole, varr. DODDYPATE, -POLL, *Obs.*

dodkin ('dɒdkɪn). Forms: 5 **doydekyn, doykyn,** 6 **dodkyn,** 6–7 (9) **dotkin,** 6– **dodkin,** (7–9 **doitkin**). [15th c. *doydekyn, doykyn*, a. MDu. *duytken*, dim. of *duyt, doyt*: see DOIT.]

1. An early name for the DOIT, a small Dutch coin. Hence, any coin of very small value.

Only *Hist.* after 1600, except in proverbial phrases.

1415 *Act 3 Hen. V*, c. 1 §2 Les Galyhalpens & la Moneie appelle Seskyn & Doydekyn. *Ibid.* Galyhalpens, Seskyns ou Doykyns. *c* **1550** *Dice-Play* (Percy Soc.) 27 He that will not stoop a dodkin at the dice. **1577** STANYHURST *Descr. Irel.* in *Holinshed* VI. 23 At the end of his maioraltie he owght no man a dotkin. **1606** HOLLAND *Sueton.* 79 Brasen Dodkins or mites called *Asses.* **1607** COWELL *Interpr.*, *Dotkins*, a kind of coine. [ed. **1672** *Doitkin*, a base Coine, prohibited by 3 H. 5. cap. 1. Hence probably we retain that phrase when we would undervalue a man, to say, *He is not worth a Doit or Doitkin.*] **1674** JEAKE *Arith.* (1696) 77 Some..divide the Farthing into 2 Ques, the Q into 2 Cees, the C into 2 Dodkins. **1881** DUFFIELD *Don Quix.* III. xxvii. 206, I did not care two dotkins.

2. a. A bud. **b.** A pistil.

[Perh. not the same word. In b perh. a dim. of DOD[2], Du. *dodde* club.]

1578 LYTE *Dodoens* III. lx. 400 Small dodkins or springes, which are the beginning of leaues. *Ibid.* v. xxvii. 585 The flower..with a yellowe Dodkin or Pestil, lyke golde in the middle.

'**dodman**. Now *dial.* [Origin unknown: connexion with DOD *sb.*[3] has been suggested. Other local names are *hodman-dod, hoddy-doddy*.] A snail.

c **1550** BALE *K. Johan* (Camden) 7 Yt is as great pyte to se a woman wepe, As yt is to se a sely dodman creepe. **1625** LISLE *Du Bartas, Noe* 149 Two crooked lines, One like a crawling snake, one like a dodman twines. **1626** BACON *Sylva* §732 [Animals] that cast their Shell, are; The Lobster, the Crab, the Crafish, the Hodmandod or Dodman, the Tortoise. **1633** AMES *Agst. Cerem.* II. 28 Time..to pull in the hornes of this dodmons accusation. **1674** N. FAIRFAX *Bulk & Selv.* 125 A Snayl or Dodman..is not only not warm, but to our feeling, very cold. **1674** RAY *S. & E.C. Words* 65 A *Dodman*: a shell-snail or Hodmandod, *Norf.* **1848** DICKENS *Dav. Copp.* vii, 'I'm a reg'lar Dodman', said Mr. Peggotty, by which he meant snail.

dodo ('dəʊdəʊ). [a. Pg. *doudo* simpleton, fool, as *adj.* silly.] An extinct bird, *Didus ineptus*, belonging to the order *Columbidæ*, formerly inhabiting the island of Mauritius; it had a massive clumsy body, and small wings of no use for flight; *transf.* and *fig.*, an old-fashioned, stupid, inactive, or unenlightened person. Phr. (*as*) ***dead as the*** (or *a*) ***dodo***: see DEAD *a.* 32 b.

1628 E. ALTHAM *Lett. to Sir Edw. Altham* 18 June in *Proc. Zool. Soc.* (1874) 448 A strange fowle, which I had at the Iland mauritius, called by ye portingalls a DoDo. *Ibid.* [P.S.] Of m^r perce you shall receue a iarr of ginger..and a bird called a DoDo, if it live. **1634** SIR T. HERBERT *Trav.* 347 Mauritius..here and here only and in Dygarroys, is generated the Dodo [**1638** a Portuguize name it is, and has reference to her simplenes] which for shape and rarenesse may Antigonize the Phœnix of Arabia. **1638** *Ibid.* 21 Like the Dodoes wings, more to looke at, then for execution. *c* **1650** H. L'ESTRANGE in *Sloane MS.* 1839. 5, lf. 54 About 1638, as I walked London streets, I [saw] the picture of a strange fowle hong out upon a cloth..went in to see it. It..was a great fowle, somwhat bigger then the largest Turkey Cock.. The keeper called it a Dodo. **1688** R. HOLME *Armoury* II. 289/1 A Dodo, or Dronte..doth equal a Swan in bigness. **1774** GOLDSM. *Nat. Hist.* III. I. vii. ¶2 Three or four dodos are enough to dine a hundred men. **1832** DE LA BECHE *Geol. Man.* (ed. 2) 163. **1886** *Pall Mall Gaz.* 11 Feb. 1/1 The old dodo at Scotland Yard, roused into a state of feverish activity..yesterday converted itself by a tremendous effort into a gigantic turkey-cock. **1896** F. HALL in *Nation* (N.Y.) LXII. 157/2 If he has not indeed gone the way of the dodo and the dinotherium. **1922** F. SCOTT FITZGERALD *Let.* 18 June (1964) 164 Tom Boyd wrote me that Bridges had been a dodo about some Y.M.C.A. man. **1950** A. WILSON (*title*) Such darling dodos.

attrib. **1874** LISLE CARR *Jud. Gwynne* II. viii. 177 He belongs to the Dodo race of real unmitigated..Toryism.

Dodonæan, -ean (dəʊdəʊ'niːən), *a.* [f. L. *Dōdōnæus*, a. Gr. Δωδωναῖος, f. Δωδώνη Dodona.] Of or pertaining to Dodona in ancient Epirus, where there was a famed oracle of Zeus situated in a grove of oaks. Also †**Dodonian** (dəʊ'dəʊnɪən).

1569 SPENSER *Visions of Bellay* v. in *Theat. Worldlings*, Then I behelde the faire Dodonian tree. **1632** LITHGOW *Trav.* I. 5 The Thespian spring, Where chatring birds, Dodonean trees do sing. **1851** THOREAU *Autumn* 84 There is mast for me too..this Dodonean fruit.

†**do'drantal**, *a. Obs. rare*—[0]. [ad. L. *dōdrāntāl-is*, f. *dōdrāns* nine-twelfths or three-fourths of a weight or measure.]

1656 BLOUNT *Glossogr.*, *Dodrantal*, of nine ounces or nine inches in length or weight. **1883** *Syd. Soc. Lex.*, *Dodrantal*, consisting of nine inches, three fourths of a foot.

dodrat, var. DOD-ROTTED *ppl. a.*

1897 *Outing* (U.S.) XXX. 173/2 This is the dodrattest place I ever struck.

dod-rot, *v. U.S. colloq.* [f. DOD- + ROT *v.*] = DODGAST *v.* Hence '**dod-rotted** *ppl. a.*

1842 *American Pioneer* I. 347 'Dod rot'em,' said the old hunter, 'I would not let them have a bushel.' **1885** 'C. E. CRADDOCK' *Prophet Gt. Smoky Mts.* vi. 121 'Dod-rot that critter,' exclaimed the sheriff, angrily. **1887** *Century Mag.* (Farmer), 'You ketch us with yer dodrotted foolin',' says he. **1911** R. D. SAUNDERS *Col. Todhunter* vii. 100 That dod-rotted old lady is a-movin' Heaven and earth to make a match.

doe (dəʊ). Forms: 1 **dá,** 2–6 **do,** (3 *pl.* **don**), 4–7 **doo,** 5–6 *Sc.* and *north.* **da,** (6 **dooe,** 7 **doa**), 6– **doe** (*Sc.* **dae**). [OE. *dá* is thought by some to be a contracted form, cognate with OHG. *tâmo, dâmo* wk. masc., MHG. *tâme*, G. *dam-* (in *damhirsch, damwild*), a. L. *dāma, damma* f., sometimes m., fallow deer, buck, doe; but there are serious difficulties. See Pogatscher *Gr. Lat. u. Rom. Lehnworte im Altengl.* §302.]

1. a. The female of the fallow deer; applied also to the female of allied animals, as the reindeer.

c **1000** ÆLFRIC *Gr.* (Z.) 309 *Damma, uel dammula*, dâ. *a* **1200** *Voc.* Wr.-Wülc. 543 Do. *c* **1290** *S. Eng. Leg.* I. 393/12 To cachche hert and bocke and don. **1388** WYCLIF *Prov.* vi. 5 Be thou rauyschid as a doo fro the hond. *c* **1400** MAUNDEV. (Roxb.) xxiii. 105 Hertez and hyndez, bukk and da. ?*c* **1475** *Sqr. lowe Degre* 324 Venyson freshe of bucke and do. **1597** MONTGOMERIE *Cherrie & Slae* 21 The hart, the hynd, the dae, the rae. **1606** SHAKS. *Tr. & Cr.* III. i. 128 For O loues Bow, Shootes Bucke and Doe. **1609** BIBLE (Douay) *Deut.* xii. 15 Lawful to be offered, as the doa and the hart. **1632** J. HAYWARD tr. *Biondi's Eromena* 127 He tooke it for a Doe, where it was more likely some..Chamoy. **1674** tr. *Scheffer's Lapland* 130 These horns are proper only to the Buck [Reindeer], the Doe having much less and fewer branches. **1807–15** WORDSW. *White Doe Rylst.* VII. 96 A doe most beautiful, clear-white. **1810** SCOTT *Lady of L.* I. iii, Close in her covert cowered the doe.

†**b.** Applied generically to both sexes, like L. *dāma.* Hence **doe-buck**, a male deer. *Obs.*

c **1475** *Pict. Voc.* in Wr.-Wülcker 759 *Hic damus*, a dobuk. *Hic vel hec dama*, a doo.

2. The female of the hare or rabbit; sometimes *dial.* of other animals, e.g. the rat.

1607 TOPSELL *Four-f. Beasts* (1658) 87 One that kept tame Conies..had Does which littered three at a time, and within fourteen daies after, they littered four more. **1741** *Compl. Fam. Piece* II. i. 300 They are distinguished by the Names of Bucks and Does; and the Males are usually call'd Jack Hares. **1837** M. DONOVAN *Dom. Econ.* II. 99 A doe [rabbit] when suckling, will drink milk.

3. *attrib.*, as ***doe-buck, -cony, -deer, -eye*** (so ***doe-eyed*** adj.), ***-leather, -venison***; made of DOESKIN, as ***doe trousers***.

c **1455** *Golagros & Gaw.* 226 Thay drive on the da deir be dalis and doun. *c* **1475** [see 1 b]. **1611** COTGR., *Rabolliere*, a Rabbets neast; the hole wherein a Doe Conie keepeth her young ones. **1747** *Phil. Trans.* XLIV. 572 The Skin drew or stretch'd like a Piece of Doe-Leather. **1819** *Pantologia* s.v., Doe venison is not equal in estimation with buck venison. **1844** *Advt.* in *Illust. Lond. News* 22 June 407/3 Plain doe trousers, 17/6. **1933** DYLAN THOMAS *Let.* (1966) 75 A broad creature, not..to be confused with the slim, doe-eyed apparition of your green book. **1959** 'J. R. MACDONALD' *Galton Case* (1960) ii. 17 The doe-eyed girl from the badminton court. **1959** *Manch. Guardian* 2 July 5/6 A certain tendency to doe-eyed sentimentality. **1963** N. FREELING *Because of Cats* iv. 64 Big wide doe-eyes nodded, yes.

doe, obs. form of DO, DOUGH.

doe-bird, var. of DOUGH-BIRD.

dœgling ('dœglɪŋ). Also dogling. [Native name in the Faröe Islands.] The bottle-nosed whale, *Hyperoodon ampullatus*, which yields ***dœgling train oil.***

1866 H. WATTS tr. *Gmelin's Handbk. Chem.* XVII. 180 Doegling Train Oil. From the doegling (the *Balæna rostrata* of Chemnitz, *Hyperodon* of later zoologists), a kind of dolphin. **1890** ROSCOE & SCHORLEMMER *Treat. Chem.* (new ed.) III. II. 483 The glyceride of this acid forms, according to Scharling, the principal part of the dœgling train oil. **1947** *Antiquity* XXI. 87 The Bottle-nosed Whale or Dogling.

doek (dʊk). *S. Afr.* Also 9 douk. [Afrikaans, = cloth (DUCK *sb.*[3]).] A cloth, especially a head-cloth. Cf. KOPDOEK.

1798 LADY ANNE BARNARD *Jrnl.* 22 May in *S. Afr. Century Ago* (1924) II. 226, I offered her four schellings or a *doek*, viz, a handkerchief; she preferred the last. **1853** W. R. KING *Campaigning in Kaffirland* iii. 19 Gaily dressed in startling cottons, with gaudy *douks* or bandanas on their woolly heads. **1944** M. DE B. NESBITT *Road to Avalon* viii. 66 The women in neat white print dresses and 'doeks'—coloured kerchiefs wrapped around their heads. **1956** N. GORDIMER *Six Feet of Country* 43 Now she had on her head a woollen doek again, instead of one of the maids' caps Ella provided for her to wear.

doel(e, obs. early f. DOLE *sb.*[2], grief, mourning.

doen, obs. form of *done*: see DO *v.*

doer ('duːə(r)). Also 4–6 **doar,** 5 **doere,** 6 **dowar(e,** 6–7 **dooer.** [f. DO *v.* + -ER[1].]

1. One who does; one who performs some act or deed; an actor, agent.

13.. *Cursor M.* 28773 (Cott. G.) Els vnmedeful es þe dede, and makes to þe doer no mede. **1382** WYCLIF *Jas.* i. 22 Be ȝe doers of the word and not herers oneli. **1561** T. HOBY tr. *Castiglione's Courtyer* I. G iij, In peincting..they are all most excellent dooers. **1594** SHAKS. *Rich. III*, I. iii. 352 Talkers are no good dooers. **1623** COCKERAM, *Actresse*, a woman-doer. **1738** SWIFT *Pol. Conversat.* 89 Ill Doers are ill Deemers. **1832** HT. MARTINEAU *Weal or W.* iii. 28 Sympathy affords great advantage to the doers of mischief.

2. One who acts on behalf of another; an agent, factor, manager; an attorney. Now only *Sc.*

1465 *MS.* in Tytler *Hist. Scot.* (1864) II. 388 He sal warn the saidis lord kennedy and Sir Alexander, or yair doars. **1566** *Act 8 Eliz.* c. 7 §2 No maner [other] person or persons . . shall . . exercyse or frequent the sayd trade . . nor have any Factor or Doer for hym or them in the same. **1721** *Wodrow Corr.* II. 603, I had the eleven pounds from the Earl of Kilmarnock's doer. **1752** J. Louthian *Form of Process* (ed. 2) 44 Before the Day of Compearance, the Lord Advocate, or his Depute, give in the Indictment . . to the Clerk of Court, that the Prisoner's Doer may have an Opportunity of seeing the same. **1870** Ramsay *Remin.* vi. (ed. 18) 232 In Scotland it is usual to term the law-agent or man of business of any party his 'doer'. **1893** Stevenson *Catr.* 97 I'm doer for Appin and for James of the Glens.

3. (with qualifying adj.) A horse or other animal that 'does' or thrives (well or ill): see do *v.* 18.

1865 *Even. Standard* 6 Mar., He . . is a rare doer, never having been sick nor sorry since the week he was foaled.

4. *slang.* One who 'does' or cheats another.

1840 *New Monthly Mag.* LIX. 47 [School Masters] are not merely 'do-the-boys', but regular doers of their parents. **1862** A. K. H. Boyd *Recreat. Country Parson* 114 The trickster has been tricked—the doer done.

5. An eccentric, a 'character', esp. in phr. ***hard doer***, a 'hard case'. *Austral.* and *N.Z.*

a **1885** in *Penguin Bk. Austral. Ballads* (1964) 78 Many more hard doers, all gone to Kingdom Come. **1916** 'Anzac' *On Anzac Trail* 122 He is a rule, a 'hard doer'. **1919** Downing *Digger Dial.* 19 *Doer*, a person unusually humorous, reckless, undisciplined, immoral or eccentric. **1928** *Bulletin* (Sydney) 29 Feb. 21/1 Give me the real hard-doer, give me the decent chap. **1929** K. S. Prichard *Coonardoo* xxxi. 300 You know Monty, . . one of the hardest doers in the Nor'-West. **1947** *Landfall* I. 166 Struth . . a real hard doer! **1959** S. H. Courtier *Death in Dream Time* iii. 28 Laurie could have been joking. He was that kind of doer, you know.

does, 3rd sing. pres. ind. of do *v.*

doeskin ('dəʊskɪn). [f. doe + skin *sb.*]

1. The skin of a doe.

1457 *Churchw. Acc. Tintinhull* (Somerset Rec. Soc.) 187 It. in una pelle de doeskyne pro eisdem libris vij[d]. **1535** Coverdale *Exod.* xxv. 5 Goates hayre, reed skynnes of rammes, doo skynnes. **1795** *Hull Advertiser* 28 Nov. 1/1 A large assortment of prime Buck and Doe Skins. **1855** Longf. *Hiaw.* xi. 74 He was dressed in shirt of doeskin.

b. A kind of leather made from this skin.

1710 *Lond Gaz.* No. 4662/4 A pair of Doe-Skin Breeches, with Brass Buttons. **1799** *Med. Jrnl.* II. 437 Thick, soft, and elastic leather, such as doe or buck skin.

2. A highly-finished closely-cut thick black cloth, twilled, but dressed so as to show very little of the twill.

Believed to have been so named as applied to a softer and less stout cloth than that called 'buckskin', which for riding breeches took the place of real buck-skins.

1851 *Rep. Juries Gt. Exhib.* 351/2 A great variety of fancy doeskins. **1874** Knight *Dict. Mech.*, *Doeskin*, a single width fine woolen cloth for men's wear.

doest ('duːɪst), 2nd sing. pres. ind. of do *v.*, q.v.

doff (dɒf), *v.* Pa. t. and pple. **doffed** (dɒft). [Coalesced form of *do off*: see do *v.* 47. Cf. also daff *v.*[2]

In ordinary colloquial use in north of England (not in Scotl.). Elsewhere, since 16th c., a literary word with an archaic flavour. Ray noted it as a northern provincialism; Johnson, as 'in all its senses obsolete, and scarcely used except by rustics'. In 19th c., from the time of Scott, very frequent in literary use.]

1. *trans.* To put off or take off from the body (clothing, or anything worn or borne); to take off or 'raise' (the head-gear) by way of a salutation or token of respect.

c **1350** *Will. Palerne* 2342 Dof blive þis bere skyn. *c* **1400** Maundev. (Roxb.) xxv. 120 He doffez his hatte. **1401** *Pol. Poems* (Rolls) II. 107 The sacred host . . to whiche we knele and doffe our hodes. **1483** *Cath. Angl.* 103/1 To Doffe, *exuere.* **1595** Shaks. *John* iii. i. 128 Thou weare a Lyons hide! doff it for shame. **1596** Spenser *F.Q.* vi. ix. 36 Calidore . . doffing his bright armes, himselfe addrest In shepheards weed. **1621** G. Sandys *Ovid's Met.* xiii. (1626) 259 Then made him d'off those weeds. **1714** Gay *Sheph. Week* iv. 21 Upon a rising Bank I sat adown, Then doff'd my Shoe. **1768** Beattie *Minstr.* i. xxxv, The little warriors doff the targe and spear. **1808** Scott *Marm.* vi. xi, Doffed his furred gown, and sable hood. **1859** Tennyson *Enid* 1444 The . . Earl . . cast his lance aside, And doff'd his helm.

†b. Const. *off*; also *intr.* with *with. Obs. rare.*

? *a* **1400** *Morte Arth.* 1023 Þow doffe of thy clothes, And knele in thy kyrtylle. **1643** [see doffing *vbl. sb.*]. **1764** Foote *Mayor of G.* ii. Wks. 1799 I. 186 If you will doff with your boots, and box a couple of bouts.

c. *absol.* To raise one's hat (*to* a person). *rare.*

1674 N. Fairfax *Bulk & Selv.* To Rdr., To look full on a Great man standing in my way, and not to vouchsafe him worth Doffing to. **1833** Tennyson *Goose* 19 The grave churchwarden doff'd, The parson smirk'd and nodded.

2. *refl.* To undress oneself, put off one's clothes. Also *fig.* Now only *dial.*

1697 De la Pryme *Diary* (Surtees) 150 The quaker doffs him stark naked, and takeing a burning candle in his hand he goes to the church. [**1838** J. Scholes *Lanc. Witches* in Harland *L. Lyrics* (1865) 133 'Hie thi whoam an' doff thi.']

3. *transf.* and *fig.* To put off as a dress or covering; to throw off, lay aside; hence (in wider sense), to do away with, get rid of (anything associated with oneself). †Also with *off* (*obs.*).

1592 Shaks. *Rom. & Jul.* ii. ii. 47. **1599** B. Jonson *Ev. Man out of Hum.* v. v, He . . oftentimes d'offeth his owne nature and puts on theirs. **1605** Shaks. *Macb.* iv. iii. 188 Your eye . . would create Soldiours, make our women fight, To doffe their dire distresses. **1628** Earle *Microcosm.*, *Vpstart Countrey Knt.* (Arb.) 38 He ha's doft off the name of a Clowne. **1854–6** Patmore *Angel in Ho.* i. ii. x. (1879) 237 Love . . doffed at last his heavenly state. **1867** Bp. Forbes *Exp. 39 Art.* ii. (1881) 29 The Word is said to have donned human nature, never more to doff it.

†4. To put (any one) *off* (with an excuse, etc.); to turn aside: cf. daff *v.*[2] 2. *Obs.*

1622 *Shaks. Oth.* iv. ii. 176 (Qo. 1) Euery day thou dofftst [*Fol.* 1. dafts] me with some deuise, Iago. *a* **1637** B. Jonson *Sad Sheph.* i. ii, They . . strew tods' hairs, or with their tails do sweep The dewy grass, to do'ff the simpler sheep. **1658–9** *Burton's Diary* (1828) IV. 67 They doffed us off as long as they could, and then locked up their doors.

5. *Textile Manuf.* a. To strip off the slivers of wool, cotton, etc., from the carding-cylinders. b. To remove the bobbins or spindles when full to make room for empty ones. See doffer.

1825 [see doffing *vbl. sb.* b]. **1851** *Art Jrnl. Catal. Gt. Exhib.* p. iv**/2 This . . instrument doffs the cotton in a fine transparent fleece. **1864** R. A. Arnold *Cotton Fam.* 33 Spinners . . have, in technical language . . to 'doff the cops'; in other words . . to remove and relieve the spindles of the spun yarn. **1879** *Cassell's Techn. Educ.* IV. 356/2.

†**doff**, *sb. Obs. rare*[−1]. [f. prec. vb.] An act of doffing; a 'put off'.

1606 *Wily Beguiled* in Hazl. *Dodsley* IX. 276 Lelia has e'en given him the doff here.

doffer ('dɒfə(r)). [f. prec. vb.] One who or that which doffs.

1. In a carding machine, a comb or revolving cylinder which 'doffs' or strips off cotton or wool from the 'cards'; a ***doffing-cylinder***.

1825 [see doffing *vbl. sb.* b]. **1842** Bischoff *Woollen Manuf.* II. 392 When it has passed over the last cylinder on to the drum, it is taken from it by a cylinder somewhat larger than the workers, and called a doffer. **1876** J. Watts *Brit. Manuf.* III. 134 The doffer or doffing cylinder.

attrib. **1825** J. Nicholson *Operat. Mechanic* 380 The main cylinder . . is soon covered with cotton, and is divested of it by the doffer cylinder. **1854** *Illustr. Lond. News* 5 Aug. 118/4 Occupations of the People . . Doffer-plate maker. **1875** *Ure's Dict. Arts* I. 969 The doffer-knife or comb for stripping the fleecy web from the doffer.

2. A worker employed in removing the full bobbins or spindles: see quot. 1894. Also **duffer**.

1862 *Illustr. Lond. News* XLI. 558/3 The Throstle Doffer. **1875** *Ure's Dict. Arts* I. 989 This loss of time, as well as the labour of the 'doffers', is abolished. **1893** *Westm. Gaz.* 22 Apr. 3/1 There are two classes of children employed, called cagers and duffers; little children, boys and girls, who assist the spinners. **1894** *Labour Commission* Gloss., *Doffers*, boys or girls from 12 to 15 years . . employed to take off the full bobbins and to replace them on the throstle or ring frames by empty ones. **1894** *Dundee Advertiser* 27 Aug. 4 These included preparers, as they are called . . stainers . . duffers . . reelers . . and weavers.

doffing ('dɒfɪŋ), *vbl. sb.* [f. as prec. + -ing[1].] The action of the verb doff. a. The putting or taking off of clothing, etc.

1606 Holland *Sueton.* 231 To doe him the grace that he might have the D'offing of her shoes. **1643** G. Wilde *Serm. St. Maries, Oxford* 17 Those . . who think a little d'offing off the Hat . . Reverence enough for the Lords Annoynted; do not they Pillage him of his Divinity? **1847** Emerson *Poems*, *Song Nature*, Too much of donning and doffing.

b. *Textile Manuf.*: see doff *v.* 5 and doffer.

doffing cylinder: a cylinder clothed with cards which takes off the fibres from the teeth of the main cylinder of a carding machine. ***doffing knife***: a steel blade with finely toothed edge, which takes off the carded wool from the teeth of the doffer. So ***doffing-plate***.

1825 J. Nicholson *Operat. Mechanic* 380 The doffer or taker-off, having affixed to it the steel comb called the doffing-plate. **1851** *Art Jrnl. Catal. Gt. Exhib.* p. iv**/2 A fine fleece of cotton . . shorn or combed off from the opposite side of the cylinder by the vibratory action of the doffing knife. *Ibid.*, A smaller drum card . . called the doffer (stripper) or doffing cylinder . . covered . . with fillet cards. **1875** *Ure's Dict. Arts* I. 989 One of the most recent improvements in the throstle frame is that of Bernhardt's 'doffing-motion'.

dog (dɒg), *sb.*[1] Forms: 1 docga, 3–7 dogge, (3, 6 doggue, 6 *Sc.* doig), 6–8 dogg, 3– dog. [late OE. *docga* (once in a gloss); previous history and origin unknown. (The generic name in OE., as in the Teutonic langs. generally, was *hund*: see hound.) So far as the evidence goes, the word appears first in English, as the name of a powerful breed or race of dogs, with which the name was introduced into the continental languages, usually, in early instances, with the attribute 'English'. Thus mod.Du. *dog*, late 16th c. *dogge* ('een dogghe, vn gros matin d'Engleterre, *canis anglicus*', Plantijn *Thesaur.* 1573), Ger. *dogge*, in 16–17th c. *dock, docke, dogg* ('englische Dock', *Onomast.* 1582, 'eine englische Docke', 1653), LG. *dogge*, Da. *dogge*, Sw. *dogg*; F. *dogue* ('le genereux dogue anglais', Du Bellay 15 . .), It., Sp., Pg. *dogo*, Pg. also *dogue*; in all the languages applied to some variety or race of dog.]

I. The simple word.

1. a. A quadruped of the genus *Canis*, of which wild species or forms are found in various parts of the world, and numerous races or breeds, varying greatly in size, shape, and colour, occur in a domesticated or semi-domesticated state in almost all countries. These are referred by zoologists to a species *C. familiaris*; but whether they have a common origin is a disputed question.

c **1050** *Prudentius Glosses* (Recd. 148/1) [Gloss to] *canum* [gen. pl.] docgena. *a* **1225** *Ancr. R.* 288 His [the devil's] teð beoð attrie, ase of ane wode dogge. Dauid, ine sauter, cleopeð hine dogge. *Ibid.* 290 Þet tes dogge of helle kumeð. *c* **1290** *S. Eng. Leg.* I. 307/281 A teie doggue. *a* **1300** *Cursor M.* 13658 (Cott. & G.) Þai scott him als a dog Right vte o Þair synagog. **1393** Langl. *P. Pl.* C. x. 261 Thi dogge dar nat berke. **1460** Capgrave *Chron.* (1858) 281 Thei seide pleynly that it was no more trost to the Pope writing than to a dogge tail. **1568** Tilney *Disc. Mariage* D viij b, Dogs barke boldely at their owne maisters doore. **1586** B. Young *Guazzo's Civ. Conv.* iv. 179 Like the Sheepheards good Dog. **1601** Shaks. *Twel. N.* ii. iii. 154 If I thought that, Ide beate him like a dogge. **1686** Horneck *Crucif. Jesus* xxii. 682 The dog teaches thee fidelity. **1732** Pope *Ess. Man* i. 112 His faithful dog shall bear him company. **1869** W. P. Mackay *Grace & Truth* viii, The dog in the East is not as here domesticated, but . . outside the cities, is more like a wolf prowling for prey.

†b. Used *spec.* as the name of some particular variety; see quots. *Obs.*

1398 Trevisa *Barth. De P.R.* xviii. xxvi. (1495) 786 A gentyll hounde . . hath lesse flesshe than a dogge and shorter heere and more thynne. *c* **1440** *Promp. Parv.* 125/1 Dogge, shyppe-herdys hownde, *gregarius.* **1530** Palsgr. 214/2 Dogge, a mischevous curre, *dogue.*

c. *esp.* A dog used for hunting; a hound.

a **1307** *Pol. Songs* (Camden) 239 A doseyn of doggen Ne myhte hyre drawe. **1398** Trevisa *Barth. de P.R.* xviii. ciii. (1495) 847 Brockes . . ben huntyd and chassyd wyth hunters dogges. ? *c* **1475** *Hunt. Hare* 26 Ychon of hus hase a dogge or too; For grehowndes have thou no care. **1649** Bp. Reynolds *Hosea* iii. 38 The Dogge in hunting of the Deere. **1748** N. Salmon *Comp. Univ.* 14 Some gentlemen of the Town always keep a Pack of Dogs.

d. *fig.*; *esp.* in Shaksperian phr. ***the dogs of war.***

a **1225** [see 1]. **1601** Shaks. *Jul. C.* iii. i. 273 Caesars Spirit ranging for Reuenge, With Ate by his side . . Shall in these Confines . . Cry hauocke, and let slip the Dogges of Warre. **1667** Milton *P.L.* x. 616 See with what heat these Dogs of Hell advance. **1842** S. Lover *Handy Andy* ii, Let loose the dogs of law on him. **1860** Trollope *Framley P.* xliii, The dogs of war would be unloosed.

e. With qualifications denoting variety or use, as bandog, bull-dog *sb.*, cur-dog, etc., q.v. in their alphabetical places or under the first element. Also ***buck-***, ***cattle-***, ***field-***, ***parlour-***, ***shore-***, ***toy-dog***.

a **1225** Kur-dogge [see cur 1 c.]. **1633** T. James *Voy.* 93 Bucke Dogs, of a very good race. **1672** Josselyn *New Eng. Rarities* 15 The Indian Dog is a Creature begotten 'twixt a Wolf and a Fox. **1813** Col. Hawker *Diary* (1893) I. 89 My Newfoundland dog . . had decamped. **1870** B. Clayton *Dog-Keeper's Guide* 6 Field dogs are used for field purposes only. **1889** St. J. Tyrwhitt in *Univ. Rev.* 15 Feb. 253 Society kept him . . painting toy dogs. **1893** Edith Carrington *Dog* vi. 52 Very famous cattle dogs.

f. ***the dogs***: a greyhound race meeting (see also 17 a). *colloq.*

1927 *Daily Mail* 28 July 7/4 'Going to the dogs' has . . lost . . its old suggestion of a descent to dissipation and ruin. Since greyhound racing at the White City . . came into existence the expression has suggested a good adventure. **1928** A. P. Herbert *Trials of Topsy* 52 (*heading*) Going to the Dogs. Well Trix darling at last I've been to these *contagious* greyhounds. **1936** W. Holtby *South Riding* i. v. 54 Pretty little painted sluts minced . . off to the pictures or dogs. **1959** *Economist* 13 June 1016/3 He . . failed his Bar examinations because he preferred horse-racing, the 'dogs' and dancing.

2. In distinguishing sex, the male of this species; a male hound; opp. to bitch. Also, a male fox, dog-fox.

1577 B. Googe *Heresbach's Husb.* iii. (1586) 154 b, The Dogge is thought better than the Bitche. **1768** G. Washington *Writ.* (1889) II. 248 Four puppys, that is 3 dogs and a bitch. **1882** *Society* 21 Oct. 19/2 If this is your fox, Jack, he's an unmistakable old dog. **1890** *Sat. Rev.* 1 Feb. 134/2 The man who knows and loves his hound only uses the word dog, as he does the word bitch, to denote sex.

3. Applied to a person; a. in reproach, abuse, or contempt: A worthless, despicable, surly, or cowardly fellow. (Cf. cur 1 b.)

c **1325** *Coer de L.* 4518 Jhon Doyly . . slowgh hym . . And sayde: 'Dogge, ther thou ly!' **1382** Wyclif *2 Sam.* xvi. 9. *c* **1440** *York Myst.* xix. 106 A! dogges, þe deuell ȝou spede. **1591** Shaks. *1 Hen. VI*, i. ii. 23. **1596** —— *Merch. V.* i. iii. 129 You spurn'd me such a day; another time You call'd me dog. **1653** H. Cogan tr. *Pinto's Trav.* xx. 72 Such feeble slaves, as these Christian Dogs. **1712** Addison *Spect.* No. 530 ¶4 Had not my dog of a steward run away as he did, without making up his accounts. **1820** Scott *Ivanhoe* vii, Dog of an unbeliever . . darest thou press upon a Christian? **1880** Tennyson *Revenge* ii, If I left them . . To these Inquisition dogs and the devildoms of Spain.

b. playfully (usually in humorous reproof, congratulation, or commiseration): A gay or jovial man, a gallant; a fellow, 'chap'. Usually with *adj.* such as *cunning*, *jolly*, *lucky*, *sad*, *sly*, etc. ***to be old dog at***: see 17 i.

a **1618** Q. Anne *Let. to Buckingham* in Ellis *Orig. Lett.* Ser. i. III. 101 My kind Dog . . You doe verie well in lugging the Sowes eare [Jas. I], and I . . would have yow doe so still upon condition that yow continue a watchfull dog to him. **1711**

Budgell *Spect.* No. 67 ¶9 An impudent young Dog bid the Fiddlers play a Dance called Mol. Patley. **1719** De Foe *Crusoe* i. vi, I was an unfortunate dog. **1814** L. Hunt *Feast Poets* 14 Poems (1832) 144 The dog had no industry. **1836** Dickens *Sk. Boz* 2nd Ser. 200 He had been a sad dog in his time. **1844** [see lucky *a.* 7]. **1847** Dickens *Dombey* xxvi. 266 Well! we *are* gay dogs, there's no denying. **1884** W. E. Norris *Thirlby Hall* ix, A sad dog. **1900, 1910** [see gay *a.* 2 a].

c. = bull-dog *sb.* 2.

1847 Tennyson *Princ.* Prol. 113 He had climb'd across the spikes..he had breath'd the Proctor's dogs.

d. = watch-dog b. (*Schoolboys' slang.*)

1870 *Chambers's Jrnl.* Oct. 676/1 The boys withdrew..to read the forbidden prints, three taking their turn at a time, whilst three more 'played dog'—that is, stood ready to bark a warning should a pion be seen approaching. **1959** I. & P. Opie *Lore & Lang. Schoolch.* xvii. 373 In Kirkaldy watch-dog [*i.e.*, a boy keeping lookout] becomes either 'watchie' or 'dog'.

e. An informer; a traitor; esp. one who betrays fellow criminals. *U.S.* and *Austral. slang.*

1846 *Nat. Police Gaz.* (U.S.) 21 Feb. 210/2 Dick White has been playing the 'dog', and he and the 'coppers' are now within ten minutes of the house. **1888** 'R. Boldrewood' *Robbery under Arms* I. v. 69 Are you going to turn dog, now you know the way in? **1901** E. Dyson *Gold Stealers* xix. 231 'Tell me how you come to be in the Stream drive that night.' Dick..answered nothing. 'Come on, old man, I won't turn dog.' **1969** *Telegraph* (Brisbane) 11 Oct. 1/1 A 'dog' is the term applied by prisoners to fellow-prisoners who turn informer.

f. Something poor or mediocre; a failure. *U.S. slang.*

1936 *Metronome* Feb. 21/4 *Dog*, something [*i.e.* a song] that's kicked around. **1952** *N.Y. Times Bk. Rev.* 10 Aug. 8/3 '[The book will have] a record-breaking sale.' 'Yes, unless of course the book turns out to be a dog.' **1968** L. O'Donnell *Face of Crime* ix. 118 I'd be a fool not to take advantage. I had a real dog on my hands. **1970** *New Yorker* 15 Aug. 65/1 Audiences are in a mess... They don't know what they want... So many movies are *dogs*.

g. A horse that is slow, difficult to handle, etc. *slang.*

1944 P. Kendall *Service Slang* 5/2 *Dog*, affectionate term for cavalryman's horse, also called a job. **1945** Baker *Austral. Lang.* ix. 175 A *dog* is a horse difficult to handle. **1955** T. Rattigan *Separate Tables: Table by Window* iii, Is it going to be dry at Newbury?.. Walled Garden's a dog on heavy going. **1958** J. Hislop *Start to Finish* xii. 132 A 'dog' means a horse who cannot be relied upon to do his best..a horse may be a 'dog' because there is something wrong with him.

4. *Astron.* **a.** The name of two constellations, the ***Great*** and ***Little Dog*** (*Canis Major* and *Minor*) situated near Orion; also applied to their principal stars Sirius and Procyon: see dog-star. **b.** ***the Hunting Dogs***, a northern constellation (*Canes Venatici*) near the Great Bear.

1551 Recorde *Cast. Knowl.* (1556) 268 Northe almost from this Dogge is ther a constellation of 2 only starres named Canicula, the lesser Dogge. **1577** B. Googe *Heresbach's Husb.* i. (1586) 210 b, The greate heate of the Sunne..is most extreame at the rysyng of the lesser Dogge. **1611** Beaum. & Fl. *Maid's Trag.* iv. i, The burnt air, when the Dog reigns. **1718** Rowe tr. *Lucan* 428 'Till the hot Dog inflames the Summer Skies. **1890** C. A. Young *Uranogr.* §41 Canes Venatici (The Hunting Dogs). These are the dogs with which Bootes is pursuing the Great Bear.

5. Applied, usually with distinctive prefix, to various animals allied to, or in some respect resembling, the dog:

e.g. ***burrowing-dog***, the coyote or prairie-wolf, *Canis latrans*; ***hunting-dog***, a kind of hyena (see hunting-dog); ***pouched dog***, a dasyurine marsupial of Tasmania, *Thylacinus cynocephalus*, also called *zebra-wolf*; ***prairie-dog*** (also *colloq.* called simply *dog* in Western U.S.), a North American rodent (see prairie-dog).

6. Short for dogfish.

1674 Ray *Words, (Sea) Fishes* 98 Picked Dogs, *Catulus spinax*. **1848** C. A. Johns *Week at Lizard* 241, I..fished in five or six different spots..there were 'dogs', as they are called, everywhere..but nothing else. **1860** Wood *Reptiles, Fishes, Insects* 71 The destructive..fish..known by the names of.. Penny Dog, or Miller's Dog. **1861** Couch *Brit. Fishes* I. 49 The Picked Dog is the smallest but far the most abundant of the British Sharks.

7. A name given to various mechanical devices, usually having or consisting of a tooth or claw, used for gripping or holding. Among these are:

a. A clamp for supporting something (*e.g.* part of a building), or fastening or holding it in place. †**b.** An instrument for extracting teeth (*obs.*). **c.** An implement for drawing poles out of the ground (see also hop-dog), or for extracting roots of broom, furze, etc. (cf. dog *v.* 6 b, and see *broom-dog*, broom *sb.* 6). **d.** A grappling-iron for raising the monkey of a pile-driver, or clutching and withdrawing tools used in well-boring or mining. **e.** A grappling-iron with a fang which clutches an object, as a log, barrel, etc. to be hoisted, or a log to be secured in position for sawing. **f.** *pl.* Nippers used in wire-drawing. **g.** At the Mint, a device consisting of two levers mounted on a small carriage running on wheels along the draw-bench, and so arranged as to constitute a pair of pincers which seize the fillet and draw it through the opening at the head of the draw-bench. **h.** One of 'the converging set screws which establish the bed-tool of a punching-press in direct coincidence with the punch' (Knight *Dict. Mech.*). **i.** A projection or tooth acting as a detent, *e.g.* in a lock; a catch or click which engages the teeth of a ratchet-wheel. **j.** In a fire-arm = dog-head 2 b [cf. F. *chien*, snaphaunce (Cotgr.); so It. *cane* (Florio), Sp. *can* (Minsheu)]. **k.** A drag for the wheel of a vehicle. **l.** 'A clamp fastened to a piece suspended on the centres of a lathe, by which the rotation of the chuck or face-plate is imparted to the piece to be turned' (= carrier 1 d). **m.** An adjustable stop placed in a machine to change direction of motion. (Webster 1864.) **n.** *Ship-building* = dog-shore. (Smyth *Sailor's Word-bk.*) **o.** 'A lever used by blacksmiths in hooping cart-wheels' (Jamieson 1825). **p.** A kind of spike used on railways for fastening flat-bottomed or bridge rails to the sleepers: = dog-nail. **q.** An appliance for toasting bread, etc.: cf. cat *sb.*[1] 9, and see Brockett *N.C. Gloss.*

a. 1458 *Churchw. Acc. St. Andrews, East Cheap* in *Brit. Mag.* XXXI. 249 To Barnard the Smyth for x doggs of Iryn for the Steple weying lxx lb. **1552** Huloet, Dogge of yron to claspe a house from fletyng, *retinaculum, trabalis clauus uel hamus*. **1649** Blithe *Eng. Improv. Impr.* (1653) 212 As a Buttress to support it, and may be as serviceable as an Iron dog as many use. **1892** *Law Times Rep.* LXV. 582/1 The posts of the gantry stand on planks, and are fixed thereto by iron dogs and dowels.

b. 1611 Cotgr., *Pelican*..a Snap, or Dog, the toole wherewith Barbers pull out teeth.

c. 1727 Bradley *Fam. Dict.* s.v., An instrument called a Dog for the more easy drawing the Poles out of the ground. **1893** C. A. Mollyson *Parish of Fordoun* xxv. 290 The dog, we presume, is still extant..We will quote..a description of the broom-dog..'It operates somewhat like a toothdrawer and eradicates the broom in an instant.'

d. 1747 Hooson *Miner's Dict.* s.v. *Boring*, For drawing up the Rods, we have..an Iron Instrument called a Bitch, and, for unscrewing them, two more we call Dogs.

e. 1740 Dyche & Pardon, *Dog*..also an utensil for coopers to carry large casks between two persons. **1750** Blanckley *Nav. Expos.* 51 *Timber Doggs*, Are drove into Timber for Horses to draw it about the Yard, or to the Saw-pits. **1825** Jamieson, *Dogs*, pieces of iron, having a zig-zag form, for fixing a tree in the saw-pit. **1840** R. H. Dana *Bef. Mast* xxix. 99 One [block] hooked to the strap on the end of the steeve, and the other into a dog, fastened into one of the beams.

g. 1859 *All Year Round* No. 10. 239 This dog is a small thin carriage, travelling upon wheels over a bench, under which revolves an endless chain. **1875** *Ure's Dict. Arts* III. 342 The chain..in its onward motion drags the dog, and causes it to bite the fillet and draw it through the opening.

i. 1853 C. Tomlinson in *Ure's Dict. Arts* III. 142 There is a dog or lever..which catches into the top of the bolt, and thereby serves as an additional security against its being forced back. **1857** Colquhoun *Comp. Oarsman's Guide* 32 The dog, or catch, prevents its running down.

j. *c* **1660** *Monckton Papers* (1884) 36, I immediately..clapt hold of the dog of the blunderbus. *a* **1684** Law *Mem.* (1818) 225 (Jam.) He lets fall the dog, the pistoll goes off. **1846** *Archæologia* XXXI. 492 (D.) A contrivance..for producing fire by the friction of the grooved edges of a steel wheel.. against a piece of iron pyrites..held in a cock or dog which pressed upon it.

k. 1795 *Trans. Soc. Arts* XIII. 255 This simple and useful contrivance, called here a Dog, or Wheel-Drag.

l. 1833 J. Holland *Manuf. Metal* II. 134 A contrivance called the dog and driver, the former being a sort of clutch screwed upon the end of the work. **1884** F. J. Britten *Watch. & Clockm.* 168 A lathe furnished with dogs.

o. 1735 *Crt. Bk. Barony Urie* (1892) 156 He saw the defenders throw a dogg at each other.

p. 1883 *Proc. Philol. Soc.* 21 Dec., *Dog* (spike used on railways), from form of head which resembles a dog's. **1892** *Labour Commission* Gloss., *Dogs*, a class of nails used for fastening down rails on sleepers. Each nail consists of a long spike, with ears on the side of the head, by means of which the nail may be wrenched up and re-used.

8. a. One of a pair of iron or brass utensils placed one on each side of a fireplace to support burning wood; = andiron; (more fully called ***fire-dogs***); **b.** a similar support for a dog grate or stove; **c.** a rest for the fire-irons.

1596 *Unton Invent.* 5 One paire of dogges in the Chymly. *a* **1661** Fuller *Worthies* ix. (R.), The iron doggs bear the burthen of the fuel, while the brazen-andirons stand only for state. **1663** Pepys *Diary* 7 Sept., Buying several things at the ironmonger's—dogs, tongs, and shovels. **1762** Franklin *Remarks* Wks. 1887 III. 184 The iron dogs, loggerhead, and iron pot were not hurt. **1862** H. Aïdé *Carr of Carrlyon* I. 140 The wood fire..burnt cheerfully on great brass dogs upon the hearthstone. *Mod. Ironfounders' Catal.*, Dog stoves.. fine polished brass dogs..fire basket sloping forward at the top. *Ibid.*, Fire Dogs..All Brass.

†**9.** An early kind of fire-arm. *Obs.*

1549 *Compl. Scot.* vi. 41 Mak reddy ȝour cannons..bersis, doggis, doubil bersis, hagbutis of croche. **1650** *Art. Reddition Edin. Castle*, 28 short brasse munkeys alias dogs.

10. Name given to various atmospheric appearances. **a.** A luminous appearance near the horizon; also *fog-dog, sea-dog*. **b.** ***sun-dog***, a luminous appearance near the sun, a parhelion. **c.** ***water-dog***, a small dark floating cloud, indicating rain.

1825–80 Jamieson, *Dog, Sea-dog*, a name given by mariners to a meteor seen, immediately above the horizon, generally before sunrise, or after sunset..viewed as a certain prognostic of the approach of bad weather..If this be seen before sunrise, it is believed that (as they express themselves) it will bark before night; if after sunset, that it will bark before morning..The *dog* has no variety of colours, but is of a dusky white. **1847–78** Halliwell, *Water-dogs*, see *Mares'-Tails*. **1867** Smyth *Sailor's Word-bk.*, *Stubb*, or *Dogg*, the lower part of a rainbow visible towards the horizon, and betokening squally weather..On the banks of Newfoundland they are considered precursors of clearer weather, and termed *fog-dogs*. **1869** *Lonsdale Gloss.*, *Dog*, a partial rainbow. 'A dog at night is the farmer's delight.' **1876** *Surrey Provincialisms* (E.D.S.), *Water-dogs*, dark clouds that seem to travel through the air by themselves, and indicate a storm. **1892** W. Pike *Barren Ground N. Canada* 97 Often a sun-dog is the first thing to appear, and more or less of these attendants accompany the sun during his short stay above the horizon.

11. Name given to a copper coin used in some islands in the West Indies; also to 'a small silver coin' (Smyth); see also black dog 1.

1797 W. Bullock in *Naval Chron.* X. 128 Negro money called stampees, or black dogs. **1811** Kelly *Univ. Cambist* (1835) I. 362 There are here [Leeward Islands] small copper coins, called Stampes, Dogs, and Half Dogs. **1888** *Star* 18 Feb. 1/4 Fees..are paid in old Spanish dollars..and in 'dogs' or French coppers struck in the reign of Louis XVI. for Cayenne.

12. Short for dog-watch.

1893 Pemberton *Iron Pirate* 151 Towards the second bell in the second 'dog' there was a change.

†**13.** = *dog-chance, dog-throw* at dice: see 20. *Obs.*

1671 H. M. tr. *Erasm. Colloq.* 441 That the throw *Cous* was a lucky one, and the *dog* was unfortunate.

14. *pl.* Short for *dog's meat*; feet. *Rhyming slang.*

1924 Wodehouse *Leave it to Psmith* x. 211 You'll pick up your dogs and run round as quick as you can make it. **1939** M. Dickens *One Pair of Hands* x. 169, I feel more like goin' to bed and sleeping for a week than prancing round the ballroom on me poor dogs. **1939** Steinbeck *Grapes of Wrath* vi. 56 We ain't gonna walk no eight miles..to-night. My dogs is burned up.

15. *pl.* Sausages. Cf. *hot dog* (hot *a.*). *slang.*

1925 Fraser & Gibbons *Soldier & Sailor Words* 80 *Dogs*, sausages. **1959** I. & P. Opie *Lore & Lang. Schoolch.* ix. 163 Sausages are 'bangers'..or 'dogs'.

II. Phrases and Proverbs.

16. ***to the dogs***: to destruction or ruin; as in ***to go, send, throw to the dogs***. So ***not to have a word to throw at a dog***.

1565–73 Cooper *Thesaurus*, *Addicere aliquem canibus*, to bequeath hym to dogs. **1600** Shaks. *A.Y.L.* i. iii. 3 *Cel.* Why Cosen, why Rosaline: Cupid haue mercie, Not a word? *Ros.* Not one to throw at a dog. **1604** —— *Oth.* iv. i. 147. **1605** —— *Macb.* v. iii. 47 Throw Physicke to the Dogs, Ile none of it. **1619** R. Harris *Drunkard's Cup* Epist. A ij b, One is coloured, another is foxt, a third is gone to the dogs. **1732** Pope *Ep. Bathurst* 66 Had Colepepper's whole wealth been hops and hogs, Could he himself have sent it to the dogs? **1770** Foote *Lame Lover* ii. Wks. 1799 II. 78, I should not have thought he had a word to throw to a dog. **1809** W. Irving *Knickerb.* vii. iv. (1849) 398 He..threw diplomacy to the dogs. **1857** Hughes *Tom Brown* i. vi, Rugby and the School-house are going to the dogs.

b. ***every dog has his day***: see day 15. ***to take a dog's leave***: see leave *sb.*[1] ***love me, love my dog***: see love *v.* ***a dog in the pot***: see pot *sb.* ***the scalded dog fears cold water***: see scalded. See also black dog, dog-in-the-manger.

17. a. ***fight dog, fight bear***: see quots. †**b.** ***a dog for (to) the bow***, 'a dog used in shooting; such dogs, being well trained and obedient, were taken to typify humble or subservient people' (Davies): cf. bow *sb.*[1] 4 d. *Obs.* **c.** ***to rain cats and dogs***: see cat and dog 2; so ***to blow cats and dogs***. **d.** ***to die like a dog***, or ***to die a dog's death***: i.e. a disgraceful or miserable death. **e.** ***a hair of the dog that bit you***: formerly reputed a specific for the bite of a mad dog; hence allusively, *esp.* of more drink used to take off the effects of drunkenness; also ellipt. ***a hair of the dog***, a drink. **f.** ***to help a (lame) dog over a stile***: see quots. **g.** ***to lead a dog's life***: i.e. a life of misery, or of miserable subserviency; so ***to lead a person a dog's life***. **h.** ***give a dog an ill name and hang him***: see quot. 1818. †**i.** ***to be old dog at*** (also ***to be dog at***): to be experienced in, or adept at. *Obs.* **j.** ***dog on it***: a form of imprecation; see also dog-gone. **k.** ***to wake a sleeping dog***, i.e. some person or influence which is for the present quiet, but if aroused will create disturbance. So, ***let a sleeping dog*** (or ***sleeping dogs***) ***lie***. **l.** ***whose dog is dead?*** also ***what dog is a hanging?*** what occasion is there for watching, or for excitement? what's the matter? **m.** ***to keep a dog and bark oneself***: see quots. **n.** ***to see a man about a dog***: used colloq. as a vague excuse for leaving or absenting oneself. **o.** In various locutions involving an unpleasant circumstance or event unfit even for a dog. **p.** ***to put on dog***: to assume pretentious airs. *colloq.* Hence *dog* (ellipt.), pretentiousness, 'side'. **q.** ***like a dog's dinner***: used of someone or something dressed or arranged in an ostentatiously smart or flashy manner. *colloq.* **r.** ***like a dog with two tails***: very pleased, delighted. **s.** In many other proverbs and phrases.

a. *a* **1642** Sir W. Monson *Naval Tracts* iii. (1704) 350/2 You must fight according to the old Saying, Fight Dog, fight Bear; that is, till one be overcome. **1831** Scott *Diary* 5 Mar., A resolution to keep myself clear of politics, and let them 'fight dog, fight bear'.

b. *c* **1386** Chaucer *Merch. T.* 770 To Ianuarie he [Damian] gooth as lowe, As evere dide a dogge for the bowe. —— *Friar's T.* 71. **1430** Lydg. *Chron. Troy*, She was made as dogge for the bowe. **1542** Udall *Erasm. Apoph.* 223 a, He ..with lacke of vitailles brought those chop-logues or greate pratlers as lowe as dogge to the bow.

c. 1738 [see cat and dog 2]. **1766** P. Thicknesse *Observ. Customs French* 106 It blows cats and dogs, as the sailors say. **1848** Col. Hawker *Diary* (1893) II. 292 It blew great guns and poured cats and dogs.

d. 1529 Rastell *Pastyme* (1811) 57 He lyved lyke a lyon, and dyed lyke a dogge. **1607** Shaks. *Timon* ii. ii. 91 Thou was't whelpt a Dogge, and thou shalt famish a Dogges death.

1894 FENN *In Alpine Valley* I. 22 To die this dog's death, out here under these mountains.

e. 1546 J. HEYWOOD *Prov.* (1867) 37, I pray the leat me and my felow haue A heare of the dog that bote us last night. 1611 COTGR. s.v. *Beste*, Our Ale-knights often vse this phrase, and say, Giue vs a haire of the dog that last bit vs. [1760 R. JONES *Treat. Canine Madness* 204 The hair of the dog that gave the wound is advised as an application to the part injured.] 1840 DICKENS *Barn. Rudge* lii, Drink again. Another hair of the dog that bit you, captain. 1936 M. MITCHELL *Gone with the Wind* x. 207 Do you think.. Miss Pittypat would be having any brandy in the house? The hair of the dog——. 1966 A. E. LINDOP *I start Counting* xviii. 224 George took Len off for a hair of the dog. 1967 N. FITZGERALD *Affairs of Death* ix. 152 What you need, Frank, is a good stiff hair of the dog.

f. 1546 J. HEYWOOD *Prov.* (1867) 32 As good a deede, As it is to helpe a dogge ouer a style. 1638 CHILLINGW. *Relig. Prot.* I. iii. §33, I once knew a man out of curtesie, help a lame dog over a stile, and he for requitall bit him by the fingers. 1857 KINGSLEY *Two Y. Ago* xxv, 'I can.. help a lame dog over a stile'—(which was Mark's phrase for doing a generous thing).

g. 15.. *Fox MSS.* in Strype *Eccl. Mem.* III. xxi. 174 Mr. Ford afterwards had a dogs life among them. 1764 FOOTE *Mayor of G.* I. Wks. 1799 I. 173 She.. domineers like the devil: O Lord, I lead the life of a dog. 1861 HUGHES *Tom Brown at Oxf.* x, They've been leading him a dog's life this year and more.

h. [1730-6 BAILEY (folio) s.v. *Dog*, He who would hang his Dog first gives out that he is mad.] 1818 HAZLITT *Table-t.*, *Nicknames* 173 Give a dog an ill name and hang him, is a proverb. A nickname is the heaviest stone that the devil can throw at a man. 1886 MISS TYTLER *Buried Diamonds* xxxix, It is a case of give a dog an ill name and hang him.

i. 1589 NASHE *Almond for Parrat* 5 b, Oh he is olde dogge at expounding, and deade sure at a Catechisme. 1591 SHAKS. *Two Gent.* IV. iv. 14 To be, as it were, a dog at all things. 1601 —— *Twel. N.* II. iii. 62, I am dogge at a Catch. 1714 GAY *What d'ye call it* Prelim. sc. 5 Ah, Sir Roger, you are old Dog at these things.

j. 1826 J. WILSON *Noct. Ambr.* Wks. 1855 I. 260 Dog on't, ye wicked auld Lucifer, hoo your een sparkle as you touzle the clergy. 1872 C. KING *Mountain. Sierra Nev.* v. 101 'Take that, dog-on-you!'

k. 1562 J. HEYWOOD *Prov. & Epigr.* (1867) 132 It is ill wakyng of a sleapyng dogge. 1607 TOPSELL *Serpents* (1658) 658 It is good therefore if you have a Wife, that is.. unquiet and contentious, to let her alone, not to wake an angry Dog. 1864 CARLYLE *Fredk. Gt.* XI. ii, Friedrich is not the man to awaken Parliamentary sleeping-dogs. 1886 H. CONWAY *Living or Dead?* xiii, Better let sleeping dogs lie.

l. 1634 MASSINGER *Very Woman* III. ii, Whose dog's dead now That you observe these vigils? *a* 1663 *Little John a Begging* viii. in Child *Ballads* v. No. 142. 189/1 'Why rings all these bells? What dog is a hanging?'

m. 1583 B. MELBANCKE *Philotimus* 119 It is smal reason you should kepe a dog, and barke your selfe. 1738 SWIFT *Polite Conv.* i. 10, I won't keep a Dog, and bark my self. 1965 J. PORTER *Dover Two* xi. 147 'What time is it?' There was a clock right opposite him on the dining-room wall but Dover didn't believe in keeping a dog and barking himself. 'Just gone nine, sir.'

n. *c* 1867 D. BOUCICAULT *Flying Scud* IV. i. in Nicoll & Cloak *America's Lost Plays* (1940) I. 221 Excuse me Mr. Quail, I can't stop; I've got to see a man about a dog. 1939 D. L. SAYERS *In Teeth of Evidence* 38 I've got to get back to London to see a man about a dog. 1963 *Amer. Speech* XXXVIII. 175 *See a man about a dog* was a Prohibition euphemism for 'buying liquor', whereas several contemporary students [at Kansas University] recognized it as a circumlocution for 'visiting a rest room'... At Johns Hopkins, the phrase served as an excuse for leaving the scene.

o. 1887 BAUMANN *Londinismen* 43/1 It isn't fit to turn a dog out. 1943 *Amer. Speech* XVIII. 46 Other examples of translated Yiddish being adopted by non-Yiddish-speaking people are, 'It should(n't) happen to a dog!' [etc.]. 1964 J. PORTER *Dover One* i. 12 The Assistant Commissioner shuddered gently as he thought of all the messes you could get into in a kidnapping case. It wasn't the sort of job you'd wish on a dog.

p. 1871 L. H. BAGG *Four Years at Yale* 44 *Dog*, style, splurge. To put on dog, is to make a flashy display, to cut a swell. 1889 W. D. HOWELLS *Hazard of Fortunes* I. 267 He's made the thing awfully *chic*; it's jimminy; there's lots of dog about it. 1915 KIPLING *Fringes of Fleet* 36 Ah! That's the King of the Trawlers. Isn't he carrying dog, too! Give him room! 1924 W. J. LOCKE *Coming of Amos* xii, I don't want to put on dog, but the Lord didn't give me physical strength for nothing. 1926 —— *Old Bridge* II. v, Young Blake puts on dog and condescends to take the order. 1940 WODEHOUSE *Eggs, Beans & Crumpets* 48 An editor's unexampled opportunities for putting on dog and throwing his weight about. 1950 W. STEVENS *Let.* 20 Feb. (1967) 670 Sweeney is completely without side or dog. 1962 'A. GILBERT' *No Dust in Attic* xiv. 190 Matron put on a lot of dog about the hospital's responsibility.

q. 1934 'C. L. ANTHONY' *Touch Wood* II. ii. 66 Why have you got those roses in your hair? You look like the dog's dinner. 1936 J. CURTIS *Gilt Kid* v. 58 The geezer.. was dolled up like a dog's dinner with a white tie and all. 1945 *Penguin New Writing* XXIII. 42 A dizzy blonde all dressed up like a dog's dinner. 1954 J. TRENCH *Dishonoured Bones* II. iii. 57 Tarting up my house and the gardens like a dog's dinner.

r. 1953 J. TRENCH *Docken Dead* v. 65 She's like a dog with two tails. 1954 P. H. JOHNSON *Impossible Marriage* III. x. 273 Ned came in.. looking scared. He was not at all like a dog with two tails. 1969 B. COBB *Scandal at Scotland Yard* iii. 34 Bagshaw didn't bear the resemblance to a dog with two tails which I had expected.

s. 1382 WYCLIF *Eccl.* ix. 4 Betere is a quyc dogge thanne a leoun dead. 1388 —— *Prov.* xxvi. 11 As a dogge that turneth aȝen to his spuyng. 1526 *Pilgr. Perf.* (W. de W. 1531) 119 Whan we.. returne to our pryde & condicyons.. as yᵉ dogge to his vomyt. 1546 J. HEYWOOD *Prov.* (1867) 64 She will lie as fast as a dogge will licke a dishe. 1586 B. YOUNG *Guazzo's Civ. Conv.* IV. 178 b, It is an olde proverbe. A staffe is sone found to beate a Dogge. 1719 DE FOE *Crusoe* II. ii, It would have made a dog laugh. 1841 COL. HAWKER *Diary* (1893) II. 210 We went to bed as tired as dogs. [Cf. DOG-TIRED.] 1843 *Ibid.* II. 236 Old C—held forth with a long speech, lying as fast as a dog would trot. 1857 KINGSLEY *Two Y. Ago* xxi, I feel his heart. There's life in the old dog yet. 1858 GRAY *Lett.* (1893) 439, I cannot promise any special instruction, and shall take no fee. 'Dog does not eat dog' is the saying, you know.

III. Combinations and attributive uses.

18. a. *attrib.* or as *adj.* Of, pertaining to, or relating to, a dog or dogs; canine.

1565 HARDING in Jewel *Def. Apol.* (1611) 81 Would he not whet his dog eloquence vpon you? *c* 1620 FLETCHER & MASS. *Trag. Barnavelt* II. iv. in Bullen *O. Pl.* II. 239 Such a den of dog whelps. 1638 FEATLY *Strict. Lyndom.* I. A iij b, Every where full of *Canina facundia*, Dogg-eloquence. 1790 BEWICK *Hist. Quadrupeds* (1824) 334 The Bull-Dog.. the fiercest of all the Dog kind. 1879 H. DALZIEL *Dis. Dogs* (1893) 38 'Specifics'.. for all dog diseases. 1880 DAWKINS *Early Man* IV. 87 In the upper Pleiocene period the.. dog family.. appear for the first time. *Mod.* The wolves, foxes, and jackals are members of the Dog Tribe.

b. With names of some animals (esp. those of the dog kind): = male (cf. 2); as in ***dog hound, hyæna, otter, puppy, tiger***; DOG-FOX, DOG-WOLF. Also humorously ***dog-cook*** = man-cook.

1555 EDEN *Decades* 96 The dogge tyger chaunsed fyrste into this pitfaul. 1687 *Lond. Gaz.* No. 2220/4 Lost lately at Newmarket, an old Dog-Hound of His Majesties. 1813 *Sporting Mag.* XLI. 136 On Saturday.. was shot.. in the river Avon, a dog-otter. *a* 1841 T. HOOK *Man of many Friends* (D.), A first-rate dog-cook and assistants. 1893 SELOUS *Trav. S.E. Africa* 184 An old dog hyæna. 1896 *Sportsman* 10 July 4/2 In beagles, the Cheshire won in the class for.. dog hounds. 1955 *Times* 14 July 5/4 The Duke of Norfolk saw the doghound championship awarded to Distaff, a 1952 entered hound from his own pack.

19. General Comb.: **a.** attributive, as ***dog-basket, -bite, -breed, -couple, -doctor, -feast, -flesh, -food, -hospital, -leash, -licence, -life, -muzzle, -pack, -show, -soap, -tax, -train, -truck, -whistle***, etc.; serving as food for dogs, as ***dog-bran, -cake***, DOG-BISCUIT, etc. Also in ref. to greyhound racing, as ***dog-race, -racer, -racing, -track***.

1842 MRS. H. M. STANLEY *Let.* 22 Sept. in N. Mitford *Ladies of Alderley* (1938) 46, I walked to Northwich to order a *dog basket & other trifles. 1726 *Dict. Rust.* etc. (ed. 3), *Dog-bite, see Biting of a Mad Dog. 1883 E. R. LANKESTER *Adv. Science* (1890) 115 Two hundred and fifty persons have gone.. to be treated for dog-bite. *a* 1661 HOLYDAY *Juvenal* 75 Thou might'st.. on base *dog-bran feed. 1652 SHIRLEY *Sisters* I. i, Led Away in *dog-couples by rusty officers. 1843 *Ainsworth's Mag.* III. 147 With his dog-couples slung across his shoulders. 1939-40 *Army & Navy Stores Catal.* 999/2 Dog Couples, medium, for spaniels, setters and pointers. 1647 R. STAPYLTON *Juvenal* 67 Thou maist.. gnaw *dog-crusts. 1771 SMOLLETT *Humph. Cl.* I. Let. i, A famous *dog-doctor was sent for. 1743 BULKELEY & CUMMINS *Voy. S. Seas* 80, I was invited to a *Dog-Feast.. It was exceeding good Eating. 1854 WOOD *Anim. Life* 133 Dog is considered a delicacy.. There are several ways in which these dog-feasts are conducted. 1807 P. GASS *Jrnl.* 146 Some.. who prefer *dog-flesh to fish. 1907 *Athenæum* 3 Aug. 119 The whale-meat taken as *dog-food was poisoning the animals. 1951 M. MCLUHAN *Mech. Bride* 77/1 The ultimate absurdity of this attitude gets frequent expression in those dog-food ads. 1889 RUSKIN *Præterita* III. 55 Kept for a day or two in a *dog-hospital. 1609 SKENE *Reg. Maj.*, *Stat. Will.* 12 He may follow his hounds within the Kings forest, as farre as he may cast his horne or his *dogleisch. 1704 N. N. tr. *Boccalini's Advt. fr. Parnass.* I. 25 A Gentleman that wanted a parcel of *Dog-muzzles. 1925 MASEFIELD *Trial of Jesus* 6 The sneered lips of the *dog-pack in men snarling. 1927 F. BRETT YOUNG *Portrait of Clare* II. xi. 201 The huntsman and his whips had clattered over from the kennels with the dog-pack. 1864 *Chambers's Jrnl.* 502/2 Betting more than you can afford upon a *dog-race. 1865 *Ibid.* 657/2 They are also fond of dog-racing. 1875 *Ibid.* 254/1 Excluded from enjoying the pleasures of bull-baiting, the Lancashire rough falls back on dog-racing or some similar sport which admits of betting. *Ibid.*, Manchester.. being the headquarters of the rabbit-courser; .. and the colliery districts generally, of the dog-racer. 1928 *Manch. Guardian Weekly* 10 Aug. 113/4 The Dog-racing bill. 1859 *Newcastle Courant* 1 July 3/1 (*heading*) Sporting *dog and poultry show. 1861 *Times* 4 Apr. 12/2 (*heading*) Fancy dog show at Birmingham. 1863 in *N. & Q.* (1963) Mar. 106/1 The International Dog Show. 1870 B. CLAYTON *Dog-Keeper's Guide* 20 One of the first dog-shows held in London. 1796 (*title*) The *Dog Tax, in Verse. 1886 *Encycl. Brit.* XX. 201/2 The imposition of a dog-tax or licence. 1928 *Observer* 25 Mar. 16/6 The Ministry of Health has decided that Wimbledon must put up with a *dog-track, however much the Council and inhabitants may resent it. 1958 *Economist* 11 Oct. 155/1 A racecourse, a dog track, and thirty-nine pubs help the men to get through the £A2,000 a year that many of them have been earning. 1897 KIPLING *Capt. Courageous* v. 121 He told them of mail-carrying in the winter up Cape Breton way, of the *dog-train that goes to Coudray. 1842 *Ainsworth's Mag.* II. 222 Their word.. is now less influential than a *dog-whistle. 1863 KINGSLEY *Water Bab.* i, I wish I were a keeper.. to.. have a real dog-whistle at my button.

b. objective and obj. genitive, as ***dog-breaker*** (see BREAKER[1] 3), ***-breeder, -breeding, -driver, -driving, -fancier, -fancying, -keeping, -lover, -owner, -owning, -seller, -skinner, -stealer, -stealing, -washing***; see also DOG-KEEPER, -WHIPPER.

1770 *Gentl. Mag.* XL. 164 To punish the dog-stealer, or the man charged with the crime of dog-stealing. 1806 *Sporting Mag.* XXVII. 194/1 (*heading*) The dog-fancyer. 1821 P. EGAN *Life in London* II. iii. 221 The dog-fancier in the corner.. sidled up to the Swells. 1845 *Zoologist* III. 1099 Dog-fanciers have become practically acquainted with these influences. 1845 *Ainsworth's Mag.* VII. 5 I'm the only honest man in the dog-fancyin' line. 1848 KINGSLEY *Saint's Trag.* I. i. 38 That a man shall keep his dog-breakers, and his horse-breakers, and his hawk-breakers, and never hire him a boy-breaker or two! 1854 WOOD *Anim. Life* 158 The whole body of quondam dog-owners. 1889 G. STABLES *Kennel Comp.* i. 10 On dog-washing days. 1895 KIPLING *2nd Jungle Bk.* 148 The boy knows something of dog-driving. 1898 *Daily News* 17 Jan. 8/5 The Admiral.. described how the two saved the life of their dog-driver.. when he 'was rapidly freezing'. 1910 H. G. WELLS *Hist. Mr. Polly* ix. 301 Drowning superfluous kittens, dog-fancying as required.

c. instrumental, parasynthetic, and similative, as ***dog-bitten, -drawn, -driven, -gnawn, -hated*** adjs.; ***dog-bright, -eyed, -footed, -furred, -haired, -hearted, -looked, -looking, -whining*** adjs. See also d below; also DOG-FACED, -HEADED, -LEGGED.

1601 HOLLAND *Pliny* II. 363 A stone which a dog hath taken vp with his mouth and bitten, wil cause debate and dissention in the company where it is.. it is growne into a common prouerbe.. when we perceiue those that dwel in one house together to be.. at variance.. to say, You have a dog-bitten stone here among you. 1605 SHAKS. *Lear* IV. iii. 47 His own unkindness.. gave her dear rights To his dog-hearted daughters. 1699 R. L'ESTRANGE *Colloq. Erasm.* (1711) 66 Out comes the Dog-looking grey-Beard again. 1829 E. ELLIOTT *Village Patriarch* I. xiii, Legless soldier, borne In dog-drawn car. *a* 1847 ELIZA COOK *Song of Spirit of Poverty* II. 3 A dog-gnawn bone. 1922 JOYCE *Ulysses* 404 Swineheaded.. or doghaired infants occasionally born. 1928 E. SITWELL 5 *Poems* 4 Beneath my dog-furred leaves you see The creeping strawberry. *Ibid.* 10 And dark green dog-haired leaves of strawberries. 1929 —— *Gold Coast Customs* 22 The dog-whining dawn light. 1931 W. DE LA MARE *7 Short Stories* 134 He looked at me.. with those dog-bright eyes. 1932 AUDEN *Orators* III. 85 A dog-hated dustman.

d. with certain adjs. = as..as a dog; thoroughly, utterly; extremely; as ***dog asleep, -drunk, -hungry, -lame, -lean, -mad, -poor, -sick, -thick*** (= intimate). See also DOG-CHEAP, -TIRED, -WEARY.

1552 HULOET, Dogge leane, *squallidus*. 1579-80 NORTH *Plutarch* (1676) 712 Cicero was dog-lean, a little eater. 1599 H. BUTTES *Dyets drie Dinner* O iv, He that saith, he is Dog-sicke, as sicke as a Dog; meaneth a sicke Dog, doubtlesse. 1611 COTGR., *Dormer en transe*, to be dog asleepe, to be in a deepe or dead sleepe. *a* 1625 FLETCHER *Hum. Lieutenant* I. i, Would I were drunk dog-drunk, I might not feel this. *c* 1645 HOWELL *Lett.* (1650) II. 47 Som of our preachmen are grown dog mad. *a* 1810 TANNAHILL *Poet. Wks.* (1846) 90 Get dog-thick wi' the parish priest. 1832 SCOTT *Jrnl.* Jan., I was dog-sick of the whole of it. 1889 BOLDREWOOD *Robbery under Arms* (1890) 59 When she [a mare] was dog-poor and hardly able to drag herself along.

e. in a contemptuous sense, = Bad, spurious, bastard, mongrel; esp. in ***dog-Latin***; so ***dog-English, dog-Greek, dog('s)-logic, dog-rime***.

1611 FLORIO, *Versaccij*, dog-rimes, filthy verses. *a* 1625 *MS. Bodl.* 30. 13 a, To begge sir Tottipate's applause in dogrime verse. 1711 SWIFT *Exam.* No. 50 ¶5 His skill in that part of learning called dog's logic. 1770 D. DALRYMPLE (Ld. Hailes) *Anc. Scot. Poems* 243 (Jam.) The alternate lines are composed of shreds of the breviary, mixed with what we call Dog-Latin, and the French, *Latin de cuisine*. 1851 THACKERAY *Eng. Hum.* vi. (1863) 289 'Nescio quid est materia cum me', Sterne writes to one of his friends (in dog-Latin, and very sad dog-Latin too). 1884 F. HARRISON in *19th Cent.* Mar. 496 Agnostic is only dog-Greek for 'don't know'. 1938 F. M. FORD *Let.* 16 Mar. (1965) 290 He will at least write comprehensible dog-English. 1961 *N.Y. Times Bk. Rev.* 22 Jan. 6/4 They have been translated into a kind of academic dog-English.

20. Special Comb. **a.** †**dog-ape**, a dog-faced baboon (Dyce), CYNOCEPHALUS; †**dog-appetite**, the disease BULIMY, or CANINE appetite (but in quot. distinguished from this); **dog-belt**, in *Coal-mining*, a strong broad belt of leather, worn round the waist, for drawing dans or sledges in the workings; †**dog-chance** = *dog-throw*; **dog-clutch**, a device for coupling two shafts in the transmission of power, one member having teeth which engage with slots in another; **dog-dance**, a dance practised by American Indians; **dog-eat-dog**, *phr.* used esp. *attrib.* of a ruthlessly competitive attitude (with allusion to the proverb 'dog does not eat dog': cf. quot. 1858 *s.v.* 17 s); **dog-end** *slang*, a cigarette-end; **dogface** *U.S. slang*, a soldier, esp. an infantryman, in the U.S. army; †**dog-flaw**, a burst of passion (FLAW *sb.*[2] 2); †**dog-flogger** = DOG-WHIPPER; †**dog-given** *a.*, addicted to dogs; **dog-grate**, a detached fire-grate standing in a fireplace upon supports called dogs (see 8); **dog handler**, a person who is in charge of a dog or dogs, esp. a police dog; **dog-hanging**, 'a wedding feast at which money was collected for the bride' (Halliwell); **dog-horse**, a worn-out horse, fit only to be made into dog's-meat; †**dog-hunger** = *dog-appetite*; **dog-ill** = DISTEMPER *sb.*[1] 4 c; **dog-in-a-blanket**, a rolled currant dumpling or jam pudding (*colloq.*); **dog-iron** = sense 8; †**dog-killer**, a person appointed to kill dogs suspected of madness; **dog-lead**, a line to lead a dog with; **dog-leader**, a servant in charge of dogs; **dog-leaved** *a. rare* = DOG'S-EARED; so ***dog-leaving***, vbl. sb.; **dog-line**, a trace for fastening a dog to a sledge; **dog-madness** = CANINE rabies, hydrophobia; **dogman**, a man in charge of dogs; in quot. *a* 1861, a dealer in dog's-meat; *Austral.* (cf. DOG *sb.*[1] 7 a), a man who gives directional signals to a crane-operator on a building-site, often riding on the goods lifted by the crane; **dog-master**; **dog-meat**, dog's flesh used as food; **dog-nap**, a short nap taken while sitting (cf. *cat-nap* s.v. CAT *sb.*[1] 18, also DOG-SLEEP); **dog-nose vice** (see quot.); **dog-paddle** *colloq.*, a stroke, or way of swimming, like a dog's; hence as *v. intr.*, to swim in this fashion; **dog-pole** (see quot.); **dog-power**, the mechanical power exerted by a dog, as in turning a spit, or driving a churn-dasher; **dog-rapper**, = DOG-WHIPPER; so *dog rapping*; **dog-robber** *slang*, (*a*) in *pl.*, civilian clothes worn by a naval officer on shore leave; (*b*) a navy or army officer's orderly; **dog-screw** (see quot. and cf. DOG-NAIL); **dog-sled, -sledge**, a sledge drawn by dogs, as in the Arctic regions; †**dog-spasm** = CYNIC spasm; **dog-stopper** *Naut.* (see quot. and STOPPER); **dog-stove** = *dog-grate*; **dog-strop** *Naut.* (see quot.); **dog tag** *U.S. slang*, a soldier's identity disc; **dog-team**, a team of dogs used for drawing a sled; **dog-tent**, a small tent, so called from its likeness to a dog's kennel; **dog-throw**, the lowest or losing throw at dice (L. *canis, canicula*); **dog-tongs** (see quot.); **dog-town** (*U.S.*), a colony of prairie dogs (see 5); **dog-trials** *pl.* (*N.Z.*), a series of tests of the skill of sheep-dogs in tending sheep; **dog tucker** *Austral.* and *N.Z.*, mutton used as food for working dogs (see quot. 1933); †**dog-wheel**, a vertical wheel turned by a dog inside as a motor. See also DOG-BOLT, -BOX, -BOY, -CART, etc.

1600 SHAKS. *A.Y.L.* II. v. 28 If euer I thanke any man, Ile thanke you: but that they cal complement is like th' encounter of two *dog-Apes. **1615** CROOKE *Body of Man* 169 In the disease called Boulimos, there is hunger without appetite, and in the *Dog-appetite, there is appetite without hunger. **1842** BRANDE *Dict. Sc., etc.*, *Dog-belt. **1613** T. GODWIN *Rom. Antiq.* (1674) 112 The losing cast, Canis or Canicula, in English a *Dog-chance. **1671** H. M. tr. *Erasm. Colloq.* 441, I always cast the unlucky dog-chances. **1907** *Westm. Gaz.* 18 Nov. 6/3 The road-wheels are mounted on the..steel valves, leaving the enclosed driving-shafts free to transmit the power, through the medium of *dog-clutches, to the hubs. **1930** *Engineering* 14 Feb. 198/2 The spindle is connected to the handwheel by a dog clutch. **1951** G. H. SEWELL *Amat. Film-Making* (ed. 2) iii. 24 A dog-clutch on the camera motor mechanism engages with the main spindle of the magazine. **1807** PIKE *Sources Mississ.* (1810) 84 In the evening we were entertained with the calumet and *dog dance. **1854** WOOD *Anim. Life* 134 There is the dog-dance, in which the liver of the dog is suspended to a pole..The Indians..commence a slow dance round the pole. **1931** 'D. STIFF' *Milk & Honey Route* xv. 169 He knows and lives the justice of the jungle as well as he knows and lives the *dog-eat-dog code of the main stem. **1959** N. N. HOLLAND *First Mod. Comedies* xiv. 168 The impression we get is of a dog-eat-dog world. **1961** *Daily Tel.* 20 Feb. 22/4 Dog-eat-dog among the Lumumbists. **1963** M. LEVINSON *Taxi* vi. 72 No woman can call herself weak if she is prepared to throw herself pell-mell into the 'dog-eat-dog' kind of driving that goes on in the West End. **1964** R. JEFFRIES *Embarrassing Death* iii. 21 You don't want to be nice for this job..it's dog eat dog. **1935** H. NEVILLE *Sneak Thief on Road* 153 'Hard-up?' '*Dog-ends,' said Yank. 'Dust, funny mixings, ten a pennies, cigarette ends out of the gutter.' **1941** *Punch* 10 Sept. 238/3 Our sojourning place was bare of everything but dust and cigarette-butts ('dog-ends', these last are called). **1955** P. WILDEBLOOD *Against Law* iii. 118 The ensuing 'dog-ends' are unpicked, re-rolled and smoked again. **1941** *Time* 13 Oct. 24 Ordinary soldiers are called '*dog-faces' by the devil-dog Marines. **1943** STEINBECK *Once there was War* (1959) 145 There are too many little religious rules and prejudices [amongst the Arabs in north Africa] that an unsuspecting dogface can run afoul of. **1958** *Newsweek* 20 Oct. 42 No dogface who dug one [*sc.* a foxhole] will ever forget his blistered hands and aching back. *a* **1625** FLETCHER *Women Pleased* III. iv, We would soon disburthen you Of that that breeds these fits, these *dog-flaws in ye. **1806** *Churchw. Acc. St. Martin's, Leicester* 5 July (1884) 228 Pd Fewkes *Dog Flogger 0 10 0. *c* **1611** CHAPMAN *Iliad* XI. 256 As a *dog-given hunter sets upon a brace of boars His white-tooth'd hounds. **1881** G. T. ROBINSON in *Art Jrnl.* (Cent.), A grate with standards, which we still call a *dog-grate. **1968** R. JEFFRIES *Traitor's Crime* i. 9 The civilian fitter..was changing a fan-belt on a *dog handler's van. **1971** *Sunday Express* 25 Apr. 17/6 Dog handler Mr. Robert Green.. receives £720 from her estate. **1698** VANBRUGH *Æsop* IV. ii, Two blind stallions, besides pads, routs, and *dog-horses. *c* **1785** T. BEWICK *Waiting for Death* in A. Dobson *B. & his Pupils* ix. (1884) 155 He..was judged to be only fit for the dogs. However, one shilling and sixpence beyond the dog-horse price saved his life. **1598** SYLVESTER *Du Bartas* II. i. III. *Furies* 451 The *Dog-hunger, or the Bradypepsie. *a* **1680** BUTLER *Rem., Miser* (1759) II. 342 His greedy appetite to riches is but a kind of doghunger that never digests what it devours. **1879** H. DALZIEL *Dis. Dogs* (1893) 41 Distemper is also known as the '*dog-ill'. **1867** MISS YONGE *Six Cushions* ix. 72 The *dog-in-a-blanket making its appearance, Clara cut three beauteous slices, with spiral rings of black currant alternating with suet. **1883** *Old Virginia Gentlem.* in *Macm. Mag.*, Brass *dog-irons of ponderous build. **1614** B. JONSON *Barth. Fair* II. i, A worthy worshipful man..who would take you now the habit of a porter, now of a carman, now of the *dog-killer, in this month of August. **1665** *Ord. Ld. Mayor Lond. Concern. Plague*, That the Dogs be killed by the Dog-killers appointed. **1826** SCOTT *Woodst.* xxix, Bevis, who was bred here when he was a *dog-leader, would not fly at him. **1886** W. J. TUCKER *E. Europe* 137 Being more thumbed, *dog-leaved, and worn than the others. **1823** SOUTHEY in *Life* (1849) I. 69 The thumbing and *dog-leaving. **1856** KANE *Arct. Expl.* I. xx. 252 The leader of the party succeeded in patching up his mutilated *dog-lines. **1715** J. DELACOSTE tr. *Boerhave's Aphorisms* 304 It's called.. because mostly proceeding from the bite of Dogs, a *Dog-madness. **1789** W. BUCHAN *Dom. Med.* (1790) 477 The *rabies canina*, or dog madness. *a* **1861** MRS. BROWNING *Napoleon III in Italy* xv, Filch the *dog-man's meat To feed the offspring of God. **1879** H. DALZIEL *Dis. Dogs* (1893) 9 It is an error of modern dog men to wean puppies too soon. **1962** R. CLARK (*title*) The dogman and other poems. **1970** *Sunday Mail Mag.* (Brisbane) 10 May 3/2 Most Sydney men will not raise their eyes beyond ladies' leg level except to see one other phenomenon—the daring dogmen on the skyhooks. **1611** BARREY *Ram Alley* IV. i. in Hazl. *Dodsley* X. 346 When did you see Sir Theophrastus Slop, The city *dog-master? **1854** WOOD *Anim. Life* 134 Another..feast, in which *dog-meat takes a prominent part. **1860** W. PHILLIPS *Speeches* (1863) 295 That sleepy crier of a New Hampshire court, who was ever dreaming in his *dog-naps that the voice of judge or lawyer was a noisy interruption, and always woke shouting 'Silence!' **1874** KNIGHT *Dict. Mech.*, *Dog-nose Vise* (*Locksmithing*), a hand-vise with long, slender, pointed jaws. Called also *pig-nose* vise. **1904** R. THOMAS *Swimming* 428 How did Beowulf swim? I should say the human stroke..popularly but incorrectly known as *dog paddle, which was the European stroke to about the year 1500. **1928** *Daily Express* 25 June 4/5 Try to push off from the side, performing the kick with a 'dog-paddle' arm stroke. **1954** *Landfall* Dec. 272 He raised him up in the water and tried to get him to dog-paddle. **1958** L. DURRELL *Balthazar* i. 21, I put the precious rose between my teeth and dog-paddled back to my clothes on the pebble beach. **1970** J. YARDLEY *Kiss the Boys* viii. 157 She dog-paddled along the tunnel behind him. Then she was out in very deep water. **1978** *Washington Post* 28 May L4/2, I learned to dog-paddle out to a log anchored in the river. **1807** P. GASS *Jrnl.* 42 An old Indian camp, where we found some of their *dog-poles ..the Indians fasten their dogs to them, and make them draw them from one camp to another loaded with skins and other articles. **1898** W. P. DRURY *Tadpole of an Archangel* 202 He was an absent-minded..young giant in..a *dogrobber suit. **1929** W. FAULKNER *Sartoris* II. 63 De Captain's dog-robber foun' whar he kep' dese here unloaded passes. **1946** G. HACKFORTH-JONES *Sixteen Bells* I. iv. 69 Numerous officers, clad in an assortment of clothing, ranging from tennis clothes to 'dog-robbers' came on deck. **1958** M. DICKENS *Man Overboard* iii. 36 Then he..changed into dog robbers and went into the town to get drunk. **1967** *Everybody's Mag.* (Austral.) 18 Jan. 36/2 A Dog-robber is a general's aide-de-camp—who, it is said, would rob a dog of his bone to please the general. **1884** F. J. BRITTEN *Watch & Clockm.* 88 *Dog Screw*, a screw with an eccentric head or with one side of the head taken off, used for attaching a watch movement to a dome case. **1810** Z. M. PIKE *Exped. Sources Miss.* 85 With my *dog-sled [I] arrived at the fort before 10 o'clock. **1889** *Pall Mall G.* 1 May 5/3 An account of a recent dog-sled trip in the North-west. **1856** KANE *Arct. Expl.* I. xvi. 185, I have been out with my *dog-sledge, inspecting the ice. **1615** CROOKE *Body of Man* 754 Those conuulsions which we call Cynicke or *Dogge-spasmes, because by the contraction of these, men are constrained to writh and grinne like Dogges. **1867** SMYTH *Sailor's Word-bk.* s.v. *Stopper of the Cable*, *Dog-stopper, a strong rope clenched round the mainmast, and used on particular occasions to relieve and assist the preceding [i.e. the stopper of the cable, or deck-stopper] when the ship rides in a heavy sea. **1881** MISS BRADDON *Asph.* vi. 71 Wide hearths and *dog-stoves. **1882** NARES *Seamanship* (ed. 6) 43 The strop round the yard is called the *dog strop, and is a single strop. **1918** *Hatchet* 22 Feb. 2/1 All that will be necessary will be to consult his finger print name and other matters of interest on the little steel tag around his neck, variously known as '*Dog Tag', 'license to live', but to the Medical Department as an Identification Tag. **1947** *Penguin New Writing* XXIX. 159 If I should die to-morrow, I suppose this is where my bones, if not my dog-tag, would lie for ever. **1856** E. K. KANE *Arctic Explorations* I. xvi. 198 They brought my *dog-team, with the restoratives I had sent for. **1928** *Publishers' Weekly* 16 June 2461 The author worked as a dog-team freighter in Alaska during the gold-rush. **1863** KINGLAKE *Crimea* III. 181 The French soldiery were provided with what they called *dog-tents—tents not a yard high, but easily carried, and yielding shelter to soldiers creeping into them. **1880** LEWIS & SHORT *Lat. Dict.*, *Canicula*..The worst throw with dice, the *dog-throw. **1891** *Rock* 2 Oct. 4 A very quaint exhibit..consisting of '*dog-tongs', formerly used for expelling dogs from churches. **1854** J. R. BARTLETT *Personal Narr.* I. iv. 70 The vast domains of this community, or '*dog-town', as they are usually called. **1873** *Gd. Words* 77 They have often seen the rattlesnake come out of holes in a dog-town, but have never seen any prairie dogs come out of the same hole. **1951** L. G. D. ACLAND *Early Canterbury Runs* ix. 303 He was also a lover of Border collies and at one time almost unbeatable at the *dog-trials. *Ibid.* 369 The expression is in frequent use at dog-trials. **1933** —— in *Press* (Christchurch) 7 Oct. 15/7 *Dog Tucker*. In the old days when Merino sheep were worth even less than they are now, it was the custom to throw in a few to the drover on delivery to make up for losses on the road. They were called *dog tucker*. E.g., 'I'll throw ten in for your dogs.' **1965** *Weekly News* (Auckland) 10 Feb. 39/4 The pup's master had thrown him a small piece of mutton, cut from the dog tucker hanging in a tree. **1756** W. TOLDERVY *Hist. Two Orphans* I. 107 A *dog-wheel, for roasting of meat.

b. Combinations with *dog's*: **dog's age** *slang* (orig. *U.S.*), a long time; **dog's breakfast** *slang*, a mess; **dog's chance**, the poorest chance; cf. *dog-chance* s.v. 20 a; also (N.Z.), *dog's show*; **dog's dinner**, (*a*) see sense 17 q above; (*b*) *slang*, = *dog's breakfast*; †**dog's face**, a term of abuse or reproach; †**dog's game**, game hunted with dogs; †**dog's hunger** = *dog-hunger* (see 20 a); **dog's-lug** (*Naut.*) = DOG'S-EAR *sb.* 2; **dog's sleep, dog's trick**, see DOG-SLEEP, DOG-TRICK. See also c and d below; also DOG'S-BODY, -EAR, -LETTER, -MEAT, -NOSE, -TAIL, -TOOTH.

1836 *Knickerbocker* VII. 17 That blamed line gale has kept me in bilboes such a *dog's age. **1916** H. L. WILSON *Somewhere in Red Gap* v. 175 Booming pained surmises through the house as to what fearful state it would get to be in if she didn't fight it to a clean finish once in a dog's age. **1919** T. K. HOLMES *Man fr. Tall Timber* v. 55, I don't get a letter once in a dog's age from any of them. **1933** M. DE LA ROCHE *Master of Jalna* xxiii. 248 She hasn't laid an offering on the altar of Jalna for a dog's age. **1937** PARTRIDGE *Dict. Slang* 231/2 *Dog's breakfast, a mess: low Glasgow (—1934). **1959** *Times* 29 Apr. 10/4 He can't make head or tail of it... It's a complete dog's breakfast. **1963** *Times* 22 Feb. 12/3 The warders..are very angry and have rejected the latest War Office offer as totally unacceptable. They feel the offer is a bit of a dog's breakfast. **1902** *Captain* VII. 542/1 They all felt that Adderman's wouldn't have a *dog's chance when Ardenwood College had got fairly going. **1939** J. B. PRIESTLEY *Let People Sing* 50 Don't suppose I've got a dog's chance really, but I have to keep on trying. **1971** J. WAINWRIGHT *Last Buccaneer* I. 35 North End is a *dog's dinner of hovels, dives and drinking dens. **1985** *Guardian* 22 Aug. 3/4 The influential Georgian Group, described the main frontage of the scheme as a dog's dinner yesterday. **1676** HOBBES *Iliad* I. 213 *Dogs-face, and Drunkard, Coward that thou art. **1610** HOLLAND *Camden's Brit.* I. 259 The Conqueror tooke away land both from God and men, to dedicate the same unto wild beasts and *Dogs-game. **1631** R. H. *Arraignm. Whole Creature* viii. 58 The disease cald the *Dogs hunger, alway eating but never satisfied. **1882** NARES *Seamanship* (ed. 6) 134 Pass in the leech from the yard-arms and *dog's-lug. **1957** I. CROSS *God Boy* (1958) vi. 46, I had to admire Bloody Jack for sitting on there even though he didn't have a *dog's show of getting any fish.

c. In names of animals (*a*) resembling dogs in some respect, or (*b*) infesting dogs: as **dog-badger** (see quot.); **dog-bat**, a species of bat having a head like a dog's, found in Java; **dog-flea**, a species of flea (*Pulex serraticeps*) infesting dogs; **dog's-guts**, a name for the fish *Harpodon nehereus*, also called BUMMALO; **dog-louse**, a kind of louse which infests dogs; also = *dog-tick*; **dog-snapper**, an American species of fish: see SNAPPER; **dog-tick**, a tick of the genus *Ixodes* infesting dogs; **dog-winkle**, the marine gastropod *Nucella lapillus*. See also DOG-BEE, -FISH, -FLY, DOG'S-TONGUE.

1741 *Compl. Fam. Piece* II. i. 297 There are two Sorts of Badgers, viz. the *Dog-Badger, as resembling the Dog in his Feet; and a Hog-Badger, as resembling a Hog in his cloven Hoofs. **1828** STARK *Elem. Nat. Hist.* I. 66 *Pteropus rostratus* ..The *Dog bat of Java. **1841** *Penny Cycl.* XIX. 117/1 Other species..have received..the names of the species they attack, such as the *dog flea (*Pulex Canis*). **1552** *Dog-louse [see *dog-tick*]. **1755** JOHNSON, *Doglouse*, an insect that harbours on dogs. **1775** ROMANS *Hist. Florida* App. 52 The fish caught here..are such as..red, grey and black snappers, *dog snappers, mutton-fish. **1552** HULOET, *Dogge tyke or louse, *ricinus*. **1849** JOHNSTON in *Proc. Berw. Nat. Club* II. No. 7. 373 My specimens were taken from the pointer, and were sent to me as the dog tick. [**1853** FORBES & HANLEY *Hist. Brit. Mollusca* III. 386 This whelk [*sc. Purpura lapillus*] is called Dog-periwinkle on many parts of the coast.] **1856** P. H. GOSSE *Man. Marine Zool.* II. 129 *Purpura* (Lamk.). Purple, or *Dog-winkle. **1901** *Westm. Gaz.* 16 Dec. 3/1 The Tyrian purple of the ancients can be obtained from the common dog-winkle (*purpura lapillus*). **1950** N. B. EALES *Littoral Fauna Gt. Brit.* (ed. 2) 196 *Nucella lapillus* (*Purpura*). Dog Winkle.

d. In names of plants (frequently denoting an inferior or worthless sort, or one unfit for human food): as †**dog's-apple**, a name for the caper shrub or berry (*obs.*); **dog-blow**, in Nova Scotia, the ox-eye daisy, *Chrysanthemum Leucanthemum*; **dog('s) cabbage** (see CABBAGE *sb.*[1] 2); **dog's camomile** (see CAMOMILE 1 b); †**dog's-caul (-call)**, Dog's MERCURY; **dog-cherry**, the fruit of *Cornus sanguinea* (Prior) = DOGBERRY[1] 1; **dog's-chop**, *Mesembryanthemum caninum* (*Treas. Bot.*); †**dog's-cods, -cullions**, various species of *Orchis* = DOGSTONES (*obs.*); **dog-daisy**, the common Daisy, *Bellis perennis*; also in some localities and now generally in books, applied to the Ox-eye Daisy, *Chrysanthemum Leucanthemum*; **dog-hip, -hep** (*dial.*), the fruit of the dog-rose; †**dog's leek, dog-leek**, an old book-name for various bulbous plants; **dog-lichen**, *Peltidea canina* (see quot.); **dog's-mouth**, the Snap-dragon; **dog('s)-parsley**, *Æthusa Cynapium*, also called Fool's Parsley; **dog-poison** = prec. (*Treas. Bot.*); **dog-standard, -stander**, a local name for Ragwort, *Senecio Jacobæa*; **dog-thistle** (see THISTLE); **dog('s)-thorn** = DOG-ROSE; **dog('s)-wheat**, a species of couch-grass, *Triticum caninum* = DOG-GRASS. See also DOGBERRY, DOGWOOD, etc.

1567 MAPLET *Gr. Forest* 36 Capers..of some it is called Dogges Bremble, of other some *Dogges Apple. **1578** LYTE *Dodoens* II. xxx. 186 The second kinde is now called.. in English..*Dogges Camomile. *Ibid.* I. liv. 77 The wilde Mercury is called..in English..*Dogges Call. **1656** EARL MONM. *Advt. fr. Parnass.* 27 Mallows, Henbane, Dogs-caul, and other pernitious plants. **1578** LYTE *Dodoens* II. lvi. 222 The first kinde is called..in Latine..*Testiculus canis*, that is to say, *Dogges Cullions, or *Dogges coddes. **1847** HALLIWELL, *Dog-daisy, the field daisy. *North.* **1888** *Sheffield Gloss.*, *Dog-daisy*, the common wild daisy, *Bellis perennis*. [So in Glossaries of Cumberland, Lonsdale, Whitby, etc.] **1894** BARING-GOULD *S. France* I. 102 The meadows were white as with dog-daisies. **1853** G. JOHNSTON *Bot. East. Borders* 75 *Rosa canina*, Dog-Rose. Briar-Rose: the *Dog-hep. **1892** *Northumberland Gloss.*, *Dog-hips* and *cat-haws* are commonly associated by children. **1548** TURNER *Names of Herbes* 21 Bulbine..maye be called in englishe *dogges Leike. *Ibid.* 57 Ornithigalum..may be called dogleke or dogges onion. **1578** LYTE *Dodoens* II. xlix.

209. **1861** H. MACMILLAN *Footnotes fr. Nat.* 105 The common *dog-lichen (*Peltidea canina*)..was formerly employed..as a cure for hydrophobia (hence its specific name). **1839** PHILLIPS in *Sat. Mag.* 18 May 190/1 It has.. received various names, as *Dog's Mouth, Lion's Snap, Toad's Mouth, and Snap-Dragon. **1866** *Treas. Bot.* s.v. *Parsley*, *Dog's P. *Æthusa Cynapium*. **1868** PAXTON *Bot. Dict.*, Dog Parsley. *c* **1750** J. NELSON *Jrnl.* (1836) 122, I do not fear the man that can kill me any more than I do him that can cut down a *dog-standard. **1694** WESTMACOTT *Script. Herb.* 29 There is a confusion of names in botanical authours about Brambles, Briars..*Dog-thorn, &c. **1776** WITHERING *Brit. Plants* (1801) II. 174 *Triticum caninum*, *dog's Wheat. Woods and hedges.

† **dog**, *sb.*[2] deformation of the word *God*, used in profane oaths. *Obs.*

c **1550** *Lusty Juventus* in Hazl. *Dodsley* II. 84 By dog's precious wounds, that was some whoreson villain.

dog (dɒg), *v.* Pa. t. and pple. **dogged** (dɒgd). [f. prec. sb.]

1. *trans.* **a.** To follow like a dog; to follow pertinaciously or closely; to pursue, track (a person, his footsteps, etc.), *esp.* with hostile intent. Also with *out*.

1519 HORMAN *Vulg.* 256 Our ennemyes..dogged vs at the backe [*a tergo instabat*]. **1601** SHAKS. *Twel. N.* III. ii. 81, I haue dogg'd him like his murtherer. **1676** WYCHERLEY *Pl. Dealer* v. i, The Bayliffs dog'd us hither to the very door. **1750** JOHNSON *Rambler* No. 16 ⁋12 Eleven painters are now dogging me, for they know that he who can get my face first will make his fortune. **1834** PRINGLE *Afr. Sk.* viii. 257 A lion was..dogging us through the bushes the whole way home. **1843** 'R. CARLTON' *New Purchase* II. 180 We'll dog out the rats now. **1851** DIXON *W. Penn* xxix. (1872) 272 Spies and informers dogged his footsteps. **1877** F. ROSS et al. *Gloss. Words Holderness* 55 *Dog-oot-ov*, to obtain by persistent importunity. **1936** M. ALLINGHAM *Flowers for Judge* ix. 140 Someone murdered him very neatly indeed... Our astute friends..dogged that much out all right.

b. *fig.* Said of immaterial agencies.

1593 SHAKS. *Rich. II*, v. iii. 139 Destruction straight shall dogge them at the heeles. **1634** MILTON *Comus* 404, I fear the dread events that dog them both. **1795** SOUTHEY *Joan of Arc* v. 174 Famine dogs their footsteps. *a* **1859** MACAULAY *Hist. Eng.* (1861) V. 245 Envy such as dogged Montague through a long career.

†**c.** To haunt (a place, etc.). *Obs. rare.*

1600 *Dr. Dodypoll* III. v. (Bullen *O. Pl.*), My mistresse dogs the banket, and I dog her. **1602** MARSTON *Antonio's Rev.* III. v, Assume disguise, and dog the court In fained habit.

2. *intr.* or *absol.* To follow close. (In quot. 1694, to continue persistently or importunately.)

1519 HORMAN *Vulg.* 265 They cam doggynge at the tayle of our hoste. **1694** R. L'ESTRANGE *Fables* cv. (1714) 121 To lie Dogging at his Prayers so Much and so Long. **1807** J. MOSER in *Spirit Pub. Jrnls.* X. 7 Should constables dog at our heels. **1837** WHEELWRIGHT tr. *Aristophanes* I. 6, I..will not hold my tongue, Unless you tell me, why on earth we're dogging.

3. *trans.* To drive or chase with a dog or dogs; to set a dog on; *fig.* to hound or drive *into*.

1591 *Bottesford* (*Linc.*) *Manor Rec.* (MS.), Dogging beast vicinorum super communem pasturam. **1601** [see DOGGING below]. **1794** T. STONE *Agric. Lincolnsh.* 62 [Sheep] being over-heated in being..dogged to their confinement. **1840** H. CLEEVE in *Jrnl. Agric. Soc.* I. III. 298 Others have dogged the animal, and worried it to exhaustion. **1847** BUSHNELL *Chr. Nurt.* II. ii. (1861) 264 He may dog his children possibly into some kind of conformity with his opinions.

4. To furnish or fill with dogs. (*nonce-use.*)

a **1661** FULLER *Worthies, Somerset* (1811) II. 276 (D.) The ancient Romans, when first (instead of manning) they dogged their Capitol.

5. To act as a dog to, to guard as a dog. *rare.*

1818 MILMAN *Samor* I. 281 Ah generous King! That sets the emaciate wolf to dog the flock; The hawk to guard the dovecote.

6. a. To fasten or secure by means of a dog (see DOG *sb.*[1] 7 a, e); also *intr.* to penetrate with a dog.

1591 in Glasscock *Rec. St. Michael's, Bp. Stortford* (1882) 65, iiij li. of leade to dog the stones together of y[e] steple windowe. **1879** *Lumberman's Gaz.* 15 Oct., We can dog directly into the hardest knot in the heaviest timber and hold the log perfectly safe and true. **1886** G. W. HOTCHKISS in *Encycl. Brit.* XXI. 345/2 When the log reached the carriage it was dogged..by the simple movement of a lever.

b. To extract or uproot with a dog (DOG *sb.*[1] 7 c).

1610 W. FOLKINGHAM *Art of Survey* I. ix. 21 Whynnes, Broome, &c...being..rooted vp by dogging or grubbing.

c. *Naut.* To fasten, as a rope, to a spar or cable in such a way that the parts bind on each other, so as to prevent slipping.

1847 A. C. KEY *Recov. H.M.S. Gorgon* 24 Another purchase was..lashed round the sheerhead..and its lower block was dogged on. **1867** SMYTH *Sailor's Word-bk.*, *Dogged*, a mode of attaching a rope to a spar or cable, in contradistinction to racking, by which slipping is prevented; half-hitched and end stopped back, is one mode.

†**7.** *Oxford Univ. slang.* (See quot., and COLLECTOR 4.) *Obs.*

1726 AMHERST *Terræ Fil.* xlii. 233 The collectors..having it in their power to dispose of all the schools and days in what manner they please..great application is made to them for gracious days and good schools; but especially to avoid being posted or dogged. *Ibid.*, The first column and the last column..(which contain the names of those who are to come up the first day and the last day, and which is called posting and dogging) are esteemed very scandalous.

8. *U.S. slang.* Used in imprecations (perhaps sometimes with a reference to sense 3). Cf. *dog on it* (DOG *sb.*[1] 17 j), DOG-GONE.

1860 BARTLETT *Dict. Amer.*, *Dogged*, a euphemistic oath; as, 'I'll be dogged if I do it'. **1884** 'MARK TWAIN' [Clemens] *Adv. H. Finn* (Farmer *Amer.*), Why, dog my cats! there must have been a house-full o' niggers in there every night.

Hence **'dogging** *ppl. a.* See also DOGGING *vbl. sb.*

1601 CORNWALLYES *Ess.* i, They are commonly hawking, or dogging fellowes.

dog, obs. form of DĀK.

dogal ('dəʊgəl), *a.* [ad. It. *dogale* ducal; in med.L. *dogālis*.] Of or pertaining to a doge.

1848 in WEBSTER. Hence in mod. Dicts.

dogan ('dəʊgən). *Canadian slang.* Also **dogun.** [Perh. f. *Dogan*, an Irish surname.] An Irish Roman Catholic.

1854 *Hamilton* (Ontario) *Gaz.* 15 May 2/7, I would be overly liberal if I estimated their number as a couple of Dogans! **1933** 'P. SLATER' *Yellow Briar* (1934) ii. 22 Many a time I got a smart clout on the lug and was told to take that for a dirty little dogan.

‖**dogana** (do'gana). [It.: see DIVAN and cf. DOUANE.] A custom-house (in Italy).

1645 EVELYN *Diary* (1889) I. 202 We were conducted to the Dogana, where our portmanteaus were visited. **1650** HOWELL *Giraffi's Rev. Naples* I. 22. **1828** [J. R. BEST] *Italy as it is* 74.

b. Customs, customs-duty, duty or impost. (In Italy and Spain.)

1822 E. E. WILLIAMS in Dowden *Life Shelley* (1887) II. 495. **1838** PRESCOTT *Ferd. & Is.* (1846) III. x. 13 The dogana, an important duty levied on the flocks of the Capitanate.

‖**doga'ressa.** [It., irreg. fem. of *doge*.] The wife of a doge.

1820 BYRON *Mar. Faliero* Pref., Towards one of her damsels, and not to the 'Dogaressa'. **1846** L. S. COSTELLO *Tour Venice* 294 The fair Dogaressa of the Morosini.

dogate ('dəʊgeɪt). [ad. F. *dogat*, Venet. *dogato*, f. *doge*.] The office or dignity of a doge; dogeship.

1727–51 CHAMBERS *Cycl.* s.v. *Doge*, The dogate is elective. **1881** *Daily News* 17 Sept. 3/3 The linen cap, or *velo ducal*, which Lewis Manin wore on the 12th May, 1797, the last day of his dogate and of the Republic of Venice.

dogbane: see DOG'S-BANE.

dog-bee. 1. A bumble bee or a drone. ? *Obs.*

1530 PALSGR. 214/2 Doggebee, *bourdon*.

2. 'A fly troublesome to dogs'.

In recent Dicts.

dogberry[1] ('dɒgbɛrɪ). [DOG *sb.*[1] 20 d.]

1. The 'berry' or drupe of the Wild Cornel or DOGWOOD. **b.** The shrub; also *dogberry-tree*.

1551 TURNER *Herbal* I. M j b, The female is called of some doge berry tree: sume call it corn tree. **1719–30** tr. *Tournefort's Compl. Herb.* 641 (Jod.) The common wild female cornus, called the dogwood, or dogberry tree. **1776** WITHERING *Brit. Plants* (1801) II. 198 *Cornus sanguinea*, Dogberry tree, Hounds tree, Hounds berry, Prick wood, Prick timber. **1879** H. DALZIEL *Dis. Dogs* (1893) 97 Among preventives of hydrophobia..in vogue one time or another ..leaves of the dog-berry tree.

2. Applied to other shrubs or trees, or their fruit. **a.** In Nova Scotia, a kind of mountain-ash, *Pyrus americana*; in U.S. the Chokeberry, *P. arbutifolia* (Cent. Dict.). **b.** Applied locally in Britain to the Guelder Rose, the Bearberry, and the fruit of the Dog-rose. (Britten & Holland.)

'Dogberry[2]. The name of a foolish constable in Shakspere's *Much Ado about Nothing*; thence, allusively, an ignorant consequential official.

1846 R. FORD *Gath. Spain* xx, There is no absurdity, no inconceivable ignorance, too great for the local Spanish 'Dogberries', who rarely deviate into sense. **1864** MISS BRADDON *Aur. Floyd* xxxviii. (Farmer), The Dogberries of Doncaster..were on the wrong scent.

Hence **Dogberrydom, Dogberryism.**

1855–81 HYDE CLARKE *Dict.*, *Dogberryism*. **1883** *Daily Tel.* 7 Dec., Is this firm government? It seems to us Dogberryism in excelsis. **1895** J. J. RAVEN *Hist. Suffolk* 206 In defiance of Dogberrydom.

'dog-biscuit. a. Biscuit for feeding dogs.

1858 SIMMONDS *Dict. Trade*, *Dog-biscuit*, coarse waste or broken biscuits sold for feeding dogs. **1870** BLAINE *Encycl. Rural Sports* §1502 Dog-biscuits are continually advertised in the London papers. **1879** H. DALZIEL *Dis. Dogs* 7.

b. *Military slang.* = BISCUIT 1 b (*b*).

1925 FRASER & GIBBONS *Soldier & Sailor Words* 79 *Dog biscuit*, an old Army term for the Army mattresses.

dogbolt, dog-bolt ('dɒgbəʊlt). Also 5 **-bolde.** [Origin uncertain; possibly sense 1 is the original, but sense 2 is known 130 years earlier.

(Johnson's surmise 'Of this word I know not the meaning, unless it be, that when meal or flower is sifted or bolted to a certain degree, the coarser part is called *dog bolt*, or flower for dogs', has no foundation.)]

†**1.** Some kind of bolt or blunt-headed arrow; perh. one of little value that might be shot at any dog. *Obs.*

1592 G. HARVEY *Pierce's Super.* 8 The dreadful engine of phrases instead of thunderboltes shooteth nothing but dogboltes and catboltes and the homeliest boltes of rude folly. **1612** T. JAMES *Jesuits' Downf.* 16 Is not this a.. sacrilegious abuse of Gods..benefits..to make them dog-bolts in every bow, and shafts in every quiver, to draw out for the managing of any impious fact?

†**2.** Applied to a person as a term of contempt or reproach. Perh. orig. = 'Mere tool to be put to any use', or 'one at the command of another'; but generally = 'contemptible fellow, mean wretch'. *Obs.*

1465 MARG. PASTON in *Paston Lett.* No. 533 II. 249 Sir John Wyndefeld and other wurchepfull men ben mad but her doggeboldes. **1579** U. FULWELL *Ars Adulandi* viii. I ij a, On mee attendeth simple Sir Iohn (a chaplayne..) who is made a doulte and dogbolt of euery seruinge man. **1584** LYLY *Campaspe* (1632) G ix, [Granichus remarks] That Diogenes that dog should have Manes that dog-bolt, it grieveth nature and spiteth art. *a* **1619** BEAUM. & FL. *Wit without M.* III. i, To have your own turn served, and to your friend to be a dogbolt. **1690** SHADWELL *Am. Bigot* III. Wks. (1720) 267 Dog-bolt, to blast the honour of my mistress. [*arch.* **1823** SCOTT *Peveril* vii, I would not be such a dog-bolt as to go and betray the girl.]

b. *attrib.* Wretched, contemptible. *Obs.*

1580 FULKE *Answers* (1848) 212 He doth nothing..but.. quarrel like a dogbolt lawyer. **1664** BUTLER *Hud.* II. i. 40 Now his dog-bolt Fortune was so low.

3. = DOG *sb.*[1] 7 a.

1824 *Archæologia* XX. 555 (D.) The beams are..fastened to the sides with bolts not unlike our dog-bolts.

4. The bolt of the cap-square over the trunnion of a gun.

1867 SMYTH *Sailor's Wd.-bk.*, *Dog-bolt*, a cap square bolt.

dog-box.

a. A box for a dog to lie in.

1815 *Sporting Mag.* XLVI. 138 A mallard belonging to Mr. Tucker..was observed to resort every evening to a dog-box in his yard.

b. A compartment in a railway truck or van for conveying dogs: cf. BOX *sb.*[2] 12.

1862 EMMA DAVENPORT *Live Toys* xiv, Shut up in a dog-box on the train.

c. *transf.* A type of railway goods wagon or compartment in a railway carriage. *Austral.* and *N.Z. slang.*

1917 E. MILLER *Diary* 19 Jan. in *Camps, Tramps & Trenches* (1939) i. 2 Our crowd moved off from headquarters in the railway goods wagons known as 'dog-boxes'. **1945** BAKER *Austral. Lang.* x., 196 The use of *dog-boxes* to describe many carriages used on N.S.W. railways.

dog-boy. A boy in charge of dogs; a huntsman's assistant.

1612 DAVIES *Why Ireland, etc.* (1747) 179 His dogges and Dog boyes. **1859** JEPHSON *Brittany* ix. 146 Three hounds, accompanied by a dog-boy.

dog-bramble. Also **dog's-.** A name for various thorny shrubs: †**a.** (*dog's bramble*) the caper-shrub, *Capparis spinosa*. †**b.** = DOG-BRIER. **c.** A kind of currant, *Ribes Cynosbati*.

1567 MAPLET *Gr. Forest* 36 Capers..called Dogges Bremble, of other some Dogges Apple. **1599** MINSHEU *Sp. Dict.*, *Escaramujo*, wilde eglantine, dogbramble. **1884** MILLER *Plant-n.*, Bramble, Dog, *Ribes Cynosbati*.

† **dog-brier.** *Obs.* [transl. of L. *sentis canis*, Gr. κυνόσβατος.] The wild brier.

1530 PALSGR. 214/2 Dogge brere. **1565–73** COOPER *Thesaurus*, *Sentis canis*, wilde Eglantine, or dogge bryer. **1591** PERCIVALL *Sp. Dict.*, *Çarça perruna*, dogge brier, *Canis rubus*. *a* **1682** SIR T. BROWNE *Tracts* 9 The Hipp-briar is also named Κυνόσβατος, or the Dog-briar or Bramble. **1840** C. F. HOFFMAN *Greyslaer* II. xi. 42 A spot where some huge rocks, covered only with dog-briers let down the light..into the forest.

dog-cart. 1. A small cart drawn by dogs.

1668 PEPYS *Diary* 13 June, Walked..through the city [Bristol]..No carts, it standing generally on vaults, only dog-carts. **1854** *Illustr. Lond. News* 8 July 7/1 The dog-cart nuisance..the use of carts drawn by dogs.

2. A cart with a box under the seat for sportsmen's dogs; subsequently, an open vehicle for ordinary driving, with two transverse seats back to back, the hinder of these originally made to shut up so as to form a box for dogs.

1803 C. K. SHARPE *Lett.* 33 July (1888) I. 178 His lordship ..keeps horses and curricles and dogs and dog-carts, and gives dinners..to all the rascality of Oxford. **1812** MISS MITFORD in L'Estrange *Life* (1870) I. 182 Our equipage, a most commodious dog-cart. **1861** *Romance Dull Life* xiii. 98 The closed carriage being better than the dog-cart, for the weather had changed, and it was cold.

dog-cheap, *adv.* and *pred. a. arch.* [See DOG *sb.*[1] 19 d and CHEAP *a.* 6.] Extremely cheap; at a very low or contemptible price.

1526 J. RASTELL *100 Merry Tales* lxxv. (1866) 126, I wyl say you .ii. gospels for one grote, & that is dog chepe. **1587** HOLINSHED *Chron. Eng.* 476 In these daies wool was dog-cheape. **1650** R. STAPYLTON *Strada's Low C. Warres* VII. 77 The Souldiers carryed most of their Plunder to Antwerp, and sold it..dogg-cheape. **1829** SCOTT *Jrnl.* 2 June, They might..have the..property for £16,000, which is dog cheap.

b. *fig.* Little esteemed; in vile repute.

1607 DEKKER *Knts. Conjur.* (1842) 38 Three thinges there [i.e. in Venice] dog-cheap, learning, poore mens sweat, and oathes. *a* **1846** LANDOR *Imag. Conv.* Wks. 1868 II. 33 Trajan ..holds all the gods dog-cheap.

dog-collar.

1. A collar for a dog's neck.

1524 *Ld. Treas. Acc. Scot.* in Pitcairn *Crim. Trials* I. 270 Hornis, leschis, and dog-collaris. **1580** HOLLYBAND *Treas. Fr. Tong, Vn collier qu'on met aus chiens*..a dog coller. **1673** in Rogers *Agric. & Prices* VI. 604 Dog collar. **1844** *Ainsworth's Mag.* VI. 352 A dagger, a green velvet bonnet, ..and a small dog-collar. **1939–40** *Army & Navy Stores Catal.* 999/1 In ordering Dog Collars, the size of dog's neck must be given.

2. a. A name given to close-fitting collars worn by men and women; *spec.* a derogatory or jocular term for the clerical collar.

1861 *Temple Bar* I. 386 The clerical High-Church nephew who wears a stiff-starched dog-collar instead of a cravat. **1883** E. C. G. MURRAY *People I have Met* 42 (Farmer) The dog-collar which rose above the black cloth was of spotless purity. **1890** *Daily News* 9 June 9/1 Another lady wore..a dog collar of pearls and diamonds. **1894** *Glasgow Her.* 6 Dec., Dr. Donald Macleod..[said that] he was first to introduce what was known as the 'dog collar'.. It was now recognised as the ecclesiastical collar. **1931** *Tablet* 21 Feb. 234/2 Jewish Rabbis..as well as Free Church pastors, are often seen wearing what the profane call 'dog-collars'. **1965** J. PORTER *Dover Two* iv. 45 His dog collar gleamed whitely in the darkness of the hall.

b. *attrib.*

1903 *Daily Chron.* 17 Oct. 8/4 The latest ornaments for the throat are of the dog-collar pattern. **1904** *Ibid.* 3 Nov. 5/6 Diamond dog-collar necklet.

'dogdayed, *a. poet. nonce-wd.* Of the dog-days (cf. next 3).

1934 DYLAN THOMAS *18 Poems* 10 There from their hearts the dogdayed pulse Of love and light bursts in their throats.

dog-days, *sb. pl.* [tr. L. *dies caniculares*: see CANICULAR.]

1. The days about the time of the heliacal rising of the Dog-star; noted from ancient times as the hottest and most unwholesome period of the year.

They have been variously calculated, as depending on the greater dog-star (Sirius) or the lesser dog-star (Procyon); on the heliacal, or (by some in modern times) the cosmical rising of either of these (both of which also differ in different latitudes); and as preceding, following, or both preceding and following, one of these epochs; and their duration has been variously reckoned at from 30 to 54 days. In the latitude of Greenwich, the cosmical rising of Procyon now takes place about July 27, that of Sirius about Aug. 11; in Mediterranean latitudes, the former is somewhat later, the latter earlier. The heliacal rising is some days later than the cosmical; and all the phenomena now take place later in the year than in ancient times, owing to the precession of the equinoxes. Thus very different dates have been assigned for the dog-days, their beginning ranging from July 3 to Aug. 15. In current almanacs they are said to begin July 3 and end Aug. 11 (i.e. to be the 40 days preceding the cosmical rising of Sirius).

The name (Gr. ἡμέραι κυνάδες, Lat. *dies caniculares*) arose from the pernicious qualities of the season being attributed to the 'influence' of the Dog-star; but it has long been popularly associated with the belief that at this season dogs are most apt to run mad; see CANICULAR 1, quot. 1601.

1538 ELYOT *Dict.*, *Canicula*..a sterre, wherof canicular or dogge days be named *Dies caniculares*. **1597–8** BP. HALL *Sat.* IV. i. 138 My double draught may quench his dog daies rage. **1660** T. M. *Hist. Independ.* IV. 52 For now (it being the Dog-dayes) the house grew so hot, that diverse members withdrew. **1712** E. COOKE *Voy. S. Sea* 397 Hotter in January, than Italy in the Dog-Days. **1842** *Penny Cycl.* XXII. 62 s.v. *Sirius*, Even at this day, when the heats of the latter part of the summer are excessive, we are gravely told that we are in the dog-days.

b. Rarely in *sing.*

1769 RUFFHEAD *Life Pope* 35 (L.) Is it necessary, to make a complaint of this kind consistent, that every day should be a dog day?

2. *fig.* An evil time; a period in which malignant influences prevail.

a **1555** PHILPOT *Exam. & Writ.* (Parker Soc.) 283 Neither that any giddy head in these dog-days might take an ensample by you to dissent from Christ's true church. **1629** N. CARPENTER *Achitophel* I. 10 What then shall wee now expect in these dogge-dayes of the worlds declining age? **1835** I. TAYLOR *Spir. Despot.* vii. 306 During the dog-days of the Romish spiritual despotism.

3. *attrib.* **dog-day**: Of the dog-days.

1719 YOUNG *Busiris* II. i, Like pois'nous vermin in a dog-day sun. **1807–8** W. IRVING *Salmag.* (1824) 223 Surely never was a town more subject to midsummer fancies and dog-day whim-whams. **1857** THOREAU *Maine W.* (1894) 315, I heard the dog-day locust here.

dogdom ('dɒgdəm). *humorous.* [see -DOM.] The domain or world of dogs; dogs collectively.

1854 *Chamb. Jrnl.* II. 280 A graduate in horse-management and dogdom. **1892** *Pall Mall G.* 11 Feb. 7/2 The Dog show..bringing together 3,000 specimens of dogdom.

†**dogdrave, -drawe.** *Obs.* Some kind of sea-fish used for food; ? cod.

[**1227** *Rotuli Litter. Clausarum* 20 Feb. II. 172 Naves piscarias quae..consueverunt ire ad piscariam de doggedragh.] **1367** in Rogers *Agric. & Prices* (1866) II. 556 Dogdrave. **14..** *Voc.* in Wr.-Wülcker 586/22 *Gerra*, a doggedraue. **1858** *Hist. Coldingham Priory* 55 There are in the accounts..references to cod and ling, dog-draves and herrings.

†**dog-draw.** *Forest Law.* The act of 'drawing after' or tracking venison illegally killed or wounded, by the scent of a dog led with the hand.

1598 MANWOOD *Lawes Forest* xviii. §9 (1615) 134 Dogge draw is, where any man hath stricken or wounded a wild beast..and is found with a Hound or other Dogge drawing after him, to recouer the same. **1708** J. CHAMBERLAYNE *St. Gt. Brit.* I. III. vi. (1743) 186 The foresters may take and arrest a man, if he be taken either at Dog-draw, Stable-stand, Back-bear, or Bloodyhand.

‖**doge** (dəʊdʒ). [a. F. *doge* (monosyll.), ad. Venetian *doge* (disyll.), repr. an It. **doce* = *duce*:—L. *duc-em* (*dux*) leader, duke.] The title of the chief magistrate in the formerly existing republics of Venice and Genoa.

1549 THOMAS *Hist. Italie* 77 a (Stanf.) They haue a Duke called after theyr maner, *Doge*. **1645** EVELYN *Diary* June (1889) I. 203 The Doge..together with the Senat in their gownes, imbarked in their gloriously painted carved and gilded Bucentora. **1776–81** GIBBON *Decl. & F.* lx. (R.), The annual election of the twelve tribunes was superseded by the permanent election of a duke or doge. **1855** BROWNING *Toccata of Galuppi's* ii, At Venice..where the Doges used to wed the sea with rings.

b. *transf.* and *fig.* Applied to any chief magistrate or leader.

1836 J. STRANGE *Germany in 1831* I. 65 This League.. whose head Doge, the burgomaster of Lubeck, received the ambassadors of emperors and monarchs. **1863** READE *Hard Cash* I. 10 Young Hardie was Doge of a studious clique.

Hence **'dogedom**, the dominion of a doge; the world of doges, doges collectively. **'dogeless** *a.*, without a doge. **'dogeship**, the office or rank of a doge; the dignity or personality of a doge.

1893 MARG. SYMONDS *Doge's Farm* 225 All the potentates of the dogedom. **1818** BYRON *Ch. Har.* IV. iv, The Dogeless city's vanish'd sway. **1677** *Govt. Venice* 181 In the Dogeship of Renier Zen..the Grand Council added four more to them. **1821** BYRON *Foscari* IV. i. 294 His Dogeship answer'd.

dog-ear, var. of DOG'S-EAR.

dogeate ('dəʊdʒeɪt). [f. DOGE + -ATE[1].] = DOGATE.

1923 J. C. POWELL in J. Buchan *Nations of To-Day, Italy* 5 In the Dogeate of Pietro Orseolo.

dogeon, obs. form of DUDGEON.

dog-faced ('dɒgfeɪst), *a.* Having a face like that of a dog; *esp.* in ***dog-faced baboon*** = CYNOCEPHALUS. (In quot. 1873, tr. Gr. κυνώπις.)

1607 TOPSELL *Four-f. Beasts* (1658) 9 He describeth them to be black haird, Dog-faced, and like little men. **1802** BINGLEY *Anim. Biog.* (1813) I. 77 The dog-faced baboon. **1836–48** B. D. WALSH *Aristoph.*, *Knights* I. iii, Before a dog-faced monkey. **1873** SYMONDS *Grk. Poets* vii. 227 Those dog-faced, Fierce-eyed, infernal ministers, dread goddesses!

dogfall, dog-fall. *Wrestling.* A fall in which both wrestlers touch the ground together.

1828 *Blackw. Mag.* XXIII. 100 It is pronounced a dog-fall—or a draw. **1858** HUGHES *Scouring White Horse* vi. 131 Both fell on their sides, and it was only a dog-fall.

dog-fennel. Also **dog's-fennel.** [From its bad smell, and fennel-like leaves.] A name for Stinking Camomile, *Anthemis Cotula*.

1523 FITZHERB. *Husb.* §20 Doggefenell and mathes is bothe one, and..beareth many white floures, with a yelowe sede. **1578** LYTE *Dodoens* II. xxx. 186 The second kind..is now called..in English Mathers, Mayweede, Dogges Camomill, Stincking Camomill, and Dogge Fenell. **1885** *Harper's Mag.* Apr. 702/2 There was no dock, nor dog-fennel, nor rag-weed.

†**b.** Also applied to Sulphur-wort, *Peucedanum palustre*. *Obs.*

1529 *Grete Herball* cccxxx. S v b, Peucedane is an herbe.. called dogfenell or swyne fenell.

'dog-fight. 1. A fight between dogs.

a **1656** BP. HALL *Rem.* 61 (T.) To clap their hands, as boys are wont to do in dog-fights. **1879** H. SPENCER *Data of Ethics* xii. §80. 215 It needs but to ask whether men who delight in dog-fights may be expected to appreciate Beethoven's *Adelaida*.

2. *transf.* A general disturbance or mêlée; *spec.* a 'scrap' between aircraft.

1880 'MARK TWAIN' *Tramp Abroad* II. 297 No information about prize fights or other dog fights, horse races, walking-matches..or other sporting matters. **1917** KIPLING *Diversity of Creatures* 208 The pitiless Whips were even then at the telephones to herd 'em up to another dog-fight. **1919** A. E. ILLINGWORTH *Fly Papers* 79 The battle develops into a 'dog-fight', small groups of machines engaging each other in a fight to the death. **1928** F. E. BAILY *Golden Vanity* xiv. 201 No dividend, reserve fund wiped out, and a dog-fight at the annual general meeting. **1928** C. F. S. GAMBLE *N. Sea Air Station* xxii. 400 It was decided that all flying-boats should have their hulls 'dazzle-painted' ..so that a pilot could, in a 'dog-fight', know at a glance who was in a particular machine. **1937** C. BOFF *Boys' Book of Flying* xvii. 190 Inevitably occasions arise in aerial warfare —as in a 'dog-fight', where several machines are milling together in whirling confusion. **1939** *Times* 3 Nov. 8/6 During the dogfight the troops and others on the ground took cover, and the only damage done was one or two holes in the roofs of barns. **1958** *Economist* 13 Dec. 967/1 Both employers and unions are to blame for the dogfight that at present passes for industrial relations at BOAC. **1970** *Globe & Mail* (Toronto) 26 Sept. 35/6 On our performance so far, we're in a dogfight for fourth.

So **dog-fighting**. Hence **dog-fight** *v. intr.*, to fight or 'scrap'; also *trans.* (*rare*).

?*c* **1475** *Hunt. Hare* 233 Sum seyd it was a beyr-beytyng, Sum seyd it was a dogg-feghttyng. **1670** EVELYN *Diary* 16 June, Cock-fighting, dog-fighting, beare and bull baiting. **1929** T. E. LAWRENCE *Lett.* (1938) 648, I live in barracks (i.e. we dog-fight promiscuously). **1934** V. M. YEATES *Winged Victory* i. 17 It was too risky to stop and fight... Dog-fighting was an amusement for rather nearer home. *Ibid.* vi. 51 They would dive and zoom..but they would never dogfight Camels. **1941** E. C. SHEPHERD *Milit. Aeroplane* 14 If the formation [of bombers] gets broken, the single machine may have to 'take evasive action', but it will not attempt to dogfight.

'dog-fish, dogfish.

1. A name given to various small sharks of the families *Squalidæ* (*Spinacidæ*), *Galeorhinidæ* (*Carchariidæ*), and *Scylliidæ*, or to the sharks of these families collectively; *esp.* in Great Britain, the Large and Small Spotted Dogfish (*Scyllium catulus*, *S. canicula*), and in New England, the Picked Dogfish (*Squalus acanthias*).

c **1475** *Pict. Voc.* in Wr.-Wülcker 765 *Hic canis*, a doke-fyche. **1530** PALSGR. 214/2 Doggefysshe, *chien de mer*. **1672** JOSSELYN *New Eng. Rarities* 33 The Dogfish, a ravenous Fish. **1766** PENNANT *Zool.* (1769) III. 77 The picked dogfish takes its name from a strong and sharp spine placed just before each of the back fins. **1861** HULME tr. *Moquin-Tandon* II. III. i. 108 Dr. Delattre has obtained it [shark-oil] from the..Lesser spotted Dogfish.

b. Applied also to the mud-fish (*Amia calva*); to the blackfish (*Dallia pectoralis*); to a kind of wrasse (*Crenilabrus caninus*); and to the mud-puppy, a batrachian reptile (*Necturus maculatus*).

1889 FARMER *Amer.*, *Dog-fish*, the mud fish of Western waters.

2. *fig.* Applied opprobriously to persons.

1589 *Pappe w. Hatchet* B ij b, Whie are not the spawnes of such a dog-fish hangd? **1591** SHAKS. *1 Hen. VI.* I. iv. 107 Puzel or Pussel, Dolphin or Dog-fish, Your hearts Ile stampe out with my Horses heeles. **1731** SWIFT *Pulteney* Wks. 1755 IV. I. 167 A pack of dog-fish had him in the wind.

Hence **dog-fishing** *vbl. sb.*, fishing for dog-fish.

1885 C. F. HOLDER *Marvels Anim. Life* 190 Everybody goes dog-fishing.

dog-fisher, an appellation given by Walton to the Otter (as a dog-like beast living on fish).

(By a strange error, explained by Johnson as 'A kind of fish'; whence in subsequent dictionaries.)

1668 WALTON *Compl. Angler* (ed. 4) 49 The Otter devours much fish..And I can tell you that this Dog-fisher, for so the Latins call him, can smell a fish in the water a hundred yards from him..and that his stones are good against the falling sickness.

dog-fly.

1. An English rendering of Gr. κυνάμυια; which writers have tried to identify with British flies troublesome to dogs: see quots.

14.. *Metr. Voc.* in Wr.-Wülcker 625 Dogflye, *ciniphex*. **1552** HULOET, Dogge flye, *cynomyia*. **1610** HEALEY *St. Aug. Citie of God* 753 Origen compareth the dogge-flye vnto thir sect. **1631** R. BYFIELD *Doctr. Sabb.* 1 Such as are these Dog-flies, such are unquiet men. **1658** ROWLAND *Moufet's Theat. Ins.* 934 Κυνομυία, *Musca canum*, in English a Dog-fly.. Isidore, and Euthymius, and Philo, suppose it to be a Wood-fly, very irksome to the ears of Dogs. **1753** CHAMBERS *Cycl. Supp.*, *Dog-Fly*, *Cynomyia*..a species of fly common in woods and among bushes, and particularly troublesome to dogs..It somewhat resembles the flat black fly so troublesome to cattle.

2. As a term of abuse [tr. Gr. κυνάμυια].

c **1611** CHAPMAN *Iliad* XXI. 366 [Mars to Minerva] Thou dog-fly, what's the cause Thou mak'st Gods fight thus?

dog-fox.

1. A male fox. (Cf. DOG *sb.*[1] 2, 18 b.)

1576 TURBERV. *Venerie* 183 The female of a foxe is called a bitche and he himselfe a doggefoxe. *a* **1659** OSBORN *Misc.* Wks. (1673) 613 A Dog-Fox and an Ordinary Bitch will generate. **1749** FIELDING *Tom Jones* X. vii, We have got the dog-fox, I warrant the bitch is not far off. **1880** *Times* 2 Nov. 4/6 A full-brushed, high-conditioned dog-fox.

b. Applied to a man.

1606 SHAKS. *Tr. & Cr.* V. iv. 12 That same dog-fox Vlisses.

2. The name of certain small burrowing animals of the family *Canidæ*, as the CORSAC, resembling both the dog and the fox.

'dogfully, *adv. humorous nonce-wd.* [f. DOG *sb.*[1], after *manfully*.] In a way worthy of a dog; with the courage or persistency befitting a dog.

1861 *Fraser's Mag.* June 770 Still he [the terrier] buckles to his work dogfully. **1880** P. GILLMORE *On Duty* 299.

doggar, var. DOGGER[3], ironstone.

dogged ('dɒgɪd), *a.* (*adv.*) Also 5 dogget, doggid, doggyd(e, 6 *Sc.* doggit. [f. DOG *sb.*[1] + -ED[2]: cf. CRABBED, which appears to be of about the same age.]

A. *adj.* **1.** *gen.* **a.** Like a dog; having the character, or some characteristic, of a dog. **b.** Of or pertaining to a dog or dogs, canine. †***dogged appetite, hunger***: = CANINE appetite, BULIMY (*obs.*). (Now *rare* in gen. sense.)

c **1440** *Promp. Parv.* 125/2 Doggyd, *caninus.* **1589** *Pasquil's Ret.* 12 This dogged generation, that is euer barking against the Moone. **1595** SHAKS. *John* IV. iii. 149 Now for the bare-pickt bone of Maiesty, Doth dogged warre bristle his angry crest, And snarleth in the gentle eyes of peace. **1608** HIERON *2nd Pt. Def. Reas. Refus. Subscript.* 121 That hunger which Phisitions cal the dogged appetite. **1658** J. JONES *Ovid's Ibis* 594 Dianas guard the Tragic poet slew, So be thou torn by a watchful dogged crew. **1740** PINEDA *Sp. Dict.* s.v. *R,* This Letter.. They call.. dogged, because it sounds like the Noise a Dog makes when he growls.

2. Having the bad qualities of a dog; currish. †**a.** Ill-conditioned, malicious, crabbed, spiteful, perverse; cruel. (Of persons, their actions, etc.) *Obs.*

a **1307** *Pol. Songs* (Camden) 199 The fals wolf stode behind; He was doggid and ek felle. *c* **1400** *Destr. Troy* 10379 Of so dogget a dede. *c* **1440** *Promp. Parv.* 125/2 Doggyde, malycyowse, *maliciosus, perversus, bilosus.* **1540** MORYSINE *Vives' Introd. Wysd.* H viij b, It is a token of a dogged harte, to rejoyce in an other mans mysfortune. **1663** BUTLER *Hud.* I. i. 632 Fortune unto them turn'd dogged. For they a sad Adventure met. **1684** *Roxb. Ball.* (1895) VIII. 40 This dogged answer cut this poor soul to the heart.

†**b.** *transf.* Of things: Awkward, 'crabbed', difficult to deal with. *Obs.*

1634 SIR T. HERBERT *Trav.* 66 The most craggie, steepe, and dogged Hils in Persia. **1677** YARRANTON *Eng. Improv.* 147 The Spanish [Iron] works tough, churlish and dogged.

c. Ill-tempered, surly; sullen, morose. Now with some mixture of sense 3: Having an air of sullen obstinacy.

c **1400** *Rom. Rose* 4028 If Bialacoil be sweete and free, Dogged and felle thou shuldist be. **1593** NASHE *Christ's T.* 55 There is vaine-glory in.. being Diogenicall and dogged. **1667** PEPYS *Diary* (1879) IV. 424 My wife in a dogged humour for my not dining at home. **1757** J. RUTTY *Diary* 5 Feb. in Boswell *Johnson,* Very dogged or snappish. **1852** MRS. STOWE *Uncle Tom's C.* xli, Legree.. looked in with a dogged air of affected carelessness, and turned away.

3. Having the persistency or tenacity characteristic of various breeds of dogs; obstinate, stubborn; pertinacious. (The current use.) Esp. in colloq. phr. ***it's dogged as does it***: persistency and tenacity win in the end.

1779 JOHNSON 1 Apr. in *Boswell,* [He commended one of the Dukes of Devonshire for] 'a dogged veracity'. **1818** SCOTT *Rob Roy* xxx, An air of stupid impenetrability, which might arise either from conscious innocence or from dogged resolution. **1855** PRESCOTT *Philip II,* I. II. viii. 229 The dogged tenacity with which he clung to his purposes. **1863** KINGSLEY *Water Bab.* vii. (1878) 323 He was such a little dogged, hard, gnarly, foursquare brick of an English boy. **1864** M. B. CHESNUT *Diary* 6 Aug. (1949) 429 'It's dogged as does it,' says Isabella. **1867** TROLLOPE *Chron. Barset* lxi, There ain't nowt a man can't bear if he'll only be dogged... It's dogged as does it. **1874** BLACKIE *Self-Cult.* 20 In this domain nothing is denied to a dogged pertinacity. **1896** *Daily News* 27 June 8/1 All his own writing seems to have been done in about three hours a day. 'It's dogged as does it,' he has been wont to explain. **1942** N. MARSH *Death & Dancing Footman* x. 195 'If we stick.. they can damn' well produce a farm animal to lug us out...' 'It's dogged as does it,' said Chloris.

4. *Comb.*, as †**dogged-sprighted** *a.*, having a 'dogged' or malicious spirit (*obs.*).

1600 ROWLANDS *Let. Humours Blood* vii. 84 Enuie's the fourth: a Deuill, dogged sprighted.

B. as *adv.* 'As a dog'; very, extremely. *colloq.* or *slang.* (Cf. DOG *sb.*[1] 19 d.)

1819 *Sporting Mag.* IV. 272 He [a horse] was dogged 'rusty' when your man passed our house. **1847-78** HALLIWELL, *Dogged,* very; excessive. *Var. dial.*

doggedly (ˈdɒgɪdlɪ), *adv.* [f. prec. + -LY[2].] In a dogged manner: see prec.

†**1.** Like a dog (in appearance or manner). *Obs.*

1591 PERCIVALL *Sp. Dict., Emperradamente,* doggedly, *Canino more.* **1638** SIR T. HERBERT *Trav.* (ed. 2) 13 Seales as big as Lyons, and.. doggedly visaged.

2. Like a dog (in bad sense); currishly.

†**a.** Cruelly, maliciously, spitefully. *Obs.*

c **1380** *Sir Ferumb.* 1289 Doggedlich y schal hem grete. *c* **1400** *Destr. Troy* 1398 And þou so doggetly has done in þi derfe hate. **1589** *Pappe w. Hatchet* (1844) 39 Then he concludes all doggedlie. **1655** HEYWOOD & ROWLEY *Fort. by Land* III. Wks. 1874 VI. 398 We have used him so doggedly.

b. Surlily, sullenly; with sullen obstinacy.

1683 KENNETT tr. *Erasm. on Folly* 57 He would not fret, nor doggedly repine. **1780** JOHNSON *Let. to Mrs. Thrale* 23 May, You cannot think how doggedly I left your house on Friday morning. **1838** LYTTON *Alice* 100 'For my part, I shall resign', said Lord Saxingham doggedly.

3. With the persistence of a dog; obstinately, stubbornly, pertinaciously.

1773 JOHNSON 16 Aug. in *Boswell,* Nay.. a man may write at any time if he will set himself *doggedly* to it. **1807** SOUTHEY *Let. to Scott* 8 Dec., It never does to sit down doggedly to correct. **1839-40** W. IRVING *Wolfert's R.* (1855) 209, I.. studied on doggedly and incessantly. **1856** FROUDE *Hist. Eng.* (1858) II. vii. 203 He doggedly adhered to his assertions of his own innocence.

doggedness (ˈdɒgɪdnɪs). [f. as prec. + -NESS.] The quality or condition of being dogged.

†**a.** Malice, spitefulness, cruelty. *Obs.*

1530 PALSGR. 214/2 Doggednesse, *cruavlté.* **1593** NASHE *Christ's T.* 4 Their disloyaltie and doggednesse. **1647** M. HUDSON *Div. Right Govt.* I. ii. 5 Hazaels.. fury and dogednesse unto them.

b. Ill temper, surliness, sullenness. Now, Sullen obstinacy; pertinacity. (Cf. DOGGED 2 c and 3.)

1611 COTGR., *Rechignement,* a powting, sullennesse, doggednesse. **1647** LILLY *Chr. Astrol.* clxxvi. 746 Inclinable to.. solitarinesse, pertinacy, and what in the vulgar English we call doggednesse. **1770** WESLEY *Jrnl.* 3 Feb. (1827) III. 376 He hides both his doggedness and his vanity. **1824** *Edin. Rev.* XL. 85 A patient and persevering doggedness of understanding in contending with difficulties. **1877** A. B. EDWARDS *Up Nile* v. 113 Our sailors, by dint of sheer doggedness, get us round the bad corner at last.

dogger[1] (ˈdɒgə(r)). [Anglo-Fr. and ME. *doggere*; also in Du. and LG. from 15th c. Origin uncertain.

The Du. word is evidently related to the obscure MDu. *dogge,* in phr. *ten dogge varen* to go to the cod-fishing; cf. also Kilian, '*dogghe-boot* cymba major'; Hexham, '*Dogge-boot,* Great-bark'. Akin to *dogge* or *dogger* is the Icel. *dugga* in same sense; with the statement cited by Vigfusson that thirty English *fiski-duggur* came fishing about Iceland in 1413, cf. our quot. 1491 and the reference there given. The *Dogger-bank* is generally supposed to be named either from this word or MDu. *dogger* trawler; cf. Kilian, '*dogger* funda, sacculus, reticulum'; Hexham, '*Dogger,* Fisher's Boat'; also 'Sling or casting net, also Satchell.']

1. A two-masted fishing vessel with bluff bows, somewhat resembling a ketch, used in the North Sea deep sea fisheries: formerly applied to English craft as well as those of other nations, but now practically restricted to Dutch fishing vessels (though out of use in Holland itself).

In the 17th and 18th c. they frequently acted as privateers.

1356 *Act 31 Edw. III,* III. c. 1 Towȝ les niefs appelles Doggeres. **1491** HEN. VII. in *Paston Lett.* No. 922 III. 367 That.. all the dogers of thos partes schuld have our licens to departe in the viage towardes Islond, as they have been accustommyd to do yerly in tyme passyd. **1566** R. MIGHELLS in A. Suckling *Suffolk* (1847) 86 Then there were thirteen or fourteen doggers belonging to the said town, and now but one. **1666** *Lond. Gaz.* No. 25/4 The Coast at Bridlington has not for 10 dayes been infested with any Capers, save onely one Dogger of 8 guns. **1680** *Ibid.* No. 1548/4 The Adventurers of the Royal Fishery, are now fitting out their Doggers from the River.. for the White Herring and Cod Fishings. *c* **1682** J. COLLINS *Making Salt Eng.* 111 The Dutch.. have out this Winter 220 Doggers. **1692** LUTTRELL *Brief Rel.* (1857) II. 494 A French dogger was brought in prize there. **1799** SIR H. PARKER in *Naval Chron.* II. 347 Two Spanish doggers, sloop rigged. **1810** *Hull Rockingham* 15 Dec. 2/1 The beautiful oak-built Dogger called the Rover. **1833** M. SCOTT *Tom Cringle* xv. (1859) 358 Like a clumsy dish-shaped Dutch dogger. **1867** SMYTH *Sailor's Word-bk., Dogger,* a Dutch smack of about 150 tons.. principally used for fishing on the Dogger Bank.

†**2.** One of the crew of a dogger = *dogger-man. Obs.*

1533-4 *Act 25 Hen. VIII,* c. 4 Suche person or persones, as.. be doggers otherwyse callid Doggermen.

3. Short for *Dogger Bank*: see 4.

1887 E. J. MATHER (*title*), Nor'ard of the Dogger.

4. *Comb.* **a.** In apposition, as †*dogger-boat, -caper, -pink, -privateer.* **b.** similative, as *dogger-built, -rigged* adjs. **c. Dogger Bank,** †**dogger-sands,** name of a great bank or shoal in the North Sea; **dogger-fish** *sb. pl.*, fish taken by doggers or on the Dogger Bank; **dogger-man,** one of the crew of a dogger (see 2).

1666 *Lond. Gaz.* No. 31/4 Some few Dogger boates plying about the *Dogger banks, whereof five labor to infest those parts. **1836** YARRELL *Brit. Fishes* (1859) I. 531 The Dogger Bank Cod. **1885** *Lyell's Elem. Geol.* vi. (ed. 4) 81 That great shoal called the Dogger-bank, about sixty miles east of the coast of Northumberland, and occupying an area about as large as Wales.. in its shallower parts is less than forty feet under water. **1662** J. SMITH *England's Improv. Rev.* 252 The Hollanders fishing for Herring, Ling, and Cod, with Busses and *Dogger-boats. **1680** *Lond. Gaz.* No. 1526/4 Pink, *Dogger built. **1703** *Ibid.* No. 3889/4 A *Dogger Caper, of 4 Guns and 45 Men, belonging to Ostend. **1356** *Act 31 Edw. III,* III. c. 2 Assiz sur le pesson de *Doggerefissh & lochefissh. **1607** COWELL *Interpr., Doggerfish*.. seemeth to be fish brought in those ships to Blackeney haven. **1703** *Lond. Gaz.* No. 3939/3 A *Dogger Pink, of about 150 Tuns. **1745** VERNON in *Naval Chron.* IX. 191 A..*dogger privateer has been taken. **1805** MITCHELL *Ibid.* XIII. 493 The.. Privateer Orestes, *Dogger rigged. **1665** *Lond. Gaz.* No. 9/2 They saw not one Man of War, but within the *Dogger-sands about twelve Dogger-Boats.

ˈ**dogger**[2]. *rare.* One who dogs: see DOG *v.* 1.

1611 COTGR., *Espie,* a spie.. obseruer, dogger of people.

dogger[3] (ˈdɒgə(r)). Also 8 *Sc.* **-ar.** [local term of uncertain origin, perh. a deriv. of DOG.]

1. *dial.* A kind of ironstone, commonly found in globular concretions; a nodule of this; = CATHEAD 2.

1670 W. SIMPSON *Hydrol. Ess.* 63 A mine, in colour much resembling that of alom.. usually called by them Doggers, or Cats-heads. **1757** WALKER in *Phil. Trans.* L. 145 Another fossil of a brown colour.. called by the miners dogger; a thin seam of which often lies in the midst of the coal. **1793** URE *Hist. Rutherglen* 253 (Jam.) The most uncommon variety of till.. is incumbent on a coarse iron-stone, or doggar. **1876** *Whitby Gloss., Scar-doggers*.. the stone nodules in the alum rock burnt for making Roman cement.

2. *Geol.* A sandy ironstone of the Lower Oolite; applied to part of the Jurassic series.

dogger-series, the series of strata resting upon the Alum Shale (Upper Lias), containing the dogger.

1822 G. YOUNG *Geol. Surv. Yorksh.* (1828) 126 This.. seam is only a few feet above the dogger. **1885** *Lyell's Elem. Geol.* xx. 311 In North-Western Germany.. The Dogger, or Brown Jura, has dark-coloured clays and ironstones.. it corresponds to the Lower Oolite.

dogger[4] (ˈdɒgə(r)). *Austral.* [f. DOG *sb.* + -ER[1].] One who hunts dingoes.

1934 *Bulletin* (Sydney) 31 Oct. 20/4 Many of the doggers, prospectors and blockholders who make the connection [*i.e.* travel] long distances by camel. **1935** H. H. FINLAYSON *Red Centre* i. 15 The dogger and prospector follow the explorer. **1946** F. DAVISON *Dusty* xviii. 204 Ask an old dogger of the western stations. **1965** E. TROUGHTON *Furred Animals of Australia* (ed. 8) 237 A Queensland 'dogger' who found it impossible to trap or poison an old-man dingo responsible for killing hundreds of sheep.

doggerel (ˈdɒgərəl), **doggrel** (ˈdɒgrəl), *a.* and *sb.* Also 4 **dogerel,** 5-7 **-ell,** 6-7 **doggerell, doggrell,** 6-9 **dogrell,** 7-8 **doggril,** 8 **dogrel.** [Origin unknown; but cf. DOG *sb.*[1] 19 e.]

A. *adj.* An epithet applied to comic or burlesque verse, usually of irregular rhythm; or to mean, trivial, or undignified verse.

c **1386** CHAUCER *Melib.* Prol. 7 Now swich a Rym the deuel I biteche This may wel be Rym dogerel quod he. **1494** FABYAN *Chron.* VII. 294 For thoughe I shulde all day tell Or chat with my ryme dogerell. **1526** SKELTON *Magnyf.* 413 In bastarde ryme after the doggrell gyse. **1589** PUTTENHAM *Eng. Poesie* II. iv. (Arb.) 89 A rymer that will be tyed to no rules at all.. such maner of Poesie is called in our vulgar, ryme dogrell. **1630** J. TAYLOR (Water P.) *Dogge of Warre* Wks. II. 226/1 In doggrell Rimes my Lines are writ As for a Dogge I thought it fit. **1711** ADDISON *Spect.* No. 60 ⁋11 The double Rhymes, which are used in Doggerel Poetry. **1789** BELSHAM *Ess.* I. xii. 233 The vile doggrel translation of Hobbes. **1868** STANLEY *Westm. Abb.* v. 397 The doggrel epitaphs which were hung over the royal tombs.

b. *transf.* Bastard, burlesque.

1550 BALE *Apol.* 93 (R.) The diuinite doggerell of that dronken papist Johan Eckius. **1873** G. C. DAVIES *Mount. & Mere* xix. 177 A doggrel form of prayer.

B. *sb.* Doggerel verse; burlesque poetry of irregular rhythm; bad or trivial verse.

1630 *Tincker of Turvey* Ep. Ded. 5 Clownes [have here] plaine dunstable dogrell, for them to laugh at. **1710** ADDISON *Whig Exam.* No. 1 ⁋14 He has a happy talent at doggrel. **1880** L. STEPHEN *Pope* iii. 71 Chapman.. sins.. by constantly indulging in sheer doggerel.

b. A piece of doggerel; a doggerel poem.

1857 O. A. BROWNSON *Convert* Wks. V. 120 The electioneering campaign of 1840, carried on by doggerels [etc.]. **1892** ANNE RITCHIE *Rec. Tennyson, etc.* III. vii. 216 A doggerel always had a curious fascination for him [Browning].

Hence ˈ**dogg(e)rel** *v.*, **-ize** *v.*, *intr.* to compose doggerel; *trans.* to turn into doggerel; ˈ**dogg(e)reler, -ist, -izer,** a writer of doggerel; ˈ**dogg(e)relism,** a doggerel manner of writing.

1680 R. L'ESTRANGE *Answ. Litter Libels* 9 His Ranging of them Together is a kinde of a Doggrilism. **1732** *Gentl. Instructed* (ed. 10) 43 (D.) Were I disposed to doggrel it, I would only gloss upon that text. **1817** *Monthly Mag.* XLIII. 421 The Scotch doggerelist. **1821** *Blackw. Mag.* X. 388 The Atys, which.. Mr. Lambe has so cruelly doggrelized. **1822** *Ibid.* XI. 363 These dabbling doggrelers. **1832** SOUTHEY *Lett.* (1856) IV. 259 Some true doggrelizers. **1850** READE *Chr. Johnstone* vi. (1853) 65 He had been doggrelling when he ought to have been daubing.

doggery (ˈdɒgərɪ). [f. DOG *sb.*[1] + -ERY.]

†**1.** Foul or obscene language. *Obs.*[—0]

1611 COTGR., *Cagnesque, Parler cagn.,* to speake doggerie.

2. Dog-like behaviour or practice; mean and contemptible action; mischievous doings.

1844 W. M. MACMILLAN *Lett.* (1893) 103 Evasive doggeries of every kind. **1886** T. HARDY *Mayor Casterbr.* xiii, 'Such doggery as there was in them ancient days.'

3. a. A company of dogs, dogs collectively. **b.** Used by Carlyle to represent F. *canaille.*

1843 CARLYLE *Past & Pr.* IV. vii. ad fin., Doggeries never so diplomaed, bepuffed, gas-lighted, continue Doggeries, and must take the fate of such. **1862** —— *Fredk. Gt.* x. ii. (1865) III. 222 As ugly a Doggery ('*infâme Canaille*' he might well reckon them), as has, before or since, infested the path of a man. **1869** *Pall Mall G.* 8 Oct. 11 With all the rabble doggery of the country after him.

4. *U.S.* (*vulgar*). A low drinking saloon.

1835 D. P. THOMPSON *Timothy Peacock* 140 (Th.), A sort of Dutch doggery, or sailor's hotel, situated near the wharf. **1860** BARTLETT *Dict. Amer., Doggery,* a low drinking-house. West and South. [Now prevalent throughout the Union (Farmer).] **1863** HOLLAND *Lett. Joneses* i. 15 To fill Jonesville with doggeries and loafers.

doggess (ˈdɒgɛs). *humorous.* [f. DOG *sb.*[1] + -ESS.] A female dog, a bitch. Also *fig.*

1748 RICHARDSON *Clarissa* (1811) VII. 131 Pretty dogs and doggesses to quarrel and bark at me. **1863** MISS POWER *Arab. Days & N.* 287 Said Pacha, determined not to give in to an unbelieving doggess.. refused to allow the terrified child to be removed. **1885** R. F. BURTON *Arab. Nts.* I. 93 *note,* Five, including the two doggesses.

dogget, obs. f. of DOCKET.

doggie: see DOGGY.

dogginess (ˈdɒgɪnɪs). [f. DOGGY *a.* + -NESS.] The quality of being 'doggy': see DOGGY *a.*

1865 MASSON *Rec. Brit. Philos.* 388 An inherent dogginess or earwigginess. **1882** MISS BRADDON *Mt. Royal* III. vi. 117 The St. Aubyn girls.. finding him a kindred spirit in horseyness and doggyness. **1884** *Sat. Rev.* 26 Jan. 111.

dogging ('dɒgɪŋ), *vbl. sb.* [f. DOG *v.* + -ING[1].] The action of DOG *v.*; *spec.* (*a*) grouse-shooting using dogs to rouse the birds, as distinguished from 'driving'; (*b*) *Austral.*, the hunting of dingoes. Also *attrib.*

1611 COTGR., *Espies*, ambushes, waylayings..treacherous dogging, of people. **1688** R. L'ESTRANGE *Brief Hist. Times* II. A vj b, The Dogging of a Plot out at Length. **1886** WALSINGHAM & PAYNE-GALLWEY *Shooting* i. 8 Wet weather is always bad for 'dogging'. **1894** *Times* 25 Aug. 3/1 Mr. Stuart-Wortley..holds the balance evenly between 'dogging' and driving. **1904** *Westm. Gaz.* 19 Aug. 4/2 On the 'dogging' moors..the actual shooting will begin as soon as it becomes legal. **1928** *Daily Tel.* 26 June 13/5 The shooting extends to 16,000 acres and is an excellent dogging moor. **1934** A. RUSSELL *Tramp-Royal in Wild Australia* iv. 37 Tuck had told me what he had made on his dogging expeditions. **1935** H. H. FINLAYSON *Red Centre* xiv. 142 More profitable is 'dogging'.

doggish ('dɒgɪʃ), *a.* [f. DOG *sb.*[1] + -ISH.]

1. Of the nature of, pertaining to, or resembling a dog; canine.

doggish appetite, a ravenous or insatiable appetite (see *dog-appetite* s.v. DOG *sb.*[1] 20 a). †***doggish letter*** (Minsheu, *Span. Gram.* 8) = DOG'S LETTER.

1530 PALSGR. 310/2 Doggysshe, of the condycions or of the nature of a dogge, *chienin.* *a* **1619** FOTHERBY *Atheom.* I. xv. §2 (1622) 156 Hee was taken..with a doggish Appetite, which called for meat almost euery moment. **1684** BUNYAN *Pilgr.* II. 29 To do to them what his Dogish nature would prompt him to. **1814** CARY *Dante, Inferno* XXXII. 70 Visages ..shap'd into a doggish grin. **1874** TROLLOPE *Lady Anna* vii, The..doggish love of fighting prevailed in the man.

2. Having or indicating a dog-like disposition or character, currish; malicious, spiteful, ill-natured; snappish, snarling, cynical. (Now *rare.*)

c **1400** *Beryn* 181 The frere, Howe he lowrith vndir his hood with a doggissh ey? *a* **1420** *Wyclif's Ecclus.* xiii. 22 *marg.* (MS. Cott. Claud. E 11) A doggische man, and siche is a chidere, and a wrathful man, and a glotoun. *a* **1536** TINDALE *Exp. Matt.* To Rdr. Wks. II. 10 Cruel and doggish hypocrites. **1553** T. WILSON *Rhet.* (1567) 77 a *note*, Diogenes doggish aunswer in despit of women. **1579** J. JONES *Preserv. Bodie & Soule* I. ii. 22 The doggish Philosopher Demetrius. **1672** EACHARD *Hobbs's State Nat.* 31 That All Men by nature were doggish, spightful and treacherous. **1863** SALA *Capt. Dangerous* II. iv. 133 You may cry Haro upon me for a Cynic or Doggish philosopher.

†**b.** Brutish, bestial, sensual. *Obs.*

1594 T. B. *La Primaud. Fr. Acad.* II. 588 These doggish epicures and atheists. **1610** ROWLANDS *Martin Mark-all* 27 Dissolute in behauiour, Apish, doggish, and Swinish.

Hence '**doggishly** *adv.*; '**doggishness**.

1576 FLEMING *Panopl. Epist.* 319, I am troubled..and doggishly dealt withall. **1592** BABINGTON *Comf. Notes Gen.* xxix. §3 Doggishnesse and currishnesse graceth neither Countrie nor people. **1866** HOWELLS *Venet. Life* vii. 113 All abuse begins and ends with the attribute of doggishness. **1905** A. BENNETT *Tales 5 Towns* I. 109 He had seldom felt less doggy... It seemed to him that doggishness was not the glorious thing he had thought. **1928** D. H. LAWRENCE in E. Rickword *Scrutinies* v. 62 The Forsyte trying to be freely sensual. He can't do it... He can only be doggishly messy. *Ibid.* v. 66 Next time I'll get properly married and do my doggishness in my own house.

doggo ('dɒgəʊ), *adv. slang.* [Of obscure origin: prob. f. DOG *sb.*[1]] ***to lie doggo***: to lie quiet, to remain hid. Also occas. with other verbs.

1893 KIPLING *Many Invent.* 259, I wud lie most powerful doggo whin I heard a shot. **1916** H. ROSHER *In R.N.A.S.* 141 In the meanwhile lie doggo and do come down this week-end. **1918** H. A. VACHELL *Some Happenings* iv. You'll play doggo and keep out of sight. **1924** *Blackw. Mag.* Sept. 352/2, I stayed doggo in the scrub. **1955** F. MACLEAN *Back to Bokhara* iii. 136 Lying doggo with an expression of angelic innocence when he came to see if she was in bed and asleep.

dog-gone (dɒg'gɒn, -'gɔːn). *U.S. slang.* Also **dog on.** [Generally taken as a deformation of the profane *God damn*: cf. *dang, darn.* But some think the original form was *dog on it*, to be compared with *pox on it!* etc.; cf. DOG *sb.*[1] 17 j. (See also *Sc. Nat. Dict.* s.v. *dag.*)]

A. *vb.* Used imperatively as an imprecation, or exclamation of impatience or the like: 'hang!'

1851 MAYNE REID *Scalp Hunt.* xxi, 'Dog-gone it, man! make haste then!' **1892** *Nation* (N.Y.) 21 Apr. 303/3, I think 'Dog gone it' is simply 'Dog on it'.

B. *adj.* or *pa. pple.* **1.** = C.

1851 MAYNE REID *Scalp Hunt.* vii, 'I'm dog-gone, Jim', replied the hunter. *a* **1860** *Southern Sketches* 33 (Bartlett) No, says I, I won't do no sich dog on thing. **1891** H. HERMAN *His Angel* 188 He ain't quite a dog-gone fool.

2. Also as *adv.* and quasi-*sb.*

1871 E. EGGLESTON *Hoosier Schoolmaster* 40 She was so dog-on stuck up. **1911** R. D. SAUNDERS *Col. Todhunter* 95 You was so dog-gone proud of the blue coat. **1933** E. CALDWELL *God's Little Acre* xviii. 266 That will be my ship coming in, and I don't give a dog-gone for the name you call it. *Ibid.*, When I get a load of it, I'll know dog-gone well my ship has come in.

C. dog-goned *adj.* or *pa. pple.*; also **dog-gauned, dog-goned**, 'confounded', 'darned'.

a **1860** T. H. GLADSTONE *Englishm. in Kansas* 46 (Bartlett) If there's a dog-goned abolitionist aboard this boat, I should like to see him. **1861** LOWELL *Biglow P.* Poems 1890 II. 23. **1868** *All Year Round* 19 Sept. 353/2 He looks the dogondest cuss ever since Jim Ford left. **1872** E. EGGLESTON *End of World* xxiii. 158 Clark township don't want none of 'em, I'll be dog-oned if it do. **1876** BESANT & RICE *Gold. Butterfly* Prol. i. **1879** TOURGEE *Fool's Err.* (1883) 672 I'll be dog-goned if I know what I do believe. **1893** T. STEWART *Miners* 203 Trade's sae dagont dull. **1908** J. LUMSDEN *Doun i' th' Loudons* 244 That dagon'd buffer o' a wife.

dog-grass, dog's-grass.

1. A name for Couch-grass, *Triticum repens*, and for the allied *T. caninum*, reputed to be eaten by dogs to produce vomiting. (Cf. Holland, *Pliny.*)

1597 GERARDE *Herbal* I. xvii. §1. 21 The common..Dogs grasse or Couch grasse. **1712** tr. *Pomet's Hist. Drugs* I. 52 The Dog grass or Quick grass. **1816** F. VANDERSTRAETEN *Impr. Agric.* p. xv, Quitch or dog-grass.

2. A local name for Dog's-tail grass, *Cynosurus.*

a **1825** FORBY *Voc. E. Anglia*, *Dog's-grass*, the common *cynosurus cristatus.* **1878** BRITTEN & HOLLAND *Plant-n.*, Dog's Grass, *Cynosurus cristatus..Hants.*; *Norf.*; *Suss.*

doggrel: see DOGGEREL.

doggy, doggie ('dɒgɪ), *sb.* [-Y, dim. suffix.]

1. A little dog; a pet name for a dog.

1825 J. NEAL *Bro. Jonathan* I. 397 Poor doggy. **1889** RUSKIN *Præterita* III. 55 The poor little..wistfully gazing doggie was tenderly put in a pretty basket.

2. *Coal-mining* (*colloq.*) A man employed by the BUTTY[1] (q.v.) to superintend the workmen in a mine.

1845 DISRAELI *Sybil* (1863) 116 A Butty in the mining districts is a middleman, a Doggy is his manager. **1860** W. WHITE *All round Wrekin* 253 The butty..employs a subordinate whose title is doggy. **1873** *Daily News* 27 Feb. 3/6 The pit was examined in the usual way by the doggy.

3. An officer's servant or assistant. Cf. *dog-robber* (b). orig. *Services' slang.*

1909 J. R. WARE *Passing Eng.* 113/2 *Doggie*,..officer's servant, especially cavalry. **1916** 'TAFFRAIL' *Carry On* 18 The captain's 'doggie'—midshipman A.D.C.—is relating certain shoregoing experiences. **1921** *Blackw. Mag.* July 50/2 Is the Admiral going to have a doggie? **1952** A. GRIMBLE *Pattern of Islands* ii. 53 My function would be to act as doggie—that is, clerical assistant and odd-job man —to..the District Officer.

4. Special Comb.: **doggy bag** chiefly *U.S.*, in a restaurant: a bag provided by the management on request, in which a diner may take left-overs home.

1964 *Time* 4 Sept. 53/2 All too frequently..guests use *doggie bags to haul off pilfered ashtrays, pepper mills, and silverware. **1975** *Courier-Mail* (Brisbane) 7 Apr. 6/9 Mrs. William Goadby Post regrets that, due to the high cost of dining out, she is obliged to approve doggy bags. **1984** *Listener* 5 Apr. 23/1 About a pound of the remains came home in a doggy bag.

doggy ('dɒgɪ), *a.* [f. DOG *sb.*[1] + -Y. (Cf. *horsy.*)]

†**1.** Having the bad qualities of a dog; malicious, spiteful; vile, contemptible. *Obs.*

1388 WYCLIF *1 Chron.* Prol., My bacbiters..gnawen me with a doggi tooth [**1382** dogge tothe]. **1583** STANYHURST *Æneis* I. (Arb.) 22 Pack hence doggye rakhels.

2. Of, pertaining to, or characteristic of a dog.

1869 *Echo* 3 June, Beasts without one doggy feeling. **1886** J. K. JEROME *Idle Thoughts* (1889) 92 The animal, whose frank, doggy nature has been warped.

3. Addicted to or conversant with dogs.

1859 PAYN *Foster Brothers* xvi. 277 Others..associate with boating men..with even doggy men. **1882** MISS BRADDON *Mt. Royal* III. vi. 102 Country people, with loud voices, horsey, and doggy, and horticultural.

4. Dashing, stylish, smart. Cf. DOG *sb.*[1] 17 p. *slang.*

1889 E. DOWSON *Let.* 26 July (1967) 95, I found it difficult to choose between the half-dozen..charming photos of Mignon... The 'doggy' ones liked me least. **1891** FARMER *Slang* II. 303/1 *Doggy*,..stylish. **1905** [see DOGGISHNESS]. **1932** A. J. WORRALL *Eng. Idioms* 6, I like your tie, it is very doggy.

5. Of Latin: debased, corrupt. (See DOG *sb.*[1] 19 e.) *colloq.*

1898 *Daily News* 3 Jan. 6/3 He spoke Latin! patristic Latin of the doggyest order.

dogh, obs. form of DOUGH, DOW *v.*[1]

dog-head. (See also DOG'S-HEAD.)

†**1.** A kind of ape with a head like a dog's; the Dog-faced Baboon, or Cynocephalus. *Obs.*

1607 TOPSELL *Four-f. Beasts* (1658) 8 Cynocephales, are a kind of Apes, whose heads are like Dogs..wherefore Gaza translateth them Canicipites, (to wit) dog-heads.

2. a. The head of a nail or spike formed by a rectangularly projecting shoulder. (Cf. DOG-NAIL.)

1793 SMEATON *Edystone L.* Plate xii, Bars in the angles.. whose dog-heads lay hold of the base of the iron work.

b. Part of the lock of a gun; the hammer.

1812 *Sporting Mag.* XXXIX. 65 A piece of steel kept firm by the screw of the doghead. **1814** SCOTT *Wav.* xxx. **1895** A. PATERSON *Man of his Word* 146 Kirk had taken a loaded rifle ..and drawn the dog-head back to the full.

dog-headed, *a.* Having a dog's head, or a head like that of a dog.

1587 GOLDING *De Mornay* viii. 105 What is to be said of Plinie with his Dogheaded men? **1834** MᶜMURTRIE *Cuvier's Anim. Kingd.* 46 The Dog-headed Monkeys..have an elongated muzzle truncated at the end. **1877** C. GEIKIE *Christ* (1879) 47 The barking, dog-headed Anubis.

dog-hole. A hole fit for a dog; a vile or mean dwelling or place, unfit for human habitation.

1579 GOSSON *Sch. Abuse* (Arb.) 16 The Schoole which I builde is narrowe, and at the first blushe appeareth but a doggehole. **1601** SHAKS. *All's Well* II. iii. 292 France is a dog-hole, and it no more merits, The tread of a mans foot. **1726** SWIFT *Epist. Corr.* Wks. 1841 II. 586 You all live in a wretched dirty doghole and prison. **1815** SIMOND *Tour Gt. Brit.* I. 324 The goblin cave was a mere dog-hole.

doghood ('dɒghʊd). [f. DOG *sb.*[1], after *manhood.*]

The condition or nature of a dog; the race of dogs, dogs collectively.

1647 TRAPP *Comm. Rom.* xii. 17 The world calls it [revenge] manhood, it is doghood rather. **1876** GEO. ELIOT *Dan. Der.* VI. xliv, A lap-dog would be necessarily at a loss in framing to itself the motives and adventures of doghood at large.

dog-hook.

†**1.** A hook used for leading a dog. *Obs.*

1571 *Bk. Revels* in Malone *Shaks.* (1821) III. 369 Money ..due for leashes, and doghookes, with staves and other necessaries..for the hunters that made crye after the fox.. in the playe of Narcissus. *a* **1631** DRAYTON *Wks.* IV. 1492 (Jod.) My doghook at my belt to which my Liam's ty'd.

2. a. A wrench for unscrewing the coupling of iron boring-rods; a spanner. (Halliwell 1847–78.)

b. An iron bar with a bent prong for securing or hoisting a log, etc.; = DOG *sb.*[1] 7 e.

1851 *Harper's Mag.* III. 519 He examines the chains.. and the dog-hook..that it lose not its grappling hold upon the tree. **1890** *Daily News* 30 Oct. 3/3 The dog-hooks.. caught the hatch, throwing the unfortunate man into the hold.

dog-house. 1. a. A house or dwelling for a dog, or for a pack of dogs; a kennel. Now chiefly *U.S.*

1611 COTGR., *Chiennerie*, a dog-house, or dog-kennell. *a* **1613** OVERBURY *Characters, Sargeant* Wks. (1856) 164 Not onely those curs at the dog-house, but those within the walls. **1822** W. IRVING *Braceb. Hall* (1823) I. 97 An unhappy cur chained in a doghouse. **1879** F. R. STOCKTON *Rudder Grange* vii. 77, I had no dog-house as yet. **1898** S. HALE *Lett.* (1919) 338 Behind the dog-house there is a warren of..four small animals. **1970** *Daily Progress* (Charlottesville, Va.) 21 Mar. C2/6 Going to paper a wall?.. Build a doghouse? Lay a patio?

b. *fig.*, ***in the dog-house***: in disgrace, out of favour. *slang* (orig. *U.S.*).

1932 *Editor* 6 Feb. 110/2 *Dog-house*: in disfavor. 'My moll caught me tryin' to make that twist, so I'm in the dog-house now.' **1940** WODEHOUSE *Quick Service* xix. 231 Already he was solidly established in the doghouse as the result of that craps business. **1955** PRIESTLEY & HAWKES *Journey down Rainbow* ii. 34 And the men, so often 'in the dog house'..are baffled and miserable, telling one another that women have always been like this, not knowing what they want, the crazy creatures. **1958** J. CANNAN *And be a Villain* iv. 83 He said to me, 'I'm in the dog-house over this.' **1963** P. H. JOHNSON *Night & Silence* ix. 55 He'd been getting bad grades, he was in the dog-house as it was.

2. a. A small structure, esp. a hut, of a shape suggesting a kennel. Usu. *colloq.* or *slang.*

1898 H. E. HAMBLEN *Gen. Manager's Story* 43 I'll have to drop off a flag, or they'll git our doghouse [*sc.* caboose, on a freight train]. **1959** *Manch. Guardian* 3 Jan. 5 At the base the staff will visit the 'greenhouse' to check the 'dog-house'. The former is a check station where simulated flights are conducted, the latter is a protuberance that houses instruments on the rocket's otherwise smooth skin. **1961** P. MOYES *Sunken Sailor* v. 74 A dog-house which gave shelter to the helmsman as he stood at the wheel. **1962** *Gloss. Terms Glass Ind.* (*B.S.I.*) 14 *Dog-house*, a small extension of a glass furnace, into which the batch is fed. **1969** *Guardian* 1 July 11/6 *Doghouse*, a small blister on the smooth skin of booster rocket, used to house instruments.

b. *slang.* A double-bass.

1923 in G. MCKNIGHT *Eng. Words* iv. 45. **1933** H. T. WEBSTER in *Forum* Dec., When the bull-fiddler plucks the strings he is slapping the doghouse. **1945** L. SHELLY *Hepcats Jive Talk Dict.* 9/2 *Doghouse*, the bass viol. **1952** B. ULANOV *Hist. Jazz in Amer.* (1958) xxv. 349 You will not find the language which was carefully attached to jazz in the first spate of general magazine articles about swing—no 'dog-house' for bass.

doght: see DOW *v.*[1]

doghter, doghty, obs. ff. DAUGHTER, DOUGHTY.

dog-hutch. A hutch for a dog; applied contemptuously to a mean dwelling; = DOG-HOLE.

1830 CARLYLE *Richter* Misc. (1872) III. 37 Would not let him occupy his own hired dog-hutch in peace. **1876** GEO. ELIOT *Dan. Der.* III. xliv. 283 A dog-hutch of a place in a black country.

dogie, dogy ('dəʊgɪ). *U.S.* [Of obscure origin.] A motherless, neglected, or undernourished calf on a cattle range. Also *attrib.*

[**1888** *Cent. Mag.* Oct. (Farmer), They were mostly Texan doughies—a name I have never seen written, it applies to young immigrant cattle.] **1892** *Outing* (U.S.) Feb. 358 A queer, pot-bellied little dogy (a calf prematurely weaned by the death of its mother and developed into a runt). **1903** A. ADAMS *Log of Cowboy* vii. 86 Before you could say Jack Robinson our dogies..were running in half a dozen different directions. **1911** H. QUICK *Yellowstone Nights* v. 124 The Old Man..was a one-lunger when this dogie enterprise started. **1920** J. M. HUNTER *Trail Drivers of Texas* 130 A dogie calf that had got into the herd. *Ibid.* 151

It took us just exactly three months and twenty days to drive a herd of southern 'dogies' from Red River. **1962** E. B. ATWOOD *Regional Vocab. Texas* 56 For a calf, particularly a 'range' calf, unaccompanied by a parent, the usual Texas term is *dogie*.. A dogie, according to various informants is 'small', 'undernourished'..or of 'inferior breed'.

ˌdog-in-the-ˈmanger. A churlish person who will neither use something himself nor let another use it; in allusion to the fable of the dog that stationed himself in a manger and would not let the ox or horse eat the hay. Also *attrib.*

[**1564** BULLEYN *Dial. agst. Pest.* (1888) 9 Like vnto cruell Dogges liyng in a Maunger, neither eatyng the Haye theim selues ne sufferyng the Horse to feed thereof hymself.] **1573** G. HARVEY *Letter-book* (Camden) 114 And as for the Syr Lowte That playdst inne and owte; A dogg in yᵉ maunger, A very ranke raunger. **1836** MARRYAT *Japhet* lxxii. (Farmer), Why, what a dog in the manger you must be—you can't marry them both. **1842** THACKERAY *Miss Lœve* Wks. 1886 XXIII. 285 That dog-in-the-manger jealousy which is common to love. **1890** *Times* 17 Sept. 7/5 A dog-in-the-manger policy is always unworthy of a nation.

Hence (*nonce-wds.*) **ˌdog-in-the-ˈmangerish, -ˈmangery** *adjs.*; **ˌdog-in-the-ˈmangerism.**

1883 C. J. WILLS *Land of Lion & Sun* 134 He was ill-mannered and dog-in-the-mangery. **1889** *Spectator* 28 Sept., To satisfy her dog-in-the-mangerish jealousy. **1894** *Sat. Rev.* 3 Mar. 234 A mere act of official dog-in-the-mangerism.

dogion, obs. form of DUDGEON.

dog-keeper. 1. One who keeps dogs; *spec.* a man appointed to take charge of a pack of dogs.

1679–88 *Secr. Serv. Money Chas. & Jas.* (Camden) 82 For building a little house in St. James's Park for the dogkeeper, and a kennell for the dogs. **1704** SWIFT *T. Tub* ii, It was written by a dog-keeper of my grandfather's. **1870** B. CLAYTON (*title*) The Dog-Keeper's Guide.

†**2.** A watch-dog. *Obs.*

1576 FLEMING tr. *Caius' Dogs* in Arb. *Garner* III. 254 The Dog Keeper..doth not only keep farmers' houses; but also merchants' mansions.

ˈdog-ˌkennel. A kennel for a dog, or dogs.

1611 COTGR., *Chiennerie*, a dog-house, or dog-kennell. **1700** DRYDEN *Fables* Pref. (Globe) 493 A certain nobleman, beginning with a dogkennel, never lived to finish the palace he had contrived. **1709** STEELE *Tatler* No. 62 ¶1, I am desired to recommend a Dog-kennel to any who shall want a Pack. **1865** KINGSLEY *Herew.* v. (1883) 110 You shall pass your bridal night in my dog-kennel.

ˈdogkind. [f. DOG *sb.*¹, after *mankind*.] The race of dogs; dogs collectively.

1888 *Pall Mall G.* 3 Mar. 2/2 A knowledge of mankind, womankind, and dogkind. **1895** *Westm. Gaz.* 10 Oct. 2/1 The *Spectator* has..earned the gratitude of all dogkind by espousing their cause and exposing their perfections.

dog-Latin. Bad Latin: see DOG *sb.*¹ 19 e.

†**dog-leech.** *Obs.*

1. A veterinary surgeon who treats dogs.

1638 FORD *Fancies* IV. i, I will once turn dog-leech. **1640** NABBES *Bride* V. i, He cured my little Shock of the mange.. an excellent Dog-leech. **1831** CARLYLE *Sart. Res.* III. v, Suspicion of 'Servility'..the very dogleech is anxious to disavow.

2. An ignorant medical practitioner; a quack.

1529 MORE *Dyaloge* II. 57 b/1 Ye myght happen vppon a dogge leche, for lacke of knowledge of the conning. **1628** FORD *Lover's Mel.* IV. ii, O these lousy close-stool empirics, that will undertake all cures, yet know not the causes of any disease! Dog-leeches! *a* **1652** BROME *Queene's Exch.* IV. Wks. 1873 III. 525 Thy Liege, Dog-leech? are you at that garb too?

ˈdog-leg, *a.* **1.** Of a bent form like a dog's hind leg; as in ***dog-leg chisel***, 'a crooked-shanked chisel used in smoothing the bottoms of grooves' (Knight); ***dog-leg fence*** (Australia), a fence made by logs or trees laid horizontally on supports crossing X-wise; ***dog-leg hole***, in *Golf*; ***dog-leg stair*** = DOG-LEGGED stair.

1889 BOLDREWOOD *Robbery under Arms* (1890) 71 A longish wing of dogleg fence. **1895** *Jrnl. R. Inst. Brit. Archit.* 14 Mar. 351 A dog-leg stair about 4 feet wide. **1903** 'T. COLLINS' *Such is Life* 75 The wild cattle having walked over the dog-leg fence. **1904** S. RUDD *Sandy's Selection* 30 A cultivation paddock enclosed with a dog-leg fence. **1907** *Daily Chron.* 17 Aug. 7/2 There are two or three very fine specimens of the dog-leg kind of hole. **1909** *Westm. Gaz.* 30 Apr. 4/2 There is the occasional variety of the 'dog-leg' hole, where the player has to go round an angle. **1935** *Bulletin* (Sydney) 16 Jan. 21/1 Companion of the dog-leg fence and huts of stringbark. **1959** *News Chron.* 14 Dec. 4/3, I had flown 650 miles on a dog-leg course. **1962** *Times* 27 Nov. 13/2 Gone are the 'dog leg' corners of the earlier wind-screen. **1967** *Listener* 9 Feb. 196/3 The dog-leg bend in the branch duct follows the wall above where the ward widens.

2. Applied to an inferior quality of tobacco. Also *ellipt.* as *sb. U.S.*

1858 *Nat. Intelligencer* (Washington) 10 July 3/3 A large quantity of 'dog-leg' tobacco and red pepper is then thrown into the tub. **1863** 'E. KIRKE' *My Southern Friends* iii. 48 The other [apartment] was densely crowded with logwood, 'dog-leg',..and cistern water. **1868** *Congress. Globe* 18 Mar., App. 287/1 Watching the neighbors pitch horseshoes for dog-leg tobacco. **1891** M. E. RYAN *Pagan of Alleghanies* ii. 25 Then the black-and-tan man treated himself to a fresh chew of 'dog-leg'.

dog-legged (ˈdɒglɛgd), *a. Arch.* **a.** Applied to a staircase, without a well-hole, the successive flights of which form a zig-zag.

1703 T. N. *City & C. Purchaser* 251 Dog-legg'd-stairs.. first fly directly forward, then wind a Semicircle, and then fly directly back again, parallel to the first flight. **1823** P. NICHOLSON *Pract. Build.* 189 Dog-legged stairs..have no well-hole. **1842–76** GWILT *Encycl. Archit.* II. ii. §2182.

b. Of a fence (see DOG-LEG *a.*). *Austral.* and *N.Z.*

1900 H. LAWSON *Over Sliprails* 95 A spidery dog-legged fence. **1935** N. R. MCKENZIE *Gael fares Forth* 88 The 'dog-legged' [type of fence]..was apparently a purely Canadian type..made with stakes of varying length and the trunks of small trees.

dogless (ˈdɒglɪs), *a.* Without a dog.

1854 WOOD *Anecd. Anim. Life* 159 A sleeping dogless man. **1887** M. BETHAM-EDWARDS *Next of Kin Wanted* I. vii. 96 A catless, dogless household.

ˈdog-like, *a.* and *adv.* Like, or in the manner of, a dog.

1605 TIMME *Quersit.* I. xv. 75 A doglike appetite. **1859** R. F. BURTON *Centr. Afr.* in *Jrnl. Geog. Soc.* XXIX. 416 The porters propping their burdens against trees, curl up, doglike, under the shade. **1874** L. STEPHEN *Hours in Library* (1892) I. iii. 123 There is something which rises to the dog-like in his affectionate admiration for Swift.

dogling (ˈdɒglɪŋ). *nonce-wd.* [f. DOG *sb.*¹ + -LING.] A little or young dog, a puppy.

1830 MISS MITFORD *Village* Ser. IV. (1863) 184 With the cat's milk these little doglings imbibed also the cat's habits.

ˈdogly, *a.* and *adv. rare.* [-LY¹, -LY².]

A. *adj.* Of the nature of a dog, canine; in quot. = CYNIC. **B.** *adv.* In the manner of a dog.

1477 EARL RIVERS (Caxton) *Dictes* 41 Dyogenes, otherwyse called dogly bycause he hadde som condicions of a dogge. **1552** HULOET, Doglye or lyke a dogge or after the maner of a dogge, *canatim.* **1829** LANDOR *Wks.* (1846) I. 470/1 Respect..to the dogly character.

dogma (ˈdɒgmə). Also 7–8 dogm(e. Pl. **dogmas** (7 -aes), **dogmata** (7 -taes). [a. L. *dogma* philosophical tenet, a. Gr. δόγμα, δογματ-, that which seems to one, opinion, tenet, decree, f. δοκεῖν to seem, seem good, think, suppose, imagine. At first used with Gr.-L. plural; the forms *dogme, dogm*, represented F. *dogme* (16th c. in Hatz.-Darm.).]

1. That which is held as an opinion; a belief, principle, tenet; *esp.* a tenet or doctrine authoritatively laid down by a particular church, sect, or school of thought; sometimes, depreciatingly, an imperious or arrogant declaration of opinion.

[*a* **1600** HOOKER *Eccl. Pol.* VIII. ii. §13 [tr. D. Stapleton] Power to proclaim, to defend, and..to preserve from violation *dogmata*, very articles of religion themselves.] **1638** SIR T. HERBERT *Trav.* (ed. 2) 267 The grosse fanatick Dogmataes of the Alcoran. **1640** G. WATTS tr. *Bacon's Adv. Learn.* III. iv. §3 Those Dogmaes and Paradoxes are almost vanished. *a* **1652** J. SMITH *Sel. Disc.* VII. iv. (1821) 350 Our dogmata and notions about justification. **1676** R. DIXON *Nat. Two Test.* 21 Prophane Dogms and impure Worship. **1704** HEARNE *Duct. Hist.* (1714) I. 400 Their Dogmata and Astrological Doctrine..we shall not enlarge upon them. **1843** RUSKIN *Mod. Paint.* I. (1844) p. lii, The dogmata of the schools of art. **1874** GREEN *Short Hist.* v. §3 (1882) 229 To assert the freedom of religious thought against the dogmas of the Papacy. **1893** J. ORR *God & World* I. 26 *note*, Dogma I take to be a formulation of doctrine stamped with ecclesiastical authority.

2. The body of opinion formulated or authoritatively stated; systematized belief; tenets or principles collectively; doctrinal system.

1791 BURKE *Fr. Affairs* Wks. VII. 13 The present..is a revolution of doctrine and theoretick dogma. **1856** EMERSON *Eng. Traits, Lit.* Wks. (Bohn) II. 111 If, going out of the region of dogma, we pass into that of general culture. **1871** KINGSLEY *Lett.* (1878) II. 368 If you wish to save Christian dogma. **1871** MORLEY *Carlyle* (1878) 191 It places character on the pedestal where Puritanism places dogma.

dogmatic (dɒgˈmætɪk), *a.* and *sb.* [ad. L. *dogmatic-us* (Ausonius), a. Gr. δογματικός, f. δόγμα, δογματ- DOGMA: cf. F. *dogmatique* (16th c.).]

A. *adj.* **1.** Pertaining to the setting forth or laying down of opinion; didactic. *rare.*

1678 GALE *Crt. Gentiles* III. Pref., To render our Discourse the lesse offensive, we have cast it into a thetic and dogmatic method, rather than agonistic and polemic. **1875** JOWETT *Plato* (ed. 2) V. 5 He is no longer interrogative but dogmatic.

2. Of, pertaining to, or of the nature of, dogma or dogmas; characterized by or consisting in dogma; doctrinal.

1706 PHILLIPS (ed. Kersey), *Dogmatical* or *Dogmatick*, relating to a Dogma, instructive. **1727–38** GAY *Fables* II. xiv. (R.), Dogmatick jargon learnt by heart. **1841** W. SPALDING *Italy & It. Isl.* II. 28 The rest of his compositions are versified treatises of dogmatic theology. **1859** MILL *Liberty* ii. (1865) 15 A..Christian in all but the dogmatic sense of the word. **1883** FROUDE *Short Stud.* IV. v. 350 No inclination to substitute dogmatic Protestantism for dogmatic Catholicism.

3. Proceeding upon *a priori* principles accepted as true, instead of being founded upon experience or induction, as ***dogmatic philosophy, medicine.***

1696 PHILLIPS (ed. 5), *Dogmatick Philosophy*, is that which [ed. 1706 being grounded upon sound Principles] positively assures a thing, and is opposed to Sceptic. **1823** CRABB *Technol. Dict.*, *Dogmatic sect* (Med.), an ancient sect of physicians, at the head of which is placed Hippocrates. **1864** BOWEN *Logic* x. 330 The foundations of all philosophy, whether dogmatic, critical, or sceptical.

4. Of persons, their writings, etc.: Asserting or imposing dogmas or opinions, in an authoritative, imperious, or arrogant manner.

1681 tr. *Willis' Rem. Med. Wks.* Vocab., *Dogmatic*, stiff in opinion. **1712** ADDISON *Spect.* No. 253 ¶7 Those criticks who write in a positive dogmatick way. **1814** D'ISRAELI *Quarrels Auth.* (1867) 458 He wrote against dogmas with a spirit perfectly dogmatic. **1868** M. PATTISON *Academ. Org.* v. 306 Not by dogmatic delivery of truths, but by scientific training in the method of enquiry. **1873** HELPS *Anim. & Mast.* viii. (1875) 200 One is afraid of being dogmatic about it, and of being dogmatically wrong.

†**b.** Of assured opinion, convinced. *Obs. rare.*

1678 CUDWORTH *Intell. Syst.* 434 (R.) From sundry other places of his writings, it sufficiently appears, that he [Cicero] was a dogmatick and hearty theist.

B. *sb.* †**1.** A philosopher of the dogmatic school; = DOGMATIST 3. *Obs.*

a **1631** DONNE *Paradoxes* (1652) 22 The Skeptike..was more contentious then..the Dogmatick. **1650** HOBBES *De Corp. Pol.* 165 All these Opinions are maintained in the Books of the Dogmaticks, and divers of them taught in Publick Chaires. **1702** tr. *Le Clerc's Prim. Fathers* 57 A Suspension [of judgment] suited not with the Dogmaticks, who can hardly confess that they know not all things.

†**b.** A dogmatic physician; see quot. 1883. *Obs.*

1605 TIMME *Quersit.* Pref. 5 Among Physitians there are Empericks, Dogmaticks, Methodici, or Abbreuiators, and Paracelsians. **1771** T. PERCIVAL *Med. & Exp. Ess.* (1778) I. 41 (*heading*) The Dogmatic; or Rationalist. **1883** *Syd. Soc. Lex.*, *Dogmatics*, an ancient sect of physicians, so called because they endeavoured to discover, by reasoning, the essence and the occult causes of diseases.

†**2.** A dogmatic person. *Obs.*

1640 HOBBES *Hum. Nat.* xiii. §4 The fault lieth altogether in the dogmatics, that is to say, those that are imperfectly learned, and with passion press to have their opinions pass every where for truth.

3. Chiefly in *pl.* form **dogmatics**: A system of dogma; *spec.* dogmatic theology.

1845 GEO. ELIOT in *Life* (1885) 137 'Dogmatik' is the idea, I believe—i.e. positive theology. Is it allowable to say *dogmatics*, think you? **1857** M. PATTISON *Ess.* (1889) II. 222 The Reformation dogmatic rests on..the exclusive sufficiency of Scripture. **1858** *Lond. Rev.* Oct. 220 To expound the polemical dogmatics of the Reformation. **1893** FAIRBAIRN *Christ in Mod. Theol.* I. I. i. 29 *note*, The book 'De Theologicis Dogmatibus', published at Paris 1644–50..the first attempt at a scientific history of dogmata, and..notable as suggesting to modern theology the term Dogmatics. **1894** MITCHELL tr. *Harnack's Hist. Dogma* i. 28 Dogmatic is a positive science which has to take its material from history.

Hence **dogˈmaticism**, dogmatic quality.

1880 FAIRBAIRN *Stud. Life Christ* ix. (1881) 156 The dogmaticism he subtly concealed.

dogmatical (dɒgˈmætɪkəl), *a.* (*sb.*) [f. as prec. + -AL¹.]

A. *adj.* **1.** Of, pertaining to, or dealing with dogmas; of the nature of dogma; = DOGMATIC *a.* 1, 2.

1604 R. CAWDREY *Table Alph.* (1613), *Dogmaticall*, that giueth instructions. **1627** MINSHEU *Ductor Ling.* (ed. 2), *Dogmaticall*, of or pertaining to a Sect or opinion. *a* **1631** DONNE in *Select.* (1840) 41 To make a true difference between problematical and dogmatical points. **1642** FULLER *Holy & Prof. St.* II. vi. 70 Their Rhetoricall hyperboles were afterwards accounted the just measure of dogmaticall truths. **1649** ROBERTS *Clavis Bibl.* 327 These Dogmatical books contain in them Doctrines. **1845** S. AUSTIN *Ranke's Hist. Ref.* III. 99 The intolerant domination of a dogmatical system. **1876** MOZLEY *Univ. Serm.* i. 11 We..look upon the judgment in its dogmatical aspect.

†**2.** = DOGMATIC 3. *Obs.*

1605 TIMME *Quersit.* I. vii. 26 The dogmatical Physitians ..are wont to refer to those qualities. **1727–51** CHAMBERS *Cycl.* s.v., In common use, a dogmatical philosopher is such a one as asserts things positively; in opposition to a Sceptic, who doubts of every thing. A dogmatical physician is he, who, on the principles of the school-philosophy, rejects all medicinal virtues not reducible to manifest qualities.

3. Asserting or maintaining dogmas or opinions; arbitrary, positive; = DOGMATIC *a.* 4.

1662 STILLINGFL. *Orig. Sacr.* I. i. §12 How uncertain the most dogmatical of them all were. **1751** JOHNSON *Rambler* No. 177 ¶3, I became decisive and dogmatical, impatient of contradiction. *a* **1852** D. WEBSTER *Wks.* VI. 148 Nothing is more apt to be positive and dogmatical than ignorance.

†**B.** *sb. pl. Obs.* **1.** = Dogmatics. (See DOGMATIC B 3.)

1605 BACON *Adv. Learn.* II. xiii. §1. 50 They hasted to their Theories and Dogmaticals. **1716** DAVIES *Athen. Brit.* II. 372 That Edition of Anselm's Dogmaticals.

2. Medicines of the dogmatic physicians.

1656 RIDGLEY *Pract. Physic* 26 Empericalls are: Earthworms provided several wayes. Dogmaticalls: Senna powder, 2 drams.

Hence **ˌdogmatiˈcality**, dogmaticalness.

1793 in L. Twining *Country Clergym. 18th C.* (1882) 175 Too much dogmaticality, too overbearing a manner.

dog'matically, *adv.* [f. prec. + -LY².] In a dogmatic or dogmatical manner.

1. By way of, in point of, or with respect to dogma or dogmas; by a dogmatic method.

1630 J. TAYLOR (Water P.) *Praise Hempseed* 49 Wks. III. 70 For he (dogmatically) doth know more Than all the learned Doctors knew before. **1651** HOBBES *Govt. & Soc.* xv. §10. 244 We..praise, and celebrate in words, when we doe it by way of Proposition, or Dogmatically. **1871** MORLEY *Voltaire* (1886) 245 Catholicism..was believed dogmatically, and therefore was to be attacked dogmatically.

2. With an assumption of positive certainty; positively or imperiously in the assertion of opinion.

1664 H. MORE *Myst. Iniq., Apol.* vii. §3. 528 Thus far we have been bold to proceed more dogmatically. **1670** *Moral State Eng.* 113 Not imposing his opinion upon any Magisterially or Dogmatically. **1796** *Phil. Trans.* LXXXVI. 500 We are not possessed of observations sufficiently decisive to enable us to speak dogmatically. *a* **1845** HOOD *Laying down Law* i, Dogmatically laying down the law.

dog'maticalness. [f. as prec. + -NESS.] The quality of being dogmatical; positiveness.

1711 SHAFTESBURY *Charac.* (1749) I. 52 The tutorage and dogmaticalness of the Schools. **1765** WESLEY *Wks.* (1872) XIII. 239 My dogmaticalness is..a custom of coming to the point at once, and telling my mind flat and plain. **1808** in *Harl. Misc.* I. *Machiavelli's Vind.* Summ. 57 He carefully avoided all dogmaticalness.

dogmatician (dɒgmə'tɪʃən). [f. DOGMATIC *a.* + -IAN.] A student or professor of dogmatics.

1846 WORCESTER cites *Q. Rev.* *a* **1849** POE *Mellonta Tauta* Wks. 1864 IV. 294 It would have puzzled these ancient dogmaticians. **1882-3** SCHAFF *Encycl. Relig. Knowl.* III. 2417 Without laying claim to being a keen critic, or a stern dogmatician.

dogmatism ('dɒgmətɪz(ə)m). [a. F. *dogmatisme* (16th c. in Hatz.-Darm.), 'the teaching, or preaching of new doctrine, the producing of a new sect' (Cotgr.), ad. med.L. *dogmatism-us* 'dissertatio, docendi ars' (Du Cange), a. Gr. type *δογματισμός, f. δόγμα, δογματ- DOGMA: see -ISM. Used by Florio in translating from French, but not in Blount, Phillips, Kersey, Bailey, Ash; used by Dr. Johnson 1751, but not given in his Dictionary.]

1. Positive assertion of dogma or opinion; dogmatizing; positiveness in the assertion of opinion.

1603 FLORIO *Montaigne* II. xii. (1632) 281 A very foolish answer: to which..Dogmatisme arriveth. **1627** MINSHEU *Ductor Ling.* (ed. 2), *Dogmatisme*, the teaching of a new Sect or opinion. **1751** JOHNSON *Rambler* No. 106 ¶3 Dogmatism has delighted in the gradual advances of his authority. **1777** PRIESTLEY *Matt. & Spir.* (1782) I. xvii. 201 A small share of natural science..generally accompanies conceit and dogmatism. **1825** MACAULAY *Milton* Ess. (1854) 19/1 Dogmatism on points the most mysterious. **1843** PRESCOTT *Mexico* App. (1864) 473 Where there is most doubt, there is often the most dogmatism.

2. With *pl.*: A dogmatic tenet or system. *rare.*

1803 *Edin. Rev.* I. 265 The theory of transcendentalism may therefore be a better dogmatism than others. **1820** L. HUNT *Indicator* No. 15 (1822) I. 114 The ethereal dogmatisms of Plotinus and Porphyry. **1871** ALABASTER *Wheel of Law* 39 These dogmatisms are not attributed to Buddha.

3. *Philos.* A system of philosophy based upon principles dictated by reasoning alone, and not relying upon experience; opposed to *scepticism*. More generally, a way of thinking based upon principles which have not been tested by reflection.

1858 WHEWELL *Hist. Sci. Ideas* II. 292 (L.) The skepticism of the uniformitarian is of force only so long as it is employed against the dogmatism of the catastrophist. **1858** MANSEL *Bampton Lect.* i. (ed. 4) 3 Theological Dogmatism is..an application of reason to the support and defence of preexisting statements of Scripture. **1877** E. CAIRD *Philos. Kant* I. 2 What Kant meant we may best understand if we consider how he opposes Criticism to two other forms of philosophy, Dogmatism and Scepticism. **1881** ADAMSON *Fichte* vi. 126 Do we explain experience as the product of the non-Ego, we have the system which may be called Dogmatism; do we explain the whole as springing from the Ego, we have Idealism.

dogmatist ('dɒgmətɪst). [a. F. *dogmatiste* (16th c.), ad. med.L. *dogmatista*, ad. Gr. δογματιστής, agent-n. from δογματίζειν: see DOGMATIZE. (The logical and chronological orders differ.)]

1. One who dogmatizes, who asserts or lays down particular dogmas; *esp.* one who positively asserts or imposes his own opinions; a dogmatic person.

1654 WHITLOCK *Zootomia* 565 That which Salomon delivered as a Dogmatist. **1661** GLANVILL *Scepsis Sci.* xxiii. (R.), I expect but little success of all this upon the dogmatist, his opinion'd assurance is paramount to argument. **1706** PHILLIPS (ed. Kersey), *Dogmatist*, one that dogmatizes, a dogmatical Teacher. **1741** WATTS *Improv. Mind* I. i. §10 A dogmatist in religion is not a great way off from a bigot. **1775** JOHNSON *Tax. no Tyr.* 16 Many political dogmatists have denied to the Mother Country the power of taxing the Colonies. **1854** KINGSLEY *Alexandria* iv. 137 Dogmatists..men who assert a truth so fiercely, as to forget that a truth is meant to be used, and not merely asserted.

†2. A propounder of new opinions or doctrines. *Obs.*

1577-87 HOLINSHED *Chron.* II. 116 A councell assembled at Oxford, whereat those dogmatists were examined upon certeine points of their profession. **1656** BLOUNT *Glossogr.*, *Dogmatist*, he that induceth any new Sect or Opinion..a forger of new Sects. **1660** BOND *Scut. Reg.* 69 With this new upstart Doctrine have our Apocryphal Dogmatists in England led the rascal rabble. **1797** SOUTHEY *Lett. fr. Spain* (1808) II. 260 What regards heretics and dogmatists.

3. One who belongs to the dogmatic school of philosophy: see DOGMATIC *a.* 3, and quot. 1858.

1603 FLORIO *Montaigne* II. xii. (1632) 294 Some have judged Plato a Dogmatist, others a Skeptike or a Doubter. **1690** DRYDEN *Don Sebast.* Ded., Of the academic sect, neither dogmatist nor stoic. **1858** MANSEL *Bampton Lect.* i. (ed. 4) 2 In the later language of philosophy..the term Dogmatists was used to denote those philosophers who endeavoured to explain the phenomena of experience by means of rational conceptions and demonstrations.

b. A physician of the dogmatic school of medicine: see DOGMATIC *a.* 3.

1541 R. COPLAND *Galyen's Terap.* 2 Biij, Some Dogmatystes which do affyrme to heale such dyseases by experyence onely without racyonall indicion. **1607** WALKINGTON *Opt. Glass* 44 The inexpert physician, I meane..the methodist or dogmatist. **1727** BRADLEY *Fam. Dict.* s.v. *Blood*, The Dogmatists make a Plaister of it..the Chymists..extract a Salt from it. **1883** in *Syd. Soc. Lex.*

dogmati'zation. *rare.* [f. next + -ATION.] The action of dogmatizing; the propounding of a dogma.

1875 GLADSTONE *Vaticanism* ii. 36 The Syllabus is part of that series of acts to which the dogmatisations of 1854 and 1870 belong, and it bridges over the interval between them.

dogmatize ('dɒgmətaɪz), *v.* [ad. F. *dogmatise-r* (13th c.), ad. med.L. *dogmatizāre* to propound dogma, ad. Gr. δογματίζειν to lay down as one's opinion, to decree, f. δόγμα, δογματ- DOGMA.]

1. *intr.* To make dogmatic assertions; to speak authoritatively or imperiously (*upon* a subject) without reference to argument or evidence.

1611 BIBLE *Transl. Pref.* 11 To admonish the Reader..not to conclude or dogmatize vpon this or that peremptorily. **1742** POPE *Dunc.* IV. 464 Prompt to impose, and fond to dogmatize. **1790** BURKE *Fr. Rev.* 37 These old fanaticks..dogmatised as if hereditary royalty was the only lawful government. **1840** CARLYLE *Heroes* i. (1872) 22 A question which nobody would wish to dogmatise upon.

†b. See quots.: cf. DOGMATIST 2, and F. *dogmatiser*, 'to teach strange doctrine..or broach new opinions' (Cotgr.). *Obs.*

1613 *Crt. & Times Jas. I* (1849) I. 262 The king..was so moved that he should dogmatize (as he called it) in his court. **1696** PHILLIPS (ed. 5), To *Dogmatize*, to teach new Opinions, to contest the Truths of Religion.

2. *trans.* To assert or deliver as a dogma; to establish as a matter of dogma; to state dogmatically; to express in the form of a dogma. Now *rare*.

1621 BP. H. KING *Serm.* 60 Hee..dogmatizes them for truth. **1626** W. SCLATER *Exp. 2 Thess.* (1629) 104 When were these dogmatized and decretally stablished for catholique doctrine? **1647** JER. TAYLOR *Lib. Proph.* xiv. §4 (L.) They would not endure Persons that did dogmatize any thing which might intrench upon their Reputation or their Interest. **1893** N. SMYTH *Chr. Ethics* I. ii. I. §2. 95 Their hope, as well as their law, had become..increasingly dogmatized.

3. ***to dogmatize away***, to do away with by dogmatic assertion.

1829 MACAULAY *Mill on Govt.* Misc. Writ. (1889) 174 He placidly dogmatises away the interest of one half of the human race.

Hence **'dogmatized** *ppl. a.*, **'dogmatizing** *vbl. sb.* and *ppl. a.*

1641 J. TOMBES *Leaven of Pharisaicall Wil-worship* (1643) 2 The Apostle condemnes dogmatizing. **1712** BLACKMORE *Creation* III. 42 Dogmatizing Schools. **1865** BUSHNELL *Vicar. Sacr.* Introd. (1866) 27 A theory or dogmatized scheme of the incarnate life.

'dogmatizer. [f. prec. + -ER¹.] One who dogmatizes; a dogmatist.

1612-20 SHELTON *Quix.* (T.), The dogmatizer and head of a bad sect. *a* **1660** HAMMOND *Wks.* II. IV. 139 (R.) The very dogmatizer, that teacheth for doctrines or commandments of God, his own dictates. **1709** SHAFTESB. *Moralist* II. i, Dogmatizers on Pleasure. **1860** S. WILBERFORCE *Addr. Ordin.* 148 Cold, quarrelsome, and unloving dogmatizers.

dogmato- [Gr. δογματο-], comb. f. of DOGMA, as in **dogma'tology** [ad. Gr. δογματολογία], the science of dogma; **dogmato'pœic** *a.* [f. Gr. δογματοποιΐα], creating dogmas.

1874 SAYCE *Compar. Philol.* viii. 341 The comparative science of religions, or, if we might coin a word, of Dogmatology. **1893** *Contemp. Rev.* Apr. 460 The people who claim this novel right of erecting new dogmatic barriers..the dogmatopœic agency, if I may be permitted to coin a word, are exclusively theologians.

†**dogmatory**, *a. Obs. rare.* [f. Gr. δογματ-: see DOGMA and -ORY.] Dogmatic.

1846 WORCESTER cites *For. Q. Rev.*

dog-nail. A nail having a solid and slightly countersunk head; also a large nail with a head projecting on one side; also = DOG *sb.*¹ 7 p.

1703 T. N. *City & C. Purchaser* 211 Dogg-nails..are proper for fastning of Hinges to Doors for..they will hold the Hinge close without the Heads flying off. **1776** G. SEMPLE *Building in Water* 87 A Ledge nailed on with Dog-nails. **1879** *Notes on Build. Constr.* III. 441 Dog nails..are used for nailing down heavy ironwork.

'dognapping, *vbl. sb. colloq.* (orig. *U.S.*). Also **dog-napping.** [f. DOG *sb.*¹ + KID)NAPPING *vbl. sb.*] The stealing of dogs, either for a reward or ransom paid by their owners, or for sale.

1939 *Sun* (Baltimore) 15 Sept. 15/2 The American Humane Association received today a plan for nation-wide identification of dogs by 'nose-printing' to eliminate 'dognapping'. **1955** W. W. DENLINGER *Compl. Boston* I. 48 This dog..sired eight champions. Among them was Champion Kid Boots Ace..who figured in a dognapping case. **1969** *New Scientist* 20 Feb. 386/3 Dog-napping, when the pet is abducted not for sale but for ransom, is also developing in the States. **1973** T. PYNCHON *Gravity's Rainbow* I. 46 Why's he here, then, assisting at yet another dognapping? **1984** *Christian Science Monitor* 5 June 25 (*heading*) Collie stars in a tale of dog-napping and danger.

Also **'dognapper**, one who steals dogs; **'dognap** *sb.*, the act of dognapping; also as *v. trans.*, to steal (a dog).

1942 BERREY & VAN DEN BARK *Amer. Thes. Slang* §461/9 *Dognaper*, one who steals dogs for the reward. *Ibid.* §490/2 *Dognap*, the theft of a dog. *Ibid.* §490/8 *Dognap*, to steal a dog, usually to hold it for the reward. **1945** *Philadelphia Inquirer* 16 Dec. s4/8 'Dog-nappers', a dishonest group which steal a valuable dog and sell for a high profit. **1947** in *Amer. Speech* (1948) XXIII. 28 Sidney [Nebraska] police believe the dog may have been dognapped but later escaped. **1969** *New Scientist* 20 Feb. 386/3 A leading authority on pets has been moved to demand the death penalty for dog-nappers. **1978** J. WAMBAUGH *Black Marble* iii. 26 There were high-wattage security lights..to safeguard Skinner Kennels from prowling dognappers.

do'gology. *nonce-wd.* [See -OLOGY.] The science or subject of dogs.

1820 *Sporting Mag.* VI. 85 A long speech on 'dogology'. **1832** *Fraser's Mag.* VI. 722 A book upon dogology.

dogoned, var. DOG-GONED *a.*

'do-good. One who or that which does good, or is of use. In modern use (orig. *U.S.*) = DO-GOODER. Also *attrib.* or as *adj.* Also **do-'gooding** *ppl. a.* and *vbl. sb.*; **do-'goodism**; **do-'goody** *a.* (all these derivatives carry the disparaging sense of DO-GOODER).

1654 WHITLOCK *Zootomia* 723 That they may be accounted somebody, and Do-goods. **1923** *Nation* 21 Nov. 569/2 There is nothing the matter with the United States except..the parlor socialists, up-lifters, and do-goods. **1936** *Sat. Rev. Lit.* 14 Mar. 5/1 'Scientific and do-gooding people from all over America' had foregathered to a Child Recovery Conference. **1951** *Manch. Guardian Weekly* 14 June 3/1 Mr. Truman..has been made aware that..anything that comes out of the State Department bears..a stigma indicating vague incompetence, sympathy to the Communists, and general 'do-goodism'. **1958** *Times Lit. Suppl.* 15 Aug. p. x/2 And the committee would, I am sure, be a snuggery of all the no-goods and do-goods whom I have spent half my life successfully avoiding. **1958** S. ELLIN *Eighth Circle* (1959) II. xiii. 141 A decision that reeked of the genteel do-goodism, of the compulsive idealism that..infected people of..[his] class and type. **1958** *Listener* 11 Dec. 1007/3 His tyrannous wife..and her do-goody brother. **1959** *Guardian* 28 Aug. 3/3 The present-day young are less interested in vague do-gooding..than in reacting to a human situation. **1968** *New Statesman* 11 Oct. 469/1 Not in a do-good social worker way ..but in a fundamental Christian way. **1969** *Listener* 23 Jan. 105/2 It contains all the do-good elements one can pack into 24 minutes: attractive, young and, of course, black war-widow, her husband having died a hero's death in Vietnam, starts life in California with her attractive young black son.

do-'gooder. orig. *U.S.* [f. *to do good* (see GOOD *sb.* 5 a) + -ER¹. Cf. prec.] A well-meaning, active, but unrealistic philanthropist or reformer; one who tries to do good. Hence **do-'goodery.**

1927 *St. Louis Post-Dispatch* 18 Jan. 14/5 The dogooder..is all the hokum, all the blather and all the babble of the modern so-called 'social movement'. **1943** *Time* 25 Oct. 32/1 Go find yourself out something about Charles P. Taft before dismissing him as famed do-gooder. **1954** KOESTLER *Invis. Writing* 250 The prim feeling of virtue of do-gooders. **1957** *Sunday Times* 12 May 8/6 [He] does not write as a sentimental do-gooder, or with primarily political motives. **1959** 'M. INNES' *Hare sitting Up* I. i. 20 An out-and-out do-gooder, full of an exalted love of..humanity. **1961** *Guardian* 25 Mar. 5/3 The boy is trapped..by do-goodery. **1968** *Daily Tel.* 11 Apr. 17/4 Amateur 'do-gooders' could slip up when certain medical attention was needed, a coroner said yesterday. **1968** N. MARSH *Clutch of Constables* i. 13 Let us examine my philanthropy. Or rather, since I have no distaste for colloquialism, my dogoodery.

dog-plate.

†1. ? A plate given as a prize in a dog-race. *Obs.*

1686 *Lond. Gaz.* No. 2166/4 There will be a Dog-Plate run for each day.

2. In a lathe, a plate which imparts rotation to the work to be turned, by means of 'dogs': see DOG *sb.*¹ 7 l.

Dogra ('dəʊgrə), *sb.* (and *a.*) Also Dogri, Dogur. [f. *Duggar* (see def.).] The name of a people inhabiting the Duggar district in north-west

India; a member of this people; also (usu. *Dogri*), their language. Also as *adj.*

1845 H. M. ELLIOT *Suppl. Gloss. Indian Terms* 238 *Dogur*, a tribe scattered over various tracts of the North-West of Hindoostan. **1870** *Proc. R. Geogr. Soc.* XV. 13 The unhappy results of the incessant feuds waged between the mountaineers (who are to a man Mahomedans) and the Dogra troops of the Kashmir Rajah. The atrocities practised by the Dogras are a disgrace to a feudatory of the British crown. **1888** KIPLING *In Black & White* (1889) 91 Sikhs, Pathans, Dogras—they're all alike, these black vermin. **1926** *Blackw. Mag.* Nov. 593/1 Dogras being high-caste Hindus are very particular. **1948** D. DIRINGER *Alphabet* vi. 373 Dogra or Dogri, a dialect of Punjabi, spoken by one and a half million people in the Jammu State and its neighbourhood. **1957** *Encycl. Brit.* VII. 503/1 Dogra, an inhabitant of the Duggar tract... The original home of the Dogra people was situated between the lakes of Siroensar and Mansar.

[dog-ray, -reie. Explained in some mod. Dicts. as: Dog-fish. App. error arising from misreading *dorrey* (see quot.), var. of DORY.

[**1577** HARRISON *England* III. x. 110/1 in Holinshed *Chron.* I, Of the first [sort of fish, the flat] are the Plaice, the Butte, the Turbut, Dorrey, Dabbe, &c.]]

Dogrib ('dɒgrɪb), *sb.* (and *a.*) Also Dog-rib, Dog-Rib. [tr. Cree *atimospikay*, perh. ult. tr. Dogrib *tłı̨chǫ*, from a legend that the peoples are descended from a dog, but the names have quite difference ranges of application.] **a.** A member of a group of Athabascan peoples of north-western Canada, inhabiting mainly the area between the Great Bear and the Great Slave lakes. Also *attrib.* or as *adj.*

[**1689** E. KELSEY *Jrnl.* 17 June in *Kelsey Papers* (1929) 25 Northern Indians Inhabiting to yᵉ Northward of Churchill river & also yᵉ dogside Nation. **1744** A. DOBBS *Acct. Countries adjoining Hudson's Bay* 19 This River comes from a country he calls *Platscotez de Chiens*, who make war against the Savannah Indians.] **1881** *Encycl. Brit.* XII. 827/2 Beavers, Dog-ribs, Strongbows, [etc.]. **1926** DOUGLAS & WALLACE tr. *Jérémie's Twenty Years York Factory 1694–1714* 20 Seal river extends up to the country of a nation called Dogribs who make war on our Maskegons. **1957** *Encycl. Brit.* IV. 700/2 The Mackenzie valley..the home of the Hares, the Dog-Ribs, the Caribou-Eaters, [etc.]. **1967** D. JENESS *Indians of Canada* (ed. 7) 392 At the end of the eighteenth century a western group of Dogrib Indians seems to have shared with the Slave the country between lac la Martre and the Mackenzie river. **1979** J. HALIFAX *Shamanic Voices* (1980) v. 148 The old and weathered Dogrib Indian shaman Adamie.

b. An Athabascan language of the Na-Dene language family, spoken by the Dogrib peoples.

1914 *Summary Rep. Anthropol. Div. Geol. Survey Canada 1913* 376 Slavey and Dogrib are closely related lexically. **1933** L. BLOOMFIELD *Language* 72 The *Athabascan* family covers all but the coastal fringe of northwestern Canada (*Chipewyan, Beaver, Dogrib, Sarsi*, etc.). **1965** *Language* XLI. 171 The study of classificatory verbs in Navaho, Chipewyan, Dogrib, [etc.]. **1981** *N.Y. Times* 1 Feb. 14/1 Herb Zimmerman is translating the Bible into an Indian language, Dogrib.

dog-rose. Also 6–8 dogs-rose. [A transl. of med.L. *rosa canina*, repr. L. *cynorrodon* (Pliny), Gr. κυνόροδον, f. κυνο- dog- + ῥόδον rose: see quots. 1597, 1830. The name is thus not of popular Engl. origin.] A common species of wild rose (*Rosa canina*), with pale red flowers, frequent in hedges.

white dog-rose, a book-name for *R. arvensis*.

1597 GERARDE *Herbal* 1088 Plinie..saith, that it is Rosa Canina—Dogs Rose. **1675** *Phil. Trans.* No. 114 (Bartholoni's Acta Med. & Phil.) A sort of Dogs-rose or Briar-bush. **1713** DERHAM *Phys. Theol.* (J.), Of the rough or hairy excrescence, those on the briar, or dogrose, are a good instance. **1778** LIGHTFOOT *Flora Scot.* (1789) I. 261 *R. arvensis*, White-flowered Dogs-rose. **1830** *Withering's Brit. Plants* (ed. 7) III. 618 *note*, By the Greeks Wild Roses were called κυνόροδον, because the root was thought to cure the bite of a mad dog; and hence the Latin *canina*, our *Dog Rose*. **1861** NEALE *Notes Dalmatia, etc.* 93 Dog-roses that skirt the country road.

'dog's-bane, 'dog-bane. [See BANE.] A rendering of the ancient names *Apocynum* and *Cynoctonum*, given to various plants reputed to be poisonous to dogs, chiefly of the orders *Asclepiadaceæ* and *Apocynaceæ*; now a book-name of the latter, and specifically of *Apocynum androsæmifolium*.

1597 GERARDE *Herbal* II. cccxxii. 755 Dogs bane is a deadly and dangerous plant, especially to fower footed beasts. **1726** *Dict. Rust.* etc. (ed. 3), *Dogs-bane*, an Herb so call'd because it kills Dogs. **1866** *Treas. Bot.*, *Dogbanes*, a name given by Lindley to the *Apocynaceæ*. *Dog's-bane*, a name for *Apocynum*; also *Aconitum Cynoctonum*.

'dog's body, dog's-body, dogsbody.

1. A sailor's name for dried pease boiled in a cloth; see also quot. 1924.

1818 'A. BURTON' *Adv. J. Newcome* ii. 76 I'll get you the Dog's-body Squeezer. **1858** GEN. P. THOMPSON *Audi Alt.* II. lxxviii. 33 What ungrateful sailors call by the harsh epithets of 'junk' and 'dog's body'. **1924** R. CLEMENTS *Gipsy of Horn* 38 Sea-biscuits soaked into a pulp with water and sugar, are known as 'dogs-body'.

2. A junior person, esp. one to whom a variety of menial tasks is given; a drudge, a general utility person. *colloq.*

1922 T. E. LAWRENCE *Lett.* (1938) 365 I'll have got used to being a dog's body. **1925** FRASER & GIBBONS *Soldier & Sailor Words* 80 Dogsbody, a Midshipman. A humorous semi-sarcastic colloquialism for any junior officer, R.N. *E.g.*, 'He's only a dogsbody sub'. **1928** *Daily Express* 3 Apr. 13/2 A midshipman is known..in the service as a 'snottie'. .. If he is a junior midshipman he is also a 'dog's body'. I defy anyone to be accurate and sentimental about a snottie who is a dog's body. **1932** H. SIMPSON *Boomerang* ix. 184 His post of dog's-body..left him no leisure at all. **1934** M. HODGE *Wind & Rain* II. i. 57 Oh, no. *I* don't understand anything! I'm just 'a dog's body'. **1942** M. DICKENS *One Pair of Feet* vii. 116 People who told me I should be a house-parlourmaid 'on Privates [*sc.* private wards]' had over-estimated. I was Dogsbody. **1950** L. A. G. STRONG *Which I Never* v. 169 As Assistant Stage Manager and general dog's body, she was grossly overworked and supremely happy. **1955** H. SPRING *These Lovers fled Away* vii. 205 My status was never defined. I was everybody's dog's-body. *Ibid.* xvii. 481 Introduced to a secretary whose dog's-body she was to be. **1967** *Listener* 14 Sept. 332/3, I was a sort of general dogsbody to begin with—assistant stage-manager, and what have you.

'dog's-ear, *sb.* [cf. next.]

1. The corner of a leaf of a book, etc. turned over like a dog's ear by constant or careless use, or to serve as a book-mark.

c **1725** ARBUTHNOT & POPE *Mem. P. P. Clerk of this Parish* (T.), I did make plain and smooth the dogs ears throughout our great bible. **1750** GRAY *Long Story* 68 Creased, like dogs-ears, in a folio. **1857** MRS. MATHEWS *Tea-Table Talk* II. 43 Dog's ears and other deteriorations..disgust the fastidious taste during perusal.

2. *U.S. Naut.* A small bight formed in the leech-rope of a sail in reefing, etc. *Hamersly's Nav. Encycl.* (1881).

1840 R. H. DANA *Bef. Mast* iv, The first [man] on the yard goes to the weather earing, the second to the lee, and the next two to the 'dog's ears'.

dog's-ear, *v.* Also dog-ear. [cf. prec.

So far as our evidence goes, the vb. is the earlier, the sense being evidently to make the leaf like the ear of a dog with its turned-down tip.]

trans. To damage or disfigure (a book, etc.) by turning or folding down the corners of the leaves.

a **1659** OSBORN *Misc.* To Rdr. (1673) 5 To ruffle, dogs-ear, and contaminate by base Language and spurious censures the choicest leaves. **1775** SHERIDAN *Rivals* I. ii, Lady Slattern Lounger..had so soiled and dogs'-eared it, it wa'n't fit for a Christian to read. **1886** J. R. REES *Divers. Bk.-worm* v. 174 [A] book..kept specially for Charles Lamb to finger and dog-ear when he came. **1891** E. GOSSE *Gossip in Library* xiii. 164 She did not dog's-ear her little library. **1903** *Westm. Gaz.* 8 Jan. 2/1 She dog-eared her book. **1940** R. STOUT *Over my Dead Body* xi. 150 He..dog-eared a page and closed the book.

Hence **dog's-eared (dog-eared)** *ppl. a.*

1784 COWPER *Tiroc.* 402 A dog's-ear'd Pentateuch. **1824** MACAULAY *Misc. Writ.* (1860) I. 125 The old schoolroom, the dog-eared grammar. **1840** DICKENS *Old C. Shop* xxiv, A few dog's-eared books upon a high shelf. **1844** —— *Chimes* 20 (Hoppe) The pockets of his trousers, very large and dog's-eared. **1895** M. PEMBERTON *Impregnable City* xv. 303 Dog-eared lilies.

dog's fennel, -grass: see DOG-F., DOG-G.

†dog's-head. *Obs.*

1. A dog-faced baboon: = DOG-HEAD 1.

1591 PERCIVALL *Sp. Dict.*, *Cabeça de perro*, dogs head.

2. A bad throw at dice: cf. *dog-chance, dog-throw* (DOG *sb.*[1] 20 a).

c **1620** FLETCHER & MASS. *Trag. Barnavelt* v. ii. in Bullen *O. Pl.* II. 304 Here are the dyce, and ile begin to ye..Dewce ace; a doggs-head!

3. A term of reproach or abuse [tr. Gr. κυνώπης].

1676 HOBBES *Iliad* I. 155 Whereof no notice (Dogshead) now you take.

dogship ('dɒgʃɪp). [f. DOG *sb.*[1] + -SHIP, after *lordship*, etc.] The personality of a dog.

1679 MRS. BEHN *Feigned Courtezans* III. i. Wks. 1724 II. 312 Yes, when your Dogship's damn'd. **1860** RUSKIN *Mod. Paint.* V. IX. iii. §21. 228 The dog..cannot understand..why she is allowed to stay, disturbing the family, and taking all their attention from his dogship.

dog-shore. Each of two blocks of timber used to prevent a ship from starting off the slips while the keel-blocks are being removed in preparation for launching.

1805 D. STEEL *Naval Archit.* II. 396 The dog-shores should be knocked down, each falling instantly. **1861** SALA *Dutch Pict.* xi. 171 The dogshores were knocked away, the frigate slid down her ways, and took the water. **1877** SPURGEON *Serm.* XXIII. 211 Useful as the scaffold to a house or the dogshores to a ship.

dog-skin. The skin of a dog, or the leather made from it; also applied to a kind of leather made from sheep-skin.

1731 A. HILL *Adv. Poets* Ep. 16 Or Mr. Lun may be out of his Dogskin? **1790** *Med. Commun.* II. 421 The whole..to be sheathed with thin dogskin. **1830** T. A. JONES *Trad. N. Amer. Ind.* II. 18 He threw the dog-skins into the fire.

b. *attrib.* Made of dog-skin.

1676 HOBBES *Iliad* (1677) 145 Meriones unto Ulysses gave His bow and quiver, sword and dogskin cap. **1710** STEELE *Tatler* No. 245 ¶2 Three Pair of oiled Dogskin Gloves.

†dog's-leather. *Obs.* [Cf. *neat's leather*.] Leather made of the skin of dogs; = prec.

1593 SHAKS. *2 Hen. VI*, IV. ii. 26 Hee shall haue the skinnes of our enemies, to make Dogges Leather of. **1611** COTGR., *Gans d'ocaigne*, Dogs leather gloues oyled in the inside to keepe the hands moist, and coole.

dog-sleep. [In reference to the light sleeping of dogs, and the difficulty of telling whether, when their eyes are shut, they are asleep or not.]

†1. Feigned or pretended sleep. *Obs.*

a **1613** OVERBURY *A Wife* (1638) 298 A jealous man sleepes dog-sleepes. *a* **1625** FLETCHER *Women Pleased* III. iv. **1711** ADDISON *Spect.* No. 184 ¶6 He is represented to have slept what the common People call a Dog's Sleep; or if his Sleep was real, his Wife was awake, and about her Business.

2. A light or fitful sleep, easily interrupted.

1708 MOTTEUX *Rabelais* IV. lxiii. (1737) 258 How one might avoid Dog-sleep. **1822** DE QUINCEY *Confess.* Wks. V. 163 My sleep was never more than what is called dog-sleep; so that I could hear myself moaning; and very often I was awakened suddenly by my own voice. **1867** SMYTH *Sailor's Word-bk.*, *Dog-sleep*, the uncomfortable fitful naps taken when all hands are kept up by stress.

dog's letter. [transl. L. *litera canina*, Persius.] A name for the letter R, as resembling in sound the snarl of a dog.

[**1592** SHAKS. *Rom. & Jul.* II. iv. 223 Doth not Rosemarie and Romeo begin both with a letter?.. Both with an R... A mocker! that's the dogs name.] **1636** B. JONSON *Eng. Gram.*, R is the dog's letter, and hurreth in the sound, the tongue striking the inner palate, with a trembling about the teeth. *a* **1670** HACKET *Abp. Williams* I. (1692) 55 Whose pamphlet is perpetuus Rhotacismus, one snarling Dogs-letter all over. **1830** *Westm. Rev.* XII. 356 There is only the difference of the dog's letter between friend and [fiend].

dog's-meat, dog's meat.

1. Food for dogs, prepared from horse-flesh or scraps of offal, etc., and sold by street dealers.

1593 NASHE *Strange News* Ep. Ded. Wks. 1883–4 II. 180 We haue cattes meate and dogges meate inough for these mungrels. **1812** COL. HAWKER *Diary* (1893) I. 54 The horses are scarcely good enough for dog's meat.

2. *transf.* and *fig.* Carrion; offal. ***to make dog's-meat of***: to kill and throw to the dogs.

1606 HIERON *Wks.* I. 43 Paul did account all things but dogs-meat, for the excellent knowledge sake of Christ Jesus. **1708** MRS. CENTLIVRE *Busie Body* v. iii, Rascals, retire; she's my Wife, touch her if you dare, I'll make Dogs-meat of you. **1837** MARRYAT *Dog-fiend* ii. (L.), Better die at once, than be made dog's meat of in this here way.

3. *attrib.*, as ***dog's-meat man***, a seller of dog's-meat.

1837 DICKENS *Pickw.* xxii, 'That's what I call a self-evident proposition, as the dog's-meat man said, when the house-maid told him he warn't a gentleman.'

dog's mercury, dog-: see MERCURY.

dog's nose, dog's-nose. A name given to a mixed liquor, compounded of beer and gin, or of ale and rum: see quots.

1812 J. H. VAUX *Flash Dict.* (Farmer). **1837** DICKENS *Pickw.* xxxiii, He is not certain whether he did not twice a week, for twenty years, taste 'dog's nose', which your committee find upon inquiry, to be compounded of warm porter, moist sugar, gin, and nutmeg. **1857** MRS. GASKELL *C. Bronte* (1862) 19 Rum, or ale, or a mixture of both called 'dog's nose'. **1863** —— *Sylvia's L.* III. 87 The serjeant.. brought up his own mug of beer, into which a noggin of gin had been put (called in Yorkshire 'dog's nose').

dog's-tail. Also dog-tail. [a transl. of Bot.L. *Cynosurus*, or Gr. κυνόσουρα.]

1. (Usually **dog's-tail grass.**) A genus of grasses, *Cynosurus*, the chief species of which is Crested Dog's-tail Grass, *C. cristatus*, so called because the flowers in each panicle all point one way, like the hairs of a dog's tail.

1753 CHAMBERS *Cycl. Supp.*, *Cynosurus*, dog's-tail, in botany, a kind of grass. **1759** B. STILLINGFL. *Misc. Tracts* (1775) 362 I have..given English names to them of my own invention... Dog's tail grass, crested. **1799** J. ROBERTSON *Agric. Perth* 208 Smooth stalked meadow-grass..and the crested dog-tail..are well adapted for dry pasture. **1806–7** A. YOUNG *Agric. Essex* (1813) I. 9 To harrow in grasses again in August..as crested dogstail, etc. **1961** R. W. BUTCHER *Brit. Flora* II. 957 The crested dogstail..is a very common plant in grassland throughout the British Isles.

2. A translation of Gr. κυνόσουρα, name of the constellation of the Little Bear: = CYNOSURE 1.

1867 SMYTH *Sailor's Word-bk.*, *Dog's tail*, a name for the constellation Ursa Minor or Little Bear.

'dog-star. [after the Gr. and L. names κύων, *canicula* (*canis*).]

1. The star Sirius, in the constellation of the Greater Dog, the brightest of the fixed stars. Also applied to Procyon (the Lesser Dog-star), a star of the first magnitude in the Lesser Dog.

The 'influence' of these, or of one of them, when rising nearly with the sun, was anciently supposed to cause excessive heat and other pernicious effects; see DOG-DAYS.

1579 E. K. *Gloss. Spenser's Sheph. Cal.* July 21 The Dogge starre, which is called Syrius, or Canicula reigneth. **1692** PRIOR *Ode Horace* III. ii. 26 Beneath the dog-star's raging heat. **1712** BUDGELL *Spect.* No. 425 ¶3 The Dog-star levelled his Rays full at his Head. **1842** *Penny Cycl.* XXII. 62 s.v. *Sirius*, In the Mediterranean latitudes, and in antient times, it was observed that the unhealthy and oppressive period coincided with the heliacal rising of the dog-star. We say *the* dog-star, without specifying whether it was Sirius or Procyon; it is uncertain which it was.

attrib. **1654** VILVAIN *Epit. Ess.* v. 50 Three Dog-star Suns in Sky somtimes are seen. **1843** MACAULAY *Lays Anc. Rome*,

Virginia 123 No fire when Tiber freezes, no air in dog-star heat.

†2. Humorously applied to a comet. *Obs.*

1712 SWIFT *Wond. Prophecy* Wks. 1755 III. I. 173 Lo! the comet appeareth!.. Think not that this baleful dog-star only shaketh his tail at you in waggery.

'dog-stone. A stone used for a millstone.

1640 in Entick *London* II. 170 Dog-stones, Marble-stones, Mill-stones, Quern-stones. **1812** J. SMYTH *Pract. of Customs* (1821) 234 Dog stones, not exceeding 4 feet in diameter, above 6 and under 12 inches in thickness,—the pair £6 3 6. **1858** SIMMONDS *Dict. Trade, Dog-stones*, rough, shaped or hewn pieces of stone imported to make millstones.

'dogstones. [transl. med.L. *Testiculvs canis* (Turner, Lyte); from the shape of the tubers.] A name for various British species of Orchis.

1597 GERARDE *Herbal* I. xcviii. 156. **1672-3** GREW *Anat. Roots* i. §8 (1682) 58 Some also have two or more Roots.. of which some are distinctly fastend to the bottome of the stalk, as in dogstones. **1773** *Gentl. Mag.* XLIII. 57 Salep is a preparation of the root of Orchis, or Dogstones.

'dog's-tongue. Also dog-. [transl. L. *cynoglossum* (Pliny), Gr. κυνόγλωσσον (Dioscorides).]

1. The genus *Cynoglossum* of boraginaceous plants, *esp.* the common species *C. officinale*; also called Hound's-tongue. (From the shape of the leaves.)

1530 PALSGR. 214/2 Doggestong or horehounde, an herbe. **1548** TURNER *Names of Herbes*, Cynaglossus the second of Plinie.. called in englishe Houndes tong or dogs tonge. **1570** LEVINS *Manip.* 167/12 Dogtong, *cynoglossus.* **1607** TOPSELL *Serpents* (1658) 730 The stalks of Dogs-tongue, the powder of the right horn of a Hart. **1860** READE *Cloister & H.* xciv, His remedies were 'womanish and weak'. Sage and wormwood.. dog's-tongue, our Lady's mantle, feverfew, and Faith, and all in small quantities except the last.

†2. A king of flat-fish, prob. *Platessa cynoglossus.*

1611 COTGR., *Pole*, the Sole-fish called a Dog's-tongue, or kind foole. **1708** MOTTEUX *Rabelais* IV. lx. (1737) 247 Dog's Tongue, or Kind-Fool.

dog's-tooth. Also dog-tooth. [transl. of med.L. *dens canis.*]

1. (Now **dog's** or **dog-tooth violet.**) The English name of the genus *Erythronium* of liliaceous plants, esp. *E. Dens-canis*, a garden plant with spotted leaves and purple flowers, which appear early in spring; so called from the teeth on the inner segments of the perianth.

1578 LYTE *Dodoens* II. xlv. 203 Dogges tooth.. hath for the most parte but two leaues, speckled with great redde spottes. **1629** PARKINSON *Paradisus* 194 It is most commonly called *Dens caninus*, and.. in English either Dogs tooth or Dogs tooth Violet. **1841** MRS. LOUDON *Ladies' Comp. Fl. Garden* 99 Dog's-tooth Violet.. is a pretty bulbous-rooted plant, with spotted leaves and purple flowers.

2. A species of grass, *Cynodon Dactylon.*

Sometimes erroneously given as a name for *Triticum caninum* (DOG-GRASS).

1600 SURFLET *Countrie Farme* I. x. 50 He shall.. plucke vp from them [the vines] the grasse called dogs tooth. **1830** *Withering's Brit. Pl.* (1837) 70 Creeping Dog's-tooth-grass. **1885** C. F. HOLDER *Marvels Anim. Life* 17 Bamboo, to which are attached bundles of fine dog's-tooth grass.

¶ See also DOG-TOOTH.

dog-tired, *a.* [See DOG *sb.*[1] 19 d.] As tired as a dog after a long chase; extremely tired, tired out.

1809-12 MAR. EDGEWORTH *Ennui* vi. Wks. 1832 VI. 47 Wretched little dog-tired creatures. **1813** JANE AUSTEN *Lett.* II. 211 It was 12 before we reached home. We were all dog-tired. **1861** HUGHES *Tom Brown at Oxf.* iii, I'm dog-tired of driving and doing the High Street.

dog-tooth. Also dog's-tooth.

1. A canine tooth or eye-tooth: see CANINE *a.* 2.

1382 [see DOGGY *a.* 1]. **1552** HULOET, Dogges teeth, *dentes canini.* **1594** T. B. *La Primaud. Fr. Acad.* II. 105 There are other twaine on each side, commonly called dogge-teeth. **1668** CULPEPPER & COLE *Barthol. Anat.* Man. IV. xii. 348 Cutters, Dog-teeth, and Grinders. **1731** ARBUTHNOT *Aliments* (J.), For dividing of flesh, sharp-pointed or dog-teeth. **1893** A. H. S. LANDOR *Hairy Ainu in Yezo* 233 Uncovering their fangs or dog teeth.

2. *dog-tooth spar*: a variety of calcareous spar, crystallizing in pointed scalenohedral forms.

1728 WOODWARD *Catal. Fossils* II. 78 They call it Dog-Tooth-Spar. **1823** H. J. BROOKE *Introd. Crystallogr.* 87 The dodecahedral variety of carbonate of lime, commonly called dog-tooth spar. **1860** PIESSE *Lab. Chem. Wonders* 33 Dogtooth crystals of carbonate of lime.

3. a. *Arch.* A pointed ornament or moulding suggesting the idea of a projecting tooth, frequent in early mediæval architecture. Also *attrib.*

1836 H. G. KNIGHT *Archit. Tour Normandy* 199 The most common mouldings are the billet.. star, rope, beak-head, dog-tooth. **1851** RUSKIN *Stones Ven.* I. xiv, English dogtooth moulding, whose sharp zigzag mingles richly with the curved edges of the tiling. *Ibid.* I. xx. §23 The four-sided pyramid.. is called in architecture a dogtooth. **1860** G. E. STREET in *Archæol. Cant.* III. 116 The label is enriched with dog-teeth. **1870** F. R. WILSON *Ch. Lindisf.* 167 Enriched with.. dogtooth ornament.

b. A broken check pattern used esp. for men's and women's suitings.

1948 *Evening Standard* 22 Mar. 6/3 A suit.. in fine dog's tooth worsted suiting. **1958** *Vogue* Jan. 41 The boldly checked tweed coat.. in brown dog's tooth checked over stone. **1958** *Spectator* 27 June 831/2 [He] displayed a certain raffish elegance in his long, dark jacket and dog-tooth trousers. **1960** *Times* 22 Feb. 13/1 A skirt of black and white dogstooth check.

4. (Also *dog's-tooth.*) 'A sharp steel punch used by marble-workers' (Knight *Dict. Mech.*).

5. *attrib. dog-tooth bit*: used as a rendering of L. *lupatum frenum*, a curb studded with jagged points like a wolf's teeth.

1894 GLADSTONE *Horace, Odes* I I His Gallic steed he doth not guide With dogtooth bit.

Hence **dog-tooth** *v. trans.*, to decorate with dog-tooth moulding: see 3.

1851 RUSKIN *Stones Ven.* I. xxiii. §12 It might easily have been dogtoothed, but the Byzantine architects had not invented the dogtooth. **1889** J. T. FOWLER *Notes on All Saints', Winterton* 11 The two [columns].. with dog-toothed, horizontal bands.

dog-tree. [app. as bearing DOG-BERRIES, q.v.; whence called by the early herbalists *dogberry-tree.*]

1. The Common Dogwood or Wild Cornel.

1548 TURNER *Names of Herbes* 30 *Cornus*.. The female is plentuous in Englande and the buchers make prickes of it, some cal it Gadrise or dog tree. **1613** PURCHAS *Pilgrimage* III. xvi. 326 The barke of the Cornell or dogge-tree.

2. Locally applied to the Spindle-tree, *Euonymus europæus*, the Elder, *Sambucus nigra*, and the Guelder-Rose, *Viburnum Opulus.*

1703 THORESBY *Let. to Ray* (E.D.S.), *Bur-tree*, an elder or dog-tree. **1878-86** BRITTEN & HOLLAND *Plant-n.*, Dog-tree..(2) *Euonymus europæus.* Warw. *Ibid.* App., Dog-tree, *Viburnum Opulus.* Warw.

dog-trick. ?*Obs.* A low or 'scurvy' trick; a treacherous or spiteful act; an ill turn.

c **1540** tr. *Pol. Verg. Eng. Hist.* (Camd. No. 36) 284, I will heere, in the way of mirthe, declare a prettie dog tricke or gibe as concerninge this mayden. **1577** HARRISON *England* III. ix. (1878) II. 64 Gewgaws for fooles, dogtricks for disards. **1612** T. JAMES *Jesuits' Downf.* 13 They haue sundrie other dogtricks of cousenage. **1690** DRYDEN *Don Sebast.* I. i, Learn better manners, or I shall serve you a dog-trick. **1803** *Times* in *Spirit. Pub. Jrnls.* (1804) VII. 364 Who scorns to resent that same dog-trick he play'd him.

dog-trot.

1. An easy trot like that of a dog.

1664 BUTLER *Hud.* II. ii. 754 They both advanc'd and rode A Dog-trot through the bawling Crowd. **1748** RICHARDSON *Clarissa* (1811) VII. 258, I hope that.. keeping on a good round dog-trot, I shall be able to overtake thee. **1861** C. BONER *Forest Creatures* 2 [The wild boar] setting off at his old dog-trot. **1868** LOSSING *Hudson* 11 Our Indian took the heaviest [boat].. and with a dog-trot bore it the whole distance.

attrib. **1830** C. CLARKE *3 Courses & Dessert* 116 Still came on at a dog-trot pace.

†b. *fig.* A steady or habitual course of action; a habit, 'way'. *Obs.* Cf. JOG-TROT.

1690 DRYDEN *Amphitryon* III. Wks. 1884 VIII. 54 I'll fall into my old dog-trot of lying again, if this must come of plain dealing. **1742** WARBURTON *Remarks Tillard* Wks. 1811 XI. 152 The common dog-trot of infidelity and free-thinking.

2. *lit.* A journey performed by dogs on the trot.

1856 KANE *Arct. Expl.* II. i. 12 A dog-trot of near one hundred miles, where your dogs may drop at any moment.

dog-vane. *Naut.*

1. 'A small vane made of thread, cork, and feathers, or buntin, placed on the weather gunwale to show the direction of the wind' (*Sailor's Word-bk.*).

1769 FALCONER *Dict. Marine* (1789), *Dog-Vane*, a small light vane, formed of a piece of pack-thread about two feet in length. **1829** MARRYAT *F. Mildmay* xiv, His head turned like a dog-vane in a gale of wind. **1859** O. W. HOLMES *Prof. Breakf.-t.* i, The fool's judgment is a dog-vane that turns with a breath.

attrib. **1825** H. B. GASCOIGNE *Nav. Fame* 51 The Dog-vane Staff the Quartermaster moves, The wind upon the Larboard Quarter proves.

2. 'Familiarly applied to a cockade.'

1785 GROSE *Dict. Vulgar Tongue*, *Dowse your dog vane*, take the cockade out of your hat. *a* **1814** DIBDIN *Bill Bobstay*, There's Nipcheese, the purser,.. The eddy of Fortune stands on a stiff breeze in, And mounts, fierce as fire, a dog-vane in his hat.

dog-violet. Also dog's violet. [transl. Bot.L.] The common name of *Viola canina* and other scentless species of wild violet. Originally merely a book-name; but now in general use.

1778 LIGHTFOOT *Flora Scot.* (1789) 508 *Viola canina.* Dog's Violet. **1801** *Withering's Brit. Plants* (ed. 4) II. 257 *V[iola] canina*, Dog's Violet. **1826** SCOTT *Woodst.* xxviii, Mistress Alice, whom I thought a very snow-drop, turned out a dog-violet! **1870** MORRIS *Earthly Par.* III. IV. 52 The pale dog-violet Late April bears.

'dogward, *adv.* (*adj.*): see -WARD.

dog-watch. *Naut.* [Cf. DOG-SLEEP.] The name given to the two short watches (of two hours each instead of four): see quot. 1840.

1700 S. L. tr. *Fryke's Voy. E. Ind.* 7 Count Maurice's Quarter hath the second Watch, and is also called the Dog-watch. **1836** E. HOWARD *R. Reefer* xxxii, About two bells in the first dog-watch the first-lieutenant decided upon furling the main-sail. **1840** R. H. DANA *Bef. Mast* iii. 5 The watch from four to eight p.m., is divided into two half, or dog-watches, one from four to six, and the other from six to eight. By this means they divide the twenty-four hours into seven watches instead of six, and thus shift the hours every night.

dog-weary, *a.* = DOG-TIRED.

1596 SHAKS. *Tam. Shr.* IV. ii. 60 O Master, master I haue watcht so long, That I am dogge-wearie. **1699** R. L'ESTRANGE *Colloq. Erasm.* (1711) 120, I was so Dog-weary of sitting. **1825** LOCKHART in *Scott's Fam. Lett.* (1894) II. 323 We are.. dog-weary every night.

dog-whelk. [See WHELK.] A member of the marine mollusc family Nassariidæ, esp. *Nassarius reticulatus*; also = *dog-winkle* (*s.v.* DOG *sb.*[1] 20 c).

1856 GOSSE *Marine Zool.* II. 129 *Nassa*, Dog-whelk. **1882** *Standard* 26 Sept. 2/2 The dog-whelk.. is likewise a great enemy to the [cockle]. **1901** E. STEP *Shell Life* xv. 257 The Dog-whelks (*Nassa*) are almost as well-known as the Purples. **1960** J. A. C. NICOL *Biol. Marine Animals* xi. 487 Another interesting case is the dog-whelk *Nucella lapillus.* **1968** N. F. MCMILLAN *Brit. Shells* 50 *Nucella lapillus*... Dog Whelk. *Ibid.* 53 Nassariidæ, or dog-whelks, are scavengers. *Ibid.*, *Nassarius reticulatus*... Dog-whelk.

dog-whip. A whip for chastising or driving a dog. Cf. *horsewhip.*

1563-87 FOXE *A. & M.* (1631) III. xii. 852/1 They did whip him about the Market with a dogge-whip, hauing three cords. **1677** MARVELL *Arg. New Parl.* Wks. 1776 II. 565 A cowardly baffled sea captain.. once whipped with a dog whip.

attrib. **1871** TENNYSON *Last Tourn.* 58 His visage ribb'd.. with dogwhip-weals.

dog-whipper.

1. An official formerly employed to whip dogs out of a church or chapel. Locally retained, as an appellation of a sexton or beadle.

1592 NASHE *P. Penilesse* Wks. (1883-4) 127 It were verie good the dogwhipper in Paules would haue a care of this. **1721** *Audit-Bk. Christ's Coll.* in Willis & Clark *Cambridge* (1886) III. 520 Paid Salmon the Dogwhipper a year ending at Mich. last 1. 0. 0. **1869** *Lonsdale Gloss.*, *Dog-whipper*, a church beadle. **1887** *Kentish Gloss.*, *Dog-whipper*, the beadle of a church, whose duty it was, in former days, to whip the dogs out of church. **1888** in *Sheffield Gloss.*

2. Humorously applied to a university proctor in allusion to his 'bull-dogs'.

1789 J. WOLCOTT (P. Pindar) *Subj. for Paint.* Wks. 1812 II. 204 Attended by each Dog-whipper called Proctor.

dog-wolf. [See DOG *sb.*[1] 18 b.] 1. A male wolf.

1557 NORTH *Gueuara's Diall Pr.* 114 b/2 Which yͤ dogge wolfe doth prouide both for the byche and her whealpes. **1674** JOSSELYN *Voy. New Eng.* 22 When the Wolves have kill'd a beast.. not a Dog-Wolf amongst them offers to eat any of it, till the she-Wolves have fill'd their paunches. **1787** *Phil. Trans.* LXXVII. 255, I happened to see a Dog-wolf.

2. = WOLF-DOG 2.

1907 *Kennel Encycl.* I. 159 At a dog show at Spa, in 1882, several 'Dog-wolves' were exhibited, and the animals so termed in the catalogue.

dogwood ('dɒgwʊd). [lit. *wood* of the DOG-TREE, q.v.]

1. The Wild Cornel, *Cornus sanguinea*, a shrub common in woods and hedgerows in the south of England, with dark red branches, greenish-white flowers, and dark purple berries.

[Turner calls it *dogberry tree*; Lyte 'Wilde Cornell tree, Houndes tree, and Hounde berie, or Dogge berie tree, and the Pricke timber tree, because Butchers vse to make prickes of it'.]

1617 MINSHEU *Ductor Ling.*, The Dogges tree, dogge-wood, or wilde cherrie tree, which Butchers make prickes of. **1753** CHAMBERS *Cycl. Supp.* s.v. *Cornus*, The dogwood, or dogberry-tree. **1824** MISS MITFORD *Village* Ser. I. (1863) 21 Promontories of dog-wood. **1859** W. S. COLEMAN *Woodlands* (1862) 124 The Dogwood, or Wild Cornel.

b. Applied to other species of the genus *Cornus*; *esp.*, in N. America, to *C. florida*, a tree bearing large white or pink flowers, and scarlet berries.

1676 T. GLOVER *Acc. of Virginia* in *Phil. Trans.* XI. 628. **1699** *Phil. Trans.* XXI. 437 We have also plenty of Pine, and Dog-wood, which is a fine Flower-bearing-Tree. **1859** LONGF. *Hyperion* II. i, The dog-wood, robed in the white of its own pure blossoms. **1877** W. MATTHEWS *Ethnogr. Hidatsa* 27 These Indians seldom use tobacco alone, but mix it with the dried inner bark of one or more species of dogwood, *Cornus stolonifera* and *C. sericea.*

2. Applied to various other shrubs and trees. a. In Jamaica, various species of *Piscidia*, a genus of leguminous trees; in New South Wales, a leguminous shrub, *Jacksonia scoparia*; in Tasmania, the shrub or small tree *Bedfordia salicina* (N.O. *Compositæ*). b. Locally and improperly applied in England to the Spindle-tree, Alder Buckthorn, Bird-Cherry, Guelder Rose, and Woody Nightshade. (Britten & Holland.) c. With defining words: **black dogwood**, Bird-Cherry, Alder Buckthorn, and *Piscidia carthaginensis.* **poison dogwood**, the Poison Sumach of N. America (*Rhus venenata*). **pond dogwood**, *Cephalanthus occidentalis* of Louisiana (Miller *Plant-n.*). **striped dogwood**, *Acer pennsylvanicum.* **white dogwood**, Guelder-Rose and *Piscidia Erythrina.*

1725 SLOANE *Jamaica* II. 275 Another sort of fishing they had with the bark of the tree called Dogwood [*Piscidia Erythrina*], which being bruised and put into standing waters.. intoxicated [the fishes]. **1838** LOUDON *Arboretum*

496 *Euonymus Europæus*.. It is called Dogwood, because a decoction of its leaves was used to wash dogs, to free them from vermin. **1847** LEICHHARDT *Jrnl.* i. 11 Ironbark ridges here and there.. with dogwood (Jacksonia).. diversified the sameness. **1866** *Treas. Bot.* 132 B[*edfordia*] *salicina*, the Dogwood of Tasmania, has beautifully marked wood, suitable for cabinet-work. **1867** *Ure's Dict. Arts* (1875) II. 764 The woods yielding good powder charcoals are black alder, poplar, spindle tree, black dogwood, and chestnut. **1878** BRITTEN & HOLLAND *Plant-n.*, Dogwood..(3) *Rhamnus Frangula*. The 'dogwood' used in the manufacture of gunpowder is produced by this shrub. *Hants.*

3. The wood of any of these; *esp.* that of *Cornus sanguinea*, which is close and smooth-grained.

1664 EVELYN *Sylva* I. xx. (1729) 108 Wild-cornel, or Dog-wood, good to make Mill-Cogs, Pestles, Bobins for Bonelace, Spokes for Wheels, &c. **1696** *Lond. Gaz.* No. 3206/4 Angle-Rods made of Foreign Dogwood. **1859** FAIRHOLT *Tobacco* (1876) 192 The tube is of dogwood such as butcher's skewers are made of. **1875** *Ure's Dict. Arts* II. 69 *Dog-wood, cornus sanguinea*.. Little splinters of this wood are used by the watch-maker for cleaning out the pivot-holes of watches, and by the optician for cleaning deeply-seated small lenses. Its peculiarity is that it is remarkably free from silex. Toothpicks are also manufactured from dog-wood. **1867, 1878** [see 2].

4. *attrib.*

1707 SLOANE *Jamaica* I. p. xii, Negroes take them [fish] by intoxicating them with Dogwood bark. **1769** W. STORK *Acc. E. Florida* 46 The ash, locust, and dog-wood-trees are here in abundance. **1875** *Ure's Dict. Arts* II. 69 *Dog-wood Bark*, the bark of the *Cornus florida*..much used in the United States as a substitute for Peruvian bark.

dogy: see DOGIE.

dohickey, var. DOOHICKEY.

dohter, -or, -ur, obs. forms of DAUGHTER.

‖**doigté** (dwate). *Fencing.* [Fr., f. *doigt* finger, DIGIT *sb.*] Fingering; the use of the fingers (see quots.) Also *fig.*

1889 POLLOCK et al. *Fencing* i. 51 The proper use of the thumb and fingers, called *doigté*, is of the greatest importance in fencing. **1931** F. C. REYNOLDS *Book of Foil* viii. 131 *Finger play or 'doigté'*. In describing the various movements of attack and parry, stress has been laid on the importance of directing the point mainly by the action of the thumb and forefinger. *Ibid.* 210 *Doigté*, the control of the point by the action of the thumb and forefinger. **1958** *Spectator* 4 July 27/2 Something missing in him as a politician, some lack in *doigté*.

doil(e, obs. var. of DOLE *sb.*², grief, mourning.

doiled, doilt (dɔɪld, dɔɪlt), *ppl. a. Sc.* Also (*north. dial.*) deyl'd, deylt. [cf. DOLD.] Stupid; foolish, crazed; affected in mind.

1513 DOUGLAS *Æneis* VIII. vi. 16 As thir beistis, or the doillit as, Thair fuid of treis did in woddis fet. **1606** BIRNIE *Kirk-Buriall* (1833) 34 It was long held as indifferent in the doylde dayes. **1659** MACALLO *Can. Physick* 23 When the body becomes heavy, lazy and doiled. **1786** BURNS *Scotch Drink* xv, Mony a poor, doylt, druken hash. **1814** SCOTT *Wav.* xxx, Ye doil'd dotard.

Hence **'doiledness**, stupidity, dullness.

1588 A. KING tr. *Canisius' Catech., Cert. Deuot Prayers* 23 O God, mak me lauly without feignednes, mirrie without lightnes, grave without doildenes.

doilful, obs. form of DOLEFUL.

doily ('dɔɪlɪ), *sb.* or *a.* Also doiley, doyly, -ley, *erron.* d'Oyley, d'oylie. [from personal surname *Doiley* or *Doyley*.

1712 BUDGELL *Spect.* No. 283 ⁋18 The famous Doily is still fresh in every one's Memory, who raised a Fortune by finding out Materials for such Stuffs as might at once be cheap and genteel. **1727** SIR H. SLOANE in *Phil. Trans.* XXXIV. 222 Mr. Doyly, (who was a great searcher after Curiosities, and gave Name to a sort of Stuffs worn in Summer). **1750–1800** PEGGE *MS. Note* (Skeat, *Philol. Trans.* 1885, 91) Doyley kept a Linnen-draper's shop in the Strand, a little West of Catherine Street.]

†**1.** *attrib.* or *adj.* The name of a woollen stuff, 'at once cheap and genteel', introduced for summer wear in the latter part of the 17th c. *Obs.*

1678 DRYDEN *Kind Keeper* IV. i, Some Doily Petticoats, and Manto's we have. **1697** *Lond. Gaz.* No. 3293/4 A sad colour Doyly Drugget new Coat. **1712** ARBUTHNOT *John Bull* I. vi, His children were reduced from rich silks to Doily stuffs. **1713** ADDISON *Guardian* No. 102 ⁋2 Summer has often caught me in my Drap de Berry, and winter in my Doily suit. **1714** GAY *Trivia* I. 43 Now in thy trunk the D'oily habit fold, The silken drugget ill can fence the cold.

2. a. *sb.* (Originally **doily-napkin**.) A small ornamental napkin used at dessert.

1711 SWIFT *Jrnl. to Stella* 23 Apr., After dinner we had coarse Doiley-napkins, fringed at each end, upon the table to drink with. **1785–95** WOLCOTT (P. Pindar) *Lousiad* II. Wks. I. 243 Who dares with Doylies des'perate war to wage. **1798** *Gentl. Mag.* LXVIII. II. 755/2 Thus also the small table napkin called a *D'Oyley*. **1802** S. ROGERS in Clayden *Early Life* (1887) 437 After dinner [in Paris] she threw about her some ugly and dirty English doyleys, which she also explained as the English fashion, and of which I felt quite ashamed. **1855** HT. MARTINEAU *Autobiog.* (1877) I. 68, I had been picking at the fringe of my doily.

b. A small ornamental mat made of paper, linen, etc., used on a plate beneath sandwiches, cakes, etc.

1864 *Hist. North-Western Soldiers' Fair* 89 [Donations] 2 cake doylies. **1905** 'P. PENNINGTON' *Woman Rice Planter* (1913) 197 You fill a basket, put a dainty doily over it. **1936** W. HOLTBY *South Riding* IV. ii. 218 The cheese cakes and lemon tarts lay on frilled netted d'oylies. **1954** J. BETJEMAN *Few Late Chrysanthemums* 95 Beg pardon, I'm soiling the doileys With afternoon tea-cakes and scones. **1958** *Times* 12 Nov. 3/4 His [*sc.* Magritte's] little painting of a figure cut out of a paper doily about to smash the head of another paper-doily figure between two very solid rocks.

doing ('duːɪŋ), *vbl. sb.* [f. DO *v.* + -ING¹.]

1. a. The action of the verb DO; action, proceeding, conduct; performance or execution *of* something. Esp. in colloq. phr. ***to take a bit of*** (or ***lot of, some***) ***doing***: to require all one's efforts; to be difficult to do.

c **1325** *Song Mercy* 129 in *E.E.P.* (1862) 122 In vre doinge. *c* **1460** FORTESCUE *Abs. & Lim. Mon.* ix, This maner off doynge hath be so ofte practised. *a* **1533** LD. BERNERS *Huon* c. 327 In the doynge is all the mater. **1638** Z. BOYD *Zion's Flowers* (1855) Introd. 40 It shall not be called your.. doeing, what shall be done..by another. **1722** WOLLASTON *Relig. Nat.* iv. 62 The faculties..necessary to the doing of any thing. **1842** TENNYSON *St. Simeon Stylites* 121 'Tis their own doing; this is none of mine. **1936** *Discovery* Oct. 332/2 The pain and swelling combined to knock Amundsen completely out for some time. And that took a lot of doing. **1964** L. NKOSI *Rhythm of Violence* II. ii. 31 *Kitty*...Did everything go according to plan? *Jimmy*. Took a bit of doing, but with talent and extremely good sense on our part we pulled it off. **1969** *Time* 28 Feb. 49 His long-suffering wife..and their six kids put up with him, which takes some doing.

b. *euphem.* Copulation.

1601 SHAKS. *All's Well* II. iii. 246. *a* **1637** B. JONSON tr. *Fragm. Petron. Arbiter* Wks. (Rtldg.) 740. **1675** COTTON *Scoffer Scoft* 117. **1869** HAZLITT *Eng. Prov.* 105.

c. A scolding; a thrashing, beating-up; a severe monetary loss. *dial.* and *colloq.*

1880 W. H. PATTERSON *Gloss. Antrim & Down* 31 *Doing off*, a scolding. **1888** G. BIDWELL *Forging his Chains* xxxviii. 418 Punishment for violence against any prison authority.. three dozen strokes of the flesh-cutting cat-o'- nine tails,.. besides the *ex officio* preliminary 'doing' by the warders. **1897** W. S. MAUGHAM *Liza of Lambeth* xi. 209 She 'as give yer a doin';..an' look at yer eye! **1909** J. R. WARE *Passing Eng.* 113/2 I've had a bad doing this week—lost thirty quid. **1923** *Hansard Commons* 13 July 1782 The hon. Member for Dundee..has given me a tremendous doing. **1959** *Times* 19 Mar. 5/5 The cops gave me a doing. **1968** B. TURNER *Sex Trap* xvii. 167 'For God's sake, man! You'd get three years if you give him a doing,' she exclaimed.

2. That which is done; a deed, act, action, performance, transaction, proceeding, piece of business. Usually (now always) in *pl.*

App. little used in 18th c.; Johnson says 'now only used in a ludicrous sense, or in low, mean language'.

c **1385** CHAUCER *L.G.W.* 1681 *Lucretia*, Th' exilynge of kynges Of Rome for here orible doinges. **1440** J. SHIRLEY *Dethe K. James* (1818) 21 That horribile doyng and faite.. at [= that] the said traitours hadde done. **1548–9** (Mar.) *Bk. Com. Prayer, Morning Prayer*, That al our doinges may be ordred by thy gouernaunce. **1603** SHAKS. *Meas. for M.* IV. i. 63 Volumes of report Run..Vpon thy doings. **1611** BIBLE *Prov.* xx. 11 Even a child is known by his doings. **1667** MILTON *P.L.* XI. 720 A Reverend Sire..of thir doings great dislike declar'd. **1799** J. JAY *Corr. & Papers* (1893) IV. 259 Our conversation here turns so much on Great Britain and (as some phrase it) her doings. **1816** SCOTT *Antiq.* xlii, You'll do this poor ruined family the best day's doing that has been done them since Redhand's days. **1818** KEATS *Let.* 13 Jan. (1958) I. 205 Lawk! Molly there's been such doings. **1825** COLERIDGE *Lett. Convers. etc.* II. 212 My thoughts, wishes, and prayers follow you in all your doings and strivings. **1923** KIPLING *Irish Guards in Gt. War* I. 216 The talk in the camps turned on great doings—everything connected with the front line was 'doings'. **1949** E. POUND *Pisan Cantos* lxxx. 92 Stewing with rage Concerning the landlady's *doings* with a lodger unnamed.

3. with adverbs or adverbial phrases: see DO *v.*

c **1340** HAMPOLE *Prose Tr.* 12 Consaile es doynge awaye of worldes reches, and of all delytes of all thyngez þat mane may be tagyld with. **1483** *Cath. Angl.* 103/1 A Doynge welle, *beneficencia*. **1814** COL. HAWKER *Diary* (1893) I. 122 The house was shabby for want of new doing up.

4. *pl.* **a.** Materials for a specified adjunct of a dish or meal; also, a made or fancy dish. *U.S. local.*

1838 E. FLAGG *Far West* II. 72 'Well, stranger, what'll ye take: wheat-bread and chicken fixens, or corn-bread and common doins?' by the latter..being signified bacon. **1843** 'R. CARLTON' *New Purchase* II. xl. 58 A snug breakfast of chicken fixins, eggs, ham-doins, and corn slapjacks. **1859** *Knickerbocker* LIII. 317 Tell Sal to..have some flour-doins and chicken-fixins for the stranger. *Ibid.* 318 Instead of 'store-tea' they had only saxifrax tea-doins, without milk. **1880** J. C. HARRIS *Uncle Remus* i. 18 Sposen' you drap roun' termorrer an' take dinner wid me. We ain't got no great doin's at our house, but I speck de old 'oman..kin sorter scramble roun' 'en git up sump'n. **1908** *Dialect Notes* III. IV. 306 *Doing(s)*,..prepared dishes, especially fancy dishes.

b. *U.S. colloq.* Lace, trimming, ornaments, etc., of a dress.

a **1847** W. T. PORTER *Quarter Race Kentucky* 84 [The girls] came pourin out of the woods.., fixed out in all sorts of fancy doins, from the broad-striped homespun to the sun-flower calico. **1856** *Knickerbocker* XLVII. 406 Pretty girl that in the black fixings and white arrangements, with blue doings.

c. Applied to any concomitant, adjunct, or 'etcetera', or anything that happens to be 'about' or to be wanted. orig. *War slang.*

1919 *Athenæum* 25 July 664/2 'Doings', practically anything: 'Pass the doings.' **1925** FRASER & GIBBONS *Soldier & Sailor Words* 80 *Doings, the*, a word with every kind of meaning and application. *E.g.*, In quarters, 'Pass the doings', might mean bread, salt, a pack of cards, or anything at hand. 'I'll have a drop of the doings' (*i.e.*, whatever drink there is going). 'Here comes Jerry with the doings' (*i.e.*, an enemy aeroplane sighted). **1927** W. E. COLLINSON *Contemp. Eng.* 101 Doings for gravy, salt, sugar, pepper, milk or anything wanted at a particular time for a particular purpose. *a* **1935** T. E. LAWRENCE *Mint* (1955) II. xvi. 144 Cook chuckled, snatched somebody's blacking-tin and with three swift passes of a boot-brush painted his doings jet-black. **1938** G. GREENE *Brighton Rock* V. i. 193 Her skirt drawn up above her knees she waited for him with luxurious docility... 'You've got the doings, haven't you?' **1938** S. V. BENÉT *Thirteen o'Clock* 248 He's got a little doin's of a black moustache.

doing ('duːɪŋ), *ppl. a.* [f. as prec. + -ING².] That does, acts, performs, etc. (see DO *v.*); *spec.* actively engaged or occupied, busy; energetic.

1576 FLEMING *Panopl. Epist.* 308 One while I wil be doing with this booke, another while with that. **1591** PERCIVALL *Sp. Dict.*, *Rebuelto, cavallo rebuelto*..a lustie doing horse. **1646** BP. MAXWELL *Burden Issachar* in *Phenix* (1708) II. 273 The active and doing men. **1792** LD. GRENVILLE in Lecky *Eng. in 18th C.* (1887) VI. 54 All that the most doing Government could do in twenty years.

†**dois.** *Sc. Obs.* [app. related to early mod.Du. *doesen* to strike with force and noise: cf. DUSH.] Shock (of bodies meeting); crash.

1535 STEWART *Cron. Scot.* (1856) II. 118 With sic ane dois togidder that tha draif, Quhill all their scheildis into pecis raif.

doit (dɔɪt). Also 7 doite, doyt. [a. early mod.Du. *duit* (in MDu. also *duyt, deuyt, doyt, deyt*), whence also Ger. *deut*. Of uncertain derivation. Kluge and Franck identify it with Norse *þveit* piece cut off, small piece of land, a unit of weight, a small coin, f. *þvíta* to cut.]

1. A small Dutch coin formerly in use, the eighth part of a stiver, or the half of an English farthing; hence (chiefly in negative phrases) as the type of a very small or trifling sum. (Cf. DENIER³.)

Also called *doitkin* or DODKIN (q.v.); it had illegal currency in England in the 15th c. It was prob. originally of silver, and afterwards of base silver; finally it was of copper.

1594 NASHE *Unfort. Trav.* 5 The pore man might haue his moderate draught..for his doit or his dandiprat. **1610** SHAKS. *Temp.* II. ii. 33 They will not giue a doit to relieue a lame Begger. **1630** J. TAYLOR (Water P.) *Wks.* Aa iij a/1 (Stanf.) They are monstrous thriuers, Not like the Dutchmen in base Doyts and Stiuers. **1638** BP. SANDERSON *Serm.* II. 104 We disburs'd not a mite, not a doyt towards it. **1755** SMOLLETT *Quix.* (1803) IV. 224, I print for profit, without which, reputation is not worth a doit. **1784** COWPER *Task* v. 316. **1850** CARLYLE *Latter-d. P.* ii. (1872) 72 Every doit of the account..will have to be settled one day.

b. Transferred to various small coins.

1728 *Episc. Ch. Rec.* in Cramond *Ann. Banff* (1893) II. 158 In French dytts and lettered bodles £9. 11. 8. **1744** *Ibid.* 159 The Thesaurer cannot get disposed of the doits belonging to the Chapel. **1882** BITHELL *Counting-ho. Dict.* (1893) 100 *Doit*, a Hindostan copper coin, 120 to a rupee. **1893** CRAMOND *Ann. Banff* II. 158 The doits on hand in 1739 were sold for £12 18*s.* Sc., and in 1743 the discount on doits..at four for a halfpenny amounted to £7 5*s.* Sc.

2. *transf.* and *fig.* A very small piece or part *of* anything; *absol.* a very little, a bit, a jot; *esp.* in phr. ***not to care a doit.***

1660 FISHER *Rusticks Alarm* Wks. (1679) 341 Many Holy Prophets Writings are lost, but not a Doit of the Doctrine. **1695** CONGREVE *Love for L.* III. v, He does not care a doit for your person. *a* **1734** NORTH *Exam.* I. ii. §83 (1740) 74 No Doit of that appears from him. **1849** MRS. CARLYLE *Lett.* II. 94 As if anybody out of the family of Friends cared a doit about W. Penn.

'doited, *a. Sc.* [Of uncertain origin: perh. a variant of DOTED. As the *oi*, however, is here a true diphthong, the form is to be distinguished from Sc. words in which *oi* was merely a fashion of spelling long *ō*.]

Having the faculties impaired, esp. by age.

c **1425** WYNTOUN *Cron.* v. xii. 4041 The doytyd dwynys off that land. **15..** *Dunbar's Tua mariit Wemen* 377 (Jam.) Full doitit was his heid [*S.T.S. ed. reads* dotit]. *a* **1605** POLWART *Flyting w. Montgomerie* 36 At mens command that laikes ingyne, Quhilke, doytted dyvours! gart thee dyte them. **1787** BURNS *Brigs of Ayr* 144 For a doited monkish race. **1823** LAMB *Elia* Ser. II. *N. Year's Coming of Age*, Which plainly shewed her old head to be little better than crazed and doited. **1825** SCOTT *Fam. Lett.* 11 Oct. (1894) II. 351 Old friends left in the bloom of youth have.. become..doited old bodies.

doitkin: see DODKIN.

ˌdo-it-your'self. [See DO *v.* 11 and YOURSELF *pron.* 3.] The action or practice of doing work of any kind by oneself, esp. one's own household repairs and maintenance, usu. as opposed to employing someone else to do it. Also *transf.* and *fig.* Freq. *attrib.* or as *adj.* Abbreviated as *D.I.Y.* Hence **ˌdo-it-him'self, ˌdo-it-your'selfer, ˌdo-it-your'selfism**, and various other nonce derivatives.

[**1616** T. DRAXE *Bibliotheca Scholastica* 163/1 If a man will haue his businesse well done, he must doe it himselfe. **1693** W. PENN *Some Fruits of Solitude* (ed. 2) 66 Have but little to do, and do it thy self. *a* **1845** BARHAM *Ingol. Leg.* (1905) 288 If it's business of consequence, *Do it yourself!* **1925** D. BEARD (*title*) Do it yourself. A book of the big outdoors. **1949** *Here & Now* (N.Z.) Oct. 17/3 Husbands who have been brought up in the do-it-all-myself tradition of the previous generation.] **1952** *Time* 30 June 45/3 Do-it-yourself has brought similar gains, and market shifts, to other industries. **1954** *N.Y. Herald Tribune* 21 Mar. IV. 17/5 There are other reasons, too, for the tidal wave of do-it-yourselfism. **1954** *N.Y. Times* 5 Sept. F1/7 To the do-it-yourselfer, plywood is as essential as paint, tools, plastics and ordinary lumber. **1955** *Pract. Householder* Dec. 203/1 A central pool such as a 'D.I.Y. Club' from which.. tools can be hired is the obvious advantage. **1957** *Times* 12 Nov. (Canada Suppl.) p. xv/4 Canadian males are great devotees of do-it-yourself. **1957** *Financial Times Ann. Rev. Brit. Industry* 51/1 A country planning a nuclear power programme has a choice of two routes: do-it-yourself and the ready-made. **1958** *Spectator* 4 July 13/2 The builder is shoving up his do-it-himself boxes. **1959** *Manch. Guardian* 13 Aug. 5/4 The.. do-it-yourself kit, complete with all necessary screws, bolts, nuts and instruction chart. **1959** V. PACKARD *Status Seekers* (1960) 76 Trimming hedges or repairing screen doors or other delights of the do-it-yourself. **1965** *Spectator* 5 Mar. 293/1 The whole of the artistic world has been debauched by the hogwash of the do-it-yourself vogue. **1966** *Guardian* 16 May 6/4 Do-it-yourselfers have been enthusiastic about.. adhesive vinyl tiles. **1966** *Listener* 24 Nov. 781/2 This chamber-music is a universe away from the stuttering *simplesse* of do-it-yourself Hemingway. **1969** *Daily Tel.* 4 Oct. 11/1 For families or parties of young people especially, who don't mind a little do-it-yourselfing, this sort of holiday is usually memorable. **1970** F. MCKENNA *Gloss. Railwaymen's Talk* 34 *Do-it-yourself kit*, diesel-age term for steam locomotives. The arrival of the diesel locomotive.. consigned the steam locomotive to the level of a do-it-yourself kit. **1970** *Guardian* 30 July 9/6 A DIY inflatable dome kit.. for £30.

‖**dojo** ('dəʊdʒəʊ, 'dəʊʒəʊ). [Japanese.] **a.** A room or hall in which judo is practised.

1942 P. LONGHURST *Jiu-Jitsu* (new ed.) 7 The *dojos*, or Judo gymnasia, would be littered with casualties. **1964** 'J. MUNRO' *Man who sold Death* iii. 27 Hakagawa's dojo, the gymnasium which was his classroom.

b. In full *dojo mat*. A padded mat on which judo is practised.

1966 P. O'DONNELL *Sabre-Tooth* iii. 41 The *dojo*, the padded mat spread in the centre of the long combat room. **1967** 'J. MUNRO' *Money that Money can't Buy*. i. 11 Their practice sessions on the dojo mat. *Ibid.* xiii. 162 In one corner.. was a dojo—a judo practice mat.

dokan, -en, obs. forms of DOCKEN.

doke (dəʊk). Now only *dial.* Also 7–8 doak. [perh. originally *dolk*, var. of DALK², DAWK: cf. EFris. *dölke* small hollow, dimple; see also DOLK.] A hollow, depression; a dint; a dimple.

1615 CROOKE *Body of Man* 621 The doke or dimple in the middest of the chin. **1674** RAY *S. & E.C. Words* 64 *Doke*, a deep Dint or furrow. **1674** N. FAIRFAX *Bulk & Selv.* 130 His two forefeet, which he had thrust so into the soft of her sides, as to make two deep doaks there. **1705** *Lond. Gaz.* No. 4156/4 Stolen.. a.. Mare.. with a Doke in her Skull over her right Eyebrow four inches long. **1866** *Spectator* 20 Jan. 72 The little doke in the end of the nose.

doke, obs. form of DUCK, DUKE.

doket, obs. form of DOCKET, DUCAT.

do'ketic, 'Doketism, etc., forms preferred by some to DOCETIC, DOCETISM, etc., as truer phonetic representatives of the Greek. See K.

1877 EADIE *Comm. Thess.* 149 The apostle had his eye on Doketic views. **1882** CAVE & BANKS tr. *Dorner's Chr. Doctr.* III. 206 The finest form of Doketism. **1882–3** SCHAFF *Encycl. Relig. Knowl.* I. 445 The doketistic Gnostics.

dokimastic, -asy, var. ff. DOCIMASTIC, -ASY.

dol (dəʊl). [f. L. *dolor* pain: see DOLOUR.] A unit of intensity of pain.

1947 J. D. HARDY et al. in *Jrnl. Clinical Investigation* XXVI. 1158/1 A scale of pain intensity is proposed, the unit of which is called a 'dol', composed of 2 just perceptible steps in discrimination of stimulus intensity. **1957** [see DOLORIMETER]. **1962** J. D. HARDY in Keele & Smith *Assessment of Pain in Man & Animals* 194 Above 8 dols, however, the intensity of pain no longer increases rapidly with skin temperature. **1964** KEELE & ARMSTRONG *Substances producing Pain & Itch* iii. 32 On this scale 'ceiling' pain intensity has a value of 10½ dols.

dol, obs. form of DAL, DOLE, DULL.

'dolabrate, *a. Bot.* [f. L. *dolābra* (see next) + -ATE².] = DOLABRIFORM. *Syd. Soc. Lex.* 1883.

†**do'labre.** *Obs. rare.* [ad. L. *dolābra* mattock, pickaxe, f. *dolāre* to chip, hew; prob. immediately from an identical OF. form.] An adze.

1474 CAXTON *Chesse* III. ii. E vj b, The carpenters ben signefyed by the dolabre or squyer.

dolabriform (dəʊ'læbrɪfɔːm), *a.* [f. L. *dolābra* pickaxe + *forma* shape, form: cf. F. *dolabriforme*.] Axe-shaped, cleaver-shaped; in *Bot.* applied to fleshy leaves having one side thick and straight, the other sharp and convex, as in *Mesembryanthemum dolabriforme*. Also, in *Entom.*, to joints of antennæ or other parts of a similar form.

1753 CHAMBERS *Cycl. Supp.*, Botany Tab. 2 Distinctions of the Leaves.. Dolabriform. **1819** *Pantologia*, *Dolabriform* .. in botany, an axe or hatchet-shaped leaf.. Compressed, roundish, obtuse.. with a sharp edge, roundish below. **1828** STARK *Elem. Nat. Hist.* II. 294 Palpi.. terminated by a dolabriform joint. **1843** HUMPHREYS *Brit. Moths* II. 119 Wings.. with broad black fascia.. which extends.. as far as the middle of the wing, where it is dolabriform.

†**do'lation.** *Obs. rare*⁻⁰. [n. of action f. L. *dolāre* to hew.] Smoothing with an adze.

1656 BLOUNT *Gl.*, *Dolation*, a smoothing or making even.

Dolby ('dɒlbɪ, 'dəʊlbɪ). [The name of Ray M. *Dolby* (b. 1933), U.S. engineer who devised the system.] A proprietary name used *attrib.* and *absol.* to designate electronic noise-reduction systems employed esp. in tape recording to reduce hiss.

1966 *Wireless World* Dec. 632/1 A new audio noise reduction or *s/n* 'stretcher' system has been developed by Dolby Laboratories of 590 Wandsworth Road, London, S.W.8. The company was set up in 1965... In the Dolby system,.. compression and expansion are carried out at a low signal level. **1970** *Official Gaz.* (U.S. Patent Office) 3 Mar. TM14/1 Dolby Laboratories Inc., New York... *Dolby System*... For noise suppressor which combats noise in transmission or recording systems. First use Oct. 30, 1966. **1970** *Wireless World* Dec. 585/3 Use of this system, called Dolby 'B' being derived from a simplification of the Dolby 'A' system.. is not limited to cassette recorders. **1973** *Daily Tel.* 24 Oct. 2 (Advt.), The reason for this encouraging news is the noise-reduction system we've built into the deck. It's a Dolby... The Dolby system.. will actually improve a poor recording on playback. **1974** *Official Gaz.* (U.S. Patent Office) 18 June TM167/2 Dolby Laboratories Inc... *Dolby*. **1975** *Gramophone* Jan. 1418/2 Even the listener without Dolby wins through less distortion. **1975** G. J. KING *Audio Handbk.* x. 234 A notable scheme is that due to Dr. Ray Dolby... This was first developed for professional studio use, and in this application is known as 'Dolby A'. *Ibid.* (*caption*) Basic principles of 'Dolby B'. All low-level h.f. signals are boosted during recording and attenuated during playback. **1975** *Trade Marks Jrnl.* 3 Dec. 2599/2 *Dolby*... Instruments and apparatus for use in sound and vision recording, sound and vision reproduction and for the reduction or suppression of noise... Dolby Laboratories Inc. **1976** *Gramophone* July 231/3 It has three heads,.. dual-capstan closed loop drive, Dolby, multiplex filter etc. **1984** *What Video?* Aug. 4/3 VHS Hi Fi is totally different from VHS Dolby stereo.

Hence **'Dolbyed, 'Dolbyized** *ppl. adjs.*, proprietary terms in Britain and the U.S. respectively applied to equipment fitted, and recordings made, with the Dolby system; (as a back-formation) **'Dolby** *v. trans.*

1971 *Pop. Photogr.* Aug. 99 Speaking of cassette recorders, with the exception of 'Dolbyized' models, you can count on one finger the number of models that have a hi-fi signal-to-noise ratio of 50 db. **1973** *Trade Marks Jrnl.* 23 May 976/1 *Dolbyed*... Apparatus and instruments, all for the reduction or suppression of noise in systems for recording, reproducing or transmitting audio or video signals; magnetic tapes and discs... Dolby Laboratories Inc. **1975** *Official Gaz.* (U.S. Patent Office) 22 Apr. TM260/1 Dolby Laboratories Inc., New York... *Dolbyized*... For pre-recorded magnetic tapes. **1975** *Ibid.* 20 May 209/1 Dolby Laboratories Inc., New York... *Dolbyized*... For pre-recorded magnetic tapes. **1977** *Gramophone* Jan. 1178/3 Companies.. are still not prepared to Dolby non-classical material. *Ibid.* Mar. 1489/1 Provision is made for the addition of a Dolby circuit board to receive Dolbyied FM broadcasts. **1983** *Financial Times* 19 Aug. I. 9/3 The soundtrack will fine down to a Dolbyised dog barking offscreen to evoke the pain and pathos of a long, lonely urban night.

dolcan ('dɒlkən). [f. It. *dolce* sweet: cf. It. *dolciano*.] A kind of organ stop (see quots.).

1852 J. J. SEIDEL *Organ* 20 Stops.. made wider at the upper end than the lower, as is the case with the.. Dolcan. **1877** HOPKINS & RIMBAULT *The Organ* (ed. 3) II. xxii. 137 Dolcan.. is a manual stop of 8 feet, the pipes of which are of larger diameter at the top than at the bottom, producing a very agreeable tone.

‖**dolce far niente** ('doltʃe far nj'ɛnte). [It.; = 'sweet doing nothing'.] Delightful idleness.

1814 BYRON in Moore *Life* (1832) III. 100 (Stanf.) Making the most of the 'dolce far niente' [at Hastings]. **1830** LONGF. in *Life* (1891) I. 187 It is there.. that the dolce far niente of a summer evening is most heavenly. **1883** W. H. RUSSELL in *19th Cent.* Sept. 490 That form of the *dolce far niente* which is termed meditation.

attrib. **1865** H. KINGSLEY *Hillyars & Burtons* i, His *dolce far niente*, insolent manner.

‖**dolce vita** (doltʃe vita, ˌdɒltʃɪ'viːtə). [It., lit. 'sweet life'.] A life of luxury, pleasure, and self-indulgence. (Freq. preceded by *the* or *la*.) Also *attrib.*

[**1960** *Times* 7 Dec. 15/5 *La Dolce Vita* is a film.. 'making up an apocalyptic fresco of seven nightmarish nights and seven sobering dawns'.] **1961** *Guardian* 30 Mar. 7/1 The grander villas, where the Roman playboys.. pursued their Dolce Vita. **1961** *20th Cent.* Mar. 311 A headstrong and muddled woman.. who combined convent education, *la dolce vita* and gambling. **1962** *Listener* 6 Sept. 367/2 His plans to abandon his *dolce vita* existence. **1970** *Times* 14 Oct. 2/6 A totally alien way of life—a dolce vita of Bicester, 1970 style.

Dolcinist, -ite: see DULCINIST.

†**dold,** *ppl. a. Obs.* [perh. orig. pa. pple. of **dol-en*, var. of *dull-en*, DULL *v.*: cf. OE. *dol* adj., dull, foolish, stupid; also Sc. *dowd*, DOW *v.*³] Stupid, inert, as through old age, cold, etc.

c **1460** *Towneley Myst.* 27 (*Noe*) Hit is wonder that I last sich an old dote Alle dold [*rime* old]. *Ibid.* 98 (*Shepherd in field by night*) What these wedirs ar cold, and I am ylle happyd; I am nere hande dold, so long have I nappyd.

doldrum ('dɒldrəm). Usually in pl. **doldrums.** [app. in its origin a slang term, prob. a deriv. of prec., or of *dol*, DULL. For the form cf. *tantrum*.]

†**1.** *slang.* A dullard; a dull, drowsy, or sluggish fellow. *Obs.*

1812 *Examiner* 7 Sept. 571/1 A *doldrum* is, we believe, the cant word for a long sleeper. **1824** SCOTT *Let. to Son* 22 Oct. in *Lockhart*, I hope you will make your way to the clever fellows and not put up with Doldrums. [*a* **1840** BARHAM *Ingol. Leg.*, *Row in Omnibus* I Doldrum the Manager sits in his chair.]

2. pl. ***the doldrums.***

a. A condition of dullness or drowsiness; dumps, low spirits, depression.

1811 *Morning Herald* 13 Apr. in *Spirit Pub. Jrnls.* (1812) XV. 175, I am now in the doldrums; but when I get better, I will send you [etc.]. **1835** MARRYAT *Jac. Faithf.* xi, 'Come, father, old Dictionary is in the doldrums; rouse him up with another stave.' **1862** *Athenæum* 30 Aug. 266 A glass of brandy-and-water is a panacea for the doldrums. **1886** C. KEENE *Let.* in G. S. Layard *Life* xi. (1892) 363 The great thing is to evade 'the Doldrums'.

b. The condition of a ship in which, either from calms, or from baffling winds, she makes no headway; a becalmed state.

1824 BYRON *Island* II. xxi, From the bluff head where I watch'd to-day, I saw her in the doldrums; for the wind Was light and baffling. **1833** MARRYAT *P. Simple* xliii, As we ran along the coast, I perceived a vessel under the high land in what the sailors called the *doldrums*; this is, almost becalmed, or her sails flapping about in every direction with the eddying winds.

fig. **1883** *Times* (weekly ed.) 16 Feb. 10 The ship of State has escaped the tornado, but seems becalmed in a kind of political and financial doldrums. **1895** SIR T. SUTHERLAND in *Westm. Gaz.* 11 July 1/3 At the present moment the trade appears to be in the doldrums.

c. An intellectually non-plussed condition.

1871 G. MEREDITH *H. Richmond* xxvii, My wits are in the doldrums. **1878** J. R. O'FLANAGAN *Irish Bar* (1879) 142 The Counsellor's questions put him in a doldrum.

3. *transf.* A region in which ships are specially liable to be becalmed; *spec.* (***equatorial doldrums***), the region of calms and light baffling winds near the equator, where the trade winds meet and neutralize each other.

(Apparently due to a misunderstanding of the phrase 'in the doldrums', the state being taken as a locality.)

1855 MAURY *Phys. Geog. Sea* x. §583 The 'equatorial doldrums' is another of these calm places. Besides being a region of calms and baffling winds, it is a region noted for its rains. **1883** E. F. KNIGHT *Cruise Falcon* (1887) 26 The sultry doldrums, where a ship may lie for weeks.. a region of unbearable calm, broken occasionally by violent squalls.

dole (dəʊl), *sb.*¹ Forms: 1 dál, 2–4 dal(e, 3 dol, 4–6 dool(e, 5 doylle, dooll, 6 *Sc.* daill, 6–7 doal(e, 3– dole. [OE. *dál*, a parallel form to *dǽl* which gives DEAL *sb.*¹ In senses 5–7, used as n. of action from DEAL *v.* See also DALE².]

†**1.** The state of being divided; division. *Obs.*

c **1000** ÆLFRIC *Exod.* viii. 23 Ic sette dal betwux þin folc & min folc. *c* **1275** *Passion Our Lord* 446 in *O.E. Misc.* 50 Hi nolden þer-of makie nones cunnes dol. *c* **1340** *Cursor M.* 23521 (Trin.) þei are in onehede so in dole.

†**2. a.** A part or division of a whole; a portion; = DEAL *sb.*¹ 1. *Obs.*

a **1000** *Guthlac* (Gr.) 25 Is þes middan-ȝeard, dalum ȝedæled. *c* **1175** *Lamb. Hom.* 47 Beo heo dal neominde of heofene riches blisse. *c* **1200** ORMIN 8266 Siþþenn wass þe kinedom O fowwre daless dæledd. *a* **1225** *Ancr. R.* 10 þe latere dole of his sawe limpeð to recluses; vor þer beoð two dolen to two manere of men þet beoð of religiun. *c* **1250** *Gen. & Ex.* 151 On four doles delen he ðe ȝer. **13..** *E.E. Allit. P.* B. 216 þer he tynt þe tyþe dool of his tour ryche. *a* **1400–50** *Alexander* 3844 As þai þe forthing-dole had of þe flode past. **1573** TUSSER *Husb.* xlviii. (1878) 104 Amongst those same hillocks deuide them by doles.

b. *Mining.* A portion of ore: see quots.

1823 CRABB *Technol. Dict.*, *Dole* (Min.), a pile of ore for sale. **1874** J. H. COLLINS *Metal Mining* 112 The piles or doles belonging to the different parties. **1880** *W. Cornw. Gloss.*, *Dole*, a parcel of copper ore; a share in a mine; mine dues. 'What dole do you pay?'

†**c.** A portion of a common or undivided field; = DALE² 1. *Obs.*

1523 FITZHERB. *Surv.* 41 They [meadows] ought to be well staked bytwene euery mannes dole. **1611** *Manch. Crt. Leet Rec.* (1885) XI. 263 One Barne and a doale of Lande. **1787** W. MARSHALL *Norfolk* II. 10 To cut and burn ant-hills off a dole belonging to his farm, upon a common.

d. A portion (conventionally fixed) for sale; a 'lot'.

1887 *Doncaster Tradesman's Advt. Bill*, We shall clear out several hundred doles of superior Wakefield Worsted at 9½d and 11½d per dole.

3. A part allotted or apportioned to one, or belonging to one by right; share, portion, lot. *arch.*

a **1225** *St. Marher.* 22 Ne schaltu habben wið me dale of heouene riche. *a* **1240** *Ureisun* 150 in *Cott. Hom.* 199 þu schalt me a ueir dol of heoueriche blisse. *c* **1325** *Chron. Eng.* 414 in Ritson *Metr. Rom.* II. 287 Made al Englond yhol Falle to ys oune dol. **13..** *E.E. Allit. P.* B. 699, I.. dyȝt drwry þer-inne, doole alþer-swettest. **1548** FORREST *Pleas. Poesye* 649 O Nobul thynge belongethe to youre Doale [*rime* soule]. **1601** SHAKS. *All's Well* II. iii. 176 What great creation, and what dole of honour Flies where you bid it. **1676** HALE *Contempl.* I. 272 Our measure and dole is given unto us. **1871** TENNYSON *Last Tournament* 556 Hath not our great Queen My dole of beauty trebled?

4. Portion or lot (in life); fate, destiny: chiefly in proverbial phr. ***happy man be his dole.*** *arch.*

?a 1500 *Parl. Byrdes* 179 in Hazl. *E.P.P.* III. 176, I woulde the hauke brake his necke, Or [were] brought vnto some myscheuous dale [*rime* tale]. 1562 J. Heywood *Prov. & Epigr.* (1867) 169 Happy man happy dole, so say sycke and hole. 1596 Shaks. *1 Hen. IV*, II. ii. 79 Happy man be his dole, say I: euery man to his businesse. 1663 Butler *Hud.* I. iii. 638 Let us that are unhurt and whole Fall on, and happy Man be's Dole. 1803 W. S. Rose *Amadis* 99 Death be his dole who worst maintains the strife. 1838 Southey *Doctor* V. 147 Happy man would be his dole, who, when he had made up his mind [etc.].

5. a. Dealing out or distribution of gifts; *esp.* of food or money given in charity.

c 1205 Lay. 19646 Six cnihtes..gan to þas kinges dale, swulc heo weoren vn-hale. 1297 R. Glouc. (1724) 165 Messagers in pouere monne wede, þat at doles in þe court her mete myd oþere bede. c 1449 Pecock *Repr.* III. xv. 375 Of the ouerplus make doole to othere. 1620 Sanderson *12 Serm.* (1637) 60 The Gifts here spoken of are distributed as it were by doale. 1653 Milton *Hirelings* Wks. (1851) 388 As he dispenses it in his Sunday Dole. 1778 *Eng. Gazetteer* (ed. 2), *Stretham, Surry*..has a charity-school, and a dole every Sunday, of 21 two-penny loaves. 1878 Browning *La Saisiaz* 59 Pleasures stinted in the dole.

†**b.** Dealing, distribution, delivery (of blows, death). *Obs.*

a 1525 (ed. Pynson) *Sir Beues* (1885) 48 *note*, Al they sayde, seke and hole, That they had ben at Beuys dole. 1587 Fleming *Contn. Holinshed* III. 1321/2 They..fought couragiouslie, as if the Greeks and Troians had dealt their deadlie dole. 1597 Shaks. *2 Hen. IV*, I. i. 169 That in the dole of blowes your Son might drop. 1621 Fletcher *Isl. Princess* IV. ii, Dealing large doles of death. 1671 Milton *Samson* 1529 What if..He now be dealing dole among his foes?

6. a. That which is distributed or doled out; *esp.* a gift of food or money made in charity; hence, a portion sparingly doled out; *spec.* (usu. ***the dole***); the popular name for the various kinds of weekly payments made from national and local funds to the unemployed since the war of 1914–18. Phr. (***to be*** or ***go***) ***on the dole***: (to be or start being) in receipt of such unemployment relief; also *transf.* and *fig.*

1362 Langl. *P. Pl.* A. III. 63 Whon ȝe ȝiuen doles. 1480 Caxton *Chron. Eng.* ccxlvi. (1482) 311 A dole to poure peple of vi shyllynges viii pens to be delyd peny mele. 1566 R. Mighells in Suckling *Suffolk* (1847) 86 There was tythe of fysche called Christs dole, paid in this manner: vidlt, of every fisher boat going to the sea, half a dole. 1635 R. Bolton *Comf. Affl. Consc.* vi. 396 Rich men cast into the Treasury large Doles, and royall offerings. 1793 Burke *Rem. Policy Allies* Wks. VII. 136 At Paris..the bread they buy is a daily dole. 1862 Merivale *Rom. Emp.* (1871) V. xl. 55 Recipients of the ordinary dole of grain. 1894 *Times* (weekly ed.) 19 Jan. 59/4 Not a penny of it was distributed until November 1, and then only in doles and driblets. 1919 *Daily Mail* 11 June 8/4 You won't draw your out-of-work dole of 29s. this week. 1923 L. A. Harker *Master & Maid* (new ed.) xx. 265 If only I'd danced an Irish jig I believe I could have got the whole of them to increase the dole. 1925 *Westm. Gaz.* 26 Mar., 3,000 Aliens on the Dole. 1928 *Britain's Industrial Future* (*Lib. Ind. Inq.*) 277 To speak of Unemployment Benefit as 'the dole' is to misrepresent the facts. 1933 W. Greenwood (*title*) Love on the dole. A tale of the two cities. 1937 *Daily Herald* 21 Jan. 4/2 Beef producers must not consider themselves as 'on the dole for ever', but must use the assistance to reorganise the industry. 1955 *Times* 29 July 5/6 The nation was on the dole, and had been for 10 years.

†**b.** Reward given to hounds. *Obs.*

1576 Turberv. *Venerie* 144 The houndes must be rewarded with the Bowels, the bloud and the feete..it is not called a rewarde but a dole. 1688 R. Holme *Armoury* II. 187/2 Dole is the reward of a Roe-Buck, given to the Hounds.

c. *transf.* and *fig.*

1642 Milton *Apol. Smect.* i. Wks. (1847) 85/1 Who made you the busy almoner to deal about this dole of laughter and reprehension? 1844 Mrs. Browning *Vision Poets* ccxvi. Poems 1850 I. 232 Hand-service, to receive world's dole.

†**7.** Dealing, intercourse; = dale² 2. *Obs.*

c 1340 *Cursor M.* 683 (Trin.) Þese beestis were so meke in dole Wiþouten hurtyng þei ȝeoden hole. 1549 Coverdale, etc. *Erasm. Par. 1 Peter* iii. 7 Yf bothe parties..refrayne from bodyly doale. 1561 *Child Marriages* (1897) 9 He had neuer any Carnall dole with her.

8. *attrib.* and *Comb.*, as in ***dole-bag***, ***-beer***, ***-cup***, ***-penny***, ***-silver***; **dole-cupboard** (see quot. 1910¹); **dole-drawer**, one who receives the dole (sense 6 a); **dole-fish** (see quot. 1641); **dole-land**, **-meadow**, **-moor**, a piece of common land, moor, etc. in which various persons have portions indicated by landmarks, but not divided off; **dolesman**, **-woman**, a man or woman who receives a dole; **dole queue**, a queue of people waiting to collect unemployment benefit; freq. as a general symbol of unemployment; **dole-window**, a window at which doles were distributed.

1610 B. Jonson *Alch.* I. i, Sell the *dole-beere to aqua-vitæ men. 1583 J. Higins tr. *Junius' Nomenclator* (N.) *Pain d'aumosne*, *dole-bread. a 1652 Brome *City Wit* IV. iv. Wks. 1873 I. 352 Five pound in dole bread. a 1845 Mrs. Bray *Warleigh* xiii, He..received the customary fee, and having drunk what was called a '*dole cup' of excellent waters, returned home. 1910 *Encycl. Brit.* VII. 634/2 The livery cupboard..was often used in churches to contain the loaves of bread doled out to poor persons... They were then called *dole cupboards. 1910 V. Tree *Let.* 9 Oct. in *Castles in Air* (1926) I. 37, I am rather inclined to sell our Dole cupboard we bought together. 1926 *Good Housekeeping* July 188/2 Profiteers, *dole-drawers and music-hall artists—in fact, the only people who have any money to-day. 1938 R. G. Collingwood *Princ. Art* xv. 333 An audience of wage-earners or dole-drawers. 1533–4 *Act 25 Hen. VIII*, c. 4 §2 No..person..shall..bie any dole or dooles of any of the maryners of any of the seid shyppe or shippes, called the maryners *Dole fysshe. 1641 *Termes de la Ley* 126 Dole-fish seemeth to bee those fishes which the fisher-men yeerly employed in the North seas, doe of custome receive for their allowance. 1805 W. Taylor in *Ann. Rev.* III. 57 The plots of field are often parcelled out like *dole-lands in petty compartments. 1881 *Times* 30 Mar. 11/4 The trustees, the *dolesmen, and the *doleswomen might be a small group of old faces well known to one another. 1726 *Dict. Rust.* (ed. 3) s.v. **Dole-Meadow*, a Meadow wherein several Persons have a share. 1825–7 Hone *Every-Day Bk.* II. 918 The two large pieces of common land called *Dolemoors. *Ibid.* 921 The Marks for allotting Dolmoors. 1686 Plot *Staffordsh.* 314 This *dole-penny is..given to all persons then residing in the parish. 1972 *Guardian* 16 Feb. 14/5 The *dole queues in the West Midlands. 1979 S. Wilson *Greenish Man* 22 In Eire, we can rely on young men..finding the patriot cause more attractive than the dole queue. 1985 *Financial Times* 21 Mar. I. 12/5 Pushing wage levels even further below the poverty line will do nothing to cut the dole queues. 1579 *Sc. Acts Jas. VI* (1814) 169 (Jam.) All landis, annuellis, obitis, *daill siluer, mailis, rentis, etc. 1859 Turner *Dom. Archit.* III. II. vii. 214 In the hall..is a low side window, called a *Dole window, formerly used for distributing alms.

dole, dool, dule (dəʊl, duːl), *sb.*² *arch.* and *dial.* Forms: α. 3–4 deol, del, (3 deil, 4 diol, dyel), 4–5 deel, dele, (deyl(le); β. 3–5 doel, (5 doell); 3–5 dol, (4–5 doul, 5 doll), 4–9 dool, dole, (4–7 doole, 6 doal(e, 7 dowle); 4 doil, 4–5 doile, doyl, doyll, 5 doylle; γ. 4 duel, dul, 4–9 dule, 4–5 duyl, 5 *Sc.* dwle, 6–7 dulle, duill; 6 deul, 6–7 dewle, 7–8 *Sc.* deule; δ. 5 duyel, dueyl, deuel, 6–7 dueil. [a. OF. *doel* (11th c.), *duel* (12–14th c.), *deol*, *diol*, *dial*, *diel*, *del* (13th c.), *dol*, *dul*, *deul* (14th c.), *duil*, *dueil* (16–17th c.), mod.F. *deuil*:—late L. *dolium* grief. The manifold forms of the OF. word are reflected in Middle English. The *deol* type, which first prevailed, and was at length reduced to *dēl*, became obs. before 1500. The *dōl*, *dole* form survived in English till the 16th c., and its normal representative in modern English is *dool*; but the word became to a great extent obsolete by 1600, and some of its modern revivers have preferred the ME. spelling *dole*. It has always been retained in Sc., where it is now regularly (døːl, dyːl), variously spelt *dool*, *duil*, *dule*; *dule* also occurred in English from 14th to 16th c., and is used in preference to *dole* or *dool* by some modern poets. In addition to these derivatives from OF., the forms *duyel*, *dueyl*, *deuel*, *dueil*, imitating later French types, occur from Caxton onwards.]

1. Grief, sorrow, mental distress.

α. c 1290 *S. Eng. Leg.* I. 42/285 Ech man hadde deol þerof. 1307 *Elegy Edw. I*, vii, For del ne mihte he speke na more. c 1320 *Cast. Love* 110 Alas whiche sorewe and dyel ther wes! 1393 Langl. *P. Pl.* C. XXI. 306 And al hus issue sholden deye with deol. c 1420 *Anturs of Arth.* xxv, Thenke quat..dele, that I inne duelle.

β. a 1240 *Wohunge* in *Cott. Hom.* 285 Leue me vnderstonde þi dol and herteli to felen sum hwat of þe sorhe. c 1320 *Seuyn Sag.* (W.) 2574 For doel therof amorewe he starf. c 1330 R. Brunne *Chron.* 165 [She] felle R[ichard] to fote gretand, þat doole him nam. c 1375 *Sc. Leg. Saints, Thomas* 250 He vald..bryne þame sene ine doile and va. c 1430 Lydg. *Bochas* I. i. (1544) 4 a, Continual sorow, dread, dole. c 1450 *Merlin* 90 The quene dide wepe as she that hadde grete doel. c 1460 *Towneley Myst.* (Surtees) 62 Alas for doylle we dy! 1579 Spenser *Sheph. Cal.* Feb. 155, I..Am like for desperate doole to dye. 1580 Sidney *Ps.* XLIII. vi, Why art thou, my soule, Cast down in such dole? a 1605 Polwart *Flyting w. Montgomerie* 526 Dryve, with doole, to death detestabill, This mad malitious monster miserabill. 1667 Milton *P.L.* IX. 894 To change Torment with ease, & soonest recompence Dole with delight. 1776 C. Keith *Farmer's Ha'* 31 They banish hence a' care and dool. 1820 Scott *Monast.* v, The Kelpy has risen from the fathomless pool, He has lighted his candle of death and of dool. 1850 Mrs. Browning *Poems* II. 87 Earth's warm-beating joy and dole.

γ. a 1300 *Cursor M.* 23975 (Cott.) Hir dule [*v.r.* dole] ne ma i noght for-dill, Bot wit hir wepeing wepe i will. c 1425 Wyntoun *Cron.* VIII. xxvii. 93 The Dwle, þat þai had in þat Fycht. 1500–20 Dunbar *Poems* xiv. 23 The dulis that communis dois sustene. 1631 A. Craige *Pilgr. & Heremite* 7 Thy duill, her delight. a 1850 Rossetti *Dante & Circ.* II. (1874) 287, I stand all day in fear and dule.

δ. 1307 *Elegy Edw. I*, i, My song, Of duel that Deth hath diht us newe. c 1477 Caxton *Jason* 18 b, Wherof their king ..hath had grete dueyl and sorowe. *Ibid.* 116 Jason demened so grete a duyel and sorow.

2. The expression of sorrow or grief; mourning, weeping, lamentation; chiefly in phr. ***to make dole***, to lament, mourn.

α. c 1290 *Beket* 645 in *S. Eng. Leg.* I. 125 Þe deol þat thomas makede: no tounge telle ne may. a 1300 *Fall & Passion* 83 in *E.E.P.* (1862) 15 Who spekiþ of deil a-ȝe þat del . neuer such nas þer none. c 1350 *Leg. Cath., Joachim & Anna* 133 Gret diol made Anne for him. 1393 Langl. *P. Pl.* C. XX. 318 Þauh men maken muche deol in here angre, And beo inpacient in here penaunces. c 1420 *Chron. Vilod.* 774 For hurre deth he made gret deylle.

β. a 1300 *Cursor M.* 10455 (Gött.) Þu blamys me for i mak dol. *Ibid.* 16752 + 97 (Cott.) Ilk a creature for his ded made doyl on þer wise. c 1380 Wyclif *Serm.* Sel. Wks. II. 99 Jesus making dool in himsilf cam to þe sepulcre. c 1450 *Merlin* 34 After the corse was made grete doel and wepynge. a 1547 Surrey *Æneid* IV. 43 Time of thy doole, thy spouse new dead, I graunt None might thee move. 1600 Shaks. *A.Y.L.* I. ii. 139 Making such pittiful dole. 1790 Burns *Bard's Epitaph* 5 Owre this grassy heap sing dool, And drap a tear. 1859 Tennyson *Elaine* 1130 She died. So that day there was dole in Astolat.

γ. c 1380 *Sir Ferumb.* 3785 Four sithes he ful a-doun y-sowe, & oþre dules made ynowe, & ofte cryede, 'Alas!' c 1425 *Seven Sag.* (P.) 710 For the dule he made ther-fore, The knyght hym selven he was for-lore. 1513 Douglas *Æneis* II. i. 25 Thair langsum duile and murnyng. 1546 *St. Papers Hen. VIII*, XI. 13 There was evensong of our Lady, very freshely, to recompense the deul bifore. 1559 Sackville in *Mirr. Mag.* Induct. xiv, The deadly dewle, which she so sore dyd make, With dolefull voice. 1567 Fenton *Fragm. Disc.* 12 Dolefull voyce, redoubled with an eccho of treble dule.

δ. c 1500 *Melusine* xxxiii. 234 He lefte & passed his deuel the best wyse that he coude. a 1656 Ussher *Ann.* vi. (1688) 95 Continual dueil, and mourning for him.

†**b.** ***clothes, habit, weeds of dole***: mourning garments, = sense 5. *Obs.*

c 1340 *Cursor M.* 10419 (Laud) Clothis of dele [*v.r.* deol] she did on thore. 1388 Wyclif *2 Sam.* xiv. 2 Be thou clothid with clooth of duyl [*v.rr.* deol, doel, deel, deyl]. 1577 Fenton *Gold. Epist.* (1582) 5 To weare attire of dule.

†**3.** Physical pain or suffering. *Obs. rare.*

c 1320 *Sir Beues* 602 Þis is þe ferste dai of ȝoul, Þe god was boren wiþ outen doul. c 1350 *Will. Palerne* 2757 He for dul of þe dent diued to þe ground.

4. That which excites sorrow, grief, or pity; a grievous or piteous thing; a grief, sorrow.

c 1290 *S. Eng. Leg.* I. 43/303 Þat deol it was to seo. 1413 *Pilgr. Sowle* (Caxton 1483) IV. xxxviii. 63 Grete doel and pyte was hit to byholde. c 1430 *Chev. Assigne* 359 Hit was doole for to se yᵉ sorowe yᵗ he made. c 1450 *Erle Tolous* 801 Grete dele hyt was to see. c 1450 *Cov. Myst.* (1841) 47 Gret doyl it is to se this watyr so wyde! 1789 Burns *To Toothache* iv, O' a' the numerous human dools.. Thou bear'st the gree.

†**5.** *transf.* Clothing or trappings worn as a sign of mourning; 'mourning'. *Obs.*

c 1500 *Melusine* xxxiv. 239 The kynge..fette the pucelle, and despoylled her of her dueyl & black clothing. 1599 *Sickness & Death Philip II*, in *Harl. Misc.* (Malh.) II. 286 My body shall be borne by eight of my chiefest servants.. all in dewle. 1636 in *Macm. Mag.* XLVI. 80 A horsse in doole. 16.. in *Q. Eliz. Acad.* (1869) 32 Sertayne gentlemen in Dowle. 1734 R. Keith *Hist. Ch. & St. Scot.* 207 (Jam.) To wear the deule for that day.

6. A funeral. *Obs.* exc. *dial.*

1548 Hall *Chron., Hen. V.* 50 The conduyt & ordre of thys dolorous dole was commaunded to sir William Philip treasorer of the kinges houshold. a 1828 Bewick *Upgetting* (1850) 13 'The spak o' the great Swire's deeth..and the number oh fwoak that went to his dhael.'

†**7.** A fanciful term for a company of doves. [From their mournful cooing.] *Obs.*

1486 *Bk. St. Albans* F vj b, A Duell of Turtillis.

8. *attrib.*, as ***dole colour***; **dole-cloth**, **-pall**, a funeral pall; **dole (dule) habit**, **weeds**, mourning clothes; **dule tree**, ? a hanging-tree, a gibbet.

1508 Dunbar *Tua Mariit Wemen* 420, I drup..with a ded luke, in my dule habit. 1535 Stewart *Cron. Scot.* III. 73 Ȝoung Alexander was crownit King efter King Williame his Fader deceissit, and tuke on him the Dule Weid, and for his Saik delt Almous Deid. 1536 Bellenden *Cron. Scot.* (1821) I. 241 Arrayit in thair dule habit, for doloure of thair husbandis. 1542 in T. Thomson *Collect. Inventories* 103 (Jam.) Item, foure doule palis of blak clayth. 1710 J. Wilson in *Collect. Dying Test.* (1806) 154 Then Zion got on her dool weed. 1870 Edgar *Runnymede* 178 The dule tree is your sure doom. 1876 *Whitby Gloss.*, *Doolweeds*, mourning attire. 1881 Stevenson *Virg. Puerisque* 165 The gibbets and dule trees of mediæval Europe.

dole, *sb.*³ [ad. L. *dol-us* deceit, cunning, trickery, a. Gr. δόλος: cf. F. *dol* (16th c.), It., Sp. *dolo*.]

†**1.** Guile, deceit, fraud. *Obs.*

1563–87 Foxe *A. & M.* (1684) II. 330 No dole, no fraud, no guile was ever found in his mouth. 1612 Ainsworth *Annot. Ps.* v. 7 Deceit, dole or guile. 1839 J. P. Kennedy *Rob of Bowl* xii. (1860) 127 What dole hath he done?

2. *Sc. Law.* 'The corrupt, malicious, or evil intention essential to the guilt of a crime' (Bell).

1753 Chambers *Cycl. Supp.* s.v., Under Dole are comprehended the vices and errors of the will, which are immediately productive of the criminal act, though not premeditated, but the effect of sudden passion. In this respect Dole differs from what the English law calls malice. 1754 Erskine *Princ. Sc. Law* (1809) 526 Capable of dole. 1795 Scott in Lockhart *Life* July, To preclude all presumption of dole. [1880 Muirhead *Gaius* III. §211 He is held to have killed wrongfully to whose dole or fault death is attributable [*cuius dolo aut culpa id acciderit*].]

dole, *sb.*⁴, variant of dool, boundary mark, etc.

dole, *v.*¹ Also 6 *Sc.* dale. [f. dole *sb.*¹]

1. *trans.* To give as a dole; to distribute by way of alms, or in charity.

1465 *Mann. & Househ. Exp.* 317 The same day my mastyr toke to mastyr Perse Baxter, to dole for my lady in almesse, x. s. 1599 Marston *Sco. Villanie* I. iv. 188 If to the Parish pouerty, At his wisht death, be dol'd a half-penny. c 1640 J. Smyth *Lives Berkeleys* (1883) I. 40 That daye shall bee doled to fifty poore men fifty loafes. 1762 Goldsm. *Cit. W.* cxii, The officers appointed to dole out public charity. 1868 Stanley *Westm. Abb.* iii. 170 The bread and meat doled out to the poor of Westminster.

2. To give *out* in small quantities; to portion or parcel *out* in a sparing or niggardly manner.

1749 Fielding *Tom Jones* XV. vi, This comfort..she doled out to him in daily portions. 1849 Macaulay *Hist. Eng.* I. 84 They accordingly doled out supplies to him very sparingly. 1886 J. R. Rees *Pleas. Bk.-Worm* v. 169 The critic ..doles out a limited number of praises.

†**3.** To deal *about*, *around*, to distribute. *Obs.*

1701 Rowe *Amb. Step-Moth.* v. ii. 2799 Thy Arts That Dold about Destruction to our Enemies. *a* **1718** —— *Wks.* (1747) II. 293 (Jod.) And Plenty doles her various bounties round. **1766** Ld. Mansfield *Sp. agst. Prerogative* (Jod.), Compensations most liberally doled about to one another.

Hence ˈ**doling** *vbl. sb.*

15.. *Aberdeen Burgh Rec.* I. 210 (Jam. Supp.) And viijs. and the daling of thair aill for the secund fault. **1876** Ruskin *Fors Clav.* VI. lxi. 2 All this temporary doling and coaling is worse than useless.

dole, *v.*² ? *Obs.* Also 4 **deol(e**, 5–6 **dool(e**, *Sc.* **dule**, 7 **duill**. [a. OF. *doleir, doloir*, mod.F. *douloir*:—L. *dolēre* to grieve. In the stem-accented forms the OF. verb had the same variety as DOLE *sb.*² (ind. pres. *dueil, duels* (*deus*), *duelt* (*deut*), *dolons, dolez, duelent*), whence the ME. variant forms.]

†**1.** *intr.* To sorrow, grieve, mourn, lament. *Obs.*

13.. *K. Alis.* 2734 Alisaundres folk deoleth, y-wis, For the knyght that is y-slawe. **1481** Caxton *Reynard* (Arb.) 68, I wente dolynge on the heeth, and wist not what to doo for sorowe. **1508** Dunbar *Tua Mariit Wemen* 450 We wemen.. We dule for na euill deid, sa it be derne haldin. **1570** Levins *Manip.* 161/11 To Doole, sorow, *dolere*. *a* **1668** Davenant *Play-House to be Let* I. Dram. Wks. 1873 IV. 27 Dismiss your doling, and let in your poet.

b. Used of the mournful cooing of doves.

1848 W. E. Aytoun in *Blackw. Mag.* LXIV. 110 The throstle's song was silenced, And the doling of the dove. **1852** *Blackw. Mag.* LXXII. 218 From the dark woods.. you hear the doling of the cushats.

†**2.** *trans.* To mourn, bewail. *Obs.*

1567 Turberv. *Poems* (Chalmers) II. 617/1 He full shrilly shright and doolde his wofull chaunce.

†**3.** To grieve. *Obs.*

a **1637** B. Jonson *Sad Sheph.* II. iii, It duills mee that I am thy mother!

Hence ˈ**doling** *vbl. sb.*

a **1668** [see 1]. **1815** L. Hunt *Feast Poets* 19 There has been such a doling and sameness. **1848–52** [see 1 b].

dole, *v.*³ *Glove-manuf.* [a. F. *dole-r* to chip, plane, etc. (12th c.), spec. to pare and thin skins for gloves:—L. *dolāre* to hew, plane.] *trans.* To pare and thin (leather or skins).

1884 *Pall Mall G.* 16 May 4/1 The kid skin.. after it has been unhaired, dressed, nourished, staked, soaked in egg yolk.. dried, stained, stretched, 'doled', or pared, and cut into shape.. is then punched. **1884** *Health Exhib. Catal.* 38 The doling or reducing the skin to an even substance.

dole: see DOOL, DOWEL, DULL.

†ˈ**doleance**. *Obs.* Also 5 **doleaunce**, 6 **dolliance, doliaunce**. [a. F. *doléance*, earlier *doliance, douliance* (13th c. in Hatz.-Darm.) f. *doleant, -iant*, ancient pr. pple. of *doloir, douloir* to grieve.]

1. Sorrowing, grieving; sorrow, grief.

c **1489** Caxton *Blanchardyn* vi. 26 Herynge the cryes, & seeynge þe wepynges, the grete sorowe & doleaunce of the vertuose and noble mayden. **1523** in Burnet *Hist. Ref.* II. 103 By way of doleance and sorrow. *a* **1639** Spottiswood *Hist. Ch. Scot.* VII. (1677) 519 Esteeming it their duty to express their doleance for that accident.

2. Plaintive utterance; complaining, complaint.

1524 *St. Papers Hen. VIII*, IV. 104 Albeit ye make some doleance in your letters. **1524** in Strype *Eccl. Mem.* I. App. xii. 30 Any motion, by way of complainte or doliaunce. **1591** Horsey *Trav.* (Hakl. Soc.) 198 All their dolliances herd and remedied. **1656** Finett *For. Ambass.* 97 The substance of these doleances, I.. imparted to the.. Ambassador.

ˈ**doleant**, *ppl. a. rare.* [f. DOLEANCE; it coincides with OF. *doliant, doleant*, pr. pple. of *doloir* to grieve.] = DOLENT.

1861 Sala *Dutch Pict.* vii. 95 She is.. a lachrymose, grumbling, doleant, miserable waiting woman.

doleful (ˈdəʊlfʊl), *a.*¹ (and *sb.*) Also **deol-, del(e)-, dul(e)-, dil-, doil-**, etc. [f. DOLE *sb.*² + -FUL. In ME. found with the variant forms of DOLE *sb.*²; but *doleful* has been the standard form since 16th c.]

A. *adj.* Full of or attended with dole or grief; sorrowful.

1. Fraught with, accompanied by, or causing grief, sorrow, etc.; distressful, gloomy, dreary, dismal.

c **1275** Lay. 6902 Ac hit was a deolful þing: þat he ne moste leng beo king. **1297** R. Glouc. (1724) 237 Þat was a deluol cas. *a* **1300** *Cursor M.* 7182 (Gött.) To doleful [*v.rr.* deleful, deolful] dede þai suld him bring. *c* **1420** *Anturs of Arth.* xiii, Lo! hou dilful dethe hase thi Dame dyȝte! *c* **1435** *Torr. Portugal* 521 Torrent toke a dulful wey, Downe in a depe valey. *c* **1440** *York Myst.* xxvi. 99 Lord, who schall do þat doulfull dede? **1500–20** Dunbar *Poems* lxxxi. 23 Scho playit sangis duilfull to heir. **1565** T. Randolph in Ellis *Orig. Lett.* Ser. I. II. 202 The deulfull daye of the buriall of her howsbande. **1568** Tilney *Disc. Mariage* D vj, The doolefull place, where he lay. **1624** Capt. Smith *Virginia* III. ii. 49 The most dolefullest noyse he ever heard. **1667** Milton *P.L.* I. 65 Regions of sorrow, doleful shades. **1725** Pope *Odyss.* XXIII. 349 In the doleful mansions he survey'd His royal mother. **1847** Emerson *Repr. Men, Shaks.* Wks. (Bohn) I. 354 Here is.. a string of doleful tragedies, merry Italian tales, and Spanish voyages.

2. Of persons, their state, etc.: Full of pain, grief, or suffering; sorrowful, sad.

c **1430** Lydg. *Thebes* III. (R.) Amphiorax they carry Set in his chaire with a doleful hert. *a* **1555** Bradford in Coverdale *Lett. Mart.* (1564) 307 For the doulefull bodies of Gods people to reste in. **1590** Spenser *F.Q.* I. vi. 9 There find the virgin, doolfull, desolate. **1647** Cowley *Mistress, Heart fled again* iii, The doleful Ariadne so, On the wide shore forsaken stood. **1829** Lytton *Devereux* II. ii, Never presume to look doleful again.

3. Expressing grief, mourning, or suffering.

c **1275** Lay. 11997 His heorte ne mihte beo sori for þane deolfulle cri. **1340** Hampole *Pr. Consc.* 6877 Þai sal duleful crying and sorow here. **1393** Gower *Conf.* III. 291 In dolfull clothes they hem clothe. **1660** F. Brooke tr. *Le Blanc's Trav.* 104 In signe of mourning: Women.. are cloathed in white, the doleful colour there. **1797** Mrs. Radcliffe *Italian* iii. (1824) 550 She would.. look up.. with such a doleful expression. **1865** Kingsley *Herew.* xiii, He went to his business with a doleful face.

B. *sb.* (*pl.*) A doleful state. *colloq.* (Cf. *dismals.*)

1822 Mrs. E. Nathan *Langreath* II. 309 You have enough of the dolefuls at Langreath. **1882** Miss Braddon *Mt. Royal* II. viii. 149 We shall be in the dolefuls all the year.

ˈ**doleful**, *a.*² *rare.* [f. DOLE *sb.*³ + -FUL.] Full of 'dole', crafty, malicious.

1617 Minsheu *Ductor*, Dolefull or craftie, *dolosus*. **1880** Muirhead *Gaius* III. §207 A depositary.. being liable only in so far as he himself has done something doleful [*si quid ipse dolo malo fecerit*].

dolefully (ˈdəʊlfʊlɪ), *adv.*¹ Forms: see the adj. [f. DOLEFUL *a.*¹ + -LY².] In a doleful manner; sorrowfully, mournfully, sadly; drearily, dismally.

c **1290** *Beket* 1481 in *S. Eng. Leg.* I. 149 Heo weopen and criden deolfulliche. **1393** Langl. *P. Pl.* C. IV. 419 Þat agag.. and al hus lyge puple Sholde deye delfulliche for dedes of here eldren. *c* **1460** *Towneley Myst.* (Surtees) 222 Behold if ever ye saw body.. thus dulfully dight. **1526** *Pilgr. Perf.* (W. de W. 1531) 303 Haue pite on hym so dolefully standyng before the. **1579** Spenser *Sheph. Cal.* Aug. 193 How dolefully his doole thou didst rehearse. *a* **1668** Davenant *Play-House to be Let* Wks. (1673) 101 They love sad Tunes, how dolefully they ring! **1797** Burke *Regic. Peace* iii. (R.) The circumstances which we so dolefully lament. **1868** Dickens *Lett.* (1880) II. 338 We.. sat dolefully staring out of window.

ˈ**dolefully**, *adv.*² *rare.* [f. DOLEFUL *a.*² + -LY².] With dole, fraud, or malice.

1880 Muirhead *Gaius* IV. §47 *note*, Was the thing deposited, and has the depositary dolefully failed to restore it?

ˈ**dolefulness**. [f. DOLEFUL *a.*¹ + -NESS.] The quality or state of being doleful; grief, sadness, sorrowfulness; dreariness, melancholy.

c **1450** *Cov. Myst.* (1841) 227 Ther had nevyr woman more doolfulness. **1530** Palsgr. 214/2 Dolefulnesse, *tristesse*. **1586** W. Webbe *Eng. Poetrie* (Arb.) 65 Wordes.. expressing wonderfully the dolefulnesse of the song. **1887** Miss Braddon *Like & Unlike* i, Sir Adrian offered no reason for dolefulness.

ˈ**dolence**. *rare.* [f. DOLENT: see -ENCE.] Mourning, expression of grief.

1861 *Temple Bar Mag.* I. 301 The song.. rises first to plaintive dolence, then to a passionate wail.

dolent (ˈdəʊlənt), *a.* (*sb.*) *arch.* Also 5 **dolant(e, dolaunt**. [a. F. *dolent* grieving, sad, suffering (11th c.), ad. L. *dolēnt-em*, pr. pple. of *dolēre* to grieve; also (in Caxton) a. OF. *dolant*, pr. pple. of *doloir, douloir* to grieve.]

A. *adj.* **1.** Sorrowing, grieving; sorrowful, sad.

c **1450** Lonelich *Grail* xxvi. 64 A sorweful womman, and ful dolente. *c* **1489** Caxton *Blanchardyn* vi. 25 The damoysell dolaunt. *c* **1530** Ld. Berners *Arth. Lyt. Bryt.* (1814) 169 All the other knyghtes were ryghte dolent for his sake. **1634** Ford *P. Warbeck* III. iv, The king is angry.. And the passionate duke Effeminately dolent. **1868** Longfellow tr. *Dante's Inferno* III. 1 Through me the way is to the city dolent! Through me the way is to eternal dole.

2. Expressing or indicating grief or sorrow; mournful, doleful.

1490 Caxton *Eneydos* xviii. 68 Dolaunte lamentacyons rewthes and complayntes. **1552** Lyndesay *Monarche* 5150 With dolent Lamentatioun. **1882** *Illustr. Lond. News* 25 Mar. 278 Why these dolent reflections?

†**3.** Attended with or causing sorrow or grief; grievous, distressing. *Obs.*

1489 Caxton *Faytes of A.* III. vii. 181 The dolent and sorowfull deth comyng oftymes sodaynly. **1572** *Satir. Poems Reform.* xxx. 7 Him.. Quhome dolent deith hes laitly done deuoir.

†**B.** as *sb.* A sorrowful or suffering person. *rare.*

1530 *Calisto & M.* in Hazl. *Dodsley* I. 82 Is this the dolent for whom thou makist petition?

Hence ˈ**dolently** *adv.*

1548 Hall *Chron., Hen. VIII* (1809) 782, I thynke never Prince tooke it more sorrowfully nor more dolently.

doler (ˈdəʊlə(r)). *rare.* In 6 **dolar**. [f. DOLE *v.*¹ + -ER¹.] One who doles; a dispenser. Also with *out*.

1593 Q. Eliz. tr. *Boethius* II. metr. ii. 10 The liberal dolar of golds plenty. **1965** *Listener* 24 June 953/1 Aaron is the speaker of smooth words, the doler-out of truth in prudent instalments.

dolerin(e (ˈdɒlərɪn). *Min.* [a. F. *dolérine*, f. Gr. δολερός deceptive + -INE.] (See quots.)

1863–72 Watts *Dict. Chem.* II, *Dolerin*, a gneissoid rock in the Alps, consisting of talc and felspar. **1878** Lawrence tr. *Cotta's Rocks Class.* 244 Dolerine is the name given by Jurine to a talc-schist with essential ingredients of felspar and chlorite.

dolerite (ˈdɒləraɪt). *Min.* [a. F. *dolérite* (Haüy), f. Gr. δολερός deceptive + -ITE: so called from the difficulty of discriminating its constituents.] A mineral allied to basalt, containing feldspar (labradorite) and augite.

1838 Lyell *Elem. Geol.* (1865) 594 The variety of basalt called dolerite. **1849** Murchison *Siluria* xii. 294 Cut through by dykes and masses of dolerite. **1879** Rutley *Study Rocks* xiii. 253 The basalts vary considerably in structure: the coarsely crystalline varieties, and those in which the different mineral constituents are sufficiently well developed to be distinguished by the naked eye, are termed dolerites.

attrib. **1880** L. Oliphant *Gilead* iii. 82 A small building of dolerite stone.. bearing the marks of extreme antiquity.

Hence **doleˈritic** *a.*, of the nature of dolerite.

1849 Murchison *Siluria* xii. 293 Basalt and doleritic trap. **1868** Dana *Min.* 343 Dolerytic and basaltic lavas.

dolerophanite (dɒləˈrɒfənaɪt). *Min.* [f. Gr. δολερός deceptive + φαν-, stem of φαίνειν to appear + -ITE. Named by Scacchi, 1873, *dolerofano*.] A form of sulphate of copper of volcanic formation, found on Mount Vesuvius.

1875 Dana *Min.* App. II. 17.

dolesome (ˈdəʊlsəm), *a.* Now *rare.* [f. DOLE *sb.*² + -SOME.] = DOLEFUL *a.*¹

1533 Bellenden *Livy* II. (1822) 155 All thingis apperit richt doulsum. **1567** *Satir. Poems Reform.* iii. 173 Hir duilsum deith be wars than Jesabell. **1586** W. Webbe *Eng. Poetrie* (Arb.) 77 In beechen groues, and dolesome shaddowy places. **1656** S. Holland *Zara* (1719) 17 The most part of the dolesom Night. **1725** Pope *Odyss.* XI. 191 The dolesome realms of darkness and of death. *a* **1849** J. C. Mangan *Poems* (1859) 135 Soon will the death-bell's knelling A dolesome tale be telling.

Hence ˈ**dolesomely** *adv.*; ˈ**dolesomeness**.

1591 Horsey *Trav.* (Hakl. Soc.) 208, 30 great.. bells.. ringinge all together.. and verie dolsomlye. **1608–11** Bp. Hall *Medit. & Vows, Death* (R.) The dolesomnesse of the grave. **1894** J. E. Vaux *Ch. Folk Lore* 119 The dolesomeness of this portion of my book.

doless (ˈduːlɪs), *a. dial.* and *colloq.* Also **doeless, do-less**. [f. DO *v.* + -LESS: app. sometimes confused with DOWLESS.] Inactive, inefficient, without energy; good for nothing, useless.

1788 E. Picken *Poems* 148 (Jam.) Hard is the fate o' ony doless tyke, That's forc'd to marry ane he disna like. **1823** Galt *R. Gilhaize* I. 135 (Jam.) Sae casten down, doless, and dowie. **1860** Bartlett *Dict. Amer.*, *Doless*, inefficient. 'He's a doless sort of fellow.' **1876** T. E. Brown *Doctor* 12 A doeless sort of a woman. **1881** B. Taylor *Ballads, Old Pennsylv. Farmer* vi, But they're a doless set. **1891** R. Mulholland *Haunted Organist* 229 It's the poor do-less pair we'd be only for our Ailsie, that's han's an' feet to us both. **1936** M. Mitchell *Gone with Wind* lv. 949 He's just a piddling, do-less, good-for-nothing. **1949** M. Mead *Male & Female* xv. 324 Too lazy, too do-less, to make an effort.

doleur, early var. of DOLOUR.

dolf, earlier form of Sc. DOWF *a.*

dolf, -en, obs. pa. t. and pple. of DELVE.

dolfin, -yn, obs. forms of DOLPHIN.

‖**doli capax** (ˌdɒlɪ ˈkæpæks), *adj. phr. Law.* [f. L. *doli*, gen. sing. of *dolus* (see DOLE *sb.*³) + *capax* capable.] Capable of having the evil intention necessary for the commission of a crime. So **doli incapax**, incapable of having such an intention: usu. applied to a person under the age of fourteen.

a **1676** Hale *Hist. Placit. Cor.* I. 22 He might or might not be guilty according to the circumstances of the fact that might induce the court and jury to judge him *doli capax, vel incapax*. *Ibid.* 26 An infant under the age of fourteen years and above the age of twelve years is not *primâ facie* presumed to be *doli capax*, and therefore regularly for a capital offense.. he is not to be convicted or have judgment as a felon. **1797** T. E. Tomlins *Jacob's Law-Dict.* II (s.v. *infant*), Also, under fourteen, though an Infant shall be *primâ facie* adjudged to be *doli incapax*; yet if it appear to the court and jury that he was *doli capax*, and could discern between good and evil, he may be convicted. **1880** *Encycl. Brit.* XIII. 3/1 After fourteen an infant is *doli capax*. **1961** *Times* 22 Feb. 11/3 Their condemnation of the *doli incapax* rule (no liability without established knowledge of wrongfulness).. has not been answered.

dolichocephal (ˌdɒlɪkəʊˈsɛfəl). [ad. mod.L. DOLICHOCEPHALI *sb. pl.*] A dolichocephalic person. Also *attrib.* or as *adj.*

1876 tr. *Peschel's Races of Man* 55 If the index [of breadth] sinks below 74, we speak of 'dolichocephal', narrow or long skulls. **1900** tr. *Deniker's Races of Man* ix. 316 In Sweden and Denmark they were dolichocephals and mesocephals. **1901** [see BRACHYCEPHAL]. **1930** C. G. Seligman *Races of Africa* vi. 132 Tall dolichocephals, with a stature about 67 inches.

dolichocephalic (ˌdɒlɪkəʊsɪˈfælɪk), *a. Ethnol.* Also **dolikho-kephalic**. [f. Gr. δολιχός long + κεφαλή head: cf. κεφαλικός pertaining to the head.] Long-headed: applied to skulls of which the breadth is less than four-fifths (or, according to Broca, three-fourths) of the length; also (less commonly) to tribes of men having such skulls: opposed to BRACHYCEPHALIC.

1849-52 TODD *Cycl. Anat.* IV. 1325/2 The first of these skulls would certainly be placed..in the 'dolichocephalic' division of Professor Retzius. **1861** HULME tr. *Moquin-Tandon* I. v. 32 The features are regular, the head dolikhokephalic. **1866** HUXLEY *Preh. Rem. Caithn.* 84 Skulls ..with the cephalic index less than 0·8 are Dolichocephalic. **1878** LUBBOCK *Preh. Times* v. 142 If we class those skulls in which the relation of the breadth to the length is less than 73 to 100 as long heads, or Dolichocephalic, those in which it is from 74-79 to 100 as medium heads. **1879** tr. *De Quatrefages' Hum. Species* 164 Tribes which were tall and dolichocephalic.

So **dolicho'cephali** *sb. pl.* [mod.L.], men with dolichocephalic skulls. **dolicho'cephalism**, the condition or quality of being dolichocephalic. **dolicho'cephalous** *a.* = DOLICHOCEPHALIC. **dolicho'cephaly** = *dolichocephalism.*

1851 D. WILSON *Preh. Ann.* (1863) I. ix. 281 [He] classes the Celts among dolichocephali. **1864** *Reader* 17 Dec. 771/1 Skull..highly dolichocephalous and prognathous. **1865** THURNAM *Brit. & Gaul. Skulls* in *Anthropol. Soc. Lond.* 477 (L.) If dolichocephalism and brachycephalism have ever, as characters, a race-value, they have it in this instance. **1866** HUXLEY *Preh. Rem. Caithn.* 112 Brachycephaly diminishing and dolichocephaly increasing with the latitude. **1871** DARWIN *Desc. Man* I. iv. 148 Welcker finds that short men incline more to brachycephaly, and tall men to dolichocephaly. **1880** *Nature* XXI. 224 Dolichocephalism and prognathism..prevail. **1881** *Ibid.* XXIII. 221 The Australians..are usually represented as black, straight-haired, dolichocephalous.

dolichocerous (dɒlɪˈkɒsərəs), *a. rare.* [f. Gr. δολιχός long + κέρας horn. Cf. F. *dolichocère.*] Having long 'horns' or antennæ; of or belonging to the *Dolichocera* a sub-tribe of *Muscides* in Latreille's classification. *Syd. Soc. Lex.* (1883).

dolichoderous (dɒlɪˈkɒdərəs), *a. rare.* Also -'dirous. [f. Gr. δολιχόδειρ-ος long-necked, f. δολιχός long + δερή, δειρή neck. Cf. F. *dolichodère.*] Long-necked. *Syd. Soc. Lex.* (1883).

dolichomorphic (ˌdɒlɪkəʊˈmɔːfɪk), *a.* [f. Gr. δολιχός long + μορφή form + -IC.] Having disproportionately long bodily members, as the head and neck.

1930 R. L. SUTTON *Long Trek* 162 In bodily conformation, the typical Mbulu is dolichomorphic. The head is considerably longer than it is wide, the neck is long, the chest is phthisical.

dolichopodous (dɒlɪˈkɒpədəs), *a. rare.* [f. Gr. δολιχόποδ- long-footed, f. δολιχός long + πούς, ποδ- foot. Cf. F. *dolichopode.*] Having long feet.

1883 in *Syd. Soc. Lex.*

‖**Dolichos** (ˈdɒlɪkəs). *Bot.* [mod.L., a. Gr. δολιχός long: named in reference to the length of the pods. Cf. F. *dolic.*] A genus of leguminous plants allied to the Haricot, widely distributed through Asia, Africa, and America.

1753 CHAMBERS *Cycl. Supp.*, *Dolichos*, in Botany, the name of a genus of plants of the papilionaceous kind. **1775** ROMANS *Hist. Florida* 130 A species of Dolichos lately introduced into Georgia from China. **1890** *Golden South* 198 Fences covered with dolichos, maurandia, and hoya.

dolichotis (dɒlɪˈkəʊtɪs). *Zool.* [f. Gr. δολιχός long + οὖς, ὠτ- ear.] A genus of long-eared South American rodents.

1893 W. H. HUDSON *Idle Days Patagonia* iii. 38 Deer, peccary, dolichotis or Patagonian hare.

‖**dolichurus** (dɒlɪˈkjʊərəs). *Gr.* and *L. Pros.* [mod.L., ad. Gr. δολίχουρος long-tailed; also in prosodic sense.] A dactylic hexameter with a redundant syllable in the last foot. Hence **doli'churic** *a.*, as a *dolichuric hexameter.*

dolie, obs. form of DOLY, *a.*

doliman: see DOLMAN.

dolina, doline (dəˈliːnə, dəˈliːn). *Geol.* [ad. Russ. *dolína* valley, plain.] A depression or basin in a karstic limestone region, esp. one that is relatively extensive and funnel-shaped.

1882 A. GEIKIE *Text-bk. Geol.* III. II. ii. 355 The ground may there be found drilled with vertical cavities (*swallow-holes, sinks, dolinas*), by the solution of the rock along lines of joint that serve as channels for descending rain-water. **1922** *Geol. Mag.* LIX. 406 The funnel-shaped hollows which are so frequently met with on the surface of the karst are termed ponors. Many of these are largely filled with red earth, formed by the decomposition of the limestone, and are then known as dolinas. **1937** *Discovery* July 214/1 Huts clustered round a very wide dolina in the shelter of the highest elevation. **1942** O. D. VON ENGELN *Geomorphology* xxii. 572 The doline, of which the swallow hole and sink hole are variants, is the initial and fundamental unit of karst topography. The type doline has the form of a funnel top and occurs in the Adriatic karst. **1962** *Nature* 16 June 1037/2 Vertically walled, knife-edged arêtes and pinnacles of bare limestone standing like battlements around dolines covered by montane forest of mossy aspect.

doling, *vbl. sb.*: see DOLE *v.*[1-3]

dolioloid (ˈdəʊlɪəlɔɪd), *a. rare.* [f. L. *dōliolum*, dim. of *dōlium* cask + -OID.] (See quot.)

1883 *Syd. Soc. Lex.*, *Dolioloid*..resembling a cask.

dolite (ˈdəʊlaɪt). *Palæont.* [ad. mod.L. *Dōlītes* (Krüger 1823), f. *Dōlium*: see below and -ITE.] A fossil shell of the genus *Dolium.*

'do-little, *sb.* and *a.* [f. DO *v.* + LITTLE.]

A. *sb.* One who does little; a lazy person. B. *adj.* Doing little; lazy.

1586 T. B. *La Primaud. Fr. Acad.* I. 190 Men borne in a fat and fertile soile, are commonly do-littles, and cowards. *a* **1654** BP. RICHARDSON *Old Test.* (1655) 281 (T.) Great talkers are commonly do-littles. **1683** KENNETT tr. *Erasm. on Folly* 41 What Woman would be content with such a doo-little Husband? **1834** FONBLANQUE *7 Administ.* (1837) III. 101 The..do-little policy which he regrets.

‖**dolium** (ˈdəʊlɪəm). [Lat.; = a cask, jar.]

1. *Rom. Antiq.* A large earthenware jar or vessel, more or less spherical, for holding wine, oil, or dry commodities, etc.; hence, in mod. use, a cask.

a **1483** *Liber Niger* in *Househ. Ord.* (1790) 29 For everey of the Kalender of the yere, a dolium of wyne. **1658** tr. *Porta's Nat. Magick* IV. xxiii. 152 For every Dolium, powder one ounce of Allome.

2. *Zool.* A genus of gastropod molluscs, having a ventricose shell; also called *tun.*

1752 SIR J. HILL *Hist. Anim.* 149 (Jod.) From the resemblance of the body of this shell to a vessel for the containing fluids, the genus has been named dolium. **1854** WOODWARD *Mollusca* (1856) 115 *Dolium*, Lam. The tun. **1878** BELL *Gegenbaur's Comp. Anat.* 361.

dolk (dɒlk). *Obs.* exc. *dial.* [In form app. the same as DALK, DOKE, as in sense 3; but sense 1 has suggested identity with OE. *dolh, dolȝ* wound, scar, gash, a Common Teut. word = OFris. *dolch*, OHG. *tolg* wound; this, however, does not account for the final *k* sound.]

†1. A wound, a scar. *Obs.*

a **1225** *Ancr. R.* 2 þe on..makeð hire efne & smeðe, wiðute knotte & dolke of woh. *c* **1250** *Gen. & Ex.* 3027 Dolc, sor, and blein on erue and man.

2. A dint; = DAB *sb.* 1 b.

1861 WYNTER *Soc. Bees, Aristocr. Rooks* 383 Put an end to by a dolk in the poll from a [crow's] beak close by.

3. = DOKE, DALK.

a **1825** in FORBY *Voc. E. Anglia.* **1893** ZINCKE *Wherstead* 251 Dolk [is used in East Anglia] for a depression, generally in the ground.

doll (dɒl) *sb.*[1] [a shortened pet-form of *Dorothy, Dor-* being modified to *Dol-*: cf. *Hal, Sall, Mall, Moll, Poll* = *Harry, Sarah, Mary.*]

1. A pet form of the name *Dorothy.* Hence given generically to a female pet, a mistress. Also, the smallest or pet pig in a litter (*dial.*).

1560 *Nice Wanton* in Hazl. *Dodsley* II. 169 But ich tell your minion doll, by Gogs body. **1578** COOPER *Thesaurus*, *O Capitulum lepidissimum*, o pleasaunt companion: O little pretie doll polle. *a* **1592** GREENE *Jas. IV*, I. i, In loving of my Doll [Dorothea], Thou bind'st her father's heart. **1597** SHAKS. *2 Hen. IV*, II. i. 176 Will you have Doll Teare-sheet meet you? *Ibid.* II. iv. 23 Enter Hostesse, and Dol. **1619** FLETCHER *M. Thomas* IV. vi, Com Doll, Doll, dizen me. **1883** *Hampsh. Gloss.*, *Doll*, the smallest pig in a litter.

2. a. An image of a human being (commonly of a child or lady) used as a plaything; a girl's toy-baby. [Cf. Sc. *Doroty*, a doll, a puppet. (Jam.)]

a **1700** B. E. *Dict. Cant. Crew*, *Doll*..also a Child's Baby. **1747** GARRICK *Miss in her Teens* II. i, I'll carry you and your doll too. **1764** O'HARA *Midas* I. v, An infant's dol. **1833** HT. MARTINEAU *Loom & Lugger* I. i, As large as my doll's saucers. **1860** *All Year Round* No. 52. 35 A laborious class Who earn painful bread by fashioning dolls' eyes.

b. A dummy used by a ventriloquist, or by a puppeteer.

1893 R. GANTHONY *Pract. Ventriloquism* IV. 138 Hand Dolls to fit on hand (à la punch)... Knee Dolls 30 inch high, dressed any character. **1950** *Oxf. Jun. Encycl.* IX. 476/2 A conventional ventriloquist's dummy is a wooden doll with large glassy eyes, enormous shutter mouth, and teeth like tombstones. **1957** *Encycl. Brit.* XIV. 906/2 To operate, put the doll on the hand like a glove. **1967** *Listener* 23 Nov. 679/1 Voices that belong not to human beings but to ventriloquists' dolls.

3. *transf.* A pretty, but unintelligent or empty person, esp. when dressed up; a pretty, but silly or frivolous woman. Also in more general sense: a woman; a girl; esp. a very beautiful or attractive woman; also *occas.*, a pleasant or attractive man. *a doll's face*, one conventionally pretty, but without life or expression. Now *slang.*

1778 F. BURNEY *Evelina* I. xxiii. 197 As to the women, why they are mere dolls. **1841-4** EMERSON *Ess.*, *Self-reliance* Wks. (Bohn) I. 32 A sturdy lad..is worth a hundred of these city dolls. **1846** *New Swell's Guide to Night Life* 29 (Partridge, *Dict. Slang* Suppl.), Soldiers and their Dolls. **1851** [see TOFF *sb.*]. **1860** *All Year Round* No. 47. 497 No worker cares to espouse a doll who costs such a deal of money to dress. **1894** BARING-GOULD *Queen Love* III. 145 You care for herself—for her doll's face and wig of yellow hair? **1903** R. L. MCCARDELL *Conversations of Chorus Girl* 53 At Vassar..a bunch of society dolls..are teaching me high kicking. **1923** G. H. MCKNIGHT *Eng. Words* iv. 61 In the vocabulary of modern youth, chivalry is dead... A girl is..a *chicken*, a *doll*, [etc.]. **1931** D. RUNYON (title) Guys and dolls. **1961** 'B. WELLS' *Day Earth caught Fire* ix. 133, I don't dig you, doll. Look we're all entitled to so much water. **1961** in WEBSTER *s.v.*, He is tall, handsome, and muscular. In short, he's a doll. **1967** I. MARDER *Paris Bit* iii. 47 He came up to me..and shook hands warmly... 'Max, doll! How *are* you?' **1971** *Scope* (S. Afr.) 19 Mar. 139/1 You don't have to do it, doll.

4. †a. A hairdresser's block. *Obs.* b. = DOLLY *sb.*[1] 4 a. c. A pair of steps, with wheels, and a stage at the top, used on coal-wharves. d. *doll's head* (in a rifle), a top-extension fitting into a mortice in the top of the standing-breech.

a **1700** B. E. *Dict. Cant. Crew*, *Doll*, a wooden Block to make up Commodes upon. **1841** *P. Parley's Ann.* II. 178 As I understand you get your living by washing, I send you a doll now..namely, a washing doll. **1881** GREENER *Gun* 216 Our new treble-bolt prevents this by keeping the doll's head firmly down in the slot in standing-breech.

5. *Comb.*, as *doll-face, -kind, -maker, -pig* (see 1), etc.; *doll-like, -sized* adjs.; †**doll-common** (the Cheater's punk in Ben Jonson's *Alchemist*) a common woman, a prostitute; **dolls' hospital** (also *N. Amer.* **doll hospital**), an establishment in which dolls are repaired and from which materials for doll-making can be bought; **doll-house** (see DOLL'S HOUSE); **doll-land**, the realm of dolls.

1610 B. JONSON *Alch.* I. i, Thou shalt sit in triumph, And not be styled Dol Common, but Dol Proper, Dol Singular. **1684** OTWAY *Atheist* v. (1735) 93 What, be a Doll-common, and follow the camp. **1884** TENNYSON *Becket* IV. ii, A doll-face blanch'd and bloodless. **1917** *Playthings* Aug. 114/2 (Advt.), Doll hospital. Attention French bisque heads. **1928** *Donaldson's Port Elizabeth & Surburban Directory* (S. Afr.) 113 Dolls' Hospital, Peel St., box 550. **1934** *Cope's Directory: Worcs.* 217/1 Bradburn A M..speciality, dolls' hospital. **1941** E. F. ACKLEY *Doll Shop of your Own* 93 A doll hospital section of your shop is a possibility... The Humpty Dumpty Doll Hospital in California is one of the best known. **1949** *Eastern Province & Midlands Directory* (S. Afr.) 90/2 Dolls Hospital. **1964** *Certificate of Incorporation* (Companies House) No. 818240, 3 Sept., Doll's Hospital Limited. **1964** A. BUTLER *Teaching Children Embroidery* ii. 22 Hair may be obtained from any Doll's Hospital shop. **1971** J. LEASOR *Love-All* ix. 155 The Dolls' Hospital... A giant red cross and red crescent painted on the glass showed ..that here was a hospital of some kind. **1871** *Monthly Packet* Oct. 392 The inhabitants of Doll-land would never have recognized the difference between these home manufactures and the best Russian sables! **1959** *Chambers's Encycl.* XIII. 709/2 An interesting adjunct of doll-land is the doll's house. **1828** MISS MITFORD *Village* Ser. III. Introd. (1863) 461 The delicate doll-like baby..is her own. **1823-5** FOSBROKE *Encycl. Antiq.* s.v. *Doll* (L.), In the middle ages the doll-maker was called coroplastes, and the dolls clothed like infants. **1843** *P. Parley's Ann.* IV. 269 The poor woman..wept as if she had lost her youngest child instead of the doll pig, which is the name usually given to the pet of the farrow.

Hence **'dollatry**, *nonce-wd.* [after *idolatry*], worship of dolls. **'dolldom**, the world of dolls. **'dollhood**, the state or condition of a doll, or of being like a doll. **'dollship**, the personality of a doll or doll-like woman.

1856 *Chamb. Jrnl.* VI. 261 To convince good Protestant mammas that 'dollatry' was not the result or the origin of Mariolatry. **1860** *All Year Round* No. 52. 35 Those limp enormities of dolldom with their pink wooden legs. **1893** *Graphic* 3 June 627/3 How a lady moving in the best circles of dolldom ought to be dressed. **18..** CARLYLE *Let.*, There is much for her to do..her whole sex to deliver from the bondage of frivolity, dollhood, and imbecility. **1876** W. BAYLISS *Witness of Art* 19 Radiant with all that real hair, and wax and rolling eyes can impart to dollhood. **1754** RICHARDSON *Grandison* (1811) VI. 104 The man who should dare to say half I have written of our dollships ought not to go away with his life.

†**doll**, *sb.*[2] *Obs.* [The same as DALLE.] The palm of the hand.

c **1460** [See DALLE]. **1570** LEVINS *Manip.* 160/10 Yᵉ Doll of the hand, *vola.* **1565** GOLDING *Ovid's Met.* VI. (1593) 138 Her babes their prettie dolles did retch.

doll (dɒl), *sb.*[3] *Horse-Racing.* Also dole. [? var. DOOL[1].] A hurdle used as a barrier (see quot. 1942).

1942 BERREY & VAN DEN BARK *Amer. Thes. Slang* §732/5 *Doles, dolls*, barrier hurdles across gallops to close them to horses and horsemen, or to mark turns on a course or gallop. **1958** J. HISLOP *From Start to Finish* vi. 49 The best going is always nearest to the bushes or dolls marking out the gallop.

†**doll**, *v.*[1] *Obs.* Also 6-9 dowl. [Deriv. unknown: it has been conjectured to be the same word as *dull* (of which *doll* occurs as a ME. form): but the Promptorium separates them.]

1. *trans.* To warm moderately; to make tepid; to mull. Hence **'dolling** *vbl. sb.*

c **1440** *Promp. Parv.* 126/1 Dollyd, sum what hotte, *tepefactus.* Dollyn' ale, or oþer drynke, *tepefacio.* *c* **1490** *Ibid.*, Dollynge (MS. K), Doolynge (MS. H), *tepefactio.* **1658** PHILLIPS, *Dolling*, warming. [So in COLES, KERSEY, BAILEY.]

2. To render stale or vapid, to deaden (drink).

1483 *Cath. Angl.* 103/2 Dollyd as wyne or ale, *defunctus, vapidus.* **1513** *Bk. Keruynge* in *Babees Bk.* (1868) 268 Loke ye gyue no persone noo dowled drynke. **1855** ROBINSON *Whitby Gloss.*, *Dowl'd* or *Dull'd*, deadened as stale liquor.

doll (dɒl), *v.*[2] *colloq.* [f. DOLL *sb.*[1] 2.] *trans.* To dress *up* finely or elaborately; to deck *up.* Also *intr.* (for *refl.*) and *transf.* So **'dolled(-up)** *ppl. a.*, **'dolling(-up)** *vbl. sb.*

1906 *Even. Standard* 31 Aug. 3/3 The time fellows spent in dolling up before taking a wheel. **1916** H. L. WILSON *Somewhere in Red Gap* ix. 378 Jeff said he'd also doll up in his dress suit and get shaved. **1917** C. MATHEWSON *Sec. Base Sloan* xix. 261 He was..all dolled up in fancy togs. **1921** *Public Opinion* 9 Sept. 252/1 Keturah dolled herself up a little but not too much. **1921** H. C. WITWER *Leather Pushers* iv. 93 He..gives himself a swift dollin' up before the mirror. **1923** E. O'NEILL *Hairy Ape* v. 46 All dis is too clean and quiet and dolled up. **1927** M. EIKER *Over the Boat-Side* 269 She had been exquisitely costumed. If she ever did run into Reverdy, she hoped it would be some time when she was dolled. **1928** *Daily Express* 11 Sept. 5/5 The look of bitter contempt and disgust that glittered out of the dolled-up servitor's eyes. **1928** GALSWORTHY *Swan Song* II. xiii. 216 He supposed his fellow-guests were 'dolling up' (as young Michael would put it) for this ball. **1932** E. WILSON *Devil take Hindmost* iv. 29 The new architecture..is a revelation of our helplessness under the industrial system... When we try to doll it up a little, the result is..the New School. *Ibid.* xxii. 234 A dolled-up blonde had called at his office. **1955** 'N. SHUTE' *Requiem for Wren* iii. 67 She could put on her Number Ones and doll herself up smartly. **1959** J. FLEMING *Miss Bones* ii. 18 Change the frames over..doll them up—you know the sort of thing that makes them sell.

† **doll**, var. of DAL (*Anglo-Ind.*), a kind of pulse; obs. f. DOLE *sb.*[2], DULL.

dollar ('dɒlə(r)). Forms: 6 **daleir, -er, dal(l)or, dalder, doler, dolor, 6–7 daller, 7–8 doller, -or, 7– dollar.** [In 16th c. *daler, daller*, a. LG. and early mod.Du. *daler* (mod.Du. *daalder*), = HG. *taler, thaler*, recorded by Alberus 1540, along with the full term *Joachimstaler*, lit. '(gulden) of Joachimsthal' (in Bohemia), where they were coined in 1519, from a silver mine opened there in 1516 (Kluge). From LG. or HG. taken into other langs. In England before 1600 modified to *dollar*.]

1. The English name for the German *thaler*, a large silver coin, of varying value, current in the German states from the sixteenth century; *esp.* the unit of the German monetary union (1857–73) equal to 3 marks. Also of coins of northern countries, bearing equivalent names, as the *rigsdaler* of Denmark, *riksdaler* of Sweden.

1553 R. MORYSIN & SIR T. CHAMBERLAYNE *Let.* 4 Apr. in E. Lodge *Illustr. etc. Edw. VI*, xxiii. (1791) I. 166 The Duke of Wirtemberg..shall have for his charges 66000 dalers. *a* **1560** *Aberdeen Reg.* V. 24 (Jam.) Twa siluer daleiris. **1560** GRESHAM in Burgon *Life & T.* (1839) I. 334 To be received of the Countie of Mansfield..300,000 dallors; which, at five shillings each, is 75,000*l.* **1577** HARRISON *England* II. xxv. (1877) I. 364 Of siluer coines..are the dalders, and such, often times brought ouer. **1588** J. READ *Compend. Method* 68 A plate..in thickenesse of a Dolor of siluer. **1601** R. JOHNSON *Kingd. & Commw.* (1603) 92, 2 dollars of money..every house one dollor. **1606** *Crt. & Times Jas. I* (1849) I. 67 The King of Denmark..hath given in court 30,000 dollars. *a* **1618** SYLVESTER *Selfe-Civil-War* 108 For Dallers, Dolours hoordeth in my Chest. **1706** PHILLIPS (ed. Kersey), *Dollar*, a foreign coin: The Zeoland, or common Dollar is worth 3 shillings sterling, the specie Dollar 5*s.* The Dollar of Riga 4*s.* 8*d.* Of Lunenburg and Brisgaw 4*s.* 2*d.* Of Hamburgh 3*s.* 2*d.* **1763** SHENSTONE *Economy* I. 218 With nice precision learn A dollar's value. **1775** WRAXALL *Tour North. Europe* 101, I tender them one of fifty copper dollars. **1865** CARLYLE *Fredk. Gt.* VII. XVII. v. 56.

2. The English name for the peso or piece of eight (i.e. eight reales), formerly current in Spain and the Spanish American colonies, and largely used in the British N. American Colonies at the time of their revolt.

1581 RICH *Farewell Milit. Profession* (Shaks. Soc.) 217 Their beardes sometymes cutte rounde, like a Philippes doler. **1634** SIR T. HERBERT *Trav.* 41 A Spanish shilling (which is a fourth part of a Dollar). **1650** BULWER *Anthropomet.* 108 As great as a silver Caroline Doller. **1767** FRANKLIN *Wks.* (1887) IV. 90 A dollar thereby coming to be rated at eight shillings in paper money of New York. **1779** R. KING in *Life & Corr.* (1894) I. 30 Could you send me three or four hundred of those good for nothing paper dollars? **1813** WELLINGTON 25 Feb. in Gurw. *Desp.* X. 143 Dollars are issued to the troops at the rate of 4/6 sterling each, which is the mint price of dollars in England. **1879** H. PHILLIPS *Notes Coins* 12 A silver dollar of Philip II of Spain bears among his other titles that of King of England.

3. a. The standard unit of the gold and silver coinage of the United States of America, containing 100 cents. Also a coin of corresponding value in Canada and some other countries. Sometimes abbreviated *dol.*, but more generally represented by the dollar-mark $ before the number. (See also ALMIGHTY *a.* 2.)

The decimal system of coinage and the dollar were adopted by the Continental Congress on 6 July 1785 (see quot.), but were not brought into use till 1794, two years after the law of 2 April 1792 establishing the mint.

[**1782** T. JEFFERSON *Notes on a Money Unit for U.S.* Wks. III. 446 The unit or [Spanish] dollar is a known coin and the most familiar of all to the mind of the people. It is already adopted from south to north.] **1785** *Resol. Continent. Congress U.S.* 6 July, Resolved, that the money unit of the United States of America be one dollar. **1796** *Amer. State Papers* For. Relat. (1832) I. 549 (Stanf. s.v. *Douceur*) Sixty thousand dollars were paid. **1821** T. JEFFERSON *Autobiog.* Writ. 1892 I. 74, I proposed..to adopt the Dollar as our Unit of account and payment. **1837** W. IRVING *Wolfert's R.* (1855) 25 The almighty dollar, that great object of universal devotion throughout our land.

b. Colloq. phrases (orig. and chiefly *U.S.*): ***bottom dollar***, see BOTTOM *sb.* 20; ***(it is) dollars to doughnuts*** (or ***buttons***, etc.), (it is) almost assured; a certainty; ***(like) a million dollars***, see MILLION.

1884 G. W. PECK *Peck's Boss Book* 130 It is dollars to buttons that..she will be blown through the roof. **1890** *Texas Siftings* 8 Nov. 6/3 It is dollars to a doughnut..That some one will start a fire. **1904** *Boston Herald* 8 Aug. 6 It is dollars to cobwebs that every such person will be disappointed. **1904** *Utica* (N.Y.) *Observer* 29 June 6 They talk of fire drills;..it is dollars to doughnuts that not an excursion boat in New York harbor ever had one. **1932** *Atlantic Monthly* Mar. 390/2 It is dollars to doughnuts not a soul will see him. **1936** J. CURTIS *Gilt Kid* xiii. 131 If he were seen it was dollars to doughnuts that he would be arrested.

4. a. Also used as a name for various foreign coins of a value more or less approaching that of the Spanish or American dollar; as the *peso* of Mexico, and of the republics of Central and South America, the *piastre* of Arabia, the *yen* of Japan, etc.

1882 BITHELL *Counting-ho. Dict.* (1893) 99 s.v. *Doblon*, The Gold Doblon of Chili weighing 7·626 grammes, ·900 fine, value 5 Chilian dollars, or 18*s.* 8·95*d.* *Ibid.* 222 s.v. *Patacon*, *Patacon.* (*a.*) The unit of value in the Argentine Republic (La Plata). It bears also the alternative names of Peso Duro, and Hard Dollar. *Ibid.* 226 s.v. *Peso*, The excellence of the Mexican peso, or dollar, renders it a favourite coin with all countries, and has given it much of the character of an international coin. *Ibid.* 228 s.v. *Piastre*, The Piastre or Mocha Dollar is the unit of value in Arabia, and is worth nearly 3*s.* 5*d.*

b. *slang.* A five-shilling piece; a crown.

5. With qualifying words. ***buzzard dollar***, a name applied, in derision of the figure of an eagle on the reverse side, to the United States silver dollar of 412½ grains, coined in accordance with the Bland Bill of 1878. ***lion dollar***, a Dutch coin bearing the figure of a lion; also current in New York in colonial times. ***pillar dollar***, a silver coin of Spain, bearing a figure of the Pillars of Hercules, formerly current in the Spanish colonies in America: cf. sense 2. ***trade dollar***, a silver dollar of 420 grains formerly coined by the United States mint for purposes of trade with eastern Asia. ***dollar of the fathers***, a phrase applied to the silver dollar, by those who advocated its remonetization, which was effected in 1878: see quot. 1889.

a **1725** WHITWORTH *Acc. Russia* (1758) 77 Of the same goodness with Lyon Dollars, viz. twelve ounces fine silver, and four ounces alloy to the pound. **1768** GOV. MOORE *To Earl of Hillsborough* 14 May (Documents relating to Colon. Hist. of N.Y. VIII. 72), The Lyon Dollars (a species of money brought here by the first Dutch settlers) are rarely now seen. **1823** CRABB *Technol. Dict.*, s.v. The former [Spanish Dollars] are called pillar dollars, because they bear on the reverse the arms of Spain between two pillars. **1877** *N.Y. Tribune* 21 July, 6 Some of the absurdities of the demand for the 'Dollar of our Fathers'. **1878** *Nation* (N.Y.) 10 Jan. 26 Linderman..was the projector of the trade-dollar. **1882** BITHELL *Counting-ho. Dict.* (1893) 301 The coinage of the Silver Trade Dollar was first authorized by the Act of Feb. 12th, 1873. **1889** FARMER *Amer.*, *Dollar of the Fathers*, a catch cry, turned by opponents into the 'dollar of the daddies', which was used during the remonetization agitation of 1877.

6. *attrib.* and *Comb.* ***dollar-bill, -earner, -earning*** adj., ***-hunt, -hunter, -hunting*** sb. and adj., ***-note***; **dollar area**, the area comprising countries where the American dollar is used as currency or as a basis for exchange, or whose sterling balances with British banks are freely convertible into dollars; **dollar-a-year man** *U.S.*, a man who serves the government for a nominal salary; also *transf.*; **dollar country**, a country in the dollar area; **dollar diplomacy** orig. *U.S.*, a foreign policy that seeks to further the financial and commercial interests of a country (*spec.* of America) abroad and often to extend its influence in international relations by means of these interests; **dollar gap**, the excess of a country's (*spec.* Britain's) receipts or imports from the United States or other countries in the dollar area over its payments or exports to those countries; **dollar imperialism** = *dollar diplomacy*; **dollar-mark**: see 3; **dollar-sign** *U.S.* = *dollar-mark*; **dollar spot**, a discoloured patch caused by disease, as on an animal or on turf; the disease itself; **dollar store** *U.S.*, a shop in which all or most of the articles are priced at a dollar or less.

1946 *Hansard Commons* 19 Nov. 688 Will the hon. Gentleman give an assurance that no goods will be purchased from the dollar area which can be purchased from the sterling area? **1918** *Lit. Digest* 11 May 11/1 While the 'dollar-a-year men' undoubtedly did good work, the delay and friction in our war-machine became glaringly evident. **1952** *Times Lit. Suppl.* 31 Oct. 702/3 This business man first turned banker; and then he turned Secretary of the Navy, and later of Defence, to serve his country as a dollar-a-year man. **1774** N. CRESSWELL *Jrnl.* (1925) 21 A considerable sum in Four, Three, Two, One, Two-thirds, One-third and 'One-Ninth' of a Dollar Bills is struck in these Bills of Credit. **1813** *Kingston* (Ontario) *Gaz.* 7 Sept. 3/3 Two hundred and fifty pounds in Dollar bills. *c* **1828** A. LAWRENCE *Diary & Corr.* (1855) 87 Dollar-bill was found in your chamber on the morning you left home. **1883** *Century Mag.* XXVI. 596/2 Folding the dollar-bills that she had brought her. **1917** H. T. COMSTOCK *Man thou Gavest* 195 He..tucked the letter and dollar bill in the breast of his shirt. **1947** *Hansard Commons* 8 July 2048 We are drawing nearly half our supplies from dollar countries. **1953** *Ann. Reg. 1952* 338 The more northerly 'dollar countries' of Venezuela, Colombia, the Dominican Republic, Cuba, and Mexico. **1910** *Harper's Weekly* 23 Apr. 8 An attempt is made..to outline..what is meant by the term 'Dollar Diplomacy', as it has come to be commonly applied to certain of the activities of Secretary Knox..in Honduras, in Liberia, [etc.]. **1940** *Economist* 31 Aug. 277/2 The Nazis reinforce Argentina's distrust of American leadership by whispering campaigns on 'dollar diplomacy'. **1958** *Times* 17 July 3/3 There were three conflicting forces... The first was international Communism, the second aggressive nationalism, and, third, and more recent—dollar doctrine and diplomacy. **1958** *New Statesman* 22 Feb. 224/3 Tourism is..our biggest single dollar-earner. **1962** *Harper's Bazaar* Aug. 13 Scotch whisky—Britain's biggest dollar-earning export. **1948** *Ann. Reg. 1947* 92 A year when the British people were introduced to a battle of the dollar gap. **1957** *Times* 18 Nov. (Annual Financial & Commercial Rev.) p. 1/1 Sterling came under such exceptional pressure in the current year, however, largely because of..the re-emergence of the dollar gap. **1892** STEVENSON & OSBOURNE *Wrecker* ix. 138 Of all forms of the dollar-hunt, this wrecking had by far the most address to my imagination. **1848** MILL *Pol. Econ.* II. IV. vi. 309 The life of the whole of one sex is devoted to dollar-hunting, and of the other to breeding dollar-hunters. **1900** *Daily News* 25 Sept. 4/6 The dollar-hunting Americans. **1964** *Daily Tel.* 12 Feb. 14 'Dollar imperialism' is condemned for disorganising or even preying on the liberation of Britain's empire. **1847** *Boston Weekly Mail* 23 Jan. 3/6 The dollar mark..is only applied, properly, to the United States coin, or currency, of that name. **1894** *Montreal Star* Almanac for 1895. 132 It was found convenient to continue the old dollar-mark in the South, and to adopt it in the North. **1831** *Deb. Congress U.S.* 22 Feb., App. p. cxxxix, Taking the issues of one, two, and three dollar notes, in the Eastern States as a guide. **1844** DICKENS *Mart. Chuz.* xxxiii, A little roll of dollar-notes fell out upon the ground. [**1857** *Hist. Mag.* I. 186 In 1784,.. Jefferson in the memorial which proposed the dollar as the American money-unit, employed the $ sign.] **1895** *Montgomery Ward Catal.* 223/3 Linen Markers Rubber Type Outfit... Consists of five printers' alphabets,.. punctuation marks, dollar sign, [etc.]. **1920** S. LEWIS *Main St.* x. 115 The dollar-sign has chased the crucifix clean off the map. **1912** J. R. MOHLER et al. tr. *Hutyra & Marek's Spec. Path. Dis. Dom. Animals* I. vi. 826 The number of the dollar spots may be considerable, even exceeding one hundred. **1922** C. R. EDMONDS *Dis. Anim. S. Afr.* 340 About the fortieth day the 'plaques' or dollar spots first appear in the skin. **1926** *Bull. U.S. Golf Assoc. Green Section* May 129 Small [brown-]patch is generally limited to about the size of a silver dollar, from which it has been commonly referred to as 'dollar spot'. **1935** *Gardeners' Chron.* 23 Feb. 129/1 Investigation of diseases of turf of lawns and greens has been prosecuted in the U.S.A. for many years, and the commonest diseases and causal organisms are well known, viz., Brown-patch, due to Rhizoctonia Solani, and Dollarspot, due to an unnamed species of Rhizoctonia. **1956** *Dict. Gardening* (R. Hort. Soc.) (ed. 2) IV. 2169/2 Dollar Spot is due to the fungus *Sclerotinia homoeocarpa*. **1872** *Harper's Mag.* June 132/2 There are ever so many good girls in factories..and in 'dollar stores' too.

Hence **'dollared** *a.*, furnished with dollars, wealthy. **'dollarless** *a.*, without dollars: cf. *penniless.* **dolla'rocracy**, *nonce-wd.*: see -CRACY. **'dollarship** (*humorously*), the personality of a dollared man.

1844 DICKENS *Mart. Chuz.* xvii. (D.) A dollarless and unknown man. **1869** H. DEEDES *America* 151 So long as their Dollarships' eyes and noses are not affected by his [the negro's] propinquity. **1884** *Longm. Mag.* Feb. 386 The dollared lady. **1889** *Pall Mall G.* 2 July 2/1 The phlegmatic assurance of dollarocracy.

'dollar-bird. An Australian bird of the genus *Eurystomus*, so called from a large round white spot on the wing.

1847 LEICHHARDT *Jrnl.* v. 156 The dollar-bird passed with its arrow-like flight.

Dollardom ('dɒlədəm). [f. DOLLAR + -DOM.] A place where the people's main aim is to amass dollars; also, the inhabitants of such a place; rich Americans collectively.

1852 *Lantern* (N.Y.) I. 109/2 My dear Dollardom, listen to a suggestion of Diogenes. **1852** *Hamilton* (Ontario) *Gaz.* 20 May 3/2 The mercurial Demon of Republicanisms, hath been urging the matrons and maidens of Dollardom to the perpetration of strangely preposterous pranks. **1920** *Blackw. Mag.* Aug. 139/1 Manhattan Dollardom trooped into the Ritz-Carlton carrying flasks.

'dollar-fish.

1. A name given to two kinds of fish, from their round form and silvery colour (in the case of the former, of the young.) **a.** *Vomer setipinnis*, called also *moonfish.* **b.** *Stromateus triacanthus*, called also *butter-* and *harvest-fish.*

2. An echinoderm of a discoid shape; a cake-urchin or sand-dollar.

18.. J. W. DAWSON in Borthwick's *Br.-Amer. Rdr.* (1860) 222 The curious flat cake-like shells of the Echinarachnius Atlanticus,—the dollar-fish of some parts of the coast.

'doll-,baby. *U.S.* [DOLL *sb.*[1] 2.] = DOLL *sb.*[1] 2 and 3; in quot. 1807, a small image of the human figure on which clothes are displayed. Also *attrib.*

1807 JEFFERSON *Writings* (1898) IX. 83 The dresses of the annual doll-babies from Paris. **1853** J. G. BALDWIN *Flush Times Alabama* 42 She never had more than a thimble-full of brains in her doll-baby head. *Ibid.* 292 The little girls.. had been petted by their fathers and mothers like doll-babies. **1896** *Harper's Mag.* XCII. 808/2, I keep on looking just the same frivolous doll-baby. **1965** H. GOLD *Man who was not with It* iv. 34 The doll-baby lashes fell shut.

dollied, -er, -ness: see after DOLLY *a.* and *v.*

dollin, obs. var. of *dolven*, pa. pple. of DELVE.

dollish (ˈdɒlɪʃ), *a.* [f. DOLL *sb.*[1] + -ISH.]

Somewhat doll-like; having characteristics of a doll.

1865 E. C. CLAYTON *Cruel Fortune* II. 237 She's rather dollish, to my taste. **1874** BURNAND *My Time* xxxii. 320 As pretty, though dollish, a blonde as you'd wish to see.

Hence ˈ**dollishly** *adv.*; ˈ**dollishness**.

1892 *Academy* 2 Jan. 9/1 A woman.. less dollishly pretty perhaps. **1893** *Nat. Observer* 437/1 Dolls both, and equal in their dollishness.

dollop (ˈdɒləp), *sb.* Also 6–9 **dallop.** [Origin obscure: cf. Norweg. dial. *dolp* lump (Ross).]

†**1.** *Farming.* A patch, tuft, or clump of grass, weeds, etc. in a field. *Obs.*

1573 TUSSER *Husb.* liv. (1878) 121 Let dallops about be mowne and had out. *Ibid.* lvii. 131 Of barlie the longest and greenest ye find, Leave standing by dallops. **1669** WORLIDGE *Syst. Agric.* (1681) 316 *Dallops*, a term used in some places for Patches or Corners of Grass or Weeds among Corn. *a* **1825** FORBY *Voc. E. Anglia*, *Dallop*, rank tufts of growing corn where heaps of manure have lain.

2. a. *colloq.* or *vulgar.* (See quots.)

1812 J. H. VAUX *Flash Dict.*, A *dollop* is a large quantity of any thing; the whole dollop means the total quantity. *a* **1825** FORBY *Voc. E. Anglia*, *Dallop*.. a clumsy and shapeless lump of any thing tumbled about in the hands. **1853** *N. & Q.* 1st Ser. VIII. 65/2 'What a dollop of fat you have given me!' **1880** BLACKMORE *Mary Anerley* xxxvi, I sent a great dollop of water into the face of the poor lieutenant.

b. An untidy woman, a slattern, trollop. *dial.*

a **1825** in FORBY *Voc. E. Anglia.* **1877** *N.W. Linc. Gloss.*

dollop (ˈdɒləp), *v. colloq.* and *dial.* Formerly also **dallop.** [f. the sb.] *trans.* To serve, put or give *out* in large quantities; to cover (something) with a large quantity. Also *fig.* (See also quots. *a* 1825 and 1860.)

a **1825** R. FORBY *Vocab. E. Anglia* (1830) I. 88 *Dallop*, to paw, toss, and tumble about carelessly. **1860** HOTTEN *Slang Dict.* 130 *Dollop*, to dole up, give up a share. **1960** R. DANIEL *Death by Drowning* i. 17 Clare dolloped a spoonful of trifle on her plate. **1961** W. BUCHAN *Helen all Alone* 168 Close-grown shrubs, all dark and dolloped with snow. **1967** *Listener* 28 Sept. 401/2 Is there either anthropological or literary virtue in mere transcription from tape, actuality dolloped out hot from a machine?

ˈ**doll's house.** Also **doll-house, dolls' house.** [DOLL *sb.*[1] 2.] A miniature toy house made for dolls; also *transf.* and *fig.*, applied esp. to a diminutive dwelling-house. Also *attrib.*

1783 LADY E. FENN *Cobwebs to catch Flies* I. 90, I have a chest at home, in my doll's house. **1840** DICKENS *Let.* 31 July (1969) II. 109, I don't believe there is anywhere such a perfect little doll's house as this... the garden flourishing, the road lively, the rooms free from creeping things. **1842** —— *Amer. Notes* I. iii. 113 Like articles of furniture for a pauper doll's-house. **1847** C. BRONTË *J. Eyre* I. iv. 47 Some picture-books and doll's house furniture. **1853** DICKENS *Bleak Ho.* vi. 57 A habitable doll's house.. would set the boy up in life. **1855** *Fraser's Mag.* July 60/2 Each of these doll-house rooms is crowded with prints, [etc.]. **1865** DICKENS *Mut. Fr.* II. IV. v. 198 'We live on Blackheath, in the charmingest of dolls' houses...' But Bella started up...'I want to be something so much worthier than the doll in the doll's house.' **1882** H. F. LORD tr. *Ibsen's Nora* p. v, The play now given to us as *Nora* is called in Norwegian *Et Dukkehjem.* To a public unused to Ibsen's surprises, *A Doll's House* is a misleading title. **1903** G. B. SHAW *Man & Superman* Ep. Ded. p. xi, Doña Juana, breaking out of the Doll's House and asserting herself as an individual. **1926** W. DEEPING *Sorrell & Son* xxiv, Christopher spent a week-end with Thomas Roland in his doll's house at Chelsea. **1959** [see DOLL *sb.*[1] 5].

dolly (ˈdɒlɪ), *sb.*[1] [f. DOLL: see -Y.]

1. A familiar pet-form of the name *Dorothy* (= DOLL *sb.*[1] 1).

1610 B. JONSON *Alch.* III. iii, (To Dol Common), So much the easier to be cozen'd, my Dolly. **1841–4** EMERSON *Ess.*, *Spir. Laws* Wks. (Bohn) I. 70 The great soul incarnated in some.. Dolly or Joan.

2. †**a.** A female pet or favourite. *Obs. slang.* **b.** A drab, slattern, useless woman. *dial.* or *colloq.*

1648 HERRICK *Hesper.*, *Lyrick to Mirth* (1869) 38 Kisse our dollies night and day. **1706** E. WARD *Hud. Rediv.* II. v. 13 And so away he led his Dolly. **1828** *Craven Dialect*, *Dolly*, a slattern. **1883** *Almondb. & Huddersf. Gloss.* s.v., 'He's got a maungy dolly for a wife.' **1873** DIXON *Two Queens* I. III. vi. 149 Puebla.. took his seat at table with these dollies and their mates.

c. A girl or woman, esp. a young, attractive one. *colloq.*

1906 E. DYSON *Fact'ry 'Ands* xiv. 181 Now I wouldn' turn it [*sc.* beer] down fer ther toffest Dolly on ther block. **1942** BERREY & VAN DEN BARK *Amer. Thes. Slang* §382/2 A female, esp. a girl or young woman,.. *dolly.* *Ibid.* §427/3 Cute girl,.. *dolly.* **1968** *Observer* (Colour Suppl.) 21 Jan. 5/1 Every bird, dolly, housewife, and career girl in Britain today owes something to the ladies on the left. **1968** *Daily Mirror* 20 Aug. 9/3 He is very gone on girls, is always falling wildly in and out of love with dishy dollies.

3. a. A pet name for a child's doll. (Also treated as the personal name of a female doll.)

1790 MORISON *Poems* 82 (Jam.) Like a dally drawn on delf Or china ware. **1865** E. C. CLAYTON *Cruel Fortune* I. 143 A ragshop, with its black dolly dangling over the door. **1884** *Health Exhib. Catal.* 137/2 Dolly as a baby, as a girl, as a young lady, as a lady.

b. *Cricket* (*colloq.*). (*a*) A donkey-drop (see DONKEY 3 b); (*b*) a very easy catch (cf. DOLLY *a.* sense b).

1906 A. E. KNIGHT *Complete Cricketer* 344 *Donkey-drop* or *dolly*, a slang term for slow, dropping bowling. **1956** N. CARDUS *Close of Play* 78 But he might give Mr. Champain an over or two of his 'dollies'. **1969** P. DICKINSON *Pride of Heroes* 40 Sir Ralph bowls me a dolly, watches me cart it for six, and records his admiration.

4. Applied to various contrivances fancied to resemble a doll in some way.

a. *dial.* A wooden appliance with two arms, and legs or feet, used to stir and twirl clothes in the wash-tub, called a ***dolly-tub***; also called ***dolly-legs*** or ***-stick***, ***peggy***, ***maiden***. The name is sometimes less correctly given to the tub, and extended to mechanical contrivances fulfilling the same purpose; also to an apparatus for agitating and washing ore in a vessel; and to a beetle for linen, beating hemp, etc.

1792 W. ROBERTS *Looker-on* No. 41 The Dumb Dolly, or a machine for washing, is recommended. **1828** *Craven Dialect*, *Dolly*.. a washing tub. **1840** SPURDENS *Suppl. to Forby*, *Dolly*, a beetle used in 'bunching hemp', as a punishment, in bridewell. **1858** SIMMONDS *Dict. Trade*, *Dolly*, in mining parlance a perforated board, placed over a tub containing ore to be washed, and which being worked by a winch-handle, gives a circular motion to the ore. **1869** R. B. SMYTH *Goldf. Victoria* 609 *Dolly*, an instrument used by diggers for dividing and mixing the tough clay or cement with water in the puddling-tub. **1877** *Holderness Gloss.* s.v., *Dolly-tub*, a barrel-shaped machine for washing clothes which are stirred about with a pronged-instrument, called a dolly-stick. **1884** *Athenæum* 26 Apr. 533/1 One sort of dolly is a barrel-formed tub, in which a beater is worked by hand up and down. **1892** *Northumbld. Gloss.*, *Dolly*, a clothes washing stick, made with feet, but otherwise like a poss-stick. **1894** *Superfl. Woman* (ed. 4) I. 159 [The] dolly-tub stood with some of the wet linen hanging on the side.

b. *Pile-driving.* A short length of timber or metal set on the top of a pile to act as a buffer between it and the ram; also used to lengthen the pile when driven out of the reach of the ram; a punch.

1838 SIMMS *Public Wks. Gt. Brit.* II. (1846) 22 Cast-iron dolleys, weighing about $1\frac{3}{4}$ cwt., were fitted to the tops of the main piles to receive the blows. **1868** *Minutes Proc. Inst. Civ. Engin.* XXVII. 318 A timber dolly was used between the pile and the ram.

c. *Austral. Gold-fields.* A rude appliance somewhat on the principle of a pile-driver, used to crush auriferous quartz.

1869 R. B. SMYTH *Goldf. Victoria* 609 *Dolly*.. a log of wood shod with iron and suspended from a sapling over a stump, and used in the early days for crushing quartz. **1880** SUTHERLAND *Tales Goldf.* 75 For the purpose of testing the quartz they employed a very primitive apparatus, which the miners call a dolly.

d. A machine for punching iron; a tool used in forming the head of a rivet.

1848 *Inv. Wallsend Colliery* (Northumbld. Gloss.), A punching dolley, $16\frac{1}{2}$ cwts. **1869** SIR E. J. REED *Shipbuild.* xvii. 340 The holder-up.. after having driven the head [of the rivet] well up by a few heavy blows, holds upon it with a large hammer or a tool called a 'dolly'. **1879** *Cassell's Techn. Educ.* IV. 134/2 A workman.. presses against the head with.. a mass of iron termed a 'dolly'.

e. A contrivance with a covering of rags, polish, etc., used in various trades for polishing.

1884 F. J. BRITTEN *Watch & Clockm.* 213 Wooden dollies of suitable shape covered with the finest doe skin and rotated in the lathe are used. **1891** *Sheffield Gloss.* Suppl., *Dolly*, a wheel covered by rags, and used by cutlers in polishing their wares.

f. *colloq.* and *dial.* A binding of rag round a hurt finger, etc.

1888 in *Berksh. Gloss.*

g. An apparatus for street gambling. (See quot. 1873.)

[**1851–61** MAYHEW *Lond. Lab.* I. 6 (Hoppe) The proprietors of Street Games, as swings.. down-the-dolly, spin-'em round, [etc.].] **1873** *Slang Dict.*, *Dolly*.. consisting of a round board and the figure of an old man or 'Dolly', down which was a spiral hole. A marble dropped 'down the Dolly', would stop in one of the small holes or pits (numbered) on the board. **1891** *Daily News* 5 Sept. 7/3 The stock-in-trade of the offenders, chiefly roulette tables and 'dollies', being destroyed by order of the Court.

h. A small platform on wheels or rollers, used as a truck or conveyance; *spec.* a mobile platform on wheels on which a film- or television-camera can be moved about; (see also quot. 1955). orig. *U.S.*

1901 MERWIN & WEBSTER *Calumet 'K'* vi. 104 Other gangs were carrying them [*sc.* planks] away and piling them on 'dollies' to be pulled along the plank runways to the hoist. *Ibid.* xiii. 246 And every stick that leaves the runway has got to go on a dolly. **1929** *Bookman* Feb. 622 'Moving in' or 'trucking up' means wheeling the camera (on a small rubber tired wagon or 'dolly') closer to the characters. **1937** *Electronics* June 14/3 The camera is mounted in a mechanically controllable mount, and this in turn may be placed on a movable platform or 'dolly' so that it can be moved about over the set. **1948** *Time* 21 June 1/2 With a heavy truck and a tractor pulling, and one of these dollies under each corner, the derrick.. was moved $3\frac{1}{2}$ miles. **1955** *Amer. Speech* XXX. 91 *Dolly*, a retractable support for a semi-trailer when it is not connected to a tractor. **1961** G. MILLERSON *Television Production* iii. 27 Two small cranes (or power-operated dollies) and two pedestal cameras will meet the reasonable demands of even an elaborate drama production. **1970** *Commercial Motor* 25 Sept. 101/2 Converter dollies for use with standard haulage semi-trailers.

i. *S. Afr.* A lure for fish (see quot. 1957).

1930 C. L. BIDEN *Sea-angling Fishes of Cape* 136 The lure or 'dolly' as the fishermen term it. **1957** S. SCHOEMAN *Strike!* 117 Professional fishermen catch thousands [of snoek] on 'dollies', which are cigar-shaped pieces of lead.. with a large barbless hook attached. A few thin strips of shark skin or pork rind or even a piece of red rag or silver paper is tied to the shank of the hook.

j. *Electr. Engin.* (See quot.)

1940 *Chambers's Techn. Dict.* 257/2 *Dolly*, the operating member of a tumbler switch; it consists of a small pivoted lever projecting through the outer cover.

5. *attrib.* and *Comb.* as ***dolly-land***; (sense 4 h) ***dolly camera***, ***-pusher***, ***shot***; **dolly-bag** = DOROTHY BAG; **dolly-bar**, 'a block or bar in the trough of a grindstone which is lowered into the water to raise the latter against the face of the stone by displacement' (Knight *Dict. Mech.*); **dolly-legs**: see 4 a; **dolly-man**, (*a*) one who keeps a dolly-shop; (*b*) one who works with a dolly; **dolly mixture**, a mixture of tiny coloured sweets of various shapes; also *transf.*, *fig.* and *attrib.*; **dolly-mop** (*slang*), a drab; **dolly-pedal**, a tool used by chainmakers in welding the ends of a link; **dolly peg** *dial.*, a wooden implement, shaped like a stool with a long handle projecting upwards from it, used for agitating clothes in a wash-tub; = sense 4 above; cf. PEGGY *sb.* 3; **dolly-shop**, a marine store, a shop where rags, bottles, etc. are bought, frequently having a black doll hanging outside as a sign, and often serving as a low or illegal pawn-shop; **dolly-tub**: see 4 a. (Cf. also DOLLY *a.* c.)

1926 R. H. MOTTRAM *Crime at Vanderlynden's* 29 She carried the day's takings clasped to her breast, in a solid little leather *dolly-bag. **1958** *Birmingham Even. Mail* 27 Mar. 6/6 Dollybags swinging from the arm. **1958** M. DICKENS *Man Overboard* ii. 30 The cameraman.. climbed up to his perch on the big *dolly camera. **1869** *Lonsdale Gloss.*, **Dolly-legs*, an implement with five or six legs for washing. **1851** MAYHEW *Lond. Labour* (1861) II. 110 A poor person driven to the necessity of raising a few pence.. goes to the *dolly-man. **1957** R. HOGGART *Uses of Literacy* vi. 167 The '*dolly-mixtures' pleasures of a constant diet of odd snippets, of unrelated scrappy facts, each with its sugary little kernel of 'human interest'. **1959** I. & P. OPIE *Lore & Lang. Schoolch.* ix. 166 Other current sweet-shop favourites appear to be the same as thirty years ago, in fact bull's eyes, jelly babies, and dolly mixture have entered schoolchild language as descriptive nouns. *Ibid.* 169 A chap who has got duck's disease is.. labelled.. dolly mixture (after a species of very small sweet). **1833** MARRYAT *P. Simple* iv, His liberty's stopped for getting drunk and running after the *Dolly Mops! **1894** DU MAURIER *Trilby* (1895) 58 A dirty, drabby, little Dolly-mop of a Jewess. **1879–81** G. F. JACKSON *Shropshire Word-bk.* 122 **Dolly-peg*, an implement similar in intention to the dolly, but differing from it in form and mode of action. **1917** *Harrods Gen. Catal.* 1111 (*caption*) Dolly Peg.. 2/9. **1987** *Spectator* 11 July 25/1 A woman came every Monday to do the household laundry with a tub and a dolly-peg. **1956** H. GRISEWOOD in A. Pryce-Jones *New Outl. Mod. Knowledge* III. 423 These various sorts of *structores* and *imaginarii* were the *dolly-pushers, the cameramen.. of the ancient world. **1851** MAYHEW *Lond. Lab.* (1861) II. 110 The *dolly-shops are essentially pawn-shops, and pawn-shops for the very poorest. **1933** in C. Winchester *World Film Encycl.* 481/2 '*Dolley shot', a moving camera shot. **1851** MAYHEW *Lond. Lab.* (1861) II. 110 The *Dolly system.. The name is derived from the black wooden doll, in white apparel, which generally hangs dangling over the door of the marine-store shops.

Hence ˈ**dollydom** = *dolldom* (see after DOLL *sb.*[1]).

1882 *Society* 30 Dec. 9/2 Dollydom is a vast study now.

‖**dolly** (ˈdɒlɪ), *sb.*[2] *Anglo-Indian.* [ad. Hindī *ḍālī.*] 'A complimentary offering of fruit, flowers, vegetables, sweetmeats and the like, presented usually on one or more trays; also, the daily basket of garden produce laid before the owner by the *Mālī* or gardener' (Yule).

1860 RUSSELL *Diary India* II. xi. 202 In the evening the Rana's dolly, or offering, was brought in. **1889** MARCHIONESS DUFFERIN *Viceregal Life in India* ii. (1890) 51 A native gentleman sent me what they call a 'Dolly', which is really a trayful of presents.

dolly (ˈdɒlɪ), *a.* [f. DOLL *sb.*[1] + -Y.] **a.** Like a doll; dollish, babyish; also, stupid, foolish.

1852 DICKENS *Bleak Ho.* (1853) 276 A dolly sort of beauty perhaps. **1865** —— *Mut. Fr.* I. iv, 'You are a chit and a little idiot.. or you wouldn't make such a dolly speech'. **1886** BAUMANN *Londinismen* 43/2 *Dolly*, dumm. **1922** JOYCE *Ulysses* 759 Grinning all over his big Dolly face.. didnt he look a balmy.

b. In games, esp. Cricket, denoting a very easy catch, shot, etc. *colloq.*

1895 *Eng. Dial. Dict.* s.v., Such a dolly-catch. **1903** JESSOP in H. G. Hutchinson *Cricket* v. 130 These simple 'dolly' catches are much more difficult to hold than those from hard drives. **1909** *Westm. Gaz.* 2 Mar. 12/2 Till then he had played a grand game, and had saved many clever shots, only in the end to be beaten by a 'dolly one'. **1955** *Times* 11 July 4/3 Lane-Fox..failed to get to the pitch of the ball and cocked up a dolly catch.

c. Usu. applied to a girl: attractive; fashionable. *colloq.*

1964 *Telegraph* (Brisbane) 6 Apr. 8/1 Take note, girls... Our London men report that you haven't really been given top-of-the-pops praise by your boyfriend unless he has called you a Dolly Bird. **1967** *Sun* 22 Feb. 6/6 *Dolly, groovy, cool, hippy*, fashionable. **1967** *Punch* 6 Dec. 872/2 It studies tradition, 'dolly girls', protest, pop, film stars, pop art and the American influence. **1970** 'D. HALLIDAY' *Dolly & Cookie Bird* vi. 89 The Chinaman..really was dolly, with a long yellow face. **1971** 'R. CRAWFORD' *Badger's Daughter* I. i. 13 You'll have to take..that dolly-bird you hide in Romford with you.

Hence **'dolliness**.

1889 MRS. ALEXANDER *Crooked Path* I. vi. 193 Her greatest charm..was her dolliness.

dolly ('dɒlɪ), *v.* orig. *dial.* and *techn.* [f. DOLLY *sb.*[1] 4.]

1. a. *trans.* To stir or wash (clothes) in a dolly-tub (see DOLLY *sb.*[1] 4 a); to beat (linen).

1847–78 in HALLIWELL. **1869** *Lonsdale Gloss., Dolly*, to wash linen, etc. with the dolly-legs.

b. *Smelting* and *Chain-making*: To beat (red-hot metal) with a hammer, dolly, etc.

1831 J. HOLLAND *Manuf. Metal* I. 85 These lumps..are drawn from the furnace and dolleyed, or beaten into cakes with hammers. **1886** [see DOLLYING below].

c. *Gold-mining.* To crush (auriferous quartz) with a dolly (see DOLLY *sb.*[1] 4 c); to obtain (gold) by this process; also of the quartz: To yield (so much gold) by this method.

1894 *Dundee Advertiser* 5 July 4 The men are now 'dollying' 1000 ounces a day. **1895** *Chamb. Jrnl.* XII. 668/1 He dollied, or ground, his little bits of rock by means of a contrivance resembling a pestle and mortar. **1896** *Daily News* 23 Jan. 9/5 This has the richest stone we have got so far, it dollies about 8 grains to the pound.

d. To prettify; to doll *up* (see DOLL *v.*[2]).

1958 *Listener* 13 Nov. 768/2 You go home and dolly them [*sc.* the songs] up a bit. **1961** C. H. DOUGLAS-TODD *Popular Whippet* 37 At all events, 'dollied up' or not, a tea-chest makes a most effective indoor kennel. **1966** *Economist* 12 Nov. 709/3 Last minute painting and dollying up is done with the flag poles in position. **1968** R. V. BESTE *Repeat the Instructions* xiii. 139, I didn't imagine you were the sort of spiv who would take a bribe however it was dollied up.

2. *intr.* (*colloq.*) To move a film- or television-camera *in* or *up* towards the subject, or *out* away from it. Cf. DOLLY *sb.*[1] 4 h. Also *fig.*

1939 L. JACOBS *Rise of Amer. Film* xxii. 442 The traveling of sound is like panning or dollying of the camera. **1957** R. LONGRIGG *Switchboard* II. 123 Dolly up a bit, Steve... Dolly *up*, you clot. **1961** *Guardian* 13 Oct. 5/2 As if this were the opening of a..television programme, you 'dolly up' to its owner. **1965** *Listener* 11 Feb. 238/3 The camera.. remains static and does not 'dolly in' for a close-up, or alternatively 'dolly out'.

3. *Cricket* (*colloq.*). *trans.* and *intr.* To toss or hit (the ball) *up* in a slow arc, offering: (*a*) an easy, playable delivery; (*b*) a simple catch. Of the ball: to present itself as a 'dolly' catch *to* a fieldsman. Also *fig.* See DOLLY *sb.* 3 b.

1963 A. ROSS *Australia 63* v. 115 He danced out to Titmus, was not quite at the pitch, and the ball, taking the outside edge, dollied up to Trueman at short extra. **1969** R. ILLINGWORTH *Spinner's Wicket* xii. 92 Brian..was waiting square in the legside field when the ball dollied to him. **1985** *Listener* 18 Apr. 29/1 Can they identify a picture of the Liverpool festival garden centre? Silence. Chairman Ray Alan dollies up an underarm 'scouse house' as an extra clue, but still there is total bafflement.

Hence **'dollied** *ppl. a.*, **'dollying** *vbl. sb.* (also *attrib.*); also **'dollier**.

1848 MRS. GASKELL *M. Barton* II. x. 138 He had been engaged in 'dollying' and a few other mischievous feats in the washing line. **1882** *N. & Q.* 28 Oct. 349/2 The soiled clothes are immersed in water in the dolly tub..then the dolly is plunged into the mass [of clothes] and worked by the dollier by both arms. **1886** *Pall Mall G.* 27 Aug. 11/1 This 'dollying' process is effected by a hammer, which by means of a spring and wooden pedal, is made to strike the already roughly joined link till the two ends are so welded together that the joining is scarcely noticeable. All hand-wrought chain above three-eighths of an inch in diameter is known as 'dollied'.

dolly, obs. Sc. form of DOWIE *a.*

Dolly Varden. [from the name of a character in Dickens's *Barnaby Rudge.*] **a.** A print dress with a large flower pattern, worn with the skirt gathered up in loops. **b.** A large hat, worn by women, with one side bent downwards, and abundantly trimmed with flowers. **c.** A Californian species of trout or char.

[**1841** DICKENS *Barn. Rudge* xix. 41 As to Dolly [Varden], there she was again..in a smart little cherry-coloured mantle, with a hood of the same drawn over her head, and.. a little straw hat trimmed with cherry-coloured ribbons.] **1872** A. DOBSON *Dial. from Plato* iv. (*St. Paul's Mag.* Dec.), Blue eyes look doubly blue Beneath a Dolly Varden. **1872** *Harper's Weekly* 25 May 407/4 Was ever any new costume more criticized than the new 'Dolly Varden'. **1872** E. WORDSWORTH *Let.* May in E. Romanes *C. M. Yonge* (1908) ix. 139 My hostess looking more like an old French *marquise* than ever in a red and black Dolly Varden dress, with pink skirt. **1876** *Vreka* (Calif.) *Union* 3 June, The first spotted trout..were given the name of Dolly Vardens by Elda McCloud. **1877** R. L. PRICE *Two Americas* 214 Large baskets of trout, among whom were many 'Dolly Vardens'. *Ibid.* 215, Convinced that the 'Dolly Varden' is a genuine trout. **1881** MRS. LYNN LINTON *My Love* I. 227 One would get one's self up to look awfully killing in a Dolly Varden. **1946** *Trail Riders Bull.* Oct. 5/1 Dr. George Rae..landed four Dolly Vardens..during a special 'time-out' for the anglers.

‖**dolma** ('dəʊlmə). [Turkish, f. *dolmak* to fill, be filled.] A Turkish dish of several ingredients (see quots.).

Widespread in various E. European countries. Pl. forms reflect local variations.

1889 *Cent. Dict., Dolma*, a Turkish dish made of vine-leaves, egg-plant, gourds, etc., stuffed with rice and chopped meat. **1935** M. MORPHY *Recipes of All Nations* 767 The *dolmas*..consists of uncooked mutton finely chopped with kidney fat, a little soaked bread, and sometimes uncooked rice, the whole highly seasoned and spiced. A teaspoon of the mixture is wrapped in either a blanched vine leaf, fig leaf, or cabbage leaf, and these are placed in a saucepan and braised. **1954** D. DODGE *Lights of Skaro* i. 17 A wooden tub full of *dolmas*, cool in their wrapping of pickled vine leaves. **1962** 'W. HAGGARD' *Unquiet Sleep* iv. 29 The delicacies craved by the Attic palate even in London —*halva, foul medames*, anari cheese, *dolmades* rolled in vine leaves, tinned. **1962** *Listener* 24 May 931/1 Among these you are certain to find *dolmathes*—vine leaves stuffed with various mixtures..and served in a tomato, or egg and lemon, sauce.

dolman ('dɒlmən). Forms 6 **dollymant**, 6–8 **dolyman, doliman**, 9 **dolman**. [orig. a. Turkish *dōlāmān* or *ḍōlāmah*, whence Pol., Boh. *doloman*, Magyar *dolmany*, F. *doliman*, (in sense 2) *dolman*, Ger. *doliman, dollman*. The disyllabic form appears to be through Fr.]

1. A long robe open in front, with narrow sleeves, worn by the Turks.

1585 T. WASHINGTON tr. *Nicholay's Voy.* III. x. 86 They are clothed with a long gowne, which they do call Dolyman, girded with a large girdle of silke. **1599** HAKLUYT *Voy.* II. I. 113 Ye great Basha..clothed with a robe of Dollymant crimson. **1702** W. J. *Bruyn's Voy. Levant* xx. 91 Over this comes on the Shirt, and over that the Doliman. **1843** MRS. ROMER *Rhone, Darro, etc.* II. 314 His haik floated loosely on his shoulders like a dolman.

2. The uniform jacket of a hussar, worn like a cape with the sleeves hanging loose.

1883 *Standard* 7 Mar. 5 (Stanf.) His Royal Highness has presented the whole of the Blücher Hussars with dolmans, which had hitherto only been worn by the Royal and Guard Regiments of Hussars.

3. A kind of mantle with cape-like appendages instead of sleeves, worn by women.

1872 *Punch* 26 Oct. 171/2 The 'dolman' is a loose jacket, with large hanging sleeves, that can be assumed or left loose at pleasure. **1876** OUIDA *Winter City* iii. 38 Perhaps it lurked in the black sable fur of her dolman.

4. In full, ***dolman sleeve***. A sleeve that is much wider at the arm-hole than it is at the wrist.

1934 C. M. BROWN et al. *Clothing Constr.* (ed. 2) xxxvi. 278 The dolman sleeve is usually set into a very low armseye. **1939** M. B. PICKEN *Lang. Fashion* 43/2 Cap-like wrap or coat with the dolman sleeve. **1941** *Amer. Speech* XVI. 68/1 Summer sleeves show that Dolmans—the very draped and opulent sleeves—are back.

Hence **dolma'nette**, a small or short dolman.

1883 *Glasgow Weekly Her.* 21 Apr. 8/4 French Pattern Dolmans, New Dolmanettes, Jackets, etc.

dolmen ('dɒlmɛn). [a. mod.F. *dolmen* (*dolmin* Latour d'Auvergne, 1796, *dolmine* Le Grand d'Aussy 1798, *dolmen, Mémoires de l'Académie Celtique* 1807).

Given by Legonidec 1821 as Breton = 'monument in form of an altar or table'; and usually explained as f. Breton *tôl* = *taol*, L. *tabula*, table + *mean, men* stone. But the Breton compound of these words would be *taolvean* or *tôlven*, and the *d* and *m* of *dolmen* are not thus satisfactorily accounted for. Borlase, *Antiq. Cornwall* (1754) called these structures *cromlêh*, but gave *tolmên*, lit. 'hole of stone', as the current Cornish name for those enormous blocks found in Cornwall and Scilly naturally poised upon two supporting points, so as to leave a 'hole' or aperture beneath, through which a man or beast may pass. There is reason to think that this is the word inexactly reproduced by Latour d'Auvergne as *dolmin*, and misapplied by him and succeeding French archæologists to the *cromlech*.]

The French name, used by some English authors, for a CROMLECH, a prehistoric structure, consisting of a large flattish stone supported upon two or more smaller upright stones.

1859 JEPHSON *Brittany* viii. 108 The dolmen appeared to me to consist of a chamber formed by gigantic unhewn granite blocks placed upon smaller ones. **1865** LUBBOCK *Preh. Times* v. (1869) 104 All over Europe..we find relics of prehistoric times..dolmens or stone chambers. **1871** TYLOR *Prim. Cult.* I. 55 Megalithic structures, menhirs, cromlechs, dolmens. **1880** JEFFERIES *Gr. Ferne F.* 150 He crawled right under the table-stone of the dolmen.

Hence **dol'menic** *a.* (*nonce-wd.*), of or belonging to dolmens, or to the race who constructed them.

1882 tr. *N. Joly's Man bef. Metals* I. vi. 158 The ethnological character..of the supposed dolmenic people.

‖**dolmus, dolmush** ('dəʊlm(j)uːʃ). [Turkish *dolmuş* a vehicle or boat which departs only when all the seats are taken, f. *dolmuş* filled.] A shared form of public transport (in Turkey), *esp.* a taxi. Also *attrib.*

1957 I. ORGA *Young Traveller in Turkey* ii. 24 *Dolmuş* means shared taxi... It's cheaper to travel *dolmuş*. **1962** J. FLEMING *When I grow Rich* iii. 44 Driving about all over Istanbul..in a packed *dolmus* (or shared taxi). *Ibid.* v. 87 They embarked in a *dolmus* rowing-boat, with two other people waiting to be rowed across. **1967** J. RATHBONE *Diamonds Bid* xii. 108 We caught a dolmush, a shared taxi, outside the New Mosque.

dolomite ('dɒləmaɪt), *sb. Min.* [In F. *dolomie, dolomite*, named 1794 after M. *Dolomieu*, a French geologist and mineralogist: see -ITE.] A native double carbonate of lime and magnesia, occurring crystalline, and in granular masses, white or coloured, called ***dolomite marble***; a rock consisting essentially of this mineral.

1794 KIRWAN *Min.* I. 111 Common Dolomite. **1799** TENNANT in *Phil. Trans.* LXXXIX. 309 The kind of marble which had been called Dolomite, from M. Dolomieu, who first remarked its peculiarity in dissolving slowly. **1862** *Chambers' Encycl.* s.v. *Dolomite*, The new Houses of Parliament are built of dolomite. **1876** PAGE *Adv. Text-b. Geol.* v. 102 Dolomite is a granular or crystalline variety of magnesian limestone.

b. pl. ***the Dolomites*** = the dolomite mountains or peaks; *spec.* those of Southern Tyrol.

1870 (*title*) Zigzagging amongst Dolomites. **1873** A. B. EDWARDS A Midsummer Ramble among the Dolomites.

c. *attrib.* and *Comb.*, as ***dolomite country, mountain, peak; dolomite-like*** adj.

1846 L. S. COSTELLO *Tour Venice* 389 The horns of the dolomite mountains. **1864** *Sat. Rev.* 8 July 58/2 The strong-hold of the Dolomite country. **1864** *Soc. Sc. Rev.* 35 Celebrated for their Dolomite peaks. **1868** DANA *Min.* §742 A fine-grained dolomite-like rock.

Hence **'dolomitize** *v.* (also **'dolomize**), to convert into dolomite; **dolomiti'zation** (also **dolomi'zation**), conversion into dolomite.

1833 LYELL in *Life* (1881) I. 397 To make up my mind about Von Buch's theory of dolomisation. **1849** DANA *Geol.* ii. (1850) 153 An instance of dolomization. **1862** G. P. SCROPE *Volcanos* 89 The frequent dolomitization of limestones. **1863** A. C. RAMSAY *Phys. Geog.* x. (1878) 149 Some modern atolls are known to become dolomitised. **1891** *Nature* 10 Sept., The limestone had been dolomitized.

'dolomite, *v.* [f. the sb.] = DOLOMITIZE *v.*

1913 V. B. LEWES *Oil Fuel* 32 The carbon dioxide dissolved in the brine under enormous pressure would slowly become absorbed in actions upon the mineral matter present, such as forming carbonates and soluble bicarbonates of magnesia, thus dolomiting the calcareous deposits.

dolomitic (dɒlə'mɪtɪk), *a.* [f. DOLOMITE *sb.* + -IC.] Of the nature of, formed of, or containing dolomite.

1832 DE LA BECHE *Geol. Man.* (ed. 2) 329 Dolomitic rocks are also found among them. **1879** RUTLEY *Study Rocks* xiv. 286 No sharp line of demarcation can..be drawn between the dolomitic limestone and the true dolomites.

dolool, var. DELOUL.

dolor, obs. f. DOLLAR; var. of DOLOUR.

†**dolo'riferous,** *a. Obs.* [f. L. type **dolōrifer*, f. *dolōr-em* DOLOUR + *-fer* bearing: see -FEROUS.] Causing pain; = next.

1599 A. M. tr. *Gabelhouer's Bk. Physicke* 73/1 Applye it on or in the doloriferous tooth. **1638** WHITAKER *Blood of Grape* 74 (T.) In such doloriferous affects in the joints.

dolorific (dɒlə'rɪfɪk), *a.* Now *rare.* [ad. med.L. *dolōrific-us*, f. *dolōr-em* pain; see -FIC.] Causing or giving rise to pain; painful, grievous.

1634 T. JOHNSON *Parey's Chirurg.* IX. xi. (1678) 223 Remedies which are contrary to the dolorifick cause. **1669** GALE *True Idea Jansen.* 144 He abhors sin, not as sin, but as dolorifick or painful. **1828** *Blackw. Mag.* XXIV. 192 Alas! for Huskisson, and his dolorific strains.

So †**dolo'rifical** *a. Obs. rare*$^{-0}$.

1623 COCKERAM, *Dolorificall*, causing sorrow.

dolorifuge: see -FUGE.

dolorimeter (dəʊlə'rɪmɪtə(r)). [f. L. *dolor* pain (see DOLOUR) + -I- + -METER.] An instrument for the measurement of pain or sensitivity to pain.

1949 *Sat. Even. Post* 3 Dec. 29/3 The instrument they developed has been christened a 'dolorimeter'. **1957** H. J. EYSENCK *Sense & Nonsense in Psychol.* vi. 238 A psychological torture instrument, the dolorimeter, which measures pain in units called dols.

doloroso (dɒlə'rəʊsəʊ), *a.*, *adv.*, and *sb. Mus.* [It. = DOLOROUS *a.*] As a direction to the performer: plaintive(ly), pathetic(ally). As *sb.*, a passage played in this manner.

1806 BUSBY *Dict. Mus.* (ed. 2), *Doloroso*,..a term by which we understand that the movement before which it is placed is to be performed in a soft and pathetic style. **1947** A. EINSTEIN *Mus. Rom. Era* xi. 143 The combination of *doloroso* and *agitato*..is typical.

dolorous ('dɒlərəs), *a.* Also 5–6 **dolerous(e, dolorouse, dolourous,** 6 *Sc.* **dolorus.** [a. OF. *doleros, -eus, doulour-, dulur-, -eus, -ous* (11th. c. in Hatz.-Darm.) mod.F. *douloureux*:—late L. *dolōrōs-us* painful, full of sorrow, f. *dolor* DOLOUR.]

1. Causing, attended by, or affected with physical pain; painful; severe, acute.

c **1400** *Rom. Rose* 5474 [Fortune] leieth a plastre dolorous Unto her hertis wounded egre. **1578** BANISTER *Hist. Man* I.

14 No Medicin may preuayle..till the same dolorous tooth be..plucked up by the rootes. **1620** VENNER *Via Recta* viii. 166 Dolorous Gouts..are not apt to be bred by parsimony. **1731** MEDLEY *Kolben's Cape G. Hope* II. 165 A very dolorous thirst. **1865** W. ROBERTS *Treat. Urin. & Renal Dis.* II. ii. (1885) 301 The dolorous sensations and irritability which constantly torment diabetic patients.

2. Causing or giving rise to grief or sorrow; grievous, distressful; doleful, dismal.

c **1450** *Merlin* 116 The archbishop gaf this scentence full dolerouse. **1548** HALL *Chron., Hen. VI* (an. 6) 105 b, Although the death of therle wer dolorous to all Englishmen. **1641** MILTON *Ch. Govt.* II. (1851) 140 When God commands to take the trumpet and blow a dolorous or a jarring blast. *a* **1711** KEN *Christophil* Poet. Wks. 1721 I. 492 Faint he sank amidst the dol'rous way. **1877** BLACK *Green Past.* xxix. (1878) 234 We had a dolorous day of rain.

3. Of persons, their feelings, state, etc.: Full of or expressing sorrow; sorrowful, sad, distressed.

1513 DOUGLAS *Æneis* XII. ii. 149 Syne confortis he his feris dolorous. *a* **1533** LD. BERNERS *Huon* lii. 174, I am ryght dolorous for the newes that I brynge you. **1667** MILTON *P.L.* VI. 658 Thir armor..wrought them pain Implacable, and many a dolorous groan. **1854** THACKERAY *Newcomes* I. 40 [His] countenance assumed an appearance of the most dolorous sympathy. **1871** R. ELLIS *Catullus* ii. 10 Might I ..my dolorous heart awhile deliver.

Hence **dolo'rosity**, dolorousness.

1835 *Tait's Mag.* II. 784, I really do not wonder at your dolorosity.

'dolorously, *adv.* [-LY².] In a dolorous manner; painfully, sorrowfully, dolefully.

c **1450** *Merlin* 544, V of tho pantoners hym toke and ledde hym forth betinge hym dolerousely. *a* **1533** LD. BERNERS *Huon* clxiii. 637 The thyrd & fourth he made doulourously to dye. **1638** SIR T. HERBERT *Trav.* (ed. 2) 176 Hearing young Soffees voyce, dolorously crying out for Fatima. **1865** E. C. CLAYTON *Cruel Fort.* III. 74 'It will not be posted now before morning', she said, dolorously.

'dolorousness. [f. as prec. + -NESS.] The state or quality of being dolorous; sorrowfulness, sadness, dolefulness.

1553 BRENDE *Q. Curtius* 41 (R.) For the dolorousness of the old woman. **1649** JER. TAYLOR *Gt. Exemp.* III. Ad §15. 95 A designe to heighten the dolourousnesse of his person. **1880** *Athenæum* 28 Feb. 272/1 Though melancholy is, no doubt, a genuine poetic mood, mere dolorousness is not fit for poetical treatment.

dolose (dəʊ'ləʊs), *a. Law.* [ad. L. *dolōs-us*, f. *dolus* craft, deceit: see DOLE *sb.*³] Characterized by criminal intention; intentionally deceitful.

1832 AUSTIN *Jurispr.* (1879) II. 1103 An act of forbearance or omission which is merely culpose (or not dolose) is not a crime or public delict. **1861** LD. CRANWORTH in *Guardian* 31 July 726 Without accusing his..learned friend of being dolose, he did accuse him of having misled their lordships.

†**do'losity.** *Obs. rare.* [a. OF. *dolosité* :—late L. *dolōsitāt-em* deceit, f. *dolōsus*: see prec.] 'Deceitfulness, hidden malice' (Bailey).

1401 *Pol. Poems* (Rolls) II. 111 Al maner of dolosité to ȝou is enditid. **1730–36** in BAILEY (folio).

dolour, dolor ('dəʊlə(r), 'dɒlə(r)). Forms: 4–6 doloure (-owre), (6 dolar, dollor, -our), 4- dolour, 6- dolor. [a. OF. *dolor*, *-our* (11th c.), mod.F. *douleur*, = It. *dolore*, Pr., Sp. *dolor*:—L. *dolōr-em* pain, grief, anger, f. *dol-ēre* to suffer pain or grief. Now unusual in spoken use; hence pronunciation varies; the historical pronunciation was as in *colour* (F. *couleur*), which is retained in East Anglia, and sometimes represented by spelling *dullor*.]

†**1.** Physical suffering, pain; also (with *pl.*), a pain, a painful affection, a disease. *Obs.*

?*c* **1370** *Robt. K. Cicyle* 59 Olyverne dyed in grete dolowre, For he was slayne in a harde schowre. *c* **1400** *Lanfranc's Cirurg.* 227 In þe chapitre of dolour of ioynctis. **1596** DALRYMPLE tr. *Leslie's Hist. Scot.* I. 24 To kure and to remeid diuers dolouris of the skin. **1612** WOODALL *Surg. Mate* Wks. (1653) 33 It easeth the dolour of the caustick medicine. **1683** SALMON *Doron Med.* I. 311 Rheumatisms and other dolors of the nerves. **1710** T. FULLER *Pharm. Extemp.* 243 In a Nephritic Fit..there's great..Dolour in the Kidneys. **1715–20** POPE *Iliad* XVI. 649 He drew the dolours from the wounded part.

2. Mental pain or suffering; sorrow, grief, distress.

13.. *K. Alis.* 5699 The Kyng therfore was in doloure. *c* **1470** HENRY *Wallace* I. 183 Mekill dolour it did hym in hys mynd. **1544** *Litany* in *Priv. Prayers* (1851) 575 Pitifully behold the dolour of our heart. **1610** SHAKS. *Temp.* II. i. 18 Dolour comes to him indeed. **1684** *Contempl. State Man* II. vii. (1699) 211 Of joy there must no mention be made in that place of dolour. **1815** SCOTT *Guy M.* xv, To leave her in distress and dolour! **1881** JEFFERIES *Wood Magic* II. ii. 66 Thus, in dolour and despair the darkness increased.

b. *pl.* Griefs, sorrows. Now *rare.*

1611 SHAKS. *Cymb.* v. iv. 80 The Graces of his Merits due, being all to dolors turn'd. **1666** BUNYAN *Grace Ab.* §163 Every Groan of that man..in his dolours. **1854** MRS. OLIPHANT *Magd. Hepburn* III. 28 Look you, dame!..I have borne with your dolours for many a day.

c. *R.C. Ch.* ***Dolours of the Virgin.***

1885 *Catholic Dict.* s.v., The seven founders of the Servite order, in the thirteenth century, devoted themselves to special meditation on the Dolours of Mary, and from them the enumeration of the Seven Sorrows (i.e. at the prophecy of Simeon, in the flight to Egypt, at the three days' loss, at the carrying of the cross, at the crucifixion, at the descent of the cross, at the entombment) is said to have come. (Hence the appellation *Our Lady of Dolours* or *Sorrows*)

†**d.** A cause or occasion of sorrow; a grievous or sad thing. *Obs. rare.*

c **1330** *Amis & Amil.* 12 To here of the childeryn twoo, How thei were in wele and woo..is grete doloure.

†**3.** The outward expression of grief; lamentation, mourning. ***to make dolour***, to lament, mourn. *Obs.*

c **1320** *Seuyn Sag.* (W.) 1270 Therefore he made gret dolour. *c* **1500** *Melusine* lvii. 338 The doleur & lamentable heuynes that men dide. *a* **1533** LD. BERNERS *Huon* lxxxi. 246 Huon..was sorowfull to se his wyfe make so grete doloure. **1634** SIR T. HERBERT *Trav.* 107 Though they saw me, they continued their dolours till the end.

†**4.** Anger, indignation, resentment. [As in L.] *Obs.*

1609 HOLLAND *Amm. Marcell.* XXIV. iv. 250 Our fighting souldiers were so enkindled with anger and dolour [*dolore*]. **1644** BULWER *Chirol.* 92 Anger, dolour, and indignation.

dolp, obs. Sc. var. of DOUP.

dolphin ('dɒlfɪn). Forms: 4–5 delfyn(e, 6–7 delphin; 5–6 dalphyn(e, 7 daulphin; 4–6 dolphyn, 5 dolfyn(e, dolphyne, 6 doulphyn, 6–7 dolphine, 6- dolphin. See also DAUPHIN. [In the form *delfyn*, *delphin*, app. directly from L. *delphin-us* (med.L. also *delfinus*, It. *delfino*, Sp. *delfin*); with the form *dalphyne*, cf. Pr. *dalfin*, OF. *daulphin*; of the latter *dolfin* appears to be a phonetic variant with *o* from *au*: Littré has an example of *doffin* in 15th c. French.]

1. A species of cetaceous mammal (*Delphinus Delphis*), having a longer and more slender snout than the porpoise, with which it is frequently confounded, so that the two names become interchanged; sometimes applied also to the grampus.

13.. *K. Alis.* 6576 Heo noriceth delfyns, and cokadrill. **1387** TREVISA *Higden* (Rolls) II. 13 þere beeþ ofte i-take dolphyns, and see calues, and baleynes. *c* **1440** *Promp. Parv.* 126/1 Dolfyne, fysche, *delphinus.* **1530** PALSGR. 214/2 Doulphyn a fysshe, *doulphin.* **1576** FLEMING *Panopl. Epist.* 353 The Dalphine feedeth her young with milke. **1601** SHAKS. *Twel. N.* I. ii. 15 Like Orion on the Dolphines backe. **1646** J. HALL *Poems* I. 41 Had but the curteous Delphins heard. **1653** HOLCROFT *Procopius, Gothick Wars* III. 102 A great number of Daulphins coming upon the mouth of the Euxine Sea. **1769** PENNANT *Zool.* III. 50 It does not appear that the dolphin shews a greater attachment to mankind than the rest of the cetaceous kind. **1885** *Encycl. Brit.* XIX. 521/2 The head [of the porpoise] is rounded in front, and differs from that of the true dolphins in not having the snout produced into a distinct 'beak'.

2. Popularly applied to the dorado (*Coryphæna hippuris*), a fish celebrated for its beautiful colours, which, when it is taken out of the water, or is dying, undergo rapid changes of hue.

1578–1628 F. FLETCHER *Drake's Voy.* (Hakl. Soc.) 32 (Yule, s.v. *Dorado*) The..great mackrel (whom the Aurata or Dolphin also pursueth). **1627** CAPT. SMITH *Seaman's Gram.* viii. 36 Fish hookes, for..Dolphins, or Dorados. **1633** G. HERBERT *Temple, Giddinesse* v. **1756** P. BROWNE *Jamaica* 443 The Dolphin. This is one of the most beautiful fishes of those seas. **1818** BYRON *Ch. Har.* IV. xxix, Parting day Dies like the dolphin, whom each pang imbues With a new colour..The last still loveliest. **1844** MRS. BROWNING *Vis. Poets* xcvi. Poems 1850 I. 215 Faint and dim His spirits seemed to sink in him, Then, like a dolphin, change and swim The current.

3. *Astron.* A northern constellation, *Delphinus.*

1430 LYDG. *Chron. Troy* II. xiv, In whiche the Egle and also the Dolphyne Haue theyr arysynge by reuolucion. **1551** RECORDE *Cast. Knowl.* 264 A lyttle from it is the Dolphine, whiche hath in it 10 starres. **1607** TOPSELL *Four-f. Beasts* (1658) 57 About the time of the Daulphins appearance. **1868** LOCKYER *Guillemin's Heavens* (ed. 3) 358 Two double stars, one of the Lion, the other of the Dolphin.

4. A figure of a dolphin (generally represented as curved) in painting, sculpture, heraldry. etc.

In early Christian art used as an emblem of love, diligence, or swiftness.

?*a* **1400** *Morte Arth.* 2054 A derfe schelde..With a dragone engowschede..Devorande a dolphyne. *a* **1440** *Sir Degrev.* 1038 He beres a dolfyn of gold. **1756–7** tr. *Keysler's Trav.* (1760) II. 20 The fish or dolphin at the side of the statue, on which some boys seem to be riding. **1851** RUSKIN *Stones Ven.* (1874) I. App. 387 A dolphin may be used as a symbol of the sea. **1895** *Chamb. Jrnl.* Aug. 449/1 Some Aldine edition, with..the sign of the well-known anchor and dolphin.

†**5.** (In full, ***dalphyn*** or ***dolphin crown.***) A French gold coin, formerly current in Scotland. *Obs.*

Prob. the Fr. *écu du Dauphiné*, weighing about 54 English grains, struck by Louis XI for the Dauphiné.

1451 *Sc. Acts Jas. II* (1597) §33 The Crown of France hauand a crowned Flowre deluce on ilk side of the Schield, ..and the Dolphin Crowne, ilk ane of them hauand course for sex shillinges aucht pennies. **1455** *Ibid.* (1597) §59 The Salute, the Rydar, the Crowne, the Dolphin, to elleven shillings.

6. Applied to various contrivances resembling or fancifully likened to a dolphin.

a. In early artillery, each of two handles cast solid on a cannon nearly over the trunnions, commonly made in the conventional form of a dolphin.

1704 J. HARRIS *Lex. Techn.* s.v. *Ordnance, Maniglions* or *Dolphins*..are the Handles placed on the back of the Piece near the Trunnions, and near the Centre of Gravity, to mount and dismount it the more easily. **1869** BOUTELL *Arms & Arm.* xi. (1874) 240 Thus the handles, *anses* (when in use in England called *dolphins*), are not infrequently made in the form of the body of some living creature; for example, in Fig. 50 they appear in the form of two dolphins.

b. *Naut.* (*a*) A spar or block of wood with a ring bolt at each end for vessels to ride by; a mooring-buoy. (*b*) A mooring-post or bollard placed at the entrance of a dock or along a quay, wharf or beach, to make hawsers fast to. (*c*) A wreath of plaited cordage fastened about a mast or yard, to prevent the latter from falling in case of the ropes or chains which support it being shot away in action.

1764 CROKER, etc. *Dict. Arts & Sc., Dolphins of the Mast.* **1833** MARRYAT *P. Simple* vi, What with dead-eyes, and shrouds, cats and catblocks, dolphins, and dolphin-strikers, I was so puzzled..that [etc.]. **1840** *Evid. Hull Docks Comm.* 90 *Q.* What is a dolphin? *A.* There is a post in the middle, and it is inclosed round by other posts, and this post in the middle is the post to make the rope fast to, and the others support it; it is for the vessels to warp into the river Hull. **1844** *Hull Dock Act* 91 Substantial hawsers..fixed to the dolphins. **1847** CRAIG, *Dolphin of the mast.* **1867** SMYTH *Sailor's World-bk., Bollard*..also a lighter sort of dolphin for attaching vessels to. *Ibid., Puddening*..a thick wreath of yarns, matting, or oakum (called a *dolphin*), tapering from the middle towards the ends.

c. *Gr. Antiq.* A heavy mass of lead, etc. suspended from a yard at the bows of a war-vessel, to be dropped into an enemy's ship when at close quarters.

1774 GOLDSM. *Grecian Hist.* I. 279 The enemy..were stopped by the yards of those ships to which were fixed dolphins of lead. **1820** T. MITCHELL *Aristoph. Knights* I. 227 Let your dolphins rise high, while the enemy's nearing. **1836–48** B. D. WALSH *Aristoph. Knights* II. iii. Quick haul up your ponderous dolphins. **1849** GROTE *Greece* II. lx. (1862) V. 262.

d. 'A technical term applied to the pipe and cover at a source for the supply of water' (Weale *Dict. Terms Arch.* 1849–50).

e. *Angling.* A kind of hook.

1854 BADHAM *Halieut.* 18.

f. (See quot.) *U.S.*

1905 *Terms Forestry & Logging* 35 *Dolphin*, a cluster of piles to which a boom is secured.

7. A black species of aphis or plant-louse (*Aphis fabæ*), very destructive to bean-plants; also called *collier* and *dolphin-fly*. Also a black coleopterous insect infesting turnips (quot. 1771).

1731 BAILEY (ed. 5), *Dolphins* (with Gardiners) small black Insects that infest Beans, etc. **1771** G. WHITE *Selborne* xxxiv. 90 The country people here call it the Turnip Fly and Black Dolphin; but I know it to be one of the coleoptera; the Chrysomela oleracea. **1846** HANNAM in *Jrnl. R. Agric. Soc.* II. II. 590 The season of 1846 has been memorable for the dolphin among the pea-crop. **1883** SUTTON *Cult. Veget. & Fl.* (1892) 382 The Bean Aphis..the Bean Plant Louse, or Black Dolphin.

†**8.** = DAUPHIN 1 *β*, q.v. (*Obs.*).

9. *attrib.* and *Comb.* as ***dolphin-colour, -family, -fish, -hue, -shoal; dolphin-borne, -drawn, -headed, -like, -torn*** adjs.; **dolphin-fat**, a fat obtained from species of *Delphinus* (DELPHIN *sb.* 2); **dolphin-flower**, the Larkspur (*Delphinium*); **dolphin-fly** = sense 7; **dolphin-oil** = *dolphin-fat* (Watts *Dict. Chem.* II. 309); **dolphin-striker** (*Naut.*), a short gaff spar fixed perpendicularly under the cap of the bowsprit for guying down the jib-boom; also called *martingale* (which name is also given to the ropes connecting it with the jib-boom).

1842 MRS. BROWNING *Grk. Chr. Poets* (1863) 1 Pang by pang, each with a *dolphin colour. **1914** W. B. YEATS *Responsibilities* 32 Paintings of the *dolphin-drawn Sea-nymphs in their pearly waggons. **1965** *Eng. Studies* XLVI. 383 If Keats did not invent the dolphin-drawn float himself he may have found this picture in..the numerous illustrators of Homer. **1513** DOUGLAS *Æneis* v. x. 88 Als swift as *dalfin fische, swymand away. **1671** H. M. tr. *Colloq. Erasm.* 510 The Dolphin fish..is a lover of man. **1846** WORCESTER, *Dolphin-fly, an insect of the aphis tribe, destructive to beans. **1846** GREENER *Sc. Gunnery* 15 The fancy cock and hammers have given place to a *dolphin-headed hammer. **1878** BROWNING *La Saisiaz* 75 Melodious moaned the other 'Dying day with *dolphin-hues.' **1606** SHAKS *Ant. & Cl.* v. ii. 89 His delights Were *Dolphin-like, they shew'd his backe aboue The Element they liu'd in. **1887** BOWEN *Virg. Æneid* v. 594 Some *dolphin shoal.. afloat on the watery plain. **1833** *Dolphin-striker [see 6 b]. **1841** MARRYAT *Poacher* xxviii, The..collision carried away our..dolphin-striker. **1867** SMYTH *Sailor's Word-bk.* s.v. *Martingale*, The spar is usually termed the dolphin-striker, from its handy position whence to strike fish. **1932** W. B. YEATS *Words for Music* 2 That *dolphin-torn, that gong-tormented sea. **1891** E. CASTLE *Conseq.* III. II. xvii. 3 Hot water bubbled..in an ancient copper *'dolphin' urn of exquisite outline.

dolphinarium (dɒlfɪ'nɛərɪəm). Pl. -ia, -iums. [f. DOLPHIN + AQU)ARIUM: cf. OCEANARIUM, SEAQUARIUM.] A large aquarium in which dolphins are kept and trained, usu. for public entertainment.

1969 *Daily Tel.* 13 Feb. 20/4 A 650-seat 'dolphinarium', where the public can watch performing dolphins and seals, may be built at Greenwich pier. **1971** *New Scientist* 15 Apr. 175/1 One can't help but have a nagging doubt about the possible consequences of this rise in dolphinaria. **1977** *Navy News* Aug. 1 (*caption*) S.S. Dolphin, the new dolphinarium, was officially opened by Cdr. Graham Laslett. **1979** *Washington Post* 3 June E3/4 We..should be learning from it rather than using it largely as a trained animal act to please crowds at dolphinariums. **1981** *Times* 16 Apr. 3/1 Two dolphins [which] arrived safely at Heathrow airport yesterday..will go on show at a dolphinarium near Liverpool. **1984** *Daily Tel.* 26 Mar. 3/3 A large number of dolphins and killer whales imported into Britain to perform tricks in dolphinaria die after only a short time in captivity.

dolphinate, -ess, obs. ff. DAUPHINATE, -ESS.

1655 FULLER *Ch. Hist.* VI. i. §9 The Dolphinate in France.

dolphined (ˈdɒlfɪnd), *a. poet.* [f. DOLPHIN + -ED[2].] Containing or having dolphins.

1934 DYLAN THOMAS *18 Poems* 19 The shades Of children ..cry to the dolphined sea.

†**dolphiˈnet.** *Obs. rare*$^{-1}$. [f. DOLPHIN + -ET[1], dimin. suffix, here exceptionally used as a feminine.] A female dolphin.

1595 SPENSER *Col. Clout* 866 The Lyon chose his mate, the Turtle Dove Her deare, the Dolphin his owne Dolphinet.

dolt (dəʊlt), *sb.* Also 6 dolte, dowlte, 6–7 doult(e. [Found with its derivatives from middle of 16th c.; perh. earlier in dialect use. App. related to OE. *dol*, ME. *dol, doll*, DULL, and to DOLD, stupid, inert of intellect or faculty. For the *-t*, cf. ME. *dult* in sense of *dulled*: see DULL *v.*]

1. A dull, stupid fellow; a blockhead, numskull.

1543 [implied in DOLTISH]. **1551** ROBINSON tr. *More's Utop.* (Arb.) 39 Thies wysefooles and verye archedoltes. *a***1553** UDALL *Royster D.* III. ii. (Arb.) 42 A very dolt and loute. **1604** SHAKS. *Oth.* v. ii. 163 Oh Gull, oh dolt, As ignorant as durt. **1658** CLEVELAND *Rustic Rampant* Wks. (1687) 417 Not only these Doults, these Sots. **1725** SWIFT *Wood the Ironmonger* 32 Wood's adulterate copper, Which ..we like dolts Mistook at first for thunderbolts. **1847** DISRAELI *Tancred* v. i, The prerogative of dolts and dullards.

2. a. *attrib.* or as *adj.* Doltish, stupid, senseless, foolish. **b.** *Comb.*, as †**dolt-head,** (*a*) a dolt, blockhead; (*b*) a stupid head (quot. 1711).

1679 DRYDEN *Troil. & Cress.* II. iii, Dolt-heads, asses, And beasts of burden. **1711** E. WARD *Quix.* I. 414 As soon as each had bolted From out his Straw, and scratch'd his Dolthead. **1828** SOUTHEY *To A. Cunningham* Poems III. 311 The dolt image is not worth its clay. **1852** R. KNOX *Gt. Artists & Anat.* 57 North Germany, the land of schnapps, and insolence, and dolt stupidity.

Hence †ˈ**doltage,** †ˈ**doltry,** the condition of a dolt; †ˈ**doltify** *v. trans.*, to make a dolt of.

1559 AYLMER *Harbor. Faithf. Subj.* G iij b, Women.. doltefied with the dregges of the Deuils dounge hill. **1581** MULCASTER *Positions* xxxix. (1887) 205 Where I see nobilitie betraid to donghillrie, and learning to doultrie. **1593** NASHE *Four Lett. Confut.* G j b, I have usually seene uncircumsised doltage have the porch of his Panims pilfries very hugely pestred with praises.

†**dolt,** *v. Obs.* [f. prec. sb.]

1. *trans.* To make a dolt of, befool; to call dolt.

1553 T. WILSON *Rhet.* 74 b, When wee would abashe a man..wee either doulte hym at the firste, and make hym beleeve that he is no wiser then a goose, or [etc.]. **1570** B. GOOGE *Pop. Kingd.* II. (1880) 26 Thus are the people dolted still, and fooles are made of fooles. **1574** HELLOWES *Gueuara's Fam. Ep.* 302 Certaine men be dolted, and charged with a thousand thoughts. **1818** TODD, *To dolt*, to make dull. I have heard the word so spoken, but know no instance of it in books.

2. *intr.* To act like a dolt, to play the fool. Hence ˈ**dolting** *ppl. a.*

1573 *New Custom* I. ii. in Hazl. *Dodsley* III. 19 More better..Than in these trifles to have dolted so much. **1593** *Tell-Troth's N.Y. Gift* 21 Touching doating or dolting Ielosy.

doltish (ˈdəʊltɪʃ), *a.* [f. DOLT *sb.* + -ISH.] Of the nature of or like a dolt; foolish, stupid, thick-headed, senseless.

1543 BALE *Course Rom. Foxe* 62 b (T.) Your argument is, as you are; unlearned, fantastical and doltish. *a***1553** UDALL *Royster D.* IV. iii. (Arb.) 63 Rather than to mary with suche a doltishe loute. *a***1677** BARROW *Serm.* Wks. 1716 III. 32 Doltish incapacity. **1851** H. MELVILLE *Whale* xxxvi. 181 A doltish stare. **1892** LUCY T. SMITH in *Hist. Rev.* Jan. 34 The man with a doltish son.

ˈ**doltishly,** *adv.* [f. prec. + -LY[2].] In a doltish manner; stupidly.

1580 HOLLYBAND *Treas. Fr. Tong, Bestement & lourdement*, beastly and doltishly. **1586** FERNE *Blaz. Gentrie* II. 98 [They] do very doltishly distinguish two kinds of adoration. **1682** BUNYAN *Holy War* 186 Thou hast perniciously and doultishly taught and maintained that there is no God.

ˈ**doltishness.** [f. as prec. + -NESS.] The quality of being doltish; stupidity.

1569 T. NORTON *Rebell. Earl Northumb.* in Strype *Ann. Ref.* I. lv. 597 The vanities, the doltishness, the borrowing without caring to pay. **1629** SYMMER *Spir. Posie* II. i. 33 It is extreame doltishnesse to deferre the practise of Wisedome. **1813** SHELLEY in Dowden *Life* (1887) I. 339 The usual doltishness of the regal race.

†**dolven,** obs. pa. pple. of DELVE *v.*: Delved, dug, buried.

*a***1225** *Ancr. R.* 292 Hud þe iðe doluene eorðe. *c***1350** *Will. Palerne* 5280 Ac he was ded & doluen. *c***1420** *Pallad. on Husb.* III. 689 In the doluen lond. *c***1440** *York Myst.* xxiv. 189 Both dede and doluen, þis is þe fourþe day.

†ˈ**doly,** *a. Obs.* or *dial.* Also 6 *Sc.* duillie, 8 dooly. [The forms *dooly* and *duillie* are clearly, and *doly* probably, from DOLE *sb.*[2]; a 16th c. *dolly* appears to be a different word: see DOWIE.] Doleful, sorrowful, sad.

1501 DOUGLAS *Pal. Hon.* I. 189 Quhidder is become sa sone this duillie hant? **1583** STANYHURST *Æneis* II. (Arb.) 57 This dolye chaunce gald vs, with blood, with slaghter abounding. **1596** LODGE *Marg. Amer.* 20 The dolie season of the yeare. **1721** BAILEY, *Doly* or *Dooly*, mourning, sad.

‖**Dom**[1] (dɒm). [In sense 1, a. Pg. *dom*, a title of honour, = Sp. *don*:—L. *domin-us* master, ruler, chief, owner; see DON *sb.*[1], DAM *sb.*[4], DAN[1]. In sense 2 an abbreviation of L. *dominus.*]

1. In Portugal and Brazil, a title of dignity prefixed to the Christian name, used by Royalty, Cardinals, Bishops, and gentlemen on whom it has been conferred by Royal authority.

1727–51 CHAMBERS *Cycl.* s.v., In Portugal, nobody is allowed to assume the title of *Dom*, which is a badge or token of nobility, without the King's leave.

2. As a shortened form of L. *dominus*, prefixed to the names of R.C. ecclesiastical and monastic dignitaries, *esp.* to Benedictine and Carthusian monks, whether priests or in minor orders.

1716 DAVIES *Athen. Brit.* II. 372 The noted French reform'd Monk Dom Gerberon. **1727–51** CHAMBERS *Cycl.*, *Dom* is likewise used in France among some orders of religious as the Chartreux, Benedictines, etc. We say, the reverend father Dom Calmet, Dom Alexis, Dom Balthasar, etc. **1822** NARES s.v. *Dan*, The *Dom* of the Benedictines. **1892** J. WICKHAM LEGG in *Trans. St. Paul's Eccl. Soc.* III. 74 Mr. Edmund Bishop, who, with Dom Aidan Gasquet, is editing the Consuetudinary of St. Mary's Abbey, York.

3. *Dom Pedro* (*U.S.*): a game at cards, a variation of don (DON *sb.*[1] 6).

1887 F. R. STOCKTON *Borrowed Month*, etc. 191 (American) Dom Pedro..a social game of cards which we generally played.

‖**dom**[2] (doːm). [mod.G. *dom* cathedral, ad. L. *domus* (*domus Dei*): see DOME. OHG. and MHG. had *tuom.*] A cathedral church.

1861 NEALE *Notes Dalmatia* ii. 35 A stroll through the city showed us..the so-called Dom..a building somewhat resembling the cathedral at Graz. **1876** FREEMAN *Hist. Sk.*, *Venetian March*, As Innsbrück never was a Bishop's see, there is no dom. **1888** *Times* (Weekly Ed.) 22 June 5/1 The Dom at Berlin.

So ˈ**domchurch** [tr. G. *domkirche*] in the same sense.

1864 KINGSLEY *Rom. & Teut.* 219 The domchurch and its organization grew up..round the body of a saint or martyr.

Dom[3] (dəʊm). [a. Hind. *Ḍōm*, f. Skr. *Ḍōma, Ḍōmba.*] A member of a menial Hindu caste. Also *attrib.* or as *adj.*

1828 H. H. WILSON in *Asiatick Researches* XVIII. 47 Nábháji..was by birth a *Dom*, a caste whose employ is making baskets and various sorts of wicker work. **1869** *H. M. Elliot's Races N.W. Prov.* I. 84 Ramgarh and Sahankot, on the Rohini, are also Dom forts. *Ibid.* 85 The Magahya Doms of Champáran are a race of professional thieves. **1872** M. A. SHERRING *Hindu Tribes* 400 The Dom is generally considered by Hindus to be the type and representative of all uncleanness. **1891** H. H. RISLEY *Tribes of Bengal: Ethnogr. Gloss.* I. 243 When a man has been ejected from his own caste for living with a Dom woman. **1937** H. W. TILMAN *Ascent of Nanda Devi* i. 7 The Doms..propitiate the local gods and demons.

dom, obs. f. DOOM, DUMB; var. f. DOUM.

-dom, *suffix.* [OE. *-dóm* = OS. *-dóm*, MDu. *-doem*, Du. *-dom*, OHG., MHG. *-tuom*, G. *-tum.*] Abstract suffix of state, which has grown out of an independent sb., orig. putting, setting, position, statute, OHG. *tuom*, position, condition, dignity, in OE. *dóm*, statute, judgement, jurisdiction, f. stem *dô-* of DO *v.* + abstract suffix *-moz*, OE. *-m*, as in *hel-m, sea-m, strea-m*, etc. Frequent already in OE. as a suffix to sbs. and adjs., as *biscopdóm* the dignity of a bishop, *cyningdóm, cynedóm*, royal or kingly dominion, kingdom, *ealdordóm* the position or jurisdiction of an elder or lord; *þeowdóm*, the condition of a þeow or slave; *fréodóm, hálizdóm, wisdóm* the condition or fact of being free, holy, or wise. The number of these derivatives has increased in later times, and *-dom* is now a living suffix, freely employed to form nonce-derivatives, not only with the sense of 'condition, state, dignity', but also with that of 'domain, realm' (*fig.*). See in their alphabetical places *alderdom, Anglo-Saxondom, boredom, Christendom, cuckoldom, dukedom, earldom, freedom, kingdom, martyrdom, popedom, sheriffdom, thraldom, wisdom*, etc. Examples of nonce-words appear in the quotations.

1885 H. PEARSON *R. Browning* 8 Pomona..to express all appledom and peardom. **1882** H. C. MERIVALE *Faucit of B.* I. I. iv. 58 Entitled him to all the honours of B.A. dom. **1887** *St. Louis Globe Democrat* 2 Feb., A real, live Dakota man.. fresh from Blizzardom. **1880** *New Virginians* I. 237 Meanwhile curdom flourishes. **1889** *Pall Mall G.* 3 Aug. 2/2 To test..the good-sailordom of the spectators. *Ibid.* 7 Oct. 2/1 Imagine Manchesterdom Protectionist. **1894** *Times* 27 Sept. 7/4 Says Mr. Labouchere, 'Liberal officialdom has wet-blanketted it.' *Ibid* 6 June 11/3 The ranks of old fogeydom. **1894** HENTY *Dorothy's Double* I. 91 A.. specimen of English squiredom. **1889** *Pall Mall G.* 26 Dec. 1/3 The classic pile which..divides clubland from theatredom. **1890** *Spectator* 18 Jan., A pervading atmosphere of topsy-turveydom.

†ˈ**domable,** *a. Obs. rare.* [ad. late L. *domābil-is* tamable, f. *domāre* to tame: cf. OF. *domable.*] Tamable. Hence †ˈ**domableness.**

1623 COCKERAM, *Domable*, easie to be tamed. **1659** D. PELL *Impr. Sea* 205 As quiet and peaceable in the world as domable, or indomable doves are. *Ibid.* 213 *note*, It is impossible to reduce this feral creature unto that domableness that young women might play with him.

domage, -eable, -eous, obs. ff. DAMAGE, etc.

†ˈ**domager.** *Obs. rare*$^{-1}$. [a. OF. pres. inf. *domager*, earlier *-ier*, to damage, used substantively.] Damage, injury.

1502 *Ord. Crysten Men* (W. de W. 1506) IV. xxi. 269 The maner of restytucyon ought to haue conformyte to the maner of the domager.

domain (dəˈmeɪn, dəʊ-), *sb.* Also 5 domayne, 7 -aine. [a. mod.F. *domaine* (1611 in Cotgr.), for earlier F. *demaine*, OF. *demeine*:—L. *dominicum*, in med.L. = 'proprietas, quod ad dominum spectat', subst. use of *dominicus* of or belonging to a lord, of the nature of private property, proper, own. See DEMESNE, which is another form of this word.

OF. *domeine, demeine*, did not come down from cl. L. *dominium* lordship, ownership, property, for that could have given only an OF. *domein, demein*; it is supposed that cl. L. *dominicum* passed in Rom. and OF. through the stages **domenio, domenië, domeine, demeine*: cf. *canonicum*, **canonio, canonië, canoine, chanoine*. But, in the intermediate stage, the form of the word naturally suggested its identity with cl. L. *dominium*, which consequently appears, beside the original *dominicum*, as the Latin equivalent in mediæval documents; the latter have also *domanium* formed on the vernacular. The *o* was in OF. regularly weakened to *e*, *demeine*, whence late AFr. & Eng. *demesne*; in *domaine* the *o* is restored after L.; in French, *domaine* is now (since *c* 1610) used in all senses; but in Eng., *demesne* has been traditionally retained in the legal use, and in senses immediately derived from it, though the two forms overlap.]

†**1.** = DEMESNE 1. Also *attrib.* in *domain lands*. *Obs. rare.*

*c***1425** WYNTOUN *Cron* v. x. 386 Octaveus..þai Deputys has slayne, And held þe kynryk in domayne. **1630** *R. Johnson's Kingd. & Commw.* 158 The rights of the Domaine are these: Rents, Feifs, Payments at alienations. *Ibid.* That is Domaine, which belongeth to the Crowne. **1876** DIGBY *Real Prop.* i. 24 This portion was called *terra dominica, terrae dominicales*, or domain lands.

2. a. *eminent domain*: ultimate or supreme lordship; the superiority or lordship of the sovereign power over all the property in the state, in accordance with which it is entitled to appropriate by constitutional methods any part required for the public advantage, compensation being given to the owner. A term chiefly used in International Law, and in the Law of the United States of America.

[**1625** GROTIUS *De Jure B. et P.* I. iii. §6 Dominium eminens, quod civitas habet in cives et res civium, ad usum publicum.] **1850** LONGF. *Ladder St. Augustine* vi, If we would gain In the bright fields of fair renown The right of eminent domain. **1894** *Harvard Law Rev.* VIII. 237 The name Eminent Domain comes from Grotius, and the subject is a prominent one with European writers on public law; but treatises on it do not exist outside of the United States. The topic develops here because it is a branch of our system of Constitutional Law. The first treatise was by H. E. Mills of St. Louis in 1879. (See also EMINENT 5.)

b. *direct domain, domain of use*, translation of the French law-phrases *domaine direct* the ownership or right of the lord, and *domain utile* the right of use on the part of a lessee, as used in the law of Lower Canada.

3. a. A heritable property; estate or territory held in possession; lands; dominions; = DEMESNE 3–5.

1601 HOLLAND *Pliny* XIII. iii. (R.), These are in the nature of a domain and inheritance, and fall to the next heire in succession. **1782** PRIESTLEY *Corrupt. Chr.* II. x. 258 Royal domains..were..made over to ecclesiastics. **1796** H. HUNTER tr. *St. Pierre's Stud. Nat.* (1799) III. 636 There are, in that Country [Russia], proprietors possessed of domains as extensive as Provinces. **1871** FREEMAN *Norm. Conq.* (1876) IV. xvii. 35 She occupied half a hide of royal domain.

b. *transf.* A district or region under rule, control, or influence, or contained within certain limits; realm; sphere of activity, influence, or dominion.

1727–46 THOMSON *Summer* 859 Ocean trembles for his green domain. **1823** LAMB *Elia* Ser. II. *Poor Relation*, He was lord of his library, and seldom cared for looking out beyond his domains. **1852** H. ROGERS *Ess.* I. vii. 407 For even an infinitude of atoms, infinite worlds in infinite space may be found domain enough.

c. Used by Pinkerton for a subdivision of the Mineral 'kingdom'.

1811 PINKERTON *Petral.* I. 132 The intrites and glutenites are classed under the several domains to which they belong. *Ibid.* I. Introd. iii–iv.

d. spec. *Austral.* (with capital initial). The name of a park in Sydney, Australia, popular for speech-making. Freq. *attrib.*

1896 E. TURNER *Little Larrikin* xiv. 163 His ideas were as sweeping and extravagant as those of a Domain orator out of work. **1904** A. B. PATERSON *Rio Grande's Last Race* 124 It's grand to be an unemployed And lie in the Domain. **1941** BAKER *Dict. Austral. Slang* 24 *Domain cocktail* (or *special*), a lethal concoction of petrol and pepper which reputedly once had a vogue among deadbeat drinkers in the Sydney Domain. *Domain dosser*, a loafer or down-and-out who frequents the Sydney Domain. **1943** K. TENNANT *Ride on Stranger* xxiii. 261 He, too, could see his old comrade, Mervyn Leggatt, across the Domain advocating the direct opposite to his own policy.

4. a. *fig.* A sphere of thought or action; field, province, scope of a department of knowledge, etc.

1764 GOLDSM. *Trav.* 97 Carried to excess in each domain, This fav'rite good begets peculiar pain. **1799** MACKINTOSH *Study Law Nat.* Wks. 1846 I. 381 Contracting..the domain of brutal force and of arbitrary will. **1828** CARLYLE *Misc.* (1872) I, Our Poet's gift in raising it into the domain of Art. **1864** BOWEN *Logic* x. 343 An actual enlargement of the domain of Science. **1866** ARGYLL *Reign Law* ii. (ed. 4) 53.

b. *Logic.* The breadth, extension, circuit, or sphere of a notion.

c. *Math.* 'In the theory of Functions, the portion of the z-plane within a circle which just does not include a singular point is called the domain of its centre' (H. T. Gerrans).

1893 FORSYTH *The. Functions* 55 If the whole of the domain of b be not included in that of a.

d. *Math.* An algebraic system with two binary operations defined by postulates stronger than those for a ring but weaker than those for a field; *esp.* (more fully ***integral domain***), a commutative ring in which the cancellation law holds for multiplication of non-zero elements and (with most writers) which has a unit element for multiplication.

1896 *Bull. Amer. Math. Soc.* III. 102 The idea of the adjunction of its root[s]..to the totality of numbers heretofore in use, viz., the rational numbers, is now developed, and the properties of rational functions of the elements of this new 'domain'..are taken up. **1904** F. CAJORI *Theory of Equations* xiii. 134 A set of numbers is called a domain of rationality or simply a domain, when the sums, differences, products, and quotients of any numbers in the set (excluding only the quotients obtained through division by o) always yield as results numbers belonging to the set. All rational numbers..constitute such a domain. **1937** A. A. ALBERT *Mod. Higher Algebra* ii. 27 The most important type of integral domain is the field. **1941** BIRKHOFF & MACLANE *Surv. Mod. Algebra* iv. 97 By a unique factorization domain (sometimes called a 'Gaussian domain') is meant an integral domain in which (i) any element not a unit can be factored into primes, (ii) this factorization is unique to within order and unit factors. **1958** ZARISKI & SAMUEL *Commutative Algebra* I. i. 22 An important class of unique factorization domains is given by the so-called euclidean domains or rings admitting a division algorithm. **1965** J. J. ROTMAN *Theory of Groups* iv. 66 A domain is a commutative ring with unit that has no divisors of zero.

e. *Math.* The set of values that an independent variable of a function can take; the graphical representation of this set; the set comprising all the first elements of the ordered pairs constituting some given set.

1902 *Encycl. Brit.* XXVIII. 545/2 The idea of a 'variable' is that of a number to which we may assign at pleasure any of the values which constitute a definite aggregate, called the 'domain' of the variable. **1914** A. R. FORSYTH *Theory of Functions of Two Complex Variables* iii. 57 A restricted portion of a field of variation is called a domain, the range of a domain being usually indicated by analytical relations. **1937** MICHELL & BELZ *Elem. Math. Analysis* I. i. 60 The parts of the plane in which N can lie are commonly called the *domain* of N and the same word is used for the corresponding aggregate of pairs of values of x, y which correspond to N. **1955** D. A. QUADLING *Math. Analysis* iii. 14 A function which is defined by means of a formula may have its domain restricted by the character of the formula itself... The domain of the function 1/x cannot include the number o. **1967** M. R. KINSOLVING *Set Theory & Number Systems* ii. 21 One might say that the domain of R is the set of all first elements appearing in the pairs (a, b) constituting R.

f. *Logic.* The class of all terms that bear a given relation to any term (see quot. 1903).

1903 B. RUSSELL *Princ. Math.* I. ix. 97 All referents with respect to a given relation form a class. It follows..that all relata also form a class. These two classes I shall call respectively the domain and the converse domain of the relation; the logical sum of the two I shall call the field of the relation. *Ibid.* 98 If paternity be the relation, fathers form its domain, children its converse domain, and fathers and children together its field. **1955** A. N. PRIOR *Formal Logic* III. iii. 277 Both the domain and the converse domain of the null relation are the null class.

g. *Math.* An open connected set of at least one point.

1906 W. H. & G. C. YOUNG *Theory of Sets of Points* ix. 178 The set of all the points inside a triangle is called a triangular domain, or the interior of the triangle, and is a simple case of a region. *Ibid.*, The points of a domain always form an open set. **1957** E. T. COPSON *Introd. Theory of Functions of Complex Variable* (rev. ed.) ii. 15 If we add to a domain its limiting points, the resulting set is called a *closed region.*

h. *Physics.* In ferromagnetic materials, a region which behaves as an elementary magnet, all the atoms or ions in a region having the axes of their permanent magnetic moments aligned in the same direction. Also *attrib.*

1926 E. C. STONER *Magnetism & Atomic Structure* xiii. 295 The size of the domains may be much smaller than the size of the actual crystalline 'grains'. **1944** *Electronic Engin.* XVII. 144/3 The assumption of a molecular field, and the sub-division of a ferromagnetic into spontaneously saturated domains, form the foundation of the modern domain theory of ferromagnetism. **1945** *Rev. Mod. Physics* XVII. 15 In a demagnetized specimen..the directions of magnetization of the individual domains are distributed at random among various possible directions. **1966** PHILLIPS & WILLIAMS *Inorg. Chem.* II. xix. 26 Ferromagnetic substances commonly exhibit a domain structure, in which each domain is permanently magnetized. **1966** CAREY & ISAAC *Magnetic Domains* i. 13 In such a case regions now exist in the crystal where the direction of the magnetization changes from one domain to the next; these regions are called domain boundaries or domain walls.

i. *Linguistics.* (See quots.)

1933 BLOOMFIELD *Lang.* xv. 247 The substitute replaces only forms of a certain class, which we may call the *domain* of the substitute. **1942** *Language* XVIII. 14 A suprasegmental phone has a Domain, defined as the type of sequence of segmental phones which it covers. **1968** P. M. POSTAL *Aspects Phonol. Theory* iii. 41 Each rule 'realizing' morphophonemic structures as phonemic ones must be defined exclusively on a domain consisting of strings of morphons.

Hence †**do'main** *v. intr.*, *Obs.* to dominate.

1589 IVE *Fortif.* 36 It must lye wholy open toward the towne, that the towne may commaund, and domaine ouer it.

do'mainal, *a.* [f. DOMAIN + -AL[1], united with the more historical word DOMANIAL by the intermediate *domainial.*] = DOMANIAL.

1857 SIR F. PALGRAVE *Norm. & Eng.* II. 551 An antient domainal palace. **1862** S. LUCAS *Secularia* 352 The domainal jurists of the eighteenth century.

do'maine-'bottled, *a.* [f. Fr. *domaine* estate + BOTTLED *ppl. a.* 2.] = *estate-bottled* (see ESTATE *sb.* 14). So ***domaine-bottling.***

1960 *Spectator* 21 Oct. 627/3 A very special Chambolle Musigny and a particularly aristocratic Clos de Vougeot, both domaine-bottled. **1961** *Guardian* 21 Nov. 15/5 A certain vogue for offering so-called domaine bottled Burgundies. **1967** E. PENNING-ROWSELL in C. Ray *Compleat Imbiber* IX. 195 The demand for authenticity, including.. domaine and château bottling. **1970** *Observer* (Colour Suppl.) 6 Dec. 74/3 The 1967 domaine-bottle Montrachet.

domal ('dəʊməl), *a.* (and *sb.*) [ad. med.L. *domāl-is* (Du Cange), f *domus* house: see DOME, etc.]

1. *Astrol.* Of or pertaining to a dome or 'house'.

1716 ADDISON *Drummer* III. i, Mars is now entering his first house, and will shortly appear in all his domal dignities. **1819** JAS. WILSON *Compl. Dict. Astrol., Domal dignity*, when a planet is in its own house.

2. Of or pertaining to houses; domestic.

1728 R. MORRIS *Ess. Anc. Archit.* 3 Templar and Domal Architecture. **1884** *Health Exhib. Catal.* 98/1 Principles of sanitation—personal, municipal, domal, etc.

3. *Phonetics.* (See quots.) Hence as *sb.*

1919 C. R. LANMAN in *Festgabe Adolf Kaegi* 101 The derivative, domal..is useable as adjective or as substantive (domals). *Ibid.*, The best English equivalent for mūrdhanya, 'produced at the dome (of the palate)', is clearly domal. **1933** BLOOMFIELD *Lang.* vi. 98 Apical articulation in the domal position (the tip of the tongue touching almost the highest point in the roof of the mouth). *Ibid.*, In Sanskrit.., postdentals..and domals..are distinct phonemes. **1943** K. L. PIKE *Phonetics* vii. 123 A *domal* sound (i.e. *cerebral*, or *cacuminal*) implies that the tongue tip articulates somewhere behind the alveolar arch. **1962** B. M. H. STRANG *Mod. Eng. Struct.* iii. 30 Positions of articulation..domal (tongue tip to dome of palate).

4. Of, pertaining to, or shaped like a dome.

1928 E. R. LILLEY *Geol. Petrol. & Natural Gas* xii. 274 The Bald Hill Dome is one of the larger domal structures that are so common in northeastern Oklahoma. **1954** W. D. THORNBURY *Princ. Geomorphology* ix. 208 Most large domal structures are of rather ancient geologic age. **1971** *Nature* 19 Feb. 538/1 A broad domal uplift of central Kenya of about 300 m in the late Miocene was suceeded by a major uplift of 1,400 m.

do'manial, *a.* Also 9 domainial. [a. F. *domanial* (16th c. in Hatz-Darm.), ad. med.L. *domaniālis*, f. *domanium.*] Of, pertaining, or relating to domain or to a particular domain.

1818 HALLAM *Mid. Ages* ii. II. (1855) I. 208 The domanial estates of the crown. *Ibid.* 221 The extent of his domanial territory. **1841** W. SPALDING *Italy & It. Isl.* II. 110 Old privileges of the domanial towns, or, as we might call them, royal boroughs. **1855** M. BRIDGES *Pop. Mod. Hist.* 405 Re-assuming those rich domainial estates. **1861** MAINE *Anc. Law* vii. (1870) 231 That..transmutation..substituted the feudal form of property for the domainial (or Roman) and the allodial (or German).

domas, obs. form of DAMASK.

domb(e, obs. ff. DUMB, DOOM.

‖**domba** ('dɒmbə). [ad. Cingalese *dombe.*] A large East Indian and Malayan tree, *Calophyllum Inophyllum*, N.O. *Clusiaceæ*, the seeds of which yield a thick dark-green strong-scented oil (*domba oil*), used medicinally and for burning.

1858 SIMMONDS *Dict. Trade.* **1866** *Treas. Bot.*

dómbóc, OE. form of DOOMBOOK.

Domdaniel (dɒm'dænɪəl). [a. F. *domdaniel*, app. f. Gr. δῶμα Δανιήλ, or L. *domus Danielis*, hall or house of Daniel.

A fictitious name, introduced in the French 'Continuation of the Arabian Nights' by Dom Chaves and M. Cazotte 1788-93, whence adopted by Southey in *Thalaba*, and so by Carlyle. It is not clear whether 'Daniel' is intended to refer to the Hebrew prophet, or to 'a great Grecian sage' of that name who appears in the tale of 'the Queen and the Serpents' in the *Arabian Nights.*]

A fabled submarine hall where a magician or sorcerer met with his disciples: placed by Cazotte 'under the sea near Tunis', by Southey 'under the roots of the ocean'; used by Carlyle in the sense of 'infernal cave', 'den of iniquity'.

1801 SOUTHEY *Thalaba* XII. xxiv, The Domdaniel rock'd Through all its thundering vaults. **1809** BYRON *Eng. Bards* 213 Next see tremendous Thalaba come on..Domdaniel's dread destroyer. **1845** CARLYLE *Cromwell* (1871) I. 41 Spain was as a black Domdaniel. *Ibid.* 64 A grisly Law Pluto.. kind of Infernal King, Chief Enchanter..in the Domdaniel of Attorneys. *Ibid.* IV. 138 Hurled..into the great Domdaniel of Spanish Iniquity in the far West. **1888** *Edinb. Rev.* Oct. 408 At ease not in Zion only but in Domdaniel.

dome (dəʊm), *sb.* Also 7 dosme, 8 doom. [In sense 1, app. directly ad. L. *dom-us* house, home; in other senses, a. F. *dome* (15-16th c.; sometimes *dosme*, whence mod.F. *dôme*), ad. It *duomo* house, house of God, 'chiefe Church or Cathedrall Church in a citie' (Florio), high cupola, dome (as a distinguishing feature of Italian cathedrals):—L. *domu-s* house.]

1. A house, a home; a stately building, a mansion. Now only as a poetical or dignified appellation.

1513 DOUGLAS *Æneis* XIII. Prol. 93 Onto my dome [= in my dwelling], I saw ȝou neuir ayr. **1553** T. WILSON *Rhet.* (1580) 166 Dated at my Dome, or rather Mansion place in Lincolneshire. **1656** BLOUNT *Glossogr., Dome*..a Town-House, Guild-Hall, a State-House, Meeting-house in a city, from that of Florence, which is so called. **1724** SWIFT *Riddles* vii. 51 Sad charnel-house! a dismal dome, For which all mortals leave their home. **1770** LANGHORNE *Plutarch* (1879) I. 74/2 They built temples..and other sacred domes. **1808** SCOTT *Marm.* VI. Introd. 121 Gladly as he we seek the dome, And as reluctant turn us home.

fig. **1812** BYRON *Ch. Har.* II. vi, Ambition's airy hall, The dome of thought, the palace of the Soul. **1818** SHELLEY *Rev. Islam* II. xliii, Hoary crime would come Behind, and fraud rebuild religion's tottering dome.

†**2.** A cathedral church; = DOM[2]. *Obs.*

1691 tr. *Emillianne's Journ. Naples* 71 The Ceremony.. Celebrated..at the Dome (so they call the Cathedral Churches in Italy). **1704** ADDISON *Italy* (1766) 46 Pope Lucius, who lies buried in the dome. **1707** *Lond. Gaz.* No. 4382/3 There was a Jew Christen'd last Sunday in the Dome of this City [Berlin]. **1753** HANWAY *Trav.* II. I. iii. 15 There is also the dome, which is a cathedral church.

3. a. A rounded vault forming the roof of a building or chief part of it, and having a circular, elliptical, or polygonal base; a cupola.

1656 BLOUNT *Glossogr., Dome*..a flat round Loover, or open roof to a Steeple, Banqueting-house, &c. Somewhat resembling the bell of a great Watch. **1660** F. BROOKE tr. *Le Blanc's Trav.* 114 The Kings Palace..was built square, with a Dome. **1712** *Lond. Gaz.* No. 5058/2 The Dome of the Cathedral was illuminated. **1756-7** tr. *Keysler's Trav.* (1760) II. 311 The roof of the Pantheon is a round doom, without pillars or windows. **1812-16** J. SMITH *Panorama Sc. & Art* II. 66 The whispering gallery in the dome of St. Paul's Cathedral, London. **1879** SIR G. SCOTT *Lect. Archit.* II. 229, I defined a dome as the covering of a circular space produced by the revolution of an arch round its central vertical axis.

b. The hemispherical roof of an astronomical observatory, made to revolve and open so as to direct the telescope towards any part of the heavens.

1865 *Chambers' Encycl.* VII. 30/2 Since the year 1852, a time-ball has been dropped on the dome of the Observatory ..at precisely one o'clock.

4. a. *transf.* The vaulted roof of a cavern or natural hollow; the concave vault of the sky; a vaulted canopy; a canopy of trees, etc.; a bee-hive.

1727 SWIFT *Gulliver* III. iii, Whence the astronomers descend into a large dome..called..the astronomer's cave. **1730-46** THOMSON *Autumn* 1182 The tender race, By thousands, tumble from their honeyed domes. **1790-1811** COMBE *Devil on 2 Sticks in Eng.* (1817) VI. 59 In a..bed, with a dome to it. **1797** MRS. RADCLIFFE *Italian* ii, The whole dome of the sky had an appearance of transparency. **1830** TENNYSON *Recoll. Arab. Nts.* 41 Imbower'd vaults of pillar'd palm..the dome Of hollow boughs. **1860** TYNDALL *Glac.* I. ii. 18 Some bubbles..had lifted the coating here and there into little rounded domes.

b. The convex rounded summit of a mountain, a wave, etc. In U.S., frequently entering into the names of rounded mountain peaks.

[**1788** SIR W. JONES *Tartars* v. Wks. 1799 I. 52 A stupendous edifice, the beams and pillars of which are many ranges of lofty hills, and the dome, one prodigious mountain.] **1851** LONGF. *Gold. Leg.* v. *At Sea*, The billows ..upon their flowing dome..poise her. **1856** STANLEY *Sinai & Pal.* x. (1858) 366 Tabor with its rounded dome. **1882** *Worcester Exhib. Catal.* iii. 58 Velvets..'studded' with polished domes. **1890** M. TOWNSEND *U.S.* 138 Carter Dome, New Hampshire; The Dome, State of New York.

c. *Geol.* Any of various kinds of geological structure resembling a dome in shape (see quots.).

[1833 C. Lyell *Princ. Geol.* III. xxi. 289 Suppose the five formations to lie in horizontal stratification at the bottom of the sea; then let a movement from below press them upwards into the form of a flattened dome, and let the crown of this dome be afterwards cut off.] 1900 *Rep. Geol. Surv. Louisiana 1899* 228 The dome of the salt is situated on the northeast of the island. *Ibid.* 229 A very distinct anticline, or better, elongated dome. 1909 J. P. Iddings *Ign. Rocks* I. I. viii. 301 Since the more siliceous lavas are generally the more viscous when extruded, they are oftener found in domes than the less siliceous ones. 1930 *Engineering* 10 Jan. 39/3 A sulphur salt dome in Louisiana has yielded 9,000,000 tons of sulphur. 1936 C. M. Nevin *Princ. Struct. Geol.* (ed. 2) iii. 46 A dome is a roughly symmetrical upfold, the beds dipping in all directions, more or less equally, from a point. 1938 *Nature* 2 Apr. 599/1 The productive domes are fairly typical of the oil fields, being of small extent but giving large yields. 1944 A. Holmes *Princ. Physical Geol.* vi. 73 Domes and basins represent the limiting cases in which the beds dip in all directions, outwards from, or inwards towards, the centre of the structure. *Ibid.* xvi. 349 Salt domes are curious structures occurring in great numbers along the Gulf Coast of the United States. 1962 E. A. Vincent tr. *Rittmann's Volcanoes* i. 26 The slowly extruded lava piles up into a dome over the mouth of the vent.

d. The head. *slang.*

1891 in Farmer *Slang* II. 305/2. 1918 C. Sandburg *Cornhuskers* 60 Your bony head.. Those grappling hooks.. The dome and the wings of you. 1923 R. D. Paine *Comr. Rolling Ocean* ix. 160 He got tired of trying to shove the book stuff into ivory domes like yours. 1959 [see bonce 2]. 1959 [see dong *v.* 2].

5. Technical senses.

a. *Manuf.* The cover of a reverberatory furnace, etc.

1706 Phillips (ed. Kersey), *Dome* ..among chymists, a kind of arched Cover for a Reverberatory Furnace. 1823 *Specif. Johnson's Patent* No. 4747. 2 The.. uppermost vessel ..must have a close dome or cover applied to it. 1854 Ronalds & Richardson *Chem. Technol.* (ed. 2) I. 127 The dome ought to be made as flat as possible consistent with durability, in order to reflect the heat down upon the coal.

b. *Cryst.* (See quot.)

1863–72 Watts *Dict. Chem.* II. 1 *Dome*, a term used to designate a trimetric, monoclinic, or triclinic prism, whose faces and edges are parallel to one of the secondary axes. 1895 Story-Maskelyne *Crystallogr.* §326 The term dome is employed not in contradistinction to the term prism or prismatid, but, like the latter term, conventionally and merely to distinguish these forms from one another.

c. In *Locomotive Engines*, the raised conical part of the boiler, forming a steam-chamber, the *steam-dome* (Weale *Dict. Terms*, 1849–50). In *Railway Carriages*, the raised roof, forming a space for ventilation and light (Knight *Dict. Mech.*, 1874).

1841 *Penny Cycl.* XIX. 259/2 The steam-dome and similar parts are double.

d. *Watchmaking.* The back part of the inner case of a watch to which sometimes the works are attached.

1884 F. J. Britten *Watch & Clockm.* 88 Used for attaching a watch movement to a dome case.

e. ***dome of silence***, the trade name of a type of castor (castor[2] 2) fitted to furniture; also *fig.*

1924 *Trade Marks Jrnl.* 12 Mar. 551 *Domes of Silence*... Metal Castors for Furniture. 1925 A. Christie *Secret of Chimneys* xvii. 170 Those boots of yours aren't exactly domes of silence, are they, Bill? 1947 G. Greene *19 Stories* 161 One of those cases of circumstantial evidence, in which you feel the jurymen's anxiety—because mistakes *have* been made—like domes of silence muting the court. 1960 *Woman* 13 Feb. 3/4 Domes of silence, small metal fittings for the legs of tables or chairs.

f. In full ***dome fastener***. A press-stud consisting of a rounded portion which clips into a socket, used esp. as a fastener for gloves.

1910 *Daily Chron.* 14 Mar. 6/4 Ladies' Kid Gloves.. with 2 or 3 dome fasteners. 1926 *Daily Colonist* (Victoria, B.C.) 17 Jan. 7/1 (Advt.), Dome Fasteners. Black or White, assorted sizes. 1966 G. W. Turner *Eng. Lang. in Austral. & N.Z.* viii. 172 Press studs are called *domes* [in New Zealand].

6. *attrib.* and *Comb.*, as ***dome-case***, ***-cover***, ***-face***, ***-form***, ***-head***, ***-span***, ***-spire***, ***-theatre***, ***-top***, ***-vaulting***; ***dome-like***, ***-shaped*** adjs; **dome-headed** *a.*, having a large, well-rounded head; **dome-light**, a dome-shaped lamp.

1797 *College* 6 Science trailed her pall Through the dome-theatre and spacious hall. 1809 A. Henry *Trav.* 128 Its [the beaver's] house has an arched dome-like roof. 1819 *Pantologia* s.v. *Dome*, Dome-vaulting.. is lighter than any that can cover the same area. 1832 G. R. Porter *Porcelain & Gl.* 60 The dome-shaped roof. 1849–50 Weale *Dict. Terms*, *Dome Cover*, in locomotive engines, the brass or copper cover which encloses the dome, to prevent the radiation of heat. 1863–72 Watts *Dict. Chem.* II. 147 When trimetric crystals are bounded only by prismatic and dome-faces. 1895 Story-Maskelyne *Crystallogr.* §328 Dome-forms with the general symbol (*okl*). 1910 H. G. Wells *Mr. Polly* vii. 158 A certain high-browed gentleman living at Highbury... This dome-headed monster of intellect alleges [etc.]. 1938 W. de la Mare *Memory* 75 A sage, dome-headed, grey, Who looked a child. 1956 *Archit. Rev.* CXIX. 354/4 The metal combined curbs and linings made for use with glass domelights. 1962 K. Orvis *Damned & Destroyed* iii. 23 She sat back under the winking domelight.

Hence **domeless** *a.*, not having a dome.

1870 *Athenæum* 20 Aug. 232/3 In that domeless Domkirche of Cologne.

dome, *v.* [f. prec. sb.]

1. *trans.* To cover with or as with a dome.

1876 Whitney *Sights & Ins.* xxv. 248 An enlarged chamber, almost domed in by the deep scooped over-leaning wall. 1885 Tennyson *Early Spring* i, [He] domes the red-plow'd hills With loving blue. 1894 Baring-Gould *Deserts S. France* II. xix. 88 To the Romans there was no necessity for doming over quadrangular spaces.

2. To make dome-shaped.

1879 *Cassell's Techn. Educ.* IV. 299/1 And brings down upon them a polished globular punch, which domes them up. 1894 Mrs. H. Ward *Marcella* I. 293 The roof had been raised and domed.

3. *intr.* To rise or swell as a dome.

1887 *Argosy* Jan. 32 The cathedral towered, or rather domed, above the ramparts. 1894 Doyle *S. Holmes* 261 His forehead domes out in a white curve.

dome, obs. form of doom, doum.

domed (dəʊmd), *a.* [f. dome *sb.* or *v* + -ed.]

1. Dome-shaped, made dome-like; vaulted.

1775 in *Lett. 1st Earl Malmesbury* (1870) I. 287 The ceiling is domed, and beautifully painted. 1871 Darwin *Desc. Man* II. xv. 164 They build a domed nest, which is a great anomaly in so large a bird. 1872 C. King *Mountain. Sierra Nev.* vii. 137 These domed mountains. 1879 *Blackw. Mag.* Aug. 152 The dark Nubians.. have domed foreheads.

2. Roofed with or possessing a dome or domes.

1855 Browning *Love among Ruins* ii, The domed and daring palace. 1863 Geo. Elliot *Romola* II. vi, He.. looked down on the domed and towered city. 1879 Sir G. Scott *Lect. Archit.* II. 7 The introduction into France of the domed architecture by a colony of Greeks.

domel, variant of dumble.

domelet ('dəʊmlɪt). [f. dome *sb.* + -let.] A miniature dome.

1883 R. F. Burton & Cameron *Gold Coast for Gold* I. i. 19 The Estrella, whose dome and domelets, built to mimic St. Peter's, look only like hen and chickens. 1892 *Athenæum* 2 July 38/2 A very low dome, or domelet.

doment ('du:mənt). *dial.* and *vulgar.* [f. do *v.* + -ment.] A performance, 'to-do': see do *sb.*[1]

1828 *Craven Dialect*, *Dooment*, deed, action, contest. 1831 *Lincoln Herald* 15 July 4/3 At the great *Do*, or *Doment*.. in honor of the Whig Ministry. 1889 *N.W. Linc. Gloss.* s.v., Ther'll be a fine doment when yung— cums at aage. Thaay kicked up no end on a doment.

†**Domes-booke.** *Obs.* = Domesday Book.

1610 Holland *Camden's Brit.* I. 234 In Edward the Confessors time (as we read in Domes-booke of England) it paied tribute.

Domesday ('dəʊmzdeɪ, 'du:mzdeɪ). [f. *dómes* genitive of *dóm* doom + day.] A Middle English spelling of doomsday, day of judgement, now commonly used as a historical term, in the following:

Domesday Book, colloquially ***Domesday***: the name applied, from the 12th c., to the record of the Great Inquisition or Survey of the lands of England, their extent, value, ownership, and liabilities, made by order of William the Conqueror in 1086. Extended to abstracts based upon that record, such as the Exon Domesday.

[The name appears to have been derived directly from *Domesday* the Day of the Last Judgement, and *Domesday Book* the Book by which all men would be judged. It originated as a popular appellation (see *Dial. de Scacc.*), given to the Book as being a final and conclusive authority on all matters on which it had to be referred to.]

1178 *Dial. de Scaccario* I. xvi, Hic liber ab indigenis Domesdei nuncupatur, id est, dies judicii per metaphoram: sicut enim districti et terribilis examinis illius novissimi sententia nulla tergiversationis arte valet eludi: sic.. sententia ejus [libri] infatuari non potest vel impune declinari. Ob hoc nos eundem librum judiciarium nominavimus. 1485 *Nottingham Rec.* II. 350 Libro de Domesday. *a* 1491 J. Ross *Hist. Reg. Angl.* (1716) 109 Redacta est dicta descriptio in unum volumen.. Nomen libri est Domesday. 1494 Fabyan *Chron.* VI. cxcvii. 202 An olde boke sometyme in yᵉ Guyldehall of London named Domys daye. 1570–6 Lambarde *Peramb. Kent* (1826) 104 The booke of the generall survey of the Realme, which William the Conquerour caused to bee made.. and to be called Domesday, bicause (as Mathew Parise saith) it spared no man, but iudged all men indifferently, as the Lord in that great day will do. 1591 —— *Archeion* (1635) 24 The Record of which Survey was then called Doomes-day Book. 1614 Selden *Titles Hon.* 232 In that which we now call Domesday, made and collected under William I. 1656 Blount *Glossogr.*, *Dooms-day-book*.. wherein all the ancient Demean Lands in this Nation are registred; It is so called, because upon any difference, the parties received their doom. 1701 De Foe *True-born Eng.* 13 Doomsday Book his Tyranny records. 1767 Blackstone *Comm.* II. 49 The compiling of the great survey called domesday-book. 1856 Emerson *Eng. Traits, Truth* Wks. (Bohn) II. 52 Down goes the flying word on the tablets, and is indelible as Doomsday Book. 1876 Freeman *Norm. Conq.* V. 476 Domesday still sets before us a most minute scale of classes.

b. Transferred to other like documents of standard authority, such as the ***Domesday of St. Paul's***, the record of a survey of the capitular estates in 1181; also *fig.* and allusively.

1742 Young *Nt. Th.* II. 271 All-rapacious Usurers conceal Their Doomsday-book from all-consuming heirs. 1749 Fielding *Tom Jones* IX. i, The vast authentic doomsday-book of nature. 1862–5 Stanley *Jew. Ch.* xii. 259 Which has made the latter half of the Book of Joshua.. the Domesday Book of the Conquest of Palestine. 1865 *Navy Docky. Expense Acc.* (*Blue Book* I. 465) Previous to the year 1858–59 the expense accounts of ships and services were transmitted annually from the Dockyards to the Surveyor of the Navy.. for recording in the 'Abstracts of Progress' or 'Doomsday Book' the expenditure incurred on account of each ship. 1869 Freeman *Norm. Conq.* (1875) III. 300 A Domesday of the conquerors was.. drawn up in the ducal hall at Lillebonne, a forerunner of the great Domesday of the conquered.

domestic (də'mɛstɪk, dəʊ-), *a.* and *sb.* Also 6–7 -ique, ick(e. [ad. L. *domestic-us*, f. *domus* house: see dome. In early form and use, immediately through F. *domestique* (14th c. in Hatz.-Darm.).]

A. *adj.*

†1. a. Having the character or position of the inmate of a house; housed. ***to be domestic with*** (*of*): to be of the household of, at home with. *Obs.*

1521 *Bradshaw's St. Werburge* 2nd Ballad to Author 21 (1887) 201 Preserue his soule, and make hym domestique Within the heuyns. 1632 Lithgow *Trav.* II. 67, I being domestick with him the selfe same time. *Ibid.* VIII. 358 [He] had turned Turke.. With whom I found Domesticke, some fifteene circumsised English Runagates. 1681 Colvil *Whigs Supplic.* (1695) 27 Mercury.. hath no dwelling of his own, But is Domestic of the Sun.

b. Intimate, familiar, 'at home'. *Obs.*

a 1612 Donne *Βιαθανατος* (1644) 42 The knowledge therof is so domestique, so neare, so inward to us, that our conscience cannot slumber in it, nor dissemble it. 1647 Clarendon *Hist. Reb.* II. §83 He.. was.. domestick with all, and not suspected by either of the.. factions. 1748 Chesterf. *Lett.* (1792) II. clxiv. 100 Domestic in the best company and the best families. 1750 *Ibid.* (1774) III. 152 An English minister shall have resided seven years at a court.. without being intimate or domestic in any one house.

2. a. Of or belonging to the home, house, or household; pertaining to one's place of residence or family affairs; household, home, 'family'.

1611 Shaks. *Cymb.* III. i. 65 Cæsar, that hath moe Kings his Seruants, then Thy selfe Domesticke Officers. 1632 Lithgow *Trav.* IV. 163 Domesticke pastimes, as Chesse, Cards, Dice, and Tables. 1664 Power *Exp. Philos.* I. 11 Of Domestick Spiders there are two sorts. 1681 Temple *Memoirs* III. Wks. 1731 I. 345, I was resolv'd to pass the rest of my Life in my own Domestick, without troubling my self further about any publick Affairs. 1764 Goldsm. *Trav.* 434 Domestic joy. 1830 D'Israeli *Chas. I*, III. vi. 110 Charles ..loved the privacy of domestic life. 1840 Dickens *Barn. Rudge* vii, Her single domestic servant.

†b. *fig.* Belonging to what concerns oneself. *Obs.*

1707 Norris *Treat. Humility* vii. 315 Domestic ignorance, the ignorance of our selves, and of what passes within our own breast.

3. a. Of or pertaining to one's own country or nation; not foreign, internal, inland, 'home'.

1545 Joye *Exp. Dan.* vii. (R.), Lo here maye ye see this beast to be no stranger.. he sitteth in the temple of God, he is therefore a domestyc enimye. 1549 *Compl. Scot.* Prol. 16, I hef vsit domestic scottis langage, maist intelligibil for the vlgare pepil. 1665 Manley *Grotius' Low-C. Warres* 859 That the contentions growing among Priests should be decided by Domestique Judges, and not at Rome. 1719 W. Wood *Surv. Trade* 7 A great Part of our Domestick Trade depends upon our Foreign Commerce. 1849 Macaulay *Hist. Eng.* II. 265 The whole domestic and foreign policy of the English government.

b. Indigenous; made at home or in the country itself; native, home-grown, home-made.

1660 Sharrock *Vegetables* 42 [It] makes the like impression upon its domestique plants. 1713 Berkeley *Guardian* No. 49 ¶8 They [glasses] are domestic, and cheaper than foreign toys. 1835 Ure *Philos. Manuf.* 77 Domestic woollens and flannels.

4. a. Of animals: Living under the care of man, in or near his habitations; tame, not wild.

1620 Venner *Via Recta* iii. 65 Domesticke or tame Ducks. 1632 J. Hayward tr. *Biondi's Eromena* 181 No small delight ..to see so timorous a creature growne so domesticke. 1856 Mrs. Browning *Aur. Leigh* I. 635 Tamed and grown domestic like a barn-door fowl. 1859 Darwin *Orig. Spec.* i. (1873) 14 The origin of most of our domestic animals will probably for ever remain vague.

†b. Of men: Having settled abodes; not nomad or wild. *Obs.*

1632 Lithgow *Trav.* VI. 291 Moores, Jews, domesticke Arabians.

5. Attached to home; devoted to home life or duties; domesticated.

1658 Davenant *Play-House to be Let* IV. Dram. Wks. 1873 IV. 85 Kings, who move Within a lowly sphere of private love, Are too domestic for a throne. 1751 Johnson *Rambler* No. 153 ¶5 To me, whom he found studious and domestick. 1837 J. H. Newman *Par. Serm.* (ed. 2) III. xx. 329 It is praiseworthy and right to be domestic.

6. ***domestic-minded*** adj.

1889 W. B. Yeats *Let.* Feb. in *Lett. to K. Tynan* (1953) 85 The poor domestic-minded swindler! 1960 *Times* 4 Mar. 13/6 The Afrikaner, being at heart a generous and very much a domestic-minded person.

7. In special collocations: ***domestic economy*** (see economy 2 a); ***domestic science***, the study or knowledge of household management, comprising cookery, laundry, needlework, etc.; = housewifery 1 a; ***domestic service***, the condition or occupation of a household servant (cf. service *sb.*[1] 1 a); ***domestic slave***, (*a*) a household slave, esp. as distinguished from a predial slave (see predial *a.* 3 a); (*b*) =

ODALISQUE; (*c*) (see quot. 1799); ***domestic slavery***, the condition of a domestic slave; also *fig.*; ***domestic workshop***, a workshop in a private dwelling-house.

1778 [see ECONOMY 2 a]. **1797** F. M. EDEN (*title*) The State of the poor, or an history of the labouring classes in England, ..in which are particularly considered, their domestic economy, with respect to diet, dress, fuel, and habitation. **1898** E. R. LUSH *Less. Domestic Sci.* I. i. 1 What do we understand by 'Domestic Economy' or 'Domestic Science' as we often prefer to call it now? **1905** *Daily Chron.* 19 May 8/1 The girls have already spent one year in a domestic economy school. **1928** Domestic economy [see *beauty culture* s.v. BEAUTY *sb.* III b]. **1897** H. CAMPBELL *Household Economics* p. xx, The directors of the 'Domestic Science' department. **1915** 'BARTIMEUS' *Tall Ship* ii. 37 Cooking and laundry, and hygiene—domestic science it's called. **1936** *Discovery* Jan. 32/2 The greatest amount of dissatisfaction was found among teachers of domestic science, art and music. **1741** RICHARDSON *Pamela* IV. xiii. 77 These duties.. inspirit every one in the Discharge of all their domestick Services. **1832** F. TROLLOPE *Domestic Manners* I. vi. 73 Young women..believe that the most abject poverty is preferable to domestic service. **1840** H. REEVE tr. *de Tocqueville's Democracy in America* IV. III. v. 39 This is not only the notion which servants themselves entertain.. domestic service is looked upon by masters in the same light. **1933** MRS. C. S. PEEL *Life's Enchanted Cup* xviii. 239 Two of these..were Ministry of Reconstruction Committees; one to enquire into the housing of the working classes..the other to enquire into conditions of domestic service. **1776** GIBBON *Decl. & F.* I. ii. 40 In the free states of antiquity, the domestic slaves were exposed to the wanton rigour of despotism. **1798** *Lady's Mag.* June 265/1 No woman of Turkish birth can be an odalik, or domestic slave. **1799** M. PARK *Trav.* (ed. 2) xxii. 287 The domestic slaves, or such as are born in a man's own house, are treated with more lenity than those which are purchased with money. **1970** *Encycl. Brit.* XX. 635/2 Manumission was..frequently granted for long and devoted services of a domestic slave, in particular to nurses who had looked after the master's children. **1818** *Public Ledger* 3 June 2/4 He proposed a return to the domestic slavery of Greece and Rome. **1825** *Kaleidoscope* 23 Aug. 57/3 We allude to that domestic slavery..to which the youth, engaged as shopmen of drapers,..are subjected. **1858** *Leisure Hour* 25 Feb. 127/1 Domestic slavery is extensively practised by the Liberians. **1970** *Encycl. Brit.* XX. 639/1 A text for the abolition of slavery..was implemented..in Algeria, where domestic slavery existed. **1878** *Act 41 Vict.* c. 16 Period of employment..for children and young persons in domestic workshop.

B. *sb.*

†**1.** A member of a household; one who dwells in the same house with another; an inmate; a member of the family (including children and relatives). (*lit.* and *fig.*) *Obs.*

1539 TONSTALL *Serm. Palm Sund.* (1823) 56 Nowe ye be not guestes and strangers, but ye be citisens and domestikes of almyghty god. **1656** FINETT *For. Ambass.* 62 From that time he had his accesses..to his Majesties presence as a Domestique without Ceremony. *a***1716** SOUTH *Serm.* II. xliii. (R.), A servant dwells..as a kind of foreigner under the same roof; a domestick, and yet a stranger too. **1737** WHISTON *Josephus' Antiq.* XVI. vii. §4 Often did he lament the wickedness of his domestics.

2. a. A household servant or attendant.

1613 SHAKS. *Hen. VIII*, II. iv. 114 Where Powres are your Retainers, and your words (Domestickes to you) serue your will. **1627** *Lisander & Cal.* VI. 103 Besides the domestics he sent for some of his tenants. **1711** ADDISON *Spect.* No. 106 ¶2 His Domesticks are all in Years, and grown old with their Master. **1845** STEPHEN *Comm. Laws Eng.* (1874) II. 228 At a month's notice like a common domestic. **1848** MAURICE *Lord's Prayer* (1861) 66 The relationship between the master of a household and his domestics.

†**b.** A domestic animal. *Obs. rare.*

1719 DE FOE *Crusoe* I. viii, My Pol..began now to be a mere domestic. **1742** J. HILDROP *Misc. Wks.* (1754) I. 215 Continue, therefore, your wonted Care..for your innocent domestics. *Ibid.* 160

†**3. a.** An inhabitant of the same country; a native, fellow-countryman. *Obs.*

1612–15 BP. HALL *Contempl., N.T.* II. vi. *Good Centurion*, If he were a foreigner for birth, yet he was a domestic in heart. **1675** *Phil. Trans.* X. 254 Supplies..afforded me both by our eminent Domesticks within his Majesties Dominions: and also by Forrainers. **1682** BUNYAN *Holy War* 313 Notable service against the Domesticks.

b. An indigenous plant. *Obs.*

1672 GREW *Anat. Plants, Idea Philos. Hist.* §8 All Exoticks ..may probably be reduced to some such Domesticks, unto which they may bear the best Resemblance.

4. An article of home produce or manufacture; *esp.*, in U.S., (*a*) home-made cotton cloth, bleached or unbleached, for common use, esp. plain cotton cloth; (*b*) *colloq.*, a kind of cigar.

1622 MALYNES *Anc. Law-Merch.* 2 When mankind was propagated into an infinite number, and the domestiques or neere hand commodities were not sufficient for their sustenance in some countries, and in other countries were ouer aboundant. **1817** M. AUSTIN *Let.* 21 July in *Austin Papers* (1924) 317 The Domesticks I expected, have Not arrived they are uncommonly difficult to obtain. **1823** W. B. DEWEES *Lett. Texas* (1852) 45 A small piece of unbleached domestic, or a bit of calico. **1846** WORCESTER, *Domestic*..a sort of American cotton cloth. **1864** R. A. ARNOLD *Cotton Fam.* 26 That large class of fabrics known in the trade as 'domestics', of which shirting and sheeting form a large part. **1865** G. A. SALA *My Diary in America* II. xvi. 375 Those eminently nasty rolls of tobacco called in New York 'domestics'. **1894** M. J. JAQUES *Texan Ranch Life* 113 The large spinning wheel, with which Mrs. B...made by hand the 'domestic' (calico) for her household. **1905** F. H. SMITH *At Close Range* 74 Sam..tilted his domestic at a higher angle, and went out to view the harbor. *Ibid.* 85 This done, he drew out a domestic from the upper pocket, bit off the end, slid a match along the well-worn seam and blew a ring out to sea. **1940** *Chambers's Techn. Dict.* 258/1 *Domestic*, a plain cotton cloth; it may be grey, coloured, or with a check pattern.

5. 'A carriage for general use' (Simmonds *Dict. Trade* 1858).

Hence **do'mesticism**, devotion to home life; **do'mesticness**, domesticity.

1643 W. GREENHILL *Axe at Root* A iij b, It's domesticknes of spirit. **1784** R. BAGE *Barham Downs* II. 344 Our happy domesticism has undergone no change. **1879** FARRAR *St. Paul* I. 509 The ignorant domesticism which was the only recognised virtue of her sex.

do'mesticable, *a.* [f. med.L. *domesticā-re* to DOMESTICATE + -BLE.] Capable of being domesticated or tamed.

1806 W. TAYLOR in *Ann. Rev.* IV. 35 The elephant and the hippopotamus..both appear domesticable. **1883** F. GALTON *Inq. Hum. Faculty* 245 All domesticable animals of any note have long fallen under the yoke of man.

do'mestical, *a.* and *sb. Obs.* or *arch.* [f. L. *domestic-us* DOMESTIC + -AL[1].] (Much used in 16–17th c.)]

A. *adj.* **1.** = DOMESTIC *a.* 2.

1459 SIR J. FASTOLF *Will* in *Paston Lett.* I. 457 My right trusty chapeleyn and servaunt domysticall. **1594** HOOKER *Eccl. Pol.* III. vi, In their domesticall celebration of the passeouer. **1664** EVELYN *Sylva* (1776) 226 Domestical utensils, as baskets, bags. **1737** WHISTON *Josephus' Hist.* I. xxii. §1 Raising him up domestical troubles. **1856** EMERSON *Eng. Traits, Relig.* Wks. (Bohn) II. 96 A massive system.. at once domestical and stately.

b. = DOMESTIC *a.* 2 b.

1586 BRIGHT *Melanch.* xii. 62 Inward and domesticall, in that it proceedeth from a natural power. **1605** TIMME *Quersit.* I. ii. 48 The domesticall enemies which are within mans body.

2. = DOMESTIC *a.* 3, 3 b.

1531 ELYOT *Gov.* II. vi. (1883) 60 We lacke nat of this vertue domisticall examples, I meane of our owne kynges of Englande. **1570–6** LAMBARDE *Peramb. Kent* (1826) 313 The domesticall and foreigne affaires of the Realme. **1610** GUILLIM *Heraldry* III. x. (1660) 149 Some [Plants] are forrein, and some Domesticall. **1655** FULLER *Ch. Hist.* VII. i. §21 Domestical dissentions of his own Subjects.

3. = DOMESTIC *a.* 4.

1562 BULLEYN *Bk. Simples* (1579) 77 Domesticall or yard foules. **1634** T. JOHNSON *Parey's Chirurg.* II. (1678) 44 The Camel is a very domestical and gentle Beast. **1677** HALE *Prim. Orig. Man.* II. ix. 208 Animals..that are domestical, and not for food, as Cats and Dogs.

b. Of plants: Cultivated, not wild.

1578 LYTE *Dodoens* IV. xviii. 473 The Domesticall, or husbandly beanes, do growe in feeldes and gardens. *Ibid.* xxii. 479 The domestical or tame Ciches.

4. Familiar, homely.

1563 WIN3ET *Agst. Hæreseis* I. xxviii. Wks. 1890 II. 60 Gif we sal begin to mixt..vncouth and strange thingis with domestical materis. **1578** BANISTER *Hist. Man* IV. 52 In our domesticall phrase. **1637** HEYWOOD *Dial.* iv. Wks. 1874 VI. 156 O Jupiter..That art domesticall and hospitable.

B. *sb.* A member of the household; a household servant; = DOMESTIC *sb.* 1, 2.

c **1540** tr. *Pol. Verg. Eng. Hist.* (Camden) I. 110 Hee tooke deliberation of his domesticalls and generallie all his princes. **1582** N. T. (Rhem.) *Eph.* ii. 19 You are citizens of the sainctes, and the domesticals of God. **1639** T. BRUGIS tr. *Camus' Mor. Relat.* 228 This youth was one of Fursees domesticals.

Hence **domesti'cality**, domestic quality.

1819 W. TAYLOR in *Monthly Rev.* LXXXVIII. 225 His very reflections have a domesticality of character.

do'mestically, *adv.* [f. DOMESTICAL *a.* + -LY[2].] In a domestic manner; in, or in reference to, the house, home, or family; with regard to domestic or home affairs; familiarly.

1576 NEWTON *Lemnie's Complex.* (1633) 80 To change that order of life, which by long use and domestically hee hath frequented. *a* **1667** COWLEY *Verses & Ess., Agric.* (1669) 104 Augustus had desir'd Mecænas to persuade him [Horace] to come and live domestically, and at the same Table with him. **1791–1823** D'ISRAELI *Cur. Lit., Introd. Tea, Coffee, etc.*, Probably, tea was not in general use domestically so late as in 1687. **1792** BURKE *Corr.* IV. 21 All is well with us, and so far as concerns us, directly and domestically. **1885** *Westmld. Gaz.* 2 Jan. 8/2 Gratified to see the Queen's youngest daughter settled domestically.

†**do'mesticant**, *a. Obs. rare*[−1]. [ad. L. *domesticānt-em*, pr. pple. of *domesticāre*: see next.] Making its home; dwelling, residing.

1642 SIR E. DERING *Sp. Relig.* 71 The power..was virtually residing and domesticant in the plurality of his Assessors.

domesticate (də'mɛstɪkeɪt, dəʊ-), *v.* [f. ppl. stem of med.L. *domesticāre* to dwell in a house, to accustom (Du Cange), f. *domestic-us* DOMESTIC: cf. F. *domestiquer* (15th c. in Hatz.-Darm.).]

1. *trans.* **a.** To make, or settle as, a member of a household; to cause to be at home; to naturalize.

a **1639** [see DOMESTICATED]. *a* **1773** CHESTERF. (Mason), Domesticate yourself there, while you stay at Naples. **1862** GOULBURN *Educ. World* in *Replies Ess. & Rev.* 9 It domesticated many of them in different parts of the heathen world. **1878** GLADSTONE *Prim. Homer* vii. 97 An element in the Greek nation originally foreign, but now domesticated.

b. *transf.* and *fig.* To make to be or to feel 'at home'; to familiarize.

1841–4 EMERSON *Ess., Art* Wks. (Bohn) I. 150, I now require this of all pictures, that they domesticate me, not that they dazzle me. **1874** SAYCE *Compar. Philol.* v. 179 The mental faculties of one people are domesticated, as it were, into the ways of thought of another.

2. To make domestic; to attach to home and its duties.

1741 RICHARDSON *Lett. Impt. Occasions* cxli. 187 Childbed *matronizes* the giddiest Spirits..it *domesticates* her, as I may say. **1748** —— *Clarissa* Wks. 1883 VIII. 437 A circumstance which generally lowers the spirit of the ladies, and domesticates them. **1863** MISS POWER *Arab. Days & N.* 130 [They] easily become domesticated (as lady-companions and housekeepers now describe themselves in advertisements to be). **1895** *Westm. Gaz.* 25 July 2/3 The efforts which are being made to domesticate the teaching.

3. To accustom (an animal) to live under the care and near the habitations of man; to tame or bring under control; *transf.* to civilize.

1641 EARL MONM. tr. *Biondi's Hist. Civ. Warres* I. iv-v. 145 Ireland, where the wisedome and valour of the Duke of Yorke had domesticated a savage people. **1805** LUCCOCK *Nat. Wool* 29 The first flock, which is minutely described.. was perfectly domesticated. **1859** DARWIN *Orig. Spec.* i. (1873) 14 There is hardly a tribe so barbarous, as not to have domesticated at least the dog.

†**4.** *intr.* (for *refl.*) To live familiarly or at home (*with*); to take up one's abode. *Obs.*

1767 H. BROOKE *Fool of Qual.* (1859) I. 305, I would rather..see her married to some honest and tender-hearted man, whose love might induce him to domesticate with her. **1796** COLERIDGE (*title of poem*) To a young friend, on his proposing to domesticate with the author. **1812** SHELLEY in Dowden *Life* (1887) I. 230, I shall try to domesticate in some antique feudal castle. **1818** KEATS *Let.* 16 Dec. (1958) II. 4 With Dilke and Brown I am quite thick—with Brown indeed I am going to domesticate—that is we⟨e⟩ shall keep house together. **1850** THACKERAY *Pendennis* II. xxi. 210 He became a good deal under the influence of his uncle's advice, and domesticated in Lady Clavering's house.

do'mesticated, *ppl. a.* [f. prec. + -ED[1].] Made domestic or familiar; tamed, naturalized.

a **1639** WOTTON in *Reliq. Wotton.* 366 (T.) Being now familiarized and domesticated evils. **1802** PALEY *Nat. Theol.* xvi. (1827) 497/1 The sheep in the domesticated state. **1838** DICKENS *Mem. Grimaldi* II, He had always been a domesticated man, delighting..in the society of his relations and friends. **1863** LYELL *Antiq. Man* 14 There are ..no signs of any domesticated animals except the dog.

do,mesti'cation. [n. of action from DOMESTICATE: see -ATION: so in F.] The action of domesticating, or the condition of being domesticated.

1774 KAMES *Sk. Hist. Man* II. 13 (Jod.) The same discipline obtains even after domestication. **1845** DARWIN *Voy. Nat.* viii. (1879) 150 Animals that readily enter into domestication. **1866** GEO. ELIOT *F. Holt* III. xliv. 192 Her domestication with this family.

do'mesticative, *a. rare.* [f. ppl. stem of med.L. *domesticāre* + -IVE.] Tending to domesticate, productive of domestication.

In recent Dicts.

do'mesticator. [agent-n. in L. form from med.L. *domesticāre* to DOMESTICATE.] One who domesticates; a tamer.

1872 BAGEHOT *Physics & Pol.* (1876) 51 Man..was obliged to be his own domesticator. **1894–5** *Q. Rev. Current Hist.* IV. 700 The domesticator of animals.

domesticity (dəʊmɛ'stɪsɪtɪ). [f. DOMESTIC *a.* + -ITY: cf. F. *domesticité* (1690 in Hatz.-Darm.).]

1. a. The quality or state of being domestic, domestic character; home or family life; devotion to home; homeliness.

1721 BAILEY, *Domesticity*, the being a servant. **1726** AYLIFFE *Parergon* (L.), Great familiarity is included under the notion of friendship and domesticity, as living together in the same house, and the like. **1827** SOUTHEY *Lett.* (1856) IV. 49 You would infer..that there is more domesticity..in Holland, than in any other country. **1874** L. STEPHEN *Hours in Library* (1892) II. iii. 74 A masculine woman, with no talent for domesticity.

b. The quality of being a domestic animal.

1830 LYELL *Princ. Geol.* (1875) II. III. xxxvi. 314 Domesticity eliminates the tendency. **1842** PRICHARD *Nat. Hist. Man* 37 The most marked sign of domesticity in our European goats.

2. *pl.* Domestic affairs or arrangements.

1824 C. J. MATHEWS in *Four C. Eng. Lett.* 550 Since you are determined to be made acquainted with our domesticities. **1843** J. MARTINEAU *Chr. Life* (1867) 165 That shelters itself amid the domesticities of life.

3. A domestic or homely expression or idiom. *rare.*

1899 WILDE *Importance of being Earnest* I. 28 Jack is a notorious domesticity for John!

domesticize (də'mɛstɪsaɪz, dəʊ-), *v.* [f. DOMESTIC + -IZE.] *trans.* = DOMESTICATE.

1656 EARL MONM. *Advt. fr. Parnass.* 63 Fair treatment doth domestichize even savage beasts. **1834** SOUTHEY *Doctor* I. xxix. 286 That most pleasant, salutiferous, and domesticising beverage [tea]. **1890** *Univ. Rev.* Jan. 13 If.. electric power as a motive force admit of being domesticized, and so bring back the system of cottage labour.

†**do'mesticly**, *adv. Obs.* [f. DOMESTIC *a.* + -LY[2].] = DOMESTICALLY.
1632 LITHGOW *Trav.* VIII. 350 Sent backe to the Governour with whom I was domesticly reserved. 1755 CHESTERF. *World* No. 151 She is..so domesticly tame.

domett ('dɒmɪt). Also **domette**. [perh. from a proper name.] A kind of textile fabric: see quots.
1835 BOOTH *Anal. Dict. Eng.* 182 A kind of plain cloth, of which the warp is cotton and the weft woollen, is called Domett, or Cotton-flannel. 1882 BECK *Draper's Dict.*, *Domett*, a loosely-woven description of flannel, with cotton warp and woollen weft, generally employed for shrouds, and sometimes in the place of wadding by dressmakers. 1895 *Montgomery Ward Catal.* 278/3 Men's Overshirts, plaid domette flannel. 1901 *Daily Chron.* 23 Nov. 8/3 Close-grained cloth coats, lined with fur, or with satin, or sandwiched with domette between it and the cloth. 1910 *Practitioner* Mar. 367 A many-tailed bandage of domette. 1939–40 *Army & Navy Stores Catal.* 412/2 Bandages... Domette, 3 in. × 6 yds.

domeykite (dəʊ'meɪkaɪt). *Min.* [Named 1845, after Domeyko, a Chilean chemist and mineralogist.] A native arsenide of copper of a greyish or tin-white metallic appearance.
1850 DANA *Min.* 513 Arseniuret of copper..corresponds with domeykite.

domic ('dəʊmɪk), *a.* [f. DOME *sb.* + -IC.] = next.
1823 P. NICHOLSON *Pract. Build.* 153 Large roofs, constructed of a domic form.

domical ('dəʊmɪkəl), *a.* [f. DOME (or its etymon) + -IC + -AL[1].]
1. Of, pertaining to, or like a dome; vaulted.
1846 WORCESTER cites LOUDON. 1849 FREEMAN *Archit.* I. I. i. 39 The curved shape..from which the domical appearance results. 1856 RUSKIN *Mod. Paint.* IV. v. App. ii, The apparently domical form of the sky. 1871 —— *Fors Clav.* vi. June 12 A white blouse..and a domical felt hat.
2. Characterized by domes or dome-like structure.
domical church, one of which the characteristic feature is a dome or series of domes.
1861 *Sat. Rev.* XI. 580/1 The wonderful domical cathedral of Perigueux. 1879 SIR G. SCOTT *Lect. Archit.* I. 76 In the celebrated domical churches of Perigord and Angoumois.
Hence '**domically** *adv.*, in the manner or form of a dome.
In recent Dicts.

†**domi'cellary**, *a. Obs. rare.* [f. med.L. *domicellāris*, *-cillāris* (Du Cange).] = DOMICILIAR.
1727–51 CHAMBERS *Cycl.* s.v. *Canon*, Domicellary Canons were young Canons, who, not being in orders, had no right in any particular chapters.

†**domicelle**. *Obs. rare.* [ad. med.L. *domicella*, also *domnicella*, dim. of *domina*; see DAMSEL.] A young lady, a damsel.
1460 CAPGRAVE *Chron.* (1858) 263 Sche broute oute of Frauns xii. chares ful of ladies and domicelles.

domicile ('dɒmɪsɪl, -saɪl), *sb.* Also 6–7 -cill(e, 7–9 -cil. [a. F. *domicile* (14th c. in Hatz.-Darm.), ad. L. *domicili-um* habitation, dwelling, deriv. of *domus* house.]
1. A place of residence or ordinary habitation; a dwelling-place, abode; a house or home. Also *transf.* the dwelling-place of an animal, and *fig.*
c 1477 CAXTON *Jason* 36 Thalyaunce of my frende and of my domycille. 1549 *Compl. Scot.* Epist. 7 Fureous mars, that hes violently ocupeit the domicillis of tranquil pace. 1599 A. M. tr. *Gabelhouer's Bk. Physicke* 55 Take..the whytest snayles, with their domicills. 1605 BACON *Adv. Learn.* II. iii. §4 That part of learning which answereth to one of the cells, domiciles, or offices of the understanding; which is that of the memory. 1794 SIR W. JONES *Ord. Menu* vi. 43 Let him have no culinary fire, no domicil. 1847 LEWES *Hist. Philos.* (1867) I. 188 That a Tub could suffice for a domicile we may guess from Aristophanes. 1871 R. ELLIS *Catullus* lxiii. 53 To be with the snows, the wild beasts, in a wintery domicile.
2. *Law.* The place where one has his home or permanent residence, to which, if absent, he has the intention of returning.
1766–80 LD. MANSFIELD in Burrows *Settlement Cases* No. 134. 421 (Jod.) The master's place of abode, his domicil, can never be supposed to be at Scarborough. 1861 W. BELL *Dict. Law Scot.* s.v., Where a company has a domicile in more than one country, the proceedings in bankruptcy in any one of the domiciles of the company comprehend the whole personal estate of the entire concern. 1875 POSTE *Gaius* III. (ed. 2) 336 Domicil is the place which a man has voluntarily chosen for his permanent residence.
fig. 1855 MILMAN *Lat. Chr.* (1864) IX. XIV. v. 200 [The] first domicile [of the new Italian language] was the court of Fredrick II.
b. The fact of being resident; residence.
1835 *Tomlins' Law Dict.* (ed. Granger) s.v. (L.), The residence of a party for forty days constitutes a domicile as to jurisdiction in Scotland. 1862 *Lond. Rev.* 30 Aug. 180 The American domicile does not take away the power which the State to which the foreigner belongs possesses of interfering for his protection. 1863 LYELL *Antiq. Man* 2 A place not only of domicile, but of sepulture.
3. *Comm.* The place at which a bill of exchange is made payable.
1892 J. ADAM *Comm. Corr.* 26 The bank or other place where a bill is made payable..is called the domicile of the bill, which is said to be domiciled there.

'**domicile** (see prec.), *v.* [f. prec. sb.]
1. *trans.* To establish in a domicile or fixed residence; to settle in a home.
1809 TOMLINS *Law Dict.* s.v. *Domicile*, The county in which he was domiciled at the time of his death. 1822 J. JEKYLL *Let.* 31 Dec. in *Corr.* (1894) 132 The Hollands were domiciled in Burlington Street. 1862 *Lond. Rev.* 30 Aug. 180 Aliens who are domiciled in America without having become citizens in the fullest sense.
b. *transf.* and *fig.*
a 1849 J. C. MANGAN *Poems* (1859) 387 Souls wherein dull Time Could domicile decay or house Decrepitude. 1874 MAHAFFY *Soc. Life Greece* ix. 278 Medicine had been long domiciled at Athens.
2. *Comm.* To make (a bill of exchange, etc.) payable at a certain place.
1809 R. LANGFORD *Introd. Trade* 18 He should write on it with his acceptance, the address where it will be honoured; such bills are termed domiciled. 1882 BITHELL *Counting-ho. Dict.*, s.v., All the Brazilian loans are said to be domiciled at Messrs. N. M. Rothschild & Sons.
3. *intr.* (for *refl.*). To have one's home, dwell.
1831 *Fraser's Mag.* V. 2 She domiciles far down in pebbled well. 1834 MEDWIN *Angler in Wales* I. 166 God forbid that the white ants should ever domicile here.
Hence '**domiciled** *ppl. a.*, '**domiciling** *vbl. sb.*; also '**domicilement**, the act of domiciling or fact of being domiciled.
1855 MILMAN *Lat. Chr.* (1864) IX. XIV. vii. 228 Each was a domiciled stranger. 1858 SIMMONDS *Dict. Trade*, *Domiciled Bill*, a bill not made payable at the residence or place of business of the acceptor, but directed for payment by the acceptor at the time of his acceptance. 1885 CLODD *Myths & Dr.* I. iv. 71 After the domiciling of the stories. 1888 *Charity Organiz. Rev.* Apr. 141 Laws of Aethelstan on the domicilement of lordless men.

†**domi'ciliar**, *a.* and *sb. Obs. rare.* [f. L. type **domiciliār-is* (see next and -AR).]
A. *adj.* Of or pertaining to one's domicile.
1655 tr. *De Parc's Francion* VIII. 27 To be brought before my Iudge natural, and domiciliar, as in an Action purely personal.
B. *sb.* Short for *domiciliar canon*, a canon of a minor order having no voice in a chapter. [cf. med.L. *domicillāris canonicus*, junior canonicus cui necdum est jus Capituli' (Du Cange).]
1761 STERNE *Tr. Shandy* IV. i, The dean of Strasburg, the prebendaries, the capitulars and domiciliars..all wished they had followed the nuns of Saint Ursula's example.

domiciliary (dɒmɪ'sɪlɪərɪ), *a.* (*sb.*) [ad. L. type **domiciliāri-us*, f. *domicilium*: cf. corresp. F. *domiciliaire* (16th. c.).]
A. *adj.* **1.** Pertaining to, relating to, or connected with a domicile or residence.
domiciliary visit, a visit to a private dwelling, by official persons, in order to search or inspect it.
1790 HEL. M. WILLIAMS *Lett. France* (1795) I. vii. 174 (Jod.) Those domiciliary visits, which were so often repeated. 1797 W. TAYLOR in *Monthly Rev.* XXIV. 495 Domiciliary visits were attempted by the police. 1849 MACAULAY *Hist. Eng.* I. iii. 287 The tax..could be levied only by means of domiciliary visits. 1885 *L'pool Merc.* 14 Aug. 5/3 To revolutionise the social and domiciliary condition of the labourers.
2. *Zool.* Of or pertaining to the general integument or structure occupied in common by infusoria or other animals of low organization.
In recent Dicts.
B. *sb.* One belonging to a domicile; a domestic.
1845 STOCQUELER *Handbk. Brit. India* (1854) 166 The two wings..are allotted to the residence of professors, pupils, and domiciliaries.

domiciliate (dɒmɪ'sɪlɪeɪt), *v.* [f. L. *domicili-um*, prob. after F. *domicilier*: cf. -ATE[3] 6.]
1. *trans.* To establish in a domicile, home, or place of residence; to domicile. Also *fig.*
1778 BURKE *Corr.* (1844) II. 244 The very good-natured ..letter..in a manner, domiciliated me already under the friendly roof you invited me to. 1808 WELLINGTON in Gurw. *Desp.* IV. 130 Subjects of France..domiciliated in Portugal. 1854 DE QUINCEY *Autobiog. Sk.* Wks. II. 190 His purpose was to domiciliate himself in this beautiful scenery.
b. *intr.* (for *refl.*)
1815 J. WILSON in *Four C. Eng. Lett.* 466 We domiciliated with many [folks in the Highlands]. 1823 LAMB *Lett.* (1888) II. 81 Just as I had learned to domiciliate there, I must come back to find a home which is no home.
2. *trans.* = DOMICILE *v.* 2.
1879 ESCOTT *England* I. 200 A foreign country in need of a loan always tries to domiciliate it in London.
†**3.** To accustom to a house or permanent dwelling-place; to domesticate (animals). *Obs. rare.*
1782 POWNALL *Study of Antiq.* 61 (T.) The propagation.. of the domiciliated animals. 1816 KEATINGE *Trav.* (1817) I. 76 Who had domiciliated the birds of the air. *Ibid.* 339 A primitive domiciliated people dwelling in hamlets.
Hence **domi'ciliated** *ppl. a.*
1782 [see sense 3]. 1819 JAS. WILSON *Compl. Dict. Astrol.*, *Domiciliated*, a planet is so called when in its house. 1849 GROTE *Greece* II. lxi. (1862) V. 310 Now began that incessant marauding of domiciliated enemies.

ˌ**domicili'ation**. [f. prec. vb.: see -ATION.]
1. The action of domiciliating, or condition of being domiciliated; settlement in a home.
1816 KEATINGE *Trav.* (1817) II. 162 As the Loire is approached, domiciliation thickens over the country. 1851 *Tait's Mag.* XVIII. 634 During my domiciliaton among them, I was received..as one of the family. 1859 MOZLEY *Ess., Indian Conversion* (1878) II. 348 This domiciliation of modern science and the useful arts in India.
†**2.** = DOMESTICATION. *Obs. rare.*
1775 ROMANS *Hist. Florida* 174 If instead of wantonly destroying this excellent beast [buffalo]..we were to endeavour its domiciliation.

domiculture ('dɒmɪkʌltjʊə(r)). *rare.* [f. L. *dom-us* house, after *agriculture*.] 'That which relates to household affairs; the art of housekeeping, cookery, etc.; domestic economy'.
1860 WORCESTER cites R. PARK.

†'**domify**, *v. Astrol. Obs.* [a. F. *domifier* (1558 in Hatz.-Darm.), ad. med.L. *domificāre* to build houses (13th c. in Du Cange), f. *domus* house: see -FY.] *trans.* To divide (the heavens) into twelve equal parts or 'houses' by means of great circles; to locate (the planets) in their respective 'houses'. Hence '**domifying** *vbl. sb.* and *ppl. a.*; also **domifi'cation** [so in Fr.].
c 1430 *Lydg. Bochas* (1554) 222, I can..in the starres search out no difference By domifying, nor calculation. 1509 HAWES *Past. Pleas.* 40 Of the vi. planettes he knewe so perfytly The operacions, how they were domified. 1603 FLORIO *Montaigne* II. xii. (1632) 315 Jugling tricks, enchantments..prognostications, domifications. 1690 LEYBOURN *Curs. Math.* 390 Alcabitius would have the xii Houses of Heaven to be divided by Domifying Circles, or Circles of Position drawn from the Poles of the World through every 30th deg. of the Equator. 1727–51 CHAMBERS *Cycl.*, *Domifying*, *Domification*.

‖**domina** ('dɒmɪnə). [L.; = mistress, lady.]
†**1.** A lady of rank (see quot.) *Obs.*
1706 PHILLIPS (ed. Kersey), *Domina*, Dame, Lady, a Title formerly given to those honourable Women that held a Barony in their own Right of Inheritance.
2. The superior of a nunnery.
1751 T. GORDON *Another Cordial for Low Spirits* II. 15 [St. Agatha] was the Domina of a Nunnery. 1819 T. HOPE *Anastasius* I. iv. 83 (Stanf.) The very domina who had excited the oracular dignity of one of the party.

dominance ('dɒmɪnəns). [f. DOMINANT *a.*: see -ANCE. Cf. OF. *dominance* (15th c. in Godef.).]
1. The fact or position of being dominant; paramount influence, ascendancy, dominion, sway.
1819 G. S. FABER *Dispensations* (1823) I. 89 That.. period, which the bishop would allot to the dominance of mere natural religion. 1881 J. PAGET in *Nature* No. 614. 327 The dominance of doctrine has promoted the habit of inference, and repressed that of careful observation and induction.
2. *Biol.* The phenomenon whereby one of a pair of alleles present in a genotype is expressed in a phenotype while the other allele is masked; the state or property of being dominant (DOMINANT *a.* 7). Also *attrib.*, as ***dominance modifier*** = DOMINIGENE.
1902 W. BATESON *Mendel's Princ. Hered.* 119 (*heading*) The facts in regard to dominance of characters in peas. *Ibid.*, The dominance of the smooth form over the wrinkled. 1916 J. WILSON *Man. Mendelism* 24 If the pairs in which the parents differ are clearly defined at the hybrid generation as regards dominance and recessiveness. 1918 BABCOCK & CLAUSEN *Genetics Rel. Agric.* v. 69 The condition of dominance..is determined by the fact that in the hybrid that character is expressed to the exclusion of its contrasted character. 1925 T. H. MORGAN *Evol. & Genetics* 151 (*heading*) The dominance of the wild type genes. 1929 R. A. FISHER in *Amer. Naturalist* LXIII. 555 The real difficulty.. is not so simple as that the selective action upon dominance modifiers is so small that there has not been time for it to have had any appreciable effect. 1937 T. DOBZHANSKY *Genetics & Origin of Species* vi. 172 It must be kept in mind that dominance versus recessiveness is a matter of degree. 1968 M. W. STRICKBERGER *Genetics* vi. 99 This phenomenon, by which one trait appears and the other does not, even though the factors for both are present, is called dominance.
3. *Ecology.* The prevalence or predominance of one or more species in a plant community.
1923 G. E. NICHOLS in *Ecology* IV. 14 A distinction is frequently made between associations in which the position of dominance is shared by two or more species..and those in which a single species is dominant. 1932 FULLER & CONARD tr. *Braun-Blanquet's Plant Sociol.* iii. 33 The measurement of the cubic volume of standing timber by the forester may be considered as a determination of dominance.

'**dominancy**. [f. as prec.: see -ANCY.]
Dominant quality, position, or condition.
1841 G. S. FABER *Provinc. Lett.* (1844) I. 82 Before the Roman [empire] came upon the stage of dominancy. 1847 *Tait's Mag.* XIV. 230 Exercising the dominancy of a superior will and intellect over his inferiors.

dominant ('dɒmɪnənt), *a.* and *sb.* [a. F. *dominant* (13th–14th c. in Hatz.-Darm.), f. L.

dominānt-em, pr. pple. of *domināri* to DOMINATE.]

A. *adj.* **1.** Exercising chief authority or rule: ruling, governing, commanding; most influential.

c **1532** DEWES *Introd. Fr.* in *Palsgr.* 1073 The qualytes principall domynant in the same. **1652** GAULE *Magastrom.* 243 Few live who, when they are born, have Saturne dominant in their horoscope. **1680** WOOD *Life* (Oxf. Hist. Soc.) II. 497 An odde feaverish sickness dominant in the Universitie. *a* **1796** REID (Mason) There are different orders of monads..the higher orders Leibnitz calls dominant; such is the human soul. **1813** SOUTHEY in *Q. Rev.* X. 102 The dominant party persecuted both in duty and in self-defence. **1871** DARWIN *Desc. Man* I. ii. 60 Dominant languages and dialects..lead to the gradual extinction of other tongues.

2. Occupying a commanding position.

1854 J. S. C. ABBOTT *Napoleon* (1855) I. xxxvi. 561 To take possession of the dominant points of the globe. **1860** TYNDALL *Glac.* I. xi. 81 We were dominant over all other mountains. **1871** —— *Fragm. Sc.* (1879) I. vi. 205 Lying in ..a bay, sheltered by dominant hills. **1891** *Nature* 23 July 267 Dominant trees, with their head well above the others.

3. *Rom. Law.* ***dominant land, tenement***: 'the tenement or subject in favour of which a servitude exists or is constituted' (Bell *Dict. Law Scot.*).

1754 ERSKINE *Princ. Sc. Law* (1809) 225 If the rent be payable in meal, flour, or malt, the grain of which these are made must be manufactured in the dominant mill. **1871** MARKBY *Elem. Law* §371 Adopting the language of the Roman Law, English lawyers call the land to which the easement is attached the dominant land, and the land over which it is exercised the servient land. **1875** POSTE *Gaius* II. (ed. 2) 166 Right of way for beast and man..over the servient tenement to the dominant tenement.

4. *Mus.* [attrib. use of B. 1 b.] Belonging or relating to the dominant or fifth of the key; having the dominant for its root, as ***dominant chord, dominant seventh***, etc.

1819 *Pantologia* s.v., The dominant or sensible chord is that which is practised upon the dominant of the tone. **1875** OUSELEY *Harmony* ii. 16. **1880** STAINER *Composition* §26 The third of the minor scale is commonly treated as a dominant discord. **1880** C. H. H. PARRY in Grove *Dict. Mus.* I. 674 The modern Dominant Harmonic Cadence..defines the key absolutely.

5. *Math.* ***dominant branch of a tree***, one containing half or more of all the knots of a 'tree'.

6. *Forestry.* Overtopping other trees; said esp. of those trees in a forest which have their crowns free to light on all sides.

1893 J. NISBET *Sel. Trees Woodland Crops* 21 Four classes of stems become distinguishable, viz., (1) predominating, (2) dominant, (3) dominated, and (4) suppressed. **1908** A. M. F. CACCIA *Gloss. Techn. Terms Ind. Forestry, Dominant*, a tree which has raised its crown above the level of the surrounding trees. **1930** *Indian Forest Rec.* XV. I. 2 Dominant Trees, including all trees which form the uppermost leaf canopy and have their leading shoots free.

7. *Biol.* [tr. G. *dominierend* (Mendel 1866, *Versuche über Pflanzenhybriden* in *Verh. d. Naturforsch. Ver., Brünn 1865* IV. 10).] Of a hereditary character: appearing to the exclusion of another character in a heterozygous organism containing alleles for them both. Hence of an allele or gene: expressed to the exclusion of another allelic gene. Const. *to, over*.

1900 W. BATESON in *Jrnl. R. Hort. Soc.* XXV. 58 In the case of each pair of characters there is thus one which in the first cross prevails to the exclusion of the other. This prevailing character Mendel calls the dominant character, the other being the recessive character. **1925** C. C. HURST *Exper. in Genetics* 246 In each pair, when crossed, Mendel found the first-named character dominant over the other. **1925** T. H. MORGAN *Evol. & Genetics* 151 The genes that arise by mutation have been found to be largely recessive to the genes already present in the original type which are said, therefore, to be dominant to the new genes. **1953** W. BRAUN *Bacterial Genetics* i. 9 When a gene derived from one parent differs from the corresponding gene contributed by the other parent, the effect of only one of the two genes may dominate, covering up the detectable effects of the other. Such genes are called dominant. **1965** BELL & COOMBE tr. *Strasburger's Textbk. Bot.* (new ed.) II. ii. 332 It is also possible for one gene to suppress the functioning of the other, i.e. one is dominant while its allele is recessive.

8. *Ecology.* Designating or pertaining to the predominant species in a plant community.

1923 [see DOMINANCE 3]. **1950** *Jrnl. Ecol.* XXXVIII. 108 Plant associations have been classified according to the 'dominant' species of the vegetation; that is, those which occur in a high proportion of quadrats.

9. ***dominant wavelength***, the wavelength or hue of a colour that determines the other colours with which it will match.

1913 W. DE W. ABNEY *Res. Colour Vision* 415/2 Dominant wave-lengths. **1957** R. W. G. HUNT *Reproduction of Colour* viii. 79 *Subjective Term*: Hue. *Objective Term*: Dominant Wavelength. *Ibid.* 193 Where θ is a correlate of the hue (in terms of dominant wavelength, for instance).

B. *sb.*

1. *Mus.* †**a.** In the ecclesiastical modes: 'The predominating sound in each mode, the note on which the recitation is made in each Psalm or Canticle tone' (Helmore in Grove *Dict. Mus.*); usually a fifth above the 'final' in the authentic modes, and a third above it in the plagal. *Obs.*

1823 CRABB *Technol. Dict.* s.v. **1880** T. HELMORE in Grove *Dict. Mus.* I. 626 To the 4 Authentic, St. Gregory added 4 'Plagal'..modes..The Dominants of the new scales are in each case a third below those of the old ones, C being however substituted for B♮ in the Hypo-mixo-lydian.

b. In modern Music: The fifth note of the scale of any key; which is of special importance in relation to the harmonies of that key. (Also *fig.*)

1819 [see 4 above]. **1855** BROWNING *Toccata of Galuppi's* viii, Hark—the dominant's persistence till it must be answered to! **1861** DORA GREENWELL *Poems* 133, I would find My soul's true Dominant. **1867** MACFARREN *Harmony* i. 24.

2. *Math.*: see quot.

1881 SYLVESTER in *Educat. Times* XXXIV. 100 The dominant of a set of numbers meaning the greatest one of them without respect to sign.

3. *Biol.* A dominant allele or character; an individual in which a particular dominant allele is expressed.

1900 W. BATESON in *Jrnl. R. Hort. Soc.* XXV. 58 In this generation the numerical proportion of dominants to recessives is..as three to one. **1905** R. C. PUNNETT *Mendelism* 10 There are dominants which breed to the dominant character, and are therefore pure. **1913** *Oxf. Univ. Gaz.* 4 June 948/2 *Hypolimnas..dubius*, Beauv., proved to be a Mendelian dominant, and *H. anthedon*, Boisd., recessive. **1930** R. A. FISHER *Genet. Theory Nat. Selection* iii. 50 If..the mutant genes are dominant just as often as they are recessive, selection will be far more severe in eliminating the disadvantageous dominants than in eliminating the disadvantageous recessives. **1965** H. E. SUTTON *Introd. Human Genetics* xvii. 213 Dominants that cannot be transmitted therefore cannot be distinguished from environmentally induced traits. **1967** *Listener* 6 Apr. 450/2 A predisposition towards depression is probably an inherited characteristic—biologically inherited, that is, as a Mendelian dominant, and not just acquired from the family environment.

4. *Ecology.* The chief constituent of a plant community.

1913 TANSLEY & ADAMSON in *Jrnl. Ecology* I. 83 It is difficult to resist the conclusion that beech is the natural dominant in the magnificent series of woods. **1916** [see ASSOCIATION 12]. **1933** *Forestry* VII. 122 There is little difference between the various stem-classes—dominants, co-dominants, and sub-dominants—as regards the distribution of form-classes. **1938** WEAVER & CLEMENTS *Plant Ecol.* (ed. 2) iv. 91 The visible unity of the climax is due primarily to the dominants or controlling species.

Hence **'dominantly** *adv.*, in a dominating way; so as to dominate or sway.

1868 *Contemp. Rev.* VII. 155 A vital factor which has dominantly entered into..national life. **1869** *Ibid.* XI. 447 The dominantly Jewish character of the population.

dominate (ˈdɒmɪneɪt), *v.* [f. L. *dominat-* ppl. stem of *domināri* to bear rule, govern, lord it, f. *domin-us* lord, master: cf. F. *dominer*.]

1. *trans.* To bear rule over, control, sway; to have a commanding influence on; to master.

1611 FLORIO, *Dominare*, to rule, to dominate, to sway. **1613** SHERLEY *Trav. Persia* 55 Hee that..can dominate his passions. **1775** tr. *Sp. Sonn.* in *Twiss' Trav.* App. (T.) He was..dominated by his step-mother. **1859** THACKERAY *Virgin.* v, Her power over him was gone. He had dominated her. **1870** HUXLEY *Lay Serm.* iii. (1878) 50 The Germans dominate the intellectual world.

2. *intr.* To bear sway, exercise control; to predominate, prevail; to lord *over*.

1818 in TODD. **1837** CARLYLE *Fr. Rev.* III. VI. i, Republicanism dominates without and within. **1837-9** HALLAM *Hist. Lit.* III. ii. (L.), The system of Aristotle..still dominated in the Universities. **1869** FARRAR *Fam. Speech* iii. (1873) 86 This was..dominated over by a small aristocracy of Aryan warriors.

b. *Rom. Law.* Cf. DOMINANT *a.* 3.

1832 AUSTIN *Jurispr.* (1879) II. l. 845 The parcel of land, the owner or occupier whereof hath the right of servitude is said to dominate over the land from the owner or occupier whereof the corresponding duty is owned.

3. *trans.* To 'command' as a height; also *fig.*

1833 L. RITCHIE *Wand. by Loire* 112 A colossal rock which dominates the whole town. **1878** BOSW. SMITH *Carthage* 420 This hill..dominates the plain, the harbours and the isthmus behind it. **1878** BROWNING *Poets Croisic* 77 From where, high-throned, they dominate the scene.

b. *intr.* To occupy a commanding position (*over*).

1816 KEATINGE *Trav.* (1817) I. 100 It is indeed the commanding ground of Madrid..but it does not dominate over the town. **1860** TYNDALL *Glac.* II. viii. 267 The moraine..rises upon its ridge of ice, and dominates..over the surface of the glacier.

Hence **'dominated, 'dominating** *ppl. adjs.*

1611 SPEED *Hist. Gt. Brit.* IX. xx. (1632) 972 A Lady, bred vp in a dominating Family. **1700** DRYDEN *Cock & Fox* 161, I..thus conclude my theme, The dominating humour makes the dream. **1885** *Athenæum* 5 Dec. 725/1 The dominating influences of a particular period. **1891** *Nature* 23 July 267 A portion of the dominated trees being removed.

domination (dɒmɪˈneɪʃən). [a. F. *domination* (12th c.), f. L. *dominātiōn-em*, n. of action f. *domināri* to DOMINATE.]

1. The action of dominating; the exercise of ruling power; lordly rule, sway, or control; ascendancy. †**b.** A lordship or sovereignty (*obs.*).

c **1386** CHAUCER *Pard. Prol. & T.* 232 In whom þat drynke hath dominacion, He kan no conseil kepe. **1483** CAXTON *Cato* A viij b, The kynges and prynces haue domynacions and lordshippes. **1490** —— *Eneydos* i. 13 Pryam was subdued and putte vnder the sharpe domynacyon of the grekes. **1585** T. WASHINGTON tr. *Nicholay's Voy.* II. ix. 43 Gave unto him..the Lordship and domination over thys yle. **1654** tr. *Scudery's Curia Pol.* 86 The people found themselves happy under his domination. **1880** G. DUFF in *19th Cent.* No. 38. 666 To keep up the horrible Turkish domination in Armenia.

†**c.** Predominance, prevalence. *Obs.*

1526 *Pilgr. Perf.* (W. de W. 1531) 3 A myxture of syluer and golde..wherin yᵉ syluer hath dominacion. **1563** W. FULKE *Meteors* (1640) 63 Upon the mixtion of these colours, or chiefe domination of them, all things have their colour.

†**2.** The territory under rule; a dominion. *Obs.*

c **1440** CAPGRAVE *Life St. Kath.* IV. 265 In what parti he dwelled of his domynacyon. **1535** *Act 27 Hen. VIII*, c. 26. §1 His subiectes of his saide dominacion of Wales. **1654** tr. *Scudery's Curia Pol.* 68 The Romans advanced not their names, nor inlarged their Dominations but by Conquests.

3. *pl.* The fourth of the nine orders of angels in the Dionysian hierachy; a conventional representation of these in art. Cf. DOMINION 4, and see note s.v. CHERUB.

[**1388** WYCLIF *Eph.* i. 21 Ech principat, and potestat, and vertu, and domynacioun [so TINDALE, *Geneva, Rhem.*].] **1398** TREVISA *Barth De P.R.* II. xii. (1495) 38 The fourth ordre is Domynacyones. **1500-20** DUNBAR *Poems* x. 9 Archangellis, angellis, and dompnationis, Tronis, potestatis, and marteiris seir. **1667** MILTON *P.L.* v. 601 Hear all ye Angels..Thrones, Dominations, Princedoms, Vertues, Powers. **1847** LD. LINDSAY *Chr. Art* I. 134 A 'throne', for instance, is seated on a throne; a 'domination' holds the balance.

dominative (ˈdɒmɪnətɪv), *a.* [ad. med.L. *dominātīv-us*, F. *dominatif, -ive* (Oresme, 14th c.); see DOMINATE and -IVE.]

1. a. Having the quality of ruling or dominating; of lordly authority.

1599 SANDYS *Europæ Spec.* (1632) 57 The Princes in Majestie and soveraigntie of power; the Nobilitie in wisedome and dominative vertue..are respectable and honourable. **1659** STANLEY *Hist. Philos.* XIII. (1701) 613 Domestic Prudence being either conjugal and paternal, or dominative and possessory. **1868** *Contemp. Rev.* IX. 77 The public feeling..ought to be dominative, determining the tone, and thus assuring acceptance for the individual.

†**b.** ***dominative argument***, transl. Gr. κυριεύων λόγος, a kind of logical fallacy. *Obs.*

1656 STANLEY *Hist. Philos.* IV. (1701) 148 Diodorus interrogated by the Dominative Argument.

c. *Psychol.* Tending to dominate; exhibiting domination (see quots.).

1937 H. H. ANDERSON in *Jrnl. Soc. Psychol.* VIII. 335 (*title*) An experimental study of dominative and integrative behavior in children of preschool age. *Ibid.* 338 Dominative behavior included the following: 1. Verbal demands to secure materials. 2. Forceful attempts to secure materials. **1953** A. K. C. OTTAWAY *Education & Soc.* vii. 137 'Dominative' behaviour is typified by autocratic methods and the attempt to dominate the will of others.

†**2.** Of predominant weight or importance. *Obs.*

1639 FULLER *Holy War* IV. v. (1840) 183 They approach.. to us in more weighty and dominative points. **1655** —— *Ch. Hist.* II. vi. §42 An Induction of the dominative Controversies, wherein we differ from the Church of Rome.

dominator (ˈdɒmɪneɪtə(r)). Also 5-7 -our. [a. F. *dominateur* (13th-14th c.), ad. L. *dominātōr-em*, agent-n. f. *domināri* to DOMINATE.] One who rules or dominates; a ruler, lord. Also of things.

c **1450** *Mirour Saluacioun* 1000 O lorde of erth dominatoure. **1588** SHAKS. *L.L.L.* I. i. 221 Sole dominator of Nauar. **1678** CUDWORTH *Intell. Syst.* I. iv. 344 The Arcadians worship their God Pan..[as] Lord or Dominator over all material substance. **1723** *State Russia* I. 259 Emperor and Dominator of all the Russias. **1817** BYRON *Manfred* I. i, The elements, whereof We are the dominators.

†**b.** *Astrol.* A planet or sign supposed to dominate a particular person or region. *Obs.*

1588 SHAKS. *Tit. A.* II. iii. 31 Madame, Though Venus gouerne your desires, Saturne is Dominator ouer mine. **1652** GAULE *Magastrom.* 4 Jupiter..Lord of the ascendant, and great dominator.

dominatory (ˈdɒmɪnətərɪ), *a. rare.* [f. ppl. stem of L. *domināri* + -ORY.] = DOMINATIVE I.

1816 KEATINGE *Trav.* (1817) I. 303 A dominatory process.

‖**domi'natrix.** *Obs.* [Lat.; fem. of *dominātor*.] A female dominator; mistress, lady.

1561 EDEN *Arte Nauig.* I. xix. 20 b, Rome..dominatrix of nations.

†**domine** (ˈdɒmɪniː), *sb. Obs.* [vocative case of L. *domin-us* lord, master.]

1. Lord, master: used in respectful address to the clergy or members of learned professions.

[*c* **900** tr. *Bæda's Hist.* III. xix. (1891) 214 Min domne hwæt is þis fyr.] **1566** GASCOIGNE III. ii, Domine, Doctor. *Ibid.* III. iv. **1609** B. JONSON *Sil. Wom.* v. i, 'Tis no presumption, domine doctor. **1616** BEAUM. & FL. *Scornf. Lady* II. i, Adieu, dear Domine! **1640** BROME *Antipodes* IV. x, [To his chaplain] You Domine where are you? **1675** WYCHERLEY *Country Wife* IV. iii, No, good Domine doctor, I deceive you, it seems, and others too.

2. A clergyman or parson; *spec.* = DOMINIE 2.

a **1679** EARL ORRERY *Guzman* iv, Are you the Domine of the Parish? **1701** C. WOLLEY *Jrnl. in N. York* (1860) 55 Two other Ministers or Domines as they were called there..one a Lutheran..the other a Calvinist. **1705** HICKERINGILL *Priest-cr.* II. ii. 26 A little Domine or Curate in the towering and topping Pulpit. *a* **1711** KEN *Lett.* Wks. (1838) 84 The Dominees are..too Calvinisticall to be in league with those who oppose you. **1892** *Critic* 12 Mar. 151/2 The Dutchman's endearing title of his pastor is properly spelled as the old Dutch documents spelled it..The 'domine' was the clergyman; a 'dominie' is a school-master.

b. A schoolmaster, etc.; = DOMINIE 1, q.v.

†**'domine**, *v. Obs.* Also 5–6 domyne. [a. OF. *domine-r*, ad. L. *dominārī* to DOMINATE.]

1. *trans.* To rule, govern, control, DOMINATE. **1481** CAXTON *Godfrey* 2 Alysaundre..domyned and had to hym obeyssaunt the vnyuersal world. **1509** HAWES *Past. Pleas.* XI. ix, The whych ryght..they myght well domyne.

2. *intr.* To rule; to prevail. **1470–85** MALORY *Arthur* v. i, That noble empyre whiche domyneth vpon the vnyuersal world. **1483** CAXTON *Gold. Leg.* 37/2 He shold domyne over them. **1509** HAWES *Joyf. Medit.* xvi, Our souerayne whiche doth nowe domyne. **1614** P. FORBES *Def. Minist. Ref. Ch.* 61 (Jam.) Hee may expell the Pope from Rome, and domine there.

3. *intr.* To predominate, prevail in importance. **1474** CAXTON *Chesse* 6 His vertues domyne aboue his vyces.

dominee ('du:mɪnɪ, 'duə-). *S. Afr.* [a. Du.: see DOMINIE.] A minister of the Dutch Reformed Church in S. Africa; = PREDIKANT. **1950** *Cape Times* 20 Sept. 16/2 The dominees of the Ring. **1959** *Ibid.* 14 Apr. 1/8 Two dominees, members of the Northern Transvaal Regional Synod. **1966** A. SACHS *Jail Diary* xvi. 136 He really is a very fine man our Dominee. He is a very good Christian, but he is a warm person.

domineer (dɒmɪ'nɪə(r)), *v.* Also 6–7 -eere, 7 -ere, -eir(e, -ier(e. [app. a. early mod.Du. *dominer-en* to rule, have domination (1573 in Plantijn), a. F. *dominer*: see DOMINE *v.*

The circumstances under which the Du. word was adopted in Eng. do not appear.]

1. *intr.* To rule or govern arbitrarily or despotically; to act imperiously; to tyrannize. Now usually (coloured by b), To exercise or assert authority in an overbearing manner, to lord it. **1588** [see DOMINEERING *ppl. a.* 1]. **1591** SIR T. CONINGSBY in *Camden Misc.* I. 62 (Stanf.) They commaund the countrie, and domineer and have their parts in any thing passinge. **1602** *2nd Pt. Return fr. Parnass.* III. i. (Arb.) 37 Craft and cunning do so dominere. **1621** BURTON *Anat. Mel.* I. ii. IV. ii. (1676) 96 Oligarchies, wherein a few rich men domineer. **1776** ADAM SMITH *W.N.* I. viii. (1869) I. 77 The mercantile company which domineers in the East Indies. **1875** W. S. HAYWARD *Love agst. World* 2 Not..disposed to domineer over his brothers or arrogate to himself a superiority. **1877** MRS. OLIPHANT *Makers Flor.* xiv. 354 With a certain conscious despotism he rules, nay domineers, over us.

†**b.** To assume lordly airs; to swagger, play the master. *Obs.* **1607** TOPSELL *Four-f. Beasts* (1658) 376 In this fashion he domineer'd a good time, until at last..a stranger..having oftentimes seen both Lions and Asses, knew it for an ass in a Lion's skin. **1678** DRYDEN *Kind Kpr.* I. i, He rants and domineers, He swaggers and swears. **1719** D'URFEY *Pills* (1872) IV. 193 When he had the money in his Purse, He domineered and vapoured. **1764** FOOTE *Mayor of G.* I. Wks. 1799 I. 173 She does now and then hector a little; and..domineers like the devil.

†**2.** To revel, roister, feast riotously. [Du. *domineren* to feast luxuriously.—Oudemans.] *Obs.* **1592** NASHE *P. Penilesse* (ed. 2) 7b, Hee can neither traffique with the Mercers and Tailers as he was wont, nor domineere in Tauernes as hee ought. **1596** SHAKS. *Tam. Shr.* III. ii. 226 Goe to the feast, reuell and domineere..Be madde and merry. **1598** B. JONSON *Ev. Man in Hum.* II. i, Let him spend, and spend, and domineere. **1691** SHADWELL *Scourers* IV, We intend to..roar and drink bloodily, and domineer in the house.

†**3.** To dominate, predominate, prevail. *Obs.* **1602** MARSTON *Antonio's Rev.* v. i, O hunger, how thou dominer'st in my guts! **1659** B. HARRIS *Parival's Iron Age* 291 Infected places, and where the small pocks domineered. **1725** BRADLEY *Fam. Dict.* s.v. *Sallet*, To suit and mingle our Sallet-Ingredients..and to adjust them that nothing may be suffer'd to domineer.

4. To tower (*over*, *above*); = DOMINATE 3 b. **1658** [see DOMINEERING *ppl. a.* 3]. **1697** DRYDEN *Virg. Georg.* I. 229 Darnel domineers, And shoots its head above the shining Ears. **1837** W. IRVING *Capt. Bonneville* I. 116 Three lofty mountains..which domineer as landmarks over a vast extent of country. **1848** DICKENS *Dombey* xxiii.

5. *trans.* **a.** To govern imperiously, tyrannize over, dominate with absolute sway. **1764** GIBBON *Misc. Wks.* (1814) V. 477 Supposing him domineered by the Metromanie in its utmost force. **1860** EMERSON *Cond. Life* i. (1861) 23 All the bloods it shall absorb and domineer. **1885** *Manch. Exam.* 7 Oct. 5/1 The people have refused to be domineered by Committees and wirepullers.

b. To tower over, 'command'; = DOMINATE 3. **1812** SIR R. WILSON *Pr. Diary* I. 136 The entrenchments ..were domineered within pistol shot. **1843** LEFEVRE *Life Trav. Phys.* III. III. ii. 98 The cathedral..situated upon a rock and domineering the whole town.

domi'neer, *sb.* [f. prec. vb.] A domineering manner or air; imperious swaggering. *a* **1768** *Sir W. Wallace* ix. in Child *Ballads* (1889) III. VI. 268/3 The captain..Did answer him in domineer. **1887** BARING-GOULD *Gaverocks* I. i. 4 There was..a selfwill in the modelling of the lips, a domineer in the cut of the nose.

ˌdomi'neerer. Now *rare.* [f. as prec. + -ER[1].] One who domineers; a tyrant, despot. **1641** SIR E. DERING in Rushw. *Hist. Coll.* III. (1692) I. 295 Away then with this Lordly Domineerer. *a* **1687** H. MORE *Death's Vis.* iv. (1713) 3 *note*, That Deadly Domineerer [Death]. **1866** ALGER *Solit. Nat. & Man* III. 147 An applauded domineerer of the forum.

domi'neering, *vbl. sb.* [f. as prec. + -ING[1].] The action of the verb DOMINEER; imperious rule, tyranny; overbearing demeanour. **1617** MORYSON *Itin.* III. 288 Women..taxed with this vnnaturall domineering over their Husbands. **1866** MRS. H. WOOD *St. Martin's Eve* xxxii, If Charlotte did remain with them, she should not stand any domineering.

domi'neering, *ppl. a.* That domineers.

1. Ruling arbitrarily or imperiously; tyrannical, despotic; overbearing, insolent. **1588** SHAKS. *L.L.L.* III. i. 179 A domineering pedant ore the Boy. **1683** A. D. *Art Converse* 105 Their unruly and domineering humour. **1868** MILMAN *St. Paul's* xv. 355 Laud in his haughty and domineering character.

†**2.** Prevailing, dominant. *Obs.* **1621** BURTON *Anat. Mel.* II. iv. I. ii. (1651) 366 The domineering and most frequent maladies of it [a place]. **1817** W. TAYLOR in *Monthly Mag.* XLIV. 325 The religion of the Abrahamites became the domineering religion of Persia.

3. Occupying a commanding position. **1658** R. FRANCK *North. Mem.* (1821) p. ix, Lofty domineering hills that over top'd the submissive shady dales.

Hence **domi'neeringly** *adv.*; **domi'neeringness.** **1684** H. MORE *Answer* C j a, He could not..act so domineeringly. **1840** *Blackw. Mag.* XLVII. 150 That is the objection to *Charles I*, as a tragedy..because too domineeringly political. **1889** *Spectator* 16 Nov., A man boiling over with energy and domineeringness.

dominial (dəʊ'mɪnɪəl), *a.* [f. L. *domini-um* lordship + -AL[1].] Of or pertaining to ownership. **1727–51** CHAMBERS *Cycl.* s.v. *Offices*, Venal offices are subdivided into two kinds; viz., dominial and casual.—Dominial, or offices in fee, are those absolutely torn off, and separated from the King's prerogative, so as not to become vacant by death, but passing in the nature of a fee, or inheritance. **1876** *Westm. Rev.* No. 98. 333 Such a right was dominial rather than marital, and belonged to a man not so much as husband but as slave-owner.

†**'Dominic**, *a.* and *sb. Obs.* [See DOMINICAN: cf. Sp. *dominico* Dominican.] = DOMINICAN. *c* **1540** *Pilgr. T.* 129 in Thynne *Animadv.*, The dominikis hold vp thomas the aquin. **1674** HICKMAN *Quinquart. Hist.* (ed. 2) 69 Reader among the Dominick-Friers.

Dominical (dəʊ'mɪnɪkəl), *a.* and *sb.* [ad. med.L. *dominicāl-is*, in F. *dominical* (1417 in Hatz.-Darm.), f. L. *dominic-us* of or belonging to a lord or master, f. *dominus* lord.]

A. *adj.* **I.** In ecclesiastical uses.

1. Of or pertaining to the Lord (Jesus Christ); Lord's. ***Dominical day***: the Lord's day, Sunday. ***Dominical year***: the year of our Lord. **1553** EDEN *Treat. Newe Ind.* (Arb.) 30 He came thether on the Sundaye called the Dominical day. **1560** BECON *New Catech.* (1844) 239 It is the dominical supper, that is to say, the Lord's. **1582** N. T. (Rhem.) *Rev.* i. 10, I was in spirit on the Dominical day. *c* **1645** HOWELL *Lett.* (1688) IV. 472 The Dominical Prayer, and the Apostolical Creed. **1743** FIELDING *J. Wild* II. viii, After the exercise of the dominical day is over. **1884** BREWER *Hen. VIII* Pref. 7 Marked with the regnal and dominical year.

2. Of or pertaining to the Lord's day or Sunday [L. *dominica (dies)*]: Sunday-. **1623** COCKERAM, *Domenicall*, belonging to the Lords day. **1649** MILTON *Eikon.* i. Wks. 1738 I. 367 That reverend Statute for Dominical Jigs and Maypoles..deriv'd from the example of his Father James. **1663** COWLEY *Cutter Coleman St.* II. iii, Grave Dominical Postures. **1891** *Times* 9 Apr. 5/5 Their demand..for a 36 hours' dominical rest, that is, rest from Saturday at 6 p.m. till Monday at 6 a.m.

b. ***Dominical letter***: the letter used to denote the Sundays in a particular year.

The seven letters A, B, C, D, E, F, G are used in succession to denote the first seven days of the year (Jan. 1–7), and then in rotation the next seven days, and so on, so that, e.g., if the 3rd January be a Sunday, the dominical letter for the year is C. Leap Year has two Dominical letters, one for the days preceding Feb. 29 (or according to some, Feb. 24; cf. BISSEXTILE), the other for the rest of the year.

1577–87 HOLINSHED *Hist. Eng.* v. ii. (R.) In the yeere of our Lord 446..the dominicall letter going by E, the prime by 10. **1594** BLUNDEVIL *Exerc.* VII. viii. (ed. 7) 660 When 28 is the number of the Sunnes Circle, A is alwaies the Dominical Letter. **1630** J. TAYLOR (Water P.) *Dog of War* Wks. II. 229/2 Some like Dominical Letters goe In Scarlet from the top to toe. **1868** *Chambers' Encycl.* III. 629 If the dominical letter of a common year be G, F will be the dominical letter for the next year.

c. *fig.* (from the printing of the Dominical letter in red, or larger type; cf. *red-letter day*.) **1632** MASSINGER *Emperor East* I. ii, At what times of the year He may do a good deed for itself, and that is Writ in dominical letters. **1644–7** CLEVELAND *Char. Lond. Diurn.* 6 For all Cromwells Nose weares the Dominicall Letter. **1651** RANDOLPH, etc. *Hey for Honesty* IV. iii, Should have scratched your face till it had been a dominical one, and as full of red letters as any Pond's Almanac in Christendom.

II. In legal and other uses.

†**3.** Belonging to a demesne or domain [med.L. *dominicum*]; domanial. *Obs.* **1540–1** ELYOT *Image Gov.* (1556) 159 He..craftily enterlaced his dominical landes with their servile possessions. **1640** SOMNER *Antiq. Canterb.* 310 Which..passe by and under the name of dominicall or desmeasnetithes.

†**4.** Of or pertaining to an absolute lord despotic. **1644** H. PARKER *Jus Pop.* 37 That Dominicall-power..is unnaturall: the very definition of it leaves the slave utterly disinherited of himself and subject to his masters sole ends. *Ibid.*, If this condition did justify Dominicall-rule.

5. Pertaining to a DOMINIE or schoolmaster; pedagogic. *nonce-use.* **1882** G. MACDONALD *Castle W.* III. iv. 58 The schoolmaster..knocking down the violator of the dominical sanctity.

†**6.** = DOMINICAN *a.*[1] *rare.* **1600** E. BLOUNT tr. *Conestaggio* 126 Least he should seeme ..to follow the advise of the dominicall Fryers.

B. *sb.* [In sense 1, ad. med.L. *dominicāle*, *-ālis*: see Du Cange.]

†**1.** *Eccl.* A garment or veil for Sundays; *spec.* a veil worn by women when receiving the Communion. *Obs.* **1565** JEWEL *Repl. Harding* 73 (R.) Wee decree that euery woman when she dooth communicate, haue her dominical. **1727–51** CHAMBERS *Cycl.* s.v., The Council of Auxerre,..decrees, that women communicate with their dominical.

†**2.** Short for *Dominical letter*: see A. 2 b. *Obs.* **1588** SHAKS. *L.L.L.* v. ii. 44 Let me not die your debtor, My red Dominicall, my golden letter. **1686** PLOT *Staffordsh.* 421 Their Dominicals and week-day Letters.

†**3.** The Lord's house; a church. *Obs. rare.* **1659** GAUDEN *Tears of Ch.* 351 Then began Christian Churches, Oratories, or Dominicals, to out-shine the Temples of the Heathen Gods.

†**4.** The Lord's day, Sunday. *Obs.* **1628** JACKSON *Creed* IX. xxiv. §3 May we Christians then call the Friday before Easter the day of our atonement, or the dominical next after it, the great Sabbath? **1673** OLEY *Pref.* to *Jackson's Wks.* (1844) I. 27 Matter proper for every dominical and festival in the year.

5. One who observes the Lord's Day, but does not treat it as representing the Sabbath of the Old Testament: opposed to *Sabbatarian*. **1861** HESSEY in *Guardian* 13 Mar. 163/1 These Dominicals (thus argue the Sabbatarians)..substitute for a Divine foundation of Sunday, one of mere human invention, the authority of the Church. **1884** W. F. CRAFTS *Sabb. for Man* (1891) 629 Those Dominicals who hold the New Testament Lord's Day, but deny the Genesis Sabbath.

Dominican (də'mɪnɪkən), *a.*[1] and *sb.*[1] [ad. eccl. L. *Dominicānus*, f. *Dominicus*, Latin form of the name of Domingo de Guzman, also called St. Dominic, the founder of an order of preaching friars: cf. F. *dominicain*.]

A. *adj.* Of or pertaining to St. Dominic or to the order of friars (and nuns) founded by him. **1680** WALLER (*title*) Narrative of the Feigned Visions..of the Dominican Fathers of the Convent of Berne. **1725–51** CHAMBERS *Cycl.* s.v. *Friars*, Dominican, or black, or preaching friars. **1756** tr. *Keysler's Trav.* (1760) III. 273 In the Dominican convent. **1845** S. AUSTIN *Ranke's Hist. Ref.* II. 13 The course taken by the court of Rome (chiefly dominican influence). **1885** *Catholic Dict.* 279/1 In Ireland ..seven convents of Dominican nuns.

B. *sb.* A friar of the order founded by St. Dominic: a Black friar. *a* **1632** WEEVER (Mason) Their rule and habit was muchwhat like that of the Dominicans. **1845** S. AUSTIN *Ranke's Hist. Ref.* I. 259 The Dominicans, who taught the strictest doctrines..had the right to enforce them by means of fire and sword.

Hence **Do'minicaˌness**, a Dominican nun. **1857** G. OLIVER *Coll. Cath. Relig. in Cornwall*, etc. 65 Two or three Dominicanesses of the Third Order.

Dominican (dɒmɪ'ni:kən), *sb.*[2] and *a.*[2] [f. *Dominica* (see def.), f. L. (*dies*) *dominica* Sunday, the day of the week on which the island was discovered in 1493, + -AN.] **A.** *sb.* A native or inhabitant of the island of Dominica in the Lesser Antilles. **1826** H. N. COLERIDGE *Six Months in W. I. 1825* 158 The Dominicans became more scrupulous, and a governor came who knew not Audain. **1898** R. T. HILL *Cuba & Porto Rico* xxiii. 236 The only true Dominicans are the inhabitants of Dominica, one of the larger islands of the Lesser Antilles. **1929** H. L. FOSTER *Combing Caribbees* v. 50 Several Dominicans had booked passage with us to Fort de France. **1968** S. HAWYS *Mount Joy* ix. 93 A favoured few Dominicans may see the interior of those yachts. **1973** *Advocate-News* (Barbados) 24 Nov. 2/4 Speakers also turned their attention to common problems facing Dominicans.

B. *adj.* Of or pertaining to Dominica or its inhabitants. **1888** J. A. FROUDE *English in W. Indies* xi. 156 Another small incident happened.., which showed the capital stuff of which the Dominican boatmen and fishermen are made. **1937** H. DE LEEUW *Crossroads of Buccaneers* 223 In this Dominican forest..the evidence of continual development is beyond the slightest question. **1969** *Word* XXV. 276 The main consonantal correspondences between Island-Carib in its Dominican (DIC) and Central American (CAIC) dialects. **1978** *Language* LIV. 225, I can say, however, that untraveled native speakers of Dominican French Creole understand very little of radio broadcasts in Haitian Creole.

Dominican (də'mɪnɪkən), *a.*[3] and *sb.*[3] [ad. Sp. *Dominicana*, f. *Santo Domingo* (see DOMINICAN *a.*[1] and *sb.*[1]), the name of one of the earliest settlements, and subsequently of the Spanish colony and Republic until 1844, and of the capital city of the Republic.] **A.** *adj.* Of or pertaining to the Dominican Republic or its inhabitants. ***Dominican Republic***, the name of an independent state in the Greater Antilles, which shares the island of Hispaniola with Haiti.

1853 B. C. CLARK *Plea for Hayti* 34 It was during the government of Boyer that the Spanish or Dominican part of the Island was united with the French part. **1862** *Chambers's Encycl.* III. 628/1 In or about 1843, it assumed a separate standing as the Dominican Republic. **1912** S. BONSAL *Amer. Mediterranean* vii. 137 Every month 100,000 dollars gold goes to New York and a handsome sum is paid into the Dominican treasury. **1959** *Chambers's Encycl.* IV. 592/1 The two dominant figures in Dominican politics in the middle of the 19th century were Santana and Báez. **1963** MRS. L. B. JOHNSON *White House Diary* 14 Dec. (1970) 17 The conversation was about recognizing the Dominican Republic. **1985** *Times Lit. Suppl.* 11 Jan. 28/1 The attempt to influence the Dominican Republic..only succeeded in forcing Dominican thinkers into a hispanophile, negrophobic and indianist mould.

B. *sb.* A native or inhabitant of the Dominican Republic.

1853 B. C. CLARK *Plea for Hayti* 35 Thus it is seen that the Dominicans adopted the Haytien Government not only voluntarily but joyfully. **1912** S. BONSAL *Amer. Mediterranean* vii. 123 Revolutionary practices had become as deeply ingrained with the Dominicans as electioneering campaigns with us. **1929** H. L. FOSTER *Combing Caribbees* xviii. 275 The Dominicans were now carrying on for themselves all the various works of sanitation and road-building. **1959** *Chambers's Encycl.* IV. 592/1 The Dominicans..tried desperately to obtain the protection of Great Columbia. **1973** *Advocate-News* (Barbados) 2 Feb. 1/5 Thousands of Dominicans watched on TV as six-inch stainless steel nails were driven through his hands and feet.

† **do'minicide.** *Obs. rare.* [ad. late L. *dominicīda*, f. L. *domin-us* master: see -CIDE.] **a.** One who kills a master. **b.** Murder of a master.

1656 BLOUNT *Glossogr.*, *Dominicide*, he that kils his Master. **1847** in CRAIG; and in mod. Dicts.

dominie ('dɒmɪnɪ). Also **domine.** [The same word as DOMINE, the final pronounced *e* being written *-ie*, as in vernacular words.]

1. a. A schoolmaster, pedagogue. (Now chiefly *Sc.*)

1612 *Two Noble K.* I. iii, But will the dainty Domine, the Schoolemaster keep touch. **1681** OTWAY *Soldiers Fort.* III. i. Wks. 1728 I. 372 Why, who am I, good Sir Dominie Doddle-pate? **1826** DISRAELI *Viv. Grey* I. vi, He then walked to the door and admitted the barred-out Dominie. **1829** SCOTT *Guy M.* Introd., Dominie Sampson..a poor, modest, humble scholar, who has won his way through the classics..But there is a far more exact prototype of the worthy Dominie. **1870** LOWELL *Study Wind.* 129 The dominie spirit has become every year more obtrusive and intolerant in Mr. C.'s writing.

b. The (male) keeper of a boarding-house or Dame's house for oppidans at Eton.

1827 J. EVANS *Excurs. Windsor* 352 The oppidans are boarded at private houses; and the title of Domine and Dame, the presiding masters and mistresses have immemorially enjoyed. **1865** W. L. C. *Etoniana* viii. 132 Formerly these houses were..kept by 'Dames' or 'Dominies'..though now the term 'Dame' applies to all without reference to sex.

2. In U.S., the title of a pastor of the Dutch Reformed Church (more historically spelt DOMINE q.v.); whence in New York, New Jersey, etc., extended colloquially to ministers or parsons of other churches. (Commonly pronounced, after Dutch, 'dəʊmɪnɪ.)

1824 W. IRVING *T. Trav.* (1849) 439 There are two family oracles, one or other of which Dutch housewives consult.. the dominie and the doctor. **1839-40** —— *Wolfert's R.* (1855) 15 An elder might be seen..apparently listening to the dominie. **1887** HAZARD *Mem. J.L. Diman* iii. 43.

3. In full ***dominie apple***. A variety of large apple. *U.S.*

1817 W. COXE *Fruit Trees* 115 The Domine was imported from England. **1876** J. BURROUGHS *Winter Sunshine* vii. 158 If they were the dominie apples..he certainly would [hasten his sermon].

dominigene (də'mɪnɪdʒiːn). *Biol.* [ad. G. *dominigen* (R. Goldschmidt 1935, in *Zeitschr. f. indukt. Abstammungs- u. Vererbungslehre* LXIX. 74), f. *domini-erend* DOMINANT *a.* + *gen* GENE.] Any gene that modifies the dominance of another gene.

1938 R. GOLDSCHMIDT *Physiol. Genetics* II. v. 107 As a short term for such modifying genes, Goldschmidt (1935*b*) has proposed the word dominigenes. *Ibid.*, Landauer (1933) found a dominigene for the frizzle character of fowl. **1940** *Nature* 9 Mar. 390/2 Two linked complementary factors for N-type are favoured by one of us..while a dominigene is the pivot of another hypothesis. **1952** C. P. BLACKER *Eugenics* x. 242 Dominance can be modified by certain genes in the genic milieu for which the term *dominigenes* has been proposed.

dominion (dəʊ'mɪnjən). [a. obs. F. *dominion* (in Godef.), ad. L. type **dominiōn-em*, deriv. of *domini-um* property, ownership f. *domin-us* lord.]

1. The power or right of governing and controlling; sovereign authority; lordship, sovereignty; rule, sway; control, influence.

c **1430** LYDG. *Thebes* II. (R.), To haue lordship, or dominioun, In the bounds of this little toun. **1494** FABYAN *Chron.* I. vi. 12 She gaue ouer yᵉ rule and domynion to hym. **1634** SIR T. HERBERT *Trav.* 29 These Moguls..got the Dominion of these Countries. **1712** ADDISON *Spect.* No. 500 ¶2 Nothing is more gratifying to the mind of man than power or dominion. **1867** FREEMAN *N.C.* (1876) I. iv. 215 Foreign dominion in any shape would soon become hateful.

fig. **1538** STARKEY *England* I. ii. 61 Fortune..hath grete domynyon and rule in al vtward thyngys. **1582** N. T. (Rhem.) *Rom.* vi. 9 Death shal no more haue dominion [WYCL. lordschip, TINDALE, etc. power] ouer him. **1751** JOHNSON *Rambler* No. 184 ¶7 Exempting them from the dominion of chance. **1875** JOWETT *Plato* (ed. 2) III. 179 For ages physicians have been under the dominion of prejudices.

2. a. The lands or domains of a feudal lord. **b.** The territory owned by or subject to a king or ruler, or under a particular government or control. Esp. a country outside England or Great Britain under the sovereignty of or owing allegiance to the English or British crown; *spec.* † (*a*) *pl.* the English possessions in America; † (*b*) the principality of Wales; (*c*) (*Hist.*) any of the larger self-governing nations in the British Commonwealth; also *attrib.* Often in *pl.*

Dominion of Canada (colloq. '***the Dominion***'), the title under which the former colonial provinces of Upper and Lower Canada, etc., in British North America, were united into one government in 1867. ***the Old Dominion*** (also ***the Ancient Dominion***), a popular name in U.S. for Virginia.

1512 *Act 4 Henry VIII*, c. 10 The Domynyons Honours Castelles Parkes..that late were to Edwarde Courteney. **1548** HALL *Chron.*, *Henry VI* (an. 14) 130 The whole dominion of Fraunce, betwene the rivers of Soame and Marne. **1605** SHAKS. *Lear* I. i. 180 If..Thy banisht trunke be found in our Dominions, The moment is thy death. **1606** *First Charter Virginia* in H. W. Preston *Doc. Illustr. Amer. Hist.* (1886) 9 The said several Colonies and Plantations,.. they being of any Realms, or Dominions under our Obedience. **1623-4** *Act 21 Jac. I* c. 3 Within this Realme or the Dominion of Wales. **1682** *Acts of Assembly Virginia* (1727) I. 142 His Majesty's Subjects, being in this his Majesty's Dominion of Virginia. **1700** *Act 11 & 12 Will. III* c. 12 §1 Commanders in Chief of Plantations and Colonies within his Majesties Dominions beyond the Seas. *Ibid.* c. 19 §7 Any Prisons..belonging to any County of this Realm, or the Dominions of Wales. **1705** F. MAKEMIE *Persuasive* (*Dedication*), To..Her Majestys Governor of the Ancient Dominion of Virginia. **1725** DE FOE *Voy. round World* (1840) 21 The King of Spain had allowed the king of France's subjects a free trade in his American dominions. **1778** *Cal. Virginia State Papers* (1875) I. 311, I should not see the old Dominion this winter. **1789** W. MACLAY *Deb. Senate* (1880) 14 The member from the ancient dominion. **1832** J. P. KENNEDY *Swallow B.* (1860) 13, I have really reached the Old Dominion. **1840** MACAULAY *Ess.*, *Clive* (1887) 529 The wide dominion of the Franks was severed into a thousand pieces. **1850** W. H. FOOTE *Sk. Virginia* 393 The Smiths came to Virginia to commence log colleges in the 'Ancient Dominion'. **1867** *Act 30 & 31 Vict.* c. 3. §3 The Provinces of Canada, Nova Scotia, and New Brunswick shall form and be One Dominion under the Name of Canada. **1901** *London Gaz.* 4 Nov., The following addition shall be made to the Style and Titles at present appertaining to the Imperial Crown of the United Kingdom and its Dependencies;..after the words 'of the United Kingdom of Great Britian and Ireland', these words, ' and of the British Dominions beyond the Seas'. **1907** *Times* 1 Mar. 10/2 They had found themselves in complete agreement with the Premiers and Ministers of Defence of the King's Dominions across the seas. *Ibid.* 22 Apr. 14/2 The Prime Ministers of the self-governing Dominions. **1910** A. H. FORBES (*title*) History of the British Dominions beyond the Seas (1558-1910). **1912** A. B. KEITH *Respons. Govt. in Domin.* III. 1313 Since the Colonial Conference of 1907 Dominion is a technical term for the self-governing Colonies. **1922** *Daily Mail Year Bk. 1923* 84/1 The terms..offered to Ireland the full dominion status of Canada. **1931** *Act 22 Geo. V* c. 4 §1 In this Act the expression 'Dominion' means any of the following Dominions, that is to say, the Dominion of Canada, the Commonwealth of Australia, the Dominion of New Zealand, the Union of South Africa, the Irish Free State and Newfoundland. **1949** *Newsweek* 1 Aug. 15/1 This constituted 'outside interference' in the affairs of the Old Dominion. **1952** *Times* 21 Feb. 3/1 The words 'British Dominions beyond the Seas' had disappeared from the Proclamations in the United Kingdom, Australia, and New Zealand... At the same time Canada had substituted 'Canada' for 'Dominion of Canada'. **1953** *Times* 8 Dec. 9/2 Her Majesty will visit three of the seven fully sovereign nations—it is significant that their only generic title of 'Dominion' is already obsolescent—which make up in the narrower sense the oversea Commonwealth. **1959** *Times* 18 Apr. 7/3 The Labour Party pamphlet suggested that they should be offered 'Dominion Status'. That is to say, they should become independent, but should be able by the act of self-determination to re-enter the Commonwealth.

fig. **1654** WHITLOCK *Zootomia* 414 The Dominions of Pen-men are of larger extent than those of Sword-men. **1821** SHELLEY *Prometh. Unb.* II. v. 86 Thy spirit lifts its pinions In music's most serene dominions.

3. a. *Law.* Ownership, property; right of possession. [= *dominium* in Rom. Law.]

1651 HOBBES *Leviath.* I. xvi. 81 The Right of possession, is called Dominion. **1682** EVATS *Grotius' War & Peace* 78 We must search into the rise or beginning of propriety, which Lawyers call Dominion. **1738** Eminent Dominion [see EMINENT 5]. **1774** T. JEFFERSON *Autobiog.* Wks. 1859 I. 138 Our Saxon ancestors held their lands..in absolute dominion, unencumbered with any superior. **1832** AUSTIN *Jurispr.* (1879) I. 50. **1885** *Law Times* 28 Mar. 386/1 Negligent dealing with goods by a bailee, which does not amount to the assertion of any dominion over them.

† **b.** *fig.* Power or right. *nonce-use. Obs.*

a **1797** H. WALPOLE *Mem. Geo. II* (1847) II. viii. 257 The King, during the whole conversation, seemed to leave open his dominion of saying or unsaying hereafter.

4. = DOMINATION 3. (Usually in *pl.*)

[**1539** BIBLE (Great) *Eph.* i. 21 Aboue all rule, and power, and might and domynion [TINSDALE dominacion]. **1611** BIBLE *Col.* i. 16 All things created..visible and inuisible, whether they be thrones or dominions [Vulg. *dominationes*, LXX κυριότητες], or principalities, or powers.] **1667** MILTON *P.L.* II. 11 Powers and Dominions, Deities of Heav'n. *a* **1711** KEN *Hymnotheo* Poet. Wks. 1721 III. 200 Dominions for supream Commands decreed.

5. *attrib.*, as ***Dominion act***. ***Dominion day***, in the Dominion of Canada, the 1st of July, observed as a general holiday in commemoration of the union of the provinces, etc., under that name in 1867.

1877 *Daily News* 3 Nov. 6/6 In violation of the Dominion Act regarding the importation of cattle from prohibited countries. **1892** W. PIKE *Barren Ground N. Canada* 167 The loyal Canadians..were..celebrating the anniversary of Dominion Day, with much rye whisky.

Hence † **do'minion** *v.*, to exercise dominion, to rule; **do'minionless** *a.*, having no dominion.

1647 *Pol. Ballads* (1860) I. 35 We shall have..But few folks, and poor, to dominion o'er. **1845** *Blackw. Mag.* LVII. 523 Dominionless over our sympathy.

‖ **do'minium.** A Latin term of the Roman Law, variously rendered lordship, ownership, property, demesne, domain, dominion; but often retained in L. form in legal use.

1823 in CRABB *Technol. Dict.* **1861** W. BELL *Dict. Law Scot.* 300 The interest vested in the superior is called the *dominium directum*, or superiority..The vassal's interest..is termed the *dominium utile*, or the property.

domino ('dɒmɪnəʊ). *Pl.* **dominoes.** [a. F. *domino* (16th c. in Hatz.-Darm.) 'a kind of hood, or habit for the head, worne by Cannons; (and hence) also, a fashion of vaile vsed by some women that mourne' (Cotgr.): cf. Sp. *domino* a masquerade garment.

Du Cange cites *domino* in L. context, in the sense of a covering of the head and shoulders worn by priests in winter: 'utantur..caputio vulgariter ung Domino', 'caputium seu Domino panni nigri'. Derived in some way from L. *dominus*; Darmesteter suggests from some L. phrase, such as *benedicamus Domino*. According to Littré, sense 3 came from the supposed resemblance of the black back of each of the pieces to the masquerade garment.]

1. a. A kind of loose cloak, app. of Venetian origin, chiefly worn at masquerades, with a small mask covering the upper part of the face, by persons not personating a character.

1719 *Free-Thinker* No. 138 ¶6 Thersites..instead of covering Himself with a Domine, dresses..in the Habit of a Running Foot-man. **1730-6** BAILEY (folio), *Domino*..the habit of a Venetian nobleman, very much in use at our modern masquerades. **1744** LADY M. W. MONTAGU *Let. to W. Montagu* 25 Mar., I went in a domino to the ball, a masque giving opportunity of talking in a freer manner than [etc.]. **1770** MAD. D'ARBLAY *Early Diary* (1889) I. 66 Miss Strange had a white satin Domino trimmed with blue. **1841** LEVER *C. O'Malley* (Rtldg.) 407 The domino which serves for mere concealment, is almost the only dress assumed.

b. Sometimes applied to the half-mask itself.

[**1837** SYD. SMITH *Ballot* Wks. (Longm.) 778 Why not vote in a domino, taking off the vizor to the returning officer only?] **1860** EMERSON *Cond. Life, Illusions* Wks. (Bohn) II. 442 The masquerade is at its height. Nobody drops his domino.

c. *fig.*

1836-9 DICKENS *Sk. Boz* (1850) 266/1 Reserve..is a bad domino which only hides what good, people have about 'em, without making the bad look better. **1870** DISRAELI *Lothair* lxxvii, As for Pantheism, it is Atheism in domino. **1875** EMERSON *Lett. & Soc. Aims, Quot. & Orig.* Wks. (Bohn) III. 221 John Wilson—who..writes better under the domino of 'Christopher North'.

2. A person wearing a domino.

1749 FIELDING *Tom Jones* XIII. vii, Jones..applied to the Domino, begging and intreating her to shew him the lady. **1866** HOWELLS *Venet. Life* viii, Motley company,—dominoes, harlequins, pantaloni, illustrissimi and illustrissime.

3. a. One of a number of rectangular pieces (usually 28) of ivory, bone, or wood, having the under side black, and the upper equally divided by a cross line into two squares, each either blank or marked with pips, so as to present all the possible combinations from double blank to double six. (Sometimes the pieces have more pips, and are more in number accordingly.) **b.** *pl.* (rarely *sing.*) A game played with these pieces, (usually) by placing corresponding ends in contact as long as this can be done, the player who has the lowest number of pips remaining being the winner.

1801 STRUTT *Sports & Past.* IV. ii. §18 Domino..a very childish sport, imported from France a few years back. **1831** DISRAELI *Yng. Duke* v. i. (L.), The menservants were initiated in the mysteries of dominoes. **1835** LONGF. *Outre-Mer* Prose Wks. 1886 I. 119 His favorite game of domino. **1870** *Modern Hoyle* 92 One of the players draws a domino.

c. *pl.* A game at cards, in which the cards as played out are laid in rows or heaps according to the suits, those of each suit following in their order; the player who first gets rid of all his cards is the winner.

d. *interjectionally*: (see quots.). Also *subst.* (see quot. 1873); ***it is domino*** (***with***), it is all up (with), it is the end (of), it is finished (for). *slang.*

1862 B. BRIERLEY *Tales & Sk. Lancs. Life* 26 What dost think abeawt Sebastypol bein' takken?.. Aw'll bet thi a quart o'ale ut it's domino wi' it neaw. **1864** HOTTEN *Slang Dict.* (ed. 3) 123 *Domino*, a common ejaculation of soldiers and sailors when they receive the last lash of a flogging. **1873** *Ibid.* (ed. 4) 147 A domino means either a blow, or the last of a series of things, whether pleasant or otherwise. **1882** *N. & Q.* 25 Mar. 229/2 Probably most Londoners have often heard 'bus conductors cry 'Domino' when an omnibus is 'full in and out'. **1891** FARMER *Slang, Domino*, an ejaculation of completion: e.g. for sailors and soldiers at the last lash of a flogging: also, by implication, a knock-down blow, or the last of a series. From the call at the end of a game of dominoes. **1894** J. T. CLEGG *David's Loom* xxi. 245 It'll be domino for me neaw. **1898** *Daily News* 10 Feb. 7/5 The young delinquent sullenly declared that James struck him first, whereupon he 'gave him domino for himself'. **1911** A. BENNETT *Hilda Lessways* v. ii. 330 I've..paid the cheque! So it's domino, now! **1927** *Chambers's Jrnl.* 45/1, I thought it was domino with me and my little schemes.

e. *pl.* The teeth. *slang.*

1828 W. T. MONCRIEFF *Tom & Jerry* II. v. 53 Sluice your dominos—vill you?.. Drink, vill you? don't you understand Hinglish? **1857** A. MATHEWS *Tea-Table Talk* II. 122 The poor destitute gentleman was still diligently seeking his lost *dominos.* **1913** *Pedagogical Seminary* XX. 436 To drink is to sluice the dominoes.

f. In full ***domino paper***. Paper printed with a design from a wood-block and coloured, used as wallpaper, etc. (see quots.). (Cf. Fr. *domino, papier dominoté.*) Also ‖**dominotier**, a maker of such paper.

1839 W. CHATTO *Treat. Wood Engraving* ii. 59 In France the same kind of cuts [*sc.* wood-cuts], probably stencil-coloured, were called 'dominos'... The word 'domino' was subsequently used as a name for coloured or marbled paper generally, and the makers of such paper..were called 'dominotiers'. **1924** N. MCCLELLAND *Hist. Wall-papers* 20 The industry which gave the *Dominotiers* their name was the making of 'domino papers', which consisted principally of marbleized papers and again of others with little figures and grotesques, crudely printed from wood-blocks and coloured by hand. These 'dominos' were made in Rouen and in other cities..of France. **1926** SUGDEN & EDMONDSON *Hist. Eng. Wallpaper* 27 In France, 'domino' papers are regarded as the real forbears of paper-hangings. *Ibid.* 28 'Domino' papers were usually small—16½ in. by 12½ in.—and all the earliest were 'marbled'.

g. *pl.* The keys of a piano (see also quot. 1889). *slang.*

1889 BARRÈRE & LELAND *Dict. Slang* I. 303/1 *Domino thumper* (theatrical), a pianist. **1891** FARMER *Slang* II. 306/1 *Dominoes*,..the keys of a piano. **1895** J. T. CLEGG *Works* I. 169 Aw con play 'God save the Queen' wi two fingers, iv aw happen to catch th' reet dominoes to start off.

h. ***to make (the) domino***: to go out at the game of dominoes; also *fig.*, to anticipate the end; to finish first.

1890 'BERKELEY' *Dominoes & Solitaire* 11 Sometimes each hand constitutes a game in itself; and when this is so, the player who makes 'domino' wins. **1892** C. SANTLEY *Student & Singer* (ed. 3) ii. 24, I did not notice the bar's rest before the 'Amen', and performed a solo, which called forth some witty remark from Benedict about the future career of the singer who made the 'domino'. **1912** 'JAR' *Dominoes* 3 A player, when he has played all the dominoes from his hand, is said to 'make domino'.

i. *Mus.* An error in performance (cf. quot. 1892 for sense 3 h). *colloq.*

1946 *Penguin Music Mag.* Dec. 50 One can get away with a 'domino' once—even thrice, but then someone starts to say: 'Poor Blank, he is beginning to slip.'.

j. *fig.* Used of a theory that a political event or development in one country, etc., will lead to its occurrence in others; also *transf.*; more freq. *attrib.*

1954 D. D. EISENHOWER in *N.Y. Times* 8 Apr. 18/1 You had broader considerations that might follow what you might call the 'falling domino' principle. You had a row of dominoes set up, and you knocked over the first one, and what would happen to the last one was the certainty that it would go over very quickly. **1965** *New Statesman* 19 Feb. 277/1 There was as much domino talk ('With the collapse of South Vietnam, Laos..would speedily be swallowed..') then as now. *Ibid.* 277/2 Even if..the domino theory works out in practice. **1965** *Guardian* 16 Dec. 9/7 The domino phenomenon...if one African country pulls out of the Commonwealth then..there is a very real possibility the others will go out in succession like dominoes. **1966** *Ibid.* 6 Sept. 8/4 The departure of Zambia would not be a freak exception, but the fall of the first domino. Tanzania would follow forthwith. **1971** *Times* 3 May 12/3 There is a 'domino theory' about the possible relaxation of drug abuse legislation in Europe and North America... By the 'domino theory', once a lead has been given, others may be encouraged.

4. A workman's ticket or 'check' given up on entering a factory.

1884 *Leisure Hour* Sept. 530/1 Every man is provided with a number stamped on a small block of wood called a domino.

5. *attrib.*, as ***domino-box***; **domino pool**, a variety of the game of dominoes, in which a stake is placed in the pool (*Mod. Hoyle*, 1870, 101).

1849 LYTTON *Caxtons* 19 A beautiful large domino-box in cut ivory, painted and gilt.

Hence **'dominoed** *a.*, wearing a domino.

1885 B. HARTE *Maruja* iii, Groups of dominoed masqueraders. **1891** *Blackw. Mag.* Jan. 46.

domitable ('dɒmɪtəb(ə)l), *a. rare.* [f. L. *domitāre* (see next) + -BLE.] Tamable.

1677 HALE *Prim. Orig. Man.* IV. viii. 369 The other are by their very nature more domitable. **1836** *Foreign Q. Rev.* XVII. 166 The carnivorous tribes he finds less domitable.

†**'domitate**, *v. Obs. rare*⁻⁰. [f. ppl. stem of L. *domitāre*, freq. of *domāre* to tame.]

1623 COCKERAM II, To Tame, *mancipate, domitate.*

domite ('dəʊmaɪt). *Min.* [f. *Puy de Dôme* in Auvergne.] A light-grey variety of trachyte.

1828 WEBSTER cites PHILLIPS. **1835** *Penny Cycl.* III. 158/2 The Puys de Dôme, formed of a particular kind of rock, which has thence been named *domite.* **1879** RUTLEY *Study Rocks* xii. 226 The name domite..has been applied to trachytes which contain a high percentage of silica.

Hence **do'mitic** *a.*, composed of domite.

1858 G. P. SCROPE *Geol. Centr. France* (ed. 2) 67 The origin of all these domitic hills. **1881** JUDD *Volcanoes* v. 126.

†**do'mition.** *Obs. rare*⁻⁰. [n. of action f. L. *domāre* (*domit-um*) to tame.] So **'domiture**.

1656 BLOUNT *Glossogr., Domition* or *Domiture* (*domitura*), a taming or breaking. [BAILEY has *Domation, domature.*]

†**domle**, *v. Obs. rare.* [Etymol. unknown.] *intr.* 'To be dull or cloudy' (Stratmann).

1340 HAMPOLE *Pr. Consc.* 1443 Now es þe wedir bright and shynand, And now waxes it alle domland.

domm, -e, obs. forms of DUMB.

dommage, obs. form of DAMAGE.

†**dommagie.** *Obs.* By-form of DAMAGE.

1556 *Aurelio & Isab.* (1608) F vj, Nether for feare nor for dommagie. *Ibid.* K iij, We do not resave anne dommagie.

dommegeable, obs. form of DAMAGEABLE.

dommerer, obs. var. DUMMERER.

domp(e, obs. var. DAMP, DUMP.

Dom Pedro: see DOM[1] 3.

Dom Pérignon (dɔm periɲɔ̃). Also **Dom Perignon**. [The name of a Benedictine monk and cellarer (1639–1715) from the monastery of Hautvilliers, who allegedly invented champagne; cf. DOM[1] 2.] A proprietary name for a celebrated brand of champagne.

1956 *Official Gaz.* (U.S. Patent Office) 19 June TM132/1 Chandon Champagne Corporation, New York... Filed Nov. 23, 1954... *Cuvée Dom Pérignon*... For champagne wines. First use November 1936. **1965** *Trade Marks Jrnl.* 17 Feb. 226/1 Moët et Chandon..Champagne Dom Perignon..Champagne wines. **1970** J. SANGSTER *Touchfeather, Too* i. 14 The steward brought me..a bottle of Dom Perignon in a silver ice bucket. **1980** M. BROADBENT *Gt. Vintage Wine Bk.* 349 There were few failures—notably two Dom Pérignons in poor condition, whose corks had not survived 22 years, though also in 1977 Laurent Perrier was showing well.

dompnation, obs. form of DOMINATION.

dompne, obs. form of DOM, or DOMINE.

a **1536** ANNE BOLEYN in Wood *Lett. Roy. & Illustr. Ladies* II. 191 One dompne John Eldmer.

dompt, *v. rare* [a. F. *dompte-r*, in OF. *danter, donter*, later *domter*:—L. *domitāre* to overcome, subdue, tame: a doublet of DAUNT.] *trans.* To tame, subdue, reduce to subjection; = DAUNT *v.*; also *intr.* (for *refl.*). Hence **'dompting** *ppl. a.*

1480 CAXTON *Ovid's Met.* XI. iii, His evyll herte myght not dompte ne make hym leve hys folye. *c* **1489** —— *Blanchardyn* li. 196 He dompted and subdewed them. **1912** GALSWORTHY *Inn Tranq.* 258 What is grievous, dompting, grim, about our lives is that we are shut up within ourselves. **1928** V. G. CHILDE *Most Anc. East* v. 115 We see a group representing a hero dompting two lions.

Hence **'dompter**, subduer, tamer.

1673 O. WALKER *Educ.* (1677) 250 Old Age—that great dompter and mortifier of our passions.

domy ('dəʊmɪ), *a.* [f. DOME *sb.* + -Y.] Having a dome or domes; dome-like.

1833 RUSKIN in *Athenæum* 26 Dec. (1891) 857/3 A thing of the domy firmament. **1890** *Temple Bar Mag.* 11 Sept., Cool summer palace and domy mosque.

Don (dɒn), *sb.*[1] Also 6 **Doen, Done.** In senses 3, 4 with small initial. [a. Sp. *don*:—L. *domin-um* master, lord.]

1. A Spanish title, prefixed to a man's Christian name.

Formerly confined to men of high rank, but now applied in courtesy to all of the better classes.

1523 WOLSEY in *St. Papers* VI. 119 The Archiduke Don Ferdinando. **1568** GRAFTON *Chron.* II. 313 Done Peter King of Spaine. **1591** SHAKS. *Two Gent.* I. iii. 39 Don Alphonso, With other Gentlemen of good esteeme. **1724** T. RICHERS *Hist. R. Geneal. Spain* 92 This prince [Pelayus] was the first, to whom was given the Title of Don, which till then, they gave only to saints. **1838** PRESCOTT *Ferd. & Is.* xvi, (Cent.), The title of Don, which had not then been degenerated into an appellation of mere courtesy.

†**b.** By extension: often humorous. *Obs.*

1588 SHAKS. *L.L.L.* III. i. 182 This signior Junios gyant dwarfe, don [*Qo.* dan] Cupid. **1599** —— *Much Ado* v. ii. 86 If Don worme (his conscience) find no impediment to the contrarie. **1619** *Pasquil's Palin.* (1877) 152 Don Constable in wrath appeares. *a* **1659** CLEVELAND *London Lady* 17 Don Mars, the great Ascendant on the Road.

c. Don Diego, a name for a Spaniard (cf. DIEGO); hence, †**Don Diego** *v.*, to cheat or 'do' (*obs.*). **Don Juan**, the name of a legendary Spanish nobleman whose dissolute life was dramatized by Gabriel Tellez in his *Convivado de Piedra*; the name was adopted in various popular imitations of this play and by Byron in his well-known poem; a rake, libertine, roué; also *attrib.*; hence, **Don Jua'nesque, Don Ju'anic, Don 'Juanish** *adjs.*, and **Don 'Juanery, Don 'Juanism. Don Pedro** (see sense 6). **Don Quixote**, the hero of a Spanish romance by Cervantes, who, from his attempt to be a knight-errant as described in the books of chivalry, has become the type of any one who attempts to do an absurdly impossible thing or to carry out an impossible ideal; also *attrib.*; hence, **Don Quixote** *v.*, **Don Quixotism**: see also QUIXOTIC, etc.

1607 WEBSTER *Hist. Sir T. Wyat* Wks. 1830 II. 298 A Dondego is a kind of Spanish stockfish, or poor John. *c* **1626** *Dick of Devon* II. iv. in Bullen *O. Pl.* II. 39 Now Don Diego ..or Don Divell, I defye thee. **1674** [Z. CAWDREY] *Catholicon* 18 The furious zeal of persons Don-Quixotted in Religion. **1709** STEELE *Tatler* No. 31 ¶8 Why you look as if you were Don Diego'd to the Tune of a Thousand Pounds. **1719** DE FOE *Crusoe* II. xiii, The state he [a Chinaman of position] rode in was a perfect Don Quixoteism being a mixture of pomp and poverty. [**1734** FIELDING *Don Quixote in England* Introd., The Audience, I believe, are all acquainted with the Character of Don Quixote and Sancho. I have brought them over into England, and introduced them at an Inn in the Country.] *a* **1845** HOOD *T. of Trumpet* xxx, The most Don Juanish rake. **1848** THACKERAY *Van. Fair* xxii. 190 Don't trifle with her affections, you Don Juan! **1855** —— *Newcomes* (1879) II. xx. 236 (Stanf.) It was the man whose sweetheart this Don Juan had..deserted. **1870** D. G. ROSSETTI *Let.* 15 Mar. (1965) II. 817 He is a complete Don Quixote in every way. **1882** STEVENSON *Fam. Stud.* 55 It is the punishment of Don Juanism. **1890** G. B. SHAW *Let.* 16 Dec. (1965) 278 An Irish Don Juan who will eventually compromise Socialism by some outrageous scandal. *Ibid.*, Those who take the Don Juan view of me. **1898** W. GRAHAM *Last Links* 33 Byron's manner was tinged with a vein of Don-Juanesque recklessness. **1900** A. CONAN DOYLE *Gt. Boer War* x. 167 His long thin figure, his gaunt Don-Quixote face. **1902** *Pall Mall Gaz.* 4 Jan. 6/3 This Don Quixote of a society has made an assault upon the most solid of windmills. **1925** D. H. LAWRENCE *Refl. on Death Porcupine* 182 It's Don Juanery, sex-in-the-head, no real desire, which leads to profligacy and squalid promiscuity. **1926** W. J. LOCKE *Old Bridge* ix. 138 Her father was a Don Juanesque clerk in a factory. **1963** AUDEN *Dyer's Hand* III. 106 B..tries to be a Don Juan seducer in an attempt to compel life to take an interest in him.

2. A Spanish lord or gentleman; a Spaniard.

1610 B. JONSON *Alch.* III. iii, A doughty don is taken with my Dol. **1659** DRYDEN *On Cromwell* xxiii, The light Monsieur the grave Don outweighed. **1797** NELSON 13 Jan. in Nicolas *Disp.* (1845) II. 326, I hailed the Don, and told him, 'This is an English Frigate'. **1880** TENNYSON *Revenge* iv, I never turn'd my back upon Don or devil yet.

3. *transf.* A distinguished man; one of position or importance; a leader, first class man. Also (*colloq.* and *dial.*) *attrib.*, and in phrase ***a don at*** something, i.e. an adept.

a **1634** RANDOLPH *Amyntas* II. v. Wks. (1875) 306 This is a man of skill, an Œdipus, Apollo, Reverend Phoebus, Don of Delphos. **1665** DRYDEN *Indian Emp.* Epil. 21 The great dons of wit. **1768–74** TUCKER *Lt. Nat.* (1852) II. 466 Quotations from the old dons of Greece. **1833** in *Westm. Rev.* Apr. 445 One of the men..was what was called a 'don workman'. **1854** *Chamb. Jrnl.* II. 280 A don at cricket.

4. Hence, in the colloquial language of the English universities: A head, fellow or tutor of a college.

1660 SOUTH *Serm.* 29 July (1843) II. 88 The raving insolence which those spiritual dons from the pulpit were wont to show [at Oxford]. **1681** THORESBY *Diary* (Hunter) I. 109 Sermons..against Arminianism, whereat many dons were offended. **1726** AMHERST *Terræ Fil.* v. 20 The reverend dons in Oxford are already alarm'd. **1882** BESANT *Revolt of Man* vii. (1883) 164 The few left were either the reading undergraduates or the dons. **1888** BURGON *Lives 12 Gd. Men* II. x. 242 An introduction to two Oxford dons.

†**5.** = DAN[1], DOM[1] 2. *Obs. rare.*

1600 *Chester Pl.* Proem i, The devise of one done Rondall, moonke of Chester abbe.

6. More fully, ***Don Pedro***, a game at cards.

The players are divided into two sides and have 6 or 5 cards each; the points scored in one game are 23:—one each for High, Low, and Jack of trumps, 5 for Game (i.e. for the side which at the end of the game scores the highest total from the cards won by them, counting 10, 4, 3, 2 and 1 for a ten, ace, king, queen and knave respectively), also 4, 3, 2 and 1 respectively for the ace, king, queen and knave of trumps, and 5 for the five or Don.

1873 *Slang Dict., Don Pedro*..was probably invented by the mixed English and Irish rabble who fought in Portugal in 1832–3. **1897** *Daily News* 16 Mar. 8/3 Two detectives.. saw the prisoners playing Don.

Hence **'dondom, 'donhood, 'donlike** *a.*, **'donly** *a.*, **'donness**, all nonce-wds. from sense 4.

1797 MRS. A. M. BENNETT *Beggar Girl* (1813) III. 122 The don was in..a truly don-like rage. **1865** *Sat. Rev.* 4 Feb. 143 In the glory of early donhood at the Universities. **1891** RODEN NOEL *Byron* 64 Juvenile verses against Cambridge Dondom. **1893** *Nat. Observer* 20 May 12/2 A very donly Don. **1895** *Ibid.* 2 Mar. 432/1 Englishwomen 'who are fairly familiar with Middle English' (who, beyond the range of donnesses, may probably be counted on fingers).

†**don**, *sb.*[2] *Obs. rare.* [a. F. *don*:—L. *dōn-um*, gift.] A donation, gift.

1524 *St. Papers Hen. VIII*, VI. 223 Whose assumpcion is undoubtedly worthy to be reputed a don and gift of God.

don (dɒn), *sb.*[3] orig. and chiefly *U.S.* Also **Don.** [a. S. It. *don*, a term of respect: cf. DON *sb.*[1]] (A respectful name for) a high-ranking or powerful member of the Mafia. Cf. CAPO[1].

1952 E. REID *Mafia* xvii. 189 Morano, boss or 'Don' of the Brooklyn Commora, was worried. **1959** F. SONDERN *Brotherhood of Evil* vii. 104 With the weight of Don Giuseppe Masseria's influence behind him..he..started a gradual expansion of the brotherhood's activities... Masseria..thought that the boys were going too far too fast and said so with all the authority of a don. **1965** J. WAINWRIGHT *Death in Sleeping City* II. vii. 129 A Mafioso must obey..any order originating from a Don or a Capo — the two senior rankings within the Mafia. **1970** [see MAFIA]. **1977** *Time* 16 May 28/3 The Mafia is overseen nationally — but loosely — by the Commission, a dozen or so dons who usually..defer to the dominant boss in New York. **1984** *Times* 29 Oct. 5 Signor Tommaso Buscetta, the former Mafia boss.., 'Don Masino' as he is known was brought under heavy guard from his place of detention. **1986** *Times* 7 Feb. 8/7 A black comedy directed by John Huston also earned a best..supporting actor nomination for William Hickey, as the ageing Mafia don.

don (dɒn), *v.*[1] *arch.* [contracted from *do on*: see DO *v.* 48.

After 1650 retained in popular use only in north. dial.; as a literary archaism it has become very frequent in 19th c.]

1. *trans.* To put on (clothing, anything worn, etc.). The opposite of DOFF.

1567 TURBERV. *Ovid's Ep.* 109 b, Do'n hornes And Bacchus thou shalt be. **1602** SHAKS. *Ham.* IV. v. 52 Then vp he rose, & don'd his clothes. **1613–16** W. BROWNE *Brit. Past.* II. iv. (R.), In Autumne..when stately forests d'on their yellow coates. **1621** QUARLES *Argalus & P.* (1678) 84 Up Argalus, and d'on thy Nuptial weeds. *a* **1764** LLOYD *Henriade* (R.), Mars had donn'd his coat of mail. **1828** SCOTT *F.M. Perth* vi, My experience has been in donning steel gauntlets on mailed knights. **1861** T. A. TROLLOPE *La Beata* II. xii. 61 To shut up his studio, and don his best coat. **1879** DIXON *Windsor* I. iii. 23 She donned the garment of a nun.

2. *transf.* To dress (a person) *in* a garment; *refl.* to dress oneself. Chiefly *north. dial.*

1801 R. ANDERSON *Cumberld. Ball.* 17 Sae doff thy clogs, and don thysel. **1845** E. BRONTE *Wuthering Heights* xix, Joseph was donned in his Sunday garments.

Hence **'donning** *vbl. sb.*

1847 EMERSON *Poems* (1857) 161 Too much of donning and doffing. **1888** ELWORTHY *W. Somerset Word-bk.*, *Donnings*, Sunday clothes, also finery.

†**don**, *v.*[2] *Obs.* [Related to DIN *v.*] *intr.* To resound, ring with sound; = DIN *v.* 1.

a **1400** *Sir Beues* (1886) 163 (MS.E.) Al þe castel donyd and rong. **1483** *Festivall* (1515) 78 b, A man sholde unneth here his folowe speke for donnynges of strokes.

don, var. form of DUN, DOWN.

don, obs. pres. inf. and pa. pple. of DO *v.*

‖**Doña** ('doɲa), **Dona** ('dəʊnə). [Sp. *doña*, Pg. *dona*:—L. *domina* mistress, lady.]

1. A (Spanish or Portuguese) lady. Also prefixed to the name as a title of courtesy.

1622 MABBE tr. *Aleman's Guzman d' Alf.* II. x. 204 We forget to goe for Doña Beatriz the new marryed Bride. *a* **1674** in *Dryden's Wks.* (1884) VIII. 513 Was there never a Dona in all Spain worthy your kindness? **1840** LONGF. *Sp. Stud.* I. i, Doña Serafina and her cousins.

2. *slang.* (in form *dona*, also vulgarly *donah*, *doner*.) A woman; a sweetheart.

1873 *Slang Dict.*, *Dona and feeles*, a woman and children. **1875** *Athenæum* 24 Apr. 545 A circus man almost always speaks of a circus woman, not as a woman, but a dona. **1887** FARRELL *How He Died* 62 Blokes and donahs..of the foulest slums. **1894** *Yellow Bk.* I. 79 The little doner.

'donable, *a. rare*[—0]. [ad. L. *dōnābilis*, f. *dōnāre* to present, DONATE.]

1727 BAILEY vol. II, *Donable*, that may be given.

donah: see DONA 2.

donary ('dəʊnərɪ). [ad. L. *dōnāri-um* repository of offerings, offering, f. *dōnum* gift.] A gift or donation; a votive offering.

1582 N. T. (Rhem.) *Luke* xxi. 5 The Temple..was adorned with goodly stones and donaries. **1621** BURTON *Anat. Mel.* Democr. to Rdr. 57 Hospitals so built and maintained, not by collections, benevolences, donaries. **1699** BENTLEY *Phal.* iii. 125 Were not Cups frequently among the Donaries presented to the Gods? **1700** J. BROME *Trav. Eng. & Scot.* ii. (1707) 53 There have been several Donaries conferred upon it [College] both in Exhibitions and Scholar-ships. **1848** WHARTON *Law Lex.*, *Donary*, a thing given to sacred uses. **1862** F. HALL in *Jrnl. Asiat. Soc. Bengal* 7 The kings..granted away land..by way of local donaries.

donat, var. of DONET, *Obs.*

'donatary. [ad. med.L. type **dōnātārius* (in F. *donataire*), f. L. *dōnāt-* ppl. stem of *dōnāre* to present: see -ARY.] The donee or receiver of a gift or donation; a DONATORY: spec. in *Sc. Law*.

1818 H. T. COLEBROOKE *Oblig. & Contr.* I. 252 The giver's preference of the donatary before his heir or presumptive successor. **1861** W. BELL *Dict. Law Scot.*, *Donatary*..In practice, the term is applied exclusively to the person to whom the Crown makes a gift, as of escheat, *ultimus hæres*, or the like. **1876** D. GORRIE *Summ. & Wint. in Orkneys* ii. 70 One of the ravenous race of crown donataries.

donate (dəʊ'neɪt), *v.* (Chiefly *U.S.*) [f. L. *dōnāt-* ppl. stem of *dōnāre* to present, f. *dōn-um*.]

1. *trans.* To make a donation or gift of; hence, vulgarly (in U.S.), to give, bestow, grant.

1845 R. W. HAMILTON *Pop. Educ.* vii. (ed. 2) 172 The sixteenth [section] is 'donated' by Congress for the support of common schools. **1862** M. HOPKINS *Hawaii* 324 Under the former tenure, all lands, to whomsoever donated, were revocable at will. **1880** MUIRHEAD *Ulpian* vi. §9 Retentions out of a dowry are competent..on account of things donated, or on account of things abstracted.

2. To present (a person, etc.) *with* something.

1862 TROLLOPE *N. Amer.* I. 197 Soldiers returning from the Mexican wars were donated with warrants for land.

donate ('dəʊneɪt), **donat** ('dəʊnæt), *sb.* [ad. med.L. *dōnātus*, *-a*, pa. pple. of *dōnāre* to give.] Name given to members or associates of certain religious orders (see quots.).

1804 L. DE BOISGELIN *Anc. & Mod. Malta* I. II. iii. 239 Those who were desirous of being received into the confraternity, and to become brothers de stage or donats in the order, presented themselves before the brother who was to receive them, fell on their knees, and placing their hands on the missal which the brother held open, pronounced the following words. **1858** G. BOWYER *Ritual of Profession of Knights & Religious Ladies* p. xiii, A Donat, or Confrère, is a member of the Order, and participates in the divine offices, benefits, prayers, Masses, and pious works of the Order. He is called Confrère, as being a member of the Confraternity of Donats. The Donats are also called in the statutes Fratres de Stagio, or Fratelli di Staggio. **1886** *Encycl. Brit.* XXI. 174/1 There was also an affiliation of religious ladies (*dames*) and of *donats* or honorary members. **1886** M. GEUDENS *Life of St. Norbert* p. xxvii, The donates, or oblates, who offer themselves to the Order, make their vows also; but they are not perpetual. **1902** BEDFORD & HOLBECHE *Order Hosp. St. John Jerus.* 207 In addition to Members there should be Honorary Associates and Donats—..the Donats being persons who, from an appreciation of the works of the Order, had contributed to its funds. **1911** *Encycl. Brit.* XXIV. 13/1 Affiliated brethren (*confratres*) and 'donats' (*donati*, i.e. regular subscribers..to the order in return for its privileges). **1925** C. S. DURRANT *Flem. Mystics & Eng. Martyrs* 45 Here [at Diepenveen] he saw about a hundred veiled nuns with no small number of lay sisters, donates, and servants.

ˌdona'tee. [f. as DONATE *v.* + -EE.] One to whom something is given; a recipient of a donation.

1716 M. DAVIES *Athen. Brit.* II. 110 Some noble Protestant Donatees. **1853** M. KELLY tr. *Gosselin's Power Pope* II. 157 From being..a donatee, you can become a donor.

donater, obs. f. DONATOR.

†**Do'natian.** *Obs.* = DONATIST.

1627 W. SCLATER *Exp. 2 Thess.* (1629) 252 As Donatians thought.

donation (dəʊ'neɪʃən). [a. F. *donation*, ad. L. *dōnātiōn-em*, n. of action f. *dōnāre* to present.]

1. The action or faculty of giving or presenting; presentation, bestowal; grant.

c **1425** WYNTOUN *Cron.* V. xii. 1207 Ðe kyng..Mad til Saynct Serf donatyowne Of þat Inch. *c* **1525** (*title*) A Treatyse of the donation or gyfte and endowment of possessyons, gyuen and graunted vnto Sylvester pope of Rhome, by Constantyne. **1597** HOOKER *Eccl. Pol.* V. lxii. §19 The grace of Baptisme commeth by donation from God alone. **1667** MILTON *P.L.* XII. 69 That right we hold By his donation. **1894** J. T. FOWLER *Adamnan* Introd. 65 Who..made to him a donation of the island of Iona.

b. *spec.* The action or right of bestowing or conferring a benefice; the 'gift'.

1540 *Act 32 Hen. VIII*, c. 44 The aduouson, donacion and presentacion of the said vicarage shall apperteyn..to the kynges hyghnesse. **1724** SWIFT *Drapier's Lett.* Wks. 1755 V. II. 145 Many principal church livings are in the donation of the crown. **1785** PALEY *Mor. Philos.* (1818) II. 222 The offices in the donation of the king.

2. *Law.* The action or contract by which a person transfers the ownership of a thing from himself to another, as a free gift.

1651 W. G. tr. *Cowel's Inst.* 106 In Lands..A Feoffment is of a Fee simple to the Donee or Feoffee, and a Donation or Gift is of an Estate taile. **1765** BLACKSTONE *Comm.* I. iii. (1793) 264 King William, queen Mary, and queen Anne, did not take the crown by hereditary right or descent, but by way of donation or purchase, as the lawyers call it. **1818** CRUISE *Digest* (ed. 2) I. 5 A feud was a tract of land held by a voluntary and gratuitous donation, on condition of fidelity and certain services.

3. That which is presented; a gift.

1577 tr. *Bullinger's Decades* (1592) 960 They..had a donatyon giuen vnto ech of them as it were a pleadge or earnest. **1630** PRYNNE *Anti-Armin.* 120 It makes all these graces..not the absolute gifts, the free donations of God. **1756–7** tr. *Keysler's Trav.* (1760) III. 197 All the gifts and donations..amounted to no more than six thousand ducats. **1895** *Daily News* 5 Dec. 3/6 The commissioners had anticipated that the donations would fall off.

4. *attrib.*, as **donation-governor**, a person constituted a governor of an institution in consideration of a donation to its funds.

1860 BARTLETT *Dict. Amer.*, *Donation Party*, a party consisting of the friends and parishioners of a country clergyman assembled together, each individual bringing some article..as a present to him..also called a *giving party*. **1894** *Daily News* 13 July 7/4 Preference to candidates recommended by a Donation Governor.

Donatism ('dəʊnətɪz(ə)m, 'dɒn-). [f. as next + -ISM (in med.L. *Donatism-us*).] The doctrine or principles of the Donatists.

1588 J. UDALL *Demonstr. Discip.* (Arb.) 64 It is a kind of Donatisme to challenge such authoritie ouer princes. **1709** J. JOHNSON *Clergym. Vade M.* II. 188 A bishop converted from Donatism.

Donatist ('dəʊnətɪst, 'dɒn-). *Eccl. Hist.* [ad. med.L. *Dōnātista*, f. *Dōnātus*: see below.] One of a sect of Christians which arose in North Africa in the year 311, out of a dispute about the election of Cæcilian as bishop of Carthage, in place of whom they elected Majorinus; they maintained that their own party was the only true and pure church, and that the baptisms and ordinations of others were invalid.

It is uncertain whether the name was derived from Donatus of Casæ Nigræ, a leading supporter of Majorinus, or from Donatus the Great, who succeeded Majorinus as bishop of Carthage.

c **1460** *Medulla* in *Cath. Angl.* 104 note, *Donatista*, a donatiste [*printed* donatrice]: *quedam heresis*. **1549** LATIMER *4th Serm. bef. Edw. VI*, (Arb.) 116 An other kynde of poysoned heretikes, that were called Donatistes. **1645** PAGITT *Heresiogr.* (1661) 68 The Separatists or Brownists agree in many things with the Donatists, who confined the holy Catholick Church to a corner of Africa, as the Brownists do confine the Church of God to their conventicles. **1873** ROBERTSON *Hist. Chr. Ch.* (1874) I. 176 *note*, At a later time, rebaptism of proselytes was practised by the Donatists.

b. *attrib.* or as *adj.*

1861 J. G. SHEPPARD *Fall Rome* vii. 372 The Donatist sectaries. **1885** *Catholic Dict.* 280 In 330 no less than 270 Donatist bishops met in council.

Hence **Dona'tistic**, **Dona'tistical** *adjs.*, pertaining to Donatism or the Donatists; **'Donatistry** = DONATISM (with implication of contempt).

1564 *Brief Exam.***** iv, This smelleth..either of Donatistrie or Papistrie. **1581** MARBECK *Bk. of Notes* 208 Both..are donatistical. **1645** PAGITT *Heresiogr.* (1647) A iv b, The Donatisticall Brownists. **1828** WEBSTER, *Donatistic*. **1889** FARRAR *Lives Fathers* II. xvii. 514 The deplorable Donatistic controversy.

donative ('dɒnətɪv, 'dəʊnətɪv), *a.* and *sb.* [ad. L. *dōnātīvus* adj., whence *dōnātīv-um* sb. donation, largess, f. *dōnāre*: see DONATE, and -IVE.] **A.** *adj.*

1. Characterized by being given or presented; of the nature of a donation: *esp.* of a benefice: Vesting or vested by donation; opposed to PRESENTATIVE.

1559 in Strype *Ann. Ref.* I. App. viii. 22 Foundations of free-chappels, and other howses ecclesiastical by the kings lycence, to be donatyve and not presentatyve. **1610** GUILLIM *Heraldry* VI. iii. (1611) 260 To these donatiue augmentations of Armes I will adde certaine Armes assumptiue. **1765** BLACKSTONE *Comm.* I. xi. 382 The deanery is donative, and the installation merely by the king's letters patent. **1875** BP. MAGEE in *Parl.* 1 June, The holder of a donative living owes no obedience to his diocesan.

†**2.** 'That is able or apt to give' (Blount *Glossogr.* 1656). *Obs.*

B. *sb.*

1. A donation, gift, present; *esp.* one given formally or officially, as a largess or bounty.

c **1430** LYDGATE *Balade of our Ladie* xi, O mirthe of martyrs, sweter then Sitole of Confessours also richest donatife. **1581** J. BELL *Haddon's Answ. Osor.* 361 b, The Graunt, & Donative of Ludovicus Pius. **1594** HOOKER *Eccl. Pol.* II. v. §7 The Romane Emperours custome was at certaine solemne times to bestow on his Souldiers a Donatiue. **1599** NASHE *Lenten Stuffe* (1871) 17 The devout oblations and donatives of the fishermen. **1728** MORGAN *Algiers* II. v. 313 Francis I gave the Grand Master a Royal Reception, accompanied with a Princely Donative. **1843** J. MARTINEAU *Chr. Life* (1867) 171 [Christ] ranked the widow's mite above the vast donatives of vanity.

2. *spec.* A benefice which the founder or patron can bestow without presentation to or investment by the ordinary.

1564 BULLEYN *Dial. agst. Pest.* (1888) 83 He would faine haue a benefice or personage of some pretie donatiue; he cannot get it at the bishoppes handes. **1686** PLOT *Staffordsh.* 297 The King can create or found a Donative exempt from the visitation of the ordinary. **1772** WARTON & HUDDESFORD *Life Hearne* 26 He was presented to the Donative or Curacy of Elsfield near Oxford. **1877** J. C. COX *Ch. Derbysh.* III. 84 This living was a donative, from the dissolution of the monasteries to the first year of Anne.

†**3.** One who is presented to a benefice. *Obs. rare*.

1651 N. BACON *Disc. Govt. Eng.* II. xxvii. (1739) 127 In their Original, Bishops were meerly Donatives from the Crown, invested by delivery of the Ring and Pastoral Staff.

Hence **'donatively** *adv.*, by way of a donation.

1827 G. S. FABER *Orig. Exp. Sacr.* II. iii. 64 Donatively presenting..sacrifices and vows and libations.

donator[1] (dəʊ'neɪtə(r)). [a. AF. *donatour*, F. *donateur*, ad. L. *dōnātōr-em*, agent-n. f. *dōnāre* to present.] One who makes a donation; a donor.

c **1449** PECOCK *Repr.* III. xix. 412 Chartours of the donatouris or of the ȝeuers. **1873** MISSES HORNER *Florence* (1884) I. v. 93 The donator and his wife kneel at the feet of the Virgin. **1894** *Tablet* 22 Dec. 974 The intention of the donator.

'donator[2]. *Sc.* Also 6 -our, 7 -ar, -er. [ad. F. *donataire* or OF. *donatoire* = next.] He to whom a donation is made; a donatory or donee.

c **1575** BALFOUR *Practicks* (1754) 23 The Kingis donatour. **1609** SKENE *Reg. Maj.* 37 Giuen..to the vse of the donatar. **1636** W. MACDOWELL *Assignation* in J. Russell *Haigs* ix. (1881) 225 Ordains the said David Haig, his heirs and donaters, my very lawful..cessioners and assignees. **1859** JAS. ANDERSON *Ladies of Covenant* 274 As donator to the forfeited estate of Coldwell, he pursued her for mails and duties.

donatory ('dɒnətərɪ, 'dəʊnətərɪ). [ad. med.L. *dōnātōrius* one to whom something is given (Du Cange), f. *dōnāre*: see -ORY.] The recipient of a gift or donation; a donatary.

a **1617** BAYNE *On Eph.* (1658) 82 A gift..must come freely from the donour, and bee greatly to the good of the donatory or receiver. **1810** SOUTHEY in *Q. Rev.* IV. 13 The donatories of crown property were to pay a double tax. **1817** *Chron.* in *Ann. Reg.* 405 The Brazilian white man..who draws his descent from the first donatory of a province. **1848** WHARTON *Law Lex., Donatory*, the person on whom the king bestows his right to any forfeiture that has fallen to the Crown.

do'natrix, *rare.* [a. L. *dōnātrix*, fem. of *dōnātor*.] A female donor or donator.

1668 *Churchw. Acc. St. Margarets, Westm.* (Nichols 1797) 69 According to the will of the said Donatrix.

†**'donature.** *Obs. rare.* [ad. L. **dōnātūra*, f. *dōnāre* to DONATE.] Donation.

1629 J. MAXWELL tr. *Herodian* (1635) 344 Being obliged to him by Donatures and all manner of honors.

do-naught: see DO-NOUGHT.

donce, donck, obs. ff. DUNCE, DANK.

doncher ('dəʊntʃə(r)). Also **doncha, dontcha, dontcher.** Colloq. representation of *don't you*, esp. in phr. ***doncher know***.

1893 E. F. BENSON *Dodo* II. xv. 309 It's an arful bore reading books, dontcherthink, what? **1897** HALL CAINE *Christian* IV. ii. 367 'Oh, let us, Glo,' cried Betty. 'I'd love it of all things, doncher know!' **1897** M. CORELLI *Ziska* i. 31 My mother has taken to 'studying character', don'cher know. **1908** A. HUXLEY *Let.* 29 June (1969) 28 We have as you so aptly put it a great many aw, ahem new *men* dontcher know. **1913** KIPLING *Diversity of Creatures* (1917) 274 You don't work any of your English on me. 'So glad to see you, doncher know——an' ta-ta!' **1957** [see DICK *sb.*[1] 1 a]. **1962** *Guardian* 31 Oct. 7/2 Don't want to spend me evenin' watching plays about incest and rape, doncher know? **1969** L. J. CHIARAMONTE in Halpert & Story *Christmas Mumming in Newfoundland* 96 Why dontcha come around with us?

†**dondaine, -dine.** [a. OF. *dom-, dondaine*, of uncertain orig. (See Godef. and Hatz.-Darm. s.v. *dondon*.)] A warlike engine for casting stones, in use before firearms.

c **1430** LYDG. *Bochas* I. iii. (1544) 6 a, Shot of arblast, nor on touche of dondine [*rime* attayne].

done (dʌn), *ppl. a.* (*sb.*) [pa. pple. of DO *v.*, q.v. for forms and participial uses.]

1. a. Performed, executed, accomplished, finished, ended, settled; also, used up, worn out: see DO *v.*

1435 MISYN *Fire of Love* I. xxx. (1896) 65 Done synnes it hidys. **1665** COTTON *Poet. Wks.* (1765) 136 She thought 't would be a done Thing Soon. **1804** J. LARWOOD *No Gun Boats* 29 What l'Eveque only contemplated as a remote probability, [he] now considers as a done thing. **1844** DICKENS *Christmas Carol* iii, It was a done thing between him and Scrooge's nephew. **1860** GEN. P. THOMPSON *Audi Alt.* III. ci. 2 A done game.

b. *absol.* That which is done or accomplished.

1855 BROWNING *Last Ride Together*, Contrast The petty Done, the Undone vast. **1872** RUSKIN *Arrows of Chace* (1880) II. 208 The condemnation given from the judgment throne..is all for the undones and not for the dones.

c. Colloq. phr. ***the done thing***: the accepted, correct, or fashionable action or mode of behaviour; = THING *sb.*[1] 15 a.

1922 C. E. MONTAGUE *Disenchantment* iv. 57 Others were anxious lest the taking of steep and thorny paths..should come to be 'the done thing'. **1940** HARRISSON & MADGE *War begins at Home* iv. 88 Interview results..show more people in favour of..the ' done thing' than written results, where people are..more candid. **1953** N. FITZGERALD *Midsummer Malice* ii. 32, I expect he made a pass at you. He still thinks it is the done thing in the theatre.

†**2.** There was in ME. a curious use of *done*, in which it was nearly synonymous with *kin* = 'kind of': thus ***many done***, many kinds of, ***what done***, 'what-kin', what sort of. At length, it took, like *kin*, a genitival *s*: thus, ***what-dones, what dons*** = 'whatkins', *cujus generis*, of what kind of. *Obs.*

[There is a certain parallelism between this and the MDu. use of the inf. *doen* (as of MLG. *dôn, dônt*, MHG. *tuon*), which has the sense-development 'doing, action, manner of doing, way of acting or being, manner, nature, wise, kind'. But in Eng. the stages by which the sense 'kind' was reached are less clear.]

1297 R. GLOUC. (1724) 112 He askede, wat God [*Trin. MS.* what Idone god; *Digby MS.* what manere god.] and wat þing Mercurius was. **1340-70** *Alex. & Dind.* 222 We discorden of dede in many done þinguus. *Ibid.* 999 Wiþ-oute diuerce dedus of many done þingus. **1377** LANGL. *P. Pl.* B. XVIII. 298 What dones man was Jhesus. *a* **1400-50** *Alexander* 2906 Quat dones man ert þou? *Ibid.* 5167 Quat dons man ert bou?..and quat dos þou here.

done, *adv. Sc.* ? *Obs.* Also 6 doyn, 8- doon, doons, dunze. [perh. adv. use of prec.; but cf. DOOMS.] Thoroughly, very, exceedingly.

1500-20 DUNBAR *Poems* lxvi. 82 Bot sa done tyrsum it is to byd it. **1536** BELLENDEN *Cron. Scot.* (1821) I. p. xliv, Thir mussillis ar sa doyn gleg of twiche and heryng. **1715** *P. Many's Truth's Trav.* in *Pennecuik's Poems* 106 (Jam.) He was not thence so doons severe. **1825-80** JAMIESON s.v. *Doyn, Doon weil*, or *dunze weil*, very well.

done, obs. form of DOWN *adv.*

donee (dəʊ'niː). [f. stem of DON-OR + -EE.] One to whom anything is given; *esp.* in *Law*, (*a*) one to whom anything is given gratuitously; (*b*) one to whom land is conveyed in fee tail; (*c*) one to whom a 'power' is given for execution.

1523 FITZHERB. *Surv.* 7 b, This donee or this purchasoure shall take [etc.]. **1598** KITCHIN *Courts Leet* (1675) 218 A Donee in tail. **1655** FULLER *Ch. Hist.* VI. vii. §16 Not sixty of the Kings Donees had sons owning their fathers estates. **1767** BLACKSTONE *Comm.* II. vii. 110 If the donee died without such particular heirs, the land should revert to the donor. **1875** MAINE *Hist. Inst.* ii. 56 The Church, as the donee of pious gifts.

Donegal ('dɒnɪgɔːl, dɒnɪ'gɔːl). The name of a county in the north-west of Ireland; used *attrib.* or *ellipt.* to designate something produced in or peculiar to the county, esp. a type of tweed or a kind of coarse, knotted carpet.

1903-4 *T. Eaton Catal.* Fall & Winter 17 Women's Trainless Suit, made of Oxford grey Donegal tweed. **1905** *Westm. Gaz.* 5 Aug. 10/2 There are some charming new tweeds this season. The Donegals are good. **1909** J. JOYCE *Let.* 27 Oct. (1966) II. 257, I send you seven or eight yards of Donegal tweed to have a new dress made from. *Ibid.* 17 Nov. 264 Irish tweeds, Donegals and suitings. **1946** J. B. PRIESTLEY *Bright Day* vi. 188 A floppy Donegal tweed hat. **1963** *House & Garden* Feb. 79/3 Donegal carpets. Hand-knotted carpets were first made in County Donegal in 1898. *Ibid.* 79/4 Those Axminster and Savonnerie carpets of the eighteenth century, whose colour and design the modern Donegal often emulates. **1968** *Guardian* 2 May 7/3 Very soft Isle of Bute tweeds and Donegals.

donek, obs. form of DUNNOCK, hedge-sparrow.

doneness ('dʌnnɪs). [f. *done*, pa. pple. of DO *v.* + -NESS.] The extent to which food is cooked; the state of being sufficiently cooked or 'done': see DO *v.* 11 b.

1968 *Good Housek. Easy-Stages Cook Bk.* 43 Remove the lid and test the rice for 'doneness'. **1968** *Listener* 16 May 650/3 The scale..marks different degrees of 'done-ness'—underdone, medium, well-done—for different joints. **1973** A. G. SEABERG *Menu Design—Merchandising & Marketing* (ed. 2) 212 South African Lobster Tail..breaded and then fried to the correct doneness. **1975** E. L. ORTIZ *Best of Caribbean Cooking* 125 To test for doneness, prick the thigh with a fork. **1983** *N.Y. Times* 11 Sept. 11NJ. 20/5 Test for doneness by opening foil and seeing if the fish flakes when prodded with a fork.

doner: see DONA 2.

doner kebab ('dɒnə(r) kə,bæb, also 'dəʊnə(r)) Also döner kebab. [a. Turkish *döner kebap*, f. *döner* ppl. a. turning, rotating (f. *dönmek* to turn) + *kebap* KEBAB.] A Turkish dish which consists of slices of lamb or mutton, layered with herbs and spices on a vertical spit and roasted as it revolves against a tall narrow grill. As the surface is cooked the meat is sliced thinly downwards and served, often with pita. Also *ellipt.* as **doner**.

The dish is also prepared (often with slightly different ingredients) outside Turkey, esp. for sale in restaurants, etc.

1958 R. HOWE *Cook's Tour* 91 *Döner Kebab*...This form of kebab needs an expert's hand and is cooked on a large vertical spit, round which the meat — always lamb or mutton, garlic flavoured — is tightly bound. **1968** C. RODEN *Bk. Middle Eastern Food* 203 In Turkey, *döner kebab* is a great favorite. Although veal cut from the leg is sometimes used, lamb is more popular. **1981** *Listener* 1 Jan. 16/1 The Chinese take-aways and doner kebab houses seem to stay open all night. **1986** J. MILNE *Dead Birds* ix. 57 A take-away doner kebab...The nice thing about doner is..enough raw onion and chili sauce on it.

†**'donet, 'donat.** *Obs.* [a. OF. *donet, donnat*, ad. L. *Dōnātus*.] The elementary grammatical treatise (*Ars Grammatica*) of Ælius Donatus, a grammarian of the 4th c.; an introductory Latin grammar; hence, an introduction to, or the elements of, any art, science, etc.

13.. *Seuyn Sag.* (W.) 181 Therinne was paint of Donet thre pars, And eke alle the seven ars. **1362** LANGL. *P. Pl.* A. v. 123 þenne I drouȝ me a-mong þis drapers my Donet to leorne. *c* **1449** PECOCK *Donet into Cristen Relig.* Introd., As the common donet berith himsilfe towards the full kunnyng of Latyn, so this booke for Goddis laws. **1509** HAWES *Past. Pleas.* v. xxv, Dame Gramer..taught me..Fyrst my Donet and then my accidence. **1535** JOYE *Apol. Tindale* 47, I had nede go lerne my donate and accidence agen.

b. *Comb.* **1483** *Cath. Angl.* 104/1 A Donett lerner ..*donatista*.

doney, var. of DHONEY.

dong (dɒŋ), *v.* [Echoic; expressing a sound of deeper tone than DING.] **1.** *intr.* To sound as a large bell.

1587 FLEMING *Contn. Holinshed* III. 1579/2 Where they might..heare the donging of the belles as they hoong in the steeples. **1954** J. MASTERS *Bhowani Junction* xxxiv. 291 A copper-smith bird donged with maddening persistence among the bushes in the garden.

2. *trans.* To hit, punch (esp. *Austral.* and *N.Z.*); to force by reiterated noise, speech, or effort. Cf. DING *v.*[1] 2 a. *colloq.*

1889 E. L. LINTON *Through Long Night* I. I. xv. 243 She had to be dinged and donged into obedience. **1928** BLUNDEN *Undertones of War* 291 The drum-tap dongs my brain To a whirring void. **1930** *Bulletin* (Sydney) 7 May 21/1, I done me block an' donged 'im proper. **1937** N. MARSH *Vintage Murder* vi. 66 It was certainly a high-class way of murdering anybody... Dong him one with a gallon of champagne. **1959** I. & P. OPIE *Lore & Lang. Schoolch.* x. 196 'Dong him on the dome' (head). **1960** N. HILLIARD *Maori Girl* III. x. 133 I'll dong you if you say it any more. **1961** P. WHITE *Riders in Chariot* xi. 410 'I will dong you one,' shouted Hannah, 'before you tear this bloody fur.'

dong (dɒŋ), *sb.*[1] [Echoic: see the vb.]

1. An imitation of the deep sound of a large bell. Cf. DING, DING-DONG.

a **1882** ROSSETTI *Wks.* (1890) II. 343 And bells say ding to bells that answer dong.

2. *Austral.* and *N.Z. colloq.* A heavy blow, a punch.

1941 BAKER *Dict. Austral. Slang* 24 *Dong*, a blow, esp. with the fist. **1965** *Telegraph* (Brisbane) 5 July 8 *Dong*, poke (punch).

Dong (dɒŋ), *sb.*[2] [Coined by E. Lear 1877 in *Laughable Lyrics*, 'The Dong with a luminous nose'.] A fabulous creature represented as having a luminous nose; also *transf.*

1927 E. BOWEN *Hotel* xi. 131 Their cigarette ends glowing and fading preceded them like a pair of luminous noses, and equidistant spots of fire advertised that other pairs of Dongs were promenading solemnly. **1954** L. MACNEICE *Autumn Sequel* 49 Egdon gives to Snark and Dong His kind attention still.

dong (dɒŋ), *sb.*[3] *coarse slang* (chiefly *U.S.*). [Origin unknown; perh. f. prec.] = PENIS.

1930 in *Amer. Speech* V. 390. **1939** J. STEINBECK *Grapes of Wrath* xvi. 245 Tell 'em ya dong's growed sence you los' your eye. **1961** PARTRIDGE *Dict. Slang* Suppl. 1124/2 Three Canadian terms for 'penis'..are *dink, dong, hammer*. **1969** P. ROTH *Portnoy's Complaint* 18, I was wholly incapable of keeping my paws off my dong.

dong(e, obs. form of DUNG.

dong(e, obs. pa. t. and pa. pple. of DING *v.*[1]

‖**donga** ('dɒŋgə). Chiefly *S. Africa.* [Native name.] A channel or gully formed by the action of water; a ravine or watercourse with steep sides. (See also quot. 1966.)

1879 *Daily News* 20 June 5/6 A donga was safely crossed. A donga..would be called..in Scotland, a gully. **1893** J. T. BENT *Ruined Cities Mashonaland* xii. 374 The culverts which they had made over the dongas. **1948** H. DRAKE-BROCKMAN in B. James *Austral. Short Stories* (1963) 2nd Ser. 102 There were..brilliant flowers in the dongas after it had rained. **1964** *Sunday Truth* (Brisbane) 9 Aug. 20/5 The Government Administration [of New Guinea] builds and supplies homes for its employees. These are called 'dongas'. **1966** BAKER *Austral. Lang.* (ed. 2) viii. 177 *Donga*, any gully or depression in which men could settle themselves in order to loaf... Also used both in Tobruk and New Guinea for a makeshift shelter... Not long after the end of World War II, the word acquired use among New Guinea's white population for a house.

†**donge.** *Obs.* A mattress.

c **1440** *Promp. Parv.* 127/1 Donge, matrasse, *culcitra, matracia*. **1448** *Bury Wills* 12, j donge optimum. **1459** *Inv.* in *Paston Lett.* No. 954 I. 485, J fedder-bedde, Item. j donge of fyne blewe. *a* **1490** BOTONER *Itin.* (Nasmith 1778) 372 Quælibet femina elimosinaria habuit..1 donge.

dongen, -eon, -eoun, obs. ff. DUNGEON.

donger, donghel, obs. ff. DANGER, DUNGHILL.

dongle ('dɒŋg(ə)l). *Computing.* [Arbitrary.] A software protection device which must be plugged into a computer to enable the protected software to be used on it.

1982 *MicroComputer Printout* Jan. 19/2 The word 'dongle' has been appearing in many articles with reference to security systems for computer software [refers to alleged coinage in 1980]. **1983** *Listener* 15 Dec. 7/1 A dongle is a kind of electronic security key without which a disc simply does not work. **1984** *New Scientist* 26 Apr. 30/1 Most dongles do not prevent programs from being copied, but they stop the copies from being used, since each copy needs a matching dongle to work. **1985** *Daily Tel.* 7 Jan. 16/4 Moneywise..uses a dongle as anti-piracy protection, so that without this plastic whatsit plugged into the back of the computer, your work will not be stored.

dongola[1]. In *dongola race*: a race in which a punt or the like is propelled by paddling, by three or four pairs (usually male and female).

1892 *Pall Mall G.* 18 July 43/3 Canadian canoe race (lady and gentleman), dongola race (four ladies, four gentlemen). **1894** *Daily News* 30 June 6/2 Dongola races for crews of eight gentlemen and mixed crews of four ladies and four gentlemen. *Ibid.* 28 July 6/5 The Dongola Race (paddling in punts)..for crews of three ladies and three gentlemen.

Dongola², **dongola** ('dɒŋgələ, dɒn'gəʊlə). [f. *Dongola*, the name of a province of the Sudan.] A type of leather resembling kid, made from goat, sheep, or calf skin. Freq. *attrib.*

1889 *Shoe & Leather Review* 10 Oct. 31/3 In twenty-eight minutes the pair of shoes were finished—a neat and perfect pair of Dongola kids. **1895** *Montgomery Ward Catal.* 270/1 Leather Clothing, commonly called Dongola Goat, is made of oil-tanned and dressed Rocky Mountain sheepskin. *Ibid.* 508/1 Ladies' Fine French Dongola Button Shoes. *Ibid.* 508/2 This shoe is made from a very fine grade of satin finish dongola. **1897** C. T. DAVIS *Manuf. Leather* (ed. 2) xxiii. 376 It is the purport of this section to treat, not of the more modern tannages, but of the earlier brands that were for a number of years..regarded as standard—we refer to the 'Dongola' and preceding tannages. *Ibid.*, The different processes through which goat-skins pass in their conversion into Dongola. *Ibid.* 424 This blacking is for..dongola. **1926** *Daily Colonist* (Victoria, B.C.) 3 Jan. 36/3 (Advt.), Ladies' Black Dongola Kid Pumps.

dongon, **-oun**, obs. forms of DUNGEON.

doni, var. of DHONEY.

† **do'niferous**, *a. Obs. rare*⁻⁰. [f. L. *dōnum* gift: see -FEROUS.] 'That carries a gift' (Blount *Glossogr.* 1656).

Donizettian (ˌdɒnɪt'sɛtɪən), *a.* and *sb.* [-IAN.] **A.** *adj.* Of, pertaining to, or characteristic of the Italian operatic composer Gaetano Donizetti (1797–1848) or his music. **B.** *sb.* An admirer or adherent of Donizetti.

1848 THACKERAY *Van. Fair* iv. 29 The eternal Donizettian music with which we are favoured now-a-days. **1955** E. DENT in H. M. van Thal *Fanfare for E. Newman* vi. 103 The opera is..rich in melody of the finest Donizettian type. **1962** *Times* 2 Feb. 13/2 Mahlerites are likely to owe their allegiance to the..gramophone records conducted by Dr. Bruno Walter.., Donizettians to Mme. Callas and Miss Schwarzkopf.

donjon ('dʌndʒən, 'dɒndʒən), archaic spelling of DUNGEON, q.v.; now usual in sense 1, 'The great tower or innermost keep of a castle', to distinguish it from the modern sense.

1300–1690, **1808** [see DUNGEON 1].

donk (dɒŋk), colloq. abbrev. of DONKEY.

1916 J. B. COOPER *Coo-oo-ee* xvi. 241 The men from Ironbark were arrested at the appearance of the long narrow lorries, and the 'donks', or donkeys, in them. **1919** *Athenæum* 8 Aug. 727/2 Mules were 'donks'. **1922** 'R. CROMPTON' *More William* (1924) xii. 206 Look out for the donk, you ole ass. **1957** BLUNDEN *Poems of Many Years* 288 The old East Window..Where Jesus used to perch On that plump donkey bound for Egypt, yes, That was a work of art, —the donk no less.

donk, dial. form of DANK.

donkey ('dɒŋkɪ). Also 8–9 **donky.** [A recent word, app. of dialect or slang origin.

As the original pronunciation apparently rimed with *monkey* (whence the spelling), suggestions have been made that the word is a deriv. of *dun* adj. (cf. *dunnock* hedge-sparrow), or, more probably, a familiar form of *Duncan* (cf. the other colloquial appellations, *Dicky*, *Neddy*).]

1. a. A familiar name for the ass. (Now in general use, exc. in scriptural or solemn language, and in Natural History.)

1785 GROSE *Dict. Vulg. Tongue*, Donkey or Donkey Dick, a he or Jack-ass. **1793** *Gentl. Mag.* II. 1083 A Donky, or a Dicky, An ass. Essex and Suffolk. **1804** MRS. BARBAULD *Wks.* (1825) II. 113, I cannot tell whether my orthography is right, but a *donky* is the monture in high fashion here [Tunbridge Wells]. *a* **1819** WOLCOTT (P. Pindar) *Wks.* (1830) 116 Peter, thou art mounted on a Neddy; Or in the London phrase, thou Devonshire monkey, Thy Pegasus is nothing but a donkey. **1838** J. L. STEPHENS *Trav. Greece, etc.* (1839) 37/1 Seven camels and the donkey were stowed in the bottom of the boat. **1859** SALA *Tw. round Clock* (1861) 45 Costermongers' 'shallows', drawn by woe-begone donkies.

b. Colloq. phrases: (*a penny*, etc., *more and*) *up goes the donkey*, used with allusion to the cry of a travelling showman (see quot. 1889); *to talk the hind leg(s) off a donkey* (see TALK *v.*).

1841 *Punch* I. 41/2 The report of Sir John Pullon, 'as to the possibility of elevating an ass to the head of the poll by bribery and corruption' is perfectly correct, provided there is no abatement in the price. Let him canvass again, and.. if he will only stand 'one penny more, up goes the donkey!' **1889** BARRÈRE & LELAND *Dict. Slang* (1897) 304/2 'Three more and up goes the donkey', that is, three pennies more and the donkey will go up the ladder. This phrase, used by mountebanks to denote that the performance will begin when the sum required is complete, is often said mockingly to a braggart to imply disbelief. **1913** M. BEERBOHM *Let.* 11 Mar. (1964) 222 They earnestly hope to raise the sum of £500; after which 'up goes the donkey', I suppose. **1970** *Brewer's Dict. Phr. & Fable* 336/2 *Two more and up goes the donkey*, an old cry at fairs, the showman having promised his credulous hearers that as soon as enough pennies are collected his donkey will balance himself on the top of a pole or ladder.

2. *transf.* **a.** A stupid or silly person.

1840 THACKERAY *Shabby Genteel Story* ix, 'What a blubbering, abthurd donkey!' said Cinqbars. **1862** MISS YONGE *C'tess Kate* xii. (1864) 212 You little donkey, you'll be off! **1878** MRS. H. WOOD *Pomeroy Abb.* I. 254 What a donkey he must be.

b. A simple card-game played with special cards.

1920 *Isis* 3 Mar. 6/1 Don't play 'donkey' with him: he is the champion of the Giler. **1959** G. AVERY *James without Thomas* xi. 195 They hastily changed to Donkey.

3. *attrib.* and *Comb.*: **a.** general, as *donkey-back* (cf. *horseback*), *-carriage*, *-cart*, *-chair*, *-path*, *-race*, *-ride*, *-track*; *donkey-breeding*, *-driver*, *-driving*, *-drubber*, *-riding*; *donkey-drawn*, *-eared*, *-like*, *-mad* adjs.

1837 J. L. STEPHENS *Trav. Holy Land* (Chambers) 116 From there we started on *donkey-back. **1884** L. OLIPHANT *Haifa* (1887) 158 A favourite method of locomotion among the women, was donkey-back. **1816** JANE AUSTEN *Let.* 9 July (1952) 459 We set off in the *Donkey Carriage for Farringdon. **1894** *Times* 23 Mar. 3/2 The Queen..went out in her donkey-carriage this morning. **1838** DICKENS *O. Twist* xxi, *Donkey-carts laden with vegetables. **1868** C. M. YONGE *Let.* 8 Oct. in C. Coleridge *C.M.Y.* (1903) 298 She had been out for a long turn in a *donkey chair. **1841** LANE *Arab. Nts.* I. 61 Three *donkey-drivers, conveying the luggage of two British travellers. **1899** *Westm. Gaz.* 18 July 3/3 This zebra-donkey combination appears to exhibit a more than *donkey-like obstinacy. **1962** I. MURDOCH *Unofficial Rose* xxvi. 250 The more owlish and donkey-like he felt himself becoming. **1855** D. G. ROSSETTI *Let.* 1 July (1965) I. 261 A *donkey-ride at Clevedon. **1894** G. DU MAURIER *Trilby* I. ii. 154 Swings, peep-shows, donkey-rides. **1825** H. WILSON *Mem.* II. 86 Fanny..doated on *donkey-riding. **1875** J. H. BENNET *Shores Medit.* I. vii. 189 The road from Castellare, a *donkey-track.

b. Special combs.: **donkey-boy**, a boy in charge of a donkey, or of a donkey-engine; **donkey-drop** *colloq.*, in cricket, tennis, etc.: a slow ball bowled or hit so that it travels in a high curve; **donkey-engine**, a small steam-engine, usually for subsidiary operations on board ship, as feeding the boilers of the propelling engines, etc.; hence *donkey-boiler*; **donkey jacket**, a thick jacket worn by workmen as a protection against rain, cold, etc., and later in more general use as a fashionable garment; **donkey-lick** *Austral. slang*, (*a*) *v. trans.*, to defeat easily (e.g. in a horse-race); (*b*) *sb.*, treacle or golden syrup; **donkey-man**, a man in charge of a donkey, or of a donkey-engine; **donkey-pump**, an auxiliary steam-pump for filling the boiler of a steam-engine, or for other subsidiary operations; **donkey-rest**, in *Paper Manuf.*, 'a frame against which the form is laid to drain' (*Cent. Dict.*); **donkey's breakfast** *slang*, (*a*) a straw mattress (see also quot. 1901); (*b*) a straw hat; **donkey-sled** *U.S.* (see quot.); **donkey's** or **donkeys' years** (occas. *ears*, with punning allusion to the length of a donkey's ears and to the vulgar pronunciation of *ears* as *years*) *colloq.*, a very long time; **donkey-work**, the hard or unattractive part of an undertaking.

1840 BARHAM *Ingol. Leg.*, *Bagman's Dog*, Little *donkey-boys your steps environ. **1894** *Times* 22 June 10/5 The mate ..and the donkey-boy..went in a boat. **1888** A. G. STEEL in Steel & Lyttleton *Cricket* iii. 128 Are *you* going to bowl your *donkey-drops? I'll hit them all out of the ground. **1906** Donkey-drop [see DOLLY *sb.*[1] 3 b]. **1927** *Daily Tel.* 14 June 9/1 He is content to play 'donkey drops' back into court, awaiting the right ball to hit. **1858** *Merc. Marine Mag.* V. 49 Hose was..put on the *donkey-engine. **1877** W. THOMSON *Voy. Challenger* I. i. 52 The donkey-engines for hoisting the dredging and sounding gear. **1929** *Morning Post* 4 Oct., Members of the City Corporation wanted to know at yesterday's meeting at the Guildhall what a *donkey jacket is... Mr. Gower explained that the jacket was one with leather shoulders and back. **1959** J. BRAINE *Vodi* xxii 237 He stood there..in his navy-blue donkey jacket and black corduroys. **1961** *Sunday Express* 19 Nov. 1/4 Mr. Osborne, wearing a fur-lined check donkey jacket over a light-weight suit, arrived 10 minutes early for the wedding. **1944** *Truth* (Sydney) 13 Feb. 4/3 Breasley saw Kintore *donkey-lick a field of youngsters in the Federal Stakes. **1945** C. MANN in *Coast to Coast* 23 The filly would donkey lick them in the second. **1953** BAKER *Australia Speaks* iii. 81 *Donkey lick* or *cocky's delight*, treacle or golden syrup. **1878** *Daily News* 26 Sept. 2/3 We also had 3 engineers and *donkeymen. **1869** *Eng. Mech.* 10 Dec. 293/2 Of the means for feeding the boiler, those in general use are the injector, *donkey-pump, and the force pump. **1901** W. C. RUSSELL *Ship's Adv.* iii, Explaining..that the term **donkey's breakfast* signified the bundle of straw which sailors who are reckless of their money ashore carry on board ship with them as a bed. **1909** J. R. WARE *Passing Eng.* 114/2 When a gent puts a donkey's breakfast a-top of his nut. **1916** 'ANZAC' *On Anzac Trail* 7 We slept on the usual 'donkey's breakfast', of course. **1935** 'J. GUTHRIE' *Little Country* vi. 131 City men in the bowler hat and in the straw hat that was called a donkey's breakfast. **1905** *Terms Forestry & Logging* 35 **Donkey sled*, the heavy sled-like frame upon which a donkey engine is fastened. **1916** E. V. LUCAS *Vermilion Box* lxxvii. 86 Now for my first bath for what the men call '*Donkey's ears', meaning years and years. **1927** H. S. WALPOLE *Great Trad.* xvi, I was at the wedding, you know,..'aving worked for Miss Janet and her sister donkey's years. **1928** S. VINES *Humours Unreconciled* ix. 121 He hasn't talked emotionally to me for donkey's years. **1955** J. I. M. STEWART *Guardians* i. 8 It was donkey's years since he had been in an English train. **1961** *Observer* 19 Mar. 3/3 American influence and financial participation have been strong here for donkeys' years. **1920** *Nat. Rev.* Apr. 145 Most of the *donkey-work of this preposterous League has fallen on British shoulders. **1928** *Sunday Dispatch* 8 July 20/5 It would never do for a player to bat and not take his share of the donkey-work afterwards! **1940** *Manch. Guardian Weekly* 15 Mar. 213 As Parliamentary Secretary to the Ministry of Health she has had to do most of the donkey work in debate.

Hence **'donkey** *v. intr.*, to ride a donkey. **'donkeydom**, condition of a donkey, stupidity, folly. **'donkeydrome** [after *hippodrome*], a course for a donkey-race. **'donkeyess**, a female donkey. **'donkeyhood**, the condition of being a donkey; donkeys collectively. **'donkeyish** *a.*, like a donkey, asinine; stupid, foolish. **'donkeyism**, the quality of being, or an act characteristic of, a 'donkey'; folly. **'donkeyship**, the personality of a donkey. (All more or less *nonce-wds.*)

1843 LEFEVRE *Life Trav. Phys.* III. III. xiii. 271 The walks ..invite to many pedestrian excursions, and to a deal of donkeying. **1889** BARING-GOULD *Pennycomequicks* (1890) 466 [It] had startled her out of this intellectual donkeydom. **1852** M. W. SAVAGE *R. Medlicott* I. v. (D.), The two charioteers being left sprawling in the dust of the donkeydrome. **1842** *P. Parley's Ann.* III. 31 Crossing the heath..with no less than seven donkeys and donkeyesses tied in a string. **1869** *Sat. Rev.* 13 Feb. 222 The typical vanity and maladroit ways of donkeyhood. **1831** *Fraser's Mag.* III. 564 We find ourselves quite donkeyish and stupid. **1855** *Househ. Words* XII. 160 [He] committed an outrageous donkeyism. **1858** O. W. HOLMES *Aut. Breakf.-t.* xii. (1891) 293 One softens down the ugly central fact of donkeyism. **1889** *St. Nicholas Mag.* Feb. 304 His donkeyship determined that he would yet have fun.

‖**Donna** ('dɒnə, It. 'dɔnna). [It. *donna*:—L. *domina* lady, mistress.] A lady; a title of honour or courtesy for an Italian or (instead of *doña* or *dona*) a Spanish or Portuguese lady.

prima, seconda donna: the principal, or the second, female singer in an opera: see PRIMA DONNA.

1670 LASSELS *Voy. Italy* I. (1698) 67 (Stanf.) To go like the Donna's of Spain. **1740** LADY M. W. MONTAGU *Let. to W. Montagu* 25 Jan., They are all well received by the gentil donnas. **1816** BYRON in Moore *Life* (1832) III. 318 (Stanf.) My 'Donna' whom I spoke of in my former epistle. **1817** —— *Beppo* xxxii, The 'prima donna's' tuneful heart would bound. **1880** GROVE *Dict. Mus.* I. 457/1 A distinguished seconda donna..of Handel's company.

donne, obs. form of DUN.

‖**donnée** (dɔne). Also **donné**. [Fr., fem. pa. pple. of *donner* to give.] The subject, theme, or motif of a story, play, etc.; a datum; a basic fact, assumption, etc.

1876 H. JAMES in *Atlantic Monthly* XXXVIII. 693/2 A silly young girl and a heavy, overwise young man who *don't* fall in love with her! That is the *donnée* of eight monthly volumes. I call it very flat. **1878** —— *Fr. Poets & Novelists* 136 The *donnée* of 'Le Père Goriot' is typical. **1885** O. WILDE in *19th Cent.* XVII. 806 There is a mention of a bodice for Eve, but probably the *donnée* of the play was after the Fall. **1896** W. JAMES *Let.* 11 June (1920) II. 37 B.'s moral atmosphere is anyhow so foreign to me, a lewdness so obligatory that it hardly seems as if it were part of a moral donnée at all. **1920** T. S. ELIOT *Sacred Wood* v. 57 It is perhaps the craving for some such *donnée* which draws us on toward the present mirage of poetic drama. **1925** *Glasgow Herald* 29 Aug. 4 In the same tale données from classical myth are also to be encountered. **1945** AUDEN *Coll. Poetry* 127 The flushed assault of your recognition is The *donnée* of this doubtful hour. **1956** *Essays in Criticism* VI. 73 Because she accepts sensation as a *donné*, Mrs Woolf accepts the flow of linear time. **1960** J. BAYLEY *Characters of Love* iv. 213 To move right away in discussion from the text and from the actual Jamesian *donnée*. **1966** *Listener* 14 July 65/1 One can see how these raw *données* could be cooked into a film—the boy's scales and sonatinas, the dockland sirens, the café radio.

'donnered, **-ard**, *ppl. a. Sc.* Also **donnart**, **-ert**, **-ort.** [f. Sc. vb. *donner* to stupefy as with a blow or a loud noise: perh. a freq. of ME. *donen* to din: cf. also DUNNER.] Stunned, stupefied, stupid 'in a state of gross stupor' (Jam.).

1722 RAMSAY *Three Bonnets* I. 63 Worthy Bristle, not sae donner'd, Preserves this bonnet, and is honour'd. **1818** SCOTT *Hrt. Midl.* vii, A donnard auld deevil! **1886** STEVENSON *Kidnapped* xxix, 'Ye donnered auld runt.'

donnish ('dɒnɪʃ), *a.* [f. DON *sb.*[1] 4 + -ISH.] Of the nature or character of a (college) don; having a pedantic stiffness or gravity of manner.

1848 J. H. NEWMAN *Loss & Gain* 7 He liked people to be natural and hated that donnish manner. **1863** *Q. Rev.* CXIV. 546 The most donnish amongst dons.

Hence **'donnishness.**

1835 J. H. NEWMAN *Lett.* (1891) II. 139 A strong specimen of donnishness. **1853** THACKERAY *Lett.* 14 Feb., A vast amount of toryism and donnishness everywhere.

donnishly ('dɒnɪʃlɪ), *adv.* [-LY².] In a donnish manner.

a **1913** F. ROLFE *Desire & Pursuit of Whole* (1934) xvi. 163 Conversation spluttered donnishly. **1924** R. MACAULAY *Orphan Island* vii. 76 Mr. Thinkwell signed to him, donnishly, with his hand, to stop talking. **1954** *N.Y. Times Bk. Rev.* 21 Nov. 6 Pater's treatment..flirted donnishly with pagan graces.

donnism ('dɒnɪz(ə)m). [f. as DONNISH *a.* + -ISM.] Action or manner characteristic of a college don.

1859 SHAIRP in W. Knight *S. & Friends* (1888) 200 Here we have no Donnism, nor any stiff academic air.

donnot: see DO-NOUGHT.

Donnybrook, donnybrook ('dɒnɪbrʊk). [The name of *Donnybrook*, a suburb of Dublin,

Ireland, once famous for its annual fair.] A scene of uproar and disorder; a riotous or uproarious meeting; a heated argument.

1852 *Blackw. Mag.* Nov. 645/2 The Irish patriots insist on having a Donnybrook to themselves. **1887** KIPLING *Plain Tales* (1888) 69 Hindus and Mohammedans together raised an aimless sort of 'Donnybrook'. **1915** *Lit. Digest* 17 Apr. 863/2 A campaign which the New York *World* called a 'Donnybrook'. **1964** *Word Study* Feb. 1/1 The lexicographical donnybrook provoked by *Webster's Third New International Dictionary*. **1966** *Economist* 12 Feb. 600/3 Imagine the Donnybrook there would be in France or Italy.

donor ('dəʊnə(r), -ɔː(r)). Also 5–7 donour, 7–8 doner. [a. AF. *donour*, OF. *doneur*, *duneor*, mod.F. *donneur*:—L. *dōnātōr-em*, agent-n. f. *dōnāre* to present.] **1. a.** One who gives or presents; a giver; *esp.* in *Law*, one who grants an estate, or power for execution. Correlative of DONEE.

1494 FABYAN *Chron.* an. 1286 (R.) The ryghtfull inheritours, or suche as were next allied vnto the firste donoures. **1531** *Dial. on Laws Eng.* I. xxviii. (1638) 50 After the death of the tenant in taile without issue, the lands shall revert to the donor. **1650** *Vind. Hammond's Addr.* xii. §32 The Creator of the World, and sole doner of life. **1755** YOUNG *Centaur* ii. Wks. 1757 IV. 138 Enjoy, but enjoy reasonably, and thankfully to the great Donor. **1876** DIGBY *Real Prop.* v. §3(2). 228 The doctrine..that a freehold interest in possession must pass instantly from donor to donee.

b. *spec.* A blood donor (see BLOOD *sb.* 21).

1910 *Johns Hopkins Hosp. Bull.* XXI. 67/1 The serum of both donor and donee is capable of agglutinating the corpuscles of the other. **1936** *Brit. Med. Jrnl.* 28 Mar. 651/2 The patient's blood should in any case be grouped... If possible suitable donors can be chosen and warned to be in readiness. **1962** 'J. LE CARRÉ' *Murder of Quality* xviii. 178 'What was Stella's blood group, do you know?' 'Mine's B. I know that. I was a donor at Branxome. Hers was different.'

c. A person, alive or dead, from whom an organ or tissue is removed for surgical transplantation; also, an animal treated in this way.

1918 *Jrnl. Med. Res.* XXXVIII. 35 In a number of cases the second lobe of thyroid from the third guinea-pig (the second donor) was transplanted into a control guinea-pig. **1930** *Physiol. Rev.* X. 549 The experiments..were mainly carried out in guinea pigs and rats and..thyroid gland and cartilage were transplanted simultaneously from donor to host in each case. **1955** *Jrnl. Clin. Invest.* XXXIV. 331/2 In two cases the kidneys came from living donors. **1963** *Brit. Med. Jrnl.* 14 Sept. 645/2 (*heading*) Renal transplantation in man: a report of five cases, using cadaveric donors. **1971** *Daily Tel.* 26 July 3/8 Doctors should only be allowed to remove an organ if the donor has given his consent in writing or if the nearest relative that it is practicable to contact, has given consent.

d. In artificial insemination: one from whom the semen is taken. Also *attrib.*

1947 [see *artificial insemination* s.v. ARTIFICIAL *a.* 5]. **1950** *Ann. Reg. 1949* 30 The Church could not condemn [artificial insemination] if the husband were the donor. **1958** *New Statesman* 18 Jan. 58/3 (*heading*) Donor Babies. *Ibid.* 25 Jan. 98/1 To afford a new legally regulated status to A.I.D. would..establish the donors as a socially approved class of persons.

2. *Chem.* and *Physics.* An atom, molecule, etc., that loses a constituent part to something else; *esp.* (*a*) an atom, etc., that gives up a valency electron pair to another atom, so forming a co-ordinate bond with it; (*b*) in a semiconductor, an impurity atom which has a higher valency than the majority of the atoms and can give up a valency electron to the conduction band of the crystal; *donor bond*, a chemical bond which can be regarded as having had some of its strength transferred to another atom.

1927, etc. [see ACCEPTOR 3]. **1946** *Trans. Faraday Soc.* XLII. 100 Here we have to consider both the electron work function of the donor and the electron affinity of the acceptor. **1952** C. A. COULSON *Valence* ix. 252 This shows that the central C-C bond is an acceptor, acquiring bond order at the expense of the two end donor bonds. **1964** GUIRARD & SNELL in Florkin & Stotz *Comprehensive Biochem.* XV. v. 173 At the stage of purity studied, the transaminase has a rather broad specificity for both amino group donors and acceptors. **1966** *Chem. in Brit.* II. 164/2 For triplet energy transfer from donor to acceptor to occur, the donor triplet must lie close to, or above that of, the acceptor. **1971** *Sci. Amer.* July 34/2 If there are more acceptors than donors, current is carried by holes (positively charged) and the material is designated a *p*-type semiconductor.

3. *attrib.*, as **donor card** orig. *U.S.*, an official card that can be carried by a person and states his or her blood group; a similar card authorizing the use of specified organs for transplant surgery in the event of the card-holder's death; **donor country** (see quot. 1959). (See also senses 1 c and d above.)

1964 *Bibliotheca Haematologica* XIX. 659 (*caption*) Rare type *donor card. **1970** *Jrnl. Amer. Pharm. Assoc.* X. 255/1 A boon to the transplantation of kidneys is now a reality. A uniform donor card now is available whereby anyone may leave all tissues and organs..to medical science upon death. *Ibid.* 256/1 Donor cards have been used by eyebanks and tissue banks..for a number of years. **1972** *Times* 15 Nov. 2/8 (*heading*) Kidney donor cards display. **1975** *U.S. News & World Rep.* 8 Sept. 66 Two organizations run nationwide programs to handle the donation of organs. Donor cards and information can be obtained from: the National Kidney Foundation, [etc.]. **1980** *Times* 29 Feb. 2 If a person carries a donor card, saying he wishes his organs to be used in the event of his death, that should overrule any objections by the coroner unless there is a reason..why the organ should not be used. **1959** *Britannica Bk. of Year* 546/1 Another political coinage [in 1958] was *donor country, a country giving financial or material aid to an underdeveloped nation. **1961** *Ann. Reg. 1960* 471 At least one donor country was realizing that aid could easily go down the drain.

do-nothing ('duːˌnʌθɪŋ), *sb.* and *a.*

A. *sb.* One who does nothing; an idler.

1579 TOMSON *Calvin's Serm. Tim.* 259/1 It is not for a do nothing that this office is ordeined. **1624** MASSINGER *Renegado* IV. i, Such a goodman Do-nothing. **1855** FARADAY in Bence Jones *Life* (1870) II. 361, I cannot imagine you a do-nothing. **1887** *Spectator* 15 Oct. 1378 A class of do-nothings who at some previous time had owned the land.

B. *adj.* That does nothing; characterized by doing nothing; idle, indolent.

1832 W. IRVING *Alhambra* II. 84 The invalids, old women, and other curious do-nothing folk. **1839** CARLYLE *Chartism* ix. 169 A do-nothing guidance; and it is a do-something World! **1876** GEO. ELIOT *Dan. Der.* IV. liv. 99 He was..very fond of yachting: its dreamy, do-nothing absolutism.

Hence **do'nothingism**, **do'nothingness**, the habit or practice of doing nothing; the condition of doing nothing; idleness; indolence.

1814 JANE AUSTEN *Mansf. Park* (1870) III. viii. 340 A situation of similar affluence and do-nothing-ness. **1839** CARLYLE *Chartism* vii. 152 Self-cancelling Donothingism. **1879** MRS. HOUSTON *Wild West* 77 Gaunt, enfeebled-looking labourers abused for their idleness, their do-nothingness. **1891** *Sat. Rev.* 5 Sept. 267/2 Dangerous apathy and donothingism.

do-nought ('duːnɔːt), **donnot** ('dɒnət). Now chiefly *dial.* [app. f. the words *do nought*: though sometimes taken as a corruption of an earlier *dow not*: cf. Ger. *taugenichts*.] One who does nothing or no good; an idler (= DO-NOTHING); a good-for-nothing.

1594 CAREW *Huarte's Exam. Wits* (1616) 12 Through griefe of seeing his sonne such a doo-nought. *Ibid.* 218 The buzzards, the sots, and the doe noughts. **1674** RAY *N.C. Words* 14 A Donnaught or Donnat..Naught, good for nothing: idle persons being commonly such. **1818** SCOTT *Hrt. Midl.* xxxii, What's brought thee back again, thou silly donnot? **1855** ROBINSON *Whitby Gloss.*, *Donnot* or *Donaught*, a good-for-nothing person..the popular designation with reference to Satan himself. **1870** MORRIS *Earthly Par.* II. III. 38 A do-nought by the fire-side.

donship ('dɒnʃɪp). [f. DON *sb.*[1] + -SHIP.] **a.** The personality of a don: used as a title. **b.** The possession of the title 'don' (quot. 1838).

c **1626** *Dick of Devon* II. iv. in Bullen *O. Pl.* II. 40 What is your Donship calld, I pray. Don John, a Knight of Spaine. **1648** GAGE *West Ind.* xv. (1655) 100 Began to answer, or more to jeer his Donship. **1772** NUGENT tr. *Hist. Friar Gerund* II. 160 For a *Monsieur* would he have changed all the Donships in the world. **1838** *Fraser's Mag.* XVIII. 231 Entitled to donship in the Basque provinces.

donsie, donsy ('dɒnsɪ), *a.* and *sb.* Chiefly *Sc.* and north *dial.* Also doncy, -cie. [Origin and primary sense unknown.] **A.** *adj.*

1. 'Affectedly neat and trim' (Jam.); nice; hence saucy, restive (as a horse). ? *Obs.*

1717 RAMSAY *Elegy Lucky Wood* iv, She was a donsie wife and clean. **1721** KELLY *Scot. Prov.* 68 (Jam.) Better rough and sonsie, than bare and donsie. **1786** BURNS *To Auld Mare* v, Tho' ye was trickie, slee, an' funnie, Ye ne'er was donsie. **1789** D. DAVIDSON *Seasons* 56 (Jam.) Come Muse! thou donsy limmer, who dost laugh, An' claw thy hough, at bungling poets. **1892** in *Northumbld. Gloss.*

2. Unlucky, untoward, unfortunate. Also, poor, dreary, low-spirited; sickly, feeble (cf. DAUNCY *a.*). *Sc.*, *north.*, and *U.S. dial.*

1720 A. RAMSAY *Familiar Epistles* 10 Has thou with Rosycrucians wandert? Or thro' some doncie Desart danert? **1786** BURNS *Address to Unco Guid* ii, Their donsie tricks, their black mistakes, Their failings and mischances. **1789** D. DAVIDSON *Seasons* 61 (Jam.) Straight down the steep they slide wi' canny care, For fear o' donsy whirl into the stream. **1805** *Lancaster* (Pa.) *Jrnl.* 2 Oct. (Th.), Citizen Lafferty must have a 'doncy' opinion of the cause, when he is afraid to bet even. **1835** J. D. CARRICK *Laird of Logan* 273 Sic an unco wastrie in the way of claiths..made me a thocht donsy. **1853** *Yale Lit. Mag.* XVII. 223 (Th.), [She brought some letters] to my room, to keep me from feeling 'donsy'. **1880** [see DAUNCY *a.*]. **1917** J. L. WAUGH *Cute McCheyne* 108 My faither was sawney an' donsie.

3. Dull or slow of comprehension; dunce-like.

1802 SIBBALD *Chron. Sc. Poetry* Gloss., *Donsie*, dunce-like, dull, stupid. **1822** GALT *Sir A. Wylie* III. xxviii. 237 Dinna heed the donsie creature.

B. *sb.* One slow of wit, a stupid; a dunce.

1825 JAMIESON, *Donsie*, *Doncie*, a stupid, lubberly fellow. *Roxb.* *c* **1826** HOGG in Wilson *Noct. Ambr.* Wks. 1855 I. 213 That poor donsy.

don't (dəʊnt), colloq. contraction of *do not* (see DO *v.* 29 and 29 b); also (now vulgar) contraction of *does not* (see DO *v.* A. 2 c. γ). Hence as *sb.* (usu. *pl.*), a prohibition; the reiteration of 'don't'. Also (*rare*) as *v. intr.*

1670, etc. [see DO *v.* A. 2 c. γ, 30 d]. **1738** [see DO *v.* 28]. **1741**, **1831** [see DO *v.* A. 2 c. γ]. **1874** HARDY *Far from Madding Crowd* vi. 76 'Whose shepherd is he?' said the equestrian...'Don't know, ma'am.' 'Don't any of the others know?' **1894** *Daily News* 23 Nov. 5/3 The plan gets rid of many 'don'ts'. *a* **1897** *Mod.* 'Don't be always don'ting!' **1902**, etc. [see DO *sb.*[1] 4]. **1919** H. L. MENCKEN *Amer. Lang.* vi. 210 *Don't* has also completely displaced *doesn't*, which is very seldom heard. 'He *don't*' and 'they *don't*' are practically universal. **1929** D. H. LAWRENCE *Pansies* 48 (*poem-title*) Dont's. **1944** *Living off Land* vi. 125 In looking after a snake bite patient.., remember the three 'dont's'.

b. don't-care, used as *adj.*, = careless, reckless. *sb.*, one who does not care (see CARE *v.* 4 a); a careless, unconcerned, or indifferent person; so **don't-care-a-damnativeness** (or **-itiveness**) (*slang*), carelessness, unconcern; So **don't-care-ism** (*nonce-wd.*); **don't-carish** *a.*; **don't-carishness**.

1841 F. A. KEMBLE *Let.* 11 Oct. in *Rec. Later Life* (1882) II. 134, I am grown old and stupid and sleepy and don't-carish. **1841** THACKERAY in K. Meadows *Heads of People* II. 169 That reckless do n't-care-a-damnativeness which leads a man to disregard all the world. **1841** *Daily Picayune* (New Orleans) 24 Feb. 2/3 He..had..all the nonchalance and dont-care-a-dam-itiveness of De Bar. **1864** *Daily Tel.* 29 Sept., There must be a deeper and more philosophic reason for this don't-carishness. **1871** *Daily News* 4 Jan., We are in the don't care mood. **1892** *Pall Mall G.* 15 Dec. 7/1 The..spirit of daring don't-careism. **1895** *Westm. Gaz.* 5 Sept. 2/1 A hearty, good-natured, don't-care sort of person. **1905** *Daily Chron.* 10 Aug. 3/7 If she is at all weak she soon becomes a 'don't care', and a street-door gossip. **1924** W. J. LOCKE *Coming of Amos* ii. 16 No nose on earth could so express the don't-care-a-damnativeness of disdain. **1955** AUDEN *Shield of Achilles* i. 29 Bloodshot images of rivers screaming, Marbles in panic, and Don't-Care made to care.

c. don't know, a person who does not know (something) or who has not reached a decision or opinion on a particular subject, esp. in answering a questionnaire or the like; hence (*nonce-wd.*) **don't knowist** (see quot. 1908).

1888 *Pall Mall Gaz.* 18 Jan. 11/2 The gospel according to 'Don't-know' is at present unfit to supersede the Synoptics. **1908** G. B. SHAW *Sanity of Art* 57 'Positivists' or 'Dont Knowists' (Agnostics). **1940** HARRISSON & MADGE *War begins at Home* xiv. 381 Their figures differ from ours in showing a lower number of Don't knows. **1959** *News Chron.* 28 Sept. 6/1 There has now been enough old-fashioned give-and-take to make the Don't Knows start thinking. *Ibid.* 6/5 The Don't Knows, the drugged, and the mindless. **1970** *Amateur Photogr.* 11 Mar. 29/1 All the questions are completely answered; there are none of those curious 'don't knows' that usually round off the totals.

dontcha, dontcher, varr. DONCHER.

donut: see DOUGHNUT.

donzel ('dɒnzəl). *arch.* Also 6–7 donsel. [ad. It. *donzello* 'a damosell, a batchelor; also a page, a squire, a waiter, a serving man' (Florio) = Pr. *donzel*, Sp. *doncel*, OF. *donzel*, *doncel*, *dancel* young man:—late L. *dom(i)nicell-us*, dim. of *dominus* lord, master: cf. DAMOISEAU.] A young gentleman not yet knighted, a squire, a page.

1592 NASHE *P. Penilesse* (ed. 2) 7 b, The high and mightie Prince of Darknesse, Donsell del Lucifer. **1610** B. JONSON *Alch.* IV. iv, Donzel, methinks you look melancholic. **1664** BUTLER *Hud.* II. iii. 572 Much may be done, my noble Donzel. *a* **1680** —— *Charact.*, *Squire of Dames*, He is Esquire to a Knight-Errant, donzel to the damsels. **1843** LYTTON *Last Bar.* I. ii, Cling to me, gentle donzel, and fear not.

‖**donzella** (dont'sɛlla). [It.; fem. of *donzello* (see prec.):—late L. *dominicella*, dim. of *domina* mistress, lady: see DAMSEL.] An Italian or Provençal damsel or young lady.

1833 CARLYLE *Misc.* (1872) V. 88 A beautiful Roman donzella. **1848** MRS. JAMESON *Sacr. & Leg. Art* (1850) 196 They bring the donzella out of the cistern alive and well.

doo, obs. form of DO, DOE; Sc. form of DOVE.

dooab, dooar: see DOAB, DOUAR.

‖**doob** (duːb). Also doub, erron. dhoop. [Hindī *dūb*, = Skr. *dūrvā*.] Native name for the dog's-tooth grass (*Cynodon Dactylon*), used as a fodder-grass in India.

1810 T. WILLIAMSON *E. India Vade M.* I. 259 (Y.) The doob..in the low countries about Dacca..this grass abounds; attaining to a prodigious luxuriance! **1835** BURNES *Trav. Bokhara* (ed. 2) II. 10 A kind of creeping grass called 'doob'. **1845** STOCQUELER *Handbk. Brit. India* (1854) 405 A thickly-matted sod of fiorin, or doob grass.

doodad ('duːdæd). Chiefly *U.S.* [Origin unknown; ? cf. DAD *sb.*[2] 2.] A 'fancy' article (of dress), a 'thingummy'; esp. a trivial or superfluous ornament.

1905, **1912** in H. WENTWORTH *Amer. Dial. Dict.* (1944) 173/2 **1920** S. LEWIS *Main Street* xxiv. 298 Have a nice square house, and pay more attention to getting a crackajack furnace than all this architecture and doodads. **1928** *Daily Express* 24 July 8/4 Men detest flounces...'More fakements and doodads! Why on earth cannot the woman keep things simple?' **1934** J. O'HARA *Appointment in Samarra* (1935) ii. 40 Decorated with Santa Claus and holly doo-dads. **1961** *Guardian* 29 Mar. 9/7 Houses with a drop of the old half timbering and the old Georgian doodads. **1966** D. ENEFER *Painted Death* viii. 76 An open lacquered box with hair clips and other doodads.

doodah ('du:dɑ:). *slang*. Also **do-da, dooda.** [From the refrain *doo-da(h)* of the plantation song 'Camptown Races'.]

1. Phr. *all of a doodah*: in a state of excitement; dithering.

1915 H. ROSHER *In R.N.A.S.* (1916) 97, I had lunch with the R—s and five daughters (swish, I was all of a doo-da!). **1918** *Chambers's Jrnl.* May 299/1, I feel all of a doo-dah, all of a wonk. **1928** S. VINES *Humours Unreconciled* xiii. 165 It was the evenings, clearly, that made her 'all of a religious doodah'. **1929** J. B. PRIESTLEY *Good Comp.* II. iii. 307, I don't care if a man's been fifty years in the business, there's the same old thrill comes back. Opening night —all of a doodah! **1952** WODEHOUSE *Pigs have Wings* i. 28 Poor old Clarence was patently all of a doodah.

2. = DOODAD.

1928 D. L. SAYERS *Unpleasantness at Bellona Club* v. 45 D'you mind stickin' all those dark-slides into one pocket and a few odd lenses and doodahs into the other? *a* **1935** T. E. LAWRENCE *Mint* (1950) III. i. 166 The old lady next me in the underground wore a flippant skirt, all doo-dahs. **1945** *Salt* 26 Feb. 16/1 A bit of a kid done up, in trousers with do-da's danging on 'em. **1957** H. CROOME *Forgotten Place* 68 They make little plastic doodahs to use in electrical machinery.

doodgean, obs. form of DUDGEON.

doodheen: see DUDEEN.

doodle ('du:d(ə)l), *sb. colloq.* [cf. LG. *dudeltopf, -dop*, simpleton, noodle, lit. night-cap.] **1.** A silly or foolish fellow; a noodle.

1628 FORD *Lover's Mel.* III. i, Vanish, doodles, vanish! **1764** FOOTE *Mayor of G.* II. i, Why, doodle, jackanapes harkee, who am I? **1845** COBDEN *Speeches* (1872) 179 The Noodles and Doodles of the aristocracy.

2. A doodle-bug. *U.S.*

1887 *Harper's Mag.* July 276/1 She wondered how the nice, fat little round 'doodles' were getting on in their tin can under the house; she never had had such a fine box of bait. **1939** *These are our Lives* (U.S.) 157 They not knowing any more than a doodle in the woods what she was saying.

3. doodle-bug a. *U.S.*, a tiger-beetle, or the larva of this or various other insects.

c **1866** G. W. BAGBY *Old Virginia Gentleman* (1910) 48 Try to tame a catbird, call doodle-bugs out of their holes. **1876** 'MARK TWAIN' *Tom Sawyer* viii. 76 Doodle-bug, doodle-bug, tell me what I want to know! **1903** S. E. WHITE *Forest* vii. 81, I never hesitate to offer them [*sc.* trout] any kind of a doodle-bug they may fancy. **1944** *Democrat* 7 Dec. 2/2 Doodlebugs are those little insects which fan out or blow out little conical shaped holes in sandy or dusty places.

fig. **1908** C. E. MULFORD *Orphan* 163 You blamed doodle bug, yu! **1918** —— *Man fr. Bar-20* xviii. 193 'Yo're a fine pair of doodle-bugs'... 'Don't you know an opportunity when you see one?' **1938** 'E. QUEEN' *Four of Hearts* (1939) I. iii. 34 She'll tell you more about these doodlebugs than they know themselves.

b. As a nickname also applied to the German pilotless plane or flying bomb of the war of 1939–45; ellipt. *doodle.*

1944 *Times* 22 June 2/1 The first fighter pilot to shoot down what the R.A.F. men call a 'doodlebug' was Flight Sergeant Maurice Rose, of Glasgow. **1944** *Aeronautics* Aug. 27/1 The most elaborate German automatic weapon, the flying bomb,..doodle-bug, or power-bomb. **1944** *N. & Q.* 9 Sept. 122/1 *The doodle-bug.*— The new weapon with which our enemy has attacked us has borne a number of names since its appearance over Southern England on 13 June... The public in London has now generally accepted doodle bug, doodle bomb or simply doodle. **1969** T. PARKER *Twisting Lane* 79, I left school in 1944, just after the doodle-bugs finished.

4. An aimless scrawl made by a person while his mind is more or less otherwise applied.

1937 R. M. ARUNDEL *Everybody's Pixillated* p. ix, A 'doodle' is a scribbling or sketch made while the conscious mind is concerned with matters wholely unrelated to the scribbling. **1938** *Life* 14 Nov. 7/2 It's a doodle picture. I've seen it dozens of times on telephone pads and what not. **1942** *Punch* 25 Feb. 158/1 Mr. Clement Attlee, the Premier's deputy, industriously drew doodles of intricate pattern. **1947** AUDEN *Age of Anxiety* (1948) i. 25 On memories stuffed With dead men's doodles. **1959** H. GARDNER *Business of Criticism* II. ii. 120 When a writer's first drafts, scraps of memoranda, and 'doodles' have been preserved, we may possibly have a limited success in tracing the workings of the creative imagination. **1961** *Times* 23 Nov. 15/2 Mr. Gwyn Thomas lets a witty pen run doodlingly on. **1970** H. BRAUN *Parish Churches* xviii. 219 Geometrical 'doodles' made with a mason's compasses are medieval.

'doodle, *v.*[1] [f. prec. sb.]

1. *trans.* To make a fool of, befool, cheat. *dial.* or *slang.*

1823 MONCRIEFF *Tom & Jerry* I. vii. (Farmer), I have been dished and doodled out of forty pounds to-day. **1834** M. SCOTT *Cruise Midge* (1859) 439 It might have doodled our whole party. **1880** *W. Cornw. Gloss.*, *Doodle*, to cheat; to deceive; to trifle.

2. *intr.* To make a doodle (sense 4); to draw or scrawl aimlessly. Also *fig.* (partly by assoc. with DAWDLE *v.*), to idle. *Colloq.*

1937 *Lit. Digest* 26 June 19/3 'But everbody doodles.' So Gary Cooper, as Longfellow Deeds, in 'Mr. Deeds Goes to Town', defended himself. He wasn't crazy because he drew squares and circles on scraps of paper —he was just 'doodling'. **1948** 'J. TEY' *Franchise Affair* xviii. 217 Robert sat doodling on..blotting-paper. A herring-bone pattern. **1955** H. SPRING *These Lovers fled Away* iv. 128 When we had changed from a main line train and were doodling across country. **1967** *New Scientist* 12 Oct. 102/1 At boring committee meetings, in common with others who doodle, I can escape with relief into the insulated world of mathematical abstraction.

Hence **'doodling** *vbl. sb.* and *ppl. a.*; **'doodlingly** *adv.*; also **'doodler** *sb.*, one who doodles.

1846 *Cornish Prov. Dial.* 55 'None of thy doodling, thee bean't St. George, no more than me.' **1937** *Manch. Guardian* 5 May 8/4 Doodling is fidgeting about pictorially with a pen or pencil at odd moments to pass the time... In Australia..[caterers] have provided special menu cards with plenty of space on them in the hope of luring doodlers into doodling on these instead of on the tablecloth. **1944** *Times* 17 Mar. 5/4 It is nevertheless a thrill to the humble 'doodling' addict to discover that Marshal Stalin himself is of the brotherhood. **1951** E. MITTELHOLZER *Shadows move among Them* III. viii. 326 He left it a doodled smear on the Penguin. **1953** C. DAY LEWIS *Italian Visit* iii. 39 Lightning sketches, Symbolic doodlings, hour by hour set down Haphazardly. **1960** *20th Cent.* Mar. 233 Poetry is not the free unfettered self-expression of the doodler.

doodle ('du:d(ə)l), *v.*[2] Chiefly *Sc.* Also **doudle.** [a. Ger. *dudeln* in same sense (of Slavonic origin: cf. Polish *dudliö*), *dudelsack* bagpipe: prob. associated with TOOTLE.] *trans.* To play (the bagpipes). Also **doodle-sack**, a bagpipe.

1816 SCOTT *Old Mort.* iv, 'I am wearied wi' doudling the bag o' wind a' day.' **1824** —— *Redgauntlet* Let. xi, 'Thou sack-doudling son of a whore!' **1846** WORCESTER cites SIR G. HEAD for *Doodle-sack.* **1847–78** HALLIW., *Doodle-sack*, a bag-pipe. *Kent.*

doodle-bug: see DOODLE *sb.* 3.

doodle-doo. Playful shortening of COCK-A-DOODLE-DOO.

1785 GROSE *Dict. Vulg. Tongue* (s.v. *Doodle*), *Doodle doo*, or cock a doodle doo, childish appellation for a cock, from its note when crowing. **1904** BARRIE *Peter Pan* (1928) v. 133 *Hook* (*slowly*). Cecco, go back and fetch me out that doodle-doo. **1907** D. O'CONNOR *Peter Pan Picture Bk.* 53 He was silenced by a shrill and piercing cock's-crow from the cabin. 'Someone must bring me out that doodledoo,' roared the Captain.

doofer ('du:fə(r)). *slang.* Also **doofah, doovah, doover.** [Prob. alteration of *do for* in such phrases as *that will do for now.*] = THINGUMMY (see also quots.).

1937 PARTRIDGE *Dict. Slang* 234/2 *Doofer*, half a cigarette: workmen's [slang]. **1941** BAKER *Dict. Austral. Slang* 25 *Doover*, any object, thingummy. **1945** —— *Austral. Lang.* viii. 153 Other words of particular note [in the 1939–45 war] were..*doover, doovah*, or *doovah-dah* used as a general utility term for a thingumebob, specifically applied to any shelter, especially a humpy, and to a hospital bottle for urination, whence, *doover-joey*, a male hospital nurse. **1945** *Salt* 2 July 43/2 Idly I lean against the parapet of our doover. **1945** C. H. WARD-JACKSON *Piece of Cake* (ed. 2) 24 *Doings*, used in place of any noun that cannot be recalled on the spur of the moment... Variants are 'Doofer' and 'Dooshanks'. **1969** 'S. TROY' *Swift to its Close* vii. 110 Mr. Turvey returns 'ome. Comes again to the Hangar in time for the doofah. **1970** P. DICKINSON *Seals* iv. 95 This is a very fancy doofer indeed... It transmits along one wavelength and receives along another.

doohickey ('du:hɪkɪ). *colloq.* (orig. and chiefly *U.S.*). Also **dohickey, doohicky.** [f. DOO(DAD + HICKEY.] Any small object, esp. mechanical; a 'thingummy' (see also quot. 1928).

1914 *Our Navy* (U.S.) Nov. 12 We were compelled to christen articles beyond our ken with such names as 'do-hickeys', 'gadgets' and 'gilguys'. **1925** FRASER & GIBBONS *Soldier & Sailor Words* 81 *Doo hicky*, an airman's term for any small, detachable fitting. **1928** *Sunday Dispatch* 30 Sept. 10/2 He offered to run me down in the old doohicky—his latest, though second-hand car. **1949** R. CHANDLER *Little Sister* vii. 45 A pencil..broke its point on the glass doohickey under one of the desk legs. **1967** A. LURIE *Imaginary Friends* iv. 44 Just unhitch that dohickey there with a wrench.

dook[1] (du:k). [Etym. unknown.] A wooden plug driven into a brick or stone wall, in order to hold a nail.

1808–18 in JAMIESON. In mod. Dicts.

dook[2]. *Sc.* The shaft of a coal mine.

1887 *Scott. Leader* 4 June 7 He was chainman in the main coal dook. **1895** *N. Brit. Daily Mail* 7 Aug. 4 The bodies of the unfortunate men may be found at the bottom of the dook, which is now full of water.

dook, obs. and Sc. form of DUCK *v.*

dool[1] (du:l), **dole** (dəʊl). Also 6 **dowe**, 7–8 **dowl(e**, 6– *Sc.* **dule.** [Corresponds to E.Fris. *dôle, dôl*, landmark, boundary-mark; a stake, stone, hole in the ground, furrow, ditch, etc., used to mark and determine the boundaries of property. Cf. also Du. *doel* aim, mark, butt, in Flemish and earlier mod.Du. (Kilian) a heap of earth, esp. that on which the mark stands at a shooting-place, which is app. related to MLG., LG. *dôle* fem., grave with the mound of earth heaped over it.]

1. A boundary or landmark, consisting of a post, a stone, or an unploughed balk or strip of land.

c **1440** *Promp. Parv.* 126/1 Dole, merke, *meta.* **1445** *Paston Lett.* No. 46 I. 58 He hath pullid uppe the doolis, and seithe he wolle makyn a dyche fro the corner of his walle.. to the newe diche of the grete cloose. **1563** *Homilies* II. *Rogation Week* (1859) 496 Accursed be he..who removeth his neighbours doles and marks. **1580** in Picton *L'pool Munic. Rec.* (1883) I. 54 The dowe stone or meire stone, which was placed and set by the Jury. **1681** WORLIDGE *Dict. Rust.*, *Dool*, a green balk or mound between the ploughed lands in common fields. *a* **1825** FORBY *Voc. E. Anglia*, *Dool, Dole*, a boundary mark in an uninclosed field. It is very often a low post; thence called a Dool-post. **1875** *Sussex Gloss.*, *Doole*, a conical lump of earth, about three feet in diameter ..and about two feet in height, raised to show the bounds of parishes or farms on the Downs.

2. *Sc.* (dyl). The goal in a game.

a **1550** *Christis Kirke Gr.* xxii, Fresch men cam in and hail'd the dulis, And dang tham doun in dailis. **1721** RAMSAY *Lucky Spence* vii, Gar the kirk-boxie hale the dools. **1783** TYTLER *Poet. Rem. Jas. I*, 187 (Jam.) When the [foot]ball touches the goal or mark, the winner calls out, Hail! or it has hail'd the dulis. **1802** SIBBALD *Chron. Scot. Poet.* II. 370 *note* (Jam.) In the game of golf..when the ball reached the mark, the winner, to announce his victory, called, Hail dule!

3. *attrib.*, as *dool-post, -stone.*

1580 *Dole-stone* [see above]. **1630** *MS. Acc. St. John's Hosp., Canterb.*, Layd out for seauen dowlstones xviijd. *a* **1825** *Dole-post* [see above]. **1887** *Kent. Gloss.*, *Dole-stone*, a landmark.

Hence **dool** *v. trans.*, to mark off by dools.

1656 in *MS. Conveyance*, As it is now dowled, and allready sett out.

dool[2], variant of DOLE *sb.*[2], grief, mourning.

dool(e, obs. form of DOLE *sb.*[1], *v.*[2]

doolally ('du:lælɪ), *a. slang* (orig. *Services*'). [Spoken form of *Deolali* (Marashtra, India) + TAP *sb.*[4]] In full *doolally tap.* Characterized by an unbalanced state of mind.

1925 FRASER & GIBBONS *Soldier & Sailor Words* 75 *Deolali tap* (otherwise *doolally tap*), mad, off one's head. Old Army. **1936** J. CURTIS *Gilt Kid* vii. 76 What's the matter with that bloke? Doolally? *Ibid.* xviii. 181 'What's up with you for Christ's sake, kid? Come doolally tap?' Scaley was getting worried... His pal seemed to have gone mad. **1936** F. RICHARDS *Old-Soldier Sahib* iv. 74 Time-expired men sent to Deolalie from their different units might have to wait for months before a troop-ship fetched them home... The well-known saying among soldiers when speaking of a man who does queer things, 'Oh, he's got the Doo-lally tap,' originated, I think, in the peculiar way men behaved owing to the boredom of that camp. **1943** HUNT & PRINGLE *Service Slang* 28 *Doolally*, very drunk or temporarily insane, without distinction.

Doolan, doolan ('du:lən). *N.Z. slang.* [Prob. f. the Irish surname *Doolan.*] A Roman Catholic; an Irish Catholic.

1940 F. SARGESON *Man & Wife* (1944) 19 It sounded pretty awful to me, that sort of praying. Because I'm a Doolan myself, and Mrs Bowman [who was doing the praying] was always down on the churches. **1947** D. M. DAVIN *Gorse blooms Pale* 186 She'll have me a doolan yet, Father. **1963** B. PEARSON *Coal Flat* iv. 63 They had called him 'the Doolan bugger'—*Doolan* on their tongues meant an Irish Catholic.

‖**doolie, dooly** ('du:lɪ). Forms: 7 **dowle, doola**, 8–9 **dooly, -ley**, 9 **doolee, dúlí**, erron. **dhooly.** [a. Hindī *ḍōlī* a litter, a kind of sedan for women, etc., dim. of *ḍōlā* swing, cradle, litter, f. Skr. *dōlā* litter, swinging cradle, f. *dul-* to swing.] A rudimentary litter or palanquin used by the lower classes in India, and as an army ambulance.

c **1625** HAWKINS in Purchas *Pilgrims* I. 435 (Y.) He sends choice Souldiers..close couered, two and two in a Dowle. **1665** SIR T. HERBERT *Trav.* (1677) 66 The Doolaes were no sooner dismounted, but that thereout issued the Amazones. **1782–3** W. F. MARTYN *Geog. Mag.* I. 264 Doolies..are only used by the very lower sorts of people, in cases of sickness or accident. **1804** A. DUNCAN *Mariner's Chron.* III. 114, I could not walk..So they put us into dooleys, or cradles, fastened together with ropes. **1869** E. A. PARKES *Pract. Hygiene* (ed. 3) 399 Order men who cannot march to be carried in waggons, dhoolies, &c.

2. *attrib.*, as *doolie-bearer.*

1862 BEVERIDGE *Hist. India* III. IX. v. 655 The dhoolie-bearers followed the example. **1883** F. M. CRAWFORD *Mr. Isaacs* xii. 253 A strong body of dooly-bearers.

dool-owl. *dial.* [f. *dool* (DOLE *sb.*[2]) + OWL *sb.*] An owl (as a symbol of gloom); in quots. *transf.*, a dull, depressing person.

1928 D. H. LAWRENCE *Lady Chatterley* (1930) xi. 196 When I look at women who's never really been warmed through by a man, well, they seem to me poor dool-owls after all. **1929** —— *Pansies* 144 The upper classes... Such bloomin' fat-arsed dool-owls.

dooly, obs. form of DOLY.

doom (du:m), *sb.* Forms: 1 **dóm**, 2–5 **dom**, 3–7 **dome**, 4–7 **doome**, (4 **dum**, *Sc.* **dowme**, 5 *Sc.* **doym**, 7 **dombe**), 4– **doom.** [Com. Teut. sb.: OE. *dóm*—OFris., OS. *dóm*, OHG., MHG. *tuom*, ON. *dómr* (Sw., Da. *dom*), Goth. *dom-s* ~:—O.Teut. **dômo-z*, lit. that which is put or set up, statute, ordinance, f. *dô-n* to place, set: see DO *v.* (Cf. Gr. θέμις, f. stem θη- to place, L. *statūtum*, f. *statuĕre.*) Used as suffix in the form -DOM.]

1. A statute, law, enactment; *gen.* an ordinance, decree. *Obs.* exc. *Hist.*

c **825** *Vesp. Psalter* ix. 26 Bioð afirred domas ðine from onsiene his. *c* **1000** ÆLFRIC *Exod.* xxi. 1 Þis synd þa domas þe þu him tæcan scealt. *a* **1340** HAMPOLE *Psalter* xiii. 1 Þai þat haf forgeten God and his domes. **1513** DOUGLAS *Æneis*

I. viii. 24 The domes of law pronuncis sche to thame then. **1669** DRYDEN *Tyrannic Love* I. i, I have consulted one, who reads Heav'n's Doom. **1844** LINGARD *Anglo-Sax. Ch.* (1858) II. xii. 220 He revised the whole code of Anglo-Saxon law, and compiled a new book of dooms. **1874** GREEN *Short Hist.* iv. §4. 191 The first Dooms of London provide especially for the recovery of cattle.

2. A judgement or decision, esp. one formally pronounced; a sentence; mostly in adverse sense, condemnation, sentence of punishment.

c **900** tr. *Bæda's Hist.* IV. v. (1891) 278 Seon heo beʒen biscopes dome scyldiʒe. *c* **1175** *Lamb. Hom.* 103 Ufele ȝitsunge..macað reaflac and unrihte domes. *c* **1205** LAY. 4271 He sculde dom þolien. **1377** LANGL. *P. Pl.* B. xv. 27 Whan ich deme domes. þen is racio my riȝt name. **1467** *Nottingham Rec.* II. 380 To obey, fulfille and perfourme the dome, ordenance and award of vs. **1596** SPENSER *F.Q.* IV. v. 16 Then was that golden belt by doome of all Granted to her. **1641** SMECTYMNUUS *Answ.* (1653) Post. 87 Thurstan refusing to stand to the Kings doom. **1709** *Tatler* No. 42 ¶5 O! Partial Judge, Thy Doom has me undone. **1808** SCOTT *Marm.* III. Introd., Whose doom discording neighbours sought. **1888** MAX MÜLLER *Nat. Relig.* vii. (1889) 173 They were not laws in our sense of the word but dooms, decisions.

†**3.** Personal or private judgement, opinion. ***as to my doom***: in my opinion. *Obs.*

a **1300** *Cursor M.* 4582 (Cott.) O þis ioseph sai me þi dome, And giue me þar-of god consail. *c* **1386** CHAUCER *Monk's T.* Prol. 49 As to my doom Thou art a maister whan thou art at hoom. *c* **1440** CAPGRAVE *Life St. Kath.* I. 314 Ye may weel suppose in yovre owen dome. *c* **1450** *Merlin* 387 Yef he and the other ne hadde not returned..by my dom, ther hadde not ascaped the halvendell. **1596** SPENSER *F.Q.* IV. x. 21 The which did seeme, unto my simple doome, The onely pleasant and delightfull place. **1624** WOTTON *Archit.* in *Reliq.* (1672) 67 The Age of the work upon which he must pass his Doom.

†**b.** The faculty of judging; judgement, discrimination, discernment. *Obs.*

c **1374** CHAUCER *Boeth.* V. pr. ii. 152 It haþ doom by whiche it discerniþ and demiþ euery þing. **1496** *Dives & Paup.* (W. de W.) II. vi. 115/1 He must haue with hym dome, that is a good and a dyscrete auysement, er he swere. **1697** DRYDEN *Virg. Georg.* IV. 565 With..unerring Doom, He sees what is, and was, and is to come.

4. Fate, lot, irrevocable destiny. (Usually of adverse fate; rarely in good sense.)

13.. *E.E. Allit. P.* C. 203 Lo þy dom is þe dyȝt, for þy dedes ille! **1375** BARBOUR *Bruce* I. 235 The angyr, na the wrechyt dome, That is cowplyt to foule thyrldome. *c* **1400** *Destr. Troy* 7123 þurgh domys of destany dreuyt to noght. **1594** SHAKS. *Rich. III*, IV. iv. 217 All vnauoyded is the doome of Destiny. **1697** DRYDEN *Virg. Georg.* III. 111 And Age, and Death's inexorable Doom. **1725** POPE *Odyss.* IV. 289 Such, happy Nestor! was thy glorious doom. **1855** KINGSLEY *Heroes* I. (1868) 7 A stranger, whom a cruel doom has driven to your land.

b. Final fate, destruction, ruin, death.

c **1600** SHAKS. *Sonn.* xiv. 14 Thy end is truth's and beauty's doom and date. **1725** N. ROBINSON *Th. Physick* 244 The Patient must fall in the Conflict, and owe his Doom.. to the too rigid Rashness of his Physician. **1860** TYNDALL *Glac.* I. xxii. 157 Irresistible dynamic energy, which moved them [glaciers] to their doom. **1874** GREEN *Short Hist.* vi. §5. 323 Both the Cardinal and his enemies knew that the minister's doom was sealed.

5. The action or process of judging (as in a court of law); judgement, trial. *arch.*

c **950** *Lindisf. Gosp.* John xii. 31 Nu is dom middangeordes. *a* **1200** *Moral Ode* 169 [167] þe dom sal ben sone idon, ne last hit nowiht longe. **1340** HAMPOLE *Pr. Consc.* 5112 Als domesman to sit in dome. *c* **1450** *Mirour Saluacioun* 2194 Thai ledde hym arely fro thens to pilates dome. **1567** *Satir. Poems Reform.* iv. 105 Hangit syne but dome. **1667** MILTON *P.L.* VI. 817 Therefore to mee their doom he hath assign'd. **1850** KINGSLEY *Alt. Locke, Song* 17 The Judge is set, the doom begun!

6. The last or great Judgement at the end of the world; also, a pictorial representation of this. *arch.* (Now chiefly in phr. ***crack of doom***.)

c **1200** *Trin. Coll. Hom.* 69 þenche we ure giltes er þe dom cume. **1393** GOWER *Conf.* I. 97 He shall for the dome finall Yef his answere. *c* **1400** MAUNDEV. (1839) x. 114 The Doom schalle ben on Estre Day, suche tyme as our Lord aroos. **1529** MORE *Dyaloge* II. Wks. 180/1, I speke of Christes.. comming to the dreadfull dome. **1605** SHAKS. *Macb.* IV. i. 117 What will the Line stretch out to' th' cracke of Doome? *a* **1800** COWPER *Heroism* 11 On a day, like that of the last doom. **1848** R. I. WILBERFORCE *Incarn. our Lord* ix. (1852) 204 When all nations shall behold Him at the crack of doom. **1874** MICKLETHWAITE *Mod. Par. Churches* 323 The.. hobgoblins of mediæval dooms.

7. ***day of doom***: the day of judgement: see DAY *sb.* 8 b, and DOOMSDAY.

1340 HAMPOLE *Pr. Consc.* 2600 Our last day þat sal falle, Our day of dome we may calle. *a* **1400–50** *Alexander* 1095 So sall to þe day of dome þi dedis be remembrid. **1526** *Pilgr. Perf.* (W. de W. 1531) 302 What answere shall ye make to your lorde at yᵉ daye of dome? **1649** JER. TAYLOR *Gt. Exemp.* II. vi. 19 The great scrutiny for faith in the day of doom. **1735** POPE *Donne Sat.* IV. 161 In sure succession to the day of doom. **1847** EMERSON *Repr. Men, Swedenborg* Wks. (Bohn) I. 331 Who, if a hail-storm passes over the village, thinks the day of doom is come.

†**b.** *transf.* The last day of one's life; the fatal day. *Obs.* (Cf. 4 b.)

1588 SHAKS. *Tit. A.* II. iii. 42. **1593** —— *Rich. II*, III. ii. 189. **1593** —— *3 Hen. VI*, V. vi. 93 Ile throw thy body in another roome, And Triumph Henry, in thy day of Doome.

†**8.** Justice; equity; righteousness. Cf. JUDGEMENT. *Obs.* (Chiefly in versions of Scripture, or allusions thereto.)

c **825** *Vesp. Psalter* xcvi. 2 Hire rehtwisnis and dom ʒerecenis seldes his. *c* **1000** *Ags. Gosp.* Matt. xxiii. 23 Ge forleton þa þing þe synt hefeʒran þære æ, dom, and mildheortnysse and ʒeleafan. **1382** WYCLIF *Prov.* xxi. 3 To do mercy and dom, more pleseth to the Lord, than sacrifices of victorie. *c* **1386** CHAUCER *Pars. T.* ¶518 Thou schalt swere in trouthe, in doom, and in rightwisnesse. **1563–87** FOXE *A. & M.* (1684) I. 458/1 David in the Sauter saith; Blessed beth they that done dome and rightfulness.

†**9.** Power or authority to judge; *gen.* power, authority. *Obs.*

c **1000** *Ags. Gosp.* John v. 22 Ne se fæder ne demð nanum menn. Ac he sealde ælcne dom þam suna. *c* **1330** R. BRUNNE *Chron.* (1810) 100 To haf þam at his dome. **13..** *K. Alis.* 2606 He sent messangers..to al that weore at his dome. **1382** WYCLIF *John* v. 22 Neither the fader iugeth ony man, but hath ȝouun al the dom to the sone.

†**10.** A judge. *Obs. rare.*

Perh. an error of transcription for DEME.

13.. *Minor Poems fr. Vernon MS.* 627 þer haunted til her hous..Two domus of þat lawe. **1502** ARNOLDE *Chron.* (1811) 162 Primate and chefe dome of cristen men.

11. *attrib.* (mostly *arch.* or *Obs.*) as ***doom-giving, -hall, -place, -storm, -word***, etc.; ***doom-laden*** adj. †**doom-house**, a judgement-hall; **doom-ring** (*Archæol.*), a ring of stones forming the boundary of the old Norse courts of judgement; †**doom-settle**, †**-stool**, judgement-seat; †**doom-stead**, place of judgement; **doom-tree**, a tree on which the condemned were hanged.

1399 LANGL. *Rich. Redeles* III. 329 At the *dome-ȝeuynge. **1870** MORRIS *Earthly Par.* III. IV. 293 Then gat he to the *doom-hall of the town..And judged the people. *c* **1000** *Voc.* in Wr.-Wülcker 145/12 *Curia*, *domhus. *c* **1440** *Promp. Parv.* 126/2 Dome howse, *pretorium*. **1938** *Times* 24 Mar., Mr. Gennadi Rozhdestvensky gave this *doom-laden symphony its full eloquence. **1382** WYCLIF *Acts* xxv. 10 At the *dom place of Cesar I stonde. **18..** WHITTIER *King Volmer & Elsie* i, Over heathen *doom-rings and gray stones of the Horg. **1893** S. O. ADDY *Hall of Waltheof* 33 The circle near the Bar Dike may have been a doom-ring. *c* **1000** *Ags. Gosp.* Matt. xxvii. 19 He sæt þa pilatus on his *dom-setle. *a* **1225** *Juliana* 55 Com..biuore þe reue as he set on his dom seotle. **1876** *Athenæum* 8 July 48 That way to the *doomstead thrones The Aesir ride each day. *a* **1225** *Ancr. R.* 306 Let skile sitten ase demare upon þe *dom stol. **1837** LOCKHART *Scott* ii, Elibank's *'doomtree' extended its broad arms close to the gates of his fortress.

doom (du:m), *v.* Also 5–6 **dome**, 6 *Sc.* **dume**, 6–7 **doome**. [f. DOOM *sb.*]

1. *trans.* To pronounce judgement or sentence upon; to judge. *Obs.* or *arch.* exc. as in 2.

c **1450** (MSS. *c*1600) *Chester Pl.* (E.E.T.S.) xxi. 354 The general Resurrection..when Christ is bowne to Dome both good and evill. **1502** ARNOLDE *Chron.* (1811) 29 The goodys and catels of alle hem that before hem be domed. **1533** GAU *Richt Vay* (1888) 15 They quhilk..Iugis or dwmis oders wranguslie. **1633** P. FLETCHER *Purple Isl.* v. xlvi. 58 There the equall Judge..dooms each voice aright. **1813** BYRON *Br. Abydos* II. xxi, No deed they've done, nor deed shall do, Ere I have heard and doom'd it too.

†**b.** with complement: To pronounce or deem.

1742 YOUNG *Nt. Th.* II. 156 Time's use was doom'd a pleasure; waste, a pain.

2. To pronounce judgement or sentence against; *esp.* to condemn *to* some fate.

1588 SHAKS. *Tit. A.* III. i. 47 Tribunes with their tongues doome men to death. **1593** —— *Rich. II*, V. i. 4 Cæsars.. Tower: To whose flint Bosome, my condemned Lord Is doom'd a Prisoner, by prowd Bullingbrooke. **1645** MILTON *Colast.* (1851) 372 He dooms it as contrary to Truth. **1849** MACAULAY *Hist. Eng.* I. 197 An act was passed which doomed him to perpetual exile. **1881** JOWETT *Thucyd.* I. 189 A decree which doomed to destruction..a whole city.

3. To destine or consign to some adverse fate or lot; also sometimes in neutral sense, to any fate, good or ill. *pa. pple.* Destined, fated.

1602 SHAKS. *Ham.* I. v. 10, I am thy Fathers Spirit, Doom'd for a certaine terme to walke the night. **1733** POPE *Ess. Man* III. 65 He..feasts the animal he dooms his feast. **1776** GIBBON *Decl. & F.* I. xii. 255 You have doomed me to a life of cares. **1860** TYNDALL *Glac.* I. ii. 19 Our hopes were doomed to disappointment. **1887** BOWEN *Virg. Æneid* I. 20 A nation..Doomed in the future ages her Tyrian towers to destroy.

4. *U.S.* (*local*): see quots.

1816 J. PICKERING *Voc. U.S.* s.v., When a person neglects to make a return of his taxable property to the assessors of a town, those officers doom him; that is, judge upon, and fix his tax according to their discretion. **1888** BRYCE *Amer. Commw.* II. II. xliii. 133 *note*, In New York..if a person makes no return the assessors are instructed to 'doom' him according to the best of their knowledge and belief.

5. To decree; to pronounce or fix as a sentence or fate; to destine; to adjudge. (With simple obj. or obj. clause.)

1588 SHAKS. *Tit. A.* IV. ii. 114 The Emperour in his rage will doome her death. **1669** DRYDEN *Tyrannic Love* II. i, The Gods adjudg'd it Parricide, By dooming the Event on Cæsar's Side. **1712–4** POPE *Rape Lock* II. 110 Whether Heav'n has doom'd that Shock must fall. **1844** LD. BROUGHAM *Brit. Const.* xv. (1862) 227 Buckingham, whose fall he perceived was doomed.

6. *intr.* To give judgement; to judge, decide. *Obs.* or *arch.*

1591 GREENE *Maiden's Dreame* xlii. 2 Doctors that well could doom of Holy Writ. **1662** COKAINE *Ovid* I. iii. Dram. Wks. (1874) 228, I shall, in my opinion, doom aright, But wish that Jove had chose some other wight. **1876** MORRIS *Sigurd* 259 They drink in the hall together, they doom in the people's strife.

Hence **doomed** *ppl. a.*, **'dooming** *vbl. sb.* and *ppl. a.*

1596 DRAYTON *Legends* IV. 62 For which immedicable Blow..Me dooming Heaven ordain'd. **1627–77** FELTHAM *Resolves* I. xv. 24 A dooming to death. **1869** FREEMAN *Norm. Conq.* (1876) III. xii. 241 The..doomed city.

doom, obs. f. DOME, DUMB; var. of DOUM.

doomage ('du:mɪdʒ). *U.S.* (*local*). [f. DOOM *v.* + -AGE.] The action of dooming (see DOOM *v.* 4); assessment in default.

1792 J. BELKNAP *New-Hampsh.* III. 284 If any person refuse to give an invoice of his rateable estate, it is in the power of the selectmen 'to set down to such person as much as they judge equitable, by way of doomage; from which there is no appeal'. **1828** WEBSTER, *Doomage*, a penalty or fine for neglect.

doombook ('du:mbʊk). Also **dome-**, **domes-**, **doomsbook**. [OE. *dóm-bóc*, book of dooms.]

1. A book or code of (Old Teutonic) laws; *spec.* that attributed to King Alfred and referred to in the laws of later West-Saxon kings. *Obs.* exc. *Hist.*

a **925** *Laws of Edward* Preamble, [Swa] hit on ðære dombec stande. *a* **940** *Laws of Athelstan* II. v. (Schmid), Bete be ðam ðe seo dom-boc secʒe. *c* **1000** ÆLFRIC *Hom.* (Th.) II. 198 Oð þæt he com to ðam dom-bocum ðe se Heofenlica Wealdend his folce ʒesette. **1660** R. COKE *Power & Subj.* 159 If any one shall not pay, let him incur the punishment expressed in the Doom-book (Laws of K. Edgar). **1765** BLACKSTONE *Comm.* I. 66 A new edition, or fresh promulgation, of Alfred's code or dome-book. **1891** ATKINSON *Moorland Par.* 218 The records..exist in the Doomsbooks..of this country and other lands in the north of Europe.

2. *transf.* A book of doom or judgement.

1837 CARLYLE *Fr. Rev.* I. II. viii, Cursed is that trade.. and is verily marked in the Doom-Book of a God!

doomer ('du:mə(r)). Now *rare.* [OE. *dómere* judge, f. *dóm* DOOM *sb.*: see -ER[1]. In later use f. DOOM *v.*] One who dooms or pronounces sentence; a judge. Cf. DEEMSTER.

c **888** K. ÆLFRED *Boeth.* xxvii. §4 Heretoʒan and domeras ..hæfdon mæstne weorþscipe. *c* **1000** *Laws of Ælfred* Introd. §18 (Schmid) Swa him domeras ʒereccen. **1589** GREENE *Tullie's Love* (1609) Kij, Be then..impartiall doomers of my sute. *c* **1590** —— *Fr. Bacon* x. 139 Fond Atè doomer of bad-boding fates. **1842** LYTTON *Zanoni* VII. x, The power which dooms the doomer.

doomful ('du:mfʊl), *a.* [f. DOOM *sb.* + -FUL.] Fraught with or involving doom; fateful.

1586 SPENSER *Sonn. to Harvey*, For Life, and Death, is in thy doomefull writing. **1630** J. TAYLOR (Water P.) *Urania* I. Wks. 1/1 Eternal God, which..at the doomefull day will once unhaspe Th' accusing booke of Subiects and of Kings. **1837** CARLYLE *Fr. Rev.* II. VI. vii, Think what a volley: reverberating doomful to the four corners of Paris.

Doomie ('du:mɪ). *R.A.F. colloq.* [f. DOOM *sb.* 4 + -IE.] A name given to an imaginary prophet of doom or giver of warnings.

1945 *Tee Emm* (Air Ministry) V. 151 (*caption*) Doomie says: Doomie-buoy says Don't shoot me. **1952** M. TRIPP *Faith is Windsock* xiii. 204 The era which produced Chads, Doomies and Gremlins. **1962** *Guardian* 30 Nov. 12/4 Pinwheel was his first name, but..he was adopted by other RAF units under the name of Doomie—and Doomie he remained until the British Army adopted him (*circa* 1943) with the new name of Chad.

dooms (du:mz), *adv. Sc.* [Origin uncertain.

Prob. from DOOM *sb.* Some have conjectured connexion with Icel. *dáindis-* pretty, rather, prefixed to adjs. and advs. Cf. also DONE *adv.*]

Very, exceedingly.

1815 SCOTT *Guy M.* xxxii, 'It was not sae dooms likely that he would go down into battle wi' sic sma' means.' **1816** —— *Old Mort.* xxiii, 'I wasna that dooms stupid.' **1893** STEVENSON *Catriona* 20 My case is dooms hard.

doomsayer ('du:mseɪə(r)). orig. *U.S.* [f. DOOM *sb.* + SAYER *sb.*[1]; cf. SOOTHSAYER 2.] A prophet of doom, esp. one of political or economic disaster.

1961 in WEBSTER. **1972** *Times* 22 May 10/5 The doomsayers conclude that there is no hope of better habits being adopted in time. **1975** *U.S. News & World Rep.* 3 Feb. 46/1 This nation of 55 million people has not lost..its perennial ability to 'muddle through' to the surprise of the doomsayers. **1985** *Washington Post* 6 Jan. 3/3 Nor does Revel quite belong in that traditional circle of doomsayers for the West: neither with Marx and Spengler,..nor quite with Max Weber, Joseph Schumpeter, and Daniel Bell.

doomsday ('du:mzdeɪ). [OE. *dómes dæʒ*, ME. *domes dei, dai*, day of judgement: see DOOM *sb.*]

1. a. The judgement day.

c **975** *Rushw. G.* Matt. x. 15 At domes dæʒe. *c* **1000** *Ags. G.* ibid., On domes dæʒ. *c* **1175** *Lamb. Hom.* 95 On his efter tocome þet is on domes deie. *a* **1225** *Ancr. R.* 58 Heo is gulti ..and schal uor his soule onswerien a Domesdei. *a* **1300** *Cursor M.* 498 (Cott.) And sua sal do to domes dai. **1533** GAU *Richt Vay* (1888) 34 Yair sal be na generacione na corrupcione efter dwmis day. **1601** SHAKS. *Jul. C.* III. i. 98 Men, Wiues, and Children, stare, cry out, and run, As it were Doomesday. **1742** YOUNG *Nt. Th.* I. 366 The present moment terminates our sight; Clouds, thick as those on doomsday, drown the next.

b. *esp.* in phr.: ***till doomsday***: to the end of the world, as long as the world lasts, for ever.

c **1200** ORMIN 17682 All þatt follc þatt fra þiss daȝȝ Till Domess daȝȝ shall wurrþenn. *c* **1330** R. BRUNNE *Chron. Wace* (Rolls) 8734 Hit myght laste til Domesday. **1553** T. WILSON *Rhet.* (1567) 103 a, If a man should aske me till Doumes daie, I would still crie silence, silence. **1606** SHAKS. *Ant. & Cl.* V. ii. 232 When thou hast done this chare, Ile giue thee leaue To play till Doomesday. **1850** CARLYLE

Latter-d. Pamph. i. 4 Questions which all official men wished..to postpone till Doomsday. **1886** FROUDE *Oceana* 233 They might have waited till Doomsday in the afternoon before [etc.].

c. *transf.* A day of judgement or trial, when sentence is pronounced. Also, a day of final dissolution, as at the end of the world.

1579 LYLY *Euphues* (Arb.) 181 Dost thou not knowe that euery ones deathes daye is his do[o]mes daye? **1594** SHAKS. *Rich. III*, v. i. 12 Why then Al-soules day is my bodies doomsday. **1642** FULLER *Holy & Prof. St.* III. xxiii. 215 This bell was taken down at the doomsday of abbeys. **1831** CARLYLE *Sart. Res.* II. vi, His sudden bereavement..is talked of as a real Doomsday and Dissolution of Nature.

2. = DOMESDAY: the usual spelling in 17–18th c., still used, esp. in fig. or transf. senses.

3. *attrib.* **doomsday machine** (see quot. 1961); also *doomsday bomb*.

1649 MILTON *Eikon.* iii. (1851) 358 The Kings admirers may..mistake this Book for a Monument of his worth and wisdom, when as indeed it is his Doomsday Booke. **1654** TRAPP *Comm. Esther* iv. 8 That dreadful day of judgement, when that doomes-day book shall be opened. **1781** COWPER *Hope* 693 Conscience..writes a Doomsday sentence on his heart. **1842** C. WHITEHEAD *Richard Savage* (1845) III. ix. 420 Long doomsday faces. **1960** H. KAHN *On Thermonuclear War* x. 489 Technology, 1969..Doomsday Machines. *Ibid.* 500 The last two items in Table 65 are probably the most important, even if not very probable. Foremost are Doomsday Machines. I am not predicting that they will be built... It is most unlikely that either the Soviet Union or the U.S. would build such machines. **1961** *New Scientist* 26 Oct. 230/1 The Doomsday Machine is a hypothetical weapon which is capable of destroying all human life. **1965** B. RUSSELL *Autobiogr.* (1969) III. iv. 211 Cobalt would be necessary for the Doomsday Bomb. **1968** *Observer* 31 Mar. 25/4 The idea of a nuclear 'Doomsday machine', capable of destroying all life on earth, is not *technically* absurd. **1970** A. DIPPER *Hard Trip* xiv. 200 It is unutterably evil, and dangerous as a doomsday bomb.

'doomsman. [early ME. *dómes man*, man of judgement: see DOOM *sb.*] A judge, deemster.

a **1200** *Moral Ode* 260 Medȝierne domes men and wrong-wise reuen. **1382** WYCLIF *Matt.* v. 25 Lest perauenture thin aduersarie take thee to the domesman, and the domesman take thee to the mynystre, and thou be sente in to prisoun. *c* **1440** *Gesta Rom.* viii. 21 (Harl. MS.) þe domys-man come to þe Cite, for to sitte vp on brekers of þe lawe. **1493** *Festivall* (W. de Worde 1515) 4 b, Our lorde Ihesu Cryste his domesman. *a* **1640** [see DOOMSTER 2]. **1708** *Termes de la Ley* 268 Doomsman, seems to be Suitors in a Court of a Mannor in Ancient Demesne, who are Judges there. **1839** BAILEY *Festus* xxx. 342 Behold in me the doomsman of your race.

attrib. **1483** *Cath. Angl.* 103/2 A domesman sete, *tribunal*.

doomster ('du:mstə(r)). In 5 domstere. [modification of *demester*, DEMPSTER, DEEMSTER, after DOOM *v.* and *sb.*]

1. A judge, doomer. *arch.*

1442 *Cursor M.* 9737 (Bedford) Fadir, rightwis domstere! **1861** LOWELL *Poet. Wks.* (1890) IV. 4 Then let him hearken for the doomster's feet! **1882** *Sat. Rev.* 11 Nov. 627 Doomsters..propounding their own construction of rubrical niceties with Sinaitic thunders.

2. In a Scottish court of law, the official (usually the executioner) who formerly read or repeated the sentence; = DEMPSTER 2.

1609 SKENE *Reg. Maj.* 158 The Domster sould be sworne. *a* **1640** JACKSON *Creed* x. xlix. §2 They will..be enforced to borrow a more fit expression of His office from our sister nation, and instyle Him to be the doomster or doomsman of the quick and the dead. **1816** SCOTT *Old Mort.* xxxvi, 'Doomster', he continued, 'repeat the sentence to the prisoner'. **1861** W. BELL *Dict. Law Scot.* s.v. *Doom*, The doom or sentence was..pronounced by the public executioner, or doomster as he was called—a barbarous practice, which was abolished by Act of Adjournal, 16th March 1773.

attrib. **1881** PALGRAVE *Visions of Eng.* 131 Before is the doomster-day, And..the shambles of Fotheringay.

doomwatch ('du:mwɒtʃ). [The name of a BBC television series first broadcast in 1970, f. DOOM *sb.* + WATCH *sb.*] Observation intended to avert danger or destruction, esp. of the environment by pollution or nuclear war; also *fig.* Freq. *attrib.*

[**1970** *New Scientist* 2 Apr. 3/2 BBC-TV's new scientific soap-opera, *Doomwatch*, has been fortunate in its first selection of topics to warn us about.] **1970** *Guardian* 23 Dec. 1/1 The Government Chemist..tested 50 tins of tuna bought throughout the country... Mr Prior said:..'We shall be getting on with this—this Doomwatch, if you like to call it that.' **1970** *New Scientist* 20 Aug. 379/2 The 'Doomwatch' bug that digests plastics to a syrupy mess as you watch is still pure science fiction. **1973** *Times* 3 July 17 In his latest piece of political doomwatch.., he..forecasts an upsurge of bloody revolt against..the 'casino society'. **1984** *Times* 20 Mar. 12/2 The CCU [*sc.* Civil Contingencies Unit] remains Whitehall's 'doomwatch' organization. It keeps constantly updated files on 16 essential industries and services.

Hence **'doomwatcher**, a person who observes or monitors evidence for the deterioration of the environment; one who prophesies ecological disaster.

1971 *New Scientist* 18 Mar. 622 (*title*) Doomwatcher incarnate. **1978** *Nature* 19 Oct. 577/2 As WMO sees it, hard evidence does little to support many of the disaster hypotheses of the doom-watchers... There is one major exception: the problem of increasing CO_2 in the atmosphere.

doomy ('du:mɪ), *a.* [f. DOOM *sb.* + -Y[1].] **a.** Of a person: depressed, sad. **b.** Of a thing: depressing, weird.

1961 G. SMITH *Business of Loving* xi. 219 The gaffer..was a doomy old nut who once or twice had talked about jagging it in. **1967** A. J. MARSHALL in L. Deighton *London Dossier* 142 The City of London... It's a doomy, forbidding place to me. **1968** *Crescendo* Jan. 22/2 Even the irrepressible Mr. Brookmeyer produces a somewhat doomy arrangement of 'Willow Weep For Me'.

doon, -e, obs. ff. DO *v.*, DONE, DOWN, DUN.

doonga ('du:ŋgə). *India.* Also dunga. [ad. Hind. *dongā*.] A flat-bottomed dug-out with a square sail.

1905 *Westm. Gaz.* 3 Jan. 2/1 A line of stretchers was winding in and out past the dungas—all laden. **1922** *Chambers's Jrnl.* 759/2 There is the house-boat, the *doonga*—a species of long canoe, with a sloping rush roof..., in which you live. **1925** *Ibid.* 77/1 At Srinagar Durrant hired a large doonga-houseboat.

door (dɔə(r)). Forms: 1 duru, 2–5 (*Sc.* 4–9) dure, 4–6 durr(e, 4–7 dur, (5 duyr), 6 *Sc.* duir(e, dwr, dourre; also 1–5 dor, 3–7 dore, (4 doer, 5 doyre, 6 dower), 6–7 doore, 7– door; also 1 dyr, 2–3 dyre. [OE. *duru*, fem. *u*-stem, not found elsewhere in Teut., but from the same base *dur-*, as the equivalent words in the other langs.: cf. OHG. *turi*, an orig. plural, which became a fem. sing., MHG. *tur*, Ger. *thür*(*e*, ODu. *duri* pl. (MDu. *döre*, *dore*, Du. *deur* fem. sing.), OS. *duri*, ON. *dyrr* fem. pl. (and n.), Sw. *dörr* f., Da. *dör*; also Goth. *daurôns* pl. weak fem. OE. had also *dor* neut., pl. *doru*, large door, gate = Goth. *daur*, OS. *dor*, OHG. *tor*, Ger. *thor* gate. The same stem *dhur-*, *dhwâr-* appears in Skr. *dvr̥*, *dwâr*, Gr. θύρα, L. *fores*. The two OE. types *duru*, and *dor* appear to have been mixed in ME., where, beside *dure* and *dor*, are also found *dur* and *dore*. *Dore* prevailed in 16th c., and is found as late as 1684; *door* appeared in 16th c., and at length supplanted *dore* in writing, though now pronounced like the latter.

The spelling *door* points to an earlier pronunciation with *ū* or ū from ME. close *ō*, which is further attested by Sc. *dure* (dør) (also in Cath. Angl. 1483), and is considered by Luick as a northern lengthening of OE. *u*. The current pronunciation may be a retention of that evidenced for 16th c. *dore* by quot. 1593 in 1 β; but it may also be a more recent modification of (duə(r)), as in the case of *floor*, and vulgar pronunciations of *moor*, *poor*, as *more*, *pore*.]

1. a. A movable barrier of wood or other material, consisting either of one piece, or of several pieces framed together, usually turning on hinges or sliding in a groove, and serving to close or open a passage into a building, room, etc.

α. in form *duru*, *dure* (*dyre*), *durre*, *dur* (after 1500 *Sc.*).

Beowulf 1447 (Th.) Duru sona on-arn fyr-bendum fæst. *c* **1000** *Ags. Gosp.* Matt. xxv. 10 Seo duru wæs belocen [*Lindisf.* ȝetyned wæs ðe dura]. *Ibid.* Mark i. 33 Eall seo burhwaru wæs ȝegaderod to þære duran [*Lindisf.* to duru *vel* to ȝæt, *Rushw.* to dore *vel* ȝeat. *c* **1160** *Hatton* Ȝe-gadered to þare dure.] *c* **1025** *Interl. v. Rule St. Benet* (1888) 78 Ætforan dyran. *c* **1175** *Lamb. Hom.* 87 And merki mid þan blode hore duren. *c* **1250** *Gen. & Ex.* 1082 Al ðat niȝt he soȝten ðor ðe dure. **1375** BARBOUR *Bruce* II. 61 Thai brak the dur. *c* **1400** *Destr. Troy* 11890 The durres to vndo. *c* **1420** *Chron. Vilod.* 931 þe durus of þ'chapelle. **1483** *Cath. Angl.* 111/1 Dure (*A.* Duyr), *hostium*. **1546** J. HEYWOOD *Prov.* (1867) 16 Ye beg at a wrong mans dur [*rime* stur]. **1562** WINȜET *Cert. Tractates* i. Wks. 1888 I. 2 Calking of the durris. **1563** —— *Four Scoir Thre Quest.* Wks. 1888 I. 87 The duiris being closit. *a* **1605** MONTGOMERIE *Sonnets* lxv. 11 To come ouir the dur. **1609** SKENE *Reg. Maj.*, *Burrow Lawes* 126 Lipper men..sall not gang fra dure to dure.

β. in form *dor* (OE. = gate, pl. *doru*), *dore* (*doer*).

c **1000** *Ags. Ps.* (Th.) xcix. 3 Gað nu on his doru. *Ibid.* cvi. 15 Æren dor. *c* **1000** *Sax. Leechd.* III. 56 Hoh ða wyrte on ..þan dore. *c* **1205** LAY. 2382 Neuer ne ferde heo wiðuten dore. **1297** R. GLOUC. (1724) 495 And the doren after hom ..loke vaste. *a* **1300** *Cursor M.* 1682 (Cott.) Mak a dor [*v.rr.* doer, dur]. **1340** HAMPOLE *Pr. Consc.* 3451 When þou spekes sharppely til þe pure, þat sum gode askes at þi dore. *c* **1386** CHAUCER *Miller's T.* 280 Whil þat þou Robyn heuest of the dore [*rime* vnderspore]. **1483** *Cath. Angl.* 104/1 Dore (*A.* Doyre), *hostium*. **1563** *Mirr. Mag.*, *Jane Shore* li. 7 To begge from dore to dore. **1593** SHAKS. *Rich. II*, v. iii. 77 Open the dore, A Begger begs, that neuer begg'd before. **1644** MILTON *Areop.* (Arb.) 59 Other dores which cannot be shut. **1684** BUNYAN *Pilgr.* II. 12 And knocked at her Dore.

γ. in forms (*dower*, *dourr*) *doore*, *door*.

1504 *Plumpton Corr.* 186 None..shall not pas the dowers. **1509–28** Wynkyn de Worde's edd. of *R. Coer de Lion* 1934 Doors and windows barred fast. **1533** GAU *Richt Vay* (1888) 61 Quhen y[e] disciplis..haid closit the dourris. **1548** HALL *Chron.*, *Hen. VIII* 3 b, At the haule doore. **1589** PUTTENHAM *Eng. Poesie* II. viii. (Arb.) 94 If one should rime to this word [Restore] he may not match him with [Doore] or [Poore] for neither of both are of like terminant. **1611** BIBLE *Gen.* iv. 7 Sinne lieth at the doore [COVERD. in the dore]. **1662** WOOD *Life* (Oxf. Hist. Soc.) I. 462 Before the west doore. **1760** FOOTE *Minor* II. Wks. 1799 I. 269 Well, do so no more, Drop, to atone, your money at the door, And, if I please,—I'll give it to the poor [*triple rime*]. **1816** KEATINGE *Trav.* I. 297 They cannot venture..to be seen beyond their own doors.

b. With various qualifications, as *chamber-*, *front-*, *hall-*, *house-*, *kitchen-*, *side-door*, etc. q.v. under their first elements; also BACK-, CHURCH-, FOLDING-DOOR, etc.

double door(*s*), a door consisting of two leaves, opening in the centre; also, two doors, one behind the other, closing the same opening, to prevent draughts, etc.; *glass door*, a door consisting mainly of glass panels; *sliding door*, a single or double door that opens by sliding into a recess.

1785 SARAH FIELDING *Ophelia* xv, The glass-door to the closet. **1840** DICKENS *Old. C. Shop* II. v. 36 This posture of affairs Mr. Brass observed through the glass-door. —— *Barn. Rudge* xxviii, Hugh closed the double doors behind him. **1871** CARLYLE in *Mrs. Carlyle's Lett.* III. 177 The double door from her bedroom went wide open.

c. With definite or indefinite numerals, expressing position in a series or row, and hence indicating the room or house to which the door belongs.

1669 STURMY *Mariner's Mag.* iv, At the Cross-daggers in Moor-fields, next door to the Popes Head Tavern. *a* **1735** ARBUTHNOT (J.), Martin's office is now the second door in the street, where he will see Parnel. **1776** *Trial of Nundocomar* 22/2 [He] lives three doors from the house I inhabited. **1885** *Law Times Rep.* LIII. 459/1 Having taken offices a few doors off.

2. The opening or passage into a building or room, which may be closed by a door; a doorway.

1382 WYCLIF *1 Kings* xix. 13 Helias..goon out, he stode in the dore of the denne. *c* **1450** *St. Cuthbert* (Surtees) 7394 þe bischope in þe dure stode. **1595** SHAKS. *Merry W.* III. v. 103 They..met the iealous knaue their Master in the doore. **1756–7** tr. *Keysler's Trav.* (1760) III. 252 On the left-hand as one enters the door. **1841** LANE *Arab. Nts.* I. 107 A door, which she entered.

3. *fig.* A means of entrance or exit (in quot. 1526 a means of closing); *esp.* in phr. *to open a door to* or *for*: to render possible the admission of; to furnish opportunity or facility for; so *to close the door upon*, and the like.

c **825** *Vesp. Psalter* cxl. 3 Duru ymbstondnisse weo[le]rum minum. **971** *Blickl. Hom.* 9 Heofonrices duru. *c* **1315** SHOREHAM 55 Inewyt hys the dore-ward, The doren wyttes fyve. **1382** WYCLIF *1 Cor.* xvi. 9 A greet dore and euident.. is openyd to me. **1526** *Pilgr. Perf.* (W. de W. 1531) 131 b, Than shall the dore of discrecyon be put to our mouth. **1570** BUCHANAN *Admonitioun* Wks. (1892) 31 Y[e] prouidence of god had closit y[e] dur to all yair wickitnes. **1648** T. GAGE *New Survey W. Ind.* xxi. 191 But this doore of hope was fast shut up. **1670** CLARENDON *Contempl. Ps.* Tracts (1727) 561 To.. open a door for the most confounding Atheism to break in. **1707** *Lond. Gaz.* No. 4342/1 Opening a Door to the French to assault us that Way. **1863** KINGLAKE *Crimea* (1876) I. xii. 195 Which left open a door to future negotiation.

4. *transf.* **a.** Anything resembling a door in its motion or use; a lid, valve; an opening, a passage.

1665 HOOKE *Microgr.* 46 How those Atoms come to be hindred from running all out, when a dore or passage in their Pores is made. **1712** J. MORTON *Nat. Hist. Northampt.* 12 Ash-Timber, for the Doors of Bellows. **1719** LONDON & WISE *Compl. Gard.* 169 A small Padlock fix'd to the Door of the Basket. **1840** GREENER *Sc. Gunnery* 259 Place on this the cap, shut the door, cock your gun.

b. One of two boards or metal plates attached to the ends of a trawl-net.

1911 *Encycl. Brit.* XXVII. 219/2 The trawl boards, or as they are frequently called 'doors', are of deal. **1928** RUSSELL & YONGE *Seas* xiii. 276 The net is hauled by two wire warps, one attached to each 'door'. **1961** *Times* 10 June 11/5 The modern trawl, with its bobbined foot rope, extra sweep between doors (French trawl).

5. Phrases. **a.** † *at door*: at the door; *out at door*, *-s*, = out of doors; *in at door*, *-s*, = indoors (*obs.*). See also A-DOORS. *in doors*: within doors, in or into the house: see INDOORS. *next door* (*to*): in the next house (to); hence *fig.* very near (to), bordering (on). *out* (†*forth*) *of door*(*s*: out of the house; in the open air, abroad; hence *fig.* out of place, lost, abroad, irrelevent, worthless (*obs.*). † *to* (*the*) *door*: out of the house or room (*obs.*). *within door*(*s*: in a house or building, indoors; also *fig.* so as not to be heard outside the door. *without doors*: out of doors.

c **1386** CHAUCER *Nun's Priest's T.* 557 Out at dores stirten they anon. *c* **1450** *Merlin* 32 Merlyn..was gon oute at dore. **1546** J. HEYWOOD *Prov.* (1867) 82 He turnde hir out at doores. **1562** WINȜET *Last Blast* Wks. 1888 I. 45 Repellit and schot to the dure. **1577** *St. Aug. Manual* 71 Love driveth feare out of doores. **1581** G. PETTIE tr. *Guazzo's Civ. Conv.* III. (1586) 156 Some fathers will not suffer their Daughters to set their foote foorth of dores. **1581** MULCASTER *Positions* viii. (1887) 53 One to be vsed within dores, and the other abroade. **1595** SPENSER *Col. Clout* 711 Out of doore quite shit. **1604** SHAKS. *Oth.* IV. ii. 144 Speake within doore. **1633** G. HERBERT *Temple, Praise* iv, May dwell next doore, On the same floore. *a* **1639** W. WHATELEY *Prototypes* II. xxxi. (1640) 118 Hee may sit without doores long enough. **1650** TRAPP *Comm. Exod.* x. 28 Destruction is at next door by. **1657–8** *Burton's Diary* (1828) II. 456 All precedents are out of doors in this case. **1682** BUNYAN *Holy War* Pref. 159 Well, now go forward, step within the dores. **1699** COLLIER *Sec. Defence* (1730) 324 A Place where Thinking is out of Doors. **1719** DE FOE *Crusoe* I. xvi, I kept ..within doors. *Ibid.* II. i, To be next door to starving. *Ibid.* II. xvi, That Objection is out of Doors. **1794** WOLCOTT (P. Pindar) *Rowl. for Oliver* Wks. II. 378 Kick the Arts and Sciences to door. **1816** KEATINGE *Trav.* (1817) I. 298 A Jew is not permitted to appear without-doors save in black. **1857** LD. HOUGHTON in Wemyss Reid *Life* (1891) II. xii. 19 These children..live..out of doors all day. **1875** E. WHITE

Life in Christ I. i. (1878) 20 It is next door to cannibalism. *Mod.* You had better remain in doors.

6. a. †*to drink* or *eat out of doors*: to bring to destitution by excessive drinking or eating: cf. EAT *v.* 4a. †*to fetch at the doors of*: to obtain from. *to lay, lie,* or *be at the door of*: to impute, or be imputable or chargeable to. †*to leap over the door*: to escape, run out. †*to set one's hand to the door*: to apply oneself diligently. †*to set behind the door*: see quot. 1552. *to darken a door*: see DARKEN 6b. *to keep open doors*: see OPEN.

1552 LATIMER *Serm. St. Andrew's Day* Wks. II. 262 They say when a man will be rich, he must set his soul behind the door; that is to say, he must use falsehood and deceit. **1579** TOMSON *Calvin's Serm. Tim.* 464/2 We must not therefore spare our selues..but set our handes to the dore, as the prouerbe is. **1658–9** *Burton's Diary* (1828) IV. 10 A part of the Commonwealth has leaped over the door. *Ibid.* 166 It is so much for your honour..to have the Scotch fetch their laws at your doors. **1659** D. PELL *Impr. Sea* 437 Many Sailors drink..wives and children out of doors. **1683** *Lond. Gaz.* No. 1835/3 The fault will lye at their doors. **1701** W. WOTTON *Hist. Rome* 299 The Blood..must all be layd to his door. **1749** FIELDING *Tom Jones* I. vii, You have in a manner laid your sins at my door. **1833** TENNYSON *Lady Clara* vi, The guilt of blood is at your door.

†**b.** *is the wind in* (*at*) *that door?* = is the wind in that quarter?, is that the tendency of affairs?

1470–85 MALORY *Arthur* VII. xxxv, 'What! neuewe, is the wynde in that dore'? **1589** *Marprel. Epit.* B iv, Is the winde at that dore with you brother deane? **1596** SHAKS. *1 Hen. IV*, III. iii. 102. **1668** DRYDEN *Evening's Love* IV. i, Is the Wind in that Door? Here's like to be fine doings.

7. *attrib.* and *Comb.* **a.** attrib., as ***door-arch***, ***-archway***, ***-catch***, ***-chain***, ***-curtain***, ***-handle***, ***-jamb***, ***-key***, ***-knob***, ***-knocker***, ***-latch***, ***-lintel***, ***-lock***, ***-panel***, ***-porch***, ***-ring***, ***-scraper***, ***-window***, etc. **b.** objective and obj. genitive, as ***door-banging***, ***-dressing***, ***-opener***, ***-warder***. **c.** ***door-like*** adj., ***-wise*** adv.

1886 WILLIS & CLARK *Cambridge* II. 162 A square-headed *door-arch. **1897** *Sears, Roebuck Catal.* 44/2 Screen *Door Catches, enameled iron with stop. **1913** MASEFIELD *Daffodil Fields* 74 A door-catch clacked. **1836** DICKENS *Sk. Boz.* 1st Ser. (1837) 81 The *door-chain was softly unfastened. **1967** *Gloss. Terms Builders' Hardware* (*B.S.I.*) IV. 14 *Door chain*, a device for preventing a door from opening beyond a limited distance, comprising a chain attached at one end to a fixing plate secured to the door frame and at the other to a stud. **1707** *Lond. Gaz.* No. 4364/4 Window-Curtains, and *Door-Curtains. **1874** KNIGHT *Dict. Mech.*, **Door-fastener*, a portable contrivance for fastening a door. **1832** F. TROLLOPE *Domestic Manners* II. xxvi. 104 A delicate silver knocker and *door-handle. **1849** GROTE *Greece* II. xxxix. V. 64 Leaving the hands still hanging to and grasping the door-handle. **1837** MARRYAT *Dog-fiend* II. iii. (L.) Leaning against the *door-jamb for support. **1838** DICKENS *O. Twist* xxvi, Fumbling in his pocket for the *door key. **1847** *Rep. Comm. Patents 1846* (U.S.) 63 Improvements in *door-knobs. **1905** *Daily Chron.* 19 July 4/7 How many door-knobs are there in this happy island? **1839** DICKENS *Nich. Nick.* xv, When Lords break off *door-knockers and beat policemen. **1678** *New Castle* (Del.) *Court Rec.* (1904) 362, 3 Iron *door Latches. **1924** J. M. MURRY *Voyage* xvii. 304 She fumbled blindly at the door-latch. **1875** W. McILWRAITH *Guide Wigtownshire* 75 Shattered *door-lintels. **1654** EVELYN *Diary* 16 July, A *dore-lock of a tolerable price. **1787** HAWKINS *Life Johnson* 123 A representation of St. John's gate..on the *door-pannel. **1535** COVERDALE *Ezek.* xlvi. 2 Then shal the prynce come vnder the *dore porche, & stonde still without by the dore cheke. **1682** MILTON *Hist. Mosc.* v. (1851) 508 Such a terrible noise, as shakes the *Door-rings of Houses..ten mile off. **1616** SURFL. & MARKH. *Country Farme* 87 It must be made higher than the *dor-window. **1907** *Westm. Gaz.* 31 Aug. 2/3 He bounded out through the wide-open French window. .. Vincent slammed the door-window behind as he jumped. **1769** *Monthly Rev.* XL. 372 A rude arch curtained *door-wise. **1798** CHARLOTTE SMITH *Young Philosopher* II. 32 One sash opening door-wise. **1898** G. B. SHAW *Arms & Man* I. 4 The window is hinged doorwise.

8. Special combs: **door-alarm** (see quot.); **door-boy**, a boy who guards the door of a passage in a mine; **door-casing**, **-facing**, **-trim** *U.S.* = DOOR-CASE; **door chimes** [CHIME *sb.*[1] 2], a chiming mechanical or electrical device acting as a door-bell; **door-fall**, the falling door of a trap; **door-frame**, (*a*) a door-case (Nicholson *Pract. Builder* 1823); (*b*) the structure forming the skeleton of a panelled door; †**door-gate**, an entrance; **door-head**, the upper part of a door-case; **door-land** (*Sc.*), a plot of ground near a door (Forsyth *Beauties Scotl.* IV. 254); **door-money**, money taken at the door of a place of entertainment; †**door-neighbour**, a near or next-door neighbour; **door-piece** †(*a*) a curtain before a door; (*b*) see quot. 1869; **door-pin**, the 'pin' or bolt of a door; **door-plane** (see quot.); **door-sign**, a sign upon a door; **door-stone**, a threshold stone, a flagstone before a door; **door-stop**, a device to stop a door from opening too widely or closing too forcibly; also, the slip of wood against which it shuts in its frame; **door-swell**, a kind of swell-box in an organ; **door-to-door** *attrib.*, (of canvassing, selling, investigating, etc.) done methodically at one house after another; (of a journey) from actual start to actual finish; **door-weed**, a name for *Polygonum aviculare* (Dunglison *Med. Lex.* 1857).

1874 KNIGHT *Dict. Mech.*, **Door-alarm*, a device attached to a door, to give an audible notice when the door is opened. **1887** M. E. WILKINS *Humble Romance* 2 He lounged smilingly against the *door-casing, jingling his scales, and waiting for the woman. **1962** A. NISBETT *Technique Sound Studio* x. 173 *Door chimes and hand-bells. **1845** W. G. SIMMS *Wigwam & Cabin* I. 99, I had been hewing out some *door-facings for a new corn-crib and fodder-house. **1877** *Congress. Rec.* 26 Nov. 705/1 This man..was sitting up in the door with his feet on the door facing. **1624** BEDELL *Lett.* iii. 59 By the most chaffie shrap that euer was set before the eyes of winged Fowle, [you] were brought to the *doorefall. **1889** R. B. ANDERSON tr. *Rydberg's Teut. Mythol.* 214 The *door-frames were covered with the soot of centuries. *a* **1529** SKELTON *Womanhod, Wanton, &c.*, 26 Of youre *doregate ye haue no doute. **1703** MOXON *Mech. Exerc.* 142 *Door-head. **1894** H. SPEIGHT *Nidderdale* 410 The *door-lintel..was..put in the door-head of the new cow-house. **1806** A. DUNCAN *Nelson's Fun.* 15 *Door-money was demanded as at a puppet-show. **1562** *Durham Depositions* (Surtees) 70 She saith she is ther *doore neighbour. **1711** *C. M. Let. to Curate* 14 Would they deny it to the Scots their door Neighbours? **1611** COTGR., *Garde-porte*, a peece of Tapistrie hung before an open dore; a *dore-peece. **1869** R. B. SMYTH *Gold-f. Victoria* 609 Door-piece—That portion of a lift of pumps in which the clack or valve is situate. *c* **1250** *Gen. & Ex.* 1078 Ðis angels two droȝen loth in And shetten to ðe *dure-pin. *a* **1300** *K. Horn* 1003 Rymenhild undude þe dure pin. **1889** W. B. YEATS *Wanderings of Oisin* 90 Raise the door-pin with alarm. **1876** GWILT *Archit.* Gloss., **Door-Plane*, the plane between the door proper, and the larger opening within which it may be placed. **1816** SCOTT *Old Mort.* viii, 'Ne'er cross the *door-stane.' **1893** M. A. OWEN *Voodoo Tales* 209 The aunties searched under every doorstone for 'tricks'. **1881** YOUNG *Every Man own Mechanic* §1285 The *door-stops may be nailed to the casing and the door hung. **1852** SEIDEL *Organ* 27 The roof or *door swell..when accurately constructed (of oak wood), is the best. **1902** *Harper's Mag.* May 1004/1 When I arrived at the house my son, the editor, had just returned from a *door-to-door sale of the *Mosquito*. **1929** 'G. DAVIOT' *Man in Queue* x. 128 You can be an ex-service man..out of a job... I don't want any door-to-door business. **1934** *Planning* II. XXXVI. 14 Apart from certain short-distance traffic which can be more cheaply and efficiently sent by road on account of the door-to-door facilities and absence of double handling, the main competition between road and rail is over certain long-distance traffic. **1943** *Our Towns* (*Women's Group on Public Welfare*) ii. 12 The door-to-door salesmanship which is one of the pests of town life. **1963** D. OGILVY *Conf. Advert. Man* v. 96 When I was a door-to-door salesman I discovered that the more information I gave about my product, the more I sold. **1905** *N.Y. Even. Post* 30 Dec. 12 (Advt.), The corridors, floors, stairways, *doortrims and walls are of marble.

doora, doorah, var. of DURRA.

†'**door-band.** *Obs.* A strip-hinge (see BAND *sb.*[1] 3); also, (?) the bolt or fastening of a door.

1379 *Mem. Ripon* (Surtees) III. 102 Et in j doreband elongand. ibidem, 1*d.* **14..** *Nom.* in Wr.-Wülcker 733/25 *Hic gumfus*, a dorbande. **1530** *Compotus* in Poulson *Beverlac* (1829) 622 Pro 4 doore bands 12*d.*

†'**door-bar.** *Obs.* [see BAR *sb.*[1] 8.] A bar of wood, iron, etc. put across a door to secure it.

13.. *Sir Beues* 1622 + 43 (MS. C) The dore barre he toke yn honde And slewe all þat he þere fonde. *c* **1425** *Voc.* in Wr.-Wülcker 667/39 *Hoc repagulum*, dorebar. **1575** J. STILL *Gamm. Gurton* v. ii. in Hazl. *Dodsley* III. 242 Onles thy head and my doore-bar kyste. **1617** *Janua Ling.* 742 The snaile creepeth beyond the doore-barres.

'**door-bell. a.** A bell in a house, connected with the door by a wire, and rung by means of a handle. **b.** A bell fixed on a door or door-case so as to be rung in opening the door; = *door-alarm*.

c **1815** JANE AUSTEN *Persuas.* (1833) II. ii. 330 Lady Russell could not hear the door-bell. **1875** TALMAGE *Around Tea-table* ii. 8 The storm was so great that the door-bell went to sleep.

'**door-case.** [CASE *sb.*[2] 5.] The case or frame lining a doorway, in which the door is hung.

1596–7 *Bond* in Ducarel *Hist. Croydon* App. (1783) 154, x *d.* the foote for the dore cases. **1665** PEPYS *Diary* 7 Sept., The window-cases, door-cases, and chimneys, of all the house are marble. **1762–71** H. WALPOLE *Vertue's Anecd. Paint.* (1786) III. 147 Door-cases of alabaster with rich foliage. **1886** WILLIS & CLARK *Cambridge* I. 489 The west door-case..appears to be of the same yellow stone.

'**door-cheek.** Now *north. dial.* [CHEEK *sb.* 9.] One of the side-posts of a door; a door-post.

1535 COVERDALE *Isa.* vi. 3 The geastes and dorechekes moued at their crienge. **1601** HOLLAND *Pliny* II. 313 The side posts or dore cheeks of any house. **1612–15** BP. HALL *Contempl. O. T.* VIII. i, The destroying angel sees the doore-cheekes of the Israelites sprinkled with red. **1818** SCOTT *Hrt. Midl.* x, 'I daur ye..to name sic a word at my door-check!' **1855** E. WAUGH *Lanc. Life* (1857) 198 A hale old man..leaned against the door-cheek.

doore, obs. f. DOOR, DOWER.

doored (dɔəd), *a.* [f. DOOR + -ED[2].] Having a door or doors; chiefly in *comb.*, as *low-doored*.

1839 BAILEY *Festus* (1854) 97 The open doored cottages. **1861** NEALE *Notes Dalmatia, etc.* 25 It is beset with..doored pews. **1892** E. REEVES *Homeward Bound* 304 Opening..by doored archways.

[**dooring,** error for *door-ring*: see DOOR 7.]

'**door-keeper,** '**doorkeeper.** One who keeps or guards a door; a janitor, porter, ostiary.

1535 COVERDALE *1 Chron.* x. [ix.] 26 Vnto these foure maner of chefe dorrkepers were the Leuites committed. —— *Ps.* lxxxiii. [lxxxiv.] 10 A dore keper in the house of my God. **1576** FLEMING *Panopl. Epist.* 354 The dogge is a diligent dorekeeper. **1608** SHAKS. *Per.* IV. vi. 126 Avaunt, thou damned door-keeper! **1809–10** COLERIDGE *Friend* (1865) 179 Privileged..to pass into the theatre without stopping at the door-keeper's box.

'**doorless,** *a.* [see -LESS.] Having no door.

a **1200** *Grave* in *Erlanger Beitr.* (1890) 11 Dureleas is ðæt hus. *a* **1200** *Worcester Fragm.* ibid. 3 On durelease huse. **1818** SCOTT *Hrt. Midl.* xii, The doorless gateway. **1876** A. ARNOLD in *Contemp. Rev.* June 41 Doorless hovels.

doorman ('dɔəmən). **1.** A farrier's assistant.

1896 *Daily Chron.* 25 Aug. 9/5 Farrier—Young man wants Job as doorman and jobbing. **1897** *Daily News* 10 May 11/5 The present scale of pay is 5*s.* a day for doormen and 6*s.* for firemen. **1901** *N. & Q.* 9th Ser. VIII. 184/2 [Advt. in provincial newspaper] Wanted, doorman, able to nail well.

2. Also **doorsman**. An attendant at the door of a shop or place of entertainment.

1858 *Evening Star* 18 June, Doorsman to a photographic artist. **1895** *Daily News* 10 Jan. 5/2 A 'doorsman,' whose business it was to..invite the patronage of the public. **1904** *Daily Chron.* 26 July 6/4 A publican whose doorman ejected a customer. **1905** *Westm. Gaz.* 27 June 9/1 Employment as porter, odd-man, lift-man, or door-man. **1927** *Blackw. Mag.* Nov. 701/1 At this moment entered the discreet white-clad doorman. **1959** *Times* 18 June 19/5 Mehmet Hassan.. doorman..was sentenced to 21 months.

door-mat. 1. a. A mat placed before a door for cleaning the shoes before entering.

1665 HOOKE *Microgr.* 6 A very convenient substance to make Bed-matts, or Door-matts of. **1808** *Med. Jrnl.* XIX. 541 Of this plant..door mats or basses are made. **1884** J. W. EBSWORTH *Roxb. Ball.* V. II. p. xi, Our jesting here upon the door-mat with the Reader.

b. *fig.* Applied to a person upon whom people 'wipe their boots'.

1861 DICKENS *Gt. Expect.* I. xii. 207 She asked me and Joe whether we supposed she was door-mats under our feet, and how we dared to use her so. **1899** *Westm. Gaz.* 15 Apr. 2/3 'Door-mat' duty was never the portion of the one who was to be four times Prime Minister. **1915** MRS. H. WARD *Eltham House* x. 172 It's no good playing doormat. You've got to make people afraid of you. **1930** *Observer* 20 Apr. 5/5 She is not such a nullity and 'doormat' as Miss Byron. **1959** M. M. KAYE *House of Shade* xii. 163 A nice kind sugar-daddy of the adoring door-mat type. **1961** WODEHOUSE *Service with Smile* vi. 90 On these occasions he ceased to be a human doormat whom an 'Oh, Clarence!' could quell.

2. *slang.* **a.** A beard or moustache. **b.** = DOOR-STEP b.

1909 J. R. WARE *Passing Eng.* 115/2 *Door-mat*, the name given by the people to the heavy and unaccustomed beards which the Crimean heroes brought home from Russia in 1855–56... By 1882 the term came to be applied to the moustache only. **1935** A. J. CRONIN *Stars look Down* I. i. 15 Here..have a doormat, do.

door-nail. A large-headed nail, with which doors were formerly studded for strength, protection, or ornamentation: now chiefly in the alliterative phr. ***as dead, deaf, dumb, dour, as a door-nail***: see DEAD *a.* 32b., DEAF *a.* 1d., etc.

(Conjectured by Todd to be 'The nail on which in ancient doors the knocker struck'. No evidence of this appears.)

c **1350** [see DEAD *a.* 32b]. **1350** in Riley *Lond. Mem.* (1868) 262, 3000 dornail..7200 dornail. *a* **1400–50** *Alexander* 4747 Dom as a dore-nayle & defe was he bathe. **1593–1680** [see DEAD 32b.]. **1854** MRS. GASKELL *North & S.* xvii, Thornton is as dour as a doornail. **1866** ROGERS *Agric. & Prices* I. 497 Door-nails, floor and roof-nails.

doorne, obs. f. DURN.

'**door-place.** A place for a door; a doorway.

1552 HULOET, Dore, place or steade, *hypothyrides.* **1681** OTWAY *Soldier's Fort.* v. i. Wks. 1728 I. 410, I have discover'd a Door-place in the wall. **1805** *Mod. Lond.* 189 A door-place now walled up, which led into the..church.

'**door-plate.** A plate, usually of metal, on the door of a house or room, bearing the name, etc. of the resident.

1823 *Spirit Pub. Jrnls.* (1824) 94 Door plates of misters and dames. **1836–9** DICKENS *Sk. Boz* (1850) 70/1 The brass door-plate. **1884** F. M. CRAWFORD *Rom. Singer* I. 23 A marble door-plate, engraved in black with his name.

'**door-post.** The post on each side of a door-way, on one of which the door is hung.

1535 COVERDALE *Ezek.* xlv. 19 The dorepostes of the ynnermer courte. **1551** CROWLEY *Pleasure & Payne* 93 Ye deafe dorepostis, coulde ye not heare? **1840** DICKENS *Old C. Shop* xviii, The landlord was leaning against the door-post.

'**door-sill.** The sill or threshold of a door.

1563–87 FOXE *A. & M.* (1596) 259/1 To Rome..to uisit the doorsels of the Apostles [*limina Apostolorum*]. **1681** W. ROBERTSON *Phraseol. Gen.* (1693) 494 A door-cill, or threshold of a door. **1758** JOHNSON *Idler* No. 15 ¶2 She.. stands gaping at the door-sill. **1861** GEO. ELIOT *Silas M.* i. (L.), He invited no comer to step across his door-sill.

doorsman, var. DOORMAN.

'**door-stead.** [STEAD, a place.] A place for a door; a doorway.

1552 [see DOOR-PLACE.] **1607** *Nottingham Rec.* IV. 283 That the doresteades be walled vp. **1617** in Willis & Clark *Cambridge* (1886) I. 204 Two doorsteedes with free stone iames and white stone heddes. **1767** WARBURTON *Lett.* (1809) 392 Did nobody clog up the King's door-stead more than I. **1849** *Fraser's Mag.* XL. 540 He was struck with lightning on his grandmother's doorstead.

b. A timber framing, like a door-case, used to support the roof of a gallery, in coal-mining. ? *Obs.*

1747 Hooson *Miner's Dict.* G iij, The Side-pieces..we call Doorsted-Forks; they have a collar on the Top-end in which the Head-tree resteth.

'door-step. **a.** The step at the threshold of a door, raised above the level of the ground outside.

1810 Cromek *Rem. Nithsdale Song* 301 (Jam.) Coupe yere dish-water farther frae yere door-step. **1840** Dickens *Old C. Shop* II. x. 74 She..sat down upon a door-step. **1874** L. Stephen *Hours in Library* (1892) II. vi. 200 The prudent person whose charity ends at his own doorstep.

b. *slang.* A thick slice of bread.

1885 *Eng. Illustr. Mag.* June 604/2 'Doorsteps', I found, were thick slices of bread spread with jam. **1924** Lawrence & Skinner *Boy in Bush* iv. 55 Everybody..chewed huge doorsteps of bread. **1933** W. de la Mare *Lord Fish* 88 The door-step [proved to be] a slab of bread with a scrimp of margarine. **1959** *Times* 5 Nov. 13/6 There is..nothing exclusive about the childish use of..' door step' for a thick piece of bread. **1969** *Listener* 17 Apr. 533/3 Won't you slice me a doorstep please?

c. *attrib.* and *fig.* (phr. ***on the*** (or ***one's***) ***door-step***, near by).

1906 *Daily Chron.* 4 Jan. 4/1 Dr. Cooper's fight is in every respect a 'doorstep' affair. **1908** *Ibid.* 20 Feb. 3/5 All the prisoners concerned in the 'doorstep' campaign. **1909** *Westm. Gaz.* 25 Oct. 9/2 We still want doorstep workers. **1909** *Daily Chron.* 30 Dec. 3/4 The Christmas-boxes that custom decrees, are as follows... This..includes only the doorstep tributes. **1949** Blunden *After Bombing* 17 Japan's young children, staring shy..From mother's back Or door-step-side. **1952** *New Statesman* 29 Mar. 370/3 Most visitors brought doorstep sandwiches and huge home-made pasties to eat with their pint-pots of tea. **1957** A. Huxley *Let.* 8 Apr. (1969) 823 The ultimate revolution..is here on our doorstep. **1958** A. White tr. *Colette's Claudine in Paris* iv. 30 Just a few yards from here, there's a delightful flat, and we'd be practically on each other's doorsteps. **1959** *Listener* 26 Nov. 945/3 Mr. Conrad Aiken has called it '..a classic right on the doorstep'. **1963** *Times* 1 Feb. 6/3 Lord Champion said hire-purchase commitments were often entered into through a stupid desire to keep up with the Joneses. This feeling was exploited by doorstep salesmen. **1970** J. Porter *Rather Common Sort of Crime* ii. 20 A wide experience of doorstep salesmen had taught her to examine life's doorstep offers with the utmost care.

†**'door-tree.** *Obs.* = door-post, door-bar.

c **1250** *Gen. & Ex.* 3155 Ðe dure-tren and ðe uuerslaȝen, wið ysope ðe blod ben draȝen. *c* **1300** *Havelok* 1806 Hauelok lifte up the dore-tre And..he slow hem thre. **1377** Langl. *P. Pl.* B. i. 185 As ded as a dore-tree.

'doorward, *sb. arch.* Also 4 **durward, -warth.** [f. OE. *weard* warden, keeper.] A door-keeper, porter, janitor. An official title under the early Scottish monarchy; = warder of the palace.

c **950** *Lindisf. Gosp.* John x. 3 Ðissum ðe duruard [*Ags. Gosp.* ȝeatweard] ontyneð. *c* **1000** Ælfric *Past. Ep.* ⁋ 34 in Thorpe *Laws* II. 378 (Bosw.-T.) *Ostiarius* is duruweard. *c* **1205** Lay. 17672 He wende to þan berhȝate..and gratte þene dureward. **1340** *Ayenb.* 121 Þe yefþe of drede is þe doreward to þe greate þreste. **1375** Barbour *Bruce* iii. 101 Thar surname wes makyne-drosser; That is al-so mekill to say her As 'the Durwarth sonnys' perfay. **1605** Camden *Rem.* (1637) 126 Dooreward, that is, Porter. **1828–40** Tytler *Hist. Scot.* (1879) I. 248 The Chamberlain, and the hostiarius or doorward. **1867** Burton *Hist. Scot.* II. 213 Nicholas de Soulis, descended of the marriage of Marjory, a natural daughter of Alexander II, to Alan the Durward.

'doorward, -wards, *adv.* (*a.*) [see -ward.] Towards the door.

c **1400** *Beryn* 477 And drowȝe to Kittis dorward to herken and to list. **1838** D. Jerrold *Men of Char.* i. (Hoppe), His landlord began to cast significant glances doorwards.

'doorway. The opening or passage which a door serves to close or open; the space in a wall occupied by a door and its adjuncts; a portal.

1799 Southey *Eng. Eclog.* vi, Sitting at evening in that open door-way. **1858** Longf. *M. Standish* ix. 57 The bridegroom went forth and stood with the bride at the doorway. **1874** Parker *Illustr. Goth. Archit.* i. iii. 59 The rich Doorways form one of the most important features of late Norman work.

attrib. **1864** Webster, *Door-way-plane*, the space between the door-way, properly so called, and the larger door-arch-way within which it is placed. It is often richly ornamented with sculptured figures.

'door-yard. *U.S.* A yard or garden-patch about the door of a house.

c **1764** in T. D. Woolsey *Hist. Disc.* (1850) 54 The Freshmen ..are forbidden to wear their hats..in the front door-yard of the President's or Professor's house. **1854** Lowell *Cambr.* (Mass.) 30 *Yrs. Ago* Prose Wks. 1890 I. 59 The flowers which decked his little door-yard. **1878** Emerson in *N. Amer. Rev.* CXXVI. 412 We send to England for shrubs, which grow as well in our own door-yards and cow-pastures. **1913** R. Frost *Boy's Will* 9 How drifts are piled, Dooryard and road ungraded. **1941** T. S. Eliot *Dry Salvages* i. 7 The rank ailanthus of the April dooryard.

doosed, doosid: see deuced *a.*

doosen, doozen, obs. forms of dozen.

doost, dooth, obs. f. *dost, doth*: see do *v.*

doote, obs. form of dote.

dooted, var. doted *ppl. a.* 2.

dooty, var. f. dhoti, loin-cloth.

doovah, doover, varr. doofer.

doo-wop ('du:wɒp). orig. *U.S.* Also **doowhop, doowop,** etc. [Imitative.] A variety of (orig. American) vocal group music, usu. performed acapella or with little instrumental accompaniment, so called from the use of nonsense phrases accompanying the vocal lead. Also *attrib.*

1969 S. Greenlee *Spook who sat by Door* x. 83 They knew the doo-waps, rock and roll, rhythm and blues. **1972** *Jazz & Blues* Nov. 26/1 It is taken from Excello/Nasco's pop repertoire, and includes the doo-wop hits *Little darlin'* and *Oh Julie.* **1973** S. Propes *Those Oldies but Goodies* 3 Long-time rhythm and blues collectors tend to attach the greatest value to the slow, sweetly romantic ballad—the so-called Do-Wop vocal group record—preferably released in the very early 50's. **1974** *Ebony* Feb. 26/2 But don't get the idea that they're among the senior citizens of soul, hobbling along on their last doowhops. **1977** *New Musical Express* 12 Feb. 31/3 From the Marcel's doowop 'Blue Moon' to Edgar Winter's 'Free Ride', all are performed with a freshness that belies their resident status. **1981** *Westindian World* 31 July 10/5 The fun-loving ninepiece doo-wop group DARTS, have not been having much success lately. **1984** *New Yorker* 9 Apr. 49 (*caption*) Welcome to an evening of doo-wop! Just kidding, folks. Now for the Berlioz.

†**dop,** *v. Obs.* [ME. *doppen*:—OE. type **dop-pian*, represented by freq. *doppettan* to dip, immerse, baptize, and sbs. *doppa, dop-enid,* doppe; f. weak grade of **deup-an*: see dip *v.* and depe *v.*]

1. *intr.* To descend or sink suddenly into water or the like, to plump or 'pop' down; to dive.

c **1380** Wyclif *Serm.* Sel. Wks. I. 246 Þei doppen now to helle. **1398** Trevisa *Barth. De P.R.* xii. xxvi. (1495) 429 The Cote highte Mergulus and hath that name of ofte doppynge and plungynge. **1579–80** North *Plutarch* (1676) 421 Like Tonny Fish they be, which swiftly dive and dop into the depth of Ocean Sea. **1682** Dryden *Unhappy Favourite* Epil. 2 We..like drowning men, But just peep up, and then dop down again.

2. To duck or suddenly drop the head or body; to curtsy.

c **1557** in Hazl. *E.P.P.* III. 126 This fained frier..dopped than, and greet this man religiously and ofte. **1635** J. Rous *Diary* (Camden) 79 He dops, ducks, bowes, as made all of joints. **1692** Dennis *Poems in Burlesque* 9, I dopt for safety as an Officer Does in a Fight, when he's a Novice.

3. *trans.* To immerse smartly, to dip (as in baptism).

1538 Bale *God's Promises* vii. in Dodsley *O. Pl.* I. 36 Preache to the people..Doppe them in water—they knowledgynge their offence. **1633** Rogers *Treat. Sacram.* i. 78 Hee should bee baptized, which word signifieth..to dip or dop the body, or some part of it, into the water.

4. *Angling.* (*trans.* and *intr.*) = dap *v.* 1.

1651 T. Barker *Art of Angling* (1653) 7 Dop your Flie behinde a Bush, which angling I have had good sport at; we call it doping. **1653** Walton *Angler* iv. 118 With these [flies] and a short line, as I showed to angle for a chub—you may dap or dop.

Hence **'dopping** *vbl. sb.* and *ppl. a.*

1398 [see 1]. **1597** *1st Pt. Return fr. Parnass.* Prol. 2 That dopping curtesie, That fawninge bowe. **1654** H. L'Estrange *Chas. I.* (1655) 96 Erecting of fixed altars, the dopping and cringing towards them.

†**dop,** *sb.*[1] *Obs.* [f. prec. vb.] A curtsy, a dip.

1599 B. Jonson *Cynthia's Rev.* v. ii, The Venetian dop this. **1650** T. Bayly *Herba Parietis* 28 Making many pretty dops, and curtchees. **1704** D'Urfey *Hell beyond H.* 94 Salutes the Punts with Bows and Dops. *a* **1825** Forby *Voc. E. Anglia, Dop,* a short quick curtsey.

dop (dɒp), *sb.*[2] [a. Du. *dop* shell, husk, cover.]

†**1.** The pupa-case or cocoon of an insect. *rare.*

1700 Leuwenhoeck in *Phil. Trans.* XXII. 640, I have seen some flies as soon as ever they came out of their Dop.

2. *Diamond-cutting.* A small copper cup with a handle, into which a diamond is cemented, to be held while being cut or polished.

1764 Croker, etc. *Dict. Arts & Sc.* s.v. *Diamond-cutting*, Diamonds, soldered into a hollow piece of metal: the workmen call them dops. **1882** *Standard* 5 Sept. 6/2 The polisher sets the diamond in a mass of solder held in a little brass cup about an inch in diameter, with a string of stout copper wire for a handle. This instrument is called a 'dop'.

dop, *sb.*[3] *S. Afr.* [Afrikaans.] **1.** In full ***dop brandy***. Cape brandy, made from grape-skins.

1889 '*Argus' Ann. & S. Afr. Directory* 338/1 Thus we obtain 'Cognac', 'Dop', and 'Cango' brandy from spirits of wine. **1895** W. C. Scully *Kafir Stories* 18 Jim..got his daily number of tots of poisonous 'dop' brandy. **1896** *Johannesburg Weekly Times* 8 Aug. 8 Several samples of whiskies, Cape dop, and Cape brandy were examined. **1896** Baden-Powell *Matabeleland Camp.* 347 We just had sufficient 'dop' (Dutch brandy) to give everybody a tot in which to drink her health. **1901** *Westm. Gaz.* 11 May 5/1 A bottle of 'Dop'—or Cape gin. **1910** 'R. Dehan' *Dop Doctor* (1913) xiii. 98 'Dop', being the native name for the cheapest and most villainous of Cape brandies, has come to signify alcoholic drinks in general. **1921** *Chambers's Jrnl.* 647/1 The Cape 'dop' bottle brought oblivion to his tortured mind. **1950** L. G. Green *At Daybreak for Isles* i. 4 Dop brandy was to be had for sixpence a bottle.

2. A tot, especially of wine as given to farm labourers in the Western Province of the Cape.

1950 *Cape Times* (Week-end Mag.) 17 June 5/4 The pay of the *mailer* is good... Added to this, there is an occasional *dop* from both shebeener and customer. **1961** *Cape Argus* 8 Aug. 2/4 He wanted to buy a 'dop'.

dop, obs. form of deep.

dopa ('dəʊpə). *Chem.* and *Biochem.* Also DOPA. [a. G. *dopa* (B. Bloch 1917, in *Arch. f. Dermatol. und Syphilis* CXXIV. 132), f. the initial letters of the formative elements of *d*i*o*xy*p*henyl*a*lanine, a former name of the compound.]

3,4-Dihydroxyphenylalanine, $C_9H_{11}NO_4$, a crystalline amino-acid which occurs naturally (not as a constituent of proteins) and is used in the treatment of Parkinsonism; in man it is a precursor of noradrenaline and of melanin, being formed by the oxidation of tyrosine in the nerves and adrenal medulla.

1917 *Jrnl. Chem. Soc.* CXII. i. 675 When a frozen section of..skin is treated with a 1‰ solution of 3:4-dihydroxyphenylalanine (termed 'dopa'), oxidation and condensation occur with the formation of a..pigment (*dopamelanin*)..owing to the action of an..enzyme, *dopaoxydase.* **1923** *Nature* 3 Nov. 675/1 The presence of 'dopa' (3,4-dioxyphenylalanin) in the cocoons of night-butterflies and sawflies causes spontaneous formation of melanine when water is admitted. **1956** *Ibid.* 3 Mar. 430/2 The mechanism of formation of melanin pigments in insects may be as follows: Phenylalanine → tyrosine → dopa → dopaquinone..→ dopachrome, [etc.]. **1962** H. Burn *Drugs, Med. & Man* xi. 115 There are..substances which can pass through the blood-brain barrier..easily. One of these is the substance out of which noradrenaline is made. It is called dihydroxyphenylalanine, and is known as dopa for short. **1968** J. W. T. Dickerson in Davison & Dobbing *Appl. Neurochem.* ii. 61 The conversion of tyrosine to DOPA is probably mainly a non-enzymic one. **1970** *Nature* 4 Apr. 21/1 During the past decade a new approach to Parkinsonism has evolved, culminating in the introduction of L-dopa. **1970** *Daily Tel.* 8 Sept. 3/3 General practitioners in the London postal area can now prescribe L-Dopa for patients with Parkinson's disease.

dopamine ('dəʊpəmi:n). *Biochem.* [f. dopa + amine.] The immediate precursor of noradrenaline in the body, found esp. in nervous and peripheral tissue and formed by decarboxylation of dopa; 3,4-dihydroxy phenylethylamine, $C_8H_{11}NO_2$.

1959 Senoh & Witkop *Jrnl. Amer. Chem. Soc.* LXXXI. 6222/1 This investigation concerns itself with related hydroxylation mechanisms of 3,4-dihydroxy-phenethylamine ('dopamine'), a biogenic amine of key importance in metabolism. **1962** H. Burn *Drugs, Med. & Man* xi. 115 When dopa enters the brain the substance dopamine is..formed. **1965** *New Scientist* 18 Mar. 719/1 Three of the key monoamines are noradrenaline, dopamine and 5-hydroxytryptamine. **1969** *New Scientist* 30 Oct. 234/2 It is thought that if dopamine is absent, there is no way of checking the excitatory action of the ACh in the caudate nucleus, and that this..results in tremor and rigidity of the muscles. **1971** *Nature* 7 May 54/1 The principal biochemical defect associated with Parkinsonism is a marked decrease in the dopamine and serotonin content of the brain.

dopant ('dəʊpənt). [f. dop(e *v.* + -ant[1].] The substance used in doping a semiconductor.

1963 Seidman & Marshall *Semiconductor Fund.* vi. 86 The melt consists of intrinsic polycrystalline germanium or silicon mixed with suitable dopants such as phosphorus, which produces an n-type melt, or gallium, which produces a p-type melt. **1969** *New Scientist* 13 Mar. 569/2 The concentrations..of dopants used during the fabrication of the circuit. **1970** *Physics Bull.* Apr. 146/2 The electrical role of implanted dopants in semiconductors.

dopchick, -eñ, obs. or dial. = dabchick.

dope (dəʊp), *sb.* [app. a. Du. *doop* dipping, sauce, etc., f. *doopen* to dip.]

1. a. Any thick liquid or semi-fluid used as an article of food, or as a lubricant. *U.S.*

18.. *Sci. Amer. Supp.* XXII. 9033 (Cent.) 'Dope', a preparation of pitch, tallow, and other ingredients, which, being applied to the bottom of the shoes, enables the wearer to lightly glide over the snow softened by the rays of the sun. **1876** *Territorial Enterprise* (Virginia City, Nev.) 13 Feb., Nothing was known of the mysteries of 'dope'—a preparation of pitch which, being applied to the bottom of the shoes, enables the wearer to glide over snow softened by the warmth of the sun. **1947** R. Peattie *Sierra Nevada* 218 They treated the running surface of the skis with 'dope', corresponding to our modern downhill wax. **1954** E. Eager *Half Magic* v. 97 Today he..had a double hot fudge dope.

b. A preparation, mixture, or drug which is not specifically named (see quots.); = stuff *sb.*[1] 6. *slang* (orig. *U.S.*).

1872 *Chicago Tribune* 24 Dec. 4/4 He..bids us beware of the sugar, for it is full of flour and sand;..of the milk, for it is compounded of dope. **1900** Flynt & Walton *Powers that Prey* 186 Give me some more o' that dope there—quick—I —I—*am*—dyin'. **1901** Ade *Forty Mod. Fables* 188 Give me some perfumed Dope that will restore a Peaches and Cream Complexion. **1912** F. A. Talbot *Moving Pictures* 53 (*caption*) Two small barrels..made all the film base, or 'dope', as it is called, in 1891. **1915** A. D. Gillespie *Let.* 4 July (1916) 222 The hay fever is better now, more because the season is passing than by reason of the doctor's 'dopes', I think. **1915** E. Poole *Harbor* 60 Joe's father vaccinated about a score of children that week. The 'dope' he used was mailed to him by a drug firm. **1924** Webster Add., *Dope*... 5. *Photogr.* A varnish used to facilitate retouching, block out portions of a negative, etc. **1928** *Sunday Dispatch* 8 July 9/5 'Dope finish' [is a slang expression] for face paint and powder.

c. A varnish applied to the cloth surface of aeroplane parts, in order to increase strength and to keep them taut and air-tight. Also, a liquid preparation applied to air-ship coverings, to increase gas-tightness.

1912 *Aeroplane* 19 Dec. 607 Cellon... The Fabric Dope used by the leading British and Continental Aeroplane and Hydro-aeroplane Builders. **1916** H. BARBER *Aeroplane Speaks 142 Strut, Dope*, a strut within a surface, so placed as to prevent the tension of the doped fabric from distorting the framework. **1917** *Times* 1 June 9/5 The King and Queen ..went on through..the seaplane department, and the 'dope' room. **1918** A. BARR in A. J. Swinton *Aeroplane Handbk.* (1920) 144 The Germans at the beginning of the war used acetate dope and covered it with transparent oil varnish. **1930** *Flight* 17 Jan. 134/2 Dope is a solution of cellulose esters in various solvents and diluents. **1967** B. ROBERTSON *Aircraft Markings* 14 The French had used a sky blue dope early in the war at the time when French uniforms were of horizon blue.

d. A substance added to petrol or other fuel, etc., to increase its efficiency; an additive.

1930 *Engineering* 11 July 31/1 A lubricant such as oleine.. or oleic acid, when added to a fuel containing metallic dope, had the effect of partially inhibiting the detonation-delaying action of the dope. **1937** *Times* 13 Apr. p. xix/4 Dopes both for petrol and for lubricating oils are now well known.

2. An absorbent material used to hold a lubricant; the absorbent element in a high explosive.

1880 *Trans. Amer. Inst. Min. Eng.* VIII. 417 Hercules powder..contains a very large proportion of nitrate of soda ..the remainder of the dope being incombustible carbonate of magnesia. **1881** RAYMOND *Mining Gloss.* s.v. *Explosives, Giant-powder*, a mixture of nitroglycerin with a dry pulverized mineral or vegetable absorbent or dope.

3. *colloq.* (orig. *dial.*). A stupid person, a simpleton, a fool. Also (*U.S. slang*), a person under the influence of, or addicted to, some drug (see sense 3 b).

1851 *Gloss. Words Cumberland* 8 *Dope*, a simpleton. **1866** E. L. LINTON *L. Lorton* II. i. 17 A 'downo-canno dope'—which meant a spiritless simpleton. *Ibid.* III. ii. 39 She was ..'a dozened lile dope'. **1909** *Sat. Even. Post* 1 May 5/1 He's an old dope, which he don't look like, or he's on. **1925** FRASER & GIBBONS *Soldier & Sailor Words* 81 *Dope*,..a fool. **1925** N. VENNER *Imperfect Impostor* ii. 17, I am just the humble dope; the clay pigeon; the simple-minded confederate. **1928** E. WALLACE *Flying Squad* xiv. 121 How many times have I told you not to frighten that girl, you poor dope? **1938** R. E. SHERWOOD *Idiot's Delight* I. 17 That wasn't an officer, that was a porter, you dope! **1948** *Chicago Daily News* 11 June 16/4 Cold tea sold to night life dopes for brandy at 75 cents a throw. **1957** J. BRAINE *Room at Top* 48 'Who's Alice?' I asked. 'You've met her, you dope.' **1959** P. CAPON *Amongst those Missing* 108 Silly dope, he can't go on dodging the Court for ever.

b. 'Opium, especially the thick treacle-like preparation used in opium-smoking' (Cent. Dict. Suppl. 1909); hence applied to stupefying drugs and narcotics in general, or to alcoholic drink. *slang* (orig. *U.S.*). (See also sense 5.)

1889 *Kansas Times & Star* 8 Oct., The oldest of the trio, an Irishman from County Cork, was very hilarious... The 'dope' made him 20 years younger and very pugnacious. **1891** T. W. KNOX in H. Campbell *Darkness & Daylight* (1892) xxviii. 570 The opium used for smoking—called by the smokers 'dope'—is an aqueous extract of the ordinary commercial gum. **1894** J. L. FORD *Lit. Shop* ix. 130 Opium-joints—those mysterious dens in which..the fumes of the burning 'dope' cloy the senses. **1896** ADE *Artie* viii. 75, I would advise you to stop smokin that double X brand of dope. **1896** *Chautauquan* Oct. 60/1 In San Francisco, large confiscations of 'dope' are made nearly every week. **1920** *Outward Bound* Oct. 38/1 The death of a fascinating actress from an overdose of 'dope'. **1922** *Public Opinion* 5 May 420/3 The cabarets in Constantinople are a meeting place for all the world's dope purveyors.

fig. **1937** *Ess. & Stud.* XXII. 146 Poetry was comparatively popular bcause it was dope, though a mild and fairly harmless dope like cigarette-smoking.

c. A medical preparation administered to a race-horse for the purpose of affecting its performance.

1900 *Westm. Gaz.* 30 Oct. 7/3 It is administered in capsules, given in a gelatine of varying thickness according to the required time when the 'dope' is desired to take effect. **1913** *Badm. Mag.* Jan. 88 A dope proper may be administered [to a horse] as a powder laid on the tongue, as a drink—usually given in old ale—or by the hypodermic syringe.

d. [Perh. arising from the ambiguity of the abbrev. *coke* = (*a*) cocaine, (*b*) Coca-Cola.] Coca-Cola or some other carbonated drink. *local U.S. slang.*

1915 *Printer's Ink* 23 Sept. 46/2 The propensity of a large portion of those who regularly drink Coca-Cola to call for their favorite drink as 'dope' or 'coke' or 'koke'. **1940** C. MCCULLERS *Heart is Lonely Hunter* (1943) II. i. 83 If she had any money she bought a dope or a Milky Way at Mister Brannon's. **1947** F. G. PATTON in *55 Short Stories from New Yorker* (1952) 224 Want a dope?.. I tried to call them cokes once.

4. Information, esp. on a particular subject or of a kind not widely disseminated or easily obtained; (a statement of) facts or essential details; also, information, a statement, etc., designed to gloss over or disguise facts; flattering or misleading talk. *slang* (orig. *U.S.*).

1901 'H. MCHUGH' *John Henry* 77 I've known Tommy for a long time, so he feels free to read his dope to me. **1904** W. H. SMITH *Promoters* iii. 72 Unless you cover your dope with a sort of angel-of-light coating that would fool Gabriel himself, you'll never get there. **1905** R. BEACH *Pardners* (1912) i. 26 He handed me the dope: 'In re Olive Troop Morrow *vs.* Justus Morroe'. **1910** S. E. WHITE *Rules of Game* (1913) II. iii. 126 Gosh! I get sick of handing out dope to these yaps. **1914** JACKSON & HELLYER *Vocab. Criminal Slang* 8 The most popular slang term in use today in the unregenerate world — 'dope' .. signifying 'news', 'intelligence', or 'meaning'. **1915** FROEST & DILNOT *Crime Club* xii. 290 Don't pull any of that dope on me. **1917** A. G. EMPEY *From Fire Step* 103, I was to send the dope to Cassell and he would transmit it to the Battery Commander as officially coming through the observation post. **1919** *Detective Story Mag.* XXVIII. I. 13, I suggested it to a detective, but he laughed at me and said the article was nothing but '*dope*'. **1920** *Public Opinion* 9 July 43/3 Your patent dialectic dope By gulps we take with zest. **1920** WODEHOUSE *Damsel in Distress* xx. 235 I could help you there. I've got the thing down fine. I've got the infallible dope! **1921** *19th Cent.* May 748 He does not quite believe that the Bolshevik leaders themselves believe in their doctrines. He strongly suspects that on their part it is mainly 'dope'. **1922** H. L. FOSTER *Adv. Trop. Tramp* x. 140 Run up to Bolivia and get the dope on this affair. **1935** AUDEN & ISHERWOOD *Dog beneath Skin* I. ii. 34 He did all the dope about the Army Contracts trial. **1945** A. CHRISTIE *Sparkling Cyanide* III. x. 136, I shouldn't dream of..denying it. You've obviously cabled to America and got all the dope.

5. *attrib.* and *Comb.*, as (sense 3 b) ***dope-addict, -dream, -merchant, -seller, -smuggler, -smuggling, -traffic, -trafficking***; **dope-book** *U.S. slang*, a book of information on any subject; also *fig.*; **dope-fiend** *slang* (orig. *U.S.*), a drug-addict; **dope-pedlar** (also **-peddler**), **-runner**, a seller of illicit drugs; hence ***dope-peddling, -running*** vbl. sbs.; **dope-ring**, a group of people engaged in obtaining, selling, and using narcotics; **dope-sheet** *U.S. slang*, a sheet of paper bearing information or instructions, esp. written or printed information about race-horses; **dope-shop**, a place where dope (sense 1 c) is applied to aeroplanes, etc.; **dope-stick** *slang* (see quot. 1918: examples are *N.Z.*).

1933 D. L. SAYERS *Murder must Advertise* xi. 188 A *dope-addict's dream. **1909** *Cent. Dict.* Suppl., **Dope-book*, a miscellaneous collection of racing information. **1918** *Amer. Mag.* Aug. 38/2 The one that invents the dope book on the female race, and the bird that holds a patent on the complete understanding of human nature. **1908** U. SINCLAIR *Metropolis* 137 What will people think..seeing you sitting there like a man in a *dope dream? **1934** H. G. WELLS *Exper. Autobiogr.* II. ix. 821, I had expected to find a new Russia stirring in its sleep..and I found it sinking deeper into the dope-dream of Sovietic self-sufficiency. **1896** *Sun* (N.Y.) Dec., 'A *dope fiend'... A victim of the opium habit. **1914** R. H. DAVIS *With Allies* (1915) 158 With the desperation of a dope fiend clutching his last pill of cocaine. **1963** *Punch* 20 Mar. 425/2 Mr. Trocchi's dopefiends. **1921** *Outward Bound* Apr. 44/2 The policy of the '*dope merchant'.. would issue in sleep, death and fossilisation. **1923** *Jrnl. Amer. Inst. Crim. Law & Criminol.* Aug. 292 No other group comes closer to the bootlegger or the *dope peddler. **1933** D. L. SAYERS *Murder must Advertise* xii. 217 You must be the dead spit of some habitual dope-peddler. **1937** A. J. CRONIN *Citadel* 388 He's nothing but a sleek dope peddler. **1959** *News Chron.* 19 Aug. 6/3 The bookies, the dope pedlars and bootleggers. **1959** P. TOWNSEND *Died o' Wednesday* x. 177 Malosti's current livelihood, the *dope-peddling organisation. **1959** F. USHER *Death in Error* ix. 143 Nothing worse than a little mild dope peddling goes on. **1929** D. HAMMETT *Dain Curse* (1930) iii. 24 What do you think he is?.. Head of a *dope ring? **1930** *Daily Express* 6 Nov. 19/4 Gangsters, dope rings, tough guys. **1957** P. MOORE *Science & Fiction* 100 Veterans whose sole mission in life was to uncover dope-rings led by unscrupulous Martians. **1933** D. L. SAYERS *Murder must Advertise* xiv. 238 He said you were a *dope-runner. **1941** A. CHRISTIE *Evil under Sun* xi. 206 The result of her getting mixed up..with the *dope-running stunt. **1953** K. TENNANT *Joyful Condemned* xxxi. 303 You used to know all about his dope-running. **1930** *New Statesman* 27 Dec. 356/2 He was using the money to finance a gang of *dope-sellers. **1903** ADE *People you Know* 111 When he arrived at the Track he gave up for a Badge and a *Dope-Sheet and a couple of Perfectos. **1959** HALAS & MANVELL *Technique Film Animation* xix. 189 His work book..must next be elaborated on a different set of printed sheets, generally known as camera-exposure charts or, in the U.S.A., as dope sheets. **1933** *Aeroplane* 26 Apr. 732/1 When the machine reaches the end of the line it is ready to go straight to the *dope shop. **1937** D. & H. TEILHET *Feather Cloak Murders* ii. 43 Wonder if your friends..know you're so companionable with a *dope smuggler, eh? **1941** A. CHRISTIE *Evil under Sun* xi. 215 The whole case hinges on *dope smuggling. **1969** M. G. EBERHART *Message from Hong Kong* xii. 104 If it's dope smuggling it's too big for me. **1918** *N.Z. at Front 1918* 132 Cigarettes! smokes, fags, weeds, *dope-sticks—they are known by many strange names. **1930** W. SMYTH *Wooden Rails* xi. 168 Pass me those dope-sticks, there's a dear. **1933** J. B. PRIESTLEY *Wonder Hero* iii. 95 He wondered which of the queer fellows..hanging about street corners were in the *dope traffic. **1933** D. L. SAYERS *Murder must Advertise* xv. 249 The crookedness of *dope-trafficking. **1954** J. SYMONS *Narrowing Circle* xii. 47 Dimmock had begun as an agent of the Barcini brothers, who got a seven-year stretch for dope trafficking.

dope, *v.* orig. *U.S.* [f. DOPE *sb.*]

1. *trans.* To administer dope to (a person, a horse); to stupefy with a drug; to drug.

1889 [implied in DOPING *vbl. sb.* below]. **1891** FARMER *Slang* II. 309/2 *Dope v.* (American), to drug with tobacco. Also *Doping* = the practice. **1900** *Westm. Gaz.* 23 Oct. 8/2 They urge a liberal investment on the American horse, and confidentially impart the information that the animal is 'doped'. **1902** H. L. WILSON *Spenders* xxxv. 429 That guy that doped me, he wa'n't satisfied with my good thirty-dollar wad. **1915** C. S. JONES *Hohenzollern* 169 The King (who, if we are to believe his fair companion, used to be liberally doped) would awake from a trance at a *séance* to find his *inamorata* in his arms. **1919** H. L. WILSON *Ma Pettengill* ii. 62 To say nothing of doping him with asperin and quinine and camphor and menthol and hot tea and soothing words. **1919** G. PAGE *Veldt Trail* xix. 200 'They must have kept him [*sc.* a horse] pretty short of food.'..' Or doped him,' suggested Birkdale. **1922** *Blackw. Mag.* May 632/2 He ladled into his nose sufficient snuff to have doped an ordinary man. **1955** *Times* 8 June 4/5 He had heard of greyhounds being doped, but not to make them run faster.

fig. **1908** G. H. LORIMER *J. Spurlock* iii. 41, I was so doped with my siren song that I steered straight for the rocks. **1928** G. B. SHAW *Intell. Woman's Guide Socialism* I. 218 Boycotting the Churches as mere contrivances for doping the workers into submission to Capitalism.

b. *intr.* To take or be addicted to drugs.

1909 in *Cent. Dict.* Suppl. **1926** N. LUCAS *London & its Criminals* xviii. 253 Doping is so prevalent in the East that the traffic in drugs appeals naturally to the Eastern crook. **1933** D. L. SAYERS *Murder must Advertise* v. 85 Did he dope?

2. To treat with an adulterant, etc.; to 'doctor'.

1898 *Let.* in *Congress. Rec.* App. 223/1 They will run their flutter mills and mixers, and dope the flour to suit themselves. **1906** in Asher & Heal *Send no Money* (1942) 95 You would like to know just where you are at before you 'dope' that kind of stock with a strange mixture. **1913** *Sunday Times* (Trenton, N.J.) 2 Mar. 1 Alternative offered to the water drinkers of Trenton: Typhoid if the water isn't 'doped' with hypochlorite of lime; an itch if it is.

b. *Electr.* To add an impurity to (a semiconductor) to produce a desired electrical characteristic.

1955 F. E. TERMAN *Electronic & Radio Engin.* (ed. 4) xxi. 753 The degree of doping is commonly expressed in terms of the conductivity (or resistivity) of the resulting material. **1956** L. P. HUNTER *Handbk. Semiconductor Electronics* VII. 7 The melt is doped with a donor (arsenic) so as to produce a low-resistivity N-type emitter. *Ibid.* VI. 26 A uniformly doped crystal will be grown. **1962** SIMPSON & RICHARDS *Junction Transistors* iii. 43 The distance that the barrier extends into the semiconductor is also smaller in the case of a heavily doped semiconductor. **1970** *Sci. Amer.* Feb. 22/3 By suitable masking and 'doping' techniques, which selectively altered the electrical behavior of small regions, several score transistors could be created on each wafer.

3. To smear, daub; *spec.* to apply 'dope' to (the outer fabric of an aeroplane or the like).

1868 *Putnam's Mag.* II. 363 With their snow-shoes thoroughly 'doped', the crowd resort to some suitable place for the contest, which begins with a grand dash. **1902** *Dialect Notes* II. 233 *Dope*, v. tr. 1. To smear, or lubricate. 2. To put salve on a wound. **1916** *Sphere* 25 Mar. 321/1 The wings are finished,..and the whole 'doped', and ready. **1917** *Times* 1 June 9/5 Some hundreds of girls were engaged in'doping' the fabric which covers the planes, rudders and ailerons. **1922** *Encycl. Brit.* XXX. 59/1 [Airship.] Cotton.. appears to have some advantages owing to its great uniformity of contraction when doped. **1928** C. F. S. GAMBLE *N. Sea Air Station* 10 The envelope was 'doped' with aluminium paint on its top side and with yellow pigment on the lower portions. **1935** H. L. DAVIS *Honey in Horn* 12 There was a salad of lettuce whittled into shoestrings..and doped with vinegar and bacon grease. **1941** *Illustr. London News* CXCIX. 198 (*caption*) A rigger dopes fresh patches of fabric over the muzzles of the guns to assist in streamlining and speed until the aircraft opens fire.

4. *to dope out.* **a.** To make out; to find out, discover; to get the truth about.

1906 'O. HENRY' *Four Million* (1916) 161 All the same, I believe it was the hand of Fate that doped out the way for me to find her. **1913** E. D. BIGGERS *7 Keys to Baldpate* ii. 31 Ther's something I haven't quite doped out. That is—who's trespassing, me or you? **1914** R. H. DAVIS *With the Allies* (1915) 10 We would study the morning papers and.. from them try to dope out the winners. **1918** C. WELLS *Vicky Van* xv. 180, I dope out all this has to be so. **1919** WODEHOUSE *Damsel in Distress* ii. 30 Nature had it all doped out for me to be the Belle of Hicks Corners. **1922** *Short Stories* Feb. 102/2 'How'd you dope it out, Kid?' asked one. 'Tell us how you could do such good detective work.' **1926** J. BLACK *You can't Win* xxiii. 367, I had all the criminal lawyers in San Francisco doped out like race horses by this time. **1943** N. MARSH *Colour Scheme* v. 94 Uncle James dopes it out that it's been Questing's idea to get this place on his own.

b. To work out; to get hold of.

1906 'O. HENRY' *Four Million* (1916) 191 He's doped out a fifty-dollar bill, anyway. **1919** *Detective Story Mag.* XXVIII. I. 6 He might have doped out a corking yarn about how the Phantom..made everybody believe that the explosion killed him. **1922** *Short Stories* Feb. 175/2, I didn't have time to dope out any plot till I got back to Denver.

Hence **doped** *ppl. a.*; **'doping** *vbl. sb.* and *ppl. a.* Also **'doper**, one who dopes; one who administers or takes drugs.

1889 BARRÈRE & LELAND *Dict. Slang* s.v., Doping is the stupifying men with tobacco prepared in a peculiar way... Nine out of ten saloons in the slums employ doping as a means to increase their illicit revenue. —*American Newspaper.* **1900** *Daily News* 14 Nov. 8/4 'Doping' meant the administration to a horse of certain medical preparations, with the object of either stimulating or retarding the animal's progress in a race. **1903** *Westm. Gaz.* 15 Sept. 5/2 The Jockey Club propose to pass a rule forbidding doping in any shape or form. **1903** *Sun* (N.Y.) 23 Nov. 12 A 'doped' cigar was given to him in a pool and billiard room, and it had pretty near the same effect on him as knockout drops. **1913** *Daily Mail* 11 Mar. 7/5 'Doped' Athletes... It is well known..that the Russian skaters take such stimulants [as strychnine]. **1913** *Badm. Mag.* Jan. 89 A doped animal will run till it is done, mad drunk with the drug. *Ibid.*, A regular doper always tries his horses at home. **1913** *Aeroplane* 13 Mar. 303/1 The shiny surface of well 'doped' wings. **1914** *Racing Calendar* 23 July, I was unable to obtain evidence of the presence of a doping agent. **1921** *Blackw. Mag.* Apr. 535/2 She rejoined the remainder of the passengers.., having in her hands a doped handkerchief. **1922** *Ibid.* Jan. 124/1 He might publish in his doped and venal press the felicitations that were showered upon him. **1923** WODEHOUSE *Inimitable Jeeves* xiv, To tell me we ought to cook Harold's food ourselves to prevent doping. **1926** *Chambers's Jrnl.* 17 July 515/1 So the old reprobate's dopings had told at long last. **1926** [see DOPE *v.* 1 b]. **1935** *Discovery* July 208/2 The 'doping' of the sample water with 'O.T.' is carried out automatically and with perfect precision. *Ibid.*, The colour of the doped solution is intermediate between those of the two permanent solutions. **1955** *Times* 7 June 3/3 A Harley Street specialist was one of three men who were alleged at the Central Criminal Court yesterday to have been concerned in a conspiracy concerning the doping of greyhounds. **1956, 1970** [see DOPE *v.* 2 b].

dopester ('dəʊpstə(r)). *slang* (orig. *U.S.*). [f. DOPE *sb.* + -STER.] **1.** One who collects information on, and forecasts the result of, sporting events, elections, etc. Cf. DOPE *sb.* 4.

1907 *Cosmopolitan Mag.* Feb. 363/1 As we talked on a corner not long ago, A Dopester..stepped up to us. **1916** *All-Story Weekly* 25 Mar. 283 The dopesters had looked up those two coast fights, and that ended the betting. **1921** *Daily Colonist* (Victoria, B.C.) 2 Apr. 10/3 America is in line for the bulk of the Davis Cup matches this summer according to the dopesters who put their pencils to work right after the recent draw. **1964** *Economist* 25 Apr. 396/1 The inside dopesters, squeezing the latest gossip about intra-party machinations out of politicians.

2. One who sells, uses, or is addicted to, drugs.

1938 J. RICE *Somers Inheritance* I. vi. 45 A dopester seldom drinks and most drinkers have not yet taken to dope.

dopey ('dəʊpɪ), *a. slang* (orig. *U.S.*). Also **dopy**. [f. DOPE *sb.* 3 b.] **1.** Sluggish or stupefied, with or as with a drug.

1896 *Sun* (N.Y.) Dec., A man who acts as if under the influence of the poppy drug is said to be dopy. **1900** ADE *More Fables in Slang* (1902) 179 A Young Man with Hair who played the 'Cello. He was so wrapped up in his Art that he acted Dopey most of the time. *a* **1909** BUCK *Handbk. Med. Sci.* VI. 686 (Cent. Dict. Suppl.), The patients are said to be 'dopey'; they are markedly prostrated, indifferent to their surroundings, and want only to be left undisturbed. **1914** R. BROOKE *Let.* Aug. (1968) 607 The general uneasiness..seems to take all the strength out of me. I feel 'dopey'. **1921** B. MATTHEWS *Ess. English* 112, I began to hear men assert that they felt *dopy, i.e.* sluggish, as though they had taken an opiate. **1924** A. J. SMALL *Frozen Gold* iii. 97 Henderson was still a bit dopey [after a blow on the head]. **1932** L. GOLDING *Magnolia St.* III. vi. 546 'Bella, you look all dopy! What's wrong?'.. Her eyes took on a far focus. **1932** J. B. PRIESTLEY *Dangerous Corner* II. 56, I took three of those tablets I have to make me sleep and now I feel absolutely dopey. **1957** E. EAGER *Magic by Lake* 71 The four children..went on being dopey and droopy and sleepy all afternoon when they *did* get up.

2. Stupid, 'dumb'.

1896 *Cincinnati Enquirer* 2 Aug. 2/1 There is an impression of truth to the rather 'dopy' proposition that makes it worthy of newspaper space. **1939** S. V. BENÉT *Tales before Midnight* 150 'He said I was a little angel.' 'Was he dopey!' said her elder, blightingly. **1947** N. MARSH *Final Curtain* v. 81 Am I dopey? I tell you I *heard* her. **1957** J. BRAINE *Room at Top* 119 It's quite unmistakable, that look—a sort of dopy joyfulness. **1957** I. CROSS *God Boy* (1958) xv. 118 'I'm off home—I don't feel like it,' I said. 'Don't be dopey,' said Joe. **1963** H. GARNER *Best Stories* 227 Step began to laugh. 'That dopey foreman. He didn't bother to check with me.'

dopiness ('dəʊpɪnɪs). *N.Z.* [f. DOPEY *a.* + -NESS.] A deficiency disease of sheep.

1932 *Discovery* Nov. 357/2 Recent investigations in New Zealand testify to..the value of top dressing of pastures with lime and superphosphate where sheep are affected with dopiness diseases. **1934** L. J. WILD *Soils & Manures in N.Z.* (ed. 3) v. 72 The sheep disease called 'dopiness' occurs notably in the Mairoa district. **1950** *N.Z. Jrnl. Agric.* July 33/3 Some green, succulent feed just before and at lambing assists in the prevention of diseases associated with lambing—dopiness (twin lamb disease or ante-partum paralysis) and milk fever.

dople, doplyt, obs. forms of DOUBLE, -ET.

†**doppe.** *Obs.* [OE. *doppa* in *dufedoppa*: see DIVEDAP, and DOP *v.*] A bird that dops or dives; a dabchick.

13.. *K. Alis.* 5776 Hy plumten doune, as an doppe, In the water, at on scoppe.

‖**doppelganger, dopple-, -gänger** ('dɒpəl,gæŋə(r), -'gɛŋə(r)). [See DOUBLE-GANGER.] = DOUBLE-GANGER I.

1851 M. A. DENHAM in *Denham Tracts* (1895) II. 79 Hell-hounds, dopple-gangers, boggleboes. **1879** C. L. DODGSON *Euclid & Mod. Rivals* I. ii, Are their Doppelgänger available? **1907** N. MUNRO *Daft Days* xxviii, Miss Macintosh is surely your doppelganger. **1940** M. LOWRY *Let.* 7 May (1967) 30 It may well be that you will observe my little doppelgänger poltergeist soul hoisting a drink in a bar in them parts. **1952** C. DAY LEWIS tr. *Virgil's Aeneid* x. 228 Not knowing that what so thrilled him was only a *doppelgänger*.

†'**dopper**[1]. *Obs.* Also 5 dooper, dowpar. [f. DOP *v.* + -ER[1].] One who or that which 'dops'.

1. A diving-bird, a didapper.

c **1440** *Promp. Parv.* 127/1 Doppar, or dydoppar, watyr byrde. **1530** PALSGR. 214/2 Doppar, byrde. **1634** W. WOOD *New Eng. Prosp.* I. viii, Snites, Doppers, Sea-Larkes.

2. A fishing-rod used in 'dopping' or dapping.

1688 R. HOLME *Armoury* III. 103/1 A Dopper is a strong long Rod very tite.

Dopper[2] ('dɒpə(r)). Also 7 doper. [ad. Du. *dooper*, dipper, baptist, f. *doopen* to dip; erroneously shortened after DOP *v.*] A (Dutch) Baptist or Anabaptist; = DIPPER 2.

1620 B. JONSON *News fr. New World* Wks. (Rtldg.) 615/2 A world of Doppers! **1625** —— *Staple of N.* III. ii, This is a Doper, a she Anabaptist!

Dopper[3] ('dɒpə(r)). *S. Afr.* Also **dopper**. [Afrikaans, of uncertain origin.] The sobriquet of a member of the 'Gereformeerde Kerk in Suid-Afrika', a strictly orthodox Calvinistic denomination, commonly regarded as being old-fashioned in ideas, manner, and dress. Hence '**Dopperdom** (*rare*), the Doppers collectively.

1850 N. J. MERRIMAN *Jrnl.* 9 Dec. in *Kafir, Hottentot, & Frontier Farmer* (1854) 96 These Doppers are a sort of Dutch Church puritans. **1859** *Queenstown Free Press* 4 May (Pettman), The *Doppers* would not be satisfied with an angel from heaven. **1881** *Daily News* 21 Jan. 5/5 Paul Kruger.. Belonging to the sect of the Doppers. **1898** W. HARCOURT *Let.* 29 Aug. in A. G. Gardiner *Life W. H.* (1923) II. xxiii. 461 It is with a view to this that A. M. [*sc.* A. Milner] wants a display of more force..to 'convince Dopperdom that *England means war*', if Kruger does not do our bidding. **1900** *Daily News* 13 Feb. 7/2 The burghers being chiefly of the 'dopper' or back-country class. **1926** *Brit. Weekly* 27 May 158/1 The charming Dutch girl lived with her old Dopper father on a nearby farm. **1958** *Cape Times* 27 Dec. 3/6 The old dopper town of Krugersdorp.

doppie ('dɒpɪ). *S. Afr.* [dim. of DOP *sb.*[3]] A grape-skin.

1948 *Cape Times* (Week-end Mag.) 24 Jan. 12/7 (Advt.), A Grape Crusher and two Wine and Doppies Pumps manufactured by Consani's for the Wine Industry. **1955** J. PACKER *Valley of Vines* i. 13 If you fell into a tank among the *doppies*—the skins—and the wine, you died.

dopping: see under DOP *v.*

Doppler ('dɒplə(r)). Also **doppler**. The name of C. J. *Doppler* (1803-53), Austrian mathematician and physicist, used *attrib.* or in the possessive to designate an effect first explained by him in 1842 (in *Abh. d. k. böhm. Ges. d. Wiss.* (1843) 5th ser. II. 465-82) and other phenomena related to it or caused by it, as ***Doppler broadening*** (of spectral lines), ***Doppler('s) principle***; **Doppler effect**, the effect on sound, light, or other waves of relative motion between the source of the waves and the observer: the observed frequency of the waves is higher or lower than the emitted frequency according as the source (or the observer) is moving towards or away from the observer (or the source); **Doppler shift**, the change of the frequency resulting from the Doppler effect. Also in equipment or procedures utilizing the Doppler effect, as ***Doppler navigation, radar***.

1871 E. ATKINSON tr. *Ganot's Physics* (ed. 5) v. i. 165 When a sounding body approaches the ear, the tone perceived is somewhat higher than the true one; but if the source of sound recedes..the tone perceived is lower. The truth of this, which is known as Doppler's principle, will be apparent from the following considerations. **1905** E. C. C. BALY *Spectroscopy* xii. 382 In order to see if the rapidly moving particles in the streamers caused any displacement in the position of the lines in the spectrum on what is known as the Doppler effect. **1926** H. MACPHERSON *Mod. Astron.* 34 The application of Doppler's principle to the measurement of the rotation and atmospheric motions of the Sun. *Ibid.* 119 The Doppler principle was first applied to the study of stellar motions as far back as 1868. **1927** A. S. EDDINGTON *Stars & Atoms* 75 Owing to the Doppler effect a moving atom absorbs a rather different wave-length from a stationary atom. **1945** *Electronic Engin.* XVII. 583 The sound of an aeroplane flying low is heard approaching, passing overhead with the attendant 'Doppler' effect, or apparent change in engine speed, then dying away into the distance. **1953** *Ibid.* XXV. 113/1 The doppler frequency of a 3·5 cm radar detecting a target of 400 M.P.H. radial velocity. **1955** *Sci. Amer.* Sept. 136/3 Special sensitive equipment makes it possible to measure the amount of this Doppler shift even though the track may last only a fraction of a second. **1956** *Nature* 18 Feb. 299/2 This spectral line enables not only the spatial distribution of hydrogen in the galaxy to be studied, but also the velocity by the Doppler displacement. **1958** *Oxf. Mag.* 8 May 418/1 Atomic beams ..were used to reduce the 'Doppler width' of spectral lines. **1959** J. L. NAYLER *Dict. Aeronaut. Engin.* 84 A Doppler radar unit is used to obtain a running record of the speed of guided missiles. **1960** *Gloss. Terms Telecomm. (B.S.I.)* 266 *Doppler radar*, a form of radar in which the radio Doppler effect is used to determine the radial component of the velocity of a target relative to the radar system. **1963** G. TROUP *Masers & Lasers* (ed. 2) iii. 38 The processes of spontaneous emission broadening, Doppler broadening and pressure broadening. **1966** *Economist* 16 Apr. 253 Marconi ..has supplied a complete airadio system (comprising communications, approach navigation, Doppler navigation and automatic direction-finding equipment). **1966** *McGraw-Hill Encycl. Sci. & Technol.* I. 164/1 Airborne radar has been used for determining drift through the Doppler principle. **1967** *Listener* 27 Apr. 544/3 In the case of the red shifts in the light from the extra-galactic nebulae we interpret these as a doppler effect. **1967** *Times Rev. Industry* Feb. 51/3 Air India has placed an order worth nearly £250,000 with the Marconi Company for Doppler navigators to fit its fleet of Boeing 707s.

Hence **Doppler-shift** *v. trans.*, to cause a Doppler shift of.

1971 *Nature* 15 Jan. 158/2 The frequency of the light undergoing Rayleigh scattering by molecules is Doppler shifted by thermal motions.

dopplerite ('dɒplәraɪt). *Min.* [Named 1849, f. *Doppler*, surname of a German physicist: see -ITE.] 'A hydrocarbon found in certain peat beds, amorphous and jelly-like when fresh, and elastic when dried, looking like black pitch' (Dana *Min.* (1854) 474).

1863-72 WATTS *Dict. Chem.* II. 345 *Dopplerite*.. occurring in layers in the peat near Aussee in Styria.

†'**doppy.** *Obs.* [ad. It. *doppia* a double, 'also a double ducket of gold' (Florio).] A former gold coin of Italy, worth, in different states, from 11*s.* 4*d.* to 21*s.*; a pistole.

1691 *Lond. Gaz.* No. 2721/2 Should pay them 1400 Doppies at two terms. **1692** *Ibid.* No. 2730/1. [**1858** SIMMONDS *Dict. Trade, Doppia*, another name for the pistole.]

†**dopt**, aphetic f. ADOPT *v. Obs.*

1631 H. CHETTLE *Trag. Hoffman* (N.), Should hee bee dopted, I would dopt him, and herrite him.

dopy, var. DOPEY *a.*

dor, dorr (dɔː(r)), *sb.*[1] Also 4-7 dorre, 5-8 dore, 7 doar. [OE. *dora*: of unknown origin.] An insect that flies with a loud humming noise.

†**1.** Applied to species of bees or flies; also ***dor-bee, dor-fly***. *spec.* **a.** A humble-bee or bumble-bee. **b.** A drone bee. **c.** A hornet. **d.** *fig.* A drone, a lazy idler. *Obs.*

a **700** *Epinal Gloss.* 119 Atticus, dora. *c* **1000** *Sax. Leechd.* II. 28 Doran huniȝ and ticcenes ȝeallan. *Ibid.*, þa ahsan ȝemenge wið dorena huniȝ. *c* **1050** *Cleopatra Glosses* in Wr.-Wülcker 351 *Adticus*, feldbeo, dora. *c* **1330** *Arth. & Merl.* 6428 So dorren don and flesche fleighen. **14..** *Lat. & Eng. Voc.* in Wr.-Wülcker 576 *Crabo*. a dore. *c* **1510** BARCLAY *Mirr. Gd. Manners* (1570) C v, If there come a hornet, a dor, or greater flye, They breake the light webbes. **1551** ROBINSON *More's Utop.* (Arb.) 38 Gentlemen which can not be content to liue idle them-selfes, lyke dorres. **1574** HYLL *Ord. Bees* xiii, If the Dorre bees be over many in the hive.. do on this maner. *a* **1613** J. D[ENNYS] *Secr. Angling* II. xxxv. in Arb. *Garner* I. 173 With brood of wasps, of hornets, doars, or bees. **1653** URQUHART *Rabelais* I. xvi, This forrest was most horribly fertile and copious in dorflies. **1658** ROWLAND *Moufet's Theat. Ins.* 894 The Dors also and Drones they kill. **1681** CHETHAM *Angler's Vade-m.* iv. §14 (1689) 45 Resembling a young Dore or Humble-bee.

2. A flying coleopterous insect or beetle; also ***dor-beetle, dor-fly***. *spec.* **a.** The common black dung-beetle or dumble-dor (*Geotrupes stercorarius*), which flies after sunset. **b.** The cockchafer or may-bug. **c.** The rose-beetle. Also, vaguely, other species, chiefly of lamellicorn beetles.

a **1450** *Fysshynge w. Angle* (1883) 26 In June take the creket & the dorre & also a red worme. **1598** YONG *Diana* 309 The dore, a little creature, so vile, and common. **1620** MARKHAM *Farew. Husb.* II. xvii. (1668) 76 The cure or prevention for these Dores, or black Clocks. **1653** WALTON *Angler* ii. 54 The Dor or Beetle (which you may find under a Cow-turd). **1711** *Phil. Trans.* XXVII. 347 The next is a pale green shining Dor. **1752** THYER *Note on Milton* 483 (Jod.) A brownish kind of beetle powdered with a little white, commonly known by the name of cockchaffer or dorrfly. **1774** GOLDSM. *Nat. Hist.* (1862) II. IV. vi. 542 The May-bug, or dorr-beetle, as some call it. **1835** BROWNING *Paracelsus* v. 144 The shining dorrs are busy. **1894** BLACKMORE *Perlycross* 192 A bat, or an owl, or a big dor-beetle.

†**3.** *fig.* Applied to persons. *Obs.*

1599 B. JONSON *Cynthia's Rev.* III. iii, What should I care what every dor doth buzze In credulous eares? **1645** MILTON *Colast.* (1851) 377 Infested, somtimes at his face, with dorrs and horsflies. **1649** G. DANIEL *Trinarch.* The Author 8 Nor..to stoope at the thicke-shell'd Dorrs of Obiection.

4. *Comb.*, as **dor-bee, dor-beetle** (see 1, 2); **dor-bug**, a name applied in America to various beetles, esp. *Lachnosterna fusca*; **dor-fly** (see 1, 2); **dor-hawk**, the goatsucker or night-jar; †**dor-head**, a stupid or blundering fellow = BEETLE[1] 4 (*obs.*).

1833 A. GREENE *Life & Adv. D. Duckworth* I. 86 It's a *dorbug! **1849** PARKMAN *Oregon Tr.* (1872) 42 The dor-bugs hummed through the tent. **1852** HAWTHORNE *Blithedale Rom.* I. iv. 55 Our fire-light will draw stragglers, just as a candle draws dorbugs. **1863** T. W. HIGGINSON *Out-door Papers* (1874) 271 The Dytiscus, dorbug of the water, blunders clumsily against it. **1668** SIR T. BROWNE *Wks.* (1848) III. 505 Have you a *caprimulgus*, or *dorhawk? **1766** PENNANT *Zool.* (1768) II. 246 The goat-sucker..feeds on moths, gnats, and dorrs or chaffers; from whence Charlton calls it the Dorrhawk. **1832** WORDSW. '*Calm is the fragrant air*' 22 The busy dor-hawk chases the white moth With burring note. **1577** tr. *Bullinger's Decades* (1592) 460 There is none so very a *dorrhead as that hee vnderstandeth not [etc.]

†**dor**, *sb.*[2] *Obs.* Also **dorre.** [Goes with DOR *v.*[1]; perh. from ON. *dár* scoff, in phr. *draga dár at* to make game of.]

Scoff, mockery, 'making game' chiefly in phrase *to give* (any one) *the dor*: to make game of, mock, subject to ridicule; so *to put the dor upon, to receive* or *endure the dor*, etc. (From quot. 1552, perh. originally a term at cards.)

1552 HULOET, Dorre at cardes. **1570** LEVINS *Manip.* 170/24 A Dorre, blanke, *argutia*. **1599** B. JONSON *Cynthia's Rev.* v. ii, Which [change of colour] if your antagonist..shall ignorantly be without, and yourself can produce, you give him the dor. [See the whole passage.] **1611** SPEED *Hist. Gt. Brit.* IX. viii. §33 The dorre, which..Hubert, did put vpon King John and his late designe. *a* **1616** BEAUM. & FL. *Lover's Progr.* I. i, I would not receive the dor. *a* **1625** FLETCHER *Love's Pilgr.* III. ii, What dor unto a doating maid this was, What a base breaking off? *a* **1625** —— *Woman Pleased* III. iii, I will never bear this, Never endure this dor. **1633** P. FLETCHER *Purple Isl.* VII. xxv, There oft to rivals lends the gentle Dor, Oft takes—his mistress by—the bitter bob. **1642** MILTON *Apol. Smect.* 82 [He] brings home the dorre upon himself. *a* **1734** NORTH *Lives* I. 361 They all thought he had put the dor, as they say, upon the chief justice. **1855** KINGSLEY *Westw. Ho!* xxxi, He has given the Lord High Admiral the dor.

† **dor**, *sb.*[3] *Obs. rare*[−1]. [perh. = ON. *dári* fool, buffoon; cf. prec. and DOR *v.*[1]] A fool.

1599 B. JONSON *Cynthia's Rev.* v. i, This night's sport, Which our court-dors so heartily intend.

† **dor**, *v.*[1] *Obs.* Also dorre. [Goes with DOR *sb.*[2]; perh. from ON. *dára* to mock, make sport of.

Gifford's conjecture that it is derived from DOR *sb.*[1], in reference to the desultory flight of the cock-chafer 'which appears to *mock* or *play* upon the passenger, by striking him on the face', appears unlikely.]

1. *trans.* To make game of, make a fool of, mock, befool, confound. *to dor the dotterel*: to cajole or hoax a simpleton: cf. DARE *v.*[2] 5.

1570 LEVINS *Manip.* 170/24 To Dorre, *arguere.* **1577** FULKE *Confut. Purg.* 368 Thinke not to dorre vs with Cyprians name. **1591** HARINGTON *Orl. Fur.* v. 39 (N.) What, hop'd you that with this I could be dor'd? **1598** B. JONSON *Ev. Man in Hum.* IV. vi, Oh that villaine dors me. **1614** —— *Barth. Fair* IV. i, Here he comes, whistle; be this sport call'd Dorring the Dotterel. **1641** 'SMECTYMNUUS' *Answ.* §10 (1653) 42 But this is but a *blind*, wherewith the Bishop would Dorre his Reader. **1675** COTTON *Poet. Wks.* (1765) 177 No more thou now shalt dorre me.

2. *intr.* To make sport, mock.

1655 tr. *Scuderi's Artamenes* VII. II. IV. 96 There was not one of them which dorred at the difficulty of the enterprize.

† **dor, dorr**, *v.*[2] *Obs.* [Cf. DURR *v.*] *trans.* To make dim or dull (in colour); to deaden.

1601 HOLLAND *Pliny* IX. xxxviii. I. 259 The lightnesse or sadnesse of the one [colour] doth quicken and raise, or els dorr and take downe the colour of the other. **1603** —— *Plutarch's Mor.* 150 By a good medly of them both to darken and dor the worst by laying the better to.

dor, obs. form of DARE *v.*[1], DEER.

Dora ('dɔərə). Also D.O.R.A. A jocular personification of the '*D*efence *o*f the *R*ealm *A*ct', the name being an acronym forming a familiar feminine proper name. The Act was first passed in August 1914 and provided the British Government with wide powers during the 1914–18 war.

1917 G. B. SHAW *London Mus. 1888–89* (1937) 382 The sixpence that went as tax to the Government, which might have stopped the performance by virtue of Dora, and didn't. **1918** 'I. HAY' *Last Million* vi. 68 We are up against official secrets again. A lady called Dora: you will become well acquainted with her. **1921** *Punch* 13 Apr. 293/2 To judge by his description, *Dora's* daughter [*sc.* the Emergency Powers Act of 1920] will be not a whit less drastic in her action than the old lady herself. **1929** P. GUEDALLA *Missing Muse* 194 These imbecile restrictions, which are the last legacy of 'Dora' to her grateful heirs. **1933** LLOYD GEORGE *War Mem.* I. vi. 177 This was the third edition of D.O.R.A., and was designed to give very greatly increased powers to the Authorities to secure munition production. **1952** H. NICOLSON *King George V* viii. 112 In spite of D.O.R.A., the principles of Magna Carta were affirmed.

‖**dorado** (dɒ'rɑːdəʊ, ‖do'rado). [a. Sp. *dorado* gilded = F. *doré*, It. *dorato*:—L. *deaurātus*, pa. pple. of *deaurāre* to gild, f. *de-* + *aurum* gold: see DORY.]

1. A fish (*Coryphæna hippuris*) celebrated for its splendid colouring and the velocity of its movements; also called *dolphin*: see DOLPHIN 2.

1604 E. GRIMSTONE tr. *D'Acosta's Hist. W. Indies* (1880) 164 They are pursued by the Dorados, and to escape them they leape out of the sea. **1626** CAPT. SMITH *Accid. Yng. Seamen* 5 Fish-hookes, for Porgos, Bonetos, or Dorados. **1796** STEDMAN *Surinam* I. i. 9 Dolphins or dorados, which beautiful fish seem to take peculiar delight in sporting around the vessels. **1852** TH. ROSS *Humboldt's Trav.* I. iii. 132.

2. A South American river fish: see quot.

1871 *Gd. Words* 720 In the deeper waters of the Uruguay are numbers of the dorado, or South American salmon..a very handsome fish, of a bright golden colour.

3. A southern constellation, also called Xiphias or the Sword-fish.

1819 in *Pantologia.* **1823** CRABB *Techn. Dict., Dorado*, a southern constellation not visible in our latitude. **1868** LOCKYER *Elem. Astron.* lxxxiv. 34.

†**4.** *fig.* **a.** A rich man. *Obs.* **b.** See EL DORADO.

1643 SIR T. BROWNE *Relig. Med.* II. §1 A troop of these ignorant Doradoes. **1660** F. BROOKE tr. *Le Blanc's Trav.* 379 He found not the sought for Dorado, a golden Prince indeed.

dor-bee, -beetle: see DOR *sb.*[1]

†**Dorbel.** *Obs.* **1.** The English form of *Dorbellus*, i.e. Nicholas de Orbellis (died 1455), a professor of Scholastic Philosophy at Poitiers, and a vehement supporter of Duns Scotus. Hence, A scholastical pedant, a dull-witted person, dolt; cf. *dunce*.

[**1533** FRITH *Answ. More* (1829) 412 Duns, Dorbell, Durand, and such draffe.] **1592** G. HARVEY *Pierce's Super.* 158 Then asse..and foole and dolt and idiot, and Dunse and Dorbell and dodipoul..and all the rusty-dusty jestes in a country. **1593** NASHE *4 Lett. Confut.* 25 Howe Dorbell comes to bee Doctour none asks. **1621** BP. MOUNTAGU *Diatribæ* iii. 305 The dotages of those Talmudicall Dorbels.

2. *Sc.* 'Anything that has an unseemly appearance.' So '**dorbelish** *a.*, stupid, awkward, clumsy; also (*nonce-wds.*) † **dor'bellical** *a.*, † '**dorbellism**, † '**dorbellist**.

1592 NASHE *P. Penilesse* E ij, Thy sheepish discourse.. was so vglye, dorbellicall and lumpish. **1593** —— *Christ's T.* 64 a, Wil you then hope to beate them [Atheists] down with fusty brown-bread dorbellisme? **1599** —— *Lenten Stuffe* Ep. Ded., Olde Iohannes de Indagines and his quire of dorbellists. **1603** H. CROSSE *Vertues Commw.* (1878) 107 They flocke to it as crowes to a dead carkasse..be they neuer so ribauld, filthie, or dorbellicall. **1847–78** HALLIWELL, *Dorbelish*, very clumsy. *Linc.*

dor-bug: see DOR *sb.*[1] 4.

dorc, obs. form of DARK.

†**dorcake.** *Obs.* A kind of cracknel.

14.. *Nominale* in Wr.-Wülcker 740/5 (*De Panibus*) *Hec colirida*, a dorcake.

Dorcas[1] ('dɔːkəs). Name of a woman mentioned in Acts ix. 36; hence, ***Dorcas Society***, a ladies' association in a church for the purpose of making and providing clothes for the poor. So ***Dorcas basket***, a basket of needlework for charitable purposes; ***Dorcas meeting***. Also *ellipt.* Hence '**Dorcas** *v. intr.*, to work for a Dorcas society (*colloq.*).

1832 F. TROLLOPE *Dom. Manners* I. xi. 154 Yet..spite of the old women and their Dorcas societies, atheism is awake and thriving. **1847–78** HALLIWELL, *Dorcas*, benevolent societies which furnish poor with clothing gratuitously or at a cheap rate. **1857** *Eleanor Clare's Jrnl.* in *Househ. Words* XVI. 199, I hope she will not bring a Dorcas basket to sew at. **1863** A. D. WHITNEY *F. Gartney* xix, There was great putting of heads together at the 'Dorcas', about it. **1866** GEO. ELIOT *F. Holt* I. v. 120 Some prime Miss,..in which Felix was no more interested than in Dorcas meetings. **1880** MISS BRADDON *Just as I am* xliv, Lizzie worked for her Dorcas society. **1894** S. BARING-GOULD *Queen of Love* II. xx. 40 Aunt Beulah will not be home for an hour. She is Dorcasing. **1900** A. UPWARD *Eben. Lobb* 39 Getting ready for a Dorcas that came to our house once a quarter to have tea and work for the heathen.

Dorcas[2] ('dɔːkəs). [mod.L. (a. the specific epithet of *Gazella dorcas*, once used as a generic name in its own right), ad. Gr. δορκάς deer, gazelle.] In full ***Dorcas gazelle***. A small gazelle, *Gazella dorcas*, found in northern Africa and western Asia.

1821 J. E. GRAY in *London Med. Repos.* XV. 307 Fam[ily] 4. Antilopidæ... Gazelle, Dorcas. Antilope Dorcas. **1860** *Proc. Zool. Soc.* 415 Additions made to the Menagerie... I Dorcas Gazelle, *Gazella dorcas.* **1893** R. LYDEKKER *Horns & Hoofs* 180 The last of the Asiatic gazelles in which the females are horned is the Dorcas gazelle. **1932** H. C. MAYDON et al. *Big Game Shooting in Afr.* vii. 177 We had passed a belt that held Addra Gazelle, and now Dorcas and Rufifrons were very common. *Ibid.* 181 Herds of Addra and Dorcas Gazelle, and an occasional Ostrich wandered amid the ravines. **1970** DORST & DANDELOT *Field Guide Larger Mammals of Afr.* 242 Dorcas Gazelle live in small herds up to 20 head.

†**dorce, dorke.** *Obs. rare.* Adapted forms of *dorcas*, Gr. δορκάς deer, gazelle.

1661 LOVELL *Hist. Anim. & Min.* 107 The curd of the Dorke is of the same vertue as that of a Hare. **1674** N. COX *Gentl. Recreat.* I. (1677) 55 We have distinct Ages for these Dorces.

dorce, dorcer, obs. forms of DORSE, DOSSER[1].

dorche, Sc. var. *duergh*, obs. f. DWARF.

dordum, var. of DIRDUM.

†**dore**, *v. Obs. Cookery.* [a. F. *dore-r* (12th c. in Littré) to gild:—L. *deaurāre*, f. *de-* + *aurum* gold: see ENDORE.] *trans.* To glaze with saffron, yolk of egg, etc.; = ENDORE.

c **1420** *Liber Cocorum* (1862) 51 þen coloure þy capon with safroune, dore With a feder. *c* **1430** *Two Cookery-bks.* 38 Dore hem with sum grene þing, percely or ȝolkys of Eyroun.

dore, obs. f. DARE *v.*[1], DOOR, DOR, DOWER *sb.*[2]

‖**doré** (dɔre), *a. Metallurgy.* [Fr., lit. 'gilded'.] Containing gold.

1887 J. A. PHILLIPS *Elem. Metall.* (ed. 2) 757 Doré silver, when it contains copper, is cupelled with lead..before parting. **1933** LIDDELL & DOAN *Princ. Metall.* x. 242 If bullion contains predominantly silver with a little gold, it is known as 'doré bullion'.

doree, dorey, var. of DORY.

dor-fly, dorhawk: see DOR *sb.*[1]

‖**doria, dorea** ('dɔərɪə). [Hindī *ḍoriyā* striped (stuff), f. *ḍor* thread, line, streak, stripe.] A kind of striped Indian muslin.

1696 J. F. *Merchant's Ware-ho.* 14 A sort of strip'd Muslings..called Doreas, it being a Musling that is a yard half quarter broad, and the broadest sorts of stripes of any Musling, and usually the coursest and cheapest of any sort. **1706** *Lond. Gaz.* No. 4284/3, 9 Chests or Bales of fine Doreas, etc. **1721** C. KING *Brit. Merch.* I. 223 From a Long Cloth or Bast to a Mulmul or Dorea. **1858** SIMMONDS *Dict. Trade, Dooriahs*, a cotton fabric made in India. **1886** *Catal. Col. & Ind. Exhib.* 16 (Stanf.) Striped muslins, or dorias, are made at Dacca, Gwalior, Nagpur.

Dorian ('dɔərɪən), *a.* (*sb.*) [f. L. *Dōri-us* (a. Gr. Δώριος of Doris) + -AN.] Of Doris or Doria, a division of ancient Greece. ***Dorian mode***, in *Music*, one of the ancient Grecian modes, characterized by simplicity and solemnity; also, the first of the 'authentic' ecclesiastical modes.

1603 HOLLAND *Plutarch's Mor.* 1021 (R.) Plato..chose the Dorian, as that which is most beseeming valiant, sober, and temperate men. **1667** MILTON *P.L.* I. 550 They move In perfect Phalanx to the Dorian mood Of Flutes and soft Recorders. **1774** BURNEY *Hist. Mus.* (1789) I. iii. 53. **1841** W. SPALDING *Italy & It. Isl.* I. 309 No Roman structures rose to contrast with the severe simplicity of the Dorian shrines. **1846** KEBLE *Lyra Innoc.* x. ix. 338 Some heart-thrilling chime, Some Dorian movement. **1867** MACFARREN *Harmony* i. 11 The Dorian is the first mode of the Ambrosian category. **1875** JOWETT *Plato* (ed. 2) I. 74 His actions, in the true Dorian mode, correspond to his words.

B. *sb.* A native or inhabitant of Doris; a member of one of the four great divisions of the ancient Hellenes or Greeks.

1662 STILLINGFL. *Orig. Sacr.* III. iv. §14 The Dorians inhabiting probably where most of the Pelasgi had been. **1837** *Penny Cycl.* IX. 89/2 The migration of the Dorians to the Peloponnese..is expressly stated to have occurred 80 years after the Trojan war, *i.e.* in 1104 B.C.

Doric ('dɒrɪk), *a.* and *sb.* [ad. L. *Dōric-us*, a. Gr. Δωρικός pertaining to Doris: cf. prec.]

A. *adj.* **1. a.** = DORIAN; of or pertaining to the Dorians.

1569 SPENSER *Visions of Bellay* ii. in *Theat. Worldlings*, Fashiond were they all in Dorike wise. **1678** CUDWORTH *Intell. Syst.* 296 Historiographers declare that Orpheus.. wrote in the Dorick dialect. **1807** ROBINSON *Archæol. Græca* v. xxiii. 534 The Phrygian mode was religious; the Lydian, plaintive; the Doric, martial.

b. Of a dialect, etc.: Broad, not refined; rustic.

1621 BURTON *Anat. Mel.* Democr. to Rdr. (1676) 5/2 Those other faults of barbarism, Dorick dialect, extemporanean style, tautologies. **1637** MILTON *Lycidas* 189 With eager thought warbling his Doric lay. **1855** J. F. F. in *J. Wilson's Noct. Ambr.* (1868) I. Pref. 17 There was a homely heartiness of manner about Hogg and a Doric simplicity in his address. **1889** *Athenæum* 2 Mar. 281/3 All this was said..in the Doric dialect of the Lake District.

2. *Arch.* The name of one of the three Grecian orders (Doric, Ionic, Corinthian), of which it is the oldest, strongest, and simplest.

[**1563** SHUTE *Archit.* E iv b, Tuscana, Dorica, Ionica, Corinthia, and Composita, increase their heightes by Diameters.] **1614** SELDEN *Titles Hon.* Ded. A ij a, Architecture of olde Temples..was either Dorique, Jonique, or Corinthian according to the Deity's seuerall nature. **1667** MILTON *P.L.* I. 714 Doric pillars overlaid With Golden Architrave. **1823** P. NICHOLSON *Pract. Build.* 491 The style of this structure is..the Grecian Doric.

B. *sb.* **1. a.** The Doric dialect of ancient Greek. **b.** A 'broad' or rustic dialect of English, as that of the North of England, Scotch, etc.

1837 *Penny Cycl.* IX. 90/2 The choruses in the Attic plays are written in a kind of Doric. **1870** RAMSAY *Remin.* v. 127 'My Lord', commenced John, in his purest Doric..'I wad hae thocht naething o't'. **1872** C. GIBBON *For the King* iii, The good doctor dropped into the broadest Doric.

2. The Doric order of architecture.

1812 J. SMITH *Panorama Sc. & Art* I. 170. **1838** J. L. STEPHENS *Trav. Greece, etc.* 18/1 A small but beautiful specimen of the pure Doric.

3. *Typogr.* (See quots.)

1857 *Spec. Printing Types (H. W. Caslon & Co.)*, Pearl Doric, No. 2... Brevier Doric, No. 1... Nonpareil Doric, No. 1... Pearl Doric, No. 1. **1888** C. T. JACOBI *Printers' Vocab.* 33 *Doric fount*, a particular kind of sans-serif type used for display work. **1900** T. L. DE VINNE *Pract. Typogr.* I. 325 Specimen No. 3, usually called doric, is really a combination of a thick-faced roman and antique. **1954** *Archit. Rev.* CXVI. 119/1 Ionic..seems to have been invented by the type-founders in contrast to *Doric*, an early name for sans [serif].

Hence † '**Dorical** *a.*, Doric; '**Doricism** (-sɪz(ə)m), a Doric form of expression.

1592 R. D. *Hypnerotomachia* 4, I heard a doricall songe. **1698** BOYLE *Bentley's Phal.* (ed. 2) 43 There is not the least shadow of Doricism. **1699** BENTLEY *Phal.* 472 Salmasius is pleas'd to prefer that Reading, as a Doricism.

Dorism ('dɔərɪz(ə)m). [ad. Gr. Δωρισμ-ός speaking Doric, f. Δωρίζειν: see DORIZE.]

1. The Dorian character of language, manners, etc.

1870 A. W. WARD tr. *Curtius' Hist. Greece* (1873) I. II. i. 219 To counteract the one-sided and inflexible Dorism, and to introduce the beneficent germs of universal Hellenic culture into Sparta.

2. A Doric form of expression; a Doricism.

1698 BOYLE *Bentley's Phal.* (ed. 2) 189 But let us hear a Second Apology that may be made for the Dorism of Dr Bentley. **1886** H. W. SMYTH in *Amer. Jrnl. Philol.* Dec. 427 Those Dorisms which appear in the Bœotian dialect.

†**dorith.** *Obs.* [related in some way to DOOR.]
c **1520** *Mem. Ripon* (Surtees) III. 204 Tremyng dorythes & lokes. *Ibid.* 206 Item for j par of gemmers [hinges] to the sayd dorith, 16*d.*

Dorize ('dɔəraɪz), *v.* [ad. Gr. δωρίζειν to imitate the Dorians, f. Δωρίς Doris: see DORIAN.]
1. *intr.* To imitate Doric manners, etc.; to speak or write in Doric.
1678 CUDWORTH *Intell. Syst.* 296 In the Writings of such as did not Dorize. *c* **1795** S. PARR *Wks.* (1828) VII. 415, I think with the lady in Theocritus, that the Dorians have a right to Dorize.
2. *trans.* To render Doric in manners, etc.
1846 GROTE *Greece* II. viii. II. 608 Ionians, but completely dorised through their long subjection to Argos. **1871** SYMONDS *Grk. Poets* v. 136 Thebes..Dorized by the Spartans.

‖**dorje** ('dɔːjɛ). [Tibetan.] A representation of a thunderbolt in the form of a short double trident or sceptre, held by lamas during prayers.
1882 *Encycl. Brit.* XIV. 501/1 In the chief of these temples is preserved the famous *Dorjé* of Buddha, *i.e.*, the *Vajra* or Thunderbolt..the symbol of the strong and indestructible, which the priest grasps and manipulates in various ways during prayer. From this *dorjé*, according to one etymology at least, comes the name of the Himalayan sanatarium *Dorjiling* or Darjeeling. **1939** M. PALLIS *Peaks & Lamas* xiii. 148 Others held a handbell..in the left hand and a *dorjé* or thunder-bolt sceptre in the right, the pair which symbolizes the marriage of Wisdom and Method.

dork (dɔːk). *slang* (chiefly *U.S.*). [Of uncertain origin: perh. var. of DIRK *sb.*, infl. by DICK *sb.*[1] 3 b.] **1.** The penis.
1964 *Amer. Speech* XXXIX. 118 The word *dick* itself serves as a model for two variants which are probably Midwestern, *dirk* and *dork*, also meaning 'penis'. **1969** P. ROTH *Portnoy's Complaint* 194 The glorious acrobatics she can perform while dangling from the end of my dork. **1975** R. H. RIMMER *Premar Experiments* (1976) i. 138 It's kind of fun to watch balls and dorks and titties bobbing in separate rhythms. **1984** *Spectator* 27 Oct. 34/1 A man with one leg and a vermilion bladder, violet stomach and testicles and a scarlet dork is seen putting it into another amputee.
2. A foolish or stupid person; also as a general term of contempt.
1972 D. WESTHEIMER *Over Edge* (1974) ii. 23 What kind of dork do you think I am? **1974** P. GZOWSKI *Bk. about this Country* 13/1 Meeting some of the famous people of the country (some of whom, confidentially are dorks). **1977** *Zigzag* Apr. 4/1 It will attract talentless dorks out for a taste of notoriety or a fast buck. **1980** P. YORK *Style Wars* 14 Sid had *stepped out of the performance* to give this poor dork a going over. **1984** *Pop. Computing* 23 Apr. 88 The same ex-rock-throwing dope smokers of the late 60s..are now slicked down dorks who brownnose every venture capitalist they see.

dork, obs. form of DARK, DIRK.

dorke: see DORCE.

Dorking ('dɔːkɪŋ), *a.* (*sb.*) [f. *Dorking*, in Surrey.] Name of a breed of poultry characterized by a long square form, and possessing five toes.
1840 *Penny Cycl.* XVIII. 476/2 The characteristics of the pure Dorking are, that it is white-feathered, short-legged, and an excellent layer. **1877** MRS. FORRESTER *Mignon* I. 59 There are only the Dorkings now, and they are all laying.

dorlach ('dɔːləx). *Sc.* Also 6–9 **dorloch,** 7 **darloch.** [Gael. *dorlach* handful, bundle, large quantity, quiver.]
†**1.** A quiver. *Obs.*
1574 *Sc. Acts Jas. VI*, (Jam.) And in the hielandis, haberschonis, steilbonnettis, hektonis, swerdis, bows and dorlochis, or culueringis. **1625–49** *Sc. Acts Chas. I*, (1814) V. 357 (Jam.) Bodin in hosteill manner with hagbutis.. bowes, dorlaches, and wther invasive wapones. **1676** W. ROW *Contn. Blair's Autobiog.* xi. (1848) 298 The Highlanders emptying their dorlachs among them.
2. 'A bundle, apparently that kind of truss, formerly worn by our Highland troops, instead of a knapsack' (Jam.); hence, a valise, portmanteau.
a **1662** R. BAILLIE *Lett.* (1775) I. 175 (Jam.) These supple fellows [the Highlanders] with their plaids, targes and dorlachs. **1814** SCOTT *Wav.* xlii, There's Vich Ian Vohr has packed his dorlach. *Ibid.* xliv, His leather dorloch wi' the lock on her was come frae Doune.

†'**dorlot.** *Obs. rare.* Also 4 **dorilot.** [a. OF. *dorelot, dorlot* knot of hair on the forehead, 'a iewell or prettie trinket...wherewith a woman sets out her apparell, or decks herselfe' (Cotgr.).] 'The head-dress of network, sometimes enriched with jewels, worn in the middle ages by ladies.' Fairholt *Costume* (1860) 437.
1340 *Ayenb.* 177 Þet hi habbe uayr dorilot. **1394** *Test. Ebor.* I. 196, j kyngll, j dorlot, j armari. *c* **1440** *Promp. Parv.* 127/2 Dorlott, *trica, caliendrum.*

†**dorm(e**[1]. *Obs. rare.* [f. stem of L. *dorm-īre* or F. *dorm-ir* to sleep: cf. DORMANT.] Sleep, slumber, a doze. *in dorme*: dormant.
1512 *Nottingham Rec.* III. 339 Letting it [a sum of money] lyg in dorme, to the gret hurte of the towne. **1637** SANDERSON *Serm.* (1681) II. 79 Not a calm soft sleep like that which our God giveth his beloved ones; but as the Slumbering Dorms of a sick man; short and..interrupted.

So **dorm** *v.*, *north. dial.*, to doze.
In Dialect Glossaries of Huddersfield, Sheffield, etc.

dorm[2] (dɔːm). Colloq. abbrev. of DORMITORY *sb.* 1.
1900 *Dialect Notes* II. 17 The student..lives in the *dorm* (dormitory). **1904** WODEHOUSE *Gold Bat* xiv. 153 It went into Rigby's dorm. So it must have been a chap in that dorm. who did it. **1927** A. MACDONALD *Dorty Speaking* iii. 22, I found Midge in the dorm when I went up to change for tea. **1936** A. HUXLEY *Eyeless in Gaza* vi. 65 It was against the school rules to go up into the dorms during the day. **1957** *Times Lit. Suppl.* 15 Nov. p. ii/1 Much of it is a sort of smouldering defence of the original Tom Brown ritual: dorm feasts, fagging, hero worship, [etc.]. **1969** C. DAVIDSON in Cockburn & Blackburn *Student Power* 342 Female students are permitted to determine how strict or 'liberal' their dorm hours might be.

†'**dorman.** *Obs.* [var. of *dormand*, DORMANT.]
1. = DORMANT *sb.* 1.
1374 in Willis & Clark *Cambridge* (1886) I. 238 Balkes summers siue dormannes giystes et etiam stures. **1579** *Ibid.* 311 One dorman xxviij foote longe xij vnch square. **1598** *Vestry Bks.* (Surtees) 274 For puttinge in of the dorman in the steeple loft, xijd. **1657** REEVE *God's Plea* 221 This is but the misery of stonework, of Arches, Dormans, Roofs.
2. a. = DORMER 2. **b.** (More fully *dorman-tile*) = DORMER-*tile.*
1703 [see DORMER 2, 4].

dormancy ('dɔːmənsɪ). [f. next, or OF. *dormance*: see -ANCY.] Dormant condition (cf. next); *spec.* of seeds and plants (see quot. 1929).
1789 N. FORSTER in *Parr's Wks.* (1828) VII. 464 The dormancy of any such prerogative. **1804** *Phil. Trans.* XCV. 18 During this dormancy, the animal may be frozen, without the destruction of the muscular irritability. **1825** LYTTON *Falkland* 37 Her only escape from misery had been in the dormancy of feeling. **1845** *Florist's Jrnl.* 158 The period of dormancy or rest should be brought on gradually. **1911** *Bot. Gaz.* LII. 455 Fawcett obtained similar results with many kinds of weed seeds, the percentage of germination being increased, and the 'period of dormancy' shortened by freezing again and again. **1916** *Amer. Jrnl. Bot.* III. 99 Dormancy in plants is common in three organs, seeds, spores, and buds. **1929** WEAVER & CLEMENTS *Plant Ecology* vi. 113 When a seed does not germinate immediately upon leaving the parent plant, it is said to be in a state of dormancy. Dormancy is not confined to seeds, however, but is also characteristic of many offshoots such as rhizomes, bulbs, tubers, etc. **1959** *New Scientist* 3 Sept. 338/3 Gibberellic acid..can also break dormancy so that freshly lifted potatoes immediately sprout when dipped in this substance and dormant seeds germinate. **1971** *Nature New Biol.* 16 June 195/1 Professor P. F. Wareing..reviewed the environmental and hormonal factors controlling seed dormancy.

dormant ('dɔːmənt), *a.* and *sb.* Also 5–6 **-and,** 5–7 **-ond, -ound.** [a. OF. *dormant* (12th c. in Hatz.-Darm.), pr. pple. of *dormir*:—L. *dormīre* to sleep.] **A.** *adj.*
1. Sleeping, lying asleep or as asleep; hence, *fig.* intellectually asleep; with the faculties not awake; inactive as in sleep.
1623 COCKERAM, *Dormant*, sleeping. **1640** G. WATTS tr. *Bacon's Adv. Learn.* Pref. 16 If we have bin too credulous, or too dormant. **1681** GREW *Musæum* (J.), His prey, for which he lies, as it were, dormant, till it swims within his reach. **1726** *Adv. Capt. R. Boyle* 285 That he only lay dormant to meditate some Mischief to me. **1858** HAWTHORNE *Fr. & It. Jrnls.* I. 132 Some Romans were lying dormant in the sun. **1869** FARRAR *Fam. Speech* iii. (1873) 104 The hitherto dormant members of the Aryan family.
b. Of animals: With animation suspended.
1772 FORSTER in *Phil. Trans.* LXII. 378 It lies dormant the greater part of the winter.
c. Of plants: With development suspended.
1863 BERKELEY *Brit. Mosses* ii. 5 In dry weather they [Mosses] are often completely dormant. **1882** VINES *Sachs' Bot.* 640 The numerous dormant buds of woody plants may long remain buried and yet retain their vitality. **1883** *Syd. Soc. Lex.*, *Dormant bud*, a bud which remains, it may be for years, undeveloped on a plant stem.
d. *Her.* Represented in a sleeping or recumbent attitude; with the head resting on the paws.
c **1500** *Sc. Poem Heraldry* 130 in *Q. Eliz. Acad.* etc. 98 xv maneris of lionys in armys..the viij dormand. **1646** SIR T. BROWNE *Pseud. Ep.* v. x. 248 Yet were it not probably a Lyon Rampant..but rather couchant or dormant. **1766** ENTICK *London* IV. 82 At his foot a cupid dormant. **1851** R. R. MADDEN *Shrines & Sepulchres* II. 37, I would rather call the ancient figures dormant.
2. In a state of rest or inactivity; quiescent; not in motion, action, or operation; 'slumbering', in abeyance.
1601 HOLLAND *Pliny* II. 597 This riuer runneth but slowly, and seemeth a dead or dormant water. **1639** EARL OF BARRYMORE in *Lismore Papers* Ser. II. (1888) IV. 39 Your lordshipps directions..must lye dormant by me. **1708** SWIFT *Abolit. Chr.* Wks. 1755 II. I. 85 What if there be an old dormant statute or two against him, are they not now obsolete to a degree? **1731** —— *Pulteney* Ibid. IV. I. 166 Thy dormant ducal patent. **1766** FORDYCE *Serm. Yng. Wom.* (1767) I. vi. 257 It is possible for original talents to lie dormant. **1792** CHIPMAN *Amer. Law Rep.* (1871) 21 Plaintiffs who have since revived a dormant claim. **1806** *Gazetteer Scot.* (ed. 2) 390 Newark..formerly gave title of Baron to the family of Leslie, now dormant. **1878** HUXLEY *Physiogr.* 203 Many volcanoes..are merely dormant.
b. *dormant commission, credit, warrant, writing*, etc., one drawn out in blank to be filled up with a name or particulars, when required to be used; *dormant partner*, a 'sleeping' partner, who takes no part in the working of a concern.
1551 *Househ. Acc. Eliz.* in *Camden Misc.* 34 Paid..unto James Russell, by warrante dormaunte..xx. *s.* *c* **1614** CORNWALLIS in Gutch *Coll. Cur.* I. 148 The warrant dormant, which all Leiger Ambassadors have, to propound and discourse of all things, which they think may tend to the encreasing of amity. **1662** MARVELL *Corr.* xxxv. Wks. 1872–5 II. 80 That you would send us up a dormant credit for an hundred pound. **1679–88** *Secr. Serv. Money Chas. & Jas.* (Camden) 101 For charge of passing a dormant privy seale, 12[li] 8[s], and of dormant l'res patents, 30[li] 2[s] 2[d]. **1714** SWIFT *Pres. St. Affairs* Wks. 1755 II. I. 221 A power was given of chusing dormant viceroys. **1716** ADDISON *Freeholder* 36 (Seager) He likewise signed a dormant commission for another to be his high admiral. **1845** STEPHEN *Comm. Laws Eng.* (1874) II. 102 Partners thus unknown to the public are said to be dormant.
c. *Mechanics.*
dormant-bolt, 'a concealed bolt working in a mortise in a door, and usually operated by a key; sometimes by turning a knob'; *dormant-lock*, 'a lock having a bolt that will not close of itself' (Knight *Dict. Mech.*).
3. Fixed, stationary. *dormant tree* = B. 1.
c **1440** *Promp. Parv.* 127/2 Dormawnte tre..*trabes.* **1703** T. N. *City & C. Purchaser* 128 *Dormant tree.* In Architecture is a great Beam lying cross a House, otherwise call'd a Summer. **1793** SMEATON *Edystone L.* §238 The dormant wedge or that with the point upward, being held in the hand, while the drift wedge or that with its point downward, was driven with a hammer. **1798** *Term Rep.* VII. 599 To the sleepers or dormant timbers they affixed railways or waggon ways. **1876** GWILT *Archit.* Gloss., *Dormant-tree* or *Summer.*
b. *dormant table*, a table fixed to the floor, or forming a fixed piece of furniture. *arch.*
c **1386** CHAUCER *Prol.* 353 His table dormant in his halle alway Stood redy couered al the longe day. **1430** LYDG. *Chron. Troy* II. xi, Eke in the hall..On eche partye was a dormaunt table. [**1448** *Inv. T. Morton* in *Test. Ebor.* III. 108 De ij mensis vocatis dormoundes.] **1610** B. JONSON *Alch.* v. v, Were not the pounds told out..vpon the table dormant. **1767** BLACKSTONE *Comm.* II. xxviii. 428 Whatever is strongly affixed to the freehold or inheritance..as marble chimney-pieces, pumps, old fixed or dormant tables, benches, and the like. **1851** TURNER *Dom. Archit.* I. ii. 54. *fig.* *a* **1635** NAUNTON *Fragm. Reg.* (Arb.) 24 She held a dormant Table in her own Princely breast.
†**4.** Causing or producing sleep. *Obs. rare.*
1654 tr. *Scudery's Curia Pol.* 66 The effects of Dormant and Narcotique remedies.
5. *dormant window*, also *dormant* = DORMER 2.
1651 CLEVELAND *Senses' Fest.* ii, Old Dormant Windows must confess Her Beams. **1727–51** CHAMBERS *Cycl.*, *Dormer* or *Dormant*, in architecture, denotes a window made in the roof of an house. **1804** *Ann. Reg.* 829 A dormant must break out in the roof. **1823** J. F. COOPER *Pioneer* x, The dormant windows in the roof.
B. *sb.* †**1.** A fixed horizontal beam; a sleeper; a summer. More fully *dormant tree* (see A. 3). *Obs.*
1453 *Paston Lett.* No. 185 I. 250 Sir Thomas Howes hath purveyed iiij. dormants for the drawte chamer, and the malthouse, and the browere. **1582** *Wills & Inv. N.C.* (Surtees 1860) 46 In the hay barne..Certaine sawen baulkes, viz., ix dormonds and j sile 10[s]. **1587** HARRISON *England* II. xii. (1877) I. 233 Summers (or dormants). **1665** *Vestry Bks.* (Surtees) 201, 2 clasps of iron for fastning the great dormond in the church, 6 s.
†**b.** The part between the opening and the top of a doorway; the tympanum. *Obs. rare.*
1723 CHAMBERS tr. *Le Clerc's Treat. Archit.* I. 102 Coach-Gates..have a Dormant (i.e. the upper part of the Gate that does not open), which Dormant, where the Gate is arch'd, commences from the Spring of the Arch.
2. = DORMER window: see A. 5.
3. A dish which remains on the table throughout a repast; a centre-piece which is not removed.
1845 J. BREGION *Pract. Cook* 25 (Stanf.) A centre ornament, whether it be a dormant, a plateau..or a candelabra.

dormer ('dɔːmə(r)). Also 6–8 **-ar.** [ad. OF. *dormeor, -ior, -or* (= F. *dortoir*):— L. *dormītōrium* sleeping-room, dormitory, f. *dormīre* to sleep.]
1. A sleeping chamber, dormitory. *Obs.* exc. *Hist.*
1605 CHAPMAN *All Fooles* IV. i. (R.), Or to any shop.. chamber, dormer, and so forth. **1666** WOOD *Life* (Oxf. Hist. Soc.) II. 98 Watson had done the great window of my dormer..then till 11 bording my dormer. **1868** FREEMAN *Norm. Conq.* (1876) II. x. 460 The foreign discipline of the common refectory and the common dormer.
†**b.** *transf.* A resting place; a repository.
c **1640** [SHIRLEY] *Capt. Underwit* II. ii. in Bullen *O. Pl.* II. 342 The gold..he put in his hocas pocas, a little dormer under his right skirt.
2. A projecting vertical window in the sloping roof of a house. Also *dormer-window.*
[Orig. the window of a dormitory or bed-room.]
1592 GREENE *Def. Conny-catch.* (1859) 19 If there were a dormar built to it..it would make the properest parlour in al the house. **1703** T. N. *City & C. Purchaser* 129 *Dorman, Dormer*, In Architecture is a Window made in the Roof of a House, it standing upon the Rafters. **1847** LONGF. *Ev.* I. i. 16 Thatched were the roofs, with dormer-windows. **1871** MISS BRADDON *Lovels* ii. 33 There were..queer little dormers in the roof.
†**3.** A beam; = DORMANT *sb.* 1. *Obs.*
1623 T. GOAD *Dolef. Euen-Song* 11 The floare..falling, by the breaking asunder of a maine Sommier or Dormer. **1758** J. CLUBBE *Wheatfield* 71 In a parlour belonging to a

farm-house..there was a remarkably large dormer of chesnut. *a* **1825** FORBY *Voc. E. Anglia, Dormer*, a large beam.

4. *attrib.* and *Comb.*, as ***dormer-roof***; ***dormer-shaped***, ***windowed*** adjs. Also, **dormer-gablet**, a small gable over a dormer-window; **dormer-tile**, one used to form a junction between the tiling on the sides of a dormer-window and that on the roof.

1703 T. N. *City & C. Purchaser* 272 *Dormar-* or *Dorman-[tile]*..These Tyles consist of a plain Tyle, and a Triangular piece of a plain Tile standing up at right Angles to one side of the plain Tyle. **1765** *Phil. Trans.* LV. 274 There is a lath and plaister wall..supporting a kind of dormer roof. **1811** *Self Instructor* 141 Dormer tiles. **1859** DICKENS *T. Two Cities* I. v, The window was dormer-shaped. **1884** *Harper's Mag.* Mar. 529/2 The roofs are.. dormer-windowed. **1886** WILLIS & CLARK *Cambridge* II. 737 The dormer-gablets..were connected by a parapet.

Hence **'dormered** *a.*, having dormers.

18.. *New Princeton Rev.* III. 112 (Cent.) A high, solid, dormered roof.

‖**dormeuse** (dɔr'mœːz). Also 8 -ouse. [Fr.; fem. of *dormeur* sleeper, applied to articles convenient for sleeping, f. *dormir* to sleep.]

†**1.** A hood or nightcap. *Obs.*

1734 MRS. DELANY *Life & Corr.* (1861) I. 479, I have sent you..a dormeuse patron. **1753** —— *Let. Mrs. Dewes* in *Life & Corr.* 260 She had not yet been able to get her dormeuse.

2. A travelling-carriage adapted for sleeping in.

1808 M. WILMOT *Jrnl.* 16 Aug. (1934) III. 363 We..set off in the Dormeuse 4 horses abreast & two before. **1825** VISC. S. DE REDCLIFFE in S. L. Poole *Life* (1888) I. 357 The two dark green carriages—a Dormeuse and Britchka, which you saw..at Windsor. **1841** LYTTON *Nt. & Morn.* (1851) 216 A dormeuse and four drove up to the inn door to change horses.

3. A kind of couch or settee.

1865 OUIDA *Strathmore* I. vi. 94 (Stanf.) He lay back in a dormeuse before the fire.

dormice, plural of DORMOUSE.

dormient ('dɔːmɪənt), *a.* [ad. L. *dormient-em*, pr. pple. of *dormīre* to sleep.] Sleeping, dormant.

1643 ? MILTON *Soveraigne Salve* 9 The peoples power ever resident in the people though dormient till it be by Parliament wakened. **1684** I. MATHER *Remark. Provid.* (1856) 3 b, How it came to lie dormient in his hands I know not. **1860** O. W. HOLMES *Prof. Breakf.-t.* i. (1883) 28 Is there a De Sauty..dormient in night-cap?

†**'dormious**, *a. Obs. rare.* [f. L. *dormī-re* to sleep + -OUS.] Sleepy.

1656 S. HOLLAND *Zara* (1719) 16 The Champion..began to grow Dormious.

†**'dormitary**, *a.* and *sb. Obs.* [f. L. *dormīt-* ppl. stem of *dormīre* to sleep: see -ARY.]

A. *adj.* Causing sleep, dormitive.

1609 DEKKER *Raven's Alm.* H, She..put the dormitarie powder that the ould wife had giuen her into the bottle.

B. *sb.* A sleep-producing medicine, a narcotic.

1547 BOORDE *Brev. Health* cxl. 52 If the pacient can nat slepe, make a Dormitary. *a* **1652** BROME *City Wit* III. iv, Sure, Sir, you use some Dormitaries.

†**dormi'tation.** *Obs.* [ad. late L. *dormītātiōn-em*, n. of action f. *dormītāre*, freq. of *dormīre* to sleep: cf. obs. F. *dormitation.*]

1. Sleeping, falling asleep, drowsiness.

1563-4 ABP. PARKER *Corr.* 202 By great considerations.. of their vigilancy and our dormitation. **1661** G. RUST *Origen* in *Phenix* (1721) I. 65 So great a Forgetfulness and Dormitation in so acute and diligent a Writer.

2. Numbness; loss of sensibility.

1543 TRAHERON *Vigo's Chirurg.* v. 170 Aliabbas nombreth vj dyseases of the teeth, payne, corosion, congelation, dormitation, fylthynes, looseness. *Ibid.* (1586) 269 b, Sometime there chanceth a certaine dormitation in the teeth, by holding cold things in the mouth.

dormition (dɔː'mɪʃən). [a. F. *dormition* (15th c. in Hatz.-Darm.), ad. L. *dormītiōn-em*, n. of action from *dormīre* to sleep.] Sleeping; falling asleep; *fig.* death (of the righteous).

1483 CAXTON *Gold. Leg.* 259/1 Thy departyng hens ne thy dormycyon shalle not be withoute wytnes. *a* **1656** BP. HALL *Wks.* (1837-9) VII. 295 (D.) Wert thou disposed..to plead, not so much for the utter extinction as for the dormitione of the soul. **1849** *Ecclesiologist* IX. 227 A large sculpture.. representing the death of our Lady; it is called the dormition or *trépas* de Notre Dâme. **1869** *Life M. M. Hallahan* (1870) 121 Her death, which in this case we may almost call her dormition.

'dormitive, *a.* and *sb.* [a. F. *dormitif, -ive* (1545 in Hatz.-Darm.), ad. L. type **dormītīv-us*, f. *dormīre* to sleep: see -IVE.]

A. *adj.* **1.** Causing sleep; soporific.

1593 NASHE *Christ's T.* 80 b, Dormatiue potions, to procure deadly sleepe. **1662** J. CHANDLER *Van Helmont's Oriat.* 338 Dormitive or Sleepifying. **1871** TYLOR *Prim. Cult.* I. 366 Accounting for opium making people sleep by its possession of a dormitive virtue.

†**2.** Sleeping through the winter. *Obs. rare.*

1694 R. BURTHOGGE *Reason* 241 In Snakes, in Dormice.. and in other Dormitive Creatures.

B. *sb.* A soporific medicine; a narcotic.

1619 LUSHINGTON *Repet. Serm.* in *Phenix* (1708) II. 490 His Presence gave them a strong Dormitive, it wrought beyond Sleep. **1700** CONGREVE *Way of World* IV. v, But for cowslip wine, poppy water and all dormitives.

dormitory ('dɔːmɪtərɪ), *sb.* [ad. L. *dormītōri-um* sleeping-place, subst. use of neuter of *dormītōrius* (see next). Cf. obs. F. *dormitoire.*]

1. a. A sleeping-chamber; *spec.* a room containing a number of beds, or a gallery or building divided into cells or chambers each having a bed or beds in it, for the inmates of a monastery, school, or other institution.

1485 CAXTON *Chas. Gt.* 33 The kyng charles beyng in his dormytorye..began to say the psaulter. **1578** T. N. tr. *Conq. W. India* 397 And lay altogither in one dormitorye as a flocke of sheepe. **1642** FULLER *Holy & Prof. St.* III. vi. 167 Thorow-lights are best for rooms of entertainment, and windows on one side for dormitories. *a* **1782** COWPER *Jackdaw*, A great frequenter of the church, Where bishop-like he finds a perch, And dormitory too. **1860-1** FLO. NIGHTINGALE *Nursing* ii. 11 Public or private schools, where a number of children or young persons sleep in the same dormitory. **1868** FREEMAN *Norm. Conq.* (1876) II. vii. 86 The canons..were made..to sleep in a common dormitory.

b. In universities and colleges: a building in which students reside; a hall of residence; a hostel. *U.S.*

1865 *Atlantic Monthly* XV. 551 He worked with them, studied with them,..slept in the same dormitory. **1892** *Univ. of Chicago Quart. Cal.* 9 Students are advised to make their residence in the dormitories. **1903** *N.Y. Even. Post* 7 Oct. 7 There are four regular dormitories or halls for women at Oxford. **1913** J. K. LORD *Hist. Dartmouth Coll.* 487 In 1899 the old home..was converted into a small dormitory for twenty men. **1964** G. B. SCHALLER *Year of Gorilla* (1965) x. 258 Through the generosity of Makerere College she was permitted to live in the girls' dormitory on the campus while I finished my work.

c. A small town, or a suburb of a large town, containing residences of those who work in the metropolitan area. Esp. *attrib.*

1923 *Westm. Gaz.* 6 Feb., The steady expansion of London's working centres and the ever-increasing sprawl of its surrounding dormitories. **1930** *Times* 12 May 9/5 Moreover, it is said, West Fulham is but a London dormitory—a place where voters sleep, and have their interests elsewhere. **1930** *Times Lit. Suppl.* 18 Sept. 736/1 Self-contained residential or 'dormitory' towns. **1949** *Here & Now* (N.Z.) Nov. 25/1 Otaki has a number of Dunlop-Rubber and Rimutaka-tunnel workers, but otherwise is a dormitory suburb. **1955** *Times* 30 June 5/1 The choice before the nation was either dormitory development, cutting into the green belts, or country town development well outside the large towns. **1961** L. MUMFORD *City in History* xvii. 549 This daily shuttling between dormitory and work-place. **1962** *Punch* 30 May 812/3 Orpington is a dormitory suburb. **1971** *Daily Tel.* 3 July 9/2 Wilmslow's commuter dormitories.

2. *fig.* A resting-place.

1634 SIR T. HERBERT *Trav.* 108 His gray haires might goe in peace to an eternall Dormitory. **1645** MILTON *Colast.* Wks. (1851) 350 Hee presumes also to cite the Civil Law, which, I perceav by his citing, never came within his dormitory. **1825** COLERIDGE *Aids Refl.* (1848) I. 1 Truths.. lie bed-ridden in the dormitory of the soul.

†**3.** A resting-place for the dead; a cemetery, vault, grave. *Obs.*

1634 SIR T. HERBERT *Trav.* 126 Our Ambassadour..died ..We obtained a Dormitory for his Body among the Armenian Christians. **1726** AYLIFFE *Parergon* 172. **1775** ADAIR *Amer. Ind.* 79 The Choktah use the like in the dormitories of their dead. **1891** ST. JOHN TYRWHITT in *Colleges Oxf.* 305 This is called 'the dormitory', being the burial-place of several deans and canons.

†**4.** A song sung to lull to sleep; a lullaby. *Obs. rare.*

1656 S. HOLLAND *Zara* (1719) 26 Soto sang this Dormitory.

5. *attrib.* (see also sense 1 c above), as ***dormitory-door***, ***-maid***; **dormitory-car** (*U.S.*), a sleeping-carriage on a railway.

1577-87 HOLINSHED *Descr. Irel.* iii. (R.), Vnder sparring the gates, and bearing vp the dormitorie doore. **1892** *Ch. Times* 1 Apr. Advt. 332 Wanted..two Dormitory Maids.

†**'dormitory**, *a. Obs.* [ad. L. *dormītōrius*, f. ppl. stem of *dormīre* to sleep: see -ORY.] Tending to or causing sleep; sleepy, drowsy.

1631 R. H. *Arraignm. Whole Creature* xii. §2. 118 Of Poppy, or Opium, or such dormitory potions. **1797** *Gentl. Mag.* I. 467 The dormitory proceedings of the American General.

Dormobile ('dɔːməbiːl). Also **dormobile.** [Blend of DORMITORY *sb.* and AUTOMOBILE (or -MOBILE).] A proprietary name for a type of motor-van with a rear compartment convertible for use as a caravan.

1952 *Trade Marks Jrnl.* 22 Oct. 977/2 *Dormobile* 710, 191. Motor land vehicles and parts thereof... Martin Walter Limited, 145 to 147, Sandgate Road, Folkestone; Manufacturers. **1962** *Times* 1 May 8/4 The eight varieties of Martin Walter Dormobile. **1966** P. WILLMOTT *Adolescent Boys* iv. 64 We're going in a big Dormobile and we'll have four chalets and a caravan. **1973** *Listener* 2 Aug. 151 As the horse-drawn carriage declined in use, so we lost the need and hence the ability to refer to the differences which 80 years ago were freely expressed by words like *phaeton*, *brougham* or *landau*... We've balanced such losses with words which distinguish between *convertibles*, *fastbacks*, *dormobiles* and *minibuses*. **1984** *Financial Times* 5 Jan. 13/6 The Chrysler Voyager or Dodge Caravan, a new mini-van.. aimed at the car market..can be used as a conventional commercial vehicle... The concept of such a vehicle has been tossed around..for many years, spawning models like the familiar old Volkswagen Dormobile.

dormond, -ound, obs. var. DORMANT *sb.*

dormouse ('dɔːmaʊs). [Origin obscure: the second element has been, at least since *c* 1575, treated as the word *mouse*, with pl. *mice*, though a pl. *dormouses* is evidenced in 16-17th c. The first element has also from 16th c. been associated with L. *dormīre*, F. *dormir* to sleep, (as if *dorm-mouse*; cf. 16th c. Du. *slaep-ratte*, *slaep-muys*); but it is not certain that this is the original composition.

(Skeat suggests for the first element ON. *dár* benumbed: cf. also dial. '*dorrer*, a sleeper, a lazy person' (Halliwell). (The F. *dormeuse*, fem. of *dormeur* sleeper, sometimes suggested as the etymon, is not known before 17th c.).]

1. A small rodent of a family intermediate between the squirrels and the mice; esp. the British species *Myoxus avellanarius*, noted for its hibernation.

striped dormouse: Pennant's name for the chipmuck, hackee, or ground-squirrel of North America.

c **1425** *Voc.* in Wr.-Wülcker 643 *Hic glis*, dormowse. *Ibid.* 700 *Hic glis, Hic sorex*, a dormows. **1523** SKELTON *Garl. Laurel* 1248 Dormiat in pace, like a dormouse. **1570** B. GOOGE *Pop. Kingd.* II. (1880) 19 And striue the Dormowses themselves in sleeping to excell. **1580** G. HARVEY in *Spenser's Wks.* (Grosart) I. 40 Slipperye Eles: Dormise. **1601** HOLLAND *Pliny* I. 233 The yong Dormice are exceeding kind and louing to their sires that begat them. **1646** J. HALL *Poems* 9 Players lay asleep like Dormouses. **1709** *Brit. Apollo* II. No. 55. 2/2 The..Toawd is as dull as a Dormouse. **1842** *Penny Cycl.* XXII. 398 The Hackee of the United States..Striped Dormouse of Pennant. **1880** HAUGHTON *Phys. Geog.* vi. 276 *note*, Extinct fossil dormice have been found as far back as the Upper Eocene of Europe.

2. *transf.* A sleepy or dozing person.

a **1568** ASCHAM *Scholem.* (Arb.) 113 Any lurking Dorm[o]us, blinde, not by nature, but by malice. **1641** MILTON *Animadv.* (1851) 245 A swashbuckler against the Pope, and a dormouse against the Devil. **1826** SCOTT *Woodst.* xx, You..attending to our patient better during your sleep, than most of these old dormice can do when they are most awake.

3. *attrib.* Dormouse-like, sleepy.

1601 SHAKS. *Twel. N.* III. ii. 20 To awake your dormouse valour. **1795** PHILLIPS *Hist. Inl. Navig.* 108 Every individual, whose state of existence is not of the dormouse kind.

dormouse, erron. f. DORMEUSE.

dormy ('dɔːmɪ), *a. Golf.* Of a player: As many holes ahead of an opponent as there are holes to play; thus, ***dormy one, two***, etc.

1887 in DONALDSON *Supp. to Jamieson.* **1892** *Pall Mall G.* 28 July 3/3 You are..'all even' so far, and only one more hole remains to be played after this. Should you lose this one, your antagonist will be 'dormy', that is to say, he will be one hole up with one to play; so that, although you may yet halve the match, you will not be able to win it. **1893** *Scot. Leader* 10 July 7 As Fernie was now dormy seven, the issue was hardly in doubt.

dorne, obs. form of DURN.

dornick[1] ('dɔːnɪk). Forms: α. 6 **dornyx(e, -ixe, -ycks, -ickes, -yk(k)es, -ikes, -eckes, 6-7 dornex, darnix, 6-8 dornix, 7 darnex, (dorninx).** β. 5 **dornewick, 6 dornik, -icke, -eck(e, -ek, (dornyth, dernyth, 7 darnisle), 7-9 darnock, darnick, dornick, 9 dornock, darnak.**

The name of a Flemish town (in French called Tournay), applied to certain fabrics originally manufactured there, and to their imitations or substitutes. †**a.** A silk, worsted, woollen, or partly woollen fabric, used for hangings, carpets, vestments, etc. *Obs.* **b.** 'A species of linen cloth used in Scotland for the table' (J.).

(In sense b often spelt *dornock*, and erroneously referred to *Dornoch* in Scotland.)

1489 *Act. Dom. Conc.* 131 (Jam.), xij cuschingis..and xij seruiotis of dornewick. **1514** *Churchw. Acc. Kingston-upon-Thames* in Lyson *Envir. Lond.* I. 230 Three yerds of Dornek for a pleyers cote. **1527** *MS. Inv. Goods T. Cromwell* (Pub. Rec. Office), ij olde qwyshyns of whyte and rede dornyx.. a hangyng of dornyxe. **1550-1600** *Customs Duties* (B. M. Add. MSS. 25097), Dornickes with silke..Dornickes with caddes..Dornickes with woll..Dornickes with thred. **1552** *Act 5 & 6 Edw. VI*, c. 24 §1 The making of Hats, Dornecks and Coverlets..of late..begun..within the City of Norwich. **1553** *Inv.* in *Rep. Hist. MSS. Comm.* I. 555 An olde white vestment of dornecke, with the albe. **1587** FLEMING *Contn. Holinshed* III. 1290/1 Over the third [loom was written] the weaving of darnix. **1625-6** in Willis & Clark *Cambridge* (1886) III. 349 For dornicks for the master's bed-chamber ix[s]. **1851** L. D. B. GORDON in *Art Jrnl. Illustr. Catal.* p. viii. **/1 Pattern-weaving..the twills and all its varieties—as dimities, dornocks..&c.

c. *attrib.* and *Comb.*

1530 J. SYMSOUN *Inv.* in *Liber S. Marie de Lundoris* (Abbotsf. Club) 32, vij seruitors of dornyth werk. **1652** *Woman's Univers* in *Montgomerie's Poems* (1887) 294 The webster with his jumbling hand, And dornick champion naperies. **1672** SHADWELL *Miser* I, A Darnock Carpet. **1725** *Lond. Gaz.* No. 6380/13 Darnick-weaver.

¶ See DANNOCKS, which in Forby's opinion 'should rather be *Dornecks*'.

dornick². *U.S. dial.* Also darnick. [Cf. Ir. *dornog* handful, small stone.] A pebble, stone, or small boulder.

1840 *Daily Pennant* (St. Louis) June 18 (Thornton), That ar man he tooks up a dornick, and made a heap of cavortins. **1869** 'MARK TWAIN' *Innoc. Abr.* xxxv, Darnick from the tomb of Abelard and Heloise. **1878** J. H. BEADLE *Western Wilds* xii. 185 He gathered a dornick, and was just drawin' back to send the strange dog where they's no fleas. **1899** ADE *Fables in Slang* 124 A big White House, with..white-washed Dornicks in front of it. **1942** C. MORLEY *Thorofare* II. xxxii. 147 You should have threw a dornick at me the other evening and put me in my place.

doronicum (dəˈrɒnɪkəm). [mod.L., ad. mod. Gr. δωρονείκον, ad. Arab. *darānaj, darūnaj*. Adopted by Linnæus in his *Systema Naturæ* (1735) as the name of a genus.] A perennial herb of the genus so named, belonging to the family Compositæ, and sometimes cultivated in gardens; LEOPARD'S BANE.

1607 TOPSELL *Four-f. Beasts* 247 That same herbe (called *Doronicum*) and of the Grecians, *Doronieu*. **1728** R. BRADLEY *Dict. Bot.* I [*s.v.* Doronicum Vulgare], The most common Doronicum of our Gardens hath divers Leaves rising from the Root. **1785** T. MARTYN tr. *Rousseau's Lett. Elem. Bot.* xxvi. 397 *Doronicum* or *Leopard's-bane*, a wild plant of the Alps, and now common among the perennials of the garden, has the scales of the calyx in two rows. **1892** S. R. HOLE *Bk. about Garden* 27 That group of iris (germanica) and doronicum reminds us of the cohorts of the Assyrians, 'all gleaming with purple and gold'. **1926** G. JEKYLL *Colour Schemes for Flower Garden* (ed. 6) 27 Tulip Chrysolora of fuller yellow, yellow Wallflowers, the tall Doronicum, and ..several patches of yellow Crown Imperial. **1970** C. LLOYD *Well-Tempered Garden* III. 310 Doronicums..will grow anywhere.

ˈDorothy bag. [f. the feminine proper name *Dorothy*.] A woman's handbag gathered at the top by a drawstring and slung by loops from the wrist.

1907 *Yesterday's Shopping* (1969) p. xxxii/3 Dorothy Bags. **1909** *Westm. Gaz.* 23 Aug. 9/1 A 'Dorothy' bag, containing a quantity of jewellery. **1923** *Daily Mail* 15 Jan. 15 An effective Dorothy bag for evenings. **1962** *Harper's Bazaar* Dec. 7/1 The matching dorothy-bag purse has an expanding frame. **1970** *Times* 22 Dec. 7/4 Languid silk tassels..decorate black satin Dorothy bags.

Dorothy Perkins (ˈdɒrəθɪ ˈpɜːkɪnz). Also simply **Dorothy**. [Personal name.] A popular variety of rambling rose which bears clusters of double pink flowers.

1903 W. PAUL *Rose Garden* (ed. 10) 262 *Dorothy Perkins*, an erect growing variety [of *Rosa wichuraiana*] of great beauty. **1908** J. H. PEMBERTON *Roses* 314 Dorothy Perkins (Wich.) Jackson & Perkins, 1901.—Shell pink, white centre. —Very vigorous pillar. **1912** H. H. THOMAS *Complete Gard.* 110 Liberties may be taken with the Dorothy Perkins class of rose that would lead to disappointment with other kinds. **1913** —— *Rose Bk.* 13 *Dorothy Perkins.*—The most popular of all wichuraiana roses, bearing large clusters of big, double, rich pink blossoms. **1915** *Star* 5 Aug. 2/6 Suburban gardens round London are aflame with blooming 'Dorothys'. **1941** L. MACNEICE *Plant & Phantom* 59 A trellis of Dorothy Perkins roses.

dorp. [a. Du. *dorp* = OE. *þorp*, Ger. *dorf* village. Cf. THORP.] A (Dutch) village; formerly more or less naturalized in sense: Village, THORP. In South Africa, a small town.

1570–6 LAMBARDE *Peramb. Kent* (1826) 377 By Thorpe, or Dorpe, [is meant by the Saxons] a village, yet used in the lower Germaine. **1583** STANYHURST *Æneis* I. (Arb.) 31 Where dorps and cottages earst stood. **1596** DALRYMPLE tr. *Leslie's Hist. Scot.* (1885) I. 106 Betuene dorpe and dorpe, and toune and toune. **1609** DEKKER *Gvlls Hornebk.* 38 Tailor's Hall that now is larger than some dorpes among the Netherlands. **1650** FULLER *Pisgah* I. vii. 18 Perizzites. By interpretation Villagers, as dwelling in dorps and Hamlets, not walled towns. **1687** DRYDEN *Hind & P.* III. 611 No neighb'ring Dorp, no lodging to be found. **1835** A. STEEDMAN *Wanderings & Adv. Interior S. Afr.* I. 103 Beaufort, therefore, generally presents a scene of activity, arising from the number of farmers, who on various accounts have frequent occasion to visit the *Dorp*. **1852** C. BARTER *Dorp & Veld* iv. 26 Maritzburg..an English town rising out of the ruins of a Dutch *dorp* or village. **1902** *Daily Chron.* 23 Apr. 7/3 The most remote 'dorp' has not been too far placed beyond the reach of the fertilising stream. **1902** J. H. M. ABBOTT *Tommy Cornstalk* 13 The dorp represented the Bush township. **1920** [see BACKVELD]. **1934** R. CAMPBELL *Broken Record* vii. 162 The radios of God have always spoken out of dorps like Medina and Nazareth. **1954** D. D'EWES *Mydorp* ii. 18 Uncle Robert and Aunt Kate..had left Mydorp..to settle themselves in a dorp down the river.

attrib. c **1611** CHAPMAN *Iliad* XI. 587 All the dorp boors with terror fled.

dorr, var. of DOR *sb.*¹ and *v.*²

dorray, dorree, dorrey, dorroy, dorry: see DORY *a.* and *sb.*¹

dorre, obs. f. DARE *v.*¹, DOR, DORY *sb.*¹

† **dorring**, obs. f. DARING *vbl. sb.*¹ and ².

1374 [See DERRING-DO]. **1618** LATHAM *2nd Bk. Falconry* (1633) 142 If she be flowne any longer, she will likewise fall to dorring, and bee lost.

dorsabdominal *a.*: see DORSO-.

dorsad (ˈdɔːsæd), *adv. Anat.* [f. L. *dors-um* back + *-ad*, suffix: see DEXTRAD.] Towards the back or dorsal aspect of the body.

1803 J. BARCLAY *New Anatom. Nomencl.* 166. **1814** J. H. WISHART tr. *Scarpa's Hernia* Mem. I. 25 Immediately behind [*note*, dorsad of] the insertion of the two tendinous pillars. **1835–6** TODD *Cycl. Anat.* I. 271/2 The tail..can be inflected dorsad.

dorsal (ˈdɔːsəl), *a.* (*sb.*) [ad. med.L. *dorsāl-is*, f. *dors-um* back: cf. F. *dorsal* (13–14th c.).]

A. *adj.* † **1.** Having a back: of a knife with one edge.

1541 R. COPLAND *Guydon's Quest. Chirurg.*, A knyfe..is of two maners; one..Dorsall bycause it hath a backe and cutteth but on the one syde, and the other is Ansall.

2. *Anat.* **a.** (*Zool.*) Pertaining to the back of an animal; situated on or near the back. (In this and b. often opposed to VENTRAL.)

dorsal fin, the fin situated near the middle of the back in fishes, etc. ***dorsal nerves***, those spinal nerves which arise in connexion with the dorsal vertebræ. ***dorsal vertebræ***, those situated between the cervical and lumbar vertebræ.

1727–52 CHAMBERS *Cycl.* s.v. *Nerve*, Dorsal Nerves are in number twelve. **1769** PENNANT *Zool.* III. 32 The dorsal and anal fins. **1846** PATTERSON *Zool.* 93 The heart [in Insects] is an elongated muscular tube, situated along the middle of the back, and hence called the dorsal vessel.

b. (*Zool. & Bot.*) Pertaining to, or situated on, the back (i.e. upper, outer, convex, or hinder surface) of any organ or part.

dorsal suture, the outer suture of a carpel or pod, corresponding to the midrib of a leaf.

1808 J. H. WISHART tr. *Scarpa's Aneurism* Mem. II. (1814) 116 The posterior [*note*, dorsal] part of the hernial sac. **1835** LINDLEY *Introd. Bot.* (1848) I. 381 Internal expansions of the dorsal or ventral suture. **1882** VINES *Sachs' Bot.* 441 The dorsal surface of ordinary leaves.

c. *Phonetics.* (Of sounds) made with the back of the tongue.

1933 BLOOMFIELD *Lang.* vi. 101 English has no dorsal spirants, but they occur in many languages. **1963** *Amer. Speech* XXXVIII. 216 The dorsal sound found in the German *ach* is very common in Armenian.

3. *gen.* Of the back; forming a ridge like the back of an animal. *rare.*

1827 LYTTON *Pelham* xxv, Warburton, from his dorsal positions, so studiously preserved, either wished to be uncivil or unnoticed. **1868** G. DUFF *Pol. Surv.* 45 The great dorsal range that in Turkey corresponds to the Apennines.

B. *sb.* **1.** *Anat.* Short for *dorsal fin* or *dorsal vertebra*: see A. 2 a.

1834 MCMURTRIE *Cuvier's Anim. Kingd.* 220 Pectorals almost imperceptible..the dorsal and anal hardly visible. **1840** G. V. ELLIS *Anat.* 124 The spines of the vertebræ.. from the sixth cervical to the third dorsal.

2. *Eccl.* = DOSSAL b.

1870 F. R. WILSON *Ch. Lindisf.* 79 The altar has an alabaster dorsal.

3. *Phonetics.* A dorsal sound.

1964 E. PALMER tr. *Martinet's Elem. Gen. Ling.* ii. 50 A dorsal may also be alveolar.

Hence **dorˈsality**; **ˈdorsalmost** *superl. adj.* [after *uppermost*, etc.], most to the back; **ˈdorsalwards** *adv.*, towards the back (= DORSAD).

1883 E. R. LANKESTER in *Encycl. Brit.* XVI. 674/1 The dorsalmost pair of tentacles. **1887** *Jrnl. R. Microsc. Soc.* Aug. 591 Nephridial tubes..projecting dorsalwards. **1951** *Archivum Linguisticum* III. 135 Plosive release, tension and dorsality.

dorsally (ˈdɔːsəlɪ), *adv.* [-LY².] In a dorsal position or direction; on or towards the back.

1839 JOHNSTON in *Proc. Berw. Nat. Club* I. No. 7. 197 Body..strengthened dorsally with a calcareous..plate. **1854** WOODWARD *Mollusca* (1856) 207 Mantle-cavity opening dorsally. **1881** J. S. GARDNER in *Nature* No. 624. 559 Sporangium of Osmunda seen dorsally.

† **dorse**, *sb.*¹ *Obs.* [ad. L. *dors-um* back.]

1. = DOSSER¹ 1.

a **1524** *Will of Sir R. Sutton* in Churton *Life* 521 (T.) A dorse and redorse of crymsyn velvet.

2. The back of a book or writing.

c **1640** J. SMYTH *Lives Berkeleys* (1883) II. 94 Without any reverse or privy seale on the dorse. **1691** WOOD *Ath. Oxon.* II. 484 Books..richly bound with gilt dorses. **1866** HORWOOD *Yearbks. 32 & 33 Edw. I.* Pref. 37 *note*, Edward the Second's letter to the Friars Preachers on the dorse of the Close Roll of 19 Ed. II.

3. *Pugilistic slang.* The back. *to send to dorse*: to throw on one's back, throw down.

1822 *Blackw. Mag.* XII. 461 Sent to dorse in a bloodless fight by Painter.

dorse (dɔːs), *sb.*² Also 7 dorce. [ad. LG. *dorsch* in same sense = ON. *torskr* codfish.] A young cod. (Formerly supposed to be a distinct species, and named *Gadus* (or *Morrhua*) *callarias*.)

1610 W. FOLKINGHAM *Art of Survey* IV. iii. 83 Base, Dorce, Mackeril, Whiteing. **1611** COTGR., *Poisson S. Pierre*, the Dorce. **1828** STARK *Elem. Nat. Hist.* I. 423 M[orrhua] *callarias*, Lin. The Dorse. Body gray, with brown spots in summer, and black in winter.

† **dorse**, *v. Obs. Pugilistic slang.* [f. DORSE *sb.*¹ 3.] *trans.* To throw on the back.

1826 J. WILSON *Noct. Ambr.* Wks. 1855 I. 40 The straight hitting..soon dorses your roundabout hand-over-head hitters.

dorse, obs. form of DOSS *sb.*² and *v.*²

dorsel: see DOSSAL, DOSSEL.

dorser: see DOSSER¹.

Dorset (ˈdɔːsɪt). The name of a county in the south-west of England, used *ellipt.* or *attrib.* in designation of things produced in or originally peculiar to the county.

1747 H. GLASSE *Art of Cookery* xxi. 164 Golden-dorset. *Ibid.*, The Golden Dacket Dauset. **1824** J. WIGHT *Mornings at Bow St.* 4 There was toast and prime Dorset, and muffins and crumpets. **1836** DICKENS *Sk. Boz* 2nd Ser. 24 Tubs of weekly Dorset, and cloudy rolls of 'best fresh'. **1891** R. WALLACE *Rural Econ. Austral. & N.Z.* xxvi. 360 The English breed..the Dorset—a close-coated, white-faced horned breed, which produces two crops of lambs within the year. **1897** H. G. WELLS *Plattner Story* 205 He wanted us to eat Dorset butter. **1940** *Chambers's Techn. Dict.* 259/1 *Dorset Down*, one of the Down breed sheep with fine close wool which is used largely for Cheviot quality woollens and for hosiery yarns. **1955** [see *blue-vinn(e)y* s.v. BLUE *a.* 13]. **1957** MANKOWITZ & HAGGAR *Eng. Pott. & Porc.* 75/1 *Dorset clay*, Poole Clay..is generally known in Staffordshire as blue clay. **1960** *Farmer & Stockbreeder* 22 Mar. 63 Mr. K. Hebditch's Dorset Down flock. **1970** *Guardian* 28 Feb. 11/1 The Dorset horn sheep is the only breed which can produce more than one set of lambs a year.

dorsi-, (dors-), combining form of L. *dors-um* back (chiefly in anatomical, zoological, and botanical terms) = 'back-; of, to, on the back'. (Sometimes less properly in the sense 'back and ——', which is correctly expressed by DORSO-.) Used in modern formations, as **dorsiˈbranchiate** *a.*, having gills on the back; belonging to the order *Dorsibranchiata* of Annelids in Cuvier's system; *sb.* a dorsibranchiate annelid. **dorsiˈcornu**, the posterior grey column or horn of the spinal cord; hence **dorsi-ˈcornual** *a.* **dorsiˈcumbent** *a.*, lying on the back, supine. **ˈdorsiduct** *v. trans.*, to bring or carry towards the back. **ˈdorsifixed** *a.*, 'fastened by the back; in Botany, used to describe an anther which is attached by its back to the filament; otherwise called *adnate*' (*Syd. Soc. Lex.*). **ˈdorsiflex** *v. trans.*, to bend (a part of the body, esp. the foot or toe) towards its dorsal surface. **dorsiˈflexion**, (*a*) (*nonce-wd.*) a bending of the back, a bow; (*b*) *Anat.*, flexion or bending towards the dorsum or dorsal surface. **ˈdorsigrade** *a.* [after *digitigrade, plantigrade*], walking upon the backs of the toes, as certain armadillos (*Syd. Soc. Lex*). **dorsi-ˈmedian** *a.*, situated in the middle line of the back. **dorsiˈmesal, dorsoˈmesal** *a.* [see next] = prec. **dorsiˈmeson** [Gr. μέσον middle], the middle line of the back (Wilder & Gage). **dorsiˈspinal** *a.*, pertaining to the spinous processes of the vertebræ. **dorsi-ˈventral** *a.*, **-venˈtrality** = DORSO-*ventral, -ventrality*.

1836–9 TODD *Cycl. Anat.* II. 411/1 The *Dorsibranchiate Annelida. **1862** DANA *Man. Geol.*, *Worms* 155 Dorsi-branchiates, or free sea worms. **1890** *Buck's Handbk. Med. Sci.* VIII. 528 The myelic cornua are strictly dorsal and ventral,..permitting the adjectives *dorsicornual and ventricornual. **1883** WILDER & GAGE *Anat. Tech.* 84 *Dorsiduct the tail of the cat. **1908** *Practitioner* Oct. 561 The ankles can be *dorsiflexed, until the dorsum of the feet touches the shin. **1823** CARLYLE in Froude *Life* I. 192 With the most profound *dorsiflexions. **1902** D. J. CUNNINGHAM *Text-bk. Anat.* 251 If posterior or dorsal surfaces be approximated by the process of bending, then the flexion becomes *posterior* or *dorsi-flexion*, as at the knee- or wrist-joints. **1967** G. M. WYBURN et al. *Conc. Anat.* vi. 186 Dorsiflexion of the foot is limited by the wedge-shaped trochlear surface of the talus. **1842** E. WILSON *Anat. Vade M.* 351 The *Dorsi-spinal veins form a plexus around the spinous..processes and arches of the vertebræ. **1882** VINES *Sachs' Bot.* App. II. 954 Sachs points out..that most monosymmetrical..organs present..dorsal and ventral halves which are of different internal structure; such organs he describes by the term *dorsi-ventral. **1959** SOUTHWOOD & LESTON *Land & Water Bugs* 51 All Amyoteinae have an abdomen capable of great volumetric increase, accomplished by *dorsi-ventral expansion. **1895** F. W. OLIVER tr. *Kerner's Nat. Hist. Plants* II. 697 The oophyte is a lobed band-like thallus with marked *dorsi-ventrality.

dorsiferous (dɔːˈsɪfərəs), *a.* [L. *-fer* bearing.]

1. *Bot.* Bearing the fructification (as a fern) upon the back (i.e. under side) of the frond.

1727–51 CHAMBERS *Cycl.*, *Dorsiferous*, or *Dorsiparous Plants*..bear their seeds on the backside of their leaves. **1835** LINDLEY *Introd. Bot.* (1848) II. 95 Polypodiaceæ, or what are more commonly called dorsiferous ferns.

2. = DORSIPAROUS b.

1755 in JOHNSON [see DORSIPAROUS]; thence in mod. Dicts.

3. = DORSIGEROUS.

In recent Dicts.

dorsigerous (dɔːˈsɪdʒərəs), *a.* [L. *-ger* carrying: see -OUS.] Carrying the young upon the back, as a species of opossum.

1839–47 TODD *Cycl. Anat.* III. 327/2 The development of the pouch..is rudimental in the Dorsigerous Opossum.

dorsiparous (dɔːˈsɪpərəs), *a.* [L. *-par-us* bringing forth.] **a.** *Bot.* = DORSIFEROUS. **b.** *Zool.* Hatching the young upon the back, as certain toads.

1727–51 [see DORSIFEROUS]. **1755** JOHNSON, *Dorsiferous, Dorsiparous*, is used of plants that have the seeds on the back of their leaves, as fern; and may be properly used of the American frog, which brings forth young from her back. **1883** *Syd. Soc. Lex.*, *Dorsiparous*, a term applied to those *Batrachia* the ova of which become inserted into the skin on the back of the parent, where they devolop.

dorsi-ventral: see *dorso-ventral* s.v. DORSO-.

dorso-, dors-, stem and combining form of L. *dorsum* back, used in comb. in the sense 'back and ——' (but sometimes improperly in other senses, where *dorsi-* is the etymological form) in modern formations, as **dorso-abˈdominal, dorsabˈdominal** *a.*, relating to the back and abdomen, or to the dorsal and ventral aspects; whence **dorsabˈdominally** *adv.* **dorso-ˈcaudal** *a.*, relating to the back and the tail; superior and posterior in direction. **dorso-ˈcervical, dorso-ˈcollar** *adjs.*, pertaining to the back of the neck. **dorso-epiˈtrochlear**, name of a muscle extending from the back to the elbow in some quadrupeds. **dorso-interˈcostal** *a.*, relating to the back and the intercostal nerves. **dorso-inˈtestinal** *a.*, situated on the dorsal aspect of the intestine (*Syd. Soc. Lex.*). **dorso-ˈlateral** *a.*, relating to the back and the side. **dorso-ˈlumbar** *a.*, relating to the back and loins; dorsal and lumbar (vertebræ). **dorso-ˈpleural** *a.*, relating to the back and the side. **dorso-ˈscapular** *a.*, relating to the back and the shoulder-blade. **dorso-ˈsternal** *a.*, relating to the back and the breast-bone. **dorso-ˈventral** *a.*, (*a*) = *dorsabdominal*; (*b*) *Bot.* (see quot. 1882); whence **dorso-venˈtrality**, dorso-ventral condition; **dorso-ˈventrally** *adv.*, in a dorso-ventral direction or situation. **dors-ˈumbonal** *a.*, 'both dorsal and umbonal, as one of the accessory valves in the family *Pholadidæ*' (Cent. Dict.).

1835–6 TODD *Cycl. Anat.* I. 170/1 These..dorso-abdominal vessels..distribute to the skin a number of ramifications. **1881** MIVART *Cat* 137 The external dorso-epitrochlear is a slender muscle which takes origin from a fascia outside the spine of the scapula. **1888** W. R. GOWERS *Dis. Nerv. Syst.* II. 750 The dorso-intercostal forms [of neuralgia], which occupy the intercostal nerves. **1835** TODD *Cycl. Anat.* I. 523/2 Dorso-lateral parts of the mantle. **1882** VINES *Sachs' Bot.* 358 A leaf springs from each of the dorso-lateral segments. **1854** OWEN in *Circ. Sc.* (*c* 1865) II. 79/2 The dorso-lumbar vertebræ. **1870** ROLLESTON *Anim. Life* 15 The lung.. occupies a much smaller space in the dorso-sternal plane than in mammals. *Ibid.* 138 The dorso-ventral muscles. **1882** VINES *Sachs' Bot.* App. II. 954 Sachs points out..that most monosymmetrical..organs present..dorsal and ventral halves which are of different internal structure; such organs he describes by the term dorsi-ventral [*sic*]. **1884** *Science* Mar. 324 Making a *T*, of which the stem represents the limb, and the cross the girdle running dorsoventrally. **1883** E. R. LANKESTER in *Encycl. Brit.* XVI. 687/2 In *Pholas dactylus* we find a pair of umbonal plates, a dors-umbonal plate and a dorsal plate.

‖**ˈdorsolum, -ulum.** *Entom.* [mod.L., dim. of *dorsum* back.] 'Kirby's name for a piece of the exoskeleton of an insect situated between the collar and scutellum, which gives insertion to the anterior organs of flight' (*Syd. Soc. Lex.* 1883).

1826 KIRBY & SP. *Entomol.* (1828) III. xxxv. 547 The anterior margin of the dorsolum is deflexed.

dorsour: see DOSSER¹.

dorst(e, obs. f. *durst*, pa. t. of DARE *v.*¹

dorstenic (dɔːˈstɛnɪk), *a. Chem.* In *dorstenic acid*, an acid obtained from *Dorstenia Contrayerva*, a tropical American plant of the mulberry tribe. So **dorstenin** (ˈdɔːstɪnɪn), a principle obtained from the same plant.

1893 *Med. Jrnl.* 30 Sept. 55 An analysis..gave..a principle which he named dorstenin, and an acid, dorstenic acid.

‖**dorsum** (ˈdɔːsəm). The Latin word for 'back', used in scientific or technical senses.

1. *Zool.* and *Anat.* **a.** The back of an animal. **b.** The upper, outer, or convex surface of a limb or organ, as the hand, nose, tongue; in *Conch.* the outer surface of a shell opposite to the opening. **c.** *Bot.* The outer surface of an organ or part (e.g. a seed), i.e. that directed away from the axis.

1840 G. V. ELLIS *Anat.* 392 On the dorsum of the hand is a venous arch, which receives..the digital veins. **1843** J. G. WILKINSON *Swedenborg's Anim. Kingd.* I. i. 30 On the dorsum of the tongue..lie obtuse papillæ. **1878** BELL *Gegenbaur's Comp. Anat.* 325 The dorsum of the Gastropoda. **1885** H. O. FORBES *Nat. Wand. E. Archip.* 195 The nose with a rather prominent and straight dorsum.

2. A ridge of hill or high ground.

1782 T. WARTON *Hist. Kiddington* 69 (T.) A similar ridge, which creeping through the deep south-east valley.. suddenly rises into a massy dorsum. **1905** W. G. HOLMES *Justinian & Theod.* I. 27 The moat..follows the trend of the ground as it rises on either side from the beach to the dorsum of the peninsula.

dors-umbonal: see DORSO-.

dorsur: see DOSSER¹.

dort (dɔːt), *sb. Sc.* [Of obscure origin; derivatives go back to *c* 1500: see DORTY, DORTINESS.] Usually in *pl.*: Sulkiness, ill-humour; sulks.

1632 RUTHERFORD *Lett.* xxiii. (1862) I. 91 Let your soul.. take the dorts (as we use to speak). **1725** RAMSAY *Gentle Sheph.* I. i, Then fare ye weel Meg-Dorts. [Cf. SCOTT *St. Ronan's* i.] **1823** MISSES CORBETT *Petticoat T.* I. 288 (Jam.) Andrew, that left you in the dorts.

Hence **dort** *v. intr.* to become pettish, to sulk; **dorted** *ppl. a.*, sulky, ill-humoured. (Jam.)

dortiness, dortiship: see DORTY.

†**ˈdortory, dortry.** *Obs. rare.* [var. of DORTOUR, *dorter*, with suffix as in *dormitory*.] = next.

1636 FEATLY *Clavis Myst.* lxii. 833 Churchyards by the Ancients are termed dormitories or dortories. **1688** R. HOLME *Armoury* III. 178/2 The Dortry or Dormitory.

†**dortour, dorter** (ˈdɔːtə(r)). *Obs.* exc. *Hist.* Forms: 3–5 dortore, 4–6 -oure, 5 -oyr, -owre, doortur, 5–7 dorture, 6– 7 -or, 7 -oir(e, 4–9 dortour, 5–9 dorter. [a. OF. *dortour, -ur, -eur*, vars. of *dortoir* (12th c. in Littré):—L. *dormītōrium* DORMITORY.] A sleeping-room, bed-chamber, dormitory; *esp.* that of a monastery.

c **1290** *S. Eng. Leg.* I. 286/278 Of þe dortore he axede him: ȝwat were þare is dede. *c* **1330** R. BRUNNE *Chron.* (1810) 256 þou may not ligge & slepe as monke in his dortoure. *c* **1386** CHAUCER *Sompn. T.* 147 His deeth saugh I by reuelacioun, Seith this frere, at hoom in oore dortour. *c* **1475** *Pict. Voc.* in Wr.-Wülcker 803/26 *Hoc dormitorium*, a dorter. **1596** SPENSER *F.Q.* VI. xii. 24 The Monckes he..pursu'd into their dortours sad. **1607** TOPSELL *Four-f. Beasts* (1658) 499 The Magicians command that the grieved party be included in his Dortor or Bed-chamber. **1666** PEPYS *Diary* (1879) IV. 214, I saw the dortoire, and the cells of the priests. **1820** SCOTT *Ivanhoe* xxxiii, Giving me somewhat over to the building of our dortour. **1891** FARRAR in *Sund. Mag.* 118 The staircase leading up to the Dorter.

attrib. **1533–4** *Act 25 Hen. VIII*, c. 12 The dorture doore was made open vnto hir by gods power. **1592** NASHE *P. Penilesse* (ed. 2) 22 b, It will make them iolly long winded to trot vp and downe the Dorter Staires.

b. *transf.* and *fig.*

1562 J. HEYWOOD *Prov. & Epigr.* (1867) 201 The mouth is assynde, to be the tounges dorter. *a* **1626** BP. ANDREWES *Serm.* (1641) 384 A cemetary, that is, a great dortor. **1641** J. JACKSON *True Evang. T.* I. 71 They are dead tenets..and we will not..call them up from their dorters againe.

Hence †**ˈdortourer**, one who has charge of a dormitory; a 'bed-maker'.

c **1430** *Pilgr. Lyf Manhode* III. xlvi. (1869) 160 But it displeseth me gretliche that she is dortowrere there, and maketh here beddes as chamberere.

dorty (ˈdɔːtɪ), *a. Sc.* [f. DORT + -Y.] Ill-humoured, pettish, sulky; saucy, haughty.

a **1605** MONTGOMERIE *Sonnets* lxv, Right dortie to come ouir the dur. **1737** RAMSAY *Scot. Prov.* (1776) 65 (Jam.) The dorty dame may fa' in the dirt. **1786** BURNS *Author's Cry & Prayer* xxiii, Though a Minister grow dorty.

Hence **ˈdortiness, ˈdortiship**, ill-humour, haughtiness, sauciness.

1513 DOUGLAS *Æneis* III. v. 86 The dortynes of Achilles ofspring. **1721** RAMSAY *Wks.* (1848) II. 192 A ferly 'tis your dortiship to see.

†**dory, dorye**, *a.* (*sb.*¹) *Obs.* Forms: 5 dorre, -ee, -ey, -oy, -y, dorye. [a. F. *doré*, pa. pple. of *dorer*:—L. *deaurāre* to gild: cf. DORE.]

1. Of a golden colour; bright yellow.

1398 TREVISA *Barth. De P.R.* v. xlv. (1495) 162 Yelowe coloure..Dorrey and cytrine and lyghte redde.

2. *Old Cookery.* Glazed with 'almond milk', 'endored': cf. DORE *v.* As *sb.* A dish so glazed.

c **1430** *Two Cookery-bks.* I. 11 Soupes dorye. *Ibid.* Soupes dorroy..Do þe dorry a-bowte. *c* **1450** *Ibid.* II. 90 Soppes Dorre. *Ibid.* II. 114 Soupes dorrees.

dory (ˈdɔərɪ), *sb.*² Forms: 5 dorre, dorray, 6 dorrey, 7 dorie, dorry, dorae, 7- doree, dory. [a. F. *dorée* 'the Doree, or Saint Peters fish; also (though not so properly) the Goldfish or Goldenie' (Cotgr.); in origin, fem. pa. pple. of *dorer* to gild.] A fish, *Zeus faber*, found in European seas, and much esteemed as food. Also called JOHN DORY, q.v.

c **1440** *Anc. Cookery* in *Househ. Ord.* (1790) 449 Salmon, fresshe and dorre rosted, or gurnard sothen. *c* **1460** J. RUSSELL *Bk. Nurture* 582 Whale, Swerdfysche, purpose, dorray, rosted wele. **1601** HOLLAND *Pliny* I. 246 The Doree or Goldfish, called Zeus and Faber. **1655** MOUFET & BENNET *Health's Improv.* (1746) 242 The Dorry is very like to a Sea-bream, of most excellent Taste. **1766** ANSTEY *Bath Guide* iv. 63 She has order'd for Dinner a Piper and Dory. **1828** STARK *Elem. Nat. Hist.* I. 478 The Dory..is said to be an excellent fish for the table.

dory (ˈdɔərɪ), *sb.*³ *W. Indies* and *U.S.* Also dorey. **a.** 'A small boat; *esp.* a small flat-bottomed boat used in sea-fisheries, in which to go out from a larger vessel to catch fish' (*Cent. Dict.*).

1726 *Trav. Capt. N. Uring* 346 We launched the Dory over the reef. **1798** COL. BARROW in *Naval Chron.* (1799) I. 247 Canoes, dories, and pit pans. **1810** *Ann. Reg.* 738 The Pip-pan being flat-bottomed, the Dory round. **1837** HAWTHORNE *Twice-told T.* (1851) II. vi. 91, I launched my dory, my little flat-bottomed skiff. **1858** O. W. HOLMES *Aut. Breakf.-t.* vii. (1891)164 A fancy 'dory' for two pairs of sculls.

b. *attrib.* and *Comb.*, as ***dory-becket, -fisherman, -fishing, -man, -mate, -roding; dory-modelled, -shaped*** adjs.

1897 KIPLING *Capt. Cour.* 154 Fiddling helplessly with a *dory-becket. **1923** T. S. ELIOT *Waste Land* 32, I had in mind the 'longshore' or '*dory' fisherman, who returns at nightfall. **1897** KIPLING *Capt. Cour.* 163 Men had met one another before, *dory-fishing in the fog. **1962** *Times* 6 Jan. 9/7 We would pass the *dorymen hauling their line. **1890** K. MUNROE *Dory Mates* 25 He delighted in being called his father's '*dorymate'. **1897** KIPLING *Capt. Cour.* 178 It's yours and welcome, Harve, because we're dory-mates. **1919** *Hist. Amer. Lit.* II. II. x. 9 The reader asks resentfully what they are doing in this *dory-modelled *galère*, painted green below with a border of blue. **1897** KIPLING *Capt. Cour.* 52 A tiny anchor..and some seventy fathoms of thin brown *dory-roding. **1897** *Outing* (U.S.) XXX. 386/2 The boat.. is *dory-shaped, nine feet long.

dos, obs. f. *does*, etc (see DO *v.*), DOSE.

dosaberd, var. of DASIBERD, *Obs.*

‖**dos-à-dos** (dozado), *adv. phr.* and *sb.* [Fr.]

A. *adv. phr.* Back to back. **B.** *sb.* A seat, carriage, or the like, so constructed that the occupants sit back to back. **C.** In Book-binding, *attrib. phr.* (see quot. 1952). Cf. DO-SE-DO.

1837 J. F. COOPER *Recoll. Europe* I. 41 Some one kindly told him that they no longer danced *dos-à-dos*. **1859** *Habits of Good Society* xvi. 349 A liberal supply of ottomans, *dos-à-dos*, and sofas. **1882** H. DE WINDT *Equator* 119 The street cab of Batavia is a 'dos-à-dos' literally so called, as the passenger sits with his back to the driver's, thus forming a mutual support. **1952** J. CARTER *ABC for Bk. Collectors* 66 *Dos-à-dos binding*, a style of binding, mostly used for devotional works, in which two volumes are bound back-to-back with a common lower board. **1970** *Sotheby's Catal. Books* 9 Nov. 28 Two modern calf gilt fitted boxes of dos-à-dos form.

dosage (ˈdəʊsɪdʒ). Also doseage. [f. DOSE *v.* or *sb.* + -AGE: cf. F. *dosage*.]

1. a. The adminstration of medicine in doses: esp. in reference to the size of the dose.

1876 BARTHOLOW *Mat. Med.* (1879) 190 As regards doseage, from fifteen to thirty grains every two, three, or four hours..is usually the necessary quantity. *Ibid.* 426[No] arbitrary rules of dosage can be laid down. **1881** *Times* 18 Apr. 10/4 Hahnemann's idea of dosage.

b. Used similarly in radiotherapy of X-rays and other ionizing radiation: see DOSE *sb.*

1893 A. S. ECCLES *Sciatica* 56 Care must be taken not to exceed the dosage either in strength or duration. **1912** BYTHELL & BARCLAY *X-ray Diagnosis & Treatment* 121 It is necessary to be extremely cautious until some idea is obtained as to the amount of dosage the skin will stand. **1918** R. KNOX *Radiogr. & Radio-Therap.* (ed. 2) II. 424 The various systems of measuring the X-ray dosage. *Ibid.* 511 The most difficult question in radium treatment is that of dosage. **1928** *New Statesman* 28 July 510/1 The most careful and experienced practitioner may sometimes cause an X-ray burn after dosages which he has used..without injury on hosts of occasions. **1938** R. W. LAWSON tr. *Hevesy & Paneth's Man. Radioactivity* (ed. 2) xxiv. 258 The maximum daily dosage of γ-rays. **1959** *Lab. Invest.* VIII. 173 This lack of certainty..of the scope of autoradiographic method for radiation dosage measurement prompted us to investigate the problem.

2. The operation of dosing; addition of a dose or doses, e.g. to wine, etc.: see DOSE *sb.* 2, *v.* 2 b.

1867 *C. A. Harris' Dict. Med. Terminol.* (ed. 3) *Dosage*, a term applied in Chemistry to a plan of analysis in which the reagent is added in measured quantities, from a graduated tube, to a measured and weighed solution of the assay. **18..** DE COLANGE I. 138 (Cent.) The dosage varies with the quality of the wine.

dosan, -and, -ain, -ayn(e, obs. ff. DOZEN.

dose (dəʊs), *sb.* Also 7 dos, doss, dosse, 7–9 doze: see also DOSIS. [a. F. *dose* (15th c. in Hatz.-Darm.), ad. med.L. *dosis*: see DOSIS.]

1. *Med.* **a.** A definite quantity of a medicine or drug given or prescribed to be given at one time.

1600 W. VAUGHAN *Direct. Health* (1633) 78 The Dose or quantity is foure or five leaves of it in a cup of Ale. **1608** T. MORTON *Pream. Encounter* 39 A dos of his Opium. **1808** *Med. Jrnl.* XIX. 248 Small dozes of tincture of digitalis. **1849** MACAULAY *Hist. Eng.* I. 441 To call his complaint a fever, and to administer doses of bark.

b. A given quantity of X-rays or other ionizing radiation, esp. considered in relation to a person receiving it; a quantity of ionizing radiation received or absorbed at one time or over a specified period (e.g. in radiotherapy or the irradiation of plants); **dose rate**, the rate at which the dose is increasing. Also *attrib.*

absorbed dose (or simply *dose*): the quantity of ionizing radiation absorbed, measured (in rads) by the energy absorbed per unit mass of material; *exposure dose* (or *exposure*): the quantity of ionizing radiation to which anything is exposed or subjected, measured (in roentgens) by the ionization it produces in a given mass of air.

1912 BYTHELL & BARCLAY *X-ray Diagnosis & Treatment* 117 Heavy doses may occasionally produce a strong skin reaction. **1918** R. KNOX *Radiogr. & Radio-Therap.* (ed. 2) II. 424 An erythema dose is one which causes slight erythema to appear within fifteen to twenty-one days. *Ibid.* 428 If the total dose is to be administered in several sittings. *Ibid.* 514 Exposures, with large quantities of radium in well-filtered doses, may be given up to twenty-four hours. **1947** *Radiology* XLIX. 283/2 Lower dose rates could not be used, as the period of fertility of mice is only eight months. *Ibid.* 352/1 Four dose levels (13, 4·3, 1·15, 0·115r) were empirically chosen. **1950** *Britannica Bk. of Year* 682/2 *Dose*, the amount of radio-active contamination received by a person, implement, or other object employed on or used in atomic energy research or utilization. **1955** *Bull. Atomic Sci.* 213/3 The biological effects of radiation are measured by the dose received, that is, by the energy absorbed by unit volume of the tissue from the radiation. **1956** *Nature* 17 Mar. 531/1 At very low dose-rates..the radiation times required would be inconveniently long. **1959** *Times* 7 Dec. (Agric. Suppl.) p. vi/5 Doses of radiation in the range 8,000–10,000 rads have been found to be sufficient for commercially acceptable sprout suppression in potatoes of several varieties. **1963** *Clin. Dosimetry* (Nat. Bur. Stand. Handbk. 87) 38/2 Numerous names were examined as a replacement for exposure dose, but there were serious objections to any which included the word dose. There appeared to be a minimum of objection to the name *exposure* and hence this term has been adopted by the [International] Commission [on Radiological Units and Measurements]... The elimination of the term 'dose' accomplishes the long-felt desire of the Commission to retain the term dose for one quantity only—the absorbed dose. **1969** *New Scientist* 24 Apr. 177/1 With high energy X-rays the dose at a depth below the surface is significantly greater than that on the surface skin. **1970** PASSMORE & ROBSON *Compan. Med. Stud.* II. xxxiii. 3/2 Such fall-out is estimated to have resulted in an average yearly dose of 2·4 mrads in the period 1954–9.

2. *transf.* and *fig.* **a.** A definite quantity or amount of something regarded as analogous in some respect to a medical prescription, or to medicine in use or effect; a definite amount of some ingredient added to wine to give it a special character.

1607 *Schol. Disc. agst. Antichr.* I. ii. 68 To banish the whole dosse of popishe doctrine. **1664** BUTLER *Hud.* II. iii. 955 Marry'd his punctual dose of Wives. *c* **1790** WILLOCK *Voy.* 55 A sufficient doze of their favorite liquor, whiskey. **1862** MERIVALE *Rom. Emp.* (1865) VI. liii. 338 To repeat and daily increase the dose of flattery. **1894** P. L. FORD *Hon. Peter Stirling* 150 'He snubbed me,'..explained Miss De Voe, smiling..at the thought of treating Peter with a dose of his own medicine.

b. An unpleasant experience.

1847 E. BRONTË *Wuthering Heights* I. 56 You have reason in shutting it up... No one will thank you for a dose in such a den! **1939** H. G. WELLS *Holy Terror* I. ii. 41 Seems he don't like the idea of this new war that's coming... *We* had a dose.

c. *a dose of salts*: a dose of aperient salts; also *transf.* and *fig.* with *like*: very rapidly.

1837 *Crockett's Almanac* 3 I'll go through the Mexicans like a dose of salts. **1953** E. SIMON *Past Masters* II. iii. 84 She went systematically through the residents, in the phrase of Monro, like a dose of salts. **1961** DOBIE & SLOMAN *Tinker* 11, If you think you're getting tired or anything, tell me and we'll be back down that bloody thing like a dose of salts. **1961** WODEHOUSE *Service with Smile* ii. 27 He boxed three years for Oxford... And went through the opposition like a dose of salts. **1968** J. WAINWRIGHT *Edge of Extinction* 31 If we don't hold 'em they'll go through this city like a dose of salts.

d. An occurrence of venereal disease.

1914 *Dialect Notes* IV. 105 *Dose*, venereal disease. **1922** JOYCE *Ulysses* 151 Some chap with a dose burning him. **1952** B. HAMILTON *So Sad, So Fresh* xix. 122 The cream of the joke is, she gave me the worst dose I've ever had. **1968** B. TURNER *Sex Trap* xi. 97 She's riddled with pox. I know four blokes who've copped a dose from her.

dose (dəʊs), *v.* [f. prec. sb.: cf. F. *doser* (16th c. in Hatz.-Darm.).]

1. *trans.* To divide into, or administer in, doses.

1713 DERHAM *Phys.-Theol.* (J.) Plants..esteemed poisonous, if corrected, and exactly dosed, may prove powerful medicines. **1733** CHEYNE *Eng. Malady* I. xi. §12 (1734) 105 Care..in dosing the proper Medicines for such ..Disorders. **1757** PULTNEY in *Phil. Trans.* L. 74 They knew how to dose it very exactly.

2. To administer doses to; to physic.

1654 GAYTON *Pleas. Notes* II. ii. 39 For the mishap, no other..was to dose it but himselfe. **1685** SOUTH *Serm.* I. 298 (T.) A bold, self-opinioned physician..who shall dose, and bleed, and kill him *secundum artem.* **1753** G. WASHINGTON *Jrnl.* Writ. 1889 I. 25 They dosed themselves pretty plentifully with it [wine]. **1824** W. IRVING *T. Trav.* I. 41 My uncle grew worse and worse, the more dosing and nursing he underwent.

b. *transf.* To add or apply a dose of something to: see DOSE *sb.* 2.

1836 J. HUME in *Ho. Comm.* 24 Mar., The dosing wines liberally with brandies and other spirits. **1884** *Fortn. Rev.* Dec. 799 This dosing with ammoniates has done more to impoverish agriculture than all the terrors of disease.

Hence **'doser**, one who (or that which) gives a dose: used contemptuously for a physician.

1888 *Poor Nellie* 162 Never met one of your dosers yet, who was anything but a quack.

dose, obs. f. *does*, etc. (see DO *v.*), DOZE.

doseberd, -beirde, var. DASIBERD, *Obs.*

do-se-do (ˌdəʊziː'dəʊ). orig. *U.S.* Also do-si-do. [Corruption of DOS-À-DOS.] A figure in square dancing in which two people pass around each other back to back and return to their places. Hence as *v. intr.* Also *transf.*

1929 D. SCARBOROUGH *Can't get Red Bird* v. 105 First couple out, round up four; Swing your pardners in a do-se-do. *Ibid.* 106 Haul six and get fixed; Do-se-do like picking up sticks. **1934** *Amer. Ballads & Folk Songs* (1957) 415 Bunch the heifers to the middle, circle stags and do-se-do. **1962** R. NETTEL *Folk-Dancing* 147 *Do-si-do.* Partners face each other and walk forward passing right shoulders, then step sideways (back to back) and return to places walking backwards and passing left shoulders. **1969** C. ARMSTRONG *Seven Seats to Moon* viii. 91 Tony Thees on J's trail in the Chevvy began to try to shake off Barry Goodrick in the Ford... They did tricky lane shifts, fast turns and do-si-dos around some blocks.

dosein, dosen, obs. forms of DOZEN.

dosel, -il, obs. forms of DOSSAL, DOSSIL.

dosemeter: see DOSIMETER.

doseper: see DOUZEPERS.

doser, obs. form of DOSSER[1].

dosh (dɒʃ). *slang.* [Origin unknown.] Money.

1953 H. CLEVELY *Public Enemy* xviii. 114 He hadn't enough dosh on him. **1959** I. & P. OPIE *Lore & Lang. Schoolch.* ix. 155 Money..is referred to as..moolah, dosh (common), sploosh, [etc.]. **1970** M. KENYON *100,000 Welcomes* xvi. 139 'America! The money's in America!' ..''Tis true. The Yankees have the dosh all right.'

dosimeter (dəʊ'sɪmɪtə(r)). Also do'someter, 'dosemeter. [f. as next + -METER.] An apparatus for measuring doses or the like; *spec.* a recording device to measure ionizing radiation, esp. one worn by a person exposed to potentially harmful radiation.

1881 *Nature* XXV. 144 An electrolytic dosometer for measuring the intensity of the current during medical application of electricity. **1944** (*title*) Photographic Film as a Pocket Radiation Dosimeter. (U.S. Atomic Energy Commission, MDDC-1065). **1957** *Financ. Times Ann. Rev. Brit. Ind.* 85/3 Dosemeters may be installed..to register.. the flux of fast neutrons..at key points. **1959** *New Scientist* 5 Nov. 872/1 Normally dosimeters employing dyes will not register any perceptible effect on a sample 1 mm. thick if the radiation intensity is below about 1,000 to 10,000 roentgen. **1969** *Times* 16 July 4 (*caption*) Dosimeter access flap.

dosimetric (dɒsɪ'mɛtrɪk), *a.* [f. Gr. δόσις (see DOSE) + -METRIC.] Relating to the measurement of doses. So **dosimetry** (dəʊ'sɪmɪtrɪ), the measurement of doses (*Syd. Soc. Lex.*).

1881 *Daily News* 11 May, The new Dosimetric method of treatment. **1883** *Syd. Soc. Lex.*, *Dosimetric medicine*, a method of treating disease..[by] the employment of simple and active remedies..in doses that are mathematically defined and administered according to certain rules. **1944** *U.S. Atomic Energy Comm. Rep. AECD-2278* (1948) (*title*) Photographic neutron dosimetry to date. **1960** *New Scientist* 2 June 1398/1 The dosimetry experiment is concerned with the..question as to precisely what dosages of radiation caused these observed effects. **1961** *Times* 17 Apr. 3/3 Appointments in the following fields:..Radiation Dosimetry. **1968** S. J. FLEMING in *Proc. 2nd Internat. Conf. Luminescence Dosimetry* 266 (*title*) The colour of spurious thermoluminescence in dosimetry phosphors.

dosin, obs. form of DOZEN.

dosi'ology, do'sology. [irreg. f. DOSE or DOSIS: see -OLOGY.] 'That branch of medicine which treats of the amounts or doses in which drugs should be given' (*Syd. Soc. Lex.*).

1678 PHILLIPS (ed. 4), *Dosology.*

dosipers, var. DOUZEPERS, *Obs.*

‖**'dosis.** *Obs.* [med.L. a. Gr. δόσις giving, n. of action from διδόναι to give.] = DOSE *sb.* (being the form in earlier use in Eng.).

1543 TRAHERON *Vigo's Chirurg.* 35 b/2 (Stanf.) The dosis of gyuing of them is .3. i. **1611** *Coryat's Crudities* Panegyr. Verses, [Thy book] a Dosis is against all Melancholy. **1655** H. VAUGHAN *Silex Scint.* II. *Joy* (1858) 146 A sugerd dosis Of wormwood, and a death's-head crown'd with roses. **1668** H. MORE *Dir. Dial.* I. 494 Too large a Dosis of Knowledge.

dosk, obs. form of DUSK.

dosology, dosometer: see DOSIOLOGY, DOSIMETER.

dosour, obs. form of DOSSER[1].

†**doss**, *sb.*[1] *Obs.* Also 5 doce. [a. F. *dos*:—late L. **dossum*, for *dorsum* back.] = DORSE *sb.*[1] 1, DOSSER[1] 1.

1482 LD. BEAUCHAMP *Will*, Doce and redoce of red velvet. *c* **1490** *Promp. Parv.* 127/2 (MS. K.) Dosse, *dossorium*. **1533** *Coronat. Q. Anne* in Arb. *Garner* (1879) II. 50 The blue 'ray cloth spread from the high dosses of the Kings Bench unto the high altar of Westminster.

doss (dɒs), *sb.*[2] *slang.* Also 8 dorse. [Prob. of same origin as DOSS *sb.*[1]: cf. DOSS *v.*[2]]

1. A place for sleeping in, a bed; *esp.* a bed in a common lodging-house. Also with suffixed *adv.*

1789 G. PARKER *Life's Painter* 165 (Farmer) Dorse, the place where a person sleeps, or a bed. **1846** *Swell's Night Guide* 77 She stalled a lushy swaddy to a doss t'other darky. **1847** G. W. M. REYNOLDS *Myst. London* III. xxv. 71/2 May she be faithful to thy doss. **1851** MAYHEW *Lond. Labour* I. 336 (Hoppe) In course the man paid..for the dos (bed). *c* **1880** BARNARDO *Taken out of Gutter* 2 The coveted 'doss', as the bed in a threepenny lodging-house is called. **1892** R. CARRICK *Romance Lake Wakatipu* iv. 16 [The bed] was accounted a luxury..compared with the doss-down the digger in pursuit of his calling was accustomed to. **1943** J. B. HISLOP *Pure Gold & Rough Diamonds* 117, I thought it a great labour-saving idea and a great place for a doss-out. **1956** E. BLYTON *Myst. Missing Man* xvii. 130 Only an old fellow who wants a doss-down somewhere.

2. Sleep.

1858 A. MAYHEW *Paved with Gold* 118 (Farmer) Into this ..retreat, the lads crept..to enjoy their doss, as, in their slang, they called sleep. **1887** *Daily News* 29 Sept. 7/2 [Bargeman] To tell you the truth, we were having a doss (sleeping) in the cabin.

3. *Comb.* **doss-house**, a common lodging-house; **doss-man**, the keeper of a 'doss-house'.

1825 C. M. WESTMACOTT *Eng. Spy* I. 380 The Duck lane doss man. **1888** *Pall Mall G.* 6 Oct. 4/1 Lord Compton's proposal for an inquiry by a Select Committee into the 'doss-houses' of London. **1891** *Spectator* 14 Mar. 385/2 Preferable..to the contamination of the doss-house.

doss (dɒs), *v.*[1] *Obs.* exc. *dial.* [Origin obscure.

It may be partly onomatopœic, under the combined influence of *dush* (or *dash*) and *toss*. Cf. also MDu. *dossen*, intens. of *dosen*, *doesen*, to strike with violence and noise (Kilian).]

1. a. *intr.* To push with the horns, as a bull. **b.** *trans.* To toss (the horns). **c.** To butt, toss, or gore (a person) with the horns. *dial.*

1583 GOLDING *Calvin on Deut.* xx. 119 [These] doe dosse with their hornes like madde bulles against all good Gouernment and policie. **1589** *Pasquil's Ret.* C iv, They are called Bulles, because they dosse out theyr hornes against the truth. **1596** H. CLAPHAM *Briefe Bible* II. 129 The Deuill ..is introduced with his Hornes, even for dossing (ey destroying) this Man-childe Jesus. *c* **1680** HICKERINGILL *Hist. Whiggism* Wks. 1716 I. 91 You may know the Nature of the Beast..by her Dossing at Men on all trivial occasions. *a* **1825** FORBY *Voc. E. Anglia*, *Doss*, to attack with the horns, as a bull, a ram, or a he-goat.

2. *Sc.* To throw *down* with force; to toss *down*.

a **1745** MESTON *Poems* (1767) 106 (Jam.) Resolv'd to make him count and reckon, And doce down. *a* **1809** *Christmas Ba'ing* in J. Skinner *Misc. Poet.* (1809) 134 (Jam.) The pensy blades doss'd down on stanes.

doss, *v.*[2] *slang.* Also 8 dorse, 9 dos. [Goes with DOSS *sb.*[2]] *intr.* To sleep; *esp.* to sleep at a common lodging-house or 'doss-house' (see DOSS *sb.*[2] 3). Also with *down*. Hence '**dossing** *vbl. sb.*; also *attrib.*

1785 GROSE *Dict. Vulg. Tongue* s.v., To dorse..to sleep. **1789** G. PARKER *Life's Painter* 165 (Farmer), I dorsed there last darkey. **1838** *Comic Almanack* Apr. (Farmer) The hulks is now my bowsing-crib, the hold my dossing-ken. **1888** EARL COMPTON *Sp. House Commons* 5 Oct., A select committee to inquire into the 'dossing' or lodging-house system. **1895** *Tablet* 14 Sept. 426 Charges of theft, begging, 'dossing out', and other juvenile misdemeanours. **1896** *N.Z. Alpine Jrnl.* II. ix. 169 Hodgkins and I 'dossed down' by the side of it. **1898** J. D. BRAYSHAW *Slum Silhouettes* 4, I was dossin' dahn at Shorty's. **1899** J. BELL *Shadow of Bush* iii. 11 There is a spare bunk in the wharé for one..and the other can doss down somewhere. **1924** *Chambers's Jrnl.* Jan. 31/2 We made a pretence of dossing down. **1932** *Daily Express* 25 June 17/6 If he wants to be on his way at daybreak he dosses down with his face to the east.

doss(e, obs. form of DOSE.

dossal, dossel ('dɒsəl). Also 7 dosel, dorsel. [ad. med.L. *dossāle*, var. of *dorsāle* a hanging behind a seat, an altar, etc., after OF. *dossel* (occas. *dossal*), f. *dos* back.]

a. An ornamental cloth forming a cover for the back of a seat: = DOSSER[1] 1. *arch.* **b.** *Eccl.* An ornamental cloth, usually embroidered, hung at the back of the altar or at the sides of the chancel.

1658–1706 PHILLIPS, A *Dosel* or *Dorsel*..a rich Canopie under which Princes sit, also the Curtain of a Chaire of State. **1848** LYTTON *Harold* v. i, The Earl's old hawk.. perched on the dossel of the Earl's chair. **1851** *Ecclesiologist* 324 A rich woven stuff suspended, as a dossel, behind the altar. **1866** F. G. LEE *Direct. Angl.* (ed. 3) 6 There should be no Cross embroidered on the Dossal where the Altar-Cross is in use. *Ibid.* 353 Dossel.

dosseberde, var. of DASIBERD, *Obs.*

dossein, dossen, obs. forms of DOZEN.

†**dossel.** *Obs.* or *dial.* Also 8–9 dorsel. [a. F. *dossel*:—late L. *dorsāle* what pertains to the back, f. L. *dorsum*, F. *dos* back.] A pannier or the like borne by a beast of burden: = DOSSER[1] 2. (In quot. 1827, an appliance for carrying burdens on the back.)

1755 JOHNSON, *Dorsel, Dorser*, a pannier; a basket or bag one of which hangs on either side a beast of burden. It is corruptly spoken, and perhaps written, *dossel*. **1791** J.

COLLINSON *Hist. Somerset* II. 34 The manure [is carried] in wooden pots called dossels. **1827** CARLYLE *Germ. Romance* IV. 44 The porter is girding the portmanteau on his dorsel.

dossel, var. DOSSAL, DOSSIL.

dosse pers, dosseperes, var. DOUZEPERS.

dosser[1] (ˈdɒsə(r)), **dorser** (ˈdɔːsə(r)). *Obs.* exc. *Hist.* Forms: α. 4–5 doser, 4–6 docer(e, 5 dossour, dosour, dosur(e, 5–7 dossar, 4– dosser. β. 4– dorser; 5 dorsere, -cere, -sur, 6 dorsour, 7 dorcer, (9 dorsar, -eur). [a. OF. *dossier, docier*, f. *dos* back: cf. med.L. *dorsārium* (f. *dorsum*), to which *dorser* is conformed.]

1. An ornamental cloth used to cover the back of a seat, esp. of a throne or chair of state, or as a hanging for the wall of a hall or room of state, or of the chancel of a church (= DOSSAL b).

α. **13..** *Gaw. & Gr. Knt.* 478 Hit watz don abof þe dece, on doser to henge. *c* **1380** *Sir Ferumb.* 1340 þe dossers were of ryche pal; y-brouded al wiþ golde. **1432** *Test. Ebor.* II. 22 A rede docer with a banquere, and all yᵉ whisshyns. **1495** *Nottingham Rec.* III. 40 Unum doser ad pendendum supra lectum cum curtenis eidem pertinentibus.

β. **1379** *Priv. Purse Exp. Eliz. of York* (1830) 242/2 Best dorser, four costers and one banker. **14..** *Lat. & Eng. Voc.* in Wr.-Wülcker 579/23 *Dorsorium*, a dorsere. **1516** *Inventories* (1815) 28 (Jam.) A frountell of ane alter of clothe of gold, a dorsour of clothe of gold. **1870** MORRIS *Earthly Par.* I. II. 555 Dorsars, with pearls in every hem.

2. A basket carried on the back, or slung in pairs over the back of a beast of burden, a pannier.

α. *c* **1384** CHAUCER *H. Fame* III. 850 Men.. maken of these panyers Or elles hottes or dossers. *c* **1449** PECOCK *Repr.* I. vi. 30 Schulde men seie.. that tho fischis grewen out of the panyeris or dossers. **1532** MORE *Confut. Tindale* Wks. 657/2 The deuil hate.. made him to fall in the diche with his docer, and breake all his egges. **1608** *Merry Devil of Edmonton* in Hazl. *Dodsley* X. 224 Turn the wenches off, And lay their dossers tumbling in the dust. **1725** BRADLEY *Fam. Dict.* s.v. *Seeds*, Seven or eight Dossers full of this earth. **1772** SIMES *Mil. Guide, Dosser*, a kind of basket.. to be carried on the shoulders, used to carry the overplus earth from one part of a fortification to another. **1850** LEITCH tr. *Müller's Anc. Art* §388 She seems to be in the act of suspending the first in a kind of dosser.

β. **1526** *Ord. Hen. VIII*, in *Househ. Ord.* (1790) 143 And that the dorsers keepe their due gage. **1625** FLETCHER & SHIRLEY *Nt. Walker* I, I may meet her Riding from Market ..'twixt her Dorsers. **1712** J. JAMES tr. *Le Blond's Gardening* 108 Dorsers or Hampers carried by Horses or Asses. **1877** WRAXALL *Hugo's Misérables* IV. xlii, A rag-picker with her dorser and her hook.

†**b.** A syphilitic swelling or bubo. *Obs.*

1547 BOORDE *Brev. Health* lxxxii. 34.

3. *attrib.* and *Comb.*, as †**dosser-head**, a foolish person; †**dosser-headed** *a.*, foolish.

1612 DEKKER *If it be not good* Wks. 1873 III. 312 That's the cause we haue so many dosser-heads. **1655** tr. *De Parc's Francion* I. 26, I find you are not dosser-headed.

†ˈ**dosser**[2]. *Obs. rare.* [f. DOSS *v.*[1] + -ER[1].] *pl.* The horns of an animal.

1565 GOLDING *Ovid's Met.* VII. (1593) 161 A ram.. Was thither.. drawne.. the medicine.. seard his dossers from his pate, And with his hornes abridgd his yeares.

ˈ**dosser**[3]. *slang.* [f. DOSS *v.*[2] + -ER[1].] One who frequents, or sleeps at, a common lodging-house. ***happy dosser***: see quot. 1884.

1866 *Temple Bar Mag.* XVII. 33 The entrance.. is usually thronged with 'dossers' (casual ward frequenters). **1884** G. R. SIMS in *Rep. Comm. Housing of Wrkg. Classes* App. 185/2 People crowd in at night, and sleep on the stairs of the houses.. they call them "appy dossers'.. "appy dosser' means a person who sleeps where he can. **1891** BOOTH *Darkest Eng.* 98 There is no compulsion upon any one of our dossers to take part in this meeting.

dosseret (ˈdɒsərɛt). *Arch.* [a. F. *dosseret*, dim. of *dossier*: see DOSSER[1].] (See quots.)

1865 *Ecclesiologist* Feb. 2 The supplementary abacus, or dosseret—that cubical block of stone, often higher than the capital itself.. so often found above the capitals of Byzantine columns. **1865** *Sat. Rev.* 182 The capitals.. have a second capital, called a dosseret, above the regular one.

dosseyn, obs. form of DOZEN.

dossiberd, var. of DASIBERD, *Obs.*

dossier (ˈdɒsɪə(r), ˈdɒsɪeɪ, ˈdɒsjeɪ). [a. F. *dossier*, in sense 'bundle of papers', which from their bulging are likened to a back (*dos*): see DOSSER[1].] A bundle of papers or documents referring to some matter; esp. a bundle of papers or information about a person.

1880 *Contemp. Rev.* 992 The dossiers of the electioneering agent. **1884** *Pall Mall Gaz.* 13 June 11/2 In neatly-docketed cabinets round his office stood the *dossiers* of all the criminals with whom he has had anything to do for the past eight years. **1885** *Spectator* 8 Aug. 1040/2 A part of the Great Hastings dossier, the case against Sir Elijah Impey. **1912** H. BELLOC *Servile State* ix. 176 A series of *dossiers* by which the record of each workman can be established. **1920** 'SAPPER' *Bulldog Drummond* xii. 300 Here's his dossier.. 'Ditchling, Charles. Good speaker; clever; unscrupulous. Requires big money; worth it. Drinks.' **1939** M. SPRING RICE *Working-class Wives* ii. 25 Questionnaires filled in by women of a better.. position... Such dossiers would have served as 'controls'. **1955** *Bull. Atomic Sci.* Apr. 129/3 A file check of government dossiers. **1967** A. S. NEILL *Talking of Summerhill* x. 125, I guessed they had rung up our Home Office to ask for my dossier.

dossil (ˈdɒsɪl). Forms: 3 dosil, 4 dosele, -eil, 5 dosel(le, -ylle, duselle, 6 dossell, 6–8 dozel(l, 7 dossill, 9 dossel, 7– dossil. [a. OF. *dosil*, now *doisil, douzil* spigot, plug, tap, cock:—late L. *duciculus* (Du Cange), dim. of *dux, duc-em*, leader. Med.L. had also *ducillus, docillus*.]

†**1.** A plug for a barrel; a spigot. *Obs.*

1297 R. GLOUC. (1724) 542 Hii caste awei the dosils, that win orn abrod. **13..** *Seuyn Sag.* (W.) 1150 And tho [= when] he hadde mad holes so fele, In ech he pelt a dosele. *c* **1425** *Voc.* in Wr.-Wülcker 659 *Hic ducellus*, dosylle. **1483** *Cath. Angl.* 111/2 A Duselle.

2. A plug of lint or rag for stopping a wound, etc.; a pledget.

1575 BANISTER *Chyrurg.* I. (1585) 262 With some dozell or fitte bowlster, layde on the place. **1676** WISEMAN *Chirurg. Treat.* 299, I dressed the Bone with Dossils dipt in a newlaid Egg. **1751** SMOLLETT *Per. Pic.* xxvii, A dossil of lint with a snip of plaister. **1805** *Med. Jrnl.* XIV. 302, I dressed the wound with small dossils, imbued with vulnerary water.

3. *dial.* (See quots.)

1828 *Craven Dialect, Dossel*, a wisp of hay or straw to stop up any aperture of a barn, &c. **1847–78** HALLIWELL, *Dossel*, the rose at the end of a water-pipe.

4. A roll of cloth for wiping off the excessive ink from the surface of a copper-plate in printing.

1874 in KNIGHT *Dict. Mech.*

dossin, -yn, obs. forms of DOZEN.

dossity, var. of DOCITY.

dossour, dosur(e, obs. forms of DOSSER[1].

dossy (ˈdɒsɪ), *a. slang.* [Cf. Sc. *doss* neat, spruce, *dossie* small, neat, well-dressed person.] Stylish, smart. Hence ˈ**dossily** *adv.*

1889 GILBERT *Brigands* in *Standard* 9 Nov. 3 (E.D.D.), We are dossy and neat From head to our feet. **1900** *Daily News* 31 July 8/2 What with the ladies' bonnets and blokes' dossy hats. **1903** 'MARJORIBANKS' *Fluff-hunters* 42 A dossy Sloane Street milliner. *Ibid.* 95 A dossily dressed girl.

dost (dʌst), 2 sing. pres. ind. of DO *v.*, q.v.

Dosto(y)evskian (dɒstɔɪˈɛfskɪən, dɒstəʊˈ(j)ɛfskɪən), *a.* Also **Dostoievskian**. [f. the name of Feodor Michaelovich *Dostoevsky* (1821–1881), Russian novelist.] Of, or characteristic of, Dostoevsky or his works.

1925 *Sat. Rev. Lit.* 12 Dec. 404 The Dostoievskian emphasis upon purification through suffering. **1929** *London Aphrodite* IV. 316 We are forced back into intellectual vicious-circles of self-scorn, and that is too dostoevskian. **1931** S. BECKETT *Proust* 62 A fine Dostoievskian contempt for the vulgarity of a plausible concatenation. **1949** KOESTLER *Promise & Fulfilment* xv. 170 The Götter-dämmerung of British rule in the Holy Land was not in the Wagnerian, but rather in the Dostoievskian style. **1959** *Times* 21 Mar. 9/5 The Dostoyevskian appreciation of the spark of the divine in every human soul. **1961** *Times* 30 Mar. 15/2 Jesus is shown as a despised Dostoevskian epileptic.

dosy, var. DOZY.

dosze-peres, var. DOUZEPERS, *Obs.*

dot (dɒt), *sb.*[1] Also 7–9 dott, 7–8 dote. [Of OE. *dott* a single instance is known in sense 'head of a boil'; otherwise the word is not known till 16th c., and not common till 18th c. The OE. word was cognate with OHG. *tutto, tutta*, mod.Ger. dial. *dütte*, nipple of the breast; perh. also with mod.Du. *dot* 'twirled knot of silk or thread', but the radical sense is not clear; if **dutto-z, dott*, was the source of *dyttan* to DIT, stop up, the original notion might be 'small lump, clot'.]

†**1.** The head of a boil. (Only OE.)

c **1000** *Sax. Leechd.* III. 40 Ȝeopeniȝe mon þonne þone dott, and binde þone cliðan to þan swyle.

2. A small lump, a clot. *Obs.* or *dial.*

[**1530** PALSGRAVE is cited by HALLIWELL.] **1570** LEVINS *Manip.* 176/24 A dot, *obstructorium*. **1611** COTGR., *Cracher vn Iacobin*, to spit out a collop, or dot of flegme. *Ibid.*, *Glagou* .. a dot or collop of flegme spet out. **1869** *Lonsdale Gloss.*, *Dot*, a small lump.

3. a. A minute spot, speck, or mark of different colour or material from the surface on which it is.

1674 N. FAIRFAX *Bulk & Selv.* 25 There being as many things to be known, as there are dotts or points in the outward immensity. **1776** WITHERING *Brit. Plants* (1796) I. 266 Receptacle globular, or oblong, with hollow dots. **1805** *Med. Jrnl.* XIV. 367 In the measles the rash is composed of circular dots partly distinct, partly set in small clusters. **1861** MISS PRATT *Flower. Pl.* III. 289 Little dots or glands of the leaves.

fig. *a* **1653** GOUGE *Comm. Heb.* iii. 4 Unless the hollow dotes of hypocrisie be made plain and even.. we can never make up a Temple for God to dwell in.

b. *Plastering*: (see quots. 1823 and 1874). **c.** *Mining*: (see quot. 1881). **d.** *Embroidery*: (see quot. 1882).

1823 P. NICHOLSON *Builder* 390 *Dots*, patches of plaster put on to regulate the floating rule in making screeds and bays. **1874** KNIGHT *Dict. Mech.* I. 722/1 *Dots* (Plastering), nails driven into a wall to a certain depth, so that their protruding heads form a gage of depth in laying on a coat of plaster. **1881** RAYMOND *Mining Gloss.*, *Dotts* or *Dott-holes*, small openings in the vein. **1882** CAULFEILD & SAWARD *Dict. Needlework* 154/2 *Dot*, an Embroidery stitch used in all kinds of fancy work, and known as Point de Pois and Point d'Or.

4. a. A minute roundish mark made with a pen or the like, or resembling one so made.

1748 *Anson's Voy.* III. ii. 315 A small island.. which is represented in the general chart.. only by a dot. **1752** J. LOUTHIAN *Form of Process* (ed. 2) 184 The Clerk marks with a Dote or Stroke of Ink, the Names of all that do appear. **1821** CRAIG *Lect. Drawing* vii. 403 Working [engraving] entirely in dots or points. **1843** PRESCOTT *Mexico* (1850) I. 91 The first twenty numbers were expressed by a corresponding number of dots.

b. *to a dot*: exactly, precisely.

1728 FIELDING *Love in Several Masques* II. ix. 27 *La. Trap.* Are you blind? they are both alike to a Tittle. *Sir Pos.* To a dot. Her Hand to a dot. **1839** *Spirit of Times* 9 Nov. 428/3 There were a large number of horses in attendance.., and amongst them were some who had the 'go along' in them to a 'dot'. **1854** M. J. HOLMES *Tempest & Sunshine* xv. 215 That was one of Tempest's capers to a dot. **1866** *Congress. Globe* 18 June 3235/3 He understands it to a dot. **1881** *Ibid.* 20 Apr. 356/1 That is the question. That is it to a dot. **1887** A. W. TOURGÉE *Button's Inn* 189 That'll suit me to a dot. **1924** KIPLING *Debits & Credits* (1926) 312 You have it!.. That's him to a dot.

c. ***the year dot*** (i.e. a date too old to be particularized), very long ago. *colloq.*

1895 W. P. RIDGE *Minor Dialogues* 166, I reckon *he* was born in the year dot, that 'orse was. **1928** E. WALLACE *Again Sanders* v. 109 He was constantly rediscovering obvious things, or revivifying theories that had been decently interred in the year dot. **1956** 'A. GILBERT' *Death came Too* xii. 132 It's.. the wife who poisons the husband, not some confederate he met in Cuba in the year dot. **1966** G. E. EVANS *Pattern under Plough* xiii. 128 'That's been the same since the *Year Dot* when *Owd Hinery* were an infant'.. and ..he explained that Owd Hinery was the Devil; 'and as "dot" comes before 1, the *Year Dot* was somewhere right back at the beginning'.

d. ***on the dot***: (lit. of the clock-face), punctually, at the precise moment. Also in similar phrases.

1909 in *Cent. Dict.* Suppl. **1923** H. CRANE *Let.* 21 June (1965) 137 From the dot of five till two in the morning. **1931** A. CHRISTIE *Sittaford Mystery* xxiii. 189 They have no idea what a curse they are to everybody with their punctuality, and everything done on the dot of the minute. **1953** W. R. BURNETT *Vanity Row* vii. 58 She's always been very scrupulous about settling her bill on the dot. **1958** R. STOUT *Champagne for One* (1959) vi. 75 At six, on the dot as always, Wolfe entered.

e. *pl.* Originally, the notes on sheet music; hence, written or printed music. *slang.*

1927 *Melody Maker* June 586, I will give you the 'dots' for them. **1956** K. BAKER in S. Traill *Play that Music* i. 22 When speaking of jazz, I mean that kind of music that is all spontaneous, fully extemporized, in other words—no 'dots'. **1968** *Crescendo* Apr. 38/2, I know of not one other guitarist in my home county.. capable of playing an arrangement.. in a manner that could be termed 'doing the dots justice'.

5. Specifically: *Orthogr.* **a.** A point used in punctuation; as in the period or full stop (.), or the colon (:). **b.** The point over the letters i and j; formerly also over y as a vowel. **c.** A point placed over, under, or by a letter or figure to modify its signification, pronunciation, or value.

1740 DYCHE & PARDON, *Dot*, a small mark or point, such as is put over an i, or at the end of a sentence. *a* **1771** G. SHARPE *Method Learn. Hebrew Lang.* i. (R.), To express thousands the Rabbins usually place two dots over the units. **1794** WOLCOTT (P. Pindar) *Rowland for Ol.* Wks. II. 380 On each superfluous letter vents a sigh, and saves the little dot upon an *i*. **1844** UPTON *Physioglyphics* 90 Ḃ represents P, but B (without the dot) is equivalent to Ph. **1887** LD. DERBY in *Pall Mall G.* 15 Nov. 14/1 He did not care to put the dots on the i's [see DOT *v.* 1 b], but he said with conviction that the difficulty which Malthus pointed out seventy years ago.. was upon us again.

d. *Mus.* A point placed for various purposes after, over, or under a note, after a rest, or before or after a double bar.

1806 CALLCOTT *Mus. Gram.* iii. 32 When it is necessary to lengthen a Note by half its value, a dot is placed after it. **1880** GROVE *Dict. Mus.* I. 431/1 Notes marked with dots should be less *staccato* than those with dashes. *Ibid.* 456/2 Dots following rests lengthen them to the same extent as when applied to notes. *Ibid.* 457/2 *Double Bar*.. when accompanied by dots indicates that the section on the same side with the dots is to be repeated.

e. *Morse telegraphy.* (See DASH *sb.*[1] 7 f.)

1838 *Ann. Electr., Magn., & Chem.* III. 146 The numbers consist of nothing more than dots made on the paper, with suitable spaces intervening. Thus .... would represent 325. *Ibid.*, The alphabetical signals are made up of combinations of dots and of lines of different lengths. **1859**, etc. [see DASH *sb.*[1] 7 f].

f. *Television.* A picture element in colour television consisting of one of the three primary colours; also, one of the corresponding areas of phosphor on the inside of the tube, which when struck by a beam of electrons fluoresce a particular colour; ***dot-sequential system***, a system of colour television in which dots of the three primary colours are formed in succession as the picture is scanned.

1937 *Discovery* Nov. 329/1 This amount of definition is determined by the number of dot elements into which the picture is arbitrarily divided. **1951** *Britannica Bk. of Year* 617/2 A dot-sequential system.. in which the colour is changed for each picture element or dot. **1957** *Encycl. Brit.*

XXI. 913/1 The superposition of the colour signal on the brightness signal signifies that areas of the order of a picture element (dots) are reproduced with a repetition rate of only 15 per second. **1959** K. HENNEY *Radio Engin. Handbk.* (ed.5) xxii. 64 The shadow-mask holes and dots are so positioned that the electron beam from, for example, the green gun can strike only green-emitting dots. **1970** *Physics Bull.* Nov. 515/2 Ciné recordings are made directly from the TV screen picture, with limitations set by phosphor dot size.

6. A little child or other tiny creature.

1859 CAPERN *Ball. & Songs* 174 Right joyous be thy lot.. My bonny bright-eyed dot. **1894** SALA *Lond. up to Date* xii. 149 Troops of children, from little dots of four and five..to big girls.

7. The act by which a dot is made by a point striking a surface.

1858 HAWTHORNE *Fr. & It. Jrnls.* I. 255 He..stumped on with a faster or slower dot of his crutch, according to our pace.

8. *Comb.*, as *dot-like* adj., *-maker*; **dot-and-dash** *a.*, formed by dots and dashes, as the Morse telegraph-alphabet, etc.; also *transf.*; and as *v. trans.*; **dot-etching** [cf. 4, quot. 1821], in photolithography, a method of modifying the colour values of a half-tone negative or positive; **dot-hole** (see sense 3 c); **dot-map**, 'a statistical map indicating, by means of dots, the relative frequency of distribution of certain statistical data over a geographical region' (Webster, 1934); **dot matrix** *Computing*, a letter-sized rectangular or square array of positions that are selectively filled to create an alphanumeric character on paper or a VDU screen; usu. *attrib.*; also *ellipt.* for *dot matrix printer* (= *matrix printer* s.v. MATRIX *sb.* 7); **dot-plant**, a plant that stands out as a conspicuous spot of varied colour in a mass of plants; **dot-punch** = CENTRE-punch; **dot-stitch**, a stitch used in making dots in embroidery; **dot-wheel**, a toothed wheel mounted in a handle, which when rolled over a surface produces a dotted line.

1876 PREECE, etc., *Telegraphy* (ed. 2) 54 Representing the one signal by a dot (.) and the other by a dash (—), we have the *dot and dash alphabet of Morse. *Ibid.* 73 Instruments employed in recording the dot and dash signals. **1901** G. B. SHAW *London Mus. 1888–89* (1937) 396 This was a more sensible system, and less harshly crushing to the singer, than the dot and dash system of using trumpets and drums. **1901** W. T. SPENCER in *Academy* 28 Sept. 266/2 Dickens..sat back in his chair, dot-and-dashing telegrams from Fancy-land. **1906** *Daily Chron.* 6 Nov. 3/3 They live in 'dot-and-dash-land', in a world of broken utterances, implied confidences, and vague memories. **1948** F. H. SMITH *Photographs & Printer* 158 The development of *dot-etching techniques for retouching screen negatives and positives has also helped the trend toward reducing the number of printings used. *Ibid.*, The screen negatives may if necessary be retouched to correct tone and colour values by dot-etching. **1960** G. A. GLAISTER *Gloss. of Book* 346/1 *Retouching*, the hand-correcting of colour separations in the photoengraving and photo-lithographic processes. This is known in America as *dot-etching*. **1968** *Gloss. Terms Offset Lithogr. Printing (B.S.I.)* 19 *Dot etching, dot reduction*, the chemical removal of silver from the edges of a half-tone dot image. **1895** *Daily News* 4 Apr. 6/1 *Dot-like irregularities. **1923** K. G. KARSTEN *Charts & Graphs* lvi. 663 *Dot-maps are often most easily made with colored map pins or map tacks. **1939** *Geogr. Jrnl.* XCIII. 274 The printing of the dot-map of the population of Australia gives some wrong impressions in detail. **1975** *Electronic Design* 1 Mar. 76/2 A *dot-matrix printer, the Model 9316, offers speeds to 173 char/s. **1979** *Sci. Amer.* Apr. 120/1 With dot-matrix printing the size and form of the characters themselves can be changed at will. **1982** *Computerworld* 31 Mar. 59/4 If characters formed from dot matrices are too large, the spaces between the dots will become evident and this..interferes with ease of readability. **1982** *Observer* 3 Oct. 21 The dot matrix..is usually cheaper and faster than printers like the daisywheel. **1984** J. HILTON *Choosing & using your Home Computer* 93 The dot matrix method..is very fast and the printers are relatively inexpensive... However, because the letter or number is made up of a series of dots, the print quality tends to be poor. **1985** *Personal Computer World* Feb. 13/2 (Advt.), ThinkJet personal computer printer is surprisingly quiet while printing 150 high quality dot-matrix characters per second. **1882** *Garden* 7 Jan. 7/2 The two last are effective as *dot' plants in large masses of Pelargoniums or dark-leaved plants.

9. Slang or dial. phr. (*to go*) *off one's dot*: (to go) out of one's senses. Cf. DOTTY *a.* 2.

1890 *Yorkshireman* 35 (E.D.D.), I have gone Completely off my dot. **1919** H. S. WALPOLE *Secret City* III. x. 391 She says he's just goin' off his dot. **1929** D. H. LAWRENCE *Pansies* 141 And you have to act up like they do Or they think you're off your dot.

‖**dot** (dɒt, dɔt), *sb.*² [a. mod.F. *dot* (dɔt), ad. L. *dōt-em* dower.] A woman's marriage portion; the property which she brings with her, and of which the interest or annual income alone is under her husband's control. See also DOTE *sb.*², which is the historical Eng. form.

1855 THACKERAY *Newcomes* (1879) I. xxxi. 354 (Stanf.) Mademoiselle has so many francs of *dot*. **1870** H. SMART *Race for Wife* ii, There would, perhaps, be some little difficulty about the *dot*. **1882** MRS. RIDDELL *Pr. Wales's Garden-Party* 37 She had a *dot* of three thousand pounds, which..brought in under a hundred a year.

dot (dɒt), *v.*¹ [f. DOT *sb.*¹]

I. 1. a. *trans.* To mark with a dot or dots; to make a dot or dots on. *dot in*, to fill in with dots.

1740 DYCHE & PARDON, *Dot*, to mark with small points, as engravers do to express *Or* in *Heraldry*. **1776** G. SEMPLE *Building in Water* 87 A third Plate..which you see dotted out. **1811** *Self Instructor* 524 To imagine that the picture was entirely dotted in. **1852** ALFORD in *Life* (1873) 211 The choice geraniums are where I have dotted my plan.

b. To put the dot (·) over the letter i or j. *to dot the i's* (*fig.*): to fill in the particulars, to particularize minutely.

1849 THACKERAY in *Scribner's Mag.* I. 557/1 I have.. dotted the i's. **1865** *Cornh. Mag.* Aug. 254 None of the i's are dotted, the dot being first used towards the end of the fourteenth century. **1885** *Manch. Exam.* 15 June 6/2 Improving the interval..to dot his i's and cross his t's. **1896** *Daily Chron.* 20 Apr. 4/7 [He] dotted our 'i's' and crossed our 't's' with a vengeance about the lack of men in the Navy.

2. To cover or diversify as with minute spots.

1818 J. MARSDEN *Amusem. Mission.* (ed. 2) 42 These em'rald isles, that Ocean's bosom dot. *a* **1859** MACAULAY *Hist. Eng.* V. 53 The whole Channel was dotted with our cruisers. **1868** MORRIS *Earthly Par.* I. 171 Meadows green Dotted about with spreading trees.

fig. **1853** J. CUMMING *Foreshadows* ix. 242 Her nation's history was dotted with judgements from the Lord.

3. To place like dots at separate points on a surface; to scatter like dots or specks.

1816 KEATINGE *Trav.* (1817) II. 25 Domestic fowls [were] dotted here and there through the other groups. **1858** LADY CANNING in Hare *Two Noble Lives* (1893) II. 464 The staff are dotted about by twos in different bungalows. **1868** MORRIS *Earthly Par.* I. 364 All about were dotted leafy trees.

4. To write *down* compendiously; to jot *down*.

1773 [see DOTTING *vbl. sb.* 2]. **1845** FORD *Hand-bk. Spain* I. 58 One word dotted down on the spot is worth a cart-load of recollections. **1860** THACKERAY *Round. Papers, Screens in Din. Rooms* (1876) 60, I had an amiable companion close by me, dotting down my conversation.

5. To hit, strike; esp. in phr. *to dot* (a person) *one*. *slang.*

1895 W. P. RIDGE *Minor Dialogues* 166 I'll dot *you* one.. if you don't keep that mouth of yourn ——. **1896** W. W. JACOBS *Many Cargoes* 239 Put your dooks up... I'm going to dot you! **1912** A. N. LYONS *Clara* xxi. 237 Some of us might dot you one. **1936** WODEHOUSE *Laughing Gas* xx. 222 This brace of thugs arguing and disputing as to which should have the privilege of dotting me. **1951** J. B. PRIESTLEY *Festival at Farbridge* 348 Any monkey tricks an' I'll dot yer one.

6. *intr.* To make a dot or dots. See next.

1755–73 JOHNSON, *Dot*, to make dots or spots.

II. The verb-stem in comb.

1. **dot and carry** (**one**). **a.** A schoolboy's expression in some processes of elementary arithmetic (subtraction, division, and addition). Hence, a name for such process; also for one who does calculations or teaches elementary arithmetic.

1785 GROSE *Dict. Vulg. Tongue, Dot-and-carry-one*, a writing master or teacher of arithmetic. **1822** SCOTT *Nigel* v, You old dotard Dot-and-carry-one that you are. **18..** LOWELL *Didactic Poetry* Poet. Wks. 1890 IV. 226 The metre, too, was regular As schoolboy's dot and carry.

b. *humorously* = 2. Also *fig.* and *transf.*

1841 LEMAN REDE *16 String Jack* I. iv, (Farmer) Of all the rummy chaps I ever did see, that dot-and-carry-one of old poetry is the queerest. **1883** STEVENSON *Treas. Isl.* IV. xvi, I know my pulse went dot and carry one.

2. **dot and go one**. An expression representing the limp of a person lame of one leg, or who has a wooden leg which makes a 'dot' on the ground for each step that the other goes. Used *subst.* for the action, and for the person; and as *adj.* and *adv.*, qualifying either. Also *fig.* and *transf.*

1772 NUGENT tr. *Hist. Friar Gerund* I. 130 The Dot-and-go-one of whom we are speaking. **1773** MAD. D'ARBLAY *Early Diary* 2 Oct., The attentive kind husband, who.. prefers a dot-and-go-one with his wife to the fiery coursers without. **1840** BARHAM *Ingol. Leg., Lay St. Nicholas* lviii, He rose with the sun, limping 'dot and go one'. **1861** T. A. TROLLOPE *La Beata* I. viii. 188 The laborious dot-and-go-one walk occasioned by his lameness. **1881** J. HAWTHORNE *Fort. Fool* I. xx, The conversation..hobbled along in the discontinuous, dot-and-go-one fashion that conversations sometimes affect.

dot, *v.*² *rare.* [ad. mod.F. *doter*, after DOT *sb.*² The historical Eng. form was DOTE *v.*²] *trans.* To dower (a bride) with a marriage portion.

1887 E. GERARD *Land beyond Forest* (1888) II. 94 The empress undertook to dot every young gipsy girl who married a person of another race.

dotage ('dəʊtɪdʒ). [app. f. DOTE *v.*¹ or *sb.*¹ + -AGE. Cf. F. *radotage*.]

1. The state of one who dotes or has the intellect impaired, now esp. through old age; feebleness or imbecility of mind or understanding; infatuation, folly; second childhood; senility. Also *transf.*

13.. *E.E. Allit. P.* B. 1425 Þenne a dotage ful depe drof to his hert. *c* **1386** CHAUCER *Wife's Prol.* 709 Thanne sit he doun, and writ in his dotage, That wommen kan nat kepe hir mariage. *c* **1430** LYDG. *Hors, Shepe & G.* 156, I trowe he be falle in Dotage. **1579** LYLY *Euphues* (Arb.) 158 Yᵉ absurde dotage of him that thinketh ther is no god. **1618** BOLTON *Florus* III. vii. (1636) 194 Hee had the reward of his dotage, for the Cretensians intercepted most part of his navie. **1766** GOLDSM. *Vic. W.* xiv, The world is in its dotage. **1855** MACAULAY *Hist. Eng.* III. 472 Now fast sinking into dotage.

b. A foolish or imbecile thought, word, or deed; a folly or stupidity.

a **1529** SKELTON *Replyc.* 272 Deullysshe pages, Full of suche dottages. **1636** PRYNNE *Unbish. Tim.* (1661) 89 This.. is a notorious dotage and untruth. **1772** FLETCHER *Logica Genev.* 47 Enemies to his antinomian dotages. **1825** COLERIDGE *Aids Refl.* (1848) I. 233 *note*, A specimen of these Rabbinical dotages.

2. The action or habit of doting upon any one; foolish affection; excessive love or fondness.

c **1440** *Partonope* 4768 She ganne no nye fall wyth hym in dotage. **1470–85** MALORY *Arthur* IV. i, Merlyn felle in a dottage on the damoisel. **1513** MORE *Rich. III* (1883) 59 For a litle wanton dotage vppon her parson. **1699** BURNET 39 *Art.* xxii. (1700) 242 A most excessive dotage upon them. **1814** BYRON *Corsair* II. xiv. 66 Oh! that this dotage of his breast would cease!

b. An object doted upon, or regarded with excessive fondness.

1662 COKAINE *Ovid* I. iii. Dram. Wks. (1874) 224 You shall..Become Jove's dotage, and be Queen of heaven. **1821** BYRON *Sardan.* II. i, He loved that gay pavilion,—it was ever His summer dotage. **1845** *Whitehall* ii. 7 Being his father's dotage.

dotal (dəʊtəl), *a.* [ad. L. *dōtāl-is*, f. *dōt-em* dowry, marriage portion, endowment; perh. immed. a. F. *dotal* (16th c.).] Pertaining to a dower, dowry, or marriage portion of a woman.

1513 DOUGLAS *Æneis* XI. vii. 182 Gif..this hald ryall Suld by thy drowry, and rich gift dotall. **1621** G. SANDYS *Ovid's Met.* XIV. (1626) 296 Nor contend..for Latinus crowne, Nor dotall Kingdome. **1722** WOLLASTON *Relig. Nat.* viii. 156 *note*, There were witnesses, and dotal writings. **1875** MAINE *Hist. Inst.* xi. 320 The well-ascertained rules supplied by the written law for dotal settlements.

†'**dotant.** *Obs. rare*⁻¹. [f. DOTE *v.* + -ANT¹. Cf. F. *radotant*, pres. pple.] = DOTARD.

1607 SHAKS. *Cor.* V. ii. 47 Such a decay'd Dotant as you seeme to be.

dotard ('dəʊtəd), *sb.* and *a.* Also 5 doterd, 5–6 dooterd, -arde, (6 dodart), 6–7 dottard, 7–8 doatard. [In sense 1, f. DOTE *v.* + -ARD. See also note to sense 2.]

A. *sb.* 1. a. An imbecile, a silly or stupid person; now, usually, one whose intellect is impaired by age; one who is in his dotage or second childhood.

c **1386** CHAUCER *Wife's Prol.* 331 For certeyn olde dotard by youre leue Ye shul haue queynte right ynogh at eue. *c* **1489** CAXTON *Sonnes of Aymon* ix. 208 Thou were an olde dooterd and a foole. **1509** BARCLAY *Shyp of Folys* (1874) I. 47 Thou blynde dodart, these wordes holde thou styll. *c* **1610** RANDOLPH *Eclog.* in Farr *S.P. Jas. I* (1848) 280 Doatard: you fowle on Pan's omniscience fall. **1725** POPE *Odyss.* xx. 433 The dotard's mind To every sense is lost, to reason blind. **1862** MERIVALE *Rom. Emp.* (1865) VI. xlvii. 13 He declared that the dying man's disposition..was the act of an incapable dotard.

†b. One who dotes (*on* something); a doter.

1602 MARSTON *Ant. & Mel.* II. Wks. 1856 I. 25 That peevish dotard on thy excellence.

†2. (Also *dottard*.) A tree that has lost its top or branches, and of which the trunk alone remains, more or less in a state of decay. Sometimes identified with *pollard*; sometimes apparently distinguished, as having lost its branches by damage or decay, and not by lopping or polling. *Obs.*

[It is doubtful whether this is the same word as sense 1; were it not that the synonymous DODDARD is known only later, it would be natural to take that as the original word, from DOD *v.*, with *dottard*, *dotard*, as variants assimilated to this word.]

a **1603** *N. Riding Rec.* (1894) 260 Warrants for the sale of dotards. **1626** BACON *Sylva* §586 We see almost all Overgrowne-Trees..are Pollards, or Dottards, and not Trees at their full Height. **1662** PETTY *Taxes* 44 The same ill husbandry, as to make fuel of young saplings, instead of dotards and pollards. **1725** BRADLEY *Fam. Dict.* s.v. *Willow*, A Willow Planted and well manag'd, may continue five and twenty Years..Old rotten Dotards may be fell'd and easily supply'd.

3. (See quot.)

1884 G. B. GOODE *Nat. Hist. Aquatic Anim.* 58 The Harbor Seal. *Phoca vitulina*. The young are there [*sc.* in Newfoundland] also called 'Rangers', and when two or three years old..receive the name of 'Dotards'.

B. *adj.* [*attrib.* use of the *sb.*]

1. Imbecile, silly; in senile decay or second childhood.

c **1386** CHAUCER *Wife's Prol.* 291 Olde dotard shrewe. **1557** NORTH *Guenara's Diall Pr.* Prol. A ij b, I never sawe a more dootarde foole than Phormio. **1795** SOUTHEY *Joan of Arc* III. 541 To please Your dotard fancies! **1876** A. D. MURRAY *Charnwood* 143 My old aunt..has been very feeble and dotard all the winter.

†2. Of a tree: Remaining as a decayed trunk without branches: see A. 2. *Obs.*

1585 BURGHLEY *Let.* in *Reg. Mert.* II. 108 The sale of some dottard trees..for their necessary fewell. **1697** LUTTRELL *Brief Rel.* (1857) IV. 202 A grant worth £20,000 of dotard trees in Needwood forest. **1797** BURNS *Eccl. Law* (ed. 6) III. 486 If dotard trees are privileged, much more ought pollards.

Hence '**dotardage**, '**dotardism**, '**dotardy** (*nonce-wds.*), the state of being a dotard; '**dotardly** *a.*, foolish, stupid; **dotard-like** *a.*

1664 H. MORE *Antid. agst. Idol.* 38 That dull and dotardly sin of Idolatry. **1831** *Lincoln Herald* 7 Oct. 4 Dotardism itself could go no further. **1859** S. WILBERFORCE in *Times* 28 Feb. 12/3 Drivelling dotardage.

dotarie, obs. form of DOTERY.

†'**dotate**, *ppl. a. Obs.* Also **-at.** [ad. L. *dōtāt-us* pa. pple. of *dōtāre*: see next.] Endowed, bestowed. Used as *pa. pple.*

1536 BELLENDEN *Cron. Scot.* (1821) I. Cosmogr. p. xxxix, Glasgu..quhare ane nobill kirk is dotat richelie in honour of Sanct Mungow. **1560** in Spottiswood *Hist. Ch. Scot.* III. (1677) 164 All things dotate to hospitality in times past.

do'tate, *v. rare.* [f. L. *dōtāre, dōtāt-* to endow, f. *dōs, dōt-em* dowry.] *trans.* To endow.

1872 *Daily News* 26 Sept., Get our bishop elected, recognised, dotated.

dotation (dəʊ'teɪʃən). [a. F. *dotation*, ad. L. *dōtātiōn-em*, n. of action f. *dōtāre*: see prec.] The action of endowing; endowment.

c **1380** WYCLIF *Agst. Begg. Friers* Sel. Wks. III. 513 Summe of hem receyven dymes and dotaciouns. *c* **1450** *Mirour Saluacioun* 4321 Haly sawles shal be dowed be treble dotacionne. **1562** WINȜET *Cert. Tractates* iii. Wks. 1888 I. 24 Amang sa gret liberalitie, and ryche dotations maid in Scotland. **1605** BACON *Adv. Learn.* II. Ded. §8. 3 This dedicating of Foundations and Dotations to professory Learning..hath..had a Maligne aspect, and influence upon the growth of Scyences. **1767** BLACKSTONE *Comm.* II. xviii. 269 The..most considerable dotations of religious houses. **1853** MERIVALE *Rom. Rep.* ix. (1867) 261 The measure embraced..a general dotation of the poorer citizens.

dotaunce: see DOUBTANCE.

‖**dotchin** ('dɒtʃɪn). Also 8 **dodgeon**, 9 **dodging.** [Corruption of the Cantonese name *toh-ch'ing* (in Court dialect *to-ch'êng*) f. *toh* to measure + *ch'ing* to weigh (N.A. Giles).] The name in the south of China for the small hand-steelyard there used.

1696 *Bowyear's Jrnl. at Cochin-China* in Dalrymple *Orient. Rep.* (1808) I. 88 (Y.) For their Dotchin and Ballance they use that of Japan. **1711** C. LOCKYER *Trade in Ind.* v. 113 Never weigh your Silver by their Dotchins, for they have usually two Pair, one to receive, the other to pay by. **1809** R. LANGFORD *Introd. Trade* 48 Dodgings..very similar to steelyards. **1833** J. HOLLAND *Manuf. Metal* II. 294 The steelyard..resembling in form the little instrument in use amongst the Chinese, called the dotchins.

dote, *sb.*[1] [f. DOTE *v.*[1]: with sense 2 cf. MDu. *dote* folly, weakness of mind.]

†**1.** A foolish or weak-minded person; a dotard. *Obs.*

a **1250** *Prov. Ælfred* 422 in *O.E. Misc.* 128 Ich holde hine for dote [*v.r.* a dote] þat sayþ al his wille. *c* **1320** *Sir Beues* 217 Aȝilt þe, treitour! þow olde dote! *c* **1460** *Towneley Myst.* (Surtees) 27 Hit is wonder that I last sich an old dote Alle dold. **15..** *Smythe & Dame* 325 in Hazl. *E.P.P.* III. 213 Come forthe, olde dote. **1630** *Tinker of Turvey, Seamans T.* 103 How did his death-bed make him a doate!

†**2.** A state of stupor; dotage. *Obs.*

1619 Z. BOYD *Last Battell* (1629) 529 (Jam.) Thus after as in a dote he hath tottered some space about, at last he falleth downe to dust.

†**3.** A piece of folly. Cf. DOTERY. *Obs.*

1643 *Plain English* 18 The votes (to them now ridiculous and call'd dotes) passed against them.

4. Decay in wood. (Cf. DOTE *v.*[1] 4.)

a **1877** KNIGHT *Dict. Mech.* I. 564/1 *Clear-stuff*, boards free from knots, wane, wind-shakes, ring-hearts, dote, sap. **1905** *Terms Forestry & Logging* 35 *Dote*, the general term used by lumbermen to denote decay or rot in timber. **1968** *Gloss. Terms Timber Preservation (B.S.I.)* 9 *Dote*..is commonly applied to timber that is slightly affected by decay and is not acceptable for certain purposes.

dote (dəʊt), *sb.*[2] *arch.* [app. a. 16th c. F. *dote*, var. of *dot*, ad. L. *dōt-em* (*dōs*) dowry, see DOT *sb.*[2]]

1. A woman's marriage portion; endowment, dowry. (Now usually superseded by *dot* from Fr.)

1515 MARY TUDOR *Let. to Hen. VIII*, in *Facism. Nat. MSS.* II. vii, I am contented..to geue you all the hoole dote whiche was delyuered with me. **1538** STARKEY *England* II. i. 151 To the dote of pore damosellys and vyrgynys. **1676** COKE *Circumcision Mustapha* in *Harl. Misc.* (1745) V. 347 Four Millions..of Dollars, which is her Dote. **1753** in Doran *'Mann' & Manners* (1876) I. xv. 353 She..insisted upon the restitution of her Dote. **1858** FROUDE *Hist. Eng.* III. xv. 278 The amount of dotes and dowries..and other legal details, were elaborately discussed.

†**2.** *fig.* (Usually in *pl.*) A natural gift or endowment. *Obs.*

1546 LANGLEY *Pol. Verg. De Invent.* Pref. 4 Through the dotes and qualities of the soule. **1580** SIDNEY *Arcadia* III. (1622) 276 Extolling the goodly dotes of Mopsa. **1656** JEANES *Fuln. Christ* 366 Cloathed with four glorious dotes, or endowments, impassibility, subtilty, agility, and clarity.

dote, doat (dəʊt), *v.*[1] Forms: 3 **dotie(n, doten,** 5 **doyt(e, doote,** 3- **dote,** 6- **doat.** [Early ME. *doten, dotien* (of which no trace is known in OE.), corresponds to MDu. *doten* to be crazy or silly, to dote. Kilian has, in same sense, *doten*, = *dutten*: cf. mod.Du. *dutten* to take a nap, to dote, *dutter* a doter, etc., also MHG. *totzen* to take a nap (:—**dottôjan*), Icel. *dotta* to nod from sleep.

The LG. stem *doten* was the source of OF. *redoter*, mod.F. *radoter* to rave, dote; the close parallelism of sense between F. *radoter, radoté*, and Eng. *dote, doted*, and the presence of Eng. derivatives with F. suffixes, as *dotage, dotant, dotery* = F. *radotage, radotant, radoterie*, show an intimate connexion between the F. and Eng. words, as if the latter were immediately from an AF. **doter* for OF. *redoter*.]

I. *intr.* **1.** To be silly, deranged, or out of one's wits; to act or talk foolishly or stupidly.

a **1225** *Ancr. R.* 224 Heo ualleð..into deop þouht, so þet heo dotie. *a* **1225** *Leg. Kath.* 2111 Hu nu, dame, dotestu? **1387** TREVISA *Higden* (Rolls) IV. 403 Me semeth þat þey doteþ [*mihi desipere videntur*]. *c* **1440** *York Myst.* xxxi. 259 Whedir dote we or dremys? **1548** UDALL, etc. *Erasm. Par. Acts* xxvi. 24 [Felix] sayd with a loude voyce, Thou dotest Paul. **1611** BIBLE *1 Tim.* vi. 4 Doting [TINDALE, *etc.* wasteth his braynes] about questions, and strifes of wordes. **1684** tr. *Bonet's Merc. Compit.* III. 71 Every evening he..doted. **1798** COLERIDGE *Fears in Solit.* v. 171 Others..Dote with a mad idolatry. **1871** R. ELLIS *Catullus* xxxv. 12 She..Doats, as hardly within her own possession.

2. Now *esp.* To be weak-minded from old age; to have the intellect impaired by reason of age. (Formerly only contextual.)

c **1205** LAY. 3294 Me þunched þe alde mon wole dotie nou nan. *c* **1330** R. BRUNNE *Chron. Wace* (Rolls) 2404 My fader in elde dotes. *c* **1440** *Promp. Parv.* 128/1 Doton, or dote for age, *deliro.* **1530** PALSGR. 525/2, I dote for age, as olde folkes do, *je me radote.* **1593** DRAYTON *Eclog.* vi. 29 Thou dot'st in thy declining Age. *c* **1710** C. FIENNES *Diary* (1888) 301 The parson..is now old and doates. **1819** CRABBE *T. of Hall* II. Wks. 1834 VI. 39 We grow unfitted for that world and dote.

3. To be infatuatedly fond *of*; to bestow excessive love or fondness *on* or *upon*; to be foolishly in love. Const. + *of* (obs. rare), *upon, on.*

1477 EARL RIVERS (Caxton) *Dictes* 129 Thyngis that a prynce ought to eschewe..the therde, dotyng of women. **1530** PALSGR. 525/2 It is a gret madnesse to dote upon an other mans wyfe. **1589** WARNER *Alb. Eng.* VI. xxx. (1612) 149 Not one but wexed amorous, yea euen Diana doted. **1591** SHAKS. *Two Gent.* IV. iv. 87 You doate on her, that cares not for your loue. **1623** MASSINGER *Dk. Milan* III. ii, A fine she-waiter..that doted Extremely of a gentleman. **1742** YOUNG *Nt. Th.* I. 277 How distant oft the thing we doat on most, From that for which we doat, Felicity! **1837** HOWITT *Rur. Life* III. iv. (1862) 255 Where lies the mother on whom I doated, and who doated on me.

4. To decay, as a tree. *Obs.* exc. *dial.* Cf. DOTED 2, DOTING *ppl. a.* 3, DOTARD 2.

c **1420** *Pallad. on Husb.* I. 752 The seed of thorn in hit wol dede and dote. **1893** E. COUES *Lewis & Clark's Exped.* 951 *note*, In North Carolina..it is said of trees dead at the top, that they are doted, or have doted.

II. *trans.* †**5.** To cause to dote; to drive crazy; to befool, infatuate. *Obs.*

1471 RIPLEY *Comp. Alch.* v. xxxiii. in Ashm. (1652) 156 Dotyng the Merchaunts that they be fayne To let them go. **1579** TOMSON *Calvin's Serm. Tim.* 652/1 Vse no babbling to dote mens heades vpon. **1580** SIDNEY *Arcadia* (1622) 103 If my miserable speeches haue not alreadie doted you. *a* **1611** BEAUM. & FL. *Maid's Trag.* III. ii, Why wilt thou dote thyself Out of thy life?

†**6.** To say or think foolishly. *Obs.*

1555 EDEN *Decades* 46 Hee openinge his mouthe..doateth that the Zemes spake to hym duryng the tyme of his traunce. **1612** T. TAYLOR *Comm. Titus* iii. 2 Whatsoeuer the Manichees haue doated to the contrarie.

†**7.** To love to excess; to bestow extravagant affection on. *Obs.*

1483 CAXTON *Gold. Leg.* 73 b/2 Whan he was olde he so doobted and loued hem. **1673** *Rules of Civility* 108 Endure a little hunger, and not dote and indulge their appetites as they do.

dote, *v.*[2] *Sc.* Now *rare.* Also 6 **dot, doit.** [a. F. *doter* (13th c.), ad. L. *dōtāre* to endow, portion, f. *dōt-em*. See also DOT *v.*[2], in mod. use.]

†**1.** *trans.* To endow *with* riches, dignities, etc.

1535 STEWART *Cron. Scot.* II. 188 And dot thame [Kirkmen] with far moir dignitie, Na euir tha had. **1549** *Compl. Scot.* xvi. 141 Pepil that ar dotit vitht rason. **1620** W. SCOT *Apol. Narr.* (1846) 39 He was not so liberally doted with vnderstanding. **1623** COCKERAM, *Doted*, endowed.

2. To grant or give as an endowment.

1535 STEWART *Cron. Scot.* II. 616 How King Malcolome foundit ane Kirk..and doittit to it mony Landis. **1636** *Scot. Canons* in *Laud's Wks.* (1853) V. 602 Lands..doted to pious and holy uses. *c* **1771** in *Spectator* 4 June (1892) 781/2 A new cup..was presented, or 'doted' to the parish. **1864** TWEEDIE *Lakes, etc. of Bible* 209 Abila was doted and confirmed to several members of the Herod family.

dote, obs. form of DOT.

doted, doated ('dəʊtɪd), *ppl. a.* Also 8 **dotted,** 9 **dooted.** [f. DOTE *v.*[1] + -ED[1]: cf. *learned.*]

†**1.** Stupid, foolish, in second childhood, dotard.

13.. *E.E. Allit. P.* C. 196 What þe deuel hatz þou don, doted wrech? *c* **1400** *Rom. Rose* 4007 She was past al that passage And was a doted thing bicomen. *a* **1533** LD. BERNERS *Huon* lxxxi. 242, I haue..meruayle that I se you so dotyd. **1621** BURTON *Anat. Mel.* II. iv. II. ii, All such as were crased, or any way doted. **1728** P. WALKER *Life Peden* (ed. 3) Pref. 25 In his dotted old Age.

†**b.** Infatuated, infatuatedly fond. *Obs.*

1550 CRANMER *Defence* 115 b, The people beyng superstitiously enamored and doted vpon the Masse. **1583** GOLDING *Calvin on Deut.* xlviii. 286 They continue doted in it.

2. Of a tree: Decayed inside, unsound. Now *dial.* and *technical.* (Cf. DOTARD 2.)

1466 in Willis & Clark *Cambridge* (1886) III. 93 White oke, not doted, nor storvyn. **1559** MORWYNG *Evonym.* 3 Woode whether it be rotten and doated, or sound. **1787** BEST *Angling* (ed. 2) 19 Found..in the hollow of these trees when doated and rotten. **1867** SMYTH *Sailor's Word-bk.*, *Dooted*, [said of] timber rendered unsound by fissures. **1883** C. F. SMITH in *Trans. Amer. Philol. Soc.* 47 *Doted*, 'decayed inside,' of a tree..quite common in..Southern States. **1893** *Westm. Gaz.* 5 June 6/3 Doated..full of large knots, ugly shakes..this class of wood is sold in large quantities at the public auctions in the City.

†'**dotehead.** *Obs. rare.* [f. DOTE *sb.*[1] + HEAD. Cf. *dolthead.*] = DOTARD A. 1.

1530 TINDALE *Pract. Prel.* Wks. (Parker Soc.) II. 265 The dotehead was beside himself and whole out his mind.

dotel(le: see DOTTLE *sb.*[1] and [2].

dotepol, var. of DODDYPOLL, *Obs.*

doter, doater ('dəʊtə(r)). [f. DOTE *v.*[1] + -ER[1]: influenced by *dotard.*] One who dotes.

1. A person of enfeebled intellect; a dotard.

1579-80 NORTH *Plutarch* (1676) 910 He had never seen a greater doter then Phormio. **1615** J. STEPHENS *Satyr. Ess.* 138 These bee the comforts of being famous: let Doaters bee ambitious of it. *c* **1720** EARL OF AILESBURY *Mem.* (1890) 607 A poor old doater. **1831** LAMB *Let.* Wks. (1865) xviii. 171 Munden dropped the old man, the doater.

2. One who dotes *on*; one foolishly fond.

1552 HULOET, Doter or folower of women, *mulierarius.* **1653** H. MORE *Antid. Ath.* I. ix. (1712) 27 Aristotle, who was no doter on a Deity. **1742** YOUNG *Nt. Th.* VIII. 570 Patron of pleasure! doater on delight! **1852** J. H. NEWMAN *Scope Univ. Educ.* 25 No doter upon the dead and gone.

Hence †'**doteress**, a female doter.

1668 EVELYN tr. *Freart's Perfect. Paint.* Pref. (R. Supp.) An old Dotaresse, who had only slaves in her service.

†'**dotery, doterie.** *Obs.* [f. DOTE *v.*: cf. F. *radoterie.*] Doting; stupidity, infatuation, folly.

1587 GOLDING *De Mornay* x. 143 God (say they) draweth the forme out of the Abilitie of the matter. Let us examine this doterie yet further. **1593** DRAYTON *Shepherds Garl.* (N.), These..spenden day and night in dotarie.

dotey ('dəʊtɪ). *Anglo-Ir.* Also **doaty, doty.** [Related to DOTE *v.*[1]] A term of endearment, esp. for a child. Also *attrib.* or as *adj.*

1892 E. LAWLESS *Grania* II. III. iii. 30 Arrah, hush, my dotey! Be easy, now, there's a good child. **1898** in *Eng. Dial. Dict.* s.v., Come here, doaty, and give me a kiss. **1919** G. B. SHAW *Heartbreak House* I. 4 *Nurse Guinness.* Never mind him, doty. *Ibid.* 9 Remember that I am Lady Utterword, and not Miss Addy, nor lovey, nor darling, nor doty. **1922** JOYCE *Ulysses* 257, I looked so simple in the cradle they christened me simple Simon.—You must have been a doaty, Miss Douce made answer. **1930** S. BECKETT *Whoroscope* 2 My squinty doaty! **1936** 'N. BLAKE' *Thou Shell of Death* xiii. 230 Ah, a dotey little love she was. **1967** S. BECKETT *No's Knife* 82 She'll say to me, Come, doty, it's time for bye-bye.

doth, (dʌθ), arch. 3rd pers. pres. ind. of DO.

dother, dial. form of DODDER.

‖**dothienenteritis** (ˌdɒθɪɛnɛntə'raɪtɪs). *Path.* Also (erron.) **dothin-.** [mod. f. Gr. δοθιήν boil, abscess + ENTERITIS.] Inflammation of certain intestinal glands, characteristic of typhoid fever.

1845 G. E. DAY tr. *Simon's Anim. Chem.* I. 289 The disease diagnosed in both instances..was dothinenteritis.

doti, var. of DHOTI, loin-cloth.

'**doting, doating**, *vbl. sb.* [f. DOTE *v.*[1] + -ING[1].] The action of the verb DOTE.

1. Action characteristic of a weak or enfeebled intellect; imbecility, stupidity; an instance of this.

c **1440** *Promp. Parv.* 128/1 Dotynge, *desipiencia.* **1548** UDALL, etc. *Erasm. Par. Acts* 85 b, Dotyng is..whan a man, through erroure of his mynde, swerueth from reason. **1586** J. HOOKER *Girald. Irel.* in *Holinshed* II. 51/2 An altercation and warre betweene the king of England and Lewes of France, through the doting of both parts. **1690** DRYDEN *Don Sebast.* Pref., I am not yet arrived to the age of doting. **1833** R. H. FROUDE *Rem.* (1838) 317 Can these [verses] be doctored into any thing available, or are they dotings?

2. The bestowal of foolish affection (*upon*); fond attachment.

1622 DONNE *Serm.* xvi. 161 Such is our passionate Doting upon this World. **1665** GLANVILL *Scepsis Sci.* 53 Dogmatizing, and fond doating upon Authorities.

Hence **doting-piece**, one who is doted on.

1741 RICHARDSON *Pamela* (1824) I. xxxii. 329 My sister B—— is my doating-piece. **1830** GODWIN *Cloudesley* I. vi. 109 He was his father's doating-piece.

'**doting, doating**, *ppl. a.* [f. as prec. + -ING[2].] That dotes.

1. Weak-minded, foolish, stupid, imbecile.

1489 CAXTON *Faytes of A.* IV. x. 257 Folysh moeuynges and dotyng opynyons. **1535** COVERDALE *Eccl.* vii. 25 The erroure of dotinge fooles. **1645** MILTON *Colast.* (1851) 366 Ignorant and doting surmises. **1797** BURKE *Regic. Peace* iii. Wks. VIII. 297 The last resource of female weakness, of helpless infancy, of doting decrepitude. **1870** MAX MÜLLER *Sc. Relig.* (1873) 273 With silly children, and doting grandmothers.

2. Foolishly or extravagantly fond.

1577 *St. Aug. Manual* (Longm.) 1 Loving and yet not dotyng. **1663** KILLIGREW *Parson's Wed.* in Dodsley *O. Pl.* (1780) XI. 497 They are still the most doting'st husbands. **1752** YOUNG *Brothers* I. i. Wks. 1757 II. 210 No picture, by the doating eye To be survey'd. **1856** MRS. BROWNING *Aur. Leigh* II. 221 You give us doating mothers.

3. Of trees: Decaying from age.

1664 EVELYN *Kal. Hort.* 32 The old wood, found commonly in doating Birches. **1726** *Dict. Rust.* (ed. 3), *Doting-Tree*..a Tree almost worn out with age. **1858** O. W. HOLMES *Aut. Breakf.-t.* xi. 109 An old doting oak.

Hence **'dotingly** *adv.*, in a doting manner or degree: infatuatedly; fondly.
1548 CRANMER *Catech.* 123 b, Thei dotyngly loued all that was their awne. **1608** T. MORTON *Pream. Encounter* 128 So dotingly vaine in ostentation of his owne wit. **1684** tr. *Agrippa's Van. Arts* lvii. 165 None more superstitious and dotingly stupid. **1839–40** W. IRVING *Wolfert's R.* (1855) 85 The duke.. became dotingly fond of his wife.

'dotish, doatish, *a. arch.* [f. DOTE *sb.*^{1} + -ISH.] Silly, imbecile, stupid, childish.
1509 BARCLAY *Shyp of Folys* (1874) I. 86 Than comys in an other with his dotysshe brayne. **1581** G. PETTIE tr. *Guazzo's Civ. Conv.* III. (1586) 145 In this dotish simplicitie, he shewed himselfe as verie a clowne. **1607** TOPSELL *Four-f. Beasts* (1658) 495 A mad dotish fellow. **1831** CARLYLE *Misc., Characteristics* (1872) IV. 30 The tongue as in doatish forgetfulness maunders low.
Hence **'dotishness,** silliness, childishness.
1598 FLORIO, *Bambolità*, childishnes, dotishnes. **1691–8** NORRIS *Pract. Disc.* 272 A great piece of dotishness and stupidity.

dotkin, variant of DODKIN, coin.

dotlet, a little or tiny dot: see -LET.

dotouse, dotrel, -elle, obs. ff. DOUBTOUS, DOTTEREL.

dotrinal, -ine, obs. ff. DOCTRINAL, DOCTRINE.

'dottable, *a.* Capable of being dotted.
1844 TUPPER *Twins* xxiv. 175 Charles' letter.. was.. less warm, less dottable with stars.

dottard, obs. or. dial. f. DOTARD, sense 2.

dotted ('dɒtɪd), *ppl. a.* [f. DOT *v.*^{1} + -ED^1.]
1. a. Formed of or traced by dots.
1869 PHILLIPS *Vesuv.* vii. 177 One such cone is represented by a dotted outline.
b. Of engraving: executed by dots instead of lines; stippled. Cf. F. (*manière*) *pointillée.*
1802 *Monthly Mag.* XIV. 59/2 Both the prints are well engraven in the dotted manner. **1821** [see Dict. 2]. **1897** R. E. GRAVES in *Dict. Nat. Biogr.* L. 58/2 He [*sc.* Ryland] adopted the 'chalk' or dotted manner of engraving. **1908** A. M. HIND *Hist. Engraving* 290 We have already noted dotted work in plates of Giulio Campagnola. **1938** *Burlington Mag.* Mar. 150/1 The importance of Cologne for the production of dotted prints.
c. *dotted line*, a line of dots or small dashes; *spec.* (on a document): one to indicate the space left for signature (and therefore acceptance, etc., of its terms). Hence *to sign on the dotted line*, to agree fully or formally.
1772–84 COOK *Voy.* II. II. vii. (R.), Some few places, which are here, and in other parts of the chart, distinguished by a dotted line. **1891** J. A. EWING *Magn. Induction in Iron* iv. 82 A cyclic process of magnetisation was gone through, the results of which are shown by the dotted lines. **1919** A. C. LESCARBOURA *Behind Motion-Picture Screen* 416 So it generally proved that the really big man who was in a position to sign the order 'on the dotted line', could not and would not spare the time for such a trip. **1921** WODEHOUSE *Indiscretions of Archie* xvi. 184, I spoke to him as one old friend to another.. and he sang a few bars from 'Rigoletto', and signed on the dotted line. **1937** *Daily Herald* 5 Feb. 19/7 When the [football] talk was of transfer and things, and when Childs.. had just signed on the dotted line for Luton. **1950** D. GASCOYNE *Vagrant* 7 Just fill in (in block letters) on the dotted line your name And number. **1958** *Times* 13 Oct. 11/6 Far from being content to 'sign on the dotted line' he [*sc.* King George VI] insists on knowing why. **1968** M. S. LIVINGSTON *Particle Physics* x. 182 These are illustrated in Weisskopf's presentation by solid or dotted lines. **1971** *Sunday Express* (Johannesburg) (Homefinder) 28 Mar. 3/3 It is enough to warrant the expense of going to have a long, lingering look before you sign on the dotted line.
2. a. Marked or covered with or as with dots.
1821 CRAIG *Lect. Drawing* vii. 404 The back-ground.. is dotted or stippled. **1828** STARK *Elem. Nat. Hist.* II. 310 Elytra a little longer than the abdomen, dotted. **1872** P'CESS ALICE *Mem.* 12 Nov. (1884) 287 The wide plateau looked dreary and sad—dotted all over with graves.
b. *spec.* Of moths.
1843 HUMPHREYS & WESTWOOD *Brit. Moths* I. 125 *(caption)* Graphiphora Baja (the dotted clay). **1845** *Ibid.* II. 17 *(caption) Cleora teneraria* (the dotted carpet). *Ibid.* 72 *(caption) Ptychopoda lividata* (the single dotted wave). **1907** R. SOUTH *Moths Brit. Isles* I. II. 187 The dotted footman (*Pelosia muscerda*). *Ibid.* 214 The dotted rustic (*Agrotis* (*Pachobia*) *simulans*). **1958** W. J. STOKOE *Caterp. Brit. Moths* (ed. 2) I. 305 The small dotted buff.. *Petilampsia minima. Ibid.* 339 The dotted chestnut.. *Dasycampa rubiginea. Ibid.* 389 The dotted fan-foot.. *Zanclognatha cribrumalis. Ibid.* II. 188 The dotted border.. *Erannis marginaria.*
3. Furnished with a dot.
1837 *Penny Cycl.* IX. 104/1 s.v. *Dot*, Thus a double dotted minim is equal to three crotchets and a quaver. **1869** OUSELEY *Counterp.* v. 27 Three minims are placed in every bar, against one dotted semibreve in the canto fermo.

dottel: see DOTTLE *sb.*^{2}

dotter ('dɒtə(r)), *sb.* [f. DOT *v.* + -ER^1.] **1.** One who or that which dots; an instrument for making dots; *spec.* a hand-instrument used in embossing letters for the blind.
1832 *Examiner* 583/1 A musician may be created on any emergency with a dotter and ruled paper. **1873** E. SPON *Workshop Receipts* Ser. I. 84/1 Put on the eyes [in bird's-eye maple] by dabbing with the dotter. **1883** N. SHEPPARD *Geo. Eliot's Ess.* Introd. 13 A dotter of I's and crosser of T's.
2. A device in which a pencil dots an oscillating target fixed to a gun when fired without ammunition, used in training gunners to take aim.
1903 *Daily Chron.* 25 June 4/5 Neither Captain Percy Scott nor his dotter were on view. **1906** *Ibid.* 5 June 2/3 Admiral Percy Scott's dotter and aiming apparatus.

'dotter, *v. Obs.* or *dial.* [Related to DODDER and TOTTER.] *intr.* To move unsteadily and infirmly; to totter; to fall in a tottering way.
c **1420** *Avow. Arth.* xvi, He began to dotur and dote Os he hade keghet scathe. *a* **1440** *Sir Degrev.* 1109 The duk dotered to the ground, On erthe swyfftly he swouned. ? **1524** in Ramsay *Evergreen* I. 213 With Grief.. I dottard owre on Sleip. **1789** DAVIDSON *Seasons* 112 (Jam.) Willy dottart by himsel Among the hens.

'dottered, *a.* App. an obsolete and dialect form of DOTARD *a.*: Decayed, tottering, or worn out with age.
1581 J. BELL *Haddon's Answ. Osor.* 358 b, Dottered Bussardly fables of Purgatory. **1884** *Gd. Words* May 324/2 To frighten crows.. is.. child's play or work for old dottered men.

dotterel ('dɒtərəl), **dottrel** ('dɒtrəl). Forms: 5–6 dotrell(e, dottrelle, 6 dotterelle, 6–7 dot(e)rel, dot(t)erell, dottrell, 7 dottril(l, 7–9 dotteril(l, 8 dotrill, 6– dotterel, dottrel. [f. DOTE *v.*^{1}, the suffix appears to be the same as in *cockerel, mongrel, pickerel*, see -REL. It is not clear whether sense 1 or sense 2 is the original: sense 1 appears to be the more frequent, and in some cases at least sense 2 is evidently treated as transf. from it.]
1. A species of plover (*Eudromias morinellus*): so called from the apparent simplicity with which it allows itself to be approached and taken.
(Collective pl. *dotterel*: cf. *snipe*, etc.)
c **1440** *Promp. Parv.* 128/1 Dotrelle, byrde, *fingus.* **1526** *Pilgr. Perf.* (W. de W. 1531) 65 b, This dotrell is a lytell fonde byrde, for it helpeth in maner to take it selfe. **1611** DRAYTON *Panegyr. Verses* in *Coryat's Crudities*, As men take Dottrels, so hast thou ta'n us. **1659** D. PELL *Impr. Sea* 243 The Dotteril, of whom they say, that whatsoever is done in the sight of her, shee will exactly imitate. **1766** PENNANT *Zool.* (1768) II. 515 The Dottrel appears in spring and in autumn. **1849** C. STURT *Exped. Centr. Australia* I. 311 We passed several flights of dotterel making to the south. **1865** KINGSLEY *Herew.* II. xi. 186 Laughing at the dottrel as they anticked on the mole hills.
2. A silly person, one whose intellect is decayed, a dotard. Sometimes with *fig.* reference to 1. (Now only *dial.*)
c **1440** *Promp. Parv.* 128/1 Dotrelle.. *idem quod* Dotarde. **1483** *Cath. Angl.* 104/2 A Dottrelle, *desipa.* **1547–64** BAULDWIN *Mor. Philos.* (Palfr.) I. x, Thy words sauour of old idle dottrels tayles. **1583** GOLDING *Calvin on Deut.* lxxx. 489 Being a misbegotten generation, they take monkes and old dotterelles for their fathers. **1681** OTWAY *Soldier's Fort.* I. i. Wks. 1728 I. 344 A paralytick coughing decrepid Dotrel. **1828** *Craven Dialect, Dotterill*, an old doating fellow.
b. *attrib.* or as *adj.* Foolish, stupid, doting.
1581 J. BELL *Haddon's Answ. Osor.* 360 b, This dottrell Ierarchy of Rome. **1607** WALKINGTON *Opt. Glass* 83 Lest the toung of it [a buckle] catch their owne dottril skins.
3. A doddered tree: so *dotterel tree.* Now *dial.*
a **1568** ASCHAM *Scholem.* II. (Arb.) 137 Som old dotterell trees. *a* **1618** SYLVESTER *Elegy Sir W. Sidney* 108 Doe not we take the timber for our turn, And leave the dotrells, in their time to burn? **1821** CLARE *Vill. Minstr.* I. 52 When he.. Has mixt with them [Shepherds] beneath a dotterel-tree. **1868** J. W. BURGON *Provinc. Bedfordsh.* in *Bedf. Times* (Mar.), *Dottrel* or *Dottle-tree*, a tree without a head, a pollard. Called a *dodder tree* in the north of the county.
Hence **'dotterelism.**
1611 COTGR., *Niaiserie*, simplicitie, sillinesse, childishnesse.. dotterelisme.

dotting ('dɒtɪŋ), *vbl. sb.* [f. DOT *v.*^{1} + -ING^1.]
1. The making of dots, or covering of a surface with dots; also, *concr.* markings so produced.
1834 MRS. SOMERVILLE *Connex. Phys. Sc.* xxxvii. (1849) 444 An exceedingly delicate and uniform dotting or stippling of the sky by points of light. **1870** RUSKIN *Lect. Art* vi. (1875) 163 The attempts to imitate the shading of a fine draughtsman by dotting. **1874** KNIGHT *Dict. Mech.* I. 722/1 *Dotting*, a form of engraving in which geographical divisions on maps are shown by interrupted lines or series of dots.
2. A jotting down (with pen or pencil).
1773 MAD. D'ARBLAY *Early Diary* Sept., I must give you this last week all in a lump, for I have no time for daily dottings.
3. *Comb.*
1874 KNIGHT *Dict. Mech.* I. 722/1 *Dotting-pen*, a pen having a roulette which makes dots or detached marks on the paper over which it is drawn.

dottle ('dɒt(ə)l), *sb.*^{1} and *a.* Now *Sc.* In 4–6 dotel. [f. DOTE *v.*^{1} or *sb.*^{1}: see -LE.]
A. *sb.* A fool or dotard; a silly person.
13.. *E.E. Allit. P.* B. 1517 þenne þe dotel on dece drank. **1562** *Burn. Paules Ch.* in *Pilkington's Wks.* (Parker Soc.) 586 A drunken dotel. **1894** J. MENZIES *Our Town* viii. 85 'Your veesits to the auld dottle.'
B. *adj.* In a state of dotage; silly, crazy. *Sc.*
1808–18 in JAMIESON. **1820** *St. Kathleen* III. 162 (Jam.) Ye dottle man. **1895** IAN MACLAREN *Auld Lang Syne* IV. i. 147 Till he be cripple an' dottle (crazy).

Hence **dottled** *ppl. a.*, (*Sc.*) in the state of dotage.
1825 in JAMIESON.

dottle, dottel ('dɒt(ə)l), *sb.*^{2} [app. dim. of DOT *sb.*^{1}: cf. DIT *v.*]
†**1.** A plug; = DOSSIL 1. *Obs.*
c **1440** *Promp. Parv.* 127/2 Dotelle, stoppynge of a vesselle (dottel, H. dossell, P.), *ducillus, ductildus.* **1743** MAXWELL *Sel. Trans. Soc. Impr. Knowl. Agric. Scot.* 284 (Jam.) Have a tub, with a small hole in the bottom of it, wherein put a cork or dottle in the under end.
2. The plug of tobacco ash remaining in the bottom of a pipe after smoking. (orig. *Sc.*)
1825 in JAMIESON. **1850** KINGSLEY *Alt. Locke* vi. (D.), A snuffer-tray containing scraps of half-smoked tobacco, 'pipe dottles', as he called them. **1890** R. KIPLING *Soldiers Three, Black Jack* (ed. 6) 84 Ortheris shot out the red-hot dottel of his pipe on the back of his hairy fist. **1894** DOYLE *S. Holmes* 214 His before-breakfast pipe, which was composed of all the plugs and dottels left from his smokes of the day before.

dottrel: see DOTTEREL.

†**'dottry.** *Obs.* [var. of DOTERY.] Doting; impairment of the intellect. So **'dottrified** *a.*, rendered doting.
1576 NEWTON *Lemnie's Complex.* (1633) 298 Losse of right wits, feeblenesse of braine, dottry, phrensie. **185.** OUTRAM *Legal & other Lyrics* (1887) 82 Dottrified senility.

dotty ('dɒtɪ), *a.* [f. DOT *sb.*^{1} + -Y^1.]
1. Consisting of or characterized by dots; dot-like.
1812 *Examiner* 30 Nov. 763/2 That dotty softness, which confers so.. natural a character on the flesh. **1879** STEVENSON *Trav. Cevennes* 80 A low dotty underwood that grew thickly in the gorges.
2. Of unsteady, uneven or feeble gait, as from stiffness or lameness. Hence *fig.*, feeble in mind, silly. *colloq.* or *dial.*
14.. in J. Glyde *New Suffolk Garland* (1866) 213 Ale mak many a mane to have a doty poll. **1870** *Sportsman* 9 Apr. (Farmer), He begins to go a little stiff in his limbs and dotty on his feet. **1884** *Daily Tel.* 9 Apr. 2/6 (ibid.) He [a race-horse] pulled up in a dotty condition. **1885** *Standard* 13 Mar. 6/6, I am not mad, drunk, or dotty. **1888** E. LAWS *Hist. Little England* 420/1 Dotty, silly from age; senile. **1896** *Evesham Jrnl.* 28 Nov. (E.D.D.), The Council hardly knows if he has not gone 'dotty'. **1936** BENTLEY & ALLEN *Trent's Own Case* vii. 73 The Englishman looked sick and a bit dotty. **1948** R. LEHMANN *Note in Music* (ed. 2) IV. 130 Quite wrapped up in herself—with something pretty rum staring out of her eyes. A bit dotty, perhaps. **1971** *Sunday Times* 16 May 32/8 Taya Zinkin, with a kind of dotty inevitability, ends as an authority on India.
Hence **'dottily** *adv.*, in a 'dotty', mad, or eccentric manner; absurdly, crazily; **'dottiness,** (*a*) unsteadiness of gait; (*b*) (*colloq.*) eccentricity, feeble-mindedness, craziness.
1888 *Matlock Visiting List* 29 Aug. 3/3 An amount of dottiness like the lurching of a landsman on a rolling steamer. **1934** WEBSTER, Dottily. **1934** WODEHOUSE *Thank You, Jeeves* xii. 162 Dotty, beyond a question. And who knew but what that dottiness might not run in the family? **1959** P. BULL *I know the Face* viii. 135, I was in the witness-box or court throughout and was drugged to the point of dottiness. **1969** Dottily [see HONEYISH *a.*]. **1978** *Economist* 4 Feb. 14/1 The cardinal hesitates... He is looking over his shoulder at his conservative fellow bishops in the Catholic hierarchy, for whom dottily enough he is not the spokesman. **1984** *Financial Times* 5 June 19/5 The fable of the Little Mermaid provides a symbolic *leitmotiv* that recurs from the opening scene when Mette's dottily genteel mother.. recalls the mortal prince loved by a sea-creature.

dotty-pol: see DODDYPOLL.

'doty, *a. dial.* Also **doaty.** [related to DOTE *v.*^{1} 4, DOTARD 2.] (See quots.) Hence **'dotiness.**
1883 *Philad. Telegraph* XL. No. 44. 8 A log may be doty in places, and even hollow, and yet have.. good timber in it. **1885** *Spons' Mech. Own Bk.* 167 'Doatiness': a speckled stain found in beech, American oak, and others. **1889** HURST *Horsham* Sussex Gloss., *Doty*, decayed with age and crumbling, said of wood. **1948** R. DE KERCHOVE *Internat. Maritime Dict.* 209/2 *Doaty*, said of the condition of timber when stained with yellow and black spots.

doty, var. DOTEY.

dou, obs. Sc. form of DOVE, DOW.

douager, -ier, obs. forms of DOWAGER.

Douai ('du:eɪ, 'daʊeɪ). Also **Douay.** The name of a town in northern France used *ellipt.* or *attrib.* to designate the English translation of the Bible completed at Douai in the early 17th century and used in the Roman Catholic Church.
1837 *Dublin Rev.* Apr. 476 To call it any longer the Douay or Rhemish version is an abuse of terms. **1847** WEBSTER, *Douay-bible*, an English translation of the Scriptures, sanctioned by the Roman Catholic Church. **1864** J. H. NEWMAN *Apol.* I. 16 Words have been running in my head, which I find in the Douay version thus. **1867** G. M. HOPKINS *Let.* 15 Aug. (1956) 41, I must check them by the Douay. **1957** *Oxf. Dict. Chr. Ch.* 419/1 *Douai-Reims Bible*, the traditional version of the Bible among English-speaking RCs... The work was begun at Douai, but owing to the migration of the college to Reims in 1578, the NT was completed in that city and published there in 1582. The OT, which did not appear till 1609, was published at Douai. **1971** 'S. WOODS' *Serpent's Tooth* 42 She repeated the oath in a nervous voice, clutching the Douay Bible that had been provided for her.

doual, douan: see DUAL, DIVAN.

‖**douane** (dwan, duː'ɑːn). [Fr.; = It. *doana*, *dogana*, lingua Franca *douana*, from Arabic: see DIVAN.] A custom-house (in France or the Mediterranean countries).

1656 BLOUNT *Glossogr.*, *Dovane*..the name of the Custom-house of Lyons; hence also any Custom or Import. **1671** CHARENTE *Let. Customs* 25 Lions..so tame, that they went up and down our Doüane, or the Christians Warehouse amongst our Antilopes. **1828** [J. R. BEST] *Italy* 74 The douane of Buffalora I found sufficiently..vexatious.

Hence ‖**douanier** (dwanje). [Fr.] A custom-house officer (in France or, by extension, elsewhere).

1739 GRAY *Let.* Poems (1775) 65 The entrance is guarded by certain vigilant dragons, called Douäniers. **1815** *Sporting Mag.* XLV. 293 You have even made the douaniers of Dover relent.

‖**douar, dowar** ('duːa(r)). Also **douwar, douah, dooar, duar.** [a. Arab. *dūār*, in F. *douar*.] A small encampment of Arab tents grouped in a circle round a central enclosure for the cattle.

1829 SOUTHEY *Sir T. More* II. 176 Those who dwell in *dou-wars* or *kraals*. **1834** *Fraser's Mag.* X. 64 Near Tuarick town and Arab douar spread. **1856** AIRD *Poet. Wks.* 168 Straight through a dowar's ground The Chieftain rode. **1899** *Daily News* 6 Nov. 7/2 At the duar of Charifin a man stole a donkey. **1908** *Westm. Gaz.* 16 Apr. 5/2 The duar or village of the Kaid of the Ouled Buziri.

douare, obs. form of DOWER *sb.*[2]

doub, var. DOOB, a kind of Indian grass.

doub(be, doubelet, obs. ff. DUB, DOUBLET.

double ('dʌb(ə)l), *a.* (*adv.*) Forms: 3–7 duble, doble, 3– double (4–7 dowble, 6–7 dubbel; with 30 variants in -bb-, -el, -il(l, -ul(l, -yl(le, etc.) [ME. a. OF. *duble*, *doble*, later *double* = Pr. Sp. *doble*, It. *doppio*:—L. *duplu-s* twice as much, double, f. *du-o* two + *-plus* from root *ple-* to fill.]

A. *adj.*

1. a. Consisting of two members, things, or sets combined; twofold; forming a pair, paired, coupled; made of two layers of material, as a garment, etc. Often, with a sing. sb., equivalent to 'two' or 'a couple of' with plural sb.

a **1300** *Cursor M.* 1528 (Cott.) Lameth..bigam was wit dubul vijfe. **1393** GOWER *Conf.* III. 125 Janus with double face. *c* **1400** MAUNDEV. (Roxb.) xiv. 60 It es wele walled aboute with a dowble wall. **1513** MORE in Grafton *Chron.* (1568) II. 830 To have a double string for his Bowe. **1590** SHAKS. *Mids. N.* III. ii. 209 Like to a double cherry..Two louely berries molded on one stem. **1611** CORYATE *Crudities* 352 The Italian when he vttereth any Latin word wherein this letter *i* is to be pronounced long, doth alwaies pronounce it as a double *e*, *viz.* as *ee*. **1666** [see YOLK *sb.*[1] 1]. **1697** DRYDEN *Virg. Georg.* III. 50 A double Wreath shall crown our Cæsar's Brows; Two differing Trophies, from two different Foes. **1711** STEELE *Spect.* No. 140 ¶5 Is Dimpple spelt with a single or double P? **1803** WORDSW. *Yarrow Unvisited* vi, Let..The swan on still St. Mary's Lake Float double, swan and shadow! **1834** MEDWIN *Angler in Wales* I. 85 Boots..of double leather. **1836** DICKENS *Sk. Boz* 1st Ser. (ed. 3) 81 The chief pastime of the children..had been..to knock loud double knocks at the door. **1838** — *Nich. Nick.* iii, Nickleby gave a double knock. **1840** [see DOOR 1 b]. **1843** *Ainsworth's Mag.* III. 153 She..assailed his nerves by means of the thundering double-knocks of postmen. **1866** [see KNOCK *sb.*[1] 1]. **1871** ROBY *Lat. Gram.* I. v. 22 After Cicero and Cæsar's time the double i had a different meaning. **1871** [see DOOR 1 b]. **1873** *Young Englishwoman* Sept. 438/2 Round eggs..[may] contain a double yolk. **1906** GALSWORTHY *Man of Property* II. xii. 256 The only thing against her was that she had not a double name. **1951** *Catal. of Exhibits, South Bank Exhib., Festival of Britain* 135/1 Double sink, stainless steel. **1953** E. SIMON *Past Masters* I. iii. 33 There was a big stove, two double sinks. **1961** *Guardian* 1 Feb. 6/4 A splendid double sink with a double drainer. **1968** J. FRASER *Evergreen Death* xix. 162 A man parks his car on a double yellow line and we can have him.

b. Folded, doubled; bent, 'doubled up', stooping much forward.

c **1450** *Bk. Curtasye* 659 in *Babees Bk.* 321 Þo ouer nape schalle dowbulle be layde. **1494** *Act 11 Hen. VII*, c. 23 Neither..should be laid double in packing. **1719** DE FOE *Crusoe* II. xii, I struck my double fist against the side. *c* **1881** *Ord. St. John, Ambulance Dept.*, *On triangular bandage*, Place a piece of lint double over the wound. *Mod.* He was bent double with pain.

c. Having some essential part double, as a two-edged axe, a carriage with two seats, an eagle figured with two heads (see DOUBLE EAGLE), etc. Also applied to a horse that carries two persons (see HORSE).

1469 *Househ. Ord.* 99 Of double horses xxxviii Of hackneyss xij. **1590** NASHE *Pasquil's Apol.* I. C ij, Mounted vppon their dubble Geldings, with theyr Wiues behinde them. *a* **1700** DRYDEN *Ovid's Met.* IX. (R.), The lance and double ax of the fair warrior queen. **1791** in Mad. D'Arblay *Diary* Aug., My daughter and I rode a double horse. **1836–9** DICKENS *Sk. Boz* (1850) 218/2 The double-fly was ordered to be at the door..at nine o'clock. **1850** *Vesper Bk.* (Burns & Oates) Pref. 12 The Office..is said to be Double when the Antiphon is sung entire both before and after each Psalm. **1894** *Jrnl. Hellenic Stud.* XIV. 123 Fifty or more 'small heads of oxen, with a double axe between their horns, cut out of gold plate'. **1957** V. G. CHILDE *Dawn Europ. Civilization* (ed. 6) ii. 28 After Middle Minoan III the single-bladed axe was ousted in Crete by the two-edged variety—the Double Axe—known also to the Sumerians and elevated to become a fetish or symbol of divine power.

d. Of flowers: Having the number of petals increased to twice the number or more by conversion of stamens and carpels into petals.

In the case of some *Compositæ*, as the dahlia: Having the ligulate florets increased at the expense of the tubular.

1578 LYTE *Dodoens* II. x. 159 By often setting they [Campions] waxe very double. **1664** EVELYN *Kal. Hort.* (1729) 198 Single and double Hepatica. **1725** BRADLEY *Fam. Dict.* s.v. *Rose Tree*, The Striped Rose does not grow so double as the Dutch. **1776** WITHERING *Brit. Plants* (1796) II. 489 Petals in several rows, resembling a double flower. **1840** HOOD *Miss Kilmansegg, Her Honeymoon* ix, A double dahlia delights the eye.

e. ***double of***: corresponding or correlative to. *rare.* (Cf. DOUBLE *sb.* 2.)

[**1611** BIBLE *Ecclus.* xlii. 24 All things are double one against another.] **1876** MOZLEY *Univ. Serm.* ix. (1877) 186 There could not be a more striking instance of things being double one of another.

2. Having a twofold relation or application; occurring or existing in two ways or respects; of two kinds; dual; sometimes = ambiguous (see also DOUBLE MEANING).

a **1225** *Ancr. R.* 70 Euerich urideie..holdeð silence, bute ȝif hit beo duble feste. *a* **1300** *Cursor M.* 660 (Cott.) O duble ded þan sal ȝee dei. *c* **1374** CHAUCER *Troylus* v. 898 With dowble wordes sleye, Swich as men clepe 'a word with two visages'. **1393** GOWER *Conf.* II. 274 He hath ordeined of his sleight Measure double and double weight. **1548** HALL *Chron., Hen. VI* (an. 36) 172 Fye on doble entendement, and cloked adulacion. **1567** MAPLET *Gr. Forest* 10 This Arsenicum is double, one ashie colour, and the other..like Golde. **1638** SIR T. HERBERT *Trav.* (ed. 2) 8 The word μῆλον, admitting a double construction, sheep and apple. **1751** JORTIN *Serm.* (1771) V. ii. 43 A double incitement to goodness. **1837** MARRYAT *Dog-fiend* lii, He..is a double traitor. **1868** LOCKYER *Elem. Astron.* iv. §26 (1879) 143 The Earth..has a double movement, turning round its own axis while it travels round the Sun.

3. Twice as much or many; of twice the measure or amount; multiplied by two. Const. *of* (formerly *over*, *to*); also *ellipt.* with prep. omitted, and thus = twice.

c **1305** *Pilate* 21 in *E.E.P.* (1862) 111 He þoȝte if he hit slowe: þat hit were doble wo. **1375** BARBOUR *Bruce* I. 5 Than suld storyss that suthfast wer..Hawe doubill plesance in heryng. **1484** CAXTON *Fables of Avian* 17 The dowble parte or as moche more ageyne. **1513** MORE *Rich. III* (1883) 123 The kyng his armie was double to all this. **1548** HALL *Chron., Hen. VI* (an. 39) 186 b, He..should have..doble wages. **1611** BIBLE *2 Kings* ii. 9 Let a double portion of thy spirit be vpon me. **1644** DIGBY *Nat. Bodies* II. (1645) 126 Let the excesse..be but..double over his that commeth next unto him. **1648** CROMWELL *Lett.* 20 Nov., Their fault who have appeared in this summer's business is certainly double to theirs who were in the first. **1712** W. ROGERS *Voy.* 5 We had now above double the number of Officers usual in Privateers. **1807** SOUTHEY *Lett.* (1856) II. 38 Offering about double pay to what the 'Annual' gives. **1838** DE MORGAN *Ess. Probab.* 147 The average error of the first..is double of that of the second. **1849** MACAULAY *Hist. Eng.* I. 592 His army..might easily have been increased to double the number.

4. a. Of (or about) twice the ordinary size, strength, value, etc., or that denoted by the simple word; of extra size, strength, or amount. Chiefly in technical names of various products, as beer, vessels, cannon, coins, sizes of paper, etc.

1472 *Mem. Ripon* (Surtees) III. 246 Clavis vocatis dowbil-spikynge. **1495** *Nottingham Rec.* III. 284, ij. dovbulle glasses. *c* **1500** *Blowbol's Test.* in Halliwell *Nugæ Poet.* 10 Sengle bere, and othir that is dowbile. *c* **1565** LINDESAY (Pitscottie) *Chron. Scot.* (1728) 108 Small artillery, that is to say myand..quarter-falcon..double-dogs. **1602** MARSTON *Ant. & Mel.* I. Wks. 1856 I. 11 Guerdoned with twentie thousand double pistolets. **1604** SHAKS. *Oth.* I. ii. 14 A voice potentiall, As double as the Duke's. **1667** *Lond. Gaz.* No. 218/4 A double shallop from Diepe bound for Nants. **1686** *Ibid.* No. 2139/4 Two double Tankards, Three single ones. **1773** WILLIAMSON in *Phil. Trans.* LXV. 100 Within the thickness of double-post paper. **1824** BYRON *Juan* XVI. lxvii, A mighty mug of..double ale. **1854** C. M. YONGE *Castle Builders* xxii. 348 Kate..continued it [*sc.* knitting] steadily when the double wool was a great deal too hot to be pleasant. **1873** *Young Englishwoman* May 247/2 Berlin Wool-work Border..it may be worked in single or double wool. **1875** *Ure's Dict. Arts* III. 497 Foolscap, 16½ by 13½ [inches]..double foolscap, 27 by 17. **1887** *Standard* 18 May 3/2 A new coin, to be called a Double-Florin.

b. *Mus.* In names of musical instruments, organ-stops, etc.: Sounding an octave lower in pitch. ***double reed***: see REED *sb.*[1] 8 a.

(A pipe, string, etc. of twice the length of another (*ceteris paribus*) gives a note an octave lower; hence this use.)

1674 PLAYFORD *Skill Mus.* I. i. 3 Those below Gam-ut are called Double Notes as Double F fa ut..being Eights or Diapasons to those above. **1876** STAINER & BARRETT *Dict. Mus. Terms* 137/1 *Double bassoon*, the deepest-toned instrument of the Bassoon family. **1880** W. H. STONE in Grove *Dict. Mus.* I. 458 *Double bassoon*..in pitch an octave below the ordinary bassoon. **1880** STAINER & BARRETT *Dict. Mus. Terms*, *Double-trumpet*, an organ reed-stop..an octave lower in pitch than the 8-ft. trumpet.

c. *Mil.* Applied to a pace in marching: see DOUBLE TIME.

5. Acting in a double manner, i.e. in two ways at different times, openly and secretly, or in profession and practice; characterized by duplicity; false, deceitful. ***to live*** (or ***lead***) ***a double life***: to sustain two different characters in life, esp. one virtuous and respectable, the other immoral or blameworthy. Often of a married man who keeps a mistress. (See also DOUBLE-DEALING.)

a **1340** HAMPOLE *Psalter* xi. 2 Dubbil hert when a fals man thynkis an & says a noþer. *c* **1374** CHAUCER *Anel. & Arc.* 87 He was double in love and nothing pleyne. **14..** *Epiph.* in *Tundale's Vis.* (1843) 121 With dowbull tongis and detraccion. **1503** HAWES *Examp. Virt.* I. xvi. (Arb.) 9 They..are..euermore fals and double. **1591** SYLVESTER *Du Bartas* I. vii. 192 God is the Judge..He sounds the deepest of the doublest heart. *a* **1715** BURNET *Own Time* (1766) I. 436 He was..either very double or very inconstant. **1866** GEO. ELIOT *F. Holt* II. 213 To act with doubleness towards a man whose own conduct was double. **1888** R. L. STEVENSON in *Scribner's Mag.* Jan. 123/2 He began..to dream in sequence and thus to lead a double life. **1892** I. ZANGWILL *Childr. Ghetto* (1893) viii. 83 Esther led a double life, just as she spoke two tongues. **1907** *Times* 19 Dec. 9/4 The woman must have been murdered by a man who was leading a double life... The prisoner had been leading a double life. **1924** E. WALLACE *Sinister Man* xxxv, She had never imagined that this gawk of a girl..could lead what was tantamount to a double life. **1953** L. P. HARTLEY *Go-Between* xi. 134 Since Marcus's return I had become vaguely aware that I was leading a double life.

6. Special Phrases, chiefly technical. **double acrostic**: see ACROSTIC *sb.* 1. **double act**: a performance by two entertainers; the entertainers themselves; also *transf.* **double action**: action in two directions, by two methods, or by the agency of two parts, etc.; *spec.* in *Steam-engine*, application of the steam power to both sides of the piston: see DOUBLE-ACTING. **double agent**: a spy who works on behalf of mutually hostile countries, usu. with actual allegiance only to one. **double album**: two long-playing records or tapes sold together as a set; cf. ALBUM[1] 6. **double algebra**: algebra which deals with two sets of quantities or relations (*e.g.* real and imaginary quantities, lengths and directions of lines, or quantities referred to two independent units). **double aspect** [ASPECT *sb.* 9]: in *Metaph.*, the two forms under which a reality may appear; also *attrib.*, as ***double-aspect theory*** (see sense C. 2 below), a philosophical theory, drawn from Spinoza, that mind and body (or matter) are the same thing viewed from two different aspects, subjective and objective; = *identity-hypothesis*. **double bar**: a species of finch found in Australia. **double bill**: see BILL *sb.*[3] 8 c. **double bind** (see quot. 1962); so ***double-binder***, a person whose action results in a double bind. **double blank**: a domino with both halves of its face blank. **double bluff**: see quot. and BLUFF *sb.*[2] 3. **double boiler**: a saucepan consisting of two pots, the upper one containing the food to be cooked, and the lower one containing water which is heated. **double bond** Chem. [BOND *sb.*[1] 13 e]: a chemical bond in which the two atoms 'share' two pairs of electrons rather than one pair. **double chair**: †(*a*) a light pleasure carriage having two seats (*obs.*); (*b*) a love-seat. **double change** (*Bell-ringing*): one in which two pairs of bells change places; = DOUBLE *sb.* 3 b. **double chin**: a chin with a fold of flesh under it (cf. *double-chinned*, quot. 1387 s.v. DOUBLE *a.* C. 1). **double chorus**: see CHORUS *sb.* 5. **double coal**: a superior kind of coal (the application varying locally). **double common time** (*Music*): time or rhythm in which each bar is equal to two bars of common time (8 crotchets in a bar). **double concerto** (see quot. 1842). **double cone** (*Arch.*): applied to a moulding composed of truncated cones joined base to base and top to top. **double consciousness**: see CONSCIOUSNESS 7. **double consonant** (*Phonology*): two of the same consonant coming together, as in *fully*; also = *double letter* (*a*) below. **double cream**: cream with a high fat-content. **Double-Crostic** orig. *U.S.*, the name for a type of word-puzzle (proprietary in the U.S.) in which the text of a famous quotation or literary passage is built up on a crossword-like grid from the letters of answers to cryptic clues, re-assembled as indicated in the puzzle. **double cube** (*Archit.*): a room of which the breadth is equal to the height and the length is twice the breadth; also *attrib.* or as *adj.* **double dagger**: see DAGGER *sb.* 8, DIESIS 2. **double date** (*U.S. colloq.*): a 'date' (DATE *sb.*[2] 2 c) involving two couples. **double decomposition** (*Chem.*): the simultaneous decomposition of two compounds in a chemical reaction accompanied by the formation of two other compounds. **double demisemiquaver**: a note of half the duration of a demisemiquaver; properly called *semidemisemiquaver* (Stainer & Barrett, 1880). **double dot** (*Mus.*): see quots. **double drummer** (*Austral.*) a noisy type of cicada. **double elephant**: see ELEPHANT 10.

double exposure (*Photogr.*) [EXPOSURE 1 e]: (*a*) an accidental exposure of the same plate or film twice; (*b*) the deliberate superimposition of a second image on an exposure already made; (*c*) *fig.* **double fault** [FAULT *sb.* 5 c]: two consecutive faults at lawn tennis, etc.. **double feast**: see FEAST *sb.* 1 b. **double feature** [FEATURE *sb.* 4 a (*c*)]: a cinema programme containing two full-length films. **double fertilization**: see quots. **double figures** (rarely *double figure*): a total or score, esp. of runs at cricket, higher than nine and less than one hundred. **double first** (*University colloq.*): a place in the first class in each of two final examinations in different subjects; one who takes such a place: see FIRST A. 7 c. **double fleece** (*Austral.* and *N.Z.*): see quot. 1933; so *double-fleecer*. **double floor**: see quot. **double frame**: (*a*) *Typogr.* = FRAME *sb.* 11 c; (*b*) *Cinemat.* and *Television*: see quot. 1959. **double-glazing** [GLAZING *vbl. sb.* 1]: the action of furnishing a window with two layers of glass to reduce the transmission of heat, sound, etc.; two layers of glass fixed in a window. **double helix**: a pair of parallel helices intertwined about a common axis: the postulated structure of the DNA molecule. **double indemnity** (*U.S.*) (see quot. 1948); also *attrib.* **double jeopardy** (*Law*): the placing of a person in jeopardy twice for the same offence, against which there is a common-law immunity. **double knitting**: (*a*) a type of knitting which is tubular and closed at both ends, used for ties, belts, borders of cardigans, etc.; (*b*) a thick knitting-wool made by doubling the yarn; also *attrib.*; hence ***double-knit, -knitted*** adjs. **double land** (*Naut.*): see quot. 1867. **double letter**: (*a*) a letter of the alphabet denoting two sounds, as *x* (= *ks*), ψ (= πσ); (*b*) in *Printing*, two letters combined in one type, as ff, fi; †(*c*) a letter written on two sheets and charged double postage (*obs.*). **double negation** in *Logic*, a statement containing two negatives which, by mathematical analogy, thereby becomes positive in meaning. **double nelson** (see quot. 1889). **double O** (*U.S. slang*) [from the resemblance to a pair of eyes]: an intense look. †**double organ**: an organ with two manuals (*obs.*). **double oxer**: an oxer with a guard-rail on each side. **double play** in *Baseball*, a play by the defence in which two runners are put out successively by throws of the basemen. **double pneumonia**: pneumonia affecting both lungs. **double point** : in the Higher Geometry, a point common to two branches of a curve, or at which the curve has two tangents (real or imaginary); a node, cusp, or conjugate point; also an analogous point on a curved surface. **double room**: a bedroom for two people. **double salt**: a salt which is composed of two simple salts and which when crystallized has physical properties different from its components but which in aqueous solution behaves as a mixture of them. **double saucepan** = *double boiler*. **double saw(-buck)** [*sawbuck*] *U.S. slang*: (*a*) twenty dollars; a twenty-dollar note; (*b*) a twenty-year prison sentence. **double shuffle**: see SHUFFLE *sb.* 5. **double sixes**: (*a*) two sixes thrown at once with a pair of dice; (*b*) the ordinary game at dominoes, in which the highest piece is the double six; (*c*) a size of tallow candles. **double snipe**: sportsman's name for the greater snipe, *Gallinago major.* **double-spacing**: see *double-spaced* s.v. sense C. 1 and SPACING *vbl. sb.* 1 a. **double spar**: a name for Iceland spar, as being double-refracting. **double-speak** = DOUBLE-TALK, DOUBLE TALK b; cf. -SPEAK and DOUBLETHINK. **double spread**: short for *double-page spread.* **double standard**, a rule, principle, judgement, etc., viewed as applying more strictly to one group of people, set of circumstances, etc., than to another; applied specifically to a code of sexual behaviour that is more rigid for women than for men. **double star** (*Astron.*): two stars so near (really or visually) as not to be separately visible without a telescope; esp. when forming a physically connected system (distinctively called BINARY). **double stem** (*Ski-ing*): a position adopted for slowing down by making a point inward angle, i.e. by spreading the rear ends of the skis and bringing the front points together. **double-stopping** (*Music*): the simultaneous sounding of two notes (strictly, of two 'stopped' notes) on two strings of a violin or other instrument of that class; notes so played are called *double-stops.* **double summer-time** (see quot. 1962 and cf. SUMMERTIME 2). **double tens** (*pl.*): name for a large kind of nail. **to work double tides**: see TIDE. **double time**: see 4 c. **double U**: (*a*) name of the letter W; (*b*) *colloq.*, short for W.C. = water-closet. **double vision**: diplopia. **double wedding** : a wedding of two couples at the same time. **double window**: see quot. 1877.

⁋Also in many other phrases, as ***double bar, d. curvature, d. entry, d. Gloucester, d. question, d. refraction, d. shuffle, d. tooth***, etc., etc., for which see the substantive element.

1905 A. BENNETT *Tales of Five Towns* II. 246 He wants me to tour with him..and do a *double act. **1952** W. GRANVILLE *Dict. Theatr. Terms* 64 *Double-act*, two vaudeville artistes, cross-talk comedians, or singers, e.g. the famous Layton and Johnson team of the 1920's. **1959** *Times* 29 May 4/2 When their double act was done, having produced 87 runs..it suited Kenyon..that he soon had Gloucestershire in again. **1935** R. P. BLACKMUR (*title*) The *double agent. **1941** KOESTLER *Scum of Earth* 79 The sensational trial..had revealed an amazing scene of plots, intrigues, spies, and double-agents. **1960** *News Chron.* 19 Feb. 3/4 A young Dutchman..said he was a double agent. He had joined the Germans only to get to Britain and there serve his country. **1970** J. LENNON in J. Wenner *Lennon Remembers* (1971) 138, I don't care about the whole concept of *Pepper*, it might be better, but the music was better for me on the *double album. **1980** *Oxford Times* 23 May 21/2 Beefheart was a friend of Frank Zappa, whose *Joe's Garage, Acts II and III*..is a double album completing the story begun in Act I. **1849** DE MORGAN *Double Algebra* v. 117 All the symbols which in single algebra denote numbers or magnitudes, in *double algebra denote lines, and not merely the lengths of lines, but their directions. **1865** J. GROTE *Moral Ideals* (1876) 267 Conscientiousness..has a *double aspect, outwards and inwards. **1870** S. H. HODGSON *Theory of Practice* I. i. 3 It was maintained that..the whole world of phenomena..had a double aspect, subjective and objective, was at once a mode of consciousness and an existing thing. **1909** A. J. NORTH *Nests & Eggs of Birds Austral.* II. 279 Stictoptera bichenovii... This Finch, the '*double-bar' of Sydney bird dealers, is another instance of a species being found in coastal as well as the inland districts of Queensland. **1933** *Bulletin* (Sydney) 13 Sept. 39/1 The grove of lemon-trees where, year after year, the double-bars had nested. **1959** J. WRIGHT *Generations of Men* 212 The garden where her pretty diamond-sparrows and double-bars and finches nested. **1956** G. BATESON et al. in *Behavioral Sci.* I. 253/2 He [*sc.* a schizophrenic] has special difficulty in handling signals of that class whose members assign Logical Types to other signals... The hypothesis which we offer is that sequences of this kind in the external experience of the patient are responsible for the inner conflicts of Logical Typing. For such unresolvable sequences of experiences, we use the term '*double bind'. **1962** *Listener* 6 Dec. 949/2 Serious troubles can arise when..a mother's normal life becomes subject to promptings from her unconscious... The child of such a parent finds himself repeatedly caught in a 'double bind', that is in a situation in which he is given simultaneous but mutually contradictory cues, so that whatever he does will be wrong. **1960** *Arch. Gen. Psychiatry* III. 359/2 The emotional importance of the *double-binder to his 'victim'. **1801** J. STRUTT *Sports & Pastimes* IV. ii. 240 One of them is a *double blank. **1868** SALA *Notes & Sk. Paris Exhib.* iv. 34 The houses..gave to the outskirts of Paris an odd affinity to a city built of dominoes set on end. The double-sixes and double-fours, with here and there a double-blank in the shape of a dead-wall. **1927** WODEHOUSE *Small Bachelor* i. 20 It has been well said of Sigsbee H. Waddington that, if men were dominoes, he would be the double-blank. **1919** J. BUCHAN *Mr. Standfast* iii. 64 His device was apparently the *Double Bluff. That is to say, when he had two courses open to him, A and B, he pretended he was going to take B, and so got us guessing that he would try A. Then he took B after all. **1879** A. D. WHITNEY *Just How* 260 Cut up and boil and mash..in a bain-marie, or *double boiler. **1950** T. S. ELIOT *Cocktail Party* I. i. 37, I suppose there must be a double boiler: Isn't there one in every kitchen? **1889** G. M'GOWAN tr. *Bernthsen's Org. Chem.* i. 49 The assumption that the affinity which becomes free at each of two carbon atoms, upon abstraction of the hydrogen, is employed in creating a '*double bond' between them. *Ibid.* i. 50 By this term 'double bond' is not, however, to be understood a closer or more intimate combination. The olefines, on the contrary, are more readily oxidized than the paraffins, being thereby attacked at the point of the double bond. **1903** WALKER & MOTT tr. *A.F. Holleman's Text-bk. Org. Chem.* I. §129. 150 The double bond must not be regarded as a mere doubling of the single one. **1944** *Hackh's Chem. Dict.* (ed. 3) 286/2 *Double bond*, a condition which exists in unsaturated compounds where two single valence bonds connect two atoms. **1964** N. G. CLARK *Mod. Org. Chem.* ii. 14 The pair of valency bonds linking adjacent carbon atoms together.. is referred to as an ethylenic or olefinic bond. When this type of linkage occurs between other atoms, it is simply termed a double bond. **1795** C. PETTIGREW *MS. Let.* 19 Sept., I think it will be best to send the *Double Chair. **1833** *Maryland Hist. Mag.* (1918) XIII. 338 Dr. Smith..and Drs negro boy left Salisbury with two easy riding horses and a double chair. **1904** P. MACQUOID *Hist. Eng. Furniture* ix. 220 Double chairs or love-seats. **1934** *Burlington Mag.* Oct. 163/1 An oak chair dated 1672..of unusual width, but hardly wide enough to be described as a double chair. **1684** R. H. *School Recreat.* 91 Make a Change..The single, by changing two Notes..the double by changing Four..which is however called One *double Change, and not two changes. **1872** ELLACOMBE *Ch. Bells Devon* iii. 39 About the year 1657, double changes came into practice. **1832** *Double chin [see CHIN *sb.* 1]. **1958** Double chin [see ASTRAKHAN b]. **1803** J. PLYMLEY *Agric. Shropsh.* 54 Coal, called the *double-coal. **1839** URE *Dict. Arts* 962 A section of the Quarrelton coal..showing the overlapped coal and the double coal. **1879–81** G. F. JACKSON *Shropsh. Word-bk.*, *Double-coal*, a good coal for manufacturing purposes, much used. **1920** W. GIBSON *Coal in Gt. Brit.* 207 The Seven Feet Coal..is the chief coal, but below it the Double and Bench coals are workable. **1894** *Times* 6 Mar. 4/3 The time of the piece is *double common time, but here and there a bar of three semibreves is put in. **1842** J. F. WARNER *Universal Dict. Mus. Terms* 26/1 We distinguish a concerto or concert for one instrument alone from a *double concerto, i.e. a concerto for two instruments together, (concerto doppio,) or indeed for several instruments together. **1958** *Listener* 30 Oct. 706/3 The double Concerto in D minor. **1871** *Public Sch. Lat. Gram.* §9 *Double Consonants, *x, z.* **1877** E. S. DALLAS *Kettner's Bk. of Table* 303 We have *double cream put in to sauces and soups. **1888** MRS. BEETON *Bk. Househ. Managem.* xxxii. 898 For whipping and making sweets it is usual to ask for *double* cream, that is thick cream that has stood on the milk for twenty-four hours instead of twelve. **1936** LUCAS & HUME *Au Petit Cordon Bleu* 161, 1 gill double cream. **1959** *Listener* 2 July 39/2 Whip the double cream until fairly stiff. **1934** *Sat. Rev. Lit.* (U.S.) 31 Mar. 598 *Double-Crostics, Number 1... This is the first of a series of ingenious literary puzzles invented by Elizabeth S. Kingsley for *The Saturday Review.* **1946** *Official Gaz.* (U.S. Patent Office) 3 Dec. 25/1 The Saturday Review Associates, Inc., New York... Double-Crostic. **1967** [see CLUE *v.* 4 a]. **1976** *Official Gaz.* (U.S. Patent Office) 24 Feb. TM219 Janet Elliott Cameron, San Francisco, Calif... Double-Crostics. **1984** T. AUGARDE *Oxf. Guide Word Games* vi. 62 Yet another type of crossword is the double-crostic, invented, by an American, Elizabeth Kingsley. **1776** A. YOUNG *Tour in Ireland* (1780) 265 He has built, besides other rooms..a drawing one.., a *double cube of 25 feet, being 50 long, 25 broad, and 25 high. **1930** H. NICOLSON *Diary* 5 July (1966) I. 51 Down to Wilton with Vita... Go with Pembroke to the Palladian bridge and look back on the house all lit up with the Van Dykes showing in the Double Cube (Room). **1969** *Guardian* 19 June 13/8, I thought..about Inigo Jones's superb double-cube room. **1969** P. DICKINSON *Pride of Heroes* 38 Beyond the hall..was the Chinese Withdrawing-room, a double cube. **1931** *Amer. Speech* VI. 204 *Double date. **1952** S. KAUFFMANN *Philanderer* (1953) ix. 140 The ultimate triumph..was more often accomplished on double dates than otherwise. **1955** M. MILLAR *Beast in View* xiv. 171 She had met Evelyn..on a double date with one of John's fraternity brothers. **1866** H. E. ROSCOE *Less. Elem. Chem.* vi. 56 The decompositions here effected may serve as the type of a very large number of chemical changes classed as *double decompositions. **1903** H. C. JONES *Princ. Inorg. Chem.* xxvii. 323 Sulphates can also be formed by double decomposition or metathesis. **1957** G. E. HUTCHINSON *Treat. Limnol.* I. x. 668 Krogh concludes that basaltic rocks in general take up CO_2, calcium carbonate and silicic acid being formed by double decomposition. **1801** BUSBY *Dict. Mus.*, **Double-Dot*, or *Dotted-Dot*, the Double-Dot consists of two points, one following the other. **1959** *Collins Mus. Encycl.* 201/1 The double dot, first suggested by Leopold Mozart in 1756.., indicates a prolongation of the normal length by three-quarters. **1927** *Austral. Encycl.* I. 269/2 In the Sydney district..the *Double Drummer (*Cyclochila australasiae*). **1952** *Chambers's Shorter Eng. Dict.* Suppl., *Double drummer*, a large brown and orange cicada, remarkable for the large, swollen drums or covers to its sound-producing organs. **1892** W. E. WOODBURY *Encycl. Photogr.* 223 **Double exposure*, an error often made by amateurs in unconsciously exposing the same plate on two occasions. **1911** D. S. HULFISH *Cycl. Motion-Pict. Work* II. ii. 91 The making of ghosts by double exposures. **1912** F. A. TALBOT *Moving Pictures* xx. 225 The fairy..having been photographed only during the second exposure, appears at first very indistinctly. The result of the double exposure is shown in the illustration; and the gradual appearance of the fairy may be followed very easily. **1939** *Amer. Speech* XIV. 271 The good pun makes a double exposure on the mind. **1958** M. L. HALL *Newnes Compl. Amat. Photogr.* iv. 54 It is common nowadays for even simple cameras to have a shutter-film wind interlock which prevents blank negatives or double exposures. **1958** *Observer* 16 Feb. 13/6 The treatment [of a film] seems a bit outmoded (all those soulful close-ups and double exposures). **1909** *Cent. Dict.* Suppl., *Double fault. **1921** A. W. MYERS *20 Yrs. Lawn Tennis* 128 A universal 'Oh!' echoed round the arena when Wilding served a double fault. *Ibid.* 156 He served half a dozen double faults and two foot-faults. **1955** *Times* 2 July 2/7 A sad double fault gave Trabert all the assurance that he might have needed. **1934** WEBSTER, *Double feature. **1945** T. WILLIAMS *Glass Menagerie* (1948) I. i. 28 *Tom*: I'm going to the movies... There's a wonderful double feature down at Loewe's State. **1909** W. BATESON *Mendel's Princ. Heredity* xv. 270 The seed of maize is formed by a **double fertilisation*. It consists of two parts, an embryo, and an endosperm... The embryo is formed by the union of one nucleus of the egg-cell with one from the pollen-tube, and the endosperm is similarly formed by the union of the united polar nuclei with another from the pollen-tube. **1916** B. D. JACKSON *Gloss. Bot. Terms* (ed. 3) 118/2 *Double fertilization*, in angiosperms, when one male cell from the pollen-tube fuses with the egg nucleus, the other with the upper polar nucleus, and this last with the lower polar nucleus. **1959** FOSTER & GIFFORD *Compar. Morphol. Vascular Plants* xix. 515 The participation of each of the two male gametes in a fusion process is uniquely characteristic of angiosperms, and is usually designated by the expression 'double fertilization'. **1860** J. E. EARDLEY-WILMOT *Remin. T. A. Smith* 251 Nor was Lord F. Beauclerk fortunate enough to mark a *double figure in either innings. **1875** *Cliftonian* IV. 93 No one scored double figures. **1884** *Boy's Own Paper* Summer No. 26 Watch the ball, keep your temper, and don't be afraid; For that is the way double figures are made. **1894** *Times* 25 May 11/3 Mr. Mitchell for once in a way failed to reach double figures. **1861** TROLLOPE *Barchester T.* xlvii, A son from college with all the fresh honours of a *double first. **1868** HOLME LEE *B. Godfrey* xxx. 158, I shall come out a double-first. **1933** *Press* (Christchurch, N.Z.) 7 Oct. 15/7 A sheep that is missed at one shearing and comes in the next has a **double fleece*. He is called a *double-fleecer*. **1904** *N.Z. Illustr. Mag.* X. 48/1 Sheep annually evaded the shearing muster and remained among the scrub..to develop into '*double-fleecers'. **1921** H. GUTHRIE-SMITH *Tutira* xxiii. 224 We lived on..the fat wild sheep and double-fleecers. **1842–76** GWILT *Encycl. Archit.* §2019 A **double floor* consists in its thickness of three tiers of timbers, which are called *binding joists* (these perform the office of girders), *bridging joists*, and *ceiling joists*. **1904** GOODCHILD & TWENEY *Technol. & Sci. Dict.* 171/1 **Double frame*, a composing frame usually made of deal and holding two pairs of cases at the same time. **1959** HALAS & MANVELL *Technique Film Animation* 338 *Double frame*, one animation drawing photographed for two frames instead of one. **1943** *Fortune* Mar. 182 *Double-glazing is quite a good insulator. **1957** *Housewife* Sept. 23/2 The north and south walls consist almost entirely of Plyglass double-glazing. **1958** *Chambers's*

Techn. Dict. 974/2 *Double-glazing*, glazing with two panes separated by spacers and a layer of dehydrated air which prevents misting. 1960 *House & Garden* May 69/2 Double-glazing prevents heat loss. 1971 D. DEVINE *Dead Trouble* vii. 65 He added a sun lounge and installed central heating and double glazing. 1954 CRICK & WATSON in *Proc. R. Soc.* A. CCXXIII. 89 (*heading*) Detailed configuration of the *double helix. 1962 T. DOBZHANSKY *Mankind Evolving* ii. 37 If the double helix separates into two single threads each can re-form an exact copy of the original double structure. 1968 J. D. WATSON (*title*) The double helix. 1968 *New Scientist* 19 Sept. 592/1 The symbol of the molecular biological age is without doubt the 'double helix' of DNA. 1924 J. B. MACLEAN *Life Insurance* xiv. 257 *Double indemnity benefits require but a few words. 1930 A. H. MOWBRAY *Insurance* xi. 170 Examination of the causes of accidents which will entitle the insured to double indemnity will disclose that these events are so spectacular..as generally to be given considerable publicity. 1948 J. B. MACLEAN *Introd. Life Insurance* I. xiii. 219 'Double Indemnity'..is a provision for payment of double the face amount of the policy if death is the result of an accident. 1969 J. WEIDMAN *Centre of Action* (1970) viii. 91 It's for her own good. With a double-indemnity clause, which comes to twenty-eight dollars a year extra, she'll be financially independent at seventy-seven. 1910 W. W. WILLOUGHBY *Constitutional Law of U.S.* I. §184. 439 It was held that by an act of Congress in 1902, the immunity from *double jeopardy for crime as provided in the Constitution had been extended to the Philippines. 1969 M. L. FRIEDLAND *Double Jeopardy* i. 3 The history of the rule against double jeopardy is the history of criminal procedure. No other procedural doctrine is more fundamental or all pervasive. 1970 H. WAUGH *Finish me Off* (1971) 194 If we charge him and the jury lets him off, there's no second chance. That's double jeopardy. 1895 *Montgomery Ward Catal.* 291/1 Fascinators, hand made, *double knit of Shetland floss. 1964 *Observer* 12 July 8/4 The double-knit jersey revolution, which has gathered in phenomenal profits for a handful of bright ladies' knitters. 1907 *Yesterday's Shopping* (1969) 243/1 Welsbach [gas] mantles..*double-knitted. 1855 MRS. GASKELL *North & South* I. xii. 146 Mrs. Thornton..liked Mrs. Hale's *double knitting far better. 1911–12 *T. Eaton & Co. Catal.* Fall & Winter 243/7 Beehive Double Knitting or Petticoat Yarn is a soft thick knitting yarn made of a fine quality of wool. 1938 M. THOMAS *Knitting Bk.* 165 *Double Knitting.* A Tubular Fabric constructed on two knitting pins is worked as follows. 1960 *Farmer & Stockbreeder* 29 Mar. (Suppl.) 9/1 3 oz. Emu Romany double-knitting or Scotch double-knitting wool. 1970 *Guardian* 24 Mar. 9/2 Regency Bainin double-knitting, for instance (used for our Aran tunic patterns) is available in twenty-four shades. 1712 W. ROGERS *Voy.* 275 The largest Island..appears to be high *double Land. 1867 SMYTH *Sailor's Word-bk.*, *Double-land*, that appearance of a coast when the sea-line is bounded by parallel ranges of hills, rising inland one above the other. 1576 FLEMING *Panopl. Epist.* 303 *note*, Simonides..devised also these *double letters in the Greeke Alphabete (namely ξ. ψ. θ). 1753 *Scots Mag.* July 328/2 The rates of double letters, are always double; of treble letters, treble. 1777 SHERIDAN *Sch. Scand.* v. ii, The postman who was just coming to the door with a double letter. 1883 F. H. BRADLEY *Princ. Logic* I. v. 131 (*heading*) The principles of identity, contradiction, excluded middle, and *double negation. 1888 B. BOSANQUET *Logic* I. vii. 324 The conclusion thus obtained ..may be *bonâ fide* arrived at through the double negation I have described, and may be at first unsupported by the direct observation. 1961 I. M. COPI *Introd. Logic* (ed. 2) ix. 282 Using the Principle of Double Negation (D.N.), which asserts that *p* is logically equivalent to ~ ~ *p*. 1969 F. I. DRETSKE *Seeing & Knowing* ii. 57 Logicians are not tempted to abandon the rule of double negation. 1889 W. ARMSTRONG *Wrestling* 233 Probably the most dangerous move in Lancashire and Cornwall and Devon wrestling..is what is called the '*Double Nelson'... To get behind an opponent, place both arms under his, and clasp your hands round the back of his neck and thus bend his head forward till his breast-bone almost gives way. 1903 J. J. MILLER *Scottish Sports* 127 So Ingram slipped on a double-Nelson, pinned him down for the requisite 30 seconds, and then politely assisted him to rise. 1917 R. W. LARDNER *Gullible's Travels* (1926) ii. 48 So then I and Bishop knocked the street-car service and President Wilson and give each other the *double-O. 1957 R. A. HEINLEIN *Door into Summer* (1960) i. 12 The cashier came over and leaned on my table, giving the seats on both sides of the booth a quick double-O. 1613 *Organ Specif. Worcester Cathedral*, Yᵉ..*double organs in yᵉ Cathedral church of Worcester. 1907 *Daily Chron.* 12 Nov. 4/4 *Double-oxers, stone-walls..and broad ditches. 1958 *Times Lit. Suppl.* 31 Jan. 63/2 Such technicalities of the chase as..double oxers. 1867 *Ball Players' Chron.* 6 June 2/3 A *double play by Willard and Shaw..caused the Lowells to retire for a blank score. 1880 N. BROOKS *Fairport Nine* ii. 36 A double play for the 'White Bears'..and not a run scored. 1968 *Washington Post* 4 July C1/7 The Yankee second baseman..grabbed the ball, stepped on second and threw to first base for a double play. 1968 *Globe & Mail* (Toronto) 10 July 26/6 McCovey then bounced into a double play. 1892 W. OSLER *Princ. Med.* 525 *Double pneumonia presents no peculiarities other than the greater danger connected with it. 1929 *Encycl. Brit.* XVIII. 100/2 Usually pneumonia affects one lower lobe but it may extend to the whole lung or even to parts of both lungs (double pneumonia). 1727–51 CHAMBERS *Cycl.*, **Double point.* 1872 B. WILLIAMSON *Diff. Calc.* xiv. (1873) §206 No cubic can have more than one double point. [1926 F. KILBOURNE *Dot & Will* (1929) 193, I would change to a single room in the hotel which was a little cheaper than the double one..we had.] 1931 *Times* 1 June 10/3 A large *double room and private bathroom. 1849 D. CAMPBELL *Inorg. Chem.* 176 These *double salts are known as manganese alums. 1948 GLASSTONE *Physical Chem.* (ed. 2) x. 807 When a double salt can exist as a solid phase the behavior on evaporation depends on whether the compound is stable in contact with water or not. 1906 MRS. BEETON *Bk. Househ. Managem.* iv. 59 The *double saucepan is especially useful for making porridge and gruel. 1961 *Guardian* 24 Mar. 12/6 Unless you have a very low heat on the top of your stove..it is really best to use a double saucepan. 1850 *Knickerbocker* XXXVI. 297 Send me the two *double 'saw-bucks'. 1925 *Writer's Monthly* June 486/1 *Double sawbuck*, a twenty dollar banknote. 1926 MAINES & GRANT *Wise-Crack Dict.* 7/2 *Double saw*, twenty dollar bill. 1929 'C. WALT' *Love in Chicago* 25 'What'd it net yuh, State Street?' I asked. 'A little over a double saw-buck, 'n' I stuffed it all on Hip-Bones, 'n' she ain't come in fur 'er oats yet.' 1936 L. DUNCAN *Over Wall* i. 21, I learned quickly that a dollar-bill was a fish-skin;..a twenty a double-saw. 1945 L. SHELLY *Jive Talk Dict.* 24 *Double sawbuck*, a twenty-year jail sentence. 1948 *Time* 17 May 87/1 Any tout or hustler around the track can usually work Eddie for a 'double sawbuck'. 1950 H. E. GOLDIN *Dict. Amer. Underworld Lingo* 61/1 *Double-saw, double-sawbuck*, a prison sentence of twenty years. 1870 HARDY & WARE *Mod. Hoyle* 91 The ordinary game—technically termed '*double sixes'—is played with 28 dominoes. 1870 *Lond. Soc.* Sept. 264 A small order for colza, or double sixes, or Souchong. 1840 HOOD *Miss Kilmansegg, Her Honeymoon* xi, A double barrel and *double snipes Give the sportsman a duplicate pleasure. 1899 J. LONDON *Let.* 7 Jan. (1966) 11 Surely the *double-spacing could not have led to a mistaken estimate of length. 1877 ROSENTHAL *Muscles & Nerves* 15 Iceland-spar or, as it is also called, *double spar. 1957 'M. BUTTLE' *Sweeniad* ii. 55 In the literary weeklies, the languages of criticism and theology have become one and book reviews all sound like sermons written in the most holy '*Double-Speak'. 1961 W. KAUFMANN in G. E. Myers *Self, Relig. & Metaphysics* 99 The theologians have a way of redefining terms in rather odd ways, and frequently engage in something best called *double-speak*: their utterances are designed to communicate contradictory views to different listeners and readers. 1970 M. PEI *Words in Sheep's Clothing* i. 1 (*heading*) Double-speak in America. 1975 *Economist* 4 Jan. 31/3 'Indicative planning' in Japan means almost the opposite of the term in current British doublespeak. In Britain planning would obviously be politically popular, because it means helping uneconomic firms to survive in uneconomic areas. In Japan it is recognised that planning would obviously be politically very unpopular..since planning means killing uneconomic industries more quickly than ordinary market forces would. 1985 *Radio Times* 28 Sept. 14/1 James Dean never consciously sought to be a god, or, indeed, a symbol for anything... The idea of heading a huge tidal wave of teenage revolt against the narrow, repressive, adult double-speak of the mid-50s did not occur to him. 1956 F. C. AVIS *Bookman's Conc. Dict.* 88/1 **Double spread*, text matter or, more usually, an advertisement stretching across the whole of two facing pages. 1951 E. PAUL *Springtime in Paris* iv. 90 Without a robust *double standard, the admittedly loose women play a losing game. 1962 *New Statesman* 16 Nov. 698/2 The greatest temptation into which the politically committed can be led is that of the double standard. 1963 AUDEN *Dyer's Hand* 3 In relation to a writer, most readers believe in the Double Standard: they may be unfaithful to him as often as they like, but he must never, never be unfaithful to them. 1968 R. AMBERLEY *Incitement to Murder* vi. 176 He no doubt follows a double standard. One for business and one for everyday life. 1968 S. HYNES *Edwardian Turn of Mind* vi. 177 The point about the double standard is made—that it is unjust of the husband to demand greater fidelity of his wife than he offers her. 1781 HERSCHEL in *Phil. Trans.* LXXII. 101 The second class of *double stars. 1890 C. A. YOUNG *Elem. Astron.* xiii. §462 Stars may be double in two ways, optically and physically.. the majority of double stars must be really physically connected. 1936 O. SCHNIEBS *Skiing for All* iii. 33 The *double-stem (snow-plow position) is the brake in skiing. 1880 P. DAVID in Grove *Dict. Mus.* I. 459 The term '*double stopping'..is..indiscriminately used for any double sounds, whether produced with or without the aid of the open strings. The playing of *double stops is one of the most difficult parts of the technique of the violin. 1943 *Times Weekly* 18 Aug. 5/2 *Double summertime ended early on Sunday, when clocks were put back an hour. 1962 E. BRUTON *Dict. Clocks & Watches* 61 *Double summertime*, introduced in Britain during the Second World War for economy. In winter the clock was one hour in advance of Greenwich mean time and in summer, two hours in advance of it. 1611 *MS. Acc. St. John's Hosp., Canterb.*, For haulfe a honndred of *dubell tennes, xd. 1717 TABOR in *Phil. Trans.* XXX. 559 Large Iron Nails..not quite so long, as those we call double Tenns. 1599 THYNNE *Animadv.* (1875) 65 The latyne, Italiane, frenche, and spanyshe haue no *doble W. 1840 HOOD *Miss Kilmansegg, Her Honeymoon* x, A double U [i.e. W. = West] wind. 1885 J. PAYN *Talk of Town* II. 232 Doubleyous and esses. 1914 C. MACKENZIE *Sinister St.* II. iv. ii. 859 The double-u is just next your bedroom. 1889 G. A. BERRY *Dis. Eye* 504 The *diplopia* or *double vision to which the condition gives rise. 1922 *Encycl. Brit.* XXX. 975/1 Paralysis of the muscles of the eye, producing diplopia or double vision. 1771 SMOLLETT *Humph. Cl.* III. 255 Every thing is now prepared for our *double wedding. The marriage-articles for both couples are drawn and executed. 1864 C. M. YONGE *Trial* II. vi. 118 There was a proposal to join forces, and have a double wedding..the two school-fellows and two young friends. 1949 D. SMITH *I capture Castle* ix. 129, I accepted him and Rose and I arranged to have a double wedding. 1819 M. WILMOT *Let.* 26 Nov. (1935) 31 We are..living at Vienna.. with stoves and *double windows in our rooms. *a*1877 KNIGHT *Dict. Mech.* I. 731/1 *Double-window*, one having two sets of sash, inclosing a body of air as a non-conductor of heat and to deaden noise. 1908 KIPLING *Lett. of Travel* (1920) 133 The double windows are brought up from the cellar. 1949 D. MACARDLE *Children of Europe* xiii. 205 The cold of winter is so intense in Hungary that people who can afford it have double windows.

B. *adv.*

1. a. To twice the amount or extent; in two ways or respects; twice, twice over, DOUBLY.

13.. *Gaw. & Gr. Knt.* 61 Þat day doubble on þe dece watz þe douth serued. 1382 WYCLIF *Matt.* xxiii. 15 ȝe maken hym a sone of helle, double more than ȝou. *c*1460 FORTESCUE *Abs. & Lim. Mon.* ix. (1885) 128 Vndir a prince double so myghty as was thair old prince. 1540 *Act 32 Hen. VIII*, c. 22 §3 Many prebendes..bene double certified by yᵉ sayd commissioners. 1567 J. SANFORD tr. *Epictetus* 14 a, Thou shalte be double as much mocked and scorned. 1601 SHAKS. *All's Well* II. iii. 254 Ile beate him..and he were double and double a Lord. 1712 *Spect.* No. 527 ¶2 Jealous ears always hear double. 1820 KEATS *Lamia* 611 Bright eyes were double bright.

b. phr. *to see double*: to see two images of one object, by an illusion or aberration of vision.

[1628 EARLE *Microcosm.*, *Self-conceited Man* (Arb.) 32 His eyes, like a drunkard's, see all double.] 1651 HOBBES *Leviath.* III. xxxix. 248* Words brought into the world, to make men see double. 1734 POPE *Ess. Man* IV. 6 Oh Happiness..O'er-look'd, seen double, by the fool, and wise. 1840 MARRYAT *Poor Jack* xxvii, It didn't prove a glass too much, or you'd have seen double.

c. In a pair or couple; two together, two at once; as in *to ride double*, i.e. two on one horse. So of a horse, etc., *to carry double*.

1599 NASHE *Lenten Stuffe* (1871) 79 As this host of feather-mongers were getting up to ride double. *a*1613 OVERBURY *A Wife* (1638) 94 He never drinks but double, for he must be pledg'd. 1678 BUTLER *Hud.* III. i. 569 Marriage is but a Beast, some say, That carries double in foul way. 1777 SHERIDAN *Sch. Scand.* II. i, Content to ride double, behind the butler. 1819 BYRON *Juan* I. cxl, To prove her mistress had been sleeping double.

d. *Mil.* In double time, 'at the double'.

1833 *Regul. Instr. Cavalry* I. 21 On the word *Double March*, the whole step off together.

†**2.** After a numeral, simply expressing multiplication: = (so many) times; -fold. (Sometimes pleonastic, as *sevenfold double* = sevenfold.) *Obs.*

*a*1325 *Prose Psalter* lxxviii[i]. 13 ȝelde to our neȝburs seven double in her bosme, her lackinge. *a*1450 *Knt. de la Tour* (1868) 113 He wolde yelde it ayenne an hundred double. 1548 UDALL *Erasm. Par. Luke* viii. 89 It..brought fruicte an hundred-fold double. 1698 J. FRYER *E. India and Persia* 99 Cover them..with a kind of Felt..two or three double.

3. With duplicity, deceitfully. *rare.*

1592 SHAKS. *Rom. & Jul.* II. iv. 179 If you should deale double with her. 1868 GEO. ELIOT *Sp. Gipsy* IV. 291 Thought played him double.

4. ***double or quit*(*s*** (Gambling): an expression implying that the stake already due is either to become double, or to be cancelled, according to the issue of another chance; hence *fig.* of a bold or desperate attempt to extricate oneself from present evils at the risk of greatly increasing them.

1580 SIDNEY *Arcadia* III. Wks. (1613) 242, I thought to play double or quit. 1626 T. H[AWKINS] *Caussin's Holy Crt.* 406 Alexandra..resolued to play at double or quit, breake the guiues of specious seruitude, or yield her necke to Herod's sword. 1798 *Geraldina* III. 205 He then offered to play double or quits. 1800 MAR. EDGEWORTH *Belinda* vii, 'I dare you to another trial—double or quit.' 1894 LD. WOLSELEY *Life Marlborough* II. lxxviii. 316 He was no gambler at the game of life, and whether winning or losing he never wagered double or quits.

C. double- in combination.

There is practically no limit to the number of combinations with *double-* in any of the four groups below, the use of the hyphen in all of them being syntactical rather than lexical, i.e. it shows that the two words which it connects are in this particular context more closely connected than would be supposed if they were written separately: thus the two words *double deck*, used attrib., are written *double-deck*, and give the parasynthetic deriv. *double-decked*; hence arise such verbs as *to double-bar*, and pa. pples. of the type *double-barred*, which again blend with the parasynthetic forms: cf. *double-hinged* with *double-barred*.

1. *Double adj.* in parasynthetic combs. (with the meaning 'having a double —, or two —s'), e.g. ***double-aspected, -barred, -battalioned, -bearded, -bedded, -bladed, -blossomed, -bodied, -bottomed, -bunched, -chinned, -columned, -curved, -decked, -doored, -dotted, -ended, -eyed, -flowered, -formed, -founted, -horned, -keeled, -lunged, -mouthed, -natured, -nostrilled, -piled, -pointed, -sensed, -sexed, -shaped, -sighted, -soled, -spaced, -tracked, -triggered, -visaged, -walled, -weaponed, -windowed, -winged***, etc.; **double-brooded**, producing two broods in the year or season, as some insects; also of birds; **double-buttoned**, having two rows of buttons (= DOUBLE-BREASTED); **double-coated**, having two coats; **double-footed**, †(*a*) two-footed (*obs.*); (*b*) = *diplopod* (see DIPLO-); **double-fronted**, having two fronts, double-faced; **double-leaded**, (printed matter) in which the lines of type are widely separated by means of double leads; **double-lived**, having two lives or manners of life; †amphibious; **double-threaded**, of a screw (also *fig.*). Hence nouns of quality, as *double-livedness, -sidedness*, etc. See also DOUBLE-BARRELLED, -BREASTED, etc.

1876 *Mind* I. 357 This *double-aspected Whole may be taken as the *larger circle* including either of the two aspects. 1767 *Byron's Voy. round World* 8 Nuns..conversing with strangers through a *double barred grate. 1933 R. TUVE *Seasons & Months* iv. 158 Janus *double-bearded (one of them forked) holds a nondescript object that is either bread or horn. 1631 WEEVER *Anc. Fun. Mon.* 220 Vnto *double Beneficed men, and Non-residents he was very strict. 1552 HULOET, *Double bodied, *bico[r]pus*. 1874 KNIGHT *Dict. Mech.*, *Double-bodied Microscope*, a microscope invented by Nachet, to enable several observers to view the same object simultaneously. 1664 EVELYN *Diary* 24 Feb., We went on board Sir William Petty's *double-bottomed vessel. 1833 B. SILLIMAN *Man. Sugar Cane* 60 His apparatus is composed of a double bottomed copper boiler, covered by a dome. 1932 E. STEP *Bees, Wasps, Ants, & c., Brit. Isles* 195 Another *double-brooded species..is *Claudius rufipes*. 1953 D. A. BANNERMAN *Birds Brit. Isles* I. 117 In the opinion of the above authority the species [*sc.* the citril finch] is..

double-brooded. *a* **1618** SYLVESTER *Maiden's Blush* 490 Upon his Camel's *double-bunched back. **1701** *Lond. Gaz.* No. 3691/4 A lightish Drabdeberry Coat *double Buttoned. **1387** TREVISA *Higden* (Rolls) I. 299 (Mätz.) Men..haueþ bocches vnder þe chyn iswolle and ibolled, as þey he were *doublechynned. **1922** R. LEIGHTON *Compl. Bk. Dog* xvii. 271 [The Cairn Terrier] must be *double-coated. **1935** *Discovery* July 190/2 Some very promising results have recently been shown by sponsors of the Brewster process, in which an imbibation printing of yellow is superposed on a toned double-coated film. **1958** T. L. J. BENTLEY in M. L. Hall *Newnes Complete Amat. Photogr.* vi. 91 With the double-coated films current in the mid-thirties acceptable prints could be obtained with camera exposures varying by as extreme a range as 2000 to 1. **1965** *Times* 30 Aug. 12/1 They become the first company to offer sheet steel coated both sides with a p.v.c. film. The double-coated steel is called Stelvetite 'R.'. **1967** KARCH & BUBER *Offset Processes* v. 192 The paper usually used for a flat is 80 lb. double-coated goldenrod stock. **1840** C. BRONTË *Let.* in Mrs. Gaskell *Life C.B.* (1857) I. 212 Recording all their sayings and doings in *double-columned close-printed pages. **1861** Double-columned [see COLUMNED *ppl. a.* 3]. **1959** *Brno Studies* I. 137 Quoted from double-columned cheap edition. **1937** *Burlington Mag.* May 258/2 The recent discovery in Shang-Yin tombs of *double-curved knives. *a* **1618** SYLVESTER *Wood-Mans Bear* xliv, That faire *double-doored port. **1837** *Double dotted [see DOTTED *ppl. a.* 3]. **1955** H. VAN THAL *Fanfare for E. Newman* v. 69 A frustrated counterpoint in jerky double-dotted rhythm. **1874** KNIGHT *Dict. Mech.*, **Double-ended Bolt*, a bolt having a screw-thread on each end. **1579** SPENSER *Sheph. Cal.* May 254 Deceitfull meaning is *double eyed. **1902** *Westm. Gaz.* 22 Oct. 12/1 A perfectly formed *double-flowered ox-eye daisy. **1552** HULOET, *Double-foted, *bipes*. **1667** MILTON *P.L.* II. 741 What thing thou art, thus *double-form'd. *Ibid.* XII. 144 The *double-founted stream Jordan. **1697** DRYDEN *Æneid* XII. 209 (Jod.) *Double-fronted Janus. **1965** *Bucks Examiner* 3 Sept. 13/2 (Advt.), A modern double-fronted Detached Bungalow. **1552** HULOET, *Double horned, *bicornium*. **1561** T. NORTON *Calvin's Inst.* Author's Pref., Their doublehorned argument. **1752** SIR J. HILL *Hist. Anim.* 567 (Jod.) The doublehorned rhinoceros. **1858** BRIGHT *Sp. For. Policy* 29 Oct., They write it down in *double-leaded columns. **1600** SURFLET *Countrie Farme* 504 Such as auncient Writers haue called *double-lived beasts, that is to say, such as liue either in or out of the water. *a* **1821** KEATS *Ode 'Bards of Passion & of Mirth'*, Bards..Double-lived in regions new! **1647** H. MORE *Song of Soul* Notes 160/1 *Dizoia*..*Double-livednesse. **1671** MILTON *Samson* 971 Fame if not double-faced is *double-mouthed. **1952** C. DAY LEWIS tr. *Virgil's Aeneid* IX. 203 The double-mouthed pipe tweedles for addicts. **1742** YOUNG *Night Thoughts* VII. 1273 Two Kinds of Life has *double-natur'd Man. **1589** R. HARVEY *Pl. Perc.* (1590) 12 In your *double pild veluet. **1833** J. RENNIE *Alph. Angling* 69 A *double-pointed spear. **1598** SYLVESTER *Du Bartas* II. ii. IV. *Columnes* 130 The Criticall and *double-sexed Seven..Which Three and Foure conteineth joyntly both. **1873** E. H. CLARKE *Sex in Educ.* 149 Double-sexed schools. **1565** GOLDING *Ovid's Met.* IV. (1593) 91 Their *double-shaped sonne. **1862** SIR H. HOLLAND *Ess., Mod. Chem.* 446 None, however, but a chemist can understand..the *doublesidedness of all the objects and relations involved in them. **1735** J. W. *Creed Expounded* II. ix. 253 Unless they are *double-sighted Folk, who see, what other People can discern nothing of. **1846** GEO. ELIOT tr. *Strauss's Life of Jesus* II. II. vi. §79. 139 What ..double-sighted beings, must Moses and Jesus have been, if they mixed with their cotemporaries without any real participation in their opinions and weaknesses. **1482** *Wardr. Acc.* in *Antiq. Rep.* (1807) I. 62, vij pair of shoon..*double soled. **1640–1** *Kirkcudbr. War-Comm. Min. Bk.* (1855) 149 Barnes' schoes, double-solled. **1956** F. C. AVIS *Bookman's Conc. Dict.* 87/2 **Double-spaced*, that style of typescript in which the inter-linear spacing equals the depth of a line of typescript. **1963** D. HEYES *12th of Never* (1964) i. 8 He then continued typing to the bottom of the double-spaced page. **1575–85** ABP. SANDYS *Serm.* (1841) 389 That triple-crowned beast, that *double-sworded tyrant. **1909** *Westm. Gaz.* 18 Mar. 4/1 The propeller is..made up of two portions of a *double-threaded screw. **1910** *Daily Chron.* 28 Jan. 6/3 'A Will in a Well' is a double-threaded mystery story. **1937** E. MUIR *Coll. Poems* (1960) 81 The double-threaded river That runs through life and death and life, Weaving one scene. **1887** C. B. GEORGE *40 Yrs. on Rail* v. 91 Accidents are reduced to a minimum, owing to good management and to the *double-tracked roads. **1967** *Times* 23 Oct. 9/4 The management should..stop spending precious capital on converting double tracked lines to a single track. **1839** Z. LEONARD *Adv.* (1904) 70 In a hurry, the one that was accustomed to the single trigger caught up the *double triggered gun. *a* **1734** NORTH *Lives* I. 178 A *double-visaged ministry, half-papist and half-fanatic. **1630** *Orders for River of Thames* in *Binnell's Descr. Thames* (1758) 66 No fisherman..shall..use or exercise any Flue, Trammel, *double-walled Net, or hooped Net. **1871** Double-walled [see WALLED *ppl. a.* 1 b]. **1903** *Dublin Rev.* July 169 The double-walled hydrogen vessel. **1965** G. MCINNES *Road to Gundagai* v. 82 It was an earthenware double-walled beehive filled with water. **1552** HULOET, *Dowble wynged, *bipennis*.

2. *Double* adj. in combination with sbs., forming **a.** adjectives or attributive phrases, in same sense as the parasynthetic compounds, as ***double-action***, ***-blast***, ***curve***, ***-cylinder***, ***-flow***, ***-furrow***, ***-motor***, ***-reduction***, ***-roller***, ***-shift***, ***-spiral***, ***-standard***, ***-zero***, etc.; **double-aspect theory**, etc. (see sense A. 6 above); **double-base powder, propellant** (see quots.); **double-beat sluice** (see quot.); **double-beat valve**, (*a*) a valve in a pump constructed to afford two openings for the water; (*b*) a device in a steam-engine consisting of two connected conical valves between which steam is admitted so as to equalize the upward and downward pressure; also called ***double-seat valve***; **double-bubble fuselage**, etc., the fuselage, etc., of a double-decked aircraft; **double-digit** orig. *U.S.*, represented numerically by two digits, i.e. between ten and ninety-nine inclusive, esp. as ***double-digit inflation***; **double-figure** = *double-digit* above; **double-gate table**, a gate-table with two hinged movable legs to support leaves; **double-pole switch** (*Electr.*) (see quot. 1940); **double-tone ink** (see quots.). **b.** substantives arising out of the absolute or elliptical use of those preceding, as DOUBLE-BARREL, -FACE, -HEAD, -LEAF, etc. **c.** substantives, as **double-man**, = DOUBLE *sb.* 2 c; **double-ripper, -runner** (*U.S.*), two sleds connected by a plank, used by boys for coasting down-hill; **double-trouble** (*U.S.*), a step of a rustic dance derived from the plantation negroes (*Cent. Dict.*).

1852 SEIDEL *Organ* 36 *Double or triple-action bellows. **1856** MRS. C. CLARKE tr. *Berlioz' Instrument.* 62 M. Erard invented..that mechanism which has given to instruments so constructed the name of double-action harps. **1879** W. JAMES in *Mind* IV. 330 The '*double-aspect' school postulate the blank form of 'One and the Same Fact'. **1909** *Hastings' Encycl. Relig. & Eth.* II. 757/1 Ward..discusses ..the Neo-Spinozism of the 'double-aspect' theory. **1931** G. F. STOUT *Mind & Matter* 82 This is the so-called double-aspect theory; according to it mind and matter are different sides or aspects of the same thing. **1960** *Discovery* Oct. 62/2 The much discussed 'double-aspect' hypothesis of mind and brain. **1951** W. LEY *Rockets, Missiles & Space Travel* vii. 172 The propelling charge in that rocket was a *double-base powder containing..nitrocellulose.. nitroglycerin..and diphenylamine added as a stabilizer. **1960** F. GAYNOR *Dict. Aerospace* 75 *Double-base propellant*, a solid propellant which consists largely of nitroglycerine and nitrocellulose. **1874** KNIGHT *Dict. Mech.* s.v., The *double-beat valve is extensively used in England for deep wells and for high lifts. **1931** F. M. DU-PLAT-TAYLOR *Reclam. Land fr. Sea* 72 Double-beat or compensated cylindrical sluices. **1832** G. R. PORTER *Porcelain & Gl.* ix. 227 The table..has fixed at its bottom a small *double-blast bellows. **1947** *Jrnl. R. Aeronaut. Soc.* LI. 142/1 The cottage-loaf design of hull—or the *double-bubble section as it applied to the landplane—was a very good form for the pressurised cabin. *Ibid.* 174/2 The Brabazon fuselage was a 16-ft. circle, and the Saunders-Roe boat had a beam of approximately 16 ft... The vices of the double-bubble fuselage did not then seem immediately apparent. **1959** J. L. NAYLER *Dict. Aeronaut. Engin.* 116 *Double-bubble fuselage*, a two-decker airliner (or fuselage) with a cross-sectional shape like a figure eight. **1927** PEAKE & FLEURE *Hunters & Artists* viii. 126 The '*double-curve' Ofnet skulls may..show us a stage in the evolution of broad-headedness. **1950** H. L. LORIMER *Homer & Monum.* v. 284 From about 600 onwards the double-curve bow appears in connexion with mythological or heroic beings. **1874** KNIGHT *Dict. Mech.*, *Double-cylinder Press..Double-cylinder Pump.. Double-cylinder Steam-engine. **1959** *Time* 31 Aug. 68 These three books were written by Shulman at the age of eight... Now Humorist Shulman, 40, has advanced into the *double-digit years. **1974** *National Observer* (U.S.) 15 June 6/1 Living with double-digit inflation has become a problem for professional economists and politicians as well as for the American consumer. **1986** *Daily Tel.* 17 June 12 Already many people in Britain have forgotten what life was like with double-digit inflation. **1966** *Sunday Times* 26 June 28/7 Doctors, judges, M.P.s, ministers and senior civil-servants, who have all had *double-figure rises. **1987** *Times* 8 Jan. 19/1 There were double-figure gains among many blue chips in the thin conditions. **1930** *Engineering* 15 Aug. 189/2 There is..a *double-flow low-pressure turbine in tandem with a high-pressure machine. **1940** *Chambers's Techn. Dict.* 260/2 *Double-flow turbine*, a turbine in which the working fluid enters at the middle of the length of the casing and flows axially towards each end. **1961** *Aeroplane* C. 394/1 Operational airline experience with the double-flow engine (this term is used here to cover both the British by-pass types and the U.S. and Russian turbofans) began just a year ago. **1807** VANCOUVER *Agric. Devon* (1813) 118 The *double-furrow plough..will plough two acres and a half per day. **1908** *Daily Report* 5 Sept. 8/2 A 3 ft. 6 in. oak *double-gate table. **1691** R. KIRK *Secr. Commw.* i. §3 (1893) 9 Some Men of that exalted Sight..have told me they have seen..a *Doubleman, or the Shape of some Man in two places. **1910** *Chambers's Jrnl.* 24 Dec. 55/2 A *double-motor aeroplane. **1920** R. E. NEALE *Whittaker's Electr. Engin. Pocket-Bk.* (ed. 4) 419 For the control of c.c. motors, *double-pole switches and fuses are commonly used. **1940** *Chambers's Techn. Dict.* 261/2 *Double-pole*, said of switches, circuit-breakers, etc. which can make or break a circuit on two poles simultaneously. **1951** *Archit. Rev.* CIX. 62/1 The two-meter unit for both power and lighting circuits has one 60 ampere switch and one 30 ampere double-pole switch. [**1922** *Encycl. Brit.* XXX. 950/1 The demands of large users of continuous-current power..are best met either by geared generators (steam turbines driving continuous-current generators through double helical reduction gearing)..or [etc.].] **1957** *Ibid.* XXI. 355/2 Later he [*sc.* Charles Parsons] followed this up by a '*double-reduction' gearing which admitted of a still greater difference in speed of rotation between the propeller and the turbine. **1962** *Economist* 10 Nov. 605/2 By re-rolling the plated steel—the double-reduction process—..American producers are making 'thin tin'. **1963** R. F. WEBB *Motorists' Dict.* 80 *Double reduction gears*, a method of increasing the number of gear ratios by the fitting of a second two-speed gearbox separated from the normal box. **1884** F. J. BRITTEN *Watch & Clockm.* 145 A *double roller escapement. **1883** *Harper's Mag.* Dec. 146/2 A large two-handed boy's sled—not what you call a *double-runner. **1884** *Manch. Exam.* 22 Feb. 5/2 Mines..worked on the *double-shift system. **1891** *Labour Commission* Gloss. s.v. *Shift*. The double or night shift system is that of working a pit both night and day, with two sets of hewers. **1928** PEAKE & FLEURE *Steppe & Sown* 96 *Double-spiral ornaments made of copper wire. **1867** J. LAING *Theory of Business* iv. 46 The *double-standard system..causes one of the two metals to be treated as bullion. **1963** *Times Lit. Suppl.* 29 Mar. 214/4 He was also a double-standard man. **1964** E. A. NIDA *Toward Sci. Transl.* viii. 158 The double-standard capacity of new literates who can decode oral messages with facility but whose ability to decode written messages is limited. **1904** MITCHELL & HEPWORTH *Inks* xi. 178 'Art shades'..are now much in vogue... A half-tone block printed in one of these inks,..appears as if produced by two printings. Such inks have been described..as **double-tone inks*. **1954** J. SOUTHWARD *Mod. Printing* (ed. 7) II. xix. 251 Doubletone inks are an adaptation of coloured inks designed for printing illustrations. These inks..impart the effect of more than one colour or shade. **1858** GREENER *Gunnery* 420 *Double-trigger revolving pistols. **1807–8** W. IRVING *Salmag.* (1824) 79 No Long-Island negro could shuffle you '*double-trouble'..more scientifically. **1914** E. POUND *Let.* 19 Jan. in *Lett. J. Joyce* (1966) II. 327 He has exactly twice as much sense as the common american editor, a sort of *double zero leaning toward the infinitesimal. **1964** A. WYKES *Gambling* ix. 214 The American double-zero wheel..*does* have a definite pattern.

3. Verbs formed from *double* adv. in comb. with verbs (or from *double* adj. with sbs.), with meaning 'to — doubly, to provide with double —s', as ***double-arm***, ***-bar***, ***-berth***, ***-board***, ***-bolt***, ***-charge***, ***-damn***, ***-darken***, ***-dike***, ***-ditch***, ***-dot***, ***-gild***, ***-glaze***, ***-hatch***, ***-load***, ***-man***, ***-moat***, ***-quickset***, ***-rack***, ***-refine***, ***-shade***, ***-trench***, ***-vantage***, etc. See also DOUBLE-BANK, -BITT, etc. **double-book** *v. trans.* and *intr.*, to make or accept two reservations, engagements, or applications for (a seat, room, etc.), esp. as an insurance against cancellation or failure of one of them (cf. OVERBOOK *v.*); to make simultaneous or overlapping appointments; hence ***double-booking*** *vbl. sb.*; **double-check** *v. trans.*, to check (something) twice, or in two ways, in order to minimize the chances of inaccuracy; **double-date** *v. intr.* (*U.S. colloq.*), to make or participate in a 'double date'; **double-declutch** *v. intr.*, see DECLUTCH *v.*; **double-dig** *v. trans.* (see quot.); so ***double-digging***; **double-dink** *Austral.* = DOUBLE-BANK *v.* 2; **double-fault** *v. intr.*, in Lawn Tennis and Squash Rackets, to serve two consecutive faults; hence ***double-faulter***; **double-iron** *v. trans.*, to shackle with irons on both legs (cf. *double-ironed* in 4); **double-shuffle** *v. intr.*, to perform a double shuffle (SHUFFLE *sb.* 5); **double-space** *v. trans.* (see *double-spaced* ((C. 1)).

1602 *How Choose a Good Wife* v. ii. in Hazl. *Dodsley* IX. 84 My uncles *double-bar their doors against me. *a* **1661** FULLER *Worthies* (1840) II. 272 He was double barred: first because an honest man..secondly because an Englishman. **1966** *Times* 27 June 10/3 Strike-bound vessels have been *double-berthed. **1874** *Rep. Vermont Board Agric.* II. 512 My plan was to *double board and cleat the main body of the barn, having a basement or cellar under the whole barn. **1748** RICHARDSON *Clarissa* (1811) IV. 54 She double-locked and *double-bolted herself in. **1970** *Times* 17 Aug. 5 Even when we *double-booked the rooms once and had to turn people away, they said 'Never mind, dear, we know it's not your fault.' **1976** *Milton Keynes Express* 4 June 18/4 Last year the show was advertised but the puppeteer had to call it off because he had double-booked. **1981** *Business Week* 7 Sept. 46/2 Some companies have already started to double-book cargo space with both NASA and the Paris-based ESA. **1983** *Economist* 6 Aug. 25/3 Clerks double-book their barristers in the hope that one of the cases will be settled before getting to court. **1978** *Aviation Week & Space Technol.* 24 July 70/1 Irresponsible passengers can well be expected to increase their *double-booking activities. **1984** *Computers & Electronics* Dec. 80/3 The calendar..alerts you to conflicts of double booking by filling in exclamation points in a disputed time slot. **1597** SHAKS. *2 Hen. IV*, v. iii. 129 Pistol, I will *double charge thee with Dignities. **1726** *Adv. Capt. R. Boyle* 24 Fired my Piece..being double charg'd. **1958** *Amateur Photogr.* 31 Dec. 2/2 (Advt.), You may..automatically *double-check your focus with your range-finder at the same time. **1969** E. LATHEN *When in Greece* ii. 13 For several hours, he and Leonard double-checked specifications. **1624** MIDDLETON *Game at Chess* II. ii, That would *double-damn him. **1656** TRAPP *Comm. Matt.* ii. 22 If Turks and Tartars shall be damned, debauched Christians shall be double-damned. **1897** G. B. SHAW *Let.* 7 Oct. (1965) 810 Damn the printer..blast him ..double-damn him! **18..** LOWELL *To G. W. Curtis* (Cent.) Such natures *double-darken gloomy skies. **1946** P. GOODIN *Clementine* xxi. 194 We'll have lots of fun—we'll be *double-dating! **1951** J. D. SALINGER *Catcher in Rye* vi. 50 I'd double-dated with that bastard a couple of times. *Ibid.* vii. 60 We once double-dated, in Ed Banky's car, and Stradlater was in the back, with his date, and I was in the front, with mine. **1952** H. WAUGH *Last seen Wearing* (1953) 12 Marlene and Peggy were double-dating that night with a couple of boys from Carlton College. **1933** *Jrnl. R. Hort. Soc.* LVIII. I. 117 The soil should be *double dug i.e. two spades deep. **1842** *Double digging [see BASTARD *a.* 8]. **1470–85** MALORY *Arthur* VII. xv, *Double dyked with ful warly wallis. **1941** BAKER *Dict. Austral. Slang*, *Double dink. **1942** E. LANGLEY *Pea Pickers* (1958) 26 We went double dinking on his white mare. *c* **1510** *Little Geste of Robin Hood* in Arb. *Garner* VI. 453 *Double ditched it was about. **1897** *Outing* (U.S.) XXIX. 377/2 Two mink had *double-dotted the course of the brook. **1921** A. W. MYERS *20 Yrs. Lawn Tennis* 136 Dixon *double-faulted in the eleventh game and lost it. **1922** W. T. TILDEN *It's All in the Game* 118 Vincey took the first point on Dave's net but double-faulted away the next. **1927** *Daily Express* 6 June 1 Tilden..double faulted. **1961** *Times* 17 Jan. 14/7 At 8—all there came five empty hands with Amin, put out off the wood, getting in again and then double-faulting above the line. **1921** A. W. MYERS *20 Yrs. Lawn Tennis* 78 The brilliant server and smasher became a *double-faulter and a snatcher at lobs. **1969** J. LOWRIE *Heating & Insulation* i. 17/1 *Double glaze French doors and other glazed doors in the same way as windows. **1977** *New Scientist* 3 Mar. 529/2 It's no good saying they ought to insulate, double glaze and buy more coal. **1566** in W. H. Turner *Select. Rec. Oxford* 314 A cup of silver, *double-gilt. **1597** SHAKS. *2 Hen. IV*, IV. v. 129 England shall double gild his treble guilt. **1704** SWIFT *Batt. Bks.* Misc. (1711) 244 The Clasps were of Silver double-gilt. **1633** SHIRLEY *Bird in Cage* III. iii, That superfluous *double-hatched rapier. **1650** FULLER *Pisgah* I. xv. 47 Places which have both flags and Asterisks..are as I may say doublehatcht with uncertainty. **1897** P. WARUNG *Tales Old Régime* 42 Here, guard! *double-iron this man. **1627** CAPT. SMITH *Seaman's Gram.* xii. 56 If they be *double-manned, that is, to haue twise so many men as would saile her. **1859** F. A. GRIFFITHS *Artil. Man.* (1862) 127 The [ropes] are double manned. **1633** G. HERBERT *Temple, Brit. Ch.* x, To *double-moat thee with his grace. **1523** FITZHERB. *Husb.* §127 *Double quyke-set it, and dyche it. *a* **1618** SYLVESTER *Spectacles* xvii, *Double-racked with two divers Tortures. **1671** MILTON *P.R.* I. 500 Now began Night..to *double-shade The Desert. **1909** M. B. SAUNDERS *Litany Lane* I. i, Toeing, tipping, *double-shuffling, hopping. **1922** JOYCE *Ulysses* 513 He.. doubleshuffles off comically. **1958** J. KERR *Please don't eat Daisies* 60 The necessity for *double-spacing the script. **1631** WEEVER *Anc. Fun. Mon.* 655 The Mannor house hath beene *double trenched. **1768** STERNE *Sent. Journ.* (1778) II. 25 The cage..was twisted and *double-twisted so fast with wire. *c* **1600** SHAKS. *Sonn.* lxxxviii, Doing thee vantage, *double-vantage me.

4. *Double* adv. in comb.: **a.** with pa. pples. or ppl. adjs., as ***double-based***, ***-distilled***, ***-glazed***, ***-lanted***, ***-loaded***, ***loathed***, ***-refined***, ***-stitched***, ***-stored***, etc.; **double-cut**, of a file = CROSS-CUT *a.* 2; **double-hung** (see quot.); **double-ironed**, loaded with irons or fetters on both legs; **double-milled**, of cloth, milled or fulled twice to make it closer and thicker; **double-screened** (see quot. 1921); **double-sided**, (*a*) that can be or has been used on both sides, cf. DOUBLE-FACED *a.* 1 c; (*b*) = DOUBLE-FACED *a.* 1; **double-struck**, of a coin or medal, showing a double impression owing to having been accidentally shifted while being struck; **double-sunk**, **double-worked** (see quots.). **b.** with pres. pples. or ppl. adjs., as ***double-biting***, ***-clasping***, ***-flowering***, ***-refracting***, ***-running***, ***-seeing***, ***-shining***, etc. **c.** with adjectives, as ***double-concave***, ***-convex***, ***-dark***, ***-double***, ***-fatal***, ***fitché***, ***-treble***, etc. **d.** with agent-nouns, as **double-breather**, an animal that breathes through two nostrils; **double-goer** = DOUBLE-GANGER.

1954 K. W. GATLAND *Devel. Guided Missile* (ed. 2) i. 34 Most of these, like cordite and ballistite, contain nitroglycerine—in which case they are known as '*double-based' propellants. **1962** SIMPSON & RICHARDS *Junction Transistors* viii. 192 The uni-junction transistor or double-based diode. **1700** DRYDEN *Palamon & A.* III. 480 His *double-biting axe, and beamy spear. **1725** POPE *Odyss.* XIX. 264 On his breast, The *double-clasping gold the King confest. **1874** KNIGHT *Dict. Mech.*, **Double-concave Lens*, a lens both of whose faces are concave. **1693** E. HALLEY in *Phil. Trans.* XVII. 965 If the Lens be *Double-Convex. **1865** TYLOR *Early Hist. Man.* viii. 199 A double-convex cross section. **1633** G. HERBERT *Temple, Sacrifice* xxxv, As Moses face was vailed, so is mine, Lest on their *double-dark souls either shine. **1705** *Lond. Gaz.* No. 4132/3 *Double Distill'd Spanish Brandy. **1845** DISRAELI *Sybil* (1863) 280 Which made him hate Egremont with double-distill'd virulence. *a* **1618** SYLVESTER *Tobacco Battered* 749 In nappy Ale, and *double-double-Beer. **1782** HERSCHEL in *Phil. Trans.* LXXII. 112 Not only double-stars, but.. double-double. **1869** DUNKIN *Midn. Sky* 160 Epsilon Lyrae is..a double-double star. **1593** SHAKS. *Rich. II*, III. ii. 117 Their Bowes Of *double fatall Eugh. **1727–51** CHAMBERS *Cycl.* s.v., A cross is denominated *double fiché, when the extremities are pointed at each angle; that is, when each extremity has two points. **1883** *Harper's Mag.* Apr. 726/1 The pure white blossoms of a *double-flowering cherry. **1910** *Westm. Gaz.* 26 Mar. 6/2 Side windows and skylights, all of which are *double-glazed, in order..to guard against changes of temperature. **1939** *Archit. Rev.* LXXXVI. 29 The double-glazed windows light the administrative offices. **1956** *Nature* 21 Jan. 111/2 Much can be done by the suitable design of houses to reduce the artificial heat load required, by double-glazed windows. **1824** *Blackw. Mag.* XVI. 57 The horrible notion of the *double-goer. **1823** P. NICHOLSON *Pract. Build.* 584/2 **Double-hung sashes*..those of which the window contains two, and each moveable by means of weights and lines. **1812** *Examiner* 23 Nov. 752/2 He has been *double ironed and handcuffed. **1630** *Tinker of Turvey* Ep. Ded., I have drunke *double-lanted Ale, and single-lanted. **1607** TOURNEUR *Rev. Trag.* I. ii. Wks. 1878 II. 18 Her *double-loathed Lord. **1831** CARLYLE *Sart. Res.* I. ix. Girt with thick *double-milled kerseys. **1631** WEEVER *Anc. Fun. Mon.* 104 Religion is *double refined, pure and spotlesse without ceremonie. **1791** T. JEFFERSON in *Harper's Mag.* Mar. (1885) 535/1 Double refined maple sugar. **1818** HAZLITT *Eng. Poets* iv. (1870) 97 A double-refined essence of wit. **1873** TYNDALL *Lect. on Light* iii. 120 The *double refracting spar. **1931** L. F. PESEL *Eng. Embroidery* I. 20 Such linens are not really satisfactory, and make this *double-running embroidery difficult. **1963** *Times* 1 June 11/7 The early double-running stitch gradually being augmented by coral-stitch, satin-stitch [etc.]. **1905** *Daily Chron.* 4 May, *Double-screened Nuts. **1921** C. E. EVANS *Hints Coal Buyers* (ed. 2) 56 Double Screened coal, indicates coal that has been screened at the Colliery, and screened also over two open screens in the spout at the Dock Tip, that is to say, 'Double Screened' at time of shipment. **1580** SIDNEY *Arcadia* (1622) 92 To see the sports of *double-shining day. **1907** *Captain* XVIII. p. xxvii (Advt.), The Best Disc Records are *Double-sided $8\frac{1}{4}$ in. **1934** *Mind* XLIII. 270 Christian philosophy is undeniably double-sided, exhibiting a rational and a religious aspect. **1936** *Burlington Mag.* Sept. 136/1 The double-sided panel from Valenciennes. **1956** *Nature* 25 Feb. 391/1 A piece of double-sided corrugated paper. **1725** DE FOE *Voy. round World* (1840) 68 We were over-manned and *double-stored. **1884** F. J. BRITTEN *Watch & Clockm.* 89 [A] *Double Sunk Dial ..[is] a dial with recesses for the hour hand and seconds hand. **1781** HERSCHEL in *Phil. Trans.* LXXII. 124 σ Orionis ..A *double-treble star, or two sets of treble stars. **18..** P. BARRY *Fruit Garden* 100 (Cent.) When we graft or bud a tree already budded or grafted, we call it *double-worked.

double ('dʌb(ə)l), *sb.* Forms: see prec. [In branch I, ellipt. use of DOUBLE *a.*; in branch II, noun of action from DOUBLE *v.*]

I. 1. A double quantity; twice as much or many; a number or magnitude multiplied by two.

a **1300** *Cursor M.* 7644 (Gött.) Dauid him þe doubil broght. **1393** GOWER *Conf.* I. 170 He saith that other have shall The double of that his felawe axeth. *c* **1430** *Art of Nombryng* (E.E.T.S.) 7 If thow truly double the halfis and truly half the doubles. *c* **1500** *Three Kings' Sons* (E.E.T.S.) 76 There were moo slayn of them by double than they were that assailed them. **1611** BIBLE *Isa.* lxi. 7 In their land they shal possesse the double. **1726** tr. *Gregory's Astron.* I. 350 The Arcs GL, LH..respectively the doubles of AE, EB. **1875** JOWETT *Plato* (ed. 2) I. 485 Ten, which is the double of five.

2. A thing that is an exact repetition of another. †**a.** A duplicate, copy, transcript (*of* a writing). *Obs.* (chiefly *Sc.*)

1543 *Sc. Acts Mary* (1814) 436 (Jam.) The auctentik dowble of thir our souerain ladeis lettrez of summondis. **1628** SIR R. BOYLE *Diary* in *Lismore Papers* (1886) II. 259 My laste will and testament, with a dowble therof, both signed. **1752** J. LOUTHIAN *Form of Process* (ed. 2) 60 Of which Warrant, the Messenger..is..ordained to give a just Double..to the Prisoner himself.

b. A counterpart; an image, or exact copy (of a thing or person). **c.** *spec.* The apparition of a living person; a wraith, fetch.

1798 *Geraldina* II. 189 Lady Withers, who is this Lady's double, and attends her constantly. **1818** TODD, *Double*..4. In modern times, used for resemblance; as, his or her double, meaning another person extremely like the party. **1826** DISRAELI *Viv. Grey* III. v, I fancy that in this mysterious..woman, I have met a kind of double of myself. **1827** HONE *Every-Day Bk.* II. 1012 The fetch or double of the Göttingen student. **1871** PROCTOR *Light Sc.* 294 The appearance of a double or 'fetch' has ever been held..to signify approaching death.

†**d.** *pl.* Two of the same kind; twins. *Obs.*

1413 *Pilgr. Sowle* (Caxton 1483) v. x. 100 Gemini that ben cleped twynnes or doubles.

3. Technical senses.

†**a.** A step in dancing (*obs.*). **b.** *Bell-ringing.* A 'change' in which two pairs of bells change places. **c.** Double-headed shot, consisting of two balls joined (cf. BAR-SHOT). **d.** Name of a small size of roofing slates. **e.** Name of a size of sheet-iron. **f.** A kind of basket for fish: see quot. **g.** *pl.* A kind of thick narrow black ribbons for shoe-strings. (Caulfeild and Saward *Dict. Needlework* (1882) 156/2.) **h.** *Printing.* An accidental duplication of a word or passage. **i.** *Mil.* A double pace: see DOUBLE *a.* 4 *c.* Esp. in phr. ***at the double***. Also *fig.* **j.** *Whist.* A game (at short whist) in which one side scores five before the other has scored three; (at long whist) in which one side makes ten and the other none; the stake in such case being doubled. **k.** *Dominoes.* A piece bearing the same number of pips on each half. **l.** *Lawn Tennis.* A game played by two players on each side; also two faults in succession. **m.** An actor or singer who takes two parts in the same piece; also an understudy or substitute. **n.** In many elliptical uses: e.g. = *double agent, bed, bedroom, event, flower, game, letter, line, snipe, star*, in which the sense is supplied by the context; also two 'tots' of whisky, two centuries scored by a batsman in one match. **o.** = *double feast* (see FEAST *sb.* 1 b). **p.** *Mus.* = VARIATION 14. **q.** *Bridge.* A call by a bidder's opponent involving doubling of the score for tricks bid and made with a bonus to the declarer if he makes overtricks and an increase of the penalty if he fails to make his contract. **r.** Double-screened coal. **s.** *Darts.* A throw on the narrow space enclosed by the two outer circles of a dart-board; the space itself.

a. **1531** ELYOT *Gov.* I. xxv, A double in daunsinge is compacte of the nombre of thre.

b. **1684** R. H. *School Recreat.* 93 Another Way of Ringing Twenty Four Changes, Doubles and Singles on Four Bells. **1880** in Grove *Dict. Mus.* I. 460.

c. **1707** *Lond. Gaz.* No. 4380/2 We gave him..our Broadside with Double and Round. **1726** *Adv. Capt. R. Boyle* 167 Firing our double and round, which kill'd 'em above fifty men.

d. **1823** P. NICHOLSON *Pract. Build.* 396 The Doubles are so called from their small size. **1876** GWILT *Encycl. Archit.* §2211*c*, Table of the Names and usual Sizes of Slates. Doubles, 13 × 10 [inches]. Ditto, 13 × 7.

e. **1887** *Daily News* 20 June 2/6 Iron sheets are £6 10*s.* for superior merchant doubles..galvanising doubles may be had at £6.

f. **1859** SALA *Tw. round Clock* (1861) 16 The 'doubles' of plaice, soles, haddock..A 'double' is an oblong basket tapering to the bottom, and containing from three to four dozen of fish.

g. **1858** SIMMONDS *Dict. Trade* 131/1 Galloon and double, a kind of silk material for shoe ties and binding.

h. **1706** PHILLIPS (ed. Kersey), *Double* (a Term in Printing) the mistake of a Compositor, that sets the same thing twice. **1784** FRANKLIN in *Ann. Reg.* Chron. (1817) 389 The outs, and doubles..are not easy to be corrected.

i. **1860** RUSSELL *Diary in India* II. 329 (Hoppe) The men cheering, broke out into a double, and at last into a regular race. **1865** *Chambers's Jrnl.* 213/1 Intellect not only marches, but marches at the 'double'. *Ibid.* 470/1 Ellsworth detailed twenty men.., and went at 'the double' down Pennsylvania Avenue. **1869** E. A. PARKES *Pract. Hygiene* (ed. 3) 393 The 'double' is never continued very long; it is stopped at the option of the commanding officer. **1883** *Army Regulations* II. x. 242 A certain number of movements are to be performed at each drill at 'the double'. **1961** NEW ENG. BIBLE *Acts* xxi. 32 He immediately took a force of soldiers with their centurions and came down on the rioters at the double.

j. **1838** DICKENS *O. Twist* xxv, That's two doubles and the rub. **1870** HARDY & WARE *Mod. Hoyle* 30 (Whist).

k. **1870** HARDY & WARE *Mod. Hoyle* 92 (Dominoes), The person holding the highest double has the 'pose' or 'down'.

l. **1894** *Times* 29 May 11/2 Lawn Tennis..yesterday, the singles competition..was played..The doubles will be played to-day.

m. **1808** S. W. RYLEY *Itinerant* I. iv. 89 When the company is *thin*, and *one* actor is obliged to do *two* parts, we call that a *double*. **1818** *Sporting Mag.* II. 14/1 It would be impossible to find what the players call '*a double*' for Mr. Stephen Kemble. **1880** E. PROUT in Grove *Dict. Mus.* I. 460 *Doubles*..singers who under-study a part in a vocal work, so as to replace the regular performer in case of need. **1891** FARMER *Slang*, *Double*..an actor playing two parts in the same piece. **1928** *Sunday Express* 8 Apr. 4 Two 'doubles' were employed..for some small scenes in which Miss Thorndike..could not appear. **1960** O. SKILBECK *Film & TV Working Terms* 42 *Double*, one who impersonates an artist (usually the star) in a shot either because of danger, or because they have superior ability in some required form.

n. **1576** FLEMING *Panopl. Epist.* 401 Brawling and wrangling..about a vowell, about a consonant, about a liquide: about a double. **1845** *Ainsworth's Mag.* VIII. 213 A very gentlemanly [Londoner]..armed with one of Purdey's first-rate doubles [*sc.* guns]. **1873** BENNETT & CAVENDISH *Billiards* 107 Doubles are seldom played for at Billiards. **1878** NEWCOMB *Pop. Astron.* IV. i. 436 Those [stars] which are catalogued as doubles. **1883** *Pall Mall G.* 15 Oct. 1/2 The doubles are charged..8*d.* a night, or 4*s.* a week. **1883** SUTTON *Cult. Veget. & Flowers* (1892) 271 Frost will not hurt the single varieties, but the doubles will not.. endure..a severe winter. **1890** C. A. YOUNG *Elem. Astron.* vi. §207 It was discovered that the line is really a close double, one of its components being due to iron, while the other is due to some unknown gaseous element. **1891** N. GOULD *Double Event* xxvi, Messrs Isaacs and Moses..were always ready to lay the double. *Ibid.*, If he loses the Derby we may go for a recovery in the cup. But..Ike is confident he will win the double. **1902** *Harmsworth London Mag.* June 438/2 The men who play both cricket and football well..the best 'first-class doubles' who were at Oxford or Cambridge. **1918** E. WALLACE *Down Under Donovan* xvi. 210 Mr. John President may yet pull off a double. **1920** *Field* 2 Oct. 488/2 There were several 'doubles' (a fish on each of the two hooks used on the line) of red gurnet and bream. **1920** G. BURRARD *Notes on Sporting Rifles* 33 A hammerless ejector double rifle is the best and quickest to reload... Next come hammerless non-ejectors, and then hammer rifles, but a double is a *sine qua non.* **1921** *Spectator* 19 Mar. 357/1 A few snipe rose. We got four of them, two being 'doubles'. **1922** J. SYRETT *Alf* 99 'You've 'ad a lot of doubles to-night, Mr. Powell,' Flo remarked... 'Don't want to go 'ome screwed again to-night, does yer?' **1929** *Star* 21 Aug. 17/1 When he reached his second hundred of the match, for no batsman before has twice done the 'double' in Test Matches. **1931** *Times* 16 Mar. 2/7 Large doubles [*sc.* bedrooms] now available. **1951** KOESTLER *Age of Longing* II. v. 264 Georges would..send him another double on the house. **1953** WODEHOUSE *Ring for Jeeves* i. 16 A double, dear lady, is when you back a horse in one race and if it wins, put the proceeds on another horse in another race. **1957** A. GRIMBLE *Return to Islands* iii. 62 Her chance of pulling off the 'double', which is to say, first the miracle of her homing, and then the crowning marvel of her safe entry into harbour. **1959** 'M. DERBY' *Tigress* i. 18 Keep an eye on her. Start off by assuming that she *is* a double. **1963** *New Yorker* 29 June 46/3 (Advt.), The famous hotel Astor Singles from $9, doubles from $14. **1969** 'A. HALL' *Striker Portfolio* viii. 93 Being not only a potential defector but a double, he had broken down. **1971** 'A. GARVE' *Late Bill Smith* i. 34 We've done very well to be left with only two singles and two doubles. That's if they all embark, of course.

o. *c* **1690** in *Month* (1882) Jan. 122 And his feast kept as a duble annually upon yᵉ 2nd of Octobre. **1759** CHALLONER *Let.* 4 May in E. H. Burton *Life* (1909) II. xxiii. 7 He..will come over to receive his consecration here: and therefore I should be obliged to you if you would obtain for him..a license to have this performed on any *double.* **1763** *Divine Office for Laity* IV. 229 The Transfiguration of our Lord. A greater Double. **1850** *Vesper Bk.* (Burns & Oates) Pref. 12 Doubles and semi-doubles have First and Second Vespers. **1885** *Cath. Dict.* (ed. 3) s.v. *Feast*, Feasts are divided, according to their rank, into doubles, semi-doubles, simples, etc.

p. **1806** BUSBY *Dict. Mus.* (ed. 2) *Double*, a word which in the old music carries the same sense as that which we now give to the term *variation.* **1962** *Listener* 26 July 153/2 'Ornamental variations' disappoint us when, as in Couperin's airs with 'doubles', the embroidering fantasy seems less developed than in previous work.

q. **1903** in 'L. Hoffmann' *Card & Table Games* (ed. 3) 276 Something fresh is always cropping up; owing, perhaps, to the Declaration or to the Double. **1905**, **1927** [see DECLARER 3 b]. **1958** *Listener* 2 Oct. 541/2 North's double conventionally asked his partner to make some unlikely lead.

r. **1931** *Times* 16 Mar. 19/7 Lanarkshire [coal]..trebles.. doubles..singles.

s. **1935** *Encycl. Sports* 221 Victory goes to the player who reduces his total exactly to nothing with a 'double'. **1936** R. CROFT-COOKE *Darts* vi. 36 *Double Top*, 40, of course, i.e. double 20. Many players..start on the double 20, score on the treble, and leave themselves the double on which to get out. **1959** *Chambers's Encycl.* IV. 381/1 The players must generally begin and finish on a double.

4. †**a.** A small copper coin (value $\frac{1}{6}$ of a sou) formerly current in France. **b.** A small copper coin current in Guernsey, value $\frac{1}{8}$ of a penny.

1586 T. B. *La Primaud. Fr. Acad.* (1589) 336 Socrates.. sent him word, that a measure of flower was sold in Athens for a Double, and that water cost nothing. **1687** A. Lovell tr. *Bergerac's Com. Hist.* I. 35 Most of them throwing a Double upon my Handkerchief. **1862** Ansted *Channel Isl.* IV. App. A. (ed. 2) 563 Copper coinage in Guernsey.. consisting of pence, half pence, farthings (called two doubles), and eighths of a penny (called one double).

II. 5. A fold; a folded piece of stuff. ? *Obs.*

1602 Marston *Ant. & Mel.* II. Wks. 1856 I. 28 Rowled up in seaven-fould doubles Of plagues. **1761** Sterne *Tr. Shandy* III. xiv, Mantles..with large flowing folds and doubles. **1784** Darwin in *Phil. Trans.* LXXV. 3 Another leaden ring..with some doubles of flannel placed under it.

6. A sharp turn in running, as of a hunted hare; also, of a river; *fig.* an evasive turn or shift in action, argument, etc. ***to give* (one) *the double***: to give the slip, evade by stratagem. Slang phr. ***to come the double***, to act in a treacherous or evasive manner; ***to put a double on*** (a person), to double-cross. See also quot. 1914.

1592 Shaks. *Ven. & Ad.* 682 With what care he [the hare] cranks and crosses, with a thousand doubles. *a* **1625** Fletcher *Woman's Prize* III. iv, All their arch-villanies and all their dobles, Which are more than a hunted Hare ere thought on. **1751** Johnson *Rambler* No. 96 ¶14 The quick retreats and active doubles which Falsehood always practised. **1813** Col. Hawker *Diary* (1893) I. 79 A fellow who had tipped the double to some bailiffs. **1820** Scott *Monast.* v, At every double of the river the shadows.. obscured the eastern bank. **1888** 'R. Boldrewood' *Robbery under Arms* II. xiii. 209, I didn't know myself that your Kate had come the double on you. **1914** Jackson & Hellyer *Vocab. Criminal Slang* 29 *Double*, a conspiracy to deceive or defraud a victim; the 'double-cross'. Example: He got the double. **1923** E. Wallace *Missing Million* xvii. 143 And I ask you..if you would think a girl who could write as this young lady wrote to me, would put a double on me as she did.

double ('dʌb(ə)l), *v.* Forms: see double *a.* [ME. *dublen, doblen, doublen*, a. OF. *dubler, dobler, doubler*, = Pr., Sp. *doblar*, It. *doppiare*:—L. *duplāre* (less common = *duplicāre*) to double, fold up, f. *dupl-us* double.]

1. a. *trans.* To make double; to make twice as many, as much, or as great; to increase or enlarge twofold; to multiply by two; to put two in place of one, as ***to double a letter*** in spelling.

c **1290** *St. Brandan* 602 in *S. Eng. Leg.* I. 236 We wolleþ þeos six dawes doubli al is wo. *c* **1385** Chaucer *L.G.W.* Prol. 522 Hire grete bounte doubelyth hire renoun. *c* **1425** *Craft Nombrynge* (E.E.T.S.) 13 Begyn at the lyft side, and doubulle 2. þat wel be 4. **1522** More *De quat. Noviss.* Wks. 78/2 He had leuer double his own payn. **1611** Bible *Rev.* xviii. 6 Double vnto her double according to her workes. **1696** Whiston *The. Earth* III. (1722) 247 Mankind do double themselves in about 360 or 370 years. **1724** De Foe *Mem. Cavalier* (1840) 103, I doubled my pace. **1825** J. Nicholson *Operat. Mechanic* 4 If either its weight or its velocity be doubled, its momentum will be likewise doubled. **1871** Roby *Lat. Gram.* I. v. 22 To denote the length of a vowel..(1) They doubled the vowel. **1875** Jowett *Plato* (ed. 2) V. 136 Ignorance doubled by conceit of knowledge.

b. *absol.* (In quot., to double the stakes.)

1669 Dryden *Tyrannic Love* III. i. Wks. 1883 III. 412 I am resolved to double till I win.

c. To amount to twice as much as.

1605 Shaks. *Lear* II. iv. 262 Thy fifty yet doth double fiue and twenty. **1666** Dryden *Ann Mirab.* cxix, The adverse fleet, Still doubling ours. **1806** *Naval Chron.* XV. 328 A number doubling that which she was calculated to carry. **1864** Tennyson *Aylmer's F.* 81 When his date Doubled her own.

d. *Mus.* To add the same note in a higher or lower octave to (a note of melody or harmony).

1731 Keller *Thorow-Bass* in Holder *Harmony* 192 On.. any..Sharp or Flat Note out of the Key, you double the 8th. **1877** Stainer *Harmony* vii. §92 The minor seventh should not be doubled. **1880** P. David in Grove *Dict. Mus.* I. 458 [The double-bass] often doubles in the lower octave the bass of the harmony.

e. ***to double a part***: to act as the double of or substitute for (another player); to play two parts in the same piece; also *fig.* Also *absol.*, to play two parts. In extended use, to become or act as a double agent (cf. double *a.* 6 and *sb.* 3 n).

1800 Mrs. Hervey *Mourtray Fam.* I. 33 When she attempted to double the part of her mother, she..failed in playing the great or the agreeable lady. **1801** *Paris as it was* II. xli. 60 Laforêt who (as the French express it), doubles Lainez, that is, performs the same characters in his absence. **1875** Lowell *Spenser* Prose Wks. 1890 IV. 319 Spenser made all his characters double their parts. **1894** *Times* 6 Mar. 4/3 Miss Rosa Green 'doubled the parts' of Martha and Siebel. **1918** H. Croy *How Motion Pictures are Made* v. 124 A young man, doubling for a leading lady in a bit of hazardous fire jumping. **1928** *Daily Express* 8 Apr. 4 Picturegoers should look out for the portions of the film in which Miss Thorndike was 'doubled' by other actresses. **1933** P. Godfrey *Back-Stage* ii. 24 The various Scottish thanes have to double and treble—soldiers, murderers, messengers, and apparitions. **1949** G. B. Shaw *Sixteen Self Sketches* vii. 39 The appointment of art critic to The World, which Archer was for the moment doubling with his regular function of dramatic critic, was transferred to me. **1959** *Times* 8 June 13/3 The umbrella, which can double as a sunshade. **1962** *Listener* 8 Mar. 253/1 His adventures at a small German court are 'doubled' and interwoven with the autobiography of a professor's cat. **1965** R. Segal *Crisis of India* iv. 204 Travelling traders, who frequently doubled as money-lenders and so could dictate terms to their debtors. **1968** 'B. Mather' *Springers* xv. 160, I was already in a Red cell. I doubled for the Russians right from the beginning.

f. *Chess. trans.* To place two pawns or two rooks one behind the other on the same file.

1750 'A. D. Philidor' *Chess Analysed* 4 He chuses rather to let you take his (Bishop)..tho' he suffers to have his Knight's Pawn doubled by it. **1806** *Chess made Easy* (ed. 5) 71 One must always strive to hinder the adversary from doubling his rooks. **1891** R. B. Swinton *Chess for Beginners* ix. 72 Sometimes it is worth while to effect an exchange of pieces, only to cause your opponent to double his Pawns in taking one of yours. **1958** H. Golombek *Instructions to Young Chess Players* ii. 18 When two pawns of the same colour are in the same file they are called 'doubled'.

g. *Bridge. trans.* and *intr.* To declare a double (double *sb.* 3 q).

1894 'Boaz' *Pocket Guide to Bridge* 6 The effect of doubling is that the value of each trick is doubled. **1898** 'L. Hoffmann' *Card & Table Games* (ed. 2) I. 312 The main elements of novelty in Bridge..may be classed under the following heads:—..3. Licence to each party alternately to double and re-double the normal value of tricks. **1902** J. B. Elwell *Bridge* 111 *Going over*... The effect of 'over', 'over', etc., is that the value of each trick point is doubled, quadrupled, etc. **1906** *Bridge Pocket Book* 13 After the trump declaration has been made by the dealer or his partner, their adversaries have the right to double. **1909** *Strand Mag.* Jan. 71/2 The fourth player will be in a fine position, either to double the forced call or to overcall it. **1912** F. Irwin *Fine Pts. Auction Bridge* 56 You can either double the two hearts or go to 'two no-trumps'. **1928** A. Waugh *Nor Many Waters* ii. 74, I called, 'Three No Trumps.' And the man on my left doubled. **1965** *Listener* 20 May 758/2 North was hoping to play in Two Hearts doubled.

h. *intr.* To play two (or more) musical instruments. So ***to double* (*on*)**: to play (an instrument) in addition to one's main instrument.

1927 *Melody Maker* May 421/1 Fred Livingstone.. belongs to the class that doubles on both saxophones and clarinet. *Ibid.* June 551/3 Miss Ivy Read leads on the piano and is supported by Miss P. Pax (violin), Miss Brightwell (banjo doubling saxophone) and Miss Sibruk (drums doubling 'cello). **1934** S. R. Nelson *All about Jazz* iii. 68 It is usual to find only one [violin] in the smaller bands, except where the saxophones both double on this instrument. **1955** L. Feather *Encycl. Jazz* ii. 64 A clarinetist would double on tenor sax.

2. a. *intr.* (for *refl.*) To become twice as much or many as before; to increase twofold.

c **1320** *Cast. Love* 1199 Þi joye doublede an hondrut folde. **1592** Shaks. *Ven. & Ad.* 521 Say, for non-payment that the debt should double. **1684–90** Burnet *Th. Earth* (J.) 'Tis observed in particular nations, that within the space of three hundred years..the number of men double. **1882** Pebody *Eng. Journalism* xix. 145 The circulation doubled, trebled, quadrupled.

b. Of flowers: To become double (see double *a.* 1 d).

1882 Vines *Sachs' Bot.* 542 When the stamens become transformed into petals (by the so-called 'doubling' of the flower). **1888** G. Henslow *Floral Struct.* 299 The starved state of the plants causes doubling.

†**3. a.** *trans.* To repeat or reiterate; to redouble; to make a copy or duplicate of (*Sc.*) *Obs.*

c **1380** Wyclif *Sel. Wks.* III. 84 Crist techiþ..to have oure wordis þus, ȝhe, ȝhe, and nai, nay..þere he doubliþ his wordis, as if he wolde seie,—ȝif ȝe seie ȝhe in ȝoure soule, seie ȝhe wiþ ȝoure mouþ. **1565** Jewel *Repl. Harding* (1611) 334 Thus he saith, and doubleth, and repeateth the same. *c* **1645** Howell *Lett.* (1650) I. 28 Pulling out the fatal steel, he doubled his thrust. *a* **1662** R. Baillie *Lett.* (1775) I. 174 (Jam.) Some of the advertisement I have caused double. **1718** *Wodrow Corr.* (1843) II. 406 I'll cause double over what account I have insert..and send up to you. **1805** Scott *Last Minstr.* I. xxvii, Cliffs, doubling, on their echoes borne, The terrors of the robber's horn.

†**b.** *intr.* or *absol.* To speak with repetition of sounds. *Obs. rare.*

1382 Wyclif *2 Sam.* iii. 34 And doublynge togidre [*congeminantes*] al the people wept upon hym. **1593** Shaks. *2 Hen. VI*, II. iii. 94 This knaues tongue begins to double. **1621** [see doubling *ppl. a.* 1].

4. *Mil.* **a.** *trans.* To increase (ranks or files) to twice their length by marching other ranks or files up into them. (The latter may also be the object.)

b. *intr.* Of ranks or files: To march up into the other ranks or files so as to double them.

1598 Barret *Theor. Warres* III. i. 37 What meane you by doubling your ranke and file? **1635** Barriffe *Mil. Discip.* xii. (1643) 45 In the doubling of Ranks, the even Ranks are to double into the odde. **1684** R. H. *School Recreat.* 55 They are held to double when the Rear is doubled into the Front. **1796** *Instr. & Reg. Cavalry* (1813) 46 No doubling up, increasing, or diminishing the front of the column, must be made after entering on a straight alignement. **1833** *Regul. Instr. Cavalry* I. 26 The left files double behind the right files.

c. *trans.* and *intr.* (*colloq.*) To couple or associate *with* (in the same quarters). Often ***double up***. In Betting, to double the stakes.

1789 W. Dyott *Diary* July (1907) I. 63, I was very unpleasantly situated, being obliged to double up with a jolly ensign, or to take lodgings in town. **1837** Major Richardson *Brit. Legion* i. (ed. 2) 23 Another Captain of my regiment is doubled up with me. **1885** W. Westall *Larry Lohengrin* iii. (Farmer), He..promised the steward a handsome tip if nobody were doubled up with him, i.e. if no other person were put into the same cabin. **1886** Morley *Stud. Lit.* (1889) 108 The scientific lawyer is doubled with the Indian bureaucrat. **1940** Wodehouse *Eggs, Beans & Crumpets* 29 You doubled up when you won, thus increasing your profits by leaps and bounds. **1952** *Times* 21 Nov. 8/3 In favour of giving students a reasonable spell of living in college, without making them 'double up' on the staircases. **1958** J. K. Galbraith *Affluent Society* xiii. 148 People cannot afford to own or rent their own homes and must double up. **1970** R. Gadney *Drawn Blanc* vii. 82 'Doubling up again, Donnelly?' someone said... The roulette wheel was spun once more.

d. *intr.* To unite in couples. ? *Obs.*

1614 T. Adams *Devil's Banquet* 27 Some double in their companies, some treble, some troupe, none goe single.

5. a. *Mil. intr.* To march in double time, go 'at the double'.

1890 R. Kipling *Willie Winkie* 19 So E Company.. doubled for the dear life.

b. To double one's effort or speed. (*colloq.*)

1887 Visc. Bury & G. L. Hillier *Cycling* 104 He doubled to his work..and left the Cantab.

6. *trans.* **a.** To add a second layer of material to (a garment); to line. *spec.* in *Her.*: see doubling *vbl. sb.* 2.

14.. *Ld. High Treas. Acc. Scot.* I. 203 (Jam. Supp.) A lang gowne to the Duk..viij elne of blak dammysk to dowbil it with. **1555** Eden *Decades* 266 A thicke vesture..well dowbeled. **1610** Guillim *Heraldry* I. iv. (1611) 14 No man under the degree of a Baron..may have his mantle doubled with Ermyne. **1766** Porny *Elem. Her.* vi. (1787) 226 The doubling of Mantlings with Furs. **1852** E. Ruskin *Let.* 26 Apr. in M. Lutyens *Effie in Venice* (1965) II. 301 Very fine looking Russians..wrapped up in immense cloaks doubled with furs.

b. To line or cover (a ship) with an additional layer of planking.

1703 T. N. *City & C. Purchaser* 203 A useful Nail in doubling of small Ships. **1820** Scoresby *Acc. Arctic Reg.* II. 190 Doubling generally consists of the application of 2 or $2\frac{1}{2}$ inches oak plank near the bow, diminishing towards the stern. **1840** *Evid. Hull Docks Com.* 222 She was obliged to be doubled; to have timber put outside her in order to make her more stationary in the water.

7. *Silk Manuf.*, *Cotton-spinning*, etc. To lay two or more filaments (of silk), or slivers (of cotton, wool, or flax), together, and compress them into one.

1831 G. R. Porter *Silk Manuf.* 204 In the operation of doubling, these bobbins are placed in front of the winding machine. **1835** Ure *Philos. Manuf.* 123 In fine spinning, the doubling of the fibres is sometimes 70,000 fold—for the purpose of producing perfect uniformity in the finished yarn. **1875** *Ure's Dict. Arts* III. 794 The raw singles are first twisted in one direction, next doubled, and then twisted together in the opposite direction.

8. a. To bend (a piece of cloth, paper, etc.) over, so as to bring the two parts into contact parallel; to fold; to bend (the body, etc.) so as to bring distant parts into proximity; to close, clench (the hand or fist). Often with *up*.

(In quot. 1589, to close (the ears).)

c **1430** *Two Cookery Bks.* 39 Take a pese of fayre Canneuas, and doble it. **1589** Puttenham *Eng. Poesie* III. xxiii. (Arb.) 282 To solace your eares with pretie conceits after a sort of long scholasticall preceptes which may happen haue doubled them. **1665** Hooke *Microgr.* 9 They double all the Stuff..that is, they crease it just through the middle.. placing the two edges, or selvages just upon one another. **1694** Dryden *Love Triumph* III. i, The page is doubled down. **1778** Mad. D'Arblay *Diary* 3 Aug., He doubled his fist at me. **1874** Blackie *Self-Cult.* 42 Bending his back, and doubling his chest. **1885** Bible (R.V.) *Exod.* xxvi. 9 Thou.. shalt double over the sixth curtain in the forefront of the tent. **1893** A. H. S. Landor *Hairy Ainu* 54 Crouched as she was, doubled up, with her head on her knees.

b. ***to double up*** (a person): to make to bend or stoop, as by a blow; hence *fig.* to finish up, cause to 'collapse'. (*slang* or *colloq.*)

1814 *Sporting Mag.* XLIV. 278 Planting a blow on the side of Perrot, which doubled him up. **1883** J. Parker *Tyne Ch.* 108 Never saw a man so doubled up [in argument]. **1891** E. W. Gosse *Gossip in Library* xxi. 275 This master of science [pugilism], who doubled up an opponent as if he were plucking a flower.

c. *intr.* (for *refl.*) To become folded together or bent over; to fold, bend.

? *c* **1650** *Don Bellianis* 164 With such terrible incounters that the knight..doubled backward upon his horse. **1875** Darwin *Insectiv. Plants* vii. 163 After 10 hrs. 15 m...the blade quite doubled up. *Mod.* His knees doubled up under him. The leaf has been folded, and tends to double over.

d. *Billiards.* (*a*) *intr.* Of a ball. To rebound. (*b*) *trans.* To cause (a ball) to rebound: cf. doublet 7.

1885 *Billiards simplified* (1889) 50 If you..hit the red nearly full, so that it doubles down the table [etc.] *Mod.* You can double the ball into the middle pocket.

9. *Naut.* **a.** (*trans.*) To sail or pass round or to the other side of (a cape or point), so that the ship's course is, as it were, doubled or bent upon itself.

1548 Hall *Chron., Hen. VIII.* 11 b, If you wil bring your shippe into the bay of Hardines, you must double yᵉ poynt of Gentilnes. **1585** T. Washington tr. *Nicholay's Voy.* I. x. 12 b, Having doubled the cape, we passed along. **1665** *Phil. Trans.* I. 42 To go into the East Indies without doubling the Cape of Good Hope. **1867** Freeman *Norm. Conq.* (1876) I. v. 295 The invaders doubled the Land's End and ravaged Cornwall.

b. *intr.* To get round. ***to double upon*** (in naval warfare): to get round to the other side of (an enemy's fleet), so as to inclose it between two fires.

1769 FALCONER *Dict. Marine* (1789) A a ij b, The lee-line .. cannot so easily double upon the van .. of the enemy. **1856** EMERSON *Eng. Traits* v. 91 Nelson's feat of 'doubling', or stationing his ships one on the outer bow and another on the outer quarter of each of the enemy's. **1867** SMYTH *Sailor's Word-bk., Doubling upon* .. a hostile fleet .. as Nelson did at the Nile. **1875** F. HALL in *Lippincott's Mag.* XVI. 751/2 I doubled nimbly round a couple of corners, and paused again.

10. a. *intr.* To turn sharply and suddenly in running, as a hunted hare; to turn back on one's course; to pursue a winding or tortuous course.

1596 DRAYTON *Legends* ii. 382 To the Covert doth himselfe betake Doubling, and creepes from Brake againe to Brake. **1690** DRYDEN *Amphitryon* IV. Wks. 1884 VIII. 75 See how he doubles, like a hunted hare. **1724** DE FOE *Mem. Cavalier* (1840) 95 He found the river fetching a long reach, double short upon itself. **1828** D'ISRAELI *Chas. I*, I. iv. 87 The negociation doubled through all the bland windings of concession and conciliation. **1864** D. G. MITCHELL *Sev. Stor.* 306 They suddenly turned to double upon their walk again.

b. *trans.* To avoid or escape by doubling; to elude, give the slip to.

1812 J. H. VAUX *Flash Dict.* s.v., To double a person .. signifies either to run away from him openly, and elude his attempts to overtake you, or to give him the slip .. unperceived. **1842** MANNING *Serm.* (1848) I. ii. 23 Skill in doubling all the changes of life, and in meeting its emergencies.

11. *fig.* (*intr.*) To make evasive turns or shifts; to use duplicity, act deceitfully.

1530 PALSGR. 525/2, I double, I varye in tellyng of my tale. .. Nay, and you double ones, I have done with you. **1578** HUNNIS *Hyveful Hunnye* Gen. xii. 25 Why hast thou dealt thus craftely And doubled so with mee? **1624** *Trag. Nero* III. iii. in Bullen *O. Pl.* I. 54 Why with false Auguries have we bin deceiv'd? What, can Celestiall Godheads double too? **1649** *Bounds Publ. Obed.* (1650) 35 Who have been .. attent not to double with their God. **1820** SCOTT *Ivanhoe* xxxv, If thy tongue doubles with me, I will have it torn from thy misbelieving jaws. **1888** 'R. BOLDREWOOD' *Robbery under Arms* III. xv. 229 How did you find out Warrigal's doubling on me?

12. *trans.* Short for DOUBLE-BANK *v.* 2. *N.Z.*

1947 *Book Miscellany* (Christchurch, N.Z.) IX. 33 After tea, he doubled me to the station. **1963** N. HILLIARD *Piece of Land* 57 A bike came past: a big boy doubling a girl on the crossbar.

‖**doublé** (duble), *a.* [Fr., = lined.] **a.** Covered *with*, folded over. **b.** Of a book lining: made with a *doublure*. **c.** Plated with gold or silver.

1848 THACKERAY *Van. Fair* iv. 25 A sort of tent, hung round with chintz of a rich .. India pattern, and *doublé* with calico of a tender rose-colour. **1890** *Catal. Exhib. Rec. Bk.-bindings Grolier Club* 11 When the inside of the cover is lined with leather it is termed *doublé*. *Ibid.* 27 Garnet morocco, with ornament in mosaic and gold; doublé, blue morocco, with border of foliage and flowers. **1901** 'L. MALET' *Hist. R. Calmady* III. x. 258 The noble house of Fallowfeild, *doublé* with all the gold of all the Barkings.

double-acting, *ppl. a.* Acting in two ways or directions, by two methods, etc.: *spec.* of a steam-engine, worked by application of steam power on both sides of the piston. (Cf. *double action* s.v. DOUBLE *a.* 6.)

1842 *Penny Cycl.* XXII. 475 The upward stroke of the piston was now produced by admitting the steam below it .. thus the engine became double-acting. **1850** CHUBB *Locks & Keys* 28 Chubb's detector being combined with the six double-acting tumblers, added very greatly to the security of the lock. **1874** KNIGHT *Dict. Mech., Double-acting Pump*, one which throws water at each stroke. **1892** LOUNSBURY *Stud. Chaucer* I. ii. 155 The assumed relationship .. had begun to perform its double-acting part.

double-bank, *v.* [Back-formation from next.] **1.** *trans.* **a.** *Naut.* To provide with two rowers on one bench for each pair of opposite oars, or with two rowers for each oar. **b.** *transf.* To work or pull with two sets of men, horses, etc. (*e.g.* a rope with men on both sides, a dray with a double team of horses); also *absol.* Also, to double; to repeat (something); *spec.* to drive (motor vehicles) in two lines abreast; to park (a motor vehicle) alongside another stationary vehicle (cf. DOUBLE-PARK *v.*). So **double-banking** *vbl. sb.*

1832 MARRYAT *N. Forster* xii, They double-banked their oars. **1859** CORNWALLIS *New World* I. 147 They started next day .. and, by good luck .. met with some chaps on the road with fresh cattle, and so double banked all the way up. **1903** R. J. CLOW *Pillar of Salt* vii. 87 'I will not call twice at the same place during the year.' .. '"Double banking" is a poor game,' continued the husky man. **1929** K. S. PRICHARD *Coonardoo* xxvi. 255 She .. stuck it when the watches [over the cattle] were double-banked for two or three nights afterwards. **1933** P. GODFREY *Back-Stage* viii. 104 This often happens when two or more first nights synchronize, and the newspaper's regular critic has to be double- or treble-banked from other members of the staff. **1936** A. THIRKELL *August Folly* i. 14 Owing to the great depth of the shelves the books were double banked. **1948** PARTRIDGE *Dict. Forces' Slang 1939–1945* 60 *Double banking*, the practice, severely discouraged, of having two parallel lines of traffic going in the same direction. **1954** *Highway Code* 11 Do not let your vehicle stand in the carriageway .. alongside a standing vehicle, thus causing 'double-banking'. **1958** *Times* 1 May 4/2 Meters were less ugly than double and triple banking of cars all over the place indiscriminately. **1961** *Guardian* 10 Oct. 18/2 Mr. Macmillan has extended his double-banking of Ministers. **1963** J. VAIZEY *Education in Class Society* iii. 10 In order to accommodate the children coming out of the sixth forms, we shall have to adopt expedients like double-banking.

2. *intr.* To ride two on a horse, bicycle, etc. Also *trans.*, to ride (a horse, bicycle, etc.) thus. Chiefly *Austral.* and *N.Z.*

1888 'R. BOLDREWOOD' *Robbery under Arms* I. xix. 267 'We must double-bank my horse .. for a mile or two.' .. He jumped up, and I mounted behind him. **1926** T. E. LAWRENCE *Seven Pillars* (1935) v. lix. 338 The man made camel-less could double-bank another, riding two-up, in emergency. **1928** 'BRENT OF BIN BIN' *Up Country* (1966) vi. 67 Bert and Tim .. double-banked on the horse, and returned to the high ground near the river. **1930** *Bulletin* (Sydney) 8 Jan. 20/4 His sister .. somehow got him on to a horse .. and double-banking to hold him on, she took him to Dr. Pirie's surgery at Liverpool. **1940** B. O'REILLY *Green Mountains* (1941) 67 Rose and I 'double-banked' on a fat round pony. **1945** BAKER *Austral. Lang.* iii. 72 It was possibly through the agency of the horse that Australia acquired .. *double-bank* .. employed mainly today when a cyclist gives another person a ride on the bar of his bicycle.

double-banked (-bæŋkt), *a.* orig. *Naut.* [parasynth. f. *double bank* + -ED.] **a.** Having pairs of opposite oars pulled by rowers on the same bench; or, having two rowers at each oar. (Said of the oars, or of the boat; also adverbially.) **b.** *double-banked frigate*: a frigate carrying guns on two decks; also called a **double-banker**.

1697 DAMPIER *Voy.* I. xv. 429 They row double-banked; that is, two Men sitting on one Bench, but one rowing on one side, the other on the other side of the Boat. **1769** FALCONER *Dict. Marine* (1780) s.v., The oars are also said to be double-banked when two men row upon every single one. **1842** *P. Parley's Ann.* III. 300 A large double-banked frigate. **1867** SMYTH *Sailor's Word-bk.* s.v. *Double-banked*, 60-gun frigates which carry guns along the gangway .. are usually styled double-bankers.

c. *transf.*

1929 F. C. BOWEN *Sea Slang* 40 *Double banked*, sleeping two in a cabin. **1964** *Times Rev. Industry* Feb. 57/3 The first 'double-banked' motor the firm has made .. (mounting two sets of five cylinders each radially round a common drive shaft). **1968** *Economist* 17 Aug. 53/1 A double-banked defence network of anti-missiles.

'double-'barrelled, -eled (-'bærəld), *a.* **1. a.** Of a fire-arm: Having two barrels.

1709 STEELE *Tatler* No. 34 ¶5 His double-barrelled Pistols. **1835** W. IRVING *Tour Prairies* 95, I discharged the double-barrelled gun to the right and left.

b. Of a telescope.

1955 *Sci. News Let.* 21 May 324/2 A double-barreled telescope that can record a golf ball's flight eight miles away will go to work for the Air Force to track guided missiles.

2. *fig.* Serving a double purpose; having a double reference; double, twofold.

1777 *Maryland Jrnl.* 9 Sept. (Th.), The event of this double-barreled scheme has been, that the colonel and his party are defeated. **1837** DICKENS *Pickw.* xxvii, This was a double-barrelled compliment. **1841** THACKERAY *Fun. Napoleon* ii, The above account .. has a double-barrelled morality. **1889** *Univ. Rev.* Nov. 345 Every one they know has a double-barrelled name and a great-grandfather of renown. **1912** W. OWEN *Let.* 24 July (1967) 151 Your sleek Thomas, Hopkins, Dixon, .. and the rest of these double-barrelled guns, whose double-barrelled names I refuse to write. **1938** *Spectator* 21 Jan. 75/2 The two minor groups are generally allowed .. to nominate one candidate in the double-barrelled constituencies. **1959** J. P. HUGHES *How you got your Name* vi. 103 In surnames the double-barrelled form does not appear before the eighteenth century. **1965** T. REESE *Bridge Conventions* 44 *Double-barrelled Stayman*, an extension of the Stayman Convention whereby both two clubs and two diamonds in response to 1 NT are conventional.

So **double-barrel** *a.* = DOUBLE-BANKED *a.*; *sb.*, (*a*) a double-barrelled gun; (*b*) a hyphenated surname (cf. DOUBLE-BARRELLED *a.* 2 above); **double-barrel** *v. nonce-wd.*, to make 'double-barrelled'.

1807 Z. M. PIKE *Acct. Exped. Mississippi* (1810) 8 Apr. 240 Visited the treasurer, who showed me the double-barrel gun given by governor Clairborne. **1811** BYRON *Hints Hor.* 556 Double-barrels .. miss their mark. **1829** FONBLANQUE *Eng. under 7 Administ.* (1837) I. 313 A double-barrel gun. **1848** THACKERAY *Bk. Snobs* xii, He double-barrelled his name, and, instead of T. Sniffle .. came out .. as Rev. T. D'Arcy Sniffle. **1952** A. POWELL *Buyer's Market* iii. 178 The double-barrel .. has really no basis whatever, beyond the surname of a remote ancestor.

double-bass ('dʌb(ə)l'beɪs). [f. DOUBLE *a.* 4 b + BASS, after the Italian name CONTRABASSO.] A musical instrument, the largest and deepest-toned of the violin class, having three or four strings, usually tuned a fourth apart.

1727–52 CHAMBERS *Cycl.* s.v. *Violone*, A double bass almost twice as big as the common bass violin. **1789** MRS. PIOZZI *Journ. France* I. 176 Girls handling the double bass. **1856** MRS. C. CLARKE tr. *Berlioz' Instrument.* 40 To double-basses belong .. the lowest sounds of the harmony.

attrib. **1816** SCOTT *Old Mort.* xvii, 'Harm them not!' exclaimed Kettledrummle, in his very best double-bass tones. **1880** P. DAVID in Grove *Dict. Mus.* I. 458 Bottesini and .. other celebrated double-bass players.

double bed. A bed to accommodate two persons. Also *attrib.* So **double-bedded** *a.*, having a double bed or two single beds.

1798 JANE AUSTEN *Let.* 24 Oct. (1952) 21 We have one double-bedded and one single-bedded room. **1839** E. A. HITCHCOCK *Jrnl.* (1930) 25 There were five double beds. **1844** *Ainsworth's Mag.* V. 407 He and his friend slept in a double-bedded room. **1910** *Bradshaw's Railway Guide* Apr. 1022 Inclusive terms .. from 15/- per day or 4½ guineas per week for double bedrooms. **1912** J. JOYCE *Let.* 22 Aug. (1966) II. 310, I have taken a double-bedded room at 21 Richmond Place. **1915** 'H. J. JAMES' (*title*) Double bed dialogues. **1925** G. BURRARD *Big Game Hunting* 280 A good warm rug or blanket, preferably double-bed size. **1931** *Times* 16 Mar. 22/1 Large double bed room. **1958** HAYWARD & HARARI tr. *Pasternak's Dr. Zhivago* I. vi. 182 They went into another room which had .. a wide double bed.

double-benched (-bɛnʃt), *a.* Having two benches; *spec.* (*Naut.*) = DOUBLE-BANKED.

1834 MEDWIN *Angler in Wales* I. 17 A double-benched cart. **1881** OGILVIE, *Double-banked, double-benched.*

double-bitt, *v. Naut.* [see BITT.] *trans.* To pass (a cable) twice round the bitts, or round two pairs of bitts instead of one.

1833 CAPT. MARRYAT *P. Simple* xv, 'Which cable was ranged last night—the best bower?' 'Yes, sir.' 'Jump down, then, and see it double-bitted and stoppered at thirty fathoms.' **1867** SMYTH *Sailor's Word-bk.* 104 In ships of war there are usually two pairs of cable-bitts, and when they are both used at once the cable is said to be double-bitted.

double-bitted, *a.* [see BIT *sb.*[1]] Having two bits (in various senses).

1816 SCOTT *Bl. Dwarf* i, A double-bitted military bridle. **1834** *Brit. Husb.* I. 345 Grubbing the roots of shrubs .. is usually performed with the .. double-bitted mattock. **1874** KNIGHT *Dict. Mech., Double-bitted Axe* .. has two opposite bits or blades. It is an ancient form of battle-axe.

double(-)blind, *a.* Applied to a test or experiment conducted by one person on another in which information about the test that may lead to bias in the results is concealed from both the tester and the subject until after the test is made; orig. used of tests for determining the efficacy of drugs.

Quots. 1937, 1948 both refer to a double-blind test.

[**1937** *Jrnl. Amer. Med. Assoc.* 26 June 2178/2 The data consisted of the patients' judgments regarding changes in pain. These data were secured in a manner relatively free of bias by the use of the 'blind test'. **1948** *Amer. Heart Jrnl.* XXXVI. 529 The study was conducted by the 'blind' method. The materials for injection .. were unknown to the observer as well as to the subject.] **1950** *Amer. Jrnl. Med.* IX. 146/1 The 'internal-evaluation' was made by skilled questioning under conditions of the 'double blind test' in which neither the physician nor the patient knew at the time whether the evaluation related to the placebo or khellin. **1954** *Proc. R. Soc. Med.* XLVII. 197 The only safe way to obtain unbiased opinions from either of them [*sc.* doctor or patient] is to make them express their opinions without knowing whether the patient received an active drug or not. This is known in America as a double blind test. **1961** *Lancet* 19 Aug. 423/1 Statistics and certain concepts, such as double-blind trials, are on everyone's mind to-day. **1968** [see EXTRA-SENSORY *a.*]. **1970** *Sci. Amer.* Mar. 62/3 To demonstrate that no cheating was involved, the experiment was repeated on a double-blind basis: neither the investigator nor the subject knew what the dot pattern contained in advance. **1971** *Nature* 12 Mar. 113/2 It should be noted that this study was not double blind and hence is subject to observer bias.

b. *ellipt.* or as *sb.*

1960 J. R. WILSON *Double Blind* i. 12 In an ordinary blind trial the patient does not know which substance he is receiving. .. There may be reasons why this information is better withheld even from the doctor himself. This is known as a double blind. **1960** *N.Y. Times* 14 Aug. 77/3 After the first few cases of improvement with griseofulvin therapy were noted, a research method known as the 'double blind' was used. **1961** *Spectator* 3 Feb. 165/1 The well designed trial avoids this unconscious conspiracy by a system known as the double-blind.

double-breasted, *a.* Of a coat, etc.: Having the two sides of the breast made alike, with buttons and button-holes, so as to button on either side. Also, having a double thickness of material on the breast, as an under-vest.

1701 *Lond. Gaz.* No. 3693/4 A light Cloth Coat double breasted. **1825** J. NEAL *Bro. Jonathan* I. 149 A loose great coat, or double-breasted surtout. **1874** BOUTELL *Arms & Arm.* iii. 54 That arrangement in a modern waistcoat which is entitled 'double-breasted'.

double cropping. [DOUBLE *a.* C.] The cultivation of land so that two or more crops are grown in one season.

1873 *Young Englishwoman* Sept. 446/2 In small gardens .. from want of space, this system of double cropping is absolutely necessary. **1918** R. E. WILLARD *Status of Farming Lower Rio Grande* 6 These 24 farms made average net incomes more than four times as great as those doing no double cropping. **1957** *Agric. Engin.* May 312/1 The practice of burning grain stubble prior to planting soybeans .. under a double cropping system in the Coastal Plain areas of the Southeast is widespread. **1977** *Sci. Amer.* Jan. 32/2 The northern limits of double cropping in the U.S. have been extended for several hundred miles by no-tillage methods of planting.

Hence **double-crop** *v. trans.*, to cultivate (land) by double cropping; also with crop as obj.; **double-crop** *attrib. phr.*; **double-cropped** *ppl. a.*

1918 R. E. WILLARD *Status of Farming Lower Rio Grande* 13 It appears that where the farm is so operated as to have from 40 to 50 per cent of the crop acres (including double-cropped land) in truck crops, better returns are made than when less truck is raised. On these farms about 40 per cent of the crop area is double-cropped. **1956** *Agric. Res.* Apr.

6/1 Southern farmers should find substantial advantages in double cropping soybeans and small grain. *Ibid.* 6/2 Results of the double-crop plan. **1969** *Listener* 12 June 814/3 They too want the peasants to build more schools, to vaccinate hogs and introduce double-crop rice farming. **1977** *New Yorker* 17 Oct. 43/1 It double-cropped most of its twenty-five thousand acres. **1980** *Christian Science Monitor* (Midwestern ed.) 4 Dec. B7/2 Because of rural labor shortages, only 30 percent is triple-cropped and 50 percent double-cropped.

ˈ**double-cross, double cross.** [f. DOUBLE *a.* + CROSS *sb.*] **1.** [CROSS *sb.* 29.] An act of treachery to both parties (orig. in gaming or sport) esp. by pretended collusion with each; more widely, betrayal of the other party in a (dishonest) transaction.

1834 W. H. AINSWORTH *Rookwood* III. IV. ii. 244 (*title of poem*) The Double Cross. **1848** *Sporting Life* 4 Mar. 4/2 All bets are off. It has..been 'rumoured', that a double cross was intended. **1874** HOTTEN *Slang Dict.*, *Double cross*, a cross in which a man who has engaged to lose breaks his engagement, and 'goes straight' at the last moment. **1887** *Referee* 21 Aug. 1/3 (Farmer), A double cross was brought off. Teemer promised to sell the match, and finished by selling those who calculated on his losing. **1896** ADE *Artie* ix. 79 Every time I see him over at the city hall he's whisperin' to one o' them red-necked boys and fixin' it to give somebody the double-cross. **1910** W. M. RAINE *B. O'Connor* 214 'Think you're getting the double-cross?' asked Leroy. **1920** A. E. W. MASON *Summons* xii, There was always a certain amount of money for the man who would work the double cross. **1930** H. G. WELLS *Autocracy Mr. Parham* I. i. 9 Espionage had never been so universal, conscientious, and respected, and the double cross of Christian diplomacy ruled the skies from Washington to Tokio. **1959** 'H. HOWARD' *Deadline* x. 80 It had to be someone on Lloyd's payroll who was working the double-X. **1970** E. MCGIRR *Death pays Wages* iv. 89 Part of the deal is that I guarantee you against a double-cross or hi-jacking.

Hence **double-cross** *v. trans.*, to give (a person or persons) the double-cross; loosely, to cheat; also *absol.*; **double-crosser**; **double-crossing** *vbl. sb.* and *ppl. a.*

1903 ADE *People you Know* 153 Although he had been double-crossed and put through the Ropes, he still had a Punch left. **1904** 'O. HENRY' *Cabbages & Kings* x. 161 'Twas thus I was double-crossed by the Tropics through a family failin' of goin' out of the way to hunt disturbances. **1910** W. M. RAINE *B. O'Connor* 240 Nothing like being on the spot to prevent double-crossing. **1915** WODEHOUSE *Something Fresh* i, A wealthy uncle who subsequently double-crossed them by leaving his money to charities. **1926** J. BLACK *You can't Win* iv. 42 This song is a favorite among negroes when in great trouble, such as..being double-crossed by a friend. **1927** *Observer* 10 July 17/5 This was apparently part of a deep-laid plot, for the Nationalists now consider they have been double-crossed. **1927** *Vanity Fair* Nov. 132/4 A 'rat' or a 'heel' is a double-crosser or a worthless person. **1928** *Hearst's International* Aug. 156/3 Are you going to be a dirty thief and a double-crosser? **1928** *Collier's* 18 Aug. 6/4 'You're a double-crossing rat,' I said. **1940** E. POUND *Cantos* lxv. 142 Congress has double XX'd me. **1942** C. S. LEWIS *Broadcast Talks* I. i. 11 Think of a country where..a man felt *proud* of double-crossing all the people who had been kindest to him. **1960** Double-crosser [see BACK-STABBER].

2. [CROSS *sb.* 28.] A cross between two hybrids each obtained by crossing two separate inbred lines, e.g. in the production of maize.

1920 *Wallaces' Farmer* 18 June 1604/2 To gain the maximum results from inbred strains it is necessary to bring together four strains in what is called a double cross. **1934** *Discovery* Feb. 52/2 The so-called double-cross technique so largely used in breeding maize in America and used to a lesser extent with swine and poultry in several countries. **1967** BRIGGS & KNOWLES *Introd. Plant Breeding* xviii. 226 Jones, in 1918, proposed the use of the double cross to produce hybrid varieties of corn. By double cross is meant the hybridization of two single crosses and the use of the F_1 as the commercial crop. *Ibid.*, Double cross hybrids.

3. Shortened form of *double* CROSS-STITCH.

[**1934** M. THOMAS *Dict. Embroidery Stitches* 63 *Double cross stitch*, a canvas stitch, consisting of a cross stitch set diagonally with another cross stitch set straight and worked over the first.] **1960** G. LEWIS *Handbk. Crafts* 38 Frequently these two are the only stitches used to the neglect of the many others which would greatly enrich many pieces of work, such as doublecross.

doubled (ˈdʌb(ə)ld), *ppl. a.* [f. DOUBLE *v.*] **1.** Made double, increased twofold, †repeated, etc.; see the verb.

c **1430** *Art of Nombryng* (E.E.T.S.) 16 Fynde a-noþer digit vnder the next figure bifore the doublede. **1571** DIGGES *Pantom.* I. xi. D iij, Ioyning to that doubled distance the heigth of your eye, ye haue the whole altitude. **1697** DRYDEN *Virg. Georg.* IV. 70 Hollow Rocks that..doubled Images of Voice rebound. **1810** SOUTHEY *Kehama* XI. xiv, Their doubled speed the affrighted Dragons try.

b. Of land: see *double land* s.v. DOUBLE *a.* 6.

1697 DAMPIER *Voy.* (1729) I. 256 The Land in the Country is high and doubled. **1712** W. ROGERS *Voy.* App. 26 The Land is white with small Hills, and in some places doubled.

2. Folded, bent: see DOUBLE *v.* 8.

1655 JER. TAYLOR *Guide Devot.* (1719) 149 Doubled knees, and Groans and Cries. **1860** MACMICHAEL *Pilgr. Ps.* 324 A small doubled piece of cloth. **1864** MRS. GATTY *Parables fr. Nat.* Ser. IV. 14 Poor Hans' doubled-up figure.

ˈ**double-dealer.** [f. next, or f. DOUBLE *adv.* 3.] One who acts with duplicity.

1547–64 BAULDWIN *Mor. Philos.* (Palfr.) VIII. i, God.. abhorreth..hypocrites, and double dealers. **1709** SACHEVERELL *Serm.* 5 Nov. 22 Thus execrable is the Traytor, and Double-Dealer. **1836** HOR. SMITH *Tin Trump.* (1876) 278 A Janus-faced double-dealer.

ˈ**double-dealing, double dealing,** *vbl. sb.* [see DOUBLE *a.* 5.] Action marked by duplicity; the profession of one thing and practice of another.

a **1529** SKELTON *Dethe Erle Northumb.* 174 Let double delyng in the haue no place. **1632** J. HAYWARD tr. *Biondi's Eromena* 133 Some..feared there was some dissembling or double dealing in this businesse. **1748** *Anson's Voy.* III. x. 403 The malice and double-dealing of the Chinese. **1830** D'ISRAELI *Chas. I*, III. iv. 45 Saville..by his double-dealing with the King and the Scots, proved himself a political traitor.

ˈ**double-dealing,** *ppl. a.* [f. prec., or f. DOUBLE *adv.* 3.] Using duplicity.

1587 GOLDING *De Mornay* xiv. 223 To be beguiled by a dubbledealing Spy. **1855** MACAULAY *Hist. Eng.* IV. 53 Lowminded, doubledealing, self-seeking politicians.

double-deck. [See DOUBLE *a.* C. 2 and DECK *sb.*] Used *attrib.* in designations of structures, vehicles, etc., having two platforms, floors, or planes one above the other. So **double-decked** *a.* [DOUBLE *a.* C. 1]; **double-decking** *vbl. sb.*

1869 *Trans. Ill. State Agric. Soc. 1867–69* VII. 460 Sheep arrive here from the west in single decked cars, but leave in double decked ones. **1894** W. T. STEAD *If Christ came to Chicago!* 186 Mr. Pullman has devised an admirable double-deck car. **1903** A. H. BEAVAN *Tube, Train, Tram, & Car* xv. 212 Electric omnibuses..double-decked. **1906** [see DECK *sb.*[1] 3 d]. **1910** A. WILLIAMS *Engin. Wonders World* II. 49/2 The makers claim that.. it [*sc.* the Scherzer Rolling Lift Bridge] could be made double-decked. *Ibid.* 267/1 The double-deck floor accommodates four elevated railway tracks. **1917** C. C. TURNER *Aircraft of To-day* ii. 34 The 'double-deck' type of rectangular planes. **1930** *Times Educ. Suppl.* 17 May p. iv/3 The building will have double-deck lifts, which will permit the taking on and discharging of passengers at two floors simultaneously. **1955** *Times* 9 May 18/1 A double-deck self-parking garage. **1956** WALLIS & BLAIR *Thunder Above* (1959) i. 6 The huge double-decked airliner. **1959** *Manch. Guardian* 29 Jan. 6/5 The proposed double-decking of the first mile of the Great West Road. **1960** BAKER & JOHNSON *Dict. Highway Traffic* 55 *Double-deck road*, a collective term for a high-level road and a low-level road that both follow the same route, one over the other. **1970** *Globe & Mail* (Toronto) 28 Sept. 17/3 A gang of youths captured a double-deck bus.

double-decker. *colloq.* [parasynth. f. *double deck* + -ER[1].] A double-decked ship, etc. **a.** 'A ship with two decks above the water-line'.

1835 *Western Monthly Mag.* June 339 The Washington is a splendid double decker, calculated to carry three hundred tons.

b. 'A street-car having a second floor and seats on top; a freight- or cattle-car with two floors' (*Cent. Dict.*). Also, a double-decked omnibus. orig *U.S.*

1867 *Terr. Enterprise* (Virginia, Nev.) 19 July 3/1 A 12-mule double-decker prairie schooner. **1878** *Design & Work* IV. 324/3 [Quoting U.S. newspaper] The car is a double-decker. **1887** *Harper's Mag.* Sept. 557/2 The street-cars are double-deckers, with seats upon the roof as well as within. **1895** *Popular Sci. Monthly* Apr. 757 The 'double decker' or two-story cars. **1908** *Westm. Gaz.* 22 Apr. 4/2 The car of the future must be a double-decker. **1955** *Times* 6 May 19/5 Our policy of substituting double-deckers for single-deckers was continued.

c. In various technical uses: a loaf baked with a smaller upper portion; a woman's dress consisting of two skirts or flounces, one above the other; a miners' cage made in two storeys; a double-decked aeroplane; two beds, one above the other; a bridge or road built on two levels; a multi-layer cake or sandwich; 'a tenement-house having two families on one floor' (*Cent. Dict.* 1889).

1877 W. WRIGHT *Hist. Big Bonanza* 301 Those [*sc.* cages in the shaft of a silver mine] with two platforms are called 'double-deckers'. **1899** DICKINSON & PREVOST *Cumbld. Gloss.* 88/1 s.v. *Curn keak*, *Double-decker*, a pastry cake baked in the oven, having a layer of currants inside it. **1902** *Fortn. Rev.* June 1008 The English 'double-decker' is a fearful and wonderful production that errs on the side of heaviness. **1902** *Westm. Gaz.* 30 Oct. 3/1 The double-decker costume sketched has each of its flounces bordered with..grey and white squirrel. **1902** *Daily Chron.* 12 Nov. 8/6 A number of workmen were being brought up out of the mine..in the double decker cage. **1917** C. C. TURNER *Aircraft of To-day* viii. 137 Chanute made 700 glides in his 'double-decker' without an accident. **1934** WEBSTER Double-decker [sandwich].

d. *attrib.*

1867 [see b]. **1881** *Harper's Mag.* Jan. 206/1 A good specimen of a 'double-decker' engine. **1906** E. DYSON *Fact'ry 'Ands* xvii. 227 She pays out double-decker 'am 'n' beef bull's-eyes. **1930** *Economist* 22 Feb. 405/2 The proposal of the Royal Commission for a double-decker rail and road bridge was rendered out of date. **1930** *Aberdeen Press & Jrnl.* 20 Mar. 7/6 Thirteen people were injured in an alarming double-decker 'bus smash. **1946** KOESTLER *Thieves in Night* 144 It is a kind of double-decker sandwich. There is a crusty top layer of apparent arrogance. **1959** *Listener* 13 Aug. 263/1, I also take a few sandwiches of the double-decker variety, that is three slices of bread and two fillings. **1963** *Times* 29 Jan. 14/4 The upswing of the past 12 months, unlike the earlier ones, has been a 'double-decker' affair.

double dip. 1. The process or result of dipping or immersing twice (freq. *attrib.*); *spec.* (*N. Amer.*), an ice-cream cone made with two scoops or portions of ice cream.

1936 *Ice Cream Rev.* Sept. 62/1 The fellows who have.. small double-dip stands..are having a hard time. **1940** R. SUTTLE *How to operate Retail Ice Cream Stores* 26a Double-Dip Cones, 18 Double-dip cones per gallon. **1965** *Tamarack Rev.* xxxiv. 6 He sprinkles orange and red and chocolate flakes of candy on top of the double-dips; this costs a nickel. **1971** *Engineering* Apr. 63/1 For large articles ..a double-dip technique may be employed; this entails immersing each half in turn.

2. *fig.* and *transf.*

1963 *Lebende Sprachen* VIII. 106/1 [Driver's vocabulary] Double dip. **1965** *Wall St. Jrnl.* 8 Jan. 2/4 The so-called 'double dip', in which some state laws permit a double payment of jobless benefits for a single period of unemployment. **1973** W. SHEED *People will always be Kind* II. v. 319 Hank Messer turned on me with Casey's extra double-dip sincere look. **1978** J. UPDIKE *Coup* (1979) v. 182 A frozen bulbousness—double-dip, Reddi-Whip accumulations of weathered lava. **1984** *Christian Science Monitor* 17 May 27/3 His double-dip soliloquy and her banana split of an answer..are some of the delights of ..[the] second act.

Hence **double-dipper, double-dipping**, esp. the practice of holding a second job, usu. in government or municipal service, (or of obtaining retirement benefit from this) while enjoying a pension from one's former employment.

1940 B. LEACH *Potter's Bk.* vi. 145, I use double dipping whenever I can grip the pot by the foot sufficiently firmly... By this method..the inside and outside of a pot are glazed with one movement. **1975** *Harper's Mag.* Sept. 28/2 At Congressional hearings called to investigate this 'double dipping', it was revealed that then FEO head William Simon had repeatedly..been urged to remove Bowen. **1976** *Graphic* (Tuscaloosa, Alabama) 19 Aug. 4A/3 Johnson, a double-dipper who gets paid by the state as a legislator and also receives state money as a school man. **1978** *Detroit Free Press* 14 Apr. 10A/2 'Double-dipping', in which retired military personnel draw their pensions while working in other government jobs, would be prohibited. **1981** *Bulletin* (Sydney) 6 Oct. 26/1 That phenomenon known as 'double dipping' whereby the individual taxpayer is given tax concessions aimed at encouraging him to provide for his own retirement only to..put himself on the pension. **1986** *N.Y. Times* 8 June IV. 6/5 The arrangement..made Admiral White a 'double dipper', paying him a Federal contract fee of $29,600 a month.

double dummy: see DUMMY *sb.* 2.

double Dutch: see DUTCH B. *sb.* 2 b.

double-dye, *v.* [f. DOUBLE *adv.* + DYE *v.*] *trans.* To dye twice; *fig.* to imbue or stain deeply.

1602 *How to Chuse good Wife* IV. iii. in Hazl. *Dodsley* IX. 77 Did he not..double-dye your coral lips with blood? **1879** G. MEREDITH *Egoist* xxxv, He is a sort of man to double-dye himself in guilt by way of vengeance.

Hence **double-dyed** *ppl. a.*, dyed twice; *fig.* deeply imbued or stained (with guilt, etc.); **double-dyeing** *sb.*, a method of dyeing mixed woollen and cotton fabrics by which the two are dyed separately.

1667 POOLE *Dial. betw. Protest. & Papist* (1735) 148 You are double-dy'd Idolaters. **1678** MARVELL *Growth Popery* 15 Some double-dyed Son of our Church, some Protestant in grain. **1870** MISS BRIDGMAN *R. Lynne* II. xii. 256 A double-dyed scoundrel.

double eagle. [f. DOUBLE *a.* + EAGLE *sb.* 5.] **1.** A gold coin of the value of twenty dollars. *U.S.*

1849 *Laws of U.S. concerning Money* (1910) 508 For all sums whatever, the double eagle shall be a legal tender for twenty dollars. **1859** BARTLETT *Dict. Amer.* (ed. 2) 185 There are also double eagles of twenty dollars. **1872** E. EGGLESTON *End of World* xxvi. 179 He..piled the double-eagles like a fortification in front of him. **1886** *Harper's Mag.* Dec. 36 Then the spokesman took a golden double-eagle from his belt. **1902** S. E. WHITE *Blazed Trail* viii. 61 His wages were twenty-five dollars a month, which his van bill would reduce to the double eagle. **1948** P. JOHNSTON *Lost & Living Cities Calif. Gold Rush* 41/1 A shower of bright double eagles clattered musically to the floor.

2. An ensign or armorial bearing, esp. in Germany.

1861 M. PATTISON *Ess.* (1889) I. 45 The Imperial double eagle..in all its ugliness. **1934** H. MILLER *Tropic of Cancer* (1948) 279 Goethe was..stamped with the German trade-mark, with the double eagle. **1936** *Burlington Mag.* Sept. 111/2 Besides the owl-jugs proper there exists another..in the form of a double-eagle. *Ibid.* 112 (*caption*) Double-Eagle Jug, with the arms of von Khuenburg of Carinthia.

double-edged, *a.* [f. *double edge* + -ED, or DOUBLE *adv.*] Having two (cutting) edges; *fig.* cutting or acting both ways.

1552 HULOET, Double edged, *anceps.* **1687** DRYDEN *Hind & Panth.* III. 192 Your Delphic sword..Is double-edged and cuts on either side. **1745** P. THOMAS *Jrnl. Anson's Voy.* 289 Pikes..headed with a double-edged Iron. **1791** BOSWELL *Johnson* I. 454 (Jod.) Strong, pointed, double-edged wit. **1866** J. MARTINEAU *Ess.* I. 196 The charge..is double-edged, and cuts both ways.

double-ˈedgedness. The quality or condition of being double-edged.

1901 J. JASTROW *Fact & Fable in Psychol.* 165 With peculiar obliviousness to the double-edgedness of his remark, he writes [etc.]. **1908** *Dublin Rev.* Oct. 281 He did not realize the double-edgedness of epigram when delivered in the wrong time and place, to the wrong person.

double-ˈender.

1. Anything having two ends alike; *spec.* a kind of gun-boat rounded fore and aft. *U.S.*

1865 *Star* 3 Feb., The double-ender Sassacus..caught one of the shells..which carried away the skylight of the cabin. **1871** PROCTOR *Light Sc.* 219 The United States double-ender 'Wateree'. **18..** *Amer. Antiquarian* IX. 370 (Cent.) It may be styled a double-ender spear, for each extremity of it is pointed in an identical manner.

2. A cross-cut sawing-machine, with two adjustable circular saws, for sawing both ends of timber.

‖**double entendre** (dubl ɑ̃tɑ̃:dr). [rare obs. F. = the usual *double entente*, double understanding, ambiguity; (an example, of 1688, is given by Littré in *Suppl.*) Cf. also *double entendement* in DOUBLE *a.* 2 quot. 1548.] A double meaning; a word or phrase having a double sense, *esp.* as used to convey an indelicate meaning.

1673 DRYDEN *Marr. à la Mode* III. i. 36 Foible, Chagrin, Grimace, Embarrasse, Double entendre, Equivoque. **1678** DUCHESS CLEVELAND in Miss Berry *Eng. & France* (1834) I. i. 92 The ambassador showed a letter, which he pretended one part of it was a double entendre. **1694** DRYDEN *Love Triumph.* Prol., No *double-entendres*, which you sparks allow, To make the ladies look—they know not how. **1709** *Brit. Apollo* II. No. 11. 3/2 A double *Entendre* By th' word is express'd. **1841** J. T. HEWLETT *Parish Clerk* I. 159 The jokes and the double entendres that were flying about.

‖**double entente** (dubl ɑ̃tɑ̃:t). [Fr.] = DOUBLE ENTENDRE.

1895 'H. S. MERRIMAN' *Sowers* (1896) xx. 163 He had a deft way..of planting a *double entente.* **1909** *Westm. Gaz.* 24 July 4/3 Our journalists have used more often the incorrect phrase *double entendre* than the French critics the phrase *double entente*, which is the term that our writers ought to employ. **1934** *Punch* 19 Dec. 692/1 There are of course occasions for laughter, the loudest laughter being very naturally given to those '*double ententes*' which are readily offered by the association of boy scouts and girl guides in camp. **1938** H. G. WELLS *Apropos of Dolores* iv. 154 There's a lot of this double-entente in French, I know. **1957** B. & C. EVANS *Dict. Contemp. Amer. Usage* 142/2 There is no use pointing out that *double entendre* does not exist in French and that the proper phrase for a double meaning, one of them usually indelicate, is *double entente.*

double entry: see ENTRY 9 b.

double event. [EVENT *sb.* 2 e.] Orig. in *Racing*, applied to the winning, by a horse, competitor, or team, of two races or matches at the same meeting or in the same season; hence *gen.* applied to two occurrences, acts, or performances of any kind. Also *attrib.*

1846 'SYLVANUS' *Pedestrian & other Reminiscences* xxiv. 221 The laying on a 'double event', when one of them remains in the bettor's power, having his victim bound in the..chain of certain..loss. **1863** *Illustr. London News* 566/3 They are not anxious to back anything for the 'double event'. **1872** *Gentl. Mag.* Dec. 696 He then 'backed himself for the double event' and went in for 'second schools', the last bar to a B.A. taking up mathematics. **1886** EARL OF SUFFOLK et al. *Racing* (1889) xiv. 268 The double-event betting. **1888** *Peel City Guardian* VI. 2/3, I was not codding, dear old boss, when I gave you the tip... Double event this time... Jack the Ripper. **1891** N. GOULD (*title*) The Double Event. **1898** *Cycling* 62 Most of the special burning oils are satisfactory, provided that 'double-event' oils are eschewed. **1899** *Chambers's Jrnl.* 25 Nov. 823/1 The reasons for a display of disgust at a 'double event' [*sc.* the birth of twins]. **1915** KIPLING *Fringes of Fleet* 30 It was a simple calculation of comparative speeds and positions, and when it was worked out she decided to try for the double event.

double-face. a. (Properly two words, *double face*) 'Duplicity; the acting of different parts in the same concern' Webster 1828. **b.** ('*double-face*), A double-faced person, a hypocrite.

1892 *Boy's Own Paper* Nov. 55/3 Then you believe that uncle is a double-face. **1910** W. B. YEATS *Green Helmet* 29 You say that, you double-face.

c. = DOUBLE-FACED 1 b. Also as *sb.*, a fabric so finished.

1873 *Young Englishwoman* Sept. 442/2 The wide sash of double-face ribbon. **1966** *Guardian* 6 Sept. 6/6 A raglan coat, of white/nutbrown doubleface.

double-faced (-feɪst), *a.*

1. a. Having two faces or aspects.

1589 GREENE *Menaphon* (Arb.) 29 Chance is like Ianus, double faced. *a* **1711** KEN *Preparatives* Poet. Wks. 1721 IV. 140 Double-fac'd Death. **1856** FROUDE *Hist. Eng.* II. 36 Double-faced as these inventions are—wearing one meaning in the apologies of theologians, and quite another to the multitude. *a* **1877** KNIGHT *Dict. Mech.* I. 726/1 *Double-faced*, a term applied to an architrave, or the like, having two faces. **1927** JESPERSEN *Mod. Eng. Gram.* III. xi. 215 Some phrases are..double-faced. **1963** VISSER *Hist. Syntax Eng. Lang.* I. ii. 99 In Old English the number of double-faced or amphibious verbs was far inferior to that of transitive verbs.

b. Of a fabric: Finished on both sides, so that either may be used as the right side.

c. Of a gramophone record: having a recording on each side (cf. *double-sided* (s.v. DOUBLE *a.* C. 4 a)).

1936 *Amer. Speech* XI. 5 The author has made ten double-faced phonograph records.

2. *fig.* 'Facing two ways'; professing different things to different people; insincere.

1575–85 ABP. SANDYS *Serm.* (1841) 64 Deep dissemblers, double-hearted, double-tongued, double-faced. **1577** *Test. 12 Patriarchs* (1604) 134 Double-fac'd men God abhorreth. **1825** T. JEFFERSON *Autobiog.* Wks. 1859 I. 63 Those whom he knew to be slippery and double-faced.

Hence **double-'facedness**, the quality of being double-faced; duplicity, insincerity.

1867 SALA *Fr. Waterloo to Penin.* II. 116 An element in Spanish statecraft..known as *doblez*, or doublefacedness. **1887** COLVIN *Keats* 79 Of double-facedness or insincerity.. Hunt was incapable.

†**'doublefold**, *a. Obs.* [loosely after *manifold*, etc.] Twofold, double.

a **1300** *Cursor M.* 6758 (Cott.) He sal again yeild duble fald. **1382** WYCLIF *Ps.* 2nd Prol., Clad with the doublefold cloth of confusion. **1577** NORTHBROOKE *Dicing* (1843) 26 The blessings are double fold to the diligent and obedient hearer. **1826** *Sporting Mag.* XIX. 70 Increased in a doublefold degree.

'double-ganger (-gæŋə(r)). [ad. Ger. *doppelgänger* or Du. *dubbelganger* double-goer.]

1. The apparition of a living person; a double, a wraith.

1830 SCOTT *Demonol. 178 note*, He..may probably find it to be his own fetch or wraith or double-ganger. **1865** KINGSLEY *Herew.* xix, Either you are Hereward, or you are his double-ganger.

2. A rendering of *amphisbæna*, the double-headed snake. *nonce-use.*

1831 WHITTIER *Double-headed Snake* 60 Urchins.. searching..for sheep or kine The terrible double-ganger heard.

'double-ˌhanded, *a.*

1. Adapted to be lifted or held with both hands; two-handled.

c **1611** CHAPMAN *Iliad* I. 566 In his lov'd mother's hand He put the double-handed cup. **1834** MEDWIN *Angler in Wales* I. 172 Do you use a single or double-handed rod?

2. Having two hands; *fig.* capable of a double use, application, or action.

1665 GLANVILL *Scepsis Sci.* (J.), All things being double-handed, and having the appearances both of truth and falsehood.

Hence **double-'handedness**, the quality of being double-handed; duplicity of action.

1883 F. M. CRAWFORD *Dr. Claudius* x, That sort of double-handedness that the Duke hated.

†**'double-head**, *sb. Obs.* **a.** The double-headed snake. **b.** Double-headed shot.

1607 TOPSELL *Serpents* (1658) 700 The Grecians call this Serpent Amphisbaina..I have called it Double-head. **1635** SWAN *Spec. M.* (1670) 440 The Amphisbena, or Double-head. **1678** *Lond. Gaz.* No. 1361/1 He..loaded his Guns with double head and round Partridge.

'double-head, *v.* orig. *U.S.* [Cf. DOUBLE-HEADER b.] *intr.* Of a train: to run with two engines. Also *pass.*, to be drawn by two engines. So **double-heading** *vbl. sb.*

1904 *Delineator* Sept. 374 A heavy freight train had double-headed up the mountain, and at the summit the leading engine had been cut off to run down ahead of the train. **1959** *Times* 5 Oct. p. iii/6 The latest electric locomotives [in Switzerland] can haul 600 tons..over the steep gradients..without any double-heading. **1970** *Railway Mag.* Oct. 541/1 The flying passage of a northbound express double-headed by 'Black Staniers'.

'double-ˌheaded, *a.* Having a double head or two heads, two-headed (*lit.* and *fig.*). Of a train: running with two engines. Of an electric locomotive (see quot. 1905).

double-headed shot: a shot consisting of two balls joined together. *double-headed serpent* or *snake*: a snake-like lizard of N. America, having the head and tail nearly alike; hence formerly supposed to have two heads; = AMPHISBÆNA 2.

1542–3 *Act 34 & 35 Hen. VIII*, c. 6 Pinnes..such as shalbe double headed. **1646** SIR T. BROWNE *Pseud. Ep.* VII. xii. 363 His favours are deceitfull and double headed, he doeth apparent good, for reall..evill after it. **1663** GERBIER *Counsel* E viij b, A double-headed-Aigle. **1678** tr. *Gaya's Art of War* 17 Double-headed Shot..are two Bullets fastned together, by a little piece of Iron, about half an inch long. **1727** A. HAMILTON *New Acc. E. Ind.* II. xxxiii. 10 This double-headed Government. **1774** GOLDSM. *Nat. Hist.* (1776) VII. 222 The Amphisbæna, or the Double Headed Serpent. **1804** *Naval Chron.* XII. 63, 13 rounds of double-headed shot. **1865** KINGSLEY *Herew.* xvii, His great double-headed axe. **1902** *Daily Chron.* 21 May 3/5 So heavy a train ..doubtless..will always be 'double-headed'. **1905** *Ibid.* 12 Jan. 8/5 The locomotive is double-headed, and controllable at either end, so that no turning is necessary. **1966** *Times* 3 Jan. 8/5 A double-headed express with 10 coaches.

double-'header. a. A kind of firework. *U.S.*

1869 ALDRICH *Story of Bad Boy* 92 The smaller sort of fireworks, such as pin-wheels, serpents, double-headers.

b. A railway train having two engines. orig. *U.S.*

1878 A. PINKERTON *Strikers* 216 'Double-headers', or freight trains composed of a larger number of cars than the single train, and drawn by two engines. **1881** *Chicago Times* 12 Mar., The..express from Chicago started out with a double-header. **1971** *Sunday Express* (Johannesburg) 28 Mar. 24/3 Steam from a ruptured locomotive boiler scalded the flesh off two railmen when their double-header jumped the rails.

c. In baseball, lacrosse, etc., the playing of two games in succession on the same day. *N. Amer.*

1896 *Cincinnati Enquirer* 30 July 2/2 In case rain should stop to-day's or to-morrow's games double headers will have to be played the next day. **1967** *Boston Herald* 8 May 16/4 Leading the New York Yankees past Kansas City, 8–3, for a split of their Sunday doubleheader. The Athletics won the opener, 4–1. **1968** C. DRUMMOND *Death & Leaping Ladies* iv. 72 The Louisiana Lancers had..won two more double-headers on Wednesday and Thursday. **1970** *Globe & Mail* (Toronto) 26 Sept. 39/5 The Detroit Tigers won the first game of the doubleheader.

d. *Logging.* (See quot.) *U.S.*

1905 *Terms Forestry & Logging* 35 *Double header*, a place from which it is possible to haul a full load of logs to the landing, and where partial loads are topped out or finished to the full hauling capacity of teams.

e. *Gambling.* A double-headed coin. *Austral.* and *N.Z.*

1948 V. PALMER *Golconda* iv. 26 'What's the trouble?' ..'Dirty work. That dago, Joe Comino, trying to ring in a ..double-header. Macy Donovan was keeping the [two-up] ring.'

'double-ˌhearted, *a.* [see DOUBLE *a.* 5.] Having a 'double heart'; deceitful, dissembling.

1552 LATIMER *Serm. & Rem.* (1845) 151 Double-hearted, speaking one thing with their tongues, and thinking another thing in their hearts. **1617** HIERON *Wks.* II. 160 Guilefull and double-hearted hypocrites. **1849** HARE *Par. Serm.* II. 227 In this doublefaced, doublehearted world.

Hence **double-'heartedness.**

1571 GOLDING *Calvin on Ps.* xii. 3 This dubblehartednesse..maketh men dubbletunged. **1888** HERON *Ch. Subapostolic Age* I. i. 21 Doubleheartedness, guile, arrogance.

double image. [f. DOUBLE *a.* + IMAGE *sb.*]

1. An optical appearance or counterpart of an object seen double in certain circumstances, esp. as a result of an affection of the eyes like diplopia.

1880 W. JAMES *Coll. Ess. & Rev.* (1920) 172 The *other eye* ..is kept covered during the experiments to prevent double images. **1890** —— *Princ. Psychol.* I. xi. 425 The increased visibility of optical after-images and of double images, which close attention brings about, can hardly be interpreted otherwise. *Ibid.* II. xx. 226 To most of us the whole [visual] field appears single, and it is only by rare accident or by special education that we ever catch a glimpse of a double image. **1966** C. L. THOMSON *Your Sight* (ed. 4) ii. 20 The person may occasionally see a double image, due to the failure of the two eyes to merge their images properly, a condition termed diplopia.

2. *Art.* (See quots.)

1939 WEBSTER Add., *Double image* (Surrealism), a representation of an object which is at the same time without deformation a representation of a different object. **1958** M. L. WOLF *Dict. Painting* 86 *Double image*, a popular device in primitive and surrealist art; any image that allows two irreconcilable interpretations simultaneously.

3. Used *attrib.* in various technical senses.

a **1877** KNIGHT *Dict. Mech.* I. 726/2 *Double-image micrometer*, suggested by Roemer about 1678; brought into use by Bonguer about 1748. *a* **1884** —— *Dict. Mech.* Suppl. 267/2 *Double image prism*, a prism of Iceland spar giving a double image of the object of complementary tints, and also used by revolving the images to measure the angle of crystals examined under the microscope. **1940** *Chambers's Techn. Dict.* 261/1 *Double-image tacheometer*, a type of tacheometer, used with a horizontal subtense bar, which gives two images of the bar in the field of view.

'doublejee, -key, -see, dubbletie, adaptations or corruptions of Du. *dubbeltje*, a coin formerly worth 10 cents, or about 2*d.* English.

1707 FUNNELL *Voy.* (1729) 201 A Doublekey, which is a piece of money that goes for two-pence. **1731** MEDLEY *Kolben's Cape G. Hope* I. 168 A Dubbletie..a twopenny piece of Dutch money. **1756** MRS. CALDERWOOD *Jrnl.* (1884) 59 Two stiver pieces called doublesees. **1889** *Blackw. Mag.* Aug. 183 We had to put a doublejee or so into the wooden shoe.

double-jointed, *a.* (Stress variable.) Having joints that permit a much greater degree of movement of parts of the body than is normal. So **double-'jointedness.**

1831 J. ROBY *Trad. Lancs.* 2nd Ser. I. 103 The knave is.. of an incredible strength, being..double-jointed. **1912** *Lancet* 19 Oct. 1077/2 A boy..with..double-jointedness... The joints were very loose, and the child took particular pleasure in forming almost circles by locking the index and middle finger of each hand. **1930** 'GREENHORN' *Tinker, Tailor* vi. 131 His double-jointed, coffee-coloured hand sent the knife hissing on its deadly way. **1961** C. H. BARNETT et al. *Synovial Joints* IV. iii. 249 Anatomists can only plead ignorance of the minor structural differences that must distinguish the normal joint from the double jointed variety.

†**'double-leaf**, *sb.* and *a. Obs.*

A. *sb.* The plant twayblade (*Listera ovata*), an orchid with two large opposite ovate leaves.

1578 LYTE *Dodoens* II. lvii. 224 The Twayblade or Doubleleaf. **1605** TIMME *Quersit.* I. xiii. 65 The salts [of] double leafe and of cardus benedictus..are diaphoricall.

B. *adj.* Having two leaves, double-leaved.

1592 LYLY *Midas* I. ii, The lips are..made for a double-leafe dore for the mouth.

ˌdouble-'lock, *v. trans.* To lock by two turns of the key, as in some forms of lock.

1592 SHAKS. *Ven. & Ad.* 448 Bid Suspicion double-lock the door. **1748** RICHARDSON *Clarissa* (1811) III. 39 How came I to double-lock myself in? **1840** DICKENS *Barn. Rudge* II. ix. 77 John had double-locked the door.

double meaning, *sb.* Double or ambiguous signification; the use of an ambiguous word or phrase, *esp.* to convey an indelicate meaning; = DOUBLE ENTENDRE. So **'double-meaning** *a.*, having a double meaning, ambiguous. **double-**

meaner *nonce-wd.*, one who deals in double meanings.

1551 T. WILSON *Logike* (1580) 8 The wily usyng of wordes, that in sense have double meanyng. 1591 SYLVESTER *Du Bartas* I. vi. 824 Th' Embassader Of Pyrrhus (whom the Delphian Oracler Deluded by his double-meaning Measures). 1601 SHAKS. *All's Well* IV. iii. 114 Has deceiu'd mee, like a double-meaning Prophesier. 1712 STEELE *Spect.* No. 504 ¶2 These are ever harping upon things they ought not to allude to, and deal mightily in double meanings..for your double-meaners are dispersed ..thro' all parts of town or city. 1840 HOOD *Miss Kilmansegg, Her Honeymoon* xiii, A double meaning shows double sense. 1853 GROTE *Greece* II. lxxxiii. XI. 36 By delicate wit and double-meaning phrases to express an offensive sentiment.

'double-minded, *a.* Having two 'minds'; undecided or wavering in mind. †Also, formerly, having two meanings, an overt and a concealed.

1552 HULOET, Dowble mynded, or of many wyttes, *altriplex.* 1611 BIBLE *Jas.* i. 8 A double minded man is vnstable in all his wayes. 1727 H. HERBERT tr. *Fleury's Eccl. Hist.* I. 161 Thou shalt not be either double-tongued or double-minded. 1834 J. H. NEWMAN *Par. Serm.* (1837) I. iii. 42 It is the double-minded who find difficulties. 1961 NEW ENG. BIBLE *James* i. 8 A man of that kind must not expect the Lord to give him anything; he is double-minded, and never can keep a steady course. *Ibid.* iv. 8 You who are double-minded, see that your motives are pure.

Hence **double-'mindedness**, the state of being double-minded (in either sense).

1608 W. SCLATER *Malachy* (1650) 29 Lameness Is hypocrisie, double-mindedness. 1646 H. LAWRENCE *Comm. Angells* 121 Insincerity and double-mindednesse. 1654 H. L'ESTRANGE *Chas. I* (1655) 71 The Amphibology, the double-mindednesse of the word 'dux'. 1881 GLADSTONE *Sp. at Leeds* 7 Oct., Feeble double-mindedness that does not see its own intention.

doubleness ('dʌb(ə)lnɪs). [f. DOUBLE *a.* + -NESS.]

1. The quality or state of being double or twofold. (In quot. 1533, A double layer or fold.)

1398 TREVISA *Barth. De P.R.* XIX. cxvi. (1495) 919 The more he passyth fro doublynesse and nygheth to symplynesse. *a*1533 LD. BERNERS *Huon* ix. 23 The stroke passyd through the doublenes of his cloke. 1665–76 RAY *Flora* 190 The Double Popy differeth only from the single field Popy in the doubleness of the flowers. 1855 BAIN *Senses & Int.* II. ii. §10 If we had..two distinct olfactory nerves, we should..have a feeling of doubleness or repetition of smells.

†**b.** Double or doubtful meaning, ambiguity.

1494 FABYAN *Chron.* VII. ccxxiii. 248 He wagged his hede, as he that conceyued some doublenesse in this reporte. 1551 T. WILSON *Logike* (1580) 8 That the doublenesse of no one woorde deceive the hearer. [1694 R. BURTHOGGE *Reason* 37 Words..often have a doubleness of meaning, and then are called Ambiguous].

c. *doubleness of mind* = double-mindedness.

*a*1628 PRESTON *New Covt.* (1634) 10 Doublenesse of mind ..when a man is distracted between God and some other object. 1863 KINGLAKE *Crimea* I. 348 That doubleness of mind which made him always prone to do acts clashing one with another.

2. The character of being 'double' in action or conduct; duplicity, deceitfulness, treachery.

*c*1374 CHAUCER *Anel. & Arc.* 159 He coude hir dowbilnesse espie. 1423 JAS. I *Kingis Q.* cxxxvi, Fy on thaire doubilnesse! 1548 HALL *Chron., Edw. IV* (an. 7) 199b, The erle began to complain..of the ingratitude and doublenes of kyng Edward. 1610 HOLLAND *Camden's Brit.* I. 602 Dissimulation and doublenesse of heart. 1792 MAD. D'ARBLAY *Diary* May, Unsuspicious..where he has met no doubleness. 1863 GEO. ELIOT *Romola* III. xxvii, What he called perplexity seemed to her sophistry and doubleness.

double-park, *v.* orig. *U.S.* [f. DOUBLE *adv.* + PARK *v.* 2 b.] *trans.* and *intr.* To place or leave (a vehicle) parallel to another vehicle parked near the side of the road. Hence **double-parker**, one who parks his vehicle in this way; **double-parking** *vbl. sb.*

1931 *Kansas City Star* 12 Aug., Manhattan and Emporia each has a local ordinance forbidding double-parking of motor cars. 1932 *Ibid.* 5 Apr. 18 Practically all of Commercial street was used by double parkers. 1936 *Amer. City* Jan. 95/1 It was a frequent occurrence for an exasperated motorist in desperation to double-park his car. 1951 I. SHAW *Troubled Air* i. 26 The police after you? Have they finally got you for double-parking? 1959 *Observer* 14 June 17/6 This forces commercial vehicles to double-park. 1959 *Encounter* Nov. 47/2 The cars are double-parked so thickly..that a moving vehicle can scarcely manœuvre. 1962 *Economist* 3 Feb. 412/1 Parked, and double-parked, cars restricted movement throughout central London. 1970 B. KNOX *Children of Mist* i. 10 The..duty car double-parked briefly outside the main entrance to let him out.

'double-,quick, *a.* (*sb.*, *adv.*) **A.** *adj. Mil.* Applied to the quickest step next to the run; = DOUBLE *a.* 4 c. Hence *gen.* Very rapid or hurried. **B.** *sb.* Double-quick pace or time; = DOUBLE *sb.* 3 i; also *gen.* ***at the double-quick***: very quickly or hastily. **C.** *adv.* In double-quick time.

In the U.S. army, according to the *Century Dict.*, double-quick time consisted of 165 steps of 33 inches (= 453¾ ft.) to the minute, which is identical with the 'double time' at present (1896) in force in the British Army. According to Funk & Wagnall the term has been superseded by 'double time': see DOUBLE TIME.

1822 G. W. MANBY *Voy. Greenland* (1823) 59, I singled out one [seal] that was marching away in double quick time. 1834 MEDWIN *Angler in Wales* II. 41 It was necessary to move on at double-quick. 1860 READE *Cloister & H.* III. 229 He took a candle and lighted it, and turned it down..till it burned his fingers; when he dropped it double quick. 1883 *Harper's Mag.* Sept. 553/1 His men were proceeding at the double-quick. 1918 *Blackw. Mag.* Mar. 293 Down go his hands on the joystick in double-quick time. 1959 J. BRAINE *Vodi* xix. 223 If we were married and I made just one mistake in business..she'd be off double-quick.

Hence **double-'quick** *v.*, *intr.* and *trans.*, to march, or cause to march, at double-quick. (*U.S.*)

1863 *Life in South* II. 294 How they marched..and marched again; and 'double quicked', they called it; thirty miles a day. 1888 *Century Mag.* XXXV. 962 Berry double-quicked his men to the point, but was too late.

doubler[1] ('dʌblə(r)). Now only *dial.* Forms: 4–5 dobler(e, dobeler(e, dub(b)lar, 5 dobbler, dowbler, *Sc.* dibler, 5– doubler, dubler, (9 *dial.* dibbler). [a. AF. *dobler, dubler,* = OF. *doblier, doublier* a kind of dish, also, a liquid measure, napkin, towel, bag, satchel:—L. *duplārium* liquid measure, bag, purse, f. *duplus* DOUBLE: see -ARIUM.] A large plate or dish.

13.. *E.E. Allit. P.* B. 1146 A bassyn, a bolle..A dysche oþer a dobler. *c*1410 LOVE *Bonavent. Mirr.* xxxix. 79 (Gibbs MS.) He þat wyth me putteþ hys honde in to þe dych or dobler. 14.. *Laws of Four Burghs* cxxv. §3 (Jam.) The heir sall haue..ane dish, ane dibler, ane charger, ane cuippie. 1562 *Wills & Inv. N.C.* (Surtees 1835) 198, ij brasse potts, iiij puder dublers. 1674–91 RAY *N.C. Words* 134 A *Dubler* or *Doubler*, a Platter or Dish. Vox per magnam Angliæ partem diffusa. 1855 ROBINSON *Whitby Gloss.*, *Dubbler*, a deep earthen dish or platter.

doubler[2] ('dʌblə(r)). Forms: see DOUBLE *a.* [f. DOUBLE *v.* + -ER[1]; cf. F. *doubleur*, prob. the immediate source of the technical sense 3 a.]

1. One who, or that which, makes double.

1552 HULOET, Dowbler, *duplicator.* 1557 in *Tottell's Misc.* (Arb.) 257 The doubler of thy gaine. 1589 PUTTENHAM *Eng. Poesie* III. xix. (Arb.) 211 One sorte of repetition, which we call the *doubler*..a speedie iteration of one word, but with some little intermission. 1869 REED *Ship-build.* i. 7 Plates, which..served as doublers to the main flat keel.

†**2.** A double-dealer: cf. DOUBLE *v.* 11. *Obs.*

1553 GRIMALDE *Cicero's Offices* (1556) 130 Gylefull, craftie, foxlike, and a verie dubbler.

3. Technical senses. **a.** A person employed in doubling (see DOUBLE *v.* 7); also, a machine for doubling cotton or silk.

1662 *Act 14 Chas. II*, c. 15 §6 Silk-winder and Doubler. 1723 *Lond. Gaz.* No. 6187/4 Elizabeth Faulkner..Silk-Doubler. *Ibid.* No. 6189/4 Katharine Jackson..Worsted-Doubler. 1879 J. ROBERTSON in *Cassell's Techn. Educ.* IV. 209/1 Carding engines, lap-machines or doublers.

b. *Electr.* An apparatus: see quot. 1788.

1788 *Phil. Trans.* LXXVIII. 8 It is Mr. Bennet's doubler that was intended..to multiply, by repeated doubling, a small, and otherwise unperceivable, quantity of electricity, till it became sufficient to affect an electrometer, to give sparks, etc. 1794 READ *Ibid.* LXXXIV. 266 When I employ the doubler to investigate atmospheric electricity. 1881 MAXWELL *Electr. & Magn.* I. 294 By means of the revolving doubler..Volta succeeded in developing..an electrification capable of affecting his electrometer.

c. *Calico-printing.* 'A blanket or felt placed between the cloth to be printed and the printing-table or cylinder' (Knight *Dict. Mech.*).

d. *Distilling.* A part or appendage of a still, for intercepting and returning the less volatile vapours to be re-distilled.

4. *slang.* A blow that 'doubles up' a person.

1811 *Morn. Herald* 10 Oct. 1812 *Sporting Mag.* XXXIX. 187 Penton was..grounded by a doubler on the left side.

5. *N.Z. slang.* (See quot.)

1871 C. L. MONEY *Knocking about N.Z.* x. 141 [We] were served out with a 'doubler', or two lots of grog in one.

double-reef, *v.* Chiefly in pa. pple. double-reefed (also 8 -rift). *trans.* To reduce the spread of (a sail) by taking in two reefs. Hence **double-reef** *sb.*, *e.g.* 'in double-reefs of the topsails' = with the topsails double-reefed.

1703 DAMPIER *Voy.* III. iii. 133 It would blow..so that we could scarce carry our Top-sails double rift. 1726 SHELVOCKE *Voy. round World* (1757) 4 At noon we set the main-sail double-reefed. 1833 MARRYAT *P. Simple* xv, We were obliged to double-reef the topsails..and the weather looked very threatening. 1857 in *Merc. Mar. Mag.* (1858) V. 8 At daylight, in double-reefs of the top-sails.

double-ruff, a game at cards: see RUFF.

doublesee: see DOUBLEJEE.

double-shot, *v. trans.* To load (a cannon) with a double quantity of shot. Also *fig.*

1824 SCOTT *Redgauntlet* ch. iii, A pair of buffers..they are double-shotted. 1830 MARRYAT *King's Own* xvi, The enemy ..poured in a double-shotted..broadside. 1853 TRENCH *Proverbs* iii. 49 [Proverbs] so rich in humour, so double-shotted with homely sense. 1859 F. A. GRIFFITHS *Artil. Man.* (1862) 60 Double shot the gun.

doublet ('dʌblɪt). Forms: 4–7 dublett(e, 4–8 dublet, (5 doubelet, -led, dobbelet, dobel(l)ett(e, dobelat, doplyt), 5–6 doblet, -ett(e, doublette, dow-, (6 *Sc.* dowblat, dwiplat), 6–7 doublett, dowblet, 4– doublet. [a. F. *doublet* (12th c. in Hatz.-Darm.) something folded, a furred coat, etc., f. *double* + dim. suffix *-et.*]

1. a. A close-fitting body-garment, with or without sleeves, worn by men from the 14th to the 18th centuries. (Rarely applied to a similar garment worn by women.) *Obs.* exc. *Hist.*

(The doublet had many changes of fashion, being at one time with, at another without, short skirts. In its various sleeved and sleeveless forms, it was the prototype of the modern coat, jacket, and waistcoat.)

1326 *Wardr. Acc. Edw. II*, 26/3 Unus doublet pro corpore Regis. 13.. *Gaw. & Gr. Knt.* 571 Dubbed in a dublet of a dere tars. 1489 CAXTON *Faytes of A.* II. xiii. 115 They hadd couertly vndre theyr lytel doublettes rasers. 1548 HALL *Chron., Hen. VI* (an. 15) 135 That it was ynough for a woman, to judge the difference betwene the shurte and the dublet of her husbande. 1627 DRAYTON *Agincourt, etc.* 158 Dublet, and Cloke, with Plush and Veluet linde. 1740 GRAY *Let.* Poems (1775) 83 We should have taken it for a red sattin doublet. 1835 URE *Philos. Manuf.* 133 George Fox.. travelled as a missionary..buttoned up in a leathern doublet with sleeves.

b. phr. ***doublet and hose***; *esp.* as the typical masculine attire; also, as a sort of undress, or dress for active pursuits, implying absence of the cloak worn for warmth and protection, or of the gown, coat, or cassock befitting age or dignity.

1598 SHAKS. *Merry W.* III. i. 46 And youthful still, in your doublet and hose, this raw-rumaticke day? 1600 —— *A.Y.L.* II. iv. 6 Doublet and hose ought to show it selfe coragious to pettycoate. 1603–4 *Const. & Canons Eccl.* §74 That in public they go not in their Doublet and Hose, without Coats or Cassocks. *a*1654 SELDEN *Table-T.* (Arb.) 38 One man can go in Doublet and Hose, when another Man cannot be without a Cloak. 1858 LONGF. *M. Standish* I. 3 Clad in doublet and hose, and boots of Cordovan leather.

†**c.** ***doublet of defence*** (or ***fence***): a body-armour composed of metal plates covered with cloth or leather; = BRIGANDINE. *Obs.*

1418 *E.E. Wills* (1882) 37 A Doubeled of defence couered with red Leþer. 1463 *Mann. & Househ. Exp.* (1841) 158 Ffusten..ffor to make doblettys off fence. 1488 *Will of Sharnebourne* (Somerset Ho.), Doblette of fence. 1885 *Fairholt's Costume in Eng.* (ed. 3) Gloss. s.v. *Brigandine.*

†**d.** ***iron*** or ***stone doublet***: a prison. *Obs. slang.*

1698 FRYER *Acc. E. Ind. & P.* 318 We say metaphorically, when any is in Prison, He has a Stone Doublet on. *a*1700 B. E. *Dict. Cant. Crew, Iron-doublet*, a Prison. *c*1720 *Lett. fr. Mist's Jrnl.* (1722) I. 227 He that will not pay his Debts when a few good Words will ballance his Accounts with his Creditor, deserves to wear a Stone Doublet all his Life-time.

2. a. One of two things precisely alike or in some way identical: one of a pair or couple; a duplicate copy; *pl.* twins. *spec.* **b.** *Philol.* One of two words (in the same language) representing the same ultimate word but differentiated in form, as *cloak* and *clock*, *fashion* and *faction*. **c.** *Printing.* A word or phrase set up a second time by mistake = DOUBLE *sb.* 3 h (Webster, 1864).

[1549 LATIMER *4th Serm. bef. Edw. VI* (Arb.) 107 For as good preachers be worthy double honour: so vnpreaching prelates be worthy double dishonoure: They muste be at theyr doublets.] 1553 T. WILSON *Rhet.* (1580) 203 Doublettes, is when we rehearse one and the same worde twise together. Ah wretche, wretche, that I am. 1681 GREW *Museum* (J.), Those doublets on the side of his tail seem to add strength to the muscles which move the tail-fins. 1869 *Contemp. Rev.* X. 160 Doublets, i.e. double and divergent derivations from a common root, as, for example, *raison* and *ration.* 1881 SKEAT *Etymol. Dict.* 175 Thus *dole* is a doublet of *deal.* 1885 *Athenæum* 9 May 594 [In] Hebrew grammar.. there is a special dual form to express doublets. 1896 T. L. DE VINNE in Moxon *Mech. Exerc.* I. p. xviii, Typographic peculiarities have been followed, even to gross faults, like *doublets.*

d. A story or saying which occurs in two different biblical contexts, and hence is regarded as derived from distinct sources.

1891 F. P. BADHAM *Formation of Gospels* 11, I subjoin tables of the doublets in S. Matthew, S. Mark and S. Luke. 1899 J. C. HAWKINS *Horae Synopticae* II. §iv. 64 The 'doublets', or repetitions of the same or closely similar sentences in the same Gospel, are of great value in supplying hints as to the sources and composition of the Gospels. 1906 F. C. BURKITT *Gospel Hist.* 14 One of the really striking features about the narrative in Genesis..is the number of Doublets, *i.e.* stories told twice over. *Ibid.* 163 At the first glance they are real doublets; *i.e.* different accounts of the same event drawn from different sources. 1927 A. H. MCNEILE *Introd. N.T.* 64 Isolated sayings in *Mark* which occur in more or less similar forms in two passages... These are often called 'doublets'.

3. *Gaming.* (*pl.*) **a.** The same number turning up on both the dice at a throw.

*c*1450 *Chester Pl.* (Shaks. Soc.) II. 56 Nowe will I begyn For to caste..Take heare, I dare laye, Are dublettes, in good faye. *a*1680 BUTLER *Rem.* (1759) II. 270 He..seldom fails to throw doublets. 1855 E. SMEDLEY *Occult Sc.* 246 Doublets must occasionally turn up if we are always casting the dice.

†**b.** An old game at tables or backgammon.

1611 COTGR., *Renette*, a game at Tables of some resemblance with our Doublets, or Queenes Game. 1628 EARLE *Microcosm.* (Arb.) 71 At tables he reaches not beyond doublets. 1684 OTWAY *Atheist* v. i. Wks. 1728 II. 85 Farewel ..Seven and Eleven, Sink-Tray and the Doublets.

4. A pair or couple. *spec.* **a.** *Sporting.* Two birds killed at once with a double-barrelled gun.

1816 COL. HAWKER *Diary* (1893) I. 146, I had eight doublets and bagged both my birds every time. 1837 *Ibid.* II. 129 Five glorious doublets.

b. A combination of two simple lenses.

1831 BREWSTER *Optics* xli. 342 Dr. Wollaston's microscopic doublet..consists of two plano-convex lenses. **1844** A. GRAY *Lett.* (1893) 325, I can..see the pollen-tubes with even my three-line doublet! **1874** KNIGHT *Dict. Mech.* s.v., Sir John Herschel's doublet consists of a double convex lens..and of a plano-concave lens..It is intended for a simple microscope. **1880** *Nature* XXI. 411 The object glasses..are doublets with a positive lens of quartz and a negative of Iceland spar.

c. A pair of associated lines occurring close together in a spectrum.

1897 J. R. RYDBERG in *Astrophys. Jrnl.* VI. 235 The constituents of the doublets and triplets of the nebulous series are built up after exact rules,..while the constituents of the sharp series, so far as we know, are simple lines. **1926** R. W. LAWSON tr. *Hevesy & Paneth's Man. Radioactivity* v. 54 Just like the *D*-line, the strongest rhodium line also consists of a doublet. **1961** *Adv. Spectrosc.* II. 228 The structure which is stable at low temperatures shows a doublet in the infra-red..as well as in the Raman spectrum.

d. The pair of words at either end of a word-ladder; in *pl.* = *word-ladder* s.v. WORD *sb.* 29 a.

1879 'L. CARROLL' in *Vanity Fair* 29 Mar. 185/2 The word 'head' may be changed into 'tail' by interposing the words 'heal, teal, tell, tall'. I call the two given words a 'Doublet'... The easiest 'Doublets' are those in which the consonants in one word answer to consonants in the other, and the vowels to vowels. **1945** [see *word-ladder* s.v. WORD *sb.* 29 a.] **1984** T. AUGARDE *Oxf. Guide Word Games* xxi. 188 All these examples illustrate one of the constant principles of Doublets: that the words being joined should either be opposites (*hate, love*) or otherwise connected in some way (*seven, eight*).

5. A counterfeit jewel composed of two pieces of crystal or glass cemented together with a layer of colour between them, or of a thin slice of a gem cemented on a piece of glass or inferior stone.

1449 *Churchw. Acc. St. George, Stamford* (Nichols 1797) 133 A gret croun..garnished with stones clepyd dublets. *c* **1530** *Pol. Rel. & L. Poems* (1866) 45 Doblettes of glasse yeue a gret euidence, Thyng countirfet wyl faile at assay. **1649** LOVELACE *Poems* Ded., Take my Garnet-Dublet Name. **1758** *Monthly Rev.* 348 Various methods of counterfeiting gems..by coloured glass, pastes, doublets. **1887** *Pall Mall G.* 28 Sept. 5/1 'Doublets' as they are called ..are topazes having a thin slice of diamond laid on the visible surface..the composite stone being sold as a diamond.

6. *Her.*

1830 ROBSON *Brit. Herald* III. Gloss., *Traverse* or *Doublet*, is a bearing..resembling the cheveron, which issues from two angles of one side of the escutcheon, and meets in a point about the middle of the other side; but without touching the line of the shield with its point.

7. *Billiards.* (See quot.)

1856 CRAWLEY *Billiards* (1859) 18 The Doublet..is produced by striking your own or the object ball against one of the cushions, so as to make it rebound to an opposite pocket or ball.

8. *attrib.* and *Comb.* (sense 1).

1513 MORE *Rich. III* (1883) 47 He plucked vp hys doublet sleue to his elbow. **1523** LD. BERNERS *Froiss.* I. ccclxxxiv, A dowblette maker of London. **1675** J. PYNCHON in Mather *K. Philip's War* (1862) 245, I pray you send down by the post my doublet coat.

Hence **'doubleted** *a.*, clad in a doublet; †**'doubleting** *sb.*, ? stuff for doublets (cf. *trousering*).

1575 *Act Gen. Assembly* in Henderson *Old World Scotland* (1893) 163 All Kinde of gowning, cutting, doubletting, or breekes of Velvet. **1858** HAWTHORNE *Ancestral Footsteps* (1883) 495 Doubletted and beruffled knightly shades of Queen Elizabeth's time.

'double-take, double take. orig. *U.S.* [TAKE *sb.*] A delayed reaction to a situation, sight of a person, etc., rapidly following an earlier inappropriate reaction; esp. a procedure in comedy, etc., in which an actor at first reacts unexpectedly or inappropriately to a given situation and then, as if more fully realizing the implications, reacts in an expected or more usual manner. Also, a second, often more detailed, look. Hence **double-take** *v. intr.*, to act in such a manner.

1938 *Chatelaine* Jan. 50/2 In case you aren't familiar with the 'double-take'—it's an exaggerated reaction to surprise. **1941** H. MACINNES *Above Suspicion* vii. 55 A young man had come out of the hotel door; he halted as he heard Frances' voice, and looked at her, giving what Hollywood has perfected as the 'double take'. **1942** BERREY & VAN DEN BARK *Amer. Thes. Slang* 595/4 *Double take*, Edward Everett Horton's specialty—first he beams at what he thinks is a compliment, then he realizes the truth and 'takes' it the second time, but not so happily. **1957** *New Yorker* 23 Nov. 43/1 The only person who recognized the former President during our stroll together happened to be a friend of ours.. who performed a double take worthy of the late Oliver Hardy. **1958** L. FLETCHER in Cerf & Carmel *24 Favorite One-Act Plays* 125/1 Duffy has been examining lunch, but double-takes suddenly on above. **1958** *N. & Q.* Feb. 65/2 The Antonio-Aquilina scenes have to be read with a 'double-take': the comedy is obvious, the ugliness must be discovered lying just below the comic surface. *Ibid.* 66/1 The play is, in effect, an extended double-take. **1959** P. MOYES *Dead Men don't Ski* xix. 260 The Colonel did a sort of double-take, as though he'd seen the others for the first time. **1961** A. WILSON *Old Men at Zoo* i. 21, I said, 'Ah!' Then I did a quick double-take, and added, 'What reporter?' **1962** *John o' London's* 10 May 460/3 Mr. Ustinov sits there..blinking, double-taking. **1969** E. MCGIRR *Entry of Death* ii. 22 The old fellow momentarily double-took, but being quick-witted darted a cunning look at the saloon bar. **1970** —— *Death pays Wages* ii. 33 'It'll be the good doctor,' said Oakley rising. Piron did a double-take, for a dazzling brunette entered.

'double-talk, double talk. orig. *U.S.* [TALK *sb.*] **a.** Deliberately unintelligible speech; speech that is a mixture of real and invented words; gibberish. **b.** Verbal expression intended to be, or which may be, construed in more than one sense; deliberately ambiguous or imprecise language; used esp. of political language that is subject to arbitrary national or party interpretation. Hence **double-talker**, one who uses such language; **double-talk** *v. intr.*; **double-talking** *vbl. sb.* and *ppl. a.*

1938 *New York Panorama* (Amer. Guide Ser.) vi. 156 Of late a humorously conceived system of language corruption called *double talk*..has made itself felt. *Ibid.* 157 *Double talk* is created by mixing plausible-sounding gibberish into ordinary conversation, the speaker keeping a straight face or *dead pan* and enunciating casually or *off the cuff*. **1941** *Time* 16 June 61/1 Thirteen recorded versions of this pandemic double-talk ballad are available. **1945** H. I. PHILLIPS *Private Purkey's Private Peace* xxii. 129 We got the right slant on bullies, greaseballs, double talkers, supermen, and dopes. **1948** AUDEN *Age of Anxiety* vi. 125 And all species of space respond in our own Contradictory dialect, the double talk Of ambiguous bodies. **1950** *Amer. Speech* XXV. 190 Back in Tsarist times Lenin and his associates inaugurated this double-talk and double-writing—especially the latter—in order to deceive the Tsarist censors and police. **1952** C. DAY LEWIS tr. *Virgil's Aeneid* IX. 203 You'll find no Atridae here, no double-talking Ulysses. **1956** *Ann. Reg. 1955* 45 The 'directive'..was itself a masterpiece of the familiar technique of double talk. Terms such as 'free elections', 'free contacts'..meant different things in East and West. **1957** *New Statesman* 19 Oct. 1/2 The Archbishop of Canterbury is the best double-talker since the Delphic oracle shut up shop. **1958** D. EWEN *Compl. Bk. Amer. Mus. Theater* 230 'Melody in Four F.', a tongue-twister relating in double talk the adventures of being conscripted into the army. **1959** *Listener* 4 June 969/2 This has meant..a certain amount of double-talk, many carefully imprecise statements of intention. **1960** *Guardian* 23 Dec. 5/3 Britain's confused and double-talking attitude to the Cyprus question. **1961** *New Left Rev.* Mar.–Apr. (*front cover*), The Labour Party has double-talked its way around the issue. **1968** *Globe & Mail* (Toronto) 13 Jan. B5/1 Spiralling costs..have inflated the price of B.C. Hydro and Power Authority's Columbia and Peace River power and flood control dams—just how much nobody is certain and Mr. Bennett has persistently doubletalked on this subject.

double-team, *v. U.S.*

1. [TEAM *sb.* 5.] *intr.* To combine two teams into one.

1843 W. T. NEWBY *Diary* 27 Sept. in *Oreg. Hist. Q.* (1939) XL. 235 We crawsed..a smawl streem. Dubeld teamed & crawsed the hill. *Ibid.* 28 Sept., We continued up the creek ..dubel teaming & passing the fork in 4 miles. **1934** H. VINES *Green Thicket World* 111 Often they had to double-team.

2. [TEAM *sb.* 3.] *intr.* To bring double force to bear *on* (or *upon*) a person.

1860 *Congress. Globe* 12 Jan. 424/2 In respect to the Senator's allusion to 'double-teaming' upon him..I do not exactly agree with my friend from Mississippi. **1865** M. B. CHESTNUT *Diary fr. Dixie* (1905) 346 Grant had double-teamed on Lee. **1904** T. WATSON *Bethany* (1920) 197 On the next day we double-teamed on one section of his army.

b. With *it*: to act in combination.

1884 'MARK TWAIN' *Huck. Finn* xix. 183 'Old man,' said the young one, 'I reckon we might double-team it together.'

'doublethink, double-think. [Coined by 'George Orwell' (see quot. 1949) from DOUBLE *a.* 5 + THINK *sb.*] The mental capacity to accept as equally valid two entirely contrary opinions or beliefs.

1949 'G. ORWELL' *Nineteen Eighty-Four* I. iii. 37 His mind slid away into the labyrinthine world of doublethink. To know and not to know, to be conscious of complete truthfulness while telling carefully constructed lies, to hold simultaneously two opinions which cancelled out, knowing them to be contradictory and believing in both of them, to use logic against logic, to repudiate morality while laying claim to it, to believe that democracy was impossible and that the Party was the guardian of democracy. **1953** *Encounter* Nov. 26/1 He will react..either with straight abuse or with devious double-think. **1957** T. KILMARTIN tr. *Aron's Opium of Intellectuals* 119 How can one condemn the Soviet Union, since the failure of the Bolshevik enterprise would be the failure of Marxism and therefore of history itself? This is an admirable piece of philosophical double-think, typical of our latter-day intelligentsia. **1959** *Daily Tel.* 13 Nov. 12/2 They ask for increases in wages which are plainly impossible; or they pretend they want a shorter working week when they really want more overtime. Their followers know double-think when they see it, as well as the employers. **1969** *New Scientist* 2 Oct. 18/1 This symposium exhibited a form of intellectual doublethink that could pay lip service to global starvation one minute, and assume Britain would always be able to import most of her food the next.

double-'thong, *v. trans.* To strike with the doubled thong of a whip. Hence **double-'thonger**, a stroke thus given (*colloq.*).

1856 WHYTE MELVILLE *Kate Cov.* xix, Double-thonging the off wheeler most unmercifully. **1890** BOLDREWOOD *Colonial Ref.* (1891) 187 With a shout, a double-thonger, half a dozen wild plunges..the team settled down..to something like racing speed.

double time. [DOUBLE *a.* 4.] **1.** *Mil.* [TIME *sb.* 11.] Formerly, a pace of 150 steps in the minute, i.e. twice the number of those in slow time. According to the regulations at present (1896) in force in the British Army it consists of 165 steps of 33 inches (= 453¾ ft.) to the minute. In the U.S. Army (according to Funk & Wagnall) *double time* has superseded *double-quick* (q.v.) and is fixed at 180 steps of 36 inches a minute.

1833 *Regul. Instr. Cavalry* I. 21 The Double March..is 150 steps in the minute, each of 36 inches. **1851** J. S. MACAULAY *Field Fortif.* 168 They are immediately to return at a double pace. **1853** STOCQUELER *Milit. Encycl.* s.v. *Pace*, In quick time, 108 paces..are taken in a minute..in slow time, seventy-five..In double time, 150.

2. *Mus.* [TIME *sb.* 12.] Double the time specified or previously used. *spec.* in *Jazz*: see quot. 1961. So **double-time** *v. intr.*

1877 W. S. GILBERT *Sorcerer* (1957) I. 217 Time was when this old heart would have throbbed in double-time at the sight of such a fairy form! **1939** D. BAKER *Young Man with Horn* i. 81 He..went into double time on the cymbal. *Ibid.*, He stayed right there double timing one-handed on the cymbal. **1961** A. BERKMAN *Singers' Gloss. Show Business Jargon* 19 *Double time*, doubling up the rhythmic beat without changing the singer's melody line.

doubleton ('dʌb(ə)ltən). *Card-playing.* [f. DOUBLE *a.*, after SINGLETON[2].] In Whist and Bridge: two cards only of one suit, in a player's hand. Also, one card of a doubleton.

1906 *Westm. Gaz.* 11 Aug. 14/1 B's ten of hearts is nearly sure to be a lead from the best of three—it cannot be a singleton... Similarly, if it is a doubleton [etc.]. **1922** *Evening News* 10 Apr. 8/6 Do not lead from a doubleton (a suit of two cards only) about which you have no information. **1927** *Observer* 20 Mar. 25 When he holds a singleton or weak doubleton of a suit. **1944** *Times* 17 May 6/3 Provision was made for revaluation after the first round of bidding to count three points for a void, two for a singleton, and one for a doubleton. **1960** T. REESE *Play Bridge with Reese* xxxiv. 118 Could the Queen of diamonds be doubleton?

†**double-tongue,** *sb. Obs.*

1. Duplicity or deceitfulness of speech. (Properly two words, *double tongue*: see DOUBLE *a.* 5.)

c **1386** CHAUCER *Pars. T.* ¶ 570 þe sinne of double tonge suche as speken faire biforn folk and wikkedly bihynde. **14..** [see DOUBLE *a.* 5].

2. *Herb.* The shrub *Ruscus Hypoglossum*; so called from the leaves springing from the middle of the leaf-like stalks or phyllodes.

1578 LYTE *Dodoens* VI. xiii. 674 Double-tongue hath.. thicke brownish leaues..vppon the whiche there groweth in the middle of euery leafe another smal leafe fashioned like a tongue. **1601** HOLLAND *Pliny* II. 284 *marg.*, *Bislingua.* Horse-tongue, or Double-tongue.

double-tongued (-tʌŋd), *a.* [cf. DOUBLE *a.* 5.] Speaking contrary or inconsistent things; deceitful or insincere in speech.

1382 WYCLIF *1 Tim.* iii. 8 It byhoueth dekenes for to be chast, not dowble tungid. **1483** *Cath. Angl.* 110/2 Dubylle-tonged, *ambiloquus..bilinguis.* **1533** GAU *Richt Vay* 17 Thay that ar doubel tungit the quhilk sais ane thing now, and sine ane oder thing. **1720** DE FOE *Capt. Singleton* xvi, Thou art but a double-tongued Christian, I doubt. **1849** GROTE *Greece* II. lxviii. (1862) VI. 114 'The double-tongued and all-objecting Zeno.'

doubletree ('dʌb(ə)ltriː). *U.S.* [f. DOUBLE *a.* + TREE *sb.*, after U.S. *single-tree* = SWINGLE-TREE.] The cross-piece to which the swingle-tree of a carriage, plough, etc. is attached.

1847 [see SINGLE-TREE]. **1952** STEINBECK *East of Eden* xiii. 121, I saw him..take the double-tree off the hay rake.

double wall. In full *double wall knot*: see WALL-KNOT. Hence **double-wall** *v.*

1801 J. J. MOORE *Brit. Mariner's Vocab.* sig. M1ᵛ, Double wall Knot. **1808** D. LEVER *Yng. Sea Officer's Sheet Anchor* 5 To Double Wall this Knot... The knot will appear.. having a double wall, and single crown. **1841** R. H. DANA *Seaman's Man.* vii. 37 Make the single wall slack, and crown it... Thus made, it has a double wall. *Ibid.* 38 It may be double walled by next passing the strands under the walling on the left of them.

doubling ('dʌblɪŋ), *vbl. sb.* [-ING[1].] The action of the verb DOUBLE, or its result.

1. a. Twofold increase, multiplication by two, dulication; †repetition (*obs.*).

1398 TREVISA *Barth. De P.R.* IX. xxiii. (1495) 361 Reflexion and reboundynge and dowblynge of the sonne bemes. **1570** DEE *Math. Pref.* 29 A Mechanicall Dubblyng of the Cube. **1603** KNOLLES *Hist. Turks* (1638) 221 To the doubling of his griefe. **1856** EMERSON *Eng. Traits, Ability* Wks. (Bohn) II. 44 The rapid doubling of the population.

b. *Brewing* and *Distilling.* (See quots.)

1743 *Lond. & Country Brew.* IV. 266 They..use their next small Wort instead of the first Water for brewing Ale or more Strong Beer from fresh Malt, which they call Doubling. **1874** KNIGHT *Dict. Mech.*, *Doubling.* 1. The second distillation of low wines.

c. *Mus.* The use by a single player of two (or more) musical instruments. Also *attrib.* (Cf. DOUBLE *v.* 1 h.)

1926 WHITEMAN & MCBRIDE *Jazz* ix. 198 Most of the players perform on many different instruments... Doubling is, then, the main strength of the jazz orchestra. **1927** *Melody Maker* May 435/2 There is no doubt that doubling is an advantage, but a player should certainly not try to play a second instrument until he is an absolute master of the one he normally uses. *Ibid.* Aug. 809/2 A violinist anxious to learn a 'doubling instrument' quickly and easily. **1955**

KEEPNEWS & GRAUER *Pict. Hist. Jazz* iii. 40 The excess of instruments on these bandstands indicates how much 'doubling' a musician was expected to do. **1968** *Melody Maker* 23 Nov. 18 Most of those at the colleges were drummers who had switched to vibes as a doubling instrument.

d. The action of DOUBLE *v.* 1 d.

1931 G. JACOB *Orchestral Technique* ix. 81 Unison doublings do not help much..except in the case of high trumpet parts being doubled in unison by clarinets. **1947** C. GRAY *Contingencies* viii. 146 The various doublings and *divisis* which are now the bread-and-butter of every orchestral composer.

2. *concr.* The lining of a garment; *esp.* in *Heraldry*.

1572 BOSSEWELL *Armorie* II. 79b, In Armes it is called Ermyne..In Mantles (as M. G. Leyghe sayeth) they are called doblinges. **1610** GUILLIM *Heraldry* I. iv. (1611) 12 Doublings or linings of roabes. **1708** J. CHAMBERLAYNE *St. Gt. Brit.* I. III. iii, A Viscount's mantle hath two doublings and a half of plain white fur. **1809** J. HOME in *Naval Chron.* XXIV. 193 A mantling gules, the doubling argent.

3. *Naut.* **a.** A piece of timber fitted on to the bitts; fir-lining. **b.** The covering or lining of a ship with an extra layer of planking; the extra layer itself. **c.** The double-seamed border or edging of a sail. **d.** *pl.* That part of a mast between the trestletrees and the cap.

1769 FALCONER *Dict. Marine* (1789), *Coussin de bittes*, the fir-lining or doubling of the bits. **1835** SIR J. ROSS *Narr. 2nd Voy.* ii. 11 Such effects are very apt to follow the doubling of vessels. **1883** *Harper's Mag.* Aug. 450/1 The lower part of the luff..laced..to the doublings of the mast.

4. *Building.* (See quots.)

1842–76 GWILT *Encycl. Archit.* Gloss., *Doubling*, a term used in Scotland to denote eaves' boards. **1874** KNIGHT *Dict. Mech.*, *Doubling*..2. The double course of shingles or slates at the eave of a house.

5. The folding of any substance; a fold.

1634 PEACHAM *Gentl. Exerc.* I. xiii. 43 Giving to every fold his proper naturall doubling. **1665** HOOKE *Microgr.* 141 A kind of hem or doubling of the leaf. **1703** MOXON *Mech. Exerc.* 9 When you double up your Iron..to make it thick enough..and..work in the doubling into one another, and make it..one..lump. **1855** BAIN *Senses & Int.* II. ii. §11 The structure is so arranged by ramifications and doublings as to present a very extensive surface to the air.

6. A sudden turn in running; *fig.* an evasion, a shift; deceitful or tricky action, double dealing.

1573 G. HARVEY *Letter-bk.* (Camden) 26 Your wurship mai the better conceive there hole dealing and dubling with me. **1611** SPEED *Hist. Gt. Brit.* IX. xii. (1632) 715 Pestred with the doublings of Lawyers. **1674** N. COX *Gentl. Recreat.* I. (1677) 92 When Hounds hunt a Female-Hare, she will use more Crossing and Doubling. **1750** JOHNSON *Rambler* No. 31 ¶8 Mean doublings to escape the pursuit of criticism. **1855** MACAULAY *Hist. Eng.* IV. 189 To trace all the turns and doublings of his course..would be wearisome.

7. *attrib.* (various technical senses: see the vb.).

1769 FALCONER *Dict. Marine* (1789), *Clous des sabords*, doubling-nails, to line the gun-ports. **1774** *Hull Dock Act* 25 Doubling planks that may be wrought upon the sides. **1875** *Ure's Dict. Arts* III. 793 (Silk Manuf.) The motions are given to the doubling-machine in a very simple way.

ˈdoubling, *ppl. a.* [f. as prec. + -ING[2].] That doubles, in various senses.

1. Making, or becoming, twice as much; increasing twofold; repeating, resounding, echoing; †stammering (quot. 1621).

1598 SYLVESTER *Du Bartas* II. i. IV. *Handy-crafts* (1621) 228 He makes the trampled ground..shake with doubling sound. **1621** QUARLES *Argalus & P.* (1678) 23 Tears..whose violence deny'd Th' intended passage of her doubling tongue. **1674** N. COX *Gentl. Recreat.* I. (1677) 13 Heads having doubling Croches, are called Forked Heads. **1711** POPE *Temp. Fame* 333 Thro' the big dome the doubling thunder bounds. **1787** CAVALLO in *Phil. Trans.* LXXVIII. 14 Experiments made with those doubling or multiplying plates. **1801** YOUNG *ibid.* XCII. 45 Doubling [= double-refracting] spars.

2. Folding, bending.

1633 G. HERBERT *Temple, Longing* i, With doubling knees and weary bones.

3. Turning suddenly in running; *fig.* evasive.

1581 MULCASTER *Positions* xxxvii. (1887) 164 Deepe dissembling and dubling hypocrisie. **1635** QUARLES *Embl.* IV. iv. (1718) 201 The hindmost hound oft takes the doubling hare. **1735** SOMERVILLE *Chase* II. 17 With Steps revers'd She forms the doubling Maze. **1755** H. WALPOLE *Let. to H. S. Conway* 15 Nov., Lord Egmont was doubling, absurd, and obscure.

doubloon (dʌˈbluːn). Also 7 doblone, dublion, 8 doublon, doblon. [a. F. *doublon*, or Sp. *doblon*, augm. of *doble* DOUBLE.] **a.** Now *Hist.* A Spanish gold coin, originally double the value of a pistole, i.e. = 33 to 36 shillings English.

1622 MABBE tr. *Aleman's Guzman d'Alf.* II. II. viii. 170, I gave him sixe Doblones of two. **1719** DE FOE *Crusoe* I. xiii, Six doubloons of gold. **1727–51** CHAMBERS *Cycl.* s.v., There are also double doubloons now current..for 3 pound 12 shillings. **1745** P. THOMAS *Jrnl. Anson's Voy.* App. 5 Dollars 540*l.* Troy and Double Loons 201. **1755** JOHNSON, *Doublon.* **1862** *London Rev.* 30 Aug. 197 A minute search is easily prevented by the influence of doubloons on Spanish officials.

b. *pl.* Money. *slang.*

1908 'O. HENRY' *Voice of City* (1916) 80 He's left his whole cargo of doubloons to a microbe. **1924** WODEHOUSE *Leave it to Psmith* i. 28 Aunt Constance keeps an eye on the doubloons and checks the outgoings pretty narrowly. **1959** P. BULL *I know the Face* v. 76, I..was anxious to lay my hands on anything that brought in the doubloons.

‖**doublure** (dublyr). [F. *doublure* lining, f. *doubler* to DOUBLE, line.] An ornamental lining, usually of leather, on the inside of a book-cover.

1886 *Pall Mall G.* 24 Nov. 6/2 With a doublure (this is the term applied to the elaborated inside faces of the cover) of crimson morocco. **1892** *Bookseller's Catal.*, Bound in Brocade of the Eighteenth Century, the cloth cover with the Artist's design in gold used as a doublure. **1895** ZAEHNSDORF *Sh. Hist. Bookbinding* 22 To Badier is assigned the first use of doublures (1703).

doubly (ˈdʌblɪ), *adv.* [f. DOUBLE *a.* + -LY[2].]

1. In a double or twofold manner or degree; in two ways, or twice as much.

c **1380** WYCLIF *Serm.* Sel. Wks. I. 386 Here we synnen doubli. *c* **1450** *Mirour Saluacioun* 1172 Two tables of the commandements dowbly in oure lady sawle ware. **1593** SHAKS. *Rich. II*, I. iii. 80 Thy blowes, doubly redoubled. **1789** MAD. D'ARBLAY *Diary* 14 Jan., I was now doubly sorry. **1834** MRS. SOMERVILLE *Connex. Phys. Sc.* xxv. 250 Doubly refracting substances.

2. With duplicity, deceitfully. ? *Obs.*

c **1430** *Pilgr. Lyf Manhode* III. xxvi. (1869) 150 False mesures she vseth doubleliche. *c* **1585** R. BROWNE *Answ. Cartwright* 2 Let him not deale doubly with vs. **1624** GEE *Foot out of Snare* 77 Hee had no reason to speak doublely. **1748** RICHARDSON *Clarissa* (1811) III. xxxi. 186 They lay a man under a necessity to deal doubly with them!

doubt (daʊt), *sb.*[1] Forms: 3–4 dut(e, (4 dote), 3–6 doute, (4–6 dowt(e, douȝt(e, dought(e, dowght), 4–7 dout, 5– doubt, (5–6 doubte, 6 dubte, dowbt). [ME. a. Of. *dute, dote, doute*, vbl. sb. f. *douter* to DOUBT. The spelling *douȝte, dought*, arose from the spoken identity, which per contra caused DOUGHTY to be spelt *doubty*. As to the mod. spelling with *b*, see DOUBT *v.*]

1. a. The (subjective) state of uncertainty with regard to the truth or reality of anything; undecidedness of belief or opinion. With *pl.*: A feeling of uncertainty as to something. *spec.* Uncertainty as to the truth of Christianity or some other religious belief or doctrine (freq. *pl.* and occas. personified).

a **1225** *Leg. Kath.* 2463 Ne beo þu na þing o dute Of al þet tu ibeden haues t. *c* **1300** *Beket* 375 Thanne was the Bischop in gret doute what were therof to done. *c* **1400** MAUNDEV. (Roxb.) xiii. 57 þou man of litil faith, whi had þou doute? **1483** *Cath. Angl.* 105/2 A Dowte, *ambiguitas, dubietas, dubitacio, dubium.* **1559** W. CUNNINGHAM *Cosmogr. Glasse* 17 Your wordes bringe me in a doubt. **1576** FLEMING *Panopl. Epist.* 17 You ought not to stand in doubt. **1585** Q. ELIZ. in *Four C. Eng. Lett.* 29, I write not this, my deare brother, for dout. **1606** SHAKS. *Tr. & Cr.* II. ii. 16 Modest Doubt is cal'd The Beacon of the wise. **1708** STANHOPE *Paraphr.* (1709) IV. 67 To remove all Remains of Unbelief and Doubt. **1779** COWPER *Hymn, 'When darkness long'* i, The folly of my doubts and fears. **1850** TENNYSON *In Mem.* xcvi, There lives more faith in honest doubt, Believe me, than in half the creeds. **1855** BROWNING *Men & Women* I. 216 What have we gained then by our unbelief But a life of doubt diversified by faith, For one of faith diversified by doubt. **1915** G. K. CHESTERTON *Poems* 98 John Grubby, who was short and stout And troubled with religious doubt. **1924** C. MACKENZIE *Heavenly Ladder* xxiv. 296 It was all right so long as I said Mass myself; I had no doubts then. **1934** H. G. WELLS *Exper. Autobiogr.* I. iv. 188, I had not yet been confirmed... I suggested that I might have 'doubts'. **1960** P. MORTIMER *Saturday Lunch with Brownings* 109 For the first time in his life..he had Doubts. **1971** *Daily Tel.* 8 Apr. 10/6 (*heading*) 3 per cent. of church-goers have doubts.

b. The condition of being (objectively) uncertain; a state of affairs such as to give occasion for hesitation or uncertainty. Phr. *to give* (an accused person) ***the benefit of the doubt***: to give a verdict of Not Guilty where the evidence is conflicting; to assume his innocence rather than guilt; hence in wider use, to incline to the more favourable or kindly decision, estimate, or the like.

a **1300** *Cursor M.* 22612 (Gött.) Saint paul it sais, it es na dute. **1375** BARBOUR *Bruce* XIV. 207 Quhill eftir myd-morne, the fichting Lestit, in-till sic ane dout. **1678** DRYDEN *All for Love* IV. i. (Seager) Like A polished glass held to the lips, when life's In doubt. **1818** JAS. MILL *Brit. India* II. v. vi. 556 It..brought in doubt the sincerity of the former professions. [**1844** C. NAPIER *Let.* 21 Feb. in W. Napier *Life* (1857) III. 48, I shall therefore..give him the benefit at your request.] **1848** *Bell's Life* 9 July 2/3 If he thought he was out, it must suffice; but he ought to have been quite certain, or..to have given the batter the benefit of the doubt. **1860** T. INMAN *On Myalgia* 104 We should more frequently give our patients the 'benefit of our doubts', and abstain from attempting to cure an inflammation [etc.]. **1892** SIR A. KEKEWICH in *Law Times Rep.* LXVII. 140/1 In a case of this kind I think I ought to give the defendant the benefit of the doubt. **1961** P. USTINOV *Loser* xi. 259 He deserved the benefit of the doubt, for old times' sake. *Ibid.* xiii. 284 Perhaps, he now thought, he had just been a microcosm of a world addled by a desperate malady... No, he deserved no benefit of any doubt.

†**2.** A matter or point involved in uncertainty; a doubtful question; a difficulty. *Obs.*

c **1374** CHAUCER *Boeth.* IV. pr. vi. 134 Whan oon doute is determined and kut awey þer wexen oþer doutes wiþouten noumbre. **1398** TREVISA *Barth. De P.R.* XVI. xlvii. (1495) 569 No man shal wene that it is doubt or fals that god hath sette vertue in precyous stones. **1581** PETTIE *Guazzo's Civ. Conv.* I. (1586) 41 b, Who will..now and then propose such doubtfull doubtes. **1693** *Col. Rec. Pennsylv.* I. 420 You doe Likewise alledge that the greatest bodie of Laws were transmitted..by Mr. penn, which is a doubt.

†**3. a.** Apprehension, dread, fear. *Obs.*

a **1225** *Juliana* 28 For dute of deaðe. **1297** R. GLOUC. (1724) 89 He nadde of no prince in þe world doute. *c* **1386** CHAUCER *Pars. T.* ¶949 Oonly for the doute of Ihesu Crist. **1411** *Rolls of Parlt.* III. 650/2, I havyng doute of harme of my body..dyd assemble these persones. *c* **1489** CAXTON *Sonnes of Aymon* iii. 81 For doubte to be blamed he spored his horse. *a* **1533** LD. BERNERS *Huon* xcv. 311 They dare not, for dought of Kyng Charlemayne. **1659** D. PELL *Impr. of Sea* 511 Being in many fears and doubts of starving.

†**b.** A thing to be dreaded; danger, risk. *Obs.*

13.. *Coer de L.* 2922 It is gret doute he schal us wynne! *c* **1400** *Lanfranc's Cirurg.* 134 If þat ilke remile peerse þe brayn panne þer is a greet doute in þe caas. **1596** SPENSER *F.Q.* v. xi. 47 How ever strong and stout They were, as well approv'd in many a doubt.

4. Phrases: **a.** ***to make doubt***: †(*a*) to hesitate, to scruple (*obs.*); (*b*) to doubt, to be uncertain. **b.** ***no doubt***: undoubtedly, doubtless. †**c.** ***out of doubt***: without doubt, doubtless (*obs.*). **d.** ***without doubt***: (*a*) certainly, undoubtedly; †(*b*) without fear, fearlessly (*obs.*).

a. 1586 T. B. *La Primaud. Fr. Acad.* I. (1589) 185 Boleslaus the seconde..made no doubt to take women by violence from their husbands. **1709** STRYPE *Ann. Ref.* I. xxii. 264, I make some doubt, whether the..Proclamation..were ever printed. **1875** JOWETT *Plato* (ed. 2) I. 320, I make no doubt that you will prove the truth of your words.

b. *c* **1380** WYCLIF *Wks.* (1880) 378 And no dowte..siluestre..schulde haue synned more greuously þan giezi did. **1576** FLEMING *Panopl. Epist.* 86 Your mother, a notable Gentlewoman (no dout). **1745** P. THOMAS *Jrnl. Anson's Voy.* 65 It was done..to the entire Satisfaction of five or six (no doubt) very disinterested Officers. **1885** *Manch. Exam.* 25 Feb. 5/1 No doubt it was adroit, but the adroitness was of a vulgar kind.

c. *c* **1340** *Cursor M.* 2276 (Trin.) þat story telleþ out of doute. **1459** *Paston Lett.* No. 323 I. 436 As I schal owt of dowght her after doo. **1577** *St. Aug. Manual* (Longm.) 111 Out of all doubt..their whole soule shall not suffise to reioise to the full. **1656** CROMWELL *Sp.* 17 Sept., Whose ends have, out of doubt, been what I told you.

d. *a* **1300** *Cursor M.* 2053 (Cott.) Cham wit-outen dout Sal be his brothers vnderlote. *Ibid.* 6557 (Cott.) Cums again, wit-vten dute. *c* **1410** *Sir Cleges* 44 Rech and pore..Schulde be there wythoutton dought. **1556** *Aurelio & Isab.* (1608) D ij, Withouten doute I sholde merite to lease yow. **1674** tr. *Scheffer's Lapland* 64 This Henricus..was without doubt..the head of the Birkali. **1895** F. HALL *Two Trifles* vii, Without doubt, in the judgment of many..he has done so.

5. *Comb.*

1649 G. DANIEL *Trinarch., Hen. V*, cxliv, His doubt-Sprung Pietie has yet a farther Quest. *a* **1656** BP. HALL *Rem. Wks.* (1660) 393 Against these doubt-mongers. **1895** *Tablet* 7 Dec. 901 The doubt-excluding certainty required.

†**doubt**, *sb.*[2] *Obs. rare*$^{-1}$. A redoubt.

c **1611** CHAPMAN *Iliad* XII. 286 This doubt downe, that now betwixt us stands.

doubt (daʊt), *v.* Forms: see DOUBT *sb.*[1] Pa. t. and pple. doubted (also 4 dutte, 4–5 dut(e, 5 doute, (dought), pa. pple. 4–5 ydouted). [ME. *duten, douten*, a. OF. *duter, doter, douter*, (14–16th c. also *doubter*):—L. *dubitāre* to waver in opinion, hesitate, related to *dubius* wavering to and fro, DUBIOUS. The normal 14th c. forms in Fr. and Eng. were *douter, doute*; the influence of Latin caused these to be artificially spelt *doubt-*, which in 17th c. was again abandoned in Fr., but retained in Eng.

Branch II 'to fear, to be in fear', a development of the verb in OF., was an early and very prominent sense of the vb. and its derivatives in ME.: cf. also REDOUBT, etc.]

I. 1. *intr.* To be in doubt or uncertainty; to be wavering or undecided in opinion or belief. Const. *of* (†*at*, †*in*).

a **1300** *Cursor M.* 21090 (Edin.) [Thomas Didymus] lange he dutid in þe richte. *c* **1325** *Metr. Hom.* 100 Of his birth douted thai noht. **1382** WYCLIF *Luke* ix. 8 He doutide, for that it was seid of sum men, for Joon roos aȝen fro deede men. **1523** LD. BERNERS *Froiss.* I. clxxxi. 216 There was none that ought to dout in hym. **1539** BIBLE (Great) *Matt.* xxviii. 17 But some douted. **1548** CRANMER *Conf. Unwrit. Verities* in Strype *Eccl. Mem.* II. App. AA. 97 The Chyrche wytnesseth them to be true..wherfore it is not lawful to doubt at them. *a* **1633** AUSTIN *Medit.* (1635) 178 Hee that never doubted, scarce ever well-beleeved. **1768** BEATTIE *Minstr.* I. xlvii, But let us hope; to doubt is to rebel. **1874** GREEN *Short Hist.* viii. §6 519 Who never doubted of the final triumph of freeedom and the law.

2. *trans.* To be uncertain or divided in opinion about; to hesitate to believe or trust; to feel doubt about; to call in question; to mistrust.

c **1340** *Cursor M.* 22811 (Trin.) Who so douteþ þis, is childe þe more. **1494** FABYAN *Chron.* II. ccxli. (R.), The lady who douted those wordes. **1513** MORE in Grafton *Chron.* II. 828 Diverse of his housholde servaunts, whome either he suspected, or doubted. **1598** SHAKS. *Merry W.* v. v. 183 Doctors doubt that. **1680** DRYDEN *Ovid's Ep., Helen to Paris* (R.), He..The beauty doubted, but believ'd the wife. **1780** HARRIS *Philol. Enq.* Wks. (1841) 461 Because Socrates doubted some things, therefore Arcesilas and Carneades doubted all. **1797** MRS. RADCLIFFE *Italian* ii, My lord, you have never yet doubted my word. **1856** EMERSON *Eng. Traits, Char.* Wks. (Bohn) II. 58 They doubt a man's sound judgment if he does not eat with appetite.

b. with clause, introduced by *whether*, *if*, *that*. (Often with *but*, *but that*, when the main clause is negative or interrogative: see BUT *conj.* 21.) †Also formerly with *inf.*

1303 BRUNNE *Handl. Synne* 857 Hys dyscyplys doutede echoun Wheþer he shulde ryse or noun. **1340** HAMPOLE *Pr. Consc.* 2965 þe saule..þat doutes whethir he sal be dampned or save. **1513** MORE in Grafton *Chron.* (1568) II.

824 Not doubtyng but that..he should finde him faythfull. **1586** A. Day *Eng. Sec.* I. (1625) 130 Doubting how to have recompence. **1664** Butler *Hud.* II. iii. 1029, I do not doubt To find friends that will bear me out. **1711** Steele *Spect.* No. 6 ¶4, I do not doubt but England is at present as polite a Nation as any in the World. **1817** W. Selwyn *Law Nisi Prius* (ed. 4) II. 1059 It never was doubted, but that one partner might bind the rest. **1858** Hawthorne *Fr. & It. Jrnls.* (1872) I. 9, I doubt whether English cookery is not better. **1871** B. Taylor *Faust* (1875) II. Pref. 5 Schiller doubted that a poetic measure could be formed capable of holding Goethe's plan. **1891** *Law Times* XCII. 107/1 The master doubted if all remedies were not barred by the lapse of time.

†**3.** To hesitate, scruple, delay: with *infinitive*.

1843 *Cath. Angl.* 105/2 To Dowte; *cunctari..herere, hesare.* **1549–62** Sternhold & H. *Ps.* l. 3 Our God shall come in hast, to speake he shall not doubt. **1576** Fleming *Panopl. Epist.* 7, I dout not to request and earnestly beseeche you, to returne. **1655** Stanley *Hist. Philos.* III. (1701) 85/2 Plato doubteth not to write in this manner. **1743** Fielding *Journ.* I. ii, Mr. Locke hath not doubted to assert, that you may see a spirit in open daylight.

4. *impers.* To cause to doubt, make doubtful.

18.. Whittier *Pr. Wks.* (1889) II. 20 This, he says, somewhat doubted him at first, as the book was not canonical.

II. 5. *trans.* To dread, fear, be afraid of.

†**a.** with simple object. *Obs.*

a **1225** *Ancr. R.* 244 þe deouel of helle duteð ham swuðe. **1297** R. Glouc. (1724) 276 Edmond..doutede God þoru alle thyng. *a* **1300** *Cursor M.* 12571 (Cott.) þai him luued and doted ai. *c* **1400** *Destr. Troy* 13834 Myche dut he his dreme, & dred hym þerfore. *a* **1450** *Knt. de la Tour* xxxiv. 48 Ye shulde love and doute your husbonde. **1523** Ld. Berners *Froiss.* I. xxix. 43 He made many to be slayne, wherby he was so doughted. *c* **1630** Risdon *Surv. Devon* §329 (1810) 339 St. Ann's Chapel is..very near the sea, yet doubts not drowning. **1664** *Flodden F.* v. 46 No English-man Scots more did doubt.

b. With infinitive phrase or objective clause: To fear, be afraid (that something uncertain will take or has taken place). *arch.* and *dial.*

a **1300** *Cursor M.* 10869 (Cott.) þis leuedi nathing doted sco þat godd ne moght his will do. *Ibid.* 15171 (Cott.) þe fleche was dutand for to dei. *c* **1450** *Merlin* 6 He dought that he myght not wynne hem. **1568** Grafton *Chron.* II. 265 They doubted to fall in their handes. **1583** Hollyband *Campo di Fior* 309, I doubt lest we are gone out of the waye. **1665** Pepys *Diary* (1879) IV. 171 Doubting that all will break in pieces in the kingdom. **1712** W. Rogers *Voy.* 237, I doubt not any ones contradicting this Journal. **1816** Scott *Antiq.* vii, But I doubt, I doubt, I have been beguiled. **1820** Shelley *Let.* Pr. Wks. 1888 II. 321, I doubt that they will not contain the latest and most important news. *Mod. dial.* I doubt we are too late.

6. In weakened sense (app. influenced by I.): **a.** To anticipate with apprehension, to apprehend (something feared or undesired).

1509 Barclay *Shyp of Folys* (1874) I. 190 Ay dowting deth by cursed gyle and treason. **1598** Grenewey *Tacitus' Ann.* II. xii, Doubting nothing more then least they should shift off the battell for feare. **1703** Rowe *Fair Penit.* II. ii. 588 Still I must doubt some Mystery of Mischief. **1810** Scott *Lady of L.* v. xi, Fear nought—nay, that I need not say—But—doubt not aught from mine array. **1838** Prescott *Ferd. & Is.* II. i. II. 365 They doubted some sinister motive, or deeper policy than appeared in the conduct of the French king.

b. To suspect, have suspicions about. *arch.*

1586 A. Day *Eng. Secretary* I. (1625) 88 Before..doubting the malicious dealings of the adverse parties against me. **1603** Knolles *Hist. Turks* (1621) 865 The defendants doubting such a matter, by diligent listening..discovered their works. **1875** Howells *Foregone Concl.* 17 Don Ippolito, whom he had begun by doubting for a spy.

c. With infin. phrase or clause: To apprehend; to suspect. *arch.*

1574 Hyll *Conject. Weather* ii, The pinne or web is likewise to be doubted to happen in that yeare. **1598** Grenewey *Tacitus' Ann.* I. iv. (1622) 6 Some perill might ensue, if he should doubt that they perceiued his dissimulation. **1705** Wesley in Hearne *Collect.* 28 Sept., My Flax [was] I doubt willfully fir'd and burnt. **1879** Trollope *Thackeray* 148, I doubt that Thackeray did not write the Latin epitaph.

†**7.** *refl.* To fear; to be afraid. [= OF. *se douter.*] Cf. fear *v.* 3. *Obs.* or *arch.*

a **1300** *Cursor M.* 6656 (Cott.) His folk..duted þam to cum him nerr. *c* **1330** R. Brunne *Chron.* (1810) 41 Doute þe of none enmys, þat comes vp on þe. *c* **1400** *Destr. Troy* 12918 Ho dout hir full deply, for drede of þe kyng. **1523** Ld. Berners *Froiss.* I. ccxviii. 278, I doubte me nothynge of them. **1607** Shaks. *Timon* I. ii. 159 Faith..would not hold taking, I doubt me. **1820** Scott *Monast.* vii, I doubt me his wits have gone a bell-wavering by the road.

†**8.** *intr.* To be fear; to be afraid *of*. *Obs.*

a **1300** *Cursor M.* 1334 (Gött.) He loked..And sau thinges þat gert him dute. *c* **1340** *Ibid.* 21870 (Trin.) Mony mon þerof shal doute. *c* **1500** *Lancelot* 1827 It..makith realmys and puple boith to dout. **1533** Gau *Richt Vay* (1888) 94 Help al men quhilk ar vexit in thair hartt doutand for thair sinnis. **1577–87** Holinshed *Chron.* II. 19 The French king who now began to doubt of the puissance of king William, as foreseeing how much it might preiudice him.

†**b.** *to doubt of*: to fear for, be in fear about.

1577 Hanmer *Anc. Eccl. Hist.* (1619) 38 Euery one doubted of his owne life.

†**9.** *impers.* To make (a person) afraid. *to be doubted*, to be afraid. *Obs.*

c **1315** Shoreham 93 Hym ne douteth of no breche Of Godes hestes healde. *a* **1400–50** *Alexander* 3555 (MS. Ashm.) All driȝtens & dewessis ere dute of my name. **1490** *Plumpton Corr.* 96, I am douted that he vary from his grant. *a* **1619** Fotherby *Atheom.* Pref. (1622) 16 It's want of reason, or it's reasons want Which doubts the minde, and Judgment so doth daunt. *a* **1625** Fletcher *Bonduca* I. ii, The virtues of the valiant Caratach, More doubts me than all Britain.

doubtable ('daʊtəb(ə)l), *a.* Forms: see doubt *sb.*[1] [ME. *doutable*, a. obs. F. *doutable* causing fear, terrible, having fear, doubtful (Godef.), ad. L. *dubitābil-is*, after *douter* to doubt: see -able.]

1. That may be doubted; doubtful, uncertain, questionable, dubitable.

c **1400** *Rom. Rose* 5413 If thee thynke it is doutable, It is thurgh argument provable. *c* **1400** Maundev. (1839) xvi. 172 To have Juggement of doutable Causes. **1483** Caxton *Gold. Leg.* 388 b/1 Answer not by doubtable wordes. **1627** Feltham *Resolves* II. (1628) 153 'Tis not doutable, but that the mind is working, in the dullest depth of sleep. **1886** W. Knight *Hume* 105 Descartes virtually said, exhaust the sphere of the doubtable.

†**2.** To be dreaded; redoubtable, dread. *Obs.*

c **1430** Lydg. *Bochas* I. xiv. (1554) 29 b, The mountain, by force he hath assured, Which for brigantes afore was ful doubtable. **1475** *Bk. Noblesse* (1860) 51 Cartage, the victorioux cite of gret renomme, most doubtable. *c* **1530** Ld. Berners *Arth. Lyt. Bryt.* (1814) 345 She hathe frendes ryghte hye and doubtable.

†**'doubtance.** *Obs.* [ME. *dot-*, *doutance*, a. obs. F. *doutance*, f. *douter* to doubt: see -ance.]

1. Doubt, uncertainty, hesitation.

[**1292** Britton III. vi. §2 Le seignur..de ceo soit en dotaunce par acun qi se profre pur dreit heir.] *c* **1325** *Chron. Eng.* 497 Thilke he spende saunt[z] dotaunce. *c* **1374** Chaucer *Troylus* IV. 1016 (1044) Out of doutaunce, I may wel maken..My resonynge. **1483** Caxton *Gold. Leg.* 110 b/1 Herof no man shold haue doubtaunce. **1529** Lyndesay *Complaynt* 5, I stand in gret dowtance.

2. Fear, dread.

13.. *Coer de L.* 1862 Have ye no doutance Of all these English cowards. *a* **1420** Hoccleve *De Reg. Princ.* 322 He that of no thyng hath dotaunce. **1484** Caxton *Chivalry* 67 Doubtance affeblysshyth strengthe of courage.

doubted ('daʊtɪd), *ppl. a.* [f. doubt *v.*]

†**1.** Feared, dreaded, redoubted. *Obs.*

c **1485** *Digby Myst.* (1882) II. 15 Most dowtyd man, I am. **1523** Ld. Berners *Froiss.* I. lxxvii. 98 The moste douted and honoured prince. **1579** Spenser *Sheph. Cal.* Oct. 41 Doubted Knights, whose woundlesse armour rusts.

†**2.** Uncertain, doubtful. *Obs.*

1563 Foxe *A. & M.* 808 a, The sayde byshoppe..in hys sayde sermon..handled them in doubted sorte.

3. Called in question; questioned, disputed.

1795 MacKnight *Apostolic Epistles* (1820) IV. 148 The doubted epistles were very early known.

Hence **'doubtedly** *adv.*, in a doubted or doubtful manner; doubtfully: opp. to *undoubtedly*.

1584 *T. Wilson's Rhet.* 108 That nothing be doubtedly [*earlier edd.* doubtfully] spoken, which maie haue a double meanyng. **1635** Pagitt *Christianogr.* I. (1646) 130 Those that are doubtedly beleevers.

'doubter. [f. as prec. + -er[1].] One who doubts; one who is uncertain or in doubt.

1603 Florio *Montaigne* II. xii. (1632) 294 Some have judged Plato a Dogmatist, others a Skeptike or a Doubter. **1682** Bunyan *Holy War* xi, Diabolus..his army consisted all of Doubters. *Ibid.*, The third captain was Captain Damnation: he was captain over the grace doubters. **1751–73** Jortin *Eccl. Hist.* (R.), Obliged to answer doubters and cavillers. **1852** Jerdan *Autobiog.* II. xix. 264 A much more respectable doubter of my statements.

doubtful ('daʊtfʊl), *a.* [f. doubt *sb.* + -ful.]

1. Of things: Involved in doubt or uncertainty; uncertain, undecided; indistinct, ambiguous.

1388 Wyclif *Ezek.* xii. 24 Nether bifor tellyng of thing to comynge schal be douteful. *c* **1440** *Promp. Parv.* 129/2 Dowtefulle, *dubius, ambiguus.* **1513** More in Grafton *Chron.* (1568) II. 762 Whereof he wist the ende was doubtfull. **1530** Palsgr. 66 Sometyme as masculynes, sometyme as femynines: and therfore I calle theym of the doutfull gendre. **1551** T. Wilson *Logike* (1580) 64 b, Deceiptfull arguments when a doubtfull worde is used. **1594** Shaks. *Rich. III*, IV. iv. 493 You haue no cause to hold my friendship doubtfull. **1669** Gale *Crt. Gentiles* I. I. x. 56 Whether he were a God or man, is doutful. **1712** Addison *Spect.* No. 470 ¶1 A doubtful Passage in a Latin Poet. **1839** Thirlwall *Greece* VI. 93 It is very doubtful whether he saw Aristotle again. **1844–57** G. Bird *Urin. Deposits* (ed. 5) 131 Highly coloured deposits..of doubtful origin.

b. Of uncertain issue.

1562 J. Shute *Cambine's Turk. Wars* 14 The battayle was so doubtefull, that of neyther syde was there seane any advantage. **1665** Manley *Grotius Low C. Warres* 673 And try the doubtful Chance of War. **1795** Southey *Joan of Arc* VI. 342 Yet the fight Hung doubtful. **1813** Scott *Rokeby* I. xix, I watched him through the doubtful fray.

c. Of questionable or equivocal character.

1838 Prescott *Ferd. & Is.* II. xvi. III. 253 She never employed doubtful agents or sinister measures. **1884** G. Allen *Philistia* I. 3 A shabby composite tenement in a doubtful district of Marylebone.

d. *Pros.* Of varying quantity; that may be either long or short.

1871 *Public Sch. Lat. Gram.* §218 Syllables which might ..be either long or short, are called Doubtful.

2. Of persons: Divided or unsettled in opinion; in doubt; undetermined, uncertain, hesitating.

1509 Fisher *Fun. Serm. C'tess Richmond* Wks. (1876) 292 Doutfull in her mynde, what she were best to do. **1526** *Pilgr. Perf.* (W. de W. 1531) 213 b, How good counseyle they haue gyuen to the doutfull. **1576** Fleming *Panopl. Epist.* 81 *note*, He was doubtfull howe Cæsar would take his doings. **1724** De Foe *Mem. Cavalier* (1840) 281 The king was doubtful, and could not resolve. **1858** Froude *Hist. Eng.* III. xiii. 122 He was doubtful of the prospects of the rebellion, and doubtful of his own conduct. **1875** Jowett *Plato* (ed. 2) V. 122 He was doubtful..whether the ideal..state could be realized.

†**3.** To be dreaded or feared; awful, dread. *Obs.*

1397–8 in *Gregory's Chron.* in *Hist. Coll. Citizen Lond.* (Camden) 98 To oure excellent ryght dowtfulle soverayne. *Ibid.* 99 Youre excellent and doughtfulle ryalle mageste. **1555–6** in W. H. Turner *Select. Rec. Oxford* (1880) 240 The unfortunate end and doubtful tragedy of T.C.

†**4.** Giving cause for apprehensions. *Obs.*

c **1400** *Lanfranc's Cirurg.* 100 A crampe..þat is douteful or dredeful to do awey. **1513** More in Grafton *Chron.* (1568) II. 822 That all thinges doubtfull should of his friendes be prudently forseen. **1637** Heywood *Royal Ship* 22 Worthily they have demeaned themselves..eyther in doubtfull discoveries, or more dangerous Naumachies or Sea-fights. **1776** Gibbon *Decl. & F.* I. 324 The consul..reported the doubtful and dangerous situation of the empire.

†**5.** Full of fear or apprehension; apprehensive. *Obs.*

1548 Hall *Chron., Edw. IV* (an. 14) 233 b, Privilie enformed of yͤ French kinges doubtfull imaginacion. **1579** Spenser *Sheph. Cal.* May 294 Home when the doubtfull Damme had her hyde. **1603** Knolles *Hist. Turks* (1621) 79 All this great fight the Constantinopolitanes beheld, with doubtfull hearts. **1723** De Foe *Col. Jack* (1840) 156, I am doubtful that you may not believe. **1791** Burke *Corr.* (1844) III. 253, I hear things which make me doubtful and anxious, though not afraid, absolutely.

6. as *sb.* A doubtful person or thing.

1589 Puttenham *Eng. Poesie* III. xix. (Arb.) 234 Aporia or the Doubtfull. **1861** Gen. P. Thompson *Audi Alt.* III. clxiv. 183 Whereby union might be effected..and the mass of doubtfuls brought into play. **1892** *Pall Mall G.* 4 Mar. 7/1 The issue of the battle might rest with the 'doubtfuls'.

'doubtfully, *adv.* [f. prec. + -ly[2].] In a doubtful, uncertain, or ambiguous manner; hesitatingly, ambiguously, indistinctly.

1483 *Cath. Angl.* 106/1 Dowtfully, *ambigue..dubie.* **1551** T. Wilson *Logike* (1580) 66 b, When sentences bee spoken doubtfully, that thei maie be construed two maner of waies. **1664** Power *Exp. Philos.* I. 2 Had our famous Muffet but seen them..he would not have spoke so doubtfully. **1804** J. Grahame *Sabbath* 168 The watcher's ear Caught doubtfully at times the breeze-borne note. **1838** Dickens *Nich. Nick.* xiii, He shook his head doubtfully.

'doubtfulness. [f. as prec. + -ness.]

1. The quality of being doubtful: **a.** Objective uncertainty of meaning or issue; ambiguity, obscurity.

1530 Palsgr. 215/1 Doutfulnesse, *ambiguité.* **1551** T. Wilson *Logike* (1580) 65 b, Of no one thyng riseth so muche controversie, as of the doubtfulnesse, and double takyng of a worde. **1640** G. Watts tr. *Bacon's Adv. Learn.* II. (R.) What are the causes and remedies of the doubtfulness and uncertainty of law? **1709** *Brit. Apollo* II. No. 77. 2/1 There is no Doubtfulness in the Case. **1885** *Law Times* 28 Mar. 387/1 The other point was of greater doubtfulness.

b. Subjective uncertainty; undecidedness of mind; want of assured opinion; distrust.

1526 *Pilgr. Perf.* (W. de W. 1531) 128 b, Dulnesse of spiryte, and doubtfulnesse in conscyence. **1663** Pepys *Diary* 24 Sept., I rather hope it is my doubtfulness of myself. **1736** Butler *Anal.* II. i. Wks. 1874 I. 151 The doubtfulness of some of the greatest men, concerning things of the utmost importance. **1829** Southey *Newman* vi, The purpose..was entertain'd With doubtfulness and fear.

†**c.** Apprehension. *Obs.*

1576 Fleming *Panopl. Epist.* 49 That whiche did not only offer unto me occasion of doubtfulnesse, but troubled me also with much feare.

†**2.** The quality of giving ground for fear. *Obs.*

1576 Fleming *Panopl. Epist.* 267 If the disease have in it much difficultie and doubtfulnesse. **1606** G. W[oodcocke] tr. *Hist. Ivstine* 94 a, Troubled with the doubtfulnesse of the danger.

'doubting, *vbl. sb.* [f. doubt *v.* + -ing[1].] The action of the verb doubt; feeling of uncertainty, hesitation; †apprehension, fear.

1375 Barbour *Bruce* XIV. 230 The gud erll had gret dowtyne That of thair men suld dronken be. **1486** *Surtees Misc.* (1890) 57 Have you no drede nor no dowting. **1531** Frith *Jdgm. upon Tracy* (1829) 247 There can be no doubting or mistrust. *a* **1628** Preston *Effectual Faith* (1631) 24 We may say of doubting as we say of Thistles, they are ill weeds, but the ground is fat and good where they grow. **1879** O. W. Holmes *Motley* xv. 94 The record of that minister's unutterable doubtings.

'doubting, *ppl. a.* [f. as prec. + -ing[2].] That doubts or is in uncertainty; of undecided opinion; †formerly also apprehensive, fearful. (See also Thomas I.)

c **1425** Wyntoun *Cron.* IX. v. 110 Ane..Sa dowtand wes in þat debate. **1715** De Foe *Fam. Instruct.* I. iii. (1841) I. 63 However doubting I am of the success. **1850** Mrs. Browning *Poet's Vow* II. v, She looked upon him silently With her large doubting eyes. **1877** Sparrow *Serm.* xxii. 297 Who would send doubting Thomas to proclaim the resurrection of Christ?

Hence **'doubtingly** *adv.*, in a doubting or uncertain manner; hesitatingly; **'doubtingness.**

a **1535** More *Wks.* 18 (R.) He that asketh doubtingly, asketh coldly. **1653** Baxter *Chr. Concord* ii. A iv b, They must act doubtingly and not in Faith. **1840** Mrs. Trollope in *New Monthly Mag.* LIX. 466 All the humility and self-doubtingness. **1842** Pusey *Crisis Eng. Ch.* 19 Churches..which, at best, own us but doubtingly.

†**ˈdoubtive, doutif,** *a. Obs.* [a. OF. *doutif, -ive,* doubtful: see -IVE, and cf. DOUBTY.] In doubt or fear; doubtful.

1393 GOWER *Conf.* III. 74 The king was doubtif [*v.r.* doutyf] of þis dom.

doubtless (ˈdaʊtlɪs), *a.* and *adv.* [f. DOUBT *sb.* + -LESS.]

A. *adj.* Free from doubt or uncertainty; undoubted, indubitable; †formerly also, free from apprehension, fear, or suspicion.

c **1440** *Promp. Parv.* 129/2 Dowteles, *indubius, sine dubio.* **1577** FULKE *Confut. Purg.* 362 This doubtlesse institution. **1595** SHAKS. *John* IV. i. 130 Pretty childe, sleepe doubtlesse, and secure. **1596** —— *1 Hen. IV,* III. ii. 20, I am doutlesse I can purge My selfe of many I am charg'd withal. *a* **1603** T. CARTWRIGHT *Confut. Rhem. N.T.* (1618) 172 You have put that..for a doubtlesse doctrine, which he maketh a doubtfull opinion. **1894** P. T. FORSYTH in *Independent* 20 Dec., It is another and a doubtless thing.

B. *adv.* Without doubt or question; unquestionably, undoubtedly, certainly. Now generally concessive of something asserted or claimed.

c **1340** *Gaw. & Gr. Knt.* 725 Nade he ben duȝty & dryȝe ..Douteles he hade ben ded. *c* **1386** CHAUCER *Man of Law's T.* 128, I wol be cristned doutelees. *c* **1400** *Destr. Troy* 3477 Ye dowtles mun degh. **1535** COVERDALE *Ps.* lvii[i]. 11 Doutles, there is a God that iudgeth the earth. **1591** SHAKS. *1 Hen. VI,* IV. vii. 44 Doubtlesse he would haue made a noble Knight. **1732** BERKELEY *Alciphr.* I. §16 Of good things, the greater good is most excellent? Doubtless. **1871** MORLEY *Voltaire* (1886) 223 He doubtless attacked many of the beliefs which good men held sacred.

b. Often in a weaker sense, implying that the speaker sees no reason to doubt the truth of an opinion or presumption uttered; = No doubt.

1664 BUTLER *Hud.* II. iii. 1 Doubtless the pleasure is as great Of being cheated as to cheat. **1728** YOUNG *Love Fame* III. Wks. (1757) 102 Since his great ancestors in Flanders fell, The poem doubtless must be written well. **1840** HOOD *Up Rhine* Introd. 1 The reader of Robinson Crusoe will doubtless remember the flutter of delight [etc.].

Hence **ˈdoubtlessness.**

1895 *Eclectic Mag.* Oct. 565 With equal doubtlessness, Bulgaria would owe her national independence to [etc.].

ˈdoubtlessly, *adv.* [f. prec. + -LY².] Unquestionably, certainly, surely; = DOUBTLESS *adv.*

c **1440** *Promp. Parv.* 129/2 Dowtelesly, *indubie.* **1556** LAUDER *Tractate* 261 Gredie Prencis, dowtleslie, Sall nocht faill to end myserablie. **1657** COKAINE *Obstinate Lady* v. vi. Dram. Wks. (1874) 109, I Doubtlessly shall consent to thy demand. **1798** PENNANT *Hindoostan* I. 203 Doubtlessly many more..have escaped the notice of travellers. **1868** ROGERS *Pol. Econ.* xxi. (1876) 283 The resources of the individual are doubtlessly diminished.

†**ˈdoubtous, doutous,** *a. Obs.* Forms: 4 dotus, dotous(e doutowse, 4–5 doutous, 5 douteouse, dowtous(e, -ows, -eus, dougheteous, doubteous, -euous(e, 4–6 doubtous(e, -uous(e. [ME. a. OF. *dutus, dotus, doutous,* mod.F. *douteux,* f. *doute* DOUBT *sb.*: see -OUS, and for the forms cf. *despitous, piteous.*]

1. Doubtful; of uncertain existence, meaning, or issue.

c **1330** R. BRUNNE *Chron. Wace* (Rolls) 14298 Merlyn seide..þat Arthures deþ was dotouse..ȝyt þe Bretons..seyn þat he lyues in lede. *c* **1380** WYCLIF *Sel. Wks.* III. 373 Counseil in doutouse þinges. **1481** CAXTON *Tulle on Old Age,* Dyvinacions to know the doubteuouse thing. **1489** —— *Faytes of A.* I. viii. 21 In the doubtouse happe of bataill. **1532** MORE *Confut. Tindale* Wks. 457/2 Scripture is..doubtouse and hard to vnderstande.

2. Full of uncertainty of mind; doubting.

c **1374** CHAUCER *Boeth.* I. pr. i. 5 Of a doutous iugement. **1483** CAXTON *Gold. Leg.* 227/2 Thenne cam he alle doubtous to the yates. **1490** —— *Eneydos* xvi. 66 He abode long in this thought doubtouse and varyable.

3. Fraught with terror; fearful, dreadful, terrible.

a **1300** *Signs bef. Judgem.* 113 in *E.E.P.* (1862) 10 þe eiȝt dai so is dotus..ful of tene and angus. ? *a* **1400** *Morte Arth.* 3968 A dowttouse derfe dede [= death], þou duellis to longe! *c* **1470** HARDING *Chron.* LXXVIII. vi, One that should yᵉ dougheteous siege acheue. *c* **1500** *Melusine* xlv. 318 My departyng fro you is more gryeuous & doubtous a thousand tymes to me than to you.

Hence **ˈdoubtously** *adv.*, doubtfully.

c **1350** *Will. Palerne* 4338 Doutusli after he stared on his stepmoder stifli a while. *c* **1400** *Lanfranc's Cirurg.* 121 Grettere maistryes..han y-writen dotousliche.

ˈdoubtsome, *a. Sc.* and *north. dial.* Also 6 doutsum. [f. DOUBT *sb.* + -SOME.] = DOUBTFUL.

1513 DOUGLAS *Æneis* VI. xi. 91 Thochtful in mynd, ne doutsum by na way. **1591** JAS. I in Farr. *S.P. Jas. I* (1848) 5 Long doubtsome fight. **1642** *Declar. Lords Secr. Counc. Scot.* 3 His generall and doubtsome faith. **1689** tr. *Buchanan's De Jure Regni apud Scotos* 35 The hazard of a doubtsome Cure. **1847–78** HALLIW., *Doubtsome,* doubtful, uncertain. *North.* [In N.W. Lincolnsh., Lonsdale, Mid-Yorksh., Whitby, Northumberland Gloss.].

Hence **ˈdoubtsomely** *adv.*, doubtfully.

1533 BELLENDEN *Livy* v. (1822) 417 Quhat maner of man this wes that spak sa doutsumlie.

†**ˈdoubty,** *a. Obs. rare.* Also 4–5 douti. [a. OF. *doutif, dotif,* nom. sing. and pl. *dotis;* the suffix being assimilated to English -Y: cf. CORSY, TARDY, etc.] Doubtful; dubious; hazardous.

c **1380** WYCLIF *Sel. Wks.* III. 381 In soche douty poyntes. **1388** —— *1 Kings* x. 1 In derk and douti questiouns. **1509** HAWES *Past. Pleas.* 17 A ful noble story, Of the doubty waye to the tower perillous. **1611** SPEED *Hist. Gt. Brit.* IX. xxi. (1632) 1014 A doubty kinde of accusation. **1679** *Hist. Jetzer* 6 This doubty controversie.

Hence †**doubtily** *adv.*, in doubt.

1654 R. WHITLOCK *Zootomia* 551, I lived..anxiously, dye doubt[i]ly, and know not whether I go.

doubty, erron. obs. form of DOUGHTY.

‖**douc** (duk). [a. F. *douc,* a. Cochin *douc, dok* monkey (Littré).] A species of monkey (*Semnopithecus nemeus*) found in Cochin China.

1774 GOLDSM. *Nat. Hist.* (1776) IV. 235 The last of the monkies of the ancient continent, is the Douc, so called in Cochin-china, of which country it is a native. **1847** CARPENTER *Zool.* §151 The Douc or Cochin-China Monkey ..is distinguished by the singular variety and brilliancy of its colours.

douce (duːs), *a.* Also, 4–9 douse, 5–8 dowse, 5–9 dowce. *β.* 5–7 doulce, 6 doulx (in sense 1). [ME. *douce, dowce,* a. OF. *dolz, dols, dous,* later *doux,* fem. *douce,* also 15–16th c. *doulce,* = Pr. *dolz, dous,* It. *dolce,* Sp. *dulce*:—L. *dulcis* sweet.]

†**1.** Sweet, pleasant. (A well-known epithet of France, from Chanson de Roland onwards.) *Obs.*

[*a* **1310** in Wright *Lyric P.* 111 Oure dame douse shal sitten hym by. **1377** LANGL. *P. Pl.* B. XIV. 122 And diues in deyntees lyued and in douce vye.] *c* **1380** *Sir Ferumb.* 1269 We buþ knyȝtes alle y-vere: y-born in douce fraunce. *c* **1420** *Liber Cocorum* (1862) 32 Powder dowce and salt also. *c* **1489** CAXTON *Sonnes of Aymon* xvi. 367 Ye shall never maye retourne in to douce Fraunce agayne. **1526** *Pilgr. Perf.* (W. de W. 1531) 22 b, Whan..sommer draweth nere, it [an apple] waxeth mellowe douce & pleasaunt. **1596** DALRYMPLE tr. *Leslie's Hist. Scot.* IV. lviii. (1887) 251 Sa douse in exhortatione. **1614** FORBES *Comm. Revelation* 126 (Jam.) The douce sounde of harpes.

β. *c* **1477** CAXTON *Jason* 18 b, To mete doulce regarde. **1531** ELYOT *Gov.* I. xiv. (1883) 154 The lawes..beyng in pure latine or doulce frenche. *c* **1540** LD. SOUTHAMPTON & BP. OF ELY in Ellis *Orig. Lett.* Ser. II. II. 111 With doulx and myld wordes. **1542** BOORDE *Dyetary* xxi. (1870) 283 Peares ..melow and doulce. *a* **1577** SIR T. SMITH *Commw. Eng.* II. iii. (1609) 43 Doulce and gentle termes.

2. Quiet, sober, steady, gently sedate; not light, flighty, or frivolous. *Sc.* and *north. dial.*

1728 RAMSAY *Adv. to Mr.* —— *on his Marriage* 16 I've given a douce advice and plain. **1776** C. KEITH *Farmer's Ha'* in Chambers *Pop. Hum. Scot. Poems* (1862) 36 The lads and lasses a' grow douse. **1816** SCOTT *Old Mort.* iv, A douce woman she was, civil to the customers. **1825** in BROCKETT *N.C. Words.* **1850** MRS. CARLYLE *Lett.* II. 129, I think the new servant will do; she looks douce, intelligent. **1868** HELPS *Realmah* vii. (1876) 158 Realmah and the Ainah talked on in the douce, quiet way.

Hence **ˈdoucely** *adv.*; **ˈdouceness.**

1621 S. WARD *Happiness of Practice* (1627) 14 Some luscious delight, yea, a kind of rauishing doucenesse there is in studying good Bookes. **1786** BURNS *Earnest Cry & Prayer* 3 An' doucely manage our affairs In parliament. **1822** GALT *Steam-Boat* 191 (Jam.) The natural douceness of my character. **1850** R. SIMPSON *Mem. of Worth* ii. 20 Mr. Hislop was riding doucely along this track.

†**douce,** *v. Obs. rare.* In 5 dowce, 7 doulce. [Aphetic f. *adoulce, adouce,* a. OF. *adoulcir, adoucir* to sweeten: see ADDULCE.] *trans.* To sweeten; to soften, mollify, soothe.

c **1420** *Liber Cocorum* (1862) 7 With sugur candy þou may hit dowce. **1600** HOLLAND *Livy* XXIII. xvi. 484 The yong mans stout heart was so doulced, mollified, and easie to bee wrought.

douce, var. of DOUSE.

doucepere: see DOUZEPERS.

doucet (ˈduːsɪt), **dowset** (ˈdaʊsɪt). Forms: *α.* 5 doucete, dowcete, -ced, -sete, 5–7 dou-, dowcette, doucet, 6–9 dowset, 7 douset, dowcet, -sett, dowlcet, doulcet. *β.* 5 dulset, 6 dulcet. [a. F. *doucet, doucette,* dim. of *doux, douce* sweet; also sb. a sweet variety of grape, of apple, etc., and in other senses. See also DULCET.]

†**1.** A sweet dish, in old cookery. *Obs.*

c **1430** *Two Cookery-bks.* 55 *Doucettes.* Take Porke..& Eyroun..& melle hem to-gederys with Hony & Pepir, & bake hem in a cofyn. **1467** *Mann. & Househ. Exp.* 399 For viij. boshelles of flour for dowsetes. **1530** PALSGR. 215/1 Dousette a lytell flawne, *dariolle.* **1593** DRAYTON *Eclogues* ix. 47 Fresh Cheese, and Dowsets, Curds and clowted Creame. **1615** MARKHAM *Eng. Housew.* II. ii. (1668) 75 An excellent Custard or Dowset. **1640** *King & Poor North. Man* (N.), Heer's dousets and flapjacks.

†**2.** A wind instrument resembling a flute. *Obs.*

α. *c* **1384** CHAUCER *H. Fame* III. 131 That craftely begunne to pipe Bothe in doucet and in riede. *c* **1430** LYDG. *Reason & Sensual.,* Trumpes and trumpettes, Lowde shallys and doucettes.

β. *c* **1450** HOLLAND *Howlat* 762 The dulset, the dulsacordis, the schalme of assay.

3. *Hunting.* (*pl.*) The testicles of a deer.

a **1611** BEAUM. & FL. *Philaster* IV. ii, He was there at the fall of a deer, and would needs..give ten groats for the dowcets. **1630** J. TAYLOR (Water P.) *Wks.* I. 93 Dewclawes, and Dowlcets. **1637** B. JONSON *Sad Sheph.* I. vi, All the sweet morsels call'd tongue, ears, and dowcets. **1638** FORD *Fancies* I. ii. Wks. 1869 II. 234, I am made a gelding, and, like a tame buck, have lost my dowsets. **1678** PHILLIPS (ed. 4), *Doulcets,* the stones of a Hart or Stag. **1686** PLOT *Staffordsh.* 255 Red and fallow deer, whose doucets if taken away..before they have hornes, will never have any at all. **1826** SCOTT *Woodst.* iii, Broiling the *umbles,* or *dowsets,* of the deer, upon the glowing embers, with their own royal hands.

doucet, early form of DULCET.

‖**douceur** (dusœːr). Forms: 4 dousour, 5 -ceour, 6– -ceur, (7 doulcure, 8 doucœur). [a. F. *douceur,* in OF. *dulcur, douçor, dousor, douçour,* = Pr. *dolzor,* Sp. *dulzor,* It. *dolciore*:—Romanic type **dolçore,* **dulçore,* for L. *dulcōr-em* sweetness, f. *dulcis* sweet. In ME. app. naturalized; but in modern use, since 17th c., a French loan-word.]

†**1.** Formerly, sweetness and pleasantness of manner; amiability, gentleness. Revived in sense 'something pleasant or agreeable'. So ***douceur de (la) vie*** or ***de vivre***: the pleasure or the sweet things of life.

13.. *E.E. Allit. P.* A. 429 For synglerty o hyr dousour, We calle hyr fenyx of Arraby. **1422** tr. *Secreta Secret., Priv. Priv.* (E.E.T.S.) 189 To Souerayns reuerence and honoure ..to fellowis company and douceoure. **1620** *Fortesc. Papers* (Camden) 126 (Stanf.) Your Majesties douceur and facilitie. **1623** ABP. WILLIAMS in Hacket *Life* I. (1692) 116, I have given special Order to the Judges for Sweetness, and Doulcure to the English Catholicks. **1700** CONGREVE *Way of World* IV. 57 My morning thoughts, agreeable wakings, indolent slumbers, all ye *douceurs,* ye *Someils du Matin adieu.* **1758** RALPH *Case Authors by Profess.* 5 All the Douceurs of Life arising from Observance and Respect will be wanting. **1793** MAD. D'ARBLAY *Let. to Mrs. Phillips* 14 May, He..answered with all his accustomed douceur and politeness. **1938** W. S. MAUGHAM *Summing Up* 294 They will not know the easy, sheltered life which makes many who were at their prime before the war look upon those years as did the survivors of the French Revolution when they looked back on the Ancien Régime. They will not know the *douceur de vivre.* **1952** W. PLOMER *Museum Pieces* 130 As if he were lamenting a *douceur de vivre* of which he had caught the last fragrance. **1958** I. MURDOCH *Bell* xxvi. 305 A curious relationship grew up between Michael and Dora, something undefined and wistful which had for Michael a certain ease and *douceur.* **1962** *Times* 13 Feb. 11/3 These institutions are sometimes a bit short of *les douceurs de la vie.* **1962** *Listener* 6 Dec. 979/2 Yet another reminder of that *douceur de vivre* which in 1939 vanished for ever. **1963** *Punch* 3 July 4/2 A certain softness,..easy-going placidity, *douceur de vie.* **1965** 'J. DARCY' *Killing in Hats* iii. 59 Between the *douceur de la vie* which was about to pass, and the tantalising future.

†**2.** An agreeable or pleasant speech; a complimentary phrase. *Obs.*

1672 DRYDEN *Marr. à la Mode* v. i, Truce with your douceurs, good servant. **1726** AMHERST *Terræ Fil.* xliv. 232 Those printed douceurs that pass between authors and their betters, vulgarly call'd dedications. **1807** *Edin. Rev.* X. 190 (Stanf.) Such elaborate douceurs as occur in the following letter..look too much like adulation.

3. A conciliatory present or gift; a gratuity or 'tip'; a bribe.

1763 H. WALPOLE *Lett.* (1857) IV. 67 (Stanf.) Her lord has ..added..little douceurs..to her jointure. **1769** in *Priv. Lett. Ld. Malmesbury* (1870) I. 174 Thirty guineas being publicly given to this last soldier, as a sort of douceur for what he had suffered. **1779** MAD. D'ARBLAY *Diary* Nov., [After] one remarkable speech in the House of Commons.. receiving some douceur to be silent ever after. **1818** R. PETERS in *J. Jay's Corr. & Pub. Papers* (1893) IV. 424 Money..devoted to secret service and douceurs to French agents. **1880** J. T. WHEELER *Short Hist. India* III. iv. 354 The commander-in-chief of the Bengal army..reckoned on receiving a handsome douceur. **1922** *Classical Rev.* XXXVI. 31/2 The Emperor..adds that a douceur will be necessary in order to get him to consent to the loan. **1965** N. GULBENKIAN *Pantaraxia* xiv. 305 On the few occasions when I have a bet, a winning one, my wife gets a little nonsense and all my servants get a little *douceur.*

douche (‖duʃ, duːʃ), *sb.* [a. F. *douche* spout, stream of water, 16th c. ad. It. *doccia* conduit-pipe, f. *docciare* to pour by drops:—L. type **ductiare,* f. *ductus* leading, lead, conduit, f. *dūcĕre* to lead.]

1. a. A jet or stream of water, or the like, applied to some part of the body, generally for medicinal purposes; the application of this; an instrument for administering it.

[**1685** COTTON tr. *Montaigne* II. 710 So the Italians have their doccie..and with them bath an hour in the morning.] **1766** SMOLLETT *Trav.* 351 This last operation called douche, is more effectually undergone in the private bath. **1835** *Penny Cycl.* IV. 33/2 A stream of water falling on the head ..It is called the *cold dash,* or *douche,* or *douse.* **1844** DUFTON *Deafness* 107 The air-press should be used, as recommended for applying the air-douche. **1866** MRS. GASKELL *Wives & Dau.* xi, It was rather like a douche of cold water on Mrs. Kirkpatrick's plans. **1894** BARING-GOULD *Deserts S. France* I. 24 To send down a douche of ice-cold air upon us.

b. *spec.* a jet of water (or a solution of water and other substances) introduced into the vagina as a means of cleansing the uterus and cervix, treating infection and haemorrhage, or *esp.* preventing conception after intercourse; (a substance for) vaginal or uterine lavage. Also with defining word, as (***intra-***)***uterine douche, vaginal douche.*** orig. *U.S.*

[**1833** Dunglison *New Dict. Med. Sci.* I. 316 The *douches ascendantes*, those administered in diseases of the uterus.] **1887** J. H. Williamson tr. *Winckel's Diseases of Women* II. iii. 131 Injections and douches are by no means so innocent as is generally supposed.. because instant death has resulted from pumping air into these cavities. **1893** *Funk's Stand. Dict.* I. 549/1 *Uterine douche*, a device to irrigate the womb. **1901** C. A. L. Reed *Textbk. Gynecol.* ii. 10 The use of the vaginal douche immediately after intercourse,.. the 'womb caps', condoms, are all damaging expedients. **1923** M. Stopes *Contraception* v. 116 Innumerable vaginal douches are on the market. **1953** G. B. Carter et al. *Dict. Midwifery* (1963) 147/2 A midwife is sometimes called upon to give an intra-uterine douche, but the treatment is unsuitable if she is single handed. **1972** M. Mead *Blackberry Winter* ix. 103 We knew that she ought not have a baby yet, and we compiled a five-page typed list of home remedies that could be used as a douche. **1987** *N.Y. Times* 4 Mar. 8/3 In addition to reducing the risk of pregnancy,.. the douche may flush virus-containing cells from the vagina.

2. *attrib.* and *Comb.*, as ***douche-bath***; **douche-bag**, (*a*) a sterile receptacle for the fluid when administering a douche; freq. applied to the whole apparatus used for douching, including rubber tubing, nozzles, etc.; (*b*) *U.S. slang*, a general term of disparagement, *esp.* for an unattractive or boring person; cf. BAG *sb.* 17 ; **douche can, glass** = *douche bag* (*a*).

1908 C. Macfarlane *Ref. Handbk. Gynecol. for Nurses* 35 Hang the *douche-bag eighteen inches above the level of the patient's hips. **1934** H. Miller *Tropic of Cancer* 109 Over the bedstead hangs a douche-bag which he keeps for emergencies. **1966** *Observer* (Colour Suppl.) 20 Mar. 41/2 A few belts, a tweed beret and a douche bag were all that was left of Eva Braun's envied wardrobe. **1967** *Amer. Speech* XLII. 228 *Douche bag, n. phr.*, an unattractive co-ed. By extension, any individual whom the speaker desires to deprecate. **1968** *Punch* 20 Nov. 718/2 'Send them away!' she hissed. 'If they are found here, those douche-bags will incriminate us all.' **1972** *Village Voice* (N.Y.) 1 June 24/5, I had begun to like the naturalistic black writer who will never live in his native land. Pollution, violence, and the douche bag of American problems have something to do with it. **1868** *Daily News* 7 Aug., A.. bath-house, with plunge-bath, *douche-bath, and shower-baths of different sorts. **1883** J. Payn *Thicker than Water* xxxv. 275, I don't mind a sprinkling; but no one likes a douche bath of it. **1908** *Practitioner* Oct. 579 At first I used an ordinary enamelled tin *douche-can. *Ibid.*, It is an advantage.. to be able to watch the limb which is being congested, and so I now use a cylindrical *douche-glass.

douche, *v.* [f. prec. sb.; cf. F. *doucher*.] **1.** *trans.* To administer a douche to; to douse.

1838 Lady Granville *Lett.* 21 July (1894) II. 261 A little douching and bathing is the best possible thing. **1864** Carlyle *Fredk. Gt.* IV. 350 Douched and drenched in dirty water. **1869** E. A. Parkes *Pract. Hygiene* (ed. 3) 618 If one or two good force pumps and hose are on board, every man should be douched.

b. *intr.* (for *refl.*) To take a douche.

1843 Sir C. Scudamore *Med. Visit Gräfenberg* 19 One.. who had regularly douched through the winter every day for eight minutes.

2. *spec.* To administer a vaginal douche (to). Also with *out*. **a.** *trans.* To apply a douche to (the vagina). **b.** *intr.* and *refl.* Of a woman: to use a vaginal douche after intercourse, as a contraceptive measure. orig. and chiefly *U.S.*

1898 H. A. Kelly *Operative Gynecol.* I. viii. 163 If there are any offensive discharges the vagina is douched out with a warm boric or carbolic solution. **1907** H. Brown *Wife Bk.* xx. 188 Neither the doctor nor nurse will douche the vagina after an ordinary labor. **1923** M. Stopes *Contraception* v. 117 'Birth Controllers' in general have encouraged women to douche daily, or often 'as an ordinary measure of hygienic cleanliness'. **1963** M. McCarthy *Group* iii. 52 Dottie would be taught how and when to douche, how much water to use, the proper height for the douche bag, [etc.]. **1969** A. Guttmacher *Birth Control & Love* (ed. 2) vi. 87 Douche immediately after intercourse. **1978** J. Irving *World according to Garp* i. 22 She wasn't going to douche, of course ... She felt more receptive than prepared soil. **1984** E. Fairweather *Only Rivers run Free* iii. 124, I douched myself out, too. Because of this womb trouble I was always being given douche bags.

Hence **'douching** *vbl. sb.*

1923 M. Stopes *Contraception* v. 116 The habit of douching is one of the three most commonly advocated methods of birth control. **1944** Miller & Bryant *Gynecol. & Gynecologic Nursing* xxvii. 265 Vaginal douching is used and abused so extensively that some comment.. is advisable. **1974** *Encycl. Brit. Macropædia* II. 1067/2 Among the methods used by women, one of the oldest is 'douching' — the practice of flushing out the vagina, generally with a liquid solution, after coitus.

doucherie, var. of DUCHERY, *Obs.*

douch-spere, corrupt sing. of DOUZEPERS.

doucht, Sc. pa. t. of DOW *v.*[1]

douchtie, -y, obs. forms of DOUGHTY.

doucimer, obs. form of DULCIMER.

‖**doucin** (dusɛ̃, 'duːsɪn). Also 6 **duseanne**. [F.; f. *douce* sweet, DOUCE.] A sweet variety of wild apple.

1589 Cogan *Haven Health* (1636) 102 The best apples.. in England are Pepins, Costards, Duseannes, Darlings. **1834** *Penny Cycl.* II. 191/2 The stocks.. employed are the wild crab, the doucin or English paradise, and the French paradise apple. **1846** J. Baxter *Libr. Pract. Agric.* (ed. 4) I. 61 There are only two kinds, according to Lindley, on which it is desirable to propagate the apple in this country—the *Wild Crab* and the *Doucin* stock.

‖**doucine** (dusin). *Arch.* [F., in 15–16th c. *doulcine*, *doucine* trumpet, f. *doux*, *douce* sweet, soft.] = *cyma recta*: see CYMA 1.

1726 Leoni *Alberti's Archit.* II. 31/2 The Cymatium, or Doucine, both upright and reversed.

douck(e, doucker, obs. ff. DUCK, DUCKER.

doud(e, obs. form of DOWD.

doudle, var. DOODLE *v.*[2], to play bagpipes.

douer, var. DOWER *sb.*[1] *Obs.*

douf, var. of DOWF *a.*

doufe, douffe, obs. forms of DOVE.

dough (dəʊ), *sb.* Forms: 1 **dáȝ, dáh**, 4 **doȝ**, 4–5 **dogh**, *north.* **dagh**, 4–8 **dow, dowe**, 6 **doughe, dowghe**, 6– **dough**, (7 **doe**, 6– *Sc.* **daigh, deawch**). See also DUFF, which represents a prevalent dialect pronunciation. [A Common Teut. sb.: OE. *dáh*, gen. *dáȝes*, = OFris. *deeg*, Du. *deg*, OHG., MHG. *teic*, Ger. *teig*, ON. *deig*, (Sw. *deg*, Da. *deig*, *dei*), Goth. *daigs*:—OTeut. **daigoz*, f. verbal stem *dig-*, *deig-*, pre-Teutonic **dhigh-* to form of clay, to knead: cf. Skr. *dih-* to besmear, L. *fig-*, *fingĕre*; cf. Gr. *τεῖχος* wall.]

1. a. A mass consisting of flour or meal moistened and kneaded into a paste, with or without leaven, ready to be baked into bread, etc.; kneaded flour; paste of bread. †SOUR-DOUGH (q.v.), leaven.

c **1000** *Sax. Leechd.* II. 342 Wyrc clam of.. daȝe. *Ibid.* III. 88 Cned hyt.. ꝧ hit si swa þicca swa doh. **1303** R. Brunne *Handl. Synne* 10099 Þe paste.. ne oghe Be made of eny maner of soure doghe. **1340** *Ayenb.* 205 Ase þe leuayne zoureþ þet doȝ. *c* **1430** *Two Cookery-bks.* 43 Take dow, & make þer-of a þinne kake. *c* **1450** Myrc 1882 Thy bred schal be of whete flour, I-made of dogh that ys not sour. **1526** Tindale *Gal.* v. 9 A lytel leven doth leven the whole lompe of dowe. **1649** Jer. Taylor *Gt. Exemp.* Pref. ¶ 25 He left this nation, as a piece of leaven in a masse of dow. **1813** Sir H. Davy *Agric. Chem.* (1814) 137 Leavened bread for use is made by mixing a little dough that has fermented, with new dough, and kneading them together. **1830** M. Donovan *Dom. Econ.* I. 351 The better and older the flour the more water it absorbs to make dough.

b. Proverb. ***(my) cake is dough, (my) meal is all dough*** (Sc.): my project has failed.

1596 Shaks. *Tam. Shrew* v. i. 145 My cake is dough, but Ile in among the rest. **1687–1708** [see CAKE *sb.* 8]. **1737** Ramsay *Scot. Prov.* (1776) 38 (Jam.) His meal's a' daigh. **1860** Reade *Cloister & H.* xxv, Dietrich's forty years weighed him down like forty bullets. 'Our cake is dough', he gasped.

2. a. *transf.* and *fig.*

1611 Cotgr., *Laudore*.. a leaden fellow, poore sneakesbie, man of dowgh. *a* **1616** Beaum. & Fl. *Wit without Money* II. ii, She has found what dough you are made of, and so kneads you. **1624** Fletcher *Rule a Wife* III. i, How unlike the lump I took him for, The piece of ignorant dow. **1788** Burns *1st Ep. to Graham* 16 She [Nature] kneads the lumpish philosophic dough. **1876** Geo. Eliot *Dan. Der.* IV. lviii. 168 The baking process which the human dough demands.

b. Money. *slang* (orig. *U.S.*).

1851 *Yale Tomahawk* Feb. (Th.), He thinks he will pick his way out of the Society's embarrassments, provided he can get sufficient dough. **1896** Ade *Artie* ii. 12 I pulled in the dough and picked up the cards. **1917** [see BOODLE[1] 2 b]. **1919** *War Slang* in *Athenæum* 22 Aug. 791/2 'Dough' denotes money, but more especially the weekly pay. **1942** Wodehouse *Money in Bank* (1946) xxvii. 241 She's got more dough than you could shake a stick at. **1943** *Coast to Coast 1942* 59 It might mean that I'll get a chance of makin' some dough. **1944** C. A. Lawrence *Narrowing Wind* 60 You're in the dough and you kin afford to live there better'n I kin. **1955** *Times* 3 Aug. 5/4 I'm going back to business and make myself a little dough.

attrib. **1904** *N.Y. Even. Post* 7 Nov. 3 This is Tammany's regular annual 'dough day'—that is, the day on which the district leaders come to Tammany Hall for election day funds. **1906** *Ibid.* 24 Oct. 4 In the country, election day without some sort of 'dough-bag' is an unheard-of thing. No 'dough-bag' means no votes.

3. Any soft, pasty mass.

1559 Morwyng *Evonym.* 220 The leaves of hempe.. Water should be poured to it, and when they are made dowe together, then to be destilled. **1623** Lisle *Ælfric on O. & N. Test.* (1638) Pref. 4 To mould the dow of artificiall marble, and bake it in killes for building. **1862** *Jrnl. Soc. Arts* X. 326/2 It [the India-rubber] may be dissolved either into 'varnish', or the more solid 'dough' , as it is called, by the digestion of the sheet in.. naphtha.

4. a. *north. dial.* (See quot. and YULE-DOUGH.)

1777 Brand *Pop. Antiq.*, *Yule Doughs* (1870) I. 293 The Yule-Dough, or Dow, was a kind of Baby, or little Image of Paste, which our Bakers used.. to bake at this season and present to their customers. *Ibid.*, *note*, Dough or Dow is vulgarly used in the North for a little cake.

b. A pudding or dumpling of dough: cf. DUFF and DOUGH-BOY.

5. *attrib.* and *Comb.*, as ***dough-bait, -cake, -pan, -pill***; ***dough-dividing, -kneaded, -like*** adjs.; **dough-ball**, (*U.S.*) ? = DOUGHNUT; **dough-balls**, the tufts of a kind of seaweed, *Polysiphonia Olneyi*; **dough-brake, -kneader, -maker, -mixer**, machines for kneading and mixing dough; **dough-cake**, (*a*) a cake made of dough; (*b*) *dial.* a simpleton, a fool; **dough-head**, (*U.S.*) 'a soft-pated fellow, a fool' (Bartlett *Dict. Amer.* 1860); **dough-raiser**, (see quot.); †**dough-rib**, an implement for scraping and cleaning the kneading-trough. Also DOUGH-BAKE, etc.

1904 *Westm. Gaz.* 19 Nov. 3/1 On the bank.. men and boys.. are fishing with quill-floats and *dough-bait, the least artistic form of sport. **1864** *Louie's last Term* (N.Y.) 168 *Dough-balls were her acknowledged passion. **1881** Farlow *Marine Algæ* 171 In its typical form P[olysiphonia] Olneyi forms dense soft tufts, sometimes called *dough-balls by the sea-shore population. *c* **1750** M. Palmer *Devonshire Dialogue* (1839) 33 How unvitty and cat-handed you go about it, you *dough-cake. **1839** F. Trollope *Dom. Manners* (ed. 5) 272 It won't convene for me to be mixing doe cakes and Johny cakes all day. **1844** Lee & Frost *10 Yrs. Oregon* xxii. 290 Becoming quite hungry we got out some flour, and baked some dough cakes. **1892** *Encycl. Cookery* I. 525/1 Small Dough Cake... Large Dough Cake. **1921** W. de la Mare *Memoirs of Midget* 8 Stuffing himself out with bread-and-dripping or dough-cake. **1854** M. J. Holmes *Tempest & Sunshine* xv. 222 He inwardly accused them all of being '*doughheads'. **1642** Milton *Apol. Smect.* (1851) 288 He.. demeanes himselfe in the dull expression so like a *dough kneaded thing. **1874** Knight *Dict. Mech.* I. 732/1 **Dough-kneader*, a pair of rollers, one corrugated lengthwise and the other transversely, working in a frame with two inclined boards. **1928** A. B. Callow *Food & Health* 25 The 'indigestibility' of very new bread is due to its *dough-like consistency. **1874** Knight *Dict. Mech.* I. 732/1 **Dough-mixer*. **1841** Lane *Arab. Nts.* I. 108 'Uncover the *dough-pan'. **1831** Carlyle *Sart. Res.* I. iii, His chief Talapoin, to whom no *dough-pill he could knead and publish was other than medicinal and sacred. **1874** Knight *Dict. Mech.* I. 732/2 **Dough-raiser*, a pan in a bath of heated water, to maintain a temperature in the dough favorable to fermentation. *c* **1325** *Gloss. W. de Biblesw.* in Wright *Voc.* 155 *Un rastuer*, a *douw-ribbe. *c* **1440** *Promp. Parv.* 129/1 Dowrys or dowrybbe, *sarpa*. **1530** Palsgr. 215/1 Dowe rybbe, *ratissevr a paste*.

dough (dəʊ), *v. rare.* [f. prec. sb.]

†**1.** *intr.* To work in dough; to make dough. *Obs.*

1631 Heywood *1st Pt. Fair Maid of W.* II. Wks. 1874 II. 277 When corne grew to be at an high rate, my father [a baker] never dowed after.

2. *trans.* To make (something) into or like dough. ***to dough in***: to mix in with the dough (see DOUGHING *vbl. sb.*).

1887 *N. & Q.* 7th Ser. III. 16/1 Doughing together the paste formed by the *yerba* and water.

Hence **'doughing**, *ppl. a.*

1883 Grant White *Washington Adams* 33 Pleasing and picturesque, and yet souring and doughing.

†**'dough-bake**. *Obs. rare*$^{-1}$. [f. DOUGH *sb.* + BAKE *v.*: cf. next.] Under-done bread; the 'crumb' of a loaf.

1573 Tusser *Husb.* lxxix. (1878) 171 Much dowebake I praise not, much crust is as ill.

'dough-baked, *ppl. a.* Now *dial.* [f. as prec.] Imperfectly baked, so as to remain doughy.

1611 Cotgr., *Pasteux*.. doughie; clammie as bread which is dough-baked. **1630** J. Taylor (Water P.) *Wit & Mirth* Wks. II. 192/1 One of the Schollers complayned vnto him that the bread were dogh-baked: Why quoth hee, so it should bee; what else is the definition of bread but dough baked? **1642** Fuller *Holy & Prof. St.* III. xx. 205 In that oven wherein dow-baked cakes shall be burnt.

b. *transf.* and *fig.* Imperfect, badly finished; deficient, esp. in intellect or sense; feeble, 'soft'.

1592 Lyly *Midas* II. ii. 22 A reason dow-baked. *a* **1613** Overbury *A Wife* (1638) 64 A very woman is a dow-bak't man. **1623** T. Scot *Highw. God* 80 A deade luke-warme indifferencie, a dow-baked zeale. **1754** Richardson *Grandison* (ed. 7) I. 84 Your milksops, your dough-baked lovers. **1809–10** Coleridge *Friend* (1865) 216 These dough-baked patriots are not however useless.

†**'dough-baken**, *ppl. a.* *Obs.* = prec.

1529 More *Dyaloge* III. 71 a/2 Yf hys brede.. be dowe baken. **1578** *Chr. Prayers* in *Priv. Prayers* (1851) 498 Who shall scrape off this dough-baken dung?

'dough-bird. Local *U.S.* Also **doe-bird**. The New England name for the Eskimo curlew (*Numenius borealis*).

18.. *Shore Birds* 12 (Cent.) Mingling freely with the golden plover are the Esquimaux curlew, or dough-birds.

'dough-boy. **1.** *Naut.* and *Colonial.* A boiled flour dumpling.

1685 Ringrose *Bucaniers Amer.* II. IV. 4 These men.. had each of them three or four Cakes of bread (called by the English *Dough-boy's*) for their provision and Victuals. **1697** Dampier *Voy.* (1729) I. v. 110 This Oil served instead of Butter, to eat with Dough-boys or Dumplins. **1880** *Blackw. Mag.* Jan. 72 Quite a gourmet in the matter of dough-boys and duff. **1887** *Pall Mall Budget* 22 Aug. 13/2 Each man had also a dough-boy made with $\frac{1}{4}$ lb. of flour, and boiled in the soup.

2. *U.S. slang.* †**a.** = ADOBE 1 (cf. DOBE). *Obs.*

1856 in *Mont. Hist. Soc. Contrib.* (1940) X. 74 The Carpenters at Work getting the Doughboy tools ready. *Ibid.* 75 The men mixed their mud in preparation for making doughboys. *Ibid.* 82 The Carpenters made.. three doughboy moulds.

b. *colloq.* An infantryman in the U.S. Army. Also *attrib.*

There have been several conjectures as to the origin of this sense (*e.g.* quots. 1887 and 1940).

[**1865** *Harper's Weekly* 25 Nov. 741/2 The battered excursionists.. were designated as 'Bummers', 'Do-Boys',

'Raiders', etc.] **1867** in E. Custer *Tenting on Plains* (1887) xvi. 516 Wasn't I glad I was not a doughboy? **1887** *Ibid.*, A 'doughboy' is a small round doughnut... Early in the Civil War the term was applied to the large globular brass buttons on the infantry uniform, from which it passed..to the infantrymen themselves. **1898** *Scribner's Mag.* Aug. 133 Horse dealers..led their ponies up and down before.. dough-boy officers. **1904** *N.Y. Times* 13 June 6 A disgusting practice which reduced a bold cavalier to the level of a 'doughboy' at once. **1918** 'I. HAY' *Last Million* ix. 134 The true exile in this war is the American born Doughboy. **1920** E. W. BOK *Autobiogr.* (1921) xxxi. 293 The amazing part of the 'show'..was the American doughboy. **1940** O. L. SPAULDING in *Dict. Amer. Hist.* II. 163/1 The word 'dough-boy'..can be traced with certainty as far back as 1854... The contemporary explanation then was, that the infantrymen wore white belts, and had to clean them with 'dough' made of pipe clay. **1966** A. LOOS *Girl like I* ix. 164 During World War I, she dressed as a doughboy in olive drab.

†'**dougher.** *Obs.* In 5 dower. [f. DOUGH *v.* + -ER[1].] One who makes dough; a baker.

1483 *Gild Bakers in Eng. Gilds* 335 All Dowers of the Cite ..[shall] grynd att the Cite-is myllis.

'**dough-face, doughface.** *U.S.*

1. A mask made of dough. Also *transf.*

1809 *Deb. Congress U.S.* 23 Feb. (1853) 1509 It is something like dressing ourselves up in a dough-face and winding-sheet to frighten others. **1820** *Massachusetts Spy* 22 Mar. (Th.), They saw their dough faces in the glass and were frightened. *a* **1833** J. RANDOLPH *Sp. in Congress* (Bartlett), They were scared at their own dough-faces. **1883** E. EGGLESTON *Hoosier School-Boy* xviii. 120 Two boys from the neighborhood, who had joined the party, agreed to furnish dough-faces for them all. **1940** C. MCCULLERS *Heart is Lonely Hunter* (1943) II. i. 98 One boy had..put on a dough-face bought in advance for Hallowe'een.

2. A dough-faced person; one who allows himself to be moulded or worked upon; formerly, in U.S. politics, applied to Northern politicians considered to yield undue compliance to the South, in the matter of slavery, etc.

[**1820** *New Brunswick Times* 13 Apr. (Th.), [John Randolph of Roanoke] said, 'I knew these would give way. They were scared at their own dough faces... We had them.'] **1830** *Boston Transcript* 6 Dec. 2/3 The protecting duty will be repealed, if the anti-tariff party can get enough dough faces to join them. **1834** WHITTIER *Let. to Sewall* Pr. Wks. 1889 III. 87 How familiar have the significant epithets of 'White slave' and 'dough-face' become! **1848** LOWELL *Biglow P.* Poet. Wks. 1890 II. 80. **1863** W. PHILLIPS *Speeches* iii. 42 Behold the great doughface cringing before the calm eye of Kossuth.

attrib. **1886** *American* XII. 279 The doughface press.

So '**dough-faced** *a.*, having a face like dough; of the character of a 'dough-face' in U.S. politics.

1792 WOLCOTT (P. Pindar) *Tears of St. Margaret* Wks. 1812 III. 81 The dough-faced Spectres crowded forth. **1848** *New York Comm. Adv.* 4 June (Bartlett) Two-third of the senate were dough-faced.

doughiness ('dəʊɪnɪs). [f. DOUGHY *a.* + -NESS.] The quality of being doughy. Also *fig.*

1616 SURFL. & MARKH. *Country Farme* 586 Any doughinesse or rawnesse in the crust. **1866** G. MACDONALD *Ann. Q. Neighb.* (1884) 243 Which made me turn and go home, regardless now of Mr. Stoddart's doughiness.

'**doughing,** *vbl. sb.* [f. DOUGH *v.* + -ING[1].] The making or dividing of dough; *attrib.* **doughing-machine**, one for dividing dough for loaves.

1882 tr. *Thausing's Beer* 412 The mixing of the malt required for one grist with water in the mash-tun at the commencement of a brewing is called *einteigen* (doughing in) or, shortly, 'mashing in'. **1884** *Engineer* 30 May 399/2 It is then passed into the doughing machine.

doughish ('dəʊɪʃ), *a.* [-ISH.] Somewhat doughy, slack-baked.

1556 WITHALS *Dict.* (1568) 44 a/1 Doughisshe breadde, not full bake, *rubidus panis.*

doughnut ('dəʊnʌt). Also donut. **1.** A small spongy cake made of dough (usually sweetened and spiced), and fried or boiled in lard. Freq. made in the shape of a thick ring.

1809 W. IRVING *Knickerb.* (1861) 90 An enormous dish of balls of sweetened dough, fried in hog's fat, and called doughnuts, or olykoeks. **1847** THOREAU in *Atlantic Monthly* June (1892) 757 The window was..the size of an oblong doughnut, and about as opaque. **1861** R. F. BURTON *City of Saints* 104 *note*, The Dough-nut is properly speaking, a small roundish cake made of flour, eggs, and sugar, moistened with milk and boiled in lard. **1870** HAZLITT *Brand's Pop. Antiq.* I. 48 At Baldock, Herts, the children call ..[Shrove Tuesday] Dough-nut Day, from the small cakes fried in brass skillets over the fire with hog's lard.

2. a. *colloq.* or *slang.* Applied to various objects with a shape resembling the toroidal shape of a doughnut, as a motor-car or aeroplane tyre or a ring-shaped float (see quots.). In *Math.*, a torus.

1925 FRASER & GIBBONS *Soldier & Sailor Words* 82 *Dough nuts*, a Navy name for the 'Carley Floats', life-saving rafts of circular shape, carried on board ships of war. **1930** *Amer. Mercury* Dec. 455/2 *Doughnut*, an automobile tire. 'We clout ten doughnuts an' call it a day.' **1931** *Flight* 13 Feb. 145/1 The 'doughnut' wheels with which the Airwork School machines are being equipped. **1936** M. ALLIS *Eng. Prelude* xxviii. 202 An occasional stone doughnut of a sheepfold tells of solitary shepherd vigils. **1955** *Times* 31 Aug. 9/4 The Air Ministry are also interested in quickly inflatable 'doughnut' buoyancy bags, which fit round the wheels like a horizontal lifebelt and can be inflated to about three times the size of a motor car tire. **1959** M. GARDNER in *Sci. Amer.* Mar. 148/2 107 We..then stretch and bend the cylinder into a torus... Every pair of antipodes on this diabolic doughnut will total 17.

b. *Nuclear Engin.* A toroidal vacuum chamber placed between the magnet poles of a betatron or synchrotron, in which electrons or protons are accelerated; applied also to similarly shaped vessels in other devices (see quot. 1958).

1941 *Physical Rev.* LX. 51/1 The central 7 cm. hole of the doughnut was formed by pushing the centers of the dished faces together and picking out the glass. **1942** *Ibid.* LXI. 94 To cut down bombardment of the inside of the vacuum doughnut..electrons are injected at 15 or 20 kilovolts for only a brief interval. **1942** *Electronics* Sept. 84/2 Prof. Kerst, inventor and designer, is shown preparing to place the doughnut vacuum tube between poles of the electro-magnet. **1949** *Times* 12 Aug. 2/3 The essential function of the synchrotron..is achieved by firing a burst of electrons.. into an evacuated 'donut'. **1958** *New Statesman* 6 Sept. 266/3 In Zeta, the heavy hydrogen particles, forming a 'plasma', are contracted into a beam which travelling round in the 'doughnut' or 'torus' (like a giant motor-tyre) is 'pinched'.

3. *Comb.*, as ***doughnut-shaped*** adj.

1941 [see BETATRON]. **1962** *Sci. Survey* VII. 108 The effect ..may be produced by toroidal (or doughnut-shaped) magnetic fields encircling the sun.

†**dought,** *sb. Obs.* [In quot. 1450 perh. for **douȝth* DOUTH valour; in 1788 app. a back-formation from DOUGHTY *a.*, on analogy of *might, mighty*, etc.] Doughtiness, might, power.

c **1450** *Merlin* 555 Yef thei knewe the dought of my brother Agravain. **1788** PICKEN *Poems* 159 (Jam.) The freckest whiles hae own't her [Fortune's] dought.

†**dought,** *a. Obs.* [app. a shortened form of DOUGHTY.] Doughty, valiant, mighty.

c **1320** *Sir Beues* 3380 (MS. A.) Lordinges..ȝe scholle þis dai be holde so douȝt. *c* **1330** R. BRUNNE *Chron. Wace* (Rolls) 13532 þat were of prowesse, & of bataille dought.

dought, pa. t. of DOW *v.*; obs. var. of DOUBT, DOUT.

doughter, obs. and dial. f. DAUGHTER.

†'**doughtihede.** *Obs.* = DOUGHTINESS.

a **1300** *Cursor M.* 848 (Cott.) Thoru his auen doghtyhede. *Ibid.* 10628 It was hir dughti-hede.

doughtily ('daʊtɪlɪ), *adv.* [f. DOUGHTY + -LY[2].] In a doughty manner; valiantly, stoutly.

a **1300** *Cursor M.* 3673 (Cott.) His moder dughtilik it dight. *c* **1380** *Sir Ferumb.* 420 He laide on Sarazyns..so doȝtilich. *c* **1440** *Gesta Rom.* xxiv. 89 (Harl. MS.) He bare him so manly, & so doutely in the turnement. **1572** BOSSEWELL *Armorie* II. 96 b, Whiche had doughtely susteined the siege. **1659** BP. WALTON *Consid. Considered* 169 To thank him for disputing so doughtily on their behalf. **1870** LOWELL *Study Wind.* 76 The battle which the English race on this continent has been carrying doughtily on.

doughtiness ('daʊtɪnɪs). [f. DOUGHTY + -NESS.] Valiantness, valour, stoutness.

c **1200** ORMIN 17582 Sawle onnfoþ att Godess hand All hire duhhtiȝnesse. *c* **1330** R. BRUNNE *Chron.* (1810) 184 His douhtynes we ken. *c* **1450** *Golagros & Gaw.* 416 Your dedis, your dignite and your doughtynes. **1509** BARCLAY *Shyp of Folys* (1570) 18 Hector..Was slayne with payne for all his doubtynes. **1526** *Pilgr. Perf.* (W. de W. 1531) 136 A discrete doughtynesse or a spyrytuall audacite, to speke or to do. **1612–20** SHELTON *Quix.* (T.), The Biscayan..perceived, by his doughtiness, his intention. **1886** LOWELL *Lett.* (1894) II. 341 Our difficulties..to test our doughtiness.

dough-trough ('dəʊtrɒf, -ɔː-). A trough or vessel in which dough is placed to rise; in modern use, also a closed vessel in which the rising of dough is promoted by the gentle heat arising from warm water beneath; = *dough-raiser*: see DOUGH *sb.* 5.

c **1440** *Promp. Parv.* 129/1 Dowe trowe, *pistralla, alveus.* **1530** PALSGR. 215/1 Doughe troughe, *husche a pestrir.* *a* **1600** *Turnam. Tottenh.* 124 A doȝ-trogh, and a pele. **1874** KNIGHT *Dict. Mech.* I. 732/2 *Dough-trough*..a water-tight, covered vessel of tin or other suitable material, with a perforated shelf across the centre.

doughty ('daʊtɪ), *a.* Forms: 1 **dyhtiȝ, dohtiȝ**, 3–5 **doȝti**, 3–6 **doȝty**, 3– **doughty**, (4 **dohty, dohuti, doghuti, douhti**, 4–5 **douȝti, dowghty**, 4– *Sc.* **douchti, -ty, dowchty**). Also 3–5 **dughti**, 4 **duhti, duȝty**, 6–7 *Sc.* **duchtie**; and 4–6 **dowtie, -ty**, 5–7 **douty**, 5–8 *erron.* **doubty**, 7– **doughty.** [The original OE. form was *dyhtiȝ*, corresp. to OHG. **tuhtîg*, MHG. *tühtec*, Ger. *tüchtig*, MDu. and MLG. *duchtich*, from an OTeut. sb. **duhti-z*, MHG. *tuht* ability, capacity, from *dugan*: see DOW *v.*[1] (If this had come down, its mod.Eng. repr. would be *dighty.*) OE. *dohtiȝ* was a later formation, of which the vowel is difficult to explain, unless perh. by assimilation to *dohte*, pa. t. of *dugan*. It came down in the ME. *doȝti, dohty, dowghty*, Sc. *dochtie, douchtie*, to the mod. spelling *doughty*, of which the expected pronunciation would be ('dɔːtɪ): cf. *bought, wrought, daughter*. Beside it, ME. had *duhtiȝ, duȝti, duhti*, 16th c. Sc. *duchtie*; and also from 14th c., *dowtie, douty*, erroneously spelt (by assimilation to another word of same sound) *doubty*; whence evidently the current spoken word ('daʊtɪ). The phonology presents many points of difficulty.]

1. Able, capable, worthy, virtuous; valiant, brave, stout, formidable: now with an archaic flavour, and often humorous. **a.** of persons.

1030 *Abingdon Chron.*, Hacun se dohtiȝa eorl. *c* **1200** ORMIN 113 Zacariȝe..haffde an duhhtiȝ wif..Elysabæþ ȝehatenn. **1297** R. GLOUC. (1724) 592 Edward, that doughty knyght. *a* **1300** *Cursor M.* 3555 (Cott.) Sir Ysaac þat dughti [*Gött.* dohuti] man. *c* **1314** *Guy Warw.* (A.) 1480 A duhti kniȝt and no coward. **1375** BARBOUR *Bruce* II. 166 For all his eldris war douchty. *c* **1380** *Sir Ferumb.* 423 Doȝty men & wiȝt. *c* **1420** *Avow. Arth.* xiv, Did as a duȝty knyȝte. *c* **1440** *York Myst.* xxxviii. 163 Sir knyghtis, þat are in dedis dowty. **1480** CAXTON *Chron. Eng.* lxxiii. 55 Kyng Arthur was.. bolde and doubty of body. **1535** STEWART *Cron. Scot.* (1858) I. 42 Lord and knycht..And mony other richt duchtie and conding. **1600** HOLLAND *Livy* XXIV. xlvi. 541 Certaine Tribunes and marshals, valourous and doubtie good men. **1609** —— *Amm. Marcell.* XIV. ix. 19 A doutie warrior. **1655** FULLER *Ch. Hist.* III. vi. §50 All the Scotish Nobility (Doughty Douglas alone excepted). **1795** SOUTHEY *Joan of Arc* v. 126 The doughty Paladins of France. **1814** D'ISRAELI *Quarrels Auth.* (1867) 263 The doughty critic was at once silenced. **1847** LEWES *Hist. Philos.* (1867) II. 98 Oxford called upon her doughty men to brighten up their arms. **1848** DICKENS *Dombey* (C.D. ed.) 115 Nor did he ever again face the doughty Mrs. Pipchin.

b. of actions, and other things.

[*Beowulf* 1287 (Z.) Sweord ecȝum dyhtiȝ. *a* **1000** *Cædmon's Genesis* 1993 Sweord ecȝum dihtiȝ.] *a* **1225** *Leg. Kath.* 782 Of mine bileaue, beo ha duhti oðer dusi, naue þu nawt to donne. *a* **1300** *Cursor M.* 2112 (Cott.) Mani contre þarin es And dughti cites mare and lesse. **1393** LANGL. *P. Pl.* C. VIII. 141 Of thyne douhtieste dedes. **1535** STEWART *Cron. Scot.* II. 510 Of his duchtie Deidis and Justice done. **1568** T. HOWELL *Arb. Amitie* (1879) 81 Nor men deserue the crowne, and doubtie diademe. **1590** SPENSER *F.Q.* I. v. 1 How that doughtie turnament With greatest honour he atchieven might. *a* **1667** JER. TAYLOR *Serm. for Year* (1678) Suppl. 185 In this doughty cause they think it fit to fight and die. **1733** CHEYNE *Eng. Malady* III. iv. (1734) 302 Another doughty Objection against a Vegetable Diet, I have heard. **1829** SCOTT *Jrnl.* 28 Apr., After this doughty resolution, I went doggedly to work.

†**2.** *absol.* = Man or men of valour. *Obs.*

c **1420** *Anturs of Arth.* i, Bothe the kyng and the qwene And other doȝti by-dene. *c* **1475** *Rauf Coilȝear* 590 Thair wald na douchtie this day for Iornay be dicht. **1800** A. CARLYLE *Autobiog.* 140, I..was going up the field to tell this when my doughty arrived.

3. *Comb.*, as ***doughty-handed*** adj.

1606 SHAKS. *Ant. Cl.* IV. viii. 5 Doughty handed are you.

doughy ('dəʊɪ), *a.* [f. DOUGH *sb.* + -Y[1].] Of the nature of dough; like dough in appearance, consistency, or character.

1601 SHAKS. *All's Well* IV. v. 3 All the vnbak'd and dowy youth of a nation. **1648** GAGE *West Ind.* xii. (1655) 53 After the Consecration many devout persons came and sticked in the dowy Image pretious stones. **1719** LONDON & WISE *Compl. Gard.* v. 76 Sometimes it grows doughy, when suffer'd to be too ripe on the Tree. **1826** SYD. SMITH *Wks.* (1859) II. 97/1 A sad, doughy lump. *a* **1827** GOOD *Study Med.* (1834) II. 161 White tongue in the morning, and a pallid doughy countenance. **1893** EARL DUNMORE *Pamirs* II. 230 The bread we had to eat was..very doughy.

Douglas[1] ('dʌgləs). [The name of David *Douglas* (1798–1834), Scottish botanist.] In full ***Douglas fir, pine,*** or ***spruce***: a large coniferous tree, *Pseudotsuga menziesii* (also known as *P. taxifolia*) or *P. glauca*, native to western North America.

[**1837** A. B. LAMBERT *Descr. Genus Pinus* III, (*heading*) Pinus Douglasii. Trident-bracted fir. *Ibid.*, I gladly adopt the name of *P. Douglasii*, in honour of the indefatigable botanist to whom I am indebted for the specimens from which I have been enabled to complete my description and plate of the species.] **1856** A. W. WHIPPLE in *Rep. Explor. Route to Pacific* (*U.S. War Dept.*) III. I. 79 *Douglass spruce* ..would afford a better material for railroad ties. **1868** F. WHYMPER *Alaska* 44 Where the Douglas pine, spruce, and hemlock had grown. **1873** G. M. GRANT *Ocean to Ocean* x. 259 The hillsides and the country beyond support a growth of splendid spruce, black pine, and Douglas fir. **1884** C. S. SARGENT *Rep. Forests N. Amer.* 209 *Pseudotsuga Douglasii.* .. Red Fir. Yellow Fir. Oregon Pine. Douglas Fir. **1931** *Discovery* Sept. 285/1 Methods of forcing the oil into the wood of refractory species, such as larch and Douglas fir, are being investigated. **1937** *Evening News* 11 Feb. 8/4 All the Office of Works stands are being constructed of Douglas Fir and Western hemlock from British Columbia. **1945** R. W. SERVICE *Ploughman* 156 The shack stood in a clearing, engulfed by Douglas pines three hundred feet high. **1947** R. PEATTIE *Sierra Nevada* 148 It is called Douglas fir or Douglas spruce indiscriminately. **1970** H. L. EDLIN *Collins Guide to Tree Planting & Cultivation* xix. 286 The green or Oregon Douglas fir, *P. menziesii*, comes from British Columbia and the neighbouring regions of Alaska, Canada, and the United States. *Ibid.*, Where there is less room, the best kind to plant is the blue or Colorado Douglas fir, *P. glauca.*

Douglas[2] ('dʌgləs). *Anat.* The name of James *Douglas* (1675–1742), Scottish physician, used in the possessive or with *of*-adjunct to designate various anatomical structures described by or named after him; ***Douglas's pouch*** (or ***pouch of Douglas***), a pouch of the peritoneum between the uterus and the rectum; the recto-uterine pouch.

1859 TODD *Cycl. Anat.* V. 706/1 The anterior wall of the recto-uterine pouch, or space of Douglas. **1864** W. SHARPEY et al. *Quain's Anat.* (ed. 7) I. 251 The deficiency thus resulting in the posterior wall of the sheath of the rectus muscle is marked superiorly by a well-defined lunated edge, whose concavity looks downwards towards the pubes—the semilunar fold of Douglas. **1878** W. TURNER *Introd. Human Anat.* xii. 841 The interval between the uterus and rectum ..is the utero-rectal pouch, or pouch of Douglas. **1880** *Lancet* 25 Sept. 494/2 Tappings through the peritoneum.. for accumulation of fluid in Douglas's pouch. **1907** *Practitioner* Apr. 472 A boggy, ill-defined, and very tender swelling present in Douglas's pouch. **1954** L. T. MORTON *Garrison & Morton's Med. Bibliog.* (ed. 2) 107 Douglas described the peritoneum in detail; his name is perpetuated in the 'pouch', 'line', and 'fold of Douglas'. **1965** L. B. AREY *Developmental Anat.* (ed. 7) xviii. 329 The pelvic cœlom is thereby subdivided into two blind bays, the recto-uterine pouch (of Douglas) and the vesico-uterine pouch. **1970** *Cumul. Index Med.* 1969 X. 5621/1 Puncture of Douglas' pouch in cytodiagnosis of ovarian neoplasms.

Douglas[3] ('dʌgləs). *Economics.* The name of Major Clifford Hugh *Douglas* (1879–1952), British engineer, used *attrib.* to designate his plan for 'social credit'. Hence **'Douglasite** *a.* and *sb.*

1933 H. G. WELLS *Bulpington of Blup* ix. 346 A lady who wanted to help forward the Douglas Scheme. *Ibid.* 369 She took up..the Douglas Plan. **1938** D. GARNETT in T. E. Lawrence *Lett.* 866 Ede had asked Lawrence's opinion of the Douglas Credit Scheme. **1939** H. G. WELLS *Holy Terror* I. iii. 73 It included everything from..single-taxers to Douglasites. *Ibid.* 75 An earnest..little man..who had swallowed the Douglas gospel whole. **1962** *Listener* 6 Sept. 357/3 Orage..became the most persuasive exponent of Douglasite economics the Social Creditors ever had.

Douglas[4] ('dʌgləs). *Austral. slang.* [Formerly a proprietary name in the U.S. for axes, hatchets, etc., produced by the Douglas Axe Manufacturing Co., East Douglas, Mass. (*Official Gaz.* (U.S. Patent Office), 1926, 13 July 326/2).] An axe. Used without art., as if personified, esp. in phr. *to swing Douglas.*

[**1876** *Internat. Exhibition: Official Catal.* (U.S. Centennial Commission) 137/1 Douglas Axe Manufacturing Co., Boston, Mass. — Axes, hatchets, adzes, picks, etc. **1896** *Australasian Ironmonger* 2 Mar. 30 D. Sharp's superior axes manufactured..by the Douglas Axe Mf'g. Co. East Douglas, Mass. U.S.A.] **1905** *Shearer* (Sydney, N.S.W.) 17 June 6/3 The squatter presents him to 'Douglas' (the axe!). **1914** *Bulletin* (Sydney) 16 Apr. 22/3 A pair of German girls (sisters) earn the elusive pin-money.. by swinging 'douglas' for the Mildura firewood supply. **1929** C. H. WINTER *Story of 'Bidgee Queen* 106 An' you graft at 'Swinging Douglas' an' you chop the limbs away. **1943** *Bulletin* (Sydney) 20 Jan. 13/2, I find myself wielding the weapons in the same manner as I wielded Douglas and banjo. **1966** 'J. HACKSTON' *Father clears Out* 160 Sometimes on a Sunday morning exhibitions of axemanship (theoretical) were given; right and wrong way to swing Douglas.

douk(e, obs. form of DUCK, DUKE.

douke, var. DAUKE, *Obs.*, carrot.

1601 HOLLAND *Pliny* XIX. v. (D.), Yellow douke or carot.

Doukhobor ('duːkəbɔː(r)). Also **Dukh-**. Pl. **-ors** or **-ortsy**. [Russ. *Dukhobór*, pl. *-bóry*, also *-bórets*, pl. *-bórtsy̆*, spirit-wrestler (see SPIRIT *sb.* 23 c).] A member of a Russian religious sect which originated in the 18th century, many of whose members emigrated to Western Canada in the late nineteenth century after persistent persecution. Also *attrib.*

1876 J. B. TELFER *Crimea* I. x. 112 The Douhobortsy fully believe the Scriptures to be the revelation of God. **1886** *Encycl. Brit.* XXI. 82/2 The 'Dukhobortsy' communities (warriors of the Spirit)..are renowned as colonizers. **1897** [see SPIRIT *sb.* 23 c]. **1899** *Westm. Gaz.* 24 Apr. 3/2 Some of the Russian Doukhobors who have been expelled for refusing to participate in war. **1899** *Daily News* 30 May 5/2 Several settlements of the persecuted sect of the Doukobohrs [*sic*] are established there [*sc.* in Canada]. **1921** R. M. JONES *Later Periods of Quakerism* II. xx. 836 The persecution of the Doukhobors in Trans-Caucasia. **1931** *Times Lit. Suppl.* 17 Dec. 1021/4 We learn that when the Dukhobor colonists marched in force to the local seat of justice to protest..'every man, woman and child in the procession was stark naked'. **1957** J. S. HUXLEY *Relig. without Revol.* vi. 135 The anti-social but extremely religious Doukhobors. **1968** WOODCOCK & AVAKUMOVIC *Doukhobors* i. 19 The name of 'Doukhobor'..was first used in anger and derision by one of their opponents, Archbishop Amvrosii Serebrennikov of Ekaterinoslav. It means 'Spirit Wrestlers', and it was intended by the archbishop, when he invented it in 1785, to suggest that they were fighting *against* the Holy Ghost. *Ibid.*, There is a central, constant element in Doukhobor Christianity.

doul, obs. var. of DOLE *sb.*[2] grief, DOWEL.

doulce, var. of DOUCE, DULCE.

doulced, doulcet(e, var. of DOUCET, DULCET.

douleia, doulia: see DULIA.

doulle, obs. form of DULL.

doulocracy, var. of DULOCRACY.

Doulton ('dəʊltən). The name of John *Doulton* (1793–1873), used *attrib.* and *absol.* to designate pottery made at the works instituted by him.

1878 L. JEWITT *Ceramic Art* 100 This ware is called 'Doulton ware', or 'sgraffito ware'. **1900** F. LITCHFIELD *Pottery & Porcelain* vii. 178 The artistic pottery may be divided into three classes,..namely, Doulton Ware, Lambeth Faience, and Impasto. **1909** H. G. WELLS *Tono-Bungay* II. iv. 229 The India-rubber plant in a Doulton-ware pot. **1966** G. BURNETT *Dead Account* iv. 27 A ceiling-high fixture..full of expensive books and Doulton and.. glass bric-a-brac.

doum (daʊm, duːm). Also **doom, dome, dom.** [Arab. *daum, dūm.*] A kind of palm (*Hyphæne Thebaica*), found in Egypt, having a dichotomously divided trunk, and an edible fruit about the size of an apple. Usually **doum-palm.**

1801 HEL. M. WILLIAMS *Sk. Fr. Rep.* II. xxxv. 170 In capitals [of columns]..the branches of the doum, and the flowers of the nelumbo, mingle together. **1830** LINDLEY *Nat. Syst. Bot.* 280 The Doom Palm of Upper Egypt and the *Hyphæne coriacea* are remarkable for their dichotomous repeatedly-divided trunk. **1849** SOUTHEY *Comm.-pl. Bk.* IV. 113 In the upper parts of Egypt they have a palm tree called the Dome. **1867** LADY HERBERT *Cradle L.* i. 34 The region of..the Theban or dôm-palm.

b. *attrib.*, as *doum-leaf, -wood.*

1788 CLARKSON *Impol. Slave Tr.* 20 The doom-wood (which the worm never enters). **1827** MOORE *Epicur.* xvi. (1839) 166 A bed of fresh doum leaves.

doum, doumb(e, obs. forms of DUMB.

douma, var. DUMA.

doun(e, obs. forms of DO, DONE, DOWN, DUN.

doung, obs. pa. pple. of DING *v.*[1]; obs. f. DUNG.

dounk, dount, obs. forms of DANK, DUNT.

doup (daʊp). *Sc.* Forms: 6 dolp, 6–9 doup, 7 doupe, 7–9 dowp. [Of Norse origin: cf. ON. *daup.*]

†**1.** A rounded cavity or hollow bottom. *Obs.*

1513 DOUGLAS *Æneis* III. x. 15 Off his E dolp the flowand blude and attir He wische away. **1641** FERGUSSON *Scot. Prov.* 7 (Jam.) Better half egg than toom dowp. **1653** URQUHART *Rabelais* I. vi, Castor and Pollux [born] of the doupe of that Egge which was laid..by Leda.

2. The posterior extremity of the body, the fundament or seat.

1653 URQUHART *Rabelais* I. xxii, At the salt doup [Fr. *au cul sallé*, the name of a game]. **1718** RAMSAY *Christ's Kirk Gr.* III. xxii, A' the skaith that chanc'd indeed, Was only on their dowps. **1817** J. SCOTT *Paris Revisit.* (ed. 4) 257 Sax and therty lashes a piece on the bare doup.

3. The bottom or end (of any thing), *e.g.* the rounded end of a candle.

1718 RAMSAY *Christ's Kirk Gr.* III. x, I' the doup o' day. **1774** T. SCOTT *Poems* 319 (Jam.), At the doup o' e'en. **1816** SCOTT *Antiq.* v, The doup o' a candle. **1894** CROCKETT *Lilac Sunb.* 72 What remained of the smooth candle 'dowp'.

b. A loop at the end.

1831 G. R. PORTER *Silk Manuf.* 285 The half leaf..passes through the upper doup of the standard.

doupt, obs. form of DOUBT.

dour (duːr), *a.* orig. *Sc.* Also 5 dowre, 6–8 doure, 6– dowr. [ad. L. *dūr-us*, or F. *dur* hard (cf. DURE).

Derivation from French is unlikely on account of the vowel, since F. *u* gives in Sc. not *ū* but *ü* (or *ö*). An early (11th or 12th c.) adoption of L. *dūr-us*, would suit phonetically; of this however we have no evidence.]

1. Hard, severe, bold, stern, fierce, hardy.

1375 BARBOUR *Bruce* x. 170 [He] wes dour & stout. *c* **1425** WYNTOUN *Cron.* VIII. xvi. 103 Dyntis dowre ware sene. **1513** DOUGLAS *Æneis* II. vi. [v.] 23 The dour Vlixes als, and Athamas. **1533** BELLENDEN *Livy* II. (1822) 166 Thir legatis wes gevin ane doure answere be Marcius. **1596** DALRYMPLE tr. *Leslie's Hist. Scot.* IV. 249 He led a dour and hard lyfe. **1794** BURNS *Winter Night* i, Biting Boreas, fell and doure. **1848** LYTTON *Harold* VI. i, Tostig is a man..dour and haughty. **1891** ATKINSON *Moorland Par.* 261 The dour, merciless intensity of a northern moorland..storm.

2. Hard to move, stubborn, obstinate, sullen.

c **1470** HENRY *Wallace* IV. 187 Malancoly he was of complexioun..dour in his contenance. **1513** DOUGLAS *Æneis* XIII. vi. 106 All our prayeris..Mycht nowder bow that dowr mannis mynd. **1572** *Satir. Poems Reform.* xxxviii. 76 Our men are dour men. **1816** SCOTT *Old Mort.* viii, 'He's that dour, ye might tear him to pieces, and..ne'er get a word out o' him.' **1854** MRS. GASKELL *North & S.* xvii, Thornton is as dour as a door-nail; an obstinate chap.

Hence **'dourly** *adv.*, with hard sternness, stubbornly, obstinately; **'dourness**, hardness of disposition, obstinacy, sullenness.

c **1375** *Sc. Leg. Saints, Jacobus minor* 337 Thai..in to durnes ay abad. *c* **1475** *Rauf Coilȝear* 918 To ding thame doun dourly that euer war in my way. **1596** DALRYMPLE tr. *Leslie's Hist. Scot.* v. 281 And fercely had fochtne thame, and dourlie dantount. **1871** C. GIBBON *Lack of Gold* iv, 'Give me those letters, father', she said dourly. **1882** *Sat. Rev.* No. 1411. 629 Scotchmen..have the same caution.. courage, and 'dourness' [as Yorkshiremen].

doura, var. DURRA, Indian millet.

doure, obs. form of DURE, to endure.

dourine ('dʊəriːn). [ad. F. *dourin.*] A contagious disease of horses transmitted by copulation and caused by the parasite *Trypanosoma equiperdum.*

1882 POWER & SEDGWICK *Lex. Med.* II, *Dourine*, the Arabic name of *Mal de coït.* **1897** M. H. HAYES *Veterinary Notes for Horse Owners* (ed. 5) xxii. 470 Dourine..was first observed in Germany by Ammon in 1796, and has since.. spread to..Germany, Austria, Russia, Italy, France, Algiers, Syria and America... It is unknown in Great Britain. **1903** *Ibid.* (ed. 6) 510 Dourine is a specific disease which at first appears as an inflammation of the surface of the genital organs, and which causes grave alterations in the nervous system of the attacked animal. *Ibid.* 511 Mares are more liable to acute dourine than stallions. **1963** JUBB & KENNEDY *Path. Domestic Animals* II. 596/2 The symptomatology of dourine can be divided into genital, cutaneous, nervous, and general manifestations which occur separately or concurrently.

†**dourlach.** *Sc.* [app. a variant of DORLACH.] 'A short sword, a dagger' (Jam.). (? An error.)

18.. SCOTT (in Jamieson s.v.), In heraldry, Highland swords are called dourlachs. **1828** —— *F.M. Perth* xvii, Manhood shall be tried by kisses and bumpers, not by dirks and dourlachs.

douro ('dʊərəʊ). Also **duro.** [Fr., ad. Sp. *duro.*] A former Spanish coin.

1870 LADY C. SCHREIBER *Jrnl.* 12 Apr. (1911) I. 105, I got for a duro a small specimen of the embossed tile. **1872** *Ibid.* 26 May 145 We gave a douro and a half (6/3). **1905** *Daily Chron.* 21 June 5/4 That the Moorish Government should pay 9,000 douros by way of compensation. **1905** *Westm. Gaz.* 12 Sept. 2/1 No, my daughter, a douro, that is sufficient. Another sou would be excessive. **1908** *Ibid.* 21 July 5/1 The new law provides that all these Seville douros shall be confiscated. **1925** *Chambers's Jrnl.* June 383/2 He proposes forty douros as a fair price... A douro is equal to five francs. **1962** R. A. G. CARSON *Coins* 317 In 1848 a new decimal coinage created new denominations... In silver the denominations were the douro and its half of 20 and 10 reals respectively.

douroucouli (duːruːˈkuːlɪ). Also **dorocouli, douracouli, douro(u)coli.** [a. S. Amer. Indian name.] Any of several S. and Central American monkeys of the genus *Aotus*, characterized by large, staring eyes, long, non-prehensile tails, and nocturnal habits; the night-monkey or owl-monkey.

1842 *Ann. Mag. Nat. Hist.* X. 256 The two species of Douroucouli are evidently distinct. **1861** *Proc. Zool. Soc.* 101 The following additions were announced to have been made to the Menagerie... 1 Douroucouli Monkey. **1891** FLOWER & LYDEKKER *Mammals* 714 The Douroucoulis. **1894** H. O. FORBES *Primates* I. 166 The Douroucoulis. **1897** *Q. Rev.* Oct. 414 The *Douracoulis* or Night Apes are truly nocturnal animals... The group ranges from Costa Rica and Nicaragua to the south of Paraguay. **1902** F. E. BEDDARD *Mammalia* 560 The Douroucouli Monkeys. **1929** *Times* 17 May 18 (caption) A pair of douroucoulis, or nocturnal owl-faced monkeys, one of the feline, the other of the three-banded species, recently acquired by the Zoo. The douroucouli is native to Guiana, Brazil, and Venezuela. **1964** *Listener* 23 July 123/1 Finnicky small mammals, such as marmosets and douroucoulis.

dousaine, -ayne, obs. forms of DOZEN.

douse (daʊs), *sb.*[1] Also 7 douze, 7– douce, dowse, 9 douss. [f. DOUSE *v.*[1]] A dull heavy blow or stroke.

a **1625** FLETCHER *Nice Valour* v. i, Souse upon Souse. Douces single. Justle sides. **1653–4** WHITELOCKE *Jrnl. Swed. Emb.* (1772) I. 137 A dowse in the neck. **1771** SMOLLETT *Humph. Cl.* I. 3 June, He gave the young man a dowse in the chops. **1821** SCOTT *Kenilw.* xxx, The porter.. started up with his club, and dealt a sound douse or two on each side. *a* **1845** BARHAM *Ingol. Leg., Jerry Jarvis*, It descended on her..head in one tremendous dowse.

†**douse, dowse**, *sb.*[2] *Obs.* [perh. subst. use of *douse*, DOUCE sweet.] A sweetheart; a 'dear'. Also *ironical.*

[*a* **1310** Dame douse: see DOUCE *a.* 1.] *c* **1460** *Towneley Myst.* (Surtees) 104 Yit is she a fowlle dowse if ye com nar. **1573** TUSSER *Husb.* x, Who looketh to marrie must laie to keepe house, for loue may not alway be plaieing with douse.

douse (daʊs), *v.*[1] Also 7– dowse, 8 dousse. [Of obscure origin: known only from 16th c. In sense 1, perh. related to MDu. *dossen*, or early mod.Du. *doesen* to beat with force and noise (Kilian): cf. also EFris. *dossen* to beat, strike, punch, knock, and Ger. dial. *dusen, tusen, tausen*, etc. to beat, strike, butt (Grimm). Senses 2 and 3 may be the same word; cf. 'to strike sail'; sense 4 is more doubtful, and may be distinct. All the senses belong to the lower strata of the language.]

†**1.** *trans.* To strike, punch, inflict a blow upon.

1559 *Mirr. Mag., Hen. VI*, iv, To death with daggers doust. **1730–6** BAILEY (folio), *To Dowse*..to give one a slap on the face.

2. *Naut.* To strike (a sail); to lower or slacken suddenly or in haste; to close (a port-hole).

1627 CAPT. SMITH *Seaman's Gram.* xiii. 60 Dowse your top-saile to salute him. **1629** —— *Trav. & Adv.* xx. 40 Very civilly they doused [*printed* dansed] their topsailes. **1769** FALCONER *Dict. Marine* (1789), *Molir une corde*, to slacken, dousse, or ease off a tight rope. **1802** in *Naval Chron.* VII.

47 Douse the ports. **1828** COL. HAWKER *Diary* (1893) I. 344 Forced to douse all sail and ease the engine.

3. To put off, doff.

1785 GROSE *Dict. Vulgar Tongue* s.v., *Dowse your dog vane*, take the cockade out of your hat. **1828** COL. HAWKER *Diary* (1893) I. 332 The latter have doused their butter-churn boots. **1841** THACKERAY *Mem. Gormand.* Wks. 1886 XXIII. 357, I..doused my cap on entering the porch.

4. To put out, extinguish, dout (a light).

1785 GROSE *Dict. Vulgar Tongue* (Farmer), *Dowse the glim* = put out the candle. **1824** W. IRVING *T. Trav.* (1849) 428 'Dowse the light'! roared the hoarse voice from the water. **1853** KANE *Grinnell Exp.* xxxiii. (1856) 294 At nine the deck-lantern was doused.

5. To throw down, table (money): = DOSS *v.*[1] 2.

1797 G. WASHINGTON *Let.* Writ. 1892 XIII. 425 Asking opinions and requiring services..without dousing my money.

6. To 'shut up', stop, cease.

1887 HALL CAINE *Deemster* xxxiii. 221 'Dowse that, Billy, and bear a hand and be quiet.'

Hence **'dousing** *vbl. sb.*; also **'douser,** (*a*) a heavy blow; (*b*) *Cinemat.* (see quots.).

1782 FRANKLIN *Wks.* (1888) VII. 411 It was allowed..to give him a rising blow. Let ours be a douser. **1837** SOUTHEY *Doctor* cxxv. IV. 248 In common use among school-boys and blackguards..the threat of giving any one a dowsing. **1921** A. C. LESCARBOURA *Cinema Handbk.* 21 *Douser*, the manually operated door in the projecting machine, which intercepts the light before it reaches the film. **1940** *Chambers's Techn. Dict.* 262/2 *Douser*, the automatic screen which cuts off the light falling on to the film from the projector arc, when it is not passing intermittently through the gate.

douse (daʊs), *v.*[2] Also 7 dou-, dowsse, douze, 7- dowse, douce. [Appears *c* 1600: origin unknown; perh. onomatopœic; cf. *souse*.

It is of course not impossible that it arose out of DOUSE *v.*[1], though connexion is not obvious.]

†**1.** *trans.* To plunge vigorously *in* water, or the like; to immerse with force. *Obs.*

1600 HOLLAND *Livy* XIX. Epit. 391 Claudius Pulcher.. commaunded the sacred Pullets to be doussed and drenched over the head in the water. **1612** T. TAYLOR *Comm. Titus* i. 16 And dowse himselfe ouer head and eares in impietie. **1643** HAMMOND *Serm.* vii. Wks. 1684 IV. 515, I have wash'd my feet in mire or ink, douz'd my carnal affections in all the vileness of the world. **1662** STILLINGFL. *Orig. Sacr.* I. iv. §11 To have heard the great noise the Sun used to make..when he doused his head in the Ocean.

2. To throw water over; to water, to drench.

1606 HOLLAND *Sueton.* 75. **1610** —— *Camden's Brit.* I. 420 A stately place..which Tanus with wandring streame doth dowsse. **1794** WOLCOTT (P. Pindar) *Remonstr.* Wks. III. 368 Well dous'd by rushing rains. **1879** SEGUIN *Black For.* x. 164 Melusina's haunt was thoroughly doused with holy water. **1893** CAPT. KING *Foes in Ambush* 26 Douse a dipper of water over him.

3. *intr.* To plunge or be plunged into water.

1603 HOLLAND *Plutarch's Mor.* 344 They joy and strive to be doussing, badling, and diving together with them. **1664** BUTLER *Hud.* II. i. 502 It is no jesting, trivial matter, To swing i' th' air, or douce in water. **1872** BROWNING *Fifine* lxv, Sowse Underneath ducks the soul, her truthward yearnings dowse Deeper in falsehood!

Hence **doused** *ppl. a.*; **'dousing** *vbl. sb.*, a drenching; also **'douser,** one who drenches.

1788 M. CUTLER in *Life, Jrnls. & Corr.* (1888) I. 416 A shower came on, and gave us a severe dousing. **1881** HENTY *Cornet of Horse* viii, A copious dousing of his face and head with water. **1883** *Gd. Words* Aug. 544/1 The 'doused' and the 'douser' being at enmity.

douse, var. of DOUCE *a.*, sweet.

douse, etc. : see also DOWSE, etc.

dousen, obs. form of DOZEN.

douseper(e)s, var. DOUZEPERS, *Obs.*

dousing-chock, -rod: see DOWSING.

douspyers, doussepers, var. DOUZEPERS.

doussemer, obs. form of DULCIMER.

†**doust.** *Obs.* [perh. a var. of DOUSE *sb.*[1]: cf. also DUST.] A firm blow, a punch.

a **1625** FLETCHER *Nice Valour* III. ii, Then there's your *souse*, your *wherrit*, and your *dowst*, *Tugs* on the hair, your *bob* o' th' lips, a whelp on't! *Ibid.* IV. i, How sweetly does this fellow take his *dowst*. **1719** D'URFEY *Pills* III. 14 Our.. Knight..gave the Dragon such a doust.

doust(e, obs. form of DUST.

dout (daʊt), *v.* Now *dial.* Also 6 dowt, (7 doubt, 9 dought). [Coalesced form of *do out*: see DO *v.* 49.] *trans.* To put out or extinguish (a fire or light).

1526 J. RASTELL *Hundred Merry Tales* (1866) 2 Dout the candell and dout the fyre. **1574** HELLOWES *Gueuara's Fam. Ep.* 357 If in the place of snuffing, we dowt the candel. **1691** ALICIA D'ANVERS *Academia* 15 It flies about And douts one's eyes and makes one cough. **1841** J. T. HEWLETT *Parish Clerk* II. 141 Grist doughted his lantern. [In nearly every Dialect Glossary from Yorkshire to Isle of Wight.]

dout, *sb.* Now *dial.* In 6 dowt. [f. prec.] A douter or extinguisher.

1573 in P. Cunningham *Revels Acc.* (Shaks. Soc.) 58 Bodkyns and dowtes for lightes..xiii *d.* **1579** *Ibid.* 160 Dowtes for Candells, vj snuffers vj paire. **1876** *Whitby Gloss.*, *Dout*, an extinguisher.

dout, -able, -ance, etc., obs. ff. DOUBT, etc.

Doutch, obs. form of DUTCH.

'douter. Now *dial.* [f. DOUT *v.*] One who or that which douts or extinguishes; an extinguisher.

1622 *Naworth Househ. Bks.* 200 For 2 tynder boxeis and 4 dooters, xxij[d]. **1798** T. JEFFERSON *Let. to J. Boucher* 23 Feb. (MS.), Dout, do out the candle—hence a Pair of Douters. **1828** *Craven Dialect*, *Douter*, extinguisher.

douter, obs. form of DAUGHTER.

†**douth** (du:θ). *Obs.* Forms: 1 duȝuþ, -oð, 2-3 duȝeð, 3 duȝeþ(e, duheð(e, doȝeþ(e, doweþ, 4 douþ(e, duþ(e, douth. [OE. *duȝuþ, -oþ* worth, virtue, excellence, nobility, manhood, force, a force, an army, people, OFris. *duged* (MDu. *döghet*, Du. *deugd*), OHG. *tugund*, MHG. *tugent*, Ger. *tugend* virtue, ON. *dygð* virtue, probity (Sw. *dygd*; a Com. Germanic deriv. of *dugan* to be good or worth: see DOW *v.*[1]]

1. Virtue, excellence, nobility, power, riches.

a **1000** *Hymns* iii. 24 (Gr.) Ealra duȝeða duȝuð, drihten hælend! *c* **1175** *Lamb. Hom.* 103 Slewðe..bið eure unȝearu to elchere duȝeðe. *a* **1225** *Juliana* 5 þe modi Maximien.. heiende heaðene maumez..wið heh duheðe. *a* **1250** *Prov. Ælfred* 177 in *O.E. Misc.* 112 Dowethes louerd.

b. Good deed, benefit.

a **1000** *Crist* 601 Secȝen Dryhtne þonc duȝuða ȝehwylcre. *c* **1205** LAY. 10438 þa duȝeðe þe he us dude whilen.

2. Manhood.

a **1000** *Andreas* 152 (Gr.) Todælan duȝuðe and ȝeoȝoðe. *a* **1250** *Owl & Night.* 634 Lutle childre..Doþ al þat in heore ȝeoȝeþe þat hi forleteþ in heore duȝeþe.

3. Men collectively; company; army, retinue.

O.E. Chron. an. 626 Se cining..wæs ȝefullod..mid eallum his duȝoðe. *a* **1000** *Cædmon's Exod.* 91 (Gr.) Duȝoþ Israhela. *c* **1205** LAY. 28005 Duȝeðe gon sturien. **13..** *E.E. Allit. P.* B. 597 þe dome of þe douþe for dedez of schame. *Ibid.* 1367 Vche duk wyth his duthe & oþer dere lordes. *c* **1340** *Gaw. & Gr. Knt.* 1815 þe douthe dressed to þe wod, er any day sprenged, to chace. *a* **1400-50** *Alexander* 2627 Sone as ser Darie þe deth of his douth sees.

4. *Comb.*, as *duȝeðe-wiht, -king, -mon.* Also **duȝeðlice** *adv.*, virtuously, worthily.

c **1205** LAY. 16844 þat heo maȝen drihten duȝeðliche hærien.

doutie, obs. form of DOUGHTY.

doutro, doutry: see DEWTRY.

douwere, -wir, var. DOWER *sb.*[1] *Obs.*

‖**douzaine** (duzɛn). [Fr. = DOZEN, q.v.] In the Channel Islands: A body of twelve men representing a parish. Hence **douzainier** (du:zə'nɪə(r)), (also 7-9 **douzenier**), a member of such a body.

1682 WARBURTON *Hist. Guernsey* (1822) 63 The Douzeniers..officiers..chosen out of the..men..in the parish. **1862** ANSTED *Channel Isl.* IV. xxiii. (ed. 2) 521 Since 1844, the douzaines have been represented in the states by deputies, who are delegates rather than representatives. *Ibid.* 521 *note*, In Guernsey, besides the douzainiers, two constables are elected by the rate-payers for each douzaine. **1889** *Clark's Guernsey News* 10 May 4/5 Douzeniers sworn-in.

douze, obs. form of DOUSE *v.*[2]

douzen, obs. form of DOZEN.

†**douzepers** ('du:zəpɛəz), *sb. pl. Obs.* or *arch.* Forms: 3 dosse pers, dosseperes, dozze pers, 3-4 dusze pers, 4 dousse pers, dosze-peres, dusze peres, duze pers, dussiperes, 4-5 dusper(e)s, 5 dosipers, -perus, doseperys, dous(se)pyers, dousepers, dozepers, duseperys, ducypers, dussepers, (doþþe peres, dugeperes, duk-peris, dowchsperys, duchepers, -peiris), 6 douseperes, dowsepers, -piers, dowsipers, dowsy peiris, (dyssypers, 7 Dutchpeeres), 9 douze peers, douceperes; also (without final *s*) 3 duzeper, 5 dozepiere, duzepere. Rarely *sing.* 4 doþþeper, 4-5 doseper, 6 dowsypere, doucepere, (douch-spere). [a. OF. *douze* (*doce, duze*) *per(s*, mod.F. *douze pairs* twelve equals, twelve peers. In English at length treated as one word, with a singular implying one of the class.]

In the *Romances*, the twelve peers or paladins of Charlemagne, said to be attached to his person, as being the bravest of his knights. In *History*, applied to the twelve great peers, spiritual and temporal, of France, supposed to represent those attributed by the romances to Charlemagne.

The historical twelve peers were orig. the Archbp. of Rheims, the Bps. of Laon, and Langres (ranking as dukes), the Bps. of Beauvais, Chalons, and Noyon (ranking as counts), the Dukes of Normandy, Burgundy, Aquitaine, the Counts of Toulouse, Flanders, Champagne. (See Du Cange s.v. *Pares Franciæ*.)

c **1205** LAY. 1622 Twelfe iferan. þa Freinsce heo cleopeden dusze pers [*c* **1275** dosseperes]. *c* **1275** *Passion our Lord* 3 in *O.E. Misc.* 37 Nis hit nouht of karlemeyne ne of þe Duzeper. *c* **1310** *Flemish Insurr.* in *Pol. Songs* (Camden) 190 The Kyng of Fraunce..anon Assemblede he is dousse pers. *c* **1330** R. BRUNNE *Chron. Wace* (Rolls) 1601 þe twelue dosze-peres of pris. **13..** *Coer de L.* 12 Off Rowelond, and of Olyver And of every doseper. **1375** BARBOUR *Bruce* III. 440 The duk-peris [*v.r.* Dutch peeres: *Wynt.* 4350 dowchsperys] wer Assegyt In-till egrymor. *c* **1400** *Melayne* 808 Erles, Dukes, & the xij duchepers Bothe barons and Bachelers. *c* **1400** *Rowland & O.* 16 His dusperes doghety. *c* **1430** LYDG. *Min. Poems* (Percy Soc.) 25 Where been of Fraunce all the dozepiere? **1494** FABYAN *Wks.* I. clv. (R.), [Charles Martel] chase xii. perys, which after some wryters, are callyd doseperys, or kyngs, of y[e] which vi. were bisshopys, and vi. temporall lords. **1503** HAWES *Examp. Virt.* VII. xcix. (Arb.) 26 Charlemayne kynge of Fraunce With his dyssypers Rowland and Olyuer. **1523** LD. BERNERS *Froiss.* I. xxi. (R.), He was crowned by the assent of the twelve dowse-piers of Fraunce. *c* **1560** A. SCOTT *Poems* (S.T.S.) ii. 12 Wes nocht so duchty deidis Amangis the dowsy peiris. **1828** SCOTT *F.M. Perth* xvi, Oliver, man? nay, then thou art one of the Douze peers already. **1864** SKEAT *Uhland's Poems* 350 King Charles with all his douceperes Across the ocean sailed.

b. Applied to other illustrious nobles, knights, or grandees. Also with *sing.*

?*a* **1400** *Morte Arth.* 66 At Carlelele a Cristynmese he haldes..Wyth Dukez and dusperes of dyvers rewmes. *a* **1400** *Gloss.* in *Rel. Ant.* I. 8 *Dolopes*, dussiperes. *a* **1400** *Octouian* 949 Ferst they sent out a doseper. *c* **1440** *York Myst.* xxvi. 8 Nowdir with duke nor dugeperes. **1550** BALE *Sel. Wks.* (Parker Soc.) 317 Prelates, priests, monks, doctors, and other spiritual dowsipers. **1590** SPENSER *F.Q.* III. x. 31 Big looking like a doughty Doucepere.

dove (dʌv), *sb.* Forms: 3-4 duve, 4-5 dofe, douf(e, douff(e, dowfe, douve, dowve, doo, (5 doyf, 6 doffe), 4- dove, (*Sc.* 5- dow, doo, 6 dou). [OE. **dufe*, not found (unless as first element in *dúfe-doppa*: see DIVE-DAP); = OS. *dûba*, OFris. *dûve* (MDu. *dûve*, Du. *duif*). OHG. *tûba, tûpa* (MHG. *tûbe*, Ger. *taube*), ON. *dúfa* (Sw. *dufva*, Da. *due*), Goth. *dúbo*:—OTeut. **dûbôn*, weak fem. Perhaps a deriv. of *dub-* to dive, dip (see DIVE): cf. the analogous connexion of L. *columba* with Gr. *κόλυμβος* diver, *κολυμβίς* diver (bird).

In OE. the native word was displaced by *culufre*: see CULVER.]

1. a. A bird of the *Columbidæ*, or pigeon family.

Formerly, and still in dialects (*dove, dow, doo*) applied to all the species of pigeon native to or known in Britain, including the Wood-pigeon, Ring-dove, or Cushat-dove, the Rock-dove or Rock pigeon, the Stock-dove, and the Turtle-dove; but now often restricted to the last, and its congeners. Most of the exotic species are called pigeons, e.g. the *Passenger-pigeon* of America, *dove* being restricted to those which in appearance or habits resemble the turtle-doves. The dove has been, from the institution of Christianity, the type of gentleness and harmlessness, and occupies an important place in Christian symbolism: cf. sense 2.

c **1200** *Trin. Coll. Hom.* 49 Buð admode alse duue.. Turtlen and duues. *a* **1300** *Cursor M.* 1901 (Cott.) [Noe] sent þe dofe eftsith. *Ibid.* 10775 (Cott.) A duu [*v. rr.* dowe, doufe, dove] þat was fra heuen send. *c* **1380** WYCLIF *Serm.* Sel. Wks. I. 78 The Spirit cam doun..and þis Spirit was þis dowfe. **1388** —— *Prov.* vi. 5 Be thou rauyschid as a doo fro the hond. *c* **1450** HOLLAND *Howlat* 231 The Dow, Noyis messinger. **1481** CAXTON *Godfrey* cxlvi. 219 They..bonde thoo lettres to the tayles of the douues, and lete them flee. *c* **1550** CHEKE *Matt.* iii. 16 He saw ye sprite of god coming down like a dow and lighting apon him. **1590** SHAKS. *Mids. N.* I. i. 171, I sweare..By the simplicitie of Venus Doues. **1678** RAY *Willughby's Ornith.* 180 The common wild Dove or Pigeon. **1712** POPE *Messiah* 12 And on its top descends the mystic Dove. **1842** TENNYSON *Gardener's Dau.* 88 Voices of the well-contented doves.

b. With prefixed word defining the species, as *ringed-, spring-dove.* **blue dove** (*Yorksh.*), the Rock dove. **bush dove,** the Stock dove. **Wrekin dove** (*Salop*), the Turtle dove. Also CUSHAT-, GROUND-, RING-, ROCK-, STOCK-, TURTLE-, WOOD-DOVE, etc., q.v. in their alphabetical places.

c **1386** CHAUCER *Sir Thopas* 59 The thrustelcock..The wodedowue. *c* **1532** DEWES *Introd. Fr.* in *Palsgr.* 911 The rynged dove, *le ramier*; the stocke dove, *le creuset.* **18..** WHITTIER *Hymns fr. Lamartine* I. vi, Thought after thought, ye thronging rise Like spring-doves from the startled wood. **1885** SWAINSON *Prov. Names Birds* 167 Stock Dove (*Columba œnas*). Bush dove. *Ibid.* 168 Rock Dove (*Columba livia*), also called..Blue dove (North Riding). *Ibid.* 169 Turtledove (*Turtur communis*), it is also called in Shropshire, Wrekin dove.

c. *Greenland-dove, sea- (turtle-) dove* = DOVEKIE. *sea-dove*, a kind of fish (see quot. 1753).

1678 RAY *Willughby's Ornith.* 326 The Greenland-Dove or Sea-Turtle. **1753** CHAMBERS *Cycl. Supp.*, *Columba Greenlandica*..called in English, the sea turtle dove. *Ibid.*, *Columba marina*, the sea dove..the name of an East Indian fish, and appearing to be a species of the orbis, or moon-fish. **1885** SWAINSON *Prov. Names Birds* 218 Black Guillemot (*Uria Grylle*), from the great attachment shown to each other by the male and female..this bird has received the names: Greenland dove (Orkney Isles), Rock dove (Ireland).

d. = *dove-colour* (5 b).

1895 *Bow Bells* 29 Mar. 322/1 Sortie-de-bals..are almost always in neutral tints—dove, gray, or fawn. **1903** *Daily Chron.* 21 Nov. 8/4 Aubergine accords with dove charmingly.

2. *fig.* and *transf.* **a.** Applied to the Holy Spirit.

[In reference to Luke iii. 22, and parallel places.]

[**13..** *Coer de L.* 5671 On hys crest a douve whyte, Sygnyfycacioun off the Holy Spryte.] **1707** WATTS *Hymn*, Come, Holy Spirit, heavenly Dove, With all thy quickening powers. **1713** WARDER *True Amazons* (ed. 2) 168 By thy sweet Dove now (from above) And always taught to pray.

1779 COWPER *Hymn, 'O for a closer walk,'* Return, O holy Dove, return. **1827** KEBLE *Chr. Y., Whit-sunday* iii, Softer than gale at morning prime, Hovered his holy Dove.

b. A messenger of peace and deliverance from anxiety, as was the dove to Noah (*Gen.* viii. 8–12).

1623 (*title*), The Essex Dove presenting the World with a few of her Olive-branches; or, a Taste of the Works of the Rev. John Smith. **1849** LYTTON *Caxtons* I. ii, He will be a dove of peace to your ark.

c. A gentle, innocent, or loving woman or child; also †an innocent or simpleton.

1596 SHAKS. *Tam. Shr.* III. ii. 159 Tut, she's a Lambe, a Doue, a foole to him. **1771** FOOTE *Maid of B.* Prol. Wks. 1799 II. 200 The gaming fools are doves, the knaves are rooks. **1850** TENNYSON *In Mem.* vi, O somewhere, meek unconscious dove, Poor child, that waitest for thy love!

d. An appellation of tender affection.

c **1386** CHAUCER *Merch. T.* 897 Rys vp my wyf, my loue, my lady free..my dowue sweete. *c* **1450** HENRYSON *Mor. Fab.* 73 The caller cryed: Hald draught, my dowes. **1535** COVERDALE *Song Sol.* v. 2 O my sister, my loue, my doue, my derlinge. **1602** SHAKS. *Ham.* IV. v. 167 Fare you well my Doue. **1764** FOOTE *Mayor of G.* I. Wks. 1799 I. 171 Shall I wait upon you, dove? **1816** SCOTT *Old Mort.* vi, Is not that worth waiting for, my dow? **1855** TENNYSON *Maud* I. xxii. 61 She is coming, my dove, my dear.

e. = *dove-marble* (5 b below). Also *attrib.*

1805 *Times* 7 Nov. 4/4 Vein, Dove, and fine Statuary chimney-pieces. **1872** *Rep. Vermont Board Agric.* 667 The first [*sc.* marble] to be mentioned is the 'Dove', it being of a dove color.

f. *Politics.* A person who advocates negotiations as a means of terminating or preventing a military conflict, as opposed to one (cf. HAWK *sb.*[1] 3) who advocates a hard-line or warlike policy. Also *attrib.* or quasi-*adj.* and *transf.*

1962 ALSOP & BARTLETT in *Sat. Even. Post* 8 Dec. 20/1 The hawks favored an air strike to eliminate the Cuban missile bases... The doves opposed the air strikes and favored a blockade. **1964** *New Yorker* 10 Oct. 108 Not one of them, whether a 'dove' or a 'hawk', took much stock in the notion of 'overkill'. **1966** *Guardian* 10 Jan. 9/8 The Republicans are themselves divided into two prongs: the liberal Javits, or doubting dove wing; and the Gerald Ford, or hawk wing, which wants a 'total win' in Vietnam. **1966** *Listener* 21 July 93/2 The term 'hawks and doves'..was put into circulation by Charles Bartlett, President Kennedy's great journalistic confidant, in the course of an apparently inspired account of what took place in the President's own National Security Council at the time of the Cuban missile crisis. *Ibid.* 6 Oct. 488/2 For the South Vietnamese there are no nice clear-cut issues, no hawk or dove solutions. **1967** *Boston Sunday Herald* 30 Apr. III. 5/3 It is unfair for the Administration and the hawks to try to compromise the patriotism of the doves. **1971** *N.Y. Rev. Books* 17 June 19/1 A perceptive columnist and long-time dove.

3. An image of a dove as a symbol of innocence, etc.; also, the vessel enclosing the pyx formerly used in the East and in France.

1513 MORE in Grafton *Chron.* (1568) II. 801 The Lorde Lisle Vicount bare the rod with the doffe, which signifieth innocencie. **1688** *Lond. Gaz.* No. 2309/3 Count Drascouitz bearing the Truncheon..Count Erdeodi the Dove. **1849–53** ROCK *Ch. of Fathers* III. ii. 203 (Cent.) There generally were two vessels: the smaller one, or the pix..the larger cup, or dove, within which the other was shut up. **1896** *Daily Chron.* 19 May 3/5 The Archbishop delivered the Sceptre to her [the Queen's] right hand, a rod, with a dove on the top, being placed by him in her left, the 'rod of equity and mercy'.

4. *Astron. dove of Noah.* (See quot.)

1837 *Penny Cycl.* VII. 363/1 *Columba Noachi* (constellation), the dove of Noah, a constellation formed by Halley, close to the hinder feet of Canis Major.

5. Combinations.

a. attrib., as ***dove-hut, -messenger, -monger, -pinion, -taker***, etc.; instrumental, as ***dove-drawn***, adj.; similative and parasynthetic, as ***dove-form, -green, -grey, -soft, -white***; ***ˈdove-feathered, -footed, -robed, -winged***, adjs.

1610 SHAKS. *Temp.* IV. i. 94, I met her deity [Venus]..and her Son *Doue-drawn with her. **1878** P. ROBINSON *My Ind. Garden* 205 The dove-drawn goddess. **1592** SHAKS. *Rom. & Jul.* III. ii. 76 Rauenous *Doue-feather'd Rauen. **1820** KEATS *Lamia* I. 42 The God, *dove-footed, glided silently Round bush and tree. **1891** MISS DOWIE *Girl in Karp.* 287 A huge bank of..*dove-grey cloud. **1650** FULLER *Pisgah* III. ix. 429 Purging of the temple from *dove-mongers. **1923** E. SITWELL *Bucolic Comedies* 44 And the miller's daughter Combs her locks, Like running water Those *dove-soft flocks. **1552** HULOET, *Doue taker, *columbarius.* **1871** SWINBURNE *Songs before Sunrise* 66 Now, to stroke smooth, the *dove-white breast of love. **1967** *New Statesman* 28 July 110/3 Their dove-white cars speed by heavy black armour contorted like paper-clips. **1867** G. M. HOPKINS *Wr. Deutschland* (1918) st. 3, My heart, but you were *dovewinged, I can tell.

b. Special comb.: †**dove-bird**, the young of a dove, a young pigeon (*obs.*); **dove-colour**, a warm grey with a tone of pink or purple; so *dove-coloured*; **dove-dock**, the coltsfoot; **dove-flower** = *dove-plant* (*Treas. Bot.*); **dove's-foot**, the plant *Geranium molle*, and some other small species of cranesbill; **dove-hawk**, the *dove-coloured falcon* or hen-harrier (*Circus cyaneus*); **dove-marble**, marble of a dove-colour; **dove orchid** or **orchis** = *dove-plant*; **dove-plant**, an orchid of Central America, *Peristeria elata*; **dove-tick**, a blind mite parasitic on pigeons; **dove tree**, *Davidia involucrata* and its varieties; **dove-wood**, the wood of *Alchornea latifolia*, a euphorbiaceous tree of the West Indies.

c **1200** *Trin. Coll. Hom.* 47 Two turtle briddes . gif hie was poure, two *duue briddes. *c* **1440** *York Myst.* xli. 250 We haue doyf-byrdes two. *c* **1475** *Pict. Voc.* in Wr.-Wülcker 760/43 *Hic pipio*, dowbyrd. **1598** FLORIO, *Colombino*, *doue colour. **1727–51** CHAMBERS *Cycl., Columbine*, a kind of violet-colour, called also dove-colour. **1727** E. DORRINGTON *Hermit* III. 227 A grave Gentle-woman..dress'd in plain *Dove-colour'd Cloathes. **1825** J. NEAL *Bro. Jonathan* II. 164 A dove-coloured silk mitten. **1876** J. S. INGRAM *Centennial Exposition* xi. 361 A very fine dove-colored or mottled marble was shown. **1812** J. HENDERSON *Agric. Surv. Caithn.* 84 (Jam.) The arable land was much infested with..the *dove-dock. **1831** *Curtis's Bot. Mag.* LVIII. 3116 (*heading*) *Peristeria elata.* Lofty *Dove-Flower. **1951** *Dict. Gardening* (R. Hort. Soc.) III. 1529/1 *P[eristeria] elata.* Dove or Holy Ghost Flower. **1548** TURNER *Names of Herbes* 100 *Douefote, *Geranium molle.* **1578** LYTE *Dodoens* I. xxxii. 47 Doue foote. **1756** WATSON in *Phil. Trans.* XLIX. 841 Doves-foot, or Doves-foot Cranes-bill. **1872** *Rep. Vermont Board Agric.* 675 The first mills at Swanton were wholly employed in the manufacture of grave-stones from the *dove-marble. **1918** *Chambers's Jrnl.* May 321/2 The '*dove' orchid, or *Espiritu Santo* flower of Central America. **1852** C. M. YONGE *Two Guardians* viii. 142 Those tropical plants..the *dove orchis or the zebra-striped pitcher-plant. **1882** *Garden* 10 June 401/3 The *Dove plant..the beautiful Holy Ghost flower of the Spaniards. **1933** A. OSBORN *Shrubs & Trees for Garden* xxxv. 324 Davidia. Chinese *Dove Tree. **1970** H. L. EDLIN *Collins Guide to Tree Planting & Cultivation* 226 When a dove tree is in bloom in May, these white bracts stand out in a bold display, as though a flock of white doves were alighting amid its bright-green foliage, and this explains the English name.

dove, *v. nonce-wd.* [f. prec. sb.] *trans.* To treat as a dove; to call 'dove'.

1864 BROWNING *Too Late* viii, Loved you and doved you.

dove (dəʊv), occasional pa. t. of DIVE *v.* See also E.D.D.

dovecot, -cote (ˈdʌvkɒt). Also 6 dowcatte, *Sc.* doocot, dooket. [f. DOVE *sb.* + COT, COTE.] A house for doves or pigeons; usually placed at a height above the ground, with openings for the doves to enter by, and internal provision for roosting and breeding.

c **1425** *Voc.* in Wr.-Wülcker 670 *Hoc columbare*, dowecote. *a* **1500** in Burton & Raine *Heminbrough* 390 A parcell of her plase to set a doufecot on. **1503** *Sc. Acts. Jas. IV* (1597) §74 Parkes with Deare, stankes, cunningares, dowcattes. **1607** SHAKS. *Cor.* v. vi. 115 Like an Eagle in a Doue-coat. **1703** MAUNDRELL *Journ. Jerus.* (1732) 3 You find here more Dove-Cots than other Houses. **1815** SCOTT *Guy M.* xxii, For the moor-fowl.. they lie as thick as doos in a dooket. *fig.* **1893** *Ch. Times* 6 Oct. 995/3 The flutter that has excited the journalistic dovecot.

†**2.** *transf.* A set or block of pigeon-holes. *Obs.*

1652 BP. HALL *Invisible World* I. vi, If a man distressed with care for the missing of an important evidence..shall be informed..in what hole of his dovecote he shall find it hid.

3. *Comb.*, as ***dovecot-breaker, -door, -pigeon***.

1847 TENNYSON *Princ.* IV. 151 When some one batters at the dovecote-doors. **1861** W. BELL *Dict. Law Scot.* s.v., Dovecot breakers, and stealers of pigeons. **1871** DARWIN *Desc. Man* II. xiv. II. 118 Dove-cot-pigeons dislike all the highly improved breeds.

ˈdove-ˌeyed, *a.* Having eyes like a dove; meek, gentle or soft-eyed.

1717 E. FENTON *Poems* 38 (Jod.) Peace, Dove-eyed, and robed in white. **1826** DISRAELI *Viv. Grey* III. vi, Dove-eyed Hope. **1895** A. DOBSON *Sundial* vii, A second lady..Dove-eyed, dove-robed, and something wan and pale.

ˈdovehouse. Also 5 duffehous, duffous, etc. A house for doves; a dovecot.

14.. *Nom.* in Wr.-Wülcker 730 *Hoc columbare*, dowfhows. **1463** *Bury Wills* (Camden) 24 The gardynes, berne, and duffous. **1530** PALSGR. 215 Dove house.. Dufhouse, *columbier.* **1615** G. SANDYS *Trav.* 175 The sides cut full of holes (in manner of a doue-house). **1887** C. W. BOASE *Oxford* 22 There had been elm walks..with dove-houses.

attrib. **1592** SHAKS. *Rom. & Jul.* I. iii. 28 Sitting in the Sunne vnder the Douehouse wall. **1807** VANCOUVER *Agric. Devon* (1813) 357 Overstocked with dove-house pigeons.

b. *fig.* A small petty house or place.

1523 LD. BERNERS *Froiss.* I. ccclxi. 587 Howe is it..that this peuysshe doue-house holdeth agaynst vs so longe?

doveish, var. DOVISH *a.*

dovekie (ˈdʌvkɪ). Also doveca, -key, -ky. [Sc. dim. of *dove*: cf. *lassikie, wifikie*, or *-ockie* (which are of 3 syllables), and see DOVE 1 c, DOVIE b.] An arctic bird, the Black Guillemot (*Uria Grylle*). Also (and now normally), the little auk (*Plautus alle*).

1821 A. FISHER *Jrnl.* 27 Another species of diver was seen today..it is called by the seamen, Dovekey. **1823** SCORESBY *Jrnl. Whale Fishery* 421 Colymbus Grylle—Tyste or Doveca. **1835** SIR J. C. ROSS *Narr. 2nd Voy.* liv. 693 The second dovekie of the season was seen. **1859** M'CLINTOCK *Voy. Fox* 95 Seals and dovekies are now common. **1917** T. G. PEARSON *Birds of Amer.* I. 31 The little Dovekies or 'Sea Doves' breed along the coasts of Greenland. **1928** W. B. ALEXANDER *Birds of Ocean* x. 251 Dovekie or Little Auk (*Alle alle*). **1954** FISHER & LOCKLEY *Sea-Birds* I. 17 Among the auks the dovekie and the Brünnick's guillemot from the north join the puffins, razorbills and guillemots in ocean wanderings.

dovelet (ˈdʌvlɪt). A little or young dove.

1825 SOUTHEY *Paraguay* I. 43 This dovelet nestled in their leafy bower. **1850** BLACKIE *Æschylus* II. 174 As the dove her dovelets nursing.

dovelike (ˈdʌvlaɪk), *a.* and *adv.* Like a dove; after the manner of a dove.

1577 tr. *Bullinger's Decades* (1592) 726 Doue-like simplicitie. **1667** MILTON *P.L.* I. 21 Thou [O Spirit].. Dove-like satst brooding on the vast Abyss. **1710** POPE *Windsor For.* 430 Where Peace..scatters blessings from her dovelike wing. **1810** COBBETT *Hist. Reform.* xiii. §381 They have not always been in the same dove-like mood. **1930** R. CAMPBELL *Adamastor* 71 With dove-like voices call the distant fillies. **1968** *Listener* 20 June 816/3 Even a journalist from the dove-like *New York Times* was seen wielding a sub-machine-gun during the Tet offensive.

ˈdoveling. [-LING.] A young dove; also, a term of affection for a little child.

a **1618** SYLVESTER *Mem. Mortalitie* II. xlix, An old Sir Tameass..to doat On Venus Dovelings. **1888** *Harper's Mag.* Apr. 748, I will be thy little mother, my doveling.

†**ˈdovely**, *a. Obs.* [-LY[1].] Dove-like; gentle.

14.. *Prose Legends* in *Anglia* VIII. 183 Wiþ an aungels contenans and douvely sympilnesse. *a* **1603** T. CARTWRIGHT *Confut. Rhem. N.T.* (1618) 300 The Douely spirit of God.

dover (ˈdəʊvə(r)), *v. Sc.* and *north. dial.* [app. a frequentative of dial. *dove* in same sense; cf. OE. *dofung* dotage, also ON. *dofna*, Goth. *daubnan*, to become heavy, flat, or dead.]

1. *trans.* To send *off* into a light slumber; to stun, stupefy. *rare.*

(But in first quot. it may be pa. pple. of the intr. sense.)

1513 DOUGLAS *Æneis* VI. vi. 12 This is the hald rycht Of Gaistis, Schaddois, Sleip, and douerit Nycht. **1853** *Fraser's Mag.* XLVIII. 695 The powder that dovers the unhappy off to sleep.

2. *intr.* 'To slumber, to be in a state betwixt sleeping and waking' (Jam.), to doze.

1806 A. DOUGLAS *Poems* 139 (Jam.) She was begun to dover. **1826** SCOTT *Jrnl.* 10 Dec., With great intervals of drowsiness and fatigue which made me, as we Scots say, dover away in my arm-chair. **1892** in *Northumbld. Gloss.*

ˈdover, *sb. Sc.* and *north. dial.* [f. prec. vb.] 'A slumber, a slight unsettled sleep' (Jam.)

1820 *Blackw. Mag.* Nov. 203 (Jam.) My mother had laid down 'th' Afflicted Man's Companion', with which she had read the guidman into a sort o' dover. **1880** J. F. S. GORDON *Bk. Chron. Keith* 32 Get a dover in the day time.

Dover's powder. *Pharm.* [Name of Thomas Dover (1660–1742), English physician.] A preparation of opium and ipecacuanha (*pulvis Doveri*) used as an anodyne diaphoretic, etc.

[**1774** *Pharm. Coll. Regii Med. Edin.* 158 Pulvis sudorificus, sive Doveri.] **1801** *Edin. New Dispensatory* (ed. 6) III. xxvi. 525/2 Compound Powder of Ipecacuanha, commonly called Dover's powder. **1834** *Boston Med. & Surg. Jrnl.* 23 Apr. 174 A grain and a half of Dover's powder ..has sometimes caused extreme anxiety for the safety of children under eight months old. **1887** *Buck's Handbk. Med. Sci.* V. 325/1 Dover's Powder..: Powdered Opium 10 parts, Ipecac. 10 parts, Sugar of Milk 80 parts. **1951** A. & E. F. GROLLMAN *Pharmacol. & Therapeutics* xxiv. 492 Opium is often added in order to further allay coughing by depressing the center, the well-known Dover's powder being a favorite prescription for this purpose. **1971** D. CLARK *Sick to Death* v. 92 You can get it [*sc.* ipecacuanha] in Dover's Powders.

dove-ship, *nonce-wd.*: see DOVE and -SHIP.

a **1656** BP. HALL *Serm. Beauty, &c. Church* (T.), Let our dove-ship approve itselfe in meeknesse of suffering.

†**ˈdovess, dovese.** *Obs.* [f. DOVE *sb.* + -ESS.] A female dove.

1432–50 tr. *Higden* (Rolls) V. 71 A dovese come and sate on his hedde.

dovetail (ˈdʌvteɪl), *sb.*

1. Something in the shape of a dove's tail.

[**1616** SURFL. & MARKH. *Country Farme* 436 Hang in some high place vvith a vvire, or doues-tayle of yron, a glasse vessell.] **1703** MOXON *Mech. Exerc.* 52 A Dufftail, is a Figure made in the form of a Doves-tail.

b. *spec.* A tenon cut in the shape of a dove's tail spread, or of a reversed wedge, to fit into an indenture or mortise of corresponding shape; also, a mortise shaped to receive such a tenon.

1674–91 RAY *N.C. Words* 22 A Dootle; a Notch..Doo tail, i.e. Dovetail, because like a Pigeon's tail extended. **1793** SMEATON *Edystone L.* §82 The blocks themselves were.. formed into large dovetails..so as mutually to lock one another together. **1880** MISS BIRD *Japan* I. 64 Very beautifully joined by mortices and dovetails.

2. = *dovetail joint*: A fastening or joint composed of tenons cut in the shape of an expanded dove's tail, fitting into mortises of corresponding shape.

1565–73 COOPER *Thesaurus, Securicla*..A swallowe tayle or dooue tayle in carpenters workes, which is a fastning of two peeces of timber or bourdes togither that they can not away. **1594** PLAT *Jewell-ho.* III. 26 Make a foure square box ..close the sides well with doue tailes or cement. **1731–7** MILLER *Gard. Dict.* s.v. *Wine Press*, These cross Pieces are placed upon the Posts which are joined into the Ground-plate by a Dove-tail. **1876** GWILT *Archit.* Gloss., *Dove-tail*, a joint..is the strongest method of joining masses, because the tenon or piece of wood widens as it extends, so that it cannot be drawn out.

b. *Her.* (See quot. 1766.)

1688 R. Holme *Armoury* I. 19 [This form of line] is termed patée or Dovetail, from a term of art used by the joiners. **1766** Porny *Elem. Her.* Gloss., *Dove-tail*, term..to denote a kind of Partition, wherein the two different Tinctures are set within one another, in such a manner, as to represent the form of the tails of Doves or Wedges reversed.

3. *attrib.* and *Comb.*, *as* ***dovetail fashion***, ***dovetail-wise*** adv.; of the shape of a dovetail, as ***dove-tail groove***, ***key***, ***mortise***, ***rail***, ***socket***, ***tenon***, ***wedge***: employed in making dovetails, as ***dovetail-cutter***, ***-marker***, ***-plane***, ***-saw***; **dovetail-file**, a thin file with a tin or brass back, like that of a dovetail saw; **dovetail-hinge**, a hinge having the outer edges of the leaves wider that the hinging edges; **dovetail-joint**, (*a*) *Joinery*: a tenon-and-mortise joint, in which the tenons are shaped like a dove's tail; (*b*) *Anat.*: a serrated articulation or suture, as in the bones of the skull; hence ***dovetail-jointed*** adj.; **dovetail-moulding**, *Arch.*, an ornament consisting of a moulding arranged in the form of a series of figures like dove-tails; the triangular fret moulding; **dovetail-plate** (see quot.); **dovetail-wire**, a wire wedge-shaped in cross-section.

1885 *Fortnt. in Waggonette* 26 Sketchit and I dispose of our legs in *dovetail fashion. **1776** G. Campbell *Philos. Rhet.* II. 412 (R.) After the invention of *dove-tail joints. **1848** C. C. Clifford *Aristoph. Frogs* 30 Well put together, *dovetail-jointed. **1853** Sir H. Douglas *Milit. Bridges* (ed. 3) 323 Pieces of timber..fastened together by *dovetail keys and wedges. **1846** Parker *Gloss. Arch.* (1875) 158 Mouldings..the Double Cone, the *Dovetail, the Embattled, [etc.]. *c* **1850** *Rudim. Navig.* (Weale) 115 *Dove-tail plates. Metal plates formed like dovetails, and used to confine the heel of the stern-post and keel together. **1812-16** J. Smith *Panorama Sc. & Art* I. 107 The *dove-tail-saw is used by joiners and cabinet-makers in dove-tailing drawers [etc.]. **1876** Routledge *Discov.* 24 A hammer face is attached to the bottom of the cylinder by a kind of *dovetail socket. **1679** Evelyn *Diary* 23 July, Some of the rooms [were] floored *dove-tail-wise without a nail. **1793** Smeaton *Edystone L.* §82 Cut dovetail-wise.

ˈdovetail, *v.* [f. prec. sb.]

1. *trans.* To fit together or join by means of dovetails, or by a similar method. Const. *in*, *into*, *to*.

1657 R. Ligon *Barbadoes* (1673) 103 That the girders be strong, and very well Dove-tayld, one into another. **1765** Ludlam in *Phil. Trans.* LV. 207 Into this is dove-tail'd the upright back KK. **1842-76** Gwilt *Archit.* §2285 e, Steps and risers mitred to cut string, and dovetailed to balusters. **1855** Ramsbottom *Obstetr. Med.* 17 The bones are not dove-tailed into each other as in the adult.

2. *fig.* To unite compactly as if by dovetails; to adjust exactly, so as to form a continuous whole.

1815 *Sporting Mag.* XLVI. 71 The difficulty of dove-tailing the component parts of the farce into each other. **1826** E. Irving *Babylon* I. iii. 213 We have..as it were, dove-tailed it [book of Revelation] with the Prophecy of Daniel. **1861** Geikie *E. Forbes* x. 293 The readiness with which Forbes had begun to dovetail zoology and geology.

3. *intr.* To fit into each other, so as to form a compact and harmonious whole or company.

1813 *Theatrical Inquisitor* II. 111 The various compartments of the dialogue dove-tailed into each other. **1817** Keats *Lett.* Wks. 1889 III. 99 Several things dove-tailed in my mind, and at once it struck me what quality went to form a man of achievement. **1833** T. Hook *Parson's Dau.* III. ix. 451 The guests did not seem to me to dovetail. **1886** Stubbs *Lect. Med. & Mod. Hist.* ii. 31 The professorial and tutorial systems have not yet dove-tailed into one another.

Hence **ˈdovetailed** *ppl. a.*, fitted together or compacted by dovetailing; **ˈdovetailedness**, dovetailed condition; **ˈdovetailing** *vbl. sb.* and *ppl. a.*; also **ˈdovetailer.**

1656 Blount *Glossogr.*, *Dovetaild*, is a term among Joyners. **1703** T. N. *City & C. Purchaser* 33 Fasten the..pieces of Timber well together..with..Dove-tailing. **1775** Romans *Hist. Florida* 200 A comfortable house of square cypress timber, dove-tailed. **1821** T. D. Fosbroke *Berkeley MSS.* 224 A very dove-tailing analogy. **1823** *New Monthly Mag.* VII. 2 Manufacturers of tragedy and dovetailers of melodram. **1825** J. Nicholson *Operat. Mechanic* 588 There are three sorts of dovetailing; viz. common, lap, and mitre. **1835-6** Todd *Cycl. Anat.* I. 736/1 [The cranial bones] are united..by the dove-tailing of their edges. **1838** Dickens *Nich. Nick.* xxiv., A kind of universal dove-tailedness with regard to place and time. **1864** *Sat. Rev.* 31 Dec. 789 A 'dovetailed and tesselated' Cabinet.

ˈdovetailed, *a.* [f. dovetail *sb.* + -ed[2].]

1. Having a tail like a dove; shaped like a dove's tail; having a dovetail.

1721 Perry *Daggenh. Breach* 53 There is no other way..to secure the said bad Ground but by driving Dovetail'd Piles. **1726** Leoni *Alberti's Archit.* I. 50/2 Cramps..of Wood are..secured by their shape, which is..such..that for resemblance, they are call'd Swallow, or Dove-tail'd. **1838** Jas. Grant *Sk. Lond.* 163 Some coal-heaver rejoicing in a dove-tailed hat, which overspreads his neck and shoulders.

2. *Her.* Broken into dovetails, as a dividing line; cf. dovetail *sb.* 2 b.

1868-82 Cussans *Her.* ii.

dovie, dovey (ˈdʌvɪ). [Dim. or pet-form of dove: see -ie, -y.] A term of affection: Little or dear dove. **b.** A local name of the dovekie.

1769 *Public Advertiser* 18 May 4/2 The domestic Lovies and Dovies. **1819** *Metropolis* III. 252 My dearest love—lovey, dovey! **1885** Swainson *Prov. Names Birds* 218 Black Guillemot..Sea dovie (Forfar).

ˈdovish, *a.* Also doveish. [f. dove + -ish.] Of or pertaining to the dove; dovelike. Now freq. in *Politics* (cf. dove *sb.* 2 f).

1537 Latimer *Serm. bef. Convoc.* 8 It is like the policie of the serpent, and is joyned with douish simplicitie. **1546** *Confut. N. Shaxton* G iv b (T.) Contempte of thys world, doveyshe simplicitie, serpentlike wysdome. **1966** *Listener* 6 Oct. 488/1 They tend to take up strong positions, 'hawkish' or 'doveish'. **1967** *Guardian* 14 Oct. 6/5 This sudden upsurge of doveish voices in the Republican ranks. **1968** *Ibid.* 19 Mar. 9/1 He does not take a particularly dovish line himself on Vietnam. **1971** *Ibid.* 23 June 2/1 'Dovish' sponsors of the initial proposal contended that it was meaningless after the Administration succeeded..in making the nine-month withdrawal contingent upon a full release of all prisoners.

dow (daʊ), *v.*[1] Now *Sc.* and *north. dial.* Forms: *Pres. t.* 1 and 3 *sing.* 1. **déaȝ**, **déah** [= Goth. *dauh*, OHG. *touc*, OS. *dôg*]; 1-3 **deȝ**, 2 **dæh**, 3 **deh**, **degh**, 3-4 **deih**, 4-7 **dowe**, 5- **dow** (7 **dou**); in 3rd *sing.* 4 **dowes**, 8-9 **dows**; *plural* 1 **duȝon** [= OS. *dugun*, OHG. *tugun*]; 2-3 **duȝen**, 4 **douwe(n**, 4-7 **dowe**, 5- **dow**. *Pa. t.* 1 **dohte** [= Goth. **dauhta*, OHG. *tohta*]; 3 **douhte**, 4 **dought(e**, **doht**, **doght**, **duȝt**, **dught**, 4- **dought**, **dowed**, *Sc.* 5- **docht**, **doucht**, **dowcht**, 6 **ducht**. [One of the original Teutonic preterite-present verbs (see can, dare, may): OE. *duȝan* to avail, be strong, good, worthy, of use, = OS. *dugan*, OFris. *duga* (MDu. *döghen*, Du. *deugen*), OHG. *tugan*, (MHG. *tugen*, Ger. *taugen*), Goth. *dugan*, ON. *duga* (Sw. *duga*, Da. *due*):—OTeut. *dugan*. The original inflexion *déaȝ* (:—OTeut. *daug*) of the singular present was in 14th c. supplanted by *dow* from the plural, the 3rd sing. being sometimes made *dows*. For the original pa. t. *dohte* (:—OTeut. *duhta*) retained in Sc. as *docht*, *dought*, a levelled form *dowed* is occasional from 14th c. Both forms are used by Scott in sense 5.]

†**1.** *intr.* To be good, strong, valiant, vigorous, manly, virtuous. Only *OE.*

Beowulf (Th.) 1057 Ðeah ðu heaðo ræsa ȝehwær dohte. *a* **1000** *Father's Instr.* 4 (in *Exeter Bk.*) Do á þætte duȝe. *a* **1000** *Satan* 283 (Gr.) Se ðe his heorte deah.

†**2.** To be valid, or of value; to be worth or good for anything. *Obs.*

c **1200** Ormin 4872 Icc amm þatt þing þatt nohht ne dæh. *a* **1275** *Prov. Ælfred* 506 in *O.E. Misc.* 132 On him þu maist þe tresten, yif [h]is troȝþe degh. *Ibid.* 546. 133 Hwile þine daȝes duȝen. *c* **1300** *Havelok* 703 Al he solde, þat outh douthe [= ouht douhte]. *c* **1320** *Sir Tristr.* 1126 Neuer no douȝt him day For sorwe he hadde oniȝt. *c* **1330** R. Brunne *Chron.* (1810) 133 Thebald nouht ne deih. **1508** Dunbar *Tua Mariit Wemen* 370 Eftir dede of that drupe, that docht nought in chalmir. **1530** Lyndesay *Test. Papyngo* 69 It dowe no thyng bot for to be deiectit. **1788** W. Marshall *Yorksh.* Gloss., *Dow*, to..be useful; as 'he dows for nought', he is good for nothing.

†**3.** To be of use or profit to any one; to avail. Chiefly *impersonal*. *Obs.*

c **950** *Lindisf. Gosp.* Matt. xvi. 26 Huæt forðon deȝ menn? *a* **1100** *O.E. Chron.* an. 1006 Ðet him naðor ne dohte ne innhere ne uthere. *a* **1300** *Cursor M.* 10771 (Cott.) Quen ioseph sagh na hide ne dught [*rime* broght]. **13..** *E.E. Allit. P.* B. 374 Noȝt dowed bot þe deth in þe depe stremez. *Ibid.* C. 50 What dowes me þe dedayn, oþer dispit make? *c* **1400** *Destr. Troy* 5001 Iff yow do þus in dede, hit doghis the bettur. **1513** Douglas *Æneis* viii. Prol. 1 Of drefling and dremis quhat dow it to endyt? **1590** R. Bruce *Serm. on Sacr.* G vij. (Jam.) So this argument dow not.

†**4.** To be good, fitting, or proper for any one; to become, befit, behove. Usually *impers.*

a **1225** *Leg. Kath.* 2228, & biburiede hire as hit deh martir. *a* **1225** *Juliana* 51 Milde and meoke..as meiden deh to beonne. *a* **1225** *Ancr. R.* 420 Swuch þing þet ou ne deih forto habben. **14..** *Tundale's Vis.* 907 As wemen doght. *c* **1450** *Merlin* 47 Blase axed what he ought to do.

5. To have the strength or ability, to be able (to do something).

a **1300** *Cursor M.* 23771 (Cott.) Fight he aght ai quils he dught, and fle quen he langer ne moght. *a* **1400-50** *Alexander* 4058 Vnde[d]lynes to dele I dowe be na ways. **1500-20** Dunbar *Poems* xviii. 14 Thocht he dow not to leid a tyk. **1573** *Satir. Poems Reform.* xxxix. 38 Scho..dang the frenchmen, quhilk we docht not do. **1637** Rutherford *Lett.* (1862) I. 203 Ye may not, ye cannot, ye dow not want Christ. **1645** *Munim. Burgh Irvine* (1891) II. 58 Our inhabitants who ducht not win away by sey. **1724** Ramsay *Tea-t. Misc.* (1733) I. 2 She doughtna let her lover mourn. **1786** Burns *Earnest Cry & Prayer* Postscr. iii, They downa bide the stink o' powther. **1816** Scott *Antiq.* xxiii, I never dowed to bide a hard turn o' wark in my life. **1818** —— *Hrt. Midl.* xxiii, As well as a woman in her condition dought.

6. To do well, thrive, prosper.

1674 Ray *N.C. Words* 13 To Daw or Dou: to thrive..He'll never dow, i.e. He will never be good. *a* **1758** A. Ramsay *Poems* (1877) II. 174 Unty'd to a man..We never can thrive or dow. **1811** Willan *W. Riding Gloss.* (E.D.S.), *Dou*, *dau*, to do well, to prosper. **1855** Robinson *Whitby Gloss.*, March grows Never dows.

Hence **ˈdowing** *ppl. a.*, †valiant, virtuous (*obs.*); thriving.

c **1175** *Lamb. Hom.* 109 Swa swa þan alden bihouað duȝende þewas. *c* **1205** Lay. 4123 Dunwale þat was þe duȝende mon. **1825** Jamieson s.v., A dowing bairn.

†**dow,** *v.*[2] *Obs.* Also 4-5 doue, dowe. [a. F. *doue-r* (12th c.):—L. *dōtāre* to portion out, bestow, f. *dōs*, *dōt-em* dowry.]

1. *trans.* To enrich with property; = endow 2.

1297 R. Glouc. (1724) 520 And the churche ifounded in a mory place, called Muryfelde, and Idowed of the pryuylege of the citee by kyng Henry. **1362** Langl. *P. Pl.* A. xv. 519 Constantyn..holykirke dowed With londes and ledes. **1382** Wyclif *Exod.* xxii. 16 He shal dowe hir and he shal have hir to wijf. **1403** *York Manual* (Surtees) p. xvi, Wyth my gyftys I dow the. **1483** Caxton *Gold. Leg.* 431 The abbay of royalmonte whyche he founded and dowed with grete reuenewe and rentes.

2. To invest *with* something; = endow 3 a.

c **1420** *Anturs of Arth.* lii, Here I doue the as Duke. *c* **1450** *Mirour Saluacioun* 3750 She was dowyd with eterne cristis ffruycionne.

3. To bequeath, give as an endowment.

c **1374** Chaucer *Troylus* v. 230 O lady myn..To whom for eueremo myn herte I dowe.

Hence **ˈdowing** *vbl. sb.*, endowment, dower.

1382 Wyclif *Exod.* xxii. 17 He shal ȝeeld the money after the maner of dowyng that maydens weren wont to tak. *c* **1450** *Mirour Saluacioun* 4323 Dampned sawles and the bodies shal haf no swilk dowyng.

dow (daʊ), *v.*[3] *Sc.* and *north. dial.* [Deriv. doubtful; possibly a Sc. form of dull *v.* or a ME. **doll-en*: cf. dowie = *dolly*, dully.]

intr. To lose brightness or freshness; to fade; to become dull or musty; to fall into a sleepy state. Chiefly in *pa. pple.* **dowed**, **dow'd**, become dull, faded, etc.

1502 *Ord. Crysten Men* (W. de W. 1506) v. iv. 386 People blynded and dowed in theyr synnes. **1653** Dorothy Osborne *Lett. to Temple* (1888) 59 I was so tired with my journey, so dowd with my cold. **1737** Ramsay *Sc. Prov.* (1776) 21 (Jam.) Cast na out the dow'd water till ye get the fresh. *c* **1746** J. Collier (Tim Bobbin) *View Lanc. Dial.* Gloss., *Dowd*, flat; dead; spiritless. **1845** Ainslie in *Whistle-binkie* (Sc. Songs) Ser. iii. 95 The day begins to dow. **1853** Ballantine in *Whistle-binkie* (1890) II. 292 As dowed the outward rind The core it grew the dearer. **1875** *Lanc. Gloss.*, It's as dowd as dyke wayter.

†**dow,** *v.*[4] *Obs.* [Used by Caxton to render MDu. *duwen*.] *trans.* To press, squeeze, wring.

1481 Caxton *Reynard* (Arb.) 61, I dowed [*ic duwede*] the cony bytwene his eeris that almost I benamme his lyf from hym. *Ibid.* 111 The sore wryngyng that the foxe dowd [*duwede*] and wronge his genytours.

dow, obs. form of dough; Sc. var. of dove.

dow, earlier and more correct form of dhow.

Dow: see Dow-Jones.

dowable (ˈdaʊəb(ə)l), *a. Law.* [a. AF. *dowable*, f. F. *douer* to portion, dow *v.*[2]] Capable of being endowed; entitled to dower.

[**1292** Britton v. i. §5 Femmes dowables des terres et des tenementz.] **1535** *Act 27 Hen. VIII*, c. 10. §7 Her husbandes tenementes or hereditamentes, whereof she was before dowable. **1613** Sir H. Finch *Law* (1636) 36 If the heire indow the ancestors wife, though she were not dowable, yet she shall hold in dower. **1767** Blackstone *Comm.* II. viii. 131 A seisin in law of the husband will be as effectual as a seisin in deed, in order to render the wife dowable. **1858** Ld. St. Leonards *Handy Bk. Prop. Law* xviii. 131 Is my wife dowable of any part of it?

†**ˈdowage.** *Obs. rare.* [a. obs. F. *douage* dowry, f. *douer*: see prec.] Dower, dowry.

1538 Leland *Itin.* II. 55 A Park wont to be yn dowage to the Quenes of Englande. **1608** *Merry Devil Edmonton* in Hazl. *Dodsley* X. 220 Thy revenues cannot reach To make her dowage of so rich a jointure As can the heir of wealthy Jerningham.

†Hence **ˈdowageable** *a. Obs. rare*, dowable.

1655 Gayton *Charity Triumph.* 7 Your Virgin, whom I shal labour to make as famous as your Honour has made her Dowagable.

dowager (ˈdaʊədʒə(r)). Also 6 do-, dou-, dowagier, douager. [a. OF. *douagere*, *-iere*, *douaygere*, *dowaigiere*, *doagiere* widow enjoying a dower, fem. of *douaigier*, etc. (= mod.F. *douairier*), f. *douage* dower + *-ier*, -er[2] 2.]

A woman whose husband is dead and who is in the enjoyment of some title or some property that has come to her from him. Often added to the title so enjoyed, as ***princess-***, ***queen-dowager***, ***dowager-duchess***, ***-queen***, ***-lady***, etc.

(App. first used of Mary Tudor, widow of Louis XII; then of Catherine of Arragon, styled 'Princess Dowager'.)

1530 Palsgr. Ep. to Hen. VIII, Your..most entirely beloved suster quene Mary douagier of France. **1542** *Fabyan's Chron.* Contn. vii. 700 In January dyed lady Katherine princes dowager [*printed* -yer]. **1558** Forrest *Grysilde Sec.* (1875) 93 They gaue her to name Ladye Douager. **1590** Shaks. *Mids. N.* i. i. 157, I haue a Widdow Aunt, a dowager, Of great reuennew. **1613** —— *Hen. VIII*, ii. iv. 180 Respecting this our Marriage with the Dowager Sometimes our Brothers Wife. *a* **1674** Clarendon *Hist. Reb.* xiii. §154 The two Dowagers, his mother and grandmother, having great joyntures out of the estate. **1701** *Lond. Gaz.* No. 3745/2 She was accompanied by the Dutchess of Savoy, her Mother, and by the Dutchess-Dowager. **1754** Hume *Hist. Eng.* I. xii. 277 He espoused Eleanor, dowager of William Earl of Pembroke. **1809** *Naval Chron.* XXII. 276 Mrs. Innes, Dowager, of Sandside. **1867**

FREEMAN *Norm. Conq.* (1876) I. vi. 411 A marriage with their dowager aunt.

†**b.** Loosely used. (In Drayton, app. = 'lady holding in dower'.) *Obs.*

1611 SPEED *Theat. Gt. Brit.* xxxii. (1614) 63/1 Kathren of Spaine, wife and dowager to K. Henry the eight. *a* **1631** DRAYTON *Eng. Hist. Ep.*, As Charles his daughter..As Henry's Queen..By France's conquest and by England's oath, You are the true made dowager of both.

c. *familiarly.* An elderly lady of dignified demeanour.

1870 DICKENS *E. Drood* iii, Like the legendary ghost of a dowager in silken skirts. **1881** 'RITA' *My Lady Coquette* v, Anxious dowagers are giving longing glances at the provision-basket.

d. *transf.* and *fig.* Of men or animals.

1819 *Metropolis* III. 71 Our..dowager generals, those who, from old men are scarcely better than old women. **1840** LADY C. BURY *Hist. of Flirt* xiv, A couple of stout post-horses were..preferable to their own quiet dowagers.

Hence (*nonce-wds.*) '**dowager** *v. intr.*, to play the dowager; '**dowagerdom**, '**dowagerhood**, '**dowagerism**, '**dowagership**; **dowa'gerian**, '**dowagerish**, '**dowagerly** *adjs.*

1733-4 MRS. DELANY *Autobiog. & Corr.* (1861) I. 426 Bury him decently in Westminster, and enjoy the dowagership most gallantly. **1825** J. JEKYLL *Let.* 6 Oct. in *Corr.* (1894) 150, I dowager daily in the carriage. **1843** *Tait's Mag.* X. 286 Sober dowagerly entertainments. **1848** THACKERAY *Van. Fair* xlvi, Mansions that have passed away into Dowagerism. **1891** *Blackw. Mag.* CXLIX. 553/1 The well-preserved dowagerhood of Hampton Court.

dowannee, obs. var. of DEWANI.

dowarie, -ry, obs. forms of DOWRY.

dowb, dowbart, obs. ff. DUB *v.*, DULBERT.

dowbill, -ble, -bul, etc., obs. ff. DOUBLE.

dowcare, obs. Sc. form of DUCKER, diver.

dowcemere, obs. form of DULCIMER.

dowcet(e, obs. forms of DOUCET, DULCET.

Dowche, dowchery, obs. ff. DUTCH, DUCHERY.

dowchsperys, corrupt f. DOUZEPERS, *Obs.*

dowd (daʊd), *sb.*[1] [Of uncertain origin. In mod. use appar. a back-formation from DOWDY *a.*

The ME. rimes with *shroud* show that the ME. vowel was (uː) = Fr. *ou* or OE. *ú*; this separates it from DOW *v.*[2] (which besides appears later); it also eliminates Wedgwood's suggestion of connexion with *dawdle* and Sc. *dawdie*. The mod.Sc. *dooda* ('dudə) may be related.]

A person, usually a woman, whose dress and appearance are devoid of smartness and brightness.

c **1330** R. BRUNNE *Chron. Wace* (Rolls) 11255, I trowe þer were many doude þat proudly spak for noble schroude. *c* **1425** WYNTOUN *Cron.* III. 795 In sege a sot to se, Or do a dowde in dignite. *c* **1460** *Towneley Myst.* (Surtees) 312 If she be neuer so fowlle a dowde, With hir kelles and hir pynnes ..The shrew hir self can shrowde. **1542** UDALL *Erasm. Apoph.* 309 b, To begette soche foule babies and oule faced doudes. **1607** BRETON *Murmure* C vij, Doest thou being Faire murmure at the preferment of a foule one and in thy rage call her foule Dowde? **1814** MAD. D'ARBLAY *Wanderer* III. 199, I go such a dowd here, that it's enough to frighten you. **1899** *Westm. Gaz.* 30 Oct. 3/2 She's a dowd to-day. **1904** *Ibid.* 23 June 4/2 Only a duchess may dare to be a dowd just now. **1930** *Time & Tide* 13 Sept., To confound the shallow-pates who complained that a suffragist must be a dowd, the leader of the W.S.P.U. appeared on platforms clothed in Paris frocks. **1950** *John o' London's* 24 Nov. 629/3 A homely and devoted dowd like some of the later translations by Victorian writers.

†**dowd**, *sb.*[2] *Obs.* or *dial.* A woman's cap or night-cap.

1749 R. GOADBY *Carew* (ed. 2) 42 Having..pinn'd a large Dowde under his Chin. *Ibid.* 223 He..puts on a long Dowde. **1808-80** JAMIESON, *Doud*, a *kelled mutch*, or woman's cap with a caul, considered as a dress cap. **1847-78** HALLIWELL, *Dowd*, a night-cap. *Devon.*

dowd, dowed, *ppl. a.*: see DOW *v.*[3]

dowdily ('daʊdɪlɪ), *adv.* [f. DOWDY *sb.*[1] and *a.* + -LY[2].] In a dowdy fashion.

1887 T. A. TROLLOPE *What I remember* II. ix. 156 The two girls..were dressed exactly alike and very dowdily.

dowdiness ('daʊdɪnɪs). [f. DOWDY *sb.*[1] and *a.* + -NESS.] The quality of being dowdy; shabby ugliness of dress or personal appearance.

1842 EMERSON *Nat., Transcendent.* Wks. (Bohn) II. 290 The Beautiful..appears to us the golden mean, escaping the dowdiness of the good, and the heartlessness of the true. **1862** TROLLOPE *Orley F.* xii, There was nothing of the dowdiness of the lone lorn woman about her.

dowdy ('daʊdɪ), *sb.*[1] and *a.* Also 6 **doudie**, 7 **dowdie**, 7-9 **doudy.** [A deriv. of DOWD.

(It would be natural to regard the adj. as the primary form, from DOWD *sb.* with suffix *-y* as in *need-y*, etc.; but the sb., being known earlier, may be a diminutive formation, as in *daddy*, and the adj. an attributive use.)]

A. *sb.* A woman or girl shabbily or unattractively dressed, without smartness or brightness.

1581 RICH *Farew. Milit. Prof.*, If plaine or homely, wee saie she is a doudie or a slut. **1592** SHAKS. *Rom. & Jul.* II. iv. 42 Dido, a dowdie: Cleopatra, a Gipsie. **1660-1** PEPYS *Diary* 8 Mar., Among others the Duchesse of Albemarle, who is ever a plain homely dowdy. *a* **1700** B.E. *Dict. Cant. Crew*, *Doudy*, An ugly coarse hard favored Woman. **1774** ANNE GRANVILLE in *Mrs. Delany's Corr.* Ser. II. II. 49 Her hair not ..suffered to grow too low on her forehead..it makes all the children look like dowdys. **1883** BESANT *All in Garden Fair* I. ii, To be gracious and sympathetic..you must be nicely dressed; a dowdy cannot be gracious.

B. *adj.* (Almost always of a woman or her dress.) Shabbily dull in colour or appearance; without brightness, smartness, or freshness.

1676 SHADWELL *Virtuoso* iii, Little dowdy strumpets. **1684** T. BURNET *Th. Earth* II. 221 Female angels..of a far more charming beauty than the dowdy daughters of men. **1774** ANNE GRANVILLE in *Mrs. Delany's Corr.* Ser. II. II. 48 A very dowdy fashion. **1865** TROLLOPE *Belton Est.* i. A thick black silk dress..not rusty or dowdy with age. **1869** —— *He knew* xcvii, A plain, silent, shy, dowdy young woman. **1887** R. N. CAREY *Uncle Max* xxx. 238 In your nurse's livery.. black serge, and a horrid dowdy bonnet.

dowdy, *sb.*[2] *Obs.* or *dial.* = DOWD *sb.*[2] (see quots.).

1778 F. BURNEY *Evelina* II. ii. 35 'Perhaps Lady Howard may be able to lend you a cap...' 'Do you think I'd wear one of her dowdies?' **1880** W. H. PATTERSON *Gloss. Antrim & Down* 32 *Dowdy cap*, same as *dowd*. **1905** WRIGHT *Eng. Dial. Dict.* Suppl. 91/1 *Dowdy*. Hmp. The linen bonnet worn by women when working in the field.

dowdyish ('daʊdɪɪʃ), *a.* [f. DOWDY *sb.*[1] and *a.* + -ISH.] Somewhat dowdy; inclined to dowdyism.

1817 BYRON *Beppo* lxvi, A fifth's look's vulgar, dowdyish, and suburban. **1854** HAWTHORNE *Eng. Note-Bks.* II. 71 The girls were all dressed in..a very dowdyish attire.

dowdyism ('daʊdɪɪz(ə)m). [f. as prec. + -ISM.] The character or quality of a dowdy.

1859 O. W. HOLMES *Prof. Breakf.-t.* vi, Dowdyism is..an expression of imperfect vitality. **1860** *All Year Round* No. 71. 495 A sorry sort of dowdyism in the matter of female finery.

dowee (daʊ'iː). [f. DOW *v.*[2] + -EE: cf. F. *doué* endowed.] A person endowed or holding a dower.

1865 NICHOLS *Britton* I. 272 The dowee may answer by herself.

dowel ('daʊəl), *sb.* Forms: 4-6 **dowle**, 7-8 **doul(e**, 8 **dowl**, (**dole**), 9 **dowel, -ell.** [Of doubtful derivation; perh. answering to MLG. *dovel*, Ger. *döbel*, MHG. *tübel*, OHG. *tubili* plug, tap (of a cask, etc.). Still closer in form is OF. *doelle*, *douelle* barrel-stave, dim. of mod.F. *douve* in same sense; but the transference of sense is unexplained.]

1. A headless pin, peg, or bolt, of wood, metal, or other material, serving to fasten together two pieces of wood, stone, etc., by penetrating some distance into the substance of the connected pieces.

c **1340** *Cursor M.* 21270 (Fairf.) Þe quelis ar ioyned with mani a dowle. **1388** WYCLIF *1 Kings* vii. 33 The extrees..the spokis and dowlis [**1382** felijs; Vulg. *modioli*] of the wheelis. **1483** *Cath. Angl.* 105/1 A Dowle of a whele; *stellio.* **1794** W. FELTON *Carriages* (1801) I. 112 The felly with the pins or dowels on the end, by which it is kept secure at the joints. **1862** *Sat. Rev.* 15 Mar. 303 An immense block of stone.. bolted into sockets in the masonry below by bronze dowels fixed into its lower face. **1876** GWILT *Encycl. Archit.* Gloss., *Dowel*, a pin of wood or iron used at the edges of boards in laying floors to avoid the appearance of the nails on the surface.

2. A plug of wood driven into a wall to receive nails; a dook. [Ger. *döbel, dübel.*]

1864 in WEBSTER. **1874** in KNIGHT *Dict. Mech.*

3. *Comb.*, as **dowel-bit**, a boring-tool of semi-cylindrical form terminating in a conoidal edge; also called a *spoon-bit*; **dowel-hole**, a hole into which a dowel is or may be inserted; **dowel-joint**, a junction formed by means of a dowel or dowels; **dowel-pin** = sense 1; **dowel-pointer**, a tool for pointing or chamfering the ends of dowels; **dowel-ways** *adv.*, in the manner of a dowel.

a **1661** FULLER *Worthies* III. (1662) 20 Having every stone ..shaped Doule-wayes, or in the form of a Cart-nail. **1707** T. N. *City & C. Purchaser* 187 They cleave these Bolts (with their Dowl-Ax) by the Felt-grain. **1743** *Lond. & Country Brew.* II. (ed. 2) 108 There are Joints, down-right Pegs, or Dole-pins. **1885** *Academy* 21 Nov. 326/1 The floor has raised edges, in which are visible the dowel-holes to hold wooden panels.

dowel ('daʊəl), *v.* [f. prec. sb.] *trans.* To fasten with a dowel or dowels.

1713 WARDER *True Amazons* 108 You must doule or nail together on the under Side, 2 Boards. **1792** *Acc. Buggesses* in *Ann. Reg.* 66 Dowling the planks together, as coopers do the parts that form the head of a cask. **1883** GORE in *Glasgow Weekly Her.* 7 July 2/7 These [columns] are not cemented but dowelled with iron clamps in the centre.

Hence **dowelled** *ppl. a.*, **dowelling** *vbl. sb.*

1805 *Times* 7 Nov. 4/2 Excellent dowelled flooring. **1823** P. NICHOLSON *Pract. Build.* App. 76 To lay dowelled floors. **1879** *Cassell's Techn. Educ.* III. 183/2 The method of uniting boards in a flat surface, called 'dowelling'.

†**do-well.** *Obs.* [f. DO *v.* + WELL adv.] The action of doing well; well-doing. (In Langland freq. personified, together with *Do-bet*, *Do-best.*)

1362 LANGL. *P. Pl.* A. VIII. 156 Þe preost..diuinede þat Dowel Indulgence passede. *Ibid.* 158 Dowel on Domesday Is digneliche I-preiset. **1377** *Ibid.* B. ix. 12 Dobet is hir damoisele sire doweles douȝter. **1628** GAULE *Pract. The. Panegyr.* 52 His Doe-well to vsward exceeds our Say-well of him.

dowelle, obs. form of DWELL.

†**dowen**, *ppl. a. Obs.* [app. for *dollen*, *dolven*, pa. pple. of DELVE.] Buried.

c **1450** *Mirour Saluacioun* 1484 Cristis flesshe dede & dowen nevere to corrupcionne slade.

†**dower**, *sb.*[1] *Obs.* Also **dover, douwere, douwir, dwer, duer.** [Cf. OF. *douvre*, var. of *douve* ditch, dyke, 'caverne que les habitants des bords de la Loire creusent dans le roc pour s'y loger.'] A burrow (of rabbits, or the like).

1398 TREVISA *Barth. De P.R.* XVIII. lxviii. (1495) 824 Conyes..make them dowers and dennes vnder erthe. *c* **1420** *Pallad. on Husb.* IV. 654 Outher in gourdis grene Make euery fige a douer in to crepe. *c* **1440** *Promp. Parv.* 128/2 Dower yn the erthe (dovwere, H. douwir, P.), *cuniculus.* *c* **1490** *Ibid.* 135/2 (MS. H), Dowere, or deen.

dower ('daʊə(r)), *sb.*[2] Forms: 4-6 **dowaire, -ayr(e, dowere**, 5 **dowar, dowyer**, 6 **douare, dore, doore**, 6-7 **dowr(e**, 4- **dower.** [a. OF. *douaire*, *doaire*, *douayre*, ad. late L. *dōtārium* (Du Cange), f. L. *dōt-em* dower, *dōtāre* to endow.]

1. The portion of a deceased husband's estate which the law allows to his widow for her life. ***tenant in dower***, the widow who thus holds land. †***lady of dower***, dowager lady.

[**1292** BRITTON I. vi. §5 Et voloms qe les femmes as felouns ne tiegnent nule terre en dowayre de nul tenement qe lour fust assignee par teus barouns.] **1439** *E.E. Wills* (1882) 115 Her part and dowyer of my godes. **1470-85** MALORY *Arthur* v. xii, The kyng..assigned certayn rentes for the dower of the duchesse & for her children. **1523** LD. BERNERS *Froiss.* I. cclxix. 399 He was before the castell of Perides, where as the Lady of Dowaire was. **1528** *Test. Ebor.* (Surtees) V. 267 To Margarete, my wif, hir hoole dore of all my landes. *a* **1626** BACON *Max. & Uses Com. Law* (1636) 58 Yet he was not such a tenant as to be seized of the land, so as his wife could have dower. **1767** BLACKSTONE *Comm.* II. vii. 116 The wife of the tenant in tail shall have her dower, or thirds, of the estate-tail. *Ibid.* 129 Tenant in dower. **1879** HESBA STRETTON *Through a Needle's Eye* II. 40 Of course it will be burdened by a dower of £500 a year to our mother.

2. a. The money or property which the wife brings to the husband; = DOWRY 2.

c **1386** CHAUCER *Clerk's T.* 751 Thilke dowere that ye broghten me Taak it agayn. **1483** CAXTON *Cato* G iv b, Thou oughtest not to take a wyf ne to coueyte hyr for hyr dowayr. **1548** HALL *Chron., Hen. VIII* (an. 19) (R.) He offereth to take to wife, Elianor Quene Dowager of Portyngall, without any dower, yea, in hir kirtell. **1601** SHAKS. *All's Well* v. iii. 328 Choose thou thy husband, and Ile pay thy dower. **1794** MRS. RADCLIFFE *Myst. Udolpho* xiii, She..offered to give Emily a dower. **1869** LECKY *Europ. Mor.* II. i. 83 Epaminondas was accustomed to ransom captives and collect dowers for poor girls.

†**b.** *transf.* Money or value given by the man to his bride's relatives for her; = DOWRY 3. *Obs.*

1382 WYCLIF *Gen.* xxxiv. 12 What thing ȝe ordeyne Y shal ȝyue; eche ȝe dower, and aske ȝe ȝiftis..oonly ȝyf ȝe to me this damesele to wijf. **1635-56** COWLEY *Davideis* III. 938 He ..A double Dowre, two hundred Foreskins brought. **1791** COWPER *Iliad* IX. 180 From him I ask No dow'r, myself will such a dow'r bestow As never father on his child before.

3. *fig.* Endowment; = DOWRY 4.

c **1375** *Myrour of Lewed Men* (MS. Egerton 927) In thes four dowers sal thi body be sa parfit. **1413** *Pilgr. Sowle* (Caxton 1483) v. iii. 94 Subtilite Clerte Inpassibilite and Agylyte ben cleped the dowerys of the body. **1592** DAVIES *Immort. Soul* Ded. iii, The richest Mind, both by Art's Purchase, and by Nature's Dower. **1807** WORDSW. *White Doe Rylstone* VII. 282 A mortal Song we sing, by dower Encouraged of celestial power. **1871** J. MILLER *Songs Italy* (1878) 50 She was damned with the dower of beauty.

4. *Comb.*, as **dower-chest**, (*a*) = *wedding-chest* (WEDDING *vbl. sb.* 4 b); (*b*) *U.S.* = *hope chest* (HOPE *sb.*[1] 5); **dower-house, -land.**

1881 C. C. HARRISON *Woman's Handiwork* III. 142 Carved *dower-chests from Spain and Italy. **1921** *Daily Colonist* (Victoria, B.C.) 19 Oct. 17/1 Carved Oak Dower Chest. **1922** *Daily Tel.* 12 June 20/1 Antique walnut cabinets, dower chest. **1925** N. VENNER *Imperfect Impostor* iv, There was an old oak dower chest, curiously carved. **1927** *Daily Tel.* 14 June 3/1 A fine old carved dower chest of the Henry VIII. period. **1862** H. MARRYAT *Year in Sweden* II. 409 A *dower-house built for Countess Christina. **1880** MRS. OLIPHANT *He that will not* xxxviii, There was a dower-house ..to which perhaps it would be well for her to retire. **1769** WASHINGTON *Diary* 16 May (1925) I. 325 Rid over my *dower Land in York. **1862** H. MARRYAT *Year in Sweden* I. 418 The dower-lands of the Princess Mary.

dower ('daʊə(r)), *v.* [f. DOWER *sb.*[2]]

1. *trans.* To give a dowry to; to endow.

1605 SHAKS. *Lear* I. i. 207 Will you..Dow'rd with our curse..Take her? **1847** LYTTON *Lucretia* 43 When she marries, I will dower her. **1883** S. C. HALL *Retrospect* II. 266 Amply dowered..her suitors were doubtless many.

b. To give as a dower or dowry.

1814 BYRON *Let. to Moore* 14 Oct., Part of them are settled on her; but whether that will be *dowered* now, I do not know.

2. To endow or furnish *with* any 'gift', talent or power of mind or body.

1793 SOUTHEY *Triumph Woman* 46 Three youths whom Nature dower'd with every grace. **1830** TENNYSON *Poet* i,

The poet..Dower'd with the hate of hate, the scorn of scorn. **1884** *Daily News* 7 Feb. 3/2 The volcanic peaks.. were dowered with soft reds and deep purples.

3. *intr.* To take or receive dower.

1848 WHARTON *Law Lex.* 196/2 The widow cannot dower out of estates of joint-tenants, because of the right of survivorship. *Ibid.*, She may dower out of the same [land].

Hence **'dowered** *ppl. a.*

a **1756** WEST *Phineus* (Seager) I led Your dower'd sister to my spousal bed. **1822** SCOTT *Nigel* iii, Taking a pretty, well-dowered English lady.

'doweral, *a. rare.* [f. DOWER *sb.*² + -AL¹.] Of or pertaining to a dower; dotal.

1781–2 POTTER *Euripides' Iphig.* v. 659 (R. Suppl.) Take the dow'ral gifts Brought with me for the Virgin.

† **'doweress.** *Obs.* Also 6 dowares(se, 9 dowress. [f. DOWER, with fem. suffix -ESS. Cf. *jointress.*] A widow holding a dower; DOWAGER.

1519 in Hall *Chron.* (1809) 601 The..Kyng of Englande ..with his bedfelowe the Quene, and his Sister the dowares of France. **1818** CRUISE *Digest* (ed. 2) I. 192 Before the abolition of military tenures, the dowress was attendant on the heir..for the third part of the services. **1823** P. NICHOLSON *Pract. Build.* 287 Some misunderstanding has subsisted between the noble doweress and the present proprietors.

dowerless ('daʊəlɪs), *a.* [f. DOWER *sb.*² + -LESS.] Without a dower; portionless.

1605 SHAKS. *Lear* I. i. 259 Thy dowerlesse Daughter. **1768** SIR W. JONES *Solima* 46 Ye friendless orphans, and ye dowerless maids. **1864** BOUTELL *Heraldry Hist. & Pop.* xiv. 139 The Princess being absolutely dowerless.

dowf, douf (daʊf), *a.* (*sb.*) *Sc.* and *north. dial.* Also 6 dolf, (8 doof). [The 16th c. form is constantly *dolf*, but it is prob. that the *ol* here (as in 16th c. *rolp* = *rope*, ROUP, *nolt* = *nowt, nout*, ON. *naut*) merely stands for *ow*, and that *dowf* is etymological. Perh. a. ON. *dauf-r* deaf; cf. Du. *doof* deaf, benumbed, faint. The notions of 'deaf' and 'dull' frequently interchange: cf. Du. *dof* 'hollow, smothered, dull, faint, heavy', related to *doof.*]

A. *adj.* Dull, flat; wanting in spirit or energy; inactive, spiritless. Of sound: Dull, flat, hollow.

1513 DOUGLAS *Æneis* III. iv. 97 Dolf wox thair spretis. *Ibid.* v. vii. 59 The dasyt bluid..Walxis dolf and dull throw myne vnweildy age. **1560** ROLLAND *Crt. Venus* I. 413 Thy dolf hart for dredour ay deuaillis. **1721** RAMSAY *Prospect Plenty* x, How dowf looks gentry with an empty purse! **1785** BURNS *Sec. Ep. to Lapraik* iv, Her dowff excuses pat me mad. **1814** SCOTT *Wav.* xliii, The lad can sometimes be as dowff as a sexagenary like myself.

b. *Comb.*, as *dowf-hearted* (*dolf-*).

1513 DOUGLAS *Æneis* IX. ii. 50 The dolf hartit Troianis.

B. *sb.* A dull spiritless fellow.

c **1430** LYDG. *Min. Poems* (Percy Soc.) 56 To have a galle, and be clepid a douffe. [**1724** RAMSAY *Gentle Sheph.* IV. i, He get her? slaverin doof!]

Hence **dowf** *v. trans.*, to make 'dowf', deprive of energy. **'dowfness,** dullness; want of spirit.

1513 DOUGLAS *Æneis* XI. xiv. 21 Huge dolfnes, and schamful cowardice. **1818** HOGG *Brownie of B.* II. 38 (Jam.) There was a kind o' doufness and melancholy in his looks. **1838** JAS. STRUTHERS *Poetic Tales* 77 Auld age douffs down the spirit.

dowghter, dowghty, obs. ff. DAUGHTER, DOUGHTY.

dowie, dowy ('daʊɪ, 'dɒwɪ), *a. Sc.* and *north. dial.* Also 5–6 **dolly.** [The identity of *dowie* with 16th c. *dolly* appears to be proved by the treatment of the two as variants in Gawain Douglas. Probably a deriv. of ME. *dol, doll*, OE. *dol*, DULL, with *-y* or *-ly*; cf. also DULLY, used in same sense, and OE. *hál, hálig*, holy.] Dull and lonely, melancholy, dreary, dismal.

1508 DUNBAR *Tua Mariit Wemen* 412 Now done is my dolly nyght, my day is vpsprungin. **1513** DOUGLAS *Æneis* VII. Prol. 51 The dowy dichis [*ed.* **1553** dolly dikis] war all donk and wait. *Ibid.* x. iv. 73 The dolly tonys [*ed.* **1553** dowy tones] and lays lamentabill. *Ibid.* XIII. x 102 And end his dolly dayis, and dee. *c* **1581** SEMPILL *Complaint on Fortoun* 171 In Striuiling toun, out of his dowie den..thai fyrit him in his nest. ? **16..** *The Dowie Dens of Yarrow* xv. (in *Minstr. Sc. Border*), She kiss'd them, till her lips grew red, On the dowie houms of Yarrow. **1724** RAMSAY *Tea-t. Misc.* (1733) I. 26 What dowy hours I thole by your disdain. **1790** BURNS *Highland Harry* ii, I wander dowie up the glen. *a* **1851** MOIR *Poems, Disenchantment* xiii, The dowie dens of Yarrow. **1890** *Scot. Liberal* 14 Feb. 11 Dark valleys and dowie dens of ignorance.

Hence **'dowily** *adv.*, **'dowiness.**

? **17..** *Twa Brithers* xi. in Child *Ballads* (1884) II. xlix. 439/2 Sae dowilie alane. **1801** MACNEILL *Poet. Wks.* (1844) 107 Lying down dowylie, sighed by the willow tree.

dowing, *vbl. sb.* and *ppl. a.*: see after DOW *v.*

dowitcher ('daʊɪtʃə(r)). [Iroquois.] Any of several long-billed waders (genus *Limnodromus*) of North America, belonging to the family Scolopacidæ and resembling the sandpiper, esp. the red-breasted snipe (*Limnodromus griseus*).

1841 *Spirit of Times* 9 Jan. 529/3 The mellow attenuated trill of the soaring dowitcher. **1872** COUES *Key N. Amer. Birds* 252 Brown-back. Dowitcher. **1888** LEES & CLUTTERBUCK *B.C. 1887* xvii. 182 The long-billed dowitchers are very much like a large snipe, of a pale cinnamon colour. **1934** I. W. HUTCHISON *North to Rime-Ringed Sun* xiii. 136 They had been shot..and were Dowitchers, a species of Arctic wildfowl. **1965** *New Scientist* 21 Oct. 163/3 Sandpiper-like American waders such as..the dowitchers..form a substantial proportion of the incomers.

Dow-Jones (,daʊ'dʒəʊnz). The names of C. H. *Dow* (died 1902) and E. D. *Jones* (died 1920), American economists, used *attrib.* to designate an index of the relative price of American securities based on the current average rates of an agreed select list of industrial and other stocks. Also in shortened form *Dow.*

1908 *Ticker* Jan. 38/1 The Dow-Jones System of Averages is simply a method of calculating the average price of 20 active railroad stocks and 12 industrial stocks. **1922** W. P. HAMILTON *Stock Market Barometer* i. 7 The Dow-Jones average is still standard, although it has been extensively imitated. **1957** *Encycl. Brit.* XVIII. 474/1 The Dow Jones averages..were based on 30 industrials, 20 railroads and 15 utilities. **1962** S. STRAND *Marketing Dict.* 44 Various ways of measuring the trend of securities prices on the N.Y. Stock Exchange, the most popular of which is the Dow-Jones average of 30 industrial stocks. *Ibid.* 45 In the case of the Dow-Jones industrial average, the prices of the 30 stocks are totaled and then divided by a divisor which is intended to compensate for past stock splits and dividends and which is changed from time to time. **1964** *Financial Times* 25 Feb. 3/1 As the Dow Jones Industrial Average approached the 800 level lively profit-taking was attracted, which limited the markets rise to mostly fractions. **1968** *Globe & Mail* (Toronto) 17 Feb. B7 Among the 30 Dow Industrials, 18 declined, 7 advanced and 5 were unchanged. *Ibid.* B8 The Dow-Jones industrial average was down 2·89 points to 836·34. **1970** *Daily Tel.* 1 June 16/2 Prices plummetted to the 'low' of 631 on the Dow in response to genuinely poor economic prospects.

dowk, var. DAUK; obs. form of DUCK.

dowl (daʊl). *Obs.* exc. *dial.* [Origin uncertain. Perhaps in some way related to DOWN *sb.*² Prof. Skeat suggests OF. *doulle* var. of *doille, douille* adj. 'soft, tender', sb. 'that which is soft.' But there is no evidence that the OF. word had any corresponding application.]

One of the filaments or fibres of a feather; the soft fine feathers or fur of birds or beasts; down, fluff.

? *c* **1400** *Plowman's T.* III. (R.), The griffen..swore by cockis herte and blode He wold him tere every doule. **1610** SHAKS. *Temp.* III. iii. 65 As well..as diminish One dowle that's in my plumbe. **1661** *Humane Industry* (T.), A certain shell-fish..called Pinna, that bears a mossy dowl, or wool, whereof cloth was spun. *Ibid.* 93 Such trees as have a certain wool or dowl upon the outside of them, as the small cotton. **1845** DE QUINCEY in *Tait's Mag.* XII. 758 No feather, or dowl of a feather, but was heavy enough for him. **1879** MISS JACKSON *Shropshire Word-bk., Dowl*, 1. the downy fibres of a feather..2. The light downy substance which collects under beds and about bedroom floors.

dowl, obs. and dial. f. DOOL¹, boundary mark; obs. form of DOWEL.

dowlas ('daʊləs). Also (? 5 douglas), 6 dolas, 6–7 doulas, 6–8 dowlass, 7 dowlace, -lasse, 8 doulace. [Named from *Daoulas* or *Doulas*, S.E. of Brest, in Brittany, like the associated *lockeram* from Locronan or Locrenan in the same vicinity.]

1. † **a.** A coarse kind of linen, much used in the 16th and 17th centuries. *Obs.* **b.** Now applied to a strong calico made in imitation of this.

[**1493** *Will of Dolyng of Taunton* (Somerset Ho.), A fyne pece of douglas.] **1529** *Act 21 Hen. VIII*, c. 14 (*title*) Of what length and bredth euery whole peece and halfe peece of dowlas and lockeram, brought into this realm, shall be. **1536** *Act 28 Hen. VIII*, c. 4 §1 Britaine, where the said linnen Cloth called Doulas and Lockeram is made. **1543** *Ludlow Churchw. Acc.* (Camden) 15, ix elles of dolas..to make ij. new albus. **1596** SHAKS. *1 Hen. IV*, III. iii. 79 Doulas, filthy Doulas..they haue made Boulters of them. *a* **1640** DAY *Parl. Bees* ix. (1881) 58 Dowlasse for saffron-bags. **1657** R. LIGON *Barbadoes* (1673) 109 Some other sorts of Linnen, as Holland or Dowlace. **1696** J. F. *Merchant's Ware-ho.* 8 Dowlas from France..being prohibited and forbidden.. therefore shall proceed with Dowlas from Hamborough. **1760** FOOTE *Minor* II. (1781) 47 A large cargo of Dantzick dowlas. **1835** URE *Philos. Manuf.* 79 Kincardine..In weaving dowlas, household linens, and a few woollens, 700 men are employed. **1882** BECK *Draper's Dict., Dowlas*..The name is still perpetuated in a strong calico made in imitation of the linen fabric.

2. *attrib.* Made or consisting of dowlas.

1550 in Strype *Eccl. Mem.* II. I. App. QQ, A yard of dowlas linnin cloth 9*d.* **1739** 'R. BULL' tr. *Dedekindus' Grobianus* 3 Throw o'er your Dowlass Shirt a Morning Gown. **1837** J. F. COOPER *Recoll. Europe* I. 38 The Channel waterman wore the short dowlas petticoat.

dowle, obs. f. DOLE *sb.*², DOOL¹, DOOLIE, DOWEL.

dowless ('daʊlɪs), *a. Sc.* [f. DOW *v.*¹ + -LESS: cf. Ger. *taugenichts.*] Without strength or energy; feeble; infirm.

1788 PICKEN *Poems* 50 (Jam.) Winter's dowless days. *Ibid.* 55 (Jam.) Dowless fowk, for health gane down. *a* **1810** TANNAHILL *Poet. Wks.* (1846) 48 Dowless eild, in poortith cauld, Is lanely left to stand the stoure.

dowly ('daʊlɪ), *a.* and *adv. North. dial.* Also 5 dauly, 5–9 **dawly.** [Perh. a doublet of Sc. DOWIE, in 15–16th c. *dolly*, to which it is exactly equivalent in meaning. The phonology is opposed to its association with DOLY *a.*, from DOLE *sb.*² In use from the Scottish Border to N. Lincolnshire.]

A. *adj.* Doleful, miserable, gloomy, lonely.

c **1400** *Destr. Troy* 13937 He fell to þe ground All dowly, for dole, in a dede swone. **1674–91** RAY *N.C. Words* 22 *Dowly*, melancholy, lonely. **1811** WILLAN *W. Riding Gloss.* (E.D.S.), *Dowly, dawly*, lonely, sorrowful. **1832** STEPHENSON *Gateshead Local Poems* 105 When trade grows slack then I Feel my lot quite dowly. **1863** HOLME LEE *A. Warleigh* I. 95 'It is a dowly, dowly spot, that it is'. **1885** *Chamb. Jrnl.* 575 'Ah sir, it was a dowly day for me'.

† **B.** *adv.* Sadly, dolefully, lamentably. *Obs.*

c **1400** *Destr. Troy* 870 Thou dawly bes dede, and I to doll broght. *Ibid.* 9522 Ded men full dauly droppit to ground. *Ibid.* 9595 Then Deffibus dauly drogh vp his Ene.

† **dowment.** *Obs.* [f. DOW *v.*² + -MENT: perh. originally in AF.] The act of endowing, endowment; the giving of dower.

1552 HULOET, Dowment, dowre and dowrie. **1574** tr. *Littleton's Tenures* 9 a, There is two other manner of dowers, ..dowemente in the church doore..dowement by the fathers assent. **1628** COKE *On Litt.* 39 b, Such dowment cannot be, but where a iudgement is giuen in the Kings Court.

† **down** (daʊn), *sb.*¹ Forms: 1 dún, 2–4 dun, 4–5 doun(e, 4–7 downe, 4– down. [OE. *dún* fem., hill = ODu. *dúna* (MDu. *dúne*, Du. *duin*, whence mod.LG. *düne* sandhill, F. *dune*). Supposed to be of Celtic origin: cf. OIr. *dún* hill, hill-fort, Welsh *din*, and place-names in *-dūnum*.

Since *dúna* must have been in use at an early date in the West Germanic dialects of Batavia and Lower Saxony, it is doubtful whether the word was brought by the Saxons from the continent, or adopted, after their settlement here, from the Britons; the former alternative is favoured by the exact correspondence in form and gender of the OE. and ODu. words, and by the fact that in local nomenclature OE. *dún* seems to have been confined to the Saxon area. It is, however, in English only that the word has given rise to an adverb and a preposition: see below.]

† **1.** A hill. *Obs.* (exc. as blending with 2).

O.E. Chron. an. 661 And ȝeherȝeade Wulfhere Pending oþ Æsces dune. **971** *Blickl. Hom.* 27 He hine lædde upon swiþe heá dune. *c* **1000** *Ags. Gosp.* Matt. xxi. 1 And com.. to Oliuetes dune. *a* **1175** *Cott. Hom.* 225 Hit ofer-stah ælle duna. *c* **1290** *S. Eng. Leg.* I. 307/256 Bi niȝte ope heiȝe dounes. *a* **1300** *Cursor M.* 7186 (Cott.) Sampson..bar þe yates o þe tun, And laid þam on a hei dun. *a* **1400–50** *Alexander* 4045 Darke in dennes vndire dounes. **1653** H. COGAN tr. *Pinto's Trav.* xlix. (1663) 194 A Creek..on the South side of the Island and invironned by a Down or Hill.

2. An open expanse of elevated land; *spec.*, in *pl.*, the treeless undulating chalk uplands of the south and south-east of England, serving chiefly for pasturage; applied to similar tracts elsewhere.

1297 R. GLOUC. (1724) 144 He wende..to þe downe of Ambresbury. **1398** TREVISA *Barth. De P.R.* XIV. xlv. (1495) 483 A downe is a lytyl swellynge or areryngе of erthe passynge the playne grounde..and not retchyng to hyghnesse of an hylle. **1470–85** MALORY *Arthur* XXI. iii, An hondred thousand layed deed vpon the down. **1563** B. GOOGE *Eglogs* iii. (Arb.) 42 To take my sheepe, and dwell vpon the downe. **1610** SHAKS. *Temp.* IV. i. 81 My boskie acres, and my vnshrubd downe. **1646** EVELYN *Mem.* (1857) I. 229 Downs of fine grass, like some places in the south of England. **1670** NARBOROUGH *Jrnl.* in *Acc. Sev. Late Voy.* I. (1711) 22 As bare as the Grass-Downs in England. **1777** *Phil. Trans.* LXVII. 386 Turf, equal to any of the finest on our sheep downs. **1842** *Penny Cycl.* XXIII. 343/2 They [tracts of poor land] are..left in down, and produce excellent pasture for the small sheep known as South Down sheep. **1856** EMERSON *Eng. Traits, Stonehenge* Wks. (Bohn) II. 123 On the broad downs..not a house was visible, nothing but Stonehenge. **1862** STANLEY *Jew. Ch.* (1877) I. iii. 53 The undulating downs of Gilead.

b. Frequent in alliterative association with *dale*: ***dale and down***, low land and upland.

c **1200**, *a* **1300**, *c* **1386** [see DALE *sb.*¹ 1]. *c* **1440** *Gesta Rom.* lxii. 220 (Harl. MS.) Thou shalt go by downys and by dalys. **1522** *World & Child* in Hazl. *Dodsley* I. 250 All is at my hand-work, both by down and by dale. **1810** SCOTT *Lady of L.* I. xxx, By dale and down We dwell, afar from tower and town.

3. A sand-hill, DUNE.

1523 LD. BERNERS *Froiss.* I. cxlv. (R.) Other by the downes by the sea syde, or elles aboue by the highe way. *a* **1608** SIR F. VERE *Comm.* 88 The space betwixt the sea and the sand-hills or Downs, was commanded by the said hills. **1677** W. HUBBARD *Narrative* (1865) II. 51 Sorely wounded on Sawco Sands or Downs. **1750** CARTE *Hist. Eng.* II. 470 Over the downs of sand by the sea side. **1837** *Penny Cycl.* IX. 117 Downs or Dunes are little hillocks of sand formed along the sea-coast..Downs sometimes intercept the flow of water to the sea.

4. ***the Downs***: the part of the sea within the Goodwin Sands, off the east coast of Kent, a famous rendezvous for ships. (It lies opposite to the eastern termination of the North Downs.)

a **1460** *Gregory's Chron.* in *Hist. Coll. Citizen Lond.* (Camden) 178 The vyntage come by londe ynne cartys unto London fro the Downys. **1548** HALL *Chron., Hen. VI* (an. 38) 175 b, Sir Simon Mondford..was appoynted to kepe the downes, and the five Portes. **1666–7** PEPYS *Diary* 2 Jan., To send all the ships we can possible to the Downes. **1773** COOK *First Voy.* Concl. (R.), About three [we] came to an anchor in the Downs, and went a-shore at Deal. **1778** *Eng. Gazetteer, Downs*, a road on the coast of Kent, through which ships generally pass, in going out and returning home. It is 6 miles long between the North and South Foreland.

5. Applied to a superior breed of sheep, raised on the chalk downs of England. Cf. SOUTHDOWN.

1831 *Lincoln Herald* 21 Oct. 1/1 Prime young Downs sell at 4*s.* to 5*s.* **1842** *Penny Cycl.* XXIII. 345/2 A heavier sort of sheep, a cross between the Somerset and the Down.

6. *attrib.* and *Comb.* (Also DOWNLAND[1].)

1807 SOUTHEY *Espriella's Lett.* I. 47 Here we left the down country, and once more entered upon cultivated fields. **1826** in Cobbett *Rur. Rides* II. 193 The down-farms in Wiltshire. **1876** *Helps Study Bible* 215 s.v. *Grass*, The bare down-grass of the limestone hills of Judæa.

down (daʊn), *sb.*[2] Also 4–7 **downe**, 5–6 **dawne**, 5–7 **doun**. [a. ON. *dún*, nom. *dúnn* down, *æðar-dún* eider-down, Sw. *dun*, Da. *duun*, whence LG. *dûne*, Ger. *daune, dune.*]

1. a. The first feathering of young birds. **b.** The fine soft covering of fowls, forming the under plumage, used for stuffing beds, pillows, etc.

c **1369** CHAUCER *Dethe Blaunche* 250 Of downe of pure doves white. **1465** *Mann. & Househ. Exp.* 321 Paid for iij. pelewes of downe, vij.*s.* viij.*d.* **1530** PALSGR. 215/1 Downe of any yong byrde, *follet.* **1600** HAKLUYT *Voy.* III. 267 (R.) Soft beds of downe or feathers. **1611** SHAKS. *Wint. T.* IV. iv. 374 This hand, As soft as Doues-downe, and as white as it. **1747** *Gentl. Mag.* 172 Iseland..Hence come the finest downs, which are the plumage of a bird called Aidur or Eider. **1870** YEATS *Nat. Hist. Comm.* 309 The development of feathers is always preceded by that of down, which constitutes the first covering of young birds.

fig. **1634** FORD *P. Warbeck* III. ii, Must I break from the down of thy embraces, To put on steel. **1750** JOHNSON *Rambler* No. 74 ¶7 To lull him on the down of absolute authority. **1827** POLLOK *Course T.* v, The silken down of happiness complete.

2. Applied to substances of the same nature or appearance: **a.** The hair as it first shows itself on the human face, or the like.

1580 BARET *Alv.*, *Doune*..the soft haires, or mossinesse in the visages of young folkes. **1597** SHAKS. *Lover's Compl.* 93 Small show of man was yet upon his chin: His phœnix down began but to appear. **1697** DRYDEN *Æneid* VIII. (R.) The callow down began To shade my chin, and call me first a man. **1874** BURNAND *My time* xvi. 136 Floyd stroked the down on his upper lip.

b. The pubescence on some plants and fruits; the soft feathery pappus of some seeds.

c **1420** *Pallad. on Husb.* XI. 219 He..most pike away the downe of al the tre. **1551** TURNER *Herbal* I. Biv b, Alopecurus..hath..a great thycke and busshy eare full of longe downes. **1652** CULPEPPER *Eng. Physic.* 184 The Cotton or Doun of Quinces. **1796** H. HUNTER tr. *St. Pierre's Stud. Nat.* (1799) I. 213 There is not a down upon a plant.. but what has it's utility. **1861** MISS PRATT *Flower. Pl.* I. 6 The Calyx..is at first a mere ring, which ultimately becomes the pappus or down.

c. Any substance of a feathery or fluffy nature.

1626 BACON *Sylva* 560 Down or Nap cometh of a subtile Spirit, in a Soft or Fat substance. **1758** A. REID tr. *Macquer's Chym.* I. 240 Nitre..effloresces..on their surface, in the form of a crystalline down. **1831** BREWSTER *Optics* xii. 101 The blackness of the surfaces arose from their being entirely composed of a fine down of quartz.

3. *attrib.* and *Comb.*, as ***down-bed, -feather, -head, -pillow, -plumage***; also ***down-covered, -headed, -like, -shod, -soft***, adjs.; **down-beard**, the pappus of the thistle; **down-thistle**, *Onopordon Acanthium* (Britten & Holland); **down-tree**, the cork-wood, *Ochroma Lagopus*; **down-weed**, *Filago germanica* (Miller).

1843 CARLYLE *Misc., Dr. Francia* (1872) VII. 18 Like an idle globular *downbeard. **1601** CHESTER *Love's Mart.*, *Cantoes* xxxix, Loving in such a *downe-bed to be placed. **1692** LOCKE *Educ.* (1693) 24 A tender weakly constitution is very much owing to Downe-Beds. *a* **1847** ELIZA COOK *Winter is here* iv, *Down-covered peaches. **1606** SHAKS. *Ant. & Cl.* III. ii. 48 The Swannes *downe feather That stands vpon the Swell. **1882** MARTIN & MOALE *Handbk. Vertebrate Dissection* II. 97 Lying beneath the contour feathers are down feathers (*plumulæ*). **1959** C. J. HYLANDER *Feathers & Flight* i. 10 Down feathers are the first body covering of baby birds. **1821** CLARE *Vill. Minstr.* II. 32 He ..perch'd on the *down-headed grass. **1835–6** TODD *Cycl. Anat.* I. 747/1 The hairs..becoming finer and more *down-like as they descend. **1863** MISS BRADDON *J. Marchmont* III. i. 6 [He] raised himself amongst the *down pillows. **1614** R. TAILOR *Hog hath lost Pearl* v. in Hazl. *Dodsley* XI. 485 The *down-soft white of lady's tempting breast. **1640** PARKINSON *Theat. Bot.* Index (Britt. & Holl.) *Down Thistle. **1562** TURNER *Herbal* II. 11 b, Cottenwede..maye be called in English *Downewede because the leafe broken is lyke Downe or cotton.

down, *sb.*[3] [DOWN *adv.*, used subst., as a name for itself, or elliptically for 'downward motion.']

†**1.** The burden of a song. (Cf. DOWN *adv.* 26.)

1611 COTGR., *Refrain d'une Balade*, the Refret, burthen, or downe of a Ballade. **1656** BLOUNT *Glossogr.*, *Refret*, the Burthen or Down of a Song or Ballad.

2. a. A going down, a descent; a reverse of fortune. Usually in phrase ***ups and downs***.

1710 *Brit. Apollo* II. No. 103. 3/2 Wit has her Up's and Downs. **1844** DICKENS *Mart. Chuz.* xvi, Fraudulent transactions have their downs as well as their ups. **1872** BLACK *Adv. Phaeton* xxvii, The ups and downs of this route.

b. An act of throwing down, as in wrestling. Also in American and Canadian football: see quots.

1840 W. G. SIMMS *Border Beagles* 134 He downed him; a fair stupid down. **1882** in P. H. Davis *Football* (1911) 470 They must give up the ball to the other side at the spot where the fourth down was made. **1893** W. K. POST *Harvard Stories* 22 After three downs Spofford dropped back. **1897** *Encycl. Sport* I. 425/1 *A down.*—The term used to indicate the number of attempts made to advance the ball. Each side has three tries in which to advance the ball five yards. The end of each try, *i.e.* when the ball is held by the opposing side, is a down. As soon as the five yards have been gained it is first down again. **1927** *Observer* 11 Dec. 16/3 After the kick-off the side that has the ball must gain ten yards in a maximum of four 'downs'. Otherwise it loses the ball. **1959** *Times* 30 Nov. (Canada Suppl.) p. xx/1 Canada has the downs system, by which a team must make 10 yards in three downs, or turns, or lose the ball. **1970** *Globe & Mail* (Toronto) 28 Sept. 18/3 Fifteen of Montreal's first downs were earned on the ground to six for the Riders.

3. *Dominoes.* (See quots.)

1870 HARDY & WARE *Mod. Hoyle, Dominoes* 92 He who draws the domino containing the smallest number of pips, wins 'the down'; [i.e.] he wins the privilege of playing first. *Ibid.* 94 In leading 'the down' from a hand consisting of a high double and several light dominoes, lead the double.

†**4.** *slang.* (See quots.) Cf. DOWN *adv.* 22. *Obs.*

1812 J. H. VAUX *Flash Dict.* s.v., *A down* is a suspicion, alarm, or discovery, which taking place, obliges yourself and *palls* to give up or desist from the business..to *put a down upon* a man, is to give information of any robbery or fraud he is about to perpetrate, so as to cause his failure or detection. **1821** D. HAGGART *Life* Gloss. 171 (Farmer) *Down*, alarm; rose the down, gave the alarm.

5. *colloq.* A tendency to be 'down *upon*'; a grudge. Chiefly in phr. ***to have a down on***: to dislike, regard unfavourably, be ill-disposed towards. orig. *Austral.*

1856 W. W. DOBIE *Recoll. Visit Port-Phillip* v. 84 The bushranger had been in search of another squatter, on whom 'he said he had a down'. **1862** C. R. THATCHER *Canterbury Songster* 10 I've got no 'down' on Travers. **1874** M. CLARKE *His Natural Life* (1875) I. II. vii. 237 He never ceased to.. find fault with him... It was evident that Mr. Frere had a 'down' on the Dandy. **1878** R. B. SMYTH *Aborig. Victoria* I. 129 Blacks never like a quarrel to be of long standing:.. nothing would make a man more miserable than to think that some of his tribe had a 'down' on him. **1893** J. A. BARRY *Steve Brown's Bunyip* 193 More especially had they a 'down' on people who wore a goatee and snuffled when they talked. **1894** MRS. H. WARD *Marcella* I. 310 Westall has a down on him. **1895** *Westm. Gaz.* 13 May 2/1 There is a remarkable 'down' on coercion just now in Europe. **1904** *Daily Chron.* 8 Dec. 8/1 Why this 'down' on an always useful, sometimes dainty, garment? **1916** *Chrons. N.Z.E.F.* 27 Dec. 199 They've got a down on arrogance and swank. **1928** S. VINES *Humours Unreconciled* xiii. 179 Somebody'd got a down on him. **1947** W. S. MAUGHAM *Creatures of Circumstance* 151 She had a down on Lady Kastellan and didn't care what she said about her.

6. A cry of *down with*; see DOWN *adv.* 25 b.

1889 *Times* (weekly ed.) 13 Dec. 17/4 The others..at once raised 'hurrahs' for him..and 'downs' for the Ministry.

7. A 'down' train or coach. *rare.*

1884 [see UP *sb.* 3].

8. The position or action of a dog lying down in response to an order to do so.

1948 E. H. S. LONGHURST *Dog Training* 158 Tests for obedience classes..Recall from Sit or Down (dog to be recalled by handler when stationary..). *Ibid.* 159 Article to be given to the handler as he leaves the ring for the 'down'.

down (daʊn), *a.* [DOWN *adv.* used attrib. with verbal sbs. as *leap*, or by ellipsis of some participial word, as *running, directed.*]

1. a. Directed downwards; descending. Also *fig.*

1647 H. MORE *Song of Soul* II. iii. III. xxxi, Binding all close with down-propensities. **1791** 'GAMBADO' *Ann. Horsem.* ix. (1809) 107 A down leap is not so very dangerous. **1858** *Advt.* in *Skyring's Builder's Prices*, Eaves gutters and down pipe. **1883** *Gentl. Mag.* July 54 He passed from the up to the down bow in those long cantabile notes. **1894** HALL CAINE *Manxman* 24 A down line for every stone weight up to eight stones.

b. Of looks or aspect: Directed downwards.

c **1565** LINDESAY (Pitscottie) *Chron. Scot.* 388 (Jam.) The kingis doun look at thame. **1580** HOLLYBAND *Treas. Fr. Tong*, *Regardeure basse*, doune looke. **1604** T. M. *Black Bk.* (Cent. Dict.) A down countenance he had. **1637** R. MONRO *Expedit.* I. 63 (Jam.) Fearing..the down-looke or frowne of his officers. **1687** *Lond. Gaz.* No. 2223/4 A low stature.. grey eyes, and a Down-look. *a* **1717** BLACKALL *Wks.* (1723) I. 158 True Religion does not consist in a peculiar Garb.. in a down Look.

c. Of a train or coach: Going 'down', i.e. away from the central or chief terminus; in Great Britain, from London. Hence *transf.* Of or pertaining to down trains, as ***the down platform***.

1840 H. COCKTON *V. Vox* v. 27 They met the 'down coach'. **1845** in J. R. PLANCHÉ *Extravaganzas* (1879) III. 48 Opening of the Down Line to the 'Bee and Orange' Station. **1846** —— *Bee & Orange Tree* v. 28 The Fairy Atmospheric down train descends rapidly and then enters the Garden. **1851** *Offic. Catal. Gt. Exhib.* I. 249 The signal.. distinguishes an 'up' from a 'down' train. **1878** F. S. WILLIAMS *Midl. Railw.* 656 To go down to the roadside station..and see the down mail pass. **1885** *Law Times Rep.* LII. 622/2 To cross the line to the down platform. **1890** BOLDREWOOD *Colonial Reformer* (1891) 131 The up coach leaving and the down one just coming in. **1892** *Daily News* 17 Oct. 2/8 Pneumatic tubes between this Central Office and ..post offices in the City and West-end, some of them having 'up' and 'down' tubes.

d. Of a payment: see DOWN *adv.* 12.

1926 *Automotive Industries* 16 Sept. 451 The dealer gets less total money on the whole transaction but permits the unpaid balance after the down-payment to be greater. **1930** *San Antonio* (Texas) *Light* 31 Jan. 14/6 Small down payment, balance like rent. **1959** J. BRAINE *Vodi* x. 138 The money for the first inescapable hundred down-payments. **1970** *New York* III. 16 Nov. 45/2 He had $1,000 for the down payment on his house.

e. ***down trip***, an unpleasant or depressing hallucinatory experience induced by the drug LSD. *U.S. slang.*

1968 [see BLOW *v.*[1] 24 j]. **1968** J. HUDSON *Case of Need* III. i. 172 She was real depressed. She took a couple of down-trips, real freaks, and it shook her up.

f. Of a crossword clue (or answer): that fills spaces down a vertical line of the puzzle. See sense 1 b of the adv. Cf. ACROSS *a.*

1925 W. MCCARTY *Noah's Word Animals* 8 No. 2 is a down word. **1963** [see ACROSS *a.*]. **1981** KURZBAN & ROSEN *Compleat Cruciverbalist* iii. 37 Work only from the Down definitions.

2. In a low condition of health or vitality. *rare.*

1690 W. WALKER *Idiomat. Anglo-Lat.* 319 An old down-man [*depontanus*]. **1885** FITZPATRICK *Life T. N. Burke* II. 225 A friend who visited [him] on one of his 'down-days' [= days of sickness].

†**3.** Downcast, dejected. *Obs.* (exc. predicatively: see DOWN *adv.* 18).

1645 QUARLES *Sol. Recant.* ii. 24 Goe winde the Plummets up Of thy down spirits.

†**4.** Downright, positive. *Obs.*

1617 FLETCHER *Valentinian* I. i, After my many offers.. And her as many down-denials. *a* **1619** FOTHERBY *Atheom.* II. iii. §4. (1622) 220 He being named from his downe Being, *I am.* [**1830** GALT *Lawrie T.* II. v. (1849) 57 He..talked even down nonsense.]

5. *Particle Physics.* Designating a quark carrying a flavour with a charge of $-\frac{1}{3}$; symbol *d* (D III. 3 c). Also as *sb.*, (a quark with) this flavour. [See note s.v. S 15. The name first appeared in print later than the symbol *d.*]

1975 *Physical Rev.* D. XII. 2108 We find m = 122 MeV for the mass of the degenerate up and down quarks. **1975**, etc. [see UP *a.* 6]. **1978** *Nature* 2 Feb. 406/2 Particles like the proton are made up of three quarks — two ups and one down for the proton itself — whereas the other class of particles called mesons..contain a quark and an antiquark. **1979** *Sci. Amer.* July 109/1 That happens in ordinary radioactivity, where an up quark is changed into a down quark or vice versa. **1981** D. WILKINSON in J. H. Mulvey *Nature of Matter* i. 24 There are 'ordinary' quarks (of two kinds called 'up' and 'down') such as go into the neutron and proton..; there are 'strange' quarks [etc.]. **1981** *Sci. Amer.* Feb. 65/1 A total of five flavors have definitely been observed (they are called up, down, strange, charm and bottom) and the existence of a sixth flavor (top) is all but certain.

down (daʊn), *adv.* Forms: 1–4 **dún**, 1–6 **dune**, 3–6 **doun(e**, (4 **dunne**, 4–5 **don(e**, **dowun**, 5 **douun**), 4–7 **downe**, 5– **down**, (9 *north. dial.* **doon**). [In late OE. *dúne, dún*, aphetic form of *adúne* ADOWN, weakened from OE. *of dúne* off the hill or height (see DOWN *sb.*[1]).] The following are the general and usual senses of the adverb; for its special combinations with verbs, as BEAR *down*, BREAK *down*, BRING *down*, BURN *down*, CALL *down*, CAST *down*, COME *down*, see under the verbs.

I. Of motion or direction in space.

1. a. In a descending direction; from above, or towards that which is below; from a higher to a lower place or position; to the ground.

It is applied to any degree of descent, from a vertical fall to the slightest slope as in a nearly level river valley, and thus passes into sense 2, in which the descent may be entirely imaginary or conventional.

a **1100** *O.E. Chron.* an. 1070 Brohton dune þæt hæcce þe þær wæs behid. **1154** *Ibid.* an. 1140 Me læt hire dun on niht of þe tur mid rapes. *a* **1300** *Cursor M.* 12962 (Cott.) Hu bot lepe dun [*v.r.* done] to the grund. **1340** *Ayenb.* 246 Þe lheddre..huerby þe angles..cliue op and doun. *c* **1385** CHAUCER *L.G.W.* 1220 *Dido*, Doun cam the reyn. **1470–85** MALORY *Arthur* XIII. viii, The teres began to renne doune by his vysage. **1548** HALL *Chron., Hen. VIII*, 26 b, He a lighted downe of his horse. **1597** MONTGOMERIE *Cherrie & Slae* 1527 Gif we gae doun. **1750** JOHNSON *Rambler* No. 15 ¶9, I was set down at my aunt's. **1808** SCOTT *Marm.* II. xiv, Where his cathedral..Looks down upon the Wear. **1889** WALLACE *Darwinism* 343 Debris brought down by rivers to the ocean.

b. Of a crossword clue (or answer): down a vertical line of the puzzle. Often after the clue number. Cf. ACROSS *adv.* 2 d.

1924 C. LAYNG *Cross-Word Puzzles* 6 Aha! we are off. No. 2, down, is a preposition. **1944, 1960** [see ACROSS *adv.* 2 d]. **1971** R. RENDELL *One Across* v. 42 The well-meaning idiot who..demands..to be told how many letters in fifteen down. **1981** KURZBAN & ROSEN *Compleat Cruciverbalist* iii. 32 Suppose your dilemma involves the word at 15 Across.., and that 7 Down is shown.

2. To some place which is conventionally viewed as lower in position; in the direction of a current, or with the wind; from the capital to the distant parts of a country; away from a university; from the House of Lords to the House of Commons or 'lower house'; to a lower or inferior court of law, etc. Also vaguely in ***up and down***, which is often = to and fro: see UP.

a **1200** *Moral Ode* 240 He..walkeð weri up and dun, se water deþ mid winde. *c* **1320** *Seuyn Sag.* (W.) 3816 Thai sold..spir in stretes, vp and downe, Efter a man of strange cuntrè. **1590** SHAKS. *Err.* I. ii. 31 And wander vp and downe to view the Citie. **1671** LADY M. BERTIE in *12th Rep. Hist. MSS. Comm.* App. v. 22 Your mourning..which Fyns sent downe a Thursday. **1678** LADY CHAWORTH *Ibid.* 44 All but six Lords disliked the Commons adresse to the King, so it was sent them downe againe. **1697** DAMPIER *Voy.* I. vii. 208 We bore down right afore the wind on our Enemies. **1726** G. ROBERTS *4 Years Voy.* 10 We took in six Cows to carry down to St. Jago. **1766** GOLDSM. *Vic. W.* xix, We caught him up accidentally in our journey down. **1769** FALCONER *Dict. Marine* (1789) F, We say, up to windward, and down to leeward. **1798** PITT in G. Rose *Diaries* (1860) I. 216, I have a scheme of running down..to Somersetshire. **1853** E. BRADLEY (C. Bede) *Verdant Green* I. xii, He won't..gate or chapel you..or send you down. **1883** *Cambridge Staircase* viii. 137, I am in college, and there I intend to remain till I go down. **1895** LD. WATSON in *Law Times Rep.* LXXIII. 636/1, I think that this case must go down for a new trial. *Mod.* I have been running up and down all the morning.

II. Of position in space.

3. a. In a low or lowered situation or position; on the ground.

1297 R. GLOUC. (1724) 29 Beter hym hadde ybe Haue bileued þer doune, þan y-lerned for to fle. **1340** HAMPOLE *Pr. Consc.* 1602 þus es þis world turned up þat es doune. **1489** CAXTON *Sonnes of Aymon* v. 132 Whan they were doun from ther horses. **1590** SPENSER *F.Q.* I. i. 34 A litle lowly Hermitage..Downe in a dale, hard by a forests side. *a* **1682** SIR T. BROWNE *Tracts* 55 When the river is down. **1726** LEONI *Alberti's Archit.* I. 28/1 Such Trees as grow..down in a Valley. **1868** HOLME LEE *B. Godfrey* xlvii. 255 The blinds were down. **1894** HALL CAINE *Manxman* 100 The tide was down, the harbour was empty of water.

b. *Theatr.* = DOWN STAGE *adv.*

1893 WILDE *Lady Windermere* I. 12 Duchess of Berwick (*Coming down C., and shaking hands*). *Ibid.* 15 Lord Darlington (*Moves up C.*)..Lord Darlington (*Coming down back of table*). *a* **1916** H. JAMES *Compl. Plays* (1949) 193 Enter Noémie Nioche and Lord Deepmere, rapidly down from centre. *Ibid.* 194 Her father has the voice of some young fellow I know. (*Coming down, left centre.*) Whose is it? **1939** N. COWARD *2nd Play Parade* 17 An ordinary bus sign R.C. [right centre] down on footlights.

4. At a place or in a locality which is considered as lower; at a distance from the capital; away in the country; away from the university.

1830 MARRYAT *King's Own* xli, He was to be down at Portsmouth in a few days. **1836** —— *Midsh. Easy* i. 5 A gentleman who lived down in Hampshire. **1883** *Cambridge Staircase* v. 81 His 'health' had compelled him to stay down for the whole of our first year.

III. Of position, posture, attitude.

5. Into or in a fallen, sitting, or overthrown position or posture. *down for the count*: see COUNT *sb.*[1] 1 c.

c **1205** LAY. 6864 Seoððen he dun læi. *c* **1300** *Havelok* 925 Sit now doun and et ful yerne. *c* **1380** WYCLIF *Serm.* Sel. Wks. I. 69 Nouȝt honge þere heedis doun. *c* **1400** MAUNDEV. (Roxb.) viii. 32 þare was sum tyme a chapell, bot now it es all doune. *c* **1450** *St. Cuthbert* (Surtees) 4725 þai knelyd doune before þe saynt. **1610** SHAKS. *Temp.* III. i. 23 If you'l sit downe Ile beare your Logges the while. **1669** STURMY *Mariner's Mag.* v. 89 Fold it down. **1678** BUNYAN *Pilgr.* I. 1, I laid me down in that place to sleep. **1700** S. L. tr. *Fryke's Voy. E. Ind.* 62 We..batter'd it down in a very little time. **1755** *Game at Cricket* 10 A Stump hit by the Ball, though the Bail was down, is out. **1799** HAN. MORE *Fem. Educ.* (ed. 4) I. 279 Christianity..pulls down their images. **1848** *Jrnl. R. Agric. Soc.* IX. II. 524 Five fields, one of which is always down to sainfoin. **1894** BARING-GOULD *Des. S. France* II. 228 He cut them down almost to a man.

6. Prostrate with sickness; 'on the sick list', ill.

1710 SWIFT *Jrnl. to Stella* 23 Dec., Write to MD when you are down. **1712** W. ROGERS *Voy.* 206 We have now about 50 men down. **1742** RICHARDSON *Pamela* III. 351 Five Children, who had been all down in Fevers and Agues. **1876** TENNYSON *Harold* II. i, When I was down in the fever, she was down with the hunger. **1892** *Times* 12 Jan. 10/1 A large number of the..household are down with influenza.

7. *to run, ride, hunt,* etc. *down*: to bring to the ground, to overtake or overthrow, by running, etc. See also the verbs.

1659 D. PELL *Impr. Sea* 137 Great care taken..who should run down one another by the board first. **1711** ADDISON *Spect.* No. 115 ⁋6 Foxes of the Knight's own hunting down. **1883** SIR M. WILLIAMS *Relig. Th. in Ind.* ix. 245 Capable of..riding down the most active demon-antagonist. **1888** *Times* 16 Oct. 10/5, I was tracked down in rather less time than it had taken me to cover the ground.

IV. Particular varieties of direction or position.

8. Below the horizon; *going down*, setting; *down*, set.

a **1300** *Cursor M.* 6800 (Cott.) Ar sun ga dun þat ilk dai. *c* **1400** *Destr. Troy* 7807 The day wex dym, doun was the sun. **1559** W. CUNNINGHAM *Cosmogr. Glasse* 18 The rysing, and goyng downe of every Planet. **1669** STURMY *Mariner's Mag.* II. 89 Far Northward or Southward..the Sun goeth not down, as they find that Sail about the North Cape. **1849** JAMES *Woodman* ii, The sun had gone down some two hours before.

9. Below the surface or to the bottom of water; into the depths of the sea: *to go down*, to sink; *to run down*, to sink (*trans.*) by running against.

1659 D. PELL *Impr. Sea* 298 One, or both of those ships..goes down with all their passengers in the very bottome. **1782** COWPER *Loss R. George* vi, When Kempenfelt went down With twice four hundred men. **1886** *Newspr.*, A boat's crew of the whaling schooner..was taken down by a whale near the Cape Verde islands.

10. To the ground-floor or floor below; downstairs, *scil.* from one's bedroom, or to the dining-room, to dinner.

1592 SHAKS. *Rom. & Jul.* III. v. 66 Is she not downe so late, or vp so early? **1766** GOLDSM. *Vic. W.* iv, Down came my wife and daughters. **1887** MRS. J. H. PERKS *From Heather Hills* II. xviii. 308 A quiet dinner-party, with a nice, sensible man to take you down.

11. Down the throat; into the stomach; *to go down*, to be swallowed; also *fig.* to please the mental palate: see GO.

1582 N. LICHEFIELD tr. *Castanheda's Conq. E. Ind.* xvii. 44 The king shuld not swallow yᵉ same downe. **1632** MASSINGER *City Madam* I. i, Butcher's meat will not go down. **1660** tr. *Amyraldus' Treat. conc. Relig.* II. vi. 241 A bitter potion that is soon down. **1766** GOLDSM. *Vic. W.* xviii, Fletcher, Ben Jonson, and all the plays of Shakespeare, are the only things that go down. **1816** KEATINGE *Trav.* (1817) I. 105 Which homely fare they wash down with a spoonful of light wine.

12. In reference to payment: (Laid) upon the table or counter; (paid) on the spot, or at the instant.

1557 in W. H. Turner *Select. Rec. Oxford* (1880) 265 Payeng vijli done. **1605** SHAKS. *Lear* I. ii. 93, I dare pawne downe my life for him. **1669** in *12th Rep. Hist. MSS. Comm.* App. v. (1890) 11 Lord Huntington's marriage..with Sir James Langham's daughter, who gives 20,000*l.* downe. **1894** WOLSELEY *Marlborough* I. 77 For a lump sum down, and a liberal annuity..Charles agreed to declare war.

13. On paper or other surface used for writing; in writing: with *write, note, set, put, take, lay,* etc. See the verbs.

1576 FLEMING *Panopl. Epist.* 83 He gathereth arguments..and setteth him selfe downe for a president or patterne to bee followed. *Ibid.* 236 In the margent, the name of the person is set downe to whome the same was directed. **1599** SHAKS. *Much Ado* IV. ii. 17 Write downe Master gentleman Conrade. **1697** DAMPIER *Voy.* I. xvi. 448 Many shoals..are not laid down in our Drafts. **171.** STEELE *Spect.* No. 155 ⁋2, I will keep Pen and Ink at the Bar, and write down all they say to me. **1712** W. ROGERS *Voy.* 248, I took down the Names. **1847** MARRYAT *Childr. N. Forest* ix, I should have put you down for eighteen or nineteen at least. **1885** *Manch. Exam.* 14 July 5/3 Mr. Stansfield's bill..was down for second reading on Wednesday.

V. Of order, time, condition, quality, or value.

14. a. From a higher to a lower point or member in any series or order.

a **1300** *Cursor M.* 1659 (Cott.) Fra þe mast dun to þe lest. **1684** R. H. *School Recreat.* 92 So by turns, 'till every Bell being hunted up and down, comes into its proper Place again. *Ibid.* 96 Whatsoever Bells you follow when you Hunt up, the same Bells in the same order you must follow in Hunting down. **1816** KEATINGE *Trav.* (1817) II. 68 Every country has its etiquettes..in Spain, down even to the taking of a pinch of snuff. **1876** TREVELYAN *Macaulay* I. i. 53 From the highest effort of genius down to the most detestable trash. **1885** *Manch. Exam.* 28 May 5/2 From the aristocracy down to the collier and quarryman.

b. (So many points, etc.) behind one's opponent in a game; opposed to *up*.

1894 *Times* 16 June 16/1 [He] lost the [golf] match by four down, and two to play. **1897** *Encycl. Sport* I. 472/2 A player is said to be down when his opponent has won one or more holes [more] than he has. **1907** H. H. HILTON *Golfing Remin.* 103 At the fourteenth hole he was one down. **1959** *Times* 28 May 4/2 He had another hard [golf] match, but was, I think, never down.

15. From an earlier to a later time; *down to date* (after UP TO DATE).

1415 HOCCLEVE *To Sir J. Oldcastle* 122 Vnto seint Petir and his successours, And so foorth doun. **1662** STILLINGFL. *Orig. Sacr.* II. i. §5 Down from the time of Moses. **1747** BERKELEY *Tar-water in Plague* Wks. III. 480 Throughout all ages down to our own. **1816** KEATINGE *Trav.* (1817) I. 228 The accounts which the ancients have handed down to us. **1889** *Cent. Dict.* II. 1461/2 *Down to date, up to date*, to the present time. **1892** 'MARK TWAIN' *Amer. Claim.* 211 I've got part of him down to date, anyway. **1897** —— *Following the Equator* xxv. 244 He was down to date with them, too. **1901** *Daily Chron.* 1 Nov. 5/2 An author of the most down-to-date ballads of the barrack-room. **1930** *Morning Post* 4 Mar. 7/5 The most down-to-date dictionaries. **1937** *Daily Tel.* 19 Nov. 22 The down-to-date traveller discovered..that without the aid of aeroplanes it was only just possible to equal Fogg's record.

16. To a lower amount; to or at a reduced rate or price.

1573 *Acc. Burgh Glasg.* 22 Aug. (Jam. Supp.) Gevin to James Andersoun..doun of his ferme be ressoun of the greit droutht, xxj li. **1678** BUTLER *Hud.* III. ii. 320 Bringing down the price of coals. **1838** MACAULAY *Temple* Ess. (1886) 434 Cutting down his salary. **1894** *Daily News* 14 Apr. 5/2 Turbot is down too.

17. a. To or in a lower or inferior condition, a state of depression, subjection, humiliation, inaction, restraint, defeat, discomfiture, annihilation.

c **1330** R. BRUNNE *Chron. Wace* (Rolls) 15736 Or hys iuel schulde brynge hym doun. *c* **1380** WYCLIF *Sel. Wks.* III. 19 Of þi myche joie þou didist doun alle yvele spiritis. **1513** DOUGLAS *Æneis* Contents 22 Rutulianis..By the deceiss of Camylla doun bett. **1596** DRAYTON *Legends* i. 357 Who can rayse him, that Fortune will have downe? **1605** BACON *Adv. Learn.* II. x. §12 The Olympian games are down long since. **1618** BOLTON *Florus* (1636) 117 Annibal, now quite downe. **1760** C. JOHNSTON *Chrysal* (1822) I. 289 She happened to look at her watch, but it was down. **1857** H. REED *Lect. Eng. Poets* viii. 274 If the spirit of a nation goes down, its poetry will go down with it. **1872** SPURGEON *Treas. Dav.* Ps. lxix. 26 If a godly man be a little down in estate.

b. With *frown, hiss, hoot, shout, talk,* etc.: to put down, reduce to silence, etc., by such action.

1590 SHAKS. *Com. Err.* III. i. 6 Here's a villaine that would face me downe He met me on the Mart. **1613** —— *Hen. VIII*, I. i. 20 The French shone downe the English. **1887** A. BIRRELL *Obiter Dicta* Ser. II. 272 He was immediately frowned down by Mrs. Snagsby.

c. Chiefly *Computing.* Of a computer system, etc.: out of action, unavailable for use. Cf. DOWNTIME and UP *adv.*[2] 13 b.

1965 *AFIPS Conf. Proc.* XXVII. 221/1 This situation arises when the system goes down before the file system has updated its assignment tables. **1971** *Ibid.* XXXVIII. 215/1 A critical situation is created when Sam [*sc.* supervisor in active mode] goes down. **1978** *Sci. Amer.* July 64/1 The usual short-distance transmission system is designed so as to ensure that it is 'down' no more than two hours per year. **1982** *Times* 23 Aug. 13/2 The phrase 'the computer's down again' is still exasperatingly familiar among data and information processors.

18. Into or in low spirits; *to be down*, to be downcast or depressed. *colloq.*

1610 B. JONSON *Alch.* IV. vii, Thou art so downe vpon the least disaster! *c* **1620** Z. BOYD *Zion's Flowers* (1855) 113 Men's hearts are downe. **1782** JOHNSON *Let. to Mrs. Thrale* 4 June, When I prest your hand at parting I was rather down. **1865** THOREAU *Cape Cod* x. (1894) 315 The Captain is rather down about it, but I tell him to cheer up.

19. To smaller size or bulk; to minute particles; to a finer consistency.

1675 WOOD *Life* (Oxf. Hist. Soc.) II. 327 He..melted it [New Coll. plate] downe. **1731** ARBUTHNOT *Aliments* (J.) To be boiled down..to a sapid fat. **1816** KEATINGE *Trav.* (1817) I. 50 Ground down into dust. **1865** LYELL *Elem. Geol.* (ed. 6) 25 Wearing down into a fine powder. **1890** ABNEY *Treat. Photogr.* (ed. 6) 76 The..liquid is..thinned down to proper fluidity.

20. From a roused, excited, or violent state; into or in a state of subsidence or calm.

1590 SPENSER *F.Q.* I. iii. 8 Downe fell his angry mood. **1591** SHAKS. *Two Gent.* II. iii. 60 If the winde were downe. **16..** *Progr. Honesty* vii. 9 You whose insipid Palat's down, Failing to relish. **1798** COLERIDGE *Anc. Mar.* II. vi, Down dropt the breeze. **1814** S. ROGERS *Jacquel.* II. 55 To walk his troubled spirit down.

21. Into a weaker, milder, or less pronounced quality; e.g. *to soften, tone down*: see the verbs.

1816 KEATINGE *Trav.* (1817) I. 250 Time softens down things by unobserved degrees. **1832** GEN. P. THOMPSON *Exerc.* (1842) II. 42 Tamed down into as harmless and beneficent a sect as the Quakers.

22. *slang.* Aware, 'wide-awake.' (See also 27 a.)

1812 J. H. VAUX *Flash Dict.*, *Down*, sometimes synonymous with *awake*, as when the party you are about to rob, sees or suspects your intention, it is then said that *the cove is down.* **1812** *Sporting Mag.* XXXIX. 285 He supposed he was *down* (had knowledge of it). **1817** *Ibid.* L. 201 Down as a nail. **1850** SMEDLEY *Frank Fairl.* iv. (Farmer) You're down to every move, I see, as usual.

VI. With ellipsis of a verb: so that *down* itself functions for the verbal phrase. (But uninflected, and therefore used only for imperative and infinitive after auxiliary verbs. Hence DOWN *v.*[2])

23. With ellipsis of *come, go, sit, kneel, lie.*

c **1388** in *Wyclif's Sel. Wks.* III. 472 His proude clerkis schal downe with ther pride. *c* **1400** *Rom. Rose* 5868 Doune shalle the castelle every dele. **1509** HAWES *Past. Pleas.* xx. vii, The warre which may sone aryse And wyl not downe. **1535** COVERDALE *Ezek.* xxxii. 19 Downe..and laye the with the vncircumcised. **1596** SHAKS. *Merch. V.* IV. i. 363 Downe therefore, and beg mercy of the Duke. **1636** SANDERSON *Serm.* II. 53 Yet down it must, subdued it must be. **1671** MILTON *Samson* 322 Down reason then, at least vain reasonings down. **1847** MARRYAT *Childr. N. Forest* iii. Down, Smoker, good dog! **1885** R. BRIDGES *Nero* I. i, That house of Rufus That blocks the way must down.

24. With ellipsis of *go*, in sense 'be swallowed.' *lit.* and *fig.*

1580 LYLY *Euphues* (Arb.) 303 There was no broth that would downe, but of hir making. **1581** PETTIE *Guazzo's Civ. Conv.* To Rdr. (1586) A vj b, Nothing will downe with them but French, Italian, or Spanish. **1692** LOCKE *Educ.* §14 (R.) If he be hungry more than wanton, bread alone will down. *c* **1708** SWIFT *Baucis & Philemon* 143 Plain *Goody* would no longer down; 'Twas *Madam*, in her grogram gown.

25. a. With ellipsis of *put*, etc.

1820 BYRON *Blues* II. 115 And down Aristotle! *c* **1860** H. STUART *Seaman's Catech.* 6 What is the necessary precaution at the word 'down oars'? **1867** SMYTH *Sailor's Word-bk.*, Down oars!..Down with the helm! **1875** BEDFORD *Sailor's Pocket Bk.* vi. (ed. 2) 215 If caught in a hard sudden squall, down helm at once.

b. In same sense, *down with*: esp. in commands. (Cf. AWAY *with.*)

1535 COVERDALE *Ps.* cxxxvi[i]. 7 Downe with it, downe with it, euen to the grounde. **1591** SHAKS. *Two Gent.* IV. i. 2 Shrinke not, but down with 'em. **1669** STURMY *Mariner's Mag.* I. 19 Down with all Hammocks and Cabins. **1708** MOTTEUX *Rabelais* IV. xxiii. (1737) 98 Down with your Sails. **1820** SHELLEY *Œdipus* I. 323 Long live Iona! down with Swellfoot! **1856** C. MACKAY *Songs for Music, Emigrants* x. i, Down with the lords of the forest! [i.e. trees.]

c. *down charge*: the order given to a setter or pointer in training to drop when the game rises and the shot is fired. So as *sb.* and *v.*; **down-charging** *vbl. sb.*

1833 *New Sporting Mag.* V. 259/1 Some sportsmen..make him down charge when the bird is missed. *Ibid.* 260/1 Call out directly, 'Down charge!' **1848** W. N. HUTCHINSON *Dog Breaking* ii. §21. 14 Your left arm..should make the young dog lie down (for the 'down charge'). **1859** 'STONEHENGE' *Shot-gun & Sporting Rifle* II. i. 129 He puts up the birds, calling out 'Down charge' at the same moment in a loud voice. **1886** LD. WALSINGHAM et al. *Shooting* I. 324 His obedience to 'down charging' being frequently enforced. *Ibid.* 334 Provided the dog is fairly cured of chasing, taught to 'down-charge', find, return, and keep at heel.

26. Used in ballad refrains, without appreciable meaning. (Cf. DOWN *sb.*[3] 1.)

1598 SHAKS. *Merry W.* I. iv. 44 I doubt he be not well, that hee comes not home: and downe, downe, adowne'a, &c. **1602** —— *Ham.* IV. v. 170 You must sing downe a-downe, and you call him a-downe-a. ? **17..** *Robin Hood & Bishop* in Evans *O.B.* (1784) I. xix. 102 Come, gentlemen all, and listen a-while, With a hey down, down and a-down. *a* **1845** Hood *Compass* xiii, Down, down, a dreary derry down.

VII. Phrases.

27. down on. a. *to be down on* (*upon*): to be aware of, to understand, to be 'up to'. *slang*. See 22.

1793 J. Pearson *Polit. Dict.*, Egad, the Baronet was down upon it. **1811** *Sporting Mag.* XXXVII. 76 Was down upon him, and clearly up to his gossip. **1865** G. Berkeley *Life, etc.* II. 103 (Farmer) I said..'I'm down on it all: the monkey never bit your dog.'

b. *to be down on* (*upon*): to fall upon, pounce upon, assail, attack (from a superior position).

1815 Scott *Guy M.* xxviii, I think we should be down upon the fellow one of these darkmans, and let him get it well. **1845** James *A. Neil* vi, We were out from the alders in a minute, down upon them. **1885** Mrs. Lynn Linton *Christ. Kirkland* II. vi. 196 The critics would have been down on the author as an absurd bungler.

c. *to be down on*: to be opposed to; to show or express disapproval of. Chiefly *U.S.*

1851 *Alta California* 5 Aug., Here the factory girls appear to be down on the style. **1854** *Daily Calif. Chron.* 26 Sept., To refuse payment of the trifling bills of a few journals who had latterly perhaps been down on them. **1874** 'Mark Twain' *Sk. New & Old* (1875) 205, I was down on sich doin's. **1883** —— *Life on Miss.* 268 If there's one thing an alligator is more down on than another, it's being dredged. **1902** W. James *Var. Relig. Exper.* xiv. 335 Some persons.. glory in saying that they are 'down' on religion altogether. **1903** *McClure's Mag.* Nov. 92 I'm down on grafting mayors and grafting office-holders. **1931** V. Palmer *Separate Lives* 111 'They're down on her for some reason or other,' he told himself. 'Angry, most likely, because she's hung on to her boy.'

28. down to. a. *to be down to*: to be attributable to (cf. *put down* s.v. PUT *v.*[1] 41 j).

1955 *Times* 5 Aug. 11/5 Wattam said: 'It's down to me, the stamps and postal orders belong to me. They are nothing to do with the wife. I've done all the jobs.' **1962** R. Cook *Crust on its Uppers* i. 24 Obscurely it's all down to Mum, who certainly does..seem to have dragged him up a bit strange. **1985** *Sunday Tel.* 26 May 11/6 The boom in Gucci and Pucci and..Lacoste 'names' on clothes, bags and other ornamentation is all down to the Yuppies.

b. *to be down to*: to be the responsibility of, to be incumbent upon; = *up to* s.v. UP *adv.*[2] 19 d.

1970 P. Laurie *Scotland Yard* 289 Down to:..*X* is down to *Y* = *X* is *Y*'s responsibility. **1986** *City Limits* 16 Oct. 41 The clothes are by Jean-Paul Gaultier, the basslines are by Blackmon, and the dancing is down to you.

29. down along: in, or to, the West Country. Also *attrib.*, and *sb.* (= the West Country). *dial.* and *slang* (see quot. 1929).

1871 Kingsley *At Last* i, Their faces lighted up at the old pass-word of 'Down-Along'; for whosoever knows Down-Along, and the speech thereof, is at once a friend and a brother. **1899** *Westm. Gaz.* 12 Jan. 3/3 The people of the 'down-along' country are slow in putting thoughts into words. **1905** E. Phillpotts *Secret Woman* III. xiii, Henceforth I shall come down-along once a year to visit you. **1907** *Westm. Gaz.* 18 Dec. 4/2 In his 'Devonshire Characters'..there is a true tang of 'Down-along' in every page. **1929** F. C. Bowen *Sea Slang* 40 *Down along*, sailing coastways down Channel.

30. down east (*U.S.*): into or in the eastern sea-coast districts of New England, esp. Maine. Also as *adj.* and *sb.* Hence **down-easter**. Also *transf.*

1825 [see AWAY *adv.* 11 b]. **1825** J. Neal *Bro. Jonathan* I. 28 A little boy from 'down-east'. *a* **1828** J. Bernard *Retrosp.* 37 This curious class of mammalia, the 'Down-Easter' as it is often called. *Ibid.* 240 He had lately quitted 'Down East', and was coming South. **1829** *Mass. Spy* 25 Nov. (Th.), 'Where the deuce is Dennis [a town]?' 'Oh, down east.' **1830** S. Smith *Major Downing* 1, Some of the down-east antiquaries. **1835** J. H. Ingraham *South-West* I. xv. 161 Miserable-looking sloops and schooners, compared to which, our 'down easters' are packet ships. **1837** W. Irving *Capt. Bonneville* I. 110 A party of regular 'down-easters', that is to say, people of New England. **1843** *Ainsworth's Mag.* IV. 426 This old lass lived 'down east' near Chiselhurst. **1867** O. W. Holmes *Guard. Angel* viii. (1891) 87 He actually had the down-east city called after it. **1883** *Harper's Mag.* Nov. 938/2 This was originated by down-east men. **1924** R. Clements *Gipsy of Horn* 84 If this ship was a 'down-easter' she'd be flauntin' a main-royal. **1945** J. C. Colcord *Sea Lang.* 68 *Down East*, a general term for Maine and the Maritime Provinces of Canada... A 'down-easter' may be either a person or a vessel hailing from that region. **1948** W. Stevens *Let.* 2 Apr. (1967) 582 We are too close to that severe Down East that is Labrador.

31. down south: into or in the south; in *U.S.* down the Mississippi; into or in the Southern States.

1852 Mrs. Stowe *Uncle Tom's C.* xii, 'Taking her down south?' said the man. Haley nodded and smoked on. *Mod.* He is now in Newcastle, but is coming down south next week.

32. down to the ground (*colloq.*): thoroughly, completely.

1867 Miss Broughton *Cometh up as a Flower* xxvi, Suited me down to the ground. **1889** T. A. Trollope *What I remember* III. 289 The occupation..suited my tastes and habits 'down to the ground', as the modern slang phrase has it.

33. down to earth: back to reality. Also freq. **down-to-earth** *adj. phr.*, interested in everyday affairs; not affectedly superior; realistic; ordinary. So ***down-to-earth*(*i*)*ness***.

1930 Wodehouse *Very Good, Jeeves!* i. 29, I had for some little time been living, as it were, in another world. I now came down to earth with a bang. **1932** *Canadian Forum* Feb. 193/3 This book is full of such 'down to earth' observations. **1934** M. Hodge *Wind & Rain* I. ii. 37 She's awfully 'down to earth', you know. **1943** J. S. Huxley *Evol. Ethics* viii. 64 The general moral principle of evolutionary purpose can come down to earth in the concrete task of achieving minimum planning. **1956** *Essays by Divers Hands* XXVIII. 80 There is still a down-to-earthness in the phrasing. **1956** L. E. Jones *Edwardian Youth* ii. 55 Julian [Grenfell] had a passion for red-blooded down-to-earthiness. **1958** A. W. Fielding *Corsair Country* viii. 163 So I call for the bill. Which brings us down to earth with an ugly thud. **1961** *Daily Tel.* 12 May 14/2 Dame Irene Ward's hope that the committee..will include ' some down-to-earth people who know something about what goes on'. **1969** *Listener* 6 Feb. 189/2 This down-to-earthness most literally strikes home in the anchoring of the play to an actual place.

34. *down at* HEEL, *down in the* HIPS, *down on* (or *in*) *one's* LUCK, *down in the* MOUTH: see the sbs. ***down with!***: see 25 b.

VIII. 35. Comparative degree †***downer***; also †***downermore*** (*obs.*). Superlative: see DOWNMOST.

13.. *K. Alis.* 6619 Ac the delfyn is more queynter, And halt him in the water douner. *c* **1391** Chaucer *Astrol.* II. §12 As the sonne clymbith vppere and vppere, so goth his nadir downere and downere. *c* **1430** *Syr Gener.* (Roxb.) 4226 Dounermore the stroke went yet. **1435** Misyn *Fire of Love* I. x. 20 Bettyr it is..þat criste..to vs say, 'frende, cum vppyrmare', þen þat he say, 'carl, go donyrmare'.

IX. down- in combination.

36. In combination with verbs, both words having their ordinary meaning. (Stress on the verb.)

Such are ***down-come***, ***down-cry*** (to cry down, decry), †***down-dagger***, ***down-darken***, ***down-droop***, ***down-go***, ***down-lay***, †***down-peize*** (to weigh down, to compensate), ***down-pour***, ***down-press***, ***down-run***, ***down-shear***, ***down-shower***, ***down-smite***, ***down-spring***, ***down-squat***, ***down-thring*** (to press down, crush), ***down-throw***, ***down-trample***, ***down-tumble***. Also DOWNBEAR, -CAST, -LIE, etc.

These are very doubtful combinations. In ME., though occasionally written as one word, the adverb and verb were usually written separately, e.g. *doun come*, *doun ryn*, but are often hyphened by editors of modern editions, e.g. *doun-come*, *doun-ryn*. Modern instances are mostly poetical, being merely examples of inversion of the prose order of verb and adverb for metrical or rhetorical purposes (e.g. *he down-throws* for *down he throws* = *he throws down*); the hyphen seems, as a rule, unnecessary.

c **1250** *Gen. & Ex.* 1608 [He] saȝ A leddre stonden, and ðoron Angeles *dun cumen and up gon. **1340** Hampole *Pr. Consc.* 4290 He sal do fire fra þe heven don com. **1883** Besant *All in Garden Fair* II. i, Those who..*downcried her beauty. **1654** Gayton *Pleas. Notes* II. i. 36 He let fly.. and with one blow, confounded and *downe-dagger'd him. *a* **1300** *E.E. Psalter* cvi. 26 Þai up stiyhen..And þai *doun ga. **1611** Speed *Hist. Gt. Brit.* VIII. iv. (1632) 404 The presence of the one, *downe-peized the absence of the other. **1340** Hampole *Pr. Consc.* 7123 Þe water þat þan salle *doun ryn Ffra þair eghen. *a* **1300** *E.E. Psalter* lxxiii. 6 Þaire yhetes with axes þai *doune schare. **1844** Mrs. Browning *Romaunt Page* xxxv, The boy *down-sprung And stood. **1513** Douglas *Æneis* I. v. 62 This Eneas..In Itale thrawart peple sall *doun thryng. **1558** Q. Kennedie *Compend. Tractive* in *Wodr. Soc. Misc.* (1844) I. 100 To invaid, oppres, and alluterlie dounthryng the Congregatioun. **1581** N. Burne *Disput.* 43 b (Jam.) Inducing subiectis to oppress and *dounthrau their maisters. **1878** Browning *Poets Croisic* 61 *Down-trampling vulgar hindrance. **1628** Ford *Lover's Mel.* III. i, One careless slip *down-tumbles him again.

37. With present participle or ppl. adj. These are practically unlimited in number, the use of the hyphen being merely syntactical. They have the stress usually on *down-* when used as adjectives, on the radical element when used as participles. Examples are: ***down-beaming***, ***down-crouching***, ***down-dragging***, ***down-drawing***, ***down-driving***, ***down-drooping***, ***down-dropping***, ***down-flowing***, ***down-going***, ***down-hanging***, ***down-rushing***, ***down-sloping***, ***down-stooping***, ***down-tumbling***, etc. Also DOWNFALLING, -LOOKING, etc.

1868 Ld. Houghton *Select. fr. Wks.* 189 *Down-beaming from the brazen Syrian skies. **1593** *Bacchus Bountie* in *Harl. Misc.* (Malh.) II. 263 To crase his crowne with a *downedriuing blow. **1840** Clough *Dipsychus* II. v. 48 The deep plough in the lazy undersoil Down-driving. **1900** Kipling in *Daily Mail* 1 May 4/5 A whispering Guardsman, half of whose larynx had been put out of commission by a *down-dropping bullet. **1936** W. Stevens *Opus Posthumous* (1957) 61 The same down-dropping fruit in yellow leaves. **1784** Cowper *Tiroc.* 361 Graced With wig prolix, *down-flowing to his waist. **1591** Sylvester *Du Bartas* I. v. 1012 As a wolf..Flyes with *down-hanging head. **1868** G. Stephens *Runic Mon.* I. 226 Another downhanging rope. *a* **1821** Keats *Fancy* 65 Acorns ripe *down-pattering. **1647** H. More *Song of Soul* II. iii. III. xxxvi, That strong *down-pulling centrall sway. *Ibid.* I. III. vii, Soft *down-sliding sleep. **1837** Longf. *Frithiof's Homestead* 3 The *down-sloping hill-sides. **1780** Cowper *Progr. Err.* 177 Night, *down-stooping from her ebon throne.

38. With past or passive participle or ppl. adj. These also are unlimited in number, the hyphen being merely syntactical; the stress varies as in prec. Examples are: ***down-bent***, ***down-borne***, ***down-burnt***, ***down-dashed***, ***down-dropped***, ***down-pressed***, ***down-put***, ***down-thrown***, ***down-turned***, etc. Also DOWNCAST, etc.

1831 Carlyle *Sart. Res.* II. iii, A *downbent, broken-hearted..martyr. **1882** L. C. Lillie *Prudence* 96 She kept her face passionately down-bent. **1597** Warner *Alb. Eng.*, *Æneidos* 317 *Down-burnt Turrets. **1832** Tennyson *Œnone* 55 With *downdropt eyes I sat alone. **1849** Clough *Life & Duty* vi. 13 With shrunk bodies and heads down-dropt. *c* **1425** *Found. St. Bartholomew's* (E.E.T.S.) 27 Oure lord ihesu criste, the whiche losith stokkid men, reysith vp *downe pressid. **1623** Penkethman *Handf. Hon.* Epist., Like downe-prest Camomile, to spring. **1840** Carlyle *Heroes* iv. (1872) 130 That downpressed mood of despair. *a* **1340** Hampole *Psalter* lxi. 3 Wall þat is withouten cyment *downput. *c* **1600** Shaks. *Sonn.* lxiv, When sometime loftie towers I see *down-rased.

39. With agent-noun (stress on *down-*), as ***down-crier***, ***-lier***, ***-puller***, ***-setter***. Also DOWN-COMER, etc.

1878 Besant & Rice *Monks of Th.* 9 *Downcriers, enviers and backbiters. **1656** S. Holland *Zara* (1719) 99 Up-risers and *Down-liers in this mighty City. **1884** Edna Lyall *We Two* ii, A mere hater, a passionate *downpuller. **1744** J. Paterson *Comm. Milton's P.L.* 386 *Down-setters; officers who set the dishes in good order upon the King's table.

40. With verbal sb. (stress on *down-*), as †***down-ganging***, ***down-going***, ***-lighting***, ***-pouring***, ***-pulling***, ***-putting***, ***-rushing***, ***-shedding***, ***-sinking***, ***-sitting***. Also DOWN-COMING, -FALLING, etc.

1641 Sir S. D'Ewes in Rushw. *Hist. Coll.* III. (1692) I. 311 To add..but one Grain to the *down-balancing of the Affairs of Christendom. **1340** Hampole *Pr. Consc.* 4779 Til þe tyme of þe son *doun-gangyng. **1398** Trevisa *Barth. de P.R.* VIII. xxviii. (Tollem. MS.) He [the sun] semeþ more in his arisinge and *doungoynge. **1846** Landor *Exam. Shaks.* Wks. II. 266 His down-goings and uprisings. **1682** R. Hamilton *Let.* 22 Aug. in M. Shields *Faithful Contendings Displayed* (1780) 40 A *down pouring of the Spirit in his fullness, be your allowance. **1871** Napheys *Prev. & Cure Dis.* I. viii. 240 There should be a liberal down-pouring of carbolic acid. **1631** Weever *Anc. Fun. Mon.* 431 This Priory Church..was preserued from..*downe pulling. **1831** Carlyle *Sart. Res.* II. vii, In our age of Downpulling and Disbelief, the very Devil has been pulled-down. *c* **1440** Hylton *Scala Perf.* (W. de W. 1494) II. xxvi, *Downe puttyng and a-lowenge of his euencristen. *c* **1565** Lindesay (Pitscottie) *Chron. Scot.* (1728) 94 To them who were the occasion of his down-putting. **1837** Carlyle *Fr. Rev.* II. v. i, The dust and *downrushing of a Bastille. **1554** Knox *Faythf. Admon.* G vij b, Of Peters *downsynckynge in ye sea. **1883** R. A. Proctor in *Contemp. Rev.* Earth Movem. Java, The upheavals and downsinkings. **1535** Coverdale *Ps.* cxxxviii. 2 Thou knowest my *downe syttinge and my vprisynge. **1816** Scott *Old Mort.* iv, They drank out the price at ae dounsitting. **1562** Winȝet *Cert. Tractates* i. Wks. 1888 I. 11 For the *dountramping of ydolatrie.

41. With noun of action (stress on *down-*), as ***downbreak***, ***down-drag***, ***downflow***, ***downgrowth***, ***downlet***, (cf. *outlet*), ***downshoot***, ***downslide***, ***down-step***, ***down-stroke***, etc. Also DOWNCAST *sb.*, -DRAUGHT, etc.

1865 Livingstone *Zambesi* 596 They must prove a *down-drag, a moral millstone on the neck. **1887** *Gd. Words* 758 The *downflow of air. **1870** Rolleston *Anim. Life* 12 The hypapophysial *downgrowths. *a* **1681** R. Allestree *Forty Serm.* I. 137 (L.) A *downlet to that bottomless pit. **1926** D. H. Lawrence *David* xiii. 100 The *downslide of his hate is great. **1966** *Listener* 8 Sept. 337/2 A downslide in foreign confidence. **1580** Sidney *Arcadia* (1622) 44 The verie first *down-step to all wickednes. **1852** Dickens *Bleak Ho.* xxi, Every up-stroke and *down-stroke of both documents.

42. Parasynthetic, as ***down-backed***, ***down-faced***, ***down-rumped***; also DOWNHEARTED, -LOOKED.

1580 Hollyband *Treas. Fr. Tong, Bossu* , *downe backed, crooke-shouldered. **1832** J. P. Kennedy *Swallow B.* xix, He was rather *down-faced and confused. **1697** *Lond. Gaz.* No. 3300/4 A bay Gelding..a little *down Rumpt.

down (daʊn), *prep.* [DOWN *adv.* construed with an object. Cf. ADOWN as *prep.*]

1. a. In a descending direction along, through, or into; from top to bottom of; from a higher to a lower part of.

1508 Dunbar *Flyting w. Kennedie* 225 Than rynis thow doun the gait. **1559** W. Cunningham *Cosmogr. Glasse* 51 Let us go downe this Hill into the Citie. **1593** Shaks. *Rich. II*, I. i. 57 Vntill it had return'd These tearmes of treason, doubly downe his throat. **1632** Milton *Penseroso* 107 Such notes as..Drew iron tears down Pluto's cheek. **1743** Bulkeley & Cummins *Voy. S. Seas* 145 Down his Sides, and all the Belly Part, is white Wool. **1895** *Manch. Guard.* 14 Oct. 5/6 The workmen have to be lowered by ropes down the face of the cliff.

b. In reference to position: At a lower part of.

1769 *De Foe's Tour Gt. Brit.* I. 225 Three Miles down the River, are the Ruins. **1816** Keatinge *Trav.* (1817) I. 26 The wines produced down the course of the Rhone. *Ibid.* II. 229 In the timbered parts of France, down the Loire.

c. ***down cellar***: in the cellar or basement. *U.S.*

1805 *Pocomtuc Housewife* (1906) 47 Put in the soapgrease barrel down cellar. **1855** M. Thomson *Doesticks* x. 84 A patent medicine palace, with a..conservatory down cellar. **1870** 'F. Fern' *Ginger-Snaps* 142 When we place a young plant down cellar and shut out light and sunshine. **1871** Stowe *Oldtown Fireside Stories* 10 Ef ye should be down cellar, and the candle should go out, now? **1877** E. S. Ward *Story of Avis* 141, I wonder if it wouldn't help you out to go down cellar and stir the ice-cream. **1947** E. H. Paul *Linden on Saugus Branch* 131, I rushed down-cellar to get our lantern.

2. a. Often with no implication of actual descent: To (or at) what is regarded as a lower part of; along the course or extent of. *up and down*: see UP. Also *fig.* (e.g. of time; cf. the adv.).

1674 N. Cox *Gentl. Recreat.* I. (1677) 94 Some Hares will go up one side of the Hedge, and come down the other. **1726** SHELVOCKE *Voy. round World* (1757) 28 He weighed, and fell down the harbour. **1816** KEATINGE *Trav.* (1817) I. 176 A steady north breeze..prevails all down this coast from the Straits. *Ibid.*, In the progress down the coast. **1859** JEPHSON *Brittany* ii. 18 Down the middle [of the room] were two.. tables. **1861** LOWELL *Poet. Wks.* (1879) 423 The echoes.. Like Odin's hounds, fled baying down the night. **1878** G. DAWSON *Serm. Disputed Points* xv. 260 Shouting down the ages, 'We did miracles!' *Mod.* Traffic passing up and down the line.

b. *down (the) wind*: In the direction in which the wind is blowing; also *fig.*: see WIND.

c. *down the course*: said of a horse which is trailing some distance behind the leaders in a race.

1920 A. E. W. MASON *Summons* xx. 202 All our horses were down the course... They weren't running in their form at all. **1923** *Daily Mail* 11 Jan. 9 Certain horses which ran second or third in the great 'chase at Aintree were 'down the course' this week at Birmingham. *Ibid.* 5 Mar. 9 What about the big and powerful stables..whose horses are down the course one day and up the next, according to the betting?

d. *down home*: at one's home, in one's native land or region; also as *sb.*, one's homeland; hence (usu. *attrib.* or *adj.*) used to designate something, esp. jazz music or blues, that is down-to-earth and unpretentious. *colloq.* (orig. *U.S.*).

[**1828** J. H. NEWMAN *Jrnl.* in *Autobiogr. Writings* (1956) v. 212 After a week's stay at Highwood, I went down home to Brighton.] **1931** *Amer. Speech* VII. 120 *Down home* [*sc.* in eastern Idaho] is Utah. **1938** *N.Y. Amsterdam News* 12 Mar. 17 Almost primal emotions, hangover from the old 'down home house rent strut' days. **1958** J. C. HOLMES *Horn* (1959) 85 Maybe later pick up gigs with a downhome band. **1966** *Melody Maker* 7 May 14/5 A measure of worldly success has not ruined their nakedly emotional down-home style.

e. *down the line*: in various lit. and fig. senses (see quots.). Also (with hyphens) *attrib.*: from one end to the other, at every point (see also quot. 1959).

1898 [see LINE *sb.*² 26b]. **1958** [see BOLT *sb.*¹ 15]. **1959** *Chambers's 20th Cent. Dict.* Suppl., *Down-the-line*, of a ballet-dancer, inconspicuously placed, unimportant. **1961** WEBSTER, *Down-the-line*, all the way; to the end (supporting the party ticket right *down-the-line*) (a *down-the-line* union man). **1962** *Listener* 1 Mar. 364/2 To others the risk is rather that consultative arrangements down the line may reinforce industry's very British predilection for cosy little get-togethers. *Ibid.* 15 Mar. 469/2 The view of many present-day mathematicians who would want to overhaul our methods all down the line. **1962** *Economist* 9 June 1000/1 Mr. Yarborough described himself as a 'down-the-line supporter' of President Kennedy. **1967** *Listener* 31 Aug. 264/1 The authorities are trying to substitute, for tight central guidance, disciplines that will ensure some down-the-line control.

f. *down the road*: in the future. *U.S. colloq.*

1964 MRS. L. B. JOHNSON *White House Diary* 17 Nov. (1970) 204 It was a sad good-by for all of us. But one good thing, we know we'll always be seeing each other down the road. **1974** G. F. NEWMAN *Price* 15 Thirty years down the road in a maximum security prison. **1979** *Arizona Daily Star* 22 July 1. 1/4 My dream is that sometime down the road we'll have students from all the nations of the world in this really non-political, non-sectarian framework. **1985** *New Yorker* 29 July 23/3 Mr. Murjani hopes to install a system resembling the electronic tellers used at banks... But this is a few years down the road. **1986** *Washington Post* 8 Aug. C12/4 I'd like to hold office myself someday, but that's down the road.

3. The preposition and its object may be used as an advb. or attrib. phrase; as in *down-lock*, *down-river*, etc. (Cf. *up-country* farmer.)

1645 RUTHERFORD *Tryal & Tri. Faith* (1845) 321 Heaven is down-ground when faith seeth it; it is, when sight faileth us, toilsome, and up the mount. **1859** SALA *Tw. round Clock* 4 p.m. ¶9 (Farmer) A knot of medical students, who should properly..have a racing and down-the-road look. **1887** *Pall Mall G.* 24 Dec. 2/1 At one of the down-river offices. **1892** *Labour Commission* Gloss., Men engaged on canal-boats on their return journey to Liverpool from Leeds..are said to be engaged on the back passage or down lock.

down, *v.*¹ *rare.* [f. DOWN *sb.*²] *trans.* To cover or line with down, to render downy.

1602 MARSTON *Ant. & Mel.* III. Wks. 1856 I. 34 O calme husht rich content..How soft thou down'st the couch where thou dost rest. **1742** YOUNG *Nt. Th.* VIII. 214 Their nest so deeply down'd, and built so high.

down, *v.*² [f. DOWN *adv.* in the elliptical uses under VI, the adv. having gradually received verbal inflexions.]

1. a. *trans.* To bring, put, throw, or knock down. *to down tools*: to cease working, to go on strike. Hence *down-tools* is used attrib. to designate such action. Also *fig.*

[**1562** TURNER *Herbal* II. 23 The rootes..helpe to down furth the birth in tyme of labor. *c* **1586** C'TESS PEMBROKE *Ps.* CXLVII. ii, To down proud wicked to the dust.] **1778** JOHNSON 29 Apr. in Boswell *Life*, He talked of one whom he did not know; but I *downed* him with the King of Prussia. **1780** —— *Let. to Mrs. Thrale* 11 Apr., Did you quite down her? **1852** R. S. SURTEES *Sponge's Sp. Tour* xxvii, His horse ..had downed him three times. **1889** GUNTER *That Frenchman* xi, The masked wrestler having downed all the professional athletes. **1898** *Westm. Gaz.* 7 Apr. 6/3 The men ..have ruined their position by..suddenly downing tools. **1915** *Daily Express* 4 Mar. 1/5 The 'down-tools' movement seems to have arisen spontaneously out of the engineers' dissatisfaction at not securing the twopence an hour increase when they asked for it. **1923** *Daily Mail* 3 Mar. 13 Yesterday some hundreds of men who did not receive their notice.. to 'down tools' on the previous day left their work. **1955** *Times* 22 June 11/6, I have been compelled..to employ the lazy and the inefficient at wages negotiated by their trade union, if not imposed under a down tools threat. **1958** *Oxf. Mail* 15 Jan. 1/2 He was 'sincerely sorry' to leave his job as Minister of Agriculture. 'I hate downing-tools in the middle of a job.' **1958** *Punch* 15 Jan. 109/1 More trouble seems to be brewing for the B.B.C., over complaints from manufacturers that after each half-hourly news bulletin workers down tools for five minutes to discuss it. **1969** *Listener* 1 May 614/1 The employer should not be able to impose sudden arbitrary action on the workers, the only remedy for which may be a down-tools strike.

b. *fig.* To overthrow, to get the better of.

1898 H. S. CANFIELD *Maid of Frontier* 43 We will have trouble in finishing the gang after Harriott is downed. **1904** F. LYNDE *Grafters* xviii. 233 'A determination to make my brag good.' 'To down the ring, you mean?' 'Yes; to down the ring.' **1909** *Westm. Gaz.* 26 July 1/2 He sees a chance of 'downing' his political opponents. **1925** W. DEEPING *Sorrell & Son* I. i. §5 The thing is not to love your neighbour, but to be able to make it unsafe for him to try and down you. **1946** K. TENNANT *Lost Haven* (1947) 7 He never missed an opportunity of downing Thorne, but Lost Haven continued to support the new store. **1970** *Globe & Mail* (Toronto) 25 Sept. 31/3 Luke Walker pitched a seven-hitter for his fifth successive victory as the Pirates downed Montreal Expos 8–0 last night. **1971** R. PRICE *Permanent Errors* II. 100, I down my own need to stop him. I grant him the rest of his respite, reward.

c. To drink down.

[**1860** O. W. HOLMES *Prof. Breakf.-t.* 52 Give a fellah a fo'-penny bun in the mornin', an' he downs the whole of it.] **1922** C. E. MULFORD *Tex* x. 145 Silently he poured out a drink and downed it mechanically. **1949** D. M. DAVIN *Roads from Home* iii. 44 John downed the two [drinks] that were waiting for him. **1954** KOESTLER *Invisible Writing* 321, I downed the sherry. **1967** W. SOYINKA *Kongi's Harvest* 22 A waiter refills his glass; he downs it. *Ibid.*, [He] downs the rest of his beer and calls for more.

2. *intr.* To come or go down, to descend.

1825 LADY GRANVILLE *Lett.* (1894) I. 360 What an odd thing life is, and how it ups and downs, and ebbs and flows.

3. *to down upon, on*: to come down upon, fall upon, assail as from a superior position.

1852 R. S. SURTEES *Sponge's Sp. Tour* (1893) 95 He would down upon her at the second or third interview. **1884** *Punch* 6 Dec. 276/2 Prove that you value me by downing..on my enemies.

4. *to down with*: to put or throw down; to have done with.

[**1599** *Broughton's Lett.* ix. 34 I dismisse you..with aduise to..downe with your traine, you Peacocke. **1659** D. PELL *Impr. Sea* Ded. 8 Let's down with swearing, if ever wee mean to prosper at Sea.] **1682** HICKERINGILL *Wks.* (1716) II. 20 Except they..down with their Dust, and ready Darby. **1713** WARDER *True Amazons* (ed. 2) 54 They down with her House. **1884** *St. James's Gaz.* 22 Nov. 3/2 Another reason for downing with the House of Lords.

down and out, *adj. phr.* orig. *U.S. colloq.* [DOWN *adv.* 5, OUT *adv.* 19c.] Completely without resources or means of livelihood; absolutely 'done'; also *transf.* (see quot. 1934). Also *absol.* ('the down and out') and as *sb.*

1889 *Kansas Times & Star* 28 Nov., The brewers, saloon-keepers and sports will meet..to provide a turkey feast for the 'down and outs' in their line. **1901** 'H. MCHUGH' *John Henry* 31 Say! I was down and out—no kidding! *a* **1910** 'O. HENRY' *Trimmed Lamp* (1916) 183 I'm down and out; but I'm no traitor to a man that's been my friend. **1917** J. FARNOL *Definite Object* vi. 49, I don't want 'em to think I'm floatin' around with a down-an'-out from Battyville. **1921** H. WALPOLE *Young Enchanted* III. vi, Everybody over forty is tired and down and out, and everybody under thirty has swelled head. **1922** G. M. TREVELYAN *Brit. Hist. 19th Cent.* xxiii. 375 France was down and out. **1923** H. L. FOSTER *Beachcomber in Orient* x. 215 Nowhere in my travels had I ever found a city so full of the down-and-out as was Singapore at that particular moment. **1924** W. B. SELBIE *Psychol. Relig.* 87 The down-and-outs converted there. **1928** H. WALPOLE *Wintersmoon* III. v, Next to Wildherne was a down-and-out with holes in his boots. **1928** GALSWORTHY *Swan Song* III. vi. 259 'You've never been down and out, I imagine, Mr. Forsyte?' 'No,' answered Soames. **1933** 'G. ORWELL' (*title*) Down and out in Paris and London. **1934** *Amer. Speech* IX. 11 *Down and out* refers to the opening lead of an Ace followed by the lead, in the order of their rank, of the next lower cards in the same suit. **1958** *Times Lit. Suppl.* 10 Jan. 15/2 After leaving school he emigrated into what he calls Fitzrovia—a world of outsiders, down-and-outs, drunks, sensualists, homosexuals and eccentrics. **1968** T. PARKER *People of Streets* 31 The assistance is for the poor people really, the ones who they call the down-and-outs. *Ibid.* 159 Billy Costello, down-and-out dosser, twenty-four years old.

Hence **down-and-out** *v. trans.*, to 'do for', destroy; **down-and-outer**, one who is 'down and out'; **down-and-outness**.

1909 *Springfield Weekly Republ.* 4 Mar. 2 Compliments from political enemies follow the most distinguished down-and-outer of his day into the seclusion of private life. **1914** G. ATHERTON *Perch of Devil* II. 298 You don't..put it over without running the risk of being shot by some sort of down-and-outer. **1916** 'BOYD CABLE' *Action Front* 186 That machine-gun upstairs is a certain invitation to sudden death and the German gunners to down and out us. **1922** H. L. FOSTER *Adv. Trop. Tramp* ii. 20 The down-and-outers of whom my old sea-captain had spoken. **1926** *Blackw. Mag.* Aug. 235/2 In the process of investigating the reason for their down-and-outness, he considered that the applicant had been a knave. **1967** *Boston* (Mass.) *Sunday Herald* 2–8 Apr. 27/2 Film..Two down and outers, looking for some rich people to marry, find each other. Down and out.

†**down'bear**, *v. Obs. trans.* To bear down, press down, cause to sink; *fig.* to oppress. Hence **down-'bearing** *vbl. sb.* and *ppl. a.*

c **1330** R. BRUNNE *Chron.* (1810) 158 A tempest on him light, His schip was dounborn. *a* **1340** HAMPOLE *Psalter* lxxxviii. 41 þou heghed þe right hand of downberand him. **1680** G. HICKES *Spirit of Popery* Pref. 5 For the Down-bearing of the Gospel. **1690** NORRIS *Beatitudes* (1694) I. 230 Such a full down-bearing Perswasion. **1834** FONBLANQUE *Eng. under 7 Administ.* (1837) III. 130 Hemmed in and downborne by an overpowering opposition.

down-beat ('daʊnbiːt), *sb.* [DOWN *adv.* 41.] A downward beat; *spec.* in *Mus.*, (the downward stroke of a conductor's baton or hand, indicating) the first or most heavily accented note of a measure; = THESIS 1.

1876 [see UP *a.* 4]. **1879** GROVE *Dict. Mus.* I. 95/2 We make the down beat for the strong accents, and raise our hand for the others. **1891** [see THESIS 1]. **1937** *John o' London's* 7 May 217 To convert the energy of a down-beat in flapping flight into that forward thrust which gives to birds their speed through the air. **1946** P. ROSENFELD tr. *R. Schumann's Music & Musicians* 169 Music itself sought to return to its origins where the laws of downbeat did not yet oppress it. **1955** G. ABRAHAM in H. van Thal *Fanfare for E. Newman* 13 Each wind instrument enters on a down-beat.

down-beat ('daʊnbiːt), *a.* orig. *U.S.* [cf. prec.] Pessimistic, gloomy, sombre; relaxed, unemphatic.

1952 *N.Y. Times Mag.* 6 Jan. 10 The visitor to Europe may be..distressed by the down-beat mood of the people. *Ibid.* 16 Mar. 22 No type of film is more chancey..than the one that is loaded with misery and ends on a note of despair. .. Such pictures have, in recent years..been tagged 'down-beat' films. **1955** *N.Y. Herald-Tribune* 19 Sept., That pictorially memorable march up the twilit hill of a dusty Southern town has an inexplicably plodding and down-beat air about it. **1958** *Times* 9 May 13/7 The checks among the men continue in down-beat tones. **1958** *Observer* 30 Nov. 16/7 It [*sc.* a play] had a nice natural down-beat ending. **1966** *Listener* 20 Jan. 88/2 Two of Austria's three goals were from half-chances driven home like a bullet. A lot of the time they cruised with typical continental down-beat deliberation.

'down-calving, *a.* [f. DOWN *adv.* 37.] (See quot. 1886.)

1886 F. T. ELWORTHY *W. Somerset Word-Bk.* 205 *Down-calving*, in calf, and near the time of calving. (Very com.) 25 Down-calving cows and heifers.—Local advertisement of sale. **1931** *Daily Express* 15 Oct. 9/4 The Dilcock challenge cup for the best down calving cow. **1952** J. M. MURRAY *Community Farm* (1953) 47 We bought six down-calving shorthorn heifers.

downcast (daʊn'kɑːst, -æ-), *v.* Now only *poet.* [f. DOWN *adv.* + CAST *v.*] *trans.* To cast down (*lit.* and *fig.*); to overthrow, demolish; to deject, dispirit. Hence **down'casting** *vbl. sb.*

a **1300** *E.E. Psalter* lxxv. 6 In ax and in thixil þai it doun-caste. *c* **1425** *Found. St. Bartholomew's* (E.E.T.S.) 9 By a cruell downecastyng. *a* **1572** KNOX *Hist. Ref.* Wks. (1846) I. 341 For the..abolishment of idolatrie, and for downcasting the places of the same. **1724** *Wodrow Corr.* (1843) III. 120 The occasion of your downcastings. **1839** LONGF. *Mass for Dying Year* xii, The stars from heaven down-cast.

downcast ('daʊnkɑːst, -æ-), *sb.* [f. DOWN *adv.* + CAST *sb.*; cf. prec. vb.]

1. The act of casting down (*lit.* and *fig.*); overthrow, demolition, ruin; downward cast (of the eyes or look). **b.** *Geol.* = DOWNTHROW 2.

a **1300** *Cursor M.* 23721 (Cott.) Dame fortune turnes þan hir quele And castes vs dun..O þat dun-cast we mai wit chance Enentis þis werld get couerance. **1612** T. JAMES *Jesuits' Downf.* 11 Exaltation of themselues, and downecast of all that side not with them. **1723** STEELE *Consc. Lovers* II. i, I saw the respectful Downcast of his Eyes. **1819** REES *Cycl.*, *Downcast*, a term among Miners and Colliers for the sinking down of the measures or strata on one side of a fault. **1881** *Q. Rev.* July 102 Upliftings and downcasts of strata.

2. The throwing down of a current of air into a coal-mine, etc.; *attrib.* in *downcast shaft*, the shaft by which fresh air is introduced into a mine, also *ellipt.* called the *down-cast*.

1816 HOLMES *Coal-mines Durham, etc.* 78 Ventilation..is accomplished by means of a stream of air which descends the Downcast Shaft and passes through the workings until it finds the Upcast Shaft, through which it ascends. **1859** *Ann. Reg.* 43 Worked by a single shaft, for both the 'up-cast' and the 'down-cast'. **1880** J. LOMAS *Alkali Trade* 150 The heat and smoke are..drawn away to the chimney by means of the downcast. **1881** *19th Cent.* No. 48. 239.

downcast ('daʊnkɑːst, -æ-), *ppl. a.* [f. DOWN *adv.* + CAST *ppl. a.*; also as pa. pple. of DOWNCAST *v.*]

1. Cast down; ruined, destroyed; *fig.* dejected.

1602 MARSTON *Antonio's Rev.* v. vi. Wks. 1856 I. 143 The downe-cast ruines of calamitie. **1611** HEYWOOD *Gold. Age* III. i. Wks. 1874 III. 42 In the repairing of your downe-cast state. **1832** HT. MARTINEAU *Homes Abroad* iii. 43 A few looked downcast. **1849** GROTE *Greece* II. lx. V. 291 A downcast stupor and sense of abasement possessed every man.

2. Of looks, etc.: Directed downwards; dejected.

1633 G. HERBERT *Temple, Ch. Militant* 86 Where first the Church should raise her down-cast face. **1718** PRIOR *Power* 787 With downcast eyelids, and with looks aghast. **1868** FREEMAN *Norm. Conq.* (1876) II. viii. 166 With downcast eyes and bated breath.

Hence **'downcastness**.

*a*1851 MOIR *Sonn., Scot. Sabbath* ii, Your doubts to chase, your downcastness to cheer.

downcome ('daʊnkʌm), *sb.* [f. DOWN *adv.* + COME *v.*; cf. *income, outcome.*]

1. The act of coming down (*lit.* and *fig.*); descent, downfall; humiliation.

1513 DOUGLAS *Æneis* III. iv. 59 At douncom of thir Harpyis. **1594** SOUTHWELL *M. Magd. Fun. Teares* 101 Love's feares will stoope to the lowest downecome. **1641** MILTON *Reform.* I. (1851) 7 Like the sudden down-come of a Towre. **1815** SCOTT *Rob Roy* xix, It's a brave kirk..It had amaist a doun-come lang syne at the Reformation. **1877** MRS. OLIPHANT *Makers Flor.* iii. 79 That sense of downcome which is, of all sensations of poverty, the most hard to bear.

b. *Hawking.* A swoop down.

1575 TURBERV. *Faulconrie* 9 Making hir downecomme, and stouping from hir wings. **1674** N. COX *Gentl. Recreat.* II. (1677) 178 The Faulcon..hath a natural inclination and love to fly the Hern every way, either from her Wings to the down-come, or from the Fist and afore-head. **1698** FRYER *Acc. E. India & P.* 219 Tropick Birds..stooping to their Game..perform it at one down-come.

2. *Metallurgy.* (See quot.)

1881 RAYMOND *Mining Gloss., Downcome*, the pipe through which tunnel-head gases from iron blast-furnaces are brought down to the hot-blast stoves and boilers, when these are below the tunnel-head.

'down-comer. **a.** One who comes down. **b.** *techn.* A pipe or tube to convey water or gas downwards (cf. prec. 2).

1868 ATKINSON *Cleveland Gloss.* **1888** *Lockwood's Dict. Mech. Engin.* 115 *Down-comer*, or *down-take*, the vertical pipe which conducts the waste gases from the top of a close-mouthed blast furnace into the blast main. **1896** *Daily News* 20 Apr. 5/2 In the Yarrow boiler there are no outside downcomers. **1910** *Chambers's Jrnl.* Jan. 60/2 At the extremities of the two drums are large tubular connections, the uptake being at the front end (where the hottest temperatures prevail), and the downcomer outside the furnace at the rear end, which is practically cool. **1950** *Engineering* 30 June 722/2 Fed from the steam and water drum through downcomer tubes.

'down-coming, *vbl. sb.* A coming down, descent (*lit.* and *fig.*): = DOWNCOME *sb.* I.

1340 HAMPOLE *Pr. Consc.* 5271 At his doun commyng. **1676** W. ROW *Contn. Blair's Autobiog.* xii. (1848) 400 Before the bishops' downcoming. **1883** BESANT *All in Garden Fair* II. vi, A sad downcoming of his lofty aims.

'down-coming, *ppl. a.* Coming down or onwards.

1851 H. MELVILLE *Moby Dick* III. xlix. 308 Starbuck and Stubb, standing upon the bowsprit beneath, caught sight of the down-coming monster. **1865** *Harper's Mag.* July 167/2 They..reached a spot where they passed the downcoming train in safety. **1922** JOYCE *Ulysses* 427 He disappears into Olhousen's the pork butcher's, under the downcoming rollshutter. **1952** L. MACNEICE *Ten Burnt Offerings* 50 Dust of down-coming houses. **1968** G. M. B. DOBSON *Explor. Atmos.* (ed. 2) v. 107 The intensity of the down-coming, cosmic radiation increases with height.

'down-country, *sb., adv.*, and *a.* [DOWN *a.* and *prep.*]

The phrase, which is current in North America, New Zealand, South Africa, etc., is to be distinguished from *down-country* s.v. DOWN *sb.*[1] 6.

A. *sb.* The flat part of a country (as opposed to the hilly regions). In the United States: see quots. 1823 and *a* 1870.

1823 J. F. COOPER *Pioneers* v, To them the road that made the most rapid approaches to the condition of the old, or, as they expressed it, the down countries, was the most pleasant. *a***1870** R. M. CHIPMAN *Notes on Bartlett* 129 *Down-country*, used in the interior to denote on or toward the seaboard; occasionally, the seaboard, or the land nearer a river's mouth. **1904** 'G. B. LANCASTER' *Sons o' Men* 192 In the down-country. **1933** ACLAND in *Press* (Christchurch) 30 Sept. 15/7 *Down country*, used (chiefly by people in the hills) to describe the localities near town or on the plains. They also speak of *down country* people or sheep. **1940** E. C. STUDHOLME *Te Waimate* (1954) xiii. 113 At Waimate we ran cross-bred sheep on the down-country and Merinos or half-breds on the hills.

B. *adv.* In or to the flat part of a country; in or to the part of a country on the plains.

1874 A. BATHGATE *Colonial Experiences* x. 135 A dozen or more horses with their pack-saddles empty..were returning down country. **1879** W. J. BARRY *Up & Down* xxiv. 263, I sent her down-country in the coach. **1945** *N.Z. Geographer* I. I. 36 They can make a better 'do' of it than on a mixed farm down-country.

C. *adj.* Situated in, belonging to, or relating to the part of a country on the plains.

1896 H. A. BRYDEN *Tales S. Afr.* iii. 68 You know I don't ..spout tall yarns for the benefit of down-country folks or bar loafers at Kimberley. **1901** KIPLING *Kim* xiii. 353 Who ever heard of these Sahibs coming into the hills without a down-country cook? **1950** *N.Z. Jrnl. Agric.* Oct. 356/3 The breed of sheep on Gleneray [high-country sheep-run] is Romney type..and it is attractive to the down-country farmer when no longer suitable for the run.

down-draught ('daʊndrɑːft, -dræft).

1. **a.** A descending draught or current of air.

1849 CDL. WISEMAN *Sense v. Sc.* Ess. 1853 III. 603 How the north wind should always drive a down-draught..into the drawing-room. **1907** *Daily Chron.* 25 Oct. 8/5 It was maddening that these harsh down-draughts of the smoke should come to help the enemy. **1961** *Manch. Guardian* 4 Sept. 1/6 The sports plane was apparently caught by a down-draught.

b. *attrib.* or as *adj.* Designating a furnace, carburettor, etc., employing a downward draught of air or gas.

1906 T. MOORE *Handbk. Pract. Smithing & Forging* ii. 6 These down-draught hearths are now being adopted in many of the modern works. **1935** *Jrnl. R. Aeronaut. Soc.* XXXIX. 503 A centrifugal fan delivers compressed air to a Stromberg down-draught carburettor. **1959** *Chambers's Encycl.* VI. 130/2 Intermittent kilns may be of the rectangular or round down-draught type. **1959** *Motor Manual* (ed. 36) iii. 51 Carburetters may be updraught, horizontal or down-draught, according to the direction in which the main mixture stream is fed into the engine.

2. **a.** A down-dragging or depressing influence. *Sc.*

*c***1788** PICKEN *Twa Rats* Misc. Poems (1813) I. 68 (Jam.) We yield To nae downdraught but perfect eild. **1850** A. M'GILVRAY *Poems* 58 Wives, and wives' friends..are..a d——d down-draught, If they be poor.

b. A ne'er-do-well; a profligate. *dial.*

1835 *Aberdeen Shaver* Jan. 125 He is..nothing better than a down-draught, or *ne'er-do-weel.* **1849** C. BRONTË *Shirley* xxii, They were chiefly 'downdraughts', bankrupts, men always in debt and often in drink.

3. The drawing or displacing of water by an object as it sinks.

1899 F. T. BULLEN *Way Navy* 24 The down-draught of the anchor had sucked him after it almost to the bottom.

So **down-draw, down-drug.** *Sc.*

*c***1788** PICKEN *Misc. Poems* (1813) I. 79 (Jam.) Poortith's sair down-draw. **1814** *North. Antiq.* 429 (Jam.) Love in our hearts will wax..Thro' crosses and down-drug.

downe, obs. f. DOWN, *done* (see DO *v.*).

downed (daʊnd), *a.* [f. DOWN *v.*[1] or DOWN *sb.*[2] + -ED[2].] Covered or lined with down.

1901 *Westm. Gaz.* 14 May 2/3 The goose has..been sitting comfortably on a downed nest. **1939** DYLAN THOMAS *Map of Love* 22 If my head hurt a hair's foot Pack back the downed bone.

downer ('daʊnə(r)). **1.** Colloq. var. DOWN *sb.*[3] 5.

1915 C. MACKENZIE *Guy & Pauline* i. 46, I knows better than go for to contradict him when he gets a downer on any plant. **1936** S. SASSOON *Sherston's Prog.* III. 224 He asserted that I'd got 'a downer' on some N.C.O.

2. *slang.* **a.** A drug (esp. a barbiturate) that has a depressant or tranquillizing effect. Cf. UPPER *sb.*[2] 1.

1966 *Observer* 25 Sept. 21/6 You know what the young take now? They take 'downers'. They want to feel depressed! **1969** FABIAN & BYRNE *Groupie* (1970) xi. 80, I asked him to describe the kind of pill he had taken, and realized from the description that he had taken a downer instead of a keep-awake. **1971** *Last Whole Earth Catal.* 97/3 Estelle had dosed herself heavily on downers. **1973** D. LANG *Freaks* xxvii. 94 None of us touched any psychedelics. It was just grass, hash, and opium, with some recourse to downers, especially valium, when one was too exhausted from doing nothing to be able to sleep. **1977** *Rolling Stone* 30 June 81/3 I'd already ingested the downers which would very quickly be taking me into dreamy nether regions. **1983** *Daily Tel.* 10 Nov. 15/6 Those that shoot dope are soon stoned and on the habit, junkies liable to write their own scripts and thieve your downers and perhaps your chinky.

b. *fig.* A depressing person or experience; a failure; a downward trend, esp. in business or the economy. Cf. UPPER *sb.*[2] 2. orig. *U.S.*

1970 *Harper's Mag.* Mar. 69/1 Depressing people were 'downers'. **1970** *Melody Maker* 12 Sept. 29 *A downer*, a depressing experience. **1971** *Oz* May 6/1 When I was in gaol they cut my hair, and that really was a downer. For four or five days I couldn't eat or sleep. I couldn't do nothing. **1975** *New Yorker* 19 May 114/2 The 'Giselle' is a downer, too, longer and slower than ever, but at least it isn't marred by witless novelty. **1976** *Forbes* (N.Y.) 1 Jan. 178/1 In the case of both the uppers and the downers, it would be a good idea to examine the companies more closely to see how meaningful these one-year trends are. **1977** *Business Week* 21 Nov. 119 The general market swoon could fall still more during the usual late-December sell-off, when investors are converting their downers to tax losses. **1982** T. BARR *Acting for Camera* III. xxii. 154 The role of a downer should not be a downer to watch.

downface, *v.* [DOWN *adv.*] *trans.* To contradict, controvert; to browbeat; to outsmart; = *to face down* (see FACE *v.* 3a). (Cf. *down-faced* s.v. DOWN *adv.* 42).

1909 G. B. SHAW *Press Cuttings* 1 She downfaces us that youve got the key of the padlock in a letter. **1922** JOYCE *Ulysses* 323 He'd try to downface you that dying was living. **1929** ST. JOHN ERVINE *First Mrs. Fraser* III. 78 A flabby sort of a fellow that lets himself be downfaced by adversity. **1938** E. BOWEN *Death of Heart* II. ii. 202 Daphne's person was sexy, her conversation irreproachably chaste. She would downface any remark by saying 'You *are* awful,' or simply using her eyes.

downfall ('daʊnfɔːl).

1. The act of falling down; sudden descent.

1450-1530 *Myrr. our Ladye* 298 The sonne knowyng no downe falle. **1594** T. B. *La Primaud. Fr. Acad.* II. 493 Those that..runne on swiftly whither they please, without feare of downe falles. **1674** N. COX *Gentl. Recreat.* II. (1677) 213 If she [the hawk] miss at the first down-fall and kill not. **1710** ADDISON *Whig Exam.* No. 2 (Seager), I never met so sudden a downfal in so promising a sentence. **1842** TENNYSON *St. Sim. Styl.* 108 'Tween the spring and down-fall of the light.

b. A fall (of water, rain, snow, etc.).

1603 KNOLLES *Hist. Turks* (1638) 31 The riuer Melas..in Winter or any other great downefall of water..right suddenly ouerfloweth his bankes. **1867** SMYTH *Sailor's Word-bk., Downfalls*, the descending waters of rivers and creeks. **1870** E. PEACOCK *Ralf Skirl.* III. 17 The weatherwise..said there would soon be 'downfall;' but no rain came.

†**2.** A steep descent, precipice; an abyss, gulf, pit. *Obs.*

1542 UDALL *Erasm. Apoph.* (1877) 151 Rockes of a down-right pitche, or a stiepe down fall. **1586** T. B. *La Primaud. Fr. Acad.* I. (1589) 231 Beware thou tumble not into some downefall. **1594** CAREW *Huarte's Exam. Wits* v. (1596) 67 These..delight to walke..thorow dangerous and high places, and to approch neere steepe down-fals. **1691** DRYDEN *K. Arthur* II. i. Wks. 1884 VIII. 153 Dreadfull downfalls of unheeded rocks. **1822** HOGG *Perils of Man* I. 63 A bit downfa' to the south.

3. Fall from high estate, ruin. (The current use.)

*a***1300** *Cursor M.* 11362 (Cott.) þis child..sal be to fel men in dun fall, And to fell in vprising. **1593** SHAKS. *3 Hen. VI*, v. vi. 64 Those that wish the downfall of our house. **1667** MILTON *P.L.* I. 116 That were an ignominy and shame beneath This downfall. **1750** JOHNSON *Rambler* No. 60 ¶2 Histories of the downfal of kingdoms. **1824** W. IRVING *T. Trav.* II. 3 The downfall of his great expectations.

†**b.** *concr.* (*pl.*) Ruins, debris. *Obs.*

1602 WARNER *Alb. Eng.* XII. lxxiii. (1612) 301 On Auentine the down-fals are of Temples store to see.

4. Something constructed on purpose to fall down.

1856 C. J. ANDERSSON *Lake Ngami* 528 To destroy the hippopotamus..by means of the downfall..consisting of a log of wood.

5. *attrib.* Falling down, descending.

1793 SMEATON *Edystone L.* §275 Protecting it..from the entrance of the downfall spray. **1807** VANCOUVER *Agric. Devon* (1813) 285 By these drains the downfall waters would immediately escape.

'down-fallen, *ppl. a.* Also 7 -fall. Fallen to the ground, or from a high estate.

1596 SHAKS. *1 Hen. IV*, I. iii. 135 The downfall [*mod. ed.* -fallen] Mortimer. **1602** CAREW *Cornwall* (J.) The land is now divorced by the downfallen steepy cliffs on the farther side. **1605** SHAKS. *Macb.* IV. iii. 4 Let vs..Bestride our downfall [*mod. edd.* -fallen] Birth-dome. **1784** COWPER *Task* VI. 144 His foe's down-fallen beast. **1817** MOORE *Lalla R., Veiled Proph.* (1854) 82 Their down-fall'n Chief.

'downfalling, *vbl. sb.* The act of falling down; downfall; †setting.

*a***1300** *E.E. Psalter* li. 6 þou loved alle wordes of doun fallinge [L. *praecipitationis*]. **1340** HAMPOLE *Pr. Consc.* 6576 Hate teres of gretyng, That the synful sal scalden in the dounfallyng. **1536** BELLENDEN *Cron. Scot.* (1821) II. 331 Ane [comet] schane ay afore the sonne-rising, and this other afore his downfalling. **1826** E. IRVING *Babylon* II. VI. 97 He sent..Jeremiah..before the downfalling of destruction.

'downfalling, *ppl. a.* Falling down; also *fig.* declining, decaying.

[*a***1300** *E.E. Psalter* xvii. 9 Koles þat ware doun falland Kindled ere of him glouand.] **1590** C. S. *Right Religion* 14 The downfalling pride of the Pope. **1659** D. PELL *Impr. Sea* 408 The Seamans high soaring *sursums*, and his down-falling *deorsums*. **1886** A. WINCHELL *Geol. Field* 60 A downfalling mass of vapour.

†**down-flat,** *a.* [cf. FLAT *a.* 6.] Downright.

1664 H. CARY *Marriage Night* III. i. in Hazl. *Dodsley* XV. 140 This is a down-flat challenge.

'downfold. *Geol.* A synclinal fold or depression. So **'down-folded** *a.*, (of strata) dipping on each side towards a common axis.

1902 H. J. MACKINDER *Britain & Brit. Seas* vi. 71 To the very top it consists of down-folded beds. *Ibid.* 80 Geographical valley and geological downfold here coincide with a precision that is rare. **1920** *Glasgow Herald* 15 Oct. 7 The oil did not come from the arches or anticlines, but from the down folds, (synclines). **1954** J. F. KIRKALDY *Gen. Princ. Geol.* ii. 25 Stratified rocks..are often seen to be folded into upfolds (anticlines) and downfolds (synclines). **1970** *Sci. Amer.* Feb. 37/2 The blocks of faulted crust in the lower part of the escarpment are tilted..in the direction opposite to what would be expected in a downfold.

†**'downgate.** *Obs.* [f. DOWN *adv.* + GATE, going.] Going down, descent, setting.

*c***1400** tr. *Secreta Secret., Gov. Lordsh.* (E.E.T.S.) 89 To þe doungate of þe sonne. **1555** WATREMAN *Fardle Facions* I. iv. 43 Certeine of theim worshippe the Sonne at his vprijste, and curse him moste bittrely at his doune gate.

downgeowne, obs. form of DUNGEON.

down-glide. *Phonetics.* A downward glide (see GLIDE *sb.* 4).

1930 H. KURATH in J. T. Hatfield et al. *Curme Vol. Linguistic Studies* 94 The up-glides and down-glides of the voice. **1932** G. E. FUHRKEN *Standard Eng. Speech* xvi. 111 In *that's his son* the down-glide coincides with the end-consonant in *son.* **1965** *Language* XLI. 475 In stressed ballistic syllables the tones high, mid, and low are actualized as rapid downglides.

down grade, down-grade, *sb.* orig. *U.S.* [see GRADE.] *lit.* A downward gradient, a descending slope (on a railway, etc.); hence *fig.* A downward course or tendency in morals, religion, etc. Also *attrib.* and as *adv.*

1858 *Harper's Weekly* 31 July 483 A train thunders along a down-grade. **1872** 'MARK TWAIN' *Roughing It* xvii. 141 A 'down grade', a flying coach, a fragrant pipe and a contented heart—these make happiness. **1872** *Newton Kansan* 19 Sept. 4/3 Greeleyism has struck the down grade. **1876** J. MILLER *Life amongst Modocs* vi. 76 He [*sc.* the stage-driver].. said:—'Boys, I am on the down grade, and can't reach the brake!' and sank down and died. And so it is that 'the down grade', an expression born of the death of the old stage-driver, has a meaning with us now. **1878** B. F. TAYLOR *Between Gates* 13 The down grade has begun. Let the engines take breath. **1885** *Harper's Mag.* Apr. 690/2 The train keeps on its rapid down-grade run. **1887** SPURGEON (*title*) Four Articles on the Down-Grade. **1888** *Pall Mall G.* 24 Apr. 11/1 The Baptist Union..both parties in the 'down-grade controversy' having marshalled their forces. **1890** *Daily News* 8 Dec. 2/1. **1895** *Westm. Gaz.* 19 Apr. 3/2 A study in the down-grade of a village girl from seduction..to prostitution. **1901** MERWIN & WEBSTER *Calumet 'K'* xi. 199 They'd all strike like a freight train rolling down grade.

down-grade, *v.* [f. the sb.] *trans.* To lower in grade, rank, status, estimation, or the like. So **down-grading** *vbl. sb.*

1930 *Sunday Times* 12 Oct. 18/4 No further down-grading of London schools should take place until the basic principles of grading have been considered. **1944** *Labor Herald* (San Francisco) 8 Dec. 6 Aircraft union join to fight downgrading pay cut drive. **1953** A. BARON *Human Kind* 97 There was a medical examination at which he was down-graded. **1955** *Times* 27 Aug. 6/6 The dispute arose from a wartime agreement under which some N.U.R. wagon shop men were upgraded to fitters. Because of the redundancy of 15 fitters, the local branch of the Amalgamated Engineering Union claimed that the N.U.R. men should be downgraded once more. **1958** *Times Lit. Suppl.* 14 Feb. 89/3 A Pordenone has been downgraded to an Amalteo. **1959** G. D. MITCHELL *Sociology* vii. 120 Non-manual employees whose subjective status is working class..have down-graded other non-manual occupations to their own estimation. **1964** F. BOWERS *Bibliogr. & Textual Criticism* v. iii. 147 A corresponding down-grading of the Folio must be made. **1969** *Times* 24 Feb. 12/5 A scientific committee.. recommended that the manned flight activities should be downgraded because they 'exaggerated' one aspect of space activity.

†**down-gyved,** *ppl. a. Obs. rare.*$^{-1}$. [f. DOWN *adv.* IX. + GYVE.] Explained by Steevens as meaning 'Hanging down like the loose cincture which confines fetters round the ancles.'

1602 SHAKS. *Ham.* II. i. 80 His stockings foul'd, Vngartred, and downe giued to his Anckle.

'downhaul (-hɔːl). *Naut.* [f. DOWN *adv.* + HAUL *v.*] (See quot. 1867.)

1669 STURMY *Mariner's Mag.* 17 All down upon your doone hall. **1727** SWIFT *Gulliver* II. i, We belayed the fore downhaul. **1840** R. H. DANA *Bef. Mast* v. 11, I..sprang forward, threw the downhaul over the windlass. **1867** SMYTH *Sailor's Word-bk., Down-haul*, a rope passing up..to the upper corner of the sail to pull it down when shortening sail. Also..to the outer yard-arms of studding-sails, to take them in securely.

b. *attrib.* ***downhaul tackle*** (see quot. 1867).

1762 FALCONER *Shipwr.* II. 319 Below the down-haul tackle others ply. **1867** SMYTH *Sailor's Word-bk., Down-haul tackles*, employed when lower yards are struck to.. prevent them from swaying about after the trusses are unrove.

†**'downhauler.** *Naut. Obs.* = prec.

1794 *Rigging & Seamanship* I. 85 The higher studding-sails..are drawn down to be furled or reefed by down-haulers. *Ibid.* 165 *Downhauler*, A rope which hoists down the stay-sails, studding-sails, and boom-sails, to shorten sail.

downhearted (-hɑːtɪd), *a.* Having the heart 'down' (see DOWN *adv.* 18); discouraged, low-spirited. ('A colloquial word.' Todd 1818.)

a **1774** GOLDSM. *Ess.* (L.), Come, my good fellow, don't be downhearted; cheer up. **1860** RUSKIN in Anne Ritchie *Rec. Tennyson, etc.* 29 Sept. (1892) 136, I am very glad to have your letter..having been downhearted lately. **1869** GOULBURN *Purs. Holiness* xxi. 199 To console many a down-hearted Christian.

Hence **down'heartedly** *adv.*; also **down-'heartedness.**

1655 GURNALL *Chr. in Arm.* Introd. v. (1669) 174, I..find it come off as weakly and down-heartedly as before. *a* **1863** THACKERAY *Haggarty's Wife* (1887) 281 His down-heartedness..surprised..his acquaintances.

†**down'held.** *Obs.* In 4 dun-, doun-, etc., -helde, -heild. [f. HELD *sb.*, slope.] A downward slope, declivity, decline, descent (*lit.* and *fig.*).

a **1300** *Cursor M.* 3822 (Cott.) Jacob..sagh þe well be a doun heild. *Ibid.* 5468 Negh seuen score yeir of eld Was þis iacob at his don heild [*Fairf.* atte his doun helde]. *Ibid.* 6431 þe sun was at dun heild [*Trin.* doun helde].

downhill (see below) *sb.*, *adv.*, and *a.*

A. *sb.* ('daʊnhɪl). [f. DOWN *adv.*]

1. The downward slope of a hill; a decline, declivity, descent (*lit.* and *fig.*).

1591 SYLVESTER *Du Bartas* I. ii. 39 Th' Icie down-Hils of this slippery Life. **1607** TOPSELL *Four-f. Beasts* (1658) 107 Some on horseback, other on foot, follow the cry..neither fearing thornes, woods, down-hils. **1795** BURKE *Regic. Peace* iv. Wks. IX. 119 It is not possible that the downhill should not be slid into. **1853** W. JERDAN *Autobiog.* III. xiv. 207 To cheer and solace the downhill of life.

†**2.** *slang.* (*pl.*) False dice which run on the low numbers. *Obs.*

a **1700** B. E. *Dict. Cant. Crew, Down-hills*, Dice that run low. **1801** *Sporting Mag.* XVIII. 100.

3. In Skiing: a downhill race.

1960 *Times* 22 Jan. 16/3 The British women's ski running championships began here to-day with the downhill.

B. *adv.* (daʊn'hɪl). [f. DOWN *prep.*] Down the slope of a hill; in a descending direction; on a decline; down-wards (*lit.* and *fig.*).

1659 *Burton's Diary* (1828) IV. 348 Whether it be up-hill or down-hill. **1719** DE FOE *Crusoe* I. xiv, A very short cut, and all down-hill. **1795** LD. AUCKLAND *Corr.* (1862) III. 313 They are going downhill..a well-concerted opposition will end the business. **1871** SMILES *Charac.* i. (1876) 17 They broke through the French and sent them flying downhill.

C. *adj.* ('daʊnhɪl). Sloping or descending downwards; declining. (Also *fig.*)

1727 POPE, etc. *Art of Sinking* 71 The gentle down-hill way to the *bathos*. *a* **1729** CONGREVE (J.), A downhill greensward. **1782** COWPER *Lett.* 11 Nov., The down-hill side of life. **1856** FROUDE *Hist. Eng.* II. 408 The monks had travelled swiftly on the downhill road of human corruption.

'downily, *adv. rare.* [f. DOWNY + -LY[2].] In a downy manner; like down or fluff.

1835 *Blackw. Mag.* XXXVIII. 639 We have detected particles of nutmeg reposing downily on the surface.

downiness ('daʊnɪnɪs). [f. DOWNY + -NESS.] The condition or quality of being downy; a downy growth or substance.

1670 W. SIMPSON *Hydrol. Ess.* 14 Vapours arise out of the iron which turn into a downiness. **1695** H. SAMPSON in *Phil. Trans.* XIX. 80 A Downyness upon her chin, unusual with those of her Sex. **1708** *Brit. Apollo* No. 88 2/1 A Hoary kind of Downyness. **1855** BROWNING *Men & Wom., Respectability*, Your lip's contour and downiness.

Downing Street. [Named after Sir George *Downing* (*c* 1624–1684), British diplomat.] A short street in London running out of Whitehall towards St. James's Park and containing the Foreign Office and the official residence (No. 10) of the prime minister; hence used as a synonym for the Government (or the prime minister, or Foreign Office) of the day.

1781 A. STORER *Let.* 1 Mar. in *15th Rep. Hist. MSS. Comm.* (1897) App. VI. 467 Even though Lord North reject my application, or neglect the good-natured interference of those friends, who..have no small weight in Downing Street. **1831** LD. PALMERSTON *Let.* 1 Mar. in H. L. Bulwer *Palmerston* (1870) II. viii. 48 The French..need not wish to have truer or warmer friends than they now have in Downing Street. **1849** THACKERAY *Pendennis* I. xxxi. 308 Look! here comes the Foreign Express galloping in. They will be able to give news to Downing Street to-morrow. **1858** *Leisure Hour* 18 Nov. 728/1 The decrees and counsels of Downing Street will be heard simultaneously in Pekin or Canton. **1920** K. JONES *Fleet St. & Downing St.* 330 Thus would Fleet Street and Downing Street at last understand one another. **1920** E. H. BEGBIE *Mirrors of Downing St.* 7 The private opposition he [*sc.* Lloyd George] encountered in Downing Street. **1971** B. GRAHAM *Spy Trap* xvi. 112 Dmitrov..instructed him to watch for a memorandum from Downing Street.

downione, obs. form of DUNGEON.

†**'downish,** *a. Obs.* [f. DOWN *a.* + -ISH.] Somewhat dejected or directed downward.

1677 *Lond. Gaz.* No. 1177/4 One Booke Bookey, of a middle stature..full fac'd, of a downish look. **1710** in *Ballard MSS.* XXXVI. No. 24 The Whigs are very downish here upon the late changes.

downk(e, obs. form of DANK.

'downland[1]. [f. DOWN *sb.*[1]; cf. OE. *dúnland.*] Land forming downs; hilly pasture-land.

[*c* **1000** ÆLFRIC *Deut.* i. 7 Feld landum & dun landum.] **1842** *Penny Cycl.* XXIII. 343/2 There are also about 50,000 acres of down-land. **1884** W. J. COURTHOPE *Addison* ii. 27 Salisbury Plain, with..its open tracts of undulating downland.

'downland[2]. [Cf. *upland.*] Land lying low, or sloping downwards; in quot. *attrib.*

1839 STONEHOUSE *Axholme* 399 Descending the downland lawns.

down lead. *Radio.* [DOWN *adv.* 41.] A wire that connects an elevated aerial or part of an aerial to a receiver or transmitter; a lead-in.

1913 *Work* 23 Aug. 413/2 The aerial..should be at least 100 ft. to 150 ft., including down leads. **1925** *Harmsworth's Wireless Encycl.* 729/1 Where the down lead enters the house care must be taken to secure perfect insulation. **1952** E. A. LAPORT *Radio Antenna Engin.* i. 38 The antenna consists of a large elevated capacitance area with two or more down leads that are tuned individually.

downless ('daʊnlɪs), *a.* [f. DOWN *sb.*[2] + -LESS.] Without down.

1598 MARLOWE & CHAPMAN *Hero & L.* v. 45 The downless rosy faces Of youths and maids. **1796** WITHERING *Brit. Plants* (ed. 3) III. 222 Doronicum..seeds of the circumference down-less and naked. **1872** J. C. JEAFFRESON *Woman in spite of Herself* I. I. iv. 59 As downless and smooth-faced as any girl of eighteen summers.

down-lie (-'laɪ), *v.* To lie down, go to bed, retire to rest. (Chiefly in pres. pple. **down-lying.**)

1526 *Pilgr. Perf.* (W. de W. 1531) 88 b, Prayer is moche necessary at all tymes, bothe vprysynge and downlyenge. *c* **1550** *Decay Eng. By Shepe* (E.E.T.S.) 98 To kepe vj. persons, downe lyinge and vprisynge in hys house. *a* **1628** PRESTON *Serm. bef. his Majestie* (1630) 74 There are so many uprising & down-lying, that must have bread and meate from day to day.

Hence **'down-lying** *vbl. sb.* (*a*) Lying down, going to bed; taking of permanent quarters. (*b*) Lying-in of a woman, confinement. (*north. dial.*)

1535 *Goodly Primer* Ps. cxxxix, My ingoing and down-lying to sleep. **1603** FLORIO *Montaigne* I. xxv. (1632) 82 What they go withall is but a conceiving, and therefore nothing neere downlying. **1637** R. MONRO *Expedit.* II. 16 What hurt the enemy was able to have done us, before our down-lying. **1848** MRS. GASKELL *M. Barton* ix, She expected her down-lying every day. **1855** ROBINSON *Whitby Gloss., Down-ligging time.*

download ('daʊnləʊd), *sb. Computing.* [f. DOWN *adv.* + LOAD *sb.*] The action or process of downloading.

1977 *Sci. Amer.* Sept. 160/1 Changes at this stage are readily achieved by a simple process of re-edit, assemble and download. **1985** *Personal Computer World* Feb. 122/1 The feature which will appeal to most telecommunications people..is the download and upload routine.

download (daʊn'ləʊd, 'daʊn-), *v. Computing.* [f. DOWN *adv.* + LOAD *v.*] *trans.* To transfer (esp. software) from the storage of a larger system to that of a smaller one.

1980 *Electronic Design* 4 Jan. 167/2 These programs are downloaded into the Microsystem Analyzer for debug and execution. **1982** *Which Computer?* June 25/3 The existing software..will be down-loaded onto the new machine. **1983** *Austral. Microcomputer Mag.* Aug. 71/1 Micromagic.. allows IBM PC users to download data from IP Sharp's online databases to the PC's files in VisiCalc format. **1984** *Daily Tel.* 9 Jan. 9/2 MicroNet 800..offers several hundred programs that can be downloaded to a home computer over an ordinary telephone line. **1986** *Sci. Amer.* Feb. 15/1 Using chess knowledge (downloaded from the oracle) relevant to the current position, the module evaluates each board.

Hence **down'loading** *vbl. sb.*; also **down'loadable** *a.*

1982 *Information Services & Use* I. 334 Quite a few online user institutions were also using a variety of means for 'downloading', on either tape or disk. **1982** *What's New in Computing* Nov. 50/4 Plain language keyboard instructions may be used to compile any application program in rom for subsequent down loading onto disc or a..cassette recorder. **1983** *Austral. Microcomputer Mag.* Dec. 110/2 Key features of the WY-300 are..extensive alphanumeric and line drawing symbols; soft downloadable character generator. **1985** *Personal Computer World* Feb. 48 (Advt.), The units stack on top of each other to provide..downloadable software and access to the international PSS network and databases such as Prestel and Micronet 800.

downlong, *prep.* and *a.* [app. coined by W. Morris; cf. *headlong.*] **A.** *prep.* Down along. **B.** *adj.* Rushing down headlong.

1876 MORRIS *Sigurd* II. 91 The rush and rattle of waters, as the downlong flood swept by. **1895** —— *Beowulf* 21 But me the sea upbore The flood downlong the tide.

†**'downlooked** (-lʊkt), *a. Obs.* [f. *down-look* see DOWN *a.* 1 b.] Having downward or downcast looks; guilty-looking; demure, sheepish.

1641 BROME *Joviall Crew* II. Wks. 1873 III. 384, I never lik'd such demure down-look'd Fellows. **1677** *Lond. Gaz.* No. 1230/4 A middle size black man, having short black brown lank hair..down-look'd. *a* **1700** B. E. *Dict. Cant. Crew, Blank*, baffled, down-look't, sheepish, guilty. **1700** DRYDEN *Palamon & Arc.* II. 489 Jealousy..Downlook'd, and with a cuckow on her fist. **1814** SCOTT *Ld. of Isles* III. xix, Men..of evil mien, Down-look'd, unwilling to be seen.

'downlooking (-lʊkɪŋ), *a.* That looks down.

1788 *Maryland Jrnl.* 9 May (Th.), Lindsey, a down-looking fellow, had on a new flaxen shirt. **1800** *Aurora* (Philad.) 23 July, A number of sneaking down-looking fellows, who occasionally assembled in a group. **1823** SCOTT *Quentin D.* ii, A..middle sized man with a down-looking visage. **1842** MRS. BROWNING *Grk. Chr. Poets* 12 Wilhelm Meister's uplooking and downlooking aspects, the reverence to things above and things below. **1881** MISS YONGE *Lads & Lasses Langley* ii. 120 The rude, clumsy, stupid, down-looking fellow he had been.

downlying: see DOWN-LIE.

down-market (stress variable), *a.* and *adv.* [DOWN *prep.*; see UP-MARKET *a.* and *adv.*]

A. *adj.* Of or relating to the cheaper end of the market; cheap, popular. Also *transf.* and *fig.*

1970 *Times* 12 May 11/6 It really is..cheering that Courtaulds, who have always seemed so determinedly down-market in their approach..should wake up to the fact that good design is..essential. **1978** *Observer* 16 Apr. 38/1 This was the down-market end of the tremendous business in antiques. **1979** J. COOPER *Class* vii. 121 Upper-class girls ..taking on a string of down-market lovers: lorry drivers one year, Negroes the next, and beards the year after that. **1983** *Economist* 2 July 66/3 Kaufhof looks like remaining the most downmarket of West Germany's stores.

B. *adv.* Towards the cheaper end of the market.

1973 *Listener* 27 Dec. 875 Readers who have asked about the matter can be told that there is no reason to believe the paper will move 'down-market' in search of popularity. **1980** *Jrnl. R. Soc. Arts* May 330/1 Some companies would claim that their particular market does not wish to buy what we might call the best design, but wants something down market. **1984** *Listener* 2 Feb. 10/2 The privatisation of the BBC and the race down-market of ITV would then be a foregone conclusion.

downmost ('daʊnməʊst), *adv.* and *a.* Also *dial.* **downermost**: cf. the obs. comparative *downermore*: see DOWN *adv.* VIII.

1790 BLAGDEN in *Phil. Trans.* LXXX. 342 So poised as that a certain part should be always downmost. **1822** COLERIDGE *Lett., Convers., etc.* II. 92 Set the jewel in the marriage ring with the speck downmost. **1849** CARLISLE in *Eng. Hist. Rev.* (1886) I. 333 The early or downmost part of the sheets had mouldered. **1879** GEO. ELIOT *Theo. Such* 307 A fowl tied head downmost.

downness (ˈdaʊnnɪs). *rare.* [f. DOWN *a.* + -NESS.] The fact or condition of being down; lowness.

1890 W. JAMES *Princ. Psychol.* II. xx. 150 Rightness and leftness, upness and downness, are again pure sensations differing specifically from each other, and generically from everything else. **1927** *Scots Observer* 1 Oct. 2/2 A friend who positively finds his happiness in responding to human downness.

down pipe, downpipe. [DOWN *a.* 1 a.] A pipe leading downward; *spec.* a pipe to carry rain-water from a roof to a drain.

1858 *Advt.* in *Skyring's Builders' Prices*, Eaves gutters and down pipe. **1904** GOODCHILD & TWENEY *Technol. & Sci. Dict.* 172/2 *Downpipe*, a rainwater pipe. **1960** *Times* 1 Aug. 10/1 Even the gutters and downpipes are of copper. **1962** *Which?* (Car Suppl.) Oct. 139/2 Connection between exhaust manifold and down pipe [was] found to be slack. **1970** *Globe & Mail* (Toronto) 28 Sept. 24/3 (Advt.), Aluminum eaves, downpipes and upper facings.

down'play, *v.* orig. *U.S.* Also **down-play.** [DOWN *adv.*: see PLAY *v.* 38.] *trans.* To minimize or make little of (a problem, rumour, etc.); to de-emphasize or play down.

1968 *N.Y. Rev. Bks.* 25 Apr. 34/3 Their chief tended to downplay the report of heavy damage. **1976** *National Observer* (U.S.) 16 Oct. 10/3 ABC has downplayed hard news for generous portions of slickness and show biz. **1977** *Rolling Stone* 24 Mar. 66/3 For the most part, vocals are down-played. **1978** R. STEVENS *Law & Politics* 103 The incredible political pressures under which he lived..caused him to neglect or at least downplay the importance of his judicial duties. **1980** I. HUNTER *Malcolm Muggeridge* v. 85 The *Guardian* drastically cut and downplayed the story. **1985** *Times* 14 Jan. 9/1 This is to..down-play the sincerity of the endorsement given him [*sc.* President Reagan] and his policies by American voters.

down-point, *v.* [f. DOWN *adv.* + POINT *sb.*[1]] *trans.* To lower the value in points of (something rationed). So **down-pointing** *vbl. sb.*

1946 *News Chron.* 5 Mar. 1 The trade would welcome the downpointing of women's coats and costumes. **1947** *Sunday Express* 7 Dec., Unless the Board of Trade downpoint the garments, hundreds of thousands of them will be left in warehouses. **1948** *Times* 26 May 4/3 Sheets over 81 in...in width will be down pointed from seven to six coupons each.

'downpour (-pɔə(r)), *sb.* A pouring down; *esp.* a heavy, continuous fall (of rain, etc.).

1811 *Agric. Survey Hebrides* 741 (Jam.) A down-pour which had persevered in deluging the island for a week. **1859** R. F. BURTON *Centr. Afr.* in *Jrnl. Geog. Soc.* XXIX. 141 The downpour is desultory and uncertain, causing frequent droughts and famine. **1872** PROCTOR *Ess. Astron.* xi. 151 A systematic and continuous downpour of missiles.

down-range, downrange, *adv.* Chiefly *U.S.* [DOWN *prep.* 3.] In a position along the course of a missile, space-vehicle, or the like. Also *attrib.*, designating a station or observation-point thus placed.

1952 *N.Y. Times* 9 Mar. 4/1 'Down-range' stations at Jupiter Inlet on the Florida coast and on Grand Bahama Island already provide instrumentation 200 miles from the missile launching sites on Cape Canaveral. **1953** *Monsanto Mag.* July 3 They seized upon the light house as a reference point. From it they worked 'down range' to establish a series of stations from which to observe the flight of missiles. *Ibid.*, A typical down range station is a little electronic city set up to track missiles, predict weather, receive telemetry signals from missiles. **1962** G. COOPER in *Into Orbit* 28 We had already worked out rescue and recovery procedures for picking up the Astronaut down-range. **1966** *Times* 28 Feb. (Canada Suppl.) p. xii/3 Some experts believe it can fire a projectile 160 miles downrange.

downright (daʊnˈraɪt, ˈdaʊnraɪt), *adv.*, *a.*, and *sb.* [f. DOWN *adv.* + RIGHT *a.* and *adv.*, in OE. *riht, rihte*: cf. ADOWNRIGHT.]

A. *adv.* (Stressed '*downright* when preceding the word it qualifies, *down'right* when following.)

†1. Straight down; vertically downwards. *Obs.*

c **1205** LAY. 25613 Þe drake..flah dun rihte, mid feondliche ræsen. *c* **1320** *Seuyn Sag.* (W.) 621 The elde tre ..Hewe him to the grounde dounright. **1426** AUDELAY *Poems* 23 He fel downe ryȝt into hel sodenly. **1538** H. MEDWALL *Nature* (1896) 40 Some shote sydelong and some down ryght. **1674** RAY *Notes Husb.* 129 That part of the root, which descends down-right. **1728** POPE *Dunc.* II. 288 He..Shot to the black abyss, and plung'd downright. **1763** *Brit. Mag.* IV. 554 Several..were seen to sink downright, by some people who were on the cliffs.

2. Thoroughly, absolutely, quite, positively, out and out, outright.

a **1300** *E.E. Psalter* cv. 18 Þe lowe it swath sinful dounright. **1377** LANGL. *P. Pl.* B. XVIII. 191 God gaf þe dome..þat Adam & Eue..Shulde deye doune riȝte. **1480** CAXTON *Chron. Eng.* ccxlvii. (1482) 314 Scottes that day were slayne doune right the substaunce of them alle. **1588** SHAKS. *L.L.L.* IV. i. 389 They'l mocke vs now downe-right. **1664** H. MORE *Myst. Iniq.*, *Apol.* 562 Unless you were down-right mad. **1724** R. FALCONER *Voy.* (1769) 141 Killed four downright, and wounded several. **1832** HT. MARTINEAU *Homes Abroad* v. 66, I was downright scared.

†3. In a direct or straightforward manner; plainly, definitely. *Obs.*

1600 SHAKS. *A.Y.L.* III. iv. 31 You haue heard him sweare downright he was. **1680** OTWAY *Caius Marius* IV. i, An honest, simple, downright-dealing Lord. **1684** T. BURNET *Th. Earth* II. 131 St. Peter..uses a plain literal style, and discourses down-right concerning the natural world.

†4. Straightway, straight. *Obs.*

1647 H. MORE *Song of Soul* II. ii. I. iii, The soul that I.. Must now pursue and fall upon downe-right. **1712** ARBUTHNOT *John Bull* II. iii, This paper put Mrs. Bull in such a passion that she fell down right into a fit.

B. *adj.* (Usually stressed '*downright*; but sometimes *down'right* at the end of a clause.)

1. Directed straight downwards; vertical; directly descending.

1530 PALSGR. 215/1 Downeright stroke, *taille.* **1578** LYTE *Dodoens* V. xiv. 566 This Hawkweede hath no deepe downeright roote. **1593** SHAKS. *2 Hen. VI*, II. iii. 92 Haue at thee with a downe-right blow. **1621** G. SANDYS *Ovid's Met.* II. (1626) 225 To iump from downe-right cliffes. **1684** BUNYAN *Pilgr.* II. 71 He gave him again a down-right blow, and brought him upon his knees. **1759** *Phil. Trans.* LI. 299 Its motion was..quite downright, i.e. perpendicular to the horizon. **1857** WHITTIER *What of the Day?* 3 Thunders.. Far-rolling ere the downright lightnings glare.

2. *fig.* a. Direct, straightforward, not circuitous; plain, definite. Of persons: Plain and direct in speech or behaviour (sometimes implying bluntness of manner). *Obs.* or *arch.*

1603 SHAKS. *Meas. for M.* III. ii. 12 After this downe-right way of Creation. *a* **1616** BEAUM. & FL. *Knight Malta* v. ii, Your downright captain still I'll live, and serve you. *a* **1626** BACON (J.), An admonition from a dead author, or a caveat from an impartial pen, will prevail more than a downright advice. **1717** SAVAGE *Love in Veil* I. i, What we call in downright English a pimp. **1733** POPE *Hor. Sat.* II. i. 52 As plain As downright Shippen, or as old Montaigne. **1856** FROUDE *Hist. Eng.* (1858) II. vii. 145 He had a certain downright honesty about him.

b. That is thoroughly or entirely (what is denoted by the sb.); nothing less than.., mere, absolute, positive, thorough, 'flat', 'out-and-out'.

1565–73 COOPER *Thesaurus*, *Autopyron*, Browne bread.. downe right bread. *a* **1628** PRESTON *Serm. bef. his Majestie* (1630) 19 To be a downe-right Papist. **1699** BENTLEY *Phal.* 267 This is no better than down-right Nonsense. **1712** STEELE *Spect.* No. 266 ¶3 [She] is not to have down-right Money, but..a Present of Plate. **1875** JOWETT *Plato* (ed. 2) I. 344 He is a downright atheist.

C. *sb.* ('*downright*). [The *adj.* used *ellipt.*]

†1. A vertical line; a perpendicular. *Obs.*

1674 N. FAIRFAX *Bulk & Selv.* 153 Brought by a sharp angle to a downright or perpendicular..with the thiller.

2. (*pl.*) Name of a quality of wool.

1793 VANSITTART *Refl. Concl. Peace* 73 Downrights £1200 per pack, Seconds £11 0 0. **1832–52** MCCULLOCH *Dict. Comm.* 1428 The best English short native fleeces..are ..divided by the wool sorter into..1. Prime; 2. Choice; 3. Super; 4. Head; 5. Downrights; 6. Seconds.

down'rightly, *adv. rare.* [f. DOWNRIGHT *a.* + -LY[2].] In a downright manner; directly; thoroughly: = DOWNRIGHT *adv.*

1642 DIGBY *Observ. Sir T. Browne's Relig. Med.* (1659) 21 Averring down-rightly, That God cannot doe contradictory things. **1679** KID in G. Hickes *Spirit of Popery* 7 Prelacy.. is destructive down-rightly to the Sworn Covenants. **1882** *Society* 7 Oct. 16/1 Persistently overbearing, if not.. downrightly insolent. **1947** DYLAN THOMAS *Let.* 5 June (1966) 310 And everybody downrightly refused to believe that *that* was the amount you got.

downrightness (daʊnˈraɪtnɪs). [f. as prec. + -NESS.] The quality of being downright; directness, straightforwardness of speech or behaviour.

1628 EARLE *Microcosm.*, *Blunt Man* (Arb.) 56 Hee is generally honest..and his downerightnesse credits him. **1809–12** MAR. EDGEWORTH *Manœuvring* vii. Wks. 1832 II. 18 They have..so much self-will, and mercantile downrightness in their manners. **1845** THACKERAY *Crit. Rev.* Wks. 1886 XXIII. 237 [To] expose their error with all the downrightness that is necessary.

†**downrights**, *adv. Obs. rare.* [f. as prec. with genitival *-es, -s.*] = DOWNRIGHT *adv.* 1.

c **1350** *Will. Palerne* 1165 Þe almauns seweden sadly & slowe doun riȝtes. **1659** D. PELL *Impr. Sea* 419 They would ..go downrights into the bottome. *Ibid.* 512 The enemy.. hath made after you to sinke you down-rights.

'downrush (-rʌʃ). Rush down, rapid descent.

1855 BRIMLEY *Ess.*, *Tennyson* 73 Like the downrush of a mighty cataract. **1893** SIR R. BALL *Story of Sun* 140 There must be a down-rush of..cooled gas from above.

downscale (stress variable), *v. U.S.* [DOWN *adv.*] To reduce in size or scale, to scale down (SCALE *v.*[3] 4 b), esp.: a. *trans.*, to render more appropriate to the lower end of the market or (social) scale; cf. DOWNSCALE *a.*; b. *intr.* and *trans.*, to reduce the size of (a business operation, etc.).

1945 *Newsweek* 2 Apr. 68 Mullikin's new crazy kitchen began as a good-will idea, aimed at the building trades, to 'downscale' futuristic advertising by means of ridicule. **1980** *Washington Post* 22 Apr. B4/3 Listen to these lunch-time bureaucrats..hashing it out..'But if you want to downscale for retrofitting...' **1981** *N.Y. Times* 30 July C2/3 The appliance business will continue to downscale, with the eventual production of the pocket washer and dryer, tiny machines convenient for laundering a single pair of underpants or socks. **1984** *Washington Post* 1 Dec. D2/6 'I think we're staying away from elegant this time,' said Deaver,..referring to the administration's plans to downscale the pomp and circumstance this time around.

'downscale, *a. U.S.* [DOWN *prep.*] At the lower end of a (social) scale; inferior, of poor quality, 'down-market'. Contr. with UPSCALE *a.*

1966 [see UPSCALE *a.*]. **1980** *New Yorker* 24 Mar. 116 Some of the dream..derives from the movie version of Edna Ferber's 'Giant': that huge Victorian house rising out of the flat Texas landscape in the middle of nowhere. The Ewings' ranch house is certainly cast in the same image, but, as the advertising people say, it is definitely downscale from 'Giant'. Large but not huge; white, serene, and grandly suburban. **1982** *Fortune* 26 July 39/2 A 35-mm camera is like a Sony Walkman, a piece of jewelry to wear around your neck. On the other hand, Kodak's name is very downscale, almost plebeian.

downset (ˈdaʊnsɛt). Also (sense 2) **-seat, -sit.**

†1. Going down or setting (as of the sun). *Obs.*

1610 HOLLAND *Camden's Brit.* II. 128 His honour and fortunes were for ever at their downe-set.

2. *Sc.* An establishment, settlement.

1818 MISS FERRIER *Marriage* I. 120 By my faith, but you have a bein downset. **1822** GALT *Entail* II. 274 (Jam.) A warm down-seat's o' far mair consequence..than the silly low o' love. **1871** W. ALEXANDER *Johnny Gibb* xxxviii. (1873) 213 He'll get a braw doonsit at Gushetneuk.

3. A setting or putting down, a rebuke.

1824 MISS FERRIER *Inher.* viii, Nowise disconcerted at the downset she had received.

'downset, *a. Her.* Of a fess: Broken so that the one half is set lower than the other by its whole width.

1847 *Gloss. Brit. Her.* 141 The best way would be to say downset on the dexter or sinister side.

'downshare, corrupt f. DENSHIRE.

1796 J. BOYS *Agric. Kent* 37 Wheat, Barley, Oats, Oats, Rye Grass..is the course after downsharing that has hitherto generally prevailed. *Ibid.* Downshare land.

downshift, *sb.* and *v.* A. *sb.* A change to a lower gear on a car. B. *v. intr.* To change to a lower gear.

1959 *Observer* 1 Mar. 21/5 Downshifts are not entirely smooth but most driving is done in top. **1961** *Engineering* 27 Oct. 530 Accelerator kick-down gives downshift to second. **1961** 'I. T. Ross' *Old Students* (1963) ii. 26, I down-shifted and concentrated on the road.

downside (ˈdaʊnsaɪd). The under side; in phr. ***downside up*** (after *upside down*). Also *advb.*: ? = downwards, or ? short for *downside up.*

1683 DRYDEN & LEE *Dk. of Guise* v. i, *A.* Since last we parted at the barricadoes, The world's turned upside down. *C.* No,' faith, 'tis better now, 'tis downside up. **1833** L. RITCHIE *Wand. by Loire* 56 The factionnaire seized the document, and looked at it upside and downside for some time. **1885** H. PEARSON *R. Browning* 13 Whether the thing shall be hung upside, downside, or endwise.

down-size, downsize (ˈdaʊnsaɪz), *v.* orig. and chiefly *U.S.* [f. DOWN *adv.* + SIZE *v.*[1]] a. *trans.* To design or build (a car) of smaller overall dimensions, esp. without reducing interior and boot capacity. Also *absol.*

1975 *Automotive Industries* 15 Oct. 10/1 The auto companies and their suppliers are turning to the job of 'downsizing' most of their cars to meet government and market demands for cars that are lighter and more economical. **1976** *Time* 13 Sept. 47 All the automakers are already at work down-sizing their cars for 1978 and later years. **1977** *Time* 1 Aug. 32/3 The drive to downsize is a result of the ever-tightening federal fuel economy standards. **1986** *Jrnl.* (Fairfax Co., Va.) 23 May C3/1 The vehicle was downsized in the late 1970s, shedding 6.5 inches of wheelbase.

b. *gen.* To reduce the size of. Also *intr.* for *pass.*, to be reduced in size.

1979 *Newsweek* 19 Nov. 79 His formal announcement in Washington was similarly down-sized. **1981** *Christian Science Monitor* 27 Apr. B3/3 The U.S. industry is investing more than $80 billion to downsize its automotive fleets across the board by 1985. **1982** *Fortune* 25 Jan. 7/1 Right now he's 'downsizing' the company, and hopes to achieve 1982 cost savings of about $600 million. **1983** *Washington Post* 10 June D8/4 Decline in demand for certain products and other factors 'make it imperative to downsize the business'. **1986** *N.Y. Times* 20 Apr. I. 47/2 New York hospitals 'will downsize'.

Hence **'down-sized** *ppl. a.*, **'down-sizing** *vbl. sb.*, esp. the practice of producing or buying smaller, more economical cars.

1975 *Automotive Industries* 15 Oct. 10/2 Downsizing will not just be a matter of switching nameplates, for example, from Chevrolet to Cadillac. *Ibid.* 1 Nov. 24/1 For the 1977 model year, when the first 'downsized' cars appear, the auto industry will increase its per-car use of aluminum by 15 to 20 lb. **1979** *Daily Tel.* 8 Feb. 6/8 The rapid 'downsizing' of American cars to meet stringent new fuel economy targets. **1982** J. MACKAY *Guinness Bk. Stamps* 22/2 Van-pooling and down-sizing helped to achieve a net saving of 10 per cent in fuel costs in 1980. **1986** *Daily Tel.* 21 Apr. 20/8 Some experts..detect a trend towards 'downsizing' to smaller but better equipped cars. **1986** *Cambrian News* 18 July 14/2 The executive saloon..is abandoning the needlessly large capacity power unit in favour of a sensibly down-sized top end engine.

downslope, down-slope (see below), *sb.*, *adv.*, and *a.* [f. DOWN *a.*, *prep.*: cf. DOWNHILL.]

A. *sb.* (ˈdaʊnsləʊp). A downward slope.

1908 *Westm. Gaz.* 5 June 2/1 We were away on the long down-slope—into California. **1914** D. H. LAWRENCE *Prussian Officer* 157 He had come in full view of the downslope. **1964** *Economist* 30 May 986/3 A frightening downslope.

B. *adv.* (ˈdaʊnˈsləʊp). Down a slope; downhill.
1928 'M. Chapman' *Happy Mountain* iii. 22 The pent roofs of tar-paper that shielded the graves' earth from washing down-slope in the rains. **1938** C. F. S. Sharpe *Landslides* Plate II A (*caption*) Trees tilted downslope by creep tend to return to vertical position during growth. **1944** A. Holmes *Princ. Physical Geol.* x. 147 There are various kinds of mass movements of surface materials downslope. **1971** *Nature* 9 July 88/1 The adult animal..could be swept down-slope by turbidity currents.

C. *adj.* (ˈdaʊnsləʊp). Directed down a slope; downhill.
1938 C. F. S. Sharpe *Landslides* iii. 21 The general term creep may be defined as the slow downslope movement of superficial soil or rock debris. **1964** *Oceanogr. & Marine Biol.* II. 31 A turbidity current is essentially a down-slope current over the bed of the sea..which is driven primarily by excess density. **1971** *Nature* 5 Feb. 399/1 The largest component of downslope creep movement is thought to be due to seasonal changes in soil water content.

Downsman (ˈdaʊnzmən). [Down *sb.*[1] 2.] A native or inhabitant of the (Sussex) Downs.
1906 *Academy* 20 Jan. 63/1 The Downsman in the city May not his home forget. **1921** S. Leslie *Manning* 44 Morning after morning in the grey mist the shepherds and downsmen could hear the bell of their vigilant pastor. **1927** *Observer* 5 June 6/3 [He] founded the Society of Sussex Downsmen. **1963** *Daily Tel.* 25 Oct. 17/7 The Society of Sussex Downsmen have protested..against a proposal that five acres of downland..should be used as an amusement area.

downsome (ˈdaʊnsəm), *a. colloq.* and *dial.* [See Down *adv.* 18, Down *a.* 3.] Inclined to be down or dispirited.
1888 F. R. Stockton *Dusantes* iii, When you left us at 'Frisco we felt pretty downsome. **1894** Blackmore *Perlycross* viii. 61 Then I just looked in at the *Bush*, because my heart was downsome.

down South, *advb. phr.* [Down *adv.* 2, 4.]
a. *U.S.* In or into the States south of the Mason-Dixon line. Also as *adj.*
1834 C. A. Davis *Lett. J. Downing* 25 Though I tell'd 'em down south my father was an Irishman,..I am as clear a Yankee..as the Major itself. **1862** 'E. Kirke' *Among Pines* i. 12 Old Abe he'se gwine to come down Souf. *Ibid.* iii. 60 Away down South in Dixie. **1884** 'Mark Twain' *Huck. Finn* xxxiii, There was plenty other farmer-preachers like that,..down South. **1905** A. H. Rice *Sandy* 23, I lived down South, clean off the track of ever' thing. **1963** *N.Y. Times* 1 Dec. 42 This winter for your Down-South vacation fly Eastern.
b. *N.Z.* In or into the South Island or its southernmost provinces, Otago and Southland.
1867 Lady Barker *Let.* May in *Station Life in N.Z.* (1870) xviii. 137 (*heading*) A Journey 'Down South'. **1873** —— *Station Amusements in N.Z.* vi. 93 All the first-class pastureland 'down South', as [Otago] was called, had been taken up long before. **1873** Trollope *Austral. & N.Z.* II. xxvi. 444 'A railway for you gentlemen down south!' says a northern member. 'Certainly,—but on condition that we have one here, up north.' **1949** P. Newton *High Country Days* vii. 69 Lofty, in happy mood, and unfailing in his praise of his native province [*sc.* Southland], delighted young Wallace with tall stories of 'down south'.

ˈdownspout. Chiefly *N. Amer.* [Down *a.* 1 a.] A pipe conveying rain-water from a roof, etc., to the ground or to a drain, etc.
1896 *Rules governing Printing of Specifications U.S. Patent Office* (rev. ed.) 49/2 Down-spout. **1912** M. Nicholson *Hoosier Chron.* xxxiv. 592 Mr. Harwood had to put a new downspout on the kitchen. **1968** *Globe & Mail* (Toronto) 3 Feb. 41/5 (Advt.), Fascia, eavestrough, downspouts, shutters. **1969** *Morning Star* 26 Aug. 2 Special non-drying paint is being put on the upper end of school downspouts in an attempt to stop vandalism.

Down's syndrome. [Named after J. L. H. *Down* (1828–96), English physician.] = Mongolism.
1961 G. Allen et al. in *Lancet* 8 Apr. 775/2 Some of the undersigned are inclined to replace the term 'mongolism' by such designations as 'Langdon-Down anomaly', or 'Down's syndrome or anomaly' or 'congenital acromicria'. **1961** *Ibid.* 21 Oct. 935/1 Our contributors prefer Down's syndrome to mongolism because they believe that the term 'mongolism' has misleading racial connotations and is hurtful to many parents. **1965** H. E. Sutton *Introd. Human Genetics* v. 37 The condition known as trisomy 21 syndrome or mongolian idiocy (sometimes referred to as Down's syndrome) had long been an enigma. **1965** *New Scientist* 2 Dec. 632/1 The chromosomal damage leading to Down's syndrome (as the 'mongol' condition is now described).

down stage, down-stage, *adv. Theatr.* [Down *prep.* 3.] At or towards the front of the stage. Also *attrib.* or as *adj.* Cf. Upstage.
1898 L. Merrick *Actor-Manager* 41 It [*sc.* her train] would fall 'down stage'. **1933** P. Godfrey *Back-Stage* i. 15 He examines these things for himself before returning to his position on the down-stage centre mark. **1936** N. R. Smith *All Star Cast* 38 Verity came down-stage to the table. **1939** L. Hellman *Little Foxes* I. 11 Downstage, right, are a high couch, a large table, several chairs. **1968** *Listener* 18 July 72/1 Rather apart from the others..was Mr. Okara, advancing down stage to meet me with outstretched hand.

downstairs (see below), *adv. phr.* (*a.*, *sb.*) Less freq. **downstair** (esp. as *adj.*).
a. *adv. phr.* (daʊnˈstɛəz). Down the stairs; on or to a lower floor or (*fig.*) 'the lower regions'.
1596 Shaks. *1 Hen. IV*, ii. iv. 112 His industry is vpstaires and down-staires, his eloquence the parcell of a reckoning. **1597** —— *2 Hen. IV*, ii. iv. 202 Thrust him downe stayres. *a* **1631** Drayton *Wks.* II. 490 (Jod.) When upstair one, downstair another, hies. **1791** Mrs. Radcliffe *Rom. Forest* x, As she went downstairs. *a* **1845** Barham *Ingol. Leg., Bros. Birchington* xxiii, Such affairs..are bruited about..'down-stairs' Where Old Nick [etc.]. **1883** Reade *Many a Slip* in *Harper's Mag.* Dec. 133/2 Down-stairs the lady did not charm.
b. *attrib.* or *adj.* (ˈdaʊnstɛə(z)).
1819 *Metropolis* I. 146 At the feet of down stairs Cinderella. **1824** Miss Mitford *Village* Ser. i. (1863) 222, I have sometimes..feared that her down-stair life was less happy. *Mod.* The downstairs rooms.
c. *sb.* (daʊnˈstɛəz). The downstairs part of a building; the lower regions.
1843 Mrs. Carlyle *Lett.* I. 254 The old green curtains of downstairs were become filthy. **1877** H. Smart *Play or Pay* (1878) 125 The accredited down stairs is so utterly overstocked with that pavement [good intentions]. **1896** *Westm. Gaz.* 23 Apr. 2/3 The magistrate could not discriminate whether upstairs or down-stairs began [the fight].

ˈdownstart. [f. Down *adv.* + *start* after Upstart *sb.*] (See quot. 1949); also, one who pretends to be of lower origin than he is. Also *attrib.*
1898 G. B. Shaw *Sixteen Self-Sketches* (1949) viii. 44 My father was an Irish Protestant gentleman of the downstart race of younger sons. **1921** —— Pref. to *Immaturity* in *Prefaces* (1934) xxiii. 627/1, I was a downstart and the son of a downstart. **1949** —— *Sixteen Self-Sketches* ii. 7 The Downstart, as I call the boy-gentleman descended through younger sons from the plutocracy, for whom a university education is beyond his father's income, leaving him by family tradition a gentleman without a gentleman's means or education, and so only a penniless snob. **1960** G. Mikes *How to be Inimitable* 21 Quite a few people assert that they are of lower origin than they..are... The place of the upstart is being taken by the downstart.

down-state, downstate. *U.S.* [Down *prep.* 3.] The part of a State outside a large city, esp. the southern part. Also as *adv.* and *adj.* Hence **down-ˈstater**, an inhabitant of downstate. Cf. Up-state *adv.*
Used in various parts of the U.S. with varying local significance.
1909 *Daily Maroon* (Chicago) 2 Oct. 1/4 Springer, a husky full-back from down-state. *Ibid.* 12 Oct. 1/1 The downstaters have always supported their men loyally. **1932** W. Faulkner *Light in August* iii. 58 She had gone to visit her people downstate. **1942** *Amer. Speech* XVII. 30 (*heading*) Pronunciation in downstate New York. **1947** *Chicago Tribune* 22 June ii. 5/6, I have had a great many letters from downstaters who want to correct the faults. **1970** *Globe & Mail* (Toronto) 25 Sept. 1/1 The New York Telephone Co., for the second day, turned on its 250 emergency generators in the downstate area.

† **ˈdownsteepy,** *a. Obs. rare*$^{-1}$. [f. Down *adv.* + Steepy *a.*] Steeply descending, precipitous.
1603 Florio *Montaigne* (1613) 97 (T.) He came to a craggy and downsteepy rock.

ˈdownˈstream, *adv.* (*a.*, *sb.*) Also **down stream, down-stream.** [Down *prep.* 3.] **a.** Down the stream, in the direction of the current, towards the mouth of a river. Also *fig.*
1706 in *Rec. Plymouth* (Mass.) (1889) I. 26 Bounded by said river..down stream unto the upper end of the meadow. **1864** Carlyle *Fredk. Gt.* IV. 560 Königstein, a little downstream of Schandau. **1865** H. B. Stowe *House & Home P.* 316 There is a general tendency to let all sorts of old forms and observances float down-stream. **1869** Blackmore *Lorna D.* vii, Even an otter might float downstream. **1878** R. L. Stevenson *Inland Voy.* 196 Canoeing was easy work..to keep the head down stream. **1929** Belloc *Joan of Arc* iii. 62 The French forces lay downstream. **1957** P. Caraman *Henry Morse* vii. 66 Across the river, about a mile downstream, a path ran from the bank.
b. as *adj.* and quasi-*sb.* Also *fig.*
1842 *American Pioneer* I. 70 Steam-boats seem almost to say, we will do your up-stream business for nothing, if you will give us your down-stream business. **1891** W. Morris *News from Nowhere* (ed. 2) ii. 8 Even the up-stream bridges ..are scarcely daintier, and the down-stream ones are scarcely more dignified and stately. **1934** J. L. Myres in E. Eyre *European Civilisation* I. ii. 115 There were certainly casual immigrants from down-stream. **1954** R. St. B. Baker *Sahara Challenge* iii. 39 The down-stream rush of water is decreased. **1963** *Economist* 21 Sept. 1042/2 Much larger 'downstream' investment.

down-street, *adv.* (*a.*) *colloq.* and *dial.* [Down *prep.* 3.] Down the street; in, into, or toward the lower part of a town, etc.; (see also quot. 1962). Also *attrib.* or as *adj.*, and as *sb.*
1828 M. R. Mitford *Our Village* III. 199 He began..to look out for a wife, up street and down... The down-street lady was a widow. **1852** H. B. Stowe *Uncle Tom* xxviii, I believe I'll go down street, a few moments, and hear the news. **1865** W. S. Banks *Provincial Words Wakefield* 76 *Up Street*, means the upper part of the town... 'Dahn street' is used in a similar manner. **1876** W. Wright *Hist. Big Bonanza* (1877) 365, I was told down street..that there was a regular row in one of the shebangs up the way. **1888** B. Lowsley *Gloss. Berkshire Words* 73 *Down-strit*, the opposite direction in the main road through a village from *up-strit.* **1962** *Amer. Speech* XXXVII. 158 One goes *down city* only if he is going to the business center; if he is going no farther than the nearest grocery store or shopping center, his destination is *downstreet.*

down-swept, *a.* [Down *adv.* 38.] Swept or curving downwards.
1927 *Daily Express* 13 Oct. 2 Much lower [car] bodies ..[are] achieved by a down-swept chassis. **1933** C. Day Lewis *Dick Willoughby* vi. 55 Her eyes observed him keenly under the down-swept lashes. **1937** *Times* 11 Dec. 4/7 The frame is of downswept box section shape. **1963** *Times* 15 Jan. 12/2 From the..front bumpers to the downswept tail.

ˈdown-swing. [Down *adv.* 41.] A downward swing; *spec.* (*a*) the descending movement of a golf-club about to hit the ball, following the back-swing; (*b*) a period of low or declining activity in trade, business, etc.
1899 [see *back-swing* s.v. Back- A. 11]. **1922** Wodehouse *Clicking of Cuthbert* viii. 192 Do shout 'Boo!' at him when he is starting his down-swing! **1935** *Economist* 2 Feb. 250/2 Mr. Crump..regards the crisis in the main as the normal downswing of the trade cycle. **1946** G. von Haberler *Prosperity & Depression* ii. 21 (*heading*) The Downswing. The reverse of the upswing. **1959** *Spectator* 11 Sept. 336/2 The sufferer should be told..about this..fluctuation in his malady, so that he doesn't get unduly discouraged during a down-swing. **1966** *Economist* 18 June p. xxx/1 After two years of popularity, clearing bank shares appear to be entering the downswing of their familiar cycle. **1970** *Nature* 21 Nov. 703/2 The present epidemic, hopefully, seems to be on the downswing.

downthrow (ˈdaʊnθrəʊ).
1. A throwing or being thrown down. *rare.*
1615 *Catascopes* in Farr *S.P. Jas. I* (1848) 352 Wars, the canker of estate, Hel's image and al commonweale's downthrow. **1891** *Times* 21 Oct. 5/3 Unable to take his downthrow philosophically.
2. *Geol.* The depression of strata below the general level on one side of a fault. (Originally a miners' term.) Also *attrib.*
1858 A. C. Ramsay *Geol. Struct. Merioneth, etc.* 5 Down the Bala valley..there runs a great fault. It is a down-throw to the north-west. **1882** Geikie *Geol. Sk.* 282 A true fault with an upthrow and downthrow side. **1889** Croll *Stellar Evol.* 54 About a mile E.S.E. of Beddgelert, there is a fault with a downthrow of 5000 feet.

down timber. *N. Amer.* A heap or tract of fallen trees, brought down by wind or storm or other natural agent.
1881 W. O. Stoddard *E. Hardery* 263 There was plenty of old 'down timber' to be cut up, and cleared away. **1895** H. S. Somerset *Land of Muskeg* 170 (*caption*) Horses in down timber. **1948** *Sierra Club Bull.* (San Francisco) Mar. 111 Up interminable slopes of down timber, where the small logs repeatedly broke under the weight of man and pack. **1951** R. P. Hobson *Grass beyond Mountains* 136 Windfalls or down timber lay piled up between the trees.

downtime (ˈdaʊntaɪm). Also **down-time, down time.** [f. Down *adv.* + Time *sb.*] **1.** Time, or an occasion, when a machine or vehicle is out of action or unavailable for use. Cf. Uptime.
1952 *Bell Telephone Syst. Monograph* No. 1972. 4/2 The amount of 'down time' due to faulty machine operation is very low. **1954** *Jrnl. Assoc. Computing Machinery* I. 194 (*table*) Number of unscheduled down times. **1966** *Economist* 2 July 56/2 All of which involves capital, labour (lugging the pieces around) and expensive down-time for the tools while the next operation is being set up. **1972** *Daily Colonist* (Victoria, B.C.) 20 Feb. 8/7 Scientific Wear Analysis can save you thousands of dollars in machine downtime and repairs. **1972** *Times* 17 Oct. (Transport Hire Suppl.) p. i/3 A spate of 'down-times' (times when trucks are not on the road for maintenance or other reasons)..these are the occasions when renting makes sense. **1983** *Belle* (Austral.) July–Aug. 102/2 Resulting downtime on the tufting machines enabled Bremworth to service and innovate its carpet-producing equipment.
2. *transf.* An opportunity for, or time of, rest; time off.
1982 *Observer* 6 June 9/4 Mr Reagan will have 'downtime' (a rest) after lunch. **1985** *English Today* Oct. 4/2 It is possible to hear people talk of 'enjoying the down-time' when they are having a break.

Downtonian (daʊnˈtəʊnɪən), *a. Geol.* [f. *Downton*, name of a locality in Herefordshire + -ian.] Of, pertaining to, or designating a stratigraphic stage or series in Europe placed at the top of the Silurian system or the bottom of the Devonian, and the age or epoch during which it was deposited. Also *absol.*
1879 C. Lapworth in *Ann. & Mag. Nat. Hist.* 5th Ser. III. Table facing 455 Silurian System: Upper Division (Downtonian). **1910** Lake & Rastall *Text-bk. Geol.* xx. 334 The Downtonian series varies little. Wherever it occurs, whether on the Welsh borders, in the Lake District or in the south of Scotland, it is essentially an arenaceous deposit and was formed in shallow water. **1938** A. K. Wells *Outl. Hist. Geol.* vii. 66 Both Downtonian and Dittonian represent successive stages in the transition from marine to continental conditions. *Ibid.* 67 The thickness of the Downtonian Stage diminishes. **1955** G. G. Woodford tr. *Gignoux's Stratigr. Geol.* iv. 110 Similar sediments are seen on the edges of the Baltic Shield... This Baltic Downtonian is attached to the Silurian by Scandinavian geologists. **1967** D. H. Rayner *Stratigr. Brit. Isles* v. 140 Molluscs..are often abundant in the lower Downtonian beds. **1971** B. W. Sparks *Rocks & Relief* viii. 295 In this account the Downtonian will be included in the Devonian.

down town, down-town, *adv.*, *a.*, and *sb.* orig. *U.S.* and chiefly *N. Amer.* Also **downtown.** [See Down *prep.* 2 b, 3.] **A.** *adv.* Into the town (from a more elevated suburb); down in the town. Cf. Up-town *adv.*
1835 Gray *Lett.* (1893) 55 To-day when I go down town I shall subscribe for the 'New York Observer' for you. **1883** *Century Mag.* XXVI. 917/1 She was down-town alone. *c* **1909** D. H. Lawrence *Collier's Friday Night* (1934) iii. 60

Well, my duck, I looked for you downtown. **1952** S. KAUFFMANN *Philanderer* (1957) vi. 91 The man who had seemed a dignified young wonder on 135th Street..looked like a pompous and overweening young ass downtown. **1968** *Globe & Mail* (Toronto) 17 Feb. 24 (Advt.), Tickets available downtown at box office prices exclusively at Moody's in the Colonnade.

B. *adj.* Of, pertaining to, or situated in the lower, or more central, part of a town or city. Cf. UP-TOWN *a.*

1836 P. HONE *Diary* (1889) I. 200 The value of down-town property. **1852** *Harper's Mag.* V. 413/2 The down-town men..slip uneasily through the brick and mortar labyrinths of Maiden-lane. **1870** J. K. MEDBERY *Men & Myst. Wall Street* 67 On these securities therefore the down-town banks make call loans. **1883** H. H. KANE in *Harper's Mag.* Nov. 944/2 In the lobby of a down-town hotel. **1891** *Congress. Rec.* 28 Jan. 1906/1 The second ward of the city of New York..is what is called a down-town ward, a business ward. **1902** *Westm. Gaz.* 12 May 2/1 Men do not doff their hats in the down-town elevators which brought her up to the big office..near the top of one of the high down-town buildings. **1911** *Daily Colonist* (Victoria, B.C.) 13 Apr. 7/5 Pedestrians in the down-town district on Friday were interested in the sight of a veritable procession of lorries loaded with high grade Pianos. **1939** C. MORLEY *Kitty Foyle* 175 His necktie was sort of downtown and Bourse-looking. **1952** B. ULANOV *Hist. Jazz* (1958) iv. 33 Squalid little clubs in downtown New York. **1958** *Times Lit. Suppl.* 10 Jan. 21/2 The account of the wild sermon in down-town Kingston, vividly conjuring up the crucifixion. **1966** *New Scientist* 14 July 103/2 Mr. Crosland writes about *downtown* schools, meaning schools in the centres of cities. Pure American, of course, and a very useful term too. **1968** *Globe & Mail* (Toronto) 17 Feb. 1/8 A downtown Ottawa office building. **1969** *Australian* 24 May 24/2 (Advt.), Your home in downtown Sydney.

C. *sb.* The lower or business part of a town or city.

1851 H. MELVILLE *Moby Dick* i, Its extreme down-town is the Battery. **1905** *N.Y. Even. Post* 4 Mar. 5 One of the diversions of downtown yesterday was watching the sure movements of a steeplejack. **1955** R. BLESH *Shining Trumpets* (ed. 3) vii. 160 New Orleans' downtown is the old quarter north of Canal Street. **1968** *Globe & Mail* (Toronto) 13 Jan. 45/1 (Advt.), At the subway stop..19 minutes from downtown.

Hence **'down-'towner**, one who lives in or frequents the down-town part of a city.

1830 J. F. WATSON *Ann. Philadelphia* 244 They were the Achilles and the Patrocles of the 'downtowners'. **1887** *Courier-Journal* (Louisville, Ky.) 8 May 12/5 Jay Gould has set down-towners to eating snails.

downtrend. [DOWN *adv.* 41.] A downward tendency, esp. in economic matters.

1926 *Dry Goods Economist* 11 Dec. 28 Retail trade is large, and no pronounced down-trend has yet developed in that quarter. **1940** *Economist* 10 Feb. 250/1 (*heading*) Down-trend in farm prices. **1960** *Times* 5 Feb. 16/3 In 1959 the seasonal downtrend was not reversed until the second week in March.

'downtrod, *ppl. a.* = next.

1596 SHAKS. *1 Hen. IV*, I. iii. 135, (Qo. 1) I will lift the down-trod [*Fols.* downfall, -faln] Mortimer. **1606** SYLVESTER *Du Bartas* II. iv. I. *Trophies* 887 [He] Wholly extirps the down-trod Iebusite.

downtrodden (daʊn'trɒd(ə)n), *pa. pple.* and ('daʊn,trɒd(ə)n), *ppl. a.*

1. Trampled down; beaten down by treading.

1568 U. FULWEL *Like Will to Like* in Hazl. *Dodsley* III. 341 Repent, repent, your sins shall be downtrodden. **1846** H. ROGERS *Ess.* (1860) I. 175 The down-trodden grass. **1875** LONGF. *Pandora* viii. 4 The flowers, downtrodden by the wind.

2. *fig.* Crushed down by oppression or tyranny.

1595 SHAKS. *John* II. i. 241 This downe-troden equity. **1641** MILTON *Reform.* II. ad fin., The most dejected..and downtrodden vassals of perdition. **1845–6** TRENCH *Huls. Lect.* Ser. I. iii. 43 All the..crushed and down-trodden of the earth. **1858** J. MARTINEAU *Stud. Chr.* 342 The down-trodden serfs of Franconia.

Hence **'down-,troddenness.**

1881 F. G. LEE *Reg. Baront.* i. 5 Their expatriation, poverty, and down-troddenness.

down-turn, downturn, *sb.* [DOWN *adv.* 41.] A turning downward; a decline, esp. in economic or business activity.

1926 *National Provisioner* 19 June 40 Most fat cows and heavy heifers lost around 25c and in instances the down-turn on better grades was even greater. **1940** *Economist* 10 Feb. 250/1 The great upturn [of prices] was basically caused by drought, and the great downturn by the breaking of the drought. **1947** DEWEY & DAKIN *Cycles* xvi. 232 The corrective economic downturn following World War II. *Ibid.* 233 The downturn in the 54-year price rhythm was hardly even noted. **1955** *Ann. Reg. 1954* 168 He asked for measures which could be used if the economic 'downturn' became a recession. **1957** *Economist* 7 Sept. 760/1 The economy has already demonstrated this year that it can suffer a mild downturn in manufacturing. **1964** L. S. HULTZÉN in D. Abercrombie et al. *Daniel Jones* 87 In some idiolects this non-finitive text shape has an arrested down-turn or slight up-turn. **1970** *Daily Tel.* 14 Jan. 19 The down-turn in stocks suggests the possibility of a lower level of importing.

down-turn, downturn, *v.* [DOWN *adv.* 36.] *trans.* To turn downwards.

1909 R. KANE *Sermon of Sea* xx. 325 The rusty green and knitted surface of the sod are gradually cloven and down-turned. **1922** JOYCE *Ulysses* 691 With solicitation, bending and downturning the upturned rug-fringe.

So **down-turned** *ppl. a.* (see DOWN *adv.* 38).

1880 *Rules on Specifications U.S. Patent Office* 25/2 The following are single words..downturned. **1909** *Westm. Gaz.* 21 June 2/3 Curve those lips..To a dismal down-turned crescent. **1942** T. S. ELIOT *Little Gidding* 10, I fixed upon the down-turned face That pointed scrutiny.

down under, *adv.* [DOWN *adv.* 4.] At the antipodes; in Australia, New Zealand, etc. Also *attrib.* and *sb.* (after a prep.).

1886 J. A. FROUDE *Oceana* 92 We were to bid adieu to the 'Australasian'...She had carried us safely *down under.* **1899** [see UNDER *adv.* 2 f]. **1908** *Daily Chron.* 31 Oct. 4/6 The Bishop of London..does not take a very active interest in the 'down under' section of his see. **1909** *Westm. Gaz.* 11 Jan. 12/1 The same could happen 'down under' if New Zealand..were bracketted with New South Wales and Queensland. **1916** *Anzac Bk.* 145/2 Macaulay's prophecy concerning the man from 'down under' sitting on the ruins of London Bridge. **1922** *Daily Mail* 9 Dec. 11 The steeplechaser Kinlark, a gift to the Prince from 'down under'. **1928** *Daily Express* 17 Feb. 4 Mr. Collins, the captain of the last visiting Australian team, was a stipendiary steward 'down under'. **1936** *Discovery* Jan. 10/2 Sydney, which proudly boasts of the finest natural harbour in the world, welcomes you to that vast Dominion 'down under'. **1941** L. A. G. STRONG *John McCormack* x. 173 The second concert in Auckland brought to an end John's first visit Down Under. **1971** *Time* 14 June 2/2 Down under may be the place to make money, but up over is the place to spend it!

downward ('daʊnwəd), *adv.* (*prep.*) and *a.* For forms see DOWN *adv.* [Primarily an aphetic form of ADOWNWARD, in OE. *adúnweard*; but subseq. referred directly to DOWN: see -WARD.]

A. *adv.*

1. Towards a lower place or position; towards what is below: with a descending motion or tendency. **a.** in reference to movement through space.

c **1200** *Trin. Coll. Hom.* 105 Ech god giue..cumeð of heuene dunward. *c* **1230** *Hali Meid.* 19 Ha..walden fallen duneward. **1297** R. GLOUC. (1724) 362 As hii þat donward come. **1398** TREVISA *Barth. De P.R.* XIII. xxiv. (1495) 456 A drope..fallyth dounwarde by his owne heuynesse. **1535** COVERDALE *2 Kings* xx. 10 It is an easy thinge for the shadowe to go ten degrees downewarde. **1641** FRENCH *Distill.* i. (1651) 40 This Oil taken inwardly worketh upward and downward. **1887** BOWEN *Virg. Æneid* I. 607 While streams downward run to the sea.

b. in reference to direction, attitude, or aspect.

c **1400** MAUNDEV. (Roxb.) xix. 87 Lukand douneward to þe erthe. *c* **1450** *Douce MS.* 55 ch. x, Tourne the brede doun-warde in the panne. **1562** J. HEYWOOD *Prov. & Epigr.* (1867) 113, I looke doneweard to my feete. **1793** SOUTHEY *Triumph Woman* 302 Why downward droops his musing head? **1855** BROWNING *Old Pictures in Florence* x, 'Tis looking downward makes one dizzy.

c. in reference to position or situation.

a **1300** *Cursor M.* 9887 (Cott.) þis castel dunward þan es it polist slight. *c* **1391** CHAUCER *Astrol.* II. §36 Thanne set I the point..downward in the same signe. *c* **1511** *1st Eng. Bk. Amer.* (Arb.) Introd. 33/2 Fro ye myddell don-warde ben they lyke the halfe neder parte of an horse. **1641** J. JACKSON *True Evang. T.* II. 115 [St. Peter] was crucified..with his head downward. **1667** MILTON *P.L.* I. 463 Dagon his Name, Sea Monster, upward Man And downward Fish. **1854** J. SCOFFERN in *Orr's Circ. Sc.* Chem. 24 Metallic cones, ranged apices downward.

2. *fig.* **a.** Towards that which is lower in order, or inferior in any way.

a **1300** *Cursor M.* 1943 (Cott.) Fra me dun-ward drogh man his thoght. *c* **1440** *Jacob's Well* (E.E.T.S.) 48 In þe lyne of kynrede dounward, þi sone to þe is in þe firste degre. **1596** DALRYMPLE tr. *Leslie's Hist. Scot.* IV. 260 The Peichtis in thair guddis and ryches downward began to declyne. *a* **1732** T. BOSTON *Crook in Lot* (1805) 160 God carries his people's circumstances downward..till they come to that point. **1847** EMERSON *Repr. Men* Wks. (Bohn) I. 351 Things seem to tend downward, to justify despondency.

b. Onward from an earlier to a later time.

1611 BIBLE *Transl. Pref.* 3 From Christes time downe-ward. **1679–1714** BURNET *Hist. Ref.* an. 1535 (R.) From the twelfth century downward. **1849** GROTE *Greece* II. lxvi, All the old laws of Athens, from Solon downward.

3. *Comb.*

1821 SHELLEY *Prometh. Unb.* II. v, Downward-gazing flowers. **1865** G. M. HOPKINS *Poems* (1948) 134 A block of copse Close-rooted in the downward-hollowing fields. **1871** BROWNING *Balaust.* 1370 The downward-dwelling people. **1878** B. TAYLOR *Deukalion* III. i. 97. **1922** JOYCE *Ulysses* 377 Exterior splendour may be the surface of a downwardtending lutulent reality. *Ibid.* 656 Slow erosions of peninsulas and downwardtending peninsulas. **1943** L. B. LYON *Evening in Stepney* 14 Fuel for the downward-bending The sod-quickening fire. **1964** J. C. CATFORD in D. Abercrombie et al. *Daniel Jones* 35 A downward-forward displacement of the hyoid bone..can easily be observed.

†**B.** *prep.* = DOWN *prep.* 1. *Obs. rare.*

c **1430** *Pilgr. Lyf Manhode* I. v. (1869) 3 A corde..he hadde set dounward þe wal.

C. *adj.*

1. Directed towards that which is lower; descending; inclined downward. **a.** *lit.*

1552 HULOET, Downewarde, *præceps.* **1592** SHAKS. *Ven. & Ad.* 1106 This foul..boar, Whose downward eye still looketh for a grave. **1697** DRYDEN *Virg. Georg.* IV. 517 The downward track. **1728–46** THOMSON *Spring* 188 In the western sky the downward sun Looks out. **1878** HUXLEY *Physiogr.* 146 The downward current of the river.

b. *fig.*

a **1586** SIDNEY (J.) At the lowest of my downward thoughts. **1700** DRYDEN *Sigism. & Guisc.* 344 Thy low fall ..Shows downward appetite to mix with mud. **1727–46** THOMSON *Summer* 1516 A Hampden..who stemmed the torrent of a downward age To slavery prone. **1869** FREEMAN *Norm. Conq.* (1876) III. xiii. 303 Steps in a downward scale.

2. Lying or situated below; lower. *rare.*

a **1300** *Cursor M.* 9926 (Gött.) þat rechis to þe donwar [*v.r.* neþemest] light. **1697** DRYDEN *Virg. Georg.* I. 341 Aurora..lights the downward Heav'n. **1824** CAMPBELL *Theodric* 138 The waste and wild Schreckhorn..frowning.. Upon a downward world of pastoral charms.

Hence **'downwardly** *adv.* = DOWNWARD *adv.*; **'downwardness.**

1839 BAILEY *Festus* iii. (1852) 26 That downwardness of soul. **1850** BROWNING *Easter Day* xv. 33 Certain rays..Shot downwardly. **1872** MIVART *Elem. Anat.* 60 The downwardly tapering condition of the coccygeal vertebræ.

downwards ('daʊnwədz), *adv.* [f. DOWNWARD with adverbial genitive *-es, -s*: see -WARDS.]

1. a. = DOWNWARD *adv.* 1 a, b.

1622 MABBE tr. *Aleman's Guzman d'Alf.* I. 120 The Light is turned down-wards. **1634** SIR T. HERBERT *Trav.* 211 Her bill is crooked downwards. **1641** WILKINS *Math. Magick* I. ix. (1648) 57 The squeezing or pressing of things downewards. **1726** *Adv. Capt. R. Boyle* 3 The Tide running downwards. **1879** LUBBOCK *Sci. Lect.* ii. 36 The hairs which cover the stalks..usually point downwards.

b. = DOWNWARD *adv.* 1 c.

c **1400** MAUNDEV. (1839) xv. 166 Þerfore make þei the halfendel of ydole of a man vpwardes, and the toþer half of an ox dounwardes. **1620** MELTON *Astrolog.* 28 The Antipodites have their feete downewards and their heads upwards as well as wee. **1756–7** tr. *Keysler's Trav.* (1760) II. 419 A small antique Venus, with a drapery from the waist downwards. **1826** DISRAELI *Viv. Grey* VI. i, He tossed..the great horn upside downwards.

2. *fig.* = DOWNWARD *adv.* 2.

a **1654** SELDEN *Table-T.* (Arb.) 69 Some of them are asham'd upwards, because their Ancestors were too great. Others are asham'd downwards, because they were too little. **1857** *Chambers' Information* I. 691 *Angling*, Wormgut varies in length from nearly two feet and downwards. **1885** L. O. PIKE *Yearbks. 12 & 13 Edw. III* Introd. 42 From the time of Glanville downwards.

'downwarp. *Geol.* [DOWN *adv.* 41.] A broad surface depression; a syncline. So **'downwarping**, the local sinking of the earth's surface to form such a depression.

1917 *Prof. Papers U.S. Geol. Surv.* XCIII. v. 110/2 From Gibson the axis of the downwarp has a general north-northeast trend to the great bend of Chaco River. **1917** *Jrnl. Geol.* XXV. 146 The downwarping of certain layers near the top of the Lockport dolomite. **1936** *Geogr. Jrnl.* LXXXVII. 165 This resistance was not however sufficient to prevent another downwarp in Southern India. **1950** F. E. ZEUNER *Dating Past* (ed. 2) vii. 280 A slow down-warping to the north is going on. **1955** BROWN & DEY *India's Min. Wealth* (ed. 3) xviii. 663 The tectonic downwarp in front of the Himalayas. **1963** D. W. & E. E. HUMPHRIES tr. *Termier's Erosion & Sedimentation* v. 108 Local downwarping or uplift can lead rivers to reverse their courses either completely or in part. **1965** A. HOLMES *Princ. Physical Geol.* (ed. 2) xxx. 1173 The primary importance of upwarping and downwarping in providing the conditions for gravitational tectonics on a spectacular scale.

'downwash. *Aeronaut.* [DOWN *adv.* 41.] The downward deflection of an air-stream by an aerofoil or other body; ***downwash angle*** (see quot. 1919). Hence (*rare*) **downwash** *v.*

1915 *Rep. & Mem. Advisory Comm. for Aeronautics, No. 196* v. 125 It appeared possible that the advantage of such increased lift might introduce a concomitant disadvantage in an increased 'downwash' in the neighbourhood of the tail planes. **1919** W. B. FARADAY *Gloss. Aeronaut. Terms* 21 *Downwash angle*, the angle through which the airstream relative to the aeroplane is deflected by an aerofoil or other body. Measured in a plane parallel to the plane of symmetry. **1922** *Encycl. Brit.* XXX. 19/2 The reaction upon the rear plane is therefore inclined backward by the angle through which the air has been 'downwashed' by the leading plane. **1931** *Flight* 20 Nov. 1148/1 The amazing control of the Autogiros, old as well as new, is very largely due to the downwash from the rotor blades. **1966** D. STINTON *Anat. Aeroplane* v. 58 To generate a given lift at a given airspeed an aerofoil of long span has to impart a smaller downwash to the air it meets than an aerofoil of shorter span.

downweigh (daʊn'weɪ), *v. trans.* To weigh down; to exceed in weight or influence, to outweigh; to depress, as with a weight.

1600 W. VAUGHAN *Direct. Health* (1633) 153 A forced sanguine complexion..might down-waigh the naturall melancholike power. **1723** *Trickology* 16 The Nod of a pretending Fop easily down-weighs the Applause of Judges competent. *a* **1851** MOIR *Poems, Message of Seth* vi, The gloom..downweighs My spirit.

†**down weight, down-weight.** *Obs.* That which weighs down the scale of a balance; full or good weight. *attrib.* Heavy enough to weigh down the scale; of full weight. Also *fig.*

c **1524** *Churchw. Acc. St. Mary hill, London* (Nichols 1797) 128, 46 oz. of silver plate, 20 downeweight, to be made into two chalices. **1591** FLORIO *2nd Fruites* 67 *A.* These your crownes are verie light. *S.* Naie, rather they are downe waight. **1638** CHILLINGW. *Relig. Prot.* I. i. §8 They will not be pleas'd without a down weight, but God is contented if the scale be turn'd. **1698** S. CLARKE *Script. Just.* xii. 61 That I may give down-weight, I shall add these Reasons more.

down wind: see WIND *sb.*[1] 19 a.

†**downwith,** *a.* and *sb. Obs.* or *Sc.* **A.** *adj.* Downward. **B.** *sb.* A downward course.

c **1470** HENRY *Wallace* IX. 911 A downwith waill the Sothroun to thaim had. **1617** MARKHAM *Caval.* VI. 9 If the fierce Horse haue..either vpwithes, inwithes or downewithes, which is that he may either runne within the side of hilles, vp hils, or downe hils. **1808–25** JAMIESON s.v., *To the downwith*, downwards. *Downwith*, descending, as, a downwith road, opposed to an acclivity.

downy ('daʊnɪ), *a.*[1] [f. DOWN *sb.*[1] + -Y[1].] Of the nature of a down; characterized by downs.

1671 *St. Foine Improved* 8 The Downy and dry parts of England and Wales. **1772–84** COOK *Voy.* (1790) III. 817 The land..was of the downy kind, without a single tree. **1867** MOTLEY *Corr.* 20 Aug., A rolling, downy country.

downy ('daʊnɪ), *a.*[2] [f. DOWN *sb.*[2] + -Y[1].]

1. a. Of the nature of or like down; feathery, fluffy.

1578 LYTE *Dodoens* V. xiv. 566 The flowers of milke Thistel..change into rounde cotton or downie bawles. **1590** SPENSER *F.Q.* II. xii. 79 On his tender lips the downy heare Did..freshly spring. **1597** SHAKS. *2 Hen. IV*, IV. v. 32 There lyes a dowlney feather, which stirres not. **1742** YOUNG *Nt. Th.* I. 4 Sleep..Swift on his downy Pinion flies. **1840** R. H. DANA *Bef. Mast* xxvi. 85 Thick downy feathers, taken from the breasts of various birds.

b. *downy mildew*: a disease of plants caused by parasitic fungi of the order Peronosporales.

1886 *Bull. Bot. Div. U.S. Dept. Agric.* II. 7 (*title*) Fungous diseases of the grape vine. I. The downy mildew. **1909** B. M. DUGGAR *Fungous Dis. Plants* x. 152 The downy mildew of the grape is one of the most important disease-producing organisms among the Peronosporaceæ. **1950** *N.Z. Jrnl. Agric.* Feb. 157/1 Downy mildew (*Perono-plasmopara cubensis*)..appears as more or less angular, yellowish spots on the leaves, on the undersides of which a scanty white downy growth develops. **1970** *Times* 14 July 10/6 The aim was to produce a variety resistant to downy mildew.

2. Made or consisting of down.

a **1592** GREENE *Alphonsus* IV. Wks. (Rtldg.) 243 Mars lies slumbering on his downy bed. **1712–4** POPE *Rape Lock* I. 19 Belinda still her downy pillow prest. **1820** *Sporting Mag.* VI. 79 The morning was truly forbidding for the swells to leave their downy dabs.

3. a. Covered or clothed with down.

1591 SHAKS. *1 Hen. VI*, V. iii. 56 So doth the Swan her downie Signets saue. **1697** DRYDEN *Virg. Past.* II. 72 For downy Peaches and the glossie Plum. **1725** BRADLEY *Fam. Dict.* s.v. *Peonie*, The Leaves are indented, downy on the Backside. **1837** LYTTON *E. Maltrav.* 20 Happiness and health bloomed on her downy cheeks.

b. Hence in specific names of plants, as ***downy ling***, ***downy oat***, ***downy willow***, etc.

1548 TURNER *Names of Herbes* (1881) 81 It [Clematis Vitalba] may be called in Englishe Heguine, or Downiuine. **1861** MISS PRATT *Flower. Pl.* IV. 193 Downy Woundwort.

c. downy woodpecker, a small species of North American woodpecker, *Dendrocopos pubescens*.

1808 A. WILSON *Amer. Ornithol.* I. 153 Downy Woodpecker. *Picus Pubescens*...is the smallest of our Woodpeckers. **1872** *Rep. Vermont Board Agric.* 321 The Downy Woodpecker (*Picus pubescens*, Linn.) a black and white bird, usually not over six inches long. **1948** *Pacific Discovery* Mar.–Apr. 18/1 A harsh *spick*! note tells of a downy woodpecker in the neighborhood. **1964** J. BULL *Birds N.Y. Area* II. 289 The Downy Woodpecker nests in open woodland, orchards, suburbs, and city parks. **1971** *Islander* (Victoria, B.C.) 13 June 13/3 There are the..downy woodpecker, flicker woodpecker, [etc.].

4. *transf.* and *fig.* Down-like, soft as down.

1602 MARSTON *Antonio's Rev.* III. ii. Wks. 1856 I. 108 Ile ..couch my heade in downie moulde. **1605** SHAKS. *Macb.* II. iii. 81 Shake off this Downey sleepe, Deaths counterfeit. **1742** YOUNG *Nt. Th.* v. 397 Time steals on with downy Feet. **1839** BAILEY *Festus* (1854) 391 A warmer beauty and a downier depth.

5. *slang.* [with sense from DOWN *adv.* 22.] Wide-awake, 'knowing'.

1821 EGAN *Tom & Jerry* (1890) 95 (Farmer) Mr. Mace had long been christened by the downies, the 'dashing covey'. **1825** C. M. WESTMACOTT *Eng. Spy* I. 379 The president must be considered a downy one. **1837** THACKERAY *Yellowplush* i. (1887) 14 I'm generally considered tolerably downy. **1873** MISS BRADDON *Strangers & Pilgr.* III. v, Hilda, you're the downiest bird—I beg your pardon, the cleverest woman I ever met with.

6. *Comb.*, as *downy-cheeked*, *-clad*, *-feathered*, *-fruited*, *-sprouting*, *-winged* adjs.

1598 SYLVESTER *Du Bartas* II. ii. III. *Colonies* 42 The feeble downie-feathered Young. **1606** *Ibid.* II. iv. II. *Magnificence* 698 Some douny-clad, some (fledger) take a twig To pearch-upon, some hop from sprig to sprig. **1791** COWPER *Iliad* IX. 553 To make me downy-cheek'd as in my youth. **1815** SHELLEY *Demon of World* 23 Downy-winged slumbers.

downy ('daʊnɪ), *sb. slang.* Also downey. [f. DOWNY *a.*[2]] A bed; so *to do the downy*, to lie in bed. Cf. DOWNY *a.*[2] 2 (and quot. 1605 for sense 4).

1846 *Swell's Night Guide* 117/2 *Dab*, a letter, doss, downey, bed. **1847** W. T. PORTER *Quarter Race Kentucky* 58 The candidate yawned, looked at his bed,..finally..seating himself upon 'the downy'. **1854** 'C. BEDE' *Further Adv. V. Green* vii. 59 This'll never do..! Cutting chapel to do the downy! **1858** TROLLOPE *Three Clerks* I. ix. 181 I've a deal to do before I get to my downy. **1868** —— *He knew he was Right* (1869) I. xlv. 347 The Colonel was lodged safe in his downey. **1906** E. DYSON *Fact'ry 'Ands* ix. 118 Er pair iv boots was stickin' out conspicuous et one end iv ther downy. **1968** *Gloss. Brit. Argot* (Paramount Pictures), *Do the downy*, remain in bed.

dowp, dowress: see DOUP, DOWERESS.

†**dowrier.** *Sc. Obs.* Also dowariar. [a. F. *douairière* a woman enjoying a dowry, a dowager, f. *douaire* DOWER, dowry.] = DOWAGER.

1533 WRIOTHESLEY *Chron.* (1875) I. 18 To be called Ladie Katherin, wife of Prince Arthur, dowarie[r] of Englande. **1555** *Sc. Acts Mary* (1597) §28 In presence of the Queenis Grace, Marie, Queene Dowrier [*ed.* 1566 Dowariar], and Regent of Scotland. **1566** *Hist. Est. Scot.* in *Wodr. Soc. Misc.* (1844) 82 The Queene Dowrier sent forth a trumpett out of the Castle. **1596** DALRYMPLE tr. *Leslie's Hist. Scot.* x. 414 Mary Quene of Scotland and Douariar of France.

dowry ('daʊərɪ). Forms: 4–5 dowary(e, doweri(e, -rye, 7 dowarie, 6 (9) dowery; 4–7 dowrie, -rey, -rye, 5– dowry. [a. AF. *dowarie* fem. = OF. *douaire* masc., dower, dowry: cf. med.L. *doāria* fem. (1273 in Du Cange), beside *doārium*, *dōdārium*, *dōtārium*, neut.: see DOWER.]

†**1.** = DOWER I. *Obs.*

[**1292** BRITTON II. xix. §3 Le garraunt de sa dowarie avaunt le assignement..de sa certeyne dowarrie. *Ibid.* v. iii. §5 Dowarie deit estre assigné entierement et ne mie par parcelerie.] *c* **1330** R. BRUNNE *Chron. Wace* (Rolls) 6538 Ffrensche wymen wolde þey non take..To haue cleym þorow heritage, Ne dowarye þorow mariage. **1418** *E.E. Wills* (1882) 32 Here Dowerye &..here parte belonging to here of al my godes. **1584** POWEL *Lloyd's Cambria* 217 Who had for her Dowrie Lhannerchheidol. **1609** SKENE *Reg. Maj.* Table 76 The dowarie or great terce, perteining to ane woman. **1713** STEELE *Englishman* No. 28. 182 His wife is deprived of her Dowry. **1841** LANE *Arab. Nts.* 76 If he replies that he accepts her, and gives her a dowry.

2. The money or property the wife brings her husband; the portion given with the wife; tocher, dot; cf. DOWER 2.

c **1400** *Cato's Morals* 58 in *Cursor M.* App. iv, Fle to take wife..take hir for na doweri. **1513** DOUGLAS *Æneis* XI. vii. 182 Gif..this hald ryall Suld be thy drowry, and rich gift dotall. **1530** PALSGR. 358 She that is good and fayre nede none other dowrie. **1644** MILTON *Jdgm. Bucer* (1851) 333 That the Husband wrongfully divorcing his Wife, should give back her dowry. **1728** MORGAN *Algiers* I. iii. 36 Augustus married her to his Royal captive, and for a Dowry bestowed on him the Mauritanian and Numidian crowns. **1874** L. STEPHEN *Hours in Library* (1892) I. vi. 221 [He] has impoverished himself to provide his daughters' dowries.

†**3.** A present or gift given by a man to or for his bride. (In quot. 1717 given by the woman.) *Obs.*

c **1450** HENRYSON *Compl. Creseide* (R.) This roiall ring set with this rubie redd Which Troilus in dowrie to me sende. **1611** BIBLE *Gen.* xxxiv. 12 Aske mee neuer so much dowrie and gift..but giue me the damsell to wife. **1717** CROXALL *Ovid's Met.* VIII. i, To his dear tent I'd fly..confess my flame And grant him any dowry that he'd name.

4. *fig.* A 'gift' or talent with which any one is endowed by nature or fortune: an endowment.

c **1440** HYLTON *Scala Perf.* (W. de W. 1494) II. iv, The body of man..shall receyue fully the ryche dowary of vndedlynes. **1596** SHAKS. *Merch. V.* III. ii. 95 So are those crisped snakie golden locks..often knowne To be the dowrie of a second head. **1625** BACON *Ess.*, *Greatness Kingd.* (Arb.) 491 Strength at Sea (which is one of the Principall Dowries of this Kingdome). **1841–4** EMERSON *Ess.*, *Prudence* Wks. (Bohn) I. 97 Beauty should be the dowry of every man and woman. **1857** H. REED *Lect. Brit. Poets* ii. 73 A taste for poetry brings a rich dowry of intellectual and moral happiness.

5. *Comb.*, as *dowry-money*; *dowryless*, *dowry-seeking* adjs.

1675 tr. *Camden's Hist. Eliz.* I. (1688) 67 Her Dowry-money not payed out of France. **1886** W. J. TUCKER *E. Europe* 267 The love-sick or dowry-seeking soldier. **1925** *Glasgow Herald* 31 Dec. 4 The 'Army man'..outraged the conventions of Breffne by marrying a dowryless maiden for love. **1949** M. MEAD *Male & Female* xv. 303 She came to be chosen in marriage for her dowryless self alone.

†'**dowry,** *v. Obs.* [f. prec. sb.] *trans.* To give a dowry to.

1588 PARKE tr. *Mendoza's Hist. China* 45 a, For to dowrie their wiues with whom they shalbe married.

dows-: see DOUC-, DOUS-.

†'**Dowsabel.** *Obs.* An English form (through French) of the female name *Dulcibella*. Perhaps first used in some pastoral song, whence applied generically to a sweetheart, 'lady-love': cf. DOLL *sb.*[1] I.

[**1585–6** in *Winterton Parish Register* as *Dussable*.] **1590** SHAKS. *Com. Err.* IV. i. 110 Where Dowsabell did claime me for her husband. **1593** DRAYTON *Eclog.* IV, He had as antique stories tell A daughter cleaped Dowsabel. *a* **1652** BROME *Eng. Moor* III. iii. Wks. 1873 II. 48 [Women] Of all conditions, from the Doxie to the Dowsabel. **1675** COTTON *Scoffer Scoft* 75 Give me her for my Dowsabel.

dowse (daʊz), *v.* Also dowze, douse. [Derivation unknown; app. a dialect term.] *intr.* To use the divining- or dowsing-rod in search of subterraneous supplies of water or mineral veins.

Hence '**dowsing** *vbl. sb.*; **dowser** ('daʊzə(r)), one who uses the divining-rod, a water-diviner; **dowsing-rod**, the rod or twig used by dowsers.

1691 LOCKE *Lower. Interest* 40 Not of the nature of the deusing-rod, or virgula divina, able to discover mines of gold and silver. **1838** MRS. BRAY *Tradit. Devonsh.* III. 260 The superstition relative to the dowsing or divining rod, and the dowsers themselves, is too well known to be noticed here. **1865** R. HUNT *Pop. Rom. W. Eng.* Ser. I. Introd. 20 The divining or dowzing rod is certainly not older than the German miners, who were brought over by Queen Elizabeth to teach the Cornish to work their mines. **1869** *Eng. Mech.* 31 Dec. 380 I The 'dowsing' or 'divining' rod is a forked stick of some fruit-bearing wood, generally hazel, held by the extremity of each prong of the fork in a peculiar way. **1888** *Standard* 22 Dec., These authorities [Hastings Board of Guardians] lately invoked the aid of a 'Dowser', or water diviner, to tell them where to sink a well. **1894** *Daily News* 28 Dec. 5/2 The dry summer of 1893 brought the Divining Rod forward..'dowsers' sought for water with the mystic 'twig', and, very often, found it. *Ibid.*, Instances are adduced of ladies who have tried..and found that they could 'dowse'.

dowsing-cheek, -chock. Also dousing-.

1849–50 WEALE *Dict. Terms*, *Dowsing cheeks*. *c* **1850** *Rudim. Navig.* (Weale) 116 *Dowsing chocks*, pieces fayed athwart the apron and lapped on the knight-heads or inside stuff above the upper deck.

'**dowsy,** *a. Sc.* [? related to DOZY.] Stupid.

1508 DUNBAR *Flyting w. Kennedie* 158 God gif this dowsy be drownd. **1529** MORE *Suppl. of Soulys* Wks. 332/1 Beeing so dowsie drunke, that he coulde neither stande nor reele. **1843** *Whistle-binkie* (Sc. Songs) (1890) II. 99 Watchin' ilka step o' your wee dousy brither.

dowt(e, etc., obs. form of DOUBT, etc.

dowter, dowtie, -y, dowve, obs. ff. DAUGHTER, DOUGHTY *a.*, DOVE.

dowy, var. DOWIE; obs. form of DOUGHY.

-dox: see DOXY[2].

doxastic (dɒk'sæstɪk), *a.* [ad. Gr. δοξαστικ-ός forming opinion, conjectural, f. δοξαστής conjecturer, f. δοξάζ-ειν to conjecture.] Of or pertaining to opinion; depending on or exercising opinion. Also as *sb.* An object of opinion.

1794 T. TAYLOR *Plotinus* Introd. 22 Different objects of knowledge were known by different gnostic powers.. sensibles by sense, doxastics by opinion. **1801** —— *Aristotle's Metaph.* Introd. 54 Subordinate to this is the doxastic energy. **1822** —— *Apuleius* I. 332 Things which may be seen by the eyes, and touched by the hand, and which Plato calls doxastic.

doxographer (dɒk'sɒgrəfə(r)). [f. mod.L. *doxographus* (Diels 1879), f. Gr. δόξα opinion + -γραφος writer: see -ER[1].] A writer who collects and records the opinions or *placita* of the Greek philosophers. Hence **doxo'graphic, doxo'graphical** *adjs.*, of or pertaining to the doxographers; **do'xography**, a collection of philosophical opinions.

1892 J. BURNET *Early Greek Philos.* 371 By the term *doxographers* we understand all those writers who relate the opinions of the Greek philosophers. *Ibid.* 374 The doxography [of the *Lucullus*] has come through the hands of Kleitomachus. *Ibid.* 375 Short doxographical summaries are to be found in Eusebios [etc.]. **1908** J. ADAM *Relig. Teachers of Greece* xiii. 267 We have doxographical testimony to show that Diogenes pronounced the soul to be imperishable. *Ibid.* 268 The doxographers sometimes ascribe to him [*sc.* Democritus] the doctrine of a single world-soul or Deity identical..with the aggregate of fiery atoms in the world. **1919** *Jrnl. Hellenic Stud.* 180 The Greek doxographers know of no astronomer before Thales. **1937** *Mind* XLVI. 248 Nor was he..blind to the possibility that doxographic statements going back to Theophrastus may sometimes originate in an Aristotelian misconception or misrepresentation. **1952** *Jrnl. Theol. Stud.* III. 123 The problem how far [Basil] knew the philosophers from their actual works and how far he was dependent on anthologies and doxographical manuals. **1952** G. SARTON *Hist. Sci.* I. x. 239 We have only fragments and the sayings of doxographers, indirectly and poorly transmitted. *Ibid.*, Doxographic books of the latter [*sc.* Theophrastos] are known only indirectly through later extracts. *Ibid.* xii. 327 We really need a new critical edition of all the Ctesias fragments and of the doxography relative to him.

doxological (dɒksəʊ'lɒdʒɪkəl), *a.* [f. DOXOLOGY + -IC + -AL[1].] Pertaining to or of the nature of a doxology; praising, glorifying.

1655 HOWELL *Lett.* IV. 123 A Doxological Cronogram including this present yeer MDCLV. **1695** G. HOOPER *Disc. Lent* 353 (T. Suppl.) The three first collects are noted to be wholly doxological. **1883** H. M. KENNEDY tr. *Ten Brink's E.E. Lit.* 42 The poet..presents a doxological opening, glorifying God.

Hence **doxo'logically** *adv.*

1891 J. E. H. THOMSON *Bks. wh. infl. our Lord* II. vi. 295 The whole Psalter closes doxologically.

doxologize (dɒk'sɒlədʒaɪz), *v.* [f. DOXOLOGY + -IZE.] To say the doxology. **b.** *trans.* To address a doxology to.

1727 BAILEY vol. II, *Doxologize*..to say the Hymn called *Gloria Patri*. *a* **1816** *Chr. Disciple* II. 295 (Pickering) No instance is to be found in which primitive Christians doxologized the Spirit of God as a Person.

†'**doxologue.** *Obs. rare.* [ad. Gr. δοξολόγ-ος: see next.] = next.

a **1617** BAYNE *On Eph.* i. (1643) 42 The manifold doxologues in Paul's Epistles.

doxology (dɒk'sɒlədʒɪ). [ad. med.L. *doxologia*, a. Gr. δοξολογία, abst. sb. f. δοξολόγ-ος uttering praise, giving glory, δόξα glory + -λογος speaking. So F. *doxologie*.]

†**a.** The utterance of praise to God; thanksgiving. *Obs.* **b.** A short formula of praise to God, esp. one in liturgical use; *spec.* the *Gloria in excelsis* or 'Greater doxology', the

Gloria Patri or 'Lesser doxology', or some metrical formula, such as the verse beginning 'Praise God from whom all blessings flow.'

1649 JER. TAYLOR *Gt. Exemp.* II. xi. 147 It is an expresse Doxology or adoration. **1660** T. WATSON in Spurgeon *Treas. Dav.* Ps. lxxxvi. 12 Doxology, or praise, is a God-exalting work. **1664** H. MORE *Myst. Iniq.* 98 That Doxologie of our Blessed Saviour, I thank, O Father [etc.]. **1720** WATERLAND *Eight Serm.* Ded., The Attempt to introduce.. New Forms of Doxology. **1894** *Times* (weekly ed.) 16 Feb. 129/4 The well-known Doxology beginning, 'Praise God from whom all blessings flow.'

doxy[1] ('dɒksɪ). Also 6 doccy, 6–7 doxe, 7 doxie, doxye, 7– doxey. [Derivation unknown: perh. like some other terms of rogues' cant, of continental origin; possibly a deriv. of DOCK *sb.*[2] 3.] Originally the term in Vagabonds' Cant for the unmarried mistress of a beggar or rogue: a beggar's trull or wench: hence, *slang*, a mistress, paramour, prostitute; *dial.*, a wench, sweetheart.

c **1530** *Hickscorner* in Hazl. *Dodsley* I. 188 Of the stews I am made controller.. There shall no man play doccy there .. Without they have leave of me. **1561** AWDELAY *Frat. Vacab.* 4 His woman with him.. which he calleth his Altham if she be hys wyfe, & if she be his harlot, she is called hys Doxy. *Ibid.* 5 So she is called a Doxy, vntil she come to yᵉ honor of an Altham [in Harman *Autem*]. **1611** SHAKS. *Wint. T.* IV. ii. 2 With, heigh the Doxy ouer the dale. **1611** DEKKER *Roaring Girle* Wks. 1873 III. 217 My doxy stayes for me in a bousing ken. **1711** STEELE *Spect.* No. 6 ¶2 The Beggar.. while he has a warm Fire and his Doxy, never reflects that he deserves to be whipped. **1825** BROCKETT *N.C. Words*, *Doxy*, a sweetheart; but not in the equivocal sense used by Shak. and other play writers. **1827** HONE *Every-Day Bk.* II. 1656 Surrounded by plough-boys and their doxeys. **1857** W. COLLINS *Dead Secret* III. i. 71 Spending all my money among doxies and strolling players.

'**doxy**[2]. *colloq.* (usually *humorous.*) [The latter part of the words *orthodoxy*, *heterodoxy*, etc., from Gr. δόξα opinion.] Opinion (esp. in religious or theological matters). (Cf. *-ism.*) So **dox**.

1730 J. ASGILL *Woolston* 2. **1756** AMORY *J. Buncle* (1825) III. 19 Orthodox and other dox. **17..** WARBURTON in *Priestley's Mem.* I. 372 'Orthodoxy, my Lord', said Bishop Warburton..'is my doxy,—heterodoxy is another man's doxy.' **1778** J. Q. ADAMS *Diary* 30 Nov., Orthodoxy is my doxy, and heterodoxy is your doxy. **1842** MRS. BROWNING *Grk. Chr. Poets, etc.* 174 [Dryden] made him [Chaucer] a much finer speaker, and not, according to our doxy, so good a versifier. **1843** *Tait's Mag.* X. 579 Heterodoxy.. does not mean cacodoxy at all.. but only another man's doxy: your doxy generally as opposed to mine. **1868** *Illustr. Lond. News* 11 Apr. 351 This is not the place for the discussion of 'doxies'.

doxycycline (dɒksɪ'saɪkliːn). *Pharm.* [f. *d(e)oxy-* (f. DE- + OXY-) + TETRA)CYCLINE.] A broad-spectrum antibiotic, $C_{22}H_{24}N_2O_8$, of the tetracycline group which has a relatively long half-life in the body.

1966 *Chemotherapia* XI. 73 Doxycycline (GS-3065), or α-6-deoxyoxytetracycline, is a new antibiotic which is prepared by the hydrogenation of methacycline. **1977** *Martindale's Extra Pharmacopoeia* (ed. 27) 1129/2 Preparations... *Vibramycin* (Pfizer). Doxycycline hydrochloride, available as capsules. **1977** *Lancet* 22 Oct. 858/2 In patients with paratrachoma, because of the associated genital infections, treatment must be systemic—tetracycline 1 g daily, doxycycline 100 mg daily, or a sulphonamide 2.3 g daily, all for 3 weeks. **1984** *Brit. Nat. Formulary* No. 8. v. 198/2 With the exception of doxycycline.. and minocycline the tetracyclines may exacerbate renal failure.

‖**doyen** (dwajɛ̃). Also 5 doien. [F. *doyen*:—L. *decān-us* DEAN. In sense 1 from OF.; in sense 2 anew from mod.French.]

†**1.** A leader or commander of ten. *Obs.*

1422 tr. *Secreta Secret., Priv. Priv.* (E.E.T.S.) 214 Euery ledere [had] ten doiens, and.. euery doiens ten men.

2. The senior member of a body. = DEAN[1] 10. Cf. DOYENNE[2].

1670 COTTON *Espernon* II. v. 242 This was he.. that was afterwards Doyen to the Council of State. **1883** *Pall Mall G.* 12 Nov. 3/2 A member of the Royal Danish Academy of Arts, of which he died the doyen. **1886** *Ibid.* 23 Sept. 3 The doyen of the Russian press.

‖**Doyenne**[1] (dwa'jɛn). Also **Doyenné**. [ad. F. *doyenné*, in full *poire de doyenné*, lit. 'deanery pear'.] In full ***Doyenne pear***. A variety of pear, esp. ***Doyenne du Comice***, a large yellow late-fruiting pear, a favourite for cultivation.

[**1666** EVELYN *Kal. Hort.* (ed. 2) 107 Pears. The Squib-pear, Spindle-pear, Doyoniere, Virgin.] **1731** MILLER *Gard. Dict.* (1733) s.v. *Pyrus* 35 Le Doyenné, *i.e.* The Deans Pear. **1822** LOUDON *Encycl. Gardening* (1824) §4437 Doyenné. *Synonym.* Dean's pear. **1858** *Trans. Ill. Agric. Soc.* III. 338 Fine crops of White Doyenne and Bartlett. **1860** R. HOGG *Fruit Manual* 181 Fruit small, roundish-obovate, or Doyenné-shaped. **1872** *Rep. Vermont Board Agric.* 109 A yearly crop of the finest Doyenne pears, in size, colour and quality, of any I have ever seen. **1958** *Listener* 20 Nov. 853/2 The best [varieties of pears] I think are Williams' Bon Chrétien, Marie Louise, Doyenne du Comice, [etc.].

‖**doyenne**[2]. [See DOYEN 2.] A female doyen; the leading or senior woman in a group, society, etc.

1905 A. BENNETT *Sacred & Profane Love* II. i. 104 That stately dowager, that impeccable *doyenne* of serious English fiction. **1926** A. HUXLEY *Let.* 10 Aug. (1969) 272 Anita Loos .. is the doyenne of Hollywood. **1958** *Times* 24 Nov. p. xvi/5 The *doyenne* of this group is that assiduous and deservedly popular writer Mazo de la Roche. **1959** P. BULL *I know the Face* i. 13 Miss Elsie Fogerty, the doyenne of The Central School of Dramatic Art.

doyk(e, obs. form of DUKE.

doyl(e, doyll(e, obs. ff. DOLE *sb.*[1] and [2].

doyld(e, doyley, -ly: see DOILED *a.*, DOILY.

doyne, doysen, obs. ff. DO *v.*, DONE, DOZEN *v.*

doze (dəʊz), *v.* Also 7 **doaze**, 7–9 **dose**. [Of late appearance in literary English; perh. earlier in dialects. The trans. sense, in which it is first known, is identical with Da. *döse* to make dull, heavy, drowsy (*dös*, dullness, drowsiness, *dösig* drowsy): cf. also rare ON. *dúsa* to doze, *dús*, *dos*, lull, dead calm, Sw. dial. *dusa* to doze, slumber.]

†**1.** *trans.* To stupefy; to muddle; to make drowsy or dull; to bewilder, confuse, perplex. *Obs.*

1647 R. STAPYLTON *Juvenal* 122 'Tis work for great soules, not [for] one dos'd about the mending of his bed. **1650** —— *Strada's Low C. Warres* VI. 7 As night and suspicion doses the mind. *a* **1656** HALES *Gold. Rem.* (1688) 17 Easily doz'd and amazed with every Sophism. **1658** FLECKNOE *Epigr. & Enigm. Char.* (1665) 82 Whose Head is so doaz'd with knocking, and Breech hardened with whipping. **1719** DE FOE *Crusoe* I. vi, The tobacco had.. dozed my head. *Ibid.* II. i, The surgeon.. gave him something to dose and put him to sleep. **1796** MACNEILL *Will & Jean* II. ix, Drams and drumming (faes to thinking) Dozed reflection fast asleep. **1818** MOORE *Fudge Fam. Paris* ii. 38 Your Lordship.. when All sovereigns else were dozed, at last Speeched down the Sovereign of Belfast.

2. *intr.* To sleep drowsily; to fall into a light sleep unintentionally from drowsiness; to be half asleep; to nod. Also *fig.* So, *to doze it* (*obs.*).

1693 W. FREKE *Sel. Ess.* xxvii. 161 The best of us dose, dote, and Slumber at times. *a* **1704** R. L'ESTRANGE (J.) There was no sleeping under his roof; if he happened to doze a little, the jolly cobler waked him. **1777** SHERIDAN *Sch. Scand.* IV. iii, I have been dozing over a stupid book. **1880** OUIDA *Moths* II. 269 A place to doze and dream in.

fig. **1855** TENNYSON *Maud* I. xxii. 48 The pimpernel dozed on the lea.

b. *to doze off* or *over*: to drop off into a doze.

1860 GEO. ELIOT *Mill on Fl.* i. 1 Before I dozed off, I was going to tell you [etc.]. **1886** STEVENSON *Dr. Jekyll* 19 The figure.. haunted the lawyer all night; and if at any time he dozed over [etc.]. **1888** E. J. MATHER *Nor'ard of Dogger* 350, I was just dozed off myself when I was aroused by a cry from the deck.

3. *trans.* (with *away*, *out*). To pass or spend (time) in dozing.

1693 R. GOULD *Corrupt. Times* 14 We doze away our Hours. **1742** POPE *Dunc.* IV. 617 Chiefless Armies doz'd out the Campaign. **1845** WHEWELL in *Todhunter's Acc. W.'s Wks.* (1876) II. 330, I.. dose away a few summer months almost in solitude.

doze, *sb.* [f. prec. vb.] A fit of dozing; a short slumber.

1731 *Lett. fr. Fog's Jrnl.* (1732) II. 209 A Doze over his Coffee. **1840** DICKENS *Barn. Rudge* vii, He fell into a doze again, and slept until the fire was quite burnt out. **1863** MRS. OLIPHANT *Salem Ch.* xiii. 224 Now and then he woke up, as men wake up from a doze.

doze, obs. form of DOSE.

dozed (dəʊzd), *ppl. a.* [f. DOZE *v.* + -ED[1].]

a. Stupefied; drowsy, sleepy. **b.** Of timber, etc.: Having lost its tenacity of fibre, as by dry rot; doted. Hence '**dozedness**, drowsiness, sleepiness.

1659 GAUDEN *Tears Ch.* 306 While they were dozed or asleep. **1669** WOODHEAD *St. Teresa* I. xxx. 216 My soul falls into a kind of dozedness. *Ibid.* II. ii. 96 It is no strange thing ..to continue dozed, and stupid for this space. **1702** C. MATHER *Magn. Chr.* VII. v. (1852) 541 The dozed conscience of the thief. **1722** NETTLETON in *Phil. Trans.* XXXII. 38 Vomiting, dosedness, startings, and sometimes Convulsions. **1776** G. SEMPLE *Building in Water* 86 Bog Oak Timber is always found to be frushey, dozed and short grained. **1825** JAMIESON, *Doz'd*.. in an unsound state; as, 'doz'd timber', 'a doz'd raip'. **1849** M. ARNOLD *Poems, New Sirens*, Slowly raising Your dozed eyelids.

dozel, obs. form of DOSSIL, plug.

dozen ('dʌz(ə)n), *sb.* Forms: 4 dozein(e, dozyne, dosain, dosene, 4–5 dozeyn(e, doseyn(e, 4–6 dosayn(e, dosein, 4–7 dosen, 5 duzan, dusan(e, dosan, dussen, 6 dousaine, -ayne, dossen, -eyn, -in, -on, dosin, -yn, doosen, dosand, 6–7 dousen, 7 doozen, dozzen, dossein, 7–8 douzen, 6– dozen. *β.* 5 disson, *Sc.* 6 desone, 8– dizzen. [a. OF. *dozeine*, *dosaine*, Fr. *douzaine* = Pr. *dotzena*, Sp. *docena*, a Com. Romanic deriv. of **dōdece*, *dotze*, *doze*, *doce*:—L. *duodecim* twelve + *-ēna*, as in *decēna*, *centēna*, etc.]

1. A group or set of twelve. Originally as a sb., followed by *of*, but often with ellipsis of *of*, and thus, in singular = twelve. Also, used colloq. in *pl.*, either indefinitely or hyperbolically, for any moderately large number; cf. HUNDRED *sb.* and *a.* 2. (Abbreviated *doz.*)

a **1300** *Cursor M.* 11407 (Cott.) Quen ani deid o þat dozein [*v. rr.* dozeine, doseyn, dozyne]. **1340–70** *Alex. & Dind.* 670 A dosain of wondrus. **1362** LANGL. *P. Pl.* A. v. 164 Dauwe þe disschere, and a doseyn oþer [B. dozeine C. dosen]. **1420** *E.E. Wills* (1882) 46 Halfe a dosen sponys. **1526** *Pilgr. Perf.* (W. de W. 1531) 118 b, A thynge done, perauenture a dosyn yere before. **15..** *A Pore Helpe* 335 in Hazl. *E.P.P.* III. 264 And feche in my cosens By the whole dosens. **1555** BRADFORD in Strype *Eccl. Mem.* III. App. xlv. 133 Halfe a dossen of grene salletts. **1670** G. H. *Hist. Cardinals* II. II. 172 Cardinals that are made by the dozens. **1726** *Adv. Capt. R. Boyle* 203 A dozen of Knives. **1734** POPE *Sober Advice from Horace* in *Poet. Wks.* (1966) 395 Dangers on Dangers! Obstacles by dozens! **1834** MEDWIN *Angler in Wales* I. 58, I saw some dozens of these little animals. **1841–4** EMERSON *Ess., Spir. Laws* Wks. (Bohn) I. 65 There are not.. more than a dozen persons. *a* **1897** *Mod.* Six dozen pencils. **1898** G. B. SHAW *Philanderer* I. III. 133 There are dozens of men who would give their souls for a look from me. **1913** D. H. LAWRENCE in *Sat. Westm. Gaz.* 6 Sept. 9/3 Dozens of men were lounging round the cart. **1961** M. KENNY *Spanish Tapestry* II. i. 125 Dozens of tailors squat over their sewing. **1986** *N.Y. Times* 23 Apr. B9/6 The new league signed dozens of high N.F.L. draft choices.

b. Elliptical (with a noun of measure, etc., understood). ***dozen of bread***: a dozen loaves. ***dozen of beer, ale, wine***, etc., i.e. a dozen pots or bottles; hence ***rump(-steak) and a dozen***: see quot. 1893. ***to give one two dozen***, i.e. lashes.

1573–80 BARET *Alv.* D 1078 A dosen of bread, *duodecim panes.* **1574** in W. H. Turner *Select. Rec. Oxford* 376 Payed for dozen of breade.. iiijᵈ. **1677** LADY CHAWORTH in *12th Rep. Hist. MSS. Comm.* App. v. 37 A dozen of Margett ale. **1815** SCOTT *Guy M.* xxxviii, 'I'll bet a rump and dozen', said Pleydell. **1835** C. SHAW *Let.* 6 Dec. in *Mem.* (1837) II. 453, I ordered them.. to receive two dozen each, being caught in the act. **1839** A. SOMERVILLE *Hist. Brit. Legion* iii. 42 He was tied up, and.. took his two dozen. **1893** *Westm. Gaz.* 4 Feb. 8/3 The stake being a 'rump-steak and a dozen'.. It was explained that it was a dinner and as much as you liked to drink.

c. With qualifying words. ***baker's dozen*** (see BAKER 6), ***devil's, long, printer's dozen***: thirteen. ***brown*** (*obs.*) or ***round dozen***: a full dozen. ***thirteen,*** (etc.) ***to the dozen***: see quots. ***to talk nineteen to the dozen***: to talk very fast, or to excess.

a **1529** SKELTON *Bowge of Courte* 393 Have at the hasarde; or at the dosen browne. **1588** *Marprel. Epist.* (Arb.) 34 Pay it you with advantage, at least thirteene to the dozen. **1598** in Lambert's *2000 years of Guild Life* (1892) 308 All the saide Company will deliver forthe theire breade.. xiijᵗᵉⁿ to the dozen. **1820** BYRON *Blues* I. 36 A round dozen of authors and others. **1831** *Blackw. Mag.* XXX. 343/2 Instead of one kick, he deserves and gets a devil's dozen. **1872** OUIDA *Fitz's Election* 210 She.. generally talked nineteen to the dozen.

†**2.** A kind of kersey or coarse woollen cloth: see quot. 1552. (Usually in *pl.*) *Obs.*

1523 *Act 14 & 15 Hen. VIII*, c. 1 Northerne whites, commonly named and called dosins. **1552** *Act 5 & 6 Edw. VI*, c. 6. §13 All Devonshire Kersies called Dozens.. shall contain in Length at the Water between twelve and thirteen Yards. **1557** *Act 4 & 5 Phil. & Mary* c. 5. §10 Every Devonshire Kersie, called Dosson. **1640** in Entick *London* (1766) II. 179 Woollen Drapery —— Devonshire dozens.. Northern dozens. **1721** C. KING *Brit. Merch.* II. 309 English Clothes called Dozens.

†**3.** The town-council of a burgh. *Sc. Obs.*

['Prob. so called because it originally consisted of twelve members' (Donaldson *Supp. to Jamieson*). Cf. also DOUZAINE.]

1416 in *Edin. Burgh Rec.* Oct. (Jam. Supp.), Aldermannus pro presenti anno, one dene of gild.. one bursator, thirty two of lie dusane. **1418** *Ibid.* Oct., The dusane is callit 'duodecim consules et limitatores'. **1492** *Ibid.* 19 Oct., Ordanit be the hale dusane of the town. **1574** in *Peebles Burgh Rec.*

†**4.** Corruptly used for Anglo-French *dizeyne* (Fr. *dixaine*) a tithing, or group of ten households. *Obs.*

[**1292** BRITTON I. xiii. [xii.] §1 Et voloms qe touz soint en dizeyne [*v. rr.* duzeyne, dozein] et pleviz par dizeyners [*v. rr.* dozeyners, dozainers].] **15..** *Act 18 Edw. II* (Berthelet 1543) If al the chiefe pledges or their dosens bee come. **1624** *Termes de la Ley* s.v. *Deciner*, Deciner is not now used for the chiefe man of a Dozein, but for him that is sworne, to the Kings peace. **1672** COWELL *Interpr.* s.v. *Deciner*, Now there are no other Dozens but Leets.

5. ***the dozens***: a Black American game or ritualized exchange of verbal insults, usu. about the family (esp. the mother) of one's opponent or opponents: (see quot. 1984 and *to play the dozens* s.v. PLAY *v.* 16 e); ***to put*** (etc.) ***in the dozens***: to subject to or involve in this form of exchange. Cf. SIGNIFY *v.* 8, SOUND *v.*[1] 3 d.

1928 R. FISHER *Walls of Jericho* 9 For it is the gravest of insults, this so-called 'slipping in the dozens.' To disparage a man is one thing; to disparage his family is another. **1935** D. L. COHN *God shakes Creation* vi. 161 Another prolific source of shootings and stabbings flows from what they call 'putting 'em in de dozens'. This is a form of Rabelaisian banter engaged in by two or more Negroes. At a gathering one Negro may begin by saying, 'Yo' mammy hists her tail like a cat.'.. Aspersion after aspersion is cast. **1942** *Amer. N. & Q.* I. 156/1 'Playing the Dozens.'.. This is a widely used phrase among the Negroes in North Carolina (and very likely in most of the South). **1962** R. D. ABRAHAMS in A. Dundes *Mother Wit* (1973) 299 One will.. find girls making dozens-type remarks. **1970** R. D. ABRAHAMS *Positively Black* iv. 88 He got your whole family in the dozens and your sister on the shelf. **1971** B. MALAMUD *Tenants* 131 'Chum,' he said,.. 'we have a game we got we call the dozens.' **1978** *Amer. Poetry Rev.* July/Aug. 44/3 All you have to do to keep them in their proper place, which is deep in the dozens, is to pat your feet and snap your fingers. **1984** *Maledicta 1983* VII. 183 Many cultures have cursing and counter-cursing games, such as the Black American ' dozens'. The purpose of the dozens is to test the participants' ability to take abuse without reacting. The participants must have a response, they must not show hurt, and they must not react with violence.

dozen ('dəʊz(ə)n), *v. Sc.* and *north. dial.* Forms: 5 doysen, 5-8 dosen, 6 dosin, 8- dozen (9 dozzen). [Prob. of Norse origin, repr. an inchoative verb in *-na*, from the stem of DOZE *v.*]

1. *trans.* To stun, stupefy, daze.

(But app. found only in pa. pple., which might belong to an intrans. vb.: cf. 2.)

1375 BARBOUR *Bruce* XVIII. 126 Mowbray..had beyne doysnyt [*v.r.* dosnyt] in the ficht. *c* **1450** HENRYSON *Mor. Fab.* 71 Both deife and dosened. *a* **1810** TANNAHILL *Poet Wks.* (1844) 86 Dorothy, dozened wi' living her lane.

2. *trans.* To make insensible, torpid, or powerless; to benumb. (Only in pa. pple.)

1576 *Trial Eliz. Dunlop* in P. H. Brown *Scot. bef. 1700* (1893) 212 The merch of the bane was consumit and the blude dosinit. **1789** BURNS *Ep. Jas. Tennent* 6 My dearest member nearly dozen'd. **1832** CARRICK in *Whistle-binkie* (Sc. Songs) (1890) I. 203 Birds Dozened sit on the frosty spray.

3. *intr.* To become torpid or benumbed.

1725 RAMSAY *Gent. Sheph.* I. ii, A dish o' married love right soon grows cauld And dozens down to nane. *a* **1774** FERGUSSON *Poems* xi. (Jam.) The birds..Dozen in silence on the bending spray.

Hence **'dozened** *ppl. a.*, benumbed, torpid.

1724 RAMSAY *Tea-t. Misc.* II. 119 Thou dosend drone. **1828** BROCKETT *N.C. Words, Dozened*, spiritless, impotent, withered. **1833** GALT in *Fraser's Mag.* VIII. 651 With a natural inclination (as all old bachelors have) to be dozened.

dozener ('dʌz(ə)nə(r)). Also 6 **dussiner**, 7 **dozinier, doziner**, (7 **decennier**, 7-9 **deciner**). [In sense 1, a. AF. *dozeyner, dozainer*, a corrupt form of *dizeyner* (DIZENER): cf. DOZEN *sb.* 4. In sense 2 prob. the same; but cf. DOZEN 3.]

1. a. A member of a tithing: see DOZEN 4. **b.** The head of a dozen.

1617 MINSHEU *Ductor* s.v. *Deciners* [tr. Britton: see DOZEN 4.] We will that all..professe themselues to be of this or that dozein, and make or offer suretie of their behauiour by these or those doziniers. **1670** BLOUNT *Law Dict., Deciners* alias *Decenniers*, alias *Doziners*. **1869** [see DECENER].

2. A name formerly borne by the constables, watchmen, or other ward-officers, in some boroughs.

1558 *Lichfield Guild Ord.* (1890) 17 Billettes Directed to the Dussiners in euery seuerall warde for the colleccion off the sommes aboue written. **1806** T. HARWOOD *Hist. Lichfield* 354 The watch..at Lichfield, used to be called 'dozeners'. *Ibid.*, The great Portmote Court of the Bailiffs and Citizens, Lords of the Manor, called anciently Le Dozener's, or Magdalen Court. **1835** *Municip. Corp. 1st Rept.* App. III. 1851 The Inspector of Pounds, called Dozener..in the borough [Derby].

dozenth ('dʌz(ə)nθ), *a. colloq.* [f. DOZEN *sb.* + -TH[1].] = TWELFTH. So ***half-dozenth*** = SIXTH.

1710 SWIFT *Jrnl. to Stella* 23 Dec., I have sent my 11th to-night..and begin the dozenth. **1840** *New Monthly Mag.* LX. 264 Every half-dozenth window might be a loophole. **1853** COBDEN in Sir L. Mallett *C.'s Pol. Writings* (1878) 202 Let me repeat it—if for the dozenth time.

dozepers, dozepiere, var. DOUZEPERS, *Obs.*

dozer[1] ('dəʊzə(r)). [f. DOZE *v.* + -ER[1].] One who dozes or sleeps drowsily.

1710 FULLER *Tatler* No. 205 ¶2 To add to my Dead and Living Men, Persons in an intermediate State..under the Appellation of Dozers. **1882** *Harper's Mag.* LXV. 633 When he aroused himself from a nap in church, arose, and looked sternly about to catch some luckless dozer.

dozer[2] ('dəʊzə(r)). Also **'dozer**. Colloq. shortening of BULLDOZER.

1942 *Infantry Jrnl.* (U.S.) Oct. 51 The blade of the dozer is not much good. **1949** *Landfall* III. 174 Come trucks and lux and tools of trade Motor tyres a dozer-blade. **1958** *Daily Mail* 16 July 6/6 These modern devices have such names as the tractor shovel, the crawler-loader, the dozer. **1959** 'J. R. MACDONALD' *Galton Case* (1960) xxvi. 204 You could of knocked me over with a 'dozer. **1971** *Engineering* Apr. 52 The whole caterpillar-built range including lift trucks, track and wheel loaders, and dozers.

doziberd(e, var. of DASIBERD, *Obs.*

dozily ('dəʊzɪlɪ), *adv.* [f. DOZY *a.* + -LY[2].] In a dozy manner; drowsily, sleepily.

1861 THORNBURY *Turner* (1862) I. 85 Quiet deer feeding dozily under the stone pines.

doziness ('dəʊzɪnɪs). [f. as prec. + -NESS.] The state of being dozy; drowsiness, sleepiness.

1679 J. GOODMAN *Penit. Pard.* II. i. (1713) 244 A mopish ineffective doziness. **1797** J. DOWNING *Disord. Horned Cattle* 9 The sleepiness or doziness to which the beast..is inclined. **1838** LD. HOUGHTON in T. W. Reid *Life* (1890) I. 232 Amid London dinners and doziness.

'dozing, *vbl. sb.* [f. DOZE *v.* + -ING[1].] The action of sleeping drowsily.

1692 BENTLEY *Boyle Lect.* i. 9 With an eternal laziness and dozing. **1879** GEO. ELIOT *Coll. Breakf. P.* 834 That border-world Of dozing, ere the sense is fully locked.

'dozing, *ppl. a.* [f. as prec. + -ING[2].] Drowsily sleeping.

1820 HAZLITT *Lect. Dram. Lit.* 6 In a dozing state. **1880** L. WALLACE *Ben-Hur* VII. iv. 451 Within arm-reach of the dozing camel.

Hence **'dozingly** *adv.*, drowsily, sleepily.

1831 TRELAWNY *Adv. Younger Son* cxvii, Trees, under groves of which they dosingly lay.

dozy ('dəʊzɪ), *a.*[1] Also **dosey, dozey**. [f. DOZE *v.* + -Y[1].]

1. a. Drowsy, sleepy. Also (*colloq.*), (mentally) sluggish; stupid; lazy.

1693 DRYDEN *Persius* iii. (R.), His lazy limbs and dozy head. **1725** POPE *Odyss.* IX. 429 The dozy fume. **1836** in R. McNab *Old Whaling Days* (1913) 451 The 4th mate..has been Sick and dozey ½ the time. **1883** A. S. HARDY *But yet a Woman* 167 A fire always makes one dozy. **1924** GALSWORTHY *White Monkey* I. vii. 50 Soames directed his gaze at the pink face of dosey old Mothergill. **1959** J. BRAINE *Vodi* iii. 51 'The swine,' Dick said. 'You're dozy,' Liphook said. 'They were damned decent, really.' **1961** J. MACLAREN-ROSS *Doomsday Bk.* vii. 75 What's funny, you dozey berk?

b. as *sb.*

1849 E. E. NAPIER *Excurs. S. Africa* II. 241 That old dozy there and myself got a fortnight's leave.

2. Of timber or fruit: In a state of incipient decay; 'sleepy'. Cf. DOZED, DOTED 2, DOTY.

1872 SCHELE DE VERE *Americanisms* 464 *Dozy* and *dozed* are said in Pennsylvania of timber beginning to decay and unfit for use, while the decay is yet hardly perceptible, but the timber already brittle. (S. S. Haldeman.) **1882** *Boston Jrnl. Chem.* 1 Feb. 19/2 The water runs in around the wood and makes it dozy, wet, and heavy. **1923** D. H. LAWRENCE *Kangaroo* viii. 166 Fatuous letters from friends in England ..as dozy as ripe pears in their *laisser aller* heaviness.

†**dozy**, *a.*[2] *Obs.* Also **dosye, dosey, dusey**. An obs. by-form of DIZZY *a.*

1530 PALSGR. 310/2 Dosye in the heed, *betourne*. **1551-68** [see DIZZY *a.* 2].

†**'dozy**, *v. Obs. rare.* [f. prec. adj.] *trans.* To make giddy or dizzy; to DIZZY.

1568 TURNER *Herbal* III. 51 Not to suffer them to lyve after they be dosyed or made dronken.

dozyne, dozzen, obs. forms of DOZEN.

dozze pers, var. DOUZEPERS. *Obs.*

†**'dozzle**, *v. Obs.* [f. DOZE *v.* with freq. suffix -LE.] *trans.* To render stupid; to stupefy.

a **1670** HACKET *Abp. Williams* II. (1692) 142 Being dozzled with fear, thinks every man wiser than himself.

dozzle ('dɒz(ə)l), *sb. Metallurgy.* Also **dozzler**. A hollow refractory brick fitted to the top of an ingot-mould to provide a reservoir of molten metal, which flows downwards to fill cavities in the ingot; = FEEDER 9 a.

1923 J. W. HALL in Harbord & Hall *Metallurgy of Steel* (ed. 7) II. i. 4 With this the fire-brick head, called in Sheffield a 'dozzler', can be lifted off. **1932** E. GREGORY *Metallurgy* ii. 51 A short fireclay cylinder, known as a *core* or *dozzle*. **1954** *Gloss. Terms Iron & Steel (B.S.I.)* II. 8 *Dozzle*, a preheated hollow refractory brick used to provide a feeder head for small ingots.

dr., abbreviation of *debtor* (in *Book-keeping*), *doctor*.

draaf, obs. form of DRAFF.

drab (dræb), *sb.*[1] Also 6 **drabe**, 6-7 **drabb(e**. [Not known before 16th c.; derivation uncertain: prob. at first a low or cant word. Evidently connected with Irish *drabog*, Gael. *drabag* dirty female, slattern; but evidence is wanting to show which is the original. Connexion with LG. *drabbe* dirt, mire, has also been suggested.]

1. A dirty and untidy woman; a slut, slattern.

c **1515** *Cocke Lorell's B.* (Percy Soc.) 11 Sluttes, drabbes, and counseyll whystelers. **1526** R. WHYTFORD *Martiloge* (1893) 36 Saynt Tabite was holden a fole and drabbe of kechyn. **1530** PALSGR. 215/1 Drabbe a slutte, *uilotiere*. *a* **1712** W. KING *Art Cookery* (T.) So at an Irish funeral appears A train of drabs with mercenary tears. **1816** SCOTT *Old Mort.* viii, A dirty drab of a housemaid. **1872** GEO. ELIOT *Middlem.* xi, Who ended by living up an entry with a drab and six children for their establishment.

2. A harlot, prostitute, strumpet.

c **1530** LD. BERNERS *Arth. Lyt. Bryt.* (1814) 403 And than shall the drabbe, my doughter, be mured vp in a stone wall. **1547** BOORDE *Brev. Health* ii. 6 b, Gyve that knave or drabbe a phylyp with a club. **1605** SHAKS. *Macb.* IV. i. 31 Birth-strangled Babe, Ditch-deliuer'd by a Drab. **1675** COCKER *Morals* 15 Drink, Dice, and Drabs, three dange'rous Dees. **1731** SWIFT *Answ. Simile* Wks. 1755 IV. I. 223 Each drab has been compared to Venus. **1856** MRS. BROWNING *Aur. Leigh* v. 789 And said 'my sister' to the lowest drab Of all the assembled castaways.

transf. **1589** *Pappe w. Hatchet* D iv b, There is no more sullen beast, than a he drab.

¶ The following are probably distinct words:

3. *Salt-making.* See quot. and cf. CRIB *sb.* 9.

1753 CHAMBERS *Cycl. Supp., Drabs*, in the English salt works, a name given to a sort of wooden cases into which the salt is put, as soon as it is taken out of the boiling pan..Their bottoms are made..gradually inclining forwards; by which means the saline liquor that remains mixed with the salt easily drains out. In some places they use cribs instead of the Drabs.

4. A small or petty sum (of money); esp. in *dribs and drabs*: see DRIB.

1828 *Craven Dial., Drab*, a small debt. 'He's gain away for good, and he's left some drabs'. **1847-78** in HALLIWELL. **1861** MAYHEW *Lond. Labour* III. 200 (Hoppe) None of us save money; it goes either in a lump, if we get a lump, or in dribs and drabs. **1888** *Daily News* 19 Apr. 3/5 It [the payment] was received in dribs and drabs.

drab (dræb), *sb.*[2] and *a.* [In early quotations app. synonymous with *drap* cloth (see quot. from Bailey, and cf. DRAP-DE-BERRY). Conjectured to have been applied to a hempen, linen, or woollen cloth of the natural undyed colour, whence attrib. in *drap* or *drab colour*, i.e. the colour of this cloth, and thus to have gradually become an adj. of colour: cf. *rose, pink, salmon*, etc. as colour names.]

A. *sb.* A kind of cloth: see quots.

1541 *Lanc. Wills* 80 Ij drabs of teir of hempe, a drab of new canvis. [**1706** PHILLIPS (ed. Kersey), *Drap* (Fr.), cloath, Woollen-cloath. **1718** *Freethinker* No. 42 ¶8 To smile on a Brocade more than upon a Brown Drap.] **1721** BAILEY, *Drap, Drab*, cloth, woollen Cloth. **1740** DYCHE & PARDON, *Drab*, an extraordinary sort of woollen cloth, chiefly worn in the winter-time. **1753** HANWAY *Trav.* II. I. v. 20 British Woollens, such as hair-list drabs..We improved some of our drabs, so as to be almost equal to the dutch cloths in the substance. [**1772** MRS. SCOTT *Test Filial Duty* II. 220 Collin, whose wedding coat is a new white drap.]

B. *adj.* **a.** Of a dull light-brown or yellowish-brown.

[**1686** *Lond. Gaz.* No. 2100/4 The one with a Drapp-colour cloth Campaigne Coat.] **1715-1768** [see *drap-coloured, drab-coloured*, in D. below.] **1775** ASH, *Drab* (adj. with clothiers), belonging to a gradation of plain colours betwixt a white and a dark brown. **1803** S. PEGGE *Anecd. Eng. Lang.* 266 Hence our drab cloth, pure and undied cloth, and they call this a drab colour in the trade. **1832** DOWNES *Lett. Cont. Countries* I. 523 The cottages..were of a deep drab hue. **1837** DICKENS *Pickw.* iii, He wore wide drab trousers. **1865** *Sat. Rev.* 12 Aug. (L.) Male Quakers have.. discarded broadbrimmed hats and drab breeches.

b. *fig.* Dull; wanting brightness or colour.

1880 MISS BROUGHTON *Sec. Th.* I. iv, The little drab day has already dropped in the maw of..night. **1892** *Pall Mall G.* 27 Feb. 1/2 The lives of the people..are dull and drab; a round of work with but little amusement.

c. In comb. with other names of colours.

1894 R. B. SHARPE *Hand-bk Birds Gt. Brit.* I. 12 Sides of neck and under surface of body drab-grey. **1905** *Westm. Gaz.* 15 May 10/2 The rather soft fur of the underparts is drab-brown.

C. *sb.* [absol. use of the adj.]

1. a. Drab colour; cloth or clothing of this colour; esp. in *pl.* = drab breeches.

1821 CLARE *Vill. Minstr.* I. 38 Milk-maids..Threw 'cotton drabs' and 'worsted hose' away. **1824** MISS MITFORD *Village* Ser. I. (1863) 38 Woe to white gowns! woe to black! Drab was your only wear. **1838** DICKENS *Nich. Nick.* xiv, A short old gentleman, in drabs and gaiters. **1884** *Pall Mall G.* 7 June 5/1 Silk gowns of Quaker drab.

b. *S. Afr.* (*pl.*) The long feathers on the part of the wing of a female ostrich near to the junction with the body. (In quot. 1896 *drab* is adj.)

1881 A. DOUGLASS *Ostrich Farming in S. Afr.* xi. 68 The little white belly feathers should have been replaced by blacks or drabs. **1896** R. WALLACE *Farming Ind. Cape Col.* xi. 235 Drab, long, and medium were about 10s. per lb. lower. **1913** C. PETTMAN *Africanderisms* 167 *Drabs*, corresponding growth from the female.

c. *fig.* A dull or lifeless appearance or character.

1903 *Daily Chron.* 31 Dec. 5/1 Despite the fact that so many of his works wore a drab, still those who knew him best recognised that the drab was the colour of his experience. **1909** *Westm. Gaz.* 4 Feb. 1/3 It is the one sustained note of colour in the dreary drab of Irish life.

2. Collector's name for a group of moths.

1819 G. SAMOUELLE *Entomol. Compend.* 370 Noctua angusta. The dark Drab. Noctua geminata. The twin-spotted Drab. **1869** NEWMAN *British Moths* 358 The clouded Drab (*Tæniocampa instabilis*).

D. *Comb.*, as ***drab-breeched, -coloured, -tinted***; **drab-coat** *a.*, wearing a drab coat, drab-coated.

1715 *Lond. Gaz.* No. 5328/4 Dark Drap colour'd Coat. **1768** STERNE *Sent. Journ.* (1775) 114 (*Mystery*) Dressed in a dark drab-colour'd coat. **1843** SYD. SMITH *Lett. on Amer. Debts* Wks. 1859 II. 330/1 Drab-coloured men of Pennsylvania. **1848** WHITTIER *Peace Con. at Brus.* Poems (1882) 149 The dull, meek droning of a drab-coat seer.

Hence **'drably** *adv.*, in drab colour; also *fig.*, without brightness or colour, dully, uninterestingly; in comb., as ***drably-clad, -tinted***; **'drabman** (*humorous nonce-wd.*), a quaker; **'drabness**, drab quality.

1860 *All Year Round* No. 66. 378 Labouring..at our target practice, long before the drowsy drabmen have moved from their pillows. **1878** MISS BRADDON *Open Verd.* viii. 60 Though the paint was mostly gone a general drabness remained. **1891** H. C. HALLIDAY *Some one must suffer* II. xii. 217 That drably-tinted lady. **1905** *Westm. Gaz.* 19 Sept. 10/1 Few guess that the dahlia..has had a drably unromantic origin. **1918** *Cornhill Mag.* June 616 The desirability of expressing thoughts fully and truly in words ..is too drably presented to the child. **1927** *Sunday Express* 1 May 9 Their novels look drably old-fashioned. **1956** *Ann. Rep. Smithsonian Inst.* 216 The sun's interior must be drably uniform.

drab (dræb), *v.* [f. DRAB *sb.*[1]] *intr.* To associate with harlots; to whore. Also *to drab it.*

1602 SHAKS. *Ham.* II. i. 26 Drinking, fencing, swearing, Quarelling, drabbing. *a* **1624** BP. M. SMITH *Serm.* (1632) 276 He is the true gentleman now adayes, that can drinke and drab it best. **1719** D'URFEY *Pills* (1872) III. 48 I'll drink and drab. **1853** *Blackw. Mag.* LXXIV. 110 He would have drunk and diced, drabbed and hunted.

Hence **'drabbing** *vbl. sb.*; †**'drabber**, a whoremonger.

a **1611** BEAUM. & FL. *Triumph of Death* vi, Drunkenness, and drabbing, thy two morals. **1632** MASSINGER *City Madam* IV. ii. A most insatiate drabber. **1820** SCOTT *Monast.* xxxv, Nothing but dicing, drinking and drabbing.

draba ('dreɪbə). *Bot.* [mod.L. (J. J. Dillenius in Linnæus *Systema Naturæ* (1735)), ad. Gr. δράβη a kind of cress.] A plant of the genus of herbs so named belonging to the family Cruciferæ, found in temperate and arctic regions, and cultivated as hardy annual, biennial, and perennial alpine plants. (See also *whitlow-grass* (WHITLOW b).)

1629 PARKINSON *Paradisi* ci. 390 Candy Tufts..is named by some, *Draba*, or *Arabis*, as Dodonæus, but *Draba* is another plant differing much from this. **1777** W. CURTIS *Flora Lond.* I. Plate 133, Vernal Draba or Whitlow Grass. **1895** S. H. VINES *Students' Text-bk. Bot.* 603 Latiseptal silicula of Draba. **1968** *Q. Bull. Alpine Garden Soc.* XXXVI. 69 There are many magnificent drabas.

‖**dra'bant.** [Sw. *drabant* attendant, satellite: in Ger. *trabant*, It. *trabante*, F. *traban*, *draban*, Boh. *drabanti*, Magyar *darabant*, Roumanian *doroban*, ad. Turkish (orig. Pers.) *darbān* porter, guard.] A halberdier; spec. a soldier of the body-guard of the kings of Sweden.

1707 *Lond. Gaz.* No. 4339/3 He was Captain-Lieutenant of the King of Sweden's Drabants. **1823** CRABB *Technol. Dict.*, *Drabants* (Mil.), a select body of men, who were commanded in person by Charles IX, King of Sweden. **1862** H. MARRYAT *Year in Sweden* II. 127 We next pass into the drabant guard-room.

†**drabbery.** *Obs. rare.* [f. DRAB *sb.*[1] + -ERY.] Drabbing, harlotry.

1570 LEVINS *Manip.* 104/12 Drabbery, *meretricium.*

drabbet ('dræbɪt, dræ'bɛt). Also **-ette.** [f. DRAB *sb.*[2] + -ET[1], dim. suffix.] A drab twilled linen, used for making men's smock-frocks, etc.

1819 J. BAXTER *Jrnl.* 16 Feb. in *Amer. Speech* (1965) XL. 198 Bot Jack a piece of Bleu Cloth for a Coat 3½ yds at 3/6 & myself a pair of Trowsers called Drabbett. **1851** *Offic. Catal. Gt. Exhib.* I. 97 Drabbetts..Fancy Drills..Grey Twills. **1874** T. HARDY *Far fr. Madding Crowd* ix, Some..in snow-white smock frocks of Russia duck, and some in whitey-brown ones of drabbet. **1885** *Chr. World* 529 Real Suffolk drabbet—one of the finest things for a workman to wear.

drabbish ('dræbɪʃ), *a.*[1] [f. DRAB *sb.*[1] + -ISH.] Partaking of the qualities of a drab; sluttish.

1566 DRANT *Horace Sat.* VIII. E, I markte the drabbishe sorcerers and harde their dismall spell. **1888** T. HARDY *Wessex T.* 171 The drabbish woman she had expected.

'drabbish, *a.*[2] [f. DRAB *a.* + -ISH.] Somewhat drab in colour; drab-looking. Also in comb.

1842 DICKENS *Amer. Notes* (1868) 89 Dressed in a dusty drabbish-coloured suit. **1870** MISS BROUGHTON *Red as Rose* I. 64 So many..are neutral-tinted, drabbish, greyish.

'drabbit! short for *'od rabbit! God rabbit!*: an imprecation: see RABBIT *v.* 2.

drabble (dræb(ə)l), *v.* [ME. *drabelen* = LG. (EFris.) *drabbeln* to walk or wade about in water or liquid mud, to paddle; to splash, bespatter: cf. *drabbe* thick dirty liquid, mire, *drabbig* muddy, miry, turbid; also early mod.Du. *drabben* to run about, tramp about.]

1. *intr.* To become wet and dirty by dabbling in, or trailing through, water or mire.

a **1400–50** *Alexander* 232 Diȝt as a Doctour in drabland wedis. **15..** *Hye way to Spyttel Hous* 116 in Hazl. *E.P.P.* IV. 28 Brechles, bare foted, all stynkyng with dyrt, With M. [= a thousand] of tatters drabblyng to the shyrt. **1565** J. SPARKE in *Hawkins' Voy.* (1878) 61 Being put vpon a hooke drabling in the water. *a* **1712** W. KING *Art of Love* IV. (R.) Who shall all this rabble meet, But Gnossy, drabbling in the street? **1807–8** W. IRVING *Salmag.* v. (1824) 74 The poor fellows who had to drabble through the..mire.

2. *trans.* To make wet and dirty by contact with muddy water or mire. Also in extended use.

c **1440** *Promp. Parv.* 129/2 Drabelyn, *paludo.* **1599** NASHE *Lenten Stuffe* 6 Spreading their drabled sailes..abroad a drying. **1792** *Trans. Soc. Arts* X. 47 Heavy showers of rain ..which has drabbled the Corn. **1867** *Jrnl. R. Agric. Soc.* Ser. II. III. II. 529 Clip off the down at the tail to prevent their being drabbled. **1903** KIPLING *Five Nations* vii, Across the sad valleys all drabbled with rain. **1923** *Chambers's Jrnl.* 89/2 Thews who..drabbled graybeards in their blood.

3. *Angling.* (*intr.*) To fish for barbel, etc. with a rod and a line threaded through a leaden bullet so that the hook may be trailed along the bottom.

1799 G. SMITH *Laboratory* II. 272 The right method of drabbling, as it is termed..for gudgeons.

Hence **'drabbled** *ppl. a.*, wet with dirty water, or with dragging in the mire; **'drabbling** *vbl. sb.* and *ppl. a.*; also **drabble-tail**, a slattern, draggle-tail; **drabble-tailed** *a.*

a **1400–50** Drabbling [see 1]. *c* **1440** *Promp. Parv.* 129/2 Draplyd (*v.r.* drablyd), *paludosus.* **1599** Drabbled [see 2]. *a* **1825** FORBY *Voc. E. Anglia*, *Drabble-tail*, a slattern, who allows her garments to trail after her in the dirt. **1825** BROCKETT *N.C. Gloss.*, *Drabbl'd*, *Drabble-tailed*, dirtied.

drabble, *sb.* [f. prec. vb.]

1. The action or process of drabbling for fish.

1799 G. SMITH *Laboratory* II. 269 When you angle for this fish at the bottom, on the drabble.

2. A contemptuous term for drabbled people.

1789 WOLCOTT (P. Pindar) *Tithe Rencounter* x. 1 Some Presbyterian rabble..Or some fierce Methodistic drabble.

drabbler, drabler ('dræblə(r)). *Naut.* [f. DRABBLE *v.*, in reference to its position.] An additional piece of canvas, laced to the bottom of the bonnet of a sail, to give it greater depth.

a **1592** GREENE & LODGE *Looking Glass* Wks. (Rtldg.) 134/2 Then scantled we our sails with speedy hands, And took our drablers from our bonnets. **1645** HEYWOOD *Fort. by Land* IV. Wks. 1874 VI. 416 Lace your drablers on. **1708** MOTTEUX *Rabelais* IV. lxiii. (1737) 256 To our Sails we had added Drablers. **1851** KIPPING *Sailmaking* (ed. 2) 182 Drabbler. **1867** SMYTH *Sailor's Word-bk.*, *Drabler*, a piece of canvas laced on the bonnet of a sail to give it more drop ..used when both course and bonnet are not deep enough.

drabby ('dræbɪ), *a.*[1] [f. DRAB *sb.*[1] + -Y.] Pertaining to, or of the nature of, a drab; abounding in drabs.

1612 W. PARKES *Curtaine Drawer* (1876) 12 The Curtaine of dishonesty..the drunken colourer of Drabby salary. **1776** COMBE *Diaboliad* (1777) 12 The wiles of drabby Drury and of low St. Giles. **1887** FRITH *Autobiog.* II. 81 They are drabby, shabby, dirty creatures.

'drabby, *a.*[2] [f. DRAB *a.* + -Y.] Rather drab; drabbish. Hence **'drabbiness.**

1862 MRS. H. WOOD *Mrs. Hallib.* II. viii, A drabby petticoat in rags. **1872** DASENT *Three to One* II. 3 While women should pass their lives in drabbiness and dowdiness. **1890** *Spectator* 25 Jan. 115/2 We do not believe in all this drabbiness,..in the modern ridicule of ceremonial. **1893** G. D. LESLIE *Lett. Marco* xxxi. 209 The want of colour that accompanies a north-east wind; sky, trees and grass all looking washed out and drabby.

drabi ('dræbɪ). [See quot. 1920.] A muleteer.

1900 *Pioneer Mail* 16 Mar. (Y.), The mule race for Drabis and grass-cutters was entertaining. **1920** *Chambers's Jrnl.* 296/2 (Indian frontier) The lot of the muleteer (or *drabi*, as he is generally called, this being the native rendering of the English word 'driver') is never a very easy one. **1920** *Blackw. Mag.* Nov. 569/2 (Mahsudland) Mule drabis. **1927** E. THOMPSON *These Men, thy Friends* 125 A fool of a *drabi*, who had left his mules and stumbled off, seeking India that lay to the east.

‖**Dracæna** (drə'siːnə). *Bot.* [mod.L., a. Gr. δράκαινα she-dragon, fem. of δράκων dragon.] A genus of *Liliaceæ*, containing the dragon-tree *Dracæna Draco*, and various other ornamental species.

1823 in CRABB *Technol. Dict.* **1870** MEADE *New Zealand* 189 Aprons of scarlet dracaena leaves. **1892** *Daily News* 21 Jan. 5/6 The rooms were charmingly embellished with white dracænas, palms, and other foliage plants.

drach, obs. f. DRAW *v.*

drac(h), drack, colloq. abbrevs. of DRACHMA 1 b.

1935 L. DURRELL *Let.* in *Spirit of Place* (1969) 31 They.. said, with uncertainty—24 dracs—1/-. *Ibid.* 33 There is a good peasant wine... It costs 6 dracks—3[d] per bottle. **1936** 'T. B. MARLE' *Candid Escort* i. 11 'Can you give me five drachs?' he asked. **1969** R. AIRTH *Snatch!* ii. 19, I stood outside the court-room in Athens with eight dracks in my pocket. **1971** P. DICKINSON *Sleep & his Brother* iii. 54 I was sitting by the yacht-basin in Iraklion wondering where my next drach was coming from.

drachm (dræm). Forms: 4–7 **dragme**, 6 **drachime**, 6–7 **drachme**, **dragm**, 7– **drachm**. See also DRAM. [a. F. *drachme*, earlier *dragme*, in OF. also *drame* = Pr. *dragma*, L. *drachma*, a. Gr. δραχμή, an Attic weight and coin, prob. orig., 'as much as one can hold in the hand', f. δράσσεσθαι (-ττ-) to grasp (cf. δράγμα).]

1. The principal silver coin of the ancient Greeks, the DRACHMA; containing 6 obols. It varied in weight and value in different places. (Also DRACHMA.)

1382 WYCLIF *Luke* xv. 8 What womman hauynge ten dragmes, ether besauntis, and if sche hath lost o dragme [etc.]. **1607** SHAKS. *Cor.* I. v. 6 These mouers, that do prize their hours At a crack'd Drachme. **1646** SIR T. BROWNE *Pseud. Ep.* VII. xi. 360 Every man of the Jews should bring into the Capitoll two dragmes. **1771** in *Phil. Trans.* LXI. 469 The current coin of Athens, was the silver Drachm.

b. Hence, the DIRHEM of the Arabs.

1554 W. PRAT *Africa* G vij a (Stanf.) .xx. Drachimes whiche is ten pens Englyshe. **1840** CARLYLE *Heroes* ii. (1872) 66 Mahomet..asked..If he owed any man? A voice answered, 'Yes, me three drachms'.

2. A weight approximately equivalent to that of the Greek coin. Hence, in Apothecaries' weight = 60 grains, or $\frac{1}{8}$ of an ounce, in Avoirdupois weight = $27\frac{1}{3}$ grains or $\frac{1}{16}$ of an ounce. (Spelt *drachm* or *dram.*) Also, the Arabic DIRHEM.

fluid drachm = $\frac{1}{8}$ of fluid ounce, = 60 minims or drops. **1398** TREVISA *Barth. De P.R.* XIX. cxxviii. (1495) 932 The leeste mesure is Coclearium and is half a Dragme. *c* **1400** *Lanfranc's Cirurg.* 153 Take..of ech two dragmis. **1590** *Recorde's Gr. Artes* (1646) 135, 3 Scruples make a Drachm or Dragme. **1704** F. FULLER *Med. Gymn.* (1711) 77 A few Drachms of Unctuous Stuff. *c* **1850** *Arab. Nts.* (Rtldg.) 584 Aladdin..desired to have half a drachm of the powder. **1894** *Lancet* 10 Nov. 1093 The catheter..drew off four drachms of albuminous urine.

3. *fig.* A small quantity; a very little. (Cf. *grain.*)

1635 J. HAYWARD tr. *Biondi's Banish'd Virgin* 4 Having.. out of the masse of our di[s]asters extracted us this dragme of comfort. **1670** G. H. *Hist. Cardinals* I. II. 48 One drachme of affliction. *a* **1729** CONGREVE (T.) The rogue has not a drachm of generous love about him. **1876** T. HARDY *Ethelberta* (1890) 306 'Now do you see the truth?' she whispered..without a drachm of feeling.

‖**drachma** ('drækmə). Also 6–7 **dragma**. Pl. **-mas**, also **-mæ**, (6–7 **-maes**). [a. L. *drachma*, a. Gr. δραχμή DRACHM. The form *dragma* is assimilated to OF. *dragme*, Pr. and med.L. *dragma.*]

1. = DRACHM 1. Also, the Jewish quarter-shekel.

1579–80 NORTH *Plutarch* 378 (R.) Small pieces of money .. called oboli, whereof six made a drachma. **1581** MARBECK *Bk. Notes* 313 A Dragma is the fourth part of a Sickle, which is to saie fiue halfe-pence. **1601** SHAKS. *Jul. C.* III. ii. 247 To euery seuerall man, seuenty fiue Drachmaes. **1614** RALEIGH *Hist. World* II. (1634) 322 Judas Macchabeus..sent thence ten thousand Dragmas. **1712** ADDISON *Spect.* No. 535 ¶7 He left him to the value of an hundred drachmas in Persian money. **1881** JOWETT *Thucyd.* I. 178 Every one of the hoplites..received two drachmae a day.

b. The standard silver coin of modern Greece, equivalent to the French *franc* and Italian *lira.*

1882 BITHELL *Counting-ho. Dict.* (1893) 196.

2. = DRACHM 2.

1527 ANDREW *Brunswyke's Distyll. Waters* Dj, Myxced with Bolo Armeno and with lapide ematitis, of eche a dragma. **1632** HEYWOOD *2nd Pt. Iron Age* v. Wks. 1874 III. 426 [They] Will scarce weigh eleauen Dragmaes. **1807** ROBINSON *Archæol. Græca* v. xxvi. 551 Grecian weights reduced to..Troy weight: Drachma = 6 dwt. $2\frac{22}{40}$ grains.

drachmal ('drækməl), *a. rare.* [f. prec. + -AL[1].] Pertaining to a drachm or drachma.

1674 JEAKE *Arith.* (1696) 105 This is sometime called the Drachmal Denary for distinction sake.

†**dracin, -ine.** *Chem.* = DRACONIN.

drack(e, obs. form of DRAKE.

dracocephalum (drækəʊ'sɛfələm). *Bot.* [mod.L. (Linnæus *Genera Plantarum* (1737) 173), f. Gr. δράκων dragon + κεφαλή head, in reference to the shape of the flower.] An annual or perennial herb of the genus so called, belonging to the family Labiatæ and native to temperate Asia and Europe; = DRAGON'S HEAD 2.

1840 J. LOUDON *Ladies' Flower-Garden Ornamental Annuals* 226 Dracocephalum... The Dragon's Head... There are several other kinds of annual Dracocephalums, but they differ very little from each other, and they are none of them common in British gardens. **1904** R. J. FARRER *Garden Asia* 237 The pallid gleam of a dracocephalum. **1957** *Q. Bull. Alpine Garden Soc.* XXV. 95 A Dracocephalum.. has flowers of a deep purple-blue.

dracoman: obs. form of DRAGOMAN.

dracone, Dracone ('drækəʊn). [f. L. *draco*, *-ōnem*, ad. Gr. δράκων dragon.] A large flexible container for transporting liquids, towed on the surface of the sea.

1956 *Trinity* (Cambr.) *Mag.* 9/2 The seas will shortly be full of Dracones. **1959** *Times* 27 Apr. (Suppl.) p. xi/4, The most spectacular of the new flexible containers are the long sausage-shaped nylon and neoprene bags called Dracones. **1963** *Daily Tel.* 20 Dec. 18/3 The dracone..has been used in Greece to bring fresh water to islands and for the transport of fuel. **1967** *New Scientist* 2 Nov. 289/1 The Dracone, a towable 'barge' made of nylon fabric coated with synthetic rubber for transporting petroleum products, drinking water, etc.

Dra'conian, *a.* [f. as DRACONIC + -IAN.] = DRACONIC 1, 2.

1876 C. M. DAVIES *Unorth. Lond.* 97 The Swedenborgian rubrics are not so Draconian. **1877** D. M. WALLACE *Russia* xiii. 206 Refraining from all Draconian legislation. **1880** *Daily Tel.* 10 Nov., In the course of one of these draconian performances..the mummer's tail came off.

Hence **Dra'conianism.**

1819 GIFFORD in Smiles *J. Murray* I. 404, I never much admired the vaunt of Draconianism, 'And all this I dare do, because I dare'.

Draconic (drə'kɒnɪk), *a.* [f. L. *draco*, *-ōnem*, ad. Gr. δράκων dragon, also f. the Greek personal name, Δράκων, Draco: see -IC.]

1. Of, pertaining to, or characteristic of Draco, archon at Athens in 621 B.C., or the severe code of laws said to have been established by him; rigorous, harsh, severe, cruel.

1708 MOTTEUX *Rabelais* v. xi. (1737) 43 Any Law so rigorous and Draconic. **1872** YEATS *Growth Comm.* 35 Their criminal code, which was Draconic in severity.

2. Pertaining to, or of the nature of, a dragon.

1680 H. MORE *Apocal. Apoc.* 118 'The great Dragon was cast out'.. This.. signified the destruction of the Empire as Draconick and Idolatrous. **1791** tr. *Swedenborg's Apoc. Rev.* xiv. §655 To whom the draconic spirit addressed the same words. **1820** SCOTT *Abbot* xv, 'Marry come up—are you there with your bears?' muttered the dragon, with a draconic silliness.

3. *Astron.* = DRACONTIC.

(Sometimes erroneously explained as 'Relating to the constellation Draco'.)

1876 G. CHAMBERS *Astron.* II. i. 174 This is termed a 'nodical revolution of the Moon.' *note.* Sometimes the Draconic Period.

†**Dra'conical,** *a. Obs.* [f. as prec. + -AL[1].] = prec. (sense 2).

1680 H. MORE *Apocal. Apoc.* 122 This Draconical power.

Dra'conically, *adv.* [f. prec. + -LY[2].] After the manner of Draco; with extreme severity.

1641 *Parall. betw. Wolsey & Laud* in *Harl. Misc.* (Malh.) IV. 465 Both of them at the Council-board, and in the star-chamber, [were] alike draconically supercilious. **1887** S. WHITMAN *Convent. Cant* 87 It is draconically prohibited.

draconiform (drə'kɒnɪfɔːm), *a.* [f. L. *dracon-, draco* DRAGON: see -FORM.] Resembling a dragon in shape.

1888 J. C. DUNLOP *Prose Fiction* I. 450 The accessory emblem of a draconiform monster.

'draconin, -ine. *Chem.* [f. L. *draco* dragon.] The colouring matter in *dragon's blood*, at first supposed to be alkaline, and named accordingly.

1837 *Penny Cycl.* IX. 118/1 Herberger.. calls this colouring matter *draconin*, and he considers it to possess rather sub-acid properties than such as denote alkalinity. **1863-72** WATTS *Dict. Chem.* II. 345 Melandri regarded the resin.. as an alkaloid, and designated it as *draconine, dracenine*, or *dracine*.

Draconism ('drækənɪz(ə)m). [f. Gr. personal name Δράκων, Draco: see -ISM.] Draconic character. (See DRACONIC 1.)

1832 *Westm. Rev.* XVII. 313 The draconism of their slave laws.

†**'draconist.** *Obs.* [f. as DRACONIC + -IST.] An adherent of the Dragon. (See Rev. xii. 3.)

1684 H. MORE *Answ.* 179 Open Draconists or Bestians.

‖**draconites** (drækə'naɪtiːz). Also 7 **dracontites, dracondite.** [L. *dracōnītis* (Pliny), f. *dracōn-em* DRAGON.] A precious stone fabled to be taken from the brain of a dragon; a dragon-stone.

1579 LYLY *Euphues* (Arb.) 124 The precious gemme *Dacromtes* [*Draconites*] that is euer taken out of the heade of the poysoned Dragon. **1608** HARINGTON *Sch. Salerne* 358 Haue in your rings.. a Draconites, which you shall beare for an ornament. **1855** SMEDLEY *Occult Sciences* 354.

draco'nitic, *a. Astron.* = DRACONTIC.

In recent Dicts.

dra'contian, *a.* [irreg. f. Gr. δράκων, -οντα dragon + -IAN.] = DRACONIC 2.

1816 G. S. FABER *Orig. Pagan Idol.* III. 282 The dracontian figure attached to the ring of Abury. **1818** —— *Hor. Mos.* I. 73 The dracontian Ahriman of the Persians.

dracontic (drə'kɒntɪk), *a. Astron.* [f. Gr. δρακοντ-, stem of δράκων dragon + -IC.] Pertaining to the moon's nodes: see DRAGON'S-HEAD, -TAIL.

1727-51 CHAMBERS *Cycl.*, *Dracontic Month*, the space of time wherein the moon going from her ascending node, called *Caput Draconis*, returns to the same. **1730-6** in BAILEY (folio). Also in mod. Dicts.

dracontine (drə'kɒntaɪn), *a.* [irreg. f. Gr. δράκων, -οντα dragon + -INE.] Of the nature of, or belonging to, a dragon.

1806 G. S. FABER *Diss. Prophecies* II. 248 Her dracontine cruelty. **1865** BARING-GOULD *Werewolves* x. 175 A gigantic man with few of the dracontine attributes remaining.

Dracula ('drækjʊlə). The name of the king of the Vampires, invented by Bram Stoker in the novel of this name (1897), used allusively to denote a grotesque or terrifying person, etc.

Prince Vlad of Wallachia, who died in 1476, was also known as 'Dracula' (spelt in various ways, e.g. Ladislaus Drakula, Wladislaus Dragwlya). *Times Lit. Suppl.* 22 Oct. 1971, p. 1336.

[**1897** B. STOKER *Dracula* iv. 51 The last I saw of Count Dracula was his kissing his hand to me; with a red light of triumph in his eyes, and with a smile that Judas in hell might be proud of. *Ibid.* xxvii. 383 We looked back and saw where the clear line of Dracula's castle cut the sky.] **1938** M. ALLINGHAM *Fashion in Shrouds* xvi. 279 If he's Dracula himself we'll get him and hang him. **1953** R. LEHMANN *Echoing Grove* 266 A real killer in disguise she must be—a real female Dracula. **1971** 'A. GILBERT' *Tenant for Tomb* xv. 252 Now that Lady Dracula is unlikely to be released.. how about our considering our own plans?

‖**dracunculus** (drə'kʌŋkjʊləs). [L. dim. of *draco* DRAGON.]

1. The muscular hair-worm *D.* (*Filaria*) *medinensis*, found in the legs and muscular parts of the arms of the inhabitants of both Indies, and other tropical countries; the Guinea-worm.

1706 PHILLIPS (ed. Kersey), *Dracunculus*.. a kind of Ulcer that eats even thro' a Nerve it self; also a long sort of Earth-worm, which frequently grows to Indians' Legs. **1727-51** CHAMBERS *Cycl.* s.v., A disease in children, wherein they feel a vehement itching; supposed to arise from little worms called *Dracunculi*. **1851-9** *Man. Sci. Eng.* 248 Why the dracunculus should be met with on the west coast of Africa. **1888** ROLLESTON & JACKSON *Anim. Life* 676 The female *Dracunculus*.. may attain a length of six feet.

2. *Ichthyol.* A fish, a dragonet or goby of the genus *Callionymus*.

1752 SIR J. HILL *Hist. Anim.* 272 (Jod.) The seadragon: this is frequent in the Mediterranean.. Ray, etc. call it dracunculus. **1753** in CHAMBERS *Cycl. Supp.*

3. *Bot.* A herbaceous genus of *Araceæ*, formerly included under *Arum*, containing the green DRAGON (q.v. 14) or DRAGONS.

1706 in PHILLIPS (ed. Kersey). **1748-52** SIR J. HILL *Hist. Plants* 596 (Jod.) Arum; this genus comprehends the arum, arisarum, colocasia and dracunculus of authors. **1753** CHAMBERS *Cycl. Supp.*, Dracunculus, *Dragons* in botany.

drad, obs. form of DREAD *a.* and *v.*

dradge, dradgy, obs. or dial. ff. DREDGE.

dradgy, Sc. form of DIRGE, chiefly in sense 3. Funeral feast.

draegerman ('dreɪgəmæn). *N. Amer.* Also **dregerman.** [f. the name of A. B. *Dräger* (1870-1928), German scientist, inventor of a type of breathing apparatus + MAN *sb.*[1]] One of a crew of men trained for underground rescue work. So ***Draeger crew.***

1918 R. DRUMMOND *Minerals & Mining, Nova Scotia* 343 Draeger men were soon ready but exploration was somewhat impeded by the jamming of the cage at the bottom of the shaft. **1936** *Ottawa Jrnl.* 20 Apr. 1/1 One of the Stellanton Draeger crew explained to bystanders. *Ibid.* 21/1 Stellanton's draegermen—a crew of rescue men trained to enter a colliery after an explosion. **1958** *Times* 25 Oct. 6/7 The dregermen.. carry about 45 lb. of oxygen equipment on their backs.

draf, obs. form of *drove*, pa. t. of DRIVE.

draff (drɑːf, -æ-). Forms: 3-5 draf, (3 drof, 4-5 draft, 5 draaf, drafe, 5-7 draffe), 5- draff, (7 draugh). [early ME. *draf*, prob. repr. an unrecorded OE. **dræf*, corresp. to MDu. and Du. *draf*, Icel. *draf*, Sw. *draf*, Da. *drav* sediment of a brewing, grains, husks, OHG. **trab*, pl. *trebir*, MHG. *treber*, Ger. *träber* grains, husks, etc.:—OTeut. type **trabaz* neuter. Cf. also Ir. and Gael. *drabh* grains of malt, prob. from English.]

Refuse, dregs, lees; wash or swill given to swine; hog's-wash; *spec.* the refuse or grains of malt after brewing or distilling; brewer's grains.

c **1205** LAY. 29256 He gon ȝeoten draf and chaf and aten. *c* **1250** *Gen. & Ex.* 3582 Moyses.. dede ðat calf melten in fir .. And mengde in water.. And gaf ðat folc drinken ðat drof. **1362** LANGL. *P. Pl.* A. XI. 11 Hogges.. draf weore hem leuere þen al þe presciouse Peerles. *c* **1380** WYCLIF *Serm.* Sel. Wks. II. 171 þei diversen fro Goddis lawe, as draf diversiþ fro clene drynke. *c* **1420** *Pallad. on Husb.* I. 580 If their appetite With draf of win be fed. **1522** MORE *De quat. Noviss.* Wks. 73/2 A sow contente with draffe durt and mire. **1671** MILTON *Samson* 573 Till vermin or the draff of servile food Consume me. **1688** R. HOLME *Armoury* II. 181/2 Washings.. necessary for keeping of Swine.. Whey Butter-milk, Dish-water, any kind of Draff. **1875** A. SMITH *Hist. Aberdeensh.* I. 559 Animals.. fed off by the dregs or draff at the Distillery.

b. *transf.* and *fig.*

c **1385** CHAUCER *L.G.W.* 312 To wryte The draf of stories, and forgo the corn. *c* **1555** HARPSFIELD *Divorce Hen. VIII* (Camden) 296 The draffs of filthy errors. **1643** MILTON *Divorce* Introd. (1851) 6 The brood of Belial, the draffe of men. **1878** DOWDEN *Stud. Lit.* 45 Examples that have survived the chaff and draff of the time.

c. *Proverbs.*

1546 J. HEYWOOD *Prov.* (1867) 22 The still sowe eats vp all the draffe. *Ibid.* 26 Draffe is your errand, but drinke ye wolde. **1598** SHAKS. *Merry W.* IV. ii. 105 Still Swine eats all the draugh. *c* **1598** D. FERGUSON *Scot. Prov.* (1785) 5 (Jam.) As the sow fills the draff sours.

d. *Comb.*, as ***draff-drink, -midden, -pock, -trough, -tub; draff-cheap*** adj. Also DRAFFSACK.

c **1450** HENRYSON *Mor. Fab.* 7 A Sow, to whom men.. Into her draffe-troch would sow precious stanes. *c* **1470** HENRY *Wallace* II. 257 Thai kest him our.. In a draff myddyn. **1568** *Wills & Inv. N.C.* (Surtees 1835) 282 One draffe tub iiij[d]. *a* **1661** RUTHERFORD *Lett.* (1765) I. l. (Jam.) The best regenerate have their defilements, and if I may speak so, their draff pock that will clog behind them all their days. **1807** TANNAHILL *Poems* 103 (Jam.) Thanks is but a draff-cheap phrase.

draffe, obs. form of DRAFF, DROVE *sb.*

'draffish, *a.* [f. DRAFF + -ISH.] Of the nature of draff, somewhat draffy; worthless.

1538 BALE *Thre Lawes* 1701 Your draffysh ceremonyes. **1543** —— *Yet a Course* 97 b (T.), The draffish declaracyons of my lorde Boner.

'draffsack. Now *dial.* [f. DRAFF + SACK *sb.* = MDu. *drafsac* lit. and fig.] A sack of draff or refuse; also *fig.* a big paunch; lazy glutton. Also *attrib.*

c **1386** CHAUCER *Reeve's T.* 286, I lye as a draf-sak in my bed. *c* **1534** SIR F. BYGOD *Treat. Impropr. Benefices*, They.. knowe none other god almost than the gret draf-sacke of Rome. *a* **1564** BECON *Humble Supplic.* Prayers, etc. (1844) 239 The priests of Baal.. pampered their idle draffsack bellies with all kind of pleasant wines and dainty dishes. **1616** DEACON *Tobacco tortured* 57 Tobacco.. the Draffe-sacks delight. **1894** CROCKETT *Lilac Sunbonnet* 171 Sleep yer ain sleeps, ye pair o' draft-sacks.

Hence †**'draffsacked** *ppl. a.*, of the nature of a draffsack; stuffed with refuse; vilely gluttonous; worthless. *Obs.*

1548 HALL *Chron.*, *Hen. VII*, 43 One of yᵉ capiteins of this donge hill and draffe sacked ruffians. **1560** BECON *Fortress Faithf.* Pref. Wks. 123 a, That gloton.. enfarcing his owne stinckyng and draffesacked belly with.. deintie dishes. *a* **1564** —— *Humble Supplic.* Prayers, etc. (1844) 228 To maintain their idle and draffsacked bellies.

'draffy, *a.* [f. as prec. + -Y[1].] Of the nature of draff, worthless; full of draff or dregs.

1621 FLETCHER *Isl. Princess* III. iii, The dregs and draffy part. **1624** GATAKER *Transubst.* 86 Such draffy stuffe as this is. *a* **1807** J. SKINNER *Tune Your Fiddles* Misc. Poetry 148 Draffy drink may please the Vicar.

draft (drɑːft, -æ-), *sb.* A modern phonetic spelling of DRAUGHT *sb.*, found in many senses of the word, and now established in the following:

1. The drawing down of one scale or end of a balance in weighing; the 'turn of the scale'; hence a deduction from the gross weight allowed for this in retailing (= CLOFF, q.v.).

[**1494-1727** see DRAUGHT 13.] **1757** W. THOMPSON *R.N. Advoc.* 39 To put his Foot into the Scale to weigh it down, to make the Draft good. **1809** R. LANGFORD *Introd. Trade* 72, 100 Hides.. Draft 1 lb. per 10 Hs. **1848** *Illustr. Lond. News* 29 Apr. 281/1 Secreting two iron hooks under his weighing-machine, thereby causing a draft of 4½ oz. against the purchaser.

2. a. The drawing off, detachment, or selection of a party from a larger body for some special (*spec.* military) duty or purpose; *spec.* (esp. in U.S.), selective conscription. Also *attrib.* and *Comb.*

[**1703-1872** see DRAUGHT 34.] *a* **1772** J. WOOLMAN *Jrnl.* (1774) v. 87 The military officers.. agreed on a draught [ed. 1900: agreed on draft]. **1780** JOSEPH JONES *Let.* 2 Dec. (1889) 58 Let an exemption from draft, or even militia duty out of the State, be offered by the law to every person who recruits a soldier for the war. **1800** WELLINGTON in Gurw. *Desp.* I. 93 If the bullocks are not occasionally recruited by drafts of fresh calves. **1813** *Ibid.* 24 Sept. XI. 140 To get nearly as many men by a draft from the militia. **1875** T. W. HIGGINSON *Hist. U.S.* 306 Soldiers were being drafted; but the draft was very unpopular. **1878** J. H. BEADLE *Western Wilds* 532 All the really valuable survivors of the volunteer army had returned to civil life;.. the draft-sneaks and worthless remained. **1918** 'CAPTAIN X' *Our First Half Million* 20 Certain newspapers in discussing the draft.. used an unfortunate word. It was 'conscript'. **1918** W. OWEN *Let.* ? 25 Mar. (1967) 542 Two companies of A 4 (boys) on Draft Leave. **1931** J. T. ADAMS *Epic of America* xi. 338 There was no draft, there were only.. volunteers. *Ibid.* xiii. 384 No reliance was placed upon volunteering.. and a universal draft act was passed. **1961** *Listener* 17 Aug. 240/1 These sermons were levelled at a nation of professional draft-dodgers. **1968** *Globe & Mail* (Toronto) 17 Feb. 1/4 The head of the Toronto Anti-Draft Program last night predicted a considerable increase in the numbers of draft-dodgers coming to Canada in the wake of new draft deferment rules for graduate students. **1968** *Listener* 6 June 733/2 Students.. were protesting against the war by turning in their draft cards. **1971** *Times* 22 Feb. (Canada Suppl.) p. v/1 Nor are more than a few of them draft-dodgers from over the United States border.

b. The party or body so drawn off or selected. Also, a person drafted for military service.

1756 G. WASHINGTON *Lett.* Writ. 1889 I. 245, I am.. convinced.. all the drafts [will] quit the service. **1780** J. REID in Sparks *Corr. Amer. Rev.* (1853) III. 20 They absolutely refuse to march the drafts to the army. **1868** *Regul. & Ord. Army* ¶515 Attention.. to the age of the men selected, so that the draft may consist of those best qualified for a change of climate. **1884** BOLDREWOOD *Melbourne Mem.* ii. 22 A draft of out-lying cattle.. rose and galloped off. **1890** *Times* 22 Sept. 4/4 The Wye.. sailed from Sheerness.. with naval drafts and stores. **1894** MASKELYNE *Sharps & Flats* 56 The 'draft'— i.e. the cards to replace those which have been discarded [at Poker]. **1916** 'BOYD CABLE' *Action Front* 110 I've seen one-half the battalion wiped out and built up with drafts. *a* **1917** E. A. MACKINTOSH *War, the Liberator* (1918) 23, I know the drafts are good men, I know they're doing well.

c. = *draft-ewe* (DRAFT *sb.* 7).

1844 H. STEPHENS *Bk. Farm* III. 1107 Drafts are ready for sale in September. **1886** C. SCOTT *Sheep-Farming* 107 Ewes and gimmers at 34/4½, being 3/- a head more than the drafts.

d. *U.S.* An act of drafting (see DRAFT *v.* 1 c).

1948 *Economist* 8 May 763/1 Many believe that General Eisenhower would yield to a draft. **1948** [see DRAFT *v.* 1 c]. **1950** *Manch. Guardian Weekly* 2 Nov. 2 He chose to yield to Governor Dewey's 'draft' and accept the nomination.

3. a. The 'drawing' of money by an order in due form. Also DRAUGHT (35 a) q.v.

[**1633-1838** see DRAUGHT 35 a.] **1833** *Act 3 & 4 Will. IV*, c. 46 §61 Such treasurer shall make no drafts on the said accounts for any private purpose.

b. A written order for the payment of money, 'drawn on' or addressed to a person holding money in trust or as an agent or servant of the drawer; a bill or cheque drawn; sometimes, *spec.*, an order for the payment of money drawn by one branch of a bank or mercantile house upon another, or by one department of an office upon another.

[**1745–1790** see DRAUGHT 35 b.] **1786** *Trials & Escapes of John Shepherd* 13 Mr. Elliot sent the draft to the bankers, which was returned unpaid. **1816** BYRON *Let. to Murray* Wks. (1846) 120/1 *note*, I have enclosed your draft. **1846** MCCULLOCH *Acc. Brit. Empire* (1854) II. 31 [They] pay them by giving a bill or draft for the sum, payable in coin at sight, or at so many days after date. **1861** GOSCHEN *For. Exch.* 31 Teas shipped from China to New York are generally paid for by a draft of the exporter on a London merchant for account of the American importer in New York. **187.** MCLEOD in Bithell *Counting-Ho. Dict.* s.v. *Draft*, If the order be addressed to a person who merely holds the money as a Depositum, as a Baillee, or Trustee, or Agent, or Servant of the writer, it is not a Bill, but a Draft.

c. *fig.* A demand, claim.

a **1817** JANE AUSTEN *Northanger Abbey* (1818) II. xi. 219 Giving ready-monied actual happiness for a draft on the future, that may not be honoured. **1866** HOWELLS *Venet. Life* 121 Their sterling honesty..has made the English tongue a draft upon the unlimited confidence of the continental peoples. **1869** LYNCH *Church & State* 14 That so great a draft should be made on our patience. **1885** *Manch. Exam.* 15 June 6/2 Her Majesty makes a thoughtless draft upon the loyalty of her Minister.

4. A plan, sketch, or drawing, *esp.* of a work to be executed; †a chart. More usually DRAUGHT (30, 31), q.v.

1697 DAMPIER *Voy.* I. v. 100 The Spaniards who first discovered them, and in whose drafts alone they are laid down. *Ibid.* ix. 272 Some of their Drafts newly made do make California to join to the main. **1703** MOXON *Mech. Exerc.* 106 A round Iron Plate which lies within the hollow ..and therefore cannot in Draft be seen in its proper place. **1727–51** CHAMBERS *Cycl.*, *Draught* or, as it is pronounced, *Draft*, in architecture, the figure of an intended building described in paper. **1809** H. CARTER *Autobiogr. Cornish Smuggler* (1894) 55 There is no draft for the Channel on board I knows nothing of the Channel. **1863** P. BARRY *Dockyard Econ.* 138 The Superintendent delivers the order, with the drafts and specifications, to the master shipwright.

5. A preliminary sketch or rough form of a writing or document, from which the final or fair copy is made.

[**1528–1831** see DRAUGHT 32.] **1769** BURKE *Corr.* (1844) I. 187, I have seen the draft of the petition. **1818** CRUISE *Digest* (ed. 2) IV. 474 A draft of the conveyance was prepared by Mr. Booth, as counsel for the purchaser. **1887** *Spectator* 9 July 921/1 The latest draft of Thames Conservancy bye-laws, now awaiting the Order of Council.

6. *Technical.* **a.** *Masonry.* Chisel-dressing at the margin of the surface of a stone to serve as a guide for the levelling of the surface. Also DRAUGHT, q.v. 43. **b.** 'The degree of deflexion of a millstone-furrow from a radial direction.' (*Cent. Dict.*) **c.** See quot. 1874.

1874 KNIGHT *Dict. Mech.*, *Draft* 6 (*Pattern-making.*) The amount of taper given to a pattern to enable it to be withdrawn from the mold, without disturbing the loam. **1878** CONDER *Tentwork Pal.* II. 81 The stones are all drafted with the real Jewish draft, broad, shallow, and beautifully cut.

7. *attrib.* **a.** Drafted or selected from the flock, as ***draft ewe***. **b.** Drawn up as a preliminary or rough form whence a fair copy is afterwards made. **c.** ***draft-cattle***, ***-horses***: see DRAUGHT 47 a.

a. 1794 URE *Agric. Surv. Roxb.* (Jam.), Those are picked out which are most unfit for breeders, and in best condition for the market. These are called *Draught* or *Cast Ewes.* **1878** *Cumbld. Gloss.*, *Draft sheep*..a selection of the best annually. **1892** *Northumbld. Gloss.*, *Draught*, the worst sheep 'drawn', or culled out from a flock. 'Draught ewes.' In parts of England these are called *culls.* **1894** *Times* 30 July 12/2 Draft ewes made up to 88s. per head.

b. 1879 E. GARRETT *House by Works* II. 153 This was but a draft will, partly filled up. **1891** *Law Times* XC. 420/1 How unreal is the publicity afforded by laying draft rules upon the table in Parliament.

d. draft tube, **†box** [DRAUGHT *sb.* 23], an air-tight tube or enclosure that at its upper end receives the discharge from a turbine and at its lower end extends below the level of the water in the tail-race; (orig. simply *draft*).

1840 PARKER & MCKELVEY *U.S. Patent 1658*, The percussion and reaction wheel..is inclosed in a box or case, which is denominated a 'draft'..the mouth of said draft-dipping into the water and being..below the level of the water in the tail-race. **1849** *Jrnl. Franklin Inst.* XLVIII. 402 The water passes from the wheels or rims into two air-tight chambers..called 'draft boxes', from which it passes into two air-tight iron tubes..called 'draft tubes', which.. discharge the water beneath the surface of the lower level. **1876** *Ibid.* CI. 285 A turbine provided with this draft tube can be placed between both levels that constitute the fall, and produce the same result as if the turbine were placed at the bottom of the fall. **1927** *Sel. Engin. Papers Inst. Civil. Engin.* xxxiv. 3 Draught-tubes for hydraulic turbines may be either straight, or curved so as to divert the direction of flow through 90 degrees between the turbine and the tail-race. **1958** *Engineering* 28 Mar. 414/2 The draft tubes for two more units have been completed.

draft (drɑːft, -æ-), *v.* [f. prec. sb. Formerly spelt DRAUGHT, which is still retained in some senses.]

1. a. *trans.* To draw off or out and remove (a party of persons, animals, or things) from a larger body for some special duty or purpose. Chiefly in *Mil.* use, and in *Stock-farming*: see quots. Also (chiefly *U.S.*), to conscript.

[**1714–1868** see DRAUGHT *v.* 1.] **1724** *Lond. Gaz.* No. 6309/2 The..Corps out of which they have been drafted. *a* **1772** J. WOOLMAN *Jrnl.* (1774) v. 86 Orders came..to draft the militia. **1833** HT. MARTINEAU *Charmed Sea* i. 6 Taddeus ..had been drafted into one of the condemned regiments. **1847** *Jrnl. R. Agric. Soc.* VIII. I. 3 Many exceedingly good animals are drafted in consequence of some little want of uniformity..It is not uncommon with the ram-breeders to draft the whole produce from a sheep that has disappointed them. **1860** G. DUPPA in S. S. Crawford *Sheep & Sheepmen of Canterbury* (1949) v. 46 Draft out rams as flock is dipped and keep them in a separate flock. **1862** O. W. NORTON *Army Lett.* (1903) 102 We want them drafted if they won't volunteer. **1863** S. BUTLER *First Year in Canterbury Settlement* x. 153 You will see fit to draft out all the lambs that are ready for weaning. **1867** ROGERS *Pref. to Adam Smith's W.N.* I. 7 Promising young Scotchmen are yearly drafted off to complete their studies at Oxford. **1889** WILLIAMS & REEVES *Colonial Couplets* 9 Dagging the hoggets, or drafting the rams. **1940** E. E. CUMMINGS *Let.* 10 Nov. (1969) 158, I avoided the American army, by visiting France with a Norton Harjes ambulanceunit, merely to have myself drafted later and serve six months at Camp Devens. **1946** F. DAVISON *Dusty* viii. 80 He and Harry were bringing a mob in to the yards to draft out some ageing ewes. **1947** 'N. SHUTE' *Chequer Board* iii. 56 When I got drafted they..put me into a construction unit. **1953** M. SCOTT *Breakfast at Six* (1960) iv. 34 Presently Larry was summoned to help draft the sheep. **1968** *Globe & Mail* (Toronto) 17 Feb. 4/8 A representative of the U.S. Office of Education said more than 150,000 prospective graduate-school students probably would be drafted.

b. More generally: To draw off or away.

1742 FIELDING *J. Andrews* IV. i, All her rents had been drafted to London, without a shilling being spent among them. *a* **1875** CARPENTER in Croll *Climate & T.* ix. 164 The cold and dense polar water..will not directly take the place of that which has been drafted off from the surface.

c. *transf.* Esp., to force or persuade (a reluctant or allegedly reluctant person) to become a candidate for office. *U.S.*

1861 J. G. HOLLAND *Lessons in Life* iii. 41 An old man.. was drafted into the grand jury. **1927** *Observer* 4 Dec. 20/7 Mr. Smith will be nominated. Mr. Coolidge will be 'drafted' by acclaim of the Convention. The Republicans will win. **1948** *Chickasha* (Okla.) *Daily Express* 4 July 1/1 Nevertheless he could be drafted, if a definite draft movement took place at Philadelphia.

2. To make a draft or rough copy of (a document); to draw up in a preliminary form, which may be afterwards perfected. Rarely *draught.*

1828 in WEBSTER. **1828** J. W. CROKER *Diary* 11 July, The Duke..read me a letter..which he had drafted. **1873** DIXON *Two Queens* I. III. ix. 168 The Articles were drafted into form and signed. **1878** SEELEY *Stein* I. 456 It is not draughting a Bill, but passing it, that is the difficulty.

3. *Masonry.* To cut a draught (or draft) on a stone: see also DRAUGHT *v.* 4.

1878 [see DRAFT *sb.* 6]. **1890** SAYCE in *Contemp. Rev.* 431 The stones of the glacis..are drafted. **1891** *Edin. Rev.* July 110 Megalithic masonry occurs on the Mole at Sidon, but it is not drafted.

Hence **'drafted** *ppl. a.*

1877 BLACK *Green Past.* iii, Some drafted bills. **1878** C. R. CONDER *Tentwork Pal.* I. 352 Drafted masonry. **1894** *Forum* Oct. 153 Drafted or pre-announced oratory.

draft, obs. form of DRAFF.

draftee (drɑːfˈtiː, -æ-). *U.S.* [f. DRAFT *v.* + -EE[1].] A conscript. Also *transf.*

1866 'F. KIRKLAND' *Pictorial Bk.* 162 The young draftee appeared a little bewildered. **1952** STEINBECK *East of Eden* xlii. 420 The draftees wouldn't look at their mothers. **1953** *Manch. Guardian Weekly* 12 Feb. 7 The American 'draftee' ..is subject to these interferences. **1964** *Economist* 1 Feb. 412/1 The third willing draftee is Mr. Richard Nixon. **1969** I. KEMP *Brit. G.I. in Vietnam* iv. 74 My companion, Bob Horton, was a draftee a little younger than myself.

drafter (ˈdrɑːftə(r), -æ-). [f. DRAFT vb.] One who drafts.

1. A man employed in drafting animals.

1829 *Sporting Mag.* XXIII. 397 It is the business of the drafter to coax and encourage the unwilling [hounds] to him. **1890** BOLDREWOOD *Col. Reformer* xviii. 227 [Cattle] keeping the drafters incessantly popping at the fence by truculent charges.

2. One who drafts or draws up a document.

1884 *Fortn. Rev.* Mar. 393 The drafters of the Constitution. **1892** *Pall Mall G.* 1 Feb. 2/1 The promoters and drafters of the Albert Charter.

3. A draught-horse; also, a horse used for drafting (animals).

Cf. **1876** F. K. ROBINSON *Gloss. Whitby*, *Draughters*, waggon-horses.

1906 *Springfield Weekly Republican* 7 Feb. 2 (Advt.), A nice lot of well-broken useful horses, consisting of all classes from the nice, pleasant driver to the large, strong, rugged drafter. **1935** *Bulletin* (Sydney) 3 Apr. 20/1 Old horses seem to be the best camp drafters.

'drafting, *vbl. sb.* [f. DRAFT *v.* + -ING[1].] The action of the verb DRAFT (in various senses).

1878 SEELEY *Stein* I. 456 Between the draughting of the Emancipating Edict, and the making it law. **1884** BOLDREWOOD *Melbourne Mem.* x. 72 Separating our cattle.. by drafting through the yard, or by 'cutting out'. **1891** *Leeds Mercury* 2 May 6/7 The unskilful drafting of the bill.

attrib. **1856** W. ROBERTS *Diary* 18 Dec. in J. H. Beattie *Early Runholding in Otago* (1947) vi. 43 There was no crush pen or drafting race. **1863** S. BUTLER *First Year in Canterbury Settlement* x. 154 The sheep are in the small yard C (which is called the drafting-yard). **1882** ARMSTRONG & CAMPBELL *Austral. Sheep Husbandry* xv. 177 A second gate hung on the inside of the race will act as a drafting gate, and, when not in use, will, when closed, leave the race secure. **1884** BOLDREWOOD *Melbourne Mem.* x. 72 We..armed ourselves with drafting sticks. **1890** —— *Col. Reformer* (1891) 217 Hitherto he had seen in drafting-yards only men used to managing breeding cattle. **1893** *Daily News* 15 Apr. 3/6 [He] submitted it to the drafting master, as well as to experts at the Treasury. **1894** *Ibid.* 17 Feb. 5/5 One or two verbal and drafting amendments having been agreed to. **1916** *N.Z. Jrnl. Agric.* 20 Sept. 229 Drafting gates 3 ft. wide. **1922** W. PERRY *Sheep Farming in N.Z.* iii. 26 It will facilitate dipping if the entrance to the dip is at the end of the drafting race. **1950** *N.Z. Jrnl. Agric.* July 7/3 *Drafting race*: This race is long and narrow, just wide enough for the sheep to pass through in single file. Its purpose is to divide a mixed flock of sheep into any required number of smaller mobs, and for this purpose the race is fitted at its exit with one or more drafting gates, which guide the sheep into several drafting pens. **1956** J. DARE *Rouseabout Jane* xxi. 167 We had to move the whole lot [of sheep] to the drafting yards. **1959** A. UPFIELD *Bony & Black Virgin* xxi. 196 Nothing there but a well and drafting yards.

'draftman. *rare.* = DRAFTSMAN 1.

1889 *Anthony's Photogr. Bull.* II. 218 Draftman's tracing paper.

draftsman (ˈdrɑːftsmən, -æ-). [Another spelling of DRAUGHTSMAN.] **1.** One who makes, or whose business it is to make, drawings or designs.

1663 GERBIER *Counsel* G j a, Good Draufts-men do express..what is to be built in Brick by a Red Line, what with Stone white. **1797** *Monthly Mag.* III. 223 Mr. Alexander, Draftsman to the late Chinese Embassy, will.. publish..a series of Plates, on the Costume of China. **1851** *Ord. & Regul. R. Engineers* §16. 62 Where there is no Draftsman, the Junior Officer..is to attend to the.. arrangement of all Plans and Models, in the Engineer Drawing Room.

2. One who drafts or draws up a document, *esp.* a legal document or a parliamentary bill or clause.

1759 FRANKLIN *Ess.* Wks. 1840 III. 179 The draftsman hath assured us, that no power..is comprised in that charter but what was the proprietary's direction. **1884** SIR H. COTTON in *Law Rep.* 26 Ch. Div. 99 The draftsman has framed this declaration of trust awkwardly.

Hence **'draftsmanship** = DRAUGHTSMANSHIP.

1882 TRAILL *Sterne* vi. 89 Sketches of travel..surpassed in vigour and freedom of draftsmanship, by the *Sentimental Journey.* **1885** *Law Times* LXXIX. 171/2 Faulty draftsmanship and highly technical construction.

†'drafty, *a. Obs.*

[In several places *drafty* is a proved misprint or misreading for DRASTY, 'of the nature of refuse, dreggy', and possibly the whole word originated in such misreading, which it was subsequently attempted to explain by association with DRAFF or with DRAUGHT *sb.* 45, 46: see DRAUGHTY 3. Scott's use, quot. 1823, is app. after an ed. of Chaucer with *drafty* erroneously for *drasty* in *Prol. to Melibeus.*]

Of the nature of refuse or garbage; rubbishy, worthless; filthy, vile.

1583 STANYHURST *Æneis* Ded. (Arb.) 9 Skauingers of draftie poetrye..that bast theyre papers with smearie larde. **1597–8** BP. HALL *Sat.* v. ii, Drafty, sluttish geere, Fit for the oven, or the kitchen fire. **1602** *2nd Pt. Return fr. Parnass.* I. ii. 195 So long As drafty ballats to the paile are song. **1823** SCOTT *Romance* Ess. (1874) 105 The poems which they recited were branded as 'drafty rhymings'.

drag (dræg), *v.* Also 5–6 dragge. [Not known before 15th c. A derivative of OE. *dragan*, or ON. *draga* (Sw. *draga*, Da. *drage*) to DRAW. Perh. a special northern dialect-form in which the *g* has been preserved instead of forming a diphthong with the prec. *a*, as in English generally: cf. Jos. Wright, Dialect of Windhill 102. See also DRUG *v.*[2]]

I. 1. a. *trans.* To draw or pull (that which is heavy or resists motion); to haul; hence to draw with force, violence, or roughness; to draw slowly and with difficulty; to trail (anything) along the ground or other surface, where there is friction or resistance.

c **1440** *Promp. Parv.* 130/1 Draggyn or drawyn, *trajicio.* **1570** LEVINS *Manip.* 10/17 To Drag, *extrahere.* **1593** SHAKS. *2 Hen. VI*, IV. iii. 14 The bodies shall be dragg'd at my horse heeles. **1611** BIBLE *John* xxi. 8 The other disciples came.. dragging the net with fishes. **1667** MILTON *P.L.* VI. 260 The arch foe subdu'd Or Captive drag'd in Chains. **1726** *Adv. Capt. R. Boyle* 244 Aligators..dragg'd him to the Bottom, and there devour'd him. **1849** MACAULAY *Hist. Eng.* I. 315 Dragging a ponderous equipage over the rugged pavement. **1883** FROUDE *Short Stud.* IV. I. x. 124 To drag him off as a prisoner. **1896** *Daily News* 9 June 9/6 A 'shot' tint..is produced by sparsely 'dragging' a little colour over the surface.

b. Said of moving the body or limbs with difficulty, or of allowing a member to trail. Also *fig.*, esp. in phr. ***to drag one's feet*** (orig. *U.S.*), to delay deliberately, hold back deliberately.

1583 GOLDING *Calvin on Deut.* xviii. 105 We dragge our winges after vs as they say. **1697** DRYDEN *Virg. Georg.* III. 644 [The Snake] retires. He drags his Tail. **1735** SOMERVILLE *Chase* III. 146 His Brush he drags, And sweeps the mire impure. **1837** W. IRVING *Capt. Bonneville* II. 228 So reduced that they could scarcely drag themselves along. **1856** KANE *Arct. Expl.* II. i. 24 Four wretched animals, who can hardly drag themselves. *a* **1897** *Mod.* I could scarcely drag one foot after the other. **1946** *Life* 20 May 69/1 The Soviets are frankly 'dragging their feet' in making the European peace in order to prolong chaos. **1948** *News Chron.* 16 Sept. 1/3 He indignantly denied that the

Government was 'dragging its feet' as it had been suggested in the American Press. 1950 *Hansard Commons* 28 Mar. 197 It is widely thought..in America that the British Government are lacking in zeal for the whole plan—'dragging their feet' is, I believe, the American expression. 1970 *Times* 24 Mar. 12/1 Many local authorities drag their feet. They wait for their sewage works to become..overloaded. 1970 *New Scientist* 4 June 480/1 Many authorities are dragging their heels in setting up the zones.

c. *Naut.* ***to drag the anchor***: 'To trail the anchor along the bottom after it is loosened from the ground, by the effort of the wind or current upon the ship.' (Crabb, 1823.)

1694 *Acc. Sev. Late Voy.* II. (1711) 11 The wind turned to North-west and west, and the single Anchor was dragg'd by the Ship. 1726 *Adv. Capt. R. Boyle* 340 [We] threw out our Anchors..but the Wind increasing, we dragg'd 'em. 1769 FALCONER *Dict. Marine* (1789), To drag the Anchors, implies the effort of making the anchor *come home*, when the violence of the wind, &c. strains the cable.

d. *intr.* for *refl.* = *passive*.

1839 MARRYAT *Phant. Ship* xxiii, The anchor still dragged, from..bad holding-ground.

e. *trans.* To take or escort (a person) to a particular place, event, etc., esp. against his will. *colloq.*

1924 P. MARKS *Plastic Age* 136 No freshman was allowed to attend the Prom, but along with the other men who weren't 'dragging women' Hugh walked the streets and watched the girls. 1925 W. DEEPING *Sorrell & Son* xxxviii. 385 'Sorry to drag you off like this.' 'Do you think I mind? —It was I who dragged you away.' 1952 J. CANNAN *Body in Beck* vii. 142 In the evening I was dragged to an Olde Tyme Dance in the Town Hall.

f. To pull *on* or *at* (a cigarette); to inhale (cigarette smoke). *colloq.* (orig. *U.S.*). (Cf. PULL *v.* 12 b.)

1919 H. LEVERAGE *White Cipher* viii. 121 He waited and dragged at the cigarette. 1926 L. H. NASON *Chevrons* (1927) x. 306 Eadie dragged on the cigarette. 1957 H. CROOME *Forgotten Place* xi. 139 He lit one cigarette from the butt of another and dragged at it nervously.

2. *fig.* Said of other than physical force, or local motion. ***to drag in*** (***into***), to introduce (a subject) in a forced manner, or unnecessarily.

1596 SHAKS. *1 Hen. IV*, IV. iii. 19 What impediments Drag backe our expedition. 1611 —— *Wint. T.* I. ii. 24 My Affaires Doe euen drag me home-ward. 1697 DRYDEN *Virg. Georg.* IV. 716 Dragg'd back again by cruel Destinies. 1725 WATTS *Logic* II. iii. §4 (3) A writer of great name drags a thousand followers after him into his own mistakes. 1853 BRIGHT *Sp. India* 3 June, Everything that could possibly be dragged into the case. 1868 FREEMAN *Norm. Conq.* (1876) II. vii. 4 His habit of dragging in the most irrelevant tales. 1875 JOWETT *Plato* (ed. 2) IV. 479 His pleasure is to drag words this way and that. 1876 F. E. TROLLOPE *Charming Fellow* II. ix. 124 To know why she must be dragged out to these people's stupid parties.

3. a. *intr.* To hang behind with a retarding tendency; to lag in the rear.

1494 FABYAN *Chron.* VI. clxxix. 176 That none shuld dragge or tary after his hoost. 1526 *Pilgr. Perf.* (W. de W. 1531) 108 They yᵗ draggeth behynde & goth but slowly forward in yᵉ iourney of perfeccion. 1530 PALSGR. 526/1 Thou draggest alwayes, *tu fais tousjours la queue*.

b. To lag behind in singing or playing.

?*a*1500 [see DRAGGER 1]. 1526 [see DRAGGING *vbl. sb.*]. 1863 *Spectator* 4 July 2203/1 The chorus..'dragged' unmistakeably in one or two passages. *Mod.* The quartet was not sung in time, the tenor dragged.

4. *intr.* To trail, to hang with its weight, while moving or being moved; to move with friction on the ground or surface.

1666 PEPYS *Diary* 12 June, Only for a long petticoat dragging under their men's coats, nobody could take them for women. 1697 DRYDEN *Æneid* VI. 753 Of sounding lashes, and of dragging chains. 1703 T. N. *City & C. Purchaser* 129 In Architecture, a Door is said to drag, when in opening and shutting it hangs upon the Floor. 1703 MOXON *Mech. Exerc.* 155 To raise the Door that it drag not. 1820 SHELLEY *Orpheus* 108 Elms, dragging along the twisted vines. 1820 HAZLITT *Lect. Dram. Lit.* 119 There is the least colour possible used; the pencil drags. 1896 *Daily News* 23 July 8/5 The overturned coach dragged along the permanent way, and suffered considerable damage.

5. *trans.* To protract or continue tediously; usually ***drag on***. Also ***to drag out***, to protract to a tedious end.

1697 DRYDEN *Æneid* II. 877 'Tis long since I..have dragg'd a ling'ring life. *a*1710 E. J. SMITH (J.), Oh; can I drag a wretched life without him? 1842 A. COMBE *Physiol. Digestion* (ed. 4) 315 Dragging out a painful existence. 1865 TROLLOPE *Belton Est.* xxvi. 308 The events of the day drag themselves on tediously in such a country house. 1878 BOSW. SMITH *Carthage* 488 [It] dragged on a wretched existence for some centuries. 1892 *Black & White* 2 Apr. 424/2 Like too many vocalists..[he] 'dragged' certain passages until all sense of time was lost.

6. *intr.* To advance or progress slowly and painfully; to be tediously protracted; to become tedious by protraction. ***to drag on, along***: to go on with painful or wearisome protraction.

1735 POPE *Ep. Lady* 29 Long open panegyrick drags at best. 1795 SOUTHEY *Vis. Maid Orleans* III. 290 He shall not drag Forlorn and friendless, along life's long path. 1816 BYRON *Ch. Har.* III. xxxii, The day drags through though storms keep out the sun. 1830 *Examiner* 472/2 He..continued to drag round the course till he had made sixty-five circuits. 1836 DICKENS *Let.* 23 Jan. (1965) I. 120, I did set to work yesterday, and dragged on as well as I could. 1861 HUGHES *Tom Brown at Oxf.* i. (1889) 5 A correspondence..had already lasted through the long vacation..without sensibly dragging.

II. To use or put a drag to.

7. a. *trans.* To draw some contrivance over the bottom of (a river, etc.), so as to bring up any loose matter; to dredge; to sweep with a dragnet; to search by means of a drag or grapnel as for the body of a person drowned. Also *fig.*

1577 in W. H. Turner *Select. Rec. Oxford* 392 Such freemen..shall..scoure, clense, and dragge..all the ryvers. 1769 FALCONER *Dict. Marine* (1789), *Draguer l'ancre*, to drag, or sweep the bottom, for an anchor which is lost. 1806-7 J. BERESFORD *Miseries Hum. Life* (1826) II. xviii, After having dragged the whole neighbourhood for every man, woman and child. 1847 TENNYSON *Princ.* IV. 136 While I dragg'd my brains for such a song.

b. *absol.* To use a grapnel or drag; to use a drag-net; to dredge.

1530 PALSGR. 526/1 Cannest thou dragge for fysshe, *scays tu bien pescher pour les poyssons?* 1630 in *Descr. Thames* (1758) 77 No Draggerman that..doth use to drag for Shrimps. 1768 G. WASHINGTON *Writ.* (1889) II. 241 Went to my Plantation..and dragd for Sturgeon & catchd one. 1790 *Trans. Soc. Arts* VIII. 84 Bricks are said to be sometimes raised by the fishermen dragging off this coast. 1867 SMYTH *Sailor's Word-bk.* s.v. *Creeper*, A small grapnel ..for dragging for articles dropped overboard.

c. *trans.* To catch with a drag-net or dredge.

1698 FRYER *Acc. E. India & P.* 49 This is the place where they drag Pearl. 1737 POPE *Hor. Epist.* I. vi. 113 Go drive the Deer, and drag the finny prey.

8. To break up (the surface of lands, clods, etc.) with a drag or heavy harrow.

*a*1722 LISLE *Observ. Husb.* (1757) 101 Ground which I had ploughed, thwarted and dragged. 1828 WEBSTER, *Drag* 2. To break land by drawing a drag or harrow over it; to harrow; a common use of the word in New-England. 1846 *Jrnl. R. Agric. Soc.* VII. I. 51 The lands are dragged with a heavy crab-harrow.

9. a. To put a drag upon (wheels or vehicles); to retard as by a drag.

1829 SOUTHEY *Lett.* IV. 156 Our endeavours must be to drag the wheels. 1884 *Law Times* 6 Dec. 97 The wheels of the waggons were chained and breaks applied, and these dragged wheels wore the road more rapidly.

b. *Austral.* and *N.Z. slang.* (See quots.)

1939 in Partridge *Dict. Slang* Suppl. (1961) 1071/2. 1941 BAKER *N.Z. Slang* v. 39 From the New Zealand shearing sheds came those effective expressions *to drag the chain* and *swing the gate*, phrases applied to the slowest and the fastest shearer in a shed respectively. 1941 —— *Dict. Austral. Slang* 25 *Drag the chain*, to be slow, to be inferior, to 'tail' the field in any work or contest. 1959 G. SLATTER *Gun in my Hand* 91 Stop dragging the chain and have one with me.

10. *Criminal slang.* **a.** To rob vehicles. Cf. DRAG *sb.* 8 a, DRAGGER 3.

1812 J. H. VAUX *Flash Dict.*, *Dragsman*, a thief who follows the game of dragging. 1936, 1938 [see DRAGGING *vbl. sb.*].

b. *trans.* To arrest.

1924 E. WALLACE *Room 13* ii. 31 After they dragged you I did some hard thinking. 1928 —— *Gunner* xxii. 185 If you particularly want him dragged, you'll tell me what I can drag him on.

11. (From DRAG *sb.* 6 a.) To follow the line of scent of (an animal); to trail.

1773 WASHINGTON *Diary* 22 Dec. (1925) II. 133 Went out after Breakfast with the Dogs, dragd a fox an hour or two, but never found [it]. 1786 *Ibid.* 9 Feb. III. 12 Never got a fox afoot, tho I dragged one to Mr. Robt. Alexander's Pocoson.

III. 12. *colloq.* ***to drag up***: to rear roughly or without delicacy: to bring up 'anyhow'.

*a*1700 B. E. *Dict. Cant. Crew*, *Dragg'd up*, as the *Rakes* call it, educated or brought up. 1802 M. MOORE *Lascelles* II. 5 Lavinia..has been wretchedly dragged up by the old curate. 1826 LAMB *Elia* Ser. II. *Pop. Fallacies*, Poor people..do not bring up their children; they drag them up. 1867 *Jrnl. R. Agric. Soc.* Ser. II. III. II. 532 They must be tenderly reared and not 'dragged up', as the saying is.

13. ***to drag along, on***: see 6; ***drag in***: see 2; ***drag on, out***: see 5.

Hence **dragged** (drægd), *ppl. a.*; esp. (*colloq.*) in sense 'physically exhausted'; also ***dragged out***.

1651 H. MORE *2nd Lash* in *Enthus. Tri.* (1656) 195 The disjoynted limbs of dragg'd Hippolytus. 1831 SEBA SMITH *Life J. Downing* (1834) 118 The poor Huntonites seemed to be a most dragged out. 1938 J. STEINBECK *Long Valley* 138 I'm kind of dragged out. 1866 LOWELL *Lett.* (1894) I. 374, I needed some more pungent food in my rather dragged-out condition. 1884 [see 9]. 1893 R. KIPLING *Many Invent.* 21 The seafog rolled back from the cliffs in trailed wreaths and dragged patches. 1962 K. ORVIS *Damned & Destroyed* vii. 49 'I'm dragged,' she said. 'Real dragged.' 1963 *Sunday Express* 13 Oct. 5/7 'She is having "dragged" walls—the latest technique in distressed paintwork.' 'Distressing' is a decorator's term for applying a top coat of the paint so that the tone of the undercoat shines through. 1965 *House & Garden* Feb. 47/2 The bedroom..has walls of pale aquamarine dragged paint.

drag (dræg), *sb.* Also 4-7 dragge, 6-7 dragg. See also DRUG *sb.*[2] [mainly f. DRAG *v.*; but some of the applications may have been originally introduced from other langs.: cf. MLG. *dragge* drag-anchor, grapnel, Sw. *dragg* grapnel, creeper, *drag-not* drag-net.]

1. Something heavy that is used by being dragged along the ground or over a surface.

a. A heavy kind of harrow used for breaking up ground or breaking clods; a drag-harrow.

1388-9 *Abingdon Acc.* (Camden) 57, ij draggis cum dentibus ferreis. 1533 J. STEVARD in Weaver *Wells Wills* (1890) 48 My dragge, olde plowe beme, my yokes and my ropes. 1552 HULOET, Dragge or instrument of husbandry with yron teeth to breake cloddes, some do cal it an harrowe. 1682 J. COLLINS *Making of Salt* 15 Then the Earth appears in Clods, which they Harrow, and bring on a Drag, and a Rowle. 1821 DWIGHT *Trav.* II. 465 A large and strong harrow; here called a drag, with very stout iron teeth. 1875 A. SMITH *Hist. Aberdeensh.* II. 1120 The drag can easily be converted into a harrow, simply by changing the tines.

†**b.** A float or raft for conveyance of goods by water: see quot. 1607. *Obs.*

?*a*1400 *Morte Arth.* 3616 Dresses dromowndes and dragges, and drawene upe stonys. 1431 *Act 9 Hen. VI*, c. 5 En Flotes autrement appellez dragges [*16th c. transl.*, flotes commonly called dragges]. 1607 COWELL *Interpr.*, *Drags* seem to be wood or timber so joyned together, as swimming ..upon the water, they may bear a..load.

c. An overland conveyance without wheels; a rough kind of sledge: see DRAY[1], and cf. DRUG *sb.*[2]

1576 *Act 18 Eliz.* c. 10 §4, Sleades, carres, or drags, furnished for..repairing..high wayes. 1611 COTGR., *Train* ..a sled, a drag or dray without wheeles. 1750 R. POCOCKE *Trav.* (1888) 135 They have drags for drawing up the side of steep fields. 1884 *Century Mag.* Jan. 446/2 Two skids fastened together make a 'drag', or 'sledge'. 1895 CAPT. KING *Under Fire* 452 The Indian households were piling their goods and chattels..on travois and drag of lodge-poles.

d. A kind of vehicle; the application has varied, and it is often not distinguished from a *brake* or BREAK; but in strict English use, applied to a private vehicle of the type of a stage coach, usually drawn by four horses, with seats inside and on the top. Cf. also DRAGSMAN 1.

1755 JOHNSON, *Drag*..a kind of car drawn by the hand. 1812 J. H. VAUX *Flash Dict.*, *Drag*, a cart. 1820 *Sporting Mag.* VI. 79 The prads are put to, and the drag is shoved forward. 1825 C. M. WESTMACOTT *Eng. Spy* I. 86 Since she put down her tandem drag. 1837 THACKERAY *Ravenswing* iii. (1887) 173 Behind her came..a drag, or private stage-coach, with four horses. *Ibid.*, The man on the drag-box said to the bugleman, 'Now!' 1865 *Derby Mercury* 1 Mar., A horse-breaker's drag or break. 1885 *Manch. Exam.* 3 June 5/4 The fine turnout of the Blues in their handsome drag at Hyde Park.

e. A motor-car. *Criminals' slang.*

1935 R. T. HOPKINS *Life & Death at Old Bailey* x. 269 When the car thief knocks off a drag (car) from some West End car park. 1947 *Sci. News* IV. 50 There he was, ready with a 'drag' to transport you both at speed. 1960 *Observer* 25 Dec. 7/6 A stately great drag..with a smart chauffeur at the wheel.

f. (See quot. 1954.) Also *attrib.*, as ***drag race, racer, racing, strip***. orig. *U.S.*

1954 *Amer. Speech* XXIX. 95 *Drag*, a race between two cars to determine which can accelerate faster. The race is over a given distance, with few exceptions a quarter of a mile. *Ibid.*, There are different types of drag racing: (1) drags from a dead stop; (2) drags from a rolling start. *Ibid.*, *Drag strip*, a straight course used in drag racing, usually an abandoned air strip. 1962 *Ibid.* XXXVII. 273 An establishment where youthful drivers congregate to plan illegal activities such as highway drag-races. 1964 *Guardian* 9 Jan. 3/2 An international drag festival is to be held in Britain... Drag racing was first seen in Britain in September when two American cars gave exhibition bouts. 1967 *Airfix Mag.* June 356/2 Any one of four separate versions can be built from the kit namely a stock, custom, saloon racing, or drag racing car. 1971 *Sunday Express* (Johannesburg) 28 Mar. 7/1 Gerry..has donated a grandstand for Margo's Rainbow dragstrip. 1971 *Capital Times* (Madison, Wis.) 15 June 29 The start of a drag race. *Ibid.*, There have been reports of drag racing by youths on country roads. *Ibid.*, The drag racers are gone.

2. Something used to drag or pull a weight or obstruction. †**a.** A hook or the like with which anything is dragged or forcibly pulled. *Obs.*

1483 *Cath. Angl.* 106/2 A Drag, *arpax, luppus, trudes.* 1577 FRAMPTON *Joyful News* I. (1596) 2 It is taken out of the Sea in great peeces with a dragge of Iron. 1610 HOLLAND *Camden's Brit.* I. 78 The executioner prepared dragges and tortures. 1783 AINSWORTH *Lat. Dict.* (Morell) II, *Uncus*.. A drag, or iron hook, to drag traitors after execution about the streets. 1789 G. VASSA *Life* (1793) 357 Leg-bolts, drags, thumb-screws..instruments of torture.

b. A DRAG-NET.

1481-90 *Howard Househ. Bks.* (Roxb.) 192 The..netter.. had sent..a dragge of viij. fadom. *c*1550 CHEKE *Matt.* iv. 18 Peter, and Andrew his broother, casting a drag into yᵉ see. 1611 BIBLE *Hab.* i. 15 They catch them in their net, and gather them in their drag. 1697 DRYDEN *Virg. Georg.* I. 214 Casting Nets were spread in shallow Brooks, Drags in the Deep. 1867 F. FRANCIS *Angling* i. (1880) 13 A drag with a coil of strings is serviceable.

c. An apparatus for cleaning out and deepening the beds of rivers, etc.; a dredging apparatus; also for collecting oysters from the bed.

1611 *MS. Acc. St. John's Hosp., Canterb.*, For mending of the dyche dragg iiijᵈ. 1769 FALCONER *Dict. Marine* (1789), *Drague*, a drag, or instrument to clear the bottom of rivers and canals; also to catch oysters. 1846 H. ROGERS *Ess.* I. iv. 162 His huge drag had brought up all sorts of fragments of antiquity.

d. An apparatus for recovering objects from the bottom of rivers or pools; esp. for recovering the bodies of drowned persons.

[1577-87 HOLINSHED *Chron. Scot.*, *Malcolme* an. 1034 (R.) Howbeit their bodies were afterwards drawne foorth of the loch with drags.] 1797 *Monthly Mag.* 163 The Lancashire Humane Society..[has] 90 stations..where the sets of apparatus, cases, drags, boards, &c. belonging to the society, are established. 1804 *Trans. Soc. Arts* XXII. 15 Premium offered by the Society of Arts for a cheap and portable drag..for the purpose of taking up..the bodies of persons who have sunk under water. 1894 DOYLE *Mem. S. Holmes* 109 We had the drags at once, and set to work to recover the remains.

e. Applied to certain agricultural implements, as a ***dung-drag*** or muck-rake, and an implement with two curving claws for pulling up turnips, etc.

1795 *Hull Advertiser* 6 June 3/3 Striking him on the head with a dung drag. **1848** *Jrnl. R. Agric. Soc.* IX. II. 501 Turnips.. are pulled up by a peculiar drag, or 'hack', as it is provincially called. **1881** MOORE & MASTERS *Epit. Gardening* 118 The drag is..a light three-pronged tool,..used for loosening the soil amongst vegetable crops.

3. Something that drags, or hangs heavily, so as to impede motion. **a.** *Naut.* (see quot.).

1708 KERSEY, *Drags*..whatever hangs over a Ship, or hinders her sailing. **1753** CHAMBERS *Cycl. Supp., Drags.* **1867** in SMYTH *Sailor's Word-bk.*

b. A drag-anchor (see 9).

1874 in KNIGHT *Dict. Mech.*

c. A device for retarding the rotation of the wheels of a vehicle when descending a hill; *esp.* an iron shoe to receive the wheel and cause friction on the ground.

1795 *Trans. Soc. Arts* XIII. 254 A Drag to prevent the Accidents..to Horses drawing loaded Carts down steep Hills. **1796** T. TWINING *Trav. Amer.* (1894) 63 The wagon descended at a great rate, for..it was not provided with a drag to keep it back. *c* **1842** SYD. SMITH *Let. to Ld. J. Russell* Wks. 1859 II. 300/1 Gently down hill. Put on the drag. **1863** MRS. C. CLARKE *Shaks. Char.* vi. 142 The drag that dishonesty claps upon the wheel of their conduct.

d. *fig.* A heavy obstruction to progress. Also, an annoyance, a bore; a dull or boring person. (Cf. quot. 1813 for sense 7 a).

1857 MRS. MATHEWS *Tea-T. Talk* I. 106 There's that drag of a husband. **1885** *Illustr. Lond. News* 9 May 492/2, I find it a drag upon me. **1892** ZANGWILL *Bow Myst.* 141 In short, she was a drag on his career. **1923** MANCHON *Le Slang* 109 *Drag*,..difficulté, embarras, partic^t une chose qui vous éprouve, vous épuise. **1936** 'F. O'CONNOR' *Bones of Contention* 157 As sure as God 'tis a drag. **1946** MEZZROW & WOLFE *Really Blues* viii. 106 They may have been a drag and a headache to their mothers. **1954** L. ARMSTRONG *Satchmo* viii. 126 Life can be such a drag one minute and a solid sender the next. **1959** C. MACINNES *Absolute Beginners* 42 Old Vern..is such a drip-dry drag that no one would ever take *him* for the male of the establishment. *Ibid.* 130 The whole thing was becoming something of a drag. **1968** *Listener* 29 Feb. 265/2, I know so many people that before they took it [*sc.* LSD] were such a drag, and when they took it, they really opened up.

e. A street, road; esp. in phr. ***the main drag***. *slang* (now chiefly *U.S.*).

1851 MAYHEW *London Lab.* I. 232/1 French news is generally liked in a fashionable drag. *Ibid.* 248/2 Another woman..whose husband has got a month for 'griddling in the main drag' (singing in the high street). **1905** [see BACK-GATE]. **1914** JACKSON & HELLYER *Vocab. Criminal Slang* 30 *Drag*, a main thoroughfare in any community; the main street... 'The boys are pivoting on the main drag', i.e. begging on the street. 'The muffs are cruising on the drag tonight', i.e. soliciting on the street. **1931** 'DEAN STIFF' *Milk & Honey Route* 204 *Drag*, hobo term for the main street of the town, as distinguished from the *main stem*. **1936** J. CURTIS *Gilt Kid* xix. 188 If he could find the main drag and jump a bus before the bogies got him, he should be able to make a clean getaway. **1962** K. ORVIS *Damned & Destroyed* v. 38 You didn't just wander in off the drag to buy coffee. **1965** J. P. CARSTAIRS *Concrete Kimono* ix. 79 We drove through..the main drag of Babaki.

f. The slow-moving portion of a cattle-herd which is being driven. Hence ***drag-driver***. *U.S.*

a **1861** T. WINTHROP *John Brent* (1883) viii. 71 Relieved from their drags, the herd frisked away with unwieldy gambolling. **1888** T. ROOSEVELT in *Century Mag.* Apr. 862/1 The rest [of the men] are in the rear to act as 'drag-drivers', and hurry up the phalanx of reluctant weaklings. **1920** J. M. HUNTER *Trail Drivers of Texas* 44, I went up the trail twice, and drove the drag both times. *Ibid.* 151 All the men were in front of the cattle except myself, the drag driver, and the cook. *Ibid.* 172 We left the drags together in another herd. **1924** W. M. RAINE *Troubled Waters* x. 101 I'm plumb fed up with the dust of the drag driver.

g. Feminine attire worn by a man; also, a party or dance attended by men wearing feminine attire; hence *gen.*, clothes, clothing. *slang.*

1870 *Reynolds's Newsp.* 29 May 5/5 We shall come in drag. **1870** *London Figaro* 23 June 3/4 Not quite so low..as going about in 'drag'. **1887** *Referee* 24 July 3/1, I don't like to see low coms. in drag parts. **1927** *Sunday Express* 13 Feb. 5/5 A drag is a rowdy party attended by abnormal men dressed in scanty feminine garments, singing jazz songs in high falsetto voices. **1942** M. MCCARTHY *Company she Keeps* (1943) iii. 80 A kind of masquerade of sexuality, like the rubber breasts homosexuals put on for drags. **1959** C. MACINNES *Absolute Beginners* 27 My Spartan hair-do and my teenage drag and all. **1959** J. OSBORNE *World of Paul Slickey* II. x. 80 You would never have the fag Of dressing up in drag You'd be a woman at the weekend. **1960** *20th Cent.* Mar. 255 Bad Taste, exemplified by..Henry Kendall in drag. This is by no means the first time that Mr. Kendall has appeared to reverse his sex. **1966** *Listener* 23 June 918/3 Laurence Olivier, doing his Othello voice and attired painstakingly in Arab drag. **1967** *Spectator* 14 July 54/1 The gear shops flip their decor as often as they do the pop tunes blaring out the newest hits as you try on the latest 'drag'. **1968** R. BAKER (*title*) Drag, a history of female impersonation on the stage.

h. Influence, 'pull'. *U.S. slang.*

1896 ADE *Artie* xii. 105 He knows I've got a drag in the precinct. *Ibid.* xvii. 160 If you've got any drag with him. **1923** HEMINGWAY *In our Time* (1926) 193 We had a big drag with the waiter because my old man drank whisky and it cost five francs, and that meant a good tip.

†**4.** A person employed to drag in or gather followers. *Obs.*

1663 HEATH *Chron.* (ed. 2) 732 Some young men and apprentices whom his drags had trepanned.

5. In various technical applications: see quots.

1823 P. NICHOLSON *Pract. Build.* 338 *Drag*, a thin plate of steel indented on the edge..used in working soft stone. [See **1876** in DRAGGING.] **1864** WEBSTER, *Drag*..(*Founding*) The bottom part of a flask;—called also *drag-box*. **1874** KNIGHT *Dict. Mech.*, *Drag*..The carriage on which a log is dogged in a veneer saw-mill. **1881** RAYMOND *Mining Gloss.* s.v., The mould having been prepared in the two parts of the flask, the cope is put upon the drag before casting.

6. *Hunting.* **a.** The line of scent left by a fox, etc.; the trail; *spec.* as in quot. 1888.

[*a* **1700** B. E. *Dict. Cant. Crew*, *Drag*, a Fox's Tail [? *read* Trail]. So in Phillips, Bailey, Dyche, etc.] **1735** SOMERVILLE *Chase* III. 47 Hark! on the Drag I hear Their doubtful Notes, preluding to a Cry More nobly full. **1741** *Compl. Fam. Piece* II. i. 295 As the Drag or Trail mends, cast off more Dogs that you can confide in. **1858** LD. RAVENSWORTH *Horace Odes* I. i, His bloodhounds snuff the drag Of timid hind or antlered stag. **1888** ELWORTHY *W. Som. Word-bk.*, *Drag*, in fox-hunting, the line of scent where a fox has been during the previous night, before he is found and started by the pack.

b. Any strong-smelling thing drawn along the ground, so as to leave a scent for animals; esp. for hounds to follow, instead of a fox.

1841 J. T. HEWLETT *Parish Clerk* I. 145 Will advised that his stockings should be well rubbed with oil of aniseed, and the hounds let out to run him as a 'drag'. **1843** LEVER *J. Hinton* xxi, He was always ready to carry a drag, to stop an earth. **1856** C. J. ANDERSSON *Lake Ngami* 127 [In trapping hyenas] A 'drag' consisting of tainted flesh, or other offal, is trailed from different points..directly up to the 'toils'. **1888** ELWORTHY *W. Som. Word-bk.* 208 A red-herring or a ferret's bed are the commonest drags used.

c. The hunt or chase with hounds following such a line of scent; a club or association for the prosecution of this sport.

1803 W. TAPLIN *Sporting Dict.* II. 486 A *train scent*, (that is, a drag across the country). **1851** *Eureka; a sequel to Lord J. Russell's Post Bag* 21 The necessity of keeping up the Drag [at Oxford]. **1869** W. BRADWOOD *The O.V.H.* v. (Farmer) He subscribed to the drag at Oxford. **1881** *Morning Post* 29 Sept. 5/5 The hounds..form two packs, one of harriers, the other for drag.

7. a. The action or fact of dragging; slow, heavy, impeded motion; forcible motion or progress against resistance.

1813 W. BEATTIE *Tales* 34 (Jam.) Washing's naething but a drag. We hae sae short daylight. **1826** *Examiner* 559/1 The first stage..was..a miserable drag through mud and holes. **1859** GULLICK & TIMBS *Paint.* 112 The 'drag' of the brush being evident. **1875** *Ure's Dict. Arts* I. 989 The strain produced by the 'drag' of the bobbin whilst being spun. **1887** in *Darwin's Life & Lett.* I. 144 He..gave one the impression of working with pleasure, and not with any drag. **1891** *Athenæum* 26 Dec. 859/1 The book is good and refined; there is no drag about it.

b. The amount by which anything drags or hangs behind in its motion.

1864 WEBSTER, *Drag*..(*Marine Engin.*), the difference between the speed of a screw-ship under sail and that of the screw when the ship outruns the screw.

c. *Billiards.* Retarded motion given to the cue-ball.

1873 BENNETT & CAVENDISH *Billiards* 194 Drag is put on by striking the ball as low as possible, No 1 strength.

d. *Angling.* A dragging motion on a fishing-line; also *concr.*, a device in a fishing reel.

1907 *Westm. Gaz.* 29 Nov. 3/1 The drag cannot be overcome—where the current fished into is far stronger than the current fished over. **1937** HEMINGWAY *To have & have Not* I. i. 23, I felt his drag. He had it screwed down tight. You couldn't pull out any line.

e. *Aeronaut.* and *Hydrodynamics.* The force resisting the motion of a body through a gas or a liquid; *esp.* the resistance along the line of flight to the motion of an aircraft, etc.

1909 A. WILLIAMS *Engin. Wonders of World* III. 12/1 To prevent the resulting drag slewing the aeroplane round, the warping mechanism is linked up with the rudder. **1918** W. E. DOMMETT *Dict. Aircraft* 19 The horizontal component of the air pressure on a wing or aerofoil is known as the drag. **1931** *Flight* 1 May 384/2 And how little headway have made such conceptions as induced drag, profile drag and span loading. **1935** P. W. F. MILLS *Elem. Pract. Flying* i. 4 The lift and drag forces act upwards and backwards respectively. **1948** *Sci. News* VII. 25 For an aerofoil it is necessary to introduce also the *induced drag*, i.e. the part of the total resistance which depends entirely on the lift. **1948** V. L. STREETER *Fluid Dynamics* iv. 67 Any body passing through a real fluid experiences a resisting force, called drag, which depends upon the form of the body and its surface roughness. **1952** *Economist* 20 Dec. 852/2 The pilot, when he lifted the nose-wheel of the aircraft off the ground, did so at a sharper angle than usual. The result of this was to give high 'drag', that is, to increase the resistance of the air to the passage of the aircraft. **1971** *Physics Bull.* Mar. 157/2 Perturbations of the orbit of an artificial satellite by the earth's oblateness and atmospheric drag.

f. *slang.* An inhalation of (cigarette) smoke; the act of smoking a cigarette. (Cf. DRAG *v.* 1 f.)

1914 JACKSON & HELLYER *Vocab. Criminal Slang* 30 *Drag*, an inhalation of smoke, tobacco or opium. **1920** F. SCOTT FITZGERALD *This Side of Paradise* (1921) I. ii. 58 The ponies took last drags at their cigarettes and slumped into place. **1926** L. H. NASON *Chevrons* (1927) x. 305 A long drag and a cloud of smoke rolled out into the aisle. **1957** C. MACINNES *City of Spades* I. v. 28, I lit up, took a deep drag, well down past the throat, holding the smoke in my lungs. **1962** *Coast to Coast 1961–62* 132 We stopped beside a little trickle of water for ten minutes' break and a drag.

g. *Cricket.* Back spin imparted to the ball by the bowler.

1920 E. R. WILSON in P. F. Warner *Cricket* 84 The two other spins which can be put on the ball are what have been called the drag (or back spin) and top spin. **1922** W. W. ARMSTRONG *Art of Cricket* i. 45 The ball on which drag has been put and which never seems to arrive as soon as it is expected.

h. A slow type of dance, or the music for this; also (*slang*), a dancing party. *U.S.*

1901 JOPLIN & HAYDEN (*title of song*) Sun Flower Slow Drag. **1928** *Melody Maker* Feb. 178 (Advt.), 'Rain' is a slow drag number. *Ibid.* 179/3 'Sugar', played in a nice drag rhythm. *Ibid.* 183/2 A fascinating *legato* drag rhythm. **1952** B. ULANOV *Hist. Jazz* (1958) x. 115 The cotillion orchestra and polite quartet that accompanied high society drags. *Ibid.* xviii. 220 The records they made ('Harlem Fuss' and 'Minor Drag') caused quite a stir.

i. *Mus.* A drum-stroke consisting of two or more grace-notes preceding a beat.

1927 *Melody Maker* Aug. 807/2 A rudimentary beat—the open drag. *Ibid.*, You must try this drag rhythm with the stick and the brush. **1931** G. JACOB *Orchestral Technique* vii. 71 The drag..may contain more than the two preliminary grace-notes (which really amount to an infinitesimally short roll). **1934** E. LITTLE *Mod. Rhythmic Drumming* 13 *The Crush Roll.* Known variously as the 'Crush', 'Press' or 'Drag' Roll, this is a 'fake' beat which has found its way into drumming for a very good reason... The stick (held fairly loosely) is 'crushed' on to the drum head, and allowed to 'bounce' a number of times. **1961** J. PREBBLE *Culloden* i. 13 The sticks of the Main Guard came down on the skins in the drag and paradiddle of the General.

8. *Criminal slang.* †**a.** Robbery of vehicles (*obs.*). **b.** A term of three months in gaol.

1781 G. PARKER *View Soc.* II. 151 Rum Drag. **1812** J. H. VAUX *Flash Dict.*, The *drag*, is the *game* of robbing carts, waggons, or carriages..of trunks, bale-goods, or any other property. *Done for a drag*, signifies convicted for a robbery of the before-mentioned nature. **1851** MAYHEW *Lond. Labour* I. 233 (Hoppe) Sometimes they are detected, and get a drag. **1891** *Daily News* 20 Nov. 6/4 Men who had actually served terms of penal servitude, 'drags' or 'sixes', as they were called, for their offences.

9. *attrib.* and *Comb.* (see also 1 f, 3 f, above), as ***drag-boat, -cart, -harrow, -horse, -hunt*** (cf. DRAG-HOUND), ***-man, -weight***; **drag-anchor**, see quot., a drift-anchor; **drag-bar, -bolt, -chain, -hook, -spring,** those by which locomotive engines, tenders, and trucks are connected; **drag-box,** (*a*) see 1 d, quot. 1837; (*b*) see 5, quot. 1864; **drag-fold** *Geol.*, a small fold in a bed that forms part of a larger fold or a fault; esp. one with the appearance of having been formed by shearing when stronger or more massive beds on each side of the folded bed moved relative to each other; **drag-line,** (*a*) *Geol.* each of a series of fainter glacial striations forming a fringe on the lee-side of an older set and produced when one glacier crosses the path of another; (*b*) an excavator having a bucket which is pulled towards the machine by a wire rope; also, the wire rope itself; also *attrib.*; **drag-link** (see quot.); **drag-mill** = ARRASTRE; **drag queen** *slang*, a male homosexual transvestite; cf. QUEEN *sb.* 12; **drag-rake** (see quot.); **drag-saw,** a saw in which the effective stroke is given in the pull, not in the thrust; **drag-seine** *U.S.*, a haul-ashore seine (*Cent. Dict.* 1890 s.v. *seine*[1]); hence **drag-seining** *vbl. sb.*; **drag-sheet** = *drag-anchor*; **drag-shoe** = SHOE *sb.* 5 f; **drag strut** *Aeronaut.*, a strut designed to strengthen a wing against forces arising from drag; **drag-twist,** see quot.; **drag-washer,** in a gun-carriage, a flat iron ring having an iron loop to which the drag-rope is attached. Also DRAG-CHAIN, -HOOK, -HOUND, -NET, -ROPE, -STAFF, DRAGSMAN.

1874 KNIGHT *Dict. Mech.*, **Drag-anchor*, a frame of wood, or of spars clothed with sails, attached to a hawser, and thrown overboard to drag in the water and diminish the lee-way of a vessel when drifting, or to keep the head of a ship to the wind when unmanageable by loss of sails or rudder. **1849–50** WEALE *Dict. Terms*, **Drag-bar*, a strong iron rod with eye-holes at each end, connecting a locomotive engine and tender by means of the *drag-bolt and spring. **1891** *Daily News* 4 Feb. 3/5 Sixteen more [bodies] were recovered by a *drag-boat. **1911** *U.S. Geol. Surv. Monogr.* LII. v. 123 A common type of fold is a *drag fold.., by which the formation becomes locally buckled along an axis lying in any direction in the plane of bedding. **1937** *Geogr. Jrnl.* XC. 124 The repeated imbricate faults, shear-plan[e]s, and drag-folds. **1942** M. P. BILLINGS *Struct. Geol.* xii. 221 The lineation results from the parallel arrangement of the crests of minute drag folds formed by the sliding of different layers over one another. **1965** G. J. WILLIAMS *Econ. Geol. N.Z.* xix. 342/2 The only folding has been in the form of drag-folds near major faults and gentle compactional folds in the lower Tertiary sediments. **1750** ELLIS *Mod. Husbandman* II. i. 49 They..harrow them in with one single *drag-harrow, as they call it. **1849–50** WEALE *Dict. Terms*, **Drag-hook and chain*, the strong chain and hook attached to the front of the engine buffer-bar, to connect it on to any other locomotive engine or tender; also attached to the drag-bars of goods waggons. **1611** COTGR., *Cheval de traict*, a *drag-horse, draught-horse, cart-horse, coach-horse. **1852** R. S. SURTEES *Sponge's Sp. Tour* vii. 32 *Drag-hunting..is not popular with sportsmen. **1886** T. C. CHAMBERLIN in *7th Ann. Rep. U.S. Geol. Surv.* (1888) 201 It clearly shows the older set by the *drag-lines on their lee sides. **1919** C. G. RAHT *Romance of Davis Mts.* 328 The intake canal was dug with..drag lines. **1922** *Glasgow Herald* 28 Sept. 7 Drag-line excavators. **1940** *Chambers's Techn. Dict.* 263/2 *Drag-line excavator*, a mechanical excavating appliance consisting of a steel scoop bucket which is suspended from a movable jib; after biting into the material to be excavated, it is dragged towards the machine by means of a wire rope. **1950** *Engineering* 17 Nov.

369/1 A drag shovel, a drag line, a grab crane. **1956** *Planning* XXII. 56 The largest type of draglines, which cost nearly £750,000, may remove ore at the rate of up to a million tons a year, depending on the depth. **1849–50** WEALE *Dict. Terms*, **Drag-link*, a link for connecting the cranks of two shafts..in marine engines. **1678** HALE *Hist. Placit. Cor.* xiv. §7 (T.) The great riots, committed by the foresters and Welsh on the *dragmen of Severn, hewing all their boats to pieces. *a* **1884** KNIGHT *Mech. Dict.* Suppl. 271/2 **Drag mill*, another name for the arrastra. **1941** G. LEGMAN in G. W. Henry *Sex Variants* II. 1164 **Drag-queen*, a professional female impersonator; the term being transferentially used of a male homosexual who frequently..wears women's clothing...While many innate male homosexuals wear women's underwear..they are not for that reason called *drag-queens*. **1973** *Nation Rev.* (Melbourne) 31 Aug. III. 1453/2 The cowboys and indians theme culminates in the sheriff..doing his drag queen act and becoming his own indian. **1984** *Listener* 31 May 25/1 He met..the prototype for Terri Dennis—the real-life drag queen being an altogether less arch, more interesting individual. **1760** in *N. & Q.* (1887) 17 Sept. 226 'Great Rakes'..are now come in general use among the farmers, and are called *drag-rakes. **1829** GLOVER *Hist. Derby* I. 188 The large drag-rake..for raking after the cart in hay and corn harvest. **1868** *Iowa Agric. Soc. Rep. 1867* 220 *Drag-saw, for cutting logs into fire-wood. **1893** *Spons' Mech. Own Bk.* (ed. 4) 355 The log is..brought under a drag-saw. **1945** B. MACDONALD *Egg & I* (1946) I. iii. 50 The drag-saw barked and smoked. **1888** GOODE *Amer. Fishes* 179 The method chiefly practiced by the colonists of New England was that of *drag-seining. **1844** J. BACKHOUSE *Narr. Visit to Mauritius & S. Afr.* vii. 138 The *drag-shoe is not used on these occasions, lest the wheel should start out of it. **1849–50** WEALE *Dict. Terms*, **Drag-spring*, a strong spring placed near the back of the tender. **1935** C. G. BURGE *Compl. Bk. Aviation* 592/2 The main planes would tend to fold back. This is prevented by dividing the space between the front and rear spars in each plane into rectangular panels by means of '*drag struts'. **1964** A. C. KERMODE *Aeroplane Struct.* (ed. 2) ix. 171 To prevent the backwards or forwards movement of the wings, the spars in the old-fashioned conventional structure were usually braced together by a system of struts and wires, the struts being called compression or drag struts. **1881** RAYMOND *Mining Gloss.*, **Drag-twist*, a spiral hook at the end of a rod, for cleaning bore-holes. **1828** J. M. SPEARMAN *Brit. Gunner* (ed. 2) 172 When a carriage is dismounted, all the small articles, such as elevating-screws, linch-pins, *drag-washers, cap-squares, &c. must be carefully collected.

†'**dragant.** *Obs.* Also 3–7 **dragagant.** [a. OF. *dragant, dragagant*, ad. late L. *tragacanthum*, (also *dragantum*), a. Gr. *τραγάκανθα* astragalus.] A gum; = TRAGACANTH. Also called *gum dragon*, and formerly ADRAGANT.

c **1265** *Voc.* in Wr.-Wülcker 559/23 *Dragagantum*, *i.* dragagant. **1542** BOORDE *Dyetary* (1870) 97, I do take Dragagant, and gumme Arabycke. **1704** *Lond. Gaz.* No. 3983/4 The Cargo..Gum Arabeck, Gum Dragant..&c.

draga(u)nce, etc., variants of DRAGONS, *Obs.*

drag-chain (-tʃeɪn).

1. A chain used to retard the motion of a vehicle; *esp.* 'a strong chain, with a large hook to hitch on the hind wheel, and keep it from turning when descending a hill' (Felton *Carriages*, 1801).

a **1791** WARTON in Boswell *Johnson* an. 1754 (Visit Oxford) He cried out 'Sufflamina'..as much as to say, 'Put on your drag chain'. **1829** GLOVER *Hist. Derby* I. 188 On arriving at the top of a steep hill, the carter takes off all his trace horses, and hooks them to the drag chain behind.

fig. **1830** GEN. P. THOMPSON *Exerc.* (1842) I. 276 The minister whose melancholy duty it is to act as a drag-chain upon the progress of liberal ideas. **1838** LYTTON *Alice* III. viii, To take from my wheels the drag-chain of disreputable debt. *a* **1871** GROTE *Plato* Pref. (1875) 9 The perpetual drag-chain..upon free speculation.

2. The strong chain by which railway wagons, etc. are coupled: see DRAG *sb.* 9.

dragdom: see -DOM.

drage, var. of DREDGE *sb.*[2]

‖**dragée** (draʒe). Also erron. **dragé.** [F. = sweetmeat, comfit: see DREDGE *sb.*[2]] 'A sugar plum or sweetmeat in the centre of which is a drug; intended for the more pleasant administration of medicinal substances' (*Syd. Soc. Lex.*). In modern use not restricted to sweetmeats serving as a vehicle for drugs; often a sugared almond. Also *attrib.* and *transf.*

1853 C. BRONTË *Villette* III. xxi. 48 He was fond of bon-bons..and..would give his 'dragées' as freely as he lent his books. **1866** *Pharmaceut. Jrnl.* Ser. II. VII. 374 A medicine called Cod-liver Dragés. **1870** *Ibid* XI. 543 On the Continent..[they] keep genuine dragées of various strengths..of rhubarb, aloes, and other simple and compound pills. **1905** A. BENNETT *Sacred & Profane Love* III. iii. 249 Alice wanted to buy him some sweets... I asked him if he would like *dragées*. **1958** *Observer* 14 Sept. 11/3 Make-up in delicate *dragée* tones.

dragence, variant of DRAGONS, *Obs.*

‖**drageoir** (draʒwar). [F. = comfit-box; cf. DRAGÉE.] A sweetmeat-box; cf. *dredge-box*, and DREDGER[2].

1861 *Our Eng. Home* 73 On the buffet of a queen were placed three drageoirs of gold. **1884** *Leisure Hour* June 375/2 The drageoirs or comfit boxes, full of perfumed confectionery, were passed about.

†'**draggage.** *Obs. rare*⁻⁰. [f. DRAG *v.* + -AGE.] The action or work of dragging.

1611 COTGR., *Tirage*, draggage; or a drawing, haling, pulling. *Ibid.*, *Droict de Tirage*, draggage; or a toll, or fee for Draggage (of salt or wine) due vnto some Lords.

dragge, draggeye, variants of DREDGE *sb.*[2]

dragger ('drægə(r)). [f. DRAG *v.* + -ER[1].]

1. One who drags: in various senses of the vb.

? *a* **1500** in *Audelay's Poems* (Percy Soc.) Notes 85 Jangler cum jasper, lepar, galper quoque, draggar. **1598** FLORIO, *Oncimatore*, a hooker or a dragger. *Ibid.*, *Sarpatore*, a puller, a drawer, a tugger, or a dragger. **1724** *Session Minutes* in Cramond *Ch. of Rathven* 60 Anent the ware draggers, there being ane act against dragging ware on Sabbath. **1854** BADHAM *Halieut.* 4 [It] Resists each pull, and 'gainst the dragger, drags.

2. *spec.* **a.** One who uses a drag or dredge. **b.** A street-seller of small wares.

1887 *Pall Mall G.* 23 Aug. 8/2 Even when the tide was quite down, the draggers encountered almost insuperable difficulties. **1896** *Daily News* 26 Feb. 6/3 These men..technically termed 'draggers', frequent the City, and..are to be found cheek by jowl with the greatest children of commerce.

†**3.** One who robs vehicles: cf. DRAG *sb.* 8. *slang.*

1781 G. PARKER *View Soc.* II. 151.

4. *Comb.*, as †*draggerman*, one who fishes with a drag-net.

1630 in *Descr. Thames* (1758) 77 [see DRAG *v.* 7 b].

dragges, obs. f. *drugs, dregs*: see DRUG, DREG.

dragging ('drægɪŋ), *vbl. sb.* [f. DRAG *v.* + -ING[1].] **a.** The action of DRAG *v.* in various senses.

c **1440** *Promp. Parv.* 130/1 Draggynge, or drawynge, *tractus.* **1526** *Pilgr. Perf.* (W. de W. 1531) 158 b, In the psalmody & hymnes..Begin al at ones, & ende all at ones..beware of tayles or draggynge. **1639** FULLER *Holy War* III. xx. (1647) 143 Mens consciences are more moved with leading then dragging or drawing. **1768** G. WASHINGTON *Writ.* (1889) II. 241 Went a dragging for sturgeon. **1812** [see DRAG *v.* 10]. **1840** R. H. DANA *Bef. Mast* xiii. 31 The ship..rode out the gale in safety, without dragging at all. **1876** GWILT *Encycl. Archit.* Gloss., *Dragging*, the operation of completing the surface of soft stone by means of an instrument called a drag, a thin plate of steel with fine teeth on one edge, moved backwards and forwards by the workman. **1876** *Encycl. Brit.* IV. 403/2 The bristles..are sorted according to thickness by a process called 'dragging', which consists in passing them through a kind of comb, which retains those that are too stout to go between the teeth. **1882** *Sydney Slang Dict.* 32 *Dragging down*, or *pulling down*, stealing articles from shop-doors. **1936** J. CURTIS *Gilt Kid* ii. 18 I'm a screwsman and not on the dragging lark. **1938** F. D. SHARPE *Sharpe of Flying Squad* 330 *Dragging*, stealing from vans. **1961** M. LEVY *Studio Dict. Art Terms*, *Dragging*, a method of applying pigment with little or no vehicle by dragging it lightly over the tacky surface of a painting, in order to produce a broken effect.

b. *concr.* The produce of dragging.

1893 *Daily News* 21 June 6/1 Scarce..equal to the draggings of a decent hay field.

'**dragging**, *ppl. a.* [f. as prec. + -ING[2].] That drags: in various senses of the vb.

1775 S. J. PRATT *Lib. Opinions* (1783) I. 158 The road..was heavy and dragging. **1787** MAD. D'ARBLAY *Diary* 15 Aug., [Mrs. Siddons] In face and person, truly noble..in voice, deep and dragging. **1883** *Manch. Exam.* 14 Dec. 4/6 A dull and dragging market.

Hence '**draggingly** *adv.*

1886 MISS BROUGHTON *Dr. Cupid* III. i. 18 Her words..come draggingly, with a little break between each.

draggle ('dræg(ə)l), *v.* Also (5 ?**drakel**), 6–8 **dragle**, 6–9 *Sc.* **draigle.** [Not certainly known before 16th c.; app. dim. and freq. of DRAG *v.*: cf. *waggle*, and see -LE.]

1. *trans.* To wet or befoul (a garment, etc.) by allowing it to drag through mire or wet grass, or to hang untidily in the rain; to make wet, limp, and dirty.

[**1499** *Promp. Parv.* 129/2 Drabelyn (drakelyn, *Pynson*), *paludo, traunlimo* (*sic*).] **1513** DOUGLAS *Æneis* VII. Prol. 76 Puire laboraris and byssy husband men Went wayt and wery draglyt in the fen. *a* **1605** MONTGOMERIE *Flyting w. Polwart* 361 Draiglit throw dirtie dubes and dykes. —— *Sonnets* lxvi, Draiglit in dirt. **1773** GOLDSM. *Stoops to Conq.* v. (Globe) 672/2 Draggled up to the waist. **1837** CARLYLE *Fr. Rev.* I. VII. xi, The wet day draggles the tricolor. **1880** WEBB *Goethe's Faust* Pref. ii. 18 If she falls, she is not draggled in the mire.

†**2.** To drag or trail (through the dirt). *Obs.*

1714 C. JOHNSON *Country Lasses* II. i, Here you have dragled me a long way. **1723** *State of Russia* II. 79 They take it by the Tail, and draggle it thrice round the Idol.

3. *intr.* (for *refl.*) To trail (on the ground), hang trailing. So † *to draggle it.*

c **1594** in Pollen *Acts Eng. Martyrs* (1891) 333 On the hurdle..one of his legs draggled on the ground as he was drawn. *c* **1660** WOOD *Life* (Oxf. Hist. Soc.) I. 300 Masters gownes long, dragling on the ground. **1775** S. J. PRATT *Lib. Opinions* (1783) IV. 16 [Man] draggles it on foot upon the polluted earth. **1815** LADY GRANVILLE *Lett.* 5 Sept. (1894) I. 78 Flounces draggling. **1859** SIR G. W. DASENT *Pop. Tales fr. Norse* 356 Such..long wool, it hung down and draggled after him on the ground.

4. *intr.* To come on or follow slowly and in a straggling train.

1577 HANMER *Anc. Eccl. Hist.* (1619) 477 The spies came dragling in after in base attire. *a* **1598** R. ROLLOCK *Wks.* (Wodrow Soc.) II. xxxii. 389 He that draigled behind will be before thee. **1809** W. IRVING *Knickerb.* (1861) 209 With heavy hearts they draggled at the heels of his troop. **1878** BOSW. SMITH *Carthage* 205 Some beasts of burden which had lagged behind..came draggling in one after the other.

Hence '**draggling** *vbl. sb.* and *ppl. a.*

a **1598** R. ROLLOCK *Wks.* (Wodrow Soc.) II. xxxii. 389 A draigling person. *Ibid.*, He or she that will persevere in draigling. **1663** BUTLER *Hud.* I. i. 449 His draggling tail hung in the dirt. **1840** THACKERAY *Cruikshank* (1869) 304 My lady with the ermine tippet and draggling feather. **1886** *Manch. Exam.* 6 Jan. 5/2 After the Speaker is chosen, several days will pass in draggling fashion.

draggle, *sb. rare.* [f. prec. vb.]

1. The action of draggling.

1894 STOPF. BROOKE *Tennyson* x. 330 The dull coarseness and the draggle of the last days of luxury and adultery.

2. One who draggles. *Sc.*

1806 TRAIN *Poet. Reveries* 64 (Jam.) To her came a rewayl'd draggle.

draggled ('dræg(ə)ld), *ppl. a.* [f. prec. + -ED[1].] Befouled with dragging through wet and mire.

1513 [see DRAGGLE *v.* 1]. **1699** GARTH *Dispens.* II. (1700) 23 The draggl'd Dignity of Scavenger. **1714** GAY *Trivia* II. 9 You'll see a draggled Damsel here and there, From Billingsgate her fishy Traffick bear. **1879** FROUDE *Cæsar* xiii. 183 A draggled trail of disreputables.

draggle-haired, *a. nonce-wd.* [f. DRAGGLE *v.* and HAIR, after *draggle-tailed.*] With hair hanging wet and untidy.

1865 DICKENS *Mut. Fr.* III. x, Draggle-haired, seamed with jealousy and anger.

draggle-tail ('dræg(ə)lteɪl). [f. DRAGGLE *v.* + TAIL *sb.*]

1. A draggle-tailed person; a woman whose skirts are wet and draggled, or whose dress hangs about her untidily and dirty; a slut.

1596 NASHE *Saffron Walden* 143 To see a..draggell taile run her taile into a bushe of thornes. **1611** SPEED *Hist. Gt. Brit.* IX. xxiii. (1632) 1135 About twenty of those bemired Souldiers were slaine, and no other cry heard, but downe with the Draggle-tailes. **1725** SWIFT *Ep. Corr.* Wks. 1841 II. 572 What a draggletail she will be before she gets to Dublin! **1881** BESANT & RICE *Chapl. of Fleet* II. iii, A well-dressed woman and a draggletail are all one to them.

2. *pl.* Skirts that drag on the ground in the mud.

1858 R. S. SURTEES *Ask Mamma* lxxv. 331 Looped-up dresses..a great improvement on the draggletails. **1871** C. GIBBON *Lack of Gold* viii, The dress..which, to avoid draggle-tails, was worn short.

3. *attrib.* = next.

1707 J. STEVENS tr. *Quevedo's Com. Wks.* (1709) 420 Draggle-Tail Jilts newly Whip'd. **1879** MISS BRADDON *Clov. Foot* xii. 108 Nice draggle-tail creatures we shall look after we have walked..under such a rain as this.

'**draggle-tailed**, *a.* Having a tail or skirt that trails on the ground in mud and wet.

1654 GATAKER *Disc. Apol.* 4 Everie draggle-tail'd Girl that comes to them. **1825** SCOTT *Jrnl.* 23 Nov., A draggle-tailed wench. **1831** TRELAWNY *Adv. Younger Son* I. 288 The draggletailed..cockatoo.

'**draggle-ˌtailedness.** [-NESS.] Draggle-tailed condition or character.

1889 E. F. KNIGHT *'Falcon' on the Baltic* iv. 62 The outrageously bad taste and gaudy draggletailedness of English girls of the same degree. **1904** *Westm. Gaz.* 2 Nov. 1/3 The terrible draggletailedness of some of the women.

'**draggly**, *a.* [f. DRAGGLE *v.* + -Y.] Inclined to draggle or trail untidily.

1850 CARLYLE in Froude *Life in Lond.* (1884) II. 65 A strange draggly-wick'd tallow candle.

draggy ('drægɪ), *a.* [f. DRAG *v.* + -Y[1].]

a. Inclined to drag or cause dragging; heavy; slow; dull.

1887 HALL CAINE *Deemster* xxix, The roads were soft and draggy. **1890** *Columbus Disp.* (Ohio) 4 Sept., The market is dull and draggy. **1891** *Sat. Rev.* 31 Oct. 501/2 One or two rather draggy episodes.

b. Boring; conventional; uncongenial; unpleasant. *colloq.* (orig. *U.S.*).

1922 S. FORD *Trilby May crashes In* iii. 43 We were both prepared to be thrilled, I expect, but we soon found that an early rehearsal is rather a draggy affair. **1964** *Punch* 4 Nov. 683/2 The 'draggy old days'. **1967** *Listener* 17 Aug. 205/2 We'll just have to ask my boss and his draggy wife to our rave. *Ibid.* 23 Nov. 668/3, I know it's draggy having the au pair feeding with us; but one has to be madly democratic if one wants to keep them. **1971** A. HUNTER *Gently at Gallop* iii. 26 Charlie was only a brewer, remember—draggy rooms made him feel comfortable.

Hence '**dragginess.**

1891 F. W. ROBINSON *Her Love and His Life* VI. ix, There was a little dragginess of gait.

dragh(en, draȝen, obs. ff. DRAW *v.*, DRAWN.

drag-hook.

1. A hook used for dragging.

1530 PALSGR. 215/1 Draghoke, *crocq.* **1653** WALTON *Angler* x. 193 You may..take it up with a drag-hook. **1848** J. A. CARLYLE tr. *Dante's Inferno* XXI. 253 They lowered their drag-hooks. **1870** BLAINE *Encycl. Rural Sports* §3038 The drag-hook is another implement for clearing away obstructions in angling..It consists of three stout iron hooks placed back to back.

2. The hook of a drag-chain: see DRAG *sb.* 9.

ˈdrag-hound. *Hunting.* A hound of a pack used to hunt with a 'drag' or artificial scent.

1884 *Times* 4 Feb. 8/2 (heading) Household Brigade Drag Hounds. **1892** *Pall Mall G.* 11 Apr. 5/2 He then hunted the draghounds for three seasons at Ballincolley.

draght, draȝt, obs. forms of DRAUGHT.

dragman[1]: see DRAG *sb.* 9.

dragman[2], obs. form of DRAGOMAN.

ˈdrag-net. [Cf. Sw. *dragg-not.*] **a.** A net which is dragged over the bottom of a river or piece of water in order to enclose all the fish, etc.; also a net used to sweep the ground game off a field.

[*c* **1000** ÆLFRIC *Gloss.* in Wright 15/13 *Tragum*, dræg-net, *vel* dræge. *Ibid.* 48/27 *Verriculum*, dræg-net.] *a* **1541** WYATT *Of meane Estate* 89 in *Tottell's Misc.* (Arb.) 87 Ye set not a dragge net for an hare. **1610** BP. HALL *Apol. Brownists* 11 Shall the Fisher cast away a good draught because his drag-net hath weedes? **1622** MALYNES *Anc. Law-Merch.* 246 It is also prouided..that no drag-net be set before March, nor vpon deeper water than foureteene fathome. **1790** BURKE *Fr. Rev.* Wks. V. 351 It has the whole draft of fishes in its drag-net. **1814** *Sporting Mag.* XLIV. 61 Preventing partridges being taken at night by drag-nets.

b. *transf.* and *fig.*

1641 MILTON *Prel. Episc.* Wks. (1847) 22/2 Whatsoever time..hath drawn down from old, in her huge drag-net.. those are the fathers. **1654** FULLER *Ephemeris* Pref. 7 The dragge-net of no diligence can be..so advantagiously cast, as to catch and hold all particulars uttered in a long speech. **1882** J. TAYLOR *Sc. Covenanters* (Cassell) 43 This act was popularly termed 'The Bishops' Drag-net'. **1906** *Daily Colonist* (Victoria, B.C.) 5 Jan. 6/5 The Police Drag-Net. —Quite a grist has been gathered to the police mill for the magistrate's sitting this morning. **1928** HECHT & MACARTHUR *Front Page* II. 73 They're throwing a drag-net around the whole North Side. **1958** *Oxford Mail* 1 Aug. 1/9 Police spread a 'dragnet' across the Jezreel Valley in a bid to recapture those who had got away.

dragoman (ˈdrægəmən). Pl. **-mans, -men.** Forms: 4, 7-8 **drogman,** 5-8 **droge-,** 6 **drag-, druga-,** 6-9 **drogue-,** 7 **dragu-, droga-, droger-, drugga-, drug-, drugoman,** 7-8 **druggerman, drogoman,** (9 **dracoman**), 6- **dragoman.** See also TRUCHMAN. [a. F. *dragoman, drogman,* in OF. *drugemen* = Sp. *dragoman,* It. *dragomanno,* med.L. *dragumannus,* late Gr. δραγούμανος, ad. OArab. *targumān,* now *tarjumān, tarjamān, turjumān,* interpreter, f. *targama, tarjama* to interpret = Chaldee *targēm,* (whence *targum*). From 14th c. commonly treated as a compound of Eng. *man* with pl. *dragomen*; in 19th c. more frequently *dragomans.*

The variants are due to the varying vocalization of the Arabic word, and the passage of Old Arabic *g* into *j*. Forms closer to the modern Arabic are Sp. *trujaman,* med.L. *turchemannus,* It. *turcimanno,* Fr. *truchement,* Eng. *toureheman, trudgeman,* TRUCHMAN, q.v.]

An interpreter; strictly applied to a man who acts as guide and interpreter in countries where Arabic, Turkish, or Persian is spoken.

13.. *K. Alis.* 3401 Alisaundre..is y-come to Arabye. So me saide a drogman. *c* **1430** LYDG. *Bochas* II. xxvii. (1554) 63 a, Cirus..All vnpurueyed of drogeman or of guide. **1506** GUYLFORDE *Pilgr.* (Camden) 56 (Stanf.) Our drogemen and guydes. **1585** T. WASHINGTON tr. *Nicholay's Voy.* IV. xvi. 131 Oftentimes they serve for Dragomans, or interpretours. **1599** HAKLUYT *Voy.* II. I. 305 The ambassador..himselfe last, with his Chause and Drugaman or Interpreter. **1606** MILDENHALL in Purchas *Pilgrims* (1625) I. III. 115 (Stanf.) For want of a Drugman. **1613** *Haga at Const.* in *Harl. Misc.* (Malh.) III. 214 Two druggermen, or interpreters. **1627** SIR T. ROE in Fennell tr. *Michaelis' Anc. Marb. in Gt. Brit.* (1882) 201 (Stanf.), I am this day sending a drogaman..to Brussia. **1656** BLOUNT *Glossogr., Drogoman* (or *Draguman*), an Interpreter or Truchman. **1782** W. F. MARTYN *Geog. Mag.* I. 106 Met..by the druggerman or interpreter. **1813** BYRON *Giaour* 592 *note,* To the horror of all the dragomans. **1821** SYD. SMITH *Wks.* (1859) I. 317/2 Our ostentatious drogueman will feel a pleasure in raising your astonishment. **1861** MRS. HARVEY *Cruise Claymore* viii. 153 Most travellers are entirely at the mercy of their dragomen. **1870** A. L. ADAMS *Nile Valley & Malta* 4 The best Maltese and Egyptian dragomans.

b. *transf.*

1690 DRYDEN *Don Sebast.* III. i. Wks. 1883 VII. 374 You druggerman of heaven, must I attend Your droning prayers? **1735** POPE *Donne Sat.* IV. 83 Pity, you was not Druggerman at Babel! **1855** MILMAN *Lat. Chr.* (1864) IX. XIV. iii. 117 Through the Jews of Andalusia &c (those Dragomen of Mediæval Science).

Hence **ˈdragomanate,** the office of a dragoman; **dragoˈmanic, ˈdragomanish** *adjs.,* of, pertaining to, or like a dragoman.

1860 *All Year Round* No. 45. 437 Grimani..looked rather grand and dragomanish. **1869** FRESHFIELD *Caucasus & Bashan* ii. 62 The usual dragomanic expenses. **1881** *Times* 19 July 9/3 To inscribe themselves..as French subjects, at the Consular Dragomanate.

dragon[1] (ˈdrægən). Forms: 3-4 **dragun,** 3-6 **dragone, dragoun(e,** 4 **dragowne,** 4- **dragon.** [a. F. *dragon*:—L. *dracōn-em* (nom. *draco*), a. Gr. δράκων, -οντα; usually referred to δρακ- strong aorist stem of δέρκεσθαι to see clearly.]

I. † **1.** A huge serpent or snake; a python. *Obs.* (exc. in etymol. use).

c **1220** *Bestiary* 759 Ðe dragunes one ne stiren nout..oc daren stille in here pit. *c* **1250** *Gen. & Ex.* 2924 And worpen he ðor wondes dun, fro euerilc ðor crep a dragun. *a* **1300** *Cursor M.* 5900 (Cott.) Dun þai kest a wand ilkan, And þai wex dragons [*v.rr.* -onis, -ownes, -ouns] son onan. *c* **1400** MAUNDEV. (1839) v. 40 It is alle deserte & fulle of Dragouns & grete serpentes. **1508** DUNBAR *Tua Mariit Wemen* 263 Be dragonis baith and dowis, ay in double forme. **1667** MILTON *P.L.* x. 529 Hee..Now Dragon grown, larger than whom the Sun Ingenderd in the Pythian Vale on slime, Huge Python. **1700** BP. PATRICK *Comm. Deut.* xxxii. 33 Many authors..say that dragons have no poison in them. **1849** KINGSLEY *Misc., Poet. Sacred & Leg. Art* I. 265 Why should not these dragons have been simply what the Greek word dragon means—what..the superstitions of the peasantry in many parts of England to this day assert them to have been—'mighty worms', huge snakes?

2. a. A mythical monster, represented as a huge and terrible reptile, usually combining ophidian and crocodilian structure, with strong claws, like a beast or bird of prey, and a scaly skin; it is generally represented with wings, and sometimes as breathing out fire. The heraldic dragon combines reptilian and mammalian form with the addition of wings.

It is difficult to separate senses 1 and 2 in early instances.

a **1225** *St. Marher.* 158 Þe deuel com to þis maide swye In aforme of a dragoun. **1297** R. GLOUC. (1724) 151 Out of the dragone's mouth twei leomes ther stode there. **1382** WYCLIF *Dan.* xiv. 28 Ȝeue to vs Danyel that distruyede Bel and slewȝ the dragoun. *c* **1400** *Destr. Troy* 166 A derfe dragon drede to be-holde. **1591** SHAKS. *1 Hen. VI*, I. i. 11 His Armes spred wider than a Dragons Wings. **1595** —— *John* II. i. 288 Saint George that swindg'd the Dragon. **1607** TOPSELL *Serpents* (1658) 705 There be some Dragons which have wings and no feet, some again have both feet and wings. **1762** H. WALPOLE *Vertue's Anecd. Paint.* I. i. (R.), On a rising ground above the tents is St. George on a brown steed striking with his sword at the dragon, which is flying in the air. **1774** GOLDSM. *Nat. Hist.* (1776) VII. 156 The Dragon, a most terrible animal, but most probably not of Nature's formation. **1813** SCOTT *Trierm.* III. xix, They..faced the dragon's breath of fire. **1895** A. H. S. LANDOR *Corea* 116 In shape, as the natives picture it, the dragon is not unlike a huge lizard, with long-nailed claws, and a flat long head.. possessed of horns and a long mane of fire.

b. Hence frequent allusions to ancient and mediæval tales of dragons, as those which watchfully guarded the Gardens of the Hesperides, those which drew the chariot of Cynthia or the moon, those fought and slain by Beowulf, St. George, and other champions.

1590 SHAKS. *Mids. N.* III. ii. 379 Night-swift Dragons cut the Clouds full fast. **1611** —— *Cymb.* II. ii. 48 Swift, swift, you Dragons of the night, that dawning May beare the Rauens eye. **1663** *Flagellum, or O. Cromwell* (ed. 2) 5 He was very notorious for robbing of Orchards..the frequent spoyls and damages of Trees..committed by this Apple-Dragon. **1837** HT. MARTINEAU *Soc. Amer.* III. 240 The other public buildings being guarded by the dragon of bigotry. **1856** EMERSON *Eng. Traits, Wealth* Wks. (Bohn) II. 75 Harder still it has proved to resist and rule the dragon Money, with his paper wings. **1860** —— *Cond. Life, Fate* II. 320 Every brave youth is in training to ride, and rule this dragon [Fate].

c. *like a dragon*: fiercely, violently.

1711 SWIFT *Lett.* (1767) III. 213 We ate roast beef like dragons. **1741** tr. *De Mouhy's Fort. Country Maid* I. 165 The poor Boy..seeing himself collar'd, fought like a Dragon. **1827** SCOTT *Jrnl.* 8 Oct., I even made a work of necessity and set to the Tales like a dragon.

3. In the Bible versions reproducing *draco* of the Vulgate and δράκων of the Septuagint, where the Hebrew has (*a*) *tannīn* a great sea- or water-monster, a whale, shark, or crocodile, also a large serpent; or (*b*) *tan* a desert mammalian animal, now understood to be the jackal, and so rendered in the Revised Version.

a **1340** HAMPOLE *Psalter* lxxiii[i]. 14 Þou angird þe heuedis of dragunys [**1382** WYCLIF dragounys, **1611** dragons, **1885** *R.V.* dragons (*marg.* sea-monsters)] in watirs. **1382** WYCLIF *Ps.* xc[i]. 13 Thou shalt to-trede the leoun and the dragoun [**1611** dragon, **1885** *R.V.* serpent]. —— *Job* xxx. 29 Brother I was of dragouns [**1611** dragons, **1885** *R.V.* jackals]. —— *Isa.* xxxiv. 13 It shal be the bed place of dragownes [**1611** dragons, **1885** *R.V.* jackals]. **1885** BIBLE (R.V.) *Ps.* cxlviii. 7 Praise the Lord from the earth, Ye dragons [*marg.* sea-monsters] and all deeps.

4. a. An appellation of Satan, the 'Old Serpent'.

1340 *Ayenb.* 174 Ine þe þrote of þe lyone of helle, and of þe dragoune þet him wyle uorzuelȝe. **1382** WYCLIF *Rev.* xx. 2 And he cauȝte the dragoun, the olde serpent, that is the deuel and Sathanas. *c* **1440** *York Myst.* xxi. 157 The dragons poure..Thurgh my baptyme distroyed haue I. **1500-20** DUNBAR *Poems* xxxviii. 1 Done is a battell on the dragon blak. **1667** MILTON *P.L.* IV. 3 The Dragon, put to second rout, Came furious down to be reveng'd on men. **1707** WATTS *Hymn 'How sad our State'* v, The old Dragon ..With all his hellish crew.

b. *transf.* A devilish person; a 'fiend'.

1508 KENNEDIE *Flyting w. Dunbar* 249 Dathane deuillis sone, and dragon dispitous. *Ibid.* 283 Corspatrick..That dampnit dragone drew him in diserth. **1715** I. MATHER *Sev. Serm.* (Boston) I. ii. 40 Has not the Dragon of France boasted, that he caused Twenty hundred thousand Persons to renounce their Religion?

c. An evil power embodied. *rare.*

c **1470** HENRY *Wallace* XI. 287 Inwy the wyle dragoun, In cruell fyr he byrnys this regioun.

5. An appellation of Death. *arch.*

1500-20 DUNBAR *Poems* viii. 17 O duilfull death! O dragon dolorous! *Ibid.* lviii. 28 Off deathe..the dragoun stang thame. **1878** BROWNING *La Saisiaz* 43 The serpent pains which herald, swarming in, the dragon death.

6. A fierce violent person; *esp.* a fiercely or aggressively watchful woman; a duenna.

dragon of virtue (F. *dragon de vertu*), a woman of austere and aggressive virtue.

1755 JOHNSON, *Dragon*..3. A fierce violent man or woman. **1837** THACKERAY *Ravenswing* vi, Lady Thrum, dragon of virtue and propriety. **1848** *Life Normandy* (1863) I. 178 She will keep her husband in as tight order as the handsome old dragon we met just now. **1887** MRS. C. READE *Maid of Mill* II. xxvii. 116 Confronted by the dragon, in her not least dragonesque mood.

7. a. A representation or figure of the mythical creature.

c **1320** *Sir Tristr.* 1042 Tristrem..Bar him þurch þe dragoun In þe scheld. *c* **1540** *Inv. Westm. Abb.* in *Trans. Lond. & Middlesex Archæol. Soc.* (1875) IV, Hym that beryth the Dragon on Easter Evyn. **1548** HALL *Chron., Hen. VII,* 1 b, A red firye dragon beaten upon white and grene sarcenet. **1766** PORNY *Heraldry* (1787) 203 The Eleventh is Or, a Dragon passant Vert. **1870** H. W. HENFREY *Eng. Coins* (1891) 38 The dragon on some of the coins [of Henry VII] was the ensign of Cadwallader, the last King of the Britons. **1888** J. T. FOWLER in *Mem. Ripon* (Surtees) III. 234 *note,* On the three Rogation Days the dragon was carried 'in principio processionis'.

†**b.** An ensign or standard, having the figure of a dragon. *Obs.*

1297 R. GLOUC. (1724) 303 Edmond ydyȝt hys standard.. And hys dragon vp yset. *c* **1330** R. BRUNNE *Chron. Wace* (Rolls) 13345 A-mong þo was þe dragoun þat Arthur bar for gonfanoun. **13..** *K. Alis.* 4300 Theo kyng dude sette out his dragoun. **1609** HOLLAND *Amm. Marcell.* XVI. xi. 74 The purple ensigne of a dragon fitted to the top of a..high launce, as if it had beene the pendant slough of a serpent.

c. *dragon china,* a kind of porcelain decorated with designs of dragons.

1786 F. TYTLER *Lounger* No. 79 ¶8 Ringing it to try if it was without a flaw, she returned it into the auctioneer's hands, declaring it a piece of true Dragon. **1853** E. M. SEWELL *Experience of Life* ix. 80 Tea came, and..the wide cups of dragon china.

d. *to chase the dragon* (*slang*): to take heroin by inhalation (see quot. 1961).

1961 HARNEY & CROSS *Narcotic Officer's Handbk.* iii. 58 The method of smoking heroin called 'chasing the dragon' or its variant, 'playing the mouth organ'... In 'chasing the dragon' the heroin and any diluting drug are placed on a folded piece of tinfoil. This is heated with a taper and the resulting fumes inhaled through a small tube of bamboo or rolled paper. The fumes move up and down the tinfoil with the movements of the molten powder, resembling the undulating tail of the mythical Chinese dragon. When a matchbox cover instead of a tube is used to assist in inhaling the vapour, that operation is called 'playing the mouth organ', which the action suggests. **1982** T. MO *Sour Sweet* vi. 50 Probably the stuff was now only twenty per cent pure. Still, good enough for 'chasing the dragon' Hong Kong style with match, silver foil, and paper tube. **1984** *Times* 8 Oct. 13/3 More [heroin] is taken by sniffing the powder—snorting; or by 'chasing the dragon'..less through intravenous injection. **1985** R. LEWIS *Blurred Reality* iii. 105 There's this myth among the kids that if they inhale the burned skag it isn't going to hurt them. Chasing the dragon, they call it.

8. *Astron.* **a.** A northern constellation, *Draco.*

1551 RECORDE *Castle Knowl.* (1556) 263 Aboute these 2 Beares is there a long trace of 31 starres, commonly called the Dragon. **1697** DRYDEN *Virg. Georg.* I. 334 Around our Pole the Spiry Dragon glides, And like a winding Stream the Bears divides. **1786-7** BONNYCASTLE *Astron.* 420.

†**b.** The part of the moon's path which lies south of the ecliptic: see DRAGON'S HEAD, TAIL. *Obs.*

c **1391** CHAUCER *Astrol.* II. §4 Whan that no wykkid planete, as..the tail of the dragoun, is in [the] hous of the assendent. **1398** TREVISA *Barth. De P.R.* VIII. xix. (1495) 330 The heed of the dragon and the taylle..meue wyth the fyrmament and folowe his course. **1594** BLUNDEVIL *Exerc.* III. I. xv. (ed. 7) 306 The Dragon then signifieth none other thing but the intersection of two Circles, that is to say, of the Ecliptique and of the Circle that carrieth the Moon..and that part towards the South is called of some the belly of the Dragon.

†**c.** Applied to a shooting star with a luminous train. *Obs.* Cf. DRAKE[1] 2.

1398 TREVISA *Barth. De P.R.* VIII. xxiii. (1495) 335 Amonge the mydle sterres of Artos fallyth downe as it were a dragon other a fleenge sterre in lykenesse of lyghtenynge. **1563** W. FULKE *Meteors* (1640) 7, 10. **1568** GRAFTON *Chron.* II. 119 Fiery dragons were seene fliyng in the ayre. **1774** GOLDSM. *Nat. Hist.* (1862) I. xxi. 134 Floating bodies of fire, which assume different names..The *draco volans,* or flying dragon, as it is called.

9. A paper kite. [Ger. *drache.*] *Sc.*

1756 MRS. CALDERWOOD *Jrnl.* (1884) 145 A peice of brocade..in the shape of a dragon the boys let fly. **1868** G. MACDONALD *R. Falconer* I. 253 The dragon broke its string ..and drifting away, went..downwards in the distance.

10. † **a.** An early fire-arm; = DRAGOON 1. *Obs.* †**b.** A soldier armed with this; = DRAGOON 2. *Obs.*

1604-28 W. YONGE *Diary* (Camden) 35 Colonel Francis his regiment, especially the soldiers called Dragons, do continually make incursions upon the enemy. **1834** PLANCHÉ *Brit. Costume* 270 The dragon received its name from its muzzle, being generally ornamented with the head of that fabled monster, and the troops who used it.. acquired the name of Dragons and Dragoons from this circumstance. **1849** JAS. GRANT *Kirkaldy of Gr.* xviii. 198. **1867** SMYTH *Sailor's Wd.-bk., Dragon,* an old name for a musketoon.

c. A very powerful armoured tractor.

1926 *Glasgow Herald* 8 Apr. 11 The tanks, dragons, light and heavy guns, cookers, etc. **1927** *Sunday Express* 1 May 7 Just as these 'tankettes' will largely supersede the infantry, so will the 'dragons' supersede horse-teams for bringing up the guns.

11. *Zool.* A lizard of the genus *Draco*, having on each flank a broad wing-like membrane, which enables it to leap some distance in the air.

1819 *Pantologia, Draco volans*, flying dragon. **1823** CRABB *Technol. Dict., Dragon* (*Zool.*) the *Draco* of Linnæus, a four-footed beast of the lizard tribe..able, by means of its lateral membrane, to support itself for a short time in the air. **1841** *Penny Cycl.* XX. 457/2 The canines of the Dragon are proportionally longer than those of Stellio. **1847** CARPENTER *Zool.* §468 The Dragons of zoologists, instead of being formidable animals, like those of poets, are of very small size, and only attack insects.

12. *Ichthyol.* (Also ***dragon-fish***.) **a.** = DRAGONET 2. †**b.** The ANGLER, *Lophius* (obs.).

1661 LOVELL *Hist. Anim. & Min.* 198 Dragon..the flesh is hard and dry, but if prepared, pleasant. **1694** *Acc. Sev. Late Voy.* II. (1711) 132 Of the Dragon-fish. **1769** PENNANT *Zool.* III. 130.

13. A fancy variety of pigeon; = DRAGOON *sb.* 3.

1867 TEGETMEIER *Pigeons* viii. 80 The Dragon most closely resembles..the Carrier, and it is stated..that it was produced by mating a Tumbler with a Horseman or a Carrier. **1895** *Daily News* 10 Oct. 5/4 A splendid collection of dragons and tumblers, both short-faced and flying.

14. (Also ***green dragon***.) The plant *Dracunculus vulgaris* (formerly *Arum Dracunculus*); = DRAGONS, DRAGONWORT. Also applied to species of *Dracontium*.

1538 TURNER *Libellus*, Dracontia latine dracunculus dicitur, anglice Dragon. **1551** —— *Herbal* I. O vj a, Dragon hath a certayne lykenes vnto aron, bothe in the lefe and also in the roote. **1626** BACON *Sylva* §632 The Spirits doe but weaken, and dissipate, when they come to the Air and Sunne; As we see it in Onions, Garlick, Dragon, &c. **1858** HOGG *Veg. Kingd.* 796 *Dracunculus vulgaris*, or Green Dragon, is a native of the South of Europe, and receives its name from spots on the stem. **1866** *Treas. Bot.*, Dragon, *Dracunculus vulgaris*; also applied to the orontiaceous genus *Dracontium*.

†**15.** A disease of the eye of the horse: see quots.

1639 T. DE GRAY *Compl. Horsem.* 94 Dimnesse of sight, filmes, pearles, pin and web, dragons, serpentines. *c* **1720** W. GIBSON *Farrier's Guide* II. xxiv. (1738) 80 Cataract..is the same which the Farriers distinguish by the different Names of a Speck, Pearl, or Dragon. *Ibid.* 81 When it is very small, and shows itself only in the Bottom of the watry humour, it is then called a Dragon.

16. (Also ***dragon cane***): see quot.

1851 *Offic. Catal. Gt. Exhib.* II. 798 From Singapore.. Ratans, dragons, and Penang lawyers are stems of various species of Calamus. *Ibid.* 800 Dragon canes mounted.

17. *slang.* A sovereign: from the device of St. George and the Dragon.

1827 MAGINN *Transl. Vidocq.* (Farmer) Collar his dragons clear away. **1859** MATSELL *Vocabulum* (Farmer).

II. *attrib.* and *Comb.*

18. *attrib.* or as *adj.* Of or as of a dragon, of the nature of a dragon; dragon-like, dragonish. ***dragon boat*** = DRAKE[1] 5.

1606 SHAKS. *Tr. & Cr.* v. viii. 17 The dragon wing of night ore-spreds the earth. **1632** MILTON *Penseroso* 59 Cynthia checks her dragon yoke. **1777** POTTER *Æschylus* (1779) I. 110 (Jod.) Fierce with dragon rage. **1822** W. IRVING *Braceb. Hall* (1823) II. 174 They..kept a dragon watch on the gipsies. **1832** TENNYSON *Dream Fair Women* 255 Those dragon eyes of anger'd Eleanor. **1848** DICKENS *Dombey* xxiii, Two dragon sentries keeping ward. **1868** TENNYSON *Lucretius* 50 Dragon warriors from Cadmean teeth. **1895** Æ. MACKAY *Fife & Kinross* I. 20 Norse Vikings whose dragon boats preyed on the coasts. **1903** *Folk-Lore* Sept. 293 A dragon-horse carrying on its back a scroll. **1937** *Burlington Mag.* Oct. 162/1 The *ch'i-lui*, also called dragon-horse, is known to us from classic writings.

19. General Combs.: **a.** attributive, as ***dragon-bought***, ***-coil***, ***-face***, ***-feet***, †***-hame*** (covering), ***-hole***, ***-killer***, ***-kind***, ***-legend***, ***-mail***, ***-race***, ***-scale***, ***-seed***, ***tooth*** (see 21 b), ***-whelp***, ***-womb***; **b.** similative, as ***dragon-green*** adj.; **c.** instrumental, as ***dragon-guarded***, ***-ridden***, ***-wardered*** adjs.; **d.** parasynthetic, as ***dragon-eyed***, ***-mouthed***, ***-penned***, ***-winged***, adjs.; also ***dragon-like*** adj. and adv.

1872 TENNYSON *Gareth* 228 The *dragon-boughts and elvish emblemings Began to move. **1711** SHAFTESB. *Charac.* (1737) I. 149 Those grotesque figures and *dragon-faces. **1820** W. TOOKE tr. *Lucian* I. 107 Hecate..stamped with her *dragon-feet. **1884** *Pall Mall G.* 1 Dec. 5/1 *Dragon-green great coats with red linings. **1901** *Daily News* 22 Feb. 6/3 Their places of captivity stand for *dragon-guarded castles. **1914** W. B. YEATS *Responsibilities* 32 In a dragon-guarded land. *a* **1400–50** *Alexander* 487 Anec[t]anabus..Did on him his *dragon-hame and drafe thurȝe þe sale. **1483** *Cath. Angl.* 106/2 A *Dragon hole. **1687** T. BROWN *Saints in Uproar* Wks. 1730 I. 81 Ten times more troublesome than..the *dragon-killer. **1963** *Times* 17 May 24/2 (Advt.), Every quarter it reviews, comprehensively and authoritatively, the latest developments in pure and applied science. It is the best dragon-killer sixpence can buy. **1848** MRS. JAMESON *Sacr. & Leg. Art* (1850) 424 The *dragon-legend of the Gargouille. **1607** SHAKS. *Cor.* IV. vii. 23 He..Fights *Dragon-like, and does atcheeue as soone As draw his Sword. **1795** SOUTHEY *Joan of Arc* VII. 392 Clad in his *dragon mail. **1886** W. J. TUCKER *Life in E. Europe* 236 The prodigious, *dragon-mouthed water-pipes. **1922** W. B. YEATS *Seven Poems* 8 Now days are *dragon-ridden. **1885** —— in *Dublin Univ. Rev.* Apr., Until afar appear the gleaming *dragon-scales. **1855** MILMAN *Lat. Chr.* IX. viii. (1864) V. 389 Had only sowed the *dragon seed of worse heresies. **1607** TOPSELL *Serpents* (1658) 709 A little *Dragon-whelp bred in Arcadia. **1605** *Play Stucley* 1191 in Simpson *Sch. Shaks.* I. 206 His dauntless *dragon-winged thoughts. **1634** MILTON *Comus* 131 The *dragon womb Of Stygian darkness.

20. Special Combs.: **dragon arum**, the plant *Dracunculus vulgaris* (sense 14); **dragon-beam**, **dragon-piece**, 'a short beam lying diagonally with the wall-plates at the angles of the roof for receiving the heel or foot of the hip-rafter' (Gwilt); **dragon-bushes**, *Linaria vulgaris* (Miller); **dragon claw** = *dragon's claw* (see 21); **dragon-fish** (see sense 12); **dragon-plant**, a name for the species of *Dracæna*; †**dragon serpentine** = DRAGONWORT; **dragon-shell** (see quot.); **dragon-stone**, DRACONITES; †**dragon-volant** (see quot.); †**dragon-water**, a medicinal preparation popular in 17th c. Also DRAGON-FLY, etc.

1703 MOXON *Mech. Exerc.* 160 **Dragon-beams*, are two strong Braces or Struts..meeting in an angle upon the shoulder of the King-piece. **1823** P. NICHOLSON *Pract. Build.* 222 **Dragon-piece*, a beam bisecting the wall-plate, for receiving the heel or foot of the hip-rafters. **1598** FLORIO, *Dragontea*, the herb dragon wort, or *dragon serpentine. **1753** CHAMBERS *Cycl. Supp.*, **Dragon-shell*..a name given ..to a species of concamerated patella or limpet. This has its top very much bent, and is of an ash-colour on the outside, but of an elegant and bright flesh-colour within. **1632** SHERWOOD, *Dragon stone, *draconite*. **1867** SMYTH *Sailor's Word-bk.*, **Dragon-volant*, the old name for a gun of large calibre used in the French navy. **1607** DEKKER *Westw. Hoe* II. ii. Wks. 1873 II. 308 Will you send her a Box of Mithridatum and *Dragon water. **1615** MARKHAM *Eng. Housew.* II. i. (1668) 6 For the Quartan Fever, Take.. Dragon water.

21. Comb. with *dragon's*. **a.** In names of plants, as **dragon's-claw**, **dragon's-herb** (= DRAGONWORT); **dragon's-mouth** (see quot.). **b.** **dragon's belly**, **dragon's skin** (see quots.); **dragon's teeth**, the teeth of the dragon fabled to have been sown by Cadmus, from which sprang armed men; also the colloquial name given to the cone-shaped anti-tank obstacles used in the war of 1939–45 (see also quot. 1971); **dragon's tongue**, ?the tongue of a buckle. See also DRAGON'S BLOOD, -HEAD, -TAIL.

1766 CROKER *Dict. Arts*, *Venter Draconis*, *Dragon's Belly, in astronomy..that part [of a planet's orbit] most remote from the nodes, that is, from the dragon's head and tail. **1832** COMSTOCK *Bot.* (1850) 424 *Corallorhiza*, *Dragon's claw. **1600** VAUGHAN *Direct. Health* (1633) 166 Rosemary, Myrrh, Masticke, Bolearmoniacke, *Dragons hearbe, Roach Allom. **1857–84** HENFREY *Bot.* (ed. 4) 301 The Snap-dragon, or *Dragon's mouth. **1884** MILLER *Plant-n.*, Dragon's-mouth, *Antirrhinum majus*, *Arum crinitum*, and *Epidendrum macrochilum*. **1865** PAGE *Handbk. Geol. Terms*, **Dragons' Skin*, a familiar term among miners and quarrymen for the stems of *Lepidodendron*, whose rhomboidal leaf-scars somewhat resemble the scales of reptiles. **1644** MILTON *Areop.* (Arb.) 35 They are as lively, and as vigorously productive, as those fabulous *Dragons teeth. **1853** MARSDEN *Early Purit.* 290 Jesuits..sowed the dragon's teeth which sprung up into the hydras of rebellion and apostasy. **1943** HUNT & PRINGLE *Service Slang* 28 *Dragon's teeth*, a form of anti-tank obstacle. **1944** *Times* 28 Nov. 4/2 Extensive minefields, road blocks, dragons' teeth, tank ditches, [etc.]. **1971** *Oxf. Univ. Gaz.* 18 Feb. 671/1 'Dragon's teeth', that is to say, sharp hinged teeth which.. protrude from the ground but can be made to sink into it for a car to pass. **1794** W. FELTON *Carriages* (1801) I. 101 The small splinter-sockets, shewing the hook, the eye and *dragon's-tongue, which are for one and the same use.

Hence '**dragonhood**, the condition or quality of a dragon; '**dragonship**, the office or occupation of a dragon (as strict guardian).

1862 E. BRADLEY (C. Bede) *College Life* 103 The same mysterious dragonship was maintained over her in-doors. **1894** G. ALLEN in *Westm. Gaz.* 23 Oct. 1/3 What are the visible signs and credentials of his dragonhood?

dragon[2]. [corruption of DRAGANT.] In ***gum dragon*** = TRAGACANTH.

1813 W. MILBURN *Oriental Comm.* I. 110 Tragacanth gum, or as it is usually called gum dragon. **1886** in *Syd. Soc. Lex.*

dragonade: see DRAGONNADE.

dragonce, var. of DRAGONS, *Obs.*

dragonesque (ˌdrægəˈnɛsk), *a.* [f. DRAGON[1] + -ESQUE.] Of the style or character of a dragon.

1881 J. ANDERSON *Scot. in E. Chr. Times* 131 Designed in fanciful dragonesque forms. **1882** R. C. MACLAGAN *Scot. Myths* 84 The dragonesque animal representing the fertilising power of water. **1887** [see DRAGON 6].

dragoness (ˈdrægənɪs). [f. as prec. + -ESS.] A female or she dragon (*lit.* and *fig.*).

a **1634** CHAPMAN *Hymn to Apollo* (R.), She gaue command ..that the dragonesse Should bring it vp. **1764** GRAY *Lett.* Wks. 1884 III. 176 Will nobody kill that dragoness? **1883** A. S. HARDY *But yet a Woman* 80 Even had she herself assumed the rôle of dragoness.

dragonet (ˈdrægənɪt). Also 6 **-ette**. [a. F. *dragonet* little dragon, f. *dragon*: see -ET[1].]

1. A small or young dragon.

13.. *K. Alis.* 602 That signifieth the dragonet. **1590** SPENSER *F.Q.* I. xii. 10 Some hidden nest Of many dragonettes, his fruitfull seede. *a* **1797** W. MASON *Ep. to Shebbeare* (R.), Each little dragonet, with brazen grin, Gapes for the precious prize and gulps it in. **1821** LAMB *Elia* Ser. I. *Witches*, From the womb of those crushed errors young dragonets would creep.

2. A fish of the genus *Callionymus*, esp. *C. dracunculus*.

1769 PENNANT *Zool.* III. 130 *Dragonet*, a name we have taken the liberty of forming, from the diminutive *Dracunculus*, a title given it by Rondeletius, and other authors. **1838** JOHNSTON in *Proc. Berw. Nat. Club* I. No. 6. 172 *Callionymus dracunculus, Linn.* Sordid Dragonet, *Penn.*

3. A South American lizard, *Crocodilurus*.

'**dragon-fly, dragon fly.**

The common name for neuropterous insects of the group *Libellulina*, characterized by a long, slender body, large eyes, and two pairs of large reticulated wings, and by their strong, swift flight. (See also quots. 1917 and 1937.)

1626 BACON *Sylva* §729 The delicate coloured Dragon Flies may have likewise some Corrosive quality. **1694** E. FLOYD in *Phil. Trans.* XVIII. 46 Wings..resembling.. those of the larger *Libellæ*, or Dragon-flies. **1782** ANDRÉ in *Phil. Trans.* LXXII. 440 The wonderful structure of the eyes of insects..most commonly illustrated by that of the *Libellula*, or Dragon-fly. **1859** TENNENT *Ceylon* I. II. vi. 247 Above the pools dragon flies, of more than metallic lustre, flash in the early sunbeams. **1917** R. J. TILLYARD *Biol. Dragonflies* i. 1 In his subdivision of the Class of Insecta, Linnaeus placed all the Dragonflies known to him in the single genus *Libellula*, forming the family *Libellulidae* of the ..Order Neuroptera. His pupil Fabricius, in re-arranging the Orders of Insects..constituted the Dragonflies as a separate Order under the name of Odonata, because of the form of their mandibles... The name Odonata persisted, and has been adopted by all subsequent writers. **1937** C. LONGFIELD *Dragonflies Brit. Isles* 6 A somewhat unfortunate situation has arisen by the double use of the word 'dragonfly'. For the past sixty years or so it has been used as the popular name for the whole Order of the *Odonata*. However, the first use of the word..only designated the large species then known to naturalists of the Sub-order *Anisoptera*, in contradistinction to the 'damsel-flies' or *Zygoptera*. **1970** *Age* (Melbourne) 22 June, Dragon-flies together with the smaller damsel-flies make up the order Odonata.

'**dragonish**, *a.* [f. DRAGON + -ISH.]

1. Of the nature or character of a dragon; fierce, severe.

1530 PALSGR. 311/1 Dragonysshe, of the nature of a dragon, *draconique*. **1549** COVERDALE, etc. *Erasm. Par. Rev.* xiii. (R.) This beastes dragonishe speache. **1852** JAMES *Pequinillo* I. 139 [She] was sufficiently 'dragonish' to make a fight for her principles. **1873** BROWNING *Red Cott. Nt.-cap* 883 A..matron—may be, maid Mature, and dragonish of aspect.

2. Somewhat like a dragon in shape.

1606 SHAKS. *Ant. & Cl.* IV. xiv. 2 Sometime we see a clowd that's Dragonish, A vapour sometime, like a Beare, or Lyon. **1880** *Daily Tel.* 16 Feb., Trees that are dragonish; trees that are like bears and lions.

'**dragonism.** [f. DRAGON + -ISM.]

†**1.** Dragonish nature; devilry. *Obs.*

1581 *Satir. Poems Reform.* xliv. 47 Vith all the properteis of Sathannis dragonisme.

2. Jealous and watchful guardianship. (See DRAGON 2 b, 6.)

1822 *Blackw. Mag.* XI. 302 Emancipated from boarding-school restraints, or the dragonism of their governesses.

'**dragonize**, *v.* [f. DRAGON + -IZE.]

1. *trans.* To turn into a dragon, render dragon-like.

1831 CARLYLE *Misc. Ess.* (1857) II. 231 Siegfried by main force slew this dragon, or rather dragonised Smith's-brother.

2. To keep guard over or watch as a dragon. Also *absol.*

c **1853** MRS. GASKELL *Let.* (1966) 857 When Meta is at home she is to dragonize & prepare French lessons. **1866** —— *Wives & Dau.* viii, Clare to dragonize..us. **1875** G. MACDONALD *Malcolm* II. x. 155 His few household goods were borne in a cart through the sea-gate dragonized by Bykes.

dragonnade (drægəˈneɪd), *sb.* Also **dragonade**, **dragoonade**. [a. F. *dragonnade* (18th c.), f. *dragon* DRAGOON: see -ADE.] In *pl.* a series of persecutions directed by Louis XIV against French Protestants, in which dragoons were quartered upon the persecuted. Hence, any persecution carried on with the help of troops. (Rare in *sing.*)

a **1715** BURNET *Own Time* an. 1686 (T.), It was supported by the authority of a great king, and the terror of ill usage, and a dragoonade in conclusion. **1781** JUSTAMOND *Priv. Life Lewis XV*, III. 25 Notwithstanding the favourable accounts given..of these Religionists, it was in agitation to renew the Dragonades. **1856** FROUDE *Hist. Eng.* I. 403 France was to go her way through Bartholomew massacres and the dragonnades to a polished Louis the Magnificent. **1870** SPURGEON *Treas. Dav.* Ps. xliv. 22 The dragoonades of Claverhouse. **1873** SMILES *Huguenots Fr.* II. i. (1881) 291 To avoid the horrors of the dragonnade.

dragoˈnnade, *v.* [f. prec. sb.] *trans.* To subject to a dragonnade; to dragoon.

1873 SMILES *Huguenots Fr.* II. i. (1881) 289 The Huguenots..refused to be converted by the priests; and then Louis XIV determined to dragonnade them.

'**dragon-root.**

†**1.** The root of dragonwort or dragons. *Obs.*

1621 BURTON *Anat. Mel.* II. iv. II. ii, These are very gentle [purgers], alyppus, dragon root, centaury, ditany.

2. In U.S. applied to the tuberous roots of various species of *Arisæma*; also to the plants themselves.

1866 *Treas. Bot.* s.v. *Arisæma*, The Dragon-root, or Indian turnip of America, is the tuber of *A. atrorubens*, which furnishes a kind of starch. *Ibid.* 427 *Dragon Root, Arisæma atrorubens*; also..*Arisæma Dracontium*. **1889** *Chambers' Encycl.* s.v., Dragon-root..of which the acrid tuber is applied to various uses in domestic medicine.

† **'dragons.** *Obs.* Forms: (1 draconze, dracentse, dracanse) 5 dragance, -ans, -auns, -ence, -onys, 5–6 dragaunce, 5–7 dragonce, 6–8 dragons. [In late ME. *dragance*, a. OF. *dragance*, var. of *dragonce* (in med.L. *dragancia, -ontia*):—L. *dracontia*, for *dracontium*, a. Gr. δρακόντιον, f. δράκων, δρακοντ- DRAGON. The Lat. word had already given late OE. *draconze, dracentse.*]

A popular name of the DRAGONWORT, *Dracunculus vulgaris* (formerly *Arum Dracunculus*).

c **1000** *Sax. Leechd.* I. 12 Herba dracontea þæt ys dracentse. *Ibid.* II. 350 Wyrc þonne drenc font wæter, rudan, Saluian, cassuc, draconzan. *c* **1440** *Promp. Parv.* 130/1 Dragaunce, herbe (dragans, P.), *dragancia*. *c* **1450** *Alphita* (Anecd. Oxon.) 48/1 Draguncea..gall. et angl. *dragaunce*. *c* **1450** *Bk. Hawking* in *Rel. Ant.* I. 301 Take the jus of dragonce. *c* **1475** *Voc.* in Wr.-Wülcker 787/8 *Hec dragansia*, a draguns. **1486** *Bk. St. Albans* C viij a, Take Juce of dragonys. **1533** ELYOT *Cast. Helthe* (1541) 11 b, Thynges good for the Lyver: Wormewode..Dragons. **1579** LANGHAM *Gard. Health* (1633) 202 Biting of a Dogge or Adder, drinke Dragons, Rue and Betony. **1607** TOPSELL *Serpents* (1658) 804 The juyce of dragons, expressed out of the leaves, fruit, or root. **1757** A. COOPER *Distiller* III. xv. (1760) 170 Take Dragons, Rosemary, Wormwood, Sage.

dragon's blood.

A bright red gum or resin, an exudation upon the fruit of a palm, *Calamus Draco*. Formerly applied also to the inspissated juice of the dragon-tree, *Dracæna Draco*, and to exudations from *Pterocarpus Draco*, *Croton Draco*, and other plants.

1599 HAKLUYT *Voy.* II. II. 331 That substance which the Apothecaries call *Sanguis Draconis*, (that is), Dragons blood, otherwise called *Cinnabaris*. **1703** T. S. *Art's Improv.* 37 When you have laid on your former Red, take Dragons Blood and pulverize it..a small Portion will extreamly heighten your Colour. **1718** QUINCY *Compl. Disp.* 97 Dragon's Blood is the Weepings of a Tree which bears a Fruit not unlike a Cherry. **1830** LINDLEY *Nat. Syst. Bot.* 282 **1887** *Pall Mall G.* 7 Mar. 6/1 The deep red varnish of Cremona is pure dragon's blood.

attrib. **1704** *Lond. Gaz.* No. 4059/4 The following Goods, viz... Jumbee Canes..Dragon's-Blood Canes. **1870** *Daily News* 6 June, The scarlet foliage of the South American dragon's-blood tree. **1884** MILLER *Plant-n.*, Dragon's-blood-plant, *Calamus Draco*. Dragon's-blood-tree, *Dracæna Draco*.

dragon's head. [See DRAGON 8 b.]

1. *Astron.* The ascending node of the moon's orbit with the ecliptic (marked ☊).

1509 HAWES *Past. Pleas.* XVIII. ii, Dyane..Entred the Crab, her propre mancyon, Than ryght amyddes of the Dragons hed. **1594** BLUNDEVIL *Exerc.* xlv. (ed. 7) 504 Subtract the place of the Dragons head from the place of the Moone. **1819** JAS. WILSON *Dict. Astrol.* 83 The place of the Dragon's Head is considered of great efficacy.

b. *Her.* The name of the tincture *tenné* or tawny in blazoning by the heavenly bodies.

1706 PHILLIPS (ed. Kersey), *Dragons head*..is..the Tenne, or Tawny Colour in the Escutcheons of Soveraign Princes. **1766** PORNY *Heraldry* Gloss., *Dragon's-head*: Part of a celestial constellation, assigned by English Heralds to express the Color Tenné in blazoning the Arms of Sovereigns.

2. *Herb.* (See quots.)

1753 CHAMBERS *Cycl. Supp.*, *Dracocephalon*, Dragon's Head, in botany, the name of a genus of plants. **1866** *Treas. Bot.*, *Dragon's-head*, name for *Dracocephalum*.

dragon's tail. [See DRAGON 8 b.]

1. *Astron.* The descending node of the moon's orbit with the ecliptic (marked ☋).

1605 SHAKS. *Lear* I. ii. 140 My father compounded with my mother vnder the Dragons taile, and my Natiuity was vnder *Vrsa Maior*. **1786–7** BONNYCASTLE *Astron.* 420. **1819** JAS. WILSON *Dict. Astrol.*

b. *Her.* The name of the tincture *murrey* or *sanguine*, in blazoning by the heavenly bodies.

1706 PHILLIPS (ed. Kersey), *Dragons-tail*..signifies the Murrey Colour in the Coats of Soveraign Princes. **1766** PORNY *Heraldry* Gloss.

2. *Palmistry.* The discriminal line.

1678 PHILLIPS (ed. 4), *Restrict Line* (in Chiromancy)..is otherwise called the *Discriminal line*, and also the Dragons tail. **1842** BRANDE *Dict. Sc.*, etc. s.v. *Chiromancy*, The dragon's tail, or discriminal line, between the hand and arm.

dragontian, -tine, bad ff. DRACONTIAN, -INE.

'dragon-tree. The monocotyledonous tree *Dracæna Draco* (N.O. *Liliaceæ*).

1611 COTGR., *Sang de dragon*..not..the bloud of a Dragon..but the Gumme of the Dragon tree opened or bruised in the dog-daies. **1640** PARKINSON *Theat. Bot.* 1531. **1712** tr. *Pomet's Hist. Drugs* I. 194 The Dragon Tree.. appears to be a kind of Date Tree. **1852** TH. ROSS *Humboldt's Trav.* I. ii. 63 *note*, Toothpicks steeped in the juice of the dragon-tree..for keeping the gums in a healthy state.

† **'dragonwort.** *Obs.*

1. The plant *Dracunculus vulgaris*; = DRAGONS.

1565–73 COOPER *Thesaurus*, *Dracontium*..Dragonwort, or dragens. **1578** LYTE *Dodoens* III. vi. 322 It is thought.. that those which carrie about them the leaues or rootes of great Dragonwurtes, cannot be hurt nor stong of Vipers and Serpentes. **1607** TOPSELL *Serpents* (1658) 594 A certain experimental unguent..made of..the roots of dragonwort.

2. *small d.*: the common Arum or Wake-robin.

1674 BLAGRAVE *Suppl. to Culpepper's Eng. Physic.* 54 *Aron maculatum*; in English, small Dragon-wort, and speckled Aron.

3. The Snakeweed, *Polygonum Bistorta. rare.*

1656 CULPEPPER *Eng. Physic.* 35 Bistort..is called Snake-weed,..Dragonwort.

dragoon (drə'guːn), *sb.* [ad. mod.F. *dragon* dragon, also in sense 2.]

† **1.** A kind of carbine or musket. So called from its 'breathing fire' like the fabulous dragon. *Obs.*

1622 F. MARKHAM *Bk. War* IV. v. 138 A lieutenant of the late invented Dragoones (being not aboue sixteene inch Barrell, and full Musquet bore). *Ibid.* v. ii. 167 If the Regiment be but Dragoones, then a Spanish Morian, and no other Armor, a light Guelding, a good sword, and a faire Dragoone. **1637** *Lanc. Wills* (1857) II. 142 To my Lord Strange one case of pistolls and a dragoone. **1659** RUSHW. *Hist. Coll.* II. II. App. 137 The arms of a harquebusier, or dragoon..are a good harquebuss or dragoon, fitted with an iron work, to be carried in a belt [etc.].

† **b.** See quot., and cf. FIRE-DRAKE 3.

1626 CAPT. SMITH *Accid. Yng. Sea-men* 32 Pots of wild fire or dragouns.

2. A species of cavalry soldier. The name was originally applied to mounted infantry armed with the firearm (sense 1). These gradually developed into horse soldiers, and the term is now merely a name for certain regiments of cavalry which historically represent the ancient dragoons, and retain some distinctive features of dress, etc.

In France, the edict of Louis XIV, 25 July 1665, ranked dragoons among infantry, and this was their status until 1784. In Montecuculi's time, *a* 1688, they still ordinarily fought on foot, though sometimes firing from horseback; when Simes wrote, 1768, they mostly fought on horseback, though still occasionally on foot. The French *règlement* of 1 Jan. 1791, confirmed by the *décret* of 21 Feb. 1793, classed them among horse soldiers, after the cavalry proper. In the British Army, the Cavalry are now (1896) divided into Life Guards, Horse Guards, Dragoon Guards, Dragoons, Hussars, and Lancers. Earlier classifications made the Hussars and Lancers subdivisions of the Dragoons. (See quot. 1836.) In the U.S. army the term is not used.

1622 F. MARKHAM *Bk. War* III. i. 83 To these Low Countries haue produced another sort of Horse-men..and they call them Dragoons which I know not whether I may returne them Foot-Horsemen, or Horse-Footmen. **1665** SIR T. HERBERT *Trav.* (1677) 283 The General following with the rest of his Horse and Dragoons. **1683** EVELYN *Diary* 5 Dec., The King had now augmented his guards with a new sort of dragoons, who carried also grenados. *a* **1694** TILLOTSON *Serm.* (1743) V. 1274 Armed soldiers, called by that name of dragons, or, as we according to the French pronunciation call them, dragoons. **1724** DE FOE *Mem. Cavalier* (1840) 286 They..lost most of their horses..and.. turning dragoons, they lined the hedges. **1768** SIMES *Mil. Medley*, *Dragoon*, is a musqueteer, mounted on horseback, sometimes fighting on foot, but mostly on horseback, as occasion requires. **1836** *Penny Cycl.* VI. 388 In the British Army [Cavalry] consists of the two regiments of Life Guards, the royal regiment of Horse Guards, seven regiments of Dragoon Guards, and seventeen regiments of Light Dragoons, of which the 7th, 8th, 10th, and 15th are Hussars, and the 9th, 12th, 16th, and 17th are called Lancers. [There are now (1896) 3 Regiments called Dragoons, 13 of Hussars, and 5 of Lancers.] **1849** MACAULAY *Hist. Eng.* I. iii. 294 The dragoon..has since become a mere horse soldier. But in the seventeenth century he was accurately described by Montecuculi as a foot soldier, who used a horse only in order to arrive with more speed at the place where military service was to be performed. **1868** FREEMAN *Norm. Conq.* II. x. 469 Riding to the field, but fighting on foot, they were *dragoons* in the earlier sense of the word.

b. As the type of a rough and fierce fellow.

1712 STEELE *Spect.* No. 533 ⁋2 What Treatment you would think then due to such Dragoons. **1856** EMERSON *Eng. Traits, Race* Wks. (Bohn) II. 27 These founders of the House of Lords were greedy and ferocious dragoons, sons of greedy and ferocious pirates.

† **c.** In the following, taken by Todd, etc., as = DRAGONNADE.

a **1691** BP. T. BARLOW *Rem.* 265 (T.) To bring men to the Catholick faith (as they pretend) by dragoons, and imprisonments.

3. A variety of pigeon, being a cross between a horseman and a tumbler.

1725 BRADLEY *Fam. Dict.* s.v. *Pigeons*, From the Tumbler and the Horseman, Dragoons. **1765** *Treat. Dom. Pigeons* 60 When the powter has laid her egg, it must be shifted under a dragoon. **1851** MAYHEW *Lond. Labour* (1861) II. 64 His pigeon-cote..is no longer stocked with carriers, dragoons, horsemen [etc.].

4. *attrib.* and *Comb.*

1688 EVELYN *Diary* 23 Mar., The dragoon missioners, Popish officers and priests, fell upon them [French Protestants], murdered and put them to death. **1688** LUTTRELL *Brief Rel.* (1857) I. 487 The duke of Grafton.. was shott at by a dragoon soldier. **1692** *Ibid.* II. 402 Rigorous proceedings against the dragoon-converts. **1745** *Gentl. Mag.* XVII. 416 A regiment of dragoon guards of 10 companies. **1828** J. M. SPEARMAN *Brit. Gunner* (ed. 2) 257 A Light Dragoon horse, mounted and accoutred complete, carries 2 cwt. 1 qr. 14 lbs. **1858** CARLYLE *Fredk. Gt.* II. xi. (1865) I. 118 [A] rugged dragoon-major of a woman.

dra'goon, *v.* [f. prec. sb.; or ad. F. *dragonner* (17th c. in Hatz.-Darm.).]

1. *trans.* To set dragoons upon, to force or drive by the agency of dragoons; to persecute or oppress, as in the DRAGONNADES.

1689 in Somers *Tracts* (1795) II. 351 The Art of Dragooning Men into Religion..the Contrivance of Lewis XIV. **1692** *Pretences Fr. Invas.* 12 To Dragoon all Men into the Kings Religion. **1738** NEAL *Hist. Purit.* IV. 566 His brother of France..was dragooning his Protestant subjects out of his kingdom. **1881** *Pall Mall G.* 3 Dec. 1/1 The necessity for dragooning the Irish or for abolishing trial by jury.

2. To force (*into* a course, etc.) by rigorous and harassing measures.

1689 PRIOR *Ep. F. Shephard* 136 Deny to have your free-born Toe Dragoon'd into a Wooden Shoe. **1794** GODWIN *Cal. Williams* 112 He dragooned men into wisdom. **1861** HUGHES *Tom Brown at Oxf.* xvi. (1889) 152 He wasn't to be dragooned into doing or not doing anything.

3. To exact free quarters from.

1753 EDWARDS in Mrs. Barbauld *Richardson's Corr.* (1804) III. 52 Nor ought I..to be..a vagrant without any fixed habitation or to dragoon my friends throughout the year.

Hence **dra'gooned** *ppl. a.*, **dra'gooning** *vbl. sb.* and *ppl. a.*; also (*nonce-wds.*) **dra'goonable** *a.*, capable of being dragooned; **dra'goonage**, the action of dragooning.

1691 *New Discov. Old Intreague* iii. 45 Domestick Heroes, whose Dragooning Hands Seek out no Forreign Wars, while they can plunder Friends. *Ibid.* vii. 3 Dragooning's ceas'd. **1717** DE FOE *Mem. Ch. Scot.* III. 78 All the French Dragooning, the Popish Burnings, the Heathen Torturings that we read of. *a* **1745** SWIFT *Wks.* (1841) II. 67 The next evil to that of being dragooned is that of living dragoonable. **1855** MACAULAY *Hist. Eng.* III. 426 That inextinguishable hatred which glowed in the bosom of the persecuted, dragooned, expatriated Calvinist of Languedoc. **1892** *Athenæum* 24 Dec. 883/3 Isaac Minet was..a witness of the 'dragooning' persecution. **1894** *Speaker* 26 May 584/1 Ecclesiastic and squirearchic almsgiving and dragoonage.

dragoonade: see DRAGONNADE.

dra'goon-bird. A Brazilian bird (*Cephalopterus ornatus*), having a large, umbrella-like crest of feathers above the bill; also called *umbrella-bird*.

1864 in WEBSTER.

† **dra'gooner.** *Obs.* Also 7 dragonier, -goner, -goneer, -gooneer. [f. DRAGOON *sb.* 1, or immediately from French. Cf. Ger. *dragoner*, in 17th c. also *tragoner, draguner*.

In German, the word was already in regular use in the Thirty Years War, and in 1617 was ridiculed as a 'fremdwort' or foreign word (Kluge). This, with the variant 17th c. English forms, and the fact that it was not a natural Eng. formation from *dragoon*, imply for the original a F. *dragonnier* 'soldier armed with a dragoon or harquebus', although this is not recorded in the dictionaries. OF. had *dragonier* in the sense 'standard-bearer', = med.L. *dracōnārius*.]

1. = DRAGOON *sb.* 2.

1639 *Lismore Papers* Ser. II. (1888) IV. 27 The dragoneers ..are commanded by one Colonell Stafford. **1642** *Decl. Lords & Com., For Rais. Forces* 22 Dec. 7 That the Dragooners be put into Companies, And that one hundred and twelve be allotted to a Company. *c* **1642** TWYNE in Wood *Life* (Oxf. Hist. Soc.) I. 68 The kynges horsemen or troopers and dragoners. **1643** *Sober Sadnes* 35 They had a power could reach him; and this was the power of the Dragooneers. **1644–7** CLEVELAND *Char. Lond. Diurn.* 2 The Emperick-Divines of the Assembly, those Spirituall Dragooners, thumbe it accordingly. **1672** T. VENN *Mil. & Mar. Discip.* iii. 7 Five several kinds of men at Arms for the Horse Service, Lanciers, Cuirasiers, Harquebuziers, Carabiniers, Dragoniers. **1705** S. WHATELY in W. S. Perry *Hist. Coll. Amer. Col. Ch.* I. 168 To raise the Dragooners and 5th men.

2. A horse ridden by a dragoon.

1642 *Ord. & Declar. Lords & Com.* 29 Nov. 11 Horses for service in the Field, Dragooners and Draught-Horses.

3. [f. DRAGOON *v.*] One who dragoons or takes part in a dragonnade; a rigid persecutor.

1688 *Reasons for Establ. Standing Army*, in *5th Coll. Papers Junct. Affairs* 14 The Dragooners have made more Converts than all the Bishops and Clergy of France. **1826** PRAED *Poems* (1865) I. 263 Who for long years had been a great dragooner.

'drag-out. *U.S. slang.* A violent fight, or one who engages in such a fight. (See also KNOCK-DOWN *sb.* 2.)

a **1859** *Southern Sketches* (Bartlett), He's a rael stormer, ring clipper, snow belcher, and drag out. **1870** *Nation* 30 June 411/2 The number of encounters,..knock-downs, drag-outs, [etc.]..in which the Representative..has been engaged.

'drag-rope (-rəʊp). A rope by which anything is dragged; *spec.* that used in dragging a piece of ordnance.

1766 ENTICK *London* IV. 345 Harness for horses, besides mens harness, drag-ropes, &c. **1893** FORBES-MITCHELL *Remin. Gt. Mutiny* 46 The sailors manned the drag-ropes of the heavy guns. **1783** in R. T. Durrett *Centenary of Louisville* (1893) 147, 4 pair drag ropes (damaged). **1856** E. E. HALE *If, Yes, & Perhaps* (1868) 147 The sled is fitted with two drag-ropes, at which the men haul. **1907** 'O. HENRY'

Heart of West 148 'He bears a drag-rope.' 'Get him and saddle him as quick as you can.'
attrib. **1853** STOCQUELER *Milit. Encycl.*, *Drag-rope Men*, ..the men attached to light or heavy pieces of ordnance, for the purpose of expediting movements in action.

dragsman ('drægzmən).
1. The driver of a drag or coach.
1812 *Sporting Mag.* XXXIX. 284 He slanged the dragsman..which means that he sneaked away from the coach, without even apologizing for his want of means of paying. **1840** THACKERAY *Shabby Genteel Story* i, He had..a nod for the shooter or guard, and a bow for the dragsman. **1885** *New Bk. Sports* 166 Men do not drive nowadays with the skill which used to characterize the gentleman dragsman.
2. *Rogues' cant.* A robber of vehicles, a dragger.
1812 J. H. VAUX *Flash Dict.*, *Dragsman*, a thief who follows the game of dragging. **1851** MAYHEW *Lond. Labour* (1862) II. 332 'Dragsmen', i.e. those persons who steal goods or luggage from carts and coaches.
3. One employed to drag a river-bed, etc.
1896 *Daily News* 15 Apr. 6/5 When every inch of the dark river bed..has been raked..the dragsmen..move round on to the towing path and begin again.

'drag-staff (-stɑːf, -æ-). A trailing pole hinged to the rear of a vehicle to check its backward movement when it stops in a steep ascent.
1769 *De Foe's Tour Gt. Brit.* II. 299 The Coach wanting a Dragstaff, it ran back, in spite of all the Coachman's Skill. **1794** W. FELTON *Carriages* (1801) II. Gloss. 6. **1806** MISS MITFORD in L'Estrange *Life* (1870) I. 53 The horses ran back on a very steep hill, and nothing but the drag-staff could have saved our lives.

dragster ('drægstə(r)). orig. *U.S.* [f. DRAG *sb.* 1 f + -STER.] (See quot. 1955.)
1954 *Amer. Speech* XXIX. 95 Dragster is one of the classifications in official acceleration competition. **1955** *Britannica Bk. of Year* 490/1 *Dragster* (drag + roadster), a 'hot rod', or car constructed from spare parts and designed to exhibit the maximum of engine efficiency and the minimum of elegance. **1961** *Engineering* 18 Aug. 200/1 His new dragster..is the first British-designed version of an American sprint car. **1967** *Times Educ. Suppl.* 13 Oct. 762 (*caption*) Some of the boys with a 'dragster' they built. **1971** B. CALLISON *Plague of Sailors* i. 43 One of those ostentatious James Bond-type dragsters that was all chrome-plated wheel spokes.

drahen, draht, obs. forms of DRAW *v.*, DRAUGHT.

draidour, var. of DREADOUR, *Obs.*

draif(f, obs. Sc. f. *drove*, pa. t. of DRIVE *v.*

draigle, Sc. form of DRAGGLE.

draiht(e: see DRETCH *v.*[1]

draik, Sc. var. of DRAKE; obs. f. DRAWK.

†**drail,** *v.*[1] *Obs.* Also drayl(e. [app. an altered form of TRAIL, influenced by *draw*, *drag*, *draggle*.]
1. *trans.* To drag or trail along.
1598 T. BASTARD *Chrestoleros* (1880) 21 First would I sterue myselfe..Or these rude chufs should drayle me through their tayles. *c* **1642** TWYNE in Wood *Life* (Oxf. Hist. Soc.) I. 82 The pike men drayled their pikes on the ground. **1664** H. MORE *Antid. Idolatry* To Rdr., He returned..drailing his sheephook behinde him.
2. *intr.* To trail, draggle, move laggingly.
1598 GRENEWEY *Tacitus' Ann.*, *Germanie* i. 259 Neither going too hastily before the horsemen, nor drailing after. *a* **1716** SOUTH *Serm.* (1737) VI. xii. (R.), Unless we have also a continual care to keep it from drailing in the dirt.

drail (dreɪl), *v.*[2] *U.S.* [f. DRAIL *sb.*] *intr.* To fish with a drail.
1636 A. SHURT *Let.* 28 June in *Mass. Hist. Soc. Coll.* (1863) 4th Ser. VI. 570 Richard Foxwill..spake with a boate of ours (draylinge for mackrell). **1873** *Rep. U.S. Bureau Fisheries* I. xiv. 248 The usual method of taking them [*sc.* bluefish] with the line is by drailing or trolling. **1888** GOODE *Amer. Fishes* 180 It is not known when the custom of drailing for mackerel was first introduced.

drail (dreɪl), *sb.* [f. DRAIL *v.*[1]]
1. A fish-hook and line weighted with lead to enable it to be dragged at a depth in the water; also, the weighted hook, and the weight, which is a conical piece of lead placed round the shank of the hook. (*U.S.*)
1634 W. WOOD *New Eng. Prosp.* (1865) 38 These Macrills are taken with drails, which is a long small line, with a lead and hooke at the end of it. **1883** *Fisheries Exhib. Catal.* 195 Jigs and drails for the capture of cod, weakfish, Spanish mackerel, bass, bluefish, and dolphin. **1894** *Youth's Companion* (U.S.) 22 Nov. 562/4 To whirl the lines..armed with weighted hooks called 'drails'.
†2. A long, trailing head-dress. *Obs. rare.*
1647 WARD *Simp. Cobler* 26 It is no marvell they weare drailes on the hinder part of their heads.
3. Part of a plough: see quot. *local.*
1794 T. DAVIS *Agric. Wilts* in *Archæol. Rev.* Mar. (1888), *Drail*, the iron bow of a plough from which the traces draw, and which has teeth to set the furrow wider or narrower. **1834** *Brit. Husb.* I. 161 The drail, by which they are now commonly attached, being at *a*.

drain (dreɪn), *v.* Also 6–7 drean(e, drayne, drane, 7–8 drein, dreyn, (dreign). [OE. *dréahnian* (*dréhnian*, *dréhnigean*), prob. for **dréagnian*, f. root *dréag-* :—OTeut. **draug-* dry.
It is remarkable that, after the OE. period, no example of this word is known to occur for 500 years, till the 16th c. (Richardson's quot. of *dreine* from Lydgate, erroneously referred here, belongs to *dereine*, DERAIGN.) The historical spelling is *drean*, pronounced in some dialects (dreːn), in others (driːn). *Drein, dreign, drain, drane*, are non-etymological representations of (dreːn), on the analogy of *rein, reign, rain, crane*: cf. *Jean, Jane*.]
I. †1. *trans.* To strain (liquid) through any porous medium. *Obs.*
c **1000** *Ags. Gosp.* Matt. xxiii. 24 Ge drehnigeað [*v.r.* drehniað; *Hatton G.* dreniеð] þone gnætt aweg. *c* **1000** *Sax. Leechd.* III. 72 Wyll swiðe well on buteran; dreahna ut þurh wyllene clað. *c* **1500** *Spir. Remedies* in Halliw. *Nugæ Poet.* 67 Drayne it and dringke it with confescione. **1615** LATHAM *Falconry* (1633) 95 Drean away what is left of the vineger. **1626** BACON *Sylva* §2 Salt-water drayned through twenty vessels. **1667** MILTON *P.L.* III. 605 Old Proteus from the Sea, Draind through a Limbeck to his Native forme.
2. To draw *off* or *away* (a liquid) gradually, or in small quantities, by means of a conduit or the like; to carry *off* or *away* by means of a drain.
1538 LELAND *Itin.* I. 99 A Causey of Stone with divers Bridges over it to dreane the low Medow Waters..into Aire Ryver. **1594** SHAKS. *Rich. III*, IV. iv. 276 A hand-kercheefe ..did dreyne The purple sappe from her sweet Brothers body. **1639** FULLER *Holy War* (1640) 2 The streams of milk and hony..are now drained drie. **1671** tr. *Frejus' Voy. Mauritania* 39 It is impossible to passe it, untill the waters ..are all dreined away. **1726** *Adv. Capt. R. Boyle* 28 A Puddle of Water, which I gave Directions to be drain'd. **1838** T. THOMSON *Chem. Org. Bodies* 621 Small trenches are cut through the field to drain off the rain. **1879** HARLAN *Eyesight* ii. 29 The ordinary flow of tears is thus drained into the nostril.
†b. To let fall in drops strained out. *Obs. rare.*
1593 SHAKS. *2 Hen. VI*, III. ii. 142 To draine Upon his face an Ocean of salt teares.
3. *transf.* and *fig.* To carry off, withdraw, take away as by a drain.
1625–8 tr. *Camden's Hist. Eliz.* an. 1596 (R.), He.. permitted those of Rome to exhaust and drain the wealth of England. **1673** MILTON *True Relig.* Wks. (1851) 412 The Pope..was wont to dreign away greatest part of the wealth of this..Land. **1818** JAS. MILL *Brit. India* II. v. iv. 433 To expend as much as it could possibly drain from its subjects.
4. To drink (a liquid) off or to the last drops.
1602 SHAKS. *Ham.* I. iv. 10 He dreines his draughts of Renish downe. *a* **1700** DRYDEN *Ovid's Met.* xv. (R.), Who.. the sweet essence of amomum drains. **1823** BYRON *Island* I. vi, [They] drain'd the draught with an applauding cheer. **1850** KINGSLEY *Alt. Locke* i, He drained the remaining drops of the three-pennyworth of cream.
5. *intr.* Of liquid: To percolate or trickle *through*; to flow gradually *off* or *away*.
1587 GOLDING *De Mornay* xiv. 207 Let the bloud dreyne out, the mouing wax weake, the sences faile. **1628** DIGBY *Voy. Medit.* (1868) 80 They..fill with fresh water; but I belieue it dreaneth thither from the higher land. **1673** RAY *Willughby's Journ. Spain* 478 The juice dreins down through the course sugar at the bottom. **1725** BRADLEY *Fam. Dict.* s.v. *Malt*, Let the Water drein well and equally from the Corn. **1878** HUXLEY *Physiogr.* 3 The vast volume of water sent down from above drains away seawards.
II. 6. *trans.* To withdraw the water or moisture from (anything) gradually by straining, suction, formation of conduits, etc.; to leave (anything) dry by withdrawal of moisture.
1577 tr. *Bullinger's Decades* (1592) 88 Bodies dreined from the dregges of all corruption. **1605** SHAKS. *Macb.* I. iii. 18 Ile dreyne him drie as Hay. **1655** MRQ. WORCESTER *Cent. Inv.* §100 Drein all sorts of Mines, and furnish Cities with water. *a* **1687** PETTY *Pol. Arith.* (1690) 66 Dutch Engineers may drain its Bogs. **1870** LUBBOCK *Orig. Civiliz.* vii. (1875) 315 In the valleys drained by the Sacramento and the San Joaquin. **1890** ABNEY *Photography* (ed. 6) 128 The emulsion may be drained..by placing it on a hair sieve. **1896** *Law Times* C. 488/1 A pipe or sewer which also drained another house.
7. To empty by drinking; to drink dry.
1697 DRYDEN *Virg. Past.* II. 53 Two Kids..drein two bagging Udders every day. **1714** POPE *Wife of Bath* 214, I drain'd the spicy nut-brown bowl. **1820** KEATS *Lamia* I. 209 Where God Bacchus drains his cups divine. **1855** DICKENS *Dorrit* I. xxiii, They had drained the cup of life to the dregs.
8. *transf.* and *fig.* To deprive (a person or thing) of possessions, properties, resources, strength, etc., by their gradual withdrawal; to exhaust.
1660 F. BROOKE tr. *Le Blanc's Trav.* 293 How the King of Fez had drained their Countrey. **1673** DRYDEN *Marr. à la Mode* III. i, You have..drained all the French plays and romances. **1762–71** H. WALPOLE *Vertue's Anecd. Paint.* (1786) I. 243 These expences..drained him so much, that he again quitted Rome. **1784** COWPER *Task* III. 784 Drained to the last poor item of his wealth, He sighs. **1844** EMERSON *Lect. Yng. Amer.* Wks. (Bohn) II. 295 The cities drain the country of the best part of its population. **1874** GREEN *Short Hist.* iv. §4. 189 The treasury..was drained by his Norman wars.
9. *intr.* To become rid of moisture by its gradual percolation or flowing away.
1664 EVELYN *Kal. Hort.* (1729) 217 Having laid them [pots] side-long to drain. **1796** MRS. GLASSE *Cookery* xviii. 288 Lay them on a coarse cloth to drain. **1864** *Jrnl. R. Agric. Soc.* XXV. I. 43 This land won't drain. **1892** W. K. BURTON *Mod. Photogr.* (ed. 10) 142 The prints, as they are taken from the washing water, are allowed to drain.
Hence **drained** (dreɪnd), *ppl. a.*
1611 COTGR., *Escoulé*, drained. **1655** in Hartlib *Legacy* 270 Trees..planted in the drained Fens..by Dutchmen. **1725** POPE *Odyss.* XVIII. 180 He..the drain'd goblet to the chief restores. **1855** TENNYSON *Maud* I. i. 20 A scheme that had left us flaccid and drain'd. *a* **1881** ROSSETTI *Spring*, Where the drained flood-lands flaunt their marigold.

drain (dreɪn), *sb.* Forms: see prec. [f. DRAIN *v.*]
1. a. A channel by which liquid is drained or gradually carried off; *esp.* an artificial conduit or channel for carrying off water, sewage, etc.
In the Fen districts, including wide canal-like navigable channels. (See *Penny Cycl.* s.v. *Bedford Level.*) Elsewhere, applied chiefly to covered sewage drains or field drains.
1552 HULOET, Drayne, *sulcus*. **1577–87** HOLINSHED *Descr. Brit.* xv. (R.), Here also it receiueth the Baston dreane, Longtoft dreane, Deeping dreane, and thence goeth by Wickham into the sea. **1580** HOLLYBAND *Treas. Fr. Tong*, *Vn Rayon*..a drane to drawe the water out of a field. **1661** PEPYS *Diary* 25 Sept., A stop at Charing Crosse, by reason of digging of a drayne there to clear the streets. **1696** *Phil. Trans.* XIX. 344 Through these Fens run great Cuts or Dreyns, in which are a great many Fish. **1739** tr. *La Pluche's Nature Display'd* III. 9 Gentlemen convert their Marshes into good fruitful Meadows by contriving large Fosses and Drains to carry off the Water. **1860–1** FLO. NIGHTINGALE *Nursing* ii. 23 Another great evil in house construction is carrying drains underneath the house. **1882** *Daily Tel.* 28 Oct. 2/4 Several drains..will be fishable tomorrow. **1895** *Westm. Gaz.* 13 Dec. 2/3 You are sometimes asked in Yorkshire to go for a picnic on the drain..you discover that 'drain' is merely the local name for canal.
fig. **1683** BURNET tr. *More's Utopia* (1684) 165 Such a leud and vicious sort of People, that seem to have run together, as to the Drain of Humane Nature.
†b. A teat. *Obs. rare.*
1587 MASCALL *Govt. Cattle* (1627) 260 Euery pigge will but sucke his drene or teate.
c. Applied to a natural water-course which drains a tract of country.
1700 DRYDEN *Fables*, *Meleager & Atal.* 93 A valley stood below: the common drain Of Waters from above, and falling rain. **1770** G. WASHINGTON *Writ.* (1889) II. 311 The little runs and drains, that come through the hills. **1876** V. L. CAMERON *Across Africa* (1885) 511 The main drain of the country is the Walé nullah.
d. *Surgery.* A tubular instrument used to draw off the discharge from a wound or abscess.
1834 *Good's Study Med.* (ed. 4) II. 106 When the case is chronic setons or some other protracted drain should never be neglected. **1880** MACCORMAC *Antisept. Surg.* 18 There was immediate union of the flaps of the wounds save where the drains emerged.
e. Colloq. fig. phr., *to go* (etc.) *down the drain*, to disappear, get lost, vanish; to deteriorate, go to waste.
[**1925** F. LONSDALE *Last of Mrs. Cheyney* 10 It is she who closes the drain on them as they go down it on the Thursday.] **1930** W. S. MAUGHAM *Breadwinner* i. 52 All his savings are gone down the drain. **1933** W. CHETHAM-STRODE in *Famous Plays of 1933* 449 We're all so down the drain no one's got anything. **1951** KOESTLER *Age of Longing* 234 Others, dozens of Leontiev's colleagues, had..collapsed or made fatal mistakes and gone down the drain. **1952** 'J. H. CHASE' *Double Shuffle* ix. 184 We had paid out good money to get those policies, and we couldn't afford to let them go down the drain. **1958** *Listener* 7 Aug. 196/1 A poor devil who goes down the drain before a temptation that he finds too strong. **1960** H. PINTER *Dumb Waiter* in *Birthday Party* 130, I thought these sheets didn't look too bright. I thought they ponged a bit... I told you things were going down the drain. **1961** *Ann. Reg. 1960* 471 It appeared that at least one donor country was realizing that aid could easily go down the drain.
f. Colloq. phr. *to laugh like a drain*, to laugh loudly.
1948 PARTRIDGE *Dict. Forces' Slang* 109 *Laugh like a drain*, to chuckle 'consumedly'; laugh loudly, especially at someone's discomfiture. (Ward-room and also Army officers'.) **1957** M. SHARP *Eye of Love* iv. 48 'What did you call me?' asked Harry Gibson—and laughed like a drain. **1958** S. GIBBONS *White Sand & Grey Sand* 222, I shall laugh like a drain if she's world-famous in another five years or so. **1966** 'K. NICHOLSON' *Hook, Line & Sinker* xv. 174 Old Hester would laugh like a drain if she could see us singing hymns over her.
2. The act of draining or drawing off, drainage; now only *fig.* constant or gradual outlet, withdrawal, or expenditure.
1721 PERRY *Daggenh. Breach* 10 Sluices or Trunks..made for the drein of the Levels. **1732** SWIFT *Propos. Paying Nation. Debts* Wks. 1761 III. 213 Remittances to pay absentees..and many other drains of money. **1796** MORSE *Amer. Geog.* II. 392 Owing..to the great drains of people sent to America. **1829** T. MOORE *Mem.* (1854) VI. 65 A sad drain upon my time. **1844–57** G. BIRD *Urin. Deposits* (ed. 5) 308 The excess of phosphates indicates the 'drain' on the nervous energies. **1849** MACAULAY *Hist. Eng.* I. 307 Which caused no drain on the revenue of the state.
3. a. That which is drained or drawn off; a small remaining quantity of liquid. b. *slang.* A drink.
1836–9 DICKENS *Sk. Boz*, *Ginshops* (D.), Two old men who came in 'just to have a drain'. **1852** —— *Bleak Ho.* xix, He stood drains round. **1868** C. H. ROSS *Bk. Cats*, A..jug ..with a drain of milk in the bottom of it.
4. a. *pl.* Dregs from which liquid has been drained. b. *dial.* Brewers' grains from the mash-tub.
1820 KEATS *To Nightingale* 3, I had..emptied some dull opiate to the drains. *a* **1825** FORBY *Voc. E. Anglia*, *Drains*, grains from the mash-tub, through which the wort has been drained off.
5. *attrib.* and *Comb.*, as *drain-digger*, *-pipe*, *-tax*, *-tile*, etc.; **drain-cock**, a cock for draining the water out of a boiler, etc.; **drain-exhauster**, a machine for pumping up the water from deep drains; **drain-grenade**: see GRENADE; **drain-**

pipe, a pipe for carrying off surplus water or liquid sewage from a building; also *attrib.* and *fig.*, esp. in *pl.*, narrow, tight-fitting trousers; **drain-plough**, a plough for cutting field-drains, a draining-plough; **drain-trap**, a trap on a drain to prevent the escape of sewer-gas; **drain-well**: see quot.

1895 PARKES *Health* 95 The escape of *drain air into the house. **1894** *Daily News* 23 Jan. 6/5 The *drain cocks blew out and the boilers emptied themselves into the vessel's bilges. **1891** S. C. SCRIVENER *Our Fields & Cities* 97 The steam-driven pump—quite a different affair from the Fen *drain-exhauster. **1857** *Chambers's Informat.* I. 494/1 The substitution of water-closets and *drain-pipes for privies and cess-pools. **1884** *Harper's Mag.* Nov. 921/2 The rage for painting on drain-pipe. **1886** BAUMANN *Londinismen* 45/1 *Drain-pipe*, Schülersprache: Makkaroni. **1903** *Daily Chron.* 4 Aug. 5/1 Sooner or later those dreadful drain-pipe structures the Charing-cross and Cannon-street bridges will have to be rebuilt. **1915** A. D. GILLESPIE *Let.* 17 Sept. in *Lett. from Flanders* (1916) 304 We have..trench-mortars, drain-pipe mortars, rifle grenades, and..every kind of shell. **1950** *Strand Mag.* Mar. 83/1 'Drain-pipes haven't caught on,' says Eddie. 'The money won't run to them. We can't wear them for work.' **1954** [see EDWARDIAN *sb.* 3]. **1955** M. BERGER-HAMERSCHLAG *Journey into Fog* xviii. 248 But even Jeff entered the class in a new outfit of that macabre character, with drainpipe trousers, both sides braided with black silk. **1960** *Times* 7 Dec. 17/4 (*heading*) The drainpipe not to be despised. *Ibid.* 17/5 What matters is..to show them that a 'drainpipe' bag with a few clubs is not to be despised. **1855** J. C. MORTON *Cycl. Agric.* I. 706 The *drain plough was first introduced into Scotland by Mr. McEwan. **1720** *Lond. Gaz.* No. 5869/3 A[n] Estate lying in Deeping Level ..subject to *Drain Taxes. **1851** J. BROWN *Forester* (ed. 2) i. 46 We are now putting a *drain-tile into the ditches and filling them up. **1940** *Chambers's Techn. Dict.* 264/1 *Drain tiles*, hollow tiles laid end to end without joints, to carry off surface or excess water. **1858** SIMMONDS *Dict. Trade*, **Drain-traps*, contrivances for preventing the escape of foul air from drains. **1874** KNIGHT *Dict. Mech.*, **Drain-well*, a pit sunk through an impervious stratum of earth to reach a pervious stratum and form a means of drainage for surface water.

drain, obs. pa. pple. of DRAW *v.*

'drainable, *a.* Capable of being drained.

1611 COTGR., *Escoulable*, drainable. **1649** BLITHE *Eng. Improv. Impr.* (1653) 48 Some great Bog or Quagmire lying so flat as is not Draynable.

drainage ('dreɪnɪdʒ). [f. DRAIN *v.* + -AGE.]

1. The action or work of draining.

1652 in Stonehouse *Axholme* (1839) 91 The works.. within the dicage and draynage of the Levell of Hatfield Chase. **1834** [see 3]. **1861** SMILES *Engineers* II. 152 Drainage by the old method of windmills, imported from Holland. **1883** *Syd. Soc. Lex.*, *Drainage, surgical*, the use of a Drainage tube, or of strands of horse-hair, silk, or other material..in a wound or suppurating cavity for the purpose of removing the fluids therein contained.

fig. **1850** W. IRVING *Goldsmith* xvi. 189 This constant drainage of the purse. **1882–3** SCHAFF *Encycl. Relig. Knowl.* II. 905/2 That drainage by Rome of the very heart-blood of his fatherland.

2. a. A system of drains, artificial or natural.

1878 HUXLEY *Physiogr.* 19 Such a line divides the western drainage of the country from its eastern drainage.

b. Porous matter, broken fragments, etc., used to drain a flower-pot. (Cf. DRAINING 3.)

1892 *Garden.* 27 Aug. 191 Pots..filled about three parts of their depth with clean drainage.

3. That which is drained off by a system of drains; sewage.

1834 in *Penny Cycl.* XXI. 314/2 Their ideas of..drainage never extended to more than taking away the surface drainage. **1857** *Chambers's Informat. for People* I. 495 The drainage..rises through a false perforated bottom covered with peat-charcoal. **1860** MAURY *Phys. Geog. Sea* §555 Lake Titicaca..receives the drainage of the great inland basin of the Andes.

4. *attrib.* and *Comb.*, as *drainage-area, -canal, -district, -line, -shaft, -system, -tent*; *drainage-soaked* adj.; **drainage-anchor, -tube**: see quots. 1883; **drainage-basin**, the area of land drained by a river and its tributaries; a catchment area; = BASIN *sb.* 12.

1883 *Syd. Soc. Lex.*, **Drainage anchor*..an india-rubber filament with laterally projecting arms..introduced within a cannula into the cavity of an abscess. **1873** J. GEIKIE *Gt. Ice Age* (1894) 549 The *drainage-area of Maggiore, Lugano, and Como. **1882** *Nation* 13 July 33/1 The topography of its immediate banks and that of its *drainage-basin..are fully set forth. **1885** A. GEIKIE *Text-bk. Geol.* (ed. 2) III. II. ii. 352 The proportion of mineral matter in river-water varies with the season... Its amount and composition depend upon the nature of the rocks forming the drainage-basin. **1965** A. HOLMES *Princ. Physical Geol.* (ed. 2) xvii. 469 A main river and all its tributaries constitute a river system, and the whole area from which the system derives water and rock-waste is its drainage basin. **1900** *Westm. Gaz.* 20 Sept. 8/1 The opening of the *drainage canal has given Chicago an excellent supply of pure water. **1966** *McGraw-Hill Encycl. Sci. & Technol.* 434/1 Drainage canals are deeply cut to facilitate the drainage of surrounding land. **1881** MOORE & MASTERS *Epit. Gard.* 143 Keeping the..soil from mixing with the *drainage crocks. **1847** *Act 10 & 11 Vict.* c. 34 §23 Separate *drainage districts. **1882** A. GEIKIE *Text-bk. Geol.* 922 The permanence of *drainage-lines is one of the most remarkable features in the geological history of the continents. **1869** R. B. SMYTH *Gold-f. Victoria* 610 The main shaft in which the pumps..are fixed..is sometimes called the water shaft, and the *drainage shaft. **1891** R. KIPLING *City Dreadf. Nt.* 6 The damp, *drainage-soaked soil is sick with the teeming life of a hundred years. **1883** *Syd. Soc. Lex.*, **Drainage tube*, a small..india rubber or coiled wire or other tube, with lateral perforations..passed through a cannula into the..cavity to be drained. **1799** G. SMITH *Laboratory* I. 69 Pumps..for carrying off the *drainage water.

drainboard ('dreɪnbɔəd). orig. and chiefly *U.S.* [f. DRAIN *v.* + BOARD *sb.* 1.] = *draining-board.*

1905 *Sears, Roebuck Catal.* (ed. 115) 542/2 Nickel plated brass strainer and 24-inch enameled iron drain board with end piece. **1945** B. MACDONALD *Egg & I* (1946) 95 Along one wall were a sink and drain-boards. **1956** 'N. SHUTE' *Beyond Black Stump* i. 24 He went into the kitchen and unloaded five small trout..on to the steel drainboard.

drainer ('dreɪnə(r)). [f. as prec. + -ER[1].]

1. One who drains; *esp.* one whose business is to construct field-drains.

1611 COTGR., *Espuiseur*, a drayner; exhauster, emptier of moisture. *a* **1661** FULLER *Worthies, Bedfordsh.* 115 The Drayners of the fenns have..secured the County against his power for the future. **1667** DUCHESS NEWCASTLE *Life Dk. of N.* IV. (1886) 224 It is a part of prudence in a common-wealth or kingdom to encourage drainers. **1717** S. SEWALL *Diary* 23 Aug. (1882) III. 136 Gave the workmen 2*s.*, Dreaners 6*d.* **1837** HOWITT *Rur. Life* VI. xv. (1862) 576 As the drainer cuts his drain in the greensward of the meadows. **1868** BROWNING *Ring & Bk.* IX. 1277 This drainer to the dregs O' the draught of conversation.

fig. **1637** WOTTON in *Reliq. Wotton.* (1672) 105, I must note the Pope's Legats and Dreyners. **1824** BYRON *Juan* XV. iv, The drainer of oblivion, even the sot.

2. That which drains; a drain; a vessel in which moist substances are put to drain.

1598 FLORIO, *Gocciolatoio*, a gutter or drainer in a house. **1662** SIR W. DUGDALE *Hist. Embank. & Drain.* (1772) 164 An old gote and drainer called Symond's gote. **1696** EDWARDS *Demonstr. Exist. God* II. 99 The gall-bladder in the hollow part of the liver, is the dreiner for choler. **1730** A. GORDON *Maffei's Amphith.* 319 He makes his Theatre to have had Drainers for Water, and a Roof. **1846** J. BAXTER *Libr. Pract. Agric.* (ed. 4) I. 208 While the curd is pressing in the drainer, it ought to be set before a good fire. **1880** LOMAS *Alkali Trade* 229 The white salt in the drainer may be washed with water.

'draining, *vbl. sb.* [f. DRAIN *v.* + -ING[1].]

1. The action of the verb DRAIN in various senses; drainage.

1565–73 COOPER *Thesaurus, Deriuatio*..a turning: a drayning. **1599** MINSHEU *Sp. Dict.*, *Esguazo*, the draining or drawing of water from a boggie or marrish ground. **1677** HALE *Prim. Orig. Man.* II. ix. 209 The drayning of the great Level in Northamptonshire. **1753** N. TORRIANO *Gangr. Sore Throat* 90 The Inside of the Nose remained perfectly clear, and free, nor was there any running or draining from thence. **1834** *Penny Cycl.* I. 225/1 The subsoil is..not wet for want of outlet or draining. **1849** COBDEN *Speeches* 73 This inordinate draining upon the prosperity of the country.

2. That which is drained off; = DRAINAGE 3.

1834 *Penny Cycl.* I. 228/1 Liquid manure..drainings of dunghills.

3. Something used to drain a flower-pot, etc.

1852 *Beck's Florist* 224 Plant them singly in a 60-size pot ..with plenty of drainings in the bottom.

4. *attrib.* and *Comb.*, as ***draining-auger, -brick, -engine, -machine, -pen*** (Sheep-farming), ***-plough, -pot, -tile, -well***, etc. **draining-board**, a grooved and sloping board on which utensils are put to drain after they have been washed; so ***draining-table***.

1874 KNIGHT *Dict. Mech.*, **Draining-auger*, a horizontal auger occasionally used for boring through a bank to form a channel for water. **1906** *Westm. Gaz.* 30 Apr. 4/2 Few sculleries are equipped with a *draining-board. **1933** *Archit. Rev.* LXXIV. 42/3 (*caption*) A typical gas-operated built-in refrigerator installed under the draining board. **1805** R. W. DICKSON *Pract. Agric.* (1807) I. 415 Another form of *draining-brick for forming larger sorts of drains. **1629** *Drayner Conf.* (1647) A ij b, A great guid in this *drayning businesse. **1874** KNIGHT *Dict. Mech.*, **Draining-machine*, a form of filter or machine for expediting the separation of a liquid from the magma or mass of more solid matter which it saturates. **1919** *N.Z. Jrnl. Agric.* 21 Apr. 224 Information is furnished..regarding the best method of finishing off the concrete floor of a sheep-dip *draining-pen. **1965** J. S. GUNN *Terminology Shearing Industry* I. 25 In the older 'dips' and also in modern 'sheep showers', this is an adjoining draining pen to which sheep go after treatment with the 'wash' or 'dip'. **1837** *Penny Cycl.* IX. 122/1 A *draining plough has been invented which..greatly accelerates the operation of forming drains. **1874** KNIGHT *Dict. Mech.*, **Draining-pot* (*Sugar-manufacture*), an inverted conical vessel in which wet sugar is placed to drain. **1895** *Army & Navy Co-op. Soc. Price List* 230/2 Plate Rack and Folding *Draining Table Combined (Patent). **1712** J. JAMES tr. *Le Blond's Gardening* 41 *Draining Wells should be made, at convenient Distances.

'drainless, *a.* [f. DRAIN *sb.* or *v.* + -LESS.]

1. That cannot be drained or exhausted; inexhaustible, exhaustless.

1817 KEATS *Sleep & Poetry*, A drainless shower Of light is poesy. **1818** SHELLEY *Rev. Islam* V. lii, Sad tears turning To mutual smiles, a drainless treasure.

2. Not provided with drains.

1902 H. RUMBOLD *Recoll. Diplomatist* I. 38 They were badly lighted and worse paved, drainless and malodorous.

draisine (dreɪ'ziːn). Also draisene, erron. draisnene. [a. F. *draisine, draisienne*, Ger. *draisine*, f. name of the inventor, Baron Drais of Saverbrun near Mannheim.] The earliest form of bicycle; = DANDY-HORSE.

1818 *L'pool Mercury* 24 Apr., Experiments with *Draisiennes* (a species of carriage moved by machinery without horses). **1879** *Lit. World* (U.S.) 30 Aug. 275/3 One of its [the velocipede's] rudimentary forms was 'the draisine', a cumbersome machine invented by Baron Von Drais, of Mannheim on the Rhine..The improved draisine soon reached America. **1884** *Longm. Mag.* Mar. 485 The dandy-horse, hobby or draisnene, was a two-wheeled vehicle.

drait, obs. pa. t. of DRITE.

drake[1] (dreɪk). Forms 1 draca, (7 drack), 3- drake. [OE. *draca*:—Com. WGer. **drako*, a. L. *draco* dragon: cf. MDu., MLG., OFris. *drake*, mod.Du. *draak*, OHG. *trahho*, MHG. *trache*, Ger. *drache*; also ON. *dreki* (Sw. *drake*, Da. *drage*).] (See also FIRE-DRAKE.)

1. = DRAGON 2. Also a representation of this used as a battle-standard. *Obs.* or *arch.*

Beowulf (Th.) 5371 þa wæs..frecne fyr-draca, fæhða ʒemyndiʒ. *a* **1000** *Martyrol.* (E.E.T.S.) 90 Of þære com gan micel draca ond abat þone þriddan dæl þæs hæðnan folces. *c* **1200** ORMIN 1842 Forr þatt he shollde fihhtenn Onnʒæn an drake. *c* **1205** LAY. 15962 þas tweie draken [*c* **1275** drakes]. *Ibid.* 27244 þa lette he sette up þene drake, heremærken unimake. **13..** *K. Alis.* 554 Theo lady gede to theo drake. *c* **1460** *Towneley Myst.* (Surtees) 259 If it were the burnand drake Of me styfly he gatt a strake. **1570** LEVINS *Manip.* 12/14 Drake, dragon, *draco.* **1597** CONSTABLE *Poems* (1859) 53 The pryde of heauen became the drake of hell. [**1892** STOPF. BROOKE *E. Eng. Lit.* iii. 71 Three hundred years before Beowulf met the drake.]

†**b.** A serpent; = DRAGON 1. *Obs.*

c **1000** *Panther* 16 (Bosw.) Is ðæt deor pandher, se is æt-hwam freond, butan dracan anum. *c* **1000** *Ags. Ps.* xc[i]. 13 (Th.) þu ofer aspide miht eaðe gangan..and leon and dracan liste ʒebyʒean.

†**c.** A monster of the waters; = DRAGON 3. *Obs.*

c **1000** *Ags. Ps.* lxxiii[i]. 13 Swylce ʒebræce þæt dracan heafod deope wætere. *Ibid.* cxlviii. 7 Heriʒen dracan swylce Drihten.

†**2.** A fiery meteor: see FIRE-DRAKE 2. *Obs.*

c **1205** LAY. 25594 þa com þer westene winden mid þan weolcen a berninge drake. **1393** GOWER *Conf.* III. 96 Lo where the firie drake alofte Fleeth up in thaier. **1610** GUILLIM *Heraldry* III. iii. (1660) 116 Fearfull..fiery Drakes, and Blazing bearded-light, Which frights the World.

†**3.** Name of a species of ordnance; a small sort of cannon. *Obs.* exc. *Hist.*

1625 J. GLANVILL *Voy. to Cadiz* (1883) 75 Wee discharged upon them some of our Drakes or field peices loaden with small shott. **1627** *Taking of St. Esprit* in *Harl. Misc.* (Malh.) III. 550 Two drakes upon the half deck, being brass, of sacker bore. **1691** LUTTRELL *Brief Rel.* (1857) II. 170 Mr. Bellingham having lately invented a sort of gun, called a drake, to serve in nature of feild peices, and may be carried behind a man on horseback. **1755** CARTE *Hist. Eng.* IV. 266 Two ships had..landed at Leith, six culverins and nine drakes. **1894** WOLSELEY *Marlborough* II. 157 Ten demiculverins, twelve drakes, two three-pounders, and some mortars.

4. An angler's name for species of *Ephemera*: the green drake is the common day-fly (*E. vulgata*). (See also *drake-fly* in DRAKE[2].)

1658 R. FRANCK *North. Mem.* (1821) 66 It was only with dracks that I killed these trouts. **1676** COTTON *Walton's Angler* viii, The drake..is to be found in flags and grass too, and indeed everywhere, high and low, near the river. **1799** G. SMITH *Laboratory* II. 282 The drake or true cad-fly, called by many the May-fly, from the month in which it is in season. **1884** G. F. BRAITHWAITE *Salmonidæ of Westmorland* vi. 26 The most beautiful species of our ephemera, the green and grey drakes.

5. A beaked galley, or ship of war of the Vikings. (Cf. ON *dreki*.)

1862 H. MARRYAT *Year in Sweden* I. 199 *note*, Those in which the vikings were buried in their drake. *Ibid.* 438 A viking was discovered at Hatuna, interred in his drake.

6. *attrib.* and *Comb.*, as *drake-head*; **drake-shot** from sense 3.

c **1205** LAY. 18231 Pendragun an Brutisc Draken hefd [*c* **1275** Drake-heued] an Englisc. *a* **1225** *Ancr. R.* 246 þu hauest forschalded..þe drake heaued. **1755** *Mem. Capt. P. Drake* II. iii. 77 A Drake Shot, otherwise a Four Pounder.

drake[2] (dreɪk). In 5 drak, 6 *Sc.* draik, (7 draig). [ME., first found in 13th c., corresponding to northern and central Ger. dial. *draak, drake, drache* (same sense); this is app. the second element in OHG. *antrahho, antrehho*, MHG. *antreche*, Ger. *enterich*, 1599 *endtrich*, Ger. dial. *endedrach, antrek, antrecht, entrach*, Sw. (from LG.) *anddrake*, the first element usually explained as *eend, end, ente, and, ant, anut* 'duck', though the OHG. forms offer difficulties. The compound form is not known in English.

If **drako*, **drakko*, **drekko* was originally the W.Ger. name of the male of the duck, the word for 'duck' may have been prefixed to distinguish it from the similar forms of DRAKE[1]. (The notion that ME. *drake* was shortened from an OE. **andrake* has no basis of fact, and the conjecture that the word contains the suffix *-ric, -rich*, 'chief, mighty, ruler', is absurd.)]

1. The male of the duck, and of birds of the duck kind.

c **1300** *Havelok* 1241 Ne gos ne henne Ne the hende, ne the drake. *c* **1385** CHAUCER *L.G.W.* 2450 *Phyllis*, Withoute lore as can a drake sweme. *c* **1450** HOLLAND *Howlat* 210 With grene almouss on hed, schir Gawane the Drak. **1500–20** DUNBAR *Poems* lxiii. 46 Huntaris of draik and duik. **1639** SIR R. GORDON *Hist. Earldom Sutherland* 3 Ther is..duke, draig, widgeon, teale..and all other kinds of wildfowl. **1871** DARWIN *Desc. Man* (1888) 393 The common drake..after the breeding-season is well known to lose his male plumage for a period of three months.

2. a. *attrib.* and *Comb.*, as ***drake-neck***, †***-nosed***, adjs.; **drake-fly**, †(*a*) an artificial fly dressed with breast feathers of a drake (*obs.*); (*b*) a may-fly, used in angling; **drake-stone**, a flat stone thrown along the surface of water so as alternately to graze it and rebound in its course.

a **1450** *Fysshynge w. Angle* (1883) 35 The drake flye, the body of blacke wull..wynges of the mayle of the blacke drake. **1575** *Appius & Virg.* in Hazl. *Dodsley* IV. 151 That drousy drakenosed drivel. **1828** De Quincey in *Blackw. Mag.* XXIV. 907 It..reappears at a remote part of the sentence, like what is called a drake-stone on the surface of a river. **1833** T. Hook *Parson's Dau.* I. v, A dab at killing trout; drake-fly, wasp-fly, or stone-fly, all one to him. **1847-8** De Quincey *Protestantism* Wks. VIII. 130 The boyish sport sometimes called 'drake-stone': a flattish stone is thrown by a little dexterity so as to graze the surface of a river. **1884** *Lit. World* (U.S.) 481/3 Bound in drake-neck blue vellum cloth. **1927** H. Williamson *Tarka the Otter* iv. 57 The summer drake-flies..hatched from their cases on the water and danced over the shadowed surface.

b. Used *attrib.* before the names of birds of the duck kind to denote the male of the species.

1889 *Daily News* 5 Jan. 5 There are few handsomer sea-fowl than the drake eider. **1907** in *Zoologist* (1908) Apr. 124 A drake Shoveler seen on the river at Eaton.

c. *Comb.* with *drake's*. **drake's tail**, (used of) unruly hair at the back of the head. Cf. *duck-tail*.

1938 M. K. Rawlings *Yearling* iii. 24 The hair grieved him..it grew in tufts at the back. 'Drake's tails', his mother called them. **1960** C. Day Lewis *Buried Day* iv. 80 It horrified me..when I first caught sight of the back of my neck..to find that I had a drake's-tail of hair.

drake, obs. form of drawk *sb.*

Dralon ('dreɪlɒn). Also **dralon**. [After nylon.] A proprietary name for an acrylic fibre used in textiles, esp. for soft furnishings, and fabric made from this.

1955 *Trade Marks Jrnl.* 21 Dec. 1266/2 *Dralon*... Textile piece goods. Farbenfabriken Bayer Aktiengesellschaft.. Bayerwerk, Leverkusen (22c), Germany. **1958** *Observer* 12 Jan. 8/1 Dralon. Only just coming into the shops. A German fibre, similar to orlon, not as strong as nylon or Terylene. **1965** *Official Gaz.* (U.S. Patent Office) 22 June TM158/1 *Dralon*... For synthetic fibers and continuous filaments for various uses in the industrial arts. **1978** *Morecambe Guardian* 14 Mar. 6/6 Sofas and chairs covered in tough Dralon velvet. **1981** *Official Gaz.* (U.S. Patent Office) 6 Jan. TM48/1 *Dralon*... For woven and knitted fabrics, including upholstery fabric, made..with synthetic fibers or filaments. **1984** S. Townsend *Growing Pains A. Mole* 179 This proof of the cruelty of fate..reduced me to silent sobs into the Dralon cushions.

dram (dræm), *sb.*[1] Also 5 **drame**, 5-7 **dramme**. [phonetic spelling of earlier drachm, *dragm*, also in OF. *drame*. See also drachma, dirhem.]

†**1.** = drachm 1, the ancient Greek coin. *Obs.*

c **1440** Hylton *Scala Perf.* (W. de W. 1494) I. xlviii, What woman..that hath lost a drame. **1526** *Pilgr. Perf.* (W. de W. 1531) 242 A certayne coyne..called a dramme.

2. A weight, orig. the ancient Greek drachma; hence, in Apothecaries' weight, a weight of 60 grains = $\frac{1}{8}$ of an ounce; in Avoirdupois weight, of $27\frac{1}{3}$ grains = $\frac{1}{16}$ of an ounce; = drachm 2. Also the Arabic dirhem, used from Morocco to Persia and Abyssinia.

c **1440** *Promp. Parv.* 130/2 Drame, wyghte, *drama, dragma*. **1555** Eden *Decades* 12 Stones of gold weighing .x. or .xii. drammes. **1601** Shaks. *All's Well* II. iii. 233 Yes good faith, eu'ry dramme of it, and I will not bate thee a scruple. **1741** *Compl. Fam. Piece* I. i. 27 A Dram of Saffron, tied in a Rag. **1892** W. K. Burton *Mod. Photogr.* (ed. 10) 17 Four ounces of sulphide of soda..one dram of citric acid.

3. a. A fluid dram (= $\frac{1}{8}$ fluid ounce) of medicine, etc.; hence **b.** A small draught of cordial, stimulant, or spirituous liquor. Also *fig.*

c **1590** *Play of Sir Thomas More* (Shaks. Soc.) 93 Thou shalt see me take a dramme..Shall cure the stone. **1592** Shaks. *Rom. & Jul.* v. i. 60 Let me haue A dram of poyson. **1611** —— *Wint. T.* I. ii. 320. **1642** Rogers *Naaman* 38 Surely ..hee must put more drammes and drugges to the Physicke. **1682** Bunyan *Holy War* (Cassell) 208, I have a cordial of Mr. Forget-Good's making, the which, sir, if you will take a dram of..it may make you bonny and blithe. **1713** Swift *Frenzy of J. Denny* Wks. 1755 III. I. 143 The dram, sir? Mr. Lintot drank up all the gin just now. **1749** Fielding *Tom Jones* xv. iv, You certainly want a cordial. I must send to Lady Edgely for one of her best drams. **1752** *Scots Mag.* July (1753) 338/2 They went in, and drunk some drams. **1768-74** Tucker *Lt. Nat.* (1852) II. 145 Unless you keep up their spirits continually with a dram of the same [variety]. **1807** *Ann. Reg.* 80 They were like a dram given to the country which for the moment might increase its power, but which would be followed by greater languor and debility. **1877** Black *Green Past.* xxxi, She to her spinning-wheel and he to his long clay and his dram.

4. *fig.* (of 2 and 3.) = drachm 3.

1566 Drant *Horace, Sat.* III. Biij, No dram he had of constancy. **1646** P. Bulkeley *Gospel Covt.* I. 77 Wrath, without any dram of mercy to allay the bitternesse of the cup. **1709** Hearne *Collect.* 11 Mar., Having not one dram of Learning.

5. *Canada* and *U.S.* A collection of 'cribs', forming a section of a raft of staves: see quot. 1892 and cf. crib *sb.* 14. (Perh. a distinct word.)

1878 *Encycl. Brit.* IV. 774/2 (*Canada*) The cribs floated from the far inland timber limits are collected into what are called drams..and so many drams form a raft. **1892** *Eng. Illustr. Mag.* Sept. 885 A raft is made into sections, or 'drams', each..about 200 feet long and fifty feet wide. About ten 'drams' make a raft.

6. *attrib.* and *Comb.* (in sense 3) ***dram-bottle***, ***-cup***, ***-dish***, ***-dose***, ***-glass***, ***-house***, ***-pot***, ***-weight***; **dram-drinker**, one addicted to drinking drams, a tippler; **dram-drinking**, tippling.

1674 *Lond. Gaz.* No. 851/4 Two Silver Beakers, and two Silver *Dram Cups. **1762** Goldsm. *Cit. W.* cii, By flourishing a dice-box in one hand, she generally comes to brandish a dram-cup in the other. **1722** *Lond. Gaz.* No. 6079/9 One small *Dram Dish. **1744** Berkeley *Siris* §108 Some tough *dram-drinker. **1855** Macaulay *Hist. Eng.* III. 554 An old dram drinker or an old opium eater. **1772** Wilmer in *Phil. Trans.* LXIV. 341 Her old custom of *dram-drinking. **1716** Addison *Drummer* III. i, I have a *dram-glass just by. **1752** *Scots Mag.* Aug. (1753) 393/2 They drank two or three drams at a *dram-house. **1691** *Songs Costume* (Percy Soc.) 197 And make themselves drunk with their *dram-pots. **1611** Florio, *Dramma*, a *Dram-waight. **1632** Rutherford *Lett.* (1862) I. 88 Sell not one dram-weight of God's truth.

dram, *sb.*[2] [Short for *Drammen*.] Timber from Drammen in Norway. Also *attrib.*

1663 Gerbier *Counsel* 64 Yellow Fur (called Dram) being very good. **1676** *Phil. Trans.* XI. 721 You must take the finest streightest grain of your Dram deal. **1858** *Skyring's Builders' Prices* 62 It is customary to allow four cuts..when cut by the load, and two to the Berwick or dram, ditto.

dram, *v.* [f. dram *sb.*[1]]

1. *intr.* To drink drams; to tipple.

1715 [see drammer below]. **1752** H. Walpole *Lett.* 28 Aug., Melancholy..is not strong enough, and he grows to dram with horror. **1755** *Connoisseur* No. 53 ¶5 To dram it by authority, and to get tipsy *secundum artem*.

2. *trans.* To give a dram or drams to; to ply with stimulants.

1770 Warton *Newsman's Verses* (D.), Dram your poor newsman clad in rags. **1855** Thackeray *Newcomes* xxviii. (1868) II. 335 The parents..are getting ready their daughter for sale..praying her, and imploring her, and dramming her, and coaxing her.

Hence **'dramming** *vbl. sb.*; also **'drammer**, **'drammist**.

1715 Cheyne *Philos. Conject. & Disc.* (L.), Habitual drinkers, drammers, and high feeders. **1755** Hales in *Phil. Trans.* XLIX. 332 The most zealous advocates for drams, even the unhappy besotted dramists themselves. **1771** Franklin *Autobiog.* Wks. 1887 I. 74 Whether they discover'd his dramming by his breath, or by his behaviour.

†**dram**, *a. Sc.* [Origin uncertain. Cf. Gael. *trom*, heavy, sad, melancholy.] Sad, melancholy.

1500-20 Dunbar *Poems* lii. 23, I pray That never dolour mak him dram. **1513** Douglas *Æneis* IV. Prol. 157 Quhat honestie or renoun is to be dram? **1570** *Satir. Poems Reform.* x. 16 Paill of the face..Deid eyit, dram lyke.

drama ('drɑːmə). Also 6 **drame**, 7 **dramma**. [a. late L. *drāma* drama, play (Ausonius), a. Gr. δρᾶμα deed, action, play, esp. tragedy, n. of action from δρᾶν to do, act, perform. In earliest use in form *drame* as in Fr. (1707 in Hatz.-Darm.).]

1. a. A composition in prose or verse, adapted to be acted upon a stage, in which a story is related by means of dialogue and action, and is represented with accompanying gesture, costume, and scenery, as in real life; a play.

1515 Barclay *Egloges* iv. (1570) C vj/1 Such rascolde drames promoted by Thais, Bacchus, Licoris, or yet by Thestalis. **1616** B. Jonson *Epigr.* cxii, I cannot for the stage a drama lay, Tragic or comic. **1636** Heywood *Loves Mistresse* Ded., Neither are Dramma's of this nature so despicable. **1641** Milton *Ch. Govt.* II. Introd., The Scripture also affords us a divine pastoral drama in the Song of Solomon. **1670** Lassels *Voy. Italy* I. (1698) 140 (Stanf.) The several Opera's or Musical Dramata are acted and sung. **1795** Mason *Ch. Mus.* i. 24 Their Tragic Dramas..being usually accompanied by Instruments. **1852** Hallam *Lit. Ess., E. European Drama* 2 The Orfeo of Politian..the earliest represented drama, not of a religious nature, in a modern language.

b. *Theatr.* = melodrama 1.

1895 G. B. Shaw *Our Theatres in Nineties* (1932) I. 106 After the exasperatingly bad acting one constantly sees at the theatres where high comedy and 'drama' prevail, it is a relief to see even simple work creditably done. **1947** —— *Shaw on Theatre* (1958) 277 To him drama meant melodrama, its technical sense on the stage.

2. With *the*: The dramatic branch of literature; the dramatic art.

1661 *Middleton's Mayor of Queenborough* Pref. Wks. (Bullen) II. 3 His drollery yields to none the English drama did ever produce. **1711** Addison *Spect.* No. 13 ¶5 The received Rules of the Drama. **1727** Pope, etc. *Art of Sinking* xvi. Wks. 1757 VI. 219 (Stanf.) The Drama, which makes so great and so lucrative a part of Poetry. **1857** H. Reed *Lect. Brit. Poets* viii. 284 The true philosophy of the drama as an imaginative imitation of life. **1861** M. Pattison *Ess.* I. 46 The lover of the Elizabethan drama.

3. A series of actions or course of events having a unity like that of a drama, and leading to a final catastrophe or consummation.

a **1714** J. Sharp *Serm.* I. xiii. (R.), It helps to adorn the great drama and contrivances of God's providence. **1775** Mason *Gray* G.'s Poems 2 That peculiar part which he acted in the varied Drama of Society. **1796** Burke *Regic. Peace* i. Wks. VIII. 78 The awful drama of Providence now acting on the moral theatre of the world. **1876** E. Mellor *Priesth.* ii. 58 That great drama which was to culminate in the death of Christ.

Dramamine ('dræməmiːn). *Pharm.* Also **dramamine**. The proprietary name of an antihistamine compound used as a drug to prevent nausea.

1949 Gay & Carliner in *Science* 8 Apr. 359/1 The dose of Dramamine was 100 mg every 5 hr and before retiring. Dramamine prevented seasickness in all but two of the 134 men. **1950** *Trade Marks Jrnl.* 7 June 516/1 Dramamine. Pharmaceutical preparation consisting of dimenhydrinate for use in the prevention and treatment of motion sickness, nausea and vomiting, and as antihistaminics. G. D. Searle & Co... United States of America. **1958** B. Hamilton *Too Much of Water* ii. 23 Edgar, beginning to feel liverish and sleepy from the dramamine tablet he had punctiliously taken an hour before sailing. **1962** I. Murdoch *Unofficial Rose* xxxvi. 344 He had provided himself with plenty of Dramamine for the trip. **1970** *New Scientist* 5 Mar. 445/2 Dramamine and hyoscine are found effective in stilling the internal turbulence.

dramatic (drə'mætɪk), *a.* (*sb.*) [ad. late L. *drāmatic-us*, a. Gr. δρᾱματικός pertaining to drama, f. δρᾶμα, δράματ- drama: (cf. F. *dramatique*).]

A. *adj.* **1.** Of, pertaining to, or connected with the, or a, drama; dealing with or employing the forms of the drama. ***dramatic soprano***: see quot. 1961.

1589 Puttenham *Eng. Poesie* I. xv. (Arb.) 49 Foure sundry formes of Poesie Drammatick..to wit, the Satyre, olde Comedie, new Comedie, and Tragedie. *c* **1680** J. Aubrey in *Shaks. C. Praise* 383 He began early to make essayes at Dramatique Poetry. **1710** C. Gildon *Life T. Betterton* p. vi, The Graces of Action and Utterance come naturally under the Consideration of a *Dramatic Writer*. **1791** Burke *Corr.* (1844) III. 196, I have never written any dramatic piece whatsoever. **1824** W. Irving *T. Trav.* I. 280 The dramatic corps. **1826** *Blackw. Mag.* XIX. 197 (*title*) On cant in dramatic criticism. *Ibid.* 198/1 Justice and honesty require, that the bread of a performer, or the character of an author, shall not be sacrificed to the dull sport or the heedless haste of paragraphs in the newspapers. These are now almost the sole vehicles of dramatic criticism. **1864** *Round Table* 2 Jan. 43/3 Dramatic critics in New York. The use of the term 'Critic' in this heading is a misuse of English, but as the persons of whom we have now to write lay claim to the honorable appelation, we venture to treat it thus badly —on this occasion. *Ibid.* 43/3 Out of this mass of moral and physical corruption has come for years the greater portion of 'Dramatic Criticism' in New York. **1879** C. E. Pascoe *Dramatic Notes* 29 That competent dramatic writer, Mr. Charles Reade. **1885** Mabel Collins *Prettiest Woman* viii, She played the part of the dramatic critic. **1907** W. Raleigh *Shakespeare, Index* 229/2 Irony, dramatic. **1926** Fowler *Mod. Eng. Usage* 295/2 *Dramatic irony*, i.e. the irony of the Greek drama... The surface meaning for the dramatis personae, & the underlying for the spectators. **1942** Partridge *Usage & Abusage* 167/2 Dramatic irony is that which consists in a situation—not in words;..when the audience in a theatre or the reader of a book perceives a crux, a significance, a point, that the characters concerned do not perceive. **1946** *Penguin Music Mag.* Dec. 44, I heard a female, who called herself a dramatic soprano, screech and bawl. **1961** A. Berkman *Gloss. Show Business Jargon* 19 *Dramatic soprano*, the strongest of the female voices, with a range up to about high C.

2. Characteristic of, or appropriate to, the drama; often connoting animated action or striking presentation, as in a play; theatrical.

1725 Pope *Odyss.* Postcr., The whole structure of that work [Iliad] is dramatick and full of action. **1778** Foote *Trip Calais* III. Wks. 1799 II. 378 There seems to be a kind of dramatic justice in the change of your two situations. **1855** Brimley *Ess., Tennyson* 9 That dramatic unity demanded in works of art. **1878** Lecky *Eng. in 18th C.* (1883) I. 176 The destruction of a great and ancient institution is an eminently dramatic thing.

B. *sb.* †**1.** A dramatic poet; a dramatist. *Obs.*

1646 G. Daniel *Poems* Wks. 1878 I. 30 Hee was, of English Drammatickes, the Prince. *a* **1680** Butler *Rem.* (1759) I. 164 No longer shall Dramatics be confin'd To draw true Images of all Mankind. *a* **1741** Gray *Lett.* Wks. 1884 II. 109 Put me the following lines into the tongue of our modern dramatics.

2. *pl.* Dramatic compositions or representations; the drama. Also *transf.* and *fig.*

1684 W. Winstanley *Eng. Worthies, Shaks.* 345-7 In all his writings hath an unvulgar Style, as well in his..Poems, as in his Drammaticks. **1711** Shaftesb. *Charac.* (1737) I. 265 We read epicks and dramaticks, as we do satirs and lampoons. **1796** G. Colman in R. B. Peake *Mem. Colman Family* (1841) II. viii. 253 They who are experienced in dramatics will, I trust, see that I have made a fair 'extenuation' of myself. **1880** C. Keene *Let.* in G. S. Layard *Life* x. (1892) 308 The prevailing mania for dramatics. **1936** L. C. Douglas *White Banners* xvi. 338 There was no need to dramatize it..; the strange chronicle furnished its own dramatics. **1957** P. Kemp *Mine were of Trouble* ix. 181 Running forward—I realize now, of course, that this was the most puerile dramatics—I seized the flag and ran back with it.

dra'matical, *a.* (*sb.*) [f. as prec. + -al[1].] = dramatic *a.* 1. (Now *rare*.)

1640 G. Watts tr. *Bacon's Adv. Learn.* II. (R.), Dramaticall, or representative [poesy] is as it were, a visible history. *a* **1652** J. Smith *Sel. Disc.* VI. iv. (1821) 221 The whole dramatical series of things. **1711** Addison *Spect.* No. 101 ¶7 A Dramatical Performance written in a Language which they did not understand. **1854** *Fraser's Mag.* L. 591 Fletcher was the dramatical parent of Congreve.

†**B.** *sb. pl.* = dramatic B. *Obs. rare.*

c **1826** Moir in *Wilson's Wks.* (1855) I. 198 Then bid Bryan Procter beat To dramaticals retreat.

dra'matically, *adv.* [f. prec. + -LY².]
a. In a dramatic manner; from a dramatic point of view. b. With dramatic or theatrical effect.
a **1652** J. SMITH *Sel. Disc.* vi. 192 The outward frame of things dramatically set forth. **1759** STERNE *Tr. Shandy* II. viii. 57 This plea, tho' it might save me dramatically, will damn me biographically. **1836–9** DICKENS *Sk. Boz* (C.D. ed.) 200 He stalked dramatically to bed.

dramaticism (drə'mætɪsɪz(ə)m). [f. DRAMATIC *a.* + -ISM.] Dramatic character or quality.
1878 T. SINCLAIR *Mount* 80 More than its dramaticism and epicism. **1890** *Athenæum* 6 Dec. 775/2 The dramaticism frequent among Nineteenth Century writers of blank verse.

dra'maticle, -icule. Also erron. -ucle. [f. L. *drāma, drāmat-* with dim. suffix.] A miniature or insignificant drama.
[**1792** T. TWINING *Recreat. & Stud.* (1882) 168 His two printed dialogues, or dramacles.] **1813** *Examiner* 15 Mar. 171/1 This admired dramatucle (if we may be allowed such a diminutive). **1851** *Beddoes' Poems* Mem. 15 'Olympian Revels,' and other dramaticles published in the 'London Magazine' of 1823. **1864** CARLYLE *Fredk. Gt.* IV. 252 Court-shows, dramaticules, transparencies. **1967** *Listener* 3 Aug. 148/1 His [*sc.* Beckett's] new play, *Come and Go*, can spare only 121 words of dialogue for its three women moving through their grim permutation-game, and so Beckett has the grace to call it 'a Dramaticule'.

'dramatism. [f. as DRAMATIST + -ISM].
1. Dramatization, dramatized form.
1834 *Autobiog. Dissenting Minister* 122 He could no longer amuse his flock with the dramatism of devotion.
2. Dramatic quality.
1880 J. H. EWING *Let.* 16 Mar. in H. Eden *J. H. Ewing* (1896) 222 Her writing is glorious—Imagination limited—Dramatism—nil! **1901** *Daily Chron.* 14 Nov. 3/1 The infamous stage management of the thing rather aided than detracted from its unspeakable dramatism.

‖**dramatis personæ** ('dræmətɪs pə'səʊniː). Abbreviated **dram. pers.** [L.; = persons of a drama.] The characters of a drama or play; the actors in a drama. *lit.* or *fig.*
1730 FIELDING *Temple Beau* I. vi. Wks. 1882 VIII. 117 There is (to give you a short Dramatis Personae) my worthy uncle [etc.]. **1806** J. JAY *Corr. & Pub. Papers* (1893) IV. 308 Whether this distant nation is to appear among the *dramatis personae* cannot now be known. **1821** BYRON *Diary* 13 Jan., Sketched the outline and Dram. Pers. of a..tragedy. **1895** *Law Times* XCIX. 547/1 His *dramatis personæ* included a low attorney.

dramatist ('dræmətɪst). [f. Gr. δρᾶμα, δραματ- DRAMA + -IST: cf. F. *dramatiste* (1787 in Hatz.-Darm.).] A writer or composer of dramas or dramatic poetry; a play-wright. (Also *fig.*)
1678 CUDWORTH *Intell. Syst.* 879 They..impatiently cry out against the Dramatist, and presently condemn the Plot. **1742** YOUNG *Nt. Th.* IX. 358 To see the mighty Dramatist's last Act..in Glory rising o'er the rest. *a* **1862** BUCKLE *Misc. Wks.* (1872) I. 483 In every country the dramatists have preceded the metaphysicians.

dramatization (ˌdræmətaɪ'zeɪʃən). [f. next + -ATION.] The action of dramatizing; conversion into drama; a dramatized version.
1796 W. TAYLOR in *Monthly Rev.* XIX. 482 The variegated list of his dramatizations. **1846** DICKENS *Lett.* (1880) I. 165, I really am bothered..by this confounded dramatization of the Christmas book. **1875** MAINE *Hist. Inst.* ix. 253 A dramatisation of the origin of Justice.

dramatize ('dræmətaɪz), *v.* [f. as DRAMATIST + -IZE.]
1. a. *trans.* To convert into a drama; to put into dramatic form, adapt for representation on the stage.
1780–83 [see DRAMATIZED]. **1810** SCOTT *Fam. Lett.* 22 Dec., They are busy dramatizing the Lady of the Lake here and in Dublin. **1884** *Law Times* 27 Sept. 358/2 The play 'Called Back,' dramatised from the novel of that name.
b. *absol.* To write dramas.
1814 *Sortes Horatianae* 125 Scrawl, dramatize..do what ye will. **1900** *Daily News* 28 May 4/1 The glorious language in which Milton sang, Shakespeare dramatised, Richard Baxter prayed, and George Whitfield thundered.
2. To describe or represent dramatically. *refl.* To behave melodramatically.
1823 ADOLPHUS in Lockhart *Scott* Aug., To exert the talent of dramatizing and..representing in his own person the incidents he told of. **1894** HOWELLS in *Harper's Mag.* Feb. 383 The men continue to dramatize a struggle on the floor below. **1934** H. G. WELLS *Exper. Autobiogr.* II. viii. 620 My mother dramatized herself, indeed, but so artlessly that I rebelled against that.
3. *intr.* (for *pass*). To admit of dramatization.
1819 SCOTT *Fam. Lett.* 15 June, The present set..will not dramatize. **1836** *New Monthly Mag.* XLVII. 235 The story would dramatize admirably.
4. *trans.* To influence by the drama. *nonce-use.*
1799 *Morn. Chron.* in *Spirit Pub. Jrnls.* (1800) III. 154 Some might take their station in the theatres, and dramatize the audience into loyalty.
Hence **'dramatized** *ppl. a.*, **'dramatizing** *vbl. sb.* and *ppl. a.* (also *fig.*); also **'dramatizable** *a.*, (Webster, 1864); **'dramatizer**, one who dramatizes.
1780–83 W. TOOKE *Russia* (Webster 1828), A dramatized extract from the history of the Old and New Testaments. **1833** *Westm. Rev.* XVIII. 226 The dramatizer of Cooper's 'Pilot'. *a* **1834** LAMB *Charac. Dram. Writers, Rowley* Wks. 530 Our delicacy..forbids the dramatising of distress. **1862** MERIVALE *Rom. Emp.* (1865) V. xli. 99 The dramatized histories of the English bard. **1875** EMERSON *Lett. & Soc. Aims* Wks. (Bohn) III. 221 A sort of dramatizing talent. **1888** MRS. H. WARD *R. Elsmere* II. xviii. 107 Oh, to fall at her feet, and ask her pardon before parting for ever! But no—no more posing; no more dramatizing. **1934** H. G. WELLS *Exper. Autobiogr.* II. viii. 620 Accident threw me in my receptive years mostly among non-dramatizing systematic-minded people.

dramaturge ('dræmətɜːdʒ). [a. F. *dramaturge* (1787), ad. Gr. δραματουργός composer of drama, f. δρᾶμα, δράματο- DRAMA + ἔργειν to work, -εργος working, worker.] = DRAMATURGIST.
[**1859** *Times* 17 Nov. 8/2 Schiller was starving on a salary of 200 dollars per annum, which he received..for his services as 'dramaturg' or literary manager.] **1870** *Athenæum* 12 Mar. 366 M. Sardou..that indefatigable dramaturge. **1882** SYMONDS *Animi Figura* 118 Fate is the dramaturge; necessity Allots the parts.

drama'turgic, *a.* [f. Gr. δραματουργ-ός (see prec.) + -IC.] Pertaining to dramaturgy; dramatic, histrionic, theatrical.
1831 BEDDOES *Let.* Jan. in *Poems* p. xcvi, So much for my dramaturgic ideas on playbills. **1845** CARLYLE *Cromwell* (1871) I. 158 Some form [of worship] not grown dramaturgic to us, but still awfully symbolical for us. **1883** *Mag. of Art* June 315/1 That lack of dramaturgic science.
So **drama'turgical** *a.*
1865 F. HALL *Daśa-rúpa* Pref. 5 To propound..a few dramaturgical definitions.

'dramaturgist. [f. as prec. + -IST.] A composer of a drama; a play-wright.
1825 CARLYLE *Schiller* II. (1845) 63 Notwithstanding..all the vaunting of dramaturgists. **1843** —— *Past & Pr.* II. ii, The World Dramaturgist has written, *Exeunt.*

'dramaturgy. [mod. ad. Gr. δραματουργία composition of dramas: cf. F. *dramaturgie* (17th c.), Ger. *dramaturgie.*]
1. Dramatic composition; the dramatic art.
1801 W. TAYLOR in *Monthly Mag.* XII. 224 Lessing's Dramaturgy. **1805** *Ibid.* XX. 41 Lessing..published a weekly paper, entitled the Hamburg Dramaturgy. **1885** *Sat. Rev.* 28 Mar. 419/2 The immortal Mac-Flecknoe, in which the 'Nursery' and its dramaturgy are annotated.
2. Dramatic or theatrical acting.
1837 CARLYLE *Diam. Neckl.* Misc. Ess. 1888 V. 184 Let her..give her past Dramaturgy the fit aspect to Monseigneur and others. **1858** —— *Fredk. Gt.* (1865) I. I. iii. 22 Sublime dramaturgy, which we call his Majesty's Government, costs so much.

Drambuie (dræm'bjuːɪ, -'buːɪ). [Proprietary term.] A whisky liqueur manufactured in Scotland.
1893 *Trade Marks Jrnl.* 20 Sept. 923 Drambuie, a Liqueur. James Ross, Broadford, Skye. **1935** A. L. SIMON *Wines & Liqueurs* 22 *Drambuie*, a Scotch liqueur, golden in colour, with the flavour of Whisky and Honey. **1962** G. THOMAS *Keep* I. 25 You took a few drinks. Why not? Anybody selling monumental masonry in..towns..where the only concession to gaiety is a striped shroud, deserves a bath in drambuie, no less.

drammer, dramming: see DRAM *v.*

drammock ('dramək). *Sc.* Also 6 drummake, 8 dramock, -uck, 8- drummock, 9 drammach. [Cf. Gael. *dramag* 'foul mixture'.] 'Meal and water mixed in a raw state' (Jam.).
1563 *Ressoning betuix Crosraguell & J. Knox* Prol. ij b, Watter & meal made i maner of a drammock. **16..** F. SEMPILL *Blythsum Bridal* in *Harp of Renfrewsh.* (1819) Pref. 63 There will be..Powsowdie and drammock and crowdie. **1786** BURNS *Scotch Bard* vii, Scarce a bellyfu' o' drummock. **1816** SCOTT *Old Mort.* xvi, The lifeless, saltless, foisonless, lukewarm drammock of the fourteen false prelates. **1886** STEVENSON *Kidnapped* xxii, We..made ourselves a dish of drammach.

'dram-shop. Chiefly *U.S.* [DRAM *sb.*¹ 3 b.] A shop or bar where spirituous liquor is sold in drams or small quantities.
1725 *New-England Courant* 8–15 Feb. 1/2 Certainly the Devil had brought himself as well as his Hogs to a fine Market, when he was thus expos'd to Sale in a Dram-Shop. **1761** J. ADAMS *Diary* in *Wks.* (1850) II. 122 Taverns and dram-shops are therefore placed in every corner of the town. **1839** *Lincoln, Boston, etc. Gaz.* 12 Feb. 3/3 A detached part of these premises is a dram-shop. **1849** F. PARKMAN *California & Oregon Trail* 445 We passed..Boone's grocery and old Vogle's dram-shop. **1875** HOLLAND *Sevenoaks* i. 2 A row of stores and dram-shops and butchers' establishments. **1951** R. CAMPBELL *Light on Dark Horse* iii. 62 The Indians ..were quite capable of boycotting his dramshop.

drane, obs. form of DRAIN, DRONE.

‖**Drang** (dræŋ). [G.] Pressure; urge, strong desire; esp. in ***Drang nach Osten*** (lit. pressure to the east), a former German imperialistic policy of eastern expansion; also *transf.*
1906 W. JAMES *Let.* 28 June in R. B. Perry *Tht. & Char. W. James* (1935) II. 471 The wide difference between your whole *Drang* in philosophizing and mine would give me a despairing feeling. **1909** V. YOVANOVITCH *Near-Eastern Problem* iii. 21 (*heading*) The 'Drang nach Osten' or the Pan-German Peril. *Ibid.* 22 The economic interests of the hour are paramount, and the real peril against which the Europe of the twentieth century must fight is the *Drang nach Osten* —in other words, the tendency of the Germans towards universal economic supremacy. **1914** H. H. MUNRO *Beasts & Super-Beasts* 153 It was, perhaps, a desire to out-distance all possible competition that influenced the management of the *Daily Intelligencer*..to transfer its offices..to Eastern Turkestan... All took part in what was popularly alluded to as the *Drang nach Osten.* **1939** H. NICOLSON *Diary* 9 Feb. (1966) 391 Berlin engineered the story about the *Drang nach Osten* in order to divert our attention from an impending drive towards the west. **1940** *Economist* 12 Oct. 450/1 A German offensive—of which the occupation of Roumania and the establishment of airfields within bombing distance of Istanbul is a first manœuvre—may well develop, following the old lines of the *Drang nach Osten.* **1941** A. HUXLEY *Grey Eminence* viii. 171 Crusading, for Wallenstein, was merely an excuse for the *Drang nach Osten.* **1951** M. LOWRY *Let.* 25 Aug. (1967) 252 A philosophy and psychological *drang.* **1967** *Economist* 18 Mar. 996/2 It is impossible not to be uncomfortably aware of the omens that support your thesis of an economic *drang nach osten* in Yorkshire.

drang, var. of DRONG, lane.

drank, pa. t. of DRINK.

[**drank**, erron. f. DRAWK *sb.*, brome-grass.]

drant, draunt (drɑːnt, -æ-), *v. dial.* [app. onomatopœic, after *drawl* or *drone* and *rant.* Recorded from Scotl. and E. Anglia. Other dialects have *drunt, drate.*] *intr.* To drawl or drone in speech. b. *trans.* To drawl or drone *out.*
1724 RAMSAY *Tea-t. Misc.* (1733) II. 141 To drivel and drant While I sigh and gaunt. *a* **1774** FERGUSSON *Poems* (1789) II. 74 (Jam.) To draunt and drivel out a life at hame. **1796** BURNS *On Life* viii, Lest you think I am uncivil To plague you with this draunting drivel. *a* **1825** FORBY *Voc. E. Anglia, Drant,* to drawl in speaking or reading; more properly *draunt* (like *aunt*). It may be connected with drone.

drant, draunt, *sb. dial.* [f. prec. vb.]
a. A droning or drawling tone. b. 'A slow and dull tune' (Jam.).
1721 RAMSAY *Lucky Spence's Last Advice* ii, Nor wi' your draunts and droning deave me. **1781** BURNS *Tarbolton Lasses* (2nd Poem) xiv, To wait on their drants. *a* **1825** FORBY *Voc. E. Anglia* s.v., He reads with a drant. **1852** AIRD *Mem. Moir* in *M.'s Poet. Wks.* I. ii. 29 A kind of rant, or drant..often fixes itself upon the public.

drap: see DRAB *sb.*² and *a.*

drap, Sc. dial form of DROP *sb.* and *v.*

‖**drápa** ('drɑːpə). Pl. drápur. [ON. *drápa*, prob. f. *drepa* to strike (cf. DREPE *v.*).] A heroic laudatory poem of the Old Norse period.
[**1843** G. W. DASENT tr. *Rask's Gram. Icelandic* xxi. 217 After [the Toglag] the Knútsdrápa, and several other laudatory poems were arranged.] *Ibid.* xxii. 223 Laudatory poems were of two kinds; a short eulogy..was called flockr ..: The longer and more stately kind of these poems were the drapur. **1913** W. A. CRAIGIE *Icel. Sagas* i. 12 It is recorded of one man, Stúf the Blind, who was himself a poet, that he could recite more than thirty long encomia (called *drápur*) and as many shorter ones (*flokkar*). **1927** E. V. GORDON *Introd. Old Norse* 297 The *drápa* had a refrain of two or four lines every two, three, or four stanzas, and usually there were several refrains. **1959** A. G. BRODEUR *Art of Beowulf* vi. 137 The tale of Hygelac's fall, which we know to be solidly historic, may have been derived..from poems of the type represented in Scandinavia by the *drápa.* **1968** G. JONES *Leg. Hist. Olaf Tryggvason* 9 The well-known Hallfred..wrote a drápa or encomium on him.

†**Drap-de-Berry.** *Obs.* Also droppe-, drape-, drab-, -du-, -Berri(e, -berry, -ie, -bure. (Printed as one or three words). [Fr.; = cloth of Berry.] A kind of woollen cloth, coming from Berry in France. Also *attrib.* and *Comb.*
1619 PURCHAS *Microcosmus* xxvii. 269 The Colours of Gingelline, Grideline, Deroy, Elderado, Droppe du Berry. **1664** J. WILSON *Cheats* II. iv Dram. Wks. (1874) 42 Drape de berry in the summer keeps out the heat. **1681** *Lond. Gaz.* No. 1585/4 Stolen..a Drabdeberry Riding Coat. **1693** SHADWELL *Volunteers* III. Wks. 1720 IX. 441 They turn it into Drabdubbery. **1700** CONGREVE *Way of World* III. iii. Plays (1887) 361 Fools never wear out—they are such drap de Berri things! **1818** SCOTT *Rob Roy* xxxi, Your rotten French camlets now, or your drab-de-berries.

drape (dreɪp), *v.*¹ [a. F. *drape-r* to weave, drape (13th c. in Hatz.-Darm.), f. *drap* cloth.]
†1. *trans.* To weave or make into cloth. *Obs.*
1436 *Libel of Eng. Pol.* in *Pol. Poems* (Rolls) II. 162 Spayneshe wolle in Fflaundres draped [*v.r.* draperd] is. *Ibid.*, By drapinge [*v.r.* drapryng] of oure wolle in substaunce Lyvene here comons. *a* **1657** SIR J. BALFOUR *Ann. Scot.* (1824–5) II. 97 All the wooll that was not drapped and made vsse off within the kingdome. **1683** *Brit. Spec.* 18 Flanders doth drape Cloth for thee of thine own Wool.
absol. **1538** LELAND *Itin.*, Baillies Sun now drapeth yn the Toun. **1622** BACON *Hen. VII*, 76 That the Clothier might drape accordingly as he might affoord.
2. To cover with, or as with, cloth or drapery; to hang, dress, or adorn with drapery.
1847 TENNYSON *Princ.* v. 54 Like some sweet sculpture draped from head to foot. **1848** LYTTON *Harold* I. i, The walls were draped with silken hangings. **1853** C. BRONTE *Villette* xxiii, She stood, not dressed, but draped in pale antique folds. **1882** MISS BRADDON *Mt. Royal* III. vi. 146 A red gown draped with old Spanish lace.
transf. and *fig.* **1872** LIDDON *Elem. Relig.* ii. 63 Draped and veiled in a phraseology so reverent and tender. **1884** W. C. SMITH *Kildrostan* 50 Abbey walls Draped with pale lichens. **1894** FROUDE *Erasmus* vii. 120 Draped in solemn inanities.

3. To arrange or adjust (clothing, hangings, etc.) in graceful or artistic folds. Also *intr.* for *refl.*

1862 *Macm. Mag.* Apr. 523 Light material that will fall around and drape itself about the figure. **1894** A. St. Aubyn *Orchard Damerel* II. ii. 59 The curtains would not 'drape' artistically.

†**4.** To reprimand. [cf. dress *v.* So in obs. F.]

1683 Temple *Mem.* Wks. 1731 I. 449 Draping us for spending him so much Money, and doing nothing.

5. To place (oneself) against or on an object or another person, *esp.* in drunken unsteadiness. *colloq.*

1943 Hunt & Pringle *Service Slang* 28 *Draped*, the worse for drink—hanging on to lamp-posts or one's friend, i.e. draped around anything available. **1958** E. Dundy *Dud Avocado* I. i. 29 The lamp-post against which I was limply draped. **1959** *Punch* 9 Dec. 559/1 Paul Drake comes in and drapes himself across the arm of an over-stuffed chair. **1960** *Times* 4 Mar. 8/1 He..draped himself round a Belisha Beacon in a thoroughly drunken fashion.

Hence **draped** *ppl. a.*

1846 Ellis *Elgin Marb.* II. 9 Draped figures. *Mod.* Is the skirt plain or draped?

drape, *v.*[2] *north. dial.* [Goes with drape *sb.*[2]] *trans.* To cull, to draft.

1641 Best *Farm. Bks.* (Surtees) 72 When the worst of the flocke are drawne out, the shepheards call this drapinge out of sheepe, and some drape out a score..by reason of theire age.

drape (dreɪp), *sb.*[1] [f. F. *drap* cloth, and drape *v.*[1]] **a.** Cloth, drapery. **b.** Draping.

1665 J. Wilson *Projectors* v. Dram. Wks. (1874) 271 My new drape. **1757** Dyer *Fleece* 107 Each glossy cloth, and drape of mantle warm. **1889** *Pall Mall G.* 27 Feb. 4/3 A dress..of pale blue velvet, with long flowing drape of white tulle.

c. *pl.* Curtains. Chiefly *N. Amer.*

[**1895** *Montgomery Ward Catal.* 13/1 Drapery Silk... Suitable for throws, sash curtains, mantel drapes, etc.] **1908** *Sears, Roebuck Catal.* 885/2 A strong, well made Nottingham Lace Curtain,..one of the most stylish and attractive drapes one could possibly desire for the parlor window. **1934** J. T. Farrell *Young Manhood of Studs Lonigan* (1936) ii. xviii. 373 He looked at a rose-green pottery lamp set on the table near the heavy blue velvet drapes. **1936** J. G. Cozzens *Men & Brethren* i. 117 The long drapes drawn together across the front windows. **1952** Granville *Dict. Theatr. Terms* 65 *Drapes*, curtains of velvet or fabric used in place of scenery in revues or in repertory productions in 'Little' theatres. **1962** *Listener* 2 Aug. 191/1 In America..they [*sc.* Venetian blinds] are frequently used with unlined 'drapes' (at the side of the window only). **1968** *Globe & Mail* (Toronto) 17 Feb. 49/4 (Advt.), Drapes for sunroom and house. **1970** *New Scientist* 7 May 269/1 The cost of moving (including items such as legal fees, new drapes, etc) is £500.

d. A suit of clothes. *slang* (orig. *U.S.*). Also *attrib.*, as ***drape suit***, a suit consisting of a long jacket and narrow trousers.

1945 L. Shelly *Jive Talk Dict.* 9/2 *Drape*, suit. **1951** [see gear *sb.* 5 e]. **1952** A. Wilson *Hemlock & After* iii. i. 201 An endless horizon of drape suits. **1957** M. Swan *Brit. Guiana* i. viii. 133 He was a..man of thirty-two, wearing gaberdine drapes and a bow-tie. **1958** E. Hyams *Taking it Easy* 238 Street-corner youths whose drape-suits and sideburns were evolving into a pastiche of Edwardian fashion. **1969** *Listener* 10 July 58/3 They wore drape-jackets with velvet cuffs and their brothel-creepers were in immaculate condition.

e. ***drape forming*** (see quot. 1964). So ***drape technique***, etc.

1958 *Times Rev. Industry* Aug. 57/2 Machine for thermo-forming heavy industrial parts..uses drape..techniques. **1964** Wordingham & Reboul *Dict. Plastics* 56 *Drape forming* (drape vacuum forming), a method of shaping a thermoplastic sheet material in which the sheet is clamped into a frame, heated and a male mould pushed into the sheet to give positive mechanical stretching. Intimate contact is obtained by applying a vacuum.

drape, *sb.*[2] and *a. local.* [Origin uncertain: cf. ON. *dráp* slaughter, f. *drepa* to strike, smite, kill, put to death.] A sheep or cow culled or drafted from the flock or herd to be fatted off for slaughter; *esp.* a cow or ewe whose milk is dried up or that has missed being with young. Used in north and north east of England.

1611 Cotgr., *Brebis de rebut*, an old or diseased sheepe thats not worth keeping..a drape or culling. **1674** Ray *N.C. Words* 15 *A Drape*, a farrow cow, or cow whose milk is dried up. **1788** W. Marshall *Yorksh.* (1796) II. 187 Dry cows—provincially, 'drapes'. **1855** Robinson *Whitby Gloss.*, *Drape*, a dry or milkless cow. **1885** *Standard* 2 May 6/4 Smaller beasts..drapes.

B. *adj.* or in *Comb.*, as ***drape cow, ewe, sheep.***

1674 Ray *N.C. Words* 15 Drape-Sheep, *oves rejiculæ.* **1851** *Jrnl. R. Agric. Soc.* XII. ii. 333 The drape-ewes (or crones) are..sold at Michaelmas. **1888** *Whitby Gaz.* 25 Feb. 4/7 The animal was a drape cow, about 9 years old.

draper ('dreɪpə(r)), *sb.* Also 4–5 drapere, 5 -ure, -ar. [a. AF. *draper* = F. *drapier* (13th c. in Hatz.-Darm.), f. *drap* cloth: see -er[2] 2.]

1. Orig., One who made (woollen) cloth. Subsequently, A dealer in cloth, and now by extension, in other articles of textile manufacture: often qualified as ***woollen, linen draper.***

1362 Langl. *P. Pl.* A. v. 123 Þenne I drouȝ me a-mong þis drapers my Donet to leorne. **1377** *Ibid.* B. v. 255 Bothe mercere & draper. *c* **1420** *Sir Amadas* (Weber) 144 Ther myght..no draper is clothe drawe. **1483** *Cath. Angl.* 106/2 A Draper, *pannarius, trapezata.* *a* **1512** Fabyan *Will* in *Chron.* Pref. 3, I Robert Fabyan, citizein and draper of London. **1572** in W. H. Turner *Select Rec. Oxford* 342 The mercers and wollen drapers shalbe incorporated to one incorporation. **1655** Fuller *Ch. Hist.* vi. i. 275 Thus the Draper may sooner sell forty ells of freeze and course cloath, than the Mercer four yards of cloath of gold. **1807** Crabbe *Par. Reg.* 13 If at the draper's window Susan cast A longing look.

2. In comb. = *-seller*: see ale-draper.

Hence **'draperess**, a female draper.

1854 *Chamb. Jrnl.* I. 226 Almost every man above the rank of a mere daily cultivator has a wife who is groceress, linen-draperess, butcheress, or confectioner.

†**'draper,** *v. Obs. rare.* [a. F. *draper* to weave, drape.] **1.** *trans.* To weave, make into cloth.

1436 *Libel Eng. Pol.* in *Pol. Poems* (Rolls) II. 168 They Cowde never drapere [*v.r.* drape, draper] here wolle. *Ibid.* [see drape *v.*[1] 1.]

2. *intr.* or *absol.* To arrange drapery, to drape.

1717 Berkeley *Tour in Italy* Wks. IV. 523 His [Perugino's] drapering every one knows to [be] of a little gout.

Hence **'drapering** *vbl. sb.*; also *attrib.*, as ***drapering-house***, one where cloth is manufactured or sold.

1436 [see drape *v.*[1] 1]. By drapryng of oure wolle. **1538** Leland *Itin.* IV. 78 This House is made by one Bell a Drapering House. **1717** [see 2 above.]

drapery ('dreɪpərɪ), *sb.* Also 4 drapreye, 4–7 draperie. [a. OF. *draperie* (12th c.), f. *drap* cloth, *drapier* draper: see -ery.]

1. Cloth or textile fabrics collectively.

a **1300** *Sat. People Kildare* xi. in *E.E.P.* (1862) 154 Hail be ȝe marchans wiþ ȝur gret packes of draperie auoir-depeise and ȝur wol sackes. **1483** *Act 1 Rich. III*, c. 8 Preamb., No Substance of fine Drapery. **1538** Leland *Itin.* I. 44 The hole profite of the Toune [Wakefield] stondeth by Course Drapery. **1622** Misselden *Free Trade* 40 The Draperies of this Kingdome are termed Old and New. By the Old; are vnderstood Broad Clothes, Bayes and Kersies: By the New; Perpetuanoes, Serges, Sayes, and other Manufactures of Wooll. **1786** *Hist. Europe* in *Ann. Reg.* 11/2 A duty..on all drapery imported into that Kingdom. **1841** Lane *Arab. Nts.* I. 122 A napkin or some other piece of drapery is suspended over the door.

2. a. The trade or business of a draper; the manufacture of cloth (*obs.*); now, the sale of cloth and other textile fabrics.

1488–9 *Act 4 Hen. VII*, c. 11 Thencres and mayntenyng of Drapery and makying of Cloth withyn this land. **1610** Holland *Camden's Brit.* I. 352 Flemings..to teach our men that skill of Draperie or weaving and making wollen cloth. *a* **1661** Fuller *Worthies, Bedfordsh.* (1662) 113 Such the use thereof [fuller's earth] in Drapery, that good cloth can hardly be made without it. *Mod. Advt.*, Millinery and Fancy Drapery. Young Lady to serve through.

†**b.** A place where cloth is made. **c.** A place where a draper's business is conducted. *Obs.*

1483 *Cath. Angl.* 106/2 A Drapyry, *pannarium.* **1598** Florio, *Drapperie*, drapery, or street where cloth is made or sold. **1610** Holland *Camden's Brit.* i. 77 The Gynegium or Draperie in Britaine in which the Clothes of the Prince and Souldiers were woven.

†**3.** See quot., and cf. cilery. *Obs.*

1552 Huloet, Draperye worcke or cylerye a kynde of caruynge or payntynge so called, *voluta.* **1611** Cotgr., *Draperie*..a flourishing with leaves, and flowers in wood, or stone, vsed especially on the heads of pillers, and tearmed by our workemen Draperie, or Cilerie.

4. The artistic arrangement of clothing in painting or sculpture.

1610 Guillim *Heraldry* vi. v. (1611) 267 Which forme of plaiting in the art of painting is termed drapery. **1634** Peacham *Gentl. Exerc.* i. xiii. 43 Drapery..principally consisteth in the true making and folding your garment, giving to every fold his proper naturall doubling and shadow. *c* **1811** Fuseli in *Lect. Paint.* iv. (1848) 448 Attitude without action..dress without drapery.

5. The stuff with which anything is draped, or artistically covered; clothing or hangings of any kind; *esp.* the clothing of the human figure in sculpture or painting. Also *fig.* Also, usu. in *pl.*, curtains (*N. Amer.*).

1686 Aglionby *Painting Illustr.* Expl. Terms s.v., *Drapery*, We say, Such a Painter disposes well the Foldings of his Drapery. **1756–7** tr. *Keysler's Trav.* (1760) II. 357 The drapery of this statue is much admired. **1771** Sir J. Reynolds *Disc.* iv. (R.), It requires the nicest judgment to dispose the drapery, so that the folds shall have an easy communication, and gracefully follow each other. **1806–7** J. Beresford *Miseries Hum. Life* (1826) iii. xviii, The muslin drapery of your fair partner. **1831** Howitt *Seasons* 315 Nature is stripped of all her summer drapery. **1859** Geo. Eliot *A. Bede* 45 There is no drapery about the window. **1895** *Montgomery Ward Catal.* 15/1 Drapery prints. For furniture coverings or draperies. *Ibid.* 351/3 Brass drapery chains. For looping back and holding in place curtains, portieres, etc. **1938** G. T. Buswell et al. *Daily-Life Arith.* iii. iii. 74 Mrs. Wilson made window draperies. **1967** L. J. Braun *Cat who ate Danish Modern* ii. 18 'There's been a delay on the draperies; the fabric manufacturer discontinued the pattern.' 'Could the photographer shoot from an angle that would avoid the missing drapes?' ..'*Never* call draperies *drapes.*' **1968** *Globe & Mail* (Toronto) 17 Feb. 46/8 Extras include..broadloom in living and dining room, draperies in living and dining room.

6. *attrib.* and *Comb.* **drapery drudge, man**, an artist employed by another artist to paint the drapery in a composition.

1712 Arbuthnot *John Bull* i. i, The Bulls and Frogs have served the lord Strutts with drapery-ware for many years. **1785** J. Trusler *Mod. Times* I. 63 Sales of linen and other drapery goods. **1861** Thornbury *Turner* (1862) II. 103 Rubensten, a drapery drudge to portrait painters. **1894** H. Gamlin *G. Romney* 90 Unlike Reynolds and Gainsborough, he employed no drapery men.

'drapery, *v.* [f. prec. sb.] *trans.* To furnish or cover with, or as with, drapery; to drape.

1824 Byron *Juan* xvi. cii, What beautiful simplicity Draperied her form with curious felicity! **1831** Carlyle *Sart. Res.* i. vii, Not only dressed, but harnessed and draperied. **1858** G. Macdonald *Phantastes* vi. 74 It was festooned and draperied with all kinds of green.

Hence **'draperied** *ppl. a.*

1816 L. Hunt *Rimini* i. 105 A sudden canopy..disparts its draperied shade. **1882** Miss Braddon *Mt. Royal* ix, The lone draperied mantel-piece.

†**'drapet.** *Obs.* [ad. It. *drappetto*, dim. of *drappo* cloth.] A cloth, a covering.

1590 Spenser *F.Q.* ii. ix. 27 Tables fayre dispred, And ready dight with drapets festivall. *a* **1799** Melmoth *Transformation Lycon & Euphormius* (R.), He op'd his gates ..a decent drapet throws O'er her cold limbs.

'draping, *vbl. sb.* [f. drape *v.* + -ing[1].] The action of the verb drape. †**a.** The action of weaving or making into cloth (*obs.*). **b.** The action of adjusting or fixing in artistic folds; manner or style of arranging the drapery.

1483 *Act 1 Rich. III*, c. 8 §1 By the meane of true makyng and drapyng and also of true dying of Wollen Cloth. **1523** *Act 14 & 15 Hen. VIII*, c. 3 The true making and draping of worstedes, sais, and stamins. **1883** *Myra's Jrnl.* Aug., The style of polonaise..owes its popularity to the grace of its draping. **1884** *Pall Mall G.* 27 Oct. 4/1 The draping is long and very simple.

draping ('dreɪpɪŋ), *ppl. a.* Hanging in graceful or 'artistic' folds.

1898 *Daily News* 7 May 8/4 A stiff collar on which are drawn folds of some softly draping stuff. **1903** R. Langbridge *Flame & Flood* xx, Vases with the draping honeysuckle.

drappie, -y (dræpɪ). *Sc.* [f. *drap* Sc. form of drop *sb.* + -ie, -y dim. suffix.] A little drop (e.g. of stimulant).

1789 Burns '*O, Willie brewed*,' We're no that fou, But just a drappie in our ee. **1795** Macneill *Will & Jean* liv, Jean, quite unhappy..Tynes a' heart, and taks a—drappy!

drapure, obs. form of draper.

†**'drasie,** *a. Sc. Obs.* [Perh. connected with drazel.] ? Phlegmatic.

1560 Rolland *Crt. Venus* Prol. 17 Flewme is flat, slaw, richt slipperie and sweir [A]nd drasie, to spit can not forbeir. *Ibid.* 74 He that hes of Watter the natoure, Is daft, and doyld, drasie with small effect.

†**'drassock.** *Obs.* Also ? drapsock, drossock. [Etym. and form uncertain.] ? A drab, an untidy woman.

1573 G. Harvey *Letter-bk.* (Camden) 117 Lowte il-favorid drapsocks died into dun. **1647** Ward *Simp. Cobler* 24 If any man mislikes a bullymong drassock [*v.r.* drossock] more then I, let him take her for all mee.

†**drast, drest.** *Obs.* Forms: *Plural* 1 dærstan, derstan, 2 dersten, 4 darstis, 4–5 drastes, -us, -ys, -en, 4–6 drestes. *Sing.* (*rare*) 4–5 dreste, drast. [OE. *dærstan* pl. (:—OTeut. type **drastjon-* or *-jôn-*), cognate with OHG. *trestir*, MHG. and Ger. *trester* pl. grounds, husks (of grapes), (app. OTeut. **drastiz-*, an *s*-stem): cf. OSlav. *droždiję* and *droštija* lees.] (*mostly pl.*) Dregs, lees; fæces, refuse, residue.

c **1000** *Ags. Ps.* (Th.) lxxiv. 8 Nyle he þa dærstan him don unbryce. *c* **1000** *Sax. Leechd.* II. 98 Getrifula wið ecedes derstan. **11..** *Semi-Saxon Voc.* in Wright 94/1 *Amurca, fex olei*, dersten. **1382** Wyclif *Ps.* lxxiv. 8 The dreste of it is not wastid out. —— *Hos.* iii. 1 Thei..louen the darstis [**1388** draffis] of grapis. **1502** Arnolde *Chron.* (1811) 165 Wel moysted at the rote wt drestis of wyne. **1530** Palsgr. 215/2 Drestes of oyle, *lie dhuille.*

fig. **1388** Wyclif *Isa.* xlix. 6 To conuerte the drastis [**1382** drestus] of Israel. **1494** Fabyan *Chron.* vii. 388 Of Troyans blode the drastes and nat sede.

draste, obs. form of *durst*, pa. t. of dare *v.*[1]

drastic ('dræstɪk), *a.* (*sb.*) [mod. ad. Gr. δραστικ-ός active, efficacious, f. δραστός, vbl. adj. of δρᾶν to do: cf. F. *drastique* (1741).]

1. *Med.* Of medicines: Acting with force or violence, vigorous; esp. acting strongly upon the intestines.

a **1691** Boyle *Wks.* II. 190 (R.) After this single taking of the drastick medicine had done working. **1789** W. Buchan *Dom. Med.* (1790) 213 All strong or drastic purgatives are to be carefully avoided. **1836** *Johnsoniana* i. 24 His friend had prescribed palliative not drastic remedies.

2. *transf.* Vigorously effective; violent.

1808 Bentham *Sc. Reform* 27 In consideration of their too extensive and too drastic efficacy. **1848** Mill *Pol. Econ.* I. 274 Occasions..in which so drastic a measure would be fit to be taken into serious consideration. **1880** McCarthy *Own Times* IV. lxiii. 424 Very comprehensive or drastic schemes.

B. *sb.* A drastic medicine; a severe purgative.

1783 F. Michaelis in *Med. Commun.* I. 318 Large quantities of the pills..acting as a drastic. **1863** Reade in *All Year Round* 3 Oct. 125/1 For want of drastics and opiates.

'drastically, *adv.* [f. DRASTIC + -AL[1] + -LY[2].] In a drastic manner; with drastic remedies or applications; with effective severity.

1850 *Fraser's Mag.* XLII. 345 The poor patient is again pilled and purged drastically. **1877** GLADSTONE *Glean.* I. 169 The spectral letters 'redistribution of seats' operate as drastically as if they were 'Mene, mene, tekel, upharsin'. **1887** *Leeds Mercury* 21 Jan. 4/7 A Bill..which..will deal drastically with the land question.

†**'drasty**, *a. Obs.* Also **dresty**. [f. DRAST + -Y[1]. In several places the *s* has been misread or misprinted as *f*, which was perhaps actually the source of DRAFTY *a.*] Dreggy; *fig.* vile, worthless, 'rubbishy'.

a **1000** *Voc.* in Wr.-Wülcker 238/20 *Feculentus, fece plenus*, dræstiȝ. *c* **1386** CHAUCER *Melib.* Prol. 5 Min eres aken of thy drasty speche. *Ibid.* 12 Thy drasty rymyng [Tyrwhitt, etc., *in both places*, drafty]. **1398** TREVISA *Barth. De P.R.* XVII. clxxxvi. (1495) 727 Erthy partyes and drasty. *c* **1420** *Pallad. on Husb.* I. 195 Olyvys..With drasty [*mispr.* 1873 drafty] wattry fruyt. **1499** *Promp. Parv.* 131/2 Dreggy (*Pynson* dresty) or fulle of drestys, *feculentus.* **1530** PALSGR. 311/1 Dresty, full of drestes, *lieux.*

drat (dræt), *int.* Also *U.S.* drot. [Aphetic f. *'od rot*, for *God rot!*: see ROT *v.* in similar use.] A vulgar form of imprecation, giving vent to annoyance or angry vexation; = 'Hang', 'dash', 'confound'.

1815 *Sporting Mag.* XLVI. 13 'Now drat that Betty', says one of the washer-women. **1857** TROLLOPE *Barchester T.* xxxix, 'Drat their impudence', said Mrs. Greenacre. **1859** THACKERAY *Virgin.* xliv, 'Drat it, Jane, kneel down, and bless the gentleman, I tell 'ee!'

β. **1834** W. G. SIMMS *Guy Rivers* II. 100 Drot the man.. who hasn't the courage to get in a passion. **1846** J. J. HOOPER *Adv. Simon Suggs* ii. 20 Drot it! what do boys have daddies for, any how? **1884** 'MARK TWAIN' *Huck. Finn* xix. 184 Drot your pore broken heart.

Hence **drat** *v.*; **'dratted** *ppl. a.* 'confounded'.

1857 TROLLOPE *Barchester T.* (1861) 326 The quintain was 'dratted' and 'bothered' and very generally anathematized by all the mothers. **1869** MRS. H. WOOD *Roland Yorke* v. (Farmer), If that dratted girl had been at her post. **1878** M. & F. COLLINS *Vill. Comedy* I. 195 The ladies are 'dratting' me, if you know what that means.

drat, obs. 3rd sing. pres. of DREAD *v.*

dratchell, drotchell ('drætʃəl, 'drɒtʃəl). Now only *midl. dial.* [Derivation uncertain. Connexion is suggested with DRETCH *v.*[2], Sc. *dratch* to go heavily and reluctantly, to linger. Cf. also Sc. *drotch* to hang negligently; and see DRAZEL, DROSSEL.] A slovenly, untidy woman; a slut.

1755-73 JOHNSON, *Drotchel*, an idle wench; a sluggard. In Scottish it is still used. **1859** GEO. ELIOT *A. Bede* xx. ¶9 She'll be a poor dratchell by then she's thirty. *Ibid.* xxxvi (end), She's not a common flaunting dratchell, I can see that.

drate: see DRITE.

drau(en, drauȝ(e, drauhe(n: see DRAW *v.*

draught (drɑːft, -æ-), *sb.* Forms: *α.* 3-4 **draht, draȝt**, 4- **draught**; (4 **draȝþe, drauht**, 4-5 **drauȝt(e**, 4-6 **draght(e, draughte, drawght(e, drawt(e**, *Sc.* 5 **drawcht**, 6 **draucht**). *β.* 6 **drafte**, (7 **drauft**), 6- **draft**. [Early ME. *draht* (prob. in OE., though not recorded), corresp. to MDu., Du. *dragt*, ? OHG., MHG. *traht*, Ger. *tracht*, Icel. *dráttr* (:—**drahtr*), verbal abstract from Com. Teut. *dragan* to *draw*. The guttural sound of *gh*, *ch*, is retained in Sc.; in late ME. the word was sometimes *drawt*, whence the frequent (drɔːt) 16-18th c. rimes, but more usually the *gh* passed in pronunciation, through *wh*, into *f*, whence the spelling DRAFT (q.v.) now established in some senses, in which the connexion with *draw* is less obvious.

All the senses in which *draught* is still the accepted or approved spelling are treated here; only those in which *draft* is established appear under that word. Many groups of senses have been derived independently from the verb, so that a satisfactory logical order is almost impossible.]

I. 1. a. The action, or an act, of drawing or pulling, esp. of a vehicle, plough, etc.; pull, traction. ***beast of draught***: a horse or other animal used for drawing a cart, plough, etc. Also *β.* rarely *draft.*

1398 TREVISA *Barth. De P.R.* XVIII. cxv. (1495) 855 The worme drawith and halyth his bodi..wyth many dyuers drauȝtes. *c* **1440** *Promp. Parv.* 131/1 Drawte, or pulle, *tractus.* *c* **1460** *Towneley Myst.* (Surtees) 220 Pulle, pulle!.. Yit a draght. **1523** FITZHERB. *Husb.* §15 The harowe..goeth by twytches, and not alwaye after one draughte. **1633** T. STAFFORD *Pac. Hib.* III. ii. 292 That bogs nor rocks, should forbid the draught of the Cannon. **1707-12** MORTIMER *Husb.* (J.), The Hertfordshire wheel-plough is the best.. and of the easiest draught. **1777** ROBERTSON *Hist. Amer.* (1778) II. VII. 318 The Llama, which was never used for draught. **1873** HELPS *Anim. & Mast.* i. (1875) 8 Beasts of draught and of burden.

β. **1801** *Trans. Soc. Arts* XIX. 295 (This Crane) having a two-fold principle..making a perpendicular draft, and discharging the load at the same time.

†**b.** Drawing of breath. *Obs.*

1490 CAXTON *Eneydos* xxii. 82 [IV. 463] This byrde.. syngyng of fyne manere in grete draughtes and of a longe brethe his right sorowfull songe.

c. Drawing motion or action.

1851 *Offic. Catal. Gt. Exhib.* I. 401 Chaff-cutter..the shaft..being within the range of the long-way of the mouth-piece, gives the knives about 24 times the usual amount of draught, and causes them to cut, instead of chopping.

2. That which is drawn. †**a.** A load. *Obs.*

a **1300** *Cursor M.* 21266 (Cott.) Four ar þai tald, þe wange-listes, þat draues þe wain þat es cristes, O þaim i sal tell.. Quat þai bitaken, and quat þair draght. *c* **1470** HENRY *Wallace* IX. 1610 Dicson suld tak..his hors..a drawcht off wod to leid. **14..** *MS. Douce* 291, lf. 7 (Halliw.) The whiche ..bere and drawe draghtes and berthennes.

b. A quantity drawn: used as a specific measure of something drawn, extracted, or taken up.

1740 DYCHE & PARDON, *Draught*..in Trade, it is so much goods as are carried upon one carriage at a time. **1847-78** HALLIWELL, *Draught*..sixty-one pounds weight of wool. **1881** RAYMOND *Mining Gloss.*, *Draught* (S. Staff.), the quantity of coal raised to bank in a given time. **1893** *Labour Commission* Gloss. s.v., In the salt industry, a draught is the quantity of salt taken out of a pan each time the pan is cleared; sometimes..this drawing takes place once or twice a day.

†**3.** A drawbridge. *Obs.*

13.. *Gaw. & Gr. Knt.* 817 þay let doun þe grete draȝt. *c* **1440** *Partonope* 1636 The porter lete the draught down falle.

4. Something used in drawing or pulling, as harness for horses to draw with: see quots.

1483 *Wardr. Acc. Edw. IV* in *Antiq. Rep.* (1807) I. 43 The chiefe chare of the Quene..with v. paire of draughts. **1552** HULOET, *Drawghte* to drawe vp water after the sorte of a gybet with a paile at the one ende. **1706** PHILLIPS (ed. Kersey). **1765** A. DICKSON *Treat. Agric.* v. (ed. 2) 173 That part of the shoulders of the horses, to which the draught is fixed. **1851** *Offic. Catal. Gt. Exhib.* I. 395 Set of box whipple-trees, or two-horse draughts.

5. A team of horses or other beasts of draught, together with that which they draw. Now only *dial.*

1523 FITZHERB. *Husb.* §22 An housbande can not conuenyentlye plowe his lande, and lode out his dounge bothe vppon a daye, with one draughte of beastes. **1644** in Rushw. *Hist. Coll.* V. 649 The officers and souldiers shall be accomodate with draughts in their march. **1774** *Beverley & Hessle Road Act* ii. 15 Any person..keeping a team or teams, draught or draughts. **1891** ATKINSON *Moorland Par.* 39 A stone waggon with a team,—a 'draught' we call it in our North Yorkshire Vernacular—of no less than 20 horses and oxen attached to it.

II. 6. *fig.* Drawing, attraction; tendency, inclination, impulse. *arch.* †*β.* also *draft.*

a **1300** *Body & Soul* 85 (Mätz.) To sunne and schame [it] was thi drauȝt. **1432** *Paston Lett.* No. 18 I. 31 For the goode reule..of the Kynges persone, and draught of him to vertue and connyng. **1758** W. RICKITT *Jrnl.* 73, I felt a draught to visit New England. **1829** CARLYLE *Misc.* (1857) II. 81 A draught towards the Deep, a commencing giddiness.

β. **1596** SPENSER *F.Q.* IV. ii. 10 He..by his false allurements wylie draft Had thousand women of their loue beraft. *a* **1775** J. CHURCHMAN *Life* (1780) 37, I felt a secret gentle draft to visit to meetings in the back parts of Chester.

III. 7. a. The act of drawing a net for fish, or (quot. 1205) for birds.

c **1205** LAY. 29259 Sparewen þerto liht. And he a þan uorme drahte Swið monie he ilahte. **1526-34** TINDALE *Luke* v. 4 Let slippe youre nettes to make a draught. **1677** HALE *Prim. Orig. Man.* II. ix. 208 Upon the draught of his Pond, not one Fish was left. *a* **1711** KEN *Hymns Festiv.* Poet. Wks. 1721 I. 362 Full three Thousand..At but one Draught he caught. **1823** J. F. COOPER *Pioneers* xxiii, Eager to witness the draught of the seine.

b. A place where a net is wont to be drawn. (Also *draft.*)

1895 *Daily News* 4 Feb. 8/5 Severn Salmon Fishing..the netting operations were greatly interfered with by masses of ice..and several favourite drafts were quite frozen over.

8. The quantity of fish taken in one drawing of the net; a take. *β.* rarely *draft.*

1387 TREVISA *Higden* (Rolls) III. 67 Som fischeres solde a drauȝte of fische wiþ þe nettis. **1526-34** TINDALE *Luke* v. 9 He was vtterly astonyed..at the draught of fisshe which they toke. **1635** PAGITT *Christianogr.* 241 This was a great draught in so short a time, and such as Saint Peter himselfe never made the like in all his life. **1833** HT. MARTINEAU *Cinnamon & Pearls* i. 13 To secure a good draught of fish.

β. **1790** BURKE *Fr. Rev.* Wks. V. 351 It has the whole draft of fishes in its drag-net.

9. A measure of weight of eels, equal to 20 lbs.

1859 SALA *Tw. round Clock* (1861) 18 Eels are sold by the 'draft' of twenty pounds weight. **1891** *Times* 28 Sept. 4/2 Live eels, 20*s.* per draught; dead eels, 14*s.* per draught.

IV. †**10.** The drawing of a bow; a bowshot; also, the distance which a bow can shoot. See also BOW-DRAUGHT. *Obs.*

c **1330** R. BRUNNE *Chron. Wace* (Rolls) 862 Wyþ þat schote his ffader he slow; Al vnwylland þat draught he drow. *c* **1400** MAUNDEV. (Roxb.) xxv. 118 þe ferthe commez behind him, as it ware ane arow draght. *c* **1400** *Destr. Troy* 1224 Lamydon..with-drogh hym A draght. **1581** STYWARD *Mart. Discipl.* I. 44 That euerie man haue a good and meete Bowe according to his draught and strength. **1605** CAMDEN *Rem.* (1637) 209 Geoffray..at one draught of his bowe.. broched three feetlesse birds called Allerions.

†**11.** The drawing or sweep of a weapon; a stroke, a blow. *Obs.*

c **1320** *Sir Beues* (MS. A) 868 Sum kniȝt Beues so ofrauȝte þe heued of at þe ferste drauȝte. *a* **1400** *Octouian* 1666 No man ne myghte with strengthe asytte Hys swordes draught. *c* **1460** J. RUSSELL *Bk. Nurture* 388, xij. draughtes with þe egge of þe knyfe þe venison crossande. **14..** *Prose Legends* in *Anglia* VIII. 109 Sche..smitith þe grounde with hir heed wiþ a meruaylous draughte.

12. The drawing of a saw through a block of wood or stone; hence a measure of sawyers' work.

1404 *Mem. Ripon* (Surtees) III. 205 *note*, In sarracione xv draghtez..11*d.* *c* **1520** *Ibid.* 205 Johanni Henryson sawying waynscottes..xxxij dragttes, 1*d.* j draghth, 16*d.* **1812** J. SMYTH *Pract. of Customs* 175 Scaleboards, from Germany, are packed in bundles, weighing 50 at each draught. **1847-8** H. MILLER *First Impr.* vi. (1859) 91 He was cutting it [a block of Sandstone], by three draughts, parallel to its largest plane into four slabs.

13. = CLOFF, q.v. (Now usually DRAFT, q.v. 1.)

1494 FABYAN *Chron.* VII. 342 Before tyme y[e] weyer vsyd to lene his draught towarde the marchaundyse, soo that the byar hadde...x. or .xii.li. in a draughte to his aduauntage. **1706** PHILLIPS (ed. Kersey), *Draught*..in Trade, an Allowance made in the weighing of Commodities. See Clough.

V. 14. a. The drawing of liquid into the mouth or down the throat; an act of drinking, a drink; the quantity of drink swallowed at one 'pull'. †*β.* rarely *draft.*

c **1200** *Trin. Coll. Hom.* 199 [þe neddre] cumeð to sum welle and drinkeð a draht swo michel þat heo chineð. **1377** LANGL. *P. Pl.* B. xx. 222 To drynke a drauȝte [C. XXIII. 223 drawt] of good ale. *c* **1440** *York Myst.* xxxvi. 240 A draughte here of drinke haue I dreste. **1555** EDEN *Decades* 220 One of these..drunke a bowl of water at a draughte. **1636** MASSINGER *Gt. Dk. Florence* II. ii. Plays (1868) 231/2 Let us take, then, Our morning draught. **1687** SHADWELL *Juvenal* Sat. x. 37 No Poyson is in Earthen Vessels brought; In Gold adorn'd with Gemms beware each draught. **1732** LEDIARD *Sethos* II. VIII. 158 Giscon drank the inflam'd potion at one draught. **1851** *Offic. Catal. Gt. Exhib.* I. 196 It forms a pleasant effervescing draught.

β. **1583** HOLLYBAND *Campo di Fior* 199 Empty thy cuppe ..there is but a litle draft left. **1659-60** PEPYS *Diary* 27 Feb., They brought me a draft of their drink in a brown bowl.

†**b.** A fanciful name for a 'company' of butlers. *Obs.*

1486 *Bk. St. Albans* F vj b, A Draught of boteleris.

15. a. A dose of liquid medicine; a potion.

a **1656** BP. HALL *Occas. Medit.* (1851) 153 On a medicinal Potion. How loathsome a draught is this! **1699** DRYDEN *To J. Driden* 94 Better to hunt in fields for health unbought Than fee the doctor for a nauseous draught. **1762** *Gentl. Mag.* 545 She spreads the couch, prepares the healing draught [*rime* unbought]. **1791** MRS. RADCLIFFE *Rom. Forest* xii, I have ordered him a composing draught. **1828** SCOTT *F.M. Perth* xv, The incipient effects of the soporific draught. **1847** TENNYSON *Princ.* II. 233 To smooth my pillow, mix the foaming draught Of fever.

b. ***black draught***: a purgative medicine consisting of an infusion of senna with sulphate of magnesia and extract of liquorice. (Also *fig.*)

1840 THACKERAY *Paris Sk.-bk.*, *Fr. Fashionable Novels*, Your dull black draughts of metaphysics. **1861** A. K. H. BOYD *Recreat. Country Parson* Ser. II. 155 As if you gave a man a large jug of pure water, and then cast into it a few drops of black-draught. **1883** MISS BRADDON *Gold. Calf* vii, One of my black draughts wanted anywhere?

16. Drawing of smoke or vapour into the mouth, inhaling; that which is inhaled at one breath.

1621 VENNER *Tobacco* (1650) 402 To take 4 or 5 draughts of this fume. **1671** MILTON *Samson* 9 The common prison ..Where I, a prisoner chain'd, scarce freely draw The air imprison'd also, close and damp, Unwholesome draught. **1835** MARRYAT *Jac. Faithf.* i, There is no composing-draught like the draught through the tube of a pipe.

17. *fig.* The 'drinking in' of something by the mind or soul; a portion of something, pleasurable or painful, 'drunk', partaken of, or experienced. (Cf. DRINK *v.*; also CUP *sb.* 9.)

1560 BECON *New Catech.* Wks. (1844) 295 Take him with the hand of thy heart, and chiefly drink him with the draught of thy inward man. **1750** JOHNSON *Rambler* No. 72 ¶1 Make the draught of life sweet or bitter. **1827** POLLOK *Course T.* IX, Quaffing deep draughts of love. **1878** GEO. ELIOT *Coll. Breakf. P.* 357 Ecstatic whirl And draught intense of passionate joy and pain.

VI. 18. The action of drawing out to a greater length, extension, stretching; *concr.* that which is drawn out or spun, a thread. *spec.* in *Cotton-spinning*, etc. the 'drawing' or elongation of the slivers by passing them between pairs of rollers revolving at different speeds. (See DRAW *v.* 56 e). *β.* sometimes *draft.*

c **1400** *Test. Love* III. (R.), The euen drauht of the wyer drawer, maketh the wyer to ben euen. **1577-87** HOLINSHED *Scot. Chron.* (1805) I. 2 The wool..is..spun so fine that it is in manner comparable to the spiders draught. **1719** J. ROBERTS *Spinster* 346 Flowered silk and worsted tammy draughts. **1875** *Ure's Dict. Arts* I. 975 The drawing operation, or draught, is..repeated in all the subsequent processes. **1877-81** W. C. BRAMWELL *Wool-carder* 44 (Cent.) What stands for 'top' in wool manufacture is called first drafts in silk-combing. **1879** *Cassell's Techn. Educ.* IV. 274/1 One yard of lap is drawn out to one hundred yards of sliver. This draught may be increased or diminished.

VII. 19. *Naut.* [See DRAW *v.* 13.] The action of 'drawing' or displacing (so much) water; the depth of water which a vessel draws, or requires to float her. *β.* sometimes *draft.*

1601 SHAKS. *Twel. N.* v. i. 58 A bawbling Vessel was he Captaine of, For shallow draught and bulke vnprizable. **1627** CAPT. SMITH *Seaman's Gram.* xi. 54 Her water draught is so many foot as she goes in the water. **1751** *Act 24 Geo. II*, c. 8 §2 Orders..touching the sizes and Draughts of all Boats, Barges and other Vessels. **1862** M. HOPKINS *Hawaii* 10 For shipping of less draught, pilots are in attendance. **1873** *Act*

36 & 37 Vict. c. 85 §3 A scale of feet denoting her draught of water shall be marked on each side of her stem.

fig. **1882** J. C. MORISON *Macaulay* 27 There was a defect of deep sensibility in Macaulay—a want of moral draught and earnestness.

β. **1796** MORSE *Amer. Geog.* II. 509 They then begin a.. march, the regularity of whose step is essential to the draft of the vessel. **1860** *Merc. Marine Mag.* VII. 115 Her draft of water..was 16 feet 7 inches aft. *Ibid.* 122 The Channel..is the least dangerous for a steamer of draft.

VIII. †20. a. The action of moving along (cf. DRAW *v.* 68); course, going, way. *Obs.*

c **1250** *Gen. & Ex.* 3745 Aȝen he maden here draȝt Al-so ðat skie haued taȝt. *c* **1330** R. BRUNNE *Chron. Wace* (Rolls) 479 Out of Grece þer cam a bole; To Paris bestes was his draught, And wiþ Parys bole he faught. **1470–85** MALORY *Arthur* XVIII. i, They loued to gyder more hotter than they did to fore hand, and had suche preuy draughtes to gyder that many in the Courte spak of hit.

†b. *fig.* Course, way of going on. *Obs.*

a **1327** *Pol. Songs* (Camden) 153 Uch a strumpet that ther is such drahtes wl drawe. *a* **1400** *Sir Perc.* 2160 Thus es the lady so wo, And this is the draghte!

†21. A 'move' at chess or any similar game. [F. *trait*:—L. *tractus.*] *Obs.*

c **1369** CHAUCER *Dethe Blaunche* 653 At the chesse with me she gan to pley, With hir fals draughtes dyvers She staale on me. ? **1370** *Robt. Cicyle* (Halliw.) 54 With a draght he was chekmate. **1412** HOCCLEVE *De Reg. Princ.* (Roxb.) 76. **1474** CAXTON *Chesse* 133 The progressyon and draughtes of the forsayd playe of the chesse. **1594** CAREW *Huarte's Exam. Wits* viii. (1596) 112 He..makes ten or twelve faire draughts one after another on the Chesse-boord. **1656** BEALE *Chess* 3 The draught of a Pawne is only one house at a time.

22. a. *pl.* A game played by two persons on a board of the same kind as that used in chess, which game it somewhat resembles, though of much simpler character, all the pieces or 'men' being of equal value and moving alike diagonally. (In U.S. called *checkers*, in Scotl. *dambrod.*) †*β.* rarely *drafts.*

c **1400** *Destr. Troy* 1622 The draghtes, the dyse, and oþer dregh gaumes. *a* **1602** W. PERKINS *Cases Consc.* (1619) 346 The games of chesse, and draughts. **1791** BOSWELL *Johnson* an. 1756, The game of draughts..is peculiarly calculated to fix the attention without straining it. **1870** HARDY & WARE *Mod. Hoyle* 105 Draughts is entirely a game of mathematical calculation. **1875** JOWETT *Plato* (ed. 2) V. 391 These pastimes are not so very unlike a game of draughts.

β. **1726** FRANKLIN *Jrnl.* Wks. 1887 I. 116, I tire myself with playing at drafts. **1796** OWEN *Trav. Europe* II. 405 The evening was passed in a variety of amusements. Some were occupied at drafts. **1816** KEATINGE *Trav.* (1817) I. 308 They play at what we call Polish drafts.

b. One of the pieces used in this game: = DRAUGHTSMAN 4. (Usually in *pl.*)

1894 'CHEQUERIST' (R. A. Williams) *How to play Draughts well* 14 The Draughts must be so turned that one man will stand on another for 'crowning'.

IX. 23. a. A current, stream, flow.

1601 HOLLAND *Pliny* I. 7 Whiles she [the moon] is turned away, all the draught of light, she casteth thither backe againe, from whence she receiued it. **1688** T. SMITH *Voy. Constantinople* in *Misc. Cur.* (1708) III. 11 There is a vast draught of water poured continually out of the Atlantick into the Mediteranean. **1751** JOHNSON *Rambler* No. 102 ¶12 The draught of the gulph was generally too strong to be overcome. **1819** JAS. WILSON *Compl. Dict. Astrol.* 161 The ..sympathy which causes..the mother to feel the draught flow into her breasts some seconds before the child awakes. **1822** J. FLINT *Lett. Amer.* 75 On approaching rapids, I was usually in the very draught of them, before I could discern the proper channel. **1883** *Syd. Soc. Lex., Draught*..in the breast of a nursing woman.

b. A stream course, a ravine (?). (Also *draft*)

1807 P. GASS *Jrnl.* 101 Having found a tolerable good road except where some draughts crossed it. *Ibid.* 231 But the snow was not so deep in the drafts between them.

c. *Hydraulics.* The area of an opening for a flow of water: see quot. (Also *draft.*)

1874 KNIGHT *Dict. Mech., Draft*..8, The combined sectional area of the openings in a turbine water-wheel; or the area of opening of the sluice-gate of a fore-bay.

24. a. A current of air, esp. in a confined space, as a room or a chimney. Phr. ***to feel the draught***: see FEEL *v.* 6 b. *β.* sometimes *draft.*

natural draught: the current of air that passes through the fire in a steam boiler, etc. without mechanical aid, as distinguished from *blast, forced draught*, that artificially increased either by rarifying the air above the fire or by compressing it below the same.

1768–74 TUCKER *Lt. Nat.* (1852) II. 478 We feel and hear the draught of air, and see the commotions it raises among the trees. **1812–16** J. SMITH *Panorama Sc. & Art* II. 315 The height of the chimney has an important effect on the draught of a wind-furnace. **1844** DICKENS *Lett.* (1880) I. 110 A sore throat; from sitting in constant draughts. **1864** WEBSTER, Blast draught..Forced draught..Natural draught. **1896** *Times* (weekly ed.) 18 Sept. 641/3 The steam trials of the Victorious, battleship, have proved remarkably successful, the contract speed for natural and forced draught having been exceeded.

β. **1812–16** J. SMITH *Panorama Sc. & Art* I. 246 The nearer the throat [of the chimney] is brought to the fire, the stronger the draft will be. **1860** TYNDALL *Glac.* I. xxvii. 207 The drafts from the doors and from the windows. **1873** LONGF. *Wayside Inn, Emma & Eginhard* Interlude 57 That draft of cold, Unpleasant night air.

b. An appliance for creating a draught in a fire-place; a blower. (Also *draft.*)

1874 MRS. WHITNEY *We Girls* vi. 129 The drafts were put on, and in five minutes the coals were red.

X. †25. The drawing of a brush, pen, pencil, or the like, across a surface, so as to make a line or mark; the mark so made; a stroke. [F. *trait*] *Obs.*

c **1250** *Gen. & Ex.* 3624 Besseleel, And eliab, he maden wel ðe tabernacle..Goten and grauen wið witter draȝt. *c* **1305** *Edmund Conf.* 224 in *E.E.P.* (1862) 77 Arsmetrike is a lore..of figours..And of drauȝtes as me draweþ in poudre. **13..** *E.E. Allit. P.* B. 1557 þer watz neuer on so wyse couþe on worde rede..What tyþyng ne tale tokened þo drauȝtes. **1548** THOMAS *Ital. Dict.* (1567), *Lineamenti*, strikes or draughtes of a figure. **1570** BILLINGSLEY *Euclid* I. def. iv. 2 A right line is the shortest extension or draught..from one poynt to an other. **1594** T. B. *La Primaud. Fr. Acad.* II. 119 It is time to draw the last draught of the pensill vpon the face. **1662** STILLINGFL. *Orig. Sacr.* I. i. §19 How to express all kind of sounds, with the several draughts of a pen.

†26. Drawing of figures; delineation. *Obs.*

1551 RECORDE *Pathw. Knowl.* I. xvii, For the manner of their draught wil declare, how many paires of parallels they shall neede. **1622** PEACHAM *Compl. Gent.* xiii. (1634) 127 For your first beginning..in draught make your hand..ready.. in those generall figures of the Circle, ovall, square, &c. **1706** *Art of Painting* (1744) 357 Had his colouring and penciling been as good as his draught. *a* **1734** NORTH *Lives* (1826) II. 211 Painters, and such as practise draught.

†27. a. That which is drawn or delineated; a representation (*of* an object) by lines drawn on the surface of paper, etc.; a drawing, picture, sketch. *β.* rarely *draft.* *Obs.* in general sense.

a **1400–50** *Alexander* 280 In þis oþir draȝt ware deuysid a dusan of bestis. **1584** PEELE *Arraignm. Paris* I. i, A dainty draught to lay her [Venus] down in blue. **1667** H. OLDENBURG in *Phil. Trans.* II. 420 Sufficiently skilled..to make a Draught of the Place. **1759** B. MARTIN *Nat. Hist. Eng.* II. 109 The Draught of an old Saxon Coin. **1779–81** JOHNSON *Ascham* Wks. IV. 621 He..embellished [his pages] with elegant draughts and illuminations.

β. **1585** T. WASHINGTON tr. *Nicholay's Voy.* IV. xxv. 141 Lively drafts of a woman of estate of Græcia, of a Turky woman of meane estate [etc.]. **1658** ROWLAND *Moufet's Theat. Ins.* 930 This sort Pennius referreth to the species of the Wasp, and so he describeth it in his drafts. **1796** STEDMAN *Surinam* (1813) I. i. 19, I took a draft of the unhappy sufferer.

†b. Representation in sculpture; a sculptured figure. *Obs.*

1646 CLEVELAND *King's Disguise* 88 Porches wrought With Sphynxes, Creatures of an Antique draught. **1658** SIR T. BROWNE *Gard. Cyrus* ii. 105 The sculpture draughts of the larger Pyramids of Ægypt. **1686** tr. *Chardin's Trav.* 246 An old Tower built of Free-stone, of which you see the Draught in the Sculpture.

28. a. *spec.* An outline, sketch, or design, preparatory to a completer work of art.

1573–80 BARET *Alv.* D 1166 The first ordinaunce, or first draught, which is done with a cole, *adumbratio.* **1579** FULKE *Heskins' Parl.* 58 The lambe [is] a shadowing figure, like the first draught of a painter. **1710** SHAFTESB. *Charac.* III. *Advice to Author* I. iii, Poetry..resembles the statuary's and the painter's [art] ..in this more particularly, that it has its original draughts and models for study and practice. **1771** SIR J. REYNOLDS *Disc.* iv. (1876) 359 A composition of the various draughts which he had previously made from various beautiful scenes and prospects. **1847** EMERSON *Poems, Day's Ration* Wks. (Bohn) I. 482 Why need I galleries, when a pupil's draught..fills and o'erfills My apprehension?

b. *fig.* Image, representation; something devised or designed like a work of art; slight or preliminary sketch or outline. †*β.* rarely *draft.*

1561 T. NORTON *Calvin's Inst.* I. v. (1634) 12 This way of seeking God..that is, to follow these first draughts which.. doe as in a shadow set forth a lively image of him. **1676** DRYDEN *Aurengz.* v. i. 2195 My Elder Brothers..Rough draughts of Nature, ill-design'd and lame. **1796** OWEN *Trav. Europe* II. 99 The Bay of Naples and its environs form a draught of higher and more finished scenery, than I have yet seen.

β. **1579** TOMSON *Calvin's Serm. Tim.* 92 Yᵉ image of God, yea, yᵉ perfect image..It is not a draft halfe drawen.

29. A sketch in words; a slight or concise account, 'outline', abstract. *β.* sometimes *draft.*

1503 HAWES *Examp. Virt.* Prol. i, The famous draughtes of poetes eloquent. **1569** T. UNDERDOWNE *Ovid's Invect. agst. Ibis* Title-p., A short Draught of all the Stories and Tales contained therein. **1665** *Epitaph at Beverley Minster*, What ere I did beleeve, what ere I tavght..*Resurgam* of them all is the fvll dravght. **1690** LOCKE *Hum. Und.* II. xxi. §73 Thus I have, in a short draught, given a view of our original Ideas. **1712** STEELE *Spect.* No. 302 ¶8 This is but an imperfect Draught of so excellent a Character. **1751** JOHNSON *Rambler* No. 151 ¶6 Unable to compare the draughts of fiction with their originals.

β. **1873** H. ROGERS *Orig. Bible* ii. (1875) 90 Drafts of the future state given by religious systems of human origin.

†30. A plan, map, chart, plot. Also DRAFT, q.v. 4. *Obs.*

1580 HOLLYBAND *Treas. Fr. Tong, Alignement*, a Carde or draught. **1635** N. CARPENTER *Geog. Del.* I. i. 2 The generall draught of the whole Iland. **1701** BOYER (*title*) The Draughts of the most remarkable Fortified Towns of Europe. **1875** TEMPLE & SHELDON *Hist. Northfield, Mass.* 15 This tract of low land was partly included in the Wells's meadow draught.

31. a. A 'plan' of something to be constructed, as a building. Also DRAFT, q.v. 4.

1577 tr. *Bullinger's Decades* (1592) 396 That..there should be lawes concerning draughts, and order of buyldings. **1662** GERBIER *Princ.* Ded., The makeing of a Sumptuous Gate at Temple-Barr, whereof a Draught hath been presented to his Sacred Majesty. **1789** P. SMYTH tr. *Aldrich's Archit.* (1818) 79 Let the architect first make a draught on paper of the intended work. *c* **1850** *Rudim. Navig.* (Weale) 116 *Elevation*, the orthographic draught or perpendicular plan of a ship, whereon the heights and lengths are expressed. It is called by ship-wrights the 'sheer draught'.

†b. A pattern, an outline drawing. *Obs.*

1594 HOOKER *Eccl. Pol.* I. iii. §4 Certaine exemplary draughts or patternes. **1610** HOLLAND *Camden's Brit.* I. 342 When the corne is come uppe a man may see the draughts of streetes crossing one another.

32. A preliminary 'sketch' or outline of a writing or document, from which the fair or finished copy is made. (Now usually DRAFT, q.v. 5.)

1528 *Test. Ebor.* (Surtees) V. 250 Where ther is a draught of a Will of myne. **1659** RUSHW. *Hist. Coll.* III. (1692) I. 238 In the Draught of the Bill..it was further specified [etc.]. *c* **1680** BEVERIDGE *Serm.* (1729) I. 263 This was the first draught of the new covenant. *a* **1715** BURNET *Own Time* (1766) I. Pref. 3 What I wrote in the first draught of this work. **1738** BIRCH *Milton* in M.'s Wks. I. 3 There are two Draughts of this Letter in his own hand writing. **1825** T. JEFFERSON *Autobiog.* Wks. 1859 I. 7, I prepared a draught of instructions to be given to the delegates. **1831** BREWSTER *Newton* (1855) II. xiv. 31 We have found several rough draughts of the changes which he intended to have made upon the scholium.

†33. Something drawn up or devised; a scheme, plan, design, device; a plot; an artifice. *β.* rarely *draft.* *Obs.*

1535 STEWART *Cron. Scot.* II. 101 Richt quietlie..that draucht wes drawin. **1631** RUTHERFORD *Lett.* (1862) I. 70 The counsels and draughts of men against the kirk. **1731** POPE *Ep. Burlington* 103 Greatness, with Timon, dwells in such a draught As brings all Brobdignag before your thought.

β. **1873** H. ROGERS *Orig. Bible* i. (1875) 21 How much this draft of morality..differs from that of heathen nations in general.

XI. 34. The withdrawing, detachment, or selection of certain persons, animals, or things from a larger body for some special duty or purpose; the party so drawn off or selected; *spec.* in military use. (Now usually DRAFT, q.v. 2.)

1703 *Lond. Gaz.* No. 3888/3 Orders..for making a considerable Draught out of our Garison, in order to some Expedition. **1708** J. CHAMBERLAYNE *St. Gt. Brit.* I. III. x. (1743) 245 The several garrisons, from whence Draughts are made for the army. **1780** T. JEFFERSON *Lett.* Writ. 1893 II. 343 We happened to have about 400 draughts raised..and never called out. **1794** T. DAVIS *Agric. Wilts* in *Archæol. Rev.* (1888) Mar., *Draughts*, hazel-rods selected for hurdle-making. **1872** YEATS *Growth Comm.* 31 Draughts of labourers were employed in Spain.

35. *Comm.* **a.** The 'drawing' or withdrawing of money from a stock by means of an order written in due form. (Also DRAFT, q.v. 3.)

1633 T. STAFFORD *Pac. Hib.* I. iii. 29 Fearing..lest some draught might bee drawen upon them. *a* **1715** BURNET *Own Time* (1766) I. 437 To get such draughts made on that bank ..that there should be no money current there. **1758** JOHNSON *Idler* No. 47 ¶3 Payments by Draughts upon our banker. **1838** PRESCOTT *Ferd. & Is.* II. xix. III. 338 Replenishing the exchequer by draughts on his new subjects.

b. A formal written order for the payment of money, 'drawn on', or addressed to, a person holding funds available for this purpose. (Now written DRAFT, q.v. 3 b.)

1730–6 BAILEY (folio), *Draught*, a bill drawn by a Merchant payable by another on whom it is drawn. **1745** FIELDING *True Patriot* Wks. 1775 IX. 335, I have sent you a draught on your tutor according to your desires. *a* **1754** —— *Ess. Char. Men* Wks. 1762 IV. 358 [He] who relieves his friend in distress by a draught on Aldgate pump. [*Note*] a mercantile phrase for a bad note. **1767** BLACKSTONE *Comm.* II. xxx. 467 In common speech such a bill is frequently called a *draught*, but a *bill of exchange* is the more legal as well as mercantile expression. **1790** in Dallas *Amer. Law Rep.* I. 195 Draughts made payable to the party himself. [**1786** —— see DRAFT 3 b.]

XII. 36. The act of drawing forth or out; drawing (as of lots). *rare.*

1807 ROBINSON *Archæol. Græca* III. xvi. 264 To take fatidical verses..written..on little pieces of paper, to put them into a vessel; out of which they drew them, expecting to read their fate in the first draught.

†37. *fig.* Extraction, derivation; something derived, an emanation. *Obs.*

1483 *Festivall* (W. de W. 1515) 76 The synne yᵗ they had of the draught of kynde of our fader Adam and Eve. **1561** T. NORTON *Calvin's Inst.* I. v. (1634) 11 Some say that Bees have part of minde divine, and heavenly draughts.

†38. A passage of a writing; an extract. *Obs.*

1382 WYCLIF *Esther* Prol., The whiche boc the comun making drawith along hider and thider with the torne drauȝtis. *c* **1385** CHAUCER *L.G.W.* 2667 *Hypermnestra*, And seyde, herof a draught, or two. **1601** HOLLAND *Pliny* II. 373 Extracts and draughts out of those authors.

†39. An extract obtained by distillation. (Also *draft.*) *Obs.*

1576 BAKER *Jewell of Health* 230 b, To the draft or substance of the hearbs let the proper water be poured.

40. The action of drawing liquor from a vessel; the condition of being ready to be so drawn.

c **1440** *Promp. Parv.* 131/1 Drawte of..lycoure owte of a wesselle. **1851** *Offic. Catal. Gt. Exhib.* I. 234 By this machine, wines, spirits, stout, &c., can be kept on draught.

41. *Cookery.* The entrails of an animal drawn out (cf. DRAW *v.* 50). *Obs.* or *dial.*

14.. *Noble Bk. Cookry* (Napier 1882) 88 Tak the draught of samon and mak it clene and put it in a pot. **1787** MRS. MACIVER in Kitchiner *Cook's Oracle* (1829) 373 Scotch Haggis..mince the draught and a pretty large piece of beef very small. **1825–80** JAMIESON, *Draucht*, the entrails of a calf or sheep, the pluck.

42. A mild blister or poultice that 'draws'.

1828 WEBSTER, *Draught*..18 A sinapism, a mild vesicatory. (So in later Dicts.)

43. *Masonry*, *Arch.*, etc. (See quots.)

1859–76 GWILT *Encycl. Archit.* Gloss., *Draught*, in masonry, a part of the surface of the stone, hewn to the breadth of the chisel on the margin of the stone according to the curved or straight line to which the surface is to be brought. *Ibid.*, In carpentry, when a tenon is to be secured in a mortise by a pin, and the hole in the tenon is made nearer the shoulder than to the cheeks of the mortise, the insertion of the pin *draws* the shoulder of the tenon close to the cheeks of the mortise, and it is said to have a *draught*. **1864** WEBSTER, *Draught*..8 The bevel given to the pattern for a casting, in order that it may be drawn from the sand without injury to the mold. **1881** YOUNG *Every Man his own Mechanic* §1313 Two chisel draughts are made at one side and the end of the stave something like what in joinery is termed a rebate.

44. *Weaving.* The succession in which the threads of the warp are inserted into the heddles of the loom in order to produce the required pattern; the plan of 'drawing' of a warp (see DRAW *v.* 8 b).

1822 A. PEDDIE (*title*), Linen Manufacturer, Weaver, and Warper's Assistant, with Tables, Drafts, Cordings, etc. **1875** *Ure's Dict. Arts* III. 979 s.v. *Textile Fabrics*, As the operation of introducing the warp into any number of leaves [of heddles] is called drawing a warp, the plan of succession is called the 'draught'. *Ibid.* 982 Fig. 1955 represents the draught and cording of a fanciful species of dimity.

XIII. [In sense 46 *withdraught* also occurs, and has been taken by some as the full word whence *draught* has been shortened.]

†**45.** (?) A cesspool, sink, or sewer. *Obs.*

1533 BELLENDEN *Livy* v. (1822) 479 Now..everie privat house hath the awin gutters and sinkes, for voiding of filthie excrementis, quhare before thay had ane commoun draucht. **1594** T. B. *La Primaud. Fr. Acad.* II. 126 Our whole body is within as it were a stinking draught or puddle that emptieth it selfe on euery side as it were by sinks and gutters. **1600** HOLLAND *Livy* I. xi. Notes (1609) 1366 The image of this Cloacina was found in a privie or draught, called Maxima. **1606** SHAKS. *Tr. & Cr.* v. i. 82 Sweet draught: sweet quoth-a? sweet sinke, sweet sure. **1703** T. N. *City & C. Purchaser* Pref. 12 Some make this Place the Draught of their Houses.

†**46. a.** A privy: also *draught-house* (see 48). *Obs.*

?*a***1500** *Wycket* (1828) 7 Christ sayde all thynges that a man eatethe..is sent downe into the draughte awaye. **1513** MORE *Rich. III* Wks. 68/1 This communicacion had he sitting at the draught [**1543** GRAFTON Drafte], a conuenient carpet for such a counsaile. **1530** PALSGR. 215/1 Draught a prevy, *ortraict*. **1607** SHAKS. *Timon* v. i. 105 Hang them, or stab them, drowne them in a draught. **1681** W. ROBERTSON *Phraseol. Gen.* (1693) 501 A draught or Jakes, *latrina*: *secessus*.

β. **1537** in W. H. Turner *Select. Rec. Oxford* 142 [He] borowed a candell.. and serched the drawft and all the chambers on the back side. **1552** HULOET, Draft or Jaques ..*latrina*.

†**b.** Evacuation. *Obs. rare.*

1659 MACALLO *Can. Physick* 6 If in the draught there be found any piece of skin, it signifies the Guts to be ulcerate.

XIV. *attrib.* and *Comb.*

47. *attrib.* **a.** Of beasts: Used for draught or drawing (see 1). *β.* also *draft.*

1466 *Test. Ebor.* II. 285 A draght ox. **1523** FITZHERB. *Husb.* §70 Melch kye and draught oxen. **1642** in Rushw. *Hist. Coll.* III. (1692) I. 777 Draught-Horses..for the Artillery and Baggage of the Irish Army. **1786** BURKE *W. Hastings* Wks. 1842 II. 141 Draught and carriage-bullocks for the army. **1832** G. DOWNES *Lett. Cont. Countries* I. 273 Strengthened with additional draught animals, both horses and bullocks, we commenced the ascent [of the Simplon].

β. **1606** SHAKS. *Tr. & Cr.* II. i. 116 Yoke you like draft-Oxen. **1681** *Lond. Gaz.* No. 1635/4 Five good Draft-Horses. **1847** LEICHHARDT *Jrnl.* Introd. 17, I purchased five draft-bullocks.

b. Of sheep: Drafted or selected from the flock; see DRAFT *sb.* 7.

c. Of liquor: On draught; drawn or ready to draw from the cask: as *draught ale, beer*, etc.

1835 DICKENS *Sk. Boz* (1837) 2nd Ser. 39 A pot of the real draught stout. **1893** *Daily News* 27 Feb. 4/7 Whisky will keep, and draft ale will not. **1971** *Daily Tel.* 13 May 13/6 Draught beer..is brewed from hops, malt and yeast and is served either by tap or by hand (suction) pump directly from the barrel.

d. Of a document: Drawn up as a preliminary or rough copy. (Commonly DRAFT, q.v. 7 b.)

1878 SEELEY *Stein* II. 293 The document resembles closely..the draught Proclamation. *Ibid.* III. 323 In the form of a draught Act of Federation.

48. *Comb.* **a.** in sense 1 (pull, traction), as *draught-bar, -equalizer, -harness, -pole, -rod, -rope, -spring*; **b.** in other senses, as *draught-phial* (15), *-player, -playing* (22), †*-raker* (46), *-furnace, -regulator* (24). **c.** Special combs. **draught-board**, the board on which the game of draughts is played; **draught-box** (see quot.); †**draught-boy** = DRAW-BOY; †**draught-breadths** *sb. pl.*, ? the traces of a vehicle; †**draught-chamber**, a chamber to withdraw or retire to, a private room; **draught-compasses** *sb. pl.* (see quot.); **draught-dog** = *draught-hound*; **draught-engine**, the engine over the shaft of a coal-pit or mine; **draught-excluder**, a device for excluding draughts; **draught-hole**, a hole by which air is admitted to a furnace; **draught-hook** (see quots.); †**draught-hound**, a hound used for tracking men or beasts by the scent [see DRAW *v.* 74]; †**draught-house**, a privy (= sense 46); **draught-line**, a line on a ship marking the depth of water she draws; **draught-net**, a net that is drawn for fish; **draught-proof** *a.*, fitted so as to be proof against draughts; hence **draught-proof** *v. trans.*; **draught-screen**, a screen for keeping off draughts; **draught-scroll**, a scroll for regulating the draught of the roving on a spinning-mule; **draught-spring**, a spring inserted between the tug or trace of a draught-animal and the car, wagon, or other load, so as to relieve the strain at starting, etc.; **draught-tube** (see *draft tube* s.v. DRAFT *sb.* 7 d); †**draught-vice**, some machine or vehicle for drawing a load; **draught-way**, a way along which something is drawn; a passage for a draught or current of air; †**draught-well**, a draw-well. Also DRAUGHT-BRIDGE, etc.

1874 KNIGHT *Dict. Mech.*, **Draft-bar*. 1. A swingle-tree. 2. The bar of a railway-car with which the coupling is immediately connected. **1726** FRANKLIN *Jrnl.* Wks. 1887 I. 104 All this afternoon I spent..at the *draft-board. *a* **1833** LAMB *Last Essays of Elia* (Ainger 218) In..books which are no books..I reckon court calendars, directories, pocket-books, draught-boards bound and lettered on the back. **1874** KNIGHT *Dict. Mech.*, **Draft-box*..an air-tight tube by which the water from an elevated wheel is conducted to the tail-race. **1687** *Lond. Gaz.* No. 2301/4 A Patent..unto Mr. Joseph Mason, for his new invented Engine, which saves all Weavers the Trouble..of a *Draft-boy. **1617** MARKHAM *Caval.* v. 54 The *draught-breadthes or Coach treates, which extend from the breast of the Horse to the bridge-tree of the Coach. **1453** MARG. PASTON in *Paston Lett.* No. 185 I. 250, I have take the mesure in the *draute chamer, ther as ye wold your cofors and cowntewery shuld be sette. **1463** *Bury Wills* (Camden) 22 The chambyr abovyn the kechene, with the drawgth chambyr longyng therto, with the esement of the prevy longgyng thereto. **1706** PHILLIPS, **Draught-Compasses*, a sort of Compasses with several moveable Points, to make fine Draughts of Maps, Charts..etc. **1656–7** in *7th Rep. Hist. MSS. Com.* App. 575/2 A couple of whelps of the blood-hound strain to make *draught-dogs. **1884** SYMONS *Geol. Cornwall* 196 To increase the efficiency of the *draught engine and to reduce the cost of fuel. **1874** KNIGHT *Dict. Mech.*, **Draft-equalizer*, a treble tree; a mode of arranging the whiffletrees when three horses are pulling abreast, so that all possess an equal leverage. **1859** G. MEASOM *Illustr. Guide Lanc. & Carlisle Railways* 118 (Advt.), *Draft excluders. **1895** *Army & Navy Co-op. Soc. Price List* 15 Sept. 187 Patent Draught Excluder. This simple invention consists of a roller covered with plushette, which revolves between two brass brackets when the door is opened or closed. **1909** *Lady's Realm* July 271/2 A most effectual draught excluder. **1548** HALL *Chron.*, *Hen. VIII*, 3 The saied Chariotes, and the *draught harnesses. **1854** RONALDS & RICHARDSON *Chem. Technol.* (ed. 2) I. 99 Above the sole of the furnace are three rows of *draught holes. **1721** BAILEY, *Draught Hooks. **1753** CHAMBERS *Cycl. Supp.* s.v., Large hooks of iron fixed on the cheeks of a cannon carriage, two on each side..called the fore and hind Draught-hooks ..Used for drawing a gun backwards or forwards by men with strong ropes, called Draught-ropes. **1853** *Catal. R. Agric. Soc. Show* 2 A neck collar for..Farm Harness..has the draft-hook attached, and requires no hames. **1598** FLORIO, *Bracco*, a beagle, a hound, a spaniell, a blood hound, a *draught hound. **1741** *Compl. Fam.-Piece* II. i. 291 Having their Harbinger, Blood-hound or Draught-hound in Readiness, they begin the Chace. **1594** J. KING *On Jonas* (1618) 69 They had..a goddesse for their *draught-houses. **1611** BIBLE *2 Kings* x. 27 They..brake downe the house of Baal, and made it a draught-house [COVERD. prevy house]. **1884** J. PAYNE *Tales fr. Arabic* I. 18 So thou mayest enter the draught-house. **1893** *Act 36 & 37 Vict.* c. 85 §3 The lower line of such..figures to coincide with the *draught line denoted thereby. *a* **1631** DRAYTON *Wks.* IV. 1495 (Jod.) With my *draught-net then I sweep the streaming flood. **1873** *Act 36 & 37 Vict.* c. 71 §14 Any person who shall shoot or work any seine or draft net for salmon. **1834** GOOD *Study of Med.* (ed. 4) III. 396 The dose of this water..was a *draught-phial full, and, consequently, about an ounce and a half. **1886** *Pall Mall G.* 17 Feb. 4/1 The inmates were sitting reading, *draught playing, or otherwise amusing themselves. **1893** *Jrnl. R. Agric. Soc.* Dec. 715 The *draft-pole is pivoted to eyes..attached to the forward face of the main frame. **1908** *Westm. Gaz.* 17 Nov. 4/2 When closed it is entirely *draught-proof. **1929** *Evening News* 18 Nov. 5/1 It seats a pilot and two passengers in an enclosed draught-proof cabin. **1960** *Farmer & Stockbreeder* 12 Jan. 107/3 Use a draught-proof surround for the first 4–5 days. **1960** *House & Garden* Oct. 119/1 Sound *draught-proofed doors and windows. **1965** E. GUNDREY *Foot in Door* xii. 90 Three burly men called on an old lady and offered to draughtproof doors. *a* **1605** POLWART *Flyting w. Montgomerie* 758 Halland shaker, *draught raiker. **1857** COLQUHOUN *Compl. Oarsman's Guide* 32 (Locks). The *draught rod connects the paddle or sluice with the lever, the rack and winch, or the crowbar [that raises it]. **1874** KNIGHT *Dict. Mech.*, *Draft-rod* (Plow.), a rod extending beneath the beam from the clevis to the sheth and taking the strain off the beam. **1907** N. MUNRO *Daft Days* xv. 129 She got him in behind the *draft-screen on the landing of the stair. **1922** F. J. NIVEN *Justice of Peace* x, Behind the draught-screen was the sound of soap-lather and water. **1968** *Listener* 20 June 798/3 He had a wooden draughtscreen..and that was elaborately painted. **1894** C. VICKERMAN *Woollen Spinning* 233 The form of the *draft-scroll has to be varied in diameter at different points to suit the twine at different portions of the draft. **1609** HOLLAND *Amm. Marcell.* XVII. iv. 84 [The Egyptian Obelisk]..beeing layed upon certaine *draught-vices and engines..was..brought into the Circus Maximus. **1835** THIRLWALL *Greece* I. i. 17 Along this line, hence called the *Diolcus*, or *Draughtway, vessels were often transported from sea to sea. **1879** *Cassell's Techn. Educ.* IV. 257/2 The metal being kept perfectly cool by the increased draughtway. *c* **1440** *Promp. Parv.* 131/1 *Drawte welle, *haurium*.

draught (drɑːft, -æ-), *v.* [f. DRAUGHT *sb.*]

1. *trans.* To draw off (a party of persons, animals, etc.) from a larger body for some special duty or purpose. (Now commonly DRAFT, q.v. 1.)

1714 *Lond. Gaz.* No. 5193/4 Who was Draughted into Sir John Gibson's Company of Invalid Serjeants. **1745** *Gentl. Mag.* 664 An order..for draughting out of the train of artillery..130 matrosses. **1758** J. BLAKE *Plan Mar. Syst.* 12 The commander..shall draught off an equal number of men ..to supply their places. **1868** E. EDWARDS *Raleigh* I. xi. 211 The soldiers..were hastily draughted off to their respective vessels.

2. To make a plan or sketch of; *esp.* to draw a preliminary plan of (something to be constructed); to design. (Sometimes *draft*.)

1828 WEBSTER, *Draft*, to draw the outline, to delineate. **1851** KIPPING *Sailmaking* (ed. 2) 138 To have a right understanding of draughting sails, geometry ought to be studied. **1863** LONGF. *Wayside Inn* I. *Building of Long Serpent* iii, Drafting That new vessel for King Olaf.

3. To treat with draughts (of medicine), administer draughts to. *rare.* (Cf. *dose* v.)

1768 FOOTE *Devil on 2 Sticks* III. Wks. 1799 II. 275 Power ..to pill..draught..and poultice, all persons.

4. *Masonry.* To cut a draught upon: see DRAUGHT *sb.* 43. (Also DRAFT, q.v. 3.)

1848 [see *ppl. a.* below]. **1888** *Daily News* 15 Sept. 3/1 They [stones] are draughted all round, but left rough on the outer face.

5. *Weaving.* To draw (the threads of the warp) through the heddles of the loom: = DRAW *v.* 8 b.

Hence **draughted** *ppl. a.*, **draughting** *vbl. sb.*; esp. = DRAUGHT *sb.* 44.

1796 H. HUNTER tr. *St. Pierre's Stud. Nat.* (1799) III. 529 The draughting of their children into the Militia. **1848** W. H. BARTLETT *Egypt to Pal.* xx. (1879) 438 The old wall.. with its large draughted stones. **1878** A. BARLOW *Weaving* 108 (Cent.) The draughting or entering of the warp threads through the headles. **1889** *Anthony's Photogr. Bull.* II. 218 Draftman's tracing paper..can be obtained of most dealers in drafting materials.

¶ For other senses, see DRAFT *v.*

†**'draught-bridge.** *Obs.* = DRAWBRIDGE.

c **1330** R. BRUNNE *Chron.* (1810) 183 Was þer non entre.. Bot a streite kauce, at þe end a drauht brigge. *c* **1380** *Sir Ferumb.* 1952 Þe ȝeates were þanne sone y-schet, & þe draȝt-brige vp y-drawe. *c* **1475** *Pict. Voc.* in Wr.-Wülcker 784/18 *Hoc superfossorium*, a drawtebrygge. *c* **1543** in Turner *Dom. Archit.* III. 78 William Clebe..hath made..at your Tour of London..a new draght brygge.

draughtman ('drɑːftmən, -æ-). *rare.*

1. = DRAUGHTSMAN: esp. in sense 4.

1865 DICKENS *Mut. Fr.* I. iv, Lavinia, rising to the surface with the last draughtman rescued. **1891** E. A. TILLETT *St. George Tombland, Norwich* 36 A bone draughtman, of the type used by the early Norsemen.

†**2.** *nonce-use*, in *morning's draught-man* = a man who indulges in a morning's draught (of liquor); a tippler. *Obs.*

1710 *Tatler* No. 241 ¶2 That the wholesome Restorative above-mentioned [Water-gruel] may be given in Tavern Kitchens to all the Mornings Draught-Men..when they call for Wine before Noon. [In some later edd. printed *morning draughtsmen*, and so quoted by Latham, etc.]

Hence **'draughtmanship** = DRAUGHTSMANSHIP.

1870 *Athenæum* 14 May 648 The artist has rendered the pathos of his subject with perfect skill in draughtmanship and modelling. **1874** *Edin. Rev.* No. 285. 179 As old as the infancy of draughtmanship.

draughtsman ('drɑːftsmən, -æ-). Pl. **-men.** See also DRAFTSMAN. [f. *draught's*, genitive of DRAUGHT *sb.* + MAN.]

1. One whose profession is to make drawings, plans, or sketches; a man employed or skilled in drawing or designing.

1663 [see DRAFTSMAN 1]. **1715** LEONI *Palladio's Archit.* (1742) I. 59 One of the best draughtsmen of our time. **1875** DAWSON *Dawn of Life* iii. 41 The..drawings were executed by Mr. H. S. Smith, the..draughtsman of the Survey. **1888** BURGON *Lives 12 Gd. Men* I. iii. 345 Though he was no draughtsman, he was the author of a large portfolio of portraits.

2. One who draws up, or makes a draft of, a writing or document; one whose office it is to draw up legal or official documents. Now more usually DRAFTSMAN, q.v. 2.

1759 [see DRAFTSMAN 2]. **1825** T. JEFFERSON *Autobiog.* Wks. 1859 I. 40 The laws of which I was myself the mover and draughtsman. **1878** SEELEY *Stein* I. 457 Jurist and parliamentary draughtsman. **1887** *Spectator* 4 June 762/1 The actual draughtsman of the Report.

3. A man employed in drawing or pulling something. *rare.* Also *draftsman*.

1795 A. ANDERSON *Narr. China* in Morse *Amer. Geog.* (1796) II. 509 Fastening one rope to the mast..the draftsmen take the rope on shore along with them.

4. One of the 'men' or pieces used in the game of Draughts; also DRAUGHTMAN, q.v. 1.

1894 'CHEQUERIST' (R. A. Williams) *How to play Draughts well* 8 The writer recommends the 'Royal' Draughtsmen of the British Chess Company, as retaining the upper man when a King is made.

draughtsmanship. Also DRAFTSMAN-. [f. prec. + -SHIP.] The function, quality, or art of a draughtsman; skill in draughting or drawing.

1846 WORCESTER cites SIR J. HERSCHEL. **1862** THORNBURY *Turner* I. 54 Turning the boy's perspective, geometry, and architectural draughtsmanship to some account. **1884** *Athenæum* 6 Dec. 739/2 In all, good, sound draughtsmanship prevails. **1886** DICEY *Eng. Case agst. Home Rule* (ed. 2) 225 Hesitations of statesmanship betrayed themselves in blunders of draughtsmanship.

ˈdraughtswoman. [as DRAUGHTSMAN.] A woman employed or skilled in drawing.

1845 *Lond. Jrnl.* I. 191 [They] are likely to become bold landscape draughtswomen. **1881** MRS. E. J. WORBOISE *Sissie* xli, She is a very fair draughtswoman.

ˈdraught-tree. ? *Obs.* The pole of a wagon or other vehicle, to which the drawing gear is attached.

1580 HOLLYBAND *Treas. Fr. Tong. Le Limon d'vn chariot* ..the beame whereon the iron hangeth in a Waine, the draught tree of a wagon, coache, or carte. *c* **1611** CHAPMAN *Iliad* XXIII. 358 His draught-tree fell to earth, and him the toss'd up chariot threw Down to the earth. **1789** MADAN tr. *Persius* (1795) 130 *note*, *Temo* signifies the beam of a wain, or the draught-tree whereon the yoke hangeth. **1793** SMEATON *Edystone L.* §109 Carts..[having] a very thick axle-tree, upon which is fixed a stout planking or platform, that terminates in a draught-tree for steerage and yoking the cattle to.

draughty (ˈdrɑːftɪ, -æ-), *a.* [f. DRAUGHT *sb.* + -Y[1].]

1. Abounding in draughts or currents of air.

1846 MRS. MARSH *Emilia Wyndham* (L.), In this draughty comfortless room I waited. **1859** R. F. BURTON *Centr. Afr.* in *Jrnl. Geog. Soc.* XXIX. 123 A filmy shade that flutters and flickers in the draughty breeze.

2. Designing, artful, crafty: see DRAUGHT 33. *Sc.*

1822 GALT *Steam-Boat* 189 (Jam.), I could discern that the flunkies were draughty fellows. **1823** —— *R. Gilhaize* I. 162 (Jam.) I'll be plain wi' you, said my grandfather to this draughty speech. **1829** HOGG *Sheph. Cal.* I. 233 Ye're a cunning draughty man.

†**3.** [Perhaps an alteration of the equivocal adj. DRAFTY.] Rubbishy; filthy. *Obs. rare.*

1602 *2nd Pt. Return fr. Parnass.* I. ii. 151 The filth that falleth from so many draughty inuentions as daily swarme in our printing house.

Hence **ˈdraughtiness**, draughty condition.

1871 *Daily News* 13 Jan., It might prove an undesirable habitation for invalids on account of its draughtiness.

drauk, obs. form of DRAWK *sb.* and *v.*

draunt, var. of DRANT.

drave (dreɪv). *Sc.* [northern form of DROVE:—OE. *dráf.*] A fishing expedition in which several men take part, each supplying a net and receiving a share of the profits made. Later, A haul (of fish); also, a shoal.

1733 P. LINDSAY *Interest Scot.* 202 Artificers, Day-labourers, and Farmers Servants that live near the Coast.. make it a Condition with their Masters, to be allowed the Drave to themselves. **1769** *De Foe's Tour Gt. Brit.* IV. 18 An Adventure of this Kind is called a *Drave*..two or three Fishermen associate five or six Landmen, for there are commonly eight or nine Men to a Boat. **1793** *Statist. Acc. Fifesh.* IX. 445 (Jam.) The Drave, as it is here called, was seldom known to fail. **1854** *Phemie Millar* I. 224 Phemie loved the stir and excitement of the great herring drave.

drave, obs. or arch. pa. t. of DRIVE *v.*

†**ˈdravel,** *v. Obs.* Also 6 dravil, drevil, drefle. [Mätzner suggests connexion with ON. *drafa* to talk indistinctly, *drafl* tattle.] *intr.* To sleep unsoundly, have troubled sleep; ? to talk in one's sleep.

13.. *Gaw. & Gr. Knt.* 1750 In dreȝ droupyng of dreme draueled þat noble. **1513** DOUGLAS *Æneis* VIII. Prol. 1 Of drefling [*ed.* **1553** dreuilling] and dremis quhat dow it to endyt? *Ibid.* X. xi. 96 Quhen mennis myndis oft in dravilling gronis. *Ibid.* XII. xiv. 52 Quhen langsum dravillyng [*ed.* **1553** dreuillyng] on the onsound sleip Our ene oursettis.

dravel, obs. form of DRIVEL.

dravick: see DRAWK *sb.*

Dravidian (drəˈvɪdɪən), *a.* and *sb.* [f. Skr. *drāvida* pertaining to *Draviḍa*, name of a province of southern India. (See TAMIL etym.)]

A. *adj.* Of or pertaining to a non-Aryan people found in southern India and Ceylon, or their languages.

1856 R. CALDWELL *Compar. Gram. Dravidian Lang.* 527 This shepherd people..gradually merged in the mass of the Drâvidian race. **1871** E. BALFOUR *Cycl. India* (ed. 2) II. s.v. *India* 39/2 That geographical distribution of the Kol and Dravidian languages. **1902** *Encycl. Brit.* XXX. 419/2 The languages spoken [in the Madras Presidency]—all of the Dravidian family—are Telugu in the north-east, Tamil in the south, Malayalam in the west, and Canarese in the central plateau. **1959** [see ASHRAM]. **1961** BURROW & EMENEAU (*title*) A Dravidian etymological dictionary.

B. *sb.* **1.** A member of this people or linguistic group.

1856 R. CALDWELL *Compar. Gram. Dravidian Lang.* 527 The builders of the cairns had settled in India earlier than the Drâvidians. **1871** E. BALFOUR *Cycl. India* (ed. 2) II. s.v. *India* 42/1 The uncivilized Dravidian speaking tribes are genuine Dravidians who have in a great measure escaped the culture which the more exposed tribes have received. **1884** D. AUBREY *Lett. fr. Bombay* 149 Every scheme appears to have been tried to draw the Hindoo, the Iranian, the Jain, the Dravidian to Christ. **1919** H. G. WELLS *Outl. Hist.* 79/1 The Himalayas etc. divided off the Dravidians from the Mongolians. **1924** A. HUXLEY *Little Mexican* 58 Two expatriated Hindus and a couple of swarthy meridional Frenchmen, who might pass at a pinch as the Aryan compatriots of these dark Dravidians. **1928** C. DAWSON *Age of Gods* iv. 82 The Dravidian was pictured as a mere jungle-dwelling savage.

2. Any of the group of languages spoken by this people.

1856 R. CALDWELL *Compar. Gram. Dravidian Lang.* 48 The Drâvidian vocabularies have borrowed largely from the Sanscrit... The Sanscrit, in some instances, has not disdained to borrow from the Drâvidian. **1862** *Jrnl. Amer. Oriental Soc.* VII. 297 We should have expected sound philological method, if anywhere, in the comparison of Dravidian and Sanskrit, considering the accessibility of the material. **1871** [see B. 1 above]. **1928**, **1934** [see C below].

C. *Comb.*, as ***Dravidian-speaking***.

1871 [see B. 1 above]. **1928** C. DAWSON *Age of Gods* iv. 83 The modern Dravidian-speaking Brahui. **1934** *Discovery* Feb. 44/1 The important distinction is that between the Aryan and Dravidian-speaking peoples, which broadly set off northern India against the south.

Dravidic (drəˈvɪdɪk), *a.* [f. *Draviḍa*: see prec. and -IC.] = prec. adj.

1888 *Amer. Antiquarian* X. 59 They first entered India, became mingled with the Dravidic race, and afterward were driven out.

draw (drɔː), *v.* Pa. t. drew (druː); pa. pple. drawn (drɔːn). Forms: see below. [A Common Teut. strong vb. of 6th ablaut series: OE. *draȝan*, *dróȝ* (*dróh*), *draȝen* = OS. *dragan*, OHG. *tragen*, ON. *draga*, Goth. (*ga*)*dragan*: only in OE. and ON. with the sense 'draw, pull'; in the other langs. with that of 'carry, bear'.

On account of the phonetic development of original *g* in English, the modern conjugation deviates much from the normal type (as in *shake*, *shook*, *shaken*); the *g* of the present stem having passed through the labialized guttural spirant (γ^w), to (w), *draȝ-*, *draȝ-*, *drauȝ-*, *drawȝ-*, *drawh-*, *draw-*. The same happened in ME. in the pa. t, where *dróȝ*, *dróh*, became *droȝ*, *drouȝ*, *drowȝ*, *drowh*, *drough*, *drow*; but this was supplanted in 14–15th c. by *drew*, app. by assimilation to the originally reduplicated verbs of the series *blow*, *blew*, *blown*, and prob. first in the northern dialect, where these verbs retained their original *-áw* (*blaw*, *blew*, *blawen*; so *draw*, *drew*, *drawen*). (Through the modern pronunciation of *ew*, after *r*, as (uː), *drew* is now pronounced as the historical *drough* would have been, if it had survived.) In OE. the 2nd and 3rd sing. pres. Ind. had umlaut, *drǽȝst*, *drǽhst*, *drǽȝþ*. This was probably the origin of the by-form *dray-* of the present stem: see A. 1 *β*. (A weak pa. t. and pple. *drawed* is occasional from 16th c., and freq. in illiterate speech.)]

A. Inflexional Forms.

1. *Present stem.* α. 1 **draȝ-**, 2–4 **draȝ**, (**drach-**), 3 **draȝh-**, **drah-**, 3–5 **drauȝ-**, 4–5 **drauh-**, **dragh-**, 5 **drawȝ-**, (4–6 **drau-**), 3- **draw-**.

c **897** K. ÆLFRED *Gregory's Past.* lvi. (1871) 431 Hit mon drǽȝþ. *a* **1000** *Guthlac* 699 (Gr.) Ongon..draȝan. *c* **1200** *Trin. Coll. Hom.* 29 And swo draȝen hem to hire. *Ibid.* 149 Louerd drah me after þe. *Ibid.* 258 Louerd drauȝ us neor þe. *c* **1200** ORMIN 15394 To draȝhenn hemm till hellegrund. *a* **1225** *Leg. Kath.* 1991 þe oþre walden drahen hit. *c* **1275** LAY. 1338 Seyles [to] drawe to toppe. *a* **1300** *Cursor M.* 21264 (Cott.) Four ar þai..þat draues [*v. rr.* draghis, draus, drawe] þe wain. *c* **1340** *Gaw. & Gr. Knt.* 1031 þere he draȝez hym on-dryȝe. **1393** LANGL. *P. Pl.* C. III. 190 Oure cart shal he drawe. **1540** *Ludlow Churchw. Acc.* (Camden) 3 To draue the clothe. **1552** HULOET, Draw as a paynter doth.

β. 3 **dreih-**, **drei-**, **drey-**, **drai-**, 5–6 **dray-**.

a **1225** *Juliana* 30 Elewsius..het..dreihen [*v.r.* dreaien] hire into darc hus. *a* **1225** *Leg. Kath.* 2237 Gultelese, leaden And dreien to deaðe. *c* **1275** *Pains of Hell* 89 in *O.E. Misc.* 149 And dreyeþ heom in-to a wel. *c* **1460** *Towneley Myst.* (Surtees) 49 When his tyme begynnys to day, I rede no man fro hym dray. **1523** FITZHERB. *Surv.* ix. (1539) 13 To dray any water like a pompe.

2. *Past tense.* α. 1 **dróȝ**, **dróh**, 2–4 **droȝ**, **droȝh**, **droh** (3 **drohh**), 3–4 **drou**, 3–5 **drow**, 4–5 **drogh**, **drouȝ**, **drowȝ**, **drowgh**, **drowh**, **drough** (**droch**, **droow**, **dro**).

c **950** *Lindisf. Gosp.* John xxi. 11 Simon Petrus..droȝ þæt nett on eorðe. *c* **1200** ORMIN 8704 Horrs off fir itt droȝhenn. *Ibid.* 11907 He drohh þær forþ þe bokess lare. *Ibid.* 14675 Abraham..droh hiss swerd. *a* **1225** *Ancr. R.* 110 Vor hore uorlorennesse þet drowen him to deaðe. *c* **1250** *Gen. & Ex.* 3909 Ðis water him on-sunder droȝ. *c* **1275** LAY. 16058 þou drohe to þe vncouþe leode. *a* **1300** *Cursor M.* 4387 (Cott.) Sco drou [*v.r.* droghe] his mantel. *Ibid.* 24056 (Edin.) þat þi son þar droch in place. **1382** WYCLIF *Jer.* xxxi. 3 Y rewende droȝ thee. *a* **1400** *Prymer* (1891) 106 He that droow me out of the wombe. *c* **1400** *Destr. Troy* 5290 And dro hym fro dethe. *Ibid.* 6207 Two dromondarys drowe hit. *c* **1430** *Pilgr. Lyf Manhode* III. lviii. (1869) 171, I..drowh my bordoun to me. **1480** CAXTON *Chron. Eng.* vi. 12 Wolues..al to drow hym. *c* **1500** *Mery Jest Mylner Abyngton* 239 in Hazl. *E.P.P.* III. 109 At that worde the clarke loughe, And by the voice to her he drough.

¶In the following either a scribal error for *droȝe*, or confused with pa. t. of DREE *v.*

a **1400–50** *Alexander* 3629 Cursoures þaim dreȝe. *Ibid.* 5554 þai dreȝe him vp to þe drye.

β. 4- **drew** (4 *Sc.* **drewch**, 5 **drw**, 5–6 **drewe**, **dreue**, **drue**).

c **1320** *Sir Tristr.* 1299 Riche sail þai drewe. *c* **1400** *Beryn* 170 þey drewȝ to dynerward, as it drew to noon. *c* **1489** CAXTON *Blanchardyn* v. 23 The wounde that drue hym toward to dethe. **1494** FABYAN *Chron.* VII. 352 Than the barons dreue towarde London. **1568** GRAFTON *Chron.* II. 24 They drewe together. *Ibid.* 155 He drue more and more of his people into the Citie. **1594** SHAKS. *Rich. III*, I. iii. 176 And with thy scornes drew'st Riuers from his eyes.

γ. **drawed.**

1619 N. BRENT tr. *Sarpi's Hist. Counc. Trent* (1676) 134 There was no..abuse which drawed not after it [etc.]. **1767** *Ann. Reg.* X. Characters 204/1 [He] wire-drawed the books of Moses into a complete system of natural philosophy.

3. *Pa. pple.* 1 **draȝen**, 2–3 **draȝen**, 4–5 **draghen**, **drauen** (4 **drauhen**, **dragh(e**, 4–6 **draun(e**, **drawen** (4–5 **-in**, **-yn**, **ydrawe**, **drawe**, **draw**), 6- **ydrawne**, 6–7 **drawne**, 7- **drawn**.

1127 *O.E. Chron.*, Eall þæt þa beon draȝen. *c* **1250** *Gen. & Ex.* 13 Ðis song is draȝen on Engleis speche. *a* **1300** *Cursor M.* 20061 (Edin.) In oþir inglis was it drawin [*v. rr.* draun, drawen]. **13..** *Guy Warw.* (A.) 4499 Toward Inglond is Gij y-drawe. *c* **1330** R. BRUNNE *Chron.* (1810) 183 Drauhen ouer þe gate. *a* **1340** HAMPOLE *Psalter* xix. 8 þai ere draghen aboute. *c* **1374** CHAUCER *Anel. & Arc.* 70 The noble folke were to the toune ydrawe. *c* **1450** tr. *De Imitatione* II. ix. 50 To be drawe oute of himself. *c* **1550** *Lucrece & Euryalus, Envoy*, Thys boke in Englysh drawe was. **1581** HOLLYBAND *Campo di Fior* 273 It shalbe drawen with horses. **1646** P. BULKELEY *Gospel Covt.* I. 110 They had drawn their curtains.

β. 3 **dreien**, 4 **drayn**, **drain**, 5 **dreyn.**

c **1320** *Sir Tristr.* 1575 Wiþ his swerd al drain. *a* **1440** *Sir Degrev.* 665 When the lordys were drawin [*rimes* leyn, aȝeyne].

γ. Weak forms.

c **1330** *Arth. & Merl.* 6828 Thai were abrod y-dreyght. **1580** T. WILSON *Logike* 58 b, Now, that we have drawed [*ed.* **1567** drawen] these wordes..so farre.

B. Signification.

General scheme of arrangement:—

I. Of traction (*Generally. **In specific applications. ***With specific objects. ****In transferred and figurative applications). II. Of attraction, drawing in or together. III. Of extraction, withdrawal, removal (*With that which is taken as the object. **With that from which the contents are taken as the object). IV. Of tension, extension, protraction. V. Of delineation or construction by drawing (*To draw a line, figure, formal document, comparison. **To draw a bill or demand note). VI. *refl.* and *intr.* Of motion, moving oneself. VII. In combination with adverbs (e.g. *draw out*).

I. Of simple traction. * *In the general sense.* (The most general word for this; other words, partly synonymous, as *drag*, *haul*, *trail*, *tug*, imply drawing in a particular manner or with special force.)

1. a. *trans.* To cause (anything) to move toward oneself by the application of force; to pull.

c **950** *Lindisf. Gosp.* John xxi. 11 Astaȝ Simon Petrus and droȝ þæt nett on eorðe. *c* **1200** ORMIN 15394 To draȝhenn hemm till hellegrund. *c* **1400** *Sowdone Bab.* 2566 The Babyloynes of his hors him drowe. **1660** F. BROOKE tr. *Le Blanc's Trav.* 140 By drawing threads out of the leaves. **1669** STURMY *Mariner's Mag.* I. 93 Draw your Sight-Vane a little lower down. **1697** DAMPIER *Voy.* I. vii. 165 Canoas.. will not last long, especially if not drawn ashore often and tarred. *Ibid.* xiv. 380 It comes off by only drawing the Cane thro your hand. **1700** S. L. tr. *Fryke's Voy. E. Ind.* 16 A Shark came up to him, and drew him under Water. **1709** ADDISON *Tatler* No. 163 ¶1 He drew a Paper of Verses out of his Pocket. **1786** MAD. D'ARBLAY *Diary* 21 May, I..drew my hat over my face. **1847** A. M. GILLIAM *Trav. Mexico* 255 The buckle of my belt was never disturbed, except to draw it tighter, when I was pinched with hunger. **1870** E. PEACOCK *Ralf Skirl.* III. 95 Drawing her father aside for an instant. **1879** DOWDEN *Southey* iii. 71 To draw the pen across six hundred lines.

b. *absol.*

c **1305** *St. Lucy* 105 in *E.E.P.* (1862) 104 Hi schoue and droȝe al þat hi miȝte. **1694** *Acc. Sev. Late Voy.* II. (1711) 131 The Rope of its own accord doth pull or draw very hard.. two such Ropes draw as much as a Man's Strength.

c. *refl.* (with adverbial or other complement). (See also *draw up*, 89 b.)

1885 G. ALLEN *Babylon* i, Mrs. Winthrop drew herself together. **1890** W. C. RUSSELL *Ocean Trag.* I. vii. 141 Wilfrid..drew himself erect. **1893** *Nat. Observer* 23 Dec. 138/1 Ermyntrude drew herself to her full stature.

d. *intr.* for *passive.* To be drawn, or to admit of being drawn. *spec.* in *Founding*, etc. = DELIVER *v.*[1] 12.

1635 QUARLES *Emblems* I. iv. 17 Thy Balance will not draw; thy Balance will not downe. **1697** DAMPIER *Voy.* I. ii. 17 The Line in drawing after him chanc'd to kink, or grow entangled. **1703** MOXON *Mech. Exerc.* 179 That the String may draw tight upon the Work. **1886** MRS. RANDOLPH *Mostly Fools* I. x. 299 The rope drew taut and parted in the middle.

2. a. To pull (anything) after one; to move (a thing) along by traction. Specifically used of a beast of draught pulling a vehicle, a plough, etc.

c **1200** [see A. 2 *a*]. *a* **1300** *Cursor M.* 11654 (Gött.) A waine ..þat drauen was wid oxen tuin. **1503** *Act 19 Hen. VII*, c. 18 Haling or drawing any such Trow, Boat, or Vessel. **1593** T. WATSON *Tears Fancie* iv. (Arb.) 180 In her Coach ydrawne with siluer Doues. **1648** GAGE *West Ind.* xii. 54 They..drew after them stones, earth, timber. **1700** S. L. tr.

Fryke's Voy. E. Ind. 263 We drew their Vessel along after us. **1889** I. TAYLOR *Orig. Aryans* 180 The Egyptians and the Hittites possessed war chariots drawn by horses. *Mod.* A locomotive drawing a long train of wagons.

b. *absol.* or *intr.* esp. of beasts of draught; also *fig.* in phr. ***to draw together***, or ***in one line*** = to 'pull together', agree (*obs.*); also ***to draw with*** = to be in like case with (quot. 1604).

1526 TINDALE *Phil.* ii. 2 That ye drawe one waye..being of one accorde. **1538** BALE *Brefe Comedy* in *Harl. Misc.* (Malh.) I. 215 Drawe only after his lyne. **1546** J. HEYWOOD *Prov.* (1867) 65 We drew both in one line. **1548** HALL *Chron., Hen. V.* 65 b, An Antlop drawyng in an horse mill. **1604** SHAKS. *Oth.* IV. i. 68 Thinke euery bearded fellow that's but yoak'd May draw with you. **1686** *Lond. Gaz.* No. 2147/4 These three [horses] have all drawn. **1775** SHERIDAN *Rivals* I. i, Does she draw kindly with the Captain? **1844** *Jrnl. R. Agric. Soc.* V. I. 171 The horses draw abreast.

c. *intr.* for *passive.*

1660 F. BROOKE tr. *Le Blanc's Trav.* 141 He..puts on a white shirt that drawes on the ground, like persons doing penance with us. **1892** *Field* 19 Mar. 415/2 The Irish outside cars..draw lighter than an ordinary English cart.

3. *transf.* **a.** With the load as object: To convey or carry in a vehicle; to cart; to haul.

c **1290** *S. Eng. Leg.* I. 39/185 Huy drowen þat bodi so mildeliche. **1362** LANGL. *P. Pl.* A. VII. 275 To drawe afeld my donge. **1592** SHAKS. *Ven. & Ad.* 153 Two strengthless doves will draw me through the sky. **1790** COWPER *My Mother's Picture* 49 Where the gardener Robin..Drew me to school..Delighted with my bauble coach. **1844** *Jrnl. R. Agric. Soc.* V. I. 282 The farmers generally draw the hay and coals for the cottagers.

b. With the beast as obj.: To employ in drawing, use for draught. ? Only in *pa. pple.*

1679 *Lond. Gaz.* No. 1423/4 One brown bay Gelding..trots all, and hath been much drawn. **1721** *Ibid.* No. 5996/10 A grey Nag, used to be drawn.

c. *absol.* Of hawks: see quot.

1486 *Bk. St. Albans* A ij, We shall say that hawkys doon draw when they bere tymbering to their nestes, and nott they beld, ne make ther nestes.

** *In specific applications.*

4. To drag (a criminal) at a horse's tail, or on a hurdle or the like, to the place of execution; formerly a legal punishment of high treason.

c **1330** R. BRUNNE *Chron.* (1810) 247 First was he drawen for his felonie, and as a þefe þan slawen, on galwes hanged hie. *c* **1400** *Destr. Troy* 1970 To be..drawen as a dog and to dethe broght. **1460** CAPGRAVE *Chron.* (1858) 287 [Serle was] condempned to be drawe thorow oute the good townes of Ynglond, and aftir to be hangen and quartered at London. **1480** CAXTON *Chron. Eng.* ccxliii. (1482) 288 Juged to be leyd on an hurdel and than to be drawe thurgh the cyte of london to Tiborne. **1548** HALL *Chron., Hen. VII*, 47 After the fassyon of treytours to be drawen, hanged and quartred. **1556** *Chron. Gr. Friars* (Camden) 18 Whane they ware drawne they had ther pardone all and their lyffes. **1568** GRAFTON *Chron.* II. 191 Because he came of the bloud royall ..he was not drawne, but was set upon an horse, and so brought to the place of execution, and there hanged. **1769** BLACKSTONE *Comm.* (1830) IV. vi. 92 That the offender [in cases of high treason] be drawn to the gallows, and not be carried or walk. **1890** T. COOPER in *Dict. Nat. Biog.* XXI. 4/1 [Garnett] was sentenced to be drawn, hanged, disembowelled, and quartered.

†**5.** To pull or tear *in pieces, asunder. Obs.*

a **1300** *Cursor M.* 9060 (Gött.), I war worthi wid hors be drauin. *c* **1420** *Sir Amadas* (Weber) 173 He seyd, the howndes schuld the flesch drawe. *c* **1489** CAXTON *Sonnes of Aymon* iii. 96 Reynawde..made Hernyer to be bounde hys foure membres..to foure horses taylles, and soo he was drawnen all quyck, and quartered in foure peces. **1530** PALSGR. 349 They had rather suffre their lymmes to be drawen in peces. **1700** TYRRELL *Hist. Eng.* II. 902 He was condemned to be drawn asunder by Horses. **1700** *Fryke's Voy. E. Ind.* 276 To be drawn in pieces with Elephants.

6. a. To contract, cause to shrink; to pull out of shape or out of place, to distort.

c **1400** *Lanfranc's Cirurg.* 99 þe crampe..in þe which sijknes cordis and þe senewis weren drawen to her bigynnynge. *c* **1450** *St. Cuthbert* (Surtees) 1074 So þat þe synnes in his ham..was drawen samen. *a* **1691** BOYLE *Hist. Air* (1692) 82 His mouth was so drawn awry, that 'twas hideous to behold. **1777** SHERIDAN *Sch. Scand.* II. ii, She draws her mouth till it..resembles the aperture of a poor's-box. **1847** TENNYSON *Princ.* VII. 114 With all their foreheads drawn in Roman scowls. **1870** SWINBURNE *Ess. & Stud.* (1875) 357 The face smiling, but drawn and fixed. **1892** *Cassell's Fam. Mag.* Apr. 279/1 Artificial teeth..are apt to draw the mouth.

b. *intr.* for *refl.* To contract, shrink.

1530 PALSGR. 527 His skynne draweth togyther lyke burned lether. **1626** BACON *Sylva* §34, I haue not yet found certainly, that the Water it selfe..will shrinke or draw into lesse Roome. **1893** *Temple Bar Mag.* XCVII. 157 Her dark brows drew together over her black eyes.

†**7.** *trans.* To bring together by sewing (edges of a rent, etc.); to mend (a rent); cf. also *draw up*, 89 c, and FINE-DRAW. *Obs.*

1592 GREENE *Upst. Courtier* in *Harl. Misc.* (Malh.) II. 242 Haue they not a drawer..to drawe & seame up the holes so cunningly, that it shall neuer be espied? **1611** COTGR., *Rentraire*..also, to draw, dearne, or sow vp a rent in a garment. *Ibid.*, *Rentraicture*..also, a drawing of rent cloth; a dearning.

*** *With specific objects.*

8. a. *trans.* To pull up (a sail, a drawbridge), pull out (a bolt, an organ-stop), haul in (a net), etc.

c **1275** LAY. 1339 Brutus heþte handli cables, seyles drawe to toppe. *c* **1385** CHAUCER *L.G.W.* 1563 *Hypsip.*, And drough his saylle and saugh hir neuer mo. **1568** GRAFTON *Chron.* II. 326 The gate was shut and the bridge drawen. **1646** JENKYN *Remora* 27 The bridge of mercy will ere long be drawn. **1869** W. LONGMAN *Hist. Edw. III*, I. xvii. 318 He then drew the bolt, the door was opened. **1881** *Scribner's Mag.* XXI. 583/2 If we..draw all the so-called 'stops' [of a great organ]. **1893** *Longm. Mag.* June 120 The net is drawn.

b. *Weaving.* To insert the threads of (the warp) into the heddles in the proper order.

1875 [see DRAUGHT sb. 44].

9. To pull back the string of (a bow) in order to bend it so as to shoot; to bend (a bow). Also, to pull back (the arrow) on the string. Also *absol.*

to draw the long bow: see BOW[1] 4 c; also LONG-BOW.

c **1330** R. BRUNNE *Chron. Wace* (Rolls) 4379 Archers drowe. *c* **1440** *Gesta Rom.* i. 2 (Harl. MS.) þe knyȝt sawe him begynne forto drawe his bowe. **1548** HALL *Chron., Hen. VII*, 19 The Englishmen y[t]..might eyther stand or drawe a bowe. **1594** SHAKS. *Rich. III*, V. iii. 339 Draw Archers, draw your Arrowes to the head. **1611** BIBLE *1 Kings* xxii. 34 A certaine man drew a bow at a venture. **1766–88** GIBBON *Decl. & F.* lvi, Exercised..to draw the bow. **1856** FROUDE *Hist. Eng.* (1858) I. ii. 173 He drew with ease as strong a bow as was borne by any yeoman of his guard.

¶ ***to draw a bead***: to take aim with a gun or rifle: see BEAD *sb.* 5 d.

10. ***to draw bit, bridle, rein***: to pull the reins in order to stop or check the horse; to stop, halt, 'pull up': also *fig.*

1664, 1782 [see BIT sb.[1] 8 d]. *a* **1690** LD. SOMERVILLE *Mem. Somervilles* (1815) II. 349 He..never drew bridle untill he came the lenth of Leads. **1828** TYTLER *Hist. Scot.* (1864) I. 55 Surrey..rode, without drawing bridle, to Berwick. **1840** BARHAM *Ingol. Leg.*, *Leech Folkestone*, Scarcely drawing bit. **1850** *Tait's Mag.* XVII. 51/2 Karolus drew rein in the square.

11. a. To pull (a curtain, veil, cloth, etc.) over something so as to cover or conceal it, or aside or off from it so as to disclose it. Also *fig.* (See also CURTAIN *sb.*[1] 1 b, VEIL *sb.*)

c **1420** *Sir Amadas* (Weber) 74 Over his heyd he drw his hode. **1509** etc. [see CURTAIN *sb.*[1] 1 b]. **1631** GOUGE *God's Arrows* I. xxv. 36 When the curtens were drawne, all the people might see it. **1632** MILTON *Penseroso* 36 And sable stole of cyprus lawn, Over thy decent shoulders drawn. **1701** DE FOE *True-born Eng.* I. 90 Satyr, be kind and draw a silent Veil. **1844** DICKENS *Mart. Chuz.* xii, In a room with all the window-curtains drawn. **1861** *Temple Bar Mag.* I. 307 Let us draw a veil over this dismal spectacle. **1891** *Longm. Mag.* Dec. 167 The sun had gone down, but the blinds had not been drawn.

b. *intr.* for *refl.* = *passive.*

1711 STEELE *Spect.* No. 240 ⁋3 Getting into one of the Side-boxes on the Stage before the Curtain drew. **1894** *Cornh. Mag.* July 38, I remember a carriage..with curtains that drew in front of it.

12. ***to draw the cloth***: to withdraw or remove the table-cloth after a meal; to 'clear away'. (Now *rare* or *arch.*) †Also, in same sense, ***to draw the board*** or ***table*** (*obs.*).

c **1320** *Sir Tristr.* 706 Cloþ and bord was drain [*rimes* bayn, fayn, etc.]. **13..** *Coer de L.* 4623 Aftyr mete the cloth was drawe. **1393** LANGL. *P. Pl.* C. IX. 289 Let hem abyde tyl þe bord be drawe. *a* **1791** GROSE *Olio* (1796) 111 Come here, Wolley, and draw the table. **1823** SCOTT *Quentin D.* xx, When the tables were drawn. **18..** THACKERAY *Haggarty's Wife* (1892) 489 When the cloth was drawn..he would retire to his own apartments. **1861** *Temple Bar Mag.* II. 307 The cloth had been drawn, as the reporters write of public dinners. **1892** *Eng. Illustr. Mag.* Dec. 192/2 People don't even 'draw cloths' any more.

13. a. Of a ship or boat: To displace (so much depth of water); to sink to a specified depth in floating. [So F. *tirer tant d'eau, seize pieds d'eau*, etc. It is not clear what the original notion is here.]

1555 EDEN *Decades* 7 The smauler vesselles which drewe no great depthe entered. **1590** WEBBE *Trav.* (Arb.) 26 She drawes but xj foot water. **1627** CAPT. SMITH *Seaman's Gram.* xi. 54 The Ships that drawes most water are commonly the most wholsome. **1634–5** BRERETON *Trav.* (1844) 5 Two feet more water than the ship drew. **1782** W. GILPIN *Wye* (1789) 59 Our barge drawing too much water to pass the shallows. **1826** *Examiner* 289/1 A boat drawing six inches water. **1892** *Blackw. Mag.* CLI. 321/2 Steamers for the Zambesi..should not draw over 18 inches.

fig. **1601** MARSTON *Pasquil & Kath.* I. 319 You may easily sound what depth of wits they draw.

absol. **1606** SHAKS. *Tr. & Cr.* II. iii. 277 Light Botes may saile swift, though greater bulkes draw deepe.

†**b.** Of the sea or river. *Obs.*

1601 HOLLAND *Pliny* I. 132 There be certaine trenches or channels in it that draw deepe water, wherein they may without danger saile.

14. In *Cricket*, To divert (the ball) to the 'on' side of the wicket by a slight turn of the bat. In *Golf*, To drive (the ball) widely to the left hand. In *Bowls*, to cause (a bowl) to travel in a curve to a chosen spot on the green. Also *intr.* (with the bowl as subject).

1843 'A WYKHAMIST' *Pract. Hints Cricket* 13 A leg-ball between these lines should be drawn or played under-leg. **1857** *Chambers's Information* II. 690 (Cricket) The proper balls to *draw* are those which are pitched somewhat short.. and come up rather within the line of your leg-stump. *Ibid.* 696/2 (Golf) *Draw*, to drive wildly to the left. **1857** HUGHES *Tom Brown* II. viii. (1880) 352. **1868** [see SHOT *sb.*[1] 11 b]. **1893** *Illustr. Sporting & Dram. News* 8 Apr. 156/3 Let him draw the ball or heel it, and the chances are he will drop into a lakelet. **1897** *Encycl. Sport* (1901) I. 126/1 Every bowl..is shaved down very carefully and evenly on one side..the effect being to cause the bowl..to incline and turn (or draw) towards the reduced side. **1902** *Encycl. Brit.* XXVI. 329/1 In drawing..the object is to draw as near as possible to the jack. **1910** *Ibid.*, III. 348/1 Should the jack be driven towards the side boundary, it is legitimate for a player to cause his bowl to draw outside of the dividing string. **1962** *Bowls* ('Know the Game' Series) 24 The drawing shot which finishes resting against the jack is sometimes called the 'dead draw'. **1962** *Times* 25 Aug. 2/6 He drew shot brilliantly.

15. *Billiards.* To cause (a ball) to recoil as if pulled back, after striking another ball.

**** *In transferred and figurative applications.*

16. *trans.* To cause to come, move, or go (from or to some place, position, or condition); to lead, bring, take, convey, put. Also *fig.* e.g. ***to draw into example, precedent, comparison, consequence, practice, allowance***, etc. *Obs.* (exc. as associated with other senses). †***to draw to death*** (also ***of*** (= from) ***life***): to put to death (*obs.*).

c **1200** ORMIN 10392 Ne nohht ne draȝhe icc upponn me To beon bridgume. *a* **1225** *Juliana* 4 Derfliche [he] droh ham to deaðe. *c* **1250** *Gen. & Ex.* 3806 And .iiii. score of liue draȝen. **13..** *E.E. Allit. P.* A. 698 Lorde þy seruaunt draȝ neuer to dome. **1375** BARBOUR *Bruce* I. 628 He in bowrch hys landis drewch. *c* **1386** CHAUCER *Pars. T.* ⁋165 To drawen in-to memorie þe goode werkes. *c* **1450** *Merlin* 17 Than the Iuges drough hem apart, and cleped these other wemen. *c* **1489** CAXTON *Blanchardyn* v. 23 The wounde that drue hym toward to dethe. *c* **1591** in *Lett. Lit. Men* (Camden) 78 Grosse practises..to drawe the wealth of the land into his treasurie. **1608** HIERON *Defence* III. 73 Kneeling..was not drawne into allowance and practise in the Church. **1638** SIR T. HERBERT *Trav.* (ed. 2) 90 Hee alters his intent, and drawes his forces against Rantas. **1832** W. IRVING *Alhambra* II. 22 He hastened to draw him from the seductions of the garden.

†**17.** To construct (a ditch, canal, wall, etc.) from one point to another; to 'lead'. (L. *ducere.*) *Obs.*

c **1400** *Destr. Troy* 11160 With dykes so depe draghen a-boute. **1603** KNOLLES *Hist. Turks* (1621) 89 A navigable ditch or cut, drawne out of the Nile. **1660** F. BROOKE tr. *Le Blanc's Trav.* 377 From this Lake they draw a Channell that sets certain Leather-Engines at worke. **1698** FRYER *Acc. E. India & P.* 37 From the first Point a Curtain is drawn with a Parapet. **1796** MORSE *Amer. Geog.* II. 26 A navigable canal has been drawn lately from Kiel..to the river Eyder.

†**18.** *Cookery.* To pass through a strainer; to bring to proper consistence (cf. *draw up*, 89 d). *Obs.*

c **1420** *Liber Cocorum* (1862) 16 Drauȝe hom thorowghe a streynour clene. *c* **1430** *Two Cookery-bks.* 13 Draw þe same brothe thorwe a straynoure. *c* **1440** *Douce MS.* 55 fol. 39 Draw it and do it in a pott. *a* **1550** in *Vicary's Anat.* (1888) App. IX. x. 227 Drawe the pulpe of them thorough a strayner.

†**19.** To render into another language or style of writing; to translate. *Obs.*

c **1250** *Gen. & Ex.* 13 Ut of latin ðis song is draȝen on engleis speche. *c* **1375** *Lay Folks Mass Bk.* (MS. B.) 32 Intil englishe þus I draw hit. **1450–1530** *Myrr. our Ladye* 2 I haue drawen youre legende and all youre seruyce in to Englyshe. *a* **1547** SURREY (*title*) The fourth Boke of Virgill..translated into Englishe, and drawen into straunge metre. **1569** FENTON (*title*) A Discourse of Ciuile warres..in Fraunce, drawne into Englishe.

†**20.** To bear, endure, suffer, undergo. *Obs.* (App. confused with DREE.)

a **1225** *Juliana* 49 Oþe pine ant te deð þat he droh for mon. *a* **1225** *Leg. Kath.* 1914 Teonen and tintreohen þe alre meast derue þat eni deadlich flesch Mahe drehen and drahen. *a* **1300** *Cursor M.* 16989 (Cott.) þe pine he for me drou [*Gött.* dregh].

†**21.** *fig.* **a.** To adduce, bring forward, appeal to for confirmation (see also *draw forth*, 81 b). **b.** To assign, attribute. **c.** To turn aside to a purpose, pervert, wrest. *Obs.*

a **1300** *Cursor M.* 14651 (Cott.) Him drau i me to mi warand. **1578** TIMME *Caluine on Gen.* 177 Paul draweth the same to all mortal men in all ages. *a* **1599** H. SMITH *Wks.* (1866–7) I. 173 If we cannot draw it to one of these, then we think it fortune. **1628** EARLE *Microcosm.*, *Lasciuious Man* (Arb.) 95 Whatsoeuer you speak, he will draw to bawdry. **1704** SWIFT *T. Tub* Apol., Passages, which prejudiced or ignorant readers have drawn by great force to hint at ill meanings.

†**22.** *Arith.* To add (*to, together*); to subtract (*out of*); to multiply (*into, in*). *Obs.*

c **1425** *Crafte of Nombrynge* (E.E.T.S.) 9 Draw 2 out of 4, þan leues 2. *Ibid.* 18 Drav þat 1 to 6..& þat 1 & þat 6 togedur wel be 7. **1660** BARROW *Euclid* I. xxxv. Schol., Draw 3 into 4, there will be produced 12. **1709–29** V. MANDEY *Syst. Math., Arith.* 13 Two Numbers given, to multiply one by the other, or to draw one into the other. **1811** HUTTON *Course Math.* II. 291 The fluxion of..the continual product of four..quantities..consisting of the fluxion of each quantity, drawn into the products of the other three.

II. Of attraction, drawing in or together.

23. a. To take in (air, etc.) into the lungs; to breathe, inhale; to cause (a draught) to enter, e.g. into a chimney or bellows. See also *draw in*, 82 c.

13.. *Coer de L.* 1780 Unnethe he might draw his blast. **1375** BARBOUR *Bruce* IV. 199 He na mocht His aynd bot with gret panys draw. **1481** CAXTON *Reynard* (Arb.) 17 He drough his breth lyke as one sholde haue deyde. **1544** PHAER *Regim. Life* (1553) D viij b, Great heate in the brest..is quenched in drawing colde ayre. **1637** MILTON *Lycidas* 126 [Sheep] Swoln with wind and the rank mist they draw, Rot inwardly. **1659** D. PELL *Impr. Sea* 271 The Male-stream-well..of Norway..draws water into it during the flood.. with such an avarous indraught. **1732** BERKELEY *Alciphr.* I. §3 Alciphron..stopped to draw breath and recover himself. **1810** SCOTT *Lady of L.* I. xxii, I ne'er before..Have ever drawn your mountain air. **1862** *Temple Bar Mag.* VI. 223 Mellish drew a deep breath.

b. *absol.* To take a draught (of liquor).

1613 PURCHAS *Pilgrimage* (1614) 348 They had their cup-quarrels, striving who should draw deepest.

24. *absol.* or *intr.* To produce or admit of a draught or current of air; said of a chimney, also of a tobacco-pipe or cigar.

1758 A. REID tr. *Macquer's Chym.* I. 269 Some chimney that draws well. 1833 MARRYAT *P. Simple* xxxvii, The fire does not draw well. 1883 *Cambridge Staircase* 100 His pipe requiring to be prodded to make it draw.

25. To attract by physical force, as a magnet; to contract, become covered or affected with (rust, heat, etc.: also *fig.*).

a 1225 *Ancr. R.* 160 Vor ne beo neuer so briht gold..ne stel, þet hit ne schal drawen rust of on þet is irusted. *c* 1315 SHOREHAM 70 So drawyth hy affinite Wyth alle thyne sibbe. *c* 1400 *Lanfranc's Cirurg.* 199 Bete þe lyme..til þou drawe blood þerto. 1413 *Pilgr. Sowle* (Caxton 1483) IV. xxxiv. 83 Bras draweth soone ruste. *a* 1533 LD. BERNERS *Huon* cix. 371 The Adamant drew so sore the Iron. 1563 W. FULKE *Meteors* (1640) 70b, Jeat and Amber draw hayres, chaffe, and like light matter, but being before chafed. 1669 STURMY *Mariner's Mag.* IV. 138 The Points of the Needle..are subject to be drawn aside by the Guns. 1880 E. KIRKE *Garfield* 25 As the rod draws the electricity from the air.

26. *fig.* To attract by moral force, persuasion, inclination, etc.; to induce to come (to a place); to attract by sympathy (to a person); to convert to one's party or interest; to lead, entice, allure, turn (*to*, *into*, or *from* a course, condition, etc.). (See also *draw in*, *on*, *off*, in VII.) **a.** a person.

c 1175 *Lamb. Hom.* 53 To draȝe lechurs to ham. *c* 1200 ORMIN 10115 Her droh Johan Bapptisste wel þe leode wiþþ hiss lare. *c* 1330 R. BRUNNE *Chron. Wace* (Rolls) 14039 He ..þy wif til hys hore haþ drawe. *c* 1450 tr. *De Imitatione* III. lix. 138 Grace drawiþ to god and to vertues. 1576 FLEMING *Panopl. Epist.* 98 I was drawn and allured ther-unto through the. 1615 J. STEPHENS *Satyr. Ess.* A vj b, [They] have.. hanged their bills up to drawe customers. 1648 GAGE *West Ind.* xii. 59 The people are drawne to their churches more for the delight of the musick. 1781 MAD. D'ARBLAY *Diary* June, He endeavoured to draw him into telling the tale. 1861 HUGHES *Tom Brown at Oxf.* iii, It is wonderful, though, how you feel drawn to a man who feeds you well.

b. The mind, desires, eyes, attention, etc.

c 1230 *Hali Meid.* 33 For to drahen his luue toward hire. *c* 1400 *Apol. Loll.* 2 þe synne of þe heldar man drawiþ..þe hertis of þe ȝungar in to dep. 1576 FLEMING *Panopl. Epist.* 358 They drawe the mindes of the people into an admiration. 1667 MILTON *P.L.* II. 308 His look Drew audience and attention still as Night. 1711 ADDISON *Spect.* No. 15 ¶5 To draw the Eyes of the World upon her. 1849 E. E. NAPIER *Excurs. S. Africa* II. 95 My attention being drawn to the spot, I saw an animal. 1884 L. J. JENNINGS in *Croker Papers* I. vi. 154 A great bereavement..drew his mind from public affairs.

27. *absol.* To exercise allurement or attractive force; to prove an attraction; to attract crowds.

1586 A. DAY *Eng. Secretary* II. (1625) 94 Such..as draw unto mischiefe. 1656 BP. HALL *Occas. Medit.* (1851) 117 All draws towards liberty and joy. 1708 PRIOR *Turtle & Sparrow* 190 Example draws, when Precept fails. 1870 LOWELL *Study Wind.* 375 Mr. Emerson always draws. 1884 *Fortn. Rev.* 1 Nov. 703 Lord Randolph Churchill..is sure to 'draw' enormously wherever he goes.

28. To influence in a desired direction, induce (*to do* something). (See also *draw on*, 86 c.)

1568 GRAFTON *Chron.* II. 205 The Spencers had so drawne the king to doe and consent to whatsoever they required. 1639 S. DU VERGER tr. *Camus' Admir. Events* 13, I say not this..to draw you to desire me for your wife. 1667 MILTON *P.L.* I. 472 Ahaz his sottish Conquerour, whom he drew Gods Altar to disparage. 1763 J. BROWN *Poetry & Mus.* xiii. 231 When I am drawn to attend more to the Singer than to what is Sung. 1892 *Argosy* May 359 When he had drawn me to love him.

29. a. To bring together, gather, collect, assemble. *Obs.* exc. as associated with other senses.

1568 GRAFTON *Chron.* II. 143 Into the marches of Wales, where they drewe to them great power. 1595 SHAKS. *John* IV. ii. 118 That such an Army could be drawne in France. 1736 LEDIARD *Life Marlborough* I. 63 An Army of about 1600 Men was drawn together.

b. *intr.* for *refl.* To come together, gather, collect, assemble (*about*, *around*, *to* some centre).

a 1300 *Cursor M.* 15911 (Cott.) Mani drou a-bote þat fire. *c* 1420 *Chron. Vilod.* 964 All his frendus..drowyn abouȝt hym theke and fast. 1538 WRIOTHESLEY *Chron.* (1875) I. 83 The great resorte of people that drue to his sermons. 1791 MRS. RADCLIFFE *Rom. Forest* ii, Our desolate party drew round it. 1849 *Tait's Mag.* XVI. 27/2 The whole party drew round the table.

30. To bring about as a result, cause to follow as a consequence, entail, induce, bring on. (See also *draw in*, 82 e, *draw on*, 86 b.)

c 1340 *Cursor M.* 26649 (Fairf.) A synne or twa vnbete þai dragh ay ma & ma. 1548 HALL *Chron., Hen. VII*, 7 The proverbe sayth, tareynge draweth and ieopardeth perell. *a* 1626 BACON *Max. & Uses Com. Law* ix. (1636) 35 Any default or laches..either in accepting the freehold, or in accepting the interest that drawes the freehold. 1869 A. W. WARD tr. *Curtius' Hist. Greece* II. III. ii 392 This act drew after it important consequences.

31. To cause to fall or come *upon*; to bring (evil, calamity, etc.) *upon*. (See *draw down*, 80 b.)

c 1340 *Cursor M.* 18729 (Fairf.) Ful grete veniaunce is on him drawe. 1628 EARLE *Microcosm., Rash man* (Arb.) 96 The occasion [that] drew this mischiefe vpon him. 1698 FRYER *Acc. E. India & P.* 113 Which drew the Forces of the Sultan his Master upon him. 1736 LEDIARD *Life Marlborough* I. 126 He drew upon Himself, immediately, that Swarm of Enemies. 1823 *Examiner* 65/2 They are drawing on themselves their own ruin. 1860 T. MARTIN *Horace* 29 Rage drew on Thyestes the vengeance of heaven.

III. Of extraction, withdrawal, removal.

* *With that which is taken as the object.*

32. *trans.* To pull out, take out, extract (*e.g.* a cork from a bottle, a tooth from the jaw, a charge from a gun, a nail, screw, etc. from what it is fixed in, bread from an oven, stone from a quarry, a root, pole, young plants, stumps at cricket, etc. from the ground, a card from the pack). Also, to bowl out a batsman. See also *draw out*, 87 a.

a 1300 *Cursor M.* 996 (Cott.) Adam..was wroght at vndern tide, At middai eue draun of his side. *c* 1400 MAUNDEV. (1839) ix. 100 Men make drawe the braunches þere of, and beren hem to ben graffed at Babiloyne. 1562 J. HEYWOOD *Prov. & Epigr.* (1867) 98 This peny father drue his purse apase. 1622 MABBE tr. *Aleman's Guzman d'Alf.* I. 46 The other Country-fellow, that was..drawing his Cards. 1703 T. N. *City & C. Purchaser* 255 Some in drawing of Stone make use of Gun-powder. 1708 MOTTEUX *Rabelais* V. xxi. (1737) 95 The Batch..in the Oven was to be drawn. 1709 STEELE *Tatler* No. 34 ¶5 To cut off Legs, as well as draw Teeth. 1752 *Scots Mag.* Aug. (1573) 402/2 Having drawn the shot of the loaded piece. 1828 *Examiner* 658/1 He would have drawn the cork. 1833 *Sporting Mag.* V. Cricketers' Reg. 13 The stumps were drawn. 1842 *Jrnl. R. Agric. Soc.* III. II. 387 A poor crop of turnips..one half of which was drawn, and the other eaten off by sheep. 1850 'BAT' *Crick. Man.* 40 The time for drawing the stumps depends..upon pre-arrangements. 1861 *Once a Week* 10 Aug. 182/1, I drew his wicket with..my second ball. 1870 HARDY & WARE *Mod. Hoyle* 156 (Besique) When a player draws two cards instead of one, he intimates the fact at once. *Mod.* That onion bed is fit for drawing [= thinning].

absol. (*Cards.*) 1870 HARDY & WARE *Mod. Hoyle* 154 (Besique) The winner of a trick is the first to draw from the pack. 1891 *Field* 28 Nov. 842/3 The dealer can only draw from the stock.

33. a. To pull out or extract (a sword or other weapon) from the sheath, etc., for fight or attack.

c 1200 *Trin. Coll. Hom.* 61 He wile his swerd draȝen. *a* 1300 *Cursor M.* 7764 (Cott.) þou dragh þi suerd and sla me her. *c* 1320 *Sir Tristr.* 1575 Ysoude to tristrem ȝode Wiþ his swerd al drain. *c* 1489 CAXTON *Sonnes of Aymon* I. 27 The barons..drewe alle theyr swerdes. 1583 HOLLYBAND *Campo di Fior* 191 Every man draw his knife. 1678 J. PHILLIPS *Tavernier's Trav., India* III. xxiv. 202 The Java Lords.. Drawing their poyson'd Daggers, cry'd a Mocca upon the English, killing a great number of them. 1700 CONGREVE *Way of World* V. x, You may draw your fox if you please, sir. 1736 LEDIARD *Life Marlborough* I. 351 They had obliged him to draw the Sword. 1852 THACKERAY *Esmond* I. xiii, Are you going to draw a sword upon your friend in your own house?

b. *absol.* (*sc.* the sword.)

1592 SHAKS. *Rom. & Jul.* I. i. 69 Draw, if you be men. 1628 J. ROUS *Diary* (Camden) 27 The Captaines..drewe upon the saylers with greate fury. 1719 DE FOE *Crusoe* II. xiv, We fired our pistols..and then drew. 1862 *Temple Bar Mag.* IV. 306 It is but ill fighting and base fence to draw upon a foe in a coach.

c. *fig.* ***to draw one's sword against***: to attack, 'take up arms' against, assume an attitude of hostility to. So ***to draw one's pen*** or ***quill against***, to attack in writing.

a 1683 SIDNEY *Disc. Govt.* II. xxiv. (1704) 153 He that draws his Sword against the Prince..ought to throw away the Scabbard. 1704 SWIFT *T. Tub* Apol., That this answerer had..drawn his pen against a certain great man. 1735 POPE *Prol. Sat.* 151 Yet then did Gildon draw his venal quill. 1759 GOLDSM. *Bee, Augustan Age* (Globe) 414/1 Many members of both houses of Parliament drew their pens for the Whigs. 1849 MACAULAY *Hist. Eng.* I. 624 The two bishops insisted on Monmouth's owning that, in drawing the sword against the government, he had committed a great sin.

34. a. To pull or take one from a number of things ('lots') so as to decide something by chance: usually in phr. ***to draw cut***(*s*, ***to draw lot***(*s* (see CUT *sb.*[1], LOT). Also *absol.*

a 1300 *Cursor M.* 16699 (Cott.) A-bute his kirtel drou þai cutt, qua suld it bere a-wai. 1386, etc. [see CUT *sb.*[1] 1]. *c* 1440 *Promp. Parv.* 131/1 Drawe lotte, *sorcior*. 1552 HULOET, Drawe cutte or lottes, *sortio*. 1634 SIR T. HERBERT *Trav.* A iij b, The World's a Lott'ry; He that drawes may win. 1832 *Examiner* 614/1 Drawing straws, for guilty or not guilty, were infinitely preferable. 1870 MORRIS *Earthly Par.* II. III. 287 The we..shared the spoil by drawing short and long. 1886 *Lesterre Durant* I. xi. 159 They had drawn for partners, and he was congratulating himself on his luck.

b. To obtain or select by lot.

1709 STEELE *Tatler* No. 124 ¶1 Neither of them had drawn the Thousand Pound. 1791 BOSWELL *Johnson* (1831) V. 215 Johnson was once drawn to serve in the militia. 1816 KEATINGE *Trav.* (1817) II. 214 The jury is drawn very fairly. 1862 *Temple Bar Mag.* IV. 251 She contributed her half-crown to a Derby sweepstakes..and triumphantly drew the winning horse.

35. To separate or select from a group or heap; *spec.* **a.** To select and set apart (sheep) from the flock, for breeding or fattening, or on account of disease or defect. **b.** To separate (seeds) from the husks. **c.** *Falconry.* To remove (a hawk) from the mew after moulting.

14.. *Tretyce* in *W. of Henley's Husb.* (1890) 54 Euery yere onys betwixt ester and whitsonday drawe your shepe and loke yeff þey be clene. 1523 FITZHERB. *Husb.* §40 To drawe shepe, and seuer them in dyuers places. 1611 MARKHAM *Countr. Content.* I. v. (1668) 36 Hawks for the field would be drawn from the mew in June. 1839 *Jrnl. R. Agric. Soc.* I. II. 169, I then proceeded..to draw forty wether hogs out of my flock of Leicesters. 1845 *Ibid.* VI. II. 373, I drew two lots of lambs on the 15th of April. 1847 *Ibid.* VIII. II. 283 The cost of 'cobbing', separating the [clover] seed from the stalks, and 'drawing', separating the seed from the husk by hand. 1866 *Ibid.* Ser. II. II. I. 165, I get all my seeds drawn by contract..It took me five days to cob and draw the 45 bushels of Anthyllis which I drew.

36. To drag or force (a badger or fox) from his hole. (See also s.v. BADGER *sb.*[2] 5.)

1834 MEDWIN *Angler in Wales* I. 272 You see this little terrier..many a fox has he drawn from earth. 1838 [see *badger-drawing* s.v. BADGER *sb.*[2] 5]. 1844 J. T. HEWLETT *Parsons & W.* iii, Bait cats and draw badgers. 1870 BLAINE *Encycl. Rur. Sports* §1751 If the fox must be drawn by a hound, first introduce a whip, which the fox will seize, and the hound will draw him more readily. 1884 LD. RANDOLPH CHURCHILL *Sp.* 28 Oct., I will..take the earliest opportunity I can find of seeing what I can do to draw the badger.

†**37.** To withdraw; in *Sporting*, to withdraw (the stakes), or to withdraw (a horse) from competing in a race. *Obs.*

1597 SHAKS. *2 Hen. IV*, II. i. 162 Go, wash thy face, and draw thy Action. 1698 LUTTRELL *Brief Rel.* (1857) IV. 365 [The match] betwixt the Yorkshire mare and Mr. Frampton's horse the Turk for 500£ is drawn by consent. 1708 *Brit. Apollo* No. 72. 2/1 We wou'd..advise the Wagerers to draw Stakes. 1809 *Brit. Press* 5 Apr. in *Spirit Pub. Jrnls.* (1810) XIII. 61 He [a horse] was drawn at the late Westminster races. 1838 J. H. NEWMAN *Lett.* (1891) II. 258 If he would specify any Tract which he wished drawn from publication..I would do so forthwith. 1857 HUGHES *Tom Brown* II. ix. (1880) 368 'Rory-o-More drawn. Butterfly colt amiss', shouted the student.

38. To leave undecided (a battle or game). Also *absol.* [Original sense unknown: see DRAWN 3.]

1837 *Penny Cycl.* VII. 51/1 (Chess) In this critical position, white having the move can draw the game by checking [perpetually]. 1871 'THOMSONBY' *Cricketers in Council* 59 To 'draw' a match by refusing to play the ten minutes necessary for finishing it is, in our opinion, a very paltry proceeding. 1878 BESANT & RICE *Celia's Arb.* v, Once or twice the battle was drawn by foreign intervention. 1892 *Graphic* 10 Sept. 302/3 The tendency to draw a match rather than gain a victory at the cost of an individual wicket or two is far less marked. 1895 *Westm. Gaz.* 2 Nov. 7/2 If First Trinity wins, it will be the first success they have had since they drew twenty-one years ago.

39. a. To take (water) from a well, etc. by hauling or pumping up. Also *absol.* **b.** *Mining.* To raise (ore) to the surface in buckets.

a 1300 *Cursor M.* 5687 (Cott.) þai war drauand watur. *a* 1300 *Vox & Wolf* 277 in *Rel. Ant.* II. 278 He com to the putte, and drou. *c* 1450 *Mirour Saluacioun* 1115 The thre stronge watere drew vpp out of a cisterne. 1549 COVERDALE, etc. *Erasm. Par. Col.* 4 Of this fountayne maye we easly drawe. 1585 T. WASHINGTON tr. *Nicholay's Voy.* II. xxii. 60 A smal bucket to draw water with. 1697 DRYDEN *Virg. Georg.* IV. 540 With Waters drawn from their perpetual Spring. 1797 *Monthly Mag.* III. 322 The engine..has been employed, ever since its erection, in drawing water, full seventeen hours per day. 1892 *Leisure Hour* Aug. 662/2 [They] congregate to draw their water at the old pump.

40. a. To cause (liquid) to flow from a vessel through an opening; to obtain (drink) from a cask, etc. by a tap or the like; to cause (blood) to come flowing through a wound. Also *absol.* to draw liquor; in quot. 1598, to exercise the trade of a 'drawer' (DRAWER[1] 2).

1393 LANGL. *P. Pl.* C. XXII. 401 Ich couþe..drawe at one hole Thicke ale and þynne ale. *c* 1400 MAUNDEV. (Roxb.) xxi. 95 þer may na maner of yrne dere him ne drawe blude of him. 1562 J. HEYWOOD *Prov. & Epigr.* (1867) 178 The butler drawth and drinkth beere. 1598 SHAKS. *Merry W.* I. iii. 11, I will entertaine Bardolfe: he shall draw; he shall tap. 1634 SIR T. HERBERT *Trav.* 24 The Toddy is drawne out of the Palmito-tree. 1697 DRYDEN *Virg. Georg.* III. 239 Their Stings draw Blood. 1737 BRACKEN *Farriery Impr.* (1756) I. 193 Blood is drawn at several Periods. 1862 *Temple Bar Mag.* VI. 529 You may draw me a mug of ale.

b. ***to draw it mild***: (*a*) *lit.*, in reference to beer; (*b*) *fig.* (*colloq.*) to be moderate in statement or behaviour; to refrain from exaggeration. So, ***to draw it strong***, in the opposite sense.

1837 THACKERAY *Ravenswing* iii, Dress quiet, sir: draw it mild. 1842 BARHAM *Ingol. Leg., Misadv. Margate*, A pint of double X, and please to draw it mild. 1864 SALA in *Daily Tel.* 6 Apr., Our ladies faithfully promised to 'draw it as mild' as possible; but when they made their appearance in most splendid array, I felt rather uncertain as to what the consequences might have been if they had drawn it strong.

41. a. To extract (a liquor, juice, etc.) by suction, pressure, infusion, or distillation.

a 1550 in *Vicary's Anat.* (1888) App. IX. iv. 222 Drawe the muscellage of them with rose-water and white wyne. 1574 HYLL *Conject. Weather* v, To drinke clarified whey simply, or drawen with cold herbes, is then very healthful. 1639 J. W. tr. *Guibert's Char. Physic.* II. 73 To draw the Juice of Cherries..take out the stones and presse them. 1730–6 BAILEY (folio) s.v., To draw as tea. 1747 WESLEY *Prim. Physic* (1762) 83 Oil of sweet Almonds newly drawn. 1836 FONBLANQUE *Eng. under 7 Administ.* (1837) III. 313 How are the gravies to be drawn, if the cook goes to church? 1838 DICKENS *Nich. Nick.* ix, He will be here by the time the tea's drawn.

b. Said *absol.* of the teapot; also *intr.* of tea.

1820 *Blackw. Mag.* VIII. 14 [The tea] took a long time to draw. 1836 *Gentl. Mag.* June 627/1, I like the teapot always to have time to draw. 1891 *Morning Post* 25 Dec. 6/5 If people buy strong Indian tea and put the same quantity into the pot as they do of China tea..the liquor draws too strong.

42. *Med.* To cause a flow of (blood, matter, 'humours') to a particular part; to promote suppuration. Also *absol.* of a poultice or blister.

c **1400** *Lanfranc's Cirurg.* 227 And leie þerto resoluyng þingis þat ben not to strong, and þat þei drawe not to harde. **1607** TOPSELL *Serpents* (1658) 808 He scarified the place, and drawed it with cupping-glasses. **1626** BACON *Sylva* §38 Rubarb draweth Choller.. Agaricke Fleagme. **1875** H. C. WOOD *Therap.* (1879) 565 In order for a blister to 'draw' thoroughly, it usually has to be left on some eight hours. **1890** BLACKMORE *Kit & Kitty* (ed. 3) III. vii. 96 As soon as his poultice began to draw.

43. To convey away (water) by a channel, etc.; to drain off; also *absol.*, and *intr.* (for *refl.*) to drain off, percolate.

1607 TOPSELL *Serpents* (1658) 766 They forsake the water when it draweth or falleth low. **1794** *Agric. Surv. Kincard.* 368 (Jam.) The sub-soil is so concreted.. that water does not draw or filter beyond a few feet of distance. **1845** *Jrnl. R. Agric. Soc.* VI. II. 573 The deep drains draw the water from a distance of 22 feet. **1856** *Ibid.* XVII. II. 488 It is a common belief that water draws better down a curved drain than a straight one.

44. a. *fig.* To take or obtain *from* a source; to derive.

a **1300** *Cursor M.* 5581 (Cott.) Of israel sede.. wald he drau his manhede. *c* **1400** *Lanfranc's Cirurg.* 193 Now we han medycyns drawen of .ij. wellis and of manie maistris. *c* **1475** *Partenay* 144 On of faire.. Of the which I am drawen lynyally. **1552** ABP. HAMILTON *Catech.* (1884) 12 Foure familiar exempills drawin fra the haly scripture. **1576** FLEMING *Panopl. Epist.* 376 The stocke from whence he draweth his descent. **1654** tr. *Martini's Conq. China* 232 Which kind of custom happily the Chineses drew from the Persians. **1758** JOHNSON *Let. to Langton* 21 Sept. in *Boswell*, The consolation which is drawn from truth.. is solid and durable. **1871** FREEMAN *Norm. Conq.* (1876) IV. xviii. 197 This incidental hint may perhaps draw some indirect confirmation from the highest evidence of all.

b. *intr.* or *absol.* To obtain supplies, resources, information, etc., *from* a source. (See also 66.)

1829 *Examiner* 772/2 His Lordship has drawn from other sources than his own brain. **1867** FREEMAN *Norm. Conq.* (1876) I. App. 702 We get a spirited account of the battle, from which I have not scrupled to draw largely.

c. *intr.* for *refl.* To be derived, spring *from.*

1847 TENNYSON *Princ.* v. 395, I know Your prowess, Arac, and what mother's blood You draw from.

45. To take, receive, or obtain (money, salary, revenues, etc.) from a source of supply.

1596 SHAKS. *Merch. V.* IV. i. 87 If euerie Ducat in sixe thousand Ducates Were in sixe parts, and euery part a Ducate, I would not draw them, I would haue my bond. **1605** —— *Lear* I. i. 87 What can you say, to draw A third, more opilent then your Sisters? **1779** J. MOORE *View Soc. Fr.* (1789) I. xxiv. 195 And draw a revenue from the poor inhabitants. **1850** *Tait's Mag.* XVII. 532/2 [He] drew his salary quarterly. **1871** MORLEY *Voltaire* (1886) 210 Neither could he forget to draw his pension from the King of Prussia. **1879** SALA *Paris Herself* (ed. 4) II. vii. 85 Ladies who have come to the Bank to draw their dividends.

46. To cause to come forth or issue; to elicit, 'fetch', call forth, evoke. *spec.* in *Cards*, To cause (a particular card or cards) to be played out.

a **1300** *Cursor M.* 1522 (Cott.) Organis harp and oþer gleu, He drou þan oute o musik neu. **1490** CAXTON *Eneydos* vii. 33 They entendyd to drawe from hir som wordes seruynge to theyr entencion. **1634** SIR T. HERBERT *Trav.* 73 Which drew aforetime many a teare from the distressed Christians. **1711** STEELE *Spect.* No. 252 ¶3 So great an Orator in this Way, that she draws from me what Sums she pleases. **1861** *Temple Bar Mag.* II. 280 He drew from me all the information I had been able to elicit. **1878** H. H. GIBBS *Ombre* 41 He draws all the trumps and wins all the tricks.

47. *colloq.* To rouse (a person) to action, speech, or anger; to induce to come forth, 'fetch'; to irritate, exasperate. (Cf. 36, also *draw out*, 87 g.)

1860 THACKERAY *Philip* vi. (Farmer), The wags.. can always, as the phrase is, 'draw' her father, by speaking of.. Waterloo, or battles in general. **1890** MRS. HUNGERFORD *Born Coquette* II. xx. 220 The hostess.. is not here to be badgered and worried and drawn. **1892** LENTZNER *Australian Word-bk.* 21 *Draw*, to vex, to infuriate.. undoubtedly a metaphor from 'drawing a badger'. **1892** *Guardian* 10 Aug. 1178/2 He has striven.. to 'draw' his opponents and to exasperate them.

48. To deduce, infer (a conclusion, etc. *from* premisses). (Cf. also 64.)

1576 FLEMING *Panopl. Epist.* 176 *note*, A conclusion.. drawne from hope and bonne esperaunce. **1693** *Hum. & Conv. Town* 132 From innocent Looks drawing what Conclusions they please. **1701** NORRIS *Ideal World* I. vii. 343 We may hence draw an argument backward for the necessity of truth. **1795** *Gentl. Mag.* 541/1 Astonished at the logick which could draw such an inference. **1847** MARRYAT *Childr. N. Forest* viii, What inference would you draw from that? **1885** S. LAING *Mod. Sc. & Mod. Th.* (1894) 146 Conclusions drawn from a totally different class of facts.

*** With that from which the contents are taken as the object.*

49. To extract something from, draw out the contents of; to empty, drain, exhaust, deplete. *to draw dry*: to empty or exhaust of liquid; also *fig.*

1576 FLEMING *Panopl. Epist.* 378 To declare.. it would.. drawe the veyne of mine invention drie. *c* **1586** C'TESS PEMBROKE *Ps.* CXV. vi, The conduites of his store, He never dry shall draw. **1589** NASHE *Pasquil & Marforius* 22 Firieouens.. and when they are drawn, they deliuer a batch for the deuils tooth. **1630** *R. Johnson's Kingd. & Commw.* 522 The Persian warre.. [has] drawne drie his Coffers. **1666–7** PEPYS *Diary* 24 Feb., Their oven was drawn by ten o'clock at night. **1844** *Jrnl. R. Agric. Soc.* V. I. 49 The calf should be allowed to draw the cow fully. *Ibid.* 281 Carrots do not draw the ground more than swede turnips. **1892** *Labour Commission* Gloss., *Drawing a Pan*, taking out of a pan the draught of salt which has accumulated there.

50. To draw out the viscera or intestines of; to disembowel (a fowl, etc. before cooking, a traitor or other criminal after hanging).

In many cases of executions it is uncertain whether this, or sense 4, is meant. The presumption is that where *drawn* is mentioned after *hanged*, the sense is as here.

c **1320** *Sir Tristr.* 1797 Sche swore bi godes rode þai schuld ben hong and drain. **1375** BARBOUR *Bruce* I. 278 Sum thai hangyt, and sum thai drew. *c* **1420** *Liber Cocorum* (1862) 35 þo crane schalle fyrst enarmed be.. Draȝun at þo syde as wodcockis. *c* **1440** *Promp. Parv.* 131/1 Drawe fowlys, or dysbowaylyn.. *eviscero.* **1465** *Paston Lett.* I. No. 99. 135, I was arestyd.. and was thretenyd to have ben hongyd, drawen, and quarteryd. **1556** *Chron. Gr. Friars* in *Monumenta Franciscana* (Rolls) II. 152 Thys yere was Roger Mortemer erle of March hangyd and drawne at Tyborne for tresoun. **1655** CULPEPPER *Riverius* I. vi. 27 Take a Goose or Duck that is fat, pluck it and draw it. **1682** S. PORDAGE *Medal Rev.* 178 Those men, whom they can neither hang nor draw. **1790** BURKE *Fr. Rev.* Wks. V. 166 We have not been drawn and trussed, in order that we may be filled, like stuffed birds in a museum, with chaff and rags. **1893** *Field* 4 Mar. 331/1 The proper mode of removing the neck, crop, and merrythought, and drawing the fowl.

51. To draw a net through or along (a river or shore) for fish. Cf. DRAG *v.* 7.

a **1440** *Sir Degrev.* 113 He drowhe reveres with ffysh. **1673** in *Descr. Thames* (1758) 83 That no Person do hereafter presume to draw the Shores in the River of Thames. **1758** *Descr. Thames* 52 Where Fishermen that draw the Shores usually resort. **1784** COWPER *Lett.* 28 Nov., When they drew the river, they presented us with a fine jack.

52. *Hunting.* **a.** To search (a wood, covert, etc.) for game. Also *absol.*

1583 STANYHURST *Æneis* IV. (Arb.) 98 When they shal in thickets thee couuert maynelye be drawing. **1686** [BLORE] *Gentl. Recreat.* II. 78 When a Huntsman beats a Wood to find a Chase, 'tis called Drawing the Covert. **1789** G. WHITE *Selborne* (1875) 319 Though the huntsman drew Harteley Wood.. yet no stag could be found. **1859** JEPHSON *Brittany* ix. 143 To open the hunting season by drawing the forest.. for wolves. **1891** *Field* 7 Nov. 693/2 Two of the.. coverts were drawn without success.

absol. **1749** FIELDING *Tom Jones* VII. v, You have lost the hare, and I must draw every way to find her. **1892** *Field* 7 May 663/3 While the hounds were drawing, a holloa.. made known the whereabouts of a fox.

b. *to draw* (a covert, etc.) *blank*: to search it without success; also *to draw a blank*, and *intr.* for *refl.*, *to draw blank.* Also *fig.*, to be unsuccessful, to fail (in a search); to be in vain. (With allusion to drawing a blank in a lottery: cf. 34 b, and BLANK *sb.* 4.)

1825 *Sporting Mag.* XVI. 25/1 One hundred sovereigns is a very pretty 'find' in any man's pocket, and particularly so in one which is sometimes drawn a blank. **1832** EG.-WARBURTON *Hunt. Songs* ii. (1883) 7 The man.. Whose heart heaves a sigh when his gorse is drawn blank. **1858** A. F. W. DRAYSON *Sporting Scenes S. Africa* 215 Some of these woods had been drawn blanks. **1874** LADY C. SCHREIBER *Jrnl.* (1911) I. 270 Drew blank the only curiosity shop. **1892** *Illustr. Sporting & Dram. News* 3 Dec. 29/3 The Laurels.. and the Willows all drew blank. **1914** *Sphere* 19 Dec. 296/1 She was worrying over Miss Titmus's probable annoyance at drawing a blank from her godchild. **1939** *Punch* 1 Nov. 484/1 Enquiries at the two houses either side of him have drawn blank. **1969** *Woman* 19 Apr. 36/2 Ask the health visitor to introduce you to other mothers.. if you.. draw a blank at the clinic.

53. *colloq.* To elicit information from (a person); to 'pump'.

1857 READE *Course True Love* 225 I'll draw the farmer! **1891** *Athenæum* 5 Sept. 330/1 It is a pity that the dramatist lets himself be drawn by the interviewer.

IV. Of tension, extension, protraction.

54. a. To pull out to a greater length or size; to stretch, distend, extend, elongate; to spin (a thread). Also *absol.*, and *intr.* for *refl.* (See also *draw abroad, draw out*, in VII.)

a **1300** *Cursor M.* 12409 (Gött.) þis tre þai droght þaim bituine. **1511–12** *Act 3 Hen. VIII*, c. 6 §1 The byer of wollen clothes.. shall not drawe.. the same clothes.. by teyntour or wynche. **1625** HART *Anat. Ur.* II. vi. 88 Any might haue drawne it.. as if it had bene some glue or birdlime. **1655** *W. Fulke's Meteors* Obs. 164 Though Gold be drawn into the smallest wire. **1742** POPE *Dunc.* IV. 590 Or draw to silk Arachne's subtile line. **1747** STOVIN in *Phil. Trans.* XLIV. 572 The Skin drew or stretch'd like a Piece of Doe-Leather. **1824** *Mirror* III. 383/2 Had we but the art of drawing threads as fine as a spider's web.

†b. To stretch on the rack; to rack. *Obs. rare.*

1481 CAXTON *Godfrey* lv. (1893) 96 They make hym to be drawen and payned to saye the trouthe. **1483** —— *G. de la Tour* cxl. 197 Rather I shold lete me drawe than I shold telle it ageyn.

55. *fig.* To extend, lengthen, prolong, protract. (See also *draw along*, 77 b, *draw out*, 87 d.)

a **1300** *Cursor M.* 791 (Cott.) Quat bot es lang mi tale to draw. **1483** *Cath. Angl.* 107/1 To Drawe on longe or on lenght, *crastinare, prolongare.* **1598** BARRET *Theor. Warres* I. i. 1, I will drawe my leisure and poore skill to the vttermost. **1619** BEAUM. & FL. *King & No King* I. i. 8 Thou drawst thy words. **1847** L. HUNT *Jar Honey* ix. (1848) 119 The sense of hushing solemnity is drawn to the finest point. **1885** *Athenæum* 23 May 661/1 The anguish of the last chapters is too long drawn.

56. *techn.* **a.** To straighten out (straw, etc.) by pulling it repeatedly lengthwise, for thatching, etc. **b.** To make (wire) by drawing a piece of metal through a succession of holes of diminishing size and thus extending it in length. **c.** To form (a glass tube or the like) by drawing molten glass out in length. **d.** To flatten out (metal) by hammering or otherwise. **e.** *Cotton-spinning*, etc. To elongate and attenuate (the slivers of cotton, wool, or flax), by passing them between successive pairs of rollers revolving at different speeds. **f.** To spread plaster over (a wall or ceiling).

1509 [see DRAWN 1]. **1606** *Durham Grassmen's Acc.* (Surtees) 33 For the carrage of yᵉ straw to yᵉ bull house and for the drawinge of yt, 14*d.* **1701** *Mem. St. Giles's* (Surtees) 98 Paid for drawing the new Whins, and spent, 8*s.* 6*d.* **1721** *Lond. Gaz.* No. 5965/4 A Work-house for.. Drawing Wyer. **1783** *Phil. Trans.* LXXIII. 450 The glass tube had been just drawn at the glass-house. **1833** J. HOLLAND *Manuf. Metal* II. 334 Wire is drawn either by hand, or by steam, water, or other power. **1837** *Penny Cycl.* VIII. 95/2 (Cotton-spinning) The next operation is called drawing.. The object.. is to complete.. the arranging of the fibres of cotton longitudinally, in a uniform and parallel direction, and to remedy all existing inequalities in the thickness of the sliver. **1841** in R. Oastler *Fleet Papers* (1842) I. xlviii. 380 Being employed in 'drawing lace', when only twenty-one months old.

57. *Naut. intr.* Of a sail: To swell out tightly with the wind.

1627 CAPT. SMITH *Seaman's Gram.* ix. 41 We haue a.. faire wind, and all sailes drawing. **1762** FALCONER *Shipwr.* II. 189 The mizen draws; she springs aloof once more. **1835** MARRYAT *Pirate* ix, The schooner had let draw her fore-sheet. **1840** R. H. DANA *Bef. Mast* xxii. 66 Her yards were braced sharp up, every sail was set, and drew well. **1893** *Harper's Mag.* Apr. 716/1 The canvas either drew full, or was absolutely slack.

†58. a. *intr.* To extend or amount *to. Obs.*

1501 *Bury Wills* (Camden) 87 As myche mony as iij quarters shall drawe to. **1563–4** in Willis & Clark *Cambridge* (1886) II. 571 Top pieces for the west wyndowe whiche drewe to xxi fote of glass.

†b. *trans.* To amount to. *Obs.*

c **1462** J. PASTON in *Paston Lett.* No. 461. II. 114 To have the seid plase and certeyn of his livelode of gretter valew than the charge of the seid college schuld drawe. **14..** *Tretyce* in *W. of Henley's Husb.* (1890) 51 Your costes done vpon þe seid acre drawithe iijd. & jd. ob.

V. Of delineation or construction by drawing.

** To draw a line, figure, formal document, comparison, etc.*

59. a. To trace (a line or figure) by drawing a pencil, pen, or the like, across a surface; to cut (a furrow) by drawing a ploughshare through the soil.

c **1305** *Edm. Conf.* 223–5 in *E.E.P.* (1862) 77 To arsmetrike he drouȝ.. And his figours drouȝ aldai.. Arsmetrike is a lore þat of figours al is And of drauȝtes as me draweþ in poudre. **1551** RECORDE *Pathw. Knowl.* I. Defin., A Straight lyne, is the shortest that maye be drawenne betwene two prickes. **1552** HULOET, Drawe a furrow with a plowe about a place. **1559** W. CUNNINGHAM *Cosmogr. Glasse* 130 Wyth th' one fote of your compasse (placinge th' other foote in K.) drawe Cycles. **1669** STURMY *Mariner's Mag.* I. 24 The Center.. from which Point all Lines drawn to the Circumference are equal. **1781** COWPER *Conversation* 380 Like figures drawn upon a dial plate. **1890** SIR S. W. BAKER *Wild Beasts* I. 159 These cuts were as neatly drawn across the skull as though done by a sharp pruning knife.

b. *to draw a* (or *the*) *line* (*fig.*): to determine or define the limit between two things or groups; in mod. colloq. use (esp. with *at*), to lay down a definite limit of action beyond which one refuses to go.

1793 *Trial of Fyshe Palmer* 42 It is difficult.. to draw the line. **1821** *Examiner* 582/1 They know how to draw the line between private and public feeling. **1832** *Blackw. Mag.* Jan. 129/1 Lord Brougham then proceeds, after stating that it was 'necessary to draw a line somewhere'. **1881** *Scribner's Mag.* XXI. 409/2 Feathers and flowers are different things. You must draw a line somewhere, an' I draw it at feathers.

60. a. To make (a picture or representation of an object) by drawing lines; to design, trace out, delineate; formerly also, to mould, model.

1526 *Pilgr. Perf.* (W. de W. 1531) 194 b, We rede that saynt Luke the euangelyst drewe and made an ymage of our Sauyour Jesu. **1654** R. CODRINGTON tr. *Hist. Ivstine* 599 He could draw the figures of men exactly [**1606** make Images] in Earth or Clay. **1659** D. PELL *Impr. Sea* 576 Will a Picture continue that is drawn upon an Ice? **1661–2** PEPYS *Diary* 1 Mar., My wife and I by coach.. to see my little picture that is a drawing. **1711** ADDISON *Spect.* No. 83 ¶5 All the Faces he drew were very remarkable for their Smiles. **1821** CRAIG *Lect. Drawing* iv. 203 The forms of the figures.. were finely imagined and correctly drawn. **1861** *Temple Bar Mag.* III. 24 He drew cartoons on wood.

b. To represent (an object) by a drawing or picture; to delineate, depict.

1581 PETTIE *Guazzo's Civ. Conv.* III. (1586) 156 b, Having to draw the singular beuties of Helen. **1602** SHAKS. *Ham.* II. i. 91 He fals to such perusall of my face, As he would draw it. **1634** SIR T. HERBERT *Trav.* 18 Here are many rare sorts of Birds.. one only I have drawne. **1833** *Mech. Mag.* 341 Those who draw the objects on wood, as well as engrave them. **1861** *Temple Bar Mag.* III. 304 Leech has drawn him in Punch five hundred times.

c. *fig.* To represent in words, describe. Also *to draw a portrait* or *picture of*, in same sense.

c **1374** CHAUCER *Troylus* II. 213 (262) And sith thend is euery tales strengthe.. What should I paint or drawen it on length. **1586** A. DAY *Eng. Secretary* II. (1625) 51 Having drawne his portraiture, I send the first counterfeit to himselfe. **1712** ADDISON *Spect.* No. 309 ¶7 Mammon's character is so fully drawn in the First Book. **1850** *Tait's Mag.* XVII. 249/1 Macaulay.. draws a flattering picture of William's capabilities. **1891** *Sat. Rev.* 19 Dec. 696/2 The character of Pamphilus.. shows how Terence could draw a young man.

d. *absol.* or *intr.* To trace the lines of a figure; to practise the art of delineation.

1530 PALSGR. 526 He draweth as well in blacke and whyte, as any man in Englande. **1732** BERKELEY *Alciphr.* I. §11 Did those great Italian masters..always draw with the same ease and freedom? **1861** *Temple Bar Mag.* III. 23 He could draw from the 'round'.

61. *Masonry. trans.* To shape (stone-work) by cutting off thin slices. (Cf. DRAUGHT *sb.* 43.)

1703 MOXON *Mech. Exerc.* 183 The work is hewed or drawn pretty near a Round.

†62. To devise, contrive; to set in order, arrange, array. *Obs.* (See also *draw up*, 89 f.)

(In quot. 1230, the sense is very doubtful.)

c **1230** *Hali Meid.* 23 þe flurs þat beoð idrahe þ[e]ron..to tellen of hare euene ne is na monnes speche. *c* **1540** tr. *Pol. Verg. Eng. Hist.* (Camden No. 29) 179 Burning with rage incredible..he drew a plot for the lord Hastinges. *a* **1586** *Satir. Poems Reform.* xxxvi. 98 Judas..any vyler draucht nor thow did neuer draw. **1587** TURBERV. *Trag. T.* (1837) 142 Straight she drew a plot to have him slaine. **1663** F. HAWKINS *Youth's Behav.* 83 The matter of any Book or Science, drawn into Indexes or Tables.

63. a. To frame (a writing or document) in due form; to compose, compile, write out. (See also *draw out*, 87 h, *draw up*, 89 g.)

a **1300** *Cursor M.* 20059 (Cott.) In sotherin englis was it draun, And turnd it haue i till our aun Langage o northrin lede. **1526** *Pilgr. Perf.* (W. de W. 1531) 1 b, I thought it necessary to drawe a treatyse for myselfe. **1548** HALL *Chron., Hen. VII*, 21 A forme of a league and amitie shoulde be drawen with condicions, clauses and covenauntes. **1596** SHAKS. *Merch. V.* IV. i. 394 Clarke, draw a deed of gift. **165.** PEPYS *Diary* (1879) IV. 92 Drawing the letter we are to send. **1722** SEWEL *Hist. Quakers* (1795) II. VII. 25 Caused an indictment to be drawn against us. **1829** *Examiner* 779/2 Acts of Parliament were drawn so negligently. **1879** L. STEPHEN *Johnson* iii. 72 Langton had employed Chambers ..to draw his will.

†b. *intr.* To write or treat *of*. *Obs.*

a **1300** *Cursor M.* 2315 (Cott.) Of abraham now wil we drau [*v.r.* draghe, drawe]. *Ibid.* 28868 And for þer mater es gode to knau, Of almus sal i for-þer drau.

64. To frame, make, formulate, lay down, institute (comparisons, contrasts, distinctions, etc.) [App. of very composite origin, having affinities in varying measure with senses 16, 48, 59 b, and 63.]

1789 MRS. PIOZZI *Journ. France* I. 136, I..drew incessant censures on his taste. **1802** MAR. EDGEWORTH *Moral T.* (1816) I. xx. 190, I..avoided drawing comparisons between your son and F. **1823** KEBLE *Serm.* ii. (1848) 31 He has been drawing, in strong colours, a contrast between the punishments and the rewards. **1831** A. FONBLANQUE *Eng. under 7 Administ.* (1837) II. 157 Praying that a distinction may be drawn between [etc.]. **1868** GLADSTONE *Juv. Mundi* i. (1870) 4 Nestor..draws a somewhat similar contrast between the heroes of his youth and those of the Greek army before Troy. **1875** JOWETT *Plato* (ed. 2) I. 21, I have heard Prodicus drawing endless distinctions about names. **1876** J. S. BREWER *Eng. Studies* iv. (1881) 201 Comparisons were drawn in his favour to the disadvantage of his brother.

** *To draw a bill or demand note.*

65. a. *Comm.* To write out in due form an order to pay money on the writer's account; to write out (a bill, cheque, or draft). Const. *on*, *upon* (the person who has to pay).

1671 CROWNE *Juliana* III, Draw bills of death, they shall be paid on sight; I will..pay as fast as you can draw on me. **1722** DE FOE *Col. Jack* (1840) 213 She should draw bills upon me. **1776** *Trial of Nundocomar* 23/2 Bollakey Doss drew a draught on Benares in favor of Lord Clive for a lack of rupees. **1817** W. SELWYN *Law Nisi Prius* (ed. 4) II. 1171 C. drew bills of exchange on B. for the price of the goods. **1861** DICKENS *Gt. Expect.* li, With instructions to draw the cheque for his signature. **1892** J. ADAM *Commercial Corr.* 24 The person who writes the 'order to pay' is said to draw the Bill.

b. *absol.* in same sense; also, less strictly, to make permitted demands *on* or *upon* (a person) for funds. ***to draw against***, to issue drafts in consideration of (value placed in the drawee's hands).

1671 [see prec.]. **1732** GAY *Let. to Swift* 16 Nov. in *S.'s Lett.* (1766) II. 171 You may now draw upon me for your money, as soon as you please. **1809** R. LANGFORD *Introd. Trade* 26, I have..taken the liberty to draw upon you for £5000. **1861** *Temple Bar Mag.* I. 504 Remit Frank his allowance without drawing on our income. *Ibid.* III. 218 She has unlimited power to draw on my banker. **1866** CRUMP *Banking* iii. 78 It is expected that the portion of the credit consisting of those documents, will not be drawn against until sufficient time shall have elapsed for them to be cleared.

66. *intr.* To make a demand or draft *upon* (a person, his memory, imagination, etc.) *for* resources or supplies of any kind.

1797 *Hist.* in *Ann. Reg.* 166/2 England, to meet the war of assignats, drew upon the finances of posterity. **1840** BARHAM *Ingol. Leg., Ghost* Introd., It is on my own personal reminiscences that I draw for the following story. **1855** H. ROGERS *Ess.* II. vii. 323 The narrative..here and there draws largely on our faith. **1859** *Jrnl. R. Agric. Soc.* XX. II. 488 [Wheat] draws less upon the natural powers of the soil. **1860** *Temple Bar Mag.* I. 41 They drew amply upon their imagination when facts failed.

VI. (*refl.* and *intr.*) Of motion, moving oneself.

†67. *refl.* ***to draw oneself***: to move oneself, betake oneself, come, go, proceed, approach *to* or *towards*; to withdraw, retire, or remove *from*. *Obs.*

c **1200** ORMIN 10656 Sannt Johan droh himm o bacch. *Ibid.* 11545 Þatt illke mann birrþ draȝhenn himm Fra gluterrnesess esstess. *c* **1205** LAY. 93 þes duc mid his drihte To þare sæ him droh. *a* **1300** *Cursor M.* 7412 (Cott.) þe men was won to drau ham nere. *Ibid.* 15904 (Gött.) A quile forward he yode, A quile him drou againe. **1388** WYCLIF *Luke* xv. 15 And he wente, and drouȝ hym to oon of the citeseyns of that cuntre. *c* **1400** *Beryn* 2322, I drowȝ me to foly, and wold nat be governed. **1530** PALSGR. 526 He begynneth to drawe hym in to companye nowe. *a* **1618** RALEIGH (J.), As their people increased, they drew themselves more westerly towards the Red sea.

†68. a. *intr.* To move, proceed, come, go. *Obs.* or *arch.* exc. as in b.

a **1000** *Guthlac* 699 (Gr.) Ongon þa leofne sið draȝan. *a* **1200** *Moral Ode* 49 Þider ȝe sculen ȝorne draȝen. *a* **1300** *Cursor M.* 22543 (Cott.) Wodd and wall al dun sal drau. *c* **1400** *Destr. Troy* 906 Iason..Drow euyn to the dragon, dressit hym to fight. *c* **1489** CAXTON *Sonnes of Aymon* ii. 66 'Where be my sonnes gone?'..'I cannot telle whether they are drawen.' *c* **1489** —— *Blanchardyn* iii. 18 So shal we leue him drawing on his waye. **1586** A. DAY *Eng. Secretary* I. (1625) 73 Why draw we not home into our owne soyle of England? **1644** CHAS. I in Ellis *Orig. Lett.* Ser. II. III. 317 Wee desire you to draw with all your forces to Bristol. **1808** SCOTT *Marm.* VI. xiii, The train from out the castle drew.

b. Now only, To move or make one's way *towards* a place, to come near, approach, to come *together*, to withdraw to one side; and in certain adverbial combinations, as *draw back*, *down*, *in*, *near*, *nigh*, *off*, *on*, *up*: see VII.

c **1250** *Gen. & Ex.* 2378 Toward here fader he gunen draȝen. *a* **1300** *Cursor M.* 6276 (Cott.) þe see drogh samen on ilka side. **1393** LANGL. *P. Pl.* C. xx. 61 Asyde he gan drawe. *a* **1533** LD. BERNERS *Huon* lxxxi. 250 They all togyther drewe a parte in to a chambre. **1563** SHUTE *Archit.* B j b, Constrained the braunches of the herbe to draw downwardes againe with a sertaine compasse. **1670** NARBOROUGH *Jrnl.* in *Acc. Sev. Late Voy.* I. (1711) 16 [Sails] all set to draw away southerly. **1697** DAMPIER *Voy.* I. v. 116 Our men immediately..drew together in a body. **1703** MAUNDRELL *Journ. Jerus.* (1732) 144 Having heard of our drawing homeward. **1766** GOLDSM. *Vic. W.* xxviii, I am now drawing towards an abode that looks brighter as I approach it. **1861** *Temple Bar Mag.* III. 535 Every believer would draw on one side. **1892** *Ibid.* Nov. 363 Drawing towards Wales and the line of the Severn. **1893** *Nat. Observer* 5 Aug. 304/1 They drew closer together.

†69. *fig.* To approach, incline, tend (to some condition, state, etc.) *Obs.*

c **1200** ORMIN 17902 All hiss hallȝhe dede Droh till þatt an, to turrnenn follc Intill þe rihhte weȝȝe. **1375** BARBOUR *Bruce* x. 781 He to sa gret vorschip dreuch, That all spak of his gret bounte. *c* **1489** CAXTON *Sonnes of Aymon* xxvi. 542 But he draweth now sore to age. **1578** LYTE *Dodoens* II. xcii. 272 The upper leaves draw towardes the proportion of the leaves of fenell. **1603** KNOLLES *Hist. Turks* (1621) 235 Of a darke colour, somewhat drawing toward a violet.

70. To draw near or approach in time.

a **1300** *Cursor M.* 22662 (Edin.) Al þing now draus til end. **1399** LANGL. *Rich. Redeles* IV. 31 Whanne it drowe to þe day of þe dede-doynge. *c* **1475** *Rauf Coilȝear* 38 It drew to the nicht. **1568** GRAFTON *Chron.* II. 410 When the time drue neere, he came to Oxforde. **1641** D'EWES in *Lett. Lit. Men* (Camden) 169 It drawes nowe towards tenn of the clocke at night. **1758** A. REID tr. *Macquer's Chym.* I. 313 The operation draws toward an end. **1821** *Examiner* 121/1 It is time I should draw to a conclusion. **1875** JOWETT *Plato* (ed. 2) I. 379 The days of Socrates are drawing to a close.

†71. ***to draw to***: to resort to, join the party of (a person); to take up with; to betake oneself to (a course of action, study, etc.). *Obs.* (exc. as associated with sense 26).

c **1205** LAY. 10530 Alle heo wulleð to me draȝen. *a* **1300** *Cursor M.* 45 (Gött.) For be þat thing men draus till, Men may þaim knaue for gode and ill. *c* **1305** *Edmund Conf.* 221 in *E.E.P.* (1862) 77 Siþþe..to arsmetrike he drouȝ. **1393** LANGL. *P. Pl.* C. IX. 190 Preestes and oþer peple to peers þei drowen. *c* **1460** *Towneley Myst.* (Surtees) 5 When Lucifer to pride drogh. **1477** NORTON *Ord. Alch.* xlv. in Ashm. (1652) 22 Heche thyng drawes to hys semblable. **1568** GRAFTON *Chron.* II. 139 Much people drewe unto them. **1893** *Nat. Observer* 13 May 643/2 Like draws to like.

†72. ***to draw after***: (*a*) to act by the advice of, follow the counsel of; (*b*) to 'take after', resemble. *Obs.*

c **1305** *St. Swithin* 32 in *E.E.P.* (1862) 44 Swithin his consailler, after wham he drouȝ. *c* **1450** *Merlin* 434 She.. draweth litill after hir moder. *c* **1475** *Partenay* 6243 He drawith after that laydy Ffro whom he is discended uerily.

†73. *intr.* To move (at chess); cf. DRAUGHT *sb.* 21. Also *trans.* with cognate obj. *Obs.*

c **1369** CHAUCER *Dethe Blaunche* 682 Whan she my fers kaught I wolde have drawe the same draught. *c* **1400** *Beryn* 1809 'Draw on', seyd the Burgeyse; 'Beryn! ye have þe wers!' *Ibid.* 1822 He drouȝe, and seyd 'chek mate!'

74. *Hunting.* **a.** Of a hound: To track game by the scent. **b.** To move slowly towards the game after pointing. Const. *after*, *on*, *upon*. See also *draw on*, 86 f.

1589 WARNER *Alb. Eng.* Prose Addit. (1612) 345 Ascanius and his Companie drawing by Parsie after the Stagge. **1590** SHAKS. *Com. Err.* IV. ii. 39 A hound that runs Counter, and yet draws drifoot well. **1617** MARKHAM *Caval.* VIII. 33 It might bee possible to make a Horse to draw dry-foot after any Man, and to distinguish Scents with his nose as well as any Bloodhound. **1730–46** THOMSON *Autumn* 365 The Spaniel..draws full, Fearful and cautious, on the latent prey. **1855** KINGSLEY *Heroes* III. (1868) 38 Thrice they snuffed round and round like hounds who draw upon a deer. **1875** 'STONEHENGE' *Brit. Sports* I. I. v. §2. 90 Many pointers are capable of drawing.

75. *Racing.* Gradually to gain *on* or get further *away from* an antagonist in running or rowing. ***to draw level***: to come up with or alongside of an antagonist; also *transf.* See also *draw out*, 87 j, *draw up*, 89 h.

1823 *Examiner* 395/2 The boat's crew still drawing on them. **1892** *Illustr. Sporting & Dram. News* 30 Apr. 249/1 They could not draw quite level, and were beaten by two to one. **1892** *Sat. Rev.* 2 July 10/1 Two drew away fast from the others, and the race appeared to be over. **1892** *Black & White* 6 Aug. 158/2 Gradually drawing upon him. **1932** *Punch* 27 Apr. 465/3 Other nations had drawn level with us. **1955** *Times* 1 Aug. 3/6 The South Africans have come from behind and surprised the favourites by drawing level in a Test rubber.

VII. In combination with adverbs.

76. draw abroad. a. See simple senses and ABROAD *adv.* **†b.** *spec.* (*trans.*) To spread (anything) over a surface; to spread out, expand. *Obs.*

c **1400** *Lanfranc's Cirurg.* 26 Whanne þe arterie is drawe abrod. *Ibid.* 53 Aboue þe wounde leie terebentine..drawen abrood bitwene two lynnen clooþis.

77. draw along. a. See simple senses and ALONG *adv.* **†b.** To stretch, extend; *fig.* to prolong, protract. *Obs.*

1362 LANGL. *P. Pl.* A. v. 124 To drawe þe lyste [*C.* þe lisure] wel along þe lengore hit semede. **1382** WYCLIF *Ps.* cxix. 5 My pilgrimaging is drawen along. *c* **1400** *Lanfranc's Cirurg.* 53 þouȝ þat þi cure be drawe along. **1613** PURCHAS *Pilgrimage* (1614) 426 This..drew me along.

78. draw back. a. *trans.* See simple senses and BACK *adv.* **b.** *Comm.* To get back or recover (the whole or part of the duty on goods) upon exportation: see DRAWBACK *sb.* 2. Also *fig.* to deduct, take off, 'discount' (quot. 1768).

1709 *Lond. Gaz.* No. 4509/3 The Sugars must pay French Duties, but on Exportation draws back all but about 2*s.* per C. **1768** STERNE *Sent. Journ.* (1775) I. 36, I always suffer my judgment to draw back something on that very account. **1776** ADAM SMITH *W.N.* IV. i. (1869) II. 24 When the home manufacturers were subject to any duty or excise, either the whole or part of it was frequently drawn back upon their exportation; and when foreign goods, liable to a duty, were imported, in order to be exported again, either the whole or a part of this duty was sometimes given back upon such exportations.

c. *intr.* (also *refl.*, *obs. rare*) To move backwards from one's position; to retire, recoil, retreat; *fig.* to withdraw from an undertaking, etc.

a **1300** *Cursor M.* 15891 (Cott.) He drogh him bak behi[nd] þe men. *c* **1340** *Ibid.* 15925 (Fairf.) Petre drogh him bakker mare. **1530** PALSGR. 526 He drewe backe and defended himselfe as well as he coulde. **1611** BIBLE *Heb.* x. 38 If any man drawe backe, my soule shall haue no pleasure in him. **1843** *Jrnl. R. Agric. Soc.* IV. I. 196 These rocks begin at last to draw back here and there from the river. **1861** *Temple Bar* I. 517 Too deeply committed to draw back.

79. draw by. a. *trans.* To draw aside. **b.** *intr.* To pass by, draw to a close.

1830 TENNYSON *Mariana* 19 She drew her casement-curtain by. **1850** —— *In Mem.* lx. 14 The foolish neighbours ..tease her till the day draws by: At night she weeps.

80. draw down. a. See simple senses and DOWN *adv.* **b.** *trans. fig.* To cause to fall or light *upon* a person, etc.; to attract, bring down.

1634 SIR T. HERBERT *Trav.* 35 These crying sinnes, have apparantly drawne downe Gods heavy judgements upon these Countries. *a* **1694** TILLOTSON (J.), The blessings it will draw down upon us. **1816** KEATINGE *Trav.* (1817) I. 164 This of course draws down French vengeance.

c. *Cookery.* To stew or boil down. **d.** *Forging.* To reduce (bars, etc.) in size by hammering.

1806 *Culina* 15 Put all those into a stew pan, with some water, and draw them down to a light brown colour.

81. draw forth. a. *trans.* See simple senses and FORTH *adv.*

c **1200** ORMIN 7413 Þatt hord tatt oppnedd wass And draȝhenn forþ. **1590** SPENSER *F.Q.* III. x. 29 Out of his bouget forth he drew Great store of treasure. **1632** J. HAYWARD tr. *Biondi's Eromena* 89 To see if they could.. draw forth into the Maine, the Sardan Galleyes. **1660** F. BROOKE tr. *Le Blanc's Trav.* 134 The Madrecon that drawes forth the Army, and ranges it in battalia. **1879** DOWDEN *Southey* iv. 86 A May morning would draw him forth into the sun.

†b. To adduce; = sense 21 a. *Obs.*

c **1200** ORMIN 11907 He drohh þær forþ þe bokess lare.

†c. To protract, prolong; to spend (time). *Obs.*

c **1305** *Edm. Conf.* 402 in *E.E.P.* (1862) 81 Þat he al day forþ drouȝ. **1589** GREENE *Menaphon* (Arb.) 57 In this sort did Pleusidippus draw foorth his infancie. **1650** TRAPP *Comm. Gen.* ix. 25 Leonard..drew forth a most poor life in the Netherlands, whither he escaped.

†d. To trace out; to design, draw up, draw out (see 60, 87 h, 89 g). *Obs.*

1551 ROBINSON tr. *More's Utop.* (Arb.) 79 Utopus him selfe..drewe furth the platte fourme of the citie.

e. To elicit, evoke, call forth.

1821 *Examiner* 780/2 [His] drollery drew forth no cordial laugh. **1849** MACAULAY *Hist. Eng.* II. 168 His bravery.. drew forth the generous applause of hostile armies.

82. draw in. a. See simple senses and IN *adv.*

1579 GOSSON *Sch. Abuse* (Arb.) 54 Eagles draw in their tallants as they sit in their nestes. **1648** GAGE *West Ind.* xiii. 81 The greedy Earth..opened her mouth to draw in Townes and Cities. *a* **1732** GAY (J.), Now, sporting muse, draw in the flowing reins. **1749** FIELDING *Tom Jones* XII. xiii, As the vulgar phrase is, [he] immediately drew in his horns. **1847** A. M. GILLIAM *Trav. Mexico* 133 Obliged to draw in his reins.

b. *trans.* To contract, draw tight; to cause to shrink.

1628 EARLE *Microcosm., Handsome Hostesse* (Arb.) 55 No Citizens wife..drawes in her mouth with a chaster simper. 1845 S. JUDD *Margaret* I. ii, Miss Gisborne's flannel..must be drawn in to-morrow. 1891 *Eng. Illustr. Mag.* IX. 192 The gown was drawn in but slightly under the arms.

c. To take into the lungs, breathe in, inhale.

1535 COVERDALE *Ps.* cxviii. [cxix.] 131, I open my mouth and drawe in my breth. 1607 TOPSELL *Four-f. Beasts* (1658) 469 All their Cattle for want of water do draw in the cold air. 1707 NORRIS *Treat. Humility* x. 402 Soft oily poisons which we incautiously draw in for common breath. 1892 *Graphic* 210/3 Hughes drew in his breath sharply.

d. *fig.* To induce to come in or take part; to allure, entice, inveigle; to ensnare, 'take in', delude. (Now only with *inf.*)

1558 in Strype *Ann. Ref.* I. II. App. iv. 6 To draw in other men of learning. 1606 *Proc. agst. Late Traitors* 74 Onely perswaded and drawen in by Catesby. 1726 *Adv. Capt. R. Boyle* 55 Smiling..to think how soon I drew in the credulous Captain. 1752 FOOTE *Taste* II. Wks. 1799 I. 24 Mecænas..has been drawn in to purchase..a cart-load of —rubbish! 1813 JANE AUSTEN *Pride & Prej.* III. xiv. 246 *Your* arts..may..have made him forget what he owes to himself and to all his family. You may have drawn him in. 1833 HT. MARTINEAU *Manch. Strike* iv. 54 He was not the man to be drawn in to do what..he disliked.

†**e.** To induce or bring as a consequence. *Obs.*

a 1450 *Knt. de la Tour* (1868) 56 One worde drauithe an other in. *a* 1704 LOCKE (J.), A view of all the intermediate ideas that draw in the conclusion, or proposition inferred.

f. *intr.* Of a day or evening: To draw to a close, to close in. Also of a succession of evenings in late summer and autumn: To become gradually shorter (as if contracting or shrinking in).

1840 R. BARHAM in *Bentley's Misc.* Mar. 274 As the evenings begin To close, or, as some people call it, 'draw in'. 1849 *Tait's Mag.* XVI. 260/2 Hours passed and the evening drew in. 1880 MISS BROUGHTON *Sec. Th.* II. x, The evenings are beginning to draw in already. 1891 H. S. MERRIMAN *Prisoners & Captives* II. iii. 55 The short winter day was drawing in.

83. draw near. *intr.* To come (gradually) near, approach (*lit.* and *fig.*).

a 1300 *Cursor M.* 21790 (Edin.) Quen he droch til his ending nere. *c* 1340 *Ibid.* 14525 (Fairf.) Halde ȝou stille & drawes nere. 1503-4 *Act 19 Hen. VII.* c. 28 Preamb., The seid parliament draweth so near to the end. 1596 SPENSER *F.Q.* VI. iii. 47 He stayd, till that he nearer drew. 1660 F. BROOKE tr. *Le Blanc's Trav.* 101 Her blossoms like Lillies broken off green, draws near to the yellow. 1712 ADDISON *Spect.* No. 523 ¶7 The time of a general peace is, in all appearance, drawing near. 1849 MACAULAY *Hist. Eng.* I. 667 Sentinels were posted to give the alarm if a stranger drew near.

84. draw nigh. = prec.

c 1330 R. BRUNNE *Chron. Wace* (Rolls) 1653 Men drowe to þeym ney. 1526 TINDALE *John* xvi. 33 The houre draweth nye. 1586 T. B. *La Primaud. Fr. Acad.* I. 138 The end of this time drew nie. 1667 MILTON *P.L.* III. 645 He drew not nigh unheard. 1842 TENNYSON *Morte d'A.* 163 My end draws nigh; 'tis time that I were gone.

85. draw off. a. See simple senses and OFF.

a 1300 *Cursor M.* 8116 (Cott.) Þe king drou of his gloue. *c* 1400 MAUNDEV. (Roxb.) x. 41 Mary Mawdelayne and Mary Cleophe, makand sorow..and drawand off þaire hare. 1697 DAMPIER *Voy.* I. iii. 37 Bark of Maho..You may draw it off either in flakes or small threads. 1711 POPE *Let. to J. C.* 19 July (1735) I. 173 Tonson's Printer told me he drew off a Thousand Copies in this first Impression. 1747 FRANKLIN *Lett.* (1887) II. 67 The wonderful effect of pointed bodies, both in drawing off and throwing off the electrical fire.

b. (*a*) *trans.* To withdraw (troops) from a particular position, or from the scene of action. (*b*) *intr.* To move off, withdraw, retire, retreat. (*c*) *Pugilism*: see quot. 1873.

1667 MILTON *P.L.* IV. 782 Half these draw off. 1697 DAMPIER *Voy.* I. iv. 84 Captain W. drew off his men. 1736 LEDIARD *Life Marlborough* I. 377 He resolved to draw off his Dragoons.

intr. *a* 1625 BEAUM. & FLETCHER *Custom of Country* I. i, Draw off a little; Here come my mistress and her father. *c* 1645 T. TULLY *Siege of Carlisle* (1840) 17 Barkley drew of sore bruised. 1865 KINGSLEY *Herew.* vii, When they were tired they drew off on both sides. 1873 *Slang Dict., Draw off*, to throw back the body to give impetus to a blow; 'he drew off, and delivered on the left drum'.

c. To turn aside, divert (the mind, attention).

1704 NORRIS *Ideal World* II. iii. 121 There is something in those objects..which draws off the mind from itself to the contemplation of them. 1834 MEDWIN *Angler in Wales* I. 187 A friend..rode after the brute, and drew off his attention to himself.

d. *trans.* To convey away (liquid) by a tap, or a channel or the like; esp. without disturbing the bottom or sediment. Also *intr.* (for *refl.*) To drain away, flow off.

1697 DAMPIER *Voy.* I. viii. 226 The Indico falls to the bottom..When it is thus settled they draw off the Water. 1737 BRACKEN *Farriery Impr.* (1756) I. 321 A Rowel is to draw off the bad or corrupt Humours from the Blood. 1840 *Jrnl. R. Agric. Soc.* I. III. 316 The water can be successfully drawn off by a catheter. 1853 *Ibid.* XIV. II. 442 It is repeatedly 'racked', or drawn off from one cask into another. 1892 *Field* 26 Nov. 802/3 Care should be taken not to disturb the lees until all the cider is drawn off.

intr. 1734 tr. *Rollin's Anc. Hist.* (1827) I. I. iv. 199 To keep back the waters which otherwise would draw off too fast. 1844 *Jrnl. R. Agric. Soc.* V. I. 9 The deposit that would be left after the water had drawn off.

86. draw on. a. See simple senses and ON.

1694 *Acc. Sev. Late Voy.* II. (1711) 162 If the Whale should draw on again. 1712 ADDISON *Spect.* No. 311 ¶5 He immediately drew on his Boots. 1847 A. M. GILLIAM *Trav. Mexico* 135 He drew on his cloak.

b. *trans.* To bring on, bring about, lead to, involve as a consequence.

1593 SHAKS. *3 Hen. VI*, III. iii. 75 Looke therefore Lewis, that by this League and Mariage Thou draw not on thy Danger, and Dis-honor. *a* 1627 HAYWARD (J.), Under colour of war, which either his negligence draws on, or his practices procured. 1672 BOYLE *On Fluids* (J.), The examination..would draw on the consideration of the nice controversies that perplex philosophers. 1736 LEDIARD *Life Marlborough* I. 55 This Beginning drew on the General Battle.

c. To entice, allure, lead on.

1605 SHAKS. *Macb.* III. v. 29 Such Artificiall Sprights, As ..Shall draw him on to his Confusion. 1648 GAGE *West Ind.* iv. 12 If I resolved to goe, my resolution should draw on an other friend of mine. 1816 J. W. CROKER in *Croker Papers* (1884) 28 Nov., If you suffer yourself to be drawn on by what you conceive to be the taste of the day. 1875 JOWETT *Plato* (ed. 2) III. 606 When he was drawing them on to speak of antiquity.

d. *intr.* To advance, approach, draw nigh.

1535 COVERDALE *Job* xxxiii. 21 His soule draweth on to destruccion. 1586 A. DAY *Eng. Secretary* II. (1625) 12 Christmasse now drew on. 1736 LEDIARD *Life Marlborough* III. 303 The Season drawing on for opening the Campaign. 1861 *Temple Bar Mag.* II. 401 Evening again drew on.

†**e.** To draw near to death, be in a dying state.

1555 WATREMAN *Fardle Facions* I. vi. 88 When any man lieth in drawing on. *a* 1577 GASCOIGNE *Flowers* Wks. (1587) 100 He lay (as some say) drawing on Untill his breath and all were past and gone.

f. *Hunting.* Of a hound: To approach game after pointing: = sense 74.

1892 *Field* 7 May 695/3 Musa pointed and drew on, but could not locate the birds. *Ibid.* 19 Nov. 797/3 The setter must often draw on and draw on, not unlike a cat creeping on its prey.

87. draw out. a. *trans.* To pull out, take out, extract, derive, etc.: see simple senses and OUT *adv.* (Also *intr.* for *pass.*)

c 1300 *Cursor M.* 19500 (Edin.) Oute he droȝ baþe wiue and man. 1393 GOWER *Conf.* II. 251 He anone the tethe out drough. *a* 1533 LD. BERNERS *Huon* xxi. 58 Than they tooke lond and drew out theyr horses. 1634 SIR T. HERBERT *Trav.* 24 Then in rage and sudden rapture drew out his knife. 1769 MRS. RAFFALD *Eng. Housekpr.* (1778) 301 Kill your pig, dress off the hair, and draw out the entrails. 1861 *Temple Bar Mag.* IV. 20 Paying in money, and drawing money out, at his employer's bank.

intr. for *pass.* 1891 *Longm. Mag.* Nov. 69 The harpoon did not penetrate sufficiently..and therefore drew out. 1893 *Field* 4 Mar. 335/1 A drawer should be fitted..so as to draw out..and shut back..in a moment.

b. *Mil.* (*a*) To lead out of camp or quarters; to call out. (*b*) To detach from the main body. (*c*) To set in array, extend in line, draw up. (*d*) *intr.* for *refl.* To march out of camp or quarters.

1638 SIR T. HERBERT *Trav.* (ed. 2) 88 Next morning drawing out his men [he] assayles him. 1724 DE FOE *Mem. Cavalier* (1840) 81 The king ordered the regiment to be drawn out. 1866 CARLYLE *Inaug. Addr.* 177 Thirty-thousand armed men, drawn out for that occasion.

intr. *a* 1616 BEAUM. & FL. *Bonduca* I. ii, To-morrow we'll draw out, and view the cohorts. 1660 F. BROOKE tr. *Le Blanc's Trav.* 10 Three score of us then drew out. 1894 WOLSELEY *Marlborough* II. 177 Some sixty or seventy Irish Dragoons 'drew out'..and took up a threatening position.

c. To stretch, extend; to flatten out (metal).

1483 *Act 1 Rich. III*, c. 8 Preamb., Clothes..ben set upon Tentours, and drawen out in Leyngh and Brede. 1694 *Acc. Sev. Late Voy.* II. (1711) 148 One may draw it out in Threads like hot Sealing-wax. 1703 MOXON *Mech. Exerc.* 9 When your Iron hath not its Form..then you must..batter it out; or, as Workmen call it..draw it out. 1754 RICHARDSON *Grandison* (1812) IV. 284 He drew out his face, glouting, to half the length of my arm. 1841 *Jrnl. R. Agric. Soc.* II. II. 222 The spores were lengthened, or drawn out into a short pedicel.

d. *fig.* To extend, protract, prolong.

1553 T. WILSON *Rhet.* (1580) 169 Dulled with overlong drawing out of a sentence. 1632 MILTON *L'Allegro* 140 In notes, with many a winding bout Of linked sweetness long drawn out. 1709 STRYPE *Ann. Ref.* I. xlvii. 515 To draw out time, and weary them. *a* 1713 ELLWOOD *Autobiog.* (1714) 30, I Prayed often, and drew out my Prayers to a great length. 1893 *Temple Bar Mag.* XCIX. 68 Breakfast was drawn out to a most unusual length.

†**e.** To utter slowly or with an effort. *Obs.*

c 1400 *Destr. Troy* 5054 Diamede full depely drough out a laughter. 1581 PETTIE *Guazzo's Civ. Conv.* I. (1586) 1 Hearing him drawe out his wordes so softlie and so weaklie.

f. To elicit, evoke, call out.

a 1586 SIDNEY (J.), To draw out more, said she, I have often wondered how such excellencies could be. 1594 HOOKER *Eccl. Pol.* IV. xiii. §10 To draw out from us an accusation of foreign churches. 1777 MAD. D'ARBLAY *Early Diary* 27 Mar., Useful in drawing out the wit and pleasantry of others. 1816 KEATINGE *Trav.* (1817) II. 215 The bench interrogating the prisoner, and drawing out indiscreet avowals.

g. To induce to talk or express opinions; to elicit speech or information from. (*colloq.*)

1778 MAD. D'ARBLAY *Diary* 23 Aug., She did not..use any means to draw me out. 1824 BYRON *Juan* XV. lxxxii, He had the art of drawing people out, Without their seeing what he was about. 1890 A. GISSING *Village Hampden* III. 295 Joice steadily resisted all efforts to draw her out.

h. To write out in proper form, draw up, (in quot. 1500, to translate, render); to make out; to trace out, delineate.

c 1500 *Lichfield Gild Ord.* (1890) 14 It ys a-Greyde that the Statutis..shalbe draue owt in-to Englyshe. 1576 FLEMING *Panopl. Epist.* 377 *note*, It passeth my capacitie to drawe out his portrayture in sufficient livelynesse. 1773 GOLDSM. *Stoops to Conq.* II. i, Bring us the bill of fare..I believe it's drawn out. 1826 *Examiner* 190/2 Leases..were drawn out and founded on the basis of that monopoly. 1861 *Temple Bar Mag.* II. 248 The [marriage] settlements were permitted to be drawn out.

i. *intr.* To extend in length, become longer.

Mod. The days are beginning to draw out.

j. *Racing.* To get gradually farther ahead.

1891 *Strand Mag.* II. 655/1 The runner..drew out in front. 1892 *Standard* 10 Aug. 7/5 The favourite drew out and won by two lengths.

88. draw over. †**a.** *trans.* To overspread.

a 1400-50 *Alexander* 4207 Draȝen ouer with hidis. 1548 HALL *Chron., Hen. VIII*, 3 Their horses trapped, in burned Silver, drawen over with cordes of Grene Silke and Golde.

b. To cause to pass over in a still; to obtain by distillation.

1676 BOYLE *On Colours* (J.), I..mixed with it essential oil of wormwood, drawn over with water in a limbeck. 1884 *N. & Q.* Ser. VI. X. 159/1 The Moslem physician Rhazes drew over a red oil by distillation called oleum benedictum philosophorum.

c. To convert to one's party or interest.

1707 ADDISON *Pres. State War* (J.), Some might be brought into his interests by money, others drawn over by fear. 1736 LEDIARD *Life Marlborough* I. 153 To draw over some of the German Princes to His Interest. 1737 WHISTON *Josephus Antiq.* Diss. i, How otherwise could he draw over so many of the Jews.

†**d.** *intr.* To extend, last, endure. *Sc. Obs.*

c 1565 LINDESAY (Pitscottie) *Chron. Scot.* (1728) 256 (Jam.) This drew over for ane space. *Ibid.* 312 Thir cumberis drew over till the king was tuelf yeires of age.

89. draw up. a. *trans.* (also *intr.* for *refl.*) See simple senses and UP *adv.*

c 1175 *Lamb. Hom.* 159 Alswa se þe sunne drach up þene deu and makeð þer of kume reines. 13.. *Coer de L.* 55 Anon the sayle up thay drowgh. 1548 HALL *Chron., Hen. VIII*, 27 And by force of engynes drewe it up. 1694 *Acc. Sev. Late Voy.* II. (1711) 174 They..draw it up also with Pulleys into the Ship. 1706 MOTTEUX *Vanbrugh's Mistake* Epil., With Glass drawn up, Drive about Covent-Garden. 1869 W. LONGMAN *Hist. Edw. III*, I. xiv. 261 The gate was shut, the bridge was drawn up.

intr. *c* 1400 *Destr. Troy* 755 Whan þe day vp droghe and the dym voidet. 1823 *Examiner* 792/1 The curtain drew up at the instant of his entrance.

b. *refl.* To assume an erect or stiff attitude.

1850 *Tait's Mag.* XVII. 342/2 The Doctor..drew himself up in offended dignity. 1866 G. MACDONALD *Ann. Q. Neighb.* xiii. (1878) 269 She drew herself up in her chair.

†**c.** To mend (a rent in a garment) by stitching so as to draw the parts together. *Obs.*

1759 STERNE *Tr. Shandy* I. x. (Hoppe), That he could draw up an argument in his sermon—or a hole in his breeches.

†**d.** *Cookery.* ?To bring to the proper consistence (as by 'drawing' through a strainer). *Obs.*

c 1430 *Two Cookery-bks.* 20 Draw hem vppe wyth the [almond] Mylke þorw a straynoure. *c* 1440 *Anc. Cookery* in *Househ. Ord.* (1790) 425 Breke hom in a morter, and drawe hom up wythe gode brothe.

e. *trans.* To bring to a stand (by pulling at the reins). *intr.* To come to a stand; to pull up, stop.

1828 *Examiner* 562/1 He drew up his gig on the wrong side. 1849 E. E. NAPIER *S. Africa* II. 26 The waggons had been drawn up so as to form a sort of hollow square. 1892 *Cornh. Mag.* July 22 She drew the horse up short.

intr. 1823 SOUTHEY *Penins. War* I. 171 A carriage with six mules drew up to the guard-house. 1859 THACKERAY *Virgin.* i, The young gentleman's post-chaise drew up at the rustic inn. 1885 *Manch. Exam.* 3 Oct. 4/7 The train drew up in the station.

f. To bring into regular order, as troops; to set in array. Also *intr.* for *refl.*

1605 SHAKS. *Lear* V. i. 51 The Enemy's in view, draw vp your powers. *a* 1671 LD. FAIRFAX *Mem.* (1699) 84 Here we drew up our army. 1776 GIBBON *Decl. & F.* i, The legion was usually drawn up eight deep. 1855 MACAULAY *Hist. Eng.* III. 243 The ranks were drawn up under arms.

intr. 1660 F. BROOKE tr. *Le Blanc's Trav.* 292 The whole Portuguese Cavalry being landed, drew up in two squadrons. 1736 LEDIARD *Life Marlborough* I. 231 They did, indeed, draw up in Order of Battle.

g. To put together in proper form; to frame, compile, compose, write out in due form.

1639 S. DU VERGER tr. *Camus' Admir. Events* Ep. Ded. A iv, The work which I have here drawne up to a translation. 1654 tr. *Scudery's Curia Pol.* 94 Those..who drew up the processe. 1693 *Col. Rec. Pennsylv.* I. 423 The Committee having drawen up their Answer to the remonstrance, doe sign it. 1711 ADDISON *Spect.* No. 60 ¶7 A List of Words.. drawn up by another Hand. 1856 FROUDE *Hist. Eng.* (1858) II. x. 440 The report was drawn up by men who had the means of knowing the truth.

h. *intr.* To come up *with*, come close *to*; in *Racing*, to gain on or overtake an antagonist.

1795 NELSON 13 Mar. in Nicolas *Disp.* (1845) II. 13 As we drew up with the Enemy. 1889 J. K. JEROME *Three Men in a Boat* 8 We drew up to the table. 1894 *Times* 17 Mar. 14/1 Then the Oxford crew began slowly but steadily to draw up.

i. To take up *with*, enter into relations *with*.

1724 RAMSAY *Tea-t. Misc.* (1733) I. 89 Gin ye forsake me Marion, I'll e'en gae draw up wi' Jean. 1821 GALT *Sir A. Wylie* III. 152 (Jam.) When I had naething I was fain to draw up wi' you. 1892 *Sat. Rev.* 9 July 32/2 There was news from Morocco that their Minister had 'drawn up' with the Sultan's dreaded rival.

draw (drɔː), *sb.* [f. DRAW *vb.*]

1. a. An act of drawing, in various senses of the vb.; draught; pull, strain; the drawing of a card from a pack, etc.

1663 *Flagellum or O. Cromwell* (1679) 45 (L.) The cavalier ..cut the ribbon which tied his murrion and with a draw threw it off his head. 1755-73 JOHNSON, *Draw*, the act of drawing. **1867** F. Francis *Angling* iv. (1880) 121 Whenever there is a draw on the baits. **1871** *Daily News* 15 Aug., The salaries..would not bear the extra draw which must necessarily ensue. **1888** Miss W. Jones *Games of Patience* xiv. 31 You are allowed 'two shuffles and a draw'.

b. An amount drawn up or out.

1847 *Jrnl. R. Agric. Soc.* VIII. I. 126 The clay being taken out one 'draw' deep. **1852** *Ibid.* XIII. I. 92 The last spit or draw being much narrower than the preceding one.

c. *Cricket.* A leg stroke in which the batsman deflects the ball so that it passes between the wicket and his legs. Also, a fieldsman placed so as to field balls so hit.

1836 *Nottingham Rev.* 30 Sept., Caught out at the draw through the ball being to the 'leg'. **1846** W. Denison *Cricket: Sketches of Players* 16 How many 'bats' have been compelled to yield up their wickets just when they fancied they had made a fine 'draw'. **1849** *Boy's Own Bk.* 78 As the ball [when drawn] generally gets away between long-stop and leg, it is advisable to place as 'draw' the fieldsman that can best be spared. **1857** *Chambers's Information* I. 690 The 'draw'..is the most elegant..of the batsman's defences. **1893** R. Daft *Kings of Cricket* v. 88 Tom Hearne..was more successful with the old-fashioned 'draw' than any batsman I can remember.

d. Short for *draw-poker* (see DRAW- a). *U.S. colloq.*

1857 *Phœnix* (Sacramento, Calif.) 20 Sept. 3/2 This mongrel, David, recently lost a sum of money, playing 'draw'. **1876** J. Miller *Life amongst Modocs* x. 133 The man ..took a quiet game of 'draw' with the boys at the Howlin' Wilderness, and won at once the title of Judge. **1891** *Scribner's Mag.* X. 278 A small game of draw shortens the dying hours. **1945** *New Yorker* 14 Apr. 21 'Dealer's choice,' said Kelly. 'Draw or stud. Fifty-cent ante on draw.'

e. A puff on a pipe, cigarette, etc., a smoke. Chiefly *dial.* and *U.S.*

1876 'Mark Twain' *Tom Sawyer* 138, I could smoke this pipe all day, but he'd keel over with just two draws on a pipe. **1881** A. Wardrop *J. Mathison's Courtship* 24 I'll jist licht my pipe, an' ha'e a bit draw. **1895** 'G. Setoun' *Sunshine & Haar* 253 After making himself quite presentable, sat down for a 'draw'. **1908** A. M'Ilroy *Burnside* v, 'You'll tak' a draw,' the host would say, taking the pipe from his mouth and handing it to his guest. **1933** P. MacDonald *Myst. Dead Police* i. 7 There's nothing like a draw to quiet a chap down. **1969** *Flamingo Mag.* (E. Afr.) x. 45/4, I lit the hemp and had a draw of it.

2. a. The drawing or bending of the bow.

1879 M. & W. Thompson *Archery* 19 Care and great practice should be given to acquiring the correct draw.

b. The act of drawing a revolver in order to shoot. *U.S.*

1857 T. H. Gladstone *Kansas* v. 54 With my hand upon the pistols..he didn't stand out long. But I felt pretty bad ..till I got the draw on him. **1903** C. T. Brady *Bishop* i. 9 He had the reputation..of being the quickest man on the draw..in the Territory. **1908** C. E. Mulford *Orphan* iii. 37 And they would have gotten it, too, only I beat them on the draw. **1947** *Chicago Tribune* 22 June (Comics) 9 She might beat me to the draw!

3. Drawing or attractive power or effect; anything having power to draw a crowd. *colloq.*

1881 L. Wagner *Pantomimes* 58 Little to do with the success or legitimate 'draw' of the entertainment. **1891** N. Gould *Double Event* 264 Smirke would have proved a big draw.

4. Drawing of lots; anything decided or arranged by drawing lots, as the order of competitors in a contest; a raffle.

1755–73 Johnson, *Draw*..the lot or chance drawn. **1885** *L'pool Mercury* 22 Dec. 115/4 The familiar raffle or 'draw'. **1892** *Daily News* 27 Jan. 7/2 Unlawfully publishing a proposal for a Christmas draw. **1894** *Times* 11 June 7/2 The following is the draw for the order of play.

5. A drawn game or match.

[**1825** J. Neal *Bro. Jonathan* I. 50 Everybody was glad when he was beaten; everybody reckoned a draw-game, as a victory over him.] **1856** Mongredien in C. Tomlinson *Chess-player's Ann.* 134 With a view to a 'draw', by bringing the Black Pawn on to a Rook's file. **1860** E. M. Cowell *Diary* 17 June in M. W. Disher *Cowells in America* (1934) 117 Of course every one knows that the fight between Sayers and Heenan was undecided—*a draw*—and both have belts given to them. **1863** *Illustr. London News* 22 Aug. 191/1 Surrey *v.* England, at the Oval..ended in a 'draw' yesterday. *a* **1871** *New York Herald* (Hoppe), He fought his last battle which ended in a draw and division of the stakes. **1885** *Manch. Exam.* 6 July 4/7 The cricket match..ended in a draw in favour of the latter county. **1887** *Times* 19 Aug. 5/2 The war..apparently has ended in a draw.

6. *Spinning.* The distance which a mule-carriage travels in drawing out the yarn; a 'stretch'.

1879 *Cassell's Techn. Educ.* IV. 396/2 So soon as the carriage has receded to the end of the 'draw' or 'stretch'—which usually extends to about sixty inches—it stops.

7. a. 'That part of a bridge which is raised up, swung round, or drawn aside; a draw-bridge or swing-bridge (*U.S.*)' (Webster 1864).

1786 *Maryland Jrnl.* 3 Nov. (Th.), A draw is placed over the deepest water, for permitting vessels to pass and repass. **1837** J. F. Cooper *Recoll. Europe* II. 243 The bridge is now permanent, though there was once a draw. **18..** Whittier *Countess*, A skipper's horn is blown To raise the creaking draw. **1889** Morse *Amer. Geogr.* 181 The draw..is designed to require the strength of two men only in raising it. **1902** G. H. Lorimer *Lett. from Self-made Merchant* 21 Our schooner was passing out through the draw at Buffalo.

b. A drawer. *U.S.*

1692 in *Connecticut Probate Rec.* (1904) I. 463, I giue to Elizabeth Thomson..one table with a draue in it. **1748** *N.H. Probate Rec.* III. 565, I give..my chist of draws to my dafter Lidea. **1775** *Essex Inst. Hist. Coll.* XIII. 188 You know I can take a Draw at a time and lay them in the same manner into Dr Gardners. **1829** in W. L. Mackenzie *Lives Butler & Hoyt* (1845) 50 That celebrated receptacle of Chancery papers..the draw or bushel-basket..of his venerable predecessor. **1862** Lowell *Biglow P.* 2nd Ser. III. 108 Once git a smell o' musk into a draw An' it clings hold. **1898** E. N. Westcott *David Harum* 143 They're in the draw there. **1929** in Wentworth *Amer. Dial. Dict.* (1944) 178/2 The draw sticks. **1971** *Amherst* (Mass.) *Record* 28 July 15/1 Wanted to Buy. Two draw file and adding machine.

8. *Clock-making.* (See quot.)

1884 F. J. Britten *Watch & Clockm.* 92 In a lever escapement the locking faces..are cut back at an angle which is called the draw.

9. A natural ditch or drain that draws the water off a piece of land. Also, a shallow valley containing a stream. *U.S.*

1882 W. A. Baillie-Grohman *Camps in Rockies* xii. 340 Among the rough and steep chains of mountains full of 'draws', 'pockets', and gulches. **1884** *Harper's Mag.* Aug. 365/1 You must..find cover in some *coulée* or draw. **1885** in A. Fryer *Gt. Loan Land* (1887) 12 The drainage of the uplands is collected by..shallow 'draws' which effectually drain the surface. **1935** W. Cather *Lucy Gayheart* II. xi. 216 In the draws, between the low hills, thickets of wild plum bushes were black against the drifts. **1953** J. Masters *Lotus & Wind* xx. 253 There was a chance they'd miss the inflow of this draw. **1959** N. Mailer *Advts. for Myself* (1961) 137 The trail rose for a few hundred feet, and then dipped into an empty draw.

10. A thing or person employed to draw a person out, to elicit from him what he knows or intends to do. Also, one from whom information, etc., may be extracted. *slang.*

1811 *Sporting Mag.* XXXVIII. 168 The pretended flat who was a *draw*, was introduced. **1860** Reade *Cloister & H.* v, This was what in modern days is called a *draw*..to elicit by the young man's answer whether he had been there lately or not. **1887** *Poor Nellie* (1888) 124 Butt was a sure 'draw' on this subject.

11. *Founding.* A cavity inside a casting produced by the shrinking of the metal during solidification; a shrinkage cavity.

1907 McWilliam & Longmuir *Gen. Foundry Pract.* xxii. 189 In this class of work, 'draws' are often met with, which constitute another class of liquid shrinkage. **1925** *Foundry Trade Jrnl.* XXXII. 552/2 Many defects described by the practical moulder as draws are in fact blows, or in some cases a combination of the two. **1962** J. G. Tweeddale *Metall. Princ. Engineers* vi. 181 Draws are very troublesome in castings.

12. a. With adverbs, as ***draw-down***; ***draw-in***, esp., in mod. usage, a roadside space out of the way of traffic where vehicles, esp. buses, may make temporary stops; cf. LAYBY; ***draw-off*** attrib., esp. in ***draw-off tap*** = *draw-tap* (DRAW- a). **b.** *Comb.*, as **draw-out** (see quot.); **draw-tender**, one who attends to a draw-bridge.

1787 Mary Wollstonecr. *Posth. Wks.* (1798) IV. 114 A *draw-down at the sides of his mouth. **1943** J. S. Huxley *TVA* ix. 55 Ingenious new methods of temporary draw-down of water-level. **1965** G. J. Williams *Econ. Geol. N.Z.* xv. 238/1 Low-permeability holes where draw-down of aquifer pressures during discharge is substantial. **1968** *Gloss. Terms Offset Lithogr. Printing* (*B.S.I.*) 27 *Drawdown*, a method of comparing or examining inks by scraping samples down a sheet or slab to produce thin graded films. **1840** *Evid. Hull Docks Comm.* 85 Is there any particular current setting into the old harbour? There is a *draw-in, like all other harbours. **1939** *Nature* 20 May 850/1 'Lay-byes' and 'drawn-ins' should be made on every few miles of highway. **1954** *Gloss. Highway Engin. Terms* (*B.S.I.*) 26 *Draw in*, a part of the highway set aside for Public Service Vehicles to draw out of the traffic lanes to pick up and set down passengers. **1909** *Westm. Gaz.* 28 Sept. 3/2 The *draw-off taps at the sink..fitted on single pipes. **1951** *Good Housek. Home Encycl.* 222/1 Only a trickle of water comes from draw-off points. **1959** *Times* 14 Mar. 9/7 Wassail bowls fitted with silver draw-off taps. **1960** G. A. Glaister *Gloss. of Book* 110/1 **Draw out*, a printing fault caused when the roller pulls out a loose type. **1883** *Harper's Mag.* Feb. 357/2 The *draw-tender..saw repeated visions of his death.

draw-, the verb-stem in combination:

a. used attrib. = drawing-, used for, in, or by drawing: as ***draw-hook***, ***-ladder***, ***-lid***, ***-mule***, ***-nail***, ***-pull***, ***-stroke***, ***-window***. **draw-arch**, a movable arch in a bridge; a drawbridge arch; **draw-beam**, a windlass; †**draw-bed**, an extensible bed, also called *drawing-bed*; **draw-bench**, a machine in which wire or strips of metal are reduced in thickness or brought to gauge by drawing through gauged apertures, also called *drawing-bench*; **draw-board**, a board adapted to be drawn up; **draw-bolt**, a coupling-pin of a railway wagon; **draw-bore**, a pin-hole through a tenon, so bored that the pin shall draw the parts together; hence **draw-bore** *v.*; **draw-box**, †(*a*) a drawer (*obs.*); (*b*) = *drawing-frame* (DRAWING *vbl. sb.* 6 a); **drawcard** = *drawing card* (see DRAWING *ppl. a.* 4); **draw-cord** = *draw-string*; †**draw-dike**, a ditch from which water can be drawn off; **draw-dock**, a creek or inlet in the bank of a navigable river into which boats or barges can be run to land cargoes, or lie in the mud at low water; **draw-farm**, a farm whence supplies are drawn; **draw-frame** = *drawing-frame* (see DRAWING *vbl. sb.* 6 a); **draw-gear**, (*a*) harness for draught animals (Phillips, 1706); (*b*) the apparatus by which railway carriages and trucks are connected together in a train; **draw-head**, (*a*) the head of a draw-bar in a railway-carriage; (*b*) part of a drawing-frame, in which the slivers are lengthened and twisted; **draw-hoe** (see HOE *sb.*[2] 1 b); **draw-horse**, a bench or support on which a drawing-knife is used; **draw-kiln**, a lime-kiln so constructed that the burned lime is drawn at the bottom; **draw-knot**, a simple knot, undone by drawing the ends of the string; **draw leaf**, a leaf of a draw-table; so **draw-leaf table** = *draw-table*; **draw-ling** (see quot.); **draw-link**, a link connecting railway carriages or trucks; **draw-loom**, the loom used in figure-weaving, in which the strings through which the warps are passed were pulled by a draw-boy; **draw-nail** (see quot. 1960); **draw-pin**, a draw-bore pin; **draw-pipe**, a pipe for drawing water from a cistern or boiler; **draw-poker**, a game of cards, also called POKER q.v.; **draw-rod**, a rod connecting the draw-bars of railway trucks; **draw-shave**, a drawing-knife for shaving spokes, etc.; **draw-sheet**, (*a*) a folded sheet placed under a patient so that it can be withdrawn without the disturbance of making the whole bed; ; (*b*) *Printing* (see quot. 1928); **draw-sluice**, a sluice opened by being drawn up a groove; **draw-spring**, the spring between a draw-bar and the truck or carriage; **draw-string**, a string slipped through the mouth of a bag, the neck or waist of a garment, etc., so as to tighten it by drawing the ends; also *attrib.*; **draw-tab**, a theatre curtain which can be pulled across the front of the stage; **draw-table**, an extending table, a table with additional pieces which can be drawn out to extend the length; **draw-tap**, a tap for emptying a pipe, cistern, etc.; **draw-taper** = DELIVERY 5 b; **draw-tongs**, a wire-drawer's tool; **draw-top (table)**, see quot. 1904; **draw-tube**, the compound tube, one part sliding within the other, which carries the object-glass and eye-piece of a microscope. Also DRAW-BAR, -BOY, -BRIDGE, etc.

1807 Sir R. C. Hoare *Tour Irel.* 197 A *draw-arch..of which all the machinery is worked under the floor of the bridge. **1611** Cotgr., *Ergate*, A Windlasse, Windbeame, or *Draw-beame. **1663** *Inv. Ld. J. Gordon's Furniture*, In the chamber next adjacent..ane stand bed with a *draw bed. **1859** Dickens in *All Year Round* 2 July 239 The fillets, or ribands of gold..are taken to a machine called a *draw-bench where their thickness is perfectly equalised from end to end. **1879** *Cassell's Techn. Educ.* IV. 298/1. Draw-bench. **1791** R. Mylne *Rep. Thames & Isis* 56 The Stone fixed weir should have a gauge-weir with *Draw-boards constructed on it. **1812–16** J. Smith *Panorama Sc. & Art* I. 120 *Draw-bore pins are used in forcing a tenoned piece into its proper place in the mortise. **1823** P. Nicholson *Pract. Build.* 232 The Draw-bore Pin, or Hook-pin [used] for draw-boring. **1662** Greenhalgh in Ellis *Orig. Lett.* Ser. II. IV. 13 In the wall..many *draw boxes, with rings at them like those in a Grocer's Shop. **1909** *Cent. Dict.* Suppl., *Draw-box*, a set of three or more pairs of rollers attached to combing- and certain other machines for attenuating, or drawing out, the sliver. **1940** *Chambers's Techn. Dict.* 264/2 *Draw-box.* This consists of two or more pairs of fluted rollers between the doffer and the coiler of a carding engine. **1959** *Times* 16 Feb. 3/7 O'Neill, who is now the *drawcard of Australian cricket. **1969** *Australian* 24 May 35/10 Yardley left St George-Budapest three seasons ago to become a top drawcard with Tranmere Rovers. **1971** *Sunday Times* (Johannesburg) (Business Section) 28 Mar. 14/1 The biggest single drawcard for overseas tourists is London. It is experiencing an unprecedented hotel boom. **1840** W. G. Simms *Border Beagles* 376 [I] have nothing to do but tie a few threads and lay a *draw-cord through the end-loops of the net. **1935** *Burlington Mag.* Aug. 92/2 Only alternate threads were controlled by draw-cords. **1936** *Ibid.* Mar. 145/2 The scale-harness is used in order to economize in the number of the drawcords on which the pattern is arranged. *c* **1470** Henry *Wallace* IX. 747 Some fell in to *draw dykis deip. **1883** *Standard* 6 Feb. 6/4 A barge..moored in the *drawdock. **1891** *Pall Mall G.* 10 Nov. 5/1 Authority to construct new drawdocks and to repair and rebuild the existing docks. **1885** R. Bagwell *Irel. under Tudors* I. p. vi, Content to look upon Ireland as a mere *drawfarm. **1897** W. S. Taggart *Cotton Spinning* II. i. 2 The full cans of sliver are taken from the card and put behind the *draw-frame, so that the sliver can be passed up in the direction of the arrows through holes in the guide-plate A. **1889** *Scribner's Mag.* Aug. 217/1 Castings daily required in the way of brake-shoes, pedestals, *draw-heads, grate-bars, etc. **1822** *Draw-hoe [see HOE *sb.*[2] 1 b]. **1961** *Amateur Gardening* 23 Dec. 13 The draw hoe is pulled towards the operator and is ideal for the larger weeds, earthing up potatoes or making seed drills. **1627** *MS. Acc. St. John's Hosp., Canterb.*, For mending on of the *drawe hoockes. **1845** S. Judd *Margaret* I. xvii. 160 Near Hash stands the *draw-horse on which he smooths and squares his shingles. **1805** Forsyth *Beauties Scotl.* II. 446 Collieries and lime-quarries were opened, *draw-kilns erected. **1894** J. Geddie *Fringes of Fife* 25 A line of cyclopean draw-kilns. **1635** Rutherford *Lett.* (1862) I. 147 To God, their belt wherewith they are girt is knit with a single *draw-knot. **1895** *Daily News* 3 May 7/6 When he..went to the premises they used a *draw-ladder, and went up into the depository where the goods were. **1932** *Daily Express* 2 July 7/6 *Draw-leaf table, size 5 ft. × 3 ft. when extended. **1955** R. Fastnedge *Eng. Furn. Styles* i. 9 Tables of joined construction..and indeed those with a draw leaf (first introduced about 1505). **1958** Osborne & Creighton *Epitaph G. Dillon* I. 11 A draw-leaf table with dining chair. **1811** Aiton *Agric. Ayrsh.* 475 Heather and the *draw-ling

(*Scirpus cæspitosus*) are the chief plants that the sheep can eat. **1856** S. C. BREES *Gloss. Terms* 153 The patent railway *draw-link..is now universally employed. **1831** G. R. PORTER *Silk Manuf.* 238 The apparatus called a *draw-loom was invented. **1851** *Art Jrnl. Illustr. Catal.* p. viii.**/1 The first step in improving the draw-loom was the substitution of mechanism for the handle and boy called a draw-boy. **1603** FLORIO *Montaigne* I. xlix. (1632) 163 They call for their fare, tie *drawmule to. **1702** in *Phil. Trans.* XXV. 1864 The Head not round..but somewhat like the modern *Draw-nails. **1960** R. LISTER *Decor. Cast Ironwork Gt. Brit.* 226 *Draw nail*, a pointed rod for driving into a pattern to extract it from its mould after ramming. Also called *draw spike*. **1703** MOXON *Mech. Exerc.* 160 *Draw Pins described..§6. **1895** *Westm. Gaz.* 12 Feb. 5/3 There were only a supply and *draw pipe, and no safety valve. **1864** SALA in *Daily Tel.* 1 Nov., Losing your money at euchre or *draw-poker. **1890** *Pall Mall G.* 24 Mar. 4/3 The great American game of draw-poker. **1886** *Badm. Library, Shooting* (1895) 60 They are now made without a *draw-pull, similar to a revolver. **1828** J. M. SPEARMAN *Brit. Gunner* (ed. 2) 17 Wheeler's Tools ..*Draw Shaves, Spoke Shaves..Drive Pins. **1870** Z. P. VEITCH *Handbk. Nurses* I. 9 Great care should be taken to arrange a macintosh and *draw-sheet in such a way that no blood or other discharge can possibly reach the under sheet. **1928** H. JAHN *Dict. Graphic Arts Terms* 75 *Draw-sheet*, the sheet drawn on over the make-ready on a press. **1960** *Guardian* 1 July 5/4 Mum replaces the draw sheet. **1721** PERRY *Daggenh. Breach* 31 There was intended *draw-sluices to be made. **1845** C. M. KIRKLAND *Western Clearings* (1846) 127 It was Miss Celestina Pye, and she certainly had no *draw-strings in her lips just then. **1872** E. EGGLESTON *End of World* xiii. 89 She pulled out the folds of the chintz curtain, hanging on its draw-string half-way up the window. **1890** *Anthony's Photogr. Bull.* III. 79 The mouth of the bag is..secured by a double drawstring. **1909** *Westm. Gaz.* 10 May 5/2 A belt of thick satin ribbon put through wide embroidered loops like a draw-string. **1955** J. CANNAN *Long Shadows* iii. 51 The striped dress with the drawstring. **1957** *New Yorker* 16 Nov. 150/2 It's a wind-resistant.. overblouse, cut straight to a drawstring waist. **1958** *Vogue* Sept. 133 Drawstring blouses solve the problem of tuck-in blouses and skirts that are constantly parting company. **1959** 'M. ERSKINE' *House of Enchantress* iii. 36 She had..a mouth pursed like the opening to a draw-string bag. **1965** C. D. EBY *Siege of Alcázar* (1966) i. 40 The city walls ran in an unbroken line across the neck of the Tagus loop like a drawstring on a sack. **1833** J. HOLLAND *Manuf. Metal* II. 333 Considerable time is lost between each *draw-stroke and the return of the pincers. **1957** J. OSBORNE *Entertainer* I. 12 Ordinary, tatty backcloth and *draw-tabs. **1904** P. MACQUOID *Hist. Eng. Furn.* iii. 96 An oak *draw-table of 1560. **1925** PENDEREL-BRODHURST & LAYTON *Gloss. Eng. Furn.* 55 *Draw table*, a term generally associated with heavy tables like the refectory table. The top is divided into three leaves, the two end ones lying under the centre leaf. **1938** *Burlington Mag.* Dec. 276/1 Celebrated drawtable from Hinton Abbey near Bath. **1895** *Daily News* 16 Mar. 3/4 A *draw tap in the supply pipe. **1904** P. MACQUOID *Hist. Eng. Furn.* iii. 93 With the invention of the *draw-top a revolution took place in tables... The top was in three pieces, the lower leaves drawing out and being supported by long armed brackets; the upper leaf dropped into its position, and so the table elongated to double its length. **1955** R. FASTNEDGE *Eng. Furn. Styles* i. 20 The draw-top table..wherein a subsidiary and additional leaf might be drawn out at each end of the table top. **1567** HARMAN *Caveat* 36 A *drawe-window of a low chamber.

b. governing an object: as **draw-blood**, he who or that which draws blood; **draw-stop**, a knob or handle in an organ by which a slider is drawn so as to admit the wind to a set of pipes.

1609 BP. HALL *Pharis. & Chr.* Wks. (1627) 409 They beat their heads against the walls, as they went, till bloud came; whence one..is called Kizai, a Pharise *draw-bloud. **1880** E. J. HOPKINS in Grove *Dict. Mus.* II. 605 The *Draw-stop action. *Ibid.* 606 The 'action' to a single stop..consists of a draw-stop rod..a movable trundle..a trace-rod..and the lever..On pushing in the draw-stop, the action of the several parts is reversed, and the stop is silenced.

'drawable, *a.* Capable of being drawn.

1647 H. MORE *Song of Soul* II. iii. II. ii, Not fixt to ought, but by a Magick might Drawable here and there. **1867** H. KINGSLEY *Silcote of Silcotes* xv. (1876) 94 Lines..which he recognised as drawable.

drawback ('drɔːbæk), *sb.* and *a.* [f. vbl. phr. *to draw back*: see DRAW *v.* 78.]

A. *sb.* † **1.** One who draws back or retires. *Obs.*

1618 BOLTON *Florus* (1636) 101 Fabius..got the nickname, to be called, The Draw-backe, or Cunctator.

2. a. An amount paid back from a charge previously made; *esp.* a certain amount of excise or import duty paid back or remitted when the commodities on which it has been paid are exported; originally, the action of drawing or getting back a sum paid as duty.

1697 LUTTRELL *Brief Rel.* IV. 200 For a drawback of the duty on exportation thereof. **1729** SWIFT *Grand Quest. Debated* 21 In poundage and drawbacks I lose half my rent. **1775** BURKE *Corr.* (1844) II. 23 To move for the account of the duties paid on tobacco imported; and also for an account of the drawback, when exported. **1874** BANCROFT *Footpr. Time* xi. 269 All imported goods are entitled to drawback whenever they are taken out of the United States. **1883** *Law Rep.* 11 Q. Bench Div. 567 The balance in hand..shall be equally divided amongst the shareholders pro ratâ per share by way of drawback.

b. *Bookselling.* A rebate of the paper tax given under certain conditions to the King's printers and the Oxford and Cambridge University presses. *Hist.*

1796 (*title*) The Poems of Ossian... Printed for A. Strahan and T. Cadell: And sold by T. Cadell Jun. and W. Davies...MDCCXCVI (Drawback). **1797** (*title*) An Historical Essay on the Ambition and Conquests of France. ..London. Printed for J. Debrett..1797. (Drawback.)

3. A deduction, a diminution.

1753 HOGARTH *Anal. Beauty* i. 15 An unnecessary weight, which would have been a draw-back from his strength. **1818** W. TAYLOR in *Monthly Rev.* LXXXV. 395 A little draw back is made from this panegyric. **1837–9** HALLAM *Hist. Lit.* I. ii. I §39. 121 The want..was a very great drawback from the utility of their compilations.

4. Anything that retards progress or advance, or that takes from or diminishes success or satisfaction; a hindrance, disadvantage.

1720 *Humourist* 59, I have..as a Drawback upon my Ambition, laid aside my Silver Buckles. **1748** RICHARDSON *Clarissa* (1811) I. xiii. 80 Daughters were but incumbrances and drawbacks upon a family. **1853** KANE *Grinnell Exp.* iv. (1856) 32 Our little vessel pursued her way without drawback. **1865** MERIVALE *Rom. Emp.* VIII. lxvii. 284 Roman citizenship had its drawbacks as well as its advantages. **1875** SCRIVENER *Lect. Text N. Test.* 6 A serious drawback to our enjoyment.

5. A movable piece or core in a mould used in iron-founding.

1843, etc. [see *false core* (FALSE *a.* 17 a)]. **1875** [see CORE *sb.*[1] 8]. **1960** LAING & ROLFE *Man. Foundry Practice Cast Iron* (ed. 3) iv. 90 When patterns are bedded in the floor, there is rarely more than one joint. Many devices are used to avoid a second, one method being the use of drawbacks.

B. *adj.* That is, or has to be, drawn back: ***draw-back lock***, a door-lock the bolt of which can be drawn back by a knob or catch inside.

1703 MOXON *Mech. Exerc.* 23 The Draw-back Spring. **1801** W. BULLOCK in *Trans. Soc. Arts* XIX. 290 An improved Drawback Lock for House-Doors. **1866** TIMMINS *Industr. Hist. Birmingham* 87 Drawback locks..resemble dead locks, except that the bolt springs and is worked by a brass knob on the inside.

draw-bar ('drɔːbɑːr).

1. The bar that bears the draw-links or couplings by which railway carriages and trucks are connected in a train. Also of other vehicles.

1839 *Jrnl. Franklin Inst.* XXIV. 156 The bumpers or elastic cushions are to be attached..to the front and rear draw-bar. **1861** *Times* 1 June, The draw-bar of one of the trucks broke, and the draw-spring fell on the rails. **1889** *Pall Mall G.* 27 Dec. 8/2 Breaking a coupling chain or a drawbar hook. **1904** *Westm. Gaz.* 30 Mar. 2/1 Two omnibuses..and four light wagons, all..connected by spring draw-bars. **1950** *Engineering* 17 Nov. 388/3 On wet heavy land, a tractor with rubber tyres..will give a drawbar performance. **1954** *Gloss. Terms Agric. Mach.* (*B.S.I.*) 8 *Drawbar*, a member fitted to a tractor for the attachment of hauled implements.

2. A bar in a fence that can be drawn out. orig. *U.S.*

1670 *Groton Rec.* (1880) 36 A gat or a sufficient pair of draw barrs to [be] Kept and maintained at the end [of] Natha[niel] Lawrences field. **1811** *Massachusetts Spy* 3 Apr. (Th.), There were a pair of draw bars about twelve or fifteen yards from [his] door. **1836** *Southern Lit. Messenger* II. 162 On every side I was met by gates, drawbars, and gaps. **1884** R. JEFFERIES *Life of Fields* 85 The gates beside the lane were not gates at all, but double draw-bars framed together.

3. *Glass-making.* (See quot. 1948.)

1948 *Amer. Ceramic Soc. Bull.* XXVII. 356/1 *Draw bar*, submerged clay block used to define the position of sheet glass during drawing. **1970** *Glass Technol.* XI. 95A, The refractory draw bar contains sealed cavities providing buoyancy in molten glass.

'draw-boy. 1. a. *orig.* The boy employed to pull the cords of the harness in figure-weaving; hence **b.** The piece of mechanism by which this is now effected.

1731 MORTIMER in *Phil. Trans.* XXXVII. 105 Mr. Le Blon's new Way of weaving Tapestry in the Loom with a Draw-boy. **1831** G. R. PORTER *Silk Manuf.* 239 This machine..from its standing in the stead of a person who was distinguished by that name..is called a draw-boy. **1835** URE *Philos. Manuf.* 339 The occupation of draw-boys and girls to harness-loom weavers..is by far the lowest and least sought after of any connected with the manufacture of cotton. **1851** [see *draw-loom* s.v. DRAW-].

2. An article exposed for sale in a shop window at a very low price to attract customers. *slang.*

1864 HOTTEN *Slang Dict.* 125 *Draw-boy*, a cunning device used by puffing tradesmen.

'drawbridge. Forms: see BRIDGE. [f. DRAW-: see also the earlier DRAUGHT-BRIDGE.]

1. A bridge hinged at one end and free at the other, which may be drawn up and let down so as to prevent or permit passage over it, or allow passage through the channel which it crosses.

The original form was the *lifting drawbridge*, used from early times to span the foss of a castle or fortification, or the inner part of it; also in more recent times to provide a passage over canals, dock-entrances, and other waterways; for this the form called a *swing-* or *swivel-bridge*, which revolves horizontally is often substituted: see also BASCULE. A drawbridge to permit the passage of vessels, sometimes forms a small section of a long permanent bridge.

13.. *K. Alis.* 1205 Heore drawbrugge they drowe ate. **1375** BARBOUR *Bruce* XVII. 757 Thai..a fyre had maid At the draw-brig, and brynt it doune. **1556** *Chron. Gr. Friars* (Camden) 87 Wyett..made a bulwarke at the bryge fotte.. and dyd no harme there..for the brygge drawebrygge was drawne agayne hym. **1673** RAY *Journ. Low C.* 2 Before we came into the Town (Graveling) we passed over five Draw-Bridges. **1722** *Lond. Gaz.* No. 6053/1 The Draw-Bridge of the..Bridge of London will be taken up in order to lay down a new one. **1808** SCOTT *Marm.* VI. xv, The steed along the drawbridge flies, Just as it trembled on the rise. **1844** *Regul. & Ord. Army* 266 The Barriers are to be shut, Draw-Bridges drawn up. **1894** *Westm. Gaz.* 11 May 2/1 It is the surface of the 'bascule'—the 'drawbridge' part of the bridge.

2. A movable bridge or gangway on a ship, etc.

1856 S. C. BREES *Gloss. Terms* 183 The floating bridge.. is a large flat-bottomed vessel..drawbridges are made at each end which let down and form roadways. **1878** BOSW. SMITH *Carthage* 93 The drawbridge..could be swung round the mast towards the point where the danger threatened, and..let fall..with its heavy weight upon the deck of the attacking ship.

Hence **'drawbridged** *a.*, having a drawbridge.

1846 DICKENS in *Daily News* 21 Jan. 6/5 Queer old towns, draw-bridged and walled.

† **draw-can-bully.** *Obs.* = next.

1698 [R. FERGUSON] *View Eccles.* 89 Whosoever steps forth as a 'Draw can bully' to stab and murther Persons in their Credit and Reputation.

Drawcansir (drɔːˈkænsə(r)). Also **'Draw-can-sir.** Name of a blustering, bragging character in Villiers's burlesque 'The Rehearsal', who in the last scene is made to enter a battle and to kill all the combatants on both sides: hence allusively, and *attrib.*

[Formed as a parody on *Almanzor* in Dryden's *Conquest of Granada*, perhaps intended to suggest *drawing* a *can* of liquor (see the references to his drinking capacity in Act iv. sc. i. 'Enter Drawcansir').]

1672 VILLIERS (Dk. Buckhm.) *Rehearsal* IV. i. (Arb.) 95 *J.* Pray, Mr. Bayes, who is that Drawcansir? *B.* Why, Sir, a fierce Hero, that frights his Mistriss..and does what he will, without regard to good manners, justice, or numbers. **1672** MARVELL *Reh. Transp.* I. 42 But it is a brave thing to be the Ecclesiastical Draw-Can-Sir. **1690** LOCKE *Govt.* II. xvi. §177 They that found absolute monarchy upon the Title of the Sword, make their Heroes..arrant Draw-can-Sirs, and forget that they had any Officers and Soldiers. **1711** ADDISON *Spect.* No. 16 ¶3, I have so much of a Drawcansir in me, that I shall pass over a single foe to charge whole armies. **1761** COLMAN *Jealous Wife* Prol. (L.), Drawcansir death had rag'd without controul: Here the drawn dagger, there the poison'd bowl. **1768–74** TUCKER *Lt. Nat.* (1852) I. 562 Such a Drawcansir, as to cut down both friend and foe. **1797** J. WARTON in *Wilkes' Corr.* (1805) IV. 335 One shall hardly see such drawcansir-work. **1800** *Rival Bards* in *Spirit Pub. Jrnls.* (1801) IV. 394 Gifford..Now struts a Drawcansir with hideous stare! **1880** MCCARTHY *Own Times* IV. xlviii. 6 Mr. Layard..a very Drawcansir of political debate, a swashbuckler, and soldado of Parliamentary Conflict.

drawcht, obs. Sc. form of DRAUGHT.

'draw-cut, *sb.* [CUT *sb.*[2]] A cut made by a drawing movement, and not by a stroke or pressure.

1833 J. HOLLAND *Manuf. Metal* II. 45 Garden shears.. amputate by a draw-cut like a knife.

† **'draw-cut,** *ppl. a. Obs. rare.* [See CUT *sb.*[1]] Done by drawing cuts or lots.

1583 STANYHURST *Æneis* I. (Arb.) 34 Shee..toyls too pioners by drawcut lotterye sorteth.

drawe, obs. inf. and pa. pple. of DRAW *v.*; obs. form of DROVE; obs. Sc. pa. t. of DRIVE *v.*

drawee (drɔːˈiː). [See -EE[1].] The person upon whom a draft or bill of exchange is drawn.

1766 W. GORDON *Gen. Counting-ho.* 346 A bill..would not make the drawee liable. **1767** BLACKSTONE *Comm.* II. xxx. 467 The person..who writes this letter, is called in law the *drawer*, and he to whom it is written the *drawee*. *Ibid.* 469 If..the indorsee cannot get the drawee to discharge it. **1878** JEVONS *Prim. Pol. Econ.* 114 If the drawer and drawee of a bill are persons of good credit, a banker will readily discount such a bill.

drawer[1] ('drɔːə(r)). [f. DRAW *v.* + -ER[1].]

1. One who draws; in various senses of the vb.

*a***1340** HAMPOLE *Psalter* xviii. 13 Puttand away þe draghere til ill. **1483** *Cath. Angl.* 107/2 A Drawer, *vector*. **1537** BIBLE *Josh.* ix. 21 Hewers of wodd, and drawers of water. **1640** *Remonstr. Troubles fr. Estates Scot.* 20 The drawers of his Majesty to this action. **1781** P. BECKFORD in Blaine *Encycl. Sports* §1719 It is a modern fashion for the huntsman..to ride into the cover..but this proceeding is apt to render hounds bad drawers. **1838** DE MORGAN *Ess. Probab.* 58 Before the drawing was made, it was three to one that the drawer should go to the first urn.

2. *spec.* One who draws liquor for customers; a tapster at a tavern. Also in comb., as ***beer-drawer***.

1567 *Triall Treas.* (1850) 32 Drawer, let us have a pinte of whyte wine and borage. **1592** SHAKS. *Rom. & Jul.* III. i. 9. **1640** *Canterbury Marriage Licences* (MS.), John Williamson of Canterbury, Beeredrawer. **1750** JOHNSON *Rambler* No. 16 ¶5 Thundering to the drawer for another bottle. **1859** DICKENS *T. Two Cities* II. iv, Bring me another pint of this same wine, drawer.

3. A name of operatives in various industries. Chiefly in comb., as ***straw-***, ***tube-***, ***wire-drawer***.

spec. In a *Coal pit*: One who draws or hauls the coal from the face to the bottom of the shaft, a hauler. In *Weaving*: A woman who puts the warp into the splits or heddles; also, a woman who draws warps through the combs and reels. In *Gasworks*: A man who draws the coke out of the ovens. (*Labour Commission's Glossary*, 1894.)

*c***1400** Wyer drawer [see DRAUGHT 18]. **1589** *Pappe w. Hatchet* 27 Weauers and Wierdrawers. **1722** DE FOE *Plague* (Rtldg.) 126 Gold and Silverwyer-drawers. **1847** *Nat. Encycl.* I. 989 The toddy-drawer selects a tree of easy ascent. **1864** *Jrnl. R. Agric. Soc.* XXV. II. 315 The straw drawers.. purchase the straw in the bulk. **1883** *Manch. Exam.* 27 Nov. 5/5 As the getters can do nothing without the drawers, the mine is stopped. **1891** *Daily News* 23 Nov. 2/7 Metal rollers and tube drawers. **1894** *Standard* 5 Apr. 3/6 A number of loomers and drawers..met the employers in conference yesterday.

4. One who draws a draft or bill of exchange. **1682** SCARLETT *Exchanges*, The Drawer when he hath made his Bill, should make the Direction on the inside of it towards the left Hand. **1767** T. HUTCHINSON *Hist. Mass.* II. ii. 191 No merchants.. would take bills, unless the drawers would make themselves responsible. **1867** TROLLOPE *Chron. Barset* I. xl. 350 The drawer of the cheque had lost it, as he thought.

5. One who makes a drawing; a draughtsman. **1579–80** NORTH *Plutarch* (1676) 410 We will not allow the drawer to leave it out altogether. **1607** TOPSELL *Four-f. Beasts* (1658) 508 The drawer made the nostrils lesse then might answer the proportion of the face. **1705** BOSMAN *Guinea* 234 For the want of a good Drawer I cannot send you Draughts of all of them. **1832** J. HODGSON in Raine *Mem.* (1858) II. 289 A good drawer and surveyor.

6. One who draws or drafts a legal document. **1776** *Claim of Roy Rada Churn* 19/1 The drawer of the affidavit. **1884** LD. BRAMWELL in *Law Rep.* 9 App. Cases 465 The drawer of this Act of Parliament. **1892** GLADSTONE in *Daily News* 22 Oct. 5/7 The drawer of the paper.. has made one omission.

7. a. An instrument, tool, or agent for drawing; an extractor. **1536** BELLENDEN *Cron. Scot.* (1821) II. 511 Ane instrument of tre, like the drawer of ane wel. **1607** TOPSELL *Four-f. Beasts* (1658) 314 Open the rift with a rosenet or drawer. *Ibid.* 322 Get out the gravel with a cornet or drawer. **1610** MARKHAM *Masterp.* II. clxxiii. 491 Iuy is a great drawer, and opener. **1737** BRACKEN *Farriery Impr.* (1756) I. 187 Such Medicaments as are.. stiled Ripeners or Drawers.

b. *Printing.* = TYMPAN 4. **1896** DE VINNE *Moxon's Mech. Exerc. Printing* 410 The pasting down of the vellum on the inner side of the tympan (now known as the drawer).

8. With adv. as ***drawer-in, -on, -out. drawer-off*** (in various trades: see Dict. Occup. Terms, 1921). *c* **1400** *Test. Love* I. Chaucer's Wks. (1561) 290 b/2 Thylke thinges been my drawers in. **1611** COTGR., *Retrayeur*, a redeemer, a fetcher or drawer back of. **1614** W. B. *Philosopher's Banquet* (ed. 2) 18 The ayre is a great.. drawer-on of health. **1847** MRS. GORE *Castles in Air* v. (Stratm.), The drawer-up of my godfather's will. **1908** *Westm. Gaz.* 9 Oct. 3/1 'Drawers-off' in saw-mills.

drawer[2] (drɔːə(r)). [f. DRAW *v.*: cf. F. *tiroir*, f. *tirer* to draw.] **a.** A box-shaped receptacle, fitting into a space in a cabinet or table, so that it can be drawn out horizontally in order to get access to it. **1580** HOLLYBAND *Treas. Fr. Tong*, *Vn escrin*.. a casket, a little chest, a drawer. **1583** —— *Campo di Fior* 145 Reache the cardes, which thou shalt finde in the drawer of the table. **1710** STEELE *Tatler* No. 245 ¶2 A small Cabinet, with Six Drawers. **1855** MACAULAY *Hist. Eng.* IV. 251 All his bookcases and drawers were examined.

b. *pl.* ***drawers*** = ***chest of drawers***: a piece of furniture made to contain a number of drawers, arranged in tiers, and having usually a flat top, used as a writing-table, toilet-table, or the like. **1677–1859** Chest of drawers [see CHEST *sb.*[1] 8]. **1697–9** DAMPIER *Voy.* an. 1688 (R.), Corners of drawers or cabinets. **1813** *Examiner* 8 Feb. 84/2 A suit of.. clothes.. happened to be on the drawers. **1850** MRS. F. VIDAL *Orphan* ii. 11, I moved away my pink ribbon off the drawers.

c. *attrib.* Also **drawerful**. **1828** MISS MITFORD *Village* Ser. III. (1863) 513 A whole drawerful of skeins. **1850** CHUBB *Locks & Keys* 14 A three-inch drawer-lock. **1919** G. B. SHAW *Heartbreak House* I. 23 He has a whole drawerful of Albert Medals. **1962** *Sunday Express* 8 July 15/3 Stockings.. by the drawerful.

drawers (drɔːəz), *sb. pl.* [From quot. 1567, app. a term of low origin, which has risen into general use: f. DRAW *v.*, prob. as things which one draws on.] A garment for the lower part of the body and legs: now usually restricted to under-hose worn next the skin. (In some early instances the word appears to mean stockings.) **1567** HARMAN *Caveat* 83 Here followyth their pelting speche.. Whych language they terme Peddelars Frenche.. A commission, a shierte; drawers, hosen; stampers, shooes. **1576** *Inv.* in *Ripon Ch. Acts* 378 A paire of drawers of mockadoo. **1611** COTGR., *Brayes*, short (and close) breeches, drawers, or vnderhose, of linnen, &c. *Ibid.*, *House*, a drawer, or course stocking worne ouer a finer, by countrey people. **1655** NEWBRUGH in *Nicholas Papers* (Camden) II. 290, I haue sent an Indian gowne and stuff for drawers. **1658** HOWELL *Part. Vocab.*, *Drawers*, le sotto calzetti, les chaussettes. **1711** STEELE *Spect.* No. 51 ¶5 Makes a Country Squire strip to his Holland Drawers. **1717** LADY M. W. MONTAGU *Let. to C'tess Mar* 1 Apr., The first part of my dress is a pair of drawers, very full, that reach to my shoes. **1791** HUDDESFORD *Salmag.* 66 Cricket, nimble boy and light, In slippers red and drawers white. **1893** SINCLAIR & HENRY *Swimming* (Badm. Lib.) 374 A skin-tight costume.. with bathing-drawers underneath of silk.

draw-file ('drɔːfaɪl), *v.* [f. DRAW- vb. -stem used adverbially.] *trans.* To file or roughen a surface by drawing the file along it longitudinally without lateral movement, as in using a spoke-shave. **1884** F. J. BRITTEN *Watch & Clockm.* 35 The bouchon.. should be previously lightly draw-filed at the end.

'drawgate. A sluice-gate; a shuttle in the gate of a canal-lock which is drawn up to let part of the water escape. **1791** *Rep. Navig. Thames & Isis* 2 Estimate 2 A new Pound Lock and Wear rebuilt with Draw-Gates. **1793** R. MYLNE *Rep. Thames* 16 A single Pair of Gates, with draw-Gates or Cloughs therein. **1861** SMILES *Engineers* II. 69 To provide them with nine draw-gates.

drawght, obs. form of DRAUGHT.

draw-glove.

†**1.** (Also *draw-gloves*.) An old parlour game, also called ***drawing (of) gloves***, which consisted apparently in a race at drawing off gloves at the utterance of certain words. *Obs.* *c* **1400** *Destr. Troy* 2938 Drawing of glovis, With comonyng in company.. Gers maidnes be mart, mariage fordone. **1598** DRAYTON *Heroic. Ep.* 370 (N.) In pretty riddles to bewray our loves, In questions, purpose, or in drawing gloves. **1648** HERRICK *Hesper.* (1869) 104 (*Draw Gloves*) At draw-gloves we'l play, And prethee, let's lay A wager, and let it be this; Who first to the summe Of twenty shall come Shall have for his winning a kisse. *Ibid.* 230. **1767** H. BROOKE *Fool of Qual.* (1859) I. 21 Here our hero was beaten hollow, as he was afterward at drawglove and shuffle the slipper.

2. An archer's drawing-glove.

drawing ('drɔːɪŋ), *vbl. sb.* [f. DRAW *v.*]

1. a. *gen.* The action of the verb DRAW in its various senses: the imparting of motion or impulse in the direction of the actuating force; pulling, dragging, draught, hauling, traction; attraction, extraction, removal, derivation; formal composition (of a document), †translation, etc. *c* **1305** *St. Lucy* 136 in *E.E.P.* (1862) 105 Summe þeȝ hit fewe beo: mid lasse drawinge wolleþ gon. **1398** TREVISA *Barth. De P.R.* IX. i. (1495) 345 The stone Adamas meuyth by strong drawinge yren. **1413** *Pilgr. Sowle* (Caxton) II. li. (1859) 54 Synne.. done.. by drawyng and inclynacion of the freel flesshe. **1450–1530** *Myrr. our Ladye* 3 Of psalmes.. ye may haue them of Rycharde hampoules drawynge. **1509** HAWES *Past. Pleas.* I. xxiii, Shotyng and drawyng of the bowe. **1548** HALL *Chron.*, *Hen. VIII*, 17 b, Beastes mete for drawyng. **1686** [BLORE] *Gent. Recreat.* II. 78 To beat the Bushes after a Fox is termed Drawing. **1712** J. JAMES tr. *Le Blond's Gardening* 209 Clay.. costs nothing but the Drawing. **1893** *Times* 14 July 11/4 At the drawing of stumps at 7 o'clock. **1894** MRS. H. WARD *Marcella* I. 176 A romantic drawing towards the stateliness and power which it all implied.

b. *concr.* That which is drawn, or obtained by drawing; *spec.* in *pl.*, the amount of money taken in a shop, or drawn in the course of business. *a* **1852** F. M. WHITCHER *Widow Bedott P.* (1883) v. 18 She sent to borrer somethin or other—a loaf o' bread—or a drawin' o' tea. **1855** T. C. HALIBURTON *Nat. & Hum. Nat.* II. 350 'I believe,' she said, 'I have a drawing of tea left,' and taking from the shelf a small mahogany caddy, emptied it of its contents. **1883** *Harper's Mag.* 829/2 To these.. is given the second drawing of the tea.

2. a. The formation of a line by drawing some tracing instrument from point to point of a surface; representation by lines, delineation; hence, 'any mode of representation in which the delineation of form predominates over considerations of colour'; the draughtsman's art.

out of drawing, incorrectly drawn, esp. in relation to the point of sight, out of proper perspective. **1530** PALSGR. 215/1 Drawyng of an ymage, *portraicture*. **1669** STURMY *Mariner's Mag.* II. 53 You must have a Gauge.. for the drawing of straight Lines on your Scale. **1769** SIR J. REYNOLDS *Disc.* ii. (1887) 21 Painting comprises both drawing and colouring. **1816** J. SMITH *Panorama Sc. & Art* II. 697 Drawing, strictly speaking, includes only the art of forming the resemblance of objects by means of out-lines; but it is usual to call those performances drawings, where only a single colour, as Indian ink, is employed to produce shades. **1859** REEVE *Brittany* 59 The building in our stereograph is.. out of drawing. **1884** *Century Mag.* XXIX. 205/2 'Drawing', though it must often be used with less precision, really implies work with the point. **1887** RUSKIN *Præterita* II. 251 The plates.. were.. the first examples of the sun's drawing that were ever seen in Oxford.

b. *transf.* The arrangement of the lines which determine form. **1753** HOGARTH *Anal. Beauty* x. 110 Legs much swoln with disease.. having lost their 'drawing', as the painters call it. **1881** GRACE *Landscape Paint.* 62 The late autumn is.. good for sketching trees, as you can see their anatomy and drawing.

3. That which is drawn; a delineation by pen, pencil, or crayon; a representation in black and white, or in monochrome; a sketch. **1668–9** PEPYS *Diary* 23 Jan., Looking on my.. pictures, and my wife's drawings. **1769** SIR J. REYNOLDS *Disc.* i. (R.), They made a variety of sketches; then a finished drawing of the whole. **1778** *Ibid.* viii. (1887) 151 A collection of drawings by great painters. **1859** GULLICK & TIMBS *Paint.* 303 We can readily understand how paintings in water colours came to be called simply 'drawings'. **1868** BROWNING *Ring & Bk.* I. 57 Modern chalk drawings.

4. In Textile manufacture, applied to various operations: see quots. Also with *-in*. **1831** G. R. PORTER *Silk Manuf.* 220 The next process is drawing or entering, which is passing each thread of the warp regularly through its appropriate loop in the heddle. **1843** *Lowell* (Mass.) *Offering* III. 215 One of the writers.. has had an opportunity to work at 'drawing in' (that is, drawing the threads through the harnesses). **1844** G. DODD *Textile Manuf.* iii. 101 Next succeed the various processes of 'winding', 'warping', 'beaming', 'drawing in', &c. **1864** R. A. ARNOLD *Cotton Fam.* 29 The tender production of the carding-engine is subjected to the drawing-frames, which give a little more consistence and much greater length to the fleecy rope, now become a 'drawing'. **1894** *Labour Commission* Gloss., *Drawing*, a number of operations from combing to spinning.. to reduce the thickness of the sliver of wool by *drawing* the warp through the 'reed'. **1927** T. WOODHOUSE *Artificial Silk* xi. 118 The weaver's beam is taken to the drawing-in department, where all the threads are drawn through the mails of the healds.. and then passed through the dents of a weaving reed. **1960** *Textile Terms & Defs.* (*Textile Inst.*) (ed. 4) 57 *Drawing-in*, the process of drawing the threads of the warp through the eyes of the healds and the dents of the reed. The operation thus includes that of reeding.

5. With *advbs.*, as ***drawing back, near, up***, etc. **1523** LD. BERNERS *Froiss.* I. ccclxxxi. (R), They haue.. good breed, and we haue the drawyng out of the chaff. **1530** PALSGR. 215/1 Drawyng nere.. *approche*. **1636** SANDERSON *Serm.* II. 53 What shrinking and drawing back! **1647** JER. TAYLOR *Lib. Proph.* iii. (R.), Little drawings aside of the curtains of peace and eternity. **1710** PALMER *Proverbs* 174 To.. insult him upon his drawing off. **1816** JANE AUSTEN *Emma* I. v. 72, I have seen a great many lists of her drawing up. **1873** HELPS *Anim. & Mast.* ii. (1875) 39 Entrusted with the drawing-up of the ultimate document.

6. *Comb.* **a.** In various senses, as **drawing account**, an account from which money can be drawn, a current account; see also quot. 1962; **drawing-awl**, an awl having an eye near the point, as to carry a thread through the hole bored; †**drawing-bed**, an extensible bed; **drawing-bench**, a bench or table in the mint on which strips of metal are drawn to the same thickness for coining; also a bench on which a cooper works with his drawing-knife; †**drawing-bridge** = DRAWBRIDGE; **drawing-engine**, a stationary steam-engine used to draw loads up an incline, the shaft of a mine, etc.; **drawing-frame**, a machine in which the slivers from the carding-machine are drawn out and attenuated; **drawing-glove**, a glove worn by archers on the right hand in drawing the bow; **drawing-machine**, a machine through which strips of metal are drawn to be made thin and even, or of a desired curve, etc.; **drawing-press**, a machine for cutting and pressing sheet metal into a required shape, as for pans, dish-covers, and the like; **drawing-rolls**, in a spinning mill, rolls between which the slivers pass in the process of 'drawing'; **drawing-string**, a string passed through a hem, casing, or eyelet holes, by which the sides of an article (as a bag) may be drawn together, or on which it may (as a curtain) be suspended instead of a rod; **drawing-table**, a table extensible by drawing out slides or leaves. **1835** *Drawing account [see DEPOSITOR 2]. **1920** H. CRANE *Let.* 30 July (1965) 41 A drawing account at the bank at my own disposal in addition to a good percentage commission on everything I sell. **1962** S. STRAND *Marketing Dict.* 223 *Drawing account*, a company's system of credit permitting withdrawals by salesmen against future commission earnings. **1439** *Will of Lochard* (Somerset Ho.), Lectos extendibiles vocatos *drawyngbeddes. **1879** *Cassell's Techn. Educ.* IV. 298/1 The drawing tool.. is a heavy block of steel with a hole in the centre, fixed upon the substantial bed of the long *drawing-bench. **1638** SIR T. HERBERT *Trav.* (ed. 2) 334 A dozen iron Gates, and *drawing Bridges. **1835** URE *Philos. Manuf.* 123 The important part which Arkwright's *drawing-frame performs in a cotton-mill. **1847** *Illustr. Lond. News* 10 July 19/3 The mill.. contained from 70 to 100 spinning and drawing frames. **1881** GREENER *Gun* 296 The thimble is then.. forced through the *drawing-machine again. **1832** J. P. KENNEDY *Swallow Barn* II. xviii. 225 Faces shortened as if with *drawing-strings. **1886** T. HARDY *Mayor of Casterbr.* 41 Dimity curtains on a drawing-string.

b. Of or pertaining to delineation, DRAWING 2, as ***drawing-box, -office, -pencil, -room, -school, -table***, etc.; **drawing-block**, a block composed of leaves of drawing-paper adhering at the edges, so as to be removable one by one when used; **drawing board**, a board on which paper is stretched for drawing on; colloq. phr. ***back to the drawing board***: used after the failure of some enterprise, an invention, etc.; **drawing-book**, a book for drawing in, wholly blank, or with designs to be copied; **drawing-compass, -es**, a pair of compasses having a pencil or pen in lieu of one of the points; **drawing-paper**, stout paper of various kinds intended for drawing on; **drawing-pen**, an instrument adjustable by a screw to draw ink lines of varying thicknesses; **drawing-pin**, a flat-headed pin used to fasten drawing-paper to a board, desk, etc. **1809** R. LANGFORD *Introd. Trade* 63, 2 Reams *Drawing Atlas [paper]. **1881** MISS BRADDON *Asph.* I. 7 Daphne produced her *drawing-block, and opened her colour-box. **1725** W. HALFPENNY *Sound Building* 26 On a *Drawing-Board, or Floor, describe.. the Arch *ABC*. **1965** *New Statesman* 9 Apr. 561/1 The super-fast giants.. are now coming on to the drawing boards. **1965** *New Yorker* 6 Nov. 122 A fiery mushroom cloud, translatable by the most cretinous moviegoer as.. 'Back to the drawing board, you plucky amoebas!' **1967** E. SHORT *Embroidery & Fabric Collage* iv. 108 Small pieces can be stretched on a drawing board; for large hangings the floor may have to be used. **1968** *Listener* 2 May 562/3 The squeaking [of some newly designed chairs] as we rolled about was too much for the sound people. So again ordinary chairs replaced them. Back to the drawing-board, Byron. **1755** (*title*) The Complete *Drawing Book, Containing many and curious Specimens. **1863** MISS WHATELY *Ragged life in Egypt* xvi. 152, I came down with a drawing-book to sit near the door. **1800** M.

EDGEWORTH *Parents' Assistant* (ed. 3) IV. I. 160 Lady Augusta's apartment, in which her writing-desk, her *drawing-box, and her piano-forte stood. **1873** C. M. YONGE *Pillars of House* II. xxiii. 264 John Harewood returned, bringing with him what Alda took for a dressing-case, and Cherry for a drawing-box. **1798** JANE AUSTEN *Let.* 18 Dec. (1952) 41, I have been forced to let James & Miss Debary have two sheets of your *Drawing paper. **1804** CT. RUMFORD in *Phil. Trans.* XCIV. 135 A circular piece of thick drawing-paper. **1706** PHILLIPS (ed. Kersey), **Drawing-pen*, an Instrument..to draw Lines finer or thicker. **1728** R. MORRIS *Ess. Anc. Archit.* Advt., Mathematical instruments ..Compasses, Drawing-Pens. **1859** F. A. GRIFFITHS *Artil. Man.* (1862) 368 Fixing it firmly by means of *drawing-pins. **1706** PHILLIPS (ed. Kersey), **Drawing-table*, an Instrument with a Frame, to hold a Sheet of Royal-Paper, for Draughts of Ships, Fortifications, etc.

'drawing, *ppl. a.* [f. as prec. + -ING[2].]

1. *gen.* That draws, in various senses of the verb.

1576 TURBERV. *Venerie* 179 We take them..with a drawing ferret when they be yong. **1659** D. PELL *Impr. Sea* 315 A deep drawing Vessel. **1890** BAKER *Wild Beasts* II. 49 With one desperate drawing cut across the throat he reached the spine.

2. *spec.* Used to draw vehicles, etc.; draught-.

1551 ROBINSON tr. *More's Utop.* II. (Arb.) 158 Drawing and bearinge beastes. **1683** *Lond. Gaz.* No. 1810/4 A brown bay drawing Gelding. **1875** R. F. MARTIN *Winding Machin.* 40 The two head-gear pulleys..at the drawing shaft.

3. That draws out purulent or foreign matter from a wound, etc.

1398 TREVISA *Barth. De P.R.* VII. lxix. (1495) 288 Thenne the leche vsyth drawynge medycynes. *c* **1400** *Lanfranc's Cirurg.* 232 þis enpostym schal be helid wiþ drawynge þingis and wastynge. **1795** *Hull Advertiser* 17 Oct. 1/4 A drawing plaister was speedily applied. **1857** DUNGLISON *Med. Dict.* 302 Substances which..promote suppuration..are vulgarly termed drawing.

4. Attractive; esp. in ***drawing card***, an attraction that attracts a large crowd, an audience, etc.

1577 FENTON *Gold. Epist.* (1582) 282 She was of goodlye personage, hir aspecte sweete and drawing. **1669** BUNYAN *Holy Citie* 181 It had a very taking and drawing Glory in it. **1887** in *Amer. Speech* (1950) XXV. 32/2 It proves as good a drawing card as ever. **1894** W. T. VINCENT *Rec. F. Leslie* I. ix. 155 A salary adequate to his 'drawing' capacity. **1906** *Westm. Gaz.* 8 Sept. 12/3 The income..varies exceedingly, depending upon the subject taught,..as well as the personal drawing-power of the teacher. **1930** *Daily Express* 6 Nov. 15/4 The biggest drawing card Europe has ever known was Georges Carpentier. **1959** *News Chron.* 9 Dec. 3/1 More than any other guest singer on the Covent Garden list, Maria Callas has the biggest drawing power and means the biggest business.

† **'drawing-chamber.** *Obs.* A drawing-room: see WITHDRAWING-CHAMBER.

1582 WHETSTONE *Heptameron* Cjb, After..Dinner.. Queene Aurelia with a chosen company, retyred her selfe, into a pleasant drawing Chamber. **1642** *Declar. Lords & Com.* 19 May 25 Meeting Mr. Jermyn in the Queens drawing Chamber. **1649** *Inv.* in *Merton Reg.* II. 361 In the Drawing chamber. **1813** in *Spirit Pub. Jrnls.* XVII. 122 For my drawing-chambers..I will have them delicately furnished.

'drawing-knife. **a.** = DRAW-KNIFE a. **b.** = DRAW-KNIFE b. **c.** (See quot. 1842–76.)

1737 BRACKEN *Farriery Impr.* (1756) I. 354 The Farrier's drawing Knife. **1794** *Rigging & Seamanship* I. 151 *Drawing Knife*..sometimes used instead of the stock-sheave, to pare off the rough wood. **1815** *Sporting Mag.* XLVI. 159 If..the drawing-knife [be] used every time he is shod, he will be tender footed. **1831** J. HOLLAND *Manuf. Metal* I. 318 A carpenter buys a drawing-knife, which is a stout blade, edged in the middle, and handled at both ends. **1842–76** GWILT *Encycl. Archit.* Gloss., *Drawing Knife*, an edge tool used to make an incision on the surface of wood along which the saw is to follow. It prevents the teeth of the saw tearing the surface.

† **'drawingly,** *adv. Obs.* [f. DRAWING *ppl. a.* + -LY[2].] In a slow, deliberate, or hestitating manner; drawlingly.

[**1561** T. HOBY *Courtier* I. Dijb, Their woordes they pronounce so drawnyngly, that a man would weene they were..yelding vp the ghost.] **1598** FLORIO, *Cacatamente*, sneakingly, drawingly..faltringly. **1626** BACON *Notes Civ. Conv.* Mor. & Hist. Wks. (Bohn) 198 To speak leisurely, and rather drawingly, than hastily. **1662** J. CHANDLER *Van Helmont's Oriat.* 18 Scarce the space, wherein any one might drawingly pronounce four syllables.

'drawing-master. A teacher of drawing. Hence **drawing-masterish** *a.*, **-mastership.**

a **1779** TWEDDELL *Rem.* lix. 273 (Jod.) Consult a drawing-master upon the subject. **1821** CRAIG *Lect. Drawing* iv. 196 The general standard of proportion which has doubtless been laid down to you by your drawing masters. **1885** *Athenæum* 12 Sept. 341/1 A sort of drawing mastership *in excelsis*. **1889** BLACK *Penance of John Logan* 207 A pretty drawing-masterish kind of a sketch.

drawing-room[1] ('drɔːɪŋruːm). [Shortened from WITHDRAWING-ROOM, which is found in 16th c. and is very common in 17th.]

1. a. *orig.* A room to withdraw to, a private chamber attached to a more public room (see WITHDRAWING-ROOM); now, a room reserved for the reception of company, and to which the ladies withdraw from the dining-room after dinner.

1642 LD. SUNDERLAND *Let. to Wife*, The king..is very cheerful, and by the bawdy discourse I thought I had been in the drawing room. **1675** BROOKS *Gold. Key* Wks. 1867 V. 579 Here are chambers, with drawing-rooms provided, not open chambers, but with doors..shut round about. *c* **1710** C. FIENNES *Diary* (1888) 239 Next this is the drawing roome of state. **1728** YOUNG *Love Fame* I. Wks. (1757) 88 Nor shoots up folly to a nobler bloom In her own native soil, the drawing-room. **1791** BOSWELL *Johnson* 25 Apr. an. 1778, We went to the drawing-room, where was a considerable increase of company. **1856** EMERSON *Eng. Traits, Manners* Wks. (Bohn) II. 51 The gentlemen..rejoin the ladies in the drawing-room, and take coffee.

b. The company assembled in a drawing-room.

[**1732** BERKELEY *Alciphr.* I. §11 In any drawing-room or assembly of polite people.] **1841–4** EMERSON *Ess., Manners* Wks. (Bohn) I. 212 The person who screams..or converses with heat, puts whole drawing-rooms to flight. **1856** MACAULAY *Johnson* Misc. Writ. (1889) 374 He would amaze a drawing-room by suddenly ejaculating a clause of the Lord's Prayer.

c. *U.S.* Formerly, a section or carriage of a railway-train more luxurious or more private than usual. Also *attrib.*

1867 *Commerc. & Financ. Chron.* V. 347/2 A new and magnificent sleeping and drawing-room car of the Pullman patent has been..placed on the Michigan Central road. **1873** 'MARK TWAIN' & WARNER *Gilded Age* 264 A lady timidly entered the drawing-room car. **1882** SALA *Amer. Revis.* (1885) 88 The Pullman 'parlor'—or, as it is called in England, 'drawing-room Car'. **1931** E. LINKLATER *Juan in Amer.* II. vi. 101 There were many so-called drawing-room compartments on the train. **1936** L. C. DOUGLAS *White Banners* xviii. 393 Uncle Thomas will still eat, and buy two tickets so he can travel in a Pullman drawing-room.

2. A levee held in a drawing-room; a formal reception by a king, queen, or person of rank; that at which ladies are 'presented' at court.

[**1673** DRYDEN *Marr. à la Mode* II. i, You shall be every day at the King's levee and I at the queen's; and we will never meet but in the drawing-room. **1706–7** FARQUHAR *Beaux' Strat.* IV. ii, Whereas, If I marry my Lord Aimwell, there will be Title, Place and Precedence, the Park, the Play, and the Drawing-Room.] **1711** SWIFT *Jrnl. to Stella* 8 Aug., There was a drawing-room to-day at court. **1714** *Lond. Gaz.* No. 5267/8 In the Evening her Highness kept a Drawing-Room, at which were all the Ladies and Persons of Distinction of this Place. **1838** COL. HAWKER *Diary* (1893) II. 148 The last Drawing Room of the season; so of course an awful crowd. **1868** Q. VICTORIA *Tours Eng. & Irel.* 183 At half past Eight we drove into Dublin for the Drawing-room. It is always held here of an evening..One thousand six hundred ladies were presented.

3. *attrib.* **a.** *gen.*

1703 *Lond. Gaz.* No. 3980/1 He met Her at Her Drawing-Room Door. **1786** MAD. D'ARBLAY *Diary* 27 July, The Queen..puts on her drawing-room apparel at St. James's. **1848** W. H. KELLY tr. *L. Blanc's Hist. Ten Y.* II. 379 The drawing-room influence thus set in motion. **1888** LOWELL *Lit. Ess.* (1892) 11 Domestic and drawing-room prose as distinguished from that of the pulpit, the forum, or the closet.

b. Used allusively to qualify a version of a story, etc., fitted by its observance of the proprieties for the society of the drawing-room.

1877 *Porcupine* 20 Jan. 676/3 It was desirable to modify the language a little, and the drawing-room version ran thus. **1885** A. EDWARDS *Girton Girl* II. ii. 22 An actor in a similar bit of drawing-room comedy. **1887** KIPLING *Under Deodars* (1888) 61 Where..did you pick up the *Chanson du Colonel*? It isn't a drawing-room song. It isn't proper. **1898, 1906** [see BALLAD 2]. **1900** G. B. SHAW *Prefaces* (1934) xxix. 709/2 Love is the one subject that the drawing room drama dare not present. **1904** *Sat. Rev.* 9 Apr. 456/1 An infinity of barren drawing-room comedy or drawing-room comedy-drama. **1909** *Daily Chron.* 23 Sept. 1/3 The Prime Minister's Birmingham version of the Budget struck me.. as having been intended for what I may call drawing-room use. **1915** ROSHER *In R.N.A.S.* (1916) 82 What do you think of this story, the latest from the trenches? It's not quite a drawing-room one! **1959** J. BRAINE *Vodi* xv. 200 The neatly-folded scarf gave him a drawing-room comedy smartness. **1966** *Listener* 15 Dec. 893/3 He contented himself within his own natural resources—classical Lieder, the standard oratorios and the best of the 'drawing-room ballads'.

Hence **'drawing-,roomy** *a.*, characteristic of the drawing-room, as being over-refined, insipid, etc.

1906 *Daily Chron.* 18 May 9/3 Miss Evelyn Millard's Desdemona was a disappointment. She was terribly drawing-roomy. **1907** *Ibid.* 18 June 6/4 The sentiment was sometimes rather drawing-roomy. **1947** N. CARDUS *Autobiogr.* I. 132 Grieg's rather drawing-roomy 'Un Rêve'.

drawing-room[2]. A room for drawing in: see DRAWING *vbl. sb.* 6 b.

drawish ('drɔːɪʃ), *a. Chess.* [f. DRAW *sb.* + -ISH[1].] Of a position, move, etc.: likely to lead to or result in a draw.

1922 *Brit. Chess Mag.* XLII. 388 Tarrasch guided the game into drawish lines. **1936** W. WINTER *Chess for Match Players* ii. 59 Black has an easy equalizing line by which he can secure a drawish position without any risk. **1974** C. H. O'D. ALEXANDER *Alexander on Chess* vi. 132 Should White play 3PxP, PxP then a dull and very drawish game results. **1981** H. GOLOMBEK *Beginning Chess* vi. 96 The opening was highly popular in the nineteenth century but lost its popularity..once it was realized how drawish violent openings tend to become.

drawk, drauk (drɔːk), *sb.* Also 4–6 **drauke**, 5–9 **drake**, 6, 9 **dravick**, (8–9 erron. **drank**), 9 **droke**. [Corresponds to OF. *droe, droue*, F. *droc*, med.L. *drauca*, MDu. *dravik*, mod.Du. *dravig*, according to Verdam *Bromus secalinus*.]

A kind of grass growing as a weed among corn; app. orig. *Bromus secalinus*, but also applied (at least in books) to *Lolium temulentum* and *Avena fatua*, and so confounded with 'cockle' or 'darnel' (*lolium, zizania*), and wild oats.

c **1325** *Metr. Hom.* 152 With gastly drauc and wit darnele. *c* **1325** *Gloss. W. de Biblesw.* in *Rel. Ant.* II. 80 Drauck, *betel.* *c* **1440** *Promp. Parv.* 130/2 Drawke, wede, *drauca.* *c* **1475** *Voc.* in Wr.-Wülcker 787/1 *Hec zizania*, a drawke. **1483** *Cath. Angl.* 107/2 Drake or darnylle. **1523** FITZHERB. *Husb.* §20 Drake is lyke vnto rye, till it begynne to sede. **1578** LYTE *Dodoens* IV. xvi. 470 *Festuca*, or as the Douchmen call it Drauick, is also a hurtfull plant, hauing his leaues and strawe not much vnlyke Rye, at the top whereof growe spreading eares..it may be also very well called..in Englishe Wilde Otes, or Drauick. **1597** GERARDE *Herbal* I. lv. (1633) 76 *Bromus Altera*, Drauke. **1802** BARRINGTON *Hist. N.S. Wales* vi. 159 The corn..was much mixed with a weed called drake. *a* **1825** FORBY *Voc. E. Anglia, Drawk*, the common darnel-grass. **1846** *Jrnl. R. Agric. Soc.* VII. II. 351 Droke is the enemy most to be dreaded in strong soils.

drawk, *v. Sc.* and *north. dial.* Also 6, 9 **draik**, 8 **drake**, 9 **drauk**. [Etymology obscure: perh. related to ON. *drekkja* to drench, drown, swamp, submerge.] *trans.* To saturate with moisture, as flour or quicklime with water.

1500–20 DUNBAR *Poems* xxxiii. 102 All his pennis war drownd and drawkit [*v.r.* draikit]. **1776** SIR J. MALCOLM in *Herd's Collect.* II. 99 (Jam.) The tail o't hang down, Like a meikle maan lang draket gray goose-pen. **1810** CROMEK *Rem. Nithsdale Song* (1880) 58 O dight, quo she, yere mealy mou', For my twa lips ye're drauking. **1825** BROCKETT *N.C. Gloss., Drawk, Drack*, to saturate with water. **1856** W. A. FOSTER in W. S. Crockett *Minstr. of Merse* (1893) 152 The muir-fowl likes the heatherbell When draiket wi' the dew.

draw-knife. **a.** A tool, consisting of a blade with a handle at each end, used for shaving or scraping a surface. **b.** A farrier's instrument. Cf. DRAWING-KNIFE.

1703 MOXON *Mech. Exerc.* 122 With the handles of the Draw-knife in both their Hands, enter the edge of the Draw-knife into the Work, and draw Chips almost the length of their Work. **1711** *Lond. Gaz.* No. 4863/4 Each fore Foot cut in three places with a draw Knife. **1868** R. TAYLOR *Past & Present of N.Z.* xiii. 292 So destructive did the natives find the [introduced] mouse that they called it the *toro naihi*, or scythe,..literally 'drawknife', a very sharp instrument used by whalers in cutting off blubber from the fish. **1881** GREENER *Gun* 249 The stock is then rounded up with a draw-knife. **1948** E. J. STOWE *Crafts of Countryside* xx. 121 Straight draw-knives are common and can be bought at any ironmonger's shop, but the curved ones are uncommon and are usually made by the blacksmith. **1959** *Times* 30 May 9/5 A farrier's rasp is a much safer instrument to use than a draw-knife. **1969** E. H. PINTO *Treen* 391 The origin of the draw-knife or shave..has never been traced.

drawl (drɔːl), *v.* Also 7–8 **draul(e**. [Appears in end of 16th c.: perh. introduced in Vagabonds' Cant from Du. or LG. Cf. Du. *dralen* to loiter, linger, delay, in Kilian (1599) *draelen* 'cunctari, morari, trahere moram' (prob. also in MDu.), LG. *drâlen*, EFris. *dralen*, in same sense; also EFris. *draueln, draulen*, LG. *draueln* (*Brem. Wb.*) to linger, loiter, dawdle. App., in origin, an intensive deriv. from the root of DRAW *v.*: cf. mod.Icel. *dralla* quasi *dragla* to loiter.]

1. a. *intr.* To move along with slow and loitering pace; to crawl or drag *along*. Now *rare* or *Obs.*

1652 BENLOWES *Theoph.* II. liii. 30 Whose..march..is slow as drawling snails. **1725** BRADLEY *Fam. Dict.* s.v. *Warren*, Suffering your Net to drawl on the Ground. **1780** MAD. D'ARBLAY *Diary* May, Charlotte..drawled towards us, and asked me why I would not dance? **1829** *Examiner* 616/2 Sporting in the moonshine, and drawling along the streets. *a* **1918** W. OWEN *Poems* (1963) 63 The blind-cord drawls across the window-sill.

b. Of words.

1597 BP. HALL *Sat.* I. vi. 8 The nimble dactils striving To out-go The drawling spondees pacing it below. **1743** R. BLAIR *Grave* 316 Duller rhymes With heavy halting pace that drawl along. **1836** T. HOOK *G. Gurney* III. 118 His words..drawled slowly over his lips.

2. *intr.* To prolong or lengthen out the sounds of speech in an indolent or affected manner; to speak slowly, by affectedly prolonging the words.

1598 SHAKS. *Merry W.* II. i. 145, I neuer heard such a drawling-affecting rogue. **1604** R. CAWDREY *Table Alph.* (1613), *Draule*, to speake slowly. **1728** POPE *Dunc.* II. 388 The clerks..in one lazy tone, Thro' the long, heavy, painful page drawl on. **1784** COWPER *Task* I. 95 The tedious Rector drawling o'er his head. **1885** *Manch. Weekly Times* 6 June 5/5 A long-winded orator..is left to drawl away by himself.

3. *trans.* To utter with lazy slowness: chiefly with *out*. Also freq. with quoted words as obj.

1663 HAWKINS *Youths Behav.* 24 If any drawl forth his words. **1795** MASON *Ch. Mus.* iii. 202 The Psalms..drawled out and bawled with..unmusical and unmeaning vehemence. **1824** L. MURRAY *Eng. Gram.* (ed. 5) I. 355 [To say] do-o-main, pul-lee, ho-lee, fu-ree, &c. protracting or drawling out the syllable. **1842** LEVER *J. Hinton* xxx, 'Them chaps always recover,' drawled out the doctor in a dolorous cadence. **1865** TROLLOPE *Belton Est.* xvi. 187 When the squire..drawled out some expression of regret. **1878** R. L. STEVENSON *New Arab. Nts.* II. vi. 66 'Ye—es,' drawled Northmour.

4. To cause to pass *on* or *away*, or move along slowly and laggingly; to drag *out*, *on*, etc.
1758 JOHNSON *Idler* No. 15 ¶7 Thus..does she constantly drawl out her time, without either profit or satisfaction. 1769 *Misc.* in *Ann. Reg.* 210/2 Their mornings are drauled away, with perhaps a saunter upon the beach. 1774 GOLDSM. *Nat. Hist.* I. 197 This languid and spiritless existence is frequently drawled on. 1825 COBBETT *Rur. Rides* (1830) I. 119 The Chancery would drawl it out till [etc.].

Hence **drawled** *ppl. a.*, **'drawling** *vbl. sb.*; also **'drawler**.
1648 MILTON *Observ. Art. Peace* Wks. (1851) 571 The common drawling of thir Pulpit elocution. 1656 S. HOLLAND *Zara* (1719) 140 A Subburb Letcher, or a drawl'd Prostitute. 1663 HAWKINS *Youths Behav.* 28. 1830 TENNYSON *To J. M. K.*, Thou art no sabbath-drawler of old saws.

drawl, *sb.* [f. prec. vb.] The action of drawling; a slow, indolent utterance.
1760 LLOYD *Actor* (R.), The white handkerchief and mournful drawl. 1781 COWPER *Hope* 199 His weekly drawl, Though short, too long. 1840 R. H. DANA *Bef. Mast* xiii. 29 They have a good deal of the Creole drawl. 1887 FRITH *Autobiog.* I. xxii. 318 In speaking, he had caught a little of the drawl affected in high life.
b. Slow loitering pace. *rare.*
1850 H. ROGERS *Ess.* II. iv. 190 It is in the epistolary compositions of the age..that the drawl of our ancestors strikes us most forcibly.

†**'draw-latch**, *sb. Obs.* [f. DRAW *v.* + LATCH. With sense 3 cf. dial. *latch*, a lazy or indolent fellow.]
1. A string hanging on the outside of a door by which a latch is drawn or raised.
1614 J. COOKE *Tu Quoque* in Hazl. *Dodsley* XI. 249 I'll pull out my tongue, and hang it at her door for a draw-latch.
2. A thief who enters by drawing up the latch; a sneaking thief; a sneak. Cf. LATCH-DRAWER.
1331 *Act 5 Edw. III*, c. 14 Roberdesmen, Wastours & Draghlacche. 1383 *Act 7 Rich. II*, c. 1 §5. c1515 *Cocke Lorell's B.* (Percy Soc.) 5 With davy drawelache of rokyngame. 1546 J. HEYWOOD *Prov.* (1867) 72 To make me Iohn drawlache, or such a snekebill. 1607 COWELL *Interpr.*, *Drawe latches*..Master Lamberd..calleth them miching theeves, as wasters.
3. Applied opprobriously, esp. to a lazy laggard.
1538 LATIMER *Serm. & Rem.* (1845) 393 If the masters be not good, but honourers of drawlatches, change them. 1583 STANYHURST *Æneis* II. (Arb.) 55 Your drawlach loytrers. 1599 *Warn. Faire Wom.* I. 394 Some heavy drawlatch would have been this month..Before he could have found my policy. *a*1610 CHETTLE *Hoffman* G j (N.), If I pepper him not, say I am not worthy to be cald a duke, but a drawlatch.
Hence †**'drawlatch** *v. intr.*, to sneak, shuffle, lag behind.
1599 NASHE *Lenten Stuffe* 59 Baw waw quoth Bagshaw to that which drawlacheth behinde.

drawlery, obs. var. DROLLERY.

drawling ('drɔːlɪŋ), *ppl. a.* That drawls.
1597 [see DRAWL *v.* 1 b]. 1645 MILTON *Colast.* Wks. (1847) 225/2 A tedious and drawling tale of burning, and burning, and lust and burning. 1727 POPE, etc. *Art of Sinking* 105 Pretty drawling words like these. 1863 HAWTHORNE *Our Old Home* 173 The drawling, snail-like slothfulness of our progress. 1869 TROLLOPE *He Knew* xxii, He seems to me always to preach very drawling sermons. 1876 DOUSE *Grimm's L.* §64. 174 A slovenly or drawling pronunciation.
Hence **'drawlingly** *adv.*; **'drawlingness**.
1742 BAILEY (ed. 10), *Draulingly*, speaking very slowly. *Draulingness*, Slowness in Speech. 1834 *Tait's Mag.* I. 643 Blarney sings drawlingly like a street singer.

'drawly, *a. Sc.* [f. DRAWL *sb.* + -Y[1].] Of the nature of a drawl, characterized by drawling.
1825 JAMIESON, *Drawlie*, slow, and at the same time slovenly. 1829 *Blackw. Mag.* XXVI. 962 For the painter to illustrate the work of the poet or proser, be it drawly or divine. 1833 M. SCOTT *Tom Cringle* xii. (1859) 285 The old don..so sedate and drawley as he was a minute before.

drawn (drɔːn). *ppl. a.* [see DRAW *v.*]
1. a. Moved by traction; dragged, hauled, pulled; attracted; extracted; protracted; strained, stretched, made thin by tension. Also in *comb.*, as *long-*, *well-drawn*; with advbs., as *drawn-up*; *drawn butter*, melted butter; *drawn-in*, (of a rug or mat) made of small cuttings of material drawn through a canvas foundation; *drawn-on* (see quot. 1940).
*c*1430 *Two Cookery-bks.* 10 Drawyn grwel. *Ibid.* 42 Take þe drawyn Eyroun. 1509 HAWES *Past. Pleas.* XVIII. xi, Her heer was bryght as the drawne wyre. 1596 SHAKS. *1 Hen. IV*, III. iii. 129 There's..no more truth in thee, then in a drawne Fox. 1648 GAGE *West Ind.* xii. 64 Ventured himselfe in a Coach with drawne curtaines. 1747 H. GLASSE *Art of Cookery* ii. 25 Have a little good drawn Gravy in a Bason. 1753 MRS. DELANY *Life & Corr.* (1861) III. 240 He has no scruple about fish or drawn gravy. 1806-7 J. BERESFORD *Miseries Hum. Life* (1826) VII. xvi, Drawn, vapid, cold tea. 1826 in *Doc. Hist. Amer. Industr. Soc. N.Y.* (1910) I. 299 Cod fish and potatoes, with drawn butter and eggs. 1864 *Jrnl. R. Agric. Soc.* XXV. II. 363 Well-drawn dry wheat-straw. 1879 Drawn butter [see BUTTER *sb.*[1] 1 d]. 1880 C. R. MARKHAM *Peruv. Bark* 247 Tall, drawn-up saplings. 1880 'MARK TWAIN' *Tramp Abr.* 281 Your brains..sloshing around in your head same as so much drawn butter. 1888 A. K. GREEN *Behind Closed Doors* ii, A long drawn-out tale. 1901 *Harper's Mag.* CII. 661/2 Her mother had only drawn-in rugs, which Ellen had watched her make. 1940 *Chambers's Techn. Dict.* 265/2 *Drawn on*, said of a book cover which is attached by gluing down the back; if the end-papers are pasted down it is said to be *drawn on solid*. 1956 F. C. AVIS *Bookman's Conc. Dict.* 88/2 *Drawn-on cover*, a separate cover glued onto a stabbed inside with flat back; as seen in most magazines.
b. *Bot.* (See quot. 1900.)
1880 W. J. MAY *Greenhouse Management* 142 The plants are kept as near the glass as possible, so that they do not become drawn. 1900 B. D. JACKSON *Gloss. Bot. Terms* 82/1 *Drawn*, applied to attenuated shoots, diminished and etiolated, often increased in length. 1962 *Listener* 26 Apr. 750/1 Do not let the seedlings become weak and drawn.
2. Of a sword: Pulled out of the sheath, naked. †Of a person: Having his sword drawn (*obs.*).
*c*1200 ORMIN 16284 þatt draȝhenn swerd wass inn an hannd. 1480 CAXTON *Chron. Eng.* clxxviii. 159 Robert the Brus pursued hym with a drawe swerd. 1590 SHAKS. *Mids. N.* III. ii. 402 Where art thou?..Here villaine, drawne and readie. 1610 —— *Temp.* II. i. 307 Hoa..why are you drawn? 1838 JAMES *Robber* vi, The stranger had in his hand a drawn sword. 1890 A. GISSING *Village Hampden* II. xi. 243 We all live now at swords drawn. [Cf. DAGGER 2.]
3. Of a battle or match: Undecided.
[The origin of this use is uncertain. It is suggested that *drawn* = *withdrawn*: cf. DRAW *v.* 37.]
1610 D. CARLETON *Let.* 17 June in *Crt. & T. Jas. I* (1848) I. 115 It concluded, as it is many times in a cock pit, with a drawn match; for nothing was in the end put to the question. 1647 N. BACON *Disc. Govt. Eng.* I. Sum. Concl. (1739) 201 A drawn battle, wherein he that continueth last in the Field, is glad to be gone away. 1650 EVELYN *Diary* 15 Oct., They shot so exact, that it was a drawn match. 1709 STEELE *Tatler* No. 18 ¶6 Our greatest Captains have been glad to come off with a drawn Battle. 1825 T. JEFFERSON *Autobiog.* (1859) I. 37 If he lost the main battle, he..regained so much of it as to make it a drawn one. 1835 MRS. CARLYLE *Lett.* I. 20 We played a drawn game at chess.
4. Traced (as a line), delineated. Chiefly in *comb.*, as *ill-drawn*.
1571 DIGGES *Pantom.* I. xxvi. Hij b, Making so many Diuisions in your drawne line, as there are Miles. 1574 HELLOWES *Gueuara's Fam. Ep.* 46 Muche difference is betwixt the drawen platte and the builded house. 1895 *Athenæum* 18 May 648/3 Deftly drawn studies of birds.
5. Disembowelled.
1789 G. WHITE *Selborne* II. xlviii. (1853) 292 My specimen, when drawn and stuffed with pepper, weighed only four ounces and a quarter.
6. Subjected to tension.
1879 E. K. BATES *Egyptian Bonds* I. vi. 130 With a white, 'drawn' look of pain on her face. 1885 MALET *Col. Enderby's Wife* VI. iv. (ed. 3) III. 147 His lips were drawn and stiff. 1894 BARING-GOULD *Queen of Love* I. 114 She looked at her father's drawn face, altered by pain.
7. Moulded by a drawing-machine. More widely, made or formed by drawing (see DRAW *v.* 5 b).
1893 *Daily News* 24 Apr. 6/6 Stamped and drawn tin-ware ..bowls, etc. are selling well for export. 1930 *Engineering* 12 Dec. 755/3 Fourcault took out his first patents in 1904, and in 1913 a machine produced a substantial quantity of drawn sheet glass at the factory at Damprémy. 1933 *Archit. Rev.* LXXIV. 130/1 Arc lamps now fitted with drawn-wire bulbs. 1940 *Chambers's Techn. Dict.* 265/2 *Drawn-wire filament*, an incandescent lamp filament, made by a wire-drawing process. 1960 *Times* 21 Sept. 9/5 Carbon steel tubes (seamless and drawn-welded). 1962 *Gloss. Terms Glass Ind.* (*B.S.I.*) 31 *Drawn glass*, glass, usually in sheet form, made by a continuous mechanical drawing operation.
8. Gathered, in needle-work.
1830 Advt. in A. Adburgham *Shops & Shopping* (1964) iv. 38 Whalebone drawn bonnets. 1852 in *Viscount Ingestre's Meliora* I. 269 They were drawn-bonnet makers. 1853 C. BEDE *Verdant Green* x, A drawn silk bonnet of pale lavender. 1894 *Daily News* 5 June 8/4 Her first bonnet..made of drawn white tulle.

'draw-net. = DRAG-NET; also 'a net with large meshes used for catching the larger varieties of fowls'.
1624 HEYWOOD *Captives* V. iii. in Bullen *O. Pl.* IV, Bee hee a Cristian or beleeve in Mawmett, I such a one this night tooke in my drawnett. 1630 in *Lex Londinensis* (1680) 201 Any Draw-net or Coulter-net. 1654 VILVAIN *Theorem. Theol.* vii. 192 The Church Militant is a mixed multitud of good and bad, as a draw-net. 1727 BRADLEY *Fam. Dict.* s.v., If you would have a Draw-Net with square Meshes. 1879 *Queen's Printers' Aids to Bible* Gloss., *Drag*, a large draw net.

'drawn-work. Also **drawn-thread work**. Ornamental work done in textile fabrics by drawing out some of the threads of warp and woof, so as to form patterns, with or without the addition of needlework, or other accessories.
1595 GOSSON *Quips Upst. Gentlewom.*, Gorgets brave with drawne-worke wrought. 1607 TOURNEUR *Rev. Trag.* II. i. Wks. 1878 II. 41 The finest drawne-worke cuffe. 1636 FEATLY *Clavis Myst.* xxxi. 401 Behold here, as in a faire samplar, an admirable patterne of drawne-worke. 1894 *Bazaar* 21 Nov. 1248/2 White linen edged with a narrow band of drawn-work. 1894 *Daily News* 28 June 6/3 Awards for smocking, baskets, embroidery, drawnthread work. 1895 *Ibid.* 23 Sept. 5/3 Beautiful drawn-thread table linen.

'draw-plate. An apparatus for reducing the thickness of wire or strips of metal, consisting of a steel plate pierced with a number of graduated apertures through which the wire or metal is drawn. Also *drawing-plate*.
1832 BABBAGE *Econ. Manuf.* xi. (ed. 3) 98 From slight imperfections in the drawplates. 1833 J. HOLLAND *Manuf. Metal* II. 332 The drawing-plate, through which the wire passes. *Ibid.* 335 A draw-plate..made of the best steel. 1884 F. J. BRITTEN *Watch & Clockm.* 92.

drawsy, obs. form of DROWSY.

drawt, obs. form of DRAUGHT.

†**drawth.** *Obs.* Also 4 **draȝthe**. [f. DRAW *v.*: see -TH[1].] **1.** A treatise; = L. *tractus*.
1340 *Ayenb.* 251 þet ich habbe hier be-uore y-ssewed.. ate ginninge of þe draȝþe of uirtue. *Ibid.* 260.
2. = DRAUGHT.
1463 *Bury Wills* (Camden) 20 The welle werke..with the drawth and the stoon werk. *a*1628 F. GREVILLE *Sidney* (1652) 219 In shipping..the drawth of water.

'draw-well. 1. A deep well from which water is drawn by a bucket suspended to a rope.
*c*1400 *Gamelyn* 372 Tho thou threwe my porter in the draw-welle. *c*1450 HENRYSON *Mor. Fab.* 78 The draw-well ..Where that two buckets seuerall suithly hang, As one came vp, the other downe would gang. 1549 *Compl. Scot.* vi. 38 He drounit in ane drau vel. 1697 E. LHWYD in *Phil. Trans.* XXVII. 467 Their Coal-works were not Pits sunk like Draw-wells. 1829 *Nat. Philos., Hydraulics* ii. 6 (U.K.S.) The Common bucket and rope..drawn up by a windlass, as in our common draw-wells.
†**2.** A deep drawer. *Obs.*
1762 STERNE *Tristram Shandy* VI. xxx, I wish for their sakes I had the key of my study out of my draw-well, only for five minutes, to tell you their names.

dray (dreɪ), *sb.*[1] Also 4-7 **draye, drey(e**. [A deriv. of OE. *dragan* to draw: cf. OE. *dræge* drag-net, also Sw. *drög* sledge, dray, (ON. *draga*, pl. *drögur* timber trailed along the ground).]
1. †**a.** A sled or cart without wheels, formerly much used for dragging wood, turf, etc. *Obs.*
[1369-70 *Abingdon Acc.* (Camden) 17 In vna dreia empta xiiijd. In rasteis vijd. ob.] 1387 TREVISA *Higden* (Rolls) III. 145 He sent it on a dreye as it were venysoun. 1398 —— *Barth. De P.R.* XVIII. xxix. (1495) 790 In stede of a slede other of a draye. 14.. *Voc.* in Wr.-Wülcker 617/10 *Traha*.. a trahendo dicta, quia rotas non habet [*anglice* a Dreye]. 1552 HULOET, Dray or sleade whych goeth without wheles.
b. A sled used in dragging logs in the woods. Also *attrib.* and *Comb. U.S.*
1902 S. E. WHITE *Blazed Trail* vii. 52 A number of pines had been felled out on the ice, cut in logs, and left in expectation of ice thick enough to bear the travoy 'dray'. 1905 *Terms Forestry & Logging* 36 *Dray*, a single sled used in dragging logs. One end of the log rests upon the sled. 1969 L. G. SORDEN *Lumberjack Lingo* 36 *Dray*, two runners with a bunk in the center to haul logs out of the woods; a single sled used in dragging logs.
†**2.** 'A little cart' or car on wheels. *Obs.*
1565-73 COOPER *Thesaurus*, *Curulis*..a little cart or drey hauing in it a chaire of estate. *c*1610-15 *Women Saints* (E.E.T.S.) 48 To fasten it to her litle cart or drey.
3. a. A low cart without sides used for carrying heavy loads: esp. that used by brewers.
1581 [implied in DRAYMAN]. 1611 COTGR., *Haquet*, a Dray; a low and open Cart, such as London Brewers vse. 1644 PRYNNE & WALKER *Fiennes' Trial* App. 32, I saw a large broad Dray..drawne into the Castle by three or foure Horses. 1703 MAUNDRELL *Journ. Jerus.* (1732) Let. ii. 1 Old batter'd Horses, such as are often seen in Drays. 1862 *Macm. Mag.* Apr. 455 A stoppage, caused by some brewer's dray.
b. Any two-wheeled cart. *Austral.* and *N.Z.*
1833 C. STURT *Exped. S. Australia* I. p. xlix, They send their produce to the market..receiving supplies for home consumption, on the return of their drays or carts from thence. 1846 A. WHISKER *Memo Book* 9 Jan. (MS.) I. 21 One of the Drays broke Down about 1 mile from the camp with shot and rum on it. 1872 C. H. EDEN *Wife & I in Q'sland* ii. 31 A horse-dray, as known in Australia, is by no means the enormous thing its name would signify, but simply an ordinary cart on two wheels without springs. 1926 J. DOONE *Timely Tips for New Australians* Gloss., *Dray*: In Australia this word denotes the springless type of cart generally being equipped with a tipping attachment.
4. *attrib.* and *Comb.*, as *dray-load*, *-track*; **dray-cart**, = sense 3 a, b; **dray-plough** (see quot. 1727); **dray-road** (see quot. 1905).
*a*1719 ADDISON (J.), Let him be brought into the field of election upon his *draycart. 1724 DE FOE *Fortunate Mistress* (1854) 3 The horses were kept at work in the dray-carts. 1848 *Handbk. N.Z.* v. 97 Dray-carts drawn by bullocks are chiefly used. 1644 PRYNNE & WALKER *Fiennes' Trial* 78 A *Dray load more of Match. 1866 M. A. BARKER *Station Life in N.Z.* (1870) vii. 49 It was preceded by two dray-loads of small rough-hewn stone piles. 1901 'M. FRANKLIN' *My Brilliant Career* xiv. 118 With stacks of love to all at home, and a whole dray-load for yourself, from your loving sister, Sybylla. 1959 J. PASCOE *N.Z. Sheep-Station* 19 Then the 'clip' of wool is baled and driven across the Rakaia in dray-loads to be taken by trucks to the wool sale down country. 1707 MORTIMER *Husb.* (J.), The *dray-plough is the best plough in Winter for miry clays. 1727-52 CHAMBERS *Cycl.* s.v. *Plough*, Dray Plough..is made without either wheel or foot. 1845 E. J. WAKEFIELD *Adv. in N.Z.* II. vi. 159 The proprietors constructed a *dray-road up the steep side. 1905 *Terms Forestry & Logging* 36 *Dray road*, a narrow road, cut wide enough to allow the passage of a team and dray. 1907 *Westm. Gaz.* 14 Dec. 14/1 For four hot and weary days I had tramped along lonely and disused dray-roads and bridle-paths that led from a little mining township in the northern part of New South Wales to the coast. 1921 H. GUTHRIE-SMITH *Tutira* xx. 188 It [*sc.* the pack-team] also, in olden days before the advent of a dray-road, played an important part in station activites. 1859 F. FULLER *Five Years' Residence in N.Z.* viii. 149 Improvements..[to] his Run ..[consist of] partial cuttings for the *dray-track where required to be made. 1866 J. MURRAY *Descr. Province of Southland* iii. 19 When such bridges, culverts and crossings as cannot be dispensed with are made, the track which is often on the line of an old bridle path, becomes a 'dray

track'. **1944** F. CLUNE *Red Heart* 81, I don't need any dray-tracks to find what I'm looking for.

Hence **dray** *v.*, to convey on a dray; also *to dray in* (*U.S.*). Hence **'draying** *vbl. sb.* Also *attrib.*

1857 *Lyttelton* (N.Z.) *Times* 13 May 8/1 Stock owners have been enabled to complete their draying operations with ease. **1858** *Richmond-Atkinson Papers* (1960) I. vii. 423, I have arranged with Johnny Jones that he shall have a large shepherd's house..and woolshed,—to be drayed up so as to have no waste timber. **1859** F. FULLER *Five Years' Residence in N.Z.* viii. 149 Such tracks may become available..for draying down the squatters' produce. **1869** LADY BARKER *Station Life N. Zealand* vi. (1874) 39 My house is being cut out in Christchurch and will be drayed to our station next month, a journey of fifty miles. **1905** *Terms Forestry & Logging* 36 *Dray in, to*, to drag logs from the place where they are cut directly to the skidway or landing. **1906** 'O. HENRY' *Four Million* 248 A single gentleman connected with the draying business. **1906** —— *Rolling Stones* (1915) 13 You can get me a bunch of draying contracts. **1942** [see BOBBING *vbl. sb.*[2]].

dray, drey (dreɪ), *sb.*[2] *local.* Also 7 draie, draye. [Origin unknown. ? Same word as prec.] A squirrel's nest.

1607 TOPSELL *Four-f. Beasts* (1658) 387 They..make their nests like the draies of Squirrels. *a* **1631** DRAYTON *Quest of Cynthia* in Campbell *Spec. Brit. Poets* (1819) III. 45 The nimble squirrel..Her mossy dray that makes. **1789** G. WHITE *Selborne* (1853) 366 Three little young squirrels in their nest or drey as it is called in these parts. **1889** *Eng. Ill. Mag.* Dec. 211 [They] lay their eggs in old nests, very often in old squirrel's drays.

dray, obs. f. DRAW *v.*; variant of DERAY.

dray(e, obs. form of DRY *a.*

drayage ('dreɪɪdʒ). [f. DRAY *sb.*[1] + -AGE.]

a. Conveyance by dray. **b.** The charge for this.

1791 T. JEFFERSON in *Harper's Mag.* Mar. (1885) 535/2 Pd. Wm. Forbes freight, storage, drayage of 13 hhds. tob°. **1860** *Times* 9 May 12/5 He then collected the drayage, and informed the agent that the person sending it would call round, pay carriage, and get a receipt.

drayff, obs. Sc. pa. t. of DRIVE *v.*

'dray-horse. [f. DRAY *sb.*[1]] A large and powerful horse used for drawing a dray. So *dray-horse* vb. (*rare*).

1709 STEELE *Tatler* No. 60 ¶10 A Discourse on the Nature of the Elephant, the Cow, the Dray-Horse. **1756** FOOTE *Eng. fr. Paris* I. Wks. 1799 I. 106 She is condemned to do more drudgery than a dray-horse. **1820** B. SILLIMAN *Jrnl. Trav.* (ed. 2) III. 86 When we speak of a London dray-horse, we must understand an animal which in size resembles an elephant rather than a horse. **1857** R. B. PAUL *Lett. fr. Canterbury, N.Z.* i. 19 One of Mr. Russell's men then mounted a dray-horse. **1896** 'MARK TWAIN' *Let.* (1917) II. 637 You have been dray-horsing over the same tiresome ground for a year. **1906** 'O. HENRY' *Four Million* 4 She lifts Tobin's hand, which is own brother to the hoof of a dray horse. **1916** J. B. COOPER *Coo-oo-ee* xix. 298 Damn ye, the dray horse wouldn't go in the shafts of that cart.

'drayman. 1. A man who drives a dray (in England, usually a brewer's dray).

1581 FLEETWOOD in Ellis *Orig. Lett.* Ser. I. II. 285 They brought unto me..vi tall fellowes that were draymen unto bruers. **1606** SHAKS. *Tr. & Cr.* I. ii. 270 A Dray-man, a Porter, a very Camell. **1710** *Lond. Gaz.* No. 4649/4 A Drayman at Mr. Truman's and Mr. Bacon's, Brewers in Spittlefields. **1844** DICKENS *Mart. Chuz.* liii, Two..burly draymen letting down big butts of beer into a cellar.

†**2.** A fisherman who uses a drag-net; cf. next and *draggerman. Obs.*

1584 in *Descr. Thames* (1758) 63 No Fishermen, Garthmen, Petermen, Draymen, or Trinkermen, shall..set up any Wears, Engines [etc.].

†**dray-net.** *Obs.* = DRAG-NET.

c **1000** ÆLFRIC *Gloss.* in Wr.-Wülcker *Voc.* 105/4 *Tragum*, drægnet *uel* dræȝe. *Ibid.* 167/13 *Uerriculum*, drægnet. **1584** in *Descr. Thames* (1758) 63 Dray Nets and Kiddels, forbidden.

draysche, drayse, obs. forms of THRESH *v.*

drazel ('dræz(ə)l). Now *dial.* In 8 drazil. See also DROSSEL. [Derivation uncertain: prob. from same root as Sc. DRASIE. Often identified with *dratchell*; but this seems improbable.] A slut.

1674–91 RAY *S. & E.C. Words* 96 A Drazel; a Dirty Slut. **1678** BUTLER *Hud.* III. i. 987 To use her as the Dev'l does Witches..That, when the time's expir'd, the Drazels For ever may become his Vassals. **1787** in GROSE *Prov. Gloss.*

dre, obs. form of DREE *v.*

dread (drɛd), *v.* Forms: 2–6 drede, (3 dræden), 4–6 dred, (4 dradde, dride, 3 pers. sing. drat, dret), 4–5 dredd(e, 4–6 dreed(e, 5–7 *Sc.* dreid, 6– dread. *Pa. t.* 3–5 dredd(e, (4 drede), 4–5 dradde, 4–6 drad, dred, 5 *Sc.* dredyt, 6– dreaded. *Pa. pple.* 4 ydred, ydradde, idrad, 4–6 dred, -de, 5–6 drad, -de, 6–7 dread(e, 6– dreaded. [Early ME. *dreden, dræden*, not found in OE.; prob. aphetic f. *adreden*, OE. *an-, ondrǽdan*: see ADREAD.]

1. *trans.* To fear greatly, be in mortal fear of; to regard with awe or reverence, venerate.

c **1175** *Lamb. Hom.* 21 Swilcne lauerd we aȝen to dreden. Þet is godalmihtin. *c* **1200** ORMIN 14686 Nu wat I þatt tu drædesst Godd. **1340** *Ayenb.* 116 Þe ybernde uer dret. *c* **1400** MAUNDEV. (Roxb.) ix. 33 Þai drede noȝt þe sowdan ne nan oþer prince. **1481** CAXTON *Myrr.* II. xxviii. 121 The thondre, whiche is moche to be doubted and drad. **1590** SPENSER *F.Q.* I. ii. 2 Nothing did he dread, but euer was ydrad. **1597** J. PAYNE *Royal Exch.* 35 Studieng no less to be ..loved then to be dreade. **1667** MILTON *P.L.* I. 464 His Temple high..dreaded through the Coast Of Palestine. **1784** COWPER *Task* IV. 129, I love thee..dreaded as thou art! **1874** GREEN *Short Hist.* iii. §7. 148 The man whom Henry dreaded as the future champion of English freedom.

†**b.** *to dread* (dative inf.): proper to dread, to be dreaded. *Obs.*

a **1300** *Signs bef. Judgem.* 16 in *E.E.P.* (1862) 8 No þing no man mai loke þat is so grisful forto drede. **1375** BARBOUR *Bruce* II. 272 Thai sall fer mar be..for to dred. *c* **1400** *Apol. Loll.* 5 It is to drede, þat..iuil comiþ to vs. *c* **1489** CAXTON *Sonnes of Aymon* xxviii. 591 [A] knyghte..that in his life was more to drede than ony man alive.

2. To have a shrinking apprehension of; to look forward to with terror or anxiety: of future or unknown events. Often with *inf.* or *subord. cl.*

a **1225** *St. Marher.* 5 Ne dredich na deð for to drehen for him. *a* **1300** *Cursor M.* 7613 He dred his kingdom to lese. *c* **1470** HENRY *Wallace* VI. 630 Wallace dredyt gyll. **1508** FISHER 7 *Penit Ps.* Wks. (1876) 26 It is to be drad leest ony preuy gyle or deceyte remayne styll in the soule. *c* **1600** SHAKS. *Sonn.* xcvii, Leaves look pale, dreading the winter's near. **1671** MILTON *Samson* 733, I came, still dreading thy displeasure. **1752** JOHNSON *Rambler* No. 203 ¶3 We..dread their intrusion upon our minds, and fly from them as enemies. **1801** MOORE *Mem.* (1853) I. 116, I sometimes dread that all is not right at home. **1802** H. MARTIN *Helen of Glenross* III. 26, I dread she is playing a dangerous fatal game. **1838** LYTTON *Alice* 31 This next visit she dreaded more than she had any of the former ones.

†**b.** To be anxious about, to fear for. *rare.*

a **1547** SURREY *Æneid* II. 966 So much I dred my burden and my feer [*comitique onerique timentem*]. **1599** SHAKS. *Pass. Pilgrim* 94 How many tales to please me hath she coin'd, Dreading my love, the loss thereof still fearing!

†**c.** To doubt. *Obs. rare.*

c **1400** *Lanfranc's Cirurg.* 96 If þat þou dredist wheþer þat it be a symple vlcus or a cankre and a foul, for þe signes..beþ doutis.

†**3.** *intr.* (or *absol.*). To be greatly afraid or apprehensive; to fear greatly. Const. *about, of, for.*

c **1205** LAY. 31164 Swiðe heo gunnen dreden of Cadwalanes deden. *a* **1240** *Lofsung* in *Cott. Hom.* 209 Ic.. am on mest ifuled of sunne ase ich drede. *a* **1300** *Cursor M.* 1810 (Cott.) Þai war ful dredand for [*Fairf.* of] þar lijf. **1382** WYCLIF *Gen.* iii. 10, I dredde, there thurȝ that I was nakid. *c* **1449** PECOCK *Repr.* 87 Drede ȝe of the effect which bifille to Bohemers. **1526** *Pilgr. Perf.* (1531) 15 God..bad them to be stronge and not to drede. **1611** BIBLE *1 Chron.* xxii. 13 Dread [**1885** *R.V.* fear] not, nor be dismayed. **1769** GOLDSM. *Rom. Hist.* (1786) II. 48 Their friends..began to dread for the consequences. **1840** J. H. NEWMAN *Lett.* (1891) II. 296, I dread about our Statutes.

†**4.** *refl.* To fear, be afraid. *Obs.*

c **1200** ORMIN 151 Ne dred te, Zacariȝe, nohht. *c* **1250** *Gen. & Ex.* 3008 Al ðis sor Saȝ pharaun, and dredde him ðor. *c* **1385** CHAUCER *L.G.W.* 1740 *Lucretia*, Drede the nat for I am here. **1470–85** MALORY *Arthur* XVIII. xii, I wold fayn do that myȝt please yow, but I drede me sore.

b. with *subord. cl. arch.*

a **1300** *Cursor M.* 3665 (Cott.), I drede me sare, for benison He sal me giue his malison. *c* **1325** *Poem Times Edw. II*, 374 in *Pol. Songs* (Camden) 340, I drede me that God us hath for-laft out of his hond. *c* **1475** *Rauf Coilȝear* 713, I dreid me sair I be begylit. **1548** HALL *Chron., Hen. VI*, 97 A felde the whiche he drade hym, might have folowed if he had long taried. **1859** TENNYSON *Elaine* 512, I dread me, if I draw it, you will die.

†**5.** *trans.* To cause to fear; to affright, terrify. (In first quot. perh. impersonal.)

c **1250** *Old Kent. Serm.* in *O.E. Misc.* 32 Wat dret yw folk of litle beliaue? **14..** *Prose Legends* in *Anglia* VIII. 141 Þe sauours þat she myghte not suffir byfore, than dredde hir not a deel. **1587** M. GROVE *Pelops & Hipp.* (1878) 42 Which sight did much appall And dread the lookers on. **1617** J. MOORE *Mappe Mans Mortal.* III. iii. 201 A blazing Starre, that dreadeth the minde by presaging ruine. **1681** R. KNOX *Hist. Ceylon* 169 The very thoughts of it would seem to dread me.

6. *Comb.*, as *dread-death, dread-devil* adjs.

1825 COBBETT *Rur. Rides* (1830) I. 48 A reader of old dread-death and dread-devil Johnson.

Hence **'dreaded** *ppl. a.*, **'dreading** *vbl. sb.*

c **1200** ORMIN 7185 He Dredinng and aȝhe sette On alle þa þatt lufenn toþþ. *a* **1325** *Prose Psalter* cx[i]. 9 Þe biginnyng of wisdome is dredyng of our Lord. **1548** UDALL *Erasm. Par. Luke* xii. (R.), If ye shal vpon the dreadyng of man, grow cleane out of kinde from the sinceritee of preaching the ghospel. **1556** Dreaded [see DREADER]. **1590** SPENSER *F.Q.* II. x. 1 My most dreaded Soueraigne. **1607** SHAKS. *Cor.* III. iii. 98 In the presence Of dreaded Iustice. **1863** FR. A. KEMBLE *Resid. in Georgia* 242 The dreaded rattlesnakes.

dread (drɛd), *sb.* Forms: 3–6 dred, drede, (4 drad, 4–5 dredde, 5–6 dreed(e, dreid(e, 6 dreade), 6– dread. [f. prec. vb.]

1. Extreme fear; deep awe or reverence; apprehension or anxiety as to future events. Rarely in *pl.*

c **1200** *Trin. Coll. Hom.* 71 Forgetelnesse, nutelnesse, recheles, shamfastnesse, drede. *a* **1340** HAMPOLE *Psalter* xiii. 9 Þai quoke for dred whare dred was noght. *c* **1400** *Lanfranc's Cirurg.* 124 Bi cause of drede lest an hoot enpostyme schulde come. **1508** FISHER 7 *Penit. Ps.* Wks. (1876) 28 The drede of god putteth awaye synne. **1663** BUTLER *Hud.* I. ii. 470 They'l straight resume their wonted Dreads. **1798** WORDSW. *Peter Bell* I. xlvii, Suspicion ripened into dread. **1828** D'ISRAELI *Chas. I*, I. iv. 67 The dread of famine. **1895** J. KIDD *Morality & Relig.* iv. 164 Dread is the extreme of anxiety on account of possible danger.

2. A person or thing (to be) dreaded; an object or cause of fear, reverence, or awe; †a danger.

c **1400** *Lanfranc's Cirurg.* 299 It is ful greet drede for to lete a child blood. **1501** DOUGLAS *Pal. Hon.* II. xlviii, He tauld..Of Dianis bair, in Callidon the dreidis. **1590** SPENSER *F.Q.* I. vi. 2 Vna his dear dreed. **1671** MILTON *Samson* 1473 Shouting to behold Their once great dread, captive and blind before them. **1725** POPE *Odyss.* IV. 980 Then Euryclea thus, My dearest dread! **1844** MRS. BROWNING *Drama of Exile* Poems 1850 I. 38 To meet the spectral Dread. **1849** MACAULAY *Hist. Eng.* I. 13 The wonder and dread of all neighbouring nations.

†**3.** Doubt, risk of the thing proving otherwise. Chiefly in phr.: ***without*** (***but out of***) ***dread***, without doubt, doubtless; ***no dread***, no fear, no doubt.

1340 *Ayenb.* 105 Hit ne is no drede þet ine þe zonge..þe ilke þet tekþ þe uoȝeles zynge, ne heþ uele notes sotiles and zuete. *c* **1386** CHAUCER *Clerk's T.* 809 To yow broghte I noght elles, out of drede, But feith and nakednesse and maydenhede. *c* **1440** *Lay Folks Mass Bk.* (MS. C.) 102 Þe tyme is nere withowten drede. *c* **1460** *Towneley Myst.* (Surtees) 105 Of that ye wolde rowne, No drede. **1556** LAUDER *Tractate* 201 Ȝe sall be plukkit frome ȝour ryngis, .. withouttin dreid.

4. a. Amongst Rastafarians: dread or fear of the Lord; also, more generally, a deep-rooted sense of alienation felt by Rastafarians towards contemporary society; extreme fear of something menacing or threatening. **b.** A Rastafarian, one who wears dreadlocks (often *contemptuous*). **c.** (*pl.*) Dreadlocks. **d.** *attrib.* or as *adj.* (esp. expressing extreme approval, dislike, etc.).

1974 COLE & ANDERSON (*song title*) Natty dread. **1976** BOOT & THOMAS *Jamaica* 44/1 That makes you a dread man, if you've got a gun. **1977** *Observer* 11 Dec. 4/7 A squat containing 15 young black men or 'dreads' and as many girls. **1978** S. CLARKE *New Planet* 26 This was the dreaded place where Rastafarians and Dreads lived. **1983** *N.Y. Times* 8 Apr. c16/6 You can't walk far on lower Second Avenue without running into at least one crowd of 'Dreads'. **1984** *Melody Maker* 6 Oct. 15/1 The Rasta leaps in the air and tosses his dreads, loosely braided at the back, over his head in a lash of black catkins.

†**dread** (drɛd), *a. Obs.* In 4 drad, 5 dred. [Aphetic f. ME. ADRAD, *ofdrad*, OE. *ofdrǽd*(*d* in same sense.] Afraid, frightened, terrified.

c **1300** *Havelok* 1669 Hauelok..was..ful sore drad, With him to ete, for hise wif. *c* **1340** *Cursor M.* 6260 (Trin.) For pharao was he not drad. **1393** LANGL. *P. Pl.* C. XVII. 310 Of deþ ne of derþe drad was he neuere. *a* **1400–50** *Alexander* 2489 Þan was ser Darius dred. *c* **1450** *St. Cuthbert* (Surtees) 5739 Theues war dred of Cuthberts wrake.

dread (drɛd), *ppl. a.* Also 5–6 drede, 5–7 drad, -de. [ME. pa. pple. of DREAD *v.*]

1. Feared greatly; hence, to be feared; dreadful, terrible.

c **1400** *Destr. Troy* 166 A derfe dragon, drede to be-holde. **1610** SHAKS. *Temp.* I. ii. 206 And make..his dread Trident shake. **1667** MILTON *P.L.* IX. 969 Death or aught then Death more dread. **1805** SCOTT *Last Minstr.* VI. xxxi, When louder yet, and yet more dread, Swells the high trump that wakes the dead! **1853** FABER *All for Jesus* 378 A bondage dreader far than death. **1868** HELPS *Realmah* ii. (1876) 21.

2. Held in awe; awful; revered.

1420 in Rymer *Foed.* IX. 883/1 Moste Dredde Soverayne Lord. **1484** CAXTON *Chivalry* 99 My redoubted naturel and most dradde sauverayne lord kyng Rychard. **1593** SHAKS. *2 Hen. VI*, V. i. 17 A Messenger from Henry, our dread Liege. **1602** —— *Ham.* III. iv. 109 Th' important acting of your dread command. **1643** *Pet. Gen. Assembly Kirk Scot.* in Clarendon *Hist. Reb.* VI. §343 Suffer us therefore, dread Sovereign, to renew our petitions. **1755** YOUNG *Centaur* I. Wks. 1757 IV. 108 That dread being we dare oppose. **1840** LYTTON *Pilgr. Rhine* xix, The dreadest ruler of men.

3. *Comb.*, adverbially, as *dread-dear, -desired, -sweet*; parasynthetic, as *dread-bolted.*

1592 SYLVESTER *Tri. Faith* IV. xlii, That drad-desired Day. **1598** —— *Du Bartas* II. i. II. *Eden* 429 And in our face his drad-sweet face he seales. **1613** —— *Microsmogr.* 7 Drad-dear Creator, new-create Thy Creature. **1605** SHAKS. *Lear* IV. vii. 33 To stand against the deep dread-bolted thunder.

†**'dreadable**, *a. Obs.* [f. DREAD *v.* + -ABLE.] To be dreaded, dreadful.

c **1490** *Manner to live* V iij in Maskell *Mon. Rit.* I. p. clvj. *note*, Sorowful and dreydabyl fygurys. **1503** *Kalender of Sheph.* (1656) xvi, At the judgement of God most dreadable. *Ibid.* ii. (T.), At the sounding of a dreadable horne.

'dreader. [f. as prec. + -ER[1].] One who dreads, or is under fear and apprehension.

1556 J. HEYWOOD *Spider & F.* vii. 20 Dred, in dred of the dreddid, the dredder driues To Judge, more or lesse, as the dreddid contriues. **1732** SWIFT *Sacramental Test* Wks. 1761 III. 297 Great dreaders of Popery. **1828** SCOTT *F.M. Perth* xvii, The old saw, that evil doers are evil dreaders.

dreadful ('drɛdfʊl), *a.* (*adv.* and *sb.*) Forms: see DREAD *sb.*; also *β.* 3–5 drefu(l, 9 *dial.* dreful. [f. DREAD *sb.* + -FUL.]

A. *adj.* †**1. a.** Full of dread, fear, or awe; fearful, terrified, timid; reverential. *Obs.*

a **1225** *Ancr. R.* 302 Schrift schal beon..hihful, edmod, scheomeful, dredful, and hopeful. **1340** *Ayenb.* 117 We byeþ þe more ymylded and þe dreduoller. *c* **1440** CAPGRAVE *Life St. Kath.* I. 844 The dreedful and seekly wolde she conforte. **1529** MORE *Dyaloge* III. 71 a/2 Ouer dredefull and scrupulous in stede of deuoute and dylygent. **1659** W.

CHAMBERLAYN *Pharonnida* III. iii, The Turks..of whom the city ladies take A dreadful view.

β. **c 1250** *Gen. & Ex.* 2590 Ghe was for him dreful and bleð. **1483** *Cath. Angl.* 107/2 Drefulle, *attonitus.*

†**b.** Const. *of* or *inf. Obs.*

c 1430 LYDG. *Bochas* II. xxvii. (1554) 62 b, The people, dreadful to bylde their mansions, For feare of death. **1590** SPENSER *F.Q.* III. i. 37 Dreadfull of daunger that mote him betyde. **1628** GAULE *Pract. The.* (1629) 370 Reuerently awfull, or desperately dreadfull of his Maiestie, and Power.

2. a. Inspiring dread or reverence; awe-inspiring; terrible, formidable; awful; to be dreaded.

c 1250 *Gen. & Ex.* 3521 Ðat dredful beames blast. **a 1325** *Prose Psalter* xlvi[i]. 2 Our Lord ys heiȝe, dredful, and michel kyng. **1447** *Will of Hen. VI*, in T. J. Carter *King's Coll. Chapel* (1867) 13 The blessed and dredeful visage of our Lord Jesu in his most fereful and last dome. **1593** SHAKS. *Rich. II*, I. iii. 135 Harsh resounding Trumpets dreadfull bray. **1667** MILTON *P.L.* x. 121 My voice thou oft hast heard, and hast not fear'd..how is it now become So dreadful to thee? **1758** C. WESLEY *Hymn, 'Lo! He comes'* ii, Robed in dreadful majesty. **1833** ALISON *Hist. Europe* (1849–50) I. i. §10. 56 The insurrection of slaves is the most dreadful of all commotions.

β. **1398** TREVISA *Barth. De P.R.* XIV. xxxvi. (Tollem. MS.), This mounte was dreful [**1535** dredful] to all men.

†**b.** Dangerous, perilous. *Obs.*

c 1400 *Lanfranc's Cirurg.* 26 Whos [the arteries'] dyuysiouns..ben nouȝt dredful to surgiens craft. *Ibid.* 129, I holde þis wey lasse dredeful þan ony oþere.

3. In weakened sense, applied to objects exciting fear or aversion. In mod. colloquial use often a strong intensive = Exceedingly bad, great, long, etc. Cf. *awful, horrid.*

1700 S. L. tr. *C. Fryke's Two Voy. E.I.* 213 The Maid..gave a dreadful Shriek. **1718** LADY M. W. MONTAGU *Let. to C'tess Bristol* 12 Sept., I intend to set out tomorrow, and to pass those dreadful Alps, so much talked of. **1775** MRS. HARRIS in *Priv. Lett. Ld. Malmesbury* I. 302, I have long wished to be in company with this said Johnson; his conversation is the same as his writing, but a dreadful voice and manner. **1864** P'CESS ALICE in *Mem.* 72 The parting from Anna three days ago was dreadful. *Mod.* It was a dreadful business. We waited a dreadful time.

B. *adv.* = DREADFULLY 2, 3. (Now *vulgar.*)

1682 CREECH tr. *Lucretius* (1683) 52 Here some..Look dreadful gay in their own sparkling blood. **1700** S. L. tr. *C. Fryke's Two Voy. E.I.* 234 We had..a dreadful violent Storm. **1713** YOUNG *Last Day* II. 297 Oh formidable Glory! dreadful bright! **1762** J. H. STEVENSON *Crazy Tales* 86 A batchellor, and old, and dredeful sly. **1870** DICKENS *E. Drood* i, The Market price is dreffle high just now.

C. *sb.* A story of crime written in a sensational or morbidly exciting style; a journal or print of such character; a 'shocker'. *colloq.*

1873 [see *penny dreadful* s.v. PENNY 11]. **1884** *World* 20 Aug. 9/2 The wicked noblemen of the transpontine melodrama or of penny dreadfuls. **1885** *Spectator* 8 Aug. 1046/1 [He] has given himself up to the writing of three-volume dreadfuls. **1886** F. HARRISON *Choice Bks.* 67 Destined to perish in shilling dreadfuls. **1888** C. M. YONGE *Our New Mistress* iv. 38 One of those cheap tales—'dreadfuls', I believe they call them—that one got at the station.

dreadfully (ˈdrɛdfʊlɪ), *adv.* [f. prec. + -LY[2].] In a dreadful manner.

†**1.** With terror, fear, awe, or apprehension. *Obs.*

1303 R. BRUNNE *Handl. Synne* 11673 [The publican] seyde wyþ herte ful dredfully, 'Lorde, þou haue on me mercy'. **c 1385** CHAUCER *L.G.W.* 2680 *Hypermnestra*, Dredfully sche quakyth. **1450–1530** *Myrr. our Ladye* 77 Mekely and dredfully knowynge oure feblenesse. **a 1553** UDALL *Royster D.* IV. vi. (Arb.) 71 I will..so make as though I ranne away dreadfully. **1603** SHAKS. *Meas. for M.* IV. ii. 150 A man that apprehends death no more dreadfully, but as a drunken sleepe.

2. So as to cause dread; terribly, fearfully, awfully.

c 1340 *Cursor M.* 21882 (Trin.) Oure soulis alle to make redy Aȝeyn his coome so dredefuly. **1593** SHAKS. *Lucrece* 444 They..tell her she is dreadfully beset. **a 1666** BROME *Ecclus.* xlii. (R.), Red burning bolts..Dreadfully bright o'er seas and earth they glare. **1802** PORTEUS *Lect. Gosp. Matt.* II. xxii. (R.), A most fatal imprecation, and most dreadfully fulfilled. **1858** FROUDE *Hist. Eng.* III. 224 Blazing martyr-piles, shining dreadfully through all after ages.

3. Colloquially used as a strong intensive = Exceedingly, 'terribly', 'awfully', 'abominably'.

1602 SHAKS. *Ham.* II. ii. 276, I am most dreadfully attended. **1697** C. LESLIE *Snake in Grass* (ed. 2) 35 This is dreadfully Astonishing! **1796** DK. LEEDS *Pol. Mem.* (1884) 220 This dreadfully interesting conversation. **1824** SYD. SMITH *Wks.* (1867) II. 42 Dreadfully afraid of America and everything American. **1881** MRS. MOLESWORTH *Adv. Herr Baby* 138 He would have liked dreadfully to come home.

'dreadfulness. [f. as prec. + -NESS.] The quality or state of being dreadful.

†**1.** The quality of having terror or dread. *Obs.*

c 1440 *Promp. Parv.* 131/2 Dredefulnesse, *idem est quod* Drede. **1604** T. WRIGHT *Passions* II. iii. §2. 71 Dreadfulnesse of infamie, and feare of diseases draw in the raynes of this inordinate affection. **1649** BP. HALL *Cases Consc.* III. i. (1654) 162 In respect of our dreadfulnesse.

2. Awfulness, terribleness, frightfulness.

c 1440 *Promp. Parv.* 131/2 Dredefulnesse, and horrybylnesse, *horribilitas, terribilitas.* **1483** CAXTON *Gold. Leg.* 431 b/1 In sygne of punycyon of his synne and terrour and dredefulnesse to alle other. **1548** UDALL, etc. *Erasm. Par. Acts* iv. (R.), Afrayed with dreadfulnes of the great judgement. **1649** ROBERTS *Clavis Bibl.* 276 The dreadfulnesse of the Lord above all gods. **1849** ROBERTSON *Serm.* Ser. I. xi. 167 The dreadfulness of death is one of the most remarkable things.

dreadingly (ˈdrɛdɪŋlɪ), *adv.* [f. *dreading* pres. pple. of DREAD *v.* + -LY[2].] With dread; apprehensively.

1589 WARNER *Alb. Eng.* VI. xxxiii. (R.), Mistrustfully he trusteth, and He dreadingly did dare. **1844** TUPPER *Crock of G.* xvii, Mary..looked on dreadingly to see the end.

'dreadless, *a.* and *adv.* [See -LESS.]

A. *adj.* Void of dread or fear; having no fear; fearless; not apprehensive. Const. *of.*

c 1340 *Gaw. & Gr. Knt.* 2334 How þat doȝty dredles deruely þer stondez. **a 1450** *Le Morte Arth.* 3262 After hys dayes fulle dredelesse..To welde Alle yngland, towre And towne. **1561** T. NORTON *Calvin's Inst.* I. 46 With a dredelesse minde to loke down vpon his enemies. **1634** PEACHAM *Gentl. Exerc.* III. 140 A haughtie courage, dreadlesse of dangers. **1762** FALCONER *Shipwr.* II. 150 At each yard-arm a dreadless sailor strides. **1854** *Tait's Mag.* XXI. 238 We await the issue..with dreadless confidence.

†**b.** Exempt from dread or apprehension of danger; secure; void of terrors. *Obs. rare.*

1591 SPENSER *World's Vanitie* x, A mighty Lyon..Safe in his dreadles den him thought to hide. **1622** S. WARD *Life of Faith in Death* (1627) 91 That which makes death so easie, so familiar and dreadlesse to a beleeuer.

†**B.** *adv.* Without doubt or apprehension of mistake; doubtless. Cf. DREAD *sb.* 3. *Obs.*

c 1369 CHAUCER *Dethe Blaunche* 1272 Dredelesse I mene none other wayes. **a 1400** *Relig. Pieces fr. Thornton MS.* 91 Thane was Orncyane dede..And sulde to delfynge be done dredles þat daye. **? a 1400** *Morte Arth.* 2043 Dredlesse with-owttyne dowtte, the daye schalle be ourez. **1535** STEWART *Cron. Scot.* (1858) I. 61 Dreidles than we man all suffer deid.

Hence **'dreadlessly** *adv.*, in a dreadless manner, fearlessly; **'dreadlessness,** fearlessness.

1580 SIDNEY *Arcadia* (1622) 68 Zelmane (to whom daunger..was a cause of dreadlesnesse). **1628** WITHER *Brit. Rememb.* IV. 670 So dreadlessly their course they did pursue. **1831** WILSON in *Blackw. Mag.* XXIX. 295 Animals who dreadlessly follow their instincts.

dreadlocks (ˈdrɛdlɒks), *sb. pl.* [f. DREAD *v.*, *sb.*, or *ppl. a.* + *locks*, pl. of LOCK *sb.*[1]] A Rastafarian hairstyle in which the hair is allowed to grow without combing, and forms into matted 'locks' which hang down from all over the head (see quot. 1966); the hair dressed in this way. Also in *sing.* (esp. *attrib.*).

1960 M. G. SMITH et al. *Ras Tafari Movement in Kingston, Jamaica* ii. 13 The plaiting of long hair by men known as the 'men of dreadlocks'... These men of dreadlocks were the Ethiopian Warriors and the self-declared Niyamen. **1966** *Guardian* 22 Apr. 13/7 An extremist fringe of members distinguished by their long twisted hair or 'dreadlocks', which were modelled after pictures of Ethiopian warriors. **1971** A. KING *One Love* 39 He..is a Dread-Locks Rastaman, who, to most people, appears as a strong half-Chinese who has neglected to cut his hair. **1975** *Globe & Mail* (Toronto) 11 June 3/5 Many [Rastafarians] wear their hair in long, matted wool-like ringlets or plaits called dreadlocks. **1980** *Daily Tel.* 13 Nov. 2/2 Employers could be influenced by young blacks who came to an interview with the long 'rasta' dreadlock hairstyle. **1981** *Times* 8 Sept. 2/7 Lord Scarman..told the inquiry that the image of the young Rastafarian with dreadlocks was based on the Masai warrior. **1984** *New Yorker* 26 Mar. 47/2 He had a Dodgers cap on top of his dreadlocks.

Hence **'dreadlocked** *a.*, wearing dreadlocks.

1977 *Sunday Times* 26 June 52/6, I have always since felt a sympathy with these dreadlocked believers in the divinity of Haile Selassie.

†**'dreadly,** *a. Obs.* Also 3 dredlich, 4 dredli. [f. DREAD *sb.* + -LY[1].] = DREADFUL 1, 2.

a 1225 *Ancr. R.* 58 þis is a swuðe dredlich word to wummen. **a 1300** *Body & Soul* 12 in *Map's Poems* (Mätz.) With dredli mod.

dreadly (ˈdrɛdlɪ), *adv.* [f. DREAD *a.* + -LY[2].]

1. In a manner inspiring dread; dreadfully, awfully, terribly.

c 1175 *Lamb. Hom.* 143 Vre drihten wile cumen dredliche in fures liche. **c 1440** *Jacob's Well* (E.E.T.S.) 25 Alle þo, þat ..dredly astonyed þe ordinaryes & here offycerys. **1605** SYLVESTER *Du Bartas* II. iii. iv. *Captains* 224 So shall you see a Cloud crown'd Hill sometime..Dreadly to shake. **1751** W. MASON *Elfrida* Poems (1773) 127 Dreadly sweeping thro' the vaulted sky. **1849** LYTTON *King Arthur* I. 11 With mangled plumes and mantles dreadly rent.

2. With dread or awe. *rare.*

1674 N. FAIRFAX *Bulk & Selv.* 181, I should go in fear of my life..and dream full dradly on't every night. **1847** R. W. HAMILTON *Disq. Sabbath* i. (1848) 18 The sabbath..was jealously reckoned and dreadly revered.

3. *Comb.*, as *dreadly deep, -glorious, -sad*, etc.

1606 SYLVESTER *Du Bartas* II. iv. II. *Magnificence* 196 Sound round the Cels of the Ocean dradly-deep.

'dreadness. [f. DREAD *a.* + -NESS.]

1. Dreadfulness, awfulness. Now *rare.*

a 1175 *Cott. Hom.* 233 He us is..hlaford for þan be [h]is ȝeie and drednesse is ofer hus. **a 1225** *Juliana* (Bodl. MS.) 69 For deaðes drednesse. **a 1300** *Cursor M.* 7544 (Gött.) Qua þat fihtes in wrangwisness It helpis him noght, his dredness. **1868** NETTLESHIP *Browning* 242 The mystery and dreadness of the hidden power.

†**2.** Dread, terror, apprehension. *Obs.*

a 1300 *Cursor M.* 11161 (Cott.) Haf na drednes. *Ibid.* 12837 (Cott.) For drednes ilk lim him quok.

dreadnought (ˈdrɛdnɔːt), *a.* and *sb.* Also **dreadnaught.**

A. *adj.* Dreading nothing, fearless.

1836 W. IRVING *Astoria* I. 301 Three Kentucky hunters, of the true 'dreadnought' stamp. **1863** MRS. C. CLARKE *Shaks. Char.* 288 The manly and dreadnought character of the seafaring man.

B. *sb.* **1. a.** A thick coat or outer garment worn in very inclement weather; also, the stout woollen cloth with a thick long pile of which such garments are made. Also *attrib.* Cf. FEARNOUGHT.

1806 A. DUNCAN *Nelson* 140 'I am Lord Nelson', replied the hero..throwing aside his green dreadnought. **1828** COL. HAWKER *Diary* (1893) I. 326 Drenched to the skin, in spite of all his 'dread-nought' garments. **1834** SOUTHEY *Doctor* lvii. II. 197 One of those dreadnoughts the utility of which sets fashion at defiance. **1842** DICKENS *Amer. Notes* (1850) 11/2 A pair of dreadnought trousers. **1870** THORNBURY *Tour Eng.* II. xxviii. 249 An artful-looking man in a dread-nought.

b. (See quot.)

1874 KNIGHT *Dict. Mech.*, *Dreadnaught*, a heavy, woolen, felted cloth, used as a lining for hatchways, etc., on board ship.

2. A fearless person.

[**1694** MOTTEUX tr. *Rabelais's Pantagruel* v. xxxvi. 179, I am as stout as Hercules... My name's William Dreadnought.] **1827** M. WILMOT *Jrnl.* 3 July in *More Lett.* (1935) 268 Our Chezy dreadnought has received him into her house. **1832** SCOTT *Redgauntlet* (Waverley ed.) I. i. 6 To recollect that the author himself..was one of those juvenile dreadnoughts, is a sad reflection to one who cannot now step over a brook without assistance.

3. (Freq. with capital initial.) The name of the first British battleship (launched on 18 Feb. 1906) of a powerful type superior in armament to all its predecessors; hence, any of a class of battleships having their main armament entirely of big guns of one calibre. (Now disused.) Also *attrib.* and *transf.*

[**1587** DRAKE *Desp.* 27 Apr. in Hakluyt *Voy.* (1904) VI. p. xiv, A great leake sprange uppon the Dreadenoughte.] **1906** *Outlook* 20 Oct. 495/2 The Atlantic Fleet will consist of three *Dreadnoughts* and five of the *Canopus* class. **1908** *Westm. Gaz.* 14 Aug. 2/2 The mysterious *Dreadnoughts* which are being built in this country for the Brazilian Government. **1909** *Daily Chron.* 23 Mar. 1/1 Our Dreadnought strength and our strength in pre-Dreadnought ships, in comparison with those of Germany. **1914** *Daily Express* 26 Nov. 2/4, 7 Dreadnought Zeppelins: Airships built for the Invasion of Britain. **1915** *Ibid.* 23 Jan. 1/5 Vessels of the Dreadnought era. **1959** *Chambers's Encycl.* IV. 634/2 All maritime powers adopted the general design and it became customary to define battleships as dreadnoughts and pre-dreadnoughts. These definitions generally lapsed as the pre-dreadnought ships became obsolete.

4. *N.Z.* The name of a strain of wheat.

1916 *N.Z. Jrnl. Agric.* 20 Apr. 306 In Canterbury and North Otago the following wheats have given a good account of themselves from the point of view of yield: Red Marvel (French), Dreadnought (French). **1959** J. M. MCEWAN *Wheat Varieties of N.Z.* 14 Dreadnought has been grown in New Zealand from 1910 and is believed to be of English origin.

dreadour (ˈdrɛdə(r)). *Sc.* Also 5–6 dreddour, 6 dred-, draid-, dreidour, 8–9 dridder, dreder, drither. [f. DREAD with F. suffix, after such words as *dolour, terror.*] Fear, dread.

1536 BELLENDEN *Cron. Scot.* (1821) I. 114 He fled with gret dredour to his tentis. **1553** *Douglas' Æneis* IX. xii. 67 With dredfull dredour [*MS.* raddour] trymbling for effray. **1570** *Henry's Wallace* x. 94 Quhen thai him saw, all dreddour [*MS.* raddour] thai forsuk. **1609** SKENE *Reg. Maj.* 83 Be reason of feare and dreadour. **1834** HOGG *Mora Campbell* 492 He..saw with dreadour and with doubt, A flame enkindling him about.

†**'dready,** *a. Obs.* In 3–4 dredi, -y. [f. DREAD *sb.* + -Y[1].] Feeling dread, fear, or awe; timid.

c 1250 *Gen. & Ex.* 872 Abram folc made him dredi. **1382** WYCLIF *Judg.* vii. 3 Who is feerful and dredy, turne he aȝen. **c 1400** *Apol. Loll.* 104 þey wil be seen a mong men dredy and just.

dreaien, obs. form of DRAW *v.*

†**dream,** *sb.*[1] *Obs.* Forms: 1 dréam, 2–3 dream, dræm, 3–4 drem(e, 4 dreem. [OE. *dréam* = OS. *drôm* mirth, noise, minstrelsy:—WGer. **draum-*. Kluge suggests that it is from the same root as Gr. θρῦλος noise, shouting.]

1. Joy, pleasure, gladness, mirth, rejoicing.

a 830 *Cædmon's Satan* 316 þær heo..moton..aȝan dreama dream mid drihtne Gode. **975** *O.E. Chron.*, Her ȝeendode eorðan dreamas Eadgar Engla cyning. **1002** *Will of Wulfric* in *Cod. Dipl.* VI. 149 God ælmihtig hine awende of eallum Godes dreame. **c 1205** LAY. 14286 Heo æten, heo drunken: dræm [*c* **1275** blisse] wes i burhȝen.

2. The sound of a musical instrument; music, minstrelsy, melody; noise, sound.

c 1000 ÆLFRIC *Hom.* (Th.) II. 86/35 He ȝehyrde micele stemne..swylce bymena dream. *Ibid.* II. 548/12 Werhades men ongunnon symle þone dream, and wifhades men him sungon onȝean. **c 1200** *Trin. Coll. Hom.* 115 þe bemene drem þe þe engles blewen. **c 1200** ORMIN 923 þe belledræm bitacneþþ ȝuw þatt dræm þatt ȝuw birrþ herenn. **c 1205** LAY. 1010 Muchel folkes dream. **a 1250** *Owl & Night.* 314 Ich singe..Mid fulle dreme and lude stefne. **a 1310** in Wright *Lyric P.* xviii. 57 Thou make me here thi suete dreem. **c 1320** *Sir Beues* 1339 (MS. A.) Saber wep and made drem. **c 1330**

Florice & Bl. (1857) 37 The leuedi . . seide here louerd with still dreme, Sire [etc.].

dream (driːm), *sb.*^{2} Forms: 3-5 **drem**, 4-6 **dreem**, **dreme**, **dreeme**, 4-7 **dreame**, 7- **dream**, (6- *Sc.* **dreim**). [Early ME. *dream*, *drém*, not recorded in OE., but pointing to an OE. **dréam* = WGer. *draum-*, OFris. *drâm*, OS., MLG. *drôm*, (MDu., Du. and LG. *droom*), OHG., MHG. *troum* (Ger. *traum*), ON. *draum* (Sw., Da. *dröm*), all in same sense. Generally thought to be a different word from DREAM *sb.*^{1}, OE. *dréam* = OS. *drôm* joy, which also points to a WGer. **draum-*. Kluge suggests that Germanic **draumo-*, dream, was for an earlier **draugmo-* or **draugwmó-*, a deriv. of the verbal series *dreug-*, *draug-*, *drug-*, to deceive, delude, Ger. *trügen*, whence ON. *draugr* ghost, apparition (cf. Zend *druj* apparition), the radical sense being 'deceptive appearance, illusion'.

It is remarkable that no trace of *dréam* in this sense appears in OE.; yet it is clear that it must have existed, since the ME. form *drêm* is regularly derived from it, and could come from no other source. It seems as if the prevalence of *dréam* 'joy, mirth, music', had caused *dréam* 'dream' to be avoided, at least in literature, and *swefn*, lit. 'sleep', to be substituted.]

1. a. A train of thoughts, images, or fancies passing through the mind during sleep; a vision during sleep; the state in which this occurs.

waking dream, a similar involuntary vision occurring to one awake.

c **1250** *Gen. & Ex.* 1179 On dreme him cam tiding. *a* **1300** *Cursor M.* 4605 (Cott.) Bath þi drems ar als an. **1388** WYCLIF *Gen.* xli. 22 Y seiȝ a dreem [**1382** sweuen]. *c* **1400** MAUNDEV. (Roxb.) vi. 22 He interpretid þe kynges dremes. **1474** CAXTON *Chesse* 2 They coude not telle hym his dreme that he had dremyd. **1594** HOOKER *Eccl. Pol.* Pref. i. §1 We have not . . permitted things to passe away as in a dreame. **1610** SHAKS. *Temp.* IV. i. 157 We are such stuffe As dreames are made on. **1673** WYCHERLEY *Gent. Dancing Master* IV. i, Ne'er fear it: dreams go by the contraries. **1752** JOHNSON *Rambler* No. 204 ¶12 Striving, as is usual in dreams, without ability to move. **1807-8** W. IRVING *Salmag.* xiv. (1860) 328 If life be but a dream, happy is he who can make the most of the illusion. **1842** TENNYSON *Locksley Hall* 79 Like a dog, he hunts in dreams. **1875** L. TOLLEMACHE in *Fortn. Rev.* Mar. 331 Large bodies of men have what may be termed waking dreams; so that, without being either authors or dupes of imposture, they declare that they have seen what they have not seen.

b. Colloq. phr. ***like a dream***: easily, effortlessly, without difficulty.

1949 R. STOUT *Second Confession* (1950) xi. 87 The engine . . starts like a dream, warm or cold. **1961** *Guardian* 28 Nov. 16/2 The Piccadilly one-way system . . worked 'like a dream' throughout the day.

2. *fig.* A vision of the fancy voluntarily or consciously indulged in when awake (esp. as being unreal or idle); a visionary anticipation, reverie, castle-in-the-air; cf. DAY-DREAM.

1581 J. BELL *Haddon's Answ. Osor.* 8b, Those be yours Osorius your owne drousie dreames. **1607** SHAKS. *Timon* IV. ii. 34 To liue But in a Dreame of Friendship. **1697** DAMPIER *Voy.* I. vi. 159 These may seem to the Reader but Golden Dreams. **1798** FERRIAR *Illustr. Sterne* ii. 24 The dreams of Rabelais's commentators have indeed discovered a very different intention. **1847** EMERSON *Repr. Men, Uses Gt. Men* Wks. (Bohn) I. 274 The search after the great is the dream of youth.

3. *transf.* **a.** An object seen in a vision.

1667 MILTON *P.L.* VIII. 292 When suddenly stood at my Head a dream. **1847** TENNYSON *Princ.* VII. 130 If you be, what I think you, some sweet dream.

b. Something of dream-like beauty or charm, such as one expects to see only in dreams.

1888 *Lady* 25 Oct. 374/1 My little dream of a place . . such a sweet, select watering-place. **1892** *Daily News* 2 May 2/1 Attired in a succession of those lovely gowns which enthusiasts delight to describe as 'a dream'.

c. An ideal or aspiration; *spec.* a national aspiration or ambition; a way of life considered to be ideal by a particular nation or group of people. Freq. with defining adj. prefixed, as ***the American dream*** (see AMERICAN A. 1 a).

1931 *N. & Q.* CLX. 107/1 If, in the course of centuries, the Russian dream comes true the history of Australia . . may seem, to students belonging to a Communist society, just as primitive, curious and exciting as to us appear the struggles within the Heptarchy. **1936** M. MITCHELL *Gone with Wind* xi. 214 He was still a young girl's dream of the Perfect Knight. **1937** L. BROMFIELD *Rains Came* Dedication, For all my Indian friends . . but for whom I should never have . . understood the Indian Dream. *Ibid.* I. xxxiii. 144 A ruler who would cherish the dream and carry it a little way farther along the way to fulfilment. **1937** KIPLING *Something of Myself* vi. 149 Rhodes . . said to me apropos of nothing in particular: 'What's your dream?' I answered that he was part of it.

4. *attrib.* and *Comb.*: **a.** Simple attrib., as ***dream-consciousness***, ***-content***, ***-habit***, ***-light***, ***-picture***, ***-play***, ***-poem***, ***-process***, ***-sequence***, ***-state***, ***-story***, ***-tide***. **b.** Pertaining to or characteristic of a dream or dreams, as ***dream-city***, ***-country***, ***-experience***, ***-fabric***, ***-figure***, ***-hall***, ***-idea***, ***-image***, ***-imagery***, ***-kingdom***, ***-landscape***, ***-language***, ***-life***, ***-lore***, ***-stuff***, ***-wish***, etc. **c.** Done in a dream, as ***dream-alliance***, ***-change***, ***-discourse***, ***-travel***, ***-vision***. **d.** Objective and obj. genitive, as ***dream-bringer***, ***-interpretation***, ***-interpreter***, ***-smith***, ***-speller***, ***-teller***; ***dream-haunting*** adj. **e.** Instrumental and locative, as ***dream-awake***, ***-awakened***, ***-born***, ***-built***, ***-created***, ***-crossed***, ***-fed***, ***-haunted***, ***-perturbed***, ***-ridden***, etc. adjs. **f.** Similative and parasynthetic, as ***dream-footed***, ***-heavy*** adjs.

1951 S. SPENDER *World within World* 310 Reader-writer walk together in a real-seeming *dream-alliance leading into gardens inhabited by Stephen Daedalus and Marcel. **1614** SYLVESTER *Bethulia's R.* v. 7 Soft, drowsie, *dream-awake. **1899** W. B. YEATS *Wind among Reeds* 35 Unknown spears Suddenly hurtle before my *dream-awakened eyes. **1881** H. PHILLIPS tr. *Chamisso's Faust* 14 Then let the *dream-born terrors selves reveal! **1845** MRS. NORTON *Child of Islands* (1846) 182 Thought, the great *Dream-bringer. **1863** HAWTHORNE *Our Old Home* 240 London the *dream-city of my youth. **1917** D. H. LAWRENCE in *Seven Arts* Mar. 443 The thin, transparent membrane of her sleep, her overlying *dream-consciousness. **1919** M. K. BRADBY *Psycho-analysis* vii. 88 There is often no clear difference in the dream consciousness between idea and act, subject and object. **1925** W. DE LA MARE *Two Tales* 15 This vision was only of his dream-consciousness. **1895** HARDY *Far fr. Mad. Crowd* (new ed.) p. vi, The horizons and landscapes of a merely realistic *dream-country. **1777** POTTER *Æschylus* (1779) II. 37 (Jod.) Oft, as short slumbers close his eyes . . The *dream-created Visions rise. **1930** T. S. ELIOT *Ash Wednesday* 20 The *dreamcrossed twilight between birth and dying. **1910** W. JAMES *Coll. Ess. & Rev.* (1920) 510, I woke again two or three times before day-break with no *dream-experiences. **1885** W. B. YEATS in *Dublin Univ. Rev.* July 137/1 Where *dream-fed passion is and peace encloses. **1919** M. K. BRADBY *Psycho-analysis* x. 123 If we fail to discover what a *dream figure symbolises, later dreams are likely to supply the clue. **1938** L. MACNEICE *Modern Poetry* ii. 46, I required poetic diction and dream-figures. **1865** LOWELL *Ode at Harvard Commem.* x, *Dream-footed as the shadow of a cloud, They [those names] flit across the ear. **1897** W. B. YEATS *Secret Rose* 2 The enchantment of his *dream-heavy voice was in her ears. **1869** G. M HOPKINS *Jrnl.* 23 Dec. (1959) 194 The *dream-images also appear to have little or no projection. **1956** W. MELLERS in A. Pryce-Jones *New Outl. Mod. Knowledge* 345 He believed art to be a dream-image, lifting us above sordid actualities. **1929** T. S. ELIOT *Dante* 65 A certain *habit* in *dream-imagery can persist throughout many changes of civilization. **1913** A. A. BRILL tr. *Freud's Interpret. Dreams* ii. 102 If the method of *dream interpretation here indicated is followed, it will be found that the dream really has meaning. **1943** *Mind* LII. 78 No dream-interpretation, no symptom analysis occurs, as it were, *in vacuo.* **1822** T. MITCHELL *Aristoph.* II. 297 The person here satirised seems to have been the diviner and *dream-interpreter of that name. **1925** T. S. ELIOT *Poems 1909–1925* 96 Eyes I dare not meet in dreams In death's *dream kingdom. **1936** *Burlington Mag.* Sept. 106/2 We detach our attention from this *dream-landscape. **1935** L. A. G. STRONG in *Amer. Mercury* Aug. 436/1 [James] Joyce . . is, throughout *Work in Progress*, assaying a *dream language. *Ulysses* dealt with day. *Work in Progress* deals with night. **1851** D. G. MITCHELL (*title*) *Dream life: a fable of the seasons. **1874** M. CLARKE *His Natural Life* (1875) II. III. v. 143 It seems to me . . that I have lived somewhere before, and have had another life— a dream-life. **1909** W. JAMES *Coll. Ess. & Rev.* (1920) 487 The will to *personate* may fall outside of the medium's own dream-life. **1940** 'G. ORWELL' *Inside Whale* 122 The idea is to give the bored factory-girl . . a dream-life. **1844** MRS. BROWNING *Lay Brown Rosary* I. ii, Forgot or unseen in the *dreamlight around her. **1890** BOLDREWOOD *Col. Reform.* (1891) 318 The *dream-palaces of a slumbering child. **1899** 'MARK TWAIN' *Man corrupted Hadleyburg* (1900) 214 A dimly connected procession of *dream-pictures. **1907** *Daily Chron.* 11 Nov. 3/4 A surprising Arabian Nights dream-picture. **1950** E. H. GOMBRICH *Story of Art* xxvii. 442 The experiment of painting dream-pictures was certainly worth making. **1897** G. B. SHAW *Let.* 4 July (1965) 779 It sounded at once serious and inexplicable, like a *dream-play. **1942** L. B. NAMIER *Conflicts* 15 There was something singularly unreal and depressingly second-hand about this dream-play of French history. **1964** C. S. LEWIS *Discarded Image* iv. 63 Every allegorical *dream-poem in the Middle Ages records a feigned *somnium.* **1944** *Mind* LIII. 179 The imagery-world into which we pass . . is just the way the *dream-process . . presents itself. **1938** W. DE LA MARE *Memory* 84 Her *dream-ridden eyes. **1856** R. A. VAUGHAN *Mystics* (1860) I. 9 But *dream-scenery of this sort is familiar to most persons. **1959** *Encounter* Oct. 53/1 A legend that has the stylised simplicity of a *dream-sequence in a Hollywood musical. **1652** GAULE *Magastrom.* 313 At this the *dream-spellers were divided in their divinations. **1899** *Westm. Gaz.* 12 Aug. 3/1 A waking and momentary *dream state. **1951** M. MCLUHAN *Mech. Bride* 10/1 Such patterns can only persist in a dream state. **1899** 'MARK TWAIN' *Man corrupted Hadleyburg* (1900) 281 The Egyptian . . rose, filled the planet with sound and splendor, then faded to *dream-stuff and passed away. **1916** D. H. LAWRENCE *Amores* 27 The dream-stuff is molten and moving mysteriously. *a* **1641** BP. MOUNTAGU *Acts & Mon.* (1642) 331 He sent for *dreame-tellers to expound his dreame. **1936** *Burlington Mag.* Aug. 85/1 His *dream-wishes should be fulfilled in reality.

g. Special combs.: **dream-boat**, **dreamboat** *colloq.* (orig. *U.S.*), an exceptionally attractive or pleasing person or thing (= DREAM *sb.*^{2} 3 b); *spec.* an extremely attractive member of the opposite sex; **dream-book**, a book containing interpretations of dreams; **dream-child**, a child seen in a dream; an imaginary child; so ***dream-son***; † **dream-doctor**, one who professes to interpret dreams; **dream-reader**, one who reads or interprets dreams; **dream ticket** orig. *U.S.*, a pair of candidates for political office ideally matched to attract widespread support for a party in an election: orig. applied to the proposed candidature of Richard M. Nixon and Nelson A. Rockefeller for President and Vice-President of the U.S.; cf. TICKET *sb.*^{1} 8; **dream-time**, (*a*) *Austral.* = ALCHERINGA; (*b*) the time for dreams, when the fancy is allowed to run freely; **dream vision**, a conventional poetic form, freq. used by medieval poets, in which the author recounts an alleged dream, the subject of which is often open to allegorical interpretation; also, a poem presenting this form; **dream-while**, the apparent duration of a dream; **dream-wise** *adv.*, after the manner of, or as in, a dream; **dream-work** *Psychol.* [tr. G. *traumarbeit*], the process by which dreams transmute their latent content into their manifest content in order to conceal their real meaning from the dreamer; **dream-world**, the world that one seems to enter in dreams; a world of dreams or illusions.

1947 BERREY & VAN DEN BARK *Amer. Thes. Slang* Suppl. 1, *Liked person.* Cheezle peezle, *dreamboat, [etc.]. **1949** in Wentworth & Flexner *Dict Amer. Slang* (1960) 162/1 [Ava Gardner] will star opposite James Mason, who she says is a 'dreamboat'. **1951** C. M. KORNBLUTH in *Galaxy Sci. Fiction* Apr. 141/1 Other cars were showing up, all of them dreamboats. **1951** T. RATTIGAN *Who is Sylvia?* II. 245, I thought you'd be quite old and staid and ordinary and, my God, look at you, a positive dream boat. **1957** *Life* 29 Apr. 137/1 (*caption*) A dream boat for hot-rodders is a chromed roadster like this one. **1960** *Woman's Own* 10 Sept. 63/2 You've been a dreamboat, and so has Robin. **1793** J. LACKINGTON *Mem.* (rev. ed.) xxxix. 415 Here you may find an old *bawd* inquiring for 'The Countess of Huntingdon's Hymn-book' . . and Dolly for a *Dream-book. **1803** M. L. WEEMS *Let.* 27 Aug. (1929) II. 272 To that list you may add . . Some dream books, dreaming Dictionaries and above all, some Pilg. Progress. **1909** J. BARLOW *Irish Ways* 17 There are fair-sized country towns, whose shops might be thoroughly ransacked without bringing to light any literary wares of more account than a dream-book. **1923** P. COLUM *Castle Conquer* x, I bought ear-rings and brooches, dream-books and fortune-books, buckles and combs. **1822** LAMB in *London Mag.* V. 21 (*title*) *Dream-Children; a reverie. **1903** *Westm. Gaz.* 28 Mar. 2/1 He's only my Dream-child. Some women have to be content all their life with Dream-children. **1545** JOYE *Exp. Dan.* v. H viij b, His sothsayers, *dreame doctours, enchaunters, sorcerers. *a* **1300** *Cursor M.* 4502 (Cott.) Welnes o welth did þis boteler For-gete ioseph, his *drem reder. **1470-85** MALORY *Arthur* I. ix, Be we wel auysed to be aferd of a dreme reder said Kyng Lot. **1879** E. ARNOLD *Lt. Asia* 3 The grey dream-readers said 'The dream is good!' **1926** M. LEINSTER *Dew on Leaf* 114 *Dream-son be all that I shall ever know. **1963** AUDEN *Dyer's Hand* 510 Prince Hal will remain his [Falstaff's] dream-son and boon-companion. **1960** *Nation's Business* June 26/1 The G.O.P. professionals in Washington began calling it the '*dream ticket'. **1983** *Sunday Tel.* 2 Oct. 1/2 Mr Kinnock, a leading left-winger, and Mr Hattersley, an outspoken figure on Labour's Centre-Right, have been described as the dream ticket because they would form a team uniting both wings of the Labour party. **1987** *Washington Post* 29 Mar. C2/1 'Dream Ticket,' says the cover of Time. 'Dream Ticket?' says the cover of Newsweek. **1910, 1965** *Dream time [see ALCHERINGA]. **1943** W. E. HARNEY *Taboo* (1944) 42 Years before, in the 'dream time' . . water poured in from the east and flooded the country. **1937** BLUNDEN *Elegy* 60 But the brain Fights *dream-time in vain. **1906** R. K. ROOT *Poetry of Chaucer* iv. 65 Its general form as a poem of the *dream-vision type associates the *Parliament of Fowls* with the essentially mediæval, French models of Chaucer's earlier period. **1929** L. POUND in Malone & Ruud *Stud. Eng. Philol. in Honor of F. Klaeber* 235 One is tempted . . to dwell upon the popularity of the Dream-Vision form in the Middle Ages as bearing relation to the dream inspiration of poetry. **1947** H. S. BENNETT *Chaucer & 15th Cent.* iii. 34 While he retains the dream-vision, he uses it in a new (if not novel) way to bring out the pathos of his story. **1957** C. MUSCATINE *Chaucer & Fr. Tradition* iv. 115 [In the *House of Fame*] Chaucer . . again adopts the dream vision as a frame. **1965** *English Studies* XLVI. 15 Chaucer's *Book of the Duchess* and his other dream-visions. **1822** LAMB *Elia* Ser. I. *Artificial Comedy*, Now and then for a *dream-while or so. **1880** WATSON *Prince's Quest* (1892) 51 When all things *dream-wise seemed to swim. **1913** A. A. BRILL tr. *Freud's Interpret. Dreams* vi. 262 The dream which we recollect upon wakening would thus only be a remnant of the total *dream-work. **1938** *Brit. Jrnl. Psychol.* XXVIII. 294 Dream-work . . enables a compromise to be reached between the satisfaction of the repressed urges and the need for sleep. **1817** COLERIDGE *Biogr. Lit.* 65 It places us in a *dream-world of phantoms and spectres. **1885** TENNYSON *Ancient Sage* x, But thou be wise in this dream-world of ours.

h. *attrib.*, passing into *adj.* Such as one dreams of or longs to have; ideal; perfect.

Some examples in senses 4a-g are not distinguishable from this use.

1896 E. TURNER *Little Larrikin* xii. 129 The dream-cottage was dearer to him than all the beautiful houses he owned. **1903** *Westm. Gaz.* 6 July 10/1 Mr. Gibson was not slow to grasp the resemblance between his dream-girl and the real. **1911** J. LONDON *Let.* 30 May (1966) 347, I am building my dream-house on my dream-ranch. **1931** J. CANNAN *High Table* xv. 220 Home at last to my Dream Girl. **1958** K. GOODWIN in P. Gammond *Decca Bk. Jazz* xiii. 149 He fronted an all-star 'dream' band for a lengthy season at the famous Birdland niterie. **1959** D. EDEN *Sleeping Bride* v. 40 She planned her dream home. **1960** *Guardian* 14 Apr. 12/4 A dream London in which there are fewer cars. **1961** *Listener* 7 Dec. 966/2 Housewives are offered dream houses with dream kitchens. **1967** WODEHOUSE *Company for Henry* iv. 66 We got engaged. The family put up a considerable beef . . because I wasn't everybody's dream girl. **1971** *Guardian* 19 Jan. 5/6 This is not a dream car just built for a motor show.

† **dream**, *v.*^{1} *Obs.* [OE. **drieman*, *drýman*, *dréman* to make music or melody, to play on an

instrument, rejoice = OS. *drômian* 'jubilare'; f. WGer. *draum-, OS. *drôm*, OE. *dréam*, DREAM *sb.*[1]] *intr.* To make a musical or joyful noise; to make melody.

a **1000** *Lamb. Psalter* xcvii. 7 (Bosw.) Dremað oððe fægniaþ on ȝesihþe cyninges. *c* **1205** LAY. 13586 Me heom brohte drinken & heo gunnen dremen. *Ibid.* 22885 Harpen gunnen dremen. *a* **1225** *Ancr. R.* 430 þet ower beoden bemen & dreamen wel ine Drihtenes earen. *a* **1240** *Ureisun* in *Cott. Hom.* 191 Murie dreameð engles biuoren þin onsene.

dream (driːm), *v.*[2] Pa. t. and pple. **dreamed** (driːmd), **dreamt** (drɛmt). Forms: see DREAM *sb.*[2] [Appears in 13th c. with the sb. Either derived from the latter, or repr. an unrecorded OE. **drïeman*, *dryman*, *dréman*, corresp. to ON. *dreyma*, OHG. *troumen*, Ger. *träumen*, an earlier deriv. of Germanic **draum-*: see DREAM *sb.*[2]]

1. *intr.* To have visions and imaginary sense-impressions in sleep. Const. *of* (†*on*), *about*, and with indirect passive.

c **1250** *Gen. & Ex.* 2067 Good is..to dremen of win. *c* **1320** *Seuyn Sag.* (W.) 2960 This lady was the same That he had so dremyd of. *c* **1470** HENRY *Wallace* XI. 1295 Tell I this in our place Thai wyll bot deym, I othir dreym or rawe. **1535** COVERDALE *Ps.* cxxv[i]. 1 Then shal we be like vnto them that dreame. **1592** SHAKS. *Rom. & Jul.* I. iv. 74 She gallops ..Ore Ladies lips, who strait on kisses dreame. **1667** MILTON *P.L.* III. 514 Jacob..Dreaming by night under the open Skie. **1726** DE FOE *Hist. Devil* II. iii. (1840) 198 To dream is nothing else but to think sleeping. **1865** TYLOR *Early Hist. Man.* i. 8 The object dreamt of. **1875** A. SWINBOURNE *Picture Logic* v. 40, I actually dreamt about Logic again.

2. *trans.* To behold or imagine in sleep or in a vision; **a.** with cognate or pronominal obj.; sometimes with simple obj. = *dream of.*

a **1300** *Cursor M.* 18985 (Cott.) Yur eldrin men sal dremes dreme. ? *a* **1366** CHAUCER *Rom. Rose* 18 That dremen in her slepe a nights Ful many things couertly. **1526** *Pilgr. Perf.* (W. de W. 1531) 36 The holy Seruauntes of god dremeth holy dremes. **1592** SHAKS. *Rom. & Jul.* I. iv. 53 They [dreamers] do dreame things true. *Ibid.* v. iii. 79 Said he not so? Or did I dreame it so? **1613** —— *Hen. VIII*, III. i. 135 One that ne'er dream'd a Ioy, beyond his [her Husband's] pleasure. **1700** DRYDEN *Fables, To D'chess Ormond* 134 The Macedon by Jove's decree, Was taught to dream an herb for Ptolemy. **1726** DE FOE *Hist. Devil* II. iii, He brought her to dream whatever he put into her thoughts. **1810** SCOTT *Lady of L.* II. xxxi, Who have..Dreamed calmly out their dangerous dream. **1813** 'ÆDITUUS' *Metrical Remarks* 32 The droning Priesthood slumber'd in their stalls, Nor dreamt the storm, which shook their fabrics' walls. **1850** TENNYSON *In Mem.* cii, On that last night..I dream'd a vision of the dead.

b. with *obj. clause.*

1393 GOWER *Conf.* II. 99, I dreme..That I alone with her mete. **1500–20** DUNBAR *Poems* xxviii. 2, I dremed ane angell came fra Hevin. **1651** HOBBES *Leviath.* III. xxxii. 196 He dreamed that God spake to him. **1815** SHELLEY *Alastor* 151 He dreamed a veiled maid Sate near him.

†**3.** Impersonal construction: with obj. of the dreamer, followed by *of*, cognate obj., or object clause, as in 1 and 2. *Obs.* or *arch.*

The regular construction in ON., and possibly the original in Eng. also. Cf. ON. *mik dreymdi draum*, or *draum dreymdi mik*, ME. *drem dremede me*; ON. *hann dreymdi þat, at hann væri*, etc., ME. *him drempte that he was*, etc. The ON. shows that there are two accusatives, which ME. from the levelling of inflexions fails to do.

c **1250** *Gen. & Ex.* 1941 Quat so him drempte ðor quiles he slep. *Ibid.* 2049 Hem drempte dremes boðen oniȝt. *Ibid.* 2059 Me drempte, ic stod at a win-tre. *c* **1300** *Havelok* 1304 Another drem dremede me ek. ? *a* **1366** CHAUCER *Rom. Rose* 51 That it was May, thus dremed me. **1377** LANGL. *P. Pl.* B. XVIII. 8 Of gerlis..gretly me dremed. *c* **1450** *St. Cuthbert* (Surtees) 7347 Me dremyd..þat I was ledd To durham. [**1854** SYD. DOBELL *Balder* xiv. 58 In the night..Methought I stood within this room..and medreamed I stood Robed like a necromancer.]

4. *trans.* To imagine or fancy as in a dream; to think or believe (a thing) to be possible; to picture to oneself.

c **1380** WYCLIF *Sel. Wks.* III. 355 Ȝit eche preest..shulde haue power to do good..but not so myche as here is dremed. **1581** MARBECK *Bk. of Notes* 197 They are farre out of the waie, that dreame in the mysticall bread and wine, a bodilie presence. **1606** SHAKS. *Cymb.* III. iii. 81 Nor Cymbeline dreames that they are aliue. **1617** SIR J. FITZEDMOND in *Lismore Papers* Ser. II. (1887) II. 83, I neuer thought or dreamed the like to doe. **1700** S. L. tr. *C. Fryke's Two Voy. E.I.* 165 [We] never dreamt that there was any thing of value within it. **1849–52** M. ARNOLD *Longing* iii, Come now, and let me dream it truth. *Mod.* Little did any one dream that such a catastrophe was at hand.

5. *intr.* with *of*, †*on*: To think *of* even in a dream or in the remotest way; to have any conception *of*; to think *of*, or contemplate, as at all possible; to conceive, imagine. Chiefly in negative sentences (express or implied).

1538 STARKEY *England* I. ii. 36 Jugyd happy and fortunate ..though he neuer Dreme of vertue. **1588** *Marprel. Epist.* (Arb) 27 Weapons, whereof they never once drempt. **1602** SHAKS. *Ham.* I. v. 168 There are more things in Heauen and Earth, Horatio, Then are dream't of in our Philosophy. *a* **1641** BP MOUNTAGU *Acts & Mon.* (1642) 539 This is..not so much as dreamed on by Baronius. **1712** BUDGELL *Spect.* No. 506 ¶12 She has discovered..accomplishments in herself, which she never before once dreamed of. **1884** G. ALLEN *Philistia* I. 167, I wouldn't dream of going to live in the place.

6. *intr.* To fall into reverie; to indulge in fancies or day-dreams; to form imaginary visions *of* (unrealities).

1533 GAU *Richt vay* To Rdr. (1888) 3 Thay thocht and dremit efter thair aune heid. **1579** TOMSON *Calvin's Serm. Tim.* 877/2 Let vs not dreame vpon rest, to say, we shall be at our ease. **1595** J. EDWARDES in *Shaks. C. Praise* 17 Poets that divinely dreampt. **1603** KNOLLES *Hist. Turks* (1621) 166 He also dreaming after the empire. **1667** MILTON *P.L.* VIII. 175 Dream not of other Worlds. **1845** LONGF. *Old Clock on Stairs* vi, There youths and maidens dreaming strayed. **1895** *Bookman* Oct. 20/2 One who..has been dreaming of future triumphs.

†**7. a.** *intr.* To act drowsily or indolently; to procrastinate. **b.** *trans.* To perform indolently like one in a dream. *Obs.*

1548 HALL *Chron., Hen. VI*, 162 b, He mindyng no longer to dreame in his waightie matter, nor to kepe secrete his right and title. *Ibid., Edw. IV*, 231 b, The Frenche kyng dremyng, and waityng like a Foxe for his praie. *Ibid.* 237 b, In all hast possible Peter not sluggyng, nor dreamyng his busines, came [etc.].

c. *intr. fig.* To hover or hang dreamily or drowsily.

1842 TENNYSON *Vision of Sin* II A sleepy light upon their brows and lips—As when the sun, a crescent of eclipse, Dreams over lake and lawn. **1858** HAWTHORNE *Fr. & It. Jrnls.* II. 284 Mist..dreamed along the hills.

8. *trans.* † ***to dream forth***: to put forth as one who tells a dream (*obs.*) ***to dream away*** or ***out***: to pass or spend in dreaming.

c **1546** JOYE in Gardiner *Declar. Art. Joye* (1546) 17 Winchester, dreamynge vs forth, his newe fayned fayth, coupleth her to an externe knouledge. **1590** SHAKS. *Mids. N.* I. i. 8 Foure nights wil quickly dreame away the time. **1687** DRYDEN *Hind & P.* III. 451 Whether [swallows] dream the winter out in caves below. **1822** LAMB *Elia* Ser. II. *Th. Bks. & Reading*, I dream away my life in others' speculations.

9. *refl.* To bring oneself in a dream.

1720 *Hum. Lett. in Lond. Jrnl.* (1721) 29 Having dreamed himself into this Importance [etc.]. **1827** R. H. FROUDE *Rem.* (1838) I. 221, I hope..that I may dream myself among lakes and mountains.

10. ***to dream up*** (occas. ***to dream out***): to picture (something) in one's mind; to think up, devise, invent.

1930 E. POUND *XXX Cantos* v. 21 And all of this, runs Varchi, dreamed out beforehand In Perugia. **1935** *Punch* 4 Sept. 262/2 The man who has a clearly formed ambition, who has dreamed *out* an ideal which his whole personality [etc.]. **1941** *Life* 3 Mar. 23/2 Ambassador Winant is about as far from the conventional picture of a..diplomat as Franklin Roosevelt could have dreamed up. **1942** *Time* 23 Mar. 60/2 Pondering Stanford's lack of a liberal arts school, Professor Dodds dreamed up one which would avoid the failings of most liberal arts colleges. **1950** *Manch. Guardian Weekly* 16 Nov. 3 A slick political trick, such as might have been dreamed up by a bright Chicago wardheeler. **1958** *Listener* 30 Oct. 680/1 This compulsory 'cooling-off period' is not something we have just dreamed up. **1964** M. MCLUHAN *Understanding Media* v. 59 Plato..failed to notice that Athens was a greater school than any university even he could dream up.

Hence **dreamed**, **dreamt** *ppl. a.*, ˈ**dreaming** *vbl. sb.*; also ˈ**dreamage** (*rare*), dream-stuff.

c **1320** *Seuyn Sag.* (W.) 3089 To hir he talde of his dremeing. **1549** CHEKE *Hurt Sedit.* (R.), They..deeme.. other mens wisedome to be but dreaminge. **1611** BROUGHTON *Require Agreem.* 53 Diana, a dreamed Goddesse of hunting. **1674** N. FAIRFAX *Bulk & Selv.* 59 This dreamt or imaginary space. **1848** CLOUGH *Bothie* IV. 127, I was walking along..Full of my dreamings. **1876** GEO. ELIOT *Dan. Der.* VII. liii, Like a dreamed visitant from some region of departed mortals. **1887** F. HALL in *Nation* (N.Y.) XLIV. 515/3 The musty dreamage which he retails.

dreamer (ˈdriːmə(r)). [f. DREAM *v.*[2] + -ER[1].]

1. One who dreams; one who has visions in sleep; a visionary; an idle speculator.

a **1300** *Cursor M.* 4111 (Cott.) Lo quar þe dremer now es cummen. *c* **1440** *Promp. Parv.* 131/2 Dremare, *sompniator.* **1533** COVERDALE *Lord's Supper* Wks. (Parker Soc.) I. 437 Unless we will be very dreamers and blockheads. **1601** SHAKS. *Jul. C.* I. ii. 24 He is a Dreamer, let vs leaue him. **1727** DE FOE *Syst. Magic* I. iv. (1840) 117 We have indeed some of Balaam's dreamers. **1855** MACAULAY *Hist. Eng.* IV. 691 He was not..the first great discoverer whom princes and statesmen had regarded as a dreamer.

2. A name given to some species of *Chelidoptera* or puff-bird.

dreamery (ˈdriːmərɪ). [f. DREAM *sb.*[2] or *v.*[2] + -ERY.] **a.** A place that favours dreams. **b.** Dream-work, 'such stuff as dreams are made of'.

1826 *Blackw. Mag.* XIX. 338 He would be..dissolved, like Sardanapalus, in that voluptuous dreamery, a hot-bath. **1838** LONGF. in *Life* (1891) I 313 One of the finest lecturers I ever heard..But it is all dreamery, after all. **1875** HOWELLS *Foregone Concl.* xviii, His whole stock of helplessness, dreamery, and unpracticality.

ˈ**dreamful,** *a.* [f. DREAM *sb.*[2] + -FUL.] Full of or abounding in dreams; dreamy.

1552 HULOET, Dreamefull or full of dreamynge, *somniculosus.* **1781** MICKLE *Siege of Marseilles* v. i. (R.), While Reason sleeps..she[Melancholy] impious leads The dreamful fancy. **1832** TENNYSON *Eleänore* 30 Into dreamful slumber lull'd. **1872** M. COLLINS *Two Plunges for Pearl* III. vii. 166 Of the Lotos-land a dreamful denizen.

Hence ˈ**dreamfully** *adv.*, dreamily.

1880 L. WALLACE *Ben-Hur* 198 As singers dreamfully play with a flitting chorus. **1887** *Century Mag.* July 412 Where dusk-green sway the pine-boughs dreamfully.

dream-hole. [? f. DREAM *sb.*[1] + HOLE.] One of 'the holes left in the walls of steeples, towers, barns, etc., for the admission of light' (Grose). Supposed (by modern archæologists) to have been originally applied to the holes in church-towers and belfries by which the sound passed out.

1559 *Churchw. Acc. Minchinhampton* in *Archæologia* XXXV. 425 For mendyne of dyuerse of the dreame-holes in the steeple, the churche porche, the north syde of the churche. **1787** in GROSE *Provinc. Gloss.* **1855** in ROBINSON *Whitby Gloss* **1876** *Mid-Yorksh. Gloss., Dream-hole*, loop-hole. **1891** ATKINSON *Last of Giant Killers* 175 He saw the dreadful-looking thing go through the narrow straitened slit or dream-hole in the tower.

ˈ**dreamily,** *adv.* [f. DREAMY + -LY[2].] In a dreamy manner; as in a dream or reverie. So ˈ**dreaminess,** the quality or state of being dreamy or given to reverie.

1795 SOUTHEY *Joan of Arc* I. 467 In that dreaminess of thought When every bodily sense is as it slept. **1835** LYTTON *Rienzi* I. i, That vague and abstracted dreaminess of eye usually denotes a propensity to reverie and contemplation. **1861** HUGHES *Tom Brown at Oxf.* x, Looking dreamily into the embers. **1866** MRS. GASKELL *Wives & Dau.* I. 298 Her dreamily abstracted eyes.

ˈ**dreaming,** *ppl. a.* [f. DREAM *v.*[2] + -ING[2].] That dreams or acts as if in a dream.

1552 HULOET, Dreaminge felowe, *somniculosus..* Dreaminge speaker, *tardiloquus.* **1681** DRYDEN *Abs. & Achit.* 529 A numerous Host of dreaming Saints succeed. **1868** FARRAR *Silence & V.* ii. (1875) 44 The cold clear light of eternity flashed suddenly upon the closed and dreaming eyes.

Hence ˈ**dreamingly** *adv.*; ˈ**dreamingness.**

1545 COVERDALE *Writ. & Transl.* (1844) 511 Allegories handled, not dreamingly or unfruitfully. **1658** A. FOX *Wurtz' Surg.* III. v. 231 They would never go so dreamingly about so weighty a matter. **1727** BAILEY vol. II, *Dreamingness*, slothfulness, acting as if in a Dream. **1891** F. W. ROBINSON *Her Love & His Life* III. VI. ix. 207 Looking out dreamingly and despondently at the dark night.

†ˈ**dreamish,** *a. Obs. rare.* [f. DREAM *sb.*[2] + -ISH.] Somewhat dreamy.

1574 J. DEE in *Lett. Lit. Men* (Camden) 38 Dremish demonstrations of places.

dreamland. [f. DREAM *sb.*[2] + LAND.] The land or country which one sees in dreams, and which exists only in imagination; an ideal or imaginary land. Also *attrib.*

a **1834** LAMB *Let. to Coleridge* (L.), They are real, and have a venue in their respective districts in dreamland. **1843** CARLYLE *Past & Pr.* II. i, This England of the Year 1200 was no chimerical vacuity or dream-land. **1847** A. C. COXE *Chr. Ballads* (1861) 30 In Dreamland once I saw a Church..And Dreamland Church was decent all. **1885** LOWELL *Pr. Wks.* (1890) VI. 74 That delightfully fortuitous inconsequence that is the adamantine logic of dreamland. **1895** *Tablet* 20 July 108 A dreamland scheme of conditional reunion.

ˈ**dreamless,** *a.* [f. as prec. + -LESS.] Without or free from dreams. Hence ˈ**dreamlessly** *adv.*

1605 CAMDEN *Rem., Names* (R.), The savages of Mount Atlas..which were reported to be both nameless and dreamlesse. *c* **1815** MOORE *Irish Mel.* Poet. Wks. II. 228 Then leave them in their dreamless sleep. **1873** OUIDA *Pascarel* I. 203, I slept all night dreamlessly.

ˈ**dreamlessness.** [-NESS.] Dreamless condition.

1905 E. F. BENSON *Image in Sand* xiii, Something that had mingled with sleep, but was previous to her deep dreamlessness. **1928** J. W. VANDERCOOK *Black Majesty* i. 2 The black peasants of Haiti have slipped ever deeper into stupor and dirt and dreamlessness.

ˈ**dreamlet.** *rare.* [f. DREAM *sb.*[2] + -LET.] A short or brief dream.

1835 *Tait's Mag.* II. 463 Is it only a dreamlet of some flower-enamoured swain? **1871** M. COLLINS *Mrq. & Merch.* II. iv. 95 She..had two or three nice dreamlets.

ˈ**dream-like,** *a.* Like a dream; unsubstantial, vague, shadowy, or ideal, as a dream.

1807 ANNA PORTER *Hungar. Bro.* vi, Her engagements became dream-like, she forgot their steadfastness. **1825** LYTTON *Falkland* 32, I can gaze upon her dream-like beauty. **1843** —— *Last Bar.* I. iv, The eyes were soft, dark, and brilliant, but dreamlike and vague. **1870** EMERSON *Soc. & Solit.* xi. 240 A new world of dream-like glory.

ˈ**dreamscape.** [f. DREAM *sb.*[2] + SCAPE *sb.*[3]] A dream-landscape (DREAM *sb.*[2] 4 b); a scene dreamed; a dream-like picture, a dream-world. Also, a (literary) description of a dream.

1959 S. PLATH in *Sewanee Rev.* LXVII. 446 The waking head rubbishes out the draggled lot Of sulphurous dreamscapes..Which seemed, when dreamed, to mean so.. much. **1966** *Life* 25 Mar. 31/2 There are psychedelic corporation presidents, military officers, doctors, teachers —each with a reason to risk a voyage on the unpredictable terrain of the deep brain dreamscape. **1967** *Guardian* 27 Dec. 5/5 The Beatles free among the dreamscapes whose poignancy their photography caught so well. **1980** *N.Y. Times* 1 June VII. 30/4 Dreams are..difficult to make convincing in fiction. There is an added problem with Kavan's dreamscapes in that they are so clearly..composed at the typewriter. **1985** *Time* 22 July 76/3 His splendid, spare, Freudian production uses a flowing white sailcloth draped about the stage to represent a snowstorm, a dreamscape, a bower and a marriage tent.

dreamt, pa. t. and pa. pple. of DREAM *v.*

dreamy ('driːmɪ), *a.* [f. DREAM *sb.*^{2} + -Y^{1}.]
1. Full of or abounding in dreams; characterized by dreaming or by causing dreams.
1567 *Triall Treas.* (1850) 6 Thou goest like a dromeldory, dreamy and drousy. **1830** TENNYSON *Mariana* vi, All day within the dreamy house, The doors upon their hinges creak'd. **1856** KANE *Arct. Expl.* I. xvi. 196 A dreamy but intense slumber. **1859** LANG *Wand. India* 196 Having spent a very dreamy night.
2. Given or pertaining to reverie or fancy.
1809 C. LLOYD in *Athenæum* 2 Mar. (1895) 282/1 In fact he [Coleridge] attends to nothing but dreamy reading & still more dreamy feelings. **1845** JAMES *A. Neil* iv, Her words were spoken in one of those strange dreamy moods, that sometimes fall upon her. **1871** L. STEPHEN *Playgr. Eur.* ix. (1894) 218 To enjoy an Alpine view properly, one should at times be dreamy and sentimental.
3. a. Characteristic of, or of the nature of, a dream; dream-like; vague, indistinct; also, of the eyes, or a colour: misty, dim, or cloudy.
1848 KEBLE *Serm.* Pref. 54 To slight it altogether, as a dreamy, unreal kind of thing. **1859** KINGSLEY *Misc.* (1860) II. 243 A single stockdove..began calling sadly and softly, with a dreamy peaceful moan. **1875** JOWETT *Plato* (ed. 2) IV. 20 He has a dreamy recollection of hearing [it]. **1884** F. M. CRAWFORD *Rom. Singer* I. 26 She has deep blue eyes, wide apart and dreamy. **1893** *Daily News* 27 Nov. 6/1 Cloth in a soft and dreamy tone of sea blue.
b. Perfect, ideal; delightful, beautiful. *colloq.* (orig. *U.S.*).
1941 *Life* 27 Jan. 79/2 Subdebs use a great many adjectives... The list merely begins with..*dreamy* and *super*. **1952** S. KAUFFMANN *Philanderer* (1953) xiv. 233 'Let us find a cool and lovely garden restaurant and have a slow, exquisite dinner...' 'O.K., Russ... Sounds dreamy.' **1953** M. DICKENS *No More Meadows* viii. 307 She said she had a date with a dreamy boy. **1958** *Spectator* 10 Jan. 38/2, I have a Ford Edsel, the first to be imported here, it's dreamy, all electric push-buttons. **1959** 'N. BLAKE' *Widow's Cruise* 67 The water's absolutely dreamy. And I bet you're a super swimmer.
4. *Comb.*, as ***dreamy-eyed, -minded***, etc.
1884 G. MOORE *Mummer's Wife* (1887) 171 The dreamy-minded musician. **1892** 'MARK TWAIN' *Amer. Claim.* 17 A dreamy-eyed young fellow. **1958** E. H. CLEMENTS *Uncommon Cold* i. 29 She looked devoted and *very* intellectual... And sensitive. Dreamy-eyed.

drean(e, obs. and dial. f. DRAIN.

drear, *sb.* Also 6 drere. [A back-formation from DREARY *a.*, by the Elizabethan archaists.]
†**1.** Dreariness, sadness, gloom. *Obs.*
1563 SACKVILLE *Induct. to Mirr. Mag.* xx, Sith sorrowe is thy name And that to thee this drere doth wel pertayne. **1590** SPENSER *F.Q.* I. viii. 40 A ruefull spectacle of death and ghastly drere. *Ibid.* II. xii. 36 The hoars Night-raven, trump of dolefull drere. **1597–8** BP. HALL *Sat.* IV. vi, His dim eyes see nought but death and drere. **1775** S. J. PRATT *Liberal Opinions* (1783) IV. 48 In the drear of December.
2. A dreary person. *colloq.*
1958 M. ALLINGHAM *Hide my Eyes* x. 101 'What an evil-eyed old drear,' he remarked. **1966** J. B. PRIESTLEY *Salt is Leaving* v. 61 He was just a miserable little drear.

drear (drɪə(r)), *a.* Chiefly *poet.* [A poetic shortening of DREARY *a.*] **a.** = DREARY *a.* 4.
1629 MILTON *Nativity* 193 A drear and dying sound Affrights the flamens at their service quaint. **1795** SOUTHEY *Vis. Maid Orleans* I. 12 A moor, Barren, and wide, and drear, and desolate. **1851** LONGF. *Gold. Leg.* I. *Crt.-yard of Castle* 18 All is silent, sad, and drear. **1968** A. CLARKE *Darkened Room* x. 127 I've bought you..a little towel—I think hospital ones are normally rather drear.
b. Rarely of persons; = DREARY 3.
a **1717** PARNELL *Fairy Tale* (R.), His heart was drear, his hope was cross'd. **1855** BROWNING *Saul* iv, So agonized Saul, drear and stark, blind and dumb. **1962** *Movie* Nov. 34/3 The Israelites are mainly drear, and the little fun comes from the performances of Anouk Aimee as the queen of Sodom and Stanley Baker as her brother.
c. *Comb.*, as ***drear-nighted, -white***.
a **1821** KEATS *Stanzas* i, A drear-nighted December. **1844** MRS. BROWNING *Drama of Exile* Poems 1889 I. 97 When he tosseth his head, the drear-white steed.
Hence **'drearly** *adv.*; **'drearness**.
1861 DORA GREENWELL *Poems* 170, I lose the drearness Of the Present. **1891** G. MEREDITH *One of our Conq.* II. xi. 270 The scene striking him drearly.

drearihead ('drɪərɪhɛd). *arch.* [See -HEAD.]
1. Sadness, sorrow; = DREARINESS 1.
c **1250** *Gen. & Ex.* 1122 So ist nu forwent mirie dale In to dririhed and in to bale. *c* **1400** *Rom. Rose* 4728 Delite right fulle of hevynesse, And dreried fulle of gladnesse. **1590** SPENSER *F.Q.* III. i. 62 Suddein feare and ghastly drerihedd. *Ibid.* III. ii. 30 What evill plight Hath..with sad dreryhead Chaunged thy lively cheare. *a* **1764** LLOYD *Progr. Envy* Poet. Wks. 1774 I. 138 Fit place for melancholy drearyhead. **1870** MORRIS *Earthly Par.* III. IV. 92 Cast somewhat off, O friend, thy drearyhead.
2. Dismalness, gloominess; = DREARINESS 2.
1591 SPENSER *Muiopotmos* 347 She grew to hideous shape of dryrihed. **1647** H. MORE *Song of Soul* I. III. xi, If't [the sun] appear In rounder shape with skouling dreryhed. **1865** G. MACDONALD *A. Forbes* vii, Other sound there was none in this land of drearihead.

'drearihood. [f. as prec. + -HOOD.] = prec.
1647 H. MORE *Song of Soul* II. I. IV. vi, Particular visibles deaths drearyhood Can seiz upon. **1817** SCOTT *Harold the Dauntless* Introd., The jolly sportsman knows such drearihood When bursts in deluge the autumnal rain. **1868** MORRIS *Earthly Par.* I. (1870) 152 So all men..Forgat him and his drearihood.

drearily ('drɪərɪlɪ), *a.* [f. DREARY *a.* + -LY^{2}.] In a dreary manner: see the adj.
c **1000** ÆLFRIC *Saints' Lives* (E.E.T.S.) II. 280 Dreorilice wepende. *a* **1225** *Leg. Kath.* 1898 þu most..3ef þu nult nawt, dreoriliche deien. *a* **1300** *Cursor M.* 22188 Siþen drerili to dei. *a* **1400** *Relig. Pieces fr. Thornton MS.* (1867) 31 We..becomes thralles dreryly to þe deuelle. **1579** SPENSER *Sheph. Cal.* Feb. 45 Breme Winter..Drerily shooting his stormie darte. **1836** W. IRVING *Astoria* II. 207 The month of December set in drearily. **1856** KANE *Arct. Expl.* I. ix. 99 A flower-growth..drearily Arctic in its type. **1885** *Manch. Exam.* 22 Feb. 5/6 One Irish member succeeded another, and went drearily over the same ground.

dreariment ('drɪərɪmənt). *arch.* [A Spenserian irreg. formation from *dreary*: cf. *merriment*, of about the same age.] Dreary or dismal condition, or the expression of it.
1579 SPENSER *Sheph. Cal.* Nov. 36 Sing of sorrowe and deathes dreeriment [*Gloss.* dreery and heauy cheere]. **1591** —— *Ruins Time* 158 Mourne my fall with dolefull dreriment. **1593** NASHE *Christ's T.* 1 Let some part of thy diuine dreariment liue againe in mine eyes. **1607** WALKINGTON *Opt. Glasse* iv. 28 Bacchus is a wise Collegian, who admits meriment, and expels dreriment. **1633** P. FLETCHER *Purple Isl.* III. xviii, The Cloudie Isle with hellish dreeriment Would soon be fill'd. **1867** CAROLINE SOUTHEY *Poet. Wks.* 110 There lay in helpless dreariment The Master loved so well. **1867** MORRIS *Jason* x. 82.

dreariness ('drɪərɪnɪs). [f. DREARY *a.* + -NESS.] The quality or state or being dreary.
†**1.** Sadness, sorrowfulness, dolefulness. *Obs.* (exc. as influenced by 2: 'desolate sadness').
a **1000** *Greg. Dial.* MS. Hatt. 5 a, 8 (Bosw.) Gif he ne ȝehulpe hire sarlican dreorinysse. *c* **1340** *Cursor M.* 22667 (Fairf.) For drerines þai salle be drad. **1382** WYCLIF *Ecclus.* iv. 8 Bowe doun to the pore thin ere without dreryness. *c* **1450** *Mirour Saluacioun* 3221 Dreryness trembling and drede cristis threfolde Orisoune. **1596** DALRYMPLE tr. *Leslie's Hist. Scot.* III. 197 He fand her lyeng..in dreirrines, lamentatioune, and mourneng sair. **1863** GEO. ELIOT *Romola* I. v, She looked with a sad dreariness in her young face at the lifeless objects around her.
2. a. Dismalness, desolateness, gloom. **b.** Oppressively uninteresting character.
1727 BAILEY vol. II., *Dreeriness*, dismalness. **1775** JOHNSON *Journ. W. Islands* Wks. X. 354 Passing on through the dreariness of solitude. **1856** KANE *Grinnell Exp.* I. 472 The dreariness of Greenland. **1886** *Athenæum* 30 Oct. 562/3 The..incessant and..gratuitous dreariness of the story.

†**'drearing.** *Obs. rare.*$^{-1}$ [A Spenserian irreg. formation from *drear*, *dreary*.] Sorrowing; grief.
1591 SPENSER *Daphn.* 189 All were my selfe, through grief, in deadly drearing.

drearisome ('drɪərɪsəm), *a.* Chiefly *dial.* [f. next + -SOME.] Of a dreary character; lonely and desolate.
1633 W. STRUTHER *True Hapines* 143 Under that drearie-some widowhood of our soule. **1828** *Craven Dialect*, *Drearisome*, dreary, solitary. **1840** BARHAM *Ingol. Leg.*, *Witches' Frolic*, Who roams the old ruins this drearysome night? **1877** BLACKMORE *Erema* i, That wearisome, drearisome, uncompanionable company.

dreary ('drɪərɪ), *a.* Forms: 1 dreóriȝ, 2 droriȝ, 2–6 dreri(e, -y, 3 dreori (drori), 3–5 druri, -y, (4 drwry, 4–5 drewry(e), 4–8 dreeri, -y, *Sc.* dreiri, (6 driery, driry, dryrye), 6– dreary. [OE. *dréoriȝ* gory, bloody, sorrowful, sad, f. *dréor* gore, falling blood, app.:—OTeut. type **dreuzo-z*; in ablaut relation to OS. *drôr*, OHG. *trôr* gore, blood (:—**drauzo-z*), and to ON. *dreyri* (:—*drauzon-*) gore, blood, whence *dreyrigr* gory, bloody. Generally referred to the verbal ablaut stem **dreuz-*, OE. *dréosan* to drop, fall. To the same verbal root is ultimately referred OHG. **trûrac*, MHG. *trûrec*, Ger. *traurig* sorrowful, sad, which is thus remotely connected in derivation with *dréoriȝ*, *dreary*.]
†**1.** Gory, bloody. *Obs.*
In OE.; the later instances are doubtful, and may belong to 2.
Beowulf (Th.) 2838 Wæter stod dreoriȝ and ȝedrefed. *a* **1300** *Cursor M.* 22462 (Cott.) A blodi rain, a dreri drift. **1590** SPENSER *F.Q.* I. vi. 45 With their drery wounds, and bloody gore.
†**2.** Cruel, dire, horrid, grievous. *Obs.*
a **1000** *Guthlac* 1085 (Gr.) þam ic ȝeorne gæst-ȝerynum in þas dreorȝan tid dædum cwemde mode and mæȝne. *a* **1225** *Ancr. R.* 106 Te Giws dutten..his deorewurde muð mid hore dreori fustes. *a* **1300** *Cursor M.* 214 (Cott.) þe dreri days fiueten þat sal cum for-wit domes day. *c* **1440** *York Myst.* xlvi. 158 What dreyre destonye me drew fro þat dede! **1600** HAKLUYT *Voy.* III. 41 (R.) To ease the ship's sides from the great and driry strokes of the yce.
3. Of persons, their actions, state, aspect, etc.: Full of sadness or melancholy; sad, doleful, melancholy: in late use, influenced by 4. *Obs.* or *arch.*
c **1000** ÆLFRIC *Gen.* xliv. 14 Hiȝ wurdon swiþe dreoriȝe. *c* **1175** *Lamb. Hom.* 97 He ifrefrað þa dr[e]oriȝan. *c* **1315** SHOREHAM 89 Drery was thy mone. **1340** HAMPOLE *Pr. Consc.* 1454 Now es he blithe, now es he drery. *c* **1386** CHAUCER *Clerk's T.* 458 Al drery was his cheere and his lookyng. *a* **1400–50** *Alexander* 2989 Sire Dary as a drery man duellis at hame. **1535** STEWART *Cron. Scot.* II. 277 Of his deid moir drerie wes ilk man. *c* **1565** LINDESAY (Pitscottie) *Chron. Scot.* (1728) 17 With sad, driry and quiet countenance. **1587** TURBERV. *Trag. T.* (1837) 53 The deaw that from thine eyes and dreerie cheekes do flow. **1613** PURCHAS *Pilgrimage* (1614) 822 Singing drerie lamentations. **1637** RUTHERFORD *Lett.* (1862) I. 224 Come and fetch the dreary passenger. **1742** SHENSTONE *Schoolmistress* 227 He, dreary caitiff! pines. **1844** MRS. BROWNING *Lay of Brown Rosary* IV. i, Only I am dreary; And, mother, of my dreariness, behold me very weary.
4. Dismal, gloomy; repulsively dull or uninteresting. (The ordinary current sense: app. a later weakening of 2.)
1667 MILTON *P.L.* I. 180 Seest thou yon dreary Plain.. The seat of desolation, voyd of light? **1718** PRIOR *Power* 401 In chains of craggy hill, or lengths of dreary coast. **1781** GIBBON *Decl. & F.* III. lxii. 560 At the dreary prospect of solitude and ruin. **1838** DICKENS *Lett.* (1880) I. 8 A house standing alone in the midst of a dreary moor. **1842** TENNYSON *Locksley Hall* 114 The light of London flaring like a dreary dawn. **1871** L. STEPHEN *Playgr. Eur.* ii. (1894) 48 It sounds a very faded and dreary commonplace. **1884** *Manch. Exam.* 14 May 5/3 The customs which made Sunday the dreariest day in the week are changing. *Mod.* A dreary speech by a dreary orator.
5. *Comb.*, as †***dreary-mood, dreary-souled***, adjs.
a **1000** *Cædmon's Gen.* 2798 Draf of wicum dreoriȝmod. *c* **1200** ORMIN 6541 Herode King Wass dreriȝmod and dreofedd. *c* **1380** *Sir Ferumb.* 1103 þan set he him doun drurymode & dropede for hure sake. **1818** MILMAN *Samor* 97 Dreary-soul'd Barbarians.

†**'dreary,** *v. Obs.* In 1 dreórȝian, 4 dreri. [f. prec. adj.] **a.** *intr.* To be dreary. (Only OE.) **b.** *trans.* To make dreary, sadden. (Only ME.)
c **1000** *Ruine* 30 (Bosw.) Ðas hofu dreorȝiaþ. *a* **1300** *E.E. Psalter* xxxvii. 7 Alle dai drerid I in-went.

dreary ('drɪərɪ), *sb. colloq.* [f. the adj.] A dreary person.
1925 N. COWARD *Hay Fever* I. 39 Damn, damn! It's those drearies. **1936** H. G. WELLS *Anat. Frustration* xiv. 165 The parade of donnish and scholastic drearies.

dreche: see DRETCH *v.*

dreck (drɛk). *slang.* Also drek. [a. Yiddish *drek* (G. *dreck*) filth, dregs, dung, f. MHG. *drec*:—Gmc. **þrekka-* repr. by OE. *þreax* rubbish, rottenness, ON. *þrekkr*, OFris. *threkk*. Ult. origin uncertain but connection with Gr. σκατός dung, στεργάνος privy, L. *stercus* excrement is generally accepted.] Rubbish, trash, worthless debris.
1922 JOYCE *Ulysses* 511 Farewell. Fare thee well. *Dreck!* **1947** *Horizon* Feb. 90 The anonymous countryside littered with heterogeneous *dreck*. **1965** E. LACY *Double Trouble* v. 58 *Drek* your dolls are!.. I wouldn't stick my customers with such junk! **1966** E. WEST *Night is Time for Listening* i. 13 'You *are* dreck,' she said. 'I hope you are killed.' **1967** O. HESKY *Time for Treason* v. 38 Meat better than the usual *drek* we get.

dred(e, etc., obs. form of DREAD, etc.

dreddour, dreder, var. DREADOUR.

dredge (drɛdʒ), *sb.*^{1} Forms: 5–6 dreg, 7 dridge, 8 drudge, 7– dredge. [Of this, and the associated verb, the Sc. form *dreg* is found *c* 1500, and in comb. in *dreg-boat* 1471; the Eng. form *dredge* appears (in the vb.) in 1576. (Cf. Sc. *seg* = *sedge*, etc.). The sb. corresponds to mod.Du. *dreg*, in 16th c. *dregghe*, *dregge* 'harpago; verriculum, euerriculum, Angl. dragge' Kilian, LG. *dregge* a dredge, F. *dreige*, *drège* (for oysters), 1584 in Hatz.-Darm. These continental words are perh. from English; and our word a derivative of the stem of DRAG *v.* The forms *dreg*, *dredge*, suggest an OE. type **dręcg* or **dręcge* from **dragjo-*, *-jôn*. The variants *dradge*, *drudge*, *dridge* appear to be perversions under the influence of other words.]
An instrument for collecting and bringing up objects from the bed of a river, the sea, etc., by dragging along the bottom; usually consisting of an iron frame with a net, bag, bucket, or other receptacle attached. **a.** *orig.* A drag-net for taking oysters, used also in pearl-fishing, etc. **b.** More recently, An apparatus for collecting marine objects for scientific investigation. **c.** A dredger for clearing the beds of rivers and navigable waters.
1471 implied in *dredge-boat*: see d. [**1561** EDEN *Arte of Navig.* Pref. ¶ iv b, Fyshermen that go a trawlyng for fyshe in Catches or mongers, and dradgies for Oysters about the sandes.] **1602** CAREW *Cornwall* 30 b, The oysters..haue a peculiar dredge, which is a thick strong net, fastned to three spils of iron, and drawne at the boates sterne. **1626** CAPT. SMITH *Accid. Yng. Seamen* 30 To the boate or skiffe belongs ..a dridge. **1709** *Lond. Gaz.* No. 4510/7 The Hoy Burthen 9 or 10 Tun..two Drudges in her with Ropes to them. **1796** MORSE *Amer. Geog.* I. 464 Mr. Culver..has constructed a Dock Drudge, which is a boat for clearing docks and removing bars in rivers. **1828** STARK *Elem. Nat. Hist.* II. 172 Sponges brought up by the dredge. **1861** GEIKIE *E. Forbes* xv. 537 Cruising..with the dredge—an instrument which he first methodized as an implement of zoological research.

fig. **1888** A. S. WILSON *Lyric of Hopeless Love* cxxvi. 360 Fancy casts her dredge in vain, To glean the secrets of the main.

d. *attrib.* and *Comb.*, as ***dredge-boat***, ***-man***, ***-net***, ***-rope***, ***-sump***, ***-wood***. Also **dredgeful**, as much as a dredge will hold.

1471 *Burgh Rec. Edin.* 16 Nov. (Rec. Soc.) (Jam Supp.), Of ilk *dreg-boat and hand-lyne bot cummand in with fisch. **1815** SCOTT *Guy M.* liv, I daresay the lugger's taken..a dredge-boat might have taken her. **1883** NORMAN *Presid. Addr. Tyneside Field Club* 27 A *dredgeful of 'Globigerina Ooze' from 2,435 fathoms. **1776** G. SEMPLE *Building in Water* 46 At low Water I set all the *Drudge and Water-men to that Corner. **1892** E. REEVES *Homewd. Bound* 160 Most of the signal-house keepers and dredge men along the canal seem French. **1875** W. MCILWRAITH *Guide Wigtownshire* 110 Persons skilled in *dredge-nets. **1773** *Hist. Brit. Dom. N. Amer.* II. xi. §12. 217 [Whale-fishing] To the further end of this stick is fastened a tow-rope, called the *drudge-rope, of about fifteen fathom. **1851** GREENWELL *Coal-trade Terms Northumb. & Durh.* 24 **Dredge Sump*, a reservoir through which a current of water is sometimes made to flow before passing to a pump, in order that any small stones or sludge may be retained.

dredge, *sb.*[2] Forms: 4–7 **drage**, 5 **drag(g)eye**, **dragie**, **-gy**, **dragge**, **dregge**, 5–6 **drege**, 5– **dradge**, 6– **dredge**, (7 **drag**). *β.* 5 **dragett**. [Late ME. *dragie*, *dragé*, also *dragett*, a. OF. *dragie*, *dragee*, mod.F. *dragée*, in Pr. and Sp. *dragea*, Sp., Pg. *gragea*, It. *treggéa* (masc.), med.L. *drageia*, *drageya*, *dragía*, *dragētum*, and *dragāta*: all supposed to derive in some way from L. *tragēmata*, a. Gr. τραγήματα spices, condiments. In Eng. the final vowel became at length mute; the form *dragett* directly represents med.L. *dragētum*.]

†**1.** A sweetmeat; a comfit containing a seed or grain of spice; a preparation made of a mixture of spices; cf. DRAGÉE. *Obs.*

c **1350** *Med. MS.* in *Archæol.* XXX. 390 Y[e] sed is good fastende to ete, And ek in drage after mete. [**1377–86** see DRUG *sb.*[1]] **1401–2** *Mem. Ripon* (Surtees) III. 208 Et in j lib. dragge empt., 5*d.* [**1402–3** dragy]. **14..** *Noble Bk. Cookry* (Napier) 27 Cast on a dridge mad with hard yolks of eggs. *c* **1440** *Anc. Cookery* in *Househ. Ord.* (1790) 454 Make thenne a dragee of the yolkes of harde eyren broken. *c* **1440** *Promp. Parv.* 130/1 Dragge (*v.rr.* dragy, dradge), *dragetum*. **1481–90** *Howard Househ. Bks.* (Roxb.) 367 Item..payed for a box of drege xx. *d.* **1530** PALSGR. 215/1 Dradge, spyce, *dragee*. **1544** PHAER *Regim. Lyfe* (1560) I vj b, By eatyng of a litle dredge, made of anyse seede and coriander. **1601** HOLLAND *Pliny* II. 108 A drage or pouder of it [thyme] with salt, brings the appetite againe. **1616** SURFL. & MARKH. *Country F.* 48 Take fasting a Dredge made of Annise, Fennell, Caraway, and Coriander seed.

β. **1470–71** *Mem. Ripon* (Surtees) III., Dragett.

2. A mixture of various kinds of grain, esp. of oats and barley, sown together. Now *dial.*

[In Fr. *dragée* is a mixture of pease, vetches, beans, lentils, sown as a forage crop.]

[**1309** in *Registr. Monast. de Winchelcumba* (1892) 304 Quatuor quarteria frumenti, et quatuor quarteria boni drageti.] **14..** *Voc.* in Wr.-Wülcker 596 *Mixtilio*, Draggeye. **14..** *Metrical Voc.* Ibid. 625 *Dragetum*, draggé, *mixtilioque*, medylde corne. *c* **1440** *Promp. Parv.* 130/1 Dragge, menglyd corne (drage, or mestlyon, P.). **1533** in Weaver *Wells Wills* (1890) 55, ij quarters of barley and ij of drege. **1573** TUSSER *Husb.* xvi. (1878) 39 Sowe barlie and dredge, with a plentifull hand. **1601** HOLLAND *Pliny* I. 534 As touching the drage called Ocymum..it is a kind of forage or prouender for horses. **1611** BIBLE *Job* xxiv. 6 *margin*, Mingled corn or dredge. **1669** WORLIDGE *Syst. Agric.* (1681) 324 *Dredge*, Oats and Barley mixed. **1888** ELWORTHY *W. Somerset Word-bk.*, *Dredge*, mixed corn of several kinds, as oats, wheat, and barley sown together; done very commonly for game feed.

fig. **1603** HOLLAND *Plutarch's Mor.* 108 (R.) Choler is a miscellane seed (as it were).. and a dredge, made of all the passions of the mind.

3. *Mining.* Ore of a mixed quality intermediate between the rich and the worthless.

1875 *Ure's Dict. Arts* II. 80 Detaching from each piece the inferior portions, and thus forming either prill or best dradge ore. **1875** J. H. COLLINS *Metal Mining* 111 A quantity of material of a mixed nature, called 'dredge', or 'roughs', or 'rows', is often separated, on the one hand from the rich ore, on the other from the worthless waste.

4. *Comb.*, as **dredge-box**, †(*a*) a box for holding dredges or comfits, etc., a drageoir; (*b*) = *dredging-box*: see DREDGE *v.*[2]; **dredge corn** (see quot.); **dredge-malt**, malt made of oats and barley; †**dredge-powder**, a powder of mixed spices, sugar, etc.

1525 LD. BERNERS *Froiss.* II. clvii. [cliii]. 434 Two *dredge boxes of golde. **1812** CHALMERS *Let.* in *Life* (1851) I. 293 Eloquent upon her favourite subject of napery inventories and dredge-boxes. **1917** *Stat. Rules & Orders 1182* 2 in *Parl. Papers* XXVI. 402 For the purposes of this Order, '*Dredge Corn' shall mean a mixture of cereals, whether or not grown together, containing more than one cereal as a main constituent. **1496–7** in Rogers *Agric. & Prices* III. 78/3 *Dregg malt. **1686** PLOT *Staffordsh.* 379 Mault of Oats, which mixt with that of barley, is call'd Dredg-mault. **1579** LANGHAM *Gard. Health* (1633) 363 A *dredge powder: take fine powder of Licoras and Anniseeds, of each one pound, suger candy to pound, pepper and ginger, of each two ounces: mixe them and vse it for most inward griefes.

dredge, *v.*[1] Also 6–7 **dreg**, **dregge**, 7–8 **drudge**, 8 **druge**. [Goes with DREDGE *sb.*[1]]

1. *trans.* To collect and bring up (oysters, etc.) by means of a dredge; to bring *up*, fish *up*, or clear *away* or *out* (any object) from the bottom of a river, etc. Also *fig.*

1508 KENNEDIE *Flyting w. Dunbar* 379 Thou sailit to get a dowcare, for to dreg it, It lyis closit in a clout on Seland cost. **1570–6** LAMBARDE *Peramb. Kent* (1826) 234 South Yenlet, notorious also for great Oisters, that be dredged thereaboutes. **1659** E. LEIGH *Eng. Descr.* 105 The salt savoury Oisters there dregged. *a* **1705** RAY *Sel. Rem.* 272 (L.) They dredge up from the bottom of the sea..white coral. **1776** G. SEMPLE *Building in Water* 34 We drudged all we could come at away. **1851** TAYLOR *Improvem. Tyne* 77 Dredging out silt. **1863** KINGSLEY *Water Bab.* vii. 265 You and I perhaps shall..dredge strange creatures such as man never saw before. **1878** HUXLEY *Physiogr.* xvii. 286 A stone celt which was dredged up from the Thames.

2. *intr.* To make use of a dredge; to fish *for* (oysters, etc.), or to remove silt, etc. from the bottom of a river, etc., by means of a dredge.

1681 COLVIL *Whigs Supplic.* (1751) 44 Some getting oyster-boats to dreg, Some making satires for to beg. **1711** *Act 9 Anne* c. 26 Such persons as shall use to fish or druge within the limits of the said Fishery as common Fishermen or Drugermen. **1764** PLATT in *Phil. Trans.* LIV. 52 To use drag-nets as they do in drudging for oisters. **1863** LYELL *Antiq. Man* 18 Mud..obtained by dredging in the adjoining shallow water.

3. *trans.* To clean out the bed or bottom of (a river, channel, harbour, etc.) by removing silt with a dredging apparatus.

1844 *Hull Dock Act* 98 Repairing, altering, dredging, or improving the said docks. **1875** J. H. BENNET *Winter Medit.* I. viii. (ed. 2) 242 The government has dredged the magnificent old port, which had been allowed to fill up.

Hence **dredged** *ppl. a.*

1867 A. BARRY *Sir C. Barry* vi. 158 The dredged bed of the river. **1894** *Daily News* 26 Nov. 5/3 Built in a dredged-out berth or dock.

dredge, *v.*[2] Also 7 **dreg**, 7–9 **drudge**. [app. f. DREDGE *sb.*[2]]

1. *trans.* To sprinkle (anything) with powder, *esp.* flour; *orig.* to sprinkle with some powdered mixture of sugar, spices, etc. Also *fig.*

1596 NASHE *Saffron Walden* 48 A continuat Tropologicall speach..all to bee-spiced and dredged with sentences and allegories. **1611** BEAUM. & FL. *Scornful Lady* II. iii, Burnt figs, dreg'd with meal and powdered sugar. *a* **1616** —— *Bloody Brother* II. i. *ad fin.*, My spice-box, gentlemen.. Dredge you a dish of plovers, there's the art on't. **1750** E. SMITH *Compl. Housew.* 19 Drudge it with a little flour. **1851** D. JERROLD *St. Giles* iv. 26 His..hair was dredged with grey.

2. To sprinkle (any powdered substance) *over* anything. Also *transf.*

1648 HERRICK *Hesper.*, *Pray & Prosper*, The spangling dew dreg'd o're the grasse. **1741** *Compl. Fam. Piece* I. ii. 98 Dredge grated Bread over it. **1853** SOYER *Pantroph.* 288 Serve, having..dredged over them a little poppy-seed.

Hence '**dredging** *vbl. sb.*; *attrib.* as ***dredging-box***.

1611 COTGR., *Rosti sanglant*, a dredging with the powder of Hares bloud. **1709** W. KING *Art of Cookery* Let. v, Basting-ladles, dripping-pans, and drudging-boxes. **1751** SMOLLETT *Per. Pic.* (1779) IV. lxxxviii. 47 This all the flour in his drudging-box had not been able to whiten. **1851** *Beck's Florist* Sept. 203 Sulphur is a well-known remedy, dusted on the leaves, while wet, from a dredging-box.

dredge, **-s**, obs. form of DREG, -S, *sb.*

dredger[1] ('drɛdʒə(r)). Also 6 *Sc.* **dregar**, **dregger**, 8 **drudger**. [f. DREDGE *v.*[1] + -ER[1].]

1. One who uses a dredge; *esp.*, in early use, one who dredges oysters.

1508 DUNBAR *Flyting w. Kennedie* 242 Rank beggar, ostir dregar, foule fleggar, in the flet. **1572** *Lament. of Lady Scot.* in *Scot. Poems 16th C.* II. 250 It is mair schame in burgh to se beggers Nor is it skaith in Crawmont to want dreggers. **1667** in Sprat *Hist. R. Soc.* 307 (Jod.) The oysters cast their spawn which the dredgers call their spats. **1723** *Lond. Gaz.* No. 6196/8 Edmund North, late of Wakerin in Essex, Oyster-Drudger. **1882** *Standard* 18 Feb. 5/2 The Whitstable dredgers feed, but do not breed oysters. **1887** *Daily News* 17 Feb. 7/2 The dragging up of the body by a dredger..[with] his dredging apparatus.

2. A boat employed in dredging for oysters.

1600 HAKLUYT *Voy.* III. 586 (R.) We..then had sight of a brigandine or a dredger, which the general tooke within one houres chase with his two barges. **1888** *Public Opinion* (N.Y.) 15 Dec., The Maryland steamer..has a two hours' fight with a fleet of oyster pirates..and runs down two of the dredgers.

3. A dredging machine: see quot. 1892.

1863 P. BARRY *Dockyard Econ.* 29 A strangely shaped anchor brought up by the dredger the other day. **1871** *Daily News* 30 June, Any tendency thereto [silting up] may be averted by the steady use of dredgers. **1892** *Labour Commission* Gloss., *Dredger*, vessels fitted with iron buckets and machinery for deepening rivers or bars and keeping harbours or docks from filling up.

'**dredger**[2]. Also **drudger**. [f. DREDGE *v.*[2] + -ER[1].] A box with a perforated lid for sprinkling powder over anything, as a ***flour-dredger***.

(In quot. 1666, some think = F. *drageoir*, OF. also *drageur*, 'a comfet box of silver', Cotgr.)

1666 PEPYS *Diary* 2 Feb., To London..and did carry home a silver drudger for my cupboard of plate. **1721** BAILEY, *Dredger*, a Flower Box. **1775** ASH, *Dredger*, *Drudger* ..the box out of which flower is thrown on roast meat. **1819** H. BUSK *Banquet* II. 189 The drudger, salt-box, cullender and skewer.

'**dredger-man.** = DREDGER[1] 1.

1696 *Lond. Gaz.* No. 3182/3 Masters of Vessels, Fishermen, Dredgermen, and other Seafaring Men. **1711** [see DREDGE *v.*[1] 2]. **1851–61** MAYHEW *Lond. Labour* II. 165 (Hoppe) The dredgermen, of the Thames, or river finders. **1887** *Daily News* 27 July 6/3 It [a Fraternity at Faversham] consisted of free fishermen and dredgermen, who had the exclusive right to dredge and sell oysters within the hundred.

'**dredging**, *vbl. sb.* [f. DREDGE *v.*[1] + -ING[1].]

a. The action of the verb DREDGE[1].

1622 R. HAWKINS *Voy. S. Sea* 227 In anno 1583..I was at the dregging of pearle oysters after the manner we dregge oysters in England. **1764** PLATT in *Phil. Trans.* LIV. 52 To use dragnets as they do in drudging for oisters. **1876** PAGE *Adv. Text-Bk. Geol.* xx. 414 So far as dredgings and soundings enable us to decide.

b. *concr.* That which is dredged up.

1881 CARPENTER *Microsc.* xii. §474 It is curious that these two forms should present themselves in the same dredging. **1891** *Law Reports* Weekly Notes 120/1 Depositing thereon dredgings from the river.

c. *attrib.* and *Comb.*, as ***dredging-bag***, ***-bucket***, ***-engine***, ***-gear***, ***-iron***, ***-machine***, etc.

1776 G. SEMPLE *Building in Water* 33 The Stones..tore and totally destroyed our Drudging-bags. *Ibid.* 29 Drudging-engines. **1830** *Mech. Mag.* XIII. 64 The dredging-machines..were invented and patented by a Mr. Israel Pownall in 1712. **1840** *Evid. Hull Docks Com.* 37 Excavation..done by the dredging-machine. **1851** *Offic. Catal. Gt. Exhib.* II. 600 Improved grappling or dredging-iron, for drawing from the water the bodies of persons.. drowned. **1872** *Porcupine* 29 June 198/3 Set the dredging-buckets to work, and scooped it all away.

dredging, **-box:** see DREDGE *v.*[2]

dredgy, **-ie**, Sc. forms of DIRGE, chiefly in sense 3, funeral feast.

dredour, var. DREADOUR.

dree (driː), *v.* Now *Sc.* and *north. dial.* or *arch.* Forms: 1 **dréoᵹan**, 2 **dreoȝen**, 2–5 **dreȝe(n**, 3 **drehe(n**, **dreȝhenn** (*Orm.*), 3–4 **driȝe(n**, 3–6 **drei(e**, 3–9 **drie**, 4 **drey(e**, **dryȝ(e**, 4–5 **dregh(e**, 4–6 **drighe**, **dry(e**, **dre** (5 **dryee**), 4– **dree**. *Pa. t.* 1 **dreáᵹ**, **dreáh**, *pl.* **druᵹon**, 2–3 **dreȝ**, *pl* **druhen**, **drehen**, 3 **dreih**, 4 **dreiȝh**, **dreȝh**, **dreyȝ**, **drey**, (**drogh**, **drow**, **drie**). *β.* 3 **drehde**, 4 **dried**, 5 **dreghit**, (6 *Sc.* **dreit**), 5– **dreed**. *Pa. pple.* 1–3 **droȝen**, 2 **idreȝen**, 4 **drowen**, (**droun**). *β.* 5– **dreed**. [OE. *dréoᵹan* (3rd sing. *dríehþ*, *drýhð*); a strong vb. of 2nd ablaut series, (OTeut. type **dreug-*, *draug-*, *drug-*), elsewhere represented only by Gothic *driugan* to do military service (*gadrauhts* a soldier), and the ON. derivative vb. *drýgja* to perform, perpetrate, lengthen, f. *drjúg-* enduring, lasting, etc. In the 13th c., a weak pa. t. is found, and the strong inflexions do not occur after 1400. The verb has lived on in Sc. and north Eng. dialects, and has been revived as a literary archaism by Sir Walter Scott and his imitators.

In ME. there was some tendency to confuse *dree* and *draw*, arising prob. from form-association of *drōȝ*, *drōgh*, *drōw*, pa. t. of *draw*, with *druȝen*, pl. of pa. t., and *droȝen*, *drowen* pa. pple., of *dree*. Hence *drogh*, *drow* occur for *dreȝ*, *dreigh*; see also DRAW *v.*

c **1340** *Cursor M.* 9398 (Trin.) Þerynne he dreyȝe aftir bale (*Laud MS.* drie, *Gött.* drow, *Cott.* drogh.)]

†**1.** *trans.* To do, perform (service, duty, any one's will); to commit (sin). *Obs.*

c **1000** *Ags. Ps.* (Th.) liv. 8 Druᵹon þæt on burᵹum, dæᵹes and nihtes. *c* **1000** *Guthlac* 386 Se þe in þrowingum þeodnes willan dæᵹhwam dreoᵹeð. *c* **1175** *Lamb. Hom.* 23 Þa sunfulle monne þe dreȝeð a heore uuele werkes. *c* **1200** *Trin. Coll. Hom.* 37 Þe wapmen and wimmen þe hordom drien. *Ibid.* 191 Neddre doð þre þing lichamliche..þe þe deuel driȝeð gostliche.

2. To endure, undergo, suffer, bear (something burdensome, grievous, or painful).

a **1000** *Cædmon's Exod.* 2978 Seo menᵹeo fæsten dreah fela missera. *a* **1200** *Moral Ode* 288 Al þat man mai here dreoȝen [*v.r.* drie]. *a* **1225** *Ancr. R.* 136 Uor þe luue of him þet dreih more uor þe. *Ibid.* 356 Wouh of scheome þet mon drihð. *c* **1230** *Hali Meid.* 37 Hare weanen þat ure alre modres drehden on us seluen. *a* **1300** *Cursor M.* 23225 (Cott.) Þe thrid pine es hard to drei [*v. rr.* drie, dreȝe, dreye]. *c* **1320** *Seuyn Sag.* (W.) 2660 He telde hire the sorewe that he dregh. *c* **1400** *Rom. Rose* 3115 For peynes gret, disese and thought, Fro day to day he doth me drye. *c* **1400** *Melayne* 1055 Pity the dole we dree for thee. **1513** DOUGLAS *Æneis* IV. x. *heading*, Quhat sorow dreis queyne Dido all the nycht. *a* **1774** FERGUSSON *Election* Poems (1845) 40 His buik has dree'd a sair, sair fa'. **1848** MRS. GASKELL *M. Barton* xxv, To dree all the cruel slander they'll put upon him. **1855** BROWNING *Old Pictures in Florence* xxv, While their pictures dree Such doom.

†**b.** with *inf.* or *subord. cl.* *Obs.*

a **1300** *Cursor M.* 1300 (Gött.) Langer to liue may he noght drei. *c* **1330** *King of Tars* 235, I nul no lengor drye That Cristene men schul for me dye. **1460** *Lybeaus Disc.* 950 (R.) Never they ne seygh Man that myghte dreygh To justy wyth Gyffroun.

c. ***to dree one's weird***: to endure one's fate, suffer or submit to one's destiny. *arch.*

13.. *E.E. Allit. P.* B. 1224 In dongoun be don to dreȝe þer his wyrdes. ?*c* **1485** *Prophecy of Waldhaue* in *Whole Prophecie of Scotland* (1603) C j b, Heere in wildernes I dwell, my weird for to dree. **1816** SCOTT *Antiq.* xxxii, 'Ohon! we're dreeing a sair weird; we hae had a heavy dispensation.' **1886** MRS. LYNN LINTON *Paston Carew* xxxv, French must dree his weird as a brave man should.

†**d.** *intr.* To suffer. *Obs.*

a 1605 MONTGOMERIE *Misc. Poems* xvi. 5 Of duill and dolour so I dry.

3. *trans.* To do, perform, suffer (penance, shrift). *arch.*

c 1175 *Lamb. Hom.* 51 Er he hefde idreȝen þet scrift. *a* 1300 *Cursor M.* 496 (Cott.) þai drei ful harde schrift. *c* 1330 R. BRUNNE *Chron. Wace* (Rolls) 16613 He schulde go to Rome.. penaunce to drye. *c* 1420 *Anturs of Arth.* xi, God hase grauntut me grace, To dre my penawunse in this place. 1596 DALRYMPLE tr. *Leslie's Hist. Scot.* IX. 210 The slaers.. sulde be banist to ffrance and drie thair pennance thair. 1810 SCOTT *Lett.* 30 Mar. (1894) I. 174, I was dreeing penance for some undiscovered sin at a family party. 1866 NEWMAN *Gerontius* v. 39 He dreed his penance age by age.

4. *intr.* To endure, last, hold out, continue. Now *Sc.* and *north. dial.*

a 1225 *Juliana* 26 Six men beateð hire hwil ha mahten drehen. *c* 1350 *Will. Palerne* 1772 Fled as fast homward as fet miȝt drie. 1375 BARBOUR *Bruce* XVIII. 53 Sall na man say, quhill I may dre, That strynth of men sall ger me fle. *c* 1460 *Towneley Myst.* (Surtees) 156 [Symeon] Welle is me that I shalle dre Tylle I have sene hym with myn ee. 1570 LEVINS *Manip.* 46/26 To Dree, last, *durare*. 1868 ATKINSON *Cleveland Gloss., Dree*, to endure, to last. 1871 WADDELL *Ps.* lxxxviii. 15, I.. kenna nae langer how till dree.

5. *trans.* To last through (time); to pass, spend, live (one's life, days); esp. with the notion of endurance. Also with *forth, out*. *Obs.* or *arch.*

c 1250 *Gen. & Ex.* 2404 An hundred ȝer.. Haue ic her droȝen in werlde wo. 1340–70 *Alisaunder* 242 With doole dried hee so his dayes. *c* 1380 *Sir Ferumb.* 5842 God lyf schalt þou drye. 1585 JAS. I *Ess. Poesie* (Arb.) 44 To drie Her voyage out. *a* 1605 MONTGOMERIE *Misc. Poems* vii. 1 Drie furth the inch as thou hes done the span. 1805 SCOTT *Last Minstr.* II. v, Would'st thou thy every future year In ceaseless prayer and penance drie.

6. To 'spin out', protract. *dial.*

1855 ROBINSON *Whitby Gloss.*, 'He dreed a lang drone', delivered a tiresome dissertation.

Hence **'dreeing** *vbl. sb.*

c 1350 *Will. Palerne* 919 For dreȝing of þis duel.

dree, *sb. Sc.* [f. DREE *v.*] The action of the verb DREE; suffering, grief, trouble. (Mostly a modern archaism.)

[*c* 1430 LYDG. *Min. Poems* (Percy Soc.) 45 The first yere wedlokk is called pleye, The second dreye, and the thrid yere deye.] 1871 WADDELL *Ps.* xxvii. 5, I' the day o' dule an' dree. 1890 R. BRIDGES *Shorter Poems* IV. 4 The half-moon.. Shrinketh her face of dree.

dree, dreigh (driː, driːx), *a.* Now *Sc.* and *north. dial.* or *arch.* Forms: 3 dreiȝ, drih, 3–5 dreȝ, 4 drye, dryȝ, 4–5 drey, 5 dregh, drie, 5– dreich, 6– dreigh, 7– dree, (8 dreech, dreegh, 8–9 driegh, 9 driche, driech). [ME. *dreȝ, dregh*:—OE. type **dréoȝ*, corresp. to ON. *drjúgr* enduring, lasting, substantial, ample, rich (Sw. *dryg* heavy, long, large, rich, etc., Da. *drøi* lasting, durable, great); from stem of DREE *v.*]

†1. Enduring, patient, long-suffering. *Obs.*

c 1200 *Trin. Coll. Hom.* 49 Lomb is drih þing and milde. *c* 1250 *Hymn Virg.* 34 *Ibid.* App. 256 Maide dreiȝ & wel itaucht.

†2. Heavy, mighty, great; doughty, fierce. *Obs.*

13.. *E.E. Allit. P.* B. 342 In dryȝ dred and daunger. *c* 1400 *Rowland & O.* 696 His dynttys were full dreghe. *c* 1400 *Destr. Troy* 5322 Dreghist in armys, And the strongest in stoure. *Ibid.* 11890 þe key.. the durres to vndo of the dregh horse. *a* 1400–50 *Alexander* 5568 þe dreȝest deele of þaim died of his dukis handis.

3. a. Long; slow, tedious, wearisome; persistent; difficult to surmount or get over, 'stiff', severe. b. Dreary, cheerless, doleful.

c 1400 *Destr. Troy* 1622 The draghtes, the dyse, and oþer dregh gaumes. *Ibid.* 3320 Elan.. driet the dropis of hir dregh teris. *a* 1400–50 *Alexander* 4441 ȝoure surfete of drinkis.. gers ȝow die or ȝoure day many dreȝe wyntir. *c* 1430 *Hymns Virg.* (1867) 22 þerof us þenkiþ þe wey to drie. ? 14.. *MS. Harl.* 2252, fo. 118 (Halliwell) A ryver brode and dreghe. 1597 MONTGOMERIE *Cherrie & Slae* 357 The craige was vgly, stay and dreich. 1674 RAY *N.C. Words* 15 *Dree*: Long, seeming tedious beyond expectation, spoken of a way. A hard bargainer, spoken of a person. *a* 1774 FERGUSSON *Leith Races* Poems (1845) 35 There's lang and dreech contestin. 1794 BURNS '*There was a lass*' i, The moor was driegh, and Meg was skiegh. 1807 J. STAGG *Poems* 19 Six dree years had Susan languish'd. 1818 SCOTT *Hrt. Midl.* xxix, 'Our minny here's rather driech in the upgang.' 1857 E. WAUGH *Lanc. Life* 207 The rains are heavy and dree upon Ashworth moors. 1886 STEVENSON *Kidnapped* xxiii, 'My life is a bit driegh.. I see little company'.

†4. At a tedious distance, far off. *Obs. rare.*

c 1330 R. BRUNNE *Chron. Wace* (Rolls) 12205 þe lasse hil was nought so drey ffro þe more, but euene ney.

dree, dreigh, *adv. Obs.* or *dial.* [ME. *dreȝe*:—OE. type **dréoȝe*.]

†1. Heavily, severely, mightily, vehemently. *Obs.*

c 1320 *Sir Tristr.* 3035 þou louest tristrem dreiȝe. *c* 1340 *Gaw. & Gr. Knt.* 2663 Hade hit [weapon] dryuen adoun, as dreȝ as he atled, þer hade ben ded of his dynt. *c* 1420 *Anturs of Arth.* (Irel.) xl, Querto draues thou so dreȝghe?

2. Persistently, 'doggedly'. *dial.*

1844 S. BAMFORD *Life of Radical* 110 The rain having set in dree. 1865 E. WAUGH *Lanc. Songs* 7 Th' rain's comin' deawn very dree.

dreed, obs. form of DREAD.

'dree-draw. An implement used in illegal fishing, being a 'stroke-haul', q.v., fastened to a line reaching across a river, and held by a man at each end.

1850 *Act 13 & 14 Victoria* c. 88 §40 It shall not be lawful.. at any Season of the Year, to use for the Purpose of taking Fish any Otter, Lyster, Spear, Strokehaul, Dree Draw, or Gaff. 1866 *Cork Constitution* (newspr.) 12 Sept., For that.. each of you did illegally use a dree-draw or goff for the purpose of taking fish in.. the Bandon River.

dreel, Sc. form of DRILL.

dreelite ('dreɪ-, 'driːlaɪt). *Min. Obs.* exc. *Hist.* Also **dréelite, dreeite.** [ad. F. *dréelite*, named by P. A. Dufrénoy (1835, in *Ann. chim. phys.* LX. 102) after E. de *Drée*: see -LITE and -ITE[1] 2 b.] The former name of a supposed sulphate of barium and calcium (see quots. 1888, 1950).

1836 *Amer. Jrnl. Sci.* XXX. 380 Dreelite, a new Mineral Species. 1888 *Jrnl. Chem. Soc.* LIV. 33 The mineral termed dreelite by Dufrénoy is shown by the angles of the cleavage planes and by the optical characters to be identical with barytes... Probably.. the percentage of calcium sulphate given by Dufrénoy was due to impurities. 1896 A. H. CHESTER *Dict. Min.*, Dreeite, Dreelite. 1950 M. H. HEY *Index Min. Species* 370 *Dréelite*,.. a mixture of baryte, gypsum, etc.

'dreely, dreighly, *adv.* Now *Sc.* and *north. dial.* [f. DREE *a.* + -LY[2].]

†1. Heavily, mightily, vehemently, stiffly. *Obs.*

13.. *E.E. Allit. P.* C. 235 Drof hem dryȝlych adoun þe depe. 13.. *Gaw. & Gr. Knt.* 1026 þay.. þe wyn dronken, Daunsed ful dreȝly wyth dere carolez. *c* 1460 *Towneley Myst.* (Surtees) 90 And thou drynk drely, in thy polle wylle it synk. *c* 1475 *Rauf Coilȝear* 217 They drank dreichlie about.

2. Slowly, persistently. *dial.*

1828 *Craven Dialect, Dreely*, slowly, though continuous. 'It rains dreely'. 1868 HOLME LEE *B. Godfrey* xlvi. 251 Father called thee dreely.

dreen, obs. and dial. form of DRAIN.

dreep, drepe (driːp), *v. Obs.* exc. *dial.* Also dreap, dreip. [In Sc. use, a dial. form of DRIP *v.*; but the 15–16th c. English examples appear to represent the OE. strong vb. *dréopan* = OS. *driopan*, OHG. *triofan*, ON. *drjúpa*:—OTeut. **dreup-, draup-, drup-* to drop. See DRIP, DROP.]

1. *intr.* To fall in drops, to drip.

a 1000 *Ags. Ps.* (Th.) lxxi[i]. 6 Dropa þe on þas eorðan up on dreopað. *c* 1430 LYDG. *Bochas* 67b, Of Diana the transmutacion, Now bright, now pale, now clere, now dreping. *c* 1450 *St. Cuthbert* (Surtees) 3198 þe terys oure hir face drepyd. 1571 GOLDING *Calvin on Ps.* xxix. 4 The Rayne dreepeth doune softly. 1594 LODGE *Wounds Civ. War* v. in Hazl. *Dodsley* VII. 183 The dreeping dimness of the night. 1681 COLVIL *Whigs Supplic.* (1751) 55 Some with spilled drink are dreeping, And some sit on a privy sleeping. 1825 BROCKETT *N.C. Gloss.* s.v., 'Dreaping o' wet'. *a* 1835 HOGG *Ringan & May* 50 Well do I like at the gloaming still, To dreep from the lift or the lowering hill.

2. To droop; *fig.* to lose courage, grow faint. (See also quot. 1825.)

c 1400 *Destr. Troy* 10795 þai drepit in dole, as þai degh shuld. *c* 1430 LYDG. *Min. Poems* 161 (Mätz.) Alcestis flower.. In stormys dreepithe. *c* 1450 *Cov. Myst.* (Shaks. Soc.) 170 In goode tyme ȝe dede downe drepe To take ȝowr rest. 1807 R. TANNAHILL *Soldier's Return* 47 Sers! how your tail, an' wings are dreeping! 1825 JAMIESON Suppl., *Dreip*,.. to walk very slowly; as, 'There she comes *dreepin*'.'.. To do any piece of business slowly, and without any apparent interest. 1894 R. REID *Poems, Songs, & Sonnets* 240 Never herriet mavis dreept sae lane and chill. 1941 L. A. G. STRONG *Bay* viii. 179 A shuffling, dreeping old crone.

dreep (driːp), *sb. dial.* [f. DREEP *v.*]

1. A wet, dripping condition; (see also quot. 1887).

1844 W. JAMIE *Muse of Mearns* 103 They danced till in a dreep wi' sweat. 1887 JAMIESON Suppl., *Dreep*, sb., drip, dripping, as from a roast, from the eaves, &c.: also, the eaves; and where drops from the eaves fall on the ground, as, 'Ye mun bide within your ain *dreep*.'

2. An ineffective, spiritless, or lugubrious person; a 'drip'.

1927 *Spectator* 5 Nov. 171 What can you expect of 'Sammy dreeps', 'dozened idiots' or 'glaikit stirks'? 1940 in *Sc. Nat. Dict.* (1952) III. s.v., That wumman's jist a dreep. I canna thole her. 1942 'P. WENTWORTH' *Danger Point* xxii. 130 'Will you give me your impression of the girl.'.. 'Oh, a long, thin dreep. No guts. The sort that whines.' 1970 'D. SHANNON' *Unexpected Death* (1971) vii. 99 She was, he thought, a dreep.

dreepy ('driːpɪ), *a. dial.* [f. DREEP *v.* or *sb.* + -Y[1].] Drooping, droopy, spiritless.

1892 R. O. HESLOP *Northumberland Words* 253 She's but a poor dreepy creetur. 1927 *Observer* 6 Nov. 15/2 A weak, dreepy-drippy sort of face, obviously belonging to a man with about as much personal force as there is in a penn'orth of suet.

dreeri, -y, obs. forms of DREARY.

†**dref**, *a. Obs. rare.* [early ME.:—OE. **dréfe* (:—*drôbjo-*), secondary form of *dróf* (:—*drôbu-*): see DROF, and cf. OHG. *truobi*, Ger. *trübe*.] Troublesome, vexatious, grievous.

c 1250 *Gen. & Ex.* 4144 Ydolatrie, ðat was hem lef, ofte vt-wroȝte hem sorȝes dref.

dref(f, obs. pa. t. and pple. of DRIVE *v.*

drefle, dreifle, obs. forms of DRIVEL.

dreful, -ly, obs. form of DREADFUL, -LY.

dreg, *sb.* Chiefly in pl. **dregs** (drɛgz). Forms: 3–4 drege, 4– dreg, (6 dredge, 7 dregge); *Pl.* 4–7 dregges, (5 -is, -ys, dregys, 6 dragges), 6–7 dreggs, 6– dregs (6–7 drags, dredges). [Probably from Norse: cf. Icel. *dreggjar* pl., Sw. *drägg* pl. dregs, lees.]

1. (Usually *pl.*) The sediment of liquors; the more solid particles which settle at the bottom of a solution or other liquid; grounds, lees, feculent matters. Also *fig.*

a 1300 *E.E. Psalter* lxxiv. 9 [lxxv. 8] Drege in him [*v.r.* his dreg; Vulg. *fæx eius*] noght is littled; drinke sal al þa sinfulle. 1377 LANGL. *P. Pl.* B. xix. 397 Whil I can selle Bothe dregges and draffe and drawe it at on hole, þikke ale and þinne ale. *c* 1440 *Promp. Parv.* 131/2 Dreggys of oyle, *amurca*. 1579 GOSSON *Sch. Abuse* (Arb.) 37 The drinke that they drawe [is] ouer-charged with dregges. 1631 GOUGE *God's Arrows* I. xliii. 70 Much corruption lieth as dreggs at the bottome. 1752 BERKELEY *Farther Th. on Tar-water* Wks. III. 493 The dregs of tar are often foul. 1809 SYD. SMITH *Two Vol. Serm.* II. 43 The bitterest dreg in the cup of God's wrath. 1825 J. NICHOLSON *Operat. Mechanic* 453 The other goes into a deep and narrow cistern, where the dreg again subsides. 1870 DICKENS *E. Drood* viii, He flings the dregs of his wine at Edwin.

b. phr. ***to drink, drain***, etc. ***to the dregs***, i.e. to the thick and turbid sediment: often *fig.*

1709 POPE *Ess. Crit.* 545 The following licence of a Foreign reign Did all the dregs of bold Socinus drain. 1762 GOLDSM. *Cit. W.* xcvii, This manner.. of drawing off a subject, or a peculiar mode of writing to the dregs. 1795 SOUTHEY *Vis. Maid Orleans* I. 260 Destined to drain the cup of bitterness, Even to its dregs. 1813 SCOTT *Trierm.* Concl. i, To require of bard That to his dregs the tale should run. 1874 J. STOUGHTON *Ch. of Rev.* xiii. 318 This strange mortal, who had drunk the dregs of Antinomianism.

†2. *transf.* Fæces, excrement, refuse, rubbish; corrupt or defiling matters. *Obs.*

a 1300 *E.E. Psalter* xxxix. 3 [xl. 2] Fra þe slogh of wrecchednes, And fra fen of dreg [Vulg. *fecis*] þat es. 1607 TOPSELL *Four-f. Beasts* (1658) 332 Because the guts be stopt with winde and dregges. 1668 CULPEPPER & COLE *Barthol. Anat.* I. xi. 26 The Dreggs or Excrements.. did lie lurking.

3. *fig.* The most worthless part or parts; the base or useless residue; the refuse or offscourings.

1531 ELYOT *Gov.* I. xiv, They.. neuer tasted other but the fecis or draggès of the sayd noble doctrines. 1546 *Supplic. Poore Com.* (E.E.T.S.) 65 Symple creatures.. taken for the dregges of the worlde. 1581 J. BELL *Haddon's Answ. Osor.* 358 Traditions of men: Mounckish vowes.. pilgrimages, and innumerable such dredge. 1675 TRAHERNE *Chr. Ethics* ix. 121 Matter is the dreg of nature, and dead without power. 1689 HICKERINGILL *Wks.* (1716) II. 495 For us who live in the Dregs of Romulus [cf. L. *in Romuli fæce*]. 1719 YOUNG *Revenge* II. i, Some dregs of ancient night not quite purg'd off. 1761 HUME *Hist. Eng.* III. lxi. 320 Low mechanics.. the very dregs of the fanatics. 1876 C. M. DAVIES *Unorth. Lond.* 66 The very dregs of the population.

4. Last remains, small remnant, residue.

1577 HOLINSHED *Hist. Scot.* 490/1 Sore hurt.. in the arme with the dredge of a caliuer shot. 1594 SHAKS. *Rich. III*, I. iv. 124 Some certaine dregges of conscience are yet within mee. 1619 MRQ. BUCKHM. in *Fortesc. Papers* 84, I will wash away that offence.. and if there shall yet remayne any dregg of it. 1685 BURNET *Life Bedell* Pref. (L.), This iron age and dreg of time. 1789 MRS. PIOZZI *Journ. France* II. 208 A dreg of the Romish superstition. 1867 G. GILFILLAN *Night* III. 76 The meteor.. left not e'en a trace or dreg behind.

b. The sequelæ of a disease.

1639 FULLER *Holy War* IV. xi. (1647) 187 The remnant-dregs of his disease. 1824 MISS FERRIER *Inher.* xxvii, The dregs of the measles are a serious thing.

5. *sing.* A small quantity or drop left; hence, *depreciatively*, a small quantity or 'drop'.

1819 SHELLEY *Cyclops* 579 Take it and drink it off; leave not a dreg. 1821 CARLYLE in *Early Lett.* (1886) II. 10 Make yourself a comfortable dreg.

Hence **'dregful** *a.*, full of dregs, dreggy; **'dregless** *a.*, free from dregs.

1552 HULOET, Dreggefull or full of dregges, *amaricosus*. 1845 LD. CAMPBELL *Chancellors* (1857) I. xiii. 197 It passed, dregless, into the vat of our memory.

†**dreg**, *v. Obs. rare.* [f. prec. sb.] *trans.* To make dreggy; to render turbid as with dregs.

1627–47 FELTHAM *Resolves* I. xcv. 298 Our much use of strong Beere, and grosse Flesh, is a great occasion of dregging our spirits. 1812 *Sporting Mag.* XXXIX. 101 So was the finish of this scene dregged with dross.

dreg, obs. form of DREDGE.

†**dregbaly.** *Obs.* ? Error for **dragbelly*: a big belly, a person with a large paunch.

1483 *Cath. Angl.* 108/1 A Dregbaly, *aqualiculus, porci est ventripotens.*

dreggish ('drɛgɪʃ), *a.* [f. DREG *sb.* + -ISH.] Of the nature of dregs or refuse; affected by the presence of dregs. Also *fig.* Base, vile.

1561 T. NORTON *Calvin's Inst.* IV. v. (1634) 535 Barbers, Cooks.. and such dreggish men. 1616 SURFL. & MARKH.

Country Farme 435 Not that which is in the bottome, because it is verie dreggish and filthie. **1716** M. DAVIES *Athen. Brit.* II. 346 The Clogging and Dreggish Menstruums of Galenick Electuaries.

dreggy ('drɛgɪ), *a.* [f. as prec. + -Y[1].] Abounding in dregs or fæces; of the nature or character of dregs; feculent; foul, impure; turbid, polluted.

c **1440** *Promp. Parv.* 131/2 Dreggy..or fulle of drestys, *feculentus.* **1574** NEWTON *Health Mag.* 48 Grapes leave much feculent and dreggie matter in the body. **1657** *Physical Dict.*, The thinner parts are evaporated, and the thicker remain black and dreggy. **1703** MOXON *Mech. Exerc.* 105 Either Draggy or..mingled with the Settlings of the Cask. **1883** *Standard* 19 May 6/2 Tallow..fine, 42*s*...dark dreggy lots, 39*s*.

b. *transf.* and *fig.*

1593 NASHE *Christ's T.* (1613) 59 Twenty thousand of these dreggy lees of Libertines. **1678** CUDWORTH *Intell. Syst.* 880 This earth..the lowest and most dreggy part of the universe! **1741** E. POSTON *Pratler* (1747) I. 33 Old Age, or the dreggy Part of Life. **1862** LOWELL *Biglow P.* Poems 1890 II. 249 A dreggy hybrid of the basest bloods of Europe.

Hence **'dreggily** *adv.*; **'dregginess.**

1607 TOPSELL *Serpents* (1658) 778 Having but little earthy dragginesse and drossy refuse. **1684** tr. *Bonet's Merc. Compit.* III. 51 The dregginess of the Ferment. **1876** WHITNEY *Sights & Ins.* II. xxxv. 638 Dim city edges that dip drearily and dreggily to the brink.

dregh, dreȝ(h, dreh(e: see DREE, DREIGH.

dregs: see DREG *sb.*

dregy, var. *dergie*, obs. Sc. form of DIRGE.

drehte, pa. t. of DRETCH *v.*[1]

drei, dreich, dreigh, dreih, obs. and dial. ff. DREE *v.* and *a.*

drei(e, obs. f. DRY.

dreid, obs. Sc. form of DREAD.

dreien, dreihen, obs. forms of DRAW *v.*

dreifle, obs. form of DRIVEL.

† **dreigh, dreich.** *Obs.* Also 4 dreh, drehi, dreih, drei, drey, 4-5 dreghe, dreȝ(e, driȝe. [? f. *dreȝe, dregh*, earlier form of DREE *a.*]

1. Long duration of space or time; length, distance, extent.

? *a* **1400** *Morte Arth.* 2916 And thus they drevene to þe dede dukes and erles, Alle þe dreghe of þe daye. *c* **1400** *Destr. Troy* 678 When the dregh was don of þe derke night. *a* **1400-50** *Alexander* 4788, viij daies be-dene þe driȝe was, and mare, Or he miȝt couire to þe copp fra þe caue vndire.

2. phr. *a-, on-, (o-) dregh*: at or to a distance, afar off; = A-DRIGH, q.v.

a **1300** *Cursor M.* 21859 (Cott.) Bi takens ferr on drei Men wat it es command nei. *c* **1470** HENRY *Wallace* v. 1079 Folow on dreich, giff that we mystir ocht. **1533** BELLENDEN *Livy* III. (1822) 213 Throw ane signe that Quincius maid on dreich, the Romanis ischit fra thair tentis. **1715** RAMSAY *Christ's Kirk* II. vi, He stood nae lang a-dreigh.

3. Tediousness, annoyance. *rare.*

a **1400-50** *Alexander* 5578 All þe dreȝe of þa deuels þai drenchid or þai past.

† **dreight, dright.** *Obs.* Also 4-5 dreght. [f. *dreȝe, dreghe*, DREE *a.* + -T.] = DREIGH 1.

c **1400** *Destr. Troy* 10633 The day of þe dreight [was] dryuyn vppo long. *a* **1400-50** *Alexander* 1112 þe dreȝt [*v.r.* droȝt] of þi days. *Ibid.* 4874 þe driȝt of daies foure score. **1557-75** *Diurn. Occurrents* (1833) 260 Thaj past throw the seynis..a dricht fra schote of the castell.

dreikanter ('draɪkantər, -kæntə(r)). Pl. dreikanter, -ers. [a. G. *dreikanter*, lit. three-edged thing, f. *drei* three + *kante* edge (see CANT *sb.*[1]) + *-er* -ER[1].] An angular, faceted pebble the surface of which has been cut by wind-blown sand; *esp.* one with three facets.

1903 *Nature* 10 Dec. 143/1 A collection of wind-worn pebbles of quartz and quartzite from an old raised beach near Waverley, North Island, New Zealand,..was exhibited by the president. They have been cut by the sand driven by the wind into the characteristic *Dreikanter.* **1938** A. K. WELLS *Outl. Hist. Geol.* xiii. 147 The quartzite and other pebbles in the Keuper in this region are not dreikanters. **1944** A. HOLMES *Princ. Physical Geol.* xiii. 258 Such wind-faceted pebbles, which often resemble Brazil nuts,..are known as dreikanter or ventifacts. **1946** F. E. ZEUNER *Dating Past* Pl. x. (*caption*) A 'dreikanter', a quartzite boulder facetted by blown sand. **1970** R. J. SMALL *Study of Landforms* ix. 301 Such abrasion is capable of..shaping individual boulders and small stone into 'ventifacts', notably the well-known 'dreikanter' with their three faceted sides.

dreint, obs. pa. t. and pple. of DRENCH *v.*

† **'dremels.** *Obs.* [a. deriv. of ME. *drem-en* to DREAM + -ELS.] A dream.

1362 LANGL. *P. Pl.* A. VIII. 138 þe Bible bereþ witnesse hou Daniel deuynede þe Dremels of a kyng. **1377** *Ibid.* B. VII. 154. *Ibid.* XIII. 14 How þat ymagynatyf in dremeles me tolde Of kynde and of his connynge.

drempt, obs. pa. t. of DREAM *v.*

drench (drɛnʃ), *sb.* Forms: 1 drenc(e, 3 dræнc, drencche, drunch, 4 drenche, drenke, 3- drench. [OE. *drenc* draught, drink, drowning:—OTeut. **draŋki-z*, f. *draŋk-* ablaut grade of *driŋk-an* to DRINK. Cf. Goth, *draggk, dragk*, OS. *dranc*, OHG. *tranch* (Ger. *trank*):—OTeut. **draŋkoᵐ*, and OHG. *trenka* fem.:—OTeut. **draŋkjâ.*]

† **1.** Drink; a draught. *Obs.* in general sense.

a **800** *Corpus Gloss.* 166 *Antedo* [*antidotum*], wyrtdrenc. *c* **1000** *Coll. Monast.* (Th.) 35 (Bosw.) Win nys drenc cilda. *c* **1205** LAY. 13435 Heo hafden drænc, heo hafden mete. **1340** *Ayenb.* 130 þer ne is noþer king ne kuene þet ne ssel drinke of deaþes drench.

2. *spec.* A medicinal, soporific, or poisonous draught; a potion. From 1600 often (after 3): A large draught or potion, or one forcibly given.

c **1000** *Sax. Leechd.* II. 56 Wyrc drenc wiþ hwostan. *c* **1000** ÆLFRIC *Hom.* II. 158 Se drenc deadbær wæs. **1297** R. GLOUC. (1724) 151 He ȝef hym a luþer drench. *c* **1380** *Sir Ferumb.* 1386 Sche fet him a drench þat noble was, & mad him drynk it warm. **1587** TURBERV. *Trag. T.* (1837) 250 A poysoned drench. **1625** B. JONSON *Staple of N.* II. Wks. (Rtldg.) 385/1 A drench of sack At a good tavern..Would cure him. **1667** MILTON *P.L.* II. 73 If the sleepy drench Of that forgetful Lake benumme not still. **1719** D'URFEY *Pills* (1872) III. 327 This muddy Drench of Ale. **1859** R. F. BURTON *Centr. Afr.* in *Jrnl. Geog. Soc.* XXIX. 286 Girls are fattened to a vast bulk by drenches of curds and cream thickened with flour. **1868** BROWNING *Ring & Bk.* II. 953 Guido..Shook off the relics of his poison drench.

fig. **1581** J. BELL *Haddon's Answ. Osor.* 324 With concubynes and drenches of Baudrye. **1641** MILTON *Animadv.* (1851) 204 To diet their ignorance..with the limited draught of a Mattin, and even song drench. **1891** E. H. HICKEY in *Athenæum* 24 Oct. 549/2 The sleepy drench of Time.

3. A draught or dose of medicine administered to an animal.

1552 HULOET, Drench or drynke for horse or other beast, *saluiatum.* **1601** HOLLAND *Pliny* II. 144 Poure this drench with an horne downe the throat of laboring jades. **1639** T. DE GRAY *Compl. Horsem.* 66 Administered by way of Drench to a horse. *a* **1748** WATTS *Ontology* x. ii. §4 A farrier constrains him to take a drench. **1864** KNIGHT *Passages Wrkg. Life* I. ii. 151 No cattle-doctor would give a drench to a cow unless he consulted the table in the Almanack.

4. The act of drenching, soaking, or wetting thoroughly; such a quantity as drenches.

1808 J. BARLOW *Columb.* I. 442 Wide over earth his annual freshet strays, And highland drains with lowland drench repays. **1850** BROWNING *Christm. Eve*, etc. 168 Quench The gin-shop's light in hell's grim drench. **1893** BARING-GOULD *Cheap Jack Z.* III. 114 A drench of rain.

5. *Tanning.* A preparation in which skins are steeped. Cf. *drenche-kive* in 6.

1853 C. MORFIT *Tanning, etc.* 410 Skins..undergo a steeping, for ten or fifteen days, in a fermenting mixture, or 'drench', of forty pounds of bran and twenty gallons of water.

6. *Comb.*, as **drench-horn,** (orig. OE. *drenc-horn* a drinking horn), a horn used for giving a medicinal drench to animals; † **drenche-kive,** a drenching vat or tub (see sense 5).

? *c* **1000** *Cod. Dipl.* 722 (Kemble) III. 361 (Bosw.) Ic ȝeann into ðære stowe ðone drenc-horn ðe ic ær [*MS.* er] æt ðam hirede ȝebohte. *a* **1300** *Sat. People Kildare* xiv. in *E.E.P.* (1862) 155 Hail be ȝe skinners wiþ ȝure drenche kiue, Who so smilliþ þer-to wo is him aliue. **1688** R. HOLME *Armoury* III. 325/2 The Farriers Drench Horn.

drench (drɛnʃ), *v.* Forms: 1 drencan, 2-5 drenchen, 3-6 drenche, (4 drensche, dr(e)inche, 4-5 drynche), 5- drench. *Pa. t.* α. 1-3 drencte, 2-5 dreint(e, 3 drengte, 3-6 dreynt(e, 4 dreynkt(e, 5 drenkte, dreyncte, 5 draynt(e, drenckt, 6-7 drent(e. β. 4-5 drenchid(e, -yd, 4- drenched, 6-7 drencht. *Pa. pple.* α. 1 drenct, 2-5 dreint, etc., 6 drent, drint, drynt. β. 4- drenched, 6-7 drencht. [OE. *drencan* = OS. *drenkian* (Du. *drenken*), OHG. *trenchen* (Ger. *tränken*), ON. *drekkja*:—*drenkja* (Sw. *dränka*):—OTeut. **draŋkjan*, f. *draŋk*, ablaut grade of *driŋkan* to drink, of which it is the causal derivative.]

1. *trans.* To make to drink; to administer drink to; now *spec.* to administer a draught of medicine in a forcible manner to (an animal).

c **1000** *Ags. Ps.* lix. [lx.] 3 Ðu..hi..mid wynsume wine drenctest. *a* **1400-50** *Alexander* 1106 þou sall be drenchid of a drinke a draȝte of vnsele. **1592** DANIEL *Compl. Rosamond* 29 Wks. (1717) 54 Take it [i.e. poison], or I will drench you else by force. **1653** HOLCROFT *Procopius, Vandal Wars* II. 55 The drink proceeding, and Gontharis being well drencht and grown bountifull, gave of his meats to the guard. **1672** J. LACY *Dumb Lady* I. Dram. Wks. (1875) 21 I'll to the wood and drench a sick horse. **1756** FOOTE *Eng. fr. Paris* I. Wks. 1799 I. 106 Madam, drenched with a bumper, drops a curtesy, and departs. **1808** SCOTT *Marm.* v. xxii, A stranger maiden..Had drenched him with a beverage rare. **1894** DALZIEL *Dis. Dogs* (ed. 3) 2 It is necessary to drench him.

fig. **1382** WYCLIF *Deut.* xxxii 42, I shal drenche myn arewis in blood, and my swerd shal deuour flesh.

† **2.** To submerge in water; to drown. Also *refl. Obs.*

c **1200** *Trin. Coll. Hom.* 175 Gif he ship findeþ, he fondeð to drenchen hit ȝif he mai. *c* **1205** LAY. 12111 Summe heo heom drengte in þere sæ deope. *c* **1300** *Havelok* 561, I shal dreinchen him in þe se. *c* **1386** CHAUCER *Frankl. T.* 650 They priuely been stirt in to a welle And dreynte [*v. rr.* drenkte, dreynt, dreinte] hem seluen. *a* **1450** *Knt. de la Tour* (1868) 55 Nor no water shulde drenche her, nor fyre brenne her. **1590** SPENSER *F.Q.* II. xii. 6 Condemned to be drent. **1621** G. SANDYS *Ovid's Met.* VIII. (1626) 165 And in the strangling waters drencht his child.

fig. *c* **1630** RISDON *Surv. Devon* §293 (1810) 302 The Dart drencheth itself into that river.

† **3.** *intr.* To sink in water; to be drowned. *Obs.*

1297 R. GLOUC. (1724) 100 þe se biset ow al a boute..ȝe mowe..drenche. *c* **1330** R. BRUNNE *Chron. Wace* (Rolls) 2008 He dreynte þerin. *c* **1485** *Digby Myst.* (1882) III. 1747 þat in þis flod we drench natt. *a* **1547** SURREY in *Tottell's Misc.* (Arb) 16 Alas, now drencheth my swete fo. **1570** ABP. PARKER *Corr.* (1853) 364, I was like to have drenched in the midst of the Thames.

fig. *c* **1374** CHAUCER *Troylus* IV. 902 (930) þough ye boþe in salte teris drenche [*Harl.* dreynte]. *c* **1385** —— *L.G.W.* 1919 *Ariadne*, And let hire drenche in sorwe & in distresse.

4. *trans.* To wet thoroughly by immersion; to steep, soak, saturate.

c **1230** *Hali Meid.* 15 His earewen idrencte of an attri haliwei. *c* **1420** *Pallad. on Husb.* I. 370 Let drenche it for a tyme in water swete. **1589** COGAN *Haven Health* ccxliii. (1636) 310 A..spunge drenched in white Vineger of Roses. **1697** DRYDEN *Virg. Georg.* III. 680 Good Shepherds after Sheering drench their Sheep. **1719** YOUNG *Busiris* v. i, I'll drench my sword in thy detested blood. **1746-7** HERVEY *Medit.* (1818) 152 The nails, which were drenched in his sacred veins.

b. *Tanning.* (See quots.)

1853 C. MORFIT *Tanning, etc.* 413 The skins are..drenched for some days in a fermenting bran-bath. **1885** *Harper's Mag.* Jan. 276/1 To 'drench'..the hides are placed for six or eight hours in vats filled with a dissolved excrement, above which a line of large wooden..wheels..in their revolution turn them over and over in the solution.

5. Now *esp.* To wet through and through with liquid falling or thrown upon the object.

1549-62 STERNHOLD & H. *Ps.* cxxxiii. 343 It weat not Aaron's head alone, but drencht his beard throughout. *a* **1656** BP. HALL *Rem. Wks.* (1660) 53 Many fields have been drencht with blood. **1714** GAY *Trivia* I. 46 And Show'rs soon drench the Camlet's cockled Grain. **1832** TENNYSON *Dream Fair Women* 85 Dark wood-walks drench'd in dew. **1871** L. STEPHEN *Playgr. Eur.* iv. (1894) 95 A thunderstorm drenched us during our descent. **1871** R. ELLIS *Catullus* ci. 9 Drench'd in a brother's tears, and weeping freshly, receives them.

† **6.** *fig.* To drown, immerse, plunge, overwhelm.

c **1374** CHAUCER *Boeth.* I. metr. i. 1 (Camb. MS.) The sorwful howre þat is to seyn the deth hadde almost dreynt myn heued. *c* **1440** *Gesta Rom.* lxvi. 303 (Harl. MS.) He drenchith þe synner in Ivill thowtis. **1560** ROLLAND *Crt. Venus* IV. 83 He..was drint into dispair. **1566** DRANT *Horace's Sat.* iv. C, His sonne is drente in debte so deepe. *a* **1628** PRESTON *New Covt.* (1630) 198 Men much drenched in worldly business. **1818** JAS. MILL *Brit. India* III. VI. i. 45 Minds drenched with terror are easily deceived.

Hence **drenched** (drɛnʃt), *ppl. a.*

c **1340** *Cursor M.* 1886 (Trin.) A drenched beest. **1589** GREENE *Menaphon* (Arb.) 27 To drie their drenched apparaile. **1660** GAUDEN *Dr. Brownrig* 212 A drenched and almost drowned man. **1885** *Harper's Mag.* Jan. 276/1 The drenched hides..are..worked over a beam.

drench: see DRENG.

'drencher. [f. DRENCH *v.* + -ER[1].] One who or that which drenches; a drenching shower; an apparatus for administering a drench to a beast.

1755 JOHNSON, *Drencher*, 1. One that dips or steeps any thing. 2. One that gives physick by force. *Dict.* **1892** *Pall Mall G.* 22 Aug. 3/1 We have just had a drencher, and the main street..is swimming. **1894** H. DALZIEL *Dis. Dogs* 3 The medicine measure and drencher..I invented.

drenching ('drɛnʃɪŋ), *vbl. sb.* [f. as prec. + -ING[1].] **a.** The action of DRENCH *v.*, various senses.

c **1380** WYCLIF *Wks.* (1880) 59 To saue a mannus bodi fro deþ or drynechyng. *c* **1386** CHAUCER *Man of Law's T.* 387 Who kepte hire fro the drenchyng in the see? **1626** BACON *Sylva* §648 Malt in the Drenching will swell. **1870** *Daily News* 25 Nov., He gives them three drenchings of varnish.

b. *Comb.*, as *drenching-horn, -staff.* **drenching-gun,** a device for giving a medicinal drench to animals.

1639 T. DE GRAY *Compl. Horsem.* 106 Holding up his head with a Drenching Staffe. **1697** DAMPIER in *Phil. Trans.* XX. 50 If it be for any Cattel, it must be..given with a Drenching Horn. **1737** OZELL *Rabelais* II. 64 A Drenching-horn serves to convey a Draught into a Horse's Mouth. **1950** *N.Z. Jrnl. Agric.* Sept. 239/1 Where a drenching 'gun' is used. **1961** B. CRUMP *Hang on a Minute* 158 On a table in the middle of the floor was a drenching-gun. **1966** *Punch* 21 Sept. 446/2 Today's stockman must be proficient with hypodermic syringe and drenching gun.

'drenching, *ppl. a.* [f. as prec. + -ING[2].] That drenches or thoroughly wets; soaking.

1757 GRAY *Descent Odin* 33 The drenching dews, and driving rain. **1860** TYNDALL *Glac.* II. xi. 292 We descended ..amid drenching rain.

Hence **'drenchingly** *adv.*

1880 MISS BROUGHTON *Sec. Th.* III. vii, It is wet—oh, drenchingly, drowningly wet.

dreng (drɛŋ). *Eng. Hist.* Also 1 drench, drengh, 3 drenche, dringche, 3-4 dring(e, *Sc.* 6-8 dring. [OE. *dreng*, ON. *drengr* young man, lad, fellow, (Sw. *dräng* man, servant, some one's 'man', Da. *dreng* boy, lad, apprentice). The modern word, had it survived in living use, would have been *dring*; but the OE. and Norse form *dreng* is retained by historical writers.] A free tenant (specially) in ancient Northumbria, holding by a tenure older than the Norman Conquest, the nature of which was partly military, partly servile. See Maitland, 'Northumbrian Tenures' in *Eng. Hist. Rev.* V. 632.

a **1000** *Battle of Maldon* 149 Forlet ða drenga sum daroð of handa, fleoȝan of folmum. **1086** *Domesday Bk.* 269 b, Hujus manerii [Neweton, Lanc.] aliam terram xv. homines quos drenchs vocabant pro xv. oris tenebant.. Modo sunt ibi vi. drenghs. *c* **1100** *Charter of Ranulph* in Murray *Dial. S.C. Scot.* 22 *note*, R[anulf] bisceop greteð wel alle his þeines & drenges of Ealondscire & of Norhamscire. *c* **1205** LAY. 12713 Androgien wes þer king; vnder him wes moni hæh dring. *Ibid.* 14700 Drenches. *a* **1300** *Cursor M.* 16022 (Cott.) All þai gadird o þe tun, bath freman and dring. *c* **1300** *Havelok* 2258 And siþen drenges, and siþen thaynes, And siþen knithes, and siþen sweynes. **1874** STUBBS *Const. Hist.* §96 (ed. 3) I. 262 Lanfranc.. turned the drengs, the rent-paying tenants of his archiepiscopal estates, into knights for the defence of the country. **1890** F. W. MAITLAND in *Eng. Hist. Rev.* V. 628 Under Richard I the thegns and drengs of Northumberland paid tallage.

b. Contemptuously: A low or base fellow. *Sc.*

1535 STEWART *Cron. Scot.* III. 278 Quhilk is knawin for ane wrache or dring. *a* **1605** POLWART *Flyting w. Montgomerie* 796 Deid dring, dryd sting! thou will hing but a sunȝie. **1799** STRUTHERS *To the Blackbird* ix, The Captive o' some dudron dring, Dull, fat an' frowsy.

drengage ('drɛŋgɛdʒ). *Eng. Hist.* [ad. med.L. *drengagium*, f. prec. + *-agium*, -AGE.] The tenure or service of a dreng. Also *attrib.*

[*c* **1250** *Testa de Nevill.* 389 Johnes de Hawilton tenet Hawilton Claverworth & Wytington in capite de domino Rege in drengagio. **1277** *P. 6 Edw. I, B.R. Rot.* 7 Drengagium est certum servicium mes nemy Service de Chivaler.] **1607–72** COWELL *Interpr.*, *Drengage, Drengagium*, the Tenure by which the Drenches held their Lands. **1890** F. W. MAITLAND in *Eng. Hist. Rev.* V. 626 Even in the fourteenth century the drengage tenants of the bishop of Durham were still nominally liable to do 'outward'. **1894** R. S. FERGUSON *Hist. Westmorld.* 94 A mere trace of Drengage is to be found in Cumberland, two tenants only, but it existed in Durham and Northumberland.

drenke, obs. form of DRENCH.

†**'drenkle**, *v. Obs.* Forms: α. 4 drenkle, -kil, 5 -kel; β. 3–5 drinkel, drynkle; γ. 4 dronkle. [A frequentative derivative from of *drink* and *drench*:—OE. type **drenclian*:—**draŋkilojan*. The form *dronkle*, if not a misreading of *drenkle*, may represent a type **draŋkulojan*; cf. *drevel*, *dravel*, DRIVEL.]

1. *trans.* To submerge, drown.

α. *a* **1300** *Cursor M.* 1652 (Gött.), I sal þaim drenkil [*Cott. & Fairf.* droun, *Trin.* drenche] in watir sone. *Ibid.* 2228 (Gött.) *c* **1330** R. BRUNNE *Chron.* (1810) 310 þe rayne.. ran doun on þe mountayns, & drenkled þe playnes.

β. *c* **1250** *Gen & Ex.* 2768 Egipte king.. ðe ðe childre so drinkelen bead. **1447** BOKENHAM *Seyntys* (Roxb.) 75 Enchauntement.. that drynklyn may the not the see.

γ. *c* **1330** R. BRUNNE *Chron.* (1810) 43 Four & tuente þousand in Temse alle at ones Wer dronkled. *Ibid.* 288 In a water stampe he was dronkled fleand.

2. *intr.* To suffer submersion or drowning.

α. *a* **1300** *Cursor M.* 1236 (Gött.) þai drenkled all in noe flode. **14..** *Songs & Carols 15th C.* (Percy Soc.) 58 His bestes drenkelyd in every dyche.

β. *a* **1300** *Cursor M.* 1796 (Gött.) þai drinklid ilkan.

γ. *c* **1330** R. BRUNNE *Chron.* (1810) 106 And dronkled by þe se side boþ William and Richard. *Ibid.* 170 þe schip þat was so grete it dronkled in the flode.

†**drent**, *ppl. a. Obs.* Also **dreint, dreynt.** [obs. pa. pple. of DRENCH *v.*] Drenched, drowned.

a **1310** in Wright *Lyric P.* xxxix. 111 He is dronke ase a dreynt mous. **1579** SPENSER *Sheph. Cal.* Nov. 37 For deade is Dido, dead alas and drent.

dreof, obs. pa. t. of DRIVE *v.*

dreoghen, dreoȝen, obs. forms of DREE *v.*

drepanid ('drɛpənɪd). *Zool.* [f. Gr. δρέπαν-ον scythe + -ID.] A fish belonging to the *Drepanidæ*, a family of scombroid acanthopterygian fishes, the typical genus of which is *Drepane*, so called from its elongated falciform pectoral fins.

From same source, **'drepaniform** *a.*, sickle-shaped, falciform. ‖**'Drepanis** [mod.L.], a genus of birds; the sickle-billed sunbirds of the South Sea Islands. ‖**dre'panium**, *Bot.* [mod.L.], 'Eichler's term for a sickle-shaped cyme, in which the lateral axes are all in the median plane and spring from the upper side of the curved axis.' **'drepanoid** *a.*, 'scythe or sickle-shaped' (*Syd. Soc. Lex.* 1883).

†**drepe**, *v. Obs.* Forms: 1 drepan, 4–5 drep(e. *Pa. t.* 1 dræp, drep, 4 drap, drop, dreped, 5 drepit. *Pa. pple.* 1 drepen, dropen, 5 drepit, -id. [A Common Teut. strong verb of ablaut series *e, a, æ, e*; OE. *drepan*, = M. and mod.LG. *drepan, drapan*, MDu. *drepan* to hit, strike, OHG. *trefan, treffan* (Ger. *treffen*), ON. *drepa* to strike, smite, kill (Sw. *dräpa*, Da. *dræbe*, to kill, slay).] *trans.* To strike, kill, overcome.

Beowulf (Th.) 3495 Under helm drepen. *Ibid.* 5753 þonne ic sweorde drep ferhð-ȝeniðlan. *a* **1300** *Cursor M.* 3602 (Cott.) þat þou mai drep [*v.r.* sle] me sum dere. *a* **1300** *E.E. Psalter* xciii[i]. 6 Step-childre þai drape al dai. *c* **1300** *Havelok* 2229 He with his hend Ne drop him nouth, that sor fend. *c* **1325** *Body & Soul* 259 in *Map's Poems* 343 The deth so deolfulliche me drap. *c* **1400** *Destr. Troy* 929 þis stone.. drepit the dragon to the dethe negh. *a* **1400–50** *Alexander* 867, I did bot my deuize to drepe him.

Hence †**'dreping** *vbl. sb.*; also †**'dreper**, one who kills: a murderer.

c **1300** *Havelok* 2684 þer was swilk dreping of þe folk. *a* **1400–50** *Alexander* 3422 þe drepars of Dary.

drepe, early form of DREEP *v.*

drere, -lie, drerie, etc., obs. ff. DREAR, etc.

Dresden ('drɛzdən). The name of a town in Saxony, used *attrib.* or *absol.* to designate a variety of white porcelain made at Meissen near Dresden, or an object made of this, characterized by elaborate decoration and figure-pieces in delicate colourings. Hence (often *attrib.*) used to designate anything of a delicate or frail prettiness.

1735 E. FINCH *Let.* 29 May in E. Burton *Georgians at Home* (1967) iv. 156 To gett either old or Dresden China. *Ibid.*, Exchang'd for a sett of Dresden. **1750** H. WALPOLE *Let.* 23 June (1941) IX. 106 On the cabinet stood a pair of Dresden candlesticks. **1752** [see CHINA *sb.*¹ 3 b]. **1753** HANWAY *Trav.* II. 226 Fourteen apartments filled with China and Dresden porcelain. **1756** [see PORCELAIN 1 a]. **1850** THACKERAY *Pendennis* I. xxxviii. 372 Wherever you sate down there were Dresden shepherds and shepherdesses convenient at your elbow. **1895** *Montgomery Ward Catal.* 9/1 Extra Fine Paris Sateens.. New artistic designs in small Dresden china effects. **1899** J. M. WARD *One Poor Scruple* I. v. 65 Madge's delicate, Dresden-china, little figure. **1905** W. HOLMAN HUNT *Pre-Raph.* I. 49 Etty was cramped by a taste for Dresden-china prettiness. **1908** *Daily Chron.* 28 Aug. 1/1 His own Dresden-china doll of a wife. **1912** C. MACKENZIE *Carnival* iv. 38 Her honey-coloured hair and Dresden cheeks fascinated the impressionable child with all the wonder of an expensive doll. *Ibid.* xv. 155 You do look like a Dresden shepherdess with your heart-shaped face and slanting eyes. **1917** T. S. ELIOT *Prufrock* 33 The Dresden clock continued ticking on the mantelpiece. **1962** G. K. HUNTER *John Lyly* iv. 233 Phebe, the Dresden-china shepherdess. **1970** D. DEVINE *Illegal Tender* i. 5 How bored she was with that face! Fair hair, big blue eyes, little pouting mouth, pink and white complexion. Like a doll. Yet Chris approved. 'A Dresden Shepherdess,' he'd called her.

†**drese**, *v. Obs. rare.* [OE. *dréosan*, to fall, go to ruin, pa. pple. (*ȝe*)*droren*, whence early ME. *ydrore*: a comm. Teut. vb. = OS. *driosan*, Goth. *driusan, draus, drusum, drusan.*] To fall.

a **1000** *Phœnix* 34 Wæstmas ne dreosað. [*c* **1275** LAY. 9245 Al he [Portcastre] gan to-drese.] **13..** *Leg. of Gregorius* 155 (Mätz.) He was to deþ ydrore.

dress (drɛs), *v.* Forms: 4 dresce, 4–6 dres, 4–7 dresse, (5 drisse, drysse), 4– dress. β. 5 dirse, dyrse, 9 *north.* derse. *Pa. t.* and *pple.* 5–6 dreste, 4– dressed, drest. [a. OF. *dresse-r* (earlier *drecier, drescer*) to arrange = Pr. *dressar, dreçar*, OSp. *derezar*, It. *d(i)rizzare*:—L. type **dīrectiāre*, f. *dīrect-us* DIRECT.]

I. To make straight or right; to bring into proper order; to array, make ready, prepare, tend.

†**1. a.** *trans.* To make straight; to erect, set *up.*

13.. *Coer de L.* 2554 He dressyd hys bak unto the maste. **1375** BARBOUR *Bruce* XVII. 372 Dressand vp ledderis douchtely. **1450–1530** *Myrr. our Ladye* 28 Myne eres shall be dressed vp, to here his prayer. *c* **1489** CAXTON *Sonnes of Aymon* xxii. 476 That the gibet be dressed all hie vpon the gate. **1530** PALSGR. 528/2, I dresse, I set upryght.. Dresse this old ymage agaynst the wall. **1585** T. WASHINGTON tr. *Nicholay's Voy.* II. iii. 73 b, To dresse up the pavillion. [**1892** *Black & White* 22 Oct. 474/2 He.. dressed his figure still more uprightly.]

†**b.** *refl.* and *intr.* To raise oneself, to rise. *Obs.*

13.. *Gaw. & Gr. Knt.* 566 He.. dressez on þe morn, Askez erly hys armez. *c* **1374** CHAUCER *Troylus* III. 22 (71) Troilus.. dressede hym vpward. **1481** CAXTON *Godfrey* cxcviii. 288 He dressyd hym on his steroppes.

†**2. a.** *trans.* To put (things) 'straight' or 'to rights' (*lit.* and *fig.*); to set in order; to manage. Also with *up. Obs.*

c **1330** R. BRUNNE *Chron.* (1810) 327 Wardeyns wise, To kepe þe lond and dres þe folk forto justise. ? *a* **1400** *Morte Arth.* 46 Danmarke he dryssede alle by drede of hym selvyne. **1570** *Satir. Poems Reform.* x. 117 All thing ȝeid weill and wes weill drest, In.. peace. **1672** *Acc. Bk. Sir J. Foulis* (1894) 9 To the wright.. for dressing some things about yᵉ house.

†**b.** To right, redress, remedy. *Obs.*

c **1560** A. SCOTT *Poems* xx. 7 Scho.. Quhilk suld thy dolour dress.

†**c.** To arrange *amongst*; to divide. *Obs.*

c **1400** *Gamelyn* 36 Dresseth my londes among my sonis thre. *c* **1400** *Destr. Troy* 2112 Till ho duly were ded & dressit in pesis. *c* **1420** *Liber Cocorum* (1862) 21 Take onyons.. And dresshe hom smalle.

†**3. a.** To place or set in position; to put on (with a connotation of adjustment). *Obs.*

c **1386** CHAUCER *Clerk's T.* 325 A coroun on hir heed thay han i-dressed. **1387** TREVISA *Higden* (Rolls) VII. 71 Gerebertus dressed hym [*se occuluit*] under a treen brugge and heng by þe armes. *c* **1400** *Melayne* 835 Thay dressede on hym a dyademe. *c* **1530** LD. BERNERS *Arth. Lyt. Bryt.* (1814) 347 How Arthur dressed downe one of the corners of her keuerchefe aboute her necke.

b. *Printing.* See quot.

1823 CRABB *Technol. Dict.*, *To Dress a Chase* (Print.) or *a Form*, to fit the pages and the chase, or form, of the matter that has been composed.

4. *Mil.* **a.** *trans.* To draw up (troops) in proper alignment.

1746 *Rep. Cond. Sir J. Cope* 54 The Artillery to have been posted on the Right of the Line, and dressed straight with it. **1796** STEDMAN *Surinam* I. viii. 185 The whole party being dressed in one rank, face to the right. **1833** *Regul. Instr. Cavalry* I. 23 No rank.. ought ever to be dressed, without the person.. appointed to dress it, determining.. a line on which the rank.. is to be formed. **1868** KINGLAKE *Crimea* (1877) III. i. 220 The battalion dressed its ranks with precision.

transf. **1840** *Evid. Hull Docks Com.* 27 Pull down the whole front of the warehouses and dress them back. **1859** F. A. GRIFFITHS *Artil. Man.* (1862) 159 The subalterns dress and correct the line of tents.

b. *intr.* To 'form' in proper alignment.

1796 *Instr. & Reg. Cavalry* (1813) 51 When marching in line, each squadron dresses to its own center. **1803** *Compl. Drill Serjeant* 10 At the word Dress, each man will cast his eyes to the point he is to dress to. **1853** STOCQUELER *Milit. Encycl.* s.v., Soldiers dress by one another in ranks, and the body collectively by some given object.

transf. **1888** *N. & Q.* 7th Ser. V. 344 All that remains of the west sides of the square.. is continued on the same plan as the brick house, and dresses with it in height.

†**5. a.** *trans.* To make ready or prepare for any purpose; to order, arrange, draw up. Also with *up. Obs.* exc. as transf. from 7.

13.. *K. Alis.* 479 Neptanabus Made so strong sorcerye, And dressed hit by the skye. **1382** WYCLIF *John* i. 23 Dresse ȝe the wey of the Lord, as Ysaye.. seyde. *a* **1400** *Pistill of Susan* 274 Nou þei dresse hire to deþ. *c* **1440** *York Myst.* xxxvi. 240 A draughte.. of drinke haue I dreste. *a* **1533** LD. BERNERS *Huon* cxvii. 422 And dresse vp tubbes with water of the see, and halowe you it, and chrysten them therin. *a* **1605** MONTGOMERIE *Minde's Melodie* Ps. lvii. 35 A ditche is drest For me—bot loe! my foes therein doe fall. **1676** *Phil. Trans.* XI. 681 Galilæus.. undertook to dress Tables of their Motions. **1763** J. BROWN *Poetry & Mus.* v. 50 There was neither History nor Philosophy.. but what was dressed by the Muses. **1834** MEDWIN *Angler in Wales* I. 34 To employ ourselves in dressing a few flies.

†**b.** *intr.* To make arrangements, arrange. *Obs.*

1596 DALRYMPLE tr. *Leslie's Hist. Scot.* x. 445 He sendis Bischop Monluch.. to handle with her, and dres anent the transporteng of the armie frome the Jnglis bordouris.

†**6.** *refl.* and *intr.* To prepare oneself, make ready; in many quots. coloured by sense 14, and so = to apply oneself, direct one's skill or energies, turn the attention *to*. Cf. ADDRESS *v.* III. *Obs.*

c **1386** CHAUCER *Man of Law's T.* 1002 Alla gan hym dresse, And eek his wyf, this Emperour to meete. *c* **1400** *Destr. Troy* 5195 þes drest for þe dede and droghen to ship. *Ibid.* 8425 Of Andromaca drem I dresse me to telle. **1526** *Pilgr. Perf.* (W. de W. 1531) 67 Let vs dresse our selfe to go forth the iourney of lyfe. **1596** DALRYMPLE tr. *Leslie's Hist. Scot.* VIII. 75 The Hammiltounis vrges the Douglas, to dres him for the morne.

7. a. *trans.* To array, attire, or 'rig out', with suitable clothing or raiment; to adorn or deck with apparel; in later use often simply, to clothe. *spec.* To make or provide clothes for (an undressed doll); to put clothes on (an undressed doll).

c **1440** *York Myst.* xvii. 91 Dresse vs in riche array. **1526** *Pilgr. Perf.* (W. de W. 1531) 201 b, The spouse.. hath many women to adorne and dresse her. **1621** BURTON *Anat. Mel.* III. ii. II. iii. (1676) 296/1 Some light housewife.. dressed like a May-lady. **1727** LD. HERVEY *Let.* 7 Nov. in *Lett. Lady M. W. Montagu* (1966) II. 88 Your pretending to be young enough to take a Pleasure in dressing Babys. **1762** GOLDSM. *Cit. W.* xiv, I was dressed after the fashion of Europe. **1800** JANE AUSTEN *Let.* 1 Nov. (1932) I. 24 My Mother is very happy in the prospect of dressing a new Doll. **1803** M. WILMOT *Let.* 31 July in *Russ. Jrnls.* (1934) I. 26, I have heard people.. regret that.. they had not collected specimens of the fashion of every year by dressing a Doll as every flash of fashion flitted by. **1825** H. WILSON *Memoirs* 22 Romping with her lovely children, dressing their dolls, and teaching them to skip. **1830** M. R. MITFORD *Our Village* IV. 213 Good Mr. Norris.. dressed his little daughter's doll. **1839** THIRLWALL *Greece* VI. xlvii. 101 He.. came out drest in white. **1844** DISRAELI *Coningsby* IV. iv. 44 Miss Millbank.. was sitting at a round table covered with working materials, apparently dressing a doll. **1864** C. M. YONGE *Trial* I. ii. 23 Ethel, are they too big for Mary to dress some dolls for them? **1866** MRS. CARLYLE *Lett.* III. 319, I was up and dressed at seven. **1968** B. DREW (*title*) Let's dress a doll.

b. *refl.* (and *pass.*) To attire oneself with attention to fashion or artistic effect; *spec.* to put on the more elaborate costume proper for a dinner or evening party or for a ceremonial occasion; also, simply, to attire oneself, put on one's clothes.

1641 J. JACKSON *True Evang. T.* II. 99 Our Saviour.. sets up little children as looking-glasses of grace to dresse ourselves in. **1667** PEPYS *Diary* 25 Mar., By and by comes Mr. Lowther and his wife and mine.. into a box, forsooth, neither of them being dressed. **1749** FIELDING *Tom Jones* XVIII. xi, He had barely time left to dress himself. **1750** JOHNSON *Rambler* No. 27 ¶4 He was come back to dress himself for a ball. **1894** BARING-GOULD *Kitty* III. 9 He saw the lawyer dressing himself and shaving.

c. *intr.* in reflexive sense. Esp. ***to dress for dinner.***

1703 ROWE *Ulyss.* Prol. 15 They.. Dress'd at Her, danc'd, and fought and.. did all that Men could do to have her. **1710** SWIFT *Lett.* (1767) III. 77 While I was dressing. **1730–6** BAILEY (folio) s.v., To dress at a person, is to dress and adorn in order to enamour or gain the affection of a person. **1741** RICHARDSON *Pamela* III. xxx. 18 The three Gentlemen rode out, and returned just Time enough to dress before Dinner. **1771** FRANKLIN *Autobiogr.* in *Writings* (1905) I. 237

One does not dress for private company as for a publick ball. **1782** L. L. DALRYMPLE *Jrnl.* (1871) 34 We are dressing for dinner. **1800** *Oracle* in *Spirit Pub. Jrnls.* (1801) IV. 23 When he gets up in the morning, let him dress off in the sprucest style. **1802** G. ROSE *Diaries* (1860) I. 505, I went up to dress for dinner. **1815** ELPHINSTONE *Acc. Caubul* (1842) II. 51 They..dress like Khyberees. **1841** F. A. KEMBLE *Let.* 28 Mar. in *Rec. Later Life* (1882) II. 67 It is close upon time to dress for dinner. **1865** TROLLOPE *Belton Est.* (1866) I. iii. 62 We'd better get ready for dinner now. I always dress, because papa likes to see it. **1885** *Manch. Exam.* 12 Jan. 6/2 The ladies..dress in blacks and drabs. **1887** *Daily News* 7 June 6/1 That section of the world that 'dresses' in contradistinction to merely wearing clothes. **1922** W. S. MAUGHAM *On Chinese Screen* xlix. 193 He always dressed, and..expected the three boys to wait at table. **1931** V. WOOLF *Waves* 129 She has not dressed, because she despises the futility of London.

d. *trans.* (and *intr.* for *refl.*) ***to dress up***: to attire elaborately, or in a manner appropriate to a superior position or to a part which one aspires to play; also *intr.*, of children: to attire oneself in a costume or in various clothes as a game. ***to dress down***: to wear clothes less formal than would be expected; to dress informally. ***to dress out*** (†***forth***): to deck out with dress.

1674 S. VINCENT *Gallant's Acad.* 29 Being neatly and Taylor-like drest up. **1721** BERKELEY *Prev. Ruin Gt. Brit.* Wks. III. 201 The direct way to ruin a man is to dress him up in fine clothes. **1749** FIELDING *Tom Jones* IV. x, Dress forth his wenches in such gaudy style. **1766** GOLDSM. *Vic. W.* iv, Down came my wife and daughters, drest out in all their former splendour. **1857** TROLLOPE *Barchester T.* III. v. 83 Them two walloping gals, dressed up to their very eyeses. **1870** L. M. ALCOTT *Old-Fashioned Girl* v. 65, I ain't going to dress up for nothing; I look so lovely, some one must admire me. **1876** TREVELYAN *Macaulay* I. i. 16 The Frenchmen..dressed out with women's gowns and petticoats. **1876** [see NINE *sb.* 6 b]. **1888** MRS. H. WARD *R. Elsmere* I. I. iv. 85 He could see her dressing up with him on wet days, reciting King Henry to his Prince Hal. **1903** *Little Folks* Feb. 115/1 We began to dress up... Humphrey had on my white flannel pyjamas with a red sash... Violet had on the lace window-curtain. **1914** C. MACKENZIE *Sinister Street* II. III. vi. 618 You'd be the first to laugh..if I dressed up.. half-a-dozen of my friends in velvet jackets. **1959** D. CAMPBELL *Evening under Lamp-Light* 21 Let's play grown-ups. Let's dress up in their clothes. **1960** *Harper's Bazaar* July 50 A predilection for dressing down at casual dinner parties. **1963** *Sunday Express* 17 Feb. 22/4, I want to be recognised as a good actress. That's why I dress down, rather than dress up. **1968** D. E. ALLEN *Brit. Tastes* vii. 175 On Tyneside the different income-groups differ less sharply than elsewhere in the styles and standard of clothing that they purchase, as if the better-off deliberately chose to dress 'down'.

e. *transf.* and *fig.* (of 7 and 7 d.)

1615 J. STEPHENS *Satyr. Ess.* A viij, Such a most busie Daw did seeme to dresse My Characters with saucinesse. **1699** BENTLEY *Phal.* 162 A sort of Declamation, to dress up and to varnish the Story of Pausanias. **1725** WATTS *Logic* III. iii. §1 They dress up the opinion of their adversary as they please. **1873** M. ARNOLD *Lit. & Dogma* (1876) 315 Dressing the popular doctrine out with fine speculations.

f. *intr.* Of a male: to allow the sexual organs to be on one side or the other of the fork of the trousers.

1966 *Guardian* 18 Mar. 10/4 You..find an amusing piece by John Morgan on Carnaby Street—'We are "dressing" in the middle this year, man,' a pop singer explains. **1967** *New Statesman* 31 Mar. 450/2, I detected some sag on the right-hand side of the trouser front and got the fitter to pin it back. 'No no no!' said Roy... 'Mr. Silver dresses to the left.' The fullness on the right was critical. **1969** *Guardian* 31 July 6/1 All those little male problems like dressing to the right or left.

8. a. To array, equip; to adorn, deck; also with *out*, †*up*. ***to dress a ship***: to deck it out with flags. ***to dress a*** (***shop***) ***window***: to decorate it with goods artistically or attractively displayed.

c **1400** *Rowland & O.* 362 Thay..dressede hym in his armours. *c* **1460** *Play Sacram.* 165, I haue dyamantis dere wourthy to dresse. **1530** PALSGR. 528/2, I dressed my house gayly against my housbandes comynge home. **1648** GAGE *West Ind.* viii. 23 The Chamber was richly dressed and hung with many pictures, and with hangings. **1769** FALCONER *Dict. Marine* (1789), *Faire la Parade*, to dress a ship, or to adorn her with flags. **1844** DICKENS *Christm. Carol* 27 It was made plain enough, by the dressing of the shops, that here too it was Christmas time again. **1879** SALA *Paris Herself Again* I. xviii. 292 His windows are not yet 'dressed'.

b. To equip or provide (a play, etc.) with the appropriate costumes.

1741 T. BETTERTON *Eng. Stage* vi. 9 The Play..was acted before the Court and very richly Drest. **1881** *Daily News* 12 Sept. 2/1 The opera will be newly dressed.

c. *Arch.* To decorate (a window, etc.) with mouldings or the like. Cf. DRESSING *vbl. sb.* 4 e.

1726 LEONI *Designs* 5/2 The Windows of the upper Apartments are dressed. —— *Alberti's Archit.* II. 57/2 A door dressed after the manner of the Doric or Ionic Order.

d. To fill (a theatre, etc.) by means of complimentary tickets. Cf. PAPER *v.* 4 b.

1896 G. B. SHAW *Our Theatres in Nineties* (1932) II. 234 The theatrical deadhead gets his ticket on the implied condition that he 'dresses the house'. If he comes in morning dress, or allows the ladies who accompany him to look dowdy, he is struck-off the free list. **1933** P. GODFREY *Back-Stage* ix. 131 A large number of complimentary tickets is distributed to keep the stalls 'dressed'. **1961** BOWMAN & BALL *Theatre Lang.* 116 *Dress the house*,..to assign seats to an audience with artful spacing so that the theatre appears to be more crowded than it really is.

9. To treat (a person) 'properly', esp. (in ironical use) with deserved severity; hence, to give a thrashing or beating to, to chastise; to reprimand severely, scold. Now usually with *down*. (App. associated with 13 f, and kindred uses.)

1423 JAS. I. *Kingis Q.* clxxiii, From day to day so sore here artow drest. **1573** *Satir. Poems Reform.* xl. 268 The Apostillis..Reioysit that for Christ sa thay were drest. **1679** *Essex Freeholders* 6 They dressed the Rogues..as they were never dressed in their lives. **1785** *Spanish Rivals* 9 He would dress my jacket, an I were to tell him on't. **1850** BLACKIE *Æschylus* II. 302 So we say allegorically to *trim* one handsomely, to *dress* him, when we mean to *punish*.

10. To treat (a wounded man or his wounds) with remedies or curative appliances.

1471 SIR J. PASTON in *Paston Lett.* No. 668 III. 3 He is hurt with an arow..and I have sent hym a serjon, whyche hathe dressid hym. **1526** TINDALE *Luke* x. 34 [He] brought hym to a commen hostry and drest him. **1603** KNOLLES *Hist. Turks* (1638) 120 The wound..had bin..well dressed by the..Surgeons. **1758** J. S. *Le Dran's Observ. Surg.* (1771) 149, I dressed him..with the common Digestive. *c* **1850** *Arab. Nts.* (Rtldg.) 156 He had his wound dressed.

11. a. To treat or prepare (things) in some way proper to their nature or character; to subject to processes requisite for cleansing, purifying, trimming, smoothing, etc. See also 13.

1480 *Wardr. Acc. Edw. IV* (1830) 225 For bynding gilding and dressing of a booke called Titus Livius. **1523** FITZHERB. *Husb.* §132 Dresse the wode and bowe it clene. **1535** COVERD. *Exod.* xxx. 7 Whan he dresseth the lampes. **1559** MORWYNG *Evonym.* 15 Hoate oyles chymistically drest and prepared. **1696** DE LA PRYME *Diary* (Surtees) 85 As her father was dressing a great pond..there was cast up out of it 60 or 80 little images. **1793** SMEATON *Edystone L.* §239 The trenails having been previously dressed with a plane. **1802** *Trans. Soc. Arts* XX. 277 These stones..require to be ..oftener dressed than French Burr-stones. **1851** *Offic. Catal. Gt. Exhib.* I. 302 The usual mode of dressing flour is to brush it through a cylinder clothed with wire. **1894** *Labour Commission* Gloss. s.v. *Dressing Lime*, The slaked lime powder is passed through a sieve to remove coarse particles, and this operation is known as dressing lime. **1879** *Cassell's Techn. Educ.* IV. 50/1 The surface..is dressed with a little oxide.

b. *intr.* = *passive*.

1802 *Naval Chron.* IX. 293 A rove-ash oar that will dress clean and light, is too pliant. **1854** H. MILLER *Sch. & Schm.* (1858) 269 It was a hard..stone, but dressed readily to pick and hammer.

12. To take away or remove (anything) in the process of preparing, purifying or cleansing.

1701 C. WOLLEY *Jrnl. in N. York* (1860) 50 They fence.. their graves about..dressing the weeds from them. **1769** MRS. RAFFALD *Eng. Housekpr.* (1778) 301 Kill your pig, dress off the hair. **1851** *Offic. Catal. Gt. Exhib.* I. 229 For the purpose of dressing the remaining sand off it [a casting]. **1858** *Jrnl. R. Agric. Soc.* XIX. I. 218 Vast quantities of the seeds of the cotton-plant are dressed out of the cottons.

13. Specific and technical uses. **a.** To prepare for use as food, by making ready to cook, or by cooking (also *intr.* = *passive*); also, to season (food, esp. a salad).

13.. *Coer de L.* 3510 Or ye come the flesch was dressyd. *c* **1430** *Two Cookery-bks.* 13 Put yn þe Oystrys þer-to, and dresse it forth. **1582** N. LICHEFIELD tr. *Castanheda's Conq. E. Ind.* iv. 10 b, To dresse their meate with salt water. **1632** MILTON *L'Allegro* 86 Their savoury dinner..Of herbs and other country messes, Which the neat-handed Phillis dresses. **1736** T. SHERIDAN in *Swift's Lett.* (1768) IV. 163 We dress them with carp sauce. **1766** GOLDSM. *Vic. W.* xxxii, A very genteel entertainment..dressed by Mr. Thornhill's cook. **1795** tr. *Moritz's Travels* 240 The sallad, for which they brought me all the ingredients, I was always obliged to dress myself. **1796–7** JANE AUSTEN *Pride & Prej.* (1813) II. xvi. 188 These two girls had been..dressing a sallad and cucumber. **1885** *Manch. Exam.* 28 May 5/1 The carcase of a..cow dressed ready for sale. **1942** C. SPRY *Come into Garden, Cook* ix. 114 It [*sc.* an American-type salad] may contain grape-fruit, orange, pineapple, grapes, peaches, and so on. Dressed with mayonnaise, it is often finished off with a sprinkling of ground nuts. *Ibid.* 115 In the happy days when..one might have little melons to serve as a first course, I have filled them with cubes of their own flesh mixed with diced cucumber and dressed them with a thin cream dressing.

1806 *Culina* 27 This dish will dress very well with the cheese of our own country. **1858** *Jrnl. R. Agric. Soc.* XIX. I. 75 Potatoes so grown..dress badly.

b. To comb, brush, and do up (the hair).

1509 HAWES *Past. Pleas.* xxx. vii, Her shining here so properly she dresses. **1663** PEPYS *Diary* 13 July, Her hair dressed *à la negligence*. **1773** JOHNSON *Let. Mrs. Thrale* 24 Sept., [She] dresses her head very high..I wish her head-dress was lower. **1835** THIRLWALL *Greece* I. viii. 333 He dressed his hair and crowned himself for a battle as others for a feast.

c. To till, cultivate, prune, or tend (a field, garden, or plant); to treat *with* manure, etc.

1526 *Pilgr. Perf.* (W. de W. 1531) 11 They laboured and dressed the vynyarde of god by holy werkes of fayth. **1593** SHAKS. *Rich. II*, III. iv. 56 He had not so trim'd And drest his Land, as we this Garden. **1635** PAGITT *Christianogr.*, *Relig. Britons* 36 Some wrought in the Gardens, others dressed the Orchards. **1727** DE FOE *Syst. Magic* I. iv. (1840) 93 In planting and dressing the Vines. **1821** DWIGHT *Trav.* II. 343 Lands, dressed with gypsum. **1843** *Jrnl. R. Agric. Soc.* IV. I. 22 The leaves are allowed to rot and dress the ground. **1881** WHITEHEAD *Hops* 8 Sets are cut in the early spring.. when the plants are dressed.

fig. **1651** HOBBES *Leviath.* I. xi. 51 This seed of Religion.. to nourish, dresse, and forme it into Lawes. *a* **1708** BEVERIDGE *Priv. Th.* II. (1730) 72 St. Paul, who had planted a Church..left him to dress and propagate it.

†**d.** To train or break in (a horse or other animal). *Obs.*

c **1400** *Destr. Troy* 6207 Two dromoudarys drowe hit, dressit þerfore. **1593** SHAKS. *Rich. II*, v. v. 80 That horse, that I so carefully haue drest. *a* **1639** WOTTON in *Reliq. Wotton.* 157 The great horse whom already dressed, no man can more skilfully manage, or better break if rough and furious. **1771** BERENGER *Hist. Horsem.* I. 169 They all having been carefully handled, dressed, or maneged.

e. To groom or curry (a horse).

1530 PALSGR. 528/2 Hosteller, dresse my horse well, and thou shalte have a penny. **1614** MARKHAM *Cheap Husb.* (1623) 61 Dress your horse twice a day, when hee rests, and once when he travels. **1789** MRS. PIOZZI *Journ. France* I. 7 The gentlemen have commonly a good horse under them, but certainly a dressed one. **1870** BLAINE *Encycl. Rur. Sports* 304 It is not only to remove dirt and to make the coat shine that we dress horses, but..to ensure their health.

f. To prepare and finish, as leather; to curry.

1511–12 *Act 3 Hen. VIII*, c. 10 Preamb., Whiche Ledder ..the same persones corye and dresse in theyr owne houses. **1607** TOPSELL *Four-f. Beasts* (1658) 113 The skins of Dogs are dressed for Gloves, and close Boots. **1791** BOSWELL *Johnson* (1831) III. 352, I observed them..dressing sheep-skins. **1837** WHITTOCK *Bk. Trades* (1842) 173 In dressing leather..the first operation on the skins is steeping them until they are thoroughly wetted.

g. To finish (textile fabrics), so as to give them a nap, smooth surface, or gloss.

1513–14 *Act 5 Hen. VIII*, c. 3 Preamb., Marchauntes should be bounden to dresse every white Cloth..on this side the See after they have bought theym. **1530** PALSGR. 528/2, I dresse an olde garment, I rayse the woll of it to make it seme newe agayne. **1570** LEVINS *Manip.* 84/33 To Dresse cloth, *concinnare*. **1879** *Cassell's Techn. Educ.* IV. 235/2 The white cloths..sent to Holland to be dyed and dressed.

h. To cleanse (corn) from chaff and the like.

1635 QUARLES *Embl.* II. x. (1718) 90 Teach me the skill To dress and chuse the corn, take those the chaff that will. **1710** PRIDEAUX *Orig. Tithes* ii. 76 Corn Threshed, Winnowed, and Dressed. **1732** *Acc. Workhouses* 79 Their bread is wheat dressed down. **1851** *Offic. Catal. Gt. Exhib.* I. 371 A machine for dressing grain, being an improved winnowing machine.

i. To prepare (ore) for smelting by the removal of the non-metallic portion.

1753 CHAMBERS *Cycl. Supp.*, *Dressing of ores*; the preparing of them as they come rough from the mine, for the working by fire. **1851** *Offic. Catal. Gt. Exhib.* I. 161 Apparatus used for dressing the inferior copper ores..for dressing the poorer portion of the mineral from the tye.

j. *Type-founding.* To finish (types or lines of type) after casting, by grooving and smoothing them and adjusting their height and alignment.

1683 MOXON *Mech. Exerc.*, *Printing* xxi. ¶2 This pair of Dressing-sticks will serve to Dress Brevier, Long-Primmer, and Pica. **1839** W. NICHOL in T. C. Hansard *Print. & Type-founding* 231 The letters are then set up in a long stick, and again dressed. **1888** *Encycl. Brit.* XXIII. 699/2 The types are then dressed and the picker takes them in hand.

k. *intr.* To weigh (a specified amount) on removal of the skin and offal.

1872 J. G. BOURKE *Jrnl.* 25 Nov. (MS.), A black tailed deer which dressed about..200 lbs. **1895** *Daily News* 12 Sept. 5/5 The sheep..should dress about 75 lbs. each.

II. To direct.

†**14. a.** *trans.* To make straight the course of (a person or thing); to turn or send in some given direction; to direct, guide. (*lit.* and *fig.*) *Obs.*

a **1325** *Prose Psalter* xxiv. [xxv.] 5 Dresce me, Lord, in thy sothenesse. *c* **1374** CHAUCER *Boeth.* IV. pr. vi. 110 (Camb. MS.) God hym self..ordeynyþ and dressyþ alle þinges to goode. **1382** WYCLIF *Num.* xxiv. 1 He..dressynge his chere aȝens the deseert..sawȝ Irael in the tentis dwellynge. *c* **1500** *Melusine* vi. 30 Yf you knowe not the way wel I shall dresse you to it. **1591** FLORIO *2nd Fruites* 75, I had beene wisely drest, if I had playd that Knight.

refl. **1556** *Aurelio & Isab.* (1608) H iij, All her entreprises ..dressethe them all unto the dishoneste parte.

†**b.** To reach or hold forth; to offer. *Obs.*

1382 WYCLIF *Matt.* vii. 9 Who of ȝou is a man, whom ȝif his sone axe breed, wher he shal dresse to hym [**1388** take hym] a stoon? —— *Luke* xxiv. 30 He took bred, and blesside, and brac, and dresside to hem. *c* **1430** LYDG. *Min. Poems* (Percy Soc.) 9 Thes ladies gan her gyftes dresse.

†**15.** *refl.* and *intr.* To direct one's course; to betake oneself, repair; to proceed, move, go. *Obs.*

13.. *Gaw. & Gr. Knt.* 1415 þe douthe dressed to þe wod. *c* **1386** CHAUCER *Clerk's T.* 951 To Grisilde agayn wol I me dresse. **1470–85** MALORY *Arthur* IV. xxviii, They dressyd to gyders and eyther gaf other suche strokes. **1500–20** DUNBAR *Poems* lxxiii. 10 Dress fro desert, draw to thy dwelling-place. **1513** DOUGLAS *Æneis* X. x. 18 Syne baldly..Agane Eneas can Tarquytus dres. **1572** FORREST *Theophilus* 1064 in *Anglia* VII, Unto the busshoppe he dreste him forth.

†**16.** *trans.* To direct (spoken words or a written message) *to* any one; to ADDRESS. *Obs.*

c **1430** LYDG. *Min. Poems* (Percy Soc.) 242 (Mätz.) Hir suster..gan unto me dresse A wooful bille. *c* **1449** PECOCK *Repr.* Prol. 2 These same wordis..bi Seint Poul dressid to Thimothe..mowe weel ynow be..dressid ferthir to ech lay persoon. *c* **1500** *Melusine* ix. 38 A knyght..dressed hys wordes toward her, & said [etc.]. **1664** *Floddan F.* ii. 17 His Letters fast he forth did dress.

dress (drɛs), *sb.* [f. prec. vb.]

†**1.** The act of dressing. *Obs.*

†**a.** A setting 'to rights'; redress.

1565 in Tytler *Hist. Scot.* (1864) III. 404 The Earls.. haue received their dress, and so are in quiet.

†**b.** Conduct (*lit.* and *fig.*).

a **1572** KNOX *Hist. Ref.* Wks. 1846 I. 434 To enter in the dresse of suche affaris. **1583** *Satir. Poems Reform.* xlv. 756

Daylie we may se his dress, When Monseir gaid vnto his mess.

†**c.** The act or fact of attiring or arraying oneself, esp. ornamentally.

1739 G. OGLE *Gualth. & Gris.* 107 Be ever on the Dress, and on the Rove. **1778** MISS BURNEY *Evelina* lxxii, She and Mrs. Selwyn were gone up stairs to finish their dress.

2. a. Personal attire or apparel: orig. that proper to some special rank or order of person, or to some ceremony or function; but, in later use, often merely: Clothing, costume, garb, esp. that part which is external and serves for adornment as well as for covering.

full dress (or, simply, '*dress*'): the more elaborate apparel proper to a public ceremony, a dinner, or an evening party.

1606 SHAKS. *Ant. & Cl.* II. iv. 5 Till I shall see you in your Souldiers dresse. **1660** F. BROOKE tr. *Le Blanc's Trav.* 93 The Merchants weare the Turkish dresse. **1693** *Hum. & Conv. Town* 35 Appeal'd to..in all nice points of Dress. **1748** RICHARDSON *Clarissa* (J.), Full dress creates dignity, augments consciousness, and keeps at distance an encroacher. **1838** DICKENS *Nich. Nick.* xix, Your black silk frock will be quite dress enough. **1856** FROUDE *Hist. Eng.* (1858) I. i. 15 Dress..was then the symbol of rank, prescribed by statute. **1868** *Daily News* 8 Aug., The male dancers were in every variety of costume..none, of course, in anything approaching to 'dress'. *a* **1876** G. DAWSON *Fr. Mem.* (1888) 249 History shows us people in full dress, biography shows them in undress, and diaries show them undressed.

b. With *a* and *pl.*: A suit of garments or a single external garment appropriate to some occasion when adornment is required; now *spec.* a lady's robe or gown made not merely to clothe but also to adorn.

1638 FORD *Fancies* III. iii, Your dresses blab your vanities! **1711** ADDISON *Spect.* No. 69 ¶4 The single Dress of a Woman of Quality is often the Product of a hundred Climates. **1773** GOLDSM. *Stoops to Conq.* II. i, Changing our travelling dresses in the morning. *a* **1821** KEATS *Sonn.* '*Keen fitful gusts*', Lovely Laura in her light green dress. **1857** RUSKIN *Pol. Econ. Art* i. (1868) 74 No good historical painting..can exist, where the dresses of the people of the time are not beautiful. *Mod.* She has had a new silk dress for the occasion.

c. *transf.* An external covering and adornment, as the plumage of birds. **d.** *fig.* The outward form under which anything is presented.

1618 CHAPMAN *Hesiod* II. 412 All the trim and dress Of those still-roaring-noise-resounding seas. **1661** BOYLE *Style of Script.* (1675) 164 Eloquence, the dress of our thoughts. **1713** DERHAM *Phys. Theol.* IV. xii. (R.), Feathers are as commodious a dress to such as fly in the air, to birds, and some insects. **1797** *Monthly Mag.* III. 147 *L'Histoire secrette de la Revolution*, which work will speedily appear in an English dress. **1871** DARWIN *Desc. Man* II. xvi. (1888) 492 The adults [birds] in their winter dress.

3. Technical senses.

†**a.** Dressing of a wound, etc. *Obs.*

1684 tr. *Bonet's Merc. Compit.* III. 76 In about six weeks from the first dress the Skull scaled. **1780** COWPER *Progr. Err.* 299 Her form with dress and lotion they repair.

†**b.** *Arch.* = DRESSING *vbl. sb.* 4 e. *Obs.*

1726 LEONI *Alberti's Archit.* II. 62/2 The Arches must stand quite clear above the water: their dress may be taken from the Ionic or..the Doric Architrave. *Ibid.* 68/1 One principal door with all the dress of the door of a Temple.

c. The arrangement of the furrows upon the surface of a millstone.

1870 *Eng. Mech.* 11 Feb. 535/1 Care must be taken to put the dress [of millstones] in the right way.

d. Finish put upon anything to improve or set off its appearance; e.g. the stiffening of a fabric with starch, glue, size, or the like.

1883 R. HALDANE *Workshop Receipts* Ser. II. 122 Boil or soak [the canvas] for an hour or so in a solution of soda and water to get out the 'dress'.

4. *attrib.* and *Comb.* **a.** Of, for, or pertaining to apparel, or to a woman's dress, as ***dress allowance, -case, -chamber, -cutting, designer, -designing, -goods, -gown, -pattern, -protector, shop, show, -silk, -skirt, -stand***, etc.; **dress agency**, an agency, shop, etc., that buys clothes privately and resells them; **dress-basket**, a travelling case for a woman's dresses; **dress-conscious** *a.*, designating a person who is sensitive and particular about clothes; **dress-form** chiefly *U.S.* (see quot. 1909); **dress-guard**, an appliance fixed to a vehicle or cycle to prevent injury to dress from the wheels; **dress house** (now *rare*), = BROTHEL *sb.* 3; **dress-improver**, a pad, cushion, etc. at one time worn by women, to make the skirt stick out at the back; = BUSTLE *sb.*[2]; **dress length**, a piece of material sufficient to make a dress; **dress-parade, dress parade**, a display of clothes by mannequins (see also sense 4 b); also *fig.*; **dress-preserver**, (*a*) = *dress-shield*; (*b*) 'a leather-covered iron frame extending from the step of a carriage upward over the rim of the wheel, designed to prevent mud or water from being thrown into the carriage' (*Cent. Dict.* Suppl. 1909); **dress reform**, a movement to make dress more practical; so *dress-reformer*; **dress rehearsal**, a rehearsal of a play in costume, esp. the final rehearsal before the first public performance; also *transf.* and *fig.*; (cf. quot. 1793 s.v. DRESSED *ppl. a.*); **dress sense** (see SENSE *sb.*); **dress-shield**, a piece of waterproof or other material fastened under the arms of a woman's bodice to protect it from perspiration; **dress-weight**, (*a*) a small lead weight placed in the hem of a dress, etc.; (*b*) cloth of a weight suitable for making into dresses. **b.** Characterized by, or pertaining to, 'full dress', as † ***dress-box; dress-ball, -boots, -coat*** (whence *dress-coated* adj.), ***cane, cloak, -clothes, -dinner, -glove, -party, -pumps, -shirt, -shoes, -suit, -sword, -uniform***, etc.; **dress-carriage**, a carriage reserved for state or semi-state occasions; **dress-circle**, a circular row of seats in a place of entertainment, the spectators in which were originally expected to be in dress-clothes; in a theatre, usually the gallery next above the floor; **dress-parade, dress parade** *Mil.*, a formal parade in which officers and men wear dress-uniforms; also *fig.*; (see also sense 4 a above). See also DRESS-MAKER, etc.

1931 W. HOLTBY *Poor Caroline* iii. 76 She inspected the garments for sale in a Court *Dress Agency, wondering who wanted to buy tarnished tinsel slippers, and stained georgette frocks. **1965** R. FERGUSON *Woman with Secret* ix. 59 A Belgian woman who ran a dress agency. **1907** A. BENNETT *Grim Smile of Five Towns* 83 A woman who had a generous *dress allowance. **1967** *Guardian* 16 Oct. 4/3 A girl ..who used two years' dress allowance to buy a pony. **1806–7** J. BERESFORD *Miseries Hum. Life* (1826) XIV. xliii, A *Dress-ball—alias a public parade of finery, dullness, and etiquette. **1894** *Country Gentlemen's Catal.* 152 Solid leather portmanteaux, ladies' *dress baskets. **1911** 'K. MANSFIELD' *German Pension* 43 A dress-basket neatly covered in a black tarpaulin. **1812** *Dramatic Censor for 1811* Feb. 99/1 The space now alloted to the *basket* to be one entire anti-room to the *dress-boxes. **1849** DICKENS *Dav. Copp.* xxiv. 383 We resolved to go downstairs to the dress-boxes. **1836** —— *Sk. Boz* I. 303 George..carried a *dress cane. **1897** *Daily News* 8 Feb. 5/4 Many of these are what one might call semi-state carriages, but are known as *Dress Carriages. **1897** *Westm. Gaz.* 9 Dec. 3/2 The travelling '*dress-case' that combines dressing-bag and trunk. **1899** *Ibid.* 3 Aug. 3/2 These..low broad dress-cases, that, if necessary, can go under a railway carriage seat. **1825** *News* 30 Jan. 36/1 In the *dress circle there was not one lady. **1845** MRS. CARLYLE *Lett.* I. 341, I kept my seat in the dress circle. **1885** E. SHERIDAN *Let.* 10 July in *Jrnl.* (1960) ii. 62 She was examining my *dress cloak and ask'd whether I thought it fit to *dance* in. **1890** C. M. YONGE *More Bywords* 161 She ran to fetch her dress cloak for Jane. **1814** C. S. M. BURY *Diary* 21 May (1838) I. 312 All the gentlemen..looked beautiful in their *dress clothes. **1831** JANE PORTER *Sir E. Seaward's Narr.* II. 201 That our dress-clothes should be brought home in time. **1929** WODEHOUSE *Mr. Mulliner Speaking* 258 He was prepared to stand or fall by his dress-clothes. **1959** N. MAILER *Advts. for Myself* (1961) 117 He was changing into his dress clothes by the time I followed him to the dormitory. **1767** J. HABERSHAM *Lett.* (1904) 61, I want a *dress Coat. **1819** M. WILMOT *Let.* 17 Dec. (1935) 40 Servants dress'd in rich embroidered dress coats. **1858** HAWTHORNE *Fr. & It. Jrnls.* II. 138 Dress-coats, and such elegant formalities. **1836–9** DICKENS *Sk. Boz, New Year*, As if we were duly *dress-coated and pumped. **1918** 'ALPHA OF THE PLOUGH' *Leaves in Wind* 146 He is as *dress-conscious as a milliner. **1958** *Spectator* 31 Jan. 130/3 Why is the bowler hat regarded by one whole class of very dress-conscious young men as untouchable? **1889** *Daily News* 18 July 3/5 Mr. J. C. Horsley, R.A., afterwards addressed the students on *dress-cutting. **1901** *Westm. Gaz.* 12 June 3/2 The tendency of the *dress designer is just now to study old pictures and prints. **1903** *Ibid.* 31 Dec. 3/1 *Dress-designing was never in a more advanced stage of development than now. **1856** EMERSON *Eng. Traits, Manners* Wks. (Bohn) II. 51 The *dress-dinner generates a talent of table-talk. **1893** *T. Eaton & Co. Catal.* Spring & Summer 97/2 Hall's patent *dress forms. **1909** *Cent. Dict.* Suppl., *Dress-form*, a frame, sometimes of wire, in the form of a woman, used in making dresses. **1916** L. I. BALDT *Clothing for Women* viii. 162 For the purpose of designing, it will be necessary to have a dress form, on which a close-fitting lining previously fitted to the person for whom the garments are to be designed, has been placed. **1836** DICKENS *Sk. Boz* II. 274 A strange chaos of *dress-gloves, boxing-gloves, caricatures, albums. **1818** SCOTT *Hrt. Midl.* xxxvii, Damage..to *dress-gowns, in consequence of its [a spaniel's] untimely frolics. **1895** *Westm. Gaz.* 3 Sept. 8/1 [A] skirt..short enough to clear cranks and pedals when the cyclist is seated, and make *dress-guards unnecessary. **1823** *Dress-house [see *accommodation house*]. **1870** W. ACTON *Prostitution* (ed. 2) ii. 9 The description of brothels called dress houses was much more prevalent a few years ago than..at present. *Ibid.* 13 The keepers of the old dress houses were mostly females of extreme avarice. **1872** *Young Englishwoman* Oct. 548 (*caption*) Horsehair *dress improver. **1884** G. MOORE *Mummer's Wife* (1887) 228 The skirts swung on the dress-improvers. **1873** *Young Englishwoman* Apr. 202/1 A *dress length of 8 metres of the best quality costs 58 francs. **1889** *Young Ladies' Jrnl.* 1 Jan. 21/1 (Advt.), A full dress-length of beautiful cloth. **1907** *Daily Chron.* 16 May 5/7 The wife of a native chief who was given a dress length by Lord Kitchener. **1847** *Army Regulations* (U.S.) 91 All company-officers and men will be present at *dress-parades. **1870** L. M. ALCOTT *Old-Fashioned Girl* xvi. 271 The dress-parade is over, and I'm ever so much obliged to you..for..showing me how to make the best of things. **1873** HOLLAND *A. Bonnic.* xiii. 210 A sort of dress parade of mediocrity. **1948** S. GILBERT tr. *Camus's Plague* II. vi. 116 Daily, round about eleven, you see a sort of dress parade of youths and girls. **1960** *Times* 14 Sept. 12/6 We were.. bundled off to a dress parade, my wife agog for the latest fashions... However, we found ourselves deposited in front of the local military academy just in time for their annual inspection. **1825** H. WILSON *Mem.* III. 386 He is going to the Duke of Devonshire's *dress party. **1844** *Lexington* (Ky.) *Observer* 25 Sept. 1/3 Just received..striped Chusans, in *dress patterns. **1895** *Chicago Tribune* 6 Apr. 1 An Eton dress pattern for 10 cents is displayed on page 16. **1907** *Yesterday's Shopping* (1969) 840/2 *Dress Preservers. **1931** J. CANNAN *High Table* xvii. 251 Mrs. Logan, already so hot that she couldn't think why dress preservers had gone out of fashion. **1951** M. KENNEDY *Lucy Carmichael* I. v. 35 Have you sewed in dress preservers?.. You know how you perspire. **1864** *Rep. Comm. Pat. 1862* (U.S.) I. 506 **Dress protector*... This article is intended for the use of infants, to protect their clothes and the dresses of their nurses. **1897** H. G. WELLS *Plattner Story* 241 Little purchases:..dress-protectors, tape, and a pair of Lisle hose. **1876** *N.Y. Tribune* 28 Sept., No man can involuntarily throw one leg over the other without a shortening of what the recent *Dress Reform convention calls the garmenture. **1889** *Kansas Times & Star* 16 Mar., Anna Jenness Miller's dress reform disciples now number about 400 here. *Ibid.* 7 Mar., Mrs. Jenness Miller, *dress reformer, is back in New York from her Western lecture tour. **1828** J. EBERS 7 *Yrs. of King's Theatre* iv. 81 On the preceding evening, a *dress rehearsal was given. **1854** A. C. MOWATT *Autobiogr. of Actress* 134 The night before that on which the play was to take place we had a dress rehearsal. **1897** *Encycl. Sport* I. 563/2 After several undress and dress rehearsals the master may venture to ask a field to meet him. **1917** *Strand Mag.* Dec. 538/1 If you'll have one dress rehearsal, I'll promise to leave you in peace for the duration of the war. **1925** *Surv. Internat. Affairs 1920–23* I. 46 The work of the Brussels Conference ..served as a 'dress rehearsal' for the First Session of the Assembly of the League of Nations. **1963** *Times* 24 May 5/1 Green's play had a slightly dress-rehearsal look about it. **1926** E. GLYN *Love's Blindness* iii. 37 She had, naturally, that *dress sense,—that perception of chic. **1943** G. BATTISCOMBE *C. M. Yonge* viii. 101 Most women..have some rudimentary feeling for dress, but Charlotte was born without dress-sense. **1884** *Queen* 9 Feb. (Advt.), You have just ruined that new dress under the arms because you did not have a Canfield *Dress Shield. **1890** *Ladies' Home Jrnl.* June 18/4 The Canfield Seamless Dress Shield. **1905** *Daily News* 26 Sept. 5/1 Sewn on the inside of the bodice were two rubber dress-shields. **1892** *Harper's Mag.* Dec. 159 Maybe it's a *dress-shirt shield. **1806** in *Doc. Hist. Amer. Industr. Soc.* III. 73, I had not long worked for him before I got on to light *dress-shoes. **1828** J. EBERS 7 *Yrs. of King's Theatre* 294 Drab pantaloons..and dress shoes. **1930** E. WAUGH *Labels* vii. 171 The *dress shops..were advertising their end of the season sales. **1971** C. WHITMAN *Death Suspended* v. 94 Neville was in advertising and Isobel ran a dress shop. **1930** *London Mercury* Feb. 320 They had had to cancel two fittings and three *dress shows. **1965** A. CHRISTIE *At Bertram's Hotel* xii. 113 The idea of patronising a dress show of any kind would not even have occurred to her. **1904** M. CORELLI *God's Good Man* 337 She had a figure which was the envy of all modellers of *dress stands. **1912** *Cassell's Penny Bk. Dressmaking* 6/1 The Dress-Stand.—There is one accessory which all home dress-makers should endeavour to procure, i.e. a padded dress-stand... Adjustable models.. are obtainable that will screw and unscrew, upon which garments may be fitted for various figures. **1806–7** J. BERESFORD *Miseries Hum. Life* (1826) XX. xlviii, A *dress-suit of clothes for a grand occasion. **1833** R. DYER 9 *Yrs. of Actor's Life* vii. 112 Presenting me with a *dress sword, with an inscription expressive of their regard. **1894** C. N. ROBINSON *Brit. Fleet* 509 Physicians and secretaries wore a dress sword with rapier blade. **1899** in A. Adburgham *Shops & Shopping* (1964) xxii. 261 *Dress weights. **1939–40** *Army & Navy Stores Catal.* 637/2 An all wool dress weight fabric. **1950** H. MCCLOY *Through Glass Darkly* (1951) iii. 25 The lead dress-weights our grandmothers wore in the hems of their long skirts. **1959** *Times* 12 Jan. 11/5 Range of Terylene and cotton mixtures..used at present for lingerie..and dress-weights.

dressage ('drɛsɑːʒ). [Fr., lit. 'training', f. *dresser* to train, drill.] The training of a horse in obedience and deportment; the execution by a horse of precise movements in response to its rider. Also *attrib.* and *fig.*

1936 *Field* 24 Oct. 1015/2 In recent years there has been considerable interest shown in the training and dressage of hacks..as witnessed in the complicated dressage test held at the recent Olympic Games. **1938** *Times* 17 May 8/7 The first international dressage tests to be held in this country will form one of the principal features of the International Horse Show. **1957** *Times* 14 Oct. 4/5 Miss Willcox and High and Mighty..duly won the open event with a dressage of 95·66. **1962** R. S. SUMMERHAYS *Elem. Riding* (ed. 4) xxvi. 145 Dressage is a series of well-defined phases or exercises in the training of a horse. **1963** *Times* 22 Apr. 8/5 Mr. Harold Wilson's Lloyd-Georgian deftness in all problems of party dressage.

dressed, drest (drɛst), *ppl. a.* [f. DRESS *v.* + -ED[1].] †Straightened (*obs.*); prepared; clothed, attired, etc. (also with *up*): see the verb.

1382 WYCLIF *Luke* iii. 5 Schrewide thingis schulen be in to dressid thingis. **1526** *Pilgr. Perf.* (W. de W. 1531) 99 Delycates or deynty dressed meates. **1612** W. STRACHEY *Virginia* (1849) II. 184/1 Apron or any kind of dressed leather. **1775** ADAIR *Amer. Ind.* 7 Shirts, made of drest deer-skins. **1793** J. WILLIAMS *Life Ld. Barrymore* (ed. 3) 20 We had a dressed rehearsal. **1798, 1815** [see UNDRESSED *ppl. a.* 8 b, 7]. **1851** *Offic. Catal. Gt. Exhib.* I. 130 Specimens of dressed oilstones. **1862** G. BORROW *Wild Wales* I. ix. 92 Whenever I go to Chester, and a dressedup madam jostles against me, I shall call her carn-butein. **1870** 'MARK TWAIN' *Sk. New & Old* (1875) 244 He murdered them 'in his splendid dresssed-stone mansion'. **1891** R. WALLACE *Rural Econ. Austral. & N.Z.* ii. 54 The best dressed mutton..was selling at 2½*d.* to 2¾*d.* per lb. **1906** L. STANFIELD (*song title*) All dressed up like a hippodrome horse. **1908–9** *T. Eaton & Co. Catal.* Fall & Winter 310/1 Fine dressed dolls, beautifully dressed. **1912** G. WHITING (*song title*) When you're all dressed up and have no place to go. **1940** W. SHEWRING *Topics* ix. 100 Isocrates and Demosthenes..are types of the pretentious bad artist—'all dressed up and nowhere to go'. **1963** 'HAN SUYIN' *Four Faces* 54 She bent to smile at the dressed total face in the mirror. **1971** *Timber Trades Jrnl.* 21 Aug. 16/1 Prior to adoption of the new standards sizes for dressed lumber have been the same regardless of the moisture content.

dresser[1] ('drɛsə(r)) Also 5 -ore, -ur(e, 5–6 -our(e, 7 -oir. [a. OF. *dresseur, dreceur, dreçor* (= mod.F. *dressoir*), f. *dresser* to DRESS: cf. med.L. *dīrectōrium* 'abacus, ministerium, ubi reponuntur vasa ad convivia' (Du Cange).]

1. a. A sideboard or table in a kitchen on which food is or was dressed; formerly also, a table in a dining-room or hall, from which dishes were served, or on which plate was displayed.

c **1420** *Liber Cocorum* (1862) 20 Powder dowce þeron þou kast Stondande at dressore on þe last. **15..** in Blount *Anc. Tenures* 100 Upon Chrystemes day he..shall go to the Dressour, and shall serve his Lordys messe. **1525** LD. BERNERS *Froiss* II. ccxxvii. [ccxxiii.] 710 All the..plate of golde and syluer that was serued..in the palays at the dresser or elswhere. **1562** LEIGH *Armorie* (1597) 123 b, What meaneth this drumme, said I. Quod he, this is to warn gentlemen of houshold to repaire to the dresser. **1596** SHAKS. *Tam. Shr.* IV. i. 166. **1608** S. HIERON *A Defence* III. 32 A dressoir whereon to marshall the dishes. **1719** DE FOE *Crusoe* I. v, I..set up some Pieces of Boards, like a Dresser, to order my Victuals upon.

b. A dressing- or toilet-table; a bureau. *N. Amer.*

1895 *Montgomery Ward Catal.* 605/1 Dresser, well made, of hardwood... Has a good 20 × 24 German beveled mirror and 3 large drawers. **1900** F. R. STOCKTON *Afield & Afloat* 263 'There,' said he, opening a dresser drawer. **1906** 'O. HENRY' *Four Million* 180 Dulcie took a last look at the pictures on the dresser..and skipped into bed. **1924** H. CROY *R.F.D. No. 3* 103 She bent over the 'dresser' to examine herself in the mirror. **1927** M. DE LA ROCHE *Jalna* xiv. 159 The tiny light of the candle, reflected in the mirror on the dresser, only faintly illuminated their faces. **1968** *Globe & Mail* (Toronto) 3 Feb. 12 (Advt.), Triple Dresser. .. $280. **1970** S. ELLIN *Man from Nowhere* iii. 13 Just tell me which dresser you want.

2. A kind of kitchen sideboard surmounted by rows of shelves on which plates, dishes, and kitchen utensils are ranged.

1552 HULOET, Cupborde or dresser, *abacus*. **1702** C. MATHER *Magn. Chr.* IV. ii. (1852) 47 It should not be fasten'd unto the wall, dresser-fashion. **1859** JEPHSON *Brittany* x. 171 The dressers were covered with brilliant copper..vessels. **1882** *Good Cheer* 48 The old black dresser with its row of shining pewter at the top.

†**3.** ? A table-cloth. *Obs. rare.*

1571 *Wills & Inv. N.C.* 360, J dresser of dyaper js.

4. *Comb.*, as †*dresser-window*; †**dresser-board**, the board or table of a dresser; †**dresser-knife**, a knife for dressing meat for the table.

14.. *Voc.* in Wr.-Wülcker 580/41 *Escaria*, dresserbord. *Ibid.* 594/15 *Machera*, a dressurcnyf. **1593** *Rites & Mon. Ch. Durh.* (Surtees) 69 Having their meat served out of the Dresser-windowe of the great Kitchen. **1676** HOBBES *Iliad* (1677) 126 The meat..on clean dresser-boards..he sets.

'dresser[2]. [f. DRESS *v.* + -ER[1].] One who or that which dresses.

1. a. One who dresses (in various special and technical senses: see DRESS *v.* 13, etc.).

1520 WHITTINTON *Vulg.* (1527) 16 b, Shermen, dressers, carders and spynners. **1526–34** TINDALE *Luke* xiii. 7 The dresser of his vyneyarde. **1583** STUBBES *Anat. Abus.* II. (1882) 36 There is great abuse in the tanners, makers, curriers, and dressers of the same [leather]. **1819** *Blackw. Mag.* V. 125 The most elegant dresser of a fly in Scotland. **1865** J. T. F. TURNER *Slate Quarries* 14 These sheets of slate are then passed to the 'dressers' or cutters.

b. *Type-founding.* An operative who finishes type after casting.

1683 MOXON *Mech. Exerc., Printing* xxi. 187 The Letter Dresser hath..his Letters Set up in Composing sticks. **1846** DODD *Brit. Manufacturers* VI. 45 The long frame, filled with a single line of type, is removed to the dresser. **1888** *Encycl. Brit.* XXIII. 699/2 The dresser..slips them into a long stick..and..cuts with a plane a groove in the bottom.

2. a. One who attires another; *esp.* a tirewoman.

a **1625** FLETCHER *Bloody Brother* IV. iii, I'le be my self thy dresser. **1631** MASSINGER *Emperor East* II. i, Command my dresser to adorn her with The robes that I gave command for. **1711** SWIFT *Jrnl. to Stella* 18 Sept., I chose to dine with Mrs. Hill, who is one of the dressers, and Mrs. Masham's sister. **1884** *Mem. P'cess Alice* 8 A former dresser of the Queen's.

b. *Theatr.* One who helps to dress an actor or actress (see quot. 1870).

1844 J. COWELL *30 Yrs. among Players* II. xii. 81/2 The domestic paraphernalia of the housekeeper and ladies'-dresser. **1851** W. K. NORTHALL *Before & Behind Curtain* 117 Carpenters, scene-shifters, gas-men, dressers and super-numeraries, all partook of the general joy. **1870** O. LOGAN *Before Footlights* 77 All theatres of any importance have 'dressers'. These help the players in change of dress, and fold up and put away their stage clothing after the piece is over. **1914** G. K. CHESTERTON *Wisdom of Father Brown* iv. 83 An aged servant or 'dresser', whose broken-down face and figure..contrasted queerly with the glittering interior of the great actress's dressing-room. **1970** K. GILES *Death in Church* v. 148 Her dresser had very pleasant memories of good Sergeant Honeybody.

3. One who attires himself (or herself) elegantly, or in any way defined by the context.

1679 CROWNE *Ambit. Statesm.* 11, He is no dresser, do but see how awkardly His damn'd crevat is tyed. **1778** MRS. THRALE in Mad. D'Arblay *Diary* 23 Aug., I don't think Mrs. Burney a very good dresser. **1837** LYTTON *E. Maltrav.* 49 The most perfect dresser that even France could exhibit. *a* **1847** MRS. SHERWOOD *Lady of Manor* III. xxi. 264 Of all the dressers I ever saw, she is the worst.

4. A surgeon's assistant in a hospital, etc., whose duty it is to dress wounds, etc.

1747 (July) *Minutes of Grand Committee St. Thomas's Hospital* (MS.), An application was made to this Committee to receive a young man as 'Pupil or Dresser' in the Hospital. **1758** (March) *Ibid.* Resolved and ordered that for the future no Surgeon, Pupil, or Dresser, be in the Wards after One o'Clock. **1861** WYNTER *Soc. Bees, George & Dragon* 60 Dressers waiting for the surgeons to make their daily round of the wards.

5. *Mil.* (See quot. 1823.)

1796 *Instr. & Reg. Cavalry* (1813) 11 Every dresser of a body in a given line, must in his own person be placed on that line, while he is directing such operation. **1823** CRABB *Technol. Dict., Dressers (Mil.)* those men who take up direct or relative points, by which a corps is enabled to preserve a regular continuity of front. **1847** *Infantry Man.* (1854) 19 On the word *March*, the dressers front, and the rear rank steps back one pace, dressing by the right.

6. Various appliances used in 'dressing' or preparing things.

a. A shoemaker's tool. **b.** A plumber's mallet to smooth down joinings in lead, etc. **c.** *Tanning*: see quot. 1853. **d.** *Coal-mining*: see quot. 1881. **e.** An apparatus for dressing corn; a winnowing machine. **f.** A tool or machine for cutting and dressing the furrows on a mill-stone. **g.** A machine for cutting and shaping geological specimens or minerals.

1600 DEKKER *Gent. Craft* iv. (1862) 15 You skoomaker, have you all your tools..a good dresser, your four sorts of awls? **1688** R. HOLME *Armoury* III. 326/1 A Plummers Dresser..a Bat of Wood made with a handle, flat at the bottom, and rounded off at the top-side. **1703** T. N. *City & C. Purchaser* 192 Having roll'd open 2 Sheets, they beat them flat with their Dresser. **1853** C. MORFIT *Tanning, etc.* 468 They [skins] are then worked with the round-knife upon the dresser..a cylindrical wooden bar fastened at a height of five feet three inches from the ground, by its two ends, to two buttresses projecting from the wall. **1881** RAYMOND *Mining Gloss., Dresser*, a large pick, with which the largest lumps of coal are prepared for loading into the skip. *S. Staffords.* **1884** *Bath Herald* 27 Dec. 6/5 After being carried through certain apparatus called detachers, the wheat passes through centrifugal dressers.

Hence **'dressership**, office of surgical dresser.

1869 *Lancet* 391/1 Certain of the dresserships..are appointed from the most diligent students.

'dressing, *vbl. sb.* [f. DRESS *v.* + -ING[1].]

1. a. The action of the vb. DRESS, in various senses.

c **1440** *Promp. Parv.* 131/2 Dressynge, *directio*. **1526** *Pilgr. Perf.* (W. de W. 1531) 201 b, The spouse..hath many women to adorne and dresse her, and yet she werketh with them to her owne dressynge. **1617** HIERON *Wks.* II. 207 One stroke may cause it [a wound], but many stirrings and dressings cannot cure it. **1712** J. JAMES tr. *Le Blond's Gardening* 105 The Words Dressing, Leveling..signify the Action of harrowing or raking the Ground, to lay it every where smooth and eaven. **1832** *Regul. Instr. Cavalry* II. 6 Dressing is a progressive operation..by which any number of men are correctly aligned. **1862** MRS. CARLYLE *Lett.* III. 101 There is no elaborate dressing for dinner here.

b. *dressing up* (see DRESS *v.* 7 d); also *attrib.*

1852 C. M. YONGE *Two Guardians* xiii. 229 What difference can my dressing up..make to any one? **1864** MRS. GASKELL *Wives & Daughters* (1866) I. xiii. 152 Molly had a private dressing-up for the Miss Brownings' benefit. **1868** L. M. ALCOTT *Little Women* 14 Meg..was as much a child as ever about 'dressing-up' frolics. **1944** M. PANETH *Branch Street* 92 We got hold of a big box full of old dressing-up material. **1950** A. WILSON *Such Darling Dodos* 130 The strange old hats and frocks in the dressing-up box in the nursery. **1957** R. HOGGART *Uses of Literacy* ii. 58 The game of dressing-up—trailing round the streets in grown-ups' cast-off clothes. **1964** D. GRAY *Devil wore Scarlet* xi. 105 A huge trunk, which was evidently the 'dressing-up' box. It was filled with old clothes of every sort. **1968** P. DICKINSON *Skin Deep* vii. 142 A good old-fashioned attic, where people have been putting things..to get them out of the way, old wickerwork cots and dressing-up clothes and iron bedsteads.

c. *Mil.* Proper alignment of troops. Cf. DRESS *v.* 4.

1792 [see ATTENTION 5]. **1802** C. JAMES *Mil. Dict.* s.v., Dressing of a battalion after the halt, is to bring all its relative parts in a line with the point..towards which it was directed to move. **1889** *Infantry Drill* I. 9 He will take up his dressing in line by moving..till he is just able to distinguish the lower part of the face of the second man beyond him. **1966** *Listener* 3 Mar. 317/3 'Come on, wake up. Get your dressing.' The familiar barks jerked their limbs into making the mechanical actions.

2. Applied to various technical processes in arts and manufactures. See quots. and the vb.

1540 HYRDE *Vives' Instr. Chr. Wom.* I. ii. (R.), The dressing of wooll hath beene euer an honest occupation for a good woman. **1611** COTGR., *Affilement*..a dressing, or stiffening with wire. **1698** FRYER *Acc. E. India & P.* 264 Hides and Leather..of their own dressing. **1745** *Gentl. Mag.* 24 A new composition for careening or dressing of ships, to preserve them from the Worms. **1792** A. YOUNG *Trav. France* 341 The corn of England, as far as respects *dressing*, that is cleaning from dirt, chaff, seeds of weeds, &c. is as much better than that of France. **1822** J. FLINT *Lett. Amer.* 7 Washing and dressing of shirts, neckcloths, &c.

3. *ironically.* A drubbing, a beating; chastisement, castigation, by blows or words. Also with *down* (see DRESS *v.* 9).

1769 in *10th Rep. Hist. MS. Comm.* App. i. 413 For this he got a very severe dressing from Ld. North. **1809** MALKIN tr. *Gil Blas* v. i. (Rtldg.) 191 His fingers itched to give me another dressing. **1854** A. FONBLANQUE in *Life* vi. (1874) 511 If our Generals do not give the enemy a dressing. **1860** THACKERAY *Round. Papers, Screens in Din. Rooms* (1876) 57 A criticism..in which an Irish writer had given me a dressing for a certain lecture on Swift. **1876** *Coursing Cal.* 223 Blucher was much faster in the stretches than Folly, who got a genuine dressing down. **1893** W. K. POST *Harvard Stories* 70 The poor man got such a dressing down that Randolph presented him with full forgiveness. **1925** E. F. NORTON *Fight for Everest, 1924* 21 The following morning, when they were coming up for a second dressing I thought I would add a little dressing down on my own account. **1956** A. L. ROWSE *Early Churchills* iv. 73 Sir Winston..gave Captain Thornhill a dressing down in open court.

4. *concretely.* That which is used in the preceding actions and processes; that with which any thing or person is dressed for use or ornament: e.g.

a. *Cookery.* The seasoning substance used in cooking; stuffing; the sauce, etc., used in preparing a dish, a salad, etc. **b.** Personal decorations; vestments, dress; trimming. **c.** *Agric.* The manure or compost spread over or ploughed into land in preparing it for a crop. **d.** *Surg.* The remedies, bandages, etc. with which a wound or sore is dressed. **e.** *Arch.* Projecting mouldings on a surface. **f.** Glaze, size, or stiffening, used in the 'finishing' of textile fabrics; etc.

a. 1504 *Nottingham Rec.* III. 319 For floure and peper, and dressing. **1853** SOYER *Pantroph.* 75 Lettuces may also be eaten with a dressing of gravy and pickles.

b. 1622 MABBE tr. *Aleman's Guzman d'Alf.* I. 26 Shee.. would..put on her dressings, and weare her attire. **1626** T. H[AWKINS] *Caussin's Holy Crt.* 11 One piece of her gaudy dressings. **1861** HUGHES *Tom Brown at Oxf.* vi, Tom began ..scrutinizing the dressings of the flies [for fishing]. **1881** BESANT & RICE *Chapl. of Fleet* I. iii, Trees..in their beautiful spring dressing.

c. *c* **1735** BERKELEY *Querist* §199 Wks. 1871 III. 371 Vegetables..ploughed in for a dressing of land. **1816** *Act 56 Geo. III*, c. 50 §11 Any Manure, Compost, Ashes, Sea-weed, or other Dressings intended for such Lands.

d. 1713 PARNELL *Guardian* No. 66 ¶2 To tear off the dressings, as I may say, from the wounds. **1861** HULME tr. *Moquin-Tandon* II. III. iii. 95 Dressings for blisters.

e. 1823 P. NICHOLSON *Pract. Build.* 584 *Dressings*, all mouldings projecting beyond the naked of walls and ceilings. **1843** in Willis & Clark *Cambridge* (1886) III. 214 The dressings round them [doors] to be of scagliola.

f. 1823 J. BADCOCK *Dom. Amusem.* 72 The dressing thereof [sail-cloth], being a compound of meal and lime. **1853** C. MORFIT *Tanning, etc.* 181 The hides..are put through the dressings, that is, subjected to the action of fermentable barley water.

5. *attrib.* and *Comb.* **a.** Employed in or connected with attiring the person, as ***dressing-bag***, ***-basket***, ***-block***, ***-boy***, ***-chair***, ***-closet***, ***-cloth***, ***-glass***, ***-jacket***, ***-maid***, ***-robe***; **dressing-bell**, **-gong**, one rung as the signal for dressing for dinner; **dressing-comb**, a comb used for dressing (see DRESS *v.* 13 b) the hair; †**dressing-plate**, silver toilet service (*obs.*); **dressing-sack** (*U.S.*), a dressing-jacket. Also DRESSING-BOX, -ROOM, -TABLE, etc. **b.** Pertaining to, or appropriated to, the treatment of various articles, as ***dressing-machine***, ***-shed***, ***-shop***; **dressing-bench**, **-floors**: see quots.; **dressing-forceps**, forceps used in applying and removing surgical dressings; **dressing-house**, a house for dressing ore; **dressing-station**, a place at which wounds are dressed. **c.** Used in preparing food: see DRESSING-BOARD, -KNIFE. **d.** For 'dressing', as ***dressing hide***, ***leather***, ***wheat***.

1865 TROLLOPE *Belton Est.* vii. 75 He..packed his coats, and *dressing-bag, and desk. **1849** MARRYAT *Valerie* xii, The *dressing-bell has rung. **1874** KNIGHT *Dict. Mech.*, **Dressing-bench*, a bricklayer's bench having a cast-iron plate on which the sun-dried brick is rubbed, polished, and beaten with a paddle to make it symmetrical. **1632** FIELD & MASSINGER *Fatal Dowry* II. ii, His *dressing-block, upon whom my lord lays all his clothes..ere he vouchsafes them his own person. **1712** STEELE *Spect.* No. 478 ¶13 A looking-glass and a *dressing chair. **1668** DAVENANT *Man's the Master* Wks. (1673) 332 Whether she be some Skeleton whose Beauties lye at night upon her *dressing-cloth. **1790** *Pennsylvania Packet* 19 Apr. 4/2 John Murduck..has likewise for Sale..*Dressing, rake, and tail combs. **1881** C. C. HARRISON *Woman's Handiwork* I. 57 Crewels..combed into fluffiness by a coarse dressing-comb. **1894** *Labour Commission* Gloss., A **dressing-floors* (not floor) is a surface works where the tin stuff as it comes from the shaft of the mine is first subjected to various crushing processes..and then 'washed'..in order that the tin may be separated from alien matter. **1826** A. C. HUTCHISON *Pract. Obs. Surg.* (ed. 2) 180 By dilating the meatus urinarius with a common pair of *dressing forceps. **1879** *St. George's Hosp. Rep.* IX. 772 Passing a pair of dressing-forceps through the joint to the lowest part of its outer aspect. **1714** *Lond. Gaz.* No. 5214/3 *Dressing Glasses, Union Suits, Dressing Boxes. **1823** J. BADCOCK *Dom. Amusem.* 121 Look for yourself in a mirror, or dressing glass. **1872** *Rep. Vermont Board Agric.* 628 The same track takes it [*sc.* the ore] to the *dressing house at the foot of the hill. **1855** MISS MANNING *Old Chelsea Bun-House* xiv. 239 Prue, in her *Dressing-Jacket. **1895** *Times* 2 Jan. 13/4 Light English sole and *dressing leather. **1795** *Hull Advertiser* 5 Sept. 2/1 Thrashing and *Dressing Machines. **1822** W. IRVING *Braceb. Hall* (1845) 29 Having been *dressing-maid..to the late Mrs. Bracebridge. **1716** LADY M. W. MONTAGU *Lett.* 16 Aug. (1887) I. 107, I had wickedness enough to covet St. Ursula's pearl necklaces.. and wished she herself converted into *dressing-plate. **1884** *Health Exhib. Catal.* 38 A *dressing shed, where the work of unhairing the skins takes place. **1894** SIR E. WOOD in *Daily News* 1 Oct. 6/2 The farm used by the doctors as a *dressing-station. **1915** A. D. GILLESPIE *Let.* 21 Mar. in *Lett. from Flanders* (1916) 61 A man who gets hit, not dangerously, with a dressing station handy, and a doctor to attend to him at once. **1709** *Wakes Colne (Essex) Overseer's Acc.* (MS.), 3 peckes of *dressinge wheat.

e. *Printing* (see DRESS *v.* 3 b): ***dressing-bench***, ***-block***, ***-hook***. **f.** *Type-founding* (see DRESS *v.* 13 j): ***dressing machine***, ***plane***, ***stick***.

1683 MOXON *Mech. Exerc., Printing* xix. 183 The Dressing-Bench. *Ibid.* ix. 31 The Dressing-Block..is to run over the Face of the Form, and..to be gently knock't upon

.., that such Letters as may chance to stand up higher than the rest may be pressed down. *Ibid.* xx. 184 The Dressing-Hook. **1888** *Encycl. Brit.* XXIII. 699/2 A machine, which produces types that do not require rubbing or dressing... The casting machine and the dressing machine are.. mounted on a common frame... The letters pass through a channel one by one into the dressing machine. **1695** in H. Hart *Century of Typography* (1900) 55 Utensils for Printing. 4 Dressing Planes. 3 Dressing Blocks. **1683** Dressing-stick [see DRESS *v.* 13j].

† **'dressing-board.** *Obs.* A board on which anything is dressed; esp. a board on which food was dressed; a dresser.

c **1440** *Promp. Parv.* 131/2 Dressure, or dressynge boorde, *Dressorium, directarium.* **1591** PERCIVALL *Sp. Dict.*, *Tajon*, a boord to cut flesh on, a dressing boord. **1694** *Acc. Sev. Late Voy.* II. (1711) 172 Puts it [the whale's fat] upon the Bench or Dressing board, where it is cut by others into less pieces. ? *a* **1700** *Sir Hugh* in Percy *Reliq.* (1765) I. 32 Scho laid him on a dressing-borde [*other versions* dressing-table, dresser-board (cf. Child *Ballads* v. 246).]

'dressing-box. = next.

1663 DRYDEN *Wild Gallant* III. ii, A fine-bred woman, with a lute, and a dressing-box. **1714** [see DRESSING 5]. **1830** MISS MITFORD *Village* Ser. IV. (1863) 181 He sports a dressing-box.. full of almond paste and violet soap.

'dressing-case. A case of toilet utensils.

1790 *Pennsylvania Packet* 10 May 4/3 A few curious morocco dressing cases for gentlemen and ladies. **1819** *P.O. Lond. Direct.* 18 Ladies and Gentlemen's Dressing-case Manufacturer. **1922** J. M. MURRY *Things we Are* 81 He wanted to know about the dressing-case; what colour it was, even, and how many bottles it contained. **1939-40** *Army & Navy Stores Catal.* 877/2 Dressing Case, in Morocco leather.

'dressing-gown. A loose gown worn while making one's toilet or when in dishabille.

1777 SHERIDAN *Trip Scarb.* I. ii, Enter Lord Foppington in his dressing-gown. **1847** MRS. CARLYLE *Lett.* II. 3, I was sitting at breakfast in my dressing-gown. **1896** 'IOTA' *Quaker Grandmother* xxiv. 280 She put the key into her dressing-gown pocket. **1909** *Granta* 11 June, I rose, put on a dressing-gown.. and went upstairs. **1971** 'E. FERRARS' *Stranger & Afraid* x. 154 She's had a habit for years of getting up quietly and going wandering about the house in her dressing-gown.

Hence **dressing-gowned** *ppl. a.*

1855 DICKENS *Dorrit* (Househ. ed.) 315/1 Mr. Dorrit, dressing-gowned and newspapered.

'dressing-knife. †**a.** A knife used in dressing food. *Obs.* **b.** A blade with two handles used in leather-dressing. Hence † ***dressing-knife-board.***

1411 *Nottingham Rec.* II. 86, j. dressyngknyf, ij d. *c* **1425** *Thomas of Erceld.* 266 (Cott. MS.) Cokes come with dryssynge knyfe. *c* **1425** *Voc.* in Wr.-Wülcker 662/18 *Hic scamellus*, dressyn-knyfbord. **1483** *Cath. Angl.* 100/2 A Dirsynge knyfe. *Ibid.* 108/1 a Dryssynge-knyffe, *spata, farcularium.* **1541** *Act 33 Hen. VIII*, c. 12. §13 The coke.. shall.. bring with him a dressing knife.

'dressing-room. A room for dressing and the toilet, usually opening from a bed-room.

1675 WYCHERLEY *Country Wife* IV. iii, I.. was made free of their society and dressing-rooms for ever hereafter. **1683** EVELYN *Diary* 4 Oct., I went.. into the Duchess of Portsmouth's dressing-room within her bed-chamber. **1803** REPTON *Landscape Gard.* (1805) 178 The present dressing-room.. added to each modern bed-room. **1875** JOWETT *Plato* I. 195 I was sitting alone in the dressing-room of the Lyceum.

'dressing-table. A toilet table. Also *attrib.*

1692 J. VERNEY *Let.* in M. M. Verney *Mem. Verney Family* (1899) IV. xii. 468 Dressing table plate. **1796** *Hull Advertiser* 3 Sept. 1/1 Ladies Inlaid Dressing Tables. **1829** MARRYAT *F. Mildmay* ix, Laying my watch.. on the dressing-table. **1899** *Daily News* 29 July 8/4 The 'dressing-table' effect, as these white muslins or lace over colour produce, is in great favour. **1960** *Farmer & Stockbreeder* 8 Mar. Suppl. 3/1 The dressing-tables had chintz frills.

dress-maker ('drɛsmeɪkə(r)). Also **dressmaker.**

a. A maker of dresses; *spec.* a woman who makes dresses for those of her own sex. Also *attrib.*, designating clothes, etc., made by a dress-maker or resembling such garments.

1803 *Morning Herald* 12 Feb. 1/2 To Milliners and Dress-makers.—Wanted immediately, two Persons who have lived as First Hands in respectable Houses of Business. **1828** in WEBSTER. **1832** W. IRVING *Alhambra* I. 289 The dress-makers, and the jewellers, and the artificers in gold and silver. **1838** DICKENS *Nich. Nick.* x, The situation I have made interest to procure.. is with a Milliner and dressmaker. **1904** *Westm. Gaz.* 28 Apr. 4/2 Robes that really look like quite expensive dressmaker frocks. **1907** *Ibid.* 5 Jan. 13/1 Perhaps I should not say tailor suit, but dressmaker cloth suit, for those charming draped bodices.. are.. more the province of the dressmaker than the tailor. **1944** *New Yorker* 7 Oct. 54/2 Simple clothes softened with a bit of dressmaker detail. **1946** *Woman & Beauty* Feb. 120/1 Black crêpe-de-chine. Lovely for dressmaker suits. **1968** J. IRONSIDE *Fashion Alphabet* 80 *Dressmaker suit*, a suit made by a dressmaker, usually softer than a tailor-made and using very little tailor's canvas.

b. ***dress-maker's dummy*** = DUMMY *sb.* 5a.

1949 D. G. SMITH *I capture Castle* ii. 13 A dressmaker's dummy of most opulent figure with a wire skirt round her one leg. **1960** D. HOLMAN-HUNT *My Grandmothers & I* i. 22 Against one wall.. stood a dressmaker's dummy.

Hence **'dress-,makership; 'dress-makery,** a dress-making establishment.

1852 R. S. SURTEES *Sponge's Sp. Tour* v. (1893) 29 In all the elegance of first-rate millinery and dressmakership. **1882** BESANT *All Sorts* viii. 75 Details of a practical nature concerning the conduct of a dress-makery.

'dress-making, *vbl. sb.* [f. DRESS *sb.* and MAKING *vbl. sb.*] The action or occupation of making (women's) dresses. Also *attrib.*

1837 WHITTOCK, etc. *Bk. Trades* (1842) 308 Dress-making came from France, i.e. Paris. **1852** MRS. STOWE *Uncle Tom's C.* xvii. 158, I can do dressmaking very well.

So **'dress-making** *ppl. a.*; **'dress-make** *v.* (*colloq.*), to make dresses.

1882 B. HARTE *Flip* iv, I must see that dressmaking sharp about it. **1884** S. O. JEWETT *Country Doctor* ii. 6 She might dress-make or do millinery work. **1885** *Times* 5 Mar. 10 A registry.. for women.. accustomed to dressmake, wash, or do charing work. **1953** E. COXHEAD *Midlanders* iii. 74 But, Connie, you know I can't dressmake.

dress-up ('drɛsʌp). [f. DRESS *v.* 7d.] The act of dressing up, esp. in one's best clothes; an occasion, gathering, etc., which demands formal dress. Also *attrib.* or as *adj.*

1865 A. D. T. WHITNEY *Gayworthys* II. vii. 132 'Will you go to meeting, Gershom?' Joanna asked him... 'I guess not, .. the dress-up takes down the devotion, rather, for me.' **1878** MRS. STOWE *Poganuc People* 52 As to that little dress-up affair over there,.. I don't think any real harm has been done. **1887** 'PANSY' *Little Fishers* iii, They are dress-up clothes. **1909** G. B. SHAW *Press Cuttings* 20 Arf of it's only ousemaidin; and tother arf is dress-up and make-believe. **1954** E. PANGBORN *Mirror for Observers* (1955) II. v. 141 It's always trousers nowadays except for evening dress-up, unfortunate for fat girls. **1965** *New Society* 8 July 12/2 The dress-up dinner party is nearly dead.

dressy ('drɛsɪ), *a.* [f. DRESS *sb.* + -Y[1].]

1. a. Fond of or attentive to dress; given to elaborate or showy dressing.

1768 GOLDSM. *Good-n. Man* I. i, One of those fine old dressy things, who thinks to conceal her age, by everywhere exposing her person. **1834** LADY GRANVILLE *Lett.* 31 Oct. (1894) II. 173, I am growing dressy.. and am learning how to unite smartness and economy. **1848** THACKERAY *Van. Fair* lix, I am a dressy man.

b. *transf.* and *fig.* Excessively elaborate.

1864 BAGEHOT *Coll. Works* (1965) II. 366 A dressy literature, an exaggerated literature, seem to be fated to us. **1941** BLUNDEN *T. Hardy* iii. 40 Hardy.. was always oddly fond of heavy, dressy expressions.

2. Of garments: Having an air of dress; stylish. Now usu., formal; (of an occasion) requiring full dress.

1785 E. SHERIDAN *Let.* 5 July in *Jrnl.* (1960) 59, I have got a Celbridge for the Honour of Ireland, these are for walks or Church, as a more dressy one I brought from London a white Persian Hat. **1818** MISS FERRIER *Marriage* I. 206 (Jam.) Black velvet gowns.. they were dressy, and not too dressy. **1845** *Blackw. Mag.* LVII. 735 Such a truly elegant boot, so gentlemanly, so dressy. **1902** in C. W. Cunnington *Eng. Women's Clothes* (1952) ii. 52 *Shoes* are more worn than boots for dressy occasions. **1954** 'L. LEWIS' *Birthday Murder* (1951) ii. 30 Victoria had planned to put on a red dress, but.. chose a short, dressy black one instead.

transf. **1882** *Garden* 28 Jan. 63/3 Anemones.. are not only very dressy, but last a long time in water. **1887** F. B. ZINCKE *Materials for Hist. Wherstead* 148 The less dressy parts of a garden.

Hence **'dressiness.**

1806 W. TAYLOR in *Ann. Rev.* IV. 249 Habits of dressiness.. are adopted. **1877** SPURGEON *Lect. to Students* Ser. II. viii. 131 A hundred years ago the dressiness of the clergy was about as conspicuous as it is now.

drest, var. pa. t. and pple. of DRESS.

drest, variant of DRAST *Obs.*, dregs, lees.

† **dretch,** *v.*[1] *Obs.* Forms: 1 drecc(e)an, 2-6 dreche, 3 dræcche, dracche, dreeche, 3-5 drecche, (4 drich), 5-6 dretch. *Pa. t.* 1 drehte, 4 draihte. *Pa. pple.* 1 (ʒe)dreht, 3-4 idrecchid (-æ-, -a-, -ee-), idraht, 4 draiht. [OE. *drecc(e)an*: unknown in the other Germanic langs.]

1. *trans.* To afflict, torment, vex; in ME. esp. to trouble in sleep.

c **900** *Bede Glosses* 27 in *O.E. Texts* 180 *Adficiens*, dreccende. *a* **1000** *Cædmon's Gen.* 2179 Mec sorʒ dreceþ. *c* **1000** ÆLFRIC *Hom.* (Th.) I. 86 ʒif he hwon hnappode, ðærrihte hine drehton nihtlice ʒedwimor. *c* **1175** *Lamb. Hom.* 77 Alle oðre men þet heuie sunnen drecheð. *c* **1205** LAY. 4521 þa þe king wes a-waht, he wes swuþe idraht. *Ibid.* 22556 þa þe king him awoc swiðe he wes idræcched [*c* **1275** idrecched]. **1340-70** *Alisaunder* 819 Hee was draiht with dreme thorou deuiles engines. *c* **1375** *Sc. Leg. Saints, Catharina* 818 þu sall drich me na mare. *c* **1386** CHAUCER *Nun's Pr. T.* 67 As man þat in his dreem is drecched soore. **1470-85** MALORY *Arthur* xx. v, We alle.. were soo dretched that somme of vs lepte oute of oure beddes naked.

2. *intr.* To be troubled in sleep. *rare.*

1421 HOCCLEVE *Complaint* 308 Lat them drem as them lyst and speke & dreche. *c* **1440** *Promp. Parv.* 131/2 Dremyn, or dretchyn yn slepe, *sompnio.* **1535** *Goodly Primer* (1834) 210 Sleeping or waking, dreaming or dreching.

Hence † **'dretching,** torment, vexation, trouble.

a **1050** *Liber Scintill.* lxxx. (1889) 217 Fram þysum lichaman butan dreccunge stiþre beon ʒenumene. *c* **1230** *Hali Meid.* 7 Deð hire in to drecchunge to dihten hus and hinen. *c* **1330** R. BRUNNE *Chron. Wace* (Rolls) 8080 Drecchynge by tymes haue þey wrought. **1470-85** MALORY *Arthur* XXI. xii, It is but dretchyng of sweuens.

† **dretch,** *v.*[2] *Obs.* In 3-5 dreche, drecche, (5 driche, dryche.) [Not known before 13th c.; in form identical with prec. vb., but, on account of diversity of sense, generally viewed as distinct.]

1. *intr.* To delay, linger, tarry.

c **1250** *Gen. & Ex.* 1420 Ne wold he ðor Ouer on niʒt drechen nunmor. *c* **1374** CHAUCER *Troylus* II. 1215 (1264) What sholde I drecche [*v.r.* dretche] or telle of his aray? *a* **1400** *Morte Arth.* 754 For drede of þe derke nyghte þay drecchede a lyttille. **1461** *Liber Pluscardensis* XI. xi. (1877) I. 399 The party.. drichit and delayit our fra yeir to yeris.

2. *trans.* To delay. **b.** To protract. *rare.*

c **1380** *Sir Ferumb.* 1602 What halt hit muche her-of to telle? to drecchen ous of our lay? **1393** GOWER *Conf.* II. 41 Than make I.. tarienges To drecche forth the longe day.

Hence **'dretching** *vbl. sb.*, procrastination, delay.

a **1300** *Cursor M.* 16390 (Gött.) Selcuth vs thinc of þe, pilate, wid dreching [*Cott.* drightin] for to drill. *c* **1330** R. BRUNNE *Chron. Wace* (Rolls) 11757 Make no long drecching þer-to. *c* **1425** WYNTOUN *Cron.* v. iii. 52 And to Rowme þet Tribwte pay Wycht-owtyn drychyng or delay. *c* **1470** HENRY *Wallace* VII. 183 Trubbill weddyr makis schippis to droune, His drychyn is with Pluto in the se.

† **dretch,** *sb. Obs.* [f. DRETCH *v.*[1]] Trouble.

13.. *Gaw. & Gr. Knt.* 1972 To sett hym in þe waye And coundue hym by þe downez, þat he no drechch had. ? **13..** *MS. Cambr.* Ff. ii. 38. 33 (Halliw.) Ye schall see a wondur dreche Whan my sone wole me fecche.

dreuch, obs. Sc. pa. t. of DRAW *v.*

† **dreve,** *v.*[1] *Obs.* Forms: 1 drœfan, dréfan, 2-3 drefe, 3 dreofe, dreaue, 3-4 dreve. [OE. *dréfan* = OS. *drôbjan, druovjan* (LG. *dröfen, dröven*, Du. *droeven*), OHG. **truobjan, truoban*, (MHG. *trüeben*, G. *trüben*), Goth. *drôbjan* to disturb; f. OTeut. **drôbu-* turbid, disturbed; perh. from an ablaut series *drab-, drôb-*, whence also DRAFF. Cf. DROVE *v.*[1], DROVY *a.*] *trans.* To trouble, disturb, agitate.

Beowulf (Th.) 2838 Water under stod dreoriʒ and ʒedrefed. *c* **1000** *Ags. Gosp.* John xiv. 1 Ne sy eower heorte ʒedrefed [*Lindisf. G.* ʒedroefed]. *c* **1200** ORMIN 147 He warrþ drefedd & forrdredd. *c* **1200** *Trin. Coll. Hom.* 195 Unbilefde folc þe wolden dreuen hem. *a* **1240** *Ureisun* in *Cott. Hom.* 193 Ne beoð heo neuer i-dreaued mid winde ne mid reine. *c* **1250** *Gen. & Ex.* 318 Ic wene ðat ic and eue sulen alle is blisse dreue. *c* **1400** *Anturs of Arth.* xxii, Alle the Duseperis of Fraunse with ȝour dyn deuyt [*Thornt. MS.* dreuede].

† **dreve,** *v.*[2] *Obs.* Also 5 *Sc.* drefe. [OE. *drǽfan* to drive, impel (:—*drâbjan*) corresp. to Goth. *draibjan* to drive, trouble, vex:—OTeut. **draibjan*, f. *draib-* ablaut grade of *dreiban*, OE. *drífan* to drive.]

1. *trans.* To drive away or apart; to separate.

c **1325** *Chron. Eng.* 406 in Ritson *Met. Rom.* II. 287 Thus wes Englond to-deled, Ant uch kyng from other dreved. *c* **1340** *Cursor M.* 5316 (Fairf.) Mony baret fra him was dreued. *Ibid.* 6766. *c* **1470** HENRY *Wallace* XI. 1330 Bot cowatice the ay fra honour drefyd [*v.r.* dreft].

absol. **1573** TUSSER *Husb.* xxxv. (1878) 83 If yee deale guilefully, parson will dreue, and so to your selfe a worse turne ye may geue.

2. *intr.* To move, proceed, tend.

a **1300** *Cursor M.* 1768 (Gött.) þe springes gan ouer al vte dreue. *c* **1400** *Destr. Troy* 7123 Thus curstly þat knighthode .. þurgh domys of destany dreuyt to noght.

dreve, drevin, -yn, obs. pa. pple. of DRIVE *v.*

drevel(l, -ill, -yll, var. of DRIVEL, *sb.*[1] *Obs.*

† **drevyll,** *v. Obs.* [f. *drevyll* early form of DRIVEL *sb.*[1]] *intr.* To drudge or slave.

1514 BARCLAY *Cyt. & Uplondyshm.* (Percy Soc.) 14 To drudge & to drevyll in warkes vyle and rude, This wyse shall ye lyve, in endeles servytude.

† **drew,** *sb. Obs.* Also 5 drewe. [Derivation unknown.]

1. A drop, a very small quantity (of liquid).

c **1430** *Hymns Virg.* (1867) 60 Whanne þe child was .vij. ȝeer olde, Passyng sowkyng of milke drewis. *c* **1450** *Mirour Saluacioun* 965 The drie erthe ferre about had noght þerof a drewe. **1501** DOUGLAS *Pal. Hon.* II. xli, Of the water I micht not taste a drew. *a* **1555** LYNDESAY *Auld Man & Wife* 87 The divill a drew sall cum in thy throte.

2. A morsel, a very small bit.

c **1450** *Cov. Myst.* (1841) 36 Of whom we have our dayly food, Ellys we had but lytyl drewe. *Ibid.* 405 Nakyd men and ffebyl of array ȝe wolde nott socowre with a lytel drewe.

drew (druː), pa. t. of DRAW *v.*

drewery, drewrie, etc.: see DRUERY.

drewin, -yn, obs. pa. pple. of DRIVE *v.*

drewry, obs. form of DREARY *a.*

drey, obs. f. DRY, DRAY[1]; var. of DRAY[2].

drey(e, dreyȝ, obs. forms of DREE *v.* and *a.*

dreyen, dreyn, obs. form of DRAW, DRAIN.

Dreyfusard ('dreɪfʊsɑː(r), -ɑːd). Now *Hist.* [Fr., f. the name of *Dreyfus* + *-ard* -ARD.] A defender or supporter of Captain Alfred Dreyfus (1859-1935), a Frenchman of Jewish

descent who was convicted of treason in 1894 and declared innocent in 1906. Also *attrib.* or as *adj.*
1898 *Westm. Gaz.* 15 Sept. 5/2 This, of course, is a sop offered to the Dreyfusards. *Ibid.*, The opinion is expressed among Dreyfusard leaders that the President is rushing to his ruin. **1905** *Book Lover* Apr. 4/2 His affiliations have not been even *Dreyfusard* in France or Bryanite in the United States. **1919** W. B. YEATS in *Irish Statesman* 23 Aug. 212/1 It was amidst Socialist and Dreyfusard controversy that he discovered his belief. **1967** *Listener* 30 Mar. 435/2 Halévy was a passionate Dreyfusard.

dreynt, obs. pa. t. and pple. of DRENCH *v.*

† **drib**, *v. Obs.* [app. an onomatopœic formation arising out of DRIP or DROP, the modified consonant expressing a modification of the notion.]
1. *intr.* To fall in drops; *fig.*, to go on little by little.
1523 *St. Papers Hen. VIII*, VI. 160 Suche drybbing warre, as hit hitherto hathe ben made by the said Princes.
2. ? To dribble, to slaver.
a **1529** SKELTON *Crowne Lawrell* (R.), Dasyng after dotterels, lyke drunkards that dribbes.
3. *trans.* **a.** To let fall or utter as in driblets.
1533 MORE *Debell. Salem* Wks. 947/1 In the second side of yᵉ .xxvi. lefe, he dribbeth in a word of spiritual dignity. **1599** NASHE *Lenten Stuffe* (1871) 107 Proverbs..which those, that have bitten with ill bargains of either sort, have dribbed forth in revenge.
b. To let fall in drops or driblets.
1682 SOUTHERNE *Loyal Brother* Prol., There's not a Butcher's Wife but Dribs her part, And pities the poor Pageant from her heart.
c. 'To crop; to cut off, to defalcate. A cant word.' (J.)
1693 DRYDEN, etc. *Juvenal* VII. 298 Merchants Gains come short of half the Mart, For he who drives their Bargains, dribs a part.
d. To lead one little by little *into* something.
a **1700** DRYDEN *Ovid's Art Love* I. (R.), With daily lies she dribs thee into cost, That ear-ring dropt a stone, that ring is lost.
4. *trans.* To shoot (an arrow) so that it falls short or wide of the mark.
1545 [implied in DRIBBER below]. **1565** GOLDING *Ovid's Met.* XIII. (1593) 295 Behold how hee..dribs his arrowes up and downe At birds. **1572** CHURCHYARD To Rdr. in J. Jones *Bathes of Bath*, At rouers they but shot theyr Shafts, and dribbed wyde a skore. **1592** LYLY *Galathea* III. iv, O Venus ..well shalt thou know what it is to drib thine arrowes up and downe Diana's leyes.
Hence **dribbed**, **'dribbing** *ppl. adjs.*; also **'dribber**, one who dribs his arrows.
1545 ASCHAM *Toxoph.* (Arb.) 94 So if a man be..neuer so wel taught in his youth to shote, yet if he giue it ouer, and not use to shote..he shal become of a fayre archer, a stark squyrter and dribber. **1581** SIDNEY *Astr. & Stella* ii, Not at the first sight, nor yet with a dribbed shot Loue gaue the wound.

drib, *sb. Sc.* and *dial.* [f. DRIB *v.*, or perh. more immediately deduced from *dribble*, *driblet*, which appear much earlier.] A drop, a petty or inconsiderable quantity; a DRIBLET.
c **1730** RAMSAY *Ode fr. Horace*, That mutchkin-stoup it hauds but dribs. *a* **1745** SWIFT *On Gibbs' Ps.* (T.), Do not, I pray thee, paper stain With rhymes retail'd in dribbs. **1819** W. TENNANT *Papistry Storm'd* (1827) 172 And gust our gabs wi' dribs o' wine. **1862** LINCOLN *Let. to McClellan* 25 May in Raymond *Life* (1864) 241 We are sending such regiments and dribs from here and Baltimore as we can spare to Harper's Ferry. **1875** *Sussex Gloss.*, *Drib*, a very small quantity of anything.

dribbet, obs. var. or misprint for DRIBLET.
1659 GAUDEN *Tears of Ch.* II. xix. 243 Pittances..slowly payd by dribbets and with infinite delayes.

dribble ('drɪb(ə)l), *v.* [freq. of DRIB *v.*; in certain uses associated with or influenced by DRIVEL *v.*]
1. *trans.* To let (anything) flow or fall in drops or a trickling stream; to give forth or emit in driblets. *lit.* and *fig.* With *out*, *forth*, *away*.
c **1589** *Theses Martinianæ* 31, I thinke it well if I can drible out a Pistle in octauo nowe and then. **1602** WARNER *Alb. Eng.* IX. lii. (1612) 236 Dribling Almes by Art. *c* **1711** SWIFT *Rules to Servants* Wks. 1778 X. 275 Let the cook..follow.. with a ladleful [of soup], and dribble it all the way up stairs. **1874** GREEN *Short Hist.* vii. 405 Elizabeth dribbled out her secret aid to the Prince of Orange.
2. *absol.* or *intr.* To let the spittle flow down over the chin, as young children and imbecile people often do. Hence also *fig.*, = DRIVEL.
1673 *Rules of Civility* 61 Snoaring, sweating, gaping, or dribling. **1731** MORTIMER in *Phil. Trans.* XXXVII. 167 He ..had no Motion to vomit, but dribbled much. **1870** DICKENS *E. Drood* 114 The Lascar laughs and dribbles at the Mouth. *Mod.* Infants generally dribble when they are teething.
3. *intr.* To flow down in small quantities or in a small and fitful stream; to trickle.
1599, **1627**, **1669**, etc. [see DRIBBLING]. **1784** R. B. CHESTON in *Med. Commun.* II. 6 She had perceived her water dribbling from her. **1802** PALEY *Nat. Theol.* xv. (1830) 185 Which receiver..allows the grain to dribble only in small quantities into the central hole in the upper mill-stone. **1878** HUXLEY *Physiogr.* 22 The water which falls upon the rock then dribbles through the little cracks.
b. *transf.* and *fig.*
1600–1672 [see DRIBBLING *ppl. a.* 3]. **1865** CARLYLE *Fredk. Gt.* VII. XVIII. v. 173 From about the end of June, the Reichs Army kept dribbling in.
4. *trans.* In *Football*, etc. To keep (the ball) moving along the ground in front of and close to one by a rapid succession of short pushes, instead of sending it as far as possible by a vigorous kick. Also *absol.*
1863 A. G. GUILLEMARD in *Sport. Gaz.* Oct. (Football), The Eton game, when the 'long-behind' is dribbling the ball before his feet slowly forward. **1868** *Football Annual* 1 'Dribbling', as the science of working the ball along the ground by means of the feet is technically termed. **1871** A. G. GUILLEMARD in *Bell's Life* Apr., The Scottish forwards 'gained not a little by their dribbling, which feature of the game is but seldom seen round London'. **1880** *Times* 12 Nov. 4/4 There is no more legitimate and scientific form of 'football' than the 'drop-kick' and that 'dribbling' with the feet which now forms a most important part of the Rugby game. **1883** F. M. CRAWFORD *Mr. Isaacs* viii. 165 To dribble it [the ball, at polo], along. **1887** *Daily News* 10 Jan. 3/5 The English forwards dribbled the ball close up to the Welsh line and nearly scored.
b. *Billiards.* To give (a ball) a slight push.
1873 BENNETT & CAVENDISH *Billiards* 253 To keep the white by the spot, and by the same stroke to dribble the red over the corner.
†**5.** in *Archery* = DRIB *v.* 4. *Obs.*
1565 GOLDING *Ovid's Met.* XII. (1593) 293 Paris dribling out his shafts among the Greekes she spide. **1603** SHAKS. *Meas. for M.* I. iii. 2 Beleeue not that the dribling dart of Loue Can pierce a compleat bosome. **1612–15** BP. HALL *Contempl.*, *N.T.* IV. i, Prayer is an arrow..if it be but dribbled forth of careless lips, it falls down at our foot.

dribble, *sb.* [f. prec. vb.]
1. A small trickling and barely continuous stream; a small quantity or drop of liquid.
c **1680** [F. SEMPILL] *Banishment Pov.* in Watson *Collect.* I. 14 (Jam.), I..stour'd to Leith To try my credit at the wine; But [ne'er] a dribble fyld my teeth. **1785** BURNS *To a Mouse* vi, The winter's sleety dribble. **1836** MARRYAT *Midsh. Easy* xxxviii, Teeth black with chewing, and always a little brown dribble from the left corner of his mouth. **1885** *Manch. Exam.* 6 June 5/4 This stream is a mere languid dribble from the side of the mountain.
b. *transf.* and *fig.*
1832 *Westm. Rev.* XVII. 403 *note*, As often as her apron-string breaks, the stones fall in such a direction as to form a dribble. *a* **1871** R. CHAMBERS *Wheesht!*, These people.. attempt to work off 'a great secret' upon me, in their quiet way, dribble by dribble. **1871** L. STEPHEN *Playgr. Eur.* xii. (1894) 294 The little dribble of Commerce..never quite ceases.
2. *Football.* An act of 'dribbling': see DRIBBLE *v.* 4.
1889 *Pauline* 34 When play was again resumed, the Modern forwards..did a good dribble into the Classical twenty-five. **1894** *Westm. Gaz.* 13 Mar. 5/3 He..collided with an opponent, who had led a dribble down the field.
3. *local.* A field drain made of broken stones between which the water trickles. Cf. RUBBLE.
1843 *Jrnl. R. Agric. Soc.* IV. II. 325 Stone drains are various; the most common here [in Wiltshire] are wall, and dribble or rubble. **1846** J. BAXTER *Libr. Pract. Agric.* (ed. 4) I. 234 The dribble is made with stones, broken about the size..used for roads, the drain about eight inches wide filled a foot high with the stones.

† **'dribblement.** *Obs. rare*[−1]. [f. DRIBBLE *v.* + -MENT.] A dribbling.
1599 NASHE *Lenten Stuffe* (1871) 23 To shun spight I smothered these dribblements.

dribbler ('drɪblə(r)). [f. DRIBBLE *v.* + -ER[1].] One who dribbles; e.g. at football.
1835 SOUTHEY *Doctor* Interchapter vii. III. 5 The aspirants and wranglers at the bar, the dribblers and the spit-fires. **1868** *Football Annual* 1 The supporters of Football appear now to have arranged themselves in two great and distinct factions..the 'dribblers', and the.. admirers of the running and hacking style. **1891** *Lock to Lock Times* 24 Oct. 13/1 The centre man is a speedy dribbler and good shot at goal.

'dribbling, *vbl. sb.* [f. DRIBBLE *v.* + -ING[1].]
1. A falling in a trickling stream or succession of drops or small quantities.
1669 PEPYS *Diary* 1 May, The day being unpleasing..and now and then a little dribbling of rain. **1728** WOODWARD *Fossils* (J.), Semilunar processes on the surface, owe their form to the dribbling of water. **1790** J. C. SMYTH in *Med. Commun.* II. 516 The dribbling of urine..ceased.
b. *concretely.* That which is dribbled, or given forth in driblets; a dropping.
1599 A. M. tr. *Gabelhouer's Bk. Physicke* 95/1 Take sixe, or seaven sheepe dribbelinges, as fresh as the sheepe avoydeth them. *a* **1666** A. BROME *Songs, Reformation* (R.), Out of all's ill-gotten store He gives a dribbling to the poor.
2. *Football.* See DRIBBLE *v.* 4.

'dribbling, *ppl. a.* [f. as prec. + -ING[2].] That dribbles (in various senses).
1. Giving forth in driblets.
1592 G. HARVEY *Pierce's Super.* 14 Pidlinge and driblinge confuters that sitt all day buzzing upon a blunt point.
2. Flowing out in a dropping stream, trickling.
1627 DRAYTON *Agincourt* 186 The Hower-glasse..whose dribbling sands..make mee too much to feele Your slackenesse hither. **1679** WOOD *Life* (Oxf. Hist. Soc.) II. 460 Dribling raine and mists. **1877** FARRAR *Days of Youth* iii. 29 It is no dribbling rivulet..but a rejoicing river.
fig. **1686** DRYDEN *Prol. Union two Companies* (R.), We'll take no blundering verse, no fustian tumor, No dribbling love from this or that presumer.
3. *fig.* Inconsiderable; made up of petty or trifling items.
1600 HOLLAND *Livy* XXVI. xvii. 597 There passed some dribbling skirmishes [*levia prœlia*] betweene the.. Carthaginians, and..the Romanes. **1630** *R. Johnson's Kingd. & Commw.* 45 A long suit for a dribling debt. **1642** MILTON *Apol. Smect.* (1851) 321 Small temptations allure but dribling offendors. **1672** E. RAVENSCROFT *Mamamouchi*, *D.* I stand indebted to you. *Cr.* A few dribbling sums, Sir.
4. That allows saliva or moisture to flow from the mouth, as *a dribbling child*.

dribbly ('drɪblɪ), *a.* [f. DRIBBLE *sb.* + -Y[1].] Tending to dribble; dribbling; characterized by dribbles.
1909 R. BROOKE *Let.* (1968) 172 A pair of dribbly dotards. **1951** DYLAN THOMAS *Let.* 12 Apr. (1966) 356 There in that English sink, intolerable, dribbly, lost. **1958** *Times* 18 Nov. 13/4 The..nature of pigment, the sort of mud-pie fascination that comes..of its liquid and dribbly aspect. **1967** D. PINNER *Ritual* xiv. 141 Those lovely dribbly dogs and those even lovelier dribbly policemen!

driblet, **dribblet** ('drɪblɪt), *sb.* [f. DRIB *v.* + -LET: association with *dribble* seems later.]
1. a. 'A small sum, odd money in a sum' (J.).
1632 QUARLES *Div. Fancies* III. xxv. (1660) 107 We crave, and crave a longer Day, Then pay in Driblets, or else never pay. **1633** T. ADAMS *Exp. 2 Peter* ii. 14 The high rate..that divers live at, can be maintained by no driblets. **1794** BURKE *Sp. agst. Hastings* Wks. XV. 41 They had received in little dribblets to the amount of ninety-five pounds. **1884** BOWEN in *Law Rep.* 28 Chancery Div. 16 A tenant who has paid his last quarter's rent by driblets under pressure.
†**b.** *esp.* A small or petty debt. *Obs.*
1591 HARINGTON *Orl. Fur.* XLIII. cxxxvi, And quite each other all old debts and driblets [*Note*—Driblets used for petty recknings]. **1600** DEKKER *Gentle Craft* 18 Ide set mine olde debts against my new driblets. **1685** DRYDEN *Thren. Augus.* xiv, So strictly wer't thou just to pay, Even to the driblet of a day. **1798** *Sporting Mag.* XI. 104 Some other driblets, called debts of honour. **1867** TROLLOPE *Chron. Barset* II. lviii. 151 A small mortgage and such like convenient but uninfluential driblets.
2. A petty or inconsiderable quantity or part of anything. ***by (in) driblets***: in petty portions at a time, little by little.
1678 PHILLIPS (ed. 4), *Dribblets* (old word), small portions or pieces. **1740** DYCHE & PARDON, *Driblet*..any small quantity or parcel of money, or any thing else. **1832** *Examiner* 34/1 It is rumoured that the creation of peers is to be by dribblets. A drop-by-drop invigoration seems.. absurd. **1862** *Macm. Mag.* Oct. 501 A hundred weight of fish to be sold in driblets, for a few pence.
3. A small quantity or dribble (of liquid).
1860 G. H. K. *Vac. Tour* 141 A driblet of sour milk. **1871** L. STEPHEN *Playgr. Eur.* iii. (1894) 77 Every driblet of water seemed to be inseparably connected in their minds with a drop of brandy.
4. *Comb.* **driblet cone**, a cone produced by the successive ejections of small quantities of lava; a hornito.
1888 J. D. DANA in *Amer. Jrnl. Sci.* CXXXV. 32 The projectile process in the basalt-volcano..makes not cinder-cones, but dribblet-cones, 15 to 40 feet high, out of the projected masses, the falling driblets becoming plastered together. *Ibid.*, Such driblet-cones are of all angles from 30° to 90°. **1939** A. K. LOBECK *Geomorphol.* xix. 675 Where gases sputter out through the side of the dome, a *spatter* or *driblet cone* may be built up 10 to 12 feet above the ground. **1969** C. D. OLLIER *Volcanoes* v. 58 Spatter may be erupted through a crack in the surface of a pahoehoe flow, and build up a small cone or spire of scoria and driblets. This is called a hornito or driblet cone. The term is usually restricted to small features perhaps 5 m high.
Hence † **'driblet** *v. intr.*, to come in driblets.
1659 GAUDEN *Tears Ch.* III. v. 276 Biting poverty..hardly to be relieved by those dribliting pittances.

driche, var. form of DREE *a.*, DRETCH *v.*[2]

drichte, -ine: see DRIGHT, DRIGHTIN.

dricksie: see DRIX, DRUXY.

driddle, *v. Sc.* [Origin obscure: cf. *diddle*, *piddle.*] *intr.* 'To work, walk, or act in a feeble, unsteady or uncertain manner.' (Jam. Suppl.)
a **1605** MONTGOMERIE *Flyting w. Polwart* 17 Thou art doeand and dridland like ane foule beast. **1785** BURNS *Jolly Beggars*, A pigmy scraper, wi' his fiddle, Wha us'd at trysts and fairs to driddle. **1786** —— *Ep. Major Logan* iii, Until you on a crummock driddle, A gray-haired carl.

dride, obs. pa. t. and pple. of DRY *v.*

dridge, obs. form of DREDGE *sb.*[1]

drie, obs. form of DREE *v.*, DRY.

driech, **driegh**, var. forms of DREE *a.*

dried (draɪd), *ppl. a.* [f. DRY *v.* + -ED[1].]
1. Deprived of moisture, desiccated. Often with *up*. *spec.* of foods: deprived of moisture so as to be capable of being preserved for a long time, often in the form of powder.
a **1340** HAMPOLE *Psalter* cl. 4 A dryid scyn. **1596** SHAKS. *1 Hen. IV* II. iv. 271 Dried neat's tongue. **1664** EVELYN *Kal. Hort.* (1729) 203 Pull off all crumpl'd dry'd Leaves. **1709** J. LAWSON *New Voy. Carolina* 29 Loblolly made with Indian Corn, and dry'd Peaches. **1737** J. BRICKELL *Nat. Hist. N. Carolina* (1743) 319 When they [*sc.* Indians] go to War or their Hunting Matches..they generally carry with them.. Bread, Indian Corn, dried Fruits, of several sorts. **1753** C. GIST *Jrnl.* (1893) 81 Got some corn and dried meat. **1771**

FRANKLIN *Lett.* Wks. 1887 IV. 403 A specimen of the American dried apples. **1816** BYRON *Ch. Har.* III. iii, I find The furrows of long thought, and dried-up tears. **1837** W. IRVING *Capt. Bonneville* III. 185 Keeping the dried meats for places where game might be scarce. **1895** *Montgomery Ward Catal.* Index. Dried fruits. **1907** H. W. WILEY *Foods & their Adulteration* II. 115 *Dried eggs.* The rapid drying of fresh eggs is perhaps an unobjectionable method of preservation. *Ibid.*, Dried products are sometimes made from decayed eggs. **1909** G. F. STILL *Common Disorders of Childhood* iv. 59 Another firm prepares a dried milk to which cream and milk sugar have been added before desiccation. **1918** *Lancet* 24 Aug. 245/1 The rôle of dried milk in infant feeding [etc.]. **1933** *Chem. Abstr.* 1919 Dried eggs may be held in storage for several months with no loss of vitamin D in the yolks. **1941** *Ann. Reg. 1940* 6 To purchase Turkish dried fruits..annually for the duration of the war. **1944** *Daily Tel.* 11 July 3 The housewife's greatest standby is Dried Eggs.

2. *transf.* and *fig.* See the verb.

1622 FLETCHER *Span. Cur.* III. ii, A man of a dride conscience. **1853** C. BRONTE *Villette* vi, A dried-in man of business. **1885** G. ALLEN *Babylon* xiii, In a dried-up Indian military tone.

driedness ('draɪdnɪs). [f. DRIED *ppl. a.* + -NESS.] Dried condition. Also *dried-up-ness*.

1907 GALSWORTHY *Country House* III. ii. 231 The strange yellow driedness of his face. **1923** *United Free Ch. Miss. Rec.* June 248/1 Dried-up-ness is of the essence of the thing.

drier, dryer ('draɪə(r)). [f. DRY *v.* + -ER[1]. The analogical spelling is *drier*, but *dryer* is app. more frequent in the technical applications in 2 and 3.] One who or that which dries.

1. a. A thing that removes moisture.

1528 PAYNELL *Salerne's Regim.* Q iv b, Olde dry nuttis are greate driers. **1686** GOAD *Celest. Bodies* I. ii. 6 Wind is a Dryer, even as Frost a Cooler. **1756** C. LUCAS *Ess. Waters* II. 73 Salt is justly deemed a drier. **1892** *Pall Mall G.* 11 Oct. 7/2 The sun and air are good enough driers.

b. A person engaged in drying. Chiefly in combination, as *fruit-drier*. Also with *up*.

1881 *Instr. Census Clerks* (1885) 64 Woollen cloth manufacture:..Drier. *Ibid.* 82 Cardboard and pasteboard making:..Dryer. **1889** F. E. GRETTON *Mem. Harkback* xii. 207 As many [hop] plantations are being gathered in about the same time, the drier has his hands full all at once. **1916** BLUNDEN *Harbingers* 24 When the dryer in his oast Had loaded up his lattice-floors. **1941** M. TREADGOLD *We couldn't leave Dinah* vi. 99 She took full possession of the sink and Mick leaned up against the table, waiting to fulfil his function as Dryer-up-in-Chief with the dish-cloth. **1944** A. THIRKELL *Headmistress* vi. 135 Captain Hornby was an excellent drier-up and Elsa was secretly much impressed by his demanding a washleather to finish off the spoons.

2. A substance mixed with oil-paints, oils, inks, etc., to make them dry quickly.

1840 *Penny Cycl.* XVII. 145/2 To all paint a little sugar of lead, or litharge (*dryers*), should be added to make it dry quick. **1859** GULLICK & TIMBS *Paint.* 208 All dryers..have in some degree a pernicious influence on colours. **1882** *Encycl. Brit.* XIV. 677/2 By slow degrees a proportion of 'dryers' is added [to linseed oil]. **1940** *Thorpe's Dict. Appl. Chem.* (ed. 4) IV. 91/1 The modern method is to heat the oil by means of closed steam coils..while the driers are employed in the soluble form. **1951** R. MAYER *Artist's Handbk. Materials* iii. 157 Driers or siccatives are metallic salts combined with materials such as oils or resins which mix with the usual paint and varnish ingredients. **1958** T. LANDAU *Encycl. Librarianship* 113/2 *Drier*, a substance used in printing inks to expedite drying by evaporation.

3. a. (*dryer*) A mechanical contrivance or apparatus used to remove moisture; a desiccator.

1874 KNIGHT *Dict. Mech.*, *Dryer*, 1. The heated tables or cylinders which expel the moisture from the just-formed paper, in the machine. 2. The oven which evaporates the moisture from ceramic work. **1890** *Kew Bulletin* 145 Gibbs' Patent Tea Dryer..is suitable for drying corn, coffee, manure, hops, brewers' grains and fruit.

b. *spec.* A hair-drier.

1937 HEMINGWAY *To have & have Not* III. xviii. 253 He put a net over it wet and put me under the dryer. **1955** *Punch* 27 Apr. 531/1 Clamped down under a drier in the Hairdressing Salon. **1961** *B.S.I. News* Sept. p. 27 The term 'hair dryer' includes the flexible cord and connectors supplied with the dryer. The dryers are classified into the three following types: *a.* Earthed dryers *b.* Double-insulated dryers and *c.* All-insulated dryers. **1961** A. WILSON *Old Men at Zoo* ii. 106, I was under the drier when this girl started on about it.

4. A substance that dries (quickly or slowly).

1886 *Longm. Mag.* VII. 379 Olive oil never dries, or at least is the worst drier known.

Hence **'drierman, 'dryerman**, a man whose business it is to manage some drying process; **'driery, 'dryery**, a drying establishment.

1880 *Daily Tel.* 24 Feb., Paper makers.—Two dryermen. **1886** *Pall Mall G.* 5 Oct. 13/2 The largest and finest peaches going to the cannery..the rest to the dryery.

drier, driest, comp. and sup. of DRY *a.*

driery, drieth, obs. forms of DREARY, DRYTH.

drieve, -en, drif(e, driff(e, obs. ff. DRIVE *v.*

drifat, var. DRYFAT *Obs.*

†**driffle, drifle**, *v. Obs.* [? Allied to DRIBBLE.]

1. *trans.* To utter in driblets.

1592 G. HARVEY *Pierce's Super.* 14 These pidlinge and driblinge confuters..with much adoe drifle-out as many sentences in a weeke as he will poure-down in an houre.

2. *intr.* 'To drink deeply' (Halliwell).

c **1645** T. TULLY *Siege Carlisle* (1840) 15 The Garrison's excessive drinking, called drifling.

3. To rain fitfully or in sparse drops, as at the 'tail' of a shower. *Sc.* Hence **driffling** *vbl. sb.*

1639 R. BAILLIE *Lett. & Jrnls.* (1841) I. 220 Some jealousies did yet remaine, as driffling after a great shower.

drift (drɪft), *sb.* [Early ME. *drift* (not recorded in OE.) corresp. to OFris. *drift* (in *ur-drift*), MDu., Du. *drift*, MHG. *trift*, G. *trift* passage for cattle, drove, ON. *drift* snow-drift, (Sw., Da. *drift*); verbal abstract from *drifan* to DRIVE.]

I. The action of driving, etc.

1. a. The act of driving; propulsion, impulse, impetus. (Now *rare* or *Obs.* exc. as in b. or 2.)

a **1300** *Cursor M.* 496 (Gött.) þar þai drey ful hard drift. *c* **1400** *Sowdone Bab.* 76 A drift of wedir us droffe to Rome. *c* **1440** *Promp. Parv.* 132/1 Dryfte, or drywynge of bestys, *minatus.* **1523** FITZHERB. *Surv.* 9 b, As the whele gothe by drifte of water. *a* **1716** SOUTH (J.), A man being under the drift of any passion, will still follow the impulse of it. **1721** PERRY *Daggenh. Breach* 26 The Breach..was stop'd by..the drift of a Row of large Piles, drove near to each other. **1858** *Jrnl. R. Agric. Soc.* XIX. II. 296 Sheep for the Smithfield Monday market had to leave their homes on the previous Wednesday or Thursday week. Such a long drift..caused a great waste of meat.

b. *Forest Law.* The driving of the cattle within the precincts of a forest to one place on a particular day, for the determination of ownership, levying of fines, etc. (Cf. DRIVE *v.* 4 b.)

1540 *Act 32 Hen. VIII*, c. 13 §4 It shalbe laufull to the said lordis owners and possessioners of the said forrestis and chaces..to make like drifte of the said forestis, chaces. **1598** MANWOOD *Lawes Forest* xv. §2 (1615) 105/1 The Officers of the Forest..did use to make two drifts of their Forest euery year. **1776** *Customs Manor Epworth* in Stonehouse *Axholme* (1839) 145 The Lord is entitled to make one drift of the commons, between May-day and Midsummer, in order to ascertain whose cattle are pasturing thereon. **1887** W. F. COLLIER *Venville Rights on Dartmoor* in *Trans. Devonsh. Assoc.* XIX. 382 The moor-man then proceeds to summon the venville tenants to join in the drift by blowing horns on the tors. **1894** *Q. Rev.* Apr. 418 Assisting at the 'drifts' in which the horned cattle and ponies are collected, branded, and the 'strays' returned to their owners.

†**c.** *Arch.* The horizontal 'thrust' of an arch.

1772 HUTTON *Bridges* 60 The thickness of the pier necessary to resist the drift of the arch. *Ibid.* 91 Drift, Shoot, or Thrust of an arch, is the push or force which it exerts in the direction of the length of the bridge. **1823** P. NICHOLSON *Pract. Build.* 338.

2. a. The fact or condition of being driven, as by a current; the action of drifting; a slow course or current. Also *fig.* ***on*** or ***upon the drift*** = ADRIFT.

1562 J. HEYWOOD *Prov. & Epigr.* (1867) 149 Beware dryft to the woorst shore. **1633** T. JAMES *Voy.* 100 We considered where we might haue the cleerest drift..and let her driue. **1659** D. PELL *Impr. Sea* 305 Anchors give way, and so [ships] are most dreadfully put upon the drift. **1721** PERRY *Daggenh. Breach* 75 A considerable Frost and drift of Ice.. that Winter. **1860** MAURY *Phys. Geog. Sea* §107 The effect of moderate winds..is to cause what may be called the drift of the sea rather than a current. Drift is confined to surface waters. **1886** *Pall Mall G.* 18 Feb. 11/1 There is a steady low-class labour drift into London.

b. *Naut.* The deviation of a ship from its course in consequence of currents; *esp.* in reference to its amount.

1671 NARBOROUGH *Jrnl.* in *Acc. Sev. Late Voy.* I. (1711) 174 True Course, Drift and all Impediments allow'd, is, [etc.] **1793** RENNELL in *Phil. Trans.* LXXXIII. 195 On the 31st of January, when lying to, 36 miles are allowed for 20 hours drift, to the north-west. **1859–62** LEWIN *Invas. Brit.* 82 The maximum drift for a single tide [in the English Channel]..is eighteen miles, and the minimum nine miles.

c. *Gunnery.* The constant deviation of an elongated rotating projectile in the direction of its rotation; = DERIVATION[2].

1864 *Daily Tel.* 4 May, The hexagonal shot is far more limited with regard to lateral drift or deflection than the other two kinds of shot. **1867** in SMYTH *Sailor's Word-bk.*

d. A slow variation of the characteristics or operation of an electric circuit or device. Also *attrib.* orig. *U.S.*

1889 in *Cent. Dict.* **1892** *Jrnl. Franklin Inst.* CXXXIV. 482 This magnification varies with the sensibility and is largest when the instrument is most sensitive. In galvanometer work this phenomenon is known as the 'drift' of the needles. **1931** *Physical Rev.* XXXVII. 396 This drift is normally very constant, so that an input current as small as 10^{-16} amp can be measured by noting the *change* in the rate of drift which it causes. **1932** *Rev. Sci. Instruments* III. 420 The degree to which the circuit is balanced is determined by noting the back and forth drift which a high sensitivity galvanometer will make, due to natural battery voltage fluctuations. **1962** SIMPSON & RICHARDS *Junction Transistors* xiii. 310 The chief problem in the design of amplifiers to pass d.c. is to reduce slow changes in the operating conditions of the transistors to a minimum. These changes..are called drifts. **1963** B. FOZARD *Instrumentation Nucl. Reactors* xi. 133 More commonly some form of automatic drift-correction circuit is used. **1970** J. EARL *Tuners & Amplifiers* ii. 31 This..is in receipt of a stabilised voltage (to avoid tuning drift).

e. *Aeronaut.* (*a*) = *head resistance*; (*b*) the horizontal deviation of an aircraft from its course in consequence of winds and air-currents; also, the rate or amount of such deviation.

1891 O. CHANUTE *Aerial Navigation* 26 How much of this new pressure..opposes forward progress, and may be denominated drift. **1896** H. S. MAXIM in J. Means *Epitome of Aeronaut. Ann.* (1910) 113 The aeroplane..in which the drift will go the greatest number of times into the lift will be considered the most satisfactory. **1909** *Westm. Gaz.* 25 Feb. 4/1 The daring plan of jumping off a hill 45 ft. high with the object of ascertaining the proportion between lift and drift. **1916** H. BARBER, *Aeroplane Speaks* 2 There's Drift, my horizontal component, sometimes, though rather erroneously, called Head Resistance. *Ibid.* 57 The Drift.. must be overcome by the Thrust in order to secure the necessary velocity to produce the requisite lift for flight. **1920** *19th Cent.* July 145 The object of camber is to obtain the maximum lift, and to reduce the drift. **1958** 'N. SHUTE' *Rainbow & Rose* ii. 41 We had about fifteen degrees of drift. **1968** G. D. P. WORTHINGTON *Airline Instrument Fying* xiii. 191 If drift has been correctly allowed for and time and rate of turn are correct, the aircraft should be on the correct track when it comes out of the turn.

f. *Astr.* Orig., any group of stars having a random distribution of velocities; usu. applied to a group of stars with an apparent systematic motion towards some point in the sky superimposed on their motion within the group, some or all of the nearest stars belonging to one or other of two such groups with opposite directions of motion.

1906 A. S. EDDINGTON in *Monthly Notices R. Astron. Soc.* LXVII. 35, I define a 'drift of stars' to be a system of stars whose velocities relative to some system of axes are quite haphazard. *Ibid.* 40 Kapteyn..found this same disagreement, and pointed out the explanation—that there are really two drifts of stars. **1928** E. A. FATH *Elem. Astron.* (ed. 2) xv. 236 The motions of the stars in any drift are not along parallel lines... But when the group is taken as a whole it shows a decided group motion toward its vertex. **1938** W. M. SMART *Stellar Dynamics* iv. 106 In most regions of the sky it is found that one drift (drift I) is usually more prominent than the other. **1968** D. S. EVANS *Observ. Mod. Astron.* iv. 137 The two drifts which describe the motion of stars relatively near the Sun are both considered to be in motion relative to the Sun.

g. In the migration of birds: the influence of wind currents.

1918 BAXTER & RINTOUL in *Ibis* VI. 255 We do not consider that the *direction* of the wind, apart from its *force*, stops birds migrating... We believe that the deviation from the direct route is largely, perhaps mainly, due to drift. **1960** E. ENNION *House on Shore* v. 66 Their capture..has gone a long way to establish the reality of 'Drift'. **1971** *Nature* 30 Apr. 580/2 Waders and waterfowl..frequently correct for drift in winds of moderate speed.

h. *Motor-racing.* A controlled slide.

1955 *Motor Trend* Jan. 33, I steer into the drift, accelerating slightly. **1957** S. MOSS *In Track of Speed* v. 61 He was a great exponent of the 'drift'. He was always fastest out of a bend, having discovered the art of pointing the car to the ensuing straight before he was fully round. **1957** *Life* (U.S.) 15 Aug. 83/1 When Fangio puts his Maserati or Ferrari into a corner in a four-wheel drift (i.e., with all wheels skidding).

3. *fig.* Natural or unconscious course, progress, process (of action, argument, †time, etc.); *esp.* in reference to direction or probable result: Tendency.

1549 COVERDALE, etc. *Erasm. Par. 2 Cor.* 61 Since the drifte of myne epistle hath brought me to the visions and reuelacions of the Lorde Jesus. **1575** LANEHAM *Let.* (1871) 46 Such a drifte of tyme was thear passed. **1594** T. B. *La Primaud. Fr. Acad.* II. 5 That Epicurean doctrine, whose only drift is..to turne men from all religion. **1796** BURKE *Regic. Peace* i. Wks. VIII. 173 The whole drift of their institution is contrary to that of the wise legislators of all countries. **1891** T. W. REID *Life Ld. Houghton* I. x. 441 The general drift of affairs on the Continent.

b. *Philol.* (See quot. 1921.)

1921 E. SAPIR *Lang.* vii. 165 The drift of a language is constituted by the unconscious selection on the part of its speakers of those individual variations that are cumulative in some special direction. **1926** *Language* II. 133 We find the same drift at work from analysis to synthesis, from monosyllabism to polysyllabism. **1961** L. F. BROSNAHAN *Sounds of Lang.* vii. 155 These great trends, or *drifts*.., are some of the most interesting phenomena of historical linguistics.

4. a. The conscious direction of action or speech to some end; the end itself; what one is 'driving at'; purpose, intention, object, aim. (Now *rare*, exc. in reference to speech or writing: see also b.)

1526 *Pilgr. Perf.* (W. de W. 1531) 168 b, To imagyn.. what is the dryfte of yᵉ kynge in his parlyament. **1602** WARNER *Alb. Eng.* IX. xlviii. (1612) 223 Our drift (quoth he) a Conquest is. **1781** COWPER *Let.* 19 Oct., My sole drift is to be useful. **1855** TENNYSON *Maud* I. IV. viii, The drift of the Maker is dark, an Isis hid by the veil.

b. Meaning, purport, tenor, scope (of a speech or writing). Now the usual sense.

1526 *Pilgr. Perf.* (W. de W. 1531) 1 Harde it is..to perceyue the processe and dryfte of this treatyse. **1655** FULLER *Ch. Hist.* IX. vii. §17 The main drift and scope of these pamphlets..was to defame and disgrace the English Prelates. **1768** GOLDSM. *Good-n. Man* III. i, I see the whole drift of your argument. **1868** HELPS *Realmah* vi. (1876) 124, I cannot see the general drift and purpose of the story.

†**5.** A scheme, plot, design, device. *Obs.*

1513 MORE in Grafton *Chron.* (1568) II. 761 That drift was by the Queene not unwisely devised. **1538** BALE *Thre Lawes* 1462 Now wyll I contryue the dryft of an other playe. **1603** KNOLLES *Hist. Turks* (1621) 647 Beware that by their wily drifts thou perish not. **1674** N. FAIRFAX *Bulk & Selv.* 193 Those..hallowed drifts, and everlasting well wishes for the happiness of..sinful man.

†6. Putting off, delay, procrastination. [Cf. DRIVE *v.* 22.] *Sc. Obs.*

a **1558** Q. Mary *Answ. Thomworth* in Keith *Hist. Ch. Scot.* (1734) App. 102 (Jam.) Scho intendit na drift of tyme. **1591** R. Bruce *Eleven Serm.* v. 5 a (Jam.) Lang drift and delay of thinges hoped for. **1632** Lithgow *Trav.* x. 484 These promises..were to be performed againe Michaelmasse..But this day come he continued his drifts.

II. That which is driven.

7. A number of animals driven or moving along in a body; a drove, herd, flock, †flight (of birds), †swarm (of bees). Rarely of persons. *Obs.* or *dial.*

c **1450** *St. Cuthbert* (Surtees) 5840 þar ran sixten men in a dryft. **1486** *Bk. St. Albans* F vj, A Dryft of tame Swyne. **1552** Abp. Hamilton *Catech.* (1884) 32 Cursit is the drift of thine Oxin. **1613** Bp. Hall *Holy Panegyrick* 45 Whole driftes of quailes. **1725** De Foe *Voy. round World* (1840) 316 Marks of cattle having passed there, as if they had gone in drifts or droves. **1816** Scott *Let. to Morritt* 16 May in *Lockhart*, To think of carrying off a drift of my neighbour's sheep. **1828** *Craven Dial.*, *Drift*, a drove of cattle.

8. a. A shower (of rain, snow, dust, etc.) driven along by the wind; a driving mass.

a **1300** *Cursor M.* 22462 þar sal fall dun fra þe lijft A blodi rain, a dreri drift. **1569** *Satir. Poems Reform.* x. 320 In snaw, sleit, drift, wind, froist, hailstanis and rane. **1595** Shaks. *John* II. i. 412 Our Thunder..Shall raine their drift of bullets on this Towne. **1725** Pope *Odyss.* VIII. 128 Drifts of rising dust involve the sky. **1842** Tennyson *Talking Oak* ii, The city lies, Beneath its drift of smoke. **1886** Ruskin *Præterita* I. 290 Exposed to drift of rain under violent.. wind.

b. An accumulation of snow, sand, etc., driven together by the wind. (In quot. 1645 applied to a bed or vein of metal.) Also *transf.*

a **1300** *Cursor M.* 9932 þis castel..quitter es þan snau drif[t]. *a* **1400–50** *Alexander* 1756 (Dubl. MS.) A flaw of fell snaw fallen..fro þe drifte. **1634** Sir T. Herbert *Trav.* 91 The sands by the fury of Tempests lies in great drifts. **1645** Quarles *Sol. Recant.* IV. 21 Hath Heaven enricht thy paynes with thriving drifts Of mighty Gold? **1698** Fryer *Acc. E. India & P.* 300 Meadows White with Drifts of Snow. **1865** Whittier *Snow-bound* 59 A smooth white mound the brush-pile showed, A fenceless drift what once was road. **1889** *Daily News* 12 Nov. 3/1 The apparent carelessness with which the folds have been drifted together..The drifts are held by clusters of ostrich feathers. **1893** *Ibid.* 10 Mar. 5/8 A drift of lovely lace fell over the large sleeves.

c. A large mass of flowering plants (see quot. 1966).

1908 G. Jekyll *Colour in Flower Garden* iii. 24 The word 'drift' conveniently describes the shape I have in mind, and I commonly use it in speaking of these long-shaped plantings. **1915** C. Mackenzie *Guy & Pauline* i. 38 Planting a drift of..deep yellow primroses. **1965** *Listener* 23 Sept. 461/2 All of these bulbs can be planted in drifts of hundreds at a time. **1966** J. Berrisford *Wild Garden* viii. 94 Plants and bulbs should be set informally in..'drift-planting'—that is in ovals of irregular outline rather like cloud formations with one or two outliers a little way off so that they look as if sown by the wind.

9. Floating matter driven by currents of water; a floating log, or mass of wood, etc. so driven. Also *fig.*

1600 Hakluyt *Voy.* (1810) III. 530 Foure leagues from the lande, you finde..many drifts of rootes, leaues of trees, [etc.]. **1627** Capt. Smith *Seaman's Gram.* ix. 43 A Drift is any thing floating in the sea that is of wood. **1666** Dryden *Ann. Mirab.* clvi, Some log perhaps upon the waters swam, An useless drift. **1856** Emerson *Eng. Traits, Voy. to Eng.* Wks. (Bohn) II. 11 We crept along through the floating drift of boards, logs, and chips. **1897** *Daily News* 3 May 4/1 They are not beggars..; they are merely human drift—men who live on 'nuffin'.

10. *Geol.* A term applied (*a*) to any superficial deposit caused by a current of water or air; also (*b*) *spec.* (*the Drift*) to Pleistocene deposits of glacial and fluvio-glacial detritus, also known as *boulder-clay*, and *till*; diluvium.

1839 Murchison *Silur. Syst.* I. xxxvii. 509 Each region of the earth has its own superficial diluvia, produced by separate and distinct action; [for these] the unambiguous word *drift* is proposed. **1851** D. Wilson *Preh. Ann.* (1863) I. i. 30 Accumulations of marine and fresh water shingle and gravel called *drift*. **1865** Lubbock *Preh. Times* Pref. (1878) 1 The Flint Implements of the Drift. **1869** R. B. Smyth *Goldf. Victoria* 609 *Drift*, loose sand or a very loose friable alluvial deposit met with in some places close to the washdirt. **1882** Geikie *Text-bk. Geol.* VI. v. i. §1. 858 This 'glacial drift' spreads over the low ground of the glaciated districts. **1892** Gardiner *Stud. Hist. Eng.* 2 These Palæolithic men of the river drift.

fig. **1878** W. P. Roberts *Law & God* 44 In the Protestant *drift* may often be found..the implements of Rome.

attrib. **1847** Emerson *Repr. Men, Plato* Wks. (Bohn) I. 288 The mountain from which all these drift boulders were detached. **1865** Lubbock *Preh. Times* 323 This drift-age cone..is about twelve times as large as that now forming. **1872** W. S. Symonds *Rec. Rocks* iv. 113 The removal of the drift deposits allows the underlying rocks to become visible.

b. drift-peat, a deposit of peat associated with a glacial drift.

1894 J. Geikie *Gt. Ice Age* (ed. 3) 308 The drift-peat and timber that underlie the Carse-deposits of the 45 to 50-ft. level.

11. a. A set of fishing-nets. **b.** A large kind of net used in the herring, pilchard, and mackerel fishery, extended by weights at the bottom and floats at the top, and allowed to drift with the tide; also called *drift-net* (see 19 c).

1834 H. Miller *Scenes & Leg.* xvii. (1857) 260 A complete drift of nets. **1844** W. H. Maxwell *Sports & Adv. Scotl.* (1855) 322 A drift of nets consists of from sixteen to twenty-six. **1854** H. Miller *Sch. & Schm.* (1858) 440 Not a herring swam so low as the upper baulk of our drift.

†**c.** A fanciful name for a company of fishers.

1481 *Bk. St. Albans* F vj b, A Drifte of fishers.

12. A series of piles driven in.

1721 Perry *Daggenh. Breach* 75 The said Drift of dove-tail'd Piles. *Ibid.* 90 A new Drift of Piles on the Thames side.

13. Technical senses. **a.** A tool used for driving or ramming something (e.g. for driving piles). **b.** A steel tool for enlarging or shaping a hole in a piece of metal; a drift-pin. **c.** 'A priming-iron used to clear the vent of ordnance from burning particles after each discharge' (Smyth *Sailor's Word-bk.*). **d.** *Ship-building* (see 1st quot. *c* 1850).

1552 Huloet, Drift, betle, or malle, to dryue pyles or stakes, *fistuca*. **1711** W. Sutherland *Shipbuilder's Assist.* 164 Term-pieces; the finishing Pieces, or those which terminate the Drifts. **1828** J. M. Spearman *Brit. Gunner* (ed. 2) 77 Needles, Quadrants, Wooden Drifts. *c* **1850** *Rudim. Navig.* (Weale) 116 *Drifts*, those parts where the sheer is raised according to the heights of the decks or gangways, and where the rails are cut off and ended by scrolls. **1850** Weale *Dict. Terms*, *Drift*, a piece of hardened steel, notched at the sides and made slightly tapering..used for enlarging a hole in a piece of metal to a particular size by being driven through it. **1864** Webster, *Drift*, a tool used in driving down compactly the composition contained in a rocket, or like firework. **1874** [see *drift-pin* in 19 c.]. **1881** [see DRIFT *v.* 6].

e. *Ship-building*. The difference between the size of a bolt and the hole into which it is driven, or between the circumference of a hoop and the circumference of the mast on which it is to be driven. (Ogilvie.)

1792 *Trans. Soc. Arts* X. 227 Being a bolt of two drifts, [it] could not be driven out. **1823** Crabb *Technol. Dict.*

III. A course or way along which something is driven.

14. a. *gen.* A track. *poetic* and *rare*.

a **1711** Ken *Hymnotheo* Poet. Wks. 1721 III. 182 Birds.. passing through the airy Drift.

b. (See quot. 1811.)

1811 T. Davis *Agric. Wilts.* (ed. 2) 269 *Drifts*, the rows in which underwood is laid when felled. **1915** J. Buchan *Thirty-Nine Steps* vii. 165, I found shelter below an over-hanging rock..where a drift of dead brackens made a tolerable bed. **1927** *Forestry* I. 33 The normal procedure is to cut the coppice..in drifts 3 feet wide and from 4 to 6 feet apart. The young trees..are planted up the middle of the drifts.

15. *Mining*, etc. A passage 'driven' or excavated horizontally, for working, exploration, ventilation, or draining; *esp.* one driven in the direction of a mineral vein. See DRIFTWAY 3.

1653 Manlove *Lead Mines* 159 They may cause [to be] open'd Drifts, and Sumps. **1667** Primatt *City & C. Build.* 5 The conveniency of driving a drift or sough, from the bottom of the hills to the sole of the Rake. **1708** J. C. *Compl. Collier* (1845) 13 A Drift or Watercourse from the old Pits. **1881** Raymond *Mining Gloss.* s.v., A drift follows the vein, as distinguished from a cross-cut, which intersects it, or a level or gallery, which may do either.

16. A lane or road along which horses or cattle are driven; = DRIFTWAY 1. *local.*

1686 Evelyn in *15th Rep. Hist. MSS. Comm.* App. I. 132 Why it should be made a common drift at all times, does not at all consist with..convenience. **1847–78** in Halliwell. **1865** W. White *E. Eng.* II. 79 I went..diagonally, across the wheatfield, and presently struck the 'drift', which has the appearance of an old pack-horse road. **1888** Rider Haggard *Col. Quaritch* i, The broad way that led to it..was a drift or grass lane.

17. *S. Africa.* [a. col. Du. *drift.*] A passage of a river; a ford.

1849 E. E. Napier *Excurs. S. Africa* II. 401 The road.. crosses two or three 'drifts' or fords. **1852** F. Fleming *Kaffraria* (1854) 46 Where the road crosses a river, what is called a drift is made..by clearing the bed of the river of large stones, and cutting a sloping roadway through the banks on either side. **1856** C. J. Andersson *Lake Ngami* 320 The passage of the Orange river..at what is called Zendlings Drift, or the missionary ford.

IV. 18. *Naut.* Length of rope paid out before a fastening is made; length that a tackle will reach from its fixed point; distance so estimated.

1860 H. Stuart *Seaman's Catech.* 47 Allow a fathom drift ..Bend it to the bunt becket, to allow the same drift as the buntlines. **1882** Nares *Seamanship* (ed. 6) 120 In ships with great drift between the fore and main yards, the boats are hoisted in..with the launches purchase.

V. 19. *attrib.* and *Comb.* **a.** *gen.*, as *drift-borer* (see 15), *-cloud*, *-current*, *-rail* (see 13 d), *-rain*, *-sand*; (sense 2 g) *drift-migrant*, *-migration*; *drift-covered*, *-strewn* adjs. **b.** *Geol.* See 10 b.

1637 R. Humphrey tr. *St. Ambrose* II. 13 The drift sand, pible stones and gravell lying on the shore. **1749** J. Smith *Voy. Disc.* II. 141 To go to the Bottom of the Bay to search for drift Fins [i.e. whales]. **1793** Smeaton *Edystone L.* §238 The dormant wedge or that with the point upward, being held in the hand, while the drift wedge or that with its point downward, was driven with a hammer. **1856** *Househ. Words* XIII. 544 Miners from Cornwall, drift borers from Wales. **1875** Bedford *Sailor's Pocket-bk.* iv. (ed. 2) 102 The Drift Current is merely the effect of the wind on the surface of the water. **1952** *Scottish Naturalist* LXIV. 12 If a drift-migrant could continue on the wing indefinitely it would pass from one weather system to another. **1959** *Listener* 22 Jan. 160/1 The average drift-migrants that make a landfall are not necessarily lost. **1960** *Brit. Birds* LIII. 325 (*heading*) Autumn 'drift-migration' on the English east coast.

c. Special combs.: **drift-anchor**, a floating wooden frame or the like, used to keep the ship's head to the wind in a gale or when dismasted (called also *drag-*, *sea-anchor*); **drift-angle**, (*a*) *Naval Arch.*, the angle of lee-way (see LEE-WAY); (*b*) *Aeronaut.* (see quots. 1951 and 1967); **drift-boat**, a boat for fishing with a drift-net; **drift-bolt** (earlier *drive-bolt*): see quot.; **drift-bottle**, a bottle used for the charting of ocean-currents; **drift-fish**, fish taken with a drift-net; so ***drift-fisher***, ***-fishery***, ***-herring***, ***-sprat***; **drift-indicator** *Aeronaut.*, a device for indicating drift (see sense 2 e, above); **drift-keel** = BILGE-KEEL; **drift-mining**, gold-mining carried on by making drifts (sense 15) along the detrital material in the channels of former rivers, now covered by more recent deposits; **drift-net** = sense 11 b (also *attrib.*); **drift-netter**, one who fishes with a drift-net; so ***drift-netting***; **drift-piece** (see quot. 1850 and sense 13 d); **drift-pile** *Canad.*, a pile of drift-wood in a river, etc.; **drift-pin**, **drift-punch** = sense 13 b; **drift plate** or **sight** *Aeronaut.* = *drift-indicator*; **drift-road** = DRIFTWAY 1; **drift-sail** (see quot. 1627); **drift-timber** = DRIFT-WOOD; **drift-weed**, (*a*) sea-weed drifted on shore by the waves; also *fig.*; (*b*) a name for the gulf-weed (*Sargassa baccifera*) and tangle (*Laminaria digitata*); †**drift-wind**, a wind that drives or impels (*obs.*). Also DRIFT-ICE, -WAY, -WOOD.

1874 Knight *Dict. Mech.*, *Drift-anchor. **1881** *Times* 27 Apr. 6/4 She had lost both her masts, and was riding to a drift anchor. **1882** W. H. White *Man. Naval Arch.* (ed. 2) xiv. 621 The angle between this tangent and the keel-line, or '*drift-angle', (*angle de dérive*) as it is termed, gradually increases. **1906** E. L. Attwood *War-Ships* (ed. 2) 237 At the point P, where OP is drawn perpendicular to the centre line of the ship, there is no drift angle, as the tangent to the circle through P is the centre line of the ship. **1935** C. G. Burge *Complete Bk. Aviation* 264/1 *Drift-angle sight*, an instrument for determining the drift-angle. **1951** *Gloss. Aeronaut. Terms* (*B.S.I.*) III. 6 *Drift angle*, the angle, at any instant, between the longitudinal axis of an aircraft and the track. **1967** *Gloss. Terms Air-Cushion Vehicles* (*B.S.I.*) 6 *Drift angle*, the angle, in the horizontal plane, between the longitudinal axis of an ACV and the instantaneous true direction of motion relative to the local meridian. **1851** *Offic. Catal. Gt. Exhib.* II. 800 Model of..the new Mevagissey *drift and fishing boat. **1883** *Leisure Hour* 697/2 A drift-boat carries from eight to twenty nets. **1867** Smyth *Sailor's Word-bk.*, **Drift-bolts*, commonly made of steel, are used as long punches for driving out other bolts. **1909** *Cent. Dict.* Suppl., *Drift-bottle. **1912** Murray & Hjort *Depths of Ocean* v. 261 In order to study the currents, drift-bottles have..been used, in which are enclosed slips of paper with directions to the finder. *Ibid.* 262 (*caption*) Results of Dr. Fulton's drift-bottle experiments in the North Sea. **1966** *McGraw-Hill Encycl. Sci. & Technol.* IX. 252/1 Even slow surface currents have been observed and measured by the drift of debris or drift bottles. **1864** *Glasgow Daily Herald* 24 Sept., I have sold *drift-fish for 12*s*...both drift herring and trawled herring would be selling for 8*s*. *Ibid.*, I was a trawler when trawling was permitted, and a *drift fisher as well. **1919** H. Shaw *Text-Bk. Aeronaut.* xiii. 169 There are two types of *drift indicator, one of which is designed for.. indicating leeway over the surface of the ground.., while the other is intended to indicate whether or not the machine is flying head to wind. **1869** Sir E. J. Reed *Shipbuild.* ii. 43 Side-keels..[also] known as '*drift-keels', 'auxiliary-keels', 'bilge-keels'. **1848** C. A. Johns *Week at Lizard* 43 At nightfall the nets are set either across or parallel to the tide and suffered to drift with it, hence they are called '*drift nets'. **1885** *Times* 25 May 9 Line and drift-net fishermen. **1889** *Cent. Dict.*, *Drift-netter. **1913** *Q. Rev.* Apr. 438 Its rapid extension so alarmed the drift-netters that an agitation was started against it. *Ibid.*, *Drift-netting is carried on by both steamers and sailing vessels. **1963** *Times* 18 May 11/1 Already there are signs that the prohibition of drift-netting will result in increased river catches. **1711** W. Sutherland *Shipbuilder's Assist.* 75 Term Pieces or *Drift Pieces sided. *c* **1850** *Rudim. Navig.* (Weale) 116 *Drift-pieces*, solid pieces, fitted at the drifts, to form the scrolls. **1927** A. P. Woollacott *Mackenzie & his Voyageurs* 37 Log-jams and *drift-piles are numerous and troublesome. **1968** R. M. Patterson *Finlay's River* 103 They found the river very swift and badly obstructed by driftpiles—dangerous piled-up jams of dead and uprooted trees. **1874** Knight *Dict. Mech.*, **Drift-pin*, a hand tool of metal driven into a hole to shape it; as the drift which makes the square socket in the watch-key. **1935** C. G. Burge *Complete Bk. Aviation* 475/1 There are many instruments in use to-day for determining this [*sc.* windage], the oldest being the *drift plate..and the most modern..the tail drift sight. **1869** Sir E. J. Reed *Shipbuild.* x. 198 When the holes are badly punched the workman drives in a steel *drift-punch..and the plate is thus forced and torn and the holes enlarged. **1627** Capt. Smith *Seaman's Gram.* vii. 31 A *Drift saile is onely vsed vnder water..to keepe the Ships head right vpon the Sea in a storme, or when a ship driues too fast in a current. **1727–51** Chambers *Cycl.*, *Drift-sail*..is generally used by fishermen, especially in the North-sea. **1935** *Drift sight [see *drift plate above*]. **1940** 'N. Shute' *Old Captivity* vii. 218 The pilot sat hunched at the wheel,..glancing from time to time down through the drift sight. **1850** Lyell *2nd Visit U.S.* II. 140 To visit the mouths of the Mississippi, and see the banks of sand, mud, and *drift timber, recently formed there. **1845** Darwin *Voy. Nat.* x. (1879) 220 The high-water mark of *drift-weed on a sea-beach. **1906** Somerville & 'Ross' *Irish Yesterdays* 223 She belonged to the drift-weed of the household. **1909** *Daily Chron.* 14 June 9/2 These dreadful drift-weeds of the great city. **1612** *Two Noble K.* v. iii, Waters, That *drift-winds force to raging.

drift, *v.* [f. prec. sb.]

1. a. *intr.* To move as driven or borne along by a current; to float or move along with the stream or wind; = DRIVE *v.* 26. **b.** Of snow, sand, etc.: To collect in heaps driven together by the wind.

?*a* 1600 *Robin Hood* 61 Cam dryfting owyr the ley. 1762 FALCONER *Shipwr.* II. 185 Drifting fast on Grecia's rocky strand. 1828 SCOTT *F. M. Perth* xxiv, We must let her drift with the current. 1869 PHILLIPS *Vesuv.* iii. 67 Columns of smoke and ashes which drifted to the south-east. 1894 J. T. FOWLER *Adamnan* Introd. 66 Beds of sand, which drift like snow.

c. *transf.* and *fig.* To move or pass passively or aimlessly; to be carried involuntarily or without effort in some course or into some condition. Also (*colloq.*), to go away, get out; to come or go casually; to wander; freq. with adverbs, as ***to drift around, by, in, out; to drift apart***, of a man and a woman: gradually to lose mutual affection, etc.

1822 HAZLITT *Table-t.* Ser. II. i. (1869) 8 Drift with the tide of nonsense. 1864 'MARK TWAIN' in Harte & 'Twain' *Sketches* (1926) 122 She can calculate on my drifting around in the course of an hour or so. 1865 R. W. DALE *Jew. Temp.* xi. (1877) 121 They..were fast drifting towards apostasy. 1874 'MARK TWAIN' & WARNER *Gilded Age* I. ix. 119 A week drifted by, and all the while the patient sank lower and lower. 1876 —— *Tom Sawyer* xxxii. 274 Villagers filed through Judge Thatcher's house..and drifted out raining tears all over the place. 1885 *Manch. Exam.* 30 Mar. 5/2 Content to let things drift. 1898 M. DELAND *Old Chester Tales* 43 Peter, with a pretty girl on his arm, drifted in out of the windy and rainy darkness. 1903 *Red Book* July 278/1 Ralph and I had drifted apart years before. 1908 [see DRIFTER e]. 1910 WODEHOUSE *Psmith in City* vi. 46 Let us drift aside into this teashop. 1925 [see DRIFTER e]. 1942 R. CHANDLER *High Window* (1943) ix. 70 'Beat it,' he said. 'Drift.' *Ibid.* xix. 134 So speak your piece and drift away. 1945 *Coast to Coast 1944* 3 Early spectators were drifting in. 1954 'N. BLAKE' *Whisper in Gloom* I. vi. 83 Well, I'll be drifting. 1958 HAYWARD & HARARI tr. *Pasternak's Dr. Zhivago* ix. 255 Tonya and I have never drifted apart and this year of work has brought us even closer together.

2. a. *trans.* To drive or carry along, as by a current of water or air; to blow into heaps (snow, sand, etc.).

a 1618 SYLVESTER *Mem. Mortalitie* II. iv, Time flits as Winde..Who knowes what ills it every moment drifteth. 1748 F. SMITH *Voy. Disc.* I. 166 In Places where the Snow is drifted by the Wind. 1856 FROUDE *Hist. Eng.* (1858) I. iv. 334 Into civil war the nation had no intention of permitting themselves to be drifted. 1869 E. A. PARKER *Pract. Hygiene* (ed. 3) 296 Can malaria be drifted to the place in any way?

b. To allow or cause (a fishing-net or -line) to be borne by the current. Also *absol.*

1850 N. KINGSLEY *Diary* 21 Apr. (1914) 118 [We] drifted the seine across the river and floated down with the current. *Ibid.* 119 They drifted once more and made up the number of 51 salmon. 1907 *Westm. Gaz.* 29 Nov. 3/1 By casting or 'drifting' the dry-fly on a long line down stream to the fish. 1963 K. MANSFIELD *Anglers' Dict.* 51 For bass the best tactics are to anchor up-tide from some buoy, quay or wharf which bass are likely to visit and drift the line down to them. 1971 *Angling Times* 10 June 3 Colin drifted his peeler crab bait around the rocks on float tackle.

c. To drive (cattle or horses) slowly (see quot. 1893). Also with *in*. *U.S.*

1893 *Funk's Stand. Dict.* 555/3 *Drift*, to drive cattle slowly, letting them feed as they go. 1903 A. ADAMS *Log of Cowboy* iv. 51 The Rebel and Blades were following, to drift in what cattle we had held on our left. *Ibid.* vii. 85 We were drifting them back towards the trail. 1920 J. M. HUNTER *Trail Drivers of Texas* 50 [They said] they would drift the horses along with two outfits instead of four.

3. *trans.* To cover with drifts (of snow, etc.); also *intr.* for *refl.* to become covered with drifts.

a 1851 MOIR *Poems, Birth Flowers* xvii, When Winter drifts the fields With snow. 1864 LOWELL *Fireside Trav.* 250 The sides of the road were drifted with heaps of wild hawthorn and honeysuckle. 1892 W. PIKE *Barren Gr. N. Canada* 105 Our tracks had drifted up.

†**4.** *trans.* To put off, delay, defer; = DRIVE *v.* 22. *Sc. Obs.*

1584 J. CARMICHAEL *Let.* in *Wodr. Soc. Misc.* (1844) 434 To drift time awhile. 1588 A. KING tr. *Canisius' Catech., Confession* 3 To drifte to do pœnance for oure sinnes quhil the houre of deathe. 1619 Z. BOYD *Last Battell* (1629) 237 (Jam.) If thou delay and drift him vntill morrow.

†**5.** To drive at, aim at, try to effect. *Obs.*

1602 WARNER *Alb. Eng.* XII. lxix. (1612) 291 Not sooner Dorcas had deuis'd, but Elenor it drifts. *Ibid., Epitome*, Which Elfrick..drifted the murther of King Edmund. *a* 1618 SYLVESTER *Cup of Consolation* 16 Dark Limbo's Potentate Drifts Man's destruction.

6. *Mech.* To form or enlarge (a hole) with a drift (DRIFT *sb.* 13 b.)

1869 SIR E. J. REED *Shipbuild.* xix. 415 Drifting unfair holes would be considered bad work. 1881 GREENER *Gun* 251 The hole is drifted from round to square by knocking in different-sized drifts.

7. (*Mining.*) *intr.* To excavate a drift (see DRIFT *sb.* 15); *trans.*, to excavate a drift in; = DRIVE *v.* 10.

1864 in WEBSTER. 1872 RAYMOND *Statist. Mines & Mining* 179 They have sunk a shaft..over 50 feet, and intend to go to a depth of 200, drifting east and west at 100 feet. 1884 *Harper's Mag.* Mar. 524/1 It is tunnelled or 'drifted' as in one of the hill-side mines.

Hence '**drifted** *ppl. a.*

1726–46 THOMSON *Winter* 285 Impatient flouncing through the drifted heaps. 1778 T. HUTCHINS *Descr. Virginia &c.* 31 The Channel is obstructed with..Islands, formed by trees and drifted wood. 1847 EMERSON *Poems* (1857) 47 Struggling through the drifted roads. 1882 *Daily Tel.* 4 May, Sprung landings held with unfair or drifted holes.

driftage ('drɪftɪdʒ). [f. DRIFT *v.* + -AGE.]

1. The process or operation of drifting.

1862 M. HOPKINS *Hawaii* 414 There is always a driftage of the [sounding] line. 1867 SMYTH *Sailor's Word-bk.*, *Driftage*, the amount due to lee-way. 1877 LE CONTE *Elem. Geol.* (1879) 135 The rate of peat-growth depends upon.. the manner of accumulation, whether entirely by growth of plants *in situ*, or partly by driftage.

2. *concr.* Drifted material. (Cf. *wreckage.*)

1768 J. BYRON *Narr. Patagonia* (ed. 2) 63 No hopes of any valuable driftage from [the wreck]. 1835 HAWTHORNE *Amer. Note-bks.* 15 June (1883) 13 Among the heaps of sea-weed there were sometimes small pieces of painted wood, bark, and other driftage.

'**driftal**, *a. rare.* [f. DRIFT *sb.* + -AL[1].] Pertaining to or of the nature of drift.

18.. ALLEN in Coues *Birds N.-W.* (1874) 10 The driftal *débris* adhering to the trees serves to mark the 'high-water' line.

drifter ('drɪftə(r)). [f. as prec. + -ER[1].]

a. *gen.* One who or that which drifts.

b. *Mining.* (*a*) A miner who excavates drifts (see DRIFT *sb.* 15); (*b*) a heavy, mounted percussion drill driven by compressed air, used in mining for horizontal working; also ***drifter drill***.

1864 *Daily Tel.* 16 Aug. The lead of rich pay dirt was lost for a short time, but..the drifters found it again. 1918 R. PEELE *Mining Engin. Handbk.* 1112 Drifters. 1921 *Engin. & Mining Jrnl.* 27 Aug. 340/1 Modern rock-drilling appliances of the hammer type fall into three well-marked groups, namely, the drifter..; the plugger..; and the stoper. 1946 G. J. YOUNG *Elem. Mining* (ed. 4) xiv. 539 For work at the face 3½-in. drifter drills..are required. 1951 S. HIGHAM *Introd. Metalliferous Mining* vii. 88 When rapid advance is desired, rigged drifters are used.

c. A boat or man engaged in fishing with a drift-net. Also, a fishing-vessel or other small boat used by the Royal Navy, esp. in wartime, for patrolling, conveying stores, etc.

1883 *Fisheries Exhib. Catal.* 79 Model of Drifter for Herring Fisheries. 1887 *Daily News* 27 Sept. 4/6 The proposal..that trawlers should fish only in the daytime, and drifters only during the nighttime. 1916 *In Northern Mists* xxiv. 97 Like all these North Sea craft, trawlers, drifters, and the rest, she is built with bows nearly twice as high out of the water as the after-part. 1917 *Times* 19 May 6/4 Light cruisers..raided the Allied drifter line in the Adriatic and succeeded in sinking 14 British drifters. 1923 *Man. Seamanship* II. 19 In home waters capital ships are generally supplied with a drifter. 1961 GRANVILLE & KELLY *Inshore Heroes* x. 108 In addition to H.M.S. *Midge*, the Coastal Forces' base, to which the M.L.s were attached, there was the base for trawlers, drifters, armed yachts and other auxiliary craft employed on anti-submarine or mine-clearance work.

d. An object which is allowed to float freely in the sea to determine ocean-currents; a drift-bottle.

1897 T. W. FULTON in *Scot. Geogr. Mag.* XIII. 637 Surface currents of the North Sea..Drifters..were used, one-ounce wide-mouthed bottles. 1900 *Geogr. Jrnl.* XV. 275 On the voyage from Iceland to Jan Mayen in 1896 twenty drifters were thrown overboard.

e. A man following an aimless, irresolute, or vagrant way of life.

1908 *Daily Chron.* 28 Sept. 4/7 The drifter drifts to California, and brings up there because..he can drift no further. 1922 *Short Stories* Feb. 25/1 The trampers ain't all hoboes, some of 'em being just drifters. 1925 W. DEEPING *Sorrell & Son* xxviii. 275 For months he had had a sense of drifting, and his character was not that of a drifter. 1971 *Guardian* 14 June 9/1 A drifter with nothing but the clothes he stands up in.

f. A wind causing snow to drift.

1922 R. J. FLAHERTY *My Eskimo Friends* 8 Then came snow, the winter's first big 'drifter', and for three days there was no land or sea or sky. 1924 A. J. SMALL *Frozen Gold* ii. 49 A confused..blur of whining blizzards, roaring drifters, flat calm cold-snaps. 1970 *Globe & Mail* (Toronto) 28 Sept. 19/8 Winds ranging from a drifter to 15 knots.

drift-ice. [f. DRIFT *sb.*] Drifting or drifted ice; *esp.* detached pieces of ice drifting with the wind or ocean currents.

1600 HAKLUYT *Voy.* III. 65 (R.) We were greatly endangered with a piece of drift yce, which the ebbe brought foorth of the sounds. 1694 *Acc. Sev. Late Voy.* II. (1711) 221 The Coast so full of drift Ice, that it is almost inaccessible. 1772–84 COOK *Voy.* (1790) V. 1892 We spent the night standing off and on, among the drift ice. 1820 SCORESBY in *Ann. Reg.* II. 1324 Drift-ice consists of pieces less than floes, of various shapes and magnitudes.

'**drifting**, *vbl. sb.* [f. DRIFT *v.* + -ING[1].]

1. a. The action of the verb DRIFT, q.v.; also *concr.* (*pl.*) that which is drifted.

1821 KEATS *Isabella* xiv, The rich-ored driftings of the flood. 1891 *Echo* 10 Mar. 3/3 The drifting has caused many roads to be impassable.

†**b.** Putting off; lapse (of time). *Obs.*

1610 J. FORBES *Certain Rec.* (1846) II. x. 496 No drifting of time sould cause them to alter.

†**c.** Scheming, machination. *Obs.*

1602 WARNER *Alb. Eng.* XII. lxxv. (1612) 313 Italian Driftings, and such Sinnes.

2. *spec.* in *Mining* (see DRIFT *v.* 7). Also *attrib.*

1853 *Harper's Mag.* VI. 447 The shafting and drifting gets only the copper which is in the immediate course of those operations. 1882 *Rep. Prec. Metals* (*U.S. Bureau of Mint*) I. 70 This mine has been worked by the drifting method. *Ibid.* III. 635 A..portion of the gravels or 'wash'..is removed by ..drifting, from underneath worthless or comparatively barren ground. 1897 *Sears, Roebuck Catal.* 50/2 Drifting picks, adze eye, oil finish. 1927 R. PEELE *Mining Engineers' Handbk.* (ed. 2) x. 500 All types of rock drill are used for drifting and crosscutting. 1952 M. H. HADDOCK *Basis Mine Surveying* vii. 259 Drifting in coal-mining has nearly always been between parallel strata with the frequently assured certainty of locating the deposit sought.

'**drifting**, *ppl. a.* [f. as prec. + -ING[2].] That drifts; see the verb.

1749 F. SMITH *Voy. Disc.* II. 43 Intensely cold, with excessive Frost and drifting Snow. 1847 EMERSON *Poems, Woodnotes* Wks. (Bohn) I. 423 Drifting sand-heaps. 1890 BOLDREWOOD *Col. Reformer* (1891) 331 The gaunt, perishing seaman on the drifting raft.

†**b.** Designing, aiming, scheming. *Obs.*

1602 WARNER *Alb. Eng.* IX. liii. (1612) 239 Ill drifting Rome and Spaine.

Hence '**driftingly** *adv.*

1859 *Chamb. Jrnl.* XI. 128 The fading clouds, all driftingly, Submerge. 1895 A. AUSTIN in *Blackw. Mag.* 639/2 To fish driftingly from one end of Lough Inagh to another.

driftland: see DROFLAND.

driftless ('drɪftlɪs), *a.* [f. DRIFT *sb.* + -LESS.]

1. Having no drift, purport, or purpose; aimless.

1806 W. TAYLOR in *Monthly Mag.* XXII. 536 The primitive meaning of ambiguous therefore is driftless. *a* 1875 H. TAYLOR *Autobiog.* (1885) I. vi. 95 A reckless and driftless conduct in life.

2. *Geol.* Free from drift: see DRIFT *sb.* 10.

1873 J. GEIKIE *Gt. Ice Age* xxxii. 465 The 'driftless region' of Wisconsin, Iowa, and Minnesota.

Hence '**driftlessness**, aimlessness.

1801 W. TAYLOR in *Monthly Mag.* XII. 582 An apparent driftlessness of the events and characters.

driftway, drift-way ('drɪftweɪ). [f. DRIFT *sb.* + WAY.]

1. A lane or road along which cattle or horses are driven to pasture or market; a drove-road: see also quot. 1884. (In local use.)

1611 *Award conc. Holland Fen, Lincolnsh.*, The said commoners..to leave a driftway for the cattle and beasts of the said Edward Dymocke. 1772 *Rhode Isl. Colonial Rec.* (1862) VII. 54 An Act empowering the several town councils..to lay out drift-ways in their respective towns. 1880 WILLIAMS *Rights of Common* 324 A way may be either a footway, or a bridleway, or a driftway for cattle. 1884 HALE *Christm. in Narragansett* xi. 41 'Driftway'..is..a cross-road to the sea by which the sea-weed..may be hauled up to their homes.

2. *Naut.* The amount by which a vessel drifts out of her course; lee-way.

1721 BAILEY, *Drift Way*, (of a Ship) is the same as Lee-way. 1867 in SMYTH *Sailor's Word-bk.*

3. *Mining*, etc. = DRIFT *sb.* 15; also, a small gallery driven in advance of a tunnel, etc.

1843 *Penny Cycl.* XXV. 371/2 The miners begin to excavate laterally by forming a heading or driftway along the level of the upper part of the tunnel. Sometimes such a drift is formed throughout the whole length of the tunnel before any part is opened out to the full size. 1861 SMILES *Engineers* I. 444 The excavations..proceeded in opposite directions to meet the other driftways..in progress.

drift-wood, 'driftwood.

1. Wood floating on, or cast ashore by, the water. Esp. wood carried down by a river. Formerly freq. *U.S.*

[1613 PURCHAS *Pilgrimage* (1614) 743 They have no wood but drift.] 1633 T. JAMES *Voy.* 26 There was great store of drift wood. 1780 COXE *Russ. Disc.* 42 Forobieff built another small vessel with drift-wood. 1785 WASHINGTON *Diary* 3 Aug. (1925) II. 396 It would probably be frequently choaked with drift wood, Ice, and other rubbish. *Ibid.* 25 Jan. (1925) IV. 79 The river there is..full of small islands occasioned by drift wood lodging on the rocks. 1821 J. FOWLER *Jrnl.* 22 Oct. (1898) 26 The men Waided over and geathered drift Wood for the night. 1840 R. H. DANA *Bef. Mast* xxiii. 72 [We] made a fire..with the drift-wood. 1848 J. F. COOPER *Oak Openings* I. iii. 47 The drift-wood choked the channel. 1850 H. C. WATSON *Camp-fires Revol.* 67 That exposed our boats to being all the time tangled in the drift-wood and bushes. 1884 'MARK TWAIN' *Huck. Finn* vii. 50 The river was coming up pretty fast, and lots of drift-wood going by on the rise.

2. *fig.* Also *attrib.*

1840 *Daily Picayune* (New Orleans) (D.A.E.), Kendall will cut a 'swell' at our next drift-wood training. 1865 J. G. HOLLAND *Plain Talks* 224 A lodging place for political drift-wood. 1907 *Daily Chron.* 23 July 4/6 The metropolis attracts human driftwood from all quarters.

drifty ('drɪftɪ), *a.* [f. DRIFT *sb.* + -Y.]

†**1.** Full of secret aims; wily. (Cf. DRIFT *sb.* 5.)

1571 CAMPION *Hist. Irel.* II. ix. (1633) 106 Ormond was secret and drifty.

2. a. Characterized by drifts, of the nature of a drift.

1730 T. BOSTON *Mem.* xii. 435 That drifty day stopt a funeral. 1785 BURNS *Winter Night* viii, Through the ragged roof and chinky wall, Chill, o'er his slumbers, piles the drifty heap! 1881 J. RUSSELL *Haigs* xi. 301 The Thirteen Drifty Days in which the storm culminated in the month of February [1674].

b. Flowing.

1897 *Daily News* 1 May 8/2 The dress..is so soft and drifty. 1962 *Sunday Express* 30 Dec. 17/5 Long drifty skirts of voile.

drifun, obs. pa. pple. of DRIVE *v.*

drige, driȝe, drigh(e, obs. ff. DRY, DREE *v.*

† **'driggle-draggle.** *Obs.* exc. *dial.* [Reduplicated f. DRAGGLE *v.*, with vowel-alternation: cf. *dingle-dangle*, etc.] A slut, slattern, drab. Also *attrib.*, slatternly.

1588 FRAUNCE *Lawiers Log.* I. vi. 33 b, If there be any driggle draggle in Shrewsbury. 1593 *Tell-Troth's N.Y. Gift* 14 Those driggell draggells (whose wicked and lascivious lives have wasted their bodies). 1611 FLORIO, *Zaccara*, a driggle-draggle strumpet. 1888 ELWORTHY *W. Somerset Word-bk.*, *Driggle-draggle*, adv. and sb., in a slovenly, slatternly manner—specially applied to women's dress; also as an epithet.

† **dright**[1]. *Obs.* In 1–3 **dryht, driht**, 5 **driȝt**. [OE. *dryht*, *driht* multitude, army, people = OS. *druht*, OHG., MHG. *truht*, ON. *drótt*; cf. Goth. *ga-drauhts* soldier; f. *dréoȝan* to do, perform, work, do military service; see DREE *v.*] A multitude, host, army.

a 1000 *Cædmon's Exod.* 78 Drihta ȝedrymost. *c* 1205 LAY. 92 þes duc mid his drihte to þare sæ him droh. *a* 1400–50 *Alexander* 3868 Dragons dryfes doun o driȝt fra þe derfe hillis.

b. *attrib.* and *Comb.*, as **drightfare**, march of a host, procession, throng; **drightfolk**, people, army; **drightman**, warrior. (OE. and early ME.)

a 1000 *Cædmon's Exod.* 34 þa wæs..deaðe ȝedrenced drihtfolca mæst. *c* 1205 LAY. 14715 Hengest gon to flonnen mid al his driht-monnen. *Ibid.* 16584 He wende in to Cuninges-burh mid his driht folke. *a* 1225 *Leg. Kath.* 1852 Wið swuch dream & drihtfare as drihtin deah to cumene.

dright[2]: see DRIGHTIN.

drighte: see DRETCH *v.*[2]

† **'drightin, -ten**, abbrev. **dright**. *Obs.* Forms: α. 1–4 **drihten**, 3 **driȝten**, (*Orm.*) **drihhtin, drittin**, 3–4 **driȝtin, drihtin**, 4 **drightinn, -un, driȝtyn, dryȝt(t)yn**, 4–5 **driȝtine, drightin(e, dryghtyn(e**, 5 **drichtine**. β. 3–4 **driht(e**, 3 **dryght**, 3–4 **drichte**, 4 **dright(e, drytte**, 4–5 **dryȝt(e**. [OE. *dryhten*, *drihten* = OS. *drohtin*, OFris. *drochten*, OHG. *truhtin*, ON. *dróttinn*, f. *dryht*, DRIGHT[1] with suffix *-ino-z*: cf. Goth. *kindins* governor, L. *dominus*, etc.] A lord, ruler, chief; *spec.* the Lord God, or Christ.

α. *Beowulf* (Th.) 2973 Geata dryhten. *Ibid.* 3113 Witiȝ Drihten rodera rædend. *c* 1000 ÆLFRIC *Exod.* xx. 10 Se seofoþa ys Drihtnes reste dæȝ þines Godes. *c* 1175 *Lamb. Hom.* 5 Iblesced he þe her cumeþ on drihtenes nome. *c* 1200 *Trin. Coll. Hom.* 109 Ure drihten christ. *a* 1300 *Cursor M.* 5217 I am driȝttyn þi faders god and al-so þine. ? *a* 1400 *Morte Arth.* 664 To dye at Dryghtyns wylle. *c* 1475 *Rauf Coilȝear* 856 Now thankit be Drichtine.

β. *c* 1200 *Trin. Coll. Hom.* 187 Manie mannisshe folȝeden ure drihte. *c* 1250 *Hymn to God* 5 ibid. App. 258 Folkes fader, heouenliche drichte. *a* 1300 *Cursor M.* 11000 Thoru grace o dright. *c* 1315 SHOREHAM 33 Bye drytte. *c* 1380 *Sir Ferumb.* 407 So helpe þe þy driȝte! *c* 1450 MYRC 1470 To burye the dede as byd owre dryȝt.

† Hence (only in OE. and early ME.): **'drightness (drihtnesse)**, majesty, godhead; **'drightful, 'drightlike (drihtlic)** *adjs.*, lordly, noble.

Beowulf (Th.) 2320 Hie..drihtlice wif to Denum feredon. *a* 1000 *Cædmon's Gen.* 1843 Him drihtlicu mæȝ..þuhte. *c* 1175 *Lamb. Hom.* 101 þreo on hadan and an god..on ane drihtnesse and godnesse. *c* 1205 LAY. 24762 Al þi drihtliche uolc. *a* 1225 *Leg. Kath.* 1123 He ne losede..undedlichnesse onont his drihtnesse. *a* 1225 *Juliana* 13 þe drihtfule godd apollo mi lauerd.

drih, drijfe, obs. ff. DREE *a.*, DRIVE *v.*

drill (drɪl), *sb.*[1] Also 5 **drylle**, 7 **dril, drille**. [In sense 2, goes with DRILL *v.*[2]; sense 1 offers difficulties, and is not certainly the same word.]

† **1.** A small draught (of liquid). *Obs. rare.*

c 1440 *Promp. Parv.* 132/1 Drylle, or lytylle drafte of drynke, *haustillus*.

2. A (? trickling) rivulet or small stream; a rill.

1641 G. SANDYS *Paraphr. Song Sol.* IV. ii, Those living Springs..Whose Drils our plants with moisture feed. 1719 DE FOE *Crusoe* I. x, Meadow-land..which had two or three ..drills of fresh water in it. 1751 R. PALTOCK *P. Wilkins* xxxiv. (1883) 93/1 Coming to my drill's mouth, I fixed my implements for a draft there. 1819 G. SAMOUELLE *Entomol. Compend.* 313 The drills in marshes should be examined.

drill (drɪl), *sb.*[2] Also 7 **dril**. [In sense 1 prob. immed. a. Du. *dril*, *drille*, in same sense (in Kilian 1599, and prob. in MDu.), f. *drillen*: see DRILL *v.*[3]; in other senses app. from the vb. in Eng.]

I. Mechanical and technical senses.

1. An instrument for drilling or boring; applied to contrivances of many kinds for boring holes in metal, stone, and other hard substances, from a pointed steel tool to an elaborate drilling machine.

1611 COTGR., *Trappan*, a Stone-cutters Drill, the toole wherewith he bores little holes in marble, &c. 1688 R. HOLME *Armoury* III. 322/1 The Drill is a shaft or long Pin of Iron with a Steel point. 1703 MOXON *Mech. Exerc.* 6 Drills are used for the making such Holes as Punches will not conveniently serve for. 1879 *Cassell's Techn. Educ.* I. 185 The drill is a revolving cutter..to form circular holes in iron or other material. 1881 RAYMOND *Mining Gloss.* s.v., The ordinary miner's drill is a bar of steel, with a chisel-shaped end.

2. A shell-fish which is destructive to oyster-beds by boring into the shells of young oysters; a borer.

1886 *Sci. Amer. Suppl.* XXII. 8868 The little *littorinas*, the destructive 'drill' which works its way into the shell of the young oysters.

3. Manner or style of drilling, or in which a hole is drilled.

1849 LONGF. *Kavanagh* 22 He..said the drill of the [needle's] eye was superior to any other.

II. Military and derived senses.

4. The action or method of instructing in military evolutions; military exercise or training; with *a* and *pl.* an exercise of this nature.

a 1637 B. JONSON *Underwoods* lxii. 29 He that but saw thy curious captain's drill, Would think no more of Vlushing, or the Brill. 1809 WELLINGTON 24 June in Gurw. *Desp.* IV. 463, I propose to give the best drilled of the seven battalions coming to Portugal, in order to assist in your drills. 1859 JEPHSON *Brittany* ii. 15 A company of soldiers..at drill.

5. One who drills (others); a drill-master.

1814 SCOTT *Wav.* lxii, Her husband was my sergeant-major..and got on by being a good drill. 1894 D. C. MURRAY *Making of Novelist* 57 The various drills laboured at him like galley-slaves.

6. *fig.* **a.** Rigorous training or discipline; exact routine; strict methodical instruction.

1815 W. H. IRELAND *Scribbleomania* 51 Thy worn quill Too often hath needed Apollo's sharp drill. 1875 EMERSON *Lett. & Soc. Aims, Eloquence* Wks. (Bohn) III. 194 This wise mixture of good drill in Latin grammar with good drill in cricket, boating, and wrestling. 1967 *Lebende Sprachen* XII. 136/2 *Drill* or *language laboratory drill*, a series of exercises devised for giving practice in teaching or testing a particular skill. It may be in the form of a two-, three-, or four-phase drill.

b. The agreed or recognized procedure, esp. on formal occasions. *colloq.*

1940 D. WHEATLEY *Faked Passports* xxii. 265 Our Generals had so little imagination that the drill was always just the same and..the Germans got quite used to it. 1943 HUNT & PRINGLE *Service Slang* 28 *The drill*, the correct way of doing a job is always referred to in this manner, or as the 'right drill'. 1957 *Listener* 5 Dec. 925/2 He would come to dinner, swallow his soup, and then fall fast asleep. The servants knew the drill and kept his other courses warm.

III. 7. *attrib.* and *Comb.* **a.** Pertaining to a drill or boring instrument, as ***drill-hole***, ***-holder***, ***-room***, ***-spindle***; ***drill-like*** adj.; **drill-barrel**, a cylinder round the shank of a drill, on which the string of the drill-bow works; **drill-bow**, a bow used for working a drill; **drill-chuck**, **-extractor**, **-gauge**, **-jar**, **-pin**, **-plate** (= BREAST-PLATE 3 b), **-press**, **-stock** (see quots.); **drill pipe** *Oil Industry*, piping which carries and rotates the bit when a hole is being drilled and conveys the circulating mud; **drill string**, (*a*) a string wound round the shank of a drill in order to rotate it; (*b*) *Oil Industry*, a column of drill pipe together with the bit and associated parts; a drilling string (cf. STRING *sb.* 15 b).

1703 MOXON *Mech. Exerc.* 6 The bigger the *Drill-barrel is, the easier it runs about, but less swift... You must..keep your *Drill-Bow straining your String pretty stiff. 1865 LUBBOCK *Preh. Times* xiv. (1869) 513 The Dacotahs used a drill bow for the purpose of obtaining fire. 1874 KNIGHT *Dict. Mech.*, **Drill-chuck*, a chuck in a lathe or drilling-machine for holding the shank of the drill. *Ibid.*, **Drill-extractor*, a tool or implement for extracting from deep borings a broken or a detached drill. *Ibid.*, **Drill-gage*, a tool for determining the angle of the basil or edge of a drill. *Ibid.*, **Drill-jar*, a..stone or well-boring tool in which the tool-holder is lifted and dropped successively. 1698 BALLARD in *Phil. Trans.* XX. 420 Little..*drill-like pieces of Steel. 1850 CHUBB *Locks & Keys* 15 The *drill pins of the locks, and the pipes of the keys. 1874 KNIGHT *Dict. Mech.*, *Drill-pin*, a pin in a lock which enters the hollow stem of a key. 1932 *Amer. Speech* VII. 266 **Drill pipe*.., (rotary equipment) heavy steel pipe which composes the column connecting the bit with the rotating apparatus at the surface. 1949 *Our Industry* (Anglo-Iranian Oil Co. Ltd.) (ed. 2) ii. 39 When a drilling bit becomes worn to such an extent that the drilling speed falls off, the whole string of drill pipe must be withdrawn in order to replace the worn bit by a new one. 1974 *BP Shield Internat.* Oct. 18/3 We might have to lift drill pipe to the drill floor. 1984 *Listener* 27 Sept. 9 This innovative device grapples with enormous lengths of drill pipe, connecting them together as drilling progresses. 1677 MOXON *Mech. Exerc.* 7 *Drill-Plate, or Breast-Plate..to set the blunt end of the Shank of the Drill in, when you drill a hole. 1864 WEBSTER, **Drill-press*, a machine-tool embodying one or more drills for making holes in metal. 1858 SIMMONDS *Dict. Trade*, **Drill-stock*, the holdfast for a metal drill. 1677 MOXON *Mech. Exerc.* 6 You may sometimes require..several *Drill-strings; the strongest Strings for the largest Drills. 1948 *Petroleum Handbk.* (Shell Internat. Petroleum Co.) (ed. 3) v. 82 The great weight needed to push the bit downward into the formations is concentrated at the bottom of the drill string. 1975 *Offshore Progress—Technol. & Costs* (Shell Briefing Service) 6 As the rig rises and falls with the heaving surface of the sea, ..constant weight must be maintained through the drillstring on the drilling bit. 1979 Drill string [see STRING *sb.* 15 b]. 1984 A. C. & A. DUXBURY *Introd. World's Oceans* iii. 83 (in figure) Acoustical sensor on drill string determines drill bit position.

b. Pertaining to or connected with military drill, as ***drill-day***, ***-ground***, ***-hall***, ***-instructor***, ***-master***, ***-purpose***, ***-room***, ***-ship***; **drill-book**, a manual of instruction in military or other drill; also *attrib.* and *transf.*; **drill order** (see ORDER *sb.*); **drill-sergeant**, a non-commissioned officer who trains soldiers in military evolutions.

1846 *United Services Mag.* II. 235 The French *drill-book. 1868 *All Year Round* 11 July 108/1 He walks in a fine drill-book style. 1900 *Daily News* 15 May 3/3 The Queensland Mounted Infantry contingent seem to have engrafted sufficient drill-book into their common-sense methods. 1906 W. WOOD *Enemy in our Midst* vii. 73 On a certain assumption which was that an enemy would work according to drill-book and rule-of-thumb. 1937 G. FAIRBANKS (*title*) Voice and articulation drillbook. 1831 JANE PORTER *Sir E. Seaward's Narr.* II. 169 After these arrangements, *drill-day came. 1844 *Regul. & Ord. Army* 120 In the Barrack-Yard or *Drill-Ground. 1878 *Chambers's Encycl.* III. 671/1 *Drill-halls, in which drill can be carried on comfortably in any kind of weather, are now common. 1891 *Scribner's Mag.* X. 565 Entertainments are also given in the drill hall every Friday evening. 1933 L. A. G. STRONG *Sea Wall* x. 120 Jerry held..a grand tournament of all his pupils, hiring for the purpose a local drill-hall. 1876 A. ARNOLD in *Contemp. Rev.* June 28 The..*drill-instructor has never before him the same body of men. 1869 SPURGEON *Treas. Dav.* Ps. xviii. 34 The Holy Spirit is the great *Drill-master of heavenly soldiers. 1803 (*title*) The Complete *Drill Serjeant. 1826 MISS MITFORD *Village* Ser. II. (1863) 265 Facing to right and left, under the command of a drill-sergeant. *a* 1865 SMYTH *Sailor's Word-Bk.* (1867) 264 **Drill-ships*, a recent establishment of vessels in which the volunteers composing the Royal Naval Reserve are drilled into practice. 1948 *Jane's Fighting Ships 1947–48* 50 *Zetland* was assigned to Solent Division R.N.V.R. as drillship.

drill (drɪl), *sb.*[3] Also 7 **dril**. [perh. ad. native name.] A West African species of baboon, *Mandrillus leucophæus*. Also *attrib.*, as ***drill baboon***, ***monkey***.

1644 BULWER *Chirol.* A iv, The dumb Ginnie Drills. 1652 —— *Anthropomet.* (1653) 439 This relation of Tulpius shows this creature to have been a kind of Ginney Drill, which this Michaelmas Terme, 1652, I saw neare Charing Crosse..which Drill is since dead, and I believe dissected. 1654 CLEVELAND *Char. Diurnal-m.* 12 A Diurnall-maker is the antemark [antimask] of an Historian, he differs from him as a Drill from a man. 1656 BLOUNT *Glossogr.*, *Dril*..a large over-grown Ape, or Baboon, so called. 1726 SWIFT *It cannot rain but it pours* Wks. 1755 III. I. 136 His ears..he can move like a drill, and turn them towards the sonorous object. 1847 CARPENTER *Zool.* §156 The Drill..is rather smaller in stature than the Mandrill..The face is black; but the beard is orange-coloured. 1898 *Westm. Gaz.* 15 Feb. 11/3 The drill monkey, the most costly and rare of its kind in the gardens. 1905 *Daily Chron.* 29 Apr. 7/1 The finest drill baboon ever seen in confinement is in the Bellevue Gardens.

drill, *sb.*[4] [Perh. the same word as DRILL *sb.*[1], in its sense of rill, runnel: cf. the senses of Ger. *rille* small furrow, drill, chamfer.]

1. A small furrow made in the soil, in which seed is sown; a ridge having such a furrow on its top; also, the row of plants thus sown.

1727 BRADLEY *Fam. Dict.* s.v. *Carnation*, The seed may be sown..in drills drawn cross a bed by a Line. 1772 T. SIMPSON *Vermin-Killer* 2, Field rats..will..run along the drills of peas. 1787 WINTER *Syst. Husb.* 184 The drills were eight inches asunder. 1834 *Penny Cycl.* I. 224/2 The seed sown by hand falls into the bottom of the drills. *Mod.* A drill of potatoes or turnips.

2. A machine for sowing seed in drills, now usually having contrivances for drawing furrows and for covering the seed when sown.

1731 J. TULL *Horse-hoeing Husb.* xxii. 147 The Drill is the Engine that plants our Corn and other Seeds in Rows; it makes the Channels, sows the Seed into them, and covers them. *a* 1740 —— in C. W. Hoskins *Occas. Ess.* (1866) 102, I composed my machine. It was named a Drill, because when farmers used to sow their beans and pease into channels or furrows by hand, they called that action drilling. 1812 CRABBE *Tales* 3 Wks. 1834 IV. 195 Corn sown by drill, or thresh'd by a machine. 1886 T. HARDY *Mayor of Casterbridge* xxiv, The new-fashioned..horse-drill.

3. *attrib.* and *Comb.*, as ***drill-box***, ***-culture***, ***-husbandry***, ***-man***, ***-system***; **drill-barrow**, a barrowlike contrivance for sowing in drills; **drill-harrow** (see quot.); **drill-machine**, **-plough** = sense 2.

1805 R. W. DICKSON *Pract. Agric.* (1807) I. 28 The *drill-barrow is..well adapted for sowing some grains and small seeds. 1753 CHAMBERS *Cycl. Supp.*, Drill, or *Drill-Box. 1847 CRAIG, *Drill-box*, the box in a drill-machine which contains the seed. *Ibid.*, **Drill-harrow*, a small harrow.. used between the drills or rows for the purpose of extirpating weeds. 1784–5 *Ann. Reg.* 59/2 *Drill husbandry is..the practise of a garden brought into the field. 1807 VANCOUVER *Agric. Devon* (1813) 120 **Drill-machines*, attached to the ploughs..or used with a horse or by hand. 1731 J. TULL *Horse-hoeing Husb.* xxiii. 166 The *Drill-Plow which makes the Channels for a treble Row of Wheat. 1847 *Jrnl. R. Agric. Soc.* VIII. I. 63 A drill-plough, which drills the seed, and covers it in with the furrow turned by the plough.

drill (drɪl), *sb.*[5] Abbreviated form of DRILLING *sb.* [Cf. Ger. *drell* (Brem. Wörterb.).]

1743 *Lond. & Country Brew.* IV. (ed. 2) 315 A Sort of Cloth called Drill. 1851 *Offic. Catal. Gt. Exhib.* I. 99 Drills, and other Twilled Linens. 1876 *Monthly Pkt.* June 570 Boys, on admission, to be..supplied with..2 suits of brown drill. 1887 *Pall Mall G.* 12 Jan. 7/1 In cotton goods.. America takes a high position in two descriptions, drills and sheetings. **1918** H. G. Wells *Joan & Peter* xiii. 664 Both the pink gingham and the white drill had been tried on. **1967** *Listener* 3 Aug. 156/2 Hugh Griffith in khaki drill and a pith helmet.

attrib. **1757** in E. W. Cunnington et al. *Dict. Eng. Costume* (1960) 253/2 Dressed in..a white drill Frock. **1882** Bret Harte *Flip* i, His light drill garments. **1899** E. W. Hornung *Amateur Cracksman* 223 A girl in a white drill coat and skirt. **1934** 'G. Orwell' *Burmese Days* vi. 96 Dressed in khaki pagri-cloth shirt, drill shorts and a pigsticker topi.

†**drill**, *v.*[1] *Obs.* (exc. *dial.*). Also 4 dril. [Appears first in ME.: origin unknown.]

1. *trans.* and *absol.* To delay, defer, put off.

a **1300** *Cursor M.* 16390 (Cott.) Selcuth vs thinc o þe, pilate, wit drightin for to drill [*Gött.* wid dreching for to drill] We haf vs chosen nu baraban, him haf algat we will. *Ibid.* 23715 þe ded ai wen we for to dril.

2. *to drill away, on, out*: to protract, lengthen *out*; to fritter *away*, spend aimlessly (time).

a **1656** Ussher *Ann.* vi. (1658) 464 Purposely drilling out the time, hoping to encline the Senate to favour his designe. **1668** Etheredge *She wou'd if she cou'd* ii. i, We must drill away a little time here. **1672** Marvell *Reh. Transp.* I. 306 They drill'd things on, till they might [etc.]. **1719** D'Urfey *Pills* (1872) V. 180 He drills on his Evil, then curses his Fate, And bewails those misfortunes himself did create. *a* **1745** Swift (Webster, 1864) This accident hath drilled away the whole summer. **1751** R. Paltock *P. Wilkins* xxx. (1883) 84/2 One pretence or other..of drilling on the time till the dark weather is over.

3. To lead, allure, or entice (a person) *on* from one point to another (in time or action); and so = to put off (cf. 1).

1669 Marvell *Corr.* iii. Wks. 1872–5 II. 270 So speedily as they may not have drilled you on beyond the time of prosecution. *a* **1688** Villiers (Dk. Buckhm.) *Poems* (1775) 141 Nor is it wit that drills the statesman on To waste the sweets of life, so quickly gone. **1711** Addison *Spect.* No. 89 ¶ 1 She has bubbled him out of his Youth;..she drilled him on to Five and Fifty, and..she will drop him in his old Age. **1752** Gray *Lett.* Wks. 1884 II. 231 He drilled him on with various pretences.

4. To draw or entice (a person) *in, into* a place; also *on, along, out of* a thing.

1662 Hickeringill *Wks.* (1716) I. 296 Drilling in the rabble with their..buffooneries. **1681** *Ibid.* 187 To drill Men out of their Estates. **1673** R. Head *Canting Acad.* 72 [He] was pickt up by a pack of Rogues in the streets and drilled into a Tavern. **1696** Aubrey *Misc.* (1721) 97 Having drill'd his Wife along 'till he came to a certain Close..he threw her by Force into the Water. **1697** Dampier *Voy.* I. v. 114 They drill'd them by discourse so near, that our men lay'd hold on all three at once.

5. *intr.* To slip away, vanish by degrees. *dial.*

c **1315** [see adrylle]. **1847–78** Halliwell, *Drill*..to slide away. *Kent.* **1887** *Kentish Dial.* (E.D.S.), *Drill*, to waste away by degrees.

†**drill**, *v.*[2] *Obs.* [Etymology of this, and the cognate drill *sb.*[1], uncertain. The verb is identical in sense with trill, frequent from Chaucer onward, and may be an altered form of it. Cf. also Ger. *trillen* to flow whirling or rolling, cited by Grimm from a 17th c. writer, and taken by him as a sense of *drillen* to turn.]

1. *intr.* To flow in a small stream or in drops; to trickle, percolate; to drip.

1603 Florio *Montaigne* i. xlix. (1632) 162 In summer they often caused cold water..to drill upon them as they sate in their dining chambers. **1609** Heywood *Brit. Troy* (N.), Swift watry drops drill from his eye. **1782** A. Monro *Anat., Bones, Nerves* 62 The liquor..drills down upon the membrane of the nose.

refl. **1634** Sir T. Herbert *Trav.* 209 Water..gently drils it selfe from the high Rocks.

2. *transf.* and *fig.* To be derived, spring, flow.

1638 Sir T. Herbert *Trav.* (ed. 2) 111 Chaldy, Arabick, and Siriack drilling from the Hebrew.

Hence '**drilling** *vbl. sb.* and *ppl. a.*

1634 Sir T. Herbert *Trav.* 214 Full of shadowing trees, and drilling Rivolets. **1665** J. Webb *Stone-Heng* (1725) 226 The drilling down of the Water..from the..Hills. **1741** Monro *Anat. Nerves* (ed. 3) 86 A constant drilling of a glairy Mucus.

drill (drɪl), *v.*[3] Also 7 dril, dryll, 9 *Sc.* dreel. [Known only from 17th c.; cf. drill *sb.*[2] All the senses are found in Du. *drillen* to drill, bore; to turn round; to shake, brandish; to drill, form to arms; to run hither and thither; to go through the manual exercise, MDu. *drillen* to bore, turn in a circle, brandish; cf. MLG. *drillen* to roll, to turn, MHG. and mod.Ger. *drillen* to turn, to round off, to bore, to drill soldiers. MHG. *gedrollen* 'rounded', *drall* '(twisted) tight', point to an old strong verb, of ablaut series ***þrell-, þrall-, þrull-**. The English verb and sb. were prob. from Dutch; they are not connected etymologically with *thrill, thirl*, OE. *þyrelian*, though sense 1 is identical in sense with it.]

I. To pierce, bore, make a narrow hole.

1. a. *trans.* To pierce or bore a hole, passage, etc. in (anything); to perforate with or as with a drill or similar tool. Also *spec.* to shoot with a gun (*colloq.*). (Said chiefly of personal agents.)

1649 G. Daniel *Trinarch., Hen. V*, clviii, The Stone dropt Sand; And the drill'd Alpes, became a Posterne which From Time lockt vp, noe foot had ever trode. **1697** Dampier *Voy.* I. xvi. 466 Twirling the hard piece between the palms of their hands, they drill the soft piece till it smoaks, and at last takes fire. **1784** Cowper *Task* i. 26 Drill'd in holes, the solid oak is found. **1808** E. S. Barrett *Miss-Led General* i. 11 It would be a terrible affair to *us*..if we should be drilled with a bullet. **1833** Marryat *P. Simple* iv, Being drilled was to be shot through the body. **1871** P. H. Waddell *Ps.* xl. 6 My lugs ye hae dreel'd. **1879** Jefferies *Wild Life in S. Co.* 213 Rabbit-holes drill the bank everywhere. **1930** *Amer. Mercury* Dec. 455/2 Go drill the mutt. He's strictly stool. **1936** M. Mitchell *Gone with Wind* xii. 223, I can drill a dime at fifty yards.

b. *intr.* To pierce *through*.

1674 N. Fairfax *Bulk & Selv.* 196 None of those rayes of other atoms..come riding or drilling through both. *Ibid.* 61.

2. To make or bore (a hole, etc.) by drilling. Also *transf.* of shooting.

1669 Sturmy *Mariner's Mag.* ii. 73 There must be a Hole drill'd. **1793** Smeaton *Edystone L.* §36 The holes..appear to have been drilled into the rock by Jumpers. **1858** Greener *Gunnery* 47 Drill a communication, and put in a nipple. **1890** *Nature* 4 Sept. 446/1 On August 28, 1859, the first well, drilled in the United States with the object of obtaining petroleum, was successfully completed. **1912** E. C. Bentley *Trent's Last Case* vi. 136 Thirty thousand men ..would have jumped at the chance of drilling a hole through the man.

II. †**3.** *trans.* To turn round and round; to whirl, twirl; in quot. 1681 to churn. *Obs.* or *dial.*

1681 R. Knox *Hist. Ceylon* 97 They skim off the Cream, and drill it in an earthen Vessel with a stick. **1847–78** Halliwell, *Drill*, to twirl, or whirl. *Devon.*

III. To train in military movements and exercise. [Found from 17th c. also in Du., Ger., Da. (Not in Kilian 1599; in Hexham 1678). Prob. from the sense 'turn round'.]

4. a. *trans.* To train or exercise in military evolutions and the use of arms. ('An old cant word.' J.)

1626 Capt. Smith *Accid. Yng. Sea-men* 37 Drilling your men..to ranke, file, march, skirmish, and retire. **1663** Butler *Hud.* i. iii. 445 The Foe appear'd, drawn up and drill'd. **1842** Macaulay *Fredk. Gt.* Ess. (1887) 695 The business of life, according to him, was to drill and be drilled. *Ibid.* 709 He drilled his people as he drilled his grenadiers.

b. *intr.* for *refl.* and *pass.*

1848 W. E. Forster in T. W. Reid *Life* I. vii. 26 May, Large numbers of men are armed and drilling nightly. *Mod.* The regiment drills regularly every day.

5. *transf.* and *fig.* To train or instruct as with military rigour and exactness. Const. *into, in, to*, and *inf.* (Also *intr.* for *refl.*)

1622 Massinger *Virg. Mart.* ii. ii, I hug thee..For drilling thy quick brains in this rich plot. **1794** Southey *Botany Bay Eclog.* iii, So I..was drill'd to repentance and reason. **1798** Edgeworth *Pract. Educ.* (1811) I. 323 Where boys are to be drilled in a given time into scholars. **1842** [see 4]. **1853** Kane *Grinnell Exp.* xxix. (1856) 254 We had drilled with knapsack and sledge, till we were almost martinets in our evolutions on the ice. **1856** —— *Arct. Expl.* I. xxix. 389 Bear-dogs..that had been drilled to relieve each other in the melée. **1873** Black *Pr. Thule* xii. 182 He had drilled her in all that she should do and say.

6. a. To order or regulate exactly. **b.** To impart by strict method (a subject of knowledge). **c.** (See quot. 1894.) **d.** *U.S. Railroads.* To shunt (carriages, engines, etc.).

1863 'Ouida' *Held in Bondage* 2 Drill Greek, and instil religious principles into them. **1877** Blackmore *Erema* lii, To be a great lady..and regulate and drill all the doings of nature. **1894** *Labour Commission* Gloss. s.v., To drill a person is to refuse him employment for a certain period, say, a fortnight, as a punishment.

Hence **drilled, 'drilling** *ppl. adjs.*; also '**drillingly** *adv.*, by way of drilling or boring.

1649 Drill'd [see 1]. **1830** [see driller[2] 2 a]. **1831** *Blackw. Mag.* XXX. 490 The moths drillingly devoured the manuscript. **1879** Froude *Cæsar* ix. 103 The superiority of the drilled Roman legions.

drill, *v.*[4] [f. drill *sb.*[4]]

1. *trans.* To sow (seed) in drills, as opposed to broadcast; to raise (crops) in drills.

a **1740** [see drill *sb.*[4] 2]. **1788** G. Washington *Let.* Writ. 1891 XI. 223 As all my corn will be thus drilled, so..I mean to put in drills also potatoes, carrots (as far as my seed will go), and turnips. **1837** *Penny Cycl.* IX. 148/2 The crops which are now most generally drilled are potatoes, turnips, beans, peas, beet-root, cole-seed, and carrots.

2. To sow or plant (ground) in drills.

1785 G. Washington *Writ.* (1891) XII. 225 A piece of ground..drilled with corn and potatoes between. **1894** *Times* 19 Mar. 11/1 He drilled two acres of land with this barley.

Hence **drilled** *ppl. a.*; **drilling** *vbl. sb.*

1766 Croker, etc. *Dict. Arts* s.v. *Wheat*, An Acre of drilled Wheat. **1767** A. Young *Farmer's Lett. People* 117 The drilling method likewise promises great advantages. **1806–7** A. Young *Agric. Essex* (1813) I. 100, I do not know that a drilled acre is superior in produce, at first, to a broadcast acre. **1846** J. Baxter *Libr. Pract. Agric.* (ed. 4) I. 241 Drilling, now styled the 'New Husbandry,' is in reality the primitive practice. **1876** T. Hardy *Ethelberta* (1890) 108 Like a drilled-in crop of which not a seed has failed.

drillable ('drɪləb(ə)l), *a.* [f. drill *v.*[3] + -able.] Capable of being drilled.

1889 *Spectator* 16 Nov., The Romans..were the most drillable of peoples. **1892** *Sat. Rev.* 5 Mar. 264/1 The German has always been an admirably drillable animal.

†'**driller**[1]. *Obs. rare*[−1]. [? f. drill *v.*[1] + -er[1].] ? One who entices or allures (*sc.* into evil).

1652 J. Tatham *Commend. Verses to Brome's Joviall Crew*, But Shakespeare the Plebean Driller, was Founder'd in 's Pericles, and must not pass.

driller[2] ('drɪlə(r)). [f. drill *v.*[3] + -er[1].]

1. One who drills holes in metal, stone, etc. **b.** A machine or contrivance for this purpose.

1835 Ure *Philos. Manuf.* 21 The dexterous hands of the filer and driller. **1870** *Eng. Mech.* 28 Jan. 480/1 A driller [*i.e.* tool].. will bore the holes.

2. a. One who drills others; a drill-master, a drill instructor. Also *transf.*

1830 Gen. P. Thompson *Exerc.* (1842) I. 251 The drillers ..were made liable to transportation..the drilled, to fine, and imprisonment. **1870** Lowell *Among my Bks.* Ser. i. (1873) 177 The great authors of antiquity..degraded from teachers of thinking to drillers in grammar.

b. One who practises military drilling.

1848 W. E. Forster in T. W. Reid *Life* (1888) I. 248 The soldiers..were called out to help the specials to arrest some drillers. **1890** C. Martyn *W. Phillips* 260 A prominent driller in the 'awkward squad'.

'**driller**[3]. [f. drill *v.*[4] + -er[1].] One who sows seed by drilling.

1788 *Trans. Soc. Arts* VI. 78 A practical Driller. **1837** *Penny Cycl.* IX. 149/2 The farmer finds horses and seed, and the driller finds the machine.

drilling ('drɪlɪŋ), *sb.* [corruption of Ger. *drillich*, MHG. *drilich, drilch* threefold, ad. L. *trilīcem* (*trilix*), f. L. *tri-* three + *līcium* thrum, thread.] A coarse twilled linen or cotton fabric used for summer clothing, etc. Also *attrib.*

1640 in Entick *London* (1766) II. 168 Gutting and spruce canvas drillinges. **1753** Hanway *Trav.* (1762) I. ii. xiv. 61 Making sail-cloth, sheetings, ravenducks and drillings. **1861** Du Chaillu *Equat. Afr.* vi. 55 A blue drilling shirt.

drilling, *ppl. a.*: see after drill *v.*[2], [3].

'**drilling,** *vbl. sb.*[1]: see after drill *v.*[2]

drilling ('drɪlɪŋ), *vbl. sb.*[2] [f. drill *v.*[3]]

1. Boring; perforation.

1698 Ballard in *Phil. Trans.* XX. 420 Bare drilling might be able to give a Polarity to a Drill. **1894** *Labour Commission* Gloss., *Drilling*, making holes in rails for the purpose of putting in bolts to fasten them to sleepers.

2. Training in military evolutions. Also *transf.*

1639 Massinger *Unnat. Combat* iii. i, There being no war, nor hope of any, The only drilling is to eat devoutly. *a* **1687** Petty *Pol. Arith.* (1690) 17 Training and Drilling is a small part of Soldiery. **1880** McCarthy *Own Times* IV. 127 Its oath of fidelity..its nightly drillings.

3. *attrib.* and *Comb.*: **a.** in sense 1, as ***drilling-engine, -machine, -tool***; **drilling-bow** = *drill-bow* (drill *sb.*[2] 7 a); **drilling-jig, -lathe** (see quots.); **drilling rig** = rig *sb.*[6] 3 a; **drilling string**: see string *sb.* 15 b. **b.** in sense 2, as ***drilling-day, -exercise***.

a. 1851 *Offic. Catal. Gt. Exhib.* I. 246 Used by watch-makers..for the *drilling-bow. **1832** Babbage *Econ. Manuf.* xix. (ed. 3) 172 The dividing and the *drilling-engine are of this kind. **1874** Knight *Dict. Mech.*, **Drilling-jig*, a portable drilling-machine which may be dogged to the work, or so handled as to be readily presented to it and worked by hand. *Ibid.*, **Drilling-lathe*, a drilling-machine on horizontal ways or shears, thus resembling a lathe. **1865** Gesner *Pract. Treat. Coal, Petrol.*, etc (ed. 2) 34 *Drilling machines which can bore nine feet per hour. **1901** J. G. McIntosh tr. *Neuburger & Noalhat's Technol. Petroleum* xxx. 396 (*caption*) Rotary oil-well *drilling rig for shallow depths. **1933** *Petroleum Handbk.* (Shell Internat. Petroleum Co.) iii. 36 The drilling rig consists of a multiple speed hoisting unit called the 'draw works' and a rotary machine for turning the drill-pipe. **1976** M. Machlin *Pipeline* i. 23 Red flames.. lighting up the sky in the direction of the Alamo Oil Company drilling rig.

b. *a* **1625** Fletcher *Love's Cure* iii. ii, I..gave him..In the artillery yard three drilling daies. **1870** Whitney *Germ. Gram.* Suppl. 3 Drilling exercises upon individual difficulties of German idiom.

drily, *adv.*: see dryly.

Drinamyl ('drɪnəmɪl). *Pharm.* Also **drinamyl.** [f. d(ext)r(o- + (amphetam)in(e + amyl[2].] The proprietary name of a preparation of dexamphetamine and amylobarbitone, used as a stimulant. Cf. purple heart 3.

1950 in *Trade Marks Jrnl.* 13 Dec. 1053/2. **1952** *Martindale's Extra Pharmacopœia* (ed. 23) 516 Drinamyl... Tablets each containing d-amphetamine sulphate 5 mg. and amylobarbitone 32 mg. For control of mental and emotional distress. **1961** *Guardian* 23 Mar. 3/1 Drinamyl, a Schedule 1 poison known in the trade as 'purple heart'. **1968** J. Blackburn *Young Man from Lima* iii. 32 Two drinamyl tablets had restored his self-confidence. **1969** *Daily Tel.* 5 Mar. 25/6 A drug addict who took drinamyl and was formerly an addict of heroin.

dring (drɪŋ), *v. dial.* [Presumably local form of thring *v.*] *trans.* and *intr.* To crowd, press, squeeze. Also *fig.* So '**dringing** *vbl. sb.*

1810 *Monthly Mag.* XXIX. i. 435/1 *Dringing*, crowding. **1825** J. Jennings *Observ. Dial. W. Eng.* 34 *To dring*, to throng; to press, as in a crowd; to thrust. **1867** W. F. Rock *Jim an' Nell* 37 A thousan' happy fancies dring. **1922** Joyce *Ulysses* 723 I'd have to dring it into him. **1923** *Chambers's Jrnl.* Apr. 309/2 'I dring through it,' he said, head up to whatever chanced.

dringe, obs. form of dreng.

†**dringle,** *v.* *Obs.* exc. *dial.* [A word of uncertain origin, varying dialectally with *drindle, drimble*: see also drumble.] *intr.* 'To

waste time in a lazy lingering manner' (Forby); to linger; to trickle sluggishly.

c **1680** HICKERINGILL *Wks.* (1716) II. 536 Condemn'd to endure the Fatigues of Life to the last dringling Sand.

drink (drɪŋk), *v.*[1] Pa. t. drank (dræŋk); pa. pple. drunk (drʌŋk). Forms: Pres. stem. 1-4 drinc-, 2- drink- (3 drinnk- *Orm.*, dringk-, 3-4 drinch-, 3-5 dring- (he dringþ), 3-6 drynk-, 4-6 drinck-); 3-7 drinke, 4- drink. Pa. t. *sing.* 1-3 dranc, 3- drank, 3 dronc, dranck, *Orm.* drannk, 3-5 drong, 4-5 dronk(e, 4-7 dranke, 6-7 drunke, 6-9 drunk; *pl.* 1 druncon, 2-4 drunken, (3 drunnkenn *Orm.*, drongken), 3-4 dronke(n, 3-5 drunke; also 3- *north.* and 5- *generally*, same as sing. Pa. pple. *α.* 1 druncen, 2- drunken, (3 *Orm.* drunnkenn, 3-6 dronken, 4 dronckyn; *Sc.* 5 drukken, 6 drokin, 7-9 druken, drucken). *β.* 3-7 drunke, (5 drownk, 5-6 dronke, droonke, droncke), 6- drunk; also 7-9 drank. [Com. Teut.: OE. *drincan* = OS. *drinkan* (Du. *drinken*), OHG. *trinkan*, *trinchan*, mod.G. *trinken*, ON. *drekka* (Sw. *dricka*, Da. *drikke*), Goth. *drigkan*:—OTeut. **driŋkan*, not found outside Germanic. The pa. t. had originally vowel change, *drank*, pl. *drunken*, *drunk(e*, but from the 13th c. in northern dial., and 15th c. generally, these were levelled under the sing. form (Caxton *we*, *ye*, *thei dranke*). Either through the retention of the pl. form in some southern dial., or from the pa. pple., *drunk* began to reappear, for sing. as well as pl., in end of 16th c., and is occasional to 19th. On the other hand, from 17th to 19th c. *drank* was intruded from the pa. t. into the pa. pple., prob. to avoid the inebriate associations of *drunk*. The full form *drunken* of pa. pple. has been since 17th c. mostly used as adj., exc. as a poetic archaism. Sc. and n. dial. *drucken* represents the ON. pa. pple. *drukkinn*.]

I. Transitive senses.

1. a. To take (liquid) into the stomach; to swallow down, imbibe, quaff.

c **1000** *Ags. Gosp.* Luke i. 15 He ne drincð win ne beor. *c* **1205** LAY. 5804 3e scullen drinken eowre blod. *a* **1300** *Cursor M.* 6354 Suetter [water] neuer þai siþen drank. *Ibid.* 12679 He dranc [*Trin.* dronk] neuer cisar ne wine. **13..** *Ibid.* 17708 (Fairf.) They fille as they had dronckyn dwale. **13..** *Guy Warw.* (A.) 318 He no may..Rest no take slepeinge, Mete ete no drinke dringe. **1398** TREVISA *Barth. De P.R.* IV. vii. (1495) 91 Yf bulles blode be dronken rawe. **1474** CAXTON *Chesse* III. i. (1883) 83 In olde tyme women dranke no wyn. **1548** HALL *Chron., Hen. VI*, 108 To tel you ..what wyne was dronke in houses. **1568** GRAFTON *Chron.* II. 116 Such a Cup of Wine as ye never dranke before. **1578** LYTE *Dodoens* I. ii. 6 Wormwood..drunken with vineger is good. **1596** SHAKS. *Tam. Shr.* Induct. ii. I ne're drank sacke in my life. **1732** ARBUTHNOT *Rules of Diet* 268 Common Water or Whey, drank in cool Air. **1747** WESLEY *Prim. Physic* (1762) 86 It should be drunk with the finest Sugar. **1761** HUME *Hist. Eng.* II. App. iii. 521 Three hundred and sixty-five hogsheads of beer were drank at it. **1795** SOUTHEY *Joan of Arc* III. 30 They..drank the running waters. **1865** SWINBURNE *Poems & Ball.*, *Triumph of Time* 26, I trod the grapes, I have drunken the wine. **1881** BESANT & RICE *Chapl. Fleet* I. 9 Which I have drunk with my parishioners.

b. *spec.* ***to drink the waters***: i.e. at a spa medicinally.

c **1681** VISCOUNTESS CAMPDEN in *12th Rep. Hist. MSS. Comm.* App. v. 56 My sister..was troubled with malincoly, so went to drinke Astrope watter. **1713** *Lond. Gaz.* No. 5130/9 The Elector intends..to drink the Waters at Pirmond. **1855** MACAULAY *Hist. Eng.* III. 699 Annandale.. retired to Bath, and pretended to drink the waters.

c. *transf.* and *fig.* in general; cf. also 3, 4.

c **1340** [see 6]. **1592** SHAKS. *Rom. & Jul.* III. v. 59 Drie sorrow drinkes our blood. **1610** —— *Temp.* v. i. 102, I drinke the air before me. **1715-20** POPE *Iliad* XI. 221 While his keen falchion drinks the warriors' lives. **1819** SHELLEY *Cenci* III. ii, When the dim air Has drank this innocent flame. **1827** POLLOK *Course T.* v. 116 Give the heart to drink.. draughts of perfect sweet. **1850** B. TAYLOR *Eldorado* i. (1862) 4, I drank in the land-wind..with an enjoyment verging on intoxication.

2. a. With *off*, *out* (now *dial.*), *up*, expressing exhaustion of the liquid; so also ***to drink dry***.

1535 COVERDALE *Job* xl. 23 Without eny laboure might he drynke out the whole floude. **1583** HOLLYBAND *Campo di Fior* 199 Drinke up all, Seeing there is but a litle left. **1592** SHAKS. *Rom. & Jul.* IV. i. 94 This distilling liquor drinke thou off. **1593** —— *Rich. II*, II. ii. 146 The taske he vndertakes Is numbring sands, and drinking Oceans drie. **1648** GAGE *West Ind.* xvii. 112 My Chocolatte, which I drunke off heartily. **1722** DE FOE *Col. Jack* (1840) 118 We drank on, and drank the punch out. **1780** COWPER *Progr. Err.* 581 He that sips often, at last drinks it up. **1816** SCOTT *Antiq.* xl, 'A' Saunders's gin..was drucken out at the burial o' Steenie.'

b. *transf.* and *fig.*

c **1374** CHAUCER *Troylus* III. 986 (1035) Pete..goodli drinkyþ vp al his distresse. **1644** CROMWELL *Let. Col. Walton* 5 July in Carlyle, Let this drink up your sorrow. **1827** POLLOK *Course T.* III. 314 Consumption..drank her marrow up.

3. *transf.* Of porous substances, plants, etc. To absorb (moisture); to suck. Often with *up* or *in*.

1530 PALSGR. 529/2, I drinke, as the yerthe dothe water, or as blottyng paper dothe ynke. **1561** HOLLYBUSH *Hom. Apoth.* 7 a, If the Aqua vite is dronke in of the herbes. **1630** *R. Johnson's Kingd. & Commw.* 82 Like barren ground, drinking up the raine. **1697** DRYDEN *Virg. Georg.* IV. 46 Let the purple Vi'lets drink the Stream. **1793** SMEATON *Edystone L.* §190 Plaster of Paris..would then drink up linseed oil plentifully. **1858** DRAYSON *Sport. S. Africa* 238 The soil that had drunk the blood of his warriors.

4. *fig.* esp., with *in*: To take into the mind, esp. by the eyes or ears, with the eager delight of one who satisfies physical thirst; to listen to, gaze upon, or contemplate with rapture.

1592 SHAKS. *Rom. & Jul.* II. ii. 58 My eares haue yet not drunke a hundred words Of thy tongues vttering. **1635-56** COWLEY *Davideis* I. 386 They sing..And with fix'd eyes drink in immortal rays. *a* **1713** ELLWOOD *Autobiog.* (1714) 18, I drank in his Words with Desire. **1859** JEPHSON *Brittany* vii. 96, I stopped for a while to drink in the beauty of the scene. **1878** BROWNING *La Saisiaz* 11 Your level path that let me drink the morning deep and slow.

†**5.** To draw in or inhale (tobacco smoke, etc.); to smoke. *Obs.*

1598 B. JONSON *Ev. Man in Hum.* III. ii, The most divine tobacco that ever I drunk. **1613** PURCHAS *Pilgrimage* IX. i. 820 Their Lords and Priests consult of warres, after they have drunke the smoke of a certain herbe. **1654** E. JOHNSON *Wond. wrkg. Provid.* 97 He was drinking a pipe of Tobacco. **1781** PENNANT *Tour Wales* II. 28 The first who smoked, or, (as they called it) drank tobacco publickly in London. [**1855** SPENCER *Turkey, Russia, &c.* xix. 278 According to the idiom of their language, they [Tatars] do not smoke the fragrant herb, but drink it.]

6. To swallow down the contents of (a cup or vessel). Also with *off*, *up*, indicating completeness, and *fig.* ***to drink the cup***, or ***chalice***, ***of joy***, ***sorrow***, ***suffering***, etc.: see CUP *sb.* 9, CHALICE 1 b.

a **1300** *Cursor M.* 15681 (Cott.), I wat wel þat i sal it drinc þis calice [*Gött.* drinck; *Fairf.* drink. *c* **1340** *Trin.* drynke þis deþ]. **1382** WYCLIF *1 Cor.* xi. 26 How ofte euere 3e schulen ..drynke the cuppe, 3e schulen schewe the deeth of the Lord. **1634** SIR T. HERBERT *Trav.* 97 Put off his Turbant, and drunke the cup off. **1750** JOHNSON *Rambler* No. 49 ¶10 He had..drank many a flaggon. **1816** J. WILSON *City of Plague* III. ii, I drank the cup of joy.

7. To swallow down (something solid) in a liquid. ***to drink candle-ends***: see CANDLE-END 1 b.

1632 LITHGOW *Trav.* VI. 278 A little of it [earth] drunke in any Liquor. **1768-74** TUCKER *Lt. Nat.* (1852) II. 35 A wasp ..may fall in [a pot] to be drank by one, whom he shall sting to death.

8. To consume or spend in drinking (money, etc.). Also with *away*, *up*.

1492 in *Burgh Rec. Edin.* I. 62 (Jam. Supp.) He sall pay for ilk defalt vj [pennies?]..to be drukken be the dusane. **1509** BARCLAY *Shyp of Folys* (1874) I. 305 If another gyue them ought of pyte, At the next alestake dronken shall it be. **1604** E. GRIMSTONE *Hist. Siege Ostend* 220 Spignola bestowed of them..forty thousand gilders to drinke. **1701** DEFOE *Trueborn Eng.* II. 31 Drink their Estates away, and Senses too. **1765** FOOTE *Commissary* I. Wks. 1799 II. 8, I hope you'll tip me the tester to drink. **1884** 'MARK TWAIN' *Huck. Finn* xliii. 437 It's likely pap's..got it [*sc.* money] all away from Judge Thatcher and drunk it up. *a* **1897** *Mod.* He drinks his whole earnings. **1964** *Penguin Bk. Austral. Ballads* 123 Between them they drank every cent.

9. *colloq.* To provide with drink.

1883 E. F. KNIGHT *Cruise 'Falcon'* (1887) 85 He could not feed us, only lodge and drink us.

II. Absolute and intransitive senses.

10. *absol.* **a.** To swallow down or imbibe water or other liquid, for nourishment or quenching of thirst. Const. †*in*, *from*, *out of* (the vessel).

c **1000** *Ags. Gosp.* Luke xiii. 26 We æton & druncon beforan þe. *a* **1225** *Ancr. R.* 44 Bitweone mete, hwo se drinken wule, sigge benedicite. *a* **1300** *Cursor M.* 3551 He ete and dranc [*Trin.* dronke] and went his wai. *c* **1420** *Chron. Vilod.* 130 And eton and drongon and made hem blythe. *c* **1489** CAXTON *Blanchardyn* viii. 31 The kynge of Fryse had nothre eten nor dronken. **1596** SHAKS. *1 Hen. IV*, II. iv. 169, I am a Rogue if I drunke to day. **1602** *Narcissus* (1893) 248 They can but bringe horse to the water brinke, But horse may choose whether that horse will drinke. **1634** SIR T. HERBERT *Trav.* 67 The Wine bottles and flat cups we drunke in, were of pure Gold. **1698** FRYER *Acc. E. India & P.* 93 Such little Glasses as we drink out of. **1780** COWPER *Progr. Err.* 466 Thou fountain at which drink the good and wise. **1876** RUSKIN *Fors Clav.* VI. lxvii. 214 Having sufficiently eaten and drunken.

b. ***to drink deep***: to take a large draught, either once or habitually; see also 10 c, 11.

a **1300** *Sat. People Kildare* xx. in *E.E.P.* (1862) 156 Men ..þat..drinkiþ dep and makiþ glade. **1393** LANGL. *P. Pl.* C. x. 145 Eremytes, That..drynke drue and deepe. **1709** POPE *Ess. Crit.* 218 Drink deep, or taste not the Pierian spring. **1820** SCOTT *Ivanhoe* v, 'Pledge me, my guests.' He drank deep, and went on.

c. Const. *of* (rarely †*upon*) the liquid or source of supply. *lit.* and *fig.* ***to drink of the cup of sorrow***, etc.: see CUP *sb.* 9.

c **1000** ÆLFRIC *Gen.* ix. 21 þa he dranc of ðam wine, ða wearþ he druncen. *c* **1200** *Trin. Coll. Hom.* 111 He dranc of deðes flode. *c* **1340** *Cursor M.* 15241 (Trin.) Drinkeþ [*Cott.* drinckes] alle of þis he seide. **1490** CAXTON *Eneydos* 4, I suppose he hath dronken of Elycons well. **1549** *Order of Communion*, Exhortation 3 To give us his said body and blood..to feed and drink upon. **1667** MILTON *P.L.* II. 584 Lethe..whereof who drinks, Forthwith his former state and being forgets. **1751** CHATHAM *Lett. Nephew* ii. 7 Drink as deep as you can of these divine springs. **1884** TENNYSON *Becket* I. iv. 75 Ye have eaten of my dish and drunken of my cup for a dozen years.

d. Proverb. ***one must drink as one brews.***

a **1300** *Cursor M.* 2848 (Gött.) Suilk as þai breu nou haue þai drunke [*Cott.* dronken]. *c* **1460** *Towneley Myst.* (Surtees) 111 Bot we must drynk as we brew, And that is bot reson. *c* **1560** A. SCOTT *Poems* xx. 64 3it man thou stand content And drynk þat thou hes brewit. *a* **1610** HEALEY *Cebes* (1636) 114 She drinketh of her owne brewing. **1647** TRAPP *Comm. Rev.* xiii. 10 Antichrist shall one day..drink as he brewed, be paid in his own coin. [See also BREW *v.* 1 d].

e. ***to drink up***, to finish one's drink. (Cf. sense 2.)

1919 C. MACKENZIE *Early Life Sylvia Scarlett* I. v. 158 Drink up and have another. **1927** HEMINGWAY *Fiesta* xiii. 150 Drink up, Harris. **1938** G. GREENE *Brighton Rock* VII. ix. 347 Drink up. We'd better get on with the good work. **1949** 'N. BLAKE' *Head of Traveller* ii. 40 Well, drink up, Jack, and we'll make a four-hand.

11. a. To take alcoholic or intoxicating liquor, either convivially, or to gratify appetite; to indulge therein to excess; to tipple; *spec.* to be a habitual drunkard. (The sense is often indicated contextually by adverbs or phrases such as *about*, *deep*, *hard*, *heavily*, *like a fish*.) Also ***to drink it***.

c **1440** *Promp. Parv.* 132/1 Drynkyn a-bowte..epoto. **1474** CAXTON *Chesse* III. vi. (1883) 130 He dranke so moche that he was veray dronke. **1500-20** DUNBAR *Poems* xxxiv. 67 The Feind me ryfe Gif I do ocht bot drynk and swyfe. **1611** BARRY *Ram-Alley* IV. (Hazl. *Dodsley*), I have been drinking hard. **1638** SIR T. HERBERT *Trav.* (ed. 2) 242 They sit long and drink soundly. **1640** FLETCHER & SHIRLEY *Nightwalker* IV. sig. H2ᵛ, Give me the bottle, I can drink like a Fish now, like an Elephant. **1701** FARQUHAR *Sir H. Wildair* II. 14 Drink like a Fish, and swear like a Devil. **1732** POPE *Ep. Bathurst* 390 His son..Who drinks, whores, fights, and in a duel dies. **1802** C. WILMOT *Let.* 2 Jan. in *Irish Peer* (1920) 24 Not forgetting I was not at Home, and consequently drinking like a Fish. **1837** *Tait's Mag.* IV. 492 I'll coach it, and dine it, and drink it till morn. **1837** [see FISH *sb.*[1] 1 c]. **1848** THACKERAY *Lett.* 28 July, We went to a barrack room, where we drank about. **1879** MISS BRADDON *Clov. Foot* vii, A woman who drank like a fish and swore like a trooper. *Mod.* Poor woman! her husband drinks.

b. ***to drink and drive***, to drive or attempt to drive a motor vehicle after taking an alcoholic drink or drinks (and while one's driving may be impaired by the after-effects of this). (Freq. as a road-safety slogan ***Don't drink and drive***.)

1944 *Cases adjudicated in Supreme Court, Florida* CLIV. 548 A resume of the evidence here would serve no useful purpose unless it might emphasize the tragic consequences resulting from the act of those who drink and drive. **1960** *Newsweek* 14 Mar. 88/3 (*heading*) If you drink and drive. **1976** *South Notts Echo* 16 Dec. 5/6, I just hope people will take notice of the warnings and do not drink and drive. **1984** *Guardian* 27 Dec. 2/7 The current Stay Low campaign..has been widely criticised for failing to push the traditional 'Don't drink and drive' message.

12. Hence *trans.* and *refl.*, with various complements, indicating the result of drinking, as **a.** *refl.* ***to drink oneself drunk***, ***sleepy***, ***tame***, ***to death***, ***into incoherence***, ***into spirit***, ***out of a situation***, etc. †**b.** *ellipt. intr.* ***to drink drunk*** (obs.). **c.** *trans.* ***to drink away one's reason***, ***one's property***, ***one's eyes out***; ***to drink down*** (i.e. quench or destroy by drinking). **d.** ***to drink*** (a person) ***out of*** or ***into*** some condition, etc; ***to drink*** (a person) ***dead drunk***, ***down***, ***to bed***, ***under the table***: said of the more seasoned toper, who sees his comrades succumb to the effect of their potations. †**e.** ***to drink the sun up***: to carouse through the night until sunrise. Also in other analogous uses.

a. 1598 SHAKS. *Merry W.* I. i. 180 The Gentleman had drunke himselfe out of his fiue sentences [= senses]. **1607** TOPSELL *Serpents* (1658) 805 The Country-people set little vessels of wine..whereunto the Vipers coming, easily drink themselves tame. **1727** DE FOE *Syst. Magic* I. iv. (1840) 95 By persuading him to drink himself drunk. **1821** BYRON *Juan* III. lxvi, A genius who has drunk himself to death. **1849** *Fraser's Mag.* XL. 384 He..drank himself diurnally into incoherence. **1879** *Lond. Soc.* Christm. No. 71/2 He drank himself out of one situation after another. **1883** STEVENSON *Treas. Isl.* I. i, Till he had drunk himself sleepy.

b. 1474 CAXTON *Chesse* III. vi. (1883) 130 And not lyue to ete glotonsly & for to drynke dronke. **1600** HOLLAND *Livy* XI. xiv. 1069 Kept my soldiours from drinking drunke. **1609** W. M. *Man in Moone* (1849) 33 Are you adicted to drink drunke? **1660** F. BROOKE tr. *Le Blanc's Trav.* 403 They gourmandize, and drink drunk after their fashion.

c. 1598 SHAKS. *Merry W.* I. i. 204, I hope we shall drinke downe all vnkindnesse. **1599** MASSINGER, etc. *Old Law* III. ii, Yet you may drink your eyes out, sir. **1679** *Essex's Excell.* 8 They will..no more suffer themselves to be..drunk out of their reason. **1701** DE FOE *True-born Eng.* II. 92 Drink their Estates away, and Senses too.

d. 1604 SHAKS. *Oth.* II. iii. 84 Why, he drinkes you with facillitie, your Dane dead drunke. **1606** —— *Ant. & Cl.* II. v. 21 Ere the ninth houre, I drunke him to his bed. **1609** *Ev. Woman in Hum.* v. i. in Bullen *O. Pl.* IV, He..will drink Downe a Dutchman. **1659** D. PELL *Impr. Sea* 437 These lads drink the Land out of quiet. *a* **1674** CLARENDON *Hist. Reb.* XI. §242 One Earl, who had drank most of the rest down, and was not himself moved or alter'd. **1720** *Humourist* 161 Drinking a Man to Death. **1813** COL. HAWKER *Diary* I. 68 We having nearly drunk the landlord out of both his English and French wine. *Mod.* To drink a person under the table.

e. *a* **1704** T. BROWN *Praise Poverty* Wks. 1730 I. 98 His best companions that have a thousand times drank up the sun with him. **1746** P. FRANCIS tr. *Horace's Sat.* I. iii. 24 He drank the Night away Till rising Dawn. **1836** DICKENS *Sk. Boz* 2nd Ser. 90 The musicians exhibit unequivocal symptoms of having drunk the new year in.

13. ***to drink to*** (a person): †**a.** To hand or present beverage for his use; to give drink to.

Obs. The cup presented was first sipped by the one who offered it, and hence

b. To salute (any one) by drinking; to invite him to drink by drinking first; to drink in his honour, wishing him health or success. Hence, in wider use, to drink in honour of (anything desired), with good wishes for its furtherance. Also *ellipt.* with the person as obj.: to pledge, toast; and in *indirect pass.*

a. *c* **1250** *Gen. & Ex.* 1660 He..dede him eten and to him dranc. **1297** R. GLOUC. (1724) 289 Vorst ych wolle to þe drynke, and suþþe þou ssalt hym yse. *a* **1300** *Cursor M.* 15263 And o mi drinc þar i sal Drinc to yow for yur mede. **1470–85** MALORY *Arthur* VIII. xxiv, Thenne they lough and made good chere and eyther dranke to other frely. **1697** DAMPIER *Voy.* I. xv. 434 When by themselves, they drink about from one to another; but when any of us came among them, then they would always drink to one of us.

b. 1530 PALSGR. 529/1, I drinke to you, *je boys a vous.* **1605** SHAKS. *Macb.* III. iv. 89, I drinke to th' generall joy o' th' whole Table. **1682** LUTTRELL *Brief Rel.* (1857) I. 186 The lord mayor was pleased to drink to Mr. North. **1758** JOHNSON *Idler* No. 5 ¶4 The gay drink to their success. **1787** BURKE *Corr.* (1844) III. 56 We drank the man we were so much obliged to in a bumper. **1833** M. SCOTT *Tom Cringle* xvi. (1859) 401 Speaking when he is spoken to, drinking when he is drunken to. **1842** TENNYSON *Vision Sin* IV. 149 Drink we, last, the public fool. **1849** MACAULAY *Hist. Eng.* I. 444 All who passed were invited to drink to the health of the new sovereign.

c. *trans.* in same sense; cf. CAROUSE *sb.* 2.

1606 SHAKS. *Ant. & Cl.* IV. viii. 34 We all would sup together And drinke Corowses to the next dayes Fate. **1682** MILTON *Hist. Mosc.* Wks. 1738 II. 145 The Emperor.. drank a deep Carouse to the Queen's Health.

14. *trans.* **to drink** (a sentiment or toast): to honour it and express a desire for its accomplishment or success by drinking.

13.. *Coer de L.* 6746 To waraunt that I have i-doo, Wesseyl I schal drynk yow too. **1600** ROWLANDS *Lett. Humours Blood* vii. (1874) 13 Drinke some braue health vpon the Dutch carouse. **1710** HEARNE *Collect.* (Oxf. Hist. Soc.) III. 35 They drunk Damnation to Dr. Sacheverell. **1742** FIELDING *J. Andrews* (1818) 297 He was drinking her ladyship's health in a cup of..ale. **1808** J. MAYNE *Siller Gun* IV. 145 'The King', and other loyal toasts..'Our fleets', and 'a' our armed hosts'; Were drank aloud. **1851** THACKERAY *Eng. Hum.* v. 244 Drinking confusion to the Pretender.

15. *intr.* To have a specified flavour when drunk. [Fr. *se boire*, refl. for pass.]

1607 HEYWOOD *Wom. kilde with Kindnesse* Epil., The wine..drunk too flat. **1697** DAMPIER *Voy.* I. xi. 314 It drinks brisk and cool. **1758** L. TEMPLE *Sketches* (ed. 2) 70 The Burgundy drinks as flat as Port. **1967** C. RAY *Compleat Imbiber* IX. 66 A vintage which was (as the wine merchants say) 'drinking very nicely now'. *Ibid.*, I sipped the wine, which drank like velvet. **1969** *Guardian* 23 May 9/3 Every one of these wines will drink well now: most of them will improve by keeping.

†**16.** *fig.* To experience, endure, suffer, pay the penalty; to 'taste the cup' of suffering, etc. (see 6, 10 c, and CUP *sb.* 9). *trans.* and *absol. Obs.*

a **1340** HAMPOLE *Psalter* x. 7 Ilk dampned man sall drynk of the sorow of hell. **1530** PALSGR. 556/1, I forgyve you for this tyme, but and you faute agayne you shall drinke for bothe. *a* **1553** UDALL *Royster D.* I. iii. (Arb.) 20 Ye will drink without a cup. **1677** W. HUBBARD *Narrative* II. 35 The dammage that side of the Country hath been made to drink thereby, is not easy to recount.

III. 17. The vb.-stem used in Comb. **drink-(and-)drive** *attrib. phr.*, of or pertaining to (the laws relating to) drink-driving.

1967 *Motor* 18 Nov. 64/1 We have introduced two of the most controversial road safety measures... The first was the 70 m.p.h. speed limit. The second..is the new *drink and drive law. **1985** *Church Times* 30 Aug. 8/3 The introduction of legislation to include imprisonment, as in Sweden, for drink-and-drive offences. **1968** *Punch* 7 Feb. 179/1 A police surgeon..says there's been a sharp rise in sexual offences since the October *drink-drive laws came in. **1973** *N. Berks. Herald* 28 June 9/7 Assaulting two policemen and failing to provide a specimen for a drink drive test. **1977** *Belfast Tel.* 22 Feb. 10/5 The..committee..urged..tougher action against..second drink-drive offenders.

†**drink**, *v.*[2] *Obs.* Aphetic f. ADRINK, to drown.

c **1425** *Seven Sag.* (P.) 3362 Hadde I than be dronken, And in the salt flod sonkyn. *c* **1440** *Jacob's Well* (E.E.T.S.) 7 3if þou fell in-to a depe pytt & schuldyst be dronchyn. **1460** CAPGRAVE *Chron.* 107 Thei were dronchin in the depe see. *Ibid.* 133 Too of the Kyngis sones..and many worthi folk.. were dronch in o schip.

drink (drɪŋk), *sb.* Forms: *α.* 1–4 drinc, drync, 3– drink, (2–4 drenc(k, 4 drenk, 3 drinck, 3–6 drynk, 5 dryng). *β.* 3 drinch, *Orm.* drinnch. *γ.* 1 drinca, 3–6 drynke, 3–7 drinke, (3 dringe). [ME. had two forms *drink* (*drinch*), and *drinke*, corresp. to OE. *drinc*, and *drinca*, f. *drincan* to DRINK; cf. Sw. *drick*, *dryck*, Da. *drik*. The normal mod. form of the sb. would be southern *drinch* (cf. *finch*, *drench*, *stench*, *bench*, etc.), northern *drink*; the latter has become the standard form, prob. under the influence of the verb.]

1. a. Liquid swallowed for assuaging thirst or taken into the system for nourishment. Also *fig.*

c **1000** *Ags. Gosp.* Matt. xxv. 37 þyrstendne & we ðe drinc sealdon. *c* **1220** *Bestiary* 206 Ðe godspel..is soule drink. *c* **1380** WYCLIF *Wks.* (1880) 14 þei 3euen not drenk to pore þristi men. **1426** AUDELAY *Poems* 7 The thorste 3if dryng. **1523** LD. BERNERS *Froiss.* I. xviii. 21 They dranke none other drynke, but the water of the ryuer. **1667** MILTON *P.L.* v. 344 For drink the Grape She crushes. **1875** JOWETT *Plato* (ed. 2) III. 319 The thirsty one, in that he thirsts, desires only drink.

b. esp. as correlative to solid nourishment (*meat*, *food*, etc.). **meat and drink**: see MEAT.

c **950** *Lindisf. Gosp.* John vi. 55 Lichoma forðon min soðlice is mett & blod min soðlice is drinca [*Rushw.* drync, *Ags. G.* drinc, *Hatton G.* drenc]. *c* **1205** LAY. 3558 Bugge him..metes & drinches. *a* **1300** *Cursor M.* 11426 þam failed neuer o drinc ne fode. **1494** *Nottingham Rec.* III. 282 Item Richard Litster dyner and drynk *jd.* ob. **1579** FULKE *Heskins' Parl.* 136 In the sacrament is drie and moyst nourishment, that is, bread and drinke. *a* **1625** FLETCHER *Love's Cure* III. ii, What's one man's poison..Is another's meat and drink. **1733** CHEYNE *Eng. Malady* II. i. §5 When the Drink is in too great a Proportion to the solid Food. **1855** MACAULAY *Hist. Eng.* IV. 516 The crews had better food and drink than they had ever had before.

c. *transf.* Liquid absorbed or drunk in.

1602 SHAKS. *Ham.* IV. vii. 182 Til that her garments, heauy with her drinke, Pul'd the poore wretch..To muddy death. **1664** EVELYN *Kal. Hort.* (1729) 224 If they [plants] shrivel and fold up, give them Drink. **1791** COWPER *Yardley Oak* 112 The scooped rind [of the oak] that seems A huge throat calling to the clouds for drink.

2. A kind of liquor for drinking; a beverage.

c **888** K. ÆLFRED *Boeth.* xv, Næron ða..mistlice.. drincas. *c* **1200** ORMIN 3212 Hiss drinnch wass waterr. *Ibid.* 15397 þuss birrleþþ defell & hiss þeww A33 werrse & werrse drinnchess. **13..** *Minor Poems fr. Vernon MS.* (E.E.T.S.) 490/219 And oþer drynkes þat weore dere In Coupes ful gret. **1585** T. WASHINGTON tr. *Nicholay's Voy.* III. x, Wyth their drinke, which they call Sorbet. **1691** TRYON *Wisd. Dictates* 4 Delight not in Meats and Drinks that are too strong for Nature. **1756** C. LUCAS *Ess. Waters* I. 154 The ancient Persians..esteemed water the best drink. **1884** GUSTAFSON *Found. Death* i. (ed. 3) 3 The fermented drinks of antiquity were but little adulterated.

3. *spec.* **a.** Intoxicating alcoholic beverage. Hence in various phrases: Indulgence to excess in intoxicating liquor; habits of intemperance, drunkenness. **in drink**: intoxicated, drunk.

1042 *O.E. Chron.*, Her 3efor Harðacnut swa þæt he æt his drinc stod. *c* **1340** *Cursor M.* 2942 (Trin.) 3yue we our fadir [Lot] ynow3e of drinke. **1553** BRENDE *Q. Curtius* 211 (R.) Hauynge then hys senses ouercome with drynke. **1596** SHAKS. *1 Hen. IV*, II. iv. 458, I doe not speake to thee in Drinke. **1605** —— *Macb.* III. vi. 13 The two delinquents.. That were the Slaues of drinke. **1659** D. PELL *Impr. Sea* 79 Take heed that your Sea-men see not the least appearance of drink in your eyes. **1887** H. R. TEDDER in *Dict. Nat. Biog.* IX. 330/2 With advancing years Caulfield took to drink. **1890** BESANT *Demoniac* iv. 46 Not a drop of drink of any kind shall be put on board that boat. **1894** HALL CAINE *Manxman* 284 Heaving into the hall like a man in drink. *Mod.* Drink's doings.

b. specifically described, as ***strong, ardent drink. small drink***: see BEER *sb.*[1] 1 b.

1526–34 TINDALE *Luke* i. 15 He..shall nether drinke wyne ner stronge drinke. **1544** PHAER *Regim. Lyfe* (1553) Bij a, Drynke onely pennye ale, or suche smalle drynke. **1648** GAGE *West Ind.* xv. 106 The great abuse of wines and strong drinks. *a* **1774** FERGUSSON *Election* Poems (1845) 40 Our Johnny's nae sma drink, you'll guess. **1890** BESANT *Demoniac* ii. 27 Ardent drinks of various kinds.

c. Colloq. phr. ***to have drink taken***, to have drunk alcoholic liquor; to be intoxicated or suffering from the effects of drink; hence in various *ellipt.* uses.

[**1914** JOYCE *Dubliners* 125 How easy it was to know a gentleman even when he has a drop taken.] **1924** KIPLING *Debits & Credits* (1926) 186, I saw 'em, sir, come out..not drunk, but all—*all* havin' drink taken. **1930** 'SAPPER' *Finger of Fate* 286 When men of Denton's calibre get into the condition of 'drink-taken', such trifles as the presence of other guests in the house do not deter them from being offensive. **1963** 'A. GILBERT' *Ring for Noose* iii. 41 You're sure he's dead, not just drink taken?

4. The action or habit of drinking (to excess); a time or occasion of drinking. *rare* exc. in colloq. phr. ***on the drink***. Cf. DRUNK *sb.*[2] 1.

1865 *Reader* No. 148. 495/1 He has been out on the drink. **1887** RIDER HAGGARD *Jess* ii, Her brute of a husband was always on the drink and gamble. **1894** R. S. FERGUSON *Charters Carlisle* xxx, There was a great drink in Carlisle that night.

5. a. A draught or portion of liquid; *spec.* a glass of wine or other alcoholic liquor.

c **1000** *Ags. Gosp.* Matt. x. 42 Swa hwylc swa sylþ anne drinc cealdes wæteres. **1297** R. GLOUC. (1724) 289 As me hym [Edward the Martyr] drynke toc. *c* **1400** MAUNDEV. (Roxb.) viii. 29 A well to þe whilk Moyses ledd þam and gafe þam a drynk þeroff. **1535** COVERDALE *Ps.* lix. 3 Thou hast geuen vs a drynke off wyne. **1752** *Scots Mag.* (1753) Sept. 450/2 He..wanted a drink very much. **1865** KINGSLEY *Herew.* xiii, Will anybody give me a drink of milk? **1888** LIGHTHALL *Yng. Seigneur* 154 He was rich, for had he not paid the drinks?

b. A medicinal potion or draught.

1362 LANGL. *P. Pl.* A. VII. 261 Leches..don men dy3en þoru3 heor drinke er destenye wolde. *c* **1400** *Lanfranc's Cirurg.* 74 þis is a perfi3t drynke to woundes of þe heed. *c* **1500** *Melusine* xxxvi. 247 A lectuary or drynk wherof ye shal be poysonned. **1611** SHAKS. *Wint. T.* I. i. 15 Wee will give you sleepie Drinkes. **1657** W. COLES *Adam in Eden* cccxxv. 601 The decoction therof in Wine, is an exceeding good Wound-drink. **1884** *Law Times* 310/2 One of the defendant's men came back with two drinks for the calf. *fig.* **1400–50** *Alexander* 1106 þou sall be drechid of a drinke, a dra3te of vnsele.

6. *colloq.* (orig. *U.S.*). A river or body of water. ***big drink***: the Mississippi; the Atlantic; the sea. Always preceded by *the*.

1832 J. K. PAULDING *Westward Ho!* I. 121 Sing dumb, or I'll throw you into the drink. **1844** *Daily Picayune* (New Orleans) 24 Mar. 2/2 There never would have been any Atlantic ocean if it hadn't been for the Mississippi, nor never will be after we've turned the waters of that big drink into the Mammoth Cave! **1844** DICKENS *Mart. Chuz.* xxxiii. 396 'He'd spill 'em in the drink:' whereby the Capting metaphorically said he'd throw them in the river. **1857** HOLLAND *Bay Path* xii. 137 So you'd better scull your dug-out over the drink again. *a* **1860** *N.Y. Spirit of Times* (Bartlett *Dict. Amer.* s.v. *Big*), Off I sot, went through Mississippi, crossed the big drink. **1873** *Roots* (1888) 47 If you don't sit steady, we shall be spilt into the drink. **1882** M. E. BRADDON *Mount Royal* II. iv. 79, I was coming across the Big Drink as fast as a Cunard could bring me. **1884** *Illustr. Lond. News* 1 Nov. 410/2 Many of the Transatlantics will doubtless take a journey across what they call 'the big drink' to hear her. **1941** *New Statesman* 30 Aug. 218/3 *The Drink*, the sea. **1942** T. RATTIGAN *Flare Path* I. 102 Down 'e goes into the drink turning and twisting. **1944** *Penguin New Writing* XX. 130 A British pilot was being pulled out of the drink. **1960** L. MEYNELL *Bandaberry* xiv. 183 [He] had fished us out of the drink just, and only just, in time.

†**7.** Barley; cf. *drink-corn* in 9. *Obs. rare.*

1573 TUSSER *Husb.* xviii. (1878) 45 Where barlie did growe, laie wheat to sowe. Yet better I thinke, sowe pease after drinke. *Ibid.* xxxiii. (1878) 75.

8. *attrib.* and *Comb.* (chiefly in sense 3). **a.** simple attrib., as ***drink-bill, -crave, -craving, -demon, -duty, -evil, -habit, -interest, -licence, -party, -table, -time, -traffic, -tray***, etc.; used for the sale or consumption of alcoholic liquors, as ***drink-house, -room, -shop, -stall***; also with *pl.* of sense 5 a, as ***drinks party***, etc. **b.** objective, as ***drink-conveyer, -giver, -maker, -seller; drink-inspiring, -prohibiting***, adjs. **c.** instrumental, as ***drink-blinded, -closed, -sodden, -washed*** adjs.

1884 *Boston (Mass.) Jrnl.* 13 Sept., The *drink-bill of Tennessee is $2,000,000 more than the wheat-crop. **1888** *Pall Mall G.* 13 Oct. 2/1 Murderous attacks..at a moment of *drink-blinded fury. **1638–48** G. DANIEL *Eclog.* III. 162 Hardly to hope That Eye (*drinke-closed still) can ever ope. **1713** COUNTESS WINCHELSEA *Misc. Poems* 57 Your self (reply'd the *Drink-conveigher) May be my Ruin. **1896** *Tablet* 1 Feb. 171 The *drink-demon in possession of a young wife. **1890** W. JAMES *Princ. Psychol.* II. xxviii. 685 The *drink-habit is only a symptom of their disease. **1960** H. EDWARDS *Spirit Healing* xi. 92 The drink habit passed away. **1883** M. DAVITT in *Contemp. Rev.* Aug. 178 The low *drinkhouse and the brothel. **1885** *Pall Mall G.* 23 July 2/2 Grocers' *drink licences. **1963** L. MEYNELL *Virgin Luck* vi. 156 Who were all those people at the *drink party? **1878** *Pall Mall G.* 13 Feb. 2/1 We might reasonably have objected to the *drinkseller voting. **1883** MISS HOWARD *Guenn* 15 Through the glass door of a *drink-shop came an orange glow. **1890** W. BOOTH *In Darkest Eng.* II. vii. 243 The disorganised, sweated, hopeless, *drink-sodden denizens of darkest England. **1904** H. G. WELLS *Food of Gods* III. iii. 240 The drink-sodden wretchedness of the painted women at the corner. **1967** L. MEYNELL *Mauve Front Door* xv. 214 The dramatist sends one of his characters to the always lavishly well-stocked *drink table. **1961** R. JEFFRIES *Evidence of Accused* v. 55 They had arrived at *drink-time. **1885** *Pall Mall G.* 28 July 2/3 His attitude towards the *drink traffic. **1964** E. BOWEN *Little Girls* III. vii. 237 He had removed the tea tray, brought in the *drink tray. **1962** E. SALTER *Voice of Peacock* xii. 127 A funeral party and a *drinks party on the agenda. **1970** C. WOOD *Terrible Hard* iii. 36 Perhaps they shouldn't have given that drinks party so soon. **1966** J. B. PRIESTLEY *Salt is Leaving* vi. 70 Alan.. followed her to the *drinks table. **1971** 'D. HALLIDAY' *Dolly & Doctor Bird* ix. 119 Johnson moved across to the drinks table, and..began to pour three neat doubles. **1966** *Observer* (Colour Suppl.) 13 Nov. 40/2 The Cocktail Hour, commonly known as *drinks time, is a mysterious 6–8 p.m. limbo. **1966** *Listener* 24 Nov. 763/3 A middle-aged couple ensconced in a lovely home: the *drinks tray, stage left, in constant use. **1963** *Harper's Bazaar* Feb. 15/1 Coiled mats of silver plate on copper..look good on the *drinks trolley.

9. Special comb.: †**drink-corn**, the grain used in brewing, barley; **drink-drowned** *a.*, intoxicated; **drink-offering**, an offering of wine or other liquid poured out in honour of a deity, a libation; hence ***drink-offerer***; **drink-penny** = DRINK-MONEY; **drink problem** = *drinking problem* s.v. DRINKING *vbl. sb.* 4 c; see PROBLEM 3 c (b).

1669 WORLIDGE *Syst. Agric.* (1681) 15 The Open [Country]..yields us the greater part of our *Drink-Corn. **1600** ROWLANDS *Lett. Humours Blood* xxii. 28 When signeur Sacke and Suger *drinke-drown'd reeles. **1824** J. SYMMONS tr. *Æschylus' Agam.* 9 In vain..the *drink-off'rers sacrifice. **1535** COVERDALE *Gen.* xxxv. 14 Jacob set vp a piler of stone ..and poured *drynkofferynges theron. **1593** DEE *Diary* (Camden) 45, I gave him a saffron noble in ernest for a *drinkpeny.

drinkable ('drɪŋkəb(ə)l), *a.* and *sb.* [-ABLE.]

A. *adj.* That may be drunk, suitable for drinking, potable.

1611 COTGR. *Potable*, potable, drinkable. ? **1690** *Consid. Raising Money* 15 A Home-Excise upon things eatable and drinkable. **1725** BRADLEY *Fam. Dict.* s.v. *Restoring of Beer*, Rendering sour Beer drinkable. *a* **1859** MACAULAY *Hist. Eng.* (1861) V. 205 A marsh where there was..neither firm earth nor drinkable water.

b. *nonce-use.* That may be drunk to or toasted.

1886 JEROME *Idle Thoughts* 127 We drink the Queen..and the Ladies, and everybody else that is drinkable.

B. *sb.* (usually *pl.*) That which may be drunk; something to drink; liquor.

1708 HEARNE *Collect.* 24 Oct., Good eatables as well as Drinkables. **1773** GOLDSM. *Stoops to Conq.* II. i, I never have courage till I see the eatables and drinkables brought upon the table. **1822** BYRON *Let. to Moore* 23 Nov., They are my favourite dish and drinkable.

Hence **drinka'bility, 'drinkableness; 'drinkably** *adv.*

1635 PERSON *Varieties* I. 25 Waters..at least drinkably fresh. **1846** WORCESTER, *Drinkableness*. **1866** FELTON *Anc. & Mod. Gr.* II. xii. 510 Words..intended to mean Champagne of the first quality, but..really meaning of the first drinkability. **1894** T. HARDY *Life's little Ironies* 271 A gallon of hot brandy and beer..kept drinkably warm.

drink-a-penny. Local (Irish) name of the little grebe, *Tachybaptes fluviatilis*.

1885 SWAINSON *Prov. Names Birds* 216.

'drinkdom. [f. DRINK *sb.* + -DOM.] The sphere of action of drink; the drink interest.

1884 R. V. FRENCH *19 Cent. Drink in Eng.* 208 The subject of comparative drinkdom. **1885** *Pall Mall G.* 28 July 2/3 The triumph of drinkdom over temperance.

drink-'driving, *sb.* (and *a.*) [f. DRINK *v.*^{1} + DRIVING *vbl. sb.*] **a.** The action of driving or attempting to drive a motor vehicle with an excessive proportion of alcohol in one's blood (esp. with an amount that exceeds a legally fixed limit).

1964 *Daily Tel.* 22 Jan. 23/5 (*heading*) 282 arrests for drink driving. **1976** *Newmarket Jrnl.* 16 Dec. 7/3 The first mention of any possible charge relating to drink-driving came after he had given a blood sample. **1984** *Daily Express* 5 Nov. 1/3 He appears..accused on three counts—assaulting a policeman, drink-driving and failing to turn up in court.

b. *attrib.*, as ***drink-driving*** (rarely ***drink-and-driving***) ***accident***, ***charge***, ***law***, ***offence***. Occas. as *adj*.

1967 *Daily Tel.* 17 May 14/3 An extensive 'educational campaign' on the effects of the new drink-and-driving laws is being prepared by the Ministry of Transport. **1971** *Reader's Digest Family Guide to Law* 513/1 The drink-driving offender faces a stiff fine, possible imprisonment, and almost certain disqualification for at least a year. **1976** *Times* 20 Mar. 3/2 Committed for trial to Knightsbridge Crown Court on a drink driving charge. **1976** *Newmarket Jrnl.* 16 Dec. 7/2 He had been fined £40 and disqualified for one year for a drink-driving offence. **1982** *Daily Tel.* 31 Dec. 30/3 The United States where 26,000 people die in drink-driving accidents every year.

drinkel, -kle: see DRENKLE.

drinker ('drɪŋkə(r)). [f. DRINK *v.*^{1} + -ER^1.]

1. a. One who drinks.

c **950** *Lindisf. Gosp.* Matt. xi. 19 Etere & drincere wines. **1398** TREVISA *Barth. De P.R.* XVII. xxxvi. (1495) 624 The rote of Carduus sod in water gyuyth appetyte to drynkers. **1520** *Caxton's Chron. Eng.* VI. 68/2 Whan one dranke to another the drynker sholde saye Wassayle. **1756** C. LUCAS *Ess. Waters* II. 125 The drinkers commonly stand to be helped with water. **1887** RUSKIN *Præterita* II. 324 As a rule sherry drinkers are soundly-minded persons.

b. *spec.* One who indulges to excess in intoxicating liquor; a tippler, a drunkard.

c **1200** *Trin. Coll. Hom.* 55 On swiche drinkeres cumeð godes curs. *c* **1290** *S. Eng. Leg.* I. 319/690 Proud and wemod, and drinkare. **1549** LATIMER *3rd Serm. bef. Edw. VI.* (Arb.) 77 Some sayed he was..a drincker, a pot-companion. **1659** D. PELL *Impr. Sea* 100 That tankard-lifting Zeno..was such a drinker, that hee would often lye as one dead.

c. Qualified by adjs. *great*, *hard*, *small*, etc., indicating the amount of liquor habitually taken.

1340 *Ayenb.* 47 Þe mochele drinkeres. **1387** TREVISA *Higden* VI. ix. (Tollem. MS.) The Danes were grete drynkers by kynde. **1616** SURFL. & MARKH. *Country Farme* VI. 614 Some say that a great drinker shall neuer become drunke, if he weare a wreath of Iua moscata about his head. **1641** BAKER *Chron.* an. 1580 (R.) The English..were hitherto the least drinkers. **1725** SWIFT *Let. to Worrall* 27 Aug. Lett. 1766 II. 49 You have been all your life a great walker, and a little drinker. **1741** RICHARDSON *Pamela* II. 179 They are horrid Drinkers. *Mod.* His father was a hard drinker.

2. (In full **drinker-moth**). The popular name of a large European moth, *Lasiocampa* (*Odonestis*) *potatoria*, of the family *Bombycidæ*, so called from its long suctorial proboscis.

1682 M. LISTER *Goedart. Albin.* pl. xvii, Drinker-Caterpillar. **1749** B. WILKES *Brit. Moths* (1773) pl. 58. **1865** WOOD *Homes without H.* xiv. (1868) 288 The fur-clad Drinker Moth. **1871** E. F. STAVELEY *Brit. Insects* 270 The downy, large-winged Drinker.

3. A drinking-trough.

1947 *All-Pets Mag.* May 5 Keeping..plenty of cool water in drinkers for them [*sc.* canaries]. **1950** *N.Z. Jrnl. Agric.* Nov. 447/2 The only satisfactory place for drinkers other than specially designed and expensive systems is outside the floor space of the [hen] house. **1960** *Farmer & Stockbreeder* 19 Jan. Suppl. 37/2 If the brooder has fitted food troughs and drinkers.

Hence **'drinkeress**, a female drinker.

1827 CARLYLE *Germ. Rom.* III. 188.

drinkery ('drɪŋkərɪ). [f. DRINK *sb.* + -ERY.] A place for the supply of (intoxicating) drink.

1840 J. P. KENNEDY *Quodlibet* 222 The Sergeant took a small frame house next door to Sim Traver's Refectory,—or rather as Sim called it, his Drinkery. **1845** T. J. GREEN *Texian Exped.* xix. 368 We wended our way up town, and called into the first open 'drinkery'. **1884** *Brit. Q. Rev.* Apr. 360 Music-hall drinkeries. **1889** *Times* 27 Dec., The public-house was the chief drinkery.

†**'drink-hail.** *Obs.* exc. *Hist.* [Early ME. *drinc hæil*, *drinc hail*, f. imperative of DRINK *v.* + HAIL *a.* = ON. *heill*: see WASSAIL. The earliest known occurrence is in Geoffrey of Monmouth VI. xii (*c* 1140). The form *hail* indicates that these phrases are of Norse, not OE. origin.] The customary courteous reply to a pledge in drinking in early English times. The cup was offered with the salutation *wæs hail* 'health or good luck to you' (see WASSAIL), to which the reply was *drinc hail*, 'drink good health or good luck'.

c **1205** LAY. 14332 Þat freond sæiðe to freonde..Leofue freond wæs hail. Þe oðer sæið drinc hail. **1297** R. GLOUC. (1724) 118 With a coppe of gold, fol of wyn..A kne to þe kyng heo [Rowena] seyde, 'lord kyng wasseyl'..Drinkhayl, quoth this kyng agen, & bed hire drinke anon. **1350–70** *Eulog. Hist.* (1863) III. v. cxxv. 110 More Saxonico salutavit, et ait: Wassayl..Rex dedit responsum: Drinkhayle, et monachus læto vultu ciphum hausit. **14..** *How Good Wyf tauȝte Douȝtir* (Trin. MS.) in *Babees Bk.* 44 Syt nat vp long At euyn As A gase with the cuppe To sey wessayle, and drynke heylle. [**1848** LYTTON *Harold* XI. xii, Leofwine..rose to propose the drink-hæl.]

drinkie ('drɪŋkɪ). *colloq.* Also **drinkie-pie, drinky**. [f. DRINK *sb.* + -IE, -Y^6.] An affected, childish, or jocular form of DRINK *sb.* 5.

1947 *Horizon* Oct. 88 'How about a little drinkie-pie?' Gwen said. **1953** D. PARRY *Going up—Going Down* V. vi. 241 We might go and have a lovely drinkie. **1962** J. CANNAN *All is Discovered* i. 18 We can have our little drinky while we choose. **1966** R. BRADDON *Committal Chamber* iii. 32 'There,' she smiled, passing him a glass of sherry. 'Drinkies.'

drinking ('drɪŋkɪŋ), *vbl. sb.* [f. DRINK *v.*]

1. The action or habit denoted by the vb. DRINK; *spec.* the use of intoxicating liquor, or indulgence therein to excess.

c **1200** *Trin. Coll. Hom.* 37 Sume men ladeð here lif on etinge and on drinkinge alse swin. *c* **1400** tr. *Secreta Secret.*, *Gov. Lordsh.* (E.E.T.S.) 58 Wythdrawe þe fro mekyl drynkynge. **1585** T. WASHINGTON tr. *Nicholay's Voy.* III. ii. 91 As for natural wine..the drinking therof is forbidden them. **1793** SMEATON *Edystone L.* §313 Finding their own provisions of eating and drinking. **1856** EMERSON *Eng. Traits, Aristocracy* Wks. (Bohn.) II. 86 Gaming, racing, drinking, and mistresses, bring them down.

2. An occasion of drinking; a convivial revel.

c **1515** *Cocke Lorell's B.* (Percy Soc.) 7 At euery tauerne in the yere, A solempne dyryge is songe there, With a grete drynkynge. **1522** *Bury Wills* (Camden) 118 A busshell and halffe of malte to be browne..to fynde a drinkinge vpon Ascention Even. **1659** D. PELL *Impr. Sea* 99 You contend in your drinkings..who should drink most.

3. *concr.* in dial. use; see quots.

1552 HULOET, Drinckinge geuen to workemen after dinner, *colosium*. **1828** *Craven Dial.*, *Drinkings*, beer given to labourers before and after dinner.

4. *Comb.* **a.** with sense 'used for drinking', as ***drinking-bowl***, ***-cup***, ***-fountain***, ***funnel*** (*N.Z.*), ***-horn***, ***-liquor***, ***-place***, ***-pool***, ***-pot***, ***-trough***, ***-vessel***, ***-water***, etc.; **b.** 'used for the sale or consumption of drink', as ***drinking-booth***, ***club***, ***-house***, ***-inn***, ***-place***, ***-room***, ***-saloon***, ***-shop***.

1796 MORSE *Amer. Geog.* II. 334 The neatness of their *drinking-booths. **1852** GROTE *Greece* II. lxxvii. X. 208 Two silver *drinking-bowls. **1967** E. PAUL *Jewels in Jeopardy* i. 11 Rather dubious entertainment in the Soho area, strip-tease clubs, *drinking clubs and so on. **1658** W. BURTON *Itin. Anton.* 121 A silver *drinking cup. **1860** DICKENS *Uncomm. Trav.* xiv. 216 A *drinking fountain..to freshen its thirsty square. **1882** Drinking fountain [see FOUNTAIN *sb.* 2]. **1968** A. MUNRO in R. Weaver *Canad. Short Stories* 2nd Ser. 260 The drinking fountain surrounded by little puddles of water. **1927** T. E. DONNE *Maori, Past & Present* vii. 76 (*caption*) *Drinking funnel for tohunga when tapu. **1955** H. J. PHILLIPPS *Maori Carving Illustr.* 9/2 Four beautifully-carved drinking funnels are on exhibition. **1552** HULOET, *Drinkinge glasse, or potte, or cuppe, *ampulla*. **1709** ADDISON *Tatler* No. 24 ¶10 Her Name is written with a Diamond on a Drinking-glass. **1552** HULOET, *Drinkynge house, *cænatiuncula*. **1654** WHITLOCK *Zootomia* 79 Thou shalt go to some drinking-house of greatest resort. **1602** *2nd Pt. Return fr. Parnass.* I. vi. 19 A *drinking Inne in Cheapside. **1727** BRADLEY *Fam. Dict.* s.v. *Ale*, A *drinking Liquor made by infusing ground Malt in boiling Water. **1853** 'P. PAXTON' *Yankee in Texas* 143 Buffaloes have a regular *drinking-place. **1870** 'F. FERN' *Ginger-Snaps* 91 The man who..takes that child to bar-rooms and drinking places. *a* **1610** HEALEY *Theophrastus* (1636) 80 Jewelled *drinking-pots. **1855** R. GLISAN *Jrnl. Army Life* (1874) 172 The lobbies and *drinking saloons at the capitol. **1875** MRS. STOWE *We & Neighbors* xli. 377 Finally we alighted before a plain house in a street full of drinking-saloons. **1855** *N.Y. Herald* 6 Nov. 5/3 A multitude of *drinking shops have already been closed. **1891** KIPLING *Light that Failed* xv, Dick entered the drinking-shop which was one source of her gains. **1814** SCOTT *Wav.* lxiii, The stone-basin seemed to be destined for a *drinking-trough for cattle. **1535** COVERDALE *2 Chron.* ix. 20 All kynge Salomons *drynkynge vessels were of golde. **1888** MISS BRADDON *Fatal Three* I. v, The *drinking-water of the house was supplied from this well.

c. Special comb., as **drinking-bout**, a fit of hard drinking; **drinking chocolate** = CHOCOLATE 1; also, the powder used for making the beverage; **drinking-club**, an association for the purpose of drinking in company; **drinking-habit**, addiction to alcoholic liquor; the drink habit; †**drinking-money**, †**-penny** = DRINK-MONEY; **drinking-nut** (see quot. 1909); **drinking problem**, an addiction to alcohol, a tendency towards alcoholism (sometimes used euphemistically); see PROBLEM 3 c (b); **drinking-song**, one written about drink or drinking; **drinking up**, the finishing of a drink; **drinking-up time**, a short period after the legal closing-time in a public house which is permitted by law for the consumption of drinks bought before it.

1672 CAVE *Prim. Chr.* III. ii. (1673) 285 Not spent upon feasts and *drinking-bouts. **1873** BLACK *Pr. Thule* (1874) 8 As if he were at a drinking-bout of the lads. **1920** *Grocer* 1 May 31/2 (Advt.), Delicious Chocolate at less money than Cocoa. Cup-Royal *Drinking Chocolate. No sugar required. **1972** J. WAINWRIGHT *Night is Time to Die* 49 His wife handed him a beaker of drinking-chocolate. **1732** BERKELEY *Alciphr.* II. §19 Most free-thinkers are the proselytes of a *drinking-club. **1899** W. JAMES *Talks to Teachers* viii. 64 They talk of the smoking-habit and the swearing-habit and the *drinking-habit. *c* **1489** CAXTON *Sonnes of Aymon* xxviii. 582 Goo to your purse & gyve vs som *drynkynge money. **1611** FLORIO, *Beueraggio*..also drinking money. **1909** *Chambers's Jrnl.* Apr. 256/1 A stalwart native..with..a dozen '*drinking-nuts' (young cocoa-nuts), the ice-creams of the Pacific. **1957** *Alcoholic Rehabilitation Commission News Let.* (Berkeley, Calif.) July 2/2 The Sobriety Foundation of San Jose has been a going concern since 1954 in the human relations venture of assisting people with *drinking problems. **1969** E. AMBLER *Intercom Conspiracy* (1970) ii. 46 He has what our American friends call a drinking problem. Not an alcoholic, but certainly a heavy drinker. **1982** *Times* 13 Apr. 5/1 It is now thought that there are 600,000 dependent drinkers in Britain alone with a further million to 1.2m with serious drinking problems. **1597** MORLEY *Introd. Mus.* 180 The slightest kind of musicke..are the *vinase* or *drincking songs. **1960** *Guardian* 30 Nov. 2/3 The proposal for an extra quarter of an hour for '*drinking up'. **1961** *Times* 29 Mar. 7/3 '*Drinking up' time of 10 minutes. **1968** 'H. CARMICHAEL' *Slightly Bitter Taste* x. 182 We stop serving at three o'clock and then there's ten minutes drinking-up time before we turn the key in the lock.

'drinking, *ppl. a.* [f. as prec. + -ING^2.] That drinks. **a.** Of persons: Addicted to drinking; *spec.* indulging freely in intoxicants. **b.** Of a material: That sucks up moisture; absorbent.

c **1175** *Lamb. Hom.* 7 Of milc drinkende childre muðe. **1583** HOLLYBAND *Campo di Fior* 339 Wast paper, Which we call, the drinking paper, which beareth no inke. **1856** OLMSTED *Slave States* 97 Drinking men, wholly unfitted for the responsibility imposed on them. **1887** *Pall Mall G.* 23 Apr. 12/1 Tobacco..known in the trade as drinking tobacco, will carry the water better.

'drinkless, *a.* [f. DRINK *sb.* + -LESS.] Without drink or liquid to quench one's thirst; dry.

13.. *Minor Poems fr. Vernon MS.* (E.E.T.S.) 621/319 Druiȝe drinkeles was his tonge. *c* **1374** CHAUCER *Troylus* II. 669 (718) He nought for-bet þat euery creature Be drynklees for alwey. **1496** *Dives & Paup.* (W. de W.) X. xiii. 389/2 Moyses was with god...xl. dayes and .xl. nyghtes metelesse & drynkeles. **1646** F. THORPE in *Hull Lett.* (1886) 143, I am now come back..meatless and drinkless. **1860** J. F. CAMPBELL *Tales West Highlands* (1890) II. 426 He was grown sick: Sleepless, restless, meatless, drinkless.

drink-money. A gratuity to be spent on drink; a douceur. Cf. G. *trinkgeld*, F. *pourboire*.

1691 A. HAIG in J. Russell *Haigs* (1881) xi. 332 A legg-dollar for parchment and drink-money. **1753** HANWAY *Trav.* (1762) I. VII. xcvii. 451 Brandy, or uncommon fees of drink-money, will induce them to travel fast. *a* **1863** THACKERAY *D. Duval* iii, He bade the man follow him to the hotel. There should be a good drink-money for him.

drink-silver, -siller. *Sc.* = prec.; a perquisite. Also *fig.*

1467 *Sc. Acts Jas. III* (1814) 87 (Jam.) And at na drinksiluer be tane be the maister nor his doaris. **1489** *Treasurer's Bks.* 10 July in Tytler *Hist. Scot.* (1864) II. 396 Given to the gunners to drink-silver, when they cartit Monss..18 shillings. **1637** RUTHERFORD *Lett.* (1862) I. 297, I cannot get a house in this town wherein to leave drink-silver in my Master's name. **1808–25** JAMIESON, *Drink-siller* is still the vulgar designation.

drink-water. *rare.* [f. DRINK *v.* + WATER *sb.*] A drinker of water.

a **1641** BP. MOUNTAGU *Acts & Mon.* (1642) 449 That *hydropotæ*, or drinke-waters were onely amongst the Rechabites.

drinky ('drɪŋkɪ), *a. colloq.* and *dial.* [f. DRINK *sb.* 3 + -Y^1.] Tipsy; drunk.

1846 J. J. HOOPER *Adv. Simon Suggs* 44 But then he was 'drinky and played careless'. **1846** —— *Taking Census* in *Adv. Simon Suggs, &c.* 166 When a little 'drinky', he was wont to exhibit very fair horsemanship. **1871** G. P. R. PULMAN *Rustic Sketches* (ed. 3) 92 *Drinky*, rather drunk. 'He was drinky, but not rigglar drunk.' **1874** HARDY *Far fr. Mad. Crowd* II. xii. 143 I've been drinky once this month already. **1901** 'M. E. FRANCIS' *Pastorals of Dorset* 52 I've seen a man as was a bit drinky-like throw off his hat and tread on it. *Ibid.* 236 He do seem to be a bit drinky.

drinky, var. DRINKIE.

driography (draɪ'ɒgrəfɪ). [f. DRY *a.* + -GRAPHY, after LITHOGRAPHY.] A lithographic printing process which dispenses with the use of water as a barrier to prevent ink from settling on non-printing surfaces. Hence **drio'graphic** *a.*

1970 *Publishers' Weekly* 14 Sept. 57/2 Traditionally, water has been required to keep non-image areas free from ink. Driography, which requires special inks, is based on fiddling with the adhesive and cohesive properties of ink. *Ibid.*, These driographic inks will also work on regular offset processes with dampening systems and conventional plates. **1971** *Brit. Printer* Feb. 62/2 The trick in driography has been to find two surfaces that are sufficiently different in 'wettability' to dispense with water completely. **1971** *Penrose Ann.* LXIV. 125/1 Dry Plate is a registered 3M brand name. The firm has adopted the words 'driography' and 'driographic' for generic description of the system its components and the presses, papers and inks involved.

drip (drɪp), *v.* Forms: 1 **dryppan**, 5–6 **dryppe**, 6 **drippe**, 6– **drip**, (*Sc.* 6–9 **dreip**, 8–9 **dreep**). [OE. *dryppan*:—OTeut. **drupjan*, from *u*-grade of ablaut-series **dreup-*, *draup-*, *drup-*, OE. *dréopan*: see DREEP *v.* Examples of *dryppen* are not known between the OE. period and the 15th c., and it is possible that the modern vb. is from Norse: cf. in same sense Da. *dryppe*.

An OE. *dryppan* seems established by the imperative *drype* in the Leechd. (5 times on p. 40); the other OE. instances in Bosw-Toller appear to belong to *dríepan*, *drýpan*, DRIPE. As to the relations of these, see the etymological note under DROP *sb.*]

1. *trans.* To let (a liquid) fall in drops; to let fall (drops; rarely other objects).

c **1000** *Sax. Leechd.* II. 40 Drype on þæt eare þone ele. *c* **1440** *Promp. Parv.* 132/2 Dryppyn, or droppyn, *stillo*, *gutto.* **1552** HULOET, Drippe, *fundere guttas.* **1606** SYLVESTER *Du Bartas* II. iv. II. *Magnificence* 448 Nectar-deaws, which Heaven drips. **1634** HEYWOOD *Witches Lanc.* I. Wks. 1874 IV. 186 I'le dresse the dinner, though I drip my sweat. *a* **1745** SWIFT (J.), The lofty barn.. Which from the thatch drips fast a shower of rain. **1830** TENNYSON *Dirge* iv, The woodbine and eglatere Drip sweeter dews than traitor's tear.

fig. **1574** tr. *Marlorat's Apocalips* 29 They bee called golden Candlestickes, bycause that they.. do drippe into mens hartes, the most pure, plaine, and naturall vnderstanding of faith.

2. a. *intr.* Of a person or object: To have moisture or liquid falling off in drops; to be so copiously wet or saturated *with* as to shed drops.

1508 KENNEDIE *Flyting w. Dunbar* 519 Thy dok of dirt dreipis. **1607** W. S[MITH] *Puritan* IV. (R.) He drips and drops poor man. **1700** T. BROWN tr. *Fresny's Amusem. Ser. & Com.* 46 Half Spent, and dripping from every Pore in his Body. **1816** SCOTT *Antiq.* xxvi, Her lang hair dreeping wi' the salt water. **1871** L. STEPHEN *Playgr. Eur.* viii. (1894) 173 Pine branches.. dripping with moisture.

transf. **1849** FREEMAN *Archit.* 396 Every arch drips with foliations hanging free like lacework.

†**b.** *absol. Falconry* = DROP *v.* 2 b. *Obs. rare.*

1696 PHILLIPS, *Dripping* [*ed.* **1706** dripping or dropping] in Faulconry, is when a Hawk muteth directly downward in several Drops.

3. *intr.* To fall in drops.

a **1670** HACKET *Abp. Williams* 166 (L.) The fat of the project dript insensibly away at a slow fire. **1676** COTTON *Walton's Angler* I. xiii. (R.) Having roasted him enough,—let what was put into his belly, and what drips, be his sauce. **1860** TYNDALL *Glac.* I. xxiii. 161 The rain.. came through the roof, and dripped from the ceiling.

transf. and *fig.* **1891** *Spectator* 21 Mar., The surplus population of Southern Europe.. drips slowly into French Africa. **1894** HALL CAINE *Manxman* 262 The moonlight was dripping down on him through the leaves of the trees.

†**4.** *intr.* To slope, slant, dip. *Obs.*

1613–39, **1740** [see DRIPPING *vbl. sb.* 3]. **1703** MOXON *Mech. Exerc.* 26 Holding your Hammer in your Right-hand, hold the Edge.. Dripping a-slope from the Right-hand outwards.

5. *Naval slang.* To complain, grumble.

1942 *Gen* 1 Sept. 13/1 When she [*sc.* a Wren] grumbles she's guilty of 'dripping'.

drip (drɪp), *sb.* [f. prec. vb.]

†**1.** A falling drop. *Obs.*

c **1440** *Promp. Parv.* 132/1 Dryppe or drope (*P.* drepe), *gutta, stilla.* **1552** HULOET, Drippe or Droppe, *gutta.*

2. a. The act or fact of dripping or falling in drops. Also redupl. ***drip-drip***. ***in a drip***: in a dripping condition, saturated.

right of drip (Law): an easement which entitles the owner of a house to let the water from his eaves drip on his neighbour's land.

1669 WORLIDGE *Syst. Agric.* vii. §1 (1681) 114 No Tree thriving under its drip. **1816** BYRON *Ch. Har.* III. lxxxvi, On the ear Drops the light drip of the suspended oar. **1855** MRS. GASKELL *North & S.* ii, Listen to the drip-drip of the rain upon the leads. **1894** HOWELLS in *Harper's Mag.* Feb. 378 He's in such a drip of perspiration.

fig. **1890** *Spectator* 8 Feb., The tedium of sitting under a drip drip of perfunctory discussion.

b. *Med.* The continuous slow introduction of fluid into the body (esp. intravenously) involving its passage drop by drop through a chamber; also, the fluid so introduced or a device for this. Also *attrib.*

1933 *Amer. Jrnl. Med. Sci.* CLXXXV. 701 The chill should be removed from the milk and the drip given continuously throughout the day and night. **1949** *Anesthesia & Analgesia* XXVII. 57 The bottle containing the solution is attached to a Murphy drip setup, and the solution injected by the anesthetist. **1961** *Lancet* 29 July 240/2 An intravenous normal saline drip was put up. **1968** J. H. BURN *Lect. Notes Pharmacol.* (ed. 9) 3 Noradrenaline is sometimes given as an intravenous drip.

3. a. That which drips or falls in drops; *pl.* drippings.

1707–12 MORTIMER (J.), Water may be procured.. from the heavens by preserving the drips of the houses. **1801** CHARLOTTE SMITH *Solit. Wand.* I. 110 But for the drip of the trees. **1866** G. MACDONALD *Ann. Q. Neighb.* xi. (1878) 227 The drip from the thatch of the mill. **1880** V. L. CAMERON *Our Future Highway* II. xii. 244 An awning.. to keep the drips off.

b. *fig.* Nonsense; flattery; sentimental drivel. *slang* (orig. *U.S.*).

1919 *Wine, Women & War* (1926) 306 Drool about duties by Navy egg, regular and hard boiled. Usual R.O.T.C. drip. **1924** P. MARKS *Plastic Age* xxiv. 297 That freshman, Larson, showed me a theme.. that Kempton had corrected. It was full of errors that weren't marked, and it was nothing in the world but drip. **1946** 'B. GRAY' *Mr. Ball of Fire* i. 10 'We'll have nothing of the sort,' interrupted Joy, putting a welcome stop to this drip.

c. A stupid, feeble, or dull person; a fool; a bore. *slang.*

1932 G. & S. LORIMER *Men are like Street Cars* v. 114 He's no drip... Ted's a darn good egg. **1936** N. MARSH *Death in Ecstasy* xviii. 215 What about that little drip Claude? **1938** J. CARY *Castle Corner* 279 Ah, ye dirty devil, and what sort of a drip are ye to be dropped in a medical hall. **1951** I. BROWN *I break my Word* 123 We now more often call a feeble, foolish creature a drip. **1951** J. CANNAN *And all I Learned* xi. 197 Of all the wet drips! **1959** I. & P. OPIE *Lore & Lang. Schoolch.* xv. 326 Someone considered over-affectionate is said to be soppy, sloppy, gormless, a drip, or a clot.

d. *slang.* A grumble, complaint. (Cf. DRIP *v.* 5.)

1945 'TACKLINE' *Holiday Sailor* v. 53 Some of you chaps, you're on the drip the whole bloomin' time. Nothing but moan, moan, moan. **1948** 'N. SHUTE' *No Highway* xii. 293 He had a bit of a drip last time because we kept him in the dark. **1970** *Guardian* 20 Aug. 1/2 One of the accused, Able Seaman Edward Kirkbride, said he remembered someone saying: 'I am going to have a drip (complaint).'

4. *Arch.* **a.** A projecting 'member' of a cornice, etc., from which the rain-water drips and so is thrown off from the parts below. **b.** An overlapping piece of lead-work; cf. *drip-joint* in 8.

1664 EVELYN tr. *Freart's Archit.* 129 A Corona or drip to the Capitel, whereof it is the Plinth and Superior. **1726** LEONI *Alberti's Archit.* II. 35/2 The mutules supporting the Drip. **1823** P. NICHOLSON *Pract. Build.* 407 Drips on Flats or Gutters.. are formed by dressing the joints of the lead as described for rolls. **1850** INKERSLEY *Romanesque Archit.* 274 Whose principal arches.. are covered with concentric drips.

†**c.** (See quot.) *Obs.*

1727–51 CHAMBERS *Cycl.*, *Drips* is also used in building, for a kind of steps, on flat roofs, to walk upon. This way of building is much used in Italy, where the roof is not made quite flat, but a little raised in the middle; with *Drips*, or steps, lying a little inclining to the horizon. **1730–36** BAILEY (folio).

5. (See quot.)

1825 BROCKETT *N.C. Gloss.*, *Drip*, stalactites, or petrifactions.

6. *Manuf.* A receptacle for waste or overflow, as in refrigerators, etc.

1880 LOMAS *Alkali Trade* 43 Only by his drips and chamber caps can an acid maker know exactly what is going on in his chambers. *Ibid.* 55 The drips of the first chamber must be kept at about 135°.

7. *Mining.* See quot., and cf. DRIP *v.* 5.

1856 S. C. BREES *Terms Archit., etc.*, *Drip* (in mining), the angle or inclination of a stratum to the horizon.

8. *attrib.* and *Comb.*, as **drip-board**, a board to carry off the drip; **drip-cock**, the tap of a 'drip' to receive condensed moisture; **drip coffee**, coffee prepared by allowing boiling water to percolate through ground coffee (cf. DRIPPED *ppl. a.*); also **drip coffee-pot, coffee-maker**, a percolating coffee-pot; **drip culture**, a hydroponic method of plant culture in which the nutrient solutions are supplied automatically by a drip-feed mechanism; **drip-cup**, a cup-shaped vessel to catch droppings of liquid; **drip-feed**, a method of feeding, lubrication, etc., whereby liquid is supplied a drop at a time; freq. *attrib.*; **drip-joint** (see quot.); **drip mat**, a small mat placed under a glass, cup, etc., to catch drips; **drip-moulding** = DRIPSTONE; **drip painting**, a method of painting by which the colour is dripped on to the canvas or other medium (not applied directly with brush or palette knife); also, a painting so produced; **drip-pan**, a pan to catch drops of liquid; **drip-pipe** (see quot.); **drip-point** *Bot.* = *drip-tip*; **drip-proof** *a.*, protected from drips; **drip-pump**, a plumbers' pump for removing water from gas-pipes, etc.; **drip-shot** (see quot.); **drip-stick**, in stone-sawing, a stick along which water is slowly led to the stone, to keep the kerf wet; = *dripping-board*; **drip-tip** *Bot.* (see quots.); **drip-tray** = *drip-pan*. Also DRIPSTONE.

1890 R. KIPLING *Phant. Rickshaw* 44 Over the mouth a wooden *drip-board projected. **1865** GESNER *Coal, Petrol., etc.* (ed. 2) 85 The *drip-cock carries off the condensed steam. **1895** G. A. SALA *Life* II. 382 The renowned '*drip' coffee.. is so strong that it is said to stain the saucer into which it is poured. **1897** *Outing* (U.S.) XXIX. 574/1 He.. produced a jar of coffee and the *drip coffee-pot. **1964** *Which?* Feb. 53/1 With most of the *drip coffee makers.. a major disadvantage was the time it took to pour the boiling water through the ground coffee. **1923** *Amer. Jrnl. Bot.* X. 559 The relative dry-weight values of the plants grown in the *drip cultures are in every instance much superior to the corresponding values for the simple cultures. **1952** C. E. TICQUET *Successful Gardening without Soil* 176/1 Drip culture. **1886** W. A. HARRIS *Dict. Fire Ins.*, **Drip-cups*.. provided to catch falling oil from bearings, and other lubricated portions of machinery. **1907** *Westm. Gaz.* 18 Nov. 6/3 The neat four-sight *drip-feed lubricator. *Ibid.* 27 Dec. 4/2 No adjustment of the drip-feed points is necessary, as the pumps send a continuous stream of oil to the various parts. **1916** *Motor Cyclists' A.B.C.* 115 Lubrication (Automatic Drip Feed). **1964** *Which?* Jan. 13/1 There were 14 drip-feed heaters—the paraffin flowed to the burner from an inverted fuel container. **1971** *Manch. Guardian Weekly* 24 Apr. 5 Contaminated hospital drip-feed solutions. **1874** KNIGHT *Dict. Mech.*, **Drip-joint*.. a mode of uniting two sheets of metal in roofing where the joint is with the current, so as to form a water conductor. **1953** *Word for Word* (*Whitbread & Co.*) 18/2 **Drip mats*, small glass or absorbent mats on which glasses are placed to prevent staining tables and counters. **1851** TURNER *Dom. Archit.* II. iii. 73 Windows.. with a *drip moulding. **1958** *Listener* 27 Nov. 888/1 The exhibition shows, as Pollock's imitators never have, the range of *drip painting. **1960** *Times Lit. Suppl.* 9 Sept. p. xlvii/5 The drip paintings of 1949–50 (probably the peak of Pollock's achievement). **1874** KNIGHT *Dict. Mech.*, **Drip-pipe*, a small copper pipe.. from the waste-steam pipe inside, to carry off the condensed steam and other hot water which may be blown into the 'trap' at the top. **1900** B. D. JACKSON *Gloss. Bot. Terms* 82/1 *Drip-point, drip-tip. **1936** F. A. WESTBROOK in H. Pender *Electr. Engineers' Handbk.* (ed. 3) IV. xvi. 14 *Drip-Proof Motors. This type of motor has the upper halves of the heads closed so that materials, including liquids, cannot fall into it. **1960** *Farmer & Stockbreeder* 15 Mar. 171 (Advt.), B.S.D. motors (drip-proof or totally-enclosed fan-cooled). **1758** ROBERTSON in *Phil. Trans.* L. 497 Under almost all the arches there are great numbers of *drip-shot piles, or piles driven into the bed of the water-way, to prevent it from being washed away by the fall. **1897** J. C. WILLIS *Flowering Plants* I. 154 The *drip-tip.. or acuminate leaf-apex. **1952** P. W. RICHARDS *Tropical Rain Forest* iv. 87 The exaggerated acumen or drip-tip so often seen in rain-forest trees has long attracted attention.

ˈ**drip-drop**, *sb.* [reduplication of DRIP or DROP.] Continuous dripping with alternation of sound. So **drip-drop** *v.*, *lit.* and *fig.*

1848 MRS. GASKELL *M. Barton* ix, The drip-drop from the roof without. **1873** BROWNING *Red Cott. Nt.-cap* 269 She patient.. wiled the slow drip-dropping hours away. **1888** W. E. HENLEY in *Pall Mall G.* 11 June 3/1 My very life goes dripping, Dropping, dripping, drip-drop-dropping, In the drip-drop of the cistern.

drip-dry (ˈdrɪpˈdraɪ), *v. intr.* Of certain synthetic or chemically treated fabrics: to dry when hung up to drip, without subsequently requiring wringing or ironing; also *trans.*, to dry (a garment, etc.) in this manner; also *absol.* Hence as *adj.*, that will drip-dry; as *sb.*, such a garment or fabric. Also *transf.* and *fig.*

[**1916** *Daily Colonist* (Victoria, B.C.) 16 July 3/5 (Advt.), Do not wring or squeeze but hang to drip dry in the open air.] **1953** *Woman* 4 Apr. 34/3 With this permanently pleated nylon nightie.. you just.. rinse out, drip dry, and you don't even think of ironing. **1954** *Sci. News Let.* 16 Oct. 252/1 It will not shrink, fade or wrinkle and it drip-dries without pressing. **1956** *World Tennis* Sept. 51/2 Dacron shorts can be drip-dried. **1957** *Woman* 16 Nov. 25/3 Cottons and rayons with a special finish—that is ones that have been made crease-resistant, drip-dry or non-iron. **1958** *Ibid.* 22 Feb. 60/2 (Advt.), The rayon which 'drip-dries' at least as well as the best 'no-iron' cottons. **1958** *Sunday Express* 23 Feb. 14/3, I wouldn't exchange the sweet scent of fresh ironing for all the drip-dry cottons from Manchester. **1959** *Woman* 4 Apr. 43/3 Drip-dries are usually resin-finished fabrics. **1959** [see DRAG *sb.* 3 d]. **1960** *House & Garden* Mar. 92/2 Plates will drip-dry without a smear. **1968** *N.Y. Rev. Books* 7 Nov. 3/2 His greying drip-dry shirts.

†**dripe**, *v. Obs. rare.* [ME. *drīpen*:—OE. *drýpan*, early WS. **dríepan*:—**draupjan*, causal from *au*-grade of ablaut series **dreup-*, *draup-*, *drup*: see DRIP *v.* and etymological Note to DROP *sb.*]

1. *trans.* To let drop, cause to fall in drops.

c **893** K. ÆLFRED *Orosius* IV. vii, þe mon nime ænne eles dropan, and drype on an mycel fyr. *c* **1000** ÆLFRIC *Hom.* I. 118 Mine handa drypton myrran. *c* **1420** *Pallad. on Husb.* II. 277 Ek of the yonge out trie Oon heer, oon theer, and elliswhere hem dripe.

†**2.** To moisten, wet with drops. *Obs.*

(In quot. 1573 prob. by ellipsis of prep. *on.*)

c **1000** ÆLFRIC *Hom.* I. 330 He bæd.. ðæt Lazarus moste his tungan drypan. **1573** TUSSER *Husb.* xxxv. (1878) 78 Ye may, for driping his fellowes, that bough cut away.

ˈ**dripless**, *a.* Without a drip; that does not drip.

1887 *Pall Mall G.* 25 Oct. 6/1 There are displays of taps, one a 'dripless'. *Mod. Advt.*, The Standard 'Dripless' Strainer. No drip to soil table-linen.

dripped (drɪpt), *ppl. a.* [f. DRIP *v.*] That has been allowed to drip or percolate, esp. (*U.S.*) of coffee so made.

1884 F. E. OWENS *Cookbook* 307 Dripped coffee. **1909** 'O. HENRY' *Options* (1916) 50 But if you're ever in the Middle West just mention my name and you'll get foot-warmers and dripped coffee.

dripper (ˈdrɪpə(r)). [f. DRIP *v.* + -ER[1].] He who or that which drips; a wet, rainy day.

1686 GOAD *Celest. Bodies* I. xii. 59 Of 261 days there are found 140 Drippers. *Ibid.* xiii. 70 Of 87 Full Moons there appear.. Seventy Five Drippers.

ˈ**dripping**, *vbl. sb.* [f. DRIP *v.* + -ING.]

1. The fall of liquid in drops; *concr.* the liquid so falling.

c **1440** *Promp. Parv.* 132/2 Dryppynge, or droppynge, *stillacio.* *a* **1635** CORBET *On J. Dawson, Butler Ch. Ch.* (R.), O ye barrels! let your drippings fall In trickling streams. *a* **1816** BP. WATSON *Anecd.* I. 121 (R.) The scanty drippings of the most barren rocks in Switzerland.

2. *spec.* The melted fat that drips from roasting meat, which when cold is used like butter. Formerly often in *pl.*

1463 [implied in DRIPPING-PAN.] **1530** PALSGR. 215/1 Drepyng of rost meate, *la gresse du rost.* **1552** HULOET, Drippinges of rost. **1601** HOLLAND *Pliny* II. 385 The dripping or grauie that commeth from a rams lights rosted. **1723** SWIFT *Poems* Wks. 1763 II. 141 For Candles she trucks her Dripping. **1826** SCOTT *Let. to Lockhart* 15 Jan., A good sirloin, which requires only to be basted with its own drippings. **1887** R. N. CAREY *Uncle Max* viii. 67 A piece of bread and dripping.

†**3.** A slope to carry off water. Cf. DRIP *sb.* 7.

1613-39 I. JONES in Leoni *Palladio's Archit.* (1742) I. 71 The Dripping of the Pavement. **1740** DYCHE & PARDON, *Dripping*..the inclination or angular slant of a pent house.

4. *attrib.* and *Comb.*, as **dripping-board**, a board from which water drips; **dripping-cake**, a cake made with dripping; **dripping crust**, a pastry crust made with dripping; **dripping toast**, toast spread with dripping; **dripping-vat** (see quot.). Also DRIPPING-PAN.

1865 I. T. F. TURNER *Slate Quarries* 16 The slab, on which, from a '*dripping-board', a continuous dropping of water washes particles of flint sand beneath the saw-plate. **1857** HUGHES *Tom Brown* II. viii, The excellence of that mysterious condiment, a *dripping-cake. **1747** H. GLASSE *Art Cookery* viii. 75 A *Dripping Crust... Beef-dripping.. work it up well into..Flour. **1906** MRS. BEETON *Bk. Household Managem.* xxxi. 883 *Dripping crust* (for plain pies and puddings). **1921** W. DE LA MARE *Crossings* 14 Maybe you'll come and have a bit of *dripping toast to your tea. **1874** KNIGHT *Dict. Mech.*, **Dripping-vat*, a tank beneath a boiler..to catch the overflow or drip, as..in indigo-factories.

'dripping, *ppl. a.* [f. DRIP *v.* + -ING².]

1. That drips; having liquid falling off in drops.

1783 COWPER *Rose* 10 A nosegay, so dripping and drowned. **1801** SOUTHEY *Thalaba* XI. xxxvi, His back and dripping wings Half open'd to the wind. **1833** HT. MARTINEAU *Cinnamon & P.* vi. 109 The other girls wrung out their dripping hair.

b. Of weather: Wet, continuously rainy.

1699 *Poor Man's Plea* 7 They had a dripping Harvest. **1792** *Trans. Soc. Arts* X. 99 In any dripping year, you will not fail of two hundred bushels to an acre. **1894** MRS. H. WARD *Marcella* III. 250 A dripping September day.

c. ***dripping eaves.*** (See quot.)

1847 CRAIG, *Dripping-eaves*, the lower edges of the roof of a building from which the rain drips to the ground. **1849** FREEMAN *Archit.* 189 The towers sometimes have octagonal spires of wood with dripping eaves.

2. quasi-*adv.* in phr. ***dripping wet.***

1840 MARRYAT *Olla Podr.*, *S.W. by W. ¾W.*, The master ..came down dripping wet.

dripping-pan ('drɪpɪŋ,pæn). [f. DRIPPING *vbl. sb.*] A pan used to catch the 'dripping' from roasting meat.

1463 *Act 3 Edw. IV*, c. 4 Hamers, pinsons, firetonges, drepyngpannes. **1552** *Bury Wills* (Camden) 142 One dryppine panne of iron. **1769** MRS. RAFFALD *Eng. Housekpr.* (1778) 95 Put them into a tin dripping-pan to bake or fry them. **1883** *Knowledge* 8 June 342/2 Inside the cylinder [of the roaster] is a cylinder to support the dripping-pan.

dripple ('drɪp(ə)l), *v.* [A frequentative formation blending *drip* and *dribble.*]

1. *intr.* = DRIBBLE *v.* 3; but connoting a lighter and brisker motion.

1821 CLARE *Vill. Minstr.* II. 106 The brook mourns drippling o'er its pebbly bed. **1838** J. STRUTHERS *Poetic T.* 59 Drippling springs romantic play.

2. = DRIP *v.* 3.

1822 BYRON *Werner* III. ii. 26 You who stood still Howling and drippling on the bank. **1863** ROBSON *Bards Tyne* 245 Drippling like some River God, he slowly left the harbour.

†**'dripplekie.** *Obs. nonce-wd.* A very small drop, a driblet.

1668 CULPEPPER & COLE *Barthol. Anat.* III. iii. 135 If you squeeze the substance thereof, many little Dripplekies of blood do sweat out.

drippy ('drɪpɪ), *a.* [f. DRIP + -Y¹.]

1. Characterized by dripping; wet, rainy.

1817-18 COBBETT *Resid. U.S.* (1822) 50 The drippy and chilly climate of England. **1868** LONGF. in *Life* (1891) III. 108 In town. Muddy, sloppy, drippy.

2. Drivelling, sloppily sentimental; having the characteristics of a 'drip' (see DRIP *sb.* 3 c); 'wet'. *colloq.* (orig. *U.S.*).

1952 *N.Y. Herald Tribune* 9 Apr. 29/1 'Isn't it too dreamingly drippy,' said Miss Temple. **1962** K. ORVIS *Damned & Destroyed* ix. 66 It was kind of drippy, me not coming back. **1963** *Times* 6 Feb. 13/4 Mr. Richard Pasco as the drippy hero. **1967** O. NORTON *Now lying Dead* iv. 63 Men get so drippy when they're over-civilized, don't they?

dripstone ('drɪpstəʊn).

1. A moulding or cornice over a door, window, etc., to throw off the rain; a label. Also *attrib.*

1812-16 J. SMITH *Panorama Sc. & Art* I. 139 The dripstone is generally clearly marked and often small. **1851** RUSKIN *Stones Ven.* I. vi. §6 The dripstone is naturally the attribute of Northern buildings, and therefore especially of Gothic architecture. *Ibid.* §9 A true dripstone moulding.

2. 'The name usually given to filters composed of porous stone' (Smyth *Sailor's Word-bk.* 1867).

1792 W. BLIGH *Voyage to South Sea* ii. 21, I also directed the water for drinking to be filtered through dripstones. **1858** in SIMMONDS *Dict. Trade.*

driry, obs. form of DREARY *a.*

drisheen (drɪ'ʃiːn). [ad. Ir. *drisín* intestine.] A kind of sausage made from sheep's blood, milk, and seasoning.

1910 P. W. JOYCE *English as we speak it in Ireland* 251 Drisheen is now used in Cork as an English word, to denote a sort of pudding made of the narrow intestines of a sheep, filled with blood that has been cleared of the red colouring matter, and mixed with meal and some other ingredients. **1914** JOYCE *Portrait of Artist* (1916) ii. 99 Mr Dedalus had ordered drisheens for breakfast. **1928** *Daily Express* 9 Mar. 11/7 Drisheen is a kind of sausage made..mainly from sheep's blood and milk. It is the Irish cousin of the Bury pudding. **1939** JOYCE *Finnegans Wake* (1964) 164 Correspondents..will keep on asking me what is the correct garnish to serve drisheens with. Tansy Sauce. Enough. **1968** T. FITZGIBBON *Taste of Ireland* 79/1 *Drisheen*, traditional name for a black or blood pudding in County Cork.

drisk. *U.S.* A drizzly mist.

1717 S. SEWALL *Diary* 27 Apr. (1882) III. 129 My Calash defended me well from the Cold Drisk. **1857** THOREAU *Maine W.* (1894) 239 We mistook a little rocky islet seen through the 'drisk'..for the steamer.

drisle, drissel, drit, obs. ff. DRIZZLE, DIRT.

drite, *v.* *Obs.* exc. *Sc.* Also 1 drítan, 5-6 drytt, 5-7 dryte, (7 *pa. t.* drait, 8 dret, *pa. pple.* drate). [Com. Teut. str. vb. **drît-an, drait, dritan-*, in ON. *drîta, dreit, dritinn*, MDu. *drîten*, Du. *drijten*, L.G. *drîten*. The strong inflexion pa. t. *drate, drait, dret*, and pa. pple. *drittin*, also *dirtin*, are retained in Sc. Hence DIRT, ME. *drit.*] *intr.* To void or drop excrement; to stool.

a **1000** *Ags. Gl.* in Wr.-Wülcker 218/11 *Degestio, i. egestio*, driting. *c* **1000** *Sax. Leechd.* I. 364 Nim eac þæt græs þær hund ȝedriteþ. *a* **1300** *Cursor M.* 22398 Sua sal he peris, al beseeten, Bath wit driten and soru beten. **1483** *Cath. Angl.* 109/1 To Dryte, *cacare, egerere.* **1508** KENNEDIE *Flyting w. Dunbar* 395, I sall ding the, quhill thow dryte and dong. *a* **1605** POLWART *Flyting w. Montgomerie* 754 And thou flyt, Ile dryt in thy gob. **1721** KELLY *Sc. Prov.* 367 (Jam.) You have dirten in your nest. **1789** DAVIDSON *Seasons* 7 (Jam.) Ere..the ducks had drate Upo' the hallan-stane.

drith(e, obs. var. of DRYTH.

drittin: see DRIGHTIN.

drivability: see DRIVEABILITY.

drivable ('draɪvəb(ə)l), *a.* [f. DRIVE *v.* + -ABLE.] Capable of being driven; suitable for driving.

1854 THOREAU *Walden* i. (1863) 49 Straight, and drivable nails. **1880** MISS BRADDON *Just as I am* liii, Within a driveable distance. **1891** ATKINSON *Moorland Par.* 359 When the snow began to be drivable. **1895** *Athenæum* 12 Jan. 52/3 That..the majority of the Scotch moors [are] 'drivable'.

drive (draɪv), *v.* Pa. t. **drove** (drəʊv); *arch.* **drave** (dreɪv). Pa. pple. **driven** ('drɪv(ə)n). [A Common Teut. vb., of first ablaut series: OE. *drîf-an, dráf*, pl. *drifon, drifen*, (corresp. to OS. *drîban*, OFris. *drîva*, Du. *drijven*), OHG. *trîban* (Ger. *treiben*), ON. *drîfa* (Sw. *drifva*, Da. *drive*), Goth. *dreiban*; *draib, dribum*; *dribans*. Not represented outside Teutonic.

The OE. inflexion is regularly represented by the current forms. In the pa. t., however, the northern *drave* long held the field (as in the Bible versions) against the southern *drove*; the ablaut plural *drĭven* became obs. in 15th c. A new pa. pple. *droven, drove*, after the pa. t., was also long used by some instead of *driven.*]

A. Inflexional Forms.

1. *Present stem.* 1 drîf-, 2-5 drif-, dryf-, (4 drijf-, 4-5 driff-, 5 dryff-, dreff-), 3- driv-, (3-6 dryv-, 4-5 dryw-, 6 driev-).

c **900** tr. *Bæda's Hist.* I. x. [xiii]. (1890) 48 Us drifað ða ellreordan to sæ. *a* **1200** *Moral Ode* 116 Hine þer to scal driue. *a* **1300** *Cursor M.* 22642 (Edin.) Drif þaim doun. *c* **1300** *Beket* 197 So moche wo he gan dryve. *c* **1400** MAUNDEV. (Roxb.) xx. 91 He herd ane dryfe bestez. **1483** *Cath. Angl.* 109/1 To Drywe (*A.* Dryffe). **1526** *Pilgr. Perf.* 179 b, Dryue hym away. **1553** EDEN *Treat. Newe Ind.* (Arb.) 13 Whiche nacion the Turke..entended to drieue out of India.

2. *Pa. t.* **a.** *sing.* α. 1 dráf, 2-4 draf, 4-7 (9 *arch.*) drave, (3 dræf, 4 *north.* 5-6 *Sc.* draif, 5 drafe, *Sc.* draiff, drayff, drawe). These forms also *pl.* from 13th c. in north, from 15th c. generally: see below c β.

a **1000** *Cædmon's Gen.* 2804 þa se wer..Draf of wicum.. his aȝen bearn. *a* **1225** *Juliana* 76 A steorm..draf ham to londe. *a* **1300** *E.E. Psalter* xlii[i]. 2 Wharfore awai drave þou me? *c* **1400** MAUNDEV. (Roxb.) xx. 92 A tempest..drafe him. **1533** BELLENDEN *Livy* v. (1822) 417 Camillus draif infinite gudis fra Capena. **1611** BIBLE *Josh.* xxiv. 18 The Lord draue out from before vs all the people. **1647** COWLEY *Mistress, Usurpation* ii, But thou, their Cov'etous Neighbour, drav'est out all. **1676** HOBBES *Iliad* I. 151 Nor ever thence my Kine or Horses drave. **1887** BOWEN *Virg. Æneid* I. 29 Now from Latium's shores Troy's exiled army she drave.

β. 3-5 drof, 4- drove, (4-5 drofe, droof(e, droff(e). These forms also *pl.* from 14th c.

c **1200** *Trin. Coll. Hom.* 39 Ure drihten drof fele deules.. ut af á man. **13..** *Coer de L.* 5092 Syx thousand..he droff hym before. *c* **1374** CHAUCER *Anel. & Arc.* 190 She..drofe him forthe. *c* **1380** WYCLIF *Wks.* (1880) 241 [Crist] droof out symonyentis. **1382** —— *Gen.* xv. 11 Abram droue hem awey. *c* **1450** *Merlin* 78 Our meynee..drof hem ageyn. **1473** WARKW. *Chron.* (Camden) 8 [He] droff oute of Lyncolnshyre Sere Thomas a Burghe. **1596** SHAKS. *1 Hen. IV*, IV. iii. 102 He..droue vs to seeke out This Head of safetie.

γ. 3 dreof, 4 dref, 4-5 drife.

c **1205** LAY. 29939 Aðelstan..dreof heom..Ut ouer Weȝen. *c* **1330** R. BRUNNE *Chron. Wace* (Rolls) 1590 In-to þe erthe his ax dref. *c* **1400** *Sowdone Bab.* 407 A Romayne drife a darte him to.

δ. 5-7 drived.

1388 driueden [see 2 c]. *c* **1400** *Melayne* 328 To the Duke a dynt he dryvede. **1685** BAXTER *Paraphr. N.T., John* iv. 46 Outward necessities..drived many to seek to Christ.

b. 2 *sing.* 1 drife.

c. *pl.* 1 drifon (dreofon), 2-3 drife(n, 3-5 drive(n, (4-5 dryve(n, dreven, -yn).

c **950** tr. *Bæda's Hist.* II. v. (1890) 112 [Hi] dreofon hine onweȝ. *c* **1000** *Ags. Ps.* lix. 9 [lx. 10] þu..ðe us swa drife. *c* **1000** *Ags. Gosp.* John ix. 35 Hiȝ hyne drifon ut [*c* **1160** *Hatton* drifen]. *c* **1205** LAY. 1673 Heo..Driuen heom on ȝeinwærd. *c* **1290** *S. Eng. Leg.* I. 39/188 Huy driue þane wayn þare as þe Quene was. **13..** *Coer de L.* 5774 That they ne dreven alle adoun. **1382** WYCLIF *Job* xxiv. 3 They dryuen awei the asse [**1388** driueden]. *c* **1420** *Chron. Vilod.* 14 þai drevyn þe Brytones houȝt and drevyn hem in to Walys. *c* **1450** *Merlin* 78 We driven the remenaunt in at the gates.

β. *pl.* from 13th c. in north, from 15th c. generally, as sing.: see 2 a, α, β.

a **1300** *Cursor M.* 4572 (Cott.) þai draf [so *Gött.*, *Fairf.* drave, *Trin.* droof] þir oþer seuen a-wai. **1480** CAXTON *Chron. Eng.* ccxxxix. 265 They..drofe oute al the prisoners. *a* **1533** LD. BERNERS *Huon* liv. 183 They..draue away al the bestes.

3. *Pa. pple.* α. 1 drifen, 3- driven, (4 drivin, y-driven, 4-6 dryven, -in, -on, -un, -yn, dreven, -in, -yn, 5 drifun, dryfen, *Sc.* drywyn, 5-6 drewin, -yn, 6 drieven).

c **950** *Lindisf. Gosp.* Luke viii. 29 [He] ȝedrifen wæs from diowlæ on woesternum. *c* **1200** ORM. 8247 He wass drifenn ut. *a* **1300** *Cursor M.* 21779 (Edin.) Nailis in his hend and fete That driuin ware. *c* **1330** *Arth. & Merl.* 6223 Y-driuen he was undir the toun. *a* **1340** HAMPOLE *Psalter* x. 7 þai ere ..dryuen in til þe pitt of hell. *c* **1340** *Cursor M.* 9454 (Fairf.) Drevyn fro his Erytage. *c* **1380** WYCLIF *Serm.* Sel. Wks. I. 187 Was dryvun þus in to helle. *c* **1400** *Destr. Troy* 12322 Dryvon fro troy. *c* **1400** *Apol. Loll.* 99 All be drifun in to þe seruice of Crist. **1535** COVERDALE *Ps.* xliii[i]. 2 How thou hast dryuen out the Heithen with thy honde. **1553** EDEN *Treat. Newe Ind.* (Arb.) 9 Drieuen into Germanie. **1556** *Chron. Gr. Friars* (Camden) 28 By tempest ware drevyne to Porchemoth havyne. **1563** WINȜET *Wks.* (1890) II. 22 The preistis dryuin away and banissit. *Ibid.* 63 This wil.. violentlie is drewin.

β. 3 ydryve, 3-6 drive (4-5 dryve, idreve, 5 idrevfe, drif, 6 dryff, dreff).

1297 R. GLOUC. (1724) 97 Mid strengþe ydryue into Yrlonde. *c* **1330** R. BRUNNE *Chron. Wace* (Rolls) 13856 Ner al slayn, and dryue bakward. *c* **1386** CHAUCER *Frankl. T.* 502 This bargayn is ful dryue. **1387** TREVISA *Higden* (Rolls) I. 133 Nilus is i-dreue aȝe. *c* **1400** *Song Roland* 1024 Or this dredfull day was drif to nyght. *c* **1485** *E.E. Misc.* (Warton Club) 43 From dale to doune I am i-dreufe. **1513** DOUGLAS *Æneis* I. Contents 2 How the..Troianis war drive on to Cartage ciete. [**1517** TORKINGTON *Pilgr.* (1884) 59 Dryff in to Barbaria. *Ibid.* 60 We war Dreff bakward.]

γ. 5-8 drove, 6-7 droven.

14.. *Amis & Amil.* 2461 (Douce MS.) When thei had.. Droue oute both broun and blake. **1557** NORTH *Gueuara's Diall Pr.* 152 b/2 To haue drouen out the Gothes. **1607** TOPSELL *Four-f. Beasts* (1658) 480 They were drove formost. *Ibid.* 517 They are not to be droven but to be carryed in a Cart. **1648** GAGE *West. Ind.* viii. (1655) 24 We thought it would [have] blown and droven us out of our beds. **1781** GIBBON *Decl. & F.* II. xxvi. 13 The victor and the vanquished have alternately drove, and been driven. **1799** NELSON 18 Feb. in Nicolas *Disp.*, The French yet may be drove out of the Kingdom of Naples.

δ. 5-7 drived.

1523 LD. BERNERS *Froiss.* I. ccclxxxvi. 658 They were driued home agayne to their losse.

B. Signification.

I. To force (living beings) to move on or away.

1. a. *trans.* To force (men or animals) to move on before one, or flee away from one, by blows or intimidation; to urge on or impel with violence. Usually with an adv. or prepositional phrase defining the direction, etc., as *away, back, down, in, off, on, out, up*; *from, to, toward, through* a place, etc. In comb. with an adv. often answering in sense to a compound verb from L.: ***drive back*** = *repel*, ***drive out*** = *expel*, ***drive in*** or ***on*** = *impel.*

c **1000** *Ags. Gosp.* Mark xi. 15 He ongann drifan [*c* **1160** *Hatton* drifen] of þam temple syllende and bicȝende. *c* **1205** LAY. 17613 Drif heom of ærde. *a* **1300** *Cursor M.* 3832 (Gött.) I se his dohutir rachell Driuand his bestes to þe well. **1413** *Pilgr. Sowle* (Caxton 1483) I. ii. 3 Michael drofe me out of heuene. *c* **1440** *Promp. Parv.* 132/2 Dryve bestys, *mino.* **1483** *Cath. Angl.* 109/2 To Drywe (*A.* Dryffe) away. **1530** PALSGR. 529/2 I drive a thyng afore me, *je chasse deuant moy.* *Ibid.* 530/1 He drave me out a dore..as I had ben a dogge. **1553** EDEN *Treat. Newe Ind.* (Arb.) 38 We droue them to flyghte. **1646** P. BULKELEY *Gospel Covt.* To Rdr. 5 To be driven up and downe the world, as a vagabond, or as dryed leaves. **1726** SWIFT *It cannot rain but it pours* Wks. 1755 III. I. 134 A flock of sheep, that were driving to the shambles. **1855** MACAULAY *Hist. Eng.* III. 333 It was impossible to drive him to bay. **1888** J. INGLIS *Tent Life in Tigerland* 35 The Indian jackal..can fight in an ugly way when driven into a corner. **1894** BARING-GOULD *Deserts S. France* II. 254 The King..drove in the Russian sharpshooters.

b. Proverb.

1532 MORE *Confut. Tindale* Wks. 557/1 He must needes go, whom the dyuel dryueth. **1556** J. HEYWOOD *Spider &*

F. lv. A a v b, Forth he must (they say) that the deuil doth driue. **1590** LODGE *Euphues Gold. Leg.* (1887) 92 He is in haste whom the devil drives. *a* **1659** CLEVELAND *Coachman* 6 The Proverb, needs must go when th' Devil drives. **1886** MRS. LYNN LINTON *Paston Carew* xxxiii, I am sorry for that little fellow..but needs must when the devil drives.

c. *transf.* To constrain or oblige to go or flee (by force of circumstances, or by an inward feeling or impulse).

c **1510** *Robin Hood* in Arb. *Garner* VI. 449 What need driveth the to green wood? **1615** J. STEPHENS *Satyr. Ess., Fidler* 425 Hope of imployment drives him up to London. **1650** TRAPP *Comm. Gen.* xlvii. 20 Stark hunger drove the wolfe out of the wood, as the proverb is. **1755** S. WALKER *Serm.* x, A Knave, or a Sot! who is drove by the Fear of an After-reckoning to the Church. **1867** *Q. Rev.* Oct. 30 Thirst for knowledge drove him to Jerusalem. **1879** *Cassell's Techn. Educ.* IV. 235/2 The persecutions..drove about 5,000 refugees to England.

2. *fig.* **a.** (with abstract object).

c **1200** *Trin. Coll. Hom.* 79 Swilch manifeald pine..driuen ut of ure þoght þe fule lustes. *a* **1300** *Cursor M.* 26865 His scrift þou agh noght to driue awai. **1484** CAXTON *Fables of Poge* (1889) 4 To dryue awey melancholye. **1576** FLEMING *Panopl. Epist.* 28 [This] drave all my sorrowes into perpetual exile. **1672** CAVE *Prim. Chr.* I. iv. (1673) 88 When he could not drive the thing he might at least banish the name. **1791** *Gentl. Mag.* 23/1 French bread having driven English from the tables of the great. **1892** *Speaker* 8 Oct. 427/1 India..has practically been driving China out of the London Market.

b. To put, bring, cause to fall (*upon* a person). *Obs.* or *arch.*

a **1300** *Cursor M.* 19335 (Gött.) Queder ȝe will driue on vs þe blam. **1535** COVERDALE *2 Sam.* xv. 14 Lest he..dryue some mysfortune vpon vs. **1885** R. BRIDGES *Nero* II. iv, Drive not the fault on him.

3. a. To cause to flee before one's pursuit; to chase, hunt, pursue, follow; also *fig. Obs.* or *arch.*

c **1200** *Trin. Coll. Hom.* 209 Þe deuel..henteð us alse hunte drieð deor to grune. **1340** *Ayenb.* 75Þe on vlyȝþ, þe oþer hyne dryfþ. **1375** BARBOUR *Bruce* VII. 66 He vist full weill that thai vald drif The kyngis trass till thai hym ta. **16..** *Chevy Chase* ii, To drive the deer with hound and horn, Earl Percy took his way. **1639** LD. DIGBY *Let. conc. Relig.* iv. (1651) 93 To drive up this belief to the Patriarkes. **1810** SCOTT *Lady of L.* VI. xxiv, Drive the fleet deer the forest through.

b. To chase or frighten the game or wild beasts of an extensive area into nets, traps, or a small area where they can be killed or captured. (See DRIVE *sb.* 1 c.)

1753 CHAMBERS *Cycl. Supp., Driving*, amongst sportsmen, a term applied to the taking of young pheasants, and some other birds, in nets of an open structure. *Driving of wild fowl*, is only practicable in the moulting time..and is to be done by means of a spaniel. **1841** J. FORBES *Eleven Y. in Ceylon* I. 125 To encircle the herd, and to await his signal to commence driving. *Ibid.* 139 We could distinctly see the progress of the people employed in driving..At last the elephants broke from the jungle. **1883** *19th Cent.* Dec. 1096 Battue shooting and grouse and partridge driving. **1890** BAKER *Wild Beasts* I. 162 Any form of shooting excepting driving is quite impossible under these conditions.

c. *absol.* To drive a tenant's cattle to the pound as a method of distraining for rent.

a **1659** CLEVELAND *Poems, &c.* 19 (T.) His landlord..hath sent His water-bailiff thus to drive for rent. **1766** GOLDSM. *Vic. W.* xxiv, My steward talks of driving for the rent. **1868** TRENCH *Realities Irish Life* vi. 82 The term 'driving' was applied to a summary process for recovering rent, which the law in these days conferred upon the landlord, whereby he could drive to the pound the cattle of any tenant who owed any rent whatever, without previous notice.

d. *trans.* and *intr.* To drive (bees) into a new hive (see quots.).

1824 T. WILKINSON *Tours to Brit. Mountains* 144 The landlord..entertained me, as we walked along, with their custom of *driving bees*.—In Autumn they turn their replenished hives the wrong side up, over which they set an empty one. The bees ascend into their new apartments; they then take them into their solitudes of heath, now in full bloom. **1875** *Encycl. Brit.* III. 502/1 Artificial swarming, the mode of proceeding for which varies according to the kind of hive in use. Considering, first, straw skeps, the common hive of the country, the operation to be pursued is known as 'driving'. **1928** C. WILLIAMS *Story of Hive* xiv. 140 The operation of driving is a simple one. A few puffs of smoke are blown into the entrance of the skep, and after a few minutes, during which the bees gorge themselves with honey, it is inverted. An empty skep is then placed above it at an angle of about forty-five degrees, and held in position by means of two driving-irons and a skewer. The sides of the lower hive are then smartly and continuously rapped until all the bees have ascended into the upper one.

4. With the place or area as verbal object: **a.** To drive off the animals, etc. from (a district); to scour, devastate, harry. **b.** *Forest Law.* To drive together all the cattle in (a forest) for purposes of identification, etc.; see DRIFT *sb.* 1 b. **c.** *Hunting.* To search (a wood, district, etc.) for game; also *absol.*

a **1400-50** *Alexander* 1198 All þe pastours and þe playnes prestly to driue, And bring in all þe bestaill, barayn and othire. **1540** *Act 32 Hen. VIII*, c. 13. §4 All forrestis..shalbe driven at the feast of Sainct Michaell. **1697** DRYDEN *Æneid* I. 745 We come not with design of wastful Prey, To drive the Country, force the Swains away. **1727** POPE, etc. *Art of Sinking* 72 They have..driven the country, and carried off at once whole cart-loads of our manufacture. **1790** R. BAGE *Hermsprong* xxiii, If I live, I will drive the country of him. **1890** BAKER *Wild Beasts & their Ways* I. 88 One day we were driving a rocky hill for a tiger. *Ibid.* 417 We were driving for any kind of animals that the jungle might produce.

5. *spec.* To urge onward and direct the course of (an animal drawing a vehicle or plough, or the vehicle itself; also, by later extension, a railway engine or train, etc.).

[*c* **1000** *Christ* 677 Sum mæȝ ofer sealtne sæ sundwudu drifan.] *a* **1250** *Prov. Ælfred* 95 in *O.E. Misc.* 108 And þe cheorl beo in fryþ..And his plouh beo i-dryue. **1382** WYCLIF *2 Sam.* vi. 3 The sones of Amynadab dryuen the newe wayn. *c* **1470** HENRY *Wallace* VI. 437 A werk man come fast, Dryfande a mere. **1553** T. WILSON *Rhet.* (1580) 206 He is a meter man to drive the cart then to serve the court. **1667** MILTON *P.L.* III. 438 Where Chineses drive With Sails and Wind thir canie Waggons light. *c* **1676** LADY CHAWORTH in *12th Rep. Hist. MSS. Comm.* App. v. 34 Sledges..are counted dangerous things and none can drive the horse that draws them about but the D. of Monmouth. **1895** *Law Times Rep.* LXXIII. 623/2 The engine-driver drove his train at the rate of..forty miles an hour.

fig. **1789** WOLCOTT (P. Pindar) *Ep. to falling Minist.* Wks. 1812 II. 116 Who driveth, Jehu-like, the church and state. **1892** MRS. H. WARD *D. Grieve* II. vii, Louie isn't an easy one to drive.

b. To carry or convey in a vehicle.

1662 J. BARGRAVE *Pope Alex. VII* (1867) 120 To be droven in a wheelbarrow. **1860** TYNDALL *Glac.* I. xxvii. 218, I was driven by my two guides in an open sledge to Sallenches. *Mod.* You can have the luggage driven to the station.

c. *absol.* To guide a vehicle or the animal that draws it, to act as driver; also, to travel or be conveyed in a carriage under one's own direction or at one's disposal. Also *intr.* (for *pass.*), of the vehicle.

One *drives* in a vehicle of which the course is under one's control, as one's own or a friend's private carriage, or a hired carriage or cab; one *rides* in a vehicle the course of which one does not control, as a public stage-coach, omnibus, or tram-car, or the cart of a friendly farmer who gives one a 'lift' on the way.

1592 SHAKS. *Rom. & Jul.* I. iv. 82 Sometime she [Queen Mab] drieth ore a Souldiers necke. **1634** SIR T. HERBERT *Trav.* 136 So that a-top might drive together sixe Chariots. **1709** BERKELEY *Th. Vision* §46, I hear a coach drive along the street. **1717** PRIOR *Alma* III. 140 The man within the coach that sits..Is safer much..than he that drives. **1793** *Regal Rambler* 83 The lady..ordered her coachman..to drive on. *c* **1838** LANDOR *Imag. Conv.* Wks. 1846 II. 14 If they do not like the price, they drive off. **1877** M. M. GRANT *Sun-Maid* ii, They drove through a shady beech-wood. **1892** *Times* 19 Jan. 7/5 The Queen drove yesterday afternoon. **1893** EARL DUNMORE *Pamirs* II. 293 A new bridge..was just finished as we drove up. *Mod.* You can ride by omnibus all the way; but, as time is an object, you had better take a cab and drive to London Bridge.

†**6.** *intr.* or *absol.* To ride hard on horseback.

c **1300** *Havelok* 2702 He cam driuende up-on a stede. *c* **1450** *Merlin* 335 Thei saugh her meyne come full harde dryuinge. **1470-85** MALORY *Arthur* VII. viii, They sawe a knyght come dryuend by them al in grene.

II. To impel (matter) by physical force.

7. a. *trans.* To cause (something) to move along by direct application of physical force; to propel, carry along (usually said of the wind, or a current of water).

a **1067** *Charter of Eadweard* in *Cod. Dipl.* IV. 221 Eall ðæt to his strande ȝedryuen hys. *c* **1200** *Trin. Coll. Hom.* 175 Storm..arereð shures fele and drieuð hem biforen him. *a* **1300** *K. Horn* 119 Þe se þat schup so faste drof. *c* **1400** *Sowdone Bab.* 76 A drift of wedir us droffe to Rome. **1582** N. LICHEFIELD tr. *Castanheda's Conq. E. Ind.* lv. 117 b, Their ships were driuen on shore, for all their Ankors. **1697** DRYDEN *Virg. Georg.* I. 125 When the light Stubble, to the Flames resign'd, Is driv'n along, and crackles in the Wind. **1762** FALCONER *Shipwr.* II. 805 Our helpless bark at last ashore is driven. **1841-71** T. R. JONES *Anim. Kingd.* (ed. 4) 696 To prevent the blood from being driven back again into the ventricle. **1862** MISS YONGE *C'tess Kate* ix, Alice and I used to drive hoops.

b. To direct the course of (timber floating down a stream). (*U.S.*, *Canada*, and *N.Z.*)

1848 THOREAU *Maine W.* (1894) 55 It was easy to see that driving logs must be an exciting as well as arduous and dangerous business. **1873** *Gt. Indust. U.S.* 822 The difficult and dangerous service of driving the logs down the rivers to the abodes of civilization. **1874** W. M. BAINES *Narr. E. Crewe* viii. 170 A million feet of timber, capable of being 'driven out' by placing a flood-dam in a suitable position. **1876** *Trans N.Z. Inst.* IX. 368 The only other practicable method I can propose for the preservation of the timber is to 'drive' the logs down to deep-water at once.

8. a. To cause to go with force; to throw, cast, send, impel in any direction; e.g. to throw *down* by force, force *asunder*, separate or dispel with force. Esp. in *Golf*; *spec.* to hit (the ball) a long distance with a driver (DRIVER 3 i); also *absol.* and *intr.* Cf. *driving-iron*, *-putter*, s.v. DRIVING *vbl. sb.* 3 b.

a **1000** *Boeth. Metr.* xxix. 57 (Fox) Hwilum þæt drige drift þone wætan. *a* **1300** *Cursor M.* 26047 Samson..þis hus skakand don dos he drijfe. *c* **1340** *Ibid.* 21143 (Trin.) Stones at him þei draue. **1398** TREVISA *Barth. De P.R.* XVI. lxii. (1495) 573 A nother kynde [of stone] forsakyth yren and dryueth it awaye fro hymself. *c* **1440** *York Myst.* xvii. 283 Hayll! duke þat dryues dede vndir fete. **1581** PETTIE *Guazzo's Civ. Conv.* I. (1586) 17 b, The Northeast winde doth not so drive in sunder the clouds. **1801** STRUTT *Sports & Past.* II. iii. 81 The game consists in driving the ball into certain holes made in the ground. **1858** A. W. DRAYSON *Sporting S. Africa* 191 He generally drove a bullet pretty straight. **1862** *Chambers's Encycl.* IV. 823/2 Crack-players will drive a ball above 200 yards. **1886** H. G. HUTCHINSON *Hints on Golf* 22 Some first-rate players have acquired the habit of 'driving off the right leg', as it is termed. **1892** [see PUT, PUTT *v.*[2] 3]. *a* **1897** *Mod. Sc. dial.* Boys driving stones at a bird in a tree. **1959** *Chambers's Encycl.* VI. 431/1 Crack players will drive a ball above 250 yards.

b. *Cricket.* To strike (a ball) with the bat held upright, so as to send it back (more or less) in the direction of the bowler. (Often with the bowler as object.) Also *intr.*; *spec.* of a bat: to be suited for driving the ball. **c.** *Baseball* and *Lawn-Tennis.* To throw or hit (a ball) very swiftly.

1827 *Sporting Mag.* Nov. 10/1 There would be comparatively no..driving forward. **1836** *New Sporting Mag.* July 197 It is a mistake to say that such [bats] are too light to 'drive' well. **1851** J. PYCROFT *Cricket Field* vii. 154 Do you ever drive a ball back from the leg-stump to long-field On? **1852** 'N. FELIX' *How to play Clarke* (1922) 8 Spring out..and drive forward with all your might. **1857** HUGHES *Tom Brown* II. viii. (1880) 358 Arthur gets the ball again, and actually drives it forward for two. **1871** 'THOMSONBY' *Cricketers in Council* 24 A very light bat rarely drives well. **1881** *Standard* 28 June 3/1 Whiting drove Studd to the off for four. **1882** *Daily Tel.* 17 May, Shaw, letting out at that bowler's next delivery, drove it to the boundary for a quartette. **1894** *Daily News* 12 June 3/4 Moorhouse, in attempting to drive Richardson was bowled. **1922** W. ARMSTRONG *Art of Cricket* i. 7 This player..is in a position to cut or drive square.

d. To separate (feathers or down) artificially by a current of air which drives away the lightest and collects them by themselves.

1604 [see DRIVEN 2]. **1696** [see DRIVING *vbl. sb.* 2]. **1755** JOHNSON, *Drive*,..18 To purify by motion: so we say to drive feathers. **1817** [see DRIVEN 2].

9. a. To force, impel, or expel, by a blow or thrust; *spec.* to force by blows (a stake, a nail, etc.) into the ground or into anything solid, so as to fix it in its place. Also *fig.* (See also NAIL *sb.* 7 b and c.)

a **1225** *Ancr. R.* 122 [Hy] driuen þuruh his four limes irene neiles. *a* **1300** *Cursor M.* 7809 Thoru his licam mi suerd i draif. **1417** *Surtees Misc.* (1890) 12 Als the stakes are dryfen. **1530** PALSGR. 530/1, I drive out the heed or bottome of any vessell, *je effonce*. **1586** B. YOUNG *Guazzo's Civ. Conv.* IV. 191 One nayle is driven out by an other. **1667** PRIMATT *City & C. Build.* 93 The ground is not firm to build on, but doth require stakes to be droven. **1698** FRYER *E. India & P.* 58 Coopers..driving home their Hoops. **1816** KEATINGE *Trav.* (1817) II. 44 [He] drove his heels into the horse's sides. **1890** BAKER *Wild Beasts & Ways* I. 147 The elephant..drove his long tusks between the tiger's shoulders.

fig. **1607** HIERON *Wks.* I. 215 That I may..driue home the naile of this exhortation euen to the head. **1891** *Law Times* XC. 459/2 The enormity of a particular case only drives home upon the public mind the evils of perjury.

b. *intr.* for *refl.* or *pass.* (of a nail, ball, etc.).

1703 MOXON *Mech. Exerc.* 123 These Hook-Pins..drive into the Pin-holes through the Mortesses and Tennants. *a* **1774** GOLDSM. *Surv. Exper. Philos.* (1776) II. 97 At twenty-six yards distance it [the ball] would drive through an oak board half an inch thick. **1793** SMEATON *Edystone L.* §239 The trenail would drive no further.

c. *transf.* (*trans.*) To drive nails into, so as to fasten; to drive the hoops upon (a cask).

1691 T. H[ALE] *New Invent.* 26 Their sheathing when laid on, and droven with Nails. **1757** W. THOMPSON *R.N. Advoc.* 18 The Casks not having been drove and filled up.

d. *to drive the centre* (*center*), *cross*, *nail*: to make a perfect shot with a gun; to hit the centre of a target; also *fig. U.S.*

1831 AUDUBON *Ornith. Biogr.* I. 293 Those who drive the nail have a further trial amongst themselves. **1835** A. B. LONGSTREET *Georgia Scenes* 276 He was very confident of..driving the cross with her [*sc.* a gun]. **1850** L. V. LOOMIS *Jrnl. Birmingham Emigr. Co.* (1928) 4 July, A shooting-match, in which..the senter was drove..several times. **1892** 'MARK TWAIN' *Amer. Claimant* xviii. 170 You've hit it; you've driven the centre; you've plugged the bull's-eye of my dream.

10. To cause (a cavity, tunnel, etc.) to penetrate any solid formation; *spec.* in *Mining*, to excavate horizontally (also *absol.*): distinguished from SINK.

c **1485** *Digby Myst.* (1882) IV. 665 A gret wounde is in your ..sid, Full deply drevyn with a..sper. **1665** *Phil. Trans.* I. 79 In the working, or driving as they call it, of Mines or Adits under ground. **1859** CORNWALLIS *New World* I. 132 To sink a square or round shaft..and then to drive or excavate horizontally, in search of the glittering ore. **1871** BROWNING *Pr. Hohenst.* 1845 Yet would fain build bridge, Lay rail, drive tunnel.

11. a. *intr.* (Also *to let drive*): To aim a blow or a missile, to strike *at*. **b.** *trans.* To aim (a blow); to strike (a person) with a thrust of the arm.

c **1380** *Sir Ferumb.* 4538 On þe heued a gerd, As harde as he may dryue. *c* **1400** *Destr. Troy* 9430 Palomydon..droffe vnto Deffibus with a dynt felle. **1566** PAINTER *Pal. Pleas.* I. 5 He let driue at him with great violence. **1596** SHAKS. *1 Hen. IV*, II. iv. 217 Foure Rogues in Buckrom let driue at me. **1713** SWIFT *Frenzy of J. Dennis* Wks. 1755 III. I. 145 [He] let drive at us with a vast folio. **1752** *Scotland's Glory* 14 Driving at him with her stool. **1894** *Westm. Gaz.* 2 Apr. 7/1 It is not the proper thing to drive a man with the elbow.

12. a. *trans.* To spread or beat out thin. (Now only as a techn. term in *Painting*: see quot. 1859.)

14.. *Noble Bk. Cookry* (Napier) 47 As thyn as ye may dryf them. **1530** PALSGR. 529/2, I drive a thyng abrode, I spred it, or make it larger, *jeslargis*..Drive this playster abrode, *eslargissez cest emplastre*. **1601** HOLLAND *Pliny* II. 553 A master and his prentise wrought in a strife and contention, whether of them could driue his earth thinnest. **1849** J. S. TEMPLETON *Guide Oil Paint.* i. (ed. 39) 44 By..scumbling is meant the driving opaque tints very thinly over parts that have already been painted. **1859** GULLICK & TIMBS *Paint.* 230 When colour is spread thinly and rapidly, it is occasionally said to be 'driven'.

b. *Printing. to drive out, over*: see quots. Also *intr.* for *pass.*: see quot. 1823.

1727–52 CHAMBERS *Cycl.* s.v. *Printing*, When an omission is to be made.. If it be but little, the compositor takes it out, and drives out the remaining matter. **1823** CRABB *Technol. Dict.* s.v., A compositor is said to drive out when he sets wide; the matter in the chace is said to drive out when, by the addition of fresh matter, it is obliged to be moved forwards into the next page. *Mod.* This word should not have been driven over.

†**13.** *to drive a buck of clothes*: see BUCK *sb.*³ 3.

1588 L. M. tr. *Bk. Dyeing* 10 Then drive them as you doe a bucke of clothes, and when they are well driven, then shall you take them foorth of the bucking tubbe. **1630** J. TAYLOR (Water P.) *Wit & Mirth* Wks. II. 181/2 A woman was driving a buck of clothes. **1648–1753** [see BUCK *sb.*³ 3].

†**14.** To dress (cloth). *Obs.*

a **1661** HOLYDAY *Juvenal* 169 A greasie cloak.. of some gross die, wᶜʰ some French weaver drove but ill.

15. a. To set in motion, set going, supply motive power for (a mill, machinery, etc.).

1596 SPENSER *F.Q.* VI. i. 21 A water-streame, whose swelling sourse Shall drive a Mill. **1654** WHITLOCK *Zootomia* 428 As good water goeth by the Mill as driveth it. **1799** J. ROBERTSON *Agric. Perth* 33 The stream that drave the machinery. **1855** LARDNER *Mus. Sc. & Art* v. 37 The machinery which the axle of the fly-wheel drives. **1891** *Times* 2 Oct. 3/1 A dynamo driven by belting from the engine.

b. *to drive a quill, a pen*: to write.

1793 *Regal Rambler* 32 Flourish thy fork, and drive thy quill. **1803** M. CUTLER in *Life, Jrnls. & Corr.* (1888) II. 131, I am compelled to write them as fast as I can drive my pen. **1878** BESANT & RICE *Celia's Arb.* vii, One of half a dozen who drove the quill for very slender wage.

III. To impel forcibly to action, or into some state; to constrain, compel.

16. To incite or impel powerfully or irresistibly; to force, compel (*to* or *into* some action, *to do* something; also, *from* a course of action, etc.).

c **1200** *Trin. Coll. Hom.* 105 He [þe deuel] me drof þerto. *a* **1300** *Cursor M.* 26262 For þou hir has to sin driuen. *c* **1449** PECOCK *Repr.* II. xvii. 253 Thouȝ ȝe be therto dryue bi peynes. **1553** T. WILSON *Rhet.* (1580) 142 [He] was driven to laugh at his owne errour. **1667** MILTON *P.L.* IV. 184 A prowling Wolfe, Whom hunger drives to seek new haunt for prey. **1751** JORTIN *Serm.* (1771) I. iv. 71 This driues him to contract unprofitable friendships. **1873** BLACK *Pr. Thule* xxii. 363 The pride of the girl had driven her to this decision.

17. a. To impel, force, or bring forcibly into some state or condition. † *to drive to scorn, to hething*: to put to scorn, make an object of scorn (*obs.*).

a **1300** *Cursor M.* 26455 His lauerd he driues to scorn. *Ibid.* 26810 þai crist till hething driue. *c* **1470** HENRY *Wallace* VI. 153 'Me think', quod he, 'thow drywys me to scorn'. **1548** HALL *Chron., Hen. VII*, 37 b, Howbeit the prolongyng of tyme drave Perkyn into a suspicion. **1576** FLEMING *Panopl. Epist.* 388 Discouraged, and driven into dumpes of doubtfulnesse. **1615** J. STEPHENS *Satyr. Ess.* 356 She drives the Parson out of Patience with her modestie. **1727** SWIFT *Gulliver* III. iii. 198 An extremity to which the prince is seldom driven. **1879** F. W. ROBINSON *Coward Consc.* II. xxii, It's enough to drive one out of his senses.

b. With adj. complement: *to drive mad, distracted, crazy*, i.e. into the state of madness, etc.

1813 SHELLEY *Queen Mab* v. 113 Or religion Drives his wife raving mad. **1841** MYERS *Cath. Th.* IV. §40. 388 Questions which drove the subtlest of their doctors almost distracted. **1852** MRS. STOWE *Uncle Tom's C.* xvi, A strange hand about me would drive me absolutely frantic.

c. With *under*: to suppress.

1920 R. MACAULAY *Potterism* v. 180, I hadn't known, until that moment, because I had driven it under, how large a part of my brain believed that Gideon had perhaps done this thing.

18. To urge on, incite to action; to force to work; to overwork, overtask.

1645 WARD *Serm. bef. Ho. Com.* in Southey *Comm.-pl. Bk.* Ser. II. (1849) 6 A field which is driven, and the heart of it worn out, whatever seed is cast in, it returns nothing. **1838** GRAY *Lett.* (1893) 79 In order that he might drive the committee a little, if it should be necessary. **1889** *Pall Mall G.* 30 Dec. 6/3 A very important matter in the training of a horse is not to drive him. I mean by that, not to over-work him, not to push him.

IV. 19. *trans.* **a.** To carry on vigorously, 'push', prosecute, conduct, practise, exercise (a custom, trade, etc.); to carry through or out, to effect; to bring to a settlement, conclude (a bargain). *to drive a hard bargain*: to be severe or uncompromising in making a bargain, settlement, etc.

c **961** ÆTHELWOLD *Rule St. Benet* lvii. (Schröer) 115 þa ðe þone ceape drifað. *c* **1200** *Trin. Coll. Hom.* 193 Talewise men, þe speches driuen, and maken wrong to rihte, and riht to wronge. *c* **1250** *Gen. & Ex.* 1681 Long wune is her driuen. **1297** R. GLOUC. (1724) 471 The King wolde, that in his court the ple solde be driue. *c* **1330** R. BRUNNE *Chron.* (1810) 1 Thorgh out Chestreschire werre gan thei dryue. *c* **1386** CHAUCER *Frankl. T.* 502 This bargayn is ful dryue [*v. rr.* dreue, drewyn]. *c* **1400** *Destr. Troy* 5600 What dede haue we don, or dryuen to an end? **1590** RECORDE, etc. *Gr. Artes* Pref. (1640) A iv, Arithmetic, by which.. all reckonings and accounts [were] driven. **1631** SANDERSON *Serm.* II. 8 Let two men.. pursue the same business, drive the same design. **1655** FULLER *Ch. Hist.* IX. i. §37 A Bargain can never be driven, where a Buyer can on no terms be procured. **1752** HUME *Ess. & Treat.* (1777) I. 204 The wife.. will still be driving some separate end or project. *c* **1795** LD. AUCKLAND *Sp. Jrnl.* in *Corr.* (1861) II. 36 The Portuguese princess spoke French sufficient to drive a conversation. **1836** DICKENS *Let.* 17 Aug. (1965) I. 165, I should be very sorry to appear anxious to drive a hard bargain. **1872** BLACK *Adv. Phaeton* vi. 81 He stuck to his business and drove a thriving trade. **1878** BOSW. SMITH *Carthage* 78 But the senate.. managed to drive a hard bargain with the Syracusan king. *a* **1953** E. O'NEILL *More Stately Mansions* 59, I want your brother to drive the hardest bargain he can.

b. with *on, through*.

1523 LD. BERNERS *Froiss.* I. ccliii. 375 The mariage.. was driuen through and agreed. **1648** *Eikon Bas.* 30 Some men driving on their private ends. *a* **1661** FULLER *Worthies* (1840) III. 490 Trading was driven on, either by the bartery or change of wares.. or else by money. **1712** SWIFT *Conduct of Allies* Wks. 1778 II. 368 We drove on the war at a prodigious disadvantage.

V. To go through, endure, pass, prolong.

†**20.** *trans.* To go through (something painful or unpleasant); to endure, suffer, undergo. (App. confused to some extent with DREE.) *Obs.*

a **1300** *Cursor M.* 7829 (Gött.) A fouler dede [= death] þan ani may driue. **1414** BRAMPTON *Penit. Ps.* xxii, Whil thou wilt here thi penaunce dryve. *c* **1430** *Hymns Virg.* 120 Bettyr.. Than soche payne for to dryve. *c* **1450** *St. Cuthbert* (Surtees) 516 þarfore sorow grete sho draue.

†**21. a.** To pass, spend (time); to cause (the time) to pass: often with *away, forth, over. Obs.*

13.. *Gaw. & Gr. Knt.* 1176 [He].. drof þat day wyth Ioy Thus to þe derk nyȝt. **1393** LANGL. *P. Pl.* C. I. 225 As dikers and deluers þat.. dryueþ forþ hure daies with '*deux saue dame emme*!' *c* **1425** *Eng. Conq. Irel.* (E.E.T.S.) 88 Anoon he wold aryse & stonde, & so dryue forth al þe meste parte of the nyght. **1484** CAXTON *Fables of Æsop* III. viii, To dryue aweye the tyme. **1500–20** DUNBAR *Poems* xxiv. 17 Quha.. dois his dayis in dolour dryfe. **1603** KNOLLES *Hist. Turks* 976 To drive out the time, untill his soldiers.. were all gathered together. **1697** DRYDEN *Virg. Georg.* III. 583 To drive the tedious Hours away.

†**b.** *intr.* Of time: To pass away, elapse. *Obs.*

c **1450** *St. Cuthbert* (Surtees) 6699 þe ȝeris of criste war our dryue Sex hundreth' thritty and fyue. *c* **1470** HENRY *Wallace* VIII. 1182 The nycht was myrk, our drayff the dyrkfull chance. **1569** MORAY *Let. to Cecil* 22 Feb. in Tytler *Hist. Scot.* (1864) III. 317 Let not time drive, but with speed let us understand her majesty's mind. **1674** N. FAIRFAX *Bulk & Selv.* 155 Two times may as well drive on by each others side.. as two everlastingnesses.

22. *trans.* To protract, prolong (time or occupation): also with *off, out, on.* Hence, to put off, defer. Also *absol.*

c **1300** *Beket* 45 He drof hire evere biheste. **1509** HAWES *Past. Pleas.* XVI. xxix, Dryve of no lenger, but tell me your mynde. **1530** PALSGR. 529/2 I drive of a thynge, I dyffar it, *je differre*. **1537** *Durham Depos.* 30 June (Surtees) 53 Dryue yt no longer. **1658–9** *Burton's Diary* (1828) IV. 140 If you drive it long, they will make it their advantage to break with you. **1705** BOSMAN *Guinea* Pref. 4, I have purposely affected Brevity, otherwise I could have drove out to a bulky Volume. **1741** tr. *De Mouhy's Fort. Country Maid* I. 209, I drove on the Time, if I may be allow'd the Expression, in Hopes [etc.]. **1828** *Craven Dial.*, *Drive*, to procrastinate, 'thou begins to drive it'. *Mod. colloq.* You had better not drive it to the last minute.

VI. To infer, conclude, deduce, derive.

†**23.** To obtain as a conclusion from premisses, or as a result from some logical process; to conclude, infer, deduce (also *drive out*). *Obs.* (Perh. sometimes associated with *derive*: cf. next, and DERIVE 7.)

1447 BOKENHAM *Seyntys* (Roxb.) 36 The fyrst yer of the secund Urban.. as cronycles dryve. *c* **1449** PECOCK *Repr.* 8 An Argument if he be ful and foormal, which is clepid a sillogisme is mad of twey proposiciouns dryuyng out of hem & bi strength of hem the thridde proposicioun. *Ibid.* IV. iv. 443. **1460** CAPGRAVE *Chron.* (1858) 9 For Enos in oure language soundith 'A resonable man'; for he drove out, be reson, that God was his makere. **1530** RASTELL *Bk. Purgat.* I. xii, Thou haste dryuen that conclusyon upon so many reasonable pryncyples. **1589** PUTTENHAM *Eng. Poesie* III. xix. (Arb.) 241 By such confronting of them together, [he] driues out thettrue ods that is betwixt them, and makes it better appeare. **1674** N. FAIRFAX *Bulk & Selv.* 141 Which upon search have been found to have been done there, as near as could be driven.

†**24.** *trans.* By confusion with *derive*: **a.** To derive, obtain from a source (= DERIVE 6); **b.** To convey (a stream) along, or divert it into, some channel (= DERIVE 1, 2). *Obs.*

1549 *Compl. Scot.* Prol. 16 Oncoutht exquisite termis, dreuyn, or rather.. reuyn fra lating. **1569** in W. H. Turner *Select. Rec. Oxford* 329 It ys.. ordered yᵗ the ffysshers do not drawe, dryve, nor turne any of the common waters of this Towne. **1571** CAMPION *Hist. Irel.* xiv. (1633) 44 S. Madoc ..with his owne hands, driued a running spring to his Monastery. **1585** JAS. I *Ess. Poesie* (Arb.) 75 Cimmerien night Drevin from a kynd of people in the East, called Cimmerij.

VII. *intr.* To drive oneself, or be driven; to move with vehemence or energy.

25. a. To move along or advance quickly; to run or come with violence; to dash, rush, hasten.

c **900** tr. *Bæda's Hist.* V. vi. (1890) 400 Ða ic hreowsende wæs, ðа ic mid ðy heafde and mid honda com on ðone stan dryfan. *c* **1205** LAY. 9367 Aruiragus him to dræf. *c* **1330** R. BRUNNE *Chron.* (1810) 25 Alfrid it herd, þidere gan he dryue. *c* **1398** CHAUCER *Fortune* 46 Abowte the wheel with oother most thou dryve. *a* **1400–50** *Alexander* 712 Doune he drafe to þe depest of þe dike bothom. **1513** DOUGLAS *Æneis* X. xiv. 102 Wyth swyft cours he Furth steris his steid, and drayf in the melle. **1697** DAMPIER *Voy.* I. xvi. 469 They.. ran away as fast as they could drive. **1798** W. CLUBBE *Omnium* 126 In swarms again they seek the Hive As fast as ever they can drive. **1817** J. SCOTT *Paris Revisit.* (ed. 4) 138 A single British battalion.. repeatedly drove at immense columns of the enemy. **1863** MRS. C. CLARKE *Shaks. Char.* xvii. 434 So he drives in between them, and plays upon the judge with his own guns.

b. *fig.* To work hard, 'go *at*' strenuously. *colloq.*

1835 W. IRVING in *Life & Lett.* (1866) III. 82 My cottage is not yet finished, but I shall drive at it as soon as the opening of spring will permit. **1842** GRAY *Lett.* (1893) 296 I have been driving away at the 'Flora', of late, very hard.

c. To play music energetically or with a strong rhythm. *colloq.* Cf. DRIVING *ppl. a.* 1 b.

1952 B. ULANOV *Hist. Jazz in Amer.* (1958) 351 *Drive*, to play with concentrated momentum. **1959** 'F. NEWTON' *Jazz Scene* 291 A band *moves* or *drives* or just *goes*.

26. a. To move along, impelled by wind, current, or other natural agency; to float along, drift.

c **1205** LAY. 28073 Ich isæh þæ vðen i þere sæ driuen. **1393** GOWER *Conf.* I. 183 She dryueth Under a castell with the floode. *c* **1475** *Rauf Coilȝear* 27 Ithand wedderis of the eist draif on sa fast. **1481** CAXTON *Reynard* (Arb.) 17 Forth he droof in the streem wel a ij or iij myle. **1526–34** TINDALE *Acts* xxvii. 15 And when the ship was caught.. we let her goo and drave with the wether [**1611** We let her drive]. **1646** SIR T. BROWNE *Pseud. Ep.* II. ii. 63 The needle.. endeavours to conforme unto the Meridian, but being distracted driveth that way where the greater & most powerfuller part of the earth is placed. **1748** THOMSON *Cast. Indol.* I. 528 Oft as he ..mark'd the clouds that drove before the wind. **1790** BEATSON *Nav. & Mil. Mem.* I. 157 By the force of the current, all three drove a great way to leeward. **1852** LONGF. *Warden Cinque Ports* 1 A mist was driving down the British Channel.

b. To fish with a drift-net.

1677 *Lond. Gaz.* No. 1245/3 This last night a small Fisher Boat, with two Men, was driving in this Bay for Herrings. **1883** *Leisure Hour* 697/1 Drift-net fishing, or 'driving', as it is technically called.

†**c.** *Metallurgy.* (See quot.) *Obs.*

1678 in *Phil. Trans.* XII. 1050 If the Lead be gone before all the Copper, 'twill rise in small red firy bubbles; then they say, the Metal Drives, and must add more Lead.

27. *fig.* **a.** To proceed in a course; to tend.

c **1460** *Towneley Myst.* (Surtees) 25 To dede may we dryfe or lif for the. *a* **1547** SURREY *Æneid* IV. 492 Ay me, with rage and furies loe I drive. *a* **1656** HALES *Gold. Rem.* (1688) 174 Christ in his preaching doth every where drive upon Parables. **1858** SEARS *Athan.* III. iv. 279 They were driving into blank universalism.

b. with *at* (formerly also †*to*): To proceed towards with definite intention, aim at, have for one's drift or aim; to mean, intend, purpose.

1579 TOMSON *Calvin's Serm. Tim.* 136/2 To this end and purpose doth the office of Magistrates driue. **1624** BP. MOUNTAGU *Gagg* To Rdr. 8 He drived directly at the church of England. **1649** MILTON *Eikon.* iii, Their intent drives to the end of stirring up the people. **1670** G. H. *Hist. Cardinals* II. III. 182 He.. is driving at the Popedom. *a* **1715** BURNET *Own Time* (1766) I. 167 The Presbyterians saw what was driven at. **1762** FOOTE *Lyar* II. Wks. 1799 I. 298 What can he be driving at now! **1865** M. ARNOLD *Ess. Crit.* ix. (1875) 387 Mankind at large.. will not listen to a word about these propositions, unless it first learns what their author was driving at. **1895** F. HALL *Two Trifles* 27, I ask you.. what you are driving at.

drive (draɪv), *sb.* [f. DRIVE *v.*]

1. a. The action or an act of driving, impelling, urging onward, etc.: see the verb. *spec.* of cattle or logs (cf. sense 3) (chiefly *U.S.* and *Canada*); also of sheep (*N.Z.*) *full drive*: at full speed; with utmost force or impetus.

1697 DAMPIER *Voy.* (1729) I. 254, 2 of our men.. rode after the Spaniards full drive. **1728** VANBR. & CIB. *Prov. Husb.* IV. i, He's coming hither full drive. **1846** T. B. THORPE *Myst. Backwoods* 14 In the excitement of the drive, horses fall, or run headlong over slow-footed cows. **1860** *Harper's Mag.* XX. 441 The stream must be cleared of obstructions for the drive [of timber] in the Spring. **1873** J. H. BEADLE *Undevel. West* xxxiii. 718 Each company comes down on a 'drive', hunting such logs as have lodged along the way. **1883** F. SEEBOHM *Eng. Village Comm.* 2 The length of the drive of the plough. **1890** *Harper's Mag.* July 240/1 They [*sc.* cowboys] have little to do when not on the drive or in branding time. **1897** I. SCOTT *How I stole 10,000 Sheep* vii. 28 There was a fair muster of sheep in the [sale] yards, ..so we did not think we should have much trouble in getting a drive. **1902** S. E. WHITE *Blazed Trail* ii. 7 Customarily a jobber is paid a certain proportion of the agreed price.. so much when the 'drive' down the waters of the river is finished. **1920** J. M. HUNTER *Trail Drivers of Texas* 53 A cheap rate.. had been perfected for.. the.. cowboys returning home after the drives. **1926** C. MAIR in J. W. Garvin *Masterworks of Canadian Authors* XIV. p. liii, To-day, when it is mainly saw-logs that are cut, the fully improved streams make the drive easy. **1949** P. NEWTON *High Country Days* v. 55 There were sufficient [sheep] to make a 'drive' out to the back.

b. An act of driving in a vehicle; a journey or excursion in a carriage driven by oneself or under one's direction.

1785 BOSWELL *Tour to Hebrides* 18 Aug., We had a dreary drive, in a dusky night, to St. Andrew's. **1823** GR. KENNEDY *Anna Ross* (ed. 6) 163 You shall have as many drives as you please in my curricle. **1849** E. E. NAPIER *Excurs. S. Africa* I. 178 After this pleasant drive of some four-and-twenty miles. **1888** BURGON *Lives 12 Gd. Men* II. vi. 73 Within two hours' drive of Oxford.

c. An urging or impelling forward of animals, so as to drive them into a net, snare, enclosure, or place where they can be killed or captured. Also of a hound in coursing.

1833 *Sketches & Eccentr. D. Crockett* 196 We were soon on foot, moving merrily forward to a small hurricane which had been agreed upon for a drive. **1843** *Amer. Pioneer* II. 55 There were four drives, or large hunts, organized during the winter. **1859** TENNENT *Ceylon* II. VIII. v. 373 Those taken in the second drive. **1876** *Coursing Calendar* 5 Dovedale got up first, through puss bearing to her side; Thunder then took a good drive and turned. **1880** *Daily News* 28 Sept. 5/3 There will be a deer drive in the forest of Invermark, and also a grouse drive. **1890** BAKER *Wild Beasts & their Ways* I. 170 After the tiger has killed a buffalo, there is much art required in the conduct of the drive.

d. A forcible blow or stroke, *esp.* in various games, as golf, base-ball, lawn-tennis, etc.: in cricket, *spec.* one which sends the ball back nearly straight in the direction of the bowler. See also quot. 1867, and *off-drive* (OFF *sb.* 3), *on-drive* (ON *sb.*). Also (*colloq.*), a forcible punch or the like.

1836 E. JESSE *Angler's Rambles* 301 He would . . shew . . the exact length which he could cover in a forward drive. **1839** *Sessions Paper* X. 16 May 33 Tighe then said, 'Give her a *drive*,' and they went off. **1845** 'N. FELIX' *Felix on Bat* I. iii. 16 A tall long-reached man could make a fine forward drive. *Ibid.* I. iv. 20 The difference between the forward play and the 'drive' being only in the additional force you must employ. **1857** HUGHES *Tom Brown* II. viii. (1880) 356 Jack Raggles . . having run one for a forward drive of Johnson's, is about to receive his first ball. **1867** *Cornh. Mag.* Apr. 493 He has two long drives and a short stroke, while I have three moderate 'drives', and get quite as far. **1867** G. H. SELKIRK *Guide to Cricket Ground* iii. 42 The ball is always endeavoured to be hit with this part of the bat [*sc.* about five inches from the bottom of the blade], which is called the 'drive'. **1879** THOMSON & TAIT *Nat. Phil* I. I. §299 In . . forces of brief duration, as in a 'drive' in cricket or golf. **1884** *Lillywhite's Cricket Ann.* 104 Rapid run-getter on a fast wicket with a strong off drive. **1894** BLACK *Highland Cousins* I. 36 He made a drive that should have sent the ball over to Lismore. **1898** S. R. CROCKETT *Standard Bearer* xxxiii. 294 He gied him aye the ither drive wi' his nieve.

e. The action of driving or state of being driven, in *fig.* senses; *esp.* the state of being hurried or overtasked, extreme pressure of work.

1854 W. ARTHUR *Let.* in Arnot *Life of J. Hamilton* (1870) 430 The constant drive of work has . . driven a postponable duty out of the way. **1892** *Pall Mall G.* 10 Nov. 2/1 The success of a manufactory will depend upon the drive and harshness of the supervision.

f. Onward course, drift, tendency.

1895 *Ch. Q. Rev.* Oct. 152 We . . believe that the tendency and drive of things is forward to a reasoned faith.

g. An organized effort to gain a particular end, esp. to raise money; an intensive campaign or effort. orig. *U.S.* Also (*U.S.*), the sale of goods or stocks at a low price.

1889 'MARK TWAIN' *Yankee* xxii. 245 She was making the honest best drive at it she could. **1890** *Ann Arbor Reg.* 1 Mar. (Advt.), Ladies, we are going to give you a Benefit and it will be the drive of the season. **1893** *Chicago Tribune* 2 July 36 A Big Cut in Waists A Big Drive in Corsets. **1921** E. L. BOGART *War Costs* 210 The four-weeks drive which ushered in the First Loan. **1928** *Britain's Industrial Future* (*Lib. Ind. Inq.*) III. xix. 258 The remarkable American 'drive' for the sale of Liberty Bonds. **1930** *Nation* 4 Oct. 10/1 The opposition of the peasantry to the 'drive' for collective agriculture assumed its most dangerous form last winter. **1933** *Granta* 19 Apr. 358/1 Anyone who has read accounts of the expulsion of the German Jews from the legal and medical professions may have wondered why no similar drive was being made against Jews in university and school appointments. **1941** *Times Weekly* 30 July 15 The export drive of the automobile industry.

h. ***whist-drive***: see WHIST *sb.*[3] b; so ***bridge-drive*** (BRIDGE *sb.*[2]). (Cf. *drive-whist* under sense 9.)

i. Energy, intensity, persistence, initiative, determination to achieve one's purpose.

1908 KIPLING *Lett. to Family* iii. 25 'Hustle' does not sit well on the national character. . . 'Drive', a laudable and necessary quality, is quite different. **1909** G. B. SHAW *Let.* 31 Dec. (1956) 161 Stella has not the drive, the zest for Hypatia. **1924** R. FRY *Transformations* (1926) 173 Roman art could become expressive when its exponent had some other qualities than Roman efficiency and drive. **1944** J. S. HUXLEY *On Living in Rev.* xv. 195 Such men seem to lack the drive and confidence needed for public life. **1955** E. HILLARY *High Adventure* 148 It seemed to us at Camp IV that there was a certain lack of drive. **1965** W. LAMB *Posture & Gesture* iii. 46 People who show drive and welcome work (or at least get down to doing it) *look* less fatigued.

j. *Mil.* A forceful advance or attack.

1911 *Encycl. Brit.* XXVII. 207/2 Lord Kitchener commenced his first drive. **1918** E. S. FARROW *Dict. Mil. Terms* 189 The drive of the Allies was costly.

k. A thrill; exhilaration, esp. resulting from the use of narcotics. *U.S. slang.*

1931 G. IRWIN *Amer. Tramp & Underworld Slang* 67 *Drive*, a thrill. Formerly that exhilaration derived from narcotics; now, any temporary pleasure or uplift of spirit. **1949** N. ALGREN *Man with Golden Arm* I. 58 *Sure* I like to see it hit. Heroin got the drive awright—but there's not a tingle to a ton.

2. a. A carriage road; *esp.* the private road leading to a house. Also, a broad path in a wood.

1816 KEATINGE *Trav.* (1817) I. 285 Four acres—for walks . . drives, produce, lawns, and plantations! **1825** C. M. WESTMACOTT *Eng. Spy* I. 238 [She] regularly sports her carriage in the drive. **1862** MRS. H. WOOD *Mrs. Hallib.* I. xiii. 65 [She] walked round the carriage drive that inclosed the lawn. **1880** R. JEFFERIES *Hodge & his Masters* I. viii. 188 There comes . . the low, dull, rushing roar of hundreds of hoofs. . . There is a block in the treacherous 'drive'. *a* **1887** —— *Field & Hedgerow* (1889) 304 The fawns fed away . . into one of the broad green open paths or drives. **1894** MRS. H. WARD *Marcella* I. 14 The window . . overlooked the long white drive. **1894** W. ROBINSON *Wild Garden* (ed. 4) ix. 94 (*heading*) Woodland drives and grass walks.

b. A course or tract over which game is driven.

3. a. A mass or quantity of timber 'driven' down a stream (*N. Amer.*): see DRIVE *v.* 7 b.

1878 *Lumberman's Gaz.* 6 Apr., [He] bid in the following drives at the prices mentioned. **1885** *Boston* (*Mass.*) *Jrnl.* 21 Apr. 1/8 A drive of 2,000,000 feet of hard and white pine logs will soon be put into the Merrimack at Boscawen.

b. (See quots.) Also *attrib.*

1899 J. BELL *In Shadow of Bush* xiv. 83 The smaller trees . . had been 'scarfed', or cut partly through in readiness, and skilfully, so that each, when struck, might again in its turn strike and bring down another. The noise of a fall or drive of this kind is like thunder. **1940** B. O'REILLY *Green Mountains* II. 76 In the felling of rain forest, much chopping may be saved . . by the use of the 'drive' system. **1948** R. ST. B. BAKER *Green Glory* xviii. 183 This fiendish practice is known as a 'drive'. The axeman will lay into the trees in such a manner that each will fall on its neighbour, when the pressure from above is set off by a big 'drive' tree on the uphill side of all the others.

4. *Mining.* A passage 'driven' or excavated horizontally; a gallery, tunnel, level; = DRIFT *sb.* 15. Chiefly *Austral.* and *N.Z.*

1857 in E. A. Cooke et al. *Fresh Evidence from Early Goldmining Pubns.* (1966) 11 A main drive shall be carried along the course of such lead or gutter. **1864** E. A. MURRAY *E. Norman* III. 58 We take this pipeclay out in tunnels called drives. **1880** H. LAPHAM *We Four* 18 There was a deserted 'drive' up on the spur. **1890** BOLDREWOOD *Miner's Right* iii. 24 The roof of the gallery, or 'drive', as it is invariably called in Australian mining parlance. **1900** M. BOYD *Our Stolen Summer* x. 93 Up ladders, down ladders, along narrow drives they went. **1912** C. PURNELL *Modern Arthur* 17 Then rushed the miners from their hollow 'drives'.

5. *Type-founding.*

1874 KNIGHT *Dict. Mech.*, *Drive*, a matrix formed by a steel punch, die, or drift. **1888** in *Encycl. Brit.* XXIII. 699/1 When the letter is perfect, it is driven into a piece of polished copper, called the *drive* or *strike*.

6. a. The means or mechanism by which something is driven; esp. a device by which power is transmitted from one part of a motor vehicle to another; a driving-gear. Freq. with defining word prefixed, as *belt drive* (BELT *sb.*[1] 6), *chain drive* (CHAIN *sb.* 19). orig. *U.S.*

1901 MERWIN & WEBSTER *Calumet 'K'* xiv. 263 He's putting in three drives entirely different from the way they are in the plans. **1902** A. C. HARMSWORTH et al. *Motors* 191 A very smooth and silent drive without the spreading or bursting action of the bevels. **1912** *Motor Man.* (ed. 14) 74 Three speeds and a reverse are provided, with direct drive on top speed. **1960** *Analog Science Fact/Fiction* Dec. 45/2 Something crunched heavily under their stern at the exact instant the drive cut out. **1961** *Listener* 7 Sept. 353/3 It [*sc.* a telescope] . . has a most efficient drive, so that the object under study is held firmly in the field of view.

b. In a motor vehicle with automatic transmission: the position of the selector lever in which the gears are automatically changed as required.

1963 *Which?* (Car Suppl.) Oct. 116/2 The selector mechanism was a little inclined to snatch at *Drive*. **1965** PRIESTLEY & WISDOM *Good Driving* v. 40 *D for Drive.* In this position, which is usual for all driving conditions, the transmission starts in first gear and automatically changes up into second and then top gear. *Ibid.* 41 With the engine running, *Drive* is selected, the handbrake released. **1967** *Times* 31 Mar. 3/7 The coroner said the selector lever must have been in 'drive'. **1970** D. MACKENZIE *Kyle Contract* (1971) 13 He drove out of Palamos. . . He shifted into drive and settled back.

c. *Computing.* = *disc drive* s.v. DISC *sb.* 8 f.

1963 *AFIPS Conf. Proc.* XXIV. 328/2 The disk storage drive is to read and write information reliably from different drives. **1968** [see *disc drive* s.v. DISC *sb.* 8 f]. **1983** *80 Microcomputing* Feb. 231/1 Once a drive has been activated it remains rotating for only 30 seconds. **1984** S. CURRAN *Word Processing for Beginners* xi. 160 It's all too easy to put the disks into the wrong drives, and copy your back-up onto your current version, instead of vice-versa.

7. *Psychol.* **a.** Any internal mechanism which sets an organism moving or sustains its activity in a certain direction, or causes it to pursue a certain satisfaction; a motive principle; any tendency to persistent behaviour directed at a goal; *esp.* one of the recognized physiological tensions or conditions of need, such as hunger and thirst. **b.** Any type of persistent behaviour or disposition that would lead to the attainment of a certain goal.

[**1888** *Mind* XIII. 165 *Trieb* (for which there is no good single equivalent in English).] **1918** R. S. WOODWORTH *Dynamic Psychol.* ii. 42 The drive is a mechanism already aroused and thus in a position to furnish stimulation to other mechanisms. *Ibid.* iii. 65 As the individual grows up, his actions are more and more controlled by inner drives. **1931** J. C. FLÜGEL in W. Rose *Outl. Mod. Knowl.* 367 It is a question rather of simultaneous 'drives' or wishes. **1931** C. J. WARDEN et al. *Animal Motivation* I. 14 By a drive we mean an aroused reaction tendency which is characterized primarily by the fact that the activity of the organism is directed toward or away from some specific incentive, such as food, water, animal of the opposite sex, etc. **1955** C. BRENNER *Elem. Textbk. Psychoanalysis* ii. 27 A drive, then, is a genetically determined, psychic constituent which, when operative, produces a state of psychic excitation or . . tension. This excitation or tension impels the individual to activity, which is also genetically determined in a general way, but which can be considerably altered by individual experience. **1958** W. STARK *Sociology of Knowl.* 234 It is not a true instinct, but what we have labelled a drive, i.e. not a tendency rooting in the body but rather an attribute of the whole personality. **1962** R. FINE *Freud* (1963) vi. 93 The individual finds it extremely difficult to recognize his unconscious emotional drives.

8. *Electr.* (See quot. 1940.) Cf. DRIVER 3 j.

1940 *Chambers's Techn. Dict.* 267/1 *Drive*, generally, the alternating voltage applied to the grid of an amplifying thermionic tube. Specially, the master oscillator circuit and its immediately subsequent amplifying stages in a transmitter using independent drive. **1959** K. HENNEY *Radio Engin. Handbk.* (ed. 5) xviii. 36 The drive for modulator tubes which are driven into grid current must have very good output-voltage regulation. **1962** SIMPSON & RICHARDS *Junction Transistors* xii. 287 The input impedance of a *CE* power stage capable of supplying 5 watts will vary typically from 80 ohms at very low drive to perhaps 15 ohms at full drive.

9. *attrib.*, as (sense 2 a) ***drive-gate***; **drive-whist** *U.S.*, progressive whist.

1903 *Westm. Gaz.* 17 Jan. 1/3 The words were painted in large letters of gold on the drive gate. **1927** F. B. YOUNG *Portrait of Clare* 127 For answer he pointed to a white drive-gate, on the left of the road. **1888** *San Juan Prospector* (Del Norte, Colo.) 15 May 3/1 Mr. Grover Allen entertained the Young Married Folks at drive whist last Monday evening.

drive-, the verb-stem used in *Comb.*: **drive-belt**, a belt that transmits torque to a mechanism, etc.; **drive-boat** (*U.S.*), a light rowing-boat used in the menhaden fishery in driving the fish into the net; **drive-bolt** = *drift-bolt* (see DRIFT *sb.* 19 c); **drive-line**, the propeller shaft and universal joints by which drive is transmitted from the gearbox of a motor vehicle to the differential and axle; **drive-off**, (*a*) *adj.* (of a ship) from which a motor vehicle can be driven; (*b*) *sb.* the act of setting off in a motor vehicle; **drive-on** *a.*, (of a ship) on to which a motor vehicle can be driven; also ***drive-on/drive-off***; **drive-pipe**, a pipe conveying water for driving machinery; **drive-screw**, a kind of screw driven by a hammer; **drive-shaft**, a shaft for communicating motion so as to drive machinery; *spec.* each of the two half-shafts in a motor vehicle that connect the differential to each driven wheel; also (*U.S.*), a propeller shaft; **drive-train** = *drive-line* above; also, the corresponding chain and sprockets of a motor cycle; **drive-wheel** = DRIVING-WHEEL; **drive-yourself** *a.* (orig. *U.S.*), designating a motor vehicle let out on hire and driven by the hirer; also *ellipt.* as *sb.* See also DRIVEWAY.

1959 *Which?* Aug. 87/2 The drive belts [on the spin drier of a washing machine] . . slipped, affecting the speed with which the drums rotated. **1967** *Lebende Sprachen* XII. 136/2 *Drive-belt*, the belt on a tape recorder for turning the reels. **1678** PHILLIPS (ed. 4), *Drivebolt*, in Navigation is a long piece used for the driving out of Tree-Nail, or the like. **1727–51** CHAMBERS *Cycl.* s.v. *Bolt*, *Drive-bolts*, used to drive out others. **1949** FRAZEE & BEDELL *Automotive Fundamentals* vii. 418 Several types of parking brake are in common use, as follows: (1) Mechanical application of service brake. . . (2) Drive line external contracting. . . (3) Drive line disk brake. **1970** *Globe & Mail* (Toronto) 25 Sept. B4/7 The 1970 models carried an extended five-year, 50,000 mile warranty on the engine, transmission and certain drive-line components. **1985** *Commercial Motor* 30 Mar. 16/2 Cab suspension and chassis suspension have been completely revised on the new [Turbostar] models, as has the driveline. **1960** *Times* 20 Jan. 9/6 Specially built drive-on/drive-off Transport Ferry ships carry loaded lorries. **1964** R. PETRIE *Murder by Precedent* vii. 103 They were to draw in the main canteen for order of drive-off. **1963** 'W. HAGGARD' *High Wire* iii. 32 Those drive-on car ferries. **1883** *Century Mag.* XXVI. 329 A drive-pipe is forced down through the earth to the rock. **1889** *Daily News* 14 Nov. 2/8 Samples of new 'drive' screws (which can be forced into wood by the blows of a hammer) were also shown. **1895** *Specif. Patent* No. 7271. 1 The drive shaft for operating the sustaining screws. [**1907** R. B. WHITMAN *Motor-Car Princ.* ix. 141 The axle end of the driving shaft follows the axle as that follows the inequalities of the road.] **1919** FRASER & JONES *Motor Vehicles* xxiv. 260 The drive shaft turns at several times the speed of the axles. **1929** NEWTON & STEEDS *Motor Vehicle* xxii. 267 In place of that cross shaft there are now two 'differential' or 'drive' shafts . . which are connected at their outer ends to the road wheels. **1967** *Jane's Surface Skimmer Syst. 1967–8* 49/2 A further shaft runs forward from the differential to a bevel gearbox from which a drive-shaft runs vertically upward to the 12-blade lift-fan. **1980** *Know about your Car* (A.A.) 56/3 The very short drive shafts necessary on front-wheel-drive and rear-engined cars. **1970** *Wall St. Jrnl.* 10 Nov. 1/4 A simple, sturdy Volkswagen engine, drive train and chassis. **1985** *Dirt Bike* Mar. 31/3 It would also remarkably free up existing engine and drive train design, as the countershaft could be placed just about anywhere within reason. **1887** C. B. GEORGE *40 Yrs. on Rail* ii. 28 The drive-wheels will slip. **1921** *Daily Colonist* (Victoria, B.C.) 2 Apr. 2/1 (Advt.), The First 'Drive Yourself' Auto Livery in Canada and it's a great success. Rent a Dodge, Overland, Chevrolet or Ford and try it yourself. **1929** D. HAMMETT *Red Harvest* xviii. 179, I found Dick Foley in a hired drive-yourself Buick. **1959** G. M. WILSON *Shadows on Landing* viii. 88 The drive-yourself car with David at the wheel. **1962** W. H. MURRAY *Maelstrom* viii. 109 He would hire a 'drive-yourself' at Tarbert.

driveability, drivability (draɪvəˈbɪlɪtɪ). [f. DRIVABLE *a.*: see -ILITY.] Capacity (of a motor vehicle, etc.) for being driven, ease of driving.

1972 *Daily Tel.* 6 Jan. 3 (Advt.), The driveability of the Dolomite . . is impressively unruffled and strain-free. **1973** *Times* 8 Feb. 31/1 These project only a millimetre or two from the tread, but totally transform a car's drivability. **1975** *Sci. Amer.* July 65 It is possible once more to tune engines for economy, drivability and performance. **1983** *Truck &*

Bus Transportation July 60/2 Response of the turbocompound plant was found to be quicker because of a more favourable turbocharger match... This resulted in both lower smoke levels and better driveability. **1984** *Guardian* 22 Oct. 23/1 Without electronic engine management of mixture and ignition, these bring risks of poor driveability during extreme conditions.

drivee (draɪˈviː). *nonce-wd.* One who is driven or conveyed in a carriage; one taken for a drive.
1882 *Pall Mall G.* 3 July 3 The cab owner is, to the majority of drivees only a dim figure in the distance. **1890** R. KIPLING in *Wit & Wisdom* 6 Dec. 63/2 Neither driver nor drivee has a thought beyond the enjoyment of a good time.

drive-in (ˈdraɪvɪn), *a.* (and *sb.*) orig. *U.S.* [f. DRIVE *v.* 5 c.] Designating a restaurant, cinema, bank, etc., into or up to which a customer can drive his car and, without leaving it, have a meal, see a film, effect a business transaction, etc. Hence as *sb.*, such a restaurant, cinema, etc.
1930 *San Antonio* (Texas) *Light* 31 Jan. 14/5 (Advt.), Drive-in drink and sandwich, with living room and bath. **1930** C. BEATON *Diary* Dec. in *Wandering Years* (1961) 189 The diehards hang on.. working at 'drive-in' quick-lunch counters. **1937** *Amer. Speech* XII. 320/1 At roadside *drive-ins*, where one may secure curb service while sitting in his car. **1941** *Time* 14 July 66 *(caption)* U.S.'s Biggest Drive-In Theater. **1950** *Archit. Rev.* CVIII. 408/1 Drive-in banks, drive-in restaurants, drive-in cinemas, drive-in shops.. are new environment elements. **1955** PRIESTLEY & HAWKES *Journey down Rainbow* 24 Drive-in movie theatres. **1959** *Listener* 5 Feb. 251/2 Britain's first 'drive-in' bank (a branch of the Westminster Bank in Liverpool). **1960** *Daily Express* 30 Aug. 7 Britain's first open-air cinema—Americans call them 'drive-ins'—is planned for Sandown Park racecourse next year. **1970** *Globe & Mail* (Toronto) 26 Sept. 50/1 (Advt.), Manager early 40's, fully experienced in drive-in restaurant.. management.

†**ˈdrivel**, *sb.*[1] *Obs.* Forms: 3–6 **drivel**, 5–6 **dryvyl(le, -ell, drevyll, -ill, -ell, drewell, -ill**, 6 **drivell**. [Early ME.: app. of Low German origin; = MDu. *drevel* scullion, turnspit, lit. 'driver, tool for driving' (OHG. *tribil*, MHG. *tribel*, mod.G. *triebel* driver), f. MDu. *drîven*, OHG. *trîben* to DRIVE.]
1. A drudge, a servant doing menial work; a 'kitchen-knave'.
a **1225** *St. Marher.* 18 The driueles unduhti swa duden. *c* **1230** *Hali Meid.* 29 And mare beon idrecchet þen eni driuel i þe hus. *c* **1440** *Promp. Parv.* 132/2 Dryvylle, serwawnte, *ducticius, ducticia.* *a* **1529** SKELTON *Agst. Garnesche* 26 A dyshwasher, a dryvyll. **1549** COVERDALE, etc. *Erasm. Par. 1 Cor.* xi. 11 To vse his wife as a vile dreuell, because she is commaunded to obeye. **1580** BARET *Alv.* D 1305 A Drudge, or driuell.. *mediastinus.*
2. Hence, opprobriously: **a.** One deficient in intelligence, an imbecile. [Prob. associated with or influenced by DRIVEL *v.* 5; cf. *driveller.*]
1478 J. PASTON in *P. Lett.* No. 812. III. 220 So the drevyll lost hys thank of us. **1509** BARCLAY *Shyp of Folys* (1874) I. 173 Blame it blynde dryull. *c* **1555** *Schole-ho. Women* 795 in Hazl. *E.P.P.* IV. 136 Called him drivel and witles man. **1597** *1st Pt. Return fr. Parnass.* IV. i. 1141 When I loved I was a drivell.
b. A dirty or foul person, a 'pig'.
1530 PALSGR. 215/2 Drivell, *sovillon.* **1580** SIDNEY *Arcadia* III. (R.) If thou didst know what a life I lead with that drivel. **1596** SPENSER *F.Q.* IV. ii. 3 That foule aged dreuill.. an incarnate deuill.
3. A driving tool or instrument.
1431–2 in Willis & Clark *Cambridge* (1886) III. 610 Item ij drewills ponderant' iiijli, vijd. **1573** *Lanc. Wills* III. 61 Twoo dryvells of iren vjd.

drivel (ˈdrɪv(ə)l), *sb.*[2] Also 5 **drevel**, 5–6 **drivil**, 6–7 **drivell**. β. 4–5 **dravel**. [f. DRIVEL *v.*]
1. Spittle flowing from the mouth; slaver, dribblings. Now *rare.*
?*c* **1325** *Old Age* ii. in *Relig. Ant.* II. 210 Moch me anueth, That my drivil druith. **1388** WYCLIF *1 Sam.* xxi. 13 His drauelis [*gloss* that is, spotelis] flowiden doun. **14..** *Voc.* in Wr.-Wülcker 599 *Orexis*, drevel. **1570** LEVINS *Manip.* 125/43 Ye Driuil at nose, *pus.* **1586** WARNER *Alb. Eng.* IV. xx. (R.) He.. clear'd the driuell from his beard. **1697** *Phil. Trans.* XX. 50 The Snivel or Drivel that comes from the Mouth of a Dog.. when mad. **1789** M. MADAN *Persius* (1795) 54 *note*, The child.. wet with drivel from the mouth. *transf.* **1780** J. T. DILLON *Trav. Spain* (1781) 211 Chequered with small hollow round grains.. which I conceive are formed by bubbles of air.. forming the drivel of the metal. [Cf. DRIVE *v.* 26 c.]
2. Idiotic utterance; silly nonsense; twaddle.
1852 BLACKIE *Study Lang.* 2 As it begins with dreams, so it must end in drivel. **1860** W. COLLINS *Wom. White* III. 474 The most abject drivel that has ever degraded paper. **1884** J. SHARMAN *Hist. Swearing* i. 21 We may have thought.. his words the drivel of idiotcy.
3. *Comb.*, as *drivel-bib*, a child's bib to intercept the drivelling.
1831 CARLYLE *Sart. Res.* I. xi. (1872) 52 Did he, at one time, wear drivel-bibs, and live on spoon-meat?

drivel (ˈdrɪv(ə)l), *v.* Forms: (1 *pr. pple.* **drefliende**), 4 **drevele**, 4–5 **dryvele**, 6 *Sc.* **dre(i)fle**, 6–7 **drivell**, 7–8 **drivle**, 6– **drivel**. β. 4 **dravel-e(n.** [ME. *drevel-en* corresponds to OE. *dreflian*; ME. *dravel-en* indicates an OE. **draflian* (not found); these prob. represent OTeut. types **drabilojan, drabulojan*, f. stem *drab-* (see DRAFF, DROF). *Drivel* is app. a later change: cf. *divel.*]
I. 1. *intr.* To let saliva or mucus flow from the mouth or nose, as young children and idiots do; to slaver, dribble.
c **1000** *Voc.* in Wr.-Wülcker 161/34 *Reumaticus*, saftriende, *uel* drefliende. **1362** LANGL. *P.Pl.* A. XI. 11 *Noli mittere* Margeri perles Among hogges.. þei don bot drauele þeron [**1377** B x. 11 dryuele; **1393** C. XII. 9 dreuele, *v.rr.* dreuel(en, dryuele, drauele, dreuely(n]. **14..** *Voc.* in Wr.-Wülcker 599 *Orexo* [*anglice* to dryvele.] **1530** PALSGR. 530/1 I drivell, I slaver.. He driveleth as he were a yonge chylde. **1616** SURFL. & MARKH. *Country Farme* 122 [A mad dog] Foming and driueling at his mouth. **1672** MARVELL *Reh. Transp.* I. 130 As oft as your nose drivles. **1822–34** GOOD *Study Med.* (ed. 4) III. 480 The patient feels a tendency to drivel at one corner of the mouth rather than the other. **1875** JOWETT *Plato* (ed. 2) III. 212 The.. nurse leaves you to drivel, and never wipes your nose.
†**2.** *trans.* To let (spittle) flow from the mouth; *transf.* to let flow *out* through a crack. *Obs.*
1571 GOLDING *Calvin on Ps.* xxxiv. 1 Too feyne himself mad by driveling doune his spittle. **1681** P. RYCAUT *Critick* 67 The rest ran furiously about this tragick Theatre, drivelling out the overflowing Bloud. **1684** tr. *Bonet's Merc. Compit.* x. 362 The Child.. driveled much Spittle. **1707** J. STEVENS tr. *Quevedo's Com. Wks.* (1709) 432 This crack'd Pot.. drivels out the Water.
†**3.** *intr.* To flow as saliva or mucus from the mouth or nose; to flow ineptly from the lips; also *transf.* of water, etc. *Obs.*
1624, 1804 [see DRIVELLING *ppl. a.* 1 b]. **1741** MONRO *Anat.* (ed. 3) 120 The Pituita drivelled down from the Emunctory of the Brain. *a* **1774** GOLDSM. *Surv. Exp. Philos.* I. 404 The water.. will not spout at all, but drivel down the side of the vessel. **1784** COWPER *Task* V. 285 Strange that such folly.. Should ever drivel out of human lips.
†**4.** *trans.* To befoul with spittle; to beslaver.
1609 W. M. *Man in Moone* (Percy Soc.) 8 Then he doth drivell his hostesse. *a* **1668** DAVENANT *News fr. Plymouth* (1673) 22, I will.. kiss Thy drivell'd Beard, though drown'd in Breda Beere.
II. *transf.* [Referring to the slavering utterance, etc. of infants, and weak-minded persons.]
5. *intr.* To talk childishly or idiotically; to let silly nonsense drop from the lips; to rave.
1362 LANGL. *P. Pl.* A. XI. 43 þus þei drauelen on heore deys þe Deite to knowe [*v.r.* dryuelen, B. x. 56 dryuele, C. XII. 40 dreuelen]. *c* **1460** J. RUSSELL *Bk. Nurture* 292 Be no lier with youre mouthe, ne lykorous, ne dryvelynge. **1704** SWIFT *Mech. Operat. Spirit* Misc. (1711) 292 Droning, and dreaming and drivelling to a Multitude.
6. *trans.* To utter in a childish, or idiotic way.
a **1754** FIELDING *Covent Gard. Jrnl.* No. 3, Nor shall it be sufficient for such critic to drivel out, 'I don't know'. **1780** COWPER *Progr. Err.* 310 Sniveling and driveling folly without end.
7. a. *trans.* To waste or fritter *away* in a childish or idiotic manner. **b.** *intr.* To go *on* in a feeble or idiotic way.
1763 CHURCHILL *Poems, Ep. Hogarth* 643 To drivel out whole years of Ideot breath. **1832** *Examiner* 66/2 Every thing has been done to drivel away the popular enthusiasm. **1878** EMERSON *Misc. Papers, Fort. Republic* Wks. (Bohn) III. 391 Drivelling and huckstering away.. every principle of humanity. **1885** *Law Times* 23 May 68/2 He drivels on from year to year, his fine abilities rusting from disuse.
Hence **ˈdrivelled** *ppl. a.*
c **1325** *Poem on Times of Edw. II*, lv. (Hardwick) 25 His hod schal hang on his brest, Riȝt as a draveled lowt. **1630** DRAYTON *Muses' Elysium* x. (R.) His staring beastly drivel'd beard. *a* **1668** [see sense 4].

†**drivelarde.** *Obs. rare*⁻⁰. [see next.]
1530 PALSGR. 215/2 Drivelarde a lyer, *baueresse.*

driveller, -eler (ˈdrɪv(ə)lə(r)). [f. DRIVEL *v.* + -ER[1].] **1.** One who drivels or slavers.
1530 PALSGR. 215/2 Drivelar that driveleth, *baueux.* **1616** SURFL. & MARKH. *Country Farme* 119 The other [cattle].. do greatly desire and delight in that which these driuelers do leaue vpon the edges of the rackes, and licke it away. **1728** MORGAN *Algiers* I. vi. 206 The proudest Arab.. never disdains to kiss the.. garments of any squalid Scoundrel, if a Natural Drivler, or a reputed Marabboth. **1841–4** EMERSON *Ess., Prudence* Wks. (Bohn) I. 98 The pitiful drivellers whom travellers describe as frequenting the bazaars of Constantinople.
2. One who talks or acts in a babyish or idiotic way; a drivelling idiot or fool.
1710 STEELE *Tatler* No. 208 ¶8 An errant Driveler. **1761** COLMAN *Jealous Wife* II. ii, Sure you imagine me an idiot, a driveller. **1790** BURKE *Corr.* (1844) III. 159 He had been.. a driveller in policy, if he had done otherwise than he did. **1825** SYD. SMITH *Wks.* (1859) II. 67/1 It is the argument of a driveller to other drivellers. **1859** MACAULAY *Biog.* (1867) 204 Pitt's.. military administration was that of a driveller.

ˈdrivelling, -eling, *vbl. sb.* [f. as prec. + -ING[1].] The action of the verb DRIVEL.
1. A running at the nose and mouth; slavering; *concr.* = slaver.
1398 TREVISA *Barth. De P.R.* VII. lxvii. (1495) 284 Yf the dreuelynge of a woode hounde fallyth in to the water, it enfectyth the water. **1563–87** FOXE *A. & M.* (1596) 740 (R.) His eyen and mouth faire closed.. without any drieuling or spurging in any place of his body. **1822–34** GOOD *Study Med.* (ed. 4) I. 407 The coryza or snuffling of old age, is precisely analogous to its ptyalism or drivelling.
2. = DRIVEL *sb.*[2] 2.
1786 tr. *Beckford's Vathek* (1868) 62 As he betrayed a villanous drivelling in his tears, the Caliph turned his back. **1842** MIALL in *Nonconf.* II. 425 The miserable drivelings of the senate.

ˈdrivelling, -eling, *ppl. a.* [f. as prec. + -ING[2].] That drivels.
1. Slavering, dribbling.
1530 PALSGR. 311/1 Drivelyng as a yonge chylde, *baueux.* **1552** HULOET, Driuelynge harlot or queane, *scraptia.* *c* **1611** SYLVESTER *Du Bartas* II. iv. IV. *Decay* 179 Stooping as she goes, With driveling mouth, and with a sniveling nose.
†**b.** *transf.* That flows or falls in drops. *Obs.*
1624 GEE *Foot out of Snare* vii. 63 Those drieuling droppes are they, which are kept in a siluer Image. **1804** *Naval Chron.* XII. 473 Gusts of wind and drivelling sleet.
2. Characterized by or given to silly childish talk or weak action; idiotic.
c **1460** [see DRIVEL *v.* 5]. **1592** SHAKS. *Rom. & Jul.* II. iv. 95 This drieuling Loue is like a great Naturall, that runs lolling vp and downe to hid his bable in a hole. **1602** MARSTON *Ant. & Mel.* V. Wks. 1856 I. 56 Can you paint me a driveling reeling song? **1728** T. SHERIDAN *Persius' Sat.* I. (1739) 21 All this drivling Stuff without Sinews or Strength. **1741** WARBURTON *Div. Legat.* IV. v. III. 222 Some driveling grecanised Mythologist. **1818** HAZLITT *Eng. Poets* iv. (1870) 105 The mere drivelling effusions of his spleen and malice. **1864** KNIGHT *Passages Wrkg. Life* I. iii. 167 A drivelling idiot called a king.
†**3.** *absol.* or as *sb.* A drab. *Obs. rare.*
1570 LEVINS *Manip.* 135/47 A Drieuling, *scraptia.*
Hence **ˈdrivellingly** *adv.*
1731 BAILEY, *Drivelingly*, sillily. **1820** W. TAYLOR in *Monthly Rev.* XCII. 62 The wording of the poetry.. is often drivellingly diffuse.

driven (ˈdrɪv(ə)n), *ppl. a.* [pa. pple. of DRIVE *v.*]
1. Urged onward, impelled, etc.: see the verb.
1641 BEST *Farm. Bks.* (Surtees) 99 If it bee not infected with a wheate called driven-wheate; which wheate hath no awnes like unto long-read. **1801** SOUTHEY *Thalaba* IX. xli, The driven air before her fann'd the face Of Thalaba. **1887** *Pall Mall G.* 3 Aug. 2/1 An amount of work such as mates of less driven steamers have no idea of.
2. Of snow: Carried along and gathered into heaps by the wind; drifted. Of feathers or down: Separated from the heavier by a current of air (see DRIVE *v.* 8 d).
1579 LYLY *Euphues* (Arb.) 89 As white as the driven snow. **1604** SHAKS. *Oth.* I. iii. 232 My thrice-driuen bed of Downe. **1668** H. MORE *Div. Dial.* III. xxviii. (1713) 251 Thin Paper.. but as strong as any Vellum, and as white as driven Snow. **1817** SCOTT *Harold the Dauntless* I. xix, More than to rest on driven down. **1823** BYRON *Juan* VI. xxv, Sheets white as what bards call 'driven Snow'.
3. *driven well* (U.S.), a tube-well.
a **1877** in KNIGHT *Dict. Mech.* **1923** M. WATTS *L. Nichols* 5 A driven well.. went dry in periods of prolonged drought.

driver (ˈdraɪvə(r)). [f. DRIVE *v.* + -ER[1].]
1. a. *gen.* One who drives (in various senses: see the verb).
14.. *Nom.* in Wr.-Wülcker 687/13 *Hic fugator*, a dryfer. *c* **1450** tr. *De Imitatione* III. lx. 142 Grace is.. þrower doun, dryuer awey of sorowe. **1570** *Act 13 Eliz.* c. 8 §4 Solicitors and Drivers of Bargains. **1625** BP. MOUNTAGU *App. Caesar* I. ix. 80 A dangerous driver at Popery and Sedition. **1767** RICHARDSON in *Phil. Trans.* LVIII. 20 The weight of a hammer did not contribute so much in driving a nail, as the quickness of the motion given it by the driver.
b. A horse trained to be driven in harness. *U.S.*
1876 *Rep. Vermont Board Agric.* III. 168 Stylish, enduring roadsters, trotters and gentlemen's drivers, standing from fifteen to fifteen and one-half hands high. **1902** A. D. MCFAUL *Ike Glidden* viii. 61 This is a pretty good driver you've got here. *Ibid.* 66 All prosperous people there keep a 'driver' and a 'trader'.
2. *spec.* **a.** One who drives a herd of cattle, etc.
1483 *Cath. Angl.* 109/1 A Drywer (*A.* Dryfer) of nawte. **1530** PALSGR. 215/2 Drivar of camelles, *chamelier.* **1844** LD. BROUGHAM *A. Lunel* II. vi. 156 All were forced to keep the same pace, in order that a single driver.. might suffice.
b. One who drives a vehicle or the animal that draws it; a charioteer, coachman, cabman, etc.; also, one who drives a locomotive engine. (Often with defining word prefixed, as *cab-driver, engine-driver*, etc., for which see the first element.) Also in Trotting. Phr. *in the driver's seat*, in a controlling position; in charge.
c **1450** *St. Cuthbert* (Surtees) 6016 All þe dryuers ware agaste þat þe sledd suld ga our faste. **1581** SAVILE *Tacitus* 93 (R.) Buffons, stage-players, and charet drivers. **1725** POPE *Odyss.* XIII. 99 Fiery coursers in the rapid race Urg'd by fierce drivers thro' the dusty space. **1812** COL. HAWKER *Diary* (1893) I. 55 An excellent chaise with a decent driver. **1923** *Nation* 18 July 49 He has swung blithely into the driver's seat and cheerfully undertaken to run the nation without knowing how. **1948** *N.Y. Times* 18 Apr. v. 2/1 Leo Durocher, after an involuntary year of exile, is back in the driver's seat. **1963** *Weekly News* (Auckland) 8 May 53/1 Two drivers were sprawled on the track after one of the worst smashes at a trotting meeting in the North Island this season. **1965** G. MCINNES *Road to Gundagai* xi. 189 'A divine Australian voice'.. with a hint of iron in it that made you feel he was in the driver's seat. **1968** *Globe & Mail* (Toronto) 15 Jan. 20/3 Wes Coke, the young driver from Petrolia, rang up three winners on the matinee card.
c. The overseer of a gang of slaves. (See also SLAVE-DRIVER.)
1796 STEDMAN *Surinam* II. xviii. 55 The prisoners.. being secured by the negro-drivers. **1823** LD. BATHURST in *Ann. Reg.* 131/1 *note*, That the whip should no longer be carried into the field, and there displayed by the driver. *a* **1843** SOUTHEY *Sonn.* iii, That inhuman driver lifts.. The .. scourge.

d. *slang.* (See quot.)

1851 MAYHEW *Lond. Labour* (1861) II. 233 'Drivers', or those who compel the men in their employ to do more work for the same wages.

e. In various other specific uses: see quots., and various senses of DRIVE *v.*

1540 *Act 32 Hen. VIII*, c. 13 §7 The same..driuours [of a forest] shal cause the same vnprofitable beastes..to be killed. **1812** *Sporting Mag.* XL. 52 The best curler, has generally the power of arranging the order of the game; and whoever is last in order gives directions to all the rest..He is called the *driver* and the first the *lead*. **1829** GLOVER *Hist. Derby* I. 58 When the holers have finished their operations, a new set of men, called hammer-men, or drivers, enter the works. **1867** *Cornh. Mag.* Apr. 492–3 There is the 'long driver' [at golf], who hits as far in two strokes as a 'short driver' does in three. **1884** *Harper's Mag.* Oct. 753/2 The..workmen wade about the vats spearing..hides as a Western river 'driver' does his logs.

f. Short for *driver-ant*.

1897 M. KINGSLEY *W. Africa* 626 Bad language, such as I am accustomed to when a lord of creation gets drivers on him. **1966** C. SWEENEY *Scurrying Bush* vi. 84 Small, reddish-brown drivers clung to my toes.

g. *Cricket.* A batsman who drives or is skilled in driving (see DRIVE *v.* 8 b).

1906 A. E. KNIGHT *Complete Cricketer* 344 The batsman who is proficient at the stroke is..a good 'driver'. **1921** P. F. WARNER *My Cricketing Life* iii. 64 Lionel Palairet..was also a fine driver on both sides of the wicket.

3. A tool or appliance for driving.

a. A bundle of osier rods used to beat the bushes in 'driving' young pheasants (see DRIVE *v.* 3 b). **b.** A mallet. **c.** A tool used by coopers in driving on the hoops of casks. **d.** *Shipbuilding* (see quot. 1850). **e.** *Weaving.* The piece of wood which drives the shuttle through the shed of the loom. **f.** A bar for tamping the powder in a blast-hole; a tamping-iron. **g.** An instrument for enlarging or altering the shape of a drilled hole; = DRIFT *sb.* 13 b. **h.** A tool for driving out the piece of a metal plate in punching. **i.** *Golf.* The *play-club*: 'a wooden-headed club with full-length shaft, more or less supple, with which the ball can be driven to the greatest distance'.

1674 N. COX *Gentl. Recreat.* III. (1706) 37 Take your Instrument called a Driver, which is made of strong white Wands or Osiers set fast in a handle..With this Driver you must make a gentle noise. **1688** R. HOLME *Armoury* III. 318/1 A Driver [is] a piece of Wood cut in the form of a Wedge..with this by the help of Blows with the Addice, all sorts of Hoops are driven fast upon Barrels. *Ibid.* 344/1 A Pavers Maul, or Mall, or Mallet..is of some termed a Driver. **1753** CHAMBERS *Cycl. Supp.*, *Driver*..used in the taking pheasant powts, in the method called driving..With this instrument the sportsman having fixed his nets, drives the young birds into them. *c* **1850** *Rudim. Navig.* (Weale) 116 *Driver*, the foremost spur on the bilgeways, the heel of which is fayed to the foreside of the foremost poppet, and cleated on the bulgeways, and the sides of it stand fore and aft. It is now seldom used. **1892** *Badm. Libr., Mountaineering* ii. 68 Forty-four inches is an average length for the golfer's driver..the longest club with which he finds he can hit accurately. **1894** *Athenæum* 24 Nov. 707/3 The bat [was] a monstrous club..wielded, as one would wield a driver at golf.

j. That part of an electronic circuit designed to supply the input signal power required by the last stage of a power amplifier, esp. a transmitter or receiver; an electrical device, as a valve or transistor (*driver transistor, tube, valve*), immediately preceding the output stage; the stage as a whole immediately preceding the output stage (called also *driver circuit, stage*).

1924 S. R. ROGET *Dict. Electr. Terms* 68/2 *Driver*, an expression sometimes used for a source of oscillations in radio telegraphy, particularly in connection with testing operations. **1938** G. E. STERLING *Radio Man.* (ed. 3) v. 213 The driver is ordinarily a class *A* 'power amplifier' stage. **1948** GLASOE & LEBACQZ *Pulse Generators* iv. 124 The driver circuit is not an oscillator in the same sense as the circuit used in television, and may more properly be referred to as a 'regenerative pulse generator'. **1948** I. A. GREENWOOD et al. *Electronic Instruments* vii. 179 Since the voltages at the potentiometer arms come from relatively high-impedance sources, precise impedance-changing circuits (drivers) are necessary to reproduce these voltages across the resolver stator windings without loading the potentiometers. **1948** J. A. PIERCE et al. *Loran* vii. 211 The pulse-output circuit and exciter driver amplify and shape the pulse that drives the local transmitter. *Ibid.* ix. 295 [This] requirement is met by the use of a c-w driver stage that amplifies the output of the 90-kc/sec generator to a level of about 20 watts. **1949** F. G. GARRATT tr. *Deketh's Fund. Radio-valve Technique* xvii. 229 The operation of valves in this manner..involves the flow of grid current and the source of grid-signal voltage has to supply a certain amount of power. To meet this, therefore, the Class-B output stage is preceded by a so-called *driver valve* capable of supplying a certain power. **1962** SIMPSON & RICHARDS *Junction Transistors* xi. 246 The fourth method, direct coupling, may be used advantageously..in the coupling of a driver to a power stage. **1970** J. EARL *Tuners & Amplifiers* ii. 51 The majority of power amplifiers have their push-pull output transistors driven direct from a pair of driver transistors.

k. *Acoustics.* A device in a horn loudspeaker that converts electrical energy into sound.

1927 *Wireless World* 16 Nov. 666/1 It is a case of arranging for the most convenient method of coupling between the driver..in this case between the diaphragm and the air within the horn, so that the imprisoned air shall be acted upon to the best advantage. **1950** H. S. KNOWLES in K. Henney *Radio Engin. Handbk.* (ed. 4) xvi. 747 The driver unit is coupled to the horn by the sound chamber. **1967** BADMAIEFF & DAVIS *How to build Speaker Enclosures* ii. 19 Every enclosure alters in some way the performance of the driver placed in it.

l. *Sheep-shearing.* (See quots.) *Austral.* and *N.Z.*

1933 L. G. D. ACLAND in *Press* (Christchurch) 14 Oct. 15/7 *Driver*, a leather strap on the handle of a pair of shears, which fits over the back of the shearer's hand. **1959** H. P. TRITTON *Time means Tucker* iv. 31/1 There is a band of leather from the heel of one blade [of shears] to the back of the other. This is the 'driver', and its purpose is to prevent the hand from slipping forward onto the blades. **1965** J. S. GUNN *Terminol. Shearing Industry* I. 25 *Driver*, a leather strap on hand shears. This fits firmly round the handle and over the back of the shearer's hand, thus allowing more drive to be given to a blow while preventing the hands from slipping over the blades.

4. A boat used in fishing with a drift-net.

1664 J. KEYMER *Observ. Dutch Fishing* in *Phenix* (1721) I. 223 The 1500 Strand-boats, Evers, Galiots, Drivers, and Tod-boats fish upon their own Coasts. **1883** *Pall Mall G.* 9 May 1/2 Drivers (i.e., boats used in the herring, mackerel, or pilchard fisheries with drift nets)..are smaller than trawlers, and are not required to sail while fishing.

5. *Naut.* †**a.** A large sail formerly used at the aftermost part of a ship in fair weather, set 'square' (i.e. transverse to the ship's length) on a yard at the end of the spanker-boom. *Obs.* **b.** Now applied to the SPANKER, a fore-and-aft sail at the same part of the ship; sometimes distinguished as a sail smaller than the spanker, but set on the same boom and gaff.

1769 FALCONER *Dict. Marine* (1789) *Driver*, an oblong sail, occasionally hoisted to the mizen peak, when the wind is very fair. **1794** *Rigging & Seamanship* I. 217 The Driver or Spanker Sail Is bent as a temporary matter. **1798** *Jrnl. of 'Vanguard'* Dec., in Nicolas *Disp. Nelson* (1845) III. 209 A very stormy passage, in which the Vanguard split her three topsails and the driver though it was brailed up. **1867** SMYTH *Sailor's Word-bk.*, *Driver*, a large sail formerly used with the wind aft or quartering..The name latterly has been officially applied to the spanker, both being the aftermost sails of a ship. **1883** (*A Coastguard says*) A driver differs from a spanker in being smaller, and is used in bad weather, being set on the same gaff and boom.

6. a. A part of machinery, usually a wheel, which communicates motion to other parts, or to which the power is directly communicated; the driving-wheel of a locomotive, etc.

1831 G. R. PORTER *Silk Manuf.* 208 The rude wooden wheels and drivers which were long used. **1847** *Engineer & Mach. Assistant* (1850) 71 When two wheels geer together, the one which communicates the motion to the other is called the *driver* or *leader*, and the wheel impelled is called the *follower*. **1879** HOLTZAPFFEL *Turning* IV. 196 Motion is transmitted by the contact of an arm or pin, the *driver*, on the chuck, with an arm or *carrier* attached to the work.

b. *front-, rear-, double-driver*: applied respectively to a bicycle or tricycle in which the driving power is applied to the front wheel, the hind wheel, or two wheels (of a tricycle).

1885 *Bazaar* 30 Mar. 1275/1 Imperial Club tricycle..front steerer, double driver. **1891** *Wheeling* 11 Mar. 455 The rear-driver can be mastered in a much shorter time. **1895** *Cycl. Tour. Club Gaz.* Dec. 372, I did not see one solitary specimen of the front driver.

7. *Comb.*, **driver-ant**, a species of ant (*Anomma arcens*) found in West Africa: see quot. 1865; **driver-boom** (*Naut.*), the boom on which the driver (sense 5) is set; **driver-yard** (see quot.).

1794 *Rigging & Seamanship* I. 84 The mizen course and driver boom sail [are set] from the mizen mast. *Ibid.* 180 The *Driver-yard* is a small yard, which expands the head of the driver without the peek of the gaff, to which it is hoisted by haliards. **1799** *Naval Chron.* I. 442 Her driver boom [is] gone. **1859** DARWIN *Orig. Spec.* viii. (1878) 232 Nest of the driver ant. **1865** WOOD *Homes without H.* xxiv. (1868) 447 They are called Driver Ants because they drive before them every living creature.

Hence **'driveress** (*nonce-wd.*), a female driver; **'driverless** *a.*, without a driver; **'drivership**, the office of a driver (sense 2 b); skill in driving.

1691 E. TAYLOR *Behmen's Theos. Philos.* 346 Not the Omnipotency, but the Driveress in or into the might. **1860** *All Year Round* No. 72. 511 They go on performing surpassing feats of drivership. **1870** *Daily News* 23 Apr., He lost all command over the horses, which dashed along driverless. **1892** *Pall Mall G.* 19 Jan. 4/3 The runaway horses had taken the driverless coach on without injury.

drive-through ('draɪvθruː), *sb.* and *a.* Chiefly *N. Amer.* Also **drive-thru**. [f. DRIVE *v.* 5 c.] **A.** *sb.* A restaurant, shop, etc., having a counter or window to which customers may drive in order to be served; cf. DRIVE-IN *sb.*; also *attrib.*, as *drive-through window*, etc. **B.** *adj.* Designating a service, restaurant, etc., affording facilities for driving through, or a place (as a wildlife park) through which one may drive.

1949 *Ann Arbor* (Mich.) *News* 9 June 19/5 When you are pointing to the Beer Vault Drive-Thru for cold refreshing beer it's good manners. **1969** *Jane's Freight Containers 1968–69* 20 Drive-through ferry service, Ardrossan/Belfast. **1975** *Americana Ann.* 52 Shuster..believed that a drive-through zoo would appeal to the American public. **1976** *National Observer* (U.S.) 21 Aug. 8/4 There's another design feature that almost all of these chains say they will adopt: drive-through windows. *Ibid.*, Now pilot tests show that reviving the drive-throughs can increase sales. **1984** *Tampa* (Florida) *Tribune* 5 Apr. 9B/2 The work includes additional production area and a drive-through canopy.

driveway ('draɪvweɪ). Chiefly *N. Amer.* [f. DRIVE *v.* + WAY.] A way along which something is driven. **a.** A course along which game are driven in hunting. **b.** A road or way along which animals or vehicles are driven; a carriage drive. Also, a private carriageway for a motor vehicle alongside, in front of, or leading to a house, garage, or other building; a drive.

1870 *Congress. Globe* 2 Feb. 966/3, I doubt as to the policy of allowing this railroad to go along exactly in the track of where we propose to have a public drive-way. **1875** TEMPLE & SHELDON *Hist. Northfield, Mass.* 46 Capturing both larger and smaller sorts by means of drive-ways and in rude traps and yank-ups. **1884** *Harper's Mag.* Jan. 184/2 Winding driveways lead up to it from the road. **1889** *Century Mag.* Dec. 227/2 The decks [of a ferry-boat] were crowded with laboring men, the drive-ways choked with teams; the women and children standing inside the cabin. **1895** H. P. ROBINSON *Men Born Equal* 16 A carriage..came down the driveway. **1935** M. M. ATWATER *Murder in Midsummer* xvi. 146 Harold was in the drive-way beside the house, about to start his car. **1945** *Chicago Tribune* 13 May VII. 1/1 Beyond the driveway that runs before her front gate, the greens start popping out of the moist earth. **1952** *Manch. Guardian Weekly* 28 Feb. 12 We twist into a driveway and have arrived. **1965** PRIESTLEY & WISDOM *Good Driving* ix. 65 It is often safer..to use a side-turning. A side-road or driveway ..will do. **1966** *Globe & Mail* (Toronto) 9 May 7/3 [I] shovelled gravel to make a new driveway. **1971** 'A. BLAISDELL' *Practice to Deceive* iv. 59, I always left the driveway light on for her.

c. A passageway for the conveyance of hay, grain, etc., into a barn.

1839 *Mass. Agric. Rep. 1838* 80 The building should be so placed that the barn floor could be laid upon the beams, and the drive-way be into the end directly under the roof. **1868** *Rep. Comm. Agric.* (*U.S. Dept. Agric.*) 242 Where it is practicable, it is best to have the drive-way for drawing in hay, grain and corn fodder enter the gable end. **1949** *Pacific Spectator* Spring 226 The upper floor, right on a level with the driveway, had a big haymow on the left.

d. A scenic highway. *Canada.*

1909 *Gow Ganda* (Ont.) *Tribune* 1 May 1/1 The advisability of spending three hundred thousand dollars in building a driveway and boulevard along the Canadian side of the Niagara River. **1927** M. DE LA ROCHE *Jalna* x. 114 They were gliding slowly along an ocean driveway in Rosamond Trent's car. **1958** *Saturday Night* (Toronto) 27 Sept. 7/1 More trees, parks and driveways as handouts from the taxpayers of Canada.

driving ('draɪvɪŋ), *vbl. sb.* [-ING[1].]

1. The action of DRIVE vb. (q.v.), in various senses.

c **1440** *Promp. Parv.* 132/2 Dryvynge, or cathchynge [*v.r.* chasinge], *minatus*. **1494** FABYAN *Chron.* VII. 461 In tyme of dryuynge..of whiche bargayne. **1549** LATIMER *4th Serm. bef. Edw. VI* (Arb.) 110 Wythout any delayes, or dryuynge of. **1580** HOLLYBAND *Treas. Fr. Tong*, *Dechassement*, a driuing away. **1611** BIBLE *2 Kings* ix. 20 The driuing is like the driuing of Iehu the sonne of Nimshi; for he driueth furiously. **1765** STERNE *Tr. Shandy* VII. xvii. (R.), All within three minutes driving. **1884** *Graphic* 20 Sept. 290/2 At private schools of a higher class the driving is even worse.

2. *concr.* That which is driven: see DRIVE *v.* 8 d.

1696 TRYON *Misc.* ii. 61 Many Feathers..are Imported from several Countries, which are the Drivings of old Beds.

3. *attrib.* and *Comb.* (Several of the combinations may also be regarded as belonging to the ppl. adj.) **a.** Relating to, adapted for, or devoted to driving in a carriage, motor vehicle, etc.

1788 MRS. HUGHES *Henry & Isabella* I. 77 Moving slowly round the driving way. **1794** W. FELTON *Carriages* (1801) Gloss., *Driving Cushion*, a deep cushion, made..for the driver to sit on. **1858** C. M. YONGE *Christmas Mummers* i. 11 Harry Mayne was perched on the driving-seat. **1882** L. C. LILLIE *Prudence* 95 To make her driving toilet. **1882** G. W. PECK *Peck's Sunshine* 24 If he don't put on an old driving coat and go out on the road occasionally. **1887** *Daily News* 16 May 2/6 The institution of the two four-in-hand driving clubs. **1891** *Pall Mall G.* 11 July 6/1 Beautiful driving weather. **1895** *Daily News* 5 July 5/3 The driving meet in Hyde Park. **1895** *Montgomery Ward Catal.* 518/1 Men's river or driving shoes. **1897** *Sears, Roebuck Catal.* 228/1 Light weight driving gloves. **1911** *Madame* 20 May 318/2 No one who has not lived in the canton for three months shall be allowed a driving licence. **1926** *Amer. Speech* I. 686/1 American..rear view mirror. English..driving mirror. **1932** KIPLING *Limits & Renewals* 135 Phil, alone in the car..shifted into the driving-seat. **1933** *Punch* 13 Dec. 662/1 Reasonable plea for a driving-test was put forward by Lord Howe. **1936** *Times* 10 Jan. 12/2 His waistcoat, containing his savings and his driving licence. **1961** *Evening Standard* 14 July 19/2 (Advt.), Driving Instructor reqd.. Motor School. **1962** N. MARSH *Hand in Glove* vi. 199, I mean his driving gloves. They're heavy leather ones with string backs. **1966** 'A. HALL' *9th Directive* xxiv. 224, I slid the driving-seat back a notch. **1966** B. KIMENYE *Kalasanda Revisited* 98 As soon as they were alone, she asked if she could take driving lessons. **1966** T. WISDOM *High-Performance Driving* xvi. 136 The driving test..in my mind is not a real *driving* test at all. It is just a traffic test. *Ibid.*, The driving-school customer is interested only in passing the test. **1968** *Autocar* 18 Apr. 26/1 Driving simulators are still a novelty. **1969** V. CANNING *Queen's Pawn* ii. 8 There was a pair of comfortable women's driving shoes down by the control pedals.

b. In names of various mechanical contrivances used for driving (see quots., and various senses of DRIVE *v.*), as *driving-block, -bolt, -cap, -chisel, -pike*; *esp.* of parts of machinery which communicate motion to other parts, as ***driving-axle***, ***-belt***, ***-gear***, ***-pulley***, ***-shaft***; or of parts in connexion with these, as ***driving-spring***; also **driving-band**, (*a*) a band transmitting motion in machinery; (*b*) (see quot. 1893); **driving-iron**, **-putter**, two clubs used in golf, the former to give great elevation to the ball, the latter to drive a very low ball against a heavy wind; **driving-stick**, a stick with which cattle, etc., are driven. See also DRIVING-BOX, -WHEEL.

1849–50 WEALE *Dict. Terms, Driving springs*, the springs fixed upon the boxes of the *driving axle of a locomotive engine, to support the weight and to deaden the shocks caused by irregularities in the rails. **1862** *Jrnl. Soc. Arts* X. 327/2 *Driving-bands..are now made largely in india-rubber. **1886** F. C. MORGAN *Handbk. Artillery Matériel* (ed. 3) vi. 56 The driving band in the newest pattern of shells is made broader, and has cannelures round it. **1893** LLOYD & HADCOCK *Artillery* ix. 230 *Driving bands.* All projectiles, except case shot, are fitted with a band of soft metal, which is cut into by the rifling of the gun, and thus forms the medium for translating the rotatory motion to the projectile. *Ibid.* 231 'Cannelures' are cut in the driving band to make room for the copper which is displaced by the rifling when the projectile is fired. **1916** 'BOYD CABLE' *Doing their Bit* v. 70 One girl..is turning the copper driving bands. **1885** *Law Rep.* 15 Q. Bench Div. 358 Leathern *driving-belts were used in working the machinery at the factory. **1849** ALB. SMITH *Pottleton Leg.* 80 The 'monkey' was the large *driving-block that falls upon a pile-head. **1769** FALCONER *Dict. Marine* (1789) *Repoussoir*, a *driving-bolt, used by shipwrights to knock out some other bolt from its station. **1890** *Driving iron [see IRON *sb.*[1] 4 e]. **1877** *Lumberman's Gaz.* 8 Dec. 362 Each man..carries a '*driving pike' or heavy pole some eight feet long. **1857** *Chambers' Inform.* II. 693/2 The *driving-putter is shorter in the shank than the play-club..The driving-putter sends 'skimming' balls, and so 'cheats the wind'. **1869** J. G. FULLER *Flower-Gatherers* 147 He took Jack's long *driving-stick. **1926** D. H. LAWRENCE *David* xii. 88, I plant this driving-stick in the soft earth.

'driving, *ppl. a.* [-ING[2].] That drives.

1. a. Impelling, setting in motion, actuating. ***driving force*** or ***power***, the force or power by which an engine or vehicle is driven; motor force or power; freq. *fig.*

(The phr. ***driving wind***, etc. may belong to sense 2.)

1297 R. GLOUC. (1724) 20 Heo..wende uorþ with god wynd & wel dryuyng flode. **1687** LUTTRELL *Brief Rel.* (1857) I. 403 So great a driving wind. **1856** EMERSON *Eng. Traits, Times* Wks. (Bohn) II. 116 The ability of its journals is the driving force. *a* **1877** KNIGHT *Dict. Mech.* I. 948/2 The great weight of this wheel is..to carry the machine over the one half of its period in which the driving-power is absent. **1895** *Ch. Q. Rev.* Oct. 156 Doubt as the driving energy of active inquiry. **1905** *Sketch* 26 July 38/1 The driving power [*sc.* of a dirigible balloon] is supplied by two 50 horse-power Bucket motors. **1909** F. HARRIS *The Man Shakespeare* 369, I always think of him as a ship over-engined; when the driving-power is working at full speed it shakes the ship to pieces. **1911** 'I. HAY' *Safety Match* i. 14 Brian Vereker would make a noble figurehead..but..the figurehead would require a good deal of imported driving-power behind it. **1927** M. PUPIN *New Reformation* 214 A cosmic stream of solar energy from which everything that lives and breathes on this terrestrial globe derives its driving-force, just as the mill on the mountain side derives its driving-power from the mountain stream. **1931** J. S. HUXLEY *What dare I Think?* vii. 246 The religious driving-force of a great many intelligent people is going to waste. **1965** *New Statesman* 30 Apr. 691/2 Hofmeyr was not only often acting prime minister but almost always the main driving force in the administration. **1967** CONDON & ODISHAW *Handbk. Physics* (ed. 2) II. iii. 23 For a given magnitude of driving force, resonance in the velocity amplitude occurs at minimum impedance. **1970** *Times* 9 Mar. 7/1 Someone persuaded the man known as the 'Driving Force' behind *Woman's Own* and *Modern Woman* to see me.

b. Energetic, dynamic, forceful. (Cf. DRIVE *sb.* 1 i.) orig. and chiefly *U.S.*

1835 J. H. INGRAHAM *South-West* II. 92 They become thorough, driving planters. **1946** R. BLESH *Shining Trumpets* (1949) xi. 257 Mitchell's cornet playing throughout is of the utmost clarity and compressed, driving simplicity. **1952** B. ULANOV *Hist. Jazz Amer.* (1958) xix. 235 Lester is also a summary example of driving, vigorous tenor saxophone.

2. Moving along rapidly, esp. before the wind; drifting; said also of a storm, in which rain or snow drives rapidly before a strong wind.

1601 SHAKS. *Twel. N.* I. ii. 11 When you..Hung on our driuing boate. **1697** DRYDEN *Virg. Georg.* III. 564 Perpetual Sleet, and driving Snow. **1802** *R. Brookes' Gazetteer* (ed. 12) s.v. *Provincetown*, The houses are..set upon piles, that the driving sands may pass under them. **1848** C. A. JOHNS *Week at Lizard* 43 The nets are set..parallel to the tide and suffered to drift with it, hence they are called 'drift nets', and the boats 'driving boats'.

†**3.** ***driving notes*** (*Mus.*): an old name for syncopated notes, as being 'driven' or prolonged through the accent. *Obs.*

1597 MORLEY *Introd. Mus.* 89 The third is a driuing waie in two crotchets and a minime, but added by a rest. **1731** KELLER *Thorough-bass* in W. Holder *Harmony* 189 The several driving Notes descend by degrees. **1858** CURRIE *Elem. Mus. Anal.* 101 Which..has so peculiar an effect in performance as to have sometimes procured for such notes the epithet of 'driving notes'.

Hence **'drivingly** *adv.*, in a driving manner.

1842 MISS MITFORD in L'Estrange *Life* (1870) III. 163 It rained drivingly.

'driving-box.

1. The box on which the driver of a carriage sits.

1794 W. FELTON *Carriages* (1801) I. 149 The driving-box ..fitted to the half top of the seat of a chaise. **1837** DICKENS *Pickw.* xiv, A couple of driving-boxes, two or three whips, and as many travelling-shawls.

2. The journal-box of a driving-axle.

1874 KNIGHT *Dict. Mech., Driving-axle*, the axle of a driving-wheel; the bearing portion rests in the driving-box. The weight of that portion of the engine is supported by a driving-spring upon the box.

driving-wheel. a. A wheel which communicates motion to one or more other wheels or machinery. **b.** Each of the large wheels of a locomotive engine, to which the power is transmitted through the connecting-rod and crank. **c.** The wheel of a bicycle or tricycle to which the force is directly applied. Also *fig.*

1838 N. WOOD *Railroads*, An engine..with driving wheels ten feet diameter. **1870** EMERSON *Soc. & Solit.* vi. 116 The men in cities who are the centres of energy, the driving-wheels of trade, politics, or practical arts.

driwerie, var. DRUERY, *Obs.*

†**drix.** *Obs.* [Origin uncertain.] Decayed wood; the decayed part (of timber).

1609 C. BUTLER *Fem. Mon.* (1634) 57 [The Wasp] worketh a Comb of the utter drix of Pales, or other Timber.

Hence **drixy**, †**dricksie** *a.*, decayed (as timber); = DRUXY, q.v.

drizzle ('drɪz(ə)l), *sb.*[1] [goes with DRIZZLE *v.*] Small, fine, spray-like rain.

1554 in Harington *Nugæ Ant.* 93 To shunne Bleak winters drizzle. **1668** WILKINS *Real Char.* 58 The Condensation of it, from a Cloud, or from a Mist, Rain, Drizle. **1806–7** J. BERESFORD *Miseries Hum. Life* (1826) VI. iii, A mist which successively becomes a mizzle, a drizzle, a shower, a rain, a torrent. **1853** C. BRONTE *Villette* xxi, It rained a November drizzle.

drizzle, *sb.*[2] A name of the young ling (fish).

1769 PENNANT *Zool.* (1776) III. 198 (Jod.) It is not reckoned a sizeable fish, and consequently not entitled to the bounty..Such are called drizzles and are in season all summer.

drizzle ('drɪz(ə)l), *v.* Also 6 **drysel**, 6–7 **drissel**, 6–8 **drizle**, **dris(s)le**, 7 **driz(z)el**. [Not known before 16th c. Origin obscure: possibly dim. and freq. of rare ME. DRESE, OE. *drēosan* to fall; with 16th c. *dryseling* cf. DRYSNING.]

1. *intr.* To rain in very fine, dense, spray-like drops: said of the weather, the day, and *impers.*; to fall, as rain, in fine drops.

1566 [see DRIZZLING *ppl. a.* b]. **1590** MARLOWE *Edw. II*, Wks. (Rtldg.) 199/2 These tears, that drizzle from mine eyes. **1637** G. DANIEL *Genius of this Ile* 7 Nor ever did the winter drissle here. **1837** CARLYLE *Fr. Rev.* I. v. ii, The morning is none of the comfortablest: raw; it is even drizzling a little. **1892** ZANGWILL *Big Bow Myst.* 89 A thin rain drizzled languidly.

fig. **1822** SHELLEY *Faust* II. 187 The magic notes, like spark on spark, Drizzle, whistling through the dark.

†**2.** *trans.* To shed in fine spray-like drops. *Obs.*

1543 [see DRIZZLING *vbl. sb.* below]. **1584** LYLY *Campaspe* III. iii, Danae, into whose prison Jupiter drizled a golden showre. **1599** SHAKS. *Much Ado* III. iii. 111 Stand thee close then vnder this penthouse, for it drissels raine. **1601** —— *Jul. C.* II. ii. 21 Fierce fiery Warriours fight vpon the Clouds ..Which drizel'd blood vpon the Capitoll. **1642** QUARLES *Div. Poems, Elegie Dr. Wilson* i, I cannot mizzle: My fluent brains are too severe to drizzle Sleight drops.

3. To sprinkle or wet with minute drops. *rare.*

1810 SCOTT *Lady of L.* IV. v, Drizzled by the ceaseless spray, The wizard waits. **1869** BLACKMORE *Lorna D.* iii, The little stubby trees..were drizzled with a mess of wet.

4. *intr.* To pick the gold thread out of tassels or embroideries into which it was woven; so ***drizzler***, ***drizzling*** (also *attrib.*).

1884 tr. *Bauer's Posthumous Mem.* II. i. 117 Prince Leopold..diligently and indefatigably drizzled. *Ibid.* 118 This 'drizzling'..was invented in Paris..during the reign of King Louis XVI... The most fashionable ladies of the court felt no compunction in asking the gentlemen of their acquaintance for cast-off gold and silver epaulettes. **1896** *Godey's Mag.* Feb. 177/2 Drizzling—which was nothing more or less than picking the gold thread out of old gold tassels, braid, [etc.]. *Ibid.* 178/1 One of the Countess's principal grievances against the Prince seems to have been that he was a confirmed drizzler; she says Leopold would sit by her hour after hour diligently and indefatigably drizzling. .. The tall Prince..bending over his elegant drizzling-box of tortoise-shell. **1969** E. H. PINTO *Treen* 310 The value of the material in gold lace led to later destruction of much of it for reclamation of the gold. In France, in the late 18th century, *parfilage* or unravelling became a social and profitable pastime. Early in the 19th century, the destructive addiction came to England under the name of drizzling.

Hence **'drizzled** *ppl. a.*, shed in spray-like drops; **'drizzling** *vbl. sb.* (in quot. 1543, *concr.*); (see also sense 4 above).

1543 BALE *Yet a Course, &c.* 97 (T.) The draffysh declaracyons of my lorde Boner, with such other dirty dryselings of Antichrist. **1590** SHAKS. *Com. Err.* V. i. 312 Sap-consuming Winters drizled snow. **1615** CROOKE *Body of Man* 499 They..auoid their water by drisling or drops. **1856** T. AIRD *Poet. Wks.* 342 A bloody drizzled shower.

'drizzling, *ppl. a.* [f. DRIZZLE *v.* + -ING[2].] That drizzles. **a.** Of rain or the like.

1579 SPENSER *Sheph. Cal.* Jan. 41 From mine eyes the drizling teares descend. **1594** —— *Amoretti* xviii, Drizling drops that often doe redound, the firmest flint doth in continuance weare. **1667** MILTON *P.L.* VI. 546 No drizling showr, But ratling storm of Arrows barbd with fire. **1743** *Lond. & Country Brew.* IV. (ed. 2) 267 Run a drisling Stream ..on a few Hops. **1863** GEO. ELIOT *Romola* III. xiv, They walked on in silence..under the small drizzling rain.

b. Of a day, climate, etc.

1566 DRANT *Horace, Sat.* II. ii. (R.), Through sletie drisling day. **1652** BENLOWES *Theoph.* II. lxxii, Thus mounts she drizling Olivet. **1741** SHORT in *Phil. Trans.* XLI. 629 All Three Days showery or drisling. **1875** J. H. BENNET *Winter Medit.* I. iii. 81 A drizzling November day in England.

drizzly ('drɪzlɪ), *a.* [f. DRIZZLE + -Y[1].] Of the nature of, or characterized by drizzling.

1697 DRYDEN *Virg. Georg.* III. 475 During Winter's drisly Reign. **1748** THOMSON *Cast. Indol.* I. 238 Falling back again in drizzly dew. **1861** DICKENS *Gt. Expect.* xxvii, Unfortunately the morning was drizzly.

dro, droch, obs. pa. t. of DRAW *v.*

droag, droan(e, obs. ff. DROG, DRONE.

drobely, drobly, drobyl, varr. DRUBLY, DRUBBLE. *Obs.*

†**drock.** *Obs.* A part of a plow (see quot.).

1753 CHAMBERS *Cycl. Supp., Drock*..is an upright piece of timber..belonging to the right side of the tail..The ground wrist of the plow is fastened to this, as also is the earth board.

†**drof, drove**, *a.* *Obs.* [OE. *drôf* turbid, disturbed, a parallel form to OS. *drôbi* (MDu. *droeve*, Du. *droef*), OHG. *truobi* (Ger. *trübe*):—OTeut. **drôbu-z* (becoming **drôbjo-*), from ablaut stem of *drab-an*, whence DRAFF. Cf. DREF.] Turbid, disturbed, troubled: physically or mentally.

c **1000** *Sax. Leechd.* III. 204 Flod drof ȝesihð æbyliiȝða hit ȝetacnað. *c* **1205** LAY. 1040 Drof he wes on mode. *Ibid.* 6588 Drof [*c* **1275** sori] him wes on heorte. *a* **1300** *Cursor M.* 13769 (Cott.) Quen þis water all droue [*v.r.* droued] war.

drof(e, droff(e, obs. ff. *drove*: see DRIVE *v.*

†**drof-land.** *Old Law.* Also ?**dryfland** and *erron.* **driftland**. [f. ME. *drōf*, OE. *drāf*, DROVE, driving + LAND.] (See quot. 1660).

1660 W. SOMNER *Gavelkind* prop. iv. 116 (Drof-land) that holden by the service of driving, as well of Distresses taken for the Lords use, as of the Lords cattel from place to place, as to and from Markets, Fairs, and the like: more particularly here in Kent of driving the Lords hogs or swine to and from the Weald of Kent. **1664** F. PHILLIPS *Mistaken Recomp.* 39 [The lords] in many or some of their manors do receive Quit-rents of their Tenants for *Berdland*, or provision of victuals for their homes; *Drofland*, for driving their Cattle to Fairs and Markets. **1848** WHARTON *Law Lex.*, Drift-land, Drofland, or Dryfland.

drog, *v.* Also 7 **droag**, 8 **drouge**. [? a back-form from DROGHER or F. *drogueur*.] *trans.* To carry in a drogher. Hence **'droging**, **'droghing**, the West Indian coasting trade; also *attrib.*

1681 *Treat. conc. E. India Trade* 4 To hope that ever we can cope with the Dutch in White Herring Fishing, Salt-droaging from St. Uvals to the East-Land, or the Russia or Greenland Trade. **1787** *Chron.* in *Ann. Reg.* 222 All the drouging vessels belonging to the island. **1805** *Naval Chron.* XIII. 6 I employed myself in drogging sugar.

drog, -arie: see DROGUE, DRUG, DRUGGERY.

droga, droger: see DAROGA.

droga-, drog(e)-, drogerman, obs. forms of DRAGOMAN.

drogat(t, drog(g)itt, obs. ff. DRUGGET.

droger, drogger, var. of DROGHER.

drogge, obs. form of DRUG.

drogh, obs. dial. f. THROUGH.

c **1425** *Eng. Conq. Irel.* lf. 4 b, Both drogh right and trowth.

drogh, droȝ, droȝghe, obs. pa. t. of DRAW *v.*

droghen, droȝen, obs. pa. pple. of DREE.

drogher ('drəʊgə(r)). Also 8–9 **drogger**, 9 **droger**, **droguer**. [a. obs. F. *drogueur* (1525 in Jal and Godef.) 'a ship which fished and dried herring and mackerel' (Jal), f. 16th c. Du. *drogher*, *drogher*, Du. *drooger*, a dryer, f. *droogen* to dry. Cf. F. *droguerie*, Du. *droogerij*, drying-place: 'ce terme se dit de la pêche et de la préparation du hareng' (Aubin 1702 in Jal).] A West Indian coasting vessel; hence transferred to other slow clumsy coasting craft.

[**1756** see DROVER 2 ¶.] **1782** *Ann. Reg.* 279/2 If they are not employed in droghers.. means shall be furnished them to depart for the neutral islands. **1790** *Phil. Trans.* LXXX. 346 Droghers, or vessels employed in carrying stores, &c. from one part of the island [Grenada] to another. **1805** *Naval Chron.* XIII. 6 A drogger is a Shallop, or Schooner, employed to convey sugar from the Plantations to the Merchantmen. *Ibid.* XIV. 73 Disguising her as a Droger.

1836 E. HOWARD *R. Reefer* xxxiv, This drogher..was a large, half-decked, cutter-rigged vessel. **1860** BARTLETT *Dict. Amer.*, *Droger* or *Drogher*..built solely for burden, and for transporting cotton, lumber, and other heavy articles.

b. *attrib.* and *Comb.*, as ***drogher-man, system.***

1873 GARDNER *Hist. Jamaica* 330 Trade..done on what is still known as the drogger system. **1889** J. J. THOMAS *Froudacity* 179 Engage the..droghermen as able seamen.

droghing: see DROG *v.*

droght(e, droȝt(e, droȝþe, obs. ff. DROUGHT.

drogoman, drogueman, varr. of DRAGOMAN.

drogue (drəʊg). Forms: 8 drug, 9 drugg, drog, dro(u)gue. [perh. orig. *drug*, var. of DRAG *sb.*, the form *drogue* arising through assimilation to *drogue*, obs. and Sc. form of DRUG *sb.*[1]]

1. *Whale-fishing.* A contrivance attached to the end of a harpoon line to check the progress of a whale when running or sounding.

A simple form consists of a piece of stout board, 12 or 14 inches square; another consists of a small wooden tub, with its concavity in the direction of the whale.

1725 DUDLEY in *Phil. Trans.* XXXIII. 263 Sometimes they will get away after they have been lanced..with Irons in them, and Drugs fastened to them, which are thick Boards about fourteen Inches square. **1858** SIMMONDS *Dict. Trade*, *Drog*, a name given in Scotland to a buoy attached to the end of a harpoon line. **1875** KINGSTON *South Sea Whaler* iii. 79 The first mate was on the point of heaving his own line overboard with a drougue fastened to it.

2. *Naut.* A hooped canvas bag towed at the stern of a boat to prevent it from broaching to.

1875 BEDFORD *Sailor's Pocket Bk.* vi. (ed. 2) 220 Towing astern a pig of ballast..or canvas bag termed a 'drogue' or drag..to hold the boat's stern back, and prevent her being turned broadside to the sea or broaching-to. **1878** *Boston Mercury* 8 June, They are provided with a novel kind of anchor (the drogue). It is a large canvas barrel-shaped bag, attached to fifty fathoms of rope. **1888** *Scott. Leader* 29 Nov. 7 The first breaker lifted the boat on her end, while the second, driving the drogue forward, slacked the rope, when the boat broached to.

3. *Aeronaut.* A truncated cone of fabric with a hoop at the larger end, used for various purposes: (*a*) a brake or anchor for aircraft, esp. seaplanes (see quot. 1919); (*b*) such a cone towed behind an aircraft as a target for gunnery practice; (*c*) a *wind-cone*; (*d*) an auxiliary braking parachute in an ejection-seat mechanism; (*e*) part of an aircraft-refuelling device (see quots. 1949 and 1966); (*f*) (see quot. 1962[1]). Also *attrib.*

1919 W. B. FARADAY *Gloss. Aeronaut. Terms* 59 *Drogue*, a fabric bag arranged to tow with its mouth open, thereby resisting passage through the water. **1931** *Flight* 13 Mar. 234/1 The manufacture of drogue targets. **1932** *Nuttall's Stand. Dict.* Suppl., *Drogue*, an open fabric bag used to show the direction of the wind at an aerodrome. **1933** *Flight* 29 June 628/1 The target is called a 'drogue' and is the same size as the fuselage of a 'Bulldog'. **1934** *Exmouth Jrnl.* 12 May 8/2 (Advt.), At every air port, you see it—the flyer's drogue. It points the right direction for air traffic to take when starting or landing. **1941** [see *air-to-air* adj. s.v. AIR *sb.*[1] B. III. 1]. **1947** *Times* 30 Aug. 2/1 The drogue steadied his upward rush, and eight seconds later the seat parachute opened. **1949** *Flight* 11 Aug. 177 The tanker aircraft trails a 65ft. fuel hose which terminates in a conical drogue. **1951** *Engineering* 30 Mar. 368/2 To..slow down the seat after ejection, a 2 ft. diameter drogue parachute..was employed. **1951** *Jrnl. Brit. Interplanetary Soc.* X. 300 The most efficient braking device is the parachute drag brake (also known as 'drogue chute' or 'parabrake'). **1962** J. GLENN et al. in *Into Orbit* 244 *Drogue*, a small parachute used to stabilize the descent of a spacecraft during re-entry. **1962** *Times* 21 Feb. 10/2 The drogue parachute opened to retard the capsule further and then the main parachute billowed out to lower Colonel Glenn into the sea. **1966** *New Scientist* 20 Jan. 142/1 Apparatus used [for refuelling a helicopter in flight] was of the standard kind—a drogue containing the cup at the end of the tanker's hose and a probe from the nose of the helicopter which is flown into the cup and locked there.

drogue, -ry, obs. and Sc. ff. DRUG, DRUGGERY.

drogulus ('drɒgjʊləs). [Coined 'on the spur of the moment' by A. J. Ayer perh. by subconscious association with DRAGON + L. *-ulus* as in DRACUNCULUS.] An entity whose presence is unverifiable, because it has no physical effects. Also *transf.*

1957 A. J. AYER in Edwards & Pap *Mod. Introd. Philos.* 608 Suppose I say 'There's a "drogulus" over there,' and you say 'What?' and I say 'Drogulus,' and you say 'What's a drogulus?' Well I say 'I can't describe what a drogulus is, because it's not the sort of thing you can see or touch, it has no physical effects of any kind, but it's a disembodied being.' **1959** L. S. PENROSE in *New Biol.* XXVIII. 98, I had difficulty in finding a suitable name for the activated complexes produced in these experiments. On showing one of them to Professor A. J. Ayer, I inquired whether it perhaps might be a 'drogulus'... He replied that it was undoubtedly a 'drogulus'.

droh, obs. pa. t. of DRAW *v.*

droich (droːx). *Sc.* Forms: 6 droiche, 7 droigh, 9 droich. [perh. a metathesis of *duerch, duergh*, or some similar form of DWARF; Gaelic has also *droich* from same source.] A dwarf.

1535 *Ld. Treas. Acc. Scot.* in Pitcairn *Crim. Trials* I. *285 To the Droiche, to lows his claithis fra the tailȝeouris. **1568** *Bannatyne MS.* lf. 173 (Jam.) Ane little Interlud, of the Droichis part of the Play. *a* **1605** MONTGOMERIE *Flyting w. Polwart* 70 Doe, droigh, what thou dow. **1818** MISS FERRIER *Marriage* II. 185 'The Englishwomen are all poor droichs,' said Nicky, who had seen three in..her life.

Hence **'droichy** *a.*, dwarfish.

1693 *Scot. Presbyt. Eloq.* (1738) 117 There was Zaccheus, a Man of a low Stature, that is, a little droichy Body.

droict, obs. form of DROIT[1].

droig, obs. var. of Sc. *drogue*, DRUG.

† **droil**, *sb. Obs.* Forms: (6 droyelle), 6–7 droyl(e, 7 droil(e. [The origin and mutual relations of this and the related DROIL *v.* are not clear. The sb. has been (very doubtfully) compared with Icel. *drjóli*, drone, sluggard. According to analogy (as well as dates), the vb. would be expected to be formed from the sb. in sense 1; the vb. however is possibly related to Du. *druilen* to loiter, slumber, in Kilian *druylen* 'suggredi, latenter siue clam ire', which answers for the form, but imperfectly for the sense. The word has prob. been influenced by *toil, moil*. Cf. also DROY.]

1. A servant of all work; a drudge.

1579 *Remedy agst. Love* Db, A bond man to his appetites, A drudge unto a droyelle. **1583** GOLDING *Calvin on Deut.* xcvi. 593 If his master would send him to the feeldes or vse him as a droyle in his house to doe whatsoeuer he had to be done. **1642** ROGERS *Naaman* 301 So they be faithfull droiles and drudges, they think more cannot be required. **1668** WILKINS *Real Char.* II. xi. §1. 264 Conditions of men.. Freeman..Slave..Bondman..Droyl, Drudge.

2. Drudgery; toil in disagreeable work.

1639 SHIRLEY *Gentl. Venice* I. ii, 'Tis I do all the droil, the dirt-work. **1645** QUARLES *Sol. Recant.* ii. 22 For what reward hath man of all his droyle.

† **droil**, *v. Obs.* Forms: 6–7 droyl(e, 7 droil(e, [goes with DROIL *sb.*, q.v.]

1. *intr.* To drudge, slave, toil in mean work.

1591 SPENSER *M. Hubberd* 157 Let such vile vassalls borne to base vocation Drudge in the world, and for their living droyle. **1635** QUARLES *Embl.* I. iii. (1718) 14 O who would droil, Or delve in such a soil! **1660** H. MORE *Myst. Godl.* v. xvii. 207 To make mill-horses of them, that they may the better droile and drudge for the satisfaction of their lusts.

2. *trans.* To subject to drudgery. *rare.*

1645 QUARLES *Sol. Recant.* i. 22 To what hopefull end Droyle we our crazy bodies?

Hence † **'droiling** *vbl. sb.* and *ppl. a.*

1607 HIERON *Wks.* I. 135 Moiling and droiling there is for the world without measure. **1641** MILTON *Reform.* I. (1851) 3 [The soul] left the dull and droyling carcas to plod on in the old rode, and drudging Trade of outward Conformity. **1674** *Govt. Tongue* ix. §13 The droiling pesant scarce thinks there is any world beyond his own village, or the neighboring markets.

droit[1] (drɔɪt, or as F., drwa). Also 5–6 droyt, 6 droict. [a. F. *droit*, earlier *dreit*:—late pop. L. **drēctum, drictum*:—L. *dīrēctum* straightened, straight, right, DIRECT; as sb. a straight or right line; in late L. right, legal right, law.]

1. a. A right; a legal claim to what is one's due; hence, that to which one has a legal claim; a due; *pl.* dues, duties, perquisites due by legal right.

Droits of Admiralty: certain rights or perquisites, as the proceeds arising from the seizure of enemies' ships, wrecks, etc., formerly belonging to the Court of Admiralty, but now paid into the Exchequer.

1481 CAXTON *Godeffroy* ccvi. 301 He sayde that they were the droytes and rightes of his chirche of the sepulcre. **1484** —— *Curiall* 8 The vertues of nature and the ryghtes and droytes of lyf humayne. **1528** SIR R. WESTON in Dillon *Calais & Pale* (1892) 92 Other casualtyes and droytes Royall belonging to the Seignorye. **1638** EARL STRAFFORD *Lett.* (1739) II. 206 As if the keeping of the Fort..had prejudiced him in the Droits of his Admiralty. **1816** KEATINGE *Trav.* (1817) II. 164 A difficulty experienced in collecting the droits or duties exacted. **1861** MAY *Const. Hist.* (1863) I. iv. 198 George III derived a considerable amount from the droits of the crown and Admiralty..and other casual sources of revenue. **1889** *Century Dict.* s.v., In American law droits of admiralty are not as such recognized.

b. ***droit(s) du*** (or ***de***) ***seigneur*** (‖drwa dy seɲœr), an alleged custom of mediæval times by which the feudal lord might have sexual intercourse with the bride of a vassal on the wedding-night, before she cohabited with her husband. Also *transf.*

[**1784** 'F. G. DESFONTAINES' (*title*) Le Droit du Seigneur. Comédie en trois actes,..mêlée d'ariettes.] **1825** H. WILSON *Mem.* III. 168 Lord Frederic Beauclerc..declares himself willing to..marry us, privately, by special licence, provided you agree to grant him les droits du seigneur. Worcester enquired what that meant. Simply, les droits du mari, for the first night. **1902** *Folk-Lore* XIII. 334 The final incident of the Wooing of Emer, proving as it does the existence of the *droit du Seigneur* among the early Irish. **1931** E. A. ROBERTSON *Four Frightened People* v. 147 The privilege, if anyone's, will be mine as the instigator of the expedition... A sort of local *droit de seigneur*. **1936** 'G. ORWELL' *Keep Aspidistra Flying* ii. 45 She exercised a sort of droit du seigneur over letters. **1961** A. WILSON *Old Men at Zoo* viii. 343 And as to your wife,..exercise the *droit de seigneur*. You're her lord and master.

† **2.** Law, right, justice; a law. *Obs.*

1480 CAXTON *Ovid's Met.* x. vii, My fader..knoweth the lawes & droytes. **1481** —— *Myrr.* I. ix. 35 The droytes and lawes by which the jugements be made. **1483** —— *Cato* C viij, It is founde in droyt canon. —— *Gold. Leg.* 175b/1 To lerne the Scyence of droyt and of the lawe. **1535–6** *Act 27 Hen. VIII*, c. 26 Preamb., The Domynyon..of Wales ..[whereof] the Kinges moost Roiall Magestie of mere droite and verye right is verie hedde King Lorde and Ruler.

3. *Comb.*, as **droit-house**, a building at a seaport for the collection of the droits of Admiralty; **droitsman**, the collector of droits.

1836 *Ann. Reg.* 31 Plaintiff was taken to the droit-house at the end of the pier. **1866** BLACKMORE *Cradock Nowell* xxxiii, The Admiralty droitsmen made an accurate inventory of the bungs and blacking bottles.

† **droit**[2]. *Obs.* [Origin unascertained.] A minute weight; the four hundred and eightieth part of a grain troy, one twenty-fourth of a 'mite'.

(Belonging to a series used in exact computations of weight of coins, before the introduction of decimals, the alternate subdivisions by 20 and 24 carrying out those of ounces and pennyweights. See *Notes & Queries* 8th S.X. 255, 278, 338.)

1601 ['Weight of Silver Coins 43 Eliz. 1601' given in 'dwt., gr., Mites, Droits, Perits, Blancs,' cited in J. MILLAN *Coins, Weights, & Meas.* 1749.] **1604** *Procl. Jas. I* in Ruding *Coinage of Gt. Brit.* 1840, I. 363. *a* **1606** *Mint & Moneta* (*MS.* in Royal Mint Lib.) iv. lf. 2, Note that..in 1 grain Subtill there are 20^ty Mites Subtill, and so further to Droites, to be devided if need shalbe. **1649** *Act Long Parlt.* c. 43 (Scobell II. 65). *Schedule or Table annexed*—Pieces of Gold: xx^s. 05 Penny weights. 20 Grains. 10 Mites.. Pieces of Silver:..1^d 00 Penny weights. 07 Grains. 14 Mites. 20 Droits. 02 Perits. 12 Blanks. —— *Memorandum*: Twelve Ounces makes a pound weight Troy;..Twenty Mites makes a Grain; Twenty four Droits makes a Mite; Twenty Perits makes a Droit; Twenty four Blanks makes a Perit. Passed 17 July. **1656** BLOUNT *Glossogr.* s.v. *Ounce.* **1658** PHILLIPS s.v. *Perit.* **1708–43** J. CHAMBERLAYNE *St. Gt. Brit.* 160. **1811** KELLY *Univ. Cambist*, The Droit of 20 Periots. **1858** SIMMONDS *Dict. Trade, Droit*, a division of the troy grain used by moneyers.

droitural ('drɔɪtjʊərəl), *a. Law.* [f. F. *droiture* (see next) + -AL[1].] Relating to a right to property, as distinguished from possession.

1850 BURRILL cited in WEBSTER. **1875** POSTE *Gaius* II. Comm. (ed. 2) 191 He might recover it for future presentations by droitural writ of right of advowson. *Ibid.* IV. 649 The old division of Real actions in English law into Possessory and Droitural.

† **'droiture.** *Obs. rare.* [a. F. *droiture* straightness, rightness:—late pop. L. **drēctūra-m*:—L. *dīrēctūra-m* a making straight (Vitruv.), f. ppl. stem of *dīrigĕre* to straighten, DIRECT.] Uprightness.

1483 CAXTON *Gold. Leg.* 246/2 Therfor remayneth his droyture perdurably whyche he fulfilled wyth holy werke.

droke (drəʊk, drʊk). Also **droch, drogue, drook.** [Of uncertain origin: see *E.D.D.* s.v. DROCK *sb.*[2] and DROKE *sb.*] **a.** *W. Country dial.* and *Newfoundland.* A furrow or groove; a ditch, a small watercourse; a (steep) narrow passageway; also, a valley.

1772 G. CARTWRIGHT *Jrnl.* 28 Mar. (1792) I. 210, I then went over Lower Table to the Droke; where I observed much old slot of deer. **1848** *Jrnl. Newfoundland House of Assembly* App. 299 Job's Cove Droke [Western Bay]. **1880** M. A. COURTNEY *Gloss. Words Cornwall* 19/1 *Droke*, a wrinkle; a furrow; a passage. **1895** J. THOMAS *Randigal Rhymes* 6 A hoss, aw have got a great droke in his cheens [hindquarters]. **1907** N. DUNCAN *Cruise of Shining Light* 269 Across the droch, lifted high above the maid and me,.. stood John Cather. **1943** *N. & Q.* 25 Sept. 202/1 *Droke*, narrow lane or passage between walls. E. Hants. (In W. of Eng. merely a groove or trench.) **1971** E. R. SEARY *Place Names Avalon Peninsula of Newfoundland* viii. 146 In Newfoundland, Droke, Drook or Drogue seems to bear four meanings: a wooded, narrow valley; a belt or clump of trees; a narrow valley or gulch; a steep path.

b. *Newfoundland.* A belt, clump, or grove (of trees).

1822 W. WILSON *Newfoundland* (1866) xiii. 331 Here and there a 'droke' of woods. **1881** W. R. KENNEDY *Sporting Notes Newfoundland* (ed. 2) 92 The country hereabouts was marshy, with belts or 'drogues' of wood. **1907** J. G. MILLAIS *Newfoundland* i. 12 The men made a comfortable camp in a 'droke' (belt) of spruce close to the water. **1944** *Saturday Night* (Toronto) 22 Jan. 3/1 Ptarmigan sheltering in leafless drokes. **1980** *Evening Telegram* (St. John's, Newfoundland) 8 Nov. 6 The moose are driven from the tucks and drokes far back into the country into the thick woods.

droll (drəʊl), *sb.* Also 7 drolle, 7–8 drol(e. [a. F. *drôle* (1584 *drolle* in Hatz.-Darm.; in 16th c. also *draule*), orig. a sb. 'a good fellow, boone companion, merrie grig, pleasant wag; one that cares not which end goes forward, or how the world goes' (Cotgr.); subseq. also an adj., and so in Eng. The origin of the F. word is uncertain: see Diez, Littré, Darmesteter.]

1. A funny or waggish fellow; a merry-andrew, buffoon, jester, humorist.

c **1645** HOWELL *Lett.* I. I. xviii, The old Duke of Main.. was us'd to play the drol with him. *Ibid.* (1650) I. 438 Dr. Dale, who was a witty kind of drole. **1658** J. HARRINGTON *Prerog. Pop. Govt.* II. v. (1700) 374 Lucian is a Drol, and intends a Jest. **1665** PEPYS *Diary* 7 June, Very merry we were, Sir Thomas Harvy being a very drolle. *c* **1672** WOOD *Life* (Oxf. Hist. Soc.) I. 201 John Lamphire..who was sometimes the natural droll of the company. *a* **1680** BUTLER *Rem.* (1759) I. 102 The worst Drols of Punchinellos Were much th' ingeniouser Fellows. **1709** STEELE *Tatler* No. 9 ¶2

Mr. Scoggin, the famous Droll of the last Century. **1768–74** TUCKER *Lt. Nat.* (1852) I. 645 The frolic gamesome droll they have seen upon Covent Garden theatre. **1847** DISRAELI *Tancred* II. viii, Mrs. Coningsby was..a fascinating droll. **1873** BROWNING *Red Cott. Nt.-cap* 328 As for the droll there, he that plays the king And screws out smile with a red nightcap on.

†**2.** A comic or farcical composition or representation; a farce; an enacted piece of buffoonery; a puppet-show. *Obs.*

1649 G. DANIEL *Trinarch.* To Rdr. 8 The frequent heapes Of Braines, from the weake sun-shine of an Eye Work Maggotts out—short Drolls—scurrilitie. **1662** TATHAM *Aqua Tri.* Introd., There are two Drolls, one of Watermen, the other of Seamen. **1711** SHAFTESB. *Charac., Enthusiasm* (1749) I. 19 They are..the subject of a choice Droll or Puppet-show at Bart'lemy Fair. **1731** MEDLEY *Kolben's Cape G. Hope* I. 10 The crew, to divert themselves, acted several Drolls. **1818** TODD, *Drollery*..2. A show; the old word for the present drolls exhibited at fairs.

†**b.** The acting of farces. *Obs.*

1817 D. HUGHSON *Walks thro' Lond.* 194 A house of public exhibition in horsemanship and droll.

†**3.** The action of making jest or sport; jesting; burlesque writing or style. *Obs.*

1670 G. H. *Hist. Cardinals* I. I. 13 The whole Sermon being but a drol and derision of Kings and their Ministers. **1698** [R. FERGUSON] *View Eccles.* Pref., To turn everything he writes of into Droll and Laughter. **1711** tr. *Werenfels' Disc. Logomachys* 164 The ridiculous Mockery and Drolls of the Vulgar. **1842** H. ROGERS *Ess.* I. i. 35 A pretty story..that affords scope for clinch and droll.

4. *attrib.* and *Comb.*, as †*droll-booth, -house*, a place where drolls were acted (*obs.*); *droll-teller.*

1706 E. WARD *Hud. Rediv.* I. viii, Like Smith-field Droll-Booth, built with Wood. **1738** WATTS *Holiness of Times* iii. Wks. 1812 III. 579 Should the senate-house..be used for a theatre or droll-house, or for idle puppet-shows. **1866** *Sat. Rev.* 11 Aug. 186/1 The droll-teller still went his rounds from hall to cottage.

droll, *a.* [f. F. *drôle*: see prec. sb.]

1. Intentionally facetious, amusing, comical, funny. †*droll painting*, caricature; *d. painter*, caricaturist.

1623 JAS. I in *Four C. Eng. Lett.* 45, I heartily thank thee for thy kind droll letter. **1756–82** J. WARTON *Ess. Pope* (ed. 4) I. ii. 51 Landschape-painting..being even preferred to single portraits, to pieces of still-life, to droll-figures. **1762–71** H. WALPOLE *Vertue's Anecd. Paint.* (1786) III. 45 Daniel Boon, Of the same country, a droll painter. **1789** BELSHAM *Ess.* I. x. 202 The droll inventions of Hogarth. **1858** LYTTON *What will He do* I. xii, He was a droll and joyous humourist. **1861** WRIGHT *Ess. Archæol.* II. xxiii. 230 Everybody has a perception of what is droll and ludicrous.

2. Unintentionally amusing; queer, quaint, odd, strange, 'funny'.

1753 MELMOTH *Cicero* IV. ix. (R.) Imitating the droll figures those gallant youths exhibited. **1790** BURNS *Tam O'Shanter* 159 Wither'd beldams, auld and droll. **1822** SCOTT *Let.* in Taylor & Raine *Mem. Surtees* (1852) 164, I have built a droll sort of house here..a pretty, though somewhat fantastical residence. *a* **1876** G. DAWSON *Biog. Lect.* (1886) 94 Charles the Second certainly was the drollest idol ever nation set up.

Hence **'drollity,** the quality of being droll; *concr.* a droll thing; **'drollness.**

1639 DAVENANT *Salmacida Spolia* Dram. Wks. 1872 II. 317 Four Grotesques or drollities. **1823** F. CLISSOLD *Ascent Mt. Blanc* (1825) 10 Excited, as he said, by the drollness of the scene. **1885** *Library Mag.* (N.Y.) July 4 The ground-cuckoo is an embodiment of drollness and absurdity.

droll, *v.* Also 7 drol, 7–8 drole. [a. obs. F. *drôler* 'to play the wag', etc. (Cotgr.), f. *drôle* sb.]

1. *intr.* To make sport or fun; to jest, joke; to play the buffoon. Const. *with, at, on, upon.*

1654 WHITELOCKE *Jrnl. Swed. Emb.* (1772) I. 130 Whitelocke drolled with them. **1665** EARL MARLEBURGH *Fair Warnings* 19 There was no greater argument of a foolish and inconsiderate person, than profanely to droll at Religion. *a* **1678** MARVELL *Wks.* III. 333 (R.) As Killegrew buffons his master, they droll on their God, but a much duller way. **1680** *Vind. Conforming Clergy* (ed. 2) 32 An Author..that drolls with every thing. **1739** MELMOTH *Fitzosb. Lett.* (1763) 227 To drole upon the established religion of a country. **1784** COWPER *Task* II. 369 He doubtless is in sport, and does but droll. **1894** R. BRIDGES *Feast of Bacchus* v. 1428 To droll on a private person.

2. *trans.* To jest (a thing) *away, off*; †to jest (a person) *out of* or *into* something (*obs.*); to bring *forth* after the manner of a jester or buffoon.

1663 R. STAPYLTON *Slighted Maid* 7 (N.) He would scarce droll away the sum he offer'd. **1679** SHARP *Serm. at St. Margarets* 11 Apr. 11 To Baffle and Droll out of Countenance those that stand up for the Reputation of Sacred things. *a* **1704** R. L'ESTRANGE (J.), Men that will not be reasoned into their senses, may yet be laughed or drolled into them. **1834** *Tait's Mag.* I. 57 The Mulgraves and Masseys..might have drolled and drivelled forth their sickening imbecility for half a century.

Hence **'drolling** *vbl. sb.* and *ppl. a.*; also **'drollingly** *adv.*; jestingly, so as to make a jest of it; †**'droller,** †**'drollist,** a professed facetious person; a jester, buffoon.

1645 EVELYN *Diary* 20 Feb., Their drolling lampoons and scurrilous papers. **1670** G. H. *Hist. Cardinals* I. I. 19 [They] use but drolling and impertinence in their Arguments. **1676** GLANVILL *Season. Refl.* i. 5 And..now he.. sets the Apes and Drollers upon it. **1681** —— *Sadducismus* II. (1726) 453 These idle Drollists have an utter Antipathy to all the braver and more generous Kinds of Knowledge. **1684** J. GOODMAN *Winter Even. Confer.* P j. (T.), To talk lightly and drollingly of it. *a* **1713** ELLWOOD *Autobiog.* (1765) 284 Something like an Epitaph, in a drolling Stile. **1847** W. IRVING 14 Apr. in *Life* IV. 3 A quiet drolling vein. **1882** TROLLOPE *Alice Dugdale, etc.* 357 There was a sound of drolling in her voice.

drollery ('drəʊlərı). Also 7 drol(l)erie, drolrie (drawlerie, drallery). [a. F. *drôlerie* (1584 in Hatz.-Darm.; also *draulerie* in Cotgr.), f. *drôle*: see -ERY.]

1. The action of a droll; waggery, jesting.

1653–4 WHITELOCKE *Jrnl. Swed. Emb.* (1772) I. 279 So they parted in much drollerye. **1681** GLANVILL *Sadducismus* II. (1726) 449 An affected humour of Drollery and Scoffing. **1743** J. MORRIS *Serm.* vi. 202 Better..than to make it the subject of their jests and drollery. **1828** CARLYLE *Misc. Ess., Burns* (1872) II. 22 This [faculty of caricature] is Drollery rather than Humour. **1873** SYMONDS *Grk. Poets* iv. 109 A humour for drollery and sarcasm.

2. Something humorous or funny: †**a.** A comic play or entertainment; a puppet-show; a puppet.

1610 SHAKS. *Temp.* III. iii. 21 What were these? A liuing Drolerie. **1614** B. JONSON *Barth. Fair* Induct., Those that beget tales, tempests, and such like drolleries. **1621** FLETCHER *Wild Goose Chase* I. ii, Our women the best linguists; they are parrots; O' this side the Alps they're nothing but mere drolleries. **1847** DISRAELI *Tancred* II. xiii, A land that has never been blessed by that fatal drollery called a representative government.

†**b.** A comic picture or drawing; a caricature.

1597 SHAKS. *2 Hen. IV*, II. i. 156 For thy walles, a pretty slight Drollery..is worth a thousand of these Bed-hangings. **1606** DEKKER *Sev. Sinnes* Ded., A Drollerie (or Dutch peece of Lantskop) may sometimes breed in the beholders eye, as much delectation, as the best and most curious master-peece excellent in that Art. **1641** EVELYN *Diary* 13 Aug., We arrived late at Roterdam, where was their annual marte or faire, so furnished with pictures (especially Landskips and Drolleries, as they call those clounish representations) that [etc.]. **1888** F. T. PALGRAVE in *19th Cent.* Jan. 85 [Dutch] pictures..were not classed in the range of serious work; they bore commonly the significant name of *Drolleries.*

c. A jest; a facetious story or tale.

1654 GAYTON *Pleas. Notes* IV. i. 170 Let it be if you please a Drawlery upon it. **1660** F. BROOKE tr. *Le Blanc's Trav.* 121 The King is very much pleased with such Fictions and Drolleries. **1871** R. ELLIS *Catullus* l. 4 Scribbling drolleries each of us together.

3. The quality of being droll; quaint humour.

1742 WEST *Let.* in *Gray's Poems* (1775) 143 Old words revived..add a certain drollery to the comic, and a romantic gravity to the serious. **1856** MACAULAY *Goldsm.* Misc. Writ. 1860 II. 255 The rich drollery of 'She Stoops to Conquer'.

Hence **dro'llerical** *a. nonce-wd.*, comical.

1656 S. HOLLAND *Zara* (1719) 15 This Drollerical Poem mightily augmented our Champion's Mirth.

drollic, *a. rare.* [f. DROLL *sb.* + -IC.] Of or pertaining to a droll or puppet-show.

1743 FIELDING *J. Wild* II. iii. (D.), At the fair of Bartholomew..Thalestris, Queen of the Amazons, Anna Bullen, Queen Elizabeth, or some other high princess in drollic story.

drollish ('drəʊlɪʃ), *a.* Somewhat droll.

1674 tr. *Scheffer's Lapland* xxiv. 108 Imposing drollish nick-names upon them. **1759** STERNE *Tr. Shandy* II. xii, A drollish and witty kind of peevishness.

drolly ('drəʊllı), *adv.* [f. DROLL *a.* + -LY[2].] In a droll manner; funnily; quaintly, oddly.

1662 PEPYS *Diary* 5 Nov., Jane..did answer me so humbly and drolly about it. **1791** BOSWELL *Johnson* 17 May an. 1775, Tom Davies described it [Johnson's laugh] drolly enough: 'He laughs like a rhinoceros'. *a* **1864** HAWTHORNE *Amer. Note-Bks.* (1879) II. 43 A tone of voice having a drolly pathetic..sound. **1880** OUIDA *Moths* II. 59 Things manage themselves drolly.

drom, obs. form of DRUM.

dromæognathous (ˌdrɒmiːˈɒgnəθəs), *a. Ornith.* [f. *Dromæus* generic name of the emeu, (ad. Gr. δρομαῖος swift-running) + γνάθος jaw: see -OUS.] Having the bones of the palate arranged as in the emu and its allies. Hence **dromæ'ognathism,** the arrangement of the palate-bone in this particular manner.

1867 HUXLEY *Classif. Birds* in *Proc. Zool. Soc.* 425 The Dromæognathous birds are represented by the single genus *Tinamus*, which has a completely struthious palate. **1875** PARKER in *Encycl. Brit.* III. 711/1 (Birds) That low kind of skull which is called 'Dromæognathous' best seen in *Dromæus* the Emeu.

drombeslade, -byllsclad, var. of DRUMSLADE *Obs.*, a drum.

drome (drəʊm). †**1.** Colloq. abbrev. of AERODROME 1. *Obs.*

1908 *Bull. Aerial Exper. Assoc. Beinn Breagh* (Nova Scotia) 30 Nov. [Contents page], Description of Drome No. 4, McCurdy's Silver Dart. **1909** *Times* 29 Mar. 8/5 The nation which possesses the best dromes will obtain.. supremacy in the air.

2. (Also *'drome.*) Colloq. abbrev. of AERODROME 2 b.

1913 in WEBSTER Add. **1915** H. ROSHER *In R.N.A.S.* (1916) xi. 41, I crashed into the atmosphere first thing this morning and flipped around for 55 minutes. By then I was as cold as——, so pitched in the 'drome. **1917** *Chambers's Jrnl.* Oct. 695/2 At the end of the drome she [*sc.* an aircraft] turns into the wind. **1930** *Flight* 27 June 714/1 Meanwhile a number of aircraft had arrived at the 'drome, some having flown from various part[s] of the country the previous day. **1940** [see BEAT-UP *sb.* and *a.*]. **1942** 'B. J. ELLAN' *Spitfire* p. ix, The aerodrome..is occasionally referred to as *the drome.*

-drome (drəʊm), combining form representing Gr. δρόμος course, racecourse, identical with δρόμος running, rel. to δραμεῖν to run, as in (*a*) AERODROME 2, HIPPODROME, LOXODROME, PERIDROME; (*b*) AERODROME 1, PALINDROME. Cf. also SYNDROME.

†**'dromed, -e.** *Obs.* [ad. late L. *dromeda*, f. class. L. *dromas, dromad-em.*] = DROMEDARY.

['*Dromeda*, quoddam genus camelorum, minoris quidem staturæ, sed velocioris' (J. de Janua in Du Cange); 'dromeda, & dromas & dromedarius, idem animal est minus camelo, sed velocius'. (*Gloss. Camberonense* in Du C.)]

c **1380** WYCLIF *Serm.* Sel. Wks. I. 340 þei camen upon dromedis. **1388** —— *Isa.* lx. 6 The lederis of dromedis [**1382** dromedaries] of Madian and Effa. **1398** TREVISA *Barth. De P.R.* XVIII. xxxvi. (1495) 797 Dromedarius is an heirde and keper of Dromedes. *c* **1410** LOVE *Bonavent. Mirr.* viii. (Sherard MS.), The dromedes þat they riden vpon. **1572** BOSSEWELL *Armorie* II. 58, G. beareth sable, a Dromede passante d'Or, gesante a branche of the Date tree propre.

dromedary ('drʌm-, 'drɒmɪdərı). Also 4–6 dromodarye, -ie (dromounday), 5 dromadayr, dromyder, drowmondere, dromond-, dromydary, (drombodary), 5–7 dromadary, 6 dromedare, -der, dromun-, drumbledary, drummi-, dromeldory, 7 dromidore, dromderrie, dromidary. [ad. OF. *dromedaire* (mod.F. *dromadaire*), late L. *dromedārius* (Vulgate, Isa. lx. 6) for **dromadārius* (sc. *camēlus*), f. *dromas, dromad-em* dromedary, a. Gr. δρομάς, δρομάδα, running, runner + Lat. suffix *-ārius*: see -ARY[1]. The *drumble-, dromel-* forms are due to popular association with vernacular words in DRUMBLE-, q.v.]

1. A light and fleet breed of the camel, specially reared and trained for riding. See CAMEL *sb.*

Usually of the Arabian or one-humped camel, but the Bactrian camel may also be improved into a Dromedary.

13.. *K. Alis.* 3407 Olifans and camailes, Dromedaries. **1382** [see prec.]. *c* **1400** *Destr. Troy* 6207 Two dromondarys drowe hit [a chariot], dressit þerfore. *c* **1400** tr. *Secreta Secret., Gov. Lordsh.* (E.E.T.S.) 111 Right swyft as dromyders. *c* **1425** *Voc.* in Wr.-Wülcker 638 *Hic dromedarius*, a drowmondere. *c* **1500** *Melusine* xxxvi. 274 Thenne came a trucheman mounted vpon a dromadary. **1570** LEVINS *Manip.* 104 A Drumbledary, *dromedarius.* **1596** SPENSER *F.Q.* IV. viii. 38 Ryding upon a Dromedare on hie, Of stature huge, and horrible of hew. **1632** LITHGOW *Trav.* VI. 298 A Dromidore, and Camel differ much in quality, but not in quantity, being of one height, bredth, and length.. the Dromidory..will ride above 80 miles in the day. **1708** MOTTEUX *Rabelais* IV. lxv, The Camels and Dromedaries of a Caravan. **1839** THIRLWALL *Greece* VI. lii. 271 Mounted on dromedaries, they crossed the desert.

†**2.** = DROMOND. *Obs.*

[Late L. had *dromeda* also as the name of a sailing vessel: 'Lembus est genus naviculæ quas Dromedas dicimus', Fulgentius, *Super Serm. Antiq.* (*c* 550).]

? *c* **1475** *Sqr. lowe Degre* 818 With lxxx shippes of large towre, With dromedarys of great honour. **1520** [see DROMOND]. **1568** C. WATSON *Polyb.* 66 b, They looked for taking certaine of their dromundaries, costed into a creek adjoining.

†**3.** A stupid, bungling fellow. *Obs.* Cf. DRUMBLE-DORE.

1567 DRANT *Horace Epist.* B ij, Because Democrites iudgd art to be more base then witte, Therefore those drummidories seeke so sleightlie after it. **1597** *Pilgr. Parnass.* II. 217 An old Stigmatick, an ould sober Dromeder. **1632** MASSINGER & FIELD *Fatal Dowry* II. ii, A soulless dromedary! *a* **1700** B. E. *Dict. Cant. Crew, Dromedary*, a Thief or Rogue..You are a purple Dromedary..You are a Bungler or a dull Fellow at thieving. **1785** in GROSE.

4. *attrib.*, as *dromedary camel, corps, hump.*

1553 BRENDE *Q. Curtius* v. 76 Dromedarye Camels that were wonderful swift. **1579–80** NORTH *Plutarch* (1676) 572 [He] had escaped..flying upon a Dromedary-Cammel. **1844** H. H. WILSON *Brit. India* II. 301 He moved against them with the third cavalry, the dromedary corps, and two companies of infantry. **1880** BLACKMORE *M. Anerley* xli, The dromedary humps of certain hills.

Hence (*nonce-wds.*) **drome'darian** *a.*, of the nature of a dromedary; *sb.*, a rider on a dromedary; also **'dromedarist.**

1706 E. WARD *Hud. Reviv.* I. xvii, On his Dromedarian Brute. **1849** LANE *Mod. Egypt.* II. ix. 135 Mohhammad Ibn Kamil the Dromedarist. **1877** *Daily Tel.* 7 Nov., Ridden by dromedarians in Egyptian costume.

dromic ('drɒmɪk), *a.* [ad. Gr. δρομικός, f. δρόμος course, race-course.] Of, pertaining to, or of the form of a race-course; applied to the basilican type of Eastern churches from its resemblance to the plan of a race-course. So also **'dromical.**

1850 NEALE *East. Ch.* I. II. i. 170 There are many [Eastern churches] of the kind called *dromic*, or *basilican*, which exhibit the early Western arrangement. **1875** *Encycl. Brit.* III. 418/2 The basilican form, or, as it was then termed, *dromical*, from its shape being that of a race-course. **1890** HUXLEY in *19th Cent.* Nov. 770 Such megalithic edifices as the dromic vaults of Maes How and New Grange.

dromioid ('drɒmɪɔɪd), *a.* (*sb.*) [f. mod.L. *Dromia* a genus of crustaceans: see -OID.] Having the form of a *Dromia*, a genus of

Anomourous Crustacea, closely allied to the true crabs. **b.** *sb.* A crustacean of this genus.

1852 DANA *Crust.* I. 50 The genus Trichia..is a transition genus between the Parthenopinea and the Dromioids. *Ibid.* 53 Three distinct grades of degradation..—i.e., the Dromioid, the Lithodioid, and the Paguroid.

dromler: see DRUMBLER.

'dromograph. [f. Gr. δρόμος course + -GRAPH.] An instrument for measuring the velocity of the blood current. Also *attrib.*

1883 in *Syd. Soc. Lex.* **1885** LANDOIS & STIRLING *Hum. Physiol.* I. 181 The dromograph curve..shews the primary elevation..and the dicrotic elevation.

Hence **dromo'graphic** *a.*

1883 *Syd. Soc. Lex., Dromographic curve*, the tracing obtained by the dromographic indicator.

dromomania (drɒmə'meɪnɪə). [f. Gr. δρόμος running: see -MANIA.] A mania for roaming or running. Hence **dromo'maniac**, one who has such a mania; (*joc.* or *slang*) an athlete.

1900 DORLAND *Med. Dict.*, Dromomania. **1907** W. JAMES in *Philos. Review* XVI. 8 Hitherto such freaks of impulse have received Greek names (as bulimia, dromamania, etc.). **1934** R. CAMPBELL *Broken Record* viii. 201 Account for a great athlete or a great poet by translating him..into..Greek..as a dromomaniac or a graphomaniac. **1967** *Listener* 30 Nov. 714/2 The American hobo, tramp, bum, vagrant, transient and dromomaniac.

dro'mometer. [f. Gr. δρόμο-ς course: see -METER.] A measurer of speed; a pocket instrument, serving to check the indications of the dromoscope.

1881 *Nature* XXIV. 225 Colonel Leboulangé will exhibit his ingenious dromometer and dromoscope for controlling the velocity of trains.

So **dro'mometry**, the measurement of velocity.

1685 PETTY in *Phil. Trans.* XVII. 658 Dromometry, and the Measures of a Ships Motions at Sea.

dromond ('drɒmənd, 'drʌmənd). *Hist.* and *arch.* Also 4–5 **dromon, dromoun, dromonde, drowmound, dromund,** 5–6 **dromounde.** [a. OF. *dromon, dromont*, AF. *dromund, -unt*, (in Cotgr. *dromant*), ad. late L. *dromōn-em*, a. Byz. Gr. δρόμων large vessel propelled by many oars, f. δρόμος racing, course.] A very large mediæval ship; according to Jal, 'a great vessel of the class of long ships'. Used both in war and commerce. In more ancient times it is said to have been 'a ship with rowers, having a single sail'.

13.. *Guy W.* (A.) 2802 A dromond he seye arïueing. **13..** *Coer de L.* 2459 The drowmound was so hevy fraught, That unethe myght it saylen aught. **13..** *K. Alis.* 90 How he scholde his fomen quelle..That comen by schip other dromouns. **1436** *Pol. Poems* (Rolls) II. 199 Whan at Hampton he made the grete dromons, Which passed other grete shippes of alle the comons. **1480** CAXTON *Chron. Eng.* cxciv. 171 He and his companye robbed two dromondes [*ed.* **1520** dromedaryes] besyde sandwyche. **1557** *K. Arthur* (Copland) v. iii, A great multytude of shyppes, galees, cogges and dromoundes. **1611** SPEED *Hist. Gt. Brit.* IX. vii. 30 A mightie Argosey, called a Dromond. **1828** SCOTT *F.M. Perth* viii, I have got the sternpost of a dromond brought up the river from Dundee. **1849** J. STERLING in *Fraser's Mag.* XXXIX. 171 Dromonds huge deep-weighed with plenteousness. **1868** MORRIS *Earthly Par.* I. Prol. 8 The great dromond swinging from the quay.

‖**Dromornis** (drəʊ'mɔːnɪs). Also **Dromæornis.** [f. δρόμος course, race, or mod.L. *Dromæus* emu + ὄρνις bird.] A genus of extinct Australian ratite birds allied to the Emu.

1872 OWEN in *Proc. Zool. Soc.* 682. **1895** C. DIXON in *Fortn. Rev.* Apr. 642 Among extinct types..we have the Dromornis of Australia, the Æpyornis of Madagascar.

‖**dromos** ('drɒmɒs). *Archæol.* [Gr. δρόμος race-course, avenue, f. vbl. stem δρεμ- to run.] An avenue or entrance-passage to a temple or other building, often as in Ancient Egypt between rows of columns or statues.

1850 LEITCH *Müller's Anc. Art* §220. 217 Alleys of colossal rams or sphinxes form the approach or dromos. **1889** C. D. BELL *Winter on Nile* vi. 57 A populous city with its palaces and temples and dromos of sphinxes. **1896** *Academy* 18 July 54/2 The tholoi with their entrance passages or dromoi excavated in the indurated clay of the hillside were..of good Mycenaean period.

dromoscope ('drɒməskəʊp). [mod. f. Gr. δρόμος running, course + -SCOPE.] An instrument to indicate the course of a ship; also, to indicate the velocity of a train or other vehicle.

1875 *Chamb. Jrnl.* No. 133. 79 The 'universal dromoscope', for correcting the course of a ship. **1876** *Catal. Sci. App. S. Kens.* §3131 *Dromoscope.* By means of this instrument the deviation of the compass, either of the course or azimuth, is indicated merely by stopping the hand. **1881** [see DROMOMETER].

dromotropic (drɒmə'trɒpɪk), *a.* [f. Gr. δρόμος running + τροπικός (see TROPIC *a.* 4).] †**a.** *Bot.* (See quot. 1890.) *Obs.* **b.** *Physiol.* [a. F. *dromotrope* (T. W. Engelmann 1901, in *Arch. Néerland. des Sci. exactes et nat.* 2nd Ser. VI. 690).] Affecting the conduction of nervous impulses through muscles of the heart. So **dro'motropism** (*rare*).

1890 C. MACMILLAN in *Amer. Naturalist* XXIV. 367 It is proposed to term the motion of twining plants—so far as that motion is the result of the specific irritability—dromotropism, and we can then speak of such twining shoots as dromotropic. **1902** *Encycl. Brit.* XXXI. 733/2 The centrifugal cardiac nerves influence the frequency, the force of contraction, and the conductivity of the excitatory wave (chrono-, ino-, and dromo-tropism of Engelmann). **1906** J. R. MURLIN tr. *Tigerstedt's Textbk. Human Physiol.* vi. 189 Engelmann describes these effects of vagus excitation as..negatively *dromotropic* (diminishing the conductivity). **1942** *Index-Catal. Libr. Surg. Gen.* 4th Ser. VII. 347/2 (*heading*) Heart nerves... Dromotropic action. **1968** DAVSON & EGGLETON *Princ. Human Physiol.* (ed. 14) vii. 169 The vagi may diminish the conduction of the excitatory process from atria to ventricles and to all parts of the ventricles (dromotropic effect).

dromslade, -slet, var. of DRUMSLADE, *Obs.*

dron, drone, obs. forms of DROWN.

'dronage. [f. DRONE *sb.*[1] + -AGE. Cf. DOTAGE.] The condition of a drone.

1846 LD. COCKBURN *Let.* in *Blackie's Biog.* x. (1895) 232 We only aggravate the drone-age of the drones. **1875** JOWETT *Plato* (ed. 2) III. 103 Many a man..is reduced into a state of dronage by him [the usurer].

drone (drəʊn), *sb.*[1] Forms: α. 1 **dran, dræn,** 2–6 (*s.w. dial.* 7–9) **drane** (6 **drayne,** 6–7 **dran**); β. ? 3 **dro(n),** 5– **drone** (6 **dron, drowne,** 6–7 **droane**). [OE. *dran, dræn* (? *drán, dræ̋n*). Cf. OS., pl. *drani* (? *drâni*), MLG. *drâne, drône*, E.Fris. *drâne*, LG. *drône*, whence mod.Ger. *drohne.* Also OHG. *treno*, MHG. *trene, tren* (Maaler 1561 *trän*), mod.HG. dial. *trehne, trene* 'drone'.

The etymological relations of these forms are difficult to make out, esp. in our ignorance whether the vowel in OE. and OS. was *a* or *â*. A short *a* would bring the OE. and OS. words together, and put both in ablaut relation to OHG. *treno*, from an ablaut series *dren- dran- drun-*, with primary sense 'to resound, boom', whence also ON. *drynja*, and mod.G. *dröhnen* (see DROUN *v.*). But an OE. *á* (:—*ai*) would not belong to the same ablaut series as OS. *á* (:—*ê*). An OE. str. fem. *dran, drane*, would regularly give ME. and mod. s.w. dial. *drane*; but it leaves unexplained the mod. *drone* (found chiefly since 1483, but app. indicated by *dro-*, in a mutilated (?) 12th c. MS. glossary, Wr.-Wülcker 543/8). On the other hand, neither are the facts explained by an OE. *drán*, since this would have given ME. *dron, droon*, mod. *drone*, Sc. *drane*; for *drane* was the ordinary ME., and is now a southern Eng., not a Sc. form.]

1. The male of the honey-bee. It is a non-worker, its function being to impregnate the queen-bee.

α. *c* **1000** ÆLFRIC *Voc.* in Wr.-Wülcker 121/10 *Fucus*, dran. *a* **1100** *Ags. Voc.* Ibid. 318/35 *Fucus*, dræn. *a* **1131** *O.E. Chron.* an. 1127, Swa drane doth in hiue. *c* **1394** *P. Pl. Crede* 726 As dranes doþ nouȝt but drynkeþ vp þe huny. *c* **1440** CAPGRAVE *Life St. Kath.* IV. 21 Dranes loue weel reste. **1531** ELYOT *Gov.* I. ii, If any drane or other unprofitable bee entreth in to the hyue. **1570** LEVINS *Manip.* 19/1 A Drane, bee, *fucus. Ibid.* 200/2 A Drayne. *Ibid.* 168/5 A Drone. **1658** ROWLAND *Moufet's Theat. Ins.* 917 The Drone called in Latine, *Fucus*..in English, a *Drone*, a *Dran.* **1880** *W. Cornwall Gloss., Drain*, a drone. **1880** ELWORTHY *W. Somerset Word-bk., Drane*, a drone.

β. **12..** *Vocab.* in Wr.-Wülcker 543/8 *Fucus*, dro(n). **1483** *Cath. Angl.* 109/2 A Drone, *asilus, fucus.* **1508** Dron [see 3]. **1523** FITZHERB. *Husb.* §122 There is a bee called a drone, and she..wyll eate the honny, and gather nothynge. **1607** HIERON *Wks.* I. 389 It helpeth not the droane, but the bee. **1637** HEYWOOD *Dial.* Wks. 1874 VI. 322 The Bee makes honey till his sting be gone, But that once lost, he soone becomes a Drone. **1720** GAY *Poems* (1745) I. 7 Some against hostile drones the hive defend. **1889** GEDDES *Evol. of Sex* 19 The drone, although passive as compared with the unsexed workers, is active when compared with the extraordinarily passive queen.

2. *fig.* **a.** A non-worker; a lazy idler, a sluggard.

a **1529** SKELTON *Agst. Scottes* 172 The rude rank Scottes, lyke dronken dranes. **1548** UDALL, etc. *Erasm. Par.* Pref. 3 Idle loiterers and verai dranes. **1570** B. GOOGE *Pop. Kingd.* I. (1880) 8 a, Droanes that greedily consume the fruites of others paine. **1599** SHAKS. *Hen. V*, I. ii. 205 The lazie yawning Drone. **1678** OTWAY *Friendship in F.* v. i, A Droan of a Husband. **1693** PRIDEAUX *Lett.* (Camden) 161 Ye preferments of ye Church were never designed for such drones. **1845** DISRAELI *Sybil* (1863) 52 The lands are held by active men and not by drones. **1940** WODEHOUSE *Eggs, Beans & Crumpets* opp. title page, In the heart of London's clubland there stands a tall and grimly forbidding edifice known to taxi-drivers and the elegant young men who frequent its precincts as the Drones Club. Yet its somewhat austere exterior belies the atmosphere of cheerful optimism and bonhomie that prevails within. For here it is that young gallants of Mayfair forgather for the pre-luncheon bracer and to touch lightly on the topics of the day. **1947** *Hansard Commons* 3 Dec. 484 The object of the [Registration for Employment] order is to compile a list of 'spivs, drones, eels and butterflies'.

b. A pilotless aircraft or missile directed by remote control. Also *attrib.*

1946 in *Amer. Speech* (1947) XXII. 228/2 The Navy's drones will be..led—by radio control, of course—to a landing field at Roi. *Ibid.*, The drone planes. **1947** *Britannica Bk. of Yr.* 840/2 *Drone*, a plane handled by remote control from a control or mother ship. **1958** *Illustr. London News* 10 May 770/3 The *C-130* will be adapted for the launching and direction of drone missiles. **1966** M. WOODHOUSE *Tree Frog* iii. 26 Nobody in their right minds would fly a drone out into that sort of radar cover. *Ibid.* v. 41 A long-range, high-altitude drone surveillance aircraft. **1970** *Daily Tel.* 7 Jan. 4 Unmanned spy aircraft—drones—are to be developed by the American armed services.

3. *attrib.* and *Comb.*, as ***drone-bee, -cell, comb, -eggs***; ***drone-like*** adj.; **drone-beetle** = DOR-BEETLE; **drone-fly**, a dipterous insect, *Eristalis tenax*, of family *Syrphidæ*, resembling the drone-bee.

1508 DUNBAR *Tua Mariit Wemen* 91 Ane bumbart, ane *dron bee, ane bag full of flewme. **1538** STARKEY *England* I. iii. 77 Much lyke vnto the drowne bees in a hyue. *c* **1540** *Pilgr. T.* 68 in *Thynne's Animadv.* (1865) App. i. 79, I thought yt had beyn the dran be. **1583** STUBBES *Anat. Abus.* II. (1882) 42 Drone bees, that liue vpon the spoile of the poore bees that labour. **1865** WOOD *Homes without H.* xxiii. (1868) 426 There are three kinds of cell in a hive..the worker-cell, the *drone-cell, and the royal-cell. **1909** I. HOPKINS *Bee-Culture* II. i. 30 The difference between worker and *drone comb is in the size of the cells. **1950** *N.Z. Jrnl. Agric.* Aug. 107/2 Large supplies of drone comb were required for insertion in nuclei so that drones could be raised from queens. **1753** CHAMBERS *Cycl. Supp.*, **Drone-fly*, or *Bee fly*, a two wing'd fly, so extremely like the common bee as to be at first sight not easily distinguishable from it. **1593** SHAKS. *Lucr.* 836, My honey lost, and I, a *drone-like bee [etc.].

drone (drəʊn), *sb.*[2] Also 6 (9 *s.w. dial.*) **drane** (6 **drene, droon,** 7 **droane**). [app. f. DRONE *v.*, though its early application to a bag-pipe or other sonorous instrument is somewhat surprising.]

I. a. A continued deep monotonous sound of humming or buzzing, as that of the bass of the bagpipe, the humming of a fly, or the like.

1500–20 DUNBAR *Poems* xv. 7 Ane fule, thocht he haif causs or nane, Cryis ay, Gif me, in to a drane [*v. rr.* rane, drene; *rime* stane]. **1641** MILTON *Animadv.* (1851) 209 Ever..thumming the drone of one plaine Song. **1751** JOHNSON *Rambler* No. 144 ¶7 The insects..that torment us with their drones or their stings. **1755** YOUNG *Centaur* ii. Wks. 1757 IV. 140 The dull drone of nominal diversion still humming on, when the short tune of enjoyment is over. **1864** MRS. GATTY *Parables fr. Nat.* Ser. IV. 131 The occasional drone of the [organ] pipes vibrating drearily through the aisles.

b. *transf.* A monotonous tone of speech.

1777 MAD. D'ARBLAY *Early Diary* (1889) II. 205 I would fain give you..some idea of the drone of her voice. **1827** MACAULAY *Misc. Poems* (1860) 416 He commenced his prelection in the dullest of clerical drones. **1888** ELWORTHY *W. Somerset Word-bk., Drane*, a drawl in speech.

c. A monotonous speaker; a drawler.

1786 BURNS *Ordination* x, We never had sic twa drones. **1834** LYTTON *Pompeii* I. ii, Some drone of a freedman..reads them a section of Cicero 'De Officiis'.

II. 2. A bagpipe or similar wind instrument.

1502 *Priv. Purse Exp. Eliz. of York* (1830) 2 A Mynstrell that played upon a droon. **1515** BARCLAY *Egloges* iv. (1570) C iij/2 Yet coulde he pipe and finger well a drone. **1530** PALSGR. 215/2 Drone, a bagpype, *cornemuse. c* **1700** *Wooing of Q. Cath.* in Evans *O.B.* (1784) I. lvi. 310 Our harps and our tabors, and sweet humming drones. **1787** BURNS *Fragm.*, '*When Guildford Good*' ix, Caledon threw by the drone, An' did her whittle draw, man. **1858** M. PORTEOUS *Souter Johnny* 30 An' sit an' smirk, an' hotch, an' swear An' blaw the drone.

3. a. The bass pipe of a bagpipe, which emits only one continuous tone.

(The modern Highland bagpipe has three drones.)

1592 LYLY *Midas* IV. i, The bag-pipe's drone his hum lays by. **1627** DRAYTON *Agincourt*, etc. 152 Then your Bagpypes you may burne, It is neither Droane nor Reed..that will serue your turne. **1663** BUTLER *Hud.* I. i. 516 This Light inspires, and plays upon The Nose of Saint, like Bag-pipe Drone. **1774** PENNANT *Tour in Scotl. in 1772*, 303 The bagpipe..had two long pipes or drones and a single short pipe. **1819** W. TENNANT *Papistry Storm'd* (1827) 90 The drone was here, the chanter yonder. **1879** W. H. STONE in Grove *Dict. Mus.* I. 123 The Irish bagpipe is perhaps the most powerful..keys producing the third and fifth to the note of the chaunter having been added to the drones.

b. On a stringed instrument: a string used to produce a continuous droning sound; the sound so produced. Also *attrib.*

1793 W. OWEN *Welsh Eng. Dict., Crŵth*,..a musical instrument with six strings, the two lowest of which are drones struck by the thumb. **1898** T. WATTS-DUNTON *Aylwin* (1899) iii. 171 Two of the strings reaching beyond the key-board, used as drones and struck by the thumb. **1954** *Grove's Dict. Mus.* (ed. 5) IV. 459/1 Three open strings, off the fingerboard, are played as an upper drone by the little finger. **1969** N. DEANE tr. *Bachmann's Orig. Bowing* iii. 91 The melody was played principally on the upper strings, with the lower strings frequently acting as a drone. *Ibid.* 99 The lower of the two strings on the *kyjak* is primarily a drone-string. **1970** *Melody Maker* 22 Aug. 7/4 The characteristic country 'drone' notes vibrating steadily in the bass strings like Eastern music.

4. The tone emitted by the drone of a bag-pipe.

1596 SHAKS. *1 Hen. IV*, I. ii. 85 I am as Melancholly as..the Drone of a Lincolnshire Bagpipe. **1623** LISLE *Ælfric on O. & N. Test.* Ded. 38 What sports they now deuise With Treble and Drone, and Bonfiers, and Bels. **1832–53** *Whistle-Binkie* (Scot. Songs) Ser. I. 54 Till the bags are weel filled, there can nae drone get up. **1879** W. H. STONE in Grove *Dict. Mus.* I. 123 A combination of fixed notes or 'drones', with a melody or 'chaunter'.

5. *attrib.*, as ***drone-bagpipe, -bass, -pipe, -reed.***

1549 *Compl. Scot.* vi. 65 The fyrst hed ane drone bag pipe. *a* **1659** CLEVELAND *Gen. Poems*, etc. (1677) 2 While his canting Drone-pipe scan'd The mystick Figures of her hand. **1781** COWPER *Conversation* 330 The drone-pipe of an humblebee. **1879** W. H. STONE in Grove *Dict. Mus.* I. 123 The drone reeds are only intended to produce a single note, which can be tuned by a slider on the pipe itself. *Ibid.* 124

An instrument..with a 'drone bass' in the strictest sense of the term.

drone (drəʊn), *v.*[1] Also 7 droan, 9 (*dial.*) drean. [f. DRONE *sb.*[1], or *sb.*[2], sense 2. (The ME. DROUN, to roar, appears to be a distinct though radically related word.)]

1. *intr.* To give forth a continued monotonous sound; to hum or buzz, as a bee or a bagpipe; to talk in a monotonous tone.

1500–20 DUNBAR *Poems* xv. 8 He that dronis ay as ane bee Sowld haif ane heirar dull as stane. **1704** SWIFT *Mech. Operat. Spirit* Misc. (1711) 292 A little paultry Mortal, droning, and dreaming, and drivelling to a Multitude. **1837** CARLYLE *Fr. Rev.* III. II. vi, From morning to night..the Tribune drones with oratory on this matter. **1849** JAMES *Woodman* xvii, The inveterate piper droned on. **1863** BARNES *Dorset Gloss.*, *Drean*, to drawl in speaking. **1868** KINGSLEY *Christm. Day* 13 Beetles drone along the hollow lane.

2. *trans.* To utter or emit in a dull, monotonous tone. Also with *out*.

1614 B. JONSON *Barth. Fair* I. iii, A dry grace, as long as a table cloth, and droan'd out by thy sonne. **1789** MRS. PIOZZI *Journ. France* II. 352 A..German organ droning its dull round of tunes. **1860** THACKERAY *Round. Papers, Week's Hol.* 203 Penitents..droning their dirges.

†**3.** [f. DRONE *sb.*[2]] To smoke (a pipe) (ludicrously compared to playing on a bagpipe). *Obs.*

1599 B. JONSON *Ev. Man out of Hum.* IV. iii, His villanous Ganimede and he ha' been droning a tobacco pipe there ever sin' yesterday noone. **1609** —— *Sil. Wom.* IV. i, As he lyes on his backe droning a tobacco pipe.

drone, *v.*[2] Also 6 drane. [f. DRONE *sb.*[1]] To act or behave like a drone bee.

1. *intr.* To proceed in a sluggish, lazy, or indolent manner. Also *to drone it*.

1509–1680 [see DRONING *ppl. a.* 2]. **1711** PUCKLE *Club* §606. 112 To which Hive every one, Bee-like, Should bring honey, and not Drone it upon the heroick labour of others. **1858** W. JOHNSON *Ionica* 87 My soul went droning through the hours. **1891** M. E. WILKINS *Humble Rom.*, *2 Old Lovers* 49 The business was not quite as wide-awake and vigorous as when in its first youth; it droned a little now.

2. *trans.* To pass *away*, drag *out*, spend (life, time) indolently and sluggishly.

1739 WESLEY *Wks.* (1872) I. 180 One that drones away life, without ever labouring. **1843** LYTTON *Last Bar.* I. iii, To..drone out manhood in measuring cloth. **1876** C. M. DAVIES *Unorth. Lond.* 361 Gentlemen who merely drone away existence in a *laisser-aller* kind of way.

droned (drəʊnd), *ppl. a.* [f. DRONE *v.*[1] + -ED[1].] Uttered or emitted monotonously. Also with *out*.

1903 KIPLING *Five Nations* 69 The palm-grove's droned lament. **1934** WYNDHAM LEWIS *Let.* 15 Dec. (1963) 230 Their droned-out nursery-melodies.

†**dronel, dronet.** *Obs.* [deriv. of DRONE *sb.*[1]: perh. one form is an error.] = DRONE *sb.*[1]

1575 *Appius & Virg.* in Hazl. *Dodsley* IV. 151 That dronel, that drousy drakenosed drivel. **1583** STUBBES *Anat. Abus.* To Rdr. (1877) 11 Like vnto dronets deuouring the sweet honie of the poore labouring bees.

droner ('drəʊnə(r)). [f. DRONE *v.*[1] + -ER[1].] One who drones. †**a.** One who plays on a drone or bagpipe. *Obs.* **b.** One who emits a monotonous sound; a monotonous speaker or reader.

a **1547** *Privy Purse Exp. Hen. VIII*, To a droner that played on the drone 10s. **1784** *Laura & Augustus* I. 127 Enough to have awakened the suspicions of any man except such an old droner. **1859** SALA *Tw. round Clock* (1861) 109, I am tempted..to summon the aid of the police, and to give one of the grinders, howlers, or droners in charge. **1893** R. F. HORTON *Verbum Dei* vi. 187 Mere droners..or reciters..of words which are merely traditional.

drong. *dial.* Also drang. [f. ablaut stem of *dring*, s.w. form of THRING, OE. *þringan* to press, compress.] A narrow lane or passage.

1787 GROSE *Prov. Gloss.*, *Drang*, a narrow lane or passage. *Devonsh.* **1830** *Mem. Gentlewoman of Old School*, Each..opening into a different street, or, I should rather say, lane; indeed, one was denominated a drang. **1863** BARNES *Dorset Gloss.*, *Drong or Drongway*, a narrow way between two hedges or walls. **1880–88** *West Cornwall Gloss. & W. Somerset Word-bk.*, *Drang, Drang-way*. **1888** T. HARDY *Wessex T.* (1889) 161 Accessible for vehicles and live-stock by a side 'drong'.

drongo ('drɒŋgəʊ). *Ornith.* [a. Malagasy *drongo* (Brisson *Ornithol.* 1760).]

1. A name originally belonging to a Madagascar bird, *Dicrurus* (*Edolius*) *forficatus*; thence extended to other species of *Dicrurus*, and in a wide sense to the numerous African and Indian species of *Dicruridæ*, also called **drongo-shrikes**. Also, an Australian bird, *Dicrurus bracteata*.

1841 *Penny Cycl.* XXI. 416 The Drongos..are fly-catching birds. *Ibid.*, The Dicrurinæ or Drongo shrikes of Le Vaillant. **1894** *Naturalist on Prowl* 178 The ever-changing..notes of the Racket-tailed Drongo. **1895** *Rep. 6th Meeting of Australasian Assoc. Adv. Sci.* 448 There being but one member of the interesting Asiatic genus *Drongos* (Dicrurinæ) in Australia, it was thought best to characterise it simply as the *Drongo* without any qualifying term. **1908** E. J. BANFIELD *Confessions of Beachcomber* I. i. 18 Drongos chatter and scold the rest of the banqueters. *Ibid.* iii. 106 The drongo is a bird of many moods. **1965** *Austral. Encycl.* III. 288/2 The drongo is common in the north of Australia and New Guinea.

2. drongo cuckoo, a species of the cuckoo genus *Surniculus*, a native of Nepaul.

3. A simpleton, a stupid person; see also quot. 1942. Hence as *adj.*, silly, foolish. *Austral. slang.*

The statement in quot. 1966 is highly speculative.

1942 A. G. MITCHELL in *Southerly* Apr., *Drongo*, an R.A.A.F. recruit. **1945** BAKER *Austral. Lang.* vi. 130 *Drongo* and *sonky*, mean silly or foolish. *Ibid.* viii. 156 *Drongo*, second-rate, worthless. *Ibid.* 160 *Drongo*, a raw recruit. **1953** R. BRADDON in I. Bevan *Sunburnt Country* 130 *Drongo*: *No-hoper*: *Galah*, all these are derogatory terms. They imply stupidity in the person at whom the word is flung. **1957** J. CLEARY *Green Helmet* 19 You're just a bloody drongo who doesn't know any better. **1960** S. H. COURTIER *Gently dust Corpse* xii. 177 Damn what you thought!.. I never realized you were such an unmitigated drongo. **1966** BAKER *Austral. Lang.* (ed. 2) vi. 135 Its popular zoological name has only the remotest link with the use of *drongo* to denote a slow-witted or stupid person. That application seems to have come from the use of Drongo as the name of a horse..[which] won a certain claim to fame by consistently finishing last or near last. **1968** K. WEATHERLY *Roo Shooter* 130 If we don't get her some dingo will, or some drongo of a holiday-shooter will murder her. **1969** *Advertiser* (Adelaide) 12 May 5/4 You Aussie coves are just a bunch of drongoes.

droning ('drəʊnɪŋ), *vbl. sb.* [f. DRONE *v.*[1] and [2] + -ING[1].]

1. Continued monotonous emission of sound, as of buzzing or humming; monotonous talk.

1704 SWIFT *Mech. Operat. Spirit* ii. Wks. 1778 II. 20 Cant and droning supply the place of sense and reason. **1878** H. M. STANLEY *Dark Cont.* xviii. 507 The monotonous droning of the one-stringed guitar. **1894** FROUDE *Erasmus* vii. 113 Mere sounds like the dronings of a barrel-organ.

2. Lazy, indolent inaction.

1825 in BROCKETT *N.C. Gloss.*

'**droning,** *ppl. a.* [-ING[2].] That drones.

1. [f. DRONE *v.*[1]] Emitting a dull, monotonous sound; having a monotonous tone or utterance.

1601 ? MARSTON *Pasquil & Kath.* I. i. 315 Along with me then, you droning Sagbut! **1697** DRYDEN *Virg. Georg.* IV. 89 Mix with tinkling Brass, the Cymbals droning Sound. **1750** GRAY *Elegy* ii, Save where the beetle wheels his droning flight. **1858** CARLYLE *Fredk. Gt.* (1865) I. I. v. 45 The endless droning eloquence of Bishops.

2. [f. DRONE *v.*[2]] Lazy, indolent, inactive, listless.

1509 BARCLAY *Shyp of Folys* (1874) I. 186 Slouth and wretchyd Idylnes By wayes remys and dranynge neglygence. **1680** DRYDEN *Sp. Friar* II. ii, A long restive race of droning kings. **1841–4** EMERSON *Ess.*, *Compensation* Wks. (Bohn) I. 46 The droning world.

Hence '**droningly** *adv.*, in a droning manner.

1887 *Advance* (Chicago) 6 Oct. 630 If he could..read it freshly like a book, not droningly and dully like a portion of the Bible. **1892** LOWELL in *Harper's Mag.* June 78/2 That droningly dreary book the *Mirror for Magistrates*.

dronish ('drəʊnɪʃ), *a.* [f. DRONE *sb.*[1] + -ISH.] Of the nature of a drone or male bee; living on another's labour; lazy, indolent, sluggish, inactive.

1580 E. KNIGHT *Trial Truth* 37 (T.) Good travelling bees..more profitable than the dronish ones. **1630** J. TAYLOR (Water P.) *Laugh & be fat* 40 Wks. II. 76/2 Each lumpish asse, and dronish noddie. **1714** ROWE *Jane Gray* III. i, The Dronish Monks, the Scorn and Shame of Manhood. *a* **1845** HOOD *Irish Schoolm.* xxix, Some dronish Dominie.

Hence '**dronishly** *adv.*, '**dronishness**.

1731 in BAILEY (both words). **1753** *Ess. on Action proper for Pulpit* 63 (L.) Flaccid dronishness of gesture.

dronk, obs. f. *drank*, *drunk*: see DRINK *v.*

dronkelew: see DRUNKELEW.

dronken, obs. f. DRUNKEN.

dronkle: see DRENKLE.

dronscellett, slade, var. DRUMSLADE, *Obs.*

‖**dronte** ('drɒnt). *Obs.* [Du. and Fr. *dronte*.] A name of the DODO, q.v.

drony ('drəʊnɪ), *a.*[1] [f. DRONE *sb.*[1] + -Y[1].] Having the characteristics of a drone; sluggish.

1781 JOHNSON in Boswell *Life* (1831) V. 3 To restrain a man from drony solitude and useless retirement. **1794** MRS. PIOZZI *Synon.* I. 169 Some stupid books were to be read by drony souls with a uniform monotony of voice.

drony, *a.*[2] [f. DRONE *sb.*[2] + -Y[1].] Characterized by a drone or monotonous tone, hum, or buzz.

1824 *Body & Soul* (ed. 4) I. 93 The bats were wheeling their drony flights. **1837** *Blackw. Mag.* XLII. 25 A couple of desperate Dutch prosers..kept up a steady, drony hum between them. **1869** LOWELL *Cathedral* Poet. Wks. 1890 IV. 52 That drony vacuum of compulsory prayer.

droof(e, obs. form of *drove*: see DRIVE *v.*

droog (dru:g). [ad. Russ. *drug* friend.]

Anthony Burgess's word for a member of a gang (see quot. 1962); a young ruffian; an accomplice or henchman of a gang-leader.

1962 'A. BURGESS' *Clockwork Orange* I. 1 There was me, that is Alex, and my three droogs, that is Pete, Georgie, and Dim. **1967** *Sunday Mail Mag.* (Brisbane) 30 Apr. 5/7 'Get in,' he said, motioning towards the car. 'I'm no droog.' **1972** *Telegraph* (Brisbane) 6 May 7/2 A world where youth gangs—the teddy boys of yesterday and the 'droogs' of tomorrow—have virtually taken over, sweeping all forms of law and order aside. **1973** *Daily Tel.* 30 Mar. 19/6 A gang of youths dressed as 'droogs' in white boiler suits, black boots and bowler hats. **1984** *Times Lit. Suppl.* 13 Apr. 402/2 How long ago it seems since the *New York Times* referred to the spray-can droogs of the subways as 'little Picassos'.

drook, var. spelling of DROUK *v.*

drool (dru:l), *v.* orig. *dial.* Also dreul, drule. [Contracted form of DRIVEL *v.*] = DRIVEL *v.*, in various senses; *spec.* = DRIVEL *v.* 5. Cf. DROUL *v.* Hence **drooled** *ppl. a.*; **drooler**; **drooling** *vbl. sb.* and *ppl. a.*

1802 'PETER PINDAR' *Middlesex Election* VI, in *Wks.* (1816) IV. 213 Old Pynsant, the mad fool, (Beginning, I suppose, to *drule*), Play'd zich a mazeg'rry trick. **1810** *Monthly Mag.* XXIX. 434/2 'Dreuling away my time'; *that is*, 'drivelling away my time'. **1847–78** HALLIWELL, *Drool*, to drivel. *Somerset.* **1854** THOREAU *Walden* iv. (1886) 124 [A frog] with his chin upon a heart-leaf, which serves for a napkin to his drooling chaps. *a* **1860** T. PARKER in Dean *Life* (1877) 159 (D.) His mouth drooling with texts. **1869** *Illinois Agric. Soc. Trans.* VII. 179 The peculiarity of the drooling which characterizes this disease is that the drooled matter is filled with air bubbles, and may be described as 'frothy' drool. **1878** A. HAMILTON *Nerv. Dis.* 290 There may be drooling of saliva and other indications of bulbar degeneration. **1879** J. D. LONG *Æneid* III. 803 Blood and morsels soaked in blood and wine Did drool. **1880** *W. Cornwall Gloss.*, *Drule*, to drivel. **1880** COURTNEY & COUCH *Gloss. Cornwall* 19/2 *Druler*, a driveller; a fool. **1923** WODEHOUSE *Inimit. Jeeves* xii. 130, I never know, when I'm telling a story, whether to cut the thing down to plain facts or whether to drool on and shove in a lot of atmosphere. **1924** *Glasgow Herald* 22 Nov. 10 The peppery leaders of the 'Morning Post', the dull-witted leaders of 'The Times', and the droolings of the 'Observer'. **1925** W. S. MAUGHAM *Painted Veil* xlix. 166 An idiot with..large vacant eyes and a drooling mouth. **1931** A. J. CRONIN *Hatter's Castle* 13 The thought of it..sent a little river of saliva drooling from the corner of her mouth. **1950** M. EDWARDS *White Riders* xii. 138 Rissa glanced up from bed-making, a quick frown on her face. 'Oh, do buck up! Drooling away!' **1964** L. NKOSI *Rhythm of Violence* II. ii. 38 An awful drooling lech!

drool (dru:l), *sb.* Also dreul, drule. [Cf. DROOL *v.*] **1.** *Sc.* (See quots.)

1825 JAMIESON Suppl. I. 352/1 *Drule*,..one who is slow and inactive, a sluggard, South of S[cotland]. **1923** G. WATSON *Roxburghshire Word-Bk.* 117 *Drool*,..a slothful person; a sluggard.

2. Drivel, spittle. *U.S. colloq.*

1869 [see DROOL *v.*]. **1947** J. STEINBECK *Pearl* (1948) iii. 36 A little thick drool of saliva issued from his lips.

b. Nonsense; foolish or empty talk; = DRIVEL *sb.*[2] 2. *colloq.* (orig. *U.S.*).

1900 in *Dialect Notes* II. 33. **1911** H. S. HARRISON *Queed* xxv. 314 Say, Doc, I been readin' them reformatory drools of yours. **1928** *Daily Express* 6 Aug. 11 That sentimental drool. **1966** N. FREELING *Dresden Green* I. 94 He switched the radio on—no short wave, and the medium band was filled with drool.

droop (dru:p), *v.* Forms: 3–4 drupe, 4 drope, 4–6 droupe, drowp(e, 6 *Sc.* drup, 6–7, (9 *dial.*) droup, 6– droop. [ME. *drupe-n*, *drowpe-n*, a. ON. *drúpa* to droop, hang the head, etc., deriv. wk. vb. f. ablaut series *dreup-*, *draup-*, *drup-*: see etymological note to DROP *sb.*]

1. *intr.* To hang or sink down, as from weariness or exhaustion; to bend, incline, or slope downward. Of the eyes: To be bent downward, with the eyelids lowered.

a **1300** *Cursor M.* 16064 Iesus stode als a lambe, His hefde druppand [*v. rr.* drupand, droupande] dun. *c* **1386** CHAUCER *Prol.* 107 Hise arwes drouped noght with fetheres lowe. **1593** SHAKS. *2 Hen. VI*, II. iii. 45 Thus droupes this loftie Pyne, and hangs his sprayes. **1602** MARSTON *Ant. & Mel.* II. Wks. 1856 I. 26 He is the flagging'st bulrush that ere droopt With each slight mist of raine. **1709** STEELE *Tatler* No. 7 ¶16 The Bridegroom's Feathers in his Hat all drooped. **1858** A. W. DRAYSON *Sporting S. Africa* 64 The elephant..male twelve feet high, droops towards the tail. **1865** DICKENS *Mut. Fr.* III. v, Bella's eyes drooped over her book.

2. To sink, go down, descend. Now only *poet.*; of the sun, day, etc.: to decline, draw to a close.

c **1400** *Destr. Troy* 9447 Er I degh, or droupe in-to helle. *Ibid.* 10407 Þe day wex dym, droupit þe sun. **1590** SHAKS. *Mids. N.* III. ii. 357 The starrie Welkin couer thou anon With drooping fogge. **1667** MILTON *P.L.* XI. 178 Laborious til day droop. **1817** SHELLEY *Rev. Islam* I. x. 5 The Eagle..as if it failed Drooped through the air. **1873** BLACK *Pr. Thule* xxvii. 452 The evening wore on, and the sun drooped in the west.

†**3.** To sink out of sight; to crouch or cower down; to lie hidden. *Obs.*

c **1420** *Anturs of Arth.* iv, The dere in the dellun, Thay droupun and daren. *c* **1440** *Promp. Parv.* 133/2 Drowpyn, or prively to be hydde. *c* **1450** HENRYSON *Test. Cres.* (R.), His eien drouped hole sonken in his heed. **1470–85** MALORY *Arthur* XX. xix, Here ben knyghtes..that wyl not longe droupe, & they are within these walles.

4. To decline in vital strength and energy; to sink in physical exhaustion, languish, flag.

c **1400** *Destr. Troy* 122 Eson..Endured his dayes drowpynge in age. *a* **1400–50** *Alexander* 734 *She..drowpys doun in swone. **1500–20** DUNBAR *Poems* xliii. 420, I drup with a ded luke. **1697** DAMPIER *Voy.* I. xviii. 524 We had not been at Sea long, before our men began to droop, in a sort of distemper that stole insensibly on them. **1709** STEELE *Tatler* No. 31 ¶3 This great Hero drooped like a scabbed Sheep. **1846** DICKENS in *Daily News* (1896) 14 Feb., When our poor infants droop.

b. *transf.* and *fig.* To flag, fail, decay.

1577 tr. *Bullinger's Decades* (1592) 34 The faith of Abraham began not to droope. **1607** DEKKER & WEBSTER *Northw. Hoe* I. D.'s Wks. 1873 III. 4 The towne droopt ever since the peace in Ireland. *a* **1618** RALEIGH *Rem.* (1644) 198 For the encrease and enabling of Merchants, which now droop and daily decay. **1880** BON. PRICE in *Fraser's Mag.* May 678 Trade languishes..the rate of interest droops.

5. To flag in spirit or courage; to become dejected, dispirited, or despondent.

a **1300** *Cursor M.* 4460 Sir, we are þe droupander [*c* **1340** *Fairf.* we droupe þe mare], For tua sueuens we sagh..to night. *c* **1330** R. BRUNNE *Chron.* (1810) 252 He drouped þerfore doune, & said þe lond were schent. *c* **1380** *Sir Ferumb.* 1103 Þan set he him doun drurymode; & dropede for hure sake. *c* **1460** *Towneley Myst.* (Surtees) 223, I dre, I drowpe, I dare in drede. **1513** DOUGLAS *Æneis* IV. Prol. 158 To droup like a fordullit as. **1633** P. FLETCHER *Poet. Misc.* 86 Why droop'st, my soul? Why faint'st thou in my breast? **1709** STEELE *Tatler* No. 159 ¶5 Must my Terentia droop under the Weight of Sorrow? **1838** [see DROOPING *ppl. a.* 3].

6. *trans.* To let hang or sink down; to bend or incline downwards; to cast down, lower, turn towards the ground (the eyes or face).

1583 STANYHURST *Æneis* I. (Arb.) 33 Thee Godes hard louring to the ground her phisnomye drowped. **1591** SHAKS. *1 Hen. VI*, II. v. 12 A withered Vine, That droupes his sappe-lesse Branches to the ground. **1602** MARSTON *Antonio's Rev.* IV. v, He droopes his eye. **1796** MORSE *Amer. Geog.* II. 34 [The reindeer] resembles the stag, only it somewhat droops the head. **1832** TENNYSON *Eleanore* vi, I cannot veil, or droop my sight. **1882** NARES *Seamanship* (ed. 6) 64 The shears being drooped, shift the..blocks.

†**b.** *nonce use* with *out*: To express by drooping.

1605 *Tryall Chev.* IV. i. in Bullen *O. Pl.* (1884) III. 319 Why wither not these trees..And every neighbour branch droup out their grief?

c. To cause to drop, fell, lay low.

1819 B. CORNWALL *Dram. Scenes, Rape Proserpine*, And if the woodman's axe should droop the tree The woodbine too must perish.

droop (druːp), *sb.* [f. DROOP *v.*]

1. The act or fact of drooping; drooping action or condition; downward bend or sinking.

1647 H. MORE *Song of Soul* I. III. xxv, Get up out of thy drowsie droop. **1852** MISS YONGE *Cameos* (1877) I. xxviii. 226 His only blemish a droop of the left eyelid. **1853** SIR H. DOUGLAS *Milit. Bridges* (ed. 3) 375 The droop of the chain is 14 feet. **1856** KANE *Arct. Expl.* I. xxx. 409 The droop of the shoulders. **1874** FORSTER *Dickens* (Househ. Ed.) 314 Such indications of a droop in his invention. **1883** STEVENSON *Treas. Isl.* xxiii, Singing a..droning sailor's song, with a droop and a quaver at the end of every verse.

2. A fool; a languid person; a 'drip'. *U.S. slang.*

1932 J. T. FARRELL *Studs Lonigan, Youth* (1936) iv. 88 He was afraid that he might be acting like a droop. **1940** in *Amer. Speech* (1942) XVII. 205/1 Don't be a droop.

3. *attrib.*, as **droop-snoot, -snooter** *Aeronaut.*, an aircraft with a down-sloping, usu. adjustable, nose; the nose of such an aircraft; also, an adjustable flap at the leading edge of a wing (see quots.). orig. *U.S.*

1945 *N.Y. Times* 5 Apr. 1/2 America's 'droop-snoot' bomber, a P-38 Lightning modified to lead standard P-38 formations in precision bombings. *Ibid.*, The 'droop-snooter', a fighter with a combined bombardier-navigator compartment added in its nose ahead of the pilot's cockpit. **1955** *Sci. News Let.* 8 Oct. 230 Nose of the Fairey Delta 2, a single-seat delta-wing research aircraft, can be lowered, rather like a drawbridge, to give the pilot a good forward view for landing, take-off and taxiing. 'Droop-Snoot' is the second British aircraft capable of supersonic speed in level flight. **1962** *New Scientist* 18 Jan. 134 The 'droop snoot'..is virtually a false leading edge, hinged so that it can be tilted downwards. **1969** *Courier Mail* (Brisbane) 21 May 1/5 Nicknamed 'Droop Snoots', the machines had been in communication with the Apollo astronauts.

droop, *a. rare.* Also 6 **drup, droup, drowp.** [The stem of DROOP *v.* used adjectively.] = DROOPING *ppl. a.*

The 13th c. instances are doubtful; they may be for *drupiest* from *drupi*, DROOPY.

[*a* **1225** *St. Marher.* 16, I..diueri ant darie drupest alre þinge. *a* **1225** *Leg. Kath.* 2050 Druicninde & dreori, & drupest alre monne.] **1508** DUNBAR *Tua Mariit Wemen* 192 Into derne, at the deid, he salbe drup [*v.r.* droup] fundin. *Ibid.* 370 Eftir dede of that drupe, that docht nought in chalmir. ?**16..** *Laird o' Laminton* xiii. in Child *Ballads* VII. ccxxi. (1890) 220/2 Droop and drowsie was the blood. **1852** *Meanderings of Mem.* I. 87 In the droop ash shade.

b. esp. in parasynthetic combs., as *droop-headed*, *-nosed*, etc.

1737 BRACKEN *Farriery Impr.* (1757) II. 29 If it [the Croupe] fall too hastily, the Horse is said to be droop-arsed. *a* **1821** KEATS *Ode to Melanch.* 13 The droop-headed flowers. **1881** A. J. EVANS in *Macm. Mag.* XLIII. 228 The ..fine aquiline nose which distinguish[es] these Serbian mountaineers from their droop-nosed lowland kinsmen.

drooped (druːpt), *ppl. a.* [f. DROOP *v.* + -ED.] Bent downward; downcast; depressed.

1873 MISS BROUGHTON *Nancy* II. 13 With drooped figure ..and swollen face. **1885** TENNYSON *Balin & Balan*, Now with droopt brow down the long glades he rode. **1891** H. HERMAN *His Angel* 72 With drooped eyes, and a face to which a hot blush was rising.

†**'droopen, droupne,** *v. Obs.* [Extended form of DROOP *v.* with suffix -EN[5], as if repr. an ON. **drúpna.*] = DROOP *v.* 5.

a **1225** *Leg. Kath.* 2048 (MS. Cott.) Al adeadet, drupninde & dreri. *a* **1240** *Sawles Warde* in *Cott. Hom.* 259 Godd iseh ow offruhte ant sumdel drupnin of þat fearlac talde of deað. *a* **1300** *Body & Soul* 1 in *Map's Poems* (Camden) [MS. Vern.] Als ich lay in Winteres niht, In a droupnynge [*MS. Auch.* droupening] to fore the day. *a* **1310** in Wright *Lyric P.* xvi. 54 For hire love y droupne ant dare. *c* **1340** *Cursor M.* 12625 (Trin.) Wiþ heuy hert & droupenyng chere.

'drooper. [f. DROOP *v.* + -ER[1].] One that droops; †one whose energy or spirit fails.

1586 STANYHURST *Ded. to Sir H. Sidney* in Holinshed *Chron.* II. 80 If the historian..be pleasant, he is noted for a jester; if he be grave, he is reckoned for a drooper. **1649** FULLER *Just Man's Fun.* 21 Let such droopers know, that.. they offend God. **1657** G. HUTCHESON *Expos. John* xiv. 15 A ..cure, which cannot be expected by lazie drowpers.

drooping ('druːpɪŋ), *vbl. sb.* [f. DROOP *v.* + -ING[1].] The action or state expressed by the verb DROOP; *lit.* downward hang or depression; *fig.* falling off, pining away; dejection.

13.. *Gaw. & Gr. Knt.* 1748 He watz in drowping depe. *c* **1400** *Destr. Troy* 3291 Sobbyng vnfaire..with drouping on nightes. **1657** AUSTEN *Fruit Trees* II. 160 To support the people of God against discouragements and droopings. **1816** BYRON *Dream* v, An unquiet drooping of the eye.

attrib. **1591** SHAKS. *1 Hen. VI*, IV. v. 5 When saplesse Age ..Should bring thy Father to his drooping Chaire.

drooping, *ppl. a.* [f. DROOP *v.* + -ING[2].]

1. Hanging or bending down; descending, declining. In names of plants = L. *nutans*.

1590 [see DROOP *v.* 2]. *c* **1600** SHAKS. *Sonnets* xxvii. 7 Keep my drooping eyelids open wide. **1633** P. FLETCHER *Purple Isl.* XXXVIII. xi, Hang down her drooping head. **1796** WITHERING *Brit. Plants* III. 144 Long stems entirely drooping. **1827** KEBLE *Chr. Y.* 2nd Sund. Advent ii, Why lifts the Church her drooping head? **1861** MISS PRATT *Flower. Pl.* V. 275 Drooping Star of Bethlehem. **1878** BRITTEN *Plant-n.*, Drooping Tulip, *Fritillaria Meleagris.*

2. Declining from vigour, prosperity, etc.; failing, decaying, flagging.

1553 T. WILSON *Rhet.* 31 b, He that is so sower of witte, and so drowpyng of braine. **1576** FLEMING *Panopl. Epist.* 210 Overburthened with drooping old age. **1747** *Gentl. Mag.* 17 Drooping cattle..recover'd to their health. **1885** *Manch. Exam.* 3 June 5/3 In the face of a drooping market.

3. Dejected, depressed, dispirited, despondent.

a **1300** [see DROOP *v.* 5]. **1470–85** MALORY *Arthur* IX. x, Fayr kny3t why sytte ye soo droupyng. **1655** *Nicholas Papers* (Camden) II. 289 To reuiue y[e] droopeing speritts of our freinds in England. **1838** THIRLWALL *Greece* IV. xxxiv. 331 To endeavour to raise their drooping spirits.

'droopingly, *adv.* [f. prec. + -LY[2].] In a drooping, hanging down, or dejected manner.

1601 DEACON & WALKER *Answ. to Darel* 200 To support our feeble hands which hang so drowpingly downe. **1814** BYRON *Lara* II. xv, That hand, so raised, how droopingly it hung! **1852** HAWTHORNE *Blithedale Rom.* xiii, She stood droopingly in the midst of us.

'droopingness. [f. as prec. + -NESS.] Drooping condition or state.

1635 J. HAYWARD tr. *Biondi's Banish'd Virg.* 220 The shackles of that benumming droopingnesse. **1864** NEALE *Seaton. Poems* 66 Where lilies hang In silver droopingness.

droopy ('druːpɪ), *a.* Forms: 3 **drupie,** 6 **droupy, -ie, droopie,** 6– **droopy.** [Early ME. *drupi*, referred to DROOP *v.*, but perh. repr. an ON. **drupag-*, f. *drupr* drooping spirits, faintness.]

1. Dejected, sad, gloomy, drooping.

a **1225** *Ancr. R.* 88 [He] makeð drupie chere. *a* **1240** *Lof song* in *Cott. Hom.* 205 Sumehwile to pleiful, to drupi oðer hwiles. ?**13..** *MS. Cantab.* Ff. II. 38. 245 (Halliw.) Sche fonde the lady alle drupy, Sore wepyng and swythe sory. *a* **1529** SKELTON *Elynour Rumming* 15 Her lothy leere is.. ugly of cheere, droupy and drowsie. **1587** GOLDING *De Mornay* iii. 35 Titans golden flame That shines by Day, and droopie Night. **1872** MARK TWAIN *Innoc. Abr.* ii. 19 Looking..droopy and woe-begone.

2. *droopy drawers* [DRAWERS *sb. pl.*], an untidy, sloppy, or depressing woman (occas., such a man). *slang.*

1939 RYERSON & CLEMENTS *June Mad* I. 25 Elmer Tut —You haven't still got *that* droopy drawers?..He looks like something whose mother was scared by a moose! **1966** 'A. GILBERT' *Looking Glass Murder* iv. 79 The neighbours round about thought what bad luck on that charming Mr. Duncan having a droopy-drawers for a wife.

Hence **droopiness**, tendency to hang down.

1828 *Blackw. Mag.* XXIV. 870 Maiden, the sleepy richness of whose eyes, and the dowdy droopiness of whose bonnet, indicate serious contemplativeness.

drop (drɒp), *sb.* Forms: 1 **dropa,** 2–7 **drope,** 4–7 **droppe,** 3– **drop** (5 **droupe,** 6– *Sc.* **drap**). [In I. repr. OE. *dropa* wk. masc. = OS. *dropo* (MDu. *droppe*, Du. *drop*), OHG. *troffo, tropfo* (MHG. *tropfe*, Ger. *tropfen*), ON. *dropi* (Sw. *droppe*):—OTeut. **dropon-* and **droppon-*, f. *u*-grade of ablaut stem *dreup-, draup-, drup-*.

The affinities of the *drop, dreep, drip, dripe, droop* family of words are here exhibited for reference from their respective places:

I. The original strong vb.: OTeut. **dreup-, draup-, drup-*; in ON. *drjúpa* (Sw. *drypa*), OHG. *triofan* (Ger. *triefen*), OS. *driopan*, OE. *dréopan*, ME. *drepe*, DREEP *v.*

II. From *au*- grade: Causal **draupjan*; in ON. *dreypa*, OHG. *troufen*, OS. **drôpian*, OE. **dríepan, drýpan*, ME. DRIPE *v.*

III. From *ū*- grade: ON. *drúpr* sb.; *drúpa* vb. (:—**drūpē-*, corresp. to a Gothic **drūpan, -aida*), ME. *droupen*, DROOP *v.*, also DROOP *a.* and *sb.*, DROOPEN *v.*

IV. From *u*- grade: 1. **dropon-* sb. (pre-Teut. **dhrubón-*), in ON. *dropi*, OHG. *troffo*, OS. *dropo*, OE. *dropa*, DROP *sb.* Thence **dropōjan*, OE. *dropian*, DROP *v.* Also **drupjan*, in OE. *dryppan*, ME. *dryppe*, DRIP *v.*

2. *-pp* forms, originating in assimilation of pre-Teut. *-bn* to *-bb*, OTeut. *-pp*, in sb. **dhrubō(n*, gen. *dhrubnós*, assimilated *dhrubbós*, in OTeut. **dropó(n, dropp-*; whence, by levelling, **droppo(n-*: in OHG. *tropfo*, OE. **droppa*, ME. *droppe*: see DROP *sb.* From this, **droppōjan*, OHG. *tropfôn*, OE. *droppian*, DROP *v.* Also **druppjan*, in ON. **dryppa*, Da. *dryppe*: see DRIP *v.*]

I. The original sb. * *Primary sense.*

1. a. The smallest quantity of liquid that falls or detaches itself, or is produced, in a spherical or pear-shaped form; a globule of liquid.

c **825** *Vesp. Psalter* xliv. 9 [xlv. 8] Myrre & dropa. *c* **1000** *Ags. Gosp.* Luke xxii. 44 And his swat wæs swylce blodes dropan [*Lindisf. G.* dropps, *Hatton* dropen] on eorðan yrnende. *c* **1000** *Sax. Leechd.* II. 34 Læt ȝedreopan on þa eaȝan ænne dropan. *a* **1225** *Ancr. R.* 184 Nout so muche ase a lutel deawes drope aȝean þe brode see. **1297** R. GLOUC. (1724) 560 An vewe dropes of reine þer velle. *a* **1300** *Fragm. Pop. Sc.* (Wright) 213 If hit is cold up an heȝ the dropen falleth to snowe. **1398** TREVISA *Barth. De P.R.* XIII. xxiv. (1495) 456 A droppe is callyd *Stilla* while it fallith, and *gutta* while it stondyth or hangyth. *c* **1400** *Destr. Troy* 3320 Elan ..driet the dropis of hir dregh teris. **1563** W. FULKE *Meteors* (1640) 49 b, Why raine falleth in round drops. **1697** DRYDEN *Virg. Georg.* III. 750 On his hanging Ears..Sweat in clammy Drops appears. **1831** BREWSTER *Optics* xxxii. 265 Drops of rain, which we know to be small spheres. **1884** BOWER & SCOTT *De Bary's Phaner.* 145 The hypodermal layer of tissue containing drops of oil and resin.

b. *fig.* Of things immaterial.

1576 FLEMING *Panopl. Epist.* 94 To instill sweete droppes of consolation, into your heart wounded with anguish. **1597** *1st Pt. Return fr. Parnass.* I. i. 319 I have bespringled them pritilie with the drops of my bountie. *a* **1687** WALLER (J.), Admiring in the gloomy shade, Those little drops of light. **1784** COWPER *Task* III. 46 To preserve thy sweets Unmix'd with drops of bitter.

c. *drop serene*, transl. of L. *gutta serena*, an old name for the disease of the eye called amaurosis.

1667 MILTON *P.L.* III. 25 So thick a drop serene hath quencht thir Orbs. **1822–34** GOOD *Study Med.* (ed. 4) III. 175 The Gutta Serena of the Arabic writers, whence the term 'Drop Serene' of our own tongue.

d. Advb. phr. *drop by drop* [BY *prep.* 25 c]: in successive drops; slowly and gradually. Also *attrib.* or as *sb.*, and *fig.*

1596 SHAKS. *1 Hen. IV*, I. iii. 134 And shed my deere blood drop by drop i'th dust. **1598** —— *Merry W.* IV. v. 100 They would melt mee out of my fat drop by drop. **1850** TENNYSON *In Mem.* lvii. 83 As drop by drop the water falls. **1878** BROWNING *La Saisiaz* 51 Life's loss drop by drop distilled. **1922** D. H. LAWRENCE *Fantasia of Unconscious* xi. 198 The agonies and ecstasies of fear and doubt and drop-by-drop fulfillment. **1948** L. MACNEICE *Holes in Sky* 20 The drop-by-drop Of games like darts or chess. **1959** *Times* 16 Sept. 11/6 The steady drop-by-drop expenditure on small items.

2. *ellipt.* or *absolutely*: = tear-drop; also drop of sweat, blood, dew, rain, according to context.

c **1000** *Azariah* 64 in *Exeter Bk.*, Þonne on sumeres tid sended weorþeð dropena dreorung mid dæȝes hwile. *c* **1400** *Destr. Troy* 7997 Achilles..warmyt in yre..That the droupes, as a dew, dankit his fas. *Ibid.* 9216 He dride vp his dropes for dymyng his ene. **1593** SHAKS. *Lucr.* 1228 The maid with swelling drops gan wet Her circled eyne. **1607** —— *Cor.* V. i. 10 I vrg'd our old acquaintance, and the drops That we haue bled together. **1620** QUARLES *Div. Poems, Jonah* (1638) 6 Tradesmen arise, and plie your thriving shops With truer hands, and eate your meat with drops. *a* **1657** LOVELACE *Poems* (1864) 157 One drop, let fall From her, might save the universal ball. **1719** DE FOE *Crusoe* I. xviii, They would be faithful to him to the last drop. **1887** BOWEN *Virg. Æneid* III. 175 Cold drops over me streaming, I leapt forthwith from my bed.

3. *spec.* In dispensing and administering medicines, etc., the smallest separable quantity of a liquid.

1772 T. PERCIVAL *Ess. Med. & Exper.* (1777) I. 97 Forty drops of the acid of vitriol. **1811** A. T. THOMSON *Lond. Disp.* (1818) p. lxxxii, The London College have introduced the last measure [minim] as a substitute for the drop, the inaccuracy of which had been long experienced; as the fluidity and specific gravity of the liquid, the thickness of the lip of the phial, and even its degree of inclination, were all liable to vary its size. **1822–34** GOOD *Study Med.* (ed. 4) I. 344 Twenty drops of turpentine, with four black drops, were given every four hours.

4. *pl.* A medicinal preparation to be taken or administered in drops. Rarely *sing.*

1726 *Adv. Capt. R. Boyle* 47 Adding some of the chymical Drops into any liquid she shall drink. **1727–51** CHAMBERS *Cycl.*, *Guttæ Anglicanæ*, English drops, volatile English drops, or Goddard's drops, a name of a medicinal liquor. **1728** SWIFT *Jrnl. Mod. Lady* 205 Here, Betty, let me take my drops. **1810** CRABBE *Borough* vii. Wks. 1834 III. 133 Tincture or syrup, lotion, drop or pill.

** *The amount of a drop, a very small quantity.*

5. a. Such a quantity as would fall in, or form, a single drop; the smallest appreciable quantity.

c **1290** *S. Eng. Leg.* I. 100/290 Nouȝt o drope of blode. *a* **1300** *Cursor M.* 16814 + 39 Þen miȝt þei..More blode fynd none, But þat sely drope þat was In his hert. *c* **1400** *Lanfranc's Cirurg.* 124 Þei comaunden to drynke a drope of water. **1581** PETTIE tr. *Guazzo's Civ. Conv.* II. (1586) 104 b, Writers: who, with one drop or two of inke, may prolong our life. **1700** S. L. tr. *Fryke's Voy. E. Ind.* 9 A man may as well steal all one's money, as a drop of Water from any one. **1786** BURNS *Sc. Drink* vii, His wee drap parritch. **1798** COLERIDGE *Anc. Mar.* II. ix, Water, water, everywhere, Nor any drop to drink. **1816** KEATINGE *Trav.* (1817) I. 163 Suspected of a drop of Moorish blood in their composition.

b. ***a drop in the*** **(*a*)** ***bucket*** or ***the ocean***: a quantity bearing an infinitesimally small proportion to the whole.

1382 WYCLIF *Isa.* xl. 15 Lo! Jentiles as a drope of a boket, and as moment of a balaunce ben holden. **1611** *ibid.*, The nations are as a drop of a bucket. **1693** W. FREKE *Sel. Ess.* xxxiii. 206 The Invisible, Infinite and Eternal Maker of all things..to whom the Whole Globe is but as a drop of the Bucket. **1844** DICKENS *Chr. C.* i, The dealings of my trade were but a drop of water in the..ocean of my business. **1853** MRS. GASKELL *Cranford* xiv. 221 That little would be but as a drop in the sea of the debts of the Town and County Bank. **1921** H. CRANE *Let.* 17 Oct. (1965) 67 Sara Teasdale, Marguerite Wilkinson, Lady Speyer, etc., to mention a few drops in the bucket of feminine lushness. **1962** D. MAYO *Island of Sin* viii. 62 Five thousand dollars, he asked for—a mere drop in the bucket, no doubt, considering the offhand manner in which the request was made. **1968** *Listener* 23 May 658/3 It's very important to me that Jennie Lee does care a lot about the provinces. But what she has given is only a drop in the ocean.

6. *spec.* A small quantity of drink or intoxicating liquor. ***to have a drop in one's eye***: to show signs of having had a glass. ***to take one's drops***: to drink hard, to tipple.

a **1700** B. E. *Dict. Cant. Crew, Drop-in-his-eye*, almost drunk. **1738** SWIFT *Pol. Conv.* i. Wks. 1778 X. 159 You must own you had a drop in your eye; When I left you, you were half seas over. **1775** SIR M. HUNTER *Jrnl.* (1894) 21 The captain's servant..liked a drop as well as his master. *c* **1793** *Spirit Pub. Jrnls.* (1799) I. 10 If I like any drop—but a drop in my eye. **1828** *Craven Dial.*, *Drops*, 'to take one's drops,' to drink hard, applied to one who drinks spirits. **1886** STEVENSON *Pr. Otto* I. iv, I have had a drop, but I had not been drinking. **1888** J. PAYN *Myst. Mirbridge* (Tauchn.) II. xi. 119, I went to the Chequers and had a drop too much.

7. *transf.* and *fig.* A minute quantity, portion, or particle of anything immaterial.

c **1398** CHAUCER *Fortune* 58 I the lente a drope of my rychesse. **1413** *Pilgr. Sowle* (Caxton 1483) IV. xx. 66 Is there in the no drope of kyndenesse. **1596** SHAKS. *Merch. V.* II. ii. 195 Take paine To allay with some cold drops of modestie Thy skipping spirit. **1607** WALKINGTON *Opt. Glass* xii. (1664) 131 Having a drop of Words, and a floud of Cogitations. **1813** BYRON *Giaour* 263 Gather in that drop of time A life of pain, an age of crime.

8. An obsolete Scotch weight, = $\frac{1}{16}$ of an ounce.

In the Scottish Troy or Dutch weight = 29·722 troy grains; in Scottish Tron weight = 37·588 troy grains (the pound of 16 oz. being in the former = 7609 gr., in the latter 9622·6 gr.).

1640–1 *Kirkcudbr. War-Comm. Min. Bk.* (1855) 35, xj spoones, Scots worke, weghtan xiij unce iij dropes. **1673** *Acc. Bk. Sir J. Foulis* (1894) 14 A quech weighting 18 unce and 10 drop. **1805** FORSYTH *Beauties Scotl.* I. 78 Archers consider an arrow of from 20 to 24 drop weight to be the best for flight.

**** Something like a drop in appearance.*

†**9.** A spot of colour (like the mark or stain of a drop); also *fig.*, spot, stain. *Obs.*

c **1420** *Pallad. on Husb.* VI. 236 O Sone of God allone, O Sapience, O Hope, of synys drope or fraude immuyn. **1548** HALL *Chron., Hen. VIII*, 80 The other all blacke, dropped w^t^ silver droppes. **1607** TOPSELL *Four-f. Beasts* (1658) 91 Their belly is parted with black strakes and drops. **1674** N. COX *Gentl. Recreat.* II. (1677) 213 The points and extremities of their Feathers full of white drops.

10. Applied to various objects resembling a drop of liquid in size, shape, or pendent character.

a. A pendant of metal or precious stone, as an ear-drop; a glass pendant of a chandelier, etc.

1502 *Priv. Purse Exp. Eliz. of York* (1830) 21 Spangelles settes..sterrys dropes and pointes..for garnisshing of jakettes. **1682** *Lond. Gaz.* No. 1750/4 A pair of Diamond Pendants, with Roses, and Knots and Drops. **1725** DE FOE *Voy. round World* (1840) 140 A pair of ear-rings..with a fine drop. **1861** *Macm. Mag.* Jan. 186 (Hoppe) Cut drops of a glass chandelier. **1885** *Scribner's Mag.* XXX. 728/1 A large silver urn bedecked with the drop-and-garland of Queen Anne's time.

b. *Arch.* (*pl.*) The frusta of cones used under the triglyphs in the architrave of the Doric Order below the tænia; also in the under part of the mutuli or modillions. (L. *guttæ.*) (Gwilt.)

1696 PHILLIPS (ed. 5), *Dropp*..an Ornament in the Pillars of the Doric Order, underneath the Triglyphs; representing Dropps or little Bells.

c. *Naut.* See quot.

c **1850** *Rudim. Navig.* (Weale) 116 Drops are..small foliages of carved-work in the stern-munnions.

†**d.** Small shot. Cf. also *drop-shot* in 23. *Obs.*

1752 MACCOLL in *Scots Mag.* Aug. (1753) 397/2 The..gun..was charged with powder and small drops. **1825–80** JAMIESON s.v. *Draps, Lead draps*, small shot of every description.

e. A lozenge or sugar-plum, originally of spherical form, but now of various shapes. Freq. with defining word prefixed, as *acid drop*, *cough-drop*, *peppermint-drop* (see the first elements). Also a cake shaped like a drop or made by dropping a mixture on to paper, etc. (cf. *drop-cake*, *-scone*).

1723 J. NOTT *Cook's & Confectioner's Dict.* §91 To make Bisket Drops. **1728** E. SMITH *Compleat Housewife* (ed. 2) 178 To make Rose Drops. **1818** KEATS *Let.* 24 Mar. (1958) I. 256 Very fond of peppermint drops. **1819** *Ibid.* 12 Apr. (1958) II. 52 As fine as barley sugar drops are to a schoolboy's tongue. **1836–9** DICKENS *Sk. Boz, Astleys*, Ma, in the openness of her heart, offered the governess an acidulated drop. **1851** *Offic. Catal. Gt. Exhib.* I. 202 Fancy chocolate in drops.

f. Name of a variety of plum, gooseberry, etc.

1883 G. ALLEN in *Colin Clout's Cal.* 197 Orleans plums, and golden drops, which differ..in their fruit.

g. Applied to flowers with pendent blossoms, as the fuchsia (*dial.*), and in *comb.*, as *snowdrop*.

1664 EVELYN *Kal. Hort.* (1729) 226 December..Flowers in Prime..Snow-flowers or Drops, Yucca, etc. **1892** *Northumbld. Gloss.*, *Drops*, the common name for fuchsia.

h. (***Prince***) ***Rupert's Drops***: see quots.

1662 MERRETT tr. *Neri's Art of Glass* 353 An Account of the Glass drops. These Drops were first brought into England by His Highness Prince Rupert out of Germany. **1753** CHAMBERS *Cycl. Supp.*, *Rupert's Drops*, a sort of glass drops with long and slender tails, which burst to pieces, on the breaking off those tails in any parts. **1833** N. ARNOTT *Physics* (ed. 5) II. I. 24 A toy called a Prince Rupert's Drop (a pear-shaped lump of glass with a slender stalk).

†**11.** A disease: in quot. 1559 (and prob. in *c* 1000) gout. (= med.L. *gutta*, F. *goutte.*) *Obs.*

c **1000** *Sax. Leechd.* I. 236 Heo ælc yfel blod and þæne dropan ȝewyldeþ. *Ibid.* 376 Wið fot adle, and wið ðone dropan nim datulus. **1559** MORWYNG *Evonym.* 241 This..cureth all scabbednes and the drop. *Ibid.*, Sod with bran and drunnken it driveth away all droppes.

II. Secondary sb., f. DROP *v.* ** The action.*

12. a. The action or an act of dropping, in various senses, e.g. the fall of a minute particle of liquid; an abrupt and clear fall or vertical descent in space; a decided descent professionally or socially: see the vb. †***to give one the drop***: to give one the slip (*obs.*).

1637 B. JONSON *Sad Sheph.* I. ii, My slow drop of tears. **1708** MRS. CENTLIVRE *Busie Body* III. v, I'll give him the drop, and away to Guardian's, and find it out. **1832** W. IRVING *Alhambra* I. 288 The..fountain with its eternal drop-drop and splash-splash. **1851** MAYHEW *Lond. Labour* (1861) III. 99 (Hoppe), I..began pitching in the street. I didn't much like it, after being a regular performer, and looked upon it as a drop. **1855** BROWNING *By Fireside* xi, The drop of the woodland fruit's begun These early November hours. **1884** *Pall Mall G.* 28 Aug. 5/1 The force of gravity, which has far greater influence than any other in determining the course of the bullet, and is called 'the drop' of the bullet.

b. *slang.* Cf. ***drop-cove***, ***drop-game*** in 23.

1812 J. H. VAUX *Flash Dict.* s.v., The game of ring-dropping is called the *drop*. **1823** in GROSE.

c. With adverbs, as *drop in*, *out*: see DROP-IN *sb.* and *a.*, DROP-OUT.

d. = DROP-KICK.

1845 [see PUNT *sb.*[3] 1]. **1864** [see TOUCH *sb.* 12]. **1897** [see CENTRE *sb.* 11 d]. **1960** E. S. & W. J. HIGHAM *High Speed Rugby* ii. 31 The method for practising the drop should be the same as described above for the punt.

e. A drop-stroke (see DROP-); see also quot. 1900.

1900 G. E. A. ROSS in A. E. T. Watson *Young Sportsman* 609 The second contact of the ball with the floor [in tennis], called the *fall*..as distinguished from its first bound or contact, called the *drop* of the ball. **1909** *Cent. Dict.* Suppl., *Drop*, in tennis, a ball so struck by the racket as to shoot sharply downward after crossing the net. **1933** *Times* 18 Nov. 5/7 Time and again his forehand drop went too low. **1960** *Times* 3 Dec. 3/4 He was pushing at attempted forehand drops.

f. In a card-game, esp. Bridge, a situation in which a particular card is dropped (see DROP *v.* 3 d).

1936 CULBERTSON *Contract Bridge Complete* xxxix. 441 Even when the odds favour a play for a drop, tactical considerations may make a finesse necessary. **1959** *Listener* 7 May 808/2 If East wins with the King the declarer must still decide whether to play the finesse or the drop on the second round. **1969** D. HAYDEN *Winning Declarer Play* (1970) I. i. 12 In the absence of any other information it is fractionally better to play for the drop.

g. *Aeronaut.* (*a*) The act of dropping men, supplies, etc., from an aircraft; cf. *air-drop* (AIR *sb.*[1] B. III. 2). (*b*) The landing of an aircraft or the like.

1943 *Time* 29 Nov. 10/1 A U.S. Supply Plane Makes a 'Drop' in the Chin Hills. **1954** A. W. FIELDING *Hide & Seek* 72 A parachute drop in an island as mountainous as Crete was always an arduous and dangerous business. **1956** 'J. WYNDHAM' *Seeds of Time* 46 The ship had..made her successful last drop to Mars. **1971** *R.A.F. Quarterly* Spring 3 Nearly every mission was flown and nearly every drop was successful.

13. *fig.* A sheer fall or descent in anything measured by a scale; e.g. in prices, values, atmospheric pressure, temperature, etc.

1847–78 HALLIWELL, *Drop*, a reduction of wages. **1883** *Daily News* 12 July 3/5 A portion of the hands..have abided by the agreement and gone in again at the drop. **1884** *Manch. Exam.* 29 Oct. 4/4 Owing to the drop in exchanges and higher rates of discount. *Mod.* There has been a great drop in the temperature since yesterday morning.

14. a. ***to get*** (***have***) ***the drop on***, *colloq.* (orig. *U.S.*): to get (have) a person at a disadvantage; orig. to have the chance to shoot before the antagonist can use his weapon. Hence ***the drop*** = the advantage.

1869 A. K. MCCLURE *Rocky Mts.* xxiv. 233 So expert is he with his faithful pistol, that the most scientific of rogues have repeatedly attempted in vain to get 'the drop' on him. **1875** J. MILLER *First Fam'lies* vii. 55 It was strange that Sandy did not pull.., at all events he had the 'drop', and could afford to wait..and see what he [*sc.* the Parson] would do. **1883** *Harper's Mag.* Jan. 208/1 The men..were always waiting to 'get the drop' on somebody. **1884** *U.S. Newspaper*, The Sheriff and his deputies..having the drop on the outlaw he surrendered quietly. **1893** MCCARTHY *Red Diamonds* II. 27 It was my own fault for letting them get the chance to have the drop on me. **1915** A. CONAN DOYLE *Valley of Fear* I. vii. 140 He'd have had the drop on me with that buckshot gun of his before ever I could draw on him. **1917** J. FERGUSON *Stealthy Terror* xiii. 288 He had got 'the drop' on us, and he knew it. **1918** C. E. MULFORD *Man from Bar-20* 149 Th' man with the drop can find a lot to say, if he's a tin-horn. **1940** 'N. BLAKE' *Malice in Wonderland* I. viii. 107 He suspects Miss Thistlethwaite..of having got the drop on him. **1959** J. CHRISTOPHER *Scent of White Poppies* ix. 147 Two of us can handle it... We shall have the drop on them. **1970** *New Yorker* 23 May 27/2 F.B.I. agents had been trying to 'crawl up through the belly of the plane either to get the drop on him [*sc.* a hijacker] or to get a shot at him'.

b. ***at the drop of a*** (occas. ***the***) ***hat***: promptly, immediately. orig. *U.S. colloq.*

1854 J. B. JONES *Life of Country Merchant* xv. 175 You said you'd marry me at the drop of a hat! **1887** M. ROBERTS *Western Avernus* 43 Ready to quarrel 'at the drop of a hat', as the American saying goes. **1901** ADE *Forty Modern Fables* 49 Every Single Man in Town was ready to Marry her at the Drop of the Hat. **1944** M. SHARP *Cluny Brown* iv. 30 Miss Cream's visit coincided with a week of superb weather. At the drop of a hat she stripped and sunbathed—or rather, a hat was the only thing she didn't drop. **1958** M. DICKENS *Man Overboard* xi. 165 The invaluable ability to write an article about almost anything under the sun at the drop of a hat.

15. The act of dropping or giving birth to young; the produce so dropped.

1891 *Australasian* 320/4 The bulk [of the lambs] consisted of this season's drop.

*** That which drops or is used for dropping.*

16. In a theatre: The painted curtain let down between the acts of a play to shut off the stage from the view of the audience; also called *act drop*, and (less technically) *drop-curtain*. Also, a piece of scenery, usu. a large flat (FLAT *sb.*[3] 11), lowered on to the stage from the flies.

1779 SHERIDAN *Critic* II. ii, The carpenters say, that unless there is some business put in here before the drop, they shan't have time to clear away the fort. **1807** [see FLAT *sb.*[3] 11]. **1859** SALA *Gaslight & D.* ii. 21 Long cylinders, or rollers, used for 'drops'. **1896** C. WYNDHAM in *Daily News* 2 May 8/2 The curtain which will fall to-night upon the drama..will not be a final curtain, but only an act drop serving to divide one section of a career, one stage of friendship from the next. **1913**, etc. [see *back-drop* s.v. BACK-B]. **1951** R. SOUTHERN in *Oxf. Compan. Theatre* 200/2 *Drop*, an unframed piece of scenery, first used about 1690, usually a canvas backcloth. It had the advantage of offering an unbroken plain surface for painting, free from any central join such as marked the alternative 'pair of flats'.

17. a. A small platform or trap-door on the gallows, on which the condemned stands with the halter round his neck, and which is let fall from under his feet. By extension, the gallows; the act of hanging.

1796 GROSE *Dict. Vulg. T.* s.v., The new drop; a contrivance for executing felons at Newgate. **1810** BENTHAM *Packing* (1821) 121 The *New Drop.* **1813** *Examiner* 18 Jan. 43/2 The drop fell. They were executed in their irons. **1843** SIR P. LAURIE in *Croker Papers* (1884) III. xxiii. 15 The first attempt at something like a drop in hanging criminals was at the execution of Lord Ferrers at Tyburn in 1760, but..it was not adopted as the general mode of execution till 1783, when ten felons were executed on the 9th of December..for the first time in front of Newgate, on a new drop or scaffold hung with black. **1846** *Swell's Night Guide* 118/1 *Drop*, the squeezer at Newgate. **1887** *Courier-Journal* (Louisville, Ky.) 1 May 20/5 The condemned walked firmly to the drop. **1924** E. WALLACE *Room 13* v. 56, I have a particular objection to Peter going to the drop. **1958** F. NORMAN *Bang to Rights* 39 It comes to the morning when he is going to get the drop.

b. = FENCE *sb.* 8 a. *Thieves' slang.*

1915 *Times* 19 Mar. 5/5 The Magistrate.—I thought that they called these men 'fences'. Mr. Pearce.—Perhaps the fashion has changed. One usually associates a 'drop' with a more serious offence. **1937** C. R. COOPER *Here's to Crime* vi. 133 All shops, whether or not they be fences or 'drops' for numerous thieves, can escape detection. **1962** K. ORVIS *Damned & Destroyed* xix. 139 You say you buy expensive jewels. You say you pay better prices than ordinary drops do.

c. A hiding-place for stolen, smuggled, or illicit goods (see quots.). *slang.*

1931 in PARTRIDGE *Dict. Underworld* (1950) 207/2 *Drop*, a hiding place for liquor; a depot where smuggled liquors are deposited to be picked up by other members of the gang or by customers. **1933** H. J. LEE *Eagle Police Manual* 147 *Drop joints*, places selected for temporarily depositing stolen goods. **1934** H. N. ROSE *Thes. Slang* iii. 20/1 *Hiding place for liquor in a car*,..a drop; trap. **1937** C. R. COOPER *Here's to Crime* xv. 332 In the transfer from dock to dock, bribed truck drivers run the shipment into a 'drop', extract the narcotics, and put real merchandise in their place. **1947** *Amer. Mercury* Apr. 430/1 The immediate problem after a trucking theft is to unload the merchandise and abandon the empty truck. For this purpose the gang must have a 'drop' where the loot can be stored until the fence can arrange for its sale and distribution. **1962** K. ORVIS *Damned & Destroyed* xxii. 164 Employing an expensive West End brothel..as a heroin drop.

d. A place, usu. secret, where letters, information, etc., may be passed on to, or left to be collected by, another person, as in espionage. *slang.*

1959 R. CONDON *Manchurian Candidate* (1960) xix. 232 An hour after Chunjin had made his report to the Soviet security drop from the red telephone booth..a meeting was called. **1960** 'E. S. AARONS' *Assignment Mara Tirana* (1966) iii. 28 An informer came to our drop in Vienna, from over in

Bratislava. **1965** I. Fleming *Man with Golden Gun* ix. 124 They had arranged an emergency meeting place and a postal 'drop'.

18. a. Variously applied to things which drop or fall from a height, and to mechanical contrivances arranged to descend, or fall from an elevated position: see quots. **b.** A movable plate covering the key-hole of a lock. **c.** The slit or aperture of a letter-box (*U.S.*).

a **1825** Forby *Voc. E. Anglia*, *Draps*, fruit in an orchard dropping before it is fit to be gathered. **1858** Simmonds *Dict. Trade*, *Drop*, a machine for lowering coals from railway staiths into the holds of colliers. **1864** Webster, *Drop*.. a contrivance for temporarily lowering a gas-jet. *Ibid.* [see *drop-press* s.v. drop-]. **1874** Knight *Dict. Mech.*, *Drop*, a swaging-hammer which drops between guides. **1879** *Postal Laws & Reg. of U.S.* 427 *Drop*, the opening in a post-office or mail apartment of a car for the mailing of letters..by the public. **1880** *W. Cornwall Gloss.*, *Drops*, window-blinds. 'I knew he was dead—the drops were down'.

d. Money, esp. when given as alms or a bribe; also, the act of giving it. *slang*.

1931 C. Massie *Confessions of Vagabond* vii. 79 A good ten minutes before the 'drop' you are forced to listen to a tale of woe. **1933** 'G. Orwell' *Down & Out* xxx. 220 A half-penny's the usual drop (gift). **1939** H. Hodge *Cab, Sir?* 222 To 'take the drop' is to accept a bribe.

*** *The space, place, or part, in which there is a fall or vertical descent.*

19. The distance through which anything drops or is allowed to fall; e.g. the distance through which a criminal drops when hanged.

1879 *Daily Tel.* 6 Sept., I would recommend the drop to be no more than $2\frac{1}{2}$ feet with ordinary sized men. **1884** A. Griffiths *Chron. Newgate* vi. 174 Sometimes the rope slipped, or the drop was insufficient. **1892** *Lit. World* 3 June 534/3 As to the length of the drop there has been prolonged controversy.

20. The depth to which anything sinks or is sunk below the general level.

1794 *Rigging & Seamanship* I. 87 *Drop* of a sail, a term sometimes used to courses and topsails instead of depth. *c* **1850** *Rudim. Navig.* (Weale) 116 *Drop*, the fall or declivity of a deck, which is generally several inches. **1864** Webster, *Drop*..the distance of a shaft below the base of a hanger. **1884** F. J. Britten *Watch & Clockm.* 143 This difference between the theoretical and actual width of the pallet is called the drop. **1889** *Century Dict.*, *Drop of stock*, in firearms, the bend or crook of the stock below the line of the barrel.

21. a. An abrupt descent or fall in the level of a surface.

1821 Clare *Vill. Minstr.* I. 62 The traveller from the mountain-top Looks down..And meditates beneath the steepy drop What life and lands exist, and rivers flow. **1891** C. James *Rom. Rigmarole* 166 Another fence loomed ahead ..the water meadow beyond it was at a considerably lower level. 'Look out!' cried Georgy. 'It's a biggish drop!'

b. *Fortification*: see quot.

1874 Knight *Dict. Mech.*, *Drop*, that part of a ditch sunk deeper than the rest, at the sides of a caponniere or in front of an embrasure.

22. An arrangement in a genealogical table, whereby names belonging to a particular horizontal line, where there is no room for them, are carried lower down. Also *drop-line*: see drop-.

1888 *Athenæum* 14 Jan. 49/3 The excessive use of 'drops' may have been necessary; we can, however, but regret the adoption of so distracting a system.

III. 23. *attrib.* and *Comb.* (See also drop- the vb.-stem.) **a.** Of, pertaining to, or consisting of a drop or drops, as *drop-earring, -fall, -falling, -ornament, -pearl*; *drop-shot* (sense 10 d); *drop-bottle* (cf. sense 10 e). **b.** Special comb.: **drop-black**, a superior quality of bone-black ground in water, formed into drops, and dried; **drop-cove** (see quot.); **drop-dry** *a.*, watertight; **drop-game** (see quot. 1891); **drop-meter**, an instrument for measuring out liquid drop by drop; **drop-sulphur, drop-tin**, i.e. that granulated by being dropped in a molten state into cold water; **drop test**, either of two tests of the strength of an object: (*a*) one in which the object is dropped in certain specified conditions; (*b*) one in which a specified weight is dropped on the object from a specified height; so **drop-testing** *vbl. sb.*

1879 *Cassell's Techn. Educ.* IV. 222/1 *Drop-black and Indian red. **1891** *Anthony's Photogr. Bull.* IV. 41, I use drop black, as it is already mixed with water, and it is very hard to make the common lamp black mix, owing to its greasiness. **1877** W. Thomson *Voy. Challenger* I. i. 16 '*Drop-bottles' manufactured for holding sweetmeats of various kinds. **1812** J. H. Vaux *Flash Dict.*, **Drop-cove*, a sharp who practises the game of ring-dropping. **1844** Cobden *Speeches* (1878) 84 The thinly thatched roofs are seldom *drop-dry. **1778** *Learning at a Loss* I. 17 Nobody can appear with a Button bigger than a *Drop Ear-ring. **1801** Mar. Edgeworth *Contrast* (1832) 180 She wore the drop-earrings. **1382** Wyclif *Ps.* lxiv. 11 [lxv. 10] In his *drope fallingus shal glade the buriounende. **1785** Grose *Dict. Vulg. Tongue*, **Drop-game*. **1891** Farmer *Slang*, *Drop-game*, a variety of the confidence trick:—The thief..pretends to pick up (say) a pocket book (snide), which he induces the greenhorn to buy for cash. **1857** Sir J. G. Wilkinson *Egyptians* 87 *Drop ornaments in necklaces. **1707** *Lond. Gaz.* No. 4383/4 Lost..two *Drop-Pearls, Weight 15 Carrets. **1698** *Ibid.* No. 3362/4 *Drop shot of all sizes. **1858** *Advt.* in Greener *Gunnery* 14 With the largest drop shot, and also with mould shot. **1851** *Offic. Catal. Gt. Exhib.* I. 122 Crude *drop Sulphur. **1890** W. M. Williams *Chem. Iron & Steel Making* xiii. 236 Prominent among the useful tests is the *drop-test, as applied to steel rails. **1947** *Shell Aviation News* No. 109, 13/1 Drop test rigs for undercarriages are in course of construction. **1960** *Farmer & Stockbreeder* 22 Mar. 131/2 For the hydraulics system alone Nuffield subjected Tractor Oils Universal to exacting bench and 'drop' tests. **1903** C. E. Wolff *Mod. Loco. Pract.* xiii. 212 One wheel out of every 20 or 24 shall be tested to destruction in a *drop testing machine. **1962** *Aeroplane* CIII. No. 2637, 4/3 A technique known as 'airborne' drop-testing has been adopted in this rig.

drop (drɒp), *v.* Pa. t. and pple. **dropped, dropt**. Forms: 1 droppian, 2–7 droppe, 4 droupe, 4–5 drope, 5 drappe (7 *pa. pple.* droppen), 6– *Sc.* drap, 3– drop. [OE. *dropian, droppian*, = MDu. *droppen*, OHG. *troffôn, tropfôn* (Ger. *tropfen*): see note to drop *sb.*]

I. Intransitive senses.

1. Of a liquid: To fall in drops or globules; to exude or distil in drops.

c **1000** *Ags. Ps.* (Th.) xliv. 10 Myrre, and gutta, and cassia dropiað of þinum claðum. *Ibid.* (Spelm.) lxxi. 6 Swa swa dropan dropende [*Lamb. Ps.* droppende] ofer eorþan. **13..** *Seuyn Sag.* (W.) 3884 He..held it vp, For water sold noght tharon drop. **1382** Wyclif *Ps.* lxvii[i]. 9 Heuenus droppeden [*Vulg.* distillaverunt] doun fro the face of God of Synay. *c* **1400** Maundev. (Roxb.) x. 38 Apon þe roche dropped blode of þe woundes. **1579** Spenser *Sheph. Cal.* Nov. 31 The kindly deaw drops from the higher tree. **1592** Shaks. *Ven. & Ad.* 958 The crystal tide that from her two cheeks..dropt. **1596** Dalrymple tr. *Leslie's Hist. Scot.* (1888) I. 47 A certane coue, quhairin water continualie drapping..turnes in a verie quhyte stane. **1659** D. Pell *Impr. Sea* 265 It will distill and drop out of the cicatrized place into the vessel. *Mod.* The rain drops incessantly from the eaves. Sweat dropped from his brow.

2. a. Of a person or thing: To give off moisture or liquid which falls in drops; = drip *v.* 2.

a **1300** *Cursor M.* 3572 þe nese it droppes [*Fairf.* droupes] ai bi-tuine. **1382** Wyclif *Job* xvi. 21 My woordi frendis, myn eȝe droppith [*Vulg.* stillat] to God. **1490** Caxton *Eneydos* xxviii. 107 The swerde dropped yet of bloode. **1553** Becon *Reliques of Rome* (1563) 226 If the chalice drop vpon the altare, let the droppe be supte vp. **1697** Dampier *Voy.* I. xviii. 499 We, who were dropping with wet. **1825** Macaulay *Ess., Milton* (1887) 14 The rabble of Comus, grotesque monsters, half bestial, half human, dropping with wine.

b. *Falconry.* (See quots.)

1615 Latham *Falconry* (1633) Vocab., *Dropping*, is when a Hawke muteth directly downeward, in seuerall drops. **1674** N. Cox *Gentl. Recreat.* ii. (1677) 167 *Sliming*, is when a Hawk muteth without dropping.

3. a. To fall vertically, like a single drop, under the simple influence of gravity; to descend.

1377 Langl. *P. Pl.* B. xvi. 79 Euere as þei [apples] dropped adown, þe deuel was redy, And gadred hem alle togideres. **1610** Shaks. *Temp.* ii. ii. 140 Ha'st thou not dropt from heauen? **1700** S. L. tr. *Fryke's Voy. E. Ind.* 14 One of the Master's Boys..dropt into the Sea. **1756–7** tr. *Keysler's Trav.* (1760) III. 140 Birds flying over it dropt down dead. **1890** *Lloyd's Weekly* 30 Nov. 6/2 You could have heard a pin drop. *Mod.* The sword dropped out of his hand.

b. *fig.*

1654 Jer. Taylor *Real Pres.* 62 That we may not think this doctrine dropt from S. Austin by chance, he again affirmes [etc.]. **1676** Hobbes *Iliad* i. 237 His words like Honey dropped from his tongue. **1871** Roby *Lat. Gram.* i. viii. 49 This ablatival *d* has dropped off also from the adverbs *supra, infra*, &c. *Mod.* The second *t* has now dropped out.

c. To have an abrupt descent in position.

1769 Falconer *Dict. Marine* (1789) s.v., Her maintopsail drops seventeen yards. **1883** Stevenson *Silverado Sq.* 74 In front the ground drops as sharply as it rises behind.

d. Of a card (in Bridge, etc.): to be played in the same trick as a higher card, esp. because of the need to follow suit. Also *trans.*, to play (a card) thus; to cause (a card) to be so played.

1933 Culbertson *Contract Bridge Blue Bk.* (ed. 2) i. iv. 60 Declarer's chances of dropping the outstanding Queen and Knave on the Ace and King leads are proportionately increased. **1936** —— *Contract Bridge Complete* xxxix. 441 The ten of spades is led. East covers with the Queen, South wins with the Ace, and West drops the seven. *Ibid.* 444 The Queen will not drop, for East has followed to three rounds of each suit. **1958** *Listener* 23 Oct. 669/2 For me, the Queen of trumps never drops in a grand slam. **1960** T. Reese *Play Bridge* 115 All follow to the Ace and King of hearts but the Queen does not drop. **1969** D. Hayden *Winning Declarer Play* (1970) i. i. 12 Do you finesse, or do you play the ace hoping the king will drop? *Ibid.* ii. x. 183 The chances of dropping a singleton queen are $\frac{1}{6}$ of 15 percent, or about $2\frac{1}{2}$ percent.

4. a. To sink to the ground like inanimate matter; to fall exhausted, wounded, or dead.

a **1400** *Octouian* 567 Neygh to dede we gan drappe. **1597** Shaks. *2 Hen. IV*, i. i. 169 It was your presurmize, That in the dole of blowes, your Son might drop. **1635** J. Hayward tr. *Biondi's Banish'd Virg.* 226 [They] were ready to drop downe for griefe. **1700** S. L. tr. *Fryke's Voy. E. Ind.* 76 Tho' thousands of their Men dropt, they would not give ground an Inch. **1841** J. Forbes *11 Y. in Ceylon* I. 141, I fired; the elephant dropped on his knees. **1856** C. J. Andersson *Lake Ngami* 371 A..giraffe..dropped dead to the first shot.

b. Of a setter, etc.: To squat down or crouch abruptly at the sight of game. Also *trans.*, to cause or order (a dog) to drop.

1840 *New Monthly Mag.* LX. 176 Few French pointers and setters are taught to back or drop. **1870** Blaine *Encycl. Rur. Sports* §2545 After standing some considerable time, she [a pointer] would drop like a setter, still keeping her nose in an exact line, and would continue in that position until the game moved. **1892** *Field* 7 May 695/3 Druid had birds before him and Blanch a rabbit; the one dropped to wing and the other to fur. **1951** C. R. Acton *Dog Annual* 55 Always 'drop' the puppy before ordering him to retrieve.

c. *drop dead*: a slang (orig. *U.S.*) exclamation expressing emphatic dislike or scorn of the person addressed. (Cf. quot. 1856 for sense 4 a.)

1934 J. O'Hara *Appointment in Samarra* vi. 181 'Let's put snow on his face.' 'Oh, drop dead,' said Whit. **1953** W. R. Burnett *Vanity Row* v. 40 'It's a pleasure I'm sure,' said Roy. 'For who?' said the girl. 'Drop dead.' **1957** J. Osborne *Look Back in Anger* iii. i. 78 Why don't you drop dead! **1959** 'O. Mills' *Stairway to Murder* xxvi. 256 'Drop dead,' he instructed two equally bruised and breathless corporals. **1959** I. & P. Opie *Lore & Lang. Schoolch.* iii. 46 The well-worn sentiments..'Do me a favour—drop dead.' **1969** J. Weidman *Centre of Action* (1970) xxiii. 238 'I mean,' I said, 'I don't really know what to say.' *Drop dead* seemed singularly inappropriate.

5. a. Of a person or thing: To fall or pass involuntarily or mechanically *into* some condition.

1654 Whitlock *Zootomia* 411 Many other Townes.. silently drop into Dung Hills, without the least mention in History. **1710** Prideaux *Orig. Tithes* v. 278 They had drop'd into absolute oblivion. **1833** Ht. Martineau *Manch. Strike* vi. 66 For fear you should drop asleep again. **1877** A. B. Edwards *Up Nile* xxii. 706 We soon dropped back into the old life of sight-seeing and shopping.

b. *fig.* To die. See also *drop off*, 28 d.

1654 Whitlock *Zootomia* 410 A small Cottage, that hath, as it were, lived and dyed with her old Master, both dropping down together. **1722** Digby *Let. to Pope* 1 Sept., Nothing, says Seneca..so soon reconciles us to the thought of our own death, as the..prospect of one friend after another dropping round us. **1848** Thackeray *Van. Fair* xi, I lay five to two, Mathilda drops in a year. **1889** Anstey *Pariah* v. i, I shall have the old place some day, when the old governor drops.

6. To come to an end through not being kept up; to cease, lapse; to fall through.

1697 T. Smith in *Lett. Lit. Men* (Camden) 257 We must ..let our correspondence drop for the present. **1705** Hearne *Collect.* 31 July, The matter was let drop. **1855** Macaulay *Hist. Eng.* III. 498 The Bill of Rights..in the last Session, had..been suffered to drop. **1896** *N. & Q.* 8th Ser. IX. 161/2 The search after him was not allowed to drop.

7. To fall in direction, condition, amount, degree, force, or pitch; to sink, become depressed.

1729 Swift *Libel on Delany* 15 His visage drops, he knits his brow. **1798** Coleridge *Anc. Mar.* ii. vi, Down dropt the breeze. **1866** Rogers *Agric. & Prices* I. xiii. 191 The prices slightly dropping afterwards. **1881** Besant & Rice *Chapl. of Fleet* i. v, His voice had dropped to the lower notes.

8. a. To allow oneself to be carried quietly down stream; to descend without effort, with the tide or a light wind.

1772–84 Cook *Voy.* (1790) II. 378 The Resolution.. dropped down the river as far as Woolwich, at which place she was detained by contrary winds. **1798** Coleridge *Anc. Mar.* i. vi, Merrily did we drop Below the Kirk, below the Hill, Below the light-house top. **1840** R. H. Dana *Bef. Mast* xvii. 47 We made sail, dropping slowly down with the tide and light wind. **1894** Hall Caine *Manxman* 425 At the turn of the tide the boats began to drop down the harbour.

b. To let oneself fall *behind* or *to the rear* by making no effort to keep ahead or to the front.

1823 Crabb *Technol. Dict.*, *Drop astern*, [used] to denote the retrograde motion of a ship. **1834** Medwin *Angler in Wales* II. 117 Toby then dropped to the hind part of Tickler ..and some thought passed the winning post before Idris. **1847** *Infantry Man.* (1854) 86 The officers drop to the rear. **1867** Smyth *Sailor's Word-bk.*, *Drop astern, to*, to slacken a ship's way, so as to suffer another one to pass beyond her.

9. a. To come or go casually, unexpectedly, or in an apparently undesigned manner (*into* a place, *across, on, upon* any person or thing casually met with); to fall upon. Also with adverbs, as *by, over, up*, etc. See also *drop in*, 27.

a **1633** Austin *Medit.* (1635) 73 Not dropping into Towne, (like men, that follow their private affaires, and no body lookes after them): but, they make their entrance in a publike manner. **1709** Steele *Tatler* No. 47 ¶5, I looked into Shakespear. The Tragedy I dropped into was, Harry the Fourth. **1853** Bright *Sp. India* 3 June, The gentlemen who drop down there for six..months. **1862** Mrs. H. Wood *Mrs. Hallib.* i. iii, He's sure to drop across somebody that.. wants it. **1877** Mrs. Forrester *Mignon* I. 11 We shall probably drop upon a stray couple of lovers. **1879** Farrar *St. Paul* II. 584 *note*, When the Church grew, and heathens dropped not unfrequently into its meetings. **1887** *Lantern* (New Orleans) 12 Nov. 3/2 If Superintendent Adams will accidentally-on-purpose drop up there some night perhaps he'll ketch them. **1893** 'Mark Twain' in *Authors Club Bk.* I. 158, I only just dropped over to ask about the little madam. **1930** L. Hughes *Not without Laughter* xix. 216 Drop by Sunday and lemme know for sure. **1935** F. M. Ford *Let.* 27 Sept. (1965) 244 Wouldn't it be better if you dropped over here for a little and we could talk about the book.

b. Slang phr. *to drop* (*down*) *to* or *on* (*to*): to come casually or accidentally to knowledge of (something); to understand, become aware of, recognize. Also *absol.*

1819 Vaux *Vocab. Flash Lang.* 168 To drop down to a person is to discover or be aware of his character or designs. **1859** G. Matsell *Vocabulum* 54 The copper..could not drop to my chant or mug,..the officer..could not recollect my name or face. **1876** *Coso Mining News* (Darwin, Cal.) 3 June 4/6 Drop on yourself Lent, you are out of season. **1886** *Lantern* (New Orleans) 6 Oct. 2/2 The crowd dropped to his little game. **1887** *Ibid.* 17 Sept. 2/3 The boys..ain't never dropped onto the way of Ed Vaz. **1888** 'R. Boldrewood' *Robbery under Arms* I. x. 118, I could see him..watching me when I put on the whole box and dice of the telegraph business. He 'dropped', I could see. **1895** J. ROBERTS *Diary* 31/1, I dropped down to it after a bit. **1901** M. E. RYAN *Montana* viii. 118 As I slipped out through the back door before your visitors left, I dropped to the fact that you had some damage done to that left arm. **1964** R. BRADDON *Year Angry Rabbit* xv. 136 It was the only place we *could* live—without being caught that is. Surprises me you never dropped to it, Mr Prime Minister, sir.

10. To come down *upon*, *on* with a surprise, a check, or forcible reproof; to 'pitch *into*'. *colloq.*

1852 DICKENS *Bleak Ho.* xxiv. 217 (Farmer) He's welcome to drop into me, right and left. **1857** *Sessions Paper* 9 Apr. 762 If you give me in custody you will be *dropped upon* for it. **1877** *Five Years' Penal Serv.* iv. 268 (Farmer) Do the police ever drop upon the parties and frustrate their plans? **1894** WILKINS & VIVIAN *Green Bay Tree* I. 48 The poor Pigeon will get dropped on. **1894** G. MOORE *Esther Waters* i. 4 You'll have to mind your p's and q's or else you'll be dropped on. **1919** *Strand Mag.* Apr. 290/2 He'll get dropped on one of these days. **1959** *Listener* 2 Apr. 603/3 The present system creates in the minds of people who are prosecuted the feeling that it is unfair that they have been dropped on and other people have not.

II. Transitive senses.

11. To let fall or shed (liquid) in drops or small portions; to distil; to shed (tears). Also *fig.* ? *Obs.*

a **1340** HAMPOLE *Psalter* Prol., þai drope swetnes in mannys saule. **1387** TREVISA *Higden* (Rolls) I. 101 Herbes groweþ þeron þat droppeþ gom. *a* **1400–50** *Alexander* 3801 A litill drysnyng of dewe was droppid fra þe heuen. **1548** UDALL, etc. *Erasm. Par. Matt.* iii. (R.), That the thyng . . be stilled, & as it wer dropped into the heartes of men. *a* **1626** BP. ANDREWES *Serm.* (1641) 429 If these eyes of Iob have droppen many a teare. **1741** *Compl. Fam.-Piece* I. i. 14 Drop in it thirty or forty of Jones's Drops. **1798** JANE AUSTEN *Let.* 27 Oct. (1952) 23, I had the dignity of dropping out my mother's laudanum last night.

absol. **1393** GOWER *Conf.* III. 36 Sende Lazar . . that he his finger wete In water, so that he maie droppe Upon my tonge. **1588** SHAKS. *Tit. A.* III. i. 19 In summers drought Ile drop vpon thee still.

12. To sprinkle with or as with drops; to bedrop; to spot; to dot with spots of colour. *arch.*

c **1430** *Pilgr. Lyf Manhode* I. ci. (1869) 55 The scrippe thus dropped with this blood. *c* **1430** *Stans Puer* 57 in *Babees Bk.* (1868) 31 Droppe not þi brest with seew & oþer potage. **1548** HALL *Chron., Hen. IV*, 12 The flancardes droped and gutted with red. **1667** MILTON *P.L.* VII. 406 Their wav'd coats dropt with Gold. *c* **1820** S. ROGERS *Italy* (1839) 253 Fish Innumerable dropt with crimson and gold.

13. a. To let fall (like a drop or drops). Also *fig.*

c **1315** [see DROPPING *vbl. sb.* 2]. *a* **1400–50** *Alexander* 1363 þe kyng . . Devynez deply on days, dropes mony willes. **1530** PALSGR. 530/1, I droppe a wyle, as a crafty man dothe, *jaffine* . . Let me alone with hym, I shall droppe a wyle to begyle him. **1588** SHAKS. *Tit. A.* II. iv. 50 He would haue dropt his knife and fell asleepe. **1600** —— *A.Y.L.* III. ii. 250 It may wel be cal'd Ioues tree, when it droppes forth fruite. **1697** DRYDEN *Virg. Past.* VI. 24 His rosie Wreath was dropt not long before. **1830** TENNYSON *Poems* 149 Furl the sail! drop the oar! Leap ashore! **1837** WHEWELL *Hist. Induct. Sc.* (1857) II. 43 Bodies . . dropt from an elevated object.

b. ***to drop anchor***: to let the anchor down, to cast anchor. See ANCHOR *sb.*[1] 6 c. Also *absol.*

1634 SIR T. HERBERT *Trav.* 27 Tyding up with streame-Anchors, each sixe houres weighing and dropping. **1682** PEPYS *Diary* VI. 143 Dropped presently her anchor, and is . . come safe in harbour. **1772** *Ann. Reg.* 151/1 Soon after the Venus had dropped, the master of the ceremonies and the captain . . were sent on board. **1890** H. M. STANLEY *In darkest Africa* I. 373 The steamer dropped anchor in the baylet of Nyamsassi.

c. To form by dropping from a shot-tower into a water-cistern.

1892 W. W. GREENER *Breech-Loader* 165 Lead shot is of two kinds: that which is moulded, as large buckshot, and that which is 'dropped', as the ordinary small shot.

d. ***to drop a brick, clanger***: see BRICK *sb.*[1] 5 c, CLANGER.

14. To let fall in birth; to give birth to (young); to lay (an egg). The usual word in reference to sheep. Also *absol.*

1662 PEPYS *Diary* 22 June, A Portugall lady . . that hath dropped a child already since the Queen's coming. *c* **1709** PRIOR *2nd Hymn Callimachus* 64 Ewes, that erst brought forth but single lambs, Now dropp'd their twofold burthens. **1749** F. SMITH *Voy. Disc.* II. 17 The Does passing to the South-ward to Fawn or drop their Young. **1816** KEATINGE *Trav.* (1817) II. App. 263 At the time the ewes drop. *Ibid.* II. 11 Mares drop their foals in January. **1834** R. MUDIE *Feathered Tribes* (1841) I. 46 The eggs are not . . dropped till toward the end of May.

15. a. To let fall (words, a hint, etc.); to utter casually or by the way. Also with *obj. clause.*

1611 BIBLE *Amos* vii. 16 Prophecie not against Israel, and drop not thy word against the house of Isaac. **1668** CULPEPPER & COLE *Barthol. Anat.* Man. IV. i. 337 Both these Authors can somtimes drop leasings. **1706** HEARNE *Collect.* 23 Jan., Keile dropt . . by chance, y[t] my Ld. Pembroke was inform'd. **1772** H. WALPOLE *Last Jrnls.* (1859) I. 15 She never dropped a syllable which intimated her expecting death. **1888** BURGON *Lives 12 Gd. Men* II. x. 268 Quoting short Latin sayings, without dropping a hint as to their authorship.

b. To let (a letter or note) fall into the letter-box; hence, to send (a note, etc.) in a casual or informal way.

1769 G. WHITEFIELD *Let.* 5 Sept. in *Wks.* (1771) III. 392 Although I could not write to you whilst ashore, yet I must drop you a few lines now I am come aboard. **1777** J. Q. ADAMS in *Fam. Lett.* (1876) 234 I will drop a line as often as I can. **1889** E. DOWSON *Let.* 25 Mar. (1967) 57 If you can dine with me to-night somewhere drop me a wire to Bridge Dock before 5. **1945** *Bristol* (New Hampshire) *Enterprise* 15 Feb. 3/4 Just drop a card to your county agent.

16. *slang.* **a.** To give, lose, or part with (money). Also *absol.*, to lose or give away money.

1676 WYCHERLEY *Pl. Dealer* III. i, After a tedious fretting and wrangling, they drop away all their money on both sides. **1812** J. H. VAUX *Flash Dict.* s.v., He dropp'd me a quid, he gave me a guinea. **1849** THACKERAY *Pendennis* xliii. (Farmer), We played hazard . . And I dropped all the money I had from you in the morning. **1876** BESANT & RICE *Gold. Butterfly* xxxi, Tommy is dropping pretty heavily [at écarté]. **1893** LADY BURTON *Life Sir R. Burton* I. 590 He was afraid he would drop several thousand pounds. **1916** E. WALLACE *Clue Twisted Candle* (1918) xvii. 194 'Did she drop?' asked the other eagerly... 'She hasn't got the money,' he said, 'but she's going to get it.' **1931** C. MASSIE *Confessions of Vagabond* vii. 79 Such men frequently 'drop' generously. **1939** H. HODGE *Cab, Sir?* 222 To tip well is to 'drop heavy'.

b. To pass (counterfeit money, cheques, etc.). *slang.*

1938 F. D. SHARPE *Sharpe of Flying Squad* xiv. 150 'Dropping' the forgers' cheques. **1962** *Daily Tel.* 23 June 9/1 Both lots of notes were printed on the Continent and are being 'dropped' in this country. **1968** L. BLACK *Outbreak* xiii. 131 The known value of counterfeit fivers dropped is more than double that.

c. To swallow or take (a drug); esp. in phr. ***to drop acid***: see ACID *sb.* 1 c. *slang.*

1966 ALPERT & COHEN *LSD* (inside cover) *Drop a cap*, swallow a capsule of LSD. **1967** R. BRONSTEEN *Hippies' Handbk.* 13, I dropped my first acid in Paris. **1969** *Guardian* 3 Dec. 9/1 She had dropped some LSD and had been tripping for an unknown number of hours. **1971** 'E. MCBAIN' *Hail, Hail, Gang's All Here* ii. 170, I realized he was on an acid trip... I tried to find out what he'd dropped. **1973** M. AMIS *Rachel Papers* 183, I was using the Mandrax my dentist had given me, surreptitiously dropping one at ten thirty. **1984** S. BELLOW in *Vanity Fair* Feb. 110/2 Some kids are dropping acid, stealing cars. **1985** S. VANAUKEN *Under Mercy* iv. 81 We obtained two six-hit caps and, recklessly, decided to drop the lot.

17. ***to drop a curtsy***: to make a curtsy by lowering the body; so, ***to drop a nod***.

1694, etc. [see CURTSY *sb.* 3]. **1880** G. MEREDITH *Trag. Com.* (1881) 280 Tresten dropped a nod.

18. To bring or throw to the ground by a blow or shot; to fell with a blow, 'floor'.

1726 *Adv. Capt. R. Boyle* 199, I . . dispatch'd two of 'em immediately, and I had made a shift to drop a third. **1812** *Sporting Mag.* XXXIX. 243 The coachman dropped his man the first round. **1813** J. Q. ADAMS *Wks.* (1856) X. 54 The wood-cutter . . was puzzled to find a tree to drop. **1834** MEDWIN *Angler in Wales* II. 151, I . . planted my fist . . under his jaw-bone, and dropped him at once. **1872** H. M. STANLEY *How I found Livingstone* (1890) 460, I . . fired at it; but . . did not succeed in dropping it.

19. To deposit from a ship or vehicle; to set down; also, to leave (a packet) at a person's house.

1796 NELSON 4 Aug. in Nicolas *Disp.* II. 233 So soon as he has dropped the Convoy at Naples, he will proceed on his voyage. **1856** KANE *Arct. Expl.* II. xxix. 296 [He] promised to drop us at the Shetland Islands. **1859** MRS. CARLYLE *Lett.* II. 395, I will drop this at your door in passing for my drive. **1878** S. WALPOLE *Hist. Eng.* II. 551 He would . . stop his coach to drop a friend at his own door.

20. To omit (a letter or syllable) in pronunciation or writing.

1864 TENNYSON *Sea-dreams* 192 Dropping the too rough H in Hell and Heaven. **1871** ROBY *Lat. Gram.* I. viii. 49 The preposition *prod* always drops the *d* in composition except before a vowel. **1872** O. W. HOLMES *Poet Breakf.-t.* ii. (1885) 36 He does not drop his *h's*. **1883** S. C. HALL *Retrospect* II. 191 The son of a celebrated clown, Gomery, who had dropped the aristocratic syllable Mont.

21. To let droop or hang down.

1842 L. HUNT *Palfrey* I. 149, I blush, dear uncle; I drop mine eye-lids. **1894** BLACKMORE *Perlycross* 51 The fair Tamar dropped her eyes, and hung her head.

22. a. To let move gently with the tide. **b.** ***to drop astern***: to leave in the rear.

1805 W. HUNTER in *Naval Chron.* XIII. 24 Admiral H. . . ordered me to drop the Cutter up-abreast of Common Hard. **1867** SMYTH *Sailor's Word-bk.*, *Drop astern, to* . . distancing a competitor. **1887** *Daily Tel.* 10 Sept. 2/5 A couple of . . catboats . . were dropped astern at a great rate.

23. To lower (the voice) in pitch or loudness.

1860 MRS. GASKELL *Right at Last*, He dropped his voice.

24. *Rugby Football.* **a.** To obtain (a goal) by a drop-kick.

1882 *Standard* 20 Nov. 2/8 B. then dropped another goal.

b. *intr.* To make a drop-kick.

1905 A. CONAN DOYLE *Return of S. Holmes* 310 He couldn't drop from the twenty-five line, and a three-quarter who can't either punt or drop isn't worth a place for pace alone.

25. To cease to keep up, or have to do with; to have done with; to leave off or let alone; to break off acquaintance or association with. ***drop it!*** (*colloq.* or *slang*) Have done! leave off!

1605 SHAKS. *Macb.* III. i. 122 Certaine friends . . Whose loues I may not drop. **1700** T. BROWN tr. *Fresny's Amusem. Ser. & Com.* 75 Let us drop that Matter. **1700** RODERICK in *Ballard MSS.* 23. 23 The . . bill is likely to be dropt. **1711** ADDISON *Spect.* No. 89 ¶ 1 She will drop him in his old Age, if she can find her Account in another. **1767** WESLEY *Jrnl.* 20 Nov., I save at least eightpence by dropping tea in the afternoon. **1844** DICKENS *Mart. Chuz.* xx. 250 Drop it, I say! . . Drop it—now and for ever. **1872** *Public Opinion* 24 Feb. 241 He looked at me angrily, and briefly answered, 'drop it'. **1873** BLACK *Pr. Thule* xxiv. 403 So the subject was discreetly dropped. **1882** BLUNT *Ref. Ch. Eng.* II. 88 A custom which had once been universal, and had never been entirely dropped. **1889** FROUDE *Ch. of Dunboy* xxvii, 'Drop that . . or . . I will drive a bullet through the brain of you.'

III. With adverbs.

26. drop away. *intr.* To fall away drop by drop, or one by one.

1601 R. JOHNSON *Kingd. & Commw.* (1603) 18 Then began they to drop away one by one, leaving the camp so disordered. **1720** DE FOE *Capt. Singleton* xix. (1840) 324 The men might drop away, and . . betray all the rest. **1882** LECKY *Eng. in 18th C.* IV. xv. 252 If the war continued much longer, America would almost certainly drop away.

27. drop in. *intr.* **a.** See simple senses and IN *adv.* **b.** To come in unintentionally; to come in or call unexpectedly or casually; to pay a casual visit.

c **1600** SHAKS. *Sonn.* xc, Join with the spite of fortune, make me bow, And do not drop in for an after-loss. **1667** PEPYS *Diary* 28 Oct., Mr. Pierce, the surgeon, dropped in. **1754** RICHARDSON *Grandison* (1781) I. i. 2 He dropt in upon us as we were going to dinner. **1850** W. IRVING *Goldsmith* xiii. 166 Many dropped in uninvited. **1887** JESSOPP *Arcady* ii. 34 The younger neighbours drop in to have a talk.

c. To come in one by one or at intervals.

1697 DAMPIER *Voy.* I. viii. 219 These . . came dropping in one or two at a time, as they were able. **1879** FROUDE *Cæsar* xxiv. 417 The other legions dropped in slowly.

d. To fall casually into one's hands or disposal, to become vacant.

1770 MRS. J. HARRIS in *Priv. Lett. Ld. Malmesbury* (1870) I. 189 Till a larger patent place in the West Indies . . drops in.

e. To meet casually *with*, to fall in *with*.

1802 MRS. E. PARSONS *Mysterious Visit* IV. 217 The party Lord Lymington accidentally dropped in with.

f. *Surfing.* (i) To obstruct another surfer by beginning one's surf ride in his path. (ii) To slide down the face of the wave immediately after take-off.

1965 P. L. DIXON *Compl. Bk. Surfing* (1966) 195 *Drop in*, a big surf term meaning to continue the slide down the face of the wave to gain speed. **1967** *Surfabout* IV. III. 27/1 Most of you are still beginners, so before taking-off on a wave, check carefully to see that no one has picked up a wave farther along, and is coming straight for you. This is usually termed 'dropping in' and you won't find yourself particularly popular if you are caught doing this. **1968** *Surfer Mag.* Jan. 52/1 Martinson dropped in with one stroke. **1968** W. WARWICK *Surfriding in N.Z.* 17/2 Don't drop in on other surfers on a wave. **1971** *Studies in English* (Univ. Cape Town) Feb. 26 It is a mark of a gremlin or gremmy to drop in (i.e., to take off on the outside of someone who has already started to take off).

28. drop off. *intr.* **a.** See simple senses and OFF *adv.* **b.** To withdraw or retire one by one, or by degrees.

1709 STEELE *Tatler* No. 149 ¶ 2, I . . found the [others] . . drop off designedly to leave me alone with the eldest Daughter. **1824** BYRON *Juan* XVI. viii, The banqueteers had dropp'd off one by one. **1890** *Century Mag.* Nov. 112/1 The membership of the Society began dropping off.

c. To fall asleep.

1820 B'NESS BUNSEN in Hare *Life* (1879) I. v. 159 He put his arms round his own mother's neck . . and dropped off. **1861** DICKENS *Gt. Expect.* xiii, Whenever they saw me dropping off, [they] woke me up.

d. To die; = 5 b.

1699 J. JACKSON in *Pepys' Diary* VI. 213 He is . . extremely ill, and could not do a greater service to strangers than to drop off at this juncture. **1771** FOOTE *Maid of B.* III. Wks. 1799 II. 230 He dropped off in six months. **1884** G. ALLEN *Philistia* II. 56 He . . would probably drop off quietly with suppressed gout.

e. To become less frequent or assiduous *in*.

1827 *Examiner* 684/1 The defendant began to drop off in his visits.

29. drop out. **a.** *intr.* (See simple senses and OUT *adv.*) **b.** To withdraw or disappear from one's (or its) place in a series, group, etc.; to disappear from public notice; *spec.* to 'opt out' from society.

1660 F. BROOKE tr. *Le Blanc's Trav.* 100 The shell opens, and the nut drops out. **1865** J. D. WHITNEY *Rep. Geol. Survey Calif.: Geology* I. x. 422 If the bottom of the Yosemite did 'drop out' . . it was not all done in one piece. **1883** 'MARK TWAIN' *Life on Miss.* li. 507, I asked him to hold my musket while I dropped out and got a drink. **1932** A. J. WORRALL *Eng. Idioms* 69 One of the runners soon dropped out. **1933** P. GODFREY *Back-Stage* iii. 38 Sometimes a player drops out through illness or accident. **1952** G. W. BRACE *Spire* (1953) xx. 195 Hadn't you better drop out and make a new start in the autumn? **1962** *Sunday Times* 21 Jan. 24/6 They say to me: Of course you remember So-and-So; and of course I say I do; but I really don't, it's somebody who's dropped right out. **1967** *Listener* 31 Aug. 273/3 Drop out of school, because schools' education today is the worst narcotic drug of all. Don't politic, don't vote... Drop out—tune in with natural things. **1970** *Daily Tel.* (Colour Suppl.) 17 Apr. 9/4 He had started a university course in San Francisco but dropped out for reasons not yet known.

c. *Rugby Football.* To make a drop-kick (see DROP-OUT 1).

1917 A. WAUGH *Loom of Youth* II. ii. 127 In a state of feverish panic Livingstone dropped out.

d. *Photogr.* To eliminate (something) from a negative, plate, etc.; *spec.* to eliminate the highlight dots from (part of a half-tone negative or plate). Also *absol.* or *intr.* Cf. DROP-OUT 3.

1948 [see DROP-OUT 3]. **1951** F. PREUCIL in *Progress in Photogr.* I. xi. 390 Special copy preparation to drop out highlights is used. **1967** KARCH & BUBER *Offset Processes* iv. 125 Modification is possible to . . drop-out shadows in Benday screens.

30. drop short. *intr.* **a.** To fall short; usually with *of*, to fail to reach or obtain. (In quot. *a* 1726, *to drop* simply, in same sense.)

1688 BUNYAN *Heavenly Footm.* (1886) 143 Many eminent professors drop short of a welcome from God into this pleasant place. *a* **1726** COLLIER (J.), Often it drops or overshoots by the disproportions of distance or application. *c* **1850** *Rudim. Navig.* (Weale) 152 A strake which drops short of the stem.

b. *colloq.* or *slang.* To die.

1826 *Sporting Mag.* XXII. 327 One of these days he must drop short.

drop-, the verb-stem used in *Comb.* **a.** *attrib.* with sb., in the sense 'dropping', 'used in dropping', 'arranged so as to drop', forming substantives or adjectives; as ***drop-ladder, -leap, -ring, -shade, -stile, -wave***; also, 'arranged so as to drop or let down', as ***drop-end, -front, -shelf, -side, -window*** (also *attrib.*, esp. of parts of furniture); **drop-arch** (see quot.); **drop-bar**, (*a*) one of the vertical bars connecting the chain and the roadway in a suspension bridge; (*b*) (*Printing*), a bar or roller for running the sheet into the machine; **drop-bottom** (see quots.); **drop-box**, in figure-weaving looms, the shuttle-box containing shuttles carrying wefts of various colours; **drop-cake** orig. *U.S.*, a small cake made by letting batter drop from a spoon into hot fat, or on a greased pan to be baked in an oven; **drop-cannon** *Billiards*, a variety of cannon; **drop-curls** (*dial.*), dropping curls, ringlets; **drop-curtain** = DROP *sb.* 16; **drop-down** *a.*, designed to drop or let down (see also quot. 1940); **drop-drill**, a drill which sows seed and manure together; **drop-flue** *a.*, of a boiler, in which the flues drop or descend; **drop-fly** (*Angling*), see quot. (= DROPPER 3); **drop-foot** = *foot-drop* (FOOT *sb.* 35); **drop-forging** *vbl. sb.*, forging in which a heavy weight is repeatedly dropped on to heated metal, forcing it into a die; also, a forging made by this method; so ***drop-forge*** v. trans. (in quot. *transf.*), ***drop-forged*** ppl. adj., ***drop-forger***; **drop-frame**, (*a*) a frame designed to drop or let down; (*b*) a bicycle frame having the top bar lowered or depressed; so ***drop-framed*** adj.; **drop-glass**, a dropping tube or pipette used for dropping liquid into the eye or other part; **drop-hammer** = *drop-press*; **drop-handle** *a.*, applied to a form of needle-telegraph instrument which is operated by a handle directed downward; *sb.*, a handle to a drawer, door, etc., that hangs down when it is not held in the hand; **drop-handlebars**, bicycle handlebars which have the handles lower than the rest of the bar (cf. quot. 1898 s.v. HANDLE *sb.* 5 and DROPPED *ppl. a.* 1 d); **drop-head** orig. *U.S.*, (*a*) a device for lowering a sewing-machine, typewriter, etc., into its cabinet or desk so as to leave a flat surface; (*b*) an adjustable canvas roof to a car; freq. *attrib.*; **drop-initial** (see quot. 1951); **drop-keel**, a movable keel which can be lowered below the bottom of a boat; a centre-board; **drop-knee** *Surfing* (see quot. 1967); **drop-lamp**, (*U.S.*), a portable gas-burner, connected with the gas-fittings by a flexible tube, usually in the form of a lamp, which can stand on a table; cf. DROP *sb.* 18, quot. 1864; **drop-leaf** *a.*, designating a table or desk having a hinged flap at the end or side which can be raised to extend the surface area; **drop-light**, (*a*) = *drop-lamp*; (*b*) an electric light suspended from the ceiling; **drop-line**, (*a*) = DROP *sb.* 22; (*b*) *U.S.* a hand-line used in fishing; **drop-off**, an act of dropping off (see DROP *v.* 28); *spec.* a diminution; also *attrib.*; **drop-pattern** (see quot.); **drop-press, drop-repeat** (see quots.); **drop-roller** = *drop-bar* b; **drop-scone** (see SCONE *sb.* 1); **drop-service** *Lawn Tennis*, a service which causes the ball to drop sharply after it passes the net; **drop-shot** = *drop-stroke* (see also DROP *sb.* 23 a); **drop-shutter**, a device for securing very brief exposure in instantaneous photography; see quot.; **dropsonde**, a radiosonde dropped from an aircraft to measure weather conditions during its descent; **drop-stitch**, an openwork pattern in knitted garments made by dropping a made stitch at intervals; **drop-stroke**, in tennis, rackets, badminton, etc., a stroke that causes the ball or shuttlecock to drop sharply after crossing the net or striking the wall; **drop-table** (see quot.); **drop-tank** *Aeronaut.*, a (fuel-)tank that can be detached and dropped in flight; **drop-title**, a title which is set comparatively low on the page; **drop-volley**, a volleyed drop-stroke; **drop-wrist**, = *wrist-drop* (WRIST 5 d) (cf. quot. 1893 s.v. DROPPED *ppl. a.* 1 a). **b.** In verbal comb. with object, as †**drop-piss**, strangury; **drop-seed**, a grass that readily drops its seed, spec. *Muhlenbergia diffusa* (*Treas. Bot.* 1866). **c.** In adverbial combination with an adj., as **drop-ripe** *a.*, so ripe as to be ready to drop from the tree; also *fig.*

1848 RICKMAN *Archit.* 50 *Drop arches..have a radius shorter than the breadth of the arch. **1853** SIR H. DOUGLAS *Milit. Bridges* (ed. 3) 375 The *drop bars are rods of iron.. which fall through the joints of the main chains. **1887** *Clowes Printing Mach.* in *Proc. Inst. Civil Eng.* LXXXIX. 111, The dropbar feeding arrangement..a revolving steel bar, on which are fastened two disks..which can by means of screws be shifted to any position..to suit the sheet to be printed. **1794** W. FELTON *Carriages* (1801) II. Gloss., **Drop Bottom*, the bottom of a coach, chariot, or chaise body, when sunk deeper than the surface of the framing, to give more room. **1835** URE *Philos. Manuf.* 44 It raises the coals..and delivers them on an elevated railway platform into a waggon —through the drop-bottom of which they are duly distributed among the range of hoppers attached to Stanley's ingenious furnace-feeding machines. **1860** *All Year Round* No. 53. 63 Robert Kay..invented the *drop-box, by means of which three spindles of different coloured wefts could be used successively. **1835** *Liberator* (Boston) 5 Dec. 196/5 The travellers on whom I bestowed your **drop cakes*. **1879** M. E. BRADDON *Vixen* II. ix. 151 Trimmer's drop-cakes..are always capital. **1904** S. A. MUSSABINI *Mannock's Billiards* I. 336 The plain '*drop cannon' which is employed to gather the balls between the two top pockets. **1909** *Westm. Gaz.* 2 Feb. 12/3 He unexpectedly missed a rather wide drop-cannon from hand. **1880** *W. Cornwall Gloss.*, **Drop-curls*, ringlets. **1832** *Examiner* 85/1 There is a new *drop-curtain, painted in crimson. **1857** DICKENS *Lett.* 17 Aug., In order that the piece may be played through without having the drop curtain down. **1934** H. ADDISON *Textbk. Appl. Hydraulics* viii. 137 (*heading*) Falling surface or *drop-down curves. **1940** *Chambers's Techn. Dict.* 267/2 *Drop-down curve* (Hyd. Eng.), the longitudinal profile of the water surface in the case of non-uniform flow in an open channel, when the water surface is not parallel to the invert. **1951** *Catal. of Exhibits, South Bank Exhib., Festival of Britain* 36/2 Gas cooker..with drop-down door. **1847** RAYNBIRD in *Jrnl. R. Agric. Soc.* VIII. I. 215 Using a *drop-drill. **1928** *Daily Mail* 31 July 1/2 Settee has *drop end. **1960** *Measurement of Spectacles* (*B.S.I.*) 18 Dimensions of drop-end sides. **1874** KNIGHT *Dict. Mech.*, **Drop-flue Boiler* ..the object being to cause [the heat] to leave the boiler at the lower part, where the feed-water is introduced. **1870** BLAINE *Encycl. Rur. Sports* §2969 When more than one fly is used in fly-fishing, the additional one is called a *drop-fly, and by some a bob..As these flies drop or hang down from the line, so they gain their name of drop-flies. **1921** *Newcastle-upon-Tyne Med. Jrnl.* Apr. 118 (*title*) Tendon fixation of *drop foot. **1924** *Jrnl. Amer. Med. Assoc.* LXXXII. 30/1 (*caption*) Shoe modified for the drop-foot brace. **1925** *Ibid.* LXXXV. 1927/1 Drop-foot is the inability to dorsiflex the ankle joint or foot, and is the result of any agent that impairs or abolishes the muscular power in the anterior group of leg muscles. **1962** D. V. & F. DAVIES *Gray's Anat.* (ed. 33) 1212 Paralysis of all the dorsiflexor and evertor muscles of the foot..producing a 'drop foot'. **1925** *Glasgow Herald* 15 Jan. 8 A mass of dough, kneaded, *drop-forged, or otherwise assembled into a solid entity. **1895** *Montgomery Ward Catal.* 555/2 Cold drawn steel tubing, with steel *drop forged crown. **1897** *Westm. Gaz.* 7 Jan. 7/2 Cleeks and irons made of drop-forged steel. **1957** *Economist* 7 Dec. 897/1 The *drop forgers and specialised ironfoundries. *a* **1884** KNIGHT *Dict. Mech.* Suppl. 277/2 **Drop forging*, one made in that form of press in which the blow is by impact instead of by mere pressure. **1897** *Outing* (U.S.) XXX. 278/2 The hammers that are pounding out the drop-forgings. **1909** *Engineer* CVII. 277 Drop forgings are cheaper and more accurate than hand forgings. **1925** *Jrnl. Iron & Steel Inst.* CXI. 527 Recent developments in drop-forging practice. **1959** *Ibid.* CXCI. 94/3 Calculating the power required in drop forging. **1895** *Montgomery Ward Catal.* 555/1 This machine..has our patent duplex *drop frame for ladies' use. **1898** *Westm. Gaz.* 18 Nov. 9/1 In Professor Lilly's triangulated frame will be found an attempt by a skilled engineer to overcome the 'drop'-frame difficulty. **1906** *Bazaar, Exch. & Mart.* Suppl. 12 Oct. 1481/2 Gentleman's cycle, 23 in. drop frame. **1928** *Daily Tel.* 16 Oct. 7 Another feature demanded by lady drivers is a drop-frame for the divisional window between the front and rear seats. **1898** *Cycling* 91 The *drop-framed safety. **1934** WEBSTER, **Drop-front* adj., of a desk, having a part of the front formed by a hinged lid or cover which may be lowered to form a writing table. **1951** *Good Housek. Home Encycl.* 74/2 Two types of door, the drop-front and the side opening, are available. **1876** PREECE, etc. *Telegraphy* §48 There are two forms of the single needle instrument in use, viz. the *drop-handle and the pedal or tapper form. **1895** *Montgomery Ward Catal.* 383/2 Drawer drop handles. **1898** J. P. ARKWRIGHT *Cabinet-Making* 84/2 Brass drop handles ..look well. **1940** *Antiquity* XIV. 69 Three angons were actually pushed through the drop handle of the larger bowl. **1967** *Gloss. Terms Builders' Hardware* (*B.S.I.*) IV. 11 *Drop handle*, any handle pivoted to a plate or spindle so that it falls by gravity to a vertical position when not in use. **1937** M. ALLINGHAM *Dancers in Mourning* xix. 243 He then turned the bike sideways, showed off the *drop handlebars with the special grips. **1895** *Montgomery Ward Catal.* 264 Our improved high arm in the new *drop head case. **1903** *Sears Catal.* (ed. 113) 420 We recommend the drop head cabinet for the reason that it serves as a protection for the head, and when closed you have in it a handsome stand or table. **1932** *Autocar* 28 Oct. 7 (Advt.), Romney 2-seater Drop-head Coupé. **1934** *Times* 16 Oct. 7/3 This all-weather car has a patented drop-head which can be folded back by one person without leaving the car. **1936** J. G. COZZENS *Men & Brethren* II. 191 Bill Jennings sat at the battered drophead desk. **1951** *Bookman's Gloss.* (*R. R. Bowker Co.*) (ed. 3) 54 **Drop initials*, initial letters as tall as two or more lines of text, which lines are indented to allow room. **1963** *Punch* 9 Oct. 528/2 Elegant drop-initials three inches deep. **1896** *Westm. Gaz.* 12 May 2/1 To steady the boat still further, it carries a water ballast, or a *drop-keel. **1967** J. SEVERSON *Great Surfing* Gloss., **Drop-knee*, a type of turn where both knees are bent—the trail leg crossed behind the lead leg with the trail-leg knee dropped closer to the board than the knee of the lead leg. **1970** *Surf '70* (N.Z.) 37/2, I found I had to change from a drop knee turn to a turn with both knees bent and my weight behind my legs. **1895** *Westm. Gaz.* 28 Sept. 2/1 The *drop-ladder was all burnt now, an' the flames pouring out of the trapdoor. **18..** MRS. SPOFFORD *Pilot's Wife*, When dark came we would light the *drop-lamp. **1895** *Montgomery Ward Catal.* 609/2 Men's *drop leaf desk. **1966** A. W. LEWIS *Gloss. Woodworking Terms* 45 The hinge is recessed into the face of the job, e.g. on bureau falls and on drop-leaf tables. **1886** BURTON *Arab. Nts.* I. 5 [He] sprang with a *drop-leap from one of the trees. **1861** *Harper's Mag.* Nov. 815/2 The dark, bright Spanish woman, on the alabaster shade of the *drop-light. **1874** KNIGHT *Dict. Mech.*, *Drop-light.* **1890** *Century Mag.* Mar. 764/1 Reading a calf-bound volume at a drop-light. **1902** *T. Eaton & Co. Catal.* Spring & Summer 218/4 Electric drop-light shade. **1904** K. C. THURSTON *John Chilcote* viii, The drop-light from the ceiling being directly above his head. **1847** C. LANMAN *Summer in Wilderness* xxvi. 158, I..with a *drop-line have taken, in twenty minutes, more trout than I could eat in a fortnight. **1882** CUSSANS *Handbk. Her.* xxi. 282 It frequently happens when Pedigrees are printed, that space forbids such an arrangement, and that *drop-lines are obliged to be used... The drop-line..shows that Margaret is sister to John and William. **1925** *Duo-Art Service Manual* 14 *Drop-off screw. **1952** *Time* 21 Apr., *Drop-off point*, place where copies of *Time* come off a plane, train or truck. **1958** *College English* XX. 16/2 There is no drop-off in volume. **1959** *Times* 31 Jan. 6/1 The rocket engines are fuelled by a mixture of liquid oxygen and ammonia representing about half the drop-off weight of 31,275 lb. **1897** STEPHENSON & SUDDARDS *Textbk. Orn. Design Woven Fabrics* iv. 49 This placing or 'dropping' of one diamond below another..gives the essence of the *drop pattern. **1578** LYTE *Dodoens* I. xxviii. 41 The roote [of Dropwort] boyled in wine and dronken is good against the *Droppisse, or Strangury. **1864** WEBSTER, **Drop-press*, a machine for embossing, punching, etc., consisting of a weight guided vertically, to be raised by a cord and pulley worked by the foot, and to drop on an anvil; called also drop-hammer, or simply a drop. **1888** W. CRANE *Arts & Crafts Catal.* 42 One way of concealing the joints of the repeat of the pattern is by ..a *drop-repeat, so that, in hanging, the paper-hanger, instead of placing each repeat of pattern side by side, is enabled to join the pattern at a point its own depth below, which..arranges the chief features or masses on an alternating plan. **1883** *Standard* 28 Mar. 5/2 Thence it [bearing-rein] passes through the *drop-ring. **1724** *Wodrow Corr.* (1843) III. 152 He was *drop-ripe for heaven. **1829** CUNNINGHAM in *Anniversary* 6 Lips like drop-ripe cherries cleft. **1898** KENNEDY & COHEN in W. A. Morgan '*House*' *on Sport* 420 Saunders..relied on his..*drop service. **1962** *Times* 8 Jan. 3/7 His cramping drop-service..just gave him the edge. **1887** *Scribner's Mag.* I. 632/1 The *drop-shades were of thick light-blue paper. **1905** *Daily Chron.* 16 Feb. 8/5 A *drop-shelf, with chains attached to one of the panels. **1908** *Captain* Aug. 453/1 They never practice its [*sc.* the lob's] antithesis, the *drop-shot. **1927** *Observer* 20 Mar. 27/3 Mixing up deep drives and clever drop-shots. **1963** *Times* 19 Jan. 3/3 He reached the first drop shot only at its second bounce. **1890** ABNEY *Treat. Photogr.* (ed. 6) 235 The principle of a *drop-shutter is the passing of an elongated aperture, cut in a board, over the front of the lens. **1907–8** *T. Eaton & Co. Catal.* Fall & Winter 243/3 Child's iron and brass cot,..*drop sides with brass top rails. **1959** *B.S.I. News* Apr. 18/1 Suitable forms of fastening devices for the drop side have been specified, with the intention of preventing the child from lowering it. **1962** *Engineering* 28 Dec. 839 Dropsides and tailboards for lorries have been made from bonded metal. **1963** *Which?* Jan. 13 A drop-side cot is probably used more continuously than any other piece of nursery furniture. **1946** *Bull. Amer. Meteorol. Soc.* XXVII. 162/1 Droppable radiosondes..can be dropped by parachute; they emit radio signals... The accuracy of the resulting..data is comparable with similar data from the usual radiosondes... These '*drop-sondes' should be quite valuable. **1951** in *Meteorol. Abstr.* (1952) III. 6 (*title*) Dropsonde observations. **1963** *New Scientist* 14 Nov. 396/3 A 'dropsonde' to measure low densities and temperatures. **1968** G. M. B. DOBSON *Explor. Atmos.* (ed. 2) ii. 19 The instrument is carried up on a small rocket to a height of about 70 km and there released, when it descends on a large parachute... Such instruments are sometimes known as drop-sondes. **1791** W. JESSOP *Rep. River Witham* 14 Gates and *Drop-stiles in the cross Fences. **1890** in *Amer. Mail Order Fashions* (1961) 12 Ladies' Black Spun Silk Hose, *drop stitch. **1905** *Smart Set* Oct. 9/2 Kind o' openwork, like a lady's drop-stitch sock. **1923** *Daily Mail* 29 June 1/2 (Advt.), French Lisle Thread Stockings..Dropstitch design. **1897** *Encycl. Sport* I. 621/2 **Drop-stroke*, a stroke by which the ball is made to drop dead, just clearing the net. **1898** COCKAYNE & GOWER in W. A. Morgan '*House*' *on Sport* 254 A 'drop' stroke [in rackets] is a return so soft that it hardly comes off the front wall at all. **1864** WEBSTER, **Drop-table*, a machine for lowering weights, and especially for removing the wheels of locomotives. **1946** TAYLOR & ALLWARD *Spitfire* 102/2 By carrying a belly *drop tank the range could be increased to around 2,000 miles. **1961** B. FERGUSSON *Watery Maze* xvi. 397 Drop tanks full of water were flown by a Skyraider from H.M.S. *Albion.* **1971** *Air Pictorial* XXXIII. 135/1 In-flight refuelling capability and up to six 600-gal. external drop-tanks can probably double this figure. **1893** WISE & SMART *Bibliography of Ruskin* I. 189 There is no title-page, the '*drop-title' on page 1 reading 'Memorandum of Association of the Guild of St. George'. **1907** *Westm. Gaz.* 9 Nov. 12/3 The *drop-volley.. was one of her favourite strokes. **1927** *Daily Express* 4 May 13/7 She would leap forward and summarily cut short the rally with a deft drop-volley. **1879** J. M. DUNCAN *Lect. Dis. Women* xxxiii. 276 There may be on one side no..rhythmic *drop-wave. **1901** *Daily News* 3 Jan. 6/4 A door with window, and on either side of the latter a *drop window. **1926** *Glasgow Herald* 26 June 9 The drop-windows permit of ready means of ventilation on warm days. **1860** R. J. JORDAN *Dis. Skin* 18 Painters..become affected with 'lead-colic' and '*drop-wrist', from having to do with white lead. **1902** H. J. STILES in D. J. Cunningham *Textbk. Anat.* 1203 The condition known as '*drop-wrist*', the result of paralysis of the extensor muscles of the forearm.

‖**dropax** ('drəʊpæks). ? *Obs.* Also 7 dropace. [mod.L., a. Gr. δρῶπαξ pitch-plaster, f. δρέπ-ειν to pluck. In F. *dropace*, Cotgr.] A pitch plaster, a depilatory. Hence '**dropacism, -ist** (see quots.).

1621 BURTON *Anat. Mel.* II. v. III. i. (1651) 401 Piso [prescribes] Dropaces of pitch, and oile of Rue, applyed at certain times to the stomach, to the metaphrene. **1656** BLOUNT *Glossogr.*, *Dropacist*, one that pulls off hair, and makes the body bare. **1678** SALMON *Lond. Disp.* 774/1 A Dropace.. is made of Pitch mixt with Oyl. **1706** PHILLIPS, *Dropax*, or *Dropacismus*.. of Pitch and Oil. **1721** BAILEY, *Dropacism*.. an Ointment for anointing the Members of the Body. **1883** *Syd. Soc. Lex.*, *Dropax, Dropacism* (old terms).

drop-bolt. [In sense 1, f. the stem of DROP *v.*; in sense 2, f. DROP *sb.*]

1. A bolt constructed so as to drop into a socket.

1786 MISS A. SEWARD *Lett.* I. 225, I lifted the drop-bolt.

2. The bolt of the drop on a gallows.

1890 R. KIPLING *Phantom Rickshaw* (ed. 3) 9 As a condemned criminal might speak ere the drop-bolts are drawn.

dropcy, dropecy, -sy, obs. ff. DROPSY.

†**dropic,** *a. Obs. rare.* [Aphetic f. *hydropic*, *edropic*: cf. DROPSY.] Affected with dropsy.

c **1425** *Found. St. Bartholomew's* 29 A Certeyne dropik man that bare his surname of the happe of this siknes.

drop-in, *sb.* and *a.* [DROP *v.* 27.]

A. *sb.* **1.** An unexpected or casual visit or visitor. *colloq.*

1819 *Metropolis* I. 234 D-s-y gave us a drop in for a few minutes, just long enough to be perceived. **1942** BERREY & VAN DEN BARK *Amer. Thes. Slang* §363/5 *Drop-in, happen-in*, a chance social call. **1970** M. MILLAR *Beyond this Point* (1971) iii. 32 Some of the people were drop-ins who had no real interest in the case.

2. (See quot. 1940.) *U.S. slang.*

1937 D. RUNYON in *Collier's Weekly* 16 Jan. 9/3 Nicely-Nicely commences to figure this is about as soft a drop-in as anybody can wish. **1940** *Amer. Speech* XV. 117/2 *Drop-in*, something which is easy; easy money. So-called because a fat *mark* may sometimes 'drop in' to a confidence-game without being steered.

3. A place or function at which one may drop in casually: see DROP *v.* 27 b. *colloq.* (chiefly *U.S.*).

1948 LAIT & MORTIMER *New York: Confidential!* v. 48 Many of the furnished rooms.. provide drop-ins for youths ..seeking..marijuana revels. **1970** *Guardian Weekly* 21 Feb. 20 Alice's Restaurant, a drop-in for dropouts. **1974** *Belton* (S. Carolina) *News* 18 Apr. 1/5 Upstairs, from 3:30 to 5:30 p.m., there will be a drop-in for patrons of the library. The public is invited and urged to attend. **1979** 'A. HAILEY' *Overload* IV. ii. 299 This evening she had promised to go to two parties, one a 'drop in', early.

B. *adj.* **1.** Designed to drop into position; *spec.* of a seat (see quot. 1960).

1921 *Spectator* 16 Apr. 485/2 Above this French window is a drop-in fanlight. **1960** A. QUINTON in G. Lewis *Handbk. Crafts* 232 Any type of 'drop-in' seat: i.e. one which can be lifted from its frame and has no springs. **1962** L. S. SASIENI *Princ. Optical Dispensing* viii. 195 There are three main types of these supplementary fronts: 'clip-on' fronts, 'grab' fronts, and 'drop-in' fronts.

2. At which one may 'drop in' (see DROP *v.* 27 b). *colloq.*

1958 *Listener* 27 Nov. 860/1 Mr. Walter Reuther's United Auto Workers runs night schools, 'drop-in' centres for retired members, recreation halls. **1962** *Guardian* 24 July 5/1 We were entertained..by the Federation of Lace Makers to a drop-in (bar ouvert toute la journée) view of the laces used in the show.

drop-kick. *Rugby Football.* [f. DROP- + KICK *sb.*] (See quot. 1896.) So **drop-kicking** *vbl. sb.*

1857 HUGHES *Tom Brown* I. v, Vigorous efforts to accomplish a drop-kick. **1880** [see DRIBBLE *v.* 4]. **1882** *Field* 28 Jan., The drop out was well returned, and some good drop-kicking took place. **1896** *Laws of Football* 2 A Drop-kick is made by letting the ball fall from the hands, and kicking it the very instant it rises.

'**dropless,** *a. rare.* [-LESS.] Free from drops.

1798 COLERIDGE *Picture* 40 Ye that now cool her fleece with dropless damp.

'**droplet.** [-LET.] A minute drop. ***droplet infection***, infection conveyed by fine droplets of mucus sprayed into the air when a person opens his mouth to speak, cough, etc.

1607 SHAKS. *Timon* v. iv. 76 Our humane griefes..those our droplets, which From niggard Nature fall. **1788** *Trifler* xxv. 323 They are also to be..taken internally by droplets. **1878** HUXLEY *Physiogr.* 45 When these droplets run together, they produce drops too heavy for suspension. [**1904** *Westm. Gaz.* 20 Sept. 7/2 In the act of loud speaking, fine droplets of mucus are sprayed from the mouth into the air... It has been shown that by reading aloud for half an hour B[acillus] prodigiosus may be disseminated from the mouth to a distance of 24 ft. in front.] **1907** J. C. M'VAIL *Prevention Infect. Dis.* 275 When a patient is out of doors in a solitary place droplet infection may on occasion be disregarded. **1932** *Times Educ. Suppl.* 17 Sept. 358/1 Droplet infection was responsible for the spread of sore throat.

drop-letter. *U.S.* **1.** A letter posted in any place merely for local delivery (formerly called *box-letter*); a 'local' letter.

Originally applied to letters sent from a distant place by some other mode of conveyance, and 'dropped' into the post office box at the place of destination for delivery there.

[**1841** *Rep. Postmaster-General* (U.S.) 452 Letters have frequently been dropped into this [Philadelphia] office, from Boston, New York [etc.], for deliverance by our carriers.] **1844** *Ibid.* 688 'Drop-letters'..This is a class of letters which are usually sent from one place to another by private conveyance, and are 'dropped' or deposited in the post-office for delivery. **1845** (Mar. 3) *U.S. Statutes at Large* V. 733 Drop letters, or letters placed in any post-office, not for transmission by mail, but for delivery only. [The term *drop matter* is common in American post offices, meaning matter for local delivery, without passing from one post-office to another.]

2. (See quots.) Cf. *drop-initial* s.v. DROP-.

1894 *Amer. Dict. Printing* 149/1 *Drop letters*, two-line letters, the top being as high as the top of a line of an advertisement or of reading matter, the remainder dropping down to the next line. This expression is not used in America, the equivalent being a two-line letter. **1950** *Dict. Printing Terms* (*Porte Publ. Co.*) (ed. 5) 53/2 *Drop-letter*, a large letter used for ornamentation at the beginning of a chapter or article.

†'**dropling.** *Obs.* [-LING.] A little drop.

1605 SYLVESTER *Quadrains of Pibrac* xiii, A dropling of th' Eternall Fount. **1782** ELPHINSTON tr. *Martial* III. lxxxii. 170 His guests to accept a few droplings he asks.

†'**drop-meal,** *adv. Obs.* [OE. *drop-mǽlum*, f. DROP *sb.*: see -MEAL.] In drops, drop by drop.

c **1000** ÆLFRIC *Hom.* I. 508 Yrnþ dropmælum swiðe hluttor wæter. *a* **1225** *Ancr. R.* 282 In hire he heldeð nout one dropemele, auh ȝeoteð vlowinde wellen of his grace. **1398** TREVISA *Barth. De P.R.* XI. vii. (1495) 393 Rayne fallyth..thenne and thenne and dropmele. **1647** TRAPP *Comm. Acts* xii. 8 As the cloud dissolves drop-meal upon the earth.

b. Often with *by*: = prec. Hence as sb.

1561 T. NORTON *Calvin's Inst.* I. 1 These good things that are as by dropmeale poured into vs from heauen. **1577** HARRISON *England* III. viii. (1878) II. 58 To them that make their water by dropmeales. **1601** HOLLAND *Pliny* II. 40 Physicians vse to instill the juice of the Radish by drop-meale into the eares. **1607** TOPSELL *Four-f. Beasts* (1658) 440 Which..cannot void his water but by drops-meal.

drop-out. Also dropout. [DROP *v.* 29.]

1. *Rugby Football.* A drop-kick made from within the defending side's twenty-five-yard line in order to restart play after the ball has gone dead.

1882 [see DROP-KICK]. **1896** *Laws of Football* 3 *Drop-out* is a drop-kick from within 25 yards of the kicker's goal line. **1896** *Durham Univ. Jrnl.* 21 Mar. 69 The drop-out was well followed up. **1905** *Westm. Gaz.* 12 Dec. 9/2 From the drop-out Cambridge began an attack. **1960** E. S. & W. J. HIGHAM *High Speed Rugby* xiii. 157 The kick-off, drop-out, penalty and free kick.

2. A person who 'drops out' (see DROP *v.* 29 b), esp. from a course of study or from society; also, the act of withdrawing. Also *attrib. colloq.* (orig. *U.S.*).

1930 *Sat. Even. Post* 1 Mar. 110/2 The drop-outs are usually those with inferior mental capacity. **1960** *Times* 21 Nov. (Canada Suppl.) p. xviii/4 The bored students—mostly boys—and the 'drop outs'. **1962** *Guardian* 19 Jan. 8/5 The brilliant woman..becomes an embarrassing statistic in the academic 'drop-out' rate... Dr. Bunting was a 'drop-out' for six years when her children were young. **1966** *Listener* 29 Sept. 454/3 The older teachers are resigned to the low standards and the high rate of drop-out. **1967** *New Statesman* 15 Dec. 838/2 An international gathering of misfits and drop-outs, smoking pot and meditating in the Buddhist temples. **1970** *New Society* 5 Feb. 231/3 He seems to imagine that, with the exception of the drop-outs, the working class has been entirely absorbed in 'co-operative economic production and consenting political citizenship'. **1971** *Brit. Med. Bull.* XXVII. 5/1 Experience suggests a high drop-out rate for those being treated.

3. *Photogr.* The elimination of highlight dots from part of a half-tone negative or plate; also, a half-tone having such an area eliminated, or the area itself. Also *attrib.*

1948 FLADER & MERTLE *Mod. Photoengraving* p. xxi/2 *Dropout*, a highlight halftone negative or printing plate; 'dropping-out' is the elimination of highlight dot formations. **1967** KARCH & BUBER *Offset Processes* v. 179 The drop-out halftone..is made where it is desirable to eliminate the highlight background of an illustration. **1968** *Gloss. Terms Offset Lithogr. Printing* (*B.S.I.*) 11 *Drop-out*, the areas of a picture which are clear of printing image. *Ibid.* 17 *Drop-out mask*, a photographic mask of sufficient density and contrast to separate non-printing areas from the first printing tones.

4. In tape-recording, a momentary decrease in the amplitude of the recorded signal due to a flaw in the tape; also, such a flaw.

1955 *Jrnl. Audio Engin. Soc.* III. 31 Tape squeal, sticking, and level variations have been caused by deposits on the head due to the shearing of imperfections in the oxide. Because of the effect of level variation in the computer field, the latter phenomenon has generally been referred to as 'dropout'. **1958** *Engineering* 7 Mar. 310/2 When the signal amplitude falls below this limit, faulty reproduction of the signal occurs. This is called 'drop-out'. **1962** A. NISBETT *Technique Sound Studio* iv. 85 Where there is a slight flaw, such as a drop-out, making a simple joint (and removing the flawed scrap of tape) will save time. **1967** D. F. ELDRIDGE in C. B. Pear *Magn. Recording* iii. 101 Once the first permanent dropout is formed, additional dropouts in increasing numbers will follow rapidly.

droppable ('drɒpəb(ə)l), *a.* [f. DROP *v.* + -ABLE.] Capable of being dropped; fit to be dropped or discarded.

1908 W. DE MORGAN *Somehow Good* xli. 446 Sally held tight to her groundless opinion long enough for the previous question to be droppable, without effrontery. **1965** *Language* XLI. 392 An informationless operator..would be droppable.

dropped, dropt (drɒpt), *ppl. a.* [f. DROP *v.*]

1. a. Fallen, lowered; allowed to drop or fall. *spec.* in *Rugby Football*, designating a goal scored by a drop-kick.

1600 SHAKS. *A.Y.L.* III. ii. 248 Vnder a tree like a drop'd Acorne. **1797** MRS. A. M. BENNETT *Beggar Girl* (1813) V. 235 With distended eyes, dropped jaws, and shaking limbs. **1811** BYRON *Hints from Hor.* 314 Till the dropped curtain gives a glad release. **1844** MRS. BROWNING *Drama of Exile* Poems 1850 I. 62 With dropt looks. **1893** *Times* 16 Dec. 9/5 Lead paralysis with its special feature of 'dropped wrist', or paralysis of the muscles of the arm. **1896** *Durham Univ. Jrnl.* 29 Feb. 46 Winners..by 1 dropped goal [i.e. obtained by a drop-kick]. **1933** *Times* 4 Dec. 5/6 Norris increased Cheltenham's lead with a splendid dropped goal from a distance of 30 yards. **1971** *Times* 15 Feb. 9/2 Bushell put Sidcup ahead with a superb dropped goal from 30 yards.

b. Of eggs: Fried or poached, 'dropped into the frying pan' (Jam.).

1824 SCOTT *Redgauntlet* ch. x, A roasted chucky and a drappit egg. **1884** MARY E. WILKINS in *Harper's Mag.* July 306/2 Martha was..eating her toast and a dropped egg.

c. ***dropped head***: a head (see HEAD *sb.* 13) at the beginning of a chapter, etc., placed lower down the page than the first line on ordinary pages.

1904 in GOODCHILD & TWENEY *Technol. & Sci. Dict.* 176/1. **1906** E. JOHNSTON *Writing* xvi. 343 It would not be necessary for the first page of a chapter to have the ordinary dropped head and blank upper space.

d. ***dropped handlebars*** = *drop-handlebars* (see DROP-).

1913 *Boy's Own Bk. Outdoor Games* 218 A warning regarding the use of 'dropped' handle-bars will not be out of place. These are only necessary in racing, and while sacrificing comfort are not conducive to fast riding. **1970** *Morning Star* 18 Aug. 4 One sees young lads on bicycles in a busy city bent over dropped handlebars on which the brake levers are right at the end of the bars.

e. ***dropped scone*** (see SCONE *sb.* 1).

†**2.** Marked with spots or specks. *Obs.*

1611 COTGR., *Gouët, faulcon gouët*, whose feathers are ill marked, mailed, or coloured..a dropt Hawke.

3. Abandoned, allowed to lapse.

1886 FROUDE *Oceana* 16, I resumed my dropped intention.

4. *Comb.*, as ***dropped-eared***.

1688 *Lond. Gaz.* No. 2308/4 A Sorrel Mare, dropt Ear'd.

†**droppell.** *Obs. rare.* [a. MLG. and MDu. *droppel*, Ger. *tröpfel* small drop.] In ***droppell-piss, -pysse***, strangury.

1527 ANDREW *Brunswyke's Distyll. Waters* B iij b, Good for the Strangury or droppell pysse named Stranguria.

dropper ('drɒpə(r)). [f. DROP *v.* + -ER[1].]

1. a. One who drops or lets fall in drops; in quot. 1700 = distiller (*slang*). **b.** One who drops seeds into the holes made by a dibbler.

a **1700** B. E. *Dict. Cant. Crew*, *Rum-dropper*, a Vintner. **1768–74** TUCKER *Lt. Nat.* (1852) II. 415 The greatest droppers of beads were often the worst men. **1770–4** A. HUNTER *Georg. Ess.* (1804) II. 356 An active dibbler..with three droppers at seven-pence per day. **1789** *Trans. Soc. Arts* (ed. 2) II. 45 With two dibbers and seven droppers.

c. One who passes counterfeit money, cheques, etc. (cf. DROP *v.* 16 b). *slang.*

1938 F. D. SHARPE *Sharpe of Flying Squad* xxix. 297 These [cheques] are then passed on to other members of the gang..known as 'droppers'. Their job is to present the cheques at the banks. **1959** 'C. HARE' *Best Detective Stories* 236 The functionary whose mission it is to put forged currency into circulation is known technically as a dropper.

d. One who delivers goods, liquor, etc., from market or store to retailers; a 'shop-dropper'. *local Austral.* and *N.Z. colloq.*

1949 F. SARGESON *I Saw in Dream* II. xv. 255 [The Police] reckoned they'd got her [sly-grogging] this time, because they'd found out a dropper had been through the town a few nights before on his lorry. **1957** *Courier-Mail* (Brisbane) 26 Nov. 2 A shop owner has only to telephone an order to a 'dropper' and within a few hours it is delivered to his door.

2. A dog that drops down when it sights game; a setter. Cf. DROP *v.* 4 b.

3. *Angling.* An artificial fly adjusted to a leader above the stretcher fly. Also *drop-fly, dropper-fly.*

1746 BOWLKER *Angling* (1833) 112 The first dropper about a yard from the leading fly; the second dropper about eighteen inches above the first. **1875** 'STONEHENGE' *Brit. Sports* I. v. iv. §3. 350 If more than two droppers are used, the single gut length is increased to eight feet.

4. dropper-in: one who drops in or pays a casual visit.

1805 *Ann. Rev.* III. 58 The laundress is a costly dropper in. **1825** *New Monthly Mag.* XVI. 264 Endless, purposeless visitants; droppers in, as they are called. **1898** *Elizabeth & her German Garden* 37 Either you or the dropper-in will say something..better left unsaid. **1941** V. WOOLF *Between Acts* 48 Uninvited, unexpected, droppers-in, lured off the high road. **1969** J. COOPER *How to stay Married* 44 The droppers-in will be so embarrassed that they'll apologise and make themselves scarce.

5. a. A pendant; cf. DROP *sb.* 10 a. **b.** A glass tube with an india-rubber top on one end, and a small opening at the other, for dropping liquid. **c.** A contrivance in some reaping-machines for depositing the cut grain in gavels on the ground; also the machine itself. **d.** *Mining.* (See quot. 1864.)

c **1825** *Houlston Juv. Tracts* No. 18 *Imag. Troubles* 4 She had..a ring on her finger, and long droppers in her ears. **1864** WEBSTER, *Dropper (Mining)*, a branch vein which drops off from, or leaves, the main lode. **1869** R. B. SMYTH *Goldfields of Victoria* 609 Dropper, a spur dropping into the lode. A feeder. **1874** KNIGHT *Dict. Mech.* I. 754/2 Simultaneously with the bringing into action of the dropper, a cut-off is brought down to arrest the falling grain till the platform is reinstated. **1886** *Sci. Amer.* LV. 373/3 Grain.. cut with a 'dropper' or a self-raking reaper. **1889** *Anthony's Photogr. Bull.* II. 12 The dropper is filled with alkali solution from the wide-mouthed bottle.

e. *Hort.* A young bulb of certain bulbous plants, *esp.* a small bulb developed at the apex of a downward shoot growing from the base of the parent bulb.

1900 B. D. JACKSON *Gloss. Bot. Terms, Dropper*, the young bulb of a tulip, not of flowering size. **1907** *Ann. Bot.* XX. 429 The 'Droppers' of *Tulipa* and *Erythronium*. **1929** A. D. HALL *Bk. Tulip* 22 Occasionally also it will be noticed..that a stolon has started away from the base of the old bulb, turned downward and formed a bulb at the extremity... These bulbs are called 'droppers' and differ in no respect from other offsets. **1951** *Dict. Gardening* (R. Hort. Soc.) IV. 2163/1 A peculiar type of natural propagation is seen in the 'droppers' which are sometimes formed.

f. A vertical member of a fence or the like; *spec.* a light lath used between the main uprights of a fence to keep the wires spaced. Chiefly *Austral.*, *N.Z.*, and *S. Afr.*

1904 'G. B. LANCASTER' *Sons o' Men* 93 [He] had prayed for slotted droppers [in the fence]. *a* **1935** G. L. MEREDITH *Adventuring in Maoriland* vii. 68 Between the posts the wires are stapled to 'droppers', consisting of about three by one battens. **1950** *N.Z. Jrnl. Agric.* Nov. 458/3 The materials are likely to be more easily obtained than wooden droppers. **1967** *Coast to Coast 1965–6* 150 'D'you know what a Mallee gate is, Bob?' 'Yes, it's a short loose panel, just droppers and wires.'

6. *Comb.*, as ***dropper-fly*** = 3.

1834 MEDWIN *Angler in Wales* II. 113 Select..a small gentle, and apply it at the end of his dropper fly. **1875** 'STONEHENGE' *Brit. Sports* I. v. iv. §3. 350 Take a few turns round the dropper-gut to make all secure.

dropping ('drɒpɪŋ), *vbl. sb.* [f. DROP *v.* + -ING[1].] The action of the vb. DROP.

1. a. The action of falling or letting fall in drops.

c **1000** *Ags. Ps.* (Th.) lxiv. 11 þurh dropunge deawes and renes. *c* **1386** CHAUCER *Melib.* ⁋120 Thre thynges dryuen a man out of his hous, that is to seyn Smoke, droppyng of Reyn, and wikked wyues. **1530** PALSGR. 215/2 Droppyng of lycour, *distillation.* **1607** TOPSELL *Serpents* (1658) 789 The watering or dropping of the Eyes. **1611** BIBLE *Prov.* xxvii. 15 A continual dropping in a very rainy day and a contentious woman are alike. **1860** PUSEY *Min. Proph.* 308 Forbidding God's word as a wearisome dropping.

b. See quot.

1823 CRABB *Technol. Dict., Dropping (Vet.)*, a name given to that disease in a cow, which is analogous to the puerperal fever in women.

2. The action of falling or descending vertically; also, of letting anything fall.

c **1315** SHOREHAM 17 So habbeth..Crystnynge, Her signe, droppynge in the water. **1599** H. BUTTES *Dyet's drie Dinner* D iv, Plantes..that are subject..to his leaves-dropping. **1874** JOHNS *Brit. Birds* 180 It begins to descend..by a series of droppings with intervals of simple hovering.

3. The action of discontinuing or abandoning.

1813 *Examiner* 10 May 300/1 The dropping of such a work ..would be a loss to the country. **1859** J. CUNNINGHAM *Ch. Hist. Scot.* II. x. 409 A dropping of the method of queries in processes of error.

4. Falling, dropping off, dying.

1768 *Woman of Honor* III. 240 By the unexpected dropping of two elder brothers, he is..come to an estate.

5. *concr.* **a.** That which drops or falls in drops, as rain, melting wax, etc.; the fat that drops from roasting meat, dripping. (In quot. 1398 = rheum.)

1398 TREVISA *Barth. De P.R.* III. xix. (1495) 66 They that haue droppyng and rewme fallyng to the brest. *c* **1430** *Pilgr. Lyf Manhode* III. lxi. (1869) 172 This kowuele i haue set vnder for to take the droppinges. **1585** T. WASHINGTON tr. *Nicholay's Voy.* II. vi. 36 The Mastic is the teare or droppings of the Lentiscus. **1663** GERBIER *Counsel* 11 The Rain and Droppings of the Thatch. **1837** WHITTOCK *Compl. Bk. Trades* (1842) 348 Rape oil, which obtains the term 'droppings'. **1861** T. A. TROLLOPE *La Beata* II. xiv. 124 Collecting the droppings from the great wax candles.

b. *pl.* The waste material cast off from a machine in certain processes of textile manufacture.

1902 W. I. HANNAN *Textile Fibres of Commerce* 115 The primary impurities from each of the two processes of opening and scutching are known as the droppings.

6. Dung of animals. (Now only *pl.*)

1596 HARINGTON *Metam. Ajax* D iv, Do you not..tell of springing a pheasant and a partridge, and find them out by their dropping? **1846** J. BAXTER *Libr. Pract. Agric.* (ed. 4) II. 80 Fresh droppings from the stables. **1890** *Pall Mall G.* 29 Sept. 5/1 The only combustible we had was the droppings of the wild yaks.

†**7.** The eaves from which water drops. *Obs.*

1597 GERARDE *Herbal* II. xlvii. §2. 262, I founde it vnder the dropping of the bishops house at Rochester. *c* **1710** C. FIENNES *Diary* (1888) 181 The meeteing house..being under the Dropings of ye Cathedrall.

8. *attrib.* and *Comb.*, as (sense 6) ***dropping(s) board, pit***; **dropping-bottle** (see quot. 1864); **dropping field, -point, zone**, a place prepared for the dropping of supplies, troops, bombs, etc., from aircraft; †**dropping-meal** *adv.* = DROP-MEAL; †**dropping-pan** = DRIPPING-PAN; **dropping-tube** (see quot.); **dropping-well**, a well formed by the dropping of water from above.

1916 *N.Z. Jrnl. Agric.* 21 Aug. 100 Those who are not prepared to pay regular attention to cleaning are advised not to have *dropping boards. **1950** *Ibid.* June 531/3 Droppings boards or wired-in droppings pits are coming back into use again [in hen-houses]. **1827** FARADAY *Chem. Manip.* vi. 185 It is proper to have a smaller *dropping-bottle ready for use. **1864** WEBSTER, *Dropping-bottle*, an instrument used to supply small quantities of a fluid to a test-tube or other vessel. **1889** *Anthony's Photogr. Bull.* II. 427 A combined minim-measure and dropping-bottle. **1942** *Times Weekly* 9 Sept. 2 He had to walk two miles back to the '*dropping' field. **1398** TREVISA *Barth. De P.R.* VII. lv. (1495) 268 Stranguria whan a man pissyth wyth dyffyculte *droppinge mele. **1463** *Bury Wills* (Camden) 23 A *droppyng panne. **1672** A. HAIG *Inventory* in J. Russell *Haigs* (1881) 475 A great fraying pan and a great droping pan. **1947** J. MULGAN *Report on Experience* 80 They ran to a schedule and knew the *dropping-points as intimately as their aerodromes. **1883** *Syd. Soc. Lex.*, **Dropping tube*, the tubulated stopper of the Dropping-bottle. **1652** J. FRENCH (*title*) The Yorkshire Spaw; or a Treatise of four famous Medicinal Wells..the *Dropping, or Petrifying Well. **1850** TENNYSON *In Mem.* lxxxiii, Laburnums, dropping-wells of fire. **1945** *By Air to Battle (H.M.S.O.)* 39 It was left to the battalion commander ..to share with the pilot the responsibility of choosing the *dropping zone from the air. **1956** J. TICKELL *Moon Squadron* viii. 83 In ten minutes, we would be over the DZ or dropping zone. **1968** A. J. JACKSON *Blackburn Aircraft* 469 The rear doors were removed for a demonstration over an Army dropping zone at Amesbury, Wilts.

dropping, *ppl. a.* [f. as prec. + -ING[2].]

1. Falling in drops; distilling.

?*a* **1400** *Morte Arth.* 4054 Derefulle dredlesse with drowppande teris. **1583** *Leg. Bp. St. Andrews* Pref. 71 in *Satir. Poems Reform.* xlv, Fra they gat the drapping grise they wanted. **1667** MILTON *P.L.* IV. 630 Those Blossoms also, and those dropping Gumms. **1790** BURNS *Elegy Henderson* xi, Frae my een the drapping rains Maun ever flow.

b. Having moisture falling off in drops, dripping. Of the weather: rainy, wet.

a **1415** LYDG. *Temple of Glas* 394 Oft also, aftir a dropping mone, The weddir clereþ. **1587** MASCALL *Govt. Cattle, Oxen* (1627) 13 If your cattell haue dropping Nostrils. **1648** GAGE *West Ind.* xv. 105 To wipe their dropping brows. **1775** SHAW *Hist. Moray* 151 (Jam.) A misty May, and a dropping June. **1790** A. WILSON *Morning* Poet. Wks. 1846 2 From every bush and every dropping tree.

c. quasi-*adv.* in ***dropping wet***.

1591 SYLVESTER *Du Bartas* I. v. 201 Dropping wet..I return to land Laden with spoyls. **1770** WESLEY *Jrnl.* 16 Apr., We..got into a Scotch mist, and were dropping wet.

2. Falling vertically, falling to the ground.

1715–20 POPE *Iliad* XIV. 546 The dropping head first tumbled to the plain. **1832** TENNYSON *On a Mourner* 9 The swamp, where hums the dropping snipe. **1892** *Pall Mall G.* 25 Mar. 2/1 The 'warm corner' is alive with rising and dropping birds.

3. Falling detachedly, desultory, not continuous.

1708 *Lond. Gaz.* No. 4467/3 The Major..and a Captain ..were kill'd, the former by a dropping Shot. **1814** SCOTT *Wav.* xxxvi, A few dropping shots fired about the spot. **1890** *Century Mag.* July 447/2 A dropping fire of musketry.

4. Falling in value, or in any scale.

1894 *Times* 23 Apr. 13/3 Small occupiers..were.. benefited by dropping prices.

'droppingly, *adv.* [f. prec. + -LY[2].] In a dropping manner; drop by drop; one by one.

c **1400** *Lanfranc's Cirurg.* 278 If he makiþ watir droppynli and a litil at oonys. **1611** SPEED *Hist. Gt. Brit.* IX. ix. (1632) 629 They came droppingly in, and became good Subiects. **1844** MRS. BROWNING *Vision of Poets* Concl. vi, The dew sliding droppingly From the leaf-edges.

dropple. *rare.* [Arbitrary dim. of DROP *sb.*] A little drop.

1821 CLARE *Vill. Minstr.* I. 132 The gudgeons..Startling as each nimble eye Saw the rings the dropples made.

droppy ('drɒpɪ), *a.* Now *dial.* [f. DROP *sb.* + -Y[1].] Given to dropping; dripping, rainy.

1635 SWAN *Spec. M.* v. §2 (1643) 130 A bow of many colours; appearing in a dewie, dark, droppie, and hollow cloud. **1828** *Craven Dial., Droppy*, wet, rainy. 'We've hed a vara droppy time'. **1834** WILSON in *Blackw. Mag.* XXXV. 789 It is dewy and droppy, and mild and misty.

'drop-scene. A term used loosely or incorrectly for *drop* or *act-drop* (DROP *sb.* 16); also for the final scene of a play or drama in real life, that on which the curtain drops.

1815 tr. *Paris Chit-Chat* (1816) I. 191 In order to make a drop-scene. **1831** BREWSTER *Nat. Magic* vi. (1833) 146 An impression very similar to that..produced by the drawing up of a drop scene in the theatre. **1849** E. E. NAPIER *Excurs. S. Africa* II. 412 Such..was the drop-scene of his Excellency's memorable Campaign—the finale of his administration. **1880** G. MEREDITH *Trag. Com.* (1881) 282 She was hoping that with Alvan's eruption the drop-scene would fall.

†**'dropsic**, *a. Obs. rare.* [f. DROPSY.] = next.

1651 WITTIE tr. *Primrose's Pop. Err.* II. vi. 96, I have seene dropsick persons whom the people have thought to be in a consumption.

dropsical ('drɒpsɪkəl), *a.* [f. DROPSY + -IC + -AL[1], after *hydropical.*]

1. Of, pertaining to, or of the nature of dropsy.

1688 *Lond. Gaz.* No. 2323/1 Dangerously ill of a Dropsical Distemper. **1727** BRADLEY *Fam. Dict.* s.v. *Flower de Luce*, The Juice..evacuates dropsical water. **1807–26** S. COOPER *First Lines Surg.* (ed. 5) 372 Hydrophthalmia, or a dropsical enlargement of the [eye]. **1846** G. E. DAY tr. *Simon's Anim. Chem.* II. 280 Dropsical symptoms.

2. Affected with or subject to dropsy.

1678 H. SAMPSON in *Phil. Trans.* 437. **1725** N. ROBINSON *Th. Physick* 180 Dropsical People are generally observ'd to sweat much, but perspire little. **1845** *Florist's Jrnl.* 153 *Anasarca*, a diseased condition of plants, resembling that of dropsical subjects.

3. *transf.* and *fig.* **a.** Swollen, enlarged. **b.** Overcharged with water.

1721 *Lett. from Mist's Jrnl.* (1722) II. 226 In dropsical bombast Expressions. **1831** CARLYLE *Misc.* (1857) III. 6 Inflates itself into a dropsical boastfulness and vainglory. **1845** —— *Cromwell* (1873) I. 19 The Country to the East is all Fen..and still of a very dropsical character. **1864** LOWELL *Fireside Trav.* 321 Puffy with a dropsical want of proportion.

Hence **'dropsically** *adv.*; **'dropsicalness**.

1727 BAILEY vol. II, *Dropsicalness*, having a dropsy. **1785** *Eugenius* I. 84 He..was somewhat dropsically disposed. **1865** DICKENS *Mut. Fr.* I. iii, That stood dropsically bulging over the causeway.

dropsied ('drɒpsɪd), *a.* [f. DROPSY *sb.* + -ED[2].] Having the dropsy; swollen with or as with water; watery; inflated, turgid.

1601 SHAKS. *All's Well* II. iii. 135 Where great addition swells, and vertue none, It is a dropsied honour. *a* **1631** DRAYTON *Noah* in Farr *S.P. Jas. I* (1848) 119 The dropsied clouds, see, your destruction threat. **1762–9** FALCONER *Shipwr.* II. 640 Our dropsied ship may founder by the lee. **1793** W. ROBERTS *Looker-on* No. 65 III. 14 An infant with a dropsied head.

†**'dropstone.** *Obs.* [f. DROP *sb.* or *v.* + STONE.] An old popular name for stalactites and stalagmites, formed by the dropping of water.

1695 WOODWARD *Nat. Hist. Earth* IV. (1723) 211 The common *Stalactites*, *Lapis Stillatitius*, or *Drop-stone*.. hanging down from the Tops and Sides of Grotto's. **1708** *Phil. Trans.* XXVI. 79 Stalagmites. The Drop-stone. **1762** tr. *Busching's Syst. Geog.* V. 211 A spacious and very humid cavern, with a variety of figures in it in dropstone.

dropsy ('drɒpsɪ), *sb.* (*a.*) Forms: 3–5 **dropesie**, 4 **dropecy, -sy(e**, 5 **dropsye**, 6 **dropcy**, 6–7 **dropsie**, 4– **dropsy.** [aphetic form of ME. *i-*, *ydropsy*, HYDROPSY, q.v.]

A. *sb.* **1. a.** A morbid condition characterized by the accumulation of watery fluid in the serous cavities or the connective tissue of the body.

c **1290** *S. Eng. Leg.* I. 364/10 Some fullen in-to þe dropesie. **13..** *Cursor M.* 11829 (Cott.) Ydropsi [*Gött.* þropsi, *Fairf.*, *Trin.* þe dropesy] held him sua in threst. **1388** WYCLIF *Luke* xiv. 2 A man sijk in the dropesie [**1382** syk in ydropesie]. *c* **1440** *Gesta Rom.* xviii. 54 (Harl. MS.) A man that hath the dropcy. *c* **1491** *Chast. Goddes Chyld.* 21 They fall in to dropesie. **1538** STARKEY *England* I. iii. 79 In a dropcy the body ys vnweldy, vnlusty and slo. **1667** MILTON *P.L.* XI. 488 Dropsies, and Asthma's and Joint-racking Rheums. **1789** W. BUCHAN *Dom. Med.* (1790) 567 A dropsy of the brain. **1857** BULLOCK *Cazeaux' Midwif.* 297 Dropsy of the Cellular Tissue is quite a frequent occurrence.

fig. **1611** RICH *Honest. Age* (1844) 37 Pampered vppe in.. the very dropsie of excesse. **1645** MILTON *Colast.* Wks. (1851) 345 The gout and dropsy of a big margent, litter'd and overlaid with crude and huddl'd quotations.

b. 'In *fish-culture*, a disease of young trout.' (*Cent. Dict.*)

c. A disease in succulent plants, from an excess of water; anasarca.

1846 in WORCESTER. **1864** WEBSTER cites WRIGHT.

†**2.** *fig.* An insatiable thirst or craving. *Obs.*

1548 J. HALES in Strype *Eccl. Mem.* II. App. Q. 50 The great dropsy and the insatiable desire of riches of some men. **1612** DEKKER *It be not good* Wks. 1873 III. 358 Seas could not quench his dropsie. **1717** L. HOWEL *Desiderius* (ed. 3) 41 Ambition..will prove an insatiable Dropsy.

3. *Comb.*, as ***dropsy-breeding, -dry, -like, -sick*** adjs.

1570 LEVINS *Manip.* 54/37 Dropsyseke, *hydropicus.* **1603** J. DAVIES *Microcosm.* (1876) 25 (D.) Many dropsy-drie forbeare to drinke Because they know their ill 'twould aggravate. *a* **1618** SYLVESTER *Memorials of Mortalitie* I. xx, As one dropsie-sick. **1619** R. HARRIS *Drunkard's Cup* 14 This Dropsilike disease is almost incurable.

4. Money, *esp.* paid as a tip or as bribery. Cf. DROP *sb.* 18 d. *slang.*

[**1616** T. DRAXE *Bibliotheca Scholastica* 33/1 He hath the siluer dropsie.] **1930** 'GREENHORN' *Tinker, Tailor* xi. 253 [He] lived only for tips, or 'dropsy' as it's called in the vernacular. **1934** P. ALLINGHAM *Cheapjack* ix. 94, I always thought he took the dropsy. If you'd made it half-a-dollar he might have taken it. **1955** P. WILDEBLOOD *Against Law* 103 A nice bit of dropsy to a copper usually does the trick. **1969** J. GARDNER *Compl. State of Death* ii. 18 'The clients immediately think if you're a wop you'll be a push-over for dropsy.' 'Dropsy?' 'Payola...'

†**B.** *attrib.* or as *adj.* **a.** = Dropsical. *Obs.*

1499 *Promp. Parv.* 133/1 (Pynson) Dropsy man or woman, *ydropicus.* **1557** *Tottell's Misc.* (Arb.) 137 The dropsy dryeth that Tantale in the flood Endureth. **1617** HIERON *Wks.* (1619–20) II. 219 Like a dropsie-man, who the more hee drinks, the more he desires to drinke. **1678** *Yng. Man's Call.* 80 It was their cups which..brought the dropsie corpse so soon thither.

†**b.** *fig.* Charged with water. *Obs.*

1598 SYLVESTER *Du Bartas* II. ii. I. *Ark* 523 All th' Earth's dropsie vapours. **1683** CHALKHILL *Thealma & Cl.* 160 Anon a Dropsie cloud Puts out the Sun.

'dropsy *v.*, to render swollen as with dropsy.

c **1817** FUSELI in *Lect. Paint.* xi. (1848) 548 Goltzius and Spranger..dropsied the forms of vigour, or dressed the gewgaws of children in colossal shapes.

† **drop vie, drop-vie,** *vbl. phr. Obs.* [f. DROP *v.* + VIE *sb.*: but sometimes treated as a compound vb.] To drop pieces of money or the like in competition or rivalry, trying which can outdo the other; to compete in alternate efforts, to bid against each other, to vie.

1598 FLORIO, *Rinuitare*, to reuye it againe at any game, to drop vye, to bid againe. **1599** NASHE *Lenten Stuffe* 19 For numbers..of honest housholders..and substantiall graue Burgers, Yarmouth shall droppe vie with them to the last Edward groate they are worth. **1605** CAMDEN *Rem.* 191 When two Monkes were at drop-vied Bezantines..before him for an Abbey. **1613–16** W. BROWNE *Brit. Past.* I. i, He there would sit, and withe the well drop vie That it before his eyes would first run drie.

Hence †**drop-vie** *sb. Obs.*, a competition in which each tries to outdo the other.

1598 FLORIO, *Rinuito*, a reuye, a drop vye at any game.

dropwise ('drɒpwaɪz), *adv.* [see -WISE.] In the manner of a drop; drop by drop.

1673 *Phil. Trans.* VIII. 6156 His urine coming from him drop-wise. **1859** TENNYSON *Vivien* 272 I cull'd the spring That gather'd trickling dropwise from the cleft.

dropwort ('drɒpwɜːt). [f. DROP *sb.* + WORT; in reference to L. name *Filipendula*, i.e. pendulous threads.] A name applied to certain plants having tuberous root-fibres.

1. ***common, field,*** or ***mountain dropwort***, a plant, *Spiræa Filipendula*, belonging to the same genus as Meadowsweet, but scentless. Extended, with defining words, to other species of Spiræa.

1538 TURNER *Libellus, Phellandryon*..uulgus Filipendulam & Droppewort nuncupat. **1578** LYTE *Dodoens* I. xxviii. 40 Of filipendula or Dropworte..The rootes be small & blacke, whereon is hanging certaine small knops or blacke pellets, as in the rootes of the female Pionye, sauing yᵗ they be a great deale smaller. **1863** BUCKMAN in *Gard. Chron.* 23 May 493 The Field Dropwort is a denizen for the most part of dry uplands on calcareous soils. **1879** MISS PLUES *Rambles Wild Flowers* (ed. 3) 102 The Willow-leaved Drop-wort (*S. salicifolia*) is..frequent in shrubberies.

2. A name for species of *Œnanthe* (esp. *Œ. fistulosa*), often distinguished as ***water dropwort, hemlock (water) dropwort***, *Œ. crocata*.

1597 GERARDE *Herbal* 901 There be divers sorts of Dropwoorts, some of the champion or fertill pastures..and some of the water..3 Narrow-leaved Dropwoort. 4 Homlocke Dropwoort. 5 Water Dropwoort. **1747** *Gentl. Mag.* 566 Four children had eaten the roots of the *Oenanthe aquatica cicutae facie* (hemlock-dropwort). **1835** HOOKER *Brit. Flora* 131 *Oenanthe*, Water Drop-wort.

† **drosen.** *Obs.* Forms: 1 drósna (*pl.*), 4 drosen, 5 drowsyn. [see DROSS.] Dregs.

c **1000** ÆLFRIC *Gram.* xlvii. (Z.) 271 Hi druncon ðð ða drosna. **11..** *Voc.* in Wr.-Wülcker 549 *Fex*, drosne. **1393** LANGL. *P. Pl.* C. IX. 193 Drosenes and dregges drynke for menye beggeres. *c* **1475** *Voc.* in Wr.-Wülcker 808 *Hec amurca*, drowsyn.

drosera ('drɒsərə). *Bot.* [mod.L. (Linnæus *Systema Naturæ* (1735)), f. Gr. δροσερός dewy.] An insectivorous herb of the genus so called, = SUNDEW; also, the dried and powdered plant, formerly used as a remedy for respiratory diseases.

1801 SMITH & SOWERBY *Eng. Bot.* XIII. 867 Every *Drosera* hitherto discovered grows in boggy situations. [**1812** J. STOKES *Bot. Mat. Med.* II. 189 Drosera.] **1846** J. LINDLEY *Veget. Kingd.* 433 The common Droseras are rather acid. **1907** *Yesterday's Shopping* (1969) 510/3 Homoeopathic pilules or tinctures...Drosera. **1922** *Chem. Abstr.* 3730 *Drosera* is used in medicine principally as a sedative in the treatment of whooping cough and bronchitis. **1928** MARTINDALE & WESTCOTT *Extra Pharmacop.* (ed. 19) 854 Drosera *not* found specific. **1962** *Amateur Gardening* 3 Mar. 8/2 Droseras do not require much warmth, but plenty of moist fresh air.

‖**droshky** ('drɒʃkɪ), **drosky** ('drɒskɪ). Also **droitzschka, drojeka, droshka, -ke, -ki, droska, droskcha.** [ad. Russ. *drozhki*, dim. of *drogi* waggon, hearse; properly pl. of *droga* perch, or 'reach' of a four-wheeled vehicle. So Fr. *droschki*, Ger. *droschke*.]

A kind of vehicle: orig. and prop. a Russian low four-wheeled carriage without a top, consisting of a narrow bench on which the passengers sit astride or sideways, their feet resting on bars near the ground; hence transferred to other vehicles in use elsewhere; in some German towns the name of the ordinary four-wheelers or fiacres plying for hire.

1808 SIR R. K. PORTER *Trav. Sk. Russ. & Swed.* (1813) I. iii. 23 A sort of hireable machine..denominated a Drojeka. *Ibid.* II. xxviii. 20 The vehicle being a droshky, there was no other servant but the coachman. **1826** SCOTT *Jrnl.* 25 June, [At Blair-Adam] We drove in the droskie and walked in the evening. **1855** *Englishwoman in Russia* 255 They were taken home by the police in droshskies. **1872** FREEMAN in Stephens *Life* (1895) II. 58 At Frankfurt..to get on the Bavarian line you have to take a droschke. **1882** STRATHESK *Bits fr. Blinkbonny* xiii. 294 He met the drosky containing Mrs. Barrie and the children.

attrib. **1838** J. L. STEPHENS *Trav. Greece*, etc. 71/1 The drosky boy..dressed in a long surtout..sits on the end.

drosometer (drəʊ'sɒmɪtə(r)). [mod. f. Gr. δρόσος dew: see -METER. In F. *drosomètre*.] An instrument for measuring the quantity of dew deposited.

1825 W. HAMILTON *Dict. Arts, etc.* (Worc.) **1866** L. P. CASELLA in W. C. Wells *Ess. Dew* 7 To measure the quantity of dew deposited each night, an instrument is used called a drosometer.

drosophila (drə'sɒfɪlə). *Ent.* [mod.L. (C. F. Fallén *Geomyzides Sveciæ* (1823) 4), f. Gr. δρόσος dew + φίλος loving.] A fruit-fly of the genus so called, much used as an experimental subject in the study of genetics.

1829 J. CURTIS *Guide Arrangement Brit. Insects* 235 Drosophila. **1877** *Encycl. Brit.* VII. 256/2 The destruction of..various culinary plants by *Psila*,..*Drosophila*, &c. **1910** T. H. MORGAN in *Science* 22 July 120/1 (*title*) Sex limited inheritance in Drosophila. *Ibid.*, In a pedigree culture of *Drosophila* which had been running for nearly a year through a considerable number of generations, a male appeared with white eyes. The normal flies have brilliant red eyes. **1932** J. S. HUXLEY *Probl. Rel. Growth* ii. 63 The increase in total size of Drosophila caused by low temperature is accompanied by a decrease in wing-size. **1938** *Ann. Reg. 1937* 346 A new technique of artificial fertilisation of Drosophila opened up fresh vistas in genetic research. **1962** G. CREMER-BARTELS in A. Pirie *Lens Metabolism Rel. Cataract* 443 Pteridines..from the red eyes of a drosophila fly. **1969** *Times* 28 Mar. 6/8 Experiments with the fruit fly *Drosophila*.

drosophyllum (drəʊsə'fɪləm). *Bot.* [mod.L. (H. F. Link 1806, in *Neues Jrnl. f. d. Botanik* I. II. 51), f. Gr. δρόσος dew + φύλλον leaf.] An insectivorous plant of the genus of plants so named, belonging to the family Droseraceæ and consisting of a single species, *Drosophyllum lusitanicum*, found in southern Spain, Portugal, and north Africa.

1875 C. DARWIN *Insectivorous Plants* xv. 335 The glands of Drosophyllum, without being stimulated, continually secrete, so as to replace the loss by evaporation. **1894** F. W. OLIVER tr. *Kerner's Nat. Hist. Plants* I. 154 It is not surprising to find *Drosophyllum* covered at the same time with remains of besmeared dead bodies. **1901** *Daily News* 5 Jan. 9/1 The lecturer..told how the drosophyllum went in for a sticky exudation that acted not as a deterrent, but as an actual death-trap. **1909** *Daily Chron.* 18 Feb. 7/5 Portuguese farmers use the fly-catching drosophyllum instead of mechanical flytraps to clear their houses of insects. **1942** F. E. LLOYD *Carnivorous Plants* viii. 102 *Drosophyllum* exercises its own proper power of digestion.

dross (drɒs), *sb.* Also: 1–6 dros, 5–7 drosse. [OE. *drós* = MLG. *drôs*, MDu. *droes* dregs. A lengthened form, DROSEN, ME. *drosne*, OE. *drósna*, corresponds to OHG. *truosana*, MHG. *truosen*, Ger. *drusen* pl. husks of grapes, lees, dregs. See *Kuhn's Zeitschr.* XXXIV. 513 (1896).]

1. The scum, recrement, or extraneous matter thrown off from metals in the process of melting.

c **1050** *Voc.* in Wr.-Wülcker 353 *Auriculum*, dros. *a* **1225** *Ancr. R.* 284 Gold and seoluer clenseð ham of hore dros iðe fure. **1340** HAMPOLE *Pr. Consc.* 3339 Als gold, þat shynes clere and bright..Whar it put in fire to fyn mare Yhit suld it leve sum dros þare. *c* **1440** *Promp. Parv.* 133/1 Drosse of metalle, *scorium*. **1598** HAKLUYT *Voy.* I. 91 (R.) As hard as the drosse of iron. **1678** *Phil. Trans.* XII. 952 There swims on the Metal..a Scum, which they call Dross; much like to Sclag or Dross of Iron. **1725** DE FOE *Voy. round World* (1840) 239 Separate the gold by fire from the dross and mixture. **1830** TENNYSON *Poems* 123 Turn..dross to gold with glorious alchemy. **1881** RAYMOND *Mining Gloss.*, *Dross*, the material skimmed from the surface of freshly melted, not perfectly pure metal.

†**b.** Volcanic scoria. *Obs. rare.*

1811 PINKERTON *Petral.* II. 307 Above are great masses of sand, red drosses, and puzzolana.

1875 *Ure's Dict. Arts* III. 73 Fresh quantities of litharge or pot dross..are from time to time thrown in. **1879** *Cassell's Techn. Educ.* IV. 81/1 The first step..is to convert the lead into..protoxide, which is more usually called 'dross' by the workmen than litharge or massicot.

d. An alloy incidentally formed in the zinc-bath, by the action of the zinc on the iron pot and iron articles dipped. (Wahl *Galvanopl. Manip.* 1884).

2. Dreggy, impure, or foreign matter, mixed with any substance, and detracting from its purity; e.g. the dregs or lees of oil or wine, the chaff of corn, etc.

c **1440** *Promp. Parv.* 133/1 Drosse of corne, *acus, criballum*. **1594** PLAT *Jewell-ho.* II. 12 You shall find a fourth or fifth part of drosse in the best butter. **1616** SURFL. & MARKH. *Country Farme* 39 She shall reserue the drosse of the Grapes shee presseth. *Ibid.* 46 Take the drosse of oyle of Linseed. **1812** J. SMYTH *Pract. Customs* (1821) 379 Report what allowance ought to be made for dross and dirt on the Bees-wax.

b. A miner's name for iron pyrites in coal; also, small or waste coal, the screenings of the coalhills.

1829 GLOVER *Hist. Derby* I. 234 Many of the coal-seams..have considerable quantities of brasses or drosses in them, which are lumps of iron pyrites. **1854** *Encycl. Brit.* VII. 117/1 A heap of dross or small coal. **1872** *Daily News* 12 Oct., Great black mounds of coal dross. **1892** *Labour Commission* Gloss., *Dross*, 'small coal' [*Ibid.* s.v. *Coal*, the duff, slag, or waste, which arises from the sorting of the large coal into nuts, and which passes through the screen bars]. **1894** *Times* 16 Apr. 4/3 Quietness rules in the coal trade..Dross is scarce and dearer.

c. *Salt-making.* 'The refuse or marl left after dissolving rock-salt in water.' *Chester Gloss.* 1884.

3. *fig.* from 1 and 2. (Cf. *dregs*, DREG 3.)

1526 *Pilgr. Perf.* (W. de W. 1531) 5 Our lorde wolde not that we sholde take the drosse of the lawe of Moyses. **1677** W. HUBBARD *Narrative* 119 The Dregs and Lees of the Earth, and Drosse of Mankinde. **1745** A. BUTLER *Lives of Saints* (1836) 104 The seventh general persecution, permitted by God to purge away the dross of his flock. **1810** SCOTT *Lady of L.* II. xxii, A human tear From passion's dross refined and clear.

4. In general: Refuse; rubbish; worthless, impure matter.

c **1440** *Promp. Parv.* 133/1 Drosse, or fylthe..qwat so it be, *ruscum, rusculum*. **1596** DALRYMPLE tr. *Leslie's Hist. Scot.* IX. 200 His chambre..with the tempest was dung in dros. **1632** G. FLETCHER *Christ's Tri.* 26 So tinne for silver goes, and dunghill drosse for gold. **1671** MILTON *P.R.* III. 23 All treasures and all gain esteem as dross. **1742** YOUNG *Nt. Th.* IV. 428 The stars, tho' rich, what dross their gold to thee. **1876** GEO. ELIOT *Dan. Der.* I. i, He was of different quality from the human dross around her.

5. *attrib.* and *Comb.*, as ***dross heap, iron; dross-full, dross-rich*** adjs.

1428 in *Surtees Misc.* (1888) 2 And iiijᵉ and mo peces of fals drosseyren. **1598** SYLVESTER *Du Bartas* II. *Ded.* 14 Such sparks may flame..A higher pitch, then dross-full Vanity. **1881** W. T. ROSS *Poems* 69 The dross-rich earthling leaves life's stage. **1893** PEEL *Spen Valley* 13 Having stood for a long time on the edge of a dross heap.

dross, *v.* [f. prec. sb.]

†**1.** *trans.* ***dross out***: to sift out as dross. *Obs.*

1641 BEST *Farm. Bks.* (Surtees) 105 In every bushell of meale..there is very neare a pecke of chizell drossed out.

†**2.** To render drossy or impure; to corrupt. *Obs.*

1648 EARL WESTMLD. *Otia Sacra* (1879) 69 Of full Power to refine the deed Our Parents Dross'd by their Corruption.

3. To convert (lead) into 'dross' or protoxide.

1891 *Address Brit. Assoc.* in *Nature* 27 Aug., In 'drossing' molten lead, the oxidation of the lead is greatly promoted by the presence of a trace of antimony.

4. To free from dross, remove dross from.

1884 W. H. WAHL *Galvanopl. Manip.* 529. (*Cent. Dict.*)

† **drossard, -art.** *Obs.* [a. mod.Du. *drossaard*, a transformation (through *drossaet, drossaert*, Kilian, 1599) of MDu. *drossâte* = MLG. *drossête, drotzête* (mod.LG. *droste*, Du. *drost*), MHG. *truhtsæze*, OHG. **truhtsâzzo, truhsâzzo, trutsâzo*:—OTeut. type **druhtisætjon-*, f. *druhti-, truhti-*, people, company, retinue + *sætjon-* one who sits; hence, 'he who sits or presides at the meals of the *druht*'. See Kluge s.v. *Truchsetz*, Franke s.v. *Drossaard*.]

A steward, high bailiff, prefect.

1678 *Lond. Gaz.* No. 1287/3 The Drossarts and Bailiffs of the several places in the Country of Waes, are summoned to Ghent, to swear Fealty to the French King. **1685** *Ibid.* No. 1998/2 The Provost of the Court, the Drossart of Brabant, and the Mareschal-General, are commanded to have their Companies abroad for the executing the said Placeat.

†**'drossel, drosell.** *Obs.* [Origin obscure: cf. DRAZEL, DRATCHELL.] A sloven, a slut.

1581 NUCE *Seneca's Octavia* iv, That drosell dyre, that furious slut, Erin. **1602** WARNER *Alb. Eng.* IX. xlvii. (1612) 219 Now dwels each Drossell in her Glasse. **1617** MINSHEU *Ductor, Panguts*..an vnweldie Drossell, nothing but guts.

drosser ('drɒsə(r)). *Glass-making.* [Corrupted from F. *dressoir*, dresser, frame, etc.] A separating iron frame placed between sets of tables in the annealing kiln.

1856 H. CHANCE in *Jrnl. Soc. Arts* 15 Feb. (*On Glass*) Iron frames or drossers, which divide the tables into sets, the first drosser leaning against the wall of the kiln, the second against the first, and so on.

drossiness ('drɒsɪnɪs). [f. DROSSY *a.* + -NESS.] The quality or condition of being drossy.

1639 ROUSE *Heav. Univ.* ix. (1702) 121 Purge thy soul from carnal drossiness. **1652–62** HEYLIN *Cosmogr.* IV. (1682) 60 The Myrrha of these parts had the name of Barbara, from the drossiness and coarseness of it. *a* **1691** BOYLE *Wks.* I. 275 (R.) To refine us from our earthly drossiness.

'drossless, *a.* [see -LESS.] Free from dross.

1846 WORCESTER cites STEVENS.

drossock, var. of DRASSOCK.

drossy ('drɒsɪ), *a.* [f. DROSS *sb.* + -Y.]

1. Of metals, etc.: Characterized by containing dross or scorious matter, or waste and worthless material; of the nature of dross; dreggy, feculent.

c **1420** *Pallad. on Husb.* x. 106 Yf thi mede is drossy, bareyn, olde, Let plough hit eft. **1592** Davies *Immort. Soul* Introd. xl, So doth the Fire the drossy Gold refine. **1667** Milton *P.L.* v. 442 The Empiric Alchimist Can turn.. Metals of drossiest Ore to perfet Gold. **1757** A. Cooper *Distiller* I. xx. (1760) 83 The recrementitious or drossy Parts of the sugar. **1870** Morris *Earthly Par.* II. III. 158 As kingly gold To our thin brass, or drossy lead.

2. *transf.* and *fig.* Impure, mixed with impurities.

1579 J. Stubbes *Gaping Gulf* A vij, Yet shal papistes be to light and to drossie to marry with vs. **1627–77** Feltham *Resolves* I. lxx. 106 Words being rather the drossie part, Conceit I take to be the principal. **1854** Faber *Growth in Holiness* xii. (1872) 205 We find our actions to be.. only the drossy compound of nature and grace.

‖**drosty.** *S. Africa.* Also **drostdy.** [Du. *drosty, drostij*, f. *drost* bailiff: cf. DROSSARD.] The official residence of a *land-drost* (no longer in use in Cape Colony).

1812 Miss Plumtre tr. *Lichtenstein's S. Africa* I. 172 The Drosty at Zwellendam was built of like materials. **1834** Pringle *Afr. Sk.* ix. 296 The source of the Ghamka, where the drostdy, or district village of Beaufort had been recently erected.

drot, *U.S.* var. DRAT *int.* and *v.*

†**drote,** *v. Obs.* [Etymology unknown.] *intr.* To stammer, stutter. Hence †**droting** *ppl. a.* and *vbl. sb.*; †**drotingly** *adv.*; †**droter,** a stutterer.

c **1440** *Promp. Parv.* 133/2 Drotare, *traulus, traula.* Drotyn yn speche, *traulo.* Drotynge, *traulatus.* Drotyngly, *traule.*

‖**dróttkvætt** ('drouhtkvait). Also 8 **droquæt,** 9 **drottkvædi, -kvæði.** [ON. *drótt-kvæði*, f. *drótt* king's household + *kvæði* poem.] Court metre, a complex verse-form employed by the scaldic poets of early Scandinavia.

1779 J. Strutt *Chron. Engl.* II. III. 253 The droquæt.. was most generally used, each verse of which consisted of six syllables. **1843** G. W. Dasent tr. *Rask's Gram. Icelandic* v. 218 Dróttqvæði has three trochees, or properly spondees in each line; but dactyls may also be used in the two first places. **1870** G. Bayldon *Elem. Gram. Old Norse* v. 115 The metre usual in laudatory poems is called *Drótt-kvæði*.. or 'heroic verse'. **1881** *Encycl. Brit.* XII. 623/1 The change in the phonesis of the language is well illustrated by the new metres as compared with the old Icelandic *Drott-kvædi* in its varied forms. **1911** *Ibid.* XXVII. 1046/1 In Icelandic poetry there was a highly artificial verse-system known as court-verse (*dróttkvaett*), which consisted of alliterative groups of two lines each, arranged in staves of eight lines. **1927** E. V. Gordon *Introd. Old Norse* 295 The favourite metre of the skalds was *dróttkvætt* (also called *dróttkvæðr háttr*). **1951** G. Turville-Petre *Heroic Age of Scandinavia* xv. 165 The most popular of the scaldic verse-forms was called the Court Metre (Dróttkvætt)... The line of the Court Metre contained three stresses, and these were generally distributed between six syllables.

drou, drough, drouȝ, obs. pa. t. of DRAW *v.*

drouery, var. DRUERY, *Obs.*

droug, drougge, obs. ff. DRUG.

drought (draʊt), **drouth** (draʊθ, *Sc.* druːθ). Forms: α. 1 **drúȝað, -oð,** 3 (*Orm.*) **druhhþe,** 4 **druȝþe, drouhþe, droȝþe,** 5 **droughþe, drouȝth,** 6–8 **drougth,** 7–8 **droughth;** 4–7 **drouthe,** 5 **drowþe,** 5–8 **drowth,** (6 **droutht**), 4– **drouth** (now *dial.* or *arch*). β. 3–4 **druȝt(e,** 4 **droȝt(e, drohut,** 4–5 **drouȝt(e,** 4–6 **droght(e, drught,** 5 **droughte, drowghte, drouht, drowte,** 4– **drought.** [OE. *drúȝað, -oð*, f. *drúȝ-* stem of *drýȝe* DRY, q.v. Cf. Du. *droogte*, f. *droog* dry. From an early period the final *-th* after *ȝ* varied with *-t* (cf. *highth, height*:—OE. *híehþu*), and this form is established in standard English, while *drouth, drowth* has continued in Sc. and northern dialects, and is often used by Eng. poets.]

1. a. The condition or quality of being dry; dryness, aridity, lack of moisture. *arch.*

α. *a* **1100** *Voc.* in Wr.-Wülcker 317/24 *Siccitas*, druȝað, oððe hæð. *c* **1400** *Lanfranc's Cirurg.* 17 It bryngiþ vnkindly drowþe to woundis. **1658** Evelyn *Fr. Gard.* (1675) 91 The drouth of the ground. **1672** Petty *Pol. Anat.* (1691) 48 The Heat, Coldness, Drowth, Moisture.. of Air. **1833** Tennyson *Fatima* 13, I look'd athwart the burning drouth Of that long desert to the south. *a* **1846** Landor *Imag. Conv.* Ser. I. xiii. Wks. 1846 I. 68 Grubs.. which die, the moment they tumble out of the nutshell and its comfortable drouth.

β. *a* **1300** *Cursor M.* 6365 Ne for na drught ne for na wat. **1398** Trevisa *Barth. De P.R.* IV. iii. (1495) 81 Droughte and moysture ben contrary. *c* **1440** *Promp. Parv.* 133/2 Drowte, *siccitas*. **1589** Cogan *Haven Health* clxi. (1636) 154 Old doves for their.. drought and hardnesse of digestion, are to bee eschewed. **1643** Lightfoot *Glean. Ex.* (1648) 28 Called *Horeb*, from the rocky drought of it. **1727** W. Mather *Yng. Man's Comp.* 27 Drought, a driness.

b. *fig.* (With quot. 1652 cf. DRY *a.* 15.)

1622 Mabbe tr. *Aleman's Guzman d'Alf.* I. 203 The great drought that we suffer in our soules. **1642** Milton *Apol. Smect.* Wks. 1738 I. 118 The sluce.. that feeds the drowth of his Text. **1652** J. Hall *Height Eloquence* p. vi, All men naturally aim at high things, and ambitiously avoid the imputation of drought or weaknesse. **1872** G. Macdonald *Wilf. Cumb.* I. xxviii. 286, 'I daresay', returned Charley, with drought.

2. *spec.* Dryness of the weather or climate; lack of rain. (The current sense.) ***absolute drought, partial drought*** (see quot. 1963).

α. *c* **1200** Ormin 8625 Forr þatt te land wass driȝȝedd all And scorrcnedd þurrh þe druhhþe. **13..** *E.E. Allit. P.* B. 524 Ne hete, ne no harde forst, vmbre ne droȝþe. *c* **1449** Pecock *Repr.* I. xviii. 108 In tyme of drouȝth. **1535** Coverdale *1 Kings* xvii. Contents of Ch., A greate drouth & derth in Elias tyme. **1673** Temple *Obs. United Prov.* Wks. 1731 I. 75 There happen'd.. a mighty Drowth in the Beginning of the Summer. **1865** Swinburne *Song in Time of Revol.* 22 The tender dew after drouth.

β. *c* **1250** *Gen. & Ex.* 2348 So sal druȝte ðe feldes deren. *c* **1386** Chaucer *Prol.* 2 Whan that Aprille with hise shoures soote The droghte of March hath perced to the roote. ? *a* **1500** *Metr. Prov.* in *Rel. Ant.* I. 323 After droght commyth rayne.. after rayne, Commyth drought agayne. **1666** Dryden *Ann. Mirab.* cx, As in a drought the thirsty creatures cry And gape upon the gathered clouds for rain. **1727–46** Thomson *Summer* 1446 Streams unfailing in the Summer's drought. **1883** H. Drummond *Nat. Law in Spir. W.* v. (1884) 148 Subject to occasional and prolonged droughts.

1881 G. J. Symons in *British Rainfall 1880* 112, (1) 'Absolute Droughts', or all periods of 14 or more consecutive days absolutely without rain; and (2) 'Partial Droughts', or all periods of 28 days or upwards in which the total fall was less than a quarter of an inch. **1899** *Daily News* 12 June 7/2 With all the dry weather we had last year there was not one case of an absolute drought in London. **1963** *Meteorol. Gloss* (Met. Office) (ed. 4) 83 An 'absolute drought' is a period of at least 15 consecutive days, to none of which is credited 0·01 in., or 0·2 mm, or more of rainfall. A 'partial drought' is a period of at least 29 consecutive days, the mean daily rainfall of which does not exceed 0·01 in., or 0·2 mm.

fig. **1620** Middleton *Chaste Maid* v. i, A drouth of virtue, And dearth of all repentance. **1640** Fuller *Joseph's Coat* Serm. i. (1867) 104 The drowth and scorching heat of persecution. **1877** L. Morris *Epic Hades* II. 82 A secret spring of joy, Which mocked the droughts of Fate.

†**3.** Dry or parched land, desert. *Obs. rare.*

a **1000** *Ps. Lamb.* 189 a, 21 (Bosw.) Bearn Israela eodon þurh druȝoþe. **1671** Milton *P.R.* III. 274 To South the Persian Bay, And inaccessible the Arabian drouth.

4. Thirst. *arch.* and *dial.*

α. **1393** Langl. *P. Pl.* C. XVI. 253 Whenne þow clomsest for colde oþer clyngest for drouthe. **1500–20** Dunbar *Poems* xl. 28 Off wyne.. They drank twa quartis.. Of drowth sic excess did thame constrene. **1548** Hall *Chron., Hen. VII*, 53 b, He called for drynke.. one of hys chambrelaynes mervellynge, requyred the cause of hys drouth. **1671** Milton *P.R.* I. 325 His carcass, pined with hunger and with droughth. **1702** S. Parker tr. *Cicero's De Finibus* 63, I am taking it off to quench my Droughth. **1726** Leoni *Alberti's Archit.* II. 82/2 That burning drowth of the mind, which kept you waking. **1855** Browning *De Gustibus* ii, Where the baked cicalas die of drouth.

β. **1588** *Losses Span. Navy* in *Harl. Misc.* (Malh.) II. 52 Their flesh meat they cannot eat, their drought is so great. **1705** Stanhope *Paraphr.* II. 560 Feeling himself afflicted with a vehement Drought. **1847–8** H. Miller *First Impr.* xvi. (1857) 272, I asked.. [for] something to slake my drought.

5. *attrib.* and *Comb.* ***drought-proof, -resistant, -resisting, -stricken*** adjs.

c **1250** *Gen. & Ex.* 2107, vii. lene [eares].. Welkede, and smale, and druȝte numen [= drought-seized]. **1822** T. Mitchell *Aristoph.* I. 169 That I may wet my drought-parch'd mind. **1936** I. L. Idriess *Cattle King* xxxvi. 314 He hoped in time with bores to make it drought-proof. **1952** *New Biol.* XIII. 41 Drought-resistant tetraploid types. **1916** *Nature* 15 June 333/2 Special drought-resisting wheats. **1927** W. G. Kendrew *Climates of Continents* (ed. 2) 54 Drought-resisting bushes. **1881** W. D. Hay *300 Years Hence* ii. 34 Drought-stricken Indian districts. **1890** *Daily News* 1 Oct. 2/6 They traversed the same drought-stricken plain. **1911** E. M. Clowes *On Wallaby* ii. 28 Especially in drought-stricken districts.

droughty ('draʊtɪ), **drouthy** ('draʊθɪ, *Sc.* 'druːθɪ), *a.* [f. DROUGHT + -Y: cf. *mighty, weighty*.]

1. Dry, without moisture; arid.

1603 Drayton *Bar. Wars* II. xvii, Yet not one drop fall from thy droughtie eyes! **1643** Lightfoot *Glean. Ex.* (1648) 28 Out of the droughty rocke Moses.. bringeth forth water. **1708** J. Philips *Cyder* II. Poems (1763) 92 Thou must With tasteless water wash thy droughty throat. **1850** Browning *Christmas Eve* xv, His cough, like a drouthy piston, Tried to dislodge the husk that grew to him.

fig. **1818** Byron *Juan* I. ccv, Campbell's Hippocrene is somewhat drouthy. **1848** Hare *Guesses* II. (1874) 561 Men of drowthy hearts and torpid imaginations.

2. Characterized by drought; deficient in rainfall.

1605 *Play Stucley* in Simpson *Sch. Shaks.* (1878) I. 261 Preach unto the droughty earth; Persuade it, if thou canst, to shun the rain. **1669** W. Simpson *Hydrol. Chym.* 315 In droughty hot weather. **1739** Labelye *Short Acc. Piers Westm. Bridge* 5 Droughty Seasons. **1818** Scott *Hrt. Midl.* xlii, As drouthy as the weather had been.

3. Thirsty; often = addicted to drinking.

α. **1626** T. H[awkins] *Caussin's Holy Crt.* 71 The children of rich men become drouthy amongst a masse of fountaynes. **1691** Tryon *Wisd. Dictates* 115, I am never droughthy as those are that eat Flesh. **1790** Burns *Tam o' Shanter* 2 When.. drouthy neebors, neebors meet. **1879** *Temple Bar* Oct. 237 The dusty, drouthy wayfarers.

β. *a* **1713** Sloane in Derham *Phys.-Theol.* x. Note 27 (R.) A limpid.. water, or sap, as gives new life to the droughty traveller or hunter. **1812** Byron *Ch. Har.* I. lxix. (Orig. Draft), [He] droughty then alights, and roars for Roman purl. **1863** Whittier *Cobbler Keezar's Vision* 37 But that droughty folk should be jolly Puzzles my poor old wits.

Hence '**droughtiness.**

1720 Welton *Suffer. Son of God* I. Pref. 63 These Methods.. will.. refresh the Droughtiness of the Soul.

drouguist, obs. f. DRUGGIST.

drouh, obs. pa. t. of DRAW *v.*

drouk, drook (druk), *v. Sc.* and *north. dial.* Also (6 **drokke**), 9 **drowk.** [Origin uncertain: cf. ON. *drukna* to be drowned, *drukkit* drunk, and DRUNK *v.*] *trans.* To drench (as with heavy rain). Hence **drouked,** *Sc.* **droukit,** *ppl. a.*

1513 Douglas *Æneis* x. vi. 44 Bot finaly, all droukit and forwrocht, Thai salffit war, and warpit to the cost. **1619** Z. Boyd *Last Battell* (1629) 302 (Jam.) Heare how the drouked man [Jonah] sang at last. *a* **1774** Fergusson *Cauler Oysters* Poems (1845) 7 If ye hae catch'd a droukit skin. *a* **1796** Burns *Weary Pund o' Tow* ii, And aye she took the tither souk To drouk the stowrie tow. **1823** Galt *Entail* I. i. 9 Foul would hae been the gait, and drooking the shower. *c* **1836** R. Dick in Smiles *Life* (1878) 64 With the mist swooping about you and drooking your whiskers and eyebrows. **1868** Atkinson *Cleveland Gloss.*, *Drouk*, to drench. **1869** C. Gibbon *R. Gray* iv, Men and cattle were 'drookit' and uncomfortable.

drouke, var. DROWK *v.*

†**drouken,** *v. Obs. rare.* [Etymol. uncertain: perh. a. ON. *drukna* to be drowned, taken fig.] ? To be sunk in slumber or a swoon. Hence **droukening, drouknyng,** deep slumber, swoon.

a **1300** *Body & Soul* 1 (MS. Laud) Als I lay in a winteris ny[h]t in a droukening [*Roy. MS.* drouknynge, *Vernon MS.* droupnynge] bifor the day. *a* **1400** *Leg. Rood* 141 Alle þei seiden þei weore sori, Fordolled in a drouknyng dred.

†**drouking,** *vbl. sb. Obs.* [Deriv. uncertain: cf. DROWK *v.*] ? Crouching, cowering.

c **1490** *Promp. Parv.* 113 (Heber MS.) Droukynge [*Pynson* droukinge, *Harl. MS.* Darynge or drowpynge], *latitatio.*

†**droul,** *v. Obs.* or *dial.* Also **drool.** [cf. Sc. *droul* 'to bellow as a hart,' Jam.] *trans.* To utter mournfully.

a **1670** Hacket *Abp. Williams* II. 224 O Sons and Daughters of Jerusalem, droul out an Elegy for good King Josias. **1825** Jamieson, *Drool*,.. to cry in a low and mournful tone.

droumslade: see DRUMSLADE *Obs.*, a drum.

†**droumy,** *a. Obs. rare.* [? Related to Sc. DRUMLY.] Turbid.

1605 Bacon *Adv. Learn.* II. xxiii. §45 To set on fire and trouble states, to the end to fish in droumy waters. **1640** Watts tr. Lat. version of do. 421 To become an incendiarie and a perturber of states, to the end he may better fish in droumy waters [L. *turbidis aquis*]. **1847–78** Halliwell, *Droumy*, dirty, muddy. *Devon.*

†**droun,** *v. Obs. rare*$^{-1}$. [Related to ON. *drynja*, Sw. *dröna* to roar, bellow, mod.G. *dröhnen* to roar, and so to DRONE *sb.*^{1}, q.v.] *intr.* To roar.

1340–70 *Alisaunder* 985 Hee drouned as a dragon, dredefull of noyes.

droun, droup, obs. ff. DROWN, DROOP.

drounslade, -slet, etc.: see DRUMSLADE.

drourie, -ry, var. DRUERY, *Obs.*

drouse, -ze, -sie, obs. ff. DROWSE, DROWSY.

drouth, drouthy, var. of DROUGHT, -Y, q.v.

drove (drəʊv), *sb.* Forms: 1–2 **dráf,** 3 **drof,** 4– **drove,** (5 **drowe,** *north.* **drafe, draffe, drawe,** 6 **droave,** *Sc.* **drave**). [OE. *dráf*, from 2nd ablaut grade of *drífan* to DRIVE.]

I. †**1.** The action of driving. (Only OE.)

971 *Blickl. Hom.* 199 He þa se fear þæs hyrdes drafe forhoȝode.

2. A number of beasts, as oxen, sheep, etc., driven in a body; a herd, flock.

a **1121** *O.E. Chron.* (Laud MS.) an. 1016 Hi drifon.. heora drafa in to Medewæȝe. *c* **1350** *Will. Palerne* 181 Whanne he went hom eche niȝt wiþ is droue of bestis. **1483** *Cath. Angl.* 107 A Drawe of nowte [*A.* a Draffe of Nowte], *armentum.* **1555** Eden *Decades* 300 They go.. with theyr droues of cattayle. **1576** Fleming *Panopl. Epist.* 27 He had also, gathered together, as it were in a droave, much cattel. *a* **1674** Clarendon *Hist. Reb.* XI. §48 Market day, when great droves of little Horses, laden with sacks of corn, allways resorted to the Town. **1837** Lytton *E. Maltrav.* 11 He passed a drove of sheep.

b. *transf.* A crowd, multitude, shoal (of other animals, or of human beings, esp. when moving in a body; also *fig.* of things).

1014 Wulfstan *Hom.* xxxiii. (1883) 163 [Hi] drifaþ ða drafe cristenra manna fram sæ to sæ. *c* **1250** *Gen. & Ex.* 102 It mai ben hoten heuene-Rof; It hileð al ðis werldes drof. **1590** Spenser *F.Q.* III. viii. 29 Proteus.. Along the fomy waves driving his finny drove. **1596** Dalrymple tr. *Leslie's Hist. Scot.* I. 51 In draues as it war, returnes to thair awne cuntrey. **1607** Hieron *Wks.* I. 230 That olde popish rule, to follow the droue, and to beleeue as the church beleeueth. **1692** Washington *Milton's Def. Pop.* M.'s Wks. 1738 I. 494 Then a great drove of Heresies and Immoralities broke loose among them. **1724** De Foe *Mem. Cavalier* (1840) 164 The Welchmen came in by droves. **1857** Hawthorne *Fr. & It. Jrnls.* II. 260 A ghost in every room, and droves of them in some of the rooms.

3. Locally, esp. in the Fen District: **a.** A road along which horses or cattle are driven. **b.** A channel for drainage or irrigation.

934 *Charter of Æðelstan* in *Cod. Dipl.* V. 217 Of ðam hlince andlang drafæ on ðonæ hlinc æt waddænæ. [**1319** *Reg. Christ Ch. Cant.* in Cunningham *Law Dict.* s.v., Pasturas.. cum omnibus pertinentiis drovis viis semitis & fossatis.] **1664-5** *Act 16 & 17 Chas. II*, c. 11 §13 Libertie..to passe and repasse upon any..Drove or Droves in or compassing the said Fenns. **1829** [J. R. BEST] *Personal & Lit. Mem.* 456 The major rode in the middle of the Drove (so our fen roads are called). **1844** *Camp of Refuge* I. 44 Droves or cuts to carry off the increase of water towards the Wash. **1861** SMILES *Engineers* I. 67 Many droves, leams, eaus, and drains were cut. **1893** BARING-GOULD *Cheap Jack Z.* I. 58 [In the Fens] there is no material of which roads can be made. In place of roads there are 'droves'.

II. 4. A stone-mason's chisel with a broad face.

1825 JAMIESON, *Drove*, the broadest iron used by a mason in hewing stones. **1881** MORGAN *Contrib. to Amer. Ethnol.* 180 It shows no marks of the chisel or the drove.

III. 5. *Comb.*, as *drove-dike*, *-way*; **drove-road**, an ancient road or track along which there is a free right of way for cattle, but which is not 'made' or kept in repair by any authority.

1865 KINGSLEY *Herew.* xxi, He sprang up the *drove-dyke. **1823** *Blackw. Mag.* XIV. 189 The *drove-road passed at no great distance. **1892** *Spectator* 12 Mar. 355/1 The old rights-of-way known as 'drove-roads' [in Scotland]. **1895** *Daily News* 1 Oct. 6/3 The drove road in Southern Scotland is the way once used by drovers..from the extreme north. **1239-52** *Rental Glaston.* (Som. Rec. Soc. 1891) 44 Philippus bel tenet vij acras et quoddam iter quod vocatur *Drofwei. **1664-5** *Act 16 & 17 Chas. II*, c. 11 §22 The twoe Drove wayes in the said Fenns called the North drove and South drove. **1726** *Laws of Sewers* 181 Whereby Drove Ways, Bridges &c...shall be obstructed.

†**drove**, *v.*[1] *Obs.* Also 4 druve, druvy. [Early ME. *drōven*, a derivative of OE. *dróf*, DROF, turbid, troubled, disturbed. Cf. DREVE *v.*[1]]

1. *trans.* To trouble, disturb.

a **1300** *E.E. Psalter* iii. 2 Hou fele-folded are þai, þat droves me to do me wa. *a* **1300** *Cursor M.* 11974 His moder mode wald he noght droue. *a* **1340** HAMPOLE *Psalter* ii. 5 In his wodnes he sall druuy þaim. *Ibid.* vi. 2 Druuyd ere all my banes.

2. *intr.* To become troubled or overcast.

a **1300** *Cursor M.* 24418 Ouer al þe werld ne was bot night, Al droued and wex dime.

drove, *v.*[2] [f. DROVE *sb.*; or back-formation from DROVER.] To drive herds of cattle; to follow the occupation of a drover. (*trans.* and *intr.*)

1632 LITHGOW *Trav.* x. 459 Baptista the Coach-man, an Indian Negro droving out at the Sea-gate. **1805** FORSYTH *Beauties Scotl.* II. 328 Persons who drove to a considerable extent ought to have funds or friends of their own to be security for them. **1881** *Gentl. Mag.* Jan. 61 Scores of highly born and bred men live by droving cattle.

drove, *v.*[3] [f. DROVE *sb.* 4.] *trans.* To dress (stone) in parallel lines with a drove or broad chisel. Hence **droved** *ppl. a.*

1825 JAMIESON, *Drove*, to hew stones for building by means of a broad pointed instrument. **1830** GRAY *Arithmetic* 98 The Droved hewn-work of said house: the rybats and lintels of 6 windows..6 soles of ditto. **1842-76** GWILT *Archit.* §1914 In Scotland, besides the above described sorts of work, there are some other kinds, termed *droved*, *broached*, and *striped*. Droving is the same as that called random tooling in England, or boasting in London. *Ibid.* §1915 The workmen will not take the same pains to drove the face of a stone which is to be afterwards broached.

drove, pa. t. (and obs. pa. pple.) of DRIVE *v.*

drove, var. of DROF *a. Obs.*

†**droveden** ('drəʊvdɛn). *Obs.* [f. DROVE *sb.* + DEN *sb.*[1]] A wooded hollow or tract into which swine and other beasts might be driven to feed.

In the Weald of Kent neighbouring proprietors sometimes had common of pannage in these: see quots. 1778-91.

1309 *Roll of Pleas, 3 Ed. II* (in Robinson *Com. Law Kent* (1791) 269 Arbores in prædictis terris & tenementis crescentes, una cum proficuo Pannagii, ratione Drovedenn sunt ipsius Archiepiscopi. **1332** *Literæ Cantuarienses* 15 Aug. (Rolls No. 85) I. Lett. 463 Par les usages de Kent de drovedenn, le boys de cheyne et de fou deit estre le nostre, a copier, et a carier..et a entrier en noz drovedenn pur les cariages faire. **1778** HASTED *Kent* I. cxlii/2 A custom peculiar to the Weald, that the lords of whom the *drovedennes* were holden in *gavelkind*, should have all the great oaks, ash, and beech growing there, together with the pannage thereof, and the tenants only the underwoods, or at most the oaks, ash, and beech, under forty years growth. **1791** T. ROBINSON *Comm. Law Kent* II. viii. 265 It was usual in ancient Royal Donations of Manors lying out of the Weald, to render the grant more compleat by an additional Privilege of Common of Pannage..in one or more Dens in the Weald..And these Denns set out for the Agistment of Hogs and other Droves of Cattle, were thence called Drovedennes.

drover ('drəʊvə(r)). Also 5 drovare (*Sc.* dravere), 6-7 drovier. [f. DROVE *sb.* + -ER[1] 1: cf. *gardener*, *miller*.]

1. One who drives droves of cattle, sheep, etc., esp. to distant markets; a dealer in cattle.

c **1425** WYNTOUN *Cron.* VIII. xxiv. 53 The Dravere he gert, and oþir ma be examynyd, þat swne þa Tald hym, þat þe Carle þame stall. **14..** *Voc.* in Wr.-Wülcker 585/10 *Fugarius*, a dryvere or a drovare. **1552** *Act 5 & 6 Edw. VI*, c. 14 §13 Counties where Drovers have bene wonte..to buy Cattell. **1599** SHAKS. *Much Ado* II. i. 201, *Cl.* I wish him ioy of her. *B.* Why that's spoken like an honest Drouier: so they sel Bullockes. **1683** LUTTRELL *Brief Rel.* (1857) I. 254 A quarrell between some gentlemen..and a drover of sheep by Temple Bar. **1870** E. PEACOCK *Ralf Skirl.* III. 59 A little wayside alehouse..much frequented by drovers.

†**b.** *fig.* A dealer, trafficker. *Obs.*

1585 ABP. SANDYS *Serm.* (1841) 237 Having entered the temple, he findeth there..drovers and brokers making sale. **1602** *2nd Pt. Return fr. Parnass.* IV. ii. 1763 The yong drouer of liuings..that haunts steeple faires.

2. A boat used for fishing with a drift-net.

(Quot. 1465 is doubtful, although rendered 'drover' in Bolton and later edd. of Irish statutes.)

1465 *Stat. Roll Ireland 5 Edw. IV*, Art. 39 [c. 6 §1] Toutz maners vessels..del portage de xii tonelx ou desuys eiauntz une drower ou lawer [**1621** *Bolton's transl.* All maner vessels ..of the burden of twelve tunnes or lesse, having one Drover or Boate]. **1584-5** *Pat. Roll Ireland 27 Eliz.*, Every boate or drover that shall fysshe herring within the liberties of the said Towne. **1590** SPENSER *F.Q.* III. viii. 22 He woke And saw his drover drive along the streame. **1603** OWEN *Pembrokesh.* (1891) 122 The order of takeinge them [herrings] is with Drovers. **1880** *W. Cornwall Gloss.*, *Drover*, a fishing-boat employed in driving, or fishing with drift or float nets.

¶ Erroneously for DROGHER.

1756 P. BROWNE *Jamaica* 23 His goods must be shipped on board of some drover.

Hence (from sense 1) **'drovering**, **'drovership** (*nonce-wds.*), the business or occupation of a drover.

1838 *Fraser's Mag.* XVIII. 381 Far better..have taken to ploughmanship or drovership. **1860** J. F. CAMPBELL *Tales of W. Highlands* (1890) I. 338 It was at drovering they had made the money.

†**droving**, *vbl. sb.*[1] *Obs.* [f. DROVE *v.*[1]] Troubling; tribulation; disturbance.

a **1300** *E.E. Psalter* ix. 22 [x. 1] In nedinges, in drovynge [L. *tribulatione*]. *a* **1300** *Cursor M.* 22384 Wit all þe drouing he mai do ouer al þis werld.

droving ('drəʊvɪŋ), *vbl. sb.*[2] [f. DROVE *v.*[2]] The occupation of driving cattle to distant markets, etc.; the business of a drover.

1881 *Cheq. Career* 335 Droving is very wearisome work. **1896** *Westm. Gaz.* 19 June 3/3 The unconventional freedom of colonial life, with its rough riding and droving.

attrib. **1808** SCOTT *Autobiog.* in Lockhart *Life* i, He was.. active in the cattle trade..and by his droving transactions acquired a considerable sum of money. **1890** BOLDREWOOD *Col. Reformer* (1891) 83 He's not used to droving work.

droving, *vbl. sb.*[3] The dressing of stone with a drove: see DROVE *v.*[3]

†**drovy** ('drəʊvɪ), *a. Obs.* exc. *dial.* [A deriv. of OE. and ME. *dróf*, turbid, troubled, DROF, or of its deriv. vb. DROVE *v.*[1]: see -Y.] Turbid; not clear or transparent, opaque, 'drumly'; cloudy.

c **1220** *Bestiary* 523 So droui is te sees grund. **13..** *E.E. Allit. P.* B. 1016 A see..þat ay is drouy & dym, & ded in hit kynde. *c* **1386** CHAUCER *Pars. T.* ¶742 An hors that seketh rather to drynken drouy or trouble water than for to drynken water of the clere welle. **1483** *Cath. Angl.* 110/1 Drovy, *turbidus*, *turbulentus*. **1691** NICHOLSON *Gloss. Northanhymbricum* in Ray *N.C. Words* (E.D.S.) 41 *Druvy*, adj. *limosus*. **1825** in BROCKETT. **1851** *Cumbld. Gloss.*, *Druivy*, overcast, muddy.

drow (draʊ), *v.* Now only *s.w. dial.* [Aphetic f. ADROUGH, ADROW, OE. *adrūʒian*. Cf. DROUGHT.] *trans.* To dry *up*. In quot. 1393, *fig.*

1393 LANGL. *P. Pl.* C. xv. 22 Connynge and vnkynde rychesse..Droweþ vp dowel and distruyeþ dobest. *c* **1430** *Two Cookery-bks.* 38 Drow hem wyl in þe Sonne, þat þey ben drye. **1746** *Exmoor Scolding* Vocab., To *Drou*, to dry. **1888** *W. Somerset Wd.-bk.*, *Drow*, to dry. (Always.)

drow (draʊ), *sb.*[1] *Sc.* [perh. f. ppl. stem *drow-* of DREE *v.* to endure, suffer, undergo, which is phonologically suitable.] A fit of illness; a fainting fit; a qualm.

1727 WALKER *Remark Pass. Life A. Peden* 63 (Jam.) There was a drow of anxiety overwhelmed her about him. **1808-18** JAMIESON, *Drow*, a fainting fit. *Angus*. **1819** W. TENNANT *Papistry Storm'd* (1827) 175 Down he tummlet in a drow. **1883** W. JOLLY *Life J. Duncan* xxxv. 409 Inquiring..how he felt after his drow.

drow, *sb.*[2] *Sc.* 'A cold mist approaching to rain; a drizzling shower.' (Jam.)

a **1614** J. MELVILL *MS. Mem.* 115 (Jam.) Comes off the hills of Lammermoor edge a great mist with a tempestuous showre and drow..It pleased God..to drive away the showre and calm the drow, so that it fell down dead calm. **1818** SCOTT *Rob Roy* xxii, A sort o' drow in the air.

drow, obs. pa. t. of DREE; s.w. dial. f. THROW.

drow, drowgh, drowȝ, drowh, obs. pa. t. of DRAW *v.*

†**drowarie**, erron. f. DROWRIER, Sc. form of DOWRIER, dowager.

a **1557** *Diurn. Occurr.* (1833) 30 In this menetyme the quenis grace drowarie past on her fute to our Lady Laureit. *Ibid.* 34 He gat word the queenis grace drowarie was cummit out of Striveling to the Parliament.

drowe, obs. form of DROVE *sb.*

drowen, obs. pa. pple. of DREE *v.*

drowk (draʊk), *v. Obs.* exc. *dial.* Also 5-6 drouke. [Deriv. uncertain: app. a parallel formation to DROOP, ME. *drowp*; cf. DROUKING.] *intr.* To droop, as a flower or plant.

a **1502** ARNOLDE *Chron.* 165 Yf the peche tree begynne to drouke let hym be wel moysted at the rote w[t] drestis of wyne. **1820** CLARE *Rural Life* (ed. 3) 71 Drowking lies the meadow-sweet. **1821** —— *Vill. Minstr.* I. 133 Bumble-bees.. Clinging to the drowking flower.

drown (draʊn), *v.* Forms: 4-6 drun(e, droun(e, (4 drounne, druen, 4-5 drone, 5-6 drowen, *Sc.* drwn), 4-7 drowne, 4- drown. *β.* 6 dround, 6-7 drownd (now *dial.* and *vulg.*) [ME. *drūn-*, *droun-*, *drown-*, pointing to an OE. **drúnian*, not found: origin obscure.

A current conjecture is that ME. *drūn-* was a phonetic reduction of ME. *drunkn-* or ON. *drukn-* (see DRUNKEN *v.*[1]) in the same sense. But, on phonetic and other grounds, this appears highly improbable. The later variant *drownd*, so widely prevalent in dialectal and vulgar use, is parallel in development to *astound*, *bound*, *compound*, *sound*, etc.]

I. Intransitive.

Considered 'unusual' by *N.E.D.* in 1897.

1. To suffer death by submersion in water; to perish by suffocation under water (or other liquid).

a **1300** *Cursor M.* 11793 Pharaon wit al his folk..Al þai drund in þe se. *c* **1300** *Ibid.* 24867 (Edin.) Al mon we druen [*v. rr.* drun, droun]. **1375** BARBOUR *Bruce* XIV. 358 Thai in perell war till droune. **1483** CAXTON *Gold. Leg.* 256 b/1 He fylle in the water and drowned. **1549** *Compl. Scot.* vi. 38 Narcissus..for loue of eccho..drounit in ane drau vel. **1654** D. OSBORNE *Lett.* lxii. (1888) 292 If I drown by the way, this will be my last letter. **1856** GRINDON *Life* v. (1875) 59 The bird and the mammal drown if submerged in water. **1924** A. D. SEDGWICK *Little French Girl* I. viii. 70 She had the sensation of drowning yet of keeping calm while she drowned. **1928** *Manch. Guardian Weekly* 31 Aug. 152/1 Public opinion is like the crowd that watches a man drown while convinced that something ought to be done. **1970** *Which?* June 171/1 Become exhausted and drown without lifejacket.

fig. **1382** WYCLIF *1 Esdras* iii. 23 Whan of win thei drownyn. *c* **1620** Z. BOYD *Zion's Flowers* (1855) 42 Our life ..drownes in time. **1902** A. SYMONS *Poems* I. 119, I sicken with a wild desire, I drown in sweetness. **1957** S. SMITH *Not waving but Drowning* 13, I was much too far out all my life. And not waving but drowning.

†**2.** To sink and perish (as a ship); to suffer extinction or destruction by deluge or inundation. *Obs.*

a **1300** *Cursor M.* 24857 þair scip ai redi for to drun [*v.r.* droun]. *c* **1340** *Ibid.* 1532 (Fairf.) þis werlde sulde come til ende To droun or wiþ fire be brende. *c* **1470** HENRY *Wallace* VII. 182 Trubbill weddyr makis schippis to droune. **1523** LD. BERNERS *Froiss.* (1812) I. cxx. 144 One of the scafoldes drowned in ye water, and the moost part of them that were within it.

II. Transitive.

3. a. To suffocate (a person or animal) by submersion in water (or other liquid).

Mostly with personal agent, or reflexive or passive; but also said of the action of the water.

a **1300** *Cursor M.* 1652, I sal þam alle in watur droun [*v. rr.* drenkil, drenche]. *Ibid.* 5592 Pharaon þat king felun þat badd þe childer for to drun [*v.r.* droun]. *c* **1400** MAUNDEV. (Roxb.) xxxiii. 151 Sum ware drouned by violence of þe wawes. *c* **1511** *1st Eng. Bk. Amer.* (Arb.) Introd. 32/2 Ther they drowne theym self. **1533** GAU *Richt Vay* (1888) 58 Thay var drunit in ye fluid. **1548** HALL *Chron., Edw. IV*, 239 b, He..was priuely drouned in a But of Malvesey. **1632** LITHGOW *Trav.* III. 109 [He] here leaped in, and drouned himselfe. *Ibid.* v. 178 The last flood did drowne the greatest part of the Inhabitants. **1784** COWPER *Task* II. 149 The earth shall..drown him in her dry and gusty gulfs. **1847** TENNYSON *Princ.* Prol. 47 Part were drown'd within the whirling brook. **1869** C. GIBBON *R. Gray* iv, My faither's drooned.

β. **1530** PALSGR. 528/2, I dreynt (Lydgate), I drownde, *je noye*. **1644** PRYNNE *Vind. Ps.* cv. 15 (ed. 3) A iij b, God.. drownded Pharaoh and his host in the read sea. **1727** SWIFT *Past. Dial.* Wks. 1814 XIV. 195 In my own Thames may I be drownded.

b. *fig.* (Also *refl.*)

1388 WYCLIF *1 Esdras* iii. 23 Whanne thei han be drowned of wyn..thei han no mynde what thinges thei diden. **1555** EDEN *Decades* To Rdr. (Arb.) 51 Men..drowned in the deluge of erroure. **1659** D. PELL *Impr. Sea* 435 They drown themselves in drink. **1788** MAD. D'ARBLAY *Diary* 29 Nov., Her Majesty..drowned in tears. **1827** POLLOK *Course T.* VII, He drowned himself in sleep, in wine.

β. *c* **1679** *Roxb. Ball.* (1886) VI. 146 They dy'd..in Seas of sorrow Drownded. **1838** DICKENS *Nich. Nick.* v, 'Just fill that mug up with lukewarm water, William, will you?' ..'Why the milk will be drownded'.

†**4.** To sink (a ship or the like) in water; to send to the bottom. *Obs.*

c **1465** *Eng. Chron.* (Camden 1856) 43 On of the grettist carrakez..was so rent and bored in the sides..that sone aftir it was dround. *c* **1500** *Melusine* xxxvi. 270 His peuple assaylled strongly, and drowned foure of the sarasyns shippes. **1601** HOLLAND *Pliny* I. 46 Brasse and lead in the masse or lumpe sinke downe and are drowned. **1632** LITHGOW *Trav.* II. 66 In that fight [Lepanto] there was taken and drowned 180 of Turkish Gallies.

5. a. To lay under or cover with water, etc.; to submerge, flood, inundate, deluge; to drench.

a **1300** *Cursor M.* 1532 þat þis werld suld cum til end, Or drund wit watur, or wit fir brend. **1500-20** DUNBAR *Poems* lxxii. 100 My visage all in watter dround. **1556** *Chron. Gr. Friars* (Camden) 19 The watter of the Temse by excesse of floode..incresid on the londe unto Populer, and drownyd many howsys and feldes and medowes. **1696** *Phil. Trans.* XIX. 353 When the Fens are drowned. **1708** J. C. *Compl. Collier* (1845) 29 Seueral good Collieries..lye unwrought and drowned for want of such Noble Engines. **1861** W. Rankine *Steam Engine* 151 A weir is said to be drowned when the water in the channel below it is higher than its crest.

β. **1667** Primatt *City & C. Build.* 7 The works in mines of Lead or Tin Oare, are like..to be drownded.

b. *to drown out*: to put or drive out by inundation; to stop (works, etc.) or drive (people, etc.) from their habitation by flooding.

1851 S. Judd *Margaret* i. iii, Chilion fished, hunted, laid traps for foxes, drowned out woodchucks. **1888** *Pall Mall G.* 28 Aug. 3/2 The [Severn Tunnel] works were constantly 'drowned out'. **1890** Baker *Wild Beasts & their Ways* I. 186 During inundations the islands are frequently drowned out. **1894** *Daily News* 23 Nov. 6/7 Deserted cottages, whose tenants had..been 'drowned out'.

6. a. *transf.* and *fig.* To overwhelm, to overpower, by rising above like a flood; to immerse or smother; to overpower (sound) by greater loudness.

a **1300** *Cursor M.* 18361 Þou slockens al vr sin; þou has þam drund and don forfare. **1398** Trevisa *Barth. De P.R.* iii. xiii. (1495) 57 The more the resonable soule drowneth hym in to the body the more slowely and the lesse perfytely he vnderstondyth. **1538** Starkey *England* i. ii. 42 They wych haue theyr myndys drownyd in the vayn plesurys of thys lyfe. **1577–87** Holinshed *Chron.* I. 23/1 Ludsgate,.. vnto this daie it is called Ludgate, (s) onelie drowned in pronuntiation of the word. **1605** Bacon *Adv. Learn.* i. vii. §2 The sound..was drowned by some louder noise. **1665** Glanvill *Scepsis Sci.* 53 Vice drowns the noble Ideas of the Soul. **1726** Leoni tr. *Alberti's Archit.* I. 43/1 Little pieces of ..Stone..which they perfectly drowned in Mortar. **1769** Sir W. Jones *Poems* (1777) 25 His heavenly charms.. drown'd her senses in a flood of light. **1879** Froude *Cæsar* xiii. 175 Yells drowned his voice.

β. **1550** Crowley *Way to Wealth* 398 Thy curate (that otherwise wold mumble in the mouth and drounde his wordes). **1884** *Harper's Mag.* Feb. 401/2 He had a beautiful voice. He could drown out the whole choir.

†**b.** *Law.* To extinguish by merging in something greater or higher. Also *intr.* To merge. *Obs.*

1642 tr. *Perkins' Prof. Bk.* ix. §584. 254 If the estate in remainder or in reversion be such an estate wherein the particular estate may be drowned. *Ibid.* §589. 256 An estate for life cannot drown in an estate for yeares. **1661** J. Stephens *Procurations* 54 Estates in land are properly drowned or confounded, when a lesser estate concurs with a greater in the same person, and in the same right. **1818** Cruise *Digest* (ed. 2) IV. 109 The reversionary interest coming to the possession, drowns it.

drownable ('draʊnəb(ə)l), *a.* [f. drown *v.* + -able.] Capable of being drowned.

1863 Owen *Lect. Power of God* 50 Air-breathing or drownable animal species.

drownage ('draʊnɪdʒ). *rare.* [f. as prec. + -age.] Drowning, submersion.

1850 Carlyle *Latter-day Pamph.* iii. 42. **1851** —— *Sterling* i. i. (1872) 6 Drownage in the foul welter of our so-called religious..controversies.

drownd, dial. and vulgar for drown *v.*, q.v.

drowned (draʊnd), *ppl. a.* Also **drownded** (now *vulg.*) [f. drown *v.* + -ed[1].]

1. a. Killed by submersion in water.

a **1300** *Cursor M.* 1886 A druned beist þar lai flettand. **1660** Gauden *Brownrig* 212 A drenched and almost drowned man. **1789** W. Buchan *Dom. Med.* (1790) 631 The society for the recovery of drowned persons. **1896** *Westm. Gaz.* 20 June 5/2 Relatives of drowned passengers.

b. *like, as wet as, a drowned rat*: in a thoroughly soaked and dripping condition.

c **1500** *Blowbol's Test.* in Halliw. *Nugæ P.* 2 He lokyd furyous as a wyld catt, And pale of hewe like a drowned ratte. **1630** Wadsworth *Pilgr.* viii. 84, I got on shoare as wet as a drowned Rat. **1738** Swift *Polite Convers.* 17 'Take Pity on poor Miss; don't throw Water on a drownded Rat.' **1880** *New Virginians* II. 229 Looking like the drowndest of drowned rats.

2. Submerged; flooded, deluged, inundated. *spec.* in *Physical Geogr.*: designating a valley or other land-form that is partly or wholly under water as a result of a (permanent) change in the relative levels of land and sea (or lake).

1616 Norden *Surv. Kirton in Lindsey* 17 in Peacock *N.W. Linc. Gloss.*, There is much drowned lande. **1711** Shaftesb. *Charac.* Misc. ii. i. (1737) III. 46 The Measure of their yearly drounded Lands. **1865** Dircks *Mrq. Worc.* 538 The Mineral wealth was drowned treasure. **1867** F. Francis *Angling* ix. (1880) 332 A drowned line is too often a lost fish. **1874** Knight *Dict. Mech.*, *Drowned-level* (*Mining*), a depressed level or drainage-gallery in a mine, which acts on the principle of an inverted syphon. [**1889** W. M. Davis in *Nat. Geogr. Mag.* I. 213 The antithesis of this is the effect of depression, by which the lower course may be drowned, flooded or fjorded.] **1902** Ld. Avebury *Scenery of England* iv. 125 When the land is sinking..the drowned river-valleys make the coast irregular and complicated. **1902** *Geol. Atlas U.S.* lxxxiii. 17/2 Both types belong to the class known among physiographers as drowned shores, a designation which signifies that they are more deeply submerged now than they were at some shortly preceding epoch. **1908** *Ibid.* clviii. 1/3 A subsidence of the coast has transformed the lower portions of the old river valleys into deep marine channels... A shore line exhibiting these characteristics is termed a 'drowned coast'. **1937** Wooldridge & Morgan *Physical Basis Geogr.* xxi. 354 The drowned river valleys or *rias* of South-western Ireland. **1957** G. E. Hutchinson *Treat. Limnol.* I. i. 11 The northern part of Lake Victoria, with its numerous drowned valleys. **1963** D. W. & E. E. Humphries tr. *Termier's Erosion & Sedimentation* v. 126 Superficially similar phenomena, sometimes classed as fjords (but simply 'drowned valleys'), occur in regions which have never been glaciated.

drowner ('draʊnə(r)). [f. drown *v.* + -er[1].]

1. One who drowns, or who suffers drowning; that which drowns.

1545 Ascham *Toxoph.* (Arb.) 52 Ydlenesse, enemy of vertue, yᵉ drowner of youthe. **1560** Whitehorne *Arte Warre* (1573) 102 b, Welles, the which be as drowners to the same caves. **1638** Mayne *Lucian* (1664) 223. **1820** Shelley *Liberty* xix, As waves..Hiss round a drowner's head. **1827** Moore *Alciphr.* iv, As drowners cling To the last hold.

2. A manager of water-meadows. ? *local.*

1805 *Trans. Soc. Arts* XXIII. 166 The drowner, as he is generally called, or the man who has the superintendence of the water-meadows. **1834** *Brit. Husb.* I. 531 When the manager of the mead,—provincially termed 'the drowner', —begins to clean out the main drain.

drowning ('draʊnɪŋ), *vbl. sb.* [-ing[1].] The action of the verb drown, in its various senses.

c **1400** *Destr. Troy* 3673 *heading*, The Drownyng of Pollux & Castor. **1539** *Act 31 Hen. VIII*, c. 4 The ouerflowyng and drowning of the medowes. **1581** Pettie *Guazzo's Civ. Conv.* ii. (1586) 55 b, Those which put the shippe in daunger of drowning. **1626** Bacon *Sylva* §798, I call *drowning of Metals*, when that the baser Metal is so incorporate with the more rich, as it can by no means be separated again. **1661** J. Stephens *Procurations* 54 Things..which in any sort might be subject to drowning, or extinguishment by unity of possession. **1862** Shirley *Nugæ Crit.* xi. 474 The hangings, and burnings, and drownings, and Bartholomew massacres, and Spanish furies, of past times.

attrib. **1659** D. Pell *Impr. Sea* 556 In great despair, and disgustion of a drowning death. *c* **1798** Southey *Ball. Lord William*, No human ear but William's heard Young Edmund's drowning scream. **1850** Mrs. Browning *Rom. Margret* xxv, The men at sea..heard a drowning cry.

'**drowning**, *ppl. a.* [-ing[2].] That drowns.

1. Perishing from suffocation in water; suffering inundation.

c **1470** Henry *Wallace* x. 822 Drownand folk. **1821** Byron *Heav. & Earth* iii. 911 The ocean..grasps each drowning hill. **1869** W. P. Mackay *Grace & Truth* (1875) 69 As is well known, a drowning man will catch at a straw.

2. Suffocating or destroying by submersion in water; also *fig.*, overwhelming, overpowering.

1659 D. Pell *Impr. Sea* 516 Great Faith..will beleeve in an angry God, in a killing God, and in a drowning God. **1716** Cibber *Love makes Man* ii. ii, Dissolving Softness! O the drowning Joy!

Hence '**drowningly** *adv.*, so as to drown.

1818 Keats *Endymion* ii. 282 What misery most drowningly doth sing In lone Endymion's ear? **1880** Miss Broughton *Sec. Th.* II. iii. vii. 233 Drenchingly, drowningly wet.

drowrie, -ry, var. druery, *Obs.*

drowrie, -ry, drowrier, obs. Sc. ff. dowry, dowrier. [These forms seem to have arisen from a confusion of *dowery*, dowry, with *drowrie*, Sc. form of druery (sense 2). See also drowarie.]

1503 *Sc. Acts Jas. IV.* (1814) 240 (Jam.) The qwenis drowry and morwyn-gift. **1513** [see dowry 2]. **1551** *Aberdeen Reg.* V. 21 (Jam.) Quene drowrier. *a* **1835** Motherwell in *Whistle-Binkie* (Scot. Songs) Ser. ii. 13 The fisch are the deer that fill my parks, And the water waste my drurie.

drowse (draʊz), *v.* Also 6–7 **drouze**, 6–9 **drowze**, 7 **drouse**. [In current use appears in 1573: perh. a back-formation from *drowsy*, which is found earlier; perh. identical with OE. *drúsian*, to sink, become low, slow, or inactive, a derivative from the ablaut series *dreus-*, *draus-*, *drus-*, OE. *dréosan* to fall down; but the non-appearance of the verb for 600 years leaves this uncertain.]

†**1.** *intr.* (OE.) To sink, droop, become slow.

Beowulf (Th.) 3265 Laȝu drusade. *a* **1000** Cynewulf *Elene* (Gr.) 1258 Cen drusende. *a* **1000** *Phœnix* (Cod. Ex.) 368 He drusende deað ne bisorgað.

2. *intr.* To be drowsy; to be heavy or dull with or as with sleep; to be half asleep. Also with *away*, *off*.

1596 Shaks. *1 Hen. IV*, iii. ii. 81 [They] drowz'd, and hung their eye-lids downe, Slept in his Face. **1666** Pepys *Diary* (1879) III. 447, I could not hold my eyes open for an houre, but I drowsed..but I anon wakened. **1667** Milton *P.L.* xi. 131 More wakeful then to drouze. **1853** *Tait's Mag.* XX. 615 Drowsing and dreaming with half-open eye. **1886** W. W. Story *Fiammetta* ii. 39 He..now and then drowsed away into a half sleep. **1908** *Smart Set* Sept. 101/2, I must have drowsed off.

3. *fig.* To be or grow inactive, dull, or sluggish.

1573 Tusser *Husb.* lxii. (1878) 140 Ill husbandry drowseth at fortune so auke: Good husbandrie rowseth himselfe as a hauke. *a* **1679** W. Outram *Serm.* (1682) 455 The minds of men would drowze and slumber. **1847** Tennyson *Princ.* ii. 318 Let not your prudence..drowse. **1863** Hawthorne *Our Old Home* (1879) 56 *Leamington* The Leam..drowsing across the principal street beneath a handsome bridge.

4. *trans.* To render drowsy; to make heavy, dull, or inactive, as with sleep.

1600 Holland *Livy* xxxix. viii. 1027 When as wine had drowned and drowsed the understanding. **1614** Sylvester *Bethulia's Rescue* vi. 101 The Fume of his aboundant Drink, Drouzing his Brain. **1819** Keats *Otho* v. v, Nations drows'd in peace! **1881** B. Webber *In Luck's Way* i. i, Any birds which the heat has not utterly drowsed.

5. To pass *away* (time) drowsily or in drowsing.

1843 Lefevre *Life Trav. Phys.* III. iii. xii. 255 To drowse away the mornings. **1875** Browning *Inn Album* i. 171 Don't I drowse The week away down with the Aunt and Niece?

Hence **drowsed** *ppl. a.*, '**drowsing** *vbl. sb.* and *ppl. a.*; also '**drowser**.

1654 Whitlock *Zootomia* 557 The lesser snatches of Rest and Drowsings. **1667** Milton *P.L.* viii. 289 Gentle sleep.. with soft oppression seis'd My droused sense. **1796** Coleridge *Relig. Musings* 34 The drowsed Soul. **1881** T. Hardy *Laodicean* ii. iii, The drowsing effects of the last night's sitting. **1887** M. B. Edwards *Next of Kin Wanted* I. viii. 110 Unwary drowsers were severely castigated from the pulpit.

drowse, *sb.* [f. prec. vb.] The action of drowsing; a fit of drowsing; the state of being half asleep.

1814 *Prophetess* III. i, Men are seiz'd with most unnat'ral drowze. *a* **1851** Moir *Poems, Tomb of De Bruce* iii, Shaking the fetters away, which in drowse she had worn. **1856** Mrs. Browning *Aur. Leigh* vi. 593. **1859** Tennyson *Enid* 1121 Many a voice along the street..burst Their drowse.

fig. **1854–6** Patmore *Angel in Ho.* ii. ii. (1866) 259 The wealthy wheat Bends in a golden drowse.

†**drowsen.** *Obs.* Also 7 **drousen, drousson.** [A variant of drosen, OE. *drósna*, grounds, dregs.] A kind of oatmeal pottage: see quot. 1620–25.

1519 Horman *Vulg.* 152 b, A drousen tubbe: and a swynes troughe, be fayre vessellis to serue swyne. **1605** *Lond. Prodigal*, White-pot and Drowsen broth. **1620–25** Markham *Farew. Husb.* 133 Boyling Oatemeale..with barme, or the dregges and hinder ends of your Beere barrells, makes an excellent..pottage..of great vse in all the parts of the West Countrie..called by the name of drousson pottage.

drowsihead ('draʊzɪhɛd). *arch.* [f. drowsy + -head.] = drowsiness.

1590 Spenser *F.Q.* i. ii. 7 The royall virgin shooke off drousyhed. **1647** H. More *Song of Soul* iii. App. civ, Thou hast..rouz'd the soul from her dull drowsiehed. **1748** Thomson *Cast. Indol.* i. 46 A pleasing land of drowsy-head it was, Of dreams that wave before the half-shut eye. **1873** Browning *Red Cott. Nt.-cap* i. 139 And did the drowsihead So suit, so soothe the learned loving eye?

drowsihood. [f. as prec. + -hood.] = prec.

1867 Longf. *Dante's Purg.* xxxii. 69 He may, who well can picture drowsihood.

drowsily ('draʊzɪlɪ), *adv.* [f. drowsy + -ly[2].] In a drowsy manner; sluggishly, inactively.

1581 Mulcaster *Positions* xiii. (1887) 62 Talking..is thought verie fit for such, as be drousely giuen. **1601** Shaks. *Jul. C.* iv. iii. 240 What, thou speak'st drowsily? **1856** Emerson *Eng. Traits* Wks. (Bohn) II. 14 Classics which at home are drowsily read. **1871** R. Ellis *Catullus* xvii. 13 Urchin, across papa's elbow drowsily swaying.

drowsiness ('draʊzɪnɪs). [f. next + -ness.]

1. The state of being drowsy; heavy sleepiness.

1559 *Primer* in *Priv. Prayers* (1851) 33 Drowsiness take from our eyes. **1562** Turner *Herbal* ii. 46 b, They shal fall into a forgetfull and a slepishe drowsines. **1630–31** Milton *Arcades* 61 When drowsiness Hath locked up mortal sense. **1736** Butler *Anal.* i. i. 37 Drowsiness, increasing till it end in sound sleep. **1860** Froude *Hist. Eng.* V. 353 The symptoms were a sudden perspiration, accompanied with faintness and drowsiness.

2. *fig.* Intellectual or moral lethargy; sloth.

1575–85 Abp. Sandys *Serm.* (1841) 438 By the drowsiness of the husbandmen and the sloth of the cultivators. **1611** Bible *Prov.* xxiii. 21 Drousinesse shall cloath a man with ragges. **1751** Johnson *Rambler* No. 89 ⁋5 Convinced of the necessity of breaking from this habitual drowsiness. **1841** D'Israeli *Amen. Lit.* (1867) 567 His vivacity relieved the drowsiness of mere antiquarianism.

drowsy ('draʊzɪ), *a.* Also (6 **drawsy, drusye**), 6–8 **drousy**, 7–8 **drouzy, drowzy.** [Found in first half of the 16th c.; no corresponding ME. or OE. form is recorded: it is however probably related to OE. *drúsian*: see drowse *v.*]

1. Inclined to sleep, esp. at a time when one wishes, or ought, to be awake; heavy with sleepiness; half asleep, dozing.

1530 Palsgr. 311/1 Drowsy, heavy for slepe or onlusty, *pesant.* **1591** Florio *2nd Fruites* 3, *N.* Me think you are very drowsie still. *T.* I am not very well awaked yet. **1648** Gage *West Ind.* xvii. 113 It made mee more drowsie at night. **1725** Pope *Odyss.* ii. 446 Drowsy they rose, with heavy fumes opprest. **1840** Dickens *Barn. Rudge* xviii, A drowsy watchman's footsteps sounded on the pavement. **1877** M. M. Grant *Sun-Maid* i, I am very tired and drowsy.

2. Caused or characterized by sleepiness or inactivity.

a **1529** Skelton *El. Rumming* 15 Her lothy leere is..ugly of cheere, droupy and drowsie. **1562** Turner *Herbal* ii. 46 b, Pour rose oyl and vinegre vpon them that haue the drawsy or forgetfull euel. **1562** —— *Baths* 8 b, Diseases of the heade, as are the drusye euill. **1655** Culpepper *Riverius* i. ii. 9 Drouzie Diseases, called Coma, Lethargy, Carus, and Apoplexy. **1727–38** Gay *Fables* ii. xiii. 68 Till drousy sleep retard the glass. **1870** Dickens *E. Drood* i, Some..period of drowsy laughter.

3. Inducing sleepiness; lulling; soporific.

1590 Spenser *F.Q.* ii. iii. 1 [He] vprose from drowsie couch. *c* **1617** Middleton *Witch* iv. iii, I spic'd them..with a drowsy posset, They will not hear. **1706** Addison

Rosamond III. iii, The bowl, with drowsie juices fill'd. **1839-40** W. IRVING *Wolfert's R.* (1855) 3 That potent and drowsy spell, which still prevails over the valley.

4. *fig.* Heavy, dull, inactive; sluggish, lethargic.

1570 LEVINS *Manip.* 108 Drowsie, *deses.* **1584** R. SCOT *Discov. Witchcr.* I. iii. 5 In whose drousie minds the divell hath goten a fine Seat. **1590** SHAKS. *Mids. N.* v. i. 399 The dead and drowsie fier. *a* **1674** CLARENDON *Hist. Reb* x. §140 The drowsy, dull Presbyterian humour of Fairfax. **1751** JOHNSON *Rambler* No. 178 ¶14 A drowsy thoughtlessness or a giddy levity. **1855** MACAULAY *Hist. Eng.* III. 467 Sinking into a servile, sensual, drowsy parasite.

5. *Comb.*, as **drowsy-head**, a person of a sleepy or sluggish disposition; ***drowsy-headed***, ***-flighted*** adjs.

1576 FLEMING *Panopl. Epist.* 354 The drowsie headed lubber. **1577** tr. *Bullinger's Decades* (1592) 269 Slothfull drousiheades are..an vnprofitable lumpe of vnoccupied earth. **1634** MILTON *Comus* 551 The drowsy-flighted steeds That draw the litter of close-curtained sleep. **1834** MOIR in *Blackw. Mag.* XXXV. 708 The drowsyhead, man, on his bed slumbers prone.

drowsyhead, variant of DROWSIHEAD.

drowte, drowth, obs. var. DROUGHT.

†**droy**, *sb. Obs.* [This and the vb. following appear to be related in some way to DROIL.] A servant; a drudge.

1573 TUSSER *Husb.* lxxxi. (1878) 172 Good droie to serue hog, to helpe wash, and to milke. **1583** STUBBES *Anat. Abus.* I. (1879) 78 Any droye or pussle in the Cuntrey. **1592** BABINGTON *Comf. Notes Genesis* xviii. 6 Wks. (1637) 56 Every Droy in the house, yea the kitchenmaid.

†**droy**, *v.* [see prec. sb.] *intr.* To toil, drudge.

1576 GASCOIGNE *Steele Gl.* (Arb.) 68 He which can in office drudge and droy.

droyl, droyt, obs. ff. DROIL, DROIT.

Dr. Pepper (ˌdɒktə ˈpɛpə(r)). orig. and chiefly *U.S.* [f. the name of Charles *Pepper*, U.S. physician: see quot. 1986.] A proprietary name for a brand of aerated soft drinks; a bottle, can, or drink of this.

1906 *Official Gaz.* (U.S. Patent Office) 30 Jan. 1464/1 *Dr. Pepper.* Aerated tonic beverages and syrups for the same. The Dr. Pepper Co., Dallas, Tex. **1947** *Fortune* Oct. 108/1 Dr. Pepper..is a soft drink, colored ruby red, and variously described by Southerners who have been drinking it some sixty-three years as tasting like: (1) cherry, (2) almond, (3) raspberry, (4) prune juice. **1975** *Business Week* 10 Feb. 34/2 The success of Dr. Pepper, a cherry-flavored soft drink favorite of the South that went national in 1966.., could hardly go unnoticed. **1984** *Trade Marks Jrnl.* 14 Nov. 2977/2 (figure), Dr Pepper... 1,146,477. Non-alcoholic drinks and preparations for making such drinks... Dr. Pepper Company, 5523 Mockingbird Lane, Dallas, Texas, United States..Manufacturers and Merchants. **1985** *Toronto Life* Sept. 76/2 Upstairs in the second-floor common room, he pops a Dr. Pepper. **1986** *Time* 3 Mar. 67/1 Morrison,..hoping to curry favor with his beloved's father [Charles Pepper], named the new pop Dr Pepper.

drub (drʌb), *v.* Also 7 **thrub**. [Appears first after 1600; all the early instances, before Hudibras, 1663, are from travellers in the Orient, and refer to the bastinado. Hence, in the absence of any other tenable suggestion, it may be conjectured to represent Arabic *ḍaraba* (i.e. ḍaraba) to beat, to bastinado, vbl. sb. *ḍarb* (i.e. ḍarb) beating, a blow, a drub.

There are difficulties. In Persia, of which Herbert wrote, the vbl. sb. is pronounced *zŭrb*; but in Turkey it is *dŭrb*; in North Africa the Arabic dental is retained, and in Algiers, and Barbary generally, the verb is vulgarly pronounced *ḍ'rab*, *ḍ'rub*, or *ḍĕrob*. It is therefore conceivable that the form *drub* came originally from the Barbary states, where so many Christians suffered captivity, and was already known to Herbert as applied to the bastinado, when he went to the East. But of this we have as yet no evidence; while the absence of the word from the Mediterranean languages, into which it was quite as likely to pass as into English, is an element of doubt.]

1. *trans.* To beat with a stick or the like, to cudgel, flog; in early use, *spec.* to bastinado; to thrash, thump, belabour; also, to beat in a fight.

1634 SIR T. HERBERT *Trav.* 47 [He] confest and was drubd right handsomely. **1663** BUTLER *Hud.* I. ii. 1042 He that is valiant, and dares fight, Tho' drubb'd, can lose no honour by't. **1663** PEPYS *Diary* 21 Feb., He..would have got seamen to have drubbed them. **1691** tr. *Emilianne's Frauds Romish Monks* 254 Those Priests who thrub'd one another in the Place of S. Mark, for to catch the Assignations to say Masses. **1698** FRYER *Acc. E. Ind. & P.* 52. **1706** PHILLIPS (ed. Kersey), *Drub*, to beat the Soles of the Feet with a Stick, a Punishment us'd in Turkey: Also simply, to cudgel or bang one soundly. **1733** FIELDING *Quixote in Eng.* II. iv, He was most confoundedly drubb'd just now. **1835** MARRYAT *Jac. Faithf.* iv, See if I won't drub you within an inch of your life. **1887** BESANT *The World went* iii, He drubbed and belaboured his servants every day.

b. Const. ***to drub*** (a person) ***to death***, *into* or *out of* something; (a thing, a notion) *into* or *out of* a person.

1634 SIR T. HERBERT *Trav.* 98 [The Bashaw] made the Petitioner be almost drubd to death. **1638** *Ibid.* (ed. 2) 172 He is almost drubd (with many terrible bastinadoes on the soles of his feet) to death. **1687** T. BROWN *Saints in Uproar* Wks. 1730 I. 80 Let us drub these lobsters into better manners. **1716** *Lond. Gaz.* No. 5460/3 He had been barbarously drubbed to Death [in Algiers]. **1728** MORGAN *Algiers* II. iv. 269. **1751** SMOLLETT *Per. Pic.* (1779) II. lxi. 188 Those foolish notions..ought to be drubbed out of you. **1791** MAXWELL in Boswell *Johnson* (1831) I. 384 We had drubbed those fellows into a proper reverence for us. **1826** SCOTT *Woodst.* viii, If the leaven of thy malignancy is altogether drubbed out of thee.

c. *fig.* To belabour with abuse.

1811 SCOTT *Let.* 4 Apr., Pray drub your management for the..blunder. **1894** *Advance* (Chicago) 1 Feb., Drubbing the church and praising outsiders.

2. *transf.* To strike or beat with force.

1849 THACKERAY in '*Punch*' Wks. 1886 XXIV. 208 Pots were cooking, drums were drubbing. **1865** G. MEREDITH *Rhoda Fleming* xliii, To go and handle butter..as Mrs. Sumpit drubbed and patted it. **1883** HOWELLS *Register* i, Teaching the young idea how to drub the piano.

3. To beat the ground; to stamp. (*intr.* and *trans.*)

1855 THACKERAY *Newcomes* II. 227 She drubs her little foot when his name is mentioned. **1859** —— *Virgin.* xxxiii, Drubbing with her little feet. **1860** —— *Round. Papers, On being found out* 129 You..drub on the ground with your lovely little feet.

Hence ˈ**drubbing** *vbl. sb.*, a beating, a thrashing; also *transf.*, *fig.*, and *attrib.*; ˈ**drubber**, one who drubs or beats.

1650 HOWELL *For. Trav.* App. (Arb.) 85 They [the Turks] have sundry sorts of punishments that torture the sense a longer time, as drubbing, guunshing, flaying alive, impaling. **1687** CONGREVE *Old Bach.* I. v, He will take a drubbing with as little Noise as a Pulpit Cushion. **1708** PRIOR *Mice* 102 These two were sent (or I'm no drubber). **1752** HUME *Ess. & Treat.* (1777) I. 266 To hear..Jupiter threaten Juno with a sound drubbing. **1769** *Junius Lett.* xxiii. 108 *note*, Sir Edward Hawke had given the French a drubbing. **1784** *Lett. to Honoria & M.* II. 36 Who had just suffered a hearty drubbing-bout. **1814** SCOTT *Wav.* xxxiv, Beyond the capacity of the drubber of sheep-skin. **1871** J. C. JEAFFRESON *Ann. Oxford* I. xx. 313 The classical drubbings which pupils underwent. **1884** G. MEREDITH *Let.* 31 Dec. (1970) II. 755 He got well licked [at football]. A swim in the Baths afterward braced him, for victory or another drubbing. **1955** *Times* 24 May 11/3 The Communists, who are still licking their wounds after the drubbing they got in 1950. **1959** *Spectator* 21 Aug. 215/1, I shall be surprised, though, if the Establishment does not take another drubbing in the City over Harrods.

drub, *sb.* [f. DRUB *v.*] A stroke given in punishment or in fighting, esp. with a cudgel; a thump; = BASTINADO I.

1663 BUTLER *Hud.* I. iii. 751 The blows and drubs I have received. **1678** *Ibid.* III. i. 1360 The drubs he had so freely dealt. **1687** *Lond. Gaz.* No. 2237/1 A Bustangee..had, after receiving 500 Drubs, been obliged to comply with the Grand Signior's Command. **1703** MAUNDRELL *Journ. Jerus.* (1721) 30 It might cost him fifty, perhaps one hundred drubs on his bare feet. **1780-86** WOLCOTT (P. Pindar) *Odes R. Academicians* Wks. 1790 I. 8 Herculean Gentlemen! I dread your drubs. *a* **1845** HOOD *Irish Schoolm.* xix, The Pedagogue, with sudden drub, Smites his scald head.

†**drubble, druble**, *v. Obs.* Also **drobyl**. [app. an alteration of *trouble*, F. *troubler*, under the influence of native words: see next.] *trans.* To trouble, disturb.

a **1340** HAMPOLE *Psalter* ix. 6 Drubild stiryngs of pryde. *Ibid.* xxxviii. 9 Broght til drublynge of warldis werkis. *c* **1400** tr. *Secreta Secret., Gov. Lordsh.* (E.E.T.S.) 100 Wharof þe kyng was mekyll drobyld. *c* **1440** *Promp. Parv.* 133/2 Drubblyn, or torblyn watur..*turbo.* **1566** DRANT *Horace, Sat.* (I. i. 60) Him needes not draw the drubbled dreggs of fawle by durtye poole (*limo turbatam..aquam*).

†ˈ**drubly**, *a. Obs.* Also **drob(e)ly**. [app. a blending of ME. *trobly*, TROUBLY from French, and OE. *dróf*, *dróflic* (ME. **drov(e)ly*) turbid, disturbed. See also DRUMLY.] Turbid, troubled.

a **1340** HAMPOLE *Psalter* xv. 5 Warldis men drynkis..þe drubly delitis of lychery & couaitys. *c* **1400** MAUNDEV. (Roxb.) vii. 27 If þe water be clere..þe bawme es gude, and, if it be thikk and drubly, it es sophisticate. *c* **1440** *Promp. Parv.* 132/2 Drobly, or drubly, *turbulentus*, *turbidus.* **1500-20** DUNBAR *Poems* lxix. 1 Thir dirk and drublie dayis.

Hence †ˈ**drubliness**.

c **1440** *Promp. Parv.* 133/2 Drublynesse, *turbulencia*, *feculencia.*

†ˈ**drubman.** *Obs. rare.* An officer who administers the bastinado.

1629 CAPT. SMITH *Trav. & Adv.* xii. 24 The Tymor Bashaw..caused his Drub-man to strip him naked.

drucken, Sc. and north. dial. f. DRUNKEN.

drudge (drʌdʒ), *sb.* Also 6 **drugge, drug**. [The derivation of this and the associated vb. is obscure: the sb. is known *c* 1500, the vb. about 50 years later. As a rarer form of both, *drugge*, *drug* is also found 1550-1650. The forms and sense would both be satisfied by an OE. sb. **dryczea* 'labourer', from **dryze*:—**drugi-z* 'labour', from *u*-grade *drug-* of *dréozan* to work, etc. (DREE *v.*), (cf. *lyre*, *scyte*, from *léosan*, *scéotan*, etc.); or by an OE. vb. **dryczean*, W.Ger. **druggjan*:—**drugjan*, from same vb.; but of these no actual trace has been found either in OE. or ME.]

One employed in mean, servile, or distasteful work; a slave, a hack; a hard toiler.

1494 FABYAN *Chron.* VII. 497 Many they held as drudges and captyues. **1530** PALSGR. 215/2 Drudge, a woman servaunt, *druge*, *meschine.* **1579-80** NORTH *Plutarch* (1676) 791 Getting their living as drudges and slaves, to do most vile Service. **1691** WOOD *Ath. Oxon.* II. 705 He was the common drudge of the University..to make, correct, or review the Latine Sermons..before they were to be delivered. **1755** JOHNSON, *Lexicographer*, a writer of dictionaries; a harmless drudge, that busies himself in tracing the original, and detailing the signification of words. **1771** SMOLLETT *Humph. Cl.* (1815) 51, I was not born to be the household drudge. **1859** HOLLAND *Gold F.* xxvi. 326 The Pastor..is required to be the hardest drudge in his parish.

β. **1552** HULOET, Drudge, or drugge, or vile seruant in a house, whych doth all the vyle seruice. **1592** GREENE *Disput.* 31 At these wise words spoken by so base a drug as his mayd. [Cf. **1607** SHAKS. *Timon* IV. iii. 254.]

fig. **1573** TUSSER *Husb.* vi. (1878) 15, I [Husbandry] seeme but a drudge, yet..To such as can vse me, great wealth I do bring. **1632** LITHGOW *Trav.* II. 73 Destiny is no mans drudge. **1871** MORLEY *Voltaire* (1886) 13 Discrowning sovereign reason to be the serving drudge of superstition.

b. *attrib.* and *Comb.*

1742 JARVIS *Quix.* I. i. (1885) 41 Rozinante. *Note*, From *Rosin*, a common drudge-horse, and *ante*, before. **1840** MILL *Diss. & Disc.* (1875) I. 465 The..drudge-like aversion to change.

Hence (*nonce-wds.*) ˈ**drudgical** *a.*, belonging to a drudge; ˈ**drudgism**, the practice of a drudge.

1831 CARLYLE *Sart. Res.* III. x, Dandiacal Self-worship or Demon-worship, and Poor-Slavish or Drudgical Earth-worship, or whatever that same Drudgism may be.

drudge (drʌdʒ), *v.* Also 6-7 **drugge, drug**. [app. f. prec. sb. But cf. Norw. *drugga* to go laboriously, bent over and with bending knees, as under a heavy burden. (Ross.)

Both *drudge* and DRUG *v.*[1], were in early times spelt *drugge*: so that there are cases in which it is difficult to be certain which word is meant. It is esp. so with the two ME. instances (*a* 1240 and *c* 1386) which are left provisionally under DRUG *v.*[1], but of which one or both may possibly belong here.]

1. *intr.* To perform mean or servile tasks; to work hard or slavishly; to toil at laborious and distasteful work.

1548 [see DRUDGING *ppl. a.*]. **1555** W. WATREMAN *Fardle Facions* App. 343 The labouryng manne that toileth and drudgeth with his body. **1604** R. CAWDREY *Table Alph.* (1613), *Drudge*, toyle. **1654** WHITLOCK *Zootomia* 188 The World is but his Slave..to drudge to his Necessity. **1791** BOSWELL *Johnson* an. 1753 (1831) I. 215 While her husband was drudging in the smoke of London. **1868** M. PATTISON *Academ. Org.* v. 234 College-tutors do indeed work; they drudge.

2. *trans.* To subject to drudgery. *rare.*

1847 BUSHNELL *Chr. Nurt.* II. vi. (1861) 349 He will even drudge himself to serve it. **1847** R. W. HAMILTON *Disq. Sabbath* v. (1848) 163 A hardness of heart which cares not how his brother-man is drudged.

3. ***drudge out***, to perform as drudgery; ***drudge away***, ***over***, to pass in drudgery; ***drudge down***, to repress with drudgery.

1645 MILTON *Tetrach.* (1851) 254 The end of the commandment is charity..not the drudging out a poore and worthlesse duty forc't from us. **1682** OTWAY *Venice Preserved* II. (1735) 37 Rise to our toils and drudge away the day. *a* **1735** GRANVILLE (J.), What is an age, in dull renown drudg'd o'er? **1862** *Athenæum* 30 Aug. 282 Rouse the independent faculties of the student's mind,—not, as now, mechanically drudge them down.

Hence **drudged** *ppl. a.*, set to laborious or servile tasks; ˈ**drudging** *vbl. sb.*, drudgery; also ˈ**drudger**, one who drudges; †ˈ**drudge-pudding**, a kitchen drudge.

1612-15 BP. HALL *Contempl., N.T.* IV. i, Life..spent in a continual drudging for edification. **1710** *Brit. Apollo* II. No. 105. 3/2 Condemn'd to Drudging. **1737** OZELL *Rabelais* II. 225 A Kitchen-slave, a Drudge-pudding. **1755** JOHNSON, *Drudger*, a mean labourer. **1851** D. JERROLD *St. Giles* xx. 210 The drudged horse stood meek and passive in the field. **1885** MABEL COLLINS *Pre-Hist. Woman* ix, A mere drudger for daily bread.

drudge, drudger, obs. ff. DREDGE, DREDGER.

drudgery (ˈdrʌdʒərɪ). Also 6 **droudgery**, 6-7 **druggery**. [f. DRUDGE *sb.* + -ERY; cf. *slavery*.] The occupation of a drudge; mean or servile labour; wearisome toil; dull or distasteful work.

1550 CROWLEY *Inform. & Petit.* 557 To tyll the grounde and doe your other droudgery. **1633** G. HERBERT *Temple, Elixer* v, A servant with this clause Makes drudgerie divine. **1652-62** HEYLIN *Cosmogr.* II. (1682) 183 Who put them to all Drudgeries and servile Works. **1791** BOSWELL *Johnson* 10 Apr. an. 1753, He now relieved the drudgery of his Dictionary..by taking an active part in the composition of 'The Adventurer'. **1879** M. PATTISON *Milton* xii. 163 If there is any literary drudgery more mechanical than another, it is generally supposed to be that of making a dictionary. **1890** W. C. GANNETT *Blessed be Drudgery* 15 Drudgery is the gray Angel of Success.

β. **1598** FLORIO, *Marruffino*, the yoongest prentise in a house, one that is put to all druggerie. **1654** WHITLOCK *Zootomia* 297 Avaricious plenty is its own Tasker..whose Druggery and Time to serve God cannot consist together.

b. *attrib.*, as in †***drudgery work***, ***servant***.

1621 BURTON *Anat. Mel.* I. ii. I. ii. (1651) 42 Familiar spirits, which are there said to be conversant with men, and do their drudgery works. *a* **1654** SELDEN *Table-T.* (Arb.) 88 They that do drudgery-work. **1801** GABRIELLI *Myster. Husb.* IV. 119 A mere drudgery servant.

drudging, *vbl. sb.*: see under DRUDGE *v.*

drudging ('drʌdʒɪŋ), *ppl. a.* Also 6 **drugging.** [f. DRUDGE *v.* + -ING[2].] That drudges; of the nature of drudgery; toilsome, laborious.

1548 CRANMER *Catech.* 40 These small and druggynge workes. **1549** COVERDALE, etc. *Erasm. Par. 1 Pet.* 8 She was hys wyfe, & not his drudgeing hande mayde. **1632** MILTON *L'Allegro* 105 How the drudging Goblin sweat, To earn his cream-bowl duly set. **1894** W. J. DAWSON *Making of Manhood* 88 A drudging attention to details.

Hence **'drudgingly** *adv.*

1678 CUDWORTH *Intell. Syst.* 149 That He should..do all the meanest and triflingest things Himself drudgingly. **1864** *Times* 12 Aug. 4 He had collected, lovingly rather than drudgingly, the materials for a new edition.

drue, obs. form of *drew*, pa. t. of DRAW *v.*

drue, early ME. form of DRY.

†**druery, drury.** *Obs.* Forms: *α.* 3–4 druery, -rie, driwerie, drywery, -orie, 4 drew-, drou-, druwery(e; *β.* 3–5 drury, -ri, 4 dreury, drwry(e, 4–5 drurie, -rye, drewri(e, -ry, drowry, 5 droury, drewre, 6 *Sc.* drou-, drowrie, (9 *Sc.* drurie). [a. OF. *druerie, droerie, druirie* love, friendship (= It. *druderia*, med.L. *drudaria* Du Cange), f. *dru*, *drut*, friend: see DRUT.]

1. Love, *esp.* sexual love, love-making, courtship; *often*, illicit love, amour.

a **1225** *Ancr. R.* 330 Uor þe deore driwerie þet he haueð to his deore spuse, þet is, to þe cleane soule. *c* **1275** *Sinners Beware* 158 in *O.E. Misc.* 77 þeos prude leuedies þat luuyeþ drywories, And brekeþ spusynge. *c* **1300** *Cursor M.* 23786 (Edin.) A litil lust, A drewri [*v.rr.* druri, dreuri, dreury] þat es bot a dust. **1375** BARBOUR *Bruce* VIII. 498 Than mycht he weill ask ane lady Hir amouris and hir drowry. *c* **1386** CHAUCER *Sir Thopas* 184 Of ladies love and druerie Anon I wol you tell. *c* **1460** *Launfal* 995 That he never, yn no folye, Besofte the quene of no drurye.

2. A love-token, keepsake, gift, present. (In Sc. confused in sense with *dowery*: see DROWRIE.)

a **1225** *Ancr. R.* 250 þis was his driwerie þet he bileauede and ȝef ham in his departunge. **13..** *K. Alis.* 7610 By special messangere, Y wol sende hire love-drewry. ? *a* **1500** *How Marchande dyd hys Wyfe betray* 32 in Hazl. *E.P.P.* I. 197 That y myȝt the bye some ryche drewre. **1550** LYNDESAY *Sqr. Meldrum* 1003 He gaif hir ane lufe drowrie, Ane ring set with ane riche rubie. **1560** ROLLAND *Crt. Venus* IV. 562 Of thy auld Name I the deprive..To thy Drourie, and callis the Dalience.

3. A beloved person, 'love', sweetheart.

c **1315** SHOREHAM 131 Thou [Mary] art Crystes oȝene drury. **13..** *K. Alis.* 2214 Mony mon ther les his brothir.. Mony maide hire drewery. *a* **1400** *Relig. Pieces fr. Thornton MS.* (1867) 74 Jesu my dere, and my drewrye. *c* **1450** HENRYSON *Mor. Fab.* 19 You was our drowrie and our dayes darling.

4. A beloved, prized, or precious thing, a treasure.

a **1300** *Cursor M.* 21372 Quen it [the cross] had ben tua hundret yere Al vnder mold, þat druri dere..He did be funden thoru a wijf. **1340** HAMPOLE *Pr. Consc.* 7825 þare es alkyn druryes and rychesce. **1362** LANGL. *P. Pl.* A. I. 85 Treuþe is þe Beste..Hit is as derworþe a drurie as deore god him-seluen. *a* **1400** *Relig. Pieces fr. Thornton MS.* (1867) 87 So was þou daynte as drowry derely endent.

drug (drʌg), *sb.*[1] Forms: (*pl.*) (4 dragges), 4–6 **drogges, drouges,** 6 **drougges,** *Sc.* **droggis, drogis, droigis,** 6–7 **drugges,** 7 **drogues, drougs,** 8 **druggs,** 8–9 *Sc.* **drogs,** 7– **drugs;** (*sing.*) 6–7 **drugge,** 7 **drogue,** 7– **drug.** [ME. a. F. *drogue* (14th c. in Hatz.-Darm.) a Com. Rom. word (Pr. *drogua*, Sp., It. *droga*): ulterior origin uncertain.

The suggestion of Diez, that the source is Du. *droog*, MDu. *droge, drooch*, Kilian *droogh* 'dry', is doubted by Kluge and Franck. In 14–15th c. there is scribal confusion in Eng. MSS. between *drogge* and *dragge* = DREDGE *sb.*[2]]

1. a. An original, simple, medicinal substance, organic or inorganic, whether used by itself in its natural condition or prepared by art, or as an ingredient in a medicine or medicament. Formerly used more widely to include all ingredients used in chemistry, pharmacy, dyeing, and the arts generally, as still in French. In early use always in the pl.: cf. *spices*. (So in Fr.)

[**1327** *Close Roll, 1 Edw. III*, I. mem. 23 Novem balas de drogges de spicerie.] **1377** LANGL. *P. Pl.* B. xx. 173 And dryuen awey deth with dyas and dragges [*v.r.* drogges; C. XXIII. 174 drogges, *v.rr.* drouges, dragges]. *c* **1386** CHAUCER *Prol.* 428 Apothecaries To sende him drogges [3 *MSS.* drugges, *Harl.* dragges]. **1398** TREVISA *Barth. De P.R.* XVII. xix. 614 By cause of stronge drouges [(1495) *printed* dreuges]. **1513** DOUGLAS *Æneis* XII. *Prol.* 144 Hailsum of smell as ony spicery, Tryakle, droggis, or electuary. **1533** ELYOT *Cast. Helthe* II. viii. (1539) 22 b, The traffyke of spyce and sondry drouges. **1555** EDEN *Decades* 239 Apothecaries drugges. **1563** WINȜET *Wks.* (1890) II. 12 An apothecaris buyth ful of al kynd of droigis, bayth of delicat spycerie and of rady poysoun. **1577** HARRISON *England* II. xx. (1877) I. 327 Our continuall desire of strange drugs. **1611** CORYAT *Crudities* 262 All the women of Venice..vse to annoint their haire with oyle, or some other drugs. **1611** BIBLE *Transl. Pref.* 3 Men talke of Catholicon the drugge that it is in stead of all purges. **1648** GAGE *West Ind.* xvii. 113 Much Cacao, Achiotte, and drugs for Chocolatte..also Apothecary drugs, as Zarzaparilla. **1682** *Lond. Gaz.* No. 1750/4 Tea and other Drugs at reasonable rates. *a* **1704** T. BROWN *Sat. Quack* Wks. 1730 I. 63 Thy druggs alone the fatal work had done. **1727–51** CHAMBERS *Cycl.*, *Drug*, in commerce, a general name for all spices, and other commodities, brought from distant countries, and used in the business of medicine, dying, and the mechanic arts. **1776** ADAM SMITH *W.N.* I. xi. (1869) I. 215 Tea..was a drug very little used in Europe before the middle of the last century. **1842** TENNYSON *Two Voices* 56 What drug can make A wither'd palsy cease to shake?

b. *spec.* Now often applied without qualification to narcotics, opiates, hallucinogens, etc., esp. *attrib.* and *Comb.*, as ***drug-abuse, -addict, -addiction, -dependence, -evil, -fiend*** (FIEND 4c), ***-habit, -peddler, -peddling, -pusher, -pushing, -taker, -taking, -traffic.***

1883 W. BLACK *Yolande* II. xiv. 255 One of the results of using..those poisonous drugs, is that the will entirely goes. **1899** *Chemist & Druggist* LV. 1010/2 Defendant entered the house to be cured of the habit of taking drugs, and it was alleged that he had absented himself without leave, and obtained cocaine for injection. **1902** *Daily Chron.* 7 Nov. 5/6 Two remedies to the drug-evil were suggested by the Bishop of Kensington. **1905** *Ibid.* 2 May 5/7 The drug-taking Chilcote. **1906** R. BROOKE *Let.* 3 Apr. (1968) 48, I have to read stealthily.., a practice akin to that of secret drug-taking. **1907** *Daily Chron.* 3 Sept. 7/7 A drug-taker appropriated a bottle of drugs from a Brighton chemist's shop. **1907** *Chemist & Druggist* LXX. 107/2 The drug habit. Mrs. Florence Iggulden..died last week from morphine-poisoning. **1916** *Ibid.* LXXXVIII. 19/1 Narcotic drug traffic. **1916** *N.Y. Evening Post* 7 Jan., The Drug Addict, the Physician, and the Law. **1917** *Amer. Review of Reviews* LVI. 435 (*title*) Drug Addiction and the Harrison Law. **1920** [see ADDICT *sb.*]. **1922** C. E. MONTAGUE *Disenchantment* xv. 199 Drunkards, thieves, liars, sorners, drug-takers. **1925** H. G. WELLS *Christina Alberta's Father* I. vi. 156 Artists' models and drug-fiends. **1930** 'E. QUEEN' *French Powder Mystery* xxxviii. 313 A gang of drug-peddlers operating..in this city. **1945** R. KNOX *God & Atom* ix. 127 If religion, as Lenin said, is the opium of the people, he himself has done his best to make drug-fiends of us all. **1949** E. PARTRIDGE in *Good Housekeeping* June 13/1 Some years ago, the League of Nations instituted an inquiry into the drug-traffic. **1959** 'F. NEWTON' *Jazz Scene* 293 Entertainment, petty crime, prostitution, drug-pushing and the like. **1966** *New Scientist* 29 Dec. 713/1 The idea of an evil shadowy figure corrupting our youth by 'pushing' drugs is largely nonsense. *Ibid.*, It is generally accepted that the addict is a psychopath before taking up the drug. **1967** E. & M. A. RADFORD *No Reason for Murder* xv. 105 How are we concerned? We've no case of drug peddling. **1967** *Observer* 10 Sept. 17/7 Areas of..drug-pushers, prostitution and delinquency. **1968** *Listener* 14 Nov. 639/1 Some drug dependences arise from medical causes, as with a diabetic who must have his insulin. **1970** *Times* 28 May 7/5 Pot-smoking is widespread in spite of dire warnings about the dangers of 'drug abuse' repeatedly broadcast by the armed forces radio. **1971** *Time* 7 June 54/3 The dream that drugs are a short cut to truth and beauty.

2. A commodity which is no longer in demand, and so has lost its value or become unsaleable. (Now usually ***a drug in*** (now freq. ***on***) ***the market.***) Also *transf.*

[It is questionable if this is the same word. Quot. 1760 implies it; but it may possibly be only a witty play on the word: see also Fuller's contrast of *drugs* and *dainties*.]

a **1661** FULLER *Worthies* IV. (1662) 54 [He] made such a vent for Welsh Cottons, that what he found Drugs at home, he left Dainties beyond Sea. **1671** NARBOROUGH *Jrnl.* in *Acc. Sev. Late Voy.* I. (1711) 151 We might send our English Cloth, which now is grown a Drug. **1673** TEMPLE *Ess. Irel.* Wks. 1731 I. 116 Horses in Ireland are a Drug, but might be improved to a Commodity. **1704** J. LOGAN in *Pa. Hist. Soc. Mem.* IX. 278 Wheat..bears no price, and bread and flour is a very drug. **1719** DE FOE *Crusoe* I. iv, I smil'd to my self at the Sight of this Money. O Drug! said I aloud, what art thou good for? **1760** MURPHY *Way to Keep Him* I, A wife's a drug now; mere tar-water, with every virtue under heaven, but nobody takes it. **1824** W. IRVING *T. Trav.* I. 211 They told me poetry was a mere drug; every body wrote poetry. **1833** *Knickerbocker* Mar. 157 Lace veils are a drug in the market. **1840** HOOD *Up Rhine* 163 Quite a drug in the market. **1893** *Funk's Stand. Dict.* s.v., A drug on (or in) the market. **1921** GALSWORTHY *To Let* I. i. 10 Well, they wouldn't confiscate his pictures, for they wouldn't know their worth. But what would they be worth, if these maniacs once began to milk capital? A drug on the market. **1922** JOYCE *Ulysses* 192 Genius would be a drug in the market. **1944** W. S. MAUGHAM *Razor's Edge* iv. 125 He can't bear his feeling of being a drug on the market.

3. *Comb.*, as ***drug-compounder, -counter, -grinder, -house, -jar, -mill, -pot, -seller, -shop, -store, -vase,*** etc.; **drug clerk** *U.S.*, an attendant in a drug-store; **drug culture,** the subculture (sense 2) associated with and peopled by users of illegal drugs; **drug-fast** *a.* [FAST *a.* 1 h] = *drug-resistant* adj.; so *drug-fastness*; **drug-induced** *a.*, (of a mental or physical condition) brought about by the taking of a drug or drugs; **drugman,** a man who deals in drugs, an apothecary; **drug-resistant** *a.*, resisting the effects of a drug or drugs; so *drug-resistance, -resisting* adj.; **drug(s) squad,** a division of a police force appointed to investigate crimes involving the taking of or trafficking in illegal narcotic and other drugs; cf. *narcotic(s) squad* s.v. NARCOTIC *sb.*[2]

1849 *Whig Almanac 1850* 25/1 A drug clerk at $1,000. *a* **1910** 'O. HENRY' *Rolling Stones* (1916) 102 The drug clerk looks sharply at the white face half concealed by the high-turned overcoat collar. **1842** ABDY *Water Cure* (1843) 162 The drug-compounder and the plaster-spreader. **1959** *Listener* 30 July 173/1 Flaubert's drug-counters and the inexhaustible inventories of Zola. [**1968** W. SURFACE *Poisoned Ivy* 213 The drug phenomenon has produced a drug-oriented culture on the nation's campuses.] **1969** *Sunday Mail Mag.* (Brisbane) 22 June 11/3 The phrase 'turn on' comes from the 'drug culture'. **1982** *Amer. Speech* IV. 271 A large number of terms and meanings related to the drug culture have found their way into the general dictionaries. **1611** SHAKS. *Cymb.* III. iv. 15 That Drug-damn'd Italy, hath out-craftied him. **1926** *Jrnl. Infectious Dis.* XXXIX. 243 The fact that bacteria become tolerant or drug fast to various germicides in vitro immediately leads to the question of specificity. *Ibid.*, Thirty drug fast strains were tested. *Ibid.* 237 (*title*) Drug-fastness in its relation to the resistance of certain organisms toward familiar germicides. **1945** *Trans. Faraday Soc.* XLI. 363 In the case of phenol itself and of several substituted phenols, little or no adaptation or drug-fastness is in fact apparent. **1886** *Pall Mall G.* 20 Apr. 8/1 Messrs. Jordan and Co., Drug grinders. **1865** DICKENS *Mut. Fr.* I. iv, Clerk in the drug-house. **1952** *Practitioner* Mar. 235 (*heading*) Drug-induced blood disease. **1970** R. C. ZAEHNER *Concordant Discord* iii. 41 Foolhardy enough to deny the identity of drug-induced ecstasies with the more controlled raptures of the orthodox mystical traditions. **1973** [see IATROGENIC *a.*]. **1983** *Oxf. Textbk. Med.* II. xxi. 120 No more needs to be said about drug-induced tremor or Parkinsonism. **1931** G. E. HOWARD (*title*) Early English drug jars. **1960** H. HAYWARD *Antique Coll.* 102/1 *Drug jar*, pot or jar intended for use on apothecaries shelves. **1961** *Antiquaries Jrnl.* XLI. 9 (*caption*) Drug-jar with inscription from Winchester. *a* **1810** TANNAHILL *Poems* (1846) 87 Mak'st..drugmen brew the poisoning dose. **1903** R. L. HOBSON *Catal. Eng. Pott. in Brit. Mus.* 137 English Delft Ware..Drug Pot, barrel-shaped. **1910** J. F. BLACKER *ABC of collecting Old Eng. Pott.* x. 78 Zachariah Barnes..was noted as the maker of wall-tiles and druggists' jars, or drug-pots. **1932** *Brit. Med. Jrnl.* II. 668/1 (*title*) Drug resistance, with special reference to trypanosomiasis. *Ibid.*, The practical significance of the capacity of trypanosomal infections to become drug-resistant, or drug-fast, for the treatment of the infections in man..was at once recognized. **1961** *Lancet* 5 Aug. 309/2 Few new drug-resistant cases will appear. *Ibid.* 310/1 Drug resistance is already a significant problem in many areas. **1951** KOESTLER *Age of Longing* 242 Developing new and better drug-resisting strains. **1586** T. B. *La Primaud. Fr. Acad.* I. 698 Apothecarie, drug-seller and such like. **1962** Drug squad [see SQUAD *sb.*[1] 4c]. **1967** *Times* 15 Nov. 3/3 Recent successful raids by Scotland Yard drugs squad men. **1976** *Eastern Daily Press* (Norwich) 16 Dec. 3/3 The alleged 'Mr. Big' of a Suffolk drugs ring was arrested by Suffolk Drug Squad. **1985** *Daily Tel.* 9 Sept. 3/5 (*heading*) Drugs squad 'needs 214 men, not 38'. **1933** *Burlington Mag.* Mar. 108/1 South Kensington has recently acquired a drug vase.

Hence **'drugful** *a.*, full of drugs, having plenty of drugs; **'drugless** *a.*, without drugs.

1877 BLACKIE *Wise Men* 150 That so the drugful leech Might profit me the more. **1880** BROWNING *Dram. Idylls* Ser. II. *Doctor* — 99 Whether drugged or left Drugless, the patient always lived, nor died.

drug, *sb.*[2] [Allied to DRUG *v.*[1]; cf. also DRAG *sb.*]

1. A low truck for the carriage of timber and other heavy articles; cf. DRAG *sb.* 1 c and d.

1677 MOXON *Mech. Exerc.* (1703) 125 The *Drug*..is made somewhat like a low narrow Carr. It is used for the carriage of Timber, and then is drawn..by two or more Men. **1688** R. HOLME *Armoury* III. 355/2. **1787** W. MARSHALL *East Norf.* Gloss., *Drug*, a four-wheeled timber carriage. **1878** in F. S. Williams *Midl. Railw.* 499 We managed that on a drug—a four wheeled timber wagon sort of thing.

2. A drag for a vehicle; = DRAG *sb.* 3 c. *dial.*

1880 in *W. Cornwall Gloss.*

3. *Comb.* †**drug-carriage** = sense 1; †**drug-saw,** a cross-cut saw: cf. *drag-saw* (DRAG *sb.* 9).

1578 *Inv. Roy. Wardr.* (1815) 255 (Jam.) Ane little drug saw for wrichtis. **1665** J. WEBB *Stone-Heng* (1725) 214 In all likelihood, they were brought thither on Drug-Carriages. ?**17..** *Acc. Depredat. on Clan Campbell* (1816) 53 (Jam.) Drug-saw, bow saw, and others.

drug, *sb.*[3] var. of DROGUE.

†**drug,** *v.*[1] *Obs.* exc. *dial.* Also 3–6 **drugge.** [Common from *c* 1500 in Sc.; also in mod.Eng. dialects. Of uncertain origin.

In Sc. and Eng. dial. use, app. a variant of DRAG *v.*; but the two ME. instances are earlier than any known examples of *drag*, and may have some different origin. One or both may possibly belong to DRUDGE *v.*, of which, also, *drugge* was an early spelling.]

To pull forcibly, to drag. (*trans.* and *intr.*)

[*a* **1240** *Lofsong* in *Cott. Hom.* 207 Bi his owune rode, on his softe schuldres, so herde druggunge. *c* **1386** CHAUCER *Knt.'s T.* 558 At the gate he profreth his seruyse To drugge [*Camb. MS.* drogge] and drawe what so men wol deuyse]. **1500–20** DUNBAR *Poems* xxxiii. 70 Evir the cuschettis at him tuggit, The rukis him rent, the ravynis him druggit. *Ibid.* lxi. 32, I am ane auld horss, as ȝe knaw That evir in duill dois drug and draw. **1513** DOUGLAS *Æneis* II. iv. 84 And for to drug and draw wald neuer irk. **1601** ? MARSTON *Pasquil & Kath.* I. 312 If all the Brewers jades in the Towne can drugge me from loue of my selfe. **1794** T. DAVIS *Agric. Wilts* (1818) 258–68 *Drugging* timber, drawing [timber] out of the wood under a pair of wheels.

drug (drʌg), *v.*[2] [f. DRUG *sb.*[1]]

1. *trans.* To mix or adulterate (food or drink) with a drug, esp. a narcotic or poisonous drug.

1605 SHAKS. *Macb.* II. ii. 7, I haue drugg'd their Possets, That Death and Nature doe contend about them. **1828** SCOTT *F. M. Perth* xv, What would it have cost me..so to have drugged that balm, as should have made your arm rot? **1855** MOTLEY *Dutch Rep.* (1861) II. 263 Montigny's meat and drink, they said, should be daily drugged.

fig. **1871** R. ELLIS *Catullus* xliv. 11 A speech of his, pure poison, every line deep-drugg'd.

2. a. To administer drugs to (a person), esp. for the purpose of stupefying or poisoning him. Also *fig.*

a **1730** FENTON *To Knt. of Sable Shield* (R.), Whom he has drugg'd to sure repose. **1791** COWPER *Odyss.* II. 434 Some baneful herb Which cast into our cup shall drug us all. **1883** *Law Rep. 11 Q. Bench Div.* 598 No one had been drugged on the night when the house was broken into.

b. To administer something nauseous to; to nauseate.

1667 MILTON *P.L.* x. 567 Drugd as oft, With hatefullest disrelish. **1812** BYRON *Ch. Har.* I. vi, With pleasure drugg'd, he almost long'd for woe.

3. *intr.* To take or be in the habit of taking drugs; *esp.* to indulge in narcotics.

1893 *Funk's Stand. Dict.* s.v., She has drugged all her life. **1968** [see DRUGGER 3].

Hence **drugged** *ppl. a.*; **'drugging** *vbl. sb.* and *ppl. a.*

1610 B. JONSON *Alch.* II. i, Past all the doses of your drugging doctors. **1871** TYNDALL *Fragm. Sc.* (1879) I. xxii. 504 The drugged soul is beyond the reach of reason. **1875** JOWETT *Plato* (ed. 2) I. 169 The physician's use of burning, cutting, drugging, and starving. *a* **1880** GEO. ELIOT in *Pall Mall G.* (1885) 9 Feb., Brewers with their drugged ale.

drug, druggery, -ing, obs. ff. DRUDGE, etc.

drug(g)a-, druggerman, obs. ff. DRAGOMAN.

†**druggard.** *Obs.* [? f. DRUG *v.*¹] ? = DRUGGLE.

15.. *Pore helpe* 313 in Hazl. *E.P.P.* III. 263 Maister huggarde Doth shewe hymselfe no sluggarde, Nor yet no dronken druggarde.

†**druggare.** *Sc. Obs.* [perh. f. *drug*, obs. Sc. f. DRUDGE.] ? = Drudger. (But cf. prec.)

1423 JAS. I *Kingis Q.* clv, The slawe ase, the druggare beste of pyne.

drugger ('drʌgə(r)). Also 6 druggier, -eir. [f. DRUG *sb.*¹ (in senses 2 and 3 f. DRUG *v.*²) + -ER¹, -IER. Cf. F. *drogueur.*]

†**1.** A dealer in drugs, a druggist. *Obs.*

1594 NASHE *Terrors Nt.* E ij, The hungrie druggier.. agrees to anything, and to Court he goes. **1596** —— *Saffron Walden* 109 Another craftie mortring Druggeir. **1610** B. JONSON *Alch.* IV. vii, He owes this honest Drugger here seven pound..[for] Tabacco. **1628** EARLE *Microcosm., Meer dull Physician* (Arb.) 25 Then follows a writ to his drugger in a strange tongue. **1845** S. NAYLER *Reynard* Introd. 42 The prelate, the lawyer, the drugger, are here fitted to their hearts' content.

2. One who administers a drug.

1836 E. HOWARD *R. Reefer* l, I became..lethargically drowsy..They are skilful druggers. **1893** *Daily News* 16 Dec. 5/1 The child was observed by this persistent drugger ..to be 'red all over'.

3. One who takes narcotic, etc., drugs; a drug-addict. *colloq.*

1941 J. CARY *Herself Surprised* lxxxi. 204 When first I knew Lizzie I thought she was a drugger or a drinker or worse. **1968** H. R. F. KEATING *Inspector Ghote hunts Peacock* vii. 98 Your precious Peacock..was nothing but a low-down little drugger. I may smoke because I need it for my work, but she just drugged to make herself lower than she was.

druggery ('drʌgərɪ). Also (*Sc.*) 6 drogarie, 9 droguery. [a. F. *droguerie* (1462 in Godef.), f. *drogue* drug: see -ERY.]

1. Drugs collectively; medicine, physic.

1535 STEWART *Cron. Scot.* III. 279 Till all seik men or tha get drogarie. **1552** ABP. HAMILTON *Catech.* (1884) 11 Potegareis that sellis corruppit drogaris. **1611** COTGR., *Drogueries*, drugs, druggeries, confections. **1822** GALT *Sir A. Wylie* III. xxxiii. 285 Nane o' the droguery nor the roguery o' doctors for me. **1891** G. MEREDITH *One of our Conq.* I. vii. 118 Awful combinations in druggery.

2. A place where drugs are kept for sale or use.

1865 W. G. PALGRAVE *Arabia* I. 422 My druggery and consultation-room.

drugget ('drʌgɪt). Also 6 *Sc.* droggitt, drogatt, 8–9 **druggit.** [a. F. *droguet* (1555 in Hatz.-Darm.), thence, prob., Sp. *droguete*, It. *droghetto*, Ger. *droguett.* Ulterior origin unknown.

Littré suggests derivation from *drogue* drug as 'a stuff of little value'; some English writers have assumed a derivation from *Drogheda* in Ireland, but this is mere wanton conjecture, without any historical basis.]

1. a. Formerly, a kind of stuff, all of wool, or mixed of wool and silk or wool and linen, used for wearing apparel. **b.** Now, a coarse woollen stuff used for floor-coverings, table-cloths, etc.

1580 LADY ERROL *Let.* in Mrs. Pratt *Buchan* (1858) App. 322 Ane pair of drogatt courtingis. *Ibid.* 323 Ane pair of courtingis of b[l]ew & quhytt droggitt. **1672** EACHARD *Observ. Answ. Cont. Clergy*, One that is in canonical black may..see as far into a millstone, as he that wears a light drugget. **1682** *Lond. Gaz.* No. 1762/4 Several Pieces of Rich Silk Druggets, Serge-Wale, Thred Druggets. **1714** *Fr. Bk. of Rates* 378 Druggets of Wool, and Thread and Wool. **1721** SWIFT *Ep. to Play* Wks. 1755 III. II. 182 In drugget drest, of thirteen pence a yard, See Philip's son. **1727–51** CHAMBERS *Cycl.*, *Drugget*..a sort of stuff, very thin, and narrow, usually all wool, and sometimes half wool and half silk..woven on a worsted chain. **1745** *Gentl. Mag.* 99/1, I remember plain John Dryden..in one uniform cloathing of Norwich drugget. **1832** LYTTON *Eugene A.* III. iv, He wore a spencer of a light brown drugget. **1877** M. M. GRANT *Sun-Maid* i, A wide corridor, carpeted with warm crimson drugget. **1882** BECK *Draper's Dict.* s.v., Twilled druggets were..known in trade as corded druggets, but when of linen warp and woollen weft, as threaded druggets.

2. †**a.** A garment or suit of drugget. **b.** A carpet or floorcloth of drugget.

1713 STEELE *Guardian* No. 147 ¶1 He was married in a plain drugget. **1859** MRS. CARLYLE *Lett.* III. 10 Putting down the drugget in the drawing-room. **1870** MISS BRIDGMAN *Ro. Lynne* xiii, The carpets..remained hidden from sight by the cleanest of druggets.

3. *attrib.* Made of drugget.

1580 [see 1]. **1675** *Lond. Gaz.* No. 980/4 A Drugget Sute lined with green. **1836** SIR G. HEAD *Home Tour* 160 Dressed in easy loose-fitting costume, viz. a drugget pea-jacket and wide trowsers. **1873** BLACK *Pr. Thule* xxv. 427 A young lady, dressed in a drugget petticoat.

4. *Comb.*, as ***drugget-maker.***

1709 *Lond. Gaz.* No. 4594/4 Thomas Twaite, late a Drugget maker.

Hence **'druggeted** *ppl. a.*, covered or carpeted with drugget; **'druggeting** = sense 1 b.

1890 *Sale-Catal.* (Derby), Carpet..Red druggeting. **1893** *Cornh. Mag.* Jan. 29 The drawing-room..is bare of furniture, and druggeted for Edith's skirt-dancing party.

†**'druggish,** *a. Obs. rare.* [f. DRUG *sb.*¹ + -ISH.] Of the nature of a drug.

1600 W. VAUGHAN *Direct. Health* (1633) 80 Take heed of the black druggish Tobacco. **1701** J. LAW *Counc. Trade* (1751) 108 However low and drugish the price of fish might be.

druggist ('drʌgɪst). Also 7 drouguist. [a. F. *droguiste* (1549 in Hatz.-Darm.), f. *drogue* drug: see -IST.] One who sells or deals in drugs.

In Scotland and United States the usual name for a pharmaceutical chemist. ***chemist and druggist***: see CHEMIST 4.

1611 COTGR., *Drogueur*, a druggist, or drug-seller. **1639** J. W. tr. *Guibert's Physic.* I. 10 Two pennyworth of Sene.. which they may have at the Apothecaries or drouguists. **1652** GAULE *Magastrom.* 360 Two chymists had agreed upon a cheat, that one of them should turn druggist, and sell strange roots and powders. **1709** ADDISON *Tatler* No. 131 ¶3 That this new Corporation of Druggists had inflamed the Bills of Mortality and puzzled the College of Physicians with Diseases, for which they neither knew a Name or Cure. **1799** *Med. Jrnl.* II. 123 Mr. Brown, Wholesale Chemist and Druggist. **1802** *Ibid.* VIII. 247 Compounding and vending medicines in the shop of a druggist or an apothecary.

'druggister. *Obs.* exc. *dial.* [f. prec.; cf. *barrister, chorister.*] = DRUGGIST.

1632 SHERWOOD, A Druggister, *drogueur.* **1679** FILMER *Free-holder* 325 The Septuagint have translated a Witch, an Apothecary, a Druggister, one that compounds poisons. **1877** *N.W. Linc. Gloss.*, *Druggister*, a druggist.

†**druggle.** *Obs.* Also 7 druggel(l. [? f. DRUG *v.*¹] A term of contempt: app. = A heavy, stupid, spiritless, or cowardly fellow. Hence †**druggle-headed,** †**druggly** *adjs.*

1611 COTGR., *Bustarin*, a great lubber, thicke druggell. *Ibid.*, *Retroussé*, thicke and short, druggellie. **1653** URQUHART *Rabelais* I. xxv, Slapsauce Fellows, slabberdegullion Druggels, lubbardly Louts. **1708** MOTTEUX *Rabelais* IV. lxvi. (1737) 272 Thou forlorn druggle-headed Sneaks-by!

druggy ('drʌgɪ), *a.* [f. DRUG *sb.*¹ + -Y.]

1. a. Of, pertaining to, or of the nature of drugs or medicinal substances.

1583 STUBBES *Anat. Abus.* II. (1882) 55 It is hard to get anything of them [apothecaries] that is right pure and good of it selfe, but druggie baggage, and such counterfait stuffe as is starke naught. **1632** QUARLES *Div. Fancies* III. lxxxviii. (1660) 136 His loathed Potion..Whose druggy taste goes so against their mind. **1890** H. JAMES tr. *Daudet's Port Tarascon* I. vi, The druggy aroma.

b. Of, pertaining to, or characteristic of narcotic drugs or their users; consisting of drug-takers. *colloq.*

1959 J. E. SCHMIDT *Narcotics Lingo & Lore* 84 *Hoppy*—Having a peculiar 'druggy' odor. **1971** *Time* 17 May 34 It begins with that familiar buzzing, distorted guitar sound and inimitable druggy sentiments. **1972** *Village Voice* (N.Y.) 1 June 76/2 He..pronounced, in an affable druggy drawl, [etc.]. **1984** *Times* 8 Oct. 13/1, I was enmeshed in a very druggy crowd at the time.

¶**2.** Error or misprint for DREGGY.

1599 MIDDLETON *Micro-Cynicon* Wks. VIII. 116 Druggy lees, mix'd with the liquid flood. **1627–47** FELTHAM *Resolves* I. xix. 66 Transcending the sense of the druggie flesh.

druggy ('drʌgɪ), *sb. slang.* Also **druggie.** [f. DRUG *sb.*¹ + -Y⁶, -IE.] One who takes or experiments with illegal drugs, a drug-addict.

1968 *Harper's Mag.* Feb. 70/2 In the case of the new druggies, their rage for 'experience' passes over into a form of hedonism. **1970** *Globe & Mail* (Toronto) 25 Sept. 6/6 Don't look at the fathers and mothers of the druggies..; look at their schoolmates and other companions. **1972** *Times Lit. Suppl.* 7 Apr. 385/2 Jill, a juvenile druggy. **1974** *Sunday Sun* (Brisbane) 3 June 1/1 A druggie who has been ordered to be detained at Wolston Park Hospital for at least six months. **1979** *Washington Post* 30 Mar. (Weekend Suppl.) 29/1 Sherlock Holmes fans..remember his portrayal as an angstridden druggie a few years back. **1985** *Time* 29 Apr. 49/1 [A] room full of disillusioned longhairs, counterculture falconers, druggie surfers,..paranoid vets.

drughe, obs. f. *drew*, pa. t. of DRAW *v.*

drught, druȝt(e, druȝþe, obs. ff. DROUGHT.

drugman, drugoman, obs. ff. DRAGOMAN.

†**drugster.** *Obs.* [f. DRUG *sb.*¹ + -STER.] = DRUGGIST.

1611 MIDDLETON & DEKKER *Roaring Girl* II. i, With the best tricks of any drugster's wife in England. **1693** SIR T. P. BLOUNT *Nat. Hist.* 215, I have often enquired amongst our London Drugsters for Egyptian Nitre. *c* **1720** W. GIBSON *Farrier's Dispens.* I. I. (1734) 4 It is a small Knotty Root, and may be had at any Drugster's or Apothecary's. **1756** W. TOLDERVY *Hist. Two Orphans* I. 106.

'drug-store. orig. *U.S.* and chiefly *N. Amer.* Also **drugstore, drug store.** [f. DRUG *sb.*¹ + STORE *sb.* 12 a.] A pharmacy or chemist's shop, often also dealing extensively or mainly in other articles, as toilet requisites, stationery, magazines and newspapers, light refreshments, etc. Also *attrib.*, esp. as **drug-store cowboy,** a braggart, loafer, or good-for-nothing; a person who is not a cowboy but is dressed like one.

1810 *Washington* (D.C.) *Chron.* 17 Nov. 2/2 (Advt.), Cash Drug Store. **1819** H. MCMURTRIE *Sketches of Louisville* 137 There are..in Louisville..three drug stores. **1859** *Brit. Colonist* (Victoria, Brit. Columbia) 12 Dec. 2/5 (Advt.), Drugstore Government street, between Yates and Johnson. **1871** *Cincinnati Commercial* 30 Aug. 3/2 A gentleman.. stopped at a corner drug store and asked for a glass of soda water. **1883** SWEET & KNOX *Through Texas* xv. 230, I felt a sort of drug-store taste in my mouth. **1889** [see HYPO *sb.*²]. **1903** *N.Y. Even. Post* 24 Sept. 8 It hardly pays to keep the [soda] fountains going in the drugstores. **1908** *Westm. Gaz.* 18 Aug. 3/1, I took them to a chemist's or I beg pardon: a drug-store. **1925** *College Humor* Feb. 57/1 (*heading*) With the Drug Store Cowboys. **1931** W. A. MCADOO *Crowded Years* iii. 34, I gave him fifty cents to buy some medicine for me at a drugstore. **1932** E. WAUGH *Black Mischief* iv. 150 Bunting strung..across the Boulevard Amurath, from Levantine café to Hindu drug store. **1935** C. W. THURLOW CRAIG *Paraguayan Interlude* xxi. 247, I have seen men carry guns this way; they were generally new-comers and quickly became objects of derision. 'Drug-store cowboys', they are called. **1936** M. DE LA ROCHE *Whiteoak Harvest* xix. 219 Almost every day they telephoned to the drug store for a pint of delicious ice-cream. **1957** P. FRANK *Seven Days to Never* iii. 102 She married..a marijuana-smoking drugstore cowboy. **1965** A. NICOL *Truly Married Woman* i. 2 He got down the new bottle of patent medicine which one of his friends who worked in a drug store had recommended to him. **1968** *Globe & Mail* (Toronto) 17 Feb. 51 (Advt.), Pharmacist manager for busy downtown drug store. **1969** *Daily Tel.* (Colour Suppl.) 24 Jan. 13/4 There is provision for a small drugstore selling coffee, books and records.

Druid ('druːɪd), *sb.* (*a.*) Also 6–7 **Druide,** 7 **Druyd.** [a. F. *druide* (1512 in Hatz.-Darm.), ad. L. **druida*, ? *druis*, found only in pl., *druidæ, druides*, in Gr. δρυΐδαι; a. OCeltic dental-stem *druid-*, whence OIr. *drui*, dat. and acc. *druid*, pl. *druad*, mod.Ir. and Gael. *draoi* (*draoidh, druidh*, gen. *druadh*) magician, sorcerer, Welsh *dryw* (also *derwydd*, perh. not the same word). As to the ulterior etymology, see Holder, *Alt.-Celt. Sprachschatz* s.v.]

1. One of an order of men among the ancient Celts of Gaul and Britain, who, according to Cæsar were priests or religious ministers and teachers, but who figure in native Irish and Welsh legend as magicians, sorcerers, soothsayers, and the like. (The English use follows the Latin sources, whence it was derived, rather than native Celtic usage.) In early use always in plural.

1563 GOLDING *Cæsar* VI. (1565) 155 The Druides are occupied about holy things: they haue the dooing of publicke and priuate sacrifices, and do interprete and discusse matters of Religion. **1598** BARCKLEY *Felic. Man* (1631) 167 A woman..that was a Soothsayer of them which were called Druides. **1602** *Hist. Eng.* in *Harl. Misc.* (Malh.) II. 439 The Druyds, lifting up their hands towards heaven, filled the air with cries and curses. **1685** STILLINGFL. *Orig. Brit.* ii. 8 The last Age hath discovered a famous Urn of one Chyndonax, Chief of the Druids. **1728** YOUNG *Love Fame* III. Wks. (1757) 101 Like an old Druid from his hollow oak. **1782** COWPER *Table T.* 503 Every hallowed druid was a bard. **1862** *Ecclesiologist* XXIII. 279 Curious beads of coloured glass commonly called 'Druids' beads'. **1892** GARDINER *Stud. Hist. Eng.* 14 In Mona was a sacred place of the Druids.

2. Hence in some modern applications. **a.** A priest, religious minister, chaplain. **b.** A philosophic bard or poet.

1710 ADDISON *Tatler* No. 255 ¶3 Even the Christmas Pye ..is often forbidden to the Druid of the Family. *c* **1748** COLLINS *On Death Thomson* i, In yonder grave a Druid lies. **1760** JORTIN *Erasm.* II. 94 Who have endeavored to serve the public in a way not agreeable to certain Druids.

c. The appellation of some officers of the Welsh Gorsedd.

1884 *Pall Mall G.* 20 Feb. 3 Not only was Dr. Price the arch-druid loudly cheered..but [etc.].

d. ***United Ancient Order of Druids***, a secret benefit society founded in London in 1781, and having now numerous lodges called *groves* in the United Kingdom, America, the Colonies, etc.

3. *attrib.* or as *adj.* Of or belonging to the Druids, DRUIDIC.

Druid stone, sandstone, the stone of which Stonehenge is constructed, grey-weather.

1670 MILTON *Hist. Eng.* II. Wks. (1851) 31 If lastly the Druid learning honour'd so much among them, were at first taught them out of Britain. **1776** WESLEY *Jrnl.* 1 Sept., Druid altars of enormous size. **1777** WARTON *Poems* 17 (Jod.), Here Poesy..In druid songs her solemn spirit breath'd. **1848** LYTTON *Harold* I. i, Grey Druid stones gleaming through the dawn. **1871** PHILLIPS *Geol. Oxford* xvii. 446 In this way perhaps we may account for the 'Druid' sandstones, or 'Grey Weathers', or 'Sarsen stones' which lie in such abundance about Ashdown..and between Marlborough and Avebury.

†'**Druidan.** *Obs. rare.* Also 6 **drydan.** [f. L. **druida* + -AN.] = DRUID.

(The first form of the word in Eng., transl. L. *Druidæ.*) **1509** BARCLAY *Shyp of Folys* I. 292 As the Druydans [*ed.* **1570** Druidans] rennyth in vayne about In theyr mad festes.

†**Dru'idean,** *a. Obs. rare.* = DRUIDIC.

1678 T. JONES *Heart & its Right Sov.* 542 The Druidean philosophy.

Druidess ('druːɪdɪs). [f. DRUID + -ESS. Cf. mod.F. *Druidesse* (Dict. Acad. 1835). F. *druide* and Eng. *Druid* were formerly of both genders.] A female Druid; a Druidic prophetess.

1755 T. AMORY *Mem.* (1769) I. 237 Caesar..conversed here with the Dryades, and Magistri Sapientiae, the Druidesses and Druids. **1769** PENNANT *Zool.* (1776) III. 32 (Jod.) Our modern Druidesses give much the same account of the *ovum anguinum.* **1813** SCOTT *Trierm.* III. xxxv, Of merry England she, in dress Like ancient British Druidess. **1827** G. HIGGINS *Celtic Druids* 286 The Druidesses are represented to have acted like furies.

Druidic (druː'ɪdɪk), *a.* [ad. L. type **druidic-us*: see DRUID and -IC. Cf. mod.F. *druidique,* (Dict. Acad. 1835).] Of or pertaining to the Druids.

1773 *Gentl. Mag.* XLIII. 230 The remains of a stone tower, which I apprehend to be a Druidic work. **1803** W. TAYLOR in *Ann. Rev.* I. 261 The druidic or rather bardic order, among the Cimbri, was very literate. **1878** BROWNING *Poets Croisic* 16 'Scraps of Druidic lore', Sigh scholars.

Druidical (druː'ɪdɪkəl), *a.* = prec.

1755 W. COOKE (*title*) An Inquiry into the Patriarchal and Druidical Religion, Temples, etc. **1842** PRICHARD *Nat. Hist. Man* 191 Circles of upright stones, like those which in Europe are termed Druidical. **1879** LUBBOCK *Sci. Lect.* v. 167 Avebury, the most magnificent of Druidical remains.

†'**Druidish,** *a. Obs.* [-ISH.] = DRUIDIC.

Holinshed has *Druiysh,* which he derives 'from Druiyas (the originall founder of their religion)'.

1577 HOLINSHED *Descr. Brit.* viii. 7 b/2 Places where the Druiysh religion was frequented. **1723** H. ROWLANDS *Mona Antiqua* (1766) 226 The Druidish discipline in Gallia.

Druidism ('druːɪdɪz(ə)m). [f. DRUID + -ISM. Cf. F. *druidisme* (1727 in Hatz.-Darm.).] The religious and philosophical system of the Druids.

1715 M. DAVIES *Athen. Brit.* I. 287 Fabulous Legends and Poetick Druidisms. **1723** H. ROWLANDS *Mona Antiqua* (1766) 257 We date and fix the original of Druidism about the time of Abraham. **1879** FARRAR *St. Paul* (1883) 340 They [Galatians] had brought with them into Asia their old Druidism.

'**Druidry.** *rare.* [f. DRUID + -RY.] = Druidism; Druidic practices.

1868 HOLME LEE *B. Godfrey* i. 4 The spring festival of Druidry.

druie, drui3e, obs. forms of DRY.

drum (drʌm), *sb.*[1] Forms: 6 **drome, droome,** 6–7 **dromme, drumm(e, drumb(e,** 6– **drum.** [Evidenced *c* 1540, but not common before 1575: app. preceded in use by *drombyllsclad, drombeslade,* DRUMSLADE, which was very common in 16th c. It is not certain whether *drome, dromme, drumme* was an Eng. shortening of that longer name, or an independent form corresp. to MDu. *tromme,* Du. *trom,* MHG. *trumme, trumbe,* LG. *trumme,* Da. *tromme,* Sw. *trumma* drum. Nor is it clear how the English forms, app. from the beginning, have *dr-,* while all the continental langs. have *tr-.* (The forms *drumbe, drumme,* occurring in late MHG., and *dromm* in mod.HG. dialects, have no historical contact with the English word.)

MHG. *trumbe, trumme* had orig. the sense 'trumpet', the only sense of OHG. *trumba, trumpa,* corresp. to It. *tromba,* Sp. *trompa,* F. *trompe* trumpet (see TRUMP); so that the more general German sense would appear to have been 'loud-sounding or booming instrument'. Mod.G. uses for 'drum' a derivative form *trommel,* MHG. *trumbel, trumel,* Du. *trommel* (beside *trom*).]

I. 1. a. A musical instrument of the percussive class, consisting of a hollow cylindrical or hemispherical frame of wood or metal, with a 'head' of tightly stretched membrane at one or both ends, by the striking of which the sound is produced.

1541 *Nottingham Rec.* III. 384 For pleying of hys drome afore Master Mayre..vjd. **1548** HALL *Chron., Hen. VIII* (1809) 678 And sodainly strake up a Dromme or Drounslade. *a* **1553** UDALL *Royster D.* IV. vii. (Arb.) 74 Now sainct George to borow, Drum dubbe a dubbe afore. **1579** TOMSON *Calvin's Serm. Tim.* 977/2 Drommes made of their skinnes. **1590** SPENSER *F.Q.* I. ix. 41 At sound of morning droome. **1599** SHAKS. *Much Ado* II. iii. 15, I haue known when there was no musicke with him but the drum and the fife. *a* **1617** BAYNE *On Eph.* (1658) 13 We hear not the Drumb. **1691** RAY *Creation* II. (1701) 271 A membrane.. stretched like the head of a drum. **1778** JOHNSON in *Mad. D'Arblay's Diary* Nov., How should a woman who is as empty as a drum, talk upon any other subject? **1817** C. WOLFE *Burial Sir J. Moore* i, Not a drum was heard, not a funeral note, As his corpse to the rampart we hurried. **1838** LONGF. *Ps. of Life* iv, Our hearts..Still, like muffled drums, are beating Funeral marches to the grave. **1844** H. H. WILSON *Brit. India* II. 307 He entered on the following morning..with drums beating, and colours flying.

b. With various qualifications, as ***bass, big, great, little, long, tenor drum***; also KETTLE-, SNARE-DRUM, q.v. ***double-drum*** (see quot. 1874). See also ***side-drum*** s.v. SIDE *sb.*[1] 27, and sense 1 d below.

1789 WOLCOTT (P. Pindar) *Subj. Paint.* Wks. 1812 II. 154, I scarcely know The Oboe from the Double Drum. **1794** MRS. RADCLIFFE *Myst. Udolpho* xxv, [He] plays the great drum to admiration. **1804,** etc. [see BASS *a.* 3 b]. **1874** KNIGHT *Dict. Mech.* I. 757/1 The large drum, beaten at both ends, is called a *double-drum.* Those hanging by the side of the drummer are called *side-drums.* **1879** GROVE *Dict. Mus.* I. 466/2 The Tenor-drum is similar to the side-drum, only larger, and has no snares. **1880** *Grove's Dict. Mus.* s.v., When musicians talk of 'drums' they mean kettledrums, in contradistinction to the side drum or bass drum. *Ibid.,* The Bass-drum..used to be called the long-drum. **1888** tr. *Riemann's Catechism Mus. Instr.* v. 100 The tenor-drum used for rolls (tamburo rullante) has likewise no snares (strings of catgut) and sounds therefore dull and gloomy (though much higher than the big-drum). **1889** *Brit. Bandsman* Sept. 280/1 The big drum..was strapped to a tent pole. **1893** SELOUS *Trav. S.E. Africa* 59 They would beat their war drums. **1894** KIPLING *Seven Seas* (1896) 200 Oh, 'ark to the big drum callin'. **1923** J. M. MURRY *Pencillings* 239 One of those multi-musical Italian wanderers, with a big drum on their shoulders. **1940** G. JACOB *Orchestral Technique* (ed. 2) vii. 72 Such things as the tenor drum..need not be spoken of in detail.

c. Phrases: †***by the drum***: by public announcement, publicly.

1574 HELLOWES *Guevara's Fam. Ep.* 375 Unto him y[t] offered most silver..the priesthoode was given, as when a garment is sold by the drumbe. **1579–80** NORTH *Plutarch* (1676) 465 That..their Slaves should be openly sold by the Drum. **1601** F. GODWIN *Bps. of Eng.* 32 He..was woont to sell all other ecclesiasticall promotions as it were by the drum. **1602** WARNER *Alb. Eng.* IX. liii. (1612) 239 Saintish, not in Deede, but by the Dromme.

d. *fig.* and *transf.* ***to beat*** or ***thump the*** (***big***) ***drum***(***s***): to make loud or ostentatious advertisement, protest, or the like.

1611 MIDDLETON & DEKKER *Roaring Girl* III. ii, What need you, sir, To beate the drumme of my wife's infamy. **1663** BUTLER *Hud.* I. i. 11 And, Pulpit, Drum Ecclesiastick, Was beat with Fist, instead of a Stick. **1690** LOCKE *Govt.* I. Pref. Wks. 1727 II. 101 So at last all Times might not have Reason to complain of the Drum Ecclesiastic. **1907** [see THUMP *v.* 1 a]. **1930** *Church Times* 4 July 3 Even the Bishop of London hesitates when the Protestant drum is loudly beaten. **1930** J. A. WILLIAMSON *Short Hist. Brit. Expansion* (ed. 2) II. VI. v. 255 The Conference of 1911 met under the shadow of war, and there is no doubt that this was realized by its members. The effect was not a public beating of the drum, but the exact contrary. **1961** *Lebende Sprachen* VI. 100/1 His old woman really beat the drum [= scolded him]. **1967** *Boston Sunday Herald* 26 Mar. I. 30/3 The second big objection to the Weston proposal is that it involves a flagrant violation of the home rule principle for which the reform element has beaten the drums so loudly in recent years.

e. Applied to the body of a banjo, being like a drumhead and of parchment.

1889 *Pall Mall G.* 24 Jan. 7/1 The best length is twenty-seven inches from nut to drum..Fixing a skin upon a drum is a delicate operation requiring considerable patience.

f. *Zool.* A natural organ by which an animal produces a loud or bass sound; *spec.* the hollow hyoid bone of the howling monkey.

1817 [see *drum-cover* in 13]. **1840** *Penny Cycl.* XVI. 37/1 (*Mycetes*) To afford room for the bony drum formed by the convexity of the os hyoides. **1847** CARPENTER *Zool.* §159 The howling Monkeys are distinguished..by the dilatation of the os hyoides into a hollow drum, which communicates with the larynx, and gives great additional resonance to the voice.

g. *Austral. slang.* A warning, a piece of information, esp. a racing tip; freq. ***the drum,*** the facts; true or reliable information.

1941 BAKER *Dict. Austral. Slang* 25 *Drum,*..a racecourse tip. e.g., 'get (give) the drum' about a horse. **1944** L. GLASSOP *We were Rats* xvi. 88 I've got the drum from a friend in the Seventh Div. Headquarters in Melbourne. We're going to Bombay. *Ibid.* xxxiv. 193 I'm givin' ya the drum now. **1960** S. H. COURTIER *Gently dust Corpse* viii. 116 Ready to give me the drum about Cullerman yet? **1961** H. R. F. KEATING *Rush on Ultimate* i. 13, I know now all right ..but I didn't a week ago. Not until Humphrey gave me the drum. **1968** D. O'GRADY *Bottle of Sandwiches* 7 Gave us the drum on where to get hold of the particular rifles we had our eyes on.

2. The sound of the instrument; also *transf.,* a noise resembling that of a drum.

1646 F. HAWKINS *Youth's Behaviour* (1663) 2 Strike not up a Drum with thy fingers, or thy feet. **1810** SCOTT *Lady of L.* I. xxxi, And the bittern sound his drum, Booming from the sedgy shallow. **1891** *Blackw. Mag.* Nov. 649 The drum of his wings as he trees.

3. a. *Mil.* One who plays the drum; a drummer (cf. *bayonet, trumpet,* etc.). †Also, a small party (sometimes the drummer alone) sent with a drum to parley with the enemy or to carry a message (*obs.*).

1577–87 HOLINSHED *Chron.* III. 1192/1 The lord lieutenant..sent a drum vnto Monsieur Doisell to signifie to him that his soldiours had gone further without their bounds than they might doo. **1599** MINSHEU *Sp. Dial.* 62/3 Tell the drum that he sound to set the watch. **1691** LUTTRELL *Brief Rel.* (1857) II. 226 Our men..took prisoners..150 private soldiers, among whom were 6 sergeants..1 surgeon, and 3 drumms. **1711** ADDISON *Spect.* No. 165 ¶5 The Day after a Drum arrived at our Camp, with a Message. **1753** *Scots Mag.* Oct. 525/2 He was appointed Houshold Drum to K. William. **1835** J. WILSON *Autobiog.* 95 note, Amongst them [horses]..was a grey one belonging to one of the drums.

†**b.** ***Jack, John,*** or ***Tom Drum's entertainment***: a rough reception, turning an unwelcome guest out of doors. *Obs.*

1577–87 HOLINSHED *Hist. Irel.* Bij/1 (N.) Tom Drum's entertainment, which is, to bale a man in by the head, and thrust him out by both the shoulders. **1579** GOSSON *Sch. Abuse* (Arb.) 22 Plato..gaue them all Drummes entertainment, not suffering them once to shew their faces in a reformed common wealth. **1601** SHAKS. *All's Well* III. vi. 41 If you giue him not Iohn drummes entertainement. **1603** H. CROSSE *Vertues Commw.* (1878) 79 If his backe be poore ..and hath neither money nor friends, he shall haue Tom Drums entertainment. **1613** J. TAYLOR in *Coryat's Crudities* (1776) III. Cc ij, Not like the entertainment of Iacke Drum, Who was best welcome when he went his way.

II. Something resembling a drum or cylinder in shape or structure.

4. The hollow part of the middle ear; the tympanum; chiefly in phrase, ***drum of the ear.***

1615 CROOKE *Body of Man* 611 The outwarde Aire affected with the quality of the sounde runneth vpon the Membrane or Head of the Drumme. **1713** BERKELEY *Hylas & P.* I. Wks. 1871 I. 272 Motion in the external air.. striking on the drum of the ear, it causeth a vibration. **1757** BEATTIE *Wolf & Shepherds* 31 A Beau..with loud and everlasting clack, [Will] beat your auditory drum. **1879** CALDERWOOD *Mind & Br.* 71 A distinct chamber known as the Drum (*tympanum*) or *middle* ear.

5. *Machinery.* A cylinder or 'barrel' round which a belt passes or a rope is wound.

1776 G. SEMPLE *Building in Water* 36 The Spring that locks the Drum to the Shaft. **1858** LARDNER *Hand-bk. Nat. Phil., Hydrost.* 111 [The rope] is carried two or three times round a large vertical drum erected near the well. **1884** F. J. BRITTEN *Watch & Clockm.* 96 The barrel on which the driving cord in turret clocks is wound also answers to the name of drum. **1887** HOFFMAN *Tips f. Tricycl.* 8 Abandoning this form of brake for the second form—the band and drum on the centre of the axle.

6. Applied to drum-shaped parts of many machines. Such are the following:

a. *Paper-making.* A framework covered with wire gauze, having in its interior two suction-tubes by which the water, after circulating through the rags, is carried away in a constant stream. **b.** *Calico-printing.* The hollow cylinder or cask in which steam is applied to printed fabrics in order to fix the colours. **c.** A cylindrical chamber used in stoves, flues and heating apparatus. **d.** The cylindrical case which holds the coiled spring of a car-brake. **e.** A doffer in a carding-machine. **f.** The cylindrical beater of a thrashing-machine. **g.** The cartridge-holding receptacle of a machine-gun; also, the contents of one of these. See also quotations.

1747 *Gentl. Mag.* XVI. 526/2 A rotatory axis furnish'd with fans for making a wind, by turning in a drum. **1805** R. SOMERVILLE *Agric. Surv. East Lothian* 74 (Jam.) The sheaves were carried between an indented drum and a number of rollers of the same description ranged round the drum. **1846** GREENER *Sc. Gunnery* 305 Then polishing the whole in a machine termed a drum. **1853** *Catal. Roy. Agric. Soc. Show Gloucester* 30 Four-horse portable thrashing machine..The drum is of iron with six beaters. **1861** SMILES *Engineers* II. 110. **1888** *Pall Mall G.* 10 July 13/2 A joint, a pair of chickens, a piece of salmon, with vegetables, each in their separate dishes, were packed one above the other in what is called the cooking drum. **1888** *Century Mag.* XXXVI. 887/1 The drum of [a Gatling gun] contains 102 cartridges. **1890** W. J. GORDON *Foundry* 29 To the breech is fixed a drum with 104 bullets. **1916** 'BOYD CABLE' *Action Front* 198 Can you fill the cartridges into these drums while I shoot? **1928** *Daily Tel.* 24 Apr. 12/6, I gave him a drum and he went down underneath me.

7. *Archit.* **a.** The solid part or 'vase' of the Corinthian and Composite capitals. **b.** The block of stone composing one section of the shaft of a column (Gwilt). **c.** The upright part under or above a cupola. **d.** See quot. 1883.

1727–52 CHAMBERS *Cycl., Vase*..the body of the Corinthian and Composite capital; called also the *tambour,* or *drum.* **1837** *Penny Cycl.* IX. 70/1 The height of the drum [of the Dome of S. Paul's] is 62 feet. **1861** MISS BEAUFORT *Egypt. Sepulch. & Syr. Shrines* II. xxiv. 320 Forty of these columns are still standing..and the ground is strewed with their fallen drums. **1883** *Glasgow Weekly Her.* 19 May 1/6 The console or drum, as our English clockmakers call the projection from the tower [to hold a clock face].

8. Various technical applications: **a.** A sieve (see quot. 1706). **b.** A cylinder of canvas used together with a cone as a storm-signal. **c.** The cylindrical or nearly cylindrical part of an urn or other vessel.

1706 PHILLIPS (ed. Kersey), *Drum*..also a fine Sieve, made use of by Confectioners, to sift powder'd Sugar, etc. **1725** BRADLEY *Fam. Dict.* s.v. *Sieve,* A finer Sieve call'd a Drum. **1867** SMYTH *Sailor's Word-bk.* s.v. *Storm Signal,* Fitzroy's drum and cone which show the direction of the expected gale. **1875** *Chamb. Jrnl.* No. 133. 8 A drum, as well as a cone, is considered to denote a very heavy gale approaching from the direction indicated by the cone.

d. *Computing.* = *magnetic drum* s.v. MAGNETIC *a.* 5.

1948 *Math. Tables & Other Aids Computation* III. 214 The latest memory device used in this machine is a rotating drum on which magnetic impulses representing the data are impressed. **1950** [see *magnetic drum* s.v. MAGNETIC *a.* 5]. **1960** M. G. SAY et al. *Analogue & Digital Computers* viii. 249 When the access time is of prime importance, a relatively small number of digits is stored on each track, the diameter is small and the drum rotates at high speed. **1979** J. E. Rowley *Mechanised In-House Information Syst.* i. 64 Drums tend to be found only occasionally in information science applications..as they have a small capacity and are expensive as stores. **1980** C. S. French *Computer Sci.* vii. 29 Typically the drum stores between 100,000 and 8,000,000 characters.

9. A cylindrical box or receptacle.

a. A box in which figs or other dried fruit are packed, weighing from $\frac{1}{8}$ to $\frac{1}{4}$ of a cwt. **b.** A large flat tub in which cod are packed. **c.** An iron or tin case for oil or spirits.

1812 J. Smyth *Pract. Customs* 46 Bristles in drums. *Ibid.* 75 Figs, 4 drums. **1854** Wynter *Curios. Civiliz.* vi. 215 Squeezed into hurdles like figs into a drum. **1858** Simmonds *Trade Dict.* s.v., The large flat tubs in which fish are packed in New Brunswick for the Brazil markets are called drums; each drum contains exactly 128 lbs. of pressed codfish, that being the Portuguese quintal. **1881** *Price List*, Burning oils are supplied in Casks about 40 gallons each and in Iron Drums of about 10 gallons each.

†**d.** A street. *Obs. slang.*

c **1789** ? G. Parker *Sandman's Wedding* in J. S. Farmer *Musa Pedestris* (1896) 64 Just as he turned the corner of the drum, His dear lov'd Bess, the bunter, chanc'd to come. **1851** Mayhew *London Lab.* I. 217/2 We..slink into the crib (house) in the back drum (street). **1889** Barrère & Leland *Dict. Slang* I. 332/1 *Drum* means also a street, a road... It may have come directly from the English gypsy *drum* (old form *drom*), which is, truly, from the Greek δρομός, a road.

e. *slang.* A house, lodging-place, or other building; esp. (*a*) *U.S.* a drinking-place, saloon, night-club; (*b*) a brothel, low dive; (*c*) a room or flat.

1846 *Swell's Night Guide* p. iii, The..cracksman, who would screw a drum. **1851** Mayhew *London Lab.* I. 418/1 Suppose I want to ask a pal to..have a game at cards with some *blokes* at *home* with me, I should say..'Splodger, will you..have a touch of the *broads* with me and the other heaps of *coke* at my *drum*.' **1859** G. W. Matsell *Vocabulum* 28 *Drum*, a drinking-place. **1867** J. Greenwood *Unsentimental Journeys* xxvi. 204 'Come along; I shall be a pot to your pot.' 'Where shall we go?' 'Oh! to the old drum, I suppose.' **1872** G. P. Burnham *Mem. U.S. Secret Service* p. v, *Drum*, a bad house, boarding-place, or small tavern. **1899** R. Whiteing *No. 5 John St.* I. ii. 15 'That's my drum two doors beyond.' His drum was better to look at. **1903** A. H. Lewis *Boss* 32 He said the Dead Rabbit was a drum for crooks! **1908** K. McGaffey *Sorrows of Show Girl* 234 We came to a door which the gee threw open and said, 'This is your stateroom.' Honest, I never saw such a drum. **1938** D. Runyon *Furthermore* xii. 231 The bar in Good Time Charley's little drum in West Forty-ninth Street. **1966** L. Southworth *Felon in Disguise* iii. 53 They probably checked at the Probation Office as soon as they left my drum. **1967** K. Giles *Death in Diamonds* vi. 118 'You get that way running a drum,' grunted Crook... 'A drum?' 'The house that ain't a home,' said Harry.

f. = swag *sb.* 10; ***to hump one's drum***: see hump *v.* 2. *Austral.* and *N.Z. slang.*

1866 W. Stamer *Recoll. Life Adventure* I. 304 Our ci-devant millionaire..'humping his drum', [would] start off for the diggings to seek more gold. **1872** C. H. Eden *My Wife & I in Queensland* i. 17 They all chaffed us about our swags, or donkeys, or drums, as a bundle of things wrapped in a blanket is indifferently called. **1889** M. Ross *Compl. Guide Lakes Central Otago* 44 'Time's up!' is called, the 'drum' (the local for swag) hoisted on, and the final ascent begins. **1933** *Bulletin* (Sydney) 18 Jan. 20, I sees a bloke comin' along the road from Winton with 'is drum up.

g. *slang.* A tin or can in which tea, etc., is made; so **drum-up**, a making of tea; the preparation of a meal.

1919 *Athenæum* 8 Aug. 728/1 I've some sugar. If you get some tea and hot water we'll have a drum up. **1931** F. Gray *Tramp* ix. 104 He will bring his 'billy-can' or 'drum' to the door of a cottage or mansion and beg a little hot water to make his tea. *Ibid.*, A 'drum' is an old tin, say a half-pound coffee tin; two holes are made at the lip so that the string may be threaded to carry and control it. **1970** F. McKenna *Gloss. Railwaymen's Talk* 35 *Drum*, a tea-can.

III. 10. An assembly of fashionable people at a private house, held in the evening: much in vogue during the latter half of the 18th and beginning of the 19th century; a rout. (See quots.) Later, An afternoon tea-party, formerly sometimes followed by the larger assembly. Cf. kettledrum. Now *Obs.*

1745 Eliza Heywood *Female Spectator* (1748) II. 269 She told me, that, when the number of company for play exceeded ten tables, it was called a *racquet*; if under, it was only a *rout*; and if no more than one or two, it was only a *drum*. **1745** Mrs. Montagu *Lett.* (1813) III. 37, I wish we had..our vanities, as last year; that by the word Drum we understood a polite assembly, and by a Rout, only an engagement of hoop-petticoats. **1746** Smollett *Advice* 30 *note*, This is a riotous assembly of fashionable people, of both sexes, at a private house, consisting of some hundreds; not unaptly stiled a drum, from the noise and emptiness of the entertainment. **1749** Fielding *Tom Jones* xvii. vi, A drum then, is an assembly of well dressed persons of both sexes, most of whom play at cards, and the rest do nothing at all. **1779** Mrs. Barbauld *Wks.* (1825) II. 22 Do you know the different terms? There is a squeeze, a fuss, a drum, a rout, and lastly a hurricane, when the whole house is full from top to bottom. **1805** [see hurricane *sb.* 2 b]. **1824** Lady Granville *Lett.* 5 Dec. (1894) I. 317 We went last night to a drum at Rothschild's. **1866** Browning in Mrs. Orr *Life* 273, I met him at a large party..also Carlyle, whom I never met at a 'drum' before. **1883** L. Troubridge *Jrnl.* May in J. Hope-Nicholson *Life amongst Troubridges* (1966) 163 A dinner-party and after a 'drum'—lots of people we knew.

IV. 11. More fully **drum-fish**: A name of various American sciænoid fishes which have the power of making a drumming noise.

Among these are the 'salt-water drum' (*Pogonias chromis*) found on the Atlantic coast; the 'fresh-water drum' (*Haplodinotus grunniens*) of the Mississippi, and lakes of the St. Lawrence; the 'branded drum', 'organ-fish', 'red-fish', 'sea-boss' (*Sciæna ocellata*) of the Gulf States.

1676 T. Glover in *Phil. Trans.* XI. 624 There is another sort which the English call a Drum; many of which are two foot and a half or three foot long. **1683–4** Robinson *Ibid.* XXIX. 480 Many Tamburo's or Drum-Fishes. **1775** Romans *Hist. Florida* 187 The principal fish here..is the red drum, called in East Florida a bass, and in West Florida carp. *Ibid.* 188 The roes of mullets and black drum. **1863** Russell *Diary North & South* I. 210. **1891** W. K. Brooks *Oyster* 106 The drawback to East River oyster-planting..is the abundance of enemies with which the beds are infested. These consist of drum fish, skates, [etc.].

V. *attrib.* and *Comb.*

12. General comb.: **a.** Simple attrib., as ***drum-beat, -call, -cover, -dance, -kit, memory, -polka, -roll, set, -skin, -tap***, etc. **b.** Like, or of the shape of, a drum, or having a part so shaped, as ***drum-capstan, -clock, -net, -pulley, -salt, -shaft, -tower***, etc. **c.** Objective and similative, as ***drum-beating, -maker, -player; drum-like, -shaped*** adjs.

1855 Longf. *My Lost Youth* iv, I remember..the *drum-beat repeated o'er and o'er, and the bugle wild and shrill. **1893** *Athenæum* 18 Nov. 697/3 It is time the *drum-beating about the deadly peril of the exploit is estimated at that true value my brother..assigned to it. **1762–71** H. Walpole *Vertue's Anecd. Paint.* (1786) III. 151 He [Sir S. Morland] invented the *drum-capstands for weighing heavy anchors. **1884** F. J. Britten *Watch & Clockm.* 96 The escapement used in French *Drum Clocks is a continual source of trouble to English clock jobbers. **1817** Kirby & Sp. *Entomol.* II. xxiv. 405 The *drum-covers or opercula [of the cicada] from beneath which the sound issues. **1934** I. W. Hutchison *North to Rime-ringed Sun* ix. 93 The strange '*drum-dance'. **1936** *Discovery* June 186/2 A drum-dance is held [in one Kenya tribe] at which the possessed victim is danced to exhaustion. **1934** E. Little *Mod. Rhythmic Drumming* (Advt. on back cover), 'Ajax' *drum kit. **1965** G. Melly *Owning-Up* v. 47 There were always a great many very steep steps to drag the drum kit up. **1690** *Lond. Gaz.* No. 2582/4 William Grining, *Drum-maker to the Office of the Ordnance. **1954** *Jrnl. Assoc. Computing Machinery* I. 196 The 10,000-word *drum-memory electronic data handler..passed its acceptance tests..in April. **1970** O. Dopping *Computers & Data Processing* x. 145 Nowadays, the drum memory is normally a secondary memory. **1814** Southey in *Q. Rev.* XII. 185 Daffodils or any bright yellow flowers will decoy perch into a *drum-net. **1580** Hollyband *Treas. Fr. Tong*, *Tabourineur*, a *drumplaier. **1849** *Theatrical Programme* 11 June 23 The Celebrated *Drum Polka, with Solos by Mess. Kœnig, Collinet, etc. **1909** T. Hardy in *English Rev.* Apr. 4 Who now recalls those crowded rooms..Where to the deep Drum-polka's booms We hopped in boisterous style? **1875** *Ure's Dict. Arts* I. 982 Upon the main shaft is mounted a cylindrical hollow box or *drum pulley. **1887** *Pall Mall G.* 22 Nov. 3/2 You will see war..without music, without the *drum-roll [etc.]. **1688** in Willis & Clark *Cambridge* (1886) II. 114 One Silver *drum Salt with the Colledge Arms on it. **1933** *Melody Maker* 2 Dec. 22/4 (Advt.), *Drum set, £5 10s., includes 28 × 18 Ludwig D.T. bass drum [etc.]. **1959** W. Balliett *Sound of Surprise* (1960) iv. 235 The total effect, which is nearly the direct opposite of the earlier drum sets, is falsetto. **1983** *New Oxf. Compan. Mus.* I. 582/1 The precursor of the drum set is the 'trap' drummer's equipment of the music hall. **1893** E. H. Barker *Wand. by S. Waters* 125 Near to this, under a mediæval *drum-tower, is the gateway of the 'City of Happiness'. **1880** *Athenæum* 20 Nov. 678/3 Musical instruments..are yet readily reducible under three distinct types: 1. The *drum type; 2. The pipe type; 3. The lyre type.

13. Special comb.: **drum-armature**, a dynamo-armature in form of a rotating hollow cylinder; **drum-boy, -man**, the drummer in a band; **drum brake**, a type of brake in which brake-shoes fixed to the vehicle are pressed against a brake-drum fixed to the wheel; **drum camera**, a camera in which the film is mounted on a drum or cylinder which rotates during exposure (recording the motion of an object as a trace on the film); **drum-curb**, a cylindrical curb of iron or wood to support the brickwork of a shaft; **drum-drying**, an industrial drying process involving drum-shaped containers; **drum-fire** (see quot. 1918); also *transf.* and *fig.*; **drum-fish**: see 11; *v. intr.* (*U.S.*), to fish for drum-fish; so ***drum-fishing***; **drum-hole**, the sound-hole in the side of a drum with two heads; **drum-line**, a line used for catching drum-fish; also ***drum-fish line***; **drum-ring**, the annular margin of the tympanum of the ear; †**drum-room**, the room in which a 'drum' or rout is held; **drum-saw**, a cylinder- or barrel-saw for sawing curved material; **drum-sieve**, a sieve enclosed in a drum-like box, for sifting fine substances without loss or dust: cf. 8 a; †**drum-staff**, a drumstick; **drum-wheel**, (*a*) a barrel or cylinder round which a rope is coiled; (*b*) a water-raising current-wheel made in the form of a drum, a tympanum; **drum winding**, an armature winding in which the conductor is wound from end to end on or in the surface of a cylindrical core; so **drum-wound** *a.*; †**drum-wine**, ? wine sold 'by the drum': see 1 c. Also drum-head, -major, -majorette.

1890 Wormell *Electr. in Serv. Man* 269 The *drum armature usually consists of a hollow cylinder, which rotates with the shaft, and round which the wires are wound parallel with the axis of rotation. **1783** Sir M. Hunter *Jrnl.* (1894) 54 A *drumboy of ours got upon the coop with him. [**1949** Frazee & Bedell *Automotive Fundamentals* ii. vi. 355 The similarity of the band clutch to certain types of brakes has led to its being called a 'drum brake' by some designers, although this name is not entirely accurate.] **1950** Newton & Steeds *Motor Vehicle* (ed. 4) xxvii. 470 The vast majority of brakes are friction brakes and these may be sub-divided into: (1) *Drum brakes and (2) Disc brakes. **1959** *Motor Manual* (ed. 36) v. 132 The internal-expanding drum brake has been practically universal on cars. **1962** *Which?* (Car Suppl.) Apr. 49/2 With drum brakes, the brake shoes are pressed outwards against a drum on the wheel hub. **1934** *Photographic Jrnl.* LXXIV. 389/1 (*heading*) High-speed *drum camera. **1951** W. D. Chesterman *Photogr. Study Rapid Events* vi. 80 Drum cameras are of two kinds. In the type which are more generally constructed, the film is attached to the outside or the inside surface of a rapidly rotating cylindrical drum, and the images are formed successively on the film by a variety of optical and mechanical means. In another type..the film is wound on a stationary drum, and the optical images are formed in rapid succession on the film surface by rotating optical parts. **1946** *Nature* 10 Aug. 194/1 Spray-drying, flash-drying and *drum-drying have been developed with considerable success. **1917** *Times* 20 Aug. 6/4 The artillery duel increased to *drumfire. **1918** E. S. Farrow *Dict. Mil. Terms*, *Drum fire*, a common name given to the artillery barrage or curtain of fire. Continuous bombardment, like the rolling of drums. **1955** *Bull. Atomic Sci.* Mar. 98/3 We expose ourselves quite unnecessarily to a drumfire of criticism. **1818** in J. R. Commons et al. *Doc. Hist. Amer. Industrial Soc.* (1910) I. 203 Sent the boat a *Drum fishing and caught 5 Drum. **1855** *Knickerbocker* XLVI. 499 So highly enjoyed is drum-fishing among our bail-fishers. **1904** *Booklovers Mag.* III. 625/2 Senator Quay..was discovered..knee-deep in the surf at Atlantic City, drum-fishing. **1626** Bacon *Sylva* §142 In Drums, the Closenesse round about..maketh the Noise come forth at the *Drum-hole, far more loud, and strong, than if you should strike upon the like Skin, extended in the Open Aire. **1794** *Rigging & Seamanship* I. 64 *Drum-lines, for drums, have 16 threads. Drum-fish-line has 9 threads. **1867** *Athenæum* No. 2085. 458/2 A tie of triple drum line. **1811** *Self Instructor* 578 The drum-major has the command of all the *drum-men. **1877** Burnett *Ear* 42 The inner and major portion of the entire auditory passage, is developed from the so-called *drum-ring, *annulus tympanicus*. **1749** Fielding *Tom Jones* xi. ix, The bonny house-maid begins to repair the disordered *drum-room. **1581** Marbeck *Bk. of Notes* 736 The Priests wold make such a noise with *drumstaves, Timbrells, and Tabrets. **1893** Hawkins & Wallis *Dynamo* vii. 117 One loop of the *drum winding is the exact equivalent of the two loops of the ring winding. **1952** K. C. Graham *Small Commutator Motors* ii. 32 A drum winding..is the general type of armature winding used in modern armatures. **1632** Massinger *City Madam* iii. i, Yet not find a chapman That in courtesy will bid a chop of mutton, Or a pint of *drum-wine for me. **1893** W. P. Maycock *Electric Lighting* ii. vii. 196 The armature is *drum wound. **1904** R. M. Walmsley *Electricity in Service of Man* ii. i. 756 A method of arranging the connections of drum-wound armatures..consists in winding and insulating the coils separately before placing them on the core.

14. ***drum-and-trumpet history***: see history *sb.* 2.

drum, *sb.*[2] [a. Gael. and Ir. *druim* back, ridge.] A ridge or 'rigg', a long narrow hill often separating two parallel valleys: a frequent element in Scottish and Irish geographical proper names. Hence *Geol.* A term for a long narrow ridge of 'drift' or diluvial formation, usually ascribed to glacial action.

1725 R. Innes *Lett. to Bp. Nicolson* 2 June 24 The lowland of Magilligan is divided into ridges (or, as we call them, dryms) of sand. **1797** *Statist. Acc. Scot.* XIX. 342 These singular ridges of Nature called here drums. **1833** *Jrnl. Roy. Geol. Soc. Dublin* I. 37 The names Drum and Drumlin (*Dorsum*) have been applied to such hills. **1873** J. Geikie *Gt. Ice Age* ii. 17 The long parallel ridges, or 'sowbacks' and 'drums', as they are termed..invariably coincide in direction with the valleys or straths in which they lie. **1882** Geikie *Text-bk. Geol.* vi. v. §1. 889 Round the mountainous centres of dispersion it [drift] is apt to occur in long ridges or 'drums' which run in the general direction of the rock-striation.

drum, *v.* [f. drum *sb.*[1] Cf. the analogous Du. *trommen*, Da. *tromme*, Sw. *trumma*, G. *trommeln*.]

I. *intr.* **1. a.** To beat or play on a drum.

1592 Shaks. *Rom. & Jul.* i. iv. 86 Then anon [she] drums in his eares, at which he startes, and wakes. **1601** —— *All's Well* iv. iii. 331 Ile no more drumming, a plague of drummes. **1872** C. Gibbon *For the King* i, He drummed with enthusiasm. **1882** Besant *Revolt of Man* xiv. (1883) 324 [They] found..a cart containing drums. They seized them and began drumming with all their might.

†**b.** To announce by beat of drum. *Obs.*

1578 *Chr. Prayers* in *Priv. Prayers* (1851) 516 We drum, that Doomsday, now at hand, Doth call all soldiers to death's band.

2. a. To beat as on a drum; to beat or thump upon anything with a more or less rhythmical or regular noise; e.g. to thump on a piano as distinguished from playing properly.

1583 Stanyhurst *Æneis* iii. (Arb.) 87 Thee rocks sternelye facing with salt fluds spumye be drumming. **1594** Nashe *Unfort. Trav.* Wks. 1883–4 V. 185 Brauely did he [an executioner] drum on this Cutwolfes bones. **1660** tr. *Amyraldus' Treat. conc. Relig.* iii. ii. 336 Some of them drumming upon Kettles, sum upon Bucklers. **1778** Mad. D'Arblay *Diary* 23 Aug., She got a harpsichord..put herself in fine attitudes, and drummed. **1835** W. Irving *Tour Prairies* 51 They..began a low nasal chant, drumming with their hands upon their breasts, by way of accompaniment. **1861** HUGHES *Tom Brown at Oxf.* xii. (1889) 111 They soon found themselves drumming at his oak, which was opened shortly. **1862** SALA *Seven Sons* I. vii. 165 [Her] foot was drumming on the carpet.

b. Applied to the strong beating of the heart.

1593 SHAKS. *Lucr.* 435 His drumming heart cheares vp his burning eye. *a* **1700** DRYDEN (J.), Now, heart, Set ope thy sluices.. Then take thy rest within the quiet cell; For thou shalt drum no more.

3. Of birds or insects: To make a loud hollow reverberating sound, as by the quivering of the wings.

a **1813** A. WILSON *Foresters* Wks. (1846) 232 Buried in depth of woods.. Where pheasants drum. **1847** EMERSON *Poems, Woodnotes* i. Wks. (Bohn) I. 421 He saw the partridge drum in the woods. **1873** J. E. TAYLOR *Half-h. in Lanes* 2 Flies and gnats drum around you.

4. To sound like a drum; to resound.

1638 R. JUNIUS *Sin Stigm.* 38 (T.) A boiling stomach, rotten teeth, a stinking breath, a drumming ear. **1643** SIR T. BROWNE *Relig. Med.* I. §51 This indeed makes a noise, and drums in popular ears. **1831** CARLYLE *Sart. Res.* III. x, Seized with.. what I can call a drumming in my ears.

5. 'To go about, as a drummer does, to gather recruits, to secure partisans, customers, etc.; with *for*' (Webster 1864). Also, to solicit orders; to canvass. *U.S.*

1839 C. F. BRIGGS *Adv. Harry Franco* I. xiii. 90 Augustus ..had drummed in Arkansas, and collected in the lithograph cities of the west. **1860** BARTLETT *Dict. Americanisms, Drumming*, in mercantile phrase, means the soliciting of customers. **1882** *Congress. Rec.* 315/1 The merchants.. have many thousands.. drumming for business in every town. **1901** *Chambers's Jrnl.* Dec. 827/1, I was 'drumming' for one of the two great houses which divided the wool and the hides of the Argentine.

II. *trans.* **6. a.** To summon by or as by beat of drum; to call or beat *up* as by drumming. **b.** *colloq.* To obtain (custom, customers) by canvassing or solicitation; cf. DRUMMER 2.

1606 SHAKS. *Ant. & Cl.* I. iv. 29 Such time, That drummes him from his sport. **1656** J. BENTHAM *Two Treatises* (1657) 46 As if none are so dead, but dancing will drumm up. **1849** GRAY *Lett.* (1893) 362, I will then drum up subscribers for Fendler. **1883** *Fisheries Exhib. Catal.* (ed. 4) 160 The fish are drummed up by striking two shells.. together.

7. To expel or dismiss publicly by beat of drum, so as to heighten the disgrace, as ***to drum out of*** a regiment; to put *down* or silence by drumming. In more general use, to dismiss or expel someone in disgrace. Const. *out*.

1766 T. AMORY *J. Buncle* (1825) III. 254 They.. ought to be drummed out of society. **1811** *Naval Chron.* XXV. 28 You are to be drummed ashore. **1829** MACAULAY *Misc. Writ.* (1860) I. 317 Another is drummed out of a regiment. **1864** SIR F. PALGRAVE *Norm. & Eng.* IV. 580 The voice of conscience drummed down by popular excitement. **1968** A. COOKE *Talk about Amer.* xxxvi. 215 Shut your eyes and you can see Mark Twain running a newspaper only a few blocks away from Sutro till he was drummed out of town. **1970** *New Yorker* 12 Sept. 47 Confound it, Moxley! Any more of that and I'll have you drummed out of the Sierra Club!

8. a. To din or drive (a person, etc. *into* a certain state) by persistent repetition of admonition, etc.; ***to drum*** (a lesson) ***into*** (a person), to drive it into the ears or mind by incessant repetition.

1820 SHELLEY *Œdipus* I. 259, I have hummed her and drummed her From place to place, till at last I have dumbed her. **1847** BUSHNELL *Chr. Nurt.* II. vii. (1861) 368 Small children are likely to be worried and drummed into apathy by dogmatic catechisms. **1848** MILL *Pol. Econ.* III. xiii. §3 (1876) 331 This doctrine has.. been tolerably effectually drummed into the public mind. **1865** BUSHNELL *Vicar. Sacr.* III. ii. (1868) 257 The soul.. cannot drum itself to sleep in mere generalities of wrong.

b. *Austral. slang.* To inform or warn (a person); to give (someone) 'the drum' (see DRUM *sb.*^{1} 1 g). Also with *up*.

1919 V. MARSHALL *World of Living Dead* 30 He impressed upon me the exact location of the maternal abode, and proceeded to 'drum me up' with the message. **1959** BAKER *Drum* (1960) vi. 49 Look, mate, let me drum you about something. **1969** D. NILAND *Dead Men Running* iii. 86 Jesus, don't bite me, son. I was only gonna drum you.

9. a. To beat or thump (anything) as in beating a drum. *dial.* To beat or thrash.

1879 JEFFERIES *Wild Life in S. Co.* 8 It is amusing to see two of these animals drumming each other; they stand on their hind legs.. and strike with the fore-pads as if boxing. **1890** *Gloucester Gloss., A drumming*, a thrashing. **1894** *Cornh. Mag.* Feb. 153 His fingers drum the dock ledge.

b. To ring or knock on the door of (a house) to ascertain whether it is unoccupied before attempting a robbery; hence, to reconnoitre, with a view to a robbery. Also *intr.*, to steal from an unoccupied house, etc. *slang.*

1925 N. E. LUCAS *Autobiogr. of Crook* vii. 105 Crooks go 'drumming' in pairs, dressed as clerks or messengers... Should they find an office left unoccupied during the lunch hour they quickly and skilfully 'turn it over'. **1933** C. E. LEACH *On Top of Underworld* x. 138 *Drumming a place*, ringing or knocking to see if occupants are at home. **1936** J. CURTIS *Gilt Kid* ii. 23 'My God, you got the gaff weighed up good.' 'Not half. A bloke drummed it for me and put me wide.' **1962** *Observer* 25 Feb. 21/2 They were both making a steady living at drumming (housebreaking). **1967** J. WAINWRIGHT *Talent for Murder* 114 Peters was hanging around outside.. the Wallaces' residence... He was.. a police officer 'keeping observations' or a criminal 'drumming the joint'. **1970** 'B. MATHER' *Break in Line* vi. 77, I bet Chatterjee's been drumming every room in the joint.

10. To strike (the hands, feet, etc.) *upon* something, as if they were drumsticks.

1851 D. JERROLD *St. Giles* xxxiv. 353 Shall I.. drum my fingers upon the table? **1886** SIMS *Ring o' Bells*, etc. I. ii. 37 All the company waiting and drumming their heels.

11. To perform (a tune) on or as on a drum.

1864 WEBSTER, *Drum*, to execute on a drum, as a tune. **1891** H. HERMAN *His Angel* iv. 69 He drummed an unconscious rataplan on the table with his knife. **1893** MCCARTHY *Dictator* I. 9 He drummed the national hymn of Gloria upon the balcony-rail with his fingers.

III. *intr.* **12.** To give or attend social 'drums'.

1825 LADY GRANVILLE *Lett.* 30 Jan. (1894) I. 339 Little they'll heed if they see me drum on. **1837** *Ibid.* Jan. II. 221 We must begin again drumming and affronting.

13. ***to drum up***: to make tea in a billy-can or the like; also, to prepare a meal under rough-and-ready conditions (out-of-doors). Cf. DRUM *sb.*^{1} 9 g. *slang.*

1923 KIPLING *Irish Guards in Great War* I. 58 The Irish 'drummed up', which is to say, stewed their tea or rations. **1931** F. GRAY *Tramp* ix. 104 Now comes the great event of the day. He is prepared and is going to 'drum up'. **1935** 'G. ORWELL' *Clergyman's Daughter* ii. 104 After getting to Bromley they had 'drummed up' on a horrible, paper-littered refuse dump. *Ibid.* 106 They.. 'drummed up' in thickets where firewood and water were handy, and cooked strange, squalid meals. **1962** *Listener* 13 Sept. 382/2 Only at midday was there a break, when fires were lit and water boiled.. to make tea. This was know as 'drumming up'.

†**drumble**, *sb.*^{1} *Obs.* exc. *dial.* [Variant of *dumble*, DUMMEL, perh. influenced by *drone*, or *dromedary*.] An inert or sluggish person; a 'drone'.

1575 *Appius & Virg.* in Hazl. *Dodsley* IV. 118 Yea, but what am I? A dreamer, a drumble, a fire or a spark? **1879** *Shropsh. Word-bk., Drumble*, obsols., a dull, inactive person. 'The poor owd mon.. wuz al'ays a poor drumble.'

drumble, *sb.*^{2}, a dial. var. of *dumble*: cf. DIMBLE.

drumble- (also 6 dromel-, 9 drummel-, drumle-), in names of insects, a variant of DUMBLE-. [Cf. DRUMBLE *sb.*^{1}] †**drumble-bee**, a humble- or bumble-bee (*obs.*). **drumble-dore**, a clumsily-flying insect, a dor-beetle, or bumble-bee; *fig.* a heavy stupid fellow; app. sometimes associated with *dromedary*. **drumble-drone**, a drone-bee, a bumble-bee.

1567 *Triall Treas.* (1850) 6 Thou goest like a dromeldory, dreamy and drowzy. **1596** NASHE *Saffron Walden* F iij b, Your fly in a boxe is but a drumble-bee in comparison of it. **1746** *Vocab.* in *Exmoor Scold.* (E.D.S.) 65/2 *Drumble-drane*, a drone or humble bee. **1855** KINGSLEY *Westw. Ho!* (1861) 290 Since you used to put drumble-drones into my desk to Bideford school. **1881** MISS YONGE *Lads & Lasses of Langley* iv. 154 Poor Billy, he was but a drumble-dore of a boy, as his mother called him. **1894** BLACKMORE *Perlycross* 69, I must a' been mazed as a drummeldrone.

drumble, *v.*^{1} Now *dial.* [f. DRUMBLE *sb.*^{1}]

1. *intr.* To be sluggish; to move sluggishly.

1598 SHAKS. *Merry W.* III. iii. 156 Go, take vp these cloathes heere, quickly.. Look, how you drumble! **1822** SCOTT *Nigel* xxiii, Why, how she drumbles—I warrant she stops to take a sip on the road. **1826** —— *Woodst.* xviii, Why do you hesitate and drumble in that manner? **1875** H. KINGSLEY *No. Seventeen* xxvi, They, to use a Devonshire expression, drumbled on to Falmouth.

†**2.** *intr.* To drone, to mumble. *Obs.*

1579 FULKE *Heskins' Parl.* 288 How so euer M. Heskins drumbleth and dreameth of this matter, Cranmer saith truely. **1596** NASHE *Saffron Walden* 34 Graybeard drumbbling over a discourse.

†**drumble**, *v.*^{2} *Obs.* [app. freq. and dim. of DRUM *v.*: cf. Du. and Ger. *trommeln*, Da. *tromle*, Sw. *trumla* to drum.] *intr.* To sound like a drum.

1630 DRAYTON *Muses' Elysium* viii. (R.), Let the nimble hand belabour The whistling pipe, and drumbling tabor.

drumble, *v.*^{3} *Sc.* Also 9 drummle. [app. a nasalized form of DRUBBLE *v.*, parallel to *drumbly*, DRUMLY *a.* from DRUBLY; but possibly a back-formation from the adj., which occurs earlier.]

†**1.** *trans.* To trouble, disturb. *Obs.*

1637 RUTHERFORD *Lett.* (1862) I. 355 My drumbled and troubled well began to clear. **1724** RAMSAY *Dk. of Hamilton's Shooting* in *Poems on R.C. of Archers* (1726) 46 Rogues that drumble [*ed.* 1800, at] the Common Weal.

2. To make drumly or turbid.

1825 in JAMIESON. *Mod. Sc.* The flood had drummled the water.

†**drumbler, drumler.** *Obs.* Also 7 dromler. [a. early mod.Du. *drommeler* a kind of ship (Kilian); perh. a perversion of the foreign term *dromon, dromond* after a native word: cf. *drommel* a compact and dense thing, *drommeler* a square-built 'chunky' man.]

1. A name in the 17th c. for a small fast vessel, used as a transport, also as a piratical ship of war.

1598 HAKLUYT *Voy.* I. 601 (R.) She was immediately assaulted by diuers English pinasses, hoyes, and drumblers. **1604** E. GRIMSTONE *Hist. Siege Ostend* 31 Two Dromlers laden with bowes. **1611** COTGR., *Dromant*, a Drumbler, Carauell, or such like small, and swift vessell, vsed by Pyrats. **1630** J. TAYLOR *Navy of Land Ships* Wks. I. 87/2 Seuerall vessels at Sea doe make a Nauy, as Carracks.. Barkes, Pinnaces, Hoighs, Drumlers, Fregates, Brigandines.

2. A wheelbarrow.

1613 MARKHAM *Eng. Husbandman* I. II. xvi. (1635) 204 This dunge you shall bring into your Garden in little drumblars or wheele-barrowes.

'drumhead. [f. DRUM *sb.*^{1} + HEAD *sb.*]

1. The skin or membrane stretched upon a drum, by the beating of which the tone is produced.

Used also in the camp or field for various purposes as an improvised table, gaming-table, writing-desk, etc.

1622 MABBE tr. *Aleman's Guzman d' Alf.* I. 170, I did so often visit the Drum-head.. getting little, and loosing much. **1654** WHITLOCK *Zootomia* 423 The Chance of War, playeth as casually while the Drumme beats, as ever Die did on Drumme Head. **1684** *Contempl. State Man* I. vi. (1699) 66 A Soldier.. passing away his time at Dice upon a Drum head. **1802** PALEY *Nat. Theol.* iii. (1830) 32 It resembles also a drum head in this principal property, that its use depends upon its tension. **1841** JAMES *Brigand* xli, He shall have no judgment but that over the drum-head.

2. The membrane across the drum of the ear.

1664 BUTLER *Hud.* II. iii. *Heroic. Ep. to Sidrophel* 24 As if the vehemence had stunn'd And torn your Drum-heads with the Sound. **1874** ROOSA *Dis. Ear* 63 Sometimes the hairs of the canal grow to such a length as to obscure the view of the Meatus and the drum-head. **1888** *Amer. Ann. Deaf* Apr. 163 Operations for deafness by the excision of the drumhead.

3. The circular top of a capstan, into which the capstan-bars are fixed. Also, the head or top of a 'drum' in machinery.

1726 SHELVOCKE *Voy. round World* 15 We began to heave up our anchor the day before, but wrench'd the drum-head of our capstane. **1769** FALCONER *Dict. Marine* (1789) L ij, The drum-head is a broad cylindrical piece of wood, resembling a mill-stone, and fixed immediately above the barrel. *c* **1860** H. STUART *Seaman's Catech.* 54 Name the parts of a capstan. The bed,.. spindle, drum-head [etc.]. **1894** *Daily News* 4 Sept. 3/1 The boring by means of the great circular drumhead—the 'Shield'—weighing 250 tons, with a sharp cutting edge in front, and at the back of it 28 hydraulic jacks.

4. A flat-topped variety of cabbage. More fully ***drumhead cabbage***.

1797 W. GREEN in A. Young *Agric. Suffolk* 94 The sort [of cabbage] drum-head, from its flat top, and as hard as a stone. **1808** CURWEN *Econ. Feeding Stock* 50 The ground was cropped with four acres of drumhead cabbages.

5. *attrib.*, as ***drumhead court-martial***, a court-martial round an up-turned drum, for summary treatment of offences during military operations; hence ***drumhead discipline, law***, that which is dispensed at a drumhead court-martial; also *fig.*

1835, etc. [see COURT-MARTIAL 1 b]. **1847** LE FANU *T. O'Brien* 168 If your majesty were to give them drumhead law. **1870** LOWELL *Among my Bks.* Ser. I. (1873) 246 He lived to see that there was more reason in the drumhead religious discipline.. than he may have thought at first. **1899** *Westm. Gaz.* 22 Dec. 10/1 What he calls 'drum-head letters', written by soldiers at the front before and after battle. **1908** *Daily Chron.* 25 May 7/7 A drum-head service held in the camp of the Essex Imperial Yeomanry.

Hence **'drum,headed**, in ***drumheaded cabbage***, = DRUMHEAD 4.

1799 *Trans. Soc. Arts* XVII. 137 The drum-headed cabbage is the best sort.

drumler: see DRUMBLER.

drumlin ('drʌmlɪn). [app. for *drumling*, dim. of DRUM *sb.*^{2}] = DRUM *sb.*^{2}

1833 [see DRUM *sb.*^{2}]. **1833-8** J. SCOULER in *Jrnl. Royal Geol. Soc. Dublin* I. 273 These drumlins are very common in many parts of the country, and a very fine example of their nature occurs between Belfast and Lisburn. **1893** SIR H. HOWORTH *Glac. Nightmare* II. 854 Sometimes.. they are aggregated into lenticular mounds or drumlins.

drumlinized ('drʌmlɪnaɪzd), *ppl. a. Physical Geogr.* [f. DRUMLIN: see -IZE.] Formed into or covered with drumlins, or with structures shaped like them.

1907 *Bull. N. Y. State Museum* CXI. 402 Smooth ridging or ribbing making one doubtful whether to map the area as moraine or drumlinized drift. **1934** *Geogr. Jrnl.* LXXXIV. 145 The drumlinized tract on the west side. **1970** *Nature* 2 May 441/2 The bench surfaces are scoured into a drumlinized micro-topography of 1–10 cm relief.

drumlinoid ('drʌmlɪnɔɪd), *a.* and *sb. Physical Geogr.* [f. as prec. + -OID.] **A.** *adj.* Resembling a drumlin in shape. **B.** *sb.* A long, low hill of drift resembling a drumlin but of a less regular form; also, a mass of rock to which glacial action has given a drumlin-like appearance.

1898 *Geol. Survey Canada, Ann. Rep. 1896* IX. 182F High regular drumlinoid hills. **1901** A. P. BRIGHAM *Text-bk. Geol.* xiv. 270 The drumlinoid (having the form of a drumlin) is a rock structure superficially modified by ice movement. **1904** *Sci. Amer. Suppl.* 16 Jan. 23447 Some of the principal ridges present drumlinoid profiles. **1953** *Canad. Geographer* III. 19 In some places, individual drumlinoids may extend over a distance of several miles, in others they are very much shorter and resemble drumlins in form. **1968** R. W. FAIRBRIDGE *Encycl. Geomorphol.* 295/1 A 'drumlinoid'.. is a spindle-shaped hill of till or a series of 'streaks' of till not developed into the typical drumlin shape.

drumly ('drʌmlɪ), *a. Orig. Sc.* Also **drumbly**. [app. nasalized var. of DRUBLY, in same sense.]
1. Of the sky or day: Troubled; gloomy, cloudy; the opposite of clear. Also *fig.*
1513 DOUGLAS *Æneis* v. xii. 55 The drumblie schoure ȝet furth our all the air Als blak as pik. **1708** J. BLACKADER *Diary* 26 Sept. in Crichton *Life* xiv. (1824) 331 This campaign has still a strange drumly aspect. *c* **1817** HOGG *Tales & Sk.* II. 220 A glow of seriousness in his drumly looks. **1888** A. S. WILSON *Lyric of a Hopeless Love* XXVIII. 92 Above the drumly day.
2. Of water, etc.: Turbid; discoloured with matter in suspension; not clear.
1570 BUCHANAN *Ane Admonit.* Wks. (1892) 24 Gude fischeing..in drumly Watter. **1622** BP. ABERNETHY *Phys. for Soule* xix. (1630) 293 Like a stirred and drumly water. **1713** KENNEDY *Ophthalmogr.*, It mixed with the aqueous humour, which becoming drumly, the patient could no longer see. **1853** G. JOHNSTON *Nat. Hist. E. Bord.* I. 10 Its margin often miry and sedgy, its water drumly.
b. *fig.* and *transf.*
1563 WINȜET *Wks.* (1890) II. 78 Lat the cleir fayth..of our elders be na mixing of glar..be tribulit and maid drumlye. **1790** BURNS '*Kind Sir, I've read your paper through*' 6 Or what the drumlie Dutch were doin'. **1829** SCOTT *Jrnl.* 13 Feb., I wrote for several hours..but was nervous and drumlie.

'drum-,major. [See MAJOR *sb.*]
1. †**a.** The first or chief drummer in a regimental band (*obs.*). **b.** A non-commissioned officer who has command of the drummers of a regiment. **c.** An officer of a band or drum-corps, who leads it and directs its movements on the march.
1598 BARRET *Theor. Warres* IV. i. 99 He is to commaunde the drumme maior to sound the call. **1689** *Lond. Gaz.* No. 2458/4 Michael Cavendish, Drum-major in my Lord Lovelace his Regiment of Foot. **1725** *Ibid.* No. 6382/1 The Drums of His Majesty's Houshold, the Drum-Major attending. **1844** *Regul. & Ord. Army* 140 The Music for Slow and Quick Time is to be practised under the direction of the Drum-Major..until the prescribed cadence has been acquired.
†**2.** *humorous.* A large 'drum' or rout. *Obs.*
1753 *Scots Mag.* Jan. 37/1 At home. To have a drum-major and seventeen card-tables.
3. *attrib.* and *Comb.* †**drum-major-general**, a staff officer who controlled the drummers, etc.
1651 CLEVELAND *Poems* 27 These Drum-major oaths of Bulk unruly. **1679–88** *Secr. Money Chas. II & Jas. II* (Camden) 177 To John Maugridge, drumajor genˡˡ, bounty ..20 0 0. **1743** *List Govt. Officers* in J. Chamberlayne *St. Gt. Brit.* 108 Staff-Officers on his Majesty's Establishment.. Mr. John Clothier, Drum-Major-General.

,drum-majo'rette. orig. *U.S.* [f. DRUM-MAJOR + -ETTE.] A female drum-major (DRUM-MAJOR 1 c); a girl who leads or takes part in a parade or the like, twirling a baton, etc.
1938 *Life* 10 Oct. 3/1 (*heading*) Drum majorettes are latest in ballyhoo. **1940** R. CHANDLER *Farewell, My Lovely* xxi. 162 The girls wore white silk blouses and drum majorettes' shakos. **1955** J. B. PRIESTLEY in Priestley & Hawkes *Journey down Rainbow* v. 84 The purple band..marched on to the field, accompanied by drum-majorettes. **1957** *New Yorker* 5 Oct. 36/1 There was the Drum and Bugle Corps of St. Rocco's Church in Newark, led by a drum majorette in blinding scarlet, gold, and blue, her knees and sabre flashing. **1971** *Graphic* (Durban) 7 May 1/2 There will be a display by drum majorettes. **1971** *Glasgow Herald* 22 June 11/4 (*caption*) The Swedish drum majorettes marching in George Square, Glasgow.

drummer ('drʌmə(r)). [f. DRUM *v.* + -ER¹.]
1. One who beats a drum for public or military purposes; one who plays the drum in a band.
In the British army it was formerly also his duty to carry out sentences of the 'cat'. (Cf. Stocqueler *Mil. Encycl.* 1853.)
1573–80 BARET *Alv.* D 1309 A Drummer, or plaier on the drumme. **1580** *Nottingham Rec.* IV. 196 Payd to the drummer xvj d. **1593** SHAKS. *3 Hen. VI*, IV. vii. 50 Drummer strike vp, and let vs march away. **1724** DE FOE *Mem. Cavalier* (1840) 206 The preachers were better than drummers to raise volunteers. **1823** J. F. COOPER *Pioneer* iv, The lash drawing through his left, in the scientific manner with which drummers apply the cat. **1844** *Regul. & Ord. Army* 168 The proportion of Acting Drummers shall not exceed Four [to a Company]. **1890** *Times* 17 Dec. 14/4 When the order to commence was given, the first drummer went in and administered 25 lashes, told off deliberately by the drum-major, 'One, two, three', and so on.
2. *fig.* **a.** One who solicits custom or orders; a commercial traveller; cf. DRUM *v.* 5 and 6 b. orig. *U.S.*
1827 SCOTT in *C. K. Sharpe's Corr.* (1888) II. 398 The Nos. of Lodge's book..were left by some drummer of the trade upon speculation. **1860** BARTLETT *Dict. Amer.*, *Drummer*, a person employed by city houses to solicit the custom of country merchants. **1882** T. S. HUDSON *Scamper thro' America* 183 As enterprising as a Chicago drummer. **1915** LD. REDESDALE *Memories* I. xiii. 287 The boarding house chiefly used by 'drummers'—travellers of English commercial houses. **1941** BAKER *Dict. Austral. Slang* 26 *Drummer*,..a commercial traveller.
b. A thief (see quots.). *slang.*
1856 MAYHEW *Gt. World of London* I. 46 Those who hocus or plunder persons by *stupefying*; as '*drummers*', who drug liquor. **1859** HOTTEN *Dict. Slang* 34 *Drummer*, a robber who first makes his victims insensible by drugs or violence, and then plunders them. **1960** *Observer* 25 Dec. 7/6 Nobody wanted to know the drummers, those squalid daytime operators who turn over empty semi-detached villas while the housewives are out shopping. **1962** 'J. BELL' *Crime in our Time* III. 51 They knock at the doors of houses to discover if the owners are at home. The police call them 'drummers', because they drum on the doors in this way.
c. *Austral.* and *N.Z. slang.* (See quots.)
1898 *Bulletin* (Sydney) 17 Dec., *Drummer*, the laziest and therefore the slowest shearer in a shed. **1941** BAKER *N.Z. Slang* v. 39 Just as *ringer* is used for the most expert shearer, *drummer* is used for the worst. **1949** P. NEWTON *High Country Days* v. 55 Hewett, the learner, and 'drummer' of the gang, with seventeen to his credit had also shown an improvement. **1959** H. P. TRITTON *Time means Tucker* v. 42/2 It's not every man that is drummer in four sheds running.
d. *Austral.* and *N.Z. slang.* A swagman or tramp. Cf. DRUM *sb.*¹ 9 f. ? *Obs.*
1933 L. G. D. ACLAND in *Press* (Christchurch) 14 Oct. 15/7 *Drum*, swag, obviously from the shape. Hence *drummer*. **1945** BAKER *Austral. Lang.* v. 102 *Bender* (1885) and *drummer* (*circa* 1890) were once popular terms for tramps of slightly better class than the sundowner.
3. (See quot.)
1885 C. MACKESON *British Alm. Comp.* 94 Among the double meanings..Drummer for a Musician or a Blacksmith's hammer man.
4. Applied to various animals which make a drumming noise, or suggest the action of drumming.
a. A drum-fish. **b.** The large West Indian cockroach (*Blatta gigantea*) which makes a noise at night by knocking its head against the woodwork of houses. **c.** A rabbit. **d.** *Sporting slang*: see quot. 1785.
1725 SLOANE *Jamaica* II. 290 Drummer-Fish. This was taken at Old Harbour. **1785** GROSE *Dict. Vulg. Tongue*, *Drummer*, a jockey term for a horse that throws about his fore legs irregularly. **1847** CARPENTER *Zool.* §665 One of them [species of *Blatta*] is known in the West Indies by the name of drummer, from the sharp knocking sound which it produces. **1883** *Fisheries Exhib. Catal.* (ed. 4) 170 Grunts, Croakers, and Drummers..deriving their names from the sounds they utter when caught. **1894** *Blackw. Mag.* May 722 'When I wanted drummers [rabbits] I could git them for myself.'
5. *Comb.*, as ***drummer-boy***, ***-fish*** (see 4), ***-lad***.
1830 SCOTT *Demonol.* x. 365 Matcham would have deserted had it not been for the presence of a little drummer-lad. **1840** DICKENS *Barn. Rudge* lviii, The drummer-boys practising in a distant courtyard.

'drumming, *vbl. sb.* [See -ING¹.]
1. The action of the vb. DRUM, in various senses.
1583 STUBBES *Anat. Abus.* I. Pref. (1879) 11 With pyping, fluting, dromming, and such like inticements. **1663** J. SPENCER *Prodigies* (1665) 228 Apparitions, Voices, Drummings, Noises of Evil Spirits in the Heavens or Earth. **1830** GALT *Lawrie T.* I. vii, The deep and dreadful drumming of the thunder. **1831** [see DRUM *v.* 4]. **1839** CARLYLE *Chartism* v. 141 Ignominious drumming out.
2. The sport of fishing for drum-fish. *U.S.*
1889 in *Century Dict.*
3. *attrib.* and *Comb.*
a **1653** G. DANIEL *Idyll* iv. 92 As a Tam'd Hare, that Strikes a Drumming fitt. **1832** J. BREE *St. Herbert's Isle* 155 That fatal hive In which..My drumming-stick I plunged.

'drumming, *ppl. a.* [f. DRUM *v.* + -ING².] That drums or beats like a drummer.
1593–1638 [see DRUM *v.* 2 b, 4]. **1859** TENNYSON *Enid* 1022 The drumming thunder of the huger fall At distance. **1875** MISS BIRD *Sandwich Isl.* (1880) 83 There are no horrid, drumming, stabbing mosquitos.

drummock, Sc. var. of DRAMMOCK.

Drummond light. The lime-light, or oxyhydrogen light (invented by Capt. T. Drummond, R.E., *c* 1825), wherein a blow-pipe flame, e.g. of combined oxygen and hydrogen, impinges on a piece of pure lime, and renders it incandescent.
1854 J. SCOFFERN in *Orr's Circ. Sc., Chem.* 298 The combination evolves what is..known as the Drummond Light. **1870** J. C. GEIKIE *Life* (ed. 3) 211 Wisdom thinks, and makes a solar Drummond light of a point of dull lime.

drummy ('drʌmɪ), *a.* [f. DRUM *sb.*¹ + -Y¹.] Of the nature of a drum, or characterized by the drum.
1833 M. SCOTT *Tom Cringle* xi, A tolerably good band, a little too drummy. **1890** FENN *Double Knot* I. Prol. iii. 49 [His] ribs..emitted a cavernous drummy sound.

†**drumslade, dromslade.** *Obs.* Also 6 **drombyllsclad, drombeslade, dromslet, droumslade, drumslade, drumslade, -slad, -slate, -sled, -selet, -salt, dronscellett, -sselat, -slade, drounslade, -slet, drunslade.** [app. corruption of Du. or LG. *trommelslag*, Ger. *trommelschlag* drum-beat (cf. next); though it does not appear how this name of the action came to be applied to the instrument. The variety of forms (with others, as *dronsselar*, *drumsted*, which are mere copyists' errors) arose from the foreign character of the word.]
1. A drum, or some form of drum.
1527 *St. Papers Hen. VIII*, I. 224 The dayly retinue of fotemen of this towne..wel trymmed and furnished with their dromslades, trompettes, and banerettes. **1530** PALSGR. 215/2 Dromslade, suche as almayns use in warre, *bedon.* **1539** T. PERY in Ellis *Orig. Lett.* Ser. II. II. 154 They cawssyde the trompettys with dronscellettys to go abowit the Cyte. **1548** [see DRUM *sb.*¹ 1]. **1550–63** MACHYN *Diary* (Camden) 13 Trompets and bagespypes, and dronsselats [*printed* -ars] and flutes. **1552** HULOET, Drunslade, *tympanum.* **1575** TURBERV. *Faulconrie* 191 To strike uppon his Drumselet or Taberde. **1635** J. HAYWARD tr. *Biondi's Banish'd Virg.* 153 The harsh antique consort of Fifes and Drumslads.
2. A drummer; = DRUMSLAGER.
1527 *MS. Acc. R. Gibson, Master of Revels* (Publ. Rec. Off.), ij cotis for the drombyllsclads of yelowe sarsenet. *a* **1533** LD. BERNERS *Gold. Bk. M. Aurel.* (1546) Ii ij, These ydell trewandes gestours, tomblers plaiers, or dromslai[d]es. **1540** in *Vicary's Anat.* (1888) App. xii. 242 Item, for Burtill and Hans, dromslades xxxiij *s* iiij *d.* **1688** R. HOLME *Armoury* III. 44/3 The Musicians..in the Kings Majesties Household [are] 3 Drumslades. **1777** HOOLE *Comenius' Vis. World* (ed. 12) 182 The drummers, and the drumslades.. call to arms.
3. *Comb.*, as ***drumslade-player***.
1548 HALL *Chron., Hen. VIII*, 80 b, The Drumslad plaiers and other minstrels arayed in white. **1552** HULOET, Drumslade player, *symphoniacus seruus.*

†**'drumslager.** *Obs.* [ad. Ger. *drummeschläger*, earlier var. of *trommelschläger*, Du. *trommelslager*, Da. *trommeslager*, Sw. *trumslagare*, drum-beater.] A drummer.
1586 J. HOOKER *Girald. Irel.* in *Holinshed* II. 175/2 There being but one man the drumslager left aliue, who by swiftnesse of his bote escaped.

†**'drumsler.** *Obs.* [Corruption of DRUMSLAGER or DRUMSLADE.] = DRUMMER.
1583 J. HIGINS tr. *Junius' Nomenclator* (N.), The drum-player, or drumsler. **1599** *Soliman & Perseda* II. in Hazl. *Dodsley* V. 303 Fellow drumsler, I'll reward you well.

†**'drumster.** *Obs.* [f. DRUM *v.* + -STER.] A drummer.
1586 in *Stow's Surv.* (ed. Strype 1754) II. v. xxxi. 567/2 Ensigne Bearers and sergeants with a fit Drumster. **1617** MINSHEU *Ductor*, Drumster, or plaier on the Drum.

drumstick ('drʌmstɪk).
1. a. The stick having a terminal knob or padded head with which a drum is beaten.
1589 *Nottingham Rec.* IV. 226 For iiij. gunstickes and twoe drumme stickes. *a* **1691** BOYLE *Wks.* III. 25 The drum-stick falling upon the drum makes a percussion of the air, and puts that fluid body into an undulating motion. **1864** ENGEL *Mus. Anc. Nat.* 219 The Egyptians had also straight drum-sticks with a handle, and a knob at the end.
†**b.** Applied to a person. *Obs.*
1633 MARMION *Fine Companion* III. iv, What? I will not offend thee, my good drumstick.
2. *transf.* (in reference to shape.) **a.** The lower joint of the leg of a dressed fowl.
1764 FOOTE *Mayor of G.* I. Wks. 1799 I. 173 She always helps me herself to the tough drumsticks of turkies. **1831** MOORE *Summer Fête* 825 Since Dinner..Put Supper and her fowls so white, Legs, wings, and drumsticks, all to flight. **1848** THACKERAY *Bk. Snobs* xxxii, A finger, as knotted as a turkey's drumstick.
b. A popular appellation of the Knapweed (*Centaurea nigra* and *C. Scabiosa*).
1878–86 in BRITTEN & HOLLAND *Plant-n.*
c. 'The colloquial name in the Madras Presidency for the long slender pods of the *Moringa pterygosperma*, the Horse-Radish Tree of Bengal.'
d. *U.S.* The stilt-sandpiper.
e. *Cytology.* An appendage of the nucleus of a polymorphonuclear leucocyte, composed of sex chromatin and characteristic of females.
1954 DAVIDSON & SMITH in *Brit. Med. Jrnl.* 3 July 6 A solitary chromatin nodule..becomes separated off from the main nuclear lobes in a proportion of the neutrophils... This characteristic 'drumstick', which is just visible at ×90 magnification, has to be distinguished from other appendages which occur in both sexes. **1964** L. MARTIN *Clinical Endocrinol.* (ed. 4) vi. 204 The drumstick consists of an ovoid chromatin mass of 1·5 μ diameter connected to the nucleus by a thin chromatin thread. **1966** W. A. DAVIDSON in K. L. Moore *Sex Chromatin* iii. 69 The drumsticks which have been identified in animals appear to be similar in form and size to those in man.
3. *Comb.*, as ***drumstick-shaped*** adj.; also **drumstick-tree**, *Cassia Sieberiana*, so called from the shape of its pods, known in Sierra Leone as ***monkey drumsticks***.
1831 DON *Dichlamyd. Pl.* I. s.v. *Cassia Sieberiana.* **1866** *Treas. Bot.*, Drumstick Tree, *Cathartocarpus conspicua.* **1893** *Fortn. Rev.* Jan. 113 All forms of tetanus..are due to ..the drumstick-shaped bacillus of Nicolaier.

drungar ('drʌŋgə(r)). *Hist.* [ad. late L. *drungārius*, f. *drungus* a body of soldiers (Vegetius *c* 420).] The leader or commander of a troop or body of soldiers. ***drungar of the fleet*** (*Drungarius classis*), a Byzantine admiral or commander of the fleet.
1619 T. MILLES tr. *Mexia's Treas. Anc. & Mod. Times* II. 465/2 Vnto this Great Duke whom they had as chiefe Admirall, they made subiect all the Drungars of their Fleete. **1788** GIBBON *Decl. & F.* liii. (1836) 1002 They obeyed the great drungaire of the fleet.

†**drunk,** *sb.*¹ *Obs.* Also 2–4 drunch, 4 drunc, (drung). [OE. *drync* (:—**druŋki-z*), corresp. to OHG. *trunch*, MHG. *trunc*, Ger. *trunk*, f. *u*-grade of *driŋk-an* to drink. The *u* in early ME.

is ü = OE. *y*. The form *drunk* may have been assimilated to the verb.] = DRINK *sb.*

a **800** *Corpus Gloss.* 1008 *Haustum*, drync. *c* **1175** *Lamb. Hom.* 103 Gula..to deþe bringeð mid unmete drunche. *a* **1225** *Ancr. R.* 14 Of mete & of drunc & of oðer þinges þet falleð ðer abuten. *c* **1290** *S. Eng. Leg.* I. 97/171 þat no man hire mete ne ȝaf ne drunch. *c* **1325** *Song on Passion* 38 in *O.E. Misc.* 198 Of bitter drunk he senden him a sonde.

drunk (drʌŋk), *ppl. a.* and *sb.*[2] Also 4–6 **dronk(e.** [pa. pple. of DRINK *v.*, of which the earlier form was DRUNKEN. Now, in standard Eng., almost exclusively in the predicate; in Sc. and north. dial. still *attrib.* 'a drunk man'.]

A. *ppl. a.* **1. a.** That has drunk intoxicating liquor to an extent which affects steady self-control; intoxicated, inebriated; overcome by alcoholic liquor. The degree of inebriation is expressed by various adjs. and advs., as *beastly*, *blind*, *dead*, *half*, etc. ***drunk and disorderly***: the official form of a charge in police-court procedure (cf. DISORDERLY *a.* 2 b); so quasi-*sb.*, a drunk and disorderly person; the offence of being drunk and disorderly; ***drunk and incapable***: see INCAPABLE *a.* 5.

c **1340** *Cursor M.* 2021 (Trin.) Drunke [*earlier texts* drunken] he lay & slept bi his one. *a* **1450** *Knt. de la Tour* (1868) 72 One counsailed to make hym gret chere tyl he were dronke. **1532** MORE *Confut. Tindale* Wks. 591/2 We ware wanton or sowe dronke. **1585** T. WASHINGTON tr. *Nicholay's Voy.* III. ii. 91 They doe not thinke they have made good cheere..except they be made beastly drunk. **1648** GAGE *West Ind.* xix. 144 If they can get any drinke that will make them mad drunk..they never leave off, untill they bee mad and raging drunke. **1684** DRYDEN *Disappointment* Prol. 59 The doughty bullies enter bloody drunk. **1830** CARLYLE *For. Rev. & Cont. Misc.* V. 1 Trodden into the kennels as a drunk mortal. **1855** [see DISORDERLY B. *sb.*]. **1874** GREENWOOD & MARTIN *Magisterial & Police Guide* 610 *margin*, Offences. Drunk and disorderly persons. **1887** SIMS *Mary Jane's Mem.* 45 She was blind drunk in the bar parlour. **1893** T. MARRIOTT *Constable's Duty* 76 Offence Defined... Every person who..is found to be drunk and disorderly. **1922** JOYCE *Ulysses* 602 Fined ten bob for a drunk and disorderly.

b. In various proverbial phrases and locutions.

c **1386** CHAUCER *Knt.'s T.* 403 We faren as he þat dronke is as a Mous. A dronke man woot wel þat he hath an hous. **1553** T. WILSON *Rhet.* (1580) 128 As dronke as a Ratte. **1562** J. HEYWOOD *Prov.* (1867) 23 He that kylth a man, whan he is dronke Shalbe hangd when he is sobre. **1622** MASSINGER *Virg. Mart.* III. iii, Be drunk as a beggar, he helps you home. **1669** DRYDEN *Wild Gallant* II. i, He had been acquainted with you these seven years drunk and sober. **1709** *Brit. Apollo* II. Supernum. No. 8. 2/2 He's as Drunk as a Wheel-barrow. **1738** SWIFT *Pol. Convers.* iii. Wks. 1778 X. 247 He came to us as drunk as David's sow. **1832** *E. Ind. Sketch Bk.* I. 137 The man was as drunk as a fiddler. **1891** FARMER *Slang* II. 333 Drunk as a lord.

c. Intoxicated or stupefied by opium, tobacco, etc.

1585 T. WASHINGTON tr. *Nicholay's Voy.* III. xi. 91 They have another order to make themselves drunk without wine, which is with their Opium. **1698** A. BRAND *Emb. Muscovy to China* 46 They..sucking the Tobacco smoak in greedily, swallow it down with the Water. For which reason.. generally at..the first Pipe in the Morning, they fall down drunk and insensible.

d. *fig.* = Intoxicated.

1340 *Ayenb.* 251 And makeþ him dronke of holy loue. **1602** MARSTON *Antonio's Rev.* IV. i. Wks. 1856 I. 117 Most things that morally adhere to soules, Wholly exist in drunke opinion. **1605** SHAKS. *Macb.* I. vii. 35 Was the hope drunke Wherein you dress'd your selfe? **1697** DRYDEN *Virg. Georg.* IV. 77 Drunk with secret Joy, Their young Succession all their Cares employ. **1874** GREEN *Short Hist.* x. §4. 799 Napoleon was drunk with success.

†**2.** Of a thing: Drenched; saturated with as much moisture as it can take in or receive. *Obs.*

1382 WYCLIF *Ps.* lxiv. [lxv.] 10 Thou hast visitid the erthe, and maad it drunke. **1611** BIBLE *Deut.* xxxii. 42, I will make mine arrows drunk [COVERDALE dronken] with blood. **1697** DRYDEN *Virg. Georg.* III. 479 The Fleece, when drunk with Tyrian Juice, Is dearly sold.

3. Of a thing: Unsteady, uneven or erratic in its course, as the thread of a screw; = DRUNKEN *ppl. a.* 5.

1884 F. J. BRITTEN *Watch & Clockm.* 170 A sure sign that the screw is not true, but 'drunk' as it is termed.

4. *Comb.*, as ***drunk-blind***, ***-mad*** adjs.; also **drunk-driving** *U.S.* = DRINK-DRIVING *sb.*; hence **drunk-driver**; †**drunk-wort**, tobacco (*obs.*).

1633 MASSINGER *Guardian* IV. ii, To be drunk-blind like moles in the wine-cellar. **1948** *Phi Delta Delta* Mar. 223 The validity of evidence based upon blood tests for *drunk drivers is today the most controversial of all medico-legal problems. **1953** *N.Y. Times Mag.* 29 Nov. 22/4 We don't want the boys picking up sick people, like diabetics, for instance, as drunk drivers. **1977** *Washington Post* 1 Feb. C1/4 Maryland's new crackdown on speeders and drunk drivers..is called 'Operation Yellow Jacket'. **1986** *Business Week* 23 June 133/1 Judge Larry Dean Lamson..is pioneering the high-tech solution to keeping drunk drivers off the road. **1937** *Lit. Digest* 30 Oct. 8/1 In view of the rise in accidents from this cause, we will concentrate on just one thing—drunk driving. **1953** *N.Y. Times Mag.* 29 Nov. 22/3 One major reason for the paucity of convictions in drunk driving cases has been the wide range of interpretations placed upon the term 'drunkenness'. **1959** *Newsweek* 2 Mar. 20/1 A marine engineer..came up for trial on a drunk-driving charge. **1986** *N.Y. Times* 30 June A18/2 The police complain, with reason, about wasting manpower in a hopeless pursuit of speeders while they shortchange drunk-driving patrols. **1722** DE FOE *Col. Jack* (1840) 147 He had.. made himself..drunk-mad. **1617** MINSHEU *Ductor*, *Drunke-woort*, or *Drunken-woort*..Tabaco.

B. *sb.*

1. (*colloq.*) A drinking-bout; a drunken fit or orgie; a state of drunkenness.

1779 W. SMITH *Let.* 8 June in *15th Rep. Hist. MSS. Comm.* (1897) App. VI. 430 They [*sc.* American soldiers] call a month's pay, which is 53*s.* 4*d.* paper money, but *three drunks*. Rum, 30 dollars a gallon. **1839** C. F. BRIGGS *Adv. Harry Franco* II. vii. 78, I have kept money enough to have a good drunk. **1846** *Spirit of Times* 18 Apr. 92/2 In an hour after he put down two gallons more to get up the drunk. **1862** *Times* 10 Apr., Both Houses immediately adjourned, and made preparations for a 'general drunk'. **1879** HOWELLS *L. Aroostook* (1883) II. 44 When I come out of one of my drunks. **1893** CAPT. KING *Foes in Ambush* 39 He could put up with an occasional drunk in a man who promised to make as good a trooper. *a* **1909** G. E. EVANS *Coll. Verse* (1928) 266 Cows in various states of drunk were scattered all around. **1952** M. TRIPP *Faith is Windsock* iii. 55 'I went on a seven-day drunk.' 'Like muck you did.' **1966** H. NIELSEN *After Midnight* (1967) xi. 135 She was sleeping off a drunk in the bedroom.

2. An intoxicated person; a case or charge of being drunk or intoxicated.

1852 J. W. CARLYLE *Let.* 18 Oct. (1949) xvi. 236 When I got up at my usual hour (*six o'clock*), I reeled about like 'a drunk' (as Mazzini would say). **1882** BESANT *All Sorts* vii. 61 Such a brave display of disorderly drunks. **1889** *Boston* (Mass.) *Jrnl.* 26 Apr. 1/6 To show the very large percentage of drunks among the commitments. **1891** R. KIPLING *City Dreadf. Nt.* 30 The burly president of the lock-up for European drunks.

3. Special Comb. **drunk tank** *N. Amer. slang*, a large prison cell for the detention of drunks; cf. TANK *sb.*[1].

1947 Drunk tank [see TANK *sb.*[1] 4]. **1976** N. THORNBURG *Cutter & Bone* xiii. 294 Bone's stay in the county jail lasted only four hours, most of which he spent in the drunk tank.

Hence †**'drunkhead** = DRUNKENNESS. **'drunkify** *v.*, to make drunk or intoxicated. **'drunkish**, **'drunky** (*dial.*) *adjs.*, somewhat drunk. †**'drunksome** *a.*, addicted to drunkenness.

1340 *Ayenb.* 260 Ne y-charged of glotounie ne of dronkehede. *c* **1400** *Apol. Loll.* 37 Drunksum men, rauenors, fornicaters, & swilk oþer. **1664** J. WILSON *A. Comnenius* II. iv, Have ye any more that must be drunkified? **1710** *Fanatick Feast* 11 The Company having plentifully dipt their Bills, and got pretty drunkish. **1858** CARLYLE *Fredk. Gt.* (1865) II. v. ii. 58 Drinks diligently..not till he is drunk, but only perceptibly drunkish. **1863** *Tyneside Songs* 63 The Fishermen then gat drunkey, O!

†**drunk**, *v. Obs.* [f. *drunk* pa. pple. of DRINK *v.*: cf. DRUNKEN *v.*[1]]

1. *trans.* To drown. Cf. DRUNKEN *v.*[1] 2.

c **1350** *Will. Palerne* 3516 Hire sone was in þe see dronked.

2. To saturate or fill with drink, to drench, to make drunken. Cf. DRUNKEN *v.*[1] 3.

1382 WYCLIF *Isa.* xliii. 24 With the talȝ of thi victorie sacrifises thou inwardly drunkedest not me [**1388** thou fillidist not me, Vulg. *non inebriasti me*]. —— *Ecclus.* xxxii. 17 Blisse thou the Lord, that made thee, and inwardli drunkinge thee of alle his goodis. —— xxxix. 28 The vnyuersel flod drunkede [**1388** fillide greteli, Vulg. *inebriavit*] the erthe.

drunkard ('drʌŋkərd). Also 6 **droncarde, -kerd(e, dronckharde.** [f. DRUNK *ppl. a.* + -ARD.]

1. One addicted to drinking; one who habitually drinks to excess; an inebriate, a sot.

1530 PALSGR. 155 *Yuroygne*, a man droncarde; *yuresse*, a woman droncarde. **1535** COVERDALE *Ps.* lxviii[i]. 12 The dronckhardes made songes vpon me. *c* **1586** C'TESS PEMBROKE *Ps.* CVII. x, As drunckards..they stagring reele. **1712** STEELE *Spect.* No. 276 ¶1 A man that is now and then guilty of Intemperance is not to be called a Drunkard. **1875** JOWETT *Plato* (ed. 2) V. 35 A drunkard in charge of drunkards would be singularly fortunate if he avoided doing a serious mischief.

2. A local name of the Marsh Marigold.

1886 in BRITTEN & HOLLAND *Plant-n.* App. **1894** BARING-GOULD *Kitty Alone* I. 118 The large golden cups that grow by the water's edge—these we call drunkards, but they drink only water.

3. *Comb.*, as ***drunkard-curer***, ***-curing***; also **drunkard's cloak**, a tub or barrel with holes for the head and hands fitted on a drunkard like a jacket, as a punishment.

1789 BRAND *Hist. Newcastle* II. 192 *note*, In the time of the commonwealth, it appears that the magistrates..punished ..drunkards by making them carry a tub, called the drunkard's cloak, through the streets. **1892** *Daily News* 22 June 5/5 There are several rival drunkard curers in the field. **1892** *Boston* (Mass.) *Jrnl.* 18 Nov. 7/4 The new drunkard-curing institution.

Hence †**'drunkardize** *v. intr.*, to act like a drunkard.

1632 VICARS *Æneid* (N.) Her deaded heart incens'd, she raves aloud, Doth madly through the citie drunkardize.

†**'drunkelec, 'droncelec.** *Obs. rare.* [f. DRUNKE(N *ppl. a.* + ON. suffix *-leik-r* action, function.] Drunkenness.

c **1450** MYRC 31 Dronkelec [*v.r.* dronkelewe] and glotonye, Pruyde and slouþe and enuye Alle þow moste putten away.

†**'drunkelew, 'drunklew,** *a.* (*sb.*) *Obs.* Forms: 4 **drunkenlew,** 4–6 **drunkelew(e,** 4–5 **dronkelew(e, -leuh,** 5 **-lowe;** 5 **drunk-, dronklew,** 6 **dronkleu.** [f. DRUNKEN + -LEWE: cf. ME. *costlewe* and *siklewe*.]

A. *adj.* Given to drunkenness, drunken.

1362 LANGL. *P. Pl.* A. IX. 75 Ho..is not dronkeleuh ne deynous Dowel him foleweþ [*B.* dronkenlew, dronkelew; *C.* dronkelewe]. **1382** WYCLIF *Matt.* xxiv. 49 ȝif he ete and drynke with drunkenlewe [**1388** drunken] men. —— *Ecclus.* xxvi. 11 A drunkelew womman. **1398** TREVISA *Barth. De P.R.* v. ii. (1495) 104 Also heedache comyth..as it happyth in dronklew men. *c* **1450** *Bk. Hawkyng* in *Rel. Ant.* I. 298 Loke that thu be not dronkelowe. **1519** HORMAN *Vulg.* 62 The foule dishoneste of them that be dronkleu. **1532** MORE *Confut. Tindale* Wks. 824/2 If he..be..dronkelew, or rauenous, wyth suche folke doe not so muche as eate.

B. *sb.* Drunkenness.

c **1430** LYDG. *Min. Poems* (Percy Soc.) 68 Voyde al drunklew. *c* **1450** [see DRUNKELEC]. **1496** *Bk. St. Albans, Her.* (1810) F iv, To be full of drynkynge & dronklewe.

Hence †**'drunkelewness**, drunkenness.

1387 TREVISA *Higden* (Rolls) II. 173 þey woneþ hem to dronkelewnesse. **1480** CAXTON *Descr. Brit.* 38 For as moche as they vse them to dronkelewnes.

†**'drunken**, *sb. Obs.* [OE. *druncen* sb., f. *druncen* pa. pple.] Drunkenness, intoxication.

c **950** *Lindisf. Gosp.* Luke xxi. 34 Ne sie ahefiȝad hearto iuero on oferfyllo & mið druuncen [*Rushw.* druncennisse]. *a* **1000** *Imposition of Penance* in Thorpe *Laws* II. 276 (Bosw.) Gif hit þurh druncen ȝewurþe. *a* **1200** *Moral Ode* 253 þe luueden tening and stale, hordom and drunken.

drunken ('drʌŋkən), *ppl. a.* Also *Sc.* 6 **drokin,** 7– **druken, drucken.** [pa. pple. of DRINK *v.*: cf. DRUNK. The Sc. and northern *drucken* is from Norse: cf. Icel. pa. pple. *drukkinn*.]

1. Overcome by liquor; intoxicated; = DRUNK.

a **1050** *Liber Scintill.* xxviii. (1889) 107 Ealswa se druncena [*ebriosus*] win onfehð unhold. *c* **1250** *Gen. & Ex.* 871 He woren drunken and slepi. *a* **1300** *Cursor M.* 27894 þe drunken semes in his misfare Noght lik þe man þat he was are. *c* **1386** CHAUCER *Wife's Prol.* 852 Ye fare as folkes that dronken ben of ale. *c* **1450** *Mirour Saluacioun* 3642 Some.. saide thai ware dronken and fulle of must hardily. **1535** STEWART *Cron. Scot.* II. 630 How King Duncane send the Wyne and Aill browin with mukil Wort to King Sueno, quhairwith thai war all drokin. **1697** DRYDEN *Virg. Past.* VI. 23 They..seiz'd with youthful Arms the drunken God. *c* **1850** *Arab. Nts.* (Rtldg.) 494 Drunken people are never seen making disturbances in open day. **1865** RAWLINSON *Anc. Mon.* III. iv. 95 Who drink till they are drunken.

b. In proverbs and locutions.

13.. *E.E. Allit. P.* B. 1500 [He] bibbes þer-of Tyl he be dronkken as the deuel. **1562** PILKINGTON *Wks.* (Parker Soc.) 51 'A drunken man is always dry', according to the proverb. **1619** R. HARRIS *Drunkard's Cup* 13 A drunken man neuer takes harme. **1887** *Scotsman* 19 Mar., The drucken man gets the drucken penny.

c. *transf.* and *fig.*

a **1340** HAMPOLE *Psalter* xxxv. 9 þan sall þai all be drunkyn in god þat wonys in godis hows. **1382** WYCLIF *Isa.* xxix. 9 Be ȝe drunken inwardli, and not of wyn. **1526** *Pilgr. Perf.* (W. de W. 1531) 291 Inebryate or dronken with heuenly ioye. **1578** TIMME *Caluine on Gen.* 313 Dronken with the flatteries of prosperity. **1856** KANE *Arct. Expl.* I. xvi. 196 We were so drunken with cold that we strode on steadily.

2. Given to drink; habitually intemperate. (The more common current sense.)

1548 HALL *Chron., Hen. VII*, 26 b, Could neither have money nor men of the dronken Fleminges. **1610** SHAKS. *Temp.* v. i. 277 Is not this Stephano, my drunken Butler? **1769** *Junius Lett.* iii. 18 You..represent your friend in the character of a drunken landlord. **1786** BURNS *Lines on meeting w. Ld. Daer* ii, I've been at druken writers' feasts. **1849** E. E. NAPIER *Excurs. S. Africa* I. 163 Drunken, lazy, good-for-nothing fellows.

3. Of actions, etc.: Characterized by or proceeding from intoxication.

1591 PERCIVALL *Sp. Dict.*, *Bevida*, drink, a potion, a drunken match. **1594** PLAT *Jewell-ho.* I. 44 Dutch & drunken deuises, about the gaining of the grounde. **1632** MASSINGER *Maid of Hon.* I. i, To take up a drunken brawl. **1752** JOHNSON *Rambler* No. 189 ¶6 Men who..destroy in a drunken frolick the happiness of families. **1842** TENNYSON *Locksley Hall* 81 Pointing to his drunken sleep.

b. Of or pertaining to drink or drunkenness.

1607 WILKINS *Inforced Marr.* v. in Hazl. *Dodsley* IX. 556 You in riot's house, A drunken tavern, spilled my maintenance. **1791** BURKE *Th. Fr. Affairs* Wks. VII. 76 The delirium of a low, drunken alehouse club.

c. That causes drunkenness. See 6 b.

4. *transf.* Soaked or saturated with moisture; sometimes (with sense affected by 1) 'drowned'.

c **1420** *Pallad. on Husb.* IX. 34 But glad is hit [radish] to loke on drunkun ayer. **1535** COVERDALE *Deut.* xxxii. 42 I wil make myne arowes dronken with bloude. **1590** SPENSER *F.Q.* III. ii. 47 She..The drunken lampe downe in the oyle did steepe. **1697** DRYDEN *Virg. Georg.* I. 170 The.. Ploughman..Drains the standing Waters, when they yield Too large a Bev'rage to the drunken Field.

5. *fig.* Of a thing: Uneven, unsteady, reeling in motion or course; off the vertical.

1786 [implied in DRUNKENNESS c.]. **1870** *Eng. Mech.* 11 Feb. 526/2 There are no abrupt breaks to form what would be called by a screw chaser 'a drunken thread'. **1876** J. ROSE *Pract. Machinist* (1885) 106 If the tool is moved irregularly or becomes checked in its forward movement, the thread will become drunken, that is, it will not move forward at a uniform speed. **1889** *Anthony's Photogr. Bull.* II. 69 You have now..no excuse for drunken architecture.

6. *Comb.*, as ***drunkenmost*** adj., most drunken, drunkenest.

1854 H. VICARS in Miss Marsh *Mem.* vii. 143 Four hundred of the drunkenmost and wildest men in the regiment.

b. *esp.* in names of intoxicating plants, or of such as suggest drunkenness: **drunken date**, the betel-nut tree; **drunken plant, drunken rye-grass**, darnel grass, *Lolium temulentum*; †**drunken-wort**, tobacco (Minsheu *Ductor* 1617).

1597 GERARDE *Herbal* III. cxxxix. (1633) 1520 Areca sive Fausel, the drunken date tree. **1611** COTGR., *Noisette des Indes*, the drunken Date. **1891** GRIFFITH tr. *Fouard's Christ Son of God* I. 304 *note*, *L'ivraie*, drunken rye-grass.

†ˈ**drunken**, *v.*[1] *Obs.* Forms: 1 druncnian, 2-3 druncnen, druncnie (*Orm.*) drunnenenn, 4 drunken, -yn, drunkne, dronken, -in, drownkyn. [ONorthumb. *druncnia*, ON. *drukna* (:—**druŋkna*) to be drowned = Goth. **druggknan*, a neuter-passive vb. in *-nan* derived from pa. pple. **druŋk-an-* of **driŋk-an* to drink: lit. to be drunk or swallowed up (by water). Cf. Ger. *ertrinken* to swallow up, drown.]

1. *intr.* To become swallowed up or sunk in water; to suffer drowning, be drowned.

c **950** *Lindisf. Gosp.* Matt. xiv. 30 Mið ðy ongann druncnia [*Rushw.* in-gon sincan, *Ags. G.* wearð ȝedofen] cliopade cueð drihten hal mec doa. *a* **1225** *St. Marher.* 15 Ich leade ham.. into se deop dung þᵗ ha druncneð þerin. *a* **1225** *Ancr. R.* 58 Leste eni best ualle þer inne, & druncnie ine sunne. *a* **1300** *Cursor M.* 24862 Quen þe scip suld quelm and drunken [*v.r.* dronkin]. *c* **1325** *Metr. Hom.* 138 In se dronkenes folc ful fele.

2. *trans.* To swallow up in water; to drown.

c **1200** *Trin. Coll. Hom.* 39 þe swin urnen.. into þe sæ, and druncnede hem seluen. *c* **1200** ORMIN 6795 All follc wass þurrh Noþess flodd O Noþess time drunnenedd. *a* **1340** HAMPOLE *Psalter* Cant. 504 Hys chosen prynces ere drunkynd in þe rede see.

3. To drench, saturate or soak with liquid.

a **1300** *E.E. Psalter* lxiv [lxv.] 10 þou soght þe land, and dronkened it yhite. *a* **1340** HAMPOLE *Psalter* lxviii[i]. 3 þe storme me drownkynd. **1382** WYCLIF *Isa.* xvi. 9, I shal drunkne thee with my tere. *Ibid.* lv. 10 What maner cometh doun weder and snoȝ fro heuene, and.. drunkneth [**1388** fillith, Vulg. *inebriat*] the erthe.

fig. **1382** WYCLIF *Jer.* xxxi. 14 Y shal inwardly drunkne the soule of the prestus with fatnesse.

†ˈ**drunken**, *v.*[2] *Obs.* [OE. *druncnian*, f. *druncen* DRUNKEN: in later use perh. a new formation.] *intr.* To drink to excess, to become drunk.

c **1000** ÆLFRIC *Hom.* (Th.) II. 70 þonne ða ȝebeoras druncniað. **1658** A. Fox *Wurtz' Surg.* II. iii. 55 If a Patient .. fall on gourmandizing and drunkning, then no good is to be looked for. **1693** SOUTHERNE *Maid's Last Prayer* 56 The Captain has been Drunkning with my Lord all Night. **1697** *View of Penal Laws* 3 Notorious Offenders, such as continue drunkening at late and unseasonable hours.

†**drunkenhead.** *Obs.* [f. DRUNKEN *ppl. a.* + -HEAD.] = DRUNKENNESS.

a **1300** *Cursor M.* 28459 And hafe i oft in my sott-hedd dryuen oþer men to drunkenhedd. **1382** WYCLIF *Judith* xiii. 19 He lai in his drunkinhed. **1393** GOWER *Conf.* III. 20 Through her dronkenhede Of witles excitation. **1483** CAXTON *Gold. Leg.* 82 b/2.

drunkenlew: see DRUNKELEW.

ˈ**drunkenly**, *adv.* [f. DRUNKEN *ppl. a.* + -LY[2].] In a drunken manner.

1573-80 BARET *Alv.* D 1312 Dronkenly. **1593** SHAKS. *Rich. II*, II. i. 127 That blood already.. Thou hast tapt out, and drunkenly carows'd. **1598** HAKLUYT *Voy.* I. 96 (R.) They carowse for the victory very filthily and drunkenly. **1854** CDL. WISEMAN *Fabiola* 210 The Dacian's eye flashed drunkenly again. **1866** GEO. ELIOT *F. Holt* II. xxix. 218 Tottering drunkenly on the edge of the grave.

drunkenness (ˈdrʌŋkənnɪs). [f. DRUNKEN *ppl. a.* + -NESS. See also DRUNKNESS.] The state of being drunk; intoxication; the habit of being drunken or addicted to excessive drinking.

c **893** K. ÆLFRED *Oros.* I. vi. §1 Hi forneah mid ealle fordyde.. mid druncennysse. *c* **1000** *Ags. Gosp.* Luke xxi. 34 On ofer-fylle and on druncennesse [*Hatton G.* druncenesse]. *c* **1200** *Trin. Coll. Hom.* 37 þe fule floddri of drunkennesse. *a* **1300** *Cursor M.* 27897 Schortly al iuels þat es Riueli becums of drunkenness [*v.rr.* drunkynnes, drinkynnes]. **1398** TREVISA *Barth. De P.R.* XVI. ix. (1495) 557 The purpur red amatistus.. helpyth ayenst dronkenesse. **1555** EDEN *Decades* 101 His noble men in their droonkennesse had so abused their toonges. **1674** R. GODFREY *Inj. & Ab. Physic* 71 We having drunk pretty high though not to drunkenness. **1789** BENTHAM *Princ. Legisl.* xix. §15 With what chance of success for example would a legislator go about, to extirpate drunkenness.. by dint of legal punishment? **1871** NAPHEYS *Prev. & Cure Dis.* II. vii. 602 Drunkenness is frequently a disease.

b. *fig.* Intoxication of the mind or spirit.

c **1200** ORMIN 14333 To ȝifenn mannkinn.. gastliȝ drunkennesse. **1526** *Pilgr. Perf.* (W. de W. 1531) 291 This inebriacyon or heuenly dronkennesse of the spiryte. **1855** MACAULAY *Hist. Eng.* IV. 733 In the drunkenness of factious animosity. **1873** HAMERTON *Intell. Life* II. i. (1875) 45 A divine drunkenness was given to them.

c. Unsteadiness of the thread of a screw.

1786 *Phil. Trans.* LXXVI. 21 To free the screw from what workmen call drunkenness. *Ibid.*, Otherwise the curved screw would be subject to.. drunkenness.

†ˈ**drunkenship.** *Obs.* [f. as prec. + -SHIP. See also DRUNKSHIP.] = DRUNKENNESS.

c **1440** *Gesta Rom.* li. 371 (Add. MS.) They drawe to lecherye, and dronkynship. **1474** CAXTON *Chesse* 68 Dronkenshyp is the begynnyng of alle euylles. **1542** BOORDE *Dyetary* xxi. (1870) 284 Quinces.. dothe preserue a man from dronkenshyppe. **1555** in Strype *Eccl. Mem.* III. App. xlii. 113 How agreeth Christe with Belyall or dronkenshippe?

†ˈ**drunkensome**, *a. Obs.* exc. *dial.* [f. as prec. + -SOME.] Addicted to drunkenness.

a **1300** *Cursor M.* 26188 Brath, and drunkensum, and skald. *c* **1400** *Apol. Loll.* 54 Drunkunsum men, vsurers, and who euer is contrari to þe doctrin, and to þe word of God, he is anticrist. **1567** *Stat. Trin. Coll. Edin.* 249 in W. Maitland *Hist. Edin.* II. (1753) 211 Gif ony of the Beidmen be drunkinsome. **1825** JAMIESON, *Druckensum.*

†ˈ**drunker.** *Obs.* Also -kar. [f. DRUNK *ppl. a.* + -ER[1].] = DRUNKARD.

1538 STARKEY *England* II. i. 171 Al craftys men in cytys and townys wych are drunkerys.. schold be.. punnyschyd. **1539** TAVERNER *Erasm. Prov.* (1552) 62 Oure common prouerbe.. Children, drunkers and fooles, can not lye. **1608** ROWLANDS *Humors Looking Glasse* 21 Two honest Drunkars must goe drinke a pot.

drunkery (ˈdrʌŋkərɪ). [f. DRUNK *ppl. a.*: see -ERY.] A place to get drunk in; a contemptuous appellation of a public-house or drink-shop.

1836 J. LIVESEY *Malt Liquor Lect.* in Pearce *Life* (1887), While about every twentieth house is metamorphosed into a drunkery. **1869** *Daily News* 29 June, He thought it was offensive to set up a drunkery in the middle of a public park.

drunkhead, drunkify, drunkish: see after DRUNK *ppl. a.*

drunklew: see DRUNKELEW.

†ˈ**drunkness.** *Obs.* Also 2-5 **drunkenesse.** [Early ME. *druncenesse*, for *druncennesse*: the *e* of the second syllable becoming at length mute.] = DRUNKENNESS.

c **1160** *Hatton Gosp.* Luke xxi. 34 Mid druncenesse. *c* **1175** *Lamb. Hom.* 33 ȝe nulleð forleten.. ȝifernesse and druncnesse. *c* **1386** CHAUCER *Pars. T.* ¶748 Dronkenesse that is the horrible sepulture of mannes reson. **1530** RASTELL *Bk. Purgat.* II. xvi, Over come by sykenes or by dronknes. **1655** H. VAUGHAN *Silex Scint.*, *Check* iv. (1858) 85 He bids beware of drunknes, surfeits, care. **1701** DE FOE *True-born Eng.* II. 100 Drunk'ness has been the Darling of the Realm, E'er since a Drunken Pilot had the Helm.

drunkometer (drʌŋˈkɒmɪtə(r)). *U.S.* [f. DRUNK *ppl. a.* + -OMETER.] A device for measuring the alcoholic content of a person's breath.

1934 *Jrnl. Amer. Med. Assoc.* 12 May 1597/1 Exhibit of automatic demonstration of the use of the 'drunkometer', a device for detecting drunkenness by testing the subject's breath. **1955** *Times* 20 July 6/1 Lord Mancroft said that three machines, the drunkometer, the alcohmeter, and the intoximeter had been developed in the United States. **1960** *New Statesman* 23 Jan. 95/1 Since the drunkometer has been used in New York, convictions for drunken driving have increased from 30 to 85 percent.

†ˈ**drunkship.** *Obs.* Also 4-5 drunke-, dronke-. [f. DRUNK *ppl. a.* + -SHIP; or shortened as DRUNKNESS from *drunkenship*.] = DRUNKENNESS.

1393 GOWER *Conf.* II. 132 Upon his drunkeship They bounden him with cheines faste. **1474** CAXTON *Chesse* III. vi. H iv b, Ful of glotonye and dronkship. *c* **1530** *Pol. Rel. & L. Poems* 32 Drunkeshippe doyth ryght nought evynly.

b. A drunken company.

1486 *Bk. St. Albans* F vij, A Dronkship of Coblers.

drunksome, drunky: see after DRUNK *ppl. a.*

drup, obs. form of DROOP.

drupaceous (druːˈpeɪʃəs), *a. Bot.* [f. mod.L. *drūpa*: see next and -ACEOUS.] Of the nature of a drupe, or characterized by bearing drupes; belonging to the *Drupaceæ*, a subdivision of the *Rosaceæ* bearing stone-fruits.

1822 GOOD *Study Med.* VI. iii. IV. 687 In drupaceous fruits. **1830** LINDLEY *Nat. Syst. Bot.* 74 Fruit 1-seeded, hard and dry, and drupaceous. **1835** —— *Introd. Bot.* (1848) I. 163 The Peach and other drupaceous plants. **1866** *Treas. Bot.* I. 54/2 The drupaceous subdivision of the rose family.

drupe (druːp). *Bot.* [ad. mod. Bot. L. *drūpa*, a stone-fruit, L. *drūpa*, *druppa* (sc. *olīva*) over-ripe, wrinkled olive = Gr. δρύππα in same sense; cf. F. *drupe* (1798 in Hatz.-Darm.).] A stone-fruit; a fleshy or pulpy fruit enclosing a stone or nut having a kernel, as the olive, plum, and cherry.

1753 CHAMBERS *Cycl. Supp.*, *Drupe*, among botanists, a species of pericarpium, consisting of a soft, fleshy, and succulent pulp, in the center of which there is a nucleus. **1791** W. BARTRAM *Carolina* 41 From the bosom of each leaf is produced a single oval drupe. **1828** STARK *Elem. Nat. Hist.* II. 469 Jasmineæ.. Their fruit is a capsule, a drupe or a berry. *c* **1854** WHITTIER *Lay Old Time* 2 Sighing o'er his bitter fruit For Eden's drupes of gold. **1870** BENTLEY *Bot.* 305 The Drupe is a superior, one-celled, one or 2 seeded, indehiscent fruit, having a fleshy or pulpy sarcocarp.

drupel (ˈdruːpəl). *Bot.* [ad. mod.L. *drupella*, dim. of *drūpa* DRUPE.] A little drupe: such as those of which a blackberry is composed.

1835 HENSLOW *Princ. Bot.* 108 The numerous small drupes, or 'drupels' of the raspberry, and other Rubi. **1870** BENTLEY *Bot.* 308. **1872** OLIVER *Elem. Bot.* I. vii. 96 The fruit of the Blackberry.. consisting of a number of succulent little drupes (called drupels).. each drupel answering to an achene of buttercup or strawberry.

drupelet (ˈdruːplɪt). *Bot.* [-LET.] = prec.

1880 *Gray's Struct. Bot.* vii. §2. 297 The several pericarps of the aggregate blackberry and raspberry are diminutive drupes or Drupelets.

drupeole (ˈdruːpiːəʊl). *Bot.* [f. L. type **drūpeola*, irregularly formed dim. of *drūpa*: cf. mod.F. *drupéole*, *drupole*.] = prec.

1866 *Treas. Bot.*, *Drupeole*, a little drupe.

dru'piferous, *a. rare.* [f. mod.L. *drūpa* + -FEROUS: in F. *drupifère*.] Drupe-bearing.

1775 ROMANS *Hist. Florida* 85 Wild plants chiefly of the Drupiferous and Bacciferous kind.

drupose (ˈdruːpəʊs). *Chem.* [f. DRUPE + -OSE, forming names of carbo-hydrates, as *glucose*, *dextrose*.] (See quot.)

1872 WATTS *Dict. Chem.* VI. 547 *Drupose*, $C_{12}H_2O_8$, a substance produced together with glucose, by the action of boiling moderately diluted hydrochloric acid on glycodrupose, the stony concretions found in pears.. It is a greyish-red body, similar in structure and physical properties to glycodrupose.

druri, -y, obs. forms of DREARY *a.*

drurie, var. of DROWRIE, Sc. f. DOWRY.

drury, var. of DRUERY *Obs.*

druse[1] (druːz). *Min.* [a. G. *druse* = Boh. *druza* in same sense.] **a.** A crust of small crystals lining the sides of a cavity in a rock. **b.** A cavity of this description.

[**1753** CHAMBERS *Cycl. Supp.*, *Drusa*,.. a name given by some of the Saxon miners to the common pyrites, and by others to some peculiar kinds of it.] **1811** PINKERTON *Petrol.* II. 576 A hard concreted stony crust, called *druse*, adhering to the inside of the cavity. **1839** MURCHISON *Silur. Syst.* I. xx. 260 Veins and druses lined with crystals of quartz. *a* **1852** MACGILLIVRAY *Nat. Hist. Dee Side* (1855) 454 Good crystals occasionally one inch broad are found in druses of the Granite on Bennachiche.

Druse[2], **Druze** (druːz), *sb.* (*a.*) [ad. Arab. *Durūz*, a form of plural used for names of nations: see note below.] One of a political and religious sect of Mohammedan origin, inhabiting the region round Mount Lebanon in Syria.

Believed to derive their name from *Ismail al-Darazi* (i.e. the tailor), who, in A.D. 1040, supported the claims of the 6th Fatimite Caliph, Hakim Biamrillahi, to be a divine incarnation, and introduced this belief to the Lebanon.

1786 tr. *Ruffin* (title) A historical Memoir concerning the Drusis, a people inhabiting Mount Lebanon; a Catechism [etc.], translated from Drusean MSS. **1798** SOTHEBY tr. *Wieland's Oberon* (1826) I. 125 Sithence our Drusi prince is loathsome grown. **1837** *Penny Cycl.* IX. 160/1 The emir of the Druses is tributary to the pachalik of Acre, on condition that no Turk shall reside within his territories. **1895** W. WRIGHT *Palmyra & Zenobia* xxv. 298 The thick stumpy Druze women.

Hence ˈ**Drusedom**, the system of the Druses. Also ˈ**Drusian, -ean**, *sb.* (*obs.*) and *a.*

1601 R. JOHNSON *Kingd. & Commw.* (1603) 553 Sydon, now the strong receptacle of the stiffe-necked Drusians. **1613** PURCHAS *Pilgrimage* (1614) 87 A Drusian Lord, kept himselfe out of his hands. **1786** [see above]. **1877** *Encycl. Brit.* VII. 484/1 The full exposition of the Drusian creed.. would require a volume of considerable size. **1890** *Blackw. Mag.* CXLVIII. 750/2 A convert from Drusedom. *Ibid.* 762/2 The dogmas of esoteric Drusedom.

ˈ**drusiform**, *a. rare.* [f. DRUSE[1] + -FORM.] Having the form of druse.

1757 tr. *Henckel's Pyritol.* 361 Drusiform mountain-crystal.

drust, obs. form of *durst*, pa. t. of DARE *v.*[1]

drusy (ˈdruːzɪ), *a.* [f. DRUSE[1] + -Y.] Covered or lined with a crust of minute crystals.

1794 KIRWAN *Elem. Min.* (ed. 2) I. 31 A surface on which very minute crystals abound is called drusy. **1841** TRIMMER *Pract. Geol.* 83. **1869** PHILLIPS *Vesuv.* xi. 308 Occasional cavities—drusy or lined with crystals. **1879** RUTLEY *Study Rocks* x. 155 The botryoidal or mammillated forms of hematite.. line drusy cavities.

drusye, obs. form of DROWSY.

†**drut.** *Obs.* In 3 **druð**, 5 **druit.** [a. OF. *drud*, *drut*, *dru* friend, lover: see DRUERY.

The OF. word, orig. adj., = It. *drudo*, late L. *drudus* (Capitulary of Charles the Bald), is app. of German origin, corresp. to OHG. *trut* (in Otfrid *drut*, *drud*), Ger. *traut* dear, beloved: see Kluge and Diez.]

Darling, love, friend.

a **1240** *Wohunge* in *Cott. Hom.* 269 Ihesu swete ihesu mi druð mi derling. *a* **1400-50** *Alexander* 5123, I drysse ȝow here a diademe ȝoure druits to were.

druther (ˈdrʌðə(r)). U.S. dialectal alteration of (*I, you*, etc.) *would rather*. Hence ˈ**druther(s)**, ˈ**ruther(s)**, a choice, preference.

1876 [see DERN *a.*]. **1895** *Dialect Notes* I. 388 Bein's I caint have my druthers an' set still, I cal'late I'd better pearten up an' go 'long. **1896** 'MARK TWAIN' *Tom Sawyer, Detective* ix. 74 'Any way you druther have it, that is the way *I* druther have it. He—— '. 'There ain't any druthers *about* it, Huck Finn; nobody said anything about druthers.' **1941** W. A. PERCY *Lanterns on Levee* (1948) xxii. 292 'Your ruthers is my ruthers' (what you would rather is what I would rather). Certainly the most amiable and appeasing phrase in any language, the language used being not English but deep Southern.

druvy: see DROVY.

druwery, var. DRUERY.

druxy ('drʌksɪ), *a.* Also 6 **dricksie**. [formerly *dricksie*, f. DRIX + -Y.] Of timber: Having decayed spots concealed by healthy wood.

1589 PUTTENHAM *Eng. Poesie* III. xix. (Arb.) 252 We liken ..an old man who laboureth with continuall infirmities, to a drie and dricksie oke. **1711** W. SUTHERLAND *Shipbuilder's Assist.* 160 Druxy Plank or Timber decayed and spungy. **18..** *Lloyds' Reg.* in Dana *Seamen's Friend* (1856) 347 The inside planking to be..free from all foxy, druxy, or decayed planks. *c* **1850** *Rudim. Navig.* (Weale) 116 *Druxey*, a state of decay in timber with white spongy veins, the most deceptive of any defect. **1875** LASLETT *Timber & Timber Trees* 36 Producing..what is technically termed a 'druxy knot'.

druye, druyȝe, obs. forms of DRY.

drw, obs. form of *drew*, pa. t. of DRAW *v.*

drwry, var. DRUERY; rare obs. f. DREARY *a.*

dry (draɪ), *a.* (*adv.*) Forms: 1 **drýᵹe, dríᵹe**, 2–4 **driȝe, drei(e**, 3 **druie**, (*Orm.*) **driȝȝe**, 3–4 **druye, drue**, 3–7 **drie**, 4 **dryȝe, druiȝe, druyȝe, draye, dreȝe, drey(e, dri**, 4–7 **drye**, 6 **drygh, drigh**, 4– **dry**. [OE. *drýᵹe* (:—**drûgi-*) in ablaut relation with MDu. *dröghe, drōghe*, Du. *droog*, MLG., LG. *drög(e, droge, dreuge* (:—**draugi-*), f. OTeut. ablaut-series **dreug-, draug-, drug-* to be dry, whence also OE. *drúᵹian* to dry, *drúᵹað* DROUGHT, and (with formative suffix) OHG. *trochan*, Ger. *trocken* dry.]

A. *adj.* I. As a physical quality.

1. a. Destitute of or free from moisture; not wet or moist; arid; of the eyes, free from tears.

c **1000** *Ags. Gosp.* Matt. xii. 43 He gæð ᵹeond driᵹe stowa [*Lindisf. G.* dryia, *Rushw. G.* dryᵹe, *Hatton G.* dreᵹe stowa]. *a* **1175** *Cott. Hom.* 227 He hi ledde ofer sé mid dreie fote. *c* **1175** *Lamb. Hom.* 87 God hom ledde ofer þa rede se, mid druȝe fotan. **1340** *Ayenb.* 240 Ase þe desert is hard and draye. *c* **1374** CHAUCER *Anel. & Arc.* 336 Ne never mo myne eyen two bee drye. *c* **1400** *Lanfranc's Cirurg.* 125 þei leien a dreie cloop vndir. *c* **1440** *Promp. Parv.* 132/1 Dry fro moysture, *siccus.* **1529** RASTELL *Pastyme, Hist. Brit.* (1811) 155 Men [went] over a fote drye. *a* **1562** G. CAVENDISH *Wolsey* (1893) 243 Among whome was not oon drie eye. **1598** R. BERNARD tr. *Terence* (1607) 226 As dry as a kixe [= kex]. **1670** NARBOROUGH *Jrnl.* in *Acc. Sev. Late Voy.* I. (1711) 52 The Air rather sharper and dryer. **1697** DRYDEN *Virg. Georg.* IV. 542 Rub his Temples, with fine Towels, dry. **1799** *Med. Jrnl.* I. 299 Atmospheric air in the driest possible state. **1806–7** J. BERESFORD *Miseries Hum. Life* (1826) II. xviii, Till every blade is as dry as a bone. ? **1834** *Orange Song* (in *Hansard* Ser. III. XXXII. 717), Then put your trust in God, my boys, And keep your powder dry!

†**b.** In mediæval physiology: One of the fundamental qualities of elements, humours, planets, etc.; opp. to *moist*. (See COLD *a.* 6.) *Obs.*

c **888** K. ÆLFRED *Boeth.* xxxiii. §4 Sie eorþ is dryᵹe and ceald. *c* **1050** *Byrhtferth's Handboc* in *Anglia* VIII. 299 Eorðe ys ceald and driᵹᵹe. *a* **1300** *Cursor M.* 3563 His blode þan wexus dri and cald. *c* **1400** *Lanfranc's Cirurg.* 10 þe qualitees..ben foure: hoot, coold, moist and drie. **1578** LYTE *Dodoens* III. lxxviii. 426 Aconit is hoate and drie in the fourth degree. **1621** BURTON *Anat. Mel.* I. ii. III. xv. (1651) 128 Saturn and Mercury, the Patrons of Learning, are both dry Planets. **1819** J. WILSON *Compl. Dict. Astrol.* 3 Madness, melancholy..and all diseases proceeding from a dry habit.

c. Of a season or climate: Free from or deficient in rain; having scanty rainfall; not rainy.

1297 R. GLOUC. (1724) 531 Thulke ȝer was that somer so druye & so hot. **1500–20** DUNBAR *Thistle & Rose* 70 Dame Nature..bad eik Juno..That scho the hevin suld keip amene and dry. **1613** PURCHAS *Pilgrimage* (1614) 560 Mise are multiplied in drie seasons. **1626** BACON *Nat. Hist.* §807 A Drie March, and a Drie May, portend a Wholesome Summer, if there be a Showring Aprill betweene. *a* **1715** BURNET *Own Time* (1766) I. 322 The Summer had been the driest that was known of some years. *c* **1893** [see WET *a.* 2 a]. *a* **1897** *Mod.* Arable land that does fairly well in a dry year. **1932** J. S. HUXLEY *Prob. Rel. Growth* ii. 71 The wet-season and dry-season forms of certain tropical butterflies. **1964** C. WILLOCK *Enormous Zoo* vii. 113 A Rhodesian dry season track which was rarely used by vehicles.

2. a. That has given up or lost its natural or ordinary moisture; dried, desiccated, parched, withered. Now *arch.* or sunk in sense 1.

c **950** *Lindisf. Gosp.* Luke xxiii. 31 Forðon ᵹif in groene tree ðas doað, in dryᵹi huæd worðes? [*Rushw.* on dryᵹe, *Ags. G.* on þam driᵹean.] *a* **1225** *Ancr. R.* 276 Ofte druie sprintles bereð winberien? *a* **1300** *Cursor M.* 20747 His arms war al clungen dri [*v. rr.* drei, dry]. **1398** TREVISA *Barth. De P.R.* XVII. xxxvii. (1495) 625 Yf olde men ete ofte drye fygges. *c* **1450** *St. Cuthbert* (Surtees) 3523 When my mouthe was dry for thrist. **1582** N. LICHEFIELD tr. *Castanheda's Conq. E. Ind.* xxiv. 61 Greate store of drie Cinamon. **1677** *Lond. Gaz.* No. 1232/1, 3 French Prizes, laden with dry Fish from Newfoundland. **1756** C. LUCAS *Ess. Waters* I. 79 A dry tongue can no more taste, than a dry eye see..distinctly.

b. Said of a body of water, or of moisture on a surface, that has disappeared by evaporation, or by being wiped or drained away: Dried up.

c **1386** CHAUCER *Knt.'s T.* 2166 The brode Ryuer somtyme waxeth dreye. **1563** W. FULKE *Meteors* (1640) 2 b, If there be a plash of water..standing in the heate of the Sunne, it will soone be drie. **1632** LITHGOW *Trav.* VI. 279 We saw a quadrangled dry Pond. **1697** DAMPIER *Voy.* I. v. 95 Some small Rivers..are dry at certain seasons of the year. **1707** WATTS *Hymn 'Come, we that love the Lord'* x, Then let our songs abound, And ev'ry tear be dry. ? **1799** in J. W. Cole *Lives Generals Penin. War* (1832) I. ii. 78 Before the sweat was dry on his brow.

3. a. Of persons: Wanting or desirous of drink; thirsty. Cf. A-DRY. (Now only in vulgar use.) **b.** *transf.* Of things or conditions: Causing thirst.

1406 HOCCLEVE *La Male Regle* 135 The thirsty hete of hertes drie. *a* **1536** *Calisto & Mel.* in Hazl. *Dodsley* I. 79 To eat when I will, and drink when I am dry. **1657** COKAINE *Obstinate Lady* IV. iii, *Boy.* I am very dry with singing and dancing. *Jaq.* Follow me to the wine cellar! **1738** WESLEY *Hymn, 'Of Him who did Salvation bring'* viii, I drink, and yet am ever dry. **1807** PIKE *Sources Mississ.* (1810) II. 182, I returned hungry, weary and dry, and had only snow to supply the calls of nature. **1890** *Beeton's Christm. Ann.* 17 Come in, you look dry; let's have a wet. *Mod.* Better have a pint; it's dry work.

fig. **1610** SHAKS. *Temp.* I. ii. 112 So drie he was for Sway.

4. a. Not yielding water (or other liquid); exhausted of its supply of liquid.

a **1300** *Cursor M.* 310 (Gött.) He es welle þat neuer is drey. **1576** FLEMING *Panopl. Epist.* 378 It would..drawe the veyne of mine invention drie. **1642** FULLER *Holy & Prof. St.* IV. xiii. 304 It must be a dry flower..out of which this bee sucks no honey. **1874** J. T. MICKLETHWAITE *Modern Par. Churches* 160 A dry inkstand. **1883** *Century Mag.* July 323/1 Wasting large sums of money on 'dry holes' [unproductive oil-wells]. *Mod.* Our own well never runs dry.

b. *spec.* Of cows, sheep, etc.: Not yielding milk.

c **1440** *Jacob's Well* (E.E.T.S.) 37 ȝif þou paye tythe for leyse to þi mylche beestys, & noȝt of þi drye beestys. **1523** FITZHERB. *Husb.* §39 The dammes wil waxe drye, and wayne theyr lambes theym selfe. **1658** W. BURTON *Itin. Anton.* 187 (L.) At home their allowance..was no more than three milch cowes; and in case any of them became dry, the parishioners supplied them again. **1789** *Trans. Soc. Arts* (ed. 2) II. 100 What we term dry sheep (viz. wethers, barren ewes, &c.). **1890** *Daily News* 8 Dec. 26/5 Twenty thousand breeding ewes..the remainder being what are called 'dry sheep'.

5. Not under, in, or on water; not submerged (see also DRY LAND); †inland (quot. 1599); drawn or cast up on shore, as a boat or a fish.

c **1200** ORMIN 14862 Swa þatt teȝȝ o þe driȝȝe grund Wel sæȝhenn openn weȝȝe. *a* **1300** *Cursor M.* 381 Drightin..bad a dri sted suld be. **1393** GOWER *Conf.* I. 220 Came none of hem to londe drey. *c* **1460** *Towneley Myst.* 2 That at is dry the erth shalle be, The waters also I calle the see. **1599** HAKLUYT *Voy.* II. 268 Aleppo..is the greatest place of traffique for a dry towne that is in all these parts. **1699** DAMPIER *Voy.* II. II. 93 The Head of his Ketch was dry, and at the Stern, there was above 4 Foot Water. **1793** SMEATON *Edystone L.* §195 *note*, In dry work the difference of hardness ..is less apparent. **1798** R. DODD *Port Lond.* 5 Further dry arches on each shore. **1816** KEATINGE *Trav.* (1817) II. 55 The tide leaves them dry.

6. Of bread (or toast): Without butter or the like.

1579 FULKE *Refut. Rastell* 762 The words..wold not agree to drie bread. **1840** DICKENS *Old C. Shop* (libr. ed.) II. ix. 66 Making some thin dry toast. **1884** G. ALLEN *Philistia* III. 157 The meal..of dry bread with plain tea.

7. Solid, not liquid.

1722 OGLE in *Lond. Gaz.* No. 6091/1 Neither the Wine nor dry Provisions were come. **1806** HUTTON *Course Math.* I. 27 By this are measured all dry wares, as, Corn, Seeds, Roots, Fruits, Salt, Coals, Sand, Oysters, &c.

8. Of wines, etc.: Free from sweetness and fruity flavour.

a **1700** B. E. *Dict. Cant. Crew*, *Dry-wine*, a little rough upon, but very grateful to the Palate. **1706** FARQUHAR *Recruiting Officer* III. (1728) 43 Many a dry bottle have we crack'd hand to fist. **1848** THACKERAY *Bk. Snobs* xlviii, Where's the old dry wine? **1887** J. A. STERRY *Lazy Minstr.*, *Bolney Ferry* (1892) 187 In Mrs. Williams' driest sherry He toasts the Lass of Bolney Ferry!

9. *Metallurgy.* Said of copper, tin, or lead, in the brittle and coarse-grained condition which they exhibit before refining, or when insufficiently deoxidated in refining.

1875 *Ure's Dict. Arts* I. 918 When the operation of refining begins, the copper is dry or brittle..Its grain is coarse, open, and somewhat crystalline. *Ibid.* 919 Copper, in the dry state, has a strong action upon iron. **1881** RAYMOND *Mining Gloss.*, *Dry copper. Under-poled copper.* Copper not poled enough to remove all sub-oxide.

10. *transf.* Of or relating to dry substances or commodities; ***dry measure***, measure of capacity for non-liquids.

1688 R. HOLME *Armoury* III. 337/2 A Pint..is the least of dry measures. **1882** VINES *Sachs' Bot.* 703 The loss in the dry weight connected with the exhalation of carbon dioxide. **1887** *Whitaker's Almanack* 363 In dry or corn measure, eight bushels..make a quarter. **1891** *Daily News* 9 Nov. 3/6 In both wet and dry departments separate rooms are set apart for all deadly drugs.

11. Not associated or connected with liquid. **a.** Not accompanied or associated with drink; orig. in *U.S. political slang*, said of places which favour the prohibition of the liquor traffic. Also, of a person who favours prohibition; hence quasi-*advb.* in phrases ***to go*** or ***vote dry***. **b.** Of diseases, etc.: Not marked by a discharge of matter, phlegm, etc. **c.** Not accompanied with tears. †**d.** Not accompanied with bloodshed: see also f. (*obs.*) **e.** Said of processes or apparatus in which no liquid is used. **f.** phr. ***to die a dry death***: i.e. without bloodshed, or (in Shaks.) without drowning.

a. **1483** *Cath. Angl.* 108/2 A Dry feste, *xerofagia.* **1579** FULKE *Refut. Rastell* 778 The Papistes make a drie communion, when they robbe the people of the cuppe. **1591** G. FLETCHER *Russe Commw.* 13 Priviledge to drinke..at drye or prohibited times. **1599** H. BUTTES *Dyets drie Dinner* A v, A Dry Dinner..without all drinke, except Tobacco (which also is but Dry Drinke). **1667** POOLE *Dial. betw. Protest. & Papist* (1735) 198 It was not a dry Feast..they had drink with it. **1870** *Scribner's Monthly* I. 63 Dry or wet, Mr. Dort? Indifferent, eh? Adolph, a hock-glass. **1887** *Courier-Journal* 7 Feb. 1/7 Athens, in which the State university is located,..is a dry town. **1888** BRYCE *Amer. Commw.* II. liv. 350 *note*, A local option system, under which each county decides whether it will be 'wet' or 'dry' (i.e. permit or forbid the sale of intoxicants). **1888** *Detroit Evening Jrnl.* 20 Feb. (Farmer), If a county has voted on local option, and has gone dry. **1892** *Daily News* 7 Apr. 3/6 Dividing the receipts at the music-halls..as they are named in the trade 'Wet Money' and 'Dry Money' [i.e. money paid for refreshments, and for admission]. **1904** *N.Y. Even. Post* 3 Oct. 6 If every town and city in Vermont should vote 'dry' at the next election. **1908** [see WET *a.* 16 c]. **1916** *Literary Digest* (N.Y.) 1 Jan. 4/2 About as much 'dry' territory 'going wet' as there was of 'wet' territory 'going dry'. **1944** W. R. SCOTT *Revolt on Mount Sinai* xxii. 179 Many members who long had voted dry accepted the election result as a mandate from the people. **1971** *Scotsman* 20 May 20/8 If the people of Kirkintilloch could be consulted on the issue of whether they should remain 'dry' or 'wet' it was difficult to see whether they should not also be consulted on the question of whether they should enter the Common Market.

b. *c* **1400** *Lanfranc's Cirurg.* 57 þe drie discrasie þou schalt knowe bi þe..litil quytture. **1581** MULCASTER *Positions* xii. (1887) 61 Good for the drie cowghe. **1704** F. FULLER *Med. Gymn.* (1718) 182 Occasion'd by the Dry-Gripes of that Country. **1811** HOOPER *Med. Dict.* s.v. *Colica*, This is called ..from its victims, the plumbers' and the painters' colic; from its symptoms, the dry belly-ache, the nervous and spasmodic colic. **1834** J. FORBES *Laennec's Dis. Chest* (ed. 4) 83 The expression dry catarrh involves a contradiction if we look to etymology..I shall employ it..to designate those inflammations of the bronchi which are attended with little or no expectoration.

c. **1619** W. WHATELEY *God's Husb.* ii. (1622) 49 The Lord will not reiect dry sorrow, if he see it hearty and true. *a* **1700** DRYDEN (J.), Dry mourning will decays more deadly bring ..Give sorrow vent, and let the sluices go. **1852** HAWTHORNE *Blithedale Rom.* xxv, Dry sobs they seemed to be.

d. **1618** DANIEL *Coll. Hist. Eng.* 75 (D.) Thus are both sides busied in this drie warre. **1660** FULLER *Mixt Contempl.* (1841) 204 If we should be blessed with a dry peace, without one drop of blood therein.

e. **1796** KIRWAN *Elem. Min.* (ed. 2) II. 395 In the Dry way, it may be essayed when pulverized. **1816** J. SMITH *Panorama Sc. & Art* II. 386 Iron..precipitates nickel from its acid solutions, and in the dry way takes from it the sulphur which it contains. *c* **1865** LETHEBY in *Circ. Sc.* I. 127/2 The first dry-meter was patented by Mr. Malam in 1820. **1879** J. M. DUNCAN *Lect. Dis. Women* xxx. (1889) 250, I have often seen the knife used in the manner which..is called dry tapping. **1890** WALMSLEY *Electr. in Serv. Man* 108 Dry piles—that is, batteries where no fluids were used —were first constructed by Behrens (1806).

f. **1591** SHAKS. *Two Gent.* I. i. 158 Destin'd to a drier death on shore. **1610** —— *Temp.* I. i. 72, I would faine dye a dry death. **1594** *Mirr. Policy* (1599) E iij, Tyrants..goe neuer to Pluto with a drie death..without bloud and murder. **1688** R. L'ESTRANGE *Brief Hist. Times* III. 275 He dy'd rather a Dry Death, then a Bloudy.

†**12.** Of a blow, or a beating: properly, That does not draw blood (as a blow given with a stick or the fist, which merely causes a bruise); by some app. used vaguely, = Hard, stiff, severe. *Obs.*

1530 PALSGR. 306/2 Blo, blewe and grene coloured, as ones body is after a drie stroke. **1577** tr. *Bullinger's Decades* (1592) 94 A Iewe..couered with woundes and swelling drye blowes. **1590** SHAKS. *Com. Err.* II. ii. 64. **1616** SURFL. & MARKH. *Country Farme* 711 Give him many a drie bob. **1709** STEELE *Tatler* No. 38 ¶3 Many a dry Blow was strenuously laid on by each Side. **1711** *Vind. Sacheverell* 44 The Fellow..had an honest dry drubbing. *a* **1774** GOLDSM. tr. *Scarron's Comic Rom.* I. 104 Having got nothing but dry blows and empty pockets.

II. Figurative senses.

13. Feeling or showing no emotion, impassive; destitute of tender feeling; wanting in sympathy or cordiality; stiff, hard, cold. In early use, chiefly: Wanting spiritual emotion or unction.

c **1200** ORMIN 9883 Hæþenn follkess herrte Iss..driȝȝe, & all wiþþutenn dæw. *c* **1380** WYCLIF *Sel. Wks.* III. 27 Weetynge of hevenly deew to her drie hertis. *c* **1450** tr. *De Imitatione* II. viii. 48 Hov dry & hov harde þou art wiþoute ihesu! **1526** *Pilgr. Perf.* (W. de W. 1531) 87 b, Drye, dull, or vndeuoute in spirituall thynges. **1637** RUTHERFORD *Lett.* (1862) I. 440 He..is grown miskenning and dry to His poor friends. **1761–2** HUME *Hist. Eng.* (1806) V. lxxi. 321 Noted for an address so cold, dry, and distant, that it was very difficult..to soften or familiarize it. **1825** T. JEFFERSON *Autobiog.* Wks. 1859 I. 110 Lord North's answers were dry, unyielding..and betrayed an absolute indifference to the occurrence of a rupture. **1852** MRS. STOWE *Uncle Tom's C.* xxvi. 244 'Well!' said St. Clare, in a tone of dry endurance.

14. Said of a jest or sarcasm uttered in a matter-of-fact tone and without show of pleasantry, or of humour that has the air of being unconscious or unintentional; also of a person given to such humour; caustically witty; in early use, ironical.

1542 UDALL *Erasm. Apoph.* Pref. *v, Of the subtile knackes, of the drye mockes..whiche Socrates dooeth there vse. **1589** PUTTENHAM *Eng. Poesie* III. xviii. (Arb.) 199 The figure Ironia, which we call the drye mock. **1601** SHAKS. *Twel. N.* I. iii. 81, I. v. 45. **1709** *Rambl. Fuddle-Cups* 7 Keep your Flirts to your self, and your merry dry Bobs. **1818** SCOTT *Hrt. Midl.* v, [He] was..something of a humorist and dry joker. **1864** BURTON *Scot Abr.* I. iii. 129 Froissart, with a touch of dry humour, explains that their allies had no objection to speed the exit of the poorer knights.

†**15. a.** Yielding no fruit, result, or satisfaction; barren, sterile, unfruitful, jejune. (Cf. 4.) *Obs.* (or merged in sense 17).

a **1340** HAMPOLE *Psalter* vi. 6, I sall make it to bere froit, þat bifore was drye fra goed werkes. **1526** *Pilgr. Perf.* (W. de W. 1531) 67 b, He shall go drye, and for a surety haue no perfeccyon. **1590** SPENSER *F.Q.* I. i. 42 One.. whose dryer braine Is tost with troubled sights and fancies weake. *a* **1680** GLANVILL (J.), That the fire burns by heat, is an empty dry return to the question, and leaves us still ignorant.

†**b.** Of persons: Miserly, stingy; reserved, uncommunicative. (Cf. 4.) *Obs.*

1552 HULOET, Drye fellow whom some call a pelt or pinchbecke. **1604** etc. [see DRY-FIST]. **1611** COTGR. s.v. *Acquests*, He is but a drie fellow, there is nought to be got by dealing with him. **1681** W. ROBERTSON *Phraseol. Gen.* (1693) 509 Dry or reserved. **1688–9** LD. CLARENDON *Diary* (T.), He thanked me.. and said, he had not seen so particular an account of those affairs before: but he was very dry as to all things else.

16. Lacking adornment or embellishment, or some addition; meagre, plain, bare; matter-of-fact.

1626 LAUD *Wks.* (1849) II. 370 And if they say.. they believe them in the Church's sense; yet that dry shift will not serve. *a* **1637** B. JONSON *Discoveries, Precipiendi modi* (1640) 116 As wee should take care, that our style in writing, be neither dry, nor empty. **1647** H. MORE *Song of Soul* To Rdr. 7/1 Contemplations concerning the dry essence of the Deity are very consuming and unsatisfactory. **1648** GAGE *West Ind.* ii. 6 With a pension and dry title only. **1678** CUDWORTH *Intell. Syst.* Pref., Enforced thereunto, by Dry Mathematicall Reason. *c* **1714** LADY M. W. MONTAGU *Let. to Mrs. Hewet* (1887) I. 34 I would willingly return.. something more.. than dry thanks impertinently expressed. **1803** LD. ELDON in *Vesey's Rep.* VIII. 435 It is the case of a dry trust, all the debts and legacies being long paid. **1859** DARWIN *Orig. Spec.* ii, A long catalogue of dry facts.

17. Deficient in interest; unattractive, distasteful, insipid. (*fig.* from food that wants succulency.)

1621 BURTON *Anat. Mel.* I. ii. I. ii. (1651) 39 Our subtle Schoolmen.. are weak, dry, obscure. **1661** PEPYS *Diary* 12 May, Methought it was a poor dry Sermon. **1712** ADDISON *Spect.* No. 315 ¶3 These Points are dry in themselves to the generality of Readers. **1780** HARRIS *Philol. Enq.* Wks. (1841) 425 If these speculations appear too dry, they may be rendered more pleasing, if the reader would peruse the two pieces criticised. **1790** J. Q. ADAMS *Wks.* (1854) IX. 567 Mankind have an aversion to the study of the science of government. Is it because the subject is dry? **1845** M. PATTISON *Ess.* (1889) I. 14 Annals.. valuable to the antiquary, but dry and profitless to others.

18. a. *Art.* Characterized by stiff and formal outlines; lacking in softness or mellowness; frigidly precise.

1716 *Notes Dryden's transl. Du Fresnoy's Art Painting* 224 His Manner was Gothique and very dry. *Ibid.* 227 [His] manner was drier and harder than any of Raphael's School. *a* **1792** SIR J. REYNOLDS *Journ. Flanders & Holland* (R.), The fall of the Angels, by F. Floris, 1554; which has some good parts, but without masses, and dry. **1850** LEITCH *Müller's Anc. Art* §205. 195 The workmanship, however, is still drier than in the Antonines. **1876** HUMPHREYS *Coin-Coll. Man.* xxiv. 353 A dry and hard manner of execution.

b. Of acoustics: lacking in warmth or resonance.

1961 *Listener* 2 Nov. 715/2 When an orchestra broadcasts in a television studio, where the acoustic is likelier to be drier. **1962** A. NISBETT *Technique Sound Studio* ii. 53 Some modern music is now written for drier acoustics than those which sound best for Beethoven.

19. Of money, rent, or fees: Paid in hard cash, in actual coin. [Cf. F. *argent sec, perte sèche.*]

1574 HELLOWES *Gueuara's Fam. Ep.* 162 Such as shal play at Cardes or dice for drie money. **1656** J. HARRINGTON *Oceana* (1700) 36 Worth a matter of four millions dry rents. **1664** PEPYS *Diary* 30 Sept., I am fain to preserve my vowe by paying 20s. dry money into the poor's box. **1694** *Provid. God* 64 That what could not be done by dry Money, might be by Debauchery. **1713** ADDISON *Guardian* No. 97 ¶5 To Zelinda's woman.. fifteen guineas in dry money. **1725** BERKELEY *Let. to T. Prior* 12 June Wks. 1871 IV. 112 It hath cost me 130 pounds dry fees, besides expedition-money to men in office. **1885** *Standard* 3 Apr. 2/6 He had played in Defendant's house.. but not for 'dry money'.

20. *dry light* (an expression derived from a doubtful or corrupt passage in Heraclitus; ed. Bywater 30): 'Light' untinged by any infusion of personal predilection, prejudice, or fancy.

1625 BACON *Ess., Friendship* ¶7 Heraclitus saith in one of his Ænigmaes: Dry Light is euer the best. —— *Apophth.* 268 Heraclitus the Obscure sayd: The drie Light was the best Soule. Meaning, when the Faculties Intellectual are in vigour, not wet, nor, as it were, blouded by the Affections. **1870** LOWELL *Among my Bks.* Ser. I. (1873) 149 The web that looks so familiar and ordinary in the dry light of every day.

B. as *adv.* In a dry manner, dryly. (See C. 2.)

1513 *Act 5 Hen. VIII*, c. 4. §1 If the same Worsted, so dry calandred, taketh any Wet. **1710–11** SWIFT *Lett.* (1767) III. 97 I talk dry and cross to him. **1765** A. DICKSON *Treat. Agric.* xix. (ed. 2) 331 Where the land is very dry situated. **1833** MARRYAT *P. Simple* xxviii, 'He's rowing *dry*, your honour—only making bilave.'

C. Combinations.

1. Parasynthetic, as **dry-eyed** *a.*, having dry eyes, tearless, not weeping; ***dry-boned, -fancied, -handed, -leaved, -lipped, -skinned, -tongued,*** etc. adjs.; also ***dry-looking*** adj. See also DRY-FISTED, -FOOTED.

1618 BRATHWAIT *Descr. Death* in Farr *S.P. Jas. I* (1848) 271 Chop-falne, crest-sunke, *drie-bon'd anatomie. **1667** MILTON *P.L.* XI. 495 Sight so deform what heart of Rock could long *Drie-ey'd behold? **1890** *Pall Mall G.* 3 Sept. 6/2 The face.. has the drawn expression of dry-eyed grief. **1682** H. MORE *Annot. Glanvill's Lux O.* 50 Any *dry-fancied Metaphysicians. *a* **1661** HOLYDAY *Juvenal* 241 As in a *drie-mouth'd feaver. **1855** TENNYSON *Maud* I. xviii. 8 The *dry-tongued laurels' pattering talk.

2. Adverbial, in comb. with verbs and their derivatives. **a.** In a dry way; without the use of liquid; without drawing blood: as ***dry-feed, -rub, -scratch, -scrub, -wash,*** etc., vbs.; ***dry-blowing*** pres. pple.; ***dry-washing***; †**dry-bang,** †**dry-baste** *vbs.* = DRY-BEAT; **dry-clean** *v. trans.*, to clean (clothes and other textiles) without using water; also *intr.* and *transf.*; hence ***dry-cleanable*** adj., ***dry-cleaned*** ppl. adj., ***dry-cleaner, dry-cleaning*** vbl. sb. and ppl. adj.; **dry-cupping,** see CUPPING 1; **dry-cure** *v.*, to cure meat, etc. by salting and drying, as distinguished from pickling; **dry-dyeing** (see quot. 1904); **dry-grind** *v.*, to grind articles of cutlery without the use of water; hence **dry-grinder,** a workman employed in ***dry-grinding***; so **dry-pointing,** e.g. of needles and table-forks; **dry-salt** *v.* = *dry-cure*; **dry-shave** *v.*, (see quots.).

c **1600** DAY *Begg. Bednall Gr.* IV. iii, And I did not *dry bang ye all one after another I'de eat no more but Mustard. **1630** WADSWORTH *Sp. Pilgr.* vi. 58 They.. *dry-basted brother Hill and left vs. **1728–46** THOMSON *Spring* 115 If.. a cutting gale.. *dry-blowing, breathe Untimely frost. **1817** W. TUCKER *Family Dyer & Scourer* i. 20 For *dry cleaning Clothes of any Colour. **1897** *Chambers's Jrnl.* 25 Sept. 620/2 A firm of so-called 'dry-cleaners' of wearing apparel. *Ibid.*, In this dry-cleaning process the goods were immersed in a vessel of benzine. **1899** *Westm. Gaz.* 9 Mar. 3/1 A dry cleaning cloth ball. *Ibid.* 20 Apr. 3/3 The present extraordinary perfection of dry-cleaning. *Ibid.*, A good gown, dry-cleaned, is a much better thing than an inferior new one. Of course I do not pretend that all dry-cleaners are equally good. *Ibid.* 12 Oct. 3/2 How well they may dry-clean at home by the use of benzoline. **1908** *Daily Report* 27 Aug. 6/4 The conditions under which women and girls work in dry-cleaning establishments, where benzine is largely used. **1930** *Engineering* 12 Dec. 760/1 The advantages which dry cleaning [of coal] had to offer, as compared with wetwashing, were essentially financial ones... Had it been decided to wash the coal in the ordinary way instead of dry cleaning it, an additional 13 ovens would have been necessary. **1957** *New Yorker* 16 Nov. 150/2 Dry-cleanable colors include black and deep gold. **1958** Dry-cleaned [see AUTOMAT 3]. **1970** 'D. HALLIDAY' *Dolly & Cookie Bird* viii. 111 Blood was spreading over.. his cream jersey suit. It would never dry-clean. **1970** *Encycl. Brit.* VII. 709/2 Dry cleaning is the process of cleaning fabrics with liquids other than water. *Ibid.*, The dry-cleaned garment maintains its original shape and feel. For many years the dry-cleaning process was based on the use of highly flammable solvents. **1822–34** GOOD *Study Med.* (ed. 4) III. 473 The use of *dry-cupping between the shoulders. **1904** *Westm. Gaz.* 8 Sept. 4/2 *Dry-dyeing is simply dyeing with aniline dyes soluble in spirit. **1907** *Daily Chron.* 8 July 4/4 New systems of *dry-feeding young and adult stock. **1824** *Ann. Reg.* 259 His apparatus for the relief of *dry-grinders. **1832** BABBAGE *Econ. Manuf.* xix. (ed. 3) 187 *Dry-pointing, which also is executed with great rapidity. **1495** *Act 11 Hen. VIII*, c. 19 Preamb., Pillows made of.. scalded feders and *drie pulled feders to gedre. **1885** *Harper's Mag.* Jan. 278/1 Goat-skins in their raw state come to the market '*dry salted'. **1869** E. A. PARKES *Pract. Hygiene* (ed. 3) 305 On intermediate days the rooms are *dry-scrubbed. **1620** THOMAS *Lat. Dict.*, *Attondere aliquem auro*, to ridde him of his gold, to *drie shaue him. **1706** PHILLIPS, To *Dry-shave*, to chowse, gull or cheat notoriously. **1778** in *Harper's Mag.* (1883) 546/2 [He] shall be dry shaved.. and have his head dressed on the parade. **1901** KIPLING *Kim* viii. 207 The halts for prayers (Mahbub was very religious in *dry-washings and bellowings when time did not press). **1962** K. ORVIS *Damned & Destroyed* xiv. 93 He began worriedly dry-washing his hands.

b. So as to be or become dry, to dryness: as ***dry-suck, -weep*** vbs.; ***dry-burnt, -drunken, -roasted, -withering*** ppl. adjs.

1891 R. KIPLING *Light that failed* xii, The grass was *dry-burnt in the meadows. **1589** COGAN *Haven Health* (1636) 132 Except it be very *dry rosted. **1671** SHADWELL *Humourists* 111, Loins of Mutton dry-roasted. **1604** DEKKER *Honest Wh.* viii. Wks. 1873 II. 49 Thou *dry-suckst him.

3. Special attributive combs.: **dry bath** *slang*, a search of a prisoner when he has been stripped naked; **dry battery** *Electr.*, a battery of dry cells; **dry-beard,** an old man with a dry or withered beard; **dry-blower** *Austral.*, (*a*) a gold-miner; (*b*) used as a term of opprobrium; (*c*) (see quot. 1964); **dry-blowing** *Austral.* (see quot. 1894); **dry-bob** (see BOB *sb.*[7]); hence ***dry-bob*** vb.; (see also BOB *sb.*[3] 1 and 2); **dry-bone** (U.S.), a miner's name for the silicate and other ores of zinc (Dana 1868); **dry-bones,** a contemptuous or familiar term for a thin or withered person, who has little flesh on his bones; **dry brush** (see quots.); freq. *attrib.*; **dry-bulb thermometer,** one of the two thermometers of which a *dry- and wet-bulb hygrometer* consists; **dry camp** *U.S.*, a camp or halt where there is no water; **dry-castor,** 'a kind of beaver, called also *parchment-beaver*' (Webster 1864); **dry cell** *Electr.*, a voltaic cell in which the electrolyte is contained in an absorbent material or is in the form of a paste, thus preventing spilling of the contents; **dry-cooper,** a cooper who makes casks, etc. for dry goods; **dry diggings,** (*a*) (orig. *U.S.*) gold-diggings away from a river or stream; (*b*) in South Africa, diamond-diggings at which the diamondiferous material is disintegrated by exposure to the atmosphere; **dry-dike** = *dry-stone dike* (see DIKE *sb.*[1] 6 b); so ***dry-diked*** adj., ***dry-diker***; †**dry-ditch** *v. trans.*, to work at (anything) without result, like one digging a ditch into which no water flows; **dry end,** that end of a paper-making or drying-machine from which the material emerges dry; **dry farming** chiefly *N. Amer.*, farming without a good supply of water; so ***dry farm*** sb. and vb., ***dry farmer***; **dry-fly** *a.* and *v.* (*Angling*), used to describe a method of fishing in which an artificial fly floats lightly on the water; an artificial fly used in this type of fishing; **dry fuck** *U.S. coarse slang*, (*a*) a simulated act of sexual intercourse, without penetration and usu. without removing the clothes; (*b*) an unsatisfactory act of intercourse, esp. one which does not result in ejaculation or orgasm; so as *vb.*, to engage in intercourse of this kind; **dry hopping** (see quot. 1956); **dry house,** a building in which miners change their clothing (also called *drying-house*, or *dry*); **dry ice** orig. *U.S.*, solid carbon dioxide; **dry joint** *Electr.*, a soldered joint with faulty electrical continuity; **dry lodging,** lodging without board; **dry-march,** a march or boundary-line not formed by a river or water; **dry mounting,** a method of mounting photographs (see quot. 1958); **dry multure,** see MULTURE; **dry-needle** = *dry-point*; **dry offset** (see quots.); **dry pack,** see PACK; **dry-pile** *a.* (†*dripile*), with the pile dry; **dry-plate** (*Photogr.*), a sheet of glass coated with collodion subsequently sensitized and dried, or, more usually, with an emulsion of gelatine (or collodion) containing a sensitive silver salt, and exposed to the action of light in a dry state; **dry-plate clutch** *Mech.*, a plate clutch which operates without lubrication; **dry-point** (*Engraving*), (*a*) a sharp-pointed needle used for engraving without acid on a copper plate from which the etching-ground has been removed; (*b*) the process of engraving in this way, or an engraving so executed; hence ***dry-point*** vb.; **dry-point settlement, village,** one which is not liable to flooding; **dry-puddling,** see PUDDLING: †**dry-rent,** a RENT-SECK or barren rent, i.e. one reserved without clause of distress (*obs.*); **dry run,** (*a*) *U.S.* a dry creek or arroyo; (*b*) *colloq.* (orig. *U.S.*), a rehearsal, test, 'dummy run'; hence as *v. trans.*, to rehearse, practise; **dry shampoo** (see quot. 1966); **dry shaver,** an electric or other razor for use without soap and water; **dry-shearer,** a workman whose business is to shear the nap of cloth; **dry-ski** *a.*, designating a school, etc., for indoor training in ski-ing; **dry skid,** a skid of a motor vehicle on a dry surface; so **dry-skid** *v. intr.*; **dry-skin** (see quot.); **dry spell,** a period of dry weather (see quot. 1920); **dry spinning,** a method of spinning natural or artificial fibres (see quots. 1904 and 1957); hence ***dry-spin*** vb. trans., ***dry-spun*** adj.; **dry-stone** *a.*, applied to a 'dike' or stone wall built without mortar, cf. DIKE *sb.*[1] 6 b; **dry-stove,** a stove for plants, with dry heat; **dry suit,** a type of diving suit, usu. made of sheet rubber, which uses the principle of air-insulation to protect the diver from cold, and under which warm clothing can be worn; **dry valley,** a valley in which the original stream or river has disappeared; **dry wall,** a wall built without mortar; hence **dry-wall** *v. trans.* and *intr.*, to build a dry wall (around); ***dry-waller, dry-walling***; **dry wash** *N. Amer.*, the dry bed of an intermittent stream. See also DRY DOCK, etc.

1933 G. INGRAM *Stir* v. 93 The warder.. said he'd give him a *dry bath just to see. **1965** *New Statesman* 30 July 452/3 Two or three times a week the Heavy Mob rushed into our cells and gave us a 'dry bath', which adequately describes the search of a man who is standing 'starkers' in the middle of his cell. **1885** *Electrician* 10 Jan. 174/1 (*heading*) Conversion of liquid into *dry batteries. **1749** GARRICK *Lethe* I. (1798) I. 11 Well said, old *dry-beard. **1797** T. PARK *Sonnets* 66 By Pythagrean dry-beards sentenc'd. **1895** *Queenslander* 7 Dec. 1069 Every other man you meet in Coolgardie.. is either a lord, a colonel, a captain, a doctor, an expert, an agent, a sharebroker, or a sharper; all the rest are dudes, drunkards, and *dryblowers, professional liars, and loafers. **1935** *Bulletin* (Sydney) 20 Mar. 10/4 In the early days of the Westralian goldfields it gained me many friends amongst the isolated dryblowers to whom I passed on my weekly copy. **1936** F. CLUNE *Roaming round Darling* xix. 196 There we met Dryblower Tom Mitchell, awaiting the return of his camel-team, to go prospecting. **1964** R. WARD *Penguin Bk. Austral. Ballads* 208 A 'dry-blower' is a crude device, made of hessian and wooden saplings, and used in arid areas for separating gold from the ore. **1894** *Argus* 28 Mar. 5/5 (Morris), When water is not available, as unfortunately is the case at Coolgardie, '*dry blowing' is resorted to. This is done by placing the pounded stuff [*sc.* alluvial ore] in one dish, and pouring it slowly at a certain height into the other. If there is any wind blowing it will carry away the powdered stuff; if there is no wind the breath will have to be used. **1865** *Dry-bob [see BOB *sb.*[7]]. **1881** W. E. NORRIS *Matrim.* I. 73 You never used to dry-bob at Eton, did you? **1845** JAMES *A. Neil* III. xiv, Ha, old *dry-bones, have I caught thee at length? **1911** H. P. BOWIE *Laws Jap. Painting* iv. 66 Dry twig or old firewood line.. is generally used in the robes of old men and produced by what is called the *dry brush; that is, a brush with very little water mixed with the *sumi*. **1958** M. L. WOLF *Dict. Painting* 88 *Dry brush*, in Chinese art, a painting technique in which the ink is used sparingly with a minimum of moisture in the brush; known natively as *kan pi*. **1959** HALAS & MANVELL *Technique Film Animation* xix. 220 If the area common to the drawings is.. less than two-thirds, then dry brush effects can be used to join the two objects. **1882** WATTS *Dict. Chem.* III. 227 Table I. To obtain the dew-point, multiply the difference of reading of the thermometers by the factor opposite the *dry-bulb reading, and subtract the product from the dry-bulb reading. **1869** J. R. BROWNE *Adv. Apache Country* 128 We made a *dry camp till morning. **1873** J. H. BEADLE *Undevel. West* xxviii. 615 We.. find a pool with water enough for our horses, and to fill our jugs, as we must make a 'dry camp' to-night. **1887** *Outing* (U.S.) X. 4/2 We halted on an open place .. and went into dry camp. **1920** J. M. HUNTER *Trail Drivers of Texas* 312 The round up boss.. called for two or three men.. to make what is called a 'dry camp'. **1893** P. BENJAMIN *Voltaic Cell* xv. 309 *Dry cells are best adapted to circumstances where current is intermittently needed and then only for a short time. **1936** *Discovery* Sept. 285/2 Causing a current from a battery of dry cells to pass through the fine wire. **1715** *Lond. Gaz.* No. 5308/3 Mr. Henry Taylor, *Dry Cooper. **1848** *Californian* 14 Aug. 2/3 In one part of the mine called the '*dry diggins', no other implements are necessary than an ordinary sheath knife, to pick the gold from the rocks. **1853** *Househ. Words* VIII. 321/1 The dry diggings at least furnish equal proof of energy and industry. **1858** *Brit. Colonist* (Victoria, Brit. Columbia) 11 Dec. 1/2 These are in fact a species of dry diggings. **1858** W. HOWITT *Land, Labour & Gold* I. xi. 126 Next came the dry diggings; these were far enough from the stream to be free of its drainage. **1862** E. HODDER *Memories N.Z. Life* 222 There are two principal kinds of diggings: river diggings.. and dry diggings, in the conglomerate and gravel accumulated on the slope of the mountains. **1873** F. BOYLE *To the Cape for Diamonds* 123 Four 'dry diggings':—New Rush.. Old De Beers, Dutoitspan, and Bultfontein. **1889** K. MUNROE *Golden Days* x. 111 The dry diggings were those of hill-sides, or in gulches containing no steady supply of water. **1899** G. LACY *Pictures of Travel* 173 The 'dry diggings' are thirty miles to the south-east of Pniel. They are so called because the gems are not found in river-wash, but in dry tufa, which has apparently never been in contact with water. **1910** J. HART *Vigilante Girl* xxiv. 326 It had been a 'dry diggings', and the skeleton line of a long flume ran thread-like along the mountains. **1907** *Macm. Mag.* Jan. 196 The platform.. was some fifty feet above the valley, and the stones on its face, which was almost perpendicular, appeared to be irregularly *dry-dyked. **1905** *Spectator* 11 Feb. 211/1 In the Boer War the '*dry dikers' of a certain East Yorkshire regiment used to be asked to volunteer to build 'sangars'. *a* **1670** HACKET *Abp. Williams* II. (1692) 98 His adversaries did *dry-ditch their matters and digg'd in vain. **1894** J. DUNBAR *Notes Manuf. Wood Pulp & Papers* 39 The temperature of the cylinders was too high at the *dry end of the machine to produce the desired result. **1927** T. WOODHOUSE *Artif. Silk* iii. 26 The delivery-end or 'dry-end' of a pulp drying machine. **1962** F. T. DAY *Introd. Paper* iv. 36 The beginning of the paper making machine is described as the 'wet end', whilst the other end of the machine, which consists of drying cylinders and paper finishing calenders, is called the 'dry end'. **1919** E. HOUGH *Sagebrusher* xxxiii, A few scattered *dry farms, edging up close to the river in the valley far below. **1952** D. F. PUTNAM *Canadian Regions* 376/2 The extra size of the dry farms. **1971** L. DAVIDSON *Smith's Gazelle* iii. 50 The sheep could graze among the table rock and the wheat could be dry-farmed on most of the rest. **1912** R. A. WASON *Friar Tuck* iii. 36 Next came the *dry farmer. **1919** H. L. WILSON *Ma Pettengill* v. 155 The forlorn shack of a dry-farmer. **1878** J. W. POWELL *Rep. Lands Arid Region* 78 A company of Danes.. have obtained a meagre subsistence by *dry farming. **1906** *Nature* 26 July 304/2 The scientific aspect of what has been designated in the United States as 'dry-farming' consists in utilising to the best advantage all the water that falls in semi-arid regions. **1908** *Sci. Amer.* 22 Aug. 120 'Dry farming' consists in so preparing the soil in semi-arid regions that it will catch what little annual rainfall there is, and store it within reach of the roots of the plants to be grown. **1936** F. CLUNE *Roaming round Darling* xiii. 113 An Experimental Farm was started to carry out investigations with regard to cereals under dry-farming conditions. **1961** L. D. STAMP *Gloss. Geogr. Terms* 165/2 Dry farming implies a specialized technological treatment of land to overcome the short supply of water. **1846** G. P. R. PULMAN *Vade-Mecum of Fly-Fishing* (ed. 2) vii. 84 If the *dry fly be widely different in these respects, the fish will be *surprised*. **1885** *Pall Mall G.* 29 June 4/2 The beautiful and delicate art of fishing with the dry fly. **1893** *Nat. Observer* 5 Aug. 300/2 You must creep up-stream as warily as if you were dry-flying it on the Hampshire chalk. **1897** *Westm. Gaz.* 7 Apr. 3/1 Dry Fly fishing is.. using a dry and floating fly instead of a wet and sunk one. **1913** *Q. Rev.* July 66 Dry-fly fishing for sea trout is still in its infancy. [**1970** PARTRIDGE *Dict. Slang. Suppl.* 1113/1 *Dry*, adj., is, in Australia, used with the low nn. of coïtion for rape and homosexual intercourse: since ca. 1950.] **1971** E. E. LANDY *Underground Dict.* 71 **Dry fuck v.*, go through the motions of sexual intercourse without entering the vagina, usually with clothes on. Performed by junior-high-school and high-school students. *n.* The simulated act of sexual intercourse with clothes on. **1975** *Wentworth & Flexner's Dict. Amer. Slang* Suppl. 695/1 *Dry fuck* [taboo], 1 To go through the motions of sexual intercourse without penetration, usu. without removing the clothes. *Junior high-school and high-school student use.* 2 Unsatisfying sexual intercourse, as when done hurriedly or without emotional involvement, esp. when it does not result in ejaculation or orgasm. **1979** *Maledicta* III. II. 231 A *gay*.. may or may not know the following words and expressions:.. *dry fuck* (without penetration, or without KY or other lubricant such as vaseline or Crisco). **1884** *Health Exhib. Catal.* 130/1 Drawing of *Dry House where miners change their clothes. **1890** *Dry hopping [see HOPPING *vbl. sb.*[2]]. **1956** *New Biol.* XXI. 14 Dry hopping is the practice of adding hops to the barrel of finished beer before it leaves the brewery. It gives added aroma and to some degree additional biological stability. **1925** *Off. Gaz. U.S. Patent Office* 28 Apr. 850/2 Dryice Corporation of America.. **Dry Ice*, Carbon Dioxide ($C\ O_2$) in Solidified Forms, Mixtures, and Compounds. **1930** *Engineering* 17 Oct. 504/2 The oxidation of carbon-monoxide from electro-metallurgical and calcium-carbide furnaces to carbon dioxide for producing 'dry ice', or solid carbon-dioxide. **1938** *Archit. Rev.* LXXXIV. 119 Dry-ice refrigeration unit accommodating approximately 180 half-pint cartons of milk. **1968** *Times* 17 Oct. 18/6 The traps were baited with solid carbon dioxide, or dry ice, which evaporated at the rate of about three litres a minute. **1933** H. J. B. CHAPPLE *Television* ii. 38 Unless [soldering is] thoroughly understood.. a set fails to function owing to weak or *dry joints. **1940** *Amateur Radio Handbk.* (ed. 2) iii. 42/2 The best and safest flux is pure resin, although it.. needs greater care if dry joints are to be avoided. **1960** *P.O. Telecomm. Jrnl.* XII. 92/2 As 'dry' or imperfectly soldered joints may not show up until after the equipment has been in use for some time.. any operator employed on soldering should have had adequate practice. **1796** in Scott *Old Mort.* Introd., To *drye Lodginge for seven weeks, £0 4 1. **1825** *Hist. Little Pat* (*Houlston Tracts* I. xi. 3) She.. lived in one of those cellars which have 'dry lodgings' written over the door. **1820** SCOTT *Monast.* vi, The last who went south passed the *dry-march at the Ridingburn with an escort of thirty spears. **1903** *Photogram* X. 320/1 Wet or *dry mounting. **1958** V. DRUMM in M. L. Hall *Newnes' Complete Amat. Photogr.* xxxv. 329 The best method of mounting photographic prints is with the use of dry-mounting tissue in a hot press. The tissue is impregnated with shellac which melts at approximately 160 °F. *c* **1790** IMISON *Sch. Art* II. 48 The *dry needle.. is principally employed in the extreme light parts of water, sky, drapery, architecture, &c. **1958** T. LANDAU *Encycl. Librarianship* 113/2 **Dry offset*, printing by letterpress to a rubber cylinder from which impressions are taken on to paper. **1967** KARCH & BUBER *Offset Processes* ii. 30 *Dry Offset.* A shallow-etched relief plate transfers the image to a rubber blanket on a cylinder. The press needs no moistening rollers. **1600** FAIRFAX *Tasso* XX. cxxiv. 388 And loue will shoote you from his mightie bow, Weake is the shot that *dripile falles in snow. **1859** *Photogr. News* I. 296 Some difference of opinion exists as to the collodion best suited for *dry plates. **1878** ABNEY *Photogr.* (1890) 91 In the development of dry plates.. the image.. is built up from the solid silver salt in the film itself. *Ibid.*, The practical part of dry-plate processes. **1927** *Observer* 15 May 22 A.. *dry plate clutch. **1928** *Motor World* 9 Mar. 162/2 There is an enclosed dry plate clutch, a three-speed unit gear-box. **1837** WHITTOCK *Bk. Trades* (1842) 216 The *drypoint, or needle, is principally employed for the lightest parts of the engraving on the copper plate. **1883** *Athenæum* 24 Feb. 256/1 The etchings and dry-points of Venetian views which Mr. Whistler is showing. **1920** M. AUROUSSEAU in *Geogr. Rev.* X. 228 We have two special cases of arrangements governed by water supply—the extreme conditions giving rise to what we will term *wet point villages* and **dry point villages*. **1946** L. D. STAMP *Britain's Struct.* xv. 173 For a thousand years these scattered 'dry-point' settlements remained typical of the heart of what is now Greater London. **1845** J. PALMER *Jrnl. Trav. Rocky Mts.* 28 Sept. (1847) 61 We took up a *dry run for one or two miles, thence over a ridge to a running branch. **1893** *Harper's Mag.* Apr. 697/2 Arroyos, or dry runs,.. collect the storm waters. **1941** *Amer. Speech* XVI. 165/1 *Dry run*, to practice; a dress rehearsal. **1943** *Sat. Evening Post* 27 Nov. 12 She had to locate his pulse, get her watch ready and make a couple of dry runs. **1944** *Air News Yearbk.* II. 18 There is long, hard planning, endless training, repeated dry runs.. behind undertakings of this magnitude. **1958** *Spectator* 1 Aug. 167/1 A comedy series.. needs the whole benefit of dry runs, ample film facilities, innumerable scriptwriters. **1968** D. MARLOWE *Mem. Venus Lackey* i. 25, I had mentally dry-runned the sexual act a thousand times since puberty. **1970** *New Yorker* 10 Oct. 159/1 Since there might be difficulty locating the Commander's home, it would be advisable to make a 'dry run' sometime before the call. **1890** *Hairdressers' Weekly Jrnl.* 14 June 383/2 (Advt.), Niagara Foam.. an American *dry shampoo.. 20/- per gallon. **1913** *Queen* 24 May (Advt.), When you want your hair to look extra nice and bright.. just treat it to a dry shampoo with.. Hair Powder. **1928** *Ibid.* Feb. 271/2 Dry Shampoo. Carbonate of Potash 1 oz. Water 32 ozs. Saponine $\frac{1}{2}$ oz. Industrial Spirit 32 oz. Perfume, as desired. **1966** J. S. COX *Dict. Hairdressing* 49/2 *Dry shampoo.* (1) A shampoo in powder form which is applied to the head as a powder, massaged in and then brushed out... (2) A shampoo composed of industrial methylated spirit or isopropyl alcohol and water with the addition of a foaming element such as saponin. **1937** *Night & Day* 1 July 4/2 (Advt.), If you drive a car you'll shave with a Schick *dry shaver. **1963** *B.S.I. News* Feb. 33 This revision will specify the requirements for mains-operated dry shavers. **1722** CHAMBERLAYNE in *Phil. Trans.* XXXII. 161 A kind of Tumor.. as the *Dry-sheerers, or those who dress Cloth, have upon their left Hands. **1954** *Springfield* (Mass.) *Daily News* 10 Nov. 22 The *dry ski class.. will begin tonight. **1957** *Times* 25 Nov. 11/4 Dry-ski schools which help muscles to become more flexible and teach beginners the basic movements. **1958** A. HOCKING *Epitaph for Nurse* xi. 197 Taking a gravelly sharp corner at an almost reckless speed she got into a *dry skid. **1961** I. FLEMING *Thunderball* ii. 23 The Bentley dry-skidded to a stop in the gravel. **1701** C. WOLLEY *Jrnl. In N.Y.* (1860) 39 If the Blubber be not fat and free, the Whale is call'd a *Dry-Skin. **1887** *Dry spell [see SPELL *sb.*[3] 5 b]. **1920** *British Rainfall 1919* 27 A Dry Spell is a period of fifteen or more consecutive days no one of which is a 'Wet Day'. **1961** *Amer. Speech* XXXVI. 267 A sharp distinction is observed in Colorado between the relatively long *drouth* and the relatively short *dry spell*. **1864** A. J. WARDEN *Linen Trade* v. i. 697 Wet spinning differs chiefly from.. *dry spinning in having the spinning frame furnished with a receptacle for holding water. **1904** GOODCHILD & TWENEY *Technol. & Sci. Dict.* 177/2 *Dry spinning*, flax may be spun wet or dry, the latter giving a softer and more spongy yarn. **1921** T. WOODHOUSE tr. *Foltzer's Artif. Silk* iv. 23 Spinning with the aid of water,.. has been replaced by a system of dry spinning. **1957** *Textile Terms & Defs.* (*Textile Inst.*) (ed. 3) 94 *Dry spinning* is the process in which a solution of the polymer is extruded into a heated chamber to remove the solvent, leaving the solid filament. *Ibid.* 39 Dry-spun. **1963** A. J. HALL *Textile Sci.* ii. 75 Solutions which can be *dry* spun—that is, into warm air to evaporate off the solvent and leave solidified filaments behind. *c* **1702** C. FIENNES *Through Eng. on Side-Saddle* (1888) II. iii. 83 You scarce see a tree and No hedges all over y[e] Country, only *dry stone walls. **1816** SCOTT *Old Mort.* i. *note*, Called by the vulgar a dry-stane dyke. **1878** C. R. CONDER *Tentwork Pal.* 312 Siloam—a most disappointing pool with dry-stone walls and a little muddy water. **1955** R. & B. CARRIER *Dive* iv. 118 Rubber suits have been designed to protect the diver from the effects of cold water. There are two basic types.. the 'wet suit' and the '*dry suit'. *Ibid.* 120 The next best thing is.. a sealed sheet-rubber dry suit worn with one or more suits of long underwear or wool sweaters underneath. **1971** B. GRAHAM *Spy Trap* xii. 84 Crabb had bought a new black Pirelli dry suit. **1898** *Dry-valley [see BLIND *a.* 11 c]. **1927** C. C. FAGG in *Proc. & Trans. Croydon Nat. Hist. Soc.* IX. 94 The development of the dry valleys of the Chalk belongs to the more recent phases of the Denudation of the Weald. *Ibid.* 96 (*caption*) The Dry Valley Systems. **1961** L. D. STAMP *Gloss. Geogr. Terms* 166/1 The origin of the dry valleys of the Chalk. **1778** G. WHITE *Let.* 3 July in *Selborne* (1789) I. xli. 236 *Lathræa squamaria*, tooth-wort.. on the *dry wall opposite *Grange-yard*. **1828** *Craven Dial.*, *Dry-wall*, a wall without lime. **1873** H. SPENCER *Study Sociol.* iii. (1877) 48 A dry wall of the same height and stability. **1883** *Encycl. Brit.* XVI. 450/1 The materials.. may be built up alone (*dry walling*) or with the aid of mortar or hydraulic cement. **1886** F. T. ELWORTHY *W. Somerset Word-Bk.* 219 Dry-waller. **1914** G. JEKYLL *Colour Schemes for Flower Garden* (ed. 3) ix. 86 An earth bank four and a half feet high, dry-walled on both sides. **1922** *Daily Mail* 10 Nov. 8/5 A dry-waller has to be born, not made. So old William told me when I found him dry-walling. **1872** J. G. BOURKE *Jrnl.* (MS.) 25 Nov. (D.A.E.), There is a *dry wash on this road. **1926** MULFORD *Hopalong Cassidy's Protégé* ix. 110 A bridge spanned a dry-wash, dry most of the year. **1962** *Bad Lands of Red Deer River* (Board of Trade, Alberta) 25 The pieces.. are lying scattered at the base of the cliffs or in dry washes where they have been carried by run-off.

dry, *sb.* Forms: see prec. [subst. use of prec.]

1. a. Dry state or condition, *esp.* of the atmosphere; dryness, drought. With *the*: the dry season (chiefly *Austral. colloq.*).

c **1200** *Trin. Coll. Hom.* 123 He.. þoleð his unwille hwile druie and hwile wete. *a* **1300** *Cursor M.* 6365 (Gött.) For na drie ne for na wate Ne changid þai neuer þair state. **1377** *Pol. Poems* (Rolls) I. 216 Thei dredde nother tempest, druyȝe nor wete. **1414** BRAMPTON *Penit. Ps.* lxxviii, For dry myn herte to gydere is runne. **1480** CAXTON *Descr. Brit.* 5 With colde ne with hete, with weet ne with drye. **1695** WOODWARD *Nat. Hist. Earth* VI. (1723) 272 Successions of Heat and Cold, Wet and Dry. **1870** MORRIS *Earthly Par.* II. III. 279 At end of dry He cut his hay, to lie long in the rain. **1877** R. F. BURTON in *Athenæum* 3 Nov. 568/3 Dead water during the dries, and a lake with two outlets after the annual rains. **1897** [see WET *a.* 2 f]. **1908** MRS. A. GUNN *We of Never-Never* vii. 88, I—I—thought you'd reckon that travellers' water for the Dry came before your rooms. **1938** X. HERBERT *Capricornia* (1939) vii. 74 The Dry! the good old Dry—when the grasses yellowed, browned, died to tinder. **1955** J. CLEARY *Justin Bayard* xi. 172 Thinking of coming down there later in the Dry. **1968** K. WEATHERLY *Roo Shooter* 35 As the dry progressed and the heat remained constant, they stopped breeding.

†**b.** Thirst: cf. DRY *a.* 3. *Obs.*

1377 LANGL. *P. Pl.* B. XIV. 50 Ete þis whan þe hungreth, Or whan þow.. clyngest for drye. *c* **1460** *Towneley Myst.* (Surtees) 313, I dy nere for dry.

2. That which is dry. **a.** *spec.* dry land. ***in the dry***: on, or as on, dry land; not under water.

a **1300** *Cursor M.* 383 Þe dri [he] cald erth. **1382** WYCLIF *Ps.* xciv[xcv]. 5 Of hym is the se, and he made it; and the drie his hondis formeden. **1784** COWPER *Task* II. 56 When did the waves so haughtily o'erleap Their ancient barriers, deluging the dry? **1871** G. MACDONALD *Sonn. conc. Jesus* vi, When God said, 'Let the Dry appear!'

b. *Austral.* A desert area; waterless country.

1909 *Bulletin* (Sydney) 21 Jan., A seventy-five mile dry. **1938** *Observer* 30 Oct. 11/4 The swaggie's.. billy-can.. is carried full of water, so that if 'on the wallaby' over a long stretch of 'the dry' (waterless country) he can.. be sure of his .. 'billy tea'.

c. A dry wine, cocktail, etc. (see DRY *a.* 8).

1953 A. UPFIELD *Murder must Wait* xxiii. 205 We settled for a half bottle of gin and a few bottles of dry. **1958** 'J. WELCOME' *Run for Cover* vi. 108 'Good evening, Herbert. A "Dry" please.'.. Herbert's dry martinis.. were as pale as ice.

3. A drying-place, or drying-house.

1876 J. H. COLLINS in *Jrnl. Soc. Arts* 5 May 568/1 The floor or 'pan' of the dry is composed of fire-clay tiles. **1882** *Encycl. Brit.* XIV. 1/2 It is transferred to the drying-house or 'dry'.

4. *Masonry.* 'A fissure in a stone, intersecting it at various angles to its bed, and rendering it unfit to support a load' (Ogilvie).

1825 JAMIESON, *Dry* (in a stone), a flaw. *Aberd.*

5. a. A prohibitionist; a person who opposes the use of alcoholic liquors. *colloq.* (orig. *U.S.*).

1888 in A. RANDALL-DIEHL *2,000 Words & Defs.* **1896** *Chicago Record* 11 Feb. 6/5 Even though there might be some precincts where the 'wets' outnumbered the 'drys'—yet the whole county would go dry. **1920** *Eye Opener* (Calgary) 7 Feb. 1/3 The drys cannot pretend much longer that Alberta is 'prohibition'. **1930** *Daily Express* 6 Nov. 2/1 An active 'Dry'. **1965** WODEHOUSE *Galahad at Blandings* i. 13 The woman who runs the school is a rabid Dry and won't let her staff so much as look at a snifter. **1970** *Encycl. Brit.*

XVIII. 610/2 The 'drys' assumed a considerable degree of power within both the Democratic and Republican parties.

b. *Pol. slang.* A politician (esp. a member of the Conservative party) who advocates economic stringency and individual responsibility, and uncompromisingly opposes high government spending. Contrasted with WET *sb.*[1] 6.

1983 [see WET *sb.*[1] 6]. **1984** *Times* 16 Oct. 25/2 It is hard to see economic dries such as Mr. Ridley buying the channel tunnel arguments now. **1987** *Sunday Tel.* 19 July 20/7 For ten years the Tory party has been split between Wets and Dries.

6. a. The process of drying.

1957 *Economist* 16 Nov. 579 (Advt.), Soft, dry towelling that gives you a good, clean dry every single time.

b. *Theatr.* The act of 'drying up' on the stage (see DRY *v.* 5 d and 2 d).

1945 M. AGATE *Madame Sarah* ii. 22 She..adopted the English custom of the stage-manager keeping an eye on the book from the prompt-corner in case of a 'dry'. **1960** *News Chron.* 14 Oct. 10/6 When no spark is struck..the effect is as embarrassing as a theatrical 'dry'.

dry (draɪ), *v.* Pa. t. and pple. **dried** (draɪd). Forms: 1 **drýȝean**, 2-4 **driȝe(n**, 3 (*Orm.*) **driȝȝenn**, 3-4 **druye(n**, 4 **druiȝe**, **drue**, **dreiȝe**, **dri**, 4-6 **drey**, **drye**, 4-7 **drie**, 5- **dry** (*inflexions* **dries**, **drieth**, **drying**). Pa. t. 1 **dryȝde**, **driȝde**, 3-5 **dride**, 4 **dreide**, **dreyede**, **druyde**, 5 **dryed(e**, 4- **dried**. Pa. pple. 1 **ȝedriȝed**, 3 (*Orm.*) **driȝȝedd**, 4-5 **dreyed**, 4-8 **dryed**, 6-7 **dride**, 7 **dryde**, 7-8 **dry'd**, 6- **dried**; (*β.* 7 **drien**). [OE. *drýȝ(e)an*, *driȝean*, f. *drýȝe* DRY *a.*]

1. a. *trans.* To make dry (*e.g.* by wiping, rubbing, exposure to heat or air, draining, etc.); to rid, deprive, or exhaust of moisture; to desiccate.

c **888** K. ÆLFRED *Boeth.* xxxix. §13 Se hata sumor dryȝþ and ȝearwaþ sæd and blæda. *c* **1000** *Ags. Gosp.* John xi. 2 And driȝde [*Hatton G.* dreide] his fet mid hyre loccon. *c* **1200** ORMIN 8625 Forr þatt te land wass driȝȝedd all And scorrcnedd þurrh þe druhhþe. *a* **1300** *Cursor M.* 14011 Sco ..þan þam dries wit hir hare. *c* **1400** MAUNDEV. (1839) iii. 19 Thei dryen it at the Sonne. *c* **1400** tr. *Secreta Secret., Gov. Lordsh.* (E.E.T.S.) 76 þes pynges dryes and feblys þe body. *a* **1500** *Flower & Leaf* (R.), To dry their clothes yt were wringing weat. **1549-62** STERNHOLD & H. *Ps.* cxix. 313 As a skin bottel in the smoke, So am I partcht and dride. **1626** BACON *Sylva* §56 After it be dryed a little before the Fire. **1664** EVELYN *Kal. Hort.* (1729) 206 They should be dry'd in the Shade. **1726** LEONI tr. *Alberti's Archit.* I. 25/1 Wood thus dry'd..acquires a Hardness..by which means they think it is better dried. **1848** DICKENS *Dombey* v, Mrs. Chick was yet drying her eyes.

b. To remove or abstract (water or moisture); to wipe away, cause to evaporate, or drain off.

c **1350** *Barlam & Josaphat* (Bodl. MS.) 867 Whan þu myȝt heuin areche wit þin hond, and dreyȝe þe water of þe se. **1387** TREVISA *Higden* (Rolls) V. 113 Faste by the brook þat he dreyede [*v.r.* druyde]. **1551** CROWLEY *Pleas. & Pain* 482 Christe doeth drye all teares from the oppressedis eye. **1697** DAMPIER *Voy.* I. vii. 197 The Water..was now dried away. **1798** CANNING *New Morality* 89 in *Anti-Jacobin* 9 July (1852) 204 Not she, who dries The orphan's tears. **1842** TENNYSON *Audley Court* 45 Till all his juice is dried, and all his joints Are full of chalk.

c. *absol.* To dry crockery, cutlery, etc., after washing up.

1935 A. J. CRONIN *Stars look Down* I. viii. 59 'Shall I dry for you, mother?' She shook her head, dried the dishes herself. **1949** D. SMITH *I capture Castle* x. 166 Neil and Simon helped with the washing up... Ivy washed and we all dried. **1967** G. NORTH *Sgt. Cluff & Day of Reckoning* vi. 51 She piled dishes into his hands to be carried to the kitchen: 'It'll save time if you dry for me.'

2. a. *intr.* To become dry; to lose or be exhausted of moisture; to cease to yield a supply of liquid.

c **1200** *Trin. Coll. Hom.* 155 Sum of þe sed ful uppe þe ston and dride þere. *a* **1300** *Cursor M.* 310 (Cott.) He is welle þat neuer sal dri. *c* **1340** *Ibid.* 8768 (Trin.) þe tre..for elde bigon to driȝe. **1387** TREVISA *Higden* (Rolls) I. 267 His armes driede and wax al drye. *c* **1420** *Pallad. on Husb.* I. 363 The see grauel is lattest for to drye. **1538** LYNDESAY *Agst. Syde Taillis* 75 In Somer quhen the streittis dryis. **1703** MOXON *Mech. Exerc.* 259 The Morter doth not Cement..when it dries hastily. **1705** *Lond. Gaz.* No. 4114/4 It [a sandbank] drys at Low-Water. **1870** C. F. GORDON CUMMING in *Gd. Words* 138/2 Masses of apricots spread out to dry in the sun.

b. Of water or moisture: To disappear or pass away by evaporation, absorption, or draining.

?*c* **1325** *Old Age* ii. in *Reliq. Ant.* II. 210 Moch me anueþ þat mi drivil druiþ. *c* **1400** *Lanfranc's Cirurg.* 197 If þou waisschist hise lymes in watir, anon riȝt it wole drie yn. **1601** SHAKS. *All's Well* II. i. 143 Great flouds haue flowne.. and great Seas haue dried. **1648** GAGE *West Ind.* 109 The unctuous part will dry away.

c. *to dry straight*: to come right eventually. *colloq.*

1897 W. J. LOCKE *Derelicts* xxii, I shall miss you terribly —at first—but it will all dry straight, Yvonne. **1936** WODEHOUSE *Laughing Gas* xxvi. 278 Cheer up, Joseph. Things will dry straight one of these days.

d. Suddenly to forget or fail to speak one's words in a play or other performance. *colloq.*

1934 *N. Y. Herald Tribune* 2 Sept. VII. 10/2 Thumbing the pages for certain theatrical terms, we find..*fluff* (but not *dry* or *dry up*). **1941** BRAHMS & SIMON *No Bed for Bacon* xxi. 253 I'm sorry I dried at the beginning. **1953** L. A. G. STRONG *Hill of Howth* i. 8 A colleague of mine once dried in the middle of a scene. **1955** J. COATES *Linda* xv. 170 She dried in the middle of a speech. Beryl prompted her and she went on. **1967** M. SHULMAN *Kill Three* III. viii. 147 'O.K., Allan,' said the director into his microphone. 'If she fluffs badly or dries we'll go straight to Three.'

e. *to dry down*: of paint, to become dry.

1958 *Listener* 28 Aug. 323/1 Some complain that the jelly paints..dry down with a poor gloss. **1959** *Ibid.* 9 Apr. 651/1 The oil-based paints..may dry down with a patchy finish on standard hardboard.

†**3.** *intr.* To be thirsty, to thirst. *Obs.*

In ME. also *impers.* me drieth; cf. HUNGER.

1362 LANGL. *P. Pl.* A. I. 25 And drink whon þou druiȝest [B. dryest: *v.rr.* þe driȝeþ, ȝow drieth]. *a* **1541** WYATT *Poet. Wks.* (1861) 117 For thirst to death I dry.

4. a. *trans.* To render (a cow, etc.) 'dry'; to exhaust or stop the secretion of milk in. **b.** *intr.* To become 'dry', cease to give milk.

1780 A. YOUNG *Tour Irel.* (Nat. Lib. Ed.) 116 All have cows, and when they dry them, buy others. **1797** J. DOWNING *Disord. Horned Cattle* 87 The following medicine may be given to any cow you wish to dry. **1806** FORSYTH *Beauties Scotl.* III. 76 The thicker milk of those which were beginning to dry. **1828** *Craven Dial.* s.v., 'It's time to dry the cow, shoe gives lile milk'. **1894** *Times* 6 Mar. 4/2 A few farmers report that they cannot dry off their cows.

c. dry out. *intr.* Of a drug-addict: to undergo a course of treatment designed to break dependence on the drug; of an alcoholic: to undergo a similar course of systematic disintoxication. Also *trans.*, to cure (a drug addict or an alcoholic) in this way. So **dry-out** *sb.*; **drying-out** *vbl. sb.* and *ppl. a.*

1967 *Guardian* 8 Feb. 7/3 They are not only making firmer contact with the addicts..but also giving some of those they have 'dried out' a purpose. *Ibid.* 7/5 The painful process of the detoxification ward, the 'dry-out'. **1969** *New Scientist* 13 Mar. 554/1 The removal of alcohol from the blood by using the artificial kidney may be found to be the safest (and cheapest) way of 'drying out' alcoholics in a state of acute intoxication. **1969** *Maclean's* Aug. 55/2 Too often a drinker 'dries out' and his case is closed. **1970** R. HAUGHTON *Love* v. 143 A boy or girl would be pulled through a 'bad patch' (and the 'patches' of a drug-addict 'drying out' are very bad indeed). **1970** E. TIDYMAN *Shaft* (1971) iii. 41 By eight, she had undergone..the drying-out procedure in private institutions. **1971** *Daily Tel.* 2 Mar. 2 Drunks arrested by police in future may have to spend a compulsory three days in a 'drying out' centre.

5. dry up. *trans.* **a.** To suck, draw, or take up (liquid or moisture) entirely, as is done by the sun or with a cloth or the like. **b.** To exhaust (anything) of its moisture; to render quite dry; to desiccate. (Chiefly in *passive.*) Also *absol.* = sense 1 c above.

c **1385** CHAUCER *L.G.W.* 775 *Thisbe*, Phebus..Hadde dreyed up the dew of erbis wete. **1484** CAXTON *Curiall* 1 The grace of humanyte is not dreyed vp in the. **1552** HULOET, Dryed vp to be, as a cowe or yewe that goeth gelde or foremilch and geueth no mylke. **1563** W. FULKE *Meteors* (1640) 63 b, Chalke is an earth by heate concocted..and dried up. **1613** PURCHAS *Pilgrimage* (1614) 105 In Summer it [Jordan] is almost drien up. **1664** EVELYN *Kal. Hort.* (1729) 197 The sharp Easterly..Winds transpierce, and dry them [tulips] up. **1804** *Ann. Rev.* II. 81/1 One fertile source of information was dried up. **1850** MᶜCOSH *Div. Govt.* III. ii. (1874) 407 The amazon..had her breast dried up that she might fight the more fiercely. **1871** R. H. HUTTON *Ess.* (1877) I. 18 Theoretic atheism dries up the sources of personal affection. [**1932** S. GIBBONS *Cold Comfort Farm* vii. 92 She..flicked the reminders of dinner off the table with Adam's drying-up towel.] **1959** *House & Garden* Dec. 34/1 (*heading*) D for drying-up Essentially the masculine task. **1962** I. MURDOCH *Unofficial Rose* ii. 28, I was just wondering if he'd mind drying up while we're at church. **1966** 'K. NICHOLSON' *Hook, Line & Sinker* ix. 101 He seemed preoccupied while drying-up.

c. *intr.* Of water or moisture: To disappear entirely as by evaporation. Of a source: To cease to yield liquid, to become quite dry.

1535 COVERDALE *Job* xii. 15 Beholde, yf he witholde the waters, they drye vp. **1604** SHAKS. *Oth.* IV. ii. 60 The Fountaine from the which my currant runnes, Or else dries vp. **1726** LEONI tr. *Alberti's Archit.* II. 104/1 Springs.. which have dryed up. **1842** TENNYSON *Two Voices* 268 The sap dries up: the plant declines.

d. *intr.* (*slang* or *colloq.*) To stop the flow of words, cease talking; also *gen.* to stop, cease. *spec.* = sense 2 d above (cf. quot. 1884[2]). Also *trans.*, to cause (someone) to forget his words in a play or the like.

1853 *San Francisco Comm. Advertiser* 9 Dec. 2/4 She defied his Honor..and giving assurance of a disposition never to 'dry up', was carried down below to cool off. **1864** in WEBSTER. **1865** *The Index* 2 Feb. (Farmer), With which modest contribution we dry up with reference to the subject. **1884** *Cornh. Mag.* June 617 (*ibid.*) Dry up!..the slangy.. exclamation with which he cuts short..attempts of his mother to lecture him. **1884** G. MOORE *Mummer's Wife* (1887) 179 No matter how well you knew your words, you'd dry up when you got before the footlights. **1892** STEVENSON *Vailima Lett.* xxiv. (1895) 231 The rain begins..and I will do the reverse and dry up. **1923** *N. Y. Times* 9 Sept. VII. 2/1 *Dry a man up*, to give the wrong cue, or to say something aside to disconcert a fellow-actor, and so cause him to dry up. **1928** F. SCOTT FITZGERALD in *Sat. Even. Post* 21 July 8/3 'Oh, dry up!' retorted Basil. **1933** P. GODFREY *Back-Stage* iii. 34 When an actor fails to remember his lines and the scene comes to an unpremeditated stop he 'dries up'. *Ibid.* 36 We didn't dry up! No, we kept that scene going! **1934** H. N. ROSE *Thes. Slang* xii. 83/2 What's the idea of trying to dry me up in the last number? **1967** *Times* 10 May 3/8 (*headline*) Insurance to stop actor 'drying up'. **1969** *Listener* 31 July 140/3 Why is the advertising drying up? Who has stopped (or never even started) advertising in these six?

dry, obs. form of DREE.

dryad ('draɪæd). Also 6-7 **driade**. Pl. **dryads**: also in L. form **dryades** ('draɪədiːz). [ad. L. *Dryas*, pl. *Dryad-es* = G. *Δρυάς*, pl. *Δρυάδες* wood-nymphs, f. *δρῦς*, *δρυ-ός* tree.]

1. In *Gr.* and *Lat. Mythol.* A nymph supposed to inhabit trees; a wood-nymph.

1555 EDEN *Decades* 23 They supposed that they had seene those most beawtyfull *Dryades*. **1575** LANEHAM *Let.* (1871) 14 The Fawnz, the Satyres, the Nymphs, the Dryardes, and the Hamadryades. **1598** MARSTON *Fygmal., etc.* Sat. iv. 155 Summon the Nymphs and Driades to bring Some rare inuention, whilst thou doost sing. **1667** MILTON *P.L.* IX. 387 Like a Wood-nymph light, Oread or Dryad, or of Delia's Traine. **1708** PRIOR *Turtle & Sparrow* 35 The dryads all forsook the wood. **1798** COLERIDGE *Picture*, Ye Oreads chaste, ye dusky Dryades. **1859** THACKERAY *Virgin.* ii. (1878) 17 Marble fauns and dryads were cooling themselves.

2. *transf.* **a.** A maiden of the woods; a sylvan beauty. **b.** A forest-tree, a denizen of the woods.

1639 S. DU VERGER tr. *Camus' Admir. Events* 30 This young Gentleman..inflamed with the love of this Driade. **1823** BYRON *Island* II. xi, The palm, the loftiest dryad of the woods.

3. *attrib.* and *Comb.*

a **1790** WARTON *Bathing* Sonn. ii. (R.), Young Health, a Dryad-maid in vesture green..On airy uplands met the piercing gale.

Hence **dry'adic** *a.*, of, pertaining to, or resembling a dryad.

1891 C. E. CRADDOCK *In Str. Countr.* iv, Soft dryadic murmurs. *Ibid.* xii, A flitting dryadic shape.

dryas ('draɪæs). *Bot.* [L.: see DRYAD. First used as a genus-name by Linnæus, *Genera Plantarum* (1737) 148.] An evergreen sub-shrub of the genus so called, belonging to the family Rosaceæ and found in cold or alpine regions of the Northern Hemisphere. Cf. AVENS.

1798 SMITH & SOWERBY *Eng. Bot.* VII. 451 We have cultivated the *Dryas* with success under a north wall. **1872** HOGG & JOHNSON *Wild Flowers Gt. Brit.* VII. 556 Dryas Octopetala... Synonymes.—*Dryas depressa*,..*White Dryas*, English. **1927** *Glasgow Herald* 26 Mar., A thin carpet of Arctic-Alpine vegetation such as a white-flowered dryas and dwarf-willows. **1936** D. MCCOWAN *Animals of Canad. Rockies* ii. 18 Dryas spreads its lovely floral carpet in the sun. **1955** *Times* 4 July 10 That *was* Dryas, my dear fellow, for already your mountain avens is far back down the pass.

Dryasdust ('draɪəzdʌst), *sb.* and *a.* [That is, *dry as dust.*]

A. *sb.* The name of a fictitious person to whom Sir W. Scott pretends to dedicate some of his novels; hence, a writer or student of antiquities, history, or statistics, who occupies himself with the driest and most uninteresting details.

1820 SCOTT *Ivanhoe*, The venerable name of Dr. Jonas Dryasdust. **1822** —— *Nigel* Introd. Ep., Captain Clutterbuck to the Reverend Dr. Dryasdust. **1858** CARLYLE *Fredk. Gt.* I. 16 (H.) The Prussian Dryasdust, otherwise an honest fellow, and not afraid of labour, excels all other Dryasdusts yet known. *a* **1872** MAURICE *Friendship Bks.* vii. (1874) 214 The Dryasdusts may pick up real gems amidst heaps of rubbish. **1889** *Spectator* 9 Nov. 644/1 In spite of his being a fellow of the Royal Historical Society, has nothing of the Dryasdust about him.

B. *adj.* **1.** Extremely 'dry', as a writer, book, or subject of study.

1872 MINTO *Eng. Prose Lit.* II. iv. 313 The most dryasdust of the whole. **1879** E. GARRETT *House by Wks.* II. 79 Dry-as-dust antiquarian stories. **1880** MISS BRADDON *Just as I am* xlv, She considered political economy as a dry-as-dust something outside the circle of her life. **1881** —— *One Thing Needful* viii, Aged by poring over dry-as-dust books.

2. *lit.* Of climate: Extremely dry or rainless.

1889 GEIKIE *Addr. Brit. Assoc.* (*Nature* 19 Sept. 490) A dry-as-dust climate like that of some of the steppe-regions of our own day. *Ibid.*, I cannot..find..any evidence of a dry-as-dust epoch..in Europe during..the Pleistocene period.

Hence (*nonce-wds.*) **Dryas'dustic**, **Dry-as'dustish** *adjs.*; **Dryas'dustism**.

1864 CARLYLE *Fredk. Gt.* XIV. i. (1873) IV. 149 The dark Dryasdustic ages. **1888** *Glasgow Even. Cit.* 7 Sept. 2/4 The British Association, which has naturally an extensive acquaintance with dry-as-dustism. **1890** *Spectator* 31 May 767 Elaborate and yet not Dryasdust-ish disquisitions.

†**dry-beat**, *v. Obs. trans.* To inflict 'dry blows' upon (see DRY *a.* 12); to beat soundly or severely. Hence **dry-beaten** *ppl. a.*

1567 HARMAN *Caveat* (1869) 64 This drye beaten hosteler. **1589** *Pappe w. Hatchet* E iij b, A yonger brother, that meanes to drie beate those of the Elder house. **1603** HOLLAND *Plutarch's Mor.* 1281 His body..is drie beaten, brused and broken. *a* **1667** JER. TAYLOR *Serm. Rom.* ii. 4 Wks. 1831 II. 393 He by dry-beating him might make him at least sensible of blows.

dryche, var. form of DRETCH *v.*[2] *Obs.*

Drydenian (draɪ'diːnɪən), *a.* Characteristic, or in the style, of the English poet John Dryden (1631-1700). So **Drydenic** (draɪ'dɛnɪk), **Drydenish** ('draɪdənɪʃ) *adjs.*, in same sense; **'Drydenism**, a phrase, etc. characteristic of Dryden.

1687 SETTLE *Refl. Dryden* Pref. 2 The boldest Drydenism that e're came in Print. *Ibid.* 23 The greatest piece of Drydenian Nonsense that I have met with yet. *Ibid.* 41 Something Drydenish, Illnatured and unjauntee. **1868** LOWELL *Dryden* Pr. Wks. 1890 III. 141 *note*, A very

Drydenish verse. **1896** SAINTSBURY *Hist. 19th Cent. Lit.* 8 The Drydenian triplet..on which Pope had frowned.

dry dock, dry-dock. a. A dock from which the water is or may be let out, for repairing (or building) a ship: see DOCK *sb.*[3] 4.

1627 [see DOCK *sb.*[3] 4]. **1697** DAMPIER *Voy.* I. xiii. 363 They immediately hale their Ship into a dry Dock, and burn her bottom. **1803** MORSE in M. Cutler *Life, etc.* (1888) II. 129 The President's scheme of a Dry Dock at Washington, appears to me in a high degree visionary and ridiculous. **1883** *Law Rep.* 11 Q. Bench Div. 503 The owner of a dry dock used for the painting and repairing vessels.

b. *in dry dock* (fig.): inactive, unemployed; in quarantine; in hospital. *colloq.*

1927 W. E. COLLINSON *Contemp. Eng.* 58 Those who have been in close contact with the infected patient may have to remain in quarantine or dry-dock. **1929** H. A. VACHELL *Virgin* iii. 55 June found herself in dry dock, and likely to remain there, when her services were most in demand. **1930** J. DOS PASSOS *42nd Parallel* 153 Janey I'm in dry-dock girl.

Hence **'dry-dock** *v., trans.* to place (a vessel) in a dry dock for repairs.

1884 *Pall Mall G.* 12 Aug. 11 The ordinary methods by which ships are dry-docked. **1895** *Boston Her.* (U.S.) 21 Mar. 7/1 The lack of dry-docking facilities.

drye, obs. form of DREE, DRY.

dryer, var. of DRIER, freq. in techn. senses.

† **'dryfat, dry-fat.** *Obs.* Also 6 **drievat,** 6–7 **drifat(te, driefat(te,** etc.; also as two words. [f. DRY *a.* + FAT *sb.*[1] = *vat.*] A large vessel (cask, barrel, tub, case, box, etc.) used to hold dry things (as opposed to liquids): see FAT *sb.*[1] 3.

1526 *Tolls* in Dillon *Calais & Pale* (1892) 89 For evry dryfatt with merchandyce iiijd. **1540,** etc. [see FAT *sb.*[1] 3]. **1558** W. TOWRSON in Hakluyt *Voy.* (1589) 127, 2 Driefats of bread. **1577–87** HOLINSHED *Chron.* II. 196 Unlesse it come out of their owne drievat. **1625** B. JONSON *Staple of N.* III. iv, I am a broken vessell..a shrunke old Dryfat. **1677** YARRANTON *Eng. Improv.* 45 The Thread..is brought down the Elbe and Rhine in dry Fats for Holland and Flanders.

dryf(e), dryff(e), dryfen, obs. inf. and pa. pple. of DRIVE *v.*

† **'dry-fist.** *Obs.* [cf. DRY *a.* 15 b.] A niggardly or stingy person. So † **'dry-,fisted** *a.*, niggardly, miserly, stingy.

1604 DEKKER *Honest Wh.* Wks. 1873 II. 28 Of all filthy dryfisted Knights. **1607** —— *Knts. Conjur.* (1842) 76 Nash inueyed bitterly..against dryfisted patrons. **1633** FORD *Love's Sacr.* III. i, Why, wise madam Dry-fist, could your mouldy brain be so addle? [**1674** COTTON *Compl. Gamester* in Singer *Hist. Cards* (1816) 334 Throwing..at a good sum with a dry fist (as they call it); that is, if they nick you, it is theirs; if they lose, they owe you so much.]

dry-foot ('draɪfʊt), *adv.* (*a.*) Also without hyphen, and as two words: see DRY and FOOT.

1. With dry feet; without wetting the feet.

c **1200** ORMIN 10338 All common oferr driȝȝefot All alls itt waterr nære. *a* **1225** *Julianna* 32 þu leddest israeles folc þurh þe reade sea..druifot. **1387** TREVISA *Higden* (Rolls) V. 239 He wolde lede hem drie foot into þe londe of byheste. *c* **1400** MAUNDEV. (Roxb.) xi. 43 Childer of Israel passed thurgh it drie fote. **1593** NASHE *Christ's T.* 19 a, Ouer the waters of my Teares and tribulation, shee..passeth as drie-foote, as once they past ouer Iordan. **1623** LISLE *Ælfric on O. & N. Test., Evangelists,* Walked upon the sea drie-foot.

† **2.** *to draw* or *hunt dry-foot*: to track game by the mere scent of the foot. Also *fig. Obs.*

1590 SHAKS. *Com. Err.* IV. ii. 39 A hound that runs Counter, and yet draws drifoot well. **1649** G. DANIEL *Trinarch., Hen. V,* ccxlix, When we read that wonder, and have trac'd Historie, dry-foot. **1651** *Life Father Sarpi* (1676) 41 Like Dogs that draw dry-foot.

† **3.** *attrib.* or *adj. Obs.*

1608 MACHIN *Dumb Knt.* III. in Hazl. *Dodsley* X. 166, I care not for his dry-foot hunting. **1635** QUARLES *Emblemes* IV. viii, 213 And, from her sandy deepes, approach the dry-foot shore. **1672** SHADWELL *Miser* II. Wks. 1720 III. 39 Thou art like a dry-foot dog.

'dry-,footed, *a.* Having dry feet; with the feet not wetted; = prec. 1.

a **1225** *Ancr. R.* 220 þer heo eoden drui-uoted. **1398** TREVISA *Barth. De P.R.* IX. xxxi. (1495) 367 [They] passyd Iordan drye foted. **1577–87** HARRISON *England* I. x. 30 Such as a man may go into drie-footed at the full Sea. **1833** MARRYAT *P. Simple* xii, Whether he was out of his depth or not, I can't tell, although I suspect that he was not dry-footed.

b. *fig.* ? Passing lightly and dexterously over a difficulty (like one who steps lightly over a stream without wetting his feet).

[**1579** FULKE *Heskins' Parl.* 359 Maister Heskins skippeth ouer with a drye foote, that Ambrose saith..he shall not die.] **1830** COLERIDGE *Table-t.* 20 May, The explanation of Erasmus, and Clarke, and some others, is very dry-footed.

'dry-,founder, *v. trans.* To render (a horse) lame from inflammation in the hoof; = FOUNDER *v.* Chiefly in pa. pple. **dry-foundered** = FOUNDERED. ? *Obs.* (In quot. 1654 alluding to the foundering of a ship.)

1611 BEAUM. & FL. *King & no King* v. iii, If he kick thus i' the dog-days, he will be dry-foundred. **1654** H. L'ESTRANGE *Chas. I,* 131 Before these ships could be fitted to flote upon the main, they were dry-foundred at land. For the Tax being a burden, every man began to study how to decline the weight. *a* **1656** USSHER *Ann.* vi. (1658) 301 Fearing least..he should dry founder and lose all his horses.

dryȝe, obs. form of DREE, DRY.

dryght, -ȝt, -in, -yn: see DRIGHT, DRIGHTIN.

dry goods. a. A name (chiefly in N. Amer.) for the class of merchandise comprising textile fabrics and related things; articles of drapery, mercery, and haberdashery (as opposed to groceries).

1657 J. ALRICHS *Let.* 25 May in *Pennsylvania Archives* (1877) V. 285 Some of the dry goods, entirely scattered about, were wet and injured by the quantity of water in the ship. **1708** *Deplorable State New Eng.* 18 in *Sewall's Diary* (1879) II. 115* One Hog's-Head of Dry Goods. **1775** A. BURNABY *Trav.* 71 With the dry goods, which they purchase in London, they traffick in the neighbouring colonies. **1812** H. & J. SMITH *Rej. Addr., Loyal Effusion,* And raised the price of dry goods and tobaccos. **1821** DWIGHT *Trav.* I. 187 There were in New-Haven..41 stores of dry goods. **1921** *Daily Colonist* (Victoria, B.C.) 26 Mar. 6/4 Fire..worked havoc in the $40,000 stock of groceries, drygoods, shoes and general stock carried by Messrs. Malpass & Wilson. **1968** *Globe & Mail* (Toronto) 17 Feb. 31 Sellers and buyers of produce, hardware, dry goods and what-not.

b. *attrib.*, as ***dry-goods business, dealer, shop, store***; **dry-'goodsman,** one who sells dry goods.

a **1813** A. WILSON *Foresters* Poet. Wks. (1846) 233 At length we spelt this precious piece of lore; 'Pat Dougherty's Hotel and Drygood Store'. **1837** HAWTHORNE *Amer. Note-bks.* 12 Aug., Fellow-passenger, a Boston dry-goods dealer, travelling to collect bills. **1863** —— *Our Old Home* (1883) I. 160 What we should call a dry-goods store, or, according to the English phrase, a mercer's and haberdasher's shop. **1863** DICEY *Federal St.* I. 3 A number of New York and Boston dry-goods men.

† **'dryhede.** *Obs.* Also **drihed, dryehed.** [f. DRY *a.*: see -HEAD.] Dryness, drought; dry land; a dry place, desert.

a **1300** *E. E. Psalter* lxv[i]. 6 Whilk þat tornes þe se In mikel drihed for to be. *a* **1325** *Prose Ps.* lxxvii[i]. 45 Hou oft hij greued hym in wildernes; hij somond him in ire in dryhede. *c* **1440** *Jacob's Well* (E.E.T.S.) 236 In hyȝe hylles of pryde arn iiij. wyckednessys, þat arn, dryehed, hardhed, bareynhed, & a foul fall doun.

† **'dryine.** *Obs.* Also 6 **drynas.** [ad. late Gr. δρυΐνας, f. δρῦς tree, oak.] A serpent reputed to live in hollow oaks.

1591 SYLVESTER *Du Bartas* I. vi. 201 Th' Adder, and Drynas (full of odious stink). **1607** TOPSELL *Serpents* (1658) 717 Bellonius writeth, that he never saw any Serpent greater than this Dryine, which he calleth Dendrozailla.

drying ('draɪɪŋ), *vbl. sb.* [f. DRY *v.* + -ING[1].]

1. The action of the verb DRY; abstraction of moisture; desiccation. Also with *adv.*, as ***drying-up.***

1398 TREVISA *Barth. De P.R.* XVI. xxii. (1495) 560 The powdre of the whestone..hath vertue of dryenge. **1480** *Wardr. Acc. Edw. IV* (1830) 124 For wasshing and drying of ix pair of shetes. **1548** *Act 2 & 3 Edw. VI,* c. 10 §1 Except the same [Malt] have in the fatt flower stepinge and sufficient drienge. **1667** H. OLDENBURG in *Phil. Trans.* II. 417 The too hasty drying thereof spoils it. **1880** C. R. MARKHAM *Peruv. Bark* 349 The people complained bitterly of the drying up of the streams. **1889** *Pall Mall G.* 7 Nov. 3/3 Fifty years is the period..[assigned] for the practical drying-up of the ivory supply.

2. *attrib.* and *Comb.* Used in or for drying something, as ***drying-basin, -box, -case, -chamber, -closet, -cylinder, -floor, -ground, -horse, -house, -machine, -paper, -pipe, -plate, -rack, -room, -stove, -tube, -yard***; **drying day,** a sunny, windy day on which washing dries quickly.

1502 *Priv. Purse Exp. Eliz. of York* (1830) 81 To..the Quenes fotemen for thaire dryeng money. **1558** *Bury Wills* (Camden) 150 A dryeng bason. **1766** C. LEADBETTER *Royal Gauge* II. xiv. (ed. 6) 371 Hung up, on Lines..in the Drying-House. **1799** MRS. ADAMS in *Harper's Mag.* (1885) Mar. 538/1, I made a drying-room..to hang up the clothes in. **1821** in Cobbett *Rur. Rides* (1885) I. 49 Close by the road-side is the drying-ground. **1854** S. THOMSON *Wild Fl.* III. (ed. 4) 238 If you consign it [the plant] to your drying-paper. **1880** C. R. MARKHAM *Peruv. Bark* 149 The green leaves, called matu..are then spread out in the drying-yard..and carefully dried in the sun. **1884** T. C. HEPWORTH *Photogr. Amat.* xiv. 124 The skeleton drying-rack which I recommend. **1906** E. NESBIT *Railway Children* vii. 143 'I'll wash your Indian muslins at once.'..'It's a nice drying day—that's one thing.' **1934** *Archit. Rev.* LXXV. 45/1 (*caption*) Kitchenette with gas-ring, sink, drying-rack. **1971** R. RENDELL *One Across* x. 79 Mrs. Blackmore's Monday wash was flapping on the line... 'Lovely drying day!'

'drying, *ppl. a.* [f. as prec. + -ING[2].]

1. That dries or renders dry: having the quality of abstracting moisture; desiccative. In early use in Medicine.

1398 TREVISA *Barth. De P.R.* XIX. lxxix. (1495) 913 The harde yolke is dryenge and harde to passe out of the stomak. *c* **1400** *Lanfranc's Cirurg.* 291 Make fumigaciouns of dryinge þingis: as galles [etc.]. **1563** W. FULKE *Meteors* (1640) 57 b, These waters being also drying by nature. **1709** PRIOR *Paulo Purganti,* Drying Coffee was deny'd; But Chocolate that Loss supply'd. **1851** CARPENTER *Man. Phys.* (ed. 2) 93 A cold drying wind.

2. Becoming dry; having the quality of drying quickly; *spec.* of oils (see quot. 1865).

1758 A. REID tr. *Macquer's Chym.* I. 115 What is called a Spirit-Varnish, or a Drying Varnish, because it soon dries. *c* **1865** LETHEBY in *Circ. Sc.* I. 99/1 Subdivided into those which become thick or gelatinous on exposure to the air (*drying oils*), as linseed and poppy; and those which do not (*fat oils*), as olive and sperm. *c* **1865** J. WYLDE *ibid.* 418/2 Some oils, by the absorption of oxygen, become what are termed 'drying oils'. **1872** TENNYSON *Lynette* 1087 A helm With but a drying evergreen for crest.

Hence **'dryingness,** drying quality.

1840 *Æolus* 60 The air..receives..an increase of dryness, or of dryingness, which latter designation is to be preferred as more truly expressive of the fact.

dryish ('draɪɪʃ), *a.* [f. DRY *a.* + -ISH.] Somewhat dry (*lit.* and *fig.*).

1725 BRADLEY *Fam. Dict.* s.v. *Ozier,* Planted rather in a dryish than overmoist ground. **1864** BURTON *Scot Abr.* I. iv. 159 A curious and valuable collection, but rather dryish.

dry land. Also **dry-land, dryland.** [See DRY *a.* 5.]

1. Land not submerged or under water; land as opposed to sea.

a **1225** *Juliana* (Bodl. MS.) 77 And drof ham to drue lond in to champaine. *a* **1330** *Otuel* 444 Anon riȝt als roulond Hadde ikauȝt þe druye lond [etc.]. **1535** COVERDALE *Gen.* i. 10 And God called yᵉ drye londe, Earth. *a* **1626** BACON *New Atl.* (1627) 3 God..discovered the face of the Deep, and brought forth Drie-land. **1892** GARDINER *Stud. Hist. Eng.* 1 Animals could pass over on dry land.

2. orig. *U.S.* An area of low rainfall, esp. when farmed without irrigation. Cf. *dry-farming* s.v. DRY *a.* C. 3.

1893 [see sense 3 b below]. **1910** W. MACDONALD *Dry-Farming* p. v, To all those who believe in the dry-lands of the United States and the British Empire this volume is respectfully inscribed. *Ibid.* i. 34 They have already demonstrated..that the finest wheats are those grown on dry lands. **1964** *TV Guide* (U.S.) 27 June 12 Ken Curtis picked up the accent..as a boy in the dry-lands of southeastern Colorado. **1977** *Observer* 28 Aug. 4/1 The desert spreads like a skin disease, erupting..behind the margin dividing dryland from desert proper.

3. *attrib.* **a.** Of or pertaining to dry land: land-.

1696 WHISTON *Th. Earth* IV. (1722) 330 The Generation of the Dryland Animals. **1732** BERKELEY *Alciphr.* v. §33 Oxen, and other dry land animals. **1866** HOWELLS *Venet. Life* xii. 179 No horse..that type of dry-land locomotion.

b. Of or pertaining to dry lands (sense 2 above); produced by farming without irrigation.

1893 *Irrigation Age* Apr. 358/2 Nearly or quite every effort that has been made to establish a dry-land colony has ended in failure. **1917** *Eye Opener* (Calgary) 6 Jan. 3/5 Jan Johnson and Katrina Jensen married and took up a dry land homestead. **1920** *Harvey's Weekly* 24 July 11/2 Vegetables —'dry-land' and irrigated. **1953** *Canad. Geogr. Jrnl.* June 241/2 Providing a market for dry-land cattle for finishing.. and..bringing nearer to the dry-land farmer the superior service facilities of the..irrigation districts. **1976** *National Observer* (U.S.) 6 Mar. 4/1 If we don't get rain in 30 days you can write off the dry-land wheat crop. **1985** *Sci. Amer* Jan. 16/2 Broad acres of dryland grain invite machine harvesters.

c. Special Combs. **dry-land farming** orig. *U.S.*, farming in dry lands (sense 2 above); a method of farming in which moisture conservation techniques are practised so as to avoid irrigation in arid or semi-arid areas; = *dry farming* s.v. DRY *a.* C. 3; hence ***dry-land farm, dry-land farmer.***

1914 'B. M. BOWER' *Flying U Ranch* 166 The soil was not fertile enough even for the most optimistic of 'dry land' farmers to locate upon it; and this was before the dry-land farming craze had swept the country. **1953** [see sense 3 b above]. **1973** B. BROADFOOT *Ten Lost Years* iv. 38 My boy and I were farming near Manyberries and it was dryland farming. No irrigation. **1976** *Billings* (Montana) *Gaz.* 16 June 11C/7 (*Advt.*), 940 acres deeded ranch in Big Horn County... Has some good dryland farm ground. **1979** *Nature* 27 Sept. 251/3 Some good progress has certainly been made in research on dryland farming, largely aimed at reducing risks in cultivation in rainfed areas.

Hence **'drylander** chiefly *N. Amer.*, one who has settled in a dry-land area, esp. one engaged in dry-land farming.

1921 *Frontier* Feb. 11 It is good house. He build summer kitchen. None of drylanders have summer kitchen. **1943** J. K. HOWARD *Montana* 37 Neighbors helped themselves to the drylanders' abandoned house. **1963** *Time* (Canada ed.) 11 Oct. 16/2 At the Tivoli theater in Saskatoon last week, surviving drylanders could be heard telling youngsters: 'That was the way it was'.

dryly, drily ('draɪlɪ), *adv.* [f. DRY *a.* + -LY[2]. The former spelling is more analogical: cf. *shyly, slyly,* also *dryness.*]

1. In a dry manner or state; without moisture.

1562 J. HEYWOOD *Prov. & Epigr.* (1867) 216 Walke thou weatly, walke thou dryly. **1601** SHAKS. *All's Well* I. i. 176 Your old virginity, is like one of our French wither'd peares: it lookes ill, it eates drily.

2. Without emotion, sympathy, or cordiality, coldly, frigidly: see DRY *a.* 13.

1622 BACON *Hen. VII* (J.), Conscious to himself how dryly the King had been used by his council. **1693** DRYDEN *Juvenal* I. 113 Virtue is but drily Prais'd, and Sterves. **1809** G. ROSE *Diaries* (1860) II. 392 Saying drily, but civilly, that he should come. **1861** WILSON & GEIKIE *Mem. E. Forbes* iv. 115 His sympathy was but dryly expressed.

3. With quiet sarcasm or caustic humour: see DRY *a.* 14.

1430 LYDG. *Chron. Troy* II. xvi, He was bouerdyng all the long daye..So dryely that no man might espye So sober he was in his countenaunce. **1592** NASHE *P. Penilesse* (ed. 2) 14 a, A iolly lustie olde Gentleman, that will winke, and laugh, and ieast drily. **1828** SCOTT *F.M. Perth* vii, 'You saw me, neighbour Glover, at the beginning of the fray?' 'I saw you after the end of it, neighbour', answered the Glover, drily. **1838–9** HALLAM *Hist. Lit.* IV. i. IV. §16. 10 The style of Bentley was sometimes humorous and dryly sarcastic.

4. In a bare or plain style, without embellishment, baldly; in a dull or uninteresting style or manner: see DRY *a.* 16–18.

1635 J. HAYWARD tr. *Biondi's Banish'd Virg.* 103 Which for being so drily written, made them..desirous to know the occasion. **1709** POPE *Ess. Crit.* 114 Some dryly plain..Write dull receipts how poems may be made. **1759** GOLDSM. *Bee, Augustan Age* (Globe) 414/2 The poet either drily didactive ..or triflingly volatile. **1836** WHATELY *Chr. Evid.* xi, The miracles..are all related briefly, calmly, and dryly, and almost with an air of indifference.

dryness ('draɪnɛs). Forms: see DRY *a.*; also 5–6 **drines**, 6–7 **drinesse**, 7–8 **driness**. [f. DRY *a.* + -NESS.]

1. a. The quality or condition of being dry; absence or deficiency of moisture; aridity; drought.

1398 TREVISA *Barth. De P.R.* IV. iii. (1495) 83 Dryenesse spoyllyth the heed of the heer and makyth it ballyd. **1483** *Cath. Angl.* 108/2 A Drynes, *ariditas.* **1530** PALSGR. 215/2 Drinesse, *sechesse*..Drighnesse, *chaline.* **1543–4** *Act 35 Hen. VIII*, c. 10 For the drines of the earth. **1563** W. FULKE *Meteors* (1640) 19 Windes..some of them bringing raine, some drinesse. **1643** DENHAM *Cooper's H.* 207 While driness moisture, coldness heat resists. **1770–4** A. HUNTER in Winter *Syst. Husb.* (1787) 183 According to the driness or wetness of the season. **1838** T. THOMSON *Chem. Org. Bodies* 562 The milky liquid is evaporated to dryness.

†**b.** *concr.* A dry place; dry land. *Obs. rare.*

1398 TREVISA *Barth. De P.R.* XVI. lxix. (1495) 575 Nitrum ..is made ryghte as salt in drynesse in alde clyues. *c* **1450** *Chester Pl.* (E.E.T.S.) 21 That drynes earth men shall call; The gathering of the waters all Seas to name.

†**c.** The condition of being dried up; failure, cessation. *Obs.*

1625 BACON *Ess., Usurie* (Arb.) 545 This will preserue Borrowing from any generall Stop or Drinesse.

2. Thirst. *Obs.* (or only in vulgar use.)

a **1535** FISHER *Serm.* Wks. (1876) 400 How in his dryghnesse they would haue filled it with Asell and Gaule. **1559** W. CUNNINGHAM *Cosmogr. Glasse* 176 Much sweter then Hony, and most pleasantly aswageth drines.

3. *fig.* **a.** Absence of emotion, feeling, or fervour; lack of cordiality; coldness of feeling; distance of manner.

c **1450** tr. *De Imitatione* III. lx. 142 Lest my soule faile for werynes & drynes of mynde. **1526** *Pilgr. Perf.* (W. de W. 1531) 94 b, Drynesse of spiryte cometh somtyme..whan a persone gyueth hymselfe moche to worldly or bodyly myrth and pleasure. **1669** WOODHEAD *St. Teresa* I. iv. 12 God changed the driness wherein my soul had formerly been, into an extream tenderness. **1748** SMOLLETT *Rod. Rand.* (1792) I. 278 There was a dryness between the lieutenant and him on my account. **1831** *Society* I. 310 An apparent want of delicacy in his accosting her..made her manner assume a dryness very unlike its usual tone.

b. Absence of embellishment, plainness, baldness; lack of interest, dullness.

a **1637** B. JONSON *Discoveries, Præcipiendi modi*, Their new flowers and sweetness do as much corrupt as others dryness and squalor. **1709** *Tatler* No. 43 ¶5 The Learned have so long laboured under the Imputation of Dryness and Dulness in their Accounts of their Phænomena. *a* **1719** GARTH (J.), Paraphrase where penury of fancy or dryness of expression ask it. **1853** 'C. BEDE' *Verdant Green* ix. (ed. 4) 78 The dryness and daily routine of lectures.

4. The condition of being 'dry' (see DRY *a.* 11 a) or without alcohol; prohibition.

1910 'MARK TWAIN' *Speeches* 430 When the others drink I like to help; otherwise I remain dry. This dryness does not hurt me. **1920** *Contemp. Rev.* July 79 'Dryness' in America is enormously increasing the consumption [of sugar] there. **1927** *Observer* 24 July 9/2 President Coolidge will..run as a staunch champion of 'dryness'. **1944** W. R. SCOTT *Revolt on Mount Sinai* xxii. 175 The platform..ordered the drys to stop measuring candidates for Congress..by their degrees of dryness.

dry-nurse, *sb.* [Cf. DRY *a.* 4 b.]

1. A woman who takes care of and attends to a child, but does not suckle it (opp. to *wet-nurse*); formerly, also, in the general sense of 'nurse'. Phr. ***at dry nurse*** (cf. NURSE *sb.*[1] 2 a).

1598 SHAKS. *Merry W.* I. ii. 3 One Mistris Quickly; which is in the manner of his Nurse; or his dry-Nurse; or his Cooke. *a* **1618** RALEIGH *To Son* ii. in *Remains* (1661) 84 After a while thou didst love thy Drie-nurse, and didst forget the other. **1663** TUKE *Adv. 5 Hours* v. iii, There's no cook, nor dry-nurse, like a wife. **1731** SWIFT *To Gay* 8 Make a dry-nurse of thy muse? **1839** R. BARHAM in *Bentley's Misc.* VI. 640 Neglecting the poor little dear out at dry-nurse. **1848** KINGSLEY *Saint's Trag.* III. iii, To play the dry-nurse to three starving brats. **1849** C. BRONTË *Shirley* III. ix. 206 Mrs. Horsfall had him at dry-nurse.

2. *fig.* A man who is charged with 'looking after' another; *esp.* one who instructs or 'coaches' a superior in his duties.

1614 B. JONSON *Bart. Fair* I. (Rtldg.) 310/2 Well, this dry nurse..is a delicate man. *c* **1640** *Capt. Underwit* in Bullen *O. Pl.* II. 322 (Farmer) You must have a dry nurse, as many Captaines have..I can hire you an old limping decayed sergeant at Brainford. **1784** COWPER *Task* II. 371 Grand caterer and dry nurse of the church! **1820** SCOTT *Monast.* vi, The old general who, in foreign armies, is placed at the elbow of the Prince of the Blood, who nominally commands in chief, on condition of attempting nothing without the advice of his dry-nurse. **1826** WELLINGTON in *Croker P.* (1884) I. xi. 343 When the Horse Guards are obliged to employ one of those fellows like me in whom they have no confidence, they give him what is called a *second in command* —one in whom they have confidence—a kind of *dry nurse.*

dry-nurse, *v.* [f. prec. sb. or f. DRY *adv.* + NURSE.] *trans.* To bring up 'by hand', without the breast; to play the dry-nurse to (*lit.* and *fig.*); to 'coach' or instruct (a superior) in his duties.

1581 RICH *Farewell* (Shaks. Soc.) 185 Her daughter..she committed to the outlawes..who..promised to drie nurse the child so well as thei could till she should make retourne. **1663** BUTLER *Hud.* I. ii. 168 As Romulus a Wolf did rear So he was dry-nurs'd by a Bear. **1767** MRS. S. PENNINGTON *Lett.* IV. 13 A round flexible pipe might be contrived for the feeding dry-nursed children. **1840** MARRYAT *Poor Jack* ii, She had dry-nursed a young baronet. **1862** CARLYLE *Fredk. Gt.* x. iv. (1865) III. 246 Franz of Lorraine bears the title of Commander, whom Seckendorf is to dry-nurse. **1894** WOLSELEY *Marlborough* I. 282 Some regular officers who had been selected..for the purpose of dry-nursing their inexperienced colonels.

Dryopithecus (ˌdraɪəʊpɪ'θiːkəs, -'pɪθɪkəs). [mod.L. (E. Lartet 1856, in *Compt. Rend. Acad. Sci.* XLIII. 221), f. Gr. δρῦς tree + πίθηκος ape.] A genus of fossil anthropoid apes of the Miocene period in France. So **dryopithecine** (-'pɪθɪsiːn) *a.*, pertaining to this genus; **dryopithecoid** (-pɪ'θiːkɔɪd) *a.*, resembling this genus.

1862 *Geologist* V. 428 The shaft of the supposed humerus of the *Dryopithecus*, from the miocene of the South of France. **1863** C. LYELL *Antiquity of Man* xxiv. 499 Fossil apes... One of these, the Dryopithecus of Lartet, a gibbon or long-armed ape, about equal to man in stature, was obtained in the year 1856 in the upper miocene strata at Sansan, near the foot of the Pyrenees. **1912** A. KEITH *Human Body* iv. 58 The very earliest of the large fossil anthropoids which have yet been discovered is the kind now named Dryopithecus. **1937** *Nature* 20 Feb. 326/2 If *Australopithecus* is not literally a missing link between the older dryopithecoid group and primitive man, what conceivable combination of ape and human characters would ever be admitted as such? **1939** *Ibid.* 2 Sept. 451/2 A primitive dryopithecine stage. **1957** *Antiquity* XXXI. 191 The Dryopithecine canine [tooth] was too large and specialized.

dry rot, dry-rot.

1. A decayed condition of timber in confined situations, in which it becomes brittle and crumbles to a dry powder; caused by various fungi, esp. species of *Polyporus* and *Merulius*, or by slow chemical processes. Also applied to any fungus causing this.

1795 (*title*) Some Observations on the Distemper in Timber called the Dry Rot. **1803** J. PAPWORTH (*title*) An Essay on the Cause of the Dry Rot in Buildings; with some Observations on the Cure of the Dry Rot, by the Admission of Air into the Parts of Buildings affected with that Disease. **1830** LINDLEY *Nat. Syst. Bot.* 337 Of parasitical Fungi, the most important are those which are called dry rot. *a* **1835** J. MACCULLOCH *Proofs & Illustr. Attrib. God* (1837) 121 The far greater number of these imaginary cases of dry-rot are no other than this, the usual chemical decomposition of the hard vegetable fibre.

2. *fig.* A state of hidden or unsuspected moral or social decay tending to disintegration.

1821 *Examiner* 91/1 A species of political dry rot is pervading the whole community. **1881** W. PHILLIPS in C. Martyn *Life* (1890) 586 The dry-rot of legislative corruption.

Hence **dry-rot** *v. trans.*, to affect with dry rot. **dry-rotten** *ppl. a.*, decayed with dry rot.

1818 BENTHAM *Ch. Eng.* 359 *note*, The more completely and notoriously dry-rotten the whole fabric, the more money would be called for..for the support of it. **1870** LOWELL *Among my Bks.* Ser. I. (1873) 223 They are dry-rotting the very fibre of will and conscience. **1883** *American* VII. 4 Swept away as incapable and dry-rotten.

dryry, obs. form of DREARY *a.*

drysalter ('draɪˌsɒltə(r)). [app. f. *dry salt*, after *salter*.] A dealer in chemical products used in the arts, drugs, dye-stuffs, gums, etc.; sometimes also in oils, sauces, pickles, tinned meats, etc.

1707 *Lond. Gaz.* No. 4352/4 John Lawford, late of London, Dry-Salter. **1745** *De Foe's Eng. Tradesman* iv. (1841) I. 25 A. B. was bred a dry-salter..As a salter A. B.... understands very well the buying of cochineal, indigo, galls, sumach, logwood, fustick, madder, and the like. **1790** SIR W. FORDYCE *On Muriatic Acid* 7 (T.), I heard by accident of a drysalter, who had acquired a great reputation and a large fortune from possessing a secret that enabled him to send out to the Indies, and other hot countries, beef and pork, in a better state of preservation than any of the trade. **1828** *Craven Dial., Dry-salter*, a person dealing in various articles for dyeing (not in pickles, according to Mr. Todd). **1848** THACKERAY *Van. Fair* lxi, There was scarce one of the ladies that hadn't a relation a peer, though the husband might be a drysalter in the City. **1891** *Labour Commission* Gloss., *Drysalter*, one who deals in drugs, oils, potted meats, gums, etc. **1896** *Kelly's P.O. London Directory* 1816 *Drysalters.* See also Druggists—Wholesale; also Gum Merchants; also Indigo Merchants; also Merchants—General; also Oil and Color Men.

drysaltery ('draɪˌsɒltərɪ). [f. prec. + -Y: cf. *grocery*, etc.] A drysalter's store or business; the articles dealt in by a drysalter (*sing.* and *pl.*).

1848 DICKENS *Dombey* xxiii, The smell of which drysaltery impregnated the air. **1865** —— *Mut. Fr.* II. 189 A bunch of keys, commanding treasures in the way of drysaltery. **1883** *Law Times* 27 Oct. 424/2 A general dealer, selling..meat and drapery, as well as groceries, or as they are called dry-salteries. **1884** *Pall Mall G.* Extra 24 July 10/1 A collection of drugs, drysaltery, and chemicals.

drysel, obs. form of DRIZZLE.

dry-shod ('draɪʃɒd), *a.* [= *dry shoed*, with dry shoes.] Having one's shoes dry; without wetting the feet. (With *go, pass, walk*, etc.)

1535 COVERDALE *Josh.* Contents iii, The people go thorow it drye shodd. *c* **1586** C'TESS PEMBROKE *Ps.* LXVI. iii, Through Jordans streames we dry-shod waded. **1679** DRYDEN *Troilus* v. ii, And dry-shod we may pass the naked ford. **1808** SCOTT *Marm.* II. ix, Dry-shod, o'er sands, twice every day, The pilgrims to the shrine find way.

b. *attrib.* qualifying *passage*, etc.

1813 SCOTT *Trierm.* i, A dry-shod pass from side to side.

†**'drysne**, *v.* *Obs.* [OE. *drysnian*, deriv. of **drus-*, *u*-grade of **dreus-an*, OE. *dréosan* to fall; cf. DRIZZLE, in 6 *drysel.*] *intr.* To fall down, sink. Hence **'drysnyng**, falling, fall.

c **950** *Lindisf. Gosp.* Mark ix. 46 Ðer wyrm hiora ne bið dead and þæt fyr ne bið adrysned [*Rushw.* ne bið drysned]. *a* **1400–50** *Alexander* 3801 A litill drysnyng of dewe was droppid fra þe heuen.

drysse, obs. form of DRESS *v.*

dryster ('draɪstə(r)). [f. DRY *v.*: see -STER.] A workman or woman employed in drying something.

14.. *Nom.* in Wr.-Wülcker 692 *Nomina artificium mulierum..Hec siccatrix*, a dryster. **1483** *Cath. Angl.* 109 A Dryster, *dissicator, -trix.* *a* **1671** LAMONT *Diary* 180 (Jam.) Old Robert Baillie being dryster that day, and William Lundy..measter of the mille. **1825** JAMIESON, *Dryster.* 1. The person who has the charge of turning and drying the grain in a kiln. 2. One whose business is to dry cloth at a bleachfield. **1894** H. SPEIGHT *Nidderdale* 384 *note*, Throwsters and drysters were potters' craftsmen.

dryte: see DRITE.

dryth (draɪθ). Now only *south. dial.* Also 6–7 **drythe, drith(e, drieth, dryeth.** [f. DRY *a.* + -TH[1], after *warmth*, etc.] Dryness, dry condition.

a **1533** LD. BERNERS *Gold. Bk. M. Aurel.* (1546) Ll v, By heate of the sonne and drythe of the powdre. **1548** UDALL, etc. *Erasm. Par. Mark* xi. 20 By reason of the drieth of his bodye. **1610** W. FOLKINGHAM *Art of Survey* I. viii. 15 Moysture and dryeth, heat and cold. **1671** BLAGRAVE *Astrol. Physic* 10 Agreeing with heat and drith. **1686** GOAD *Celest. Bodies* I. ii. 3 Dryth and Moisture. **1711** J. GREENWOOD *Eng. Gram.* 175 Dry'th. **1889** *Temple Bar* Feb. 178 (*dial.*) 'What the old man do want is nourishing food and dryth.'

b. Dry weather, drought.

1571 FORTESCUE *Forest* 106 b, Bee you well assured of greate drieth. **1610** G. FLETCHER *Christ's Vict.* in Farr *S.P. Jas. I* (1848) 53 But now for drieth the fields were all undone. **1875** *Sussex Gloss.* s.v., Drythe never yet bred dearth. **1893** Q. [COUCH] *Delectable Duchy* 294 The end of a week's dryth.

†**c.** Thirst. *Obs.*

1557 *Tottell's Misc.* (Arb.) 137 The dropsy dryeth, that Tantale in the flood Endureth aye. **1587** M. GROVE *Pelops & Hipp.* (1878) 86 His dryth and thirst he slakes.

d. Drying.

1881 YOUNG *Every man his own Mechanic* §1588 To harden it and promote quick dryth.

drytt, drytte: see DRITE, DRIGHTIN.

dry-up ('draɪʌp). The action of drying up (see DRY *v.* 5).

1873 J. H. BEADLE *Undevel. West* 711 The plowman returns to his work without waiting for a 'dry-up'. **1891** FARMER *Slang* II. 334/2 *Dry-up* (theatrical), a failure. **1939** A. THIRKELL *Before Lunch* v. 136 The two elder ladies rapidly finished the wash-up and the dry-up. **1940** N. COWARD *Australia Visited* IV. 22 It is well over a year now since I have written anything... This..dry-up of talent is extremely painful.

dry-vat: see DRYFAT.

dryve, dryven, drywe, etc.: see DRIVE *v.*

drywery, dryworie, var. DRUERY, *Obs.*

dschikketai, dshiggetai: var. of DZIGGETAI.

dschin: see JIN.

‖**dso.** *Zool.* Also dzo. Cf. ZHO. [Tibetan.] See quot.

[**1866** H. A. JAESCHKE *Tibetan & Eng. Dict.* 33/1 *Dzo*, hybrid of yag and common cow.] **1882** *Encycl. Brit.* XIV. 197 (*Ladak*) Among domestic animals are the famous shawl goat..the yak, and the dso, a valuable hybrid between the yak and common cow. **1897** *Geogr. Jrnl.* July 36 They also breed herds of *dzo*, a very valuable hybrid between the cow and yak... The male *dzo* is used for ploughing. **1960** 'S. HARVESTER' *Chinese Hammer* vii. 71 Some dzos..highly prized as draught animals and for a high fat content in their milk. **1969** C. D. DARLINGTON *Evol. Man & Society* 625 The herdsmen stumping the hills probably came from Mongolia..bringing yaks, dzos (yak-ox hybrids) and sheep.

d-string ('diːˌstrɪŋ). *Mus.* [See D II. 2.] The string sounding the note D on instruments of the violin class; in the violin the third string.

1894 *Contemp. Rev.* Aug. 262 It sounds higher on the G-string than on the D-string of a violin.

'dswounds: see ZOUNDS.

D.T. ('diː'tiː). Also D.T.'s ('diː'tiːz). Colloq. abbrev. of DELIRIUM TREMENS.

1858 'MEGATHYM SPLENE' *Almæ Matres* 33 The disease called D.T. (heaven forbid I should write it in full). **1861** B.

HEMYNG in Mayhew *London Labour* Extra vol. (1862) 224/2, I shall soon get D.T. and then I'll kill myself in a fit of madness. **1880** G. R. SIMS *Ballads of Babylon* 79 A titled churl Who had just got round from a bad *d.t.* **1907** *Daily Chron.* 30 Aug. 7/3 'D.T.'s' without drunkenness. **1910** A. H. DAVIS *From Selection to City* ix. 82 He started to shake as if he had the d.t.'s. **1955** R. KING *No Paradise* II. iv. 168 Men, in the last stages of d.t., rend the darkness with their ravings. **1969** KESSEL & WALTON *Alcoholism* (ed. 3) iii. 34. Delirium tremens—DTs—generally begins two to five days after stopping very heavy drinking.

du, Sc. and dial. form of DO *v.*

†'**duable**, *a. Obs. nonce-wd.* [f. L. *du-o* two: see -ABLE.] Divisible into two.

1647 WARD *Simp. Cobler* 58 Whatsoever is duable or triable, is fryable.

duad ('djuːæd). Also 8 **duade**. [ad. Gr. δυάς, δυαδ-, 'the number two'; prob. influenced by L. *duo*; the normal repr. of the Gr. is DYAD.]

1. A group or combination of two; a couple, a pair.

1660 STANLEY *Hist. Philos.* IX. (1701) 378/2 The Duad is indeterminate; Monad is taken according to equality and measure, Duad according to excess and defect. **1751** HARRIS *Hermes* II. i. (1786) 226 Δυὰς ἐγνωσμένη, a known Duad, as Apollonius expresses himself. **1793** BEDDOES *Math. Evid.* 133 Lord Monboddo..reduces without hesitation, the Greek primitives to the five duads already quoted. **1797** *Monthly Mag.* III. 517 What the Pythagoreans intended to signify by monad, duad, and triad. **1848** G. A. POOLE *Eccl. Archit.* Contents x, Three Duads of Ecclesiastical Builders. **1857** DE QUINCEY *Judas Isc.* VII. 32 *note*, [Aaron] is blind; [Moses] is dumb. But, moving as a co-operating Duad, they become the salvation of Israel.

2. *Math.* A combination of two things; a pair (considered without reference to the order of the two elements: e.g. *ab* and *ba* are the same duad).

Hence **du'adic** *a.*, relating to or consisting of duads.

1879 SYLVESTER in *Amer. Jrnl. Math.* II. 94 *Duadic disyntheme*, any combination of duads..in which each element occurs twice and no oftener.

dual ('djuːəl), *a.* (*sb.*) Also 6 douale, 7 duall. [ad. L. *duāl-is* containing two, f. *du-o* two: cf. F. *duel*, and see -AL¹.] **A.** *adj.*

1. Of or pertaining to two. ***dual number*** (*Gram.*), the inflected form expressing two or a pair.

1607 BP. ANDREWES *Serm.* II. 217 In the holy tongue, the word which signifieth life is of the dual number. **1706** A. BEDFORD *Temple Mus.* iv. 75 It ought to be read..in the Dual or Plural Number. **1876** J. PARKER *Paracl.* II. Epil. 397 The great dual law which makes Adam and Eve one humanity, the dry land and the seas one globe.

2. Composed or consisting of two parts; twofold, double.

1654 H. L'ESTRANGE *Chas. I* (1655) 7 His Majesty.. conducted her to Canterbury, where the marriage was finally completed..From Canterbury his now dual Majesty took coach for White-hall. **1862** *Weldon's Register* Aug. 3 That in the dual life of man the working faculty should be married to intellectual beauty. **1871** TYNDALL *Fragm. Sc.* (1879) II. vi. 79 Truth is often of a dual character. **1886** *Pall Mall G.* 1 Dec. 3/1 They..proclaimed it as their policy to get rid of this 'dual ownership' in the land. **1891** *Daily News* 15 Apr. 6/4 The skirt was dual, and rather short.

3. In specific collocations: ***dual carriageway***, a road with separate carriageways, divided by a central strip, for up and down vehicular traffic; ***dual control***, control exercised by two parties or persons jointly; in *Aeronaut.*, the duplication of the pilot's controls for instructional purposes; similarly in a motor vehicle; freq. *attrib.*; hence ***dual-controlled*** adj.; ***dual ignition***, ignition in a motor-vehicle engine by two independent currents from a battery; ***dual key***, a system of joint control over the use of nuclear weapons deployed by one government in the territory of another, allowing the weapons to be fired only if both governments have given permission; freq. *attrib.*; ***dual personality***, two distinct personalities in one individual; ***dual-purpose*** adj., serving two purposes or bred for two purposes; *spec.* of cars, capable of carrying people and goods; ***dual-standard*** adj., pertaining to or capable of transmission or reception of television programmes using either of two different picture-densities (see quot. 1961).

1933 *Proc. Inst. Municipal & County Engineers* LX. IV. 274/2 The intention of such roads was to so design them as to enable them to carry very fast traffic safely. The only method of doing that was by providing dual carriageways with central strips which could be so treated as to make them a delightful amenity. **1957** I. MURDOCH *Sandcastle* viii. 128 A dried-up grass verge separated her from the dual carriageway. **1968** Dual carriageway [see BLUB *sb.*]. **1884** *Illustr. London News* 23 Feb. 170/2 The Dual Control... was the proximate cause of our troubles in Egypt. **1913** *Captain* Sept. 1069/2 Military influence is seen in the two or three-seated machine with dual control. **1914** *Aeroplane* 15 July 60/2 Even if the 'Herring Pond' is crossed previously by a single or dual control machine. **1944** H. C. DENT *Education Act, 1944* 21 The compromise on the 'Dual Control' of schools is one of the outstanding triumphs of the Act. **1959** *Which?* May 37/2 All lessons should be on a dual-control car. **1930** *Daily Tel.* 24 July 10/4 The machine was dual-controlled. **1909** *Westm. Gaz.* 22 July 8/3 Some system of what is known as dual ignition for the modern high-class ..motor-car. **1917** A. G. CLARK *Text Bk. Motor Car Engin.* II. 73 Having in view the high efficiency of the modern magneto, it may be accepted that the dual ignition will only be fitted on the more expensive and high-powered cars to facilitate starting up. **1979** *Economist* 27 Jan. 41/2 American cruise missiles could be put into Europe under dual-key control. **1980** *Hansard Commons* 17 June 1353 We could have a dual key if we shared in the cost and the ownership of the weapon, but we do not. **1981** *R. United Services Inst. Jrnl.* June 5/2 Various systems equipped with US nuclear weapons and operated on a dual-key basis. **1983** *Daily Tel.* 15 Feb. 2/3 The controversy over 'dual key' continued yesterday despite Mr Heseltine's assurance that, without such an arrangement, Britain could still prevent American Cruise missiles being fired from bases in England. **1905** *Strand Mag.* Apr. 451/2, I feel my dual personality rather puzzling. **1917** A. WAUGH *Loom of Youth* I. ii. 29 In the corps as Officer Commanding..and as a clerk in orders... His dual personality embodied the spirit of 'the Church Militant'. **1935** B. RUSSELL *Relig. & Sci.* v. 140 In cases of what is called dual personality..what seems to outside observation to be one person is, subjectively, split into two. **1958** 'LANCASTER' & POLING *Strangers in my Body* III. 128 This twenty-five-year-old married female patient was referred for psychological examination with diagnosis of dual personality. **1914** *Scotsman* 8 Oct. 9/1 The number of 'dual-purpose' boats, equipped to burn both coal and oil, includes 38 battleships,..and 21 light cruisers. **1925** J. T. COLE in G. F. Finlay *Cattle Breeding* II. xxxii. 431 The 'dual-purpose' Shorthorn type imported from England in the first half of last century. **1958** *Observer* 19 Jan. 5/4 Police action against owners of 'dual purpose' cars has increased sharply. **1958** *Church Times* 21 Nov. 1/2 He saw St. John's —at present a dual-purpose hall which is also dual-owned, the sanctuary belonging to the diocese and the hall to the local authority. **1961** *Which?* Nov. 301/2 A dual standard (sometimes called switchable) set, which operates at present on the 405-line system, but which is already partly converted and might need only a new tuning unit to make it capable of receiving both 405 and 625-line transmissions. **1965** *B.B.C. Handbk.* 111 A new television studio in Glasgow and a modified one in Bristol are equipped for dual-standard working.

B. *sb.* **1.** *Gram.* The dual number.

1650 REEVE *Introd. Grk. Tongue* 9 In the second and third duall, and in the second plurall. **1832** COLERIDGE *Table-t.* 7 July, It is very natural to have a dual, duality being a conception quite distinct from plurality. **1858** MAX MÜLLER *Chips* (1880) III. i. 3 Gothic. (where we still find a dual in addition to the singular and plural).

†**2.** App. a name for the two middle incisor-teeth in each jaw. *Obs.*

1541 R. COPLAND *Guydon's Quest. Chirurg.* (1579) 18 Howe many tethe ought euery persone to haue?.. In some is founde .xxxij .xvj. in euery Jawe. And in other is founde but [x]xviij. That is to wyt two douales two quadruples .viij. molares and two cassalles [*orig. L.* duo duales: duo quadrupli: et duo canini: et viii. molares et duo caysales].

3. In chess problems, a choice in White's continuations. Hence **dual** *v.* in *pass.*, to admit of a dual solution.

1875 *City of London Chess Mag.* 116 The Black Pawn on the K R file is here omitted as superfluous, and the above-mentioned duals entirely eliminated. **1903** *Daily Chron.* 11 July 8/7 Your problem is dualled by 22 17. **1906** A. C. WHITE *Tours de Force* p. xxxiii, If White is allowed a choice of continuations, such a choice is called a dual, or multiple, continuation. There are two kinds of duals: Absolute duals ..and minor duals. **1966** *New Statesman* 13 May 705/2 That beautiful piece by Sikdar..had to be disqualified because a dual was discovered and couldn't be cured.

dual ('djuːəl), *v.* [f. the adj.] *trans.* To convert (a road) into a dual carriageway.

1959 *Times* 23 Dec. 4/2 Before 1958–59, 20 miles [of the Great North Road] were already dualled and during the year a further 24 miles were completed. **1961** *Times* 15 Dec. 8 (*caption*) Trunk road to be dualled in the current programme. **1969** *Oxford Times* 18 Apr. 17 (*heading*) Northern by-pass to be dualled to Banbury Road.

dual(e, obs. form of DWALE.

dualin ('djuːəlɪn). *Chem.* Also -ine. [f. DUAL + -IN: in reference to the twofold combination with nitre.] A powerful explosive consisting of 20 parts of nitre mixed with 30 of fine sawdust, and 50 of nitro-glycerin. Also ***dualin-dynamite***.

a **1874** *Jrnl. Appl. Chem.* (in Knight *Dict. Mech.* I. 767) Dualine..contains 30 to 40 per cent of nitro-glycerine mixed with sawdust saturated with nitrate of potassia. **1879** WATTS *Dict. Chem.* 3rd Suppl. 694 *Dualin.* **1884** *Pall Mall G.* 6 May 8/1 One of the cartridges found last week under the Parliament buildings here [Toronto], has..been found to be filled with dualin.

dualism ('djuːəlɪz(ə)m). [f. DUAL + -ISM: cf. F. *dualisme* (1755 in Hatz.-Darm.).]

1. The condition or state of being dual or consisting of two parts; twofold division; duality.

1831 CARLYLE *Sart. Res.* II. ix, In Teufelsdröckh there is always the strangest Dualism. **1833** —— *Diderot* Misc. Ess. 1872 V. 53 Among the dualisms of man's wholly dualistic nature, this we might fancy was an observable one. **1841–4** EMERSON *Ess., Compensation* Wks. (Bohn) I. 41 An inevitable dualism bisects nature, so that each thing is a half, and suggests another thing to make it whole. **1877** E. CAIRD *Philos. Kant* ii. 12 A dualism between knowing and being, between the 'me' and the 'not me'.

2. *Gram.* The fact of expressing two in number.

1874 SAYCE *Compar. Philol.* vii. 276 We find many others [languages] in which the formal expression of plurality has never passed beyond that of dualism.

3. A theory or system of thought which recognizes two independent principles. *spec.* **a.** *Philos.* The doctrine that mind and matter exist as distinct entities; opposed to *idealism* and *materialism*. **b.** The doctrine that there are two independent principles, one good and the other evil. **c.** *Theol.* The doctrine, attributed by his opponents to Nestorius, that Christ consisted of two personalities.

1794 MATHIAS *Purs. Lit.* (1798) 65 Then he introduces.. the two principles or dualism (a little more French jargon) the *monde animé* and the *monde machine*. **1836–7** SIR W. HAMILTON *Metaph.* (1877) I. xvi. 293, I would be inclined to denominate those who implicitly acquiesce in the primitive duality as given in Consciousness, the Natural Realists or Natural Dualists, and their doctrine Natural Realism or Natural Dualism. **1847** BUCH tr. *Hagenbach's Hist. Doctr.* I. 93 The Gnostic doctrine of two supreme beings (*dualism*). **1864** PUSEY *Lect. Daniel* (1865) 529 The characteristic error of the Zend religion, its Dualism, was its blot from the first. **1872** LIDDON *Elem. Relig.* iv. 148 Manicheeism was the Dualism which had acquired a Christian flavour by coming into contact with Christianity. **1882** FARRAR *Early Chr.* I. 263 The dualism—the existence of matter as the source of evil apart from God—finds a distinct expression in the *Wisdom of Solomon*. **1882–3** SCHAFF *Encycl. Rel. Knowl.* I. 669 According to dualism existence itself is based on a contrariety which appears in philosophy as spirit and matter.

4. *Chem.* The theory, originated by Berzelius, now abandoned, that every compound is constituted of two parts which have opposite electricities.

1884 MUIR *Princ. Chem.* I. ii. iii. §54 Dumas' discovery of the chloracetic acids which marks the beginning of the revolt against the compound radicles of dualism.

dualist ('djuːəlɪst). [f. DUAL + -IST: cf. F. *dualiste*.]

1. One who holds a doctrine of dualism or duality.

a **1822** SHELLEY *Christianity* Pr. Wks. 1880 II. 340 The Stoic, the Platonist, the Polytheist, the Dualist, and the Trinitarian. **1845** R. BALMER *Lect. & Disc.* I. vi. 305 For a certain portion of his life he was a dualist, a believer in the doctrine of the duality of persons in the Godhead. **1872** LIDDON *Elem. Relig.* iv. 149 We of this generation are not Dualists.

attrib. **1850** DAUBENY *Atom. The.* i. (ed. 2) 49 When two kinds of matter shew an affinity one for the other, it is because they are actually penetrable.. This, which has been called the Dualist system, presents..but an obscure and imperfect image to the mind.

†**2.** A holder of two offices. *Obs. rare.*

a **1661** FULLER *Worthies, Wilts* III. (1662) 154 He was a Duallist in that Convent (and if a Pluralist, no ingenious person would have envied him).

dualistic (djuːə'lɪstɪk), *a.* [f. prec. + -IC; cf. F. *dualistique*.]

1. Pertaining to, or of the nature of, dualism.

1801 J. JONES tr. *Bygge's Trav. Fr. Rep.* v. 106 He..passed over Symmer's theory [of electricity], or the dualistic system entirely. **1817** COLERIDGE *Biog. Lit.* 57 The admission of the dualistic hypothesis. **1876** E. R. LANKESTER tr. *Haeckel's Hist. Creat.* I. ii. 33 In the usual dualistic or teleological conception of the universe, organic nature is regarded as the purposely executed production of a Creator working according to a definite plan. **1884** MUIR *Princ. Chem.* I. ii. ii. §48 Berzelius raised the structure of dualistic chemistry, which asserted that every compound, whether simple or complex, must be constituted of two parts, of which one is positively, and the other negatively electrified. **1885** J. MARTINEAU *Types Eth. Th.* (1886) I. I. xi. §8. 205 The dualistic assumption..of the mutual exclusion of extension and thought. **1892** WESTCOTT *Gospel of Life* 178 From this source [Zoroastrianism] dualistic doctrines invaded the Christian Church in Gnosticism and Manichæism.

2. Characterized by duality; dual.

1832 *Fraser's Mag.* VI. 260 Consider them as the two disjointed Halves of this singular Dualistic Being of ours. **1884** MUIR *Princ. Chem.* I. ii. ii. §48 All salts were to be regarded as dualistic structures.

Hence **dua'listically** *adv.*, in a dualistic manner; in accordance with duality.

1857 DE QUINCEY *Judas Iscariot* Wks. VII. 31 *note*, The two co-agents move in couples—move dualistically. Each is essential to the other. **1881** WILLIAMSON in *Nature* No. 618. 414 Each of them [compound atoms] was the smallest quantity of a compound, which..could be represented as built dualistically of its constituent atoms.

duality (djuː'ælɪtɪ). Also dualty. [ad. F. *dualité* (14th c.), ad. late L. *duālitās*, f. *duālis* DUAL.]

1. The condition or fact of being dual, or consisting of two parts, natures, etc.; twofold condition.

c **1400** *Test. Love* II. Chaucer's Wks. (1561) 306 b/1 This dualitie, after Clerkes determission, is founden in euery creature, bee it neuer so single of onhed. **1575** LANEHAM *Let.* (1871) 54 Wheat and barly, peaz and beanz, meat and drinke, bread and meat, beer and ale, appls and pearz. But least by such dualiteez I draw you too far: let vs heer stay, and cum neerer home. *a* **1619** FOTHERBY *Atheom.* II. x. §2 (1622) 299 Dualitie is nothing but a composition of two vnities. **1781** COWPER *Lett.* (1887) 83 The solitude, or rather the duality of our condition, at Olney. **1887** *Whitaker's Almanac* 437 In the Austro-Hungarian empire duality extends to the annual budget. **1892** WESTCOTT *Gospel of Life* 176 Zarathustra himself seems to have taught a certain duality in the one Divine Being.

†2. The holding of two benefices together. *Obs.*

1619 BRENT tr. *Sarpi's Counc. Trent* (1676) 714 Plurality of Benefices is forbid, and dualty granted when one is not sufficient. *Ibid.* 738. **1634** CANNE *Necess. Separ.* (1849) 156 Dispensations given..for non-residents..dualities, trialities, pluralities. **1647** SIR J. BIRKENHEAD *Assembly Man* (1662-3) 8 He is not against Pluralities, but Dualities.

dualize (ˈdjuːəlaɪz), *v.* [f. DUAL + -IZE.] *trans.* To make or regard as two. Hence **ˈdualized** *ppl. a.*; **dualiˈzation**, the action of dualizing.

1838 *Blackw. Mag.* XLIV. 550 The great unity of sensation, that is, the state which prevailed anterior to the dualization of subject and object. **1856** R. A. VAUGHAN *Mystics* (1860) I. III. iii. 295 *note*, It was feared that to represent God as the God of Creation and of Providence would be to dualize him. **1877** FAIRBAIRN *Stud. Philos. Relig.* 33 Man had not learned to dualize his own being.

dually (ˈdjuːəlɪ), *adv.* [f. DUAL *a.* + -LY².] In a dual or twofold capacity; in the dual number.

1650 REEVE *Introd. Grk. Tongue* 24 Dually and plurally they are declined like the Feminine Article. **1785** BURKE *Corr.* (1844) III. 44 If, therefore, we do not resolve (..if you and I *dually* do not resolve) to consult. **1881** *19th Cent.* Mar. 492 Hence it has followed that this great outside party..has come to be dually represented in the Lower Chamber.

duan (ˈduːən). [Gael. *duan* poem, canto, song. First used in Eng. in Macpherson's *Ossian*, 1765.] A poem or song; a canto of an epic or long poem.

1765 J. MACPHERSON *Ossian* II. 237 Cath-loda, Duan I. (*Note.* The bards distinguished those compositions in which the narration is often interrupted by episodes and apostrophes, by the name of *Duän*). **1785** BURNS *Vision*, Duan First. **1805** W. TAYLOR in *Ann. Rev.* III. 281 His Diarmod and his Guare may stalk on the stage, or declaim in duans. **1821** BYRON *Juan* IV. cxvii, Till what is call'd, in Ossian, the fifth Duan. **1893** H. WALKER *3 Cent. Scot. Lit.* II. 124 One epic poem of six duans or cantos, and another of eight.

duan, obs. var. DEWAN, DIVAN: so **du'anee** = DEWANI; **du'anage**, dewanship.

1669 *Lond. Gaz.* No. 415/1 Carrying a Letter to the Duan. **1766** *Hist. Eur.* in *Ann. Reg.* 29/1 The Duanage became annexed to the Nabobship. **1818** JAS. MILL *Brit. India* II. IV. i. 18 Appointed duan (or controller of the revenues) of Bengal. *Ibid.* v. 213 The duanee, or collection, receipt and disbursement of the revenue.

duant (ˈdjuːənt). *Physics.* [f. L. *duo* two + -ANT¹.] In an accelerator = DEE *sb.* 2; in an electrometer = BINANT.

1930 *Science* 10 Oct. 376/2 Semicircular hollow plates in a vacuum not unlike duants of an electrometer. **1936** [see DEE *sb.* 2]. **1936** *Nature* 22 Feb. 316/2 The cyclotron at present has a limited voltage amplification due, in part, to a space charge built up within the duants. **1938** [see BINANT].

duar, var. DOUAR.

duarchy (ˈdjuːɑːkɪ). [f. L. *duo* (or irreg. f. Gr. δύο) two, after *monarchy*, etc.] A government by two co-ordinate rulers; a diarchy.

1586 T. B. *La Primaud. Fr. Acad.* I. 582 Properly called a Duarchie, which may continue so long as those two princes agree. **1655** FULLER *Ch. Hist.* III. iii. §3 A Duarchie in the Church..being inconsistent with a Monarchie in the state. **1807** ROBINSON *Archæol. Græca* II. iv. 144 That Sparta should be careful to preserve both her Kings, and not change the duarchy into a monarchy.

So **ˈduarch**, one who shares rule with another.

1848 *Tait's Mag.* XV. 706 There will be *duarchs* for four phalanx, *triarchs* for 12, *tetrarchs* for 48, and so on.

dub (dʌb), *sb.*¹ *Sc.* and *north. dial.* Also 6 doubbe, dubbe, 6-7 dubb; see also DIB *sb.*³ [Of uncertain origin.

It has been compared with Da. *dyb* adj. deep, sb. deep, abyss; but this being a relatively recent repr. of ON. *djúp*, can hardly be connected.]

1. A muddy or stagnant pool; a small pool of rain water in a road; a puddle. (Chiefly *Sc.*)

1500-20 DUNBAR *Poems* xxxiii. 119 Thre dayis in dub amang the dukis He did with dirt him hyde. **1513** DOUGLAS *Æneis* VII. Prol. 54 The..stretis..Full of fluschis, doubbis, myre and clay. **1596** DALRYMPLE tr. *Leslie's Hist. Scot.* II. 145 Ouir dykes and dubis, sykes and seuches thay suld spang and leip. **1790** BURNS *Tam o' Shanter* 81 Tam skelpit on thro' dub and mire. **1886** STEVENSON *Kidnapped* xxiv. 243 'Here's a dub for ye to jump.'

2. A deep dark pool in a river or stream (*north. dial.*).

1535 STEWART *Cron. Scot.* III. 264 Siclike the Scottis, on the tother syde, Arrayit war thair battell for to byde..Ane mos also vpoun the tother syde, With mony dubbis that war bayth deip and wyde. **1825** BROCKETT *N.C. Words, Dub*, a small pool of water; a piece of deep and smooth water in a rapid river. **1883** *Kendal Mercury* 12 Oct. 5/3 In the neighbourhood of Tebay salmon are in the various favourite dubs in immense numbers. **1886** *Pall Mall G.* 6 Oct. 4/1 During summer and when the water becomes low the fish congregate in deep 'dubs'.

3. *Comb.*, as **dub-skelper**, one who runs through the 'dubs', 'a rambling fellow' (Jam.).

1824 SCOTT *St. Ronan's* xxviii, I'll warrant it's some idle dub-skelper..coming after some o' yoursells. **1825** BROCKETT, *Dub-skelper*, bog-trotter; applied to the borderers.

†**dub**, *sb.*² *Angling. Obs.* [f. DUB *v.*¹ 5.] An artificial fly: also ***dub-fly***.

a **1450** *Fysshynge w. Angle* (1883) 6 How ye schall make your hokes of steyl & of osmonde som for þe dub & som for þe flote. *Ibid.* 20 Yf ye se..þe trowyt or the graylyng lepe, angle to hym with a dub accordyng to the same moneth. **1681** CHETHAM *Angler's Vade-m.* ii. §11 (1689) 12 Your line for Dub-fly, Cast-fly, or Artificial fly.

dub (dʌb), *sb.*³ Also 6 dubbe. [Mainly onomatopœic (cf. *dub-a-dub*, *rub-a-dub*); but having connexions with DUB *v.*²]

1. A beat of a drum; the sound of a drum when beaten. Cf. DUB-A-DUB.

c **1572** GASCOIGNE *Fruits of Warre* Wks. (1587) 113 They ..Who followe drummes before they knowe the dubbe. **1576** TURBERV. *Venerie* 140 That drummes with deadly dub, may countervayle the blast. **1710** E. WARD *Brit. Hudibras* 86 Before the Masters of the Dub..Advanc'd a Red-fac'd squabby Fellow. **1816** KEATINGE *Trav.* (1817) I. 321 The sullen dub of two drums beaten with crooked sticks.

2. A blow struck as in drumming. *rare.*

1664 BUTLER *Hud.* II. i. 850 As skilful Coopers hoop their Tubs With Lydian and with Phrygian Dubs; Why may not Whipping have as good A Grace, perform'd in Time and Mood?

3. A short blunt dull-sounding thrust or blow.

1837 HAWTHORNE *Twice-Told T.* II. xix. 271 Jotting down each dull footstep with a melancholy dub of his staff.

dub (dʌb), *sb.*⁴ *East Ind.* [Telugu *dabba.*] 'A small copper coin, value 20 cash' (Yule).

1781 in Ld. Lindsay *Lives Lindsays* (1849) III. (Y.), The fanam changes for 11 dubs and 4 cash. **1791** J. ANDERSON *Corr.* 43 The Exchange 88 Dubs for one Rupee. **1858** SIMMONDS *Dict. Trade, Dub*..a division of the rupee in Mangalore, also called dudu, equal to about 2½*d.*

dub (dʌb), *sb.*⁵ *Criminals' slang.* [Cf. DUB *v.*³] A key, especially one used for picking locks. Hence **ˈdubsman** (or abbrev. **dubs**), a turnkey, gaoler.

a **1700** B. E. *Dict. Cant. Crew, Dub*, c. a Pick-lock-key. **1789** G. PARKER *Life's Painter* 139 A bunch of young dubs by her side. **1821** D. HAGGART *Life* 31 We seized him, took the dubs, bound, and gagged him. **1839** AINSWORTH *Jack Sheppard* II. xii, Oh! give me a chisel, a knife, or a file, And the dubsmen shall find that I'll do it in style! **1887** HENLEY *Villon's Good Night* (Farmer), You coppers' narks, and dubs, What pinched me when upon the snam. **1923** *Chambers's Jrnl.* 716/1, I pulled the dub of the outer jigger from his suck.

dub, *sb.*⁶ *slang* (orig. *U.S.*). [Perh. related to DUB *v.*¹ 11, DUBBED *ppl. a.* 4] One who is inexperienced or unskilful at anything; a duffer, fool.

1887 *Courier-Journal* (Louisville, Ky.) 20 Jan. 6/4 Dem dubs is goin' to git it in de neck. **1896** ADE *Artie* i. 4 What kills me off is how all these dubs make their star winnins. **1902** H. L. WILSON *Spenders* xxx. 353 People can talk all they want to about your bein' just a dub—I won't believe 'em. **1905** *Smart Set* Oct. 18/1 I've made up my mind that I ain't goin' to keep on bein' a common dub all my life. **1911** H. QUICK *Yellowstone Nights* 43, I was coming on pretty well for a dub. **1916** 'BOYD CABLE' *Action Front* 8 The Schmidt customer crowd didn't need to know a thing about me being here unless he was dub enough to tell 'em. **1923** J. MANCHON *Le Slang* 111 *Dub, tennis*, un joueur médiocre. **1931** T. A. HARPER *Windy Island* (1934) II. iii. 122 He was not exactly a dub at Latin and maths. **1943** K. TENNANT *Ride on Stranger* xix. 213 Quinlan wasn't such a dub as he looks. **1949** O. NASH *Versus* 40 The unassuming dub Trying to pick up a Saturday game In the locker room of the club.

dub, *sb.*⁷ [f. DUB *v.*⁵] **1.** A re-mixed version of a piece of recorded music, often with the melody line removed and including various special effects, which was developed in Jamaica and is popular esp. in REGGAE and other Black music. Freq. *attrib.*

1974 C. GILLETT *Rock File* II. 70 (*heading*) Dub wise skank: talk over. **1975** *Black Music* June 21/3 He's been collecting some heavy dubs. **1977** *Sounds* 3 Dec. 22 The first dub record was 'Travelling Man' by the Techniques. **1978** *Oxford Times* (City ed.) 13 Jan. 15 'Dub'..a peculiar Jamaican invention in which the recording is remixed with various electronic effects and alterations—reverberation, feedback, repetition—while keeping the existing bass line throughout. **1983** *Listener* 19 May 22/3 As we pull up outside a reggae shop in the Lower Clapton Road, loud and bass-heavy 'dub' music with a patois talkover 'toast' booms into the bus.

2. A type of Black performance poetry, orig. performed extempore and accompanied by dub (sense 1 above) or other recorded music, but subsequently also written down. Freq. *attrib.*, as ***dub poet***. Cf. TOAST *sb.*³

1982 D. SUTCLIFFE *Brit. Black Eng.* ii. 63 Johnson has.. brought his poetry to young Black people on record, where it becomes a kind of 'dub'. **1982** *New Musical Express* 30 Oct. 19/1, I consider Louise Bennett to be the mother of the young dub poets. **1983** *Poetry Soc. News Let.* Sept. 2 Michael Smith, Jamaica's leading dub poet, was murdered on August 17. **1986** *Daily Tel.* 24 Nov. 31/2 In this last episode Robert McNeil explores the new Englishes of Papuan tribesmen, Krio speakers in Sierra Leone, dub poets in the West Indies and Brixton, [etc.].

dub (dʌb), *v.*¹ Forms: 1 dubban, 2-5 dubben, 3-5 dobb(e, 4-6 dubbe, 4 dube, 5 doubbe, dowbe, 5-6 doub(e, 5- dub. [Appears in Eng. before 1100. Generally supposed to be from OFr., which had in this sense *aduber* (Ch. de Rol. 11th c.), *adober*, *adouber*, also (rarer, and app. only later) *duber*, *douber*. The OFr. word is Com. Rom., It. *addobbare*, OSp. and Pr. *adobar*, OPg. *adubar*; its ulterior derivation is unknown.

By Diez it was assumed to be of Teutonic origin: there is however no such Germanic verb as *dubban* to strike, and the Icel. and Sw. *dubba*, cited in support of such, are really late words for 'to dub a knight', from Eng. or Romanic. EFris. *dubben* to strike, seems, like our DUB *v.*², to be a recent onomatopœic formation. Even the relation of Eng. *dub* to the OF. word presents difficulties, since the latter would be expected to have been adopted as *adub*, which is not found till the 15th c. Branch II is presumably an extension of the same word, though some of the senses are very remote, and are perh. affected by other associations.]

I. To invest with a dignity or title.

1. *trans.* To confer the rank of knighthood by the ceremony of striking the shoulder with a sword. **a.** (with compl.) ***to dub*** (one) ***a knight*** (†***to a knight***).

1085-1123 *O.E. Chron.* (Laud MS.) an. 1085, Se cyng.. dubbade his sunu Henric to ridere þær. *c* **1205** LAY. 22497 þu..scalt..to cnihte hine dubben. *a* **1300** *K. Horn* 447 Horn..þu schalt beo dubbed kniȝt. *c* **1489** CAXTON *Sonnes of Aymon* i. 31 The kynge Charlemayne..doubed hym to a knyghte. **1559** *Mirr. Mag., Dk. of Suffolk* v, Whan my Kyng had doubed me a Knight. **1764** FOOTE *Mayor of G.* I. i, Has his majesty dubbed me a Knight for you to make me a Mister? **1865** KINGSLEY *Herew.* II. vii. 116 Thou wast dubbed knight in this church.

†**b.** (with simple obj.) *to dub* (a knight, etc.).

13.. *K. Alis.* 818 Dubbed weore an hundrud knightis. *c* **1380** *Sir Ferumb.* 1168 Charlis..him self me dobbede riȝt. *c* **1386** CHAUCER *Pars. T.* ¶693 The swerd that men yeuen first to a knyght whan he is newe dubbed. **1470-85** MALORY *Arthur* Contents XIII. i, How..a damoysel..desyred syr launcelot for to come and dubbe a knyght. **1577-87** HOLINSHED *Chron.* II. 37/1 He dubd on saint Michaell the archangels daie thirtie knights. **1596** SPENSER *F.Q.* VI. ii. 35 So he him dubbed, and his knight did call. **1617** in *Crt. & Times Jas. I* (1849) I. 467 Sir John Smith..was lately knighted..Robin Hatton..was likewise dubbed. **1685** *Lond. Gaz.* No. 2031/1 [They] were Dub'd by his Grace with the Sword of State.

2. To invest with a dignity or new title. (In later times often mockingly or humorously used.)

c **1330** R. BRUNNE *Chron.* (1810) 331 An abbot..of Scone, þat dubbid þe kyng. *c* **1340** *Cursor M.* 7328 (Fairf.) He sal be dubbed [*earlier texts* enoynted] king to be. *c* **1400** *Melayne* 304 Dubbe hym Duke in my stede. **1594** SHAKS. *Rich. III*, I. i. 82 Since that our Brother dub'd them Gentlewomen. **1737** POPE *Hor. Epist.* I. vi. 81 A Man of wealth is dubb'd a Man of worth. *a* **1745** SWIFT *Wks.* (1841) II. 76 The college ..has dubbed most of us doctors. **1758** G. WASHINGTON *Writ.* (1889) II. 6 *note*, You are pleased to dub me with a title I have no pretentions to—that is, yᵉ Honble. **1865** MISS BRADDON *Only a Clod* iv. 22 They'd hardly dub you Esquire. **1893** *Ch. Times* 6 Oct. 995/3 The marvel is that he was not dubbed F.R.S.

3. To name, style, nickname; to speak of or set down as: now usually in pleasantry or ridicule.

1599 SHAKS. *Hen. V*, II. ii. 120 To dub thee with the name of Traitor. **1607** *Schol. Disc. agst. Antichr.* I. iv. 175 The reading of homilies, which they dubb with the name of preaching. **1693** *Humours & Conv. Town* 62 A Condemning-Face..dubs any one an uncontrovertible Critick. **1713** STEELE *Englishm.* No. 40. 260 A Cobler blacks a Boot..and dubs it *La Botte Royalle.* **1773** GARRICK *Prol. to Goldsmith's Stoops to Conq.*, You..Pronounce him regular, or dub him quack. **1894** G. R. SIMS in *My First Bk.* 88 Was I to be dubbed a scribbler?

II. To dress; to trim; to crop.

†**4.** To dress, clothe, array, adorn. *Obs.*

a **1300** *Cursor M.* 28014 Yee leuedis..studis hu your hare to heu, hu to dub and hu to paynt. *c* **1325** *Metr. Hom.* (1862) 12 He..schop him bodi of hir fleyse And dubbed him wit our liknes. *a* **1450** *Alexander* 3447 He gase..vp to þe gilt trone, Dobbed in his diademe & diȝt as be-fore. **1570** LEVINS *Manip.* 181/38 To Dub the house, *exornare, putare.*

†**b.** To 'stick' (with ornaments). *Obs.*

c **1400** MAUNDEV. (1839) xxii. 24 Covered..of Plate of fyn gold, dubbed with precious stones. *c* **1400** *Destr. Troy* 6205 A cloth all of clene gold, Dubbit full of diamondis.

5. *Angling.* To dress or make up (an artificial fly), or to dress (a hook or line) *with* a fly.

a **1450** *Fysshynge w. Angle* (1883) 33 Thyse ben the xij. flyes wyth whyche ye shall angle to þe trought & grayllyng, and dubbe lyke as ye shall now here me tell. **1675** J. SMITH *Chr. Relig. App.* I. 65 He who..dubs his Hook with a counterfeit Fly, will chuse to fish in troubled Waters. **1799** *Sporting Mag.* XIII. 31 Dubbed with bear's hair of a brownish colour. **1846** *Blackw. Mag.* LIX. 310 They could neither scour a worm..nor dub a fly.

6. a. To cut off the comb and wattles of (a cock).

1570 LEVINS *Manip.* 181/39 To Dubbe a cocke, *coronare.* **1688** R. HOLME *Armoury* II. 252/2. **1828** *Craven Dial.* **1871** DARWIN *Desc. Man* xiii. (1883) 403 Cock-fighters trim the hackles and cut off the combs and gills of their cocks; and the birds are then said to be dubbed.

b. To trim or crop (trees, hedges, etc.).

1634-5 BRERETON *Trav.* (Chetham) 73 The trees, which are now cut and dubbed. **1877** *N.W. Linc. Gloss., Dubbings*, evergreens with which churches and houses are decorated at Christmas. **1884** *Cheshire Gloss., Dub*, to clip a hedge.

7. To dress (cloth) see quot. 1847. Formerly, To 'renovate' old cloth or clothes: see DUBBER¹.

[*a* **1400** *Liber Albus* IV. lf. 337a. (Rolls) 718 Item, qe nul face dubber ne fuller tielx draps, et les vendent pur novels.] **1801** *Chron.* in *Ann. Reg.* 456 For dressing or dubbing cloths, either wet or dry, otherwise than by green cards and pickards. **1847-78** HALLIWELL, *Dub*, to strike cloth with teasels in order to raise the flock or nap. *Glouc.*

8. 'To place good wares in the upper part of a basket and inferior beneath; a term still in use in Billingsgate Market.' Riley, *Liber Albus* III. 311.

[**1290** in *Liber Albus* III. III. (Rolls) 378 Et qe nulle soit des pessoners si hardi..faucementz a douber lour panyers; cestassavoir, mettre al desus panyer un demonstrance de convenable pessoun, et dessouthe en les panyers mettre pessoun desconvenable de poy de value.]

9. To smear with fat or grease. Now *spec.* to do this to leather. Cf. DUBBING *vbl. sb.* 4.

c **1611** CHAPMAN *Iliad* I. 448 All, after pray'r..kill'd, flay'd the beeves, Cut out and dubb'd with fat their thighs, fair dress'd with doubled leaves. **1615** —— *Odyss.* III. 619 Apart flew either thigh, That with the fat they dubb'd. **1831** J. HOLLAND *Manuf. Metal* I. 162 Well dressed ox or cow leather..when in use, is occasionally dubbed over with neat's oil. **1866** ROGERS *Agric. & Prices* I. xviii. 398 Grease was needed for dubbing leather.

10. To trim, or work level and smooth, with an adze. Also with *off, down, out*.

1711 W. SUTHERLAND *Shipbuild. Assist.* 160 To Dub; to work with an Addice. **1719** DE FOE *Crusoe* I. iv, I had..to cut down a Tree..hew it flat on either Side with my Ax, till I had brought it to be thin as a Plank, and then dubb it smooth with my Adze. **1789** G. KEATE *Pelew Isl.* 315 Canoes made from the trunk of a tree dubbed out. **1812** J. SMYTH *Pract. of Customs* 234 A paling board..slabbed or feather-edged and dubbed on the sappy side.

11. To beat blunt or flat.

1879 *Cassell's Techn. Educ.* IV. 298/1 The end of the tube is bent and hammered over in any rough way to pass it through..and is afterwards 'dubbed' or 'tanged'.

dub, *v.*[2] [Known only since 1500: evidently onomatopœic, imitating the sound, or suggesting the feeling of a firm blow or thrust with something blunt. Cf. EFris. *dubben* to butt, beat, strike.]

1. *trans.* To thrust: now implying a moderately firm blunt thrust or poke. †Formerly also, To stab as with a dagger; to bring down (a club) (*obs.*).

1513 DOUGLAS *Æneis* IV. xii. 109 Or that Proserpine..dubbit hir heid Onto the Stygian hellis flude of deid. *c* **1572** GASCOIGNE *Fruites Warre* Wks. (1831) 210 With bodkins dubd and doust to death. **1586** WARNER *Alb. Eng.* II. vii. (R.), He dubs his club about their pates. *a* **1659** CLEVELAND *Gen. Poems, etc.* (1677) 15 Women commence by Cupid's Dart, As a King hunting Dubs a Hart. **1836** E. HOWARD *R. Reefer* xxxiv, Pigs..were..to be seen dubbing their snouts under the gunnel.

b. *intr.* To make a thrust or dab, to poke (*at*).

1833 MARRYAT *P. Simple* xv, The slightest mistake as to time..and at this moment the flatfish would have been dubbing at our ugly carcasses. **1875** SIR G. W. DASENT *Vikings* II. 196 The flounders would now be dubbing at our limbs thirty fathoms deep.

2. Used *intr.* and *trans.* of the beating or sound of a drum. Also redupl. DUB-A-DUB, *rub-a-dub*. Cf. DUB *sb.*[3]

1588 T. DELONEY *3 Ball. Armada* II. iv. in Arb. *Garner* VII. 47 With trumpets sounding, and with dubbing drums. *Ibid.* II. xiv. 50 The warlike Armie then stood still, and drummers left their dubbing sound. *a* **1625** FLETCHER *Mad Lover* I. i, Now the drums dubbs.

dub, *v.*[3] *slang.* [? corruption of DUP *v.* = do up.]

†**1.** *trans.* To open (a door). *Obs.*

a **1700** B. E. *Dict. Cant. Crew* s.v. *Case*, Tis all Bob, and then to dub the gigg. *Ibid.* s.v. *Gigger.*, *Dub the Gigger*, open the Door with the Pick-lock.

2. To shut *up*.

1753 J. POULTER *Discoveries* 33 If the Seger is dub'd, that is, the Door lock'd or bolted. **1781** G. PARKER *View of Society* II. i. 69 *Dub the Jigger* is, in other words, *shut the door.* **1785** in GROSE. **1812** J. H. VAUX *Flash Dict., Dub up*, to lock up or secure any thing or place; also to button one's pocket, coat, etc. **1958** F. NORMAN *Bang to Rights* I. 12 Everybody in the nick had already been dubbed up for the night.

dub, *v.*[4] *slang.* [Origin obscure.] *intr.* To pay *up*; so *to dub in*, to make a contribution.

1823 'J. BEE' *Slang* 72 *Dub up*, to pay at once. **1839** *Comic Almanack 1840* 36 'Come, dub up!' roars a third; and I don't mind telling you.. that I..took out the sovereign and gave it. **1845** *Punch* Oct. 147/1 He has been compelled to 'dub up' out of his own pocket. **1846** *Swell's Night Guide* 79 A stranger may gain admission by the rum cull introducing him, and dubbing a tanner to the chairman. **1852** G. C. MUNDY *Our Antipodes* I. v. 181 The juniors are compelled to *dub up.* **1923** BLUNDEN *Christ's Hospital* 199 Five or six boys 'dub in' for a pot of strawberry jam or treacle. **1959** I. & P. OPIE *Lore & Lang. Schoolch.* x. 195 The demand to hand over has elsewhere been heard expressed in the words: 'Cough it up', 'Dish it out', 'Dub up' (North Country).

dub, *v.*[5] [Shortened form of DOUBLE *v.*] *trans.* To provide an alternative sound track to (a film or television broadcast), especially a translation from a foreign language; to mix (various sound tracks) into a single track (see quot. 1959); to impose (additional sounds) on to an existing recording; to transfer (recorded sound) on to a new record. Also with *in, on*. So **dubbed** *ppl. a.*; **'dubbing** *ppl. a.* and *vbl. sb.*[2]

1929 *N.Y. Times* 13 Oct. IX. 8/6 Dubbing, the process of re-recording from film to film, or from film to wax, or from wax to film, or from wax to wax. **1930** *Electronics* Nov. 373/2 These people are then re-photographed in silent close-ups, and then foreign players 'dub' in the same lines. **1930** PITKIN & MARSTON *Art of Sound Pictures* 270 Dubbing, a method of doubling the voice on the screen after the photographing of the picture. **1931** B. BROWN *Talking Pictures* xi. 275 Dubbing on disc is no more difficult than on film. *Ibid.* 288 Dubbing from sound track to disc was frequently employed. **1938** *Encycl. Brit. Bk. of Yr.* 421/1 'Dubbed' versions, bearing sound tracks in the native languages. **1939** *Times* 25 Mar. 10/4 Queen Mary..went into what is called the 'dubbing' theatre, where sound is recorded. **1944** *Ann. Reg. 1943* 344 The Overseas Dispatch Department..handled some 300 copies of 80 different films ..some 'dubbed' and some with foreign commentaries or foreign subtitles. **1952** *Record Year* 124 The Michelangeli set (GX 61004–7) is a dubbing, so unsuccessful as to preclude judgment on the merits of the performance. **1959** HALAS & MANVELL *Technique Film Animation* xix. 209 The final set of tracks required for dubbing are laid, and at the subsequent dubbing session these are run simultaneously and balanced together and amalgamated on to one single sound track. **1962** *Movie* Sept. 6/3 Watching a film he has previously made with the director for whom he is now working in the dubbing room. **1966** *B.B.C. Handbk.* 38 More international sound tracks for programmes were provided to allow foreign commentaries to be dubbed on.

dub-, in *Comb.* Chiefly *dial.* [cf. DUBBED 4.] Having a blunt point.

1706 E. WARD *Hud. Rediv.* II. VIII. 12 A swarthy dub-nosed Fellow, With Cheeks like rusty Bacon, yellow. **1881** *Oxfordsh. Gloss., Dub-point, dubpointed, sb.* a blunt point; *adj.* blunt at the point. [**1888** *Sheffield Gloss., Dub*, a straight-edged, round-pointed, dinner-knife blade.]

dub, dube, var. of DOOB, E. Indian grass.

dub-a-dub. [Echoic; cf. DUB *v.*[2]] The sound made in beating a drum: used, **a.** advb., or without construction, as a simple representation of the sound; **b.** as *sb.*, to name the sound, or the drummer who makes it; and **c.** as *adj.* to characterize it.

a **1553** UDALL *Royster D.* IV. vii. (Arb.) 74 Now sainct George to borow, Drum dubbe a dubbe afore. **1576** GASCOIGNE *Steele Gl.* (Arb.) 67 When drums are dumb, and sound not dub a dub. **1583** STANYHURST *Æneis* VIII. (Arb.) 137 Lowd dub a dub tabering with frapping rip rap of Ætna. *a* **1592** GREENE *Alphonsus* Wks. (Rtldg.) 242 Hark, how their drums with dub-a-dub do come! **1608** DAY *Hum. out of Br.* v. ii. (1881) 77 These drumming dub adubs loues pleasure feares. **1708** MOTTEUX *Rabelais* v. xviii. (1737) 81 The Dub-o-dub Rattling of the Drums. **1878** STEVENSON *Inland Voy.* 86 Each dub-a-dub goes direct to a man's heart.

¶ Applied, by confusion, to the accolade given in conferring knighthood.

1612 FIELD *Woman a Weathercock* I. ii. in Hazl. *Dodsley* XI. 23 The dub-a-dub of honour, piping hot Doth lie upon my worship's shoulder-blade.

So **dub-a-dub** *v.* = DUB *v.*[2] 2.

1598 FLORIO, *Tambussare*..to dub a dub, to drum. **1851** *Blackw. Mag.* Nov. 573 Trumpets and drums, blown and dub-a dubbed by fellows that..I would not trust [etc.].

dubartas, -us, obs. var. JUBARTES, a kind of whale.

‖**dubash** (duːˈbɑːʃ, -æ-). *East Indies.* Also 7 deubash, 9 debash, dubashee. [ad. Hindī *dūbhāshiya, dōbāshī*, man of two languages, f. *dō, dū* two + *bhāshā* language.] An (Indian) interpreter or commissionaire, employed in transacting business with the natives, and as a cicerone, courier, etc.

1698 FRYER *Acc. E. Ind. & P.* 30 The Moors..not vouchsafing to return an Answer by a Slave, but by a Deubash, who is the Interpreter. **1776** in *Gentl. Mag.* (1792) 14/2 Two days before our arrival at Hyderabad, I sent my Dubash on before. **1814** W. BROWN *Hist. Prop. Chr.* (1823) I. 198 The rapacious dubashes denied them full payment. **1832** MARRYAT *N. Forster* xxxviii, By inquiry of the dubashee. **1845** STOCQUELER *Handbk. Brit. India* (1854) 318 The dubashes, a superior sort of *valet de place* and cicerone.

‖**dubba, dubber.** *East Indies.* Also 7–9 dupper, 8 duppa. [Arab., Pers., and Urdū *dabbah* vessel made of raw skins.] 'A leather bottle or skin bag, used chiefly in India for holding oil, ghee, and other liquids, and capable of holding, according to size, from 20 to 80 lbs. weight' (Simmonds *Dict. Trade*, 1858).

1698 FRYER *Acc. E. India & P.* 118 Their Butter..after it has passed the Fire, they keep it in Duppers the year round. **1727** A. HAMILTON *New Acc. E. Ind.* I. 126 (Y.) Great Quantities of Butter, which they gently melt and put in Jars called Duppas. **1799** *Ann. Reg.* 26 A small quantity of wood-oil, contained in a dubber, or leathern bottle. **1845** NAPIER *Gen. Order* in J. Mawson *Rec.* (1851) 35 (Y.) What became of these dubbas of ghee.

dubbed (dʌbd), *ppl. a.* [f. DUB *v.*[1] + -ED[1].]

1. Invested with knighthood, knighted.

1552 HULOET, Dubbed, *decuriatus.* **1589** WARNER *Alb. Eng.* V. xxviii. (1612) 137 Lord of nine score dubbed knights. **1731** *Lett. fr. Fog's Jrnl.* (1732) II. 257 A dubb'd Plebeian, Fortune's Fav'rite Fool. **1825** SCOTT *Talism.* ii, A dubbed knight.

2. *Angling.* Dressed, as a hook.

a **1450** *Fysshynge w. Angle* (1883) 11 The dubbyd hoke.

3. Cropped.

1634–5 BRERETON *Trav.* (Chetham) 44 Dubbed hedges.

4. Blunted; blunt, pointless. (Now *dial.*)

17.. E. SMITH *Compl. Housewife* (1750) 8 The spurs of the pheasant cock, when young, are short and dubbed. **1796** MRS. GLASSE *Cookery* ii. 10 His spurs will be short and dubbed. **1825** *Wiltsh. Words, Dubbed*, blunt, pointless.

‖**dubbeltjie** (ˈdœbəlcı). *S. Afr.* Also dubbeltjiedoring (-ˌdʊrəŋ); duiweltjie (ˈdœʏvəlcı) and (formerly) dubbeltje(doorn).

1. [Afrikaans, of uncertain origin.] One of several South African weeds, esp. *Tribulus terrestris* or *Emex australis*; also the spiny, angular burr of any of these weeds.

1795 tr. *Thunberg's Trav.* (ed. 2) I. 148 The seed-vessels of the *rumex spinosus* (dubelties). **1827** T. PHILLIPS *Scenes in Albany & Caffer-Land* vi. 100 Our dogs were soon disabled by a prickly seed which gets into their feet..called a *dubbeltje.* **1912** *East London Dispatch* 13 Sept. 7/4 The every-increasing spread of the 'Dubbeltje Doorn' weed. **1949** *Cape Argus* (Mag. Section) 2 Apr. 2/5 A sheet of yellow dubbeltjie blossom.

2. [Afrikaans, f. Du. *dubbeltje* double stiver, double penny.] A penny; in *pl.*, money, pence. Cf. DOUBLEJEE, etc.

1822 W. J. BURCHELL *Trav. Interior S. Afr.* I. iii. 78 The only current coin, are English penny-pieces, which here pass for the value of two pence, and are called *dubbeltjes.* **1833** S. KAY *Trav. Caffraria* II. xi. 283 At last he scarcely had *dublejees* (pence) sufficient to carry him back to the Colony. **1949** L. G. GREEN *In Land of Afternoon* (1950) vii. 102 English coins became legal tender at the Cape in 1806, and the heavy 'cartwheel' penny pieces bearing the head of George III soon became known as 'dubbeltjes', as they were worth two pence.

†**dubber**[1]. *Obs.* [a. OF. *doubeur* repairer, f. *douber* to trim, dress, repair: cf. DUB *v.*[1] 7.] A renovator of old clothes.

(But the meaning in quot. 1415 is uncertain: some have conjectured 'trimmers or binders of MSS.')

1225–6 *Liber Albus* I. II. viii. (Rolls) 83 Et Paganus le Dubbour, unus vicinorum, attachiatur pro morte illa. **1240–1** *Ibid.* I. II. xxxviii. (Rolls) 103 Et Johannes Clericus, Dubbeour, et Thomas de Marisco..committantur gaolæ. **1415** *Liber Memorandorum* A/Y lf. 129b, in *York Myst.* Introd. 20 Que touz hosyers que vendront chauuces.. aueront la charge del pagyne de Moyses et Pharao..horspris les Dubbers et ceux que sount assignez a eux. **1415** *Ordo paginarum ludi Corporis Christi* lf. 245 Ibid. 26 Escriueners, Lumners, Questors, Dubbers.

dubber[2]: see DUBBA.

dubbil, -ble, -bul, etc., obs. forms of DOUBLE.

dubbin *sb.* and *v.*: see DUBBING *vbl. sb.* 4.

'dubbing, *vbl. sb.*[1] [f. DUB *v.*[1] + -ING[1].] The action of the verb DUB[1].

1. The conferring of knighthood; investment with a dignity or title.

a **1300** *K. Horn* 438 Help me to kniȝte Bi al þine miȝte, To my lord þe king, þat he me ȝiue dubbing. *c* **1315** SHOREHAM 15 A prince longeth for to do The gode knyȝtes dobbynge. *c* **1440** *York Myst.* xxvi. 7. **1586** FERNE *Blaz. Gentrie* 152 The ordering of dubbings and creations of Knights or Esquires. **1611** in Gutch *Collect. Cur.* I. 101 All Bachelor Knights of more puny dubbing. **1676** MARVELL *Mr. Smirke* 2 The Dubbing or Creating of Witts.

†**2.** Attire, dress, array. *Obs.*

a **1300** *Cursor M.* 28032 Quen þai see your dubbing ware [*i.e.* attiring gear]. *c* **1400** A. DAVY *Dreams* 76 Boþe hij hadden a newe dubbyng; Hure gray was her cloþing.

3. *Angling.* The dressing of an artificial fly; *concr.* the materials used in the process.

1676 COTTON *Walton's Angler* II. 300 To teach you..of what dubbing you are to make the several flies. **1799** G. SMITH *Laboratory* II. 290 The dubbing of the fur of a black spaniel. **1867** F. FRANCIS *Angling* vi. (1880) 214 *note*, The dubbing..of which the fly is composed.

4. A preparation of grease for softening leather and rendering it waterproof. Also **dubbin**. Hence **'dubbin** *v. trans.*, to apply dubbin to; **'dubbined** *ppl. a.*, treated with dubbin.

1781 J. RIPLEY *Orig. Lett.* 23 Take currier's dubbing, and anoint his sores. **1819** REES *Cycl.* XX, The hide or skin is then conveyed to the shade or drying-place, where the oily substances are applied, termed stuffing or dubbing. **1825** JAMIESON, *Dubbin*, the liquor used by curriers for softening leather, composed of tallow and oil. **1855** J. DAVIES in *Trans. Philol. Soc.* 230 *Dubbin*, a kind of paste used by shoemakers. **1875** *Ure's Dict. Arts* III. 96 The dubbing..is composed of tallow, brought to a soft plastic condition by being melted and mixed with cod-liver oil. **1896** *Price List*, Prout's Dubbin. **1896** J. K. SNOWDEN *Web of Old Weaver* vii. 77, I was seeking a pot of dubbin on the top shelf of her cupboard. **1897** C. T. DAVIS *Manuf. Leather* (ed. 2) xxx. 463 Dubbin them again and lay them by for a day or two. **1899** M. COBBETT *Bottled Holidays* 147 An omnibus odorous of freely-dubbined boots. **1909** C. E. BENSON *Brit. Mountaineering* ii. 30 Dubbin..keeps them [*sc.* boots] supple, and prevents the leather perishing. *a* **1918** [see BLANCO]. **1967** *Listener* 30 Nov. 702/2 Tommy grew up in the Gorbals, dubbining his football boots with bacon fat.

5. a. Working timber with an adze. **b.** *dubbing-out* (*Plastering*): see quot. 1842–76.

1823 P. NICHOLSON *Pract. Build.* 379 The expenses of dubbing-out. **1842–76** GWILT *Archit.* Gloss., *Dubbing-out* ..the bringing of an uneven surface in a wall to a plane, by pieces of tile, slate, or the like, before it is plastered over. *c* **1850** *Rudim. Navig.* 116 Dubbing, working with an adze.

6. *attrib.*

a **1300** [see 2]. *a* **1400** *Octouian* 1274 Seuen dayes ylyke hyt leste, The bredale and the dubbyng feste. **1864** WEBSTER, *Dubbing-tool*, a tool for paring down to an even surface. **1883** *Fisheries Exhib. Catal.* 51, Lines, Fly Books, and Dubbing Books.

dubbler, var. DOUBLER.

dubbletie: see DOUBLEJEE.

dubby ('dʌbɪ), *a. colloq.* and *dial.* [f. DUB *v.*[1] + -Y[1].] Blunt; short, dumpy.
1825 JENNINGS *Obs. Dial. West Eng.* 35 *Dub, dubbed, dubby*,..blunt; not pointed; squat. **1872** F. W. ROBINSON *Wrayford's Ward* III. 208 A nose that young ladies, I believe, call 'dubby'. **1904** FOWLER & FELKIN *Kate of Kate Hall* xxiii, A dubby piece of blacklead that couldn't write two consecutive words.

'duberous, 'dubersome, *a. dial.* or *vulg.* [Corruptions of DUBIOUS.] Dubious, doubtful.
1818 *Sporting Mag.* II. 17 They became a little duberous. **1830** GALT *Lawrie T.* IV. x, The squire..was duberous if his charackter would serve. **1837-40** HALIBURTON *Clockm.* (1862) 139 As if he was dubersome whether he ought to speak out or not. **1876** HOLLAND *Sev. Oaks* xx. 277 'She was ..a little dubersome about my coming to time.' **1889** BOLDREWOOD *Robbery under Arms* (1890) 109 That's what I'm dubersome about.

dubiety (dju:'baɪɪtɪ). [ad. late L. *dubietās*, f. *dubius* doubtful: see -ITY.] The condition or quality of being dubious; doubtfulness, dubiousness. **b.** An instance of this, a matter of doubt.
c **1750** RICHARDSON (T.), A state of dubiety and suspense is ever accompanied with uneasiness. **1766** W. GORDON *Gen. Counting-ho.* 32 So expressive..as to admit of no dubiety. **1821** LAMB *Elia* Ser. I. *Imperf. Sympathies*, The twilight of dubiety never falls upon him. **1892** STEVENSON *Across Plains* 286 On one point there should be no dubiety.
b. 1806-7 J. BERESFORD *Miseries Hum. Life* (1826) xx. 279 Hume's account of his own dubieties. **1845** CARLYLE *Cromwell* (1871) II. 260 A terrible dubiety to itself and to us.

dubil, obs. form of DOUBLE.

dubiosity (dju:bɪ'ɒsɪtɪ). [ad. L. type **dubiōsitās*, f. *dubiōsus* DUBIOUS: cf. It. *dubbiosità*.] = DUBIOUSNESS; with *pl.*, a doubtful matter.
1646 SIR T. BROWNE *Pseud. Ep.* I. v. 17 Men..swallow falsities for truths, dubiosities for certainties. **1821** *New Monthly Mag.* II. 299 The puzzles and the dubiosities of meaning. **1859** G. MEREDITH *R. Feverel* III. vi. 169 Distinctly and without a shadow of dubiosity.

dubious ('dju:bɪəs), *a.* [ad. L. *dubiōs-us* doubtful, f. *dubium* doubt, neuter of *dubius* doubtful.]
1. Objectively doubtful; fraught with doubt or uncertainty; uncertain, undetermined; indistinct, ambiguous, vague.
1548 HALL *Chron., Edw. IV*, 208 To abide the fortune of battayle, which is ever dubious and uncertayne. **1662** STILLINGFL. *Orig. Sacr.* I. iii. §8 In what year of his raign, is very dubious. **1725** WATTS *Logic* II. ii. §8 Dubious propositions..are distinguished into probable, or improbable. **1769** ROBERTSON *Chas. V*, III. VIII. 100 He joins a dubious friend against a known benefactor. **1813** BUSBY tr. *Lucretius* Life, The faint and dubious rays of crepuscular light. **1868** STANLEY *Westm. Abbey* iv. 350 A dubious honour.
b. Of uncertain issue or result.
1635 J. HAYWARD tr. *Biondi's Banish'd Virg.* 181 The fight was no lesse dubious than dangerous. **1667** MILTON *P.L.* I. 104 His utmost power..oppos'd In dubious Battel on the Plains of Heav'n. **1875** HELPS *Ess., Self-Disc.* 16 A dubious deadly struggle which had terminated in his favour.
†**c.** *Old Chem.* ***dubious acids***: see quot. *Obs.*
1727-51 CHAMBERS *Cycl.* s.v. *Acid, Dubious* or *Latent Acids*, are those which do not possess enough of the Acid nature to give sensible marks thereof on the taste, but agree with the manifest Acids in some other properties.
d. Of questionable or suspected character.
1860 TYNDALL *Glac.* I. iii. 25 A large bed, covered with clothes of the most dubious black-brown hue. **1884** L. J. JENNINGS in *Croker Papers* I. vi. 158 She had been absent from England..oftentimes in very dubious company. **1893** *Bookman*, June 83/1 Having got into evil odour by their dubious gains.
2. Subjectively doubtful; wavering or fluctuating in opinion; hesitating; inclined to doubt.
1632 J. HAYWARD tr. *Biondi's Eromena* 189 Though I beleeve..yet am I somewhat dubious in beleeving. **1710** NORRIS *Chr. Prud.* v. 220 Uncertain Ballancings and Fluctuations of a dubious Will. **1865** MISS BRADDON *Sir Jasper* I. ii. 40 [She] raised her eyebrows with a dubious expression. **1874** HELPS *Soc. Press.* xiv. 198 I followed them, dubious as to whether I should ultimately interfere.

'dubiously, *adv.* [f. prec. + -LY[2].] In a dubious manner; with doubt, doubtfully, hesitatingly; uncertainly, vaguely, ambiguously.
1646 SIR T. BROWNE *Pseud. Ep.* III. v. 115 Albertus magnus speaks dubiously..but Aldrovand affirmeth plainly. **1708** SWIFT *Predict. for* 1708 Wks. 1755 II. I. 152 To wander in generals, and talk dubiously. **1821** BYRON *Sardan.* III. i, How Goes on the conflict? *A.* Dubiously and fiercely. **1860** HOLLAND *Miss Gilbert* ii. 39 'I don't know where you will find it', said the doctor, shaking his head dubiously.

'dubiousness. [f. as prec. + -NESS.] The quality of being dubious; doubtfulness; doubtful character; uncertainty, ambiguity.
1651 R. SAUNDERS *Plenary Possess.* 3 All which particulars ..have difficulty and dubiousnesse in them. **1725** POPE *Odyss.* I. *note* (R.), She speaks with the dubiousness of a man, not the certainty of a Goddess. **1865** M. ARNOLD *Ess. Crit.* x. (1875) 411 The dubiousness and involved manner of the Greek. **1872** GEO. ELIOT *Middlem.* lxxiii, The dubiousness of all medical treatment.

dubitable ('dju:bɪtəb(ə)l), *a.* [ad. L. *dubitābilis*, f. *dubitāre* to DOUBT: see -ABLE, and cf. OF. *dubitable*.] Capable of being doubted; liable to doubt or question.
1624 MIDDLETON *Game at Chess* III. i. 265 The dubitable hazards Of fortune. **1657** HAWKE *Killing is M.* 30 Aristotle makes it dubitable, and disputable, whether it is better to be Ruled by a good Law, or a good Man. **1704** NORRIS *Ideal World* II. ix. 391 The consequence, which is the only dubitable one, is again proved by this enthymeme. **1893** *Nat. Observer* 30 Sept. 515/1 To put into dubitable French what he might have said..in indubitable English.
Hence **'dubitably** *adv.*, in a dubitable manner.
1864 in WEBSTER.

†**dubitancy.** *Obs.* [ad. L. **dubitāntia*, f. *dubitāre* to DOUBT: see -ANCY and cf. OF. *dubitance*.] Doubt, hesitation, uncertainty of opinion.
1648 HAMMOND *Serm. on Rom.* iv. 25 Wks. 1684 IV. 505 They are..without all dubitancy resolv'd, that all the joys of Heaven are forfeited by this choice. **1669** WOODHEAD *St. Teresa* I. Pref. 3 A certain knowledge, free from all dubitancy, of his Presence.

dubitant ('dju:bɪtənt), *a.* (*sb.*) [ad. L. *dubitāntem*, pres. pple. of *dubitāre* to DOUBT: see -ANT.] Doubting; having doubts. *absol.* One who doubts.
1821 *Blackw. Mag.* IX. 39 Why art thou..to be less dubitant and circumlocutory? **1821** CRAIG *Lect. Drawing* ii. 87 Let the dubitant take a piece of the blackest paper. **1871** LYTTON *Coming Race* x, The male is a shy and dubitant creature. **1895** *19th Cent.* Oct. 680 The Church militant rather than the Church dubitant may hold sway.

dubitate ('dju:bɪteɪt), *v. rare.* [f. L. *dubitāt-*, ppl. stem of *dubitāre* to DOUBT.] *intr.* To doubt, hesitate, waver.
1837 CARLYLE *Fr. Rev.* II. II. vi, If..he were to loiter dubitating, and not come. **1879** MAUDSLEY *Pathol. Mind* vii. 312 If it were some great thing concerning which they dubitated and wavered.
Hence **'dubitating,** *vbl. sb.* and *ppl. a.*; **'dubitatingly** *adv.*
1827 CARLYLE *Germ. Romance* I. 231 Dubitatingly. **1837** —— *Fr. Rev.* I. IV. i, What dubitating, what circumambulating. **1845** —— *Cromwell* (1871) III. 194 Answered dubitatingly.

dubitation (dju:bɪ'teɪʃən). [a. F. *dubitation* (13th c.), ad. L. *dubitātiōn-em*, n. of action f. *dubitāre* to DOUBT.] The action or condition of doubting; doubt, uncertainty; hesitation. **b.** An instance of this; †a matter of doubt (*obs.*).
c **1450** *Cov. Myst.* (Shaks. Soc.) 67 I..Alle that my progenitouris hath..seyn, ffeythfully beleve withowtyn alle dubytacion. **1570** BUCHANAN *Chamæleon* Wks. (1892) 51 The Chamæleon..eftir sum dubitatioun come to Strivelling. *c* **1645** HOWELL *Lett.* I. V. xxi, It is as true a rule, that.. dubitation is the beginning of all knowledg. *a* **1734** NORTH *Exam.* I. i. (1740) 28 Lest the Author should think himself affronted by this Dubitation touching his Story. **1814** SCOTT *Wav.* xli, 'Beyond a shadow of dubitation.' **1891** *Spectator* 14 Mar., The assertion, made with no dubitation or reserve.
b. 1545 JOYE *Exp. Dan.* xii. (R.), The trewe inuocacion of God thorow Cryst, thei haue turned it into a dowtfull dubitacion. **1683** E. HOOKER *Pref. Ep. Pordage's Mystic Div.* 99 Altercations, disputations and dubitations of, in and about Mystic Theologie. **1837** CARLYLE *Fr. Rev.* III. VII. vii, In the wreck of human dubitations, this remains indubitable, that Pleasure is pleasant.

dubitative ('dju:bɪtətɪv), *a.* [ad. L. *dubitātīv-us* (Tertull.) doubtful, f. *dubitāre*: cf. F. *dubitatif* (13–14th c. in Hatz.-Darm.).] Inclined or given to doubt; expressing doubt or hesitancy.
1615 [implied in DUBITATIVELY]. **1727-51** CHAMBERS *Cycl., Conjunctions dubitative*, those which express some doubt, or suspension of opinion.—as, *if*. **1859** GEO. ELIOT *A. Bede* liii, Turning his head on one side in a dubitative manner. **1887** JESSOPP *Arcady* 49 Your old Arcadian's style of talk is full of doubts; it is what may be called the dubitative or approximating style.
b. *absol.* A word or phrase expressing doubt.
1835 SOUTHEY *Doctor* III. xcii. 176 Some one has said that the Devil's dubitative is a negative.

'dubitatively, *adv.* [f. prec. + -LY[2].] In a dubitative or doubting manner; doubtingly.
1615 SIR E. HOBY *Curry-combe* iii. 121 This is the exposition..so dubitatiuely propounded by the Interpreters themselues. **1858** CARLYLE *Fredk. Gt.* VI. ix. II. 131 The Reichshofrath dubitatively shook its wig, for years. **1889** F. BARRETT *Under Strange Mask* I. vii. 107 'H'm—yes', said I dubitatively.

duble, dubler, dublet, obs. ff. DOUBLE, etc.

Dublin ('dʌblɪn). The name of the capital of the Republic of Ireland, used *attrib.* in **Dublin (Bay) prawn,** the Norway lobster, *Nephrops norvegicus*.
1911 *Encycl. Brit.* XVI. 838/2 The Norway lobster..is less esteemed for food than the common species. In London it is sold under the name of 'Dublin prawn'. **1949** H. SMITH *Master Bk. Fish* ix. 171 Dublin Bay prawns (*Langoustines*). .. All recipes given for prawns may be used for Dublin Bay prawns. **1951** E. DAVID *French Country Cooking* 31 Dublin Bay prawns in fritters. **1963** *Times* 19 Jan. 10/6 The Norway Lobster or the Dublin Prawn, which, as scampi, we now purchase in the anonymous form of frozen packets of shelled 'tails'. **1971** *Nature* 29 Jan. 298/2 It is the tail of this animal, also known as the Dublin Bay prawn although it is really a close relative of the common lobster, which constitutes scampi.

Dubliner ('dʌblɪnə(r)). [f. *Dublin* (see prec.) + -ER[1].] A native or inhabitant of Dublin.
1900 *Westm. Gaz.* 11 Apr. 4/1 The ceremony..which Dubliners hope the Queen will perform. **1914** J. JOYCE (*title*) Dubliners. **1961** *Observer* 22 Jan. 31/1 The other, a Dubliner I should judge by her accent, was the girl who gave her baby away to Jane Russell.

†**dubment.** *Obs. rare.* [f. DUB *v.*[1] + -MENT: cf. *adubment*.] Dubbing, adornment, array.
13.. *E.E. Allit. P.* A. 121 The dubbement dere of doun and dalez.

duboisine (dju:'bɔɪsaɪn). *Chem.* [see -INE.] An alkaloid obtained from the Australian solanaceous shrub *Duboisia myoporioides*, having qualities similar to those of atropine and hyoscyamine.
1883 in *Syd. Soc. Lex.*

Dubonnet (dybɔne). [The name of a family of French wine-merchants.] The proprietary name of a sweet French aperitif; also, a glass of this wine.
1913 *Trade Marks Jrnl.* 25 June 1022 *Dubonnet*... The Best Appetizer in the World... A Wine. La Société Anonyme Dubonnet..7, Rue Mornay, Paris, France; Merchants. **1919** W. S. MAUGHAM *Moon & Sixpence* lvii. 256 Ask *Monsieur* if he will not drink a little glass of Quinquina Dubonnet. **1930** H. CRADDOCK *Savoy Cocktail Bk.* 62 *Dubonnet cocktail.* ½ Dubonnet, ½ Dry Gin. **1960** L. COOPER *Certain Compass* 149 What will you have? A Martini, Dubonnet, whisky?

dubs (dʌbz). *local.* [Short for *doubles*.] A term used in various senses in the game of marbles (see quots.).
1823 E. MOOR *Suffolk Words* s.v., A player knocking two out of the ring cries 'dubs!' to authorize his claim to both. **1882** M. H. FOOTE *Led-Horse Claim* iv. 62 'What is it the boys say when they play marbles?'..'Fend dubs?' Hilgard suggested. **1896** *Dialect Notes* I. 220 In Missouri..dubs means, not doublets, but that the player has blundered, and by crying 'dubs' is entitled to play again. **1941** BAKER *Dict. Austral. Slang* 26 *Dubs*, marbles which are placed in a ring in a game of marbles.

dubs, dubsman: see DUB *sb.*[5]

dubu ('du:bu:). [Native name.] In full ***dubu-house***. In eastern Melanesia, a men's house or communal dwelling.
1917 *Nature* 27 Dec. 335/2 The men's club-houses, or *dubus*, have now almost died out. **1924** 'R. DALY' *Outpost* xii. 118 At the end of the main street, in front of the dubu-house, there was a raised platform.

dubul, dubylle, obs. forms of DOUBLE.

duc, obs. form of DUKE.

ducal ('dju:kəl), *a.* (*sb.*) Also 5 ducall, 7 duckal. [a. F. *ducal* (15th c. in Hatz.-Darm.) = It. *ducale*, Sp. *ducal*, ad. late L. *ducāl-is*, f. *duc-em* (*dux*) leader, DUKE.] Of, pertaining to, or characteristic of a duke or dukedom (also, of a doge).
In quot. 1626 = Of the party of the Duke (of Buckingham).
1494 FABYAN *Chron.* VII. 374 The bezaunde imperiall is worth .l. ducates, and the ducall bezaunde is worth .xx. ducates. **1626** *Crt. & Times Chas. I* (1848) I. 106 Some say my Lord of Suffolk having given his proxy to my Lord of Walden, his eldest son, and now, finding him ducal, hath revoked. **1685** *Lond. Gaz.* No. 2099/4 The Crest is a Griffins-head between two Wings, coming out of a Duckal Coronet. **1731** SWIFT *On Pulteney* 10 Produce at last thy dormant ducal patent. **1765-9** BLACKSTONE *Comm.* (1793) 106 Jersey, Guernsey, Sark, Alderney..are governed by their own laws, which are for the most part the ducal customs of Normandy. **1841** W. SPALDING *Italy & It. Isl.* I. 216 The Ducal Gallery of Florence. **1851** RUSKIN *Stones Ven.* (1874) I. i. 17 The Ducal Palace of Venice..is the central building of the world.
b. Of the rank or bearing the title of duke.
1796 MORSE *Amer. Geog.* II. 138 The offices..are hereditary to the ducal families of Ancaster and Norfolk.
c. ***ducal mantle***, (*a*) the official robe of a duke; (*b*) *Conch.* a species of mollusc, *Chlamys pallium*.
1776 DA COSTA *Conchol.* 292 The Ducal Mantle Escallop. **1819** in *Pantologia*. **1823** in CRABB *Technol. Dict.*
†**B.** *sb.* See quot. *Obs.*
1727-51 CHAMBERS *Cycl., Ducals*, the letters patent granted by the senate of Venice are called *ducals*.

ducality (dju:'kælɪtɪ). *humorous.* [f. prec. + -ITY.] Ducal rank or character; *concr.*, a ducal personage; the ducal order.
1847 LD. HOUGHTON in *Life* (1890) I. 399 The German ducalities go to Granada. **1848** *Ibid.* 408 Disraeli made an excellent use..of the ducality of his friend. **1891** *Pictorial World* 7 Mar. 307/2 The Ducality was in high good humour.

'ducally, *adv.* [f. as prec. + -LY[2].] In a ducal manner; as a duke.
1823 RUTTER *Fonthill* p. xxii, A lion rampant, Argent, ducally crowned, Or.

ducape (djuːˈkeɪp). [Origin unascertained.] ‘A plain-wove stout silk fabric of softer texture than *Gros de Naples*.

Its manufacture was introduced by the French refugees of 1685.’ Beck, *Draper's Dict.*

1678 PHILLIPS (ed. 4), *Ducape*, a certain kind of Silk used for Womens Garments. **1688** R. HOLME *Armoury* III. 98/1 Womens Hoods..made of..Sarsenet, Ducape, Vinian Sarsnet, Persia..Silk. **1773** FRANKLIN *Lett.* Wks. 1887 IV. 477, I have had it worked up..into a French grey ducape. **1842** *Penny Cycl.* XXII. 12/1 Persian, sarsenet, gros-de-Naples, ducapes, satin, and levantines are..plain silks, which vary from one another only in texture, quality, or softness.

ducat (ˈdʌkət). Forms: 4 **duket**, 5 **dokett(e, ducatt(e**, 5–6 **doket**, **duckett(e**, 5–7 **dukat**, (6 **ducade**), 6–7 **ducate**, **duccat(e**, **duckat(e**, 6–8 **ducket**, 5– **ducat**. [a. F. *ducat* (1395 in Hatz.-Darm.), ad. It. *ducato* (12th c.), in late L. *ducātus* DUCHY, also name of a coin, f. L. *dux* DUKE.]

1. a. A gold coin of varying value, formerly in use in most European countries; that current in Holland, Russia, Austria, and Sweden being equivalent to about 9*s.* 4*d.* Also applied to a silver coin of Italy, value about 3*s.* 6*d.*

Used as the name of a silver coin issued in 1140 by Roger II of Sicily, as Duke of Apulia, bearing the inscription R DX AP, i.e. *Rogerus Dux Apuliæ*; according to Falcone de Benevento ‘monetam suam introduxit, unam vero, cui Ducatus nomen imposuit’ (Du Cange, s.v.). In 1202, it appears (Pappadopoli, *Monete di Venezia*, 1893, 81) as the name of a Venetian Silver coin, usually known as the *grosso*. In 1284, the first gold ducat, also called *zecchino d'oro*, was struck at Venice under the doge John Dandolo. This coin, worth about 9*s.*, bears on one side figures of St. Mark and the Doge, and on the other a figure of Christ with the legend ‘Sit tibi Christe datus quem tu regis iste ducatus’; this, though it did not originate, may have contributed to spread the name, which was subseq. applied to the gold coins of various European countries.

c **1384** CHAUCER *H. Fame* III. 258 As fyne as ducat [*v.rr.* doket, ducket] in venyse. **1387** TREVISA *Higden* (Rolls) VI. 259 A duket þat is worþy half an Englisshe noble. **1477** *Paston Lett.* No. 804 III. 204 In mony he brengyth with hym an hundred thowsand dokets. **1494** FABYAN *Chron.* VI. clix. 148 A dukat is of sondry valuys, but ye leest in value is .iiii.*s.* iii.*d.* ob. & the best .iiii.*s.* vii.*d.* **1547** BOORDE *Introd. Knowl.* xxx. (1870) 199 In golde they [Castilians] haue duccates and doble duccates. **1555** EDEN *Decades* 176 The double ducades whiche yowre maiestie haue caused to bee coyned, are disparsed throughowte the hole worlde. **1596** SHAKS. *Merch. V.* II. viii. 15 Two sealed bags of ducats, Of double ducats. *a* **1618** RALEIGH *Rem.* (1644) 199 This Ducket currant for three ounces in Barbary, was then worth in England seven shillings and six pence. **1727–51** CHAMBERS *Cycl.* s.v., The chief gold ducats now current, are, the single and double ducats of Venice, Florence, Genoa, Germany, Hungary, Poland, Sweden, Denmark, Flanders, Holland, and Zurich. **1823** CRABB *Technol. Dict.* s.v., The Dutch ducats, which are reckoned the purest gold, are about 9*s.* 6*d.* sterling. **1835** BURNES *Trav. Bokhara* (ed. 2) III. 363 A Persian ducat now bears the value of nine kurans, or rupees. **1858** CARLYLE *Fredk. Gt.* II. xiv. I. 189 The latest existing representative of the ancient Gold Gulden is the Ducat, worth generally about a Half-sovereign in English.

†**b.** A money of account in the Venetian republic. *Obs.*

1611 CORYAT *Crudities* 286 Now whereas the Venetian duckat is much spoken of, you must consider that this word duckat doth not signifie any one certaine coyne. But many severall pieces do concurre to make one duckat, namely six livers and two gazets. **1638** ROBERTS *Merch. Map of Commerce* in Halliw. *Shaks.* V. 323 At Venice there were two sorts of duccats, the one currant in payment, which may bee valued ster. about 3*s.* 4*d.*, and the other of banco, which may be valued about 4*s.*, or 4*s.* 2*d.*

2. *loosely.* **a.** A piece of money; *pl.* Money; cash.

1775 SHERIDAN *Duenna* II. iv, I shall be entitled to the girl's fortune, without settling a ducat on her. **1853** WHYTE MELVILLE *Digby Grand* vi. (Farmer) From spendthrift King John downwards, the Christian has ever pocketed the [Jew's] ducats, and abused the donor. **1895** *Cornh. Mag.* Aug. 174 Holmes was likewise out of ducketts.

b. (Also **ducket.**) A ticket, esp. a railway-ticket or ticket of admission. Cf. DOCKET *sb.*[1] 7. *slang.*

1871 J. H. BANKA *State Prison Life* 493 Railroad ticket,.. ducket. **1874** HOTTEN *Slang Dict.* 152 *Ducket*, a ticket of any kind. Generally applied to pawnbroker's duplicates and raffle cards. **1879** *Macm. Mag.* Oct. 501/2 So I took a ducat (ticket) for Sutton in Surrey. **1935** *Sat. Even. Post* 26 Oct. 9/2 I'll slip you a workin'-press ducat. *Ibid.* 9 Nov. 76/3 It'll sell plenty ducats. Big publicity. **1970** *Guardian* 30 Nov. 8/2 My wife and I had a couple of ducketts to see the Marxes' Broadway musical, ‘Animal Crackers’.

3. ducat gold, fine gold; also applied to gilding of a brilliant colour.

1548 HALL *Chron., Hen. VIII*, 7 The garmentes were powdered with castels, and shefes of arrowes of fyne doket gold. *Ibid.* 80 b, On their faces visers, and all the berdes were fine wyer of Ducket gold. **1808** R. K. PORTER *Trav. Sk. Russ. & Swed.* (1813) I. iv. 29 The spire of this edifice is.. gilt with ducat gold.

ducatoon (dʌkəˈtuːn). Also 7 **ducaton**, **ducattoon**, **-oun**, 7–8 **duccat-**, **duckatoon**. [a. F. *ducaton* ‘a small duckat, or halfe duckat’ (Cotgr.), ? ad. It. *ducatone* (not in Florio) augm. of *ducato* (being a bigger coin than the gold ducat, *Della Crusca*): see prec. and -OON.] A silver coin formerly current in Italian and some other European states, worth from 5 to 6 shillings sterling.

1611 CORYAT *Crudities* 285 The greatest [Venetian silver coin] is the duckatoone, which containeth eight livers, that is, sixe shillings. This piece hath in one side the effigies of the Duke of Venice and the Patriarch..and in the other the figure of St. Justina. *a* **1659** CLEVELAND *Gen. Poems* (1677) 40 What mean the Elders else, those Kirk Dragoons, Made up of Ears and Ruffs like Ducatoons? **1672** PETTY *Pol. Anat.* 385 Weighty plate pieces, together with ducatoons, making about three quarters of the money now current in Ireland. **1704** *Royal Proclam.* 18 June in *Lond. Gaz.* No. 4029/1 Duccatoons of Flanders, Twenty Peny-weight and Twenty one Grains, Five Shillings and Six Pence. **1727–51** CHAMBERS *Cycl.*, *Ducatoon*, a silver coin, struck chiefly in Italy; particularly at Milan, Venice, Florence, Genoa, Lucca, Mantua, and Parma; though there are also Dutch and Flemish ducatoons..There is also a gold ducatoon, struck and current chiefly in Holland. **1827** DE QUINCEY *Murder* Wks. 1862 IV. 19 He had possessed himself of a ducatoon.

Duce (ˈduːtʃeɪ). Also **duce**. [It., = leader.] A leader; spec. ***Il*** or ***The Duce***, title assumed by Benito Mussolini (1883–1945), the creator and leader of the Fascist state in Italy.

1923 B. QUARANTA DI SAN SEVERINO *Mussolini* p. xv, Three..important elements account for the success of the ‘National Fascista Party’..above all, the personality of Mussolini himself, the ‘Duce’, as he is called. **1928** *Observer* 12 Feb. 12 Signor Mussolini makes no allusion to theocracy in his preface to Major Barnes's book. Nevertheless, it is obvious that the book is acceptable to the Duce. **1930** *Economist* 25 Oct. 748/2 The Austro-German ‘duce's’ [*i.e.* Hitler's] anxiety..to deny that the damage has been done by the Nazis. **1937** A. HUXLEY *Ends & Means* v. 34 They yet persist in taking the same roads as are taken by the Duces and Fuehrers. **1937** [see BILATERAL *a.* c]. **1965** ‘C. HIBBERT’ *Garibaldi & his Enemies* I. iv. 57 The sight of the ‘Duce’ [*sc.* Garibaldi] sitting astride his horse. **1971** R. COLLIER (*title*) Duce! The rise and fall of Benito Mussolini.

duce, obs. form of DEUCE.

†**duceˈnarious**, *a.* *Obs.* *rare*$^{-0}$. [f. L. *ducēnārius*, f. *ducēnī* two hundred (each).]

1656 BLOUNT *Glossogr.*, *Ducenarious*, pertaining to two hundred.

‖**duces tecum** (ˈdjuːsiːz ˈtiːkʌm). *Law.* [Latin phrase: more fully *sub pœna duces tecum*, ‘Under penalty thou shalt bring with thee’.] A writ commanding a person to produce in court specified documents or other things which are in his custody, and are required as evidence.

1617 MINSHEU *Ductor*, *Duces tecum*, is a Writ commanding one to appeare at a day in the Chauncerie, and to bring with him some peece of euidence, or other thing that the Court would view. **1658** in PHILLIPS. **1715** *Amer. State Papers* Misc. (1834) I. 682.

Duch(e, obs. forms of DUTCH.

duchepers, **-peiris**, corrupt ff. DOUZEPERS.

†ˈ**duchery**. *Obs.* Also 5 **douch-**, **dowch-**. [app. f. *duché*, earlier form of DUCHY + -ERY, q.v.]

1. The domain or territory of a duke; = DUCHY.

?*a* **1400** *Morte Arth.* 49 He doubbyd hys knyghtez, Dyvysyde dowcherys and delte in dyverse remmes. *c* **1475** *Rauf Coilȝear* 936 Appeirand air To twa Douchereis. **1494** FABYAN *Chron.* VII. 455 Charlis de Bloyes made his clayme to that duchery by tytle of his wyfe. **1536** BELLENDEN *Cron. Scot.* (1821) II. 291 To have the empire of Ingland, with the duchery of Normandy.

2. A duke's rule or term of office.

1387 TREVISA *Higden* VI. v. (Tollem. MS.), The fourtenthe yere of his duchery. *Ibid.* (Rolls) VII. 119 A ȝere of his ducherie. **1494** FABYAN *Chron.* VI. ccvii. 220 The .vii. yere of his dowchery, he went to Iherusalem.

duchess (ˈdʌtʃɪs). Forms: 4–6 **duches**, 4–7 **duchesse**, (5 **ducesse**, **dochesse**, **duchez**, **dukes**, 6 **dutches**, *Sc.* **duiches**), 6–9 **dutchess**, 6– **duchess**. [a. F. *duchesse* (12th c. in Hatz.-Darm.) ad. late or med.L. *ducissa*, f. *dux* (*duc-*): see DUKE. The spelling *dutchess* was usual till *c* 1810. See also DUCHESSE.]

1. a. The wife or widow of a duke. **b.** A lady holding in her own right a position equal to that of duke.

Grand (***† Great***) ***Duchess***, the wife of a GRAND DUKE, q.v.

13.. *Gaw. & Gr. Knt.* 2465 Arþurez half suster, þe duches doȝter of Tyntagelle. *c* **1385** CHAUCER *L.G.W.* 2122 *Ariadne*, Myn dere herte, Of Athenys duchesse [*v.rr.* ducesse, duches]. *Ibid.* 2127 Al softely systyr myn, quod she, Now be we duchessis bothe I and ȝe. **1447** BOKENHAM *Seyntys* (Roxb.) 145 Aftyr the dochesse of York clepyd Isabel. *c* **1475** *Voc.* in Wr.-Wülcker 792/4 *Hec duxissa*, a dukes. **1529** *Act 21 Hen. VIII*, c. 13 §28 Any Chaplaine of any Duchesse, Marquesse, Countesse, Vicountesse, or Baronesse. **1613** SHAKS. *Hen. VIII*, II. iii. 38 What thinke you of a Dutchesse? Haue you limbs To beare that load of Title? **1701** *Act 12 & 13 Will. III*, c. 2 §1 Princess Sophia, Electress and Dutchess Dowager of Hannover. **1756–7** tr. *Keysler's Trav.* (1760) II. 2 The public audiences are given by the great dutchess. **1779–81** JOHNSON *L.P.*, *Pope* Wks. IV. 74 To display the Dutchess of Marlborough under the name of Atossa. **1818** CRUISE *Digest* (ed. 2) I. 344 A court of demissions was held in the names of the duke and duchess.

2. *transf.* †**a.** Lady (as feminine of *lord*). *Obs.*

1393 LANGL. *P. Pl.* C. III. 33 Ich am hus dere douheter, duchesse of heuene. *c* **1485** *Digby Myst.* III. 515 A dere dewchesse, my daysyys Iee! **1513** BRADSHAW *St. Werburge* I. 2183 A duches of vertue as whylom was Delbora.

fig. *c* **1430** LYDG. *Min. Poems* 173 (Mätz.) Prynce! remembre..Howe vertue is of vices a duchesse.

b. *slang.* A woman of imposing demeanour or showy appearance. [Cf. F. *duchesse.*] Hence, a girl or woman, *spec.* one's mother or wife (cf. DUTCH *sb.*[2]); also as a term of address to a woman.

a **1700** B. E. *Dict. Cant. Crew*, *Rum-dutchess*, a jolly handsom Woman. **1773** GOLDSM. *Stoops to Conq.* II, This Stammer in my address..can never permit me to soar above the reach of..one of the Duchesses of Drury-Lane. **1895** *Westm. Gaz.* 9 Oct. 8/1 The dissemination of those articles of apparel amongst ‘factory ladies’ and the elderly ‘duchesses’ of Chevalierland! **1906** E. DYSON *Fact'ry 'Ands* xiii. 170 Er sorrer—eh, what? 'Tain't er little duchess, is it? **1909** J. R. WARE *Passing Eng.* 119/2 *Duchess*, mother—invariable title given between familiar friends when the mother of either is being asked after. ‘How's the Duchess, Bob?’ **1923** J. MANCHON *Le Slang* 112 *The* (or *my*) *old duchess*.., ma vieille, ma femme. **1953** K. TENNANT *Joyful Condemned* xxviii. 272 ‘Hold your noise, Duchess,’ Jimmy commanded. **1967** L. FORRESTER *Girl called Fathom* xii. 147 Start talkin', Duchess. We're gonna toss what you got into the computer..and see what comes out.

3. a. A size of roofing slate, of 24 by 12 inches.

1823 P. NICHOLSON *Pract. Build.* 396 Countesses are in size the next gradation above ladies; and Duchesses still larger. **1851** *Offic. Catal. Gt. Exhib.* I. 141 From ‘ladies’ (16 inches by 8) to ‘duchesses’ (24 by 12), the slates are sold per thousand (of 1200 slates). **1883** [see COUNTESS 2].

b. A size of writing paper (see quot.).

1923 H. A. MADDOX *Dict. Stationery* 24 *Duchess*, a fashionable small broad size of private note paper, measuring $5\frac{3}{4}$ in. or 6 in. by $4\frac{3}{8}$ in.

4. *attrib.* and *Comb.*, as ***duchess-gentlewoman***, ***-regent***; ***duchess-like*** adj.

1824 MISS MITFORD *Village* Ser. I. (1863) 52 Her beauty is duchess-like. **1826** W. E. ANDREWS *Exam. Fox's Cal. Prot. Saints* 47 The cause for which the priest-knight and the duchess-gentlewoman suffered was one and the same. **1871** FREEMAN *Norm. Conq.* IV. xviii. 178 An honourable embassy was sent to the Duchess-Regent in Normandy.

Hence ˈ**duchessship**, the rank or personality of a duchess; ˈ**duchessy** *a.*, *colloq.*, like or of the nature of a duchess; abounding in duchesses.

1607 CHAPMAN *Bussy D'Ambois* Plays 1873 II. 29, I would haue put that proiect face of his To a more test than did her Dutchesship. **1819** *Monthly Mag.* XLVIII. 415 His Princeship and her Princessship; his Dukeship and her Duchess-ship, may also find a place in his crabbed vocabulary, if he prefer it. **1870** *Contemp. Rev.* XIV. 486 ‘Lothair’ has been called a ‘duchessy’ book. **1887** SIMS *Mary Jane's Mem.* 49 A handsome nose that made her look duchessy.

duchesse (ˈdʌtʃɪs, ‖dyʃɛs). [Fr., = duchess.]

1. A kind of chaise-longue, consisting of two armchairs facing each other, with a stool connecting them. So ***duchesse brisée*** (see quot. 1937).

1794 *Cabinet-Maker* (*A. Hepplewhite & Co.*) (ed. 3) 16 (*caption*) Duchesse and Confidante. [**1803** T. SHERATON *Cabinet Dict.* 337 Duchess, a kind of bed, composed of three parts, or a chair at each end and a stool between them.] **1936** ‘R. WEST’ *Thinking Reed* i. 12 André..poured out a glass of Evian and sat back on the duchesse sofa. **1937** *Burlington Mag.* June 286/2 Our chaise-longue..consists of a *bergère* and a *bout-de-pied*. In this form it is usually called *duchesse brisée*. **1955** R. FASTNEDGE *Eng. Furnit. Styles* ix. 200 The *duchesse*..was formed by two facing ‘Barjier chairs..with a stool in the middle’.

2. ***duchesse dressing-chest***, ***-table***, a dressing-table with a swing-glass; also *ellipt.*; ***duchesse toilet-cover***, ***-set***, a cover for a dressing-table, or a set of covers usually consisting of one long runner, one smaller, and two very small mats.

1863 M. B. CHESNUT *Diary from Dixie* 10 Sept. (1905) xv. 240 The bride had a *duchesse* dressing-table, muslin and lace. **1881** C. C. HARRISON *Woman's Handiwork* III. 210 The Duchesse Dressing Table... Dear to woman's heart is the convenient little ‘Duchesse’..with its snowy draperies. **1895** *Army & Navy Co-op. Soc. Price List* 15 Sept. 1102/2 Duchesse Toilet Covers. **1906** *Lady's World* Nov. 156/1 Very dainty Duchesse toilet sets can be made by placing some of these floral squares on a foundation of coloured silk. **1922** *Daily Tel.* 12 June 20/1 Burr walnut duchesse tables and washstands. **1930** *Ibid.* 5 Apr. 21/7 Duchesse dressing chests. **1957** J. FRAME *Owls do Cry* I. xii. 54 The tweezers.. stayed in exactly the same place on the duchesse.

3. (See quot. 1878.)

[**1873** *Young Englishwoman* July 338/2 The bodice and open Duchess sleeves are also trimmed.] **1878** *Cassell's Family Mag.* IV. 168/2 For balls..there are the Duchesse and Marquise sleeves. The Duchesse covers two-thirds of the arm, and is finished off with frills..and lace.

4. ***duchesse satin***, ***satin duchesse***, a very soft, heavy kind of satin.

1878 *Cassell's Family Mag.* IV. 365/1 Duchesse satin is the widest, and at the same time far the best. **1884** *Pall Mall Gaz.* 9 Aug. 9/1 A long train of cream duchesse satin. **1894** *Times* 19 Sept. 10/4 Charged..with stealing a large quantity of silk and satin duchesse. **1895** *Army & Navy Co-op. Soc. Price List* 15 Sept. 1095/2 Coloured Satins. Duchesse. **1968** J. IRONSIDE *Fashion Alphabet* 248 *Duchesse*, a highly lustrous, heavy, firm, yet soft satin.

5. ***Duchesse lace***, a variety of Brussels pillow-lace, worked with fine thread in large sprays.

1882 CAULFEILD & SAWARD *Dict. Needlework* 166/2 Duchesse Lace is worked with a finer and different thread to that of Honiton. **1902** *Encycl. Brit.* XXX. 110/2 ‘Duchesse’ and Bruges lace are the chief pillow-made laces. **1926–7** *Army & Navy Stores Catal.* 1110/3. Duchesse and lace-trimmed blinds.

6. ***duchesse potatoes***, mashed potatoes mixed with egg and either baked or fried in small cakes or used as a decoration (see quots.).

[**1930** R. WAKEFIELD *Toll House Recipes* 172 Duchess potatoes.] **1947** I. B. ALLEN *Food for Two* 106 Pipe duchesse potato around the edge. **1948** L. MARION *Be your own Chef* xii. 209 Duchesse Potatoes... When you have a compact mash of potatoes.. add two tablespoons of grated cheese and beat in a yolk of egg.. melt a tablespoon of butter in the frying-pan.. place your little pieces in it and turn them on both sides, until they are of an even golden colour. **1951** *Good Housek. Home Encycl.* 481/1 Mashed or Duchesse potatoes may be piped into fancy shapes or borders.

ducht, pa. t. of DOW *v.*[1]

duchtie, -y, Sc. forms of DOUGHTY.

duchy (ˈdʌtʃɪ). Forms: 4–5 duche, -ee, 4–7 -ie, (5 dwche, -ie), 5–6 duchye, 6–8 dutchie, -y, 6– duchy. [a. OF. *ducheé*, later *duché*, fem. (12th c. *duchete*, *duceé* in Hatz.-Darm.), and later OF. *duché* masc. The former represents a L. type **ducitāt-em* dukeship; the latter is = Pr. *ducat*, It. *ducato*, Sp. *ducado*:—late L. *ducātus* territory of a duke; f. L. *dux, duc-em* leader, DUKE.]

1. The territory ruled by a duke or duchess.

1382 WYCLIF *Neh.* v. 18 The ȝeris frutis of my duchie [Vulg. *annonas ducatus mei*] I soȝte not. **1393** LANGL. *P. Pl.* C. IV. 245 A kyngdome oþer duche May nat be sold soþly. *c* **1400** MAUNDEV. (1839) i. 7 He holdeth.. of the reme of Roussye a gret partie, where-of he hath made a Duchee. **1568** GRAFTON *Chron.* II. 291 The French king should clerely geve unto him all the Duchy of Guyan.. And that king Edward.. should freely holde and occupie the sayde Duchie. **1601** R. JOHNSON *Kingd. & Commw.* (1603) 105 The Pope hath the cittie of Rome.. the Dutchie of Spolet. **1756–7** tr. *Keysler's Trav.* (1760) IV. 157 The dutchy of Carniola. **1782** PRIESTLEY *Corrupt. Chr.* I. IV. 396 Otho.. had erected his duchy into a kingdom.

b. In Great Britain, applied to the dukedoms of Cornwall and Lancaster (the two earliest in England) vested in the Royal Family, and having certain courts of their own, in which respect they differ from ordinary peerage dukedoms.

1480 CAXTON *Chron. Eng.* ccxxv. 229 Kyng edward made of the erledome of cornewayle a duchye. **1553**, etc. Duchy of Lancashire [see CHANCELLOR 4]. **1645** SIR R. GREENVILLE in Clarendon *Hist. Reb.* IX. §104 The Revenue of his Dutchy of Cornwal. **1703** *Act 1 Anne* Stat. I. c. 7 §5 Under the.. seals of the duchy and county palatine of Lancaster. **1895** *Whitaker's Almanack* 157 Duchy of Lancaster.. Duchy of Cornwall. [With a List of Officers of the two Duchies.]

c. A district between London and Westminster forming the precincts of the Duchy House of Lancaster.

1626 *Crt. & Times Chas. I* (1848) I. 154 St. Clement's parish, the Duchy, with the Savoy, have caused a riot.

2. *attrib.* **a.** generally, as ***duchy rights***; †**duchy-peerage**, a dukedom. **b.** *spec.* Of or relating to the duchies of Cornwall and Lancaster; as ***duchy land, manor, tenement*** (one held of the crown in either of these duchies); **duchy-chamber**, the court-room at Westminster of the **duchy-court** of Lancaster, held before the chancellor of the Duchy (see CHANCELLOR 4), or his deputy, having equitable jurisdiction over lands holden of the Crown in right of the duchy; **duchy-house**, the official London residence of the Chancellor of the Duchy.

1555 *Act 2 & 3 Phil. & Mary* c. 20 §5 The Fermes Rentes Suytes and services.. aunsweryd and paide in the Court of the Duchye Chambre at Westminster. **1607** Duchy court [see CHANCELLOR *sb.* 4]. **1609** *Crt. & Times Jas. I* (1849) I. 100 The two chancellors of the exchequer and duchy keep residence here in town: of which the last hath been.. driven from the duchy house to Lambeth by the plague. **1653** MANLOVE *Lead Mines* 193 The Dutchie Court (if just cause be) May yield relief against those verdicts three. **1659** *Rushworth's Hist. Coll.* I. 149 (Title of Act 21 Jas. I. c. 25) An Act for relief of Patentees, Tenants, and Farmers of Crown-Lands and Dutchy-Lands. **1672** LEYCESTER *Hist. Antiq.* II. iv, The dutchy office at Gray's Inne in London. **1705** *Ibid.* No. 4132/4 Exposed to Sale, a Dutchy Tenement ..being parcel of the Dutchy Manour of Tremation, and part of the Ancient Dutchy of Cornwall. **1750** CARTE *Hist. Eng.* II. 445 To shew his title to the Dutchy-peerage of Bretagne. **1768** BLACKSTONE *Comm.* III. vi, The court of the duchy chamber of Lancaster is another special jurisdiction. **1814** LYSONS *Cornwall* vii, The tenants of the duchy manors are either free tenants, or conventionary or customary tenants.

†**ˈducible**, *a.* *Obs.* [ad. med.L. *dūcibilis*, f. *dūcere* to lead.] **a.** That can be led; tractable. **b.** Able to be drawn out; = DUCTILE 1.

1633 T. ADAMS *Exp. 2 Peter* ii. 2 Here is a ducible disposition.. that will follow upon the least hint. **1657** TOMLINSON *Renou's Disp.* 427 Silver is easily ducible and liquescible.

duck (dʌk), *sb.*[1] Forms: α. 1 duce, 4 duk, 5– duck (5 dukke, 6 ducke). β. 4–5 doke (5 dooke, 6– *Sc.* duke, duk, duik (deuk). γ. 4–5 douk, 5–6 dowk. [OE. *duce* (? *dúce*), from *u-* (or *ū-*) grade of **dúcan* to DUCK, dive; cf. Da. *duk-and* lit. dive-duck (*and* = duck), Sw. *dyk-fågel* lit. dive-fowl, diver; and the synonyms under DUCKER[1].

The phonological history presents some difficulties, esp. owing to uncertainty whether the OE. vowel was *u* or *ú*, and the development of the three ME. types: *dukke, duk*, corresp. to mod. *duck*; *dōke, dook*, corresp. to mod. Sc. *duik* (dYk); *douke, dowke*. Cf., for the forms, BROOK *v.* and DOVE; and see Luick, *Untersuch. zur Engl. Lautgeschichte* (1896) §388, 553.]

I. Primary sense.

1. a. A swimming bird of the genus *Anas* and kindred genera of the family *Anatidæ*, of which species are found all over the world.

Without distinctive addition or context, the word is applied to the common ***domestic duck***, a domesticated form of the ***wild duck*** or MALLARD (*Anas boscas*). The other species (about 125 in number, distributed among some 40 genera) are distinguished by adjuncts expressing colour, appearance, or habits, as ***black, brown, crested, dusky, fishing, grey, little, long-tailed, noisy, painted, pied, red-headed, ring-necked, ruddy, sleepy, swallow-tailed, tufted, velvet, whistling, white-faced duck***, etc.; habitat, as ***channel-, creek-, mire-, moss-, mountain-, river-, rock-, sea-, shoal-, surf-, tree-, wood-duck***; native region, as ***American, English, French, German, Labrador, Norway duck***; or by more distinctive words as CANVAS-BACK-, CUTHBERT-, EIDER-, HARLEQUIN-, HERALD-, MAIDEN-, MANDARIN-, MUSCOVY- or MUSK-, MUSSEL-, PENGUIN-, SQUAM-DUCK, etc., q.v. in their alphabetical places. In its widest technical sense, the name includes the gadwalls, garganeys, golden-eyes, pintails, pochards, scaups, scoters, sheldrakes, shovellers, spoonbills, teal, whistlewings, widgeons, and other related groups; the geese and goosanders, though *Anatidæ*, are not usually called 'ducks'.

α. **967** in Kemble *Cod. Dipl.* No. 538. III. 18 Andlang Osrices pulle þæt hit cymþ on ducan seaþe; of ducan seaþe þæt hit cymþ on Rischale. **1377** LANGL. *P. Pl.* B. XVII. 62 A-syde he gan hym drawe Dredfully.. as duk [*v.r.* 5 *MSS.* doke] doth fram þe faucoun. *c* **1420** *Liber Cocorum* 5 Henneban sede duckys wylle kylle. **1483** *Cath. Angl.* 110/2 A Dukke, *anas.* **1530** PALSGR. 215/2 Ducke a foule, *canne.* Duke of the ryver, *cannette.* **1564** J. RASTELL *Confut. Jewell's Serm.* 37 b, He is more neerer a ducke then a duke. **1610** SHAKS. *Temp.* II. ii. 136 Though thou canst swim like a Ducke, thou art made like a Goose. **1699** DAMPIER *Voy.* II. II. 69 Whistling Ducks are somewhat less than our Common Duck.. In flying, their Wings make a pretty sort of loud whistling Noise. **1845** HIRST *Poems* 162 Brooding black-duck from her nest of turf In the tall sedge. **1847** CARPENTER *Zool.* §455 The Eiders are the largest of all the Ducks, being as weighty as the average of Geese.

collective pl. **1858** LD. MALMESBURY *Mem. Ex-Min.* (1884) II. 145 It would do for firing into a flock of duck.

β. **1362** LANGL. *P. Pl.* A. v. 58 He schulde.. Drinken bote with þe Doke [So B. v. 75. **1393** C. VII. 174 douke] and dyne but ones. *c* **1400** *Lanfranc's Cirurg.* 58 Hennes, goos, and dokis. **14..** *Lat. & Eng. Voc.* in Wr.-Wülcker 563 *Anas*, a doke. *c* **1440** *Promp. Parv.* 125/2 Dooke, byrde (*K.* doke), *anas.* **1486** *Bk. St. Albans* D ij b, Tame Dookes. *Ibid.* F vj, A badelyng of Dokys. **1500–20** DUNBAR *Fenȝeit Friar* 119 Thre dayis in dub amang the dukis. **1549** *Compl. Scot.* vi. 39 The dukis cryit quaik. **1630–56** SIR R. GORDON *Hist. Earls Sutherland*, Duke, draig, widgeon, teale.. and all other kinds of wildfowl. [*Mod. Sc.* duik.]

γ. **1393** [see β] **1502** ARNOLDE *Chron.* (1811) 84 Swannes, gies, or dowkes.

b. *spec.* The female of this fowl: the male being the DRAKE.

In the domestic state the females greatly exceed in number, hence *duck* serves at once as the name of the female and of the race, *drake* being a specific term of sex.

c **1386** CHAUCER *Miller's T.* 390 Thanne shal I swymme as myrie.. As dooth the white doke after hire drake. ? *c* **1475** *Sqr. lowe Degre* 320 The tele, the ducke and the drake. **1523** FITZHERB. *Husb.* §146 Take hede how thy hennes, duckes, and gees do ley. **1678** RAY *Willughby's Ornith.* III. iv. §1. 380 Between the Duck and the Drake there is this difference, that he hath growing on his Rump certain erect feathers.. which she hath not. *Mod.* A flock of ducks swimming behind their drake.

c. The flesh of this fowl.

1774 GOLDSM. *Nat. Hist.* (1776) VI. 111 Plutarch assures us, that Cato kept his whole family in health, by feeding them with duck whenever they threatened to be out of order.

d. *Antiq.* (More fully *duck-weight*.) A stone or clay figure of a duck used as a weight in ancient Assyria and Babylonia.

[**1849** LAYARD *Mon. Nineveh* Ser. I. 21 A duck, in baked clay, with.. a cuneiform inscription.. The letters may denote a numeral.] **1853** —— *Nineveh & B.* xxv. 601 *note*, The actual weight of the large ducks in the British Museum being 480 oz. troy.

2. In phrases and proverbial sayings. ***duck's weather, fine day for ducks***, etc., referring to wet weather; ***like a duck in thunder, like a (dying) duck in a thunderstorm***: having a forlorn and hopeless appearance; ***like water off*** (or ***from***) ***a duck's back, like*** (or ***as***) ***a duck (takes) to water***: easily, readily; ***does*** (or ***will, would***) ***a duck swim?***: a colloquial phrase of enthusiastic acceptance or confirmation.

1611 COTGR. s.v. *Apprendre*, (An idle, vaine, or needlesse labour) we say, to teach his grandame to grope ducks. *a* **1656** R. CAPEL in Spurgeon *Treas. Dav.* Ps. ix. 18 Money, which lying long in the bank, comes home at last with a duck in its mouth. **1785** 'P. PINDAR' *Lyric Odes for 1785* 21 Gaping upon Tom's thumb, with me in wonder, The rabble rais'd its eyes,—like ducks in thunder. **1802** C. WILMOT *Let.* 31 Jan. in *Irish Peer* (1920) 35 On asking him what fault he had to find with her, he look'd 'like a Duck in Thunder', and made me instinctively wave [*sic*] the investigation. **1822** SCOTT *Peveril* I. xi. 269 Closed her eyes like a dying fowl —turned them up like a duck in a thunder-storm. **1824** *Blackw. Mag.* XVI. 347 The thing passed off like water from a duck's back. **1840** DICKENS *Old C. Shop* ii. 81 Mr. Swiveller.. observed that last week was a fine week for the ducks, and this week was a fine week for the dust. **1842** S. LOVER *Handy Andy* iv. 35 'What do you say.. will you dine with me?' 'Will a duck swim?' chuckled out Jack Horan. **1863** KINGSLEY *Water Bab.* 188 Then he.. turned up his eyes like a duck in thunder. **1867** A. D. RICHARDSON *Beyond Mississippi* xiv. 177 He takes to them as instinctively as a young duck to water. **1871** [see WATER *sb.* 1 f]. **1880** J. PAYN *Confid. Agent* III. 161 Look less like a duck in a thunderstorm. **1885** *Boy's Own Paper* 23 May 542/3 'Perhaps you would not object to drinking the queen's health?' Would a duck swim? **1889** L. B. WALFORD *Stiffnecked Generation* (1891) 321 It had all passed off like water off a duck's back. **1891** L. T. MEADE *Sweet Girl Graduate* xvi. 133 'Do you really think that Maggie Oliphant cares for Mr. Hammond?'.. 'Cares for him!.. Does a duck swim? Does a baby like sweet things?' **1893** [see TAKE *v.* 74 e]. **1894** ASTLEY *50 Y. of Life* I. 22, I always took to shooting like a duck to water. **1906** 'O. HENRY' *Four Million* (1916) 82 'With you, Dempsey?' she stammered. 'Say—will a duck swim?' **1917** J. C. BRIDGE *Cheshire Proverbs* 72 He winks and thinks like a duck i' thunner. **1933** A. CHRISTIE *Lord Edgware Dies* xxii. 183 You did look for all the world like a dying duck in a thunderstorm. **1960** C. DAY LEWIS *Buried Day* vi. 107, I had taken to vice like a duck to water, but it ran off me like water from a duck's back. **1971** 'A. GILBERT' *Tenant for Tomb* i. 8 The Bear Lady said brightly that it was a nice day for the ducks.

II. Transferred uses.

3. a. A term of endearment.

1590 SHAKS. *Mids. N.* v. i. 282 O dainty Ducke: O Deere! **1607** MIDDLETON *Fam. of Love* I. iii, And now, sweet duck, know I have been for my cousin Gerardine's will. **1624** HEYWOOD *Captives* I. iii, For see you not too women? daynty ducks! **1840** DICKENS *Old C. Shop* xi, How is he now, my duck of diamonds? **1880** SPURGEON *Serm.* XXVI. 46 Her child.. was so much her 'duck' that he grew up to be a goose.

b. Often ***a duck of a***...; and applied to things as well as persons.

1819 M. WILMOT *Let.* 26 Nov. (1935) 31, I shall presently throw my letter into *the long drawer* at the top of my *duck of a* secretaire. **1841** *Punch* 18 Sept. 112/1 If our remarks were made with an affectionate eye to the young ladies of the satin-album-loving school, we should assuredly style this 'a duck of a picture'. **1884** W. L. REDE *Sixteen String Jack* I. ii, Oh, isn't he a duck of a fellow? **1891** FARMER *Slang* s.v., A duck of a bonnet.

c. With hypocoristic suffix *-s.* Used as a familiar form of address.

1936 J. CURTIS *Gilt Kid* viii. 81 She crossed her legs. Her thighs were white and shapeless. 'Got a fag, ducks?' **1958** E. HYAMS *Taking it Easy* 200 Talked like you 'e did, ducks. **1958** *Times* 1 Oct. 11/6 One is waited on; called 'sir', not 'ducks'. **1963** *Ibid.* 13 Feb. 11/4 The comfortable northern friendliness of the expression 'ducks' as employed by comfortable northern females to all and sundry—to warm the heart towards the species.

4. a. Short for *lame duck*: see 9.

b. A fellow, 'customer'. *U.S. slang.*

1857 *Phoenix* (Sacramento) 11 Oct. 4/1 No such 'duck' as this could *nab* the 'Ubiquitous'. **1872** 'MARK TWAIN' *Roughing It* xlvii. 331 Are you the duck that runs the gospel-mill next door? **1903** A. ADAMS *Log of Cowboy* ix. 125, I can't quite make out this other duck, but I reckon he's some big auger. **1904** W. H. SMITH *Promoters* v. 100 As you said, Goldsby, Slosher's a slick duck.

c. (See quots.) *U.S. slang.*

1938 *Amer. Speech* XIII. 156/1 *Duck*, a flying boat. **1942** E. COLBY *Army Talk* 76 *Ducks.* Air Corps men.. give the name to amphibian airplanes capable of landing on water or ground.

5. *Anglo-Ind. slang.* A nickname for soldiers of the Bombay Presidency.

1803 ELPHINSTONE in Sir E. Colebrooke *Life* (1884) I. 53 (Y. Supp.) They have neither the comforts of a Bengal army, nor do they rough it, like the Ducks. **1879** LOW *Afghan War* i. 97 The 'Ducks' (as the Bombay troops are called) enjoy it much.

6. A boy's game, also called *duckstone, duckiestone*; also one of the stones used in this game, and sometimes a player.

1821 *Blackw. Mag.* Aug. 32 (Jam.) The duck is a small stone placed on a larger, and attempted to be hit off by the players at the distance of a few paces. **1888** ELWORTHY *W. Somerset Word-bk.*, *Duck*, a game. **1893** *Cassell's Bk. Sports & Pastimes* 255 The players [at Duckstone] then, standing at home, 'pink for duck', that is, they throw their stones towards the block, and he whose stone remains farthest from the block is first duck.

7. *Cricket slang.* (Short for DUCK'S EGG). No score, nought; also, a player who fails to score.

1868 *St. Paul's Mag.* in *Daily News* 24 Aug., You see.. that his fear of a 'duck'—as by a pardonable contraction from duck-egg a nought is called in cricket-play—outweighs all other earthly considerations. **1880** *Daily Tel.* 24 Sept., Life is very much like cricket: Some get scores and some 'a duck'. **1885** *Edin. Daily Rev.* 17 Aug. 3/5 The former batter proved a duck.

8. *dial.* and *slang.* (See quots.)

1873 *Slang Dict.*, *Duck*, a bundle of bits of the 'stickings' of beef sold for food to the London poor. A faggot. **1876** *Mid. Yorksh. Gloss.*, *Duck*, a faggot.

9. ***lame duck***: a disabled person or thing: *spec.* (*Stock Exchange slang*): one who cannot meet his financial engagements; a defaulter. Also, short, *duck*.

1761 H. WALPOLE *Lett. H. Mann* 28 Dec. (1843) I. 60 Do you know what a Bull, and a Bear, and a Lame Duck are? **1771** GARRICK *Prol. to Foote's Maid of B.*, Change-Alley bankrupts waddle out lame ducks! **1806–7** J. BERESFORD *Miseries Hum. Life* (1826) XII. xviii, Attending at the Stock-exchange on settling-day amidst the quack of Ducks, the bellowings of Bulls, and the growls of Bears. **1832** MACAULAY *Mirabeau* Misc. 1860 II. 95 Frauds of which a lame duck on the Stock exchange would be ashamed. **1889** C. D. WARNER *Little Journ.* xvii, Do you think I have time to attend to every poor duck?

10. *Bombay duck* = BUMMALO.

1860 MASON *Burmah* 273 (Y.) A fish nearly related to the salmon is dried and exported in large quantities from Bombay, and has acquired the name of Bombay Ducks. **1879** F. S. BRIDGES *Round World in 6 Months* 214 'Bombay Ducks' are always served with curry. These are small dried fish of a peculiar flavour, and are quite dry and crisp.

III. *attrib.* and *Comb.*

11. a. *attrib.*, as ***duck-dance, -gun, -house, -pond, -pool, -puddle, -tribe***. **b.** objective and obj. genitive, as ***duck-decoying, -fattener, -fattening, -hunter, -hunting, -keeper, -rearer, -rearing, -shooter, -shooting***. **c.** similative, as ***duck-foot, -tail; -footed, -hearted, -like, -toed*** adjs.

1884 *Mag. of Art* Feb. 143/2 Indulging in a most ungraceful *duck-dance. **1886** *Athenæum* 21 Aug. 230/3 Most readers of sporting books have some idea of *duck-decoying. **1895** *Westm. Gaz.* 9 May 3/1 *Duck fatteners have to pay highly for sittings of eggs. **1725** DE FOE *Voy. round World* (1840) 350 They killed more fowls..of the *duck-foot kind. **1813** COL. HAWKER *Diary* (1893) I. 85 I left my *duck gun and went to Whitchurch. **1846** GREENER *Sc. Gunnery* 285 Never make duck-guns above seven-eights in the bore. **1699** DAMPIER *Voy.* (1729) II. I. 45 Like so many *Duck-houses all wet and dirt. **1730** *Index of Addison's Wks.* (Jod.) *Duckhunting, what Mr. Bayle compares to it. **1857** HUGHES *Tom Brown* II. iii, They had never been duck-hunting there since. **1696** *Lond. Gaz.* No. 3175/4 Mr. Webbs, the *Duck-keeper in St. James's Park. **1831** T. L. PEACOCK, *Crotchet Castle* 293 To live on a gravelly hill—without so much as a *duck-pond within ten miles of him. **1601** *Memorials of St. Giles's, Durham* (Surtees) 29 For castinge of the *dooke poole and for dammynge the water at giles bridge—xxd. **1893** SINCLAIR & HENRY *Swimming* (Badm. Libr.) 337 Harrow..Its swimming-pond, named the '*duck-puddle', is one of the finest open-air baths in England. **1792** SCOTT *Let.* 10 Sept. (1932) I. 22, I have turned a keen *duck shooter, though my success is not very great. **1945** C. MANN in B. James *Austral. Short Stories* (1963) 72 Even old duck-shooters have now almost got used to them. **1792** SCOTT *Let.* 30 Sept. 26, I have quite given up *duck-shooting for the season. **1859** J. CONWAY *Lett. from Highlands* viii. 73 A day's duck-shooting.

12. a. Special comb.: **duck-chicken**, one hatched by a hen; **duck-dive**, a vertical dive down into water by a swimmer; hence as *v. intr.*, to make such a dive; **duck-gravel** (see quot.); **duck-ladder**, a kind of short ladder; **duck-legged** *a.*, having unusually short legs: so ***duck-legs***; **duck-oil**, water, moisture (Halliwell); **duck('s) arse, ass** (also **anatomy, behind**) *slang*, a style of haircut in which the hair at the back of the head is shaped like a duck's tail (cf. D.A. s.v. D III. 3); **duck's** (or **ducks'**) **disease** *colloq.*, a facetious expression for shortness of leg; also ***duck-disease***; **duck-shot**, shot of a size suitable for shooting wild ducks; **duck-shover** *Austral.* and *N.Z. slang*, a cabman who does not wait his turn in the rank, but touts for passengers; also *transf.* (see quot. 1941); so ***duck-shove*** vb. intr. and trans., ***duck-shoving*** vbl. sb.; **duck's-off**, the game duck or duckstone; **duck soup** *slang* (orig. and chiefly *U.S.*), something requiring little effort; a person easy to overcome or cheat; a 'cinch'; **duck-tail, ducktail** *colloq.*, (*a*) = *duck's arse* (see above); (*b*) *S. Afr.*, a young hooligan or 'teddy-boy'; **duck-walk**, a duckboard track (see DUCKBOARD); **duck-weight** = 1 d; **duck-wife**, a woman who has charge of ducks. Also DUCK AND DRAKE, DUCK-BILL, DUCK'S BILL, EGG.

1969 N. COHN *A WopBopaLooBop* (1970) vi. 55 He looked like another sub-Elvis, smooth flesh and *duck-ass hair. **1678** T. JONES *Heart & Right Sov.* 201 Neither understood the other no more than *duck-chickens their hen-dam, recalling them from connatural element. **1928** S. VINES *Humours Unreconciled* viii. 103 Mr. Sheepshanks..soon got his host expanding a theory of the '*duck-disease', as he facetiously called the shortness of leg from which the Japanese were suffering. **1942** G. MITCHELL *Laurels are Poison* ix. 99 She..began to come upstream in a series of *duck-dives, testing the depth of the water. **1953** L. CHARTERIS in J. Merril *Off Beaten Orbit* (1959) 114 Any good swimmer can duck-dive. **1969** 'I. DRUMMOND' *Man with Tiny Head* xv. 176 Nigel took a deep breath, duck-dived and swam under water. **1885** *Daily News* 14 July 2/2 *Duck-gravel, a deposit like pumicestone, into which the ducks push their bills. Every ducker's place has a lump of this duck-gravel, a coralline stuff..like little oyster shells. **1883** *Law Times Rep.* XLIX. 139/1 He took a shorter ladder (called a *duck ladder) and placed this duck ladder against the roof. **1650** BULWER *Anthropomet.* 263 Or, why so long, doe they make men *Duck-leg'd? **1714** tr. *Adv. Rivella* 45 Conscious of his duck Legs and long Coat. **1809** W. IRVING *Knickerb.* (1861) 187 A little duck-legged fellow, was equipped in a pair of the general's cast-off breeches. **1951** *Sunday Pictorial* 29 Oct., The D.A. therefore stands for *Duck's Anatomy—or some such word. **1960** WENTWORTH & FLEXNER *Dict. Amer. Slang* 165/2 **Duck's ass*,..a boy's haircut. **1961** J. I. M. STEWART *Man who won Pools* iv. 48 His girl had..made him quit that *Duck's Behind for a straight sleeking back with oil. **1925** FRASER & GIBBONS *Soldier & Sailor Words*, **Ducks' disease*, short-legged. **1960** B. MARSHALL *Divided Lady* I. vi. 28 Plinio, the barman with duck's disease, came running up. **1960** *Spectator* 4 Nov. 677 As the leader of the [New Zealand] Opposition complained, the Government has 'dodged and *duckshoved' the issue. **1969** *Sunday Mail* (Brisbane) 31 Aug. 5/1 Some Cabinet Ministers said that most local authorities were 'duck shoving' on the State's litter problem. **1898** MORRIS *Austral. Eng.*, *Duck-shover. **1908** *Westm. Gaz.* 18 Jan. 3/2 A swanker and a duck-shover. **1941** BAKER *Dict. Austral. Slang* 26 *Duckshover*, one who adopts unfair business methods. **1870** *N. & Q.* 4th Ser. VI. 111 '*Duck-shoving'..is the term used by our Melbourne cabmen to express the unprofessional trick of breaking the rank, in order to push past the cabman on the stand for the purpose of picking up a stray passenger or so. **1896** *Otago Daily Times* 25 Jan. 3/6 (Morris), 'Duck shoving', a process of getting passengers which operated unfairly against the cabmen who stayed on the licensed stand and obeyed the by-law. **1888–9** *Longm. Mag.* XIII. 516 Another [game] named '*ducks-off' consisted in setting on a large flat stone a round stone..which from a certain distance one strove to knock off. **1912** A. H. LEWIS *Apaches of N.Y.* iv. 84 'Them Gophers are as tough a bunch as ever comes down the pike.' 'Tough nothin'!' returned Slimmy: 'they'll be *duck soup to Ike.' **1929** D. HAMMETT *Red Harvest* xxvi. 257 it was a juicy row, while it lasted—no duck soup for the coppers at that. **1966** OGILVY & ANDERSON *Excurs. Number Theory* i. 4 The number 307 comes out, in binary notation, to be 100110011 which would not have the convenience of 307 at the grocery store, perhaps, but is duck soup for the Computer. **1966** B. E. WALLACE *Murder in Touraine* xvii. 52 Now all he had to do..was to..avoid a guard: it was going to be duck soup if you were the right kind of duck. **1955** D. KEENE *Who has W. Lathrop?* (1966) xi. 129 The blond youth was in this up to his *ducktail haircut. **1959** *Chambers's 20th Cent. Dict.* Add., *Ducktail*, the white Teddy Boy of South Africa. **1960** *Guardian* 28 Mar. 1/2 He [*sc.* Dr. Verwoerd] described South Africa's overseas critics as 'the ducktails (Teddy boys) of the political world'. **1961** *Personality* 16 May 27, I have long since ceased to use the label 'Teddy boy' and now think entirely in terms of 'ducktails'. **1961** *Listener* 7 Sept. 343/2 The '*stilyagi*' with their tight trousers and duck-tail hair-dos. **1968** *N.Y. Rev. Books* 7 Nov. 3/3 He was buying a bottle of hair-oil..to soothe his ducktail. **1915** *Blackw. Mag.* Apr. 449/1 Where there are no *duck-walks, we employ planks laid across the mud. **1917** *War Illustr.* 28 Apr. 239/2 The 'duck-walk' is laid for easy crossing of difficult surfaces. **1869** BLACKMORE *Lorna D.* x, She counted them like a good *duck-wife.

b. Esp. in names of animals and plants: **duck-ant**, the white ant or termite; **duck-eagle**, a South African species of eagle; **duck-mole**, the Duck-billed Platypus; **duck-mud**, Crow-silk; **duck's foot**, a local name of Lady's Mantle; also the American May-apple, *Podophyllum peltatum*; **duck-snipe** (Bahamas), the willet, *Symphemia semipalmata*; **duck-wheat** = DUCK-BILL wheat. Also DUCK-HAWK, -WEED, etc.

1851 GOSSE *Nat. in Jamaica* 283 A fragment of the earthy nest of the *Duck-ants (*Termites*). **1731** MEDLEY *Kolben's Cape G. Hope* II. 136 There is another sort of eagle in the Cape countries which the naturalists call *Aquila anataria*, or the *Duck-Eagle. **1875** tr. *Schmidt's Desc. & Darw.* 237 The Ornithorhyncus, or *duck-mole of Tasmania. **1884** MILLER *Plant-n.*, *Duck-mud, *conferva rivularis* and other delicate green-spored Algæ. **1755** JOHNSON, **Ducks-foot*, black snakeroot, or Mayapple. **1611** COTGR., *Bled rouge*, ordinarie red wheat; called by Kentishmen, *Duck-wheat.

duck, *sb.*[2] Also 7 douke. [f. DUCK *v.*] An act of ducking.

1. A quick plunge, a dip.

1843 PRESCOTT *Mexico* (1850) I. 156 *note*, Two singular basins..not large enough for any monarch bigger than Oberon to take a duck in. **1876** *World* V. No. 113. 18 The elder women content themselves with a few ducks as the waves break over them.

2. An instantaneous lowering of head or body; a rapid jerky bow or obeisance.

1554 T. SAMPSON in Strype *Eccl. Mem.* III. App. xviii. 46 The fond nods, crosses, becks, and ducks. **1634** MILTON *Comus* 960 Without duck or nod. *a* **1652** BROME *New Acad.* I. Wks. 1873 II. 19 Be ready with your napkin, and a lower douke, maid. **1802** LAMB *J. Woodvil* II. Wks. 612 The ducks, and nods Which weak minds pay to rank. **1879** S. ST. JOHN *Life Sir J. Brooke* 268 The ball rushing over our heads, caused a most undignified duck.

duck, *sb.*[3] [Known only from 17th c.; app. a. 17th c. Du. *doeck* 'linnen or linnen cloath' (Hexham 1678); = Ger. *tuch*, Icel. *dúkr*, Sw. *duk.*]

1. A strong untwilled linen (or later, cotton) fabric, lighter and finer than canvas; used for small sails and men's (esp. sailors') outer clothing.

In the earlier half of the 19th c. much worn for trousers.

1640 in Entick *London* (1766) II. 169 Duck hinderlands, middle good headlock. **1660** *Act 12 Chas. II*, c. 4 Sched., Drilling & pack ducke ye 100 ells cont. 6 score. **1780** T. JEFFERSON *Lett.* Writ. 1893 II. 329 What is to be done for tents, I know not. I am assured that very little duck can be got in this country. **1835** MARRYAT *Jac. Faithf.* ii, A shirt of coarse duck. **1883** T. HARDY in *Longm. Mag.* July 258 The genuine white smock-frock of Russia duck and the whity-brown one of drabbet, are rarely seen now afield.

2. *pl.* Trousers of this material.

1825 *Universal Songster* 305 T'other day I saw a goose in white ducks. **1829** MISS SHERIDAN in *Lett. etc. Dk. Somerset* (1893), The boys were in white ducks, with lightish green jackets. **1849** THACKERAY *Pendennis* xxv, They must be young Pendennis's white ducks.

3. *attrib.* and *Comb.*

1745 *Gentl. Mag.* 485 Coopers, duck-weavers, hemp-dressers. **1796** MORSE *Amer. Geog.* I. 403 There is a duck manufactory at Boston. **1849** THACKERAY *Pendennis* xxxvi, In a blue frock-coat and spotless white duck trousers.

duck (dʌk), *sb.*[4] orig. *U.S.* Also D.U.K.W., dukw. [*DUKW* is a combination of factory serial letters designating certain features of the vehicle.] An amphibious vehicle (see quots.).

1943 *War Illustr.* 15 Oct. 301 'Ducks' they are called in soldier slang, and it is easy to see why. In the first place there is something duck-like about these queer motor-barges-cum-trucks which are as much at home on the sea as on the land; and then their factory serial letters placed together spell 'Dukws'. **1944** *Hansard Commons* 2 Aug. 1466 The marvellous American invention, the 'Duck', spelt D.U.K.W., is a heavy lorry which goes at between 40 and 50 miles per hour along the road, and can plunge into the water and swim out for miles to sea in quite choppy weather. **1945** [see AMPHIBIOUS *a.* 2 b]. **1945** *Manch. Guardian* 18 July 5/2 Officially known as 'Dukws'—a combination of the factory serial letters D for boat, U for lorry body, and KW for lorry chassis—they quickly became known in the Army and Navy as 'Ducks'. **1958** *Observer* 14 Sept. 1/1 Supply craft might stand offshore and disgorge their cargoes into ducks and other smaller craft.

duck (dʌk), *v.* Forms: α. 3–5 (*Sc.* 6) duke, 4–6 douke, 5–6 (*Sc.* and *north. dial.* -9) douk, dowk(e, 6 (*Sc.* 7–9) dook; β. 6 ducke, (dokk), 6– duck. [The ME. forms (= duːk), correspond to an OE. type **dúcan* = MDu., MLG. and LG. *dûken* (Da. *duiken*), OHG. *tûhhan*, MHG. *tûchen*, G. *tauchen*, a WGer. strong vb. of 2nd ablaut series (with *û* instead of *eu, iu* in pres. stem). This form is still preserved in Sc. *douk*, *dook* (duk); but about the middle of the 16th c., it was shortened in Eng. to *duck*, prob. by assimilation to DUCK *sb.*[1] Cf. however MHG. and Ger. *ducken* (MHG. also *tucken, tücken*) to duck, dive, etc.:—**dukjan*; also Sw. *dyka* to duck, dive.]

I. *intr.* **1. a.** To plunge or dive, or suddenly go down under water, and emerge again; to dip the head rapidly under water.

c **1340** *Cursor M.* 23203 (Trin.) He þat doukeþ ones þer doun. *a* **1400–50** *Alexander* 4090 It was..bred full..Of dragons..& doukand neddirs. **1481** CAXTON *Reynard* (Arb.) 60 They conne wel also duke in the water after lapwynches and dokys. **1552** HULOET, Ducke vnder the water, *vide in* dyue. **1581** MARBECK *Bk. of Notes* 182 The outward sacrament of dipping or ducking in the water. **1652–62** HEYLIN *Cosmogr.* IV. (1682) 7 Though (to avoid their Darts) he sometimes ducked, yet held he still his left hand above the water. **1855** ROBINSON *Whitby Gloss.*, *To Douk*, to bathe or plunge under water, to duck. **1890** *Spectator* 9 Aug. 167/2 It [a torpedo] will be able 'to duck' under the defensive nettings carried by men-of-war. *Mod. Sc.* To dook for apples at Hallowe'en.

b. To make a sudden descent or dive, not under water.

1513 DOUGLAS *Æneis* V. xiii. 126 Quhill all the wallis doukis to the ground, Wndir the braing quhelis and asiltre. *a* **1851** MOIR *Poems, Snow* ii, Behold the trees Their fingery boughs stretch out..As they duck and drive about. **1870** DICKENS *E. Drood* iii, Receiving the foul fiend, when he ducks from its stage into the infernal regions.

2. a. To bend or stoop quickly so as to lower the body or head; to bob; to make a jerking bow; hence, *fig.* to cringe, yield; so, *to duck under*.

1530 PALSGR. 526/1, I dowke, I stowpe lowe as a frere doth. **1535** COVERDALE *Ecclus.* xix. 24 A wicked man can behaue himself humbly, and can douke with his heade. **1539** *Surrender of Monasteries* in Rymer *Fœdera* (1710) XIV. 611 Dokkyng, Nodding and Beckynge. **1599** NASHE *Lenten Stuffe* (1871) 89 Douking on all four unto him. **1630** LENNARD tr. *Charron's Wisd.* (1658) 73 To duck and stoop to all sorts of people. **1713** POPE *Guardian* No. 92 ¶5 He never once ducked at the whiz of a cannon-ball. **1869** BROWNING *Ring & Bk.* VIII. 1407 Law ducks to Gospel here. **1872** GEO. ELIOT *Middlem.* (1878) I. III. 352 Eat cold mutton, have to ..duck under in any sort of a way. **1887** BESANT *The World went* v. 42 [I] was comforted to see the men at the guns, none of them killed, and none of them ducking.

b. To back out, withdraw; to make off, abscond; to default. *colloq.* (orig. *U.S.*).

1896 ADE *Artie* ii. 9, I think I'll have to duck on that present. **1900** —— *Fables in Slang* 42 Having delivered herself of these Helpful Remarks she would Duck. **1910** W. M. RAINE *B. O'Connor* 249 Coming through the cañon Del Oro in the night, he ducked; I reckon he's in Mexico now. **1911** H. S. HARRISON *Queed* xxi. 270 It's about over. And now I must pay for my fun—duck back to the office. **1917** H. L. WILSON *Ruggles of Red Gap* ii. 26, I duck out every morning before she's up. **1919** WODEHOUSE *Damsel in Distress* xvi, He saw me, too, and what do you think he did? Ducked down a side-street, if you please. **1968** *Globe & Mail* (Toronto) 17 Feb. 7/3 A wealthy bachelor, he ducked away from a question on the extent of his financial resources.

c. *trans.* To get away from, to avoid, dodge (a person or thing). *colloq.* (orig. U.S.).

1896 ADE *Artie* vi. 55 He was with a lot o' them Prairie avenue boys, and purty soon he ducks 'em and comes over an' touches me for two cases. **1926** J. BLACK *You can't Win* vii. 80 We'll get a passenger train out of Cheyenne, kid, if we can duck Jeff Carr. **1928** *Daily Tel.* 6 Nov. 13/3 (American Election) Both sides, he says, have 'ducked' the problems of Labour and foreign policy. **1936** 'R. HYDE' *Passport to Hell* 155 Soldiers who had ducked the church parades since the beginning of the War fell out of the lines to pray there. **1959** M. M. KAYE *House of Shade* vi. 79, I should like to duck the whole situation by getting roaring drunk. **1963** *Listener* 21 Feb. 351/1 His peculiar play certainly ducked the questions of subjective and objective judgments that he chose to raise in *Radio Times*.

II. *trans.* **3.** To plunge (a person or thing) momentarily *in, into*, or *under* water or other liquid.

a **1300** *Cursor M.* 23203 He that es duked ans dun. *c* **1450** HENRYSON *Mor. Fab.* 27 In the water either twyse or thryse

Hee dowked him. **1553** *Note* in Hakluyt *Voy.* (1589) 266 Ducked at yardes arme, and so discharged. **1582–8** *Hist. James VI.* (1804) 105 They were dukit in a deepe loche, ouer the head thrie seueral tymes. **1598** STOW *Surv.* xi. (1603) 95 Ouerthrowne, and well dowked. **1631** RUTHERFORD *Lett.* (1862) I. 78 Howbeit, ye may be ducked, but ye cannot drown. **1751** in Hone *Every-day Bk.* I. 1045 A man and woman are to be publicly ducked at Tring. **1785** BURNS *Jolly Begg.*, 4th Recit., And had in monie a well been dooked. **1790** A. WILSON *To E. Picken* Poet. Wks. (1846) 109 While I can douk in ink a quill. **1820** SCOTT *Abbot* ii. I say, duck her in the loch, and then we will see whether she is witch or not.

4. To lower (the head, etc.) suddenly and momentarily; to jerk down.

1598 E. GILPIN *Skial.* (1878) 57 But bring them to the charge, then..Though but a false fire, they theyr plumes will duck. **1617** MARKHAM *Caval.* II. 81 If..he haue taken a custome to duck downe his head, when he standeth still. **1727** SWIFT *To Delany* 3 When..first he hears The bullets whistling round his ears, Will duck his head. **1884** GILMOUR *Mongols* 240 We..ducked our heads, and hurried into the tent.

5. *duck up* (*Naut.*): To raise with a jerk, haul up (a sail that obstructs the steersman's view).

1706 PHILLIPS s.v., 'Duck up the Clew-lines of those Sails'.

6. *trans.* and *intr.* In the game of Bridge (see quots.).

1905 R. F. FOSTER *Complete Bridge* 263 Ducking..is refusing to part with the command of your own suit, and is usually resorted to in situations in which no finesse is possible. *Ibid.* 264 The dealer sees that it is impossible to catch the K, Q, 10 of spades, so he ducks the suit by leading a small card. *Ibid.* 266 As there is no card in dummy's hand but the club ace that will bring the suit into play, that card must be kept as a re-entry until the third round, and the first two rounds of the suit must be ducked. *Ibid.* 312 *Ducking.*—Refusing to win tricks when able to do so. **1928** *Daily Express* 27 Aug. 4 You can frequently make the most of a suit by deliberately losing the first trick. This method of play, called 'ducking', is founded not only on the law of average probabilities but also on the expectation that the cards are normally distributed.

duck, obs. form of DUKE, TUCK.

duck and drake. [from the motion of the stone over the watery surface.]

1. A pastime consisting in throwing a flat stone or the like over the surface of water so as to cause it to rebound or skip as many times as possible before sinking. Chiefly in phr., *to make a duck and drake, to play (at) duck and drake.* (Often in *pl.*)

1583 J. HIGINS tr. *Junius' Nomenclator* (N.), A kind of sport or play with an oister shell or stone throwne into the water, and making circles yer it sinke, etc. It is called a ducke and a drake, and a halfe-penie cake. *c* **1626** *Dick of Devon.* I. ii. in Bullen *O. Pl.* II. 14 The poorest ship-boy Might on the Thames make duckes and drakes with pieces Of eight fetchd out of Spayne. **1730** SWIFT *Vind. Carteret* Wks. 1755 V. II. 188 Scipio and Lelius..often played at duck and drake with smooth stones on a river. **1829** *Nat. Philos.*, *Hydrostatics* i. 2 (U.K.S.) The common play of making ducks and drakes, that is, throwing a flat stone in a direction nearly horizontal against a surface of water, and thus making it rebound, proves the water to be elastic. **1842** *P. Parley's Ann.* III. 15 A shot made a duck-and-drake in the water.

b. *attrib.*, as *duck-and-drake fashion, sort.*

1858 A. W. DRAYSON *Sport. S. Africa* 304 Sometimes with a duck and drake sort of progression they [fish] skipped along over the top of the pool. **1893** *Boy's Own Paper* Jan. 183/2 A cannon ball..came Skipping at a long range over the water 'duck and drake' fashion.

2. *fig.* In phrases: *to make ducks and drakes of* or *with, to play (at) duck and drake with*: to throw away idly or carelessly; to play idly with; to handle or use recklessly; to squander.

c **1600** *Timon* v. v, I will make duckes and drakes with this my golde..Before your fingers touch a piece thereof. **1768–74** TUCKER *Lt. Nat.* (1852) II. 164 A miser has it in his power to make ducks and drakes of his guineas. **1810** WELLINGTON in Gurw. *Desp.* VII. 32 His Majesty's Government never intended to give over the British army to the Governors of this Kingdom to make ducks and drakes with. **1872** TENNYSON *Last Tournament* 344 Ye..grew So witty that ye play'd at ducks and drakes With Arthur's vows. **1883** STEVENSON *Treas. Isl.* I. vi, Finding the money to play duck and drake with ever after.

b. Idle play, reckless squandering.

1614 J. COOKE *Tu Quoque* in Hazl. *Dodsley* XI. 212 This royal Cæsar doth regard no cash; Has thrown away as much in ducks and drakes As would have bought some 50,000 capons. *a* **1678** MARVELL *Poems, Char. Holland*, Nature.. Would throw their land away at duck and drake.

Hence **duck-and-drake** *v. trans.*, to make 'ducks and drakes' of; to throw away idly.

1700–32 *Gentl. Instructed* 18 (D.) I would neither fawn on money for money's sake, nor duck and drake it away for a frolick. *Ibid.* 116 Is it then no harm..like children, [to] duck and drake away a treasure able to buy Paradise?

duckat, duckatoon, obs. ff. DUCAT, etc.

ˈduck-bill, *sb.* [f. DUCK *sb.*[1] + BILL *sb.*[2]]

a. Red wheat; more fully *duck-bill wheat.*

1556 WITHALS *Dict.* (1568) 20 a/1 *Ador*, is also an other kinde of wheate..whiche we doo nowe call duckbill. **1597** GERARDE *Herbal* I. xl. §5. 60 Red Wheate is called in Kent Duckbill Wheate. *c* **1680** *Enquiries* 2/2 Wheat—Square gray with ailes, otherwise called *Dunovex*, Duck-bill Wheat, and Duke wheat. **1832** *Veg. Subst. Food* 32 The cultivation of.. Duck-Bill, or Conical-Wheat—Triticum turgidum—has been attempted in England.

b. The broad-toed shoe worn in the 15th c.

1834 PLANCHÉ *Brit. Costume* 202 When men became tired of these pointed shoes..they adopted others in their stead denominated duck-bills.

c. = Duck-billed platypus: see below.

1840 *Penny Cycl.* XVII. 28/1 *Ornithorhynchus*, Blumenbach's name for that extraordinary quadrupedal form, The Duckbill or Duckbilled Platypus. **1850** J. B. CLUTTERBUCK *Port Philip* iii. 42 *Platypus*, water-mole or duckbill.

d. *duck-bill speculum*, a speculum flattened like a duck's bill.

1879 J. M. DUNCAN *Lect. Dis. Women* ix. (1889) 55 The duck-bill speculum is the best. **1882** *Quain's Dict. Med.* 1778 Another form of speculum much used of late years.. is the 'duck-bill' speculum.

e. *duck-bill (scraper)*, *Archæol.*, a scraper (sense 4 e) flattened like a duck's bill.

1911 J. CHAMBERS *Stone Age Lake Lothing* 11 Here are disc-shaped and duckbill scrapers. **1959** J. D. CLARK *Prehist. S. Afr.* viii. 206 Another form of scraper made on a blade is known as a 'duck-bill'.

Hence **duck-billed** *a.*, having a bill like a duck. **duck-billed platypus**, the *Ornithorhynchus* of Australia, a monotrematous mammal having a horny beak resembling the bill of a duck; **duck-billed cat**, the paddle-fish (*Polyodon spatula*); **duck-billed speculum**: see DUCK-BILL d.

1822–34 GOOD *Study Med.* (ed. 4) III. 13 The platypus or ornithorhynchus as he [Blumenbach] calls it, that most extraordinary duck-billed quadruped which has lately been discovered in Australasia. **1847** CARPENTER *Zool.* §317 The Ornithorhyncus or Duck-billed Platypus, the Water Mole of the Colonist. **1859** CORNWALLIS *New World* I. 35 Know ye the land contrariety sways..Where black swans..With water-rats, duck-billed, come forth to the day?

duckboard (ˈdʌkbɔəd). [f. DUCK *sb.*[1] + BOARD *sb.*] Usually *pl.* In the war of 1914–18, a slatted timber path laid down on wet or muddy ground in the trenches or in camps; also in wider use (*spec.* see quot. 1940). Also *attrib.* Hence **ˈduck-boarded** *a.*, furnished with duckboards.

1917 *War Illustr.* 17 Mar. 109 Walking wounded are helped along the duck-boards that flank the light railways. *Ibid.* 14 July 467 They..flung duck-board bridges over the Douve river. **1920** G. K. ROSE *2/4th Oxf. & Bucks Lt. Infty.* 31 For four miles the path lay along a single duckboard track, capsized or slanting in many places. *Ibid.* 72 The day was spent in..rebuilding dug-outs or laying fresh duckboards (wooden slats to walk on in the trenches). *Ibid.* 73 A duck-boarded communication trench. **1925** FRASER & GIBBONS *Soldier & Sailor Words, Duckboard glide*, a common term for after-dark movements along the trenches, when secrecy and quietness was essential... *Duckboard harrier*, a despatch 'runner' or messenger, whose duty took him along the duckboards in the trenches. **1926** *Glasgow Herald* 9 Jan. 9 Certain underground stations are feeling the effects of the flood, particularly that of Mirabeau, where duck-boards have been laid upon the platform. **1932** E. BOWEN *To North* xix. 196 Lady Waters, in grey knitted wool, standing out on a duckboard. **1940** *Chambers's Techn. Dict.* 270/2 *Duck board*, a board which has slats nailed across it at intervals and is used as steps in repair works on roofs.

duckcoy, obs. form of DECOY.

1634 W. WOOD *New Eng. Prosp.* (1865) 47 There be convenient ponds for the planting of Duckcoyes.

duck egg: see DUCK'S EGG.

ducker[1] (ˈdʌkə(r)). Forms: 5 dokare, 5–6 dowker, 6 douker, *Sc.* dowcare, 7 doucker, 9 *Sc.* dooker, 7– ducker. [f. DUCK *v.* + -ER[1]. In sense 2 it corresponds to MDu. and MLG. *dûker*, Du. *duiker*, Ger. *taucher* diver (bird).] One who or that which ducks or dives.

1. A person who ducks or dives under water; a diver. In mod. Sc., *douker, dooker*, a bather.

1483 *Cath. Angl.* 105/1 A Dowker, *emergator.* **1508** KENNEDY *Flyting w. Dunbar* 379 Thou sailit to get a dowcare, for to dreg it. **1613** PURCHAS *Pilgrimage* V. xii. 431 Fished for by duckers, that dive into the water. **1893** *Scott. Leader* 29 Dec. 7 Glasgow Morning Dookers Holiday Races.

2. A diving bird: applied to the *Colymbidæ* or Divers generally; also *spec.* the little grebe or dabchick. **b.** A local name of the Water Ouzel.

c **1475** *Pict. Voc.* in Wr.-Wülcker 762 *Hic mergulus*, a dokare. **1565–73** COOPER *Thesaurus, Collimbris*..the birde called a Douker, or Didapper. **1691** RAY *Creation* 147 Some sorts of Colymbi or Douckers. **1694** *Acc. Sev. Late Voy.* Introd. (1711) 11 Divers Duckers, and other Sea Birds. **1805** FORSYTH *Beauties Scotl.* II. 380 [Amongst] the sea-fowls are..scarfs or black duckers. **1837** MACGILLIVRAY *Hist. Brit. Birds* II. 50 *Cinclus Europæus*..Dipper, Ducker. **1859** A. SMITH in *Macm. Mag.* I. 122 Gulls of all kinds are there, dookers and divers of every description.

†**3.** A fighting-cock that ducks its head. *Obs.*

1688 R. HOLME *Armoury* II. 252/1 A Ducker, or Doucker, is such a kind of Cock as in his Fighting will run about the Clod almost at every blow he gives.

4. 'A cringer' (J.).

¶ Meaning uncertain: Todd inserts it under 4; others would explain as = *duck-hunter.*

1611 BEAUM. & FL. *Philaster* v. iv. (1620) 60 My dainty duckers, vp with your three-pil'd spirits.

ducker[2]. [f. DUCK *sb.*[1] + -ER[1].]

1. One who breeds or rears ducks.

1885 *Daily News* 14 July 2/2 Often the eggs are sold to a 'ducker'. **1889** *Pall Mall G.* 14 May 3/1 Ducks are..dirty creatures, and if 'cleanliness be next to godliness' the Aylesbury duckers are a long way removed.

2. A ducking-gun.

1896 *Month* Mar. 390 He warned us in the most terrible manner not to get near his heavy ducker in the bows.

ˈduckery. [f. DUCK *sb.*[1] + -ERY.] A place where ducks are reared.

1745 tr. *Columella's Husb.* VIII. xv, In the middle of this duckery a lake is digged. **1791** S. ROGERS *Diary* in *Early Life* (1887), Saw the dauphin's garden and duckery.

ducket, variant form of DUCAT (see DUCAT 2 b).

duck-hawk. [f. DUCK *sb.*[1] + HAWK.]

1. A common English name of the marsh harrier or moor-buzzard (*Circus æruginosus*).

1812 *Note in Pennant's Zool.* I. 237 In some places it [the Moor Buzzard] is called duck hawk. **1876** T. HARDY *Ethelberta* (1890) 7 Another large bird, which a countryman would have pronounced to be one the biggest duck-hawks that he had ever beheld.

2. *U.S.* Applied to the American variety of the peregrine falcon (*Falco peregrinus* var. *anatum*).

1884 ROE *Nat. Ser. Story* iv, Our duck or great-footed hawk is almost identical with the..peregrine falcon of Europe..It measures about forty-five inches in the stretch of its wings, and its prevailing color is of a dark blue.

duckhood: see -HOOD.

duckie, duckey: see DUCKY *sb.*

ducking (ˈdʌkɪŋ), *vbl. sb.*[1] [f. DUCK *v.* + -ING[1].]

a. Immersion in water.

1581 [see DUCK *v.* 1]. **1626** CAPT. SMITH *Accid. Yng. Seamen* 4 Ducking at Yards arme, hawling vnder the Keele. **1628** DIGBY *Voy. Medit.* (1868) 60, I punished by ducking and other wayes a dozen..men. **1727–51** CHAMBERS *Cycl.* s.v. *Ducking*, There is also a kind of dry ducking, wherein the patient is only suspended by a rope, a few yards above the surface of the water. **1771** FRANKLIN *Autobiog.* Wks. 1840 I. 30 His ducking sobered him a little. **1886** RUSKIN *Præterita* I. 378 He ran no risk but of a sound ducking, being ..a strong swimmer.

b. Prompt bowing or bending of the head or body.

1539 T. CHAPMAN in *Chron. Gr. Friars* (Camden) p. xv, Dome ceremonyes..dokynges, nodyngs, and bekynges. **1641** SANDERSON *Serm.* II. 6 What are all our crossings, and kneelings, and duckings? **1880** MISS BRADDON *Just as I am* xxi, There was much..ducking of heads in the doorway.

ˈducking, *vbl. sb.*[2] [f. DUCK *sb.*[1]] The catching or shooting of wild ducks. Also *attrib.*, as *ducking-punt*; **ducking-gun**, a fowling-piece carrying a heavy charge a long way, so as to kill a large number of ducks in a flock at one shot.

1577 E. HOGAN in Hakluyt *Voy.* (1589) 159 His pastime in ducking with water Spaniels. **1598** B. JONSON *Ev. Man in Hum.* I. i, Keep company with none but the archers of Finsbury, or the citizens that come a ducking to Islington ponds! *a* **1640** DAY *Peregr. Schol.* (1881) 77 Their wiues drew them..into the feilds a ducking with there water spaniells in somer. **1823** J. F. COOPER *Pioneer* xxii, The French ducking gun. **1880** N. H. BISHOP *4 Months in Sneak box* 7 He constructed a new ducking-punt with a low paddle-wheel at its stern.

ducking[3]. = DUCK *sb.*[3]

1822 T. MITCHELL *Aristoph.* II. 238 Add pillow-case, sheeting, and ducking. **1904** *N.Y. Times* 10 May 4 (Advt.), Splendid selection of duckings from which to make them [*sc.* awnings]. **1920** J. M. HUNTER *Trail Drivers of Texas* 177 The silver..was placed in duckin' sacks.

ˈducking, *ppl. a.* [f. DUCK *v.* + -ING[2].] That ducks, dives into water or bows the head.

a **1400–50** [see DUCK *v.* 1]. **1530** TINDALE *Pract. Prel.* K iv, A douckynge hypocrite. **1770** ARMSTRONG *Imitations* 88 The Cyclades appear'd Like ducking cormorants.

ˈducking-pond. [f. DUCKING *vbl. sb.*[1] and [2].]

a. A pond on which ducks may be hunted or shot. **b.** A pond for the ducking of offenders. (The senses cannot always be discriminated.)

1607 MIDDLETON *Fam. of Love* IV. i, You may take your spaniel and spend some hours at the ducking-pond. **1625** *Sess. Bk. Middlesex* in *Jrnl. Chester Archæol. Soc.* (1861) VI. 224 The inhabitants of the parishe of St. James, Clerkenwell, shall erect and place a Cocqueane-Stoole on the side of the ducking ponde. **1634** W. WOOD *New Eng. Prosp.* (1865) 33 No ducking ponds can affoard more delight than a lame Cormorant, and two or three lusty Dogges. **1664** PEPYS *Diary* 27 Mar. **1765** *Universal Mag.* XXXVII. 54/1 The ducking-pond in Whitechapel. **1870** *Observer* 13 Nov., Ball's Pond, Islington, takes its name from the Ducking Pond which belonged to a person named Ball, who kept a tavern there in the reign of Charles II.

ˈducking-stool. A sort of chair at the end of an oscillating plank, in which disorderly women, scolds, or dishonest tradesmen, were tied and ducked or plunged in water, as a punishment. See CUCKING-STOOL. So **ducking tumbrel**, a ducking-stool provided with wheels.

1597 *Ipswich Chamberlain's Bk.* in Clarke *Ipswich* (1830) 299 To porters for taking down the 'Ducking Stole'. **1635** *Records of Gravesend* in *Jrnl. Chester Archæol. Soc.* (1861) VI. 225 For two wheeles and Yeekes for the Ducking-Stool. **1688** R. HOLME *Armoury* III. viii. 351 A Cuck-stool, or a Ducking Tumbrel. **1712** ARBUTHNOT *John Bull* I. xii, Once for all, Mrs. Mynx..remember, I say, that there are pillories and ducking-stools. **1777** HOWARD *Prisons Eng.* (1780) 84 The bakers at Vienna are punished for frauds by the severity and disgrace of the ducking-stool. **1780** B. WEST *Misc. Poems* in Andrews *Old Time Punishm.* (1890) 13 There stands, my friend, in yonder pool, An engine called the ducking-stool. **1831** *Gentl. Mag.* Jan. 43/1 In an apartment of the Custom-house at Ipswich, is an original ducking-stool. **1853** WHARTON *Pa. Digest* §455 The punishment of the ducking stool cannot be inflicted in Pennsylvania.

'duckling. [f. DUCK *sb.*[1] + -LING, dim. suffix.] A young duck.

ugly duckling, the cygnet, in one of Hans Andersen's tales, hatched with a brood of ducklings, and despised for its clumsiness until it grew into a swan. Hence the unpromising child in a family who turns out the most brilliant of all.

c **1440** *Promp. Parv.* 125/2 Dookelynge (*P.* birde), *anatinus.* *c* **1532** DEWES *Introd. Fr.* in *Palsgr.* 912 The ducklyns, *les annetons.* **1601** HOLLAND *Pliny* I. 299 It is sport alone to see the maner of an hen that hath sitten vpon ducks egs..how at the first she will wonder to haue a teem of ducklings about her. *c* **1709** PRIOR *Widow & Cat* 14 Nor chick, nor duckling, 'scapes, when Grim Invites the fox to dinner. **1869** DULCKEN tr. *Andersen's Little Match Girl* 45, *Ugly Duckling*, I never dreamed of so much happiness when I was still the ugly Duckling! **1883** J. H. INGRAM in *Harper's Mag.* July 226/2 The mother's fears about her 'ugly duckling'..took another turn.

†**b.** A term of endearment. *Obs.*

1629 MASSINGER *Picture* II. i, Thy dear, thy dainty duckling, bold Mathias. **1716** ADDISON *Drummer* (T.), But hark you, duckling; be sure you do not tell him that I am let into the secret.

Hence **'ducklingship**, the state of a duckling.

1830 *Fraser's Mag.* I. 740 Ducks, whether..full grown, or in the tender state of ducklingship.

duckoy, obs. form of DECOY.

duck's bill. The bill of a duck. Applied **a.** to certain instruments of this shape, chiefly in surgery. Also *attrib.*

1601 MANNINGHAM *Diary* Feb. (Camden) 23 They grope for the stone [in the bladder] with an other toole which they call a duckes bill. **1676** WISEMAN *Chirurg. Treat.* 314, I took hold of it with a Forceps Ducks bills. **1794** *Rigging & Seamanship* I. 4 *Cleats*..the thin end is shaped with a duck's bill. *Ibid.* 28 The lower ends are..thinned with a duck's-bill shape.

b. *Printing.* A tongue cut in a piece of stout paper and pasted on at the bottom of the tympan sheet.

c. *Comb.*, as **duck's-bill bit**, a form of bit for use in a brace in wood-boring; **duck's-bill limpet**, a limpet of the genus *Parmophorus.*

duck's egg. Also **duck egg. a.** The egg of a duck; hence, **b.** in *Cricket*, the zero or 'o' placed against a batsman's name in the scoring sheet when he fails to score; no runs; hence, generally in school-boy slang, 'nought'; ***to break one's duck's egg***: see BREAK *v.* 7 d.

1398 TREVISA *Barth. De P.R.* XIX. lxxxiv. (1495) 914 Duckys egges ben more thanne hennes egges. **1601** [see DUCKLING]. **1863** READE *Very Hard Cash* vii, Now you and I, at Lord's the other day..achieved..the British duck's-egg. **1868** [see DUCK *sb.*[1] 7]. **1881** *Standard* 8 July 6/1 Their captain was out for the dreaded 'duck's egg'.

c. The colour of the egg of a duck; used *attrib.* Freq. ***duck-egg blue, duck's egg blue.***

1876 T. HARDY *Ethelberta* (1890) 115 A general flat tint of duck's-egg green. **1893** COLLINGWOOD *Life Ruskin* II. 190 The walls, painted 'duck egg', are hung with old pictures. **1899** *Daily News* 13 Feb. 8/5 One of the prettiest of the new colours is a soft, duck's-egg blue. **1934** *Times* 18 July 17/6 This year pastel colours are much used, particularly a rather dark duck-egg blue. *a* **1954** F. BRETT YOUNG *Wistanslow* (1956) iv. 87 The cool duck-egg blues and greens made fashionable by the Adam brothers. **1967** *Harper's Bazaar* Mar. 8 (Advt.), Sweater... In maple..duck egg blue.

d. ***duck('s)-egg china, porcelain*** (see quots.).

1897 W. TURNER *Ceramics of Swansea* 72 Some of this ware has a greenish hue when held up to a strong light. Hence locally, it is called the 'duck's egg.' *Ibid.* 343/2 'Duck's Egg' China at Swansea. **1904** *Burlington Mag.* July 397/1 Old Swansea, or what is locally called the 'duck-egg' porcelain, has been collected, especially in South Wales, for many years. **1957** MANKOWITZ & HAGGAR *Encycl. Eng. Pott. & Porc.* 78/2 *Duck Egg Porcelain*, a much sought after variety of Swansea soft-paste porcelain showing a greenish translucency made about 1816–17.

duck's meat, duckmeat. = DUCKWEED.

1538 TURNER *Libellus*, Duckes meat. *Lens Palustris.* **1601** HOLLAND *Pliny* II. 142 There is a kind of marish or moory Lentils (called Ducks meat) growing of it selfe in standing waters. **1766** J. BARTRAM *Jrnl.* 7 Jan. 27 Having most of its surface covered with duck-meat. **1842** S. LOVER *Handy Andy* iii, There was Andy..floundering in rank weeds and duck's meat.

b. *fig.* As an epithet of contempt.

1599 MASSINGER, etc. *Old Law* III. ii. Here's your first weapon, duck's meat!

'duckweed. The common name for plants of the genus *Lemna*, which float on still water, so as to cover the surface like a green carpet.

c **1440** *Promp. Parv.* 125/2 Dockewede, *padella* (P. *paradilla*). **1591** PERCIVALL *Sp. Dict.*, *Lenteja de agua*, duck weede, *Lens palustris.* **1626** BACON *Sylva* §567 The Water also doth send forth Plants, that have no Roots fixed in the Bottome..Such is that we call Duck-Weed. **1745** *Gentl. Mag.* 418 Go to a ditch where there is a quantity of duckweed. **1840** HOOD *Up the Rhine* 35 Stagnant ditches and ponds covered with duckweed.

Comb. **1895** K. GRAHAME *Gold. Age* 20 He had rendered up his duckweed-bedabbled person into the hands of an aunt.

Hence **'duckweedy** *a.*, full of duckweed.

1883 *Harper's Mag.* Mar. 530/2 The little green duckweedy moat.

ducky ('dʌkɪ), *sb.* [f. DUCK *sb.*[1] + -Y, dim. suffix.]

†**1.** A woman's breast. *Obs.*

a **1536** HEN. VIII *Let. to A. Boleyn* in *Select. fr. Harl. Misc.* (1793) 147 Whose pritty duckys I trust shortly to kysse. **1847–78** HALLIWELL, *Ducky* (North.).

2. A term of endearment. Also **duckie.** Cf. DUCK *sb.*[1] 3.

1819 *Metropolis* III. 252 The extravaganza of 'My heart's core..my dearest love—lovey, dovey, or odious duckey'. **1908** J. MASEFIELD *Capt. Margaret* v. 124 You are afraid. You're in love with Olivia, ducky. D'ye think you're going to fight me? **1913** C. MACKENZIE *Sinister Street* I. I. iv. 61, I believe you'll miss your poor old Mrs. Frith, eh, ducky? **1945** G. MILLAR *Maquis* i. 21 You must wear it tonight, though, duckie. **1958** E. HYAMS *Taking it Easy* 54, I must have sounded disagreeable, because Matilda said, 'Don't be narky, ducky.' **1968** *Listener* 19 Sept. 370/2 'Hullo, duckies,' he said, 'guess what I'm doing.'

ducky ('dʌkɪ), *a. colloq.* [f. DUCK *sb.*[1] + -Y[1]; cf. DUCKY *sb.*] Sweet, pretty; fine, splendid. Chiefly in affected or familiar use.

1897 *Westm. Gaz.* 5 Apr. 10/1 She remembers making his first dress with its 'ducky buttons.' **1905** M. BARNES-GRUNDY *Vacil. Hazel* 111 The duckiest, little bronze beetle, ..mounted in gold. **1905** *Punch* 8 Mar. 178/1 Only see how prettily he's scratching his ducky little ear. **1927** *Ibid.* 14 Sept. 285/1 You can wear one of those ducky little lace caps. **1949** F. BROWN *Dead Ringer* ii. 16 'Is everything okay, Am?' 'Everything's ducky.' **1958** M. DICKENS *Man Overboard* xv. 248, I shall tell the tradesmen that you have no authority to give orders... That's going to make you look just ducky, isn't it?

ducquoy, obs. form of DECOY.

duct (dʌkt), *sb.* [ad. L. *duct-us* leading, conduct, command, in med.L. aqueduct, n. of action f. *dūcĕre* to lead, conduct, draw; in mod.L. in sense 6. The L. form was formerly in Eng. use.]

†**1.** The action of leading; lead, guidance. *Obs.*

a **1660** HAMMOND (J.), To obey our fate, to follow the duct of the stars. **1684** tr. *Bonet's Merc. Compit.* VI. 216 The Physician..is bound to follow Nature's duct.

†**2.** Course, direction, trend. *Obs.*

1650 BULWER *Anthropomet.* 48 The other the ductus or course of the hair turns away. **1662** GLANVILL *Lux Orient.* 146 (T.) According to the duct of this hypothesis. **1712** BLAIR in *Phil. Trans.* XXVII. 435 Observing..the Duct of its Fibres. **1718** J. CHAMBERLAYNE *Relig. Philos.* I. ix. §8 Remarks upon each Duct, or Course, of these Nerves.

†**3.** A passage, etc. leading in any direction. *Obs.*

1670 E. BROWN in *Phil. Trans.* V. 1191 The ductus's or veins of Metals, do..some-times run North and South. *a* **1711** KEN *Anodynes* Poet. Wks. 1721 III. 431, I then meet labyrinthal Ducts, Turnings and Windings, dark Retreats.

4. A stroke drawn or traced, or the manner of tracing it (cf. L. *ductus litterarum*).

1699 N. MARSH in *Lett. Lit. Men* (Camden) 297 Using.. a magnifying glass for discovering the more diminutive lines, ductuses, and appendages to the Letters. **1760** SWINTON in *Phil. Trans.* LI. 857 The ducts of the letters are drawn with so much accuracy, that they may be intirely depended upon. **1796** PEGGE *Anonym.* (1809) 278 The ducts of the letters will sufficiently justify this reading. **1954** N. DENHOLM-YOUNG *Handwriting* iv. 32 The method of tracing the strokes, and the resulting general appearance of the script can conveniently be termed the duct or *ductus.* **1957** N. R. KER *Catal. MSS. containing Anglo-Saxon* p. xxv, The change from Anglo-Saxon minuscule to caroline minuscule..involved the duct of the handwriting of all manuscripts. **1969** M. B. PARKES *Eng. Cursive Book Hands 1250–1500* p. xxvi, The duct of a hand is the distinctive manner in which strokes are traced upon the writing surface: it represents the combination of such factors as the angle at which the pen was held in relation to the way in which it was cut, the degree of pressure applied to it, and the direction in which it was moved.

5. a. A conduit, channel, or tube, for the conveyance of water or other liquid. *spec.* = INK-*trough*; also *attrib.*

1713 POPE *Guardian* No. 173 ¶7 The two fountains.. were brought by conduits or ducts. **1776** *Act 16 Geo. III*, c. 56 (T.) For making and perfecting any channel, course, main cut, or duct, through any of the grounds. **1809** A. HENRY *Trav.* 69 The [sugar-maple] trees were..tapped, and spouts or ducts introduced into the wound. **1880** *Print. Trades Jrnl.* No. 31. 10 For letterpress it has two ink ducts. **1888** *Encycl. Brit.* XXIII. 706/1 A trough, which contains the ink..is fitted with the *duct roller* of cast iron. **1968** *Gloss. Terms Offset Lithogr. Printing* (*B.S.I.*) 38 *Duct*, the trough ..which contains the supply of ink, and by means of which the ink is presented to the duct roller.

b. A pipe or tube through which air is conveyed for cooling, ventilation, etc.

1884 J. S. BILLINGS *Princ. Ventilation & Heating* xi. 190 Into this chimney empties a foul-air duct..which receives the air from lateral ducts opening beneath the foot of each bed. **1908** A. G. KING *Pract. Steam & Hot Water Heating* ix. 92 It is well to take the hot-air duct from the boxing at the end opposite to that where the cold air enters. **1930** *Engineering* 28 Feb. 279/1 The arrangement of the fans and ducts. **1947** T. N. ADLAM *Radiant Heating* xiv. 308 For circulating the air through the various offices..a system of metal ducts has been installed. **1962** *Which?* (Car Suppl.) Oct. 139/1 Demister duct trim screws [were] slack.

c. A conduit for an electric cable or the like.

1893 T. O'C. SLOANE *Stand. Electr. Dict.* 193 *Duct*, the tube or compartment in an electric subway for the reception of a cable. **1901** *Westm. Gaz.* 11 Apr. 7/2 The work of laying the cable ducts has practically finished. **1945** '*Electr. Engineer*' *Ref. Bk.* xxvi. 7 The lightest and most convenient system is probably to run the cables in open ducts. **1962** P. DUNSHEATH *Hist. Electr. Eng.* xiv. 241 The [telephone] cables were at first drawn into cast-iron pipes and later earthenware single and multiple ducts.

6. a. *Phys.* A tube or canal in the animal body, by which the bodily fluids are conveyed. Formerly used in a wide sense, so as to include the blood-vessels and alimentary canal, but now applied more strictly to the vessels conveying the chyle, lymph, and secretions. Also used *attrib.* in such phrases as ***duct-cancer, -cyst, -papilloma***, = (cancer, etc.) affecting the epithelium of the ducts of the mammary glands.

These have names expressing their position or character, or in some cases the name of their discoverer, as *biliary, choledoch, cystic, efferent, genito-urinary, hepatic, lactiferous, lymphatic, nasal, pancreatic, parotid, thoracic duct.* (See these words.) Also ***ducts of Bellini***, the excretory tubes of the kidneys; ***duct of Bartholin, ducts of Rivinus***, certain ducts of the sublingual gland; ***Steno's duct***, that of the parotid gland, which conveys saliva into the mouth; ***Wharton's duct***, that of the submaxillary gland, also conveying saliva; ***duct of Wirsung***, the principal pancreatic duct; ***Wolffian duct***, the excretory duct of the Wolffian body or primitive kidney.

1667 *Phil. Trans.* II. 579 There being peculiar ductus's, by which the bloud passeth into the Aorta. **1692** BENTLEY *Boyle Lect.* 109 All the various ducts and ventricles of the body. **1741** MONRO *Anat.* (ed. 3) 134 *Steno's* Duct may be traced some Way on the Side of these Passages next the Nose. **1748** HARTLEY *Observ. Man* I. ii. 151 The whole alimentary Duct, quite down to the *Anus.* **1767** GOOCH *Treat. Wounds* I. 327 *marg.*, The treatment of wounds of the salival ducts. **1837–9** HALLAM *Hist. Lit.* (1847) III. 219 Eustachius had observed the thoracic duct in a horse. **1845–6** G. E. DAY tr. *Simon's Anim. Chem.* I. 210 The capillary system surrounding the biliary ducts. **1864** T. HOLMES *Syst. Surg.* IV. 680 Duct-cysts. Perfectly closed cysts..but having an opening communicating with a duct. **1872** HUXLEY *Phys.* v. 131 The neck by which a gland communicates with the free surface is called its duct. **1889** *Lancet* 21 Dec. 1278/1 In duct cancer of the breast he had not observed eczematous appearances. **1910** *Practitioner* Apr. 469 When a duct-papilloma obstructs one of the large ducts near the nipple. **1966** WRIGHT & SYMMERS *Systemic Path.* I. xxviii. 982/2 Duct papilloma is considerably less frequent than fibroadenoma.

b. *Bot.* One of the vessels of the vascular tissue of plants, formed by a row of cells of which the partitions have been obliterated, and containing air, water, or some secretion; *spec.* the narrow tubular continuous cells surrounding the broad cells or utricles in the leaves of *Sphagnum.*

1858 CARPENTER *Veg. Phys.* §40 The midrib and veins.. consist of three kinds of structure;—*ducts* or canals, which are supposed to transmit fluid. **1866** *Treas. Bot.* I. 433/1 *Ducts*, tubular vessels marked by transverse lines or dots.

duct (dʌkt), *v.* [f. the sb.] *trans.* To convey through a duct; usu. in the form **ducted** *ppl. a.*, conveyed through a duct; situated or operating in a duct. Cf. DUCTING *vbl. sb.*

1936 *Aircraft Engin.* VIII. 218/3 The ideal efficiency of the ducted radiator at high speed is about 50 per cent greater. **1938** *Encycl. Brit. Bk. of Yr.* 20/2 Ducted cooling has been developed sufficiently to recover..more than one half of the radiator losses. **1945** *Jrnl. R. Aeronaut. Soc.* XLIX. 698/1 The ducted fan system of propulsion, as we understand it to-day, consists of a fairly large diameter ducted fan or axial compressor of relatively low compression ratio at the intake to the nacelle. **1945** '*Electr. Engineer*' *Ref. Bk.* xxvi. 7 Ducted cables are screened by the metal box in which they run. **1958** *Times Rev. Industry* Aug. 39/1 Compressed air is ducted from the compressors..to.. pressure jets. **1965** *Economist* 13 Feb. 670/3 A revolutionary new type of helicopter which uses hot ducted turbine exhaust gases to drive the rotor blades through tip vents.

†**duc'tarious**, *a. Obs.* [f. L. *ductārius* of or for drawing, f. *duct-*: see DUCT *sb.* and -ARIOUS.]

1656 BLOUNT *Glossogr.*, *Ductarious*, that draweth, leadeth, or guideth.

†**'ductate.** *Obs.* [Cf. DUCTION and -ATE[1].] The product of two quantities multiplied together.

1610 W. FOLKINGHAM *Art of Survey* II. viii. 61 From the medietie of the sides vnited, subduct each side seuerally; eradicate the ductat of the said medietie and remainders.

'ductible, *a.* Now *rare.* [a. obs. F. *ductible*, ad. L. type **ductibilis*, f. *duct-* ppl. stem of *dūcĕre* to lead, draw: see -BLE.] = DUCTILE.

1413 *Pilgr. Sowle* (Caxton 1483) IV. xxx. 77 The hede oweth rightwysly to be of gold, shewyng hymself tough and ductyble. **1623** COCKERAM, *Ductible*, easie to be perswaded, or drawne. **1660** W. SECKER *Nonsuch Prof.* 12 The purest gold is the most ductible. *a* **1704** T. BROWN *2 Oxford Schol.* Wks. 1730 I. 12 If any should prove more intractable or less ductible than others. **1847** LEWES *Hist. Philos.* (1867) II. 449 We must..know from experience that gold is ductible before we can predicate ductility of gold.

Hence **ducti'bility**, ductility, pliableness.

1789 COWPER *Lett.* 16 June, Ductability of temper.

ductile ('dʌktɪl, -aɪl), *a.* Also 7 -il. [a. F. *auctile* (13–14th c. in Hatz.-Darm.), ad. L. *ductilis* that may be led or drawn, f. *dūcĕre* to lead.]

1. Of metal: **a.** That may be hammered out thin; malleable; flexible, pliable, not brittle. Still frequent in literary use: for technical use, see b.

a **1340** HAMPOLE *Psalter* xcvii. 6 Syngis til oure God..in trumpys ductils [Vulg. *in tubis ductilibus*]. **1567** MAPLET *Gr. Forest* 10 It [gold] is more ductile and easie to be brought to what poynt you will then any of the other. **1601** HOLLAND *Pliny* II. 505 The other sort of copper..yeeldeth to the hammer and will be drawne out, whereupon some there be who call it Ductile, i. battable. **1676** HOBBES *Iliad* (1677) 290 Pieces for his legs of ductile tin. **1869** MRS. SOMERVILLE *Molec. Sc.* I. i. 4 Calcium is a bright ductile metal of a bronze colour. **1870** BRYANT *Iliad* II. XVIII. 229 Greaves of ductile tin.

b. Capable of being drawn out into wire or thread, tough. (The current technical use.)

1626 BACON *Sylva* §845 All Bodies Ductile (as Metals that will be drawne into Wire). **1796** PEARSON in *Phil. Trans.* LXXXVI. 430 The best English copper is accounted less tough and ductile than Swedish copper. **1826** HENRY *Elem. Chem.* I. 479 All the metals, that have been described as malleable (with the exception, perhaps, of nickel) are also ductile, or may be formed into wire. **1875** EMERSON *Misc., Parnassus* Wks. (Bohn) III. 359 A firm ductile thread of gold.

2. Of matter generally: Flexible, pliant; capable of being moulded or shaped; plastic.

1659 H. MORE *Immort. Soul* (1662) 175 The moist and ductil matter in the Womb. **1677** HALE *Prim. Orig. Man.* IV. ii. 303 The Waters were..a more ductile, and possibly a more fertil Body than the Earth. **1725** POPE *Odyss.* XII. 208 The ductile wax with busy hands I mold. **1735** SOMERVILLE *Chase* IV. 162 Potters form Their soft and ductile Clay to various Shapes. **1869** PHILLIPS *Vesuv.* viii. 209 The level interior is full of ductile sulphur.

b. *fig.* Of things immaterial.

1684 T. BURNET *Th. Earth* I. 187 The first principles of life must be tender and ductile, that they may yield to all the motions and gentle touches of nature. **1788** REID *Aristotle's Log.* iv. §3. 77 To show of what ductile materials syllogisms are made. **1842** H. ROGERS *Introd. Burke's Wks.* 46 There never was a man under whose hands language was more plastic and ductile. **1864** BURTON *Scot Abr.* I. v. 239 The Roman law..has proved extremely ductile and accommodating.

3. Of persons, their dispositions, etc: Susceptible of being led or drawn; yielding readily to persuasion or instruction; tractable, pliable, pliant.

1622 DONNE *Serm.* 15 Sept. 21 A good, and tractable, and ductile disposition. **1650** DURYE *Just Re-prop.* 16 Men of ductile spirits unto evill. **1765** JOHNSON *Obs. Shaks. Plays, Rom. & Jul.*, Whose genius was not very..ductile to humour, but acute, argumentative, comprehensive, and sublime. **1835** LYTTON *Rienzi* III. ii, The ductile temper of Adeline yielded easily. **1894** MRS. H. WARD *Marcella* II. 310 The man..was in truth childishly soft and ductile.

4. Of water: Conducted or capable of being made to flow through channels.

[*a* **1637** *B. Jonson's Fall of Mortimer* Wks. (Rtldg.) 503/2, I felt it ductile [**1640** Dactile: see DACTILE] through my blood.] **1728** POPE *Dunc.* I. 62 Ductile dulness new meanders takes. **1737** SAVAGE *Of Public Spirit* 16 Lo! ductile riv'lets visit distant towns! **1834** *Blackw. Mag.* XXXV. 177 The ductile streams, after performing their fertilizing office, bound over the rocks.

Hence **'ductilely** *adv.*; **'ductileness** (*rare*).

a **1612** DONNE *Βιαθανατος* (1644) 155 Gold..by reason of a faithfull tenacity and ductilenesse, will be brought to cover 10000 times as much of any other Mettall. **1618** —— *Serm.* lii. 524 Which shewes the Ductilenesse, the Appliablenesse of Gods Mercy. **1629** *Ibid.* cxxxvi. 439, I come into the hands of my God as pliably, as ductilely, as that first clod of Earth of which he made me in Adam.

ducti'limeter. [f. L. *ductil-is* DUCTILE + -METER: cf. mod. F. *ductilimètre* (Littré).] An instrument for measuring the ductility of metals.

1825 W. HAMILTON *Dict. Terms Arts & Sc.* cited in WORCESTER 1846.

ductility (dʌk'tɪlɪtɪ). [f. DUCTILE + -ITY, after L. type **ductilitās*: cf. F. *ductilité* (1701 in Hatz.-Darm.).] The quality of being ductile.

1. Capability of being extended by beating, drawn out into wire, worked upon, or bent; malleability, pliableness, flexibility.

1654 WHITLOCK *Zootomia* 44 This Ductility of Spirit commendeth Men, as well as that other doth Mettals. **1683** EVELYN *Diary* 19 Sept., I stepp'd into a goldbeaters workhouse, where he shew'd me the wonderfull ductilitie of that spreading and oylie metall. **1794** SULLIVAN *View Nat.* I. 435 Argillaceous earth is distinguishable from..a certain viscidity and ductility, which proceed from its power of retaining water. **1816** J. SMITH *Panorama Sc. & Art* II. 364 The ductility of platina is such, that it has been drawn into wire of less than the two-thousandth part of an inch in diameter. **1881** LUBBOCK in *Nature* No. 618. 407 Supposing that glacier ice enjoys a kind of ductility.

b. *transf.* and *fig.*

1654 [see prec.]. **1734** tr. *Rollin's Anc. Hist.* III. IX. i. 164 Never was there ductility of genius equal to his. **1849** MACAULAY *Hist. Eng.* II. 202 Greater ductility and energy of language.

2. Capability of being easily led or influenced; tractableness, docility.

1654 WHITLOCK *Zootomia* 220 Calling Obstinacy, Solidity; and humble Ductility after further Reason, and Discovery, Sceptick Inconstancy. **1768** STERNE *Sent. Journ.* (1778) I. 46 (*Remise Door*) As I led her on, I felt a pleasurable ductility about her. **1880** KINGLAKE *Crimea* VI. ix. 247 A spirit of servile ductility.

ducting ('dʌktɪŋ), *vbl. sb.* [f. DUCT. *sb.* + -ING 1 g.] A system of ducts; material in the form of a duct or ducts.

1945 E. MOLLOY *Princ. Heating & Ventilation* xiv. 263 They are available as wall fixtures where no ducting is necessary on the motor side of the fan. **1955** *Archit. Rev.* CXVIII. 340/3 A system of telephone ducting embedded in the floor screen has been provided throughout the building. **1957** *Times* 19 Aug. 2/7 Grain..can be ventilated..in heaps by means of portable ducting. **1958** *New Scientist* 16 Jan. 16/2 A length of ducting in which noise level can be measured. **1969** F. G. THOMPSON *Electr. Installation* II. iv. 73 Ducting is used to provide a network of cable ducts in concrete floors.

†**'duction.** *Obs.* Also 5 ducciouns. [ad. L. *ductiōn-em*, n. of action f. *dūcĕre* to lead.] The action of leading or bringing. *lit.* and *fig.* (In quot. 1430 = multiplication.)

c **1430** *Art of Nombryng* (E.E.T.S.) 11 Oft of ducciouns of figures in cifres nought is the resultant, as here, wherof it is evident and open, yf that the first figure of the nombre to be multipliede be a cifre, vndir it shalle be none sette. **1627-77** FELTHAM *Resolves* II. lxvi. 299 By the but meanly wise and common ductions of bemisted Nature, it would haue been no very powerful Oratory. *a* **1696** SCARBURGH *Euclid* (1705) 36 Euclide only means a Mental Duction, or Position of that strait line between any two points.

'ductless, *a.* [-LESS.] Having no duct.

ductless glands, 'term applied to several bodies which present the general character of glands, but possess no excretory ducts. They are the thymus and thyroid bodies, the spleen, adrenals, and the vascular, carotic, coccygeal, and pituitary bodies.' *Syd. Soc. Lex.*

1849-52 TODD *Cycl. Anat.* IV. 1112/1 The ductless glands. **1880** *Libr. Univ. Knowl.* IX. 89 The liver, in one of its functions, is a ductless gland. **1881** MIVART *Cat* 237 The Thyroid Body or gland is another ductless structure of unknown function.

ductor ('dʌktə(r), -ə(r)). [a. L. *ductor* leader, agent-n. from *dūcĕre* to lead.] A leader.

†**1.** 'The leader of a band of music, an officer belonging to the court' (Halliw.) *Obs.*

15.. *Househ. Ord. Edw. III* in *Househ. Ord.* 9 Mynstrelles, ductors or centeners, everye man by the daye ..0. 0. 12.

†**2.** A line which 'leads' in some direction. *Obs.*

1658 SIR T. BROWNE *Gard. Cyrus* ii. 115 The..Lozenge figure..being most ready to turn every way..having its ductors..at each Angle.

3. *Printing.* A roller which conveys the ink from the ink-fountain to the distributing-rollers. Cf. DOCTOR *sb.* 7 a. Also *ductor-roller.*

1851 *Offic. Catal. Gt. Exhib.* I. 283 [A] trough formed of an iron roller, called the ductor, against which..an iron plate rests, and, by its pressure, regulates the quantity of ink ..The ink is conveyed by the ductor-roller to the table.

†**ductory.** *Obs. rare.* [f. L. *duct-*: see above and -ORY.] A conducting instrument or appliance.

1678 WANLEY *Wond. Lit. World* III. xliv. §15. 226/1 I did therefore put words into this ductory of the voice.

ductule ('dʌktju:l). *Anat.* [f. L. type **ductulus*, dim. of *duct-us.*] A minute duct.

1883 FOSTER & BALFOUR *Embryol.* I. vi. 18 (Cent.) As the ductules grow longer and become branched, vascular processes grow in between them. **1924** H. E. JORDAN *Textbk. Histol.* (ed. 3) xv. 502 The ductuli aberrantes are blind tubules... The superior ductule opens into the epididymis ..; the inferior opens at the globus minor. **1939** E. R. A. COOPER *Human Histol.* xii. 203 Interlobular ducts continue into intralobular ones, from which terminal ductules communicate with collections of secretory cells known as alveoli. **1951** H. A. CATES *Primary Anat.* (ed. 2) viii. 222/2 Each efferent ductule, finer than the lead of a pencil, is highly coiled and, when unraveled, about eight inches long. **1967** G. M. WYBURN et al. *Conc. Anat.* i. 15 Twelve to sixteen small ducts, the efferent ductules, connect the testis to the head of the epidi[d]ymis.

†**'ducture.** *Obs.* [ad. L. type **ductūra*, f. *dūcĕre* to lead: see -URE.]

1. Leading, guidance, direction.

1644 J. GOODWIN *Innoc. Triumph.* (1645) 84 Willingly and by the ducture of their own inclinations. *a* **1677** MANTON *Wks.* 1871 II. 332 Observe the ducture and leading of Providence. *a* **1716** SOUTH *Serm.* (1737) IX. v. (R.), To steer our practice according to the ducture of the universal church.

2. Extension or movement in some direction.

1675 TRAHERNE *Chr. Ethics* xxii. 328 A melodious song, a delicious harmony..by ductures scarce perceivable in the throat. **1691** T. H[ALE] *Acc. New Invent.* p. v, Lines are Artificially made by the ducture of some point.

3. A duct or channel.

1670 MAYNWARING *Vita Sana* vi. 81 Aliene matter..sent forth by the next convenient ducture, or emunctory.

ductus ('dʌktəs). [L. (see DUCT).] **1.** *Anat.* In various (mod.) Latin phrases = DUCT 6 a.

1699 M. LISTER *Journey to Paris* 72 The same happens to the *Ductus Bilaris* in its insertion into the Guts. **1722** W. CHESELDEN *Anat. Humane Body* (ed. 2) IV. iii. 232 When the Umbelical-Vein is stop'd, the Ductus Venosus soon shrinks and Disappears, having no longer any Blood flowing through it. **1811** *London Dissector* (ed. 3) viii. 178 The aorta ..is connected to the pulmonary artery by a ligament, which in the fœtus, was a large canal, the Ductus Arteriosus. **1846** *Dublin Q. Jrnl. Med. Sci.* II. 505 Fungous Growth round the Orifice of the Ductus Choledochus. *Ibid.*, The ductus communis was greatly dilated, but the obstruction to the flow of the bile had never been complete. **1927** HALDANE & HUXLEY *Animal Biol.* iv. 97 Ductus arteriosus, derived from part of the embryonic arterial arch system, and connecting pulmonary artery with..the aorta. **1962** DAVSON & EGGLETON *Princ. Human Phys.* (ed. 13) xiii. 297 As the arterial blood of the umbilical vein passes from the placenta, the greater part of it traverses the ductus venosus and enters the inferior vena cava. *Ibid.* 299 About 78% of the right ventricular output passes into the descending aorta via the ductus arteriosus. *Ibid.* lxiv. 1480 The vasa efferentia lead to a single long duct, the ductus epididymis.

2. = DUCT 4; the method of making strokes with the pen, etc.

1922 *New Internat. Encycl.* (ed. 2) X. 11 The Bulgarian ductus of the Glagolitsa is round, while the Croatian is more angular. **1933** *Burlington Mag.* July 23/1 The 'ductus' appears to me to be absolutely that of Dürer's own pen. **1934** PRIEBSCH & COLLINSON *German Lang.* II. ix. 404 The script is round Anglo-Saxon, though of a more or less cursive ductus. **1954** [see DUCT *sb.* 4].

‖**ductus litterarum** ('dʌktəs lɪtə'rɑ:rəm). [mod.L., f. L. *ductus* (see prec.) + *litterarum*, gen. pl. of *littera* letter.] The general shape and formation of letters and their combinations in manuscripts, study of which may make possible the restoration of true readings in a corrupt text.

1888 *Athenæum* 7 Jan. 25/1 Of all our literature there is none more carelessly printed than our early drama—none in which conjecture, founded on the *ductus literarum*, comes more legitimately into play for the correction of its errors. **1899** A. W. WARD *Hist. Eng. Dram. Lit.* (ed. 2) II. 175 The extraordinary blunders of a printer, who when he could not read a word substituted another that most readily suited the *ductus literarum* without reference to meaning. **1926** *Daily Colonist* (Victoria, B.C.) 16 July 4/6 It [*sc.* a hypothesis] may be rejected on various grounds; the ductus litterarum may not satisfy some purists. **1966** *English Studies* XLVII. 272 The standard methods of textual criticism (analysis of ductus litterarum, minimum errors, common types of misprints).

ductwork ('dʌktwɜ:k). [f. DUCT *sb.* + WORK *sb.*] A system of ducts for the conveyance of liquids, gases, etc.

1934 E. L. JOSELIN *Ventilation* v. 70 When considering a length of ductwork whose sizes are not yet determined, it is usual to assume an allowance for bends, etc. **1941** SHELDON & FARQUHAR *Progress Sci.* 23 Air washers or finned coil banks with separate supply fans are provided, connected to guest rooms through systems of ductwork. **1959** *Times* 5 Jan. 2/3 The flow of liquids or gases through branched ductwork systems and steam power cycles. **1960** R. W. MARKS *Dymaxion World of B. Fuller* 34/1 Ventilation was provided by a small fan located under the lavatory; air was drawn from the nearest room and exhausted through ductwork to the outside. **1971** *Engineering* Apr. 127 Automatic viscous filters and ductwork.

ducypers, var. DOUZEPERS, *Obs.*

dud (dʌd). Chiefly *pl.* **duds** (dʌdz). *colloq.* and *dial.* Also 5-7 **dudde.** [Origin unknown.]

1. †An article of clothing, a coarse cloak (*obs.*). Usually (now always) *pl.* = Clothes. (*slang* or *colloq.* depreciatory or humorous).

14.. *Voc.* in Wr.-Wülcker 568 *Birrus vel Birrum, i. grossum vestimentum*, a dudde. *c* **1440** *Promp. Parv.* 134/2 Dudde, clothe, *amphibilus.* **1567** HARMAN *Caveat* 86 We wyll fylche some duddes. *a* **1605** MONTGOMERIE *Flyting w. Polwart* 345 When thy duddes are bedirtten. **1651** RANDOLPH, etc. *Hey for Honesty* III. i. Wks. (1875) 431 By these good stampers, upper and nether duds, I'll nip from Ruffmans of the Harmanbeck. **1790** BURNS *Jolly Beggars* 8th Recit., They toom'd their pocks, an' pawn'd their duds. **1831** SCOTT *Jrnl.* 5 Mar., I promised to shake my duds and give them a cast of my calling. **1861** RAMSAY *Remin.* Ser. II. 126 He's mair need o' something to get duds to his back. **1866** MRS. STOWE *Lit. Foxes* 26 Girls knit away small fortunes..on little duds that do nobody any good. **1881** TROLLOPE *Marian Fay* iii. (Farmer), To see her children washed and put in and out of their duds.

attrib. *a* **1529** SKELTON *Poems agst. Garnesche* 46 In dud frese ye was schryned With better frese lynyd.

b. *slang* and *dial.* Effects in general, 'things'.

1662 HEAD & KIRKMAN *Eng. Rogue* (Farmer) All your duds are binged avast. *a* **1700** B. E. *Dict. Cant. Crew, Dudds*, Cloaths or Goods. **1780** R. TOMLINSON *Slang Pastoral* ix. 2 No duds in my pocket, no sea-coal to burn. **1877** E. PEACOCK *N.W. Linc. Gloss., Duds*, workmen's tools, clothes, personal possessions of small value.

2. *pl.* Rags, ragged clothes, tatters. (Rarely *sing.*)

1508 KENNEDIE *Flyting w. Dunbar* 384 Cryiand *caritas* at durris..Bairfut, brekeles, and all in duddis vpdost. **1768** ROSS *Helenore* 40 (Jam.) A hair-brain'd little ane wagging a' wi' duds. **1822** SCOTT *Nigel* v, A ragged rascal, every dud upon whose back was bidding good-day to the other. **1823** GALT *R. Gilhaize* I. 81 (Jam. s.v. *Cuff*) He fell into the corner of the room like a sack of duds. **1880** BESANT & RICE *Seamy Side* xix, She..was clothed in nothing but old rags and duds. **1889** BESANT *Bell of St. Paul's* III. 21.

3. Applied contemptuously to a person. *rare.* (In quot. 1870, perh. = scarecrow: see DUDMAN)

1825 JAMIESON s.v., Applied to a thowless fellow..'He's a soft dud.' *Roxb.* **1840** CARLYLE *Let.* in Froude *Life in Lond.* I. vii. 186 A wretched Dud called —, member for — called one day. **1870** *Putnam's Mag.* Feb. (Farmer), Think of her? I think she is dressed like a dud; can't say how she would look in the costume of the present century.

4. A counterfeit thing, as a bad coin, a dishonoured cheque; in the war of 1914–18 applied *spec.* to an explosive shell that failed to explode; hence (cf., however, sense 3) applied contemptuously to any useless or inefficient person or thing. (Cf. next.)

1897 *Daily News* 14 Jan. 2/2 He admitted that he knew that he ought not to have sold the piracies, and that such works were known as 'Duds'. **1908** *Westm. Gaz.* 28 Jan. 4/1 Gambling with 'Duds'... A 'dud' car is a worthless contraption, which.. has arrived at a stage when it would be dear at any price. **1908** *Captain* Apr. 23/2 We want talent, not duds. **1915** *Blackw. Mag.* Feb. 141 Our weary hearts rejoice When Silent Susan sends us down a dud! **1915** 'BOYD CABLE' *Between Lines* 254 One of these [shells] was a dud an' didn't burst. **1920** *Punch* 1 Sept. 168/1 He.. has.. been irritated by his school-boy son derisively addressing him as an 'old dud'. **1923** *Public Opinion* 30 Nov. 531/1 All the torpedoes they carry are duds. **1928** GALSWORTHY *Swan Song* III. xvi. 345 It's when you don't understand that you feel such a dud. **1951** R. GRAVES *Poems & Satires* 39 An expert on shell-fish, otherwise a dud.

Hence **'dudman**, a scarecrow. *dial.*

1674 BLOUNT *Glossogr.* (ed. 4), *Dudman*, a Maulkin or Effigies set up to fright Birds from Corn or Grain sowed. **1787** GROSE *Prov. Gloss., Dudman*, a scarecrow, also a ragged fellow. **1825** in BROCKETT *N.C. Gloss.* **1844** J. T. HEWLETT *Parsons & W.* x, He was just like a dudman.

dud (dʌd), *a.* [app. adj. use of DUD 3, 4.] Counterfeit; failing to answer to its description or to perform its function; worn out; useless; unsatisfactory.

1903 *Daily Chron.* 29 July 9/4, I.. got him to give me half a crown for a dud ring. **1904** *Ibid.* 13 May 6/3 Wanted comedy and dramatic sketches. Something with life and go in it. No Dud stuff required. **1908** [see prec.]. **1915** H. ROSHER *In R.N.A.S.* (1916) 130 As luck would have it, the weather was dud. **1917** *Blackw. Mag.* May 803/2 It was soon afterwards that our engine went dud. **1917** 'CONTACT' *Airman's Outings* 267 They wanted a plan of some new defences on which the Hun had been busy during the spell of dud weather. **1918** W. J. LOCKE *Rough Road* xviii, 'It's a dud sort of a place, Durdlebury,' said he. 'Dud?' He laughed. 'It never goes off.' **1929** *Star* 21 Aug. 14/4 Hitherto, he has met with rotten luck in Africa. Seemed to strike one dud patch after another. **1948** J. BETJEMAN *Coll. Poems* (1958) 159 'You going to the Hanks's hop to-night?' ..'It's pretty dud though,—only lemonade.' **1958** *Times Lit. Suppl.* 7 Feb. 73/4 The dud violinists rehearsing in the next room.

[**duddels**, given in some Dicts. = duds; but probably a misprint for *puddles*.

1562 PILKINGTON *Exp. Abdiam.* Pref. Aa viij, As he that ripes in a dungehyll, is infect with the smell therof.. so good men, now searchinge the festerd cankers and riping the stinking duddels of Poperi, for a time smell evil.]

dudder ('dʌdə(r)), *v. Obs.* exc. *dial.* [var. of DIDDER.] *intr.* To shudder, shiver.

a **1658** FORD, etc. *Witch Edmonton* II. i, I dudder and shake like an aspen leaf. *a* **1846** SPURDENS *Suppl. Forby's Voc. E. Anglia, Dudder*, to shiver with cold, or with fear; to shudder; but a more expressive word.

'duddery. *dial.* [f. DUD + -ERY.] A place where woollen cloth is sold or manufactured.

a **1552** LELAND *Collect.* (1774) II. 444 (Stourbridge) Sacellum & inditia ruderum domus veteris eo loco ubi nunc pars fori lanarii, Angl. *the Duddery*. **1778** *Eng. Gazetteer* (ed. 2) s.v. *Stourbridge*, Great store of serges, duroys, druggets, &c. from Exeter, Taunton, Bristol.. and some too from London: so that the Duddery, an area of 80 or 100 yards square, in which the clothiers unload, resembles Blackwell-Hall. **1806** in Hone *Every-day Bk.* I. 1306 In this duddery [at Stourbridge fair].. 100,000*l.* worth of woollen manufacture has been sold in less than a week. [A correspondent says that a large woollen factory at Haverhill in Suffolk goes by the name of the Duddery.]

† **duddle**, *sb. Obs. rare.* A teat, nipple.

1708 T. WARD *Eng. Ref.* (1716) 242 To his lips Madge held the Bottle, On which he suckt, as Child at Duddle.

† **duddle**, *v. Obs.* [cf. DODDLE *v.* and DIDDLE *v.*[3]] *trans.* To confuse, muddle.

1548 W. PATTEN *Exped. Scotl.* in Arb. *Garner* III. 129 Howbeit because the riders were no babies, nor their horses any colts, they could [with their rattles] neither duddle the one nor affray the other. **1575** LANEHAM *Let.* (1871) 47 So duddld with such varietee of delyghts.. [they] coold not.. tend their work a whyt.

† **'duddroun.** *Sc. Obs.* [? f. DUD.] An opprobrious epithet: ? One clad in duds.

1500–20 DUNBAR *Poems* xxvi. 71 Mony slute, daw, and slepy duddroun. **1536** LYNDESAY *Answ. Kingis Flyting* 59 To indyte, how that duddroun was drest, Drowkit with dreggis, quhimperand with mony quhryne.

duddy ('dʌdɪ), *a. Sc.* [f. DUD + -Y[1].] Ragged.

1725 RAMSAY *Gentle Sheph.* I. i. Song v, Little love or canty cheer can come Frae duddy doublets, and a pantry toom. **1818** SCOTT *Hrt. Midl.* xxx, There isna a wheen duddie bairns to be crying after ane. **1845** MRS. CARLYLE *Lett.* I. 306 That two-year-old duddy child.

Hence **'duddiness** (Jam. 1825).

dude (dju:d), *sb. U.S.* [A factitious slang term which came into vogue in New York about the beginning of 1883, in connexion with the 'æsthetic' craze of that day. Actual origin not recorded.]

1. A name given in ridicule to a man affecting an exaggerated fastidiousness in dress, speech, and deportment, and very particular about what is æsthetically 'good form'; hence, extended to an exquisite, a dandy, 'a swell'.

1883 *Graphic* 31 Mar. 319/1 The 'Dude' sounds like the name of a bird. It is, on the contrary, American slang for a new kind of American young man.. The one object for which the dude exists is to tone down the eccentricities of fashion.. The silent, subfusc, subdued 'dude' hands down the traditions of good form. **1883** *North Adams* (Mass.) *Transcript* 24 June, The new coined word 'dude'.. has travelled over the country with a great deal of rapidity since but two months ago it grew into general use in New York. **1883** *American* VII. 151 The social 'dude' who affects English dress and the English drawl. **1883** *Harper's Mag.* LXVII. 632 The elderly club dude. **1884** in Bryce *Amer. Commw.* (1888) II. App. 642 Dudes and roughs, civil service reformers and office-holding bosses.. join in midnight conferences. **1886** A. LANG in *Longm. Mag.* Mar. 553 Our novels establish a false ideal in the American imagination, and the result is that mysterious being 'The Dude'.

2. A non-westerner or city-dweller who tours or stays in the west of the U.S., esp. one who spends his holidays on a ranch; a tenderfoot; **dude ranch**, a ranch which provides entertainment for paying guests and tourists; so **dude rancher**, one who owns a dude ranch. Chiefly *U.S.*

1883 *Prince Albert Times* (Saskatchewan) 4 July 5/1 The dude is one of those creatures which are perfectly harmless and are a necessary evil to civilization. **1921** *Scribner's Mag.* Mar. 343/1 'Is this Scott Lawson's dude ranch?' soberly inquired the rider of the pinto. **1924** H. CROY *R.F.D. No. 3* 148 I'm going to put up the finest cattle barn in the state —that is, belonging to a real dirt farmer, not to one of them city dudes. **1940** E. FERGUSSON *Our Southwest* vi. 108 Every dude rancher saw his profits disappear underground in pumps, pipes, and septic tanks. **1949** 'J. TEY' *Brat Farrar* xiii. 116 There was paint galore at the dude ranch, but there was also a tradition of toughness. **1967** *Boston Sunday Herald* 14 May II. 13/1 It features in abundance the attractions that people who want to live in high, wide and handsome fashion will appreciate in its various seasons—riding, fishing, hunting, golfing, skiing, dude ranches and plush hotels.

Hence **'dudedom, 'dudeness, 'dudery, 'dudism** (*nonce-wds.*), the state, style, character or manners of a dude; **'dudess, dudine** (-'i:n), a female dude; **'dudish** *a.*, characteristic of a dude; foppish.

1883 *Philad. Times* No. 2892. 2 Not.. to encourage the development of the dude or the dudine in his dominion. **1885** *Weekly New Mexican Rev.* 28 May 2/5 The dudes and dudesses of Vegas are rehearsing for the opera entitled 'The Doctor of Alcantara'. **1885** *Boston* (Mass.) *Jrnl.* 15 June 2/3 The intense dudeness of Lord Beaconsfield in his early days is illustrated by a letter written in 1830. **1889** 'MARK TWAIN' *Yankee* viii. 80 Reverence for rank and title.. had disappeared—at least, to all intents and purposes. The remnant of it was restricted to the dudes and dudesses. **1889** *Bookworm* 237 Any dudish Anglo-maniac or Fifth Avenue 'bud'. **1889** *Voice* (N.Y.) 2 May, The Pharisaical dudery which presumes to deny her [woman] a place in the world.. equal with man. **1890** *Teacher* (N.Y.) Sept. 101 Are we traveling the way of the Greeks?.. Is dudism becoming more contagious among us than philanthropy? **1891** A. WELCKER *Woolly West* 69 Joe then went east, and.. married a young dudine out there. **1894** DICKSON *Life Edison* 230 A dudish applicant, with an overweening sense of his own self-importance. **1894** *Forum* (U.S.) May 345 [It] would relegate its champion to the realms of dudedom.

dude (dju:d), *v. colloq.* (orig. *U.S.*). Also dood. [f. the sb.] *intr.* With *up*: to dress oneself as or like a dude; also *refl.* Usu. in phr. ***duded up***.

1899 B. TARKINGTON *Gentleman fr. Indiana* xiii. 240 Why should Cale Parker be wearing a coat, and be otherwise dooded and fixed up beyond any wedding? **1924** D. MARQUIS *Old Soak's Hist.* xxv. 124 If I gotto be all duded up ..I'm a goanto dude myself up. **1958** *New Statesman* 22 Feb. 243/1 The country cousins duding up to impress less snappy dressers back home. **1960** *Guardian* 8 Nov. 1/6 The two men, shaved and rested and all duded up.

dude, obs. pa. t. of DO *v.*

dudeen (du:'di:n). Also **dhudheen, dodeen, doodheen, doudeen, dudheen.** Irish name for a short clay tobacco-pipe; in the late 19th c. generally known in Great Britain, and esp. in the British Colonies and U.S.

1841 LEVER *C. O'Malley* cvii, A short dudeen graced his lip. **1842** THACKERAY *Fitz-Boodle's Conf.* Wks. 1869 XXII. 215, I found the Irish doodheen and tobacco the pleasantest smoking possible. **1853** 'C. BEDE' *Verdant Green* viii. 67 A great consumption of tobacco was going on, not only through the medium of cigars, but also of meerschaums, short 'dhudheens' of envied colour, and the genuine yard of clay. **1867** P. KENNEDY *Banks Boro* xxiv, Their hands went into their pockets more than once in search of the treacherously-consoling *dhudheen*. **1880** SENIOR *Trav. & Trout in Antipodes* 100 [He] knocks the ashes out of his dudheen. **1905** *Daily Chron.* 7 July 5/7 Removing his clay dhudheen from his lips.

† **dudgen**, *sb.* and *a. Obs.* [perh. the same as DUDGEON *sb.*[1]: a dagger with a handle of this material being cheap and often regarded as an inferior, unreliable weapon; cf. quots. 1581 and 1590 in DUDGEON *sb.*[1] 3.]

A. *sb.* 'Poor stuff', trash.

1592 G. HARVEY *Pierce's Super.* 139 The stalest dudgen or absurdest balductum that they.. can invent.

B. *adj.* **1.** Mean, poor, contemptible.

1589 NASHE *Almond for Parrat* 5 a, We talkt euen now of a dudgen destinction from which my Bedlam brother.. with the rest of those patches, striue to derive theyr discipline disobedience. **1593** DRAYTON *Idea* 427 Think'st thou, my Wit shall keepe the pack-Horse Way, That ev'ry Dudgen low Invention goes?

2. ? Ordinary, homely.

1613 BEAUM. & FL. *Captain* II. i, Though I am plain and dudgeon, I would not be an ass. *c* **1618** FLETCHER *Q. Corinth* II. iv, Tell him I.. would request to see him presently: Ye see I use old dudgen phrase to draw him.

dudgeon ('dʌdʒən), *sb.*[1] Forms: 5–6 dogeon, 5 dogean, dojoun, dugion, 6 dogen, -ion, dugyon, 6 doodgean, 6–7 dudgen, -in, -ion, 6– dudgeon. [Occurs as *digeon* in AF.: the form of the word suggests a French origin; but no corresp. word has been found in continental French.]

† **1.** A kind of wood used by turners, esp. for handles of knives, daggers, etc. *Obs.*

(According to Gerarde 1597 = boxwood. The same sense has been attributed to *dudgin* in the following quot. from Holland's Pliny, where however the Latin is obscure, and the English a very rude rendering of it.)

1601 HOLLAND *Pliny* XVI. xvi, Now for the Box tree, the wood thereof is in as great request as the very best: seldom hath it any grain crisped damask-wise, and neuer but about the root, the which is dudgin and ful of work. For otherwise the grain runneth streight and euen without any wauing. [PLINY: In primis vero materies honorata buxo est raro crispanti nec nisi radice, de cetero lenis quies est materiæ silentio quodam et duritie ac pallore commendabilis, in ipsa vero arbore topiario opere.]

1380 *Ordinance for Cutlers, Lond.*, in *Lett. Bk.* H. lf. cxviii, Qe nulles manches darbre forsqe digeoñ soyent colourez. [tr. in Riley *Mem. London* (1868) 439 No handle of wood, except dogeon.] **1439** *Test. Ebor.* (Surtees) III. 96 De j dagger, cum manubrio de dogeon. **1443** *Ibid.* II. 88 Unum par cultellorum cum manubrio de dugion. *c* **1440** *Promp. Parv.* 436/2 *Ronnyn*, as dojoun, or masere, or oper lyke. **1502** ARNOLDE *Chron.* (1811) 245 All my stuf beyng in my [Cutler's] shoppe, that is to saye, yuery, dogeon, horn, mapyll. **1535** in Maddison *Linc. Wills* (1888) 11 A pare of beads of dogeon. **1550–1600** *Customs Duties* (B.M. Add. MS. 25097) Dogen, the c peces containing v[xx] xs. **1562** TURNER *Herbal* II. 71 b, The wilde ashe.. can scarsly be knowen from dudgyon and I thynke that the moste parte of dogion is the root of the wilde ashe. **1597** GERARDE *Herbal* (1633) 1225 (L.) Turners and cutlers.. doe call this woode [box woode] dudgeon, wherewith they make dudgeon-hefted daggers. **1660** *Act 12 Chas. II*, c. 4 Sched., Dudgeon the hundred peeces cont. five score, j. li.

† **2.** The hilt of a dagger, made of this wood: cf. *dudgeon-haft* in 4. *Obs.*

1605 SHAKS. *Macb.* II. i. 46, I see.. on thy Blade, and Dudgeon, Gouts of Blood.

3. Hence **dudgeon-dagger**, and in later use **dudgeon**: A dagger with a hilt made of 'dudgeon'; also, a butcher's steel. *arch.*

1581 J. BELL *Haddon's Answ. Osor.* 10 b, Upon the whiche when you rushe with your doodgean daggar eloquence. **1590** GREEN *Wks.* (1882) VIII. 199 Loose in the haft like a dudgin dagger. *a* **1687** COTTON *Poet. Wks.* (1765) 83 With Dudgeon Dagger at his Back. **1826** SCOTT *Woodst.* vii, Bid me give him three inches of my dudgeon-dagger.

1638 BROME *Antipodes* V. v. Wks. 1873 III. 328 Take your dudgeon, Sir, I ha done you simple service. **1663** BUTLER *Hud.* I. i. 379 It was a serviceable Dudgeon, Either for fighting or for drudging. *Ibid.* ii. 769 That Wight With gauntlet blue and Bases white And round blunt Dudgeon [*some later edd.* truncheon]. **1837** CARLYLE *Fr. Rev.* II. III. v, And still the dudgeon sticks from his left lapelle. **1882** SHORTHOUSE *J. Inglesant* (ed. 2) II. xix. 372.

4. *attrib.* and *Comb.*, as ***dudgeon-knife***; † **dudgeon-dagger**: see 3; **dudgeon-haft**, the hilt of a dagger, made of 'dudgeon'; hence **dudgeon-hafted** *a.* (*arch.*); † **dudgeon-tree** = 1.

1559 *Will of J. Gryffyn* (Somerset Ho.), My dagger w[t] the *dudgen hafte gilte. **1611** COTGR., *Dague a roëlles*, a Scottish dagger; or Dudgeon haft dagger. *a* **1612** HARINGTON *Epigr.* IV. 11 A gilded blade hath oft a dudgen haft. **1634–5** BRERETON *Trav.* (1844) 108 [I] bought in Edinburgh.. a dudgeon-hafted dagger, and knives, gilt. **1816** SCOTT *Old Mort.* xxxvi, I'll dash your teeth out with my dudgeon-haft! **1841** BORROW *Zincali* (1872) 213 I'd straight unsheath my *dudgeon knife And cut his weasand through. **1861** THORNBURY *True as Steel* (1863) III. 20 Cutting out the heavy lead window frame with a short heavy dudgeon-knife. **1551** *Aberdeen Reg.* V. 21 (Jam.) Certane *dugeon tre coft be him. **1602** DEKKER *Satirom.* Wks. 1873 I. 195, I am too well rancht.. to bee stab'd With his *dudgion wit.

dudgeon ('dʌdʒən), *sb.*[2] and *a.* Forms: 6 dudgion, duggin, 6–7 dudgen, (7 dodgeon, dudgin, -ing), 7– dudgeon. [Origin unknown; identical in form with prec.; but provisionally separated as having, so far as is known, no connexion of sense. Cf. ENDUGINE.

A conjectural derivation from Welsh *dygen* malice, resentment, appears to be historically and phonetically baseless.]

A feeling of anger, resentment, or offence; ill humour. Almost always in phr. ***in dudgeon***, and esp. with qualifying adj., as ***high, great, deep***.

1573 G. HARVEY *Letter-bk.* (Camden) 28 Who seem'd to take it in marvelus great duggin. **1592** GREENE *Disput.* 6 Taking it in dudgion, that they should be put down by a Pesant. **1663** BUTLER *Hud.* I. i. 1 When civil dudgeon first grew high. **1687** CONGREVE *Old Bach.* II. ii, I hope you are not going out in dudgeon, cousin? **1781** MAD. D'ARBLAY *Diary* May, I returned without.. any remaining appearance of dudgeon in my phiz. **1816** SCOTT *Antiq.* v, They often parted in deep dudgeon. **1862** TROLLOPE *Orley F.* xxvii. (1873) 195 You must not be in a dudgeon with me. **1865** LIVINGSTONE *Zambesi* ix. 197 He went off in a high dudgeon. **1885** *Manch. Exam.* 23 Feb. 5/3 [He] resigned his position as reporter of the Committee in high dudgeon.

† **B.** *attrib.* and *adj.* Resentful, spiteful; ill-humoured. *Obs.*

[**1589** *Pappe w. Hatchet* C b, If such a one doo but nod, it is right dudgin and deepe discretion.] **1599** NASHE *Lenten Stuffe* (1871) 5 Those dull-pated pennifathers, that in such dudgeon scorn rejected him. **1625** LISLE *Du Bartas, Noe* 128 Another speaketh low, one dudgen is and spightful.

Hence **'dudgeon** *v.*, to be in dudgeon. *rare.*
1859 G. MEREDITH *R. Feverel* xxxviii, You've never been dudgeoning already.

dudine, dudish, dudism: see DUDE *sb.*

dudleyite ('dʌdlɪaɪt). *Min.* [f. *Dudleyville*, a town in Alabama, U.S.] A hydrous mica formed by the transformation of margarite.
1873 in *Proc. Amer. Phil. Soc.* XIII. 404. **1875** *Dana's Min.* App. ii. 17 Dudleyite..has the form of margarite.

dudman: see DUD.

due (dju:), *a.* and *adv.* Also 4-6 **dew, dewe, dwe,** 5 **deu, diewe, dwwe, duewe,** 5-6 **du,** 7 **dueue.** [ME. a. OF. *deü*, later *dû*, orig. pa. pple. of *devoir* to owe:— late L. **debūt-um* for *debitum*: cf. It. *dovuto*, formerly *devuto*, owed, due.]

A. *adj.* **1. a.** That is owing or payable, as an enforceable obligation or debt.
c **1340** *Cursor M.* 68 (Trin.) For þere shal mede wiþouten let Be sett to him for dew [*Gött.* duel] dett. *c* **1380** WYCLIF *Sel. Wks.* III. 312 ȝif tiþes when dewe bi Goddis comaundement. **1413** *Pilgr. Sowle* (Caxton) v. xiv. (1859) 79 Owre raunson were superhaboundaunt, ouer that was due. **1596** SHAKS. *Merch. V.* IV. i. 411 Three thousand Ducats due vnto the Iew. **1616** SIR F. KINGSMILL in *Lismore Papers* Ser. II. (1887) II. 18 Bouth confesse the dueue debt but I can gett itt of neyther. **1674** N. COX *Gentl. Recreat.* II. (1677) 160 It must speedily die, and pay the Debt that's due to Nature. **1848** WHARTON *Law Lex.* s.v., A debt is said to be *due* the instant that it has existence as a debt; it may be *payable* at a future time. **1874** GREEN *Short Hist.* v. §4. 238 The amount of service due from the serf had become limited by custom. **1891** *Law Times* XC. 509/1 The whole of those sums remained due.

b. Of a person: That owes. Now *dial.* or *colloq.*
1413 *Pilgr. Sowle* (Caxton 1483) IV. vii. 61 They ben due to payen this dette. **1812** INGRAM *Poems* 73 (Jam.) He.. strives to pay what he is due Without repeated craving.

c. Phrases. ***to fall*** or ***become due***: to become immediately payable, as a bill on reaching maturity. ***to grow*** or ***accrue due***: to be in process of maturing for payment.
1682 SCARLETT *Exchanges* 96 The Time must precisely be ..written in every Bill of Exchange, that the Drawer may certainly know when they fall due. **1695** in Picton *L'pool Munic. Rec.* (1883) I. 263 Now due or accrewing due. **1818** CRUISE *Digest* (ed. 2) IV. 224 Nor for what estate the rent was to be paid, nor when or on what days it was to grow due. **1882** BITHELL *Counting-ho. Dict.* (1893) 89 The bill really becomes due on the third day of grace, and not earlier, unless it fall upon a Sunday, Christmas Day, Good Friday, or a day of public fast or thanksgiving, in which cases the bill becomes due the day *before.* If on a Bank Holiday, the day *after.* **1896** *Law Times* C. 509/1 Income which has become due and has not yet been paid over.

†**2.** Belonging or falling *to* by right. *Obs.*
c **1400** *Destr. Troy* 61 Dites full dere was dew to the Grekys, A lede of þat lond & logede hom with. **1553** EDEN *Treat. Newe Ind.* (Arb.) 32 Whatsoeuer..vnknowen landes shoulde be discouered in the Easte partes the same to be dewe to the Portugales. **1648** GAGE *West Ind.* ii. 6 In Rome there is an other preferment successively due to Dominicans, from the time of Dominicus de Guzman. **1655** M. CARTER *Hon. Rediv.* (1660) 26 A new Coat..which is due to the descendents onely of his body.

†**3.** Belonging or incumbent as a duty. *Obs.*
c **1385** CHAUCER *L.G.W.* 603 *Cleopatra*, Hym thoute there nas to hym no thyng so dewe As Cleopatras for to love and serve.

†**4.** Pertaining or incumbent as a necessity. *Obs.*
c **1386** CHAUCER *Knt.'s T.* 2186 To maken vertu of necessitee, And take it weel, that we may nat eschue, And namely that to vs all is due [*i.e.* death]. *c* **1400** *Destr. Troy* 2673 It was desteynid by dome, & for due holdyn. **1491** *Act 7 Hen. VII*, c. 12 Preamb., Deth is due to every creature born in this world.

5. Owing by right of circumstances or condition; that ought to be given or rendered; proper to be conferred, granted, or inflicted. **a.** with *to.*
1393 GOWER *Conf.* II. 18 To pursue Thing, which that is to love due. **1393** *Ibid.* I. 19 There is a helle, Whiche unto mannes sinne is due. *a* **1450** *Knt. de la Tour* (1868) 14 For to grete [people] ye make curtesie of right, the whiche is dew to hem. *a* **1533** LD. BERNERS *Huon* lxiii. 219 Honoure is dew to them that dyserueth it. **1648** GAGE *West Ind.* iii. 8 Absolved ..from all sinne, and from their Purgatory and Hell due unto it. **1651** HOBBES *Leviath.* I. xiv. 68 He that winneth Meriteth, and may claime the Prize as Due. **1711** STEELE *Spect.* No. 262 ⁋9 The first Place among our English Poets is due to Milton. **1712** *Ibid.* No. 426 ⁋1 The Care of Parents due to their Children. **1838** LYTTON *Alice* 7 So much is due to the wishes of your late husband.

b. *simply.* Merited, appropriate: proper, right.
13.. *E.E. Allit. P.* C. 49 ȝif me be dyȝt a destyne due to haue, What dowes me þe dedayn, oþer dispit make? **1489** CAXTON *Faytes of A.* I. i. 3 Warres and bataylles shold be acursed thyng and not due. **1500-20** DUNBAR *Poems* xlviii. 77 Full law inclynnand with all due reuerens. **1591** SPENSER *M. Hubberd* 1237 Hell, his dewest meed. **1611** BIBLE *Luke* xxiii. 41 We receiue the due reward of our deeds, but this man hath done nothing amisse. **1633** BP. HALL *Hard Texts* 321 The Lord..shall execute due vengeance upon Satan. **1635** BRATHWAIT *Arcad. Pr.* Ded., Your Honours in duest observance Ri: Brathwait. **1657** J. SMITH *Myst. Rhet.* 67 He useth a decent and due Epithet, thus, Honourable Judge, Honoured Sir. **1807** CRABBE *Par. Reg.* II. 154 Silent, nor wanting due respect, the crowd.

6. a. Such as ought to be, to be observed, or to be done; fitting; proper; rightful.
c **1325** *Poem temp. Edw. II* (Percy) I, Knygts shuld were clothes Ischape in dewe manere. *c* **1400** *Apol. Loll.* 15 [It] procediþ in dewe ordre. *c* **1440** *York Myst.* xxx. 61, I do but þat diewe is. **1562** WINȜET *Cert. Tractates* i. Wks. 1888 I. 4 The passage and dew course is partlie tyll vs knawin. **1651** HOBBES *Leviath.* II. xxix. 173 At last reduceth the people to their due temper. **1688** R. HOLME *Armoury* III. 146/1 In the working of Landskips..observe a due distance of things. **1728** T. SHERIDAN *Persius* ii. (1739) 29 You may offer these Prayers in due Form. **1762** KAMES *Elem. Crit.* xviii. (1833) 315 A beauty that results from a due mixture of uniformity [etc.]. **1806** A. KNOX *Rem.* I. 35 It will produce its due effects. **1841** MYERS *Cath. Th.* III. xxxviii. 136 The due use of some human gift. **1885** *Act 48 & 49 Vict.* c. 54. §4 Such certificate shall be conclusive evidence of the due election of the person therein mentioned.

b. Of time.
c **1385** CHAUCER *L.G.W.* Prol. 364 (MS. Gg. 4. 27) To heryn here excusacyons..In duewe tyme whan they schal it profre. *c* **1400** *Destr. Troy* 6584 Troilus was takyn..And don out of daunger for the due tyme. **1535** COVERDALE *Prov.* xv. 23 O how pleasaunt is a worde spoken in due season? **1551** T. WILSON *Logike* (1580) 45 b, Thynges, that in due tyme followe the causes that went before. **1611** BIBLE *Gal.* vi. 9 In due season we shall reape, if we faint not. **1667** MILTON *P.L.* XII. 152 This Patriarch blest, Whom faithful Abraham due time shall call. **1711** BUDGELL *Spect.* No. 77 ⁋1, I left him to be convinced of his Mistake in due time. **1876** BLACK *Madcap V.* vii. 69 In due course of time they got into the hot air of London.

7. Such as is necessary or requisite for the purpose; adequate, sufficient.
c **1400** *Destr. Troy* 12867 þat þe pepull..shuld send ffor Dyamed the dughty, with his du helpe. *c* **1400** *Lanfranc's Cirurg.* 112 [Veins] bryngen lijf and dewe norischinge and cordialle spiritis. **1464** *Paston Lett.* No. 483 II. 147 Ye havynge dooe swerte [surety] both in obligacions and pleggs. **1563** W. FULKE *Meteors* (1640) 65 b, They have not the due quantity of brimstone. **1664** EVELYN *Kal. Hort.* (1729) 197 To bring them to a due stature, and perfect their seed. **1747** WESLEY *Prim. Physic* (1762) p. xx, A due Degree of Exercise. **1844** LD. BROUGHAM *Brit. Const.* ix. §1. (1862) 115 Upon due consideration.

†**8.** Of a person: Proper, right; genuine, real, true.
1399 LANGL. *Rich. Redeles* III. 60 But þan þe dewe dame ..ffostrith hem fforthe. *c* **1450** HOLLAND *Howlat* 575 The forest of Ettrik, and vthair ynewe With dynt of his derf swerd, the Dowglass so dewe Wan wichtly of weir.

9. To be ascribed or attributed: **a.** as a quality or attribute *to* its possessor (*arch.* or *obs.*); **b.** as a thing *to* its author or introducer; **c.** as an effect or result *to* its cause or origin; owing to, caused by, in consequence of. *rare* bef. 19th c.; according to Johnson 'proper, but not usual'.
1661 BOYLE *Hist. Fluidity* I. xxiv. Wks. 1772 I. 395 The motion of the oily drops may be in part due to some partial solution made of them by the vinous spirit. **1669** EARL ORRERY *Tryphon* v, That Guilt is to Aretus due. **1706** E. WARD *Hud. Rediv.* II. viii, All the Ills that happen in it, Are due to them that did begin it. **1847** TENNYSON *Princ.* IV. 293 Jonah's gourd, Up in one night, and due to sudden sun. **1861** M. PATTISON *Ess.* (1889) I. 38 His delay in setting out was due to pure procrastination and dilatoriness. **1870** TYNDALL *Notes Lect. Electr.* 5 This beautiful experiment is due to Grove. **1875** JOWETT *Plato* (ed. 2) IV. 136 The.. difficulty in the Philebus, is really due to our ignorance of the philosophy of the age. **1886** *Lancet* 15 May 947/2 The albuminuria was due to a bacterial nephritis.

d. ***due to***, as prepositional phr. = *owing to* (OWING *ppl. a.* 3 b).
Described as 'erroneous' by W. A. Craigie in the *Dict. of Amer. Eng.*, and said by H. W. Fowler in *Mod. Eng. Usage* (1926) to be 'often used by the illiterate as though it had passed, like *owing to*, into a mere compound preposition', this use is now widely current though still firmly rejected by many grammarians.
1897 S. T. CLOVER *Paul Travers' Adv.* 190 [The Koturah] was taxed to her capacity, due to the fact that..she was advertised to go first to Adelaide. **1926** in Fowler *Mod. Eng. Usage* 123/2 The old trade union movement is a dead horse, largely due to the incompetency of the leaders. **1953** *Sat. Even. Post* 5 Dec. 173 So far, due to engineering controls, more precise than any known to industry, this has never happened. **1955** *Times* 25 July, Largely due to the defence efforts of the Western Powers, Europe was in a state of stalemate. **1957** ELIZABETH II in *Times* 15 Oct. 10/6 Due to inability to market their grain, prairie farmers have for some time been faced with a serious shortage of funds to meet their immediate needs.

10. Under engagement or contract to be ready, be present, or arrive (at a defined time); reckoned upon as arriving; as *the train is already due* = ought, according to the time-tables, to be already here (or *at* such a place).
1833 MOORE *Mem.* (1854) VI. 336 Bills coming in at Christmas, and my History due at the same time. **1865** DICKENS *Mut. Fr.* I. vi, Williams, Bob Glamour, and Jonathan, you are all due. *a* **1872** B. HARTE *Lost Galleon* i, Due she was, and over due—Galleon, merchandise, and crew. **1896** *Times* 13 Jan. 7/1 She is due at Ascension on February 11, and is to leave for England again on February 21..being due at Sheerness on March 19. *Mod.* The train is due in London at 5 a.m. He is due at his office next Monday. I must go; I am due at Mr. B.'s at seven o'clock.

11. Phrases and Comb., as **due-bill** (*U.S.*) (see quot. 1864); **due date**, the date on which a bill falls due and is payable; so †**due day**, the day on which any payment falls due.
a **1617** HIERON *Wks.* (1620) II. 457 There is a due day put in vpon the lease to be payd to him that is thy lord. Darest thou deale..with him in that duty, as thou dealest with God in His due-day? **1843** [*Due date* is remembered in ordinary business use]. **1864** WEBSTER (citing BURRILL), *Due-bill*, a brief written acknowledgment of a debt not made payable to order, and not transferable by indorsement, like a promissory note. **1877** *Banker's Mag.* 53 In case the bill is not taken up by the acceptor on the due date. **1887** J. E. WORDSWORTH (*title*) Tables for calculating the Due-Dates of Bills of Exchange.

B. *adv.* **1.** = DULY, in various senses. *arch.*
1597 SHAKS. *2 Hen. IV*, III. ii. 330 Euery third word a Lye, duer pay'd to the hearer, then the Turkes Tribute. **1606** SYLVESTER *Du Bartas* II. iv. II. *Magnificence* 1342 Of this great Frame, the parts so due-devis'd. **1667** MILTON *P.L.* V. 303 And Eve within, due at her hour prepar'd For dinner savourie fruits. **1800-24** CAMPBELL *Caroline* II. *To Even. Star* ii, So due thy plighted love returns, To chambers brighter than the rose.

2. With reference to the points of the compass: Properly; right, straight; directly. (Orig. *Naut.* Allied to 6.)
1601 SHAKS. *Twel. N.* III. i. 145 There lies your way, due West. **1604** —— *Oth.* III. iii. 455 The Ponticke Sea, Whose Icie Current.. Neu'r keepes retyring ebbe, but keeps due on To the Proponticke. **1634** SIR T. HERBERT *Trav.* 45 Tis from Ormus Ile forty leagues due South. **1720** DE FOE *Capt. Singleton* vi. (1840) 103 We went due east. **1810** SCOTT *Lady of L.* I. xxvi, Due westward, fronting to the green, A rural portico was seen. **1878** HUXLEY *Physiogr.* xx. 345 This.. does not take the shape of a due north wind.

3. *Comb.*, as ***due-distant***, at due distance; †***due-timely***, in due season, duly (*obs.*).
1605 SYLVESTER *Du Bartas* II. iii. *Abraham* 1002 Their extreme thirst due-timely to refresh. **1725** POPE *Odyss.* XIX. 120 A seat..prepare, Due-distant for us both to speak and hear. **1742** YOUNG *Nt. Th.* VI. 595 By some due-distant eye ..seen at once.

due (dju:), *sb.* Also 5-6 **dew(e.** [subst. use of DUE *a.*: cf. F. *dû* sb., in 14th c. *deü*, from *dû* pa. pple.]

†**1.** That which is due; a debt. *Obs.* (exc. as in 2-4.)
1439 *E.E. Wills* (1882) 127 And all othir dueez and governances for the performyng of his wyll. *c* **1460** *Towneley Myst.* (Surtees) 311 Thow can of cowrte thew, Bot lay downe the dewe. **1607** SHAKS. *Timon* II. ii. 16 My Lord, heere is a note of certaine dues. **1682** GREW *Anat. Plants* IV. Ep. Ded., The Performance whereof..is to be looked upon, as a Due to the Authority which Your Judgment hath over me.

2. a. That which is due or owed to any one; that to which one has a right legal or moral: with possessive of the person to whom owed.
1582 N. T. (Rhem.) *Rom.* xiii. 7 Render therfore to al men their dew [**1611** their dues]. **1593** SHAKS. *Lucr.* 1183 Which ..shall for him be spent, And as his due writ in my testament. **1612** ROWLANDS *More Knaues Yet?* 32 The cursed crew, That will not cheate the hangman of his due. *a* **1704** T. BROWN *Two Oxf. Scholars* Wks. 1730 I. 9 When I come to demand my dues..I shall find it a hard matter to get them. **1726** *Adv. Capt. R. Boyle* Ded. A ij, Though Praise is the just Due of Merit. **1770** LANGHORNE *Plutarch* (1879) I. 118/2 It was no more than his due. **1838** THIRLWALL *Greece* V. 249 He charges them with having defrauded the masters under whom he studied of their dues.

b. ***to give (a man) his due*** (fig.): to treat him or speak of him with justice, to do justice to any merits he may possess. ***to give the devil his due***: to do justice even to a person of admittedly bad character or repute (or one disliked by the speaker).
1589 *Pappe w. Hatchet* D ij, Giue them their due though they were diuels. **1596** SHAKS. *1 Hen. IV*, I. ii. 59 *Prin.* Did I euer call for thee to pay thy part? *Fal.* No, Ile giue thee thy due, thou hast paid al there. *Ibid.* 133 He was neuer yet a Breaker of Prouerbs: He will giue the diuell his due. **1642** *Prince Rupert's Declarat.* 2 The Cavaliers (to give the Divell his due) fought very valiantly. **1698** FRYER *Acc. E. India & P.* 38 Fryers; who, to give them their due, compass Sea and Land to make Proselytes. **1879** HOWELLS *L. Aroostook* x, 'Well', observed the captain..with the air of giving the devil his due, 'I've seen some very good people among the Catholics'.

3. That which is due or owed by any one: with possessive of the person owing.
1738 WESLEY *Hymn, 'Infinite Power, Eternal Lord'* vi, Shall Creatures of a meaner Frame Pay all their Dues to Thee? **1823** SCOTT *Peveril* v, Independent so long as my dues of homage are duly discharged. **1832** HT. MARTINEAU *Ireland* i. 14 There was no chance of paying the rent..even if Sullivan had been answerable for nobody's dues but his own. **1878** B. TAYLOR *Deukalion* II. i. 54 Pay your dues And make them debtors.

4. *spec.* **a.** A payment legally due or obligatory; a legal charge, toll, tribute, fee, or the like. Chiefly in *pl.* Often with attrib. word, expressing the nature of the charge, as *admiral, dock, Easter, harbour, light, market, Sound, tonnage dues*, etc.; see these words.
1546 *Suppl. Poore Comm.* (E.E.T.S.) 86 Tyll the poore people..had begged so moch as the pristes call theyr dwe. **1653** MILTON *Hirelings* Wks. 1738 I. 570 To seize their pretended priestly Due by force. **1660** F. BROOKE tr. *Le Blanc's Trav.* 213 Who have not paid the King dues for their harvest of silk. **1709** STEELE & SWIFT *Tatler* No. 66 ⁋1 The Parson of the Parish goes to Law for half his Dues. **1753** *Scots Mag.* Apr. 204/2 The produce of herring caught last season..was, after deducing 16*s.* 8*d.* per boat for admiral dues, 2028*l.* 9*s.* 2*d.* **1809** BAWDWEN *Domesday Bk.* 414 And it still pays all customary dues except gable and toll. **1875** *Act 38 & 39 Vict.* c. 39. §1 The bar-master or other local officer, if any, employed to collect the dues or royalty. **1879** FARRAR *St. Paul* II. 263 The question as to the payment of civil dues leads St. Paul naturally to speak of the payment of other dues.

b. *pl.* The fee for membership or use of a college, club, etc.

1670 in *Publ. Col. Soc. Mass.* (1925) XV. 52 To require the College dues from him forthwith. **1790** *Let. to V. Knox* 10 The Collegiate and University dues are peculiarly trifling. **1937** *Discovery* June p. xlix/2 Annual dues, 5 dollars. **1966** *Rep. Comm. Inquiry Univ. Oxf.* I. v. 168 There are only small variations in those charges, if dues and establishment charges are added to those made for board and lodging.

c. *fig.* (pl.). Responsibilities or obligations; esp. in phr. *to pay one's dues*, to fulfil obligations, undergo hardships, or gain experience. *U.S. slang.*

1943 'S. G. Wolsey' *Call House Madam* xiv. 403 She was mixed up later in one of the rottenest shooting messes ever staged in Hollywood, but she got away with her end of it and never paid her dues. **1961** N. Hentoff *Jazz Life* (1962) ii. 29 'Paying dues' is the jazz musician's term for the years of learning and searching for an individual sound and style while the pay is small and irregular. **1968** *Crescendo* Apr. 12/3, I guess I've, as they say, paid my dues. Looks like I'm still paying 'em. **1969** *Down Beat* 17 Apr. 19/2 Duke, Thad, Mel and myself, we've paid considerable amounts of dues in trying to get this thing off the ground.

†**5.** That which is due to be done; duty. ***of due***, as a matter of duty. *Obs.*

c **1430** Lydg. *Chorle & Bird* 101 in *Min. Poems* (Percy Soc) 182 To synge agayne, as was his due. —— *Min. Poems* 19 Of dew os thei oughte to doo, On procession withe the kyng to goon. **1548** Gest *Pr. Masse* 71 To the full discharge of my bonden dew herin. **1549–62** Sternhold & H. *Ps.* lxxxii. 3 Whereas of due you should defend The fatherlesse and weake. **1615** Chapman *Odyss.* I. 658 Euryclea, that well knew All the observance of a handmaid's due. **1697** Dryden *Æneid* XII. 318 All dues perform'd which holy Rites require.

†**6.** A right; *of (by) due*, by right, by just title.

1594 Carew *Huarte's Exam. Wits* x. (1616) 143 Whereas of due, a good wit and sufficiencie should rather encline a man to vertue and godlinesse. **1605** Bacon *Adv. Learn.* I. iv. §12. (1873) 37 Let great authors have their due, as time.. the author of authors, be not deprived of his due, which is.. further to discover truth. **1667** Milton *P.L.* II. 850 The key of this infernal Pit by due.. I keep. **1669** W. Simpson *Hydrol. Chym.* 122 That which should of due have been separated.

†**7.** Due quality or character, propriety. *Obs.*

1594 Carew *Huarte's Exam. Wits* (1616) 49 If the same grow hot or cold beyond due. **1600** *Trial Sir C. Blunt* in Cobbett *State Trials* (1809) I. 1422 For the honour of the Indictment and manifesting the due of their proceedings.

8. *Naut.* What is duly or thoroughly done: in phrase ***for a full due*** = thoroughly, for good and all; so that it will not need to be done again.

1830 Marryat *King's Own* xiii, Desire the carpenter to nail up the hatchway-screens.. We'll keep them up for a *full due*. *c* **1860** H. Stuart *Seaman's Catech.* 32 How will you turn in the lower rigging when it is marked off for a full due? **1867** Smyth *Sailor's Word-bk.*, *Full due*, for good; for ever; complete; belay. **1884** Luce *Seamanship* 116 (Cent.) The stays and then the shrouds are set up for a full due.

†**due**, *v.*[1] *Obs.* [variant of dow *v.*[2]: cf. endue = *endow*.] *trans.* To endow, invest, endue.

c **1394** *P. Pl. Crede* 776 Fraunces founded hem nouȝt to faren on þat wise, Ne Domynik dued hem neuer swiche drynkers to worþe. **1591** Shaks. *1 Hen. VI*, IV. ii. 34 This is the latest Glorie of thy praise, That I thy enemy, dew thee withall.

†**due**, *v.*[2] *Obs. rare.* [f. due *a.*] *impers.* To be due, to fall due; to be proper or fit.

1603 Drayton *Odes* VI. 16 Which when it him deweth, His Fethers he meweth.

due, obs. form of dew.

dueful ('dju:fʊl), *a. arch.* [f. due *a.* + -ful: an anomalous Spenserian formation, prob. on some such analogy as *right*, *rightful*.] Due, duly belonging, appropriate.

1596 Spenser *F.Q.* IV. xi. 44 To doe their dueful service, as to them befell. *Ibid.* VII. vi. 35 Of my desert, or of my dewfull Right. [Also IV. i. 6; VI. x. 32.] **1855** Singleton *Virgil* I. 84 Ere to the furrows you consign Their dueful seeds. *Ibid.* 316 For the altars he The dueful sacrifices slew.

dueil, obs. f. dole *sb.*[2], after later French.

duel ('dju:əl), *sb.* Also 7 duell. [a. F. *duel*, ad. It. *duello* or med.L. *duellum*, an ancient form of L. *bellum*, retained in archaic lang. and by the poets, and app. appropriated in late or med.L. to the fight of two combatants. The L. *duellum* was also in earlier Eng. use.

Isidore c. 600 says 'Bellum antea duellum vocatum, eo quod sunt duæ dimicantium partes, vel quod alterum faciat victorem et alterum victum'.]

1. A regular fight between two persons; a single combat. *spec.* †**a.** A judicial single combat; trial by wager of battle. *Obs. exc. Hist.*

[**1284** *Act 12 Edw. I* (Stat. Walliæ) c. 8, Placita de terris in partibus istis non habent terminari per duellum, neque per magnam assisam. **1299** see fine *sb.* 6. **1397** W. Wyrc. *Ann.* in *Wars Eng. in Fr.* (Rolls) II. II. 754 Duellum inter Henricum ducem Lancastriæ, appellantem, et comitem Norfolche, defendentem. **1600** Abp. Abbot *Exp. Jonah* 550 How many lawes did Moses make, but none for the *duellum* or combat betweene two?] **1611** Speed *Hist. Gt. Brit.* IX. vi. 23 Were it not for his function, he would enter the Duell or Combat with them in the field, to acquit himselfe both of Treason and Perjury. **1709** Steele *Tatler* No. 31 ¶1 When a Man is sued, be it for his Life or his Land, the Person that joins the Issue, whether Plaintiff or Defendant, may put the Trial upon the Duel. **1875** J. Fowler in *Yorks. Archæol. Jrnl.* III. 270 A certain man.. was vanquished in a duel.

b. In current use: A private fight between two persons, pre-arranged and fought with deadly weapons, usually in the presence of at least two witnesses called seconds, having for its object to decide a personal quarrel or to settle a point of honour.

[**1606** Bryskett *Civ. Life* 65 This kind of chalenging and fighting man to man, vnder the name of *Duellum*, which is vsed now a dayes among souldiers and men of honour, and by long custome authorized, to discharge a man of an iniury receiued.] **1611** Coryat *Crudities* 506 They fought a Duell, that is, a single combat in a field hard by Spira. *a* **1616** Beaum. & Fl. *Fr. Lawyer* I. i, Private Duells which had their first originall from the French. *a* **1683** Sidney *Disc. Govt.* III. xxviii. (1704) 353 When Duels were in fashion (as all know they were lately). **1727** Swift *What passed in Lond.* Wks. 1755 III. I. 186 A duel was fought.. between two colonels. **1840** Dickens *Barn. Rudge* xi, He and Mr. Haredale are going to fight a duel.

c. A sustained fight between two animals.

1890 Baker *Wild Beasts & their Ways* I. 287, I never.. witnessed a duel between this dog and a leopard. *Ibid.* 303 During this duel [of two bucks] the herd of females stood entranced.

2. Duelling, as a practice having its code of laws.

1615 Tomkis *Albumazar* IV. vii, Understand'st thou well nice points of duel?.. by strict laws of duel, I am excus'd To fight on disadvantage. **1822** Shelley tr. *Calderon's Magico Prod.* I. 247, I know little of the laws of duel.

3. Any contest between two persons or parties.

1591 Sylvester *Du Bartas* I. iii. 802 If he [Aconite] finde our bodies fore-possest With other Poyson.. with his Rivall enters secret Duel. **1612–15** Bp. Hall *Contempl.*, *N.T.* II. iii (Christ tempted), This duel was for us. **1671** Milton *P.R.* I. 173 Victory and triumph to the Son of God Now entering his great duel. **1781** Cowper *Convers.* 84 Preserve me from .. A duel in the form of a debate. **1839** Alison *Hist. Europe* (1849–50) VII. xlii. §27. 110 It was a duel between France and England, and France had succumbed. **1888** *Pall Mall G.* 1 Aug. 1/1 The duel between Mr. Parnell and Mr. Chamberlain hardly came up to general expectation.

4. *Comb.*, as ***duel-cut***, ***-trial***.

1631 in Cobbett *St. Trials, Ld. Uchiltrie* III. 474 If his majesty is pleased to admit torture before a duel-trial the pannel is ready.. to bear out the torture. **1871** Carlyle in *Mrs. C.'s Lett.* I. 33 Big German refugee.. scarred with duel-cuts.

duel ('dju:əl), *v.* [f. prec. sb.: cf. med.L. *duellāre*.]

1. *intr.* To fight a duel; to engage in single combat. Also ***to duel it***.

c **1645** *Vox Turturis* 8 Dimicare, to duell or fight. *a* **1661** Fuller *Worthies* I. (1662) 179 The thirty English, who for the honour of the Nation, undertook to duel with as many Britons. *a* **1679** Earl Orrery *Guzman* I, Nay, if you will duel it, you shall do it without Seconds. **1795** S. Rogers *Poems, Written for Mrs. Siddons* 99 The Sires.. Knelt for a look, and duelled for a smile. **1886** W. J. Tucker *E. Europe* 61 'We duel a great deal, and must be ready, on the slightest provocation, to defend our honour'.

†**2.** *trans.* To encounter in a duel or combat.

a **1659** Cleveland *Gen. Poems, etc.* (1677) 152 This is an Heresie where you stand alone, and.. with your single Valour duel an Army. **1698** B. F. *Modest Censure* 31 Dr. Whitby and Mr. Norris, who have duell'd one another about the Love of the Creature. **1703** Maundrell *Journ. Jerus.* (1721) 38 The Stage on which St. George duell'd and kill'd the Dragon.

†**b.** To overcome or kill in a duel. *Obs.*

1673 O. Walker *Educ.* 60 How many have bin murthered, more duelled, upon play-quarrels! *a* **1716** South *Serm.* (1737) II. vi. 215 He might so fashionably and genteelly.. have been duelled or fluxed into another world.

Hence **'duelling** *ppl. a.*

1837 Ht. Martineau *Soc. Amer.* III. 58, I was talking over the correspondence with a duelling gentleman.

duel, obs. f. dole *sb.*[2], grief; obs. f. dwell.

dueliche, duelie, obs. forms of duly.

†**'duellary**, *a. Obs. rare.* [f. L. *duell-um* (see duel) + -ary.] Relating to duels or duelling.

1613–18 Daniel *Coll. Hist. Eng.* (1626) 38 No more then would the Lumbards forsake their duellary Lawes in Italy.

†**due'llation.** *Obs. rare.* [n. of action f. med.L. *duellāre* to duel.] Combat of two antagonists.

1502 *Ord. Crysten Men* (W. de W. 1506) IV. xxi. 250 Torneys duellacyon or the fight of two men.

dueller, dueler ('dju:ələ(r)). [f. duel *v.*]

1. One who duels; a duellist.

1628 Earle *Microcosm.*, *Sceptick in Relig.* (Arb.) 67 His conscience interposes itself betwixt Duellers. **1741** Richardson *Pamela* II. 297, I have been accused as a Dueller, and now as a Profligate. **1842** Miall in *Nonconf.* II. 81 Gamesters, duelers, adulterers, scoffers, the foes of God and the pests of men.

fig. **1668** Dryden *Evening's Love* III. i, These perpetual talkers, disputants,.. and duellers of the tongue!

2. A duelling pistol or revolver.

1836 E. Howard *R. Reefer* xxxvii, His long-barrelled Manton duellers.

duelling, dueling ('dju:əlɪŋ), *vbl. sb.* [f. as prec. + -ing[1].] The fighting of duels.

1654 W. Mountague *Devout Ess.* II. xi. §3 (R.) I have character'd this spirit of duelling as ugly and deform'd as I could. **1711** Hearne *Collect.* (Oxf. Hist. Soc.) III. 163 The House of Commons have brought in a Bill to prevent Duelling and make it Felony. **1857** Buckle *Civiliz.* I. ix. 584 Duelling has from the beginning been more popular in France than in England.

attrib. **1697** Collier *Ess. Mor. Subj.* I. (1703) 143 Religion will not endure the duelling principle. **1842** S. Lover *Handy Andy* iii, Engaged in cleaning the duelling pistols.

†**du'ellion.** *Obs. rare.* [ad. med.L. *duelliōn-em* = *duellium*, *duellum*.] A duel.

1728 Rawlinson *Hist. Sir J. Perrott* 228 The recital of privat Quarrells, Duellions, or contentions.

†**'duellism.** *Obs. rare.* [f. duel + -ism; prob. after *duellist*.] A duel, contest between two.

c **1609** Donne *Let. to Sir H. G.* Wks. (Alford) VI. 313 Those single Duellisms between Rome and England.

duellist, duelist ('dju:əlɪst). Also 7 dualist. [f. duel *sb.* + -ist; prob. after F. *duelliste* (16–17th c. in Hatz.-Darm.), ad. It. *duellista*.] One who fights duels, or practises duelling.

1592 Shaks. *Rom. & Jul.* II. iv. 33 He fights as you sing pricksong, keeps time, distance, and proportion, he rests his minum, one, two, and the third in your bosom: the very butcher of a silk button, a Dualist, a Dualist. **1616** B. Jonson *Epigr.* I. xlviii, He hath no honour lost, our Due'llists say. **1753** Hanway *Trav.* (1762) II. I. i. 2 Many worthy men have been in the sad case of the surviving duellist. **1815** Scott *Guy M.* xvi, What I have written will not avail.. the professed duellist.

fig. **1676** Boyle *Alcali & Acidum* vii. Wks. 1772 IV. 291 The Duellists (or the two jarring principles of alkali and acidum). *Ibid. passim.* **1706** in Phillips (ed. Kersey). **1856** Froude *Hist. Eng.* II. xi. 499 The blind wrestling of controversial duellists.

Hence **due'llistic** *a.*, pertaining to a duellist.

1873 H. Curwen *Hist. Booksellers* 147 He escaped all duellistic dangers. **1881** *World* 12 Jan. 6 Mr. Irving's duellistic performance as Fabian dei Franchi.

†**'duellize**, *v. Obs.* [f. duel + -ize.] *intr.* To engage in a duel or combat.

1632 Vicars *Æneid* v. (N.), The furious duellizing chariots swift Burst from their bounds. **1661** K. W. *Conf. Charac., Courtier* (1860) 22 That makes him so duellize and quarrell for the one. *a* **1693** Urquhart *Rabelais* III. xlii. 350 The Lists of a Duellizing Engagement.

‖**duello** (du:'ɛləʊ). [It. (du'ello) = duel.]

1. Duelling, as a custom having its laws and rules; the established code of duellists.

1588 Shaks. *L.L.L.* I. ii. 185 The Passado hee respects not, the Duello he regards not. *a* **1613** Overbury *A Wife* (1638) 243 But observes not the lawes of the Duello. **1842** S. Lover *Handy Andy* iii, The most accomplished regulator of the duello. **1863** H. Kingsley *A. Elliot*, Under the infernal, devil-invented system of the duello.

†**2.** A duel (*lit.* and *fig.*). *Obs.*

1612 Field *Woman a Weathercock* II. in Hazl. *Dodsley* XI. 44 Setting this duello of wit aside. *a* **1625** Fletcher *Nice Valour* III. ii, And spurn out the duelloes out o' th' kingdom. **1826** Scott *Woodst.* xxv, None shall fight duellos here.

duelly, duely, duelye, obs. forms of duly.

duelsome ('dju:əlsəm), *a.* [f. duel *sb.*, after *quarrelsome*.] Given or inclined to duelling.

1840 Thackeray *Paris Sk.-book* ii. (1872) 21 Being incorrigibly duelsome on his own account.

‖**duende** (dw'ende). [Sp.] **a.** A ghost, an evil spirit. **b.** *transf.* Inspiration, magic, 'fire'.

1924 *Contemp. Rev.* Jan. 98, I never heard of the existence of any good fairies, but *duendies* or bad ones abound... Often when a man has laid down his axe.. a *duende* will seize it. **1960** E. Sitwell in R. Campbell *Coll. Poems* III. 5 Roy Campbell had this '*duende*'. **1967** McCormick & Mascareñas *Compl. Aficionado* v. 167 According to good Mexican and Spanish aficionados, Manolete and Belmonte possessed both angel *and* duende, hence their extraordinary interest. **1967** 'La Meri' *Sp. Dancing* (ed. 2) vi. 76 The most important part of gypsy dancing is the *duende*, the emotional motivation. The word *duende* means, literally demons or poltergeists. The dancer, then, must be possessed. **1968** G. Household *Dance of Dwarfs* 64 For Pedro they were real... For Geronimo they are clearly duendes. Yet his treatment of the subject differed from the matter-of-fact way in which he usually describes the various spirits which surround us. **1970** *Daily Tel.* 31 Mar. 12/1 His own dancing was polished but lacking in what Spaniards call *duende*—the demoniacal intensity which sweeps audiences off their feet.

dueness ('dju:nɪs). [f. due *a.* + -ness.] The quality of being due: in various senses of the adj.

1621 W. Sclater *Tythes* (1623) 153 There is.. a Parochicall or particular duenesse of Tithes. **1646** *Ord. Lords & Com. Susp. Tryers* 9 The duenesse of their election. **1651** Baxter *Inf. Bapt.* 175 The promise determineth of the dueness of the reward. The threatening determineth of the dueness of the Penalty. *a* **1679** T. Goodwin *Exp. 1 Eph.* Wks. I. II. 199 When God had dissolved that dueness, that debt, (as I may call it,) that obligation. **1862** Ruskin *Unto this Last* 98 The.. dueness of wages. *a* **1866** J. Grote *Exam. Utilit. Philos.* viii. (1870) 142 The rational recognition of duty or dueness.

duenna (dju:'ɛnə). Also 7 douegna, 8 duegna, duena. [Sp. *dueña* ('dweɲa), formerly spelt *duenna*, married lady, mistress (fem. of *dueño* master):—L. *domina* lady, mistress.]

1. a. The chief lady in waiting upon the queen of Spain. **b.** An elderly woman, occupying a position between governess and companion, and having charge over the girls of a Spanish family.

1668 R. L'Estrange *Vis. Quev.* (1708) 64 I am call'd (says she) Douegna, or Madam the Gouvernante. **1681** Dryden *Sp. Friar* I. ii, Enter Elvira's Duenna, and whispers to her. **1715** C'tess D'Anois Wks. 141 One of my Lady Constable's Duegna's desir'd to speak with her. **1761** H. Walpole *Lett. to Mann* 10 Sept. (1857) III. 435 Kitty Dashwood.. living in the palace as Duenna to the queen. **1832** W. Irving

Alhambra I. 293 The Princesses hung round their old duenna, and coaxed, and entreated.

2. Any elderly woman whose duty it is to watch over a young one; a chaperon.

1708 MRS. CENTLIVRE *Busie Body* II. ii, You are her duenna. **1820** W. IRVING *Sketch Bk.* (1859) 111 There is no duenna so rigidly prudent, and inexorably decorous, as a superannuated coquette. **1827** SCOTT *Jrnl.* 18 Jan., He used ..to have a duenna of a housekeeper to sit in his study with him while he wrote. **1877** RITA *Vivienne* VI. i, Her home is guarded by a dragon-like duenna.

3. *Comb.*, as ***duenna-like*** adj.

1802 H. MARTIN *Helen of Glenross* I. 188, I never had Duenna-like talents.

Hence (*nonce-wds.*) **duennadom**, the realm of duennas; **duennaship**, the position or office of a duenna; **duenna-ish, duennesque** *adjs.*, like or characteristic of a duenna.

1821 *Examiner* 205/1 Her voice and eye were..not at all Duenna-ish. **1876** BESANT & RICE *Gold. Butterfly* III. 123 The ancient dames of duennadom may purse their withered lips. **1881** DUFFIELD *Don Quix.* III. xxxviii. 320 When the duennesque squadron had finished coming in. **1884** HUNTER & WHYTE *My Ducats & My Dau.* xi. (1885) 154 Camilla's aunt..regulated Mr. Arden's household affairs, and exercised a shadowy duennaship over his daughter.

duer, var. DOWER *sb.*[1] *Obs.*, burrow.

duerch, duergh, duerwe, duery, obs. forms of DWARF.

duere, rare obs. form of DEAR *a.*[1]

duesse: see DEWESS, goddess.

duet, duett (djuːˈɛt), *sb.* [ad. It. *duetto*: see below.] A musical composition for two voices or two performers.

1740 DYCHE & PARDON, *Duet.* **1757** (*title*) Apollo's Cabinet..an accurate Collection of English and Italian Songs, Cantatas, and Duetts. **1797** MRS. RADCLIFFE *Italian* i. (1826) 10 They..opened the serenade with a duet. **1884** F. M. CRAWFORD *Rom. Singer* I. 47 You can..take me to her house to sing duets, as part of her lesson.

transf. **1840** DICKENS *Barn. Rudge* xxii, When Miggs had finished her solo, her mistress struck in again, and the two together performed a duet. **1876** MISS BRADDON *J. Haggard's Dau.* II. 92 The two young women performed a sobbing duet. **1890** *Daily News* 13 Sept. 3/1 Two sisters.. wore recently an original duet of gowns in these colours.

attrib. and *Comb.* **1819** *Metropolis* I. 156 Your duet singer. **1836** SYD. SMITH *Mem.* (1855) II. 383, I have fallen into the duet life, and it seems to do very well.

du'et, -ett, *v.* [f. prec.] *intr.* To perform a duet.

1822 BYRON *Let. to Moore* 12 July, You can spare time from duetting. **1879** G. MEREDITH *Egoist* II. ii. 29 As accordantly coupled..as a drum duetting with a bass-viol.

duete(e, -ie, y(e, obs. forms of DUTY.

‖**duettino** (duetˈtino, djuːɛˈtiːnəʊ). [It.: dim. of *duetto* DUET.] 'A duet of short extent and concise form' (Grove *Dict. Music* 1879).

1839 LONGF. *Hyperion* IV. iv, Ariettas and duettinos succeed each other. **1842** *Musical World* XVII. 83/3 (*title*) Three Duettinos for the Cornet à Pistons.

duettist (djuːˈɛtɪst). [f. DUET *sb.* + -IST; cf. *soloist.*] One who takes part in a duet.

1876 J. GOULD *Letter-press Printer* 100 Mr. and Mrs. J. H. will be the duettists. **1887** *Daily News* 8 July 3/7 Well known in music-hall circles as a duettist and dancer.

‖**duetto** (duˈetto, djuːˈɛtəʊ). [It. *duetto*, dim. of *duo* a duet: see DUO.] = DUET; also *transf.*

1724 *Short Explic. For. Words in Music Bks.* (Stanf.) *Duetti*, or *duetto*, are little Songs or Airs in two Parts. **1731** MRS. PENDARVES in *Mrs. Delany's Life & Corr.* 275 They agreed to sing a duetto out of yᵉ Beggars' Opera. **1815** W. H. IRELAND *Scribbleomania* 55 *note*, The literary pretensions of this once metrical and corresponding duetto. **1820** SCOTT *Monast.* xviii, They then..set off in a sort of duetto, enumerating the advantages of the situation.

duff (dʌf), *sb.*[1] [orig. a northern pronunc. of DOUGH: cf. *enough*.] **a.** Dough, paste. (*dial.*) **b.** A flour pudding boiled in a bag.; a dumpling.

1840 R. H. DANA *Bef. Mast* iv. 7 To enhance the value of the Sabbath to the crew, they are allowed on that day a pudding, or, as it is called, a 'duff'. **1847–78** HALLIWELL, *Duff*, dough, paste. *North.* *a* **1870** J. P. ROBSON *Wor Mally Torned Bloomer* (Northumb. Gloss.), Aw wesh'd the currans, wey'd the duff. **1872** C. KING *Mountain. Sierra Nev.* vii. 139 Crowning the repast with a duff, accurately globular. **1880** BESANT & RICE *Seamy Side* I. 8 Two helps of minced veal and two of currant duff.

Comb. **1883** *Chamb. Jrnl.* 142 The sailors' duffbags.

duff (dʌf), *sb.*[2] *local.* [Possibly the same as prec.; but more prob. onomatopœic, or associated with the sound made in striking a soft spongy substance.]

1. *Sc.* **a.** 'The soft or spongy part of a loaf, a turnip, a new cheese, etc.' **b.** 'A soft spongy peat.' (Jam.).

2. *Sc.* and *U.S.* The decaying vegetable matter (fallen leaves, etc.) which covers forest ground.

1844 W. H. MAXWELL *Sports & Adv. Scotl.* xvi. (1855) 150 Dung, mixed with duff-mould. **1878** *Pop. Sc. Monthly* XIII. 289 (Cent.) This duff (composed of rotten spruce-trees, cones, needles, etc.) has the power of holding water almost equal to a sponge. **1886** *Rep. Forest Comm. State N.Y.* 102 (Cent.) I have seen the smoke from fires in the duff even after the snow has fallen.

3. Coal dust or smaller coals, after separation of the nuts; slack, dross. Also ***duff coal.***

1865 JEVONS *Coal Quest.* (1866) 363 We could hardly prohibit the burning of duff and slack coal on the colliery heaps. **1867** W. W. SMYTH *Coal & Coal-mining* 248 The extended use..of slack and the smaller varieties of screened coal (pease and duff). **1887** *Pall Mall G.* 2 Nov. 6/1 One ton of common duff coal..has generated as much steam as two tons of good bituminous coal. **1892** [see DROSS *sb.* 2 b].

4. Something worthless or spurious; counterfeit money; smuggled goods; also, the passing or selling of such things. *slang.*

1781 G. PARKER *View of Society* II. 158 Sham leggers. The duff. Whispering dudders. **1879** *Macm. Mag.* XL. 502/1 Men at the duff (passing false jewellery). **1895** H. L. WILLIAMS *Love & Lockjaw* 7 Lucky my money won't do him any good. It is duff that I carry for a hold-up. **1935** G. INGRAM *Cockney Cavalcade* viii. 120 'That's all duff,' he proceeded. The announcement that so much was rubbish, as it consisted of imitation jewellery [etc.].

duff (dʌf), *v.*[1] *slang* or *colloq.* [A word of thieves' slang. Evidently closely related to DUFFER *sb.*[1] from which (appearing so much later) it may be a back-formation.]

1. *trans.* To dress or manipulate (a thing) fraudulently, so as to make it look like new or to give it the appearance of something which it is not; to 'fake up'.

c **1838** J. VAILL in *Mem.* (1839) 26 My pillow was a duffed great coat. **1870** W. B. SANDERS in *31st Rep. Dep. Keeper Public Rec.* p. vi, Some of these..MSS. were so very bad that it would have been impossible to duff them. **1892** *Edin. Evening News* 3 Mar. 2 A good deal of the old plate was 'duffed'.

2. (*Australia*). To alter the brands on (stolen cattle); to steal (cattle), altering the brands.

1869 E. C. BOOTH *Another Eng.* 138 The man who owned the 'duffing paddock' was said to have a knack of altering cattle brands. **1881** *Cheq. Career* 306 In such districts 'duffing' cattle is thought rather a smart thing to do. **1890** BOLDREWOOD *Squatter's Dream* xiv. 162 He'd think more of duffing a red heifer than all the money in the country.

3. To cheat, do *out of* fraudulently.

1863 SALA *Capt. Dangerous* III. ix. 305 Allowing him to duff me out of a few score pieces at the game of Lansquenet.

4. to duff up. a. *intr.* To become foggy or hazy (see also quot. 1876). *colloq.* or *dial.*

1876 F. K. ROBINSON *Gloss. Whitby* 58/1 *Duff up*, to drift like road dust on a hot day. **1942** I. GLEED *Arise to Conquer* x. 94 The weather looks O.K... If it duffs up, Derek, give us a shower of Verey lights to show us the way to come home.

b. *trans.* To beat (someone) up, to thrash. Hence **duffing-up**, a thrashing. *slang.*

1961 *Technology* May 131/1 Jeff and Bill was duffed up on saterday at st Albans drillhall. **1967** *Listener* 31 Aug. 261/3 He may have been taught—either through a fine he couldn't pay or a duffing-up he couldn't sustain—that this age has rid itself of some semantic taboos only to enthrone others. **1968** R. LAIT *Chance to Kill* i. 3 They had been duffed up at the police station. **1970** A. DRAPER *Swansong for Rare Bird* i. 11 Even when I was getting a good duffing up I just kept on going; as a result I never lost a punch-up.

Hence **'duffing** *vbl. sb.*; also *attrib.*

1851 MAYHEW *Lond. Labour* I. 380 'Duffing' and all that is going down fast. **1858** FONBLANQUE *Life & Labours* (1874) 279 Duffing..is the art of giving such a gloss and air of novelty to old clothes as to pass them off for new. **1869** [see 2]. **1881** *Cheq. Career* 329 'Cattle-duffing' and free-bootery. **1889** BOLDREWOOD *Robbery under Arms* (1890) 27 It was a duffing yard, sure enough.

duff, *v.*[2] [Back-formation f. DUFFER *sb.*[2]] *trans.* and *intr.* In Golf, to perform (a shot) badly (see quot. 1897). Also *transf.*, to make a mess of (something), to muff. Hence **duffed** *ppl. a.*, **duffing** *vbl. sb.* and *ppl. a.*

1897 *Encycl. Sport* I. 469/1 The verb 'to duff' does not mean..to play as a 'duffer' or hopelessly bad player, but simply to hit the ground first, behind the ball, so that the ball is struck with the upper edge of the face, and sent only a short way into the air. *Ibid.* 469/2 Duffing is very frequently caused by the player having his ball too near his right foot. **1906** *Westm. Gaz.* 8 Sept. 3/1 At the first duffed shot. **1909** *Ibid.* 30 Apr. 12/2 Mayo duffed his approach. **1909** J. R. WARE *Passing Eng.* 119/2 'He duffs everything he touches.' 'He is the most duffing duffer that ever duffed.' **1924** *Glasgow Herald* 15 June 11 He made one solitary slip when he duffed his putt on Wee Bogle. **1927** *Sunday Express* 29 May 21/6 The ninth provided Landale's crowning error, for he duffed two mashie shots.

duff (dʌf), *a. colloq.* [f. DUFF *sb.*[2]; cf. DOWF *a.*] Worthless, spurious, false, bad, 'dud'.

1889 BARRÈRE & LELAND *Dict. Slang* I. 336/2 *Duff* (thieves), spurious. **1910** *Sessions Paper* CLIV. 24 Nov. 82, I rang it [*sc.* a coin] on the counter; he said 'Break it up—it is duff.' **1944** G. NETHERWOOD *Desert Squadron* 10 It was said by the erks that he once sold rock on Blackpool sands. This was just 'duff gen'. **1956** R. ROBINSON *Landscape with Dead Dons* ix. 79 Pity we got off to a duff start. **1965** J. LYMINGTON *Green Drift* i. 8, I went down to the pub because the play was so duff. **1967** *Crescendo* June 24/1 A duff piano player will still sound duff on a Bosendorffer Grand.

‖**duffa'dar.** *E. Indies.* Also daf(f)adar. [Pers. and Urdū *dafaɛdār* a subaltern of cavalry.] 'A petty officer of native police; and in regiments of Irregular Cavalry, a non-commissioned officer corresponding in rank to a corporal' (Yule).

1800 WELLINGTON *Disp.* (1844) I. 109 (Stanf.) 2¼ pagodas for a maistry or duffadar. **1849** E. B. EASTWICK *Dry Leaves* 69 A Dafadār of Captain Christie's corps. **1892** *Pall Mall G.* 15 Mar. 5/3 Two native officers, two Kote Duffadars, and three others. **1921** *Glasgow Herald* 25 Mar. 7 A force of one dafadar and ten sowars of mounted police. **1951** J. MASTERS *Nightrunners of Bengal* 337 The three-striped non-com was havildar (inf.) or daffadar (cav.).

duffel: see DUFFLE.

duffer (ˈdʌfə(r)), *sb.*[1] *slang.* [Connected with DUFF *v.*[1] From the date of the words and senses, it may be inferred that *duffer* in senses 1 and 2 (the relative priority of which is uncertain) is the starting-point in Eng.; that DUFF *v.*[1] is a back-formation from this, to express the action of the *duffer* (in a somewhat later application), and that sense 3 of the sb. is, in turn, an agent-noun from the vb. Cf. also DUFFING *ppl. a.*, and DUFFER *sb.*[2]]

I. 1. One who sells trashy goods as valuable, upon false pretences, e.g. pretending that they are smuggled or stolen, and offered as bargains.

1756 W. TOLDERVY *Hist. Two Orphans* III. 61 These two fellows..are being duffers, or some such thieves. **1756** FIELDING in *Gentl. Mag.* XXVI. 565 Another set of gamblers..call'd duffers..invite you to go down some alley, and buy some cheap India handkerchiefs. **1781** R. KING *Mod. Lond. Spy* 65 One of the people called Duffers, who pretend to sell smuggled goods, such as silk handkerchiefs, and stockings. **1832** *Examiner* 268/1 On being searched, a complete stock-in-trade of a duffer was found upon him. His hat was crammed with rings, brooches, seals, &c...and a couple of watches, apparently of immense value..but got up in reality for the purposes of fraud. **1844** DICKENS *Mart. Chuz.* xxxvii. **1851** MAYHEW *Lond. Labour* I. 324 Duffers, who vend pretended smuggled goods..also, the sellers of sham sovereigns and sham gold rings for wagers.

2. A pedlar or hawker: see quots.

[**1763** SIR S. T. JANSSEN *Smuggling laid open* 19 These Duffers supply the Hawkers, who carry it about the Town, and sell it to the Consumers.] **1795** *Fortn. Ramble* 22 You have been dealing with a duffer..they carry none but the worst of wares, and charge three times the value of them. **1847–78** HALLIWELL, *Duffer*, a pedlar; applied exclusively to one who sells women's clothes. *South.* **1884** S. DOWELL *Hist. Taxation* III. I. i. iii. 38 A class of persons termed 'duffers', 'packmen', or 'Scotchmen', and sometimes 'tallymen', traders who go rounds with samples of goods, and take orders for goods afterwards to be delivered..These duffers were numerous in Cornwall.

II. 3. [f. DUFF *v.*[1] 1, 2.] **a.** One who 'fakes up' sham articles. **b.** (*Australia*) One who 'duffs' cattle.

1851 MAYHEW *Lond. Labour* (1861) II. 70 The 'Duffer' in English birds disguises them so that they shall look like foreigners. **1889** BOLDREWOOD *Robbery under Arms* (1890) 32 No cattle-duffer in the colonies could have had a better pair of mates. **1890** —— *Col. Reformer* xxv. 352 What's a little money..if your children grow up duffers and planters?

'duffer, *sb.*[2] *colloq.* and *slang.* [The evident association of the word with DUFFING *ppl. a.*, 'a duffer' being = 'a duffing fellow', 'a duffing coin or article', appears to connect the word with DUFF *v.*[1] It is possible, though our quots. do not show it, that the application to things, e.g. to a counterfeit or base coin, is the earlier, and that the term was thence transferred to a man who is similarly 'no good'. Less probable, though not out of the question, are the suggestions that a duffer is a man of *duff* or dough, or 'spongy substance' (see DUFF *sb.*[1], [2]), or that the word is the same as Sc. *duffar*, *duffart* 'a blunt stupid person', *dofart*, *doofart*, *dowfart*, 'a dull heavy-headed inactive fellow' (Jamieson).]

1. *colloq.* **a.** A person who proves to be without practical ability or capacity; one who is incapable, inefficient, or useless in his business or occupation; the reverse of an adept or competent person. Also more generally, a stupid or foolish person.

1842 LD. HOUGHTON *Let.* in Wemyss Reid *Life* (1891) I. 284, I do not think him the mere duffer that most people make him out. *a* **1845** HOOD (O.), 'Duffers' (if I may use a slang term which has now become classical, and which has no exact equivalent in English proper) are generally methodical and old. **1873** BLACK *Pr. Thule* xxv. (D.), 'Do you get £800 for a small picture?'..'Well, no'..'but then I am a duffer'. **1887** MISS BRADDON *Like & Unlike* xvii, I was always a duffer at dancing. **1889** J. K. JEROME *Three Men in Boat* 171 'Is it all right?'..'Lovely..You are duffers not to come in'. **1891** A. LANG *Angling Sketches* 8 Next to being an expert, it is well to be a contented duffer.

b. ***duffer's*** (or ***duffers'***) ***fortnight***, a fortnight of the angling season during which trout are supposed to be caught easily.

1927 *Observer* 19 June 27/4 That period of imbecility the so-called 'duffer's fortnight'. **1928** *Daily Express* 28 May 4/5 This annual festival of the Mayfly inaugurates the 'Duffers' Fortnight'.

2. *slang.* A counterfeit coin or article; any article that is 'no good'. Cf. DUFF *v.*[1] 1.

1875 JEVONS *Money* xxi. 289 The cheques, bills [etc.] are regarded by thieves as 'duffer', with which they dare not meddle. **1876** *World* V. No. 115. 19 He had purchased a veritable 'duffer' and could get no redress. **1881** *Standard* 2 Sept. 5/3 The [picture] gallery of a wealthy but uncritical collector came to the hammer, when..nine-tenths of it were adjudged to consist of 'duffers'. **1889** *Answers* 29 June 66/1 (Farmer) If the note is a genuine one the water-mark will then stand out plainly. If a duffer it will almost disappear.

3. *Australian* and *N.Z. Mining.* A claim or mine which proves unproductive. Also *attrib.*

1861 T. McCombie *Austral. Sk.* 193 It was a terrible duffer anyhow, every ounce of gold got from it cost £20 I'll swear. **1863** V. Pyke in *App. to Jrnls. House of Reps. N.Z.* D vi. 3 The place was rushed by about 500 men, who speedily deserted it, and declared the Waitahuna to be a 'duffer'. **1864** Rogers *New Rush* ii. 33 Reposing here, the son of quartz and clay Forgets the duffer he has sunk to day. **1869** R. Waite *Narr. Disc. West Coast Goldfields* 15 Those first arrivals chose to call the expedition a duffer rush. **1890** *Melbourne Argus* 9 Aug. 4/6 We struck the reef at Christmas, but it was a duffer. *a* **1928** D. McK. Wright in Currie *Centennial Treasury Otago Verse* 54 We had sunk a hundred holes that was duffers.

Hence (*nonce-wds.*) **'dufferdom, 'dufferism,** the style, character, or condition of a duffer.

1893 *Field* 10 June 832/1 There is no wilful misconduct, but only hopeless dufferism. **1895** *Tablet* 20 July 96 Aspirations to escape from dufferdom.

'duffer, *v. Australian* and *N.Z. Mining.* [f. DUFFER *sb.*² 3.] *intr.* Of a mine: To prove a 'duffer', become unproductive or exhaustive, give *out.* Also *fig.*

1885 Finch-Hatton *Advance Australia* 279 The lode had 'duffered out', and..it was useless to continue working. **1890** Boldrewood *Miner's Right* vi. 58 'So you're duffered out again, Harry!' she said. **1894** C. J. O'Regan *Voices of Wave & Tree* 10 Life's claim is almost duffered. **1897** D. McK. Wright *Station Ballads* 111 A good bit of ground duffers out.

duffer, variant of DOFFER.

duffing ('dʌfɪŋ), *ppl. a. slang.* [f. DUFF *v.*¹]

1. That passes off a worthless article as valuable.

1862 *Lond. Herald* 27 Dec. (Farmer) Houses..run up by the 'duffing' builder, merely for sale.

2. Counterfeit, rubbishy and offered as valuable.

1851 Mayhew *Lond. Labour* (1861) II. 19 Dealers in 'duffing fiddles'. These are German-made instruments, and are sold to the Street-folk at 2*s.* 6*d.* or 3*s.* each. **1873** *Times* Jan. (Farmer) We know now that so-called 'duffing' jewellery is scattered far and wide. **1883** *Sword & Trowel* July 355 'Duffing' canaries, or painted sparrows.

3. Incompetent, inept, stupid, duffer-like.

1881 J. Grant *Cameronians* I. iii. 39 A little brilliant singing, which Hew..secretly stigmatised as 'the most duffing caterwauling!'

duffle, duffel ('dʌf(ə)l). Also 7–8 duffield, 7–9 duffil. (The more common form is now **duffle.**) [Named from Duffel, a town of Brabant, between Antwerp and Mechlin.]

1. a. A coarse woollen cloth having a thick nap or frieze.

1677 Plot *Oxfordsh.* 279 These Duffields, so called from a Town in Brabant, where the trade of them first began.. otherwise called shags, and by the Merchants, trucking cloth. **1693** *Lond. Gaz.* No. 2914/4 Broad-Cloths, Serges half thicks, Duffils, Kerseys. *c* **1695** J. Miller *Descr. N. York* (1843) 42 Indian goods, as duffels, shirts. **1769** *De Foe's Tour Gt. Brit.* II. 283 Witney..They likewise make here the Duffield Stuffs, a Yard and three Quarters wide, which are carried to New-England and Virginia, and much worn even here in Winter. **1802** Wordsw. *Alice Fell* 53 Let it be of duffil grey. **1856** Mrs. Carlyle *Lett.* II. 289 If you weren't satisfied with the duffle. **1864** Carlyle *Fredk. Gt.* xi. iv. (1865) IV. 66 Muffled-up in a dressing-gown of coarse blue duffel.

b. Short for *duffle coat.*

1957 C. MacInnes *City of Spades* 108 You'd better buy yourself a duffel. **1957** M. Spark *Comforters* v. 112 Caroline pulled their spare duffle from the back seat and arranged it over her head and shoulders. **1959** J. Verney *Friday's Tunnel* ix. 85 Instead of a duffle, he wore a bright scarlet roll-neck pullover.

2. *U.S.* Change of flannels; personal effects taken by a sportsman or camper-out.

1884 G. W. Sears *Woodcraft* 4 (Cent.) Every one has gone to his chosen ground with too much impedimenta, too much duffle. **1889** *Anthony's Photogr. Bull.* II. 188 His dainty craft has room for little beyond her crew and a limited amount of duffle.

3. a. *attrib.* Made or consisting of duffle. So **duffle bag** orig. *U.S.*, a cylindrical canvas bag for carrying personal belongings; **duffle coat,** a coat made of duffle; *spec.* a short coat with a hood and fastened at the front with toggles.

1684 in *New Jersey Archives* (1880) 1st Ser. I. 459 He.. gave them [*sc.* Minisinck Indians] four Duffle Coats &ca. **1699** J. Dickenson *Jrnl. Trav.* 70 He gave each of them a Duffel Blanket. **1759** G. Washington *Writ.* (1889) II. 138 Light duffil Cloak with silver frogs. **1791** Newte *Tour Eng. & Scot.* 246 Duffle great coats. **1856** Mayhew *Rhine* 260 A long grey great-coat like a duffle dressing-gown. **1863** Mrs. Gaskell *Sylvia's Lovers* ii. 20 She was going..to buy a bran new duffle cloak all for herself. **1915** 'Bartimeus' *Tall Ship* vi. 105 The hood of his duffel-suit fell back. **1917** E. E. Cummings *Let.* 1 Oct. (1969) 37, I had a duffle-bag, chuck full. **1919** W. Lang *Sea-Lawyer's Log* x. 124 The guns' crews, wrapped in thick, blanket-like garments known as duffle coats. **1939** A. Keith *Land below Wind* xx. 312 There were our two brief-cases..and the duffle bag. **1953** P. Frankau *Winged Horse* iii. i. 181 He wore a duffle coat and corduroys. **1957** M. Spark *Comforters* v. 114 Laurence could not see her face, it was behind the duffle-coat. **1961** L. van der Post *Heart of Hunter* i. vii. 114 In the end the suitcase and duffle bag we had given Dabé were nearly bursting with presents. **1968** J. Ironside *Fashion Alphabet* 38 *Duffel coat,* a warm coat of heavy cloth... The front is fastened with toggles. This 'fashion' originated in the Navy when duffel-coats were worn as protection against the elements.

b. *Comb.*, as ***duffle-clad, -coated, -dressed*** adjs.

1901 Kipling *Kim* xiii. 330 The sallow, greasy, duffle-clad people. **1957** *Times Lit. Suppl.* 18 Oct. 629/4 Amorous students and duffle-clad professors. **1953** E. Taylor *Sleeping Beauty* iv. 56 Wind-nipped, duffle-coated, they climbed out of what they called their vintage Bentley. **1958** P. Mortimer *Daddy's gone a-Hunting* i. 8 A pillioned girl with hair streaming, duffle-coated arms clasped tightly round his waist. **1776** J. Trumbull *M'Fingal* (1826) iii. 89 Call'd forth each duffil-dress'd curmudgeon.

duffous, obs. form of DOVEHOUSE.

dufftail, duftail: see DOVETAIL.

dufoil ('djuːfɔɪl). *Her.* [f. L. *duo* two + FOIL leaf; cf. *trefoil, cinquefoil.*] A two-leaved flower; the plant Twayblade (*Listera ovata*).

1688 R. Holme *Armoury* ii. iv. §2. 58 He beareth Argent, a Dufoile or Twyfoile, Vert, flowered, Purpure. The Flower is like that which we commonly call Dogstones,..but more spireing. **1889** Elvin *Heraldry* Gloss., *Dufoil,* or *Twyfoil,* having only two leaves.

dufrenite (djuː'frɛnaɪt). *Min.* [Named 1833 after M. Dufrénoy, a French mineralogist.] Hydrous phosphate of iron, occurring in dull-greenish nodules and fibrous masses.

1850 Dana *Min.* 450 Dufrenite.

dufrenoysite (djuːfrɪ'nɔɪzaɪt). *Min.* [Named 1845 after M. Dufrénoy: see prec.] An arsenical sulphuret of lead, occurring in highly modified prisms, of grey colour and metallic lustre.

1848 *Amer. Jrnl. Sc.* Ser. ii. V. 268 Dufrenoysite is an arsenical sulphuret of lead. **1868** Dana *Min.* 92.

‖**dufter** ('dʌftə(r)). *E. Indies.* Also 8 -ur. [Arab., Pers., Urdū *daftar* record, register, ad. Gr. διφθέρα skin.] **a.** A bundle of official papers; a register, record. **b.** A business office.

1776 *Trial of Joseph Fowke* 18/1 The said Kialanders entered false records in the Duftur. **1803** Wellington *Disp.* (1844) I. 761 (Stanf.), I refer you to the papers upon this subject, which you will doubtless find in the dufter. **1817** M. Wilks *Hist. Sk. S. Ind.* xxv. II. 33 The business of the treasury was conducted in two dufters or departments.

dufterdar, var. DEFTERDAR.

dug (dʌg), *sb.*¹ Also 6–7 dugge. [Not known before 16th c.: origin obscure. Perh. radically connected with Sw. *dægga*, Da. *dægge* to suckle (a child).] The pap or udder of female mammalia; also the teat or nipple; usually in reference to suckling. As applied to a woman's breast, now contemptuous.

1530 Palsgr. 280/1 Tete, pappe, or dugge, a womans brest. **1583** Stanyhurst *Æneis* i. (Arb.) 34 Her dug with platted gould rybband girded about her. **1592** Shaks. *Ven. & Ad.* 875 Like a milch doe, whose swelling dugs do ache. **1607** Topsell *Four-f. Beasts* (1658) 519 The number of young Pigs..I finde to be so many as the Sow hath dugs for. *a* **1628** Preston *New Covt.* (1630) 477 The promises are full of comfort as a dugge is full of milke. **1713** Derham *Phys. Theol.* iv. xv. 256 With Duggs and Nipples placed in the most convenient part of the Body of each Animal. **1878** H. M. Stanley *Dark Cont.* II. iii. 75 The enormous dugs which hung down from the bosoms of the women.

b. *transf.* and *fig.*

1670 Lassels *Voy. Italy* I. 131 Lye hidden a while, at the dug of the booke. **1774** Goldsm. *Nat. Hist.* (1776) VII. 253 Nature has supplied this animal [spider] with..five dugs or teats for spinning it into thread. **1866** B. Taylor *Poems, Mondamin,* The savage dugs of fable.

†**c. dug-tree,** an old name of the Papaw-tree (*Carica Papaya*), apparently from the milky juice exuded by all parts of the tree when wounded.

1640 Parkinson *Theatr. Bot.* xvii. cxxix. 1649 *Manoera mas & femina.* The male and female Dugge tree.

†**dug,** *sb.*² *Obs. Angling.* A kind of red worm used as a bait. More fully called **dug-worm.**

1607 Topsell *Serpents* (1658) 811 Some are red, (which we Englishmen call Dugs). **1653** Walton *Angler* iv. 93 Others [breed] amongst or of plants, as the dug worm. **1674** N. Cox *Gentl. Recreat.* iv. (1677) 60 Baits for the Angler; the Earth-worm, the Dug-worm, the Maggot or Gentle.

dug (dʌg), *ppl. a.* [pa. pple. of DIG *v.*]

1. Obtained by digging, excavated, thrust into something, etc.: see the verb.

1715 Leoni *Palladio's Archit.* (1742) I. 4 All dug Stones are better..than gather'd ones. **1885** Tennyson *Balin & Balan* Wks. (1894) 374/2 Now with slack rein..Now with dug spur..he rode. **1892** A. E. Lee *Hist. Columbus* (Ohio) I. 29 Several excavations or 'dugholes', from which material.. seems to have been taken.

2. ***dug-in,*** entrenched; firmly established in a position; (see also quot. 1948). Cf. DIG *v.* 11.

1919 W. H. Downing *Digger Dial.* 21 *Dug in,* in a safe or comfortable position. **1944** *Times* 6 July 4/6 From a ridge behind the airfield dug-in German tanks have a clear field of fire. **1948** Partridge *Dict. Forces' Slang* 62 *Dug-in job,* a base job; such a job within a unit..as carried certain privileges.

dugarde: see DIEU-GARDE.

dugeperes, corrupt f. DOUZEPERS, *Obs.*

†**duggishly,** *adv. Obs. nonce-wd.* [f. ***duggish** adj. (f. DUG *sb.*¹ + -ISH) + -LY².]

1611 Cotgr., *Mammellement,* duggishly, breast-fashion, pap-like. **1653** Urquhart *Rabelais* i. vii. (1694) 24 This point hath been found duggishly scandalous.

†**duggy,** *a. Obs. rare*⁻⁰. [f. DUG *sb.*¹ + -Y.]

1611 Cotgr., *Tetassier*..duggie, hauing great..dugs.

dughtie, -y, obs. forms of DOUGHTY.

dugion, obs. form of DUDGEON *sb.*¹

†**dugon.** *Sc. Obs.* Also 6 dogone. [perh., as Jamieson suggests, a. F. *doguin* 'a filthie great old curre' Cotgr., dim. of *dogue* dog.] A worthless fellow: a term of contempt.

1508 Dunbar *Tua Mariit Wemen* 458 Thir damysellis.. That dogonis haldis in dainte, and delis with thaim so lang. **1820** Hogg *Wint. Even. T.* I. 292 (Jam.) When ane comes to close quarters wi' him, he's but a dugon.

dugong ('duːgɒŋ). [a. Malay name *dūyong.* Barchewitz, 1751, gives *dugung* as the name in the Philippine isle of Leyte; this was adopted 1765 by Buffon (*Hist. Nat.* XIII. 374) as *dugon,* and by Gmelin, *Linn. Syst. Nat.* ed. 13, 1788, as *dugong.*]

A large aquatic herbivorous mammal (*Halicore dugong,* order *Sirenia*) inhabiting the Indian seas.

1880 G. Shaw *Gen. Zool.* I. 239 Trichecus Dugong (*Gmel.*). Dugon (*Buffon*). Indian Walrus (Pennant *Quadr.*). This species, in the Philippine Islands, is said to be called by the name of *Dugung.* **1820** Sir S. Raffles in *Phil. Trans.* CX. 174 (*title*) Some account of the Dugong. *Ibid.* 180 The Malays..distinguish two varieties, the duyong *bamban,* and the duyong *bantal*; the latter much thicker and shorter in proportion. **1835** Kirby *Hab. & Inst. Anim.* II. xxiv. 496 The Dugong..is the only animal yet known that grazes at the bottom of the sea. **1849** *Sk. Nat. Hist., Mammalia* III. 126 We have..alluded to the dugong or duyong, and the lamantin..belonging to the pachydermatous order. **1889** H. H. Romilly *Verandah in N. Guinea* 189 On the surface of the water there were several dugong asleep.

dug-out, *ppl. a.* and *sb.* [See DUG *ppl. a.*, and *dig out,* DIG *v.* 13 b.]

A. *ppl. a.* Hollowed out by digging, excavated.

1886 *Athenæum* 24 Apr. 556/3 In some cases the station was completely insulated, and reached only by means of dug-out canoes. **1887** *Archæologia* L. 370 Dug-out boats of more or less rude construction. **1889** *Spectator* 14 Dec. 838 Ordinary dug-out canals like that of Suez.

B. *sb.* (chiefly *U.S.*) **1.** A canoe made by hollowing out the trunk of a tree.

1819 J. A. Quitman in Clairborne *Life* (1860) I. 42 At Wheeling..we purchased a small canoe, called here a 'dug-out', or 'man-drowner'. **1839** Marryat *Diary Amer.* Ser. i. II. 57 We had no boat with us, not even a dug-out. **1887** *Archæologia* L. 370 Ship-building..of a very superior kind to these rude dug-outs.

2. a. A rough kind of dwelling formed by an excavation in the ground (usually in a slope or bank), roofed with turf, canvas, etc. Also *attrib.*

1855 in J. A. Thomson *80 Yrs'. Remin.* (1904) I. 171, I live in a dug-out tent [at Balaklava], which is pretty warm, with a capital fire-place made out of potato tins! **1860** *Jrnl. Discourses* VIII. 293/1 When you have built splendid habitations, be as willing to leave them as you would to leave a dug-out. **1873** J. H. Beadle *Undevel. West* xxxi. 685 The unhappy traveler, if compelled to seek shelter in winter, will find it in a Swedish 'dug-out'. **1881** *Chicago Times* 16 Apr., Instead of 'dug-outs' on the prairies, he found the farmers living in large, handsome frame houses. **1883** *Leisure Hour* 281/2 The Kansas 'dug-outs' consist..of a square hole dug in the ground, roofed either by a canvas waggon-cloth or.. with sods.

b. *spec.* Applied to the roofed shelters used in trench warfare. Also *attrib.*

1904 *Westm. Gaz.* 7 Dec. 7/1 The following telegram from General Sakharoff..has been received at St. Petersburg:.. Our troops, thanks to their dug-outs, warm clothing, and plentiful food, do not suffer from the cold. **1914** D. O. Barnett *Lett.* (1915) 19 A dug-out in the reserve trenches. *a* **1917** E. A. Mackintosh *War the Liberator* (1918) 23 And I shall see no more The gallant friendly faces Framed in my dug-out door. **1919** G. K. Rose *2/4th Oxf. & Bucks Lt. Infty.* 26 Desire Trench..was a shallow disconnected trough upholstered in mud and possessing four or five unfinished dug-out shafts. *Ibid.* 63 A bombed dug-out is the last word in 'unhealthiness'.

3. A person of out-dated appearance or ideas; *spec.* a superannuated officer, etc., recalled for temporary military service. *slang.*

1912 *Blackw. Mag.* June 805/2 From his turn-out, he was probably a prehistoric 'dug-out', a 'was-bird' of 'weird' early Victorian ideas. **1915** (*title*) Tales of a 'dug-out'. *Ibid.* 5 [Publishers' note], These War Stories are written by an Officer—a 'dug-out', returning to the Service after 20 years' absence. **1916** H. G. Wells *Mr. Britling* ii. ii. 232 A new untried man—usually a dug-out in an advanced state of decay—is stuck into the job. **1918** W. J. Locke *Rough Road* vii. 75 The Colonel was immensely proud of them and sang their praises to any fellow dug-out who would listen to him. **1920** *Q. Rev.* July 139 Retired officers and civilians, the much sneered at 'Dug-outs'..saved the situation. **1939** A. J. Toynbee *Study Hist.* VI. 98 These 'elder statesmen' are the last people to whom a community can safely commit its destinies in an emergency, since..these 'dug-outs' are doubly incapacitated. **1958** P. Kemp *No Colours or Crest* iii.

31 The Assistant Provost Marshal.. was a dug-out major of a famous cavalry regiment.

'dug-up, *a.* [See DIG *v.* 14.] Exhumed; unearthed. Usu. *fig.*

1897 *Daily News* 23 Jan. 5/5 When the loud laughter which greeted this dug-up relic had died away. **1900** *Westm. Gaz.* 20 Jan. 4/2 The facts which this 'dug-up' material discloses are all to Thackeray's credit. **1921** GALSWORTHY *To Let* I. xii. 106 Thought her father had some 'ripping' pictures and some rather 'dug-up'.

duhti, obs. form of DOUGHTY.

‖**duiker**[1], **duyker** ('daɪkə(r)). [Du. *duiker* ('dœykər):—MDu. *dûker* = Ger. *taucher* ducker or diver: see DUCKER[1].] In full, *duikerbok*: A small South African antelope, *Cephalopus mergens*; so called from its habit of plunging through the bushes when pursued.

1777 G. FORSTER *Voy. round World* I. 84 The duyker or diving antelope.. is not yet sufficiently known. **1786** SPARRMAN *Voy. Cape G.H.* II. 224 As for the duyker-bok, or diving goat, I have only had a single glimpse of it. **1834** PRINGLE *Afr. Sk.* 23 And the duiker at my tread Sudden lifts his startled head. **1895** *Longm. Mag.* July 263 Dainty steinboks and timid duykers.. began to feed.

‖**duiker**[2] ('daɪkə(r), 'dœykər). *S. Afr.* [Afrikaans, f. Du.: see DUIKER] Any of several cormorants of the genus *Phalacrocorax*, esp. *P. carbo*.

1838 D. MOODIE tr. *Record* I. 13 The yacht returned from Robben Island, bringing about an hundred black birds, called *duikers*, (cormorants) of a good flavour. **1856** C. J. ANDERSSON *Lake Ngami* ii. 16 The way in which the 'duikers' (cormorants and shags) obtain their food is not uninteresting. **1950** L. G. GREEN *At Daybreak for Isles* iii. 129 Besides the trek-duiker and white-breasted duiker, there is a species on the islands known as the bank duiker... The reed duiker.. also nests on the islands; but this is really a fresh-water bird. *Ibid.* iii. 29 The shy duikers, the cormorants that can only be approached on their nests or in the darkness.

duil, duill, obs. or Sc. forms of DOLE *sb.*[2], grief.

duillie, Sc. form of DOLY *Obs.*, doleful.

duir, -e, obs. Sc. forms of DOOR, DURE *a.*, hard.

†**duistre**. *Obs. rare.* [a. AF. *duistre*, var. of OF. *duitre* (obj. case *duitor*):—L. *dūctor*, *dūctōrem*, leader.] A leader, conductor.

1393 GOWER *Conf.* I. 76 (Fairf. MS.) That þei be Duistres of þe weie.

†'**duity**. *Obs. rare.* [f. L. *duo* two; after *unity*.] Twofold nature or condition; duality.

1645 M. CASAUBON *Orig. Temp. Evils* 16 Plutarch.. writeth, that he the said Pythagoras called.. the unity, God; and the.. duitie daemon. [Cf. **1642** H. MORE *Life of Soul* xxvi. 7 But he [Dæmon]'s the fount of foul duality.]

duiweltjie, var. DUBBELTJIE.

duk, duke, obs. Sc. forms of DUCK.

‖**duka** ('duːkə). [Swahili, = shop, store, business.] In Kenya, a shop, store. Also *attrib.*

1924 *Chambers's Jrnl.* Jan. 12/2 He revels in exploring the *duka's* stock of caps, hats, shirts, cotton vests, and drill trousers. **1942** *E. African Ann.* *1941–2* 88/2 Stock.. can usually be depended upon to give fair.. returns on the capital which it represents, and which is always bringing in something with which to pay the wages and the duka bill. **1963** *Listener* 21 Mar. 485/1 They [*sc.* the Asians] have played a vital part in Kenya's development, pushing retail trade out into the tribal areas through their little shops, their *dukas*. **1966** D. BENNETT *Stranger in Grave* xviii. 148 Simbega Town was comprised of an Indian 'duka', an administrative building.. and an African market.

duk-duk ('dʊkdʊk). [Native name.] A secret society among the natives of New Britain, Bismarck Archipelago, which executes justice on the rest of the tribe and practises sorcery and mysterious rites; also, a member of this society.

1883 W. POWELL *Wand. Wild Country* 61 The Duk-duk.. may be spoken of as the administration of law, being judge, policeman, and hangman all in one. **1884** *Encycl. Brit.* XVII. 372/2 Justice is executed, and tabus, feasts, taxes, &c., arranged, by a mysterious disguised figure, the 'duk-duk'. **1896** A. J. BUTLER tr. *Ratzel's Hist. Mankind* I. 133 The weak chiefs of Melanesia, in order not to be quite powerless, apply the mystic Duk-Duk system to their own purposes. **1908** *Athenæum* 11 Apr. 444/2 The Dukduk of Melanesia. **1929** E. A. WEBER (*title*) The Duk-Duks. Primitive and historic types of citizenship.

duke (djuːk), *sb.* Forms: 2–6 duc, (3 dux), 3–4 duk, 4– duke. (Also 3–5 duyk, 3–6 duck, -e, 4 douk, -e, douc, deuk, 5 dukke, dwk, -e, doke, doyk, duche, 5–6 dewke, duque, duce, *Sc.* duik.) [ME. *duc*, *duk*, a. F. *duc*, in OF. nom. *dux*, *ducs*, *dus* (11–12th c. in Littré), early ad. L. *dux*, *duc-em*, leader, commander, general. (If the Latin word had come down in OF., its form would have been *dois*, *doix*: cf. *croix*, *noix*, OF. *crois*, *nois*:—L. *crucem*, *nucem*.)]

†**1. a.** A leader; a leader of an army, a captain or general; a chief, ruler. *Obs.*

c **1205** LAY. 264 þe ȝet leouede Asscani, þe on þan londe was duc. *Ibid.* 268 þa sende Asscani, þe wes lauerd and dux. *a* **1300** *Cursor M.* 17979 Sathan.. duke of deeþ & prynce of helle. *c* **1380** WYCLIF *Sel. Wks.* I. 340 A duk þat shal reule my folk of Israel. *Ibid.* III. 137 Jesus Crist duke of our batel. **1382** —— *Ps.* lxxix. 10 [lxxx. 9] Duke of the weie thou were in his siȝt. **1398** TREVISA *Barth. De P.R.* XVIII. iii. (1495) 749 The ramme that is duke and defender of other shepe. **1430–40** LYDG. *Bochas* VII. ix. (1554) 173 a, Duke Moses, by god was made their gyde. *c* **1449** PECOCK *Repr.* IV. vii. 460 Dukis and reulers of the chirche. **1460** CAPGRAVE *Chron.* 237 The Comones risen ageyn the kyng and the lordes.. Her duke was Wat Tyler, a proude knave and malapert. **1533** BELLENDEN *Livy* IV. (1822) 339 Na man may be callit duke, bot he alanerlie be quhias avise the army is led. **1591** SYLVESTER *Du Bartas* I. i. 346 The great Duke, that (in dreadful aw) Upon Mount Horeb learn'd th' eternall Law. [**1869** *Daily News* 26 Jan., Now-a-days *Dukes* do not *lead*. *Dux a non ducendo* is the true political etymology of the title.]

b. Rendering L. *dux*, a provincial military commander, under the later emperors.

1652 NEEDHAM tr. *Selden's Mare Cl.* 234 The Counts or Dukes of the Midland parts and the Count of the Sea-Coast or Saxon Shore, had distinct charges. **1781** GIBBON *Decl. & F.* xvii. II. 44 Under their orders thirty-five military commanders were stationed in the provinces.. All these provincial generals were therefore *dukes*; but no more than ten among them were dignified with the rank of *counts* or companions, a title of honour, or rather of favour, which had been recently invented in the court of Constantine. **1836** *Penny Cycl.* V. 445/2 Three other principal officers are mentioned—the *Comes littoris Saxonici per Britanniam*.. the *Comes Britanniarum* (Count of Britain), and the *Dux Britanniarum* (Duke of Britain). We have translated the words *Comes* and *Dux*, by *Count* and *Duke*, after Horsley.

c. In O.T. rendering *dux* of the Vulgate, ἡγεμών of LXX, in sense 'chief or leader of a tribe'.

1382 WYCLIF *Gen.* xxxvi. 40 Thes thanne the names of the dukis [**1388** duykis] of Esau.. the duke [*v.r.* duyk] Thanna, the duke Alua, the duke Jezeth [etc.].. thes the dukys [*v.r.* duykis] of Edom, the dwellers in the loond of his empire. [So **1611** and *R.V.* **1885**; COVERD. has 'prynce, prynces'.]

2. a. In some European countries: A sovereign prince, the ruler of a small state called a duchy.

Five dukes (with six *grand-dukes*) ruled states included in the German Empire after 1870. Two Italian dukes (and one grand-duke) remained as rulers of independent states down to 1860.

(In this sense, the name is partly derived from the late Roman use of *dux* (1 b), partly the English rendering (through med.L. *dux*, F. *duc*, It. *duca*) of Ger. *herzog*, OHG. *herizogo*, OE. *heretoga*, lit. 'leader of warlike host'. Throughout the Frankish empire, the Merovingian kings appointed *duces* to superintend several frontier *comitatus* (the *dux* being superior to the *comes*). These *duces* of Aquitaine, Allemania, etc. were purely official. But in the half of Germany not under the Franks there still existed 'dukes' of another kind. The Teutonic *herizogo* was originally the temporary war-chief of a tribe, as opposed to the civil chief or king. He occasionally made himself permanent head of the *volksstam*, while still retaining his title (e.g. in Bavaria). In Germany, this class of 'duke' came to an end when Charlemagne destroyed the last independent German states. Under the Carolingians, the *dux* was, east and west of the Rhine alike, an *official* ruling a province. But, in the decay of this dynasty, the dukes everywhere became hereditary and practically independent. Hence came, in the West, the dukes of Aquitaine, Burgundy, Normandy, etc.; in the East, those of Franconia, Saxony, Suabia, etc. In France, however, the monarchy gradually reabsorbed the duchies, which by 1500 were all amalgamated with the crown, the title of 'duke' having become merely that of the highest rank of nobility, with no sovereign rights. (See sense 3.) In Germany, on the other hand, the Duke of Bavaria or of Saxony was practically independent, the emperor having little or no power over him. The early Italian *duca* came direct from the Old Teutonic *herizogo*, the dukes of Benevento and Spoleto having been chiefs of Lombard war-bands who carved new states out of Roman Italy. In England, before the Norman Conquest, *dux* was an ordinary translation of *ealdorman* in L. charters; but did not become vernacular. From the Conquest till Edward III, *ealdorman* or *eorl* was rendered by *comes*, and *dux*, *duc*, *duk*, was known only as a foreign title; even William and Robert are known to the Old English Chronicle only as 'earls' of Normandy.)

[**1066** *O.E. Chron.*, Wyllelm eorl of Normandiȝe. **1124** *Ibid.* þes eorles sunu Rotbert of Normandi.] **1129** *O.E. Chron.*, Mid him helden ða of Rome . and se duc of Sicilie. **1297** R. GLOUC. (Rolls) 7498 þys noble duc Willam hym let crouny kyng At Londone amidewinter day. **13..** *Guy W.* (A.) 2372 þe douke wers bifallen is, For miche of his folk he les. *c* **1489** CAXTON *Sonnes of Aymon* xxii. 477 Wenynge that reynawd had not durst hange the duche richarde. **1568** GRAFTON *Chron.* II. 1 William the Conquerour, Duke of Normandie.. began his dominion over this Realme. **1610** SHAKS. *Temp.* I. ii. 58 Thy father was the Duke of Millaine and A Prince of power. **1756–7** tr. *Keysler's Trav.* (1760) IV. 217 The emperor Leopold I. and John III. king of Poland, met.. attended by a great number of electors, dukes, princes, and nobles, to congratulate each other after they had successfully raised the siege of Vienna. **1839** *Penny Cycl.* XV. 295/1 The government of Modena is the most absolute in Italy.. the present duke, Francis IV. of Este, is .. the last descendant of the houses both of Este and Cibo. *Mod.* H.R.H. Alfred Ernest Albert, Duke of Edinburgh, and Duke of Saxe-Coburg-Gotha.

†**b.** Used to render the Venetian DOGE. *Obs.*

1547 BOORDE *Introd. Knowl.* xxiv. (1870) 183 The Duke of Venys is chosen for terme of hys lyfe. **1604** SHAKS. *Oth.* IV. i. 230 The Duke, and the Senators of Venice greet you. **1643** HERLE *Answ. Ferne* 45 What better is His Majesty then a Duke of Venice? **1820** BYRON *Mar. Fal.* I. ii, 'Tis not well in Venice' Duke to say so.

c. Loosely used as the translation of the Russian *knyaz*, prince: see F. *duc*. See also GRAND DUKE.

1614 SELDEN *Titles Hon.* 208 Remember what is in the first booke of the Duke of Muscouie, for a Duke vncrowned, yet supreme Prince. **1618** FLETCHER *Loyal Subj.* Dram. Pers., Great Duke of Moscovia. *Ibid. passim.*

3. a. In Great Britain and some other countries: A hereditary title of nobility, ranking next below that of prince.

royal duke, a duke who is a member of the royal family, taking precedence of the other dukes.

(After the great feudatory dukes of France, or most of them, had come to be merely the greatest nobles of the country, the title was imitated in England and other countries. In England it was introduced by Edward III, who in 1337 created the Prince of Wales, Duke of Cornwall, and in 1351 the king's cousin Henry, Duke of Lancaster, which title at his death in 1361 was conferred on his son-in-law, John of Gaunt, the king's third surviving son, the title of Duke of Clarence being at the same time conferred upon the second son Lionel. Under Richard II and in subsequent reigns, the dignity was gradually extended outside the Royal Family, this being especially the case after the death of Queen Elizabeth, under whom the rank had been for some time extinguished.)

[**1337** *Rot. Cart. 11 Edw. III*, No. 60 in *Lord's Jrnls.* (1829) LXI. 743 Pro Edwardo duce Cornubie. *Ibid.*, Eidem filio nostro nomen & honorem ducis Cornubie de communi assensu & consilio.. dedimus. **1352** *Patent Roll 25 Edw. III*, I. m. 18 *ibid.* 748 Pro Henrico duce Lancastrie. *Ibid.*, Prefato Henrico nomen ducis Lancastrie inponimus et ipsum de nomine ducis dicti loci.. investimus. **1351–2** *Act 25 Edw. III*, stat. v. Preamb., Nostre Seignur le Roi del assent des Prelatz, Ducs, Countes, Barons, & de tout le comunalte de son Roialme dEngleterre [etc.]]. **1389** in *Eng. Gilds* (1870) 23 Duckes, Erles, Barouns, and Bachelers of ye londe. **1399** *Rolls of Parlt.* III. 452/1 The Lordes.. ajuggen.. that the Dukes of Aumarle Surrey and Excestre.. lese and forgo fro hem and her heirs thes names that thei have now as Dukes. **1472** J. PASTON in *P. Lett.* No. 715 III. 75 To the right hyghe and myghty Prince.. my Lord the Dwke of Norffolk. **1556** *Aurelio & Isab.* (1608) L iij, The Quene and manney Duques, earles, and grete lordes besoughte him. **1556** *Chron. Gr. Friars* (Camden) 7 Thys yere sir Edmonde Langle and sir Thomas Wodstoke ware made duckes. *Ibid.* 52 The dewke of Norffoke and the yerle of Sorré hys sonne ware comyttyd unto the tower of London. **1593** SHAKS. *2 Hen. VI*, I. i. 124 For Suffolkes Duke, may he be suffocate, That dims the Honor of this Warlike Isle. **1765** BLACKSTONE *Comm.* I. xii. 397. **1850** FONBLANQUE in *Life & Labours* i. (1874) 106 The Duke of Wellington, the 'Iron Duke', the 'hero of a hundred fights'. **1852** TENNYSON *Ode Wellington*, Bury the Great Duke With an empire's lamentation.

b. *slang.* A man of showy demeanour or appearance.

a **1700** B. E. *Dict. Cant. Crew*, *Rum-duke*, a jolly handsom Man. **1763** *Brit. Mag.* IV. 372, I.. soon acquired the appellations of a rum duke, a queer dog, and a choice spirit. **1785** in GROSE *Dict. Vulg. Tongue*.

c. Phr. ***Duke of Exeter's daughter***: see DAUGHTER 6 c. ***to dine with Duke Humphrey***: see DINE *v.* 1 b.

†**4.** The castle or rook at chess. *Obs.*

1624 MIDDLETON *Game at Chess* Induct. 54 Dukes? they're called Rooks by some. **1656** BEALE *Chess* 7 The Rocks, Rookes, or Dukes walk forward, backward, and side-wayes.

†**5.** The great eagle-owl (*Bubo maximus*). *Obs.*

1656 W. D. tr. *Comenius' Gate Lat. Unl.* §137. 41 The boading Owl, the Horn-Owl, or Duke, the mournful Howlet, the sad Scrietch-Owl.

6. Name of a kind of cherry.

1664 EVELYN *Kal. Hort.* (1669) 64 June.. Cherries.. Duke, Flanders, Heart (Black, Red, White). **1727** BRADLEY *Fam. Dict.* s.v. *Cherry*, The Duke and archduke on a good wall are most years ripe before the end of the month. **1883** G. ALLEN in *Colin Clout's Cal.* 117 The common dwarf cherry.. is the ancestor of morellos, dukes, and the Kentish kind.

7. *slang.* The hand or fist. Usu. *pl.* Also **dook**.

1874 HOTTEN *Slang Dict.* 153 'Put up your *dooks*' is a kind invitation to fight. **1879** *Macm. Mag.* XL. 501 (Farmer), I said I would not go at all if he put his dukes (hands) on me. **1894** ASTLEY *50 Y. my Life* I. 142 There were many officers in the Guards well known to be fairly clever with their 'dukes'. **1898** J. D. BRAYSHAW *Slum Silhouettes* i. 3 'E could 'andle 'is dooks, an' no error: the way 'e set abaht Bill was a fair treat. **1952** PARTRIDGE *From Sanskrit to Brazil* 4 He can handle his fives or *dooks*.. or hands, i.e. he can box well. **1963** J. MITFORD *Amer. Way Death* vi. 191 The funeral men are always ready with dukes up to go to the offensive.

Hence **duke** *v.* (*nonce-wd.*) *trans.*, to make a duke or leader of; *intr.* (also ***to duke it***), to play the part of a duke, act as a duke; to court dukes.

c **1450** *Golagros & Gaw.* 1072 Thow salbe.. dukit in our duchery. **1603** SHAKS. *Meas. for M.* III. ii. 100 Lord Angelo Dukes it well in his absence. **1605** SYLVESTER *Du Bartas* II. iii. *Captaines* 1 Just-Duked Josuah cheers the Abramides To Canaan's Conquest. **1690** CROWNE *Eng. Friar* III. Dram. Wks. 1874 IV. 70 Ay, sister, as young maids go a-maying we'll go a-squiring, a-knighting, a-lording, a-duking. **1894** WOLSELEY *Marlborough* I. 293 During his [Monmouth's] previous visit to the West, during what was locally known as 'The Dukeing Days'.

dukedom ('djuːkdəm). [f. DUKE *sb.*; see -DOM.]

1. The state or territory ruled by a duke; a duchy.

1460 *Lybeaus Disc.* 1723 Of alle thys dukdom feyr That ylke lady ys eyr. **1475** *Bk. Noblesse* 30 The ducdom of Normandy. **1535** COVERDALE *2 Esdras* i. 39 Yᵉ people.. vnto whom I wyll geue the dukedome of Abraham, Isaac and Iacob. **1593** SHAKS. *3 Hen. VI*, IV. vii. 9 What then remaines .. But that we enter, as into our Dukedome? **1665** MANLEY *Grotius' Low C. Warres* 399 In the Dutchy of Burgundy.. the Guisian Faction.. to whom there was nothing left Fortified in that Dukedom, but Chalons sur la Saone. **1756–7** tr. *Keysler's Trav.* (1760) III. 218 This whole tract of land belongs to the dukedom of Urbino. **1861** PEARSON *Early & Mid. Ages Eng.* 89 When chaos gave way to order, and the dukedoms were swallowed up in kingdoms.

2. The office or dignity of a duke.

1534 MORE *Treat. Passion* Wks. 1286/2 With the honour of a Dukedome also to him and hys heires for euer. **1593** SHAKS. *3 Hen. VI*, II. i. 93. **1642** W. BIRD *Mag. Honor* 30 All that is before spoken concerning the Duke and the Dukedom of Lancaster. **1710** *Lond. Gaz.* No. 4781/1 The Marquisate of Moravia, and the Dukedom of Silesia. **1818** CRUISE *Digest* (ed. 2) VI. 502 Thomas..who became Duke of Norfolk..died without issue, whereby the dukedom descended to Henry. **1885** *Manch. Exam.* 27 Feb. 4/6 It is considered probable that the Marquis..will have a dukedom conferred upon him.

Hence †**dukedomship** (*Obs. rare*) = prec.

1547 BOORDE *Introd. Knowl.* xvi. (1870) 164 Saxsony is [a] Dukedom-shyp, And holdeth of hym selfe. *Ibid.* xxiv. 183 [He] shall not clayme no inheritaunce of the dukedomshyp.

†**dukehood.** *Obs. rare.* In 5 **duchehode**. The office of a duke; dukedom, dukeship.

c **1449** PECOCK *Repr.* IV. iii. 429 Holi Scripture approueth weel Princehode and Duchehode..to be ouer and aboue the comoun peple.

'dukelet. *nonce-wd.* [see -LET.] = next (sense 1).

1870 *Daily News* 16 Dec., Very serviceable in teaching some dukelets and their good ladies better manners.

dukeling ('dju:klɪŋ). [see -LING.]

1. A little or petty duke. (Contemptuous; in quot. 1634, One who claims to be a duke.)

1634 FORD *P. Warbeck* II. iii, This dukeling mushroom Hath doubtless charm'd the king. *Ibid.* V. ii, Urswick, command the dukeling and these fellows, To Digby, the Lieutenant of the Tower. **1890** H. M. STANLEY *Darkest Africa* I. xiv. 363 No proud dukeling in England could regard a pauper with more pronounced contempt.

2. A duke's child.

1612 SYLVESTER *Lacrymæ* 139 For Savoy's Dukelings, or the Florentine, Hee [Prince Henry] wedds his Saviour of a Regall Line. **1618** FLETCHER *Loyal Subj.* II. v, The duke gone thither, do you say?..And all the ducklings too. **1690** CROWNE *Eng. Friar* III. Dram. Wks. 1874 IV. 70 Little squirelings, and knightlings, and lordlings, and dukelings. **1794** WOLCOTT (P. Pindar) *Rowl. for Oliver* Wks. II. 411 Duke, Dukeling, Princess, Prince, consign'd to jail!

dukely ('dju:klɪ), *a. nonce-wd.* [f. DUKE + -LY[1].] Belonging to or befitting a duke.

1826 *Examiner* 119/2 Making somewhat free with his dukely character. **1827** SOUTHEY *Lett.* (1856) IV. 48 The Duke has sent them to me, with a dry and dukely note.

dukery ('dju:kərɪ). Also 6 *Sc.* **duikrie**. [f. DUKE *sb.*: see -ERY, -RY.]

1. †**a.** The office or dignity of a duke, a dukedom (*obs.*). **b.** The territory ruled by a duke, a duchy. (Now only as *nonce-wd.*)

c **1565** LINDESAY (Pitscottie) *Chron. Scot.* (1728) 9 To give him the dukery of Turine. **1596** DALRYMPLE tr. *Leslie's Hist. Scot.* x. 338 He hechtis the forsaid duikrie to the Guernour. **1855** CARLYLE *Prinzenraub* Misc. Ess. 1872 VII. 162 The Albertine line..made apanages, subdivisions, unintelligible little dukes and dukeries of a similar kind.

2. The residence or estate of a duke; *spec.* (usually *pl.*, ***the Dukeries***) a district in Nottinghamshire containing several ducal estates.

1837 SOUTHEY in *Q. Rev.* LIX. 291 A Rookery has been demolished, and a Dukery planted in its stead. **1879** *Standard* 8 Dec. (D.), The Dukeries still exist, but they are little more than a geographical expression. Welbeck Abbey is the last of those palaces for which this part of England was formerly famous. **1884** L. J. JENNINGS in *Croker Papers* III. xxv. 166 Thoresby, the second of the three famous 'Dukeries' which comprise within their domains the scenes of Robin Hood's most popular exploits.

dukeship ('dju:kʃɪp). [f. DUKE *sb.* + -SHIP.] The office or dignity of a duke. Also (with possessive pronoun) as a humorous title for a duke.

? *a* **1500** *Nine Ladies Worthie* in *Chaucer's Wks.* (1561) II. (R.), Yᵉ dukeship of Diamedes & dignitie. **1636** MASSINGER *Gt. Dk. Florence* IV. ii, Will your dukeship Sit down and eat some sugar-plums? **1850** *Tait's Mag.* XVII. 619/2 'Tis for killing English game, your Dukeship.

Dukhobor, var. DOUKHOBOR.

duk-peris, corrupt form of DOUZEPERS, *Obs.*

D.U.K.W., dukw: see DUCK *sb.*[4]

dul, obs. var. of DOLE *sb.*[2]; obs. f. DULL.

dulace, obs. form of DOWLAS.

1552 *Berksh. Ch. Goods* 22 A pece of Dulace.

dulbert ('dʌlbət). *Sc.* and *north. dial.* Also 6 *Sc.* **dowbart**, 7 **dullberd**, 9 **dulbard**. [The first element is app. DULL *a.*; the second is possibly *beard*: cf. Ger. *dummbart*.] A dull or stupid person; one slow of comprehension.

1508 DUNBAR *Flyting w. Kennedie* 66 ȝe, dagone, dowbart, thairof haif thow no dowt! **1681** W. ROBERTSON *Phraseol. Gen.* (1693) 510 Very flockpates, dullberds. **1809** T. DONALDSON *Poems* 45 in *Northumbld. Gloss.* s.v., To learn your exercise be quick, An dinna be a dulbard. **1825** BROCKETT *N.C. Gloss.*, *Dullbirt, Dulburt, Dulbard*, a stupid person, a block-head.

†**dul'cacid**, *a. Obs. rare*[−0]. [ad. late L. *dulcacid-us*, f. *dulcis* sweet + *acidus* sour.]

1656 BLOUNT *Glossogr.*, *Dulcacid*, that which hath a mingled taste with sweet and sower.

‖**dulcamara** (dʌlkə'mɛərə). *Herb.* and *Pharm.* [med.L. = bittersweet, f. L. *dulc-is* sweet + *amāra* bitter (sc. *herba*).] The Woody Nightshade or Bittersweet, *Solanum Dulcamara*; the pharmaceutical preparation of this plant.

1578 LYTE *Dodoens* III. lvii. 397–8 The learned men of our age do cal this herbe..in Latine *Dulcamara* or *Amara Dulcis* ..Dulcamara is of complexion hoate and drie. **1828** STARK *Elem. Nat. Hist.* II. 479 The Belladonna, Stramonium, and Dulcamara, are active poisons. **1847** E. J. SEYMOUR *Severe Dis.* I. 146 Washing the parts..twice daily with the decoction of dulcamara. **1876** HARLEY *Mat. Med.* (ed. 6) 500 Dulcamara..has been distinctly known only since the time of Tragus.

Hence **dulca'marin**, *Chem.*, the glucoside $C_{22}H_{34}O_{10}$, obtained from dulcamara; converted by dilute acids into **dulcama'retin** (see quot.) and glucose.

1863–72 WATTS *Dict. Chem.* II. 347 *Dulcamarin.* **1883** *Syd. Soc. Lex.*, *Dulcamaretin*, $C_{16}H_{26}O_6$, a brown, resinous, tasteless substance obtained from dulcamarin, along with glucose, by the action of dilute acids.

†**dul'carnon.** *Obs.* [a. med.L. *dulcarnon*, corrupted from Arabic *ðū'lqarnayn* two-horned, *bicornis, cornutus*; lit. 'lord or possessor of the two horns'.]

1. A dilemma (= med.L. *cornutus*, CORNUTE *sb.* 5); a non-plus; ***at dulcarnon***, at one's wit's end.

According to Neckham (*De Nat. Rerum*, Rolls, 295) and others, *Dulcarnon* was also a mediæval appellation of the Pythagorean theorem, Euclid I. 47 (it is supposed, from its somewhat two-horned figure). In Pandarus's reply to Cressida (quot. 1374), *Dulcarnon* appears to be confounded with *Elefuga* or *Eleofuga*, an appellation of the *pons asinorum*, Euclid I. 5, mediævally explained as *fuga miserorum*, 'flemyng of wrechis'. See *N. & Q.* (1887) 7th s. IV. 130, and references there given.

c **1374** CHAUCER *Troylus* III. 882 (931), I [Crisseide] am til god me betire mynde sende, At [*v.r.* A] dulcarnoun ryȝt at myn wittis ende. Quod Pandarus, ȝa nece, wele ȝe here: Dulcarnoun clepid is flemyng of wrechis. It semyþ hard for wrechis nil it lere. **1534** MRS. M. ROPER in *More's Wks.* 1441/2 In good fayth father qd. I, I can no ferther goe, but am, (as I trowe Cresede saith in Chaucer) comen to Dulcarnon euen at my wittes ende.

2. A person in a dilemma; one 'halting between two opinions'.

1577 STANYHURST *Descr. Irel.* in Holinshed (1587) II. 28/1 S. Patrike considering, that these sealie soules were (as all dulcarnanes for the more part are) more to be terrified from infidelitie through the paines of hell, than allured to christianitie by the ioies of heauen.

†**dulce** (dʌls), *a. (adv.) Obs.* Also 6 **dulse**. [ad. L. *dulcis* sweet: or a refashioning of DOUCE after the L., through the intermediate *doulce*.]

1. Sweet to the taste or smell.

1500–20 DUNBAR *Poems* xlviii. 47 This garth, most dulce and redolent Off herb and flour. **1597** J. PAYNE *Royal Exch.* 41 To make it dulce and pleasant in the taste.

2. Sweet to the eye, ear, or feelings; pleasing, agreeable, soothing.

1501 DOUGLAS *Pal. Hon.* I. xliv, Thair musick tones war mair cleir And dulcer than..Orpheus harp. **1545** RAYNOLD *Byrth Mankynde* Prol. (1634) 8 Dulse and sugred eloquence. **1572** J. JONES *Bathes Buckstone* 4 a, The dulce, or delectable Bathes, or Welles of Buckstone. *a* **1605** MONTGOMERIE *Misc. Poems* xvii. 57 With blinkis dulce and debonair. **1659** D. PELL *Impr. of Sea* 259 Of that sugred and dulce aspect. [**1709** STRYPE *Ann. Ref.* I. xliv. 479 Which two means, if they should seem to him and his associates too dulce.]

B. *adv.* Sweetly.

1549 *Compl. Scot.* vi. 64 The musician amphion..sang sa dulce, quhil that the stanis mouit. *a* **1562** G. CAVENDISH *Wolsey* (1893) 87 My lords mynstrells, who played there so connyngly and dulce.

dulce, *sb.* [In 1 f. prec. adj.; in 2 = Sp. *dulce*.]

†**1.** Sweetness, gentleness. *Obs.*

1659 D. PELL *Impr. Sea* B vj, The goodness, candor, and dulce of your nature. **1728** NORTH *Mem. Musick* (1846) 88 His lesser peices imitated the dulce of Lute-lessons.

‖**2.** A sweet substance; sweet wine, must.

1844 G. W. KENDALL *Narr. Santa Fé Exped.* II. i. 31 Among the higher order of Mexicans the dinner finishes with fruits, dulces or sweetmeats. **1846** R. FORD *Gatherings from Spain* xi. 130 The sweet hams of the *Alpujarras*..are called *dulces* or sweet, because scarcely any salt is used in the curing. **1870** J. ORTON *Andes & Amazons* II. xxxviii. (1876) 518 [Cacao] yielding, besides chocolate..a wine, and a dulce. **1923** J. HERGESHEIMER *Bright Shawl* 127 Minute fragile dulces, cakes, glazed in green and pink, and ornamental confections of almond paste.

†**dulce**, *v. Obs.* [Refashioned from DOUCE, *doulce v.*: cf. DULCE *a.*] *trans.* To sweeten; to soften, soothe, appease. Hence **dulcing** *vbl. sb.*

1579–80 NORTH *Plutarch* (1676) 83 To dulce and soften the hardned hearts of the multitude. **1603** HOLLAND *Plutarch's Mor.* 54 (R.) For the dulcing, taming, and appeasing of the soul. **1610** —— *Camden's Brit.* I. 68 This Albinus..dulceth and kindly intreateth the men.

dulce, var. form of DULSE.

†**'dulcean**, *a. Obs. rare*[−1]. [f. DULCE *a.* or L. *dulc-is* + -AN.] Dulcet, sweet.

1606 J. RAYNOLDS *Dolarney's Prim.* (1880) 66 With dulcean straynes of heauenly melody.

†**'dulcely**, *adv. Obs.* [f. DULCE *a.* + -LY[2].] In a 'dulce' manner; sweetly; soothingly.

1508 KENNEDIE *Flyting w. Dunbar* 339, I..dulcely drank of eloquence the fontayne. *a* **1577** SIR T. SMITH *Commw. Eng.* III. viii. (1612) 120 They can handle their husbands so well and dulcely. **1592** G. HARVEY *Four Lett.* Sonnets, Nothing so dulcely sweet or kindly dear.

†**'dulceness.** [-NESS.] Sweetness.

c **1535** FISHER *Wks.* (E.E.T.S.) II. 436 By the dulcenes of loue, whiche the holy gost hath put in our hartes. **1605** BACON *Adv. Learn.* II. xxiii. §32 (1873) 238 By too much dulceness, goodness, and facility of nature.

†**'dulceous**, *a. Obs. rare.* [irreg. f. DULCE *a.* or L. *dulc-is* sweet + -OUS.] Sweet.

1688 R. HOLME *Armoury* II. 387/2 The Dulceous [is a] Luscious, or sweet tast.

[**dulcerate, -ation**, erron. ff. DULCORATE, etc.]

†**dul'cescate**, *v. Obs. rare*[−1]. [irreg. f. L. *dulcesc-ĕre* to become sweet + -ATE[3].] *trans.* To sweeten.

1657 TOMLINSON *Renou's Disp.* 370 Art..dulcescates the acid.

dulcet ('dʌlsɪt), *a.* and *sb.* Forms: α. 5–7 **doucet**, 5 **dowcet**; β. 5 **dulcette**, 6 **doulcet(e**, (6–7 **dulced**, 7 **doulced**), 6– **dulcet**. [A refashioning of *doucet* (from F.), after L. *dulcis* sweet: cf. It. *dolcetto*, dim. of *dolce*. See also DOUCET.]

†**1.** Sweet to the taste or smell. *Obs.* or *arch.*

α. *c* **1430** *Two Cookery-bks.* 33 Seson it with Sugre, & loke þat it be poynant & doucet. *c* **1440** *Promp. Parv.* 128/1 Dowcet mete, or swete bake mete. *c* **1475** *Partenay* 972. **1664** EVELYN *Kal. Hort.* (1729) 196 Doucet Pippins.

β. **1398** TREVISA *Barth. De. P.R.* V. xl. (1495) 156 The other partyes..arne the swetter and more dulcette. **1505** *Tower of Doctr.* 49 in *Percy's Reliq.*, Thys dulcet water. **1528** PAYNEL *Salerne's Regim.* H ij, All doulcet wynes. **1623** COCKERAM, *Dulced*, sweet. **1667** MILTON *P.L.* v. 347 And from sweet kernels prest She tempers dulcet creams. **1742** SHENSTONE *Schoolmistress* 312 Whose art did first these dulcet cakes display. **1854** LONGF. *Catawba Wine* vi, But Catawba wine Has a taste more divine, More dulcet, delicious, and dreamy.

2. Sweet to the eye, ear, or feelings; pleasing, agreeable; soothing, gentle. Now chiefly of sounds.

α. **14..** *Prose Leg.* in *Anglia* VIII. 178 Wiþ doucet not and ryme. *c* **1475** *Partenay* 877 Doucet songes hurde of briddes enuiron. *Ibid.* 1008 Fair melusine, the suete doucet made [= maid].

β. **1477** NORTON *Ord. Alch.* v. in Ashm. (1652) 53 With doulced [*MS. in margin* dowcet] speech. **1503** HAWES *Examp. Virt.* v. (Arb.) 20 Her delycate and doulcete complacence. **1567** DRANT *Horace, Ep. to Mæcenas* D iij, He will see the my dulcet frinde. **1607** WALKINGTON *Opt. Glass* xi. 118 It is a dulcet [*ed.* **1664** dulcid] humour. **1667** MILTON *P.L.* I. 712 Dulcet Symphonies and voices sweet. *c* **1750** SHENSTONE *Elegies* vii. 52 Still to her dulcet murmurs not a foe. **1837** DISRAELI *Venetia* II. iii, Her dulcet tones seemed even sweeter than before.

3. *Comb.*, as ***dulcet-chinking, -eyed, -streaming***.

a **1784** JOHNSON *Parody Transl. Medea* ii, With dulcet-streaming sound. *a* **1821** KEATS *Fancy* 81 Dulcet-eyed as Ceres' daughter. **1864** SIR F. PALGRAVE *Norm. & Eng.* III. 23 Five dulcet-chinking pennies.

B. *sb.* †**1.** A dulcet note or tone. *Obs.*

1575 LANEHAM *Let.* (1871) 61 Mine Italian dulcets, my dutch houez, my doobl releas.

†**2.** ? = DOUCET 3. *Obs.*

1583 STANYHURST *Æneis* I. (Arb.) 24 Thee stags vpbreaking they slit to the dulcet or inchepyn.

3. †**a.** A wind instrument: see DOUCET 2. *Obs.* **b.** An organ stop resembling the Dulciana, but an octave higher in pitch; = ***dulciana principal***.

1876 HILES *Catech. Organ* ix, Dulcet, a delicate stop of 4 feet, small scale metal pipes. **1880** E. J. HOPKINS in Grove *Dict. Mus.* II. 598 In the organ made..Green..included [in the Swell] not only a Dulciana but also its octave, the Dulcet or Dulciana Principal.

Hence **'dulcetly** *adv.*, **'dulcetness.**

1528 PAYNEL *Salerne's Regim.* H b, The doulce wynes (for theyr doulcetnes) are vehemently drawen. **1536** *Primer Hen. VIII*, lf. 149 Jesu, the author of buxomnes..Of dulcednes the well of grace. *a* **1555** BRADFORD *Wks.* (Parker Soc.) 338 The..short time that we have to use them should assuage their dulcetness. **1832** L. HUNT *Sonnet* Poems 209 His brow with patient pain dulcetly sour.

dulcian ('dʌlsɪən). *Mus.* [f. L. *dulcis* sweet: cf. next and OF. *doulçaine, doulcine, doucine*, an ancient musical instrument, 'a sort of flute' (Godefroy).] An organ reed-stop; = BASSOON 2.

1852 SEIDEL *Organ* 95 Dulcian is the same as 'bassoon', the latter having originated in an old instrument called the dulcian. **1876** HILES *Catech. Organ* x, Dulcian..is a free-reed [organ stop] of 16 feet.

‖**dulciana** (dʌlsɪ'ɑ:nə, -æ-). *Mus.* [ad. med.L. *dulciana*, 'musici cantus dulcioris species', f. *dulcis* sweet: cf. prec.] An 8-foot organ stop of a soft string-like tone, introduced in 1754 by Snetzler. ***dulciana principal***: = DULCET *sb.* 3 b, q.v.

1776 SIR J. HAWKINS *Hist. Mus.* IV. I. x. 149 The organ at Haerlem is said to have 60 stops, many of them little known to the English workmen, among which are the.. Dulciana, [etc.]. **1870** NELSON in *Eng. Mech.* 11 Feb. 534/1 The organ..by Johannes Snetzler..bears the date 1754. It was the first organ that ever had a dulciana stop, which was Snetzler's invention. **1876** HILES *Catech. Organ* ix, Dulciana, an open stop..It is generally of metal.

†'**dulciary.** *Obs. rare.* [ad. late L. *dulciāri-us* making sweetmeats, f. *dulcis* sweet, *dulcia* sweets.]

1657 *Physical Dict., Dulciaries*, sweetners, such things as sweeten. **1696** in PHILLIPS.

†**dulcid,** *a.* and *sb. Obs.* [A modification of *dulcet, dulced*, after words like *rapid.*]

a. *adj.* Dulcet, sweet. **b.** *sb.* A sweet substance.

1657 TOMLINSON *Renou's Disp.* 19 All dulcid things are agreeable to the Lungs. **1658** R. FRANCK *North. Mem.* (1821) 314 Some with honey and other dulcids have sweetly allured him. **1698** FRYER *Acc. E. India & P.* 182 Tartness.. excellently qualified by a dulcid Sapor.

dul'cific, *a. rare.* [f. L. type **dulcific-us*, f. *dulcis* sweet + *-ficus* making.] Sweetening.

1772 T. NUGENT tr. *Hist. Friar Gerund* I. 50 These narcotic, emolient and dulcific remedies avail not.

dulcification (ˌdʌlsɪfɪ'keɪʃən). [n. of action f. L. *dulcificāre* to DULCIFY.]

1. The action of dulcifying, sweetening, or correcting; *spec.* in *Old Chem.*: see DULCIFY 2.

1612 WOODALL *Surg. Mate* Wks. (1653) 270 Dulcification is the correction of mineral medicaments by ablutions, and the like. **1641** [see DULCORATION]. **1683** PETTUS *Fleta Min.* I. (1686) 126. **1770** *New Dispens.* 457/2 The dulcification of the spirit of salt. **1852** ROSS *Humboldt's Trav.* II. xix. 204 The dulcification of the amylaceous roots.

2. The softening (of a sound) to the ear.

1826 *Examiner* 612/1 A sort of Tuscan dulcification of the *ch.*

'**dulcified,** *ppl. a.* [f. DULCIFY + -ED[1].]

1. Sweetened; *spec.* in *Old Chem.*: see DULCIFY 2.

1612 WOODALL *Surg. Mate* Wks. (1653) 43 A little well dulcified Mercury. **1743** *Lond. & Country Brew.* III. (ed. 2) 234 A Pint of dulcified Spirit of Wine. **1800** *Phil. Trans.* XC. 221 Boiled with dulcified spirit of nitre.

2. Softened in sound.

1789 MRS. PIOZZI *Journ. France* I. 176 In their dulcified pronunciation.

dul'cifluous *a. rare.* [f. L. *dulcis* sweet + *flu-us* flowing + -OUS.] Sweetly or softly flowing.

1727 BAILEY vol. II, *Dulcifluous*, flowing sweetly. **1839** LADY LYTTON *Cheveley* (ed. 2) I. xii. 272 His dulcifluous anathemas against all existing laws. **1895** W. WATSON *On Landor's Hellenics* Poems 33 With beakers rinsed of the dulcifluous wave.

dulcify ('dʌlsɪfaɪ), *v.* [ad. L. *dulcificāre*, f. *dulcis* sweet: see -FY. Cf. F. *dulcifier* (17th c.).]

1. *trans.* To render sweet to the taste, sweeten.

1599 A. M. tr. *Gabelhouer's Bk. Physicke* 152/1 You may ..dulcify it with Suger. **1664** EVELYN *Pomona* Gen. Advt. (1729) 95 One Pound of broad Figs slit, is said to dulcify an Hogs-head of cider. **1727** BRADLEY *Fam. Dict.* s.v. *Birch Tree*, This Wine..may be dulcify'd with Raisins. **1822** LAMB *Elia* Ser. I. *Roast Pig*, Intenerating and dulcifying a substance..so mild and dulcet as the flesh of young pigs.

†**b.** To purify from acidity or other distempered condition. *Obs.*

1673 O. WALKER *Educ.* (1677) 99 Such medicines as dulcify the blood. **1710** *Brit. Apollo* II. Quarterly No. 1. 12/1 Crab's Eyes..Dulcify the Blood.

†**2.** *Old Chem.* To wash the soluble salts out of a substance; to neutralize the acidity of.

1610 B. JONSON *Alch.* II. v, Can you sublime, and dulcefie? calcine? **1662** HOBBES *7 Problems* vi. Wks. 1845 VII. 48. **1683** PETTUS *Fleta Min.* I. (1686) 126 Pour the Aqua fortis off, and dulcify the Gold with warm water. **1696** *Phil. Trans.* XIX. 350 The Astroites..will not only stir in Vinegar, but also Dulcifie it. **1789** J. KEIR *Dict. Chem.* 32/2 Their..oily part, which dulcifies the acid.

†**b.** *intr.* for *pass.*

1686 W. HARRIS tr. *Lemery's Course Chym.* I. x, The oftner it is sublimed, the more it does dulcify, and becomes proper to apply to flesh, where we would gently corrode.

3. *transf.* and *fig.* To sweeten in temper; to render gentle, soften, mollify; to appease.

a **1669** TRAPP in Spurgeon *Treas. Dav.* Ps. cxix. 122 There are that render the words thus, 'Dulcify, or, delight thy servant in good'. **1694** CROWNE *Married Beau* IV. Dram. Wks. 1874 IV. 301, I am mollified; I will go home, and be dulcified. **1770** J. LOVE *Cricket* 1 This Title might have been dulcified; and..rendered extremely polite and unintelligible. **1831** *Blackw. Mag.* XXX. 217 Time had not dulcified the tempers of the three elder.

4. *intr.* To speak in dulcet or bland tones.

1839 LADY LYTTON *Cheveley* (ed. 2) III. iii. 87 As she had dulcified sufficiently with..the duchess. **1856** *Chamb. Jrnl.* V. 44 'Waiter', dulcifies an urbane gentleman.

Hence '**dulcifying** *vbl. sb.* and *ppl. a.*; '**dulcifier**.

1727–51 CHAMBERS *Cycl., Dulcifying*, a term used in physic, for rendering a fluid less acid, and rough. **1816** SCOTT *Antiq.* i, The pleasure of this discourse had such a dulcifying tendency. **1847** *Tait's Mag.* XIV. 163 A kind of general dulcifier of all acerbities.

dulciloquent (dʌl'sɪləkwənt). *a.* [f. L. *dulcis* sweet + *loquens*, pres. pple. of *loqui* to speak.] Speaking sweetly.

1656 BLOUNT *Glossogr., Dulciloquent* (*dulciloquus*), that speaks sweetly. **1840** *New Monthly Mag.* LIX. 248 Most dulciloquent and incomparable Miss Camilla.

†**dul'ciloquy.** *Obs. rare.* [ad. L. **duciloquium* sweet speech; cf. L. *soliloquium* soliloquy.] A soft or pleasant manner of speaking.

1623 COCKERAM, *Dulciloquie*, sweet speaking. **1731** BAILEY, *Dulciloquy.* **1846** WORCESTER cites MAUNDER. Hence in mod. Dicts.

dulcimer ('dʌlsɪmə(r)). Also 6 douci-, dousse-, dowcemer, (7 dulcimel). [a. OF. *doulcemer* (Roquefort), *doulcemele, doulz de mer* (Godef.) = obs. Sp. *dulcemele*, It. *dolcemelle* (Florio); supposed to represent L. *dulce melos* sweet song, tune, or air. (The L. in this application is not known.)]

1. A musical instrument, in which strings of graduated lengths are stretched over a trapezoidal sounding board or box and struck with two hammers held in the hands.

Considered to be the earliest prototype of the pianoforte.

? *c* **1475** *Sqr. lowe Degre* 1075 With fydle, recorde, and dowcemere. **1509** HAWES *Past. Pleas.* XVI. xi, Cymphans, doussemers, wyth claricimbales glorious. **1662** PEPYS *Diary* 23 May, Here among the fiddlers I first saw a dulcimere played on with sticks knocking of the strings, and is very pretty. **1667** MILTON *P.L.* VII. 596 The solemn Pipe, And Dulcimer, all Organs of sweet stop. **1879** STAINER *Music of Bible* 45 The dulcimer became a genuine string-instrument constructed without a neck.

b. It has sometimes been applied erroneously to wind-instruments. In Dan. iii. 5, etc. it is used to render *sûmpōnyâh*, Gr. συμφωνία, which was a kind of bagpipe; while the word rendered 'psaltery' in the same passage signifies 'dulcimer'. *Oxf. Helps to Study of Bible.*

1567 MAPLET *Gr. Forest* 42 The Elder..Hereof are made ..a kind of Symphonie whiche the common sort call a Pipe: the learned and more civil kinde of men name it a Dulcimer. **1611** BIBLE *Dan.* iii. 10 The sound of the cornet, flute, harpe, sackbut, psalterie, and dulcimer [COVERD. Symphonies, *R.V. marg.* or bagpipe].

attrib. **1801** MAR. EDGEWORTH *Good French Governess* (1832) 195 The little boy belonging to the dulcimer man.

†**2.** A kind of bonnet. *Obs.*

a **1790** WARTON *High-St. Trag.* (R.), With bonnet trimm'd and flounced withal, Which they a dulcimer do call.

dulcin ('dʌlsɪn). *Chem.* Also dulcine. [f. L. *dulcis* sweet + -IN[1].] **a.** = DULCITE, DULCITOL.

1862 H. WATTS tr. *Gmelin's Hand-bk. Chem.* XV. 384 Dulcite $C_{12}H_{14}O_{12}$... Dulcose (Laurent); Dulcine (Jacquelain). **1920** C. T. KINGZETT *Pop. Chem. Dict.* 116 Dulcitol or Dulcin or Dulcite ($C_6H_{14}O_6$).

b. A synthetic crystalline derivative of phenetidine which has been used as a sweetening agent; *p*-ethoxyphenylurea, $C_9H_{12}N_2O_2$; *p*-phenetylurea.

1893 J. ATTFIELD *Chem.* (ed. 15) 514 Para-phenetol-carbamide or dulcin is a body having a very powerful sweet taste, and proposed for use, like saccharin, in place of sugar. **1912** *Jrnl. Chem. Soc.* CII. II. 104 Detection and identification of 'saccharin' and 'dulcin' in beverages, foods, drugs, cosmetics, etc. **1948** GARDNER & COOKE *Chem. Synonyms* (ed. 5) 187/1 Dulcine..is 200 times sweeter than cane sugar. **1959** S. DAVIDSON et al. *Human Nutrition & Dietetics* lvii. 788 The use of dulcin as an alternative sweetening agent to saccharin..was found to cause liver tumours in animals.

‖**Dulcinea** (dʌl'sɪnɪə, dʌlsɪ'niːə). [Sp. deriv. of *dulce* sweet.] The name given by Don Quixote to his mistress in Cervantes' romance; hence, A mistress, sweetheart, lady of one's devotion.

1748 SMOLLETT *Rod. Rand.* (1812) I. 40 His dulcinea.. persuaded him. **1777** G. FORSTER *Voy. round World* I. 404 Our sailors..took it for granted that their dulcineas were all of one name. **1815** W. H. IRELAND *Scribbleomania* 134 *note*, The fables of knights errant and their persecuted dulcineas. **1829** LONGF. in *Life* (1891) I. 171.

[**dulciness,** in Webster 1828 and later Dicts., attributed to Bacon; an error for DULCENESS, q.v.]

Dulcinist ('dʌlsɪnɪst). Also **dolcinist.** [ad. med.L. *Dulcinistæ* (pl.), followers of *Dulcinus* or *Dulcino*: see -IST.] One of a religious sect, identical with the Apostolicals, who opposed the papacy and rejected oaths, marriage, and rites and ceremonies generally. So '**Dulcinite**.

1721 BAILEY, *Dulcinists*, a sort of Hereticks. **1884** *Ch. Q. Rev.* XVIII. 351 Nor does the defence of the Dolcinists in the 13th century, afford a capable brief to the assailant of Christianity.

†**dul'cisonant,** *a. Obs. rare*[−0]. [f. L. type **dulcisonānt-em*, f. *dulcis* sweet + *sonāre* to sound.]

1656 BLOUNT *Glossogr., Dulcisonant* (*dulcisonus*), that sounds sweetly.

dulcite ('dʌlsaɪt). *Chem.* [f. L. *dulc-is* sweet + -ITE.] A saccharine substance ($C_6H_{14}O_6$) similar to and isomeric with mannite, obtained from various plants, and known in the crude state as Madagascar manna. Also called **dulcin, dulcitol, dulcose**.

1863–72 WATTS *Dict. Chem.* II. 349 Dulcite (from Madagascar) crystallises in colourless highly lustrous prisms of the monoclinic system.

Hence '**dulcitaˌmine**, the amine or compound ammonia of dulcite $C_6H_8(OH)_5.NH_2$. '**dulcitan**, the anhydride of dulcite, $C_6H_{12}O_5$, a very viscid neutral syrup. '**dulcitaˌnide**, a compound of dulcitan with an acid, analogous to the mannitides and glycerides, as ***benzo-, butyro-dulcitanide***.

1863–72 WATTS *Dict. Chem., Dulcitan*..the anhydride of dulcite ($C_6H_{14}O_6 - H_2O$), obtained by heating dulcite for some time to near 200°C. *Ibid., Dulcitanides*..may be regarded as dulcitan, in which 2 or 4 at. H are replaced by acid radicles. **1873** *Fownes' Chem.* (ed. 11) 632 Dulcite.. heated with organic acids forms ethers called dulcitanides.. yielding by saponification, not dulcite, but dulcitan.

dulcitol ('dʌlsɪtɒl). *Chem.* [f. DULCIT(E + -OL.] = DULCITE.

1884 *Jrnl. Chem. Soc.* XLVI. 1284 Dulcitol is neutral to litmus. **1938** *Thorpe's Dict. Appl. Chem.* (ed. 4) II. 296/1 Haas has detected both dulcitol and sorbitol in a red seaweed. **1970** R. W. MCGILVERY *Biochem.* xxvi. 639 Some infants have defects of galactose metabolism... If the kinase is missing..the accumulation of galactose leads to formation of cataracts through reduction to the corresponding hexitol, dulcitol.

dulcitone ('dʌlsɪtəʊn). [f. L. *dulcis* sweet + TONE *sb.*] A keyboard instrument in which steel forks are struck by hammers (see quot. 1888).

1888 T. MACHELL *Brit. Pat. 4071* 1 My invention, which I call 'The Dulcitone', has been designed to meet the want now generally felt of a portable keyboard percussion instrument... In the 'Dulcitone' the sound producers (hereinafter referred to as forks) are bars of steel bent into a U form, the forks being of graduated lengths for the various musical notes. **1909** *Chambers's Jrnl.* Mar. 206/2 The dulcitone is a musical instrument on the lines of the pianoforte. **1923** R. NOBLE *Shakespeare's Use of Song* 17 The dulcitone, which is portable and is capable of being performed upon by an actor or actress of moderate musical accomplishment. **1970** R. SMITH BRINDLE *Contemp. Percussion* 63 The dulcitone, as its name suggests, is soft and sweet, with a bell-like sound not unlike the celesta.

dulcitude ('dʌlsɪtjuːd). [ad. L. *dulcitūdo* sweetness, f. *dulcis* sweet.] Sweetness.

1623 COCKERAM II, *Sweetnesse*, Dulcitude. **1652** F. KIRKMAN *Clerio & Lozia* 127 The charming dulcitude of a fair reputation. **1847** L. HUNT *Men, Women, & B.* II. iv. 55 The sweeter it, for preserving its dulcitudes as it did.

†'**dulcity.** *Obs.* [ad. L. *dulcitās* sweetness, f. *dulcis* sweet.] Sweetness.

1623 COCKERAM, *Dulcitie*, Sweetnesse. **1634** SIR T. HERBERT *Trav.* 183 Which seeme to have dulcitie and acrimony mixt together. **1657** TOMLINSON *Renou's Disp.* 38 The austerity..expelled, dulcity succeeds.

†**dulcoacid,** *a. Obs.* [irreg. f. L. *dulcis* sweet + ACID.] = DULCACID.

1657 *Physical Dict., Dulcoacid*, sweet, and yet sharp, as syrup of lemons. **1657** TOMLINSON *Renou's Disp.* 165* If dulcoacid, incide..and prepare viscous and crasse Phlegme.

†**dulcoamare,** *a. Obs.* [irreg. f. L. *dulcis* sweet + *amārus* bitter.] Bitter-sweet.

1657 *Physical Dict., Dulcoamare*, bitterish sweet. **1657** TOMLINSON *Renou's Disp.* 165* If dulcoamare, deterge, coct and expurgate.

†**dulcor, -our.** *Obs.* [a. L. *dulcor* sweetness, f. *dulc-is* sweet.] Sweetness, pleasantness.

c **1450** *Mirour Saluacioun* 153 A full swete voice..full of all dulcoure. **1552** LYNDESAY *Monarche* 584 Withouttin dolour, dulcore and delyte. **1599** A. M. tr. *Gabelhouer's Bk. Physicke* 116/2 Suger mixed therwith..accordinge as we desire the dulcor therof. **1675** L. ADDISON *State of Jews* 176 (T.) That by its colour and dulcour they might be remembered of the purity and delightfulness of the law.

†'**dulcorate,** *a. Obs. rare.* [ad. L. *dulcōrāt-us*, pa. pple. of *dulcōrāre*: see next.] Endowed with sweetness; sweet.

1501 DOUGLAS *Pal. Hon.* II. v, The ladyis sang in voices dulcorait.

†**dulcorate** ('dʌlkɒreɪt), *v. Obs.* [f. ppl. stem of L. *dulcōrāre* to sweeten, f. *dulcor*: see prec.] *trans.* To sweeten, DULCIFY; to free from acridity.

1566 PAINTER *Pal. Pleas.* II. 145 b, To dulcorate and make sweet the bitter gall of griefe. **1620** VENNER *Via Recta* (1650) 258 A few Aniseeds dulcorated with white Sugar Candie. **1669** EVELYN *Vintage* (1675) 47 Some dulcorate, and sweeten their wines..with raisins of the sun. **1675** E. BORLACE *Reduct. Irel.* 174 Conducing to dulcorate the humour apt to ferment with so much virulency.

Hence '**dulcorating** *vbl. sb.*; **dulco'ration**.

1626 BACON *Sylva* §358 In the Dulcoration of some Metalls; as *Saccharum Saturni. Ibid.* §465 The Ancients for the Dulcorating of Fruit, doe commend Swines-dung, aboue all other Dung. **1641** FRENCH *Distill.* i. (1651) 10 Dulcoration, or dulcification is either the washing off the salt from any matter that was calcined therewith..or it is sweetening of things with sugar or honey, or syrup.

†'**dulcorous,** *a. Obs. rare*[−1]. [f. L. *dulcor* sweetness + -OUS.] Sweet.

1675 EVELYN *Terra* (1729) 28 Some [Plants] are acid, other more dulcorous and sweet.

dulcour, var. of DULCOR, *Obs.*

dule, var. f. DOLE *sb.*[2] grief; Sc. f. DOOL, landmark: obs. and dial. f. DEVIL.

duledge (ˈdjuːlɪdʒ). [Cf. DOWEL.] A dowel or peg for connecting the felloes of the wheels of gun-carriages.

1721 in BAILEY. **1753** CHAMBERS *Cycl. Supp.*, *Duledge*, in gunnery, a peg of wood which joins the ends of the six fellows, which form the round of the wheel of a gun-carriage; and the joint is strengthened on the outside of the wheel by a strong plate of iron, called the Duledge plate.

dulful(l, obs. form of DOLEFUL.

duli, var. DOOLIE; obs. form of DULY.

‖**dulia** (duːˈlaɪə). Also **douleia**. [med.L., a Gr. δουλεία slavery, servitude, f. δοῦλος slave, bondsman.] Servitude, service; *spec.* the inferior kind of veneration paid by Roman Catholics to saints and angels; opposed to LATRIA.

[**1613** PURCHAS *Pilgrimage, Descr. India* (1864) 15 The Iesuites distinction of *douleia* and *latreia*.] **1617** COLLINS *Def. Bp. Ely* II. ix. 369 Austen patronizeth not your dulia to Saints. **1623** COCKERAM, *Dulia*, seruice of a bondman, worship to Saints. **1844** LINGARD *Anglo-Sax. Ch.* (1858) II. x. 10 The worship of *latria* due to God, and that of *dulia*, the respect which may justly be shewn to his creatures. **1865** *Union Rev.* III. 404 The hyperdulia and dulia due respectively to our Blessed Lady and the Saints coregnant with Christ.

Hence (*nonce-wds.*) ˈ**dulian** *a.*, pertaining to dulia; ˈ**dulically** *adv.*, by way of dulia.

1617 COLLINS *Def. Bp. Ely* II. ix. 368 Austen neuer said that we may adore a creature..with a relligious adoration, no not vnder latria, or neuer so dulically. **1635** PAGITT *Christianogr.* II. vii. (1636) 68 The Romists say that they give to the Saints one kinde of worship, to wit, Dulian.

dulipan, early form of TURBAN.

1600 J. PORY tr. *Leo's Africa* III. 160 On their heads they wear a black dulipan.

dull (dʌl), *a.* Forms: 3–6 dul, 4–6 dulle, (5 dol(e), 6 *Sc.* doll, 4– dull. See also DILL *a.* [ME. *dul*, *dull*, found once in 13th c., but not usual bef. 1350; beside which *dil*, *dill*, *dylle*, is found in same sense 1200–1440. The two appear to point to an OE. **dyl*, **dylle*:— **duljo-*, a parallel form to OE. *dol* foolish (:— **dulo-*) = OS. and Du. *dol*, OHG. *tol* (Ger. *toll*), from the Germanic *dul-*, ablaut-form of *dwel-* to be foolish.]

1. Not quick in intelligence or mental perception; slow of understanding; not sharp of wit; obtuse, stupid, inapprehensive. In early use, sometimes: Wanting wit, fatuous, foolish.

[*c* **940** *Seafarer* 106 Dol biþ se ðe him his Dryhten ne ondrædeþ. *c* **975** *Rushw. Gosp.* Matt. v. 22 Seðe þanne cwæþe dysiȝ *vel* dole [Vulg. *fatue*; *Ags. G.* þu stunta] he biþ scyldiȝ helle fyres.] *a* **1000** *Riddles* xii. 3 Ic..dole hwette. *a* **1250** *Leg. Kath.* 1268 Wacre þen eni wake! of deað & of dul [*earlier MSS.* dult] wit! *c* **1340** HAMPOLE *Prose Tr.* (1866) 40 If thi herte be dulle and myrke and felis noþer witt ne sauour ne deuocyone for to thynke. **1362** LANGL. *P. Pl.* A. I. 129 'Þou dotest daffe' quaþ heo 'Dulle are þi wittes'. **1398** TREVISA *Barth. De P.R.* XVIII. i. (1495) 735 The oxe is slowe and stable and the asse dull of wytte. **1413** *Pilgr. Sowle* (Caxton 1483) IV. xxiv. 70 She fond the soo dulle and soo lothe to hir wordes. **1494** FABYAN *Chron.* 2 To my dull wytte it is nat atteynaunt. **1576** FLEMING *Panopl. Epist.* 269 The blunt and dull capacities of them that give judgement. **1651** HOBBES *Leviath.* II. xxv. 135 Feare of appearing duller in apprehension. **1690** LOCKE *Hum. Und.* II. i. (1695) 44, I confess myself to have one of those dull Souls, that doth not perceive it self always to contemplate Ideas. **1751** JORTIN *Serm.* (1771) VI. ii. 32 The Israelites were a dull and a carnal people. **1833** HT. MARTINEAU *Briery Creek* i. 8 He was rather a dull child—usually called uncommonly stupid.

2. a. Wanting sensibility or keenness of perception in the bodily senses and feelings; insensible, obtuse, senseless, inanimate. In dialect use, *esp.* Hard of hearing, deaf.

c **1340** *Cursor M.* 3564 (Trin.) His body waxeþ drye & dulle [*Gött.* dall; *not in Cott.* or *Fairf.*]. **1500–20** DUNBAR *Poems* xv. 9 And he that dronis ay as ane bee Sowld haif ane heirar dull as stane. **1526–34** TINDALE *Matt.* xiii. 15 Their eares were dull of herynge. **1590** SPENSER *F.Q.* I. x. 18 She ..opened his dull eyes, that light mote in them shine. **1613** SHAKS. *Hen. VIII*, III. ii. 434 And when I am forgotten.. And sleepe in dull cold Marble. *a* **1791** GROSE *Olio* (1796) 115 By dull I only mean hard of hearing. **1830** TENNYSON *Poet's Mind* 35 You never would hear it; your ears are so dull. **1878** J. P. HOPPS *Jesus* iv. 18 The light came again into the poor dull eyes.

b. Of pain or other sensation: Not keen or intense; slightly or indistinctly felt.

1725 N. ROBINSON *Th. Physick* 165 A heavy, dull Pain generally affects the Patient, either on the Right or Left Side. *Mod.* A sharp pain, followed by a dull ache.

3. a. Slow in motion or action; not brisk; inert, sluggish, inactive; heavy, drowsy.

1393 GOWER *Conf.* III. 6 My limmes ben so dull, I may unethes gon the pas. **1530** PALSGR. 311/1 Dull at the spurre as a horse is, *restif*. **1590** SPENSER *F.Q.* I. vii. 5 Thenceforth her waters wexed dull and slow. **1625** J. GLANVILL *Voy. Cadiz* (1883) 56, I gott a dull and ill paced horse. **1699** DAMPIER *Voy.* II. II. 20 Our Ketch, even when light, was but a dull Sailer. **1788** FRANKLIN *Autobiog.* Wks. 1840 I. 222 When we came to sea she proved the dullest of ninety-six sail. **1849** E. E. NAPIER *Excurs. S. Africa* II. 9 The long whips could not urge the dull, lean teams into a quicker pace. **1869** HAZLITT *Eng. Prov.* 49 All work and no play makes Jack a dull boy.

b. Of trade: Sluggish, stagnant; the opposite of *brisk*. Hence *transf.* of goods or merchandise: Not much in demand, not easily saleable.

1705 BOSMAN *Guinea* 73 Trade being extremely dull at that time. **1729** FRANKLIN *Ess.* Wks. 1840 II. 275 If raising wheat proves dull, more may proceed to the raising and manufacturing of hemp, silk, iron. **1797** T. JEFFERSON *Writ.* (1859) IV. 182 Flour is dull at $7·50. **1863** FAWCETT *Pol. Econ.* I. iv. 43 Dull trade is always prejudicial to them. **1892** E. REEVES *Homewd. Bound* 205 This being the dull season, we arranged terms at about half price. **1895** *Times* 17 Jan. 4/1 In the Market..Consols opened dull at 104½.

4. Of persons, or their mood: Having the natural vivacity or cheerfulness blunted; having the spirits somewhat depressed; listless; in a state approaching gloom, melancholy, or sadness: the opposite of *lively* or *cheerful*.

c **1393** CHAUCER *Scogan* 45 Scogan þat knelist at þe wellis hed Of grace of alle honour and worþynesse In þe ende of wich strem I am dul as ded. *c* **1475** *Lerne or be Lewde* in *Babees Bk.* (1868) 9 To Dulle, ne to Dredefulle, ne Drynke nat to offte. **1590** SHAKS. *Com. Err.* v. i. 79 Sweet recreation barr'd, what doth ensue But moodie and dull melancholly? **1709** STEELE *Tatler* No. 45 ¶7 You are dull to Night; prithee be merry. **1840** DICKENS *Barn. Rudge* vii, When other people were merry, Mrs. Varden was dull. **1877** SPURGEON *Serm.* XXIII. 103 They say they are 'dull' if they have to be quiet for a while.

5. Causing depression or ennui; tedious, uninteresting, uneventful; the reverse of exhilarating or enlivening.

1590 SHAKS. *Com. Err.* II. i. 91 Are my discourses dull? Barren my wit? **1693** *Hum. & Conv. Town* 63 Some admirable Passage in the last dull Prologue. **1716** LADY M. W. MONTAGU *Let. to Mrs. Thistlethwayte* 26 Sept., I have already said too much on so dull a subject. **1798** DK. CLARENCE 1 June in Nicolas *Nelson's Disp.* III. 10 *note*, I trust the Campaign..will be less dull than you imagine. **1838** LYTTON *Alice* 23 Good curates generally are dull. **1892** *Bookseller* 18/2 There is no fear of Sunday being a dull day for the little ones.

6. Not sharp or keen; blunt (in *lit.* sense).

[*c* **1400** *Destr. Troy* 10548 Parys cast at the kyng..þre darttes noght dole.] *c* **1440** *Promp. Parv.* 135/1 Dulle of egge, *obtusus*. **1594** SHAKS. *Rich. III*, IV. iv. 226 No doubt the murd'rous knife was dull and blunt, Till it was whetted on thy stone-hard heart. **1633** G. HERBERT *Temple, Time* i, Meeting with Time, Slack thing, said I, Thy sithe is dull; whet it for shame. **1719** DE FOE *Crusoe* I. v, I had three large axes..but with much chopping and cutting..they were all full of notches, and dull. **1835** WHITTIER *Mogg Megone* II. iv, Time..Wielding the dull axe of Decay.

7. a. Of or in reference to physical qualities, as colour or luminosity, sound, taste: Not clear, bright, vivid, or intense; obscure, dim; indistinct, muffled; flat, insipid. **b.** Of the weather: Not clear or bright; cheerless, gloomy, overcast. (Here there is app. some mixture of sense 5.)

c **1430** LYDG. *Min. Poems* 151 (Mätz.) Al is dul shadwe, whan Phebus is doun goon. **1552** HULOET, Dulle or sadde coloure, *rauus* [printed *raucus*] *color*. **1599** SHAKS. *Hen. V*, III. v. 16 Is not their Clymate foggy, raw, and dull? **1611** —— *Cymb.* II. iv. 41 Sparkles this Stone as it was wont, or is't not Too dull for your good wearing? **1694** *Acc. Sev. Late Voy.* II. (1711) 4 On the 19th we had a dull Sun-shine. **1699** DAMPIER *Voy.* II. II. 66 Of a dull grey. **1816** J. SMITH *Panorama Sc. & Art* II. 826 The alloys of platina with silver give only a dull metal. **1836** DUBOURG *Violin* i. (1878) 11 In character of sound, the viol instruments were decidedly sweet, but comparatively dull. **1860** TYNDALL *Glac.* I. xxvii. 195 The dawn was dull, but the sky cleared as the day advanced.

8. *Comb.*, as ***dull-disposed***, ***-looking***, ***-making***, ***-smelling*** adjs.; parasynthetic, as ***dull-brained***, ***-browed***, ***-coloured***, †***-conceited***, ***-edged***, ***-eyed***, ***-featured***, ***-hearted***, ***-scented***, ***-sighted***, ***-spirited***, ***-surfaced***, ***-voiced*** adjs.; also **dull emitter**, a thermionic valve in which the filament operates at a relatively low temperature, and so does not glow brightly; also, such a filament; also *attrib.*; hence ***dull-emitting*** adj.; † **dull-house** [*transl.* Du. *dolhuis*, in Kilian *dulhuys*], a mad-house. See also DULL-HEAD, -HEADED, etc.

1594 SHAKS. *Rich. III*, IV. iv. 332 *Dull-brain'd Buckingham. **1644** QUARLES *Barnabas & B.*, *Sensual Man* (T.), A pitch beyond the reach of *dull-browed sorrow. *a* **1592** H. SMITH *Wks.* (1867) II. 369 They cannot be so sottish or *dull conceited. **1599** B. JONSON *Cynthia's Rev.* IV. i, The most melancholick and *dull-disposed creature upon earth. *a* **1631** DRAYTON *Wks.* III. 1176 (Jod.) *Dull-edg'd tools. **1922** *Wireless World* 30 Sept. 858/2 The set has been designed that either R or '*Dull Emitter' valves can be fitted, the latter permitting of the operation of the set from dry cells. **1923** *Ibid.* 5 May 137/2 The dull-emitting filaments of the valves are made from thoriated tungsten and ..if thoriated tungsten had not proved useful in electric lamp manufacture, there would not exist to-day the 'dull-emitter' valve. **1923** *Exper. Wireless* Nov. 97/2 The object of the dull emitter is to obtain the same filament emission with only a fraction of the energy previously required to render the ordinary filament sufficiently incandescent. **1970** D. F. SHAW *Introd. Electronics* (ed. 2) x. 209 Oxide-coated cathodes..glow a dull red and they are therefore called dull emitters, contrasted with tungsten filaments which are bright emitters. **1596** SHAKS. *Merch. V.* III. iii. 14 Ile not be made a soft and *dull ey'd foole. **1870** MORRIS *Earthly Par.* II. III. 121 This helped him through his dull-eyed woe. **1622** T. SCOTT *Belg. Pismire* 79 Their Bedlams and *Dul-houses for distracted people. **1581** SIDNEY *Apol. Poetrie* (Arb.) 72 If ..you be borne so neere the *dull making Cataphract of Nilus, that you cannot heare the Plannet-like Musick of Poetrie. **1552** HULOET, *Dulle sighted or poreblinde, *rauos oculos habens*. **1686** *Lond. Gaz.* No. 2188/4 A light Grey Gelding..dull Sighted, especially in the right Eye. **1616–61** HOLYDAY *Persius* (1673) 335 Whether he buy *dull-smelling cinnamun. **1597** HOOKER *Eccl. Pol.* v. xxx. §4 To play vpon *dull-spirited men.

dull (dʌl). *v.* Also 4 doulle. [f. DULL *a.*]

I. *trans.* To make dull, in various senses.

1. To render sluggish or inert; to deprive of quickness, sharpness, or activity; to stupefy (a person, or the mind, understanding, wits, etc.).

c **1392** CHAUCER *Compl. Venus* 76 Ffor eelde þat in my spiryt doulleþe me. *c* **1440** *Promp. Parv.* 135/1 Dullyn, or make dulle in wytte, *hebeto*. **1571** GOLDING *Calvin on Ps.* xxxix. 8 They wilfully dull themselves, that they may sleepe soundly in their owne vanitie. **1604** SHAKS. *Oth.* II. iii. 394 Dull not Deuice, by coldnesse, and delay. **1625** BACON *Ess.*, *Usury* (Arb.) 543 Vsury..doth Dull and Dampe all Industries..wherin Money would be Stirring, if it were not for this Slugge. **1678** R. BARCLAY *Apol. Quakers* v. §21. 165 Man is dull'd by an evil habit. **1877** E. R. CONDER *Bas. Faith* ii. 89 Without dulling their responsiveness to each new impression.

†**b.** To pass *away* in sloth or inactivity. *Obs.*

1682 SIR T. BROWNE *Chr. Mor.* I. §33 Dull not away thy days in slothful supinity.

†**2.** To render dull of mood; to make listless, or somewhat gloomy: the opposite of to enliven. *Obs.*

c **1386** CHAUCER *Can. Yeom. Prol. & T.* 540 Of his falshede it dulleth me to ryme. *c* **1400** *Destr. Troy* 11314 Youre dedis me dullis, & dos out of hope. **1576** FLEMING *Panopl. Epist.* 64 My desire is not to dull you, if I can not delight you. *c* **1600** SHAKS. *Sonn.* cii, I would not dull you with my song. *a* **1611** BEAUM. & FL. *Philaster* III. i, The nobles and the people are all dulled With this usurping king.

3. To render less sensitive; to take away the keenness of, blunt (the bodily senses or organs).

1552 HULOET, Dulle or darken with ouer muche lyght, *perstringo*. **1578** LYTE *Dodoens* IV. xxx. 488 If one eate to muche thereof, it dulleth the sight. **1633** BP. HALL *Hard Texts* 292 Their ears shall be dulled and deafened. **1812** J. WILSON *Isle of Palms* II. 161 Each sense is dull'd! *a* **1822** SHELLEY *M.N. Post. Fr.* 16 For passion's voice had dull'd their listless ear.

b. To render (feeling) less keen or intense.

1651 HOBBES *Govt. & Soc.* i. §2. 4 That the Appetite, of present matters, be dul'd with the memory of things past. **1832** TENNYSON *To J.S.* 40 Weep, weeping dulls the inward pain.

4. To take off the sharpness of, to blunt (an edge or point, or something edged or pointed). Often *fig.* in phr. ***to dull the edge of*** = 3 b.

c **1400** *Destr. Troy* 5131 Þen Vlixes..The derfe wordis of Diamede dullit with speche. *c* **1440** *Promp. Parv.* 135/1 Dullyn, or make dulle in egge toole, *obtundo*. **1591** SYLVESTER *Du Bartas* I. i. 128 My Reason's edge is dull'd in this Dispute. **1607** TOPSELL *Four-f. Beasts* (1658) 359 Leopards..and Lions, do hide their clawes within their skin when they go or run, that so they might not be dulled. *a* **1716** SOUTH *Serm.* IV. ii. (R.), How quickly the edge of their valour was dulled. **1821** B. CORNWALL *Mirandola* II. ii, Your sword is dulled With carnage, I am told.

5. To take away the brightness, clearness, vividness, or intensity of; to make dim or indistinct; to tarnish. Also *fig.*

c **1386** CHAUCER *Pars. T.* ¶159 Þe goode werkes þat he dede..ben amortised and astoneyed and dullid by ofte synnynge. *c* **1425** WYNTOUN *Cron.* II. x. 24 Swa suld I dulle hale yhoure Delyte. **1596** SPENSER *F.Q.* VI. iii. 13 In which they [the sun's beams] steeped lay All night in darkenesse, duld with yron rust. **1630** DAVENANT *Cruel Bro.* III. Dram. Wks. 1872 I. 157 Foreste is the man That dulls your reputation with the Duke. **1870** MORRIS *Earthly Par.* III. IV. 185 The swift footfalls Were dulled upon the marble floor By silken webs from some far shore. **1872** BLACK *Adv. Phaeton* xvii. 237 A sort of mist..dulling the rich colours of the glen. **1892** WESTCOTT *Gospel of Life* 220 The image of God in man if dulled has not been destroyed.

II. *intr.* To become dull, in various senses.

6. To become stupid, inert, blunt, dim, etc.; to lose force, intensity, keenness, or clearness.

c **1374** CHAUCER *Boeth.* I. metr. ii. 3 (Camb. MS.) Allas how the thowt of man dreynt in ouerthrowynge depnesse dulleþ and forletiþ his propre cleernesse. *c* **1450** *Cov. Myst.* (Shaks. Soc.) 343 Myn heed dullyth, Myn herte ffullyth Of sslepp. **1509** FISHER *Fun. Serm. C'tess Richmond* Wks. (1876) 305 Her heryynge sholde haue dulled. **1591** SYLVESTER *Du Bartas* I. vi. 230 A pregnant Wit; Which rusts and duls, except it subject finde Worthy it's worth, whereon itself to grinde. **1633** T. JAMES *Voy.* 22 The winde duld something. **1862** G. P. SCROPE *Volcanos* 35 The lava was visible at a white heat, gradually dulling to a faint red. **1871** BLACK *Dau. Heth* III. ii. 24 The day had dulled somewhat.

†**b.** To be inactive or sluggish; to drowse. *Obs.*

1430 LYDG. *Chron. Troy* II. xx, My counsayle is our ankers up to pulle In this matter no longer that we dulle. *c* **1440** *Jacob's Well* (E.E.T.S.) 281 Þat þou schalt noȝt dullyn and slawthyn in þi labour of þi prayers.

†**7.** To become dull, listless, or somewhat gloomy; to grow weary, tire (*of* something). *Obs.*

[*c* **1220** *Bestiary* 383 in *O. Eng. Misc.* 12 Ðus is ure louerdes laȝe, luuelike to fillen, her-of haue we mikel ned, ðat we ðar-wið ne dillen.] *c* **1374** CHAUCER *Troylus* IV. 1461 (1489) That ye shul dullen of þe rudenesse Of vs sely Troians. *c* **1440** *Gesta Rom.* xx. 68 (Harl. MS.) He dradde moche of the forseid world, and gretly dullid therwith.

†**8.** To be tedious; to urge tediously. *Obs.*

1540 HYRDE tr. *Vives' Instr. Chr. Wom.* (1592) P vij, Many women..with their ungodly crying and unreasonable calling, craving, and dulling upon them, driveth them to seeke unlawfull meanes of living.

dullard ('dʌləd), *sb.* and *a.* Also 5–6 dullarde, 6 dullarte, dullerde. [f. DULL *a.* + -ARD.]

A. *sb.* A dull or stupid person; a dolt, dunce.

c **1440** *Promp. Parv.* 114 Dastard, or dullarde, *duributcius.* **1561** T. NORTON *Calvin's Inst.* Table Script. Quot., Ps. xcii. 7 A dullard doth not know this, neither doth a foole understand it. **1613** PURCHAS *Pilgrimage* (1614) 342 To steale cunningly wins great reputation..and they which cannot doe it, are holden dullards and blockes. **1831** CARLYLE *Sart. Res.* I. viii, But indeed man is, and was always, a blockhead and dullard. **1880** L. STEPHEN *Pope* v. 135 Cibber..might be a representative of folly, but was as little of a dullard as Pope himself.

B. *adj.* Stupid, inert, dull.

1583 HOLLYBAND *Campo di Fior* 255 In a moment he is become the most dullard and ignorant. **1598** MARSTON *Pygmal.* sat. ii. 143 These darke Enigmaes..passe my dullard braines intelligence. *a* **1748** THOMSON *Hymn to May* (R.), The dullard earth May quick'neth with delight. **1894** GLADSTONE *Horace* III. xxi. 13 Thou prickest on the dullard sense Yet gently.

Hence **'dullardism, 'dullardness.**

1840 *Tait's Mag.* VII. 666 Dullardness and stagnation of soul. *a* **1846** MAUNDER (cited in WORCESTER), Dullardism.

dulle, obs. f. *dule*, DOLE *sb.*², and DULL.

dulled (dʌld), *ppl. a.* [f. DULL *v.* + -ED¹.] Made dull (in various senses: see DULL *v.* 1–5).

c **1480** *Crt. of Love* 477 And not to wander liche a dulled asse. **1514** BARCLAY *Cyt. & Uplondyshm.* (Percy Soc.) 16 Thy dullyd reason can not perceyve the same. **1549** *Compl. Scot.* vi. 68 My dullit brane. **1590** SPENSER *F.Q.* I. xi. 35 The deadly dint his dulled sences all dismaid. **1794** COLERIDGE *To Yng. Ass* 5 What thy dulled Spirits hath dismayed? **1866** DK. ARGYLL *Reign Law* vii. (1871) 384 We look on the facts of Nature and of human life through the dulled eyes of Custom and Traditional Opinion.

† **'dullen**, *ppl. a. Obs. rare.* [irreg.] = prec.

1602 DAVISON *Rhapsody* (1611) 70 And beating oft my dullen weary braine.

dullen ('dʌlən), *v. rare.* [f. DULL *a.* + -EN⁵.] *trans.* To make dull, to dull.

1832 L. HUNT *Sir R. Esher* (1850) 464 His glossy locks were now dullened and mixed with grey.

duller ('dʌlə(r)). *rare.* [f. DULL *v.* + -ER¹.] One who or that which dulls.

a **1611** BEAUM. & FL. *Philaster* II. ii, Fresh pork, conger, and clarified whey..are all dullers of the vital spirits.

dullery ('dʌlərɪ). *nonce-wd.* [f. DULL *a.* + -ERY.] Dullness; stupidity; unenlivened condition.

1653 URQUHART *Rabelais* II. xi, Master Antitus..had passed his degrees in all dullery and blockishness. **1841** LADY F. HASTINGS *Poems* 190 And victim she to all a housewife's dullery Visited eke the kitchen and the scullery.

† **'dull-head.** *Obs.* [cf. next.] A dull-headed or slow-witted person; a fool, a blockhead.

1549 COVERDALE, etc. *Erasm. Par. Titus* iii. 3 Now for foles and dulleheddes, we be made sobre and wise. *a* **1568** ASCHAM *Scholem.* (Arb.) 76 Fooles and dul-hedes to all goodnes. **1624** GATAKER *Transubst.* 146 Neither I, nor any such dull-heads as I am..can easily understand.

dull-headed ('dʌl,hɛdɛd), *a.* [parasynthetic f. *dull head* + -ED².] Having the head dull or stupid; slow-witted; obtuse in intellect.

1552 HULOET, Dulle headed, *capitosus.* **1571** GOLDING *Calvin on Ps.* xiv. 2 Wee be monstruously dullheaded, if his majestie strike us not in feare. **1635** *Gram. Warre* D vij, Some are obserued so dull-headed and doltish. **1840** DICKENS *Barn. Rudge* liv, The very uttermost extent of dull-headed perplexity supplied the place of courage.

dullify ('dʌlɪfaɪ), *v. colloq.* [see -FY.] *trans.* To render dull, to dull. So **dullifi'cation** *nonce-wd.* (in quot., something that makes one dull).

1657 TOMLINSON *Renou's Disp.* 38 Watry humidity doth ..dullify the strength of every sapour. **1838** MRS. CARLYLE *Lett.* I. 104 Preternatural intensity of sensation..which I study to keep down with such dullifying appliances as offer themselves. **1846** MOORE *Mem.* (1856) VIII. 20 The long and dullyfying dose. **1855** DORAN *Hanover. Queens* II. vii. 275 The princess called her mother's court a 'Dullification'.

dulling ('dʌlɪŋ), *vbl. sb.* [f. DULL *v.* + -ING¹.] The action of the verb DULL, q.v.

1581 MULCASTER *Positions* v. (1887) 33 The dulling of the childe, and discouraging of the maister. **1684** BAXTER *Twelve Argts.* xvi. 24 The dulling of Affection in hearing still the same words. **1894** *Athenæum* 24 Nov. 719/2 A general dulling of the field [of the telescope].

'dulling, *ppl. a.* [f. as prec. + -ING².] That dulls: see the verb.

1592 BP. ANDREWES *Wks.* (1843) V. 486 So hath His temptation a dulling force to the devil. **1696** TRYON *Misc.* ii. 42 Strong Drinks..send dark and dulling fumes into the Head. **1822** LAMB *Let. to Wordsw.* 20 Mar., I have a dulling cold. **1841** CLOUGH *Early Poems* vii. 144 The dulling clouds.

dullish ('dʌlɪʃ) *a.* [f. DULL *a.* + -ISH.] Somewhat dull, rather dull.

1399 LANG. *Rich. Redeles* III. 127 And ffor her dignesse endauntid of dullisshe nollis. **1581** SAVILE *Tacitus' Hist.* II. lxxvii. (1591) 98 The other through pride and breach of discipline waxe dullish. **1660** HOWELL *Parly of Beasts* 12 (D.) They are somewhat heavy in motion and dullish. **1751** R. PALTOCK *P. Wilkins* (1884) II xi. 115 A dullish glass. **1866** MRS. GASKELL *Wives & Dau.* xxxvii, I haven't read it myself, for it looked dullish.

dullness, dulness ('dʌlnɪs). [f. DULL *a.* + -NESS. The former spelling is more in accordance with general analogies, as in *smallness, illness, stillness, drollness*, though the latter has hitherto been more prevalent.]

The state or quality of being dull.

1. Slowness or obtuseness of intellect; stupidity.

1398 TREVISA *Barth. De P.R.* v. xii. (1495) 118 It is a token of dulnesse and of slowe wytte. **1483** *Cath. Angl.* 111/1 A Dullnes, *ebitudo.* **1561** T. NORTON *Calvin's Inst.* I. 25 Possessed with dullnesse, yea ouerwhelmed with grosse ignorance. **1651** HOBBES *Leviath.* I. viii. 32 A slow Imagination, maketh that Defect..which is commonly called Dulnesse. **1728** POPE *Dunc.* I. 11 Dulness o'er all possess'd her ancient right, Daughter of Chaos and eternal Night. **1881** JOWETT *Thucyd.* I. 190 Dulness and modesty are a more useful combination than cleverness and licence.

2. Sluggishness, inertness, inactivity; drowsiness.

1526 *Pilgr. Perf.* (W. de W. 1531) 128 b, Theyr ende is drynesse of deuocyon, dulnesse of spiryte. **1610** SHAKS. *Temp.* I. ii. 185 Thou art inclinde to sleepe: 'tis a good dulnesse, And giue it way. **1665** GLANVILL *Scepsis Sci.* 75 Such a Dulness and inactivity of humor. **1852** GROTE *Greece* II. lxxii. IX. 309 From the general dullness of character pervading Spartan citizens.

3. Gloominess of mind or spirits: now esp. as arising from want of interest.

c **1369** CHAUCER *Dethe Blaunche* 879 Dulnesse was of hir a-drad. *c* **1400** *Destr. Troy* 9854 Lette no dolnes you drepe, ne your dede let. **1500–20** DUNBAR *Poems* lxxviii. 10 My heid.. Dullit in dulness and distress. *c* **1600** SHAKS. *Sonn.* lvi, Do not kill The spirit of love with a perpetual dullness. **1654** WHITLOCK *Zootomia* 32 Mirth endeth in Dulnesse, if not Sadnesse.

4. Irksomeness; uninteresting character or quality.

1751 JOHNSON *Rambler* No. 141 ¶5 A man of parts, who wanted nothing but the dulness of a scholar. **1781** COWPER *Conversat.* 609 Grave without dulness. **1871** L. STEPHEN *Playgr. Eur.* x. (1894) 231 The deadly dulness of the grounds that surround a first-class family mansion.

5. Want of sensibility or acuteness (of the senses); want of sharpness, clearness, brightness, distinctness, or intensity (of physical qualities); bluntness, dimness, etc.: see DULL *a.* 2, 6, 7.

c **1440** *Promp. Parv.* 135/1 Dulnesse of egge, *obtusitas.* **1567** MAPLET *Gr. Forest* 3 b, Through yᵉ dulnesse of his owne colour. **1833** J. RENNIE *Alph. Angling* 50 Sport.. depending..on the brightness or dulness of the water.

† **'dull-pate.** *Obs.* = DULL-HEAD. So **'dull-,pated** *a.*, dull-headed.

15.. *Doctour doubble ale* 47 in Hazl. *E.P.P.* III. 304 They folowe perlowes lechis, And doctours dulpatis, That falsely to them pratis. **1580** LYLY *Euphues* (Arb.) 439 Grose and dull pated. **1590** SWINBURNE *Testaments* 39 b, For his dull capacity he might worthily bee tearmed *Grossum caput*, a dulpate or a dunse. **1668** CULPEPPER & COLE *Barthol. Anat.* I. xxiv. 59 Blockheads and dull-pated Asses. **1705** HICKERINGILL *Wks.* (1716) III. 218 Dul-pates.

'dullsville, *sb.* (and *a.*) *slang* (orig. *U.S.*). Also **Dullsville.** [f. DULL *a.* 5: see -VILLE.] An imaginary town characterized by extreme dullness or boredom; hence, a state, environment, or condition of extreme dullness. Cf. SQUARESVILLE. Also *attrib.* or as *adj.*

1960 *N.Y. Times Mag.* 28 Feb. 94/4 *-ville*, suffix connoting a superlative notion and tacked on to words at will to intensify them..as in..'He's from Dullsville'. **1966** *Time* 7 Oct. 17 Johnson is square, folksy and dullsville, sounding ..like dozens of boring politicians from the past. **1967** 'T. WELLS' *Dead by Light of Moon* xviii. 183 It was dullsville, that apartment. Decadent, like. **1969** *Guardian Weekly* 23 Jan. 4 Style-wise..it looks like backward to Dullsville for the next four years in the nation's capital. **1978** *Oxford Times* 13 Jan. 11/6 January and February are traditionally 'dullsville' months in restaurants and pubs and clubs. **1980** *Times* 5 Dec. 1390/1 All his life he's been a citizen of the East Midlands... By the metropolis's jeering estimates, of course, these are..a series of worthy, yes, but oh how meanly parochial dullsvilles.

dull-witted ('dʌl,wɪtɪd), *a.* [parasynthetic f. *dull wit* + -ED².] Having a dull wit; stupid.

1387 TREVISA *Higden* (Rolls) III. 467 Dyvers manere of soules..beeþ witted in a cleer day, and dul witted in an hevy. **1553** EDEN *Treat. Newe Ind.* (Arb.) 22 Dulle witted, of no strength, and Idolaters. *a* **1680** BUTLER *Rem.* (1759) II. 476 Dull-witted Persons are..the fittest Instruments for Wisemen to employ. **1887** W. GLADDEN *Parish Probl.* 404 The average boy..is [not] duller-witted..now than I was then.

dully ('dʌlɪ), *sb. colloq.* [f. DULL *a.* + -Y: cf. *softy*.] A dull or stupid person.

1883 *My Triv. Life & Misfort.* xliv, I was lucky in my dully, since he could entertain himself. Most dullies can't! **1887** *Poor Nellie* (1888) 12 Any..gentleman or useful dully.

dully ('dʌlɪ), *a. poetic.* [In sense 1, a Sc. variant of *dolly*, DOWIE, or of DOLY; in sense 2, f. DULL *a.* + -Y (cf. *vasty*).]

†**1.** Doleful, gloomy, dreary. *Sc. Obs.*

1500–20 DUNBAR *Poems* x. 37 Passit is ȝour dully nycht. *Ibid.* l. 15 Amang thai dully glennis. **1528** LYNDESAY *Dreme* 320 That dully den, that furneis infernall.

2. Faint, indistinct.

1832 TENNYSON *Palace Art* lxix, Far off she seem'd to hear the dully sound Of human footsteps fall.

dully ('dʌllɪ), *adv.* [f. DULL *a.* + -LY².] In a dull manner.

1. Without quickness of understanding; stupidly.

1533 MORE *Debell. Salem* Wks. 1029/1 In fayth that is spoken very dully. **1682** SHADWELL *Medal* Ep. A, He..has perform'd it so dully, that if you put him away..No body else will take him. **1706** HEARNE *Collect.* 7 Jan., A dully stupid Creature. **1895** M. CORELLI *Sorrows of Satan* 7 So I thought, dully.

2. Without energy or activity; sluggishly, inertly, drowsily.

1591 SHAKS. *Two Gent.* I. i. 7 Liuing dully sluggardiz'd at home. **1698** CROWNE *Caligula* v. Dram. Wks. 1874 IV. 419 They..in the lap of fortune dully dose. **1731** *2nd Add. on Bowman's Serm.* 6 Preaching the Word, not triflingly and dully, but with a warmth of affection. **1853** KINGSLEY *Hypatia* xi, He who cannot pray for his brothers..will pray but dully.

3. Gloomily, sadly (*obs.*); with ennui; irksomely, tediously; without interest or enlivenment.

1599 SHAKS. *Much Ado* II. i. 380 I warrant thee Claudio, the time shall not goe dully by vs. **1699** GARTH *Dispens.* v. 61 He's always dully gay, or vainly grave. **1766** GOLDSM. *Vic. W.* xx, All honest joggtrot men, who go on smoothly and dully. **1772** MRS. DELANY *Lett.* Ser. II. I. 538 The park very fine indeed, the house dully magnificent. **1882** STEVENSON *New Arab. Nts.* (1884) 76, I trust you did not find the evening hang dully on your hands.

4. In reference to the bodily senses, or to physical qualities: Bluntly, indistinctly, obscurely, dimly; not keenly, clearly, or brightly.

1430–40 LYDG. *Bochas* I. xi. (1544) 23 a, He gan dully to heare their mocions. **1486** *Bk. St. Albans* D iij, And thay be brokyn thay wyll sowne full dulli. **1626** BACON *Sylva* §375 The Aire, if it be Moist, doth in a Degree quench the Flame ..and..maketh it burne more dully. **1658** SIR T. BROWNE *Hydriot.* ii. (1736) 18 Many urns are..dully sounding. *a* **1680** BUTLER *Rem.* (1759) II. 385 A Crocodile sees clearly in the Water, but dully on Land. **1879** PROCTOR *Pleas. Ways Sc.* i. 25 Dully glowing sodium vapour.

dully, obs. form of DULY.

† **'dulman.** *Obs.* [f. DULL *a.* + MAN.] A dull or stupid person; humorously as a proper name.

1615 J. STEPHENS *Satyr. Ess.* 38 And then right harmeles Dulman doth inchant the Scæne. **1635** *Gram. Warre* D vij, These bussards of Barbary, Ignoramus and Dulman his Clearke. *a* **1666** A. BROME *To Friend J. B. on his Trag.* (R.), I dare not do't, lest any dulman says We by consent do one another praise.

dulness: see DULLNESS.

dulocracy (dju:'lɒkrəsɪ). Also doulo-. [ad. Gr. δουλοκρατία (Josephus), f. δοῦλος slave + -κρατία rule: see -CRACY.] Government by slaves; the rule of slaves. Hence **dulo'cratical** *a. rare*⁻⁰.

1656 BLOUNT *Glossogr.*, *Dulocracy*, *Dulocratical.* **1824** (*title*) Dreams of Dulocracy. **1836** HARE *Guesses* (1867) 232 We should be the sport of chance and caprice, as has ever happened to a people when fallen under a doulocracy.

dulosis (dju:'ləʊsɪs). *Ent.* [mod.L., ad. Gr. δούλωσις, f. δουλοῦν to enslave, f. δοῦλος slave.] The practice, exhibited by certain genera of ants, of enslaving other ants or colonies of ants. So **du'lotic** *a.*, slave-holding.

1904 *Biol. Bulletin* VI. 257 Dahl is mistaken in supposing that *L. bismarckensis* is a dulotic ant, as a perusal of the above quoted passages from Wroughton's work will suffice to show. **1905** W. M. WHEELER in *Bull. Amer. Mus. Nat. Hist.* XXI. 2 This observation, taken in connection with the close taxonomic affinities of *pergandei* with *sanguinea*, forcibly suggests dulosis. **1925** A. D. IMMS *Gen. Textbk. Entom.* 571 From temporary social parasitism the next step is exhibited by dulosis or slavery. **1928** W. M. WHEELER *Social Insects* 289 Yet another Myrmicine genus, Harpagoxenus..must be included among the dulotic, or slave-making ants. **1970** BROWN & TAYLOR in *Insects of Australia* (C.S.I.R.O.) xxxvii. 955/1 The special type of permanent parasitism known as dulosis, or slave-making, in which workers of the 'slave' component are constantly replenished by the addition of pupae acquired through mass raids on neighbouring pure nests of the host species, is so far not known to occur in Australia.

† **dulsa'cordis.** *Obs.* [Ultimately f. L. *dulcis* sweet + ACCORD *sb.* 4 or L. *chorda* string.] Some kind of musical instrument.

c **1450** HOLLAND *Howlat* 762 The dulset, the dulsacordis, the schalme of assay.

dulse (dʌls). Forms: 7– dulse; also 7 duleasg, 8 dulish, *Ir.* delisk, *Sc.* dilse, 9 dellish, dulce, dul(l)esh, dylish, *Ir.* dillesk, -isk, -osk, dilex, *Sc.* dilce, dills. [ad. Ir. and Gael. *duileasg*, in W. *delysg*.] An edible species of seaweed, *Rhodymenia palmata*, having bright red, deeply divided fronds. In some parts applied to *Iridæa edulis.*

[**1547** SALESBURY *Welsh Dict.*, *Dylysc*, Tang.] **1684** O'FLAHERTY *West Connaught* (1846) 99 Duleasg, or salt-leafe, is a weed growing on sea-rocks. **1698** M. MARTIN *Voy. St. Kilda* (1749) 58 They boil the Sea-Plants, Dulse and Slake. **1707** SLOANE *Jamaica* I. 49 From this concretion.. sticking to the leaves of the Delisk..it is that that plant is made delightful to the Irish palats. **1724** RAMSAY *Tea-t. Misc.* (1733) I. 91 Scrapt haddocks, wilks, dulse and tangle. **1732** ARBUTHNOT *Rules of Diet* 257 Dilse, a Sea-Plant, antiscorbutick. **1807** J. HALL *Trav. Scot.* II. 351 Farmers collecting the dilce (as they name it). **1859** Longf. in *Life* II. 387 The tide is low, and the purple dulse is lovely. **1875** *Ure's Dict. Arts* I. 67 *Rhodomenia palmata* passes under a variety of names, dulse, dylish, or dellish. **1883** J. B. Bloomfield in N. Okoshi *Fisheries Japan* (Fish. Exhib. Publ.) 27 A kind of seaweed called dilex, which they found upon the rocks. **1889** Barrie *Wind. Thrums* iv, Dulse is roasted by twisting it round the tongs fired to a red-heat.

b. *Comb.*, as ***dulse-dealer***, ***-green***, ***-man***.

1854 *Illustr. Lond. News* 5 Aug. 118/4 Occupations of the People.. Dulse-dealer. **1883** *Century Mag.* Sept. 730/2 Variously coloured tiles.. dark leaden gray for mud.. and dulse-green for sea-weed. **1889** Barrie *Wind. Thrums* iv, The dulseman wheeled his slimy boxes to the top of the brae.

dulsome ('dʌlsəm), *a. Obs.* exc. *dial.* [f. DULL *a.* + -SOME: cf. *darksome*, etc.] Of a dull character or quality; dreary, dismal.

1614 Lodge *Seneca's Epist.* 486 Darksome night Begins to spread her sad and silent eye Upon the dulsome earth. *a* **1770** C. Smart *Hop Garden* (R.), What time Aquarius' urn impends To kill the dulsome day. **1877** E. Peacock *N.W. Linc. Gloss.* s.v., 'It's strange dulsome weather for August'. 'He looks strange an' dulsome'.

† **dult**, *a. Obs.* [? related to DULL.] Blunt; *fig.* dull, stupid.

a **1225** *Ancr. R.* 292 Idoluen mit te dulte neiles.. þe neiles weren so dulte þet heo duluen his flesch. *a* **1225** *Leg. Kath.* 1268 Of ded and of dult [*v.r.* dul] wit! [*hebetatis sensibus*] Nu is ower stunde! *a* **1240** *Ureisun* in *Cott. Hom.* 203 þurh driuen fet and honden wið dulte neiles.

dult (dʌlt), *sb. Sc.* = DOLT; a dunce; the boy at the bottom of a class or form.

1825 in Jamieson. **1831** *Blackw. Mag.* XXX. 115 Agamemnon should have been sent to school for a dult. **1837** Lockhart *Scott* iii, The stupidity of some laggard on what is called the dults' bench.

dul'willy. [? = *dull Willy*.] A provincial name for the Ringed Plover, *Ægialitis hiaticula*.

1802 G. Montagu *Ornith. Dict.* (1833) 141.

duly ('dju:lɪ), *adv.* Forms: 4–5 **duelich(e**, **dulich(e**, 5–8 **duely**, 5– **duly** (5 **duli**, **dueli**, **dewli**, **dwly**, **deuly**, **diewly**, **dieulie**, **dulye**, 5–6 **dewly**, 6 **deulie**, **dulie**, **duelye**, 7 *Sc.* **dewlie**). [f. DUE *a.* + -LY^2.] In due manner, order, form, or season.

1. In a manner agreeable to obligation or propriety; as is due; rightly, properly, fitly.

1382 Wyclif *Num.* xxix. 27 And the sacrifices.. duelich [**1388** riȝtfuli] ȝe shulen halwe. **1399** Langl. *Rich. Redeles* I. 106 But had ȝe do duly, and as a duke oughte.. He shulde have hadde hongynge on hie on the fforckis. *c* **1430** *Pilgr. Lyf Manhode* I. cli. (1869) 76 Whan thou puttest thee oother weys than dueliche. *c* **1440** *York Myst.* i. 11 Vnto my dygnyte dere sall diewly be dyghte A place. **1477** *Certif.* in *Surtees Misc.* (1888) 36 Dieulie sworn & examyned. **1531** Elyot *Gov.* II. x, Well and duely employed. **1609** Skene *Reg. Maj.*, *Stat. Robt. III*, c. 45 §5 Gif they doe dewlie their office. **1613** Shaks. *Hen. VIII*, IV. ii. 150 That they may haue their wages, duly paid 'em. **1769** Robertson *Chas. V*, III. VII. 28 Persons duely qualified. **1875** Jowett *Plato* (ed. 2) I. 349 A set oration duly ornamented with words and phrases. **1891** *Law Rep.* Weekly Notes 70/1 These persons had never been duly appointed directors.

2. To the extent or degree that is due; adequately, sufficiently, fully.

1393 Gower *Conf.* III. 245 Whan kinde is dueliche served. *c* **1532** *Remedie of Love* (R.), Not to much, but duely mending Both praise and blame. **1611** Shaks. *Cymb.* I. i. 27, I do extend him (Sir) within himselfe, Crush him together rather than vnfold His measure duly. *c* **1680** Beveridge *Serm.* (1729) I. 514 Whosover duely considers it. **1742** Young *Nt. Th.* II. 97 The Man Is yet unborn, who duly weighs an Hour. **1816** Keatinge *Trav.* (1817) I. 108 Just duly sufficient to shade this.

3. At the due time; in due season, time, or order.

1494 Fabyan *Chron.* 2 Manyfolde storyes, in ordre duely sette. **1552** Huloet, Duelye or in due season, *tempestiue*. **1596** Dalrymple tr. *Leslie's Hist. Scot.* VII. xcviii. (1895) 24 From their first beginning, continuall successioun, dulie descending, all ordourlie. **1628** Digby *Voy. Medit.* (1868) 40 The brize comes from the sea duely euerie day about noone. **1638** Cowley *Love's Riddle* II. i, What day did e'er peep forth In which I wept not dulier than the Morning? **1712** Steele *Spect.* No. 263 ¶6, I will have my Rent duly paid. **1865** Dickens *Mut. Fr.* II. i, And duly got to the Surrey side.

duly, anglicized form of DULIA.

1674 Brevint *Saul at Endor* xvi. 352 Devotion.. whether Duly or Hyperduly.

dum, obs. form of DOOM, DUMB.

duma ('du:mə). Also (in Fr. form) **douma**. [Russ. *dúma*.] In Russia, an elective municipal council. ***the Duma***, an elective legislative assembly (*Gosudárstvennaya Dúma*), which was established in 1905 by a ukase of Tzar Nicholas II and lasted until the Revolution of 1917. Hence '**dumaist**, a member of a duma or the Duma.

1870 *Nation* 1 Dec. 364/2 Municipal Reform in Russia... The city is governed by a city council (*duma*) and a city regency (*uprava*). **1886** *Encycl. Brit.* XXI. 70/2 Since 1870 the municipalities have had institutions like those of the zemstvos... The executive is in the hands of an elective mayor and an *uprava* which consists of several members elected by the *duma*. **1905** *Daily Chron.* 16 Feb. 5/1 The Douma will consist of delegates of the district councils, each sending five. **1905** *Outlook* (N.Y.) 12 Aug. 892/2 [The plan] was received with derision by the zemstvoists and dumaists at their Congress in July. **1905** *Times* 19 Aug. 7/2 The *Duma* is established for the preliminary study and discussion of legislative propositions which.. will be submitted to the supreme autocratic authority by the Council of the Empire. **1906** G. Meredith *Let.* 9 July (1970) III. 1565 The members of the Duma.. have shown a memorable self-control. **1906** *Daily Chron.* 2 Aug. 1/7 M. Herzenstein, a wealthy Dumaist,.. has been shot dead.. in Finland. **1955** G. B. Carson *Electoral Practices in U.S.S.R.* 2 The most important electoral machinery was that created for elections to the imperial duma.

† '**dumal**, *a. Obs. rare*$^{-0}$. [ad. L. *dūmāl-is*, f. *dūmus* bramble.]

1656 Blount *Glossogr.*, *Dumal*, pertaining to Bryers.

dumb (dʌm), *a.* (*sb.*) Forms: 1– **dumb**; also 3–5 **doumb(e**, 3–6 **domm(e**, (4 **doum**, **doump**), 4–7 **domb(e**, **dumbe**, 5 **doom**, **dowmb(e**, **dowm(e**, **dume**, 5–6 **dome**, 5–7 **dum**, **dumm(e**. [A Com. Teut. adj.: OE. *dumb* = OS. *dumb* (MDu. *domp*, *dom*, Du. *dom*, LG. *dum*), OHG. *tumb*, *tump* (MHG. *tump*, *tum*, early mod.G. *thumb*, mod.G. *dumm*), ON. *dumbr* (Sw. *dumb*), Goth. *dumbs*. In Gothic, Old Norse, and OE. only in sense 'mute, speechless'; in OHG. it shared this sense with those of 'stupid' and 'deaf'; in the other langs. and periods, generally in sense 'stupid', though early mod.Ger. had also that of 'deaf': see Grimm. These diverse applications suggest as the original sense some such notion as 'stupid', 'not understanding', which might pass naturally either into 'deaf' or 'dumb'.]

A. *adj.* **1. a.** Destitute of the faculty of speech. ***deaf and dumb***: see DEAF *a.* 1 e.

c **1000** *Ags. Gosp.* Matt. ix. 32 Hiȝ brohton hym dumbne man [*Rushw. G.* monnu dumb and deaf]. *c* **1000** Ælfric *Hom.* I. 202 Beo ðu dumb oðþæt þæt cild beo acenned. *c* **1200** *Trin. Coll. Hom.* 125 þus bicom þe holi man dumb. **1297** R. Glouc. (1724) 131 þe maistres sete stille y now, ryȝt as heo doumbe were. *c* **1380** Wyclif *Serm.* Sel. Wks. I. 29 A deef man and a doumbe was helid of Crist. *c* **1450** *Merlin* 172 Thei were alle stille and mewet as though thei hadde be dombe. **1523** Skelton *Garl. Laurel* 82 Better a dum mouthe than a brainles scull. **1535** Coverdale *Hab.* ii. 18 Therfore maketh he domme Idols. **1613** Sir H. Finch *Law* (1636) 103 Diuers may haue vnderstanding by their sight onely, though dumb and deafe. **1678** *Yng. Man's Call.* 284 Worshippers of dum idols. **1785** Mad. D'Arblay *Diary* 16 Dec., It appears quite as strange to meet with people who have no ear for music.. as to meet with people who are dumb. **1865** Tylor *Early Hist. Man.* iv. 66 Every deaf and dumb child is educated, more or less, by living among those who speak.

absol. *c* **1000** Ælfric *Hom.* I. 544 Hi forȝeafon.. dumbum spræce. *c* **1200** *Vices & Virtues* (1888) 75 þe blinde, ðe dumbe, ðe deaue, ðe halte. **1382** Wyclif *Prov.* xxxi. 8 Opene thi mouth to the dumbe. **1611** Bible *Isa.* xxxv. 6 The tongue of the dumbe [shall] sing. **1884** tr. *Lotze's Logic* 14 The ideas of the deaf and dumb.

b. Applied to the lower animals (and, by extension, to inanimate nature) as naturally incapable of articulate speech. Esp. in phrases ***dumb chum***, ***dumb friend***, applied to domesticated animals.

a **1000** *Andreas* 67 (Gr.) Swa þa dumban neat. *a* **1225** *Ancr. R.* 134 Of dumbe bestes & of dumbe fueles leorneð wisdom & lore. *a* **1300** *Cursor M.* 11222 He.. did þe dumb asse to speke. **1340** Hampole *Pr. Consc.* 49 þe creatours þat er dom, And na witt ne skille has. *c* **1489** Caxton *Sonnes of Aymon* iii. 82 They slewe the one thother, as domm bestes. **1593** Q. Eliz. *Boeth.* (E.E.T.S.) 31 That the divine Creature.. should no otherwise florish, but that it neede possession of dom [L. *inanimatæ*] ware? **1697** Dryden *Virg. Georg.* I. 644 Dumb Sheep and Oxen spoke. *Ibid.* III. 722 A Plague did on the dumb Creation rise. **1849** Lytton *Caxtons* XVIII. ii, To waste on a dumb animal what.. many a good Christian would be.. glad of. **1870** *Animal World* July 163/1 My considerable experience.. combined with the affection I still feel for the dumb friends of my childhood, induces me to note down a few reminiscences of favourites. **1927** Wodehouse *Meet Mr. Mulliner* iii. 80 The dog.. stood there, barking... 'Having a little trouble with the dumb friend, bish?' he asked genially. **1934** —— *Right Ho, Jeeves* i. 13 He retired to the depths of the country and gave his life up to these dumb chums. **1940** 'N. Blake' *Malice in Wonderland* I. vii. 84 Don't leave your dumb friends at home! Bring them to Wonderland and instal them in our superbly equipped Pets' Corner! **1957** R. Campbell *Portugal* 62 Cassius's dumb-chum, the moray, adored him.

c. Without the power of making their voice effectively heard; without any voice in the management of affairs.

1856 Olmsted *Slave States* 215 The dumb masses have often been so lost in this shadow of egotism, that [etc.]. **1878** Morley *Carlyle* 191 He talks of the dumb millions in terms of fine and sincere humanity.

d. In proverbial phrases.

c **1340** *Cursor M.* 13739 (Fairf.) þai wex doumbe as stane. **1382** Wyclif *Isa.* lvi. 10 Doumbe dogges not mowende berken, seende veyne thingus, slepende, and loouende sweuenus. *c* **1384** Chaucer *H. Fame* II. 148 Dombe as any stoon Thou sittest at another booke. *a* **1400–50** *Alexander* 4747 Dom as a dore-nayle and defe was he bathe. *c* **1440** *York Myst.* xxxiii. 65 Domme as a dore gon he dwell. *a* **1607** J. Raynolds *Proph. Obad.* ii. (1613) 29 The ignorance of many, that are dumbe dogges, and cannot barke. **1770** Foote *Lame Lover* I. Wks. 1799 II. 61 A whole family dumb as oysters. *c* **1793** *Spirit Pub. Jrnls.* (1799) I. 13 When Pitt, as a fish, in the Commons was dumb.

2. Temporarily bereft of the power of speech, from astonishment, grief, or some mental shock.

a **1300** *Cursor M.* 24308 (Gött.) For murning al dumb war þai. **1388** Wyclif *Ps.* xxxviii. 10 [xxxix. 9], I was doumbe, and openyde not my mouth; for thou hast maad. **1513** Douglas *Æneis* IV. i. 1 Enee half wod and doum stude. **1635** J. Hayward tr. *Biondi's Banish'd Virg.* 29 Strucken dumbe remain'd Feredo with this.. dishonest proposition. **1714** Miss Vanhomrigh in *Swift's Lett.* (1766) II. 287 There is something in your looks so awful, that it strikes me dumb. **1870** Emerson *Soc. & Solit.*, *Clubs* Wks. (Bohn) III. 95 Men of a delicate sympathy, who are dumb in a mixed company. **1888** J. Inglis *Tent Life in Tigerland* 31, I was struck dumb with astonishment for the minute.

3. a. That does not or will not speak; that remains persistently silent; little addicted to speech; taciturn, reticent.

1406 Hoccleve *La Male Regle* 433 The prouerbe is 'the doumb man no lond getith'. **1581** G. Pettie tr. *Guazzo's Civ. Conv.* II. (1586) 119 That they be neither to talkative, nor to dumbe. **1602** Shaks. *Ham.* I. i. 171 This Spirit dumbe to vs, will speake to him. **1629** Milton *Nativity* 173 The Oracles are dumb. **1719** De Foe *Crusoe* II. xiv, He was dumb all the rest of the way. **1742** Young *Nt. Th.* IV. 717 Nature is dumb on this important point. **1843** Carlyle *Past & Pr.* III. v, The English are a dumb people.

† **b.** Const. *from*, *of*. *Obs.*

c **1380** Wyclif *Wks.* (1880) 60 [þei] ben doumb fro þe gospel, and tellen here owen lawis. *Ibid.* 420 His herdis.. be doump of lore of lif and lore of word to helpe þer sheepe.

c. ***to sing dumb***: to be silent, hold one's peace.

1715 *Auld Stuarts back again* in *Jacobite Songs* (1871) 27 We'll either gar them a' sing dumb, Or 'Auld Stuarts back again'. **1725** Ramsay *Gentle Sheph.* II. iii, I'll tell them tales will gar them a' sing dumb. **1752** *Scotland's Glory, etc.* 54 When this is answered I'll sing dumb.

4. Of things or actions: Not characterized by or attended with speech or vocal utterance. ***dumb crambo***: see CRAMBO 1 b. See also DUMB SHOW.

dumb cake, a cake made in silence on St. Mark's Eve, with numerous ceremonies, by maids, to discover their future husbands (Halliwell).

1538 Starkey *England* I. iv. 103 So long as the kyng ys lyuely reson.. so long.. he ys aboue hys lawys, wych be but, as you wyl say, rayson dome. **1580** Sidney *Arcadia* I. iii. (1590) 10 b, His countenance could not but with dumme Eloquence desire it. **1592** Shaks. *Ven. & Ad.* 359 All this dumbe play had his acts made plain. **1610** —— *Temp.* III. iii. 39 Expressing.. a kinde Of excellent dumb discourse. **1725** De Foe *Voy. round World* (1840) 344 Doing all by signs and dumb postures. **1814** Mrs. J. West *Alicia De Lacy* I. 30 Her employ is making dumb cakes, and tying girdles round the bed-posts to dream of her sweet-heart. *Ibid.* III. 214. **1865** Dickens *Mut. Fr.* II. xii, Pleasant answered with a short dumb nod.

5. a. Not emitting sound, unaccompanied or unattended by sound of any kind; silent, mute; unheard, from the sound being drowned by a louder one.

[*c* **1000** Ælfric *Gram.* iii. (Z.) 6 þa oðre niȝon *consonantes* synd ȝecwedene *mutæ*, þæt synd dumbe.] **1606** Shaks. *Ant. & Cl.* I. v. 50 What I would haue spoke, Was beastly dumbe [*mod. edd.* dumbed] by him. *a* **1680** T. Brooks in Spurgeon *Treas. Dav.* Ps. cxxvii. 2 Written with א, a quiet dumb letter. **1724** Ramsay *Tea-t. Misc.* (1733) II. 149 This is the dumb and dreary hour When injur'd ghosts complain. **1805** Wordsw. *Waggoner* 39 All the while his whip is dumb. **1819** Shelley *Peter Bell* I. xiii, Its thunder made the cataracts dumb. **1822–34** Good *Study Med.* (ed. 4) I. 385 The trachea is straight in the tame or dumb swan. **1842** Tennyson *Sir Galahad* 52 The streets are dumb with snow. **1891** R. Kipling *Eng. Flag* xvii. in *Nat. Observer* 4 Apr. 511/1 The dead dumb fog hath wrapped it.

b. ***dumb peal***: a muffled peal of bells.

1799 *Naval Chron.* II. 264 A dumb or mourning peal.. was rung. **1837** *Boston Advertiser* 10 Jan. 2/1 [He] was greeted on his return home with a dumb-peal.

c. Giving no sound on percussion, as a tumour.

1879 J. M. Duncan *Lect. Dis. Women* i. (1889) 3 The ear may find it dumb, or may find a souffle or a pulse. *Ibid.* xv. 112 The tumour is rounded, dull on percussion, dumb, slightly displaceable.

6. Applied to mechanical contrivances which take the place of a human agent. See DUMB-WAITER.

dumb borsholder: see Hasted (as cited), L. J. Jennings *Rambles among the Hills* (1880) 299.

1782 Hasted *Hist. Kent* II. 284/2 Electing a Deputy to the *Dumb Borsholder of Chart*, as it was called. **1793** B. Edwards *Hist. W. Indies* in Burrowes *Cycl.* X. 286/1 The canes are turned round the middle roller by a piece of frame work of a circular form, which is called in Jamaica, the dumb-returner. **1853** (*title*) Specif. S. Blackwell's Patent for.. 'constructing a certain article of saddlery denominated a dumb jockey'.

7. a. Saying nothing to the understanding; inexpressive, meaningless; stupid, senseless. Now *rare*.

1531 Tindale *Exp. 1 John* (1537) 53 They wyl breake in to thy conscience, as the byshop of Rome doeth with his domme traditions. **1542–5** Brinklow *Lament.* lf. 18 b, A popishe Masse.. is to the people a domme, yea a deade ceremonye. **1643** Sir T. Browne *Relig. Med.* I. §17 'Twas not dumbe chance, that.. contrived a miscarriage in the Letter.

b. Foolish, stupid, ignorant (chiefly of persons); spec. ***dumb blonde***, a conspicuously attractive but stupid blonde woman; ***dumb bunny***, a stupid person; ***dumb Dora***, a stupid girl; ***dumb ox***, a stupid, awkward, or uncommunicative man (cf. sense 1 b above); *spec.* a nickname for St. Thomas Aquinas. *colloq.*

Possibly reinforced by G. *dumm* or Du. *dom*.

[*c* **1323** P. Calo *Vita* in D. Prümmer *Fontes Vitae S. Thomae Aquinatis* (1912) I. 78 Cœperunt eum Fratres vocare bovem mutum.] **1756** A. BUTLER *Lives Saints* I. 393 His [*sc.* St. Thomas's] school-fellows thought he learnt nothing, and, on account of his silence, called him *The dumb Ox.* *Ibid.*, Albertus not able to contain his joy and admiration, said, 'We call him the dumb ox, but he will give such a bellow in learning as will be heard all over the world.' **1823** J. F. COOPER *Pilot* II. iii. 39 'They're a dumb race' said the cockswain,.. 'now, there was our sargeant, who ought to know something.' **1851** LONGF. *Golden Leg.* VI. 271 To gather in piles the pitiful chaff That old Peter Lombard thrashed with his brain, To have it caught up and tossed again On the horns of the Dumb Ox of Cologne. **1888** F. R. STOCKTON *Dusantes* 124 The Grootenheimers always was the dumbest family in the township. **1892** *Harper's Mag.* Feb. 441/1 My, but men are dumb. A woman would have caught on long ago. **1914** R. BROOKE *Let.* 15–17 Aug. (1968) 609 This is a badly-written, dumb, letter. **1919** F. HURST *Humoresque* 259, I been so dumb not to right away see it. **1922** *Dialect Notes* V. 141 *Dumb-bunny* [in College slang], a somewhat stupid person... 'My dear, you are the preshest old dumb-bunny.' *Ibid.* 147 *Dumbdora*, a stupid girl. **1930** [see BALL *sb.*[1] 18]. **1932** 'A. BRIDGE' *Peking Picnic* xx. 255 He is that dumb, if you'll pardon the word, madam, that not a bit of sense could I get out of him. **1936** 'J. TEY' *Shilling for Candles* vi. 62 A sulky fair girl, who played 'dumb' blondes from year's end to year's end. **1938** E. BOWEN *Death of Heart* I. i. 25 One has got to see just how dumb Mr. Quayne was. He had not got a mind that joins one thing and another up. **1945** L. SHELLY *Jive Talk Dict.* 24 *Dumb bunny*, stupid person. **1947** *Times Lit. Suppl.* 15 Nov. 594/2 The cult of 'dumb-ox' individualism is certainly unsuitable for New Zealand, where the individual has rarely bulked as large as the State. **1959** 'M. DERBY' *Tigress* ii. 88 The dumb blonde to whom all instruments and machinery were insoluble riddles. **1959** *Listener* 16 July 110/3 An amiable dumb-ox. **1965** G. MCINNES *Road to Gundagai* ix. 145 They [*sc.* hens] would then wait expectantly, heads cocked on one side with a sort of dumb-Dora inquisitive chuckle.

c. Of a computer terminal: not intelligent (INTELLIGENT *a.* 5); without any independent data-processing capability.

1976 *Telecommunications* Nov. 39/2 The totally nonintelligent, or dumb, or basic terminal is one thing that can be defined nonsubjectively. **1983** *Your Business Computer* Oct. 6/3 The dumb terminal relies on the host CPU for all processing, and is effectively a video monitor with a keyboard. **1985** *Which Computer?* Apr. 119/3 Dentron provides a central microcomputer to which 'dumb' terminals are attached (they are dumb in the sense that all the clever processing goes on in the central computer).

8. Lacking some property, quality, or accompaniment, normally belonging to things of the name.

dumb ague, one in which the paroxysms are obscure; also, an irregular form of malarial fever, which lacks the usual chill; also ***dumb chill, fever***. ***dumb arch***: cf. BLIND *a.* 10. ***dumb chamber***, one having no outlet. ***dumbfish***: cf. DUNFISH. ***dumb nettle***, the DEAD-NETTLE: cf. BLIND-NETTLE. ***dumb nut*** (*Sc. dial.*), a deaf nut. ***dumb piano***, a contrivance having a set of keys like a piano and used for exercising the fingers. Also DUMB BARGE, -BELL, CRAFT.

1638 SIR T. HERBERT *Trav.* (ed. 2) 131 Musick, three kettle drummes, and six dumb Musquets. **1792** J. BELKNAP *New-Hampsh.* III. 214 Large thick fish, which after being properly salted and dried, is kept alternately above and under ground, till it becomes so mellow as to be denominated dumb fish. **1793** *Trans. Amer. Philos. Soc.* III. p. iv, Fever and ague..also visits the borders of limpid streams. The lesser degree of it generally called *dumb ague*, is not rare in the most salubrious places during the months of September and October. **1832** R. BAIRD *Valley Mississippi* viii. 73 These maladies are intermitting and remitting bilious fevers..which..have received the names of 'ague', 'dumb ague', and 'chill and fever'. **1853** G. BIRD *Urin. Deposits* (ed. 4) 435 Imperfect paroxysms, the 'dumb-ague' as they are often..called..appear again. **1859** BARTLETT *Dict. Amer.* (ed. 2) 133 *Dumb chill*, or *dumb ague*, an expression common in malaria regions to denote that form of intermittent fever which has no well defined 'chill'. **1866** MITCHELL *Hist. Montrose* viii. 80 The dumb overarched spaces where the letters are put in. **1871** SIR T. WATSON *Princ. & Pract. Med.* (ed. 5) II. xxxv. 763 This state is commonly known..as the *dumb* ague, or the *dead* ague; the patient is said not to *shake out*. **1888** GOWERS *Dis. Nervous Syst.* II. 674 Gymnastic exercises are often useful ..for which with advantage a 'dumb piano' may be used. **1893** DARTNELL & GODDARD *Gloss. Wiltshire* 49 'Tis what 'ee do caal the dumb-agey. **1894** W. M. F. PETRIE *Hist. Egypt* I. 185 A long staircase, which ended in a dumb chamber.

†**9.** Lacking brightness; dull, dim. *nonce-use.*

1720 DE FOE *Capt. Singleton* xviii. (1840) 315 Her stern.. was painted of a dumb white, or dun colour.

B. *absol.* or as *sb.* †**1.** A dumb person. *Obs.*

[*c* **1000** *Ags. Gosp.* Matt. ix. 33 Utadrifene þam deofle, se dumbe spræc.] **1596** DALRYMPLE *Leslie's Hist. Scot.* (1888) I. 122 A murthirer, a dum [*mutus*], or vngrate to his parents.

†**2.** A dumb state; a fit of dumbness. *Obs.*

1640 NABBES *Bride* II. ii, Suddaine dumbs: Whence are they? *c* **1678** *Roxb. Ball.* (1882) IV. 358 Can you cure a Woman of the Dumb?

3. *N. Amer.* A foolish or stupid person. Also ***dum(b)-dum(b)***. *colloq.*

1928 *Daily Express* 4 Dec. 10/3 A 'dumb' is a stupid person, and if he's dumb enough he'll probably drive you 'cuckoo' or crazy. **1970** L. SANDERS *Anderson Tapes* xxxi. 81 You're no dumdum, are you? **1970** *Calgary Herald* 24 Aug. 9/1 Better they should employ some dumb-dumb.

C. *Comb.* **a.** general, as ***dumb-born, -cowed, -discoursive, -doggish, -mad, -stricken, -struck***, etc.

1580 SIDNEY *Arcadia* III. 244 Thus would hee..bee dumb-stricken when her presence gave him fit occasion of speaking. **1594** DRAYTON *Ideas* xxxv, A dumb-born muse made to express the mind. *a* **1613** OVERBURY *Characters, Distaster of Times* Wks. (1856) 128 He is often dumb-mad, and goes fetter'd in his owne entrailes. **1852** THACKERAY *Esmond* I. ix, Poor young Esmond was so dumb-stricken that he did not even growl. **1887** SIR R. H. ROBERTS *In the Shires* vi. 104 For a few moments he remained dumb-struck. **1887** RUSKIN *Præterita* II. 332 Affectionate in a dumb-doggish sort. **1890** R. KIPLING *Willie Winkie* 63 They were openly beaten, whipped, dumb-cowed, shaking and afraid.

b. Special combinations: **dumb-chalder** or **-cleat**, a metal cleat, bolted to the back of the stern-post for one of the rudder-pintles to rest on (Smyth *Sailor's Word-bk.*); **dumb-drift**, an airway conveying foul air to the upcast shaft of a mine, past and not through the ventilating furnace, called when so arranged a **dumb-furnace; dumb-pintle**, a peculiar kind of pintle or rudder-strap; **dumb-play** = DUMB SHOW 2; **dumb-scraping**, 'scraping wet-docks with blunt scrapers' (Smyth); **dumb sheave**, a sheaveless block having a hole for a rope to be reeved through; **dumb singles**, a kind of silk merely wound and cleaned (Simmonds *Dict. Trade*); **dumb-sound** *v.*, to deaden the sound or noise of; **dumb-tooling** (*Book-binding*) = *blind tooling*; **dumb well**, a well sunk into a porous stratum, to carry off surface water or drainage; also called *blind well, dead well.*

1881 RAYMOND *Mining Gloss.*, **Dumb-drift*, an air-way conveying air around, not through, a ventilating furnace to the upcast. **1874** KNIGHT *Dict. Mech.*, **Dumb furnace.* *c* **1850** *Rudim. Navig.* (Weale) 137 Sometimes one or two are shorter than the rest, and work in a socket-brace, whereby the rudder turns easier: the latter are called *dumb-pintles. **1867** SMYTH *Sailor's Word-bk.* s.v. *Pintles*, The rudder is hung on to a ship by pintles and braces..a dumb pintle on the heel finally takes the strain off the hinging portions. **1920** *Chambers's Jrnl.* 374/1 A violent *dumb-play of smoothing the hair and arranging the coats of pyjamas. **1921** *Glasgow Herald* 10 Feb. 6 Certain M.P.'s did take the part of actors and were duly taken and their dumb-play shown on the screen. *c* **1860** H. STUART *Seaman's Catech.* 74 There is a live sheave for the working top pendant, and a *dumb one for the hawser. **1882** NARES *Seamanship* (ed. 6) 32 It is rove over a dumb sheave in the flying jib-boom end. **1882** *Even. Standard* 3 Feb., To compel the Company to '*dumb-sound' and make water-tight a bridge which they propose building across Montpellier Road. **1895** J. ZAEHNSDORF *Short Hist. Bkbind.* 11 Great aptitude for receiving impressions of *dumb or blind tooling. **1878** J. T. BUNCE *Hist. B'ham* I. 325 The contents of water-closets..pass.. into *dumb wells. **1888** *Law Rep.* Ch. Div. XXXIX. 272 A dumb well, viz. a well into which waste water flows through a pipe and thence percolates into the soil, is not a 'drain or watercourse' within the meaning of the Highway Act 5 & 6 Wm. IV. c. 50 §67.

dumb, *v.* [f. prec. adj. (OE. had, in sense 1, *adumbian.*)]

†**1.** *intr.* To become dumb, speechless, or silent.

[*c* **1000** *Ags. Gosp.* Mark i. 25 A-dumba and ga of þisum men.] *a* **1300** *E.E. Psalter* xxxviii[i]. 3 I doumbed [*v.r.* ic a-dumbade] and meked, and was ful stille. *a* **1340** HAMPOLE *Psalter* xxxviii[i]. 13, I dumbid, and i oppynd not my mouth.

2. *trans.* To render dumb, silent, or unheard.

1608 SHAKS. *Per.* v. Prol. 5 Deep clerks she dumbs. *a* **1618** SYLVESTER *Sonn. late Mirac. Peace* xxv. 3 Deafning the winds, dumbing the loudest thunders. **1650** W. BROUGH *Sacr. Princ.* (1659) 219 It..dumbs the mouth to prayer. **1885** BURTON *Arab. Nts.* (1887) III. 14 A splendour that dazed the mind and dumbed the tongue. **1895** *Daily Tel.* 22 Aug. 5/1 Sounds at sea..becoming arrested, and, as it were, dumbed by new strata of air.

dumb barge. [see DUMB *a.* 8.] A barge without mast or sails. On the Thames applied to the ordinary lighters which travel up and down river by means of the tide. (See also quot. 1886, and cf. DUMMY *sb.* 4 c.)

1869 *Daily News* 24 May, There are, we believe, some four thousand 'dumb' barges belonging to the port, and 2,385 sailing barges. **1884** W. C. RUSSELL *Jack's Courtship* xix, Didn't you notice the dumb-barge right in the road of the tug? Those things are the curse of the river. **1886** *N. & Q.* 7th Ser. I. 28 (Editor) A dumb barge used to signify a barge used as a pier, and not for the conveyance of merchandise. **1891** *Daily News* 3 Oct. 3/8 The dumb barge Athens, laden with sugar, was proceeding up the Thames. **1896** *Letter fr. London Ship-owner*, The barges used for wrecks are large dumb barges, but the word would have to be qualified in some way to convey any other meaning here than an ordinary cargo lighter.

dumb-bell ('dʌmbɛl), *sb.*

1. a. Formerly, An apparatus, like that for swinging a church-bell, but without the bell itself, and thus making no noise, in the 'ringing' of which bodily exercise was taken. **b.** Also, applied to a similar apparatus, used in learning bell-ringing.

1711 ADDISON *Spect.* No. 115. ¶7, I exercise myself an Hour every Morning upon a dumb Bell, that is placed in a corner of my room..My Landlady and her daughters.. never come into my room to disturb me while I am ringing. **1747** *Gentl. Mag.* XVII. 77. **1784** WESLEY *Wks.* (1872) XI. 520 If you cannot ride or walk abroad, use, within, a dumb-bell, or a wooden horse. **1888** J. DIXON in *N. & Q.* 7th Ser. VI. 282. **1895** R. S. FERGUSON in *Archæol. Jrnl.* LII. 45 A contrivance or machine at Knole, called the 'Dumb Bell', which stands in an attic called the 'Dumb Bell Gallery'. **1896** *Ibid.* LIII. 23 Two instances of actual dumb bells, that is of dumb bells used for the purpose of teaching beginners the art of change-ringing.

2. a. An instrument of wood or iron, consisting of a short bar or slender connecting-piece weighted at each end with a roundish knob; used in pairs, which are grasped in the hands and swung for exercise.

[**1711** ADDISON *Spect.* No. 115 ¶8 (Described under the name of σκιομαχία).] **1785** F. TYTLER *Lounger* No. 24 ¶ 3. It was Peter's province..to attend me at noon with the dumb-bells, and measure out my hour of exercise. **1824** MISS MITFORD *Village* Ser. I. (1863) 208 Talking..is nearly as good to open the chest as the dumb-bells. **1894** HALL CAINE *Manxman* 426 A stone like a dumb-bell, large at both ends and narrow in the middle.

b. [After DUMB *a.* 7 b.] = DUMBHEAD. Also *attrib. slang* (orig. *U.S.*).

1920 *Collier's* 3 July 8/1 The gent..stands alone as the Crown Prince of dumb-bells. **1922** S. LEWIS *Babbitt* xviii, 227 The poor old dumb-bells that you can't get to dance. *a* **1930** D. H. LAWRENCE *Etruscan Places* (1932) i. 21 They gave the usual dumb-bell answer. **1936** *Punch* 15 Apr. 430/3 Next came one of those series of Dumb-bell Letters which seem to be very popular, a dumb-bell being the kind of person who writes to the manufacturer asking him to replace a gadget that has been lost, and then adds a postscript telling him not to bother as the missing gadget has just been found.

3. An object of the shape of a dumb-bell or of two rounded masses with a narrowed connecting part. **a.** Applied to microscopic crystals of oxalate of lime, etc. found in the urine. **b.** A name for a diplococcus.

a. [**1844** G. BIRD *Urin. Deposits* 127 In a very few cases the oxalate is met with in very remarkable crystals shaped like dumb-bells or rather like two kidneys with their concavities opposed. *Ibid.* 128 Large 'dumb-bell' crystals.] **1864** G. HARLEY in *Med. Times & Gaz.* II. 535 Lithates may be found as dumb-bells.

b. 1885 E. KLEIN *Micro-Organisms & Dis.* (1886) 58 Between the individuals of a dumb-bell there is always noticeable a short pale intervening bridge.

4. *attrib.* and *Comb.*, as ***dumb-bell-shape, -shaped*** adj. **dumb-bell nebula**, a nebula of this shape in the constellation Vulpecula.

1826 R. H. FROUDE *Rem.* (1838) I. 83 This is the third day I have practised a dumb-bell exercise. [**1833** SIR J. HERSCHEL *Catal. Neb.* in *Phil. Trans.* CXXIII. 465 A nebula shaped like a dumb-bell.] **184.** NICHOL *Archit. Heav.* (1851) 81 The celebrated 'Dumb Bell' nebula of Sir John Herschel. **1867–77** G. F. CHAMBERS *Astron.* VI. iv. 536 A curious object near the 5th-magnitude star 14 Vulpeculæ..usually known as the 'Dumb-bell' nebula. **1844–57** G. BIRD *Urin. Deposits* (ed. 5) 29 A very thick double convex lens excavated at the sides into a kind of dumb-bell shape. **1870** ROLLESTON *Anim. Life* 77 A dumb-bell-shaped mass.

Hence **'dumb-bell** *v.*, (*a*) *intr.* To practise with dumb-bells; (*b*) *trans.* To exercise or drill with dumb-bells. So **'dumb-beller.**

1827 *Mirror* II. 274/2 Gymnasticating, dumb-belling, and dancing-mastering, will not put quicksilver into a man's neck. **1881** MISS BRADDON *Asph.* I. 144 How I have been.. governessed..and back-boarded..and dumb-belled. **1891** DU MAURIER *Peter Ibbetson* II. in *Harper's Mag.* July 177/1 A..persevering dumb-beller and Indian-clubber.

dumb cane. A West Indian araceous plant, *Dieffenbachia Seguine*, so called from the effect of its acrid juice upon the tongue: see quot 1830.

1696 *Phil. Trans.* XIX. 296 The Dumb Cane..is not properly any Species of Reed or Cane, but of Arum or Wake-Robin. **1707** SLOANE *Jamaica* I. 168. **1750** G. HUGHES *Barbadoes* 252. **1830** LINDLEY *Nat. Syst. Bot.* 287 The Dumb Cane..has the power, when chewed, of swelling the tongue and destroying the power of speech.

dumb cluck, 'dumb-cluck. *slang* (orig. *U.S.*). [f. DUMB *a.* 7 b + CLUCK *sb.* 5.] A dull or stupid person; a fool.

1929, 1931 [see CLUCK *sb.*]. **1934** J. M. CAIN *Postman always rings Twice* vi. 59 This Greek had had a fracture of the skull, and a thing like that don't happen to a dumb cluck like him every day. **1939** C. MORLEY *Kitty Foyle* 164 They're just dumb clucks, and they haven't any ambition to go off on their own. **1944** *Coast to Coast 1943* 125 She had to get up and speak, and tell these dumb-cluck women they'd just got to pull their weight. **1945** D. WHEATLEY *Man who missed War* vi. 62 Do I look the kind of dumb-cluck who would be wastin' her time joy-ridin' in this boat instead of gettin' her a liner? **1958** *Economist* 1 Nov., There emerges an elite of Top People (no longer encumbered with hereditarily privileged dumb-clucks) in the 140-and-up IQ range. **1960** O. MANNING *Great Fortune* ii. 15 For the last half-hour I've been telling these dumb clucks to find me a bloke who can speak English.

dumb craft. [see DUMB *a.* 8, CRAFT 9.]

a. In some places = DUMB BARGE. **b.** More particularly, A heavy boat, hulk, or 'hopper' without sail or propelling power, used for weighing up and raising sunken ships, or heavy matter from the sea-bottom or river-bed. (So in regular use on the Tyne.) **c.** 'An instrument somewhat similar to the screw-jack, having wheels and pinions which protrude a ram, the point of which communicates the power.' (Ogilvie.) ? *Sc.*

1867 SMYTH *Sailor's Word-bk.*, *Dumb-craft*, lighters, lamps, or punts, not having sails. Also, a name for the screws used for lifting a ship on a slip.

dumbfound, dumfound (dʌm'faʊnd), *v.* [app. f. DUMB *a.* + *-found* in CONFOUND.] *trans.* To strike dumb; to confound, confuse; to nonplus.

1653 URQUHART *Rabelais* I. vi. (1694) 22, I beseech you never Dum-found or Embarrass your Heads with these idle Conceits. **1681** OTWAY *Soldier's Fort.* II. i, He has but one eye, and we are on his blind side; I'll dumb-found him (strikes him on the shoulder). **1762** STERNE *Tr. Shandy* VI. ii, To cramp and dumbfound his opponents. **1861** DARWIN in *Life & Lett.* (1887) II. 361, I cannot wriggle out of it; I am dumbfounded.

Hence **dumb'founded** *ppl. a.*, **dumb'founding** *vbl. sb.* and *ppl. a.*

1682 *Epil.* to *Mrs. Behn's False Count*, Among all the follys here abounding, None took like the new Ape-trick of Dumfounding. **1690** DRYDEN *Prol.* to *Beaum. & Fl.'s Prophetess* 47 That witty recreation, call'd dumb-founding. **1770** C. JENNER *Placid Man* II. 139 That kind of dumb-founding astonishment. **1815** MOORE *Mem.* (1853) II. 70 The dum-founded fascination that seizes people.

dumb'founder, dumfounder, *v.* [f. prec.: assimilated to FOUNDER *v.*] = prec.

1710 *Fanatick Feast* 16 Both which Blockheads..I could dumb-founder with a single syllogism. **1741** RICHARDSON *Pamela* (1824) I. 181 Poor Beck, poor Beck; 'fore gad, she's quite dumb-founder'd. **1848** C. BRONTË *J. Eyre* (1857) 156 I..stood..dumbfoundered at..her miraculous self-possession. **1859** G. RAWLINSON *Herodotus* VI. cxxix, Hippoclides, who quite dumbfoundered the rest, called aloud to the flute-player, and bade him strike up a dance.

dumb'foundered *ppl. a.*; **dumb'founderment.**

1880 *Blackw. Mag.* Mar. 368 A state of body and mind made up one-half of benumbment, the other half of dumb-founderment. **1883** A. S. SWAN *Aldersyde* I. x. 160 In dumfoundered amazement.

'dumbhead. *U.S.* and *Sc. slang.* [f. DUMB *a.* 7 b + HEAD *sb.*, after G. *dummkopf*, Du. *domkop.*] A blockhead.

1887 H. FREDERIC *Seth's Brother's Wife* 339 We wouldn't elect such a dumb-head to be a hog-reeve. **1895** S. R. CROCKETT *Men of Moss-Hags* xxxix. 278 What a dumbhead I was, to bide with an empty belly in a place where at least there must be plenty of fish near at hand. **1921** C. E. MULFORD *Bar-20 Three* xi. 125 Have I got to do *all* the thinking for this crowd of dumbheads?

dumb-iron ('dʌmaɪən). [See DUMB *a.* 8.] A carriage-spring composed of two half-elliptic springs joined at the ends. In the chassis of a motor car, each of the pair of curved forward ends of the frame-side members to which one end of each front spring is fixed. (See also quot. 1963.)

1907 *Westm. Gaz.* 19 Dec. 4/2 The distinctive frame is of pressed steel, slightly narrowed from the dashboard, tapered, and turned down in front so as to form its own dumb-irons, thus making the connexion for the forward ends of the springs. **1920** *London Mag.* June 334/1 The sharp dumb-irons dug into the bank, and the car reared itself on end. **1928** *Daily Tel.* 16 Oct. 17 Sankey's tool box ..which fills the usual blank space between the dumb irons, curved to follow the line of the dumb iron. **1963** R. F. WEBB *Motorists' Dict.* 86 *Dumb irons*, the portions of the chassis of a car which carry the shackles for the front springs. Recently the term has also come to mean the iron or steel supports carrying the fenders or bumpers.

dumble ('dʌmb(ə)l). *dial.* A dumbledore.

1893 in DARTNELL & GODDARD *Gloss. Wilts.* 50. **1909** HARDY *Time's Laughingstocks* 67 The dumbles thin their humming.

dumble-, in names of insects, app. the same as DUMMEL; but varying with *bumble-*, *drumble-*, *humble-*.

†**dumble bee.** *Obs. rare.* [see prec.] A drone.

1577 NORTHBROOKE *Dicing* (1843) 71 To liue, like the ydle dumble bee in the hyue, vpon..other mennes labours.

dumbledore, dumble-dore ('dʌmb(ə)ldɔə(r)). *local.* [f. DUMBLE- + DOR *sb.*[1]: see also DRUMBLE-*dore.*] A humble-bee or bumble-bee; also *dial.* a cockchafer.

1787 GROSE *Prov. Gl.*, *Dumble-dore*, an humble, or bumble-bee. **1799** SOUTHEY in Robberds *Mem. W. Taylor* I. 264 Is it not the humble-bee, or what we call the 'dumble dore',—a word whose descriptive droning deserves a place in song? **1837** —— *Doctor* IV. Interch. xvi. 383 Of Bees, however, let me be likened to a Dumbledore, which Dr. Southey says is the most goodnatured of God's Insects. **1856** MISS YONGE *Daisy Chain* I. xxvi. (1879) 276 Buzzed and hummed over by busy, blacktailed yellow-banded dumbledores. **1863** G. KEARLEY *Links in Chain* iii. 57 In Hampshire these insects [humble bees] are Dumbledors, in other districts Bumble bees, and hummel bees. **1880** *Cornwall Gloss.*, *Dumbledory*, cockchafer.

dumbly ('dʌmlɪ), *adv.* [f. DUMB *a.* + -LY[2].] In a dumb manner; speechlessly, mutely.

1552 HULOET, Dombely, *mute.* **1592** SHAKS. *Ven. & Ad.* 1059 Dumblie she passions, frantikely she doteth. **1593** —— *Rich. II*, v. i. 95 One Kisse shall stop our mouthes, and dumbely part. *a* **1845** HOOD *Bridge of Sighs* xvii, Cross her hands humbly, As if praying dumbly. **1859** TENNYSON *Enid* 1177 Your wretched dress..dumbly speaks Your story, that this man loves you no more.

dumbness ('dʌmnɪs). [f. as prec. + -NESS.]

1. The quality or condition of being dumb; inability to speak; speechlessness; silence, muteness.

c **1380** WYCLIF *Wks.* (1880) 126 To displese god bi suffrynge of opyn synne & domnpnesse. *c* **1440** *Promp. Parv.* 135/1 Dumnesse, *mutitas, taciturnitas.* *c* **1450** *Cov. Myst.* (Shaks. Soc.) 125 The plage of dompnesse his lippis lappyd. **1565** JEWEL *Def. Apol.* 553 (R.) This therefore is no spiritual dumbenesse. **1611** SHAKS. *Wint. T.* v. ii. 14 There was speech in their dumbnesse, Language in their very gesture. **1861** O'CURRY *Lect. MS. Materials Irish Hist.* 253 The spell of his dumbness was broken, and the young man spoke.

2. Stupidity; ignorance (cf. DUMB *a.* 7 b). *U.S. colloq.*

1858 THOREAU *Jrnl.* 10 Oct. in *Autumn* (1892) 94, I see dumb-bells in the minister's study, and some of their dumbness gets into his sermons. **1924** *Chicago Tribune* 26 Oct. (Comics) 6 You can tell me how to take some of the dumbness outta the kid.

dumbo ('dʌmbəʊ). *slang* (orig. *U.S.*). [f. DUMB *a.* 7 b + -O[2].] A slow-witted or stupid person.

1960 WENTWORTH & FLEXNER *Dict. Amer. Slang* 166/2 *Dumbo*, a stupid person. **1951**: 'Edison was a dumbo in school' Radio station WHK, Cleveland, Jan. 27. **1978** *Washington Post* 3 Feb. (Weekend Suppl.) 16/1 Laurel and Hardy used routines of the dumbo bouncing Falstaffian antics off the straight man. **1982** *Observer* 18 July 6/3 Senators were..frequently inept in their questioning. 'They're dumbos,' said a committee official. **1984** S. TOWNSEND *Growing Pains A. Mole* 106, I am sharing a book with three dumbos who take half an hour to read one page.

dumb show.

1. In the early drama, A part of a play represented by action without speech, chiefly in order to exhibit more of the story than could otherwise be included, but sometimes merely emblematical.

1561 NORTON & SACKV. *Gorboduc* (1847) 94 The Order of the domme shewe before the firste Acte, and the Signification therof. **1602** SHAKS. *Ham.* III. ii. 14 Groundlings, who (for the most part) are capeable of nothing, but inexplicable dumbe shewes, and noise. *a* **1628** F. GREVILLE *Sidney* (1652) 77 Both stood still a while, like a dumb shew in a tragedy. **1674** S. VINCENT *Gallant's Acad.* 20 You have heard..nothing but the Prologue, and seen no more than a Dumb Show: Our *Vetus Comedia* steps out now. **1887** SAINTSBURY *Hist. Elizab. Lit.* vii. (1890) 275 The recourse to dumb show (which, however, Webster again permitted himself in *The Duchess*).

2. Significant gesture without speech.

1588 SHAKS. *Tit. A.* III. i. 31 Or shall we bit our tongues, and in dumbe shewes Passe the remainder of our..dayes? **1611** COTGR., *Emparle silence*, a dumbe shew, or speaking by signes. **1711** ADDISON *Spect.* No. 123 ¶5 Expressing in dumb Show those Sentiments of..Gratitude that were too big for Utterance. **1888** FRITH *Autobiog.* III. v. 109 A great master in the art of conveying a story by dumb-show.

3. *attrib.*, as ***dumb-show-man.***

1812 J. NOTT *Dekker's Gvlls Horne-bk.* 56 *note*, A sort of dumb-show-man stands forth between the acts, holding up a board on which is inscribed the business of the act about to commence.

dumb-waiter. [see DUMB *a.* 8.]

1. An article of dining-room furniture, intended to dispense with the services of a waiter at table.

In its typical form, an upright pole bearing one or more revolving trays or shelves. On these are placed dishes and other table requisites, which can thus readily be got at as required. Other simpler forms have also been used.

1749 J. CLELAND *Mem. Woman Pleasure* I. 156 A bottle of Burgundy, with the other necessaries, were set on a dumb-waiter. **1755** *Mem. Capt. P. Drake* II. iii. 49 As soon as Supper was over, Glasses and a Bottle of Burgundy with a Flask of Champaign, was laid on the Table, with a Supply of those Wines on a Dumb-Waiter. **1779** BOSWELL in Fitzgerald *Life* (1891) 265 We dined in all the elegance of two courses and a dessert, with dumb waiters. **1824** SCOTT *Let. to Ld. Montagu* 14 Apr. in *Lockhart.* **1861** DICKENS *Gt. Expect.* xxvi, A capacious dumb-waiter, with a variety of bottles and decanters on it. **1884** SHORTHOUSE *Schoolmaster Mark* II. vii, Dumb waiters..were placed by the table's side, and the servants left the room.

2. 'A movable frame, by which dishes, etc. are passed from one room or story of a house to another.' (Webster, 1864.) orig. *U.S.*

['So called in my father's house.' F. Hall.]

1847 WEBSTER 372/2 When the kitchen is in the basement, the dumb-waiter is made to rise and fall by means of pulleys and weights. **1876** J. S. INGRAM *Centenn. Exposition* iii. 69 The general kitchen whence the food is distributed throughout the upper stories by means of dumb waiters. **1903** A. H. LEWIS *Boss* vi. 69 There's a dumb waiter from the bar to send up beer and smokes. **1960** H. PINTER *Dumb Waiter* 16 Disclosed is a serving-hatch, a 'dumb waiter'. A wide box is held by pulleys.

dumby, earlier form of DUMMY.

dum casta (dʌm 'kæstə). *Law.* [L.; short for *dum sola et casta vixerit* as long as she shall live alone and chaste.] A clause in a legal instrument conferring on a woman a benefit which is to cease should she cease to lead a chaste life, or should she marry or remarry.

[**1628** E. COKE *First Pt. Inst. Laws Eng.* III. 234[v] *Dum*, also maketh a limitation, as if a Lease be made, *Dum sola fuerit*, or *Dum sola & casta vixerit.*] **1883** J. M. LELY *Wharton's Law Lex.* (ed. 7) 280/2 This proviso is termed the 'dum casta clause'. **1905** *Law Jrnl. Rep.*, *Prob.* LXXIV. 3/1 The main subject to be regarded is the temptation to which the wife may be exposed; and in this respect it appears a material precaution that the limitation *dum casta* should be inserted. **1906** *Westm. Gaz.* 29 Mar. 7/2 The question..was whether it was a condition of the allowance of £100 that a *dum casta* or chastity clause should be inserted. **1960** *Times* 15 Jan. 15/7 The defendant..forfeited..her right to maintenance ..by committing a breach of the *dum sola et casta* clause in the order.

dum-dum ('dʌmdʌm). Also Dum Dum, Dum-Dum. [f. *Dum-Dum*, name of a town and arsenal near Calcutta, where they were first produced.] In full ***dum-dum bullet***: a metal-cased bullet with a soft core uncovered at the point, which expands on impact. Hence '**dum-dum** *v. trans.*, to convert into a dum-dum bullet.

1897 *Westm. Gaz.* 14 Dec. 7/3 The piper hero, Findlater, was wounded in the ankle with a Dum Dum bullet. **1898** *Ibid.* 25 Mar. 3/1 That the War Office authorities are not responsible directly for Dum-dumming the Lee-Metford bullets. **1899** *Ibid.* 25 Nov. 6/1 Any man can 'Dum-Dum' his own cartridges in a very few minutes by merely filing the nickel envelope off the nose of the bullet. **1906** *Ibid.* 27 Mar. 9/2 It is impossible that the Kaiser can know or approve of the adoption of the dum-dum. **1968** *Peace News* 12 Apr. 8/3 Dum-dum bullets were outlawed by 22–2 votes. **1970** *Daily Tel.* 9 Jan. 3/7 Use of the dum-dum has been classified as a war crime by a number of international conventions, including the Hague Declaration of 1907.

dume, obs. f. DUMB; obs. Sc. f. DOOM *v.*

dumetose (djuːmɪ'təʊs), *a. Bot.* [f. L. *dūmētum* thicket (of thorn-bushes), f. *dūmus* thorn-bush, bramble: see -OSE.] Bush-like.

a **1864** HENSLOW is cited by Webster.

dumfound, -er: see DUMBFOUND, -ER.

‖**dumka** ('dʊmkə, 'duːmkə). *Mus.* Pl. **dumkas, dumky.** [Czech. = plaintive song, elegy.] An alternately melancholy and gay piece of music, found chiefly in the work of Slavonic composers.

[**1886** A. DVOŘÁK (*title*) Dumka a Furiant.] **1895** W. H. HADOW *Stud. Mod. Mus.* 2nd Ser. 221 Even more distinctive is his [*sc.* Dvořák's] treatment of the Dumka or 'Elegy', a complex form which, like a sonnet-sequence, holds in combination a series of separate poems. **1947** A. EINSTEIN *Mus. Rom. Era* xvii. 302 Dvořák was less regionally limited than Smetana; although he still wrote polkas, dumkas, and furiants, he also wrote waltzes and mazurkas.

dummel ('dʌməl), *a.* (*sb.*) *dial.* [app. a deriv. of DUMB, with the more general sense seen in Ger. *dumm*, Du. *domm.*]

A. *adj.* Stupid, dull, slow. **B.** *sb.* A dumb person; a stupid, dull person.

1570 LEVINS *Manip.* 55 A Dumel, *stupidus*..A Dummel, *mutus.* **1847–78** HALLIWELL, *Dummil*, a slow jade. *Salop.* **1878** JEFFERIES *Gamekeeper at H.* 155 Severe weather, which makes all wild animals 'dummel'. **1881** *Leicestersh. Gloss.*, *Dummel*, a dolt; a blockhead. **1883** *Hampsh. Gloss.*, *Dumble*, stupid. *Dummell*, slow to comprehend. **1888** *Berksh. Wds.*, *Dummle*, in animals, sluggish.

†**'dummerell.** *Obs. rare*$^{-1}$. [f. DUMB *a.*] A dumb person; a dummy.

1592 G. HARVEY *Pierce's Super.* 185 Is it not impossible for Humanity to be a Spittle-man, Rhetorique a dummerell ..History a bankrowt?

†**'dummerer.** *slang.* (*obs.* exc. *arch.*) Also 6 **dommerar,** 7 **-er.** [f. DUMB *a.*] The cant name for a beggar who pretended to be dumb.

1567 HARMAN *Caveat* xii. (1869) 57 The Dommerars are lewd and most subtyll people; the moste part of these are Walch men. **1615** J. STEPHENS *Satyr. Ess.* 274 It is thought he will turne Dummerer, he practises already, and is..many times taken speechlesse. **1622** FLETCHER *Beggar's Bush* II. i, Higgen your orator..That whilom was your Dommerer. **1725** in *New Cant Dict.* **1834** H. AINSWORTH *Rookwood* III. v, The dummerar, whose tongue had been cut out by the Algerines. **1931** J. BUCHAN *Blanket of Dark* xvi. 304 There was a troop of crowders in the little town, and as many cozeners and dommerers as if it had been an abbey-gate.

dummify ('dʌmɪfaɪ), *v. nonce-wd.* [f. DUMMY + -FY.] *trans.* To make a dummy of.

1893 LADY FL. DIXIE in *Mod. Rev.* I. v. 461 Royalty, mummyfied by custom and dummyfied by law.

'dumminess. *rare.* [f. DUMMY *sb.* + -NESS.] The quality of being a dummy.

1852 C. A. BRISTED *Eng. University* (ed. 2) 235 *note*, A little anecdote..which..strikingly illustrates the dumminess of a certain class of the English population.

‖**dummkopf** ('dʊmkɒpf). *colloq.* (orig. *U.S.*). Also dom cop, dum(b)kopf. [G., see DUMBHEAD.] = DUMBHEAD.

1809 'D. KNICKERBOCKER' *Hist. N.Y.* II. v. ii. 16 As great a dom cop, as if he had been educated among that learned people of Thrace, who..could not count beyond the number four. **1834** CARLYLE *Sart. Res.* II. vii. 59/1 Not being born purely a Loghead (*Dummkopf*), thou hadst no other outlook. **1894** G. DU MAURIER *Trilby* I. II. 166 Great big she-fool that you are—sheep's head! Dummkopf! Donnerwetter! **1923** M. WATTS *L. Nichols* 15 All I got to do is wait on dumkopfs! **1951** M. LOWRY *Lett.* (1967) 237 He was..as brilliant a teacher as I was a dummkopf of a pupil. **1968** *Listener* 31 Oct. 567/3 They may turn out, after all, to have been fall guys, dumbkopfs, dupes of their own chicanery.

dummy, ('dʌmɪ), *sb.* Also 6–7 *Sc.* **dummie, dumbie,** 8 **dummee,** 9 **dumbee, dumby.** (The usual modern form is **dummy.**) [f. DUMB *a.* + -Y. Cf. BLACKY, DARKY.]

1. a. A dumb person. *colloq.*

1598 FERGUSON *Scot. Prov.* (1785) 10 (Jam.) Dummie canna lie. **1619** BOYD *Last Battell of Soule* (1629) 1049 (Jam.) All men are lyers, but Dummie cannot lye. **1681** COLVIL *Whigs Supplic.* (1751) 120 Like to dumbies making signs. **1823** MOORE *Fables* 26 The wise men of Egypt were secret as dummies. **1826** J. WILSON *Noct. Ambr.* Wks. 1855

I. 117 Tongue-tied like a dumbie. *a* **1849** HOR. SMITH *Addr. Mummy* ii, Speak! for thou long enough hast acted dummy.

b. A deaf-mute; a tramp or beggar who pretends to be deaf and dumb. *slang.*

1874 in HOTTEN *Slang Dict.* **1918** 'A No. 1' in N. Anderson *Hobo* (1923) vii. 100 *Dummy*. Pretends to be deaf and dumb. **1926** J. BLACK *You can't Win* vi. 70 What do you do if you bump into a natural dummy when you're D. D.ing? **1940** C. MCCULLERS *Heart is Lonely Hunter* (1943) I. iv. 47 But a dummy!.. 'Are there any other deaf-mute people here?' he asked.

2. a. At *Whist*, An imaginary player represented by an exposed 'hand', managed by and serving as partner to one of the players; a game so played.

double dummy, a game in which two 'hands' are exposed, so that each of the two players manages two 'hands'.

1736 SWIFT *Proposal for Regul. Quadrille* Wks. 1824 VII. 374 She shall not handle a card that night, but *Dummy* shall be substituted in her room. **1825** LAMB *Lett.* (1888) II. 140 We have a corner at double dumbee for you. **1826** DISRAELI *Viv. Grey* (L.) He proposed that we should play double dummy. *a* **1839** PRAED *Poems* (1864) II. 181 He'll see her, silent as a mummy, At whist, with her two maids and dummy. **1856** *Whist-player* (1858) 70 Dummy cannot revoke. **1860** *Bohn's Hand-bk. Games* IV. 178 He who draws the lowest card takes Dumby as his partner.

b. In auction or contract Bridge, the hand of the declarer's (in the old type of Bridge, of the dealer's) partner, which is displayed and is played by the declarer; also, the player whose cards are thus displayed; *double dummy* (see quot. 1964). Also *attrib.*

1886 *Biritch, or Russian Whist* 2 No suggestions as to play may be made by the one standing out (Dummy) to the dealer. **1894** 'BOAZ' *Pkt. Guide to Bridge* 5 After the first player has played a card, the dealer plays his partner's hand, which, like Dummy, is placed face upwards on the table. **1901** R. F. FOSTER *Bridge* 17 After laying down his cards.. the dummy takes no further part in the play, and is not allowed to make any remarks or suggestions. **1901** W. DALTON *Bridge Abridged* 23 With very bad cards in your own hand, there is a slightly increased possibility of an exceptional hand in your Dummy. *Ibid.*, After the first card is led the Dummy hand is exposed. **1903** [see BRIDGE *sb.*[2] b]. **1904** *Bridge & Progressive Bridge* 18 Dummy Bridge, or Bridge for three players, can be played in several ways. The following is the best system:—The player who cuts the lowest card takes Dummy against the other two players.. and the Dummy hand is placed opposite to him. *Ibid.* 22 Double Dummy Bridge, or Bridge for two players, is not at all a bad game. **1910** W. DALTON *'Saturday' Bridge* (9th imp.) 14 After exposing Dummy, the dealer's partner has no part whatever in the game. *Ibid.* xvi. 230, Z leads to the first trick, and A's hand is exposed on the table, and A becomes the dummy for that deal. **1936** E. CULBERTSON *Contract Bridge Complete* xxxix. 443 South leads a small trump and dummy's Queen is taken by East's King. **1955** *Times* 6 July 4/7 It is not a double-dummy problem to find the best line of play by the declarer. **1964** *Official Encycl. Bridge* 131/1 *Double dummy*, play of a hand that could not be improved upon, as though declarer were looking at all four hands... It can also be used to refer to perfect play by the defenders. Originally, double dummy was a two-handed form of whist in which each player had a dummy. Some players exposed all four hands, thus giving rise to the modern usage. **1969** E. H. PINTO *Treen* 224 Playing card stands.. are used in double dummy bridge.

3. A person who has nothing to say or who takes no active part in affairs; a dolt, blockhead.

1796 MRS. M. ROBINSON *Angelina* II. 61 Those who take you for a dummy will be out of their reckoning. **1840** DICKENS *Barn. Rudge* lxi, If the chief magistrate's a man and not a dummy. **1856** MISS MULOCK *J. Halifax* (ed. 17) 219 Half the House of Commons is made up of harmless dummies.

4. One who is a mere tool of another; a 'man of straw'; in *Australia*, a man employed to take up crown-land as if for himself, but in reality for another person who is not entitled to do so.

1866 ROGERSON *Poems* 23 The good selectors got most of the land The dummies being afraid to stand. **1880** C. H. PEARSON in *Victorian Rev.* I. 527 No doubt this will reduce the area upon which dummying is profitable, and the average profits of dummies. **1885** *Law Times Rep.* LI. 687/2 The petitioner was from first to last a mere dummy in the hands of Mr. Tassie.

5. A counterfeit object made to resemble the real thing, as a sham or empty package, drawer, etc. in a shop, made as though containing goods; a substitute used to mark or occupy a space in an arrangement of articles, etc.; *spec.*, **a.** A block, model, or lay figure on which clothes, hair, etc. are displayed. (See also *tailor's dummy* s.v. TAILOR *sb.* 6 b.) **b.** A figure representing a man in rifle or artillery practice. **c.** A floating landing-stage, or dumb barge. **d.** A hatter's pressing-iron. **e.** A set of sheets or leaves of paper made to resemble a book or document. See also quots. 1858, 1864, 1964, and cf. 6. So *in dummy*, in dummy form.

a **1845** HOOD *Tale Trumpet* vii, She was deaf as any tradesman's dummy. **1850** THACKERAY *Hobson's Choice* ii. Wks. 1886 XXIV. 228 A dark green suit.. purchased at an establishment in Holborn, off the dummy at the door. **1851** *Illustr. Lond. News* 53 Attempted to jump on to the 'dummy' before the vessel had got quite alongside. **1856** S. C. BREES *Gloss. Terms*, *Dumby*, a floating barge connected with a pier. **1857** MRS. MATHEWS *Tea-T. Talk* I. 341 Like the dummies on a young lawyer's shelf. **1858** SIMMONDS *Dict. Trade*, *Dummy*.. a name given by firemen to the jets from the mains or chief water pipes. **1864** WEBSTER, *Dummy*, 1. A dumb-waiter (*Colloq.*).. 5. A locomotive with condensing engines, and, hence, without the noise of escaping steam. **1870** *Illustr. Lond. News* 24 Sept. 327 On Friday the small gun was again fired, at various ranges, from 1200 down to 400 yards, at targets and at dummies.. making the same targets and producing the like destructive effect among the dummies. **1871** *Daily News* 28 Apr. (Farmer), The Bill is not yet in the hands of members or public, the document placed on the table of the Lords being what is, in parliamentary slang, called a 'dummy'. **1893** *Leeds Mercury* 19 May 5/2 Mr. Acland.. laid the new Evening School Code in dummy form on the table of the House of Commons. **1898** A. J. BALFOUR in *Hansard Commons* 20 June 768 The Report has been presented in dummy, and is now being proceeded with. **1929** F. W. CARTER *Secrets of your Daily Paper* 59 They are supplied with what is known as a 'dummy' or a 'make-up'. **1964** *Gloss. Letterpress Rotary Print. Terms* (*B.S.I.*) 12 *Dummies*, blank or printed copies usually made up for editorial or production purposes. **1967** *Times Rev. Industry* Aug. 69/1 A mammoth *Encyclopaedia of Education*, the dummy of which looks most impressive even though not all the contents are in it.

f. In full *dummy teat*. An indiarubber teat put into a baby's mouth to soothe it. Also *fig.*

1903 *Science Siftings* 22 Aug. 269/1, I never saw the child but it had a dummy in its mouth. **1906** *Chemist & Druggist* LXIX. 648/2 There has been little progress in the shape of the 'dummy teat'. **1915** D. H. LAWRENCE *Let.* 12 Feb. (1962) I. 316 He [*sc.* E. M. Forster] sucks his dummy—you know, those child's comforters—long after his age. *a* **1930** —— *Last Poems* (1932) 273 The British Public.. gets bigger and bigger.. and its dummy-teat has to be made bigger and bigger and bigger.

g. (Rugby) Football. *to give* (or *sell*) *the* (or *a*) *dummy*: to feign to pass the ball so as to deceive one's opponent. *colloq.*

1907 'OLD INTERNATIONAL' *Rugby Guide* 27 Feinting, 'giving a dummy', or pretending to pass is a useful adjunct to the numerous other qualifications of a good centre. *a* **1914** J. E. RAPHAEL *Mod. Rugby Football* (1918) 125 A little judicious 'dummy' giving might be very effective in securing an opening. **1920** *Times* 8 Nov. 6/3 R. C. Pickles 'sold the dummy' really cleverly to score again for Gloucestershire.

h. The punishment cell in a prison. *N.Z. slang.*

1936 'R. HYDE' *Passport to Hell* iii. 60 It is always dusk in the Dummy, which lies underground. *Ibid.* iii. 65 Twenty-one days on bread and water in the Dummy. **1945** O. BURTON *In Prison* vii. 107 The aggressor in this case was promptly led off and incarcerated in the 'dummy'.

i. A figure representing a human being, animal, etc., used by a ventriloquist. Cf. DOLL *sb.*[1] 2 b. Also *fig.*

1936 E. SITWELL *Victoria* xix. 229 The miserable, hallucinated ventriloquist-dummy hero of one of the most notorious murder trials. **1950** [see DOLL *sb.*[1] 2 b]. **1960** *Economist* 8 Oct. 175/1 Is he no more than the ventriloquist's dummy for any scientific pressure group that is not getting its way with the Treasury?

j. In a double bail in a milking shed, the structure which separates the foreparts of the two cows, keeps them in position for milking, and serves as a stand for parts of the milking machine. *N.Z.*

1950 *N.Z. Jrnl. Agric.* Apr. 378/3 The use of galvanised iron piping or iron piping for erection of internal dummies and partitions. *Ibid.* May 479 (*caption*) A small dairy with suspended dummy and bucket milking machine for one cow.

k. *Computing.* An instruction or a sequence of data that merely occupies space, used either to regularize the position of other items or to allow a later insertion. Usu. *attrib.*

1948 GOLDSTINE & VON NEUMANN in *Coll. Wks. J. von Neumann* (1963) V. 158 The three *a*'s must obtain numbers of the same parity. This may necessitate the insertion of dummy (ineffective, irrelevant) orders in appropriate places. **1951** M. WILKES et al. *Preparation of Programs for an Electronic Digital Computer* 148 Order 13 is I F during input of punched digits, T F for dummy zeros which make up remainder of 10 digits. *c* **1964** *KDF9 Programming Man.* iv. 22 Any instruction preceded by an asterisk will be compiled as the first instruction in a new word, any redundant spaces in the preceding word being filled with dummy instructions. **1969** LEHMAN & BAILEY *Digital Computing* x. 193/2 The function might be defined as SUM(A,B,C,D) = A + B + C + D. In this case, the dummy variables are A, B, C, and D. When the function reference is executed, these dummy variables take on the values of the variables named in the reference. **1970** F. STUART *Fortran Programming* (ed. 2) ix. 203 All arguments mentioned as dummies may be duplicated in other subprograms or in the main program, without causing error.

6. *slang.* A pocket-book.

1785 in GROSE *Dict. Vulg. Tongue* (Farmer). **1812** in J. H. VAUX *Flash Dict.* **1834** H. AINSWORTH *Rookwood* III. v, Then out with the dummy.

7. a. *attrib.* or *adj.* Counterfeit, sham: see 4. *dummy whist*: see 2.

1843 LEFEVRE *Life Trav. Physic.* III. III. xi. 234, I found three gentlemen playing a rubber of dummy whist. **1846** *Punch* XI. 185 (Farmer) A Dummy list of Causes has long since been preferred. **1870** READE *Put yourself*, etc. I. xi. 275 A very beautiful organ that had an oval mirror in the midst of its gilt dummy pipes. **1872** O. W. HOLMES *Poet Breakf.-t.* i. (1885) 13 The dummy clock-dial. **1892** STEVENSON *Across the Plains* 15, I have.. enjoyed some capital sport there with a dummy gun. **1971** J. LEASOR *Love-All* i. 6 Now for the flat, number 1792... Floor 17, flat two. The nine was just a dummy digit to make the building seem more important... Some people did that with their names and added an extra initial.. Harry S. Truman for example. **1971** *Listener* 22 Apr. 521/2 Of 91 human volunteers, 47 received three grams of ascorbic acid daily for nine days, and 44 others took dummy tablets.

b. *Comb.* **dummy-head(ed)** *a.*, applied to a torpedo which is provided with a thin copper head and filled with water for target practice; **dummy run** *colloq.*, orig. *Naval slang* (see quots. 1916 and 1929); hence, a practice attack, exercise, landing, etc.; a 'trial run', a rehearsal.

1906 *Daily Chron.* 8 Sept. 5/3 A large proportion of the dummy-headed torpedoes struck her hull. **1923** *Daily Mail* 22 June 5 The 'planes released six dummy-head aerial torpedoes. **1916** *In Northern Mists* xvi. 60 At certain firing practices the ship steams along a buoyed course, aiming the guns at the target but not actually firing, as a rehearsal or dummy run. **1929** F. BOWEN *Sea Slang* 42 *Dummy run*, a practice evolution in the Navy. **1943** C. H. WARD-JACKSON *Piece of Cake* 27 *Dummy run*, a bombing raid or target approach during which no bombs are dropped. **1959** *Punch* 6 May 604/1 A man of my known and respected equanimity was considered the ideal vehicle for a dummy run. **1962** *Listener* 31 May 942/1 The pied wagtails made dummy runs over the hawks' heads. **1967** E. GRIERSON *Crime of one's Own* vii. 57 It was a dummy run... What I saw today was part of the cover story.

dummy, *v.* [f. prec. sb.] **1.** *trans.* To select or take up (land) in one's own name, but really in the interest of another person who is not himself entitled to do so. Also *absol.* *Australia.*

1873 TROLLOPE *Austr. & N.Z.* vi. 101 The.. system is generally called dummying—putting up a non-existent free selector—and is illegal. **1880** C. H. PEARSON in *Victorian Rev.* I. 527 A cry is raised.. that land is dummied for rich men. *Ibid.* 531 A man who has dummied 320 acres. **1885** MRS. C. PRAED *Head Station* 15 The expediency of doing a little 'dummying'.

2. *intr.* *to dummy up*: to refuse to talk or give information; to keep quiet. *U.S. slang.*

1926 J. BLACK *You can't Win* xix. 282 He dummies up on the natives an' in a couple of days they let him go. **1942** R. CHANDLER *High Window* (1943) xx. 145 You can't dummy up on a murder case. **1962** K. ORVIS *Damned & Destroyed* xii. 84 All right, dummy up, then.

3. *trans.* To prepare a dummy (DUMMY *sb.* 5 e) of (a book, document, etc.). Also *intr.* (with *in*) of copy: to fit into a lay-out. *U.S.*

1928 in *Funk's Stand. Dict.* **1952** *Time* 21 Apr., *Dummy* (v.t.), to lay out a sample issue of the magazine, showing where editorial material and ads will be printed. **1967** L. J. BRAUN *Cat who ate Danish Modern* iv. 33 The copy dummied in perfectly, cut-lines spaced out evenly.

4. *trans.* In Football, to feint (a pass); to deceive (an opponent) by means of a feigned pass, a body-swerve, etc. Also *intr.* So *to dummy one's way.* Cf. DUMMY *sb.* 5 g.

1958 *Times* 13 Oct. 15/1 Once Ridd nearly dummied his way through a wall of humanity. **1960** E. S. & W. J. HIGHAM *High Speed Rugby* xviii. 262 The fly-half dummies a pass to him and then slips the ball back inside to the blindside wing. **1960** T. MCLEAN *Kings of Rugby* 148 Jackson made dummying runs which lightened the gathering gloom. **1961** *Times* 8 May 4/6 Smith.. dummied King one way, swivelled the other and on the turn cracked a fierce shot to the roof of the Leicester net. **1967** *Ibid.* 9 Oct. 13/8 A typically brilliant try by Pickering, who dummied his way over near the posts.

So **ˈdummyism**, the practice of dummying land.

1875 *Spectator* (Melbourne) 19 June 80/2 'Larrikinism' was used as a synonym for 'blackguardism', and 'dummyism' for 'perjury'. **1877** M. CLARKE *Hist. Australia* 211 It contains powers to prevent dummyism, and gives concessions to Crown lessees. **1880** C. H. PEARSON in *Victorian Rev.* I. 532 In Victoria.. the system specially favours dummyism.

dummygrane, var. of DEMIGRAINE, *Obs.*

1568 *Satir. Poems Reform.* xlviii. 76 With vlis to renew it ..And gar it glanss lyk Dummygrane.

dumortierite (djuːˈmɔːtɪəraɪt). *Min.* [Named 1881 after M. Dumortier.] A silicate of alumina, occurring in minute crystals in gneiss, and showing unusual dichroism.

1881 *Amer. Jrnl. Sc.* Ser. III. XXII. 157 Dumortierite.. has a bright blue color.

dumose (djuːˈməʊs), *a.* *rare.* [ad. L. *dūmōs-us* bushy, f. *dūmus* thorn-bush, bramble.] **a.** Full of bushes. **b.** *Bot.* Having a compact bushy habit of growth.

[**1623** COCKERAM, *Dumosous*, full of bushes.] **1721** BAILEY, *Dumose*, full of Brambles and Briers.

Hence **duˈmosity**.

1656 BLOUNT *Glossogr.*, *Dumosity*, that hath many, or is full of Brambles or Bryers. (Sic.)

dumous (ˈdjuːməs), *a.* = DUMOSE, a.

1847 in CRAIG.

dump (dʌmp), *sb.*[1] Also 6 **dompe, doompe, dumppe**, 6–7 **dumpe**. [First found early in 16th c.; derivation obscure.

In form it corresponds to MDu. *domp* exhalation, haze, mist; and possibly the original notion might be a mental haze or mist, in which the mind is befogged; but connecting links are not known, and the sense-development in Eng. does not quite favour such a starting-point. Cf. also the Ger. adj. *dumpf*, LG. *dump*, dull, flat, hollow (in sound), dead, obtuse; mentally depressed, clouded, dazed, or dulled, having the sensations blunted (Grimm); gloomy (silence) (Flügel); but this is known only from middle of 18th c., and has no corresponding sb.]

†**1.** A fit of abstraction or musing, a reverie; a dazed or puzzled state, a maze; perplexity,

amazement; absence of mind. (Often in *pl.*) *Obs.*

1523 SKELTON *Garl. Laurell* 14 So depely drownyd I was in this dumpe, encraumpyshed so sore was my conceyte, That, me to rest, I lent me to a stumpe of an oke. **1530** [see DUMP *v.*[2] 1]. **1586** J. HOOKER *Girald. Irel.* in *Holinshed* II. 17/1 [They] were in a great dumpe and perplexitie, and in a maner were at their wits end. **1611** COTGR., *Donner la muse à*, to put into a dumpe, to make to studie, or pause about a matter. **1663** BUTLER *Hud.* I. ii. 973 To rouse him from lethargic dump, He tweak'd his nose, with gentle thump. *c* **1698** LOCKE *Cond. Underst.* §45 The shame that such dumps cause to well-bred people, when it carries them away from the company.

2. A fit of melancholy or depression; now only in *pl.* (*colloq.* and more or less *humorous*): Heaviness of mind, dejection, low spirits.

1529 MORE *Comf. agst. Trib.* I. Wks. 1140/2 What heapes of heauynesse, hathe of late fallen amonge vs alreadye, with whiche some of our poore familye bee fallen into suche dumpes. **1555** W. WATREMAN *Fardle Facions* II. viii. 179 Nor lacke throwe men into desperate doompes. **1582** T. WATSON *Centurie of Loue* xi. (Arb.) 47 Into howe sorrowfull a dumpe, or sounden extasie he fell. *c* **1600** *Chevy Chase* 198 For Witherington needs must I wayle As one in doleful dumpes. **1664** BUTLER *Hud.* II. i. 85 His head, like one in doleful dump, Between his Knees. **1714** *Swift's Corr.* Wks. 1841 II. 513 He tells me that he left you [Swift] horridly in the dumps. **1785** GROSE *Dict. Vulg. Tongue* s.v., *Down in the dumps*, low spirited, melancholy. **1850** THACKERAY *Lett.* 23 Apr., If I am dismal don't I give you the benefit of the dumps?

†**3.** A mournful or plaintive melody or song; also, by extension, a tune in general; sometimes app. used for a kind of dance. *Obs.*

a **1553** UDALL *Royster D.* II. i. (Arb.) 32 Then twang with our sonets, and twang with our dumps, And heyhough from our heart, as heauie as lead lumpes. *a* **1586** SIDNEY *Sonn.* in Arb. *Garner* II. 180 Some good old dumpe, that Chaucers mistresse knew. **1591** SHAKS. *Two Gent.* III. ii. 85 To their Instruments Tune a deploring dumpe. **1610** HOLLAND *Camden's Brit.* I. 421 The funerall Song or Dump of a most ancient British Bard. **1706** ADDISON *Rosamond* I. iv, What heart of stone Can hear her moan, And not in dumps so doleful join? *a* **1852** MOORE *Vision* ii. 33 Like..an Irish Dump ('the words by Moore') At an amateur concert screamed in score.

dump, *sb.*[2] [Not known before the latter part of 18th c., some time later than DUMPY *a.*[2], from which it is prob. a back-formation.]

A term familiarly applied to various objects of 'dumpy' shape.

a. A roughly-cast leaden counter, used by boys in some games. (In quot. 1859 applied to the disk of metal or 'blank' before being coined.) **b.** A name of certain small coins; *esp.* a coin worth 1*s.* 3*d.* formerly current in Australia, made by punching a disk out of the middle of a Spanish dollar and milling the edge. Hence (*slang* or *colloq.*) used allusively for a small coin or amount; and in *pl.* for money in general. Colloq. phr. ***not to care a dump***: not to care at all; to regard as unimportant. **c.** A kind of bolt or nail used in ship-building (also ***dump-bolt, dump-nail***); see quots. **d.** A kind of quoit made of rope for playing on board ship. **e.** A local name for a short thick skittle; *pl.* the game played with these. **f.** A globular sweetmeat, a 'bull's-eye'. **g.** Applied to a short and stout person.

a. 1770–90 D. KILNER *Village School* ix. in Miss Yonge *Storehouse of Stories* (1870) 369, I could buy..a top too, and some dumps, and a new skipping-rope. **1785** GROSE *Dict. Vulg. Tongue* s.v., Dumps are also small pieces of lead, cast by schoolboys in the shape of money. **1825** HONE *Every-day Bk.* I. 253 The capons were leaden representations of cocks and hens pitched at by leaden dumps. **1827** HOOD *Retrospect. Rev.* v, My dumps are made of more than lead. *a* **1845** —— *Tale Trumpet* xxxvi, Playing at dumps, or pitch in the hole. **1859** *All Year Round* No. 10. 239 The golden dumps that are passed into the Weighing Room..are distributed amongst the balances.

b. 1821 *Bank of N.S. Wales Notice* 5 May, in Hyman *Coins Austral.* (1893) III. 59 The following Description of illegal Coin is much in Circulation:—Dollars and Dumps that are not Silver. **1842** BARHAM *Ingol. Leg., Sir Rupert*, When a gentleman jumps In the river at midnight for want of 'the dumps'. **1843** *Ainsworth's Mag.* IV. 315 Mrs. Dodger didn't care a 'dump' if she didn't. **1844** J. T. HEWLETT *Parsons & W.* xxxv, It's all gone, every dump. **1852** J. WEST *Hist. Tasmania* II. 141 Dumps struck out from dollars. **1870** HENFREY *Guide Eng. Coins* (1891) 293 The pieces (halfpence and farthings) of 1717 and 1718 are much thicker and smaller than those of the following dates, and generally go by the name of dumps. **1892** A. BIRRELL *Res Judicata* iv. 116 One of those questions..that..does not matter a dump. **1908** G. K. CHESTERTON *All Things Considered* 70, I do not care a dump whether they know the alphabet.

c. 1794 *Rigging & Seamanship* I. 7, *Nails, Dump*, are round, and have long flat points. **1867** SMYTH *Sailor's Word-bk.*, *Dump-bolt*, a short bolt driven in to the plank and timber as a partial security previous to the thorough fastenings being put in. **1879** *Cassell's Techn. Educ.* IV. 60/1 The fastenings..in the deck-planking..consist of nails or dumps (short bolts) driven into, not through the beams.

e. 1895 *W. Sussex County Times* 4 May 8/5 A game known as 'dumps'.

f. 1869 BLACKMORE *Lorna D.* ii. 5 Some of us..having sucked much parliament and dumps at my only charges. **1894** —— *Perlycross* 2 The big Tom Waldron supplied the little Phil Penniloe with dumps and penny-puddings.

g. 1840 E. HOWARD *Jack Ashore* xviii. (Stratm.), Her dump of a daughter. **1867** CARLYLE *Remin.* II. 53 A puffy, thickset, vulgar little dump of an old man. **1887** C. HAZARD *Mem. Diman* v. 94 The little dump of a rector made an eloquent address on the importance of observing the laws.

dump, *sb.*[3] *local.* [perh. of Norse origin: cf. Norw. *dump* pit, pool, also dial. Ger. *dumpf*, *dümpfel*, *dümpel*, a deep place in flowing or standing water, an abyss (Grimm); Du. *dompelen* to plunge, dive, dip.] A deep hole in the bed of a river or pond.

1788 W. MARSHALL *E. Yorksh.* Gloss., *Dump*, a deep hole of water; feigned at least to be bottomless. **1868** ATKINSON *Cleveland Gloss.*, *Dump*, a deep hole in the bed of a river, or in a pool of water. **1887** RUSKIN *Hortus Inclusus* 28 An Alpine stream..becomes a series of humps and dumps wherever it is shallow.

dump, *sb.*[4] [f. DUMP *v.*[1], senses 2, 3.]

1. a. (Chiefly *U.S.*) A pile or heap of refuse or other matter 'dumped' or thrown down. *spec.* A pile of ore, earth, etc., which accumulates during mining operations; esp. *U.S.* and *S. Afr.* Cf. *mine-dump* (MINE *sb.* 6).

1865 *Harper's Mag.* Feb. 287/1 A number of Mexicans were at work getting out the ore and..I took a seat a little on one side of the 'dump'. **1871** *Rept.* in *Daily News* 21 Sept., The dump is being overhauled and the pay ore selected for the company's mill. **1883** STEVENSON *Silverado Sq.* 81 A canyon..was here walled across by a dump of rolling stones. **1883** *Blackw. Mag.* Jan. 49 *note*, A 'dump' is the mass of refuse matter which gathers at the mouth of a mine. **1885** C. F. HOLDER *Marvels Anim. Life* 8 It was pointed out as an ash-dump from a steamer. **1895** *St. James' Gaz.* 10 Sept. 16/1 Small chips of quartz which I took from the dump of this working. **1909** *Westm. Gaz.* 11 Feb. 3/3 Such statements as that..a mine dump can contain 40,000 tons, and that such a dump consists of 10 per cent. of pitchblende. **1931** J. MOCKFORD *Khama* xxiii. 155 The grey dumps of the world's greatest gold mines. **1948** A. PATON *Cry, Beloved Country* II. viii. 174 He..looked out over the veld, out to the great white dumps of the mines, like hills under the sun. **1956** H. G. DINES *Metalliferous Mining Region S.W. Eng.* I. iv. 117 The dumps were being worked over for uranium ores in 1907.

b. The practice of dumping goods (see DUMP *v.*[1] 2 c); also, the goods dumped.

1884 *Congress. Rec.* 1 May 3663/1 It is this dump that we want to stop; it is protection against this dump that the protective system seeks to accomplish. **1908** *Westm. Gaz.* 8 Apr. 9/2 The present 'dump', which has assumed such amazing proportions in the eyes of the alarmists.

c. A collection of provisions, ammunition, equipment, etc., deposited in a convenient place for later use; also, the place where such supplies are deposited.

1915 *Daily Mail* 30 Dec. 4/6 The Dump! Just a pile of old clothes, battered helmets, decrepit boots, kit bags, shirts, socks, boots—all the little personal properties of soldiers. **1916** J. BUCHAN *Battle of Somme* 55 That same day we..took a 'dump' of German stores. **1918** E. M. ROBERTS *Flying Fighter* 61 One night about six o'clock I received orders to report at an engineers' dump known as Hyde Park Corner. **1919** R. H. REECE *Night Bombing with Bedouins* 6 The gunners may be called upon to fire at certain targets, such as cross-roads or houses used as infantry headquarters or ammunition and stores dumps. **1925** E. F. NORTON *Fight for Everest: 1924* 353 A dump for stores..would seem to be essential half-way between Camps II and III. *Ibid.* 361 To provide dumps of reserve cylinders on the mountain. **1926** T. E. LAWRENCE *Seven Pillars* (1935) III. xxxi. 178 The collection of the necessary food-dumps for the army. **1937** *N. & Q.* CLXXIII. 19/2 Should the Air Ministry succeed in establishing their ammunition 'dump' at Acorn Bank [etc.]. **1939** [see *arms-dump* s.v. ARM *sb.*[2] V].

d. An act of defecation.

1942 BERREY & VAN DEN BARK *Amer. Thes. Slang.* §124/1 *Defecation*,..call of nature, crap, dump. **1966** AUDEN *About House* 26 To start the morning With a satisfactory Dump is a good omen All our adult days.

e. *Computing.* The process or result of dumping data (see DUMP *v.*[1] 5); a printout of stored data; *spec.* a complete listing of the contents of a computer's memory, obtained when a program cannot be fully executed and used to help locate program errors. Freq. *attrib.*

1956 *Computers & Automation* Jan. 15/2 *Dump check*, a check which usually consists of adding all the digits during dumping, and verifying the sum when retransferring. **1959** *Jrnl. Assoc. Computing Machinery* VI. 129 The most generally used debugging technique is the post-mortem (static) dump. **1965** *AFIPS Conf. Proc.* XXVII. 220/2 A weekly dump is prepared of all files which have been used within the last M weeks. **1972** *Computer Jrnl.* XV. 192/1 The incremental dump tapes can..be re-used as soon as the next complete dump has taken place. **1978** J. MCNEIL *Consultant* xxi. 188, I bet you've never had to interpret a dump of a totally unfamiliar program! **1981** *80 Microcomputing* Nov. 276/3 When a large system can't figure out what the heck your program is trying to do, it spits it out as a dump. **1983** *Your Computer* (Austral.) Nov. 20/1 You can keep dumps of source listings on paper while your compiled versions are kept on electronic media.

2. a. (Orig. *U.S.*) A place where refuse material, *esp.* from a mine or quarry, or that collected from domestic refuse bins, is deposited.

1872 RAYMOND *Statist. Mines & Mining* 68 Natural advantages for the construction of dumps and undercurrents. **1883** *Century Mag.* Jan. 327/1 To use [the cañon] as a 'dump' or depository for the 'tailings' or débris of his sluices. **1891** *Boston* (Mass.) *Youth's Comp.* 9 July 13/1 Thrown by housekeepers into the domestic ash-barrel, and from there..taken to the town or city 'dump'.

b. A place, building, house, etc.: usu. as a pejorative or contemptuous term. *colloq.* (orig. *U.S.*).

1899 'J. FLYNT' *Tramping with Tramps* 393 *Dump*, a lodging-house or restaurant; synonymous with 'hang-out'. **1903** *Cincinnati Enquirer* 9 May 13/1 *Dump*, a house; saloon, hang-out for a gang. **1914** JACKSON & HELLYER *Vocab. Criminal Slang* 30 *Dump*, a rendezvous; an establishment of any kind; a hangout; a joint; a meeting place. **1919** F. HURST *Humoresque* 321 You never got in your life to live in a worse dump. **1929** P. JOHNSON *Four Plays* 26 We'll see what's doin' in this bloody dump. **1932** WODEHOUSE *Hot Water* i. 27 Do you think if I had any money I'd be living in a dump like the Château Blissac? **1941** K. TENNANT *Battlers* xxviii. 192 Commercial travellers..were hurrying through these little 'dumps' of towns. **1942** *Daily Express* 8 Jan. 2/7 A uniformed cop patrolled the bar... I didn't think that mattered much at a dump like this. **1959** J. BURKE *Echo of Barbara* ii. 13 We'll go and have an evening in the town here. Not much of a dump, but you'll find quite a good crowd there.

3. a. A dull abrupt blow, a thud; a bump, as of a heavy body falling.

1825 JAMIESON, *Dump*, a stroke [with the feet]. *a* **1859** L. HUNT *Robin Hood* II. xxviii, As in a leathern butt of wine.. Stuck that arrow with a dump. **1894** MRS. CROKER *Mr. Jervis* I. 211 Mrs. Brande..was now let down with a dump.

b. *Surfing.* = DUMPER d.

1935 *Bulletin* (Sydney) 9 Jan. 11/3 It gave the Duke of Gloucester his first experience of a dump, in the Mooloolaba surf. **1963** *Observer* 13 Oct. 15/3 A rider..must be able to.. escape the 'dump' by flicking back off the top of the wave or sliding across to some section where the water is too deep for the wave to break. **1967** J. SEVERSON *Great Surfing* Gloss. 153 *Dump*, a wipe-out in surfing.

4. *attrib.* and *Comb.*, as ***dump-heap, dump-pile*** = sense 1a above; esp. used *attrib.* (chiefly *U.S.*) to designate vehicles having a body that tilts or opens at the back for unloading materials, as ***dump car, cart, truck, wagon***; **dump condenser** (see quot. 1960); **dump tank**, a tank used for receiving a sudden discharge of liquid from a reactor or for storing radioactive liquids while they are dangerous; **dump valve**, a valve which releases the contents of a container quickly.

1912 *Out West* Feb. 133/1 The small *dump cars were wont to carry the yellow gravel from the cut. **1868** *Mich. Agric. Rep.* VII. 347 Joram Priest, Detroit, [manufactured the] 2 *dump carts. **1958** *Nuclear Power* III. 170 Instrumentation system of a typical gas-cooled reactor ..*dump condenser. **1960** *Gloss. Atomic Terms (H.M.S.O.)* 20 *Dump condenser*, a water-cooled steam condenser which allows the heat output of a power reactor to be 'dumped' into the cooling water system should the turbine system become inoperative. **1884** J. G. BOURKE *Snake Dance of Moquis* xxvi. 286 On the outskirts of the town are great *dump-piles. **1959** *Nuclear Energy Engineer* XIII. 337 Reactor for Chalk River... *Dump tanks. **1964** C. F. BONILLA in *Reactor Handbk.* (ed. 2) IV. iii. 122/1 Dump tanks in any of the coolant systems may receive hot discharge from the system at any time. **1930** *Water Works & Sewerage* Dec. 24/3 Where to buy..*Trucks, Dump. **1936** J. STEINBECK *In Dubious Battle* xv. 295 Up the road from Torgas a huge Mack dump-truck rolled. **1959** *New Scientist* 29 Oct. 801/1 Dump trucks..shifted, on an average, over 500 yards an hour. **1930** *Flight* 4 July 760/1 It is intended to let air into this reservoir quickly when the safety *dump valve is used. **1955** *Jrnl. Brit. Interplanetary Soc.* XIV. 16 To give a clean shut-down a dump valve was fitted to the cooling jacket which drained overboard any fuel remaining in it. **1869** *Rep. Comm. Agric. 1868* (U.S.) 357 Wheel-barrows, carts, or *dump-wagons will be necessary. **1969** *Islander* (Victoria, B.C.) 9 Nov. 2/1 There were no trucks as today, 120 mules and 50 to 60 dumpwagons on the move from dawn till dark did the trick.

dump, *a. rare.* [In sense 1, app. f. DUMP *sb.*[1] In sense 2, perh. related to LG. and EFris. *dump* damp, moist, heavy, close, hollow in sound, etc.]

†**1.** In a 'dump', amazed, perplexed; ***to strike dump***, to strike with amazement. (But perhaps an error for to ***strike dumb***.) *Obs.*

1616 S. WARD *Coale from Altar* (1627) 31 How can hee chose but be strucke dumpe? **1622** MABBE tr. *Aleman's Guzman d'Alf.* I. 53 He was strooken so dumpe, and so full of wonder, to see what I had show'd him, that hee had not a word to say. [Cf. *Ibid.* I. 79 Whil'st they were thus strucken into their dumps and doubts.]

2. Of the consistence of dough or dumpling; without elasticity or spring.

1852 *Meanderings of Mem.*, An heiress doughy-like and dump. **1866** J. B. ROSE *Ecl. & Georg. Virg.* 83 The more we knead, the denser will it grow, Adhesive like to pitch and dump as dough.

dump (dʌmp), *v.*[1] Also 4 domp(e. [perh. of Norse origin: cf. Da. *dumpe*, Norw. *dumpa*, Sw. dial. *dompa*, to fall suddenly or with a rush, to fall plump; also in same sense the Sw. str. vb. *dimpa, damp, dumpit*; which may show the primary ablaut series. But the sense of the word has evidently received onomatopœic modification, from its suggestiveness of a dull abruptly-checked blow or thud, and of the action producing this: cf. *thump*.]

†**I.** in ME. use.

†**1. a.** *intr.* To fall with sudden force; to plunge.

13.. *E.E. Allit. P.* C. 362 Vp-so-doun schal ȝe dumpe depe to þe abyme. **1333–52** MINOT *Poems* (1887) x. 24 Kene men sall þe kepe, And do þe dye on a day, and domp in þe depe. *c* **1400** *Destr. Troy* 10713 But I degh of þi dynt, and dump into helle. *Ibid.* 13289 The folke in the flete felly þai drownen:—þai dump in the depe and to dethe passe.

†**b.** *trans.* To cast or fling down forcibly, to plunge down. *Obs.* (exc. as in 2).

a **1300** *Cursor M.* 22643 And driue þam dun all vntil hell, And dump [*Gött.* bete] þe deuels þider in.

II. in modern use.

2. a. *trans.* (orig. *U.S.*) To throw down in a lump or mass, as in tilting anything out of a cart; to shoot or deposit (rubbish, etc.); to fling down or drop (anything) with a bump; to make a dump of (DUMP *sb.*[4] 1 c). Also *fig.*

1784 J. HILTZHEIMER *Diary* 16 Mar. (1893) 62 The Street Commissioners selected sites to dump the dirt from the streets. **1828** WEBSTER, *Dump, v.t.*, to throw or drop, as a load from a cart. **1856** OLMSTED *Slave States* 387 Loading them [carts] with dirt, and dumping them upon the road. **1870** EMERSON *Soc. & Solit., Civilization* Wks. (Bohn) III. 13, I see..California quartz-mountains dumped down in New York. **1879** MACCOOK *Nat. Hist. Agric. Ant Texas* 139 Presently the carcasses..were carried up and dumped into the water. **1880** EARL DUNRAVEN in *19th Cent.* Oct. 593 The houses..are..dumped down anywhere. **1882** *Standard* 9 Dec. 3/6 The tip system..by which manure..can be dumped..with no further labour than working a crank handle to give the..cart body the necessary inclination. **1882** SALA *Amer. Revis.* (1885) 128 A baggage porter 'dumps' trunks and portmanteaus down on the pavement as though he were delighted with the noise they made in falling. **1887** *Westm. Rev.* CXXVIII. 349 Hundreds of thousands of the poorest and least educated peasantry in..Europe were all at once dumped upon the American seaboard. **1890** G. B. SHAW *Fab. Ess. Socialism* 189 To dump four hundred and fifty millions a year down on the Exchequer counter. **1919** A. P. HERBERT *Secret Battle* viii. 165 Philpott..accused him hotly of dumping the rations carelessly anywhere. **1919** G. K. ROSE *2/4th Oxf. & Bucks Lt. Infty.* 35 A pile of logs dumped in the wrong place. **1925** E. F. NORTON *Fight for Everest: 1924* 52 To prepare the camp and dump tents and stores for it. **1961** NEW ENG. BIBLE *Acts* xxvii. 38 They lightened the ship by dumping the corn in the sea.

b. *intr.* for *refl.* To deposit oneself, drop down.

1891 *Daily News* 10 Jan. 3/3 Down we dump in the dead rushes, buckle on our own skates, and are presently flying away with the rest of them.

c. *trans.* To export, or throw on the market, in large quantities and at low prices; *spec.* to offer for sale (surplus goods), esp. abroad, at less than the ordinary trade prices. Also *absol.* Often in *ppl. adjs.* and *vbl. sb.*

1868 *Commerc. & Financ. Chron.* VI. 326/1 New stock secretly issued [was] 'dumped' on the market for what it would fetch. **1884** *Congress. Rec.* 1 May 3663/1 The surplus dumped from foreign pauper markets is the great bane of our industries. **1903** *Westm. Gaz.* 8 Sept. 2/2 Those who base their case on (*a*) decreasing exports, and (*b*) the dumped state of iron and steel. **1903** *Daily Chron.* 25 Sept. 3/7 'Dumping' is in our eyes a great sin. **1904** *Treasury* Oct. 8/1 The..capitalists desire this, as it..enables them to dump their surplus production on foreign countries. **1908** *Westm. Gaz.* 30 Mar. 10/2 As for the dumping scare,..there is nothing in it. *Ibid.* 4 May 2/2 You appear to think that he dumps for the sake of dumping. **1916** *Economist* 4 Mar. 458/1 We hear of large stocks of cheap manufactures that will be dumped upon us. **1928** *Britain's Industr. Future* (*Lib. Ind. Inq.*) I. v. 50 They showed that the practice of dumping demoralises the world-market to the ultimate disadvantage of all concerned. **1957** *Act 5 & 6 Eliz. II* c. 18 (*title*) Customs Duties (Dumping and Subsidies) Act. *Ibid.*, For the purposes of this Act imported goods shall be regarded as having been dumped..if the export price from the country in which the goods originated is less than the fair market price of the goods in that country. **1970** *Financial Times* 13 Apr. 12/6 Continental companies could 'dump' steel in the U.K. if there are no tariff barriers.

d. To discard, abandon, get rid of. *colloq.*

1919 *Athenæum* 15 Aug. 759/1 'To dump' a thing that it is a nuisance to carry means to get rid of it. **1944** *Korero* (N.Z.) 9 Oct. 27 The pony will try..to 'dump' its burden [the rider]. **1946** D. STIVENS *Courtship of Uncle Henry* 29 You've dumped plenty of fellows before. *Ibid.* 30 Dumping me like this for a couple of dumb sailors.

e. Of a wave: to hurl (a swimmer or surfer) down. Cf. DUMPER d. Chiefly *Austral.*

1938 J. MOSES *Nine Miles fr. Gundagai* 88 W'en de breakers dumped Me at Curl Curl. **1963** *Observer* 13 Oct. 15/4 The wave traps and dumps the rider, burying him for half a minute or longer and churning him over and over on the ocean floor. **1966** *Surfer* VII. 54 A really good body surfer got banged up pretty bad when a Yokohama wave dumped him right on the reef.

f. *intr.* Chiefly *N. Amer.* In slang phr. ***to dump on*** (occas. ***all over***) (a person), to criticize or abuse (someone); to better in argument; so ***to be dumped on***, to be defeated in argument or in a game.

[**1963** *Amer. Speech* XXXVIII. 171 [Kansas University] Many of the responses referring to one party's rejection of another, as, for example, a girl breaking a previously arranged date with a boy, are figurative expressions of excremental activities. A boy so treated is said to have been *dumped on.*] **1967** *Ibid.* XLII. 228 *Dump on*, to have one's arguments continually defeated by a particular opponent. 'He is dumping on you' (i.e. 'He bettered your arguments'). 'You've been dumped on' (i.e., 'You've had your arguments beaten'). The phrase evidently derives from *dump shit on* or *dump a load of shit on.* **1968–70** *Current Slang* (Univ. S. Dakota) III–IV. 42 *Dump on*, to criticize.—College students, both sexes. New Hampshire. **1975** *Saturday Night* (Toronto) July–Aug. 20/1 Last year, after a frustrating and unsuccessful try at settling a dispute between Air Canada and its pilots, Hartt dumped on both sides. **1977** *New Yorker* 28 Feb. 27/1 When Ron's first ball flopped, Kerry was candid. 'Well, you got dumped on with a mere one hundred and fifty-one'. **1985** *Woman's Own* 22 June 36/3 One minute I'm with a woman who makes me feel like a man, the next I'm with someone who's dumping all over me.

3. a. *trans.* To thump, beat, strike. *Sc.*

1808–18 JAMIESON, *Dump*, to strike with the feet. **1832–53** J. BALLANTYNE in *Whistle-Binkie* (Sc. Songs) Ser. II. 74 He thumpit the blacksmith hame to his wife, He dumpit the butcher, who ran for his life.

b. *intr.* To strike with a dull abrupt thud.

1832 L. HUNT *Boileau Battle Bks.* 115 The book, like butter dumps against his head.

4. *trans.* To compress (wool-bales), as by hydraulic pressure. *Australia.*

1872 C. H. EDEN *My Wife and I in Queensl.* 68. **1896** MORRIS *Austral English* s.v., Bales are often marked 'Not to be dumped'.

5. *Computing.* To copy (stored data) to a different location, usu. to an external storage medium from an internal one, e.g. to check a program or safeguard data; to reproduce the contents of (a store) externally.

1956 *Computers & Automation* Jan. 15/2 *Dump*, to transfer all or part of the contents of one section of computer memory into another section. **1959** *Jrnl. Assoc. Computing Machinery* VI. 132 There are three 'information macros' which enable the programmer to specify the area of core, drum, or tape storage to be dumped. **1964** [see BYTE]. **1969** G. B. DAVIS *Computer Data Processing* x. 229 Rerun the program until it hangs up and then obtain information on contents of registers,..etc... The entire memory may, in certain instances, be listed, or dumped. **1972** *Computer Jrnl.* XV. 191/2 A simple application of this principle in the case of a disc-base filing system is to dump the entire disc on to magnetic tape at suitable intervals. **1978** *Nature* 10 Aug. 567/2 Optical burst 1 occurred while SAS 3 was dumping data to a ground station and so no X-ray data are available. **1982** *80 Microcomputing* Nov. 464/2 Economically, it's very easy to dump an entire newspaper into a data base. **1983** *Austral. Microcomputer Mag.* Nov. 109/2 This device is suited ideally to word processors—for example, a document can be dumped to the printer via the spooler in seconds.

†dump, *v.*[2] *Obs.* [f. DUMP *sb.*[1]]

1. *intr.* **a.** To fall into, or be in, an abstracted or absent state of mind; to muse. **b.** To be in the dumps; to be sad or downcast in spirit.

1530 PALSGR. 531, I dumpe, I fall in a dumpe or musyng upon thynges, *je me amuse*..He dumpeth nowe a days more than he was wont to do. **1583** STANYHURST *Æneis* II. (Arb.) 46 With Colericque fretting I dumpt and ranckled in anguish. **1590** GREENE *Orl. Fur.* (1599) 17 He knows the Countie (like to Cassius) Sits sadly dumping, ayming Cesars death. **1590** —— *Never Too Late* G, I thought either Diana sate musing on the principles of her modesty, or Venus malcontent, dumping on her amours.

2. *trans.* To cast into melancholy, sadden, grieve, cast down. (Sometimes blending with DUMP *v.*[1])

c **1585** CARTWRIGHT in R. Browne *Answ. to Cartwright* 87 The greater nomber of them being dumped with dumbe ministerie. **1599** NASHE *Lenten Stuffe* 45 The gods..were so dumpt with this miserable wracke [of Hero and Leander], that they beganne to abhorre all moysture. **1614** FORBES *Def. Lawfull Ministers* 66 (Jam.) Which..hath dumped in a deep sorrow all true hearts of both the ilands.

'dumpage. *U.S.* [f. DUMP *v.*[1] + -AGE.] The work of dumping or emptying out refuse, ballast, etc.; the privilege of doing this on a particular piece of ground; the fee paid for this privilege.

1864 in WEBSTER.

dumper ('dʌmpə(r)). [f. DUMP *v.*[1] + -ER[1].] **a.** One who 'dumps' or deposits rubbish, etc. **b.** A dumping-cart or truck.

1856 *Trans. Mich. Agric. Soc.* VII. 334 There are on the road..20 gravel dumpers. **1881** RAYMOND *Mining Gloss.*, *Dumper*, a tilting-car used on dumps. **1958** *Engineering* 7 Feb. 165/3 Designed for a payload of 28 short tons, the end-tip dumper can travel at 24 m.p.h. **1967** *Guardian* 18 July 3/7 A dumper driver.

c. One who, or a country or community which, dumps goods (DUMP *v.*[1] 2 c).

1903 *Daily Chron.* 24 Oct. 5/2 They would not have supported the fiscal policy of Mr. Chamberlain, for they were 'dumpers', who sold shoes to the poor below cost-price. *Ibid.* 21 Nov. 6/3 How long do you think that the dumpers will be content with only dumping unfinished goods? **1919** *Economist* 11 Oct. 568/2 Germany as a 'Dumper'.

d. A large wave which breaks suddenly and hurls a swimmer or surfer down with great force. *Austral.* and *S. Afr.*

1933 *Bulletin* (Sydney) 5 Apr. 11/3 One morning he arrived totally gummy in the lower jaw... 'Done them in in a dumper yesterday at the surf,' he told us. **1956** S. HOPE *Diggers' Paradise* 166 The dumper is a wave that builds up into a solid mass of water that advances closer inshore without breaking. **1963** A. ROSS *Australia 63* ii. 51 On the surf beaches beyond Manly, the dumpers thunder in. **1970** *Studies in English* (*Univ. of Cape Town*) I. 27 The most popular expression in South African surfing idiom would appear to be *dumper*. A 'dumper' occurs most often when there is an abrupt rise of the ocean bottom to the shore. The wave thus breaks in shallow water and, instead of breaking slowly from the top, falls suddenly in an arc.

dumpily ('dʌmpılı), *adv.* [f. DUMPY *a.*[2] + -LY[2].] In a dumpy manner or form.

1880 WATSON in *Jrnl. Linn. Soc.* XV. No. 82. 126 Another specimen is more dumpily conical.

dumpiness ('dʌmpınıs). [f. as prec. + -NESS.] The state or quality of being dumpy.

1824 MISS MITFORD *Village* Ser. I. (1863) 128 A very little inclined to clumsy dumpiness. **1883** MISS BRADDON *Gold. Calf* xi. 147 Girls with nineteen inch waists, before whom I felt myself a monster of dumpiness.

dumping ('dʌmpıŋ), *vbl. sb.*[1] [f. DUMP *v.*[1] + -ING[1].] **1. a.** The action of the verb DUMP; flinging down in a heavy mass; depositing of rubbish, etc.; *concr.* a heap of material flung down or deposited. (See also DUMP *v.*[1] 2 c.)

1883 HOWELLS *Woman's Reason* xii, The Common, where for three months past the monumental dumpings of the icy streets had dismally accumulated. **1894** SALA *Lond. up to date* xvii. 210 Noises of the hammering of rivets, and the dumping down of huge sheets of metal.

b. *attrib.* Used for dumping or depositing loads, as ***dumping-bucket***, ***-car***, ***-cart***, ***-machine***, ***-place***, ***-reel***, ***-sled***, ***-wagon***. **dumping-ground**, a place where refuse, etc., is deposited; also *transf.* and *fig.*

1857 *N.Y. Tribune* 18 May (Bartlett), There is much difficulty in getting dumping grounds for the dirt from the streets. **1874** KNIGHT *Dict. Mech.*, *Dumping-reel*, an arrangement in a harvester for dropping the gavels of grain. **1883** *Harper's Mag.* May 829/1 Dumping-place for city refuse. **1885** *Pall Mall G.* 2 Jan. 3/1 A 'dumping ground' for all the human garbage collected in the moral cesspools of the [French] Republic. **1899** *Westm. Gaz.* 17 May 3/1 A corrupt young married woman..whom the mother finds a convenient dumping-ground for this too mature daughter. **1936** J. C. BEAGLEHOLE *New Zealand* i. 15 England needed a new dumping-ground for convicts. **1969** J. MANDER *Static Soc.* viii. 269 The sub-continent is being used as a dumping-ground for obsolescent weaponry.

2. *Path.* The abnormally rapid emptying of the stomach via the bowels such as sometimes occurs after partial gastrectomy. Freq. *attrib.* and as *ppl. a.*, esp. in ***dumping syndrome*** (see quot. 1970).

1922 C. L. MIX in *Surg. Clinics N. Amer.* II. 617 Patient suffering from severe gastric disturbance following gastro-jejunostomy. Fluoroscopic examination revealed a 'dumping stomach'. **1935** G. B. EUSTERMAN et al. *Stomach & Duodenum* x. 241 In performing gastro-enterostomy, the stoma should be neither too large nor too small... If too large, so-called 'dumping' results with precipitant evacuation of gastric content. *Ibid.* lix. 845 Too rapid emptying of the stomach, 'dumping stomach', following gastro-enterostomy or gastric resection may cause a train of disturbances, chiefly intestinal. **1954** *Brit. Med. Jrnl.* 13 Nov. 1131/2 Serious 'dumping'..happens to have been associated with bilious regurgitation. *Ibid.*, It is customary ..to suggest that the 'dumping' syndrome subsides..within a few months of [gastrectomy] operation. **1970** PASSMORE & ROBSON *Compan. Med. Stud.* II. xvii. 3/2 After surgical removal of part of the stomach, patients sometimes suffer from attacks of sweating and flushing, weakness and occasionally fainting together with intestinal discomfort and explosive diarrhoea. These symptoms..are known as the dumping syndrome.

†dumping, *vbl. sb.*[2] *Obs.* [f. DUMP *v.*[2] + -ING[1].] Mental stupefaction.

1542 UDALL *Erasm. Apoph.* 114 b, To note the brutish grossenesse and dumping of the minde.

†dumping, *sb. Obs.* [f. DUMP *v.*[1] (sense 1) + -ING, or (in form *dompyng*) a nasalized form of *doppyng*, f. DOP *v.* Cf. the synonym *dompus*, app. a nasalized form of *doppes*, DOPPE *sb.*] A dabchick or didapper.

1393 LANGL. *P. Pl.* C. XIV. 169 In mareis and in mores in myres and in wateres Dompynges [*v. rr.* dumpynges, doppynges, dompus] dyueden.

dumpish ('dʌmpıʃ), *a.* [f. DUMP *sb.*[1] + -ISH.]

†1. Dull, stupid, slow-witted; inactive, inert, spiritless; destitute of sensation; abstracted, insensible to outward things; dull, uninteresting. *Obs.*

1545 ASCHAM *Toxoph.* (Arb.) 28 Base and dompysshe wittes can neuer be hurte with continuall studie. **1558** PHAER *Æneid* VI. Q j b, Combrous Age of dompishe yeeres. **1562** BULLEYN *Dial. Soarnes & Chir.* 41 b, A dumpische priuation of sense. **1603** FLORIO *Montaigne* II. xii. (1632) 258 She was but in a deepe study, and dumpish retracting into herselfe. *c* **1682** HICKERINGILL *Wks.* (1716) II. 3 Let such busie Censurers use their own Lumpish Dumpish grave way.

2. Sad, melancholy; dejected, 'in the dumps'.

1562 J. HEYWOOD *Prov. & Epigr.* (1867) 182 I am dumpyshe to see thee play the drabbe. **1595** SOUTHWELL *Mæoniæ* 23 Dolefull tunes for dumpish cares. **1627** BP. HALL *Heaven upon Earth* §23 It is a false slander raised on christianitie that it maketh men dumpish and melancholicke. **1684** BUNYAN *Pilgr.* II. 17 She will..be dumpish or unneighbourly. **1779** MAD. D'ARBLAY *Diary* Jan., On Monday..I was wofully dumpish. **1847** EMERSON *Eng. Traits* xix. (1856) 310 In prosperity they were moody and dumpish, but in adversity they were grand.

b. Such as to put one 'in the dumps'.

c **1717** *Lett. fr. Miot's Jrnl.* (1722) I. 89 The Day and Weather being as sad and dumpish as old Saturn himself.

'dumpishly, *adv.* [f. prec. + -LY[2].] In a dumpish manner; dejectedly, gloomily.

c **1621** S. WARD *Life of Faith* (1627) 47 If thou liuest dumpishly, and yet say thou liuest by Faith. **1648** BP. HALL *Select Th.* §61 (R.) One so dumpishly sad, as if he would freez to death in melancholy.

'dumpishness. [f. as prec. + -NESS.]

†1. Sluggishness, inertness, insensibility. *Obs.*

1573–80 BARET *Alv.* D 1356 A Dumpe, or dumpishnesse, *torpor.* *a* **1665** J. GOODWIN *Filled w. the Spirit* (1867) 444 That which is born of the flesh hath all the properties of the flesh, heaviness and dumpishness. **1677** HORNECK *Gt. Law Consid.* v. (1704) 307 What means that..strange dumpishness, when God courts and beseeches my soul?

2. Dejection; tendency to be in the dumps.

1548 HALL *Chron., Edw. IV* (an. 15) 237b, What should signifie, that dumpishenes of mynde, and inward sighyng. **1653** BOGAN *Mirth Chr. Life* 194 Making pictures in his fancy..out of pensivenesse and dumpishnesse. **1864** H. BRADSHAW in *Life* (1888) 116 Never allow yourself more than five minutes..for the luxury of dumpishness.

dumple ('dʌmp(ə)l), *v. rare.* †**a.** [nonce-formation from *dumpling.*] *trans.* To make or cook, as a dumpling. *Obs.* **b.** [? f. DUMPY².] To bend or compress into a dumpy shape.

1625 MASSINGER *New Way* III. ii, *Greedy.* Without order for the dumpling? *Over.* Let it be dumpled Which way thou wilt. **1827** SCOTT *Diary* 17 Jan. in *Lockhart,* He was a little man, dumpled up together, and so ill made as to seem almost deformed. **1868** BROWNING *Ring & Bk.* VIII. 65 Let law come dimple Cinoncino's cheek, And Latin dumple Cinarello's chin.

dumpling ('dʌmplɪŋ). Also 7–9 dumplin. [prob. f. same source as DUMP *a.*: see -LING.]

1. A kind of pudding consisting of a mass of paste or dough, more or less globular in form, either plain and boiled, or inclosing fruit and boiled or baked. (Originally attributed to Norfolk.)

c **1600** DAY *Begg. Bednall Gr.* II. ii. (1881) 35 When mine Hostis came up to call me, I was as naked as your Norfolk-Dumplin. **1608** ARMIN *Nest Ninn.* (1842) 17 He lookt like a Norfolke dumpling, thicke and short. **1688** R. HOLME *Armoury* III. 293/2 A Dumpling, or Pot-Ball is made either long or round, as the maker pleaseth. **1709** STEELE *Tatler* No. 19 ¶2 An Esquire of Norfolk eats Two Pounds of Dumplin every Meal. **1791** MAXWELL in Boswell *Johnson* an. 1770 (1831) I. 391 A clergyman of small income.. brought up a family very reputably, which he chiefly fed with apple dumplings. **1831** CARLYLE *Sart. Res.* I. i, Now, to many a Royal Society, the Creation of a World is little more mysterious than the cooking of a Dumpling; concerning which last, indeed, there have been minds to whom the question, How the apples were got in, presented difficulties.

b. *transf.* A pasty mass like a dumpling.

1743 *Lond.& Country Brew.* III. (ed. 2) 199 Mix them up ..into a Mass, out of which form Dumplins. *Ibid.* 240 Oyster-shell-powder, Pebble-stone-powder..one Quartern of French Brandy, and two Ounces of powder'd Ginger; Knead all together into four or five Dumplins.

2. A dumpy animal or person, short and of rounded outlines.

1617 MINSHEU *Ductor* s.v. *Dwarfe,* A dwarfe, dumplin, a Nobodie. **1641** BEST *Farm. Bks.* (Surtees) 5 Short runtish sheepe..of the shepheardes callede dumplinges, or grasse belly'de lambes. **1828** *Craven Dial., Dumpling,* a little fat child or person, as broad as long. **1848** DICKENS *Dombey* ix, You ought to have a nice little dumpling of a wife.

3. *attrib.* and *Comb.*

1726 ARBUTHNOT *Diss. Dumpling* 21 Why should Dumpling-Eating be ridicul'd, or Dumpling-Eaters derided? **1852** R. S. SURTEES *Sponge's Sp. Tour* (1893) 180 A young dumpling-shaped doctor. **1865** MISS BRADDON *Sir Jasper* iv. 36 She had no idea that there could be any prettiness in a dumpling figure.

dumpoked ('dʌmpəʊkt), *a. India.* [ad. Hind. *dampukht,* f. Pers. *dam* breath + *pukhteʰ* cooked.] Applied to a steamed dish of boned and stuffed meat. Hence '**dumpoke,** a steamed dish of this kind, especially a boned and stuffed chicken or duck.

1696 OVINGTON *Voy. Suratt* 397 A dumpoked Fowl. **1698** J. FRYER *Acc. E. India & P.* 93 These Eat highly of all Flesh Dumpoked, which is Baked with Spice in Butter. *Ibid.* 404 Baked Meat they call Dumpoke which is dressed with sweet Herbs and Butter, with whose Gravy they swallow Rice dry Boiled. **1879** MRS. A. E. JAMES *Ind. Househ. Managem.* 89 *Dumpoke* is a boned chicken, its form preserved, only all the bones extracted; it is stuffed with a rice forcemeat, and you cut it through in slices. **1954** G. S. RAO *Indian Words in Eng.* iii. 17 Indian dishes figured on their tables: cabob, pilau, dumpoked fowl, curry, kedgeree.

dumps, dial. var. of DIMPS.

dumpty ('dʌmptɪ), *a.* (*sb.*) By-form of DUMPY *a.*² (See also HUMPTY-DUMPTY.)

1847–78 HALLIWELL, *Dumpty,* a very short person. *West.* **1857** KINGSLEY *Two Y. Ago* xxv, Mary comes in; a little dumpty body with a yellow face and a red nose. **1879** F. W. ROBINSON *Coward Consc.* I. iii, The dumpty wooden lighthouse. **1891** *Dawn of Day* 158 The 'dumpty dolly'..is a piece of muslin twisted up with a lump of sugar inside it, which some mothers give their children to suck.

dumpy ('dʌmpɪ), *a.*¹ [f. DUMP *sb.*¹ + -Y.] Melancholy, dejected, 'in the dumps'.

a **1618** SYLVESTER *Tobacco Battered* 643 For Dumpier none then the Tobacconer; None sadder then the gladdest of their Host. **1825** BROCKETT *N.C. Gloss., Dumpy,* sullen. *a* **1845** HOOD *John Trot* vi, And left her to her widowhood, Of course more dumpy still.

dumpy ('dʌmpɪ), *a.*² (*sb.*) [Appears in middle of 18th c.: not in Johnson 1755–87, nor in Ash 1775; in Todd 1818. Its form is that of a derivative from a sb. *dump* (cf. *lump-y, stump-y*); but the sb. DUMP², with which it goes, is known only later, and appears to be a back-formation from this adj. It is not obvious how these words can be connected with the other sbs. and vbs. of same form.]

Short and stout; deficient in length or stature.

1750 *Student* II. 225 Short, dumpy, gouty, crooked fingers. **1808** SCOTT *Let. to G. Ellis* 23 Feb. in *Lockhart,* The 5th canto of a certain dumpy quarto, entitled Marmion. **1819** BYRON *Juan* I. lxi, Her stature tall—I hate a dumpy woman. **1856** MAYHEW *Rhine* 44 Everlasting rows of dumpy willows.

b. ***dumpy level***: a spirit-level used in surveying, having a short telescope with a large aperture.

1838 P. BRUFF *Engineer. Field-work* 137 Gravatt's Improved Level, commonly called (from its appearance) the Dumpy Level. **1885** *Athenæum* 23 May 664 On levelling and the use of the dumpy level.

B. *sb.* **a.** A dumpy person or animal; *spec.* one of a breed of very short-legged fowls; in *pl.* a nickname for the Nineteenth Hussars. **b.** Short for *dumpy level*; see above.

1808–18 JAMIESON, *Dumpy,* adj. Short and thick; also used as a sb. **1868** *Who breaks, pays* (Tauchn.) 39 (Hoppe) The daughter is a dumpy. **1878** TRIMEN *Regiments Brit. Army* 38 [The Nineteenth Hussars] nicknamed 'the Dumpies' when raised, from the diminutive size of the men. **1885** *Bazaar* 30 Mar. 1267/2 Dumpies' eggs, genuine Scotch breed.

dun (dʌn), *a.* Also 4–6 dune, donne, 5 don, 5–7 dunne, 6 doon. *β. Sc.* 6 dyn, 9 din. [OE. *dun(n,* perh. from Celtic: cf. Irish and Gael. *donn* brown, Welsh *dwn* 'subfuscus' (Davies).]

1. Of a dull or dingy brown colour; now *esp.* dull greyish brown, like the hair of the ass and mouse.

953 *Charter of Eadred* in *Cod. Dipl.* V. 325 Ðanne to ðan redan hole; and ðanne to ðan dunnan hole. *c* **1000** ÆLFRIC *Voc.* in Wright 46 *Nomina colorum. Dosinus uel cinereus,* asse dun. *Natius,* dun. ? *a* **1366** CHAUCER *Rom. Rose* 1213 She was not broune ne dunne of hewe [*qui nestoit ne brune ne bise*]. **1388** WYCLIF *Gen.* xxx. 32 What euer thing schal be dun and spottid. **1434** *E.E. Wills* (1882) 98 My Don Bullok. **1548** HALL *Chron., Henry VIII,* an. 5 (1550) 28 On the toppe of the pauilions stode the kynges bestes holdynge fanes, as the Lion, the Dragon, the Greyhounde, the Antelope, the Donne kowe. **1562** J. HEYWOOD *Prov. & Epigr.* (1867) 139 The dun Asse hath trode on both thy feete. **1567** *Trial Treas.* in Hazl. *Dodsley* III. 279 May the devil go with you and his dun dame! **1698** FRYER *Acc. E. India & P.* 118 A Buffola is of a Dun Colour. **1709** ADDISON *Tatler* No. 148 ¶1 Guy Earl of Warwick, who is well known to have eaten up a Dun Cow. **1820** SCOTT *Ivanhoe* xvi, Among the herds of dun deer that feed in the glades. **1830** —— *Demonol.* iv. 132 Her colour..is now of a dun leaden hue. **1852** MISS YONGE *Cameos* (1877) IV. iii. 38 The dun cow was a cognizance of the Earldom of Richmond. **1863** HUXLEY *Man's Place Nat.* I. 22 Its dun or iron-grey colour.

β. The Sc. form *dyn, din,* has now esp. the sense of *dingy-coloured* as opposed to *white* or *fair.*

1553 *Douglas' Æneis* VIII. ix. 26 Ane dyn [*MS.* dvn] lyoun skyn with nalis of gold. **1814** *Saxon & Gael* I. 107 (Jam.) As din as a docken, an' as dry as a Fintrum speldin. *a* **1876** *Binórie O an Binórie* x. in Child *Ballads* I. x. (1882) 133/2 But ye was fair and I was din.

2. More vaguely: Dark, dusky (from absence of light); murky, gloomy. Cf. BROWN. (Chiefly *poetic.*)

a **1300** *Cursor M.* 22510 þe sun þat es sa bright..It sal becum..dune [*Gött.* dim] and blak sum ani hair. *c* **1374** CHAUCER *Troylus* II. 859 (908) Whit thingis gan to wexe donne For lak of light. *a* **1415** LYDG. *Temple of Glas* 30 Certein skyes donne. **1634** MILTON *Comus* 127 Tis only daylight that makes sin, Which these dun shades will ne'er report. *c* **1748** COLLINS *On Death Thomson* ix, Dun Night has veil'd the solemn view. **1801** CAMPBELL *Hohenlinden* 22 Scarce yon level sun Can pierce the war-clouds, rolling dun. **1827** KEBLE *Chr. Y.* 23rd Sund. Trinity, Chill and dun Falls on the moor the brief November day. **1851** LONGF. *Gold. Leg.* v. *At Sea* 31 Athwart the vapours, dense and dun.

fig. **1797** ANNA SEWARD *Lett.* (1811) V. 11 Frowning like herself, in dun cogitation.

3. *Comb.* **a.** With adjs. of colour, as ***dun-brown, -olive, -red, -white, -yellow.*** **b.** Parasynthetic, as ***dun-belted, -coloured*** adjs.

1783 LIGHTFOOT in *Phil. Trans.* LXXV. 11 All of one uniform *dun-brown colour. **1882** E. O'DONOVAN *Merv Oasis* I. 336 The air is thick with dun-brown dust. **1674** N. COX *Gentl. Recreat.* I. (1677) 41 Of the Dun-Hound..there are few *dun-coloured to be found bad. **1868** DARWIN *Anim. & Pl.* I. ii. 55 The English race-horse..is said never to be dun-coloured. **1798** COLERIDGE *Picture,* With *dun-red bark The fir-trees..Soar up. **1822–34** GOOD *Study Med.* (ed. 4) I. 516 The *dun yellow colour of the middle coat. **1851** MAYNE REID *Scalp Hunt.* xxiii, [The mare] of that *dun-yellowish colour known as 'clay-bank'.

c. Special Combs.: **dun-bar,** collector's name for a dun-coloured moth (*Cosmia trapezina*), having two bars or transverse lines on the fore-wings; **dun courses** (see quot.); **dun cow,** local name for a fish, the shagreen ray, *Raia fullonica* (Yarrell *Brit. Fishes* II. 578); **dun cur** [see CUR 3], local name of the pochard = DUN-BIRD; **dun cut, dun drake, dun hackle,** names of artificial flies used in angling; †**dun-kite,** †**dun pickle,** obsolete names for the moor-buzzard (*Circus æruginosus*); **dun land** (see quot.); †**dun-row,** name given to a dun-coloured stratum.

1819 G. SAMOUELLE *Entomol. Compend.* 433 *Noctua trapezina.* The *Dunbar. **1869** NEWMAN *Brit. Moths* 381 The Dun-bar. **1881** E. A. ORMEROD *Injurious Insects* (1890) 241 The carnivorous caterpillars of the Dunbar Moth.. doing great good in clearing away this attack. **1877** A. H. GREEN *Phys. Geol.* vii. §2. 276 Ribs of Magnesian Limestone are met with in the Carboniferous L. of Yorkshire where they are known as **Dun Courses.* **1802** G. MONTAGU *Ornith. Dict.* (1833) 142 Dunbird and *Duncur. Names for the Pochard. *a* **1450** *Fysshynge w. Angle* (1883) 34 The *donne cutte: the body of blacke wull and a yelow lyste after eyther syde. **1799** G. SMITH *Laboratory* II. 291 The Duncut. Dub with bear's-cub fur, and a little yellow and green crewel. **1799** G. SMITH *Laboratory* II. 302 The brown-fly or *dun-drake. *Ibid.* 301 *Dunhackle: Body, dun coloured silk, with a dun cock's hackle. **1577** HARRISON *England* III. v. (1878) II. 31 The bussard, the kite, the ringtaile, *dun-kite. **1810** J. T. in *Risdon's Surv. Devon* p. iv, **Dun land*..is furnished..by the decomposition of the Schistus rock on which it lies. **1802** G. MONTAGU *Ornith. Dict.* (1833) 146 **Dunpickle,* a name for the Moor Buzzard. **1825** HONE *Every-day Bk.* I. 535 The dun-pickles or moor buzzards alight. **1712** F. BELLERS in *Phil. Trans.* XXVII. 542 A black Substance, called the *Dun-Row-Bat. *Ibid.,* A hard grey Iron Oar, called the Dun-Row Iron-Stone.

dun (dʌn), *sb.*¹ [subst. use of DUN *a.*]

1. Dun colour: see DUN *a.* 1.

1568 *Satir. Poems Reform.* xlviii. 11 Dun dippit in ȝello ffor mony gud fallo. **1686** PLOT *Staffordsh.* 111 They will certainly change the colour of their coat to a whitish-dun. **1819** BYRON *Juan* II. xcii, Baptized in molten gold, and swathed in dun. **1894** *Superfluous Woman* (ed. 4) I. 171 Silvery grays and duns.

2. A dun horse. Formerly a quasi-proper name for any horse (see also 5).

c **1386** [see 5]. *c* **1460** *Towneley Myst.* (Surtees) 18 Gif Don, thyne hors, a wisp of hay. **1840** E. E. NAPIER *Scenes & Sports Foreign Lands* I. ii. 27 In India..four-legged duns are as much disliked as those of the biped species. **1892** R. KIPLING *Barrack-r. Ballads, East & West* 21 The Colonel's son has taken a horse, and a raw rough dun was he.

3. A name for various dusky-coloured flies used in angling, and for artificial flies imitating these.

1681 CHETHAM *Angler's Vade-m,* xxxiv. §26 (1689) 200 Angle with the smallest gnats, Browns and Duns you can find. **1760** HAWKINS in *Walton's Angler* I. xvii. *note,* Ash-coloured duns of several shapes and dimentions. **1799** G. SMITH *Laboratory* II. 290 The little-dun. The dubbing of a bear's dun-hair, whirled upon yellow silk. **1833** J. RENNIE *Alph. Angling* 36 Various species of day flies known to anglers by the various names of duns, drakes, and may flies.

4. (See quot.) = DUN-ROW in DUN *a.* 3c.

a **1843** SOUTHEY *Comm-pl. Bk.* (1849) IV. 407 A thin stratum near the coal called duns.

5. Proverbial Phrases. ***dun*** [the horse] ***is in the mire*** (see 2): (*a*) a phrase denoting that things are at a stand-still or dead-lock; (*b*) an old Christmas game (called also ***drawing dun out of the mire***), in which a heavy log was lifted and carried off by the players. ***dun's the mouse***: a phrase 'alluding to the colour of the mouse, but frequently employed with no other intent than that of quibbling on the word *done*' (Nares). ***the devil upon dun,*** i.e. (app.) on horseback: see DEVIL *sb.* 22n, quots. 1708. *Obs.*

c **1386** CHAUCER *Manciple's Prol.* 5 Ther gan our hoost for to lape and pleye, And seyde, sires, what Dun is in the Myre. *c* **1440** CAPGRAVE *Life St. Kath.* II. 1046 For as wyth me, dun is in the myre, She hath me stoyned and brought me to a bay. She will not wedde, she wil be stylle a may! *c* **1550** *Schole-ho. Women* 461 in Hazl. *E.P.P.* IV. 122 One and other little ye care..Though dun and the pack lye in the mire. **1592** SHAKS. *Rom. & Jul.* I. iv. 40, 41 The game was nere so faire, and I am done. Tut, duns the Mouse, the Constables owne word, If thou art dun, weele draw thee from the mire. **1620** *Two Merry Milkmaids* (N.), Why then 'tis done, and dun's the mouse, and undone all the courtiers. **1640** SHIRLEY *St. Patrick for Irel.* (N.), Then draw Dun out of the mire, And throw the clog into the fire. **1801** STRUTT *Sports & Past.* IV. iv. 355. **1887** E. GILLIAT *Forest Outlaws* 252 Merry games at barley-break and dun-in-the-mire.

dun, *sb.*² Also 7 dunne. [Goes with DUN *v.*³

The evidence does not decide whether the sb. or the vb. is the starting-point. If sense 1 below is (as appears in the quotation) earlier than sense 2, we should naturally expect it to be the source of the vb. as in *Burke, to burke,* and the like; sense 2, on the other hand, would as naturally be a noun of action from the vb. as in *to kick, a kick.* See the vb.; also the following:

1708 *Brit. Apollo* No. 60. 2/1 The word *Dun*..owes its birth to one *Joe Dun,* a famous Bailif of the Town of Lincoln ..It became a Proverb..when a man refused to pay his Debts, Why don't you *Dun* him? That is why don't you send Dun to arrest him?.. It is now as old as since the days of King Henry the Seventh.]

1. One who duns; an importunate creditor, or an agent employed to collect debts.

1628 EARLE *Microcosm.* xlv. (Arb.) 74 An Vniversitie Dunne..Hee is an inferiour Creditor of some ten shillings or downwards. Hee is a sore beleaguerer of Chambers. **1712** ARBUTHNOT *John Bull* II. iv, To be pulled by the sleeve by some rascally dun. **1812** COMBE *Picturesque* XXIII. I've just enough the duns to pay. **1881** BESANT & RICE *Chapl. of Fleet* I. x, Here I live free of duns and debt.

2. An act of dunning or importuning, esp. for debt; a demand for payment.

1673 F. KIRKMAN *Unlucky Cit.* 210 [To] endure the frequent Duns of his Creditors. **1691** *Islington Wells, or Threepenny-Acad.* 7 Who..Kickt their Taylors, For giving Dun at Chamber Door. **1751** SMOLLETT *Per. Pic.* (1779) III. lxxxiv. 312 The debtor..Finding himself waked with such a disagreeable dunn. **1847** A. M. GILLIAM *Trav. Mexico* 149 The..crowd let us pass to our rooms, without our receiving a single dun for alms.

3. *Comb.,* as ***dun-driven, -haunted, -racked*** adjs.

1839 J. R. DARLEY *Introd. Beaum. & Fl.'s Wks.* I. 13 As fast as a dun-driven poet. **1840** DICKENS *Barn. Rudge* xv, Dun-haunted students.

‖**dun** (dʌn), *sb.*³ Also doon. [Irish and Gaelic *dun* (dun), hill, hill-fort, fortress, W. *din* hill-fort.

A frequent element in Celtic proper names in Scotland and Ireland, as in Dunkeld, Gael. *Dunchaillein* hill fort of the woods, *Dumbarton*, the dun of the Britons.]

An ancient hill-fortress or fortified eminence (in the Highlands of Scotland, or in Ireland). Sometimes also applied to a *brough* or BROCH.

1605–74 CAMDEN *Rem.* (ed. 7) 196 (Jam.) The Dune or Tower of Dornadilla in the parish of Diurnes. **1774** PENNANT *Tour Scotl. in 1772*, 293 These fortresses are called universally in the Erse, Duns. **1794** *Statist. Acc. Scotl.* XIII. 334 There are several duns in this parish, most of which were built by the Danes. **1851** D. WILSON *Preh. Ann.* (1863) II. III. iii. 87 This class of strongholds or Duns, as they are locally termed, pertain to a people whose arts were still in their infancy. **1873** O'CURRY *Mann. Anc. Irish* III. 3 The Dun was of the same form as the Rath, but consisting of at least two concentric circular mounds or walls, with a deep trench full of water between them. **1875** W. MCILWRAITH *Guide Wigtownshire* 138 Here are the remains of a doon, or of a circular tower of some sort. **1888** *Archæol. Rev.* Mar. 70.

dun (dʌn), *v.*¹ [OE. *dunnian*, f. *dun(n*, DUN *a.*]
1. *trans.* To make dun, dusky or dingy; to darken or dull the colour of.

c **888** K. ÆLFRED *Boeth.* iv, Se mona mid his blacan leohte þæt þa beorhtan steorran dunniaþ on þam heofone. *a* **1415** LYDG. *Temple of Glas* 252 Riȝt as þe sonne Passeþ þe sterres and doþ hir stremes donne. **1765** *Projects* in *Ann. Reg.* 135/2 Smoke..disfigures the furniture..and duns the complexion. **1832–53** *Whistle-binkie* (Sc. Songs) Ser. III. 103 Afore the Lammas' tide Had dun'd the birken-tree.

b. In New England, To cure (codfish) in a particular way, by which they become of a dun colour, and are termed *dunfish*.

'They are first slack-salted and cured, then taken down cellar and allowed to "give up", and then dried again.' (*Century Dict.*)

1828 in WEBSTER s.v. *Dunning*. **1873** CELIA THAXTER *Isles of Shoals* 83 The process of dunning, which made the Shoals fish so famous a century ago, is almost a lost art, though the chief fisherman at Star still 'duns' a few yearly.

†**2.** *intr.* To become dun or dull-coloured.

c **1300** *Cursor M.* 23695 (Edin.) Flures..þat neuir mar sal dunne ne dwine. *a* **1400** in *Pol. Rel. & L. Poems* 221 Wonne ..þin hew dunnet; and þi sennewess starket.

†**dun**, *v.*² *Obs.* In 4–5 don(n-, 5 dunn-en. [app. a. ON. *duna* to thunder, give a hollow sound, f. Germanic root *dun-*, whence also DIN *sb.* and *v.*] *intr.* To sound, ring with sound, resound; = DIN *v.* 1.

Hence **dunning** *vbl. sb.*

13.. *Coer de L.* 4975 The erthe donyd hem undyr. *c* **1345** *Orpheo* 275 The kyng..Com to hunte all aboute, With dunnyng and with blowyng. *a* **1400** *Sir Beues* (E.E.T.S.) p. 163 (MS. E.) Al þe castel donyd and rong Off here merþe and off here song. **14..** *Sir Raynborwn* (MS. Cantab. Ff. 2. 38, lf. 224), Soche strokys gaf the knyghtys stowte, That the hylle donyed all abowte. *c* **1440** *Promp. Parv.* 135/1 Dunnyn in sownde, *bundo*. **1483** *Festivall* (1515) 78 b, A man sholde unneth here his folowe speke for donnynges of strokes.

dun (dʌn), *v.*³ [First found after 1600, when quoted by Bacon, from the old besom-maker at Buxton; to Blount 1636–56 it was a 'fancy' word recently taken up. Origin uncertain.

It is generally assumed to be identical with DUN *v.*², or to be a variant of DIN *v.*, of which it may possibly have been a dialect form. But cf. the cognate DUN *sb.*²]

1. *trans.* To make repeated and persistent demands upon, to importune; *esp.* for money due.

a **1626** BACON *Apophth.* in *Baconiana* (1679), The advice of the plain old man at Buxton that sold besoms..'Friend, hast thou no money? borrow of thy back, and borrow of thy belly, they will never ask thee again: I shall be dunning thee every day'. **1656** BLOUNT *Glossogr.*, To *Dun*, is a word lately taken up by fancy, and signifies to demand earnestly, or press a man to pay for commodities taken up on trust, or other debt. **1681** *Trial S. Colledge* 73, I dunn'd him for money and could not get it. **1706–7** FARQUHAR *Beaux' Strat.* III. iii, I remember the good Days, when we cou'd dun our Masters for our Wages. **1831** *Lincoln Herald* 16 Dec. 4/6 Ministers are again dunning the king for more Peers. **1862** MRS. H. WOOD *Channings* viii, There's a certain tradesman's house down there that I'd rather not pass; he has a habit of coming out and dunning me.

2. *transf.* To pester, plague, assail constantly.

1659 *Shuffling, Cutting & Deal.* 5, I am so dun'd with the Spleen, I should think on something else all the while I were a playing. **1711** *C.M. Let. to Curat* 72 I'm so dunn'd with your Author's *demonstrations*, that they can take no effect upon me. **1720** *Wodrow Corr.* (1843) II. 486, I am dunned with letters upon all hands from London and Edinburgh, urging us to meet, and do somewhat.

3. Associated with DIN *v.*

1753 *School of Man* 24 Ismena..concealed her desire, whilst Philemon was dunning everybody's ears with his. **1818** *Sporting Mag.* II. 189 His teeth chattered and his head was dunned. **1821** *Joseph the Book-Man* 116 You brute my ears thus will you dun!

dun, obs. f. DOWN *sb.*¹

dun, var. DHOON.

dunam ('dʊnəm). Also dunum. [mod.Heb., f. Turkish *dönüm*.] A measure of land, used esp. in Israel, equal to 1,000 sq. metres or about a quarter of an acre.

1920 *Glasgow Herald* 31 Dec. 8 The [Zionist] Commission has assisted in the planting and draining of 1600 duna[m]s of land. **1922** JOYCE *Ulysses* 60 They plant a dunam of land for you. **1930** *Economist* 1 Nov. 796/2 An area of at least 130 'dunums' is required in order to maintain an Arab peasant family. **1946** KOESTLER *Thieves in Night* 23 In Khubeira they paid six pounds for the dunum and another five hundred to the Mukhtar. **1962** *Economist* 28 Apr. 345/2, 2½ million dunams (something over half a million acres) of land have been distributed [in Iraq]. **1971** L. DAVIDSON *Smith's Gazelle* iii. 50 The 5,000 dunams, 1,250 acres, were basically suitable for a mixed sheep/wheat economy.

dun-bird. [f. DUN *a.* + BIRD *sb.*] The pochard or red-headed duck, *Fuligula ferina*. Also, locally (Essex), the Scaup Duck, *Fuligula marila*.

1766 PENNANT *Zool.* (1776) II. 600, These birds..are much sought for in the London markets where they are known by the name of dun birds. **1802** G. MONTAGU *Ornith. Dict.* (1833) 142 Dunbird and Duncur. Names for the Pochard. **1813** COL. HAWKER *Diary* (1893) I. 86 The geese, dunbirds and wigeons were in myriads. **1831** T. WRIGHT *Hist. Essex* I. 25 In a decoy at Goldhanger the fowls called dun birds are exceedingly numerous. **1896** *Blackw. Mag.* May 769.

dunce (dʌns), *sb.* Also 6–7 duns(e. [An application of the name of John *Duns* Scotus, the celebrated scholastic theologian, called 'Doctor Subtilis' the Subtle Doctor, who died in 1308.

His works on theology, philosophy, and logic, were textbooks in the Universities, in which (as at Oxford) his followers, called *Scotists*, were a predominating Scholastic sect, until the 16th c., when the system was attacked with ridicule, first by the humanists, and then by the reformers, as a farrago of needless entities, and useless distinctions. The *Dunsmen* or *Dunses*, on their side, railed against the 'new learning', and the name *Duns* or *Dunce*, already synonymous with 'cavilling sophist' or 'hair-splitter', soon passed into the sense of 'dull obstinate person impervious to the new learning', and of 'blockhead incapable of learning or scholarship'.

1530 TINDALE *Answ. to More* Wks. (1573) 278/1 Remember ye not how..the old barkyng curres, Dunces disciples & lyke draffe called Scotistes, the children of darkenesse, raged in euery pulpit agaynst Greke Latin and Hebrue. **1553** T. WILSON *Rhet.* (1567) 101 a, Vse the quiddities of Dunce, to set forth Gods misteries: & you shal se thignorant either fall a slepe, or els bid you farewell. **1679** HOBBES *Behemoth* I. Wks. 1840 VI. 214 Peter Lombard, who first brought in..the learning called School-divinity..was seconded by John Scot of Duns..whom any ingenious reader, not knowing what was the design, would judge to have been two of the most egregious blockheads in the world, so obscure and senseless are their writings. **1691** WOOD *Ath. Oxon.* I. 673 That the said Winter should study the Dunces Logick Questions, meaning I suppose the Logick Questions of John Dunse.]

†**1.** The personal name *Duns* used attrib. ***Duns man***, a disciple or follower of Duns Scotus, a Scotist, a schoolman; hence, a subtle, sophistical reasoner. So ***Duns learning***, ***Duns prelate***. *Obs.*

1527 TINDALE *Par. Wicked Mammon* Wks. (1573) 88 A Duns man would make xx. distinctions. *a* **1540** BARNES *Free Will* Wks. (1573) 267 Now where will our Duns men bring in their *Bonum conatum*? **1546** *Confut. Shaxton* F iij (T.), The pure worde of God, voied of all the dregges of Dunsse learning and man's traditions. **1581** MARBECK *Bk. of Notes* 479 The Dunce-men and Sophisters..the inuenters and finders, yea, and the verie makers of Purgatorie. **1626** W. SCLATER *Exp. 2 Thess.* (1629) 184 That selfe-conceited dunce criticke. **1641** MILTON *Ch. Govt.* v. (1851) 115 It were a great folly to seeke for counsell..from a Dunce Prelat.

†**2.** A copy of the works of Duns Scotus; a textbook of scholastic theology or logic embodying his teaching; a comment or gloss by or after the manner of Scotus. *Obs.*

1530 TINDALE *Pentat.* To Rdr. 3 They which in tymes paste were wont to loke on no more Scripture then they founde in their duns or soch like develysh doctryne. **1536** LEYTON *to Cromwell* in *Suppr. Monast.* (Camden) 71 We have sett Dunce in Bocardo, and have utterly banisshede hym Oxforde for ever, with all his blinde glosses. *Ibid.*, The second time we came to New College..we found all the great quadrant court full of the leaves of Dunce, the wind blowing them into every corner. **1607** MARSTON *What You Will* II. i, My spaniel slept, whilst I bausd leaves, Tossd ore the dunces, por'd on the old print Of titled wordes. **1607** TOURNEUR *Rev. Trag.* III. iv. Wks. 1878 II. 78 A villanous Duns upon the letter, knauish exposition. **1620** MIDDLETON *Chaste Maid* III. ii, Brought him in league with logicke, And red the Dunces to him. **1633** T. STAFFORD *Pac. Hib.* II. ix. (1810) 333 I will write as I have read in my dunses of Logicke.

3. A disciple or adherent of Duns Scotus, a Duns man, a Scotist; a hair-splitting reasoner; a cavilling sophist. *Obs.* exc. *Hist.*

1577 STANYHURST *Descr. Irel.* i. in *Holinshed* (1587) 9/2 Duns, which tearme is so triuiall and common in all schools, that whoso surpasseth others either in cauilling sophistrie, or subtill philosophie, is forthwith nickenamed a Duns. **1611** FLORIO, *Scotista*, a follower of Scotus, as we say a Dunce.

†**4.** One whose study of books has left him dull and stupid, or imparted no liberal education; a dull pedant. *Obs.*

1579 LYLY *Euphues* (Arb.) 47 If one be hard in conceiuing, they pronounce him a dowlt: if giuen to studie, they proclaime him a dunce. **1592** G. HARVEY *Pierce's Super.* 25 You that purpose with great summes of study and candles to purchase the worshipfull names of Dunses and Dodipoles may closely sitt or sokingly ly at your bookes. **1614** T. ADAMS *Devil's Banquet* 322 When a man courts to be a Doctor in all Arts, hee lightly proues a dunce in many. **1642** FULLER *Holy & Prof. St.* III. xviii. 199 A dunce, void of learning but full of books. **1742** POPE *Dunc.* IV. 90 A wit with dunces, and a dunce with wits.

5. One who shows no capacity for learning; a dull-witted, stupid person; a dullard, blockhead.

1577–87 HOLINSHED *Chron. Scot.* 461/1 But now in our age it is growne to be a common prouerbe in derision, to call such a person as is senselesse or without learning a Duns, which is as much as a foole. **1611** COTGR., *Lourdaut*, a sot, dunce, dullard. *Viedaze*,..an old dunce, doult, blockhead. **1669** STURMY *Mariner's Mag.* IV. 202 I confess the greatest Dunces have commonly the best Imployments, and many abler men before the Mast. **1712** ARBUTHNOT *John Bull* IV. i, Blockhead! dunce! ass! coxcomb! were the best epithets he gave poor John. **1852** BLACKIE *Stud. Lang.* 21 Let the hopeless dunce of the Grammar School be tried with Natural History. **1866** R. W. DALE *Disc. Spec. Occ.* ii. 39 As some boys remain dunces though they are sent to the best schools.

6. *attrib.* and *Comb.*, as ***dunce-corps***; †***dunce-table***, a table provided for duller or poorer students in some inns of court; ***dunce's cap***, a cap of conical shape, sometimes marked with a capital D, and placed on the head of a dunce at school.

1624 FORD *Sun's Darling* V. i, His father, me thinks, should be one of the Dunce-table, and one that never drunk strong beer in's life, but at festival-times. **1840** DICKENS *Old C. Shop* xxiv, And on a small shelf, the dunce's cap. **1847** MARY HOWITT *Ballads*, etc. 383 Or, learning's serf, puts day by day, Dunce-corps through classic exercises.

†**dunce**, *v. Obs.* [f. prec. sb.] *trans.* To puzzle, pose, prove to be a dunce; to make a dunce of.

1611 COTGR., *Metagraboulizé*, puzzled in, dunced vpon. *Metagraboulizer*, to dunce upon, to puzzle, or (too much) beat the braines about. **1649** R. HODGES *Plain. Direct.* 66 Boys may be easily taught the Latine. Why should children therefore be wearied and dunced out many yeares, and yet in the end fail? **1658** GURNALL *Chr. in Arm.* verse 14. vi. 71 'Tis time for the Scholar to throw off his gown..when every Schoolboy is able to dunce and pose him. **1662** *Ibid.* verse 17. xxiv. 202 Thy own reason..which is dunced and pozed with so many secrets in Nature.

†**duncecomb.** [f. DUNCE, after *coxcomb*.]

1630 J. TAYLOR (Water P.) *To T. Coriat* Wks. III. 15/2 I am no Duncecomb, Coxecombe, Odcomb Tom.

duncedom ('dʌnsdəm). [see -DOM.] The domain of dunces; dunces collectively; a dunce's condition or character.

1829 CARLYLE *Voltaire* Misc. Ess. 1872 II. 151 In the midst of that warfare with united Duncedom. **1829** —— *Novalis* ibid. 197 Their far-famed campaign against Duncedom, or that which called itself the 'Old School' of Literature. **1865** *Pall Mall G.* 21 Apr. 110 One who displays the true characteristic of Duncedom.

duncehood ('dʌnshʊd). [f. as prec. + -HOOD.] The quality, condition, or character of a dunce or dunces; mental opacity.

1829 *Blackw. Mag.* XXVI. 561 The seal of supreme dunce-hood. **1837** *Tait's Mag.* IV. 728 The caution or dunce-hood of modern booksellers. **1868** M. PATTISON *Academ. Org.* v. 231 A habit of dunce-hood which has been acquired by the passive resistance of the mind to the reiteration of the same matters.

duncely ('dʌnslɪ), *a. rare.* [f. DUNCE + -LY¹.] Like or of the nature of a dunce.

1826 *Examiner* 407/1 Duncely scribes and clerks.

'**duncely**, *adv. rare.* In 6 dunsly. [f. as prec. + -LY².] As a dunce; †in the way of the scholastic philosophy.

c **1535** LATIMER *Wks.* (Parker Soc.) II. 374 He is wilfully witted, Dunsly learned..zealous more than enough.

dunce-man, duns-man: see DUNCE *sb.* 1.

†'**duncer**, '**dunser**. *Obs.* [f. *Duns*, DUNCE + -ER.] An adherent of Duns Scotus, a Scotist; a follower or teacher of the scholastic divinity and logic; = DUNCE 3.

c **1550** BECON *Jewel of Joy* 9 [Latimer's teaching] whyche thynge dyuers drowesy dunsers wyth certayne fals fliynge flateringe Friers coulde not abyde. *Ibid.* 10 Drowned in the dirty dregges of the drowsy dunsers.

duncery, dunsery ('dʌnsərɪ, 'dʌnsrɪ). [f. DUNCE: see -ERY.]

†**1.** The practice, style, or character of a Scotist or Schoolman. *Obs.*

1560–70 SIR T. SMITH *Orat.* iv. in *Life* (1698) App. 81 Here you come with your fine and logical Distinction..as tho' we were in a School of Dunsery. **1641** MILTON *Ch. Govt.* II. (1851) 148 Prelaty, under whose inquisitorious and tyrannical duncery no free and splendid wit can flourish. **1683** KENNETT *Erasm. on Folly* (1709) 75 The more of duncery they have, the more of pride, and the greater is their ambition. **1687** *Refl. Dryden's Hind & P.* 25 The Author of *Pax Vobis*..your brother in Scholastick Duncery.

2. The state, character, or practice of a dunce or dullard; intellectual dullness, stupidity.

1615 SIR E. HOBY *Curry-combe* i. 17 He shewed more foolery then Philosophy, more Dunsery then Diuinity. **1715** PRIDEAUX *Art. Reform. in Universities* xxiv. in *Life* (1748) 216 To the discouragement of learning, and the encouragement of duncery and idleness. **1881** SWINBURNE in *Fortn. Rev.* Feb. 151 The detestable duncery of sham Pindarics.

dunch (dʌnʃ), *v.* chiefly dial. Also **dunsh**. [Derivation unknown.

Mätzner suggests connexion with Icel. *dunka* to resound, give a hollow sound, Sw. *dunka*, Da. *dunke* to beat, knock, thump, throb; but these are modern forms, having no historical connexion with English.]

trans. To strike or push with a short rapid blow, now esp. to jog with the elbow.

a **1240** *Wohunge* in *Cott. Hom.* 283 Þat tai þe dunchen and þrasten þe forðward swiðe toward ti dom. *c* **1440** *Promp. Parv.* 135/1 Dunchyn, or bunchyn, *tundo*. **1789** D. DAVIDSON *Seasons* 49 (Jam.) The unco brute much dunching dried Frae twa-year-alls and stirks. **1802** R. ANDERSON *Cumberld. Ball.* 25 When Trummel cleek'd her on his knee, She dunch'd and punch'd, cried, 'fuil, let be!' **1827** *Ann. Reg.* 198, I felt his skull had been dunched in. **1887** SIR W. G. SIMPSON *Art Golf* 132 A bad ball, which can ..be dunched along the ground a short distance with a brassy. *Mod. Sc.* Do not dunch me while I am writing. **1930** W. S. MAUGHAM *Cakes & Ale* ii. 23 Verbs that you only know the meaning of if you live in the right set (like 'dunch'). **1963** *Times* 9 Jan. 4/3 It [*sc.* mud] catches one in the eye when a [golf] shot is 'dunched'.

dunch, *sb. Sc.* and *north. dial.* [f. prec. vb.] A jog, a push with the elbow, a smart shock.

c **1440** *Promp. Parv.* 135/1 Dunche, or lonche..*sonitus, stepitus..bombus*. *c* **1490** *Ibid.* (MS. K.) Dvnche (*P.* dunchinge), *tuncio, percussio*. **1811** AITON *Agric. Ayrsh.* Gloss. 691 *Dunch*, a smart push. **1886** STEVENSON *Kidnapped* xiii. (1888) 118 She..struck the reef with such a dunch as threw us all flat upon the deck.

dunch, *a. Obs.* exc. *dial.* [Derivation uncertain: cf. DUNNY *a.*[2]] Dull or inert in the senses, or in composition.

1. Deaf. ***dunch down***: see quot. 1578.

1574 HELLOWES *Gueuara's Fam. Ep.* (1577) 75, I haue spoken with Perianes..and as he was deafe and moste dunch, I cried out more in speaking vnto him, than I do vse in preaching. **1578** LYTE *Dodoens* IV. liii. 513 This herbe is called..in Latine *Typha*..in Englishe..Dunche downe, bycause the downe will cause one to be deafe, if it happen to fall into the eares. **1787** GROSE *Provinc. Gloss., Dunch*, deaf. *W.* **1888** *Berkshire Gloss., Dunch*, deaf.

2. Blind.

?**16..** *Clown's Journey to London* (Somerset dial.) *MS. Ashmole* 36 lf. 112 What with the zmoke and what with the criez, I waz amozt blind and dunch in my eyes. **1888** *Berkshire Gloss., Dunch passage*, a *cul de sac*; the term 'blind passage' is sometimes used in this sense.

3. Heavy or doughy, as bread.

1842 AKERMAN *Wiltsh. Gloss., Dunch-dumpling*, a hard dumpling, made of flour and water. **1879** JEFFERIES *Wild Life in S.C.* 129 Priding herself that [the batch of bread] is never 'dunch' or heavy. [Hence prob., in midland dialects, *dunch* sb., dumpling.]

4. Stupid, slow of comprehension; dull.

1845 *Ainsworth's Mag.* VII. 368 The boy is either so dunch..or he is so sharp that you can scarcely trust him out of your sight. **1889** A. GISSING *Both of this Parish* I. xv. 324 William Stretch be a trifle dunch in some of his faculties. **1927** M. SADLEIR *Trollope* 169 *The Autobiography* contains a number of judgments on novels, and..they are 'dunch' and unconvincing.

Dunciad (ˈdʌnsɪæd). [f. DUNCE *sb.*: see -AD c.] The epic of dunces: name of a well-known poem by Pope. Also, the world or commonwealth of dunces. Hence **Dunciaˈdean**, *a. nonce-wd.*

1728 POPE (title) *The Dunciad*. **1742** —— *Dunciad* IV. 604 Tyrant supreme! shall three Estates command, And make one Mighty Dunciad of the Land! **1799** *Morn. Her.* in *Spirit Pub. Jrnls.* (1800) III. 169 Dunciadean critics.

duncical (ˈdʌnsɪkəl), *a.* and *adv.* Now *rare*. Also dunsical. [f. DUNCE *sb.* + -IC + -AL[1].]

A. *adj.* †**1.** Of or pertaining to the Scotists or to the Scholastic system. *Obs.*

1546 COVERDALE tr. *Calvin on Sacrament* Pref. A ij, Romisshe idolatrers and diligent studentes of duncicall dregges. **1588** FRAUNCE *Lawiers Log.* I. i. 3 b, Miserable Sorbonists and dunsicall Quidditaries. **1625** *Gonsalvio's Sp. Inquis.* 140 All that Sophisticall and Dunsicall diuinitie.

2. Of or pertaining to a dunce; dull-witted, stupid, blockheaded.

1588 J. HARVEY *Disc. Probl.* 65 Botched vp..after a rude, and dunsicall sort. **1655** FULLER *Ch. Hist.* VIII. ii. §26 This neck-question..the most dull and duncicall Commissioner was able to aske. **1708** MOTTEUX *Rabelais* IV. liii, Students sottish and duncical. **1748** RICHARDSON *Clarissa* Wks. 1883 VIII. 303, I have no patience with the foolish duncical dog. **1841** *Tait's Mag.* VIII. 7 Mathematics might be flogged into them..as readily as into our own dunsical natures.

B. as *adv.* for *duncically*.

1624 RAND *Epil. to Skelton's El. Rummyng*, King Henry the Eight Had a good conceit Of my merry vaine, Though duncicall plaine.

Hence †**dunciˈcality**.

1588 FRAUNCE *Lawiers Log.* Ded. ¶iij, If this be all the Dunsicalitie you talke of, you are farre more nyce then any Vniversitie man of mine acquaintance.

ˈduncify, *v. rare.* [f. DUNCE *sb.*: see -FY.] *trans.* To make a dunce of. Hence **duncified** *ppl. a.*, constituted as a dunce.

1597 *1st Pt. Return fr. Parnass.* IV. i. 1222 Let this duncified worlde esteeme of Spencer and Chaucer, I'le worshipp sweet Mr. Shakspeare. **1759** WARBURTON *Lett. to Hurd* (1809) 286 A fellow ten thousand times more duncified than dunce Webster.

duncish (ˈdʌnsɪʃ), *a.* [f. DUNCE *sb.* + -ISH.] Of the nature of a dunce; dunce-like. Hence **ˈduncishly** *adv.*; **ˈduncishness**.

1825 FONBLANQUE in *Westm. Rev.* IV. 377 A sentence of impenetrable duncishness. **1831** *Examiner* 162/1 Stupid by nature, and dunceish by education. **1833** T. HOOK *Widow & Marquess* x, The 'duncish curate', as his lordship called him. **1834** FONBLANQUE *Eng. under 7 Administ.* (1837) III. 161 Men, who read the broad signs of the times so duncishly.

duncur: see *dun cur* s.v. DUN *a.* 3 c.

Dundee (dʌnˈdiː). [Name of a Scottish city on the Firth of Tay.] **1.** Used *attrib.* to designate a variety of rambling rose.

1837 T. RIVERS *Rose Amateur's Guide* 43 The Ayrshire Rose (Rosa Arvensis Hybrida)... Dundee Rambler, is the most double, and one of the best in this division. **1899** G. JEKYLL *Wood & Garden* vii. 79 What a fine thing, among the cluster roses, is the old Dundee Rambler!

2. ***Dundee marmalade***: a kind of marmalade manufactured in Dundee (registered as a trade-mark by James Keiller & Son in 1880). Also *ellipt.*

1856 DICKENS in *Household Words* 28 June 555/2 Anchovy Paste, Dundee Marmalade, and the whole stock of luxurious helps to appetite. **1962** *Housewife* Apr. 92/2 Their silver-topped jar of Dundee marmalade. **1963** C. MACKENZIE *My Life & Times* II. 59, I do not remember ever seeing him eat any other preserves than Beech's strawberry jam and Keiller's Dundee marmalade. **1964** WODEHOUSE *Frozen Assets* iii. 51 The marmalade, too, had a tang which even Henry Blake-Somerset's imported Dundee could not have rivalled.

3. Used *attrib.* or *absol.* to designate a kind of rich fruit cake, usually decorated with split almonds.

1892 T. F. GARRETT *Encycl. Pract. Cookery* I. 234/2 Dundee Cake. Put 1 lb. of butter into a basin..loaf sugar.. flour..candied peel..and lastly thirteen eggs. **1920** 'K. MANSFIELD' *Jrnl.* Sept. (1954) 218 A paper parcel that held a very large wedge of cake—of the kind known as Dundee. *Ibid.*, 'This is the last of our precious Dundee,' said she,.. cutting it so tenderly that it almost seemed an act of cannibalism. **1928** M. LOWRY *Let.* (1967) 3, I heard the girl opposite me order some more Dundee cake. **1938** E. BOWEN *Death of Heart* II. i. 187 Portia ate doughnuts, shortbread and Dundee cake. **1943** G. GREENE *Ministry of Fear* I. i. 8 He had always liked cakes, especially rich Dundees.

dunder (ˈdʌndə(r)). [Corrupted from Sp. *redundar* to overflow.] The lees or dregs of cane-juice, used in the West Indies in the fermentation of rum; = DANDER *sb.*[2]

1793 EDWARDS *W. Indies* v. ii. II. 241 The use of dunder in the making of rum, answers the purpose of yeast in the fermentation of flower. *Ibid.*, Dunder..is the lees or feculencies of former distillations. *Ibid.* 240 To provide a dunder-cistern of at least 3000 gallons. **1795** SIR J. DALRYMPLE *Let. to Admiralty* 5 The miserable ferment called Dunder, which is the only one used in the West Indies.

dunder, var. of DUNNER *v. Sc.*

dunderbolt, dial. f. THUNDERBOLT, a belemnite; a flint arrow-head.

dunderhead (ˈdʌndəhɛd). [The origin of *dunder* in this and the following words is obscure.

It may possibly be connected with DUNNER *v.* and *sb.*[1] (which also occur as *dunder*): cf also Sc. *donner* to stun as with a blow or loud noise: see DONNERED. Some association between *dunder* and *blunder* appears to be indicated by the change of Du. *donderbus* to *blunderbuss*.]

A ponderously stupid person; a blockhead, a numskull.

a **1625** FLETCHER *Elder Bro.* II. iv, Oh, thou dunderhead! Wouldst thou be ever in thy wife's Syntaxis? **1629** MASSINGER *Picture* II. i, Recover, dunder-head! *a* **1700** B. E. *Dict. Cant. Crew, Dunder-head*, a dull heavy Creature. **1767** STERNE *Tr. Shandy* IX. xxv, Shall I be called as many blockheads, numsculls, doddypoles, dunderheads..and other unsavoury appellations. **1894** J. N. MASKELYNE *Sharps & Flats* i. 6 There are so many dunderheads of all nationalities who can never realise the truth of that simple maxim.

Hence **ˈdunderheadism**, practical stupidity.

1846 POE *Wks.* (1864) III. 115 Utter and inconceivable dunderheadism. **1881** SALA in *Illustr. Lond. News* 21 May 491 Bureaucratic and police dunderheadism.

ˈdunder-headed, *a.* [f. as prec. + -ED.] Ponderously stupid, thick-headed.

1825 COBBETT *Rur. Rides* (1885) II. 37 The poor scolded broken-hearted boy..becomes dunder-headed and dull for all his life-time. **1836** WAKLEY *Sp. in Ho. Com.* 15 Mar., Any illiterate and dunder-headed police officer. **1872** GEO. ELIOT *Middlem.* xlv, He regarded it as a mixture of jealousy and dunderheaded prejudice.

Hence **ˈdunderˌheadedness**, gross stupidity.

1870 *Sat. Rev.* 15 Jan. 80/2 This dunderheadedness of crime which is brought home to our senses by reports like these.

dunderpate (ˈdʌndəpeɪt). = DUNDERHEAD.

1809 W. IRVING *Knickerb.* III. i. (1849) 140 A dunderpate, like the owl, the stupidest of birds. **1829** J. JEKYLL in *Corr.* 16 Mar. vii. (1894) 194 When the Republic, like Great Britain at this day, was overrun by dunderpates.

†**ˈdunderwhelp**. *Obs.* [see above.] A dunderheaded 'whelp', a contemptible blockhead.

1621 FLETCHER *Wild-Goose Chase* III. i, What a purblind puppy was I!.. What a dunder-whelp, To let him domineer thus! *a* **1625** —— *Women Pleased* II. vi, You know what a dunder-whelp [*Folio* 1, dundierwhelp] my master is.

dun-diver. [f. DUN *a.* + DIVER 2.] **a.** The female and young male of the goosander (*Mergus merganser*). **b.** *U.S. local.* The ruddy duck.

1678 RAY *Willughby's Ornith.* 333 The Dun-Diver or Sparlin-fowl, *Merganser fæmina*. **1766** PENNANT *Zool.* (1776) II. 556 The Dun Diver or female is less than the male. **1829** DARWIN in *Life & Lett.* (1887) I. 175 I shot whilst in Shrewsbury a Dundiver (female Goosander, as I suppose you know).

Dundonian (dʌnˈdəʊnɪən). [f. DUNDEE, after ABERDONIAN *a.* and *sb.*] A native or inhabitant of Dundee.

1898 *Westm. Gaz.* 6 Oct. 10/1 It is common for Dundonians wishing salmon from their own river to send for it to London. **1965** *Guardian* 26 Nov. 9/2 Some Dundonians harbour a continuing misgiving about the implications [etc.].

Dundreary (dʌnˈdrɪərɪ). [Name of Lord *Dundreary*, a character in T. Taylor's comedy *Our American Cousin* (1858).] In allusive attrib. uses, esp. ***Dundreary whiskers***, long side whiskers worn without a beard. Also *absol.*, usu. in *pl.* (See also quot. 1864[2].)

1862 *Englishwoman's Dom. Mag.* Aug. 183 Bodger..came to understand (in a Dundreary manner) a little more about Bradshaw. **1864** *Chambers's Jrnl.* 17 Sept. 595/2 It was only a summer scarf, of the sort that is called Dundreary. **1864** HOTTEN *Slang Dict.* 127 *Dundreary*, an empty swell. **1867** 'PIPS' *Lyrics & Lays* 141 Full proud is he, I ween, Of his Dundreary whiskers. **1882** 'F. ANSTEY' *Vice Versa* xvii, Bushy black whiskers, more like the antiquated 'Dundreary' type than modern fashion permits. **1894** C. G. HARPER *Revolted Woman* ii. 39 This fashion was the 'Piccadilly-weeper' variety of adornment, known at this day—chiefly owing to Sothern's impersonation of a contemporary lisping fop—as the 'Dundreary'. **1906** GALSWORTHY *Man of Property* I. i, His cheeks, thinned by two parallel folds, and a long clean-shaven upper lip, were framed within Dundreary whiskers. **1929** C. H. SMITH *Bridge of Life* ii. 38 The older men wore beards, Dundrearys or side whiskers; the middle-aged, mustaches.

dunducketty (dʌnˈdʌkɪtɪ, -ətɪ), *a. colloq.* or *dial.* Also -ety, -ity. [app. f. DUN *a.* + DUCK *sb.*[1]] In phr. ***dunducketty mud-colour***: (of) a dull, drab colour.

1818 LADY MORGAN *Let.* 26 Aug. in *Autobiogr.* (1859) 29 A colour I have supplied her with (not from the rainbow), dun-ducketty mud colour. [**1847** HALLIWELL, *Dunduckity-mur*, an indescribable colour, but rather dull. *Suffolk*.] **1897** M. KINGSLEY *Trav. W. Africa* 420 It is better than all white, or dunduckety mud-colour paint.

dune (djuːn). [a. mod.F. *dune* (13th c. in Hatz.-Darm.), a. ODu. *dûna*, MDu. *dûne* (Du. *duin*, mod.LG. *düne*) = OE. *dún*: see DOWN *sb.*[1]]

a. A mound, ridge, or hill of drifted sand on the sea-coast (or, rarely, on the border of a lake or river); applied esp. to the great sand-hills on the coast of France and the Netherlands, but used more widely of any mound of drifted sand; also, a similar ridge or mound of clay formed by the action of wind. In earlier English use, *down* occurs: see DOWN *sb.*[1] 3.

1790 ROY in *Phil. Trans.* LXXX. 184 Supposing the extremities of the base between Fort Revers and the Dunes to be accurately known. **1830–33** LYELL *Princ. Geol.* xxi. (1847) 312 By the aid of embankments and the sand dunes of the coast. **1832** DE LA BECHE *Geol. Man.* (ed. 2) 79 Indurated dunes occur in various parts of the world: they have been noticed by Peron in New Holland. **1855** LONGF. *Hiaw.* xvi. 10 On the dunes of Nagow Wudjoo..Stood the lodge of Pau-Puk-Keewis. **1878** K. JOHNSTON *Africa* ii. 23 The Sahara presents now a stretch of sand, then hills and ravines, Marshes and dunes. **1879** *Encycl. Brit.* X. 266/1 Captain Sturt found vast deserts of sand in the interior of Australia, with long lines of dunes 200 feet high. **1883** SYMONDS *Italian Byways* vii. 222 A handful of horned poppies from the dunes. **1909** *Jrnl. Geol.* XVII. 754 These 'clay dunes' were almost always associated with a lagoon. **1926** T. E. LAWRENCE *Seven Pillars* IV. xliv. 256 The ground was flat and featureless till five o'clock, when we..found ourselves..amid sand-hills coated slenderly with tamarisk. .. The bushes and the dunes broke the wind. **1944** A. HOLMES *Princ. Physical Geol.* xiii. 264 One of the most remarkable features of desert dunes is their apparent power of collecting all the sand in their neighbourhood. **1961** *Jrnl. Sedimentary Petrol.* XXXI. 246/2 Clay dunes are..limited to the shores of clay-floored saline playas and tidal mud flats. **1963** *Ibid.* XXXIII. 766/2 The eolian particles become fixed in the dune when the clay regains moisture from the air or from rain.

b. *attrib.* and *Comb.*, as *dune-like* adj.; **dune-bedding** (see quot. 1940); **dune buggy** orig. *U.S.* = *beach buggy* s.v. BEACH *sb.* 4; **dune sand**, sand formed into dunes by the wind; **dune-slack** = SLACK *sb.*[1] 2.

1940 *Chambers's Techn. Dict.* 271/2 *Dune bedding, that type of current bedding commonly exhibited by sand dunes and interpreted in sandstones as evidence of desert conditions. **1946** L. D. STAMP *Brit. Struct. & Scenery* xxii. 229 The Permian Mauchline Sandstones..are believed to represent desert sand-dunes for they exhibit dune-bedding on a huge scale. **1965** *Hot Rod* Apr. 75/1 (*caption*), With front wheels on ground for a change, *dune-buggy gets a once-over from owner. **1969** *Daily Tel.* (Colour Suppl.) 17 Oct. 57/1 To date, 137 independent manufacturers and distributors are shoving Dunebuggies on to the American asphalt as fast as nuts can be spun on bolts. **1976** *National Observer* (U.S.) 22 May 18/2 Visitors can rent a dune buggy, pack a picnic lunch, and spend several days exploring the mountains and beaches of Mahe. **1853** KANE *Grinnell Exp.* xxxi. (1856) 270 Rolling *dune-like hills. **1792** A. YOUNG *Trav. France* 74 Mons. le Brun has an improvement on the Dunes, which he very obligingly shewed me. Between the town and that place are..one or two fields inclosed of most wretched blowing *dune sand. **1916** *Jrnl. Geol.* XXIV. 242 Red dune sands are exceptional rather than the rule in the desert regions of today. **1967** *Oceanogr. & Marine Biol.* V. 132 So far as the various environments along the shore are concerned, beach sands and dune sands have been distinguished by several authors. **1938** *Nature* 7 May 817/2 The parallel ridges often rest on a relatively impermeable substratum, and the water, of which the dune ridges are the catchment area, drains into the intervening hollows and sometimes forms what are known as '*dune slacks'... The dune slacks are the especial home of the bog pimpernel. **1964** V. J. CHAPMAN *Coastal Vegetation* vi. 152 Most of the species to be found in dune slacks are common or reasonably common.

dune, obs. f. DIN, DOWN, DUN *sb.*[3]

'dunfish, dun-fish. *U.S. local.* (New England). [f. DUN *a.*] Cod cured by dunning (see DUN *v.*[1] 1 b).

[Cf. **1792** *Dumb-fish* s.v. DUMB *a.* 8.] **1828** WEBSTER, *Dunfish.* **1873** CELIA THAXTER *Isles of Shoals* 83 A real dunfish is handsome, cut in transparent strips, the color of brown sherry wine. The process is a tedious one.

dun-fly. [f. DUN *a.*] **a.** A kind of artificial fly used in angling. **b.** A kind of gadfly.

a **1450** *Fysshynge w. Angle* (1883) 33 The donne flye: the body of the donne woll. **1653** WALTON *Angler* iv. 97, I will name..the dun flie, the stone flie, the red flie [etc.]. **1829** GLOVER *Hist. Derby* I. 177 *Oestrus Curvicauda*, Gadbee or Dun Fly.

dung (dʌŋ), *sb.* Forms: 1– dung, (3 ding), 4–6 dunge, dong(e, 4–7 doung(e, (6 dungue, doong, 6–7 dongue). [OE. *dung* = OFris. *dung*, OHG. *tunga* manuring, mod.G. *dung* and *dünger* manure. Cf. also Sw. *dynga* dung, muck, Da. *dynge* heap, hoard, mass, pile, mod.Icel. *dyngja* heap, dung. The original sense is uncertain: see Kluge s.v.]

1. Excrementitious and decayed matter employed to fertilize the soil; manure.

c **1000** ÆLFRIC *Gloss.* in Wr.-Wülcker 104/9 *Fimus*, dung. *c* **1160** *Hatton Gosp.* Luke xiii. 8 Ic hine beweorpe mid dunge. **1362** LANGL. *P. Pl.* A. IV. 130 Þat lawe schal ben a laborer and leden a-feld dounge. *c* **1420** *Pallad. on Husb.* I. 276 The lond aboute a roote is to be moued Al vpsodoun, and flekis shal we make Of donge and molde. *c* **1440** *Promp. Parv.* 127/1 Donge, mucke, *fimus, letamen.* **1583** STUBBES *Anat. Abus.* II. (1882) 44 What kind of dung is best to fatten the same [barren ground] againe. **1616** SURFL. & MARKH. *Country Farme* 533 It will be good to spread Quicklime vpon the plowed ground..the haruest after it is more plentifull, than after anie other dung that a man can inuent. **1727** BRADLEY *Fam. Dict.* s.v. *Garden*, Dung made of Leaves that are well rotted. **1875** *Ure's Dict. Arts* III. 213 All the essential fertilising substances of a large mass of home-made dung.

2. (As constituting the usual manure) The excrement or fæces of animals (rarely of human beings): as *cow-dung, horse-dung, pig's-dung*, etc.

1297 R. GLOUC. (1724) 310 In to a chambre forene þe gadelyng gan wende..& in þe dunge þar Hudde hym þere longe. *a* **1300** *Sarmun* 6 in *E.E.P.* (1862) 2 A sakke ipudrid ful wiþ drit and ding. *c* **1400** MAUNDEV. (Roxb.) xiv. 64 Þai dight þaire mete with dung of bestez dried at þe sonne. *c* **1420** *Pallad. on Husb.* I. 527 Donge of fowlis is ful necessary To londtiling. **1523** FITZHERB. *Husb.* §17 Horse-donge is the worste donge that is..And the dounge of douues is best, but it muste be layde vppon the grounde verye thynne. **1535** COVERDALE *2 Kings* xviii. 27 That they maye eate their owne donge and drynke their owne stale. **1611** BIBLE *Job* xx. 7 Yet he shall perish for euer, like his owne doung. **1796** H. HUNTER tr. *St. Pierre's Stud. Nat.* I. 262 Now this dung was entirely the produce of the fishes on which those fowls constantly fed. **1817** J. BRADBURY *Trav.* 135 Having collected a sufficient quantity of dry buffaloe's dung, we made a fire.

3. *transf.* and *fig.* Applied to that which is morally filthy or defiling; or to matter that is vile, contemptible, or loathsome.

a **1225** *Ancr. R.* 140 Heo mot..upholden ham, þet heo ne uallen iðe dunge of sunne. *c* **1325** *Rel. Ant.* II. 191 Loverd king, to hori ding what makith man so hold? **1413** *Pilgr. Sowle* (Caxton 1483) III. viii. 55 They were fallen and leyen defyled in the donge of synne. **1526–34** TINDALE *Phil.* iii. 8 For whom I have counted all thynge losse, and do iudge them but donge. **1577** NORTHBROOKE *Dicing* (1843) 76 This dung and filth of ydlenesse. **1583** STUBBES *Anat. Abus.* II. (1882) 95 For greedinesse of a little mucke or dung of the earth, (For monie is no better). *a* **1677** BARROW *Serm.* Wks. 1716 I. 16 The dust of pelf, the dung of sensuality. **1858** CARLYLE *Fredk. Gt.* I. i. (1865) I. 12 The noteworthy Dead is sure to be found lying under infinite dung, no end of calumnies and stupidities accumulated upon him.

4. *Tailor's slang.* A term of obloquy, applied to journeymen who submit to the masters' terms, working by the piece instead of by the day, or working while others are on strike. Cf. DUNGHILL 2 d.

1764 *Chron.* in *Ann. Reg.* 66/2 Who, refusing to comply with the masters' terms..call themselves *Flints*, in contradistinction to those who submit, and are in derision called by the first *Dungs.* **1824** *Ibid.* 80 The whole body of journeymen tailors is divided into two classes, denominated Flints and Dungs: the former work by the day and receive all equal wages; the latter work generally by the piece. **1837** WHITTOCK, etc. *Bk. Trades* (1842) 430 (Tailor) Any man being declared a 'dung' for working too fast. **1867** *Morning Star* 6 Aug. 7/1 He said, 'I know by your walk you are a "dung!"' (A term applied to men who work for a shop where the hands are on strike.)

5. *attrib.* and *Comb.* **a.** attrib., as ***dung-barge, -bed, -boat, -cake, -drag, -mere, -mixen*** (i.e. dung-heap), ***-pike, -pit, -yard***, etc.

1751 SMOLLETT *Per. Pic.* (1779) IV. xcvi. 188 The rudder of a *dung-barge. **1845** *Florist's Jrnl.* 47 The preference of a small [hot] house over a *dung-bed. *a* **1667** COWLEY *Answ. Invit. Cambridge* Wks. 1711 III. 63 The Quondam *Dung-boat is made gay. **1901** KIPLING *Kim* iv. 91 For luxury's sake, Kim bought a handful of *dung-cakes to build a fire. **1929** [see CHOOLA]. **1949** M. L. DARLING *At Freedom's Door* 213 There is one feature of village life which is so universal that I have hardly mentioned it—the dung cakes. **1795** *Hull Advertiser* 6 June 3/3 Striking him on the head with a *dung drag. **1706** PHILLIPS (ed. Kersey), **Dung-Meers*, are Places or Pits where Soils, Dungs, Weeds, etc. are mix'd and lie and rot together for some time, for the Improvement of Husbandry. **1480** *Robt. Devyll* 38 So into a foule *donge myxen he her caryed. **1861** MUSGRAVE *By-roads* 12 Road-side laystalls and dung-mixens removed out of sight. **1530** PALSGR. 214/2 *Donge pyke, *fourche a fiant.* **1658** ROWLAND *Moufet's Theat. Ins.* Ep. Ded., Oyl Beetles..rowl up and down a *dung-pil. **1870** RAMSAY *Remin.* v. (ed. 18) 86 Their dung-hills or *dung-pits. **1707–12** MORTIMER (J.), Any manner of vegetables cast into the *dungyard.

b. objective, instrumental, etc. as ***dung-eater, -finding; dung-bred, -feeding*** adjs.

a **1631** DRAYTON *Poems* IV. 1271 (Jod.) I scorn all earthly *dungbred scarabees. **1845** DARWIN *Voy. Nat.* (1889) 490 Many kinds of *dung-feeding beetles. **1610** HEALEY *St. Aug. Citie of God* 691 Stercutius, who was deified for *dung-finding.

c. Special combs.: **dung-bath** (*Dyeing*), a mixture of dung, usually that of cows, with chalk in warm water, used to remove superfluous mordant from printed calico; **dung-beetle**, a name for the dor-beetle or dumble-dore; also a general name for the group of beetles which roll up balls of dung; **dung-bird**, (*a*) the hoopoe; (*b*) = *dung-hunter*; **dung-chafer** = *dung-beetle*; **dung-cistern, -copper**, a vessel containing a dung-bath; †**dung-farmer**, one who contracts to remove dung and refuse; **dung-fly**, a two-winged fly of the genus *Scatophaga*, feeding in ordure; **dung-gate, -port**, a gate through which dung and refuse are removed; in O.T., the name of a gate of Jerusalem; the anus; **dung-hunter, -teaser**, the Dirt-bird or Dirty Allan: (see quots.); †**dung-wet** *a.*, as wet as dung, wet through; **dung-worm**, a worm or larva found in cow-dung, used as bait. Also DUNG-CART, -FORK, etc.

1836 *Penny Cycl.* VI. 153/2 The chalk occasionally added to the *dung-bath serves to neutralize the acids as they are evolved from the mordants. **1863–72** WATTS *Dict. Chem.* II. 353 The dung-bath is now almost wholly superseded by the solutions of certain salts, viz. the double phosphate of soda and lime, arsenite and arsenate of soda, and silicate of soda. **1634** MOUFET *Theat. Ins.* 153 *Dung-beetle, Sharnbugg. **1828** DARWIN in *Life & Lett.* I. 172 A bluish metallic-coloured dung-beetle. **1816** KIRBY & SP. *Entomol.* (1843) II. 280 The common *dung-chafer..flies with great rapidity and force. **1836** *Penny Cycl.* VI. 154/1 The goods must be..winched through a fresh *dung-cistern (commonly called a *dung-copper). **1598** E. GILPIN *Skial.* (1878) 26 He'le cry, oh rare, at a *Dongfarmers cart. **1599** HAKLUYT *Voy.* II. II. 69 The dungfermers seek in euery streete by exchange to buy this durtie ware. **1616** *Crt. & Times Jas. I* (1849) I. 414 They say a dung-farmer gave him his death's wound. **1658** ROWLAND *Moufet's Theat. Ins.* 947 Merdivora or *Dung-flies are of divers sorts. **1535** COVERDALE *Neh.* xii. 31 On the righte hande of the wall toward the *Donggate. **1657** W. RAND tr. *Gassendi's Life Peiresc* II. 152 The Excrement..in that part which was near the Dung-gate. *a* **1661** FULLER *Worthies* I. (1662) 144 Searching into the pedigree of Paper, it cometh into the world at the doungate, raked thence in Rags. **1766** PENNANT *Zool.* (1768) II. 423 This species [of Gull] is likewise called by some the *Dung Hunter. **1885** SWAINSON *Prov. Names Birds* 210 Richardson's Skua ..[called] from the vulgar opinion that the gulls are muting, when, in reality, they are only disgorging fish newly caught ..Dung bird or Dung hunter. **1535** COVERDALE *Neh.* ii. 13, I rode by nighte vnto the valley porte..and to the *Dongporte. **1841** SELBY in *Proc. Berw. Nat. Club* I. No. 9. 256 Arctic skua, better known..by the name of the *dung teazer. **1599** NASHE *Lenten Stuffe* in *Harl. Misc.* (1808–12) VI. 180 (D.) Fishermen cowthring and quaking, *dung-wet after a storme. **1603** KNOLLES *Hist. Turks* (1621) 723 The duke of Alva (wonderfully wearied in the late skirmish, and dung wet). **1753** CHAMBERS *Cycl. Supp.*, **Dung-worms*..found in great plenty among cow-dung in September and October.

dung (dʌŋ), *v.* Forms: 1 dyngian, 4–6 dong(e, (5 doong, 6 doung), 4–7 dunge, 4– dung. [In OE. *dyngian* from *dung* sb.; cf. OFris. *donga, denga*, MHG. *tungen*, Ger. *düngen*. In ME. assimilated to, or formed anew from the sb.]

1. a. *trans.* To manure (ground) with dung; to dress with manure.

c **1000** ÆLFRIC *Gloss.* in Wr.-Wülcker 104/8 *Stercoratio*, dingiung. *c* **1380** WYCLIF *Serm.* Sel. Wks. I. 99 Digge aboute þe vyne rotis and dung hem wel. *c* **1440** *Promp. Parv.* 127/1 Dungen, or mukkyn londe, *fimo.* **1502** *Caxton's Chron. Eng.* I. (1520) 7/1 He taught men to donge theyr feldes. **1548** LATIMER *Ploughers* (Arb.) 19 The ploughman.. tilleth hys lande..and sometyme doungeth it. **1648** GAGE *West Ind.* xviii. 135 The best way to husband or dung their ground. **1770–74** A. HUNTER *Georg. Ess.* (1803) I. 313 They miss a crop by dunging an improper soil.

fig. **1709** STEELE *Tatler* No. 35 ¶2 To improve and dung his Brains with this prolifick Powder [snuff].

b. Predicated of animals.

1574 tr. *Littleton's Tenures* 15 b, If I deliver to a man mye sheepe to dong or marle his land. **1607** DEKKER *Westw. Hoe* II. i. Wks. 1873 II. 294 Doe Iack-dawes dung the top of Paules Steeple still? **1759** tr. *Duhamel's Husb.* I. iv. (1762) 9 The land is well dunged by them.

c. Predicated of the manure.

1562 TURNER *Herbal* II. 52 b, Medic fother muste be sowen in April..It dongeth the ground well. **1589** *Pasquill's Ret.* 5 The carkases of the deade did dunge the grounde.

2. a. *intr.* Of animals: To drop or eject excrement. Also of human beings.

c **1470** HARDING *Chron.* XXI. iv, In [the whiche time] no horsse maye dunge. **1523** FITZHERB. *Husb.* §18 Let them [shepe] stande stylle a good season, that they maye donge. **1699** DAMPIER *Voy.* II. II. 105 He grases on the Shore, and dungs like a Horse. **1791** J. WHITAKER *Rev. Gibbon's Hist.* 256 (R.) He dungs upon it at last from the dirty tail of Mahometanism. **1846** [see DUNGING *vbl. sb.* 2]. **1865** H. J. HUNTER *Rep. Med. Off. P.C. 1864* App. VI. 183 in *Parl. Papers* XXVI, The women and children dung into pots.., the men dunging away from home. **1928** E. & C. PAUL tr. *Marx's Capital* II. 761 A house whose 'tenants dunged against the house-side'.

†**b.** *trans.* ***dung out***, to pass as excrement. *Obs.*

1641 BEST *Farm. Bks.* (Surtees) 8 Till such time as the lambe beginne to dunge out the milke which it hath gotten of her [an ewe].

3. *Calico-printing.* To immerse in a dung-bath in order to remove superfluous mordant.

1836 [see DUNGING]. **1875** *Ure's Dict. Arts* I. 626 In dunging calicoes. *Ibid.* 628 A solution of arseniate of soda, containing from 10 to 50 grains arsenic acid per gallon, according to the strength and nature of the mordants to be dunged.

Hence **dunged** *ppl. a.*, covered or mixed with dung; manured; **dunger**, an animal that dungs (Cotgr. s.v. *Grumer*).

c **1420** *Pallad. on Husb.* I. 151 In donged lond. **1597–8** BP. HALL *Sat.* V. i. 116 To see the dunged folds of dag-tayled sheepe. **1626** BACON *Sylva* §500 An Infusion of the Medecine in Dunged Water. **1651** R. CHILD in *Hartlib's Legacy* (1655) 11 Dung'd land.

dung, pa. t. and pple. of DING *v.*[1]

dunga, var. DOONGA.

dungaree (ˌdʌŋgəˈriː). Also **dungeree.** [ad. Hindī *dungrī.*] **a.** A kind of coarse inferior Indian calico.

[**1613** CAPT. SARIS in Purchas *Pilgrimes* (1625–6) I. 363 (Y.) The sorts requested, and prices that they yielded.. Dongerijns, the finest, twelve.] **1696** J. F. *Merchant's Ware-ho.* 14 Dungarees is another sort of Callico which is course, but something whiter than the former, yet not so fine, but is much stronger than the Derribands. **1759** *Lond. Mag.* XXVIII. 604 A sail-cloth called Dungaree. **1868** MISS FRERE *Deccan Days* p. xxiv. (Y.), Such dungeree as you now pay half a rupee a yard for.

b. *pl.* Trousers of this material. Now usually made of blue dungaree or similar material.

1891 R. KIPLING *City Dreadf. Nt.* 40 He's got his dungarees on. **1928** *Granta* 2 Nov. 74/2, I myself, as a matter of fact, sweated through nine dungarees. **1940** *Geogr. Jrnl.* XCV. 260 Dressing more and more in..American mass-produced dungarees.

c. *attrib.* and *Comb.*

1849 E. E. NAPIER *Excurs. S. Africa* II. 230 Blue dungaree trowsers. **1890** W. C. RUSSELL *My Shipmate Louise* III. xxxiii. 103 Clad in shirts and duck or dungaree breeches.

'dung-cart. A cart used to convey manure.

c **1386** CHAUCER *Nun's Pr. T.* 216 He..fond A dong Carte as it went for to donge lond. **1523** FITZHERB. *Husb.* §146 To helpe her husbande to fyll the mucke wayne or donge cart. **1606** *Choice, Chance, etc.* (1881) 48 What a spight it was to see a horse of seruice drawe in a doung-cart. **1865** TROLLOPE *Belton Est.* xiii, If I thought that no one would see me, I'd fill a dung-cart or two.

fig. **1624** HEYWOOD *Captives* I. i, Whele about thou dung cart of diseases. **1636** B. JONSON *Discov.* Wks. (Rtldg.) 764/2 Reducing all wit to the original dung-cart.

Hence **dung-cartful**, as much as fills a dung-cart.

1598 *Mucedorus* in Hazl. *Dodsley* VII. 235 I have kill'd a dungcartful at the least. *a* **1659** CLEVELAND *Chym. Magic* 18 Guts at least a Dung-cart full.

dungeon (ˈdʌndʒən), *sb.* Forms: α. 4–5 dongeoun, -goun, -gon, -gen, -gyn, doun-, dungoun, *Sc.* dwngeoune, -geown, downgeowne, 4–6 dongeon, dungion, 5–6 doungeon, -gen, 6 dongion, -gyon, 4– dungeon. β. 4–9 Donjon (4 dunjon, 4–5 donjoun(e, 9 donjeon). [a. F. *donjon* (12th c. in Littré), in OF. also *danjon, dangon* = Pr. *donjon, dompnhon*:—late L. *domniōn-em* in same sense, f. *domnus* (for *dominus*) lord; thus essentially a doublet of DOMINION.]

1. The great tower or keep of a castle, situated in the innermost court or bailey. (To this the archaic spelling donjon is now usually appropriated.)

α. **1375** BARBOUR *Bruce* XVII. 224 Bath the castell and the dwngeoune. *c* **1385** CHAUCER *L.G.W.* 937 *Dido*, The noble tour of Ylion That of the citee was the cheef dongeon. *c* **1430** LYDG. *Bochas* I. iii. (1544) 6 a, A thousand arblastes, bent in his doungeoun. *c* **1489** CAXTON *Sonnes of Aymon* i. 23 Lohier ..mounted vp vnto the dongeon of the castell. **1568** GRAFTON *Chron.* II. 288 Come on Sirs, ye shal enter into the Dungeon, for then shall ye be sure to be Lordes of the Castell. **1705** *Lond. Gaz.* No. 4164/3 The Governor.. retired into the Dungeon, which is a small Fort within the great one. **1797** MRS. RADCLIFFE *Italian* vii, The keep or dungeon of the ancient fort.

β. a **1300** *Cursor M.* 9926 þe thrid [colur]..castes lem ouer al sa bright, þat reches to þe dunjon light. *c* **1330** R. BRUNNE *Chron.* (1810) 121 Steuen..did reise in þat coste a stalworth donjon. **1475** *Bk. Noblesse* 12 The castelle and donjoune held still. **1678** tr. *Gaya's Art of War* II. 116 Donjon, a place of Retreat in a Town or Place, to capitulate in with greater security in case of Extremity. **1691** *Lond. Gaz.* No. 2727/2 After this we fixed our Miners to the Donjon or Tower within the Castle. **1813** SCOTT *Trierm.* II. x, Nor tower nor donjon could he spy. **1894** BARING-GOULD *Deserts S. France* II. xvi. 38 A cylindrical donjon, with ancient buildings grouped about it.

b. More fully, ***donjon-*** (***dungeon-***) ***keep***, ***-tower***.

1808 SCOTT *Marm.* I. i, The battled towers, the Donjon keep. **1813** —— *Rokeby* II. ii, By Brackenbury's dungeon-tower. **1849** JAMES *Woodman* xi. **1855** MOTLEY *Dutch Rep.* VI. iii. (1866) 828 It was in the donjon keep of the castle.

c. *Arch.* (See quot.)

1823 CRABB *Technol. Dict.*, *Donjon* (Archit.), a small wooden pavilion raised above the roof of the house, where anyone may command a fine view.

2. A strong close cell; a dark subterranean place of confinement; a deep dark vault.

13.. *E.E. Allit. P.* A. 1186 So wel is me in þys doel doungoun. **13..** *Coer de L.* 728 That thou dwelle in a fowle dongon. *c* **1325** *Body & Soul* 471 in *Map's Poems* (Camden) 345 The eorthe closede hit self aȝeyn, And the dungoun was for-dit. **1512** *Act 4 Hen. VIII*, c. 8 Preamb., The said Richard was taken and imprisoned in a doungen and a depe pytt under grounde. **1604** SHAKS. *Oth.* III. iii. 271, I had rather be a Toad, And liue vpon the vapour of a Dungeon. **1667** MILTON *P.L.* II. 317 The King of Heav'n hath doom'd This place our dungeon. **1713** BERKELEY *Guardian* No. 39. ¶3 Beneath the castle I could discern vast dungeons. **1871** MORLEY *Voltaire* (1886) 7 When the fortunes of the fight do not hurry the combatant to dungeon or stake.

3. *transf.* and *fig.*

1340 HAMPOLE *Pr. Consc.* 2835 'In helle', he says, 'es na raunceon'. For na helpe may be in þat dungeon. *c* **1430** LYDG. *Min. Poems* 251 (Mätz.) That worldly waves with there mortal deluge Ne drowne me nat in ther dreedful dongoun. **1549** COVERDALE, etc. *Erasm. Par. Col.* 2 In the deepe doungeon of ignorance. **1671** MILTON *Samson* 156 Thou art become..The dungeon of thyself. **1832** G. R. PORTER *Porcelain & Gl.* 68 Palissy..confined within the dungeon of his own breast, those feelings of bitterness. **1871** R. ELLIS *Catullus* lxviii. 102 Strangely the land's last verge holds him, a dungeon of earth.

†**b.** A habitation, mansion: also *fig. Obs.*

1430-40 LYDG. *Bochas* VIII. xxiv. (1554) 194 b, Up to the rich sterry bright dongeon..Called Arthurs constellacion. —— *Lyke thyn Audience etc.* in *Pol. Rel. & L. Poems* (1866) 25 Dyogenes lay in a smalle dongeon, In sondre wedyrs which turnyd as a balle. **1443** —— *Prospect Peace* in *Pol. Poems* (Rolls) II. 211 Briht was the sterre ovir the dongoun moost, Wher the hevenly queen lay poorly in jesyne.

c. Applied to a person of profound learning or wisdom: = 'deep mine or receptacle.' (*Sc.* and *north. dial.*)

1773 in Boswell *Jrnl. Tour Hebrides* 22 Oct., Lady Lochbury said, 'he was a dungeon of wit'. **1832-53** *Whistle-binkie* (Sc. Songs) Ser. III. 81 Although he's a dungeon o' Latin and Greek. **1855** ROBINSON *Whitby Gloss.* s.v. *Dungeonable*, 'He's a dungeon o' wit', very shrewd. *Mod. Sc.* He is a perfect dungeon of learning.

4. *attrib.* and *Comb.*: Of or belonging to a dungeon, as ***dungeon-bolt***, ***-cell***, ***-door***, ***-floor***, ***-fortress***, ***-gate***, ***-vault***, etc.; **dungeon-keep**, **-tower** (see 1 b). Also *dungeon-like* adj.

1813 SCOTT *Rokeby* IV. xxii, A fearful vision..Of *dungeon-bolts and fetters worn. **1814** —— *Ld. of Isles* III. iv, From lowest *dungeon cell To highest tower. *a* **1743** SAVAGE *Wks.* (1775) II. 107 (Jod.) Where *dungeon damps arise Diseas'd he pines. *c* **1440** CAPGRAVE *Life St. Kath.* v. 720 The gayleris were sore afrayde of certeyn light at the *dongeon-doore. **1645** MILTON *Tetrach.* Wks. (1847) 183/2 This is that grisly porter, who..claps the *dungeon-gate upon them. **1864** A. MCKAY *Hist. Kilmarnock* 98 Above were two *dungeon-like apartments. **1856** W. E. AYTOUN *Bothwell* (1857) 2 They riot o'er my *dungeon-vault. **1810** MONTGOMERY *Poems, Old Man's Song* viii, To burst these *dungeon-walls of clay.

Hence **'dungeonable** *a.* (*north. dial.*), 'deep', shrewd, knowing (cf. 3 c). **'dungeonly**, **'dungeony** *a.*, dungeon-like.

1593 NASHE *Christ's T.* (1613) 42 None but the God of heauen may..returne Conquerour from that dungeonly Kingdome. **1674-91** RAY *N.C. Words* 22 A Dungeonable Body; a shrewd person, or, as the vulgar express it, a divelish Fellow. **1823** in *Life of Dean Hook* I. 360 Unaired dungeony rooms of a bachelor's house. **1855** ROBINSON *Whitby Gloss.*, *Dungeonable*, deep, knowing.

dungeon ('dʌndʒən), *v.* [f. prec. sb.] *trans.* To put or keep in a dungeon or cell; to imprison; to shut *up* in, or as in, a dungeon.

1615 T. ADAMS *Blacke Devill* 76 If he once recovers him into his prison he will dungeon him. **1645** BP. HALL *Remedy Discontents* 124 Are we dungeon'd up from the sight of the Sun? **1819** SHELLEY *Cenci* II. i, You said nothing Of how I might be dungeoned like a madman. **1884** TENNYSON *Becket* V. ii. 193 They..Kill'd half the crew, dungeon'd the other half In Pevensey Castle.

Hence **'dungeoned** *ppl. a.*, **'dungeoning** *vbl. sb.* and *ppl. a.*; also **'dungeoner**, one who or that which dungeons.

1633 T. ADAMS *Exp. 2 Peter* ii. 4 The prisoner that is allowed to walk abroad, though with his keeper, is not so miserable as the dungeoned. **1795** SOUTHEY *Vis. Maid of Orleans* I. 30 A dungeon'd wretch. **1820** *Examiner* No. 650. 620/1 The dungeonings and ironings of Reformers. *a* **1821** KEATS *Lines to Fanny* 33 That most hateful land, Dungeoner of my friends.

'dung-fork.

1. A three- or four-pronged fork used to lift or spread dung; a kind of pitchfork.

c **1430** LYDG. *Chorle & Byrde* (Roxb.) 13 To a chorle a dongforke in his honde. **1530** PALSGR. 214/2 Donge forke, *fourche a fian.* **1669** WORLIDGE *Syst. Agric.* (1681) 324 A Dung-fork is a Tool of 3 Tines or Pikes, for the better casting of Dung. **1834** *Brit. Husb.* I. x. 254 The manure.. so far rotted as to be easily divisible by the dung-fork. **1875** TENNYSON *Q. Mary* II. ii, The reeking dungfork master of the mace!

attrib. **1674** FLATMAN *To Mr. Austin* 9 Our Noddles understand them can No more, than read that dung fork, pothook hand That in Queen's Colledge Library does stand.

2. *Entom.* The anal fork on which the larvæ of certain coleopterous insects carry their excrement; a fæcifork.

'dung-heap. A heap of dung, a dunghill.

a **1310** in Wright *Lyric P.* xxxvii. 103 Ne fyndest thou non so fyl dung-heep. **1393** [see next 1]. *c* **1430** *Pilgr. Lyf Manhode* II. liii. (1869) 96 Eche wight is strong on his owen dung hep, and tristeth to his cuntree; He is heere in his cuntree, on his dung hep. **1843** CARLYLE *Past & Pr.* II. v, 'Dungheaps' lying quiet at most doors.

dunghill ('dʌŋhɪl), *sb.*

1. A heap or hillock of dung or refuse.

c **1320** *Seuyn Sag.* (W.) 2417 To-delue anon in thi donghel. **1377** LANGL. *P. Pl.* B. xv. 109 For ypocrysie in latyn is lykned to a dongehul [**1393** C. XVII. 265 dounghep]. **1484** CAXTON *Fables of Æsop* I. i, As a Cok ones sought his pasture in the donghylle he fond a precious stone. **1697** SIR T. P. BLOUNT *Ess.* 29 Raking of Dunghills is an Employment more fit for a Scavenger than a Gentleman. **1776** ADAM SMITH *W.N.* II. iii. (1869) I. 352 One half, perhaps, of these provisions is thrown to the dunghill. **1843** LEVER *J. Hinton* xx, Mud hovels, with their dunghills.. around them.

b. In proverbs and locutions.

1546 J. HEYWOOD *Prov.* (1867) 25 But he was at home there, he might speake his will, Euery cock is proude on his owne dunghill. **1581** SIDNEY *Apol. Poetrie* (Arb.) 43 Alexander and Darius, when they straue who should be Cocke of thys worlds dunghill. **1857** TROLLOPE *Three Clerks* xl, Mr. Chaffanbrass was the cock of this dung-hill. **1879** FROUDE *Cæsar* xv. 233 What he [Cicero] could not say in the Forum he thought he might venture on with impunity in the Senate, which might be called his own dunghill.

2. *transf.* and *fig.* **a.** A heap or repository of filth or rubbish; often applied depreciatively to the earth, and to the human body. Also as the type of the lowest or most degraded situation.

1526 *Pilgr. Perf.* (W. de W. 1531) 147 b, Yᵉ foule & fylthy donghyll of this world. **1540** MORYSINE *Vives' Introd. Wysd.* C ij, The fayrest body is nothing els but a doungehyll covered in white and purple. **1559** *Mirr. Mag.*, *Salisbury* ix, And buryed in the dounghil of defame. **1617** MIDDLETON & ROWLEY *Fair Quarrel* II. i, More to be loath'd than vileness or sin's dunghill. **1692** WASHINGTON tr. *Milton's Def. Pop.* v. (1851) 133 For matter of Books there is no body publishes huger Dunghils than you. **1768** *Woman of Honor* II. 40 Considering the condition from which this son of a dunghill sprung. **1785** GROSE *Dict. Vulg. Tongue* s.v., Moving dunghill, a dirty filthy man or woman. **1817** COBBETT *Wks.* XXXII. 40 Those who have risen suddenly from the dunghill to a chariot.

b. Applied opprobriously to a person of evil life, or of base station.

1553 BECON *Reliques of Rome* (1563) 105 Shal yᵉ vile dong-hills of the earth presume to alter and chaunge the blessed and euerlasting Testament of yᵉ only begotten sonne of God? **1595** SHAKS. *John* IV. iii. 87 Out, dunghill! dar'st thou braue a Nobleman? **1665** J. SPENCER *Vulg. Proph.* 49 Paracelsus..was a walking Dunghil (so offensive and corrupt his life).

c. With reference to the *dunghill cock* (see 3 d), a man who is not 'game ', a coward or spiritless fellow. *to die dunghill*, to die as a coward, not to die 'game'. **d.** = DUNG 4.

1756 W. TOLDERVY *Hist. Two Orphans* IV. 52 Submit, be a wretch, and die dunghill. **1761** *Brit. Mag.* II. 358 There would be no sport, as the combatants were both reckoned dunghills. **1785** GROSE *Dict. Vulg. Tongue*, *Dunghill*, a coward; a cockpit phrase, all but game cocks being stiled dunghills; *to die dunghill*, to repent or shew any signs of contrition at the gallows. **1820** SCOTT *Ivanhoe* xliii, To see.. whether the heroes of the day are, in the heroic language of insurgent tailors, flints or dunghills.

3. *attrib.* and *Comb.* **a.** Of or pertaining to a dunghill, as ***dunghill beetle***, ***raker***, etc. **b.** Fit for or vile as a dunghill. **c.** Cowardly, or showing no fight, as the dunghill cock.

c **1430** LYDG. *Min. Poems* 192 (Mätz.) A downghille doke as deynte as a snyghte. **1548** HALL *Chron.*, *Hen. VII.* 7 A donghyll knave and vyle borne villeyne. **1583** STUBBES *Anat. Abus.* II. (1882) 39 This dunghill trade of Brokerie. **1601** CORNWALLYES *Ess.* xxv, Many Dung-hill Birdes have maintained infinite labours, assisted onely with the fame of making their sonnes Gentlemen. **1633** BP. HALL *Hard Texts* 423 Rich offerings..were made to that dunghill Deity. **1658** ROWLAND *Moufet's Theat. Ins.* 1009 Some call the Pilularius the dunghill Beetle, because it breeds from dung and filth. **1670** BROOKS *Wks.* (1867) VI. 54 God never loves to lift up the light of his countenance upon a dunghill-spirited man. **1684** BUNYAN *Pilgr. Progr.* II. 55 The Dunghil-raker, Spider, Hen, The Chicken too to me Hath taught a Lesson. **1794** SOUTHEY *Wat Tyler* III. ii, My liege, 'twas wisely ordered, to destroy The dunghill rabble. **1889** SWINBURNE *Study of Ben Jonson* 70 Some dunghill gazetteer of this very present day.

d. Special combs.: **dunghill-cock**, **-fowl**, **-hen**, common barndoor fowls, as distinguished from the game-cock, etc.; so **dunghill craven**.

1580 G. HARVEY *3 proper wittie Lett.* 29 [There are] Asses in Lions skins; *dunglecocks. **1774** GOLDSM. *Nat. Hist.* (1776) V. 163 The game-cock being by no means so fruitful as the ungenerous dunghill-cock. **1711** SHAFTESB. *Charac.* (1737) III. 218 The difference..between the game-cock, and the *dunghill-craven. **1796** MORSE *Amer. Geog.* I. 112 A few *dung-hill fowls were also found on these islands. **1611** COTGR., *Vne poule de pailler*, a *dunghill henne, a henne thats fed at the barne doore.

Hence (chiefly *nonce-wds.*) **'dunghill** *v. trans.*, to make *up* into a dunghill; in quot. *fig.*; †**'dunghillry**, vile condition or practice; **'dunghilly** *a.*, like or characteristic of a dunghill; vile, ignoble.

1581 MULCASTER *Positions* xxxix. (1887) 205 Where I see nobilitie betraid to donghillrie, and learning to doultrie. **1632** MASSINGER & FIELD *Fatal Dowry* IV. i, Poor, degenerate, dunghilly blood and breeding. **1662** J. CHANDLER *Van Helmont's Oriat.* 115 It hides part of a stinking or Dunghilly ferment under the soureness of the milk. **1860** *All Year Round* No. 45. 438 Where all the lees of Stamboul were dunghilled up into one reeking mass of infamy.

dunging ('dʌŋɪŋ), *vbl. sb.* [f. DUNG *v.* + -ING[1]. Cf. Ger. *düngung*.] The action of the verb DUNG.

1. The manuring of land; *concr.* manure, dung.

c **1000** [see DUNG *v.* 1]. *c* **1420** *Pallad. on Husb.* I. 238 Lupyne and ficchis slayn, and on their roote Vpdried, are as dongyng, londis boote. **1562** TURNER *Herbal* II. 74 b, Dungyng hurteth Date trees. **1708** J. CHAMBERLAYNE *St. Gt. Brit.* I. I. iii. (1743) 11 The soil is so rich that it..will bear good Barley for almost 20 years without dunging.

2. Dropping of excrement.

1617 MARKHAM *Caval.* III. 24 Which you shall know by his dunging. **1725** BRADLEY *Fam. Dict.* s.v. *Pheasant taking*, If you perceive by their dunging and scraping, that they frequent any Place. **1846** J. BAXTER *Libr. Pract. Agric.* (ed. 4) II. 109 By eating, by treading, by dunging, by staling.

3. *Calico-printing.* The operation of passing the cloth through a dung-bath. Also *attrib.*

1836 *Penny Cycl.* VI. 153/2 The dunging is..one of the most important..processes in calico-printing. **1875** *Ure's Dict. Arts* I. 627 Dunging salts, or liquors, are now made by the manufacturing chemist.

†**'dungish**, *a. Obs. rare.* [f. DUNG *sb.* + -ISH.] Of the nature of dung; vile.

1550 BALE *Apol.* 46 Dongysh and fylthie tradicions. **1628** GAULE *Pract. The.* (1629) 126 No lesse dungish and brutish.

†**dunglecock.** *Obs.* = DUNGHILL *cock*.

†**'dungled**, *ppl. a. Obs.* ? = *dunghilled*, thrown on a dunghill.

1606 WARNER *Alb. Eng.* XIV. To Rdr. 332 As if a dungled Asse should die.

dung-pot. Now *dial.* A tub for carrying manure, etc., of which a pair is borne by a pack-horse; also a low-wheeled cart for the same purpose.

1388-9 *Abingdon Acc.* (Camden) 58, Ij wylpottis..j dung-pot. **1552** HULOET, Dunge cart or dunge potte made of wickers, *scirpea*. **1575-6** *Act 18 Eliz.* c. 10. §1 Everye person ..shalbe charged to finde..one Carte..Tumbrell, Dounge Pott or Courte..for..repayringe of the Highe wayes. *c* **1710** C. FIENNES *Diary* (1888) 171 A horse wᶜʰ draws a sort of carriage, the wheeles like a Dung-pott. **1881** in *Isle of Wight Gloss.* **1888** in ELWORTHY *W. Somerset Word-bk.*

dungy ('dʌŋɪ), *a.* [f. DUNG *sb.* + -Y[1].]

1. Of the nature of dung; abounding in dung.

1606 SHAKS. *Ant. & Cl.* I. i. 35 Our dungie earth alike Feeds Beast as Man. **1675** EVELYN *Terra* (1729) 21 The best dungy compost.

2. Foul or filthy as dung; vile, defiling.

c **1430** *Pilgr. Lyf Manhode* III. xlvii. (1869) 160, I am foule ..stinkinge and dungy. **1599** MARSTON *Sco. Villanie*, *To Detraction* 165 My mind disdaines the dungy muddy scum Of abiect thoughts. **1611** BIBLE *Deut.* xxix. 17 Their idols [*marg.* dungy gods], wood and stone. **1860** PUSEY *Min. Proph.* Hosea ix. 10 Scripture gives disgraceful names to the idols (as abominations, nothings, dungy things).

dunite ('dʌnaɪt). *Min.* (See quot. 1879.)

1868 DANA *Min.* 258 Dunyte. **1874** DAWKINS *Ess.* v. 137 The peridot rock of New Zealand known as dunite. **1879** RUTLEY *Study Rocks* xiii. 265 Dunite (so named from Dun Mountain in New Zealand, which consists in great part of this rock and serpentine) is a crystalline-granular aggregate of olivine and chromic-iron.

‖**duniwassal** ('duːnɪ'wasəl). Also duniwassel, -waisle, dunni-, dunnie-wassal, dhuine-, dunniwassel. [Gael. *duine uasal* lit. gentleman, = *duine* man + *uasal* gentle, noble, well-born.] A (Highland) gentleman; a gentleman of secondary rank, below the chief, a yeoman; a cadet of a family of rank.

c **1565** LINDESAY (Pitscottie) *Chron. Scot.* (1814) 357 (Jam.) The king..caused many of the great Duny vassalis to shew thair holding. **1639** DRUMM. OF HAWTH. *Consid. to Parlt.* Wks. (1711) 187 That..the overseers of ministers, deacons and elders, be named duniwassels of the kirk. **1681** COLVIL *Whigs Supplic.* (1751) 60 Though some, Sir, of our duniwaisles Stood out, like Eglinton and Cassils. **1802** SCOTT *Bonny Dundee* viii, There are wild Duniewassals three thousand times three, Will cry hoigh! for the bonnet o' Bonny Dundee. **1814** —— *Wav.* xvi, His bonnet had a short feather, which indicated his claim to be treated as a *Duinhé-Wassell* or sort of gentleman. **1884** *Times* 18 Mar. 7 The feathers..indicated gentility..the 42nd being duinnie-wassals, or small gentry. **1905** *Daily Chron.* 7 July 5/7 Scottish Dhuine wassels with aggressive feathers in front of their Tam o' Shanter caps. **1920** *Blackw. Mag.* Apr. 517/1 Kilted Hebridean dhuine-wassels.

dunk (dʌŋk), *v. orig. U.S.* [Pennsylvanian G. *dunke* to dip (cf. G. *tunken*).] **1.** *trans.* To dip (bread, cake, etc.) into a beverage or other liquid. Also *absol.*, *transf.*, and *fig.*

1919 *Quill* Feb. 12 (*title*) Some notes on dunking. *Ibid.* 16 It should be remembered that the really fastidious dunker never burns his thumb. **1927** *Dialect Notes* V. 474 Them young-uns is allus a-dunkin' their bread in th' bottom-sop. **1931** *Daily Progress* (Charlottesville, Va.) 21 Feb. 10 The pone should be 'dunked' in the likker. **1940** in *Amer. Speech* (1941) XVI. 147/2 Dunk your nylons in rich suds of neutral soap. **1941** 'R. WEST' *Black Lamb & Grey Falcon* II. 311 Constantine sat dunking a roll in his coffee. **1951** M. MCLUHAN *Mech. Bride* 4/2 The same man would rather dunk himself in the newspaper than have any esthetic or intellectual grasp of its character and meaning. The incorrigible dunker would perhaps do well to skip the next few pages. **1958** G. MITCHELL *Spotted Hemlock* xvi. 187 'For heaven's sake, don't stop eating,' said Miss Paterson, herself dunking a doughnut. **1959** M. M. KAYE *House of Shade* iii. 36 'He's a one, isn't he? Your gentleman friend,' said the blonde, dunking Dany's head into a basin. **1959** *Manch. Guardian* 26 June 5/3 Nylon sheets..can be 'dunked' along with underclothes or put in a washing machine. **1971** *Nature* 26 Feb. 597/1 But the possibility that the RNA picks up basic proteins when dunked in the cytoplasm cannot be disregarded.

2. *Basketball.* To push (the ball) down through the basket, esp. by jumping so that the hand is above the level of the ring.

1937 F. C. ALLEN *Better Basketball* vii. 82 The tall offensive player may tip-in, dunk, or push the ball into the basket. **1956** J. MCCREARY *Winning High School Basketball* iv. 43 A player who cannot 'dunk' the ball—get above the goal and drop the ball through—must use the board on a straight drive-in shot. **1979** *Arizona Daily Star* 5 Aug. I. 5/4 What most of these players have in common..is their belief in the dream that shows them hitting home runs or dunking the winning shot in front of thousands of applauding fans. **1985** *N.Y. Times* 10 July A17/1 He dunks the ball quite well.

Hence **'dunker, 'dunking** *vbl. sb.*

1919 [see sense 1]. **1931** *Daily Progress* (Charlottesville, Va.) 21 Feb. 4/8 No information is given about dunking. *Ibid.* 2 Mar. 10 Governor Long..is champion of the dunkers. **1937** F. C. ALLEN *Better Basketball* vii. 82 Dunking does not display basketball skill—only height advantage. **1940** *Chambers's Techn. Dict.* 271/2 *Dunking*, a colloquialism for the process of dipping the [cinematographic] film into chemical solutions for any stage of processing. **1960** *Times* 30 Nov. 13/6 In naval parlance a 'dunker' never becomes immersed except in dire emergency, and only a part of his equipment, in the form of a sonar buoy, is lowered into the sea. This is the device which enables the helicopter crew to 'listen in' for submarines. *Ibid.*, My interest in dunking arose through my being in the aero engine business. **1975** *Oxf. Compan. Sports & Games* 67/1 In N.C.A.A. rules only, the method of scoring known as 'dunking', whereby a player takes the ball above the ring and forces it downwards into the basket, is prohibited.

dunk, *sb. Basketball* (orig. *U.S.*). [f. DUNK *v.* 2.] **1.** A shot made by jumping high into the air and pushing the ball down through the basket from above the level of the ring. Cf. *slam dunk* s.v. SLAM *sb.*[1] 5.

[**1966**: see sense 2 below.] **1971** HOLLANDER & PADWE *Basketball Lingo* 32 Dunk: a crowd-pleasing shot made popular by big men. **1976** *Sunday Tel.* 13 Mar. 36/7 The dunk is a clever and exhilarating scoring shot. **1979** *Time* 13 Aug. 34/1 Herb Williams, 21, a forward from Ohio State, slammed home a fearsome dunk against Yugoslavia and shattered the backboard in the process. **1982** S. B. FLEXNER *Listening to Amer.* 58 The dunk was banned from college play..in 1968. **1985** *N.Y. Times* 1 July C9/4 One of dozens of basketball camps.., this one seems to be more than merely a showcase for dunks and behind-the-back passes.

2. *Comb.* **dunk shot** = sense 1 above.

1966 J. WOODEN *Pract. Mod. Basketball* iii. 97 Not too many years ago I frowned on the use of the '*dunk' shot. **1973** P. TAMONY *Americanisms* (typescript) No. 34. 4 In the 1940s efforts were made to neutralize the height advantage of 6.9 *goons*..through the..elimination of the center jump ..and the 'dunk' shot. **1978** J. KRANTZ *Scruples* iii. 72 Spider Elliott had lost his virginity in his senior year in high school to a horny, big-breasted girls' basketball coach who admired his dunk shots only less than the fit of his gym shorts, which one of his sisters had shrunk three sizes. **1982** S. B. FLEXNER *Listening to Amer.* 58 Though to *dunk* had meant to shoot the ball through the basket in any way since the 1930s, tall, agile offensive players developed the modern *dunk shot* in the mid 1960s and the *slam dunk* in the early 1970s.

dunkadoo (dʌŋkə'du:) [Echoic: from the bird's cry.] Popular name in New England of the American bittern (*Botaurus mugitans*).

Dunkard ('dʌŋkərd). *U.S.* = DUNKER[1].

1784 J. BROWN *Hist. Brit. Ch.* I. xii. 336 Dunkards, whose men and women live in separate communities. **1896** *Chr. World* 21 May 403/1 The Dunkards are to be found in twenty of the United States, the total membership being about 75,000. *Ibid.*, A Dunkard minister made a speech.

Dunker[1] ('dʌŋkə(r)), **Tunker** ('tʌŋkə(r)). [ad. Ger. *tunker*, f. *tunken* (*dunken*) to dip.] A member of a body of German-American Baptists, who administer baptism only to adults, and by triple immersion.

They settled in Pennsylvania early in the 18th c., whence they spread into Ohio and other states.

1756 G. WASHINGTON *Lett.* Writ. 1889 I. 354 The Dunkers (who are all Doctors) entertain the Indians who are wounded here. **1785** J. Q. ADAMS *Wks.* (1854) IX. 533 The Quakers and Moravians, Dunkers, Mennonites, or other worthy people in Pennsylvania. **1796** MORSE *Amer. Geog.* I. 281 The words Tunkers and Tumblers have been corruptly written Dunkers and Dumplers. **1858–60** GARDNER *Faiths World* I. 770/1 The Dunkers hold that celibacy is not binding..but that it is to be commended as a virtue. **1886** BLUNT *Dict. Sects* 602/1 Settlements were formed by the emigration of married Tunkers to other parts.

Dunker[2], corruption of DUNKIRK: see next.

1631 FITZ-GEFFRAY *Curse of Corn-horders* 14 Suffered to be a prey to Dunkers abroad, and to as bad at home.

Dunkirk. **1.** ('dʌnkɜ:k) Name of a town on the coast of French Flanders; hence, a privateer vessel of that town. Also *transf.* and *fig.*

1602 DEKKER *Satirom.* Wks. 1873 I. 200 Ile march through thy dunkirkes guts for shooting jestes at me. **1607** WALKINGTON *Opt. Glass* 89 Like to roving Dunkirkes, or robbing pyrats. *a* **1625** FLETCHER *Elder Bro.* IV. ii, Quite shot through 'tween Wind and Water by a she-Dunkirk. **1629** *Churchw. Acc. Kirton-in-Lindsey* in *Antiquary* (1888) Dec. 21 A trawler..that was taken with Dunkerkes. **1888** *Athenæum* 17 Mar. 335/1 Of persons robbed on the sea by Dunkirks we have several examples [in the Doncaster records].

2. (dʌn'kɜ:k). The (scene of the) evacuation of the British forces from Dunkirk between 29 May and 3 June 1940; hence used allusively for any similar withdrawal, crisis, etc.; so *to do a Dunkirk*, to make such a withdrawal. Also *attrib.*, esp. in ***Dunkirk spirit***.

1941 *Time* 9 June 9/2 In far too many items we are still lagging behind and..there may well be more Dunkirks. **1941** *New Statesman* 20 Sept. 275/1 America can look for no Dunkirk To underline the warnings Presidential. **1943** *Hutchinson's Pict. Hist. of War* 4 Aug.–26 Oct. 21/2 Evacuation of some of the enemy's forces, harassed by allied aircraft and naval units, has already begun, but it remains to be seen how successful this minor 'Dunkirk' will be. **1944** *Amer. Speech* XIX. 278, I have heard 'to do a Dunkirk'. **1948** *Hansard Commons* 28 Mar. 2853 He asked me to bring about what he called a 'Dunkirk evacuation' of Palestine. **1955** *Times* 8 Aug. 3/3 The Navy had saved the situation, and Dunkirk had become 'D' Day. **1956** J. CHRISTOPHER *Death of Grass* vii. 113 If the country only shows the Dunkirk spirit, we can pull through. **1961** *Listener* 19 Oct. 589/1 The Dunkirk spirit of only starting to try hard when it becomes really necessary is deeply ingrained in the British character. **1961** H. WILSON in C. Booker *Neophiliacs* (1969) ix. 249, I myself have always deprecated..appeals to the Dunkirk spirit as an answer to our problems. **1969** *Guardian* 18 July 20/8 The Church of England faces 'an ecclesiastical Dunkirk' unless it recognises the contribution young people can make.

'Dunkirker. [f. prec. + -ER[1].] A privateer belonging to Dunkirk, or one of its crew.

1603 *Crt. & Times Jas. I* (1849) I. 4 The Dunkirkers have been very busy with us of late, and..took three pinks coming from Flushing. **1625** *Crt. & Times Chas. I.* (1848) I. 50 There are brought into Plymouth three long boats full of Dunkirkers. **1659** FULLER *App. Inj. Innoc.* (1840) 373 A Dunkirker, who delights to prey on poor merchants' ships.

dunkle ('dʌŋk(ə)l), *v. Sc.* Also dunckle. [A parallel form to DUNTLE, DIMPLE: cf. the parallel forms *crimple*, *crumple*, *crinkle*, *crunkle*, *dingle*, *dimble*.] *trans.* To make a dint or pit in; to dint.

1822 GALT *Sir A. Wylie* III. xxxiii. 284 We think his harnpan's surely dunklet. **1830** —— *Lawrie T.* II. i. (1849) 42 Without very deeply dunkling the truth.

dunkle ('dʌŋk(ə)l), *sb. Sc.* [Goes with prec. vb.] 'The dint made or cavity produced by a blow, or in consequence of a fall' (Jam.).

1821 GALT in *Blackw. Mag.* X. 6 [It] would have left both cloors and dunkles in her character.

dunlin ('dʌnlɪn). [dial. form of *dunling*, f. DUN *a.* + -LING. Cf. *dunnock*.] The red-backed sandpiper (*Tringa alpina* or *variabilis*), a European migratory bird, abundant at certain seasons on the sea-coast. Also an American species or subspecies (*T. pacifica*).

1531–2 in Rogers *Agric. & Prices* III. 185/1. **1678** RAY *Willughby's Ornith.* III. xii. 305 The North-Country Dunlin ..is about the bigness of the Jack-Snipe. **1766** PENNANT *Zool.* (1776) II. 471 *Dunlin*, this species is at once distinguished from the others by the singularity of its colours. **1877** BESANT & RICE *Son of Vulc.* I. xiii, A flock of ox-birds, or dunlins, digging out the juicy slugs from the mud.

Dunlop ('dʌnlɒp). Also Delap, Dulap, Dunlap. The name of a parish in Ayrshire, Scotland, used (chiefly *attrib.*) to designate an unskimmed-milk cheese originally made there.

1821 J. GALT *Annals of Parish* vi. 66 They have, under the name of Delap-cheese, spread far and wide over the civilized world. **1825** J. C. LOUDON *Encycl. Agric.* III. VII. v. 990 Dunlop cheese, so named from the parish..where it was originally made. *c* **1842** in *Scottish Hist. Soc. Misc.* (1939) VI. 271 Who has not heard..of Dunlop cheese. **1864** J. B. GREENSHIELDS *Annals Lesmahagow* xvii. 278 Sweet milk cheese, known as 'Dunlop', is the staple commodity. **1878** *Chambers's Encycl.* II. 786 Dunlop Cheese..is now manufactured in the dairy districts of Scotland generally. **1905** W. H. SIMMONDS *Pract. Grocer* III. 79 The Dunlop is a rather rich cheese, similar in general quality to Derbyshire or Gouda, but larger in size. **1966** P. V. PRICE *France* 94 Take a pound of Double Gloucester, Lancashire, Dunlop, or a whole baby Cheddar.

dunnage ('dʌnɪdʒ), *sb. Naut.* [In 17th c. *dynnage*, *dinnage*: origin unascertained.

Cf. Du. *dun*, LG. *dün* thin, *dünne twige* brushwood.]

1. Light material, as brushwood, mats, and the like, stowed among and beneath the cargo of a vessel to keep it from injury by chafing or wet; any lighter or less valuable articles of the cargo used for the same purpose.

1497 *Naval Accts. Hen. VII* (1896) 251 For xxxvj shegge Shevys layed alow in John Millers crayer for donage. **1623** WHITBOURNE *Newfoundland* 75 Mats and dynnage vnder the Salt, and Salt Shouels. **1755** MAGENS *Insurances* II. 101 To take Care of the requisite Dunnage and Bavins at the Bottom. **1840** R. H. DANA *Bef. Mast* xxix. 98 We covered the bottom of the hold..with dried brush, for dunnage. **1863** READE *Hard Cash* I. 198 He had stowed his dunnage, many hundred bundles of light flexible canes from Sumatra and Malacca.

attrib. *c* **1850** *Rudim. Navig.* (Weale) 116 *Dunnage battens*, pieces of oak or fir, about two inches square, nailed athwart the flat of the orlop, to prevent wet from damaging the cables, and to admit air. **1860** *Merc. Marine Mag.* VII. 73 Dunnage wood 26*d.* per 100 pieces. **1867** SMYTH *Sailor's Word-bk.*, *Dunnage gratings*, express gratings placed on a steamer's deck to place cargo upon, serving as dunnage. **1893** *Westm. Gaz.* 1 Feb. 4/2 They store there the dunnage mats used for the cargo. *Mod.* When guano was shipped in bulk at the Chincha Islands, the hold was lined with guano in bags, called *dunnage-bags*, to protect the rest and for better packing; so with various other commodities.

¶ Loosely used for miscellaneous baggage; *slang*, a sailor's or tramp's clothes.

1851 MAYHEW *Lond. Lab.* (1861) I. 262. **1873** *Slang Dict.*, *Dunnage*, baggage, clothes. **1885** C. A. NEIDÉ *Cruise of Aurora* 105 (Cent.) Some of the dunnage and the tent would need to be dried before being packed. **1887** *Pall Mall G.* 9 Apr. 2/1 The other dunnage was a curious mixture of odds and ends, such as a sextant, a little mahogany sea chest, strings of candles, bread bags, rusty scissors, knives, forks, and spoons.

2. dunnage bag, a kit-bag.

1904 *Chicago Evening Post* 23 Aug. 7 A dunnage bag..is a sack of heavy brown canvas nearly four feet long... In it the aspiring mountaineer may pack fifty pounds of necessities. **1925** FRASER & GIBBONS *Soldier & Sailor Words* 86 *Dunnage bag*, kit bag (Navy). **1929** M. DE LA ROCHE *Whiteoaks* xxviii. 381 The dogs..trotted without rest from point to point of interest—the dunnage bag, the provisions, the weapons.

'dunnage, *v. Naut.* [f. prec. sb.] *trans.* To stow or secure with dunnage. Also *intr.* for *refl.*

c **1860** H. STUART *Seaman's Catech.* 63 Dunnage as high as the kelson..to prevent water getting to the casks. **1865** J. LEES *Laws Brit. Shipping* (ed. 9) 190 The vessel must also be properly dunnaged in the bottom and at the sides of the hold, in order to raise up the loading. **1867** SMYTH *Sailor's Word-bk.* s.v., A vessel dunnages below the dry cargo to keep it from bilge-water. **1884** *American* VIII. 382 Vessels fraudulently 'dunnaged' for the purpose of reducing their tonnage.

dunnamany ('dʌnə,mɛnɪ), colloquial form of (*I*) *don't know how many*. So **'dunna,much**, (I) don't know how much. Cf. DUNNO.

1831 R. LOWER *Tom Cladpole's Jurney to Lunnun* 14 So arter dun-a-much more talk, He said he must be gwyn. **1853** W. D. COOPER *Gloss. Sussex* (ed. 2) 43 *Dunnamany* and *Dunnamuch*, corruptions of *I don't know how many* or *much*. **1906** KIPLING *Puck* 267 Justabout tore the gizzards out of I dunnamany. *Ibid.* 273 The Pharisees just about flowed.. down the beach to the boat, *I* dunnamany of 'em. **1946** G. HEYER *Reluctant Widow* iii. 41 Your lordship knows I've been with Mr. Hitchin a dunnamany years.

†**'dunned,** *ppl. a. Obs.* [f. DUN *v.*[1] + -ED[1].] Made dun; of a dark or dusky colour: = DUN *a.* 1.

c **1440** *Promp. Parv.* 135/1 Dunnyd of coloure, *subniger.* **1530** PALSGR. 311/1 Dunde gray as a horse is. **1542** *Richmond. Wills* (Surtees) 37 One great donnyed cow. **1643** *St. Trials, Essex Witches* (R.), That the impe, which the said Joyce Boanes sent was a dun'd one like unto a mouse.

dunner ('dʌnə(r)), *sb.*[1] *Sc.* Also **dunder.** [Belongs to DUNNER *v.*] A resounding or reverberating noise; a blow causing vibration.

1780 J. MAYNE *Siller Gun* II. 127 But a' this time, wi' mony a dunder [= dunner], Auld guns were brattling aff like thunder [= thunner]. **1789** DAVIDSON *Seasons* 18 (Jam.) His Maggy on his mind Did sometimes gie a dunner. **1850** J. STRUTHERS *Poet. Wks.* I. Autobiog. 129 The dunner of the engine..has ceased.

dunner, *sb.*[2] [f. DUN *v.*[3] + -ER[1].] One who duns or importunes another, esp. for money due; a dun.

a **1700** B. E. *Dict. Cant. Crew*, *Dunner*, a Sollicitor for Debts. **1712** STEELE *Spect.* No. 454 ¶5 [They] serve the Owners in getting them Customers, as their common Dunners do in making them pay. **1822** T. THOMAS *To Occupiers of Land* 14 A fine till'd wheaten Field That Owner will from Debts and Dunner shield.

dunner, *v. Sc.* [perh. in origin freq. of DUN *v.*[2]; but with onomatopœic associations.] *intr.* To make a reverberating noise, to resound; to fall or strike with vibration and reverberating noise.

1802 in SIBBALD *Chron. Sc. Poetry* Gloss. **1819** W. TENNANT *Papistry Storm'd* (1827) 180 As down he dunner'd on the ground. **1820** *Edin. Mag.* June 533 (Jam.) It gard the divots stour aff the house riggins and every caber dunner.

dunness ('dʌnnɛs). [f. DUN *a.* + -NESS.] The quality of being dun; duskiness, dinginess.

1610 MARKHAM *Masterp.* I. lxvi. 140 When Baynesse turnes to dunnesse, blackes to duskishnes. **1616** SURFL. & MARKH. *Country Farme* 205 Spots or dunnesse of the skinne. **1848** LYTTON *Harold* v. vii, The dunness of the clouds.

†**dunning**, *vbl. sb.*[1]: see DUN *v.*[2]

dunning ('dʌnɪŋ), *vbl. sb.*[2] [f. DUN *v.*[3]] The action of importuning for debt, etc.

1714 MANDEVILLE *Fab. Bees* (1725) I. 246 Without taking notice of their dunning. **1726** AMHERST *Terræ Fil.* xxxiii. 176 The continual dunnings and insolent menaces of their creditors. **1753** *Scots Mag.* XV. 36/2 The importunate dunnings of a gamester.

dunning (of codfish): see DUN *v.*[1] 1 b.

'**dunning**, *ppl. a.* [f. DUN *v.*[3] + -ING[2].] That duns, or importunes for debt, etc.

1816 'QUIZ' *Grand Master* v. 116 Surrounded by these dunning devils. **1848** THACKERAY *Van. Fair* xlviii, Madame Bobinot is writing dunning letters for the money.

dunnish ('dʌnɪʃ), *a.* [f. DUN *a.* + -ISH.] Somewhat dun or dusky; inclining to a dun colour.

1551 TURNER *Herbal* I. G iij, The sede is donnysh blak. **1676** *Lond. Gaz.* No. 1134/4 A dunish gray Mare. **1753** *Stewart's Trial* App. 27 Dressed in a dunnish-coloured great coat.

dunno ('dʌnəʊ, də'nəʊ), also **dunna(w)**, etc., colloquial forms of *(I) do not* (or *don't*) *know*. See DO *v.* 29 and cf. DUNNAMANY.

1842 G. P. R. PULMAN *Rustic Sketches* 34 There I vlounder'd like a zow, An' ramm'l'd out I dun-no how. **1848** LOWELL *Biglow Papers* 1st Ser. vii, I dunno as it's ushle to print Poscrips. **1867** P. KENNEDY *Banks Boro* xxiii, Now indeed I *dunna* what to do. **1868** [see BLOW *v.*[1] 12 b]. **1888** B. L. BURNETT *Stable Boy* ii, I dun naw wat ta du! **1902** J. MASEFIELD *Salt-water Ballads* 85 Dunno a heap about the what an' why, Can't say's I ever knowed. **1926** R. MACAULAY *Crewe Train* I. ii. 10 If you had asked her why, she would have replied, 'Dunno. It's a bother speaking to people when you're out.' **1938** C. MORGAN *Flashing Stream* II. ii. 186 He'll begin to say to himself: 'Well, I dunno. P'raps I'm wrong.' **1946** [see GET *v.* 42 g]. **1966** P. MOLONEY *Plea for Mersey* 22 A sed 'Wharar thee wack?' 'A dunno,' she said back.

dunnock ('dʌnək). Also 5 **donek, dunoke,** 7 **dunneck,** 9 **dinnick** (sense 2). [app. f. DUN *a.* + -OCK dim. suffix; from the dusky brown colour of the plumage. Cf. *dunlin*.]

1. The hedge-sparrow or hedge-warbler (*Accentor modularis*).

c **1475** *Pict. Voc.* in Wr.-Wülcker 761/38 *Hec lonefa*, a donek. **1483** *Cath. Angl.* 111/1 A Dunoke..*curuca*. **1611** COTGR., *Verdon*, a Dunneck, Dike-smowler, Hedge-sparrow. **1824** FORSTER *Perenn. Calend.* in Hone *Every-day Bk.* II. 119 The dingie dunnock, and the swart colemouse. **1847** E. BRONTE *Wuthering Heights* iv. (D.), Hareton has been cast out like an unfledged dunnock.

2. (form *dinnick*) Applied in Devonshire to the Wryneck (*Jynx torquilla*).

1863 *Q. Rev.* July 245 Either the cuckoo or the cuckoo's servant, the dinnick, as it is called in Devonshire. **1885** SWAINSON *Prov. Names Birds* 104 Wryneck..Dinnick (Devon). From its brown plumage.

dunny ('dʌnɪ), *a.*[1] [f. DUN *a.* + -Y.] Somewhat dun or dusky brown.

a **1529** SKELTON *El. Rummyng* 400 I were skynnes of conny, That causeth I loke so donny. **1610** W. FOLKINGHAM *Art of Survey* I. x. 28 Lime made of a dunny gray stone. **1715** LANCASTER 16 Jan. in *Ballard MSS.* XXI. 59 Paper of the same Dunny Colour. **1819** T. THOMPSON in *Coll. Songs, Comic and Satirical* (1827) 10 Tyneside seem'd clad wiv bonny ha's An furnaces sae dunny. **1951** J. FRAME *Lagoon* 38 The house with..its dunny roses on the trellis-work.

'**dunny**, *a.*[2] (*sb.*[1]) *dial.* [possibly f. DUN *v.*[2]; and if so, meaning originally 'having a ringing or resonance in the ears'; cf. also DUNCH *a.*] **A.** *adj.* Dull of hearing, deaf; dull of apprehension, stupid.

1708 KERSEY, *Dunny*, somewhat deaf, deafish. **1775** MRS. DELANY *Life & Corr.* Ser. II. II. 97 My eyesight grew dimmer, my ears more dunny. *a* **1791** GROSE *Olio* (1796) 105 What the devil are you dunny? won't you give me no answer? **1826** SCOTT *Woodst.* iii, My old Dame Joan is something dunny. **1882-8** [In Dialect Glossaries of Berkshire, Worcestersh., etc.].

†**B.** *sb.* A stupid fellow; a dunce. *Obs.*

1709 *Brit. Apollo* II. No. 29. 3/2 Should a School-boy do so, he'd be whip'd for a Dunny.

Hence '**dunnily,** '**dunniness.**

1731 BAILEY, *Dunnily*, deafishly. *Dunniness*, deafishness.

dunny ('dʌnɪ), *sb.*[2] Also **danna, dunikin, dunnakin, dunnee, dunniken, dunnyken.** [Origin unknown, but cf. DUNG *sb.* and KEN *sb.*[2]] **1.** *dial.* and *slang.* An earth closet, (outside) privy (see also quot. 1859). Also *attrib.* (Freq. in *Austral.* and *N.Z. slang.*)

a **1790** H. T. POTTER *New Dict. Cant* (1795) 26 *Dunnakin*, a necessary. **1812** J. H. VAUX *Flash Dict.* 184 *Knapping a jacob from a danna-drag.* This is a curious species of robbery ..; it signifies taking away the short ladder from a nightman's cart, while the men are gone into a house, the privy of which they are employed emptying, in order to effect an ascent. **1846** *Swell's Night Guide* 57 'Where's the plant, cully?'..'Fenced, in a dunniken.'..'What? Fenced in a crapping ken?' **1859** HOTTEN *Dict. Slang* 29 *Danna*, excrement. *Danna drag*, a nightman's or dustman's cart. *Ibid.* 35 *Dunny-ken*, a watercloset. **1943** *Horizon* VIII. 156 The crazy dunikins, outside w.c.s listing away from the prevailing wind. **1947** [see BUGGER *v.* 2 b]. **1952** J. BAXTER in Chapman & Bennett *Anthol. N.Z. Verse* (1956) 258 Cigarette stink from a hole in the rushes Dark as a dunny. **1960** N. HILLIARD *Maori Girl* I. iii. 19 She delighted in giving cheek to the boys and taking refuge in the girls' dunny. **1962** C. ROHAN *Delinquents* 137 How is the dunny? .. Does it have a chain? **1965** G. MCINNES *Road to Gundagai* iii. 38 The lavatory, or the 'dunny' as Dad used to call it. **1970** *Private Eye* 16 Jan. 16 It seems a bit crook for old bazza to spend the night in the dunnee!

2. *Sc.* [Perh. a different word.] An underground passage or cellar, common in old tenement buildings.

1918 N. MUNRO *Jaunty Jock* ii. 24 Flat on flat it rose for fourteen stories, poverty in its dunnies (as they called its cellars), poverty in its attics. **1922** J. BUCHAN *Huntingtower* vii. 152 Sleepin' in coal-rees and dunnies and dodgin' the polis. **1947** *Forward* 4 Jan. 3 Broken-down sewage system which periodically overflows into the dunnies and back-courts.

dunpickle: see DUN *a.* 3 c.

duns, dunse, etc., obs. forms of DUNCE, etc.

†**dunship.** *Obs. nonce-wd.* [f. DUN *sb.*[1] + -SHIP.] As a humorous title, referring to the saying 'Dun is in the mire': see DUN *sb.*[1] 5.

1678 BUTLER *Hud.* III. iii. 110 Ralph himself, your trusty Squire, Wh' has drag'd your Dunship out o' th' Mire.

Dunstable ('dʌnstəb(ə)l), *a.* and *sb.* [The name of a town in Bedfordshire.]

†**1. a.** *attrib.* in phr. ***Dunstable way***, app. referring originally to the road from London (Edgware Road) to Dunstable, a part of the ancient Roman Road called Watling Street, notable for its long stretches in direct line, and for its general evenness; used proverbially as a type of directness and plainness. *Obs.*

1549 LATIMER *2nd Serm. bef. Edw. VI* (Arb.) 56 Some.. that walked in the kynges highe waye ordinarilye, vprightlye, playne Dunstable waye. **1596** HARINGTON *Metam. Ajax* (1814) 122 Indeed for the device, I grant it as plain as Dunstable highway. *a* **1661** FULLER *Worthies, Prov. Bedfordsh.* I. (1662) 114 As plain as Dunstable Road. It is applied to things plain and simple, without welt or guard to adorn them, as also to matters easie and obvious to be found, without any difficulty or direction. **1719** D'URFEY *Pills* VI. 132 'Tis of the making of Dunstable way, Plain without turning. **1744** WARBURTON *Rem. Sev. Occas. Refl.* 128, I would advise him to return again as fast as he can into the old Dunstable Road of Moses and a future State for ever.

[Cf. also the following:

1611 B. JONSON *Introd. Verses to Coryat's Crudities*, Here up the Alpes (not so plaine as to Dunstable) Hee's carried like a cripple. **1614** W. B. *Philosopher's Banquet* (ed. 2) A ij b, Whilst pathes vntraced former steps vntroad, Become as Dunstable, more worne, more broad.]

†**b.** Hence as *adj.*: Direct, straightforward, plain, downright. (Often preceded by *plain, downright*.)

1589 NASHE *Almond for Parrat* 19 a, A good old dunstable doctor here in London. **1598** FLORIO, *Carlóna*, plainly, dunstable way, homelie fashion. **1607** R. C. tr. *Estienne's World of Wonders* 21 Men who vsed old and ancient simplicitie, and were (as a man would say) plaine Dunstable. **1672** EACHARD *Hobbs's State Nat.* (1705) 11 The old plain Dunstable stuff that commonly occurs in those that have treated of Policy and Morality. **1754** RICHARDSON *Grandison* (1812) VI. 177 (D.) Your uncle is an odd, but a very honest, Dunstable soul. **1817** SCOTT *Lett.* 17 Mar. (1894) I. 422 Now Morritt (who is 'Downright Dunstable') would not have let this sentence slip him.

†**c.** as *sb.* in phr. ***plain*** (or ***downright***) ***Dunstable***: plain speaking or language. *Obs.*

1597 BRETON *Miseries of Mavilla*, Plaine Dunstable is the high way, and yet there are many holes in it. **1737** BRACKEN *Farriery Impr.* (1757) II. 87 Their Fore-fathers..lov'd plain downright Dunstable. **1748** RICHARDSON *Clarissa* (1811) I. xxxii. 239 That's the plain dunstable of the matter, Miss! **1824** SCOTT *Redgauntlet* ch. xvii, If this is not plain speaking, there is no such place as downright Dunstable in being!

2. *attrib.* Applied to a kind of straw plait made at Dunstable, or to the method of plaiting it. Hence *ellipt.* as *sb.* (Formerly also a straw bonnet.)

1849 LONGF. *Kavanagh* (1851) 424 A milliner, who sold 'Dunstable and eleven-braid, open-work and coloured straws'. **1851** *Offic. Catal. Gt. Exhib.* II. 377 Plait straw is the straw of the wheat..grown on dry chalky lands, such as those about Dunstable..'Whole Dunstable', signifies that the plait is formed of seven entire straws, and 'patent Dunstable', that it consists of fourteen split straws. *Ibid.* 581 A coarser kind of material than the Dunstable.

†**dunster** ('dʌnstə(r)). *Obs.* A woollen cloth, so called from a small town in West Somersetshire.

1601 *Act 43 Eliz.* c. 10 Preamb., Dunster Cotton hereafter shalbe by this presente Acte intended and taken to be of like weighte, lengthe, and breadth as Taunton and Bridgewater Cloth. **1607** *Act 4 Jas. I*, c. 2 Dunsters made in the Westerne parts of Somersetshire. **1887** ROGERS *Agric. & Prices* V. 95.

†'**dunstery.** *Obs.* [var. of *dunsery*, DUNCERY.]

1616 S. WARD *Coal from Altar* (1627) 50 The dunstery of the Monkes made Erasmus studious.

†'**dunstical,** *a. Obs.* [var. of DUNCICAL.]

1563-87 FOXE *A. & M.* (1596) 47/2 All those decretall letters, nothing sauouring of that age, but rather of the latter dunsticall times that followed. **1581** J. BELL *Haddon's Answ. Osor.* A ij b, As Sophisters use to argue of moates in the Sunne in their triflyng and Dunsticall Schooles. **1674** S. VINCENT *Gallant's Acad.* 8 Those silly and ridiculous Fashions, which the Old dunstical world wore, even out at Elbows.

Hence '**dunstically** *adv.*

1611 A. STAFFORD *Niobe* II. 195 (T., s.v. *Dunce*), One speaks fluently, but writes dunsticallie.

dunstone ('dʌnstəʊn). *Mining* and *Geol.* [f. DUN *a.*; cf. also *dun-courses, dun-row*, s.v. DUN *a.* 3 c.] Stone of a dun or dull brown colour; applied locally to different sedimentary rocks, as magnesian limestone, ironstone, sandstone, and sometimes to igneous rocks, such as dolerite.

1777 G. FORSTER *Voy. round World* I. 20 A few..of the kind which the Derbyshire miners call dunstone. **1807** VANCOUVER *Agric. Devon* (1813) 19 The soil generally consists of a hazel-coloured loam, or free dunstone. **1870** R. S. HAWKER *Prose Wks.* (1893) 1 One wide, wild stretch of rocky moorland, broken with masses of dunstone. **1887** H. B. WOODWARD *Geol. Eng. & Wales* (ed. 2) 577 Dolerites are exposed west of St. Austell..In places they are called 'Dunstones'.

dunt (dʌnt), *sb.*[1] Chiefly *Sc.* and *dial.* Also 5-6 **dount.** [app. a phonetic variant of DINT *sb.*, perh. modified to express the duller sound implied. Cf. also Sw. dial. *dunt* in same sense. (In early ME. *dunt* (-y-) is merely a southern spelling of *dynt*, DINT.)]

1. a. A firm but dull-sounding blow or stroke.

c **1420** *Chron. Vilod.* 183 Wt ouȝt ony stroke, dount, or wound. **1513** DOUGLAS *Æneis* XI. xvii. 60 Full hastely doun swakkis, dunt for dunt. **1535** STEWART *Cron. Scot.* II. 572 All with ane dunt the dur sone vp tha dang. *c* **1690** *Roxb. Ball.* (1888) VI. 616 And double dunts upon their rumps, the lads began to fa' then. **1788** BURNS *Naebody* 12 I'll tak dunts frae nae-body.

b. A wound produced by such a blow.

1886 STEVENSON *Kidnapped* vii. 56 My visitor..set himself to wash and dress the wound upon my scalp. 'Ay', said he, 'a sore dunt'. **1894** CROCKETT *Raiders* (ed. 3) 279 Wi' a three-cornered dunt on his broo.

c. A beat or palpitation of the heart.

1768 ROSS *Helenore* 62 (Jam.) Dunt for dunt, her heart began to beat. **1789** DAVIDSON *Seasons* 52 (Jam.) Ilk rowt the twa gave thwart the burn Cam o'er her heart a dunt.

d. *R.A.F. slang.* (See quot. 1924.)

1924 *Jrnl. R. Aeronaut. Soc.* Mar. 198 Special temperature conditions are brought about by vertical currents of air. The vertical currents usually consist of a hot stream of air rising or a cold stream falling. In flying into such a current the airship will experience a 'dunt'. The 'dunt' received will depend on two actions—one the dynamic action of the current, and the other the sudden change in lift due to change in temperature. **1928** E. F. SPANNER *Gentlemen prefer Aeroplanes* vi. 43 Moderate clouds—unavoidable temperature 'dunts'—and so on. *Ibid.* x. 71 When the vessel meets 'temperature "dunts"' and other atmospheric irregularities.

2. ***dunt-about***, a person or thing knocked about, ill-used, or made a convenience of.

1825-80 in JAMIESON. **1892** *Northumbld. Gloss.*, s.v., 'Aye, poor thing, she's a fair dunt-aboot.'

dunt, *a.* and *sb.*[2] *dial.* [perh. f. root of DUN *v.*[2]: cf. *dunch, dunny*.]

A. *adj.* Stupid, dizzy, or giddy, from an affection of the brain: said especially of sheep or calves.

1787 GROSE *Provinc. Gloss.*, *Dunt*, stupified, numbed. *Norf.*.. A dunt sheep, one that mopes about, from a disorder in his head. **1794** VANCOUVER *Agric. Surv. Cambr.* 33 Dying dunt (as the shepherds term it) that is dizzy. *a* **1825** FORBY *Voc. E. Anglia, Dunt*, stupid; or dizzy. A dizzy calf with water in the head is said to be dunt. **1893** ZINCKE *Wherstead* 276 Dunt [in East Anglia, means] chronically stupid from some affection or lesion of the brain.

B. *sb.* The gid or sturdy, in sheep, etc.

1784 YOUNG *Ann. Agric.* II. 436 *Dunt*, a distemper [in sheep] caused by a bladder of water gathering in the head; no cure. **1822-34** GOOD *Study Med.* (ed. 4) I. 355 The staggering or vertiginous disease which is provincially known by the name of dunt.

dunt (dʌnt), *v.*[1] *Sc.* and *dial.* [f. DUNT *sb.*[1], or variant of DINT *v.* (sense 1): cf. also Sw. dial. *dunta* to strike, shake.]

1. *trans.* To knock with a dull sound, as with the fist in the back or ribs. Also *absol.* or *intr.*

1570 *Henry's Wallace* x. 285 Duschyt in dros, duntit [*MS.* in gloss, dewyt] with speris dynt. *c* **1610** SIR J. MELVIL *Mem.* (1735) 393 The dunting of Mells and Hammers. **1789** DAVIDSON *Seasons* 59 (Jam.) The pliant foot..Dunting, oppressive, on the verdant path. **1806** *Jamieson's Pop. Ball.* I. 304 (Jam.) He dunted o' the kist, the buirds did flee. **1895** CROCKETT *Men of Mosshags* 38 The sound of my mother's roller..'dunt-dunting' on the dough. *Mod. Sc.* It's too good a hat to be dunted about every day.

b. ***to dunt out***: to drive out by knocking; to thresh or beat out. Also *fig.*

1768 Ross *Helenore* 115 (Jam.) Ae thing I'd hae dunted out. **1823** Galt *R. Gilhaize* II. 220 (Jam.) Fearing the wrathful ram might dunt out the bowels, or the brains..of the young cavalier. **1871** W. Alexander *Johnny Gibb* xiii. (1873) 81 Johnny's principle of action, as regarded differences between himself and others, was always to 'dunt it oot' as he went along.

2. *intr.* Of the heart: To beat violently.

1724 Ramsay *Evergreen* (1824) II. 17 Neir dunt again within my Breist. **1795** Burns *To Mitchell* 11 While my heart wi' life-blood dunted. **1801** Macneill *Poet. Wks.* (1844) 111 His proud heart it dunted.

dunt, *v.*[2] *dial.* [Belongs to dunt *a.*] *trans.* To drive stupid; to deafen or stun with noise.

1787 Grose *Provinc. Gloss.* s.v., How you dunt me, saying of a mother to a crying child. *a* **1825** Forby *Voc. E. Anglia*, *Dunt*, to stupify.

dunt, early ME. form of dint.

dunter ('dʌntə(r)). *local.* [In sense 1 prob., in 2 certainly, f. dunt *v*[1].]

1. A local name of the eider-duck (app. originally in Orkney and Shetland). Also ***dunter-goose***, ***-duck***.

1693 J. Wallace *Orkney* 16 Plenty both of wild and tame fowls..Dunter-Goose, Claik-Goose. **1768** Wales in *Phil. Trans.* LX. 126 There are various sorts of the geese, as..the brant, the dunter..The gander of the dunter kind is..one of the most beautiful feathered birds that I have ever seen. **1866** Crichton *Nat. Rambles Orcades* 97 We could distinguish one eider duck or dunter, as they are here termed.

2. A porpoise (*Northumbld.* and *south Scotld.*).

1825 in Jamieson. **1825** in Brockett *N.C. Gloss.*

†**duntibour**. *Sc. Obs.* Also dont-, dount-, duntebor. [Derivation uncertain.] ? A lady of the bed-chamber.

1538 Lyndesay *Supplic. agst. Syde Taillis* 176 Quod Lindesay in contempt of the syde taillis, That duddrounis & duntibouris throu þe dubbis traillis. *a* **1572** Knox *Hist. Ref.* iv. (1644) 307 The old Duntebors, and others that had long served in the Court, and hoped to have no remission of sins, but by vertue of the Masse. *Ibid.* 363 Certain Duntiberis, and others of the French Menȝie. *Ibid.*, Madame Baylie, Mistris to the Queens Dountibures (for maids that Court would not then well bear).

duntle ('dʌnt(ə)l), *v. dial.* [perh. dim. and freq. of dunt *v.*: but see also dunkle.] *trans.* To knock; to dent with a blow.

1852 R. S. Surtees *Sponge's Sp. Tour* xxvii. 167 It was between these places that I got my head duntled into my hat. **1857** Kingsley *Two Y. Ago* Introd. (1879) 6 His cap is duntled in: his back bears fresh stains of peat.

duo ('dju:əʊ). Pl. duos. [It. *duo* duet, a. L. *duo* two.] **1.** *Mus.* A duet.

1590 T. Whithorne (*title*) His Songs for 2 voyces, of the which some be plaine and easie..the rest of these Duos be made for those that be more perfect in Singing or Playing. **1665** Pepys *Diary* 15 Oct., Tried to compose a duo of counter point. **1781** J. Moore *View Soc. It.* (1795) I. 189 A Duo performed by an old man and a young woman. **1880** *Grove's Dict. Mus.* I. 468 Some writers use the form 'Duet' for vocal, and 'Duo' for instrumental compositions; this distinction, however, is by no means universally adopted. *transf.* and *fig.* **1802** Marian Moore *Lascelles* I. 232 She usually had a female friend staying with her, to interrupt these tedious duo's. **1872** Geo. Eliot *Middlem.* x, The talking was done in duos and trios more or less inharmonious.

2. Two people; a couple; esp. a pair of entertainers. Also *fig.* (Cf. quot. 1872, sense 1 above.)

1887 *Lantern* (New Orleans) 16 July 2/2 The morals of this duo were very much impaired. **1930** *Amer. Speech* VI. 115 (*newspaper headline*) Date set for bank theft trial of duo. **1942** Berrey & Van den Bark *Amer. Thes. Slang* §583/33 *Pop duo* or *trio*, a popular team of two or three [entertainers].. **1958** *Times* 23 Sept. 3/4 They [*sc.* two Spanish dancers] are a delightfully matched duo. **1958** *Listener* 16 Oct. 595/2 Richards..ejected the poet, leaving a duo of poem and reader. **1969** *Stage* 18 Sept. 23/2 (Advt.), Organ-drums duo with vocals.

duo-, L. *duo* = Gr. δύο (*dyo*), 'two', as an initial element, forms composite numbers. It is sometimes improperly used to form other modern compounds where bi- (or in Greek words di-) is the proper formative; e.g. **duo'cameral** = bicameral; **duo'centenary** = bicentenary or ducentenary; **'duoglott** = diglott; **duo'literal** = biliteral; **du'opedal** = bipedal.

1828 Webster cites Stuart for *Duoliteral*. **1850** (*title*) The Duoglott Bible comprising the Holy Scriptures in the Welsh and English Languages. **1859** Sala *Gas-light & D.* xxviii. 318 Forced to assume the duopedal attitude by the cudgel of his master. **1879** *Sat. Rev.* 4 Oct. 412/1 Duocentenaries, tercentenaries, and quin-centenaries have all lately taken place. **1894** *Daily Graphic* 19 Mar. 7/3 It has helped to illustrate..the utility of the Duocameral system. **1894** *Daily Tel.* 23 Aug. 4/7 Many thousands of the 'duoglot' babies have been reduced by a stroke of his autocratic pen to 'monoglots'.

duo'decad, -ade. [ad. late L. *duodecas* the number twelve: cf. decade.] A group of twelve; a period of twelve years; = dodecade.

1621 Bp. Mountagu *Diatribae* i. 258 Ogdoades, Duodecads, Triacontads..and all the Æones, blasphemous speculations [of the Gnostics]. **1866** *Contemp. Rev.* III. 57 The changes necessitated by a duodecade of eventful years.

duo'decagon, -'hedron = dodecagon, -hedron. **duodeca'hedral** *a.* = dodecahedral.

a **1696** Scarburgh *Euclid* (1705) 173 From the bisection of an Hexagonal Arch, may be inscribed..a Duodecagon. **1828** Webster, *Duodecahedral, Duodecahedron.*

duodecane: see duodecyl.

duodecennial (ˌdju:əʊdɪ'sɛnɪəl), *a.* [f. L. *duodecennium* period of twelve years, f. *duodecim* twelve + *annus* year: see -al[1].] Of twelve years.

1656 in Blount *Glossogr.* **1865** *Morning Star* 12 Apr., The next duodecennial period commences next July.

duodecim-, L. *duodecim* twelve, an initial element in some 19th-c. technical terms: **duode'cimfid** *a.* [L. *-fidus* cleft], divided into twelve parts or segments (Webster, 1828); **duode'cimlobate** *a.* [Gr. λόβος lobe], divided into twelve lobes (*Syd. Soc. Lex.* 1883).

duodecimal (dju:əʊ'dɛsɪməl), *a.* and *sb.* [f. L. *duodecim-us* twelfth, f. *duodecim* twelve: see -al[1]. Cf. F. *duodécimal* (1801 Hauy).]

A. *adj.* Relating to twelfth parts or to the number twelve; proceeding by twelves.

1727 J. Jordaine (*title*) Duodecimal Arithmetick and Mensuration improved. **1749** F. Smith *Voy. Disc.* II. 56 A duodecimal Progression. **1857** *Sat. Rev.* III. 448/1 A strictly duodecimal coinage.

B. *sb. pl.* **duodecimals**, a method of multiplying together quantities denoting lengths given in feet, inches, twelfths of an inch, etc., without reducing them to one denomination; also called *cross-multiplication*.

The method is essentially that of long multiplication, but in the duodecimal scale instead of the decimal. The successive terms of the result denote square feet, twelfths of a square foot, square inches, etc.

1714 S. Cunn (*title*) A new and complete Treatise of the Doctrine of Fractions..with an Epitome of Duodecimals. **1802** P. Barlow (*title*) On the Method of Transforming a Number from one Scale of Notation to another, and its Application to the rule of Duodecimals. **1859** Barn. Smith *Arith. & Algebra* (ed. 6) 167 This method is styled Cross Multiplication or Duodecimals, and it is generally employed by painters, bricklayers, &c., in measuring work.

Hence **duo'decimally** *adv.*

1847 Craig, *Duodecimally*, by duodecimals.

duo'decimary, *a.* [f. L. *duodecim* twelve: see -ary.] Having twelve parts or sections.

1837 *Fraser's Mag.* XV. 27 In the course of one month, by the mere disposal of cards, divided into twelve compartments, as tickets for so many lessons, he pocketed about fifty pounds..[He] only desired that they would take his duodecimary cards, and pay for them.

‖**duodecimo** (dju:əʊ'dɛsɪməʊ). [L. (*in*) *duodecimō* in a twelfth (*sc.* of a sheet), abl. of *duodecimus* twelfth.]

1. The size of a book, or of the page of a book, in which each leaf is one-twelfth of a whole sheet: usually abbreviated 12mo.

1658 Phillips s.v., A book is said to be in *Duodecimo*, when it is of twelve leaves in a sheet. **1688** *Catalogus Librorum..per Benj. Walford* 137 English Miscellanies in Octavo and Duodecimo. **1759** Dilworth *Pope* 47 His miscellanies in duodecimo. **1837-9** Hallam *Hist. Lit.* (1847) I. 451 The book is in duodecimo, and contains but eighty-five pages. **1878** Browning *Poets Croisic* 56 Some fifty leaves in duodecimo. *fig.* **1832** *E. Ind. Sketch Bk.* I. 49 Mrs. Erskine was a beauty in duodecimo.

2. A book or volume of this size.

1712 Addison *Spect.* No. 529 ⁋1 The Author of a Duodecimo. **1807** *Director* II. 348 Some of the duodecimos of our circulating libraries. **1851** Carlyle *Sterling* iii. iii. (1872) 190 A tiny duodecimo without name attached. *fig. a* **1839** Praed *Poems* (1864) I. 282 Those delicious things, Which constitute Love's joys and woes In pretty duodecimos.

3. *attrib.* or *adj.*

1781 W. Mason *Let.* 29 Mar. in *Walpole's Lett.* (1858) VIII. 18 *note*, A hundred duodecimo pages. **1791** Boswell *Johnson* an. 1750, It was published in six duodecimo volumes. **1824** L. Murray *Eng. Gram.* I. Pref. 3 The last Duodecimo edition of his Grammar. **1837-9** Hallam *Hist. Lit.* I. iii. i. §148 The duodecimo division of the sheet. **1850** W. Irving *Goldsmith* xxx. 296 An abridgement in one volume duodecimo.

b. *fig.* Applied to a person or thing of minute or diminutive size.

1777 Sheridan *Sch. Scand.* ii. ii, Lady Betty..was taking the dust in Hyde Park, in a sort of duodecimo phaeton. **1833** *New Monthly Mag.* XXXVII. 46 All the little monarchies and duodecimo princedoms. **1860** *All Year Round* No. 38. 283 He bent, and bowed, and touched his heart with his hand, like a little duodecimo Lord Chesterfield.

duo'decuple, *a.* [f. L. *duodecim* twelve, after decuple.] Twelvefold.

1727 Arbuthnot *Coins* (J.), To establish the duodecuple proportion.

duodecyl (dju:'ɒdɪsɪl). *Chem.* [f. L. *duodecim* twelve + -yl.] The twelfth member of the series of hydrocarbon radicals having the formula C_nH_{2n+1}; the monatomic alcohol radical $C_{12}H_{25}$. Used *attrib.* in ***duodecyl chloride***, ***compound***, ***hydride***. So **du'odecane**, **duo'decylene**, the paraffin and olefine of this series. Also *dodecyl*, *dodecane*, etc.

1872 Watts *Dict. Chem.* VI, *Duodecyl compounds*.. *Duodecane* or *Duodecyl Hydride* $C_{12}H_{26}$, is one of the constituents of American petroleum..*Duodecyl chloride*, $C_{12}H_{25}Cl$, is a faintly yellowish, nearly inodorous liquid..*Duodecylene*, $C_{12}H_{24}$, is one of the hydrocarbons obtained by Warren and Storer by destructive distillation of the lime-soap of Menhaden oil; also from Rangoon tar.

duodenal (dju:əʊ'di:nəl), *a.*[1] [ad. mod.L. *duodēnālis*. f. *duodēnum*: see below; cf. F. *duodénal*.] Pertaining or relating to the duodenum.

1843 J. G. Wilkinson *Swedenborg's Anim. Kingd.* I. v. 149 The duodenal artery. **1870** Rolleston *Anim. Life* 15 In the concavity of the duodenal fold.

duo'denal, *a.*[2] *rare.* [f. L. *duodēnī* twelve each + -al[1].] Composed of twelve members.

1817 G. S. Faber *Eight Diss.* (1845) II. App. v. 275 The southern Duodenal Confederacy of the Turseni. *Ibid.* 286 Duodenal Federations.

duo'denal, *sb. Mus.* The symbol of the root of a duodene.

1874 A. J. Ellis *Proc. R. Soc.* XXIII. 20 The duodenal will direct the player to the mode of arranging the manual.

duodenary (dju:əʊ'di:nərɪ), *a.* and *sb.* [ad. L. *duodēnārius* containing twelve.]

A. *adj.* **1.** *Arith.* Pertaining to twelve; proceeding by twelves.

1857 *Sat. Rev.* III. 448/1 The use of the duodenary division of the shilling. **1864** Webster s.v., *Duodenary arithmetic*, that system in which the local value of the figures increases in a twelve-fold proportion from right to left. **1890** *Times* (weekly ed.) 17 Jan. 15/1 The duo-denary system of calculation.

2. *Mus.* Relating to duodenes.

1874 A. J. Ellis in *Proc. R. Soc.* XXIII. 21 The fingering..on manuals constructed on the duodenary theory.

B. *sb.* †**1.** A period of twelve years. *Obs.*

1681 H. More *Exp. Dan.* 224 In the beginning of the Duodenary.

2. *Mus.* A keyboard constructed according to duodenes. See A 2.

1874 A. J. Ellis in *Proc. R. Soc.* 28 The hand would on the duodenary..dip between high digitals to strike octaves of low digitals.

'duodenate, *v. Mus. intr.* To modulate by duodenes. So **duode'nation**.

1874 A. J. Ellis *Proc. R. Soc.* XXIII. 21 If..a piece in †B♭ duodenated much to the left..we could play it as A♯. *Ibid.* 19 To consider modulation as taking place by duodenes, and hence consisting of duodenation.

duodene ('dju:əʊdi:n). *Mus.* [f. med.L. *duodēna* a dozen, a group of twelve, f. L. *duodēnī* twelve each: cf. late L. *centēna*, etc.] Name given by A. J. Ellis to a group of twelve notes having certain fixed relations of pitch, in a proposed scheme for obtaining exact intonation on a keyboard instrument.

1874 A. J. Ellis in *Proc. R. Soc.* XXIII. 16 A *duodene*.. consists of 12 tones, forming four *trines* of major Thirds arranged in three *quaternions* of Fifths.

duodenectomy (ˌdju:əʊdɪ'nɛktəmɪ). *Surg.* [f. duoden(um + -ectomy.] Partial or total excision of the duodenum.

1908 *Practitioner* Sept. 454 Codivilla is the only surgeon, who, operating on the pancreas, has performed a duodenectomy. **1962** *Lancet* 22 Dec. 1308/1 A further partial gastric resection, partial pancreatectomy, and duodenectomy with node dissection.

duodeno- (dju:əʊ'di:nəʊ), comb. form of duodenum, as in **duodeno-jejunal** *a.*, pertaining to the duodenum and the jejunum.

1886 *Buck's Handbk. Med. Sci.* II. 537 Duodenocholecystostomy. **1887** *Ibid.* V. 606 The little pocket which lies behind this (duodeno-jejunal recess). **1890** Billings *Med. Dict.* 417/1 *Duodeno-renal*, relating to duodenum and kidney. **1900** Dorland *Med. Dict.* 215/1 *Duodenocholecystostomy*, the operation of forming a communication between the gall-bladder and the duodenum. *Duodeno-choledochotomy*, surgical incision of the duodenum and bile-duct. *Duodeno-enterostomy*, the artificial creation of a passage from the duodenum to another part of the small intestine. **1906** *Practitioner* Dec. 761 The duodeno-jejunal junction. **1908** *Ibid.* Nov. 712 The duodenopyloric constriction. **1966** *Lancet* 24 Dec. 1391/1 The whole of the intestine from 2 ft. below the duodenojejunal flexure to the mid-transverse colon was grossly ischæmic. **1968** S. Taylor et al. *Short Textbk. Surg.* (ed. 2) xxviii. 427 After the stomach contents have been aspirated a duodenoduodenostomy is performed.

‖**duodenum** (dju:əʊ'di:nəm). *Anat.* In 6 also **duodene**. [med.L. (so called from its length, = *duodēnum digitōrum* space of twelve digits, inches, or finger's breadths), f. *duodēnī* twelve each (see duodene). Used in Fr. in 1514 (Hatz.-Darm.).]

The first portion of the small intestine immediately below the stomach, commencing at the pylorus, and terminating in the jejunum or second portion, at the second lumbar vertebra.

1398 Trevisa *Barth. De P.R.* v. xlii. (1495) 158 The fyrste gutte of the thre subtyll guttes hyghte duodenum, for in his lengthe by the mesure of euery man he conteynyth twelue ynches. *c* **1400** *Lanfranc's Cirurg.* 168 þe firste gutt is maad fast to þe lower mouþ, and þis gutt is clepid duodenum.. for he is of þe lengþe of xij. ynchis. *Ibid.* 171 Wiþ a gutt þat is clepid duodeno. **1594** T. B. *La Primaud. Fr. Acad.* II. 349 The first is called Duodene, because of the length of it, which is without any folding or turning. **1699** *Phil. Trans.* XXI. 237 The greatest part of the Food, that is thus broken and concocted, is by the Contraction of the Fibres of the Stomack press'd into the Duodenum. **1767** GOOCH *Treat. Wounds* I. 398 The small intestines.. consisting of the *Duodenum*, *Jejunum* and *Ileum.* **1878** T. BRYANT *Pract. Surg.* I. 603 The duodenum is rarely ruptured, its position protecting it.

Hence **duode'nitis**, inflammation of the duodenum; **duode'nostomy** [Gr. στόμα mouth], **duode'notomy** [Gr. -τομία cutting]: see quots.

1854–67 C. A. HARRIS *Dict. Med. Terminol.*, Duodenitis. **1866** FLINT *Princ. Med.* (1880) 450 Duodenitis.. separately, or in connection with gastritis and enteritis. **1883** *Syd. Soc. Lex.*, *Duodenostomy*, the opening of the duodenum through the abdominal walls, and its attachment to them so as to make an artificial mouth or entrance for food, as in cancer of the pylorus. *Ibid. Duodenotomy*, the opening of the duodenum through the abdominal parietes, as in cancer of the pylorus, to introduce nutriment.

duo'drama. [ad. It. *duodramma* (= F. *duodrame*), f. L. or It. *duo* + DRAMA.] 'A dramatic piece for two performers only: cf. DUOLOGUE.

In recent Dicts.

duologue ('djuːəlɒg). [irreg. f. L. *duo* or Gr. δύο (*dyo-*) two, after *monologue*.] A conversation between two persons, a dialogue; *spec.* a dramatic piece spoken by two actors. Also *attrib.*

1864 *Home News* 19 Dec. 21/1 The dramatic monopolists .. are now taking steps to stop a 'dualogue entertainment' at Weston's Music Hall. **1865** MISS BRADDON *Sir Jasper* v, [He] was fain to let the conversation lapse almost into a duologue between his daughter and his guest. **1894** *Athenæum* 3 Mar. 288/1 'Fashionable Intelligence', an original duologue.. is promised at the Court Theatre.

duomachy (djuː'ɒməkɪ). *nonce-wd.* [irreg. f. L. *duo* or Gr. δύο two + -μαχια fighting.] A fight of two; single combat.

1885 R. F. BURTON in *Academy* Aug. 69/1 To run away.. rather than engage in a Waki' al-isnayn or duomachy.

‖**duomo** ('dwɔmo). Also 6–8 **domo.** [It. *duomo, domo* cathedral: see DOME *sb.*]

1. A cathedral church (in Italy): cf. DOM.[2]

1549 THOMAS *Hist. Italie* 188 b, The *Domo* of Myllaine. **1644** EVELYN *Diary* 19 Oct., The Duomo, or Cathedral.. is a superb structure. **1672** CROWNE *Chas VIII*, v. Dram. Wks. (1873) I. 214 The Duchess, Sir! Bleeding and faint is from the Domo led. **1855** TENNYSON *Daisy* 46 In bright vignettes.. Of tower or duomo, sunny-sweet.

attrib. **1851** MRS. BROWNING *Casa Guidi Windows* 94 We chased the Archbishop from the duomo door. **1856** —— *Aur. Leigh* VIII. 44 The duomo-bell Strikes ten.

†**2.** = DOME 5 a. *Obs.*

1693 SALMON *Bate's Dispens.* (1713) 94/1 Open the Cover to the Duomo, and increase the Fire more and more.

†**du'opolize**, *v. Obs. nonce-wd.* [f. L. *duo* or Gk. δύο two, after *monopolize.*] *trans.* To engross between two.

1659 GAUDEN *Tears of Ch.* 440 Some rigid Presbyterians and popular Independents affect with great Magistery to Duopolize all Church-power.

duopoly (djuː'ɒpəlɪ). [f. DUO- + Gr. πωλ-εῖν to sell, after MONOPOLY.] A condition in which there are only two suppliers of a certain commodity, service, etc.; the domination of a particular market by two firms. Hence **du'opolist**, one member of a duopoly.

1920 A. C. PIGOU *Econ. of Welfare* xii. 232 Cournot decided.. that the resources devoted to production under duopoly are a determinate quantity, lying somewhere between the quantity that would have been so devoted under simple competition and under simple monopoly respectively. **1951** J. R. WINTON *Dict. Econ. Terms* 29 When the total supply of a commodity is produced by two firms or individuals, that state of affairs is known as 'duopoly'. **1961** *Guardian* 28 Jan. 1/1 He.. believes.. monopoly is.. preferable to the present duopoly—the domination of the magazine industry by two powerful groups. **1965** SELDON & PENNANCE *Everyman's Dict. Econ.* 132 If a duopolist moves his price above or below the monopoly price he will be worse off because profits are maximized at the monopoly price.

b. *transf.* Control or domination by two persons or groups.

1959 *Listener* 1 Jan. 4/2 The party duopoly of Britain. **1959** *Economist* 22 Aug. 525/2 As we move from nuclear duopoly to nuclear oligopoly, the range of circumstances in which these weapons could be rationally used becomes narrower.

duorow, obs. form of DWARF.

duosecant (djuː'ɒsɪkənt), *a. Cryst.* [non-etymol. f. L. *duo* two + *secāntem* cutting.] (See quot.)

1851 *Offic. Catal. Gt. Exhib.* I. 121 Any plane of any crystal whatever must belong to one or other of the three.. forms.. Trisecant. Cutting all three gubernatorial axes. Duosecant. Cutting only two axes, and therefore parallel to the third. Ultimate. Cutting only one.

duotone ('djuːəʊtəʊn), *sb.* [f. DUO- + TONE *sb.* 10.] A half-tone illustration printed in two colours from two plates made from the same original, but using different screen angles; also, the process by which such an illustration is printed. Also *attrib.*

1907 AMSTUTZ & JENKINS *Hand-Bk. Photoengraving* viii. 406 *Duo-tones*, the printing of two superposed impressions from one engraved half-tone plate, in two colors, one a black and the other a tint, placing them slightly out of register, but in alignment; or the printing of two superposed colors from two separate plates. **1913** *Dial* 16 Dec. 530/1 Of the numerous illustrations.. some are 'collotype plates',.. and ..others.. are 'duo-tone illustrations'. **1967** KARCH & BUBER *Offset Processes* v. 174 A true duotone is a two color reproduction made by two halftone negatives at two different screen angles, with the halftone plates printed in complementary colors. **1971** *Publishers' Weekly* 23 Aug. 63 The extensive coverage in this issue of 'The New Gift and Art Books',.. including a 16-page duotone picture portfolio of outstanding books.

Passing into general use as *adj.*

1934 WEBSTER, *Duotone*, having or yielding two tones or colours. **1966** 'A. HALL' *9th Directive* vi. 61 The duotone Chevrolet in the main parking area was moving away.

duotype ('djuːəʊtaɪp). [f. DUO- + TYPE *sb.*[1]] A half-tone illustration printed from two plates made from the same monochrome negative, but etched differently to give two sets of colour-values; also, the process used to print such an illustration.

1913 S. H. HORGAN *Halftone & Photomechanical Processes* 207 *Duotype*, two half-tone plates made from the same negative, but etched differently. **1967** KARCH & BUBER *Offset Processes* v. 176 A duotype is a two color halftone made from one halftone negative.

dup (dʌp), *v. dial.* or *arch.* [contr. from *do up* (see DO *v.* 52): cf. *doff, don, dout*, and see DUB *v.*[3]] *trans.* To open.

1547 BOORDE *Introd. Knowl.* i. (1870) 122 Dup the dore, gos! **1564** EDWARDS *Dam. & Pithias* in Hazl. *Dodsley* IV. 69 Will they not dup the gate to-day? **1602** SHAKS. *Ham.* IV. v. 51 Then vp he rose, and don'd his clothes, and dupt the chamber dore. **1673** R. HEAD *Canting Acad.* 14 If we.. dup the Giger. **1785** in GROSE *Dict. Vulg. Tongue.* **1865** S. EVANS *Bro. Fabian* 5 'Now dup the gate', quoth the king's men, 'So quickly as ye may'.

dup, -e, obs. forms of DEEP.

dupable ('djuːpəb(ə)l), *a.* Also **dupeable.** [f. DUPE *v.*[1] + -ABLE.] Capable of being duped; gullible. Also as *sb.* Hence **dupa'bility**, gullibility.

1833 CARLYLE *Cagliostro* Misc. Ess. 1872 V. 104 That same blubbery oiliness.. the very gift of a fluent public speaker to Dupeables. *Ibid.* 122 Some boiling muddle-heads of the dupeable sort. **1835** SOUTHEY *Doctor* lxxxvii. III. 119 Man is a dupeable animal. **1840** CARLYLE *Heroes* (1858) 366 Napoleon.. believed too much in the Dupeability of men. **1856** R. S. VAUGHAN *Mystics* (1860) II. VIII. ix. 99 Behold that grand Magnet for all the loose and dupable social particles in every class and country.

†'**du,parted**, *a. Her. Obs.* [f. *du-* (= DUO-) + *parted.*] = BIPARTED.

1688 R. HOLME *Armoury* III. 270/2 Some blazon this.. Duparted and Biparted, if it end in two points.

dupe (djuːp), *sb.*[1] [a. F. *dupe*, †*duppe* (15th c.) deluded person: in 1426 said to belong to 'the manner of speaking that they call *jargon*'.]

A person who allows himself to be deceived or deluded; one who is misled by false representations or notions; a victim of deception. Const. *of*, rarely *to.*

1681 TEMPLE *Mem.* II. Wks. 1731 I. 344 They were other Mens Dupes, and did other Mens work. **1759** DILWORTH *Pope* 39 But Dennis was the dupe of his credulity. **1772** PRIESTLEY *Inst. Relig.* (1782) II. 304 Dupes to the most fatal delusion and self deceit. **1830** SCOTT *Demonol.* x. 356 The ready dupe of astrologers and soothsayers. **1845** M. PATTISON *Ess.* (1889) I. 22 But Gregory was not the dupe of this stratagem.

Hence '**dupedom**, '**dupism.**

1798 ANNA SEWARD *Lett.* (1811) V. 171 That single instance of dupism. **1843** CARLYLE *Past & Pr.* IV. i. (1845) 322 Imbecile Dupedom.

dupe (djuːp), *sb.*[2] *colloq.* [Abbrev. of DUPLICATE *sb.*] A duplicate; *spec.* in *Cinemat.*, a duplicate negative made from a positive print (see quots.). Also *attrib.* or as *adj.*

1916 E. W. SARGENT *Technique Photoplay* (ed. 3) 361 *Dupe*, a pirated print of a film. Made by passing a genuine positive print through a printer in company with negative film whereby an imperfect duplicate of the negative is obtained from which prints are made. **1937** A. BUCHANAN *Film Making* iii. 51 Frequently a 'dupe' negative is made... A dupe is created by printing a special lavender positive print from the original negative, and from that a second or duplicate negative is made in the laboratory. **1948** [see DUPE *v.*[2]]. **1969** C. YOUNG *Todd Dossier* 152 Rosen.. sent me down to 326 to pick up a dupe file copy of Todd's surgery report.

dupe, *v.*[1] [a. F. *dupe-r* (17th c. in Hatz.-Darm.); or f. DUPE *sb.*[1]] *trans.* To make a dupe of; to deceive, delude, befool; to cheat.

1704 SWIFT *T. Tub* §9 Those entertainments and pleasures we most value in life, are such as dupe and play the wag with the senses. **1771** *Junius Lett.* li. 264, I will not concur to dupe and mislead a senseless multitude. **1825** LYTTON *Zicci* 26, I am not to be duped by these solemn phrases. **1855** MACAULAY *Hist. Eng.* III. 480 William had too much sense to be duped. **1895** F. HALL *Two Trifles* 14, On his faith, I have been duped.. into imagining myself able to [etc.].

Hence **duped** (djuːpt), *ppl. a.*

1756 C. LUCAS *Ess. Waters* I. Pref., The duped populace. **1855** LEWES *Goethe* I. II. iv. 91 One of those duped dupers who still clung to the great promises of Alchemy.

dupe (djuːp), *v.*[2] *Cinemat. colloq.* [f. DUPE *sb.*[2]] *trans.* To make a 'dupe' of. Hence **duped** *ppl. a.*, '**duping** *vbl. sb.* Cf. DUPE *sb.*[2]

1912 F. A. TALBOT *Moving Pictures* xviii. 206 His most successful subjects were seized by American houses and 'duped'—as unauthorized reproduction is called in cinematographic parlance in that country. **1923** *Ibid.* (ed. 2) x. 134 These 'duped' (duplicated) films were highly indifferent. **1933** A. BRUNEL *Filmcraft* 158 A duped negative has until recently always given prints considerably inferior to positives taken from an original negative. **1948** E. LINDGREN *Art of Film* 205 *Duping print*, special soft print.. made from an original negative so that a dupe negative can subsequently be made from it. **1963** *Movie* July/Aug. 33/1 Fleapit projectionists.. duping and scratching the first sequence of cut-up film to make it look old. **1969** J. ELLIOT *Duel* III. ii. 233 She went to the cutting-rooms to learn the mysteries of.. fine grain duping prints.

dupeable, var. spelling of DUPABLE.

duper ('djuːpə(r)). [f. DUPE *v.*[1] + -ER[1].] One who dupes; a deceiver, deluder.

1792 MAD. D'ARBLAY *Diary* 24 Sept., The duped and the dupers. **1868** BROWNING *Ring & Bk.* v. 1361 The waggish parents who played dupes To dupe the duper.

dupery ('djuːpərɪ). [f. DUPE *v.*[1] + -ERY: cf. F. *duperie* (1690 in Hatz.-Darm).] **a.** The action or practice of duping; deception, trickery. **b.** The condition of one who is duped.

1759 ADAM SMITH *Mor. Sent.* VI. i. (R.), [Machiavel].. has much contempt for the dupery and weakness of the sufferers. **1791–1823** D'ISRAELI *Cur. Lit.* (1859) II. 163 The whole displays a complete system of dupery. **1816** MAD. D'ARBLAY *Let.* 28 Oct., While thus open to dupery.. he is so fearful of ridicule that [etc.]. **1830** *Fraser's Mag.* I. 418, I was.. continually exposed to the dupery of cunning.

'**dupion** ('djuːpɪən). Also **doupion, douppion, duppion.** [ad. F. *doupion* = It. *doppione*, f. *doppio* double.] **1.** 'A double cocoon formed by two silk-worms' (Simmonds *Dict. Trade* 1858).

1828 in WEBSTER. **1933** T. WELFORD *Textile Student's Man.* vi. 61 *Dupions*, double cocoons.

2. A rough silk fabric woven from threads from double cocoons; such a thread. Now also applied to imitations of such fabric made by other processes.

1922 A. F. BARKER *Textiles* (ed. 2) xv. 329 Not many of the Chinese or Japanese duppions are exported, being reserved for native use. **1938** *Times* 28 Feb. 19/4 For cruising frocks there is a douppion flamella at 7s. 11d. **1961** *Times* 13 Feb. 13/3 Available in silk twills, chiffon and duppions. **1968** J. IRONSIDE *Fashion Alphabet* 226 *Dupion* (*Douppion*).. is a silk thread made from two cocoons which have been so closely 'nested' that a coarse double filament results. The double thread is always woven as one and the resultant silk fabric is irregular and slub-like. The yarn is now simulated in rayon and acetate fibres. **1971** *Scotsman* 20 May 6/4 The carpet is a Wilton-weave twist pile in Grecian olive and the curtains are in turquoise dupion.

†'**duplar**, *a. Obs. rare.* [ad. late L. *duplār-is* containing double, f. *duplus* DUPLE] Double, duple: see quot.

1610 HOLLAND *Camden's Brit.* 783 Duplar or Duple Armaturæ they were called in those daies, who had Duble alowances of Corne; Simplar, that had but single.

†'**duplat**, *a. Sc. Obs. rare.* [ad. L. *duplāt-us*, pa. pple. of *duplāre* to double.] = DUPLE *a.*

1501 DOUGLAS *Pal. Hon.* I. xli, Proportionis.. Duplat, triplat, diatesseriall.

duplation (djuː'pleɪʃən). [ad. L. *duplātiōn-em*, n. of action f. *duplāre* to double.] The operation of doubling.

c **1425** *Craft Nombrynge* (E.E.T.S.) 12 This is the chapture of duplacioun.. Duplacioun is a doublyng of a nombre. *Ibid.* 13 Do away þe figure þat was dowblede, and sett þere þe digit þat comes of þe duplacioun. **1542** RECORDE *Gr. Artes* (1575) 167 Duplation is nothing else but multiplying by 2. **1861** F. HALL in *Jrnl. Asiat. Soc. Bengal* 6 The originals in all cases double consonants which have *r* over them. I have simplified this duplation.

duple ('djuːp(ə)l), *a.* (*sb.*) [ad. L. *duplus* double, f. *duo* two + *-plus*, from root *ple-* to fill.]

A. *adj.* Double, twofold. *Obs.* in *gen.* sense: in *Math.* applied to the proportion of two quantities one of which is double of the other; in *Music*, to 'time' or rhythm having two beats in the bar.

1542–3 *Act 34 & 35 Hen. VIII*, c. 27 §47 If it.. be with a duple voucher, then sixe shillinges and .viii. *d.* **1609** DOULAND *Ornith. Microl.* 19 For example sake 6 and 12 will make a duple reason [= ratio]. **1656** STANLEY *Hist. Philos.* v. (1701) 162/2 By finding two mean proportionals between two right lines in a Duple proportion. **1664** BUTLER *Hud.* II. ii. 269 A breach of Oath is Duple And either way admits a Scruple. **1725–52** CHAMBERS *Cycl.* s.v. *Time*, Common or duple Time is of two species. The first, when every bar or measure is equal to a semi-breve... The second, where every bar is equal to a minim. *a* **1763** BYROM *Robbery Camb. Coach* (R.). Made the red-rugg'd collector's income duple.

1881 W. S. PRATT in Gladden *Par. Probl.* 460 Duple and quadruple rhythms are the best.

†**B.** *sb.* A double; = DOUBLE *sb.* 1. *Obs.*

1609 DOULAND *Ornith. Microl.* 61 You shall find it a Duple. **1650** BULWER *Anthropomet.* 63 The proportion of a half part to a duple. **1726** LEONI tr. *Alberti's Archit.* II. 88/2 Four..the Duple of two. **1787** SIR J. HAWKINS *Johnson* 535 Mathematical ratios of a duple and triple.

†**'duple,** *v. Obs.* [ad. L. *duplāre* to double, f. *dupl-us* DUPLE.] *trans.* To double; to make twice as much or many.

c **1425** *Found. St. Bartholomew's* (E.E.T.S.) 63 Rehersyng, and duplynge prayers. **1654** VILVAIN *Epit. Ess.* VI. lxxxii, That dupled force. **1694** HOLDER *Harmony* (1731) 116 Dupling the Terms of the Ration.

'duplet. [f. DUPLE, after *doublet*: see -ET[1].]

†**1.** = DOUBLET 3 a. *Obs. rare.*

1668 DRYDEN *Evening's Love* III. i, To throw with three dice, till duplets, and a chance be thrown; and the highest duplet wins.

2. *Physics.* A pair of electrons with opposite spins, esp. one forming a covalent or co-ordinate bond between two atoms.

1921 I. LANGMUIR in *Science* LIV. 60/2 According to Postulate 1, the first complete layer in any atom consists of two electrons close to the nucleus. Let us call this stable pair of electrons a *duplet* and let us broaden the definition of duplet to include any pair of electrons which is rendered stable by its proximity to one or more positive charges. We may now state the second postulate... Two atoms may be coupled together by one or more duplets held in common by the completed sheaths of the atoms. **1940** GLASSTONE *Textbk. Physical Chem.* i. 8 Sharing of electrons occurs in pairs, each pair or duplet being equivalent to one conventional chemical bond.

3. *Mus.* A group of two notes or beats; *spec.* (see quot. 1938). (Cf. TRIPLET 2 c.).

1922 S. GREW *Art of Player-Piano* v. 73 We are..able to take the duplet-division of the beat. **1938** *Oxf. Compan. Mus.* 273/1 A duplet is a group of two [notes] or its equivalent, to be performed in the time of three.

duplex ('dju:plɛks), *a.* [a. L. *duplex* twofold, f. *duo* two + *plic-* to fold. Not in Webster 1828.]

1. a. Composed of two parts or elements; twofold.

1817 T. L. PEACOCK *Melincourt* II. 51 A poet and a critic—in which *duplex* capacity he had first deluged the world with torrents of execrable verses—and then written anonymous criticisms to prove them divine. **1841** MIALL in *Nonconf.* I. 29 A double definition is required; because we are endeavouring to express a duplex idea. **1877** TYNDALL in *Daily News* 2 Oct. 2/4 Social progress is for the most part typified by this duplex or polar action.

b. In various technical applications.

duplex escapement, one in which the escape-wheel has both spur and crown teeth; ***duplex gas-burner***, one having two jets so arranged as to combine the two flames into one; ***duplex lamp***, one with two wicks; ***duplex lathe***, one having a cutting-tool at the back opposite to that in front, and in an inverted position; ***duplex process***, a process for making steel in which the charge undergoes treatment by two of the standard processes or in two furnaces in succession.

1851 *Offic. Catal. Gt. Exhib.* III. 1266 Gold hunting watch..style of regulator with duplex escapement. **1883** MISS BRADDON *Gold. Calf* xxv. 281 In the mellow light of a duplex lamp. **1889** FINDLAY *Eng. Railway* 114 A duplex steam hammer of 30 tons, and one of 10 tons. **1902** *Jrnl. Iron & Steel Inst.* LXI. 589 The quantities of slag made were also very great..compared with 0·1 ton of slag in the present duplex process. **1926** *Ibid.* CXIII. 571 This is a continuous duplex process carried out in two tilting open-hearth furnaces. **1939** J. DEARDEN *Iron & Steel Today* vii. 101 Duplex processes..are designed to combine the advantages of the Bessemer and open-hearth processes, while avoiding their disadvantages. **1951** G. R. BASHFORTH *Manuf. Iron & Steel* II. xii. 353 Duplex processes usually employ a high percentage of hot metal.

c. Designating paper or board which is formed by uniting two separate layers of paper, or which is coloured differently on either side.

1901 *Brit. Pat. 22,418* 2 In making duplex papers that is papers that may be white on one side and coloured on the other, or be coloured on one side and coloured with a different colour on the other side, a brass or metal roller D would be used for spreading the colour. **1914** E. A. DAWE *Paper* xvii. 120 Duplex Papers may be made of two layers of differently coloured papers brought together in the wet state and rolled together, or may be coated with different colours, after the paper is made, as duplex art papers. **1962** F. T. DAY *Introd. to Paper* iv. 46 In the case of Duplex tinted boards, different coloured pulps are used to produce a board with a different colour on each side.

d. Of an eye: having pigment on the anterior surface of the iris as well as on the posterior surface, as in eyes that are a colour other than blue.

1908 C. C. HURST in *Proc. R. Soc.* B. LXXX. 86 The eyes in which two kinds of pigment are present; the one, yellow-brown in colour, deposited on the outer or anterior surface of the iris; the other, blue-black in colour, deposited on the inner or posterior surface of the iris. Such eyes I propose to call *duplex. Ibid.*, To the duplex type belong the various shades of eyes with both anterior and posterior pigments. **1911** A. D. DARBISHIRE *Breeding & Mendelian Discov.* 276 Duplex eyes are those which have a layer of brown pigment in front of the iris. **1946** R. R. GATES *Human Genetics* I. v. 88 Hurst..classified eyes as duplex or simplex.

e. *Biol.* Of a polyploid organism: having the dominant allele of any particular gene represented twice.

1923 A. F. BLAKESLEE et al. in *Bot. Gaz.* LXXVI. 345 The convenient terms nulliplex, simplex, duplex, triplex, and quadriplex, can be used in regard to the number of chromosomes containing a given gene, without thereby admitting the amount of so-called dominance of the factors in question. **1963** LEWIS & JOHN *Chromosome Marker* IV. iii. 327 Thus, a tetraploid of the type *AAaa* (duplex) can produce gametes of three kinds—*AA*, *Aa* and *aa*.

f. *Biochem.* Applied to a molecular structure, or part of one, in which two polynucleotide strands are linked together side by side, as in a DNA molecule.

1969 *Nature* 22 Nov. 771/1 There should be a unique sequence of complementary material in each strand giving rise to a single, homogeneous set of duplex regions in the heteroduplex molecules. **1970** *Proc. Nat. Acad. Sci.* LXVI. 197 It was predictable that the flow of biological information in the living cell, postulated to start with the transcription of the duplex DNA to yield a series of messenger RNA species, must originate from only one of the two complementary DNA strands. **1971** *Nature* 19 Feb. 530/1 The enzyme shows a strong preference for single stranded DNA, which it degrades about 150 times faster than duplex DNA.

2. *Electric Telegraphy.* **a.** Applied to any system by which two messages can be sent along the same wire at the same time: now called DIODE. **b.** Now restricted to systems in which two messages are sent simultaneously in opposite directions: opp. to DIPLEX, q.v.

1873 *Telegraphic Jrnl.* I. 59 The term duplex telegraphy has recently been applied to the system by which two messages may be sent along the same wire at the same time. **1879** G. PRESCOTT *Sp. Telephone* p. iii, In 1872 Stearns perfected a duplex system, whereby two communications could be simultaneously transmitted over one wire.

'duplex, *v. Electric Telegraphy.* [f. prec. 2] *trans.* To render duplex; to arrange (a wire or cable) so that two messages can be sent along it at the same time.

1880 *Daily News* 27 Dec. 3/4 The Duplexing of Submarine Cables. **1882** *Sat. Rev.* 18 Mar. 330/2 Duplexing had been known and used on land lines for some time before it could be applied to long deep-sea cables. **1883** *Daily News* 30 May 7/3 Science had enabled them to duplex their cables. **1894** *Times* 30 Apr. 3/4 There are two systems of duplexing—the one called the 'differential', where you balance two currents against one another, and the 'bridge' system, where you balance two electric pressures or tendencies to drive a current.

duplex ('dju:plɛks), *sb.* [f. the adj.] **1.** orig. *U.S.* A house or other building so divided that it forms two dwelling-places; also, a flat occupying two floors. Also *attrib.* or as *adj.*

1922 *Daily Ardmoreite* (Ardmore, Okla.) 6 Jan. 9/1 For Rent—6 room duplex bungalow. **1931** 'D. STIFF' *Milk & Honey Route* iii. 32 You live in a duplex with ten baths, or a cold-water walk-up flat, according to your ability to pay rent. **1936** *Archit. Rev.* LXXX. 101 It consists of an office for the architect-owner on the ground floor, and on the upper floors two 'duplex' (i.e. self-contained two-storey) apartments, one of which is occupied by the architect. **1937** *Sunday Dispatch* 28 Feb. 2/7 A duplex is a house of two storeys, with its own front door on the ground floor. **1938** *Archit. Rev.* LXXXIV. 165 *(caption)* Duplex (two-storey) flats occupy the centre portion. **1959** *Observer* 15 Nov. 18/3 We do not live in a spacious house..but a Chelsea duplex. **1968** *Globe & Mail* (Toronto) 17 Feb. 49/1 (Advt.), 3 bedroom duplex or equivalent. **1969** *Sydney Morning Herald* 24 May 37/1 (Advt.), The owner has had plans drawn for a very impressive duplex. **1971** *Rand Daily Mail* (Home Owner) 27 Mar. 7/2 City dwellers are gravitating towards high density living (flat complexes, town houses, duplex..and so on).

2. *Biochem.* A double-stranded or duplex polynucleotide molecule (see DUPLEX *a.* 1 f).

1963 *Proc. Nat. Acad. Sci.* L. 910 No evidence for an RNA-replicating duplex, analogous to that of the single-stranded DNA virus $\phi X174$, has thus far appeared, despite the fact that RNA-RNA duplexes are known to be very stable structures. **1967** I. H. HERSKOWITZ *Basic Princ. Molec. Genetics* iii. 31 Hybrid DNA-RNA duplexes (each composed of one DNA strand and one RNA strand) can be made. **1969** *Prog. Nucleic Acid Res.* IX. 304 The stability of the duplex is affected both by the base composition and by the sequences of bases along the individual strands.

duplexer ('dju:plɛksə(r)). [f. DUPLEX *a.* + -ER[1].] A device by means of which signals are alternately transmitted from and received by a single radar or radio aerial.

1952 REINTJES & COATE *Princ. Radar* (ed. 3) i. 10 The use of a single antenna for both transmission and reception in nearly all radar sets is made possible by a *transmit-receive device*..also called a *duplexer* and a *receiver-protective* device. **1954** H. C. MINNETT in E. G. Bowen *Textbk. Radar* (ed. 2) ix. 294 An aerial duplexer or TR/RT switch is an electronically operated switching device, which enables the same aerial to be used for both transmitting and receiving in pulsed radar equipments. **1962** *Engineering* 5 Oct. 434 Discussions on valves..will cover..magnetrons, modulators, duplexers.

'duplexing, *vbl. sb. Metallurgy.* The utilization of a duplex process (see DUPLEX *a.* 1 b).

1918 *Iron Age* 30 May 1398/1 'Reversed Duplexing'..consisted of making steel in electric furnaces..at least one of which was run with basic lining, and the rest of the furnaces were to be run with acid lining. **1959** *Economist* 9 May 557/1 One can use hot-metal in them [*sc.* electric furnaces] by 'duplexing', blowing the hot iron in a Bessemer convertor..before feeding it into the arc furnace.

duplexity (dju:'plɛksɪtɪ). *rare.* [f. DUPLEX *a.* after *complexity*.] The quality of being double; doubleness. (Used occasionally instead of DUPLICITY (sense 2), to avoid the suggestion of sense 1.)

1856 DOVE *Logic Chr. Faith* VI. vi. 405 In the duplexity of method may be found the key. **1885** HUXLEY *Phys.* Index, Nervous apparatus, duplexity of.

‖**duplex querela** ('dju:plɛks kwɪ'ri:lə). [Law Latin, lit. twofold complaint.] (See quot. 1763.)

1713 E. GIBSON *Codex Juris Ecclesiastici Anglicani* XXXIII. viii. 823 He may appeal to the immediate Superiour..and thereupon obtain an Instrument directed to the Ordinary, and called *Duplex Querela*. **1763** R. BURN *Eccl. Law* I. 113 When the bishop doth..refuse, or unduly delay to admit and institute a clerk to the church to which he is presented, the clerk may have his remedy against the bishop in the ecclesiastical court..complaining to the judge of appeals thereof; the judge is wont to write to the bishop in the form of law, and this writing they call a duplex querela. This duplex querela is to contain a monition to the bishop. **1845** H. W. CRIPPS *Pract. Treat. Laws rel. Ch. & Clergy* v. i. 480 Where a refusal is appealed against, the dean of the arches, or other judge or judges of the court of appeal, sends a letter to the bishop so refusing, which letter or rescript is called *duplex querela*. **1895** J. WILLIAMS *Briefless Ballads* 62 Aid me, Muses!..for *duplex querela* is an uninviting theme. **1931** *Church Times* 20 Feb. 223/1 The Clerk might have commenced proceedings by *Duplex querela* in the Arches Court, but for weighty reasons this was turned down.

†**'duplic.** *Obs.* In 6 -icke, 7 -ique. [a. F. *duplique* sb. (1512 in Hatz.-Darm.), med.L. *duplica* 'iterata responsio in litigiis' (Du Cange), f. F. *dupliquer*, L. *duplicāre*, to double.] = DUPLY *sb.*, DUPLICATION 3.

1563-87 FOXE *A. & M.* (1596) 984/2 Then after, at the daies appointed, went forth with replication duplicke, with other answeres ech to other in writing what they could. **1682** *Lond. Gaz.* No. 1747/2 Making a Duplique to the last Reply of the French Ambassadors.

†**duplicament.** *Obs. rare.* [f. L. *duplicā-re* to double: see -MENT.] A duplicate, a copy.

1574 in H. Hall *Soc. in Eliz. Age* (1886) 161, I delivered him the Duplycamente of his Accompte. *Ibid.*, Wch sayde Duplycamente is enrolled before Mr. Fanshawe.

dupli'cand, 'duplicando. *Sc. Law.* [L. *duplicando* (in feu charters written in Latin) 'with or by doubling', used in Engl. context with sense 'doubling', and now usually anglicized as *duplicand*.] The doubling of feu-duty for one year, on the occasion of the admission of an heir or assignee, or at certain specified intervals, as e.g. at the 20th, 25th, or 30th year; a double feu-duty so paid.

1769 *Morrison's Dict. of Decisions* 15059 'Necnon duplicando dictam feudifirmam primo anno introitus cujuslibet heredis aut assignati.' **1777** *Ibid.* 15053 The superior is bound to enter an heir..for a mere *duplicando* of the feu-duty. **1804** *Ibid.* 15040 On payment of the *duplicando* or other composition. **1838** DUFF *Feudal Convey.* ii. ii. §56 ¶4 With respect to the *duplicand* or *relief* due by an heir, it ought to be expressed in the charter. *Ibid.* The duplicand or casuality of relief may be renounced. **1892** *Scottish Feu Charter*, 'As also paying to me and my foresaids a duplicand or additional sum of one pound ten shillings sterling at the expiration of every period of twenty years from Whitsunday..1892.'

duplicate ('dju:plɪkət), *a.* and *sb.* [ad. L. *duplicāt-us* doubled, pa. pple. of *duplicāre* to double: see next.]

A. *adj.* **1. a.** Double, twofold, consisting of two corresponding parts; that is made or exists in two corresponding examples.

1432-50 tr. *Higden* (Rolls) I. 125 Galile is a region betwene the Iewery and Palestine, whiche is duplicate, the superior and inferior. **1533-4** *Act 25 Hen. VIII*, c. 21 §12 No man..shal pay any more..then shalbe..limitted in the saide duplicate bokes of taxes. **1657** HOBBES *Absurd Geom.* Wks. 1845 VII. 382 Euclid has but one word for double and duplicate. **1670** W. SIMPSON *Hydrol. Ess.* 152 Nitro-aluminous, or duplicate salt. **1856** DOVE *Logic Chr. Faith* v. i. §1. 248 Astronomy is a science of duplicate origin. **1882** PEBODY *Eng. Journ.* xx. 148 The *Standard* is a morning and an evening paper, and is the only London newspaper which now appears in this duplicate form.

b. ***duplicate ague***: see DUPLICATED 3.

1822-34 GOOD *Study Med.* (ed. 4) I. 607 The fifth species [i.e. complicated ague] is distinguished from the rest by its peculiar complexity, consisting of double tertians, triple tertians, unequal tertians, duplicate tertians.

2. Double, doubled; consisting of twice the number or quantity.

1548 HALL *Chron., Hen. VII*, (an. 6) (1550) 23 The estates of Bruges little doubted to admit so small a nombre into so populous a company, ye though the numbre were duplicate. **1883** *Syd. Soc. Lex.* s.v., Double, duplicate. Applied to flowers having a double row of petals.

3. That is the exact counterpart or 'double' of something already in existence: applied to any number of such copies or specimens of a thing.

1812 J. SMYTH *Pract. of Customs* App. (1821) 375 Sometimes..goods..are included with other goods, in a warrant passed in the Wood Farm Office; in which case the Landing Waiter is furnished with a duplicate warrant from thence, as his authority for the delivery. **1847** EMERSON *Repr. Men, Montaigne* Wks. I. 341 The duplicate copy of Florio, which the British Museum purchased. **1863** P. BARRY *Dockyard Econ.* 194 For each ship of war there are duplicate boilers, either in store, in hand, or in contemplation. **1895** *Stanley Gibbons' Stamp Catal.* 593 A convenient means of keeping duplicate or superfluous stamps.

4. ***duplicate proportion, ratio***: the proportion or ratio of squares, in relation to that of the radical quantities.

1678 HOBBES *Decam.* v. 57 'Tis because all heavie Bodies Naturally descend with proportion of swiftness duplicate to that of the time. **1794** SULLIVAN *View Nat.* II. 386 All the particles of matter attracting one another in the reciprocal duplicate ratio of their distances. **1827** HUTTON *Course Math.* I. 330 If any number of quantities be continued proportionals; the ratio of the first to the third, will be duplicate or the square of the ratio of the first and second. **1831** BREWSTER *Newton* (1855) I. xii. 309 He must have been acquainted with the duplicate proportion before his conversation with Hooke.

5. ***duplicate bridge, whist***, a type of bridge or whist in which the hands are replayed by different persons.

1891 J. T. MITCHELL (*title*) Duplicate whist. Its rules and methods of play. **1894** R. F. FOSTER *Duplicate Whist* 27 The theory of duplicate whist, or Rejoué,.. is that the play of each of the competitors.. shall be contrasted with that of the others, by giving to each the same cards, with the same advantages or disadvantages of position at the table, an equal number of times. **1929** M. C. WORK *Bridge Pointers & Tests* 184 *Duplicate Auction Bridge*, a form of the game in which the hands are played more than once (*i.e.*, over-played). **1959** *Listener* 13 Aug. 262/1 In duplicate bridge 50 points are added for all part-score contracts.

6. *Genetics.* Designating one of two or more non-allelic genes having indistinguishable effects.

1914 G. H. SHULL in *Zeitschrift für Induktive Abstammungs- und Vererbungslehre* XII. 96 (*heading*) Duplicate genes for capsule-form in *Bursa bursa-pastoris*. *Ibid.* 120 By 'duplicate' determiners I understand those which, when separated from each other, produce characters so like that they can not be distinguished from one another. **1949** DARLINGTON & MATHER *Elem. Genetics* 410 Two genes of identical but non-cumulative effect are said to be *duplicate*. **1951** *Cold Spring Harbor Symp. Quant. Biol.* XVI. 162/1 We also assume that the component genes are not identical; i.e., that they do not represent duplicate genes which have yet to diverge in function.

B. *sb.* [absol. use of the adj.; in F. *duplicata*, a. med.L. *duplicata* (*charta*, etc.)]

1. One of two things exactly alike, so that each is the 'double' of the other; especially, that which is made from or after the other. **a.** A second copy of a letter or official document, having the legal force of the original: whether made along with it, for separate custody or transmission, or prepared subsequently to take the place of the other in case of loss. **b.** The second copy of a bill drawn in two parts; a 'second of exchange'. **c.** A pawnbroker's ticket.

1532 SIR J. RUSSELL in Ellis *Orig. Lett.* Ser. II. I. 303, I do send a post unto your Highnes with the duplicate of these my said Lettres who goyth by Alemaignie. **1575** in W. H. Turner *Select. Rec. Oxford* (1880) 374 Two duplicats thereof to be signed. **1641** *Termes de la Ley* 130 Duplicat is a second letters Patents graunted by the Lord Chancellour, in case where hee hath graunted the same before, and therefore they are held void by M. Crompton. **1648** CROMWELL *Let.* 2 Oct. in *Carlyle*, Duplicates of all which I have sent to the Committee at Derby House, and therefore forbear to trouble you with the things themselves. **1683** *Col. Rec. Pennsylv.* I. 20 That a transcript or Duplicate of all lawes, be transmitted to the privy Councell. **1818** CRUISE *Digest* (ed. 2) VI. 113 The original and duplicate being but one will, they must stand or fall together. **1828** WEBSTER s.v., A second letter or bill of exchange exactly like the first is called a duplicate. **1836-9** DICKENS *Sk. Boz, Pawnbroker's Shop* (D.), This elegantly attired individual is in the act of entering the duplicate he has just made out in a thick book. **1838** —— *O. Twist* xxxviii, 'It was a pawnbroker's duplicate'. **1862** C. STRETTON *Chequered Life* II. 147 The moment you have cashed your duplicate, which you are certain to receive by next mail.. go to the office.. and take your berth for Liverpool. **1874** STUBBS *Const. Hist.* I xi. 379 The rolls of the treasurer and chancellor were duplicates.

2. a. Generally, a thing which is the exact counterpart or 'double' of another reckoned the original or primary specimen; one of two or more specimens of anything exactly or virtually alike: in this sense there may be any number of 'duplicates'.

1701 NORRIS *Ideal World* I. ii. 50 So that one man is but the duplicate or counterpart of another. **1705** HEARNE *Collect.* 3 Dec., We will part with duplicates [of coins]. **1762-71** H. WALPOLE *Vertue's Anecd. Paint.* (1786) II. 23 He commonly made duplicates of his pictures, reserving one of each for himself. **1771** SWINTON in *Phil. Trans.* LXI. 350 It is so similar to the former.. that it may almost.. pass for a duplicate of the same coin. **1820** LAMB *Elia* Ser. I. *Oxford in Vac.*, As if a man should suddenly encounter his own duplicate. **1890** OGILVIE *Postage Stamps* 11 Friends.. will soon supply you with plenty of duplicates which you can utilize for exchanges.

b. A word which is in sense exactly the same as another; a synonym.

1839 H. ROGERS *Ess.* II. iii. 147 These languages, more especially the Latin, have furnished us with duplicates of many words of common objects, which add much to the variety and harmony of expression.

3. ***in duplicate***: in two exactly corresponding copies or transcripts.

[**1627** SIR N. HYDE in *St. Trials* (1735) VII. 140/1 This was certified under the hands of all the Judges.. in a duplicate, whereof the one was delivered to the Lord Chancellor, and the other to the Lord Treasurer. **1660** PEPYS *Diary* 21 July, I.. went to get Mr. Spong to engross it [the agreement] in duplicates.] **1884** *Harper's Mag.* June 61/1 Receipts for refunds are taken in duplicate.

4. *ellipt.* for *duplicate bridge, whist* (see sense A. 5 above). Also *attrib.*

1894 R. F. FOSTER *Duplicate Whist* 23 'Duplicate' is looked upon as the coming game. **1898** C. E. LEIBOLD *Woman Proposes* xvi. 171, I am primed for a spirited game of duplicate. Come, get ready. **1929** M. C. WORK *Complete Contract Bridge* 237 *Duplicate*, a form of the game in which the hands are played more than once (i.e., overplayed). **1963** *Listener* 17 Jan. 137/1 This point is dealt with in a different manner in the Duplicate Laws.

duplicate ('djuːplɪkeɪt), *v.* [f. L. *duplicāt-*, ppl. stem of *duplicāre*, f. *duplex*, *duplicem*, double.]

1. *trans.* To double; to multiply by two; to make double or twofold; to redouble.

1623 COCKERAM, *Duplicate*, to double. **1650** BULWER *Anthropomet.* 101 To duplicate the analogy. *a* **1652** J. SMITH *Sel. Disc.* iv. 100 Requiring them to duplicate the dimensions of Apollo's altar. **1660** F. BROOKE tr. *Le Blanc's Trav.* 308 Their wailings and lamentations, which they duplicate when they come together. **1674** JEAKE *Arith.* (1696) 24 As 4372 duplicated.. is.. 8744. **1884** *Pall Mall G.* 16 Oct. 5/2 The Eastern Extension Telegraph Company.. have decided to duplicate the cables which are not duplicated over their lines.

2. To make or provide in duplicate; to make the double or exact copy of; to repeat.

1860 EMERSON *Cond. Life, Fates* (1861) 14 Copying or duplicating his own structure. **1880** *Times* 27 Dec. 9/4 To provide against the possibility of a breakdown.. all the vital parts are duplicated. **1883** H. DRUMMOND *Nat. Law in Spir. W.* x. 330 It is a case which is being duplicated every day in our own country. **1895** *Tablet* 7 Dec. 900 Many of the official pieces were almost certain to be duplicated.

†**3.** *intr.* for *refl.* To become doubled. *Obs.*

1646 SIR T. BROWNE *Pseud. Ep.* III. xx. 156 If we abduce the eye unto either corner, the object will not duplicate. **1649** JER. TAYLOR *Gt. Exemp.* v. §6 The desires of man.. if they pass upon an end or aim of difficulty or ambition,.. duplicate and grow to a disturbance.

†**b.** To double or fold on itself. *Obs.*

1638 SIR T. HERBERT *Trav.* (ed. 2) 325 Pepper.. in the growth supported by poles or canes, about which it entwines and duplicates with many embraces.

4. *Eccl.* (*absol.*) To celebrate the Eucharist twice in one day.

1865 F. G. LEE *Direct. Angl.* (ed. 2) 196 If the Priest has to duplicate, i.e. to celebrate twice in one day, he must not drink the ablutions. **1881** T. E. BRIDGETT *Hist. Holy Eucharist* II. x. 132 Rebuking priests who said mass frequently, sometimes duplicating out of avarice.

Hence '**duplicating** *ppl. a.*

1805-17 R. JAMESON *Char. Min.* (ed. 3) 79 Iceland or duplicating spar.

'**duplicated**, *ppl. a.* [f. prec. + -ED¹.]

1. Doubled, made in duplicate, repeated.

1643 PRYNNE *Sov. Power Parl.* II. 30 Sundry duplicated deepe Asseverations. *a* **1661** FULLER *Worthies* II. (1662) 274 Single flowers are observed much sweeter than.. such flowers which are duplicated. **1801** HOOKE in *Phil. Trans.* XCII. 40 This confused or duplicated pulse.. does produce on the retina, the sensation of a yellow. **1896** T. MARTIN *Æneid* IV. (470) When he sees.. two suns And duplicated Thebes before him rise.

†**2.** Doubled back. *Obs.*

1741 MONRO *Anat. Nerves* (ed. 3) 73 The Edges of the.. Valves are duplicated with a muscular Corpuscle in the Middle. **1741** —— *Anat. Bones* (ed. 3) 210 The duplicated Tendon of the *Musculus descendens abdominis*.

3. *Pathol.* 'Applied to intermittent fevers in which two paroxysms occur during the time in which one is usual; the two paroxysms being unlike to each other, but each like the corresponding one of the following period' (*Syd. Soc. Lex.*, 1883).

'**duplicately**, *adv. rare.* [f. DUPLICATE *a.* + -LY².] In a double or twofold manner or measure.

1660 tr. *Paracelsus' Archidoxis* II. 145 If there happens a twofold need.. of Medicine.. then administer also duplicatly to the Paralitick.

'**duplicating**, *vbl. sb.* [f. DUPLICATE *v.*] The action of the vb. Also *attrib.*, as ***duplicating machine*** (cf. *writing engine*), ***paper***.

1659 FULLER *App. Inj. Innoc.* (1840) 316 Who.. hath represented all my faults in a duplicating glass. **1893** J. T. DAVIS *U.S. Pat.* 494,060 4/2 The duplicating machine writes and spaces simultaneously with the initial machine. **1914** E. A. DAWE *Paper* xvii. 120 *Duplicating papers*, unsized or half-sized papers used for taking copies on cyclostyle, mimeograph and similar duplicating machines. **1962** A. NISBETT *Technique Sound Studio* ii. 40 Use a fairly stiff paper (duplicating paper is quite good). **1969** D. TRIESMAN in Cockburn & Blackburn *Student Power* 153 A minority report which the Executive turned out on some duplicating paper.

duplication (djuːplɪ'keɪʃən). [a. F. *duplication* (13th c. in Godef.), ad. L. *duplicātiōn-em*, n. of action from L. *duplicāre* to double.]

1. The action of doubling. †**a.** *Arith.* Multiplication by two. *Obs.*

c **1430** *Art Nombryng* (E.E.T.S.) 7 Duplicacioun is agregacion of nombre þat me may se the nombre growen. In doublynge ay is but one ordre of figures necessarie. **1674** JEAKE *Arith.* (1696) 24 Duplication is nothing else but to double every figure of the Multiplicand.

b. The making anything twice as many or as much; the repetition of an action or thing; division into two by natural growth or spontaneous division.

1590 SWINBURNE *Testaments* 168 There be duplication of notable members, as to haue four armes, or two heades. **1649** JER. TAYLOR *Gt. Exemp.* v. Ad sect. vii. §1 The duplication of their joys. **1770** SWINTON in *Phil. Trans.* LXI. 86 A duplication of consonants, in writing, having been unknown to the most ancient Etruscans. **1831** BREWSTER *Nat. Magic* vi. (1833) 154 It could only have been produced by a duplication of one of the figures produced by unequal refraction. **1847** GROTE *Greece* II. xlvii. (1862) IV. 149 The alleged duplication of the tribute. **1869** ROSCOE *Elem. Chem.* 291 This duplication of the carbon element.. by a combination of one of the four combining units of one atom with one of the four units of the other atom.

c. *Math.* ***duplication of the cube***: The problem of finding the side of a cube having double the volume of a given cube; the DELIAN (*a.*¹) problem, q.v.

duplication formula, a formula for obtaining the sine or other trigonometrical function of the double of an angle from the corresponding function of the angle itself.

1660 STANLEY *Hist. Philos.* IX. (1701) 435/2 Amongst his Geometrical Inventions also must be remembered the Duplication of a Cube. **1754** *Dict. Arts & Sc.* II. 992 The duplication of a Cube is a problem famous in antiquity. **1837** *Penny Cycl.* IX. 203.

d. *Music.* See DOUBLE *v.* 1 c.

e. *Genetics.* The existence in a set of chromosomes of two copies of a particular chromosome segment; the process by which this comes about; also, the duplicated segment.

1917 C. B. BRIDGES in *Genetics* II. 454 As evidence that pieces may be lost bodily from chromosomes and that fragments may join together, there may be offered two distinct cases of 'duplication' (unpublished), a phenomenon, the explanation of which seems to be that a section taken from the mid-region of one X has become attached to the end of the other X, its mate. **1945** *Genetics* XXX. 161 The position effect, here, would appear to extend over a distance at least as great as the length of the duplication. **1949** DARLINGTON & MATHER *Elem. Genetics* v. 105 Heterozygous deficiencies and duplications are.. for segments what monosomics and trisomics are for whole chromosomes. **1965** PEACOCKE & DRYSDALE *Molec. Basis Heredity* vii. 77 These results are those expected if the interphase chromosome before duplication contains two components each of which remains intact.. during chromosome duplication. **1965** A. M. SRB et al. *Gen. Genetics* (ed. 2) vii. 198 Extra parts of chromosomes are called duplications. Various kinds of duplications have been observed. Some exist attached to the chromosome whose segments are 'repeated'; some are attached to different chromosomes; others may exist as independent fragments.

2. A duplicate copy or version; a counterpart.

1872 HARDWICK *Trad. Lanc.* 219 Appears to be but a duplication of the Tarquin legend. **1893** J. INGLIS *Oor Ain Folk* iv. (1894) 41 There were numberless duplications of Jeems Wright.

3. a. *Civil* and *Canon Law.* A pleading on the part of the defendant in reply to the replication, corresponding to the rejoinder at common law.

1622 MALYNES *Anc. Law-Merch.* 476 The courts of Equitie beyond the seas, after bill and answere, replication and reioynder, and sometimes duplication, and at last conclusion [etc.]. **1726** AYLIFFE *Parergon* 251 Duplications are those Exceptions, which the Defendant made use of to repel the Plaintiffs Replication. **1880** MUIRHEAD *Gaius* IV. §127 [If] a replication.. operates inequitably against the defender; in that case an additional clause is added on his account, which gets the name of duplication.

b. *transf.*

1621 BURTON *Anat. Mel.* Democr. to Rdr. 11 To haue written in controuersie, had bin to cut off an Hydra's head, *lis litem generat*, one begets another, so many duplications, triplications, and swarmes of questions.

†**4.** *Anat.* **a.** A folding, a doubling; *concr.* a fold.

1578 BANISTER *Hist. Man* VII. 90 The Cause of this duplication [of the pleura]. **1676** WISEMAN *Surgery* (J.), The peritonæum is a strong membrane, every where double; in the duplications of which all the viscera of the abdomen are hid. **1748** tr. *Renatus' Distemp. Horses* 170 A Ganglion is a Tuber or Tumour which is formed of the Duplication of a Nerve.

†**b.** = DIPLOE 1. *Obs.*

1615 CROOKE *Body of Man* 447 To the duplication of the skull, that is to the porie substance between the tables thereof.

5. *Eccl.* 'A second celebration by the same priest on the same day.'

1866 F. G. LEE *Direct. Angl.* (ed. 3) 354.

duplicative ('djuːplɪkətɪv), *a.* and *sb.* [f. L. *duplicāt-*, ppl. stem of *duplicāre* to double + -IVE.]

A. *adj.* Having the quality of doubling; producing two instead of one.

c **1870** CARPENTER (O.), The multiplication of cells by duplicative subdivision.

B. *sb.* A doubling addition.

1884 *Athenæum* 23 Aug. 235/2 Clack, near Bradenstock, is the Celtic *cleg*, a hill.. Clay Hill.. is simply *cleg*, with a duplicative to make it intelligible.

'**dupli,cato-**, combining adverbial form of L. *duplicātus* doubled, prefixed to adjs. in the sense 'doubly'; esp. in *Botany*, as ***duplicato-dentate***, ***-pinnate***, ***-serrate***, ***-ternate***, applied to toothed, pinnate, etc. leaves, of which the teeth, pinnæ, etc. are themselves again dentate, pinnate, and so on.

1753 CHAMBERS *Cycl. Supp.* s.v. *Leaf, Duplicato-ternatea Leaf*, one consisting of leaves, which are themselves composed of three leaves each. 1845 LINDLEY *Sch. Bot.* i. (1858) 9 In like manner we have the terms bicrenate and bidentate, or rather duplicato-dentate.

duplicator ('dju:plɪkeɪtə(r)). [agent-n. in L. form f. DUPLICATE *v.*: see -OR.] A machine for producing copies. Also *attrib.*

1893 J. T. DAVIS *U.S. Pat.* 494,060 (*title*) Combined type-writing machine and duplicator. 1894 *Westm. Gaz.* 1 Jan. 7/2 The matter being closely type-written on six foolscap pages and the copies produced by a duplicator apparatus. 1916 'BOYD CABLE' *Doing their Bit* ii. 36 You know what a duplicator is? Thing for printing copies off a typed stencil sheet. 1939–40 *Army & Navy Stores Catal.* 327/1 A compact duplicator... Will copy Handwriting, Typewriting, Drawings, Plans.

† **duplicatory**, *a. Obs. rare.* [f. as prec. + -ORY.] Having the quality of doubling; in quot. used for: Double, twofold.

1659 D. PELL *Impr. Sea* 562 A duplicatory reason of this desire; 1: For... 2. For...

duplicature ('dju:plɪkeɪtjʊə(r)). [a. F. *duplicature* (16th c.), f. L. *duplicāt-*, ppl. stem of *duplicāre* to DUPLICATE: see -URE.] A doubling; a fold. (Chiefly in *Anat.*)

1686 SNAPE *Anat. Horse* I. xx. 42 Seeing it is onely a Duplicature of the common coverings of the Body. 1727–51 CHAMBERS *Cycl.* s.v. *Duplication*, The Duplicature of the cube. 1796 MORSE *Amer. Geog.* I. 203 A duplicature of the skin connects the fore and hinder legs together. 1854 WOODWARD *Mollusca* II. 279 The internal muscular ridges are produced by duplicatures of the shell-wall.

duplicidentate (,dju:plɪsɪ'dɛntət), *a. Zool.* [f. L. *duplici-*, comb. form of *duplex* (see DUPLEX) + DENTATE: cf. F. *duplicidenté*.] Belonging to the *Duplicidentata*, a division of rodents characterized by two pairs of upper incisor teeth.

duplicipennate (-'pɛnət), *a. Entom.* [f. as prec. + L. *pennātus* winged.] 'Having the wings folded longitudinally when in repose' (*Syd. Soc. Lex.*).

duplicity (dju:'plɪsɪtɪ). Also 5–6 -te, 6–7 -tie. [a. F. *duplicité* (13th c.), ad. L. *duplicitāt-em*, n. of quality f. *duplex, duplic-em*: see DUPLEX.]

1. The quality of being 'double' in action or conduct (see DOUBLE *a.* 5); the character or practice of acting in two ways at different times, or openly and secretly; deceitfulness, double-dealing. (The earliest and still the most usual sense.)

c 1430 LYDG. *Min. Poems* 165 (Mätz.) In symulacioune is false duplicite. 1503 HAWES *Examp. Virt.* v. (Arb.) 19 Wo worth the man full of duplycyte. 1597 J. PAYNE *Royal Exch.* 14 Suche ys the choyce that these make of duplicitie and hypocrisie. 1650 BULWER *Anthropomet.* 143 Whether this Duplicity of Tongue be in them *Lusus Naturæ*, or a meer Device of Art. 1771 *Junius Lett.* lii. 267 I am astonished he does not see through your Duplicity. 1828 D'ISRAELI *Chas. I*, I. vi. 206 We have here complete evidence of the duplicity of the King's conduct.

2. *lit.* The state or quality of being numerically or physically double or twofold: doubleness.

1589 PUTTENHAM *Eng. Poesie* III. xviii. (Arb.) 205 Because of the darkenes and duplicitie of his sence. 1688 BOYLE *Final Causes Nat.* iv. 163 Nature has furnished men with double parts..where that duplicity may be highly useful. 1764 REID *Inquiry* vi. §13. Wks. I. 165/2 We as invariably see two objects unite into one, and, in appearance, lose their duplicity. 1863 C. PRITCHARD in *Smith's Dict. Bible* III. 1375 The duplicity of the two stars must have been apparent. 1867–77 G. F. CHAMBERS *Astron.* VIII. 769 The duplicity of Saturn's ring. 1892 MIVART *Ess. & Crit.* I. 403 Due to non-appreciation of our duplicity in unity.

3. *Law.* The pleading of two (or more) matters in one plea; double pleading.

[1628 COKE *On Litt.* 304 The Plea that containes duplicity or multiplicity of distinct matter to one and the same thing ..is not allowable in Law.] 1848 WHARTON *Law Lex.*, *Duplicity.* See *Double Pleading.*

Hence **du'plicitous** *a.*, showing duplicity, deceitful.

1961 in WEBSTER. 1966 *New Statesman* 11 Mar. 350/3 Peggy Mount, as the duplicitous washerwoman,..subdues her comic extravagance. 1969 G. LEFF *Hist. & Soc. Theory* ii. 44 Whether John was contrite or merely duplicitous in acceding to the barons' demands in 1215 is irrelevant to the meaning of Magna Carta.

† **duplify**, *v. Obs.* [f. L. *duplus* double: see -FY.] *trans.* To make double, to double.

1509 HAWES *Past. Pleas.* 122 Wherfore by reason I must be duplyfyde. 1602 W. BAS *Sword & Buckler* B ij b, Your slight regard and recompence of this, So duplifies the bondage of our state. 1649 BULWER *Pathomyot.* II. i. 73 Duplifying the single motion.

Hence **duplifi'cation**, the action of doubling.

1821 GALT *Ann. Parish* xlviii. 157 I was pleased to see the duplification of well-doing, as I think marrying is.

duplo- ('dju:pləʊ). [L. *dupl-us* double.] Used in chemical nomenclature with the sense 'double' or 'twofold', as ***duplo-carburet***, twofold carburet.

1872 WATTS *Dict. Chem.* VII. 442 *Duplosulphacetone.*

duply (dju:'plaɪ), *sb. Sc. Law. Obs.* exc. *Hist.* Usually in *pl.* [f. med.L. *duplica* 'iterata responsio in litigiis' Du Cange; cf. F. *duplique*, and *reply* = F. *réplique*.] A second reply; a defender's rejoinder to a pursuer's reply. (Now abolished.)

1609 SKENE *Reg. Maj.*, *Forme of Proces* 121 Quhen ane exception onely, or ane exception with ane duply, is admitted to probation of the defender. *a* 1693 URQUHART *Rabelais* III. xxxix. 326 Duplies, Triplies, Answers to Rejoinders. 1760 in *Scotsman* (1885) 20 Aug. 5/3 Having considered the petition of the Magistrates..answers thereto, replies, duplies, and triplies with the writs produced. 1881 J. RUSSELL *Haigs* viii. 210 Counsel on both sides, with many replies, duplies, and triplies, discussed the question of its relevancy.

b. *transf.* In a controversy, the rejoinder that comes fourth in order after the original assertion.

1638 (*title*) Duplyes of the Ministers and Professors of Aberdene to the Second Answeres of some Reverend Brethren. 1676 W. ROW *Contn. Blair's Autobiog.* xi. (1848) 340 Replies were made by Monks and duplies by them. 1820 SCOTT *Abbot* i, Answers, replies, duplies, triplies, quadruplies, followed thick upon each other. 1873 BURTON *Hist. Scot.* VI. lxxi. 235 To the Demands there were 'Answers', to these came 'Replies' by the Doctors, and then second Answers, and finally 'Duplies' by the Doctors.

Hence **du'ply** *v.*, to make a duply.

1631 in Cobbett *State Trials* III. 444 (Trial Lord Uchiltrie), It is duplyed for the Pannel by his Prolocutors, as to the particulars contained in my Lord Advocate's Answer. 1818 SCOTT *Hrt. Midl.* xii, *Advocatus* for Lackland duplies that..the pursuer must put his case under the statute.

dupondius (dju:'pɒndɪəs). *Roman Antiq.* Earlier also **dipondius**. Pl. **dupondii**. [L.] A bronze or brass coin of the value of two asses.

1601 HOLLAND *Pliny* XXXIII. iii. II. 462 Like as the weight in brasse of two pound, they named Dipondius. 1853 H. N. HUMPHREYS *Coin Collector's Man.* II. 378 The second bronze, which was called the dupondius, or double as, was ..exactly half the sestertius. 1937 *Oxoniensia* II. 67 The large bronze coins, *sestertii, dupondii* and *asses*, which are representative of the first two centuries of Roman occupation.

duporthite (dju:'pɔːθaɪt). *Min.* [Named 1877, from Duporth in Cornwall: see -ITE.] A silicate of alumina and other bases, occurring in greyish fibres in serpentine.

1877 *Min. Mag.* I. 226 Duporthite, a new asbestiform mineral.

duppa, dupper, var. DUBBA.

duppion, var. DUPION.

duppy ('dʌpɪ). [Understood to be of African origin.] Name among West Indian negroes for a ghost or spirit.

1774 LONG *Hist. Jamaica* II. 416 They firmly believe in the apparition of spectres. Those of deceased friends are *duppies*; others..like our raw-head-and-bloody-bones, are called *bugaboos*. 1834 M. G. LEWIS *Jrnl. West Ind.*, The negroes are..very much afraid of ghosts, whom they call the duppy. 1885 LADY BRASSEY *The Trades* 215 After dark nothing would induce them to pass the mangrove-swamps or cockle-ponds, for fear of 'Duppies'. 1896 N. DARNELL DAVIS (Br. Guiana) in *Letter*, Only last Saturday morning, my butler was told by a man that 'the Duppies had been troubling the telephone wire'.

Dupuytren (dypɥitrɛn). The name of Baron Guillaume *Dupuytren* (1777–1835), French surgeon, used in the possessive to designate certain conditions observed or appliances, etc., invented by him. **Dupuytren's contraction** or **contracture**, a painless disorder of the fibrous tissue of the palm that leads to fixed flexion of one or more fingers and affects chiefly old people; **Dupuytren's fracture**, fracture of the fibula just above the malleolus; **Dupuytren's method** (see quot. 1887); **Dupuytren's paste** (see quot. 1886); **Dupuytren's splint**, a splint to prevent eversion in Pott's fracture.

1876 O. W. MADELUNG (*title*) The causes and operative treatment of Dupuytren's finger contraction. 1880 *Brit. Med. Jrnl.* 19 June 919/1 (*title*) Dupuytren's fracture of the fibula. 1883 HOLMES & HULKE *Syst. Surg.* (ed. 3) I. 1093 Dupuytren's splint is often used, and is good when properly applied. 1886 *Buck's Handbk. Med. Sci.* II. 7 Dupuytren's paste was made of from six to ten parts by weight of arsenic, and one hundred of calomel. *Ibid.* III. 159 Dupuytren's Finger-contraction.—This deformity is dependent chiefly upon chronic disease and contraction of the palmar aponeurosis. 1887 *Ibid.* V. 197 Dupuytren's Method. A method of amputating at the shoulder-joint. 1895 *Treves's Syst. Surg.* I. 870 Dupuytren's splint..a 'long splint' in miniature, should be padded with increasing thickness from the knee down to the ankle. 1908 *Practitioner* Feb. 279 Treatment of Dupuytren's contraction by thiosinamine. 1947 E. B. KRUMBHAAR tr. *Castiglioni's Hist. Med.* (ed. 2) xix. 713 Baron Guillaume Dupuytren... His descriptions of varicose aneurysms, of fracture of the lower end of the fibula (Dupuytren's fracture, 1819) and the characteristic flexion of one or more fingers due to contraction of the palmar fascia (Dupuytren's contraction,..) are classic. 1966 WRIGHT & SYMMERS *Systemic Path.* II. xxxviii. 1447/2 Fibromatosis of the plantar fascia of the feet is much less frequent than Dupuytren's contracture.

dur, obs. form of DARE *v.*[1], DOOR.

dura[1] (djʊərə). [L. *dūra* adj. fem. 'hard'.]

1. Short for DURA MATER.

1882 WILDER & GAGE *Anatom. Technol.* 447 Notwithstanding its feminine form, *dura* is frequently employed without the substantive *mater*. 1886 *Med. News* XLIX. 536 The dura was universally adherent on both hemispheres. 1890 F. P. FOSTER *Med. Dict.* 2166 *Ligamentum dentatum*..Its outer edge is serrated, the serrations being adherent to the inner surface of the spinal dura.

2. = DURAMEN.

dura[2], var. DURRA, DHURRA.

durability (djʊərə'bɪlɪtɪ). [a. obs. F. *durabilité*, ad. late L. *dūrābilitāt-em* (Palladius), f. *dūrābilis* DURABLE.] The quality of being durable.

1. Continuance; lastingness, permanence.

c 1374 CHAUCER *Boeth.* III. pr. xi. 78 (Camb. MS.) By the whiche is sustenyd the longe durablete of mortal thinges. *c* 1400 tr. *Secreta Secret., Gov. Lordsh.* (E.E.T.S.) 67 þat all delitable þinges of þys world..þat þay ben alle for long-lastynge of durabilyte..lyflode for lastynge ys to be had, and noght durabilite for liflode. *a* 1677 BARROW *Serm.* Wks. 1687 I. 164 The Prophets..assign the character of perpetual durability thereto. 1812 D'ISRAELI *Calam. Auth.* (1867) 224 Pope hesitated at deciding on the durability of his poetry. 1891 *Spectator* 27 June, Nor has there ever been an explanation of this durability in the Jew..which in the least satisfies or convinces any reflecting mind.

2. Capability of withstanding decay or wear.

a 1600 HOOKER (J.), Stones, though in dignity of nature inferior unto plants, yet exceed them in..durability of being. 1794 G. ADAMS *Nat. & Exp. Philos.* II. xx. 370 Colours..greatly superior both in beauty and durability. 1860 TYNDALL *Glac.* I. xx, The great density and durability of the rock. 1879 *Cassell's Techn. Educ.* III. 184 Where doors are required to combine strength, beauty and durability.

durable ('djʊərəb(ə)l), *a.* [a. F. *durable* (11th c. in Littré) = It. *durabile*, Sp. *durable*, ad. rare L. *dūrābilis* lasting, durable, f. *dūrāre* to last, endure, hold out, f. *dūrus* hard, unyielding.]

1. Capable of lasting or continuing in existence; persistent, lasting; not transitory, permanent.

c 1386 CHAUCER *Pars. T.* ¶965 To han thynges espiritueel and durable and somtyme temporele thynges. *c* 1450 tr. *De Imitatione* III. xxxv. 103 Wiþoute me is noon availyng..ner durable remedie. 1582 N. LICHEFIELD tr. *Castanheda's Conq. E. Ind.* xxvi. 65 b, They thought this kinde of weather was alwayes durable there. 1667 MILTON *P.L.* v. 581 Time ..measures all things durable By present, past, and future. 1754 HUME *Hist. Eng.* I. x. 204 The compunction of Richard for his undutiful behaviour was durable. 1839 ALISON *Hist. Europe* (1849–50) VII. xli. §58. 63 Comparing his durable designs with the temporary expedients of the statesmen who ..followed him.

2. a. Able to withstand change, decay, or wear.

1398 TREVISA *Barth. de P.R.* XVII. lxxxiii. (Tollem. MS.) The tre þerof [of Ilex] is durable and stronge, and nyȝe nouȝt able to rote. 1470–85 MALORY *Arthur* XVII. vi, The best wood and moost durable that men maye fynde. 1555 EDEN *Decades* 42 To dye clothe with a more fayre and durable colour. 1638 SIR T. HERBERT *Trav.* (ed. 2) 134 Sun-burnt bricks, hard and durable. 1703 MOXON *Mech. Exerc.* 238 They make a good Pavement, and are very Durable. 1874 MICKLETHWAITE *Mod. Par. Churches* 225 Inscriptions are more durable incised than in relief.

b. *spec.* Designating a class of goods the usefulness of which continues over a period of time, as distinguished from goods produced for immediate consumption. Hence as *sb. pl.* (rarely *sing.*), goods of this kind (cf. *consumer durable* s.v. CONSUMER 2 c).

1930 *Economist* 31 May 1206/2 It includes an estimate of the value of services rendered to their owners by durable, direct or consumers' goods. 1948 G. CROWTHER *Outl. Money* (rev. ed.) v. 142 Some of them are for immediate consumption, the rest are goods whose value will last beyond the immediate present. These two categories can be called current goods and durable goods. 1951 *N.Y. Times* 14 Oct. F. 1 (*headline*) Production eases on some durables. 1957 *Economist* 7 Sept. 777/2 One can trace the rapid growth of engineering exports in the immediate postwar years, while investment and consumption of metal 'durables' grew more slowly. 1958 *Spectator* 12 Sept. 353/3 The spending on 'durables'—cars, refrigerators, television and radio sets and household furniture—increased by 64 per cent. 1959 *Listener* 15 Jan. 92/1 Bicycles, sewing machines, radio sets, three-piece suites, and all the various sorts of durable consumption goods that help to make life tolerable for Africans like the rest of us.

† **3.** Able to endure toil, fatigue, etc. *Obs.*

1540–1 ELYOT *Image Gov.* (1556) 4 Stronge and durable to susteigne peynes. 1596 DALRYMPLE tr. *Leslie's Hist. Scot.* I. 63 Thair horses ar verie litle..bot in labour meruellous durable. 1616 SURFL. & MARKH. *Country Farme* 708 French Goshawkes..are..neither so valiant, sound or durable, as those which are bred in Ireland.

† **4.** Capable of being endured, endurable. *Obs.*

1509 BARCLAY *Shyp of Folys* (1874) I. 194 A small diseas which is ynoughe durable At the begynnynge.

durableness ('djʊərəb(ə)lnɛs). Now *rare.* [f. prec. + -NESS.] The quality or condition of being durable.

1. = DURABILITY 1.

1587 GOLDING *De Mornay* ix. (1617) 141 The measuring of durablenesse..they call Time. **1668** H. MORE *Div. Dial.* IV. xxv. (1713) 350 *marg.*, The Apostacy of the Church, how consistent with the durableness of God's Kingdom. **1725** BRADLEY *Fam. Dict.* s.v. *Pease*, Pease, everlasting, so call'd because of its durableness. **1754** SHERLOCK *Disc.* (1764) II. 243 Speculating on the Durableness of Things without themselves.

2. = DURABILITY 2.

1579–80 NORTH *Plutarch* To Rdr. 1 (R.) There is neither picture, nor image of marble, nor arch of triumph..that can match the durableness of an eloquent history. **1669** WORLIDGE *Syst. Agric.* (1681) 90 No Timber natural to our English Soil exceeds the Oak, for its Plenty, Strength, and Durableness. **1776** ADAM SMITH *W.N.* I. xi. III. (1869) I. 221 The durableness of metals is the foundation of this steadiness of price. **1778** *Eng. Gazetteer* s.v. *Barrington*, A quarry of free-stone..noted for its durableness.

†**3.** Power of endurance. Cf. DURABLE 3. *Obs.*

1737 BRACKEN *Farriery Impr.* (1757) II. 50 He..exceeds our English Horse as to Durableness in travelling.

durably ('djʊərəblɪ), *adv.* [f. as prec. + -LY².]

1. In a durable or lasting manner; lastingly.

a **1586** SIDNEY (J.), Monuments engraved in marble, and yet more durably in men's memories. **1646** SIR T. BROWNE *Pseud. Ep.* VII. xvi. 374 Yet did not his Successors durably inherit that scruple. **1775** PRIESTLEY *On Air* I. 320 A durably elastic Vapour. **1831** LYTTON *Godolphin* 7 The habits of his mind were durably formed. **1868** E. EDWARDS *Raleigh* I. xv. 294 The play and the publication of the book strongly and durably affected Queen Elizabeth.

†**b.** Continually; continuously. *Obs.*

1555 ABP. PARKER *Ps.* xlv. 134 The people so shall durably, To thee aye thankes pronounce. **1688** BOYLE *Final Causes Nat. Things* i. 59 That weariness, which..that durably constrained posture would be sure to give them. **1797** HOLCROFT tr. *Stolberg's Trav.* (ed. 2) III. lxvii. 48 The mountain ceased to repeat its quick successive claps of thunder, and continued to roll it durably.

2. So as to withstand wear or decay.

1809 PINKNEY *Trav. France* 125 Others being more durably constructed, were still habitable.

†**duracine**, *a.* (*sb.*) *Obs.* [a. F. *duracine* (16th c. in Littré, first as adj.) stone fruit with hard pulp, ad. L. *dūracin-us* hard-berried, f. *dūrus* hard + *acinus* berry.]

A. *adj.* Applied to stone-fruit: Having a hard pulp. **B.** *sb.* A cherry with a hard pulp.

1578 LYTE *Dodoens* v. xl. 710 That kinde [of peach] whiche will not easily be separated from the stone, are called *Duracina.* **1601** HOLLAND *Pliny* I. 448 The Duracine Cherries be the soueraign, which in Campaine are called Pliniana. **1655** MOUFET & BENNET *Health's Improv.* (1746) 294 Duracines, or in French *Cœurs*, or Heart-Cherries,.. are the firmest of all other.

durain ('djʊəreɪn). [f. L. *dūrus* hard + *-ain* as in FUSAIN (sense 2).] A type of hard, compact coal forming a dull layer in a bituminous seam.

1919 [see CLARAIN]. **1930** *Engineering* 18 July 92/1 Vitrain and durain belonged to the former [coking coal] and fusain to the latter [non-coking coal] class. **1950** WILSON & WELLS *Coal, Coke, & Coal Chemicals* iii. 59 Exact correlation of the Bureau of Mines and the British terminologies, particularly the clarain and the durain of the latter, is not possible on account of the different bases for the classification. **1961** W. FRANCIS *Coal* (ed. 2) vi. 312 Generally American coals appear to contain much less durain than British coals.

†**'dural**, *a.*¹ *Mus. Obs.* [f. It. *duro* hard, harsh, in Music also 'sharp'.] = DURE *a.* 2.

1609 DOULAND *Ornith. Microl.* 14 The Scale ♮ Durall is a Progression of Musicall Voyces, rising from A to ♮ sharpely, that is, by the Voyce *Mi.* [**1753** CHAMBERS *Cycl. Supp.*, *Durale* or *Duro*, in the Italian music..This name is given to B natural, by reason its sound is sharp, when compared with B mol, or flat.]

dural ('djʊərəl), *a.*² [f. DURA¹ (*dura mater*) + -AL¹.] Of or pertaining to the dura mater.

1888 *Medical News* LII. 430 The dural vessels were well injected externally and internally. **1890** F. P. FOSTER *Med. Dict.*, *Dural*, pertaining to the dura.

dural ('djʊərəl), *sb.* Abbrev. of next.

1937 *Jrnl. R. Aeronaut. Soc.* XLI. 495 Standard dural tanks weigh approximately 0·47 to 0·38 lb. per gallon. *Ibid.* 588 Before these plastic materials can be considered as being on a par with steel, dural, or spruce. **1951** 'N. SHUTE' *Round Bend* 145 A seating scheme of long, hard dural benches.

Duralumin (djʊ'ræljuːmɪn). Also **duralumin**, **duraluminium**. [Perh. f. L. *dūrus* hard + ALUMIN(IUM: but see note below.] The proprietary name of a number of heat-treatable wrought aluminium alloys which contain copper and other elements and are comparable to mild steel in strength and hardness but are much lighter.

The name may have been derived from the German placename *Düren.* Heat-treatable light aluminium alloys were first produced by the Dürener Metallwerke Aktien Gesellschaft.

1910 *Blackw. Mag.* July 4 In this airship, and in the Barrow ship, another aluminium alloy called duralumin is employed. **1910** *Trade Marks Jrnl.* 7 Dec. 1941 Duralumin... An aluminium alloy. The Electric and Ordnance Accessories Company, Limited,..Aston, Birmingham. Manufacturers. **1917** A. G. CLARK *Motor Car Engin.* II. 53 A metal which has recently come into prominence on account of remarkable properties that it possesses is duralumin, which is manufactured by Vickers, Limited... This material combines lightness with great strength, has an excellent elongation, and may be forged. **1920** ANDREWS & BENSON *Aeroplane Design* 15 Duralumin is composed of aluminium, copper, manganese, and magnesium. **1921** *Glasgow Herald* 8 July 8/4 The aerohydrotor parts will be made chiefly of duraluminium wire stayed. **1925** E. F. NORTON *Fight for Everest, 1924* 131 The duralumin carriers. **1928** C. F. S. GAMBLE *N. Sea Air Station* 10 This hull was twelve-sided, the framework being built of the alloy duralumin. **1958** *Engineering* 7 Feb. 164/3 A skin of Duralumin..should be adequately resistant to meteoric particles. **1968** E. R. PETTY *Physical Metall. Engin. Materials* viii. 153 The true high strength alloys are the duralumins and the aluminium-copper-magnesium-zinc type.

‖**dura mater** ('djʊərə 'meɪtə(r)). *Anat.* [Med.L. = hard mother; literal translation of the Arabic *umm al-γalīdah* or *umm al-jāfīyah* (Bocthor) in the same sense, in accordance with the Arabic use of 'father', 'mother', 'son', etc. to indicate relations between things.] The dense, tough, outermost membranous envelope of the brain and spinal cord.

c **1400** *Lanfranc's Cirurg.* 112 An hard pannicle þat is to seie a cloop þat is vndir þe brayn panne..þe which pannicle ..is clepid dura mater. **1525** tr. *Brunswyke's Surg.* A iv b/1 (Stanf.) Than within be ij. small fleces named dura mater and pia mater, than the substance of the braynes. **1717** PRIOR *Alma* III. 157 How could I play the commentator On dura and on pia mater? **1767** GOOCH *Treat. Wounds* I. 270 The Dura Mater is an inelastic membrane, about the thickness of parchment. **1873** MIVART *Elem. Anat.* ix. 365 The solid structures which protect the cerebro-spinal axis are lined by a dense membrane—the dura mater.

‖**duramen** (djʊ'reɪmɛn). *Bot.* [rare L. *dūrāmen* hardness; a hardened or ligneous vine-branch (Columella), f. *dūrāre* to harden.] The central wood or heart-wood of an exogenous tree.

1837 *Penny Cycl.* IX. 205/1. **1839** CARPENTER *Princ. Gen. & Comp. Phys.* §329 The deposition of the products of secretion which gives strength and firmness to the duramen, destroys or greatly diminishes its power of transmitting fluid. **1882** VINES *Sachs' Bot.* 133 The inner layers of alburnum are gradually transformed into duramen..the cell-walls assuming a darker colour, from saturation with resin, colouring-substances, etc. The distinction between alburnum and duramen is very clear and well-marked in the oak, walnut, cherry, elm..brazil wood, etc.

durance ('djʊərəns). [a. OF. *durance* duration, f. *durer* to last, DURE: see -ANCE.]

†**1.** Continuance, duration; lastingness. *Obs.*

1494 FABYAN *Chron.* I. cv,. Some wryters accompt the terme of the duraunce of this kyngdome from Cerdicus to Egbert, and some to the last yere of Aluredus. **1599** A. M. tr. *Gabelhouer's Bk. Physicke* 29/2 Let it soe rest in a sellar the durance of 14 dayes. **1698** FRYER *Acc. E. India & P.* 271 Had not that Instigator of Ills..forbid its Durance by maliciously sowing Tares.

†**2.** Lasting quality, durability. *Obs.*

1599 T. M[OUFET] *Silkwormes* 69 That compar'd with this is nought so fine..Nor of like durance. **1663** GERBIER *Counsel* 108 Precious Wood..both for Colour, Aromatick smell and Durance. **1703** *Art Vintners* 23 It acquires a better durance and taste. **1847** EMERSON *Poems, Astræa* Wks. (Bohn) I. 444 The durance of a granite ledge.

†**3.** A stout durable cloth. (Cf. DURANT *sb.*) *Obs.*

1583 in *North. N. & Q.* I. 77 A payr of blew paynd hosse, drawin furthe wᵗ Dewrance. **1588** *Acc.-bk. of W. Wray* in *Antiquary* (1896) Feb. 54 Ii pece cremosynge Duraunce.. and one pece blacke duraunce. **1601** CORNWALLYES *Ess.* (1632) xiii, I refuse to weare buffe for the lasting, and shall I be content to apparrell my braine in durance? **1709** MRS. CRACKENTHORPE *Female Tatler* in Malcolm *Anecd. 18th C.* (1808) 133 Shallons, durances, and right Scotch plaids.

4. Endurance (of toil or fatigue). *arch.*

1579 SPENSER *Sheph. Cal.* Epil. 2 That..time in durance shall outweare. **1611** SPEED *Hist. Gt. Brit.* v. vii. §5. 38 Their hardinesse..partly naturall, and partly acquired by practise of their bodies to durance. **1881** R. BUCHANAN *God & Man* III. 31 Many a man..had saved himself from..madness by the hard durance of toil.

5. Forced confinement, imprisonment; constraint. Now esp. in phr. ***in durance vile.*** Cf. DURESS 3.

1513 MORE in Grafton *Chron.* (1568) II. 773 Those that have not letted to put them in duraunce without colour, will let as little to procure their destruction without cause. **1568** GRAFTON *Chron.* II. 82 His mother, which as yet was in durance in Englande. **1597** SHAKS. *2 Hen. IV*, v. v. 36 Thy Dol..is in base Durance, and contagious prison. **1637** SANDERSON *Serm.* II. 62 St. Paul being at durance in Rome. **1663** BUTLER *Hud.* I. iii. 995 Him they release from durance base. **1770** BURKE *Pres. Discont.* Wks. 1842 I. 130 This royal servitude and vile durance. **1791** MACKINTOSH *Vind. Gallicæ* Wks. 1846 III. 9 To deliver the peerless and immaculate Antoinetta..from the durance vile in which she has so long been immured in the Tuilleries. **1794** BURNS *Esopus to Maria* 57 A workhouse!..In durance vile here must I wake and weep. **1841** BORROW *Zincali* I. 246 The writer, who..was in durance for stealing a pair of mules.

†**durancy.** *Obs. rare.* [see -ANCY.] = prec. 1.

1647 H. MORE *Song of Soul* II. i. II. xlvii, A never fading durancie Belongs to all hid principles of life. **1653** —— *Conject. Cabbal.* (1662) 119 The permanency and stable durancy of the world.

durand, -ly, obs. north. forms of DURING, -LY.

durangite (djʊ'ræŋgaɪt). *Min.* [Named 1869, from Durango in Mexico.] A fluo-arsenate of aluminium and sodium, in orange-red crystals.

1869 *Amer. Jrnl. Sc.* Ser. II. XLVIII. 182, I propose for it the name Durangite.

durant ('djʊərənt), *a.* and *sb.* [a. F. *durant*, pres. pple. of *durer* to last, continue, DURE.]

†**A.** *adj.* Lasting, continuous; current, present.

1455 *Paston Lett.* No. 237 I. 325 [To hear of his] durant prosperite and welfare. **1494** FABYAN *Chron.* 2 Of names of tymes, and of the duraunt yere. **1652** MARBURY *Comm. Habak.* i. 2 Christ's so frequent, so durant prayers. **1653** J. HALL *Paradoxes* 97 Can he..suppose the greatnesse of his Master were constant and durant.

B. *sb.* A woollen stuff called by some 'everlasting' (Webster, 1828); a variety of tammy.

1766 W. GORDON *Gen. Counting ho.* 428 Superfine black durants. **1851** *Offic. Catal. Gt. Exhib.* I. 98 Fabrics composed entirely of Wool..Durants and Buntings. **1883** BECK *Draper's Dict.* s.v., Both Tamies and Durants were hot-pressed and glazed, but the former were kept at the full width of the cloth, while the latter were creased.

‖**durante** (djʊ'ræntiː), *pres. pple.* and *prep.* The Latin pres. pple. *dūrāns* enduring, in ablative singular, used in absolute constructions.

a. In Latin phrases ***durante beneplacito***, during pleasure; ***durante vita***, life enduring, during life.

1621 *Debates Ho. of Lords* (Camden) 63 Whether to be degraded *durante vita.* *a* **1627** MIDDLETON *Anyth. for Quiet Life* IV. i. E iij, I cannot longer merit their *durante bene placita.* **1676** WYCHERLEY *Pl Dealer* v. iii, To have the priviledges of a Husband, without the dominion: that is *Durante beneplacito.*

†**b.** Hence, in English context, = DURING. *Obs.*

1556 *Aurelio & Isab.* (1608) L viij, To take plesour durante thy lyfe. *a* **1641** BP. MOUNTAGU *Acts & Mon.* (1642) 101 *Durante* the minority of Ioas surviving. **1832** J. P. KENNEDY *Swallow B.* xvi. (1860) 147 It was a grant *durante* the existence of the mill-pond.

duration (djʊ'reɪʃən). [a. obs. F. *duration*, ad. late L. *dūrātiōn-em*, n. of action f. *dūrāre* to harden, endure: see DURE *v.* Used by Chaucer, and then after 1600; not in Shaks.]

1. a. Lasting, continuance in time; the continuance or length of time; the time during which a thing, action, or state continues.

c **1384** CHAUCER *H. Fame* III. 1024 And yaf hem eke duracioun. *c* **1386** —— *Knt's T.* 2138 That same prince.. Hath stablissed in this wretched world adoun Certeyne dayes and duracioun [*Corp., Petw., Lansd.* dominacioun] To al that is engendrid in this place. **1614** JACKSON *Creed* III. xxx. §5. 283 The actuall visibilitie of colours wholly depends vpon the light, as well for existence as duration. **1677** GALE *Crt. Gentiles* IV. 287 What is Duration, but the persevering of a thing in its existence? **1685** BOYLE *Salub. Air* 80 Their duration was unequal, some lasting ten or fifteen days, and others longer. **1711** ADDISON *Spect.* No. 94 ¶5 That Space of Duration which we call a Minute. **1783** COWPER *Let.* 24 Feb., The peace will probably be of short duration. **1862** SIR B. BRODIE *Psychol. Inq.* II. iv. 118 The average duration of human life in the agricultural districts is beyond that of the great cities.

†**b.** Lasting in use; endurance of wear; durableness, permanence. *Obs.*

1637 EARL MONM. tr. *Malvezzi's Romulus & Tarq.* 139 That Magistracy in States is of duration, which is content to execute as a Minister, not to command as a Lord. **1665** SIR T. HERBERT *Trav.* (1677) 380 Date..a Tree which both for quality, duration, and fruit is [etc.]. **1712** J. JAMES tr. *Le Blond's Gardening* 212 A Bason..of Ciment, is preferable to all for its Duration. **1753** HANWAY *Trav.* (1762) I. III. xxxiv. 157 The brick..appears to be ill prepared for duration.

c. *Phonetics.* The quantity or length of a sound.

1888 H. SWEET *Hist. Eng. Sounds* 9. §21 A sound which can form a syllable by itself is called *syllabic.* Syllabicness implies an appreciable duration and force. **1933** BLOOMFIELD *Lang.* vii. 109 *Duration* (or *quantity*) is the relative length of time through which the vocal organs are kept in a position. **1957** S. POTTER *Mod. Ling.* iii. 60 Many degrees of *length, duration* or *quantity* may be detected by observation and experiment in most languages. **1962** A. C. GIMSON *Introd. Pronunc. Eng.* 24 We shall..refer later to the 'long' vowels of English such as those of *bean* and *barn*, as compared with the 'short' vowel in *bin.* But, in making such statements, we shall not be referring to absolute duration values.

d. The time during which a war lasts, used first of the 1914–18 war from the term of enlistment 'for four years or the duration of the war'; esp. in phr. ***for the duration***, until the end of the war; hence, for a long or an unconscionably long time. Also *attrib.*

1916 *Punch* 12 July 51 'I've got a lot of contracts to finish.' 'How long will they take?' 'Oh, about three years—or the duration of the War.' **1925** FRASER & GIBBONS *Soldier & Sailor Words* 86 *Duration, for the*, a phrase often used colloquially to express weariness and impatience. Men, for instance, whose relief was long overdue might be heard complaining, 'Are we going to stop here for the duration?' **1930** *Times Lit. Suppl.* 17 Apr., Nothing so prosaic as 'doing one's bit' would have kept an Italian heart up 'for the duration'. **1939** *Punch* 1 Nov. 483/1 Miss Dodge's motor-bicycle..has been laid up for the duration. **1940** *New Statesman* 19 Oct. 381 We have received a number of letters from country readers offering week-end hospitality for those who must work in London, or 'duration' hospitality for their children. **1941** M. TREADGOLD *We couldn't leave Dinah* xi. 176 That ought to keep you busy for the duration. **1960** L. DURRELL *Clea* II. iii. 157 The war had intervened... The Brigadier was pinned down..'for the duration'.

†**2.** Hardening. *Obs.*

1612 WOODALL *Surg. Mate* (1653) 270 Duration is either when things mollified at the fire are set in a cold place to harden: or by boyling..do waxe hard. 1657 TOMLINSON *Renou's Disp.* 75 The doctrine of Mollition and Duration.

3. *Comb.*, as **duration-block** (see quots.).

1890 W. JAMES *Princ. Psychol.* I. xv. 610 The unit of composition of our perception of time is a *duration*, with a bow and a stern, as it were—a rearward- and a forward-looking end. It is only as parts of this *duration-block* that the relation of *succession* of one end to the other is perceived. 1935 *Mind* XLIV. 33 There is no such thing as a simple present; the present, to use William James's expression, is a 'duration-block' made up of 'succeeding' parts.

Hence **du'rational** *a.*, pertaining to duration.

1881 SPOTTISWOODE in *Nature* No. 623. 549 The durational character of this former is very much more marked than that of this latter. 1930 F. R. BLAKE in *Curme Vol. Ling. Studies* 38 There is only one temporal durational case. 1942 *Mind* LI. 150 Only when they have been redigested and creatively synthesized as metaphysical derivatives of eternal action can their durational causality be discovered.

durationless (djʊˈreɪʃənlɪs), *a.* [f. DURATION + -LESS.] Having no duration.

1919 A. N. WHITEHEAD *Enquiry Princ. Nat. Knowledge* i. 2 The ultimate fact embracing all nature is distribution of material throughout all space at a durationless instant of time. 1933 *Mind* XLII. 308 The absurd suggestion of everything being contained in a single durationless instant.

durative (ˈdjʊərətɪv), *a.* [f. DURAT(ION + -IVE.] Continuing; not completed; *spec.* in *Gram.* applied to a form which marks action as going on. Also as *sb.* Hence **ˈduratively** *adv.*, **duraˈtivity**.

1889 W. R. MORFILL *Russ. Gram.* 40 Durative verbs on taking a prefix become perfective. 1895 [see PERFECTIVE *a.* 3]. 1904 *Expositor* 6th Ser. X. 360 In οἱ ἀπολλύμενοι, strongly durative though the verb is, we see its perfectivity in the fact that the goal is *ideally* reached. *Ibid.* 361 Ἀγωνίζεσθαι is only used in the durative present. *Ibid.* 444 The effective aorist κατήντησαν is very different from a durative like ἐπορεύοντο. *Ibid.* 441 Other futural presents..have no lack of durativity about them. 1912 WRIGHT *Compar. Gram. Gk. Lang.* §424 (2) An action is said to be cursive, durative or imperfective when it denotes continuous action without any reference to its beginning or end, as in English *I am striking* compared with *I strike.* 1921 H. POUTSMA *Char. Eng. Verb* 5 Iterative ..distinguished into..duratively iterative. 1924 [see ASPECT *sb.* 9b]. 1932 *Jrnl. Eng. & Gmc. Philol.* XXXI. 251 The durative aspect indicates duration: 'He *is working* in the garden.' 1935 [see EFFECTIVE *sb.* 3]. 1957 *Essays in Crit.* VII. 121 *Je vais* is not quite the same as the durative present 'I am going'.

‖**durbar** (ˈdɜːbɑː(r)). *East Indies.* Also **darbār**. [Pers. and Urdū *darbār* court.]

1. The court kept by an Indian ruler; a public audience or levee held by a native prince, or by a British governor or viceroy in India.

1609 HAWKINS in Purchas *Pilgrims* (1625) I. IV. 432 (Y.) An inner court where the King keepes his Darbar. 1665 SIR T. HERBERT *Trav.* (1677) 98 This Noble Prince shews himself in the Durbar and Jarneo to the people not so oft as was expected. 1804 WELLINGTON in Owen *Wellesley's Desp.* 298 To lay these communications before the Peishwa's Durbar. 1862 BEVERIDGE *Hist. India* III. VIII. vi. 475 The Maharanee held durbars daily. 1881 SIR W. HUNTER in *Encycl. Brit.* XII. 811 On January 1, 1877, Queen Victoria was proclaimed Empress of India at a *darbár* of unequalled magnificence, held on the historic 'ridge' overlooking the Mughal capital of Delhi. 1887 *Times* (weekly ed.) 12 Aug 1/2 A grand Durbar was held..by Mr. Crosthwaite the Commissioner at Mandalay.

attrib. 1867 *Evening Star* 7 Dec., The beautiful durbar-tent of red and yellow silk.

2. The hall or place of audience.

1793 HODGES *Trav. India* 105 In the inner court are the remains of the durbar, or hall of public audience. 1888 *Quiver* July 673/1 The Durbar, a large audience hall, which forms a part of every Eastern palace.

‖**durchkomponiert** (ˌdurçkɔmpoˈniːrt, ˈdʊəxkɒmpəʊniːət), *a. Mus.* [G., f. *durch* through + *komponiert* composed.] Of songs, etc.: having a different musical setting for each verse, stanza, or strophe; through-composed.

1897 J. S. SHEDLOCK tr. *Riemann's Dict. Mus.* 209/1 *Durchkomponirt* (Ger., 'through-composed'), a term applied to a song, when the different strophes of the poem have each their own melody, and are not, as in the volk-song and simple art-song, sung to one and the same melody. 1957 E. T. CONE in N. Frye *Sound & Poetry* 10 Schubert..made the decision to renounce the simple quatrains of Goethe's ballad in favor of a *durchkomponiert* design following the climactic narrative. 1958 *Listener* 20 Nov. 850/3 Puccini's *Girl of the Golden West*..is more completely *durchkomponiert* than his earlier operas.

durdum, var. of DIRDUM.

dure (djʊə(r)), *v. arch.* and *dial.* Also 4 **duyre**, **dyre**, 4–6 **dour(e**, 5 **deure**, **dewre**, **dowre**, 6 **duer**. [a. F. *dure-r* to last, continue, persist, †extend:—L. *dūrā-re* to harden, be hardened, endure, hold out, last, f. *dūr-us* hard.]

1. *intr.* To last, continue in existence. *arch.*

c1275 LAY. 26708 Al þane day long durede þat fiht strong. c1315 SHOREHAM 3 Hy ne moȝe naȝt dury. c1330 R. BRUNNE *Chron.* Pref. (1810) 189 þare biriels he þouht to honoure With som þing þat ay myght doure. 13.. *Minor Poems fr. Vernon MS.* xxxvii. 793 Monnes lyf nis bote schort: Sone wol hit go; Bote þe sely soule Duyreþ euermo. c1450 *Merlin* 32 As longe as the worlde dureth shall thi boke gladly ben herde. 1526–34 TINDALE *Matt.* xiii. 21 Yet hath he no rotts in him selfe, therfore dureth but a season. 1533 BELLENDEN *Livy* IV. (1822) 321 Thare empire durit nocht lang. 1575 CHURCHYARD *Chippes* (1817) 97 This bickring duerd, foure hours and more at lest. 1664 EVELYN *Sylva* (1776) 261 The wood being preserved dry, will dure a very long time. 1669 WORLIDGE *Syst. Agric.* (1681) 247 You may change for the other, and so make your sport dure the longer. 1871 R. ELLIS *Catullus* xcvi. 6 In thy love dureth a plenary joy. 1882 in *W. Worc. Gloss.*

†**2.** To persist, 'hold out' in action; to continue in a certain state, condition, or place. *Obs.*

1297 R. GLOUC. (1724) 181 He þoȝte..to wynne ȝut al Europe, ȝyf he myȝte dure. 13.. *Coer de L.* 2937 The Sarezynes myghten nought doure, And flowen into the heye toure. c1477 CAXTON *Jason* 8b, [They] persecuted them with their arowes as long as they dured. a1510 DOUGLAS *K. Hart* 469 For so in dule he micht no langar dure. a1541 WYATT *Despair counselleth*, etc. Poet. Wks. 97 Against the stream thou mayst not dure. 1573 *Satir. Poems Reform.* xlii. 639 As the body can not dure, Except in sesoun men procure Fude in dew tyme it to sustene.

†**3.** To continue or extend onward in space. *Obs.*

a1300 *Floriz & Bl.* 210 Babilloine..Dureþ abute furten-niȝt ȝonde. c1400 MAUNDEV. (1839) vi. 67 There begynnethe the Vale of Ebron, that dureth nyghe to Jerusalem. 1481 CAXTON *Myrr.* I. xvii. 52 Lyke as a flye goth round aboute a round apple In like wyse myght a man goo rounde aboute therthe as ferre as therthe dureth. c1500 *Melusine* xxxvi. 281 Nygh therby was a forest that dured a myle.

†**4.** *trans.* To sustain, undergo, bear (pain, opposition, etc.); to endure. *Obs.*

1297 R. GLOUC. (1724) 335 ȝyf heo yt may dure. c1400 *Ywaine & Gaw.* 2634 Might thare none his dintes dour. a1533 LD. BERNERS *Huon* lxvii. 232 Durynge grete sorow in yᵉ horryble pryson. 1594 MARLOWE & NASHE *Dido* IV. iii. I may not dure this female drudgery. 1598 MARSTON *Pygmal.* Sat. I. (1764) 138 He that..arm'd in proofe, dare dure a strawes strong push.

5. To harden: see DURING *vbl. sb.* 2.

dure (djʊə(r)), *a. arch.* Also 4 dur, 5 deure, 6 *Sc.* duire. [a. F. *dur, dure*:—L. *dūrus* hard: cf. also DOUR.]

1. Hard. *lit.* and *fig.*

c1375 *Sc. Leg. Saints, Andreas* 621 Gyf þat þu sa dur wil be þat þu wil nocht consent to me. 1412–20 LYDG. *Chron. Troy* I. vi, His bryght skales were so hard and dure. 1567 *Satir. Poems Reform.* iv. 155 As the woirme that workis vnder cuire At lenth the tre consumis that is duire. 1567 TURBERV. *Ovid's Epist.* 47 That place with dure and deadly dinte hath Cupid crased earst. 1664 *Flodden F.* viii. 80 Blows with bils most dure was delt. 1848 LYTTON *Harold* IX. i, In reply to too dure a request. 1885 R. F. BURTON *1001 Nts.* I. 111 The last judgment will deal them durer pains and more enduring.

†**2.** *Mus.* Sharp. (In quot. applied to the note now called B natural, as distinguished from B flat.) [cf. F. *dur*, formerly used in same sense.]

1609 DOULAND *Ornith. Microl.* 15 The Scale of ♮ dure, and where the Mutations are made. *Ibid.* 16 For ♮ dures are not changed into *b* mols, nor contrarily.

Hence **ˈdurely** *adv.*; **ˈdureness**, stubbornness.

c1375 *Sc. Leg. Saints, Jacobus (minor)* 337 þe Iowis..wald [not] mend þar wikit liffis..bot in to durnes ay abad. c1477 CAXTON *Jason* 102 He made his heed hurtle ayenst his crawpe right sore and durely.

dure, obs. form of DARE, DEER, DOOR.

†**duree, dure**, *sb. Obs.* [a. F. *durée* (12th c. in Hatz.-Darm.) duration, f. *durer* to endure.]

a. Power of endurance. **b.** Duration.

c1330 R. BRUNNE *Chron.* (1810) 16 þe kynges folk was litelle, it had no dure. On the nyght he fled away, þat non suld him se. —— *Chron. Wace* (Rolls) 14123 þen myghte Moddred haue no duree, Ne no fot helden his meynee.

†**ˈdureful**, *a. Obs.* [f. DURE *v.* + -FUL.] Lasting, continuing, durable.

1594 SPENSER *Amoretti* vi, The durefull Oake, whose sap is not yet dride. 1596 —— *F.Q.* IV. x. 39 Neither pretious stone, nor durefull brasse. 1614 RALEIGH *Hist. World* I. (1634) 56 A durefull continuance.

†**ˈdureless**, *a. Obs.* [f. as prec. + -LESS.] Not lasting, unenduring, transient.

1614 RALEIGH *Hist. World* I. (1634) 23 The false and dureless pleasures of this Stage-play World. 1636 FEATLY *Clavis Myst.* xlv. 664 As lasting as the other is dureless.

Dureresque (dyrəˈrɛsk), *a.* [see -ESQUE.] In the style or manner of Albert Dürer (1471–1528), the most distinguished Renascence artist of Germany, famous both as painter and as engraver on copper and on wood.

1860 RUSKIN *Mod. Paint.* V. IX. ii. §13. 213 Trace this fact ..through Greek, Venetian, and Dureresque art. 1893 *Nation* (N.Y.) 23 Mar. 221/1 Nor does he rely upon Greek drapery or Düreresque handling for success as book decorator. 1896 *Westm. Gaz.* 23 Mar. 2/1 Dureresque as it is in its treatment.

duress, duresse (djʊˈrɛs, ˈdjʊərɪs), *sb.* Forms: 4–9 **duresse**, 4 **duresce**, (5 **dwresse**, **dewresse**), 5–7 **dures**, 7– **duress**. [a. obs. F. *duresse, -esce, -ece*, hardness, oppression, constraint:—L. *dūritia* (= *dūritiēs*), n. of quality f. *dūr-us* hard.]

†**1.** Hardness; roughness, violence, severity; hardiness of endurance, resistance, etc.; firmness.

c1400 *Test. Love* I. i, By duresse of sorowe. c1440 *Promp. Parv.* 135/2 Dwresse, or hardenesse, *duricies*. c1460 Ross *La Belle Dame* 463 in *Pol. Rel. & L. Poems* (1866) 67 An herte of suche duresse..ye wynne al this diffame by cruelte. 1651 N. BACON *Disc. Govt. Eng.* II. ii. 13 What he did was done by duress of mind.

†**2.** Harsh or severe treatment, infliction of hardship; oppression, cruelty; harm, injury; affliction.

[1292 BRITTON V. iii. §1 Sauntz duresce fere.] c1320 *Seuyn Sag.* (W.) 2189 Ac yif thou do thi sone duresse. c1350 *Will. Palerne* 1074 þe duresse þat he wrouȝt. c1430 LYDG. *Min. Poems* 118 (Mätz.) The wolfe in fieldis the shepe doth grete duresse. 1508 DUNBAR *Gold. Targe* 170 Thair scharp assayes mycht do no dures To me. 1673 in *Jackson's Wks.* (1844) IX. 271 Taught to hunt counter for pleasure, and seek delights in difficulties and duresses.

3. Forcible restraint or restriction; confinement, imprisonment; = DURANCE 5. **b.** Harshness or strictness of confinement (cf. senses 1 and 2).

c1430 *Life St. Kath.* (Roxb. 1884) 13 She wyl..put me in duresse as þouȝ I were a faytour. c1470 HARDING *Chron.* (Prose add. Harl. MS.) cxcvi. 353 Kynge Richarde vnder dures of prison in the Toure of London. 1577–87 HOLINSHED *Chron.* II. 40/1 He was suddenlie apprehended ..and kept in duresse, by reson that he was suspected to be of no sound religion. 1651 N. BACON *Disc. Govt. Eng.* II. lix. 188 He kept the whole Synod in duress to have their votes for the election of his Son to be his successor. 1800 WELLINGTON in Gurw. *Desp.* I. 249 What, then, is the degree of duresse which is to constitute imprisonment? 1857 TOULMIN SMITH *Parish* 376 Persons in prisons, workhouses, asylums, hospitals, or under any form of duress. 1880 McCARTHY *Own Times* IV. lvi. 222 Some of the missionaries had been four years in duresse.

4. Constraint, compulsion; *spec.* in *Law*, Constraint illegally exercised to force a person to perform some act.

Such compulsion may be by actual imprisonment, by threat of imprisonment or of loss of life or limb, or by physical violence. A deed or contract made under duress is voidable on a *plea of duress* at a subsequent trial.

1596 SPENSER *F.Q.* IV. xii. 10 If he should through pride your doome undo, Do you by duresse him compell thereto, And in this prison put him here. 1601–2 FULBECKE *1st Pt. Parall.* 3 If an infant make..a lease by dures, if the lessee enter, the infant may haue an assise. 1643 PRYNNE *Sov. Power Parl.* II. 78 A Marriage, Bond, or deed made by Duresse or Menace, are good in Law, and not meerly void, but voidable only upon a Plea and Tryall. 1765 BLACKSTONE *Comm.* I. i. 131 The constraint a man is under in these circumstances is called in law *duress*, from the Latin *durities*, of which there are two sorts; duress of imprisonment, where a man actually loses his liberty..and duress *per minas*, where the hardship is only threatened and impending. 1768–74 TUCKER *Lt. Nat.* (1852) I. 550 The man was under duresse, and his act not voluntary, but imposed upon him by force. 1876 DIGBY *Real Prop.* x. §1. 369 Similar principles apply to conveyances by persons under *duress*, that is, under pressure of illegal bodily restraint, or of danger to life or limb. 1896 W. T. STEAD *Pref. to Keble's Chr. Y.* 2, I made the omissions with reluctance, under duress from the inexorable printer.

b. *ellipt.* for *plea of duress.*

1613 SIR H. FINCH *Law* (1636) 10 One imprisoned till he bee content to make an obligation..being at large, yet he shall auoid it by dures of imprisonment.

†**duˈress**, *v. Obs.* [f. prec. sb.] *trans.* To subject to duress, constraint, or oppression. Hence †**duˈressor**, he who subjects another to duress.

a1626 BACON *Max. & Uses Com. Law* xxii. (1636) 81 If the party duressed doe make any motion or offer. *Ibid.*, If it had beene moved from the duressor, who had said [etc.].

‖**du reste** (dy rɛst), *adv. phr.* [Fr.] Besides, moreover.

1827 M. WILMOT *Jrnl.* 14 Aug. in *More Lett.* (1935) 285 Du reste he only drank one cup of weak tea. 1889 E. DOWSON *Let.* 3 Feb. (1967) 32 The scenery is everything that could be desired & the dresses excellent. *Du reste*, I am still suffering from it. 1919 W. S. MAUGHAM *Moon & Sixpence* xxii. 96 *Du reste*, it has still to be proved that this friend of yours has merit.

†**duret.** *Obs.* [Etym. obscure. (cf. OF. *duret* dim. of *dur* hard.)] A kind of dance.

1612 BEAUM. & FL. *Masque at Gray's Inn* Stage Direct., The knights take their ladies to dance with them galliards, durets, corantoes.

‖**duˈretto.** *Obs.* Also **-etta, -ette, -etty.** [a. It. *duretto*, dim. of *duro* hard:—L. *duru-m* hard.] A coarse or stout sort of stuff; app. so named from its durable quality. Also *attrib.*

1619 PURCHAS *Microcosm.* xxvii. 269 The new deuised names of Stuffes and Colours..the lying names of Perpetuano and Duretto. 1638 SIR T. HERBERT *Trav.* (ed. 2) 27 These Mohelians..are cut and pinckt in several works, upon their duretto skins, face, armes, and thighs. 1639 MAYNE *City Match* I. v. in Hazl. *Dodsley* XIII. 222, I never durst be seen Before my father out of duretta and serge. 1641 L. ROBERTS *Treas. Traff.* 41 Grograme-yarne of which is made Iames [? Janes], Grograms, Durettes, silke-mohers. 1660 *Act 12 Chas. II*, c. 4 Sched., Durance or Duretty.

Durex (ˈdjʊərɛks). Also **durex**. [Orig. uncertain, but see quot. 1982.] **a.** A proprietary name for a contraceptive sheath. **b.** Hence, any condom.

1932 *Trade Marks Jrnl.* 16 Nov. 1462/2 Durex.. Instruments, apparatus, and contrivances, not medicated, for surgical or curative purposes, or in relation to the health of men or animals, but not including surgical adhesive tape. .. The London Rubber Company, London. 1963 *Which? Contraceptives Suppl.* 15 Nov. IV. 37 Durex Gossamer was found in almost every shop, and Durex Protectives were found nearly as often. 1971 B. THORNBERRY tr. *Hansen &*

Jensen's Little Red School Bk. (ed. 2) 98 Boys use sheaths, sometimes called durex, skins, or French letters. **1973** M. AMIS *Rachel Papers* 155, I was conversant with Durex lore, however, having naturally peed and wanked into them a good deal as a youngster. **1977** *Spare Rib* June 26/3 You know that joke about durex. **1982** A. ROOM *Dict. Trade Name Origins* 69 *Durex* (contraceptives by LRC International). The name was devised by the former chairman of LRC, Mr. A. R. Reid, to whom it came 'out of the air' when he was travelling one evening in 1929 on his usual train home from London. **1986** *N.Y. Times* 5 Jan. III. 10/5 London International, whose Durex brands account for 96 percent of Britain's condom sales.

‖**durgah** (dʌrgɑː). *E. Indies.* Also durgaw. [Pers. *dargāh* royal court; gate, door, large bench.] In India, 'The shrine of a (Mohammedan) saint, a place of religious resort and prayer.' (Yule.)

1793 HODGES *Trav. India* 87 On some of the highest of these hills I observed durgaws, or burial places, with little chapels annexed, belonging to the Mussulmans. **1845** STOCQUELER *Handbk. Brit. India* (1854) 293 In a durgah, or mosque outside the town, lie the bones of Chanda Sahib.

ˈ**durgan, -en.** *dial.* [This and dial. *durgy* dwarfish, are app. derived from some of the forms mentioned under DWARF.] An undersized person or animal; a dwarf.

1706 PHILLIPS (ed. Kersey), *Durgen*, a little thick and short Person; a Dwarf. **1730** FIELDING *Tom Thumb* II. v, And can my princess such a durgen wed [*i.e.* Tom Thumb]? **1890** *Gloucester Gloss., Durgan*, a name for an undersized horse in a large team.

Durham (ˈdʌrəm). [Name of a town and a county in the north of England.] **a.** Used to designate a breed of shorthorn cattle originating in Durham, now generally called shorthorns.

1810 J. BAILEY *Agric. Durham* xiv. 230 The Durham Ox was bred by Mr. Charles Colling, of Ketton, in the year 1796. **1855** *Poultry Chron.* III. 391/2 Amongst them [*sc.* breeds of cattle] were to be seen short horns, Durhams, Devons, and others in great perfection. **1861** GEO. ELIOT *Silas M.* vi. 89 P'rhaps you didn't say the cow was a red Durham. **1902** *Encycl. Brit.* XXV. 190/2 The Shorthorn.. is still termed the Durham breed in most parts of the world except the land of its birth.

b. Durham Mustard, ground mustard orig. produced by a Mrs. Clements in Durham in the 18th century.

1799 *Times* 1 June 1/4 Best Durham mustard 2s. **1861** MRS. BEETON *Bk. Househ. Managem.* 216 From the circumstance of Mrs. Clements being a resident at Durham, it obtained the name of Durham mustard. **1911** *Encycl. Brit.* XIX. 98/1 The bright yellow farina.. produced under the name of 'Durham mustard' pleased.. George I. **1970** SIMON & HOWE *Dict. Gastronomy* 274/1 In 1729 she [*sc.* Mrs. Clements] hit on the idea of grinding mustard seeds... It is said she made a small fortune selling what became known as Durham mustard.

‖**durian** (duːˈriːən, ˈdʊərɪən). Also 6- durion, 6-7 duryoen, 7 duroyen, 8 durean, 9 dorian. [Malay *durian*, f. *dūrī*, thorn, prickle: so called from its prickly coat (Marsden).] The oval or globular fruit of *Durio zibethinus*, N.O. *Sterculiaceæ*, a tree of the Indian Archipelago; it has a hard prickly rind and luscious cream-coloured pulp, of a strong civet odour, but agreeable taste; also the tree itself.

1588 PARKE tr. *Mendoza's Hist. China* 393 There is one, yᵗ is called in the Malaca tongue Durion, and is so good that.. it doth exceede in savour all others that euer they had seene, or tasted. **1634** SIR T. HERBERT *Trav.* 184 The Duroyen.. may be called an Epitome of all the best and rarest fruits. **1697** DAMPIER *Voy.* I. xi. 319 The Trees that bear the Durians, are as big as Apple Trees.. the Fruit.. as white as Milk, and as soft as Cream, and the taste very delicious. **1727** A. HAMILTON *New Acc. E. Ind.* II. xxxix. 81 The Durean is another excellent Fruit, but offensive to some Peoples Noses, for it smells very like human Excrements, but when once tasted the Smell vanishes. **1884** *Q. Rev.* Apr. 332 Loftiest in height as unrivalled in excellence of flavoured fruit, the royal durion. **1887** ANNA FORBES *Insulinde* 111 The durian, of which Mr. Wallace says that it is worth a voyage to the East to taste it.

duricrust (ˈdjʊərɪkrʌst). *Geol.* [f. L. *dūr-us* hard + -I- + CRUST *sb.*] A hard crust formed at or near the surface in a semi-arid climate by the accumulation of mineral matter, esp. silica or iron oxides, deposited as ground water rises by capillary action and evaporates; *esp.* such a crust in Australia.

1928 W. G. WOOLNOUGH in *Jrnl. & Proc. R. Soc. N.S.W.* LXI. 27 From the fact that.. the chemically formed covering.. always appears as a relatively hard 'armour plate', protecting softer, decomposed rock residue beneath it, I propose to group together all the representatives of the hard crust, in every part of Australia where they can be shown to have formed in the same manner, during the same geological period, under the name of the duricrust... [*Note*] This name was suggested to me by Professor Todd, Professor of Latin in the University of Sydney. **1954** W. D. THORNBURY *Princ. Geomorphol.* iv. 83 Under the present arid conditions which prevail today [in Australia] duricrusts are not forming in a significant amount but rather are undergoing destruction. **1955** P. A. BUXTON *Nat. Hist. Tsetse Flies* xi. 390 The thicket grows on a clay cement or duricrust, which may well be too hard for the larva to enter. **1962** L. C. KING *Morphol. of Earth* vi. 172 The duricrust often grades down through a zone of weathered rock into the bedrock itself. **1977** A. HALLAM *Planet Earth* 85 At other times (pluvials), average rainfall may have been markedly greater so that.. bedrock became deeply weathered to give striking weathering crusts (duricrusts). **1978** T. LANGFORD-SMITH *Silcrete in Australia* i. 2 Differences in the type of duricrust.. were regarded by Woolnough as a reflection of changes in the rock type, so that whether a duricrust happened to be ferruginous or siliceous was a measure of the underlying parent material.

Hence ˈ**duricrusted** *a.*, covered with a duricrust.

1962 L. C. KING *Morphol. of Earth* vi. 172 Most duricrusted lands are subject to an annual period of drought (Africa, Australia). **1978** T. LANGFORD-SMITH *Silcrete in Australia* i. 2 Woolnough's conception of a single duricrusted surface was over-simplified.

during (ˈdjʊərɪŋ), *vbl. sb.* [f. DURE *v.* + -ING[1].]
1. The action of the verb DURE: duration.

c **1374** CHAUCER *Boeth.* IV. pr. iv. 99 (Camb. MS.) Yif they weere of lengere duryinge. **1382** WYCLIF *1 Esdras* iv. 40 Mageste of alle duringis aboue time [*aevorum*]. **1526** *Pilgr. Perf.* (W. de W. 1531) 241 How shorte they [rychesse] be in during. *a* **1661** FULLER *Worthies* III. (1662) 38 Long the during thereof.

2. Hardening; induration. In quot. *attrib.*

1804 *Hull Advertiser* 30 June 2/3 A Bark-Mill, three Leather-houses, two During-shades.

ˈ**during,** *ppl. a.* [f. as prec. + -ING[2].] That dures; lasting, continuing.

1398 TREVISA *Barth. De P.R.* VII. x. (1495) 230 Fallynge euylles ben moost duringe and harde to heele. **1568** T. HOWELL *Arb. Amitie* (1879) 51 Nor canst thou.. stop the trumpe, that sounds hir during fame. **1601** WEEVER *Mirr. Mart.* Dj, Marble.. and during Adamant. **1633** BP. HALL *Hard Texts, N.T.* 226 Charity is a during and perpetual grace. **1850** BLACKIE *Æschylus* II. 15 Close-linked chains of during adamant.

during (ˈdjʊərɪŋ), *pres. pple.* and *prep.* (*conj.*) Also 5 dewer-, 6 duering.

†**1.** The *pres. pple.* of DURE *v.* = enduring, lasting, continuing, was used in Fr. and Eng. in a construction derived from the Latin 'ablative absolute'; thus L. *vita durante*, OF. *vie durant*, Eng. *life during*, while life endured or endures.

c **1440** *Jacob's Well* (E.E.T.S.) 271 Sche was comoun to alle þat wolde haue here, xv. ȝere durynge. **1480** CAXTON *Chron. Eng.* lxxxviii. 72 She neuer was seyn among folke hir lyf durynge. **1523** LD. BERNERS *Froiss.* I. xxxviii. 52 This sege durynge, ther were many skirmysshes. **1542-5** BRINKLOW *Lament.* lf. 12, I.. will continuallye, my lyfe duringe, praye vnto the euerlyuinge God.

The participle also often stood before the sb., e.g. L. *durante bello*, F. *durant la guerre*, Eng. *during the war*; in which construction *during* came in the modern langs. to be treated as

2. *prep.* Throughout the whole continuance of; hence, in the course of, in the time of.

c **1385** CHAUCER *L.G.W.* Prol. 283 (MS. Gg. 4. 27) Stedefaste wedewys durynge alle here lyuys. *a* **1400-50** *Alexander* 1118 In damaging of Darius durand [*Dublin* endurand] his lyfe. **14..** *Epiph.* in *Tundale's Vis.* 103 This contynued duryng mony a yere. **1548** HALL *Chron., Edw. IV*, 221 An annuitie of an. C. l. [£100] duryng his lyfe. **1585** T. WASHINGTON tr. *Nicholay's Voy.* I. xxii. 29 Al that which during our voyage was happened unto us. **1648** *Bury Wills* (Camden) 203 Dureing the terme of her naturall life. **1670** J. SMITH *Eng. Improv. Reviv'd* 77 Trees may live during the world. **1678** LADY CHAWORTH in *12th Rep. Hist. MSS. Comm.* App. v. 49 Judge North, who supplies the Lord Chancelors place during his being sicke. **1754** HUME *Hist. Eng.* (1812) I. iv. 281 During the course of seven hundred years. **1860** TYNDALL *Glac.* I. xxiii. 161 During the night the rain changed to snow. **1885** *Act 48 & 49 Vict.* c. 58 §2 The hours during which the offices.. shall be open.

†**3.** *conj.* While; until. (Also *during that.*) *Obs. rare.* [cf. F. *durant que, pendant que.*]

1595 T. BEDINGFELD tr. *Macchiavelli's Florentine Hist.* 192 During that these matters.. were handled in Toscana. **1653** *Cloria & Narcissus* I. 308 To remaine.. during a necessary conveniency might also be had for the repairing of her own ship. **1693** *Mem. Cnt. Teckely* IV. 32 During the Christians and the Turks were seeking one another for fighting.

†ˈ**duringly,** *adv. Obs.* [f. DURING *ppl. a.* + -LY[2].] Lastingly, continuously; for a long time.

1413 *Pilgr. Sowle* (Caxton 1483) IV. xxvii. 72 Yeuen hym only to kepen hym duryngly. *c* **1440** *Jacob's Well* (E.E.T.S.) 246 þe meke seruyth smertly, & lyȝtly, & strongly, and duryngly. *c* **1475** *Rauf Coilȝear* 17 The deip durandlie draif in mony deip dell.

duritike, obs. (erron.) form of DIURETIC.

†**durity** (ˈdjʊərɪtɪ). *Obs.* [ad. L. *dūritās*, n. of quality f. *dūrus* hard. Cf. F. *dureté* (13th c.), earlier OF. *durté.*] Hardness. *lit.* and *fig.*

1543 TRAHERON *Vigo's Chirurg.* II. iv. 19 Apostemes whyche encline to corruption thorough durittees and hardenes. **1623** COCKERAM, *Duritie*, harshnesse, crueltie, hardnesse. **1646** SIR T. BROWNE *Pseud. Ep.* II. i. 55 [Chrystall].. commeth short of their [gemmes'] compactnesse and durity. **1772** T. NUGENT tr. *Hist. Friar Gerund* I. 533 What motive could induce.. to such durity severe. **1795** tr. *Mercier's Fragments* I. 154 Physical durity.. engenders moral durity.

durk, -e, obs. forms of DIRK, DARK.

Durkheimian (dɜːkˈhaɪmɪən), *a.* and *sb.* [f. the name of Émile *Durkheim* (1858-1917), French sociologist + -IAN.] **A.** *adj.* Of, pertaining to, or characteristic of Émile Durkheim or his sociological theories. **B.** *sb.* A follower or supporter of Durkheim.

1915 C. E. GEHLKE *Durkheim's Contrib. to Sociol. Theory* iii. 68 To admit a 'psychological' explanation of the social phenomenon would be to waive the central requirement of the whole Durkheimian sociology. **1936** B. MALINOWSKI in R. Firth *We, the Tikopia* p. vii, In confirmation of that Durkheimian principle of solidarity personified in *l'Etre Moral.* **1938** R. H. LOWIE *Hist. Ethnol. Theory* xii. 223 Radcliffe-Brown agrees not only with other Durkheimians. **1951** PARSONS & SHILS *Toward Gen. Theory of Action* II. v. 239 A Durkheimian 'theory of social facts'.

durling, -yng, obs. forms of DARLING.

durmast (ˈdɜːmɑːst, -æ-). [A recent word. The first element is doubtful (see Note below); the second is MAST, fruit of forest tree.] A sessile-flowered sub-species or variety of oak (*Quercus pubescens*, or *Q. sessiliflora*): see quot. 1866. (Usually ***durmast-oak.***)

1791 T. NICHOLS *Obs. on Oak Trees* 24 There are two different sorts of oak growing in the [New] forest, one the true english.. the other is called by the woodmen in the forest the dur mast oak, which I believe to be the second sort of oak, described by Mr. Miller.. the wood of which is not so strong. **1792** MARTYN *Flora Rust.* I, A branch.. received from Mr. Nichols out of the New Forest, where it is known by the name of the *Durmast Oak.* **1841** *Penny Cycl.* XIX. 212/2 What is called the Durmast oak.. seems to us a slight variety of *Q. sessiliflora*, with the leaves pubescent on the under side. **1866** *Treas. Bot.* 949 The wood of *Q. sessiliflora*, or Durmast as it is called, is described as darker, heavier, and more elastic than that of *Q. pedunculata*, less easy to split, not so easy to break, yet the least difficult to bend.

[*Note.* The original authority for 'durmast' appears to be Nichols, on whose information Martyn inserted it in his ed. of Miller's Dictionary, whence it has passed into general book use. According to W. Atkinson in *Trans. Hort. Soc.* (1833) I. 336, the name appears to have been mistaken: he says 'The woodmen in the Forest call certain oaks that have dark-coloured acorns *Dun-mast*, but those dun-coloured acorns are found both of the *Q. pedunculata* and *Q. sessiliflora*; I have raised trees from them, and consider them as only accidental varieties, and that the colour of the acorns may be occasioned by something peculiar in the soil'. (No ground has been found for connecting 'durmast' with F. *durelin* or Ger. *dürreiche*, varieties of the oak. Welsh *derw* is, of course, out of the question.)]

durn (dɜːn). Now *dial.* Forms: 4-7 dorne, 5 dirn, dyrn, 6 doorne, 6-7 durne, 7 dourne, 9 dern, durn. [Widely used in dialects, Lincolnshire to Cornwall: app. from Norse. Cf. in same sense OSw. *dyrni*, Norw. *dyrn*, Sw. dial. *dörne*:— **durnja-* deriv. of **durŭn*, *durn* (Goth pl. *daurons*, Crim-Goth. *thurn*) door, f. *dur-* DOOR.]

a. A door-post, when made of solid wood; usually in *pl.* The framework of a doorway.

c **1325** *Gloss W. de Biblesw.* in Wright *Voc.* 170 E entre la teste la suslyme [*Gloss.* over-slay, *MS. Cambr.* hover-dorne]. **1408** *Nottingham Rec.* II. 58 Unum hostium cum dirnis de chelario.. unum hostium et unum par de dyrnes. **1503** *Churchw. Acc. Yatton* (Somerset Rec. Soc.) 127 For hewyng of yᵉ dornenys of yᵉ seyd dor. **1591** PERCIVALL *Sp. Dict., Batiente de puerta*, the doornes of a doore, *anta.* *c* **1600** NORDEN *Spec. Brit., Cornw.* 59 The fayre freehewed stone wyndowes, the Durnes and wrowght Dorepostes, are converted to private mens purposes. **1630** *Churchw. Acc. Tavistock* in Worth *T. Par. Acc.* (1887) 44 Paid Stephen Browne the mason for makinge of new durnes. **1787** GROSE *Provinc. Gloss., Durn*, gate-posts. N[orth]. **1855** KINGSLEY *Westw. Ho!* xiv. (1861) 237 So I just put my eye between the wall and the dern of the gate, and I saw him come up to the back door. **1880** *E. Cornwall Gloss., Derns*, the wooden frame in which a door swings. **1886** COLE *W. Lincolnsh. Gloss.* s.v. *Door-dern*, I am sure the doors were in, leastways the derns were. **1888** ELWORTHY *W. Somerset Word-bk., Durns*, the frame of a door *in situ*.. applied to a solid door-frame. *Ibid.*, *Durn-head*, the cross piece at the top of a door-frame.

b. *Mining.* **durns** (as a *sing.*), A frame of timbering; also called DOOR-STEAD (b).

1778 PRYCE *Min. Cornub.* 166 If the ground is very loose on all sides, they make a Durns.. which for a Shaft is square like the frame of a window, and for an Adit is the same as a door case. **1877** tr. *Callon's Lect. Mining* I. 257 (Cent. s.v. *Set*), A gallery requires what are called frames (sets or durnzes) for its proper support.

durn: see DARE *v.*[1]

durn, *U.S.* var. DARN *sb.*[2], *adv.*, *a.*, and *v.*[2] Cf. DERN, DURNED.

1835 A. B. LONGSTREET *Georgia Scenes* 18 Old Boler's.. broke a dish and two plates all to durn smashes! **1866** C. H. SMITH *Bill Arp* Durn the staff and Joe Brown, too. **1867** G. W. HARRIS *Sut Lovingood* 32, I can't say that es a human shut [shirt] I'd gin a durn fur a dozin ove em. **1888** *Portland Transcript* (Farmer), I'll bet I could make as good-lookin' a burst as any o' these,—an' mebbe a durn sight better. **1898** H. S. CANFIELD *Maid of Frontier* 176 It was as much as a man's life was worth to say 'durn' out loud. **1918** *Sat. Even. Post* 5 Jan. 12 If I'd been as big as you be they wouldn't have cared a durn about my eyes. **1936** W. FAULKNER *Absalom, Absalom!* 44 Boys, this time he stole the whole durn steamboat!

durned, var. of DARNED, euphem. for DAMNED.

1876 BESANT & RICE *Gold. Butterfly* viii, It was the durndest misbegotten location.. that ever called itself a city. **1895** *Harper's Mag.* Mar. 648/1 Palaces be durned! Excuse my French.

‖**duro** ('duro). [Sp.: for *peso duro* hard or solid piastre.] The Spanish silver dollar, or piastre.

1832 W. IRVING *Alhambra* 39 (Stanf.) A peseta (the fifth of a duro, or dollar). **1869** in *Mem. & Rem. J. D. Burns* v. 81 The talk of the Brazilians was of Spanish duros, bales of cotton, and yellow fever.

duro, var. DOURO.

†**'durous**, *a. Obs. rare.* [f. L. *dūr-us* hard + -OUS.] Hard.

1666 J. SMITH *Old Age* (ed. 2) 186 They [glandules] all of them vary much from their primitive tenderness and bigness, and so become more durous.

†**duroy** (də'rɔɪ). *Obs.* Also 7 deroy. [Of uncertain origin: perh. Fr. *du roi* of the king. *Glossaire* to *Encyclopédie Méthodique* (1790) vol. II gives '*Duroi*, étoffe de laine, rase et sèche, dans le genre de la tamise, mais moins large et plus serrée'.]

A kind of coarse woollen fabric formerly manufactured in the west of England; akin to the stuffs called *tammies*. (Not the same as *corduroy*.)

1619 PURCHAS *Microcosm.* xxvii. 269 The Colours of Gingelline, Grideline, Deroy, Elderado, Droppe du Berry. **1722** *Lond. Gaz.* No. 6089/4 Wearing a grey Duroy Coat and Wastcoat. **1722** DE FOE *Col. Jack* (1840) 331 Fine silk drugget and duroys. **1769** *De Foe's Tour Gt. Brit.* I. 93. **1778** *Eng. Gazetteer* (ed. 2.) s.v. *Somersetshire*, The manufactures are chiefly fine cloths, druggets, duroys, shalloons, serges. **1807** VANCOUVER *Agric. Devon* (1813) 385 Those [manufactures] formerly carried on at North and South Molton, consisted chiefly of duroys, serges, and other light cloths.

‖**durra, dhurra** ('dʊrə). Also dourra, doura(h, dura, doora(h, durrah, dhourra. [Arabic *ðurah*, *ðurrah*.] A kind of corn, Indian Millet (*Sorghum vulgare*).

1798 MALTHUS *Popul.* I. x. (1806) I. 214 A little flat cake of barley or dourra. **1832** *Veg. Subst. Food* 117 Panicled Millet is the species most usually cultivated.. In India it is called jovaree; in Egypt and Nubia dhourra. **1867** BAKER *Nile Tribut.* 77 The dhurra.. is the grain most commonly used throughout the Soudan. **1876** S. MANNING *Land of Pharaohs* 67 Riding through some fields of doorah and vetch. **1877** A. B. EDWARDS *Up Nile* vi. 140 The strip of cultivated soil, green with maize or tawny with doora. **1925** *Blackw. Mag.* Sept. 423/2 Largesse was forthcoming in the shape of increased rations, both meat and dura. **1926** *Spectator* 24 Apr. 757/1 The only agriculture carried on was the cultivation of 'dura'. **1966** C. SWEENEY *Scurrying Bush* xii. 177 A man from the village of Korongo Tabanya was walking along a path.. to his field of *dura*.

attrib. **1834** *Penny Cycl.* II. 212/1 Dates, durra-bread, and fish. **1883** V. STUART *Egypt* 27 Coarse, reed-like dourra straw. **1885** *Times* 3 Jan. 12 The whole district is busy just now with the durrah harvest.

durre, obs. f. DARE *v.*[1], DOOR.

Durrellian (dʌ'rɛlɪən), *a.* [See -IAN.] Of or pertaining to the English writer Lawrence *Durrell* (born 1912), or his style. Also **Durre'llesque** *a.*

1961 *New Statesman* 21 July 92/3 In the background there is that damned baroque sea, going through its daily transformations in a spray of Durrellian metaphors. **1961** *Spectator* 22 Dec. 922 The Durrellesque fantasy of a Coptic-Zionist alliance. **1966** *Economist* 17 Sept. 1152/3 One or two of the portraits, notably that of the old Imam Ahmad of the Yemen, are almost Durrell-ian gems. **1970** *Guardian* 26 Mar. 11/6 The usual Durrellian whirligig of allusions and illusions, quotes and echoes.

durrie, durry, varr. DHURRIE.

durst, pa. t. (and *dial.* pa. pple.) of DARE *v.*[1]

durt, durwe, obs. forms of DIRT, DWARF.

durum ('d(j)uːrəm). [f. L. *durum*, neut. of *dūrus* hard, used as the specific epithet of *Triticum durum* (R. L. Desfontaines *Flora Atlantica* (1798) I. 114).] In full ***durum wheat***. A species of wheat, *Triticum durum*, or one of its varieties, characterized by hard seeds rich in gluten and yielding a flour used in the manufacture of spaghetti, etc.

1908 P. T. DONDLINGER *Bk. Wheat* i. 8 There are several kinds of the less common wheats, such as Polish wheat, spelt and durum wheat. **1911** *Encycl. Brit.* XIV. 276/2 A wonderful region for growing the *durum* or macaroni wheat. **1921** *Nature* CVII. 251/1 The common wheats, such as Marquis, were susceptible, the durums such as Kubanka, 'commercially resistant'. **1961** *Economist* 26 Aug. 822/1 Durum wheat, an extremely hard wheat normally grown in hot climates and used to make pasta dishes like spaghetti and macaroni, has risen steeply in price.

durwan (dɜː'wɑːn). *India.* Also 8 derwan, dirwan, door-van, 9 darwan. [Hind. (a. Pers.) *darwān*.] A porter or door-keeper.

1773 E. IVES *Voy. to India* 50 Derwan. These are properly porters, who sit at the gate to receive messages, &c. **1781** *Bengal Gaz.* 14 Apr. (Yule), A Door-van is well known to be the alarm of the House. **1784** in W. S. Seton-Karr *Sel. fr. Calcutta Gaz.* (1864) I. 12 A most extraordinary and horrid murder was committed upon the Dirwan of Thomas Martin, Esq. **1874** *Calcutta Rev.* LIX. 207 In the entrance passage.. is a raised floor with one or two open cells in which the *darwáns* (or door keepers) sit, lie and sleep. **1926** *Blackw. Mag.* June 726/2 His durwan.. refused to awaken a sleeping man.

durward, -warth, obs. forms of DOORWARD.

†**durze**, *v. dial. Obs.* Also durse. *intr.* Of corn: To shed the grains, as when over-ripe. *trans.* To shake or beat out (corn) from the ear.

1641 BEST *Farm. Bks.* (Surtees) 50 If they [mowers] shoulde not follow the corne, and goe with the winde, the oates woulde slipe and durze extreamely with the cradles. *Ibid.* 52 [They] remove things out of the way, fey up dursed corne, and lye strawe on the floores. **1674-91** RAY *N.C. Words* 23 *Durz'd* or *Dorz'd out*; it is spoken of Corn, that by Wind turning of it, etc. is beaten out of the Straw. *Ibid.* 57 Corn—so dry that it easily durses out.

durzee ('dɜːziː). *India.* Also derzie, -y, dhirzee, dhurzee, dirge, dirgee, dir(d)jee, dirzie, durjee. [Hind. (a. Pers.) *darzī* (Pers. *darz* sewing, hem).] A tailor.

1812 M. GRAHAM *Jrnl. Resid. India* 30 The *derdjees*, or taylors, in Bombay, are Hindoos of a respectable caste. **1834** A. PRINSEP *Baboo* II. x. 180 The milliners and durzees of the City of Palaces. *a* **1847** M. M. SHERWOOD *Life* (1854) xvi. 300 We took other servants, Dirges, and Dobes. **1848** *Alfred in India* 18 The needlework of the family is done by a *durzie*, or tailor. **1884** D. AUBREY *Lett. fr. Bombay* 204 Their parents have no wish to make 'dirzees' or tailors of them. **1894** M. DYAN *Man's Keeping* i, Manufacturing, with the incompetent aid of her durzee, a gown for the ball. **1922** *Blackw. Mag.* Feb. 183/2 The regimental dhurzee. **1969** *Islander* (Victoria, B.C.) 6 July 2/3 And the names! Ayahs, kansamahs, chuprassis, peons, chowkidars, durzis, dhobis, kitmutgars. Wonderful names and each with a different job.

dus, obs. form of *does*, etc.: see DO *v.*

dusan(e, obs. form of DOZEN.

duschet, obs. Sc. f. DOUCET (sense 2), a kind of pipe or flute.

1583 *Leg. Bp. St. Androis* 88 in *Satir. Poems Reform.* xlv, Bot for to tell what text he tuike, Dysertis Duschet was the buike. *Ibid.* 270 Vpon his duschet vpe he played.

duseanne, obs. form of DOUCIN.

duseliche, obs. form of DIZZILY.

†**duseling.** *Obs.* [app. f. Ger. *duseln* to be dizzy. Cf. DOZZLE.] Dizziness, giddiness.

1561 HOLLYBUSH *Hom. Apoth.* 36 a, If it is a hote humor ..he hath a duselynge.

duselle, obs. form of DOSSIL.

duseperys, var. DOUZEPERS, *Obs.*

dusey, dusie, obs. forms of DIZZY.

dush (dʌʃ), *v. Obs.* exc. *Sc.* Forms: 4 dusshe, 4-6 dusche, 6- dush. [Found in 14th c.: perh. a modification of DASH, expressing the same kind of action with a suggestion of more muffled sound: cf. *crash*, *crush*. But there are similar continental words, as Ger. dial. *duschen*, *düschen*, *dussen*, to beat, strike, knock, box (see Grimm, s.v. *Dusen*[2]); E. Fris. *dössen* to beat, etc. Cf. *Douse*.]

†**1.** *intr.* To move with violent impulse or collision; to rush or strike forcibly against something; to fall with a thud. *Obs.*

13.. *E.E. Allit. P.* B. 1538 Such a dasande drede dusched to his hert. *c* **1400** *Destr. Troy* 6410 He dusshet, of þe dynt, dede to þe ground. *c* **1450** HENRYSON *Mor. Fab.* 37 For dread of death hee dushed ouer ane Dyke And brack his neck. **1513** DOUGLAS *Æneis* x. vi. 109 Owt throw the scheyld ..Duschit the dynt.

2. *trans.* To push or throw down violently.

1785 BURNS *Vision* i. 45, I glowr'd as eerie's I'd been dusht In some wild glen. **1825** BROCKETT *N.C. Gloss.*, *Dush*, to push with violence. **1892** *Northumb. Gloss.*, *Dush*, to thrust, to strike. (*Obs.*)

Hence **'dushing** *vbl. sb.*

1340 HAMPOLE *Pr. Consc.* 7351 Raumpyng of devels and dyngyng and dusching.

†**dush**, *sb. Obs.* exc. *Sc.* Also 4-6 dusch(e, dosche. [f. prec. vb.] A violent blow, stroke, or impact; the sound of violent collision.

1375 BARBOUR *Bruce* XIII. 147 [Thai] with axis sic duschis gaff. *c* **1400** *Melayne* 470 A fire þan fro þe crosse gane frusche, And in the Saraȝene eȝhne it gaffe a dosche. *c* **1425** WYNTOUN *Cron.* IX. xxvii. 407 Dusch for dusch, and dynt for dynt. **1513** DOUGLAS *Æneis* v. iii. 82 With mony lasche and dusche, The carteris smat thar horsis fast in teyn. **1819** W. TENNANT *Papistry Storm'd* (1827) 144 Heav'n rattles wi' the dunnerin' dush.

†**dusi**, *a. Obs.*, foolish: see DIZZY *a.* 1.

†**'dusilec.** *Obs.* [Early ME., f. *dusi*, DIZZY + *-lec*, *-leke*, *-leche*, suffix of action or function.] Foolishness, folly.

a **1225** *Leg. Kath.* 425 Nis bute dusilec al þæt ha drihteð.

†**'dusischip.** *Obs.* [as prec. + -SHIP.] = prec.

a **1225** *Leg. Kath.* 1817 To longe we habbeð idriuen ure dusischipes. *a* **1225** *Ancr. R.* 182 Nout þet [sicnesse] sum keccheð þuruh hire owune dusischipe.

dusk (dʌsk), *a.* and *sb.* Forms: 3 deosc, deosk, dosc, 3-6 dosk, 5-6 duske, doske, 6- dusk. [Origin and phonetic history obscure.

OE. had in the same, or an allied sense, *dox*, which, if = **dosc*, would repr. an OTeut. **dusko-z*:—Aryan **dhuskos*, to which Kluge refers also L. *fuscus*. The relation of mod. *dusk* to OE. *dox*, **dosc*, presents some difficulties, both as to the vowel, and, still more, in regard to the final consonant-group. Few of our words in *-sk* are of OE. origin; OE. *-sc* normally gives *-sh* in later English, e.g. in *ash*, *dish*, *fish*, *bush*, *rush*; so that from OE. *dosc* we should expect *dosh*, or, at least, as in the case of *ask* and *tusk*, ME. and mod. forms in *-sh*, and *-x*, beside the *-sk* form.]

A. *adj.* (Now largely supplanted by *dusky*.)

1. Dark from absence of light; dim, gloomy, shadowy; dark-coloured, blackish; dusky. (Now usually in reference to twilight: cf. B. 2.)

[*a* **1000** *Aldhelm Gloss* (*Anglia* XIII. 28 No. 8) *Furva*, dohx. —— *OE. Gloss.* in Wr.-Wülcker 239/35 *Flava specie*, of glæteriendum *vel* scylfrum hiwe *vel* doxum.] *a* **1225** *Ancr. R.* 94 þe sihðe þæt is nu deosc her. *a* **1240** *Sawles Warde* in *Cott. Hom.* 259 Aȝein þe brihtnesse ant te liht of his leor, þe sunne gleam is dosc. *a* **1450** *Fysshynge w. Angle* (1883) 34 The body of doske wull. **1496** *Bk. St. Albans, Fishing* 9 Yelowe: grene: browne: tawney: russet: and duske colours. **1513** DOUGLAS *Æneis* VII. Prol. 63 The grund stude barrand, widderit, dosk and gray. **1667** MILTON *P.L.* XI. 741 Vapour and Exhalation, dusk and moist. **1703** MAUNDRELL *Journ. Jerus.* (1732) 72 As soon as it grew dusk. **1832** HT. MARTINEAU *Ireland* v. 79 Every evening, as it became dusk. **1847** TENNYSON *Princess* II. 5 As rich as moths from dusk cocoons.

fig. **1573-80** BARET *Alv.* D 1375 Wisedome is made duske, or dimme by drinking of wine: it is obscured and darkened.

†**2.** Obscure, veiled from sight or understanding.

a **1225** *Ancr. R.* 148 þis word is deosk. **1583** STANYHURST *Æneis* II. (Arb.) 62 My mother, the godesse (who was accustomed algats Eare this tyme present to be dusk).

B. *sb.*

1. The quality of being dusk; that which is dusk; duskiness, shade; gloom (as of a forest).

1700 DRYDEN *Palamon & A.* III. 77 Freckles.. Whose dusk set off the whiteness of the skin. **1705** STANHOPE *Paraphr.* I. 25 Frail Mortality will always have some Remains of Shadow and Dusk. **1850** TENNYSON *In Mem.* ii, And in the dusk of thee [Old Yew], the clock Beats out the little lives of men.

2. a. The darker stage of twilight before it is quite dark at night, or when the darkness begins to give way in the morning.

1622 MABBE tr. *Aleman's Guzman d'Alf.* II. 313 In the duske of the evening. **1726** *Adv. Capt. R. Boyle* 218, I would not fail waiting on her the Sunday following, after Dusk. **1833** J. RENNIE *Alph. Angling* 21 Light colours in the dusk of morning or evening, and dark colours in.. bright weather. **1893** *Law Times* XCV. 268/2 The gardens of Lincoln's Inn will.. be thrown open.. from three until dusk.

fig. **1755** YOUNG *Centaur* v. Wks. 1757 IV. 233 To grope out our weary way, through the dusk of life, to our final home.

b. *attrib.*, as ***dusk-hour***, ***-light***, ***-time***.

1881 A. B. & S. EVANS *Leics. Words* 143 **Dusk-hour*, late evening twilight. 'Ah shouldn' like to mate his oogly mug upo' *dusk-hour* in a daa'k leane.' **1937** W. DE LA MARE *Poems*, Perhaps 'twas the talk of chance farers.. In the *dusk-light clear? **1957** J. KEROUAC *On Road* (1958) IV. vi. 300 We saw all of Mexico City stretched out.. spewing city smokes and early dusklights. **1890** J. D. ROBERTSON *Gloss. Gloucester* 42 **Dusk time*, evening.

Hence **'duskly** *adv.*; **'duskness.**

1382 WYCLIF *Job* xxiii. 17 Dusknesse couerede my face. **1531** ELYOT *Gov.* III. xxii, Paynfull diseases and sickenesses ..duskenesse of sight. **1844** MRS. BROWNING *Drama of Exile* Wks. 1889 I. 42 Shapes which have no certainty of shape Drift duskly in and out between the pines. **1864** NEALE *Seaton. Poems* 68 Duskness and dreariness around. **1880** W. WATSON *Prince's Quest* 58 An eagle with wide wings outspread Athwart the sunfire hovering duskly red.

dusk, *v.* [f. DUSK *a.*; OE. had *doxian*, from *dox*. See Kluge *Engl. Studien* XI. 511.]

1. *intr.* To become dusk or dim; to grow dark.

[*a* **1000** *Vercelli MS.* lf. 2 b, þonne wannað he [dead body] and doxaþ; oðre hwile he bið blæc and schiwe.] *c* **1230** *Hali Meid.* 35 þine ehnen schulen doskin. *c* **1386** CHAUCER *Knt.'s T.* 1948 Dusked hise eyen two and failled breeth. *c* **1430** LYDG. *Bochas* I. iv. (1544) 6 b, By process of yeres Their memory hath dusked. **1876** MORRIS *Sigurd* III. 217 The even dusketh o'er that sword-renowned close. **1888** G. GISSING *Life's Morning* xi. (1890) 169 When it began to dusk, Hood descended and supper was prepared.

b. To exhibit a dusky appearance.

1832 TENNYSON *Lady of Shalott* i, Little breezes dusk and shiver. **1889** MRS. RANDOLPH *New Eve* I. Prol. 2 A copse of aspens dusked and shivered near the brink.

2. *trans.* To make dusky or somewhat dark in colour; to darken, obscure; to dim.

c **1374** CHAUCER *Boeth.* I. pr. i. 2 (Camb. MS.) The whiche clothes a dirknesse of a forletyn and a despised Elde hadde dusked and derked. **1549** CHALONER *Erasm. on Folly* Q iv b, They goe about to duske mens eies with smoke. **1577** STANYHURST *Descr. Irel.* in *Holinshed* (1807-8) VI. 51 You must not think that.. you may so easilie duske or dazell our eies. **1601** HOLLAND *Pliny* I. 9 That shadow which dusketh the light of the Moone. **1869** LOWELL *Cathedral* xiii, Poet. Wks. 1890 IV. 47 The painted windows.. Dusking the sunshine which they seem to cheer.

b. *fig.* To obscure, darken, cloud, sully.

c **1394** *P. Pl. Crede* 563 þe.. poyntes of scheldes Wiþdrawen his deuocion & dusken his herte. *a* **1533** LD. BERNERS *Gold. Bk. M. Aurel.* (1546) C vij b, The onely vnderstandyng, which is dusked in errours. **1680** *Counterplots* 33 [It] would.. dusk the lustre of his Name. **1848** LYTTON *K. Arthur* XII. lv, One appalling silence dusk'd the place As with A demon's wing.

Hence **'dusked** *ppl. a.*; **'dusking** *vbl. sb.* and *ppl. a.*

c **1430** LYDG. *Min. Poems* 204 (Mätz.) Hire cote armure is duskyd reed. **1533** ELYOT *Cast. Helthe* (1541) 72 b, Duskynge of the eyes, head aches, thyn reumes. **1566** DRANT *Horace's Sat.* v. D iij, The worlde is bliearde with duskyng shoes [= shows]. **1820** KEATS *Hyperion* II. 375 Who travels from the dusking East.

dusken ('dʌsk(ə)n), *v. rare.* [f. DUSK *a.*: see -EN⁵.] **a.** *trans.* To make dusk or obscure. **b.** *intr.* To grow dusk.

1550 NICOLLS *Thucyd.* 163 The sayd Epigrame was not vtterly defaced, but onely duskened or so rased, that it myght be redde, thoughe..with..difficultie. **1870** LOWELL *Study Wind.* I. 10 Till twilight duskened into dark.

†**'dusketly**, *a. Obs. rare.* [? erroneous form.] ? Of somewhat dusky colour.

1486 *Bk. St. Albans. Her.* A iij a, An Ametisce a dusketli stone, brusk hit is calde in armys.

duskily ('dʌskılı), *adv.* [f. DUSKY *a.* + -LY².] In a dusky, dim, or obscure manner; dimly.

1611 COTGR., *Obscurement*, obscurely, darkly..duskily. **1797** MRS. RADCLIFFE *Italian* vii, Those arches that stand duskily beyond the citadel. *a* **1851** MOIR *Poems, Deserted Churchyard* iv, Or the crow that..Sail'd through the twilight duskily. **1872** BLACK *Adv. Phaeton* xvi.

duskiness ('dʌskınıs). [f. as prec. + -NESS.] The quality of being dusky; partial darkness or blackness; dimness, gloom.

1611 COTGR., *Obscurité*, obscuritie, darknesse.. duskinesse. **1659** HAMMOND *On Ps.* xci. 5 Duskyness or twilight. **1775** BOSWELL *Let. to Johnson* 18 Feb. in *Life*, One of them [manuscripts]..does appear to have the duskyness of antiquity. *a* **1851** MOIR *Poems, Matin Carol* ii. **1861** L. L. NOBLE *Icebergs* 141 A gloomy duskiness drapes the cape.

duskish ('dʌskıʃ), *a.* [f. DUSK *a.* + -ISH.] Somewhat dusk or dusky; blackish; partly obscure.

1530 PALSGR. 310/2 Doskysshe of colour, *soubz brun.* **1576** FLEMING *Panopl. Epist.* 47 As duskish cloudes do darken dayes. **1624** WOTTON *Archit.* (1672) 61 Let them have rather a Duskish Tincture, then an absolute black. **1741** RICHARDSON *Pamela* (1824) I. 91 To return as soon as it was duskish. **1840** T. HOOK in *New Monthly Mag.* LX. 290 It was getting duskish. **1842** D. R. HAY *Nomencl. Colours* (1846) 36 Described as a duskish red.

¶ Used as *sb.* The time when it is near dusk.

1696 S. SEWALL *Diary* 25 Oct. (1878) I. 436 About duskish we know there is a house on fire. **1745** *Gentl. Mag.* 105 At duskish the Dreadnought was about 7 miles astern.

duskishly ('dʌskıʃlı), *adv.* [f. prec. + -LY².] In a duskish manner; duskily; obscurely.

1589 FLEMING *Virg. Georg.* IV. 65 Purple hew..dooth somwhat duskishly shine in the leaues. **1626** BACON *Sylva* §369 To burn duskishly. **1664** PEPYS *Diary* 27 Dec., The Comet appeared again to-night, but duskishly.

duskishness ('dʌskıʃnıs). [f. as prec. + -NESS.] The quality of being duskish or slightly dark; slight obscurity or dimness.

1533 ELYOT *Cast. Helthe* (1541) 52 a, Fumositie ascendynge up into the head..causeth..duskyshness of the sight. **1604** HIERON *Wks.* I. 497 Men in the duskishness of ignorance. **1769** WINTHROP in *Phil. Trans.* LIX. 356 There seemed to be a duskishness in the place of contact.

duskly, duskness: see after DUSK *sb.*

dusky ('dʌskı), *a.* [f. DUSK *a.* (or ? *sb.*) + -Y¹. The normal source of an adj. in -*y* is a sb.; but the substantival use of *dusk* is not known so early as the appearance of *dusky*, so that the latter would appear to be one of the rare instances of a secondary adj.: cf. the parallel *worth, worthy, murk* (*mirk*), *murky*; also *ready*.]

1. Somewhat black or dark in colour; dark-coloured; darkish.

Also used to specify animals or plants characterized by this colour, as ***dusky ant, crane's-bill, duck, grebe, lark, petrel***, etc.

1558 PHAER *Æneid* v. (R.), A showre aboue his head there stoode, all dusky blacke with blew. **1590** GREENE *Never too late* (1600) 34 No duskie vapour did bright Phœbus shroude. **1626** BACON *Sylva* §554 It is not greene, but of a duskie browne Colour. **1763** E. STONE in *Phil. Trans.* LIII. 199 Of a light brown, tinged with a dusky yellow. **1827** POLLOK *Course T.* v, Afric's dusky swarms. **1860** TYNDALL *Glac.* I. iii. 30 The peaks in front deepened to a dusky neutral tint. **1861** MISS PRATT *Flower. Pl.* II. 36 Dusky Crane's-bill.. flowers..of a dingy, purplish black colour. **1865** WOOD *Homes without H.* vii. (1868) 125 The Dusky Ant..generally prefers banks with a southern aspect.

2. Somewhat dark or deficient in light; not bright or luminous; dim, obscure.

1580 SIDNEY *Ps.* XXXIII. ix, Who dwell in duskie place. **1591** SHAKS. *1 Hen. VI*, II. v. 122 Here dyes the duskie Torch of Mortimer, Choakt with Ambition of the meaner sort. **1667** MILTON *P.L.* v. 667 Midnight brought on the duskie houre Friendliest to sleep and silence. **1775** ROMANS *Hist. Florida* 95 As soon as it is dusky they make a fire of dry pitch pine. **1826** SCOTT *Woodst.* iii, One end of this long and dusky apartment. **1876** DAVIS *Polaris Exp.* vi. 168 From 4 to 5 in the evening, it is quite dusky.

3. *fig.* Gloomy, melancholy.

1602 MARSTON *Ant. & Mel.* Induct., Wks. 1856 I. 3 Why looke you so duskie? *Ibid.* III. ibid. 41, I..fill a seat In the darke cave of dusky misery. **1692** BENTLEY *Boyle Lect.* 24 That dusky scene of horror, that melancholy prospect. **1762** FALCONER *Shipwr.* I. 195 Here no dusky frown prevails.

4. *Comb.*, as ***dusky-faced, -raftered, -tinted***, etc.

1730–46 THOMSON *Autumn* 1088 The dusky-mantled lawn. **1825** LONGF. *Spirit Poetry* 9 The..dusky-sandaled Eve. **1848** WALSH *Aristoph., Clouds* I. iii, Dusky-faced clouds.

Hence '**duskyish** *a.*, somewhat dusky.

1794 MRS. RADCLIFFE *Myst. Udolpho* xxv, Too far off to see him, if it was pretty duskyish.

†**dusky**, *v. Obs.* [f. DUSKY *a.*] *trans.* To make or render dusky.

1567 MAPLET *Gr. Forest* 19 It is not so soone dulled or duskied as many other be.

dusodile, erroneous form of DYSODYLE.

duspers, dussiperes, var. DOUZEPERS.

dussel, obs. form of DOSSIL, plug.

14.. *Voc.* in Wr.-Wülcker 579/11 *Docillus*, a dussel.

dussen, -on, obs. forms of DOZEN.

‖**dusserah** ('dʌsərɑː). *E. Indies.* Also **dusrah, desserah, dasserah.** [a. Hindī *dasahrā*, Marāṭhi *dasrā*, Skr. *daçaharā*.] A Hindu annual festival extending over nine nights (or ten days) in the month Jaishṭha (Sept.–Oct.).

1799 SIR J. MALCOLM in *Trans. Bombay Lit. Soc.* (1820) III. 73 (*title*) On the institution and ceremonies of the Hindoo Festival of the Dusrah. **1813** J. FORBES *Oriental Mem.* IV. 97 (Y.) This being the desserah, a great Hindoo festival..we resolved to delay our departure and see some part of the ceremonies. **1849** *Benares Mag.* II. 1 Our friends ..are coming over to spend the Dasserah with us. **1889** *Daily News* 7 Oct. 5/6 The Mahommedans have built a mosque in a street through which the Hindoo procession passes on the occasion of the Dusserah festival.

dussie, obs. Sc. var. DOUCET (sense 2), a kind of pipe or flute: cf. DUSCHET.

1583 *Leg. Bp. St. Androis* 180 in *Satir. Poems Reform.* xlv, He toned his dussie for a spring.

dussiner, obs. form of DOZENER.

dust (dʌst), *sb.*¹ Forms: 1– **dust**: also 3 (*Orm.*) dusst, 3–5 doust(e, 4 dost, 4–6 duste. [OE. *dúst* (later prob. *dust*) = OFris. and EFris. *dûst*, OLG., MLG., LG. *dust*, MDu. *donst, dunst, dûst* fine flour, Kilian *duyst, donst, dûst*, mod.Du. *duist* meal-dust, bran, ON. *dust* dust, Da. *dyst* mill-dust. All these go back to an earlier *dunst*, whence also Ger. *dunst* vapour; the primary notion being app. that which rises or is blown in a cloud, like vapour, smoke, or dust. See Kluge, and Franck.]

1. a. Earth or other solid matter in a minute and fine state of subdivision, so that the particles are small and light enough to be easily raised and carried in a cloud by the wind; any substance comminuted or pulverized; powder. (Rarely in *pl.*)

Often extended to include ashes and other refuse from a house: cf. DUST-BIN, etc.

c **825** *Vesp. Psalt.* xvii[i]. 43 Swe swe dust biforan onsieme windes. *c* **1000** *Sax. Leechd.* I. 290 Ʒedriȝede & to swyðe smælon duste ȝecnucude. *c* **1205** LAY. 27646 þenne he þat dust [*c* **1275** doust] heȝe Aȝiueð from þere eorðe. **1340** *Ayenb.* 108 Of motes and of doust wyþ oute tale. **1398** TREVISA *Barth. De P.R.* XVII clix. (1495) 708 To clense houses of duste. *c* **1450** *Two Cookery-bks.* 112 Bray hem al to doust in a morter. **1583** HOLLYBAND *Campo di Fior* 367 Beate these upper hose that the dust maye come out. **1620** *Nottingham Rec.* IV. 367 Presentmentes..for castinge theire dust and ashes into the highe way. **1760** WESLEY *Jrnl.* 19 Aug., We had..showers, which..laid the dust. **1886** A. WINCHELL *Walks & Talks Geol. Field* 212 Clouds of cosmic dust intervene between us and the sun. **1894** *Daily News* 26 June 8/3 Of the whole of the dusts tested, that from the Albion Colliery..excelled all others in violence and sensitiveness to explosion.

b. The fine or small particles separated in any process: cf. *sawdust*; *spec.* (see quot. 1828).

1552 HULOET, Duste of corne, mettall, or anye other thinge that commeth of wyth fylynge and clensing. **1598** *Sc. Acts Jas. VI* (1814) 179 (Jam.) Paying alss deir for dust and seidis as gif the samyn wes guid meill. **1644** DIGBY *Nat. Bodies* (1645) I. 22 It will..swimme upon the water like dust of wood. **1794** T. DAVIS *Agric. Wilts* in *Archæol. Rev.* (1888) Mar., *Cave*, or *dust*, the chaff of the wheat and oats which is generally given to the horse. **1828** *Craven Dial.*, *Dust*, the small particles separated from the oats in the act of shelling.

c. Applied to the pollen of flowers.

1776 WITHERING *Brit. Plants* I. xxii, The fine dust or meal that is contained in the Tips, is thrown upon the Summit of the Pointal. **1807** J. E. SMITH *Phys. Bot.* 272 The Pollen, or Dust, is contained in the Anther. **1894** H. DRUMMOND *Ascent of Man* 301 The butterfly and the bee..carry the fertilizing dust to the waiting stigma.

2. With *a* and *pl.* **a.** A grain of dust, a minute particle of dry matter; **b.** in *Cookery*, etc., a small 'pinch' of something in the form of powder.

1593 SHAKS. *Rich. II*, II. iii. 91 Why haue these banish'd ..Legges Dar'd once to touch a Dust of Englands Ground? **1595** —— *John* IV. i. 93 A graine, a dust, a gnat, a wandering haire. **1674** N. FAIRFAX *Bulk & Selv.* 105 'Tis impossible to put so much as one jot or dust unto bulk, beyond a set or bounded number. **1701** WATTS *Horæ Lyr., True Monarchy* 52 Wealth and fame A bubble or a dust. **1784** M. UNDERWOOD *Treat. Dis. Children* (1799) I. 54 With, or without, a dust of grated nutmeg. *a* **1854** C. B. SOUTHEY *Poet. Wks.* (1867) 50 If a mote, a hair, a dust prepond On Inclination's side, down drops the scale.

c. (With *a*) A cloud of dust floating in the air, such as is raised by a vehicle driven or a crowd walking over dusty ground, or by sweeping, etc.

1570–81 [see 4 and 5]. **1659** D. PELL *Impr. Sea* 188 Oh what a dust do I raise. **1806** *Oracle* in *Spirit Pub. Jrnls.* (1807) X. 53 To kick up the d——l of a dust in Rotten-row. *Mod.* What a dust you are making!

3. *transf.* and *fig.* (from 1.) **a.** That to which anything is reduced by disintegration or decay; *spec.* the 'ashes', or mouldered remains of a dead body. Also in phrases denoting the condition of being dead and buried (***laid in the dust***, etc.).

? *a* **1000** *Martyrol.* (E.E.T.S.) 74 þæt hi mihton mid heora handum ræcan ond niman þæs halȝan dustes. *c* **1350** *Will. Palerne* 4124 Many a day hade i be ded and to dust roted. **1388** WYCLIF *Ps.* xxi[i]. 16 Thou hast brouȝt forth me in to the dust of deth. **1602** SHAKS. *Ham.* v. i. 225 Why may not imagination trace the Noble dust of Alexander, till he find it stopping a bunghole? **1676** I. MATHER *Hist. K. Philip's War* (1862) 38 That Great Author, unto whose dust..I owe a sacred Reverence. **1750** GRAY *Elegy* xi, Can Honour's voice provoke the silent dust? **1803** *Med. Jrnl.* IX. 263 One, without whose friendly aid the hand which writes this would long since have been in the dust. **1869** FREEMAN *Norm. Conq.* III. xi. §2. 40 Worthier dust lies east and west of him.

b. Applied to the mortal frame of man (usually in reference to Gen. ii. 7, iii. 19).

c **1000** ÆLFRIC *Gen.* iii. 19 For þan þe þu eart dust, and to dust wyrst. *Ibid.* xviii. 27 Nu ic æne begann to sprecanne to minum Drihtene þonne ic eom dust and axe. *a* **1175** *Cott. Hom.* 223 þu ært dust, and þu awenst to duste. **1388** WYCLIF *Ps.* cii[i]. 14 He bithouȝte that we ben dust. *c* **1450** tr. *De Imitatione* III. ix. 76 þouȝ I be dust & asshen. **1548–9** (Mar.) *Bk. Com. Prayer, Burial*, Earth to earth, asshes to asshes, dust to dust. **1613** PURCHAS *Pilgrimage* (1614) 11, How covetous, how proude is dust and ashes of dust and earth. **1814** CARY *Dante, Par.* II. 133 The soul, that dwells within your dust. **18..** SIR R. GRANT *Hymn*, '*O worship the King*' v, Frail children of dust, And feeble as frail.

c. In phrases denoting a condition of humiliation.

a **1340** HAMPOLE *Psalter* Cant. 501 Raysand þe nedy out of dust. **1535** COVERDALE *Ps.* lxxi[i]. 9 His enemies shal licke the dust. **1591** SHAKS. *1 Hen. VI*, v. iii. 29 Now France, thy glory droopeth to the dust. **1667** MILTON *P.L.* IV. 416 The Power..That rais'd us from the dust and plac't us here. **1718** WATTS *Ps.* li. III. vi, My soul lies humbled in the dust. **1850** TENNYSON *In Mem.* Prol. iii, Thou wilt not leave us in the dust. **1894** C. N. ROBINSON *Brit. Fleet* 186 The Navy that..humbled to the dust the pride of France.

d. As the type of that which is worthless.

a **1300** *Cursor M.* 23786 For a littel lust, A druri þat es bot a dust. **1576** FLEMING *Panopl. Epist.* 282 Thus whiles they search for gold and silver, they search for dust and sand. **1694** *Acc. Sev. Late Voy.* II. (1711) 168 A Long-boat he [the whale] values no more than Dust. **1818** JAS. MILL *Brit. India* II. IV. ix. 296 The rights conferred by charter [were] treated as dust.

e. In other figurative uses.

1620 T. GRANGER *Syntag. Logic.* 382 Besprinkled with the powder, or dust of veniall imperfections. **1682** EARL OF ANGLESEA *Pref. to Whitelocke's Mem.*, The dust of action [had] never fallen on his gown. **1699** BENTLEY *Phal.* (1836) II. 29 The very dust of his writings is gold.

f. ***dust and ashes*** (in allusion to the legend of the Dead Sea Fruit): used to indicate severe disappointment or disillusionment.

1902 W. JAMES *Var. Relig. Exper.* vi. 143 Trustful self-abandonment to the joys that freely offer has entirely departed from both Epicurean and Stoic; and what each proposes is a way of rescue from the resultant dust-and-ashes state of mind. **1911** BEERBOHM *Zuleika D.* xxi. 310 But there was no spark of triumph now in her eyes; only a deep melancholy; and in her mouth a taste as of dust and ashes. **1930** A. HUXLEY *Vulgarity in Literature* iii. 13 The spirit of the time..demands that we should 'press with strenuous tongue against our palate' not only joy's grape, but every Dead Sea fruit. Even dust and ashes must be relished. **1945** —— *Let.* 2 Apr. (1969) 518 The most wildly romantic adventures all turned into dust and ashes.

4. Phrases. ***to shake the dust off one's feet*** (in allusion to Matt. x. 14, etc.). ***to throw dust in the eyes of***: to confuse, mislead, or dupe by making 'blind' to the actual facts of the case. ***to bite the dust***: to fall to the ground; *esp.* to fall wounded or slain (see also BITE *v.* 16). For other phrases, see senses 3 and 5.

c **1000** *Ags. Gosp.* Matt. x. 14 Asceacaþ þæt dust of eowrum fotum. **1382** WYCLIF *Matt.* x. 14 Ȝee goynge forth fro that hous, or citee, smytith awey the dust fro ȝoure feet. **1581** PETTIE *Guazzo's Civ. Conv.* I. (1586) 27 b, They doe nothing else but raise a dust to doe out their owne eies. **1612** *Crt. & Times Jas. I* (1849) I. 169 To countermine his underminers, and, as he termed it, to cast dust in their eyes. **1767** FRANKLIN *Wks.* (1887) IV. 79 It required a long discourse to throw dust in the eyes of common sense. **1856** C. J. ANDERSSON *Lake Ngami* 94 In the course of half an hour, he had twice bitten the dust. *Ibid.* 363 He..had made numerous lions bite the dust. **1862** COLENSO *Pentateuch* 6, I was not able long to throw dust in the eyes of my own mind and do violence to the love of truth in this way.

5. a. *fig.* (from 2 c.) Confusion, disturbance, commotion, turmoil (as of a conflict in which much dust is raised); formerly chiefly in phr. ***to raise a dust***, to make a disturbance; now only with conscious reference to the literal sense (exc. as in b).

c **1570** *Marr. Wit & Science* v. v. in Hazl. *Dodsley* II. 390 A doughty dust these four boys will do. **1649** BP. HALL *Cases Consc.* (1650) 220 This particular concerning Tithes hath raised no little dust in the Church of God. **1700** T. BROWN tr. *Fresny's Amusem. Ser. & Com.* 118 That quarrel and raise a Dust about nothing. **1784** COWPER *Task* III. 161 Great contest follows, and much learned dust Involves the combatants. **1845** M. PATTISON *Ess.* (1889) I. 4 Entering heart and soul into the dust and heat of the Church's war with the world.

b. Hence (*slang* or *colloq.*) A disturbance, uproar, 'row', 'shindy'.

1753 A. MURPHY *Gray's-Inn Jrnl.* No. 50 Mr. Buck..will ..then adjourn to kick up a Dust. **1774** *Westm. Mag.* II. 380

Several of the company, not satisfied .. in the language of the Bucks, kicked up a dust. **1805** F. D. ROMNEY in *Naval Chron.* XIV. 493 This dust has cut me up. **1859** DE QUINCEY *Ceylon* Wks. XII. 16 Soon there would be a dust with the new master.

6. *slang.* Money, cash; *esp.* in phr. ***down with the*** (†***your***) ***dust.***

[**1526** *Pilgr. Perf.* (W. de W. 1531) 23 b, Neuer wery to labour for this erthly dust & rychesse.] **1607** G. WILKINS *Miseries Enforced Marr.* IV. in *Hazl. Dodsley* IX. 531 Come, down with your dust. **1691** H. MAYDMAN in *Naval Chron.* XV. 210 He .. is not willing to down with his dust. **1753** SMOLLETT *Ct. Fathom* (1813) I. 122, I have more dust in my fob than all these powdered sparks put together. *a* **1845** HOOD *Dean & Chapter* ii, And make it come down with the dust.

7. = DUST-BRAND.

In recent Dicts.

8. *Comb.* **a.** *attrib.* Consisting of or relating to dust, as ***dust-atomy, -bath, -cloud, -haze, -heap*** (also *fig.*), ***-particle, -screen, -spout, -whirl***; used for the reception or conveyance of dust, as ***dust-basket, -cart, -cellar, -wharf, -yard*** (also *fig.*). **b.** objective and obj. genitive, as ***dust-catcher, -collector, -contractor, -shovelling, -sifter, -sifting, -throwing; dust-catching, -free, -laying, -licking, -producing, -proof, -raising*** adjs. **c.** instrumental and locative, as ***dust-begrimed, -born, -clogged, -covered, -creeping, -filled, -laden, -polluted, -soiled*** adjs. **d.** similative, as ***dust-dry, -grey, -white*** adjs.; also ***dust-like*** adj.

1839 BAILEY *Festus* vi. (1848) 59 Are not all equal as *dust-atomies? **1626** T. LOATE in *12th Rep. Hist. MSS. Comm.* App. IV. 478 George's desk, and his sword, and a *dust basket. **1891** C. JAMES *Rom. Rigmarole* 33 Taking a *dust-bath there in the centre of the roadway. **1870** BRYANT *Iliad* I. XI. 339 Blood-stained and *dust-begrimed. **1598** SYLVESTER *Du Bartas* II. i. II. *Imposture* 483 Till .. Death .. Thy *dust-born body turn to dust again. **1776** ENTICK *London* I. 187 A tumbrel or *dust-cart. **1812** *Sporting Mag.* XXXIX. 21 Every species of carriage from the chariot to the dust-cart. **1939** D. R. G. CRAWFORD *Gas Producer Operator's Handbk.* v. 70 The simple gas-cleaning plant .. is for use .. where a clean cool gas is required... Where hot raw gas is required the complete cleaning plant is replaced by a static *dust-catcher. **1940** *Chambers's Techn. Dict.* 273/1 *Dust catcher*, a chamber in which dust is extracted from furnace gases by causing a sudden change in the direction of the gas stream. **1953** D. J. O. BRANDT *Manuf. Iron & Steel* viii. 64 This will normally lead direct to the dust-catcher. **1902** *Encycl. Brit.* XXVII. 428/1 A *dust-catching apparatus has been .. erected at Edinburgh. **1894** H. NISBET *Bush Girl's Romance* xxxi. 293 The bushranger's *dust-clogged brow became corrugated. **1849** WHITTIER *Wife of Manoah* 16 The thick *dust-cloud closed o'er all. **1851** MAYHEW *Lond. Lab.* (1861) II. 188 (Hoppe) The *dust-contractors are likewise the contractors for the cleansing of the streets. *a* **1847** ELIZA COOK *Old Clock* i, Thy *dust-covered face. **1580** SIDNEY *Arcadia* (1622) 97 Such a *dust-creeping worme as I am. **1879** BROWNING *Ned Bratts* 4 Ponds drained *dust-dry. **1908** *Westm. Gaz.* 25 July 3/2 A man with a *dust-filled throat. **1925** SHAW & OWENS *Smoke Probl. Gt. Cities* xi. 211 When breathing dust-laden air, it is only after long periods of quiet breathing that the air from the deep parts of the lungs is *dust free. **1934** *Discovery* July 184/1 Bringing the surfaces together in a clean and dust-free condition. **1882** OUIDA *Maremma* I. 51 The misty scorching *dust-grey shores. **1925** SHAW & OWENS *Smoke Probl. Gt. Cities* x. 197 Smoke or dust is normally dispersed in an upward direction .. and it is evident from ordinary observations of *dust haze that the upper limit is sometimes very well defined. **1945** *Finito! Po Valley Campaign* 36 In the dust-haze .. factories .. collapsed in ruins. **1654** TRAPP *Comm. Ps.* xiii. 8 Such *dust-heaps are found in every corner. **1901** *Westm. Gaz.* 1 May 3/2 The Salvation Army deserves to be helped in its work of sifting the dust-heap of our lowest social strata. **1940** R. G. COLLINGWOOD *Ess. Metaphys.* 120 The distinction between truth and falsehood is part of that antiquated lumber which has at last .. been thrown on the dust-heap. *a* **1847** ELIZA COOK *Grandfather's Stick* xi, The *dust-laden carpets. **1899** *Westm. Gaz.* 18 July 2/1 Water-carts sprayed the road with grateful *dust-laying streams. **1902** *Ibid.* 11 Sept. 7/3 Oil is the latest dust-laying agent. **1808** R. A. D. *To France* in *Poet. Reg.* 1806–7, 170 Blood-drinking tyrants, or *dust-licking slaves! **1621** LADY M. WROTH *Urania* 227 *Dust-like Dispaire may with me liue. **1887** *Pall Mall G.* 10 Aug. 5/1 Operatives engaged in *dust-producing trades. **1869** *Rep. Comm. Agric. 1868* (U.S.) 15 The museum has been partly filled with absolutely *dust-proof cases. **1882** *Leisure Hour* 414/2 The fittings are massive and dust-proof. **1888** J. SOUTHWARD *Mod. Printing* I. iv. 26 One of the most useful recent innovations is to make the racks 'dust-proof'. **1903** Dust-proof [see BENNY[1]]. **1934** *Archit. Rev.* LXXV. 142/2 Dust-proof electric light fittings are available. **1903** B. HARRADEN *Kath. Frensham* 272 A long, straggling, *dust-raising line of about 50 conveyances. **1908** *Westm. Gaz.* 22 Dec. 4/2 On the mere off-chance of minimising in an infinitesimal degree their dust-raising propensities. **1963** P. DRACKETT *Motor Rallying* i. 10 There were even dust-raising tests and noise checks. **1899** W. H. MAXWELL *Removal of Town Refuse* vii. 175 *Dust screens are ineffective. **1918** W. OWEN *Let.* 15 June (1967) 559, I have now a waterproof tent with long grass & buttercups all round to act as dustscreens. **1889** *Pall Mall G.* 5 Mar. 3/1 The female *dust-sifters had just completed their ablutions. **1926** T. E. LAWRENCE *Seven Pillars* (1935) III. xxxv. 205 Two *dust-spouts, tight and symmetrical chimneys, advanced. **1937** A. HUXLEY *Let.* 3 June (1969) 422 Western Texas, which we crossed in the midst of a premature heatwave (dust-spouts in a temperature of 105° in the shade). **1890** *Pall Mall G.* 26 Aug. 2/3 The Ottoman art of *dust-throwing in the eyes of Europe. **1887** *Courier* 16 June 2/2 To let or sell to the Board a *dust-wharf. **1886** *Jrnl. Franklin Inst.* CXXI. 247 (Cent.) The formation of a *dust-whirl as it suddenly bursts upon you in the open street. **1923** E. SITWELL *Bucolic Comedies* 48 And in the street *dust-white and lean, Two black apes bear her palanquin. **1938** W. DE LA MARE *Memory* 16 Dust-white hedge. *a* **1852** MAYHEW *London Labour* (1861) II. 216/1 The *dust-yards must not be confounded with the 'night-yards'. **1854** DICKENS *Hard T.* II. ix. 232 Her father was usually sifting and sifting at his parliamentary cinder-heap in London .. and was still hard at it in the national dustyard. **1904** *Daily Chron.* 27 Sept. 8/2 In a few odd corners of London there still exist dustyards in which the refuse of the great city is sifted and sorted.

e. Special combs.: **dust-ball**, a concretion of the dust of corn sometimes formed in the intestine of the horse, and giving rise to disease; **dust-bowl** orig. *U.S.*, a region subject to drought where, as a result of the loss or absence of plant cover, the wind has eroded the soil and made the land unproductive; hence, any region that is arid or unproductive; also *attrib.*; **dust-brush**, a brush for removing dust from furniture, etc.; **dust-cap**, a cap (CAP *sb.*[1] 12) to protect something from dust; **dust-chamber** (in an ore-roasting furnace), a closed chamber in which the heavier products of combustion are collected; **dust-cloak** , a cloak worn to keep off the dust (so ***dust-coat, -gown, -wrap***); **dust-cloth**, (*a*) a cloth for wiping off dust (= DUSTER 1); (*b*) a cloth placed over something to keep off dust; **dust-coat**: see *dust-cloak* above; **dust-colour**, the colour of the ordinary dust of the ground, a dull light brown; hence ***dust-coloured*** adj.; **dust-core** *Electr.*, a core of magnetic powder in which the insulating properties of the binding agent result in reduced core losses; **dust-counter**, an instrument for counting the dust particles in a known volume of air; **dust-cover, dust cover**, a cover to protect something from dust; *spec.* a detachable paper cover or jacket in which a new book is normally issued and which often contains information about the book or its author; also *fig.*; **dust-cup** (see quot.); **dust-destructor**: see DESTRUCTOR 2; **dust-devil**: see DEVIL 11; **dust-flow**, a stream or landslide of volcanic ashes saturated with water; †**dust-gold**, gold dust; **dust-gown**: see *dust-cloak* above; **dust-guard**, a contrivance to keep off dust from the axle and bearings of a wheel, or on a bicycle from the dress of the rider; **dust-hole**, a hole or receptacle in which dust and refuse are collected, a dust-bin; **dust-jacket, dust jacket** = JACKET *sb.* 2 b (cf. *dust-cover*); **dust-louse**, an insect of the genus *Psocus*; **dust-pan, dustpan**, a utensil for catching dust as it is swept from a floor, etc.; hence **dustpanful**, as much as a dust-pan will hold; **dust-plate** (see quot.); **dust-sheet**, a sheet for covering furniture or the like to keep off dust (cf. quot. 1888 *s.v.* SHEET *sb.*[1] 1 a); hence **dust-sheeted** *a.*, covered or provided with a dust-sheet; **dust-shoot**, a place where dust and refuse are shot or deposited; **dust-shot**, the smallest size of shot; †**dust-spawn**, offspring or progeny of the dust; **dust-storm**, a tempest in which large clouds of dust are raised and carried along; †**dust-tempered** *a.*, mingled or composed of dust; **dust-thread, dust-way** (*nonce-wds.*), applied to the stamens and pistils of flowers, as respectively producing and conveying the pollen (see 1 c); **dust-trap**, something in or on which dust collects; also *attrib.*; **dust-wind**, a wind bringing dust-storms; **dust-woman**, a woman employed in sifting dust and refuse; †**dust-worm**, a 'worm of the dust', a mean or grovelling person; **dust-wrap**: see *dust-cloak* above; **dust-wrapper** = WRAPPER *sb.* 1 b (cf. *dust-cover*). See also DUST-BIN, etc.

1936 *Durant* (Okla.) *Daily Democrat* 26 Mar. 1/7 The panhandle '*dustbowl' was outside the path of the wind. **1936** *Dallas Morning News* 26 Dec., They say he nearly defeated himself by urging Landon's election among the dust bowl farmers. **1937** *Ann. Reg. 1936* 288 Some pastoral areas where over-feeding of live-stock had completely killed the pasturage were called 'dust-bowls'. **1951** B. RUSSELL *New Hopes for Changing World* 33 Will all the arable land be turned into dust-bowls as it has been in large parts of the United States? **1959** *Listener* 20 Aug. 276/1 A more depressing picture, widely supported at the present time, is that Venus is an arid dust-bowl. **1828** WEBSTER, **Dust-brush.* **1898** *Springtime* Apr. 103/1 There are .. five separate pieces in the *dust-cap alone. **1930** *Engineering* 16 May 647/1 After screwing down the needle valve, disconnecting the pump and screwing on the dust cap, the strut is ready for use. **1883** *Truth* 31 May 768/1 With our *dust-cloaks and some yards each of brown gauze, we defied the great Dust Demon. **1727** BRADLEY *Fam. Dict.* s.v. *Draught horse*, They must with a *Dust-cloth wipe off all the Dust that lies on the Horse. **1884** TENNYSON *Becket* v. ii, A slut whose fairest linen seems Foul as her dust-cloth, if she used it. **1702** C. FIENNES *Journeys* (1947) 261 The wind soone dry'd my *dust coate. **1872** *Punch* 6 July 7/1 He arrives in a white dustcoat. **1916** H. G. WELLS *Mr. Britling* I. iii. 80 A lady in a motoring dust coat. *Ibid.* 86 The dust-coat lady. **1968** J. IRONSIDE *Fashion Alphabet* 39 *Dust-coat*, any lightweight coat worn mainly to protect the clothes and not necessarily for warmth. **1607** TOPSELL *Four-f. Beasts* (1658) 3, Apes .. both red, black, green, *dust-colour, and white ones. **1798** BLOOMFIELD *Farmer's Boy* (1837) 14 The small *dust-coloured beetle. **1861** DICKENS *Gt. Expect.* xliii, A man in a dust-coloured dress. [**1920** *U.S. Pat. 1,523,109* Telephone loading coil cores of the so-called 'dust' type.] **1924** S. R. ROGET *Dict. Electr. Terms* 70/1 **Dust core*, an iron core for induction in telephone lines in which eddy current and hysteresis losses are negligible. **1928** *Trans. Amer. Inst. Electr. Engin.* XLVII. 436/2 The commercial use of permalloy-dust-core loading coils .. has brought about a number of very important improvements. **1954** E. MOLLOY *Radio & Telev. Engin. Ref. Bk.* xxx. 11 Cores made of ferrites .. are commercially available now, and but for their high cost would have replaced the dust core over the frequency range in which they are advantageous. **1970** D. F. SHAW *Introd. Electronics* (ed. 2) v. 87 These materials [*sc.* ferrites] have many advantages over the earlier 'dust-core' materials. **1892** J. AITKEN in *Proc. R. Soc. Edinb.* XVIII. 39 A simple pocket *dust-counter. **1936** *Discovery* Nov. 348/1 The Aitken dust-counter has been considered by some to give counts too high for the actual dust particles. **1902** D. SALOMONS in A. C. Harmsworth et al. *Motors* vi. 95 Every car should have mackintosh raincovers .. ; also *dust-covers, which are useful on many occasions. **1921** *Sat. Westm. Gaz.* 17 Sept. 14/1 The dust-cover .. suggests that the book will be of service not only in schools but also as 'an entertainment for home-reading'. **1923** *Times Lit. Suppl.* 22 Feb. 126/1 The lurid dust cover. **1942** 'N. SHUTE' *Pied Piper* 49 Dozing uneasily in the chair, half-covered by the dust-cover from the bed. **1962** *Which?* (Car Suppl.) Oct. 138/2 Rubber dust covers on front brake cylinders disintegrated. **1968** *Listener* 1 Aug. 144/2 Soon after you came back from your recent honeymoon, your wife was quoted in one newspaper as saying that she must help you to take the dust covers off certain areas of your personality. **1884** F. J. BRITTEN *Watch & Clockm.* 99 [The] *Dust Cup .. a guard fitted round the fusee arbors of watches and chronometers to exclude dirt. **1888** KIPLING *Plain Tales fr. Hills* 43 The wheeling choking '*dust-devils' in the skirts of the flying storm. **1892** R. KIPLING *East & West* 31 in *Barrack-r. Ballads* 77 It's up and over the Tongue of Jagai, as blown dust-devils go. **1926** T. E. LAWRENCE *Seven Pillars* (1935) III. xxxv. 205 At last I saw that part of the yellow cloud off Serd was coming slowly against the wind in our direction, raising scores of dust devils before its feet. **1955** H. KLEIN *Winged Courier* vii. 46 The airmen experienced a new African flying hazard in the form of dust devils, some of which rose as high as 8,000 ft. **1904** *Science* 1 July 24/2 Clouds of steam rising from the crater, accompanied from time to time by *dust-flows. **1665** *Phil. Trans.* I. 117 A .. way of washing out very small *Dust-gold. **1802** MRS. J. WEST *Infidel Father* I. 23 Her homespun *dust-gown. **1888** *Engineer* LXV. 297 The *dust-guard is made of sycamore wood, and is either in one or two parts. **1811** L. M. HAWKINS *C'tess & Gertr.*, *Dust hole. **1836–9** DICKENS *Sk. Boz, Streets* i. A rakish-looking cat .. bounding first on the water-butt, then on the dusthole. **1928** *S. J. Looker's Booklover's Catal.* Jan. 5 The Life and Letters of Emily Dickinson .. in *dust jacket. **1928** *Observer* 24 June 8 The book is sent out by Constable's in a particularly attractive dust-jacket. **1957** *Times* 25 Nov. 11/3 Henry Fielding's *Tom Jones* in a practical transparent dust jacket at 12s. 6d. **1785** F. HOPKINSON *Misc. Essays* (1792) II. 158 It was soon after swept out with the common dirt of the room, and carried in a *dust pan to the yard. **1857** DICKENS *Dorrit* xxv. 125 Ladies would fly out at their doors crying, 'Mr. Baptist—tea-pot!' 'Mr. Baptist—dust-pan!' **1861** —— *Gt. Expect.* xii, She .. got out the dustpan .. and began cleaning up to a terrible extent. **1966** J. BETJEMAN *High & Low* 17 Brooms and plastic dustpans hang from the ceiling. **1882** F. A. KEMBLE *Rec. Later Life* I. 60 Three and four *dustpanfuls a day would be swept away. **1965** M. ECHARD *I met Murder* (1967) xvii. 137 The maid told me she swept up dead roaches by the dustpanful. **1881** RAYMOND *Mining Gloss.*, **Dust-plate*, a vertical iron plate, supporting the slag-runner of an iron blast furnace. **1854** MRS. GASKELL *Let.* 17 May (1966) 290 Not even a book to beguile the time—five fathoms deep they lie beneath *dust-sheets. **1907** *Westm. Gaz.* 17 Aug. 4/3 The big town-house was depressing in its shroud of dust-sheets. **1928** *Daily Mail* 25 July 4/2 Hundreds of dust sheets, 2 yards wide by $2\frac{3}{4}$ yards long, for covering furniture, are being sold by a West End firm. **1936** W. DE LA MARE *Wind blows Over* 159 Having muffled the furniture with their sepulchral dust-sheets. **1917** C. S. LEWIS *Let.* 18 July (1966) 38 Some of the rooms were all *dust-sheeted. **1883** *Pall Mall G.* 27 Dec. 12/1 Each tenement has a separate .. coal-place, copper and *dust-shoot. **1800** *Sporting Mag.* XVI. 273 Used to kill small birds for their plumage, with *dust shot. **1863** BATES *Nat. Amazon* xi. (1864) 352 Mine was a double-barrel, with one charge of BB, and one of dust-shot. **1598** SYLVESTER *Du Bartas* II. ii. II. *Babylon* 178 See .. these *dust-spawn, feeble dwarfs. **1879** MRS. A. E. JAMES *Ind. Househ. Managem.* xii. 82 *Dust-storms come on often very quickly. **1936** 'F. GERALD' *Millionaire in Memories* ii. 42 At Port Pirie a dust-storm swept down upon us. **1627–47** FELTHAM *Resolves* I. xi. 30 Poore *dust-tempered man. **1879** JAS. GRANT in *Cassell's Techn. Educ.* IV. 95/1 He showed that the stamina, or *dust-threads, were the male, and the pistilla, or *dust-ways, the female parts of the plants. **1905** *Daily Chron.* 17 Apr. 8/2 Fussy, *dust-trap trimming near the hem. **1906** *Westm. Gaz.* 15 Jan. 2/1 Hailstones, the slowly falling flakes of snow, drops of rain, are literally dust-traps. **1967** R. RENDELL *New Lease of Death* i. 8 The primrose venetian blinds .. were dust-traps. **1901** *Geogr. Jrnl.* XVIII. 91 Observations, outline and relief of the region, .. temperature in the interior, *dust-winds, temperatures of wells and springs [etc.]. **1851** MAYHEW *Lond. Labour* (1861) II. 162 The calling of the dustman and *dustwoman is not so much as noticed in the population returns. **1621** BURTON *Anat. Mel.* I. ii. III. xii. (1651) 116 Never satisfied, a slave, a *dust-worme. **1932** *Book-Collector's Q.* Apr.–June 10 The somewhat more humble '*dust-wrapper' is to be found in the catalogues of the greater and more conscious booksellers. **1934** *Punch* 24 Oct. 476/2 The love-interest which I guessed (from the dust-wrapper) must be contained somewhere.

† **dust**, *sb.*[2] *Obs. rare.* [cf. DUST *v.*[2]: also DOUST.] A stroke, blow.

1611 COTGR., *Excez de main non garnie* .. a cuffe, or dust with the fist.

dust, *v.*[1] [f. DUST *sb.*[1]: cf. ON. *dusta* to dust. The connexion of senses 7 and 11 is obscure, and it is not certain that they belong here. Cf. DUST *v.*[2]]

†**1.** *intr.* To be dusty; to rise as dust. *Obs.*

a **1225** *Ancr. R.* 314 ȝif hit dusteð swuðe, heo vlaskeð water þeron, & swopeð hit ut awei.

†**2. a.** *trans.* To reduce to dust, or to small particles like dust. **b.** *intr.* To crumble to dust.

c **1440** *Promp. Parv.* 135/2 Dustyn, *pulverizo.* **1580** HOLLYBAND *Treas. Fr. Tong*, *Pouldrer*, to dust. **1636** W. DENNY in *Ann. Dubrensia* (1877) 16 When thy name fades; Marble pillars shall Dust into nothing. **1686** GOAD *Celest. Bodies* III. ii. 417 He can crumble a Showr into a Drisle, or Dust it into a Fog.

3. a. *trans.* To sprinkle with dust or powder.

1592 GREENE *Art Conny Catch.* II. 19 He being thus dusted with meale. **1764** HARMER *Observ.* XXIX. vi. 288 Shimei's behaviour..who..threw stones, and dusted him with dust. **1769** MRS. RAFFALD *Eng. Housekpr.* (1778) 33 Dust them with flour. **1859** TENNENT *Ceylon* II. VIII. v. 367 Dusting themselves with sand.

b. *refl.* Of birds; also *intr.* for *refl.*

1789 G. WHITE *Selborne* II. ix. (1853) 185 Let me hear.. whether skylarks do not dust. **1872** BLACK *Adv. Phaeton* x. 144 The partridges that were dusting themselves in the road. **1884** SPEEDY *Sport* xv. 267 [Partridges] prefer, as a rule, places where they can 'dust' and bask in the sun.

c. ***to dust the eyes of*** (fig.: see DUST *sb.*[1] 4); also (slang or colloq.) *to dust*, in same sense.

1814 *Stock Exchange Law Open* 11 This is termed 'Dusting the public'. **1867** FROUDE *Ess.* 401 Instead of dusting our eyes with sophistry.

4. a. To soil with dust; to make dusty.

1530 PALSGR. 530/2 You have dusted your cappe, let one go brusshe it. **1624** R. SKYNNER in *Ussher's Lett.* (1686), Dust thy self in the dust of their Feet. **1848** FROUDE *Nemesis of Faith* (1849) 154 We go out..and dust our feet along its thoroughfares. **1886** A. LANG *Lett. Dead Authors* 194 Dusting your ruffles among the old volumes on the sunny stalls.

†**b.** *intr.* To become dusty. *Obs.*

1625 J. PHILLIPS *Way to Heaven* 52 The Booke..lay dusting and out of vse.

5. To strew or sprinkle as dust.

1790 WEDGWOOD in *Phil. Trans.* LXXX. 314 *note*, A little of it is applied, or even dusted only, on the bottom of a small cup made of clay. **1806** *Culina* 74 Dust in a little flour. **1884** G. H. BOUGHTON in *Harper's Mag.* Sept. 528/1 We never dusted on enough [pepper] to please him.

6. a. To free from dust; to wipe or brush off the dust from.

1568 NORTH *Gueuara's Diall Pr.* (1619) 708/2 The French riddles (with which they dust their corne). *a* **1577** GASCOIGNE *Flowers, etc.* Wks. (1587) 180 Yea when he curried was and dusted slike and trimme. **1713** STEELE *Guardian* No. 60 ¶2 It became my province once a week to dust them [books]. **1843** MRS. CARLYLE *Lett.* I. 267 I went about sweeping and dusting. **1894** HALL CAINE *Manxman* 52 [She] was..dusting the big shells on the mantelpiece.

b. ***to dust a person's coat, jacket***, etc.: to beat him soundly. *colloq.* (Cf. sense 7.)

1690 W. WALKER *Idiomat. Anglo-Lat.* 154 I'll dust your coat for you. **1698** FARQUHAR *Love & a Bottle* v. ii, Tell me presently..sirrah, or I'll dust the secret out of your jacket. **1771** SMOLLETT *Humph. Cl.* I. 3 June, With a good oak sapling he dusted his doublet. **1807** *Eagle* (Staunton, Va.) 28 Aug. 4/2 Go in peace, or I will dust thy jacket with this horse-whip. **1842** BARHAM *Ingol. Leg.* 2nd Ser. 52 Old Shylock was making a racket, And threatening how well he'd dust every man's jacket. **1884** L. J. JENNINGS in *Croker Papers* II. xiv. 49 The threat to dust the author's jacket, for the gratification of private malice. **1895** 'ROSEMARY' *Under Chilterns* i. 31 Master told me as 'ow 'ee'd dusted 'is jacket for 'im.

7. a. *trans.* To beat, thrash. Now *colloq.* or *dial.* **b.** *intr.* To strike, hit.

[But the place of these is doubtful: cf. DUST *v.*[2]]

1612 tr. *Benvenuto's Passenger* (Farmer) If..she be good, to dust her often hath in it a singular..vertue to make her much better. *c* **1612** CHAPMAN *Iliad* XVI. 544 Another stony dart As good as Hector's he let fly, that dusted in the neck Of Sthenelaus. **1884** 'MARK TWAIN' *Huck. Finn* xxxix. 395 So she took and dusted us both with the hickry [*sic*]. **1950** *Time* 30 Jan. 14/2 [Miners] dusted one of [the district leader's] lieutenants with an old shoe for trying to talk them back to work. **1970** H. E. ROBERTS *Third Ear* 6/2 *Dust* v., beat up.

8. *trans.* To brush, shake, or rub off as dust.

1775 S. J. PRATT *Lib. Opinions* (1783) IV. 63 Boy, dust away the crumbs with your hat. **1887** STEVENSON *Underwoods* I. xxxviii, A strenuous family dusted from its hands The sand of granite.

9. To pass (any one) on the road, so as to expose him to the dust of one's horse or wheels; to make one 'take the dust'; to outride. *U.S.* and *Colonial.*

1890 BOLDREWOOD *Col. Reformer* (1891) 419 I could have dusted any of 'em with Ben.

10. *intr.* To ride or go quickly, hasten, hurry, make *off*; also, *to dust it.* (Chiefly *U.S. slang* or *colloq.*)

1655 H. VAUGHAN *Silex Scint.* I. *Rules & Lessons* (1858) 75 Stick thou To thy sure trot..Let folly dust it on, or lag behind. **1860** *Mesilla* (Ariz.) *Times* 18 Oct. 1/2 The 'gold seekers' thought prudence the better part of valor and 'got up and dusted'. **1884** A. A. PUTNAM *10 Years Police Judge* xvii. 166 He's throwing dust, but he dusted off with the horse all the same. **1888** 'R. BOLDREWOOD' *Robbery under Arms* II. xi. 190 And you're a going to dust out right away, you say? **1909** J. R. WARE *Passing Eng.* 120/2, I quickly got inside, locked the door, and dusted out the back way.

†**11.** *trans.* To drink quickly, 'toss off' (liquor).

1673 SHADWELL *Epsom Wells* III. Wks. 1720 II. 241 Clodpate is to dust his stand of ale, and he must be bubbled. *a* **1680** BUTLER *Rem.* (1759) II. 447 A Prodigal..dusts his Estate, as they do a Stand of Ale in the North. *a* **1700** B. E. *Dict. Cant. Crew*, *Dust it away*, drink quick about.

12. to dust off. a. *intr.* (See sense 10) **b.** *trans.* = sense 6 a (orig. *U.S.*).

1948 A. HUXLEY *Ape & Essence* (1949) 127 The charvessels can dust off the tables and wash the floors. **1959** *Economist* 18 Apr. 218/1 The clerics are..dusting off their copies of Fox's *Book of Martyrs.*

c. To bring to ruin, defeat, kill; to discard, get rid of. *slang* (orig. *U.S.*).

1938 H. ASBURY *Sucker's Progress* xii. 385 He had been dusted off by Vanderbilt. **1942** BERREY & VAN DEN BARK *Amer. Thes. Slang* §27/5 Eliminate; discard; get rid of,..*dust off.* *Ibid.* §118/3 Kill; murder,..*dust off.* **1960** *Times* 13 Dec. 4/1 They have always been dusted off in the inter-zone matches.

†**dust**, *v.*[2] *Obs.* Pa. t. 3–4 **duste, deste.** [A ME. word, of which the earlier history does not appear.

The pa. t. *deste* beside *duste*, and the rime in Ferumbras, show that the *u* was *ü*, pointing to an OE. **dystan* (:—**dustjan*), of which, however, no examples have been found. The Norse words cited by Mätzner, Icel. *dust* a 'tilt', Sw. *dust* a 'brush' with any one, Da. *dyst* 'tilting, fighting, shock', appear to be later words, and are app. not related. Of an OE. *dystan*, early ME. *düsten*, the normal mod. Eng. repr. would be *dist*; but *dust* (cf. BLUSH) would also be possible; in which case senses 7 and 11, under DUST *v.*[1], may possibly belong here, though the wide chronological gap is against this.]

1. *trans.* To cast forcibly or violently, fling, dash.

a **1225** *St. Marher.* 12 Ant duste him adunriht to þere eorðe. *Ibid.* 18 þa warð þe reue wod, ant bed..dusten hire into þe grunde. *a* **1225** *Leg. Kath.* 984 þu underfes þet an half, and dustes adun þet oðer. *Ibid.* 1094 He is godd seolf, þe duste deað under him. *a* **1225** *Juliana* 38 Ant te þreo children..beon idust in þe fur of þe ofne. *c* **1315** SHOREHAM 52 Thet..non harm hyne don deste, In mode.

b. *intr.* To dash, throw oneself violently.

c **1320** *Sir Tristr.* 2393 Vrgan lepe vnfain, Ouer þe bregge he deste.

2. To strike or hit with violence. See also DUST *v.*[1] 7.

a **1225** *Leg. Kath.* 2025 þis wes uneaðe iseid, þat an engel ne com..And duste hit [the wheel] a swuch dunt þat hit bigon to claterin. *c* **1380** *Sir Ferumb.* 2855 [He] heuid vp ys honde, & þar-wiþ an þe heued him duste [*rime* vuste 'fist'].

dust-bin, 'dustbin. 1. A bin or receptacle for the dust, ashes, and other refuse of a house.

1848 DICKENS *Dombey* xvii, The Captain's nosegay was swept into the dust-bin next morning. **1895** PARKES *Health* 37 The old-fashioned brick dustbin.

fig. and *attrib.* **1901** M. BEERBOHM in *Sat. Rev.* 23 Feb. 234/2 The Drama of the Dustbin. This phrase was not coined by me... Mr. Clement Scott issued it into our currency as a description of 'Mr. & Mrs. Daventry'. **1930** C. DIXON *This Way to Paradise* I. 29 Wasn't it just one of the usual dust-bin experiences? *Ibid.* 30 The whole of existence is an affair of dust-bins. **1931** R. GRAVES *Poems 1926–1930* 53 He leads the sick words into parliament To rule a dust-bin world with deep-sleep phrases. **1940** *Times* 25 Apr. 8/7 When two..men were summoned..for removing refuse from dustbins without authority..solicitor for the prosecution said, 'This offence is known as "dustbin totting".' **1958** E. H. CARR *Socialism in one Country* I. iv. 148 Trotsky relegated his defeated opponents to the dustbin of history. **1959** *Times* 23 May 5/6 Plainly the *Ulysses* of James Joyce is the great source of the modern dustbin drama.

b. Special Comb. **dustbinman**, a refuse collector; = BINMAN 2.

1969 *TV Times* 18 Sept. 8/2 He recited the formal caution: 'The *dustbinman never solicits gratuities, never 'tots' or sells scrap on the side, and he is never discourteous'. **1982** *Times* 9 Dec. 7/7 Rubbish continued to pile up on the streets and pavements of Paris yesterday as the dustbinmen's strike entered its fifth day.

2. A gun-turret of an aircraft, esp. the one beneath the fuselage. *slang.*

1934 *Flight* 15 Feb. 160/1 Our photographer..took his photographs from the 'dustbin', the retractable and rotatable turret for a Lewis gun beneath the fuselage. **1942** *Gen* 1 Sept. 14/1 The rear gunner's turret is the 'dust bin'. **1967** C. H. BARNES *Shorts Aircraft* 377 Here there had originally been mounted a twin-Browning F.N. 25 retractable ventral turret..; this 'dust-bin' turret was deleted from early production Stirlings.

dust-box.

1. A box from which 'dust', i.e. fine sand or powder, is sprinkled on something (e.g. on writing, for the purpose now served by blotting-paper; also, on a prepared photographic plate).

1581 MULCASTER *Positions* iii. (1887) 34 Incke and paper, ..a deske and a dustboxe. **1894** *Brit. Jrnl. Photog.* XLI. 33 Place some pulverised asphaltum in a 'dust-box', agitate it, and allow the particles to settle down upon the plate.

2. A box or receptacle for the dust of a house.

1896 E. TURNER *Little Larrikin* ii. 17 On the footpaths there were dust-boxes twice a week. **1906** E. DYSON *Fact'ry 'Ands* xvi. 219 They've dumped Toucher in ther dust-box for immedjit removal.

3. (See quot. 1893.)

1893 *Funk's Stand. Dict.*, *Dust box*, a box supplied with dust for the use of poultry, to aid them in expelling lice. **1894** *Vermont Agric. Rep.* XIV. 176 Fix a dust box so that biddy can take a bath every day.

dust-brand. [f. DUST *sb.*[1] + BRAND *sb.* 7: cf. Ger. *staub-brand.*] A disease of corn, in which the ears become filled with a black powder; the fungus which causes this. Also called *smut.*

1861 H. MACMILLAN *Footn. fr. Nat.* 268 By farmers it is familiarly called smut or dust-brand. **1866** *Treas. Bot.* 435 Dust brand, *Ustilago.*

dusted ('dʌstɪd), *ppl. a.* [f. DUST *v.*[1] + -ED[1].]

1. Sprinkled with dust or powder; powdered.

1643 *5 Years of K. James* in *Select. Harl. Misc.* (1793) 293 Yellow bands, dusted hair, curled, crisped, frizzled, sleeked skins. **1806** J. GRAHAME *Birds Scot.* 28 The spacious door White-dusted tells him, plenty reigns around. **1870** MORRIS *E. Par.* IV. 383 The purple-dusted butterfly.

2. Cleansed or freed from dust.

1686 N. COX *Gentl. Recreat.* v. 59 A handful of clean dusted Hempseed.

duster ('dʌstə(r)). [f. DUST *v.*[1] or *sb.*[1] + -ER[1].]

1. a. A cloth for removing dust from a surface; a dust-brush. Cf. *feather-duster* (FEATHER *sb.* 19).

1576 TURBERV. *Venerie* 30 A litele brush or duster to rubbe and duste his houndes. **1611** COTGR., *Vistempenard*, a Duster made of a Fox-taile fastened vnto a staffe. *a* **1748** WATTS *Educ. Children & Youth* xi, We were..well instructed in the conduct of the broom and the duster. **1862** LYTTON *Str. Story* I. 163 The housemaid was forbidden to enter it with broom or duster. **1895** *Montgomery Ward Catal.* 104/2 Duster, 8-inch handle, all dark down, 7 × 9 inch, double faced brush. **1939–40** *Army & Navy Stores Catal.* 110/3 Household brushes... Turnover Library Duster, White Lily bristles.

b. A machine for removing dust (by rubbing, etc.) in various mechanical processes.

2. a. A contrivance for removing dust by sifting; a sieve. **b.** An apparatus for sifting dry poisons upon plants to kill insects.

1667 *Hist. Gunpowder* in Sprat *Hist. R. Soc.* (1702) 283 (T.) The lower sieve is called the dry duster, and retains the small corns..and lets fall the dust into the bin.

3. A person who dusts, or wipes off dust.

1850 HASTINGS *Life of J. Wilson* II. ii. 255 A cobweb here and a little dust there which have escaped the vigilance of the duster. **1888** *Pall Mall G.* 17 Sept. 6/2 Employed as an assistant 'duster' for the stalls at the Italian Exhibition.

4. a. A light cloak or wrap worn to keep off dust; = *dust-cloak* (see DUST *sb.*[1] 8 e). Chiefly *U.S.*

1864 SALA in *Daily Tel.* 13 Oct., The citizen in the straw hat and the 'duster' or overcoat of yellow Spanish linen. **1870** LOWELL *Lett.* (1894) II. xi. 77 Rose discovered your thin coat, which she called a 'duster'. **1883** GRANT WHITE *W. Adams* 114 Whether it was an overcoat that he was wearing as a duster, or a duster doing service as an overcoat. **1962** 'S. RANSOME' *Without Trace* ix. 98 A dark-haired woman..was wearing a duster while hanging the family wash on a line.

b. In full ***duster coat***: a woman's loose light casual full-length coat.

1959 W. CAMP *Ruling Passion* xviii. 154, I adore that duster coat, but it's at least a couple of inches longer than your frock. **1960** *Guardian* 25 June 10/3 The Princess wore a royal blue duster coat over a..flowered frock.

5. *Naval slang.* An ensign or flag; ***the red duster*** (see quot. 1929).

1904 *Eastern Morn. News* 27 June, A regatta..of the duster boats for the championship of the Humber. **1918** *Punch* 27 Mar. 206/1 She's dipped her dingy duster in the spray of all the seas. **1929** F. C. BOWEN *Sea Slang* 111 *Red Duster*, the Red Ensign.

dustering ('dʌstərɪŋ). [f. DUSTER + -ING[1].] Material such as is used for dusters.

1910 H. G. WELLS *Mr. Polly* ii. 47 He was now hanging long strips of grey silesia and chilly-coloured linen dustering.

dustifit, dustifute: see DUSTYFOOT.

dustily ('dʌstɪlɪ), *adv.* [f. DUSTY + -LY[2].] In a dusty manner or condition.

1577 B. GOOGE *Heresbach's Husb.* IV. (1586) 177 If they bee heavy, looke lothsomely, and dustelie. **1863** *Cornh. Mag.* Jan. 102 The regiments in homespun gray and butter-nut that trail dustily through the high streets.

dustiness ('dʌstɪnɪs). [f. as prec. + -NESS.] Dusty condition.

1577 B. GOOGE *Heresbach's Husb.* II. (1586) 65 The craft is perceived by the dustinesse thereof. **1772** GRAVES *Spirit. Quixote* III. 2 (T.) The heat of the weather, dustiness of the roads. **1858** MORRIS *Sir Peter Harpdon's End* Poems 105 High up in the dustiness of the apse.

dusting ('dʌstɪŋ), *vbl. sb.* [f. DUST *v.*[1] + -ING[1].]

1. a. The action of the verb DUST, q.v., in various senses: usually, that of freeing from dust.

1623 COCKERAM II, Dusting, *pulueration.* *Ibid.* I. *Pulueration*, a beating into powder. **1726** AMHERST *Terræ Fil.* x. 47 Dusting of cushions. **1837** DICKENS *Pickw.* xii, Mrs. Bardell resumed her dusting.

b. The sprinkling of powdered insecticide, fertilizer, etc., on crops, usu. from the air. Usu. in form ***crop dusting.***

1926 H. H. ARNOLD *Airman & Aircraft* 212 (*index*) Crop 'dusting' by planes. **1930** *Flight* 17 Oct. 1151/1, 11 engaged on crop dusting. **1958** *Times Rev. Industry* July 76/2 The prototype of the Wirraway war-time trainer, rebuilt for crop-dusting.

c. With *adv.*, as ***dusting-on.***

1879 *Telegraphic Jrnl.* 15 Oct. 344/2 The 'dusting-on' process [of phosphorescent photography] consists in coating a plate with a preparation of dextrine, honey, and bichromate of ammonia which..becomes hardened.. remaining tacky where it is protected from..light.

2. A beating, thrashing; also used by sailors of rough or stormy weather. (*colloq.* or *slang.*)

1799 *Naval Chron.* II. 542 They did not venture a dusting with the *Naiad.* **1821** *Sporting Mag.* VII. 285 So his men fac'd about..and gave all the rogues a good dusting. **1895** *Daily News* 14 Sept. 6/4 When we got beyond the shelter of the islands we should have a rough time of it—what the skipper calls 'a dusting'.

3. *attrib.* and *Comb.* Used for dusting, as ***dusting-brush***, ***-cloth***, etc.; also **dusting-colours**, colours in the form of powder to be dusted over adhesive varnish; **dusting-powder**, a powder, usually antiseptic, for dusting over wounds, etc.; also = *talcum powder*.

1667 *Hist. Gunpowder* in Sprat *Hist. R. Soc.* (1702) 281 (T.) The bin, over which the sieve is shaken, called the dusting bin. **1686** N. Cox *Gentl. Recreat.* v. 28 Your Curry-combs, Brushes, Dusting-cloaths, Oyntments. **1851** *Offic. Catal. Gt. Exhib.* I. 101 The Feathers..made into dusting-brooms. **1907** *Yesterday's Shopping* (1969) 358/1 Typewriter sundries... Dusting Brushes. *Ibid.* 506/1 Dusting Powder for wounds..tin 0/10½. **1926** *Toilet Goods Economist* 12 June 59 Bath salts, face powders, dusting powders. **1947** E. H. Young *Chatterton Square* xxiii. 158 She had bathed and changed and smelt faintly of dusting powder. **1951** 'J. Tey' *Daughter of Time* i. 11 The Midget smelt of lavender dusting powder.

dusting, *ppl. a.* That dusts: see DUST *v.*[1]

1890 *Spectator* 27 Sept., Partridges are a good example of the dusting birds, and are most careful in the selection of their dust-baths.

† **dustish**, *a. Obs. rare.* Somewhat dusty.

1646 J. Hall *Poems* I. 45 Sooner, yond dustish mulberry In her old white shall cloathed be.

dustless ('dʌstlɪs), *a.* [f. DUST *sb.*[1] + -LESS.] Free from dust.

a **1618** Sylvester *Mayden's Blush* 577 The Wayes so dust-lesse, and so dirtlesse faire. **1861** W. F. Collier *Hist. Eng. Lit.* 405 Blue morocco books in dustless regularity. **1904** *Westm. Gaz.* 9 Aug. 1/3 An August morning that..is sunnily cool, and breezily fresh and deliciously dustless. **1970** *Sunday Tel.* 11 Oct. 21/2 The council's automatic dustless loading bins have made the dustmen's lot a happier one. **1970** *Interior Design* Dec. 767/4 Little progress seems to have been made in finding a dry writing/erasing system, acceptable to lecturers, which is dustless.

† **'dustling.** *Obs. nonce-wd.* [f. as prec. + -LING.] A small grain or particle; cf. DUST *sb.*[1] 2 a.

1674 N. Fairfax *Bulk & Selv.* 60 Now Gods Almightiness is within the least *punctum physicum*, or dustling of body.

dustman ('dʌstmən). [f. as prec. + MAN.]

1. A man whose occupation it is to collect and cart away dust and refuse from dust-bins, etc.

1707 J. Stevens tr. *Quevedo's Com. Wks.* (1709) 399 The Dust-men were not idle. **1714** Gay *Trivia* II. 37 The dustman's cart offends thy cloaths and eyes. **1850** Mrs. Browning *Poems* II. 191 The dustman's call down the area-grate.

2. *colloq.* A personification of sleep or sleepiness; in allusion to the rubbing of the eyes as if there were dust in them.

1821 P. Egan *Tom & Jerry* 111 (Farmer) Till the dustman made his appearance and gave the hint to Tom and Jerry that it was time to visit their beds. **1891** Farmer *Slang* s.v., 'The dustman's coming' = you are getting sleepy.

3. *slang.* A preacher who uses violent action; a 'cushion-thumper'.

1877 Blackmore *Cripps* (1887) 368 Sitting under the most furious dustman that ever thumped a cushion.

‖ **dustoor** (dʌ'stʊə(r)). *East Ind.* Also 8 dastoor, 9 dustour. [Pers. and Urdū *dastūr* custom, privilege, perquisite.] **a.** Custom, usage, fashion. **b.** Customary commission; = DUSTOORY.

1680 *Fort St. Geo. Cons.* 2 Dec. in *Notes & Extracts* II. 61 (Y. Supp.) [To] be content with the Dustoor..of a quarter anna in the rupee, which the merchants and weavers are to allow them. **1785** in Seton-Karr *Sel. fr. Calcutta Gaz.* I. 130 (Y.) No Commission, Brokerage, or Dustoor is charged by the Bank, or permitted to be taken by any Agent or Servant employed by them. **1887** Fife-Cookson *Tiger Shooting* 14 A handsome profit in commission which is called in Hindustani, 'dustour', literally meaning 'that which is customary'. **1888** J. Inglis *Tent Life Tigerland* 57 The claims of custom, the tyranny of dustoor. **1909** M. Diver *Candles in Wind* viii, It was *dastur*; and there was no more to be said. **1926** *Blackw. Mag.* June 756/1 It was his custom —*dastur*—respected by his people and the British Resident.

‖ **du'stoory** (dʌ'stʊərɪ). *East Ind.* Also 9 **-ree, -ri, dasturi.** [a. Pers. and Urdū *dastūrī* what is customary, f. *dastūr*: see prec.] A commission or perquisite by custom paid to or taken by an agent.

1681 *Fort St. Geo. Cons.* 10 Jan. in *Notes & Extracts* III. 45 (Y. Supp.) For the farme of Dustoory on cooley hire at Pagodas 20 per annum. *a* **1826** Heber *Journ. Upper Prov. India* (1844) I. 198. **1866** Trevelyan *Dawk Bungalow* 217 (Y.) Of all taxes small and great the heaviest is dustooree. **1886** Kipling *Departmental Ditties* (ed. 2) 7 Roused his Secretariat to a fine Maratha fury, By a Hookum hinting at supervision of *dasturi.* **1909** M. Diver *Candles in Wind* i, Is the *zubbardusti*' gentleman up there a toll-gate keeper that we should offer him *dasturi*?

† **dust-point.** *Obs.* A boy's game in which 'points' were laid in a heap of dust, and thrown at with a stone.

1611 Cotgr. s.v. *Darde*, Our boyes laying their points in a heape of dust, and throwing at them with a stone, call that play of theirs, *Dust-point.* *a* **1625** Fletcher *Captain* III. iii, He looks Like a great school-boy that had been blown up Last night at Dust-Point. **1630** Drayton *Nymphal* 6 (N.) Down go our hooks and scrips, and we to nine holes fall At dust-point or at quoits. **1675** Cotton *Scoffer Scoft* 50 To play at Dust-point, Span-counter, Skittle-pins.

‖ **dustuck, dustuk** ('dʌstʌk). *East Ind.* Also 8 dustick. [a. Pers. and Urdū *dastak* passport.] A passport; applied esp. to the passports granted by the covenanted servants of the East India Company.

1748 in J. Long *Sel. fr. Rec. Govt.* (Fort William) (Y.), The Zemindar..stopped several boats with English Dusticks. **1783** Burke *Rep. Indian Affairs* Wks. XI. 173 Persons, who had not the protection of the Company's dustuck. **1862** Beveridge *Hist. India* I. III. xii. 673 The European officials..availed themselves of the dustuks or passports of their employers, to smuggle goods.

dust-up ('dʌstʌp). *colloq.* [f. DUST *sb.*[1] + UP *adv.*[1]] A quarrel, fight, disturbance; = DUST *sb.*[1] 5 b.

1897 *Daily News* 6 Mar. 7/3 They turned at the Lasher, and after a dust-up for about a minute in Iffley Reach did a nice piece of paddling back to the raft. **1897** S. L. Hinde *Fall Congo Arabs* 152 An American nigger said..they ain't had such a dust-up in this hole since creation. **1926** D. L. Sayers *Clouds of Witness* i. 31 [He] had thought Wednesday evening's dust-up none of his business. **1930** H. Tomlinson *All our Yesterdays* v. i. 391 Some fellows always thought they'd pulled it off..if they got out of a dust-up on the cheap. **1944** 'N. Shute' *Pastoral* v. 123 He had a bit of a dust up with one of his girl friends.

dustward ('dʌstwəd), *adv. nonce-wd.* [f. DUST *sb.*[1] + -WARD.] Towards the dust; towards death or the grave.

18.. Lowell *Extreme Unction* ii, This fruitless husk which dustward dries Hath been a heart once, hath been young.

dusty ('dʌstɪ), *a.* [f. DUST *sb.*[1] + -Y.]

1. a. Full of, abounding with, or strewn with dust.

a **1225** *Juliana* 79 And weorpð þat dusti chef to hellene heate. **1499** *Promp. Parv.* 135/2 (Pynson) Dusty, *pulverulentus.* *a* **1586** Sidney *Fear of Death*, Our life is but a step in dustie way. **1602** *2nd Pt. Return fr. Parnass.* v. iv. (Arb.) 72 Farewell musty, dusty, rusty, fusty London. **1605** Shaks. *Macb.* v. v. 23. **1725** Pope *Odyss.* XIII. 99 Urged by fierce drivers through the dusty space. **1849** Macaulay *Hist. Eng.* I. 532 In the dusty recesses of a few old libraries. **1891** *Labour Commission* Gloss. s.v. *Money*, *Dusty money*, a special allowance per quarter made when the corn to be unloaded at docks is dusty.

b. Of wine: containing sediment.

1886 J. Noble *Handbk. Cape Gd. Hope* 275 Notwithstanding the large amount of alcohol which they [*sc.* Cape wines] contain, they are not clear and always somewhat 'dusty'.

2. Consisting of, or of the nature of, dust; powdery.

1552 Huloet, Dustye, or of dust, *pulverius.* *c* **1586** C'tess Pembroke *Ps.* LXVI. iii, A field of dusty sand. **1606** Shaks. *Tr. & Cr.* III ii. 196 When..mightie States characterlesse are grated To dustie nothing. **1748** F. Smith *Voy. Disc.* I. 157 We had a Fall of small dusty Snow. **1890** *Nature* 20 Mar. 473 A dusty material of a scaly form.

3. Of colour, etc.: Having the appearance of being strewn with dust. Also *advb.* qualifying adjs. of colour.

1676 *Lond. Gaz.* No. 1148/4 A dusty brown Gelding. **1679** *Ibid.* No. 1419/4 A dusty black Gelding. **1701** *Ibid.* No. 3703/4 A black dusty-colour Mare. **1843** Carlyle *Let. to Emerson*, A great shock of rough, dusty-dark hair.

4. In various *fig.* senses: † **a.** Soiled or stained as with dust, smirched (*obs.*). **b.** Mean, worthless, vile (cf. DUST *sb.*[1] 3 d); now only in slang phr. ***not (or none) so dusty*** = 'not so bad'. **c.** Obscured as with a cloud of dust. **d.** 'Dry as dust', uninteresting. Also, unsatisfying, inconclusive, poor; esp. in phr. ***dusty answer***.

c **1610** *Women Saints* 168 She knew her dayes to haue beene..dustie and deceitfull. *a* **1649** Drumm. of Hawth. *Fam. Ep.* Wks. (1711) 144 Yet should they not envy silly men a dusty honour. **1847** L. Hunt *Men, Women, & B.* I. ix. 172 What, to his dusty apprehension, appeared the most confused..story in the world. **1856** F. E. Smedley *Harry Coverdale* xlii. 312 None so dusty that—eh? for a commoner like me? **1860** Hawthorne *Marble Faun* (1879) I. v. 56 Hard and dusty facts. **1862** G. Meredith *Modern Love* 82 Ah, what a dusty answer gets the soul When hot for certainties in this our life! **1864** Hotten *Slang Dict.* 128 'What do you think of this?' 'Well, it's not so dusty,' *i.e.*, not so bad; sometimes varied to 'none so dusty'. **1893** R. Kipling *Many Invent.* 148 B Company has come up very well, I said..They're none so dusty now, are they? **1926** Galsworthy *Escape* I. i, Out of Germany! Cripes! That was none so dusty! **1927** R. Lehmann (*title*) Dusty answer. **1929** J. B. Priestley *Good Compan.* I. i. 16 'You're a swell tonight all right!'..'Not so dusty, Mar,' said Leonard. **1936** 'I. Hay' *Housemaster* xix. 235 The applicants met with what is technically known as a dusty answer.

5. *Comb.*, as ***dusty-footed*** adj.; **dusty boy** *Naval slang*, a naval stores rating; **dusty miller**, (*a*) a popular name of the auricula (*Primula Auricula*), from the fine powder on the leaves and flowers; also of *Senecio Cineraria* and *Cerastium tomentosum*; (*b*) a kind of artificial fly used in angling; (*c*) any of several noctuid moths with speckled markings on their wings (*U.S.*); † **dusty-poll**, a nickname for a miller.

[**1909** J. R. Ware *Passing Eng.* 120/2 *Dusty*, a ship's steward's assistant.] **1916** 'Taffrail' *Pincher Martin* vii. 114 Puts on a lot o' swank fur a bloomin' *dusty boy. **1835** Thirlwall *Greece* I. 417 Conipodes, the *dusty-footed. **1825** Jamieson, **Dustie-miller*, the plant Auricula. **1867** F. Francis *Angling* x. (1880) 355 The Dusty Miller..has become a capital general fly. **1888** *Chambers' Encycl.* I. 581 The auricula has..the popular name in Scotland of 'Dusty Miller'. **1909** G. Stratton-Porter *Girl of Limberlost* xii. 243 Small insects of night gathered, and at last a little dusty miller, but nothing came of any size. *c* **1515** *Cocke Lorell's B.* 3 A myller *dusty-poll than dyde come. *a* **1600** J. T. *Collier of Croydon* IV. i. in Hazl. *Dodsley* VIII. 446 Now, miller, miller dustipoll I'll clapper-claw your jobbernole.

† **dustyfoot.** *Sc. Obs.* In 6 dustifit, 7 dustifut(e. [A transl. of med.L. *pede pulverosus* 'dusty of foot' = *vagans* wandering, travelling, in AF. *piépoudreux*: see PIEPOWDER.]

A wayfarer, traveller; *spec.* a travelling pedlar or merchant. (In quot. 1570 applied to Death personified.) *Obs.* exc. *Hist.*

a **1400** *Leg. Quat. Burg. Scot.* xxix, (*Stat. Scot.* I. 361) Vagans, qui vocatur piepowdrous, hoc est Anglice Dustiefute. [*tr.* Beand vagabund in þe contre þe quhilk is callit pipouderus.] **1570** *Satir. Poems Reform.* xxii. 56 At thy last funerall, Quhen Dustifit to dance sall furth the call. **1609** Skene *Reg. Maj.*, *Burrow Lawes* 134 Burgesses, Merchands, and Dustifutes (*Cremars*) quhen they passe forth of the foure Portes of their burghs. **1861** W. Bell *Dict. Law Scot.* s.v., According to Lord Kames, courts of *Pie-Powder* are so called, because fairs are generally composed of pedlars or wayfaring persons, who in France bear the name of *Pied Poudreux*, and in Scotland of *Dusty-Foot.* **1872** E. W. Robertson *Hist. Ess.* 131 The *Negotiatores*, the chapmen and dustyfeet of our old laws.

Dusun ('du:sən), *sb.* and *a.* [a. Mal. *dusun* orchard, village.] **A.** *sb.* **1.** doosoon, dusun. In Malaysia, a village or settlement; (an area of) cultivated land.

1783 W. Marsden *Hist. Sumatra* 49 The *doosoons* or villages..are always situated on the banks of a river or lake. **1845** *Encycl. Metrop.* XXV. 247 Each dúsun or village is governed by a dúpati or head-man. **1914** *Oxf. Survey Brit. Empire* II. xii. 381 The Malay orchard, or 'Dusun', indeed, is a curious combination of the efforts of man and nature. **1964** J. C. Jackson in Wang Gungwu *Malaysia* xvii. 265 In more recent schemes the allocation has been 8 acres of rubber, 2 acres of *dusun*, and a ½-acre house-lot.

2. a. (A member of) a Dyak people inhabiting the Malaysian state of Sabah (formerly North Borneo).

1836 *Penny Cycl.* V. 188/2 In the interior [of Borneo] are the Kayan, the Dusun, the Marut, the Tataoeli, &c., but they are not farther known. **1858** *Geogr. Jrnl.* II. 347 The inhabitants of this region, the Dusuns, or, as they are also sometimes called by the Malays, Idäan, are, for the most part, a fine, well-made, and not unhandsome race. **1881** [see Murut]. **1924** *Chambers's Jrnl.* XIV. 73/2 The Dusuns are great gamblers. **1968** *Encycl. Brit.* III. 966/1 Other aboriginal groups to be noted are the Murut and a subdivision known as the Dusun of North Borneo. They are wet-rice cultivators. **1974** *Encycl. Brit. Macropædia* XI. 372/1 Some groups, such as the Melanaus of Sarawak and the Dusuns of Sabah, have abandoned the longhouse settlement form.

b. The West Indonesian language spoken by the Dusun people.

1922 O. Rutter *British N. Borneo* iii. 64 He much appreciates your being able to say a word or two of Dusun and will then recognize you as a friend indeed. **1965** K. G. Tregonning *Hist. Mod. Sabah* iii. 32 Dusun-speaking descendants of Chinese produced sago and pepper. *Ibid.* ix. 176 Schools teaching Chinese and Dusun or Malay. **1972** *Bk. of Thousand Tongues* (rev. ed.) 110/2 Dusun, with Tagal, shows affinities with the Philippine tongues.

B. *adj.* Of or relating to the Dusun people or their language.

1851 *Jrnl. Indian Archipelago* 49 Dusun knife..used by the Dusuns or Hill Tribes. **1897** *Jrnl. Straits Branch R. Asiatic Soc.* July 2 The Dusun (Kadasan) language contains some very old forms of words. **1960** K. G. Tregonning *N. Borneo* i. 7, I was loaded..on to a small decrepit launch, along with..three Dusun porters. **1974** *Encycl. Brit. Macropædia* XVII. 230/1 In Sabah..rural Dusun women coming as nurse trainees to the capital city discover that their 'native law and custom' does not apply.

dusy, obs. form of DIZZY.

dusze pers, var. DOUZEPERS, *Obs.*

dut, obs. f. *doubt*, *doubted*: see DOUBT *sb.* and *v.*

dut, var. of DUTE, *Obs.*

Dutch (dʌtʃ), *a.*, *sb.* (*adv.*) Also (4 duchyssche, 5 duysshe), 5–7 duch(e, 6 dou(t)che, dowche, duitch, dutche. [a. MDu. *dutsch*, *duutsch*, *duutsc*, 'Hollandish, or, in a wider sense, Netherlandish, and even German' (Verdam), in early mod.Du. *duytsch*, now *duitsch*, 'German', = Ger. *deutsch*, MHG. *diutsch*, 'German', OHG. *diutisc*, popular, vulgar.

OHG. *diutisc*, OS. *thiudisc*, OE. *þéodisc*, Goth. **þiudisks*:—OTeut. **þeudisko-z*, meant 'popular, national', f. OTeut. **þeudâ-*, Goth. *þiuda*, ON. *þjóð*, OS. *thioda*, *thiod*, OE. *þéod* (ME. THEDE), OHG. *diota*, *diot*, people, nation. In

Germany, the adj. was used (in the 9th c.) as a rendering of L. *vulgaris*, to distinguish the 'vulgar tongue' from the Latin of the church and the learned; hence it gradually came to be the current denomination of the vernacular, applicable alike to any particular dialect, and generically to German as a whole. From the language, it was naturally extended to those who spoke it (cf. *English*), and thus grew to be an ethnic or national adjective; whence also, in the 12th or 13th c., arose the name of the country, *Diutisklant*, now *Deutschland*, = Germany. In the 15th and 16th c. 'Dutch' was used in England in the general sense in which we now use 'German', and in this sense it included the language and people of the Netherlands as part of the 'Low Dutch' or Low German domain. After the United Provinces became an independent state, using the 'Nederduytsch' or Low German of Holland as the national language, the term 'Dutch' was gradually restricted in England to the Netherlanders, as being the particular division of the 'Dutch' or Germans with whom the English came in contact in the 17th c.; while in Holland itself *duitsch*, and in Germany *deutsch*, are, in their ordinary use, restricted to the language and dialects of the German Empire and of adjacent regions, exclusive of the Netherlands and Friesland; though in a wider sense 'deutsch' includes these also, and may even be used as widely as 'Germanic' or 'Teutonic'. Thus the English use of *Dutch* has diverged from the German and Netherlandish use since 1600.]

A. *adj.*

† **1.** Of or pertaining to the people of Germany; German; Teutonic. *Obs.* exc. as a historical archaism, and in some parts of U.S.: see B 1 and DUTCHMAN.

High Dutch, of or pertaining to the South Germans who inhabit the more elevated parts of Germany, High German; ***Low Dutch***, of or pertaining to the Germans of the sea coast, and flatter districts in the north and north-west, including the Netherlands and Flanders.

c **1460** *Towneley Myst.* (Surtees) 311 Hie barnes bredeles. A horne and a duch ax, his slefe must be flekyt. **1480** CAXTON *Chron. Eng.* ccxli. 266 Lordes and knyȝtes of hir countre of beme and of other duche tonges. **1530** PALSGR. 31 In propre names commyng out of the Greke or doutche tong. **1563** SHUTE *Archit.* A iij a, French and dowche writers. **1570** LEVINS *Manip.* 195/35 Dutche, *Teutonicus*. **1599** MINSHEU, *Gente Alemāna*, the high Dutch people, the high Germans. **1601** R. JOHNSON *Kingd. & Commw.* (1603) 132 When the Dutch knightes were Lordes of the countrey [Poland]. **1611** CORYAT *Crudities* 376 The Dutch word Zurich signifieth two kingdomes. **1788** M. CUTLER in *Life, Jrnls. & Corr.* (1888) I. 404 We baited our horses..at the first house, a Dutch cabin [in Pennsylvania]. **1884** *Sat. Rev.* 14 June 785/2 The High-Dutch practice of ennobling every substantive with a capital.

2. a. Of, pertaining to, or characterizing the 'Low Dutch' people of Holland and the Netherlands.

Dutch school, a school of painters and style of painting which attained its highest development in the Netherlands, in which commonplace subjects, chosen from ordinary or low life, received consummate artistic treatment.

[**1568** (*title*) Propositions or Articles drawn out of Holy Scripture, showing the Cause of continuall Variance in the Duch Church in London.] **1606** DEKKER *Sev. Sinnes* (Arb.) 37 The short waste hangs ouer a Dutch Botchers stall in Vtrich. **1611** MIDDLETON & DEKKER *Roaring Girl* II. ii, You'll have the great Dutch slop. **1617** MINSHEU *Ductor* s.v. *Duchman*, The Duch nation aboue all other haue had the glorie and fame..for their valour in warre..fortunate battels both by land and sea. **1742** POPE *Dunc.* IV. 198 Each fierce Logician..dash'd thro' thin and thick On German Crouzaz, and Dutch Burgersdyck. **1822** SCOTT *Pirate* xxvi, Brenda..ran from her like a Spanish merchantman from a Dutch caper. **1838** *Murray's Hand-bk. N. Germ.* 16 The collections of pictures of the Dutch school. **1842** TENNYSON *Gardener's Dau.* 188 A Dutch love For tulips.

b. *S. Afr.* Of, pertaining to, or designating South Africans of Dutch descent; Afrikaans-speaking.

1731 MEDLEY tr. *Kolben's Pres. State Cape of Good Hope* v. 58 The Terror of the *Dutch* Arms was spread through all the Nations about the Cape. **1791** G. CARTER *Narr. Loss Grosvenor* xvii. 50 They had got out of the country of the Caffrees, and had reached the northermost of the Dutch settlements. **1852** C. BARTER *Dorp & Veld* vi. 52 Dutch families on their way to Maritzburg for the half-yearly 'Nacht maal' or sacrament. **1871** J. MACKENZIE *10 Yrs. North of Orange River* i. 18 The 'Nachtmaal', or celebration of the Lord's Supper, by the Dutch Church, takes place several times in a year. **1954** D. D'EWES *Mydorp* xii. 70 He attended the Dutch Reformed Church regularly every Sunday. **1970** *Cape Times* 28 Oct. 1/5 He had never had much hope in the liberal movement there, but had contacts with Dutch Reformed Church ministers and had never found them completely impervious to suggestion.

3. a. Of or belonging to the Dutch; native to, or coming from, Holland; first used, introduced, invented, or made by the Dutch.

1592 NASHE *P. Penilesse.* [As hoary as Dutch butter]. **1667** WOOD *Life* (Oxf. Hist. Soc.) II. 131 A. W. did transcribe on Dutch paper. **1681** *Trial S. Colledge* 36 There was an Original drawn with a Pencil, upon Dutch Paper. **1695** CONGREVE *Love for L.* IV. xxi, Dreams and Dutch almanacs are to be understood by contraries. **1698** *Lond. Gaz.* No. 3358/4, 5 Cane Chairs, 3 Dutch Chairs. **1840** DICKENS *Old C. Shop* x, Late as the Dutch clock showed it to be. **1881** *Syd. Soc. Lex., Camphor, Dutch.* Japan camphor is so called because it was introduced into commerce by the Dutch.

b. Often distinguishing a particular sort of article, originally made in or imported from Holland: e.g. **Dutch barn, brick**: see quots.; **Dutch cap**, (*a*) a woman's cap of lace or muslin with a triangular piece rolled back at each side; (*b*) a type of contraceptive pessary; = DIAPHRAGM *sb.* 2 b; **Dutch carpet, case, cheese, clinker**: see quots.; **Dutch doll**, a jointed wooden doll; **Dutch door** (see quot. 1890); **Dutch drops**: see quots.; **Dutch elm disease**, a fungous disease of elms, first discovered in Holland, caused by *Ceratocystis ulmi*; **Dutch foil**, a very malleable alloy of 11 parts of copper and 2 of zinc, beaten into thin leaves, and used as a cheap imitation of gold-leaf; **Dutch garden** (see quots.); **Dutch gilding, gilt, gold** = *Dutch foil* above; **Dutch hoe** (see HOE *sb.*[2] 1 b); **Dutch interior**, a painting of the interior of a Dutch room or house, esp. by the Dutch painter Pieter de Hooch (1629–83); also *transf.*; **Dutch leaf** = *Dutch foil* above; **Dutch liquid, oil**, Ethene dichloride, 2 (CH_2Cl), a thin oily liquid, having a sweetish smell and taste; **Dutch metal** = *Dutch foil* above; **Dutch mill**, an oil mill for rape oil; **Dutch oven** (see OVEN *sb.* 2 a); also *slang*, a person's mouth; **Dutch pen**: see quot.; **Dutch pink** [PINK *sb.*[5]], a yellow lake pigment; also *slang*, blood; **Dutch pins, rubbers**, a form of nine-pins or skittles; **Dutch pump**: see quot.; **Dutch roll**, (*a*) a roll in ice-skating, executed by gliding with the feet parallel and pressing alternately on the edges of each foot; (*b*) *Aeronaut.* (see quot. 1960); **Dutch sauce**, a sauce served with fish; = HOLLANDAISE; **Dutch tile**, a kind of glazed tile frequently painted in colours; **Dutch white**, a pigment consisting of one part of white lead and three parts of barium sulphate; **Dutch wife** (see quots. and sense 4 below).

1743 W. ELLIS *Mod. Husb.* June x. 76 In order to enjoy his Hay finer than his Neighbours, he built him a **Dutch* Barn, in 1738. **1886** W. A. HARRIS *Techn. Dict. Fire Ins., Dutch barn*, a protection for hay, straw, &c., having the supports and framework of a barn, without the side and end boarding. **1657** R. LIGON *Barbadoes* (1673) Index 84 *Dutch Bricks, which they call Klinkers. **1890** A. RIMMER *Summer Rambles Manchester* 35 Red 'Dutch' bricks in 'Flemish bond'. **1726** MRS. JOHNSON *Let.* Oct. in E. Hamilton *Mordaunts* (1965) vii. 145 Misses coat fitts her very well, the *Dutch cap Miss Mordaunt is not at all reconciled to but will wear it if her Cosens doe. **1857** D. H. STROTHER *Virginia* 68 His head..was surmounted by a tiny Dutch cap. **1922** M. STOPES in *Lancet* 12 Aug. 357/2 Recourse may then be had to the inverted or Dutch cap. **1943** J. H. PEEL *Textbk. Gynæcol.* xxiii. 342 The best and most widely applicable is undoubtedly the Dutch cap pessary. **1960** C. WATSON *Bump in Night* iv. 44 Don't ever again describe bridesmaids as wearing Dutch caps. **1962** 'H. LOURIE' *Question of Abortion* iv. 34 One patient..had proved not to be pregnant...she had come back for a Dutch cap. **1967** M. DRABBLE *Jerusalem the Golden* vii. 155 Spread before her on the floor was a..dutch cap, an instruction leaflet, and various other accoutrements of contraception. **1858** SIMMONDS *Dict. Trade*, **Dutch-carpet*, a mixed material of cotton and wool, used for floor-coverings. **1874** KNIGHT *Dict. Mech.*, **Dutch-case* (*Mining*), a shaft-frame composed of four pieces of plank, used in shafts and galleries. **1700** S. L. tr. *Fryke's Voy. E. Ind.* 7, 5 *Dutch Cheeses. **1858** SIMMONDS *Dict. Trade*, *Dutch-cheese*, a small round cheese made on the Continent from skim milk. **1856** S. C. BREES *Gloss. Terms*, **Dutch clinkers*, a description of brick employed for paving stables and yards, being exceedingly hard. **1797** LADY A. BARNARD *Let.* 10 July (1901) ii. 57 What they [*sc.* Dutch ladies] most want is shoulders and manners. I know now what is meant by a '*Dutch doll'; their make is exactly like them. **1824** SCOTT *Redgauntlet* Let. iii, All thy motions, like those of a great Dutch doll, depending on the pressure of certain springs. **1926** W. DEEPING *Sorrell & Son* vii, Her head was as neat as the head of a Dutch doll. **1890** WEBSTER, **Dutch door*, a door divided into two parts, horizontally, so arranged that the lower part can be shut and fastened, while the upper part remains open. **1945** NELSON & WRIGHT *Tomorrow's House* v. 57 The kitchen also opens into the main room by way of..a Dutch door. **1844** DICKENS *Mart. Chuz.* xxiv, A bottle of *Dutch Drops. **1858** SIMMONDS *Dict. Trade*, *Dutch-drops*, a balsam or popular nostrum, prepared with oil of turpentine, tincture of guaiacum, nitric ether, succinic acid, and oil of cloves. **1927** *Gardeners' Chron.* 19 Feb. 133/3 (*heading*) The *Dutch Elm Disease... The disease was first observed in Holland in September, 1919. **1931** *Science* 30 Oct. 437/1 After the identification of the Dutch elm disease in Ohio, during the summer of 1930. **1968** *New Scientist* 5 Sept. 489/1 The beetles that carry Dutch elm disease are attracted to dead or dying trees for egg laying. *a* **1772** T. WHATELY *Obs. Mod. Gardening* (new ed.) (1801) iv. 153 To get too, as far as can be, the advantage of natural prospects, the artificial mounts of the flat *Dutch gardens should here be introduced. **1872** A. SMEE *My Garden* 584 The chief peculiarities of a Dutch garden may be said to consist in its being seen at one glance;..in the utmost symmetry being observed in all its parts..; in its trees being clipped sometimes into curious shapes and figures..; in its having long serpentine or straight walks..; [etc.]. **1899** S. R. HOLE *Our Gardens* 277, I asked an old gardener whether he could tell me anything about Dutch Gardens, and he made answer, 'They be bits o' beds with edgings o' box, and gravel walks, and four sloping banks forming a square outside, and they be pratty toys for children, and very snug for varmint.' **1902** H. I. TRIGGS *Formal Gardens* pl. 58 Holland House, Kensington. The Dutch Garden. **1928** L. ARCHER-HIND tr. *Gothein's Hist. Garden Art* II. xiii. 218 People were misled by the term 'Dutch garden', as it came to be used derisively in the eighteenth century. *Ibid.* 230 The Dutch garden must be reckoned as of the French school. **1759** SYMMER in *Phil. Trans.* LI. 375 A piece of paper, covered on one side with *Dutch gilding. **1825** HONE *Every-day Bk.* I. 51 Their..ware has leaves of untarnished *dutch-gilt stuck on. *Ibid.* 1170 The gingerbread stalls..were..fine, from the *dutch gold on their..ware. [**1816** M. BRYAN *Dict. Painters & Engravers* I. 559 His [*sc.* P. de Hooch's] favourite subjects were the interiors of Dutch apartments..the sun shining through a window.] **1886** BRYAN & GRAVES *Dict. Painters & Engravers* I. 370/1 *Dutch Interior [by P. de Hooch]; a Lady playing the lute and singing, whilst a cavalier accompanies her. **1913** E. WHARTON *Custom of Country* I. v. 73 The hall, with..the quiet 'Dutch interior' effect of its black and white marble paving. **1940** 'F. O'CONNOR' (*title*) Dutch interior. **1966** M. CATTO *Bird on Wing* ix. 131 The lights were dim. It made an intimate picture. Like one of those cosy Dutch interiors: the burgher at home with his wife. **1970** V. C. CLINTON-BADDELEY *No Case for Police* iii. 63 Like some picture of a 'Dutch Interior', the open door revealed a hall, and, beyond that, another open door... Only the traditional distant figure was lacking. **1848** FOWNES *Elem. Chem.* III. (ed. 2) 404 Pure *Dutch liquid is a thin colourless fluid, of agreeably fragrant odour, and sweet taste. **1851** *Offic. Catal. Gt. Exhib.* I. 191 Dutch liquid, chloride of olefiant gas, a new anæsthetic agent, said to be less irritating than chloroform. **1877** WATTS *Fownes' Chem.* (ed. 12) II. 69 *Dutch liquid* having been discovered by four Dutch chemists in 1795. **1825** HONE *Every-day Bk.* I. 1245 Instead of leaf gold..they were covered..with *Dutch metal. *c* **1865** URE in *Circ. Sc.* I. 99/2 These mortars and press boxes constitute what are called *Dutch mills. **1769, 1849** *Dutch oven [see OVEN *sb.* 2 a]. **1922** JOYCE *Ulysses* 419 O, cheese it! Shut his blurry Dutch oven with a firm hand. **1968** *Islander* (Victoria, B.C.) 11 Aug. 7/2 Other relics of trail days, which time has not completely erased, are three beehive Dutch ovens built from native stone. **1727–52** CHAMBERS *Cycl.* s.v. *Pen*, **Dutch Pens*, are those made of quills which have been passed through hot ashes, to take off the grosser fat and moisture thereof. **1758** *Dutch pink [see PINK *sb.*[5]]. **1835** Dutch pink [see *English pink* s.v. ENGLISH *a.* 2 e]. **1853** 'C. BEDE' *Verdant Green* II. iv, That'll take the bark from your nozzle, and distil the Dutch pink for you, won't it? **1881** J. BELL *Anal. Foods* I. 22 The leaves were slightly coloured with Dutch pink to impart a bloom. **1801** STRUTT *Sports & Past.* III. vii. §10 *Dutch-pins is a pastime much resembling skittles; but the pins are taller and slenderer, especially in the middle pin, which is higher than the rest, and called the king-pin. **1809** *Sporting Mag.* XXXIV. 236 A match at Dutch-pins for 100 guineas. **1867** SMYTH *Sailor's Word-bk.*, **Dutch pump*, a punishment so contrived that, if the prisoner would not pump hard, he was drowned. **1893** *Durham Univ. Jrnl.* X. 103 Others have in spite of honourable endeavour been obliged to content themselves with mediocre achievement and *Dutch roll. **1939** *Jrnl. R. Aeronaut. Soc.* XLIII. 795 Lateral oscillations, or 'Dutch roll', as they are sometimes called. **1960** *Electronic Engin.* XXXII. 407 A 'dutch roll' is the characteristic short period lateral oscillation of an aircraft, involving yaw, roll and sideslip, which is excited either by rudder application, or a lateral gust. **1801** STRUTT *Sports & Past.* III. vii. §4. 238 Some call this game [long-bowling] *Dutch-rubbers. **1573** 'C. HOLLYBAND' *French Schoolemaister* fol. 55ᵛ Will you eate of a Pike with a high *dutche sauce? **1893** T. F. GARRETT *Encycl. Pract. Cookery* II. 387/2 Dutch or Holland Sauce (à la Hollandaise). **1955** *Oxf. Jun. Encycl.* XI. 396/2 *Hollandaise* (or Dutch sauce) is made entirely of butter emulsified with egg-yolks and lemon juice—a sort of butter mayonnaise served warm. **1727–41** *Dutch tile [see TILE *sb.*[1] 1 c]. **1753** H. WALPOLE *Let.* 12 June (1903) III. 168 A cool little hall..hung with paper to imitate Dutch tiles. **1844** Dutch tile [see TILE *sb.*[1] 1 c]. **1862** ROSSETTI *Let.* 9 Jan. (1965) II. 435, I have had the fireplace covered with real old blue glazed Dutch tiles. **1957** *Granta* 9 Mar. 19/3 He walked over the steeply pitched, loose Dutch tiles of the roofs as if he were on a dance-floor. **1968** L. O'DONNELL *Face of Crime* i. 11 The fireplace faced with authentic Dutch tiles in the traditional pale lavender depicting scenes from the Bible. **1886** H. C. STANDAGE *Artists' Man. Pigments* i. 5 White lead (known also as Ceruse, Cremnitz, *Dutch, Flemish, Hamburg, Venetian, or Roman White). **1891** FARMER *Slang* II. 349 *Dutch-wife, a bolster. **1965** W. YOUNG *Eros Denied* xxvii. 271 We call..a masturbation machine a Dutch husband or wife. **1966** G. BLACK *You want to die, Johnny?* vi. 114 'What's this great long bolster for?..' 'Colonial invention. For the hated Imperialists. Known as a Dutch wife.' **1967** *Guardian* 19 May 9/6 He will liberate man from dependence on the opposite sex by constructing what seems to be known in Japan as a 'Dutch Wife'; a kind of life-size mechanical doll with built-in electric heating and all the other refinements.

c. In names of trees and plants, of species or varieties introduced from Holland, or common in that country; or sometimes merely to distinguish them from the common English variety or species; e.g.

Dutch agrimony, beech, clover, elm, honeysuckle, medlar, mezereon, myrtle, violet, willow, etc.; see these words. **Dutch mice**, Carmele, *Lathyrus tuberosus*. **Dutch rushes**, a species of *Equisetum* or Horse-tail used for polishing; shave-grass.

1548 TURNER *Names Herbes* A vj b, Albucum..groweth in gardines in Anwerp, it maye be named in englishe whyte affodil, or duche daffodil. *Ibid.* D v b. *Ibid.* E v. **1640** PARKINSON *Theat. Bot.* 1156 Sweet Dutch grasse with a tufted head. **1731–45** MILLER *Gard. Kalendar* 79 Imperial, Cos and Brown Dutch Lettuces. *Ibid.*, The large-rooted Dutch Parsley. **1829** LOUDON *Encycl. Plants* 208 *note, Ulmus suberosa*, often called the Dutch Elm. *Ibid.* 891 *note*, *Equisetum hyemale* is imported from Holland under the name of Dutch rushes. **1849** CARPENTER *Veg. Phys.* §757 Minute particles of silex or flinty substance, whose presence renders one species,..the 'Dutch Rush', valued for its use in polishing furniture and pewter utensils. **1860** *Gardener's Chron.* 774/2 *Lathyrus tuberosus*..is occasionally cultivated under the name of Dutch Mice. **1888** G. S. BOULGER *Fam. Trees* Ser. II. 142 The Dutch Elm..was introduced by William III. for clipped hedges, on account of its rapid growth.

4. Characteristic of or attributed to the Dutch; often with an opprobrious or derisive application, largely due to the rivalry and enmity between the English and Dutch in the 17th c.

Often with allusion to the drinking habits ascribed to the 'Dutch'; also to the broad heavy figures attributed to the Netherlanders, or to their flat-bottomed vessels. Sometimes little more than = foreign, un-English.

Dutch auction (so ***auctioneer***), ***bargain, concert, courage, gleek, nightingale, uncle***: see AUCTION, BARGAIN, etc. ***Dutch comfort, consolation, defence, feast, palate, reckoning, widow***: see quots. ***Dutch act*** (see sense B. 4 below); ***Dutch***

lunch, party, supper, treat (orig. *U.S.*), one at which each person contributes his or her own share; ***Dutch wife***, an open frame of ratan or cane used in the Dutch Indies, etc. to rest the limbs upon in bed.

1859 SALA *Tw. round Clock* 21 The sale is conducted on the principle of what is termed a '*Dutch auction', purchasers not being allowed to inspect the fish in the doubles before they bid. **1872** *Daily Tel.* 30 Nov. (Farmer) The old Dutch auction, by which an article was put up at a high price, and, if nobody accepted the offer, then reduced to a lower, the sum first required being gradually decreased until a fair value was attained. **1830** *Virginia Lit. Museum* 632 A *Dutch auctioneer, whose practice is to set up his wares at the highest price, and thence bid downwards till he meets with a purchaser. **1654** WHITLOCK *Zootomia* 28 The contract..is not (like *Dutch Bargains) made in Drinke. **1796** GROSE *Dict. Vulg. T.*, **Dutch Comfort*, thank God it is no worse. **1773** BARRINGTON in *Phil. Trans.* LXIII. 267 What is commonly called a *Dutch concert, when several tunes are played together. **1867** SMYTH *Sailor's Word-bk.*, **Dutch consolation.* 'Whatever ill befalls you, there's somebody that's worse'; or 'It's very unfortunate, but thank God it's no worse'. **1888** *All Year Round* 9 June 542 (Farmer) The expression often heard, 'Thank Heaven, it is no worse', is sometimes called Dutch consolation. **1749** FIELDING *Tom Jones* IX. vi, I am afraid Mr. Jones maintained a kind of *Dutch defence, and treacherously delivered up the garrison without duly weighing his allegiance to the fair Sophia. *a* **1700** EVELYN *Diary* 25 Nov. an. 1682 (1955) IV. 296, I was exceedingly afraide of Drinking, (it being a *Dutch feast). **1785** GROSE *Dict. Vulg. T.*, *Dutch feast*, where the entertainer gets drunk before his guests. **1904** *Columbus Post-Dispatch* 21 Aug., Dancing was enjoyed by all as was the *Dutch lunch which was partaken of at intervals during the evening. **1954** J. SYMONS *Narrowing Circle* xxv. 107 'Shall we make this a Dutch lunch?'..He was all there when it came to money. **1678** NORRIS *Coll. Misc.* Pref. (1699) 3 Fit only for a Tavern entertainment; and that too among Readers of a *Dutch Palate. **1927** *Observer* 8 May 13/3 *Dutch parties are rather more elaborate, in that while the hostess provides the dance floor, music, table, service, and cutlery, her friends bring along the drinks and the viands, raiding their family cellars and larders. *a* **1700** B. E. *Dict. Cant. Crew*, **Dutch-Reckoning*, or *Alte-mall*, a verbal or Lump-account without particulars. **1867** SMYTH *Sailor's Word-bk.*, *Dutch reckoning*, a bad day's work, all in the wrong. **1904** *Dallas Morning News* 10 Sept. 6 Depriving themselves of money they need to buy plug-cut and *Dutch suppers with. **1887** *Lippincott's Mag.* Aug. 191 'You'll come along too, won't you?' Lancelot demanded of Ormizon. '*Dutch treat vous savez.' **1937** *Sunday Express* 14 Feb. 25/3 Are you a 'Dutch treat' addict? (In a Dutch treat every one buys his or her own drinks.) **1945** 'L. LEWIS' *Birthday Murder* (1951) iii. 39 It's Dutch treat; he pays his own way and makes the women pay theirs. **1958** 'A. GILBERT' *Death against Clock* 81 We arranged to go to the pictures next night. Dutch treat. **1608** MIDDLETON *Trick to catch Old One* III. iii, *Hoord.* What is that Florence? a widow? *Dra.* Yes, a *duch widdow. *Hoo.* How? *Dra.* Thats an English drab sir.

5. *Comb.* (parasynthetic and adverbial), as ***Dutch-bellied, -built, -buttocked*** (see note to 4); ***Dutch-cut*** (like yews, etc. in Dutch gardening).

1672 R. WILD *Declar. Lib. Consc.* 7 Such a Dutch-bellied, blundering, boreal Month as this March. **1676** *Rep. French Capers* 4 Aug. in Marvell *Growth Popery* (1678) 59 Whether (as is imputed) all the Ships taken are Dutch built? **1823** MOORE *Fables* ii. 8 Some wished them tall; some thought your dumpy, Dutch-built the true Legitimate. **1868** DARWIN *Anim. & Pl.* II. xii. 8 The farmers continued to select cattle with large hind-quarters, until they made a strain called 'Dutch-buttocked'. **1893** T. C. FINLAYSON *Ess.* etc. 97 Many allow themselves to be 'Dutch-cut'.

B. *sb.* [Elliptical uses of the adj.]

1. The German language, in any of its forms. *Obs.* exc. in ***High Dutch*** = German [*Hoch Deutsch*]; ***Low Dutch*** = Low German [*Platt Deutsch*], that of the north and north-west (including Netherlandish: see next), which has not undergone the High German consonant-mutation, and thus is in form nearer to English and Scandinavian.

Pennsylvania Dutch, a degraded form of High German (orig. from the Rhine Palatinate and Switzerland) spoken by the descendants of the original German settlers in Pennsylvania.

c **1380** WYCLIF *Sel. Wks.* III. 100 Wheþer it be..wryten in Latin in Englyssche or in Frensche or Duchyssche [*v.r.* Duche]. **1485** CAXTON *Pref. to Malory's Arthur*, Bookes..as wel in duche ytalyen spaynysshe and grekysshe as in frensshe. **1547** BOORDE *Introd. Knowl.* xv. (1870) 163 In Denmark..theyr speche is Douche. **1548** TURNER *(title)* The names of herbes in Greke, Latin, English, Duch and Frenche. **1578** LYTE *Dodoens* v. xxxi. 590 Called..in high Douche, Melaunen: in base Almaigne, Meloenen: in Englishe, Melons. *a* **1634** CHAPMAN *Alphonsus* II. Plays 1873 III. 219 Good Aunt, teach me so much Dutch to ask her pardon. *Empress.* Say so: *Gnediges frawlin vergebet mirs* [etc.]. **1682** R. WARE *Foxes & Firebrands* II. 11 Translated out of Low-Dutch. **1721** DE FOE *Mem. Cavalier* (1840) 60, I spoke high Dutch. **1756–7** tr. *Keysler's Trav.* (1760) IV. 326 A chronicle of Nurenberg, in High-Dutch, written in the year 1585. **1871** EARLE *Philol. Eng. Tongue* §17 The Saxons were a border people, and spoke a Low Dutch strongly impregnated with Scandinavian associations.

2. a. The language of Holland or the Netherlands.

[**1647** H. HEXHAM *(title)*, A copious English and Netherduytch Dictionarie.] *a* **1706** DORSET (Mason), Thy plays are such I'd swear they were translated out of Dutch. **1871** EARLE *Philol. Eng. Tongue* §470 The pronoun of the second person singular is lost in Dutch. **1872** R. MORRIS *Hist. Outl. Eng. Accid.* §9 To the Low German division belong the following languages:—(1) Gothic..(2) Frisian..(3) Dutch..(4) Flemish..(5) Old Saxon..(6) English.

b. ***double*** (**†*high***) ***Dutch***: a language that one does not understand, gibberish.

1789 DIBDIN *Poor Jack* ii, Why 'twas just all as one as High Dutch. **1876** C. H. WALL tr. *Molière* I. 116 (Farmer) Though I have said them [prayers] daily now these fifty years, they are still double Dutch to me. **1879** SPURGEON *Serm.* XXV. 297 The preacher preaches double Dutch or Greek, or something of the sort.

c. *S. Afr.* = AFRIKAANS *sb.*; in full, ***Cape Dutch*** or ***South African Dutch***.

1731 MEDLEY tr. *Kolben's Pres. State Cape of Good Hope* iii. 26 The People far up the Country, on the Appearance of Strangers, are us'd to say in *Dutch, wat Volk*, i.e. *What People?* **1798** LADY A. BARNARD *Jrnl.* 11 May in *Lives of Lindsays* (1849) III. 437, I doubt much if my whole stock of Dutch amounts to two dozen of words. **1849** N. J. MERRIMAN *Kaffir, Hottentot & Frontier Farmer* (1854) 51 He knew Dutch well, and between the three tongues we contrived to make ourselves intelligible. **1936** F. R. THOMPSON *Matabele Thompson* i. 25, I..became proficient in Dutch, and in the various native languages that I came across.

d. ***High Dutch*** (S. Afr.) [tr. Afrikaans *Hooghollands*], Netherlands (literary) Dutch as distinguished from Cape Dutch or Afrikaans.

1901 LOGEMAN & VAN OORDT *How to speak Dutch* (ed. 3) I. 31 The main points of difference between so-called 'High Dutch' and Cape-Dutch phonetics and spelling may be enumerated as follows. **1911** H. H. FYFE *S. Afr. To-Day* viii. 96 High Dutch..is not the language of the Dutch people in South Africa..the 'taal'..is the common speech. **1936** HAARHOFF & VAN DEN HEEVER *Achievement of Afrikaans* i. 13 While we tried to write in High Dutch our thoughts were cast in rigid moulds;..and the result was often secondhand rhetoric. **1958** L. VAN DER POST *Lost World Kalahari* iii. 60 In High Dutch I wrote: 'I have decided to-day.'

3. ***the Dutch*** (*pl.*) **†a.** The Germans. *Obs.* **b.** The people of Holland and the Netherlands; formerly called also ***Low Dutch***. (†Rare pl. ***Dutches***.)

1577 *Remembr. Life Gascoigne* (Arb.) 19 Wel plaste at length, among the drunken Dutch [*margin* He served in Holland]. **1601** R. JOHNSON *Kingd. & Commw.* (1603) 155 Of mercenary soldiers..he had 4300 Polonians: of chirchasses (that are under the Polonians) aboute 4000, Dutches and Scottes aboute 150. *Ibid.* 257 He is served by the Swizzers and the Dutch. **1631** T. POWELL *Tom all Trades* (1876) 164 When our acquaintance tooke first life with those of the Low Countries..the Dutch..askt him [our Embassador] what handicraft our King was brought up unto. **1648** H. HEXHAM *Netherdutch & Eng. Dict.* Pref., Having of late compiled a large English and Netherdutch Dictionarie..for the accommodation of the Netherdutches who are desirous to attaine unto the knowledge..of our English Tongue. **1666** DRYDEN *Ann. Mirab.* clxvii, The toils of war we must endure, And from the injurious Dutch redeem the seas. **1777** WATSON *Philip II* (1839) 345 The success of Philip's arms..excited in the Dutch and Flemings the most alarming apprehensions. *c* **1826** G. CANNING (in *Lyra Elegantiarum* 1867. 148) In matters of commerce, the fault of the Dutch Is giving too little and asking too much. **1831** SIR J. SINCLAIR *Corr.* II. 180 The Dutch are distinguished by a great desire for cleanliness.

c. ***to beat the Dutch***, to do something extraordinary or startling. ***that beats the Dutch***, that beats everything. *U.S. colloq.*

1775 *Revolut. Song* in *New Eng. Hist. Reg.* Apr. (1857) 191 (Bartlett) Our cargoes of meat, drink, and cloaths beat the Dutch. **1906** M. E. W. FREEMAN *By Light of Soul* xx. 277 Well, you women do beat the Dutch. **1939** *Amer. Speech* XIV. 267 If it is startling news, it 'beats the Jews' or 'beats the Dutch'.

d. *S. Afr.* The Afrikaans-speaking people; the South Africans of Dutch descent.

1731 MEDLEY tr. *Kolben's Pres. State Cape of Good Hope* v. 57 There are at this Time the strictest Alliance and the closest Friendship subsisting between the Dutch and the several Hottentot Nations. **1776** MASSON *Phil. Trans. R. Soc.* 305 There is another species of animal called by the Dutch Bles-moll. **1850** J. W. APPLEYARD *Kafir Lang.* 10/2 The Dutch language as generally spoken..by the Dutch themselves in the country districts, is very different from the Dutch as used in Holland. **1897** [see HOTTENTOT 1 a].

4. Slang phrases (orig. *U.S.*): (*a*) ***in Dutch***, in disfavour, disgrace, or trouble; (*b*) ***to do a*** (or ***the***) ***Dutch*** (***act***), to desert, escape, run away; also, to commit suicide.

1904 H. HAPGOOD *Autobiogr. of Thief* vi. 112 A week later Dal was found dead in his cell, and I believe he did the Dutch act (suicide). **1909** J. R. WARE *Passing Eng.* 120/2 We did a dutch with everything—even down to the coalhammer. **1912** A. H. LEWIS *Apaches of N.Y.* iv. 70, I don't want to put you in Dutch with your fleet. **1948** M. ALLINGHAM *More Work for Undertaker* xxv. 286 He'll be in dutch if there's nothing to show at the end of it. **1953** P. FRANKAU *Winged Horse* II. iv. 134 Maybe Baron'll fire me when he knows I'm in Dutch with his family. **1958** M. A. DE FORD in J. Macdonald *Lethal Sex* (1962) 115 You can't face it..so you're doing the Dutch and leaving a confession. **1959** E. FENWICK *Long Way Down* xx. 155 Scare the poor kid to death, probably—and get her in dutch with her people, too. **1965** 'R. L. PIKE' *Police Blotter* (1966) ii. 37 The day Caper Connelly does the dutch, my guess is it'll be against somebody else. **1968** J. DOS PASSOS *Best Times* ii. 69 While I plodded around..trying to explain my position and getting myself deeper in Dutch every time I opened my face, I saw marvellous scenes.

C. *adv.* **†1.** In Dutch (or German) fashion. *Obs.*

a **1601** ? MARSTON *Pasquil & Kath.* II. 364 Drinke Dutch, like gallants, let's drinke vpsey freeze.

2. With each person paying for his own food, drink, etc.; esp. in phr. ***to go Dutch*** (cf. ***Dutch lunch***, etc., under sense A. 4 above). orig. *U.S.*

1914 S. LEWIS *Our Mr. Wrenn* v. 63 We'll go Dutch. **1957** *Economist* 5 Oct. 14/1 To suggest a free trade area to any of them in such circumstances looks rather like proposing to a teetotaller that you and he go dutch on daily rounds of drinks. **1962** *Ibid.* 29 Sept. 1213/3 There is 'Dutch auction', 'Dutch uncle', to eat out 'Dutch' with one's friends, and many more.

Hence **ˈDutchlike** *a.*; **ˈDutchly** *adv.*, in a Dutch fashion, like the Dutch.

1599 H. BUTTES *Dyets Dry Dinner* P. v, On English foole: wanton Italianly:..Duchly drink: breath Indianly. **1818** W. ALLSTON in *W. Irving's Life & Lett.* (1864) I. 397 Impenetrably, and most Dutchly grave. **1889** HISSEY *Tour in Phaeton* 203 Flat Dutchlike country.

dutch, *sb.*[2] *slang.* [Abbrev. of DUCHESS.] A costermonger's wife; *gen.* a wife; often ***old Dutch***.

a **1889** MITCHELL *Jimmy Johnson's Holiday* (Barrère & Leland), He made a vow he'd never row With his old Dutch again. **1889** BARRÈRE & LELAND *Dict. Slang* I. 341/2 *Dutch* (popular), a wife. **1893** A. CHEVALIER *My Old Dutch*, There ain't a lady livin' in the land As I'd 'swop' for my dear old Dutch! **1901** R. C. LEHMANN *Anni Fugaces* 128, I detected a coster..with some one to act as his Dutch. **1926** *Calgary Daily Herald* 7 June, Joe Brown, Sal Gratton, and the rest of the quaint coster characters of 'My Old Dutch' come to life and live over their romantic story at the Strand theatre.

dutch, *v.* [f. DUTCH *a.*] *trans.* To clarify and harden (quills) by plunging them in heated sand or rapidly passing them through a fire.

1763 *Lond. Chron.* 3–6 Sept. 231/1 Advt., The whole art of Dutching, Clarifying, and Making of Quills perfectly clear and hard. **1768** *Woman of Honor* III. 215 Hardened like a quill, by being Dutched. **1837** WHITTOCK, etc. *Compl. Bk. Trades* (1842) 373 We imported vast quantities of quills from Hamburgh, Rotterdam, etc., and these were clarified or Dutched.

ˈDutcher[1]. *rare.* [f. DUTCH, after Ger. *deutscher*.] A Dutchman; in earlier use, a German.

1671 CROWNE *Juliana* II. Dram. Wks. 1873 I. 45 There have I..boarded the French-man, the high Dutcher, the Spaniard, the Grecian. **1818** *Blackw. Mag.* III. 402 Reviled the Dutchers as Poltroons and Shirks.

ˈdutcher[2]. [f. DUTCH *v.*] (See quot.)

1875 *Ure's Dict. Arts* II. 333 (*Feathers*) Quills are dressed by the London dealers..the principal worker is called a Dutcher.

dutchess, obs. form of DUCHESS.

Dutchify (ˈdʌtʃɪfaɪ), *v.* [f. DUTCH *a.* + -FY.] *trans.* To make Dutch; to render Dutch-like.

1680 *Hon. Cavalier* 13 So much Dutchified, as to understand the Phrase Hogan-Mogan. **1774** J. Q. ADAMS *Diary* 11 Sept. Wks. II. 379 We..heard..a Dutchified English prayer and preachment. **1811** COLERIDGE *Lect. Shaks.* ix. (1856) 115 In modern poems, where all is so dutchified, if I may use the word, by the most minute touches, that the reader naturally asks why words, and not painting, are used. **1890** *Murray's Mag.* Apr. 452 The admixture tends to Anglicize the Dutch rather than to Dutchify the English.

†Dutchkin, *a. nonce-wd. Obs.* [f. DUTCH + -KIN: cf. *alkin*, etc.] Of 'Dutch' or German kind or sort.

1576 GASCOIGNE *Steele Gl.* Epil. 31 (Arb.) 83 What be they? women? masking in mens weedes? With dutchkin dublets, and with Ierkins jaggde? With Spanish spangs, and ruffes set out of France?

Dutchland (ˈdʌtʃlænd).

†1. [= Ger. *Deutschland.*] Germany. *Obs.*

Divided into ***High Dutchland*** and ***Low Dutchland***, the latter including, and sometimes definitely meaning, the Netherlands.

1547 BALE *Sel. Wks.* (1849) 243 Both in England and Dutchland also. **1561** J. WYTHERS tr. *Calvin's Prof. Treat.* Title-p., In France, Dutchland, Spaine. **1563** SHUTE *Archit.* B j a, Trier in lowe Doutcheland. **1599** MINSHEU *Sp. Dict.*, *Alemaña*, Germanie, high Dutchland. *a* **1634** CHAPMAN *Alphonsus* Plays 1873 III. 206 Brave Duke of Saxon, Dutchland's greatest hope.

2. Holland, the Netherlands. *rare.*

1617 MINSHEU *Ductor*, *Duchland* or Low Countries. **1865** MRS. HAWTHORNE in Bridge *Pers. Recoll. N. Hawthorne* (1893) 194 Do we not like to see even a common object of still life truthfully represented by the great masters of Dutchland?

Dutchman (ˈdʌtʃmən). [f. DUTCH *a.* + MAN.]

1. †a. A German; a man of Teutonic race. *Obs.* exc. locally in *U.S.*

1387 TREVISA *Higden* (Rolls) I. 253 Þe woodnesse of Duchesmen [*furorem Teutonicorum*]. **1413** *Pilgr. Sowle* (Caxton 1483) IV. xxx. 80 Be it duysshe man or lumbard or ony other nacion. **1538** WRIOTHESLEY *Chron.* (1875) I. 90, 3 men and 1 woman, all Duchemen borne. **1570** LEVINS *Manip.* 21/2 Dutchman, *Teutonicus*. **1599** SHAKS. *Much Ado* III. ii. 33 To bee a Dutchman to day, a Frenchman to morrow. **1617** MINSHEU *Ductor*, A *Duchman* or German. Vi[de] *German*. **1788** M. CUTLER in *Life, Jrnls. & Corr.* (1888) I. 404 This is a good house, kept by a Dutchman [in Pennsylvania]. **1871** E. EGGLESTON *Hoosier Schoolm.* (1872) vii. 74 The robbery at 'the Dutchman's' (as the only German in the whole region was called). **1931** 'D. STIFF' *Milk & Honey Route* iii. 38 Germans of all kinds are 'Dutchmen', 'square-heads' or 'Heines'.

b. A European; a foreigner (see quots.). *colloq.*

1857 J. D. BORTHWICK *3 Yrs. in California* 311 Europeans..save French, English, and 'Eyetalians' are in California classed under the general denomination of Dutchmen, or more frequently 'd—d Dutchmen', merely for the sake of euphony. **1892** STEVENSON & OSBOURNE *Wrecker* xii. 194 In sea-lingo (Pacific) *Dutchman* includes all Teutons and folk from the basin of the Baltic. **1907** *Daily Chron.* 21 Dec. 6/6

'Only fifty years ago,' he remarked, 'we gave the generic name of Dutchman to all the representatives of Western civilisation in the Far East.' **1910** G. C. EGGLESTON *Recoll.* 3 To us in the West, at least, all foreigners whose mother tongue was other than English were 'Dutchmen'. **1925** FRASER & GIBBONS *Soldier & Sailor Words, Dutchman*, the British seafarers' name for sailormen in general, natives of Northern Europe: Dutchmen proper, Danes, Swedes, Russians, Germans. Finns are excepted. **1928** *Daily Express* 20 July 2/7 British sailors refer to foreigners employed on vessels as 'Dutchmen'.

2. a. An inhabitant of Holland or the Netherlands.

1596 *Edward III*, III. i. 25 In Netherland, Among those euer-bibbing Epicures, Those frothy Dutch men, puft with double-beer. **1617** MINSHEU *Ductor*, A *Duchman*, or one of the Low Countries. **1700** S. L. tr. *Fryke's Voy. E. Ind.* 66 A Gill of Brandy (the best thing in the World to inspire Courage into a Dutch-man). **1873** F. C. BURNAND *My Time* i, Uncle Van Clym was a Dutchman. *Mod.* Is he a German or a Dutchman?

b. Phr. ***I'm a Dutchman***, i.e. some one that I am not at all: as the alternative clause to an assertion or questioned hypothesis. *colloq.*

1837 THACKERAY *Ravenswing* iii, If there's a better-dressed man in Europe..I'm a Dutchman. **1856** READE *Never too late* lii, If there is as much gold on the ground of New South Wales as will make me a wedding-ring, I am a Dutchman. *Mod.* It is my brother, or I'm a Dutchman.

3. A Dutch ship.

Flying Dutchman: **a.** A legendary spectral ship supposed to be seen in the region of the Cape of Good Hope; also, the captain of this ship, said to have been condemned to sail the seas for ever. **b.** Applied to a particular express train on the Great Western Railway running between London and Bristol.

1657 R. LIGON *Barbadoes* (1673) 19 There was a Dutch man that lay there but three dayes, and in that little stay lost two Anchors. **1676** DRYDEN *Aurengz.* Ded., They..give it no more Quarter, than a Dutch-Man would to an English Vessel in the Indies. **1813** SCOTT *Rokeby* II. xi. *note*, A fantastic vessel, called by sailors the *Flying Dutchman.* **1839** MARRYAT *Phant. Ship* ix, I fear no Flying Dutchman. **1870** BRADWOOD *The O.V.H.* 25 The Flying Dutchman from Paddington.

4. In technical applications (see quots.). Chiefly *U.S.*

1859 BARTLETT *Dict. Amer.* 134 *Dutchman*, a flaw in a stone or marble slab, filled up by an insertion. **1874** KNIGHT *Dict. Mech., Dutchman* (*Carpentry*), a playful name for a block or wedge of wood driven into a gap to hide the fault in a badly made joint. **1905** *Terms Forestry & Logging* 36 *Dutchman*, a short stick placed transversely between the outer logs of a load to divert the load toward the middle and so keep any logs from falling off. **1909** *Cent. Dict.* Suppl., *Dutchman*, a layer of suet fastened with skewers into a roast of lean beef or mutton. **1957** *Brit. Commonwealth Forest Terminol.* 64 *Dutchman*, a prop used in logging for such purposes as preventing the binding of a saw when crosscutting, or for supporting the coupling of an arch while it is being hooked to a tractor. **1960** *New Yorker* 3 Sept. 20/3 He mended the [marble] lion by cutting recesses several inches deep wherever the stone was damaged, and fitting new pieces of stone therein. These pieces are known in the trade as dutchmen.

5. *Comb.*, as **Dutchman's breeches**, (*a*) a name in U.S. of the plant *Dicentra Cucullaria*; (*b*) *Naut.* (see quot. 1867); **Dutchman's laudanum**, a climbing shrub allied to the passion-flower, *Passiflora Murucuja* (*Murucuja ocellata*); also, a narcotic prepared from this; **Dutchman's pipe**, (*a*) 'an American name for *Aristolochia Sipho*' (*Treas. Bot.* 1866); (*b*) the nest of the South American wasp.

1756 P. BROWNE *Jamaica* 328 The Bull-hoof or Dutchman's Laudanum..a climber, whose fruit is..about the size of a large olive. **1857** DUNGLISON *Med. Lexicon* 315 Dutchman's Pipe, *Aristolochia Hirsuta.* **1865** WOOD *Homes without H.* xxiii. (1868) 421 The South American wasp, which makes the nest popularly called the 'Dutchman's pipe'. **1866** *Treas. Bot.* 400/1 *Dicentra Cucullaria*, is known in the United States as Dutchman's Breeches, from the shape of the spurred flower. **1867** SMYTH *Sailor's Wordbk., Dutchman's breeches*, the patch of blue sky often seen when a gale is breaking, is said to be, however small, 'enough to make a pair of breeches for a Dutchman'.

Hence **Dutchman-like**, *a.*

1612 W. SCLATER *Christians Strength* 5 That same vnmeasurable and Dutchmanlike drinking.

dutchpeeres, corrupt f. DOUZEPERS, *Obs.*

'Dutchwoman. [See DUTCHMAN.] †**a.** A German woman. *Obs.* exc. locally in *U.S.* **b.** A woman of Holland or the Netherlands.

1788 M. CUTLER in *Life, Jrnls. & Corr.* (1888) I. 400 His wife is the handsomest, smartest, and most delicate Dutchwoman we have seen on the road..she was born in Germany, and came over when a child. *Mod.* Mrs. L. is a Dutchwoman, a native of Haarlem.

Dutchy ('dʌtʃɪ), *sb. colloq.* (orig. *U.S.*). Also **Dutchee, Dutchie.** [f. DUTCH *a.*, *sb.* + -Y⁶.] A familiar or contemptuous name for a Dutchman or a German.

1835 C. F. HOFFMAN *Winter in West* II. 165 Where's Yankee and Dutchee? the bacon and greens are smoking on the table. **1864** J. T. TROWBRIDGE *Cudjo's Cave* (1868) iv. 18 See here, Dutchy! ye hain't been foolin' us, have ye? **1888** M. GRIGSBY *Smoked Yank* xvi. 139 Then some one behind would yell: 'Go it, Dutchie.' **1901** *Daily Chron.* 12 Aug. 6/1 The captain of the ship insulted him by saying, 'Here's another Dutchy who wants to be an American.' **1949** *Sci. Monthly* July 44 Among Western 'civilized' peoples we hear the constant use of such terms as..'nigger', 'Dutchy', 'flip', 'greaser', [etc.]. **1959** *Amer. Speech* XXXIV. 225 Nicknames in Australian lower-class society... *Dutchy*, a German.

'Dutchy, *a.* [f. DUTCH + -Y¹.] Dutch-like.

1862 A. GRAY *Lett.* (1893) 495, I was..copying out Grisebach's manuscripts for the printer (for the printer won't touch the Dutchy-looking thing). **1893** J. H. ROSS in *King's Business* (New Haven, Conn.) 127 The faces [in Rembrandt's Scripture pictures] are not ideal but Dutchy.

dutchy, obs. form of DUCHY.

†**dute.** *Obs.* Shortened form of *dedute*, DEDUIT, enjoyment, pleasure.

a **1300** *Fall & Passion* 24 in *E.E.P.* (1862) 13 Of paradis þe grete dute. *c* **1305** *Land Cokaygne* 9 ibid. 156 þoȝ þer be ioi and grete dute. **13..** *Gaw. & Gr. Knt.* 1020 Much dut watz þer dryuen þat day.

dute, obs. form of DOUBT.

duteous ('djuːtɪəs), *a.* Also 6–7 dutious. [f. DUTY + -OUS; cf. the earlier *beauteous.*] Characterized by the performance of duty to a superior; dutiful, submissive, obedient, subservient. (Of persons and their actions, etc.)

1593 SHAKS. *Lucr.* 1360 And yet the duteous vassal scarce is gone. **1594** —— *Rich. III*, II. i. 63, I intreate true peace of you, Which I will purchase with my dutious seruice. **1605** —— *Lear* IV. vi. 258 Duteous to the vices of thy Mistris. **1645** MILTON *Tetrach.* Wks. (1847) 190/2 But the law can compel the offending party to be more duteous. **1698** DRYDEN *On a Lady who died at Bath* 35 A daughter duteous, and a sister kind. **1742** YOUNG *Nt. Th.* I. 417 And only wish, As duteous sons, our fathers were more wise. **1805** SCOTT *Last Minstr.* I. iii, Nine-and-twenty yeomen tall Waited, duteous, on them all.

Hence **'duteously** *adv.*; **'duteousness.**

1660 JER. TAYLOR *Duct. Dubit.* III. v. (R.), Whatever dutiousness or observance comes afterwards. **1814** WORDSWORTH *Excurs.* VII. 667 Once every day he duteously repaired To rock the cradle of the slumbering babe. **1822** SCOTT *Nigel* xxvii, Kneeling duteously down. **1839** J. STERLING *Ess. etc.* (1848) I. 311 (Carlyle) Without faith, affectionateness, duteousness, truth.

‖**du théâtre** (dy teɑtr), *adj. phr.* [Fr.] 'Of the theatre'; characteristic of or suited to the theatre; theatrical.

1895 G. B. SHAW *Our Theatres in Nineties* (1932) I. 7 His plays are *du théâtre* when the right people are in the theatre. **1911** M. BEERBOHM *Let.* 6 Dec. (1964) 211 You who are so very *du théâtre* and love being behind the scenes among T-lights and properties.

dutiable ('djuːtɪəb(ə)l), *a.* [f. DUTY + -ABLE.] Liable to duty; on which a duty is levied.

1774 A. YOUNG *Pol. Arith.* (L., s.v. *Excise*), The number of dutyable articles. **1858** HAWTHORNE *Fr. & It. Jrnls.* II. 201 He inquired whether I had any dutiable articles. **1884** *Chamb. Jrnl.* 26 Jan. 58/2 Goods now comprised in the tariff as 'dutiable'.

dutied ('djuːtɪd), *a. U.S.* [f. DUTY + -ED².] Subjected to duty; on which duty is charged.

1771 T. JEFFERSON *Let.* Writ. 1892 I. 394 Everything but the dutied articles. **1866** A. L. PERRY *Elem. Pol. Econ.* (1873) 522 Goods into which dutied goods have entered.

dutiful ('djuːtɪfʊl), *a.* [f. DUTY + -FUL.]

1. Full of 'duty', i.e. that which is due to a superior; rendering the services, attention, and regard that are due.

1552 HULOET, Dutifull or dewtifull, *officiosus.* **1590** J. SMYTH in *Lett. Lit. Men* (Camden) 57 With all duetifull respect unto your Lordship. **1704** J. TRAPP *Abra-Mulé* II. i. 401 How can I pay dutiful Allegiance To him? **1748** RICHARDSON *Clarissa* (1811) I. xviii. 134 If words were to pass for duty, Clarissa Harlowe would be the dutifullest child breathing. **1844** H. H. WILSON *Brit. India* I. 511 Dutiful and loyal subjects of the King of Great Britain.

†**2.** Relating to duty or obligation. *Obs. rare.*

1588 A. KING tr. *Canisius' Catech.* 177 Quhilk [cardinal] vertues ar also called official or dewetifull, for that of thame proceids al kynd of offices and dewties.

dutifully ('djuːtɪfʊlɪ), *adv.* [f. prec. + -LY².] In a dutiful manner; with the regard and observance that is due.

1552 HULOET, Dutifullye or dewtifullye, *officiose.* **1579–80** NORTH *Plutarch* 195 (R.) Citizens, whose persons and purse did dutifully serve the commonwealth in their wars. **1632** LITHGOW *Trav.* v. 171 Having dutifully taken my Counge of many worthy friends. **1816** SOUTHEY *Poet's Pilgr.* Proem, Ye Nymphs..Whom I have dutifully served so long.

dutifulness ('djuːtɪfʊlnɪs). [f. as prec. + -NESS.] The quality of being dutiful; the habit of due performance of obligations to superiors.

1576 FLEMING *Panopl. Epist.* 329 The auncient duetifulnesse, which I owe to your reverence. **1611** SPEED *Hist. Gt. Brit.* IX. xix. (1632) 932 We doe it rather out of a sense of our dutifulnesse. **1748** RICHARDSON *Clarissa* (1811) I. xxxvi. 264 A dutifulness so exemplary. **1888** BURGON *Lives 12 Gd. Men* I. ii. 277 His dutifulness..to his Parents.

dutiless ('djuːtɪlɪs), *a.* [f. DUTY + -LESS.]

1. Wanting in the performance of duty; undutiful. *Obs.* or *arch.*

1592 *Nobody & Someb.* in Simpson *Sch. Shaks.* (1878) I. 298 To be so dutilesse unto the Queene. *a* **1603** T. CARTWRIGHT *Confut. Rhem. N.T.* (1618) 155 Wee are not so dutilesse to endevour any such thing. **1889** SWINBURNE *Stud. in Prose & P.* (1894) 202 The heartless and dutiless young king.

2. On which duty has not been paid. (*nonce-use.*)

1894 CROCKETT *Raiders* 37 The lads who bring over the dutiless gear from Holland and the Isle of Man.

‖**du tout** (dy tu), *adv. phr.* [Shortening of Fr. *pas du tout* not at all.] Not at all; by no means.

1824 T. CREEVEY *Let.* 23 Sept. in *Creevey Papers* (1903) II. iii. 82 'Do you know what happened last night?'—'Du tout,' says I. **1904** H. O. STURGIS *Belchamber* vii. 91 'It is very good of you to take an interest.'..'Oh, *du tout*,' she said suavely. **1936** A. CHRISTIE *ABC Murders* ix. 70 'Mr. Poirot ..[would] like to see it.' '*Du tout*,' said Poirot quickly. 'You misunderstand me.'

dutra, -troa, -troy, -try, var. DEWTRY, *Obs.*

dutte, obs. form of DOUBT, and of DIT *v.*

duttee, dutty, obs. form of DHOTI.

duty ('djuːtɪ). Forms: 3 deuyte, 4 **dewete**, (dwete), 4–5 duete(e, duyte, 4–6 deute, dewte(e, 5 dutee, (dywte), dwte, 5–6 dute, dutye, 5–7 dutie, 6 deuty, duitie, *Sc.* deuitie, dewite, 6–7 dew(e)tie, -y(e, duetie, -y(e, 6– duty. [a. AF. *dueté, duité, deweté*, f. *du, due* DUE: see -TY, and cf. *beauty, fealty.* Not recorded in continental French: cf. DEVOIR.]

1. a. The action and conduct due to a superior; homage, submission; due respect, reverence; an expression of submission, deference, or respect.

1297 R. GLOUC. (1724) 316 þe kyng..gret deuyte tolde of hem, vor her gentryse. *c* **1386** CHAUCER *Knt.'s T.* 2202 That goode Arcite..Departed is with duetee and honour Out of this foule prisonne of this lyf. *c* **1485** *Digby Myst.* (1882) IV. 994 To do hym reuerence & dewtee. **1551** T. WILSON *Logike* (1580) 70 [To] dooe his dutie with his Cappe of to his better. **1588** SHAKS. *L.L.L.* IV. ii. 147 Stay not thy complement, I forgiue thy duetie, adue. **1602** —— *Ham.* I. ii. 252 Our duty to your Honour. **1703** ROWE *Fair Penit.* Ded., What Duty, what Submission shall they not pay to that Authority? **1851** HT. MARTINEAU *Hist. Peace* (1877) III. v. ix. 383 Before noon came the lord mayor, with aldermen and other members of the Corporation, to offer their duty on behalf of the city of London. **1875** PRINCESS ALICE in *Mem.* 15 June (1884) 337 Many, many kisses from all children, and William's respectful duty.

b. *spec.* An action due to a feudal superior or lord of a manor. Cf. also 3 c.

1893 ELTON & MACKAY *Law of Copyholds* App. v. No. 17. 502 To have and to hold..according to the custom of the manor, by and under the rents, duties, and services therefor due and of right accustomed.

†**2.** That which is owing to any one; (one's) due; a debt; a charge, fee, etc. legally due; a due portion or allowance. *of duty*: as a debt or thing due. *Obs.* **a.** with possessive of the person to whom it is due.

c **1386** CHAUCER *Friar's T.* 54 His maister had not half his duetee. *Ibid.* 93 To reysen vp a rente That longeth to my lordes duetee. *c* **1440** *Generydes* 2016 He and his ayeris claymeth it of dewte. **1476** SIR J. PASTON in *Paston Lett.* No. 779 III. 166 Dyverse have lost mony er they cowde gete ther dywtes owte off the Staple. **1487** *Act 3 Hen. VII*, c. 4 [5] Preamb., To defraude ther creditours of their duties. **1526–34** TINDALE *Matt.* xx. 14 Take that which is thy duty. —— *Luke* xii. 42 To geve them their duetie of meate at due season. **1541** BARNES *Wks.* (1573) 231/1 To him that worketh is the rewarde not geuen of fauour, but of duetye. **1642** tr. *Perkins' Prof. Bk.* xi. §755 A stranger by his act without my assent shall not take away my duty.

b. with possessive of the person by whom it is due.

c **1430** LYDG. *Min. Poems* 141 (Mätz.) How may this be that thou art froward To hooly chirche to pay thy dewtee. **1540** HYRDE tr. *Vives' Instr. Chr. Wom.* (1592) B b viij, To pay their duty unto nature, as their creditor. **1573** *Satir. Poems Reform.* xlii. 198 Kirkis..dois also pay Thair dewtie alsweill as thay. **1628** COKE *On Litt.* 291 a, If *A.* be accountable to *B.* and *B.* releaseth him all his duties.

3. A payment due and enforced by law or custom.

c **1489** CAXTON *Sonnes of Aymon* vi. 150 He sholde be free of all maner of duytes the space of x. yeres. **1581** MARBECK *Bk. of Notes* 559 Therewith were they quite of all duetyes, both of rent, custome, tribute, and tolle.

spec. †**a.** Payment for the services of the church. Chiefly *pl. Obs.* (superseded by *dues*).

1431 *E.E. Wills* (1882) 88 Y wille that my parisshe chirches haue alle here duetees. **1514** *Test. Ebor.* (Surtees) V. 53, I will that the parrysh prest and the parrysh clerke have ther dewty as they by custome have hadde aforetyme. **1546** *Supplic. Poore Commons* (E.E.T.S.) 86 These charitable men..woulde not take the paynes to bury the dead corps, onlesse they had theyr dutye, as they call it. **1552** *Bk. Com. Prayer, Matrimony*, The man shal geue vnto the woman a ring, laying the same vpon the boke with the accustomed duty to the priest and clerke [so also in 1662]. **1562** *Child Marriages* (E.E.T.S.) 139 That they shuld resort to their owne parish churche..and pay their duties accordingly.

b. A payment to the public revenue levied upon the import, export, manufacture, or sale of certain commodities, the transfer of or succession to property, licence to use certain things or practise certain trades or pursuits, or the legal recognition of deeds and documents, as contracts, receipts, certificates, protests, affidavits, etc. Applied to the payments included under the several heads of customs, excise, licences, stamp-duties, probate and succession duties (death duties), inhabited house duty.

In general, 'duties' differ from other taxes in that they are levied upon specific articles or transactions, and not upon persons whether by capitation or in proportion to their income or possessions. But the distinction is not strictly observed in language; a 'window-tax' and 'dog-tax' are duties, as much as the inhabited house duty, or the duty on men-servants.

1474 CAXTON *Chesse* 120 The costumes, tolles, scawage, peages and duetees of the cytees. **1509–10** *Act 1 Hen. VIII*, c. 20. §1 Yf eny concelement be founde in the merchaundez of the dewetye aforeseid [= poundage]. **1530** PALSGR. 216/1 Dutie or exaction, *exaction*. **1644** EVELYN *Diary* 11 Oct., Here, having payd some small duty, we bought some trifles offer'd us by the souldiers, but without going on shore. **1660** *Act 12 Chas. II*, c. 4 Sched. of Rules r. 4, Any kind of Wines wch formerlie have paid all the dutyes of the Tonnage inwardes. **1669** *Sc. Acts Chas. II*, c. 9 The tolls customes and other dewties belonging to the said yeerlie fair and weeklie mercat. **1705** *Lond. Gaz.* No. 4154/4, 86 Hogsheads of.. White Wine.. to be deliver'd free of all Duties, except the Orphans Duty. **1711** SWIFT *Jrnl. to Stella* 2 Oct., Cards are very dear: there is a duty on them of sixpence a pack. **1711** *Act 10 Anne*, c. 19. §34 The said Books, Prints, and Maps as are to pay the said Duties *ad Valorem*. **1712** ADDISON *Spect.* No. 445 ¶3, I am informed by my Bookseller he must raise the Price of every single Paper to Two-pence, or that he shall not be able to pay the Duty of it. **1766** FRANKLIN *Exam.* Wks. 1887 III. 447 By taxes they [the American colonists] mean internal taxes; by duties they mean customs. **1825** MCCULLOCH *Pol. Econ.* III. viii. 387 High duties were laid on foreign corn when imported. **1894** *Act 57 & 58 Vict.* c. 30. §34 Duties of income tax granted by this act. **1894** HARCOURT *Sp. Ho. Commons* 16 Apr., The death duties have grown up piecemeal and bear traces of their fragmentary origin.. There exist at present five duties, and there is a wide distinction between them that may be illustrated by the Probate and Legacy Duty.

c. *Sc. Law.* A payment made in recognition of feudal superiority; hence, the rent of a feu or lease-hold tenement (perpetual or for a term of years). ***mails and duties***: see MAIL.

1536 BELLENDEN *Cron. Scot.* XI. viii. (Jam.), He dischargit thame of all malis and dewteis aucht to hym for v. yeris to cum. *c* **1565** LINDESAY (Pitscottie) *Chron. Scot.* (1728) 169 Constrained to pay the yearly duty and mails of the said lands. **1606** *Sc. Acts Jas. VI*, c. 13 (*title*), Act in favouris of his Majesteis vassellis for payment of their blenshe dueties. **1669** *Sc. Acts Chas. II*, c. 5 But preiudice to Superiors, to vse poinding against their Vassalls for their few duties. **1723** Blench-duty [see BLANCH *sb.* 3 c]. **1861** W. BELL *Dict. Law Scot.* s.v., *Feu-duty*.. The feu-duty is truly a rent in cattle, grain, money, or services, generally agricultural; varying in amount from an adequate to a merely elusory rent.

4. a. Action, or an act, that is due in the way of moral or legal obligation; that which one ought or is bound to do; an obligation. (The chief current sense.)

c **1385** CHAUCER *L.G.W.* Prol. 360 (MS. Gg. 4. 27) Hym owith o verry duetee.. wel to heryn here excusacyons. *c* **1489** CAXTON *Sonnes of Aymon* xiv. 324 Yet have I lever to serve you, as mi dute is for to doo. **1526–34** TINDALE *Luke* xvii. 10 We have done that which was oure duetye to do. **1530**, etc. Bounden duty [see BOUNDEN 5] . **1560** BIBLE (Genev.) *Eccl.* xii. 13 Feare God and kepe his commandments: for this is the whole dutie of man. **1651** HOBBES *Leviath.* II. xxxi. 186 The entire Knowledge of Civill duty. **1748** BUTLER *Serm.* Wks. 1874 II. 317 Economy is the duty of all persons, without exception. **1805** (21 Oct.) NELSON in J. K. Laughton *Nelson* xi. (1895) 221 (Signal at Trafalgar) 'England expects that every man will do his duty.' **1845** M. PATTISON *Ess.* (1889) I. 15 To do one's duty thoroughly is not easy in the most peaceable times. **1876** MOZLEY *Univ. Serm.* ix. (1877) 183 The New Testament says comparatively little about duties to equals, and enlarges upon duties to inferiors.

b. Absolutely: Moral obligation; the binding force of what is morally right. (Sometimes personified.)

1579 LYLY *Euphues* (Arb.) 195 Where duetie can haue no shewe, honestie can beare no sway. **1671** MILTON *P.R.* III. 172 Zeal and duty are not slow, But on Occasion's forelock watchful wait. **1732** LAW *Serious C.* ix. (ed. 2) 132 Out of a pious tender sense of Duty. **1805** WORDSW. *Ode to Duty* i, Stern Daughter of the Voice of God! O Duty! **1869** LOWELL *Parting of Ways* 8 The figure of a woman veiled, that said, 'My name is Duty, turn and follow me'. **1894** WOLSELEY *Marlborough* II. xci. 445 In England the noble, selfless word 'duty' has long been the motto of her most famous warrior sons.

5. a. The action which one's position or station directly requires; business, office, function.

1375–89 in *Eng. Gilds* 5 ȝif eny.. haue dwellid in þe bretherhede vij. ȝer, and done þerto alle þe duytes with-in þe tyme. **1393** GOWER *Conf.* I. 12 Which is the propre duetee Belongend unto the presthode. **1512** *Act 4 Hen. VIII*, c. 1, §2 If.. Constables do not theire dutie as is aforesayd. **1535** COVERDALE *1 Chron.* x. 27 Their dewtye was to geue attendaunce to open euery mornynge. **1698** FRYER *Acc. E. India & P.* 102 Other Fakiers (whose Duty it is daily to salute the Sun at his Height, Rising, and Setting, with their Musick). **1847** MARRYAT *Childr. N. Forest* iii, His father.. was.. too aged to do the duty [of forest ranger].

b. *Eccl.* Performance of the prescribed services or offices of the church; in *R.C. Ch.*, attendance at the public services, confession, communion, etc.

ministerial or ***clerical duty***, or (with contextual indication) simply *duty*: the regular ministration and service of a clergyman.

1526 *Pilgr. Perf.* (W. de W. 1531) 158 b, Whan ye synge or say your duty. **1692** *Covt. Grace Conditional* 71 Persons that have cast off Sabbaths, Duties, Ordinances. **1796** JANE AUSTEN *Pride & Prej.* xiii. (1813) 55 Provided that some other clergyman is engaged to do the duty of the day. **1814** —— *Mansf. Park* xxv. (D.), Edmund might, in the common phrase, do the duty of Thornton, that is, he might read prayers and preach. **1843** LEVER *J. Hinton* xix. (1878) 132 He [a priest] asked why Tim didn't come to his duties. **1891** E. PEACOCK *N. Brendon* II. 197 A papist always going to her duties. *Mod.* He lived in my rectory and took duty for me last August. He does Sunday duty in a neighbouring parish.

c. *Mil.* Prescribed or appointed military service (now, other than actual engagement with an enemy: see quot. 1853).

1590 R. WILLIAMS *Disc. Warre* (ed. 2) 30 Considering the number of hands that come to fight, and to doo duetie. **1607** SHAKS. *Cor.* I. vii. 1 Keepe your Duties As I haue set them downe. **1712** STEELE *Spect.* No. 493 ¶1 A Regiment which did Duty in the West-Indies. **1849** MACAULAY *Hist. Eng.* II. 585 It had been wisely determined that the duty of the capital should be chiefly done by the British soldiers in the service of the States General. **1853** STOCQUELER *Milit. Encycl.*, *Duty*, the exercise of those functions which belong to a soldier, with this distinction, that duty is counted the mounting guard, etc., where no enemy is to be engaged; but when any body of men marches to meet the enemy, it is strictly called *going upon service*.

d. *School work.* The service other than teaching performed by an assistant master, consisting in taking charge of the pupils out of school hours, superintending preparation of lessons, keeping order in corridors and dormitories, and the like.

Sometimes this work is shared among the members of the staff, some of whom are thus *on* while others are *off* duty; sometimes it is done entirely, or nearly so, by a ***duty-master***.

e. phr. ***on duty***: engaged in the performance of one's appointed office, service, or task. ***off duty***: the opposite of this; not officially engaged.

1667 MILTON *P.L.* I. 333 Men wont to watch On duty. **1698** FRYER *Acc. E. India & P.* 134 Killing Two of the Watch on Duty. **1700** S. L. tr. *Fryke's Voy. E. Ind.* 298, I was upon Duty in the Fort Galture. **1791** MRS. RADCLIFFE *Rom. Forest* i, On duty with his regiment in Germany. **1852** THACKERAY *Esmond* II. ii, When off duty.. Captain Dick often came to console his friends.

f. Of things: ***to do duty***, to discharge a function; to serve or stand *for* something else.

1825 H. WILSON *Mem.* II. 175 Such a thing on his head, doing duty for a hat! **1871** EARLE *Philol. Eng. Tongue* §289 Observe that *ought* once did duty for both these senses. **1873** TRISTRAM *Moab* ii. 28 A railway reading lamp did duty for footlights. **1878** BOSW. SMITH *Carthage* 198 With historians and other prose writers, stock epithets almost always do duty.

g. ***to do*** (***one's***) ***duty***: euphemism for 'to defecate, urinate'.

1935 A. J. CRONIN *Stars look Down* III. iv. 509 The lamb ran away and stood in the middle of the field doing duties at an adjacent haystack. **1938** I. GOLDBERG *Wonder of Words* vi. 108 The child.. never defecates or urinates; he.. does his 'duty'.

6. *Mech.* The measure of effectiveness of an engine, expressed by the number of units of practically effective work done per unit amount or weight of fuel. (See also quot. 1890.)

1827 D. GILBERT in *Phil. Trans.* CXVII. 26 Duty, a term first introduced by Mr. Watt, in ascertaining the comparative merit of steam-engines. **1874** J. H. COLLINS *Metal Mining* 102 Good Cornish engines.. in water-works, whose 'duty' averages nearly, or quite, 100,000,000 foot-lbs., or in other words, which lift one hundred million pounds of water one foot high, by the consumption of each hundredweight of coal. **1876** TAIT *Rec. Adv. Phys. Sc.* vi. 151 The duty of an animal engine is much larger than the duty of any other engine, steam or electro-magnetic. **1890** J. W. POWELL in *Century Mag.* 770/2 The amount of water which is needed to serve an acre of land. This is called the 'duty' of water, and in the United States it varies widely.

7. a. *attrib.* and *Comb.*, as ***duty call***, ***dance***, ***man***; ***duty-doing***, ***-monger***; (in sense 3 c) ***duty-fowl***, ***-ore***; also **duty-bound** *a.*, bound by duty; morally or legally obliged (cf. quot. 1591 *s.v.* BOUND *ppl. a.*[2] 7 a); **duty cycle** (see quot. 1924); **duty-paid** *a.*, on which customs or excise-duty has been paid; **duty-pay**, a bonus paid for work done outside the ordinary routine work (see also quot. 1879); **duty-sergeant**, a sergeant who has the charge of seeing that military duty (5 c) is done; **duty-sounding**, the sounding of a trumpet for some special military duty.

1908 HARDY *Dynasts* III. III. i. 93, I was *duty-bound To let him know. **1957** H. ROOSENBERG *Walls came tumbling Down* viii. 191 This Dutch officer.. would be duty-bound to stop it. **1864** C. M. YONGE *Trial* viii. 142 Forgetting her has not been easy to the payers of *duty calls. **1905** *Daily Chron.* 2 Aug. 4/6 When he [*sc.* the Kaiser] made his duty-call to the Danish capital. **1924** S. R. ROGET *Dict. Electr. Terms* 70/2 **Duty cycle*, the cycle of operation (starting, running and stopping) which a motor on intermittent duty performs each time it runs. *Duty cycle factor*, the ratio of the equivalent constant current during a duty cycle to the steady running current of the motor. **1962** SIMPSON & RICHARDS *Junction Transistors* xvi. 419 Such low duty-cycle devices as radio beacons. **1971** *Nature* 19 Mar. 160/2 The higher pulse repetition rate of the radar does not increase the accuracy if the signal-to-noise ratios and overall duty cycles (fraction of time that the transmitter is on) are equal in the two cases. **1850** B'NESS TAUTPHŒUS *The Initials* (Bentley Ed.) 325 Released from what he probably considered a *duty dance. **1881** 'RITA' *My Lady Coquette* viii, I am marked out for.. duty-dances for the rest of the evening. **1563** FOXE *Life Latimer* in *Serm. & Rem.* (1845) p. xvi, Detaining him from his *duty-doing. **1802** MAR. EDGEWORTH *Rosanna* i. (1832) 301 Notice that they must pay all the *duty-fowl and duty-geese. **1906** *Westm. Gaz.* 15 Sept. 4/1 Prepared to join the suggested training battalion for a further period of six months, as non-commissioned officers and '*Duty-men'. **1942** *Gen* 1 May 42/1 Special dutymen to your stations! **1692** *Covt. Grace Conditional* 71 Calling them, *Duty-mongers, Men of an Old Testament Spirit. **1881** RAYMOND *Mining Gloss.*, **Duty-ore* (*Cornw.*), the landlord's share of the ore. **1879** *Cassell's Fam. Mag.* V. 103/2 '*Duty pay' (*i.e.* extra pay awarded to men whose work is of a specially onerous or responsible kind). **1879** C. MARVIN *Our Public Offices* 67 Most of these extras in the way of nomenclature had something handsome attached to them in the shape of gratification money or 'duty-pay'. **1893** *Times* 13 June 9/4 A large export of *duty-paid Irish spirits. **1890** *Pall Mall G.* 13 Sept. 3/1 There should.. be more sergeants to a battalion, so as to give four *duty-sergeants to each company. **1799** *Instr. & Reg. Cavalry* (1813) 281 Trumpet *Duty Soundings. 1. Reveillé. 2. Stable Call—For stable duties. **1844** *Regul. & Ord. Army* 140 The Duty-Soundings of every Regiment are to be invariably performed on Trumpets in the Key of E flat.

b. *attrib.* or quasi-*adj.* Designating a visit, work, etc., undertaken as a duty (opp. to the same undertaken voluntarily or for pleasure); also applied to a person whom one visits, etc., as a duty. Cf. *duty call*, *dance*

1806 M. EDGEWORTH *Leonora* II. xlii. 4 If it be duty-work kindness, I would not give thanks for it. **1852** GEO. ELIOT *Let.* 5 June (1954) II. 32 Mrs. M[ackay] is disagreeably nervous and wanting in ease. One feels very glad when she has done her duty-talk. **1873** C. M. YONGE *Pillars of House* IV. xxxix. 151 Their grandson never went near them if he could help it, only enduring a duty-visit by the help of shooting. **1939** C. ISHERWOOD *Goodbye to Berlin* 268 It was more probably a duty-party, given once a year, to all the relatives, friends and dependents of the family. **1941** M. TREADGOLD *We couldn't leave Dinah* iv. 64 Dreary duty-visits to the tall sombre house in Eaton Square. **1946** A. CHRISTIE *Hollow* i. 13 We had him to lunch with some other Duty people. **1953** J. MASTERS *Lotus & Wind* vii. 97 Her father circled sedately from time to time with duty-partners. **1970** P. MOYES *Who saw her Die?* i. 14 I'll go and have a duty dinner with Kitty Prestwether. She's been pestering me ever since we got here.

duty-free, *a.*, *adv.*, and *sb.* [See DUTY 3 b.] **A.** *a.* and *adv.* **a.** Free of duty; exempt from payment of duty.

1689 *Order in Council* 12 Dec. in *Lond. Gaz.* No. 2514/1 The Term allowed for the Importation of Provisions and Necessaries into Ireland Duty-free. **1793** T. JEFFERSON *Writ.* (1859) IV. 43 Where a treaty does not give the principal right of selling, the additional one of selling duty free cannot be given. **1861** M. PATTISON *Ess.* (1889) I. 43 The Hanseatic traders.. imported their goods duty-free.

b. *Comb.* **duty-free shop**, a shop at an airport, on a boat, etc., at which duty-free goods can be bought.

1965 *Which?* May 150/1 Not all airports have duty-free shops. **1969** *Ibid.* Mar. 79/1 Some 'duty-free' shop prices are too high. **1970** *New Yorker* 16 May 44/2 Maybe I should get him a gift at the duty-free shop. **1971** P. PURSER *Holy Father's Navy* iv. 22 We were already on the second of the two bottles we'd bought at the duty-free shop.

B. *sb.* A duty-free article; freq. used in *pl.*, esp. of cigarettes, alcoholic drinks, etc., bought and imported free of duty by those returning from or travelling abroad; also, a duty-free shop. *colloq.*

1958 *Times* 16 Sept. 10/7 The meagre stub in his mouth had burnt out and I offered him one of my duty-frees. **1980** J. GARDNER *Garden of Weapons* III. xii. 349 I'm going to march you into the duty free at Tegel and make you buy them. **1982** *Economist* 21 Aug. 64/1 A sample shopping basket of duty-frees costs almost twice as much on LB-Färjorna lines as it does at.. Schiphol airport. **1985** *Sunday Times* 10 Mar. 12/1 (Advt.), During the flight, our cabin staff will be coming round with drinks and Duty-Frees.

duumvir (djuːˈʌmvə(r)). Pl. **-virs**, or in L. form **-viri** (-vɪraɪ). [L. *duumvir* lit. 'man of the two', 'one of the two men'; in pl. originally *duovirī* 'the two men', later *duumvirī* after the sing.] In *Rom. Hist.*: One of the *duumviri*, the general name given to pairs of co-equal magistrates and functionaries in Rome and in her coloniæ and municipia. Hence, in modern use, one of two colleagues in authority.

1600 HOLLAND *Livy* I. xxvi. 19 b, The king [Tullus Iostilius].. assembled the people together and said: 'I ordaine Duumvirs to sit upon Horatius.. to judge him according to the law'. **1727–51** CHAMBERS *Cycl.* s.v., The antient Romans.. had almost as many Duumviri as they had officers joined two by two in commission. **1794** BURKE *Sp. Impeach. Hastings* (Bohn) II. 33 Here is a compact of iniquity between these two duumvirs [Wheler and Hastings]. **1838** ARNOLD *Hist. Rome* I. 312 *note*, The two supreme magistrates in the municipia.. whose office was analogous to that of the consuls at Rome, were called duumvirs.

† **duˈumviracy**. *Obs. rare.* [f. as DUUMVIRATE: see -ACY.] = DUUMVIRATE.

1659 GAUDEN *Tears Ch.* 438 A cunning complicating of Presbyterian and Independent principles and interests together, that they may rule in their Duumviracy.

duumviral (djuːˈʌmvɪrəl), *a.* [ad. L. *duumvirāl-is*, f. *duumvir*.] Of or pertaining to duumvirs.

1828 in WEBSTER.

duumvirate (djuːˈʌmvɪrət). [ad. L. *duumvirāt-us*, f. *duumvir*: see -ATE[1].]

1. The position or office of the Roman duumvirs; the joint office or authority of two.

1656 BLOUNT *Glossogr.*, *Duumvirate*, the Office of the Duumvir in Rome, or of two in equal Authority, and may be taken for the Sheriffship of the City of London, or of any other place, where two are in joynt Authority. **1727–51** CHAMBERS *Cycl.* s.v., The duumvirate lasted till the year of

Rome 388, when it was changed into a decemvirate. **1831** *Fraser's Mag.* III. 137 A Swift and Pope can even found an imperious Duumvirate. **1894** W. K. Hill *Life of W. H. Widgery*, title p., The government of children is a duumvirate of teacher and parent.

2. A coalition of two men; a pair of officials or of men associated in any office or position.

1771 *Magna Charta* in Newell *Inquest Jurymen* (1825) 104 The livery..had made a resolution to walk before this illustrious Duumvirate [two Magistrates released from confinement] to the Mansion-House. **1807** Sir R. Wilson *Jrnl.* 28 June in *Life* (1862) II. viii. 283 The duumvirate were three hours together. *a* **1828** H. Neele *Lit. Rem.* (1829) 29 That highly gifted duumvirate, Beaumont and Fletcher.

So (in sense 1) † **du'umvirateship** (*obs.*).

1679 Penn *Addr. Prot.* 197 It is a sort of Duumvirateship in Power, by which the Civil Monarchy is broken.

duv(e, obs. forms of DOVE.

‖ **duvet** (dyvɛ). [F. *duvet* down, earlier *dumet*, dim. of OF. *dum* down.] **1.** A quilt stuffed with eider-down or swan's-down.

1758 Johnson *Idler* No. 40 ⁋4 There are now to be sold ..some duvets for bed-coverings. **1880** M. V. G. Havergal *Mem. F. R. Havergal* xv. 299 Her pet kittens on her duvet. **1967** R. Petrie *Foreign Bodies* ii. 22 Marian..turned back the sheets, heaping the plump feather *duvet* over a chair. **1970** *Cabinet Maker & Retail Furnisher* 31 July 169 Continental quilt or duvet? Call it what you will, this is a market with potential. **1971** *Guardian* 3 May 9/5 The cult of the Duvet is undoubtedly spreading even if there are those who find continental quilts..too..hot.

2. A downy growth.

1934 in Webster. **1957** M. Sharp *Eye of Love* x. 88 A slight *duvet* of black hair by comparison softened them [*sc.* her forearms].

Duvetyn ('djuːvɪtiːn, 'dʌvtɪn). Now usu. with lower-case initial. Also **-tine, -tyne.** [f. Fr. *duvet* down.] The trade name of a soft material of worsted and silk with a fine downy nap, used for women's coats and dresses. Also *attrib.*

1913 *Trade Marks Jrnl.* 10 Sept. 1434 Duvetyn..Silk Piece Goods. **1921** *Glasgow Herald* 19 Feb. 5 The upper part, which had a high calyx collar buttoned at the left side, was of dark duvetine. **1922** *Tatler* 18 Oct. Advts. p.w, This Hat can also be copied in Duvetyn, in all shades, at 2½ Gns. *Ibid.* 130/2 A new fabric known by the name of crocodile duvetyn. **1923** G. G. Denny *Fabrics & how to know Them* 41 The so-called silk duvetyn usually has a fine mercerized cotton warp and spun silk filling. **1924** *Scribner's Mag.* Aug. 200/2 She was wearing a new dark blue duvetyne suit. **1939** Joyce *Finnegans Wake* I. 148 Your delighted lips, love, be careful! Mind my duvetyne dress above all! **1960** *Times* 25 July 13/4 Pale sage green duvetyn.

dux (dʌks). [a. L. *dux*; leader.]

1. A leader, chief; *spec.* the head pupil in a class or division in a school: chiefly in Scotland.

1808 Scott *Autobiog.* in Lockhart *Life* i, Our class contained some very excellent scholars. The first Dux was James Buchan, who retained his honored place almost without a day's interval all the while we were at the high school. **1870** Ramsay *Remin.* (ed. 18) p. xxix, 'I'm second dux'..means in Scottish academical language second from the top of the class. **1876** Grant *Burgh Sch. Scotl.* II. v. 213 *note*, A gold medal [is given] to the dux of the [Aberdeen grammar] school.

2. *Mus.* The subject of a fugue (the 'answer' being called *comes*). Also, the subject of a canon; the leading voice or instrument in a fugue or canon.

1740 J. Grassineau *Mus. Dict.* 68 *Dux*, in fugues is the first voice or instrument that begins, and serves as a guide to the other parts, which are called *comes*, or followers. **1819** *Pantologia* citing Busby, *Dux*, in music, the name formerly given to the leading voice or instrument in a fugue. **1838** *Penny Cycl.* XI. 2 s.v. *Fugue.* **1880** Grove *Dict. Mus.*, *Dux*, an early term for the first subject in a fugue—that which leads; the answer being the *comes* or companion. **1885** G. B. Shaw in *Mag. Music* Nov. 178/3 Gounod often gives us a few pretty bars in canon, or a theme, with a bold skip or two at the beginning, introduced and answered in the rococo 'dux and comes' style. **1938** *Oxf. Compan. Mus.* 135/1 The voice first entering with the melody in a canon is called *Dux* ('leader') or *Antecedent*.

Hence **'duxship,** the position of dux.

1845 R. W. Hamilton *Pop. Educ.* viii. (ed. 2) 192 In Scotch schools very generally..Places are taken, tickets are given, and notices of the duxship are recorded.

Duxeen ('dʌksiːn). [Patented by the *Dux* Chemical Solutions Co., Bromley-by-Bow, London. See -EEN[1].] A paper used as a book covering, made in imitation of bookbinders' cloth.

1920 in *Trade Marks Jrnl.* 24 Nov. 2215. **1921** *Caxton Mag.* XXIII. 127 (Advt.), Duxeen is a strong, flexible hard-surfaced fibre. **1927** in *Longman's Class. Catal. Educ. Works* 11. **1956** *Bookman's Conc. Dict.* 90 *Duxeen*, a patented form of bookbinding material, simulating cloth.

duxelles (‖ dyksɛl, 'dʌksəlz). Also **d'Uxelles.** [f. the name of the Marquis *d'Uxelles*, 17th-c. Fr. nobleman.] A seasoning (see quots.). Also *attrib.*

1877 E. S. Dallas *Kettner's Bk. of Table* 162 Duxelles is the name given to a combination of mushrooms, parsley, and shalots, which are chopped together finely and used for flavouring. *Ibid.* 163 The name of Duxelles.. commemorates..La Varenne..[who] was lord of the kitchen of the Marquis d'Uxelles. *Ibid.* 164 Duxelles Sauce is made by adding Duxelles to about six times as much of Brown or Spanish sauce. **1964** L. Joyce-Cowen *Million Menus* 223/1 Duxelles is made of mushrooms..chopped and sautéed with..onion and parsley. **1964** A. Launay *Caviare & After* 130 *Duxelles*, small cuts of meat garnished with mushrooms pounded into a hash with onions and shallots cooked in a white wine.

duxite ('dʌksaɪt). *Min.* [Named by Dölter 1874, from *Dux* in Bohemia, where it is found.] A dark brown resin found as a layer on lignite.

1879 Watts *Dict. Chem.* VIII. 695.

duyel, duyl, var. DOLE *sb.*[2], grief, mourning.

duyker: see DUIKER[1].

duyn(e, duyr, duyre, obs. forms of DWINE *v.*, DOOR, DURE *v.*

duzan, obs. form of DOZEN.

duzeper(e, duzze peres: see DOUZEPERS.

DOMI MINA
NVS TIO
ILLV MEA